WHO WAS WHO

VOL. II

1916–1928

WHO'S WHO

AN ANNUAL BIOGRAPHICAL DICTIONARY

FIRST PUBLISHED IN 1848

WHO *WAS* WHO

VOL. I. 1897–1915

VOL. II. 1916–1928

VOL. III. 1929–1940

VOL. IV. 1941–1950

VOL. V. 1951–1960

PUBLISHED BY

ADAM & CHARLES BLACK

WHO WAS WHO
1916-1928

A COMPANION TO

WHO'S WHO

**CONTAINING THE BIOGRAPHIES
OF THOSE WHO DIED DURING
THE PERIOD 1916–1928**

ADAM & CHARLES BLACK
LONDON

FIRST PUBLISHED 1929
SECOND EDITION 1947
THIRD EDITION 1962
FOURTH EDITION 1967

A. AND C. BLACK LIMITED
4, 5 AND 6 SOHO SQUARE LONDON W.I

© 1967 A. & C. BLACK LTD

PRINTED IN GREAT BRITAIN

PREFACE TO THE FOURTH EDITION

A NUMBER of minor corrections, which have come to light since the volume was last printed, have been incorporated in this fourth edition.

PREFACE TO THE THIRD EDITION

THIS volume contains the entries, as they appeared in *Who's Who* for the last time, of those who died during the years 1916–1928, brought up to date and with the date of death added. The number of children shown in an entry is the number living at the date of the last issue of *Who's Who* in which the entry appeared.

When this volume was first published in 1929 a certain number of entries were omitted as it was not then known to the publishers that those concerned had died. In this third edition such entries have been included in an enlarged Addenda on pages xv–xxxii and cross-references have been added at the foot of those pages on which such entries would have appeared alphabetically in the volume itself.

ABBREVIATIONS

A1	.	First Rate (at Lloyd's).
A.A.G.	.	Assistant-Adjutant-General.
A.B.	.	Bachelor of Arts; able-bodied seaman.
Abp.	.	Archbishop.
A.C.	.	*Ante Christum* (before Christ).
A.C.A.	.	Associate of the Institute of Chartered Accountants.
Acad.	.	Academy.
A.C.G.I.	.	Associate of City and Guilds of London Institute.
A.C.I.S.	.	Associate of the Chartered Institute of Secretaries.
A.C.S.	.	Additional Curates Society.
A.D.	.	Anno Domini.
A.D.C.	.	Aide-de-camp.
Ad eund.	.	*Ad eundem gradum* (admitted to the same degree).
Adj.	.	Adjutant.
Ad lib.	.	*Ad libitum* (at discretion).
Adm.	.	Admiral.
A.D.O.S.	.	Assistant Director of Ordnance Stores.
Adv.	.	Advocate.
A.D.V.S.	.	Assistant Director of Veterinary Services.
Advt.	.	Advertisement.
Æt., Ætat.	.	*Ætatis* (aged).
Aft.	.	Afternoon.
A.G.	.	Attorney - General; Adjutant-General.
A.G.I.	.	Associate of the Institute of Certificated Grocers.
A.I.F.	.	Australian Imperial Forces.
A.I.G.	.	Adjutant-Inspector-General.
A.K.C.	.	Associate of King's College, London.
Ala.	.	Alabama (U.S.)
Alta.	.	Alberta.
A.L.I.	.	Argyll Light Infantry.
A.M.	.	*Ante Meridiem* (before mid-day); *Anno Mundi* (in the year of the world); Master of Arts; Alpes Maritimes.
A.M.I.C.E.	.	Associate Member of Institute of Civil Engineers.
A.M.I.E.E.	.	Associate Member of Institute of Electrical Engineers.
A.N.A.	.	Associate National Academician (America).
Anat.	.	Anatomy; Anatomical.
Anon.	.	Anonymously.
A.O.D.	.	Army Ordnance Department.
A.P.D.	.	Army Pay Department.
A.P.S.	.	Aborigines Protection Society.
A.Q.M.G.	.	Assistant-Quartermaster-General
A.R.A.	.	Associate of the Royal Academy.
Ar. Agt.	.	Army Agent.
A.R.A.M.	.	Associate of the Royal Academy of Music.
A.R.C.A.	.	Associate Royal Cambrian Academy.
A.R.C.E.	.	Academical Rank of Civil Engineers.
Archt.	.	Architect.
A.R.C.O.	.	Associate Royal College of Organists.
A.R.C.S.	.	Associate Royal College of Science.
A.R.E.	.	Associate of Royal Society of Painter Etchers.
A.R.I.B.A.	.	Associate of the Royal Institute of British Architects.
Ark.	.	Arkansas (U.S.)
A.R.M.S.	.	Associate of the Royal Society of Miniature Painters.
A.R.S.A.	.	Associate Royal Scottish Academy.
A.R.S.M.	.	Associate Royal School of Mines.
Art.	.	Artist.
A.R.W.S.	.	Associate Royal Society of Painters in Water-Colours.
A.S.	.	Anglo-Saxon.
A.S.A.M.	.	Associate of the Society of Art Masters.
A.S.C.	.	Army Service Corps.
Ass. or Assist.		Assistant. [General.
Ass. Commiss. Gen.		Assistant-Commissary-
Assoc.Sc.	.	Associate in Science.
Astr.	.	Astronomy.
Ath.	.	Athabasca (Canada).
A.U.C.	.	*Anno urbis conditæ* (from the foundation of the city) (Rome).
A.V.	.	Authorised Version.
Av.	.	Avenue.
A.V.D.	.	Army Veterinary Department.
Avoird.	.	Avoirdupois.
B.	.	Baron.
b.	.	born; brother.
B.A.	.	Bachelor of Arts.
B.A.I.	.	Bachelor of Engineering.
B.A.O.	.	Bachelor of Obstetrics.
Ball.	.	Balliol.
bar.	.	Barometer.
Barr.	.	Barrister.
Bart. or Bt.		Baronet.
Batt. or Batn.		Battalion.
B.C.	.	Before Christ; British Columbia.
B.Chir.	.	Bachelor of Surgery.
B.C.L.	.	Bachelor of Civil Law.
B.C.S.	.	Bengal Civil Service.
B.D.	.	Bachelor of Divinity.
Bd.	.	Board.
B.E.	.	Bachelor of Engineering.
Beds	.	Bedfordshire.
Berks	.	Berkshire.
B.Litt.	.	Bachelor of Letters.
B.M.A.	.	British Medical Association.
B.M.J.	.	British Medical Journal.
B.N.C.	.	Brasenose College.
Bom. C.S.		Bombay Civil Service.
Bom. S.C.		Bombay Staff Corps.
Bot.	.	Botany; Botanical.
B.P.	.	British Public.
Bp.	.	Bishop.
Brev.	.	Brevet.
Brig.	.	Brigade; Brigadier.
B.S.	.	Bachelor of Surgery.
B.S.C.	.	Bengal Staff Corps.
B.Sc.	.	Bachelor of Science.
B.Th.	.	Bachelor of Theology.
B.V.M.	.	Blessed Virgin Mary.
Bucks	.	Buckinghamshire.
(C.)	.	Conservative; 100.
c.	.	Cents; centimes; child.
C.A.	.	County Alderman; Chartered Accountant (Scotland).
Cal.	.	California (U.S.)
Cambs	.	Cambridgeshire.
Cantab.	.	Of Cambridge University.
Capt.	.	Captain.
Cav.	.	Cavalry.
C.B.	.	Companion of the Bath; Confined to Barracks.
C.B.E.	.	Commander Order of the British Empire.
C.B.S.A.		Clay Bird Shooting Association.
C.C.	.	County Councillor; Cricket Club; Cycling Club; County Court.

vii

C.C.C.	Corpus Christi College.		D.C.	District of Columbia (U.S.)
C.C.S.	Ceylon Civil Service.		D.C.L.	Doctor of Civil Law.
C.E.	Civil Engineer.		D.D.	Doctor of Divinity. [plies.
C.E.T.S.	Church of England Temperance Society.		D.D.M.S.	Deputy Director of Medical Sup-
			D.D.S.	Doctor of Dental Surgery.
C.F.	Chaplain to the Forces.		deg.	Degree.
Cf.	Compare.		Del.	Delaware (U.S.)
C.H.	Companion of Honour.		del.	(L. *delineavit*), he drew.
Ch.	Chief.		Dele. or d.	Cancel.
Chanc.	Chancellor ; Chancery.		D.Eng.	Doctor of Engineering.
Chap.	Chaplain.		Dep.	Deputy.
Ch.B.	Bachelor of Surgery.		Depart.	Department.
Ch.Ch.	Christ Church.		D.F.C.	Distinguished Flying Cross.
Ch.Coll.	Christ's College.		D.G.	(*Dei Gratia*), by the grace of God
Ch.M.	Master of Surgery.			Dragoon Guards.
Chm.	Chairman.		D.G.M.W.	Director - General of Military
C.I.	Imperial Order of the Crown of India.			Works.
			Dioc.	Diocese ; Diocesan.
C.I.D.	Criminal Investigation Department.		Diplo.	Diplomatic.
C.I.E.	Companion of the Order of the Indian Empire.		Dist.R.	District Railway.
			Ditto or do.	(It.), the same.
Cir.	Circus.		Div.	Division ; Divorced.
Circ.	Circa.		D.L.	Deputy-Lieutenant.
C.I.V.	City Imperial Volunteers.		D.L.I.	Durham Light Infantry.
Civ. Serv.	Civil Service.		D.Litt. or D.Lit.	Doctor of Literature.
C.J.	Chief Justice.		Do. or $	Dollar.
C.L.	Commander of Order of Leopold,		D.O.M.	Deo Optimo Maximo.
Cl.	Class.		Dom.	Dominus.
C.M.	Church Missionary.		Dow.	Dowager.
C.M.	Master in Surgery.		D.P.H.	Diploma in Public Health.
C.M.	Certificated Master.		Dr.	Doctor ; Debtor.
C.M.G.	Companion of St. Michael and St. George.		dr.	Drachm.
			Dr. Univ. Par.	Doctor of University of Paris.
C.M.S.	Church Missionary Society.		D.Sc.	Doctor of Science.
C.O.	Commanding Officer.		D.S.O.	Companion of the Distinguished
C.O.	Colonial Office.			Service Order.
Co.	County ; Company.		d.s.p.	died without issue.
Col.	Colony ; Colonel.		D.Theol.	Doctor of Theology.
Coll.	College ; Collegiate.		D.V.	(L. *Deo volente*), God willing.
Colo.	Colorado (U.S.)		dwt.	pennyweight.
Col.-Sergt.	Colour-Sergeant.		12mo	duodecimo (folded in 12).
Comdg.	Commanding.			
Comdt.	Commandant.			
Com.-in-Chf.	Commander-in-Chief.		E.	East ; Earl.
Comm.	Commander.		Ebor.	(Eboracensis) of York.
Comr.	Commissioner.		E.C.	East Central (postal district).
Comy.-Gen.	Commissary-General.		Eccl.	Ecclesiastical.
Conn.	Connecticut (U.S.)		E.C.U.	English Church Union.
Corp.	Corporal.		Ed.	Editor.
Corr. Mem. or Fell.	Corresponding Member or Fellow.		Edin.	Edinburgh.
			Educ.	Educated.
C.O.S.	Charity Organisation Society.		Edw.	Edward.
C.P.R.	Canadian Pacific Railway.		E.E.	Early English.
Cr.	Crown.		e.g.	(L. *exempli gratia*), for example.
cr.	created.		E.I.	East Indian.
Cres.	Crescent.		E.I.C.S.	East India Company's Service.
C.S.	Civil Service.		Ency. Brit.	Encyclopædia Britannica.
C.S.C.	Conspicuous Service Cross.		Eng.	England.
C.S.I.	Companion of the Order of the Star of India.		eng.	Engineer.
			esp.	especially.
C.SS.R.	Congregation of the Most Holy Redeemer (Redemptorist Order).		E. & W.L.R.	East and West London Railway
			Ext.	Extinct.
C.T.C.	Cyclists' Touring Club.			
C.U.	Cambridge University.		f.	fathoms.
C.U.A.C.	Cambridge Univ. Athletic Club.		F.A.	Football Association.
C.U.B.C.	Cambridge University Boating Club.		Fahr.	Fahrenheit.
C.U.C.C.	Cambridge University Cricket Club.		F.A.I.	Fellow of Auctioneers' Institute.
C.U.F.C.	Cambridge Univ. Football Club.		F.A.S.B.	Fellow of Asiatic Soc. of Bengal.
C.V.O.	Commander of the Royal Victorian Order.		F.B.A.	Fellow of the British Academy.
			F.B.O.U.	Fellow British Ornithologists'
Cwt.	Hundredweight.			Union.
			F.C.A.	Fellow of the Institute of Chartered Accountants.
D.	Duke ; 500 (Roman numerals).		F.C.G.I.	Fellow of City and Guilds of
d.	Pence ; died ; daughter.			London Institute.
D.A.A.G.	Deputy-Assistant-Adjutant-General.		F.C.I.S.	Fellow of the Chartered Institute of Secretaries.
D.A.D.Q.	Deputy Assistant Director of Quartering.		Fcp.	Foolscap.
			F.C.P.	Fellow College of Preceptors.
D.A.G.	Deputy-Adjutant-General.		F.C.S.	Fellow of the Chemical Society.
D.A.Q.M.G.	Deputy - Assistant - Quartermaster-General.		F.C.T.B.	Fellow of the College of Teachers of the Blind.
D.B.E.	Dame Commander Order of the British Empire.		F.E.I.S.	Fellow of the Educational Institute of Scotland.

P.E.S.	.	Fellow of Entomological Society.
F.F.A.	.	Fellow of Faculty of Actuaries.
F.F.P.S.	.	Fellow of the Royal Faculty of Physicians and Surgeons (Glasgow).
F.G.I.	.	Fellow of the Institute of Certificated Grocers.
F.G.S.	.	Fellow of the Geological Society.
F.I.A.	.	Fellow of Institute of Actuaries.
F.I.C.	.	Fellow of Institute of Chemistry.
F.I.D.	.	Fellow of Institute of Directors.
F.I.Inst.	.	Fellow of the Imperial Institute.
F.J.I.	.	Fellow of Institute of Journalists.
Fla.	.	Florida (U.S.).
F.L.S.	.	Fellow of the Linnean Society.
F.M.	.	Field-Marshal.
Fo.	.	Folio (a sheet of paper folded once).
F.O.	.	Foreign Office.
F.O.	.	Field Officer.
f.o.b.	.	Free on board.
F.P.	.	Fire-plug.
F.P.S.	.	Fellow of Philosophical Society; also of Philharmonic Society.
F.R.A.I.	.	Fellow of the Royal Anthropological Institute.
F.R.A.M.	.	Fellow of the Royal Academy of Music.
F.R.A.S.	.	Fellow of the Royal Astronomical Society.
F.R.B.S.	.	Fellow of the Royal Botanic Society.
F.R.C.I.	.	Fellow of the Royal Colonial Institute.
F.R.C.O.	.	Fellow of the Royal College of Organists.
F.R.C.P.	.	Fellow of the Royal College of Physicians.
F.R.C.P.E.	.	Fellow of the Royal College of Physicians of Edinburgh.
F.R.C.S.	.	Fellow of the Royal College of Surgeons.
F.R.C.V.S.	.	Fellow of the Royal College of Veterinary Surgeons.
F.R.F.P.S.	.	Fellow of Royal Faculty of Physicians and Surgeons.
F.R.G.S.	.	Fellow of the Royal Geographical Society.
F.R.Hist.S.	.	Fellow of Royal Historical Socy.
F.R.Hort.S.	.	Fellow of the Royal Horticultural Society.
F.R.I.B.A.	.	Fellow of the Royal Institute of British Architects.
F.R.M.S.	.	Fellow of the Royal Microscopical Society.
F.R.Met.S.	.	Fellow of the Royal Meteorological Society.
F.R.N.S.A.	.	Fellow Royal School Naval Architecture.
F.R.P.S.	.	Fellow of the Royal Photographic Society.
F.R.S.	.	Fellow of the Royal Society.
F.R.S.A.	.	Fellow of the Royal Society of Arts.
F.R.S.C.	.	Fellow of the Royal Society of Canada.
F.R.S.E.	.	Fellow of the Royal Society of Edinburgh.
F.R.S.G.S.	.	Fellow of the Royal Scottish Geographical Society.
F.R.S.L.	.	Fellow of the Royal Society of Literature.
F.S.A.	.	Fellow of the Society of Antiquaries.
F.S.A.A.	.	Fellow of the Society of Accountants and Auditors.
F.S.A.S.	.	Fellow of the Society of Antiquaries of Scotland.
F.S.I.	.	Fellow of Surveyors' Institution.
F.S.S.	.	Fellow of the Royal Statistical Society.
F.S.Sc.A.	.	Fellow of the Society of Science and Art of London.
F.T.C.D.	.	Fellow of Trinity College, Dublin.
F.Z.S.	.	Fellow of the Zoological Society.

F.Z.S.Scot.		Fellow of the Zoological Society of Scotland.
Ga.	.	Georgia (U.S.)
Gal.	.	Gallon.
G.B.E.		Knight or Dame Grand Cross Order of the British Empire.
G.C.B.	.	Knight Grand Cross of the Bath.
G.C.H.	.	Knight Grand Cross of Hanover.
G.C.I.E.		Knight Grand Commander of the Indian Empire.
G.C.M.G.	.	Knight Grand Cross of St. Michael and St. George.
G.C.R.	.	Great Central Railway.
G.C.S.I.	.	Knight Grand Commander of the Star of India.
G.C.V.O.		Knight Grand Cross of Royal Victorian Order.
Gdns.	.	Gardens.
Gen.	.	General.
gen.	.	genus = kind.
G.E.R.	.	Great Eastern Railway.
G.F.S.	.	Girls' Friendly Society.
Gib.	.	Gibraltar.
G.L.	.	Grand Lodge.
Glos.	.	Gloucestershire.
G.N.R.	.	Great Northern Railway.
Goth.	.	Gothic.
Gov.	.	Governor.
Govt.	.	Government.
G.P.O.	.	General Post Office.
Gr.	.	Greek.
Gram. Sch.	.	Grammar School.
g.s.	.	Grandson.
G.W.R.	.	Great Western Railway.
H.A.C.	.	Honourable Artillery Company.
Hants.	.	Hampshire.
Harv.	.	Harvard.
H.B.M.	.	His Britannic Majesty.
h.c.	.	honoris causa.
H.E.	.	His Excellency.
H.E.I.C.	.	Honourable East India Company.
H.E.I.C.S.	.	Honourable East India Company's Service.
Heir app.	.	Heir apparent.
Heir pres.	.	Heir presumptive.
Herts.	.	Hertfordshire.
H.F.A.R.A.	.	Honorary Foreign Associate of the Royal Academy.
H.F.R.A.	.	Honorary Foreign Member of the Royal Academy.
H.H.	.	His (or Her) Highness.
H.I.H.	.	His (or Her) Imperial Highness.
H.I.M.	.	His (or Her) Imperial Majesty.
H.L.I.	.	Highland Light Infantry.
H.M.	.	His (or Her) Majesty.
H.M.I.	.	His Majesty's Inspector.
H.M.S.	.	His Majesty's Ship.
Hon.	.	Honourable.
(Hon.)	.	Honorary.
h.-p.	.	half-pay.
h.p.	.	horse-power.
H.Q.	.	Headquarters.
(H.R.)	.	Home Ruler.
H.R.C.A.	.	Honorary Royal Cambrian Academician.
H.R.H.	.	His (or Her) Royal Highness.
H.R.H.A.	.	Honorary Member of Royal Hibernian Academy.
H.R.S.A.	.	Honorary Member of Royal Scottish Academy.
H.S.H.	.	His (or Her) Serene Highness.
Hum.	.	Humanity, Latin.
Hunts.	.	Huntingdonshire.
Ia.	.	Iowa (U.S.)
I.A.	.	Indian Army.
Ib. or Ibid.	.	Ibidem (in the same place).
Icel.	.	Icelandic.
I.C.S.	.	Indian Civil Service.
Id.	.	Idaho (U.S.).
id.	.	idem (the same).

I.D.B.	illicit diamond buying.	
i.e.	*id est* (that is).	
Ign.	*ignotus* (unknown).	
I.H.S.	*Jesus Hominum Salvator* (Jesus the Saviour of Men), more correctly IHΣ, the first three letters of the name of Jesus in Greek.	
Ill.	Illinois (U.S.)	
I.L.P.	Independent Labour Party.	
Imp.	Imperial.	
I.M.S.	Indian Medical Service.	
Incog.	*Incognito* (in secret).	
Ind.	Indiana (U.S.)	
Insp.	Inspector.	
Inst.	Instant ; Institute.	
I. of M.	Isle of Man.	
I.O.G.T.	International Order of Good Templars.	
I.O.O.F.	Independent Order of Oddfellows.	
I.O.P.	Inst. Painters in Oil Colours.	
I.O.U.	I owe you.	
I.S.C.	Indian Staff Corps.	
I.S.O.	Imperial Service Order.	
I.T.	Indian Territory (U.S.)	
Ital. or It.	Italian.	
ital.	italics.	
I.W.	Isle of Wight.	
J.A.	Judge-Advocate.	
Jas.	James.	
Jes.	Jesus.	
Joh. Jno.	John.	
J.P.	Justice of the Peace.	
Jun.	Junior.	
Jun. Opt.	Junior Optime.	
K.	King.	
Kans.	Kansas (U.S.)	
K.B.	Knight of the Bath (seldom used now) ; Knight Bachelor.	
K.B.E.	Knight Commander Order of the British Empire.	
K.C.	King's Counsel.	
K.C.B.	Knight Commander of the Bath.	
K.C.C.	Commander of Order of Crown, 'Belgian and Congo Free State.	
K.C.H.	Knight Commander of Hanover.	
K.C.I.E.	Knight Commander of the Indian Empire.	
K.C.L.	King's College, London.	
K.C.M.G.	Knight Commander of St. Michael and St. George.	
K.C.S.I.	Knight Commander of the Star of India.	
K.C.V.O.	Knight Commander of the Royal Victorian Order.	
K.D.G.	King's Dragoon Guards.	
Keb.	Keble College, Oxford.	
K.G.	Knight of the Order of the Garter.	
K.H.	Knight of Hanover.	
K.H.C.	Hon. Chaplain to the King.	
K.H.P.	Hon. Physician to the King.	
K.H.S.	Hon. Surgeon to the King ; Knight of the Holy Sepulchre.	
K.-I.-H.	Kaiser-i-Hind.	
Kil.	Kilometre.	
Kilo.	Kilogramme.	
K.O.S.B.	King's Own Scottish Borderers.	
K.P.	Knight of the Order of St. Patrick.	
K.R.R.	King's Royal Rifles.	
K.S.	King's Scholar.	
K.S.G.	Knight of St. Gregory.	
K.T.	Knight of the Order of the Thistle.	
Kt. or Knt.	Knight.	
Ky.	Kentucky (U.S.)	
(L.)	Liberal.	
L.	50 (Roman numerals).	
£	Pounds (sterling).	
l.	left.	

L.A.	Literate in Arts ; Liverpool Academy.	
La.	Louisiana (U.S.)	
L.A.C.	London Athletic Club.	
L.-Corp. or Lance-Corp.	Lance-Corporal.	
Lancs	Lancashire.	
Lat.	Latin.	
lat.	latitude.	
lb.	pounds (weight).	
L.C.C.	London County Council.	
L.Ch.	Licentiate in Surgery.	
L.C.J.	Lord Chief Justice.	
L.C.P.	Licentiate of the College of Preceptors.	
L. Div.	Licentiate in Divinity.	
L.D.S.	Licentiate of Dental Surgery.	
L.F.P.S.	Licentiate of the Faculty of Physicians and Surgeons.	
L.H.D.	(*Literarum Humaniorum Doctor*) Doctor of Literature.	
L.I.	Light Infantry.	
Lic. Med.	Licentiate in Medicine.	
Lieut.	Lieutenant.	
Linc or Lincs	Lincolnshire.	
Lit.	Literature ; Literary.	
lit.	literally.	
Lit. Hum.	Classics.	
Litt.D.	Doctor of Letters.	
L.J.	Lord Justice.	
L.L.A.	Lady Literate in Arts.	
LL.B.	Bachelor of Laws.	
LL.D.	Doctor of Laws.	
LL.M.	Master of Laws.	
L.M.	Licentiate in Midwifery.	
L. of C.	Lines of Communication.	
long.	longitude.	
Loq.	*Loquitur* (speaks).	
L.R.C.P.	Licentiate of the Royal College of Physicians.	
L.R.C.P.E.	Licentiate Royal College of Physicians, Edinburgh.	
L.R.C.S.	Licentiate of the Royal College of Surgeons.	
L.R.C.S.E.	Licentiate of the Royal College of Surgeons, Edinburgh.	
L.R.C.V.S.	Licentiate of the Royal College of Veterinary Surgeons.	
L.S.A.	Licentiate of the Society of Apothecaries.	
£. s. d.	Pounds, shillings, and pence ; Money.	
Lt.	Light (*e.g.* Light Infantry).	
Lt. or Lieut.	Lieutenant.	
Lt.-Col.	Lieutenant-Colonel.	
Lt.-Gen.	Lieutenant-General.	
L.Th.	Licentiate in Theology.	
(L.U.)	Liberal Unionist.	
L.U.O.T.C.	London University Officers' Training Corps.	
L. & N.W.R.	London and N.-Western Railway.	
L. & S.W.R.	London and South-Western Railway.	
L. & Y.R.	Lancashire and Yorkshire Railway.	
L.B.&S.C.R.	London, Brighton, and South Coast Railway.	
L.C.&D.R.	London, Chatham, and Dover Railway.	
LXX	Septuagint.	
M.	Marquess ; Member ; Monsieur ; 1000.	
m.	married.	
M.A.	Master of Arts.	
M.A.B.Y.S.	Metropolitan Association for Befriending Young Servants.	
Mag.	Magnetism or Magazine.	
Magd.	Magdalen ; Magdalene.	
M.A.I.	Master of Engineering (*Magister in Arte Ingeniaria*).	
Maj.-Gen.	Major-General.	
Man.	Manitoba (Canada).	
M.A.O.	Master of Obstetric Art.	
Marq.	Marquis.	
Mass.	Massachusetts (U.S.)	
Math.	Mathematics ; Mathematical.	

M.B.	Bachelor of Medicine.
M.B.E.	Member of the Order of the British Empire.
M.B.O.U.	Member Brit. Ornithologists' Union.
M.C.	Military Cross.
M.C.C.	Marylebone Cricket Club.
M.Ch.	Master in Surgery.
M.C.M.E.S.	Member of Civil and Mech. Engineers' Society.
M.Com.	Master of Commerce.
M.C.S.	Madras Civil Service.
M.D.	Doctor of Medicine.
Md.	Maryland (U.S.)
Me.	Maine (U.S.)
M.E.	Mining Engineer.
M.E.C.	Member of Executive Council.
Mech.	Mechanics.
Med.	Medical.
Mem.	Memorandum.
M.Eng.	Master of Engineering.
Met.R.	Metropolitan Railway.
M.F.H.	Master of Foxhounds.
M.G.I.	Member of the Institute of Certificated Grocers.
M.H.A.	Member of House of Assembly.
M.H.R.	Member House of Representatives
Mich.	Michigan (U.S.)
M.I.E.E.	Member of Institute of Electrical Engineers.
M.J.I.	Member of Institute of Journalists.
Mil.	Military.
M.I.M.E.	Member of Institute of Mining Engineers.
M.I.Mech.E.	Member Institution of Mechanical Engineers.
M.I.M.M.	Member of Institute of Mining and Metallurgy.
Min.	Minister.
Minn.	Minnesota (U.S.)
M.Inst.C.E.	Member of Institution of Civil Engineers.
M.Inst.M.E.	Member of Institution of Mining Engineers.
M.I.N.A.	Member of Institution of Naval Architects.
M.Inst.W.E.	Member of the Institution of Water Engineers.
Miss.	Mississippi (U.S.)
M.J.S.	Member of the Japan Society.
M.L.	Licentiate in Medicine.
M.L.A.	Member of Legislative Assembly.
M.L.C.	Member of Legislative Council.
Mlle.	Mademoiselle (Miss.)
M.L.S.B.	Member London School Board.
Mme.	Madame.
M.M.S.	Member of Council, Institution of Mining Engineers.
Mngr.	Monsignor.
Mo.	Missouri (U.S.)
Mods.	Moderations (Oxford).
M.O.H.	Master of Otter Hounds; Medical Officer of Health.
Mon.	Montana (U.S.)
Most Rev.	Most Reverend (of an Archbishop).
M.P.	Member of Parliament.
M.P.P.	Member of Provincial Parliament.
M.R.	Master of the Rolls; Midland Railway.
M.R.A.S.	Member of Royal Asiatic Society.
M.R.C.P.	Member of the Royal College of Physicians.
M.R.C.P.E.	Member of the Royal College of Physicians, Edinburgh.
M.R.C.S.	Member Royal College of Surgeons.
M.R.C.S.E.	Member of the Royal College of Surgeons, Edinburgh.
M.R.C.V.S.	Member of the Royal College of Veterinary Surgeons.
M.R.I.A.	Member of the Royal Irish Academy.
M.R.U.S.I.	Member of the Royal United Service Institute.
M.S.	Master of Surgery.

MS., MSS.	Manuscript, Manuscripts.
M.S.C.	Madras Staff Corps.
M.Sc.	Master of Science.
M.S.H.	Master of Stag-hounds.
M.S.I.	Member of Sanitary Institute.
M.S.& L.R.	Manchester, Sheffield. and Lincoln- Railway.
Mt.	Mountain.
Mus.B.	Bachelor of Music.
Mus.D.	Doctor of Music.
Mus.M.	Master of Music. [Order.
M.V.O.	Member of the Royal Victorian
(N.)	Nationalist.
N.	North.
n.	noun; nephew.
N.B.	North Britain; (L. Nota Bene, notice); New Brunswick.
N.B.A.	North British Academy.
N.B.R.	North British Railway.
N.C.	North Carolina (U.S.)
N.C.U.	National Cyclists' Union.
N.D.	No date.
N. Dak.	North Dakota (U.S.)
N.E.	North-east.
Neb.	Nebraska (U.S.)
nem. con.	Nemine contradicente (no one contradicting); unanimously.
N.E.R.	North Eastern Railway.
net, nett	(It.) Netto (free from all deductions).
Nev.	Nevada (U.S.)
New M.	New Mexico (U.S.)
N.H.	New Hampshire (U.S.)
N.I.	Native Infantry.
N.J.	New Jersey (U.S.)
N.L.F.	National Liberal Federation.
N.N.E.	North-north-east.
N.N.W.	North-north-west.
non seq.	Non sequitur (it does not follow).
Northants	Northamptonshire.
Notts	Nottinghamshire.
N.P.	Notary Public.
N.R.A.	National Rifle Association.
N.S.	Nova Scotia; New Style in the Calendar (in Great Britain since 1752); National Society.
N.S.A.	National Skating Association.
N.S.P.C.C.	National Society for Prevention of Cruelty to Children.
N.S.W.	New South Wales.
N.T.	New Testament; Northern Territory of South Australia.
N.U.T.	National Union of Teachers.
N.U.T.N.	National Union of Trained Nurses.
N.U.W.W.	National Union of Women Workers.
N.W.	North-west.
N.W.P.	North-Western Provinces.
N.W.T.	North-Western Territories.
N.Y.	New York—City or State.
N.Y.C.	New York City.
N.Z.	New Zealand.
O.	Ohio (U.S.)
o.	only.
O. & O.	Oriental and Occidental (Steamship Co.)
ob.	Died.
O.B.E.	Officer Order of the British Empire.
o.c.	only child.
O.C.	Officer Commanding.
O.D.	Ordinary seaman.
O.F.M.	Order of Friars Minor.
O.H.M.S.	On His Majesty's Service.
O.L.	Officer of the Order of Leopold.
O.M.	Order of Merit.
O.M.I.	Oblate of Mary Immaculate.
Ont.	Ontario.

O.P.	Ordinis Prædicatorum = of the Order of Preachers (Dominican Ecclesiastical Title).
o.p.	opposite prompter.
O.S.	Old Style in the Calendar (in Great Britain before 1752).
o.s.	only son.
O.S.A.	Ontario Society of Artists.
O.S.B.	Order of St. Benedict.
O.S.F.C.	Franciscan (Capuchin) Order.
O.S.N.C.	Orient Steam Navigation Co.
Ore.	Oregon (U.S.)
O.T.	Old Testament.
O.U.	Oxford University.
O.U.A.C.	Oxford University Athletic Club.
O.U.B.C.	Oxford University Boating Club.
O.U.C.C.	Oxford University Cricket Club.
O.U.F.C.	Oxford University Football Club.
Oxon	Oxfordshire; Of Oxford.
Oz.	Ounces.
8vo	Octavo (folded in eight).

P.	Prince.
Pa.	Pennsylvania (U.S.)
Parl. Agt.	Parliamentary Agent.
P.A.S.I.	Professor Associate Surveyors' Institution.
P.C.	Privy Councillor; Police Constable; Perpetual Curate.
p.c.	per centum (by the hundred); post-card.
P.C.M.O.	Principal Colonial Medical Officer.
P.D.G.	President Dudley Gallery.
P.F.	Procurator-Fiscal.
Ph.D.	Doctor of Philosophy
Phil.	Philosophical.
Phys.	Physical.
pinx.	(He) painted it.
Pl.	Place; Plural.
Plen.	Plenipotentiary.
P.M.	Post Meridiem (after mid-day); Pacific Mail.
P.M.G.	Postmaster-General; Pall Mall Gazette.
P.M.O.	Principal Medical Officer.
P.M.S.	President Miniature Society.
P. & O.	Peninsular and Oriental Steamship Co.
P.O.	Post Office; Postal Order.
P.O.O.	Post Office Order.
Pop.	Population.
P.P.	Parish Priest.
Pp.	Pages.
P.P.C.	Fr. Pour prendre congé (To take leave).
P.Q.	Province of Quebec.
P.R.	Prize ring (The).
P.R.A.	President of the Royal Academy.
Preb.	Prebendary.
Pres.	President.
P.R.I.	President of the Royal Institute of Painters in Water Colours.
Prin.	Principal.
Proc.	Proctor.
Prof.	Professor.
Pro tem.	Pro tempore (for the time being).
Prov.	Provost.
Prox.	Proximo (next).
P.R.S.	President of the Royal Society.
P.S.	Postscriptum (postscript); prompt side.
p.s.	passed School of Instruction (of Officers).
p.s.c.	passed Staff College.
P.S.N.C.	Pacific Steam Navigation Co.
Pt.	Pint.
Pte.	Private (soldier).
P.T.O.	Please turn over.
P.W.D.	Public Works Department (roads, buildings, Gov. railways, telegraphs, etc.)

Q.	Queen.
Q.C.	Queen's Counsel.

Q.E.D.	Quod erat demonstrandum (which was to be demonstrated), applied to a theorem.
Q.E.F.	Quod erat faciendum (which was to be done), applied to a problem.
Q.H.P.	Queen's Honorary Physician.
Q.M.G.	Quartermaster-General.
Qr.	Quarter.
Qt.	Quart.
Qto.	Quarto (folded in four).
Queensl.	Queensland.
Q.U.B.	Queen's University, Belfast.
Q.U.I.	Queen's University in Ireland.
q.v.	quod vide (which see).

(R.)	Radical.
R.	Rector.
r.	right.
R.A.	Royal Academician; Royal Artillery.
R.A.C.	Royal Agricultural College.
R.A.M.	Royal Academy of Music.
R.A.M.C.	Royal Army Medical Corps.
R. Art.	Royal Artillery.
R.A.S.	Royal Astronomical or Asiatic Society.
R.B.	Rifle Brigade.
R.B.A.	Royal Society of British Artists.
R.B.C.	Royal British Colonial Society of Artists.
R.B.S.	Royal Society of British Sculptors
R.C.	Roman Catholic.
R.C.A.	Member Royal Cambrian Academy
R.C.V.S.	Royal College of Veterinary Surgeons.
R.D.	Rural Dean; Royal Naval Reserve Decoration.
Rd.	Road.
R.E.	Royal Engineers; Royal Society of Painter Etchers.
R. Eng.	Royal Engineers.
Rear-Adm.	Rear-Admiral.
Rect.	Rector.
Reg. Prof.	Regius Professor.
Regt.	Regiment.
Res.	Resigned; Reserve.
Rev.	Reverend.
R.F.A.	Royal Field Artillery.
R.G.A.	Royal Garrison Artillery.
R.H.A.	Royal Hibernian Academy; Royal Horse Artillery.
R.H.G.	Royal Horse Guards.
R.H.S.	Royal Humane Society.
R.I.	Royal Institute of Painters in Water Colours; Rhode Island.
R.I.B.A.	Royal Institute of British Architects.
R.I.E.	Royal Indian Engineering (Coll.)
R.I.M.	Royal Indian Marine.
R.I.P.	Requiescat in pace (May he or she rest in peace).
R.M.	Royal Marines; Resident Magistrate.
R.M.A.	Royal Marine Artillery.
R.M.A.	Royal Milit. Academy, Woolwich.
R.M.C.	Royal Military Coll.. Sandhurst.
R.M.L.I.	Royal Marine Light Infantry.
R.M.S.	Royal Microscopical Society; Royal Mail Steamer; Royal Society of Miniature Painters.
R.N.	Royal Navy.
R.N.R.	Royal Naval Reserve.
Rock. The.	Gibraltar.
R.O.I.	Royal Institute of Oil Painters.
Roy.	Royal.
R.S.A.	Royal Scottish Academy.
R.S.E.	Royal Society of Edinburgh.
R.S.L.	Royal Society of Literature.
R.S.O.	Railway Sub-Office.
R.S.P.C.A.	Royal Society for Prevention of Cruelty to Animals.
R.S.V.P.	Fr. Répondez s'il vous plaît (Please answer).

R.S.W.	Royal Scottish Water Colour Society.	
Rt. Hon.	Right Honourable.	
Rt. Rev.	Right Reverend (of a Bishop).	
R.T.S.	Religious Tract Society; Royal Toxopholite Society.	
R.U.	Rugby Union.	
R.U.I.	Royal University of Ireland.	
R.U.S.I.	Royal United Service Institution.	
R.V.	Revised Version.	
R.W.A.	Member of Royal West of England Academy.	
R.W.S.	Royal Society of Painters in Water Colours.	
R.Y.S.	Royal Yacht Squadron.	

T.D.	Territorial Decoration.
T.F.	Territorial Forces.
T.R.H.	Their Royal Highnesses.
Temp.	Temperature; Temporary.
Tenn.	Tennessee (U.S.A.)
Ter. or Terr.	Terrace.
Tex.	Texas (U.S.)
Tn.	Ton.
T.O.	Turn over.
tr.	transpose.
T.R.C.	Thames Rowing Club; Tithes Rent Charge.
Trin.	Trinity.
T.Y.C.	Thames Yacht Club; Two-Year-Old Course.

(S.)	Socialist.
s.	succeeded; South; Saints.
s.	son; shillings.
S.A.	South Australia; South Africa.
Salop	Shropshire.
Sarum	Salisbury.
S.C.	South Carolina (U.S.)
s.c.	Student at the Staff College.
S.C.A.P.A.	Society for Checking the Abuses of Public Advertising.
Sc.D.	Doctor of Science.
Sch.	Scholar.
S.C.L.	Student in Civil Law
scr.	scruple.
sculps.	sculpsit (he engraved).
Sculpt.	Sculptor.
S. Dak.	South Dakota (U.S.)
S.D.F.	Social Democratic Federation.
S.E.	South-east.
Sec.	Secretary.
Selw.	Selwyn Coll. Cambridge.
S.E.R.	South-Eastern Railway.
Serjt.	Serjeant.
S.G.	Solicitor-General.
S.J.	Society of Jesus (Jesuits).
S.L.	Serjeant-at-Law.
S.M.E.	School of Military Engineering.
Soc.	Society.
Sovs.	Sovereigns.
s.p.	sine prole (without issue).
S.P.C.C.	Society for the Prevention of Cruelty to Children.
S.P.C.K.	Society for Promoting Christian Knowledge.
S.P.G.	Society for the Propagation of the Gospel.
S.P.Q.R.	Senatus Populusque Romanus (The Senate and People of Rome).
S.P.R.C.	Society for Prevention and Relief of Cancer.
Sq.	Square.
SS.	Steamship; Saints.
S.S.C.	Solicitor before Supreme Court (Scotland).
S.S.M.	Society of the Sacred Mission.
St.	Street; Saint.
St. Alb. Hall.	St. Alban Hall.
S.T.D.	Sacræ Theologiæ Doctor.
St. Edm. Hall.	St. Edmund Hall.
Stip.	Stipend; Stipendiary.
S.T.L.	Sacræ Theologiæ Lector (Reader or a Professor of Sacred Theology).
S.T.M.	Sacræ Theologiæ Magister.
S.T.P.	Sacræ Theologiæ Professor (Professor of Divinity, old form of D.D.)
Supt.	Superintendent.
Surg.	Surgeon.
Surv.	Surviving.
S.W.	South-west.
Syn.	Synonymous; synonym.

T.	Telephone.
T.A.	Telegraphic Address.
Tasm.	Tasmania.
T.C.D.	Trinity College, Dublin.

(U.)	Unionist.
u.	uncle.
U.C.	University College.
U.F.	United Free Church.
U.K.	United Kingdom.
Ult.	Ultimo (last).
Univ.	University.
U.P.	United Presbyterian.
U.S.	United States.
U.S.A.	United States of America.

V.	Five (Roman numerals); Version; Vicar; Viscount; Vice.
v.	Versus (against).
v. or vid.	Vide (see).
V.A.	Victoria and Albert.
Va.	Virginia (U.S.)
V.C.	Victoria Cross.
V.D.	Volunteer Officers' Decoration.
Ven.	Venerable (of an Archdeacon).
Very Rev.	Very Reverend (of a Dean).
Vet.	Veterinary.
Vice-Adm.	Vice-Admiral.
Vict.	Victoria.
Visc.	Viscount.
Viz.	Videlicet (namely).
V.L.	Vice-Lieutenant.
V.M.H.	Victoria Medal Horticulture.
Vol.	Volume; Volumes.
V.P.	Vice-President.
V.R.	Victoria Regina (Queen Victoria).
V.R. et I.	Victoria Regina et Imperatrix (Victoria Queen and Empress).
Vt.	Vermont (U.S.)

W.	West.
W.A.	West Australia.
Wadh.	Wadham.
Wash.	Washington State (U.S.)
W.I.	West Indies.
Wilts	Wiltshire.
Wis.	Wisconsin (U.S.)
W.L.F.	Women's Liberal Federation.
Wm.	William.
W.O.	War Office.
W.S.	Writer to the Signet.
W.S.P.U.	Women's Social and Political Union.
W. Va.	West Virginia (U.S.)
Wyo.	Wyoming (U.S.)

X.	Ten (Roman numerals).
Xmas.	Christmas.
yds.	yards.
Yeo.	Yeomanry.
Y.M.C.A.	Young Men's Christian Association.
Yorks	Yorkshire.
Yrs.	Years.
Y.W.C.A.	Young Women's Christian Association.

ADDENDA

ADAMS, William Henry, I.S.O. 1902; late First Clerk, Teachers' Pension Office, Treasury Remembrancer's Department, Dublin Castle; *b.* July 1844; *s.* of William Henry Adams, Dublin; *m.* 1st, 1866, Barbara, *d.* of William Greene (*d.* 1892); 2nd, 1893, Jane C., *d.* of John F. Ruthven, Dublin; two *s.* three *d. Educ. :* Private schools. Entered office of Commissioners of National Education, 1858; transferred to Teachers' Pension Office, 1879. *Recreations:* cycling and photography. *Address:* 148 Tritonville Road, Sandymount, Dublin.

(*Died 30 Oct. 1928.*)

ALLBON, Charles F., A.R.E., 1886, water-colour painter, black and white artist and etcher; *s.* of C. F. Allbon; *b.* 1856. *Educ.:* Mr. Hudson's Academy. Joined School of Art, Croydon, 1870; all his art studentship free—won by scholarships; came to London, 1880; elected a member of the Langham, 1885; exhibited Old Post Office, Beddington, Suffolk Street, and engraved in Pictorial World, 1874. *Publications:* The Seasons; Castle Elly in the Olden Time; Breezy Weather; Old Chrome and Chepstow Castle; Evening in Hertfordshire. *Recreations:* reading, chess, backgammon, and cards. *Address:* Cheshunt Cottage, Chingford Green, Essex. [*Died 14 June 1926.*

BAILLIE-GROHMAN, William A.; Justice of the Peace, B.C., Canada ; Author ; *b.* 1 Apr. 1851 ; *m.* 1887, Florence, *d.* of T. Nickalls, Patteson Court, Nutfield, Surrey ; one *s.* one *d. Educ. :* Austria, England, France. *Publications ;* Tyrol and the Tyrolese, 1875 ; Gaddings with a Primitive People ; Camps in the Rockies ; Sport in the Alps ; Fifteen Years' Sport and Life in Western America ; Das Jagdbuch Kaiser Maximilian I. ; edited with his wife and Theodore Roosevelt, the Master of Game, the oldest English Book on Hunting, by Edward, 2nd Duke of York ; The Land in the Mountains, 1907 ; Tyrol, 1908 ; Sport in Art, 1913 ; Contributor to Badminton Library Big Game Vols., Sport in Europe, Quarterly, Nineteenth Century Reviews, and other principal magazines of England and America ; since Majuba Hill disclosures strong advocate of improved National rifle training ; started with Lord Bryce, Sir Martin Conway, and others, the Tyrolese Relief Fund. *Recreations :* big game shooting in the Alps and Rocky Mountains ; rifle shooting (winner of upwards of seventy prizes on the Continent, England, and America) ; historical researches concerning history of the chase, and collecting books and prints relating to this subject, collection consisting of more than 4000. *Address :* (Temp.) Boxley Abbey, Maidstone ; Schloss Matzen, Brixlegg, Tyrol. *Clubs ;* Alpine, Royal Societies. (*Died 27 Nov. 1921.*)

BARRY, Edward, J.P. Co. Cork ; *b.* 1852 ; *m.* Marian, *d.* of late Timothy Sullivan, 1882. *Educ.:* St. Vincent's College, Castleknock ; M.P. (N.) S. Cork Co., 1892-1910. *Address:* Rathbarry, Rosscarbery, Cork.

(*Died 7 Dec. 1927.*)

BARRY, Richard Fitzwilliam; late Crown Solicitor, King's County; *b.* 11 Sep. 1861 ; *o. surv. s.* of late Capt. William Fitzjames Barry, J.P., Resident Magistrate, and Annette Thelaire, *o. d.* of Edmond Hore, Liverpool; *m.* 1890, Catherine Frances, *d.* of late Frederick Augustus White, County Inspector, Royal Irish Constabulary; five *s.* four *d. Educ. :* Trin. Coll., Dublin. B.A. 1888 ; LL.B. 1891 ; claimant to dormant title of Viscount Buttevant, to which his grandfather, James Redmond Barry, lodged a claim, the hearing of which was adjourned, before the Committee of Privileges of the House of Lords, 1825. *Address:* Johns Place, Birr, King's County ; Glandore, Co. Cork. *Clubs:* University, Dublin ; King's County and Ormond. Birr. (*Died 16 June 1916.*)

BARTON, Rt. Hon. Sir Edmund, G.C.M.G., *cr.* 1902 ; P.C. 1901 ; Order of Rising Sun (Japan) First Class, 1903 ; K.C., M.A. ; Hon. D.C.L. Oxon., Hon. LL.D. Cantab. and Edin. ; Fellow of Senate, University of Sydney ; Senior Puisne Judge, High Court of Australia, since 1903 ; *b.* Glebe, Sydney, 18 Jan. 1849 ; *m.* 1877, Jean Mason, *d.* of David Ross ; four *s.* two *d. Educ. :* Public School, Fort Street ; Sydney Grammar School ; Univ., Sydney. Barr. 1871 ; M.L.A. Sydney Univ., 1879-80 ; Wellington, 1880-82 ; East Sydney, 1882-87 and 1891-94 ; and Hastings-Macleay, 1898-99 ; Speaker Legislative Assembly, N.S.W., 1883-87 ; M.L.C. 1887-91, 1897-98 ; Attorney-General, N.S.W., 1889, and again 1891-93 ; Member Federal Convention, Sydney, 1891 ; Senior Representative, N.S.W., to Federal Convention, 1897 ; Leader of Federal Convention, Adelaide, Sydney, Melbourne, 1897-98 ; Leader, N.S.W. Opposition, 1898-99 ; Leader of Delegation to London with Australian Commonwealth Bill, 1900 ; Prime Minister and Minister for External Affairs, first Australian Federal Cabinet, 1901-3 ; Hon. Bencher Gray's Inn, 1902 ; received freedom of City of Edinburgh, 1902. *Recreation:* literature. *Address:* Avenel, Darling Point, Sydney, N.S.W. (*Died 1920.*)

BELFIELD, Major William Seymour, C.M.G. 1919; *s.* of late T. D. Belfield, Torquay; *m.* 1924, Doris Evelyn, *d.* of Rev. George Thompson, Rector of North Bovey, South Devon. Served European War, 1914-19 (despatches, C.M.G.). *Address:* c/o Lloyds Bank, Cox and King's Branch, 6 Pall Mall, S.W.1.

(*Died 3 Nov. 1924.*)

xv

BELL, Ven. John White, M.A.; Archdeacon of Emly, 1918; Incumbent of Cappamore, 1878; Rural Dean, Doone, 1894. *Educ.:* Trinity College, Dublin. Canon and Treasurer of Cashel Cathedral, 1900; retired, 1920. *Address:* 10 Summer Hill, Kingstown, Co. Dublin.
(Died July 1928.)

BERUETE Y. MORET, Aureliano de, Directeur du Musée du Prado since 1918; *b.* 1878; *s.* of late Aureliano Beruete; *m.* 1921, Isabel Regoyos; one *s. Educ.:* Madrid. Docteur en Philosophie et Lettres; écrivain, critique d'art; membre de l'Académie Royale de l'Histoire; owner of a picture gallery. *Publication:* Goya as a portrait painter. *Address:* Celle Genova 19, Madrid. *T.:* 1546-T *M.:* 3049 M. *Clubs:* Athénié, Caviar de Madrid, Gran Pêna, Madrid. *(Died 10 June 1922.)*

BLOOMFIELD, Maurice; Professor of Sanskrit and Comparative Philology, Johns Hopkins University; *b.* Bielitz, Austria, 23 Feb. 1865; *m.* Rosa Zeisler, 1885. *Educ.:* Chicago University; Furman University, South Carolina (M.A. 1879); Yale University; Johns Hopkins University (Ph.D. 1879). Hon. LL.D. of Princeton University, 1896; Furman University, 1898; Doctor of Humane Letters, University of Chicago, 1916; Hon. Doctor, University of Padua, 1922. Edited for the first time from the original Sanskrit manuscripts, the Grihyasamgraha of Gobhilaputra (Leipsic, 1881), and the Sûtra of Kâuçika (New Haven, 1890); translated the Atharva-Veda in the Sacred Books of the East (edited by Max Müller); author of the Atharva-Veda and the Gopatha-Brâhmana, (Strassburg, 1899); joint-editor (with Professor Richard Garbe of the University of Tübingen) of the chromo-photographic reproduction of The Kashmirian Atharva-Veda, the so-called Pâippalâda, 1900; author of Cerberus, The Dog of Hades, 1905; A Concordance of the Vedas (Harvard Oriental Series), 1907; Religion of the Veda, 1907; Rig-Veda Repetitions (Harvard Oriental Series; two volumes), 1916; The Life and Stories of the Jaina Savior, Pârçvanatha, 1919; contributor to numerous learned journals and reviews on subjects connected with the history, religions, mythology, and literature of Ancient India; on Sanskrit, Greek, Latin, and Comparative Grammar; on Ethnology and Science of Religions; Vice-President and President of the American Oriental Society 1905-1910; President of the Linguistic Society of America; Member of the American Philological Association; German Oriental Society; Member and Councillor of the American Philosophical Society; Member of the Committee on International Congresses for the History of Religions; Advisory Council of American Spelling Reform Association; National Institute of Social Sciences; Fellow of the American Academy of Arts and Sciences; Foreign Member of the Royal Bohemian Society of Prague; Hon. Member Finno-Ugrian Society of Helsingsfors; Hardy prize of the Royal Bavarian Academy of Munich, 1908. *Address:* 861 Park Avenue, Baltimore, U.S.A. *T.:* Mount Vernon 4560 W. *Clubs:* University; Johns Hopkins, Baltimore. *(Died 13 June 1928.)*

BONSALL, Arthur Charles; newspaper proprietor and editor since 1880; *b.* 1859; *y. s.* of Isaac Bonsall, Dole Hall, Aberystwith; *m.* 1880, Jane, *e.d.* of J. R. Swift, Lincoln's Inn. *Educ.:* private school and tutor. Proprietor Burlington Publishing Company. *Recreations:* shooting, fishing, golfing, motoring. *Address:* Kennet Lodge, Theale, Berks. *M.:* BL 7076.
(Died April 1924.)

BOTTOMLEY, Col. Herbert, C.M.G. 1900; Imperial Light Horse; *b.* Natal, 18 July 1866; parents both from Yorkshire, England; *m.* 1902, Helena Emma, *d.* of late Captain Barnes, R.N., and *widow* of Mr. Graham. *Educ.:* Diocesan College, Rondebosch, Cape Town. Matriculated, 1884. Entered the law, 1885, and threw it up, 1886; proceeded to Barberton, and spent 3 years prospecting for gold; proceeded to Johannesburg in 1890, and took up gold-mining; was mine manager of Village Main Reef; joined the I.L.H. 1889, as lieutenant; attained rank of colonel, 1901; served South African War, 1899-1902 (C.M.G.); Deputy Inspector of Mines, Transvaal, 1902; Commanded 12th S.A.I. German East Campaign, 1916 (despatches). 1902. *Club:* Rand, Johannesburg. *(Died 20 Sept. 1926.)*

BOURCARD, Gustave (Amaury René); *b.* Rennes (Ille-et-Vilaine), 12 Oct. 1846; writer on art; originaire de Bâle (Suisse) de la grande et vieille famille Christophe Burckhardt 1494, dont il possède le grand arbre généalogique; il est le dernier Bourcard de la branche française. Président d'Honneur de la Société des Amis des Arts de Nantes; Membre d'Honneur de la Société des Peintres-Graveurs Français; Membre d'Honneur de la Société des Peintres Lithographes; Honorary Foreign Fellow of the Royal Society of Painter-Etchers and Engravers; a fait la campagne 1870-71 dans l'armée de Paris. *Publications:* Les Estampes du XVIII siècle 1885; Les Françaises du XVIII siècle, portraits gravés; en collaboration du marquis de Granges de Surgères, 1887; Dessins gouaches estampes et tableaux du XVIII siècle 1898; Felix Buhot, catalogue descriptif de son œuvre gravé, 1899; A travers cinq siècles de gravures, 1903; Graveurs et gravures, essai de bibliographie, 1910; La Cote des Estampes, 1912. *Address:* 24 rue Crébillon, Nantes (Loire-Inférieure), France. *(Died 17 June 1925.)*

BOVELL, John Redman, J.P., I.S.O., 1908; Director of Agriculture, Barbados, B.W.I., 1919; retired under age limit, 31 March 1925; *b.* 31 Dec. 1855; *s.* of late John Bovell, Barbados; *m.* 1897, Annie Louisa, *d.* of late Benjamin T. Bovell, Barbados; one *s. Educ.:* private schools; Lodge School and Harrison College, Barbados. Trained as a sugar planter; Superintendent Botanical Station, 1886; went to Antigua, 1890, to start Skerrett's Training School; Vice-President, Windward District Agricultural Society, 1890; Member of Commission to inquire into sugar-cane borers, 1893; Chairman Emigration Committee, 1895; Superintendent of Agriculture, Barbados, B.W.I., 1898; went to Antigua and St. Kitts to start sugar-cane experiments, 1899; one of the Barbados representatives at the various agricultural conferences held by Imperial Commissioner of Agriculture; sent to St. Vincent to report on damage done in Carib country by volcanic eruptions of 1902-3, 1907; went to Porto Rico, 1909, to report on sugar cane diseases occurring on a number of sugar plantations; went to Saint Croix in 1910 at the request of the Governor of that island to formulate a scheme for a Department of Agriculture; went to Guadeloupe and Martinique in 1917 at the request of the Governors of those Colonies, and with the consent of the Governor of Barbados to report on the sugar industry of those two islands; went to Santo Domingo with consent of the Governor of Barbados, to report on a large sugar estate, 1924. *Publications:* reports and papers in connection with the agriculture of Barbados. *Recreation:* reading. *Address:* Paradise House, Tacarigua, Trinidad, B.W.I. *(Died 23 Nov. 1928.)*

BOWEN, Rev. David, Prebendary of St. Davids. *Address:* Monkton, Pembroke.
(*Died 6 Nov. 1928.*)

BROADBENT, A., R.B.S. *Address:* 436 Fulham Road, S.W.6. (*Died Sept. 1919.*)

BURROWES, Thomas Cosby; *b.* 1856; *s.* of late James Edward Burrowes and Mary Anne, *y. d.* of John Nesbitt of Lismore; *m.* 1885, Anna Frances Maxwell, *s.* of 10th Baron Farnham; *S.* uncle, 1886; J.P. Co. Cavan; High Sheriff, 1888. *Address:* Lismore, Cavan.
(*Died 20 Feb. 1925.*)

BURTON, Maj.-Gen. Benjamin, C.B. 1900; C.M.G. 1917; R.A.; *b.* 10 Mar. 1855; *s.* of Rev. Benjamin Burton. *Educ.:* Eton; R.M.A., Woolwich. Entered army, 1874; Lieut.-Colonel, 1900; served South Africa, 1900-1 (despatches, medal with five clasps, C.B.). *Clubs:* Naval and Military, Cavalry; Kildare Street, Dublin.
(*Died 6 Aug. 1921.*)

CHAPLIN, 1st Viscount, *cr.* 1916, of St. Oswalds, Blankney, in the county of Lincoln; **Henry Chaplin,** P.C. 1885; J.P., D.L.; *b.* 22 Dec. 1840; *e. s.* of late Rev. H. Chaplin and Caroline Horatia, *d.* of Wm. Ellice; *m.* Florence, *d.* of 3rd Duke of Sutherland, 1876 (*d.* 1881); one *s.* two *d. Educ.:* Harrow; Christ Church, Oxford. Hon. LL.D., Edinburgh, 1890. M.P. Mid Lincolnshire, afterwards the Sleaford Division of Lincolnshire, 1868-1906; Chancellor of Duchy of Lancaster, 1885-1886; President of Board of Agriculture, 1886-92; President of Local Government Board, 1895-1900; Member of Royal Commission on Agriculture, 1881 and 1893; Member of Royal Commission on Horse Breeding, 1887; Member of Royal Commission on Gold and Silver, 1889; Member of Royal Commission on Supply of Food and Raw Material in Time of War, 1903; Member of Tariff Commission, and Chairman of its Agricultural Committee, 1904; M.P. (U.) Wimbledon Div. Surrey, 1907-16. *Recreations:* sport of all kinds—hunting, racing, deerstalking, shooting. *Heir: s.* Hon. Eric Chaplin, *q.v. Address:* 6 Charles Street, Berkeley Square, W.1; *T.:* Gerrard 7184; Hall Farm, Brixworth. Northants. *Clubs:* Athenæum, Carlton, Marlborough, Turf, Jockey.
(*Died 29 May 1923.*)

CHURCHILL, William; Officier de l'Ordre de Leopold II., 1920; *b.* Brooklyn, New York, 1859; *e. s.* of William Churchill and Sarah, *d.* of Rev. John Starkweather; married; no *c. Educ.:* Yale University. United States Consul-General for Samoa, 1896; Judge of Consular Court with exclusive jurisdiction over American citizens; Senior Member of the Consular Board in execution of the Berlin General Act; acted jointly with British and German Consuls as adviser to Malietoa Laupepa, King of Samoa; Receiver and Custodian of Revenues of Samoa; President of the Municipality of Apia; commission extended as Consul-General for Tonga at Nukualofa, 1897; Division of Visé of Federal Committee of Public Information, 1917; special agent Department of State, 1918; Corresponding Member Hawaiian Historical Society, 1898; Corresponding Member Polynesian Society, 1899; Member American Philological Association, 1910; Fellow Royal Anthropological Institute, 1912; Hon. Member Polynesian Society, 1913; Corresponding Member American Geographical Society, Member Association American Geographers, 1914; Member Institut Suisse d'Anthropologie Générale, 1914; Member American Association for the Advancement of Science, 1916; Member American Ethnological Society, 1916; Member Archæological Institute of America, 1916; Research Associate in Primitive Philology of the Carnegie Institution of Washington, 1915; Associate of the Carnegie Institution, 1917; National Geographic Society, 1920; Honorary Consulting Ethnologist, Bishop Museum Honolulu and Dominick Pacific Exploration Fund, 1920. *Publications:* A Princess of Fiji, 1892; The Polynesian Wanderings, Tracks of the Migration deduced from an Examination of the Proto-Samoan Content of Efaté and other Languages of Melanesia, 1910; Beach-la-Mar, the Jargon or Trade Speech of the Western Pacific, 1911; Easter Island, Rapanui Speech and the Peopling of South-east Polynesia, 1912; The Subanu, Studies of a Sub-Visayan Mountain Folk of Mindanao (with Colonel John Park Finley, United States Army), 1913; Sissano, Movements of Migration within and through Melanesia; Samoan Kava Custom, 1916; Club Types of Nuclear Polynesia, 1917; editor Malayo-Polynesian section Standard Dictionary, 1913; editorial contributor New International Encyclopædia, 1914; many monographs on ethnological and philological topics. *Clubs:* Cosmos. Washington; Yale, New York.
(*Died 9 June 1920.*)

COLLIER, James; *b.* Dunfermline, Scotland, 1846; *m.* 1905, Florence, *d.* of Sir W. Durrant, 5th Bart. *Educ.:* Universities of St. Andrews and Edinburgh, 1863-68. Assistant to Herbert Spencer, 1871-80. *Publications:* joint author, with Spencer, of Descriptive Sociology, and with Prof. Royce, Harvard, of volume on Spencer; author of Sir George Grey: an Historical Biography; The Pastoral Age in Australasia; The Evolution of Colonies, etc.; editor of Collins's English Colony in N.S. Wales, and Wakefield's Art of Colonization; etc. *Address:* St. Helena. Manly, Sydney, Australia. (*Died 1925.*)

CRAIGHEAD, Edwin Boone. M.A., LL.D., D.C.L.; *b.* Ham's Prairie, Missouri 1861; *m.* 1889, Kate Johnson; two *s.* one *d. Educ.:* Westminster College, Central College, Mo.; Vanderbilt University; Leipzig; Sorbonne. Professor of Greek, Wofford College, S.C., 1890-93; President Clemson College (South Carolina A. and M. College), Clemson, S.C., 1893-97; Central College, Fayette, Mo., 1897-1901; Missouri State Normal School, Warrensburg, 1901-4; Tulane University, N.O., 1904-1912; President University of Montana, 1912-15; Commissioner of Education, North Dakota, 1915-17; Editor and Owner Billings Star, Weekly and Daily New North-West, Missoula, Mont.; member of American Board, The Hibbert Journal; member Board of Trustees Carnegie Foundation for the Advancement of Teaching; Fellow American Scientific Association; Commissioner of Education for schools of higher education in North Dakota. *Publications:* Skepticism as an Element of Progress; John C. Calhoun; Medical Education in the South; Functions and Limitations of Governing Boards; Inaugural Address at Tulane University and others. *Address:* Missoula, Montana.
(*Died 1920.*)

CUNNINGHAM, Rt. Rev. John F., D.D., Bishop of Concordia since 1898; *b.* Mountcoul, Ireland, 1842. *Educ.:* Listowrie, Co. Kerry. Parish of Irremore, Ireland; Atchison, Kans., Milwaukee, Wis. Missionary at Fort Scott, Kans., and south-east part of the State, and five Counties in State of Missouri; Pastor, Laurence, Kans.; three years collecting in the country for the Leavenworth Cathedral, and Kansas sufferers; Pastor of Topeka; Vicar-General of the Diocese of Leavenworth, 1881 Rector of the Leavenworth Cathedral; Administrator of the Diocese in absence of the Ordinary Precognised Bishop of Concordia, 1882. *Ad*

dress: Concordia, Kansas, U.S.A.
(*Died 23 June 1919.*)

DAVIS, Major William Hathaway,
D.S.O. 1918 ; M.C. ; M.A.; ; Headmaster of the William Ellis School, N.W.5, since 1919 ; *b.* 1881 ; *s.* of A. J. Davis, Brandesburton, Hull ; *m.* Isabelle Kathleen Watkins, *d.* of T. Watkins Baker ; one *s.* *Educ.:* Hyner's College, Hull ; The Yorkshire College, Victoria University. B.A. 1903 ; M.A. 1906 ; Victoria University, Salt Scholar : Gladstone Prizeman; Editor of Gryphon ; Chairman of Union ; Assistant Master at Leeds Central High School, 1904-6 ; Second Master of Normanton Grammar School, 1906-14 ; served European War, 1914-19 ; commissioned to K.O.Y.L.I. 1914 ; transferred to Machine Gun Corps, 1916 ; service in France as O.C. Machine Gun Company with rank of Major, 1916-17 (M.C., despatches, D.S.O.). *Address:* 141 Woodstock Avenue, N.W.11. *T.:* Speedwell 4616. (*Died 7 Dec. 1928.*)

DAWNAY, Hon. Eustace (Henry),
J.P., D.L. ; 5th *s.* of 7th Viscount Downe ; *b.* 15 April 1850 ; *m.* 1883, Lady Evelyn de Vere Capel, *g.d.* of 6th Earl of Essex ; one *s.* [Capt. Cuthbert Dawnay, M.C. ; *m.* 1921, Marjorie, *o. c.* of Reginald Loder], two *d.* Late Lieutenant Coldstream Guards ; served Egypt, 1882 (medal and star). *Address :* 9 Sussex Square, W.2. *T. :* Paddington 1858. *Clubs :* Guards' Arthur's, Bath. (*Died 15 Dec. 1928.*)

DEACON, Col. William Thomas, C.B. 1900 ; retired ; late of 13th Australian Light Horse Regt. (Queensland Mounted Infantry) ; *b.* Ipswich, Queensland, 10 July 1850 ; *s.* of W. T. Deacon and Louisa Shenton ; *m.* 1st, 1874, Elvina Buglar; one *s.* two *d.* ; 2nd, 1884, Isabella M'Nevin ; one *d.* *Educ.:* private schools ; Collegiate School, Ipswich. Served South Africa, 2nd in Command 4th Queensland Imperial Bushmen Contingent subsequently in command (despatches twice, C.B., Queen's medal, four clasps). *Address :* Bellemount, Ipswich, Queensland. *Club:* United Service, Brisbane.
(*Died 4 May 1916.*)

DE LEMOS, Charles Herman, I.S.O. 1915 ; *b.* 1855 ; *m.* 1885, Guillermina Clemencia, *d.* of John Dalton, Consul, U.S.A. ; one *d.* *Educ.:* private tutor ; Continent. British Vice-Consul at Ciudad, Bolivar, 1887-99 ; H.M. Consul for the States of Bolivar, Apure, etc. (Venezuela), 1899 ; retired, 1915. *Address:* 11 St. John's Road, Harrow. *T. :* Harrow. 0574. *Club:* Union. (*Died 27 Nov. 1928.*)

DENNEHY, William Francis ; has edited Irish Catholic since 1888, and sole proprietor since 1912 ; late Editor of Irish Daily Independent and Nation, Dublin ; was Editor of the Nation from 1896 until the period of its amalgamation with the Independent in 1900 ; *b.* Kingstown, Co. Dublin ; *e. s.* of late Alderman Cornelius Dennehy, J.P., of Dublin, and Newtown Cashel, Co. Longford. Secretary to Lord Mayor of Dublin, 1886-87 ; originated the Irish Institute of Commerce and Industries, 1903 ; in the same year launched the project of an Irish International Exhibition, to be held in Dublin in 1906, under the patronage of the King ; has devoted much attention to the study of Irish economic and commercial problems ; hon. secy. Irish Institute of Commerce, and also of the Irish International Exhibition of 1907 ; acted as an hon. sec. of the Citizens' Committees for the reception of King Edward VII. and of King George V. on their first visits to Dublin after their accession to the Throne ; publicly thanked by H.E. Cardinal Logue, 1915, on behalf of the

Bishops of Ireland for his services in securing appointment of sufficiency of catholic chaplains in Army and Navy ; a Governor, Royal Hospital for Incurables. *Publications:* The Story of the Union told by its Plotters ; and many contributions to English and American reviews and journals. *Address:* 28 Leeson Park, Dublin. (*Died 2 March 1918.*)

DOREZ, Léon Louis Marie, Librarian in the Department of Manuscripts of the Bibliothèque nationale, Paris, since 1905 ; *b.* Villemaur, Aube, France, 17 July 1864 ; *m.* 1887, Berthe Marie Louise Dorez; one *d.* *Educ.:* École des Hautes Études ; Sorbonne ; École des Chartes. Member of the French School at Rome, Palazzo Farnese, 1890-93 ; entered the National Library, Paris, as an assistant, 1893 ; Hon. LL.D. St. Andrews, 1911 ; Editor of the Revue des Bibliothèques (26 vol.), and of the Bibliothèque littéraire de la Renaissance (17 vol.). *Publications:* more than one hundred papers in different French and Italian reviews on the artistic, literary, and political history of the Renaissance in France and Italy ; Chronique d'Antonio Morosini, 4 vol. ; Itinéraire de Jérôme Maurand d'Antibes à Constantinople ; La Canzone delle Virtù e delle Scienze di Bartolomeo di Bartoli ; Les manuscrits à peintures de Lord Leicester à Holkham Hall, Norfolk ; Pétrarque, Vie de César ; Le Psautier de Paul III ; Pontifical peint pour le cardinal Giuliano Della Rovere par Francesco dai Libri de Vérone ; Notice sur un recueil de poésies latines et un portrait de l'humaniste véronais Leonardo Montagna ; Tables des Monuments et Mémoires de la Fondation Piot ; Catalogue de la Collection Alexandre Bixio ; Nouvelles recherches sur Michel-Ange et son entourage ; Léonard de Vinci au Service de Louis XII. et de François I. ; Léonard de Vinci et Jean Perréal, etc. *Address:* 10, rue Littré, Paris (6e) ; Villemaur-sur-Vanne, Aube.
(*Died 25 Jan. 1922.*)

DOTTIN, Henri Georges ; professeur à l'Université de Rennes ; conseiller municipal de Rennes ; *b.* Liancourt (Oise), 29 oct. 1863 ; fils de Charles Henri Dottin, homme de lettres ; *m.* Marie Delaunay, fille du professeur à l'Université de Rennes ; two *s.* *Educ.:* lycée de Laval. Etudiant à la Faculté des lettres de Rennes, 1888-84 ; étudiant à la Sorbonne, élévé à l'Ecole des Hautes Etudes, 1884-91 ; agrégé de grammaire, 1890 ; docteur ès lettres, 1897 ; Maitre de conférences à la Faculté des lettres de Dijon, 1891-92 ; Maître de conférences de grammaire et philologie, 1892-1903, puis Professeur de grec à la Faculté des lettres de Rennes, 1903 ; doyen de la Faculté des Lettres, 1910 ; correspondant de l'Institut de France, 1919. *Publications:* Les Formations verbales en-r en sanskrit, en italique et en celtique, 1896 ; De eis in Iliade inclusis hominum nominibus quao non unice propria nomina sunt, 1896 ; Glossaire des parlers du Bas-Maine, 1899 ; Contes irlandais traduits du gaélique, 1901 ; Contes et légendes d'Irlande traduits du gaélique, 1901 ; Glossaire du parler de Pléchâtel (Ille et Vilaine), 1901 ; Manuel pour servir à l'étude de l'antiquité celtique, 1906, 2nd ed. 1915; Louis Eunius ou le Purgatoire de Saint Patrice, mystère breton, 1911 ; Manuel d'irlandais moyen, 1913 ; Les Anciens Peuples del'Europe, 1916 ; La langue gauloise, 1920 ; Les Littératures celtiques, 1924 ; L'épopée irlandaise, 1925. *Address:* 39, boulevard Sévigné. Rennes.
(*Died 11 Jan. 1928.*)

DRUMMOND, His Honour Judge Michael, K.C. Ireland ; County Court Judge, Cos. Meath, Westmeath, Longford, and King's County, 1914-24 ; County Court Judge and

Chairman of Quarter Sessions, Cos. Cavan and Leitrim, 1904-14; *b.* 1850. Irish Bar, 1872; Inner Bar, 1891; Bencher of King's Inns, Dublin, 1899. *Address:* 22 Upper Fitzwilliam Street, Dublin. *(Died 1921.)*

DUGAS, Hon. Francois Octave, B.C.L., K.C.; *b.* St. Jacques, Co. Montcalm, 12 Apr. 1857; *s.* of Aimé Dugas and Sophie Poirier; *m.* 1882, Marie Alix Godin; two *s. Educ.:* St. Mary's Coll., Montreal; McGill University. Town Councillor of Joliette, 1890-1900; Crown Prosecutor for district of Joliette, 1887-92 and 1897-1909; a Puisne Judge of the Superior Court for Province Quebec, 1909; M.P., Canada, 1900-9. *Address:* Joliette, Quebec, Canada. *(Died 23 June 1918.)*

ELWELL, Colonel Francis Edwin, Sc., S.A.R.; Commissioned Speaker for League of Nations; Sculptor and Writer on Art; *b.* Concord, Mass., 15 June 1858; Scotch-English; *s.* of John W. Elwell and Clara Farrar-Elwell; *m.* 1st; two *s.*; 2nd, Annie Marion Benjamin-Elwell, British subject before her marriage; one *s. Educ.:* Concord, Mass.; Paris. Highest award at Columbia Exposition for Statue of Dickens and Little Nell; five medals, one from the King of Belgium; Hon. Member of the Dickens Fellowship of London; Hon. Member Cincinnati Art Club; Hon. Colonel 7th Rhode Island Infantry; Delegate for the State of New Jersey for the Atlantic Congress for the League of Nations; for some years Curator of Ancient and Modern Statuary, Metropolitan Museum of Art, New York City; worked in two Aeroplane Plants, one Ammunition Plant, and unofficial worker in Navy Intelligence Bureau, U.S.N., European War; lectured at Harvard and other Universities; newspaper and editorial work; first to write about the Reuniting of the Anglo-Saxon Race before the war. *Works:* thirty or forty statues and works in Sculpture—three in Europe. *Recreations:* prayer, work, play, and sleep. *Address:* Darien, Fairfield County, Connecticut. *T.:* Stamford 2723. *Clubs:* Cincinnati Art, Sons of the American Revolution, New York. *(Died 23 Jan. 1922.)*

EVANS, Maurice Smethurst, C.M.G. 1902; J.P.; *b.* 30 July 1854; *s.* of E. H. Evans, Manchester; *m.* 1886, Elizabeth Fairweather Murray, Edinburgh; went to Natal, 1875; Member Legislative Assembly, 1897. *Publications:* Black and White in South-East Africa; The Native Problem in Natal; Problem of Production in Natal; Studies in the Southern States from a South African Point of View. *Address:* Hillcrest, Ridge Road, Durban, Natal. *Club:* Durban. *(Died 8 April 1920.)*

EVERARD, Captain Andrew Robert Guy, J.P.; late 54th Regiment; *s.* of late R. G. Everard, High Sheriff and D.L. for Somerset; *m.* Louisa Emily, *d.* of Rev. H. Townend; one *s.* four *d. Educ.:* Eton. Lord of the manors of Otterhampton, Exton; and patron of the living of Otterhampton, Somerset. *Address:* Hill House, nr. Bridgwater; Stone Lodge, Exton, Dulverton.
(Died June 1925.)

FAWCETT, Lieut.-Col. P. H., D.S.O., retired; Royal Artillery; *b.* Torquay, 1867; *s.* of E. B. Fawcett, Torquay, and *g.s.* of Henry Fawcett, of Broadfields, York, and Myra, *d.* of Col. A. M. McDougall, Bengal Army; *m.* Nina, *d.* of G. W. Paterson, Ceylon Civil Service; two *s.* one *d. Educ.:* Newton College, S. Devon; Westminster (Exhibitioner); R.M.A., Woolwich. Joined R.A., 1886; served Ceylon, England, Malta, Hong Kong, Ireland, in R.G.A. and Staff;

received R.G.S. Diploma, 1900, for surveying; mission interior Morocco, 1901; lent to Bolivian Government as Boundary Commissioner, 1906-1910; retired from Army, 1910, continuing exploration in S. America, returning for War, close 1914; commanded Brigade R.F.A. Heavy Artillery, and was C.R.S.O. in France till 1919 (D.S.O., despatches four times); returned S. America, 1919-22, for exploration; received Founder's Medal, R.G.S., 1917. *Publications:* geographical, travel, and journalistic articles in newspapers and magazines. *Recreations:* all sports, exploration, surveying and prospecting, artist (exhibitor Royal Academy in black and white), archæology, philosophy, yacht designing building, and navigating, motoring. *Address:* c/o Royal Bank of Canada, Rio de Janeiro, Brazil, S. America. *M.:* FJ 1867. *(Died 1925.)*

FERGUSON, Hon. William Nassau; Justice of Appeal in Supreme Court, Ontario, since 1916; 3rd *s.* of Isaac Ferguson of Cookstown, Ontario, who came to Canada from Killoughter, County Cavan, Ireland, and Emily J., *d.* of late Lieut.-Col. Ogle R. Gowan, M.P. for Leeds and Grenville, Ont.; *b.* Cookstown, 31 Dec. 1869; unmarried. *Educ.:* Upper Canada College and Osgoode Hall, Toronto. Called to bar, 1894; Bencher, Law Society, Upper Canada, 1916; K.C. 1908; member of Board of Governors, Wycliffe College, Toronto, and of Board of Governors of Hospital for Sick Children, Toronto; Anglican; Conservative. *Recreations:* Has been identified with outdoor sports. *Address:* 244 St. George Street, Toronto. *T.A.:* Rallim, Toronto. *T.:* Hillcrest 1724 and Adelaide 4101. *Clubs:* British Empire; Albany, York, National, Royal Canadian Yacht, Ontario Jockey, Toronto Hunt, Toronto Golf, Toronto. *(Died 9 Nov. 1928.)*

FISET, Hon. Jean Baptiste Romuald, M.D.; *b.* St. Cuthbert, P.Q., 7 Feb. 1843; *s.* of Henri Fiset of St. Cuthbert; *m.* 1st, 1869, Aimée, *d.* of late Honoré Plamondon of Quebec; 2nd, Emelina Loranger, widow of Captain H. Pouliot; five *s.* three *d. Educ.:* Montreal College, classical course; Laval University, Quebec, as M.D., 1868. Is a Governor of the College of Physicians and Surgeons of Quebec; has been Councillor and subsequently Mayor of Rimouski, Quebec, 1871; took his certificates of Captain, Military School, Quebec, 1865; served Fenian raids, 1865-66 and 1870; Surgeon of 89th Batt. Rimouski, 1871; Surgeon-Major, 1895; retired, 1899, with rank of Lieut.-Col.; Member for Rimouski, Quebec, House of Commons, 1872-82, 1887-91, and 1896; Senator, 1897; Liberal. *Recreations:* hunting and fishing. *Address:* Rimouski, Province of Quebec, Canada. *Club:* President of Fishing and Game Club, Rimouski, Quebec. *(Died 6 Jan. 1917.)*

FORNERET, Ven. George Augustus, M.A.; D.D., Queen's, Kingston; Rector All Saints' Church, Hamilton, Ontario; Archdeacon of Hamilton; Chaplain and Hon. Lt.-Col., 13th Royal Regt.; *s.* of Lt.-Col. C. Alexr. Forneret, J.P. of Berthier-en-haut, Que.; *g. s.* of Maj. Forneret, 60th Regt. Imperial Army; *m.* Adelaide Robbins; one *s.* one *d. Educ.:* Berthier Grammar School; Bishop's College School; M'Gill University; Montreal Diocesan Theological College. Curate Christ Church Cathedral, Montreal, 1875; S.P.G. Missionary Diocese Saskatchewan, 1877-79; Rector Dunham, P. Que., 1879-81; Curate St. Thomas Church, St. Catharine's, Ont., 1881-82; Curate-in-Charge St. James', Dundas, Ont., 1882-85; Rector All Saints', Hamilton, 1886; Has served as Rural Dean of Hamilton. *Publication:* How Shall I Give? *Recreation:* militia.

Address: 13 Queen Street, South Hamilton, Ontario, Canada. *T.*: 153. *Club:* Military Institute, Toronto. *(Died 1927.)*

FOWKE, Frank Rede; late Assistant Secretary, Board of Education ; *b.* 17 March 1847 ; 2nd *s.* of Captain Francis Fowke, R.E., and Louisa Charlotte, *e.d.* of Rev. Robert Rede Rede ; *m.* 1870, Isabella Langdale, 4th *d.* of Sir Henry Cole, K.C.B. ; three *d. Educ.:* Eton, and by tutor. On the staff of L'Exposition Universelle de 1867 à Paris ; after serving temporarily in the Department of Science and Art (subsequently merged in the Board of Education), joined its permanent staff, 1868 ; Hon. Secretary of the Committee on Solar Physics throughout its duration, 1879-1918. *Publications:* The Bayeux Tapestry reproduced in Autotype Plates, with Historic Notes, published under the sanction of the Science and Art Department of the Committee of Council on Education, by the Arundel Society, 1875 ; partially reprinted in Ex Libris Series and in Bohn's Library. *Recreations:* painting, books. *Club:* Chelsea Arts. *(Died 2 Jan. 1927.)*

FRASER, Mrs. Hugh, novelist and writer of travels ; *b.* Rome ; *d.* of Thomas Crawford, sculptor, and Louisa Cutler Ward ; *sis.* of late Marion Crawford ; *m.* Hugh Fraser, late H.M. Minister to Japan. *Educ.:* Bonchurch, by Miss E. M. Sewell, and in Rome. Accompanied her husband to China, South America, and Japan, as well as to various Courts of Europe ; has travelled much in the United States ; became a Catholic in 1884 ; and a widow in 1894. *Publications:* The Brown Ambassador, 1895 ; Palladia, 1896 ; A Chapter of Accidents, 1897 ; The Looms of Time, 1898 ; A Diplomatist's Wife in Japan, 1899 ; The Customs of the Country, or, Tales of New Japan, 1899 ; The Splendid Porsenna, 1899 ; A Little Grey Sheep ; Marna's Mutiny, 1901 ; The Stolen Emperor : a Tale of Old Japan, 1903 ; The Slaking of the Sword, 1904 ; A Diplomatist's Wife in many Lands, 1911 ; Further Reminiscences of a Diplomat's Wife, 1912 ; Captain Corbeau's Adventure, 1913 ; Italian Yesterdays, 1914 ; Seven Years on the Pacific Slope, 1915 ; Storied Italy, 1916. *Recreations:* reading old books, seeing old friends, Drama of the day. *(Died 7 June 1922.)*

FRASER, Sir John George, Kt., *cr.* 1905 ; M.L.C. ; LL.D. Aberdeen ; *b.* Beaufort West, S.A., 17 Dec. 1840 ; *s.* of Rev. Colin Mackenzie Fraser, minister of Dutch Reformed Church ; *m.* 1866, Dorothea, 2nd *d.* of A. A. Ortlepp, Colesberg ; three *s.* six *d. Educ.:* Free Church Inst., Inverness ; Marischal and King's Colleges, Aberdeen. Returned to South Africa, 1861 ; fought in Basuto War ; was Secretary to Sir John Brand ; Registrar of High Court, Secretary to Volksraad, and Master of Orphan Chamber, Orange Free State ; retired from Government service, 1877 ; represented Bloemfontein in Volksraad, 1880-99 ; stood for President, 1896 ; M.L.C. Orange River Colony, 1902 ; Member Inter-Colonial Council, O.R.C. and Transvaal, 1904 ; Member of Parliament and Leader of Opposition in Parliament, O.R.C. ; Senator, Union Parliament of South Africa, 1910-20. *Address:* Clach-na-Cuddin Lodge, Bloemfontein. *(Died June 1927.)*

GARSTIN, John Ribton, F.S.A. (Lond. and Scot.) ; ex-President Royal Society Antiquaries of Ireland ; ex-Vice-President Royal Irish Academy ; D.L., J.P.; a Visitor of the National Museum Dublin, and Governor of Armagh Library and Observatory: *o. c.* of William Garstin of Dublin ; *b.* 27 Dec. 1836 ; *m.* 1864, Martha (*d.* 1910), *o. d.* of J. A. Durham of Elm Lodge, Hampton, Middlesex : three *d. Educ.:*

Cheltenham College; Dublin Univ., M.A., LL.B. and B.D. Dublin. Educated for Holy Orders: purchased the family estate in the Co. Louth, 1877 ; High Sheriff, Co. Louth, 1879. *Recreations:* reading, bibliography, and public duties. *Address:* Braganstown, Castlebellingham, Co. Louth. *(Died 16 June 1917.)*

GRIGGS, Hon. John William ; *b.* New Jersey, 10 July 1849. *Educ.:* Lafayette University. Admitted to Bar, 1871 ; Member General Assembly, N.J., 1876-77 ; State Senator, 1882-88 ; President Senate, N.J., 1886 ; Governor of New Jersey, 1896-1898 ; Attorney-General, 1898-1901. Republican. *Address:* Paterson, New Jersey. *[Died 28 Nov. 1927.*

GWYNN, Rev. John, D.D. Dublin ; D.C.L. Oxon. ; Regius Professor of Divinity, Dublin University, 1888-1907 ; *b.* Larne, 28 Aug. 1827 ; *e.s.* of Rev. Stephen Gwynn ; *m.* 1862, Lucy (*d.* 1907), *e. d.* of late Wm. Smith O'Brien, of Cahirmoyle, Co. Limerick ; six *s.* two *d. Educ.:* Royal School, Enniskillen ; Trinity Coll. Dublin. Fellow 1853-1864 ; Warden of St. Columba's, 1856-64 ; Rector of Tullyaughnish, 1863-82 ; Dean of Raphoe, 1873-82 ; Rector of Templemore and Dean of Derry, 1882-83 ; Archbishop King's Lecturer in Divinity (Dublin Univ.), 1883-88. *Publications:* Commentary on Epistle to Philippians, with Introduction (in Speaker's Commentary), 1881, and several articles in Smith and Wace's Dictionary of Christian Biography, and in Hermathena ; also, The Apocalypse in a Syriac Version hitherto unknown, with critical notes, etc. ; with Introductory Dissertation on the Syriac Versions of the Apocalypse, 1897 ; Selections from Ephraim and Aphrahat, translated from the Syriac, with Introduction, 1898 ; Remnants of the later Syriac Versions of the Old and New Testament, 1909 ; the Book of Armagh, with Introduction, 1913. *Address:* Trinity College, Dublin ; Ashbrook, Clontarf. *[Died 2 April 1917.*

HANDS, Rev. John Compton, J.P. ; Hon. Canon, St. Paul's Cathedral, St. Helena, 1895-1910 ; *b.* Daventry, May 1842 ; *m.* 1869, Alice Mary Metcalfe ; two *s.* two *d. Educ.:* private schools, Banbury, and other places ; St. Augustine's College, Canterbury. Ordained, 1868 ; Curate of St. Matthew's Longwood, 1868-75 ; Vicar of St. Matthew's, 1875-1910 ; Curate of St. John's, Jamestown, 1892-1900 ; Vicar-General of St. Helena, 1890-91, 1904-5, 1909 ; Acting Chaplain to Forces, 1884-1906. *Recreation:* driving. *Address:* Willow Bank, Island of St. Helena. *[Died Nov. 1928.*

HARE, Francis, M.D. Durham ; M.R.C.S. England ; Medical Superintendent, Oaklands, Beckenham ; late Medical Superintendent, Norwood Sanatorium ; *b.* Dublin, 12 Feb. 1858 ; *s.* of Matthias Hare, LL.D., and Frances Louisa Everard ; *m.* 1902, Ethel Maud Bell ; one *s. Educ.:* Fettes College, Edinburgh. Surgeon, P. and O. S.N. Co. ; Surgeon-Superintendent Queensland Immigration Service ; Resident Medical Officer, Brisbane General Hospital ; Medical Superintendent and acting Medical Superintendent, Brisbane General Hospital ; Medical Superintendent, Charters Towers District Hospital, Queensland ; Inspector-General of Hospitals for Queensland ; Medical Superintendent and Visiting Physician, Diamantina Hospital for Chronic Diseases, Queensland ; Consulting Physician, Brisbane General Hospital. *Publications:* The Cold-Bath Treatment of Typhoid Fever ; The Food Factor in Disease ; On Alcoholism : its clinical aspects and treatment. *Recreations:*

various. *Address:* Oaklands, 15 The Avenue, Beckenham, Kent. *(Died 9 Dec. 1928.)*

HAY, Sir William Henry, 8th Bt., of Alderston, *cr.* 1703; *s.* of William Thomas Hay (*s.* of 6th Bt.), and Isabella, *d.* of Robert Charles, Melbourne; *b.* 30 May 1867; *S.* uncle, 1916. *Heir: b.* Edward Hamilton, *b.* 30 May 1870 (did not prove his succession, or use the title; *d.* 1936). *[Died 3 July 1927.*

HAYES, Hugh, a practising solicitor, since 1882; M.P.(C.U.), West Down, 1922. *Address:* Lurgan, Co. Down. *(Died 5 Sept. 1928.)*

HAYFORD, John Fillmore, Director, College of Engineering, Northwestern University, since 1909; *b.* Rouse's Point, New York, 19 May 1868; *s.* of Hiram Hayford and Mildred Alevia Fillmore; *m.* 1894, Lucy Stone, of Charlotte, New York. *Educ.:* Cornell University. Computer U.S. Coast and Geodetic Survey, 1889; Assistant Astronomer to International Boundary Commission, U.S. and Mexico, in charge of one of field parties, 1892-93; with U.S. Coast and Geodetic Survey, 1894-95; Instructor, Civil Engineering, Cornell University, 1895-98; Expert Computer and Geodesist, U.S. Coast and Geodetic Survey, 1898-99, and Inspector of Geodetic Work and Chief of Computing Division, 1900-9; Member National Advisory Com. for Aeronautics; Fellow A.A.A.S.; Member National Acad. Sciences; Am. Philos. Soc., Am. Astron. Soc., Am. Soc. C.E., Western Soc. Engrs. *Publications:* Geodetic Astronomy, 1898; numerous monographs in reports of U.S. Coast and Geodetic Survey. *Address:* 574 Ingleside Park, Evanston, Ill., U.S.A. *(Died 10 March 1925.)*

HERBERT, Hilary A., LL.D.; lawyer in Washington, D.C., U.S.A.; *b.* South Carolina; *s.* of Thos. E. and Dorothy T.; *m.* 1867, Ella B. Smith, Selma, Alabama (*d.* 1885); one *s.* one *d.* *Educ.:* Universities of Alabama and Virginia. Was Col. 8th Alabama Confederate Volunteers; disabled at Wilderness; practised law at Greenville and Montgomery, Alabama; was sixteen years representative in Congress from Alabama; Secretary U.S. Navy, 1893-97. *Publications:* Why the Solid South, a History of Reconstruction; The Abolition Crusade and its Consequences; magazine articles. *Recreations:* fishing, hunting. *Address:* 1612, 21st Street, Washington, D.C. *Clubs:* Metropolitan, Army and Navy, Washington. *(Died 6 March 1919.)*

HOARE, Edward Wallis, F.R.C.V.S.; Practising Veterinary Surgeon; *b.* 9 Oct. 1863; *s.* of late Capt. Wm. Jesse Hoare of Carrigrohane Castle, Co. Cork (late 7th Royal Fusiliers); *m.* 1899, Emily, B.A., N.U.I., *d.* of late H. L. Helen, Dublin; one *s.* five *d.* *Educ.:* privately, New Veterinary College, Edinburgh (M.R.C.V.S. 1886, and passed the Fellowship Examination, 1892); Lecturer in Veterinary Science, University College, Cork; late Member of the Board of Examiners, Royal College of Veterinary Surgeons; late External Examiner in Veterinary Jurisprudence, Toxicology, and Sanitary Law, University of Liverpool; Hon. Member of the American Veterinary Medical Association; Editor of the Veterinary News. *Publications:* A System of Veterinary Medicine, in 2 volumes, 1916; Veterinary Therapeutics 3rd edition, 1916; various papers on Veterinary Science. *Recreation:* horticulture. *Address:* 18 Cook Street, Cork; Clover Hill, Blackrock. *T.A.:* Hoare V. S., Cork. *T.:* 65 Y. *(Died 26 Nov. 1920.)*

HOFMEYR, George Morgan, B.A. (Cape University); Rector of Grey University College, Bloemfontein, since 1928; *b.* Montagu, Cape Colony, 3 July 1867; *s.* of Rev. S. Hofmeyr, D.D., and Anna Morgan, *d.* of Rev. George Morgan; *m.* Anna E., *d.* of Prof. P. J. G. de Vos; one *s.* one *d.* *Educ.:* Victoria College, Stellenbosch. Devoted more than seven years to teaching; admitted as an Attorney-at-law, Notary Public, and Conveyancer of the Transvaal High Court, 1897; practised at Johannesburg and Germiston until 1906; served as Registrar and Treasurer to the Victoria College; Secretary for Education Union of South Africa, 1910-27; retired, 1927. *Recreations:* gardening, etc. *Address:* Grey University College, Bloemfontein, S.A. *(Died 31 Oct. 1928.)*

HOLBOROW, Col. William Hillier, C.M.G. 1896; late M.L.C. of N.S.W.; commanded a regiment of New South Wales Infantry; *s.* of late Daniel Holborow of Cromall, Gloucester; *b.* 1841; *m.* 1864, Maria Amelia, *d.* of late William Town, N.S.W. *Address:* Gadshill, Croydon, New South Wales. *(Died 10 July 1917.)*

HOZUMI, Baron Nobushige, Vice-President of the Privy Council, Japan; LL.D.; Barrister of Middle Temple; Honorary Professor of the Imperial University of Tokyo; President of the Imperial Academy; Judge of the Permanent Court of Arbitration, Hague; *cr.* Baron, 1915; *b.* 11 July 1855; *m.* 1882, *d.* of Baron Shibusawa. *Educ.:* Tokyo University; Middle Temple (1st Class Scholarship); Berlin University. Member House of Peers, 1890-92; with two colleagues drafted present Japanese Civil Code. *Publications:* Ancestor Worship and Japanese Law (English); The New Japanese Civil Codes as Material for the Study of Comparative Jurisprudence (English); Hoten-ron, or Treatise on Codification (Japanese); Inkyo-ron, or Treatise on Retirement from House-headship (Japanese); Gonin-gumi, or the System of Mutual Help and Supervision among Five Families (Japanese); Horitsu Shinka Ron or The Evolution of Law, 2 vols. (Japanese), etc., etc. *Address:* 9 Haraikala Machi, Ushigome, Tokyo. *(Died 1926.)*

HUBBARD, Robert Richard, Bey, Commander, R.D., R.N.R. (retired); Captain, Imperial Ottoman Navy; *b.* Ramsgate, 18 Mar. 1843; 3rd *s.* of late John Hubbard and Mary Hill, of Canterbury; *m.* 1st, 1886, Lizzie (*decd.*), 2nd *d.* of Rev. George Sydenham, M.A., vicar of Farewell, Staffordshire, and later of Montreal, Canada, one *s.*; 2nd, 1912, Agnes, *d.* of late Henry Cornelius, Mountrath, Queen's County, Ireland. *Educ.:* private school. Entered Mercantile Marine, 1857; master of sailing ships, 1866-70; joined steamships, 1870; served as an officer and in command of all classes of steamers; entered Royal Naval Reserve as Sub-Lieutenant, 1877; Lieutenant, 1886; retired Commander, 1898; served as Lieutenant of H.M.S. Arethusa, Benbow, Forth, and Venus, 1893-97. While in command of H.M. hired cruiser Kimberley towed gunboat Gadfly from Portsmouth to Simon's Bay (6000 miles), war with Russia imminent, 1884 (despatches); also conveyed on deck of the same steamer for the relief of General Gordon, H.M. Nile steamer Albert from Chatham to Alexandria, 1885; was in Port Morant, Jamaica, during Negro rebellion, 1864; served in the Transport Service at the Cape during the Kaffir, Zulu, and Boer Wars, 1872-81; commanded tourist steamer Barracouta, 1886-90; Ceylon, 1894; and Norse-King, 1898; twice visited the West India Islands under the auspices of the Secretary of State for the Colonies in the interest of the development of the minor industries, and submitted to the Colonial Governments his scheme for faster communication with the United States and

Great Britain; rescued a large number of people from drowning and shipwreck (medal and clasp, two diplomas, Liverpool Shipwreck and Humane Society; Medal d'Honneur and Diplomee from the French Government; silver binocular glasses and vote of thanks from the Canadian Government); Founder of the Annual National Service for Seafarers in St. Paul's Cathedral, 1905; Founder of the National Maritime Club, 1909; acted as Senior Officer in convoying two Turkish transports from Southampton to Constantinople, 1906; Order of the Osmanieh, 4th class; Order of the Medjidieh, 4th class; was offered and accepted service in the Imperial Ottoman Navy with the rank of Captain, and was appointed to H.I.M.S. Tirri-Mujgan; F.R.G.S.; F.R.S. of St. George; Younger Brother, Trinity House. *Publications:* Turkish Characteristics; In the Forbidden Mosque; Service under the Sultan; French Humanity; A Story of a Rescue in Mid Ocean; Wrecks and their Remedy; The Power of Bacsheesh in Turkey; In the Hands of the Turks; The Merchant Service a National Maritime Service; short stories. *Recreations:* boat-sailing, rowing, swimming. (*Died 21 Dec. 1926.*)

HUDON, Lt.-Col. Joseph Alfred George, C.M.G. 1902; retired, 1918; *b.* Quebec City, 7 June 1858; *s.* of F. E. Hudon and H. Couillard Dupuis; *m.* 1881, Alphonsine, *d.* of Charles Joncas, Quebec; two *s.* two *d.* *Educ.:* Elementary School; Seminary and Commercial Academy, Quebec. Joined Militia, 1878; Royal Canadian Artillery, 1883; served North-West Rebellion, 1885 (medal with clasp); South Africa, 1900, command of C Battery Royal Canadian Artillery (despatches, medal with clasps, C.M.G.). *Address:* Kingston, Ontario, Canada. *T. :* 120.
(*Died 22 Sept. 1918.*)

HUME, Alexander Williamson; Editor Hobart Critic since 1911; J.P.; Councillor Municipality of Clarence; *b.* 20 May 1850; *s.* of late Alexander Hume, Linlithgow, Scotland; *m.* 1873, Amelia, 2nd *d.* of late Alex. Clark of Hobart; one *s.* two *d.* *Educ.:* Hutchins School, Hobart. Engaged in law for nine years; took up journalism, 1879; joined Hobart Mercury, 1883; leader of staff Tasmanian News, 1887-1900; Editor Tasmanian News, 1900-11. *Publication:* Old Time Reminiscences of Tasmania. *Recreations:* in youth cricket, aquatics, football, now gardening. *Address:* Lindisfarne, Hobart, Tasmania. *T.A.:* Hobart Critic, Argyle Street.
(*Died 16 Feb. 1925.*)

JEFFERY, Edward Turner; President Denver and Rio Grande Railway since 1891; *b.* Liverpool, 6 April 1843; *m.* 1877, Virginia Osborne, *d.* of James C. Clarke, M.A., Frederick, Maryland. Emigrated to America 1850; entered employ of Illinois Central Railroad Co., 1856; general superintendent, 1877; general manager, 1885; resigned, 1889. *Address:* 165 Broadway, New York City, N.Y. (*Died 24 Sept. 1927.*)

JESSE, Richard Henry; President of University of Missouri 1891-1908; *b.* Ball Farm (birthplace of Washington's mother), Lancaster, Co. Va., 1 Mar. 1853; *s.* of W. T. Jesse and Mary Claybrook; *m.* Addie Henry Polk of Princess Anne. Md., 1882; three *s.* three *d.* *Educ.:* Hanover Academy; University of Virginia; Europe. LL.D., Tulane University, 1891; University of Wisconsin, 1904; South Carolina College, 1905; Missouri Valley College, 1906; Washington University, 1907; University of Missouri, 1908; Instructor in French and Mathematics, Hanover Academy, 1875 76; Dean of Academic Department, University of Louisiana, 1878-84; Professor of Latin, Tulane

University, New Orleans, 1884-91; a member of the Committee of Ten, 1891 (National Educational Association); Chairman, Section Higher Education, N. E. A., 1898; President State Teachers Association of Missouri, 1899; President Southern Association Colleges and Secondary Schools, 1903 and 1905; awarded medal for services to Education; President of National Association of State Universities, 1905-6; delegate from United States to first International Congress of Radiology in Belgium, 1905; offered retirement on Carnegie Foundation; offer accepted after July 1, 1908; Emeritus Professor of Ancient and Mediæval History, University of Missouri, 1909. *Publications:* Missouri Literature (with E. A. Allen), papers in transactions of various societies, etc. (*Died 1921.*)

JOGLEKAR, Rao Bahadur Ramchandra Narayan, I.S.O. 1913; B.A.; Chief Land Officer Tata Hydro-electric Department Bombay; Collector, Baroda State, 1917-20; Deputy Collector, 1st grade, and Native Assistant to the Commissioner, Central Division, 1901-1916; sometime General Adviser to the Chief of Inchalkaranji; *b.* Satara, 8 Dec. 1858; *e. s.* of late Narayan Bhikaji Joglekar, retired Deputy Collector; four *s.* four *d.* *Educ.:* Deccan Coll., Poona. Held non-gazetted appointments in Nasik, Satara, Ahmednagar, Poona, and Sholapur Districts, 1883-1899; Deputy Collector. 1899. *Publications:* The Court-Fee Manual; Alienation Manual; the annotated Bombay Land Revenue Code, Act 5 of 1879, revised and brought up to 1 Oct. 1920 and Watan Act. *Address:* 203 Kala Haud, Shukrawar, Peth, Poona City. *Club:* Dekkan Gymkhana. (*Died 16 April 1928.*)

JOHNSON, Rt. Rev. Joseph Horsfall, D.D., S.T.D.; Bishop of Los Angeles, California, U.S.A.; *b.* 7 June 1847; *s.* of Hon. Stephen Hotchkiss Johnson and Eleanor Horsfall; *m.* 1881, *d.* of Hon. Isaac Davis of Worcester, Mass.; one *s.* *Educ.:* private schools. Graduate in Arts, 1870, Williams College, General Theological Seminary, New York, 1873. Rector successively of Holy Trinity, Highland, N.Y.; Trinity, Bristol, R.I.; St. Peter's, Westchester, N.Y. City; Christ Church, Detroit, Michigan. *Publications:* Pamphlets and Sermons. *Address:* Cathedral House, 615 S. Figueroa Street, Los Angeles, California. (*Died 18 May 1928.*)

JOHNSTON, Rt. Rev. James Steptoe, D.D.; *b.* 9 June 1843; *s.* of James and Louisa C. B. Johnston; *m.* 1865, Mary M. Green; two *s.* two *d.* *Educ.:* Oakland College, Miss.; University of Va. Four years in Confederate Army (Lee's), Co. I. 11th Miss. Regt. till 1862; after that 2nd Lieut. Stuart's Cavalry; Deacon, 1869; Priest, 1871; Rector of St. James Church, Port Gibson, Miss., 1870-76; Ascension Church, Mt. Stirling, Ky., 1876-80; Trinity Church, Mobile, Ala., 1880-88; Bishop of West Texas, 1888-1914. *Publications:* sermons and articles in church and secular papers. *Address:* 517 E. Myrtle Street, San Antonio, Texas (*Died 4 Nov. 1924.*)

JORDAN, Edwin Oakes, Ph.D.; Andrew MacLeish Distinguished Service Professor Emeritus of Bacteriology, University of Chicago; *b.* 28 July 1866; American parentage; *m.* 1893; two *s.* one *d.* *Educ.:* Mass. Institute of Technology, S.B. 1888; Ph.D., Clark Univ., 1892; Sc.D., Univ. of Cincinnati, 1920; Member, International Health Board, 1920-27; Board of Scientific Directors of the Rockefeller Foundation, 1930-34; Editor of The Journal of Infectious Diseases, The Journal of Preventive Medicine, The Newer Knowledge of

Bacteriology and Immunology, 1928 ; President American Society of Bacteriologists,1905; President American Epidemiological Society,1930-31 ; President Chicago Institute of Medicine,1932-33; Sedgwick Medal, 1935 ; Nat. Acad., 1936. *Publications:* Translation of Hueppe's Bacteriology ; A Text-Book of General Bacteriology (11th edition); Food Poisoning (2nd edition), 1931 ; Epidemic Influenza, 1927 ; special monographs in Journal of the American Medical Association, Journal of Infectious Diseases, Journal of Experimental Medicine, Journal of Hygiene, etc. *Recreations:* travel, golf. *Address:* University of Chicago, Chicago, Ill.

(*Died 2 Sept 1926.*)

KENNEDY, George, M.A., LL.D., K.C. 1902 ; *b.* Bytown (now Ottawa), 1 March 1838 ; *s.* of Donald Kennedy and Janet Buckham; *m.* 1883, Sarah Jackson Watson (*d.* 1910); no *c. Educ.:* Casleton Co. Grammar School ; University of Toronto. First Classical Schoolmaster; subsequently first class Honours in Classics, Mathematics, Metaphysics, and Ethics, Modern Languages, and Natural Sciences ; B.A. 1857, gold medal ; M.A. 1860 ; LL.B. 1864 ; called to Bar, Osgoode Hall, 1865 ; M.D. 1877 ; practised profession at Ottawa, 1866-71 ; Law Clerk of the Department of Lands, Forests, and Mines of the province of Ontario, 1872 ; Law Examiner in University, 1878-80; Ex-President, Hon. Member, and thirty years Editor of the Transactions of the Canadian Institute ; Ex-President and Hon. Member of the St. Andrew's Society ; Ex-President of the Caledonian Society ; Ex-President of the Burns Literary Society. *Publications:* Scottish - Canadian Poets (joint editor); Alexander M'Lachlan's Poems (joint editor); Science and English Law ; Digest of Crown Lands Cases ; Analysis of the Public Land Laws of Canada, etc. *Clubs:* National, Madawasha, Toronto. (*Died June 1916.*)

KEOGH, Martin Jerome, LL.D. ; Justice, Supreme Court of New York, 1896-1909 and 1910-12 ; *b.* Ireland, 1855 ; *m.* 1894, Katharine Temple Emmet, New Rochelle. *Educ.:* New York University. Admitted to bar, 1875 ; practised at New York, 1875-95. *Address:* New Rochelle. New York. (*Died 24 Oct. 1928.*)

KING, Oliver ; Professor of the Pianoforte, Royal Academy of Music, since 1893 ; *b.* London, 1855. *Educ.:* under Sir Joseph Barnby and W. H. Holmes ; Conservatorium, Leipzig. Pianist to Princess Louise ; in Canada during Governor-Generalship of Lord Lorne ; gained Philharmonic Society's prize for best overture, 1883 ; Precentor, St. Marylebone Church, 1884-6 ; has made several tours as a solo player in Germany, Holland, England, Ireland, America, and Wales. *Publications:* Symphony Night, 1880 ; overture Among the Pines, 1883 ; concerto for Pianoforte and Orchestra, 1885 ; violin concerto, cantatas, organ suites, piano solos, violin solos, many songs, duets, and trios, also part-songs, and fifty anthems and church-services, etc. *Recreation:* organ building. *Address:* 10 Rostrevor Road, S.W. (*Died about 1923.*)

KITTSON, Rev. Henry, M.A., D.C.L., Canon, Christ Church Cathedral, Ottawa ; Canon Missioner Diocese of Ottawa ; *b.* 15 Nov. 1848 ; *s.* of Norman Kittson ; *m.* 1875, Flora Grant (deceased) ; one *s.* two *d. Educ.:* Berthier Grammar School and Bishop College University, Lennoxville, Quebec. Missionary in Diocese of Montreal, 1871-82; Rector of St. John's Church, St. Paul, Minn., U.S., 1882-86 ; Rector, Church of Advent, Montreal, 1886-1901. *Publications:* Church History from Archives ; A Study of Early Canadian Church ; sermons and papers. *Recreations:* chiefly yachting and canoeing.

Address: Berthier, Que., Canada.
(*Died 23 July 1925.*)

KOHLSAAT, Herman H., proprietor and editor Chicago Record Herald ; *b.* Edwards County, Illinois, 22 March 1853 *s.* of Reimer Kohlsaat, *b.* 1809, Brunsbuttel, Holstein, Denmark, Officer in Danish Army, and Sarah Hall, Surrey, England ; *m.* 1880, Mabel E., *d.* of E. Nelson Blake, leading member and former President Chicago Board of Trade ; two *d. Educ.:* Public and private schools, Galena and Chicago. Bought the Chicago Inter-Ocean, 1891 ; sold it, 1894 ; purchased the Times-Herald and Evening Post, 1895. Republican ; took active part in election of President M'Kinley and in drafting gold plank in Republican platform of 1896. *Clubs:* Chicago, Commercial, Union League, Press.
(*Died 17 Oct. 1924.*)

KRAUS, Adolf; Lawyer ; *b.* 1849 ; *m.* ; three *s.* one *d. Educ.:* Rokycan, Bohemia. Was President Board of Education, City of Chicago : Corporation Counsel, City of Chicago; President, Civil Service Commission ; Knight of the Order of Francis Joseph ; was International President, Order of B'nai B'rith, for twenty years. *Publications:* was owner and editor Chicago Times. *Recreation:* golf. *Address:* East End Park Hotel, Chicago. *T.A.:* Kragos, Chicago. *Clubs:* Covenant, Athletic, Standard, Chicago. (*Died 22 Oct. 1928.*)

KUTLEHR, Raja Ram Pal of, C.S.I. 1904 ; head of an ancient family of Rajputs who formerly ruled, according to the local traditions, for over two hundred generations ; judicial powers were granted in 1878 ; *b.* 22 Nov. 1849 ; *s.* of Raja Narain Pal ; *m.* 1st, *sis.* of Raja Sham Ser Singh of Rampur Bushahr State ; 2nd, *d.* of Raja Mahendra Sein of Keental State, Simla; one *s. Educ.:* Shastri (nagri), Persian and English. Sub-Registrar of Kutlehr, 1867 ; Judicial Powers granted, 1875 ; Judicial Powers, First Class, 1877 ; a Sanad for good conduct and morality, 1877 ; a letter of thanks for offer of military service in Afghan war, 1879 ; silver and gold medal Delhi Coronation Durbar, 1903 ; numerous Sanads for services during European War; life member of St. John Ambulance Association. *Address:* Kutlehr, Kangra, Punjab.
(*Died 21 Nov. 1927.*)

LAMB, Sir Richard Amphlett, K.C.S.I., *cr.* 1911 ; C.S.I. 1909 ; C.I.E. 1901 ; *b.* 4 Apr. 1858 ; *s.* of late William Lamb, Indian Vet. Department ; *m.* 1901, Kathleen, 2nd *d.* of Lt.-Colonel J. P. Barry, I.M.S. ; four *s. Educ.:* Highgate Grammar School. Joined I.C.S. 1879 ; served as assistant collector and magistrate ; as forest settlement officer, Khandesh ; as Deputy Commissioner, Burmah, 1887-90 (medal with clasp) ; subsequently assistant collector, acting collector, and collector and magistrate, Bombay ; Chairman Poona Plague Committee, 1897 ; Secretary and Acting Chief Sec. to Govt. of Bombay, 1904 ; Commissioner Central Division, 1905 ; Member, Indian Excise Committee, 1905-6 ; Chief Secretary, 1907 ; Member of Executive Council, Governor of Bombay, 1910 ; retired 1915 ; Kaiser-i-Hind medal (1st class), 1900. *Address:* Tudor House, Broadway, Worcs. *Clubs:* East India United Service ; Club of Western India, Poona.
(*Died 27 Jan. 1923.*)

LANGLEY, Walter, R.I. ; painter ; *b.* Birmingham, 1852 ; *m.* 1896. *Educ.:* National School, Birmingham. Served apprenticeship as lithographer, studying art in local School of Art in evenings ; obtained National Scholarship and studied at South Kensington 2 years ; finally took up painting as profession ; settled in Newlyn, Cornwall, 1882 ; gold medal for painting at

Paris and Chicago; painted an autograph portrait, by invitation of the Directorate, for the gallery of the Uffizi, Florence. *Exhibited:* R.I. (water colours)—Among the Missing; Departure of the Fleet; Disaster; After the Storm, etc.; R.A. (oil paintings)—Never morning wore to evening but some heart did break; Motherless; Bread-winners; Wandering Musicians; Between the Tides, etc. (*Died 1922.*)

LARIVIÈRE, Hon. Alphonse Alfred Clément; 3rd *s.* of late Abraham C. La-Rivière of Montreal, and Adélaide Marcil of Longueuil; *b.* Montreal, 24 July 1842. *Educ.:* St. Mary's College, Montreal. Elected President of the Board of Arts and Manufactures for the Province of Quebec, the Institut des Artisans Canadiens, and the Cercle St. Pierre of Montreal; President of the Selkirk County Agricultural Society; Superintendent of the Catholic Schools; Joint Secretary of the Board of Education, and a member of the Council of the University of Manitoba; contested St. Anne in the Manitoba Legislative Assembly, 1874; elected for St. Boniface, 1878, 1879, 1881; Provincial Secretary, 1881; Minister of Agriculture, Statistics and Health, 1883-86; Provincial Treasurership, 1886; elected to represent Provencher in the Dominion House, 1889; three times re-elected; was called to the Senate, 1911. *Address:* St. Boniface, Manitoba, Canada. (*Died 20 Sept. 1925.*)

LATHROP, Rose Hawthorne (Mother Mary Alphonsa Lathrop), superioress Dominican Community of Third Order, and directress of Charitable Home; *b.* Lenox, Mass., 20 May 1851; *d.* of Nathaniel Hawthorne; *m.* 1871, George Parsons Lathrop, author. Devoted to betterment of cancerous and destitute men and women unable to find care in any existing hospital. Established in 1898 St. Rose's Free Home for Cancer, 426 Cherry Street, New York, and in 1901 Rosary Hill Home, Hawthorne, Westchester Co., New York, for country annexe; built new City Home for 90 patients, St. Rose's, Corlaer's Park, and Jackson Street, New York, 1912. *Publications:* (poems) Along the Shore; A Story of Courage; Memories of Hawthorne. *Address:* 71 Jackson Street, near Corlaer's Park, New York. (*Died 9 July 1926.*)

LEMASS, Peter Edmund, I.S.O. 1903; L.R.C.S.I., 1880; *b.* Dublin, 6 March 1850; *s.* of late P. J. Lemass; *m.* 1883, Maria Patricia, *d.* of late Michael Scallan, Dublin; one *s.* three *d.* *Educ.:* Public and private schools; Ledwich School of Medicine; St. Vincent's Hosp., Dublin. Studied surgery and medicine, 1875-80; was Senior Secretary to Board of National Education, Ireland, till 1915, when he retired. *Recreations:* walking, music, theatres. *Address:* 3 Clifton Terrace, Monkstown, Co. Dublin. (*Died 20 March 1928.*)

LIDDELL, Colin, I.S.O. 1913; *b.* 8 Feb. 1862; *s.* of Walter George Liddell, sugar planter. Entered Public Service, 1881; Surveyor-General, Jamaica, 1894. *Address:* Hazeldean, South Camp Road, Kingston, Jamaica. (*Died Oct. 1916.*)

McCOMB, Col. Robert Brophy, C.B. 1900; A.S.C.; retired; *b.* 22 Nov. 1855. Entered army, 1874; Colonel, 1900; served Egyptian War, 1882 (medal and Khedive's star); Bechuanaland Expedition, 1884-85; Zululand, 1888; South Africa, 1899-1902, as Assist. Adjt.-Gen. (despatches, Queen's medal, King's medal two clasps, C.B.). *Address:* c/o Lloyds Bank, Ltd. (Cox's Branch), 6 Pall Mall, S.W.1. (*Died 18 Nov. 1925.*)

McCUBBIN, Lt.-Col. Thomas, C.M.G. 1900; J.P.; late Durban Light Infantry. Served South Africa, 1899-1901, in command of Durban Light Infantry (despatches twice, Queen's medal with clasp, C.M.G.). *Address:* Durban, Natal. (*Died 15 Dec. 1925.*)

MACDONNELL, Col. William, C.B. 1891; retired; *b.* 7 June 1831; *s.* of William Macdonnell; *m.* 1878, Annie Jessie, *d.* of Col. C. J. Cox of Fordwich, Kent. *Educ.:* privately in Dublin. Ensign, 1848; and served in the 55th, 14th, and 88th Regiments; joined the Army Pay Department as Staff Paymaster, 1878; became Chief Paymaster, 1881; sometime Chief Paymaster Home District. *Decorated* for long and meritorious service. *Recreation:* riding. *Address:* Via Castillfidardo, 47, Rome. (*Died 12 July 1919.*)

M'EACHRAN, Duncan, F.R.C.V.S., V.S. Edin.; LL.D. and D.V.S. McGill; J.P.; *b.* Campbeltown, Argyllshire, Oct. 1841; *o. s.* of David M'Eachran and Jean Blackney; *m.* 1868, Esther, 3rd *d.* of Timothy Plaskett of St. Croix, West Indies. *Educ.:* Edinburgh. Was invited to join in the establishment of a course of lectures in connection with the Board of Agriculture of Ontario at Toronto, 1862; removed to Montreal, where he inaugurated the Montreal Veterinary College in connection with the Medical College of McGill University, 1866, which, 1890, became the Faculty of Comparative Medicine and Veterinary Science, of which he became Dean, and held that position till his retirement, 1903; organised the Cattle Quarantine System of Canada, 1876; after twenty-six years he resigned the active duties of the position and became Honorary Veterinary Adviser to the Government; represented Canada at scientific congresses at Baden Baden, at London (Tuberculosis Congress, 1901), and in all international discussions and agreements bearing on animal diseases; was largely instrumental in raising the Strathcona Horse, sent to South Africa during the Boer War; President of the New Walrond Cattle Ranch in the Rocky Mountain region of Canada. *Publications:* Handbook on the Diseases of Horses, 1866; Notes of a Trip to Bow River, 1881; Notes of a Visit to the Scientific Institutions of France, Germany, and Denmark, 1898; numerous scientific bulletins on Contagious Diseases for the information of agriculturists and stock-breeders, issued by the Government. *Recreations:* principally spending two or three months annually on the foothills of the Rocky Mountains, where in early days he hunted buffalo and other game; devotes himself to the breeding of high-class agricultural horses. *Address:* Ormsby Grange, Ormstown, P. Que. *Clubs:* Authors'; St. James's, Montreal, Ranchman's, Calgary.
(*Died 13 Oct. 1926.*)

McKENZIE, Hon. Robert Donald, O.B.E., J.P.; *b.* Maldon, Victoria, Australia, 19 March 1865; 2nd *s.* of Hugh McKenzie, J.P.; *m.* 1895, Emma Mary, *e. d.* of James Widgery, Sydney, N.S.W.; three *s.* one *d.* *Educ.:* St. Paul's Grammar School, Melbourne. Arrived in West Australia with the advent of gold discoveries, 1892; a pioneer of Kalgoorlie; largely interested in mining and commercial pursuits; first Senior Councillor of Kalgoorlie, afterwards Mayor; Member of Legislative Council for North-East Province, 1904-16; served on three Royal Commissions in connection with mining industry in West Australia; founded Kalgoorlie Chamber of Commerce, elected first President, 1910-11; Hon. Minister and Member of the Executive Council of West Australia, 1910-11; hon. Red Cross work in France, 1915-18 (despatches). *Recreations:* golf, bowls. *M.:* CT 1. *Clubs:* Perth, Hannans, Kalgoorlie. Masonic, Perth. (*Died 1928.*)

M'KINNON, Rev. W., Minister, Gairloch; ex-Moderator General Assembly Free Church of Scotland, 1908; *b.* Strath, Skye, 1848. *Educ.:* Free Church School, Strath; Normal Training College, University, and Free Church College, Glasgow. Minister at Ballachulish, 1873; North Uist; Glenmoriston. *Address:* Gairloch, Scotland. *(Died 13 Feb. 1925.)*

M'LEOD, Hon. Donald, late Member Legislative Assembly, Victoria; *b.* Caithness; *m.*; four *s.* four *d. Educ.:* John Knox's Grammar School, Melbourne. Went to Victoria as a child, 1850; trained as a chemist; followed agricultural and mining pursuits for many years; Town Clerk, Daylesford, and Official Assigner Insolvency, etc., for twenty-five years; M.P. Daylesford, 1899; Hon. Member Irvine Government, 1902; Minister Mines and Forests, 1904; Acting Minister of Water Supply and Acting Treasurer, 1909; Chief Secretary and Minister of Health, Victoria, 1915-18; Member of the Executive Council of Victoria; of Melbourne University Council; President Daylesford Hospital, etc. *Address:* 244 Beaconsfield Parade, Middle Park, Melbourne. *T.:* Windsor 2905. *Clubs:* Stock Exchange, Freemasons, Melbourne. *(Died about 1918.)*

McSWEENY, George, K.C. 1911; H.M. Third Serjeant-at-Law in Ireland, 1913; Second Serjeant since 1919; Crown Counsel for Co. Cork; *b.* 1865; *m.* 1919, Kathleen, *widow of* late F. D. Matthews, Bombay; one *d. Educ.:* National Schools; University College, and Trinity College, Dublin. Called to Irish Bar, 1896. *Address:* Lochlin, Howth, Co. Dublin. *T.:* Howth 62. *(Died 14 Nov. 1923.)*

MACVICAR, Hon. John; Mayor, City of Des Moines, 1928; Commissioner-General International Municipal Congress and Exposition, Chicago, 1911; *b.* Galt, Ontario, 1859; *s.* of John MacVicar, Scotland, and Mary M'Ewen, Scotland; *m.* 1884, Nettie M. Nash; one *s.* two *d. Educ.:* Public Schools, Erie, Pennsylvania. Recorder Town of North Des Moines, Ia., 1888; Mayor, 1889; Mayor, City of Des Moines, Ia., 1896-1900, and since 1916; Pres. League of American Municipalities, 1897; Member of the City Council and Superintendent of Department of Streets and Public Improvements, Des Moines, under Commission form of city government, 1908-12; Plattsburg Training Camp, 9th Regiment, 1916; commissioned Captain Quartermaster, Officers' Reserve Corps, U.S.A., 7 Feb. 1917; assigned to active duty as Assistant to the Quartermaster. Fort Douglas, Utah, 18 May 1917; discharged 6 March 1919; Superintendent, Department Public Safety, Des Moines, 1922-23. *Publications:* several articles on Municipal affairs. *Address:* Des Moines. Iowa. U.S.A.
(Died 15 Nov. 1928.)

McWEENEY, Edmond J., M.A., M.D., M.Ch., M.A.O., Royal University of Ireland; F.R.C.P.I.; D.P.H. of the Conjoint Royal Colleges in Ireland; Professor of Pathology and Bacteriology at Univ. Coll., Dublin; *b.* Dublin, 9 Mar. 1864; *s.* of Theophilus M'Weeney, journalist (Freeman's Journal), of Beaumont, Rathgar, Co. Dublin, and Margaret, *d.* of late Jonathan Kendellen of Castlebar, Co. Mayo; *m.* 1891, Emilie, *d.* of late Simon Brazil of Kingstown, Co. Dublin. *Educ.:* Coll. St. Bertin, St. Omer (France); Cath. University, Dublin. Entered at the first Matric. Exam. held by the then newly created Royal University of Ireland, Nov. 1881, and gained exhibition; scholar (£150) in Mod. Lit. 1882; B.A. with 1st Hon. and £50 Prize and Studentship (£500) in Mod. Lit. 1884; M.A. 1885. Meanwhile worked at medicine and graduated M.B. with hons. and exhibition, 1887; M.D. 1891; devoted himself to Pathology and Bacteriology, and worked in Vienna 1888 under Kolisko, and in Berlin 1889 under C. Fraenkel and von Esmarch; in 1894 gained the studentship in these subjects (£400); appointed Pathologist to the Mater Misericordiæ Hospital, Dublin, 1889; and Bacteriologist to the Irish Local Gov. Board, 1900, which positions he continues to hold; President of Pathological Section, Royal Academy of Medicine, in Ireland; Consulting Pathologist to the Troops in Ireland. *Publications:* translator and joint-author of Tappeiner's Chemical Methods of Clinical Diagnosis, as well as of numerous papers on human and vegetable pathology and bacteriology in various medical journals and in the transactions of the Royal Academy of Medicine in Ireland. *Recreations:* golf, cycling, swimming, botanising (Fungi). *Address:* 84 St. Stephen's Green, S. Dublin. *T.:* 2017.
(Died 20 June 1925.)

MATSUMURA, Jinzo, D.Sc., Hon. LL.D. (Aberd.); Professor of Botany and Director of Botanic Gardens, Imperial University, Tokio; *b.* 1856 (Samurai); *m.* 1879; one *s. Educ.:* began self-study in botany, 1877; Universities of Würzburg and Heidelberg, 1886-88; Assistant Professor, 1883; Professor, 1890. *Publications:* Conspectus of the Leguminosæ found growing wild or cultivated in Japan, Loochoo, and Formosa, 1902; Nippon Shokubutsu mei-i, or Nomenclature of Japanese Plants in Latin, Japanese, and Chinese, 1884; Catalogue of Plants in the Herbarium of the College of Science, Imperial University, 1886; Names of Plants and their Products in English, Japanese, and Chinese, 1892; Shokubutsu mei-i : Enumeration of selected scientific names of both native and foreign plants, with romanised Japanese names, and in many cases Chinese characters, 1900; Index Plantarum Japonicarum sive Enumeratio Plantarum omnium ex insulis Kurile, Yezo, Nippon, Sikoku, Kiusiu, Liukiu, et Formosa hucusque cognitarum systematice et alphabetice dispositu (Cryptogamæ), 1904; (Phanerogamæ), 1905; Ito and Matsumura—Tentamen Floræ Lutchuensis, 1899; Revisio Alni Specierum Japonicarum, 1902; Matsumura and Hayata—Enumeratio Plantarum in insula Formosa sponte crescentium, 1906; Chinese Names of Plants, 1915; A Classified Etymological Vocabulary of the Japanese Language Ancient and Modern, 1915; An Etymological Vocabulary of the Yamato Language, 1921; retired, 1922. *Address:* 16 Akebonocho, Hongo, Tokio, Japan.
(Died 4 May 1928.)

MAXWELL, Lawrence, B.S., A.M., LL.B., LL.D.; Lawyer, Cincinnati; *b.* Glasgow, 4 May 1853; *s.* of Lawrence and Alison Crawford; *m.* 1876, Clara Barry Darrow; twc *d. Educ.:* University of Michigan; Cincinnati Law School. Admitted to Bar, 1875; Solicitor-General of the U.S. 1893-95; Lecturer, Cincinnati Law School, 1896-1916; Non-Resident Lecturer, Law Department University of Michigan, 1909-16; Chairman of Section of Legal Education of American Bar Asscciation, 1905; Chairman Bar Committee on Revision of the Equity Rules of Supreme Court, U.S.A., 1911; Commemoration Orator at the 75th anniversary of the founding of the University of Michigan, 1912; President, Cincinnati Musical Festival Association. *Recreation:* music. *Address:* Union Central Building, Cincinnati, Ohio, U.S.A. *T.A.:* Maxwell, Cincinnati. *Clubs:* Queen City (Pres. 1915-24), Commercial, Country, University, Optimists, Cincinnati; Metropolitan, Washington; University, New York.
(Died 18 Feb. 1927.)

MEARS, Thomas Lambert, M.A., LL.D. (Lond.); of the Inner Temple; Barrister-at-law; called 1868; South-Eastern Circuit; Member of the Senate (retired 1915) and Representative of the University of London on the Essex Education Committee, and on the Territorial Force Association for the County of London; Lieut.-Col., formerly commanding 5th Midx. R.V.; A.K.C., London; for many years Reporter to the Law Reports of Admiralty cases in the Court of Admiralty and Court of Appeal; Fellow of Geographical and Zoological Societies, and Fellow and Member of Council of Botanical Society; Member of the Royal Institution of Great Britain; a Governor and Member of the Board of Management of the Middlesex Hospital; *b.* New York, of English parents; *m.* 1875, Alice Catherine, *e. d.* of late J. H. Westcar Peel of Watlington, Oxfordshire; two *s.* one *d. Educ.*: King's and University Colleges. Has twice circumnavigated the globe, visiting N. and S. America, Sandwich Islands, Australia, Tasmania, New Zealand, Ceylon, Burma, Siam, China, Japan, etc. *Publications:* an Analysis of Ortolan's Roman Law; a translation with notes of the Institutes of Gaius and Justinian; editor of several handbooks of Travel, and of editions of Practical Forms and Forms of Agreement, and joint-author of the last edition of Admiralty Law and Practice. *Address:* 1 St. Andrew's Place, Regent's Park, N.W.
(Died 10 Jan. 1918.)

MEREDITH, Rev. Richard; Prebend of Tullowmagimma and Canon of Leighlin Cathedral since 1906; *s.* of Richard Duke Meredith, B.A., T.C.D. *Educ.:* Trinity College, Dublin (M.A. and Div. Testl.). Ordained, 1869; Curate of Clonenagh, 1869-76; Incumbent of Killaban, 1876 - 1919; Rural Dean of Aghade, 1913. *Address:* 28 Corrig Avenue, Kingstown, Co. Dublin. *(Died Dec. 1928.)*

MEYER, Kuno, Ph.D.; Professor of Celtic at the University of Berlin since 1911; Member of the Royal Prussian Academy; *b.* Hamburg, 20 Dec. 1858; *y. s.* of Dr. Edward Meyer, Classical Master at the Johanneum. *Educ.:* Gelehrtenschule of the Johanneum, Hamburg. Studied Germanic and Celtic Philology at the University of Leipzig, 1879–83; Lecturer in Teutonic Languages at University College, Liverpool, 1884, Professor, 1895–1915; founded the Zeitschrift für Celtische Philologie, 1895, and, jointly with Whitley Stokes, the Archiv für Celtische Lexikographie, 1898; founded the School of Irish Learning, Dublin, 1903; Hon. D.Litt. Wales, Oxford, and St. Andrews. *Publications:* Eine irische Version der Alexandersage, 1883; The Battle of Ventry,1884; The Irish Odyssey, 1885; A German Grammar (Parallel Series),1888; The Vision of MacConglinne, 1892; The Voyage of Bran,1894; Hibernica Minora,1895; Early Relations of the Brython and Gael, 1896; King and Hermit, 1901; Liadain and Curithir, 1902; Four Songs of Summer and Winter, 1903; The Age and Origin of Shelta, 1892; The Law of Adamnan, 1904; Ancient Irish Poetry, 1911; Contributions to Irish Lexicography, etc. *Address:* Niebuhrstr. 11A, Charlottenburg.
(Died 11 Oct. 1919.)

MOSSOP, Joseph Upjohn, D.S.O. 1902; farmer; *b.* Grey Town, Natal, 27 April 1872; *s.* of an Englishman who came to Natal, 1840; *m.* 1904, Clarissa, *d.* of Henry M. Meek of Wakkerstroom District, Natal; three *s.* one *d. Educ.:* Grey Town; private tutor. Was a burgher of the Transvaal; despatch rider to Generals C. and L. Botha and T. Smuts during early part of Boer War; surrendered to Gen. Buller, May 1900; caught and imprisoned by Boers; escaped

and became guide to Generals Dartnell and Buller; made intelligence officer in Col. Stewart's column of J.M.R.; joined Gen. Hamilton's column; assisted in capture of Gen. C. Emmett. *Address:* Brooklyn Farm, P.O. Machadodorp, Eastern Transvaal, South Africa. *[Died 26 June 1928.*

MULJI, Vasanji Trikamji, Rao Sahib Sir, Kt., *cr.* 1911; J.P.: Hon. Magistrate; Member Bombay Cotton Exchange; Member Bombay Panjrapole, etc.; *b.* 8 July 1866.
(Died 12 Jan 1925.)

MUMTAZUD DOWLAH MUHAMMAD FAIYAZ ALI KHAN, Nawab of Pahasu; K.C.V.O., *cr.* 1911; Minister, Jaipur State, Rajputana; *b.* 4 Nov. 1851; *s.* of late Nawab Sir Faiz Ali Khan Bahadur, K.C.S.I. (family traces origin to Rama, King of Ajodhya); married; one *s.* one *d.* Late member of the Supreme and Provincial Legislative Councils; Hon. Magistrate of Pahasu; President of Board of Trustees, M.A.O. College, Aligarh. *Address:* Nawab's House, Jaipur, Rajputana. India.
(Died March 1922.)

MURFREE, Mary Noailles (pen-name Charles Egbert Craddock), novelist; *b.* Murfreesboro', Tennessee; *d.* of late William L. Murfree, lawyer; *g. -g.d.* of Colonel Hardy Murfree of Murfreesboro, North Carolina, who served with conspicuous gallantry throughout the American Revolution, 1775-82 (the town of Murfreesboro', Tennessee, was named in his honour). *Publications:* In the Tennessee Mountains, 1884; Where the Battle was Fought, 1884; Down the Ravine, 1885; The Prophet of the Great Smoky Mountains, 1885; In the Clouds, 1886; The Story of Keedon Bluffs, 1887; The Despot of Broomsedge Cove, 1888; In the Stranger-People's Country, 1891; His Vanished Star, 1894; The Phantoms of the Footbridge, 1895; The Mystery of Witch-face Mountain, 1895; The Juggler, 1897; The Young Mountaineers, 1897; The Story of Old Fort London, 1899; The Bushwhackers, 1899; The Champion, 1902; A Spectre of Power, 1903; The Storm Centre, 1905; The Frontiersmen. 1905; The Amulet, 1906; The Windfall, 1907; The Fair Mississippian, 1908; The Ordeal, 1912; The Raid of the Guerrilla, and other Stories, 1912; The Story of Duciehurst, 1914. In 1878 began to contribute fiction to magazines under pen-name of "Charles Egbert Craddock," real identity not known until 1885. *Address:* Murfreesboro', Tennessee, U.S.A.
(Died 1 Aug. 1922.)

NANAK CHAND, Masheerud-dowal Rai Bahadur, C.S.I. 1911; C.I.E. 1901; Pensioner, 1st class, Sirdar and Jagirdar of Indore State; *b.* 1860; Hindu by religion, Vaish by community; *e. s.* of Masheerud-dowla Rai Bahadur Omeid Singh, tutor and adviser to Chief of Indore; two *s. Educ.:* Delhi and Indore. Received his father's title of Masheerud-dowla Rai Bahadur from Indore State at age 13; Judicial Secretary to Minister, 1886; State Treasurer, 1886-1891; Deputy Minister. 1891-1895; Residency Vakil as well in 1893, and Minister, 1895-1913 (except for ten months); holds Kaiser-i Hind Medal, first-class, for services in the famine of 1898-99; after retiring he travelled round the world, and visited Ceylon, China, Japan, America, England, France, Switzerland and Italy. *Publications:* edited J'Khairkhah-i-Vaish', a monthly paper in Urdu, for four years; wrote Moortibhooshan and Vidhwa-Vivah in Nagri on idolatry and widow marriage; and Hinduism in English. *Recreation:* tennis. *Address:* Santoshkuti, Indore; Mohalla Dassa, Delhi. *(Died 29 March 1920.)*

NAPIER, Colonel Wm., C.M.G. 1896; Member of the firm of Napier & Weir, merchants; b. Scotland, 1861; served as trooper in Natal Carbineers for four years; entered service of B.S.A. Co., 1891; joined Victoria Rangers as a subaltern, 1892; commanded a troop under Maj. Alan Wilson during advance into Matabeleland, 1893; present at all engagements which led to subjugation of Lobengula's forces; in command of whole of armed forces in Rhodesia, 1895; commanded all local forces engaged in suppressing Matabeleland rebellion, 1896, up to arrival of Sir Richard Martin (despatches, Matabele Medal for 1893); commanded A Squadron of the Southern Rhodesia Reserve Force for a few months, Boer War, 1899-1900. *Address:* Hillside, Bulawayo. *Clubs:* Junior Constitutional; Bulawayo.

(Died 29 Jan. 1920.)

NORWOOD, Rev. Reginald, M.A., Vicar of All Souls', Heywood, Manchester, since 1924; 5th s. of late Rev. R. P. Norwood, B.A., Vicar of Fritwell, Oxon; b. 3 Jan. 1874; m. 1902, Charlotte Eveline, o. d. of Rev. Canon O'Flaherty, Prebend of Kilbragh; one s. one d. *Educ.:* private school and Trinity College, Dublin (Senior Moderator and Gold Medallist; Prizeman in French, in German, and in Italian; Prize Essayist in French and in English). Formerly Headmaster of Inverness College, of Lutterworth Grammar School and of Sandringham School, Southport; Vicar of Wimbish, 1919; Originator of the Moderators' (War) Memorial, T.C.D., 1918. *Recreations:* formerly tennis, tives, Badminton, Rugby football. *Address:* All Souls' Vicarage, Heywood. Lancs.

(Died April 1928.)

OBEYESEKERE, Hon. Sir Solomon Christoffel, Kt., cr. 1911; M.L.C., M.R.C.I.; Vice-President of the Ceylon Branch of the Royal Asiatic Society; Member of the British Empire League; Vice-President of the Board of Agriculture, Ceylon; an incorporated Trustee of the Anglican Church in Ceylon; a Member of the Executive Committee of the Synod of the Church of England in Ceylon; President of Christian Literature Society, Ceylon; Member of the Committee of the British and Foreign Bible Society, Colombo; President of the Sinhalese Sports Club, Colombo; Member of the Ceylon Turf Club; Patron of the Ceylon Plumbago Merchants' Union; landed proprietor; Representative of the Low Country Sinhalese in the Legislative Council of Ceylon; Member of the Colombo Friend in Need Society; b. 12 Feb. 1848; s. of late D. B. F. Obeyesekere, Mudhjar of Talpe Pattoo, and Cornelia Susannah Dias Bandaranaike; m. 1878, Ezline Maria, 2nd d. of late Hon. James Alwis. M.L.C.; one s. three d. *Educ.:* Colombo Academy (Queen's College); St. Thomas' College. Passed the District Courts Proctor's Examination as 1st in order of merit, 1872; devoted his time more to cocoanut planting and improving his estates than practising at the Bar; representing the Low Country Sinhalese community in the Legislative Council of Ceylon since 1900; presented with the gold Victoria Diamond Jubilee Medal, 1897; visited England for Coronation of King Edward VII.; presented with gold Coronation Medal of King Edward VII., 1902; and again as an authorised representative of Ceylon at the Coronation of King George V., presented with the Coronation Medal of King George V. and Queen Mary, 22 June 1911. *Recreations:* shooting, tennis, cricket. *Address:* Hill Castle, Colombo, Ceylon. *T.A.:* Freloquet, Colombo. *Clubs:* Corona: Sinhalese Sports, Turf, Colombo.

(Died 14 Oct. 1926.)

O'DONOGHUE, David J., biographer and editor; Librarian of University College, Dublin, 1909; b. Chelsea, 22 July 1866; m. Florence White; three d. Began to write for press in 1886; has written largely for Dublin papers; writes chiefly on Irish literary subjects; Vice-President of National Literary Society, Dublin. *Publications:* Ireland in London (with F. A. Fahy), 1887; The Poets of Ireland, a Biographical Dictionary, 1891-1893; new and enlarged edition, 1912; Irish Humorists, 1892; Minor Irish Poets, 1893; Humour of Ireland, 1894; introduction to Reliques of Barney Maglone, 1894; Irish Poetry of the Nineteenth Century, 1894; List of 1300 Irish Artists, 1894; Fardorougha the Miser (introduction to), 1895; Writings of James Fintan Lalor, 1895; Life of William Carleton, 2 vols., 1896; edited Traits and Stories of the Irish Peasantry, 4 vols., 1896-1897; Life and Writings of James Clarence Mangan, 1898; edited Works of Samuel Lover, 6 vols., 1898-99; also The Black Prophet, by Carleton, 1898; Bibliographical Catalogue of Collections of Irish Music, 1899; Richard Pockrich, an Irish Musical Genius, 1899; Life of Robert Emmet, 1902; Poems of James Clarence Mangan, 1904; Prose Writings of the same, 1903; Sir Walter Scott's Tour in Ireland, 1905; Geographical Distribution of Irish Ability, 1906; Memoir of John Keegan, in collection of Legends and Stories, by Keegan, 1907; Essays of Thomas Davis, 1915; also author of numerous articles in Dictionary of National Biography, Catholic Cyclopædia, etc. *(Died 1917.)*

OLIVER, Charles Nicholson Jewel, C.M.G. 1905; b. 1848. Joined the Public Service, Department of Lands, 1866; Under-Secretary for Lands, New South Wales, 1880; Railway Commissioner, 1888; Chief Commissioner for Railways, 1897; retired, 1907. *Address:* Camira, Pennant Hills, nr. Sydney, N.S.W. *(Died 14 June 1920.)*

O'NIAL, Surgeon-General John, C.B. 1881, L.R.C.S.I.; retired, 1887; b. 1827. Assist.-Surgeon, 1852; Surgeon, 1859; Surgeon-Major, 1872; Surgeon-General, 1885; served Kaffir War, 1852-53 (medal); Afghan War as P.M.O. (despatches, medal with clasp); Nile, 1884-85 (despatches, promoted, medal with clasp, Khedive's star); Soudan, 1885-86. *Club:* Naval and Military. *(Died 1 Sept. 1919.)*

O'SHEA, Sir Henry, Kt., cr. 1916; Lord Mayor, Cork; J.P.; b. 8 July 1858; m. 1882, Bridget, d. of John Blewitte; four s. six d. *Educ.:* National School, Kilbrin. Member of Cork Corporation, 1898; High Sheriff, 1901; Alderman, 1908; Lord Mayor, 1911-16. *Address:* Old Court, Rochestown. Co. Cork. *(Died 1926.)*

OUIMET, Hon. Joseph Alderic; b. 20 May 1848; m. 1874, Marie Therese (d. 1897), d. of late J. F. A. Chartier La Rocque, Montreal; three s. three d. *Educ.:* Victoria University, Cobourg. Advocate, 1870; K.C. 1880; M.P. (C.) Laval, 1873-96; Speaker, 1887-91; Minister of Public Works, 1892-96; Puisne Judge, Court of King's Bench, 1896-1906. *Clubs:* Mount Royal, Canadian, Montreal.

(Died 12 May 1916.)

OVEREND, Walker, M.A., M.D. Oxon; Chief Assist. X-Ray. Dept., St. Bartholomew's Hospital; Hon. Radiologist to East Sussex Hospital, Hastings; late Physician to Prince of Wales' Hospital, N. *Address:* 29 Eversfield Place, St. Leonards. *(Died 10 Feb. 1926.)*

PALADINI, Grande Ufficiale Prof. Carlo, Professor of English and Italian literature at the Reale Istituto Tecnico Galileo, and of literature relating to forestry at the Reale Istituto Superiore Forestale Nazionale, Florence; *b.* near Lucca, 1864; *m.* Maria Pagani, Milan; three *c.* Almost entirely self-taught; learned reading and writing from the parish priest of his native village; at sixteen joined a party of sellers of plaster casts, with whom he wandered about the world; in the United States he took to journalism, and wrote for many of the chief periodicals; lived at New Orleans, Salt Lake City, then in Gautemala, British Honduras, Hawaii, and Hong Kong; on returning to Italy he contributed to the daily papers and reviews; Crispi sent him to accompany Gladstone on the English statesman's last visit to Italy, the result of this journey being a volume entitled Gladstone e Dufferin in Italia —Lord Dufferin being at this time British Ambassador in Rome; was private secretary to two ministers of Public Instruction—Bianchi and De Marinis,—also to the Prime Minister, Alessandro Fortis; Commendatore of the Crown of Italy, Cavaliere dei S.S. Maurizio e Lazzaro and Officier d'Academie of the French Republic. *Publications:* Novelle Cinesi, 1900; Interviste, a series of Interviews with Gladstone, Cecil Rhodes, Chamberlain, Lord Salisbury, Jefferson Davis, Edwin Booth, etc., 1902; San Francesco d' Assisi nell' arte e nella storia lucchese, 1900; L'Isola di Montecristo, 1908; Il Turdus Musicus; Impero e Libertà nelle Colonie inglesi, 1916; The United States, Wilson and Italy, 1918; Un occasione perduta; L'alleanza anglo-italiana in Egitto, 1918; Lenin, 1920; Francesco Carrara cittadino lucchese e plebeo; Paese de vai lucchese de trovi; Il corvo di San Gemiguano; La volpe di Fiorini. *Recreations:* shooting, philately, and art collection. *Address:* Villa Paladini, Massa Pisana, near Lucca, Tuscany. *(Died 10 July 1922.)*

PARKER, Rt. Rev. Edward Melville, D.D., D.C.L.; Bishop of New Hampshire since 1914; *b.* Cambridge, Mass., 11 July 1855; *s.* of Henry M. Parker, Lawyer, and Fanny C. Stone; *m.* 1st, 1885, Grace (*d.* 1888) *d.* of Prof. J. J. Elmendorf, Racine, Wisconsin; one *s.*; 2nd, 1914, Isabella, *d.* of Rev. James B. Goodrich of Concord, N.H.; two *s.* one *d. Educ.:* St. Paul's School, Concord, New Hampshire; Keble College, Oxford; 2nd class Mathematic Moderations and Theology; M.A. A master at St. Paul's School, 1879-1905; D.D. Berkely Divinity School, 1905; D.C.L. Bishop's College, Lennoxville, Canada, 1906; D.D. Dartmouth College, 1914; Bishop Coadjutor of New Hampshire, U.S.A., 1906-14. *Address:* Concord. New Hampshire, U.S.A. *(Died 22 Oct. 1925.)*

PASCAL, Jean Louis, architect; Inspecteur général des Bâtiments civils; Member of the Institute of France and of the Académie des Beaux Arts; Commander of Legion of Honour; Officer of Public Instruction; King's Gold Medal, 1914; Gold Medal of the Institute of American Architects, 1914; *b.* 4 June 1837. *Educ.:* Ecole des Beaux Arts; Villa Medici (Grand Prix de Rome); Atelier Gilbert, Questel. *Works:* (monuments) Colonel d'Argy, at Saint Louis-des-Français, Rome; Michelet, at Père-Lachaise; Carnot, at Bordeaux; Victor Hugo, and Garnier, in Paris; (new buildings) Château du Doux, Corrèze; Château de Maubuisson, Clairefontaine; Villa Renouard, Pau; numerous houses and hotels; (restorations, additions, etc.) at Bibliothèque Nationale, Paris; Faculté de Médecine et de Pharmacie, Bordeaux. *Address:* 8 Boulevard Saint-Denis, Paris *(Died 16 May 1920.)*

PATTERSON, George, M.A., K.C. 1909; Master and Referee of the Court of King's Bench, Manitoba, since 1911; Registrar in Bankruptcy since 1921; *b.* Perth, Ont., 20 April 1846; *s.* of James and Jane Patterson; *m.* 1st, 1870, Annie G. Baker (*d.* 1897); 2nd, 1908, Viola G. Geddes; three *s.* two *d. Educ.:* Perth High School; University of Toronto. Gold Medallist in Mathematics; First-class Military School Certificate, Toronto, 1867; in action at Ridgway, Ont., Fenian Raid; Mathematical Master at Hamilton and Galt Collegiate Institutes, 1867-1872; called to Bar at Toronto, 1874; practised law in Hamilton, Ont., till 1882, when moved to Winnipeg; Deputy Attorney-General of Manitoba, 1898-1911. *Publications:* Editor Manitoba Law Reports, and of Digest of volumes i.-xxi. of the same reports. *Recreations:* lawn bowling, canoeing, skating, golf. *Address:* Court House, Winnipeg, Manitoba. *T.:* N 40-841; F 1879 *Club:* Canadian, Winnipeg.
(Died 23 Aug. 1925.)

PILLANS, Charles Eustace, I.S.O. 1907; J.P.; Horticultural Assist., Cape Colony, since 1905; *b.* Rosebank, Cape Colony, 26 Feb. 1850; *s.* of Chas. Stuart Pillans and Alida Dorothea Colyn; *m.* 1883, Mary Eliza Siddons Porter; one *s. Educ.:* Diocesan College, Rondebosch, Cape. Third-class clerk, Audit Office, 1873; Resident Magistrate's clerk, Wynberg, 1875; transferred to General Post Office, 1876; served as Lieut. and Acting Adjutant to Frontier Light Horse (Carrington's) during Gaika-Gealeka Kaffir War, 1877-78 (Kaffir War medal) and in the D.E.O.V. Rifles during Basuto War. 1880-81 (Basuto War medal); Surveyor, Provincial Post Offices, 1884; Agricultural Assistant, 1899. Director of Information Bureau, 1902; Director of Government Labour Bureau and Immigration Officer, 1902; attached to Excise Branch, Treasury, 1904; Stamping Commissioner, 1904. *Publications:* Manual of Orchard Work at the Cape. *Recreations:* gardening, collecting and growing Cape succulent plants. *Address:* Rosedale, Rosebank, Cape Colony. *(Died 15 March 1919.)*

PITTI, Sir Thyagaraya Chetti Garum, Diwan Bahadur, Kt., *cr.* 1920; President of the Madras Corporation.
(Died 28 April 1925.)

PRINCE, J.-E., A.B., LL.D., K.C., Advocate; retired; *b.* St. Célestin, district of Three Rivers, 15 May 1851; *m.* 1884, Miss Rivard, Quebec; five *d. Educ.:* Nicolet Seminary; Laval Univ. Admitted at the Quebec Bar, 1879; late teacher of Roman Law and Civil Procedure, now of Economics at Laval University. *Publications:* several writings on divers topics and public lectures. *Recreations:* literature, music, etc. *Address:* 81 Dorchester Street, Quebec. Canada.
(Died 6 June 1923.)

PROUT, Henry Goslee; formerly Editor of Railroad Gazette, New York, and President and General Manager of companies manufacturing engineering products; late Governor of provinces of the Equator, Africa: Colonel of General Staff and Major of Engineers, army of Khedive; .C.E. (Univ. of Michigan); A.M. (hon., Yale Univ.); LL.D. (hon. Univ. of Michigan); Corresponding Member American Geographical Society. *Publications:* Life of George Westinghouse; numerous fugitive pieces. *Address:* Nutley, New Jersey. *Club:* Century, New York. *(Died 26 Jan. 1927.)*

QUINN, John, Lawyer; *b.* Tiffin, O., 24 April 1870; *s.* of James W. Quinn and Mary Quinian; unmarried. *Educ.:* University of Michigan; LL.B. Georgetown U., Washington, D.C., 1893; LL.B. Harvard, 1895; Private Secretary to Hon. Charles Foster, Sec. of Treasury in

Harrison Cabinet, 1890-93 ; associated in practice in N.Y. City with Gen. Benjamin F. Tracy, 1895-1900 mem. law firm Alexander & Colby, 1900-6 ; head own law office since 1906 ; del. Dem. Nat. Conv., Denver, 1908, Baltimore. 1912. Member Am. Bar Association, N.Y. State Bar Association, Association Bar City of New York ; New York Co. Lawyers' Association, Contemporary Art Soc., Société de Cent Bibliophiles, etc. One of organisers of International Exhibition of Modern Art, New York, 1913 ; hon. Fellow for life Met. Mus. of Art, New York, in recognition of services in the cause of free art ; an authority on modern Irish literature and drama, and possesses valuable collection of modern art ; conducted campaign which resulted in removal of all duty on modern works of art ; Chevalier Legion of Honour, France, for services during the War. *Publications :* Essays on Literature and Art. *Address :* 58 Central Park W., New York ; 31 Nassau Street, New York. *Clubs :* Harvard, Manhattan.

(*Died 28 July 1924.*)

RALPH, William, I.S.O. 1903 ; late Secretary to Registrar-General for Scotland ; three times Superintendent of Scottish Census. *Address :* Nethersole, Wymynswold, Canterbury.

(*Died 29 June 1928.*)

RANSOME, Arthur, M.D., M.A., F.R.C.P., F.R.S. ; Hon. Fellow Caius College, Cambridge ; Consulting Physician Manchester Hospital for Consumption, and Diseases of the Chest and Throat, and Royal Victoria and West Hants Hospital ; Vice-President of M. and S. Sanitary Association ; Fellow of College of State Medicine ; *b.* Manchester, 11 Feb. 1834 ; *e.s.* of late Joseph Atkinson Ransome (*d.* 1868), and Eliza, 3rd *d.* of Joseph Brookhouse, Derby ; *m.* 1862, Lucy Elizabeth Fullarton (*d.* 1906) ; three *s.* four *d.* *Educ. :* Manchester ; Trin. Coll. Dublin ; Caius Coll. Camb. ; St. George's Hospital, London ; Paris. Caian scholar in Anatomy ; Mecklenberg Scholar in Chemistry ; Senior Optime in Math. Tripos ; 1st class Nat. Science Tripos, 1856 ; Lecturer on Biology, 1857-61. Lecturer and afterwards Professor of Hygiene and Public Health at the Owens College, 1880-95 ; Examiner in Sanitary Science at the Cambridge and Victoria Universities ; Milroy Lecturer to the College of Physicians on the Causes and Prevention of Phthisis, 1890 ; Weber-Parkes Prize Essayist on Tuberculosis, 1897. *Publications :* Stethometry, 1876 ; Prognosis in Lung Disease, 1882 ; Causes of Consumption, 1884 ; Causes and Prevention of Phthisis, 1890 ; Treatment of Phthisis, 1896 ; Researches on Tuberculosis ; The Principles of Open-Air Treatment of Phthisis and Sanatorium Construction, 1903 ; A Campaign against Consumption, 1914. *Recreations :* bacteriology, photography. *Address :* Sunnyhurst, Bournemouth. *T. :* Bournemouth 55. *Club :* Bournemouth.

[*Died 25 July 1922.*]

REID, George Ogilvy, R.S.A. since 1898. *Address :* 11 Carlton Street, Edinburgh. *Club :* Scottish Arts, Edinburgh.

(*Died 11 April 1928.*)

RENALS, Sir James Herbert, 2nd Bt., *cr.* 1895 ; Lieutenant for City of London ; *b.* 5 Nov. 1870 ; *s.* of 1st Bt. and Mary, *d.* of Alfred Wilson ; *S.* father, 1907. *Heir :* *s.* Herbert, *b.* 29 Sep. 1919. (*Died April 1927.*)

RENTELL, Henry William Sidney, A.M.I.E.E., F.Z.S. ; Editor Electricity ; Managing Director S. Rentell & Co., Limited, publishers ; *b.* 1864 ; *m.* 1899, Sophie, *d.* of

Geo. Strohmenger ; two *s.* two *d.* *Educ. :* Philological School, London ; Neuenheim College. Heidelberg ; Finsbury Technical College. After several years of engineering practice acquired and edited Electricity ; subsequently founded the publishing firm bearing his name. *Recreation :* freemasonry. *Address :* Haroldene, 61 Tytherton Road, Tufnell Park, N.19. *T. :* North 1148.

(*Died 22 Oct. 1927.*)

RICHARDS, Theodore William, Prof. of Chemistry, Harvard Univ., since 1901 ; Director of Walcott Gibbs Memorial Laboratory since 1912 ; S.B. (Haverford, 1885), A.B. (Harvard, 1886), A.M., Ph.D. (Harvard, 1888), Hon. Sc.D. (Yale, 1905), Hon. LL.D. (Haverford, 1908, Pittsburgh, 1915), Hon. Chem.D. Clark, 1909), Hon. Ph.D. (Prague, 1909), Hon. Sc.D. (Harvard, 1910) ; Hon. M.D. (Berlin, 1910) ; Hon. D.Sc. (Cambridge, Oxford, Manchester, 1911) ; Hon. Ph.D. (Christiania, 1911) ; Hon. LL.D. Pennsylvania, 1920 ; Hon. Sc.D., Princeton University, 1923 ; *b.* 31 Jan. 1868 ; *s.* of late William T. Richards, 1833-1905, and Anna Matlack ; *m.* 1896, Miriam S., *d.* of Prof. Joseph Henry Thayer ; two *s.* one *d.* *Educ. :* Haverford College, Pa. ; Harvard University ; Göttingen ; Dresden ; Munich ; Leipzig. Assistant in Chemistry, Harvard, 1889-91 ; Instructor. 1891-94 (Member of Faculty of Arts and Sciences of Harvard, 1892) ; Assistant Professor, 1894 1901 ; Chairman of Division of Chemistry, 1903-1911 ; Visiting Professor at University of Berlin, 1907 ; Research Associate, Carnegie Institution of Washington, since 1902 ; Lecturer, Lowell Institute, 1908 ; Davy Medallist, Royal Society, 1910 ; Faraday Lecturer, 1911 ; Willard Gibbs Medallist, 1912 ; Nobel Prize for Chemistry, 1914 ; Franklin Medallist, 1916 ; Le Blanc and Lavoisier Medallist, 1922 ; Member of International Commissions on Atomic Weights, Elements, etc. ; Officier de la Légion d'Honneur, 1925 ; Member National Academy of Sciences ; Foreign Member of the Royal Society of London ; Hon. and Foreign Member of Chemical Society of London ; Hon. Member of Royal Institution of Great Britain ; Hon. Fellow, Royal Society of Edinburgh ; Membre d'Honneur de la Soc. Chim. de France ; Foreign Member of Royal Swedish Academy, R. Accad. dei Lincei, and Hon. Member Royal Irish Academy ; Corresponding Member Royal Bologna Academy, Royal Danish Academy of Science ; Royal Prussian Academy of Sciences ; Fellow of American Academy of Arts and Sciences (Pres. 1919-21) ; Member of American Philosophical Society ; Fellow of American Association for Advancement of Science (Pres. 1917) ; Hon. Member of American Chemical Society (Pres. 1914), etc. ; Member of various committees and advisory boards connected with use of chemistry in the war. *Publications :* about three hundred papers on chemical and physical topics. *Recreations :* sketching, golf, sailing. *Address :* 15 Follen Street, Cambridge, Mass., U.S.A. *T.A. :* Professor Richards, Cambridge, Mass. *T. :* University 8117. *M. :* Mass. 118286. *Clubs :* Saturday, Colonial, Oakley Country, Harvard Union, Harvard, Tavern (Hon.), Boston ; Chemists, New York.

(*Died 2 April 1928.*)

ROBERTS, Martin, M.Inst.C.E., M.I.E.E., F.C.S. ; consulting engineer ; *b.* Lichfield, 21 Nov. 1853 ; *s.* of late William Roberts of Charlton Kings, Gloucestershire ; *m.* 1879, Alice, *d.* of Jaques Hein of Erfurt ; two *s.* one *d.* *Educ. :* Bayley Hall, Hertford ; King's College, London. Entered Engineering Department, Post Office, 1871 ; Inspecting Engineer, 1873 ; Superintendent of Factories, 1880 ; Assistant Engineer-in-Chief, 1898 ; retired from Post Office, 1909 ; designed Post Office Factories, Post Office Power

Stations, and engineering work for Post Office London Telephone System; Member of Engineering Standards Committee and of Physical Standards Committee; an authority on telegraph and telephone engineering, and the design of electrical power stations. *Publications:* contributions to journals of Institution Civil Engineers and Institution Electrical Engineers. *Recreations:* yachting, golf, fishing. *Club :* Reform. (*Died 22 Feb. 1926.*)

ROSS, Hon. William Roderick, M.A., K.C.; *b.* Fort Chipewyan, Alberta, 29 March 1869; *s.* of Donald Ross and Anna M'Kenzie (both Scotch); father's family employed by Hudson's Bay Company for two or three generations back; *m.* 1892, Leila Young; two *s.* three *d. Educ.:* St. John's College, Winnipeg, Man.; B.A., M.A., Barrister-at-law; practised in Fernie, B.C., for several years; (C.) Provincial Assembly, 1903, 1907, 1909, 1912-16; Minister of Lands, British Columbia, 1910-16. (*Died 4 Feb. 1928.*)

SAUZIER, Anatole; *b.* Mauritius, 20 July 1849; *m.* 1879; six *s.* two *d. Educ.:* Royal College, Mauritius; Edinburgh Academy. Called to Scottish Bar in Edinburgh, 1873; practised as barrister in Mauritius until 1882; District Magistrate in Mauritius, 1882-88; Judicial Vice-Consul at Tamatave, Madagascar, 1888; Acting Consul, 1889-97; Consul, 1897-1910. *Address:* Curepipe, Mauritius.
(*Died April 1920.*)

SHAH, Khan Bahadur Sir Sayyid Mehdi, K.C.I.E., *cr.* 1924; C.I.E. 1921; O.B.E. 1919; Honorary Magistrate and Pres., Municipal Committee, Gojra; Senior Vice-Chairman District Board; Member Sanitary Board, Punjab; Member N.W. Railway Advisory Board; Member Provincial Cotton Committee. *Address:* Gojra, Lyallpur District, Punjab. (*Died 5 Oct. 1927.*)

SHAMSHER SINGH, Sir Sardar, Sardar Bahadur, K.C.I.E., *cr.* 1917; C.I.E. 1911; Chief Minister Jind State since 1903; *s.* of Sardar Jaimal Singh of Raipur, Ludhiana District, Punjab; *b.* 1860. *Educ.:* Jullundur and Hoshiarpur High Schools, and at Government College, Lahore. Served during Afghan War, 1879-80, with march from Kabul to Kandahar (medal, bronze star); was Secretary to the Maharaja of Jind, 1885-87; Postmaster-General and Secretary to Council of Regency, Jind State, 1887-99, and Chief Judge of State, High Court, 1899-1903; received personal title of Sardar Bahadur, 1906; Coronation medals, 1903 and 1911. *Address:* Sangrur, Jind State, Punjab.
(*Died 8 March 1920.*)

SMITH, Alfred John, F.R.C.S.I., M.B., M.Ch., M.A.O., R.U.I.; late Vice-Pres. British Gynæcological Society; late President Obst. Sect. Royal Academy of Medicine; ex-Assistant Master, Rotunda Hospital; Prof. of Midwifery and Gynæcology, National Univ.; Consultant Gynæcologist, St. Vincent's Hospital, Dublin; *b.* Kevit Castle, Nov. 1865; *e. s.* of late Philip Smith, J.P., of Kevit Castle, Crossdoney, Cavan; unmarried. *Educ.:* St. Patrick's College, Cavan; Dublin; Leipsic; Vienna. *Publications:* large contributor to various societies and journals on questions of interest to gynæcologists and laparotomists. *Recreations:* golf, fishing, shooting, motoring. *Address:* 30 Merrion Square, Dublin. *T. :* 1295 Dublin. *M. :* RI 839. *Club:* Stephen's Green, Dublin.
(*Died 20 Feb. 1925.*)

SOMERSET, John Henry William; late Principal Clerk of the Private Bill Office, House of Commons; *b.* 1848; *y. s.* of late Rev. Villiers Henry Plantagenet Somerset, *s.* of late Lord

Charles Somerset; *m.* 1st, 1889, Mary de Chair (*d.* 1892), *d.* of Rev. W. C. Denshire, of Thetford House, Lincoln; 2nd, 1893, Isabel Maud, *d.* of Frederick Courtney; one *d. Educ.:* Marlborough. *Address:* Westfield, Cheltenham.
(*Died 2 March 1925.*)

SPENCER, Ven. George, Incumbent of North Goulburn, 1908 - 12 ; Archdeacon of Young, 1903. *Educ.:* Moore College, N.S.W. Ordained, 1867; Curate of St. Stephen's, Ballarat, 1867-69; Incumbent of St. Stephen's, 1869-72; of St. Saviour, Tarnagulla, 1872-75; Adelong, 1875-77; Tumut, 1877-85; Bega, 1885-94; St. Nicholas, Goulburn, 1894-97; St. Matthew, Albury, 1897-1903; Canon of Goulburn, 1894-1912. *Address:* Neath, 315 Miller Street, North Sydney, New South Wales. (*Died 1926.*)

STOKER, George, C.M.G. 1901; L.M.C.S.I.; J.P. for Co. Kerry; M.R.C.P.I. and M.R.C.S. England; Physician, London Throat Hospital; Medical Officer, Oxygen Hospital; *b.* 20 July 1855; 5th *s.* of late Abraham Stoker of Dublin Castle; *m.* 1882, Agnes, *e. d.* of Richard, The M'Gillycuddy of The Reeks, Co. Kerry. *Educ.:* Dublin. Hon. Associate of Order of St. John of Jerusalem in England; Vice-President (formerly President) of British Laryngological Association ; Fellow of Medical Society of London ; Member of Pathological and Clinical Societies; Physician to London Throat Hospital, and Hon. Medical Officer of Actors' Benevolent Fund ; formerly Surgeon to Hospital for Diseases of the Throat (Golden Sq.) ; Surgeon in Imperial Ottoman Army; was Medical Officer of Bulgarian Relief Fund, 1877 ; acted as Chef de l'ambulance du Croissant Rouge during Turko-Russian War 1876-78 (special medal for Champcharee, 4th class Medjidie) ; was through the sieges of Shipka, Plevna, and Erzeroum, and as Stafford House Commissioner during Zulu War, 1879-80 (medal) ; initiated and organised Civil Hospital in S. Africa, 1899-1900 ; and served as 2nd Surg. Irish Hosp. (despatches, medal with three clasps) *Publication:* With the Unspeakables. *Recreation:* golf. *Address:* 14 Hertford Street, Mayfair, W.1. *Club:* Princes Golf, Mitcham.
(*Died 23 April 1920.*)

STRUBEN, William Charles Marinus, C.M.G. 1900; Natal Guides; *b.* 12 May 1856; *s.* of Capt. Struben, of Pretoria; *m.* 1882, Helen *d.* of A. K. Murray. Served Zulu War, 1879-80 Boer War, 1880-81; South Africa (despatches medal). *Address:* Glen Athol, near Charlestown. Natal. (*Died 25 April 1928.*)

SWANN, Harry Kirke; F.Z.S., M.B.O.U. Corr. Fellow Amer. Orn. Union; Managing Director of Wheldon & Wesley, Ltd.; *b.* 18 March 1871. *Educ.:* privately. Has made ornithological researches in Spain, Roumania and other parts of Europe, as well as in North America. *Publications:* A Monograph of the Birds of Prey ; Two Ornithologists on the Lower Danube: A Dictionary of English and Folk-names of British Birds; a Synopsis of the Accipitres; The Birds of London ; A Concise Handbook of British Birds; Nature in Acadie H. Kirke White (Canterbury Poets), etc. (with W. H. Mullens) A Bibliography of British Ornithology; formerly Editor of The Naturalist's Journal, The Ornithologist, The Naturalists' Directory, etc., and Editor and Literary Adviser to W. C. Nimmo ; Vice-President Barnet Boy Scouts Assoc. ; Member, International Ornithological Committee. *Recreations* ornithology, oology, foreign travel. *Address* Thorncombe, Lyonsdown Road, New Barnet Herts ; 2, 3 and 4 Arthur Street, New Oxford Street, W.C.2. *Club:* Authors.
(*Died 14 April 1926.*)

SWEENEY, Hon. Francis J., K.C.; *b.* 1862. *Educ.:* St. Joseph's College, New Brunswick. Was for some years a school teacher; called to Bar, 1902; Member Westmorland, New Brunswick, 1903; Member Provincial Government, 1903 - 4; Member, Executive Council, New Brunswick, 1905; Solicitor-General, 1904 - 5; Surveyor - General, 1905 - 8. *Address:* Moncton, New Brunswick, Canada.
(Died 2 May 1921.)

TAVEGGIA, Rt. Rev. Santino; Bishop of Dinajpur since 1927; Bishop of Krishnagar, 1906-27; *b.* Italy, 1855. Went to India, 1879. *Address:* Dinajpur, North Central Bengal.
(Died 2 June 1928.)

THULRAI, Taluqdar of, Rana Sir Sheoraj Singh Bahadur of Khajurgaon, K.C.I.E., *cr.* 1911; Rai Bareli District; *b.* 1865; *s.* of Hon. Rana Sir Shankur Bux Singh Bahadur, K.C.I.E.; *S.* father, 1897; *m.* 1st, *d.* of Bahu Amarjit Singh, *y. b.* of the Raja of Majhonli; 2nd, *d.* of Raja Somesurdutt Singh, a Raja of Kundwar; 3rd, *d.* of the Raja of Bijaipur District, Mirzapur; two *s.* five *d. Educ.:* Government High School, Rai Bareli. Hon. Magistrate and a Munsif; holds about 150 villages, and maintains a dispensary, an upper Primary Village School and Coronation Anglo-Sanskrit Pathshallaat Khajurgaon; the house descends from King Sahvahan, whose Sumvat Era is current in India, and so the Rana is a Bais Rajput. *Recreations:* hunting and sports, etc. *Heir:* Kunwar Lal Eina Natti Singh Bahadur. *Address:* Thulrai, Khajurgaon, India. *T.A.:* Dalman District, Rai Bareli.
(Died 14 April 1920.)

TRAPANI, Lt.-Col. Alfred, M.V.O. 1912; late Royal Malta Artillery; *b.* Malta, Jan. 1859; *s.* of G. B. Trapani, LL.D., C.M.G.; *m.* Mary, *e. d.* of Professor A. Mifsud, M.D.; three *d. Educ.:* private school. Commissioned as 2nd Lieutenant, 1877; Lieutenant, 1880; Captain, 1885; Major, 1896; Lt.-Col. 1909; served Egyptian Campaign, 1882 (Queen's Medal, Khedive's bronze star); retired, 1915. *Address:* 314 S.S. Paolo, Valletta, Malta.
(Died 9 Dec. 1928.)

TRICKETT, William, A.M., D.C.L., LL.D.; Dean of Dickinson School of Law since 1890; *b.* Leicester, 9 June 1840. *Educ.:* Dickinson College, Carlisle, Pennsylvania. For five years Professor, Dickinson College; Member of Bar of Pennsylvania, 1875. *Publications:* The Law of Boroughs; Law of Highways; Law of Liens; Law of Limitations; Law of Witnesses; Guardians; Landlord and Tenant; Criminal Law; Partition; also many articles in Law Reviews. *Address:* Carlisle, Pennsylvania.
(Died 1 Aug. 1928.)

WATKINS, Frederick Henry, I.S.O. 1904; O.B.E. 1925; *b.* Edgbaston, Birmingham, 1859; *m.* Marion Charlotte, *d.* of late Rev. Canon Connell of St. Vincent; one *d. Educ.:* St. Olave's, Southwark; Switzerland, Italy, and Germany. Private Secretary to Sir Roger Goldsworthy, Administrator of St. Lucia, 1882; Inspector of Schools, St. Vincent, 1883-89; Inspector of Schools of the Leeward Islands, 1889-99; Adjutant of St. Christopher Nevis Defence Force, 1897-99; Commissioner of Montserrat, 1900-6; Commissioner and Acting Judge of Turks and Caicos Islands, 1906-14; Colonial Secretary of Grenada, 1914; retired, 1915; in Foreign Censorship Department, War Office, 1915; Acting Scientific Assist. Imperial Dept. of Agriculture, West Indies, 1917; Acting Colonial Secretary of the Leeward Islands, 1917 - 20; Magistrate, Nevis, 1920-25; retired, 1925. *Publications:* Educational Works; Lives of Comenius Pestalozzi, Froebel, and Locke; Daily Thoughts from Horace; Handbook of the Leeward Islands, 1924. *Address:* Antigua, West Indies. *(Died 8 July 1928.)*

WATSON, Ven. W. C., M.A. (Durham); Rector of All Saints', St. Thomas, Danish West Indies, since 1916; Canon of St. John's Cathedral, Antigua, B.W.I., since 1911; Archdeacon of the Virgin Islands, 1916; *b.* Barbados, 26 May 1867; *s.* of Rev. W. C. and Mrs. C. M. S. Watson; *m.* 1891, Edith Hutson, *e. d.* of H. J. Inniss, owner of Welches Plantation, St. Thomas, Barbados; three *s.* two *d. Educ.:* Harrison College and Codrington College, Barbados. Acting Headmaster of the Grammar School and Inspector of Schools in St. Vincent, B.W.I., 1890; ordained, 1890; Curate of St. George's, Grenada, B.W.I., 1890; Priest-in-charge of St. Paul's, St. Croix, D.W.I., 1893; Curate of St. John's Cathedral, Antigua, 1894. *Recreations:* boating, fishing, motoring; also proof-reading. *Address:* All Saints' Rectory, St. Thomas, Danish West Indies. *T.A.:* Watson, St. Thomas. *(Died 1916.)*

WELSH, Rev. Thomas; Professor St. Mary's College, Blairs, Aberdeen; Editor of Catholic Directory for Scotland. *Address:* St. Mary's College, Blairs, Aberdeen. *(Died 1920.)*

WILMER, Canon John Kidd; *b.* Portsmouth, England; *e. s.* of late George Wilmer; *m.* Georgina, 2nd *d.* of late Thomas Gorringe; two *d. Educ.:* Private school, England; Christ's College, Canterbury, New Zealand. Ordained 1872; Curate of Ellesmere, 1872-1875; Fernside, 1876-78, both in New Zealand; Incumbent of Green Ponds, 1879-1881; Rector of Brighton, 1881-98; of Devonport, 1898-1904; of Kingston, 1904-1911; of Carrick, 1911-19; Rural Dean, 1895-1905, all in Tasmania; Canon of S. David's Cathedral, Hobart, Tasmania; Chaplain Australian Commonwealth Military Forces (Capt.). *Address:* 218 Charles Street, Launceston, Tasmania. *[Died 1928.*

WILSHERE, Alfred Henry, C.M.G. 1913; *b.* 23 Aug. 1854; *s.* of Rev. H. M. M. Wilshere; *m.* 1882, Annie Florence Isabelle, *d.* of Captain A. H. Richetts, late of 2nd Somersetshire Light Infantry Militia; three *s.* five *d. Educ.:* Diocesan College, Rondebosch. Clerk Colonial Secretary's Office, 1872; Clerk Customs, East London, 1873; Sub-Collector Customs, East London, 1900; Controller of Customs, Capetown, and Registrar of Shipping, 1901-14; Chairman of Table Bay Harbour Board, 1902-9; J.P. Cape Colony; Member Game Protection Association. *[Died 28 Feb. 1927.*

WILSON, P. Macgregor; R.S.W.; artist; *b.* Glasgow; *m.;* one *d. Educ.:* University Glasgow and London. Travelled extensively America, all Europe, Egypt, India, Arabia, Russia, etc.; rode 1000 miles through Persia; painted the late Shah's portrait at Teheran; exhibited in Antwerp, Munich, Berlin, Copenhagen, Edinburgh, and Glasgow; upon two occasions President Glasgow Art Club; member of Committee, International Exhibition, Glasgow. *Publications:* various articles on the East; Autotypes; The North Sea, etc. *Recreations:* travel, patentee of engine for steam launches. *(Died 25 Sept. 1928.)*

YOUNG, Ernest Herbert, B.M.; Assistant Superintendent, Hospital for Insane, London, Ontario, since 1916; President, Canadian Hospital Association, since 1914; Member of the Canadian Medical Association; Member of American Psychological Association; *b.* Guelph, 1878; *s.* of William Young; *m.* 1912, Florence Williamson, B.A., Kingston. *Educ.:* Guelph; Toronto Univ. Graduated in Medicine, 1907; appointed Clinical Assistant at Toronto Asylum, 1907; Assistant Physician, Rockwood Hospital, Kingston, 1908; Assistant Superintendent, 1912; Professor of Psychiatry, Queen's Univ. 1912; Associate Professor of Psychiatry, Western University, London, 1916; Captain C.A.M.C., No. 10 Stationary Hospital, Western University Unit, C.E.F., 1916; Officer Commanding Coburg Military Hospital, Aug. 1916. *Address:* Hospital for Insane, London, Ontario. (*Died 8 Aug. 1921.*)

SUPPLEMENTARY ADDENDUM

DALY, John Archer Blake-, J.P., D.L.; *b.* 1835; *s.* of late Andrew William Blake, of Furbough, Co. Galway, and Maria Julia, *d.* of Malachy Daly of Raford: *m.* 1864, Lady Anne Elizabeth Charlotte Nugent (*d.* 1907), *d.* of 9th Earl of Westmeath. High Sheriff, Galway, 1866; late Lieut.-Col. and Hon. Col. 4th Batt. Connaught Rangers; assumed name of Daly under the will of his maternal grandfather. *Address:* Raford, Kiltulla, nr. Athenry; Furbough, Galway. (*Died 13 June 1917.*)

WHO WAS WHO, 1916-1928

A

ABBAY, Rev. Richard, M.A., Hon. Canon of Norwich since 1906 ; Rector of Earl Soham, Suffolk, 1880-1912 ; *b.* Aldborough, Yorkshire, 11 Feb. 1844 ; *m.* 1880, Janet Norman, *d.* of Canon C. F. Norman, Mistley Place, Essex ; two *s.*, three *d. Educ. :* St. Peter's School, York ; Exeter College, Oxford. (Scholar) ; 1st class Math. Mods. 1865 ; 1st class final Math. School, 1867 ; Lecturer and Demonstrator in Physics, King's College, London, 1868 ; Fellow of Wadham College, Oxford, 1869 ; member of Eclipse Expedition, S. Spain, 1870 ; S. India, 1871 ; member of French Transit of Venus Expedition, New Caledonia, 1874 ; chaplain, Kandyan Province, 1872-74 ; Rector of Little Bromley, Essex, 1878 ; Rural Dean of Loes, 1893 ; County Council, East Suffolk, 1900 ; Alderman, 1911. *Publications :* papers in the Royal Astronomical, Geological, Physical, Linnean Societies' Journals ; Castle of Knaresburgh, a tale in verse of the Civil War ; Life, a Mode of Motion, in verse. *Recreation :* cricket. *Address :* Earl Soham, Framlingham.

(Died 11 Dec. 1924.)

ABBE, Prof. Cleveland, A.M., LL.D., F.R. Ast. Soc., F.R. Met. Soc., U.S. National Acad. of Science. Professor of Meteorology, U.S. Weather Bureau, since 1871 ; Lecturer on Meteorology, Johns Hopkins University, since 1895 ; *b.* New York City, 3 Dec. 1838 ; *s.* of George Waldo Abbe and Charlotte Colgate, and descended from purely English families ; *m.* 1st, 1870, Frances Martha, *d.* of David Neal and Calista Lane ; three *s.* ; 2nd, 1909, Margaret Augusta, *d.* of W. Geo. Halman Percival of St. Kitts, W.I. *Educ. :* College of the City of New York, 1851-57; University of the State of Michigan, 1858-60 ; Harvard University, 1860-64 ; Central Nicolas Observatory, Poulkova, near St. Petersburg, Russia, 1864-66. *Career :* Instructor in Mathematics, Trinity Parish School, New York, 1857-1858 ; in Engineering, Michigan State Agricultural College, 1859 ; and in University of the State of Michigan, Ann Arbor, 1859-60 ; Aid in U.S. Coast Survey (under B. A. Gould), 1860-64 ; Resident at the Central Nicholas Observatory, 1864-66 ; Aid at the U.S. Naval Observatory, 1867-68 ; Director of Cincinnati Observatory, 1868-73 ; started the reform in standards of civil time reckoning by even hours of longitude from Greenwich ; conducted the Harrison expedition to observe the solar eclipse of August 1869 at Sioux Falls City, Dakota and the Signal Service expedition to observe the solar eclipse of July 1878 from Pike's Peak ; Signal Service Delegate First Forestry Congress, Cincinnati, 1872, and U.S. Electrical Conference, 1884, where he moved the formation of the American Institute of Electrical Engineers ; U.S. Delegate International Congress on Standard Meridian and Time, Washington, 1884 ; Meteorologist to the U.S. Scientific Expedition to the west coast of Africa, 1889-90 ; U.S. delegate to the International Meteorological Congress, Munich, 1891 ; associate-editor of the American Meteorological Journal, 1891-94, and of the Beiträge zur Physik der freien Atmosphäre, 1905 ; founder and editor of Monthly Weather Review, 1893-1909 and since 1914, and of Bulletin, Mt. Weather Research Observatory, 1908-1913 ; Professor of Meteorology, George Washington University, Washington, 1885-1910 ; Adviser in Meteorology to the Carnegie Institution of Washington ; Founder of the Abbe Meteorological Library of the Johns Hopkins University ; delegate to the Kelvin Jubilee, 1896 ; to the Benjamin Franklin Bicentenary, 1906 ; Symons' medallist R. Met. Soc., 1912, *Publications :* numerous writings in Astronomy and Meteorology, since 1859. *Recreations :* none. *Address :* U.S. Weather Bureau, Washington. *T.A. :* Clevabbe, Washington. *(Died Oct. 1916.)*

ABBOTT, Rev. Edwin Abbott, M.A., D.D., student and author ; Hon. Fellow of St. John's College, Cambridge, 1912 ; Fellow of the British Academy, 1913 ; *b.* London, 20 Dec. 1838 ; *s.* of Edwin Abbott, Headmaster Philological School, London ; *m.* 1863, Mary Elizabeth Rangeley (*d.* 1919) ; one *s.* one *d. Educ. :* City of London School ; St. John's College, Cambridge. Senior Classic ; Chancellor's Classical Medallist, Cambridge, 1861 ; Fellow of St. John's College, Cambridge, 1862 ; Assistant Master King Edward's School, Birmingham, 1862-64 ; Clifton College, 1865 ; Headmaster of City of London School, 1865-89 ; Hulsean Lecturer, Cambridge, 1876 ; Select Preacher, Oxford, 1877. *Publications :* Bible Lessons, 1872 ; Cambridge Sermons, 1875 ; Through Nature to Christ, 1877 ; Oxford Sermons, 1879 ; article on "Gospels" in 9th ed. of Encyclopædia Britannica ; The Common Tradition of the Synoptic Gospels (with Mr W. G. Rushbrooke), 1884 ; Shakespearian Grammar, 1870 ; English Lessons for English People (with Prof. J. R. Seeley), 1871 ; How to Write Clearly, 1872 ; Latin Prose through English Idiom, 1973 ; The Good Voices, or A Child's Guide to the Bible, and Parables for Children, 1875 ; How to Tell the Parts of Speech, and How to Parse, 1875 ; edition of Bacon's Essays, 1876 ; Bacon and Essex, 1877 ; Philochristus, 1878 ; Via Latina, 1880 ; Hints on Home Teaching, 1883 ; Francis Bacon, an Account of his Life and Works, 1885 ; The Latin Gate, 1889 ; Onesimus, 1882 ; Flatland, or A Romance of Many Dimensions, 1884 ; The Kernel and the Husk, 1886 ; Philomythus, 1891 ; The Anglican Career of Cardinal Newman, 1892 ; The Spirit on the Waters, 1897 ; St. Thomas of Canterbury, his Death and Miracles, 1898 ; Clue, a Guide through Greek to Hebrew Scripture, 1900 ; Corrections of Mark adopted by Matthew and Luke, 1901 ; From Letter to Spirit, 1903 ; Paradosis, or, In the Night in which He was (?) Betrayed, 1904 ; Johannine Vocabulary, A Comparison of the

Words of the Fourth Gospel with those of the Three, 1905; Johannine Grammar, 1906; Silanus the Christian, 1906; Apologia, 1907; Notes on New Testament Criticism, 1907; Indices to Diatessarica, 1908; The Message of the Son of Man, 1909; The Son of Man, Contributions to the Study of the Thoughts of Jesus, 1910; Light on the Gospel from an Ancient Poet, 1912; The Fourfold Gospel, Introduction, 1913; Miscellanea Evangelica (I.), 1913; The Fourfold Gospel, The Beginning, 1914; The Fourfold Gospel, The Proclamation of the New Kingdom, 1915; Miscellanea Evangelica (II.), Christ's Miracles of Feeding, 1915; The Fourfold Gospel, The Law of the New Kingdom, 1916; The Fourfold Gospel, The Founding of the New Kingdom, 1917. *Address:* Wellside, Well Walk, Hampstead, N.W. 3. *(Died 12 Oct. 1926.)*

ABBOTT, Frank Frost, A.B., Ph.D., A.M.(Hon.); Kennedy Professor of the Latin Language, Princeton University; Trustee American Academy in Rome; ex-President American Phil. Association; *b.* 27 Mar. 1860; *s.* of Thaddeus Marvin Abbott and Mary Jane Frost; *m.* Jane Harrison, New Haven, Conn. *Publications:* Roman Political Institutions; A Short History of Rome; The Toledo Manuscript of the Germania of Tacitus; Society and Politics in Ancient Rome; The Common People of Ancient Rome; Selected Letters of Cicero; Roman Politics; The Spanish Pleas of Alberico Gentili, 2 vols. *Recreation:* fishing. *Address:* Princeton University, Princeton, New Jersey, U.S.A. *(Died 23 July 1924.)*

ABBOTT, Brig.-Gen. Henry Alexius, C.B. 1898; I.A., 15th Sikhs; *b.* Allahabad, 22 Jan. 1849; 4th *s.* of late Maj.-Gen. Augustus Abbott, C.B., Bengal Artillery; *m.* 1883, Isabella Agnes, 2nd *d.* of Robert Laing of Kinder, Kirkcudbrightshire, and Queensborough Terrace, Hyde Park, W. *Educ.:* King William's Coll., Isle of Man. Joined 37th Foot, 1868; Indian Staff Corps (15th Sikhs), 1870; Afghan War, 1878-80; actions of Ahmed Khel, Urzoo, and Kandahar; General Roberts' march Cabul to Kandahar (despatches, medal, 2 clasps, bronze star); Soudan, 1885; actions of Hasheen, Tofrek, and Tamai (despatches, medal, 2 clasps, bronze star, brevet of Major); 2nd Miranzai Expedition, 1891 (despatches, medal and clasp); operations of Flying Column in Kurrum Valley, 1897; Tirah, 1897-98; actions of Chagru Kotal and Dargai, capture of Sampagha and Arhanga Passes, Saransar and Waran Valley, and action of 16th Nov., twice severely wounded (despatches, medal with 3 clasps, C.B.); Colonel 15th Sikhs, 1913. *Address:* H. S. King and Co., 9 Pall Mall. S.W. *(Died 26 June 1924.)*

ABBOTT, Rev. Lyman, D.D., LL.D., L.H.D.; editor-in-chief of The Outlook since 1893; *b.* Roxbury, Mass., 18 Dec. 1835; *s.* of Jacob and Harriet Vaughan Abbott; *m.* 1857, Abby Frances Hamlin (*d.* 1907); four *s.* two *d. Educ.:* New York Univ. Entered Bar, 1856, New York; after three years' practice left the law for the ministry; and since the spring of 1860 has been engaged in ministerial, literary, and editorial work; Pastor, Plymouth Church, Brooklyn, N.Y., 1888-99. *Publications:* Jesus of Nazareth; A Layman's Story; Illustrated Commentary on the New Testament, 1875; In Aid of Faith, 1891; Life of Christ, 1894; Evolution of Christianity, 1896; Christianity and Social Problems, 1897; The Theology of an Evolutionist, 1897; The Life and Letters of Paul, 1898; The Life and Literature of the Ancient Hebrews, 1900; The Rights of Man, 1901; Henry Ward Beecher, 1903; The Great Companion, 1904, 1905; The Other Room, 1904; Christian Ministry, 1905; Personality of God, 1905; The Home Builder, 1908; The Temple, 1909; The Spirit of Democracy, 1910; My Four Anchors, 1911; America in the Making, 1911; Letters to Unknown Friends, 1913; Reminiscences, 1915; The Twentieth-Century Crusade,

1918; What Christianity Means to Me, 1921. *Recreations:* driving, walking, travel. *Address:* Cornwall on Hudson, New York; The Outlook, 381 Fourth Avenue, N.Y.-City. *Clubs:* Century, National Arts, Union League, Aldine Association, Post-Graduate, N.Y. City.
(Died 22 Oct. 1922.)

ABBOTT, Rt. Rev. Robert Crowther; *b.* 1869; *s.* of Rev. A. R. Abbott, late Vicar of Gorleston. *Educ.:* Marlborough College; Trinity College, Cambridge (Scholar). 7th Wrangler, 1891; Assistant Master Marlborough College, 1892, 1907; Chaplain, 1904-7; Principal of Salisbury Theological College and Canon in Salisbury Cathedral, 1907-13; Vicar of Great St. Mary's with St. Michael's, Cambridge, 1913-14; of Holy Trinity, Weymouth, 1914-16; of Gillingham, Dorset, 1916-25; Chaplain to Bishop of Salisbury, 1912; Canon in Salisbury Cathedral, 1917; Examining Chaplain, 1918; Bishop of Sherborne, 1925-27.
(Died 25 Nov. 1927.)

ABBOTT, Thomas Charles, J.P. for the City of Manchester, and Alderman; *b.* Blackburn; *m.* Anna Pye of Fulwood, Preston; one *s.* one *d.* President Library Association, 1921-1922; Chairman Manchester Public Libraries Committee; Governor of the John Rylands Library; Member of Lancashire Asylums Board and Chairman of Mental Defectives Committee; Member of Board of Overseers, township of Manchester; Vice-President Manchester and Salford Sanitary Association; Vice-President Manchester Playgoers' Club; Member of Council, Workers' Educational Association lectures for Working Men's Clubs Association Organiser and Lecturer, Altrincham centre Oxford University Extension Lectures; Commander of the Order of George I. (Greece); has contributed many articles to periodicals, etc. some of which have been reprinted. *Recreations:* golf, music. *Address:* 20 Pall Mall, Manchester. *Clubs:* Royal Societies; Clarendon Manchester. *(Died 26 Jan. 1927.)*

ABDY, Brig.-Gen. Anthony John, C.B. 1911; C.B.E. 1918; *b.* 26 April 1856; *s.* of J. T. Abdy, Regius Professor Civil Laws, Cambridge and Marian, 2nd *d.* of J. H. Hollway; *m.* 1888 Laura, *d.* of J. Bonham-Carter, of Adhurst, Petersfield; one *s.* one *d. Educ.:* Charterhouse; R.M.A. Woolwich. Entered R.A., 1876; Captain, 1884 Major, 1892; Lt.-Col., 1901; Col., 1904; Secretary R.A. Institution, 1891-98; served S. Africa 1899-1900 (slightly wounded, despatches, brevet Lt.-Col., queen's medal with clasp); commanded R.H.A. and R.F.A. South Africa 1908-12; A.M.S. Southern Command, 1916-18 retired. *Recreations:* cricket, travel, fishing *Address:* Woodbridge, Suffolk. *Club:* Naval and Military. *(Died 4 July 1924.)*

ABDY, Sir Henry Beadon, 4th Bt.; *b.* 1850; *b.* 13 June 1853; *s.* of 1st Bt. and Harriot *d.* of Rowland Alston of Pishiobury, Herts; brother 1921; *m.* 1891, Anna Adele Coronna one *s.* one *d. Heir: s.* Robert Henry Edward *b.* 11 Sep. 1896. *Address:* 100 Eaton Square S.W.; *T.:* Victoria 5969; Albyns, Romford Essex; Foss House, Pitlochry, Perthshire.
(Died 1 Dec. 1922.)

A'BECKETT, Hon. Sir Thomas, Kt. c 1909; Puisne Judge of the Supreme Court of Victoria since 1886; *b.* London, 31 Aug. 1837; *e. s.* Hon. Thomas Turner A'Beckett; *m.* 1875, Isabell *d.* of Sir Archibald Michie, K.C.M.G., Q.C. *Educ* King's College. Called to Bar after winning the Law Studentship of the Hon. Society of Lincoln Inn; member of the Council of the Melbourne University, 1887. *Recreation:* travelling. *Address:* Karbarok, Orrong Road, Armidale, Melbourne. *Club:* Melbourne. *(Died 24 June 1919.)*

ABEL-SMITH, Geoffrey Samuel, C.M.G. 1917; D.S.O. 1915; 3rd *s.* of late Reginald Albert Smith, of Wendover, Bucks; *m.* 1st, 1911 Marjorie (*d.* 1918), *d.* of Rev. Chas. Garnett Rector of Ardtrea, Co. Tyrone, and Lady Elizabeth

2

3rd *d.* of 4th Earl Castlestewart ; 2nd, 1923, Lilias, *d.* of Major M. A. Close ; one *d.* ; added Abel to surname by deed-poll, 1922. Served South African War, 1902, and World War, 1914-18, Lt.-Col. New Zealand Imperial Forces. *Address:* 44 Stanford Road, Kensington Court, W.8. *T.:* Western 3896.
(*Died 17 Sept. 1926.*)

ABERCROMBIE, Capt. Alexander Ralph, D.S.O. 1916; M.C. ; 1st Batt. The Queen's (Royal West Surrey) Regiment ; *b.* 14 Oct. 1896. *Educ.:* Haileybury ; Sandhurst. Entered Army, 1914; served European War in France, 1914-18, including engagements of Hill 60, Belgium, 19-21 April 1915 (wounded, Military Cross); Hohenzollern Redoubt, 13 Oct. 1915 (D.S.O.); Vimy (Bois-en-Hache), April 1917; Locon (Battle of Lys), 9-16 April 1918. *Address:* 34 Gloucester Terrace, Hyde Park, W.
(*Died 31 Dec. 1918.*)

ABERCROMBY, 4th Baron (*cr.* 1801), **George Ralph Campbell Abercromby;** *b.* 23 Sep. 1838 ; *S.* father 1852 ; *m.* Lady Julia Janet Georgina Duncan, V.A. (*d.* 1915), *d.* of 2nd Earl of Camperdown, 1858. Owns about 16,000 acres. *Heir: b.* Hon. John Abercromby. *Address:* 41 Brompton Square, S.W. ; *T.:* Western 3601 ; Tullibody Castle, Clackmannan. *Club:* Turf. (*Died 30 Oct. 1917.*)

ABERCROMBY, 5th Baron, *cr.* 1801 ; **John Abercromby,** LL.D. ; F.R.S.E. ; 2nd *s.* of 3rd Baron Abercromby and Louisa Penuel, *d.* of Lord Medwyn ; *b.* 15 Jan. 1841 ; *S.* brother 1917 ; *m.* 1876, Adele Wilhemine Marika, *d.* of Chevalier Charles von Heidenstam (marriage dissolved 1879) ; one *d.* Entered Army, 1858 ; retired as Lieut. Rifle Brigade, 1870 ; Vice-President, Folklore Society ; ex-President; Society of Antiquaries of Scotland ; Hon. Member, Finno-Ougrian Society of Helsingfors, and of Finnish Archæological Society. *Publications :* A Trip through the Eastern Caucasus ; Pre- and Proto-Historic Finns (2 vols.); Bronze Age Pottery of Great Britain and Ireland (2 vols.), 1912. *Heir:* none. *Address :* 62 Palmerston Place, Edinburgh. *Clubs :* Athenæum ; New, Edinburgh.
(*Died 7 Oct. 1924.*)

ABERGAVENNY, 2nd Marquess of (*cr.* 1876), **Reginald William Bransby Nevil,** J.P. ; Baron Abergavenny, 1450 ; Earl of Abergavenny and Viscount Nevill, 1784 ; Earl of Lewes, 1876 ; *b.* 4 March 1853 ; *s.* of 1st Marquess and Caroline, *d.* of Sir John Vanden-Bempde-Johnstone, 2nd Bt. ; *S.* father, 1915. *Educ.:* Eton. Conservative. Owns about 50,000 acres. *Heir: b.* Lord Henry Nevill. *Address:* 7A Eaton Square, S.W. *T.:* Victoria 2324 ; Eridge Castle, Tunbridge Wells.
(*Died 13 Oct. 1927.*)

ABINASH CHANDRA SEN, Rai Bahadur, C.I.E. 1921 ; *b.* Oct. 1870 ; *s.* of late Rao Bahadur Sansar Chandra Sen, C.I.E., M.V.O. ; *m.* 1886. *Educ.:* Jaipur ; Bombay. Assistant in the office of Private Secretary, 1901-6; Assistant Private Secretary, 1906-12 ; Private Secretary to the Maharaja, 1912-18 ; Member of the State Council, 1918, and of the Cabinet, 1920; title of Rai Bahadur, 1916; is an estate holder and one of the First-class nobles. *Address:* Huthroi Villa, Jaipur, Rajputana, India. (*Died Dec. 1923.*)

ABINGDON, 7th Earl of (*cr.* 1682), **Montagu Arthur Bertie ;** Baron, 1572 ; *b.* 13 May 1836 ; *m.* 1st, 1858, Caroline (*d.* 1873), *d.* of Charles Towneley ; two *d.* ; 2nd, 1883, Gwendeline, *d.* of Lieut.-Gen. Hon. Sir J. C. Dormer, and *sis.* of 13th Baron Dormer ; two *s.* two *d.* ; *S.* father, 1884. *Educ.:* Eton. *Heir: g.s.* Lord Norreys. *Address:* Oaken Holt, Oxford. *Club:* Travellers'.
(*Died 10 Mar. 1928.*)

ABINGER, 5th Baron (*cr.* 1835), **Shelley Leopold Lawrence Scarlett,** J.P.; late Capt. 3rd Batt. Bedfords Regt.; *b.* 1 Apr. 1872 ; *s.*

of late Lieut.-Col. L. J. Y. C. Scarlett, *g. s.* of 1st Baron Abinger, and Bessie Florence, *d.* of Edward Gibson of Spring Vale, Isle of Wight, niece and adopted *d.* of Sir Percy F. Shelley, 3rd Bart., and Lady Shelley ; *S.* cousin 1904. Appointed Hon. Attaché to H.B.M.'s Legation at Berne, 1894; transferred to Stockholm, 1897 ; *m.* 1899, Lila Lucy Catherine, *o. d.* of late Rt. Hon. Sir William White, G.C.B., G.C.M.G., sometime British Ambassador in Constantinople, and *widow* of late Kammerherr C. E. de Geijer, of the Swedish Diplomatic Service. Owns about 41,000 acres. *Heir: b.* Hon. Robert Brooke Campbell Scarlett. *Address:* Rownhams House, Rownhams. *M.:* 342. *Clubs:* Carlton, Junior United Service, Wellington, Garrick, Marlborough R.Y.S., Cowes. (*Died 23 May 1917.*)

ABINGER, 6th Baron (*cr.* 1835), **Robert Brooke Campbell Scarlett ;** Barrister, Inner Temple ; Assist. Paymaster R.N.R. ; Lieut. R.N.V.R ; *b.* 8 Jan. 1876 ; *s.* of late Lieut.-Col. L. J. Y. C. Scarlett, *g.s.* of 1st Baron Abinger, and Bessie Florence, *d.* of Edward Gibson of Spring Vale, Isle of Wight, *niece* and adopted *d.* of Sir Percy F. Shelley, 3rd Bart., and Lady Shelley ; *S.* brother, 1917 ; *m.* 1917, Jean Marguerite *J.* of late Edouard Japy and *widow* of M. Steinheil, Paris. *Educ.:* Wellington. *Heir: b.* Major Hon. Hugh R. Scarlett. *Address:* Brookehurst, Ewhurst, Surrey; Inverlochy Castle, Inverness-shire. *Club:* Conservative. (*Died 10 June 1927.*)

ABNEY, Sir William de Wiveleslie, K.C.B., *cr.* 1900; C.B., D.Sc., D.C.L., F.R.S. 1876. Adviser to the Board of Education (Science Department) since 1903 ; Member of the Advisory Council for Education to the War Office, 1903 ; *b.* Derby, 24 July 1843 ; *e. s.* of Canon Abney ; *m.* 1st, 1864, Agnes Mathilda (*d.* 1888), *d.* of E. W. Smith of Tickton Hall, Yorks ; one *s.* two *d.* ; 2nd, 1890, Mary Louisa, *d.* of late Rev. E. N. Meade, D.D., of St. Mary's Knoll, Scarborough on Hudson, U.S.A. ; one *d. Educ.:* Rossall. Lieut. R.E. 1861 ; Capt. 1873; President, Royal Astronomical Society, 1898-95 ; President, Physical Society, 1895-97 ; Chairman, Society of Arts, 1904. Principal Assistant Secretary, Board of Education, South Kensington, 1899-1903 ; *Publications:* Instruction in Photography, 1870; Treatise on Photography, 1875 ; Colour Vision, Colour Measurement and Mixture, 1893 ; Thebes and its Five Great Temples, 1876 ; The Pioneers of the Alps (with C. D. Cunningham), 1888 ; Trichromatic Theory of Colour, 1914. *Recreations:* painting, golf, shooting. *Address:* Measham Hall, Leicestershire ; Rathmore Lodge, South Bolton Gardens, S.W. *T.:* Western 4203 ; Measham 7. *M.:* AY 8060. *Club:* Athenæum.
(*Died 2 Dec. 1921.*)

ABRAHAM, Phineas Simon, M.A., M.D., B.Sc., F.R.C.S.I. ; Associate Royal College of Science, Ireland ; Consulting Dermatologist, West London Hospital; late Lecturer on Dermatology to West London Post Graduate College; President W. London Medico-Chirurgical Society, 1910-11 ; President Derm. Section, B.M.A. London Meeting, 1910 ; Ex-President, Irish Medical Schools and Graduates' Association, and of the New London Dermatological Society ; Fellow Royal Society of Medicine ; *b.* Falmouth, Jamaica ; *s.* of late Phineas Abraham, J.P., formerly of that island ; *m.* Ellen, 2nd *d.* of late Wm. Chard of Longford, Middlesex ; one *d. Educ.:* University College, London (First Honours, B.Sc.); Royal College of Science, Dublin (Royal Exhibitioner and Prizeman); Trinity College, Dublin (First Senior Moderator and Large Gold Medallist in Natural Science, Erasmus Smith Scholar, and M.A. Stip. Con. Hon. Causa); St. Bartholomew's Hospital ; Ecole de Medicine, Paris ; Clausthal in Germany. Qualified as a chemical and mining engineer ; obtained the Science Exhibition and the 1st Scholarship of the year, St. Bartholo-

3

mew's Hospital, 1876 ; Curator of the Museums of the Royal College of Surgeons, Dublin, 1879, and subsequently Member of Court of Examiners ; Lecturer on Physiology and Histology, Westminster Hospital Medical School, 1885 ; Medical Secretary of the National Leprosy Fund, 1889 ; represented this country at the International Lepra Conference, Berlin, 1897 ; one of the principal founders of the Royal Academy of Medicine of Ireland, and of the Dermatological Society of Great Britain and Ireland ; member of Council, Royal Drawing Society ; P.G.D. in Masonry. *Publications:* The Journal of the Leprosy Investigation Committee ; Articles on Leprosy and various Diseases of the Skin in Professor Clifford Allbutt's System of Medicine ; Skin Affections in Syphilis (Oxford System) ; numerous papers on pathological and dermatological subjects in the Transactions of various learned Societies. *Recreations:* motoring, gardening. *Address:* 66 Harley Street, W.1. *T.:* Mayfair 522. *M.:* LN 3468. *Clubs:* Savage, Royal Automobile, Wigwam.
(Died 23 Feb. 1921.)

ABRAHAM, Rt. Hon. William, P.C. 1911 ; LL.D.; M.P. (R.) Glamorganshire (Rhondda Valley), 1885-1918, Rhondda, West Div. 1918-20 ; *b.* 1842 ; *s.* of a working miner ; *m.* 1860, Sarah Williams (*d.* 1900) ; three *s.* three *d. Educ.:* Carnarvon National School. Known as "Mabon" ; Miners' agent from 1873 ; Ex-President South Wales Miners' Federation. *Address:* Bryn-y-Bedw, Pontre, Pontypridd. *T.A.:* Mabon, Pentre. *T.:* P.O. Pentre 85.
(Died 14 May 1922.)

ABRAHAMS, Israel ; author and lecturer ; reader in Talmudic and Rabbinic Literature in University of Cambridge ; formerly Senior Tutor at Jews' College, London ; first President of the Union of Jewish Literary Societies ; President, Jewish Historical Society of England, 1905 ; Hon. President, Univ. of Glasgow Theological Society, 1907 ; first Lewisohn Lecturer, New York, 1912 ; President Society of Historical Theology, Oxford, 1921 ; *b.* London, 26 Nov. 1858 ; *m.* Frederica, *o. d.* of late Rev. S. Singer, minister of New West End Synagogue ; two *d. Educ.:* Jews' Coll., London ; University Coll., London ; M.A. London and Cambridge ; Lit.D. Western Pennsylvania ; D.D. Hebrew Union College, Cincinnati. *Publications:* The Jewish Quarterly Review from 1889 till 1908 ; Aspects of Judaism, 1895 ; Jewish Life in the Middle Ages, 1896 ; Chapters on Jewish Literature, 1899 ; contributions to Encyclopædia Biblica, 1900 ; Hebrew Lessons, 1903 ; Maimonides, 1903 ; Festival Studies, 1905 ; A Short History of Jewish Literature, 1906 ; Judaism, 1907 ; edited Literary Remains of S. Singer 3 vols., 1908 ; Macaulay on Jewish Disabilities, 1909 ; Rabbinic Aids to Exegesis, 1910 ; Jews and other articles in Encyclopædia Britannica, 1911 ; The Book of Delight, 1913 ; Annotated Hebrew Prayer Book, 1914 ; Jews, in Hutchinson's History of the Nations, 1915 contributions to Encyclopædia of Religion, 1916 ; Studies in Pharisaism, 1917 ; Essays on the Future of Palestine, 1918 ; By-paths in Hebraic Bookland, 1920 ; Poetry and Religion 1921 ; Permanent Values, 1923 ; Studies in Pharisaism, 2nd series, 1924. *Recreation :* photography. *Address:* Christ's College, Cambridge. *(Died 6 Oct. 1925.)*

ABRAHAMS, Sir Lionel, K.C.B., *cr.* 1915 ; C.B. 1908 ; *b.* London, 9 Dec. 1869 ; *o. s.* of M. Abrahams ; *m.* 1896, Lucy, *d.* of N. S. Joseph ; one *s. Educ.:* City of London School ; Balliol College, Oxford (Scholar, 1888-1892 ; Exhibitioner, 1892-96 ; Arnold Prize, 1894). Entered India Office, 1893 ; Assistant Secretary to Indian Currency Committee, 1898 ; Assistant Financial Secretary, 1901 ; Financial Secretary, 1902-11 ; Member of Departmental Committees on Indian Railway Administration and Finance, 1907-8, and West African Currency, 1912, and of the

Indian Wheat Committee, 1915 ; Assistant Under-Secretary of State, India Office, 1911-17. *Publications:* The Expulsion of the Jews from England in 1290 ; contributions to the Dictionary of Political Economy. *Address:* 18 Porchester Terrace, W. *T.:* Paddington 8854. *Club:* Athenæum. *(Died 30 Nov. 1919.)*

ABRAHAMS, Louis Barnett ; Order of Mercy ; *b.* Swansea, 3 Oct. 1839 ; *s.* of Rev. Barnett Abrahams, minister of the Jewish community of that town ; *m.* Fannie, *e. d.* of late Ephraim Moseley of London ; one *d. Educ. :* Jews' School, London ; Univ. Coll ; B.A. London. Principal assistant master, vicemaster, and headmaster of Jews' Free School, Spitalfields, E. ; editor for three years of the Jewish Record ; one of the founders of the Jewish Education Board ; vice-president of the League of Mercy ; Hon. Captain, Jewish Lads' Brigade ; member of various Care Committees of the L.C.C. *Publications:* Chronological History of England ; Manual of Scripture History ; translator of the Standard Hebrew Prayer Book. *Recreations :* literary pursuits. *Address :* 3 Seaforth Road, Westcliff-on-Sea. *Clubs:* University of London, Maccabæans.
(Died 3 June 1918.)

ABRAM, Sir George Stewart, Kt., *cr.* 1922 ; B.A., M.B., B.C. (Cantab), M.R.C.S., L.R.C.P., J.P., Physician Royal Berks Hospital ; Major R.A.M.C. (T.) ; *b.* 18 Mar. 1866 ; *m.* 1893, Ethel May, *d.* of late T. F. Rider, M.V.O. ; one *s.* two *d. Educ. :* Merchant Taylors' School ; Cambridge ; University College Hospital, London. Mayor of Reading, 1919-20. *Publications:* Medical in Lancet. *Recreations :* golf and lawn tennis. *Address:* 106 London Road, Reading. *T. :* 268. *M.:* DP 2926. *(Died 24 Oct. 1928.)*

ACHESON, Maj.-Gen. Hon. Edward Archibald Brabazon ; late Coldstream Guards ; *b.* 22 May 1844 ; *bro.* of 4th Earl of Gosford ; *m.* 1869, Clementina, *d.* of late Gen. Sir J. Gaspard le Marchant, G.C.S.I., K.C.B. ; four *d. Educ.:* Harrow. Served Egypt, 1882 (medal with clasp, Khedive's Star). *Clubs:* Travellers', Guards'. *(Died 3 July 1921.)*

ACHURCH, Janet (Janet Achurch Sharp) ; *b.* Lancashire ; *m.* Charles Charrington. First appeared in London with Genevieve Ward ; toured in provinces, playing over a hundred parts ; played in Harbour Lights ; and with Mr. Beerbohm Tree through run of three pieces ; appeared as Nora Helmer in A Doll's House, 1889 ; first English actress to visit Khedivial theatre, Cairo ; toured with own company in Australia, India, and America played Rita Allmees in Little Eyolf, Cleopatra in special Manchester production afterwards given at matinées in London ; and Candida in play of that name ; also original Lady Cicely in Capt. Brassbound's Conversion ; Merete Beyer in The Witch, Anna Redvers in A Secret Woman Mrs. Alving in Ghosts. *Publications:* several short stories. *Recreations:* travelling, seeing new places and people. *Address:* c/o Th Stage, 16 York Street, W.C.*(Died 11 Sept. 1916.)*

ACKLAND, Robert Craig, C.B.E. 1920 M.R.C.S.; L.R.C.P., L.D.S.; Dental Surgeon to St. Bartholomew Hospital ; Medical Officer in Charge of the Red Cross Hospital for Facial Injuries, 78 Brook Street, W., and 24 Norfolk Street, W. ; *s.* of late Robert Ackland, Exeter *m.* Ruth, *d.* of late Edmund Macrory, K.C. two *d. Educ. :* Torquay ; Charing Cross Hospital. *Publications:* Diseases of the Teeth Quain's Dictionary of Medicine, etc. *Recreations:* shooting, golf, etc. *Address:* 54 Brook Street, W.1 ; The Hill, Winterton, Norfolk. *T.* Mayfair 2433. *M.:* T 512. *Clubs:* Bath ; Denham Golf ; Great Yarmouth Golf. *(Died 6 Aug. 1925.)*

ACKLOM, Major (Temp. Lieut.-Col Spencer, D.S.O. 1917 ; 1st Batt. The Highland Light Infantry ; Commanding 22nd Northumberland Fusiliers (3rd Tyneside Scottish *m.* 1909. Lucie, *e. d.* of Mountford Spencer, Th

Hill, Teignmouth, Devon. *Educ.*: R.M.C., Sandhurst. Joined 2nd Batt. H.L.I. 1902; transferred to 1st Batt. 1905; adjutant of the 9th (T.F.) Battalion H.L.I. (The Glasgow Highlanders), 1913; proceeded to France with that battalion on 4 Nov. 1914; posted to 22nd N.F. (3rd Tyneside Scottish) as second in command, May 1916, and appointed to command that battalion with temporary rank of Lieut.-Col., 2 July 1916 (despatches thrice, D.S.O., M.C.). *Recreations:* golf, polo, racquets, etc. *Club:* Junior Naval and Military.
(*Died 30 Mar. 1918.*)

ACLAND, Rt. Hon. Sir Arthur Herbert Dyke, 13th Bt.; *cr.* 1644; P.C., M.A.; Hon. LL.D. (Leeds); *b.* 1847; 2nd *s.* of Rt. Hon. Sir T. D. Acland, Bt., and first wife, Mary, *d.* of Sir Charles Mordaunt, 8th Bt.; *S.* brother, 1919, *m.* 1873, Alice Sophia, *e. d.* of Rev. Francis Cunningham; one *s.* one *d.* *Educ.:* Rugby; Christ Church, Oxford. Formerly Steward and Senior Student of Christ Church; was Senior Bursar, and is now Honorary Fellow of Balliol; Vice-President, Committee of Council on Education, 1892-95; M.P. Rotherham, Yorks, 1885-99; late Chairman Executive Committee, Imperial College of Science and Technology. *Publications:* Handbook of Political History of England; Working Men Co-operators; Patriotic Poetry of William Wordsworth, 1915. *Heir:* s. Rt. Hon. Francis Dyke Acland. *Address:* 85 Onslow Square, S.W.7. *Club:* Athenæum.
(*Died 9 Oct. 1926.*)

ACLAND, Sir (Charles) Thomas Dyke, 12th Bt.; *cr.* 1644; M.A.; J.P., D.L., Somerset, Devon, Cornwall, etc.; *b.* 16 July 1842; *e. s.* of Rt. Hon. Sir Thomas Dyke Acland, 11th Bt.; *S.* father 1898; *m.* 1879, Gertrude, *sis.* of 1st Baron Waleran. *Educ.:* Bradfield; Eton; Christ Church, Oxford. 3rd class Classics, 1866. Lieut.-Col. late Devon Yeomanry Cavalry; Deputy Warden of the Stanneries; Barr.; M.P. East Cornwall, 1882-85; N.E. Cornwall, 1885-92; Parliamentary Secretary to Board of Trade and Ecclesiastical Commissioner, 1886; County Alderman, Devon; Chairman of Technical Education Committee of Devon County Council from its commencement, 1890 till 1910; V.P. Bath and West of England and Southern Counties Agricultural Society, in which Society he has been for some years chairman, or acting-chairman, of the Journal Committee, Experiments Committee, and Dairy Committee; Sheriff of Devon, 1903-1904. *Heir:* b. Rt. Hon. A. H. Dyke Acland, M.P. *Address:* Killerton, Exeter; Holnicote, Taunton. *Clubs:* Athenæum, Travellers'; Cavendish, Cobden; Devon and Exeter, Exeter; Somerset County, Taunton. (*Died 18 Feb. 1919.*)

ACLAND, Sir Reginald Brodie Dyke, Kt., *cr.* 1914; K.C. 1904; Recorder of Oxford since 1903; Judge - Advocate of the Fleet, 1904; *b.* 18 May 1856; 6th *s.* of Sir Henry Wentworth Acland, 1st Bt., K.C.B., M.D., sometime Regius Professor of Medicine in the University of Oxford; *m.* 1885, Helen, *d.* of Rev. Thomas Fox, Rector of Temple Combe, Somerset; two *s.* two *d.* *Educ.:* Winchester; University College, Oxford. Called to the Bar, 1881; Junior Counsel to the Admiralty, 1897-1904; Counsel for Great Britain, North Sea Enquiry, 1905; formerly for many years Member of the General Council of the Bar; late Treasurer, Barristers' Benevolent Association; has taken interest in hospital work in London; Chairman Hospital Saturday Fund, 1890-98; Recorder of Shrewsbury, 1901-1903; J. P. Berks; Chairman Quarter Sessions. *Recreations:* gardening and all country pursuits. *Address:* 2 Hare Court, Temple, E.C.4. *T.:* Central 2722; Cold Ash, Newbury. *Club:* United University. (*Died 18 Feb. 1924.*)

ACLAND, Admiral Sir William Alison Dyke, 2nd Bt., *cr.* 1890; C.V.O. 1903; J.P. Oxfordshire and Devon; *b.* Ox-

ford, 18 Dec. 1847; *e. s.* of Sir Henry W. Acland, 1st Bart.; *m.* Emily Anna, *d.* of late Viscountess Hambleden and late Rt. Hon. W. H. Smith, 1887 (Hon. Lady Acland is the author of several novels); two *s.* *Educ.:* private schools. Entered H.M.S. Britannia as Cadet, 1861; Lt. 1868; Comdr. 1879; Capt. 1885; attached to 1st Brigade Chilian Army in campaign against Peru, 1881 (medal, two clasps); Deputy Commissioner Western Pacific; A.D.C. to the Queen, 1896-99; Jubilee Medal, 1897; Captain of Dockyard Reserve at Devonport, 1897-99; Rear-Admiral, 1899; 2nd in command Channel Squadron, 1901-1902; Superintendent, Gibraltar Dockyard, 1902-1904; Vice-Admiral, 1904; Admiral, 1908; retired, 1911. *Recreations:* fishing, boat-sailing. *Heir:* s. William Henry Dyke (*b.* 16 May 1888; *m.* 1916, Margaret Emily, *d.* of late Theodore Barclay, of Fanshaws, Herts; two *d.* Capt. Devon Yeomanry and late Major R.A.F.; served European war (Military Cross, Air Force Cross, 4th Class Order of St. George). *Address:* Barnes Wood, Welwyn. *Clubs:* Bath, Athenæum]. *Address:* Wilmead, Torquay. *T.:* Torquay 695. *M.:* T 289. *Club:* United Service.
(*Died 26 Nov. 1924.*)

ACTON, 2nd Baron (*cr.* 1869), **Richard Maximilian Dalberg-Acton,** Bt., *cr.* 1643; K.C.V.O., *cr.* 1916; M.V.O. 1901; *b.* 7 Aug. 1870; *s.* of 1st Baron and Countess Marie Arco-Valley, of Munich; *m.* 1904, Dorothy (*d.* 1923), *d.* of late T. H. Lyon, of Appleton Hall, Cheshire; two *s.* seven *d.*; *S.* father, 1902. *Educ.:* Magdalen Coll., Oxford. Entered Foreign Office, 1894; 3rd Secretary Diplomatic Service, Berlin, 1896; 2nd Secretary, 1900; 2nd Secretary, Vienna, 1902; Berne, 1903; Madrid, 1906; The Hague, 1907; Lord in Waiting to H.M., 1905 - 15; 1st Secretary Diplomatic Service; Charge d'Affaires, Darmstadt, 1911-14; Councillor of Embassy, 1914; Consul-General, Zurich, 1917-19; Envoy to Finland, 1919-20. *Heir:* s. Hon. John Emerich Henry; *b.* 15 Dec. 1907. *Address:* Aldenham Park, Bridgnorth. *Club:* Athenæum.
(*Died 16 June 1924.*)

ACTON, Fitzmaurice, C.M.G. 1918; *b.* Feb. 1874; *s.* of Colonel and Mrs. Hampden Acton, of Chalet Lucia, Pau, France; *m.* 1910, Ruby, widow of Lieut. P. Crabtree, R.N.; one *s.* Joined Britannia, 1887; Commander, 1908; Naval Attaché, Paris, 1915-17; Naval Attaché, Tokyo, since 1918; Acting Captain, 1915; Officer Legion of Honour, Order of the Rising Sun 3rd class. *Recreations:* fishing, shooting. *Address:* Rathmullen, Donegal. *Club:* United Service. (*Died 7 Aug. 1921.*)

ACWORTH, Sir William Mitchell, Kt., *cr.* 1921; K.C.S.I., *cr.* 1922; barrister; *b.* 22 Nov. 1850; 3rd *s.* of Rev. W. Acworth of the Hall, South Stoke, Bath; *m.* 1st, 1878, Elizabeth Louisa Oswald (*d.* 1904), *e. d.* of James Brown of Orangefield, Ayrshire; 2nd, 1923, Elizabeth Learmonth, *yr. d.* of late Thomas Wotherspoon, Hundleshope, Peebles. *Educ.:* Uppingham; Christ Church, Oxford, M.A. 1875. Member London County Council, 1889-92; Unionist Candidate for Keighley Division of West Riding, 1906, 1910, 1911; member of many Royal Commissions and Committees on British Railways; Royal Commission of Enquiry into Canadian Railways, 1916; S. Rhodesian Railways, 1918; Chairman of Committee on Indian Railways, 1921; reported on Austrian Railways for the League of Nations, 1923; on German Railways for the Reparations Commission, 1924; member of Council of the Royal Economic Society and of the Institute of Transport; Director of the Underground Electric Railways of London, Limited, and other companies. *Publications:* Railways of England, 1889; Railways of Scotland, 1890; Railways and the Traders, 1891; Railway Economics, 1905; State Railway Ownership, 1920. *Address:* The Albany, Pic-

cadilly, W.1. *T.:* Regent 696 ; Underwood, Ide Exeter. *Clubs:* Brooks's, Reform.
(Died 2 April 1925.)

ADAIR, Admiral Charles Henry; *b.* 2 July 1851 ; 2nd *s.* of General Sir Charles W. Adair, K.C.B., R.M.L.I.; *m.* 1893, Annette C., *d.* of W. H. Wilson of Nortonsea, Waterloo, Lancashire ; two *s.* one *d.* Entered Royal Navy, 1864 ; Lieut. 1874 ; Commander, 1886 ; Captain, 1893 ; Rear-Admiral, 1905 ; Vice-Admiral, 1909 ; Admiral, 1913 ; has served continuously at sea in all parts of the world ; Suakim, 1884 (Egyptian medal and star) ; retired, 1913. *Address:* Hendon, Regents Park, Southampton. *Club:* United Service. *(Died 9 Mar. 1920.)*

ADAIR, Mrs. Cornelia, *e. d.* of Gen. Wadsworth, of New York (*d.* 1864), and Mary, *d.* of late William Wharton ; *m.* 1st, 1858, Col. Montgomery Ritchie (*d.* 1864) ; 2nd, 1867, John George Adair, of Rathdaire (*d.* 1885). *Address:* 11 Portman Square, W. ; *T.:* Mayfair 4760; Glenveagh Castle, Churchill, Co. Donegal.
(Died 22 Sept. 1922.)

ADAIR, Rear-Admiral Thomas Benjamin Stratton, Head of the Ordnance Department of W. Beardmore & Co. Ltd., Parkhead Steelworks, Glasgow; *s.* of late Gen. Sir Charles William Adair, K.C.B.; *b.* Gosport, 6 Nov. 1861. Entered Navy, 1874 ; retired,1906; Member of the Ordnance Committee, 1900-1902; M.P. (C.U.) Shettleston Division of Glasgow, Dec. 1918- Oct. 1922. *Address:* 45 St. George's Road, S.W.1. *T.:* Victoria 5802. *Club:* United Service. *(Died 12 Aug. 1928.)*

ADAM, Sir Charles Elphinstone, 1st Bt., *cr.* 1882 ; D.L., J.P. Kinross and Fife. Barr. Inner Temple and Lincoln's Inn, 1885 ; Convener Kinross-shire, 1893-1910 ; Chairman Kinross Territorial Association, 1908 ; Lord-Lieut. Kinross-shire, and President Territorial Assoc. 1909-11; *s.* of late Rt. Hon. W. P. Adam, Governor of Madras, and Emily Eliza, *d.* of Gen. Sir W. Wyllie, G.C.B. ; *b.* 7 Aug. 1859 ; *m.* 1912, Edith, *d.* of late W. Dobson, Victoria, British Columbia. *Educ.:* Eton ; Christ Church, Oxford. Private Sec. to Parliamentary Secretary of Treasury, Lord Privy Seal and Chancellor of Duchy of Lancaster(Lord Tweedmouth),1892-5 ; Volunteer Long Service Medal, 1904 ; served with R.N.V.R. (A.A.C. Gun Stations), June 1915-Dec. 1916 ; Lieut. in Army, and Train Conducting Officer (France), 1916 - 18. Owns 4250 acres; no heir to title. *Publication:* editor of Political State of Scotland in the Last Century, 1887. *Address:* Blair-Adam, Kinross-shire ; 5 New Square, Lincoln's Inn, W.C. *Clubs:* Brooks's, United University, National Liberal.
(Died 6 Dec. 1922.)

ADAM, Rev. David Stow, M.A., D.D., Professor of Systematic Theology and Church History at Ormond College, University of Melbourne, since 1908 ; *b.* Langside, near Glasgow, 9 Feb. 1859 ; *s.* of George Adam, teacher in Glasgow Normal Seminary, and Jane Constable of Perth ; *m.* 1892, Mary Grace, *d.* of John Paterson, Skirling Mains, Biggar; four *s.* one *d. Educ.:* Langside Academy ; Glasgow University ; Free Church College ; Erlangen University. M.A. with first-class Honours in Mental Philosophy, 1881 ; B.D., 1884 ; D.D., 1912 ; Scott Scholar, Glasgow University, 1881 ; Eglinton Fellow and Lecturer in Logic and Mental Philosophy, Glasgow University, 1882-3 ; Stevenson Scholar, Freeman Fellow, and Hebrew Tutor, Glasgow F.C. Theological Hall, 1882-6 ; Minister at Banchory, Deeside, 1886-90 ; Kelso, 1890-95 ; St. Andrews, Greenock, 1895-1907 ; President of Council of Churches, Victoria, 1910 ; Chairman of Church - Union Committee of Australia since 1916. *Publications:* Cardinal Elements of the Christian Faith, 1911 ; various articles in Hastings' Dictionaries. *Recreations:* golf, fishing. *Address:* Ormond College, Melbourne. *T.:* Cent. 6419.*(Died 31 Jan. 1925.)*

ADAM, Eric Graham Forbes, C.M.G. ; 1st Secretary in the Foreign Office ; *b.* Bombay, 3 Oct. 1888 ; 2nd *s.* of Sir Frank Forbes Adam, Bt. ; *m.* 1918, Agatha Perrin, *e. d.* of Dr. R. W. Macan; one *s. Educ.:* Eton (K.S.); King's College, Cambride (Scholar). First class in Parts I. and II. of the History Tripos ; passed first into the Foreign Office, 1913 ; 3rd Secretary in British Peace Delegation, Paris, 1919; London and San Remo Conferences, 1920 ; 1st Secretary, 1922; 1st Secretary in British Delegation, Lausanne Conference, 1922-23. *Address:* c/o British Embassy, Constantinople. *Club:* 1917.
(Died 7 July 1925.)

ADAM, Sir Frank Forbes, 1st Bt., *cr.* 1917 ; Kt., *cr.* 1890 ; C.I.E. 1888 ; C.B. 1919 ; LL.D. Vict. ; J.P., D.L. ; *b.* 1846 ; *m.* 1888, Rose Frances, *d.* of C. G. Kemball, late Judge High Court, Bombay; three *s.* one *d. Educ.:* Loretto. Went to India 1872 as a merchant ; President Bank of Bombay; President Chamber of Commerce ; Member of Port Trust; Member of Legislative Council; returned to England 1890; President of Manchester Chamber of Commerce, 1894 and 1903-5 ; Chairman of Council of Manchester University ; Chairman of Manchester Royal Infirmary Board, 1900 - 1902 ; Chairman of St Mary's Hospitals Board ; Chairman, Territorial Force Association since 1914 ; Chairman Manchester and County Bank ; Member Commercial Intelligence Committee. *Recreation:* golf. *Heir:* *s.* Col. R. F. Adam. *Address:* The Palace Hotel, Buxton. *T.A.:* Wilmslow. *Club:* Union.
(Died 22 Dec. 1926.)

ADAM, Maj.-Gen. Frederick Archibald, C.B. 1913 ; *s.* of Archibald MacIndoe Adam, of Glasgow, and Sophia Catherine Gillespie ; *b.* 8 Aug. 1860 ; *m.* 1884, Florence, *d.* of late Maj.-General Thomas James Watson, Bengal Cavalry ; two *d. Educ.:* Fettes College, Edinburgh Royal Military College, Sandhurst. Joined 40th Regiment in India, 1880; served S. Africa, 1900-2 ; commanded 1st Batt. South Lancashire Regt., 1901 (despatches twice, Brevet Lt.-Col.) ; 2nd South Lancashire Regt., 1906-10 ; North Lancashire Infantry Brigade (T.F.), 1910-13 ; the Infantry Brigade, Malta, 1913-14. *Recreations:* shooting, cricket, music, natural history. *Address:* Dunain, Inverness.
(Died 5 Mar. 1924.)

ADAM, Capt. Herbert Algernon, C.B.E. 1919 ; R.N. ; Captain for Coastguard Duties on Staff of C.-in-C. Nore ; *b.* 3 Jan. 1872 ; *s.* of late Rev. B. W. Adams, D.D., Rector of Santry, Co. Dublin ; *m.* 1898, Emily Banner Clough, *d.* of Captain S. J. Johnstone, R.N. ; one *s. Educ.:* H.M.S. Britannia ; Royal Naval College, Greenwich. Assumed original name of Adam by Deed Poll, 1901 ; served in Witu Expedition, 1890 (medal and clasp) ; Egyptian Waters during Dongola Expedition (medals, British and Egyptian) ; was in command of H.M.S. Barham at Messina Earthquake (medal and Chevalier of the Order of St. Maurice and St. Lazarus for services) and at S maliland Blockade, 1909 ; Flag Captain to Admiral Sir Cecil Thursby in command of H.M.S. Queen at the Dardanelles, and landed the Anzac Division at Gallipoli, Easter Sunday, 1915 ; P.N.T.O. at Salonica, and in command of H.M.S. Cornwall on North Atlantic Convoy work and employed bringing over U.S. Troops (desp tches). *Recreations:* riding, driving, motoring, gardening, poultry-rearing. *Address:* The Chillies, Uckfield, Sussex. *T.:* Crowborough, 211. *Clubs:* United Services ; Union, Malta. *(Died 27 Sept. 1920.)*

ADAMI, John George, C.B.E. 1919 ; F.R.S. 1905 ; M.A., M.D. (Camb.), F.R.C.P. Lond., F.R.C.S. Eng., F.R.S.S. Edin. 1898, Canada 1902, M.A., M.D. (ad eundem), McGill, 1899 ; M.D. (Hon.) Belfast, 1921; LL.D. (New Brunswick), 1900 : (Toronto) 1912 ; (Manchester) 1923

Sc. D. (T.C.D.) 1912; Vice-Chancellor of the University of Liverpool since 1919; b. Manchester, 12 Jan. 1862; s. of late John George Adami of Manchester and Ashton-upon-Mersey, Cheshire, and Sarah Ann Ellis; d. of Thomas Leech of Urmston, Lancs; m. 1st, 1894, Mary Stuart (d. 1916), d. of James Alexander Cantlie and Eleonora Stephen of Montreal; one s. one d.; 2nd, 1922, Marie, er. d. of Rev. T. W. Wilkinson, The Vicarage, Litherland, Lancs. Educ.: Owens College, Manchester; Christ's College, Cambridge (Scholar); Breslau and Paris. 1st cl. 1st pt. Natural Science Tripos, 1882; 1st cl. 2nd pt. 1884; Darwin Prizeman, 1885; House Physician, Manchester Royal Infirmary, and Demonstrator of Pathology, Univ. of Camb., 1887; John Lucas Walker Student of Pathology, 1890; Fellow of Jesus Coll., 1891; President Association American Physicians, 1911-12; Canadian Association Prevention of Tuberculosis, 1909 - 12; Montreal City Improvement League, 1909-16; Montreal Child Welfare Exhibition, 1912; Colonel C.A.M.C.; Medical Historical Recorder, Canadian Expeditionary Force, A.D.M.S.; Strathcona Professor of Pathology and Bacteriology, McGill University, Montreal, 1892-1919; Fothergillian Medallist, Medical Soiety, London, 1914; Hon. Fellow of Christ's College and Jesus College, Camb., 1920; Member Consultative Committee of Minister of Education. Publications: The Principles of Pathology, 1908; Medical Contributions to the Study of Evolution, 1918; Charles White of Manchester, and the Prevention of Puerperal Fever, 1922; numerous papers upon pathological subjects in journals and transactions; articles on Inflammation, Allbutt's System of Medicine. Address: The University, Liverpool. Clubs: Athenæum; University, Exchange, Athenæum, Conservative, Reform, Liverpool. (Died 29 Aug. 1926.)

ADAMS, Rev. Arthur, Hon. Canon of Truro since 1912; Vicar of Crowan since 1904; b. 11 Oct. 1852; s. of William Adams, Bridge House, East Molesey. Educ.: Sherborne; St. John's College, Cambridge; Cuddesdon Theological College. Ordained, 1875; Curate of Camborne, 1875-81; Vicar of St. Colan, 1881-1883; of Tuckingmill, 1888-1904. Address: Crowan Vicarage, Praze, Cornwall.
(Died 13 Feb. 1926.)

ADAMS, Brooks; b. Quincy, Massachusetts, 24 June 1848; y. s. of Charles Francis Adams; g.s. of John Quincy Adams; m. 1889, Evelyn Davis. Educ.: Harvard; graduated class of 1870. Lawyer and literary. Publications: Emancipation of Massachusetts. 1887; Law of Civilisation and Decay, 1895 (translated into French and German); The Gold Standard, 1894; America's Economic Supremacy, 1900 (translated into German); The New Empire, 1902 (translated into German and Russian); two chapters in Centralisation and the Law, 1906; Railway as Public Agents, 1910; Theory of Social Revolutions, 1913; The Degradation of the Democratic Dogma (with Henry Adams), 1919; numerous addresses, etc. Address: 84 State Street, Boston, Mass.
(Died 13 Feb. 1927.)

ADAMS, George Burton, Ph.D., Litt.D.; LL.D.; Professor of History in Yale University since 1888; b. Fairfield, Vermont, 3 June 1851; s. of Rev. Calvin Carlton and Emeline Nelson Adams; m. 1878, Ida, d. of Mills de Forest Clarke. Educ.: Beloit Coll.; Yale and Leipzig Universities. Professor of History in Drury College, 1877-88; president of the American Historical Association, 1907-8; one of the editors of the American Historical Review, 1895-1913; member of the American Antiquarian Society, Corresponding Member Royal Historical Society, Massachusetts Colonial Society, and Massachusetts and Vermont Historical Societies, etc. Publications: Civilisation during the Middle Ages; The Growth of the French Nation; European History; Vol. II. in Hunt and Poole's Political History of England; The Origin of the English Constitution; Outline of English Constitutional History; The British Empire; Constitutional History of England; editor of Duruy's Middle Ages; Bémont and Monod's Medieval Europe; and with Prof. H. Morse Stephens of Select Documents of English Constitutional History; and author of many articles and addresses. Recreations: fishing, boat sailing. Address: 57 Edgehill Road, New Haven, Conn. Clubs: Graduates. Elizabethan, New Haven.
(Died 26 May 1925.)

ADAMS, George Francis, C.B.E., 1919; M.Inst.C.E.; Chief Inspector of Mines in India since 1910; b. 6 May 1870; s. of late George Frederick Adams, M.Inst.C.E., Cardiff; m. 1904, Margaret Elizabeth, d. of late Cornelius O'Connor, London; one d. Educ.: Harrow; Bedford. H.M. Assist.-Inspector of Mines, South Wales District, 1894-1902; Inspector of Mines in India, 1902-10. Publications: Various reports on Mining and Mining Education. Recreation: golf. Address: Hirapur House, Dhambad, India. T.A.: Mines, Dhambad. Clubs: Sports: Bengal United Service, Calcutta.
(Died 10 Jan. 1921.)

ADAMS, Henry Carter, Ph.D., LL.D. Professor of Political Economy and Finance, University of Michigan. since 1887; Associate Editor International Journal of Ethics; b. Davenport, Iowa, 31 Dec. 1851; m. 1890, Bertha H. Wright, Port Huron, Michigan. Educ.: Iowa College; Johns Hopkins University; Heidelberg; Berlin; Paris; Andover Theological Seminary. Publications: Outline of Lectures on Political Economy, 1881, 1886; State in Relation to Industrial Action, 1887; Taxation in the United States, 1787-1816, 1884; Public Debts, 1887; The Science of Finance, 1888; Statistics of Railways, 1888-1910; Economics and Jurisprudence, 1897; Description of Industry, 1918; American Railway Accounting, 1918. Address: Ann Arbor, Michigan, U.S.A.
(Died 11 Aug. 1921.)

ADAMS, Capt. Joseph Ebenezer, R.A.M.C.(T.); Surgeon to St. Thomas's Hospital; Senior Surgeon East London Hospital. for Children; b. 7 Feb. 1878; 5th s. of William Adams, merchant in City of London; m. 1913, Muriel Emma, y. d. of late Harry Webb, of. Southland, Chislehurst. Educ.: City of London School; St. Thomas's Hospital (Entrance Scholarship); qualified M.R.C.S., L.R.C.P., 1902. House Surgeon, Clinical Assist. in Throat Department; M.B., B.S. London, 1904; F.R.C.S., 1904; Beaney scholar in Surgery and Surgical Pathology, St. Thomas's Hospital, 1904; Surgical Registrar and Resident Assistant Surgeon, 1905-9; Hunterian Professor, Royal College of Surgeons, 1913; same year appointed Surgeon in charge of out-patients at St. Thomas's; besides above appointments is conducting research in abdominal surgery. Publications: Acute Abdominal Diseases; Peritoneal Adhesions, Lancet, 1913; Intestinal Obstruction, Practitioner, 1913; Observations on Operations for Appendicitis, Practitioner, April 1917; many other publications in Medical Journals. Recreations: golf, lawn tennis. Address: 19 Harley Street, W.1; T.: Langham 2108; Holt's Crest, Fordcombe, Kent; T.: Fordcombe 19. M.: XA 8523.
(Died 22 Dec. 1926.)

ADAMS, Joseph Robert George, General Secretary, Public Library, Museum, and Art Gallery of South Australia since 1909; b. Melbourne, Victoria, 17 May 1859; e. s. of late Joseph Adams, Hawthorn, Victoria; m. 1884, Alice, y. d. of late Robert Downing, Melbourne; one s. four d. Educ.: Scotch College, Melbourne, Victoria. Assistant Librarian of the South Australian Institute,

1879 ; Assistant Librarian of the new Institution, 1884, when the South Australian Institute developed into the Public Library, Museum, and Art Gallery of South Australia ; Librarian, 1896 ; Principal Librarian and Secretary, 1904. *Publications:* articles in Library Record of Australasia and Proceedings of Library Association of Australasia; ed. Proceedings of Library Association of Australasia for 1900. *Recreations :* angling, walking, and gardening. *Address :* Public Library, Adelaide, South Australia.
(*Died 16 Aug. 1919.*)

ADAMS, Rev. Reginald Samuel, Hon. Canon of Chester, 1913. *Address: 222* Hale Road, Hale. (*Died 6 July 1928.*)

ADAMS, Maj.-Gen. Sir Robert Bellew, K.C.B., *cr.* 1912 ; C.B. 1898 ; V.C. ; *b.* 26 July 1856 ; *s.* of late Major R. Adams, I.S.C. Entered army, 1876 ; Captain, 1887 ; Major, 1896 ; Bt. Lt.-Col. 1896 ; Bt. Col. 1901 ; Lt.-Col. 1902 ; Col. 1904 ; Brig.-Gen. 1904 ; Maj.-Gen. 1906; served Afghan War, 1879-80, including operations round Kabul, engagement at Charasieh (medal with clasp); Chitral Relief Force, in command Queen's Own Corps of Guides, cavalry, 1895 (despatches, Brevet Lieut.-Col., medal with clasp): North-West Frontier, 1897 (despatches, V.C.); operations Bajaur (despatches) ; commanded troops Rustam and Persai in Buner Expedition (despatches, C.B., two clasps). Brig. Commander Commanding Derajat Brigade, 1906 - 9 ; commanded Corps of Guides, Mardan ; retired, 1911. *Decorated* for rescue (with others) of Lieut. Greaves under heavy fire, 17 Aug. 1897, Upper Swat. *Club :* East India United Service. (*Died 13 Feb. 1928.*)

ADAMSON, John, R.B.A. ; *b.* Aug. 1865 *s.* of Sir William Adamson. *Educ.:* Sher borne ; Royal Academy of Arts. *Address:* 3 Steele's Studios, Haverstock Hill, N.W.
(*Died 12 Dec. 1918.*)

ADAMSON, Sir William, Kt., *cr.* 1907 ; C.M.G. 1897 ; merchant ; *s.* of Ebenezer Adamson of Glasgow ; *b.* 1832 ; *m.* 1859, Margaret, *d.* of Andrew Hamilton. A merchant of the Straits Settlements, and for many years a resident at Singapore ; has on several occasions been a member of the Legislative Council of the Colony ; a director of the Peninsular and Oriental Steam Navigation Company. *Decorated* for public services in connection with the Colony. *Address:* Rothbury, Avenue Road, Highgate, N. *T.:* Hornsey 85.
(*Died 11 Mar. 1917.*)

ADCOCK, Sir Hugh, Kt., *cr.* 1901 ; C.M.G. 1897 ; late Persian Consul, Florence ; first-class Star of Lion and Sun with cordon, 1897 ; first - class Gold Star from Imperial College, Teheran, presented by the late Shah, Nasr-e-Din, 1898, for services during the severe cholera epidemic, 1892 ; consulting physician-in-chief to H.I.M. the Shah of Persia ; *b.* London, 1847 ; 4th *s.* of Christopher Adcock, surgeon, and Catherine Elizabeth of Church Hill House, Hunstanton, Norfolk, and of London ; *m.* 1st, Elizabeth, *d.* of William Watkin of New Town, Wales, 1866 ; 2nd, 1908, Florence Beatrice (*d.* 1911), *d.* of Lt.-Colonel J. S. G. Manera, Indian Army, retired ; two *s. Educ.:* privately, London and Cambridge. L.S.A. Lond. ; L.R.C.P.E. L.M.Ed., 1869 ; M.R.C.S. Eng., 1872. In private practice at Heacham, Norfolk, 1870-72 ; London, 1872-88 ; chief physician to H.I.H. Mouzaffer-e-Din, Vali-ahd, at Tabreez, Persia, 1889-97, when Mouzaffer-e-Din ascended the Persian throne. *Decorations:* Legion of Honour, 4th class, France ; Iron Crown, 2nd class, Austria ; Medjidie, 1st class, Turkey ; Orders of Civil Merit—1st class, Bulgaria ; St. Sava, 1st class, Servia ; Leopold, 2nd class, Belgium ; Orange, 2nd class, Holland. *Recreations :* hunting, shooting. *Address:* Nymet House, Nymet Rowland, N. Devon. *Club:* Royal Societies.
(*Died 13 April 1920.*)

8

ADDIS, Rev. William E., M.A. ; Vicar of All Saints, Ennismore Gardens, S.W., since 1910; *b.* Edinburgh, 9 May 1844 ; *s.* of F.C. minister there ; *m.* Miss Flood, Sydenham, 1888 ; one *s.* one *d. Educ.:* Merchiston Castle School, Edin. ; Glasgow Coll. ; Balliol Coll. Oxford. Snell Exhibitioner ; 1st class in Class. Mods. and Final Classical Schools. Became R.C. 1866; joined London Oratory, 1868 ; ordained priest, 1872 ; parish priest of Sydenham, 1878 - 88 ; returned to Church of England, 1901 ; permission to officiate as priest in Church of England granted by Primate, 1907 ; Curate of St. Martin and All Saints, Oxford, 1909 ; Professor of Old Testament Criticism, Manchester College, Oxford, 1898-1910 ; Master of Addis Hall, 1900-1910. *Publications:* Catholic Dictionary in conjunction with Thomas Arnold (fourth ed.), 1884 ; Documents of Hexateuch (2 vols.), 1893-98 ; Christianity and the Roman Empire, 1893 ; Hebrew Religion and the Rise of Judaism under Ezra, 1906 ; various pamphlets, reviews, articles in Encyclopædia Biblica, Ency. Brit., etc. *Recreations :* walking, study of Gothic architecture. *Address:* 34 Rutland Gate, S.W.
(*Died 20 Feb. 1917.*)

ADENEY, Walter Frederick, M.A. London; D.D. St. Andrews ; *b.* Ealing, Middlesex, March 14, 1849 ; *s.* of late Rev. G. J. Adeney, of Reigate ; *m. d.* of late W. Hampton, Reigate; four *s.* four *d. Educ.:* New Coll., London. Seventeen years Congregational Minister at Acton ; fourteen years Professor of New Testament Exegesis and Church History at New Coll., London, and Lecturer at Hackney Coll., London ; Principal Lancashire Independent College and Lecturer in History of Doctrine at the University of Manchester, 1903-13 ; Chairman of Congregational Union, 1912. *Publications :* The Hebrew Utopia ; From Christ to Constantine ; From Constantine to Charles the Great ; Theology of the New Testament, which has been translated into Japanese (Theological Educator); Ezra, Nehemiah, and Esther ; Canticles and Lamentations (Expositor's Bible); Women of the New Testament ; How to Read the Bible (translated into Welsh) ; A Century's Progress ; St. Luke, and Galatians and Thessalonians (Century Bible); History of the Greek and Eastern Churches (International Theological Library) ; The New Testament Doctrine of Christ ; The Christian Conception of God ; Faith To-Day ; joint author of The Bible Story and also of Biblical Introduction ; Editor of Century Bible. *Recreation:* gardening. *Address:* The Croft, Southover, Lewes. (*Died 1 Sept. 1920.*)

ADKINS, Sir (William) Ryland Dent, Kt., *cr.* 1911 ; M.P. (L.) Middleton Division Lancs (S.E.), 1906-23 ; Recorder of Birmingham since 1920 ; *b.* 11 May 1862 ; *o. surv. s.* of late William Adkins, J. P., of Springfield, Northampton, and Harriet, *y. d.* of John Dent, Manor House, Milton, Northampton. *Educ.:* Mill Hill School ; University Coll. London; Balliol Coll., Oxford (Exhibitioner). Called to Bar, 1890 ; K.C. 1920 ; Recorder of Nottingham, 1911-20 ; Chairman Northants C.C. since 1920 ; Vice-Chairman Northants Territorial Force Association ; Chairman Executive Council of County Councils Association ; D.L. Northants ; J.P. Northants and Northampton. *Recreations :* shooting, gardening, history, literature. *Address:* 5 Paper Buildings, E.C.4 ; Springfield, Northampton. *T.:* Central 507. *Clubs :* Athenæum, Reform, Bath. (*Died 30 Jan. 1925.*)

ADRIAN, Alfred Douglas, C.B. 1895 ; K.C. 1904 ; *b.* 1845 ; *s.* of late E. Adrian of Local Government Board ; *m.* 1885, Flora, *d.* of Charles Howard Barton ; one *s. Educ. :* London University. Late Assistant Secretary Local Government Board, 1883 ; Legal Adviser to Local Government Board, 1899-1910. *Address:* 40 Elsworthy Road, Hampstead, N.W. (*Died 18 April 1922.*)

ADAMS, William Henry. See page xv.

ADY, Mrs. Henry (Julia Cartwright); *b.* Edgcote, Northamptonshire ; 2nd *d.* of Aubrey Cartwright and Hon. Mrs. Cartwright, *d.* of Lord Cottesloe ; *m.* 1880, Rev. W. H. Ady, Rector of Ockham (*d.* 1915); one *d.* *Educ.:* home. *Publications:* The Pilgrims' Way, 1892 ; Sacharissa, 1893 ; Madame : the Life and Letters of Henrietta, Duchess of Orleans, 1894 ; Life and Work of Sir Edward Burne-Jones, 1894 ; Raphael in Rome, 1895 ; J. F. Millet : his Life and Letters, 1896 ; Life and Work of G. F. Watts, 1896 ; Bastien-Lepage, 1895 ; Christ and His Mother in Italian Art, 1897 ; Beatrice d'Este, Duchess of Milan, 1899 ; The Painters of Florence, 1901 ; Isabella d'Este, a Study of the Renaissance, 1903 ; Sandro Botticelli, 1904 ; Raphael, 1905 ; The Perfect Courtier ; Life and Letters of Count B. Castiglione, 1908 ; Hampton Court, 1909 ; Christina of Denmark, 1913 ; Italian Gardens of the Renaissance, 1914 ; The Journals of Lady Knightley of Fawsley, 1915 ; besides many volumes of fiction and magazine articles. *Recreations:* travelling, motoring. *Address:* 40 St. Margaret's Road, Oxford.

(Died 28 April 1924.)

AFFLECK, Sir James Ormiston, Kt., *cr.* 1911 : F.R.S.E. ; LL.D. Edin. ; M.D., M.B., C.M., F.R.C.P.E., F.R.C.S.E., Consulting Physician Royal Infirmary, Edinburgh ; Physician, Royal Edinburgh Hospital for Incurables. *Address:* 38 Heriot Row, Edinburgh.

(Died 24 Sept. 1922.)

AFFLECK, Sir Robert, 7th Bt.; *cr.* 1782 ; J.P., D.L., Suffolk ; *b.* 4 March 1852. *Educ.:* Eton ; Oxford. *S.* father 1882 ; *m.* 1886, Julia Georgina [who *div.* him 1914], *d.* of John Sampson Prince. Owns about 4000 acres. *Heir:* b. John De Linden [*b.* July 18, 1850 ; *m.* 1895, Blanche Euphemia, *d.* of Alexander A. Robson, Sydney, N.S.W.].

(Died 4 Dec. 1919.)

AFLALO, Frederick George, F.R.G.S., Editor of the Encyclopædia of Sport, the Angler's Library, The Cost of Sport, the Young Naturalists' Library, Sport in Europe, Sports of the World, The Sportsman's Handbook for India ; Half a Century of Sport in Hampshire ; Fishermen's Weather ; The Call of the Sea (a prose anthology) ; A Book of Fishing Stories ; *b.* London, 17 Aug. 1870 ; *m.* 1895 ; one *d.* *Educ.:* Clifton College ; Rostock University. Mecklenburg. In 1891 studied in Italy ; founded the British Sea Anglers' Society (now over 1000 strong), 1893 ; travelled in Australia, particularly in Queensland, 1895, and in Morocco and the Atlas, 1899 ; visited every important fishing port on the English coast from Berwick-on-Tweed round to the Solway Firth, 1903 ; Madeira and Porto Santo, 1905 ; Florida and West Indies, 1906 ; California and Canada, 1908 ; Near East, Holy Land and Caucasus, 1909 ; Cape Breton Island and Nova Scotia, 1910 ; Russia, 1911 ; British East Africa, Uganda, and Sudan, 1913-14 ; India, 1915 ; War Service (Red Cross) in Volknyia, 1916 ; British Vice-Consul at Bâie, 1917. *Publications:* Sea-Fishing on the English Coast, 1891 ; Hints and Wrinkles on Sea-Fishing, 1894 ; A Sketch of the Natural History of Australia, 1896 ; A Sketch of the Natural History (Vertebrates) of the British Islands, 1897 ; Sea Fish, 1897 ; Types of British Animals, 1899 ; A Walk through the Zoological Gardens, 1900 ; Sea and Coast Fishing, 1901 ; Fifty Leaders of Sport, 1904 ; The Sea Fishing Industry of England and Wales, 1904 ; Salt-water Fishes (Woburn Library), 1904 ; The Salt of My Life, 1905 ; Sunshine and Sport in Florida and the West Indies, 1907 ; Sunset Playgrounds, 1909 ; Regilding the Crescent, 1910 ; An Idler in the Near East, 1910 ; A Fisherman's Summer in Canada, 1911 ; Behind The Ranges, 1911 ; Our Agreeable Friends, 1911 ; A Book of the Jungle and Wilderness, 1912. *Recreation:* fishing. *Address:* Teignmouth. *Clubs:* Sports ; East

Devon and Teignmouth, Teignmouth.

(Died 7 Dec. 1918.)

AGNEW, Sir Andrew Noel, 9th Bt., *cr.* 1629 ; *b.* 14 Aug. 1850 ; *s.* of 8th Baronet and Lady Louisa, *d.* of 1st Earl of Gainsborough. *Educ.:* Harrow ; Trinity Coll., Camb.; *m.* 1889, Gertrude, *d.* of Hon. G. C. Vernon, and *g.d.* of 1st Baron Lyveden ; *S.* father, 1892. Barr. Inner Temple, 1874. Vice-Lieut. Wigtowns.; M.P. (L.U.) South Edinburgh, 1900-6; late Captain 1st Ayrshire and Galloway Volunteer Artillery ; Member of Royal Company of Archers (King's Body Guard for Scotland) ; former President Royal Scottish Arboricultural Society. *Publications:* An Introduction to Forestry ; A Guide to Wigtownshire. *Heir:* b. Major Charles Hamlyn [*b.* 21 June 1859 ; *m.* 1897, Lilian Ann (whom he divorced, 1908), *d.* of Lt.-Gen. Sir J. Wolfe Murray ; one *s.* Late 4th Hussars. *Clubs:* Naval and Military, Brooks's, Cavalry.] *Recreations:* shooting, forestry, golf. *Address:* Lochnaw Castle, Stranraer, Wigtownshire. *Clubs:* Brooks's ; New, Edinburgh.

(Died 14 July 1928.)

AGNEW, Sir Patrick Dalreagle, K.B.E., *cr.* 1920 ; C.B.E. 1918 ; Knight of Grace of the Order of St. John of Jerusalem ; M.A. (Hon.) Oxford ; *s.* of William Henry and Janet Moubray Agnew ; *b.* Victoria, Australia, 26 Apr. 1868 ; *m.* 1897, Elizabeth Frances Seaton, *d.* of Lt.-Col. C. F. Massy, Indian Army, of Granstown, Tipperary ; one *d.* *Educ.:* Bedford Grammar School ; Balliol College, Oxford. Joined Indian Civil Service in 1889 ; Assistant Commissioner in the Punjab till 1898 ; Deputy Commissioner, 1898 ; Divisional Judge, 1910 ; Officiating Judge, Chief Court, 1913 ; retired, 1914 ; Managing Director and Vice-Chairman Central Prisoners of War Committee, 1916-19. *Recreation:* golf. *Address:* 8 Northmoor Road, Oxford. *Club:* East Indian United Service.

(Died 5 Sept. 1925.)

AGNEW, Sir Stair, K.C.B., *cr.* 1895 ; F.R.S.E. ; *b.* 1831 ; *s.* of Sir Andrew Agnew of Lochnaw, 7th Bt. *Educ.:* Trin. Coll. Camb. (B.A. 1855 ; M.A. 1858) ; *m.* Georgina, *d.* of George M. Nisbett, 1870. Late Lt. 9th Regt. : Scotch Barr. 1860 ; Legal Secretary to Lord Advocate, 1861 -3, 1868-70 ; Queen's Remembrancer for Scotland, 1870-81 ; Registrar-General for Scotland, and Keeper of Records, Scotland, 1881-1909. *Recreations:* rowed in Oxford and Cambridge boat race, 1854. *Address:* 22 Buckingham Terrace, Edinburgh. *Clubs:* Reform ; New, Edinburgh.

(Died 12 July 1916.)

AGNEW, William Lockett, J.P. ; Head of Thomas Agnew and Sons ; *s.* of Thomas Agnew, Manchester ; *b.* 1858 ; *m.* 1884, Augusta, *d.* of late F. Sheil of Bearforest, Mallow. *Address:* 10 Chesterfield Street, Mayfair, W. ; *T.:* Mayfair 1124; Hallingbury Place, Bishops Stortford.

(Died 15 Feb. 1918.)

AGOSTINI, L. B., K.C. ; late Attorney-General Trinidad and Tobago, West Indies ; *b.* 1853. *Educ.:* Stonyhurst College ; Downside College ; University College, London. Called to Bar, Lincoln's Inn, 1874. *Address:* Port of Spain, Trinidad, West Indies.

(Died 7 Aug. 1918.)

AGUET, Gustave Charles, C.B.E., Chairman Nestlé and Anglo-Swiss Condensed Milk Co. *Educ.:* University of Lausanne. *Recreations:* golf, shooting, fishing. *Address:* 42a Great Cumberland Place, W.1 ; Kiln Cottage, Holmwood, Surrey. *Clubs:* Reform, Ranelagh.

(Died 19 Feb. 1927.)

AHMAD, Hon. Ahsanuddin, C.S., I.S.O., 1915 ; Commissioner of Excise and Salt, Inspector-General of Registration, Registrar-General of Births, Deaths, and Marriages, and Registrar of Joint Stock Companies, Bihar and Orissa ; Additional Member, Bihar and Orissa Legislative Council ; President, Bihar and Orissa

9

Provincial Haj Committee; *b.* Calcutta, 16 Aug. 1859; 3rd *s.* of late Nawab Amir Ali Khan Bahadur, C.I.E.; *m.* 1881; three *s. Educ.*: Balliol, Oxford; Doveton College, Calcutta. Bar, Inner Temple; nominated to Bengal Covenanted Civil Service; Assistant Magistrate and Collector at Monghyr, Bengal; Joint Magistrate; acted for 6 or 7 years as District and Sessions Judge; Elected Executive branch of the Service; acted as Collector and Magistrate in different districts; Fishery Commissioner for Bengal; Durbar Medal. *Recreations:* plays racquets, tennis, golf and auction bridge. *Address:* Ranchi, B.N.R., India. *Clubs:* Calcutta, Calcutta; Ranchi, Ranchi; Bankipur, Bankipur. (*Died 3 July 1918.*)

AICARD, Jean, Membre de l'Academie Française; président d'honneur de la Société des Gens de Lettres; président de l'Union Française; poète, romancier, auteur dramatique; Officer of the Legion of Honour; *b.* Toulon, 1848. *Educ.*: Lycée de Mâcon; Lycée de Nimes. *Publications.*— *Poèmes:* Les Jeunes Croyances; Rébellions et Apaisements; Poèmes de Provence, 1873; Chanson de l'enfant; Miette et Noré; Visite en Hollande, 1879; Le Dieu dans l'homme, 1885; Le Livre des petits, 1886; Le Livre d'heures de l'amour, 1887; Au bord du désert, 1888; Jésus; Don Juan, 1889; Le Jardin des enfants, 1913; Le Témoin, 1915; Le Sang du sacrifice, 1917. *Romans:* Roi de Camargue; Pavé d'amour; Fleur d'abime; Melita; L'Ibis bleu; Diamant noir; Notre Dame d'amour; Tata; Arlette des Mayons; Gaspard de Besse; L'Âme d'un enfant; Arlette des Mayons; Maurin des Maures and L'Illustre Maurin (traduit en anglais). *Critique:* Alfred de Vigny; La Vénus de Milo. *Divers:* Des Cris dans la mêlée. *Théâtre:* Le Père Lebonnard; Smilis; La Légende du cœur; Le Manteau du roi; La Milésienne, Gaspard de Besse. *Address:* Paris, 40 rue Guynemer; La Garde, Var, Villa les Lauriers-roses; Solliès-le-Vieux, Var, France. (*Died May 1921.*)

AIKMAN, Sir Robert (Smith), Kt. *cr.* 1910; M.A.; Hon. LL.D., St. Andrews; *b.* 18 July 1844; *s.* of A. Aikman, St. Andrews; *m.* 1st, 1877, Mary (*d.* 1914), *e. d.* of late J. Craig, J.P., Three Crofts, Kirkcudbrightshire; three *d.*; 2nd, 1916, Catherine Maud, *d.* of Mr. Richards, Burton-on-Trent. *Educ.*: Madras College, St. Andrews; St. Andrews and Edinburgh Universities. Entered Indian Civil Service, 1867; retired 1909; for fifteen years Puisne Judge of the High Court of the North-Western Provinces; for three years Vice-Chancellor of the Allahabad University. *Address:* c/o H. S. King and Co., 9 Pall Mall, S.W. (*Died 6 April 1917.*)

AILWYN, 1st Baron, *cr.* 1921, of Honingham, Norfolk; **Ailwyn Edward Fellowes;** P.C. 1905; K.B.E., *cr.* 1917; K.C.V.O., *cr.* 1911; D.L., J.P. Norfolk; *b.* 1855; 2nd *s.* of 1st Lord de Ramsey; *m.* 1886, Hon. Agatha Eleanor Augusta Joliffe, *d.* of 2nd Lord Hylton; three *s. Educ.*: Eton; Trin. Hall, Camb. Vice-Chamberlain of Queen Victoria's Household, 1895-1900; a Junior Lord of the Treasury, 1900-1905; President Board of Agriculture, 1905-6; M.P. (C.) Hunts, Ramsey, 1887-1906; Chairman of Norfolk County Council; late Chairman of Agricultural Wages Board; Deputy-Chairman G.E. Railway. Owns 4500 acres. *Heir: s.* Major Hon. Ronald T. Fellowes. *Address:* Honingham, Norwich. *T.:* Honingham 2. *Club:* Carlton. (*Died 23 Sept. 1924.*)

AINGER, Arthur Campbell, M.A., M.V.O. 1908; *b.* 4 July 1841; *s.* of Rev. Thomas Ainger, Prebendary of St. Paul's and Incumbent of Hampstead, Middlesex; unmarried. *Educ.*: Eton; Trinity College, Cambridge. First class Classics, 1864; Assistant Master at Eton, 1864-1901; Hon. Secretary Old Etonian Association, 1900; Eton Memorial Buildings, 1902. *Publications:* Eton Songs (including Carmen Etonense.

Vale, etc.); various school books (Clivus, English Latin Verse Dictionary, with H. G. Wintle, M.A., etc.); Eton, an Anthology in Prose and Verse, 1910; Memories of Eton Sixty Years Ago, 1917; sundry Hymns (including "God is working His purpose out," etc.). *Address:* Mustians, Eton, Bucks. *Club:* United University. (*Died 26 Oct. 1919.*)

AINSLIE, Rev. Richard Montague, M.A., T.D.; Vicar of Childwall since 1903; Hon. Canon of Liverpool; *b.* 23 Jan. 1858; *m.* 1st, 1887, Mabel Bower Forwood (*d.* 1893); 2nd, 1895, Euphemia Brown Fortune; one *s.* four *d. Educ.*: St. Peter's School, York; Pembroke College, Cambridge. Deacon, 1884; Priest, 1885; Curate of Witton, Northwich, 1884-87; Vicar of St. Saviour's, Liverpool, 1887-1903; Chaplain of 1st Batt. King's Liverpool Regt. 1890; Chaplain 5th Batt. K.L.R. 1908; Secretary of Liverpool Hospital Sunday Fund since 1893; Secretary of Liverpool Diocesan Church Building Society since 1902; Secretary of Diocesan Conference since 1893; Member of Liverpool Cathedral Committee; Territorial Decoration, 1912. *Recreations:* Shooting and fishing. *Address:* Childwall Vicarage, Liverpool. *T.A.*: Vicarage, Broad Green. *T.:* Gateacre 69. *Club:* Athenæum, Liverpool. (*Died 23 Dec. 1924.*)

AINSWORTH, Sir John (Stirling), 1st Bt., *cr.* 1916; D.L.; J.P.; *s.* of late Thomas Ainsworth of The Flosh, Cleator, Cumberland, and Mary Laurie, *d.* of John Stirling, D.D., of Craigie, Ayrshire; *b.* 30 Jan. 1844; *m.* 1879, Margaret Catherine (*d.* 1918), *d.* of Robert Reid Macredie; one *s.* two *d. Educ.*: University College School and University College, London, M.A., LL.B. Sheriff of the county of Cumberland, 1891; commanded the 3rd Volunteer Batt. Border Regt. 1898-1902; contested Barrow-in-Furness, 1886; Argyllshire, 1900; M.P. (L.) Argyllshire, 1908-18. *Heir: s.* Thomas [Lieut. 11th Hussars; *b.* 8 Feb. 1886; *m.* 1911, Lady Edina Dorothy Hope, 4th *d.* of 4th Marquess Conyngham; one *s.* one *d.*]. *Address:* Ardanaiseig, Loch Awe, Argyllshire; Harecroft, Gosforth, Cumberland. *Club:* Reform. (*Died 24 May 1923.*)

AIREY, Paymr. Rear-Adm. Frederick W I., C.B. 1920; R.N.; *b.* 3 June 1861; *s.* of late Rev. John A. L. Airey, M.A., Rector of St. Helen's Church, Bishopsgate Street, E.C., and Mary Lumb; *m.* 1899, Katherine Mary, *yr. d.* of William Parham, Bath; no *c. Educ.*: Merchant Taylors' School, London. Joined Royal Navy, 1877; served in Egyptian Campaign of 1882; Soudan Campaign, 1884-85; Boxer Insurrection in China, 1900; European War, 1914-1918; retired from Royal Navy, 1919. *Publication:* Pidjin Inglis Tails, and others. *Recreations:* tennis, golf. *Address:* c/o Admiralty, S.W.1. *Club:* Royal Dorset Yacht, Weymouth. (*Died 18 Aug. 1922.*)

AIRY, Rev. Basil Reginald, M.A., T.D.; Prebendary of Exeter Cathedral; Vicar of St. John's, Torquay, since 1886; *s.* of Rev. William Airy, M.A., Vicar of Keysoe, Beds., and nephew of Sir George Biddell Airy, K.C.B., late Astronomer Royal; *b.* Keysoe, 20 April 1845; *m.* 1874, Emma, *d.* of Shepley Watson, of York; two *s.* two *d. Educ.*: King Edward's School, Birmingham; Trinity College, Cambridge. Deacon, 1868; Priest, 1869; Curate of Wisbech St. Mary, 1868; Stretham, nr. Ely, 1870; Kirkby Misperton, 1871; Vicar of Whitwell, Yorks, 1873; Chaplain to Devon and Somerset Engineers (Vol.), and to Devon Royal Engineers (Territorial) for 24 years; Chaplain to High Sheriff of Yorkshire, 1890. *Address:* St. John's Vicarage, Torquay. (*Died 15 Jan. 1924.*)

AIRY, Osmund, LL.D. St. Andrews, 1899; M.A.; J.P. Berks; *b.* Royal Observatory, Greenwich, 29 Oct. 1845; *y. s.* of late Sir

G. B. Airy, K.C.B., Astronomer - Royal, and Richarda Smith, *e. d.* of Rev. C. Smith, Edensor, Derbyshire; *m.* Emily Josephine, *d.* of late Canon Miller, D.D., 1873; one *s.* three *d. Educ.:* Blackheath Proprietary School; Trinity Coll., Cambridge. 27th Wrangler, 1868. Assist. Master Blackheath Proprietary School, 1868; Assist. Master Wellington College, 1868-76; H.M. Inspector of Schools, 1876; Divisional Inspector, and Inspector of Training Colls., 1904; retired, 1910. *Publications:* Treatise on Geometrical Optics, 1870; Selections from Addison's Spectator, 1874; historical and other articles in various Reviews, Encyclopædia Britannica, and Dict. of Nat. Biog.; Louis XIV. and the English Restoration (Epochs of Modern History), 1888; edited Lauderdale Papers, 3 vols. (Camden Society), 1884, 1885; Essex Papers (Camden Soc.), 1890; Text Book of English History, 1893; Burnet's History of His Own Time (Charles II.), 2 vols., 1897-99; Biography of Charles II. (Goupil), 1901. *Address:* Crowthorne, Berks.

(Died 30 Nov. 1923.)

AIRY, Wilfrid, B.A., M.I.C.E. *Publications:* Levelling and Geodesy; Weighing Machines. *Address:* White House, Croom's Hill, Greenwich, S.E. *(Died 8 Oct. 1925.)*

AITCHISON, Gen. Charles Terrington, C.B., 1875; *b.* 28 May 1825; *m.* 1854, Annie, *d.* of Alexander Colquhoun. Entered army, 1842; Captain, 1855; Major, 1858; Lieut.-Col. 1864; Colonel, 1869; Major-Gen. 1881; Lieut.-Gen. 1884; General, 1889; retired; served South Mahratta country, 1844-45 (wounded, despatches); Persian Expeditionary Force, 1856-57 (despatches, thanks of Governor-General, medal with clasp, brevet of major); Southern Mahratta country during Mutiny, 1857-58 (medal). *Address:* 48 Duke Street, St. James's, S.W.

(Died 5 Jan. 1919.)

AITKEN, George Atherton, M.V.O. 1911; Assist. Secretary, Home Office; *b.* Barkingside, Essex, 19 March 1860; *o. s.* of late John Aitken and Mary Ann Elizabeth. *d.* of William Salmon; *m.* 1903, Emma, *d.* of John Cawthorne. *Educ.:* King's Coll. School; University Coll London. Entered the Secretary's Office, General Post Office, 1888; private secretary to the Permanent Secretary, Sir Arthur Blackwood, K.C.B., 1890; transferred to the Home Office, 1892; Secretary to Reformatory and Industrial Schools Departmental Committee, 1895, and to Inebriate Reformatories Committee, 1898; private secretary to Sir Kenelm Digby, K.C.B., Permanent Under Secretary of State, 1896-1901; member of Home Office Committee on grants to Reformatory and Industrial Schools, 1905; Chairman of Committee on Superannuation of Officers of Reformatory and Industrial Schools, 1914; British Delegate at International Conferences at Paris on White Slave Traffic, etc., 1910, and at International Congress at Brussels on the Protection of Child Life, 1913: Life Governor of University College, 1902. *Publications:* Life of Richard Steele, 2 vols. 1889; Life and Works of Dr. John Arbuthnot, 1892; editions of Marvell, 1892; Burns, 1893; Steele's Plays, 1893; Defoe's Romances and Narratives, 16 vols. 1896; Spectator, 8 vols. 1898; Tatler, 4 vols. 1899; Swift's Journal to Stella, 1901; contributions to Dictionary of National Biography and Cambridge History of English Literature. *Recreations:* walking, book-collecting. *Address:* 21 Church Row, Hampstead, N.W. *Club:* Athenæum. *(Died 16 Nov. 1917.)*

AITKEN, Hon. J. G. W., M.L.C.: Moderator, Presbyterian Church, New Zealand, 1917. *Address:* Wellington, New Zealand.

(Died Aug. 1921.)

AITKEN, John, LL.D., F.R.S., F.R.S.E.: 4th *s.* of late Henry Aitken, Darroch, Falkirk. *Educ.:* Grammar School, Falkirk; Glasgow University. Served apprenticeship as marine

engineer in the works of R. Napier and Sons, Lancefield, Glasgow. *Publications:* has investigated and written papers in the publications of the Royal Society, London, and Royal Society of Edinburgh, on Colour and Colour Sensation; Rigidity produced by Centrifugal Force; Dust Fogs and Clouds; Colour of Water; Dew; Apparatus for Counting the Dust Particles in the Air; Observations of the Number of Dust Particles in the Atmosphere of Different Places in Europe; Hazing Effect of Atmospheric Dust; Cloud Particles; Cyclones and Anticyclones, The Sun as a Fog-Producer, etc. Has invented instruments for counting the dust particles in the atmosphere, chromomictors and the koniscope. *Recreations:* trout and salmon fishing, photography, gardening, wood and metal work. *Address:* Ardenlea, Falkirk, N.B.

(Died 13 Nov. 1919.)

AITKEN, John Hobson, I.S.O. 1916; *b.* 28 March 1851; *s.* of late Richard Aitken, formerly of Aberdeen; unmarried. In Government Office, Isle of Man, 1870; retired as Chief Clerk, 1914; has been Private Secretary to successive Lieut.-Governors; Secretary to Local Government Board of Isle of Man, 20 July 1894 to 31 Dec. 1894; acted as Insular Registrar General, two months, 1910. *Address:* Farnley, Beverley Mount, Douglas, Isle of Man.

(Died 21 Mar. 1923.)

AITKEN, Sir Robert, Kt., *cr.* 1918; Managing Governor, Imperial Bank of India; *b.* 13 May 1863; *s.* of John Aitken of West Linton, Peeblesshire; *m.* Carolina Mary, *d.* of Theophilus Lobb, Ex-Engineer, P.W.D., India; two *s.* one *d. Address:* Kinellan, Malabar Hill, Bombay. *Club:* Oriental.

(Died 18 April 1924.)

AITKEN, Colonel William, C.B. 1896; A.D.C. to H.M. 1900-3; *b.* 24 Feb. 1846; 4th *s.* of late James Aitken of Gartcow's, Falkirk, N.B.; *m.* Susan Elizabeth, *y. d.* of George A. Coventry, Shanwell, Kinross-shire, N.B. 1894; one *s.* one *d. Educ.:* Edinburgh Academy; Heidelberg. Entered R.A. 1867; Captain, 1878; Major, 1884; Brevet Lieut.-Col. 1887; Bt. Col. 1897; served Afghan War, 1878-9-80 (despatches, medal); Mahsud Waziri Expedition, 1881; Burmah Expedition, 1885-87 (despatches, Bt. Lieut.-Col.); Chitral Relief Force, 1895 (despatches, C.B.); A.D.C. to Queen Victoria, 1897; Malakand Field Force, Mohmand and Buner Expeditions, 1897-98; commanded Mountain Artillery, Rawal Pindi, Punjab, to 1899; Col. on Staff commanding R.A. Scottish District, 1899-1903; retired, 1903. *Recreations:* shooting, golf. *Address:* Kemback, Cupar, Fife. *Clubs:* Army and Navy; New, Edinburgh; Royal and Ancient Golf, St. Andrews. *(Died 11 Jan. 1917.)*

AITKEN, Reverend William Hay Macdowall Hunter, M.A.; Canon Residentiary of Norwich Cathedral since 1900; General Superintendent of the Church Parochial Mission Society since 1876; *b.* Grove Street, Liverpool, 21 Sept. 1841; *y. s.* of late Rev. Robert Aitken, Vicar of Pendeen, Cornwall, and his second wife, Wilhelmina Day Macdowall Grant, of Arndilly, Banffshire, N.B.; *m.* 1867, Eleanor Marian Barnes of Arkley Barnet; two *s.* four *d. Educ.:* at home; Wadham Coll., Oxford. Second Class Lit. Hum., B.A. 1865, M.A. 1867. Ordained 1865 to curacy of St. Jude's, Mildmay, N.; took prominent part in Twelve Days' Mission, 1869; Incumbent of Christ Church, Great Homer Street, Liverpool, 1871; resigned to be a Mission-Preacher 1875; was the means of founding Church Parochial Mission Society, 1876 (originally the Aitken Memorial Fund, being a memorial to his father); visited the United States on a Mission Tour 1886, and again 1895-6, when he worked also in Canads, the tour extending over six months; was invited by the Bishop of London to take part in the

Fulham Conference on the subject of the Confessional, January 1902. *Publications :* Mission Sermons, 3 Series ; Newness of Life ; What is your Life ? The School of Grace ; God's Everlasting Yea ; The Glory of the Gospel ; The Highway of Holiness ; Around the Cross ; The Revealer Revealed ; Temptation and Toil ; Eastertide ; The Love of the Father ; The Romance of Christian Work and Experience ; Soul - Difficulties ; The Doctrine of Baptism ; The Divine Ordinance of Prayer ; The Mechanical Versus the Spiritual ; Apostolical Succession ; Life, Light, and Love—Thoughts on the First Epistle of St. John. *Address :* The Close, Norwich. *T.A. :* Canon Aitken, Norwich.

(Died 28 Oct. 1927.)

AKELEY, Carl Ethan, taxidermist, inventor, sculptor, ; *b.* Orleans Co., N.Y., 19 May 1864 ; *s.* of Daniel Webster Akeley and Julia M. Glidden. *Educ. :* State Normal School, Brockport, N.Y. With Field Museum, Chicago, 1895-1909 ; American Museum of Natural History, New York, since 1909. Served as Consulting Engineer, Division of Investigation, Research and Development, Engineering Department, United States Army ; also as Special Assistant, Concrete Department, Emergency Fleet Corporation. Inventor of Cement-gun, Akeley camera, etc. ; medallist Franklin Inst. ; big-game hunter ; made four trips to Africa for study and collection of big game. *Publication :* In Brightest Africa. *Address :* American Museum of Natural History, 77th Street and Central Park W., New York. *Clubs :* Century, Boone and Crockett, Explorers, African Big Game, Camp Fire of America, Wilderness, Ends of the Earth, New York ; Camp Fire, Adventurers, Chicago.

(Died 29 Nov. 1926.)

ALBEE, Ernest, Professor of Philosophy in Cornell University ; *b.* Langdon, N.H., 8 Aug. 1865 ; *s.* of Solon Albee and Ellen Lucilla Eames ; *m.* 1911, Emily Humphreys Manly. *Educ. :* University of Vermont (A.B., 1887) ; Clark University ; Cornell University (Ph.D., 1894). Fellow in Psychology, Clark University, 1891 ; Fellow in Philosophy, Cornell Univ., 1892 ; Teacher of Philosophy in Cornell Univ. since 1892 ; co-editor of the Philosophical Review, 1903-8. *Publications :* A History of English Utilitarianism, 1902, and articles on philosophical subjects. *Recreations :* golf and walking. *Address :* 207 Kelvin Place, Ithaca, New York, U.S.A. *Clubs :* Authors ; City, New York.

(Died May 1927.)

ALCOCK, Capt. Sir John William, K.B.E. *cr.* 1919 ; D.S.O. 1919 ; late R.A.F. Decorated for first crossing the Atlantic in an aeroplane (Vickers-Vimy Atlantic), Newfoundland to Clifden, Ireland, 4.28 P.M. June 14-8.40 A.M. June 15, 1919. *(Died 18 Dec. 1919.)*

ALDEN, Henry Mills, A.M., LL.D. ; Editor Harper's Magazine since 1869 ; *b.* 11 Nov. 1836, at Mt. Tabor, near Danby, Vermont, U.S.A. ; *m.* 1st, 1861, Susan Frye Foster of North Andover, Mass. ; 2nd, 1900, Ada Foster Murray of Norfolk, Va. *Educ. :* Graduated at William's Coll. 1857 ; Andover Theological Seminary, 1860. Lecturer before Lowell Institute, 1863-1864, subject "The Structure of Paganism" ; Managing Editor Harper's Weekly, 1863-69. *Publications :* God in His World, 1890 ; A Study of Death, 1895 ; Magazine Writing and the New Literature, 1908. *Address :* Metuchen, New Jersey. *Club :* Authors', New York.

(Died 7 Oct. 1919.)

ALDERSON, Lt. - Gen. Sir Edwin Alfred Hervey, K.C.B., *cr.* 1916 ; C.B. 1900 ; *b.* 8 Apr. 1859 ; *o. s.* of late Edward Mott Alderson, Poyle House, Ipswich ; *m.* 1886, Alice Mary, 2nd *d.* of late Rev. Oswald P. Sergeant, Vicar of Chesterton, Oxon. Entered Royal West Kent Regiment, 1878 ; Capt. 1886 ; Major, 1896 ; Bt. Lt.-Col. 1897 ; Bt. Col. 1900 ;

Col. 1903 ; Maj. - Gen. 1906 ; Lt. - Gen. 1914 ; Adjutant, Mounted Infantry, 1887-91 ; R. West Kent Regt. 1890-4 ; D.A.A.G. and commanding M.I. Aldershot, 1897-99 ; Brigadier-General Commanding 2nd Infantry Brigade, Aldershot 1903-7 ; commanded 6th (Poona) Division, S. Army, India, 1908-12 ; served with M.I. Boer War, 1881 : Egyptian War, with M.I., 1882, including Kassassin (both actions) and Tel-el-Kebir (medal with clasp, Khedive's star) ; Nile Expedition, with M.I. Camel Regt., 1884-85 (two clasps) ; South Africa, 1896 ; in command of M.I. and expedition which relieved Salisbury, and finally in command of troops in Mashonaland, 1896 (despatches, brevet of Lt.-Col., medal) ; commanded Mounted Infantry in South Africa, 1900-1 ; Inspector-Gen. M.I., S. Africa, 1900-2, rank Br.-Gen. (despatches three times, two medals with seven clasps, A.D.C. to the King, brevet of Col., C.B.) ; served European War, 1914-18, commanding 1st Canadian Division and subsequently the Canadian Army Corps (despatches, K.C.B., Commander Legion of Honour) ; awarded bronze medal of Royal Humane Society, 1885 ; A.D.C. to Queen Victoria and King Edward VII. 1900-6. *Publications :* With the Mounted Infantry and Mashonaland Field Force, 1896 ; Pink and Scarlet, or Hunting as a School for Soldiering, 1900 ; Lessons from 100 Notes made in Peace and War. *Recreations :* Hunted the Shorncliffe Drag Hounds, 1891-93 ; the Staff College Drag Hounds, 1894-95 ; Cape Jackal Hounds and Salisbury Hounds, 1896 ; Alderson's Hounds, Pretoria, 1902 ; Poona and Kirkee Hounds, 1910 ; S. Shropshire Foxhounds, 1914-23 ; owns several racing and other yachts. *Clubs :* Marlborough, Naval and Military ; Royal Norfolk and Suffolk Yacht ; Royal Canoe. *(Died 14 Dec. 1927.)*

ALDERSON, Sir George Beeton, K.B.E., *cr.* 1922 ; engineer ; *b.* 8 Jan. 1844 ; *s.* of Frederic Henry Alderson, of Ingham House, Ipswich, Suffolk ; *m.* 1st, 1869, Ellen Owen Wells ; 2nd, 1906, Helen, *d.* of Dr. Andrew Pouzetta. *Address :* Norland House, Ramleh, Egypt. *Club :* Union, Alexandria.

(Died 2 Dec. 1926.)

ALDINGTON, Charles, C.B.E. 1918 ; General Manager, Great Western, Railway, 1919-21 ; late Superintendent of the Line. *Address :* 53 Eastbourne Terrace, W.2.

(Died 15 Oct. 1922.)

ALDRICH - BLAKE, Louisa Brandreth, M.S., M.D., M.B. (1st class hons.), B.S. (1st class hons.) ; Dean, London School of Medicine for Women ; Senior Surgeon, Elizabeth Garrett Anderson Hospital, Euston Road ; Consulting Surgeon with beds, Royal Free Hospital, Gray's Inn Road ; Fellow, Royal Society of Medicine ; late Anaesthetist and Surgical Registrar, Royal Free Hospital. *Publication :* Abdomino - Perineal Excision of the Rectum by a New Method. *Address :* 17 Nottingham Place, W.1. *T. :* Mayfair 371. *Clubs :* University Women's, London University.

(Died 28 Dec. 1925.)

ALDRIDGE, Very Rev. John Mullings, Dean of Clonfert since 1907 ; Rector of Donanaughta, 1898-1906 and since 1911 ; Canon of St. Patrick's, Dublin, 1914. *Educ. :* Trinity College, Dublin (M.A.). Ordained 1870 ; Incumbent of Donanaughta, 1871-1886 ; Rector of St. John, Forfar, 1886-92 ; West Bridgford, 1892-94 ; Charton, 1894-95 ; Meyseyhampton, 1895-98 ; Rector of Creagh, 1906-11. *Address :* Rectory, Eyre Court, Co. Galway.

(Died 18 Mar. 1920.)

ALEXANDER, Alexander, F.R.G.S., 2nd *s.* of W. C. Alexander of Glanmire and Liverpool ; *b.* Liverpool, 14 May 1849 ; *m.* Emily Adelaide, *d.* of late John and Mary Smith of Ranelagh, Dublin ; one *s.* *Educ. :* Liverpool College and Liverpool Institute. Apprenticed

to John Hulley, gymnasiarch, 1862; trained by James Mace (Champion of England), Andre Durbec (Paris), and J. Beckton (Cumberland); Public Demonstrator of Physical Training at Liverpool Gymnasium, 1864; took to the road, 1870, and as a pioneer of physical training gave lectures and demonstrations at the various public schools and military stations throughout the United Kingdom; Prof. of Gymnastics at Trinity College, Dublin, 1875; Director of the Liverpool Gymnasium, 1880; invented and patented (which was not renewed) bent handles for cycles; founded with Lord Gladstone the National Physical Recreation Society, 1886; at the invitation of King Oscar of Sweden he took over a team of English athletes to Stockholm to introduce athletic sports, 1896; in same year, at request of H.M. Government, visited the principal colleges and military stations of Europe with the view of ascertaining the relative values of the various systems of physical training in vogue; about the same period his advice in physical training was sought by the French, South African, Canadian, and Australian Governments; Vice-President of International Board of Education, U.S.A.; holder of many prizes, including Military Gymnastic Championship, National Physical Recreation Societies Challenge Shield, and first prize for activity and strength, Stockholm 1896. *Publications:* Musical Drill, 1882; Modern Gymnastic Exercises, 1884; Advanced Gymnastics, 1888; Physical Training at Home, 1890; Physical Training of all Nations, 1896; British Physical Education, 1903; A Holiday Romance, 1904; Robin Hood, 1908; Pirates' Hoard, 1908; A Wayfarer's Log, 1919; A Wayfarer's Caravan, 1921. *Recreations:* chess, draughts, reading, music, walking. *Address:* Innisfallen, Birkdale, Lancs.
(Died 23 May 1928.)

ALEXANDER, Col. Aubrey de Vere, D.S.O. 1903; retired; late Officiating Col. on Staff, Rawal Pindi; *b.* 28 May 1849; *s.* of late G. H. M. Alexander, I.C.S.; *m.* 1875, Mary Georgina Carter, *d.* of late General Sir James Brind, G.C.B. *Educ.:* Wellington College. Entered army, 1869; Captain, 1881; Major, 1889; Lieut.-Col. 1895; Bt.-Col. 1899; served with Khyber Field Force in Afghan War, 1879-80 (medal); China Field Force, 1900-1901, (despatches, D.S.O.); European War, 1914-19, Intelligence Department, War Office. *Address:* c/o Cox & Co. Charing Cross. S.W.1.
(Died 11 Sept. 1923.)

ALEXANDER Lt.-Col. Boyd Francis, late Rifle Brigade; *b.* 1834; 3rd *s.* of Boyd Alexander of Ballochmyle, Ayrshire, and Sophia, 3rd *d.* of Sir B. Hobhouse, 1st Bart.; *m.* Mary, *d.* of D. Wilson; two *s.* one *d.* *Educ.:* Harrow. Served with the Rifle Brigade in Turkey, 1854; Indian Mutiny, 1857-8; Battle of Cawnpore; siege and capture of Lucknow; Oudh campaign; action at Nawabgunge; commanded storming party at attack on Fort Birwah (twice wounded, despatches, Bt. Major, medal and clasp); in Canada, Fenian Raid, 1870 (medal). *Address:* Swifts Place, Cranbrook. *T.A.:* Alexander, Swifts, Cranbrook. *Club:* Carlton.
(Died 19 Aug. 1917.)

ALEXANDER, Charles McCallon, M.A.; Evangelist; *b.* Oct. 24, 1867; *e. s.* of late John D. Alexander of Maryville, Tennessee, U.S.A.; *m.* 1904, Helen, *d.* of late Richard Cadbury of Birmingham. Engaged in evangelistic work, singing, organising and conducting large chorus choirs for 8 years; made an evangelistic tour of the world with Rev. R. A. Torrey, 1902-6; made the Glory Song famous throughout the world at this time; second tour of the world with his wife 1906-7; conducted the largest evangelistic choir ever organised (4000 members) for two months daily in the Royal Albert Hall,

London; compiler of Alexander's hymns; worked with Dr. J. Wilbur Chapman of New York in evangelistic work, 1908-18, conducting united missions in Australia, Philipine Islands, China, Japan and Korea; also in America and Great Britain. *Address:* Tennessee, Moor Green Lane, Birmingham; 158 Fifth Avenue, New York City, U.S.A. *T.A.:* Bible, Moseley. *T.:* South 310. *(Died 13 Oct. 1920.)*

ALEXANDER, Conel W. O'D. L., M.Sc., B.E., Assoc. M.Inst.C.E.; Professor of Civil Engineering, University College, Cork, since 1906; *b.* Imlick, Co. Donegal, 6 June 1879; *s.* of Joseph Alexander, J.P.; *m.* 1907, Hilda Barbara Bennett; two *s.* one *d.* *Educ.:* Foyle College, Derry; Friars School, Bangor; Queen's University, Belfast; Birmingham University. Graduated in Royal University, 1901, and in Birmingham University, 1905; Engineer-Assistant to City Engineer of Birmingham, 1902-6; won James Forrest Medal, Miller Scholarship, and Birmingham Students' Medal, Institution of Civil Engineers, 1904, Heslop Medal, Birmingham University, 1906, and Mullins Medal, Institution of Civil Engineers of Ireland, 1913; Dean of Faculty of Engineering of Nationa University of Ireland since 1909; Examiner to National University, to Institution of Civil Engineers, and to the Civil Service Commissioners; President, Irish Rugby Football Union, 1909-10, and member of Committee since 1909. *Publications:* Fluid Friction in Pipe Bends; Reinforced Concrete; Hydraulic Diagrams; and several technical papers. *Recreations:* Rugby football, cricket, and gardening. *Address:* Tyrconel, Perrott Avenue, Cork.
(Died 17 Dec. 1920.)

ALEXANDER, David Lindo, K.C. 1892; J.P.; *b.* 1842; *s.* of J. Alexander; *m.* Hester (*d.* 1913), *e. d.* of S. J. Joseph. *Educ.:* Trinity Hall, Cambridge (B.A.). Called to Bar, Lincoln's Inn, 1866; Bencher, 1895. President of Jewish Board of Deputies *Address:* 11 York Gate, Regent's Park, N.W.1. *T.:* Mayfair 592.
(Died 29 April 1922.)

ALEXANDER, Edwin, R.W.S.; R.S.A. 1918; artist; *b.* Edinburgh, 1870; *s.* of late Robert Alexander, R.S.A.; father Scotch, mother English; *m.* 1904. *Educ.:* Edinburgh. Studied in the Edinburgh School of Art, at the Royal Scottish Academy's life class, and in Paris; has exhibited chiefly in the Royal Scottish Academy, and the R.W.S. *Address:* Links Lodge, Musselburgh, Midlothian. *Club:* Scottish Arts, Edinburgh. *(Died April 1926.)*

ALEXANDER, Sir George, Kt., cr. 1911; J.P., (Hon.) LL.D.; actor and manager St. James's Theatre; *b.* Reading, 19 June 1858; *m.* Florence Théleur. *Educ.:* Dr. Benham's, Clifton; Relton's, Ealing; High School, Stirling. Started in the City, but being an enthusiastic amateur actor, soon took to the stage. Theatre Royal, Nottingham, in 1879; then on tour with Robertsonian Comedy, till, in 1881, joined Mr. Irving at the Lyceum; played there and at other leading theatres. He opened own management with Dr. Bill, at Avenue Theatre, 1890, and migrated to the St. James's Theatre in 1891. Represented South St. Pancras in London County Council, 1907-13; president of Royal General Theatrical Fund; vice-president and active associate of Actors' Benevolent Fund; admitted Freeman of Turners' Company, 1908. *Recreations:* riding, bicycling, golfing. *Address:* 57 Pont Street, S.W.; Little Court, Chorleywood, Herts. *T.A.:* Ruritania, London. *Clubs:* Carlton, Garrick Beefsteak, Green Room.
(Died 16 Mar. 1918.)

ALEXANDER, Colonel John Donald, D.S.O., C.B.E., M.B., B.Ch., A.M.S. (retired); *b.* 1867; *e. s.* Very Rev. John Alexander, Dean of Ferns; *m.* 1906, Georgina Eleanor, *d.* of Alexander Going of Altavilla, Cahir; no *c.* *Educ.:* St. Columba's College; Trinity College,

13

Dublin. Gazetted to the Army Medical Service, 1892, serving till 1920; served Tirah and N.W. Frontier of India, 1907-8 (despatches, medal and 2 clasps); South African War, 1899-1902 (despatches twice, 2 medals and 7 clasps); European War on Western Front, 1914-1918 (despatches four times, D.S.O., C.B.E., Chevalier de l'Ordre de Leopold, 4 British medals, Croix de Guerre, France and Belgium). *Address:* Landcross Grange, Bideford. *T.A.:* Landcross Bideford. *T.:* Bideford 2X2. *M.:* XF 4691. *Club:* University, Dublin. *(Died 9 July 1922.)*

ALEXANDER, Joseph Gundry, LL.B. Lond.; retired barrister; Hon. Secretary of Society for the Suppression of the Opium Trade since 1894; Member of Permanent International Peace Bureau, Berne; J.P., Kent; *b.* Bath, 1848; *s.* of Samuel Alexander and Sarah Gundry; *m.* 1881, Josephine Crosfield; four *s.* *Educ.:* private Friends' Schools, Brighton and Weston-super-Mare. Business at Leominster, 1863-71; called to Lincoln's Inn, 1874; practised as an equity draftsman and conveyancer till 1890; Hon. General Secretary of International Law Association, 1883-1905; Secretary of Society for the Suppression of the Opium Trade, 1890; accompanied the Royal Opium Commission to India and Burma, 1893-94, afterwards visiting China; Chairman of International Peace Congress, London, 1908. *Address:* 3 Mayfield Road, Tunbridge Wells. *T.:* Tunbridge Wells 950. *Club:* National Liberal. *(Died 16 Feb. 1918.)*

ALEXANDER, Reginald Gervase, M.A. Cantab, M.D., F.L.S.; J.P. Yorks; K.C.V.O., *cr.* 1908; C.V.O. 1905; *b.* 1859; *o. s.* of 1st Lord Alington and Lady Augusta Bingham, *d.* of 3rd Earl of Lucan; S. father 1904; *m.* Lady Feodorowna Yorke, *d.* of 5th Earl of Hardwicke, 1883; two *s.* two *d.* *Educ.:* Eton; Christ Church, Oxford. Formerly Lieut. Dorset Yeomanry; M.P. (C.) Dorset, E. 1891-1904. Owns about 18,000 acres. *Heir:* s. Hon. G. P. M. Sturt. *Address:* Crichel, Wimborne; 38 Portman Square, W. *Clubs:* Carlton, Turf, Marlborough, White's.

(Died 14 Feb. 1916.)

ALEXANDER, Robert, R.S.A. *Address:* Hailes Cottage, Slateford, W. Edinburgh.

(Died Aug. 1923.)

ALEXANDER, Lt.-Col. Robert Donald Thain, D.S.O. 1917; O.B.E. 1919; T.D. 1919; The London Scottish (T.F. Reserve); Executive Engineer Railway Branch Indian Public Works Dept.; *b.* 29 Sept. 1878; *e. s.* of Thomas Alexander, Jamaica Constabulary; *m.* 1914, Lilian Margaret Beatrice, *e. d.* of A. J. W. Storie, advocate, Aberdeen; one *s.* *Educ.:* Dulwich College; King's College, London University. Trained in Engineering Works in America and England; entered Indian Public Works Dept. (Railway Branch), 1904; engaged on construction of the Nagda-Muttra State Railway, Frontier Surveys and the Lower Ganges Bridge, Bengal; served throughout European war in India and Mesopotamia (despatches four times, D.S.O., O.B.E., T.D.); Lieut.-Col. Apr. 1917, and appointed Assistant Director of Inland Water Transport, Mesopotamian Expeditionary Force; served in Mahsud Campaign (Waziristan) 1920; Assistant Secretary Railway Board (India) 1920-21; Services lent by Government as Chief Engineer, Bengal Nagpur Railway, 1921. *Recreations:* Rugby football, cricket, golf, shooting, tennis. *Address:* c/o The Railway Board, Simla, India. *Clubs:* Caledonian; Bengal.

(Died 14 Nov. 1924.)

ALEXANDER, William, C.I.E. 1917; Traffic Dept., Great Indian Peninsula Railway, Bombay. *Address:* Wadi Bunder, Bombay.

(Died 3 Mar. 1921.)

ALEXANDER, William Cleverly; *b.* 1840; *y. s.* of late George William Alexander, of Woodhatch, Surrey; *m.* 1861, Rachel Agnes,

14

d. of Jeffery Lucas of Hitchin. Herts; one *s.* six *d.* *Address:* Heathfield Park, Sussex; Aubrey House, Kensington, W. *Club:* Burlington Fine Arts. *(Died 17 April 1916.)*

ALFORD, Rev. Henry Powell; Rector of Worthen, Shrewsbury; Prebendary of Hereford; 3rd *s.* of late Richard Alford, F.R.C.S.; *m.* Amy, *d.* of Major Joseph Rimington, Indian Army. *Educ.:* Clifton College; New College, Oxford. Vicar of Woodbury Salterton; Rural Dean of Aylesbeare; Rural Dean of Montgomery. *Address:* Worthen Rectory, Shrewsbury.

(Died 18 Jan. 1921.)

ALFORD, Rev. Josiah George, C.B.E. 1919; V.D.; T.D.; M.A.; Canon Residentiary and Sub-Dean of Bristol; Hon. Chaplain to Bishop of Bristol; Personal Chaplain to late Bishop; *b.* 1 Jan. 1847; 2nd *s.* of late Charles Richard Alford, D.D., Bishop of Victoria; *m.* Catherine Mary, *d.* of late Colonel Leslie, C.B.; one *s.* three *d.* *Educ.:* King's College, London; Corpus Christi College, Cambridge. Graduated, 1869; ordained 1870, as Curate of St. Leonards-on-Sea; Assistant to Archbishop's Inspector of Training Colleges, 1872-75; Minor Canon of Bristol Cathedral, 1873; Vicar of St. Nicholas, Bristol, 1880; Vicar of Stoke Bishop, 1895; Hon. Canon, 1897; Rural Dean, 1905; Bishop's Commissioner since 1882; Governor under the Colston Trust since 1887; Chaplain to the Lord Mayor of Bristol, 1893; Chaplain (1st class, ranking as Colonel), Territorial Force; mobilised 1914-19, S.C.F. Bristol; later S.C.F. No. 2 Area, Southern Command; Surrogate for the Diocese, and Diocesan Trustee; Member of the Education Committee for Bristol, 1903-1913; Proctor in Convocation, 1919-21; Member of the Royal United Service Institution. *Address:* 5 Richmond Hill, Clifton, Bristol; Park Cottage, Cleeve, nr. Bristol.

(Died 12 Jan. 1924.)

ALINGTON, 2nd Baron (*cr.* 1876), Humphrey Napier Sturt, J.P., D.L.; K.C.V.O., *cr.* 1908; C.V.O. 1905; *b.* 1859; *o. s.* of 1st Lord Alington and Lady Augusta Bingham, *d.* of 3rd Earl of Lucan; S. father 1904; *m.* Lady Feodorowna Yorke, *d.* of 5th Earl of Hardwicke, 1883; two *s.* two *d.* *Educ.:* Eton; Christ Church, Oxford. Formerly Lieut. Dorset Yeomanry; M.P. (C.) Dorset, E. 1891-1904. Owns about 18,000 acres. *Heir:* s. Hon. G. P. M. Sturt. *Address:* Crichel, Wimborne; 38 Portman Square, W. *T.:* Paddington 389. *Clubs:* Carlton, Turf, Marlborough, White's.

(Died 30 July 1919.)

ALINGTON, Admiral Arthur Hildebrand, J.P., Lindsey, Lincs.; Lord of the Manor of Swinhope; Patron of Livings of Swinhope and Stenigot, Lincs.; *b.* 1889; 3rd *s.* of late George Marmaduke Alington of Swinhope, Lincs., D.L., J.P.; *m.* 1870, Charlotte Mary (*d.* 1913), *d.* of Rev. Charles Moore of Garlenick, Cornwall; two *s.* one *d.* *Educ.:* Dr. Lovell's, Winslow Hall, Bucks. Entered Royal Navy, 1852; served throughout Russian war in Baltic and Black Sea, 1854-56; Lieut. commanding H.M.S. Britomart on Lake Erie during Fenian troubles, 1866-68; Commander of H.M.S. Boxer on West Coast Africa; Niger Expedition; Captain of Conqueror, Dreadnought, and Superb battleships; 2nd in command Channel Fleet, 1895-96; flagships Empress of India and Magnificent; retired, 1899. *Recreations:* fishing, shooting, cycling, and motoring. *Address:* Swinhope House, near North Thoresby, Lincs. *T.A.:* Swinhope, Binbrook. *M.:* BE 419. *Club:* United Service.

(Died 7 Dec. 1925.)

ALISON, Sir Archibald, 3rd Bt.; *cr.* 1852; *b.* 20 May 1862; *s.* of Sir A. Alison, 2nd Bt., and Jane, *d.* of late James Black, Dalmonach; S. father 1907; *m.* 1888, Georgina,

y. d. of late J. Bond Cabbell of Cromer Hall, Norfolk; two *s. Educ.:* Eton; Sandhurst. Capt. 5th Batt. Rifle Brigade, 1885-95; Colonial Secretary, Bermuda, 1888-1900. *Heir: s.* Archibald, Lieut.-Commander, R.N. [*b.* 5 Nov. 1888; *m.* 1919, Isa Margery Tyrrell, *d.* of C. Tyrrell Giles]. *Address:* Possil, Budleigh Salterton, Devon. *Club:* Boodle's.
(Died 7 Nov. 1921.)

ALLAN, Arthur Percy, M.D., B.S. (Lond. Univ.); medical practitioner; for five years Editor of the General Practitioner; *b.* Chislehurst, 1868; 7th *s.* of late John Allan; *m.* Margaret, *d.* of late Richard Clark, Amersham. *Educ.:* Private schools, Hanover; Birkbeck College; Guy's Hospital, London. Formerly Clinical Assistant, Assistant House Physician and House Physician, Guy's Hospital; Vice-President University of London Graduates' Association. *Publications:* Contributions to Times, Kent Messenger, Lancet, British Medical Journal, British Journal of Children's Diseases, General Practitioner, Clinical Journal. *Recreations:* walking, gardening, and billiards. *Address:* Crogdene, Croham Road, Croydon. *T.:* Croydon 1369. *T.A.:* Dr. Allan, South Croydon. *(Died 2 Sept. 1927.)*

ALLAN, Maj.-Gen. William, Colonel, Welsh Regiment, since 1904; *b.* 22 June 1832; *s.* of Alex. Allan, of Hillside, Edinburgh; *m.* 1st, 1870, Anne Campbell Penney (*d.* 1876), *d.* of Lord Kinloch; 2nd, Jane Husey, *d.* of Rev. James Senior, afterwards Husey-Hunt. Entered army, 1850; Maj.-Gen. 1889; retired, 1894; served Crimea with the 41st, The Welsh Regt., at the battles of the Alma and Inkerman, both assaults on the Redan, siege and fall of Sevastopol, 1854-56 (medal with three clasps, Knight of Legion of Honour, Turkish medal); Brig.-Gen. commanding troops, Cyprus, 1890-94. *Address:* Hillside, Bidborough, Kent. *Clubs:* Army and Navy; New, Edinburgh.
(Died 12 July 1918.)

ALLANBY, Ven. Christopher Gibson; *b.* Flimby Park, Sorell, Tasmania; 5th *s.* of John William Allanby, formerly of Cross Canonby, Cumberland, England; *m.* Alice Mary, 2nd *d.* of Sidney James Fletcher of Moreland Road, Croydon, England; two *d. Educ.:* Moore College, New South Wales. Ordained Deacon, 1862; Priest, 1864, by the Bishop of Melbourne (Dr. Perry); appointed Curate of St. Paul's, Ballarat, 1862; Archdeacon of the Wimmera, 1885; Archdeacon of the Loddon, 1894; Incumbent of Brown Hill, Ballarat, 1866-1914; Archdeacon to the Bishop of Ballarat, 1902-14; retired 1914. *Address:* 55 Morland Road, Croydon, Surrey.
(Died 13 Jan. 1917.)

ALLBUTT, Rt. Hon. Sir (Thomas) Clifford, P.C., 1920; K.C.B., *cr.* 1907; M.A., M.D., Hon. LL.D. Cantab., Hon. D.Sc. Oxon., Hon. M.D., Hon. LL.D., F.R.S., F.L.S., F.S.A. D.L.,; Fellow of Caius College; Regius Professor of Physic, Cambridge University, since 1892; Hon. Colonel Eastern Div. R.A.M.C. *b.* 20 July 1836; *s.* of Rev. Thomas Allbutt; *m.* Susan, *d.* of late Thomas England of Headingley. *Educ.:* St. Peter's, York; Caius Coll., Cambridge. 1st class Natural Science Tripos, 1860. Consulting Physician Leeds General Infirmary, Belgrave Hospital for Children, and King Edward VII Sanatorium, Midhurst; Physician Addenbrookes Hospital, Cambridge; Commissioner in Lunacy, 1889-92; Member of Council of Royal Society, 1896-98 and 1914-16; Vice-President, 1914-16; Hon. Fellow Royal Society of Medicine; Member of Committee of Home Office on Trade Diseases, Nat. Med. Research, and other Government and Royal Society Committees; Hon. Member American Association of Physicians; Foreign Hon. Member American Academy of Arts and Sciences. *Publications:* The Ophthalmoscope

in Medicine, 1871; Goulstonian Lectures (On Visceral Neuroses), 1884; On Scrofula, 1885; The Lane Lectures on Diseases of the Heart, 1896; Science and Medieval Thought, 1901; The Historical Relations of Medicine and Surgery, 1905; editor of Systems of Medicine and Gynæcology, 1896-99-1907; Fitzpatrick Lectures on Greek Medicine in Rome, 1909-10; Greco-Roman Med. and other historical essays, 1921; Diseases of the Arteries and Angina Pectoris, 1915; Science in the School, 1917; Notes on Composition of Scientific Papers, 3rd ed., 1923. Inventor of Short Clinical Thermometer. *Recreations:* Alpine Club, cycling. *Address:* St. Radegund's, Cambridge. *T.:* Cambridge 307. *Clubs:* Alpine, Athenæum. *(Died 22 Feb. 1925.)*

ALLCOCK, Rev. Arthur Edmund, M.A.; Headmaster of Highgate School 1893-1908; *b.* Harborne, Staffs, 16 Feb. 1851; *s.* of late Thomas Allcock. *Educ.:* King Edward's School, Birmingham; Emmanuel Coll. Camb. Assistant Master King Edward's School, Birmingham, 1874-80; Wellington Coll. 1880-93; ordained 1889. *Recreations:* cricket, fives, golf. *Address:* 46 Carpenter Road, Edgbaston, Birmingham. *(Died 23 Dec. 1924.)*

ALLDRIDGE, Thomas Joshua, F.R.G.S., F.R.C.I., F.Z.S.; I.S.O.,1905; District Commissioner of Sherbro, West Coast of Africa (retired); *b.* 1847; *y. s.* of late R. W. Alldridge, Old Charlton. *Educ.:* City of London School; Blackheath Proprietary School. F.R.G.S. and awarded the Cuthbert Peek grant (1900) for geographical work in the interior of the colony of Sierra Leone, West Coast Africa; presented with the Life Fellowship of the Zoological Society, London, 1884; Acting United States Consular Agent at Sierra Leone, 1871-72; travelling commissioner for that colony, 1889; Hon. Inspector Police; Justice of the Peace; Commissioner of the Court of Requests; Coroner, etc.; Pioneer into Upper Mendi, Bandi, and Bundi countries, and made numerous treaties on behalf of the British Government with the paramount chiefs; sent on special mission by the Government to Robari, and succeeded in stopping war and making peace between the Timinis and Yonnis; convened meeting of 3000 chiefs and people at Bandasuma, Barri country, to meet the Governor, Sir Francis Fleming, K.C.M.G., by direction of Secretary of State; as topographical and astronomical observer accompanied His Excellency Sir F. Cardew, K.C.M.G., 1894, upon his first interior tour of 617 miles, occupying 52 days; special mission to Sama country, 1894; through the Mendi Rising, 1898 (medal and clasp). *Publications:* The Sherbro and its Hinterland, 1901; A Transformed Colony (Sierra Leone), 1910. *Address:* Oak Mount, Bagshot, Surrey. *Club:* Royal Societies. *(Died 28 June 1916.)*

ALLEN, Col. Sir Charles, Kt., *cr.* 1908; V.D., J.P.; *b.* 1852; widower. Late Col. Commanding 3rd Brigade West Riding R.F.A., and 2/5th North London Brigade, R.F.A.; Chairman of Sir Henry Bessemer and Co.; Chairman Ebbw Vale Steel, Iron, and Coal Co., Ltd.; Local President I.C. and M. Bank, Ltd., Sheffield. *Address:* 10 Gladstone Road, Fulwood Road, Sheffield. *Club:* Junior Carlton.
(Died 13 April 1920.)

ALLEN, Charles Francis Egerton, J.P. *b.* 14 Oct. 1847; *s.* of Charles Allen of Tenby and Mary, *d.* of James Allen of Freestone, parish of Carew, County of Pembroke; *m.* 1891, Elizabeth Georgina, *d.* of William Wilcox of Whitburn, near Sunderland; no *c. Educ.:* Eton; St. John's College, Cambridge; Senior Optime, Mathematical Tripos, 1870. Called to Bar, Inner Temple, 1871; joined the Northern Circuit, afterwards the North Eastern; went to India. 1873; practised in Calcutta and Rangoon; law lecturer, Presidency College;

15

ALLBON, Charles F.   See page xv.

Judge in Calcutta Court of Small Causes; went to Rangoon as Government Advocate, 1877 ; officiated as Recorder of Rangoon ; returned, 1888 ; retired from practice; M.P. (L.) Pembroke and Haverfordwest District Borough, 1892-95 ; lived at Tenby ; served as Borough Magistrate, 1896-1905 ; served for a time on the Town Council and as Guardian on the Pembroke Union Board. *Recreations:* wasting his time dabbling in heraldry, genealogy, local history, local politics. *Address:* Norton House, Tenby. *Clubs:* Tenby and County; Pembrokeshire County, Haverfordwest.

(Died 31 Dec. 1927.)

ALLEN, George Berney; *b.* 11 Sep. 1862 ; *e. s.* of late Sir George Allen, K.C.I.E., founder of the Indian Pioneer newspaper. *Educ.:* Clifton College. Head of Allen Bros. & Co., East India Agents, London, and is connected with other businesses in India ; Managing Proprietor of The Near East and The Indiaman, weekly newspapers. *Address:* Freechase, Warninglid, Sussex. *Club:* White's. *(Died 19 June 1917.)*

ALLEN, Sir Harry Brookes, Kt., *cr.* 1914 ; Professor of Pathology, 1906 - 24, and Dean of Faculty of Medicine, University of Melbourne ; Pathologist Melbourne Hospital ; Chairman Executive and Finance Committee Australian Red Cross Society (B.R.C.S) ; *b.* 13 June 1854 ; 2nd *s.* of late Thomas Watts Allen, Geelong, Victoria ; *m.* 1891, Ada, *e. d.* of late Henry Mason, H.M. Customs, Liverpool ; three *d. Educ.:* Flinders' School, Geelong ; Church of England Grammar School, Melbourne ; Melbourne University ; M.B. 1876 ; M.D. 1878 ; B.S. 1879 ; Hon. LL.D. Edin. 1912 ; LL.D. Adel. 1914. Demonstrator of Anatomy, Melbourne University, and Pathologist, Melbourne Hospital, 1876; Lecturer, 1881, Professor, 1882, of Anatomy and Pathology ; President, Professorial Board, 1895-1897 ; Editor, Australian Medical Journal, 1879-83 ; Hon. Secretary, Medical Society of Victoria, 1879-87 ; Member Tuberculosis in Cattle Board, 1883-84, and joint author of report ; Member of Central Board of Health, 1883-84 ; drafted Model Bye-Laws for Local Boards, etc. ; advised meat-preserving companies to revolutionise construction of freezing chambers, 1883 ; created Museum of Pathology in Melbourne University ; President, Royal Commission on Sanitary state of Melbourne, and of Intercolonial Rabbit Commission, 1888 1889 ; Gen. Secretary, Intercolonial Medical Congress, 1889 ; visited Europe and obtained recognition of Melbourne Medical Degrees, 1890 ; drafted Deed of Union of Medical Societies of Victoria under British Medical Association ; President, Old Melburnians, 1897 ; Member of Council, Melbourne University, 1898 ; President, Australasian Medical Congress, 1908 ; Member Executive Committee International Medical Congress, 1913. *Publications:* Typhoid Fever and Milk Supply, 1889 ; Reports to Victoria Government on Hospital Construction, Sewerage Works, Tuberculin, etc., 1891 ; Address as President of Medical Society of Victoria, 1892 ; Medical Periodicals in Melbourne, 1893 ; Tumours of Kidney, 1896 ; Address on Cancer and Cancer Statistics in Australasia, 1902 ; Tumours, 1903 ; Tubercle of Joints, 1904 ; Address as first Pres. of United Medical Societies of Victoria, 1908 ; Specific Disease, 1908 ; Address as Pres. of Australasian Med. Cong., and various papers, 1908 ; Address on Vaccines, Aust. Med. Cong., 1911 ; Report to Commonwealth Government on Health Conditions at Panama, 1913 ; on Risks of Middle Age and Specific Diseases, 1916 ; Pathology, Lectures and Demonstrations, 1920. *Address:* The University, Melbourne.

(Died 28 Mar. 1926.)

ALLEN, Henry Seymour, J.P., C.C., D.P.; *b.* 30 Aug. 1847 ; *s.* of late Seymour and Lady Cathrine Allen ; unmarried. *Educ.:* Harrow.

Recreations: hunting, shooting, cycling, skating. *Address:* Cresselly House, Cresselly, Begelly, Pembrokeshire. *Clubs:* Brooks's, Naval and Military, Eighty.

(Died 25 Feb. 1928.)

ALLEN, James Lane, American Author ; *b.* Kentucky, 1849. *Educ.:* Transylvania Univ. *Publications:* A Kentucky Cardinal ; The Choir Invisible ; A Summer in Arcady ; Flute and Violin ; The Blue Grass Region of Kentucky ; The Increasing Purpose ; Aftermath : second part of A Kentucky Cardinal ; The Mettle of the Pasture, 1903 ; The Bride of the Mistletoe, 1909 ; The Doctor's Christmas Eve, 1910 ; A Heroine in Bronze, 1912 ; The Sword of Youth, 1915 ; A Cathedral Singer, 1916 ; The Emblems of Fidelity, 1917 ; The Kentucky Warbler, 1918. *Address:* 66 5th Avenue, New York.

(Died 18 Feb. 1925.)

ALLEN, Richard William, M.A. (N.Z.), M.D. (London); Capt. New Zealand Medical Corps ; *b.* Auckland, New Zealand, 28 Nov. 1876 ; *s.* of James and Jessie Balfour Allen ; *m.* 1909, Beatrice Mary Harston ; one *s.* two *d. Educ.:* Auckland College and Grammar School ; University College, Auckland ; Guy's Hospital, London. Junior and Senior University Scholar, and Master of Arts ; 1st class honours of University of New Zealand ; entrance Science Scholar Guy's Hospital, 1899 ; Wooldrige Memorial Scholar in Physiology, 1902 ; gold medallist in Materia Medica University of London, 1902 ; M.B.B.S. 1st class honours in medicine, 1905 ; Gull student in Pathology, 1904 ; late Pathologist to Royal Eye Hospital ; late Director of Vaccine Therapy Department Mount Vernon Hospital for diseases of chest ; Fellow of Royal Society of Medicine. *Publications:* late editor Journal of Vaccine Therapy ; Practical Vaccine Treatment for the General Practitioner ; Vaccine Therapy (4th edition) ; Bacterial Diseases of Respiration ; numerous monographs in chemical and medical sciences. *Recreations:* football, cricket, running, fishing, yachting. *Address:* 128 Harley Street, W.1. *T.:* Mayfair 3086 ; 2 Carlton Houses, Westgateon-Sea. *(Died 28 Aug. 1921.)*

ALLEN, Col. Robert Franklin, D.S.O. 1905 ; Royal Engineers; *b.* 21 Feb. 1860 ; *s.* of late Major R. Austen Allen, M.D., A.M.S. ; *m.* 1886, Alice Gordon, *d.* of late Surgeon-General Inkson ; one *s.* Entered army, 1879 ; Captain, 1889; Major, 1897 ; served Manipur, 1891 (despatches, medal with clasp); East Africa, 1904 (despatches, medal with two clasps, D.S.O.) ; retired, 1909. *Address:* c/o Cox and Co., Charing Cross, S.W.

(Died 20 Nov. 1916.)

ALLEN, Very Rev. Thomas, A.M., T.C.D.; Rector of Killoran and Kilvarnet, Diocese of Achonry, since 1904 ; Canon of St. Patrick's Cathedral, Dublin, since 1904 ; Dean of Achonry since 1916 ; member of the Diocesan Council of Killala and Achonry ; Examining Chaplain to Bishop of Tuam, 1923 ; Diocesan Secretary for Temperance ; *b.* 2 Nov. 1873 ; *e. s.* of William Allen, Camp Hill House, Ballymena, Co. Antrim. *Educ.:* Model School, and Collegiate and Intermediate School, Ballymena ; Trinity College, Dublin. 1st class exhibitioner—Junior Grade Intermediate Educ. Board ; 1st class Divinity Testimonium, T.C.D.; Ryan Prizeman, T.C.D., B.A. 1897 ; M.A. (1900) of T.C.D. ; curate of Maryborough, Queen's Co., 1897-1900 ; senior curate of Galway, 1900-4 ; Diocesan Inspector of Religious Education, Tuam, 1903 - 4. *Address:* The Rectory, Coolaney, Co. Sligo. *(Died 16 May 1927.)*

ALLEN, Thomas Carleton, LL.B., D.C.L., K.C. ; Registrar Supreme Court of New Brunswick, Deputy Attorney - General, and Clerk of the Crown ; *b.* Fredericton, N.B., 9 Nov. 1852 ; *s.* of Sir John Campbell Allen; *m.* Louisa L. Wetmore; two *s.* one *d.* Mayor of Fredericton, 1890-93. *Recreations:* golf, tennis,

16

hunting. *Address:* Fredericton, N.B.
(*Died Sept. 1927.*)

ALLEN, Wilfred Baugh; late C. C. Judge, Nottingham, resigned Dec. 1917 ; J.P. Cos. Pembrokeshire and Nottingham ; *b.* 14 Nov. 1849; 2nd *s.* of George Baugh Allen of Cilrhiw, Co. Pembroke ; *m.* 1883, Anne Sophia, *d.* of late Rev. Robt. Wedgewood of Dumbleton, Gloucs. ; one *s. Educ.:* Rugby ; Trin. Coll. Camb. Called to Bar, Inner Temple, 1882 ; Member of S.E. Circuit. *Publications:* (joint) Forms of Endorsement of Writs of Summons and Pleadings in Queen's Bench Division ; Criminal Evidence Act. *Address:* Cilrhiw, Narberth, Pembrokeshire ; Rosemount, Tenby. *Club:* Notts County, Nottingham.
(*Died 10 June 1922.*)

ALLEN, William Henry, D.L., J.P. ; Bedfordshire High Sheriff, 1904-5 ; Member of the Territorial Association ; Chairman of W. H. Allen, Sons & Co. Ltd., Bedford ; *b.* 1844 ; *s.* of late William George Allen of Cardiff ; *m.* 1st, Annie Mary Pemberton, *d.* of Richard Thomas Howell of Bryn-Caeran Castle, Carmarthenshire ; six *s.* four *d.* ; 2nd, Madeline, *d.* of W. J. Fedden, Clifton, Bristol ; one *d. Educ.:* under John Elwell, Wallescote House, Weston-super-Mare. Educated as an engineer ; founded The Queen's Engineering Works, Bedford. Member of Royal Institution, of Institution of Civil Engineers ; Vice-President, Institution of Mechanical Engineers ; Member of Council of Institute of Metals. *Publication:* paper read before Institution of Civil Engineers on Auxiliary Machines for large steamships. *Recreations:* all games, including hunting and shooting, gardening, farming, and organ-playing. *Address:* Bromham House, Bromham, near Bedford. *M.:* MB 27. *Club:* Athenæum. (*Died 3 Sept. 1926.*)

ALLENDALE, 1st Viscount, *cr.* 1911, **Wentworth Canning Blackett Beaumont;** 2nd Baron (*cr.* 1906) ; M.A.; D.L.; M.P. (L.) Hexham Division Northumberland, 1895-1907 ; Vice-Chamberlain H.M.'s Household, 1905-7 ; Capt. of H.M.'s Bodyguard of the Yeomen of the Guard, 1907-11 ; Lord-in-Waiting to H.M. 1911-16; ChairmanTerritorial Force Association, Northumberland, 1908-19; *b.* Bywell Hall, Northumberland, 1860 ; *e. s.* of 1st Baron and Margaret, 4th *d.* of 1st Marquess of Clanricarde ; *S.* father, 1907 ; *m.* 1889, Lady Alexandrina Louisa Maud (Aline) Vane-Tempest, *d.* of 5th Marquess of Londonderry ; two *s.* three *d. Educ.:* Eton ; Trinity College, Cambridge. *Heir : s.* Capt. Hon. W. H. C. Beaumont. *Recreation:* hunting. *Address:* 144 Piccadilly, W. 1; Bywell Hall, Stocksfield - on - Tyne ; Bretton Park, Wakefield. *Clubs:* Brooks's, Travellers', Turf. (*Died 12 Dec. 1923.*)

ALLERTON, 1st Baron of Chapel Allerton (*cr.* 1902), **William Lawies Jackson,** P.C., F.R.S. ; J.P. ; Chairman of G.N. Railway Co. ; *b.* 1840 ; *s.* of late W. Jackson, Leeds ; *m.* Grace (*d.* 1901), *d.* of G. Tempest, 1860 ; two *s.* five *d.* Contested Leeds, 1876 ; Financial Secretary to Treasury, 1885-86, 1886-91; Chief Secretary for Ireland, 1891-92 ; M.P. (C.) Leeds, N., 1880-1902. *Heir : s.* Hon. George H. Jackson. *Address:* 41 Cadogan Square, S.W.; *T.:* Kensington 810 ; Allerton Hall, Chapel Allerton, Leeds. *Clubs :* Carlton, Athenæum. (*Died 4 April 1917.*)

ALLERTON, 2nd Baron, of Chapel Allerton, *cr.* 1902, **George Herbert Jackson,** *b.* 1867 ; *e. s.* of 1st Baron Allerton and Grace, *d.* of G. Tempest ; *S.* father, 1917 ; *m.* 1899, Katherine Louisa, *y. d.* of W. W. Wickham, J.P., of Chestnut Grove, Boston Spa ; one *s.* one *d. Educ.:* Rugby. *Heir : s.* George William Lawies Jackson, *b.* 1903. (*Died 29 Jan. 1925.*)

ALLETSON, Major G. C., D.S.O. 1917 ; Remount Service ; *s.* of G. H. Alletson, Ewloe Wood, Northop, Flintshire ; *m.* 1902, Norah, *g.c.* of late Charles Trevor-Roper, Plas Teg,

Flintshire ; one *s.* one *d. Educ.:* privately. Served in South African War, Denbighshire Yeomanry ; then Lieut. in Prince of Wales Light Horse, and finally Capt. Remount Service, 1900-2 ; Adjutant, Flintshire National Reserve, 1912-14 ; Capt. in Remount Service, France and Italy, Oct. 1914; Major, May 1915 (D.S.O., despatches). *Recreations:* shooting, fishing. *Address:* Clun, Lee-on-Solent, Hants.
(*Died 14 May 1928.*)

ALLGEYER, Bishop Emile Auguste, Bishop of Ticelia and Apostolic Vicar of Zanzibar and British East Africa, 1906-13 ; *b.* Rixheim, Alsace, near Mulhouse, 14 April 1856 ; *s.* of Benoit Allgeyer and Genevieva Haby. *Educ.:* at home ; Blackrock College, Dublin ; Bretagne ; Philosophy and Theology in Paris. Priest, 1885 ; Professor at St. Mary's College, Port-of-Spain, Trinidad, W. Indies, 1885 ; Parish Priest at Newton, Port-of-Spain, 1890-96 ; St. Andrews, Grenada, 1896-97 ; Bishop of German and British East Africa, 1897-1906 ; erected a Cathedral in Zanzibar ; founded seven new centres of mission in German East Africa ; four convents for the education of Negro girls ; and in British East Africa six new missions and an English high boarding school at St. Austin's Mission, near Nairobi. *Recreations:* has been thrice in Europe on business and twice in Natal for his health. *Address:* Kilana, Tang Territory, East Africa. (*Died 9 April 1924.*)

ALLHUSEN (Augustus) Henry (Eden), J.P., D.L.; *b.* 20 Aug. 1867 ; *s.* of late Henry Christian Allhusen and Alice, *d.* of late Thos. Eden, Norton Hall, Gloucestershire ; *g. s.* of Christian Allhusen, J.P., D.L., Stoke Court, Bucks, chemical manufacturer, Newcastle - on - Tyne ; *m.* Dorothy Stanley, *d.* of Lady St. Helier and her 1st husband Col. Hon. J. C. Stanley, Grenadier Guards, 2nd *s.* of 2nd Baron Stanley of Alderley, 1896; two-*d. Educ.:* Cheltenham Coll. ; Trin. Coll. Camb. (B.A. 1890). Formerly Lieut. Bucks Yeomanry ; M.P. (C.) Salisbury, 1897-1900 ; Central Hackney, 1900 - 6 ; High Sheriff, Bucks, 1913 ; Chairman of Magistrates and Guardians at Slough. *Address:* Stoke Court, Stoke Poges, Bucks. *T.:* Farnham Common 68. *Clubs:* Carlton, White's, Boodle's. (*Died 2 May 1925.*)

ALLHUSEN, Beatrice May, wife of W. H. Allhusen, *d.* of late Col. Thomas Bromhead Butt, 79th Highlanders. *Publications:* Miss Molly ; Ingelheim ; An Episode on a Desert Island ; The Great Reconciler. *Address:* 35 Kensington Palace Gardens, W. *Clubs:* Ladies' Athenæum, Writers'.
(*Died 29 July 1918.*)

ALLHUSEN, William Hutt; *b.* 16 Sept. 1845 ; *s.* of late Christian Allhusen of Stoke Court ; *m.* Beatrice May (*d.* 1918), *d.* of late Col. T. Bromhead Butt, 79th Highlanders. *Educ.:* Cheltenham College ; Carlsruhe ; Magdalen College, Cambridge. *Recreation:* motoring. *Address:* 15 Kensington Palace Gardens, W.; Lemoenfontein, Beaufort West, Cape Colony. *Clubs:* Wellington, Royal Automobile ; Civil Service, Royal Automobile, Cape Town. (*Died 25 Aug. 1923.*)

ALLIES, Mary H. A., *b.* 2 Feb. 1852 ; *e. d.* of Thomas William Allies, K.C.S.G., and Eliza Hall, 2nd *d.* of Thos. Harding Newman of Nelmes, Essex. *Educ.:* The Convent of the Holy Child, St. Leonard's-on-Sea ; Visitation Convent, rue d'Enfer, Paris. Published her first book in 1875 under the guidance of her father, who formed and directed both her studies and her pen. *Publications:* Life of Pope Pius VII., 1875 ; Three Catholic Reformers of the 15th Century, 1878 ; Leaves from St. Augustine, 1886 ; Leaves from St. John Chrysostom, 1889 ; Letters of St. Augustine, 1890 ; History of the Church in England, 1892-97, 2 vols. ; The Heiress of Cronenstein, adapted from the German of

Countess Hahn-Hahn, 1900; Treatise on Holy Images (Greek, St. John Damascene), 1898; Thomas William Allies, 1907; How to help the Dead (de Cura gerenda pro Mortuis), 1914; Thomas William Allies, *secundo*, 1924; numerous articles, notably for the Catholic World and Dublin Review, occasionally in French. *Address:* Berkeley Lodge, 7 Melina Place, St. John's Wood, N.W.   (*Died 27 Jan. 1927.*)

ALLINGHAM, Helen (Mrs. William Allingham); Water-colour Painter; *b.* 26 Sep. 1848; *d.* of A. Henry Paterson, M.D.; *m.* William Allingham, the Irish poet, 1874; two *s.* one *d. Educ.:* Royal Academy Schools. Drew in black and white for Graphic, Cornhill; A.R.W.S. 1875; R.W.S. 1890. Holds occasional exhibitions of English cottage and rural subjects, in the Fine Art Society's rooms. *Publications:* Happy England, 1903 (with M. B. Huish); The Homes of Tennyson (with Arthur Paterson), 1905; The Cottage Homes of England (with Stewart Dick), 1909; (edited) William Allingham, a Diary; Letters to William Allingham; By the Way, by William Allingham. *Recreation:* country walks and drives. *Address:* Eldon House, Lyndhurst Road, Hampstead, N.W.   (*Died 28 Sept. 1926.*)

ALLISON, Sir Robert Andrew, Kt., *cr.* 1910; J.P., D.L.; *b.* 5 March 1838; *m.* 1st, 1867, Laura Alicia (*d.* 1892), *d.* of J. M. Atkinson of Thorp Arch, Yorks.; two *s.* two *d.*; 2nd, 1897, Sara Eudora, *d.* of Canon Slater, Branksome Park, Bournemouth. *Educ.:* Rugby; Trinity College, Cambridge. M.P. (R.) North Cumberland, 1885-1900. *Publications:* Essays and Addresses, 1913; Five Plays of Plautus, 1914 (translated); Belgium in History, 1914; Cicero on Old Age, in verse 1916; Lucretius on the Nature of Things, translated, 1919; Translations mainly from the Greek Anthology. *Address:* Scaleby Hall, Carlisle. *T.A.:* Kirklinton. *Club:* County, Carlisle.   (*Died 15 Jan. 1926.*)

ALLISON, William, The Special Commissioner, The Sportsman; Barrister-at-Law; Managing Director of The International Horse Agency and Exchange, Ltd. (Lessees of the Cobham Stud, Cobham, Surrey); *b.* 30 Apr. 1851; *s.* of late J. P. Allison, Kilvington, Thirsk, Yorkshire, and Maria, *d.* of late William Whitehead; *m.* 1876, Frances, *d.* of late James Leslie Walker; one *s.* one *d. Educ.:* Rugby; Balliol College, Oxford (M.A.). *Career:* The Law, Inner Temple and N.E. Circuit, and Sporting Journalism. *Publications:* Blair Athol; A Tory Lordling; The Parson and the Painter (illustrated by Phil May); The British Thoroughbred Horse; My Kingdom for a Horse; Blairmount, Memories of Men and Horses, 1922, etc. *Recreation:* golf. *Address:* 50 Harrington Gardens, S.W.7; 46A Pall Mall, S.W.1; Cobham Stud, Cobham, Surrey. *T.A.:* Ciliary, London. *T.:* Regent 49. *Club:* Sports. (*Died 15 July 1925.*)

ALLIX, Charles Peter, J.P., D.L., M.A.; landed proprietor; *b.* 21 Feb. 1842; *s.* of late Col. Charles Allix, Grenadier Guards, and Mary C. E., his cousin, *d.* of late Chas. Allix of Willoughby Hall, Lincolnshire; *m.* 1866, Laura A. W., *d.* of R. L. Bevan, Brixworth Hall, Northants; two *s.* three *d. Educ.:* Harrow; Trinity College, Cambridge. Appointed J.P. 1864, and has served continuously to the present time; Vice-Chairman of the Cambridgeshire Quarter Sessions; Chairman of the Bottisham Petty Sessional Division; Chairman of the Swaffham and Bottisham Fen Drainage District Commissioners; served as a representative of the diocese of Ely in the Canterbury House of Laymen, 1889-96; also Deputy Chairman of the Ely and Bury St. Edmunds Light Railway Company authorised by Act of Parliament in 1875, in which capacity he promoted the construction of the Cambridge and Mildenhall Railway, subsequently constructed by the Great Eastern

Railway Company in 1884. *Heir:* Charles Israel Loraine, J.P., D.L. (*b.* 1872; *m.* 1906, Hon. Hilda Strutt, 3rd *d.* of 2nd Lord Belper; two *d. Educ.:* Eton; Trin. Coll. Camb., M.A.] *Publications:* Papers read before the Cambridge Archæological Society:—St. Mary's Church, Swaffham-Prior; A Primitive Neolithic Dwelling discovered on the estate; The Escape of Allix the Huguenot from France in 1685. *Recreations:* shooting, fishing, landscape gardening, carving, and carpenter's work; archæology and geology. *Address:* Swaffham - Prior House, near Cambridge. *Clubs:* Junior Carlton; Cambridge County, Cambridge.   (*Died 10 June 1926.*)

ALLMAN, Robert, C.M.G. 1901; L.R.C.S.I., L.R.C.P.I.; Principal Medical Officer Oil Rivers Protectorate (now Southern Nigeria) since 1891, and organised Medical Department; *b.* 11 Sept. 1854; *s.* of late Rev. William Allman, M.A., M.D., of Lurgy Vale, Kilmacrenan, Ireland; *m.* 1893, Constance Maude, 2nd *d.* of late Edmund Murphy, J.P.; one *s.* three *d.* P.M.O. Cross River, Eket, Okrika Expeditions, 1895-96; P.M.O. Protectorate troops, Benin City Expedition, 1897 (despatches, medal and clasp, thanks of Sec. of State); P.M.O. Oron, 1897, Ekuri, 1897-98 (despatches); Ubium and Ishan 1899 Expeditions; Aro Expedition, 1901-1902 (medal and clasp); Member of Committee at Colonial Office for Reorganisation of the West African Medical Staff, 1901 (thanks of Sec. of State). *Address:* 2 Cowper Villas, Palmerston Park, Dublin.   (*Died 16 Nov. 1917.*)

ALLNUTT, Rev. Geo. Herbert, R.D.; Rector St. Paul's, Cobbitty, and St. Thomas, Narellan, since 1883; Rural Dean Liverpool and Camden, since 1904; Hon. Canon of St. Andrew's Cathedral, 1911; *b.* London, 1843; *e. s.* of late Rev. Thos. Allnutt, B.D. Rector of Stibbard, Norfolk; *m. o. d.* of late John Cash Neild, M.D. Ch.D., Sydney; one *s.* two *d. Educ.:* Queen Elizabeth's Grammar School, Ipswich. Third Master of Chesterfield Grammar School, 1862; emigrated to Queensland, 1864; engaged for some years in station work, and sugar making, Queensland and N.S.W.; Catechist at St. Paul's, Sydney, 1874; entered Moore Theological College, 1875 (1st class and prizeman); ordained, 1876; incumbent of Milchester and Charters Towers, N. Queensland, 1876-8; Rector of Mulgoa, N.S.W. 1878-83. *Address:* The Rectory, Cobbity, N.S.W.   (*Died 28 July 1919.*)

ALLSOPP, Hon. Frederic Ernest; *b.* 1857; *e. surv. s.* of 1st Baron Hindlip. Late Capt. R.A.; served Afghan War, 1879-81 (despatches, medal and two clasps); Suakin Campaign, 1885 (medal and clasp); Burma Campaign, 1886-7 (despatches, medal and clasp)   (*Died Dec. 1928.*)

ALLSOPP, Capt. Hon. Herbert Tongue, late 10th Hussars; *e. surv. s.* of 1st Baron Allsopp; *b.* 1855; *m.* 1891, Edith Mary, *d.* of late H. C. Okeover. Served Afghan War, 1878-80 (medal with clasp); Egypt, 1884 (medal with clasp, bronze star). *Address:* Walton-Bury, Stafford.   (*Died 31 Jan. 1920.*)

ALLSUP, Major Edward Saunders, D.S.O. 1917; R.A.; Commanding 8th Field Battery R.A., Edinburgh; *b.* 27 Nov. 1879 *s.* of late William James Allsup; unmarried. *Educ.:* Monkton Combe School, Bath. First Commission, 1900; Captain, 1913; Major, 1915 served North-West Frontier, India, Mohmand Field Force, 1908 (medal and clasp), European War, 1914-18 (D.S.O., 1914 Star). *Address* Lloyds Bank, Ltd., Cox's Branch, 6 Pall Mall S.W. *Club:* Junior United Service.   (*Died 22 Feb. 1928.*)

ALLWORK, Rev. Robert Long, M.A. Vicar of Epping since 1906; Hon. Canon of Chelmsford; Rural Dean of Chigwell; Surrogate for the Diocese of Chelmsford; Chaplain to the Epping Union; *y. s.* of late C. L. Allwork Surgeon, of Maidstone; *b.* 1863; *m.* Helen Margaretta, *d.* of late C. W. Chaldecott, Surgeon

of Dorking ; one d. *Educ.*: Tonbridge ; Corpus Christi College, Cambridge. Curate of S. Botolph, Bishopsgate, 1886-87 ; S. Ann, Stamford Hill, 1887-97 ; S. Mary's, Southampton, 1897-1900 ; Vicar of S. Saviour's, Walthamstow, 1900-6. *Recreations*: music and mechanics. *Address*: The Vicarage, Epping, Essex.
(*Died 15 Mar. 1919.*)

ALMOND, W. Douglas, R.I. ; Member of the Artists' Society and the Langham Sketching Club ; Member of the Royal Institute of Oil Painters. *Address*: 188 Regent's Park Road, N.W. *Club*: Savage. (*Died 12 Mar. 1916.*)

ALSOP, James Willcox, O.B.E. ; Hon. LL.D. Liverpool ; Solicitor, practising in Liverpool ; Pro-Chancellor of University of Liverpool since 1909 ; Chairman of Liverpool Education Committee (member since 1903) ; Deputy Chairman, London and Lancashire Insurance Co., Ltd. ; *b.* Birmingham, 6 June 1846 ; *e. s.* of Rev. James Alsop, and Mary, *d.* of William Willcox, Birmingham ; *m.* 1886, Constance, 2nd *d.* of Charles Grey Mott, J.P. of Harrow Weald, Middlesex ; no *c. Educ.*: Hope St. British Schools, Liverpool ; Liverpool Institute ; Queen's College, Liverpool. B.A. (London), 1867, with 1st class Honours in English Language and Literature (University Exhibition), and in Logic and Mental and Moral Philosophy ; President of Liverpool Incorporated Law Society, 1892-93 ; Life Governor of University College, Liverpool, from its Incorporation, 1882 ; Life Governor of University of Liverpool from its Incorporation, 1903 ; Vice-President of University Council, 1903-9 ; President, 1909-18 ; Member of Liverpool City Council since 1899. *Publications*: various papers and addresses. *Recreations*: golf, travel. *Address*: Ulverscroft, Bidston Road, Birkenhead ; 14 Castle Street, Liverpool. *T.A.*: Jurist, Liverpool. *T.*: Birkenhead 835 ; Liverpool Bank 865. *Clubs*: Reform ; University, Exchange, Liverpool. (*Died 19 May 1921.*)

ALTON, Sir Francis (Cooke), C.B. 1902 ; C.M.G. 1917 ; K.B.E., *cr.* 1919 ; Paymaster Rear-Adm. ; retired ; *b.* 24 Aug. 1856 ; *s.* of late Francis Cooke Alton, Chief Inspector of Machinery, R.N. ; *m.* 1884, Lina (*d.* 1919), *d.* of Ernest Barclay ; one *s.* one *d.* Secretary to Admiral Seymour, Commander-in-Chief, China, 1898-1901 ; took part in Naval Expedition for relief of Legations at Pekin during Boxer outbreak in China, 1900 (promoted Fleet Paymaster) ; Secretary to Admiral of the Fleet Sir Edward Seymour when British Representative at Hudson Fulton Celebration, New York, 1909 ; has served as Secretary to several Naval Commanders-in-Chief ; retired, 1914 ; served European War as Secretary to Principal Naval Transport Office, France, 1914-17 (despatches).
(*Died 27 Mar. 1926.*)

ALVORD, Clarence Walworth ; Historian ; *b.* Greenfield, Mass., 21 May 1868 ; *s.* of Daniel Wells Alvord and Caroline Betts Dewey ; *m.* 1st, 1893, Jennie Kettell Blanchard (née Parrott) (*d.* 1911) ; 2nd, 1913, Idress Head, St. Louis. *Educ.*: Williams College ; University of Berlin ; University of Chicago ; Ph.D., University of Illinois, 1908. Instructor Milton (Mass.) Academy, 1891-93 ; Instructor Preparatory School, University of Illinois, 1897-1901 ; Instructor in History, 1901-6 ; Associate, 1906-1907 ; Assistant Professor, 1907-9 ; Associate Professor, 1909-13 ; Professor, 1913-1920 ; Professor Univ. of Minn., 1920-23 ; Gen. Editor Illinois Historical Collections, 1906-20 ; President Mississippi Valley Historical Association, 1908-1909 ; Member American Historical Association, Massachusetts Historical Society (Hon.), Missouri Historical Society of St. Louis (hon.), American Antiquarian Society (hon.) ; Corresponding Member Missouri State Historical Society, Nebraska Historical Society, Chicago Historical Society, Minnesota Historical Society

(life) ; Fellow Royal Historical Society ; Managing Editor Mississippi Valley Historical Review, 1914-23 ; Editor-in-chief Illinois Centennial History ; Unitarian. *Publications*: Mississippi Valley in British Politics (2 vols.), 1917 (Loubat prize, 1917) ; The Illinois Country, 1919 ; Lord Shelburne and the Founding of British-American Goodwill, the Raleigh Lecture on History, 1925 ; contributions to Historical periodicals. Editor of Cahokia Records (Illinois Historical Collections), 1906 ; Invitation Serieuse aux Habitants des Illinois (with Dr. C. E. Carter), 1908 ; Governors' Letter-Books (with Dr. E. B. Greene) (Illinois Historical Collections), 1909 ; Kaskaskia Records (Illinois Historical Collections), 1909 ; Early Explorations of the Virginians in the Trans-Alleghany Region (with Lee Bidgood), 1912 ; (with C. E. Carter), The British Series, vols. i., ii., iii. (Illinois Historical Collections), 1915-25. *Recreations*: golf, gardening. *Address*: American University Union, 50 Russell Square, W.C.1 ; 56 Clarence Ave., Minneapolis, Minn., U.S.A.
(*Died 25 Jan. 1928.*)

AMEER-ALI, Rt. Hon. (Syed), P.C. 1909 ; C.I.E. 1887 ; Hon. LL.D. Cambridge ; D.L. (Calcutta Univ.) ; D.Litt. (Aligarh Univ.) ; Member of the Judicial Committee of the Privy Council ; *b.* 6 April 1849 ; 4th *s.* of late (Syed) Saâdut Ali of Mohan, Oudh ; *m.* Isabelle Ida, 2nd *d.* of late H. Konstam, 64 Gloucester Place, Portman Square, W. ; two *s. Educ.*: Hooghly College ; called to Bar, Inner Temple, 1873 ; Lecturer on Mahommedan Law at the Presidency College, 1873-78 ; President of the Committee of Management of the Mohsin Endowment, Bengal, 1876-1904 ; Member of the Commission to enquire into the affairs of the ex-King of Oude, 1879 ; Magistrate and Chief Magistrate of Calcutta, 1878-81 ; Member of the Bengal Legislative Council, 1878-83 ; Tagore Law Professor, 1884 ; President of the Faculty of Law, Calcutta University, 1891-92 ; Member of the Imperial Legislative Council of India, 1883-85 ; a Judge of His Majesty's High Court of Judicature at Fort William in Bengal, 1890-1904. *Decorated* for services in the Imperial Legislative Council of India. *Publications*: Critical Examination of the Life and Teachings of Mohammed ; Spirit of Islam ; Ethics of Islam ; A Short History of the Saracens ; Personal Law of the Mahommedans ; Mahommedan Law, in 2 vols. ; Student's Handbook of Mahommedan Law ; joint author of The Law of Evidence Applicable to British India ; of a Commentary on the Bengal Tenancy Act ; The Code of Civil Procedure, etc. *Recreations*: riding and shooting. *Address*: 2 Cadogan Place, S.W.1 ; *T.*: Sloane 4430 ; Pollingfold Manor, nr. Rudgwick, Sussex. *T.A.*: Ameer-Ali, London. *Club*: Reform. (*Died 3 Aug. 1928.*)

AMES, Frederick ; *b.* 1836 ; *s.* of G. H. Ames, Cote House, Gloucestershire ; *m.* Letitia, *d.* of Geo. Fillingham of Syerston, Nottinghamshire. *Educ.*: Brighton Coll. Late Rifle Brigade. *Recreation*: hunting. *Address*: Hawford Lodge, Worcester. *T.A.*: Fernhill Heath, Worcester. *Club*: Junior United Service.
(*Died 3 June 1918.*)

AMES, Lt.-Col. Oswald Henry, J.P. Norfolk ; *s.* of Lionel Ames, of The Hyde, Bedfords ; *b.* 3 January 1862 ; *m.* 1901, Violet, 2nd *d.* of late Lord Francis Cecil of Stocken Hall, Rutland ; one *s.* one *d. Educ.*: Charterhouse. Entered Herts Militia, 1881, and 2nd Life Guards, 1884 ; retired, 1906 ; rejoined Aug. 1914. *Address*: Durfold Hall, Dunsfold, Surrey. *T.*: Dunsfold 19. *Club*: Guards'.
(*Died 6 Nov. 1927.*)

AMES, Percy W., LL.D., F.S.A., Secretary of Royal Society of Literature, 1890-1917 ; lecturer on literary and scientific subjects ; *b.* Kirkstall, Yorks, 1853 ; *y. s.* of late John William Ames, schoolmaster ; *m.* 1879, Isa-

bella, d. of late George Neville Turner of Croydon, and g. d. of late William Rushton of Liverpool; two s. three d. Hon. LL.D. Wilberforce University. *Publications:* Obituary —Sir Patrick Colquhoun, The Eagle, Camb. 1891; edited, with Introductory Address, Afternoon Lectures on English Literature, 1893; Papers in Transactions R.S.L.: Positivism in Literature, vol. xvii. 1894; Supposed Source of The Vicar of Wakefield, vol. xix. 1897; Racial and Individual Temperaments, vol. xx. 1898; Edmund Spenser, vol. xxv. 1904; edited, with Historical Sketch of the Princess Elizabeth and Margaret of Navarre, The Mirror of the Sinful Soul, 1897; edited, with Introduction and one lecture, Chaucer Memorial Lectures, 1900; edited, with Introduction, Milton Memorial Lectures, 1908; various articles and addresses uncollected. *Address:* 77 Primrose Mansions, Battersea Park, S.W. 11. *Club:* Authors'.
(*Died 11 Feb. 1919.*)

AMHERST, 4th Earl (cr. 1826), **Hugh Amherst.** Baron Amherst of Montreal, 1788; Viscount Holmesdale, 1826; b. 30 Jan. 1856; 6th s. of 2nd Earl; m. 1896, Hon. Eleanor Clementina St. Aubyn, d. of 1st Baron St. Levan; two s. two d. Joined Coldstream Guards, 1875; Captain, 1887; served Nile, 1884-85, with Guards' Camel Regiment (medal with two clasps, Khedive's star). S. brother, 1910. *Heir:* s. Viscount Holmesdale. *Address:* 1 Wilton Crescent, S.W.1. *Club:* Carlton, Travellers'.
(*Died 7 Mar. 1927.*)

AMHERST of Hackney, Baroness (cr. 1892), **Mary Rothes Margaret Cecil;** d. of 1st Baron and Margaret Susan, only child of Admiral Robert Mitford; b. 25 April 1857; S. father, 1909; m. 1885, Lord William Cecil;   three s. Lady of Justice, St. John of Jerusalem. Owns about 10,000 acres. *Heir:* g.s. William Alexander Evering Cecil. *Address:* Stow Langtoft Hall, Bury St. Edmunds.
(*Died 27 Dec. 1919.*)

AMHERST, Hon. Sybil Margaret, 2nd d. of 1st Baron Amherst of Hackney; Lady of Justice, St. John of Jerusalem. *Address:* Foulden Hall, Brandon, Norfolk. *Club:* Ladies' Automobile.
(*Died 21 June 1926.*)

AMOS, Major Herbert Gilbert Maclachlan, D.S.O. 1900; K.O.S.B.; b. 28 April 1866; s. of Rev. James Amos of St. Ibbs, Hitchin, Herts; m. 1893, d. of Gen. Stratton; one d. Entered army, 1890; Adjutant, 1898; Captain, 1900; served South Africa (despatches twice, D.S.O.); European War, 1914-17. *Address:* St. Ibbs, Hitchin, Herts. *T.:* Hitchin 145. *Club:* Junior United Service.
(*Died 30 June 1924.*)

AMPHLETT, Major Charles Grove, D.S.O. 1900; Reserve of Officers, North Staffs Regt.; J.P. Salop and Staffordshire; b. 8 March 1862. Entered army, 1884; Capt. 1893; Major, 1901; commanded the 1st Mounted Infantry Regt. in the S. African Campaign. *Address:* Four Ashes Hall, near Stourbridge. *Club:* Naval and Military. (*Died 18 Aug. 1921.*)

AMPHLETT, His Honour Richard Holmden, J.P.; Judge of County Court of Birmingham since 1908; b. 24 April 1847; e. s. of late Samuel Holmden Amphlett and Mary Georgiana, d. of George Edward Male, and nephew of late Rt. Hon. Sir Richard P. Amphlett of Wychbold Hall; m. 1877, Sophy Emily, 2nd d. of John Shapter, Q.C.; three d. *Educ.:* Eton; Trin. Coll., Camb.; M.A. 1873. Called to Bar at Lincoln's Inn, 1871; Bencher, 1903; Q.C. 1895; Vice-Chairman of Quarter Sessions; Recorder of Worcester, 1891-1908. *Address:* Wychbold Hall, Droitwich. (*Died 25 Nov. 1925.*)

AMUNDSEN, Captain Roald, Leader of the Norwegian Polar Expedition which reached the South Pole; b. Borge, Smaalenene, 16 July 1872; s. of Jens Amundsen, shipowner (d. 1886). *Educ.:* Christiania. Student, 1890;
20

two years study medicine; went to sea; Examen 1st officer at the Christiania public sailors' school; Mate with the Belgica, Capt. de Gerlache, 1897-9; Ice navigation in the north, 1901-2; First voyage with the Gjoa hunting and making deep-water observations, Spitzberg-Greenland; 2nd Gjoa Expedition North Magnetic pole and North-West Passage, 1903-1906; The Norwegian Antarctic Expedition with the Fram, 1910-12; The Maud Expedition North-East Passage, 1918-21; The Airplane Flight to 87° 44' N. latitude, 1925; The Transpolar Flight from Spitzbergen to Teller Alaska over the North Pole, 1926. *Publications:* The North-West Passage; The South Pole; The North-East Passage; The First Flight Across the Polar Sea; My Life as an Explorer, 1927. *Address:* Oslo, Norway. *T.:* 1911.
(*Died June 1928.*)

ANDERSON, Maj.-Gen. Alexander Dingwall, R.A.; b. 19 Mar. 1843. Entered army, 1859; Maj.-Gen., 1897; retired, 1897; served Afghan War, 1878-79 (medal).
(*Died 13 Mar. 1916.*)

ANDERSON, Sir Arthur Robert, Kt., cr. 1918; C.B.E. 1917; C.I.E. 1915; b. 28 July 1860; s. of late James Anderson, Auchendarroch, Argyllshire; m. 1891, Gertrude (decd.), d. of late J. D. Fraser, J.P., Tiverton; one s. one d. *Educ.:* Glasgow Academy and University. Educated as a Civil Engineer; Chief Engineer Madras and Southern Mahratta Railway, 1897-1908; General Manager, 1908-14; Member Railway Board, Government of India, 1914-17; President, 1919-20; Member of Indian Railways Committee to enquire and report on working of Indian Railways, 1921; retired 1921; Director Madras and Southern Mahratta Railway, 1921. *Address:* Rotley Place, Faygate, Horsham. *Club:* Caledonian.
(*Died 24 Sept. 1924.*)

ANDERSON, Lt. - Col. Barton Edward, D.S.O. 1916; 59th Royal Scinde Rifles, F.F.; b. 15 Sep. 1881; s. of Beresford Anderson, late Chief Engineer, Madras Railway, and Dora, d. of late Michael O'Shaughnessy, Q.C. Served N.W. Frontier, Bazaar Valley, and Mohmand Expedition, 1908 (despatches); European War, 1914-18 (despatches three times, Bt. of Major, D.S.O.); 3rd Afghan War, 1919; Mesopotamia Rebellion, 1920; Waziristan, 1920-22 (despatches). *Club:* United Service. (*Died 23 May 1927.*)

ANDERSON, Daniel Elie, M.D. Lond. and Paris; B.A., B.Sc. Lond.; M.R.C.S. Eng.; L.R.C.P., L.S.A., F.R.S.E., F.R.G.S.; Lecturer and Research Scholar to the Honyman Gillespie Trust in London in Tropical Diseases; b. Mauritius; 4th s. of , ohn Anderson, Glasgow, and Euphémie Elie Bourelly; m. Marion, d. of D. Munro Drysdale, Liverpool; one s. two d. *Educ.:* Royal College of Mauritius; University College and Hospital, London; Examiner of Recruits and Assessor of Pensions during the war; Paris University; School of Tropical Medicine, London. Late Physician Assistant, University College Hospital, and Obstetric Assistant; late Deputy Medical Officer Parish of Hampstead; Liston Gold Medal University College Hospital; late Superintendent of McAll Medical Mission, Paris 1886-89; Physician Hertford British Hospital Paris, and practised in Paris for 22 years; returned to London, 1908; went on scientific mission to Mauritius; to Chile and West Indies 1913; has travelled extensively; Fellow of the Roy. Medical Society; Fellow of the Roy. Tropical Society of Medicine; Member of the British Medical Association. *Publications:* Fever after Operations (in French); Epidemics of Mauritius Notes on Tropical Disease; Atlas of Venomous Snakes; Atlas of Fly Carriers of Diseases Scientific Mission to Chile, Peru, Panama, and the West Indian British Possessions; Sunday

Stories for Children; contributions to medical and scientific journals. *Recreations:* travelling abroad. *Address:* 3 North Grove, Hampstead Lane, Highgate, N.6; *T.:* Hornsey 734; 26 Harley Street, W.1; *T.:* Padd. 2192; Cannes, France (Jan. to April).   (*Died 23 Jan. 1928.*)

ANDERSON, Dr. Elizabeth Garrett, M.D. (Paris); Mayor of Aldeburgh, 1908; *b.* 1836; *d.* of Newson Garrett of Aldeburgh, Suffolk; *m.* 1871, J. G. S. Anderson, J.P. (*d.* 1907); shipowner and managing director of Orient Line of Royal Mail steamers; one *s.* one *d. Educ.:* privately. Began to study medicine in 1860; Colleges of Surgeons and Physicians refused to admit her to their examinations; was admitted to the examinations of the Society of Apothecaries and obtained its license to practise in 1865; passed the medical examinations of University of Paris and received M.D. degree, 1870; elected to first School Board for London, 1870; from 1866 to 1890 Senior Physician to New Hospital for Women; Dean of the London Sch. of Medicine for Women, 1883-1903; Lecturer on Medicine ditto, 1876-98; President of East Anglian Branch of British Medical Association, 1896-97; first woman elected as mayor in England; Hon. Sec. Imp. Vaccination League. *Recreations:* travelling, gardening. *Address:* Alde House, Aldeburgh, Suffolk.
    (*Died 17 Dec. 1917.*)

ANDERSON, Lt.-Col. Francis, D.S.O. 1917; M.C.; Royal Highlanders; *b.* 1888; *m.*; one *s.* one *d.* Served European War, 1914-18 (despatches, D.S.O., M.C.). *Address:* Diana Lodge, Sandhurst.   (*Died 17 May 1925.*)

ANDERSON, Brig.-Gen. Sir Francis James, K.B.E., *cr.* 1919; C.B. 1917; Chairman, Army Sanitary Committee, and attached General Staff; 3rd *surv. s.* of late Dep. Inspector-General of Hospitals, Robert Carew Anderson; *m.* 1886, Frances Alice, *e. d.* of late Major Purcell O'Gorman, M.P. for Waterford; one *s.* one *d. Educ.:* privately; R.M.A., Woolwich. Has served as Colonial Engineer and Member of Executive and Legislative Councils of the Straits Settlements; commanded Queen Victoria's Own Sappers and Miners; served as Assistant Director at the War Office. *Recreations:* yachting, shooting, fishing. *Address:* 4 Trebovir Road, Earl's Court, S.W.5.
    (*Died 6 Mar. 1920.*)

ANDERSON, Sir George, Kt., *cr.* 1905; Treasurer of the Bank of Scotland, 1898-1917; *b.* Fraserburgh, Aberdeenshire, 26 March 1845; *s.* of John Anderson, who resided there; *m.* 1870, Mary, *y. d.* of Alexander Anderson, London. *Educ.:* Fraserburgh. Entered service of North of Scotland Bank as apprentice at the Fraserburgh Branch, 1857; Accountant, 1860; Accountant at Banff Branch, 1863; Elgin Branch, 1866; Peterhead Branch, 1868; Agent at Huntly Branch, 1873; Dundee Branch, 1879; Assistant-Manager at Head Office, Aberdeen, 1888; General Manager, 1889; Convener and Chairman of the Scottish Bank Managers, 1898-1917; President of Institute of Bankers in Scotland, 1903-7; J.P. Aberdeenshire and Midlothian; attended Coronations 1902 and 1911, Courts at Holyrood 1903 and 1911 as Deputy-Usher of White Rod of Scotland; a Director of Scottish Widows' Fund; a Governor of Donaldson's Hospital; and one of Walker Trustees. *Address:* Beechmount, Murrayfield, Midlothian. *T.:* Edinburgh Central 7817. (*Died 1 Dec. 1923.*)

ANDERSON, Gen. Harry Cortlandt, C.B. 1907; Hon. Col. 4th Rajputs, Indian Army, since 1904; *b.* 28 May 1826; *m.* Alice Forbes (*d.* 1911). Entered army, 1842; Gen. 1894; U.S. List, 1886; served Sutlej campaign, 1846 (medal with clasp); Indian Mutiny, 1857-1858 (despatches, medal, Brevet-Major). *Address:* Harrington Road, S. Kensington, W.
    (*Died 20 Sept. 1921.*)

ANDERSON, Major Henry Graeme, M.B.E. 1919; M.D., Ch.B., F.R.C.S. (England); Consulting Surgeon to the Royal Air Force; Surgeon to St. Mark's Hospital for Diseases of the Rectum; Senior Assistant Surgeon to the Belgrave Hospital for Children; *b.* Scotland, 1882; *yr. s.* of Nicol Anderson; *m.* 1921, Gladys, *er. d.* of Charles Hood.; one *d. Educ.:* Glasgow University; King's College; London Hospital. Fellow of Royal Society of Medicine; House Surgeon, St. Mark's Hospital, 1907-8; Surgical Registrar to Metropolitan Hospital, Cancer Hospital, and to Royal National Orthopædic Hospital, 1909-12; joined Royal Navy as Surgeon-Lieutenant, Aug. 1914; attached as Surgeon to original R.N. Air Service Expeditionary Force; served at Antwerp, Ypres, and Belgian and Northern France Coasts (1914 Star); attached R.N. Air Station, Eastbourne, and R.N. Airship Station, Polegate, 1916; gained Aviator's certificate, No. 3758, of Royal Aero Club, 26 Oct. 1916; at Eastbourne on Maurice Farman; Surgeon to British Flying School, Vendome, France, 1917; Surgeon to Central R.A.F. Hospital, 1918-19; transferred from Royal Navy to Royal Air Force as Major R.A.F.M.S. *Publications:* The Medical and Surgical Aspects of Aviation; The Rectum—Encyclopædia of Surgery; Combined Operations for Excision of Rectum—System of Operative Surgery; Operative Treatment of Hæmorrhoids—British Medical Journal; Aeroplane Accidents—Journal R.N. Medical Service; numerous articles on Surgery, and Aviation. *Recreations:* aviation, tennis, dancing. *Address:* 75 Harley Street, W.1. *T.:* Langham 2772. *M.:* RI 7703. *Clubs:* Royal Air Force, Royal Aero.   (*Died 28 June 1925.*)

ANDERSON, Sir Hugh Kerr, Kt., *cr.* 1922; M.A., M.D., F.R.C.P., F.R.S.; Master of Gonville and Caius College, Cambridge, since 1912; *b.* Hampstead, 6 July 1865; *s.* of James Anderson and Eliza, *d.* of Surgeon-General John Murray; *m.* Jessie, *d.* of Surgeon-General F. W. Innes, C.B.; one *s.* one *d. Educ.:* Harrow (Sayer Scholar); Gonville and Caius College, Cambridge (Scholar); St. Bartholomew's Hospital; Fellow of Gonville and Caius College, 1897-1912; member of Royal Commission on Oxford and Cambridge Universities, 1919, and of the University of Cambridge Statutory Commission, 1922; a Governor of Harrow School. *Publications:* papers on physiological subjects. *Recreations:* fishing, gardening. *Address:* The Lodge, Gonville and Caius College, Cambridge. *T.:* Cambridge 860. *Club:* Athenæum.
    (*Died 2 Nov. 1928.*)

ANDERSON, James Drummond, M.A., Litt.D.; University Lecturer on Bengali, Cambridge; *b.* Fort William, Calcutta, 11 Nov. 1852; *s.* of James Anderson, M.D., and Ellen Garstin; *m.* Frances Louisa, *d.* of Captain S. Cordue; five *s.* one *d. Educ.:* Cheltenham College; Rugby. Was in the Indian Civil Service, 1875-1900; served mostly in Assam. *Publications:* Kachari Folk Tales, a collection of Chittagong Proverbs, and other works on languages of N.E. India; The Peoples of India (Cambridge Manuals); Indira and Other Stories (translation from B. C. Chatterjee); A Manual of the Bengali Language; Papers on linguistic subjects in Journal Royal Asiatic Society and elsewhere. *Address:* Mostyn House, Brooklands Avenue, Cambridge.   (*Died 24 Nov. 1920.*)

ANDERSON, James Maitland; Hon. LL.D. (St. And.), 1912; Librarian, University, St. Andrews, 1881-1924; Hon. Keeper of the University and College Records since 1924; *b.* Rossie, Fifeshire, 22 Oct. 1852; *e. s.* of James Anderson, gardener to Capt. James Maitland, R.N.; *m.* 1880, Margaret Elizabeth, *e. d.* of John Bain, Brisbane, Queensland; two *d. Educ.:* Free Church School, Giffordtown; Parish School, Auchtermuchty; private study. Began life as a cow-herd, thereafter gradually drifted, through business occupations, into journalism ; reported for various newspapers ; contributed to several minor periodicals in English and German ; edited the Phonographic Standard, 1872-1874 ; appointed assistant librarian, University of St. Andrews, 1874 ; was also Secretary of the University, 1878-99 ; Quæstor, 1881-92 ; Registrar and Secretary of the General Council, 1881-99. *Publications*: Historical Sketch of the University of St. Andrews, 1878 ; Heraldry of the University, 1895 ; Register of Students at St. Andrews, 1747-1897, 1905 ; Handbook to the City and University of St. Andrews, 1911 ; Writings and Portraits of George Buchanan, 1906 ; Matriculation and Graduation Rolls of St. Andrews University, 1413-1579, 1926 ; articles in Cyclopædias, etc. ; editor of the St. Andrews University Calendar, 1882-99, and of the Library Bulletin, 1901-24. *Recreations*: reading and walking daily ; antiquarian rambles at home or abroad, occasionally ; collector of books on academical and local history. *Address*: Kinnessbank East, St. Andrews.

(*Died 25 Aug. 1927.*)

ANDERSON, James Wallace, M.D., F.R.F.P.S.G. ; Physician ; Hon. Associate of the Order of St. John of Jerusalem in England ; *b.* Glasgow, 20 Oct. 1848 ; *e. s.* of Hugh Locke Anderson and Helen Willox, Glasgow ; *m.* 1886, Mary (*d.* 1916), *d.* of late James Ramsay Orr, Montreal ; no *c.* *Educ.*: Langside Academy ; Glasgow University ; Dublin ; Berlin. Connected with the Glasgow Royal Infirmary as Student, Resident Physician, Physician, Hon. Consulting Physician, and Manager since 1866 ; late Lecturer on the Practice of Medicine, Queen Margaret College, University of Glasgow. *Publications*: Medical Nursing ; Home Nursing and Hygiene (joint author) ; The Power of Nature in Disease ; Four Chiefs of the G.R.I., and various medical papers. *Recreation*: music. *Address*: 41 Falkland Mansions, Hyndland, Glasgow.

ANDERSON, Sir John, K.C.B., *cr.* 1913 ; G.C.M.G., *cr.* 1909 ; K.C.M.G., *cr.* 1901 ; C.M.G. 1898 ; Hon. LL.D. Edin. 1911 ; Governor and Commander-in-Chief of Ceylon since 1916 ; *b.* 23 January 1858, Gartly, Aberdeenshire ; *o. s.* of John Anderson, Supt. Gordon Mission, Aberdeen ; married. *Educ.*: Aberdeen University. M.A., 1st class honours in Mathematics ; gold medal as most distinguished graduate of year ; Hon. LL.D. 1907 ; 2nd class clerk Colonial Office, 1879 ; Bacon scholar, Gray's Inn, 1887 ; Inns of Court studentship, 1888 ; private secretary to late Hon. Sir R. Meade (Under-Secretary of State), 1892 ; attached to staff for the Behring Sea Arbitration in London and Paris, 1892-93 ; 1st class clerk, 1896 ; principal clerk, 1897 ; secretary to Conference of Colonial Premiers with Mr. Chamberlain, June and July 1897 ; and to Conference of 1902 ; with Prince of Wales on Colonial Tour ; Governor Straits Settlements and High Commissioner Federated Malay States, 1904-11 ; High Commissioner, State of Brunei, 1906-11. Permanent Under-Secretary of State for the Colonies, 1911-16. *Publications*: editor of Colonial Office List, 1885-97. *Address*: Queen's House, Colombo, Ceylon.

(*Died 24 Mar. 1918.*)

ANDERSON, Sir John, Kt., *cr.* 1912 ; attorney of Guthrie & Co., Ltd., East India merchants ; *b.* Rothesay, March 1852 ; *m.* 1901, Winifred Ethel Dunbar-Pope. *Educ.*: Raffles Institution, Singapore. Arrived Singapore, 1859 ; in Government Service at Singapore till 1871, when commenced mercantile career ; Siamese Consul-general for Singapore, 1880-1910 ; Member Legislative Council, Straits Settlements, 1886-8 and 1905-8. *Address*: 5 Whittington Avenue, E.C. ; Eastcote Place, nr. Pinner. *Clubs*: Bath, City Carlton. (*Died 18 Dec. 1924.*)

ANDERSON, John William Stewart, C.B. 1918 ; M.V.O. 1911 ; an Assistant Secretary, Secretary's Department, Admiralty, since 1917 ; *b.* 22 April 1874. *Address*: 28 Argyll Road, Kensington, W. *T.*: Park 3641.

(*Died 28 May 1920.*)

ANDERSON, Joseph, LL.D. ; Keeper of the National Museum of Antiquities, Edinburgh, 1870-1913, and Assistant-Secretary of the Society of Antiquaries of Scotland ; *b.* Arbroath, Forfarshire, 1832 ; *m.* Jessie Dempster (*d.* 1913). *Educ.*: St. Vigeans Parish School ; Educational Institution, Arbroath. Teacher in East Free School, Arbroath, 1852-56 ; in English School, Hasskioy, Constantinople, 1856-59 ; editor of John O'Groat Journal, Wick, Caithness, 1860-69. Edited The Orkneyinga Saga, 1873 ; The Oliphants in Scotland, 1879 ; Drummond's Ancient Scottish Weapons, 1881. Was Rhind Lecturer in Archæology to the Society of Antiquaries of Scotland, 1879-82, the subject of the four courses of lectures being Scotland in Early Christian and in Pagan Times, subsequently published in 4 vols., 1881-86 ; again Rhind Lecturer in 1892, the subject being The Early Christian Monuments of Scotland, published by the Society, with an illustrated descriptive list of the Monuments, by J. Romilly Allen, 1903 Is an Honorary Member of the Royal Society of Northern Antiquaries, Copenhagen ; of the Society of Antiquaries, Stockholm ; of the Royal Irish Academy ; and Honorary Professor of Antiquities to the Royal Scottish Academy. *Publications*: numerous papers in the Proceedings of the Society. *Address*: 8 Great King Street, Edinburgh.

(*Died 27 Sept. 1916.*)

ANDERSON, Rev. K. C., D.D. ; retired Minister ; *b.* Jedburgh, Roxburghshire ; *s.* of George Anderson and Isabella Cranston ; *m.* Robina Fisher ; one *s.* one *d.* *Educ.*: Jedburgh Grammar School ; Middlebury College, Vermont, U.S.A. ; Yale Theological Seminary. Congregational Minister at Fairhaven, Vermont, U.S.A. ; Milwaukee, Wis. ; Oskkosh, Wis. ; Troy, N.Y. ; Bradford, Yorkshire ; Dundee, Scotland ; D.D. Union College, Schenectady. *Publications*: The Larger Faith ; The New Theology.

ANDERSON, Peter John, M.A., LL.B. ; Librarian to the Univ. of Aberdeen since 1894 ; Clerk of the General Council since 1907 ; Registrar since 1918 ; *s.* of Peter Anderson, solicitor, Inverness. *Educ.*: Inverness Royal Academy ; Universities of Aberdeen and Edinburgh. Has held various posts in connection with the University of Aberdeen. *Publications*: Fasti Academiæ Mariscallanæ, 3 vols., 1889-98 ; Charters and other Writs illustrating the History of the Royal Burgh of Aberdeen, 1890 ; Inventories of Ecclesiastical Records in the N.E. Synods of Scotland, 1890 ; Historical Notes on the Libraries of the Universities of Aberdeen, 1893 ; Officers and Graduates of King's College, Aberdeen, 1893 ; Aurora Borealis Academica, 1899 ; Records of Aberdeen Universities Commission of 1716-17, 1900 ; Roll of Alumni of King's College, Aberdeen, 1900 ; Rectorial Addresses at the Universities of Aberdeen, 1902 ; Studies in the History of the University, 1906 ; Record of Quatercentenary, 1907 ; Bibliography of the University, 1907 ; Aberdeen Friars, 1909 ; Bibliography of Inverness-shire, 1917. *Address*: The University, Aberdeen. (*Died 12 May 1926.*)

ANDERSON, Sir Robert, 1st Bt., *cr.* 1911 ; Kt., *cr.* 1903 ; *b.* 1837 ; *s.* of James Anderson of Ballybay, Co. Monaghan, and Elizabeth, *d.* of Andrew Ker of Newbliss ; *m.* 1890, Wilhelmina, *d.* of Rev. Andrew Long, M.A., of Moureagh, Co. Donegal. Chairman of Anderson and M'Auley, Ltd., Arnott & Co., Ltd., Vulcanite, Ltd., City Estates, Ltd., Milfort Weaving and Finishing Co., Ltd., William Ross & Co., Ltd., Spinners, Baltic Firewood Co., Ltd. ; Alderman and

J.P. City of Belfast; High Sheriff of Belfast, 1908; Lord Mayor, 1907-8-9; retired from Corporation, 1918; High Sheriff Co. Monaghan, 1911; J.P. Co. Antrim. *Heir:* none. *Address:* Parkmount, Belfast; Mullaghmore, Co. Monaghan. *(Died 16 July 1921.)*

ANDERSON, Sir Robert, K.C.B., *cr.* 1901; LL.D.; Barrister-at-law (Dublin and Middle Temple); J.P. for London; *b.* 29 May 1841; *s.* of Matthew Anderson, Crown Solicitor, Dublin; *m.* Lady Agnes A. Moore, sister of 9th Earl of Drogheda, 1873; three *s.* one *d. Educ.:* Trinity Coll. Dublin; B.A. 1862; LL.D. 1875. Home Office as adviser in matters relating to political crime from 1868; late Assistant Commissioner of Police of the Metropolis, and Head of Criminal Investigation Department from 1888, resigned 1901. *Publications:* The Coming Prince; Human Destiny; The Gospel and its Ministry; Daniel in the Critics' Den; The Silence of God, 1897; The Buddha of Christendom, 1899; The Bible and Modern Criticism, 1902; Pseudo-criticism, 1904; For Us Men, 1905; The Way, 1905; Sidelights on the Home Rule Movement, 1906; In Defence: a Plea for the Faith; Criminals and Crime, 1907; The Bible or the Church? 1908; The Lord from Heaven, 1910; The Lighter Side of my Official Life, 1910; The Hebrews Epistle, 1911; The Honour of His Name, 1912; Forgotten Truths, 1913; The Entail of the Covenant, 1914; Misunderstood Texts of the New Testament, 1916. *Address:* 39 Linden Gardens, W. *Club:* National.
(Died 15 Nov. 1918.)

ANDERSON, Sir Robert Rowand, Kt., *cr.* 1902; LL.D., F.R.S.E., H.R.S.A., F.R.I.B.A.; architect; *b.* 1834; *s.* of James Anderson, solicitor, Edinburgh, and Margaret Rowand; *m.* 1863, Mary, *d.* of Henry Ross of Kinnahaird, Co. Ross. *Educ.:* Edinburgh. *Address:* 16 Rutland Square, Edinburgh; Allermuir House, Colinton, Midlothian. *Clubs:* Royal Societies; Conservative, Edinburgh.
(Died 1 June 1921.)

ANDERSON, Thomas, I.S.O.; late Superintendent of Registry Board of Trade; retired, 1910; *b.* 24 Feb. 1844. *Address:* The Chálet, Gipsy Lane. Putney, S.W.15.
(Died 28 Mar. 1926.)

ANDERSON, Thomas Scott, M.D., J.P., M.F.H.; *b.* 1858; *s.* of Thomas Anderson, M.D., Selkirk, and Joan M'Laurin; *m.* 1876, Joan A., *d.* of Thomas Shaw, Woolwyrite, Australia. *Educ.:* Merchiston Castle School; Edinburgh University; Ecole de Médecine, Paris. Practised profession for a short while in Australia, and afterwards travelled, forming a collection of Australian birds. Returned home and took to sheep-farming. *Publications:* Holloas from the Hills; Hound and Horn in Jedforest, 1909; a book of hunting verses and other contributions to sporting magazines over the signature of Teviotdale. *Recreations:* fox-hunting, shooting, natural history. *Address:* Ettrick Shaws, Selkirk, N.B. *Clubs:* Nimrod; Scottish Conservative, Edinburgh. *(Died June 1919.)*

ANDERSON, William C., M.P. (Lab.) Attercliffe Division of Sheffield since 1914; *m.* 1911, Mary R. Macarthur; one *d.* Member National Administrative Council Independent Labour Party; Contested Parliamentary Elections, Hyde, 1910; Keighley, 1911. *Recreation:* reading. *Address:* 7 Mecklenburgh Square, W.C. *T.:* Holborn 2485. *(Died 25 Feb. 1919.)*

ANDERSON, Col. William Campbell, F.R.G.S.; D.S.O. 1900; late Lt.-Col. 3rd Cameronians (Scottish Rifles); *b.* 14 Dec. 1868; *m.* 1894, Elizabeth, *d.* of late Edward Barnes. *Educ.:* Harrow. Formerly Capt. 15th Hussars.; served S. Africa 5th Batt. Imperial Yeomanry (despatches twice, 2 medals and clasps); served Gold Coast and Nigeria (W. African medal and clasp). *Club:* Naval and Military.
(Died 21 Dec. 1926.)

ANDERSON, Colonel Wm. Patrick, C.M.G. 1913; *b.* Levis, Quebec, 4 Sep. 1851; *e. s.* of late Thomas Anderson, Edmonton, Alberta; *m.* 1876, Dorothea Susannah, *e. d.* of late Henry Beaumont Small; four *s.* one *d. Educ.:* University of Lennoxville; University of Manitoba. Entered Civil Service of Canada as Assistant Engineer, Department of Marine and Fisheries, 1874; Chief Engineer, 1880; superannuated, 1919; has erected over 900 lighthouses and 80 fog-alarm installations; is a Past President of the Engineering Institute of Canada, a member of the Institution of Civil Engineers, and F.R.G.S.; Chairman of the Geographic Board of Canada, and a member of the Lighthouse Board of Canada; was in command of the 43rd Regt. Canadian Militia up to 1892 (Fenian raid medal, with two clasps, V.D.); and has been in command of the Canadian Bisley Team; represented Canada at the International Congress of Navigation, 1912; and at the National Waterways Congress, Washington, 1913. Established in 1885, and for two years edited, Canadian Militia Gazette; contributor to Encyclopædia Britannica, etc. *Recreations:* golf, curling. *Address:* 64 Cooper Street, Ottawa. *T.:* Queen 1910. *Clubs:* Royal Ottawa Golf, Rideau Curling, Governor-General's Curling, Ottawa.
(Died Feb. 1927.)

ANDERSON - MORSHEAD, Acting Lt.-Col. Rupert Henry, D.S.O. 1918; 2nd Batt. Devonshire Regt.; *s.* of John Y. Anderson-Morshead, Barrister, Salcombe Regis, Sidmouth; *m.* 1914, Lucy Helen, *d.* of William Carstares-Dunlop, Gairbraid, Scotland. *Educ.:* Wellington College; Royal Military College, Sandhurst. Served European War, 1914-18 (D.S.O.). *Recreations:* cricket, tennis, fishing, and shooting. *Address:* Wayside, Lingfield, Surrey. *T.A.:* Wayside, Dormansland, Surrey. *T.:* Longfield 8X. *Club:* Junior Army and Navy. *(Died 27 May 1918.)*

ANDREWES, Major (Acting Lt.-Col.) Francis Edward, D.S.O. 1916; R.A.; *b.* 8 May 1878; *s.* of Rev. Nesfield Andrewes and Katherine Phillipps; *m.* 1905, Margaret Agnes Malden; four *s.* one *d. Educ.:* Bradfield College. Served South African War, 1899-1902 (Queen's and King's medals, 5 clasps), European War, 1914-16 (D.S.O.); Brevet Lt.-Col. Jan. 1919. *Address:* 15 Mount Avenue, Ealing, W. *Club:* United Service. *(Died 29 Mar. 1920.)*

ANDREWES, Rev. John Brereton, M.A.; Canon of Chelmsford, 1916. *Address:* The Vicarage, Harlow, Essex.
(Died 1 April 1920.)

ANDREWS, Charles William, B.A., D.Sc., F.R.S. 1906; Assist.-Keeper in the Geol. Department of the British Museum (Natural History); *b.* Hampstead, 1866. *Educ.:* private school. B.A. (Lond.) 1887; B.Sc. (Lond.) Hons. in Zoology, 1890; D.Sc. (Lond.) and Sherbrooke Scholarship, 1900; member of the staff of the Geological Department, British Museum, 1892; awarded Lyell Fund of Geological Society, 1896; visited Christmas Island and Cocos-Keeling Islands on a collecting expedition, 1897-98; made several expeditions to the Fayùm, Egypt, collecting fossil vertebrates, 1900-6; made a second expedition to Christmas Island, 1908. *Publications:* A Descriptive Catalogue of the Tertiary Vertebrata of the Fayùm, Egypt; part author of A Monograph of Christmas Island (Indian Ocean); Catalogue of the Marine Reptiles of the Oxford Clay, vols. i. and ii.; numerous papers on fossil vertebrates. *Recreations:* walking and reading. *Address:* Natural History Museum, S.W.7. *Clubs:* Athenæum, Savage.
(Died 25 May 1924.)

ANDREWS, Edward Gordon, I.S.O. 1909; Treasurer, Kingston, Jamaica. *Address:* Kingston, Jamaica. *(Died 11 Nov. 1915.)*

ANDREWS, Hon. Elisha Benjamin, Ph.D., D.D., LL.D.; Chancellor Emeritus University of Leunoxville —

versity of Nebraska since 1909; *b.* Hinsdale, N.H., 10 Jan. 1844; *s.* of Erastus and Almira Bartlett; *m.* 1870, Ella Anna Allen. *Educ.:* Brown Univ.; University of Berlin; University of Munich; Newton, Mass., Theological Institution. Private, Corporal, Sergeant, and Lieutenant in First Conn. Heavy Artillery in Civil War, 1861-64; student in Brown University, 1866-70; ordained Bapt. ministry, 1874; pastor, Beverly, Mass., 1874-75; President Denison University, Ohio, 1875-79; Professor in Newton Theological Institution, 1879-82; Prof. of History and Political Economy in Brown University, 1882-88; Professor of Political Econ. and Finance in Cornell University, 1888-89; President Brown University, 1889-98; Supt. Chicago Public Schools, 1898-1900; Chancellor University of Nebraska, 1900-8; member Loyal Legion, Grand Army of the Republic, American Economic Association; member International Monetary Conference, Brussels, 1892; member Gen. Educ. Board until 1912. *Publications:* Institutes of Constitutional History, English and American; Institutes of General History; Institutes of Economics; History of the United States; History of Last Quarter Century in United States; History of the United States in our Own Time; Outlines of the Principles of History (translated); Eternal Woods (sermons); Wealth and Moral Law; An Honest Dollar; The Problem of Cosmology (translated); The Call of the Land. *Address:* Interlachen, Fla., U.S.A. *(Died 30 Oct. 1917.)*

ANDREWS, Rev. Prof. Herbert T., D.D.; Professor of New Testament Exegesis and Criticism, New and Hackney Colleges, University of London, since 1903; *b.* Oxford, 22 Dec. 1864; *m.* 1st, 1891, Edith Mary Birt; one *s.* one *d.*; 2nd, 1915, Jessie Caroline, *o. d.* of late Rev. Dr. Forsyth *Educ.:* Oxford High School; Magdalen (Classical Demy) and Mansfield Colleges, Oxford; 1st Class Honours Classical Moderations, 1885; 2nd Class Literæ Humaniores, 1887; Senior Septuagint (Hall-Houghton) Prize, 1889; Ellerton Essay Prize, 1889; Denyer and Johnson Scholarship, 1890. Entered Congregational ministry at Chingford, Essex, 1890; removed to Swansea, 1892; Professor of Church History and Historical Theology at Cheshunt College, 1895. *Publications:* Commentary on Acts in the Westminster New Testament, 1908; Century Bible Handbook on Apocryphal Books, 1908; The Value of the Theology of St. Paul, 1915; contributed an article on the Social Principles and Effects of the Reformation to Christ and Civilisation, and articles for the 11th edition of the Encyclopædia Britannica, Chambers's Encyclopædia, and the Universal Encyclopædia, etc.; edited the Epistle of Aristeas for the Oxford Apocrypha and Pseudepigrapha, 1913; contributed several sections in Peake's Commentary on the Bible, 1920, also articles for Contemporary Review, Expositor, etc. *Recreation:* golf. *Address:* 283 Willesden Lane, N.W. *Club:* Neasden Golf. *(Died 1 Jan. 1928.)*

ANDREWS, Hugh, J.P.; *s.* of late Hugh Andrews of Fortview; *m.* Isabel, *e. d.* of late John Sowerby of Benwell Tower, Northumberland. High Sheriff, Northumberland, 1891-92. *Address:* 18 Rutland Court, Rutland Gardens, S.W.; Toddington Manor, Winchcombe, R.S.O., Gloucestershire. *T.A.:* Andrews, Toddington, Winchcombe. *T.:* Toddington 1. *Clubs:* White's, Aero, Royal Automobile: Royal Yacht Squadron, Cowes.
(Died 25 May 1926.)

ANDREWS, James Frank, I.S.O. 1913; J.P.; late Secy. to New Zealand Cabinet, Clerk of the Executive Council, and Secretary to the Prime Minister, Dominion of New Zealand; *b.* Plymouth, 26 June 1848; *s.* of late Henry John Andrews, surgeon H.I.C.S.; widower; one *s.* *Educ.:* Church of England Grammar School,

Auckland (scholarship). Six years in Customs Department, nine in Telegraph Department; Private Secretary to late Hon. John Ballance, Prime Minister: thirteen years Private Secretary to late Rt. Hon. R. J. Seddon, and three years to Rt. Hon. Sir J. G. Ward, Prime Minister. *Address:* 35 Bidwell Street, Wellington, New Zealand. *T.:* 927 and 913 A.
(Died 10 Dec. 1922.)

ANDREWS, Right Hon. Thomas, P.C. Ire. 1903; D.L., Co. Down; flax spinner; *b.* Comber, 26 Feb. 1843; 4th *s.* of late John Andrews, J.P., of Comber, and Sarah, *o. d.* of late Dr. Wm. Drennan of Cabin Hill, Co. Down; *m.* Lizzie, *o. d.* of late James A. Pirrie of Little Clandeboye, Co. Down, 1870; three *s.* one *d.* *Educ.:* Royal Academical Institution and Queen's College, Belfast. President Ulster Liberal Unionist Association since 1892; one of promoters of Great Ulster Convention, 1892; member of Ulster Defence Union, 1893; member of Recess Committee, 1895; chairman of Belfast and Co. Down Railway Company since 1895; member of Appeal Commission under Local Government (Ireland) Act, 1898; chairman Co. Down County Council since 1902; member of Arterial Drainage Commission, Ireland, 1905; High Sheriff of Down, 1912. *Address:* Ardara, Comber, County Down, Ireland. *T.A.:* Andrews, Ardara, Comber. *T.:* 1 Comber. *Clubs:* Ulster Reform, Ulster, Belfast; County, Downpatrick.
(Died 16 Sept. 1916.)

ANDREWS, Rt. Hon. William Drennan, P.C. (Ireland), 1897; *b.* 24 Jan. 1882; 2nd *s.* of late John Andrews, Comber, Co. Down; *m.* 1857, Eliza (*d.* 1901), *d.* of late John Galloway, Monkstown, Co. Dublin. *Educ.:* Royal Belfast Academical Institution; Trin. Coll., Dublin. LL.D. 1860; a senior gold medallist in Ethics and Logic. Barr. Ireland, 1855; Q.C. 1872; Hon. Bencher, King's Inns, Dublin, 1910; Judge in the Exchequer Division of the High Court of Justice, Ireland (since merged in the King's Bench Division), 1882 - 1910. *Address:* 51 Lower Leeson Street, Dublin. *(Died 3 Dec. 1924.)*

ANGELL, Col. Frederick John, C.B.E. 1918; late Assistant Director of Ordnance Services Southern Command; late Col. Royal Irish Fusiliers; *b.* 1861; served Egyptian Expedition, 1884; Bechuanaland Expedition, 1884-85; retired pay, 1921. *(Died Jan. 1922.)*

ANGELL, James Burrill, LL.D.; President of the University of Michigan 1871, President Emeritus, 1909; *b.* Scituate, Rhode Island, 7 Jan. 1829; *m.* Sarah S., *d.* of President Caswell, of Brown University, 1855; two *s.* one *d.* *Educ.:* Brown University and in Europe. Professor of Modern Languages, Brown University, 1853-60; editor Providence Journal, 1860-66; President Univ. of Vermont, 1866-71; Minister of United States to China, 1880-81; member of Fisheries Commission of U.S. and Great Britain, 1887; member of Deep Waterways Commission, Canada and U.S. 1896; United States Minister to Turkey, 1897-98; President Emeritus, 1909. *Publications:* Reminiscences; Selected Addresses; numerous articles in leading American Reviews. *Address:* Ann Arbor, Michigan, U.S.A. *T.A.:* Ann Arbor. *T.:* 40. *(Died 1 April 1916.)*

ANGERS, Hon. Sir Auguste Réal, Kt., *cr.* 1913; K.C.; LL.D.; P.C.; Knight Grand Cross of St. Gregory the Great; *s.* of François Réal Angers, Quebec, Barrister; *b.* Quebec 8 Oct. 1837; *m.* 1st, Julia Marguerite (*d.* 1879), *d.* of late Senator Chinic; 2nd, 1890, Emilie, *d.* of late Alexander Le Moine, Notary. *Educ.:* College of Nicolet and Laval University. Barrister; admitted at Bar, 1860; Member of Legislative Assembly, 1874, and Leader of House until 1878; elected a member of the House of Commons of Canada; appointed one of the Justices

of the High Court of the Province of Quebec; resigned in 1887 to accept Lieutenant-Governorship of the Province; at the expiration of term entered Sir John Thompson's administration, Ottawa, and continued in office under Sir MacKenzie Bowell; in 1896 entered Sir Charles Tupper's administration; was defeated at the general election of June 1896, and retired from office. *Address:* City of Westmount, near Montreal; 35 St. James Street, Montreal.
(*Died April 1919.*)

ANGST, Sir Henry; K.C.M.G., *cr.* 1906; C.M.G. 1902; H.B.M. Consul-General in Switzerland (unpaid) 1896, resigned 31 March 1916; Hon. F.S.A.; *b.* Regensberg (Zurich), 18 October 1847; widower. *Educ.:* Zurich at the Gymnasium; Federal Polytechnic School. Doctor Philosophiæ, honoris causa, University of Zurich; Hon. LL.D. Harvard. Vice-Consul, Zurich, 1886; Consul for German and Italian speaking Cantons of Switzerland, 1886; Director of Swiss National Museum, Zurich, 1892-1903. *Publications:* Annual Illustrated Museum's Reports, and various publications on ancient Swiss art. *Address:* Regensberg (Canton of Zurich). *Club:* Athenæum.
(*Died 14 May 1922.*)

ANGUS, Henry Brunton, M.B., M.S. Durh., F.R.C.S. Eng.; Honorary Surgeon, Royal Victoria Infirmary, Newcastle-on-Tyne; Professor of Surgery, University of Durham; *b.* Dec. 1867; *s.* of J. Acworth Angus, M.R.C.S., L.S.A.; *m.* Marian, *d.* of late J. Arnison, Sandyford, Newcastle-on-Tyne; two *d.* *Educ.:* University of Durham; St. Bartholomew's Hospital. House Surgeon, Royal Infirmary, Newcastle-on-Tyne; Southport Infirmary, Lancashire; Resident Medical Officer, Newcastle-on-Tyne Dispensary; Hon. Assistant Surgeon, Royal Infirmary, and Hon. Surgeon, Royal Victoria Infirmary, Newcastle-on-Tyne; Professor of Surgery, University of Durham College of Medicine. *Publications:* A Method of treating Damaged Intestine without Resection; Case of Subcortical Cerebral Tumour, tuberculous in nature, removed by operation, recovery, The Lancet, March 8, 1913. *Recreations:* fishing, shooting, golf. *Address:* 5 Eslington Road, Newcastle-on-Tyne. *T.:* 373 Jesmond.
(*Died 4 Oct. 1927.*)

ANGUS, Richard Bladworth, Director, Bank of Montreal and Canadian Pacific Railway; *b.* 28 May 1831; went to Canada, 1857; General Manager, Bank of Montreal, 1869-79. *Address:* 240 Drummond Street, Montreal.
(*Died 17 Sept. 1922.*)

ANNALY, 3rd Baron (*cr.* 1868), **Luke White;** G.C.V.O., *cr.* 1917; K.C.V.O., *cr.* 1912; C.V.O. 1908; D.L.; Hon. Col. Northants Yeomanry; M.F.H. Pytchley, 1902-14; *b.* 25 Feb. 1857; *S.* father 1888; *m.* Hon. Lilah Georgiana Augusta Constance Agar-Ellis, *d.* of 3rd Viscount Clifden, 1884; one *s.* two *d.*; formerly Capt. Scots Guards; Permanent Lord-in-Waiting to the King; served in Egyptian Campaign, 1882. *Heir:* *s.* Hon. Luke Henry White. *Address:* 43 Berkeley Square, W.; *T.:* Gerrard 3768; Holdenby House, Northampton. *Clubs:* Turf, Marlborough. (*Died 15 Dec. 1922.*)

ANNANDALE, (Thomas) Nelson, C.I.E. 1923; B.A. (Oxon.), D.Sc. (Edin.), F.L.S.; corresponding member of the Zoological Society of London, and the Natural History Society of Saratow; Fellow of the Asiatic Society of Bengal; Director of the Zoological Survey of India, 1916; Superintendent of the Indian Museum and Secretary to the Trustees 1906-1916; President, Asiatic Society of Bengal; *e. s.* of late Prof. Thomas Annandale, F.R.C.S.; unmarried. *Educ.:* Rugby; Edinburgh University; Balliol College, Oxford. Travelled in the Malay Peninsula, 1899, 1901-2, and 1916; Research Fellow in Anthropology in the University of Edinburgh, 1902-4; Deputy Super-

intendent of the Indian Museum, 1904; investigated the fauna of the Sea of Galilee, 1912. *Publications:* The Faroes and Iceland: Studies in Island Life, 1905; with other authors, Fasciculi Malayenses, Zoology and Anthropology, 1903; many papers on zoological and anthropological subjects in scientific periodicals; has edited the Records and the Memoirs of the Indian Museum since their foundation in 1907, and also The Indian Museum: 1814-1914, 1914. *Recreation:* travelling and Official Correspondence. *Address:* Indian Museum, Calcutta. *Clubs:* Royal Societies; Bengal United Service, Calcutta. (*Died 10 April 1924.*)

ANNESLEY, Lt.-Col. James Howard Adolphus, C.M.G. 1917; D.S.O. 1900; *cousin* of 5th Earl Annesley; *b.* 3 Mar. 1868; *s.* of Capt. F. C. Annesley, 28th Rgt.; *m.* Hélène Marie, *d.* of late C. E. Johnston. *Educ.:* Eastman's Royal Naval Academy. Joined 15th Hussars, 1893; served as A.D.C. to G.O.C. Tirah Field Force through the expedition, 1897-98 (despatches, medal with two clasps); Adjutant of Bethune's Mounted Infantry from beginning of Boer War, 1899 (D.S.O.), and on the Staff (despatches, Queen's medal and six clasps, King's medal and two clasps). *Clubs:* Army and Navy, Cavalry. (*Died 22 April 1919.*)

ANNINGSON, Bushell, M.D., M.A., M.R.C.S.; Lecturer in Medical Jurisprudence, Cambridge University, since 1884; Medical Officer of Health for Districts in Cambridgeshire, Herts, and Hunts; Examiner in Sanitary Science, Birmingham and Cambridge; Fellow and Member of Council, Royal Sanitary Institute. *Educ.:* King's College, London; Caius College, Cambridge. *Publications:* Evolution of Human Communities in Relation to Disease; Origin and Progress of Sanitary Endeavour; etc. *Address:* Walt-hamsall, Barton Road, Cambridge. *T.:* 0393. (*Died 19 July 1916.*)

ANSCOMB, Major Allen-Mellers, I.S.O. 1911, V.D. 1898, K.I.H. 1904; Government (India) Civil pensioner; Municipal Commissioner, Quetta; Commandant of the Baluchistan Rifles, Indian Defence Force; *b.* 27 Feb. 1849; *s.* of late John Anscomb, of Appleby, Derbyshire; *m.* 1885, Alice, *d.* of late Alfred Booth, of Horninglow, Staffordshire. *Educ.:* Appleby Grammar School. Joined Indian Uncovenanted Civil Service, 1875; has served in Baluchistan since 1881; raised the Baluchistan Volunteer Rifle Corps, 1883, and was its Commandant for more than 20 years; Kaisar-i-Hind Medal, 1904; Treasury Officer at Quetta, 1892-96; and City Magistrate, Quetta, 1896-1911; selected to represent the Baluchistan Volunteers at Coronation of King George V. in London, 1911. *Address:* Quetta, Baluchistan. *Club:* Junior Army and Navy.

ANSELL, William James David, I.S.O. 1907; Chief Collector of Customs and Excise and Superintendent of Ports, Cyprus, since 1898; *b.* 19 May 1858. Assistant Superintendent Larnaca Port, Cyprus, 1880-81; Deputy Harbourmaster, 1881-2; Government and Municipal Inspector Weights and Measures, 1892-98; Assistant Collector Customs and Excise, 1894-96; has passed examination in Modern Greek. *Educ.:* St. Martin's, Jersey. *Address:* Larnaca, Cyprus. (*Died 16 June 1920.*)

ANSON, Major-General Sir Archibald Edward Harbord, K.C.M.G.; *cr.* 1882; R.A., retired; J.P. Sussex; *b.* London, 1826; *s.* of Gen. Sir William Anson, Bt., K.C.B.; *m.* 1st, 1851, Elizabeth (*d.* 1891), *d.* of Richard Bourchier; one *s.* one *d.*; 2nd, 1906, Isabelle Jane (*d.* 1923), *d.* of Robert Armitstead of Dunscar, Lancs. R.A. 1844; R.H.A. 1848; employed in right and left siege trains in Crimea in the bombardments of 6 and 18 June 1855; Inspector-General of Police, Mauritius, 1858-67; employed Mission to the King of Madagascar,

25

1862 ; Lieut.-Governor. Penang, 1867 ; Administrator of Government of the Straits Settlements, 1871-72, 1877, 1879 ; had charge of Expedition in Sungie Ujong, and Negri Sambilan, Malay Peninsula, 1875-76. *Publications :* About Others and Myself, 1745-1920, 1920. *Recreations :* horticulture, carpentry, and other works. *Address :* Southfield, Silverhill, St. Leonards-on-Sea.   *(Died 26 Feb. 1925.)*

ANSON, Hon. Frederic (William), J.P. ; 4th *s.* of 2nd Earl of Lichfield ; *b.* 4 Feb. 1862 ; *m.* 1st, 1886, Florence Louisa Jane (*d.* 1908), *d.* of Lieut.-Col. John Henry Bagot Lane of Kings Bromley, Staffordshire ; two *s.* three *d.* ; 2nd, 1915, Edith, *d.* of E. S. Rowland, Bramlyns, Horsham. Director London and South-Western Bank, Ltd. *Address :* 8 Pall Mall, S.W. ; *T. :* Gerrard 3652 ; Cell Barnes, St. Albans. *Club :* Arthur's.   *(Died 2 April 1917.)*

ANSON, Sir John Henry Algernon, 5th Bt. ; *cr.* 1831 ; Sub-Lieutenant R.N. ; *b.* 13 Jan. 1897 ; *s.* of late Rear-Adm. Algernon Horatio Anson, 4th *s.* of 2nd Bt., and Hon. Adela Vernon, *d.* of 6th Baron Vernon ; *S.* cousin 1914. *Heir :* *b.* Edward Reynell, *b.* 31 Jan. 1902.
     (Died 10 Mar. 1918.)

ANSTEY, Percy, B.Sc. (Econ.) London ; Principal of the Sydenham College of Commerce and Economics, Bombay, since 1914 ; *s.* of Captain Adolph Page, 2nd Queen's Regiment, and Mary, *e. d.* of Alexander Anstey, whose name he took by deed-poll ; *b.* Paris, 25 Feb. 1876 ; *m.* 1913, Vera, *d.* of James Powell, Reigate ; two *s.* one *d. Educ. :* Felsted ; St. Paul's School ;. Vienna University ; London School of Economics. After studying abroad, joined the stage in 1898, and acted till 1906 with Forbes Robertson, the German Theatre in London, Tree, Martin Harvey, etc. ; studied at London School of Economics, 1906-10 ; a Lecturer on Economics, Sheffield University, 1910-11 ; Head of Economics Department, Bristol University, 1911-14 ; elected first Chairman of the Indian Economic Association, 1914. *Publication :* The Abuse of the Psychological Method in Sociology. *Recreations :* tennis, mountaineering. *Address :* Dungarsi Road, Malabar Hill, Bombay. *Clubs :* Bombay Yacht, Orient, Bombay.   *(Died 23 Nov. 1920.)*

ANSTICE, Lieut.-Col. and Hon. Col. Sir Robert Henry, K.C.B. *cr.* 1910 ; *b.* 17 Aug. 1843 ; *s.* of late J. Anstice, Madeley Wood Hall, Shropshire. *Educ. :* Rugby ; St. Leonards-on-Sea ; Oxford (M.A.). Ensign 29th Regt. 1866 ; Lieut., 1869 ; Captain, 1879 ; exchanged to 55th (2nd Batt. Border Regt.), 1881 ; Major, half-pay, 1885 ; Adjutant, 1st Aberdeenshire Royal Engineers (Volunteers), 1884 ; placed on retired pay, 1889 ; Commanding 1st Aberdeenshire Royal Engineers (Volunteers), 1891-1904 ; Hon. Colonel, Highland Division, R.E. (Terr.), 1914. *Address :* Norfolk Hotel. Brighton. *Clubs :* Junior United Service, Junior Army and Navy.   *(Died 9 April 1922.)*

ANSTIE, James, K.C. 1882 ; *b.* 1836 ; *m.* 1867, Sarah, *d.* of Lindsey Winterbotham. Called to Bar, Lincoln's Inn, 1859, Bencher; holds Certificate of Honour. *Address :* Millandreath, 87 Southbourne Road, Stourwood, Bournemouth.   *(Died Oct. 1924.)*

ANSTRUTHER, Colonel Charles Frederick St. Clair, M.V.O. 1905 ; D.S.O. 1900 ; J.P., D.L. Fife ; Officer of Legion of Honneur ; Knight Commander of the Sword of Sweden ; Knight Commander of Isabel la Catolica ; Esquire of St. John of Jerusalem ; *b.* 6 May 1855 ; *e. surv. s.* of John Anstruther-Thomson of Charleton, Fife ; *m.* 1882, Agnes, 3rd *d.* of late James A. Guthrie of Craigie ; one *d.* Entered army, 1874 ; Major, 1895 ; served South Africa, 1899-1900 (despatches, medals, 6 clasps, D.S.O.) ; commanded 2nd Life Guards ; retired, 1907. *Address :* Charleton, Fife ; Rutland House, Rutland Gardens, S.W.7. *T. :* Kensington 3152.

Clubs : Bachelors', Travellers'; New, Edinburgh.   *(Died 21 Oct. 1925.)*

ANSTRUTHER, Henry Torrens, member of the Administrative Council Suez Canal Co. since 1903; J. P. Co. Bucks and Co. Fife ; Alderman, L.C.C., 1905-10 ; 2nd *s.* of Sir Robert Anstruther, 5th Bt., M.P. ; Director of the North British R. Co., 1900-23 ; *b.* 1860 ; *m.* 1889, H on. Eva I. H. Hanbury-Tracy ; one *s.* one *d. Educ. :* Eton; Edinburgh University. Advocate, Eton ; Edinburgh University. Advocate, Edinburgh, 1884 ; M.P. (L.U.) St. Andrews District, 1886-1903 ; a Lord of the Treasury, 1895-1903. *Address :* Old Court House, Whitchurch, Aylesbury. *Club :* Brooks's.
     (Died 5 April 1926.)

ANSTRUTHER, Sir Windham Frederick Carmichael-, 11th Bt., *cr.* 1694 and 1798 ; Hereditary Carver to Royal Household in Scotland ; one of the Hereditary Masters of the Household for Scotland ; *b.* 30 April 1902 ; *S.* father, 1903 ; *s.* of 10th Bt. and Sylvia, *d.* of late Right Hon. Sir Frederick Darley, G.C.M.G., P.C. [she married 2nd, 1905, late Maj. Hon. A. H. C. Hanbury-Tracy]; *m.* 1925, Katharine Mary, *d.* of late D. A. Neilson, of Westbridge House, Pontefract, Yorks. *Heir :* *c.* Windham Eric Francis, *b.* 1900. *Address :* Carmichael House, Thankerton R.S.O., Scotland ; 66 Upper Berkeley Street, W.1.
     (Died 29 Nov. 1928.)

ANTHONISZ, James Oliver, C.M.G. 1914 ; retired from Civil Service, Straits Settlements, 1914 ; *b.* Galle, Ceylon, 15 Jan. 1860 ; 2nd *s.* of late James Edmund and Eliza Sarah Caroline Anthonisz ; *m.* 1894, Florence Lowndes ; three *d. Educ. :* Ceylon ; St. John's College, Cambridge ; B.A. Math. Tripos, 1882. Cadet, Straits Settlements Civil Service, 1883 ; Magistrate, Singapore ; Official Assignee, S.S. ; District Judge, Singapore ; President, Singapore Municipality ; Colonial Treasurer, Straits Settlements ; Acting Resident Councillor, Penang ; Acting British Resident, Selangor ; the currency of the Colony was placed on a gold basis during tenure of office as Treasurer ; President of a Commission to enquire into the working of the Municipalities of the Colony, 1910. *Recreation :* golf. *Address :* The Cottage, Dynevor Road, Richmond.   *(Died 28 May 1921.)*

ANTRIM, 11th Earl of (*cr.* 1620), **William Randal M'Donnell** ; Viscount Dunluce, 1785 ; *b.* 8 Jan. 1851 ; *S.* father 1869 ; *m.* 1875, Louisa Jane, V.A., *d.* of late Gen. Hon. Charles Grey, Lady of the Bedchamber to the Queen ; two *s.* one *d.* Owns about $35,000 acres. *Heir :* *s.* Viscount Dunluce. *Address :* Glenarm, Castle, Larne, Antrim.   *(Died 19 July 1918.)*

ANTROBUS, John Coutts, J.P. ; *e. s.* of Gibbs Crawfurd Antrobus and 1st wife Jane, 2nd *d.* of Sir Coutts Trotter, 1st Bart. ; *b.* 1829 ; *m.* 1st, 1855, Frances (*d.* 1863), 2nd *d.* of late Clement Swetenham, of Somerford Booths, Cheshire, one *s.* three *d.* ; 2nd, 1865, Mary Caroline (*d.* 1872), *d.* of late Geoffrey Joseph Shakerley, three *s.* one *d.* ; 3rd, 1875, Mary Egidia, *y. d.* of late Gen. Hon. Sir James Lindsay, K.C.M.G. ; four *s.* one *d. Educ. :* Eton ; St. John's College, Cambridge ; M.A. Called to Bar, Lincoln's Inn, 1857 ; High Sheriff, Cheshire, 1868 ; patron of two livings ; Hon. Lieut.-Col. retired, Earl of Chester's Yeomanry Cavalry. *Address :* Eaton Hall, Congleton. *Club :* United University.   *(Died 19 Dec. 1916.)*

APLIN, Col. Philip John Hanham, D.S.O. 1904 ; *b.* 18 Dec. 1858 ; *m.* 1st, 1905, Mary Bertha, *d.* of Brig.-Surg. C. F. Oldham of The Lodge, Gt. Bealings ; one *s.* one *d.* ; 2nd, 1920, Martha Lyon, *d.* of late George Edward Barnard. *Educ. :* Sherborne School. Entered army, 1878 ; Capt. 1889 ; Major, 1898 ; Lt.-Col. 1904 ; served Afghanistan, 1879-80 (medal) ; Burmah, 1885-89 (medal with two clasps) ; East

Africa, 1904 (despatches, D.S.O.) ; retired, 1919.
(Died 10 May 1927.)

APPERLEY, Newton Wynne, M.V.O., 1908 ; Private Secretary to successive Marquises of Londonderry since 1879, including three years' service as Assist. Private Secretary to the 6th Marquis as Lord-Lieut. of Ireland 1886-89 ; J.P. Co. Durham ; Chairman Durham (County) Petty Sessional Division, and Chairman of Visiting Justices ; Member of Standing Joint Committee ; *b.* Australia, 29 July 1846 ; 4th *s.* of Col. W. W. Apperley (4th Bengal Cavalry) of Morben, Machynlleth, Montgomeryshire, N. Wales, and of Esther, *d.* of Brig.-Gen. Wallace, killed at Ferozeshah ; *m.* 1880, Mary, *o. d.* of A. W. Hutchinson of Hollingside, Durham ; two *s.* three *d. Educ.* : Dr. Huntingford's School, Eagle House, Hammersmith ; Rev. F. Faithfull's, Headley Rectory, near Epsom. Cornet in the Montgomeryshire Yeomanry Cavalry, 1868 ; served in it twenty years, and retired with the rank of Major. *Publications :* The Nimrod Game Book ; Sport in Wales Thirty Years Ago ; An Old Coaching Road ; Various Hunting Diaries ; etc. *Recreations :* hunting and shooting. *Address :* South End, Durham. *T.A. :* Durham. *T. :* Durham No. 284. *Club :* Junior Constitutional ; County, Durham. *(Died 21 Jan. 1925.)*

APPLEGARTH, Robert ; M.I.E.E. ; retired from business after an interesting career as a Trade Unionist, and as Agent for Submarine and Mining Engineers ; *b.* Kingston-on-Hull, 26 Jan. 1834 ; *s.* of a mariner, who afterwards went as quartermaster on the "Terror" to the North Polar regions. Received but a scanty education ; at 19 was in Sheffield, the next year, 1854, went to the U.S.A., and spent some time at Galesburg, Knox County, Illinois ; his spare time, both in the U.S.A. and afterwards in Manchester and Sheffield, was spent in self-education ; led early to study economic and industrial questions, with special regard to the condition of workmen in those days. Member of the Amalgamated Society of Carpenters and Joiners from the first ; General Secretary, 1862-71 ; member of the Sheffield No. 1 Branch of the A.S.C. and Joiners ; politician and reformer, and promoter of popular education ; took up electric lighting ; was member of the Royal Commission of Inquiry into the C.D. Acts, the first workman so appointed ; member of the Reform League, of the London General Council of the International Working Men's Association of the London Chamber of Commerce, and a delegate to the International Congress at Basle in 1869 ; was war correspondent in the Franco-Prussian War, 1870 (Sheffield Independent, the Scotsman, and the New York World). *Publications :* Letters to the Sheffield Independent in 1869, on Schools in Switzerland. *Recreation :* work, more work, and still again more. *Address :* 23 Parchmore Road, Thornton Heath, Surrey. *Club :* National Liberal. *(Died 13 July 1924.)*

ARBER, Edward Alexander Newell, M.A., Sc.D., F.L.S., F.G.S. ; Demonstrator in Palæobotany in the Univ. of Cambridge since 1899 ; Hon. Member New Zealand Institute ; *b.* 5 Aug. 1870 ; *e. s.* of late Professor Edward Arber, D.Litt. ; *m.* 1909, Agnes, *d.* of H. R. Robertson ; one *d. Educ. :* King Edward's High School, Birmingham ; Trinity College, Cambridge. *Publications :* Monograph of the Glossopteris Flora (British Museum Catalogue) ; Plant Life in Alpine Switzerland ; The Natural History of Coal ; The Coast Scenery of North Devon ; author or joint-author of numerous botanical papers contributed to various scientific journals. *Recreations :* gardening, music, and photography. *Address :* The Sedgwick Museum, and 52 Huntingdon Road, Cambridge. *(Died 14 June 1918.)*

ARBUTHNOT, Charles George, M.A., Director of Bank of England ; *b.* Oct. 1846 ; *s.* of

John Alves Arbuthnot, of Coworth Park, Berks. *Educ. :* Eton ; Merton College, Oxford. After leaving Oxford, travelled abroad, and has since been mainly occupied in banking house of Messrs. Arbuthnot, Latham & Co., of which he has been a partner for many years. *Address :* 69 Eaton Square, S.W.1. *T. :* Victoria 2933. *Clubs :* Athenæum, Carlton, Wellington, Burlington Fine Arts. *(Died 27 Sept. 1928.)*

ARBUTHNOT, Ven. George, D.D. ; Archdeacon of Coventry since 1908 ; *b.* 24 May 1846 ; *s.* of George Clerk Arbuthnot of Mavisbank, Midlothian ; *m.* 1885, Margaret Evelyn, *e. d.* of Very Rev. H. M. Luckock, late Dean or Lichfield. *Educ. :* Eton ; Christ Church, Oxford (M.A.). Read with Dr. Vaughan at the Temple ; ordained to the Curacy of Arundel, Sussex, 1872 ; Vicar, 1873 ; Vicar of Stratford-on-Avon, 1879 ; Surrogate for the Diocese of Worcester, 1883 ; Proctor for the Clergy in Convocation, 1906. *Publications :* The Passion of Christ ; A Plain Guide to Holy Communion ; Sermons on Disestablishment, etc. ; Editor Shakespeare Sermons. *Recreation :* travelling. *Address :* Comyn House, Leamington. *T. :* 121 Leamington. *Club :* United University. *(Died 9 Nov. 1922.)*

ARBUTHNOT, Gerald Archibald ; *b.* 19 Dec. 1872 ; *o. s.* of late Major-General William Arbuthnot, 14th Hussars, and Selina, 7th *d.* of Sir Thomas Moncreiffe, 7th Bart. of Moncreiffe ; *m.* 1894, Dulce Johanna, *d.* of late Charles Oppenheim, 40 Great Cumberland Place, W. ; three *d. Educ. :* privately ; H.M.S. Britannia. Left Navy, 1892 ; Private Secretary to Rt. Hon. Walter H. Long, M.P., 1894 ; served in that capacity during Unionist governments of 1895 and 1900 at the Board of Agriculture, Local Government Board, and Irish Office ; contested Burnley, 1906 ; Vice-Chairman Budget Protest League, 1909 ; Chairman of the Lancashire and Cheshire Federation of Junior Unionist Associations ; M.P. (U.) Burnley, 1910 ; Vice-Chancellor, Primrose League, 1912. *Publications :* various magazine and newspaper articles. *Recreations :* mountaineering and golf. *Address :* 43 Princes Gardens, S.W. *T. :* 60 Western. *Club :* Carlton. *(Died Sept. 1916.)*

ARBUTHNOT, Major-Gen. Henry Thomas, C.B. 1907 ; Royal Artillery, retired ; *b.* 16 Oct. 1834 ; *s.* of George Arbuthnot, Assist. Secretary H.M.'s Treasury ; *m.* 1862, Anna Jane (d. 1909), *d.* of B. H. Mowbray of Surbiton, Surrey ; one *s. Educ. :* Royal Military Academy, Woolwich. Joined Royal Regiment of Artillery as 2nd Lieut., 1853 ; served Crimean War, 1854-56, including affair of Mackenzie Farm, Repulse of Sortie, 26 Oct. 1854, Battles of Alma and Inkerman and Siege and Fall of Sebastopol (medal and clasps for Alma, Inkerman, and Sebastopol, Knight of Legion of Honour, Turkish medal) ; Indian Mutiny, 1857-59, Action of Secundra, Siege and Capture of Lucknow, Capture of forts Rehara and Koorlee (despatches, medal and clasp for Lucknow, Brevet-Major) ; Assistant Superintendent Royal Small Arms Factory, Enfield and Birmingham, 1862-72 ; Captain of the Company of Gentlemen Cadets, Royal Military Academy, Woolwich, 1875-79 ; Superintendent Royal Small Arms Factory, Enfield, 1880-87 ; retired with rank of Major-General, 1887 ; Chairman of the Aerial League of the British Empire, 1912 ; J.P. borough of Sutton Coldfield. *Publications :* articles on Military Subjects in Chambers's Encyclopædia. *Address :* Ramsay House, Shooters Hill, S.E.18. *Club :* United Service. *(Died 3 May 1919.)*

ARBUTHNOT, James Woodgate ; *e. surv. s.* of late George Arbuthnot and Maria, *d.* of James Thomas, Madras Civil Service ; *b.* 1848 ; *m.* 1877, Anne Susan Charlotte, *d.* of Sir Charles Jackson, Judge of the High Court of Calcutta. *Educ. :* Eton. Formerly a banker in Madras ; retired, 1884 ; J.P. Surrey. *Address :* Elderslie, near Dorking. *Club :* Athenæum. *(Died 21 Oct. 1927.)*

27

ARBUTHNOT, Robert Edward Vaughan, C.S.I. 1922; Indian Civil Service; Financial Commissioner, Burma, since 1919; *b.* 1871; *s.* of late Rev. Robert Keith Arbuthnot, vicar of St. James, Ratcliff, E.; *m.* 1899, Ethel Mary, *d.* of late Major Charles Wyndham, Bengal Cavalry; one *d. Educ.:* Merchant Taylor's School; St. John's College, Oxford (Scholar). Appointed I.C.S. 1802, and posted to Burma; Acting Secretary to Burma Govt., 1899; Under Secretary to Govt. of India in Revenue and Agricultural Dept., 1900-1904; Revenue Secretary to Burma Govt., 1905-7, and 1910-13; Acting Chief Secretary to Burma Govt., 1913-14; Member Imperial Legislative Council, 1914-15; Commissioner of Settlements, Burma, 1915-19; Member Burma Reforms Committee, 1921. *Publication:* Settlement Report of the Hanthawaddy District, 1910. *Address:* Rangoon; 20 Via de Bardi, Florence, Italy. *Clubs:* Athenæum, East India United Service.
(Died 22 Oct. 1922.)

ARBUTHNOT, Rear-Admiral Sir Robert Keith, 4th Bt.; *cr.* 1882; M.V.O. 1904; R.N.; *b.* 23 March 1864; *m.* 1897, Lina, *d.* of Col. A. C. Maclesy, C.B.; one *d. S.* father 1889. Entered Navy, 1877; Commander, 1897; Captain, 1902; Rear-Admiral, 1912; Rear-Admiral 2nd Battle Squadron, 1913-14. *Heir: b.* Major Dalrymple Arbuthnot, R.F.A.; *b.* 1 April 1867. *Recreations:* motor-cycling, cricket. *Address:* 51 Elsworthy Road, Hampstead, N.W. *Clubs:* Travellers', Royal Automobile.
(Died 31 May 1916.)

ARBUTHNOTT, 12th Viscount (*cr.* 1641), **William Arbuthnott**; Baron Inverbervie, 1641; *b.* 24 Oct. 1849; 4th *s.* of 9th Viscount and Lady Jean Graham Drummond Ogilvy, *d.* of 6th Earl of Airlie; S. *b.* 1914. *Heir: c.* Lt.-Col. W. C. W. Arbuthnott. *Address:* Arbuthnott House, Fordoun, Kincardineshire.
(Died 8 Nov. 1917.)

ARBUTHNOTT, 13th Viscount, *cr.* 1641; **Walter Charles Warner Arbuthnott;** *b.* 2 Oct 1847; *g.s.* of 8th Viscount; S. cousin, 1917; *m.* 1878, Emma Marion Hall, *d.* of Rev. J. H. Parlby; two *s.* two *d. Heir: s.* Hon. John Ogilvy, Master of Arbuthnott [*b.* 15 Sep. 1882; *m.* 1914, Dorothy, *d.* of Adm. Charles L. Oxley, The Hall, Ripon. *Address:* Spotted Lake Ranche, Alberta]. *Address:* Arbuthnott House, Fordoun, Kincardineshire.
(Died 9 Aug. 1920.)

ARBUTHNOTT, John Campbell, C.I.E. 1898; I.C.S., retired; President Assam Legislative Council since 1921; *b.* 6 April 1858; *s.* of late Lieut.-Col. Hon. Hugh Arbuthnott, 3rd *s.* of 8th Viscount Arbuthnott; *m.* 1887, Jeannie, *d.* of Robert Hamilton of Elmhirst, Kent; one *s.* three *d.* Entered Indian Civil Service, 1879; served in Bengal as Assistant-Magistrate and Collector; transferred to Assam, 1883; Deputy Commissioner, 1890; Commissioner, Surma Valley and Hill Districts, Eastern Bengal and Assam, 1905-14; retired 1914; Member of the Legislative Council, Eastern Bengal and Assam; Additional Member Imperial Legislative Council, 1913-14. *Publication:* Report on the Conditions of Tea Garden Labour in the Duars of Bengal, Madras, and Ceylon. *Address:* Shillong, Assam, India.
(Died 20 May 1923.)

ARCH. Joseph, *b.* 10 Nov. 1826; widower; *s.* of a labourer; worked in fields for living; self-educated by reading; founded National Agricultural Union, 1872; after an unsuccessful contest, M.P. (R.) N.W. Norfolk, 1885-86, 1892, 1895-1900. *Address:* The Cottage, Barford, Warwick.
(Died 12 Feb. 1919.)

ARCHAMBEAULT, Hon. Sir Horace, Kt., *cr.* 1914; LL.D., K.C.; Chief-Justice of the Court of King's Bench of the Province of Quebec since 1911; puisne-judge of same court since 1908; Professor of Commercial
28

and Maritime Law at Laval University, Montreal, since 1881; *b.* 6 March 1857; *m.* 1882, Elizabeth, *d.* of Roger Lelievre, Quebec. *Educ.:* L'Assomption College; studied law at Laval University, Quebec (LL.L. (Summa Cum Laude), 1878, LL.D. 1886). Called to bar 1878, and has since practised his profession in Montreal. Called to Legislative Council, 1888; Member of Council of Public Instruction, 1890; Batonnier General of the Bar, Province of Quebec, 1901-1902; Attorney-General, Quebec, 1897-1905; and Speaker of the Legislative Council, 1897-1908. Roman Catholic: Liberal. *Address:* Quebec. *(Died 26 Aug. 1918.)*

ARCHDALE, Rt. Hon. Edward, P.C. 1913, J.P., H.M. Lieutenant for Co. Tyrone; head of the Archdale family; landowner; *b.* 22 March 1850, *s.* of Rev. Henry Montgomery Archdale, and Sarah, *d.* of Blackwood Price of Saintfield House, Co. Down; *m.* 1908, Elizabeth, *d.* of late Nicholas Harwood, H.M. Dockyard, Pembroke, and widow of Captain Wingfield Clark, Leicestershire regiment; no *c. Educ.:* Marlborough College; Keble College, Oxford; B.A. 1871. Civil Engineer; engaged in submarine cable laying in various parts of the world up to 1880; succeeded his uncle the late William H. Mervyn Archdale, 1899; High Sheriff, Co. Fermanagh, 1902; Co. Tyrone, 1906; Foreman of Co. Fermanagh Grand Jury; a Liberal in politics. *Recreations:* riding, yachting, shooting, motoring, croquet, billiards, golf. *Address:* Castle Archdale, Irvinestown. *M.:* I.L. 122. *Clubs:* Fermanagh Co.; Tyrone Co. Club. *(Died 4 July 1916.)*

ARCHDALE, Brig.-Gen. Hugh James, C.B., 1902; C.M.G. 1918; Royal Welsh Fusiliers and Lincolnshire Regt.; *b.* 15 Jan. 1854; 2nd *s.* of late Capt. Mervyn Edward Archdale; *m.* 1st, Minnie (*d.* 1888), *e. d.* of Capt. Hugh Montgomery Archdale, late 52nd Light Infantry; 2nd, 1894, Helen Evelyn Trevor, *e. d.* of Captain B. T. Griffith Boscawen of Trevalyn Hall, Rossett, N. Wales; one *d. Educ.:* Cheltenham College. Entered army, 1875; Captain, 1885; Major, 1892; Lieut.-Col. 1900; Col. 1904: served Soudan, 1884-85 (medal with clasp, Khedive's star); Burmah, 1886-87, with 1st Batt. Royal Welsh Fusiliers (medal with clasp); Crete, 1897-98, with 2nd Batt. Royal Welsh Fusiliers; South Africa (despatches, Queen's medal, 5 clasps, King's medal, 2 clasps, C.B.), 1899-1902; Commandant, Imperial Yeomanry Discharge Depot, Aldershot, 1908; Commanding a Division, 1907-11; retired, 1911. *Club:* Naval and Military.
(Died 31 Aug. 1921.)

ARCHDALE, Major Theodore Montgomery, D.S.O. 1900; R.F.A.; *b.* 24 Sep. 1873; *y. s.* of late Nicholas Montgomery Archdale of Crock na Crieve, Co. Fermanagh; *m.* 1901, Helen Alexander, *d.* of late Alexander Russel. Entered R.A., 1894; served South Africa (despatches, D.S.O.); European War, 1914-15 (despatches, wounded). *Address:* c/o Cox and Co., Charing Cross, S.W. *Club:* Army and Navy.
(Died 10 Oct. 1918.)

ARCHDALE, Rev. Thomas Hewan, Hon. Canon of Durham. *Address:* Tanfield Vicarage, Tantobie, Durham.
(Died 23 June 1924.)

ARCHER, Major Henry, D.S.O. 1917; R.F.A.; Brigade-Major, Royal Artillery, 51st Division, B.E.F.; *b.* 17 April 1883; *s.* of H. C. Archer, Cenis Lodge, Wimbledon, S.W.; *m.* Sybil Mary, *d.* of late Rev. A. H. Cooke of Quethiock; one *d. Educ.:* Oundle; Royal Military Academy, Woolwich. Commissioned, 1902; 1st Lieut., 1905; Captain, 1914; Major, 1916; joined 128th Battery R.F.A. on first commission; served in 128th Battery six years; Adjutant 4th East Lancs Brigade R.F.A. 1909-13; joined 126th Battery R.F.A. on outbreak of war; commanded 125th Battery R.F.A. Sep. 1915-

Feb. 1917; served continuously in France since Aug. 1914 (D.S.O.). *Recreations:* hunting, golf. *Address:* Cox & Co., 16 Charing Cross, S.W.1. *Club:* Junior Army and Navy.
(*Died 17 Dec. 1917.*)

ARCHER, Walter E., C.B. 1911; F.R.S.E.; Assistant Secretary Board of Agriculture and Fisheries, 1903-12; *b.* 4 July 1855; *s.* of late Captain Clement R. Archer, 4th Dragoon Guards; *m.* 1878, Alice Lina, *d.* of late Robert Hay Murray, Spinfield, Bucks; three *s.*, three *d. Educ.:* Eton. Engaged in salmon research, 1884-92; for this purpose acquired entire control of two rivers and intervening sea-coast in Norway; publicly thanked in 1890 for improvement effected in economic condition of the Norwegian fishermen in the county of Stavanger; Inspector of Salmon Fisheries for Scotland, 1892-98; Chief Inspector of Fisheries to the Board of Trade, 1898-1903; British Delegate to the International Conference for the Investigation of the Sea, 1899; Member of the Royal Commission appointed to inquire into the Salmon Fisheries of Great Britain, 1900-1902; Member of the Tethyological Research Committee, 1901; British Delegate to the International Council for the study of the sea since 1904; President of that Council since 1908; Fellow, Statistical Society, London. *Publications:* Salmon Fishery Reports of the Fishery Board for Scotland, 1892-98; Sea and Salmon Fishery Reports of England and Wales since 1898. *Recreations:* fishing and yachting. *Address:* 17 Sloane Court, S.W.; Sand, Stavanger, Norway. *T.:* 3592 Vic. *Club:* Union.
(*Died 19 Aug. 1917.*)

ARCHER, William; *b.* Perth, Scotland, 23 Sep. 1856; *s.* of Thomas Archer, C.M.G., of Gracemere, Queensland, formerly Agent-General for Queensland in London. *Educ.:* Edinburgh University (M.A.). Barr. Middle Temple, 1883; journalism, in Edinburgh, 1875; travelled in Australia, 1876-77; came to London, 1878; dramatic critic of London Figaro, 1879-81; travelled in Italy, 1881-82; dramatic critic of World, 1884-1905; afterwards of the Tribune, the Nation, and of the Star. *Publications:* edited Ibsen's Prose Dramas, 5 vols., and Collected Works of Ibsen, 11 vols.; translated with his brother, Lt.-Col. Charles Archer, Ibsen's Peer Gynt; wrote Life of Macready; Masks or Faces: a Study in the Psychology of Acting; The Theatrical World, 1893-97, 5 vols.; Study and Stage, a Yearbook of Criticism, 1899; America To-day, 1900; Poets of the Younger Generation, 1901; Real Conversations, 1904; Through Afro-America, 1910; The Life, Trial, and Death of Francisco Ferrer, 1911; Play-making, 1912; The Great Analysis, 1912; The Thirteen Days, 1915; 501 Gems of German Thought, 1917; God and Mr. Wells, 1917; India and the Future, 1917; The Peace President, 1918; War is War (a drama), 1919; The Green Goddess (a drama), 1921; The Old Drama and the New, 1923; *with H. Granville Barker, A National Theatre Scheme and Estimates, 1907. *Address:* 27 Fitzroy Square, W.1. *T.:* Museum 664. *Club:* Reform.
(*Died 27 Dec. 1924.*)

ARCHIBALD, Very Rev. John, M.A., Canon of Inverness Cathedral since 1894; Rector of Trinity Episcopal Church, Keith, 1876-1912; *b.* Musselburgh, Midlothian; *m.* Miss Boyd, of Peterhead. *Educ.:* University of Aberdeen; Trinity College, Glenalmond. Ordained Deacon, 1870; Priest, 1871; Curate, St. John's Church, Darwen, Lancs; Incumbent, St. John's Church, Wick; Dean of the United Diocese of Moray, Ross, and Caithness, 1902-12; Synod Clerk Moray Diocese. *Publications:* History of the Episcopal Church at Keith in 17th, 18th and 19th Centuries, 1889; Historic Episcopate in Columbian Church and Diocese of Moray, 1892; A Ten Years' Conflict, 1907. *Address:* Northfield, Worcestershire.
(*Died 10 Sept. 1916.*)

ARCHIBALD, Sir William Frederick Alphonse, Kt. *cr.* 1917; M.A., F.S.S.; Barrister-at-Law; *b.* 1846; *g.s.* of late Hon. S. G. W. Archibald, LL.D., Master of the Rolls and Speaker of the House of Assembly, Nova Scotia, and *s.* of late Hon. Sir Thomas Dickson Archibald, one of the Judges of the Court of Queen's Bench and afterwards of the Common Pleas Division of the High Court; *m.* 1873, Florence, *d.* of late C. W. H. Wallroth of Lee, Kent; four *s.* three *d. Educ.:* Repton School; St. John's College, Oxford (Fereday Fellow); Civil Engineer; was Assoc. Inst. C.E.; Underground Surveyor of the Metropolitan Board of Works, employed on the Drainage of London; called to the Bar, 1874; Master of the Supreme Court, King's Bench Division, 1890-1916; Chairman of the Royal National Mission to Deep Sea Fishermen; late Hon. Treasurer of the Religious Tract Society, etc.; late Chairman of the Scrivenery Board R.C.J.; late Chairman of the London Prescribed Officers under the Poor Persons Rules, 1914; Board of Trade nominated member of the Committee of the Seamen's National Insurance Society. *Publications:* Practice at Judge's Chambers; The Country Solicitor's Practice; Joint-Author of Archibald's Metropolitan Police Guide issued by the Home Office and Editor of Brom's Common Law; Editor of Articles on Courts and Interpleader in the Laws of England. *Address:* Moorside, Hindhead, Surrey. *T.:* Hindhead 53; Royal Courts of Justice, W.C. *T.A.:* Courts Justice, London. *Club:* Oxford and Cambridge.
(*Died 31 Mar. 1922.*)

ARDEN, Lt.-Col. John Henry Morris, D.S.O. 1915; Worcester Regiment (Reserve of Officers); Commandant, No. 2 R.F.C. Cadet Wing; *b.* 2 Feb. 1875; *s.* of late Rev. A. H. Arden. Entered army, 1897; Captain 1900; retired 1912; Bt. Major, 1915; served South Africa, 1899-1902 (Queen's medal 3 clasps, King's medal 2 clasps); Sudan, 1912 (medal and clasp, 2nd Class Osmanieh); European War, 1914-16 (D.S.O., despatches twice). *Club:* Royal Automobile.
(*Died Aug. 1918.*)

ARDRON, John, C.B., 1906; A.I.E.E.; *s.* of John Ardron of Queniborough, Leicesters.; *b.* 1843; *m.* 1873, *d.* of J. J. Ridge, M.D., Gravesend; Retired Assistant Secretary, G.P.O. Identified with the progress and organisation of the telegraph service of the country since it was taken over from the private electric telegraph companies, 1870; also with telephone and wireless telegraph services; Vice-Chairman, International Telegraph Conference, 1903; Commander of the Danish Order of the Dannebrog. *Address:* "Nordra," Stanmore. *Club:* Stanmore Golf.
(*Died 4 Dec. 1919.*)

ARENBERG, Auguste Louis Alberic, Prince D'; Member of the Institute; *b.* 15 Sep. 1887. President of the Suez Canal Company; Vice-Pres. of the Paris-Orleans Railway Company; Chef des Battalions during War of 1870-71. *Address:* Rue de la Ville-l'Eveque 20, Paris VIIIᵉ; Menetou-Salon, Cher. *Club:* Jockey, Paris.
(*Died 24 Jan. 1924.*)

ARGLES, Rev. Canon George Marsham, Rector of St. Clement's, York, 1871-1919; *b.* 1841; *s.* of late Dr. Argles, Dean of Peterborough; *m.* Mary Ann, *d.* of Thos. Harrison of Singleton Park, Kendal, 1870; three *s.* four *d. Educ.:* Harrow; Balliol Coll. Oxford. 2nd class Final Classical School; Denyer and Johnson Univer.-theological scholar. Curate of Christ Church, Doncaster, 1865-71; Canon of York, 1888; Proctor in Convocation for the Archdeaconry of York, 1896; Examining Chaplain to the Bishop of Peterborough, 1897. *Publication:* Instructions for Confirmation. *Address:* The Old Residence, York; Hawbarrow, Milnthorpe. Westmorland. *T.A.:* York. *T.:* 595 York *M.:* EC 6 and EC 74.
(*Died 22 Feb. 1920.*)

ARKWRIGHT, Frederic Charles, J.P., D.L., Vice-Lieutenant of Derbyshire; Hon. Lt.-Col. Volunteer Force, 1918; *o. s.* of late Frederic Arkwright of Willersley; *b.* 7 Nov. 1853; *m.* 1883, Rebecca Olton, 3rd *d.* of late Sir John G. N. Alleyne, 3rd Bt.; one *s.* one *d. Educ.:* Eton; Christ Church, Oxford. Sheriff, 1887; Capt. 2nd Derbyshire R.V. 1882-87; contested (C.) West Derbyshire, 1885. *Address:* Willersley, Matlock. *T.A.:* Cromford. *T.:* Matlock 75. *Club:* United University.
(Died 18 July 1923.)

ARKWRIGHT, Richard; *b.* 1835; *m.* 1862, Lady Mary Caroline Charlotte Byng, *d.* of 2nd Earl of Strafford. *Educ.:* Harrow; Cambridge (M.A.). Barrister, Oxford Circuit; Revising Barr. for Monmouthshire, Gloucester, and Cheltenham, 1865; M.P. (C.) Leominster, 1866-1875; D.L. Herefordshire. *Publications:* Queen Anne's Gate Mystery; Driven Home. *Address:* Herne House, Windsor. *Club:* Carlton.
(Died 14 Nov. 1918.)

ARKWRIGHT, William; *o. s.* of late Major William Arkwright, 6th Dragoons, and Fanny Susan, 2nd *d.* of Edward Thornewill, of Dovecliff, Co. Stafford; *b.* 21 April, 1857; *m.* 1884, Agnes Mary, *e. d.* of Hon. John J. T. Somers-Cocks. *Educ.:* Eton; Christ Church, Oxford. High Sheriff, Co. Derby, 1890. *Publications:* The Pointer and his Predecessors; Knowledge and Life; The Trend; Utinam. *Address:* Thorn, Knighton, S.O., Plymouth; 28 Brompton Square, S.W. *Club:* White's.
(Died 19 Feb. 1925.)

ARMAGHDALE, 1st Baron, *cr.* 1918; **John Brownlee Lonsdale,** 1st Bt., *cr.* 1911; Lord Lieutenant, Co. Armagh, since 1920; *b.* Armagh, 23 March 1850; *s.* of James Lonsdale, D.L., of Armagh, and Jane, *d.* of William Brownlee; *m.* Florence, *d.* of William Rumney of Stubbins House, Lancashire. High Sheriff, 1895; M.P. (C) Mid Armagh, 1900-18; Hon. Secretary and Whip of the Irish Unionist Party, 1901-16; Chairman until 1918; a Conservative. *Heir:* none. *Address:* 18 Prince's Gardens, S.W.7; The Dunes, Sandwich. *T.:* Kensington 44. *Clubs:* Carlton, Bachelors'.
(Died 8 June 1924.)

ARMITAGE-SMITH, George, D.Lit., M.A. (Lond.); Principal of Birkbeck College, 1896-1918, and Lecturer on Economics and Mental Science; Dean of the Faculty of Economics, University of London, 1904-8; Fellow of the Royal Statistical Society; Member of the Council of the Royal Economic Society. *Publications:* The Citizen of England, 1895; The Free Trade Movement, 1898; Principles and Methods of Taxation, 1906; and numerous articles and reviews on social and economic subjects in magazines, journals, encyclopedias. *Address:* 8 Albert Terrace, Regent's Park, N.W.
(Died 10 Jan. 1923.)

ARMITSTEAD, Rev. John Richard, Vicar of Sandbach, Cheshire, since 1865; Hon. Canon of Chester; *b.* 11 May 1829; *e. s.* of Rev. John Armitstead, Vicar of Sandbach; *m.* 1866, Frances Mary, *e. d.* of W. H. Hornby, M.P. for Blackburn; five *s.* two *d. Educ.:* Westminster; Christ Church, Oxford. Formerly Incumbent of Goostrey, Cheshire; afterwards Rector of Wendlebury, Oxfordshire; Member of Cheshire County Council since 1895; Alderman, Cheshire County Council, 1912. *Recreations:* fond of farming, and outdoor sports generally. *Address:* The Vicarage, Sandbach, Cheshire. *T.A.:* Sandbach. *(Died 19 Sept. 1918.)*

ARMOUR, Rev. James Brown, M.A., Minister Trinity Church, Ballymoney, 1869-1925; *b.* 31 Jan. 1842; *m.* 1883, Jennie Staveley Hamilton, *d.* of Rev. A. M. Staveley, St. John, Canada; three *s. Educ.:* Royal Academical Institution; Queen's Colleges, Belfast and Cork. Took active part in Land, Home Rule and Catholic University controversies; long

30

interested in primary, secondary and university education; sometime Senator, Queen's University, Belfast; Lecturer in Classics, Magee College, Londonderry; Carey Lecturer; Hon. Chaplain to Lord-Lieutenant of Ireland, 1906-1915. *Publications:* articles, including A Presbyterian View, in the New Irish Constitution. *Recreation:* formerly golf. *Address:* Ballymoney, Co. Antrim, Ireland.
(Died Feb. 1928.)

ARMOUR, Jonathan Ogden, Pres. Corporation of Armour & Co., packers; *b.* Milwaukee, 11 Nov. 1863; *s.* of late Philip Danforth Armour; *m.* Lolita Sheldon; one *d. Educ.:* Yale. *Publication:* The Packers and the People, 1906. *Address:* 3724 Michigan Avenue, Chicago. *(Died 16 Aug. 1927.)*

ARMOUR-HANNAY, Samuel Beveridge; Sheriff-Substitute of Fifeshire since 1898; *b.* 4 March 1856; *s.* of John Armour of Kirktonfield, Renfrewshire; *m.* 1899, Robina Anne Marjory, *o. d.* of Colonel George Hannay of Kingsmuir and Dalgairn, Fifeshire. Assumed name of Hannay on wife succeeding to the estate of Kingsmuir. *Educ.:* Madras College, St. Andrews; Edinburgh Academy and University (M.A. 1877). Passed for Scottish Bar, 1880; appointed Sheriff-Substitute of Caithness, Orkney, and Zetland, 1887. *Publication:* Valuation of Property for Rating in Scotland, 1892 (Second Edition, 1912). *Recreations:* golf, shooting, yachting. *Address:* Dalgairn, Cupar, Fife. *(Died 30 Mar. 1919.)*

ARMSTRONG, Sir Andrew Harvey, 3rd Bart.; *cr.* 1841; *b.* 23 May 1866; *s.* of 2nd Bart. and Alice, *d.* of W. W. Fisher; *S.* father 1899. Formerly Capt. 3rd Batt. Leinster Regt. (Royal Canadians); served with Imperial Yeomanry in South Africa; joined 5th Service Batt. The Connaught Rangers, 19 Sep. 1914. *Heir:* b. Nesbitt William [*b.* 8 July 1875; *m.* 1910, Clarice Amy, *d.* of John Carter Hodgkinson, Maryborough, Victoria, Australia; one *s.* one *d.*]. *Address:* Gallen Priory, Ferbane, King's County. *(Died 3 June 1922.)*

ARMSTRONG, Edmund Clarence Richard, M.R.I.A., F.S.A.; Keeper of Irish Antiquities Collections, National Museum, Dublin, since 1914; *b.* 1879; *e. s.* of Captain Andrew Charles Armstrong, 2nd Queen's and 3rd Batt. Leinster Regiment, an Inspector of Factories, 3rd *s.* of Sir Andrew Armstrong, Bt., of Gallen Priory, and Alice Maria, *y. d.* of Sir T. W. C. Murdoch, K.C.M.G., sometime Chief Secretary for Canada; *m.* 1906, Mary Frances, 2nd *d.* of late Sir Francis R. Cruise, M.D., D.L.; two *s.* one *d.* For a short time in business, afterwards temporary assistant to Mr. George Coffey, Keeper of Irish Antiquities, in the National Museum, Dublin; permanent Assistant for Irish Antiquities, 1907; an Honorary General Secretary Royal Society of Antiquaries of Ireland, 1909-15; Vice-President, 1915-19, and since 1921; Honorary Treasurer, 1919-21; Margaret Stokes Lecturer, Alexandra College, 1921; External Examiner in Archaeology, National University of Ireland, 1922; inherited property in Galway and Limerick, which was sold under the Wyndham Act. *Publications:* Numerous papers on Irish Archaeological subjects in Proceedings Royal Irish Academy, and Journal Royal Society of Antiquaries of Ireland, etc. *Address:* 73 Park Avenue, Sydney Parade, Dublin. *Club:* Kildare Street, Dublin.
(Died 29 Mar. 1923.)

ARMSTRONG, Edward, M.A.; F.B.A. 1905; Fellow, Queen's College, Oxford; Hon. Fellow of Exeter College; *b.* 3 Mar. 1846; *s.* of John Armstrong, D.D., first Bishop of Grahamstown, South Africa, and Frances Whitmore; *m.* 1st, Mabel (*d.* 1920), *d.* of J. W. Watson, D.Sc.; 2nd, 1921, Geraldine Prynne, 3rd *d.* of late Rev. J. A. Harriss. *Educ.:* Grahamstown; Bradfield; Exeter College,

Oxford (scholar); first, Class. Mods., 1866; first, Final Litt. Hum., 1869; Fellow, Queen's College, 1869; tutor, 1870; assistant master Rugby School, 1871-73; at Queen's College from 1875 (Bursar, 1878-1911); Pro Provost, 1911-22; Warden of Bradfield College, 1910-25; Lecturer to the University in Foreign History, 1902-4; for the Dante sexcentenary, 1921; Serena Medal, British Academy, 1926. *Publications:* Elisabeth Farnese; The French Wars of Religion; Lorenzo de' Medici; the Emperor Charles V., 2 vols.; has contributed to Cambridge Modern History, Edinburgh, Quarterly, Church Quarterly, English Historical Reviews, History, and other periodicals. *Recreations:* gardening, travelling. *Address:* Queen's College and The Red House, Oxford. *T.:* Oxford 1158. *M.:* FC 8005. *Club:* Athenæum.
(*Died 14 April 1928.*)

ARMSTRONG, Maj.-Gen. Edward Francis Hunter; *b.* 1834; *m.* 1st, Matilda, *d.* of late Major James Fitzgerald, Indian Army; 2nd, Florence (*d.* 1890), *d.* of late Henry Colbeck, Indian Army. Late 11th Madras Native Infantry and Deputy Commissioner, Mysore. *Address:* 31 Clarendon Villas, Hove.
(*Died 2 Jan. 1917.*)

ARMSTRONG, F. A. W. T., R.B.A. 1895; R.W.A.; landscape painter; *b.* Malmesbury, 15 Feb. 1849; *e. s.* of Francis Armstrong of Cannobie, Dumfriesshire, and Elizabeth Ann Leonard of Stonehill, Malmesbury, Wiltshire. *Educ.:* privately. Exhibitor at Paris (Salon), Berlin, Dusseldorf, etc. *Publications:* assisted in illustrating the Edition de Luxe of Mr. Blackmore's Lorna Doone; also Art Journal, Portfolio, etc. etc. *Recreation:* fly fishing. *Address:* 42 St. Michael's Hill, Bristol.
(*Died 1 Dec. 1920.*)

ARMSTRONG, Francis Edwin, M.Sc., Assoc. M.Inst.C.E.; Mining Engineer; Professor of Mining at the Univ. of Sheffield since 1913; *b.* Nottingham, 1879, *s.* of late Rev. R. A. Armstrong, Liverpool; unmarried. *Educ.:* Giggleswick Grammar School; University College, Liverpool. Articled pupil to Arnold Lupton, M.I.C.E., at Tinsley Park Colliery, Sheffield; held several positions as assistant at Midland Collieries; Engineer to the Askern Coal and Iron Co., Ltd., Doncaster, 1910-13; Head of Labour and Wages Section Coal Mines Dept. Board of Trade, 1917-18; Member of Home Office Committee on Miners' Safety Lamps, 1919. *Address:* 40 Elmore Road, Sheffield. *T.:* 4705 Central. *M.:* LU 6695.
(*Died 28 Oct. 1921.*)

ARMSTRONG, Rev. James, Incumbent of Castle Rock since 1868; Canon of Derry since 1900. *Educ.:* Trinity Coll., Dublin. Ordained 1865. *Address:* Castle Rock, Co. Derry.
(*Died 30 April 1928.*)

ARMSTRONG, Surgeon-Dentist John Alexander, C.B.E. 1919; C.M.G. 1918; *b.* 26 Nov. 1862; *s.* of Thomas Armstrong and Jane Beatty; *m.* 1890, Ida G. Spittal (*d.* 1904); one *s.* *Educ.:* Ottawa Collegiate Institute, Ottawa; Royal College of Dental Surgeons and Toronto University, Toronto. Captain, 43rd D.C.O.R., Canada; Chairman Ottawa Public School Board; Member of Ottawa, Canada, Public School Board for ten years; organised the Canadian Army Dental Corps in May 1915, and brought the Corps overseas, June 1915; first Army Dental Corps ever organised; Director of Dental Services, Overseas Military Forces of Canada, 1915-19. *Publications:* several papers at Dental Conventions and in Dental Magazines. *Recreations:* member of several athletic, rowing, and football clubs in Canada; Chairman 43rd D.C.O.R. Rifle Association, 1907-14. *Address:* 102 James Street, Ottawa, Canada. *T.:* Queen 7940. *Clubs:* Overseas Officers, National Liberal, Sports; Laurentian, Wellington, Canadian, Ottawa.
(*Died 2 Nov. 1928.*)

ARMSTRONG, Thomas Mandeville Emerson, Barrister-at-Law, Lincoln's Inn; *b.* 1869; 4th *s.* of late Edward Armstrong and Emma Saunderson of Tanderagee, Co. Armagh; *m.* 1904, Jean, *d.* of Robert M. Young, J.P., Rathvarna, Belfast, and *g. d.* of Rt. Hon. Robert Young, P.C.; four *s.* two *d.* President Insurance Institute of London, 1916; General Manager Commercial Union Assurance Co. since 1920; formerly Manager Ocean Accident Insurance Company, Ltd. *Address:* Limpsfield, Surrey. *T.:* Oxted 5. *Clubs:* Union; Addington and Littlestone Golf. (*Died 21 Aug. 1922.*)

ARMSTRONG, Sir Walter, Kt.; *cr.* 1899; J.P.; Hon. R.H.A.; B.A. Oxon.; *b.* Roxburghshire, 7 Feb. 1850; *s.* of Walter Armstrong, of Ennismore Gardens; *m.* 1873, Emily Rose, *d.* of C. C. Ferard, J.P., of Ascot Place, Berks; two *s.* three *d.* *Educ.:* Harrow; Exeter Coll. Oxford. Art critic on staffs of Pall Mall Gazette, St. James's Gazette, Manchester Guardian, Guardian, Manchester Examiner, 1880-92; Director National Gallery of Ireland, 1892-1914. *Publications:* Life of Alfred Stevens; Life of Peter de Wint; Life of Thos. Gainsborough; Life of Velazquez; Notes on the Nat. Gallery; Scottish Painters; co-editor of Bryan's Dictionary of Painters; Gainsborough and his Place in English Art, 1898; Sir Joshua Reynolds, 1900; J. M. W. Turner, 1901; Sir Henry Raeburn, 1901; Art in Great Britain and Ireland, 1909; Life of Sir Thos. Lawrence, 1913. *Recreations:* photography, golf, etc. *Address:* 63 Carlisle Mansions, S.W. *T.:* Victoria 2206. *Clubs:* Junior Athenæum, Burlington Fine Arts, Cosmopolitan. (*Died 8 Aug. 1918.*)

ARMYTAGE, Sir George John, 6th Bt.; *cr.* 1738; D.L.; F.S.A.; High Sheriff of Yorkshire, 1907-8; Chairman Lancashire and Yorkshire Railway; *b.* 26 April 1842; *s.* of 5th Bt. and Eliza Matilda Mary, *d.* of Sir Joseph Radcliffe, Bt., Rudding Park, Yorks; *S.* father 1899; *m.* 1st, 1871, Ellen (*d.* 1890), *d.* of Rev. A. Fawkes of Farnley Hall, Yorkshire; two *s.* one *d.*; 2nd, 1893, Mary Georgiana, *d.* of late Henry A. Littledale, of Bolton Hall, Yorkshire; Chairman of Council and one of founders of Harleian Society. *Publications:* edited several volumes of Harleian Society's publications. *Recreations:* shooting, golf. Owns about 3500 acres. *Heir: s.* George Ayscough, Brigadier-General [*b.* 2 March 1872; *m.* 1892, Aimée, *d.* of Sir L. M. Swinnerton-Pilkington, 11th Bt.; two *s.* one *d.* *Club:* Carlton]. *Address:* Kirklees Park, Brighouse, Yorks; 27 Cambridge Square, W. *T.A.:* Armytage, Brighouse; Armytage, Edge, London. *T.:* Brighouse 16; Paddington 1391. *Club:* Windham.
(*Died 8 Nov. 1918.*)

ARNAUD, Emile; President of the Ligue Internationale de la Paix et de la Liberté since 1891; Vice-Président du Bureau international permanent de la Paix, de Berne; *b.* 1864, La Chape (Isère), France. Active speaker and writer on behalf of Peace; editor of Les États-Unis d'Europe; President of the 12th International Peace Congress, Rouen, 1903. Has attended all the present series of Congresses which began in 1889. Notaire, Président de la Chambre des Notaires de Pontoise, plusieurs fois Vice-Président du Congrès des Notaires de France, Vice-Président de la Caisse de Retraites des Notaires de France et d'Algérie, Capitaine Commandant une Compagnie du Génie pendant la guerre 1914-17. *Address:* Luzarches, Seine et Oise, France. *T.:* 5. (*Died 11 Dec. 1921.*)

ARNHEIM, Edward Henry Silberstein Von, I.S.O. 1911; late Deputy Master, Royal Mint, Sydney. *Club:* Union, Sydney.
(*Died 25 Nov. 1925.*)

ARNOLD, Edward Vernon, Litt.D.; late Fellow of Trinity College, Cambridge; Professor of Latin at the University College of North Wales, 1884-1924; *s.* of late Rev. C. M. Arnold,

M.A., Vicar of St. Mark's, South Norwood ; *b.* 18 July 1857 ; *m.* 1894, Violet, *d.* of late Lieut.-Col. R. D. Osborn ; three *s.* two *d.* *Educ. :* Westminster School ; Trinity College, Cambridge ; University of Tübingen. 1st class Classical and Mathematical Triposes, 1879. *Publications :* Historical Vedic Grammar, 1897 ; Forum Latinum, a first Latin reading-book, 1899 ; The Rigveda, in D. Nutt's Popular Studies in Folk-lore and Mythology, 1900 ; Vedic Metre, 1905 ; Aeneae facta, a Stepping-stone to Virgil, 1907 ; Cothurnulus, 1907 ; Basis Latina, 1908 ; Roman Stoicism, 1910 ; (with J. W. E. Pearce) Cornelia, 1912 ; War-Time Lectures, 1916 ; The Ferment of Revolution, 1917. *Address :* Bryn Seiriol, Bangor. (*Died 19 Sept. 1926.*)

ARNOLD, George Frederick, I.C.S., C.I.E. 1912 ; Deputy Commissioner, 1st grade, Burma ; *s.* of Dr. G. B. Arnold, Mus.Doc. (Oxon.), of the Close, Winchester. Unmarried. *Educ. :* Merchant Taylors' School ; Queen's College, Oxford (open scholarship) ; 2nd class in Moderations and 1st class in Literæ Humaniores, 1892. Entered Indian Civil Service, 1893 ; was Assistant Secretary and Under Revenue Secretary to Government of Burma, Sessions Judge in Burma, and officiating Deputy Secretary to Government of India Legislative Department, 1906 ; Revenue Secretary to the Government of Burma, 1906-11 ; Member of the Burma Legislative Council, 1909-11. *Publication :* Psychology applied to Legal Evidence and other Constructions of Law. *Recreations :* lawn tennis ; champion of Burma, 1910 and 1911. *Address :* 47 Southgate Street, Winchester. *Clubs :* East India United Service ; United Service, Simla ; Pegu, Rangoon.
(*Died 3 April 1917.*)

ARNOLD, Henry Fraser James Coape-, Commissioner of Land Tax, Warwickshire ; M.A. and member of the Senate of the University of Cambridge ; *b.* 27 Feb. 1846 ; *s.* of James Coape, J.P., of Mirables, Isle of Wight, and Georgeana, *o. d.* and heiress of G. H. Arnold, J.P., of Ashby St. Ledgers, Northamptonshire, and Wolvey Hall, Warwickshire ; *m.* Mary G., *e. d.* of Rev. C. J. Cummings, rector of Cheadle, Cheshire ; five *s.* five *d.* *Educ. :* St. John's College, Cambridge. A co-heir of the abeyant Baronies of de Morley, *cr.* 1299 ; Marshal, 1309 ; and Monteagle, 1514. *Address :* Wolvey Hall, near Hinckley. *T.A. :* Wolvey Hall, Bulkington.
(*Died July 1923.*)

ARNOLD, Rev. Henry James Lawes, M.A., Rector of North Creake since 1911 ; Hon. Canon of Norwich ; *b.* 20 May 1854 ; *s.* of Walter Brown Arnold ; *m.* 1892, Nora, *d.* of Charles Hope of Shorestone Hall, Northumberland. *Educ. :* Pembroke College, Cambridge. Mathematical Honours, 1877 ; Assistant Master at Walton Lodge School ; ordained to Tarporley, Cheshire, 1881 ; curate in charge St. James', Yarmouth, 1887-88 ; Vicar of Dereham, 1888-1911. *Recreations :* rowed in College Boat and played in College Eleven. *Address :* North Creake Rectory, Fakenham. *Club :* Alpine.
(*Died 13 June 1928.*)

ARRHENIUS, Professor Svante August, Dr. phil. juris et med. ; Director of the Physico-Chemical Department of the Nobel Institute since 1905 ; *b.* Wijk, near Upsala, Sweden, 19 Feb. 1859 ; *s.* of the engineer Svante Gustaf Arrhenius and Carolina Thunberg ; *m.* 1st, 1894, Sophia, *d.* of Colonel-Lieutenant Carl Rudbeck ; 2nd, 1905, Maria, *d.* of Curate Johansson ; two *s.* two *d.* *Educ. :* Cathedral School and University, Upsala. Dr. phil. at Upsala University, 1884 ; Privatdocent, 1884 ; Teacher of Physics, University, Stockholm, 1891 ; Professor of Physics at the same University, 1895 ; Rector, 1897-1902 ; Director of the Nobel Institute, subordinate to the Academy of Sciences, 1905 ; Davy Medal, 1902 ;

Nobel Prize, 1903 ; Faraday Medal, 1914 ; Dr. med. hon. causa, Heidelberg, 1903 ; Groningen, 1914 ; Dr. sc. hon. causa, Oslo, 1904, Oxford and Cambridge, 1908 ; Dr. ph. hon. causa, Leipzig, 1909 ; Hon. LL.D., Birmingham, 1913 ; Hon. Member of Chemical and of Physical Societies of London, of Royal Society and Royal Institution ; Member of a great number of academies and learned societies in Europe and America ; originator of the theory of electrolytic dissociation, 1884 and 1887, whereby the chemical processes are explained as dependent on the electric conductivity of the reacting solutions. *Publications :* Lehrbuch d. kosm. Physik, 1903 ; Electrochemistry, transl. by M'Crae, 1901 ; Immunochemistry, 1906 ; Theories of Chemistry, 1906 ; Worlds in the Making, 1908 ; Life of the Universe, 1909 ; Quantitative Laws in Biological Chemistry, 1915 ; The Destinies of the Stars, 1918 ; Chemistry and Modern Life, 1919 ; all originally written in Swedish, and translated into different languages. *Address :* Nobel Institute, Experimentalfältet, near Stockholm. (*Died 2 Oct. 1927.*)

ARTHUR, Sir Allan, Kt. *cr.* 1900 ; merchant, Calcutta ; member of the Viceroy's Legislative Council, 1898-1902 ; *b.* 3 April 1857 ; *s.* of Allan Arthur, of Henry Monteith & Co., Glasgow, and Margaret Hamilton Thomson, Hawick ; unmarried. *Educ. :* Glasgow Academy ; Merchiston Castle School, Edinburgh. President of the Bengal Chamber of Commerce, 1894-95, 1896-97, part of 1898, 1899-1900 ; Sheriff of Calcutta, 1898. *Recreations :* fishing, shooting, polo, golf. *Clubs :* Oriental ; Western, Glasgow ; Bengal, Calcutta. (*Died 9 Oct. 1923.*)

ARTSIBASHEV, Michel Petrovitch ; *b.* 18 Oct. 1878 ; [his great-grandfather on the maternal side was Kosciusko]. *Educ. :* grammar school, school of art. *Publications :* Millionen und andere Novellen ; Sanine, 1909 ; Tales of the Revolution, 1917 ; Jealousy, 1914 ; The Millionaire, 1915 ; Breaking-Point, 1915 ; War, 1918. (*Died 3 Mar. 1927.*)

ARUNACHALAM, Sir Ponnambalam, Kt., *cr.* 1914 ; J.P. ; *b.* Colombo, Ceylon, 14 Sep. 1853 ; 3rd *s.* of A. Ponnambalam, Mudaliyar of the King's Gate, and Sellachchi, *d.* of A. Coomara Swamy, Mudaliyar of the King's Gate and M.L.C. ; nephew of Sir Mutu Coomara Swamy, Kt., M.L.C. ; *m.* Svarnam, *d.* of S. Namasivayam, Mudaliyar ; two *s.* four *d.* *Educ. :* Colombo Academy (now Royal College) ; Christ's Coll., Cambridge (Foundation Scholar and Ceylon Government Scholar) ; B.A. 1875 ; M.A. 1879 ; called to Bar, Lincoln's Inn, 1875 ; entered Ceylon Civil Service, 1875 ; held various judicial and administrative offices ; for many years Registrar-General of Ceylon ; received thanks of the Government for reorganising the Registrar-General's Department and for organising and reporting on Ceylon Decennial Census of 1901 ; Victoria Diamond Jubilee Gold Medal, 1897 ; M.L.C. 1906-13 ; member of the Executive Council, Jan. 1912 ; retired from Civil Service, July 1913 ; served on various Ceylon Commissions ; author of various Consolidating Statutes now in force ; President of the Royal Asiatic Society (Ceylon Branch) since 1917 ; President of the Ceylon University Association, 1906-13, of the Ceylon Social Service League, 1915-17, Ceylon Reform League, 1917-19, Ceylon Saiva Paripalana Sabha and Sen Tamil Paripalana Sabha (Societies for the advancement of the Hindu religion and of Tamil Literature) ; President of the Ceylon National Congress, 1919-20, and of the Ceylon Workers' Federation, 1920-21 ; Vice-President, Ceylon Agricultural Society, 1904-21 ; member of various learned societies in England, France, and Germany. *Publications :* Codification of the Ceylon Civil Law ; Decennial Census of Ceylon, 1901 ; Ceylon Vital Statistics ; Ceylon History and Antiquities ; Indian Re-

ligions and Philosophies. *Recreations:* literature and agriculture. *Address:* Ponklar, Colombo; Brindabana, Waga, Kelani Valley; Tillai, Walahapitiya, Chilaw—all in Ceylon.
(*Died Feb. 1924.*)

ARUNDELL of Wardour, 14th Baron (*cr.* 1605), **Edgar Clifford Arundell;** Count of the Holy Roman Empire, 1595; *b.* 1859; *S. c.* 1907; descended in the fifth generation from the 6th Baron; *m.* 1895, Ellen, widow of Melbourne Evans. Conservative. Family has never ceased to be Roman Catholic since mediæval times. *Property:* about 500 acres sold since the last "Domesday" Survey. Cornish property sold, with reservation of Manors of Lanherne, Treloy, Tresithney, and Bossuen. A picture gallery; but several valuable pictures sold, and gone out of the country, since passing of Finance Act of 1894: mediæval deeds and MSS. the old castle a ruin. *Heir:* b. Gerald Arthur Arundell. *Address:* Wardour Castle, Tisbury, Wiltshire.
(*Died 8 Dec. 1921.*)

ARUR SINGH, Sir Sardar Bahadur Sardar, K.C.I.E., *cr.* 1921; C.I.E. 1913. Member Amritsar Municipality, Vice-Chairman Amritsar District Board; Hon. Magistrate, 1st Class, and Civil Judge; *b.* 25 April 1863; *s.* of late Sardar Harnam Singh; *m.* four times; two *s.* one *d.* Manager, Golden Temple, Amritsar, 18 years. *Address:* Naushera Nangli, Amritsar, Punjab. (*Died 21 Mar. 1926.*)

ASCROFT, Sir William, Kt., *cr.* 1908; Solicitor; Chairman of the Harris Orphanage, Preston; J.P., County Borough of Preston and County of Westmorland; *b.* Preston, 24 Aug. 1832; *e. s.* of Robert Ascroft of Preston, Solicitor, and Town Clerk of Preston, and Isabella Noble; *m.* 1858, Christiana (*d.* 1907), *d.* of Charles Walker of Whitley Lower, Yorkshire, and Christiana Fawell; two *s.* four *d.* *Educ.:* The Grammar School, Preston. Admitted a Solicitor, 1855; since practised at Preston in partnership with his father, afterwards with his brother, Alfred Edward Ascroft, J.P., and now with his sons, Robert Walker Ascroft, M.A., B.C.L., J.P., and William Fawell Ascroft, M.A. *Recreations:* reading and enjoyment of the Lake District scenery. *Address:* Overleigh House, Preston; The Wyke, Grasmere. *T.:* 579 Preston, 7 Grasmere. *Clubs:* Winckley, Preston; Westmorland County, Kendal. (*Died 29 Sept. 1916.*)

ASH, Major William Claudius Casson, D.S.O. 1916; 1st Batt. Middlesex Regiment.; Temp. Lieut.-Colonel 23rd Batt.; *b.* 6 Feb. 1870; *e. s.* of W. H. Ash, of 51 Hamilton Terrace, N.W., and of Heathfield, Sussex; *m.* 1894, Edith Learoyd, 2nd *d.* of late Edward W. Barnett, Selly Oak, Worcestershire; two *d.* *Educ.:* Westminster School. Played cricket for Westminster School; entered Army, 1892; Captain, 1900; Adjt. Middlesex Regiment, 1902-7; Major, 1909; served South African War (Queen's medal 3 clasps); European War, 1914-16 (despatches, D.S.O.). *Recreations:* cricket, rackets, music. *Address:* Rock House, Aldershot. *Clubs:* Army and Navy, M.C.C.; Union, Malta. (*Died 29 Sept. 1916.*)

ASHBROOK, 8th Viscount (*cr.* 1751), **Robert Thomas Flower,** Baron of Castle Durrow, 1773. *b.* 1 April 1836; 3rd *s.* of 5th, and *b.* of 6th Viscount Ashbrook; *m.* 1866, Gertrude Sophia (*d.* 1911), *y. d.* of Rev. S. Hamilton; two *s.* three *d.* Formerly Hon. Lieut.-Col. 4th Batt. Prince of Wales's Leinster Regt. (Royal Canadians). *S. b.* 1906. Owns about 23,000 acres. *Heir:* s. Hon. Llowarch Robert Flower. *Address:* Castle Durrow, Co. Kilkenny. (*Died 9 Mar. 1919.*)

ASHBURNER, Lt.-Col. Lionel Forbes, D.S.O. 1900; M.V.O.; 1st Batt. Royal Fusiliers; Brig.-Major, Nasirabad, 1909-1914; *b.* 18 Sep. 1874; *m.* 1907, Ethel Hermione,

2nd *d.* of Sir Charles Bayley. *Educ.:* Cheltenham College. Joined Durham Light Infantry 1895; served South Africa (despatches, D.S.O.); European War, 1914-15 (despatches five times, Bt. Lt.-Col.). *Club:* Army and Navy.
(*Died 19 Jan. 1923.*)

ASHBURNHAM, 6th Earl of (*cr.* 1730), **Thomas Ashburnham.** Baron of Ashburnham, 1689; Viscount St. Asaph, 1730; late 7th Hussars; 5th *s.* of 4th Earl of Ashburnham and Katherine Charlotte, *d.* of George Baillie of Jerviswood, Co. Lanark; *b.* 8 Apr. 1855; *S.* b. 1913; *m.* 1903, Maria Elizabeth, 2nd *d.* of W. H. Anderson, Fredericton, N.B. Knight of the Medjidie; was A.D.C. to Lord-Lieut. of Ireland; served Egypt, 1882; retired, 1889; extra A.D.C. to Lords Carnarvon and Aberdeen, Viceroys of Ireland. Owns about 24,000 acres. *Heir:* None. *Address:* Ashburnham Place, Battle; Barking Hall, Needham Market, Suffolk; Pembrey, Carmarthenshire. (*Died 12 May 1924.*)

ASHBURNHAM, Sir Cromer, K.C.B. 1882; Col. Commandant K.R.R.C.; *b.* Guestling, Sussex, 13 Sept. 1831; *s.* of Rev. Sir John Ashburnham, 7th Bt., of Broomham, Sussex, Chancellor and Prebendary of Chichester; *m.* Urith, *d.* of Capt. G. B. Martin, C.B., R.N., 1864. Served in Mutiny Campaign, 1857-58, medal and clasp; in Afghanistan Campaign, 1878-80, medal and clasp; commanded 2nd Batt. Rifles; commanded 3rd Batt. Rifles throughout Boer War, 1881; A.D.C. to Queen Victoria; com. 3rd Batt. Rifles in Egyptian Campaign, 1882; commanded a brigade, Tel-el-Kebir; medal and clasp, bronze star and 3rd class of the Medjidie; commanded 3rd Batt. Rifles in campaign in Eastern Soudan, 1884, 2 clasps; appointed Governor of Suakim. *Recreation:* shooting. *Address:* 165 Coleherne Court, S.W. (*Died 25 Feb. 1917.*)

ASHBY-STERRY, Joseph; *b.* London; *o. s.* of late Henry Sterry, Moss Grange, Sydenham Hill; unmarried. *Educ.:* privately. First ambition to be a painter; at 19 he was painting life-size oil portraits and drawing on the wood for Punch and other papers; drifted into journalism, and eventually abandoned the pencil for the pen; was the versatile Lazy Minstrel of Punch and at one time a constant contributor to its pages; originated the popular Bystander column in the Graphic, and wrote it over eighteen years (till 1909); art-critic Daily Graphic, 1891-1907. *Publications:* Shuttlecock Papers, Tiny Travels, Boudoir Ballads, Snailway Guides, Cucumber Chronicles, The Lazy Minstrel (which is now a book of perpetual new editions), Nutshell Novels, A Naughty Girl, A Tale of the Thames, The Bystander, or Leaves for the Lazy (1900), and the popular edition of A Tale of the Thames, with much additional matter and numerous fresh Sketches in Song (1908); The River Rhymer, 1913. *Recreations:* rowing or sailing in little dinghey "The Shuttlecock" on the Thames, which stream he has closely studied from his childhood, and is said to know every inch of it from the source in Trewsbury Mead to the Buoy at the Nore. His knowledge of London is "extensive and peculiar," and one of his favourite recreations is the minute explorations that he makes of all parts of it, old and new. *Address:* 8 St. Martin's Place, Trafalgar Square. *Clubs:* Garrick Beefsteak. (*Died 1 June 1917.*)

ASHCOMBE, 1st Baron (*cr.* 1892), **George Cubitt,** P.C.; *b.* 4 June 1828; *m.* 1853, Laura (*d.* 1904), *d.* of Rev. James Joyce, vicar of Dorking; one *s.* five *d.* *Educ.:* Trin. Coll. Camb. (M.A. 1854). M.P. W. Surrey, 1860-85; Mid-Surrey, 1885-92; 2nd Church Estate Commissioner, 1874-79; is a member of the Council of Selwyn College; and Hon. Col. 2nd V.B. Queen's Royal West Surrey Regiment. *Heir:* s. Hon. H. Cubitt. *Address:* 17 Prince's Gate, S.W.; Fallapit, East Allington, S. Devon. *Club:* Carlton. (*Died 26 Feb. 1917.*)

3

ASHDOWN, Sir George Henry, K.B.E., cr. 1920; C.B.E. 1918; I.S.O. 1915; Legion of Honour, 1919; D.S.O. of U.S.A., 1919; Director of Stores, Admiralty, 1918-20; b. 1857; m. 1884, Edith, d. of William Haines. *Address:* Waratah, Effingham Road, Surbiton.
(*Died 3 Dec. 1924.*)

ASHFORD, Hon. William George, Minister for Lands and Forests, 1915 - 20; b. 9 Aug. 1874; m. 1904; four s. *Educ.:* State Public Schools. Engaged all life in rural pursuits; elected State Parliament, 1910; Minister for Agriculture, 1914. *Recreations:* cricket, rifle-shooting, tennis. *Address:* Ruby Street, Mosman, New South Wales.
(*Died 24 Mar. 1925.*)

ASHLEY, Lt.-Col. Frank, C.B.E. 1918; British Red Cross Commissioner, Malta (Croix de Guerre); b. 1870; m. 1903, Cecilia, d. of F.C. Walker. *Educ.:* Clifton College.
(*Died 16 Oct. 1923.*)

ASHLEY, Sir William (James), Kt., cr. 1917; Ph.D., M.A., M. Com.; b. London, 25 Feb. 1860; m. 1888, Margaret (d. 1922), d. of Geo. Birkbeck Hill, D.C.L.; one s. two d. *Educ.:* St. Olave's School, Southwark; History Scholar of Balliol College, Oxford; 1st class History, 1881; Lothian prize, 1882. Fellow and Lecturer of Lincoln College, Oxford, 1885-88; Professor of Political Economy, Toronto University, 1888-92; Professor of Economic History, Harvard, 1892-1901; Professor of Commerce, Birmingham University, 1901-25; now Emeritus Professor; Vice-Principal, 1918-25; a Vice-President Royal Economic Society; Corresponding Mem. Mass. His. Society and Assoc. Acad. Roy. Belg.; Examiner in History, Economics, or Commerce, between 1899 and 1920, in the Universities of Cambridge, London, Durham, Wales, and Ireland; Pres. Econ. Section Brit. Assoc. 1907, 1924; President Econ-Hist. Section of International Historical Congress, 1913; Ball Lecturer at Oxford, 1922; Member Committee on Coal Prices, 1915; Huth Jackson Committee, 1916; Food Prices Committee, 1917; Consumers' Council, 1918; Cost of Living Committee, 1918; Royal Commission on Agriculture, 1919; Glassware Committee, 1921; Agricultural Tribunal, 1923; Tariff Advisory Committee, 1923; Committee on Industry and Trade, 1924. *Publications:* Introduction to English Economic History and Theory; pt. i. The Middle Ages, 1888; pt. ii. The End of the Middle Ages, 1893 (trans. into German, French, and Japanese); Surveys, Historic and Economic, 1900; Adjustment of Wages, 1903; The Tariff Problem, 1903 (4th ed. enlarged, 1920); Progress of the German Working Classes, 1904 (trans. into German); The Rise in Prices, 1912 (trans. into German and Swedish); Gold and Prices, 1912; Economic Organisation of England, 1914 (trans. into French); The Christian Outlook, 1925; ed. Economic Classics, and translated therein Turgot, Reflections, and Schmoller, Mercantile System; ed. British Industries, 1903, British Dominions, 1911, and Mill's Political Economy, 1909; joint author of Report of Unionist Social Reform Committee on Industrial Unrest, 1914. *Address:* 3 St Stephen's Road, Canterbury. *Club:* Authors'. (*Died 23 July 1927.*)

ASHLIN, George C., R.H.A., F.R.I.B.A., ex - President, Royal Institute of Architects of Ireland; 3rd s. of J. M. Ashlin, J.P., Rush Hill, Surrey; b. Carrigrenane House, County Cork, 1837; m. d. of late Augustus Welby Pugin; one d. *Educ.:* College of St. Servais, Liège; Oscott College, near Birmingham; student of Royal Academy, London, 1858; pupil of the late E. Welby Pugin, 1856-60. Practised as an architect in Ireland in partnership with the late E. W. Pugin, 1860-70, afterwards independently; principal buildings—SS. Peter and Paul's Church, Cork, Queenstown

Cathedral, and about 50 other churches in Ireland; gained many competitions, including Portrane Asylum, which cost about £900,000. *Recreations:* sketching, cycling, golf. *Address:* St. George's, Killiney, Co. Dublin; 7 Dawson Street, Dublin. *Club:* Stephen's Green, Dublin.
(*Died 10 Dec. 1922.*)

ASHMAN, Sir Frederick Herbert, 2nd Bart., cr. 1907; b. 16 Jan. 1875; s. of 1st Bt. and Lizzie, d. of Frederick George Lorenzen; S. father 1914; m. 1898, Alice Ethel, d. of late William Ansell Todd, J.P., Portishead, Somersetshire. *Heir:* none. *Address:* Clarence Croft, Weston-super-Mare, Somerset.
(*Died 22 Dec. 1916.*)

ASHTON, Arthur Jacob, K.C. 1906; Judge of Appeal, Isle of Man, since 1921; b. 4 Feb. 1855; e. s. of late Walter Ashton of Warrington, Lancashire; m. 1890, Emma, d. of Dr. Thomas Burnie of Nottingham; one s. two d. *Educ.:* Manchester Grammar School; Balliol College, Oxford (Classical Scholar); first class in Classical Moderations and Final Schools. B.A. 1878; called to Bar, Inner Temple, 1881; Bencher, 1914; Recorder of Manchester, 1914. *Address:* 43 Montagu Square, W.1.; *T.:* Paddington 3873; 2 Mitre Court Buildings, Temple, E.C. *T.:* City 99; Lavender Walk, Rye, Sussex. *Clubs:* Garrick, Reform. (*Died 23 Mar. 1925.*)

ASHTON, Sir Ralph Percy, Kt., cr. 1911; Major (retired); partner, Kilburn Brown & Co., London, and Kilburn & Co., Calcutta; b. Darwen, 1860; s. of late Ralph Shorrock Ashton, J.P.; m. 1000, Emma, d. of late Robert Francis Rendell, of Kingston House, Staverton; one s. *Educ.:* Uppingham; Owens College. Additional Member of Legislative Council of India, 1901-2; has been Trustee for Port of Calcutta, for Victoria Memorial of India, and for Indian Museum; President Mining and Geological Institute of India, 1911. *Address:* Beechwood, Reigate; *T.:* 360; Orient House, New Broad Street, E.C.; *T.:* City 20. (*Died 28 Jan. 1921.*)

ASHTON, Rt. Hon. Thomas, P.C. 1917; J.P. City of Manchester; Miners' General Secretary, 1881-1918; b. Openshaw, Manchester, 1844; father a coalminer and mother daughter of a miner; m. 1865; two s. four d. *Educ.:* self-educated. Commenced working in the pit at an early age; Branch Secretary for the Bradford and Clayton Miners, 1865; left the pit to commence check-weighing on the pit bank; 1873; Secretary Ashton - under - Lyne and Oldham Miners' Association, 1879; General Secretary of the Lancashire and Cheshire Miners' Federation, 1881; General Secretary of the Miners' Federation of Great Britain, 1889-1919; Joint Secretary of the International Miners' Federation, 1890-1902; then General Secretary; Joint Secretary with Sir Thomas Ratcliffe Ellis of the Conciliation Board for the English and North Wales Federated Area since its formation, 1894. *Address:* Almas House, Droylsden Road, Droylsden, Manchester. (*Died 13 Oct. 1927.*)

ASHWORTH, Philip Arthur, LL.D., M.A.; e. s. of late Rev. John A. Ashworth, M.A., Rector of Didcot, Berks; b. 1853. *Educ.:* Sherborne School; New College, Oxford (Honours Classics and Law, 1875); Universities of Bonn and Leipzig (LL.D. with honours, University of Würzburg); barrister at-law, Inner Temple, 1881; Advocate of the Cyprus Courts; m. 1879, Emma, Baroness von Estorff. Editor of 5th, 6th, and 7th editions of Taswell Langmead's Constitutional History of England; translator from the German, of Rudolph von Gneist's History of the English Constitution; Leopold von Ranke's History of the Latin and Teutonic Nations; Baron von der Goltz's Nation in Arms; Rudolph von Ihering's Battle for Right; author of Das Witthum (Dower im englischen Recht; contributor of various articles to the Encyclopædia Britannica (10th and 11th editions). *Recreations :* walking and foreign travel.   (*Died Nov. 1921.*)

ASKEW, Claude Arthur Cary, 2nd *s.* of late Rev. John Askew, M.A.; *m.* 1900, Alice, *o. surv. d.* of late Col. Henry Leake, 44th and 70th Regiments; one *s.* one *d. Educ.:* Eton; Continent. Took up a literary career after his marriage; writes only in collaboration with Mrs. Askew; their first book, the Shulamite, was published in 1904, and in 1906 this novel was dramatised by Mr. Claude Askew and Mr. Edward Knoblauch and produced at the Savoy Theatre by Miss Lena Ashwell. *Publications :* The Shulamite; Eve and the Law; The Premier's Daughter; Anna of the Plains; Jennifer Pontefract; The Etonian; The Baxter Family; The Love Stone; Lucy Gort; The Plains of Silence; The Path of Lies; The Orchard Close; Not Proven; Felix Stone; Testimony; The Sporting Chance; The Rod of Justice; The Woman Deborah; Destiny; The Englishwoman; The King's Signature; Through Folly's Mill; Freedom; Trespass; The Stricken Land, 1916. Serial and short stories in many periodicals. *Club :* Union.   (*Died 5 Oct. 1917.*)

ASLETT, Alfred; *s.* of Alfred Aslett, late District Superintendent, Great Northern Railway; *b.* York, 3 July 1847; *m.* 1877, Emma Mary, *o. d.* of late Edward Francis Rimbault, LL.D. *Educ. :* York and Peterborough Grammar Schools. In service of Great Northern Railway Company, 1862-81; Manager of the Eastern and Midlands Railway, 1884-91, now the joint Midland and Great Northern; Secretary and General Manager of the Cambrian Railways, 1891 - 95; Secretary and General Manager of the Furness Railway, 1895-1918. J.P. Borough of Barrow-in-Furness; ex-Pres. Barrow-in-Furness Chamber of Commerce; P.P.G. Warden for West Lancashire (Masonic). *Recreations :* golf and tennis. *Address :* Stanyan Lodge, Ulverston, Lancs. *T.A.:* Aslett, Ulverston. *T. :* 18 Ulverston. *M. :* B 231. *Clubs :* National Liberal; County, Barrow-in-Furness; North Lonsdale, Ulverston.   (*Died 28 April 1928.*)

ASPINALL, Lt.-Col. Robert Lowndes, D.S.O. 1900; Commanding 11th Battalion Yorkshire Regiment; late Captain 15th Hussars; *b.* 3 Mar. 1869; *s.* of late Robert Augustus Aspinall. *Educ. :* Eton; Sandhurst. Served as A.D.C. to Sir John French in South Africa, 1900-1902 (despatches, Queen's medal, 5 clasps, King's medal, D.S.O.). *Recreations :* coaching, hunting, etc. *Address :* 37 Greycoat Gardens, S.W. *Club :* Army and Navy   (*Died 2 July 1916.*)

ASQUITH, Raymond, Lieut. Grenadier Guards, 1915; *e. s.* of Rt. Hon. H. H. Asquith, and Helen, *d.* of Frederick Melland of Rusholme; *b.* 6 Nov. 1878; *m.* 1907, Katharine, *d.* of Sir John Horner, K.C.V.O., of Mells Park, Somerset. two *d. Educ. :* Winchester College (Scholar); Balliol College, Oxford (Scholar). 1st Class Classical Moderations, 1899; 1st Class Lit. Hum. 1901; 1st Class Jurisprudence, 1902; Craven, Ireland, Derby and Eldon Scholarships; President Oxford Union; Fellow of All Souls, 1902; Called to Bar, Inner Temple, 1904; Junior Counsel for Great Britain in North Atlantic Fisheries Arbitration at the Hague, 1911; Junior Counsel to the Inland Revenue, 1914; 2nd Lieut. 3/16th County of London Regt., 1914. *Recreations :* shooting, golf, tennis. *Address :* 49 Bedford Square, W.C. *T. :* Museum 783. *Clubs :* Brook's, Athenæum; Hampshire County; Prince's Tennis. (*Died 18 Sept. 1916.*)

ASTBURY, Rev. George, M.A.; Hon. Canon, Birmingham, 1906; *m. Educ. :* Christ's College, Cambridge. Curate of Redditch, 1873-1884; Perpetual Curate of Smethwick since 1884. *Address :* Old Church Vicarage, Smethwick, Staffs.   (*Died 23 April 1926.*)

ASTELL, Captain Somerset Charles Godfrey Fairfax, D.S.O. 1900; late North Staffords Regt.; retired; J.P. for Transvaal and Dorset; *b.* West Lodge, 15 July 1866; *s.* of late Gen. C. E. Astell and *g.-s.* of W. Astell, M.P., and H. D., *d.* of F. Spaight, Derry Castle, Tipperary; *m.* 1903, Fredericka Beatrice, *o. c.* of James F. Roberts. *Educ. :* St. Columba College, Dublin. Joined service, 1887; promoted, 1895; Soudan (Dongola), 1896 (two medals—Queen's and Khedive's); South Africa, 1900; Intelligence Officer, Wakkerstroom, April 1901; in charge of Johannesburg Criminal Investigation Department, 6 June 1900 to 25 Feb. 1901 (D.S.O.); Adjutant 4th North Staffords, quarters Lichfield, 1902-3. *Recreations :* hunting, shooting, fishing. *Address :* West Lodge, Dorchester, Dorset. *T.A. :* Piddlehinton.   (*Died 24 Mar. 1917.*)

ASTLEY, Hubert Delaval, J.P., M.B.O.U., F.Z.S.; *b.* 14 July, 1860; 2nd *s.* of late Francis Le Strange Astley, Lieut.-Col. Norfolk Artillery, and late Mrs. Frankland Russell Astley of Chequers Court, Bucks; *m.* 1895, Constance, *d.* of late Sir Vincent Rowland Corbet, 3rd Bart., and *widow* of Sir Richard F. Sutton, 5th Bart.; one *s.* one *d. Educ. :* Eton; Christ Church, Oxford (M.A.). *Recreations :* ornithology, gardening, sketching, etc. *Publication :* My Birds in Freedom and Captivity. *Address :* Brinsop Court, Herefordshire. *T. :* Burghill 10.   (*Died 26 May 1925.*)

ASTOR, 1st Viscount, *cr.* 1917, of Hever Castle, **William Waldorf;** Baron, *cr.* 1916; *b.* New York, 31 Mar. 1848; *o. c.* of John Jacob Astor and Charlotte Augusta Gibbes; *m.* 1878, Mary Dahlgren (*d.* 1894), *d.* of James W. Paul, Philadelphia, Penn., U.S.A.; two *s.* one *d. Educ. :* private tutors. Barr. 1875; Legislature of State of New York, 1878, 1881; United States Minister to Italy, 1882 - 1885; Naturalised British subject, 1899. *Publications :* Valentino, 1886; Sforza, 1889; Pharaoh's Daughter, and Other Stories, 1900. *Heir. :* *s.* Hon. Waldorf Astor. *Address :* Hever Castle, Kent. *Clubs :* Marlborough, Carlton.   (*Died 18 Oct. 1919.*)

ATCHISON, Major Charles Ernest, D.S.O. 1915; Shropshire Light Infantry, attached 3rd Batt.; *b.* 12 May 1875. Entered army, 1895; Captain, 1902; served South Africa, 1899 - 1902 (Queen's medal, 3 clasps, King's medal, 2 clasps); European War, 1914 - 15 (D.S.O.).   (*Died 24 Aug. 1917.*)

ATCHLEY, Chewton, C.M.G. 1911; I.S.O. 1902; *b.* 23 Feb. 1850; *s.* of Wm. Henry Atchley, formerly of H.M.'s Treasury; *m.* Alice, *d.* of Henry Whitehouse, of Highgate, N., 1879; one *s.* one *d. Educ. :* privately. Entered Colonial Office, 1868; Librarian, 1880-1915; retired, 1915. *Publications :* Lucas's Historical Geography of the British Colonies, vol. ii., West Indies, second edition; numerous articles in Supplement to Dictionary of National Biography. *Recreations :* interested in most forms of sport except golf and bridge.   (*Died 29 Dec. 1922.*)

ATHERTON, Colonel Thomas James, C.B. 1900; C.M.G. 1918; retired; late 12th (the Prince of Wales's Royal) Lancers; *b.* 19 Aug. 1856; *s.* of late Sir W. Atherton, M.P., Attorney-General; *m.* 1892, Mabel Louisa (*d.* 1919), 3rd *d.* of Sir Edward Dean - Paul, 4th Bart.; one *s. Educ. :* Charterhouse; Cambridge. Entered army, 1880; Captain, 1887; Major, 1893; Lieut.-Col. 1900; Colonel, 1904. Served South Africa, 1899-1902 (despatches); European War, 1914 - 18 (C.M.G.). *Club :* Naval and Military.   (*Died 27 Sept. 1920.*)

ATHILL, Charles Harold, M.V.O. 1911; F.S.A.; Clarenceux King of Arms, 1919; *m.* Catherine Mildred, *d.* of late Ven. B. F. Smith, Archdeacon of Maidstone, and Canon of Canterbury Cathedral. Entered College of Arms

35

as Bluemantle Pursuivant of Arms, 1882; Richmond Herald, 1889-1919; Norroy King of Arms, Jan. to Sept., 1919; Registrar of the College of Arms, 1911-19. *Address:* College of Arms, Queen Victoria Street, E.C.; The Firs Sevenoaks, Kent. *(Died 27 Nov. 1922.)*

ATHOLL, 7th Duke of *(cr.* 1703), **Sir John James Hugh Henry Stewart-Murray,** K.T. Lord Murray of Tullibardine, 1604; Earl of Tullibardine, Lord Gask and Balquhidder, 1606; Earl of Atholl, 1629; Marquess of Atholl, Viscount Balquhidder, Lord Balvenie, 1676; Marquess of Tullibardine, Earl of Strathtay, Earl of Strathardle, Viscount Glenalmond, Viscount Glenlyon, 1703—all in the Peerage of Scotland. Lord Strange of Knockyn (England), 1628; Lord Percy (by writ), 1722; Earl Strange and Lord Murray of Stanley. 1786,—all in the Peerage of Great Britain. Lord Glenlyon of Glenlyon (U.K.). Lord-Lieut. of county of Perth since 1878; Hon. Colonel 3rd Batt. The Black Watch, 1903; Chancellor of the Order of the Thistle, 1913; *b.* 6 Aug. 1840; *S.* father 1864; *m.* 1863, Louisa *(d.* 1902), *d.* of Sir Thos. Moncreiffe, 7th Bt.; three *s.* three *d. Educ.:* Eton. Late Lieut. and Capt. Scots Fusilier Guards. Owns about 202,000 acres. *Heir: s.* Marquess of Tullibardine. *Address:* Blair Castle, Blair Atholl, and Dunkeld, Perthshire; 84 Eaton Place, S.W. *T.:* Victoria 3282. *Clubs:* Carlton, Marlborough, Guards', Bachelors'. *(Died 20 Jan. 1917.)*

ATKINS, Major-General Sir Alban Randell Crofton, K.C.B., *cr.* 1919; C.B. 1917; C.M.G. 1915; *b.* 29 June 1870. Entered army, 1889; Captain, 1898; Major, 1905; Bt. Lt.-Col. 1913; Bt.-Col. 1915; Deputy Assistant Director War Office, 1911-14; Assistant Director of Transport, 1914; served Ashanti, 1895-96 (star); Sierra Leone, 1899-1900 (despatches, Bt. Major, Queen's medal 2 clasps); European War, 1914-18 (C.M.G., K.C.M.G., prom. Maj.-Gen.); retired pay, 1920; holds 3rd Class Order of White Eagle, Serbia. *Club:* United Service.
(Died 29 April 1926.)

ATKINSON, Hon. Cecil Thomas, K.C. 1913; a Puisne Judge of the High Court of Behar and Orissa since 1915; *e. s.* of Baron Atkinson; *b.* 28 Oct. 1876; *m.* 1903, Florence, *d.* of Godfrey Lovelace Taylor of Grangeville, Co. Wexford; one *s.* two *d. Educ.:* Trinity College, Dublin, B.A. Called to the Irish Bar, 1901. *Recreations:* golf, riding, and shooting. *Address:* Patna, India.
(Died 20 Nov. 1919.)

ATKINSON, Charles Milner, M.A., LL.M.; Stipendiary Magistrate for Leeds since 1894; *b.* 6 Nov. 1854; *e. s.* of late J. G. Atkinson, M.D., of The Grange, near Rotherham; *m.* Mary Josephine *(d.* 1915). *Educ.:* Clare Coll. Cambridge, scholar and exhibitioner; Sixteenth Wrangler, 1877; M.A., LL.M. Barr. Inner Temple, 1878; went N. E. Circuit and West Riding Sessions; appointed by Lord Macnaghten to act as his registrar under the Portsea Island Building Society's Act, 1893; J.P. for West Riding of Yorks. *Publications:* The Magistrate's Practice, 13th ed., 1916; Jeremy Bentham; His Life and Work, 1905; Translation of Dumont's *Traités de Législation,* 1914. *Address:* 47 Frognal, Hampstead, N.W.; Town Hall, Leeds. *Club:* New University. *(Died 5 Dec. 1920.)*

ATKINSON, Major Edward William, D.S.O. 1915; 1st Batt. R. Inniskilling Fusiliers; *b.* 12 Aug. 1873; *e. s.* of Edward Atkinson, Ashfield, Moynalty, Kells, Co. Meath; *m.* 1907, Louise H. S., *y. d.* of John Power Oliver, Indian Medical Service; no *c. Educ.:* Trinity College, Dublin; B.A. Served in 3rd Batt. Royal Inniskilling Fusiliers (Fermanagh Militia) 1893-96; entered army, 1896; Captain, 1902; Major, 1915; Adjutant, 6th Batt. Notts. and Derby Regt., 1906-11; Hythe (Extra), 1893; Signalling Cert. Instructor, 1906;

Provisional Course, 1911; served South Africa, 1900-2 (Queen's medal, 3 clasps, King's medal, 2 clasps); in Dardanelles, European War, 1914-15 (despatches, D.S.O.). *Club:* Army and Navy. *(Died 27 July 1920.)*

ATKINSON, Rev. Canon Henry Sadgrove, M.A., Surrogate; Canon of York and Prebendary of Givendale since 1908, Rural Dean of Pontefract, 1900-23, and Vicar of Darrington since 1892; *o. s.* of Henry Hayes Atkinson, late of Brixton, Surrey; *m.* 8 Nov. 1871, Elizabeth Frances, *e. d.* of Dr. Owen Daly, F.R.C.P., of Hull; three *s.* one *d. Educ.:* Jesus College, Cambridge. Curate of the Parish Church, Hull, 1870-74; Vicar of Royston, Yorks, 1874-92. *Address:* Darrington Vicarage, Pontefract. *T.:* Pontefract 250 Y2. *M.:* DN 440. *(Died 25 May 1927.)*

ATKINSON, His Hon. Judge Henry Tindal; Judge of Courts; Courts Assessor since 1901; *s.* of late Henry Tindal Atkinson, Serjeant-at-Law and County Court Judge; *m.* 1873, Marian, *e. d.* of H. Hale Lewin, of Holly Hill, Wanstead; one *s.* four *d.* Called to Bar, Middle Temple, 1865; Bencher, 1896; J.P. Hertfordshire. *Address:* 3 Clanricarde Gardens,.W.; 3 Dr. Johnson's Buildings, Temple, E.C. *Club:* Reform. *(Died 14 Mar. 1918.)*

ATKINSON, John Mitford, M.B. (Lond.), D.P.H. Cambridge, etc.; *b.* 3 Dec. 1856; *s.* of late Rev. Samuel Atkinson, M.A.; *m.* 1898, Clara, *e. d.* of James Eastmond, of Puddington, Devon; two *s. Educ.:* Queen's College, Taunton; London Hospital. Resident Medical Officer, St. Mary Abbot's Infirmary, Kensington, 1878-85; Superintendent Government Civil Hospital, Hong-Kong; Medical Officer to Small-pox Hospital and the Government Lunatic Asylums, 1887; J.P. 1890; received thanks of Secretary of State for services during plague, 1896; Member Executive Council, Hong-Kong, 1903-12; Principal Civil Medical Officer, Hong-Kong, 1897-1912; Fellow Royal Sanitary Institute, Colonial Institute and Society of Tropical Medicine. *Publications:* contributions to Lancet and British Medical Journal. *Recreations:* cricket, tennis, and golf. *Address:* 37 Welbeck Street, W.; *T.:* Mayfair 1094; 107 Comeragh Road, West Kensington, W.; *T.:* Hammersmith 797. *Clubs:* Thatched House, Queen's.
(Died 23 May 1917.)

ATKINSON, Maj.-Gen. John Richard Breeks, Indian Army; *b.* 8 April 1844; 2nd *s.* of Rev. John Breeks Atkinson, Rector of Kingston, I.W., Vicar of Cowes, I.W., and Jane Isabella Atkinson; *m.* 1887, Margaret Augusta, *d.* of J. L. Turner and Mrs. Turner, Coombe House, Backwell, Somerset. Went to India from Addiscombe College, 1861; retired, 1895; served in 1st Punjab Cavalry, Punjab Frontier Force, 1866-94; Maj.-Gen. 1894; served Afghan War, 1878-80 (despatches thrice, medal with clasp, Brevet Major and Lieut.-Col.). *Address:* Elm House, Rodwell, Weymouth. *T.:* Weymouth 247. *Club:* Royal Dorset Yacht, Weymouth. *(Died 27 Nov. 1926.)*

ATKINSON-WILLES, Admiral Sir George (Lambart), K.C.B., *cr.* 1905 (took the additional surname of Willes in compliance with the will of his uncle, Admiral Sir George Willes, G.C.B.); Commander-in-Chief, East Indies, 1903-6; *b.* 13 July 1847; 2nd *surv. s.* of late Rev. Thomas Atkinson, Rector of Kirby Sigston, Yorkshire, and Henrietta J., *d.* of Capt. George W. Willes, R.N.; *m.* Alice, *y. d.* of late Thomas Sutcliffe Mort of Greenoakes, Darling Point, Sydney, one *s.* three *d. Educ.:* Leamington College; R.N. Academy, Gosport. Entered navy, 1861; captain, 1886; admiral, 1901; served Abyssinian War in Naval Brigade, including action of Arogee and storming of Magdala, 1868 (despatches, promoted to Lieut., medal); as commodore commanded Training Squadron, 1895-97; Dockyard Reserve,

36

Chatham, 1898-1900 ; A.D.C. to H.M. Queen Victoria, 1899-1901, and to King Edward until promoted Rear-Adml. ; Rear-Admiral in command Home Squadron and second in command of Home Fleet, 1902-3 ; Commander-in-Chief, East Indies, 1903; directed the operations of a mixed naval and military force which captured the Dervish stronghold of Illig, 1904 ; as Commander-in-Chief was present on Somali Coast, 1904, during the operations against the Mullah ; retired 1912. *Address :* The Stroud, Haslemere. *Clubs :* United Service, Travellers'.
(*Died 25 Dec. 1921.*)

ATTERBURY, Sir Frederick, K.C.B., *cr.* 1917 ; C.B. 1910 ; Barrister-at-law ; Controller of H.M. Stationery Office, and King's Printer of Acts of Parliament since 1913 ; *b.* 19 Oct. 1858 ; 2nd *s.* of Benjamin John Atterbury, Hampstead ; *m.* 1889, Charlotte, *e. d.* of Thomas Lawrence Forbes, Hampstead ; one *s. Educ. :* North London Collegiate School. First place in open competition for Civil Service, 1872 ; Inland Revenue, Accountant and Comptroller-General's Office, 1872 ; Secretary's Office, 1875 ; Comptroller of Stamps and Taxes for Ireland, 1901-3 ; Secretary to Board of Inland Revenue, Controller of Stamps, and Registrar of Joint Stock Companies, 1909-13. *Publications :* articles on Taxation, etc., in Dictionary of Political Economy. *Recreation :* golf. *Address :* 2 Upper Terrace, Hampstead Heath, N.W. *T. :* 6746 P.O. Hampstead. *Club :* Union.
(*Died 10 Feb. 1919.*)

ATTHILL, Major Anthony William Maunsell, M.V.O. 1907 ; O.B.E. 1919 ; Chairman Royal Norfolk Veterans' Association ; *b.* 10 Aug. 1861 ; *e. s.* of Henry Maunsell Atthill ; *m.* ; two *s.* two *d. Educ. :* King Edward VI. School, Norwich. Founded Royal Norfolk Veterans' Association, 1898 ; Recruiting Officer 9th Regimental District, 1900 ; served with 2nd Battalion Norfolk Regiment in South African War, 1901-2 ; operations in the N.W. Transvaal (medal with 5 clasps) ; Captain Reserve of Officers, 1902 ; decorated by King Edward VII. at Sandringham, May 1907, for services in connection with the Veterans of Norfolk ; Capt. A.S.C. 1914 ; Major, 1915 ; served with British Force in Egypt and Mediterranean Expeditionary Force in Gallipoli (despatches, O.B.E., 1914-15 Star, and medals). *Publications :* From Norwich to Lichtenburg via Pretoria, 1910. *Address :* Hillcrest, Bourne Hall Road, Bushey, Herts. (*Died 28 Feb. 1926.*)

AUBREY, William Hickman Smith, LL.D., M.J.I.; author and journalist; *b.* London, 9 Dec. 1858. *Educ :* privately. LL.D. University of the City of New York and Rutgers Coll., New Brunswick. Sub-editor and then leader-writer on Morning Advertiser ; editor Barrow Daily and Weekly Times ; editor Capital and Labour, 1873-82 ; on leader staff and reviewer Daily News ; descriptive and social articles Illustrated London News ; vice-president London Institution, Finsbury Circus ; trustee of Croydon Charities ; Chairman, Croydon Board of Guardians ; Chairman, Surrey Joint Poor Law Committee for the Mentally Defective ; London letter on politics, literature, art and society to syndicate of American papers ; contributed numerous articles on literary, social, and economic subjects to reviews and magazines ; visited U.S. and Canada seven times on lecturing tours ; candidate (L.) North Hackney, 1886 ; Honiton Division, Devonshire, 1892. *Publications :* The National and Domestic History of England, three editions, 3 vols., 1886-90 ; London's Roll of Fame, 1884 ; The Rise and Growth of the English Nation, four editions and eight American and Colonial editions, 3 vols., 1896-1912. *Recreations :* collection of literary "ana" and historical portraits ; incessant work, varied by change of subject. *Address :* 13 Canterbury Road,

Croydon. *Club :* National Liberal.
(*Died 11 Feb. 1916.*)

AUCKLAND, 5th Baron (*cr.*—Irish barony, 1789 ; British, 1793), **William Morton Eden ;** *b.* 27 Mar. 1859 ; *s.* of 4th Baron and Lucy Walbanke, *y. d.* of John Walbanke Childers of Cantley, Co. York ; *S.* father 1890 ; *m.* 1891, Sybil, *d.* of late Col. G. M. Hutton, C.B. ; one *s.* Late Capt. 2nd Batt. Dorset Regt. *Heir : s.* Hon. Frederick Colvin George Eden, *b.* 1895. *Recreations :* shooting, fishing. *Clubs :* Carlton, Naval and Military.(*Died 31 July 1917.*)

AUDEN, Rev. Thomas, M.A., F.S.A., *s.* of William Auden, of Rowley Regis, Co. Stafford ; *b.* 1836 ; *m.* 1861, Anne (*d.* 1905), 2nd *d.* of William Hopkins of Dunstall, Co. Stafford ; four *s.* three *d. Educ. :* St. John's College, Cambridge. B.A., 1858 ; M.A., 1861 ; Deacon, 1859 ; Priest, 1860 ; Headmaster of Wellingborough Grammar School, 1863-69 ; Vicar of Ford, Salop, 1869-79 ; St. Julian's, Shrewsbury, 1879-92 ; Condover, Salop, 1892-1908 ; Prebendary of Lichfield, 1905 ; Rural Dean of Condover, 1906 ; Proctor in Convocation for the Diocese of Hereford, 1908-10 and 1911-16 ; one of Secretaries of Church Congress at Shrewsbury, 1896 ; Chairman of Atcham Board of Guardians, 1905-10 ; Vice-Chairman of Education Committee of Salop County Council ; Chairman of Council of Shropshire Archæological Society. *Publications :* Shrewsbury, School History of Shropshire, and other books and papers on local history. *Address :* Alderdene, Church Stretton, Salop. *Clubs :* Royal Societies ; Shropshire. (*Died 11 Nov. 1920.*)

AULARD, Alphonse, Professeur honoraire a l'Université de Paris ; président de la Société de l'Histoire de la Révolution. *b.* Montbron (Charente) ; *b.* 19 juillet 1849. *Educ. :* collège de Lons-le-Saunier ; lycée Louis-le-Grand et Ecole normale supérieure. Professeur aux lycées de Nîmes et de Nice ; aux Facultés d'Aix, Montpellier, Dijon, Poitiers ; au lycée Janson de Sailly ; à la Sorbonne. *Publications :* Les idées et l'inspiration de Leopardi ; Les Orateurs de la Révolution ; Le culte de la Raison et la culte de l'être suprême ; La Société des Jacobins ; Paris sous le Directoire, le Consulat et l'Empire ; Etudes et leçons sur la Révolution ; Recueil des actes du Comité de salut public ; Histoire politique de la Révolution Française ; Taine historien de la Révolution Française ; Napoléon 1er et le monopole universitaire ; La guerre actuelle commentée par l'histoire ; La Révolution française et le Régime féodal ; Le patriotisme français de la Renaissance à la Révolution ; Le Christianisme et la Révolution française. *Address :* Place de l'Ecole, No. 1, Paris 1er area. (*Died Oct. 1928.*)

AUMONIER, Stacy, author ; *b.* 1887 ; *s.* of William Aumonier, architectural sculptor ; *m.* Gertrude Peppercorn ; one *s. Educ. :* Cranleigh. Began career as a decorative designer and landscape painter ; exhibited frequently at the R.A., the R.I., and the International ; in 1908 became a Society Entertainer, giving many recitals of his own original character sketches, and performing at the Comedy, the Criterion, and other theatres ; began writing in 1913, and has contributed a great number of short stories to all the leading magazines of England and America ; during the war served as a private in the A.P.C., and afterwards as a maker of charts at the Ministry of National Service. *Publications :* Novels—Olga Bardel, Just Outside, The Querrils, One after Another ; Heartbeat, 1922 ; volumes of short stories—Three Bars' Interval, The Love-a-duck ; Miss Bracegirdle and Others ; Odd Fish ; Overheard ; The Baby Grand, 1926 *Recreation :* gardening. *Address :* 35 Marlborough Hill, St. John's Wood, N.W.8. *T. :* Primrose Hill 1089. *Clubs :* Savage, St. John's Wood Arts, Pen.
(*Died 21 Dec. 1928.*)

AUNG, Maung Myat Tun, C.I.E. 1911 ; Deputy Commissioner, Provincial Civil Service, since 1908. *Address :* Kyaukpyu, Burma.
(Died 1920.)

AUSTEN-LEIGH, Charles Edward ; *b.* 1833 : 2nd *s.* of Rev. James Edward Austen of Tring. *Educ. :* Harrow ; Balliol Coll. Oxford. Principal Clerk of Committees, House of Commons 1892-97. *Recreations :* shooting, fishing, stalking, golf. *Address :* Frog Firle, Berwick Station, Sussex. *Club :* Oriental.
(Died 3 April 1916.)

AUSTIN, Hon. Austin Albert, Member South-Western Province Legislative Council of Victoria ; *b.* 23 Nov. 1855 ; *s.* of Thomas and Elizabeth Philips Austin ; *m.* Winifred Cameron of Morgiana, Hamilton, Victoria ; two *s.* three *d.* *Educ. :* Church of England Grammar School, Geelong. Captain of School cricket and football teams, 1872-1873. *Address :* Larundel, Elaine, Victoria, Australia. *Club :* Geelong.
(Died 29 July 1925.)

AUSTIN, Michael, member of late Labour Commission ; *b.* 1855 ; *s.* of late J. Austin, Cork ; *m.* 1885, Jane, 2nd *d.* of Peter Moriarty, The View, Orrery Hill, Cork. *Educ. :* Christian Brothers' School, Cork. Takes a keen interest in industrial matters ; M.P. (N.) Co. Limerick, W. 1892-1900. *(Died 18 Feb. 1916.)*

AVERY, Sir William Eric Thomas, 2nd Bt., *cr.* 1905 ; Capt. (Temp. Major) A.S.C., S.R. ; *b.* 16 Mar. 1890 ; *s.* of 1st Bt. and Anna Louisa, 4th *d.* of Francis Bell. *Educ. :* Winchester ; University College, Oxford. *S.* father 1908 ; served European War, 1914-18 (M.C.). *Heir :* none. *Recreations :* rowing, motoring. *Address :* University College, Oxford. *Club :* Conservative. *(Died 20 Nov. 1918.)*

AVES, Ernest, M.A., F.S.S. ; Chairman of Trade Boards : *b.* Cambridge, 1857 ; *y. s.* of late William Owen Aves ; *m.* 1897, Eva, *y. d.* of late Frederick Maitland ; two *d.* *Educ. :* private schools ; Trin. Coll. Cambridge. First class Moral Sciences Tripos, 1883 ; Fellow of the Royal Statistical Society since 1893 ; member of the Council of the Royal Economic Society since 1897 ; resident at Toynbee Hall, 1886-97 ; Secretary to the Council of the Universities' Settlement Association, 1889-1901; acting sub-warden of Toynbee Hall, 1890-97. Commissioner (Home Office) to investigate and report on Wages Boards, Industrial Conciliation and Arbitration Acts, etc., of Australia and New Zealand (1907-8) ; Special Enquiries (Board of Trade), 1909-11. *Publications :* contributed several chapters to vols. iv., v. and ix. of Mr. Charles Booth's inquiry into the Life and Labour of the People ; Co-operative Industry ; has written articles on Wages and Hours of Labour in Ency. Brit. (new vols.) and various papers on Economics and Sociology, mostly for the Economic Journal. *Recreations :* fond of mountaineering, golf, cycling, walking, etc. *Address :* 12 Thurlow Road, Hampstead, N.W. *T. :* Hampstead 5366. *Clubs :* Alpine Royal Societies. *(Died 29 April 1917.)*

AWDRY, Sir Richard Davis, K.C.B., *cr.* 1902 ; C.B. 1894 ; *b.* 1843 ; *s.* of Rev. Charles R. E. Awdry ; *m.* 1st, 1868, Annie Martha (*d.* 1900), *d.* of T. Allgood ; 2nd, 1901, Katherine Louise James, adopted *d.* of Herbert Worthington, late of Brithdir Hall, Berriew, Montgomery; two *s.* one *d.* *Educ. :* Marlborough. Accountant-General of the Royal Navy, 1896-1904. *Address :* 63 Victoria Road, Kensington, W. *Club :* St. Stephens. *T.A. :* 1315 Western.
(Died 4 Oct. 1916.)

AYLESFORD, 8th Earl of (*cr.* 1714), Charles Wightwick Finch. Baron of Guernsey, 1703 ; *b.* 7 June 1851 ; *S.* brother 1885 ; *m.* 1st, 1873, Georgiana (*d.* 1874), *d.* of 3rd Lord Bagot ; 2nd, 1879, Ella Victoria, *d.* of John Ross, Benena, and widow of Captain James Wingfired Linton of Hemingford, Abbots, Hunts ; three *s.* two *d.* *Educ. :* Eton. Owns

about 9000 acres. *Heir* g.s. Lord Guernsey. *Address :* Packington Hall, Coventry ; Diddington Hall, Coventry ; The Friars, Aylesford. *Clubs:* Carlton, Marlborough, Cavalry.
(Died 16 Sept. 1924.)

AYLMER, 8th Baron (*cr.* 1718), Matthew Aylmer ; Bt. 1662 ; President Kootenay Gold Mines, Ltd. ; *b.* 28 March 1842 ; *s.* of 7th Baron and Mary, *d.* of Edward Journeaux ; *S.* father, 1901 ; *m.* 1875, Amy Gertrude, *d.* of Hon. John Young ; three *s.* two *d.* Lt. 7th R. Fus. 1864 : served Fenian Raids (medal, 2 clasps, general service medal) ; entered Canadian Militia ; served as District Paymaster A.A.G., etc. ; in command of Canadian Contingent, Queen Victoria's Diamond Jubilee ; Hon. Col. 11th Hussars, 1903 ; Inspector-General, 1904 ; retired, Major-General, 1907. *Heir : s.* Hon. J. F. W. Aylmer. *Address :* Queen's Bay, Kootenay, B.C. *(Died 11 June 1923.)*

AYLMER, Sir Arthur Percy Fitzgerald, 13th Bt., *cr.* 1621 ; *b.* 2 Mar. 1858 ; *e. s.* of late Fenton John Aylmer, 97th Regt., and Isabella Elinor, *e. d.* of late George Darling, Fowberry Tower, Northumberland; *m.* 1st, 1878, Annie, *d.* of John Sanger (*d.* 1884) ; 2nd, 1885, Anne (who obtained a divorce, 1886), *d.* of J. Douglas Reid, of New York, and divorced wife of George Stelle, Chicago; *S.* grandfather, Sir Arthur Percy Aylmer, **12th Bt.**, 1885. *Recreations :* music, gardening, travelling. *Heir : b.* Sir Fenton John Aylmer.
(Died 5 Dec. 1923.)

AYRTON, Hertha ; the only woman member of the Institution of Electrical Engineers ; *b.* Portsea ; *d.* of Levi and Alice Marks ; *m.* 1885, Prof. W. E. Ayrton (*d.* 1908) ; one *d.* *Educ. :* private school ; Girton College, Cambridge. Invented and constructed a line divider ; assisted in the completion of a series of experiments on the electric arc for Prof. Ayrton during his absence in America, 1893; has carried out several series of experiments on the same subject since ; discovered the connection between current length and pressure in the arc, the cause and laws of hissing in it, etc. ; has carried out various researches connected with the motion of water, and has discovered causes and process of formation of sand-ripples on the sea-shore ; nominated for Fellowship of Royal Society, 1902, but, on counsel's opinion, the Council had no power to elect a woman ; Hughes medal awarded by the Royal Society, 1906. *Publications :* The Electric Arc, 1902 ; twelve papers on the Electric Arc in The Electrician, 1896 ; papers before the British Association, 1895, 1897, 1898 ; the Institution of Electrical Engineers, 1899 ; the International Electrical Congress, 1900 ; La Société Française de Physique, 1911 ; the Royal Society, 1901, 1904, 1908, 1911, 1915, 1919 ; Afternoon Lecture before British Association, 1904 ; invented in 1915 and presented to the War Office for the duration of the War, Anti-Gas Fan, of which over a hundred thousand were used at the Front. *Recreations :* novel reading and sketching. *Address :* 41 Norfolk Square, W.2. *T. :* Paddington 3109. *(Died 26 Aug. 1923.)*

AYSCOUGH, John (Rt. Rev. Mgr. Count Bickerstaffe-Drew, *q.v.*) ; *s.* of Rev. Harry Lloyd Bickerstaffe. *Educ. :* Lichfield Grammar School. Entered Catholic Church while an undergraduate at Oxford. *Publications :* Rosemary ; Mezzogiorno ; Marotz ; Dromina ; San Celestino ; Hurdcott ; Admonition ; Mr. Beke of the Blacks ; A Roman Tragedy ; Outsiders and In, Faustula ; Levia Pondera, Gracechurch, Monksbridge, French Windows, The Tideway, Jacqueline, Fernando, A Prince in Petto, Abbotscourt, The Foundress, First Impressions in America, Pages from the Past, 1922, Mariquita, etc. ; an essayist and contributor to Magazines and Reviews. *Recreation :* literary work. *Club :* Authors'.
(Died 3 July 1928.)

AYSCOUGH, Rev. Thos. Ayscough; Prebendary of Hereford; *b.* 11 Sep. 1880 ; *s.* of Ayscough Smith, Leesthorpe Hall, Melton Mowbray ; *m.* 1858, Ethel Anna, *d.* of J. P. Fearon, Ockenden, Cuckfield. *Educ.:* Rugby ; Trinity College, Cambridge—B.A. 1853, M.A. 1856. Curate of Skipsea, dio. York, 1854-56 ; Loughborough, 1856-60 ; Vicar of Tenbury, 1860-1892 ; Rector of Cradley, near Malvern, 1892-1917. *Address:* Pinehurst, Evesham Road, Cheltenham.   *(Died 18 April 1920.)*

AZOPARDI, Sir Vincent Frendo, Kt., *cr.* 1912 ; LL.D., C.M.G. 1908 ; Chief Justice and President of H.M.'s Court of Appeal, and Vice-President of the Council of Government of Malta, 1915 ; *b.* 6 Jan. 1865 ; *s.* of Pasquale Frendo Azopardi, LL.D.; *m.* 1892, Caterina, *d.* of late M. A. De Giorgio, LL.D.; LL.D. Malta Univ.; Bar. Malta, 1887 ; Advocate for the Poor, Malta, 1895 ; Professor of Law, Malta University, 1899-1905 ; Magistrate of Judicial Police, 1900 ; Assistant Crown Advocate, 1903 ; Crown Advocate and Govt. Legal Adviser to Naval and Military Authorities (with seat in Executive and Legislative Councils), 1905. *Address:* Valetta, Malta.   *(Died June 1919.)*

B

BABBAGE, Major-General Henry Prevost ; retired ; *y. s.* of late Charles Babbage, F.R.S.; *b.* 1824 ; *m.* Mary, *d.* of late Colonel P. W. A. Bradshawe; two *d.* *Educ.:* University College School and University College, London. East India Company's Bengal Army, 1843 ; passed Interpreters' Examination, 1845 ; served in Sutlege Campaign, 1846 ; services placed at disposal of the Bengal Government for employment in Assam, 1847 ; resigned, 1849 ; commanded expedition against the Abor tribe, 1848 ; Adjutant and acting 2nd in command Shekhawatte Battalion, 1850 ; furlough to England, 1854-57 ; interpreter to his regiment, Mutiny, 1857 ; Assistant Commissioner in the Punjab, 1857 ; J.P. Punjab, 1859 ; Member of the Senate, Lahore University; resigned the Service, 1874, with rank of Major-General; served at Bromley, in Kent, six years on the Bromley Town Council, and three years as Guardian of the Poor; Elective Auditor at Cheltenham, 1904-5 ; Member of Royal Asiatic and the Royal Statistical Societies. *Publications:* On Mechanical Notation, British Association, 1856 ; Magistrates' Handbook of Special Laws, Post Office, Railways, Excise, etc., etc., 1863, in India ; Occulting Lights, 1889 ; Babbage's Calculating Machines, 1889 ; Scheme of Accounts for Municipal Boroughs, 1906 ; Thoughts on Income Tax by C. Babbage, 4th ed., 1907 ; Calculating Machine, British-Japan Exhibition 1910, Coronation Exhibition 1911, Science Museum, South Kensington, 1912. *Address:* Mayfield, Lansdown Place, Cheltenham. *Club:* New, Cheltenham.   *(Died 29 Jan. 1918.)*

BABTIE, Lieut.-Gen. Sir William, V.C. 1899 ; K.C.B., *cr.* 1919 ; K.C.M.G., *cr.* 1916 ; C.B., 1912 ; C.M.G., 1899 ; Hon. Surgeon to H.M., 1914-19 ; a Knight of Grace of the Order of St. John of Jerusalem in England ; *b.* 7 May 1859 ; *e. s.* of late John Babtie, J.P., of Dunbarton ; *m.* 1903, Edith Mary, *d.* of late W. H. Barry, J.P., of Ballyadam, Co. Cork, and widow of Major P. A. Hayes ; one *d.* *Educ.:* Univ. of Glasgow ; M.B., 1880 ; LL.D. 1919. Entered Army Medical Service, 1881 ; Assistant Director-General, 1901-6 ; Assist. Med. Officer Eastern Command, 1906-7 ; Inspector of Medical Services, 1907-10 ; Deputy-Director-General Army Medical Service, 1910-14 ; Director,

Medical Services in India, 1914-15 ; served during international occupation of Crete as senior medical officer, 1897-98 (C.M.G.); in South Africa on Staff of Natal army, present at all the actions for the relief of Ladysmith and subsequent operations in Natal and Eastern Transvaal, 1899-1900 (despatches, promoted Lieut.-Col., medal with five clasps, V.C.); during European War as Principal Director, Medical Services, Mediterranean, during operations in Gallipoli, Egypt, and Salonika, 1915-16 (despatches, K.C.M.G.); and as Director and later Inspector Medical Services, War Office, 1916-19 (K.C.B.). *Address:* 7 Campden Hill Gardens, W. *Club:* Junior United Service.   *(Died 11 Sept. 1920.)*

BACK, Ven. Hugh Cairns Alexander, Rector of Hampton-Lucy since 1924 ; Archdeacon of Warwick since 1923 ; Hon. Canon of Coventry ; Proctor in Convocation, 1919 ; Rural Dean ; *b.* 26 Aug. 1863 ; *m.* Maud E., *d.* of Colonel and Lady Harriet Fletcher of Kenward, Kent ; one *s.* one *d.* *Educ.:* Trinity College, Cambridge (M.A.). Deacon, 1887 ; Priest, 1888 ; Curate of Ulverston, 1887-89 ; Kidderminster, 1889-92 ; Rector of Brandiston, 1892-97 ; Vicar of Rostherne, 1897-1903 ; Rector of Berkswell, 1903-24. *Address:* Hampton-Lucy Rectory, Warwick.   *(Died 27 Dec. 1923.)*

BACKHOUSE, Sir Jonathan Edmund, 1st Bt.; *cr.* 1901 ; J.P., D.L. ; Director of Barclay and Co., Ltd. ; *b.* 1849 ; *e. s.* of late Edmund Backhouse, M.P., and Juliet Mary, *d.* of Charles Fox; *m.* 1871, Florence (*d.* 1902), *d.* of Sir John S. Trelawny, 9th Bt.; four *s.* one *d.* *Educ.:* Rugby School ; Trinity Hall, Cambridge. *Heir:* *s.* E. T. Backhouse. *Address:* The Rookery, Middleton Tyas, Yorks.
     (Died 27 July 1918.)

BACON, Edwin Munroe, M.A.; *b.* Providence, Rhode Island, 20 Oct. 1844 ; editor of Time and the Hour, 1892-1900. Formerly Editor successively of Boston Globe, Boston Advertiser, and Boston Post. *Publications:* Boston Illustrated ; Bacon's Dictionary of Boston ; Walks and Rides in the Country round about Boston ; Historic Pilgrimages in New England ; Literary Pilgrimages in New England ; Boston : a Guide Book ; The Connecticut River and the Valley of the Connecticut ; English Voyages of Adventure and Discovery (Retold from Hakluyt) ; The Boy's Drake ; Manual of Ship Subsidies ; Manual of Navigation Laws ; Direct Elections and Law-Making by Popular Vote : The Initiative—The Referendum—The Recall—Commission Government for Cities—Preferential Voting (latter in association with Morrill Wyman). *Address:* 36 Pinckney Street, Boston, U.S.A.   *(Died 24 Mar. 1916.)*

BACOT, Arthur William, F.E.S. ; Entomologist to the Lister Institute of Preventive Medicine ; Hon. Entomologist to War Office ; Member W. O. Sanitary Committe ; *b.* London, 1866 ; *s.* of Edmund Alexander Bacot ; unmarried. *Educ.:* Birkbeck School. Student of Entomology for many years ; worked in Sierra Leone for Yellow Fever Commission. *Publications:* numerous contributions concerning Lepidoptera to Entomological Magazine and Tutt's British Lepidoptera ; many papers dealing with Insects and Disease in Journal of Hygiene, Parasitology ; report of Yellow Fever Commission, British Medical Journal, etc. *Recreations:* gardening, cycling, skating. *Address:* 19 York Hill, Loughton, Essex.   *(Died 12 April 1922.)*

BADCOCK, Brig-Gen. Francis Frederick, D.S.O. 1892 ; late Commandant 2nd Batt. 6th Ghoorka Rifles; *b.* 13 Sep. 1867 ; *s.* of late General Sir A. R. Badcock ; *m.* 1896, Eleanor Sara Austen, *d.* of late Rev. G. F. de Gex ; one *s.* one *d.* *Educ.:* Wellington College. Entered army, 1886 ; Captain, 1897 ; served Hazara Expedition, 1891 (despatches, clasp) ; Miranzai

Expedition, 1891 (clasp) ; Hunza-Nagar, 1891-92 (wounded, despatches, D.S.O., clasp) ; Waziristan Field Force, 1894-95 (clasp) ; Tirah Expeditionary Force (severely wounded, medal with two clasps) ; N.W. Frontier of India, Zakka Khel Expedition (medal with clasp) ; retired, 1920. *(Died 9 July 1926.)*

BADCOCK, Jasper Capper, C.B. 1899 ; *b.* 2 Sept. 1840 ; *e. s.* of late John Badcock of Chelsea ; *m.* 1864, Mary, *d.* of E. G. Burton. *Educ.:* private school. Appointed clerk in General Post Office, 1858 ; Assist.-Controller London Postal Service, 1882 ; Vice-Controller, 1887 ; Controller London Postal Service, 1892-1905 ; retired, 1905. *Address:* Springfield, 37 Brodrick Road, Upper Tooting, S.W. 17. *(Died 25 May 1924.)*

BADDELEY, Col. Charles Edward, C.B. 1919 ; C.M.G. 1916 ; R.E. ; *b.* 27 July 1861 ; *s.* of late Col. W. H. C. Baddeley ; *m.* Kathleen, *d.* of Rev. M. Chaplin. Served Burmese Expedition, 1885-87 (despatches, medal with clasp) ; N.W. Frontier, India, 1897-98 (despatches, medal with clasp) ; Tirah, 1897-98 ; capture of Sampagha and Arhanga Passes ; Operations in Bazar Valley (clasp) ; European War, 1914-18 (C.M.G., C.B.). *(Died 23 April 1925.)*

BADDELEY, Sir John James, 1st Bt., *cr.* 1922 ; Kt., *cr.* 1909 ; J.P. ; Alderman, Farringdon Within ; Member of the Common Council since 1886 ; Chairman of Cripplegate Foundation, 1907, and of many Committees ; *b.* 22 Dec. 1842 ; *e. s.* of John Baddeley, Hackney ; *m.* 1st, 1868, Mary, *d.* of William Locks, Hackney ; five *s.* four *d.* ; 2nd, 1912, Florence, *d.* of J. Douglass Mathews. Sheriff of the City of London, 1908-9 ; Lord Mayor of London, 1921-22 ; Commander Swedish Order of Wasa, of Russian Order of St. Anne, and Crown of Belgium. *Publications:* A History of St. Giles's Church, Cripplegate ; A History of the Guildhall ; The Aldermen of the Cripplegate Ward from 1275 ; Cripplegate Ward, 1921. *Recreation:* fishing. *Heir: e. s.* John William [*b.* 24 Aug. 1869 ; *m.* 1892, Kate, *d.* of John Shaw, Clapton]. *Address:* Lakefield, 32 Woodberry Down, Stoke Newington, N.4. *T.:* Clissold 1343. *(Died 28 June 1926.)*

BADEN-POWELL, Warington, K.C. ; Lieutenant Royal Naval Reserve ; *m.* 1913, Cicely Hilda Farmer ; went to sea and served in various parts of the world, 1860-73 ; Barr. Inner Temple ; practises in Admiralty Court, Wreck Court, and Northern Circuit. *Recreations:* yachting, canoeing, salmon fishing, shooting. *Address:* 1 Chelsea Court, Chelsea Embankment, S.W. *Clubs:* Athenæum, Royal Thames Yacht. *(Died 24 April 1921.)*

BAGGALLAY, Rev. Frederick ; *b.* 16 May 1855 ; *s.* of Rt. Hon. Sir Richard Baggallay, Lord Justice of Appeal ; *m.* 1885, Emily Cecile (*d.* 1920), *e. d.* of Wilson Fox, M.D., F.R.S., Physician in Ordinary to Queen Victoria ; one *s.* *Educ.:* Rugby ; Gonville and Caius Coll., Camb. (Scholar). Ordained, 1880 ; Curate of Great Yarmouth ; Clerk in Orders at St. George's, Hanover Square, 1888 ; Vicar of St. Peter, Mancroft, Norwich, 1884 ; Holy Trinity, Weymouth, 1890 ; Oakham, 1894 ; Hon. Canon of Peterborough, 1903-5 ; Rural Dean of Rutland, 1897 ; Rector of Pulborough, 1904-21 ; prebendary of Ferring in Chichester Cathedral, 1915-21 ; Proctor in Convocation for Diocese of Chichester, 1918-21 ; Licensed Preacher, Diocese of Rochester, 1921. *Address:* The Vicarage, Bickley, Kent. *T.:* Ravensbourne 1001. *Club:* Overseas. *(Died 3 Dec. 1928.)*

BAGGE, Sir Alfred Thomas, 3rd Bt. ; *cr.* 1867 ; Capt. R.N. (retired 1893) ; *b.* 5 July 1843 ; 2nd *s.* of 1st Bt. and Frances, *d.* of Sir Thomas Preston, Bt. ; *m.* Millicent, *d.* of J. Grant Morris, Allerton Priory, Liverpool, 1872 ; three *s.* one *d.* S. brother 1881. Entered R.N. 1857 ; served throughout China War, 1857-61. *Heir: s.* Alfred

William Francis [*b.* 14 Sept. 1875. *Educ.:* Eton ; King's Coll. Camb. ; B.A., LL.B. *Address:* St. Faith's Lane, Norwich ; 4 Temple Gardens, E.C. *Club:* Oxford and Cambridge]. *Address:* Stradsett Hall, Downham Market, Norfolk. *T.A.:* Fincham. *(Died 16 Feb. 1916.)*

BAGHOT DE LA BERE, Stephen ; *b.* Dec. 1877 ; *s.* of Kinard Baghot de la Bere of Burbage Hall, Leicestershire, and Catherine Leahy. Unmarried. *Educ.:* Ilkley College, Yorkshire. Studied in London and France; Exhibitor R.A., Paris, Madrid, etc. ; illustrated various books ; black and white work for leading magazines and periodicals ; 2nd Lt. R.G.A. (S.R.) ; served in France, 1917. *Recreations:* golf, motoring, fishing, etc. *Address:* 52 Sydney Building, Bath. *Clubs:* Chelsea Arts, London Sketch. *(Died 29 July 1927.)*

BAGNALL - WILD, Ralph Bagnall, M.A., J.P., C.C. ; *b.* 1845 ; 2nd *s.* of William Kirkby ; assumed the surnames of Bagnall-Wild by Royal Licence, 1868, on succeeding to estates of late Samuel Bagnall-Wild ; *m.* 1871, Alice, *d.* of R. A. Pfeil of Guildford ; one *s.* one *d.* *Educ.:* Ruabon School ; Gonville and Caius College, Cambridge. Senior Open Scholarship, 1864 ; rowed in college boat ; 18th Wrangler, 1868 ; B.A. 1868 ; M.A. 1871 ; a pupil of Arthur Cohen, K.C., P.C., and of late Thos. Lewin ; called to Bar, Inner Temple, 1870 ; practised Northern Circuit and Liverpool Sessions ; in the Lawn Tennis world he was known by introducing the system of "draw" in matches known as the "Bagnall-Wild" system ; J.P. Co. Notts ; *Address:* Manor House, Costock, Loughborough. *T.A.:* Bagnall-Wild, East Leake.
(Died 11 Oct. 1925.)

BAGOT, Sir Alan Desmond, 1st Bt., *cr.* 1913 ; Lieut. Royal Horse Guards ; *b.* 20 Feb. 1896 ; *s.* of Lt.-Col. Josceline Fitzroy Bagot and Lady Theodosia Bagot. *Heir:* none. *Address:* 71A Duke Street, Grosvenor Square, W.1 ; *T.:* Mayfair 5894 ; Levens Hall, Milnthorpe, Westmorland. *Clubs:* Bachelors', Wells. *(Died 11 Jan. 1920.)*

BAGOT, Richard ; novelist ; Grand Officer and Commendatore of the Order of the Crown of Italy ; a Knight of Honour of the Sovereign Order of Malta ; *b.* 8 Nov. 1860 ; 2nd *surv. s.* of late Col. Charles Bagot, Grenadier Guards, and Sophy Louisa, *d.* of Admiral Hon. Josceline Percy, *s.* of the Earl of Beverley, and brother of 5th Duke of Northumberland ; succeeded to the Levens and Kilburn estates on death of his nephew, Sir Alan Bagot, Bt., of Levens, 1920. *Educ.:* privately. Private Secretary to the late Sir Frederick Napier Broome, when Governor of Western Australia, 1882-88 ; member of Royal Institution ; hon. member of Società Leonardo da Vinci, Florence. *Publications:* A Roman Mystery, 1899 ; Casting of Nets, 1901 ; The Just and the Unjust, 1902 ; Donna Diana, 1903 ; Love's Proxy, 1904 ; The Passport, 1905 ; Temptation, 1907 ; The Lakes of Northern Italy, 1907 ; Anthony Cuthbert, 1908 ; The House of Serravalle, 1910 ; My Italian Year, 1911 ; The Italians of To-day, 1912 ; Darneley Place, 1912 ; The Gods Decide, 1918 ; articles in reviews (British and Italian) on political and literary subjects ; was presented in 1917 with an Illuminated Address from the Italian nation, signed by the Members of the Government, Senate, and Chamber, and by the leading representatives of Italian Science, Literature, Art, and Industries, and Mayors of the chief cities, as a tribute to his literary, international and other services to Italy. *Recreations:* fishing, travelling, etc. *Address:* Levens Hall, Westmorland ; Tripalle, Crespina, Italy. *Clubs:* Travellers', Bachelors', Authors'. Athenæum, Royal Automobile. *(Died 11 Dec. 1921.)*

BAGOT, Major Hon. Walter Lewis, D.S.O. 1900 ; General Manager, The Victoria Falls and Transvaal Power Company, Ltd., and

Chairman of Rand Mines Power Supply Co., Ltd. (Johannesburg); *b.* Blithefield, Rugeley, 22 Apr. 1864; *s.* of 3rd and *heir-pres.* of 4th Baron Bagot; *m.* 1892, Margaret Jane Caroline, *d.* of Hon. F. W. Cadogan, *s.* of 3rd Earl Cadogan; one *d. Educ.:* Eton; R.M.C., Sandhurst. Entered Grenadier Guards. 1884; A.D.C. to Governor of S. Australia, 1890; served Soudan, 1898 (British medal, Khedive's medal and clasp); retired 1898; recalled as D.A.A.G. Imperial Yeomanry, 1900; South Africa (despatches, Queen's medal three clasps, King's medal two clasps, Brevet Major, D.S.O.); served on staff of G.O.C. 4th Army Corps in France, Nov. 1914–June 1915, and as a Director in Ministry of Munitions of War, June 1915–Jan. 1916. *Address:* P.O. Box 2671, Johannesburg. *Club:* Travellers'.
(*Died 26 May 1927.*)

BAGSTER, Robert, F.S.A., F.Z.S.; Chairman and Managing Director, Samuel Bagster & Sons, Ltd.; *b.* 1847; *s.* of head of Bagster & Sons, Publishers; *m.* C. J Toms, Chard; one *d. Educ.:* Brighton. Printer and Publisher; Freeman of City of London; Ambulance Section during War; Treasurer British Archæological Association, etc. *Address:* 15 Paternoster Row, E.C.4. *T.A.:* Bagster Cent. London. *T.:* Central 3172. *M.:* XP 2669. *Clubs:* Constitutional; Conservative, Edinburgh. (*Died 20 Nov. 1924.*)

BAGWELL, Richard, J.P. and D.L. Co. Tipperary; J.P. Co. Waterford; *b.* 9 Dec. 1840; *e. s.* of John Bagwell, M.P., Clonmel, 1857-74; *m.* 1873, Harriet, *d.* of P. J. Newton, Dunleckney; one *s.* three *d. Educ.:* Harrow; Christ Church, Oxford. Called to Bar, Inner Temple; Special Local Government Commissioner, 1898-1903; Commissioner of National Education since 1905; Hon. Litt.D., Dublin University; Oxford University, 1917; a Unionist and has been an active speaker and writer for that cause. *Publications:* Ireland under the Tudors, 3 vols.; Ireland under the Stuarts, 3 vols. *Address:* Marlfield, Clonmel. *Clubs:* Brooks's, Athenæum, Oxford and Cambridge; Kildare Street, Dublin. (*Died 4 Dec. 1918.*)

BAIKIE, Brig.-Gen. Sir Hugh Archie Dundas Simpson-, K.C.M.G., *cr.* 1919; C.B. 1915; late R.A.; *b.* 18 Mar. 1871; *s.* of F. Simpson-Baikie; *m.* 1907, Marion Evelyn, *d.* of C. Miller; one *d.* Served Nile Expedition, 1899 (despatches, 4th Class Medjidie, Egyptian medal, 2 clasps); S. Africa, 1900-1902 (despatches twice, Queen's medal, 4 clasps, King's medal, 2 clasps); France, 1914-15; Dardanelles, 1915 (despatches, C.B., Officer Legion of Honour), France, 1916 (despatches); Salonica, 1917 (Bt. Colonel, despatches); Egypt and Palestine, 1917-18 (K.C.M.G., despatches 4 times). *Club:* Army and Navy. (*Died 6 Mar. 1924.*)

BAILEY, Captain Arthur Harold, D.S.O. 1900; late South Lancs Regt.; *b.* 24 Aug. 1873; *s.* of W. H. Bailey. Entered army, 1894; Adjutant, 1899; served Matabeleland, 1896; South Africa, 1900 (despatches twice, Queen's medal, five clasps, Queen's medal two clasps, D.S.O.). (*Died 17 Feb. 1925.*)

BAILEY, Lt. - Col. E. Wyndham - Grevis, J.P. Co. Kent; late commanding 3rd Bt. Royal West Kent Regt.; *m. o. d.* of Capt. Jas. Evelyn, Grenadier Guards; one *s. Educ.:* privately. Joined the West Kent Militia, 1876; served in Malta with the Regt. during the S. African War, 1900; the Regt. being the first to leave England and volunteer for service; Lord of the Manors of Ightham, Wrotham, and Stansted. *Recreations:* shooting and hunting. *Address:* Ightham Court, Kent. *Club:* Junior United Service; Kent County, Maidstone.
(*Died 1920.*)

BAILEY, Rt. Hon. Wm. Frederick, P.C. Ireland, 1909; C.B. 1906, B.A., F.R.G.S., M.R.I.A., Estates Commissioner under the Irish Land Act, 1903, and one of the Irish Land Commissioners; Governor of the National Gallery; *b.* Castletown Conyers, Co. Limerick, 1857; *e. s.* of W. Bailey, M.D., R.N. *Educ.:* Trinity College, Dublin; a first senior moderatorship and large gold medal in History and Political Science; was auditor and gold medallist in oratory of the College Historical Society; called to Irish Bar and joined the Munster Circuit, 1881; was Barrington Lecturer in Political Economy; examiner in English under the Intermediate Education Board; appointed one of the Secretaries to the Royal Commission on Irish Public Works, 1886; became a Legal Assistant Commissioner under the Irish Land Acts, 1887; for many years Secretary of the Statistical and Social Inquiry Society of Ireland, and was elected President of the Society, 1902. *Publications:* The Slavs of the War Zone, 1916; The Law of Franchise and Registration in Ireland; Local and Centralised Government in Ireland; Ireland Since the Famine; Report on the Condition of Peasant Purchasers in Ireland; editions of Gray's Poems, Coleridge's Ancient Mariner, etc., and various papers in Reviews, etc., and in the Irish Statistical Society's Journal. *Recreations:* golf, cycling, motoring, photography, and travel. Has been in every European country, and has travelled extensively in North, Central and South America, North and South Africa, India, Transcaucasia, and Palestine. *Address:* 3 Earlsfort Terrace, Dublin. *Clubs:* Reform, Royal Automobile; University, Dublin.
(*Died 16 April 1917.*)

BAILEY, William Henry, I.S.O. 1905; *b.* 10 July 1855; *s.* of Wm. R. Bailey of Barbadoes; *m.* 1882, Isabella, *d.* of late I. K. Brown, Comptroller of Customs; four *s.* two *d.* 3rd Clerk, Customs Department 1875; 2nd Clerk, 1876; Chief Clerk, Colonial Secretary's Department, 1882; acted Auditor-General on several occasions; Registrar of the Courts, 1898; Colonial Postmaster, 1900; acted as a member of the Legislative Council, 1912-13 and 1919; Manager Savings Bank, Aug. 1919; Auditor - General, Feb. 1920; resigned, May 1920. *Address:* Bridgetown, Barbados.

BAILHACHE, Hon. Sir Clement Meacher, Kt., *cr.* 1912; LL.B.; K.C. 1908; Judge of the High Court since 1912; *s.* of a Baptist minister; *b.* Leeds, 2 Nov. 1856; *m.* 1881, Fanny Elizabeth, *d.* of Herman Liebstein; two *d. Educ.:* City of London School; London University. Practised for some years as a Solicitor; Bar, Middle Temple, 1889; joined South Wales and Chester Circuit. *Address:* Trevanion, Totteridge, Herts.
(*Died 8 Sept. 1924.*)

BAILIE, Maj.-General Thomas Maubourg, J.P.; *b.* 16 Aug. 1844; *m.* 1886, Amy, *d.* of Sir William Miller of Manderston, 1st Bt. Entered army, 1862; Maj.-Gen., 1893; retired, 1896. *Address:* 54 Sloane Street, S.W.; Caldecot House, Abingdon. *Club:* Naval and Military. (*Died 5 April 1918.*)

BAILLIE, Sir Duncan (Colvin), K.C.S.I., *cr.* 1914; C.S.I. 1910; I.C.S.; retired; *b.* Inverness, 27 Nov. 1856; *s.* of late Peter Baillie, ship-owner, Inverness; *m.* 1887, Julia Luisa, *d.* of late Rev. Henry Stern, Rector of Brampton, Norwich; one *s.* one *d. Educ.:* Inverness Academy; Glasgow Academy; Edinburgh University. Entered I.C.S. 1879; Assist. Settlement Officer, 1886-89; Superintendent of Provincial Census, 1890-92; Dy.-Commissioner and Settlement Officer of Rai Bareli, 1892; Director of Land Records and Agriculture, 1895; Magistrate and Collector, 1896; Secretary to Board of Revenue, 1896; Opium Agent, Benares, 1899; Commissioner, Benares, 1903; has been officiating and subsequently permanent member of the Board of Revenue since 1907 except whilst employed in the Punjab as Member and subsequently President of a Committee on the Canal Colony Administration, 1907-8 ; Member Lt.-Governor's Council, 1909 ; officiated as Lieut.-Governor U.P. in 1913 ; retired, 1914. *Publication* : Census Report of 1891. *Recreation* : golf. *Address* : 89 Queen's Gate, S.W.   *T.* : Kensington 6422. *Club* : East India United Service.

(*Died 30 Aug. 1919.*)

BAILLIE, Sir Frank, K.B.E., *cr.* 1918 ; President, Bankers Investments, Ltd., and Burlington Steel Co. Ltd. ; *b.* Toronto, 9 Aug. 1875 ; *s.* of John Baillie and Marian Wilton ; *m.* 1900, Edith Julia, *d.* of late Aubrey White, C.M.G., Deputy Minister of Lands and Mines for Ontario ; three *s.* two *d.* Commenced business career as clerk with the Central Canada Loan & Savings Co., Toronto ; became private secretary to the late Senator George A. Cox ; accountant, Central Canada Loan & Savings Co. 1896 ; Secretary, 1898 ; Assistant Manager, 1901 ; General Manager, Metropolitan Bank, Toronto, 1902 ; formed the firm of Baillie, Wood & Croft, members of Toronto Stock Exchange, 1903 ; organised the Burlington Steel Co. Ltd., Hamilton, 1910, the Bankers Bond Co. Ltd., Toronto, 1912, and Dominion Steel Foundry Co. Ltd., Hamilton, 1912 ; shortly after the commencement of the European War in 1914, organised the Canadian Cartridge Co. Ltd., Hamilton, to manufacture brass cartridge cases for the British Government and later Anti-Aircraft Cases for U.S.A. Government ; Director of Aviation for Canada, Imperial Munitions Board, Dec. 1916, same month acting for the British Government, organised and became President of Canadian Aeroplanes, Ltd., which Company manufactured aeroplanes for the Royal Air Force in Canada, and flying boats for the American Government. Anglican. Independent (Politics). *Recreations* : golf, motoring, curling, yachting. *Address* : Lisonally Farm, Oakville, Ontario, Canada. *Clubs* : Albany, Lambton Golf and Country, Mississauga Golf, National, Royal Canadian Yacht, Toronto ; Victoria, Hamilton, Hamilton Golf, Hamilton, Ontario ; Los Angelos, Country, Beverly Hills, Cal. (*Died 2 Jan. 1921.*)

BAILLIE, Gen. James Cadogan Parkison, Bengal Infantry ; *b.* 8 Sept. 1835. Entered army, 1852 ; General, 1894 ; served Indian Mutiny, 1857-59 (twice wounded, once severely, medal). *Club* : East India United Service.

(*Died 31 Mar. 1923.*)

BAILLIE - GROHMAN, W. A. See Addenda, page xv.

BAILLIE-HAMILTON, Sir William Alexander, K.C.M.G. ; *cr.* 1897 ; C.B. 1892 ; C.M.G. 1887 ; Officer of Arms Order of St. Michael and St. George, 1901 ; Gentleman Usher of the Blue Rod, 1911 ; Chief Clerk of the Colonial Office, 1896-1909 ; Lt.-Col. and Hon. Colonel (retired) Lothians and Berwickshire Imperial Yeomanry ; *b.* 1844 ; *s.* of the late Adm. W. A. Baillie - Hamilton and Lady Harriet, *o. sister* of 1st Duke of Abercorn, K.G. ; *m.* Mary Aynscombe, *d.* of late Rev. John Mossop, 1871 ; two *s.* Barr. Inner Temple, 1871 ; Sec. to Colonial Conference, 1887 ; Private Secretary to Secretaries of State for Colonies, 1886 - 92. *Recreations* : hunting, shooting, fencing, field sports generally. *Address* : 55 Sloane Street, S.W. *Clubs* : Carlton ; Scottish Conservative, Edinburgh. (*Died 6 July 1920.*)

BAINBRIDGE, Francis Arthur, M.A., M.D., D.Sc., F.R.C.P. (Lond.), F.R.S. ; Pro-

fessor of Physiology, University of London ; *b.* Stockton-on-Tees, 1874 ; *s.* of R. R. Bainbridge ; *m.* 1905, Hilda Winifred, *d.* of Rev. Thornton Smith ; one *d.* *Educ.* : The Leys, Cambridge ; Trinity College, Cambridge (Scholar) ; St Bartholomew's Hospital, London. 1st Class Natural Sciences Tripos, Part I. (1895) and Part II. (1897), and Horton Smith Prize (1904), Cambridge ; Shuter Scholarship, House Physician and Casualty Physician, St. Bartholomew's Hospital ; Demonstrator in Physiology and Pharmacology, St. Bartholomew's Hospital ; Gordon Lecturer in Pathology, Guy's Hospital ; Assistant Bacteriologist, Lister Institute of Preventive Medicine ; Arris and Gale lecturer, Royal College of Surgeons, 1908 ; Milroy Lecturer, Royal College of Physicians, 1912. *Publications* : Numerous papers on physiological and bacteriological subjects. *Recreations* : walking, tennis. *Address* : St. Bartholomew's Hospital, E.C.   *Club* : Reform.

(*Died 27 Oct. 1921.*)

BAINBRIGGE, Rev. Philip Thomas, M.A. ; Prebendary of Reculversland in St. Paul's Cathedral, 1918 ; Vicar of St. Thomas, Regent Street, W., since 1888 ; *o. s.* of Major-Gen. Bainbrigge, R.E. ; *m.* 1st, 1884, Helen Jane (*d.* 1904), *d.* of Alexander Gillespie of Biggar Park, Lanarkshire ; one *d.* ; 2nd, 1905, Beatrice Eleanora, *d.* of Francis Borthwick of Haslieburn, Peeblesshire ; one *s.* *Educ.* : Hailey-bury ; Pembroke College, Oxford. Six years in business in the City, between School and College ; 2nd Class Theo. Schs. 1874 ; Curate of Oakham, 1875-78 ; St. Peter's, Leicester, 1878-80 ; St. Philip's, Regent Street, 1880-3. *Publications* : The Day Dawn from on High ; The Use and Abuse of the Word Protestant ; The Credulity of Unbelief, and other pamphlets. *Recreations* : golf, chess. *Address* : 12 Kingly Street, W.1. *Clubs* : Athenæum ; Walton Heath Golf. (*Died 1 Nov. 1919.*)

BAINES, Lieut.-Colonel J. C., D.S.O., T.D., A.R.I.B.A. ; practising architect ; *b.* 8 Sep. 1876 ; *s.* of S. C. Baines of Leicester ; *m.* E. S. Britten, *d.* of Vicar of Somerby ; two *s.* Served S. African War in Volunteer Service Coy. 1st Leicester Regt. ; European War, commanded 2/5 Sherwood Foresters and 14th Leicester Regt. (badly wounded, despatches 3 times). *Address* : Barn Close, Oadby, near Leicester. *T.* : Oadby 141. *M.* : NR 6486 and BC 6893. *Club* : Leicestershire, Leicester.

(*Died 26 Jan. 1928.*)

BAINES, Sir Jervoise Athelstane, Kt., *cr.* 1905 ; C.S.I. 1894 ; Indian Civil Service, retired ; Alderman, L.C.C., 1892-1902 ; Councillor, Oxon C.C., 1917-22 ; President (Gold Medallist), Royal Statistical Soc. 1909-10 ; *b.* Bluntisham, Hunts, 17 Oct. 1847 ; *s.* of Rev. Edward Baines and Catherine Eularia Baines, *d.* of John Baines of Eltham ; *m.* Constance, *d.* of late Henry Pyne, barrister, 1874 ; one *s.* one *d.* *Educ.* : Rugby ; Trin. Coll. Cantab. India Civil Service, Bombay, 1870-89 ; Census Commissioner under Government of India, 1889-93 ; employed at India Office and as Secretary to Royal Commission on Opium, 1894-95 ; retired, 1895. *Decorated* for Census Administration. *Publications* : Official Reports on Provincial Administration, on Indian Census Operations, 1881 - 91 ; on Indian Progress (Parliamentary), 1894 ; Many papers, ethnographic and statistical, for London Societies. *Address* : Home Close, Kidlington, Oxon. *Clubs* : Reform, Unionist. *M.* : BW 323.

(*Died 26 Nov. 1925.*)

BAINES, Matthew Talbot, M.A., J.P. ; late agent for the Marquess of Lansdowne, K.G. ; formerly Senior Small Holdings Commissioner for the Board of Agriculture and Fisheries ; *e. s.* of late L. T. Baines, of Westbrook, Horsham ; *b.* 1863 ; *m.* 1892, Eveleigh, *e. d.* of W. R. Holden, of Victoria Park, Dover ; two *s.* *Educ.* : Harrow ; Trinity Hall, Cambridge. Land agent since 1886. *Recreations* : cricket, lawn tennis, shoot-

ing, fishing. *Address:* Westbrooke Hall, Horeham, Sussex. *Club:* New University.
(*Died 6 May 1925.*)

BAINES, William, Composer of Music; *b.* Horbury, near Wakefield, 26 March 1899. At the age of seventeen had written a symphony, a pianoforte quartette, two pianoforte trios, sonatas, etc.; later his works have been chiefly for the pianoforte. *Publications:* for piano—Paradise Gardens; Seven Preludes; Silverpoints; Milestones; Tides; Four Poems; Coloured Leaves. *Address:* 91 Albemarle Road, The Mount, York.
(*Died 6 Nov. 1922.*)

BAIRD, Sir Alexander, 1st Bt.; *cr.* 1897; Lord-Lieut. of Kincardineshire since 1889; *b.* Scotland, 22 Oct. 1849; *e. s.* of John Baird, of Lochwood and Urie; *m.* 1873, Hon. Annette Palk, *d.* of 1st Baron Haldon (*d.* 1884); two *s.* three *d. Educ.:* Harrow. Sent to Upper Egypt to relieve the famine in the provinces of Girgeh, Kenneh, and Esneh, 1879. *Heir: s.* John Lawrence. *Address:* Urie, Stonehaven, N.B. *M.:* SU 30. *Clubs:* Carlton, Turf. (*Died 21 June 1920.*)

BAIRD, Edith Elina Helen. "Queen of Chess"; *o. surv. d.* of late T. Winter Wood, of Hareston, Devon; *wife* of late Deputy-Inspector-General W. J. Baird, M.D., R.N.; one *d. Educ.:* privately. From early childhood displayed more taste for the intellectual side of life than for the social. At the age of five she was taken to the Crystal Palace by her parents to put together puzzles purposely cut by an expert, which she did in a given time in the presence of numerous spectators. Her taste for chess developed when she was very young, inheriting it from her parents, who are known chess-players. She has composed and published upwards of a thousand problems, and with them has won many prizes; invented and introduced the Twentieth Century Retractor, 1902. *Publications:* Seven Hundred Chess Problems; The Twentieth Century Retractor and Chess Novelties, 1907. *Recreations:* archery and painting. *Address:* Hareston, Paignton, S. Devon. (*Died 1 Feb. 1924.*)

BAIRD, Rear-Adm. Sir George Henry, K.C.B., *cr.* 1924; C.B. 1918; R.N.; Commanding the Destroyer Flotillas of the Atlantic Fleet since 1923; *e. s.* of Alexander Baird of The Willows, Wickhambreaux, Canterbury, J.P.; *b.* 1871; *m.* 1908, Frances Josephine Sharp; three *d.* Entered Britannia naval cadets training ship at Dartmouth, 1885; midshipman, 1887; passed first in the examination of all midshipmen afloat, 1889; Lieutenant for meritorious examinations, 1892; Commander, 1903; Captain, 1909; Commodore, 1st class, 1918; Rear-Admiral, 1920. Served European War, 1914-19 (despatches, C.B., Legion of Honour, Rising Sun, Crown of Italy); Director of Mobilisation Department, Admiralty, 1921-3. *Address:* Littlebourne Court, near Canterbury. *M.:* XN 7222. *Club:* United Service. (*Died 22 Oct. 1924.*)

BAIRD, Hon. George Thomas, Senator of Dominion of Canada since 1895; *b.* Andover, Victoria Co., New Brunswick, 3 Nov. 1847, of Scotch descent; *m.* 1879, Ida J., *d.* of Capt. D. W. Sadler; two *s.* one *d. Educ.:* Carleton Co. Grammar School. Began life, after having spent his boyhood on a farm, by teaching; taught a superior school in Andover, N.B., 1870-74; moved to Perth, N.B., where he carried on lumber and general store business, 1874; represented Victoria County in the Local Legislature at Fredericton, 1884-95; appointed to Legislative Council, 1891; voted to abolish the Council, which was done in 1892, when he was again elected and sat until 1895; Episcopalian; Conservative. *Address:* Andover. New Brunswick, Canada. (*Died 21 April 1917.*)

BAIRD, John George Alexander, D.L. *b.* Rosemount, Ayrshire, 31 May 1854; 3rd *s.* of William Baird, Gartsherrie, and Janet Johnston;

m. 1880, Susan Georgiana, *e. d.* of Rt. Hon. Sir J. Fergusson, 6th Bt.; two *d. Educ.:* Eton; Christ Church, Oxford. Joined 6th Dragoon Guards, 1877, and 16th Lancers six months afterwards; left army, 1882; M.P. Central Division, Glasgow, 1886-1900 and 1900-1906. *Publication:* The Private Letters of the Marquis of Dalhousie, 1910. *Address:* 89 Eaton Square, S.W.; Wellwood, Muirkirk, N.B. *Clubs:* Carlton, Naval and Military.
(*Died 6 April 1917.*)

BAIRD, William, J.P., D.L.; *b.* 1848; *e. s.* of late William Baird of Elie; *m.* 1883, Caroline Muriel, *d.* of late John Alex. Burn Callander of Preston Hall, Midlothian; one *s.* two *d.* Hon. Col., late Lieut.-Col. and Hon. Col. Commanding Fife R.G.A. Militia. *Address:* Deanscroft, Oakham, Rutland. *Clubs:* Carlton, Turf, Conservative. (*Died 29 June 1918.*)

BAIRD, Sir William James Gardiner, of Saughton Hall, Midlothian, 8th Bt.; *cr.* 1695; *b.* 23 Feb. 1854; *S.* father 1896; *m.* Hon. Arabella Rose Evelyn Hozier (*d.* 1916), *d.* of 1st Baron Newlands, 1879; one *s.* one *d.* Late Lieut. 7th Hussars; J.P. for Mid and East Lothian; Lieut.-Col. and Hon. Col., retired, Lothians and Berwickshire Yeomanry Cavalry. *Heir: s.* James Hozier Gardiner [*b.* 25 Nov. 1883; Capt. 4th Batt. Argyll and Sutherland Highlanders; retired; rejoined the army as Captain 4th Bedfordshire Regiment, 1914 (wounded at Neuve Chapelle, despatches, Military Cross).]. *Address:* Glendalough, North Berwick, N.B. *T.:* 55 North Berwick. *Clubs:* Carlton; New, Edinburgh. (*Died 19 April 1921.*)

BAKER, Major Arthur Brander, D.S.O., 1900; Brigade Major, Commonwealth Military Forces; *b.* 4 Aug. 1868; *s.* of late Capt. Arthur Baker, R.N.; Secretary Vancouver Club, British Columbia. Entered army 1st Battalion The Royal Sussex Regt., 1887; served Hazara, 1888 (medal and clasp); South Africa, 1899-1902, with New South Wales Bushmen and raised and commanded Colonial Light Horse (D.S.O. despatches, Queen's medal with five clasps, and King's medal with two clasps); European War, 1914-16 (wounded).
(*Died 23 Sept. 1918.*)

BAKER, Sir Augustine FitzGerald, Kt., *cr.* 1903; M.A. Trinity College, Dublin; admitted Solicitor in Ireland, 1878; President of the Incorporated Law Society of Ireland, 1903; *b.* 1851; *y. s.* of Hugh Baker, of Lismacue, Tipperary. *Address:* 56 Merrion Square, Dublin. *Clubs:* Constitutional; University, Dublin; Royal Irish Yacht. (*Died 7 Oct. 1922.*)

BAKER, Vice-Adm. Casper Joseph; retired; *b.* 8 May 1852; 3rd *s.* of Admiral James Vashon Baker; *m.* 1886, Harriet Penuel, *y. d.* of Professor John Hutton Balfour of Edinburgh; two *s.* three *d. Educ.:* Clifton College. Entered Britannia as Naval Cadet, 1865; Sub-Lieut. 1872; Lieut. 1875; Commander, 1891; Capt. 1898; retired, 1907; Rear-Admiral, 1908; Vice-Admiral, retired list, 1913; when First-Lieut. of Egeria, at anchor in the Friendly Islands, a seaman fell overboard and was stunned, he and Quartermaster Bulloch jumped overboard and rescued him; served as Commander in Persian Gulf for three years in command of H.M.S. Sphinx; served as Capt. in Blake; Astraea (China Station); Flora (Pacific); Edgar and Ramillies. *Address:* Oaklands, South Petherton, Somerset.
(*Died 3 Aug. 1918.*)

BAKER, Lieut.-Col. Edward Mervyn, D.S.O. 1916; *b.* 1875. Entered Royal Fusiliers (City of London Regt.), 1897; Capt. Manchester Regt., 1901; Major R. Fusiliers, 1915; Bt. Lt.-Col., 1917; served S. Africa, 1899-1901 (despatches, Queen's medal with five clasps); Yola Expedition, 1901 (despatches, medal with clasp); Kontagora Expedition, 1902 (medal with clasp); European War, 1914-17 (despatches, D.S.O., Bt.

Lt.-Col., Order of Redeemer of Greece); retired. *Address:* Neatham Grange, Alton, Hants.
(*Died 19 Oct. 1925.*)

BAKER, His Honour Sir George Sherston, 4th Bt.; *cr.* 1796; County Court Judge, Circuit 17, since 1901; Recorder of Barnstaple and Bideford since 1889; J.P. Lincs, City of Lincoln, Great Grimsby, Boston, Barnstaple, and Bideford; *b.* London, 19 May 1846; *S. cousin* 1877; *m.* 1st, 1871, Jane Mary (*d.* 1909), *d.* of late F. J. Fegen, R.N., C.B., Ballinlonty, Tipperary; two *s.* three *d.*; 2nd, 1912, Mary Josephine (*d.* 1919) of The Manor House, Lillington, Warwickshire, *y. d.* of late Henry Bacchus; 3rd, 1920, Emmeline, *d.* of James Andrews, M.I.C.E., Dublin. Barrister Lincoln's Inn and Middle Temple; Examiner to Inns of Court, 1895-1901; Examiner in Equity to Birkbeck Institute, 1880-1897; Standing Counsel to Hon. Society of the Baronetage, 1898-1901. *Publications:* Halleck's International Law, 2nd ed. 1878, 3rd 1893, 4th 1908; The Laws relating to Quarantine, 1879; The Office of Vice-Admiral of the Coast, 1884; Law Reports, Digest of Cases, 1881-85; editor of Law Magazine and Review, 1895-98; Archbold's Quarter Sessions, 5th ed. 1898; First Steps in International Law, 1899; many Magazine Articles and Reviews. *Recreation:* late Inns of Court R.V. *Heir: s.* Col. Dodington Sherston Baker, I.M.S. [*b.* 22 July 1877; *m.* 1906, Irene Roper, *y. d.* of Sir Roper Parkington; one *s.* one *d.*] *Address:* Castle Moat House, Lincoln. *Club:* Devonshire.
(*Died 15 Mar. 1923.*)

BAKER, James, Kt. of Imperial Order of Francis Joseph, 1908; F.R.G.S., F.R.Hist.S., Corresponding Member Royal Academy of Arts Madrid, 1911; Hon. Sec. British International Association Journalists since 1906; and International Press Conference, 1909; *b.* 1 Jan. 1847; *s.* of James Baker; *m.* Agnes Anne, *d.* of J. Hallett, Swell Court, Somerset; three *s.* three *d.* *Educ.:* by his father. Has travelled in Greece, Russia, Lapland, Egypt, etc.; made a special study of Bohemia, was voted Great Silver Medal of Prague by Senate for literary work; in 1899 travelled in Tunis and Sicily and studied technical and commercial education in Prussia, Poland, Galicia, and Bohemia, to write a report thereon for the Education Department, published 1900; Travelled in Georgia and Palestine, 1903; Bohemia, 1905; Spain, 1906-9; Bosnia, 1907; Bukovina, 1911; Guest of City of Prague at Palacky and Sokol Commemoration, 1912; lectured throughout Britain on the War, Bohemia, Roumania, 1914-1918; to Army on Front, 1919. *Publications:* Quiet War Scenes: Poems and Translations, 1879; Days Afoot and European Sketches, 1881; John Westacott, 1886; By the Western Sea, 1889; Our Foreign Competitors, 1892; Mark Tillotson, 1892; A Forgotten Great Englishman, 1894; Pictures from Bohemia, 1894; The Gleaming Dawn, 1896; The Cardinal's Page, 1898; A Double Choice, 1901; A National Education to National Advancement, 1904; The Inseparables, 1905; A plea for power for the Church of England 1906 Anglicanus; The Harrogate Tourist centre, 1906; Literary and Biographical Studies, 1908; Austria: her People and their Homelands, 1912; Reminiscent Gossip of Men and Matters, 1913; Bohemia and her People: a Buffer State against Berlin, 1917; A Leader of Men (Mayor S. Harold Baker), 1919; has written for the principal magazines. *Recreations:* foreign travel, music, glee-singing, archaeology. *Address:* Sewelle Villa, Clifton. *Clubs:* Savage, Authors'; University, Musical, Bristol.
(*Died 24 June 1920.*)

BAKER, James H., M.A., LL.D.; President University of Colorado 1892-1914; President-Emeritus since 1914; *b.* Harmony, Maine,

13 Oct. 1848; *m.* Jennie V. Hilton, 1882; one *s.* one *d.* *Educ.:* Bates College, Lewiston, Maine. Principal of Yarmouth High School, 1873-1875; Principal of Denver High School, 1875-1892; President National Council of Education, 1892; President of National Association of State Universities, 1907; author of movement that resulted in national investigation of "Committee of Ten" on secondary schools; chairman of N.E.A. Committee on Economy of Time in Education (Report published by U.S. Government); member of N.E.A. Committee on A National University and of National Association of State Universities Committee on The Standards of American Universities; Fellow American Association for the Advancement of Science. *Publications:* Elementary Psychology; Education and Life; American Problems; Educational Aims and Civic Needs; American University Progress and College Reform relative to School and Society; After the War—What?; Of Himself and Other Things. *Clubs:* University, Denver; Colorado Mountain.
(*Died 10 Sept. 1925.*)

BAKER, John Gilbert, F.R.S., F.L.S., M.R.I.A. 1902; *b.* 13 Jan. 1834, Guisbro', Yorks; *m.* Hannah Unthank, 1860; one *s.* one *d.* *Educ.:* public schools of Society of Friends, Ackworth and York. First assistant, Herbarium of Royal Gardens, Kew, 1866; Keeper, 1890-99; Victoria Medallist of the Royal Horticultural Society, 1897; Gold Medallist of the Linnean Society, 1899; Veitch Gold Medal for Horticulture, 1907. *Publications:* North Yorkshire; Flora of English Lake District; Synopsis Filicum (with Sir W. J. Hooker); Flora of Mauritius; Handbooks of Fern Allies, Irideæ, Amaryllideæ, and Bromeliaceæ. *Recreations:* walking, botanising. *Address:* 3 Cumberland Road, Kew. (*Died Aug. 1920.*)

BAKER, Joseph Allen, M.P. (L.) Eastern Finsbury since 1905; member, L.C.C., 1895-1906; Chairman, Baker and Sons, Ltd., Willesden; *b.* Canada, 1852; *m.* 1873, Eliz. B. Moscrip of Roxburghshire, N.B.; three *s.* four *d.* *Educ.:* Trenton High School. Entered his father's business (engineering) in 1876, came over to London, establishing his business here. Has been prominently connected with tramway extension in the L.C.C.; published special reports on tramway traction and recommended the conduit system for London; acted as Chairman of Highway Committee; initiated and organized interchange of visits between representatives of the Christian churches of Great Britain and Germany in the interests of international peace and closer friendship; Chairman, Executive Committee of British Council of the Associated Councils of Churches in the British and German Empires for fostering Friendly Relations; contested East Finsbury, 1900; Chairman, Executive Committee British Group of the World Alliance of Churches for promoting International Friendship. *Address:* Donnington, Harlesden, N.W. *T.A.:* Bakers, London. *T.:* 1138 Willesden. *M.:* A 3. *Club:* National Liberal. (*Died 3 July 1918.*)

BAKER, Lawrence James; *b.* 1827; *e. s.* of Capt. John Law Baker and Caroline Brown; *m.* 1st, 1857, Ellen Catherine Thompson; 2nd, 1871, Susan Taylor. M.P. Somerset (Frome Div.), 1885-86; High Sheriff of Surrey, 1898. *Heir: s.* Lawrence Ingham, J.P. [*b.* 1862, *m.* 1885, Helen Agnes, *y. d.* of Sir S. M. Peto, 1st Bt.; one *s.* *Address:* Brambridge Park, Eastleigh, Hants. *Club:* Reform. (*Died 10 June 1921.*)

BAKER, Sir Thomas, K.B.E., *cr.* 1920; ex-Mayor of Plymouth; Freeman of the Borough of Plymouth; J.P. Plymouth, 1919. *Address:* The Crossways, Yelverton, S. Devon. *T.:* Yelverton 37. (*Died 17 Dec. 1926.*)

BAKER, William, M.A., LL.B., F.R.H.S., Hon. Director and Chairman of Council of Dr. Barnardo's Homes: National Incorporated Asso-

16

ciation; *b.* 23 April 1849; 3rd *s.* of late Hugh Baker of Lismacue, Bansha, Co. Tipperary, Ireland; *m.* 1882, Annie Austin (*d.* 1901). *Educ.:* Trinity College, Dublin. Called to Bar, 1875; practised at the Chancery Bar; joined Dr. Barnardo's Committee, 1887; became Honorary Director on the death of Dr. Barnardo in 1905. *Address:* 18-26 Stepney Causeway, E. *T.A.:* Waifdom, Step, London. *(Died 17 Nov. 1920.)*

BAKER, Ven. William George, Vicar of Brightwater since 1894; Archdeacon of Waimea since 1909; *m.* Ordained, 1872; Curate of Stalbridge, Dorset, 1882-84; St. John, Wakefield, New Zealand, 1884-91; Holy Trinity, Richmond, New Zealand, 1891-94. *Address:* Brightwater, New Zealand. *(Died 4 Oct. 1923.)*

BAKST, Leon, Artiste Peintre; *b.* St-Pétersbourg, 1868; *m.* 1903, Mademoiselle Trétiakoff, fille du maire de Moscou; one *s. Educ.:* Collège de Pétrograd, puis École des Beaux-Arts à Pétrograd. En 1897 délégué par l'Etat russe pour assister et peindre "L'Arrivée de l'Amiral Avellan à Paris" (tableau au musée de la Marine à Petrograd). En 1900 participé à la fondation de la société artistique "Mir Iskousstva"; en 1905 Sociétaire du Salon d'Automne à Paris; en 1907 Chevalier de la Légion d'Honneur; en 1909 peint les ballets "Schéhérasade" et 'Cléopâtre." En 1910 première médaille d'or de la section russe à l'Exposition Universelle à Bruxelles; exposition pavillon Marsan en 1911 à Paris (musée du Louvre); en 1912 peint ballets "L'Après-midi d'un Faune" et "Hélène de Sparte," de Verhaeren; puis "St Sébastien" de d'Annunzio. En 1913 peint "La Pisanella" de d'Annunzio et en juillet 1913, en 1920 "Dames de bonne humeur," en 1923 "La Nuit ensorcellée" à l'Opéra de Paris, 1923 Exposition Knoedler New York, 4 tableaux acquis Albert et Victoria Museum 1922; et 3 tableaux acquis 1923 Metropolitan Museum New York; Officier de la Légion d'Honneur; membre de l'Académie Impériale russe de Beaux Arts, 1916; Membre de l'Académie Royale de Bruxelles. Par ligne directe descendant des familles Scheryra (d'Espagne) du sang du roi David de Judée. *Publications:* article "Les Problèmes de l'art nouveau" Nouvelle Revue 1910, Paris. A Londres et a Paris en 1913 édition d'art: "L'Art décoratif de Léon Bakst," par Arsène Alexandre; La Vie de Léon Bakst, monographie par A. Levinson; L'Œuvre de Léon Bakst pour La belle au bois dormant. *Recreations:* escrime et gymnastique. *Address:* 112 boulevard Malesherbes, Paris.
(Died 27 Dec. 1924.)

BALDWIN, Hon. Simeon Eben, A.M. (Yale), LL.D. (Harvard, Columbia, Wesleyan, and Yale); Professor of Law, Yale University, since 1872; Governor of Connecticut, 1911-15; *b.* 5 Feb. 1840; *s.* of Hon. Roger Sherman Baldwin, LL.D., Governor of Connecticut and U.S. Senator; *g.s.* of Hon. Simeon Baldwin, Judge of the Supreme Court of Errors; *m.* Susan Winchester of Boston, 1865. *Educ.:* Hopkins Grammar School of New Haven; Yale College; and Yale and Harvard Law Schools. Member of State Commissions to revise Education Laws, 1872; General Statutes, 1873-74; Civil Procedure Laws, 1878-79; Taxation, 1885-87 and 1915-17; Associate Justice, Supreme Court of Errors, Connecticut, 1893-1907; Chief Justice, 1907-10; Director, Bureau of Comparative Law of the American Bar Association, 1909-19; Member of the American Antiquarian Society, the American Philosophical Society, and of the National Institute of Arts and Letters; Corresponding Member of the Massachusetts Historical Society; the Colonial Society of Massachusetts; and of the Institut de Droit Comparé, of Brussels; Fellow of the American Academy of Arts and Sciences, and of the American Association for the Advancement of Science; Associate of the Institut de Droit International. *Publications:* Baldwin's

Connecticut Digest; Modern Political Institutions; Baldwin's Illustrative Cases on Railroad Law; American Railroad Law; The American Judiciary; The Relations of Education to Citizenship; The Young Man and the Law; co-author of Two Centuries' Growth of American Law. *Address:* 44 Wall Street, New Haven, Conn., U.S.A. *Clubs:* Yale, New York City; Graduates, New Haven. *(Died 30 Jan. 1927.)*

BALE, Edwin, R.I.; Art Director, Cassell and Co., Ltd., 1882-1907; Secretary, Artists Committee for Promoting Art Copyright Bill; *b.* London, 1838; *m.* 1878, Julia Dalton (*d.* 1901). *Educ.:* South Kensington Schools; the Academy of Arts, Florence. Member of Royal Institute of Painters in Water Colours, 1877; contributed articles to Ency. Brit. on Artistic Copyright and Process; 1st Chairman Imperial Arts League, 1909-12; Editor of the Journal of the League, 1910-19. *Recreations:* painting, gardening. *Address:* 11 Grove End Road, St. John's Wood, N.W. *Club:* Arts'.
(Died 9 April 1923.)

BALFOUR of Burleigh, 6th Baron (cr. 1607), **Alexander Hugh Bruce,** K.T., P.C.; G.C.M.G., cr. 1911; G.C.V.O., cr. 1917; *b.* Kennet, Alloa, N.B., 13 Jan. 1849; *s.* of R. Bruce, Kennet; title attainted 1716 for rising of 1715, and only restored to present possessor in 1869; *m.* Lady Katherine Hamilton-Gordon, sister of 7th Earl of Aberdeen, 1876; one *s.* three *d. Educ.:* Loretto; Eton; Oriel Coll. Oxford. B.A. with honours, 1871; M.A. 1872. Church of Scotland. Conservative. Member Factory Commission, 1874-75; member Endowed Institution Scotland Commission, 1878-79; Chairman Educational Endowments Commission, 1882-89; Chairman Welsh Sunday Closing Commission, 1889; Chairman Metropolitan Water Supply Commission, 1893-94; Chairman Rating Commission, 1896; Lord-in-Waiting to Queen, 1888-89; Parliamentary Secretary to Board of Trade, 1889-92; Lord Rector Edinburgh University, 1896-99; Chancellor of St. Andrews University, 1900; Chairman Royal Commission on Food Supply in Time of War, 1903; D.C.L. 1904; LL.D., Universities of St. Andrews, Aberdeen, Glasgow, and Edinburgh, and of the Welsh University; Secy. for Scot. (in the Cabinet) 1895-1903; Chairman Royal Commission on Closer Trade Relations between Canada and West Indies, 1909; Chairman of Committee on Commercial and Industrial Policy after the War, 1916-17; Lord Warden of the Stannaries since 1904. Owns about 3000 acres. *Heir: s.* Major Hon. George Bruce. *Address:* Kennet, Alloa, N.B.; 47 Cadogan Square, S.W. *T.:* Kensington, 800. *Clubs:* Carlton, Athenæum; New Conservative, Edinburgh; Western, Glasgow.
(Died 6 July 1921.)

BALFOUR, Ven. Andrew Jackson, M.A., D.C.L., Archdeacon of Quebec since 1906; *b.* Waterloo, Quebec, 31 Dec. 1845; *m.* 1910, Edith Marina, *d.* of late Alexander Marling. *Educ.:* Bishops' University, Lennoxville. Ordained, 1869; Curate at Levis, P.Q., 1869-72; Incumbent of Hatley, 1872-81; Rector of Richmond, 1881-88; Rector of St. Peter's, Quebec, 1888-1906; Canon of Quebec Cathedral, 1902-6; Archdeacon of St. Francis, 1906-9. *Address:* Church House, 2 Donnacona Street, Quebec, Canada. *(Died 6 Oct. 1923.)*

BALFOUR, Charles Barrington, of Balgonie, Fife, and Newton Don, Kelso; C.B. 1919; Lord-Lieutenant, Berwickshire, 1917; J.P. Roxburghshire and Berwickshire; County Councillor, Berwickshire, and Chairman of Finance Committee; President and Chairman, Berwickshire Territorial Force Association, and Chairman Berwickshire National Health Insurance Committee; Director, Barclay's Bank and Scottish Widows' Fund Life Assurance Society; *b.* 20 Feb. 1862; *s.* of Charles Balfour of Balgonie and Newton Don, and Hon. Adelaide

Barrington; *m.* 1888, Lady Nina McDonnell, *d.* of 5th Earl of Antrim; four *s.* Formerly Lieutenant, Scots Guards, 1881-1890; Captain, Royal Guards Reserve Regt. 1900-1901; served Egyptian Campaign, 1882; contested Roxburghshire, 1885; Berwickshire, 1892, 1894, 1895; Southport Division of Lancashire, 1899; M.P. (C.) Hornsey Div. of Middlesex, 1900-7; President of National Union of Conservative Associations for Scotland, 1894-95. *Heir: s.* Capt. Charles James Balfour, Scots Guards [*b.* 8 Feb. 1889; *m.* 1917, Hon. Aurea Vera Baring, 2nd *d.* of 5th Baron Ashburton]. *Address:* Newton Don, Kelso, Scotland; *T.:* Kelso 21; 14 Grosvenor Crescent, S.W.1; *T.:* Gerrard 1807. *Clubs:* Carlton, Guards', Bachelors', Royal Automobile; New, Edinburgh. (*Died 31 Aug. 1921.*)

BALFOUR, Edward, J.P., D.L.; *e. surv. s.* of late Col. John Balfour, Balbirnie, and Lady Georgiana Isabella, 2nd *d.* of 1st Earl of Cawdor; *b.* 23 Jan. 1849; *m.* 1879, Isabella Weyman Hooper, Boston, U.S.A.; one *s.* two *d.* *Address:* 2 Grosvener Crescent, S.W.1; *T.* Sloane 4270; Balbirnie, Markinch, N.B. *Clubs:* Turf, Marlborough; New, Edinburgh. (*Died 10 Sept. 1927.*)

BALFOUR, Rt. Rev. Francis Richard Townley; Assistant Bishop of Bloemfontein since 1910; *b.* Sorrento, 21 June 1846; *s.* of late Blayney Townley Balfour and Elizabeth Catherine Reynell, Townley Hall, Co. Louth, Ireland. *Educ.:* Harrow; Trinity College, Cambridge; Cuddesdon Theological College, Oxon. B.A. 1869, 3rd class Classical Tripos; M.A. 1872; Deacon, 1872; Curate of Buckingham; Priest, 1874; chaplain to the Bishop of Bloemfontein, 1876; missionary in Basutoland; canon of Bloemfontein, 1884; chaplain to the British South Africa Company's Police on the Pioneering Expedition from Bechuanaland to Mashonaland, 1890; missionary in Mashonaland, 1890-92; director of the Mission at Sekubu, Basutoland, 1894-1898; Archdeacon of Bloemfontein, 1901-1906; of Basutoland, 1907-22. *Address:* Mafeteng, Basutoland, S. Africa. (*Died 3 Feb. 1924.*)

BALFOUR, Sir Isaac Bayley, K.B.E., *cr.* 1920; M.D., D.Sc., LL.D., M.A., F.R.S.; *b.* Edinburgh, 31 Mar. 1853; *s.* of John Hutton Balfour, Professor of Botany, University of Edinburgh, 1845-79; *m.* Agnes, *d.* of late Robert Balloch, Glasgow; one *d.* *Educ.:* Edinburgh Academy; Universities of Edinburgh, Strassburg, and Würzburg. Transit of Venus Expedition to Rodriguez, 1874; Regius Professor of Botany, University of Glasgow, 1879-84; explored Island of Socotra, 1880; Sherardian Professor of Botany, University of Oxford, and Fellow of Magdalen College, 1884-1888; King's Botanist in Scotland, 1888-1922; Regius Keeper of Royal Botanic Garden, Edinburgh, 1888-1922; Professor of Botany, University of Edinburgh, 1888-1922. *Publications:* Botanical. *Address:* Courts Hill, Haslemere. *T.:* Haslemere 113. *Club:* Athenæum. (*Died 30 Nov. 1922.*)

BALL, Sir Charles Bent, 1st Bt.; *cr.* 1911; Kt., *cr.* 1903; M.D., M.Ch., F.R.C.S.I.; Hon. F.R.C.S. Eng.; Regius Professor of Surgery, Univ. of Dublin, and Surgeon, Sir Patrick Duns Hospital; Consulting Surgeon, Steevens, Monkstown, and Orthopædic Hospitals; Hon. Surg. to the King in Ireland; Member General Medical Council; *b.* 21 Feb. 1851; *y. s.* of late Robert Ball, LL.D., Dublin; *m.* Annie J., *e. d.* of late D. Kinahan, J.P., Roebuck Park, Dublin; three *s.* four *d.* *Educ.:* Trin. Coll. Dublin. Medical Scholarship, senior Moderatorship, and gold medal Natural Science; Surgical Travelling Prize, University of Dublin; Lane Lecturer at San Francisco, 1902; late Member of Advisory Board for Army Medical Service; Erasmus Wilson Lecturer, Royal College of Surgeons of England, 1903; Lord Chancellor's Consulting Visitor in Lunacy;

Medical Referee under Workmen's Compensation Act; late Commissioner for Education, Ireland; Temp. Lt.-Col. R.A.M.C. 1914. *Publications:* various surgical works. *Heir: s.* Charles Arthur Kinahan, M.D. [*b.* 29 Mar. 1877; *m.* 1907, Elizabeth, *d.* of Joseph S. Wilson, Berkeley, California; no *c.* *Address:* 22 Lower Fitzwilliam Street, Dublin]. *Address:* 24 Merrion Square, Dublin; White House, Killybegs, Co. Donegal. *T.:* 1076. *Clubs:* Constitutional; Kildare Street, University, Dublin. (*Died 17 Mar. 1916.*)

BALL, Rev. Charles Richard, M.A.; late Vicar of All Saints, Peterborough; Hon. Canon of Peterborough; Rural Dean of Peterborough, No. 1 Deanery; *b.* Clifton, Bristol; *s.* of Joseph and Rebecca Ball; *m.* Mary Eliza, 3rd *d.* of Very Rev. A. P. Saunders, D.D., late Dean of Peterborough, and formerly Headmaster of the Charter House; one *s.* four *d.* *Educ.:* Christ's Coll. Camb. Curate of Trentham, Staffordshire; Belgrave, Leicestershire; St. John's, Leicester; St. Andrew's, Leicester; appointed to the Vicarage of St. Paul's, Peterborough, and to an Hon. Canonry in the Cathedral by Bishop Magee; Rural Dean of Peterborough, 1st Deanery, by Bishop Creighton; elected one of the Proctors for the Diocese of Peterborough to Convocation. *Publications:* Lessons on our Lord's Life and Ministry; The Promised Seed; The Apostle of the Gentiles; The Dispensation of the Spirit; Plain Instructions on the Church Catechism; The Blankthorpe Papers; Plain Thoughts on a Great Subject (Salvation); The Faith in Outline; Confirmation Before and After; Character: its Signification and its Outcome; The Chosen People and the Promised Christ; Preliminary Studies on the Books of the New Testament in the probable order of their writing; The Holy Communion in Substance and Shadow; The Voyage of Life. *Address:* Madeley House, Peterborough. (*Died 20 May 1918.*)

BALL, Ernest. *Publications:* (Songs) Mother Machree, When Irish Eyes are Smiling, Love Me and the World is Mine, Till the Sands of the Desert Grow Cold, Will you Love me in December as you did in May? A Little Bit of Heaven, Down the Trail to Home, Sweet Home, Let the Rest of the World Go By, Ten Thousand Years from Now, Saloon. (*Died May 1927.*)

BALL, James Barry. M.D., F.R.C.P.; Consulting Physician Department for Diseases of Throat, Nose, and Ear, West London Hospital; Consulting Physician for Diseases of Throat and Ear SS. John and Elizabeth Hospital; formerly Lecturer on Diseases of Throat, Nose, and Ear, West London Post-Graduate College; Ex-President. Laryngological Society of London; *m.* Clare, *d.* of Joseph Weld. *Publications:* Hand-book of Diseases of the Nose and Pharynx; Intubation of the Larynx; and various contributions to medical journals and Transactions of Societies. *Address:* 12 Upper Wimpole Street, W.1; *T.:* Paddington 826; 65 Stert Street, Abingdon, Berks. (*Died 2 Oct. 1926.*)

BALL, Sir James Benjamin, Kt., *cr.* 1918; Civil Engineer, M.Inst.C.E., M.Inst.M.E.; Past President Permanent Way Institution; Major, Engineer and Railway Staff Corps; *b.* 9 March 1867; *m.* 1st, Emily Françes Alexandra, *d.* of late Edward Spencer Shapley, Torquay; three *d.*; 2nd, Julia, widow of late Robert Hill, Melbourne; one *s.* *Educ.:* privately. Entered service Great Northern Railway, 1890; Engineer Lancashire, Derbyshire, and East Coast Railway, 1899; New Works Engineer Great Central Railway, 1907; Engineer-in-Chief Great Central Railway, 1912; London, Brighton, and South Coast Railway, 1917; services lent to Government in May 1917 by L.B. and S.C. Company and appointed by President of the Board of Trade as Controller of Timber Supplies; has been responsible for design and carrying out of heavy railway and dock works involving large expenditure; Telford Gold Medal, Inst. Civil Engineers. *Publications:* several technical papers presented to the Institution of Civil Engineers. *Club:* Reform. *(Died 16 Sept. 1920.)*

BALL, James Dyer, I.S.O., M.R.A.S., M. China Br.R.A.S.; Hong-Kong Civil Service (retired); Director L.M.S.; on Committee S.S.U.; on Committee Anti-Opium Society; Editor, Friend of China, 1915-17; *b.* Canton, 4 Dec. 1847; *s.* of Rev. Dyer Ball, M.A., M.D. and Isabella Ball; *m.* 1885, Gertrude Jane, *d.* of Rev. Samuel Joseph Smith; two *s.* one *d. Educ.:* Home; King's College, London; University College, Liverpool. Thirty-five years in the Hong-Kong Civil Service as Chief Interpreter, Sheriff, Registrar-General and Protector of Chinese; Member of Civil Service Board of Examiners; Commissioner for Oaths; J.P.; Editor China Review, 1900-1; Member Oxford Local Board of Examiners, Hong-Kong, etc.; literary work for the Admiralty, 1916-18; work for the W.O. 1917-18. *Publications:* Things Chinese; The Chinese at Home; The Religious Aspect in China; The Pith of the Classics; The Cantonese made Easy Series; Hakka made Easy; How to Write Chinese; Macao; and articles in Encyclopædia of Religion and Ethics, etc. *Recreations:* numismatics and philately. *Address:* Belstone, Alexandra Grove, North Finchley, N.12. *(Died 21 Feb. 1919.)*

BALL, Thomas, C.M.G. 1901; *b.* Hull, 12 Dec. 1846; *m.* 1st, 1869, Emily Joanna, *d.* of John Dunkley; 2nd, 1890, Louise, *d.* of John Wilson, and widow of Oscar Branmuller; three *s.* two *d.* Mayor of Cape Town, 1898, 1899, 1900; President Mayoral Congress, South Africa, 1899, 1900, 1901, 1902, 1903, 1904, and 1905. *Address:* Rondebosch, Cape Town. *(Died 16 Mar. 1922.)*

BALL, Very Rev. Thomas Isaac, LL.D.; examining Chaplain to Bishops of Argyll since 1884; Provost of Cathedral Chapter and College Cumbrae since 1891; Rector of St. Andrew, Millport, since 1892. Ordained 1865; served in the Diocese of Brechin till 1874; Domestic Chaplain to late Earl of Kinnoull 1874-1876; served in the diocese of Edinburgh from 1876; Rector of St. Michael's, Edinburgh, 1888-1891; LL.D. degree *honoris causâ* by St. John's College, Annapolis, Maryland. *Publications:* A Plea for Simplicity in Eucharistic Teaching; The Royal Supremacy over the Church of France in 1789; English Catholic's Vade Mecum (compiled); A Pastoral Bishop: Memoir of Bishop Chinnery-Haldane; numerous articles and literary contributions in various periodicals; translations of Latin hymns; compiler and translator, or co-compiler of many works of liturgical interest. *Address:* Millport, R.S.O., Buteshire, Scotland. *T.A.:* College, Millport. *(Died 4 Aug. 1916.)*

BALL, Walter William Rouse, M.A.; Barrister; Fellow Trinity College, Cambridge, and University College, London; *b.* 1850: *m.* 1885, Alice Mary Ball (*d.* 1919). *Educ.:* University College, London; Trinity College, Cambridge. Honours in Philosophy and Mathematics, University of London; Second Wrangler and First Smith's Prizeman, University of Cambridge; Deputy Professor for J. K. Clifford, London, 1877; Lecturer, Trinity College, Cambridge, 1878; Director of Mathematical Studies of College, 1891; Senior Tutor and Chairman of College Education Committee, 1898; Representative of University of Cambridge on Borough Council, 1905; member of Governing Bodies of Westminster School and the Cambridge Perse School; has examined on various occasions in the Tripos and other examinations, and has served on numerous Boards and Syndicates; owner of the largest collection in Great Britain of portraits of mathematicians. *Publications:* A History of Mathematics, and a

Primer of the same subject; Mathematical Recreations and Essays; The Genesis and History of Newton's Principia; History of Mathematics at Cambridge; Text-Book on Algebra; A Guide to the Bar; History of Trinity College, Cambridge; A History of the First Trinity Boat Club; Records of Admission to Trinity College, 1546-1900; etc.; and various memoirs in Mathematical Journals. *Address:* Trinity College and Elmside, Grange Road, Cambridge. *Clubs:* New University, Junior Constitutional. *(Died 4 April 1925.)*

BALL, Wilfrid, R.E.; painter in water-colours and etcher; Member of Council, Royal Society of Painter Etchers; *b.* London, 4 Jan. 1853; *m.* Florence, *d.* of H. Brock-Hollinshead, 1895. *Educ.:* Grammar School, Hackney. Began life as public accountant in London; studied art at Heatherley's School; exhibited in R.A. since 1876; bronze medal, Paris Exhibition 1900, for etching. *Publications:* Paper on Mezzotint Engraving; Sussex; Hampshire. *Recreations:* holder of London Athletic Club challenge cup for walking, 1876; rowing. *Address:* Sunnerset, Lymington, Hants. *Club:* Arts. *(Died 14 Feb. 1917.)*

BALLANTYNE, John William, M.D., C.M., F.R.C.P., Edin., F.R.S.E.; Hon. Fellow Glasgow Obstetrical and Gynaecological Society; Hon. Fellow American Association of Obstetricians and Gynaecologists; Hon. Member American Child Hygiene Association; Socio Honorario Soc. Scientifica Protectora da Infancia (Brazil); Extra Physician, Royal Maternity Hospital, Edinburgh (in charge of Antenatal Department); Lecturer on Midwifery and Gynaecology (to women students) in the University of Edinburgh and in the Edinburgh Post-Graduate Courses in Medicine; Examiner in Midwifery in the Universities of Glasgow and Liverpool; Hon. Librarian Royal College of Physicians, Edinburgh; obstetric physician and gynaecologist in private practice; *b.* Eskbank, Dalkeith, 4 June 1861; *o. s.* of late John Ballantyne, nursery and seedsman, of Dalkeith and Birkdale, Windermere, and Helen Pringle, *e. d.* of Walter Mercer, Silk-Mercer, Edinburgh; *m.* 1889, Emily Rosa (*d.* 1914), 2nd *d.* of late George Mathew, of Worsted Lodge, Cambridgeshire; no *c. Educ.:* Bonnington Park School, Peebles; George Watson's College, Edinburgh; Edinburgh University. M.B., C.M. Edin., 1883, with Buchanan Scholarship in Midwifery and Gynaecology; M.D., 1889, with gold medal and Gunning Simpson Prize in Obstetrics; Cullen Prize, R. C. Physicians, Edinburgh, 1902; Senior Assistant to the Professor of Midwifery in the University of Edinburgh, 1885-1890; Lecturer on Midwifery and Gynaecology, School of Medicine of the Royal Colleges and School of Medicine for Women, Edinburgh, 1890-1916; Examiner in Midwifery in the Universities of Aberdeen 1895-99, and Edinburgh, 1901-5; Edinburgh University Lecturer in Antenatal Pathology and Teratology, 1899-1900, and Lecturer on Midwifery to Women Students, 1916; President, Edinburgh Obstetrical Society, 1906-7; President, Edinburgh Medical Missionary Society, 1907-12. *Publications:* Diseases of Foetus, 2 vols., 1892-95; Teratogenesis, 1897; Manual of Antenatal Pathology and Hygiene, 1902-4; Diseases of Infancy, 1891; Essentials of Obstetrics, 1904; Essentials of Gynaecology, 1905; Expectant Motherhood, 1914; editor of Teratologia, 1894-95, of two issues of Green's Encyclopedia and Dictionary of Medicine, of second edition of Encyelopaedia Medica, and of Quinquennium of Medicine and Surgery; sub-editor for Scotland of the International Clinics; over four hundred articles. *Recreations:* literary research in medicine and addressing brotherhood meetings. *Address:* 19 Rothesay Terrace, Edinburgh. *T.A.:* Antenatal, Edinburgh. *T.:* Central 2235. *(Died 23 Jan. 1923.)*

BALLARD, Henry, C.M.G. 1901; Port Captain, Durban, 1884-1904; *b.* 1840; *s.* of Henry James Ballard, of Southampton; *m.* 1st, 1868, Harriet E. J. Richardson; 2nd, 1877, Sarah Eugenie Wroe, 3rd *d.* of James Wroe of London. *Educ.:* Southampton. Went to sea, 1854; made first voyage to Black Sea during Crimean War; served 25 years in the Union Steamship Company, Cape Mail Service; last ship command S.S. Mexican. *Address:* Inchanga, Howard Road, Southampton. *(Died 30 Jan. 1919.)*

BALRAMPUR, Maharaja Bahadur of, Sir Bhagwati Prasad Singh, K.C.I.E.; K.B.G.; Member of the Legislative Council of the U.P. of Agra and Oudh; Hon. Fellow of the University of Allahabad for life; Chairman Municipal Board, Balrampur; Special Magistrate; *b.* 19 July 1879; *S.* 1893. *Educ.:* European and Indian tutors. Contributed large sums towards objects of charity and public utility in War Funds; invested about 30 lacs in War Loans; fond of sports; motorist, possessing nine cars of different makes; owning over a hundred elephants. *Address:* District Gonda, Oudh. *(Died 25 May 1921.)*

BALZANI, Count Ugo; President of the Reale Società romana di storia patria; Member of the Reale Accademia dei Lincei, and of the Istituto Storico Italiano; Hon. Litt.D. Oxford; Corresponding Fellow of the British Academy; *b.* Rome, 5 Nov. 1847; *s.* of Count Andrea Balzani; *m.* Mary Augusta Simon Agnew (*d.*), of Kilwaughter Castle, Ireland. *Educ.:* University of Rome. *Publications:* Le Cronache Italiane nel Medio Evo; Il Regesto di Farfa di Gregorio di Catino; The Popes and the Hohenstaufen; Il "Chronicon Farfense"; Sisto V.; besides many contributions to the transactions of the various institutions, Italian and foreign, of which he is a member. *Recreations:* walking and climbing. *Address:* 9 Via Po, Rome. *Club:* Athenæum. *(Died 27 Feb. 1916.)*

BAMBER, Capt. Wyndham Lerrier, C.B.E. 1919; R.N.; was Drafting Commander and Assistant Director Mobilisation Division, Admiralty, during European War (C.B.E.). *Address:* 23 Vineyard Hill Road, S.W. 19. *T.:* Wimbledon 1438. *Club:* Junior United Service. *(Died 14 Jan. 1924.)*

BAMBRIDGE, Rev. Joseph John, M.A., M.R.A.S.; Vicar of St. Mary Bredin, Canterbury, since 1895; Rural Dean of Canterbury, 1909-19; Hon. Canon of Canterbury Cathedral; *m.*; one *d.* *Educ.:* Durham University. C.M.S. Missionary in Sindh, India; Fellow of and Examiner in the University of Bombay, 1881-91. *Address:* St. Mary Bredin Vicarage, Canterbury. *(Died 28 April 1923.)*

BAMFORD, Major Edward, V.C. 1918; D.S.O. 1916; R.M.; Instructor of Small Arms, Hong-Kong, since 1926; *b.* 28 May 1887; *s.* of late Rev. Robert Bamford and Mrs. Myers; unmarried. *Educ.:* Sherborne School. 2nd Lieut. Royal Marine Light Infantry, 1905; Lieut., 1906; served in H.M.S. Bulwark, Magnificent, Britannia, Chester, Royal Sovereign and Highflyer; temp. Captain, 2 May 1916; Captain, 1 Sep. 1916; present at Battle of Jutland and operations at Zeebrugge, 23 April 1918 (D.S.O., V.C., Bt.-Major). *Recreations:* golf, hockey, lawn-tennis, boat-sailing and fishing. *Address:* Hong-Kong. *(Died 29 Sept. 1928.)*

BANBURY. Brig.-Gen. Walter Edward, C.M.G. 1916; Indian Army; retired; *b.* 25 Dec. 1863. Served Burma, 1885-87 (medal with clasp); N.W. Frontier, India, 1897-1898 (despatches, medal with clasp); European War, 1914-17 (despatches, C.M.G., Bt.-Col.). *Address:* St. Cuthbert's, Ledbury. *T.:* Ledbury 61. *Club:* East India United Service. *(Died 2 Dec. 1927.)*

BANCROFT, Lady (*née* Marie Effie Wilton), *d.* of late Robert Pleydell Wilton, a member of one of the oldest Gloucestershire families, who left home to become an actor; *m.* 1867, Sir Squire Bancroft. After acting as a child in provinces, first appeared in London in Sep. 1856, as the boy in Belphegor; then chiefly at Strand Theatre until 1865, when the memorable management of the old Prince of Wales's Theatre began with production of the Robertson Comedies; migrated to Haymarket in 1880; retired from an exceptional career of successful management in 1885; has only occasionally acted since. *Publications:* joint-author of Mr. and Mrs. Bancroft On and Off the Stage, 1888; and sole author of A Riverside Story, 1890; My Daughter, 1892; A Dream, 1908; The Shadow of Neeme, 1912. *Address:* A1 The Albany, W.; Underlea, Sandgate. *(Died 22 May 1921.)*

BANCROFT, Sir Squire Bancroft, Kt., *cr.* 1897; Hon. LL.D.; *b.* London, 14 May 1841; *m.* 1867, Marie Effie Wilton, the famous actress (*d.* 1921); one *s.* [*b.* 1868; *m.* 1898, Effie Lucy, *d.* of late Sir John Hare]. *Educ.:* private schools, England and France. First appeared on the stage at Birmingham in 1861; acted afterwards at leading provincial theatres with all the prominent "stars" of the stage; twenty years manager old Prince of Wales's and Haymarket Theatres, during which modern revival of stage was started; retired from an exceptional career of successful management, 1885; acted afterwards with Irving, but rarely since; was knighted by Queen Victoria for notable services to his profession; has devoted much time to "Readings" for Hospitals throughout the country, and by which he raised £20,000; President of the Royal Academy of Dramatic Art; a member of the Lord Chamberlain's Advisory Board for the Licensing of Plays. *Publication:* joint-author of Mr. and Mrs. Bancroft On and Off the Stage: written by themselves, 1888; author of the Bancroft Recollections of Sixty Years, 1909, and Empty Chairs, 1925. *Address:* A1 The Albany, W.1. *T.:* Gerrard 3206. *Clubs:* Athenæum, Garrick, Green Room (Pres.). *(Died 19 April 1926.)*

BANCROFT, Claude Keith; Assistant-Director of Science and Agriculture, and Government Botanist, British Guiana, since 1918; *b.* 1885; *s.* of Joseph Richard and Helena Blanche Bancroft; *m.* 1909, Irene Mary, *d.* of George Ernest Boorman, Faversham, Kent; two *s.* *Educ.:* Harrison College, Barbados (scholar); Trinity College, Cambridge (major scholar, prizeman); First Class Natural Sciences Tripos, 1908. For some time research student in mycology, Royal Gardens, Kew; Mycologist and Botanist, Federated Malay States, 1910-13; Deputy-Chairman, Board of Agriculture, British Guiana, 1913. *Publications:* various, dealing with botany, mycology, and agricultural subjects in the Annals of Botany, Journal of Board of Agriculture, England, Kew Bulletin, and publications of Tropical Departments of Agriculture. *Recreation:* cricket. *Address:* Botanic Gardens, Georgetown, British Guiana. *Club:* West India. *(Died Jan. 1919.)*

BANCROFT, Edgar Addison; American Ambassador to Japan, since 1924; *b.* Galesburg, Ill., U.S.A., 20 Nov. 1857; *m.* 1896, Margaret Healy (*d.* 1923), Brooklyn, N.Y. A.B. Knox College, 1878; LL.D. 1882; LL.B. Columbia University, 1880. Solicitor for Ill. of A.T. and S.F. R.R. Co., 1892-95; V.-P. and general solicitor Chicago and Western Ind. R.R. Co. and the Belt R.R. Co., 1895-1904; member law firm Scott, Bancroft, Martin & McLeish, 1904-24; General Counsel International Harvester Co., 1907-20; Pres. Ill. State Bar Assn., 1910; ex-Pres. of Law Club and of Chicago Bar Assn.; orator on numerous patriotic, academic and festive occasions; gave the main addresses of welcome to various

World-War Commissioners and heroes from Europe visiting Chicago at different times. *Publications:* The Chicago Strike of 1894; The Moral Sentiment of the People the Foundation of National Greatness; Destruction or Regulation of Trusts; The Mission of America; Belgium; Why we Are in the War; Marshal Foch, and other War-time Addresses; Chairman of the Commission that published The Negro in Chicago: a Study of Race Relations and a Race Riot, 1922. *Recreations:* golf and hunting. *Address:* 134 S. La Salle Street, Chicago, Ill.; American Embassy, Tokio, Japan. *Clubs:* Chicago, Union League (Pres. 1904-5), University, Literary, Merchants (Pres. 1899), Commercial (Pres. 1919-20), City, Cliff Dwellers, Onwentsia, Old Elm.

(Died 28 July 1925.)

BANCROFT, Elias, R.C.A. *Address:* 10 Acomb Street, Manchester. *(Died 22 April 1924.)*

BANCROFT, Hubert Howe, historian; *b.* Granville, O., 5 May 1832; *s.* of Ashley Bancroft, Massachusetts, and Lucy Howe, Vermont; *m.* 1876, Matilda Griffing (*d.* 1910), New Haven, Conn.; three *s.* one *d.* Entered book-store of his brother-in-law, Geo. H. Derby, Buffalo, N.Y. 1848; went to establish a branch in San Francisco, 1852; collected as materials for Pacific coast history a library of 60,000 vols. (now in possession of California University), and with aid of a staff of collaborators, has written and published an historical series of 39 vols., covering the western part of N. America, comprising the Native Races of the Pacific States, History of Central America, History of Mexico, and of various other districts; Popular Tribunals, Essays, and Miscellany, Literary Industries; other works: The Book of the Fair, The Book of Wealth, Resources of Mexico, The New Pacific and Retrospection, etc. *Address:* 2898 Jackson Street, San Francisco. *T.:* West 904. *(Died 3 Mar. 1918.)*

BANDON, 4th Earl of (*cr.* 1880), **James Francis Bernard.** Baron Bandon, 1793; Viscount Bandon, 1795; Viscount Bernard, 1800. Irish Representative Peer; H.M.'s Lieutenant of Co. Cork since 1874; Kt. of the Order of St. Patrick; *b.* 12 Sep. 1850; *S.* father 1877; *m.* 1876, Hon. Georgiana Dorothea Harriet Evans-Freake, C.B.E. 1920, *o. c.* of 7th Baron Carbery. *Educ.:* Eton. Owns about 41,000 acres. *Heir:* cousin, Percy Ronald Gardner Bernard, *b.* 1904. *Address:* Castle Bernard and Durras Court, Bantry, Co. Cork. *Club:* Carlton.

(Died 18 May 1924.)

BANERJEA, Sir Surendranath, Kt., *cr.* 1921; B.A.; editor of The Bengalee; Professor of English Literature, Ripon College; *b.* 10 Nov. 1848; 2nd *s.* of late Dr. Durga Churn Banerjea, Physician; *m.* 1867; one *s.* five *d.* *Educ.:* Doveton College, Calcutta; University College, London. Entered I.C.S., 1871; left the service, 1874; Professor of English Literature, Metropolitan Institution of Calcutta, 1875; founded Indian Association, 1876; founded Ripon College, Calcutta, 1882; was twice President of the Indian National Congress; for eight successive years was a Member of the Bengal Legislative Council; again elected, 1913; Member of the Imperial Legislative Council, 1913-20; President of the Moderate Conference, 1918; appointed a Member of the Franchise Committee in connection with Montagu-Chelmsford Scheme of Reforms for India, 1918; went to England and gave evidence before the Joint Parliamentary Committee of both Houses on Indian Reforms, 1919; Member of the Bengal Legislative Council under the Reforms Scheme, 1921; appointed Minister to the Government of Bengal in charge of Local Self-Government and Public Health. *Recreation:* gardening. *Address:* Bengalee Office, Calcutta. *(Died 6 Aug. 1925.)*

BANERJEE, Sir Gooroo Dass, Kt., *cr.* 1904; M.A., D.L., Ph.D.; retired High Court Judge; *b.* Narikeldanga, Calcutta, Jan. 1844; *e.s.* of late Babu Ram Chandra Banerjee; *m.* 1861, 3rd *d.* of Pandit Pitambar Tarkapanchanan; four *s.* two *d.* *Educ.:* Hare School; Presidency College, Calcutta. Junior, Senior, and Burdwan Scholarships; B.A. 1864; Gold Medal for Mathematics; B.L. Gold Medallist, 1866; Vakil of the Calcutta High Court, 1866; Assistant Lecturer in Mathematics, Presidency College, 1865; Law Lecturer in the Berhampur College 1866-72; Tagore Law Lecturer, 1878; Fellow of Calcutta University, 1878; Vice-Chancellor, 1889-91; Municipal Commissioner for the Suburbs of Calcutta, 1886; Presidency Magistrate, 1887; Member of the Bengal Legislative Council, 1888; Judge of the Calcutta High Court, 1889-1908; President of the Central Text-Book Committee, 1896-99; Member of the Indian Universities Commission, 1902; Hon. Ph.D. 1908. *Publications:* The Elements of Arithmetic, 1879; The Tagore Law Lectures on the Hindu Law of Marriage and Stridhana, 1879; A Note on the Devanagari Alphabet, 1893; A Few Thoughts on Education, 1904; Elementary Geometry, 1907; Siksha (in Bengali); Juan O Karma (in Bengali), 1910; Saral Patiganit (in Bengali), 1914; Saral Vijarganit (in Bengali), 1914; Saral Jyamiti (in Bengali), 1914; The Education Problem in India, 1914. *Address:* 23 Sastitala Road, Narikeldanga, Calcutta.

(Died 1919.)

BANFIELD, Col. Rees John Francis, C.B., 1900; late The Welsh Regiment; passed Staff College; *b.* 10 Oct. 1850; *e.s.* of late Rees Silvanus Price Banfield of Chiswick, W.; *m.* 1877, Marie Louise, *d.* of late J. G. Upton, Esq., of the East India Company; three *s.* one *d.* Entered army, 1871; Capt. 1881; Maj. 1886; Lieut.-Col. 1896; served S. Africa, 1899-1900 (severely wounded, despatches, medal with 5 clasps, C.B.); A.A.G., Chief Staff Officer, and Brig.-Gen. in charge of Administration, Gibraltar; commanded South Wales Territorial Brigade, 1906-10; retired, 1910. *Address:* Park View, Poole Road, Bournemouth.

(Died 15 Jan. 1926.)

BANGS, John Kendrick, author; *b.* Yonkers, New York, 27 May 1862. *Educ.:* Columbia University, New York. Managing Editor, Life, 1884-88; Editorial Staff, Harpers' Magazine, 1888-1900; Editor of Harpers' Weekly, 1900-2; Vice-President Board of Education, Yonkers, N.Y. 1895; President Halstead School, Yonkers, 1895-1903; Candidate for Mayor of Yonkers, 1894. *Publications:* Coffee and Repartee; A House-Boat-on-Styx; Mr. Bonaparte of Corsica; Ghosts I Have Met; Mollie and the Unwise Man; Alice in Municipaland; and about thirty other books. *Recreations:* golf, gardening, and travel. *Address:* Ogunquit, Maine; 7 West 43rd Street, New York City. *Clubs:* Century, Players, New York. *(Died 21 Jan. 1922.)*

BANISTER, Col. Fitzgerald Muirson, C.M.G. 1917; retired pay, R.F.A.; *b.* 17 Sep. 1853; 3rd *s.* of late Surg.-Gen.G. Banister, I.M.S.; *m.* 1888, Caroline Margaret (*d.* 1921), *d.* of Gen. R. E. Hamilton, R.E. *Educ.:* Wellington College; R.M.A. Entered Army, 1872; Lt.-Col. 1897; Bt. Col. 1901; retired, 1904; served Afghan War, 1879 (medal); rejoined, 1914; B.E.F. 1915-17 (despatches twice, C.M.G.). *Address:* 58 Westbourne Terrace, W.2. *T.:* Padd. 2738. *(Died 28 June 1928.)*

BANISTER, Rt. Rev. William, D.D.; *b.* Walton le Dale, Lancashire, 31 May 1855; *m.* Alice, *d.* of T. Grime Preston, Lancashire. *Educ.:* privately; C.M.S. College, Islington. Ordained deacon, Bishop of London, 1879; priest, Bishop of London, 1880; curate, Balderstone, Blackburn, Lancashire, 1879-80; C.M.S. Missionary, Foochow and Ku Cheng, Fuh-Kien Mission, 1880-93; Principal, C.M.S. Theological College, Foochow, 1893-96; secretary, C.M.S. Hong-Kong,

1897; Archdeacon of Hong-Kong, 1902-9; Commissary to Archbishop of Canterbury during vacancy in See of Victoria, Hong-Kong, 1906-7; Bishop of Kwangsi-Hunan, China, 1909-1923; retired. *Publications:* Scripture Catechism for the Young, Chinese; Notes on 1st Corinthians, in Chinese. *Address:* c/o Church Missionary Society, Salisbury Square, E.C.
(*Died 26 Feb. 1923.*)

BANKES, Ralph Vincent, K.C. 1910; Metropolitan Police Magistrate, S. Western Police Court, since 1917; *y. s.* of late J. Scott Bankes, Soughton Hall, Flint; *m.* Ethel Georgina, 2nd *d.* of late W. G. Mount, Wasing Place, Berks, many years M.P. for Newbury Division, Berks; two *s. Educ.:* Winchester; University College, Oxford. Called Inner Temple, 1890. *Address:* 39 St. George's Square, S.W. *T.:* Vict. 2134. *Club:* Oxford and Cambridge.
(*Died 25 Oct. 1921.*)

BANKS, Rev. John Shaw, D.D., Edin. 1903; Theol. Prof. Emeritus, Leeds, 1880-1910; *b.* Sheffield, Oct. 8, 1835; *m.* Charity A. Hill, Plymouth; two *s.* two *d. Educ.:* King Edward's Branch School, Birmingham. Missionary in South India, 1856-64; laboured in Plymouth, Dewsbury, London, Manchester, Glasgow, 1865-80. President of the Wesleyan Conference, 1902. *Publications:* Manual of Christian Doctrine; Science of Religion (Fernley Lecture); Development of Christian Doctrine, 2 vols.; Tendencies of Modern Theology; Central Questions of Faith; The New Testament Books; Translations from German of works by Philippi, Dorner, Monrad, Delitzsch, etc. *Address:* 3 Richmond Road, Leeds. (*Died 17 Mar. 1917.*)

BANNATYNE, Rev. Prof. Colin A., M.A.; Professor of Church History and Principles, College of the Free Church of Scotland, Edinburgh, since 1905; *b.* 5 June 1849; *s.* of late Rev. Archibald Bannatyne, Oban; unmarried. *Educ.:* Edinburgh University and New College. Graduated at Edinburgh University; ordained minister Culter Free Church, 1876; Moderator of Free Church, 1900 and 1906. Took leading part in famous law case, Bannatyne *v.* Overtoun, appealed to and twice heard before House of Lords, decided in favour of the Free Church of Scotland, 1904. *Address:* 11 Bright's Crescent, Edinburgh.
(*Died 23 Nov. 1920.*)

BANNERMAN, Maj.-Gen. William Burney, C.S.I. 1911; K.H.P. 1913; F.R.S.E.; M.D., D.Sc., I.M.S. (ret.); *b.* 6 July 1858; *s.* of late Rev. James Bannerman, D.D., Abernyte, Perthshire, Professor of Theology, New College, Edinburgh, and D. A. Douglas; *m.* 1889, Helen, *d.* of late Rev. R. Boog Watson, LL.D., late Chaplain H.M. Forces; two *s.* two *d. Educ.:* Edinburgh Academy and University. M.B., C.M., Edinburgh, 1881, entered I.M.S. 1883; in military employ till 1891; Burmese Campaign, 1886-1889 (medal, two clasps); in civil employ since 1891; Deputy Sanitary Commissioner, Madras; Superintendent, Plague Research Laboratory; Director, Bombay Bacteriological Laboratory, Parel; Surgeon-General, Madras, 1911-18; Associate Fellow College of Physicians, Philadelphia; corresponding member, American Society Tropical Medicine; Fellow Royal Society, Edinburgh; *Publications:* Serum Therapy of Plague in India; Production of Alkali by Plague Bacillus in Liquid Media; Scientific Memoirs of Government of India; various papers on Plague in Journal of Hygiene; Treatment of Snake-Bite with Potassium Permanganate, Indian Journal of Medical Research, 1914-15, etc. *Recreations:* motoring, golf. *Address:* 11 Strathearn Place, Edinburgh. *Club:* University, Edinburgh. (*Died 3 Feb. 1924.*)

BANNISTER, Rev. Henry Marriott, M.A., D.Litt.; Acting Sub-Librarian of the Bodleian; *b.* 18 Mar. 1854; *s.* of Henry Powell Bannister, M.R.C.S., and Hannah Maria

Marriott; unmarried. *Educ.:* Epsom College; Pembroke College, Oxford; 2nd Class Classical Moderations, 1875; 2nd Class Theology, 1877; Deacon, 1877; Priest, 1878; Assistant Curate of St. Mary-Charterhouse, 1877-83; Mission Priest of St. John the Baptist, Newport, Mon., 1883-84; Vicar of Winterbourne Down, Bristol, 1884-87. *Publications:* Editor of Analecta Hymnica Medii Aevi, vol. xl.; co-editor of vols. xlvii., liii., liv.; Editor of Missale Gothicum, Henry Bradshaw Society, vol. lii.; author of Catalogo sommario della Esposizione Gregoriana, Rome, 1904; Introduction to Ye Solace of Pilgrims, London, 1911; Monumenti Vaticani di Paleografia Musicale, 1913; contributor to English Historical Review, Journal of Theological Studies, Rassegna Gregoriana. *Address:* 205 Woodstock Road, Oxford. *T.:* Oxford 69. *Clubs:* Union, Deal; Union, Rome; Oxford and County, Oxford. (*Died 16 Feb. 1919.*)

BARBÉ, Louis A., B.-ès-L. Univ. Gall.; Officier d'Académie. Professor of Modern Languages (retired) and author; on the editorial staff of Blackie & Son; reviewer on the Glasgow Herald since 1887; *b.* 15 Nov. 1845; *s.* of Charles Barbé, Commissaire de Marine, Cherbourg; *m.* 1880, Alice Rosa, *d.* of John George Allen, Guernsey; one *s. Educ.:* France. Began his scholastic career as Professor of English at the Collège Jean-Bart, Dunkerque; for six years tutor to the Princes of Schaumburg-Lippe; Headmaster of the Modern Languages department in the Glasgow Academy, 1884-1918; additional Examiner in French, University of Edinburgh, 1901; and in Modern Languages to the Faculty of Advocates. *Publications:* The Tragedy of Gowrie House, 1887; Kircaldy of Grange, and Viscount Dundee (Famous Scots Series); The Bass Rock and its Story (with his son, the late Lieut. Adrien E. Barbé, R.A.F.); In Byways of Scottish History, 1912; Margaret of Scotland and the Dauphin Louis, 1917; Sidelights on the Political, Social, and Industrial History of Scotland, 1919; has contributed many articles to various magazines and journals. *Address:* May View, Dunbar, Haddingtonshire.
(*Died Sept. 1926.*)

BARBENSON, Nicholas Peter Le Cocq, Ex-Judge and President of the States of Alderney; *b.* 2 May 1838; *e. s.* of Thomas Nicholas Barbenson, late Judge of Alderney, and Margaret Le Cocq; *m.* 1869, Elizabeth Isabella Charlotte, *e. d.* of Commissary-General David Gibbons; two *s.* two *d. Educ.:* Queen Elizabeth College, Guernsey; studied Law subsequently at Caen in the University of France (diploma of Bachelor of Law and Licentiate at Law in 1857-59). Called to Alderney Bar, 1860; Attorney-General, 1878. *Recreation:* yachting. *Address:* 7 Banister Road, Southampton. (*Died 3 Aug. 1928.*)

BARBER, Ohio C., Chairman Board of Directors Diamond Match Co. since 1881; *b.* Middlebury, O., 20 April 1841; *s.* of George Barber and Eliza Smith; *m.* 1866, Laura L., *d.* of Daniel Brown of Akron, O. (*deceased*), lineal descendant of Cotton Mather; *m.* 1915, Mary, *d.* of Wilbur Orr, Akron, Ohio. *Educ.:* Akron, O., common schools, until 16 years of age, then began selling matches for his father (who was a match manufacturer), travelling in Ohio, Ind., Mich., and Pa. When he became of age, had entire management of the business; in 1881 he arranged consolidation of a number of leading match manufacturers, and formed Diamond Match Co.; built up and developed Barberton now a town of fully 18,000 population; is interested in various large corporations. Director of Babcock & Wilcox Co. and Bryant & May Co., Ltd., President and Director of American Steam Board Co. Is interested in many other manufacturing industries. *Address:* Barberton Ohio, U.S.A. (*Died 4 Feb. 1920.*)

BARBER, William Charles, M.B., M.D., C.M.; Superintendent and Managing Director of Simcoe Hall Sanatorium, Barrie, Ont., Canada; Canadian-Irish parentage; *m.* 1896, Susan C. Graham, Toronto. *Educ.:* private tuition; Toronto Collegiate Institute, University of Toronto. After serving 21 months Senior House Surgeon Toronto General Hospital entered Ontario Government Hospital for Insane service; 10½ years Assistant Superintendent Mimico Hospital; 9½ years Rockwood Hospital, Kingston. *Recreation:* fishing and shooting. *Address:* Simcoe Hall, Ltd., Barrie, Ont., Canada. *T.:* 441. *Club:* Albany, Toronto.
(*Died 13 Dec. 1921.*)

BARBER, Sir (William) Henry, 1st Bt., *cr.* 1924; *b.* 9 Nov. 1860; *s.* of late William Henry Barber, Edgbaston; *m.* 1893, Martha Constance, *o. c.* of Simon Onions, Bourne Bank, Earls Croom, Worcestershire. A Life Governor of Birmingham University. *Heir:* none. *Address:* Culham Court, Remenham, Berks. *Clubs:* Boodle's; Union, Brighton.
(*Died 2 July 1927.*)

BARBER-STARKEY, William Joseph Starkey, J.P.; *o. s.* of late Rev. Wm. Henry Barber, of Darley Dale, Derbyshire, and Mary, 3rd *d.* of late John Starkey, of Wheat House, Yorkshire; *b.* 1847; *m.* 1873, Margaret Aimée, 3rd *d.* of Sir George Kinloch, 1st Bart., of Kinloch, Perthshire; three *s.* four *d.* *Educ.:* Rugby; Trinity College, Cambridge. Called to the Bar, Inner Temple, 1877. *Address:* Knockshannoch, Glen Isla, Forfarshire; Aldenham Park, Bridgnorth, Shropshire. *Clubs:* Athenæum, Royal Automobile.
(*Died 10 July 1924.*)

BARBIER, Paul, officier d'Academie, officier de l'Instruction publique, Univ., Gall., Professor of French language and literature, University of Wales, Cardiff; *b.* Colombier Chatelot, Doubs, France; 2nd *s.* of late Pasteur G. Barbier, French Protestant Church, London; *m.* Euphémie, *e. d.* of Prof. Bornet, Aubonne, Lausanne. *Educ.:* École de la Confession d'Augsbourg, Paris. Read for the ministry; appointed French master at Felstead Grammar School, then in the Manchester Grammar School; permanent lectureship in French language and literature, 1888, which was raised to the status of a professorship in the University College of South Wales and Monmouthshire, Cardiff; past examiner-in-chief, University of London, etc.; has taken a leading rôle in bringing the Keltic branch of France and the Welsh together; has been, by a singular literary coincidence, identified with the Paul Barbier of Mrs. Humphry Ward's novel David Grieve. *Publications:* school editions of French classics. *Address:* University College, Cardiff. (*Died 24 Sept. 1921.*)

BARBOUR, A. H. Freeland, M.A., B.Sc., M.D., F.R.C.P. Edinburgh, LL.D.; F.R.S.E.; J.P.; Hon. Gynecological Physician, Royal Infirmary; Consulting Physician Royal Maternity Hospital, Edinburgh; *b.* 7 Jan. 1856; *s.* of G. F. Barbour of Bonskeid and Gryffe; *m.* 1889, Margaret Nelson, *e. d.* of Hon. George Brown of Toronto; two *s.* three *d.* *Publications:* (with Dr. Berry Hart) Manual of Gynecology; Spinal Deformity in its Relation to Obstetrics; Atlas of the Sectional Anatomy of Labour; The Sectional Anatomy of Labour, and its Bearing on Clinical Work; (with Professor Watson) Gynecological Diagnosis and Pathology; Gynecological Treatment. *Address:* 4 Charlotte Square, Edinburgh. *T.:* 2414.
(*Died 11 June 1927.*)

BARBOUR, Sir David Miller, K.C.M.G., *cr.* 1899: K.C.S.I., *cr.* 1889; *b.* 1841; *s.* of late Miller Barbour of Calkill, Ireland; *m.* 1883, Katherine Constance, *d.* of late Thomas Gribble; three *s.* one *d.* Member of Royal Commission on Gold and Silver, 1886; Financial Member of Council of Governor-General of India, 1887-

1893; Member of Royal Commission on Financial Relations of Great Britain and Ireland, 1898; Member of Royal Commission on Sugar-Growing Colonies of the West Indies, 1897; of Indian Currency Committee, 1898; Commissioner to inquire into the finances of Jamaica; Chairman of Committee on the Currency of the West African Colonies, 1899; Special Commissioner to inquire into the finances of the Orange River Colony and the Transvaal, 1900; Chairman of the Committee on the Currency of the Straits Settlements, 1902; Chairman of the Royal Commission on London Traffic, 1903; Member of the Royal Commission on Shipping Rings, 1907. *Publications:* The Theory of Bimetallism; The Standard of Value; The Influence of the Gold Supply on Prices and Profits. *Address:* Tiltwood, Crawley Down, Sussex. *Clubs:* Athenæum, East India United Service.
(*Died 12 Feb. 1928.*)

BARBOUR, George, M.A., J.P., D.L.; *o. s.* of late Robert Barbour and Janet Andrew, *d.* of late William Fleming, of Sawnillfield, Glasgow; *b.* 1841; *m.* 1869, Caroline Easton, *d.* of late Robert Andrew Macfie, of Dreghorn Castle, Midlothian; one *s.* six *d.* *Educ.:* Harrow; Trinity College, Cambridge. Called to Bar, Inner Temple, 1865; High Sheriff, Cheshire, 1890; Patron of one living; Hon. Major late Earl of Chester's Yeomanry Cavalry. *Heir: o. s.* Robert [Major Earl of Chester's Yeo.; *b.* 1876; *m.* 1909, Ida Lavington, *o. d.* of Arthur Lavington Payne; two *s.* *Educ.:* Harrow; Trinity College, Cambridge]. *Address:* Bolesworth Castle, near Chester. *Clubs:* Carlton, New University.
(*Died 3 Nov. 1919.*)

BARBOUR, Major Robert, M.A., J.P., D.L.; T.D.; *o. s.* of late George Barbour and Caroline Easton, *d.* of late Robert Andrew Macfie, of Dreghorn Castle, Midlothian; *b.* 1876; *m.* 1909, Ida Lavington, *o. d.* of Arthur Lavington Payne; three *s.* *Educ.:* Harrow; Trinity College, Cambridge. Major, Earl of Chester's Yeomanry; High Sheriff Cheshire, 1925; served South African War, 1900-1; European War, 1914-18. *Heir: s.* George Richard, *b.* 1911. *Address:* Bolesworth Castle, near Chester. *Clubs:* Carlton, Junior Carlton.
(*Died 3 Sept. 1928.*)

BARCLAY, Florence L., *b.* 2 Dec. 1862; *m.* Rev. Charles W. Barclay; two *s.* six *d.* *Publications:* The Wheels of Time, 1908; The Rosary, 1909; The Mistress of Shenstone, 1910; The Following of the Star, 1911; Through the Postern Gate, 1912; The Upas Tree, 1912; The Broken Halo, 1913; The Wall of Partition, 1914; My Heart's Right There, 1914; In Hoc Vince, 1915; The White Ladies of Worcester, 1917; Returned Empty, 1920. *Address:* Little Amwell Vicarage, Hertford-Heath, Hertford, Herts; The Corner House, Overstrand, Norfolk. *T.A.:* Hertfordheath. *M.:* AR 2230.
(*Died 10 Mar. 1920.*)

BARCLAY, Sir George Head, K.C.S.I., *cr.* 1913; K.C.M.G., *cr.* 1908; C.V.O. 1906; H.M. Minister at Bucharest since 1912; *b.* 23 Mar. 1862; 3rd *s.* of late Henry Ford Barclay of Monkhams, Woodford; *m.* 1891, Beatrix Mary Jay, *d.* of late Henry G. Chapman of New York; one *d.* *Educ.:* Eton; Trinity College, Camb. Attaché. 1886; appointed to Washington, 1888; to Rome as 3rd Secretary, 1891; transferred to Madrid, 1894, where he was acting Chargé d'Affaires, 1897 and 1898; transferred to Constantinople, 1898; First Secretary of Legation at Tokyo, 1902-5; Councillor of Embassy, 1905; and again Constantinople, 1906; Minister at Constantinople, April to July 1908, and at Tehran, 1908-12. *Address:* British Legation, Bucharest. *Clubs:* Travellers'. St. James's.
(*Died 26 Jan. 1921.*)

BARCLAY, Rev. James, D.D.; Minister of St. Paul's Church, Montreal, 1883-1910; *b.* Paisley, 19 June 1844; 3rd *s.* of late James

Barclay of Edinburgh; *m.* 1873, Marian Simpson of Dumfries. *Educ.*: Paisley Grammar School; Merchiston Castle, Edinburgh; Glasgow University. Minister at Dalbeattie, 1870; Canonbie, 1874; Linlithgow, 1876; St. Cuthbert's, Edinburgh, 1878. *Clubs:* St. James's University, Montreal. (*Died 18 May 1920.*)

BARCLAY, Robert Buchanan, I.S.O. 1902, General Superintendent of Poor, Local Government Board for Scotland (retired); *s.* of Hugh Barclay, LL.D., Sheriff-Substitute of Perthshire; *b.* 24 Feb. 1843; *m.* 1875, Margaret, *d.* of Bailie Binnie of Glasgow. *Educ.:* Perth Academy. *Address:* 17 Inverleith Gardens, Edinburgh. (*Died 26 Dec. 1919.*)

BARCLAY, Sir Thomas, Kt., *cr.* 1908; J.P. for Birmingham, Warwickshire, Worcestershire; *b.* Sunderland, 30 Aug. 1839; 2nd *s.* of James and Margaret Barclay of Felling, Co. Durham; *m.* 1st, 1861, Mary Anne (*d.* 1891), 2nd *d.* of late Robert Jaques, M.R.C.S.; 2nd, Mary Dingley, 2nd *d.* of late Edward D. Pethybridge, J.P., Banker, Launceston, Cornwall; two *s.* five *d.* *Educ.:* private tuition. Was the first Managing Director of Southall Bros. & Barclay, Ltd., Birmingham, which position he still holds; was for 8 years member King's Norton School Board, and 9 years member of the Birmingham City Council, during that time he was a member of the Water Committee and one of the pioneers of the scheme for bringing the Welsh water to Birmingham; represented British Pharmacists at the International Congress, 1881; after several years' agitation, commencing 1877, succeeded in abolishing the compulsory collection of Income Tax, Land Tax Grants, by unwilling collectors; was the Founder of the Chemists' and Druggists' Trade Association of Great Britain, 1876. *Publications:* The Future Water Supply of Birmingham (3 editions); The Class Leader at Work. *Recreations:* golf, travelling. *Address:* The Uplands, Blackwell, nr. Bromsgrove. *T.A.:* Uplands, Bromsgrove. *T.:* 20 Barnt Green. *M.:* AB 640 and AB 4260. *Club:* National Liberal. (*Died 23 Dec. 1921.*)

BARDSLEY, Rev. Joseph Udell Norman, M.A.; Vicar and Rural Dean of Lancaster; *b.* 13 Dec. 1868; *s.* of Rev. S. Bardsley, M.A., Rector of Finchley; *m.* 1895, Annie Mabel Killick, Beech Mount, Aigburth, Liverpool; two *s.* four *d.* *Educ.:* St. Paul's School; Gonville and Caius College, Cambridge. Ordained 1892; Curate of St. Leonard's, Bootle; St. Anne, Aigburth; St. Philip, Litherland; Rector of Ulverston, 1896; Vicar of Lancaster and Chaplain to the Bowerham Barracks, 1909; Proctor in Convocation, 1907-10; Rural Dean, 1911; Proctor in Convocation, 1919; Hon. Canon of Blackburn, 1927. *Publication:* The Church of England and her Endowments, 1912. *Recreation:* golf. *Address:* The Vicarage, Lancaster. *T.:* Lancaster 87. (*Died 8 July 1928.*)

BARE, Captain Arnold Edwin, M.V.O. 1916; 1st Artists Rifles; *b.* 1880; *s.* of Thomas Edwin Bare, Past President Quantity Surveyors' Association; *m.* 1906, Janie H. Stormont; one *s.* two *d.* *Educ.:* Emanuel School. Quantity Surveyor; member of firm, Bare, Leaning & Bare; Fellow of The Surveyors' Institution; enrolled in Artists' Rifle Volunteers, 1897; to France with B.E.F. Oct. 1914. *Address:* Rokra, Bushey Grove Road, Bushey, Herts. *T.:* Holborn 5675.
(*Died 30 Oct. 1917.*)

BAREFOOT, Lt.-Col. George Henry, C.B. 1916; C.M.G. 1915; late R.A.M.C.; *b.* 29 Nov. 1864; entered army, 1886; Maj. 1898; Lt.-Col. 1906; served Hazara Expedition, 1888 (despatches, medal with clasp); European War, 1914-18,(despatches, C.M.G., C.B.); retired pay, 1919. (*Died 15 Sept. 1924.*)

BARFF, Henry Ebenezer, C.M.G., M.A.; Warden and Registrar, University of Sydney,

since 1914; *b.* Tahaa, Society Islands, 9 July 1857; *s.* of Rev. John Barff, of the L.M.S.; *m.* 1899, Jane Foss, *d.* of H. C. Russell, C.M.G., B.A., F.R.S., Govt. Astronomer of N.S.W.; one *d.* *Educ.:* Camden College School; Sydney University. B.A. 1876; M.A. 1882; Master of Studies, University of Sydney, 1876; Acting Registrar, 1880; Registrar, 1882. *Publication:* A Short Historical Account of the University of Sydney. *Recreation:* golf. *Address:* Cotham, Newcastle Street, Rose Bay, Sydney, N.S.W. *T.:* Sydney F7017. *Clubs:* University, Royal Sydney Golf, Sydney. (*Died 2 May 1925.*)

BARFF, Rev. Henry Tootal, M.A.; Canon of Gibraltar since 1894; *b.* Wakefield, 1834; *m.* Mary, *d.* of Rev. J. Matthews, Vicar of Sherburn; two *s.* one *d.* *Educ.:* Trinity Hall, Camb.; 2nd Class Classical Tripos. Ordained 1858; Incumbent of Hawkley, Hants, 1862-65; Curate of Holy Trin. Maidstone, 1868-70; Hythe, Kent, 1870-71; Assistant Chaplain, Nice, 1872-1875; Chaplain at Naples, 1875-1904. *Address:* Nailsea House, Nailsea, Somersetshire. *T.A.:* Nailsea. (*Died 4 April 1917.*)

BARING, Major Hon. Guy Victor, Reserve of Officers; M.P. (C.) Winchester since 1906; *b.* 1873; 4th *s.* of 4th Lord Ashburton; *m.* 1903, Olive, *y. d.* of Hugh C. Smith, Mount Clare, Roehampton; four *s.* one *d.* *Educ.:* Eton; Sandhurst. Joined Coldstream Guards, 1893; served with 2nd Batt., S. Africa, 1899-1900 (medal, three clasps); present with the Imperial Representative Corps at the Inauguration of the Australian Commonwealth, Sydney, 1901; served with Ogden Punitive Force, 1901 (medal, clasp). *Recreation:* travel. *Address:* 16 Cadogan Square, S.W.; St. Cross Mill, Winchester. *Clubs:* Carlton, Guards'. (*Died 15 Sept. 1916.*)

BARING, Harold Herman John, M.B.E., *e. s.* of late Thomas Charles Baring, M.P., and Susan Carter, *d.* of Robert Bowne Minturn, of New York; *b.* 4 March 1869; *m.* 1898, Mary, *d.* of John Augustus Churchill, New York. *Address:* High Beech, Loughton, Essex. *T.:* Loughton 102. (*Died 10 Dec. 1927.*)

BARING, Hon. Windham; Managing Director of Baring Brothers & Co., Ltd., and Director of The Buenos Ayres Great Southern Railway Co., Ltd.; served in European War as Lieut. R.N.V.R.; *b.* 29 Sep. 1880; 2nd *s.* of 1st and *b.* of 2nd Earl of Cromer; *m.* 1913, Lady Gweneth Frida Ponsonby, *y. d.* of 8th Earl of Bessborough; three *s.* *Educ.:* Eton; Christ Church, Oxford. *Recreations:* shooting, golf. *Address:* 57 Portland Place, W.; *T.:* Mayfair 2627; Woodcock, Little Berkhampstead, Hertford; *T.:* Essendon 16. *Clubs:* Turf, Brooks's, Bath. (*Died 23 Dec. 1922.*)

BARING-GOULD, Sabine, M.A., J.P.; Hon. Fellow of Clare College, Cambridge; Rector, Lew-Trenchard; *e. s.* of Edward Baring-Gould, Lew-Trenchard, and Charlotte Sophia, *d.* of Admiral F. Godolphin Bond, R.N.; *b.* 28 Jan. 1834 at Exeter; *m.* 1868, Grace (*d.* 1916), *d.* of Joseph Taylor, Horbury, Yorkshire. *Educ.:* Clare College, Cambridge. Travelled in Iceland, 1861; various parts of Europe; Curate, Horbury, Yorkshire, 1864; Vicar, Dalton, Yorkshire, 1866; Rector of East Mersea, Essex, 1871; inherited family estates, Lew-Trenchard, 1872, on death of father; presented himself to Rectory of Lew-Trenchard on death of his uncle, 1881. Owns 3000 acres. *Publications:* The Path of the Just, 1854; Iceland, its Scenes and Sagas, 1862; Post-Mediæval Preachers, 1865; book of Were-Wolves, 1865; Curious Myths of the Middle Ages, 1866, 1868; The Origin and Development of Religious Belief, 1869-70; The Golden Gate, 1870; The Silver Store, 1870, 1888; In Exitu Israel, 1870; Legendary Lives of Old Testament Characters, 1871; One Hundred Sermon Sketches for Extempore Preachers, 1872; Secular *v.* Religious Education, 1872; Lives of the Saints, 1872-77;

Village Conferences on the Creed, 1873 ; The Lost and Hostile Gospels, 1874 ; Some Modern Difficulties, 1875 ; Village Sermons for a Year, 1875 ; The Mystery of Suffering, 1877 ; Mehalah, 1880, 1885 ; John Herring, 1883-86 ; Court Royal, 1886-88 ; Red Spider, 1887-88 ; The Gaverocks, 1887-88 ; Richard Cable, 1888 ; Eve, 1888 ; The Sacristy, a Quarterly Review of Ecclesiastical Art and Literature, 1871-73 ; Germany, Present and Past, 1879, 1883 ; Sermons to Children, 1879 ; The Preacher's Pocket, 1880 ; The Village Pulpit, 1881, 1887 ; Village Preaching for a Year, 1884 ; Church Songs, 1884 ; The Seven Last Words, 1884 ; The Passion of Jesus, 1885, 1886, 1887 ; The Nativity, 1885 ; Germany (Story of the Nations Series), 1886 ; Our Parish Church, 1886 ; The Resurrection, 1888 ; Our Inheritance, a History of the Holy Eucharist in the First Three Centuries, 1888 ; The Pennycomequicks, 1889 ; Arminell, 1889 ; Historic Oddities and Strange Events, 1889-91 ; Old Country Life, 1889 ; History of the Church in Germany, 1891 ; Urith, 1890 ; In Troubadours' Land, 1890 ; Conscience and Sin, 1890 ; Songs of the West, 1891 ; In the Roar of the Sea, 1892 ; The Tragedy of the Cæsars, 1892 ; Curious Survivals, 1892 ; Mrs. Curgenven, 1893 ; Cheap Jack Zita, 1893 ; The Deserts of Southern France, 1894 ; The Queen of Love, 1894 ; A Garland of Country Song, 1894 ; Old Fairy Tales Retold, 1894 ; Noémi, 1895 ; The Old English Fairy Tales, 1895 ; Napoleon Bonaparte, 1896 ; The Broom Squire, 1896 ; A Study of St. Paul, 1897 ; Guavas the Tinner, 1897 ; Bladys, 1897 ; The Sunday Round, sermons, 1898 ; Domitia, 1898 ; Pabo the Priest, 1899 ; A Book of the West, 1899 ; Furze-Bloom, 1899 ; The Crock of Gold, 1899 ; Winefred, 1900 ; A Book of Dartmoor, 1900 ; In a Quiet Village, 1900 ; Virgin Saints and Martyrs, 1900 ; The Frobishers ; A Book of Brittany ; Royal Georgie, 1901 ; Miss Quillet ; Nebo the Nailer, 1902 ; Brittany, 1902 ; A Book of N. Wales, 1903 ; Chris of All Sorts, 1903 ; A Book of Ghosts, 1904 ; In Dewisland, 1905 ; A Book of S. Wales, 1905 ; A Book of the Riviera, 1905 ; A Memorial of Nelson, 1905 ; A Book of the Rhine, 1906 ; A Book of the Pyrenees, 1907 ; The Restitution of all Things, 1907 ; A Book of the Cevennes, 1908 ; Devonshire Characters, 1908 ; Cornish Characters, 1909 ; Family Names, 1910 ; The Land of Teck, 1911 ; Cliff Castles and Cave Dwellings, 1911 ; The Church Revival, 1914 ; The Evangelical Revival, 1920 ; Early Reminiscences (1834-1864), 1923. *Address:* Lew-Trenchard House, N. Devon. *T.A.:* Lew, Down.
                         (Died 2 Jan. 1924.)

BARKER, Arthur Edward James, Professor of Surgery, University College, since 1898 ; Surgeon, University College Hospital, London, since 1885 ; Consulting Surgeon to the Queen Alexandra Military Hospital, Millbank, S.W. ; Consulting Surgeon to Osborne Convalescent Home for Officers R.N. and Army ; Lieut.-Colonel, R.A.M.C. ; Consulting Surgeon to the Southern Command ; *m.* 1880, Emilie Blanche, *d.* of Julius Delmege of Rathkeale, Co. Limerick ; one *s.* four *d. Publications:* Manual of Operative Surgery, 1887 ; Diseases of Joints (Treves's System of Surgery), 1896 ; Address in Surgery, British Medical Association, 1909 ; Operations for Hernia in System of Operative Surgery, edited by F. F. Burghard, 1909. *Recreations:* yachting, cricket, lawn-tennis, golf. *Address:* 144 Harley Street, W. *T.:* 1547 Paddington.   *(Died 8 April 1916.)*

BARKER, Col. Charles Wm. Panton, C.B.E., 1920 ; V.D. ; Solicitor, Clerk to Justices ; Notary Public ; *b.* 15 Sep. 1857 ; *m.* 1884, Mary (*d.* 1922), 2nd *d.* of Jun Carr Tone, Grange House, Sunderland ; two *s.* two *d. Educ.:* Crow Tree House, Sunderland. Law, Society's Prizeman, 1878 ; Durham R.G.A. (T.), 1877-1910 ; 160th R.F.A. (Wearside) Brigade 1915. *Address:* The Hawthorns, Sunderland. *T.:* Sunderland 863, 974. *Club:* Sunderland.   *(Died 21 Mar. 1926.)*

BARKER, Edward Harrison ; British Vice-Consul for Tréport and Eu, France, since 1904 ; *b.* 19 Feb. 1851 ; *s.* of Benjamin Barker, *g.-s.* of Thomas Barker, painter of The Woodman, etc. ; *m.* 1876, Mary Isabel, *d.* of late Captain Kitching, E.I.C.S., Inspecting Commander of H.M. Coastguard ; two *s.* two *d. Educ.:* Bath Grammar School. Editor of Bath Argus at age of 21 ; subsequently on editorial staff of Galignani's Messenger and Paris Correspondent of London and other newspapers ; contributed frequently to Temple Bar and various magazines ; British Vice-Consul at Pauillac, 1900. *Publications:* Wayfaring in France ; Wanderings by Southern Waters ; Two Summers in Guyenne ; France of the French ; A British Dog in France, etc. *Recreation:* natural history. *Address:* Le Tréport, Seine Inférieure, France.
                       (Died 31 Oct. 1919.)

BARKER, Sir Francis (Henry), Kt., *cr.* 1917 ; Director Vickers, Ltd. ; *b.* 18 June 1865 ; 2nd *s.* of late Alfred Barker of Constantinople and Elmfield, Esher ; *m.* 1897, Aimée, *e. d.* of late Arthur de Vere ; two *s. Educ.:* private tutors ; Clifton College. Vice-Chairman of Metropolitan-Vickers Electrical Co., Ltd. ; President of British Russia Club ; Chairman of Executive Council of Russo-British Chamber of Commerce ; has travelled all over Europe and Asia Minor. *Recreations:* shooting and riding. *Address:* Lowndes House, Lowndes Place, Belgrave Square, S.W. ; *T.:* Victoria 6854 ; Burnt Stub, Chessington, Surrey ; *T.:* Esher 227. *T.A.:* Barkonia, London. *Clubs:* Marlborough, St. James's, Royal Automobile.
                       (Died 28 Jan. 1922.)

BARKER, Colonel Sir Francis (William James), Kt., *cr.* 1906 ; R.A., retired ; *b.* 29 Apr. 1841 ; *e. s.* of late William Barker, F.R.C.Ph.I., ex-President of Royal College. of Physicians, Ireland ; *m.* 1873, C. Jessie, *o. d.* of late John Foster ; four *s.* two *d. Educ.:* Trinity College, Dublin ; Royal Military Academy, Woolwich. Entered R.A. 1868 ; Major, 1883 ; Lt.-Col. 1890 ; Col. 1896 ; retired from Army, 1898 ; served Abyssinian Expedition, 1867-8, including assault and capture of Magdala (medal) ; Instructor in Gunnery, 1873-6 ; Inspector of Warlike Stores, 1878-84 ; Assistant Superintendent, Royal Gunpowder Factory, 1885-92 ; Acting Superintendent, 1892 ; Superintendent, Royal Small Arms Factory, Birmingham, 1892. *Recreations:* yachting, boating, and fishing. *Address:* 1 Westbourne Mansions, Folkestone. *Club:* Radnor, Folkestone.   *(Died 3 Mar. 1924.)*

BARKER, Hon. Sir Frederic Eustace, Kt., *cr.* 1913 ; Chief Justice of the Supreme Court of New Brunswick 1908-14 ; *b.* 27 Dec. 1838 ; *s.* of Enoch Barker of Sheffield, county of Sunbury ; *m.* 1st, Julia (*d.* 1874), *d.* of Edward Lloyd of the R.E. Civil Staff ; 2nd, Mary Ann, *d.* of late B. E. Black of Halifax ; one *s.* four *d. Educ.:* Sunbury Grammar School ; University of New Brunswick. B.A. with honours, 1856 ; M.A. 1858 ; B.C.L. 1861 ; D.C.L. 1866. Called to Bar, 1860 ; Q.C. 1873 ; Judge of the Supreme Court of New Brunswick, 1893 ; member House of Commons for City of St. John, 1885 ; Administrator of the Government during absence of Lieutenant-Governor Fraser, 1896 ; some years a member of the University Senate ; one of the Commissioners to revise the Provincial Statutes, 1866 ; was Chairman of the St. John School Board, etc. *Recreation:* fishing. *Address:* The Cedars, Mount Pleasant, St. John, N.B. *Club:* Union.
                       (Died 15 Dec. 1916.)

BARKER, Maj.-Gen. John Stewart Scott, C.B. 1903 ; R.A. ; commanding Royal Artillery, Malta since 1912 ; *b.* 13 Sept. 1853 ; *s.* of Sir George Barker ; *m.* 1885, Agnes Mary, *y. d.* of late Major Peel of Aylesmore, Gloucs. Entered army, 1872 ; Captain, 1882 ; Major, 1889 ; Lt.-Col., 1898 ; Col., 1902 ; served

8. Africa, 1901-1902 (despatches, twice; medals with 5 clasps, brevet-Col.); Brig.-Gen. commanding Jhansi Brigade, 1907-12. *Address:* Malta.
(Died 20 April 1918.)

BARKER, Very Rev. Joseph, D.D.; *b.* 23 Oct. 1834; *s.* of John Perkins Barker, 1875; *m.* 1st, 1853, Elizabeth Annie White (*d.* 1869) of Huntley, Gloucestershire; six *d.*; 2nd, 1870, Isabel S. Fannin; one *s.* one *d. Educ.:* Kidderminster Diocesan School; private tuition as Pupil Teacher, St. Mary's National School; in 4th year, acting Master during vacancy. Arrived in Natal, 1853; ordained, 1857; Curate of Ladysmith, 1857-61; Canon of St. Saviour's Cathedral, Maritzburg; Incumbent of St. Patrick's, Umzinto, 1861-87; Archdeacon of Durban, 1878-87; Vicar of Ladysmith, 1887-1906; Archdeacon of Maritzburg, 1887-1908; Dean of Maritzburg and Archdeacon, city of Maritzburg, 1906; Vicar of St. Saviour's, Maritzburg, 1913; Retired on pension, 1915. *Address:* The Deanery, Maritzburg, Natal.
(Died 25 June 1924.)

BARKER, Lt.-Col. Randle Barnett-, D.S.O. 1916; Commanding 22nd Batt. Royal Fusiliers; *b.* 1870; *e. s.* of late Major J. B. Barnett-Barker, 5th Fusiliers; *m.* 1897, Ellinor Gertrude, *e. d.* of Richard Hobson, J.P., D.L., The Marfords, Bromborough, Cheshire; two *s. Educ.:* privately. Joined Royal Welsh Fusiliers, 1891; Brigade Major, Cheshire Brigade, 1907-12; retired from Army; Commandant prisoners of war, Aug. 1914; raised the 22nd Batt. Royal Fusiliers in Kensington, Sep. 1914; afterwards commanded them when they embarked for France (despatches 4 times, Brevet Majority, June 1917, D.S.O. (immediate reward) for gallantry on the Somme, Bar to D.S.O. (immediate reward for gallantry at Arras, 1917); in following actions: Vimy Ridge, 1916; Delville Wood, 1916; Beaumont-Hamel, 1916; Ancre advance and Miraumont battle, 1917; Arras, April 1917. *Recreations:* shooting and fishing; won many point-to-point races. *Address:* Cae Kenby, Abergavenny. *Club:* Naval and Military. *(Died 24 Mar. 1918.)*

BARKER, Rev. Rowland Vectis, Hon. Canon of St. Edmundsbury and Ipswich; Hon. Chaplain to the Bishop; Proctor in Convocation for Archdeaconry of Suffolk, 1906-19; *b.* 1846; *y. s.* of John Barker, J.P., D.L., of Albrighton Hall, Shifnal, and Cleveland House, Wolverhampton; *m.* 1883, Elizabeth, *d.* of late Sir R. H. Inglis Palgrave, F.R.S.; three *s.* one *d. Educ.:* Shrewsbury School; Christchurch, Oxford, M.A. Ordained, 1871; Curate of Gt. Yarmouth, 1871-5; Nantwich, 1877-9; Vicar of St. Paul's, Preston, 1879-85; Vicar of St. Mark, Lakenham, Norwich, 1885-94; Vicar of Bramford with Burstall, Suffolk, 1894-1904; Rector of Henstead, Suffolk, 1904-18; Organising Secretary S.P.G. for Archdeacon of Suffolk, 1898-99; Rural Dean of Bosmere, 1898-1904. *Address:* The Lodge, Woodbridge, Suffolk. *T.A.:* Woodbridge. *M.:* DX 2240. *(Died 8 Nov. 1926.)*

BARKER, Very Rev. William, D.D., Oxford; Dean of Carlisle since 1908; Hon. Chaplain to the King; Prebendary of St. Paul's; Rural Dean, 1905; *b.* London, 1 Dec. 1838; *s.* of Joseph Charles Barker; *m. o. d.* of Adm. Sir James Ross, Arctic explorer; two *s.* one *d. Educ.:* private tutors; Worcester Coll. Oxford. B.A. 1861, M.A. 1863; ordained Deacon, 1862; Priest, by Bishop of London, Dr. Tait, 1863; Curate of Hanover Church, St. George, Hanover Square (the church has recently been pulled down), 1862-64; Chaplain to Royal Ophthalmic Hospital, Moorfields; Assistant Minister, Curzon Chapel, 1867-70; Organising Secretary of Curates' Augmentation Fund, 1870-73; Vicar of St. Mary's, West Cowes, 1873-1882; Chaplain to the Queen, 1874-99; member of London School Board, 1882-88; Rector of St. Marylebone to 1908; Chaplain to the

"Foresters"; Hon. Chaplain in ordinary to the King, 1902. *Publications:* no book; writings chiefly articles; once sub-editor of the old English Churchman. *Recreations:* fishing, golf, foreign travelling. *Address:* The Deanery, Carlisle. *T.A.:* Deanery, Carlisle. *T.:* 427. *M.:* LB 9094. *Club:* Felixstowe Golf.
(Died 28 Jan. 1917.)

BARKER, Lt.-Col. William Arthur John, D.S.O. 1916; late Commanding 8th South Stafford Regt.; *b.* 22 Aug. 1879; 2nd *s.* of Col. Sir Francis Barker. Entered South Staffordshire Regt. 1899; served South Africa, 1900-2 (Queen's medal, 3 clasps; King's medal, 2 clasps); European War, 1914-16 (wounded three times, despatches thrice, D.S.O., Croix de Guerre with palms); resigned, 1909; rejoined, 1915. *Address:* 1 Westbourne Mansions, Folkestone. *(Died 25 Aug. 1924.)*

BARLOW, Adm. Charles James, D.S.O. 1887; R.N.; *b.* 11 Aug. 1848; *m.* 1892, Elizabeth Hume, *d.* of Arthur Dight of Queensland and N.S.W., Australia. Entered navy, 1862; Capt. 1889; served Egypt, First Lieut. H.M.S. Inflexible, bombardment of Alexandria and ashore, 1882 (medal, Alexandria clasp, Khedive's star, 4th class Osmanieh); Burmah, 2nd in command Naval Brigade, 1885-86 (despatches, D.S.O., India medal, clasp); 2nd in command Channel Fleet, 1905; 2nd in command Home Fleet, 1904; Admiral Superintendent Devonport Dockyard, 1905-8; retired, 1911. *(Died 25 Aug. 1921.)*

BARLOW, George Thomas, C.I.E. 1915; Chief Engineer and Secretary, Government Irrigation Branch, U.P., India; *b.* 11 March, 1865; *s.* of Rev. J. M. Barlow, Ewhurst Rectory, Guildford; *m.* 1891, A. S. Anthony; two *s.* two *d. Educ.:* Haileybury; R.I.E. College. Appointed P.W.D., India, 1886; after a year's practical course in England went to India as Irrigation Engineer; employed at various posts on Ganges Canal till 1901; Executive Engineer, 1897; Superintending Engineer, 1911; has been working since 1901 in the trans-Jumna Tract, U.P., known as Bundel-Khund, or prospecting on the Survey and on the construction of numerous reservoirs and large masonry dams and canals. *Publications:* a few text-books. *Recreations:* tennis, big game shooting. *Address:* Allahabad, U.P., India. *(Died 9 April 1919.)*

BARLOW, Jane, Hon. D.Litt. Dublin; *b.* Clontarf, Co. Dublin, *e. d.* of J. W. Barlow. *Educ.:* at home. *Publications:* Bogland Studies, 1892; Irish Idylls, 1892; Kerrigan's Quality, 1893; The End of Elfintown, 1894; The Battle of the Frogs and Mice, 1894; Maureen's Fairing, 1895; Strangers at Lisconnel, 1895; Mrs. Martin's Company, 1896; Creel of Irish Stories, 1897; From the East unto the West, 1898; From the Land of the Shamrock, 1900; Ghost-Bereft, 1901; The Founding of Fortunes, 1902; By Beach and Bog Land, 1905; Irish Neighbours, 1907; The Mockers, 1908; Irish Ways, 1909; Mac's Adventures, 1911; Flaws, 1911; Doings and Dealings, 1913. *Recreation:* music. *Address:* The Cottage, Raheny, Co. Dublin. *T.A.:* Barlow, Raheny. *T.:* 47 Clontarf.
(Died 17 April 1917.)

BARLOW, Col. John, M.V.O. 1909; V.D.; Vice-President National Rifle Association. *Address:* N.R.A. School of Musketry, Bisley Camp.
(Died 30 Sept. 1924.)

BARNARD, 9th Baron (cr. 1698), Henry de Vere Vane; F.S.A., J.P., D.L.; Hon. D.C.L. Durham; Provincial Grand Master Durham Freemasons since 1900; Hon. Col. 4th (Special Reserve) Batt. Durham L.I.; Chairman Tees Fishery Board; a Governor of Shrewsbury School; *b.* 10 May 1854; *s.* of Sir Henry Morgan Vane; *S.* kinsman, 4th and last Duke of Cleveland, in Barony of Barnard, 1891; *m.* Lady Catharine Sarah Cecil (*d.* 1918), *d.* of 3rd Marquess of Exeter, 1881; three *s. Educ.:* Eton; Brasenose

College, Oxford (B.A. 1876). Barr. 1879; Northamptonshire Militia, 1876-84; served in Charity Commission, 1881-91; Private Secretary to Chief Commissioner, 1885-90. *Heir: s.* Hon. Christopher William Vane, M.C. [Capt. Westmorland and Cumberland Yeomanry; *b.* 28 Oct. 1888. Served European War (wounded)]. *Address:* 20 Belgrave Square, S.W.; Raby Castle, Darlington. *Clubs:* Brooks's, Oxford and Cambridge.   *(Died 28 Dec. 1918.)*

BARNARD, Andrew Bigoe, C.I.E. 1911; Deputy Director of Criminal Intelligence with the Government of India, 1905-14; retired, 1914; *b.* 26 July 1862; 2nd *s.* of late Colonel W. A. M. Barnard, Grenadier Guards and 96th Regt.; *m.* 1903, Florence Anne, *e. d.* of James Worrall, J.P., of Westwell, Tenterden, Kent; one *s.* two *d.* *Educ.:* Bedford School. Entered Bengal Police as Assistant-Superintendent, 1881; Deputy Commissioner of Police, Calcutta, 1889; Assistant Inspector-General Government Railway Police, 1897; Deputy Inspector-General of Police, 1906; Commandant Prisoner of War Camp, with rank of Major, 1916. *Address:* Withersdane Hall, Wye, Kent. *T.:* Wye 12. *Club:* Windham.   *(Died 16 Feb. 1928.)*

BARNARD, Rev. Charles William; Rector and Rural Dean of Sutton Coldfield since 1909; hon. canon of Birmingham; proctor of Convocation, 1905-19. *Educ.:* Oriel College, Oxford (M.A.). Ordained, 1879; curate of St. George, Barrow-in-Furness, 1879-82; St. Mary's, Beverley, 1882-85; vicar of Rowley Regis, Staffs., 1885-88; rector of Churchill, Worcester, 1888-93; hon. canon Worcester, 1904-5; vicar of Kings Norton, 1893-9; Rural Dean of Kings Norton, 1907-9; Deputy Provincial Grand Master and Grand Superintendent of Freemasonry in Warwickshire. *Address:* Merlewood, Leamington Spa. *Club:* Fly Fishers'.

    (Died 18 Aug. 1928.)

BARNARD, Sir Herbert, Kt., *cr.* 1898; J.P. London, Middlesex, and Surrey; late Chairman of Public Works Loan Commission; *b.* 1 Oct. 1881; *s.* of John Barnard, Cornhill, London, banker; *m.* 1854, Ellen, *d.* of William Wyndham of Dinton, Wilts, M.P.; three *s.* nine *d.* *Educ.:* Eton. *Address:* 23 Portland Place, W. *Club:* Union.   *(Died 30 June 1920.)*

BARNARD, Major-General William Osborne; *b.* 1838; 3rd *s.* of late George Barnard, who was *g.-s.* of Sir Frederick Augusta Barnard; *m.* 1872, Isabella, *d.* of late Francis Tucker, Bengal Civil Service. *Educ.:* Charterhouse. Joined 96th Regiment, 1856; Captain, 1859; Major, 1878; Lieut.-Col., 1881; commanded, 1882-86; commanded 53rd Regimental District, 1887-88; Brig.-General commanding Nerbudda District, 1888-93; Maj.-Gen. commanding Mauritius, 1895-96; Maj.-Gen. 1896; Maj.-Gen. commanding 2nd Infantry Brigade, Aldershot, 1896-99; retired, 1899; Col. the Manchester Regt. 1904. *Recreations:* ordinary. *Address:* 5 Montagu Mansions, W. *T.:* Paddington 4493. *Clubs:* Army and Navy, United Service; Union, Brighton.

    (Died 15 Jan. 1920.)

BARNARD, William Tyndall, K.C. 1905; Registrar of the Divorce Court; *e. s.* of W. T. Barnard, Barrister, and Charlotte Jane, *g.-d.* of Richard Jeune; *m.*; one *s.* Student, Gray's Inn, 1875. Called to Bar, 1879. *Address:* 13 King's Bench Walk, Temple, E.C.; Somerset Lodge, The Manor Way, Blackheath.

    (Died 30 Sept. 1923.)

BARNARDISTON, Col. Nathaniel; J.P. Essex and Suffolk; D.L. Suffolk; County Councillor, West Suffolk (Chairman), 1889-99; Chairman, Quarter Sessions, 1876-1909; *b.* 24 April 1832; *s.* of N. C. Barnardiston; *m.* 1858, Lady Florence Legge, 5th *d.* of 4th Earl of Dartmouth; four *s.* five *d.* *Educ.:* Harrow. Entered 27th Inniskilling Regt. 1851; served in India; Brigadier-General Commanding Harwich Volun-

teer Brigade, 1890-1900. *Heir: s.* Maj.-Gen. N. W. Barnardiston. *Address:* The Ryes, Sudbury, Suffolk.   *(Died 12 Feb. 1916.)*

BARNARDISTON, Maj.-Gen. Nathaniel Walter, C.B. 1918; M.V.O. 1904; J.P.; Commanded H.B.M.'s Forces in North China, 1914-15; *b.* 29 Nov. 1858; *e. s.* of late Col. Nathaniel Barnardiston of The Ryes, Sudbury, Suffolk, and Lady Florence Legge (*d.* 1917), *d.* of 4th Earl of Dartmouth; *m.* 1892, Sarah Hall, *d.* of late Hon. D. R. Floyd-Jones, of Fort Neck House, Massapequa, Long Island, U.S.A., sometime Secretary of State and Lieut-Governor of New York; one *d.* *Educ.:* privately; Merton College, Oxford (matriculated 1877). Joined 77th (Duke of Cambridge's Own) Regiment from West Suffolk Militia, 1878; was Adjutant 2nd Batt. Middlesex Regiment, 1882-86; passed Staff College, 1888; A.D.C. to Governor of Bermuda (Sir E. N. Newdegate, K.C.B.), 1889; D.A.A.G. Eastern District, 1894-97; Staff Captain Intelligence Division, War Office, 1898-99; D.A.A.G., 1899-1901; served in South African campaign as second in command 2nd Batt. Middlesex Regiment, 1901-2 (South African medal with 4 clasps); commanded British Troops at capture of Tsingtao, 1914 (prom. Maj.-Gen.); commanded a Division, 1915-18; Chief of British Military Mission to Portugal, 1916; Military Attaché Brussels and The Hague, 1902, and to the Scandinavian Courts, 1904; Assistant-Commandant, Royal Military College, Sandhurst, 1906-10; Assistant-Director of military training and Substantive Col., War Office, 1910-14; coronation medals, 1902 and 1911; holds the 2nd class of the Order of the Rising Sun, conferred upon him by the Emperor of Japan for his services in the Tsingtao Expedition, and 1st class of the Order of Aviz, and is a Commander of the Orders of the Osmanieh, Dannebrog, Sword, Leopold, and St. Olaf. *Recreations:* shooting, hunting, tennis, golf. *Address:* The Ryes, Sudbury, Suffolk. *Club:* Naval and Military.

    (Died 18 Aug. 1919.)

BARNARDISTON, Lt.-Col. Samuel John Barrington, D.S.O. 1900; the Suffolk Regt.; *b.* 19 Aug. 1875; 5th *s.* of late Nathaniel Barnardiston of The Ryes; *m.* 1919, Mlle van Riemsdyk. *Educ.:* Haileybury. Entered army, 1897, from 3rd Batt. Suffolk Regt.; Adjutant, 1900; served South Africa (despatches); served in European War, 1914. *Club:* Junior United Service.

    (Died 31 Jan. 1924.)

BARNE, Major Miles, D.S.O. 1917; Suffolk Yeomanry; *e. s.* of late Frederick St. John Newdegate Barne and late Lady Constance Adelaide Seymour, 5th *d.* of 5th Marquess of Hertford; *b.* 15 Mar. 1874; *m.* 1904, Violet Ella, *e. d.* of Sir Archibald Orr-Ewing, 3rd Bt.; three *s.* one *d.* Late Capt. Scots Guards; served South Africa, 1900-2; Seconded July 1915 from Suffolk Yeomanry to Scots Guards; European War, 1914-17 (D.S.O.). *Address:* Grey Friars, Dunwich; Sotterley Hall, Wangford, Suffolk; May Place, Cragford, Kent. *Clubs:* Carlton, Guards'. *(Died 17 Sept. 1917.)*

BARNES, Alexander, I.S.O. 1915; *b.* 1855; *m.* 1st, 1885, Ellen Nevison (*d.* 1914), *d.* of Rev. E. Hammond; one *s.*; 2nd, 1915, Ella Mary, *d.* of Thomas Holland; two *s.* one *d.* *Educ.:* Wells Grammar School. Entered Board of Trade, 1873; Accountant, 1909; Accountant-General, 1915-19. *Address:* 22 Park Hill, Ealing, W.5. *T.:* Ealing 145. *Clubs:* National Liberal, Alpine; W. Middlesex Golf. *(Died 2 Mar. 1924.)*

BARNES, Capt. Charles Roper Gorell, D.S.O. 1915; Rifle Brigade; General Staff Officer, 3rd grade, June 1917; *b.* 1 July 1896; *e. s.* of Sir Frederic Gorell Barnes. *Educ.:* Stubbington House, Fareham; R.N.C. Osborne and Dartmouth; Pembroke College, Cambridge (Scholar). Joined Lord Kitchener's 1st Army, and served with 14th Division in the European War, May

1915-Sep. 1916; 2nd Lieut. 1914; Lieut. 1915; Adjutant, 1915 (despatches twice, D.S.O., Military Cross). *Address:* Eyot Wood, Shiplake, Oxon. (*Died 17 April 1918.*)

BARNES, Henry, O.B.E., M.D., LL.D., F.R.S.E., Fellow Royal Society of Medicine; *b.* 1842; 3rd *s.* of Joseph Barnes, Aikton, Cumberland; *m.* 1873, Emily Mary, *d.* of Thomas Barnes, Bolton, Lancs; one *s.* one *d.* *Educ.:* St. Bees School, Cumberland; Edinburgh University, graduating with first-class honours in 1864. Has practised as a physician in Carlisle since 1866; is consulting physician to the Cumberland Infirmary, Cumberland and Westmorland Convalescent Institution, and Border Counties Home for Incurables; is President Border Counties Home for Incurables; is Vice-President Cumberland Infirmary; is Vice-President of the British Medical Association, and was President, 1896-97; has been twice President of the Border Counties branch of the Association, and is Vice-President of Cumberland and Westmorland Antiquarian and Archæological Association; is Vice-President Royal Society of Medicine (History of Medicine section); Vice-President Royal Medical Benevolent Fund; J.P. for Carlisle and Cumberland, and Chairman of Cumberland Ward Justices. *Publications:* The Medical History of Carlisle; On Roman Medical Inscriptions found in Britain; various papers and addresses on medical and archæological subjects. *Recreations:* walking, hill climbing, travel. *Address:* 6 Portland Square, Carlisle. *T.:* 240. *Club:* County, Carlisle. (*Died 12 April 1921.*)

BARNES, John Frederick Evelyn, C.M.G., 1901; *b.* Innistiogue, Co. Kilkenny, 1851; *s.* of late Frederick Piers Barnes, Firgrove, Co. Kilkenny, and Matilda, *d.* of late Rev. George Armstrong, Listerlin, Co. Kilkenny; *m.* 1879, Mary Sanbach, *d.* of E. E. Graves; one *d.* *Educ.:* Trin. Coll. Dublin. M.Inst.C.E.; 1889. Practised as civil engineer in Ireland; engineer and surveyor Duke of Abercorn's estates for several years prior to 1879; went to Natal, 1880; Gov. surveyor until 1882, then borough engineer, Durban; carried out waterworks and many municipal improvements; in Government Public Works Department, 1888, till retirement, 1910; Acting Colonial Engineer for periods totalling 3 years with seats on Executive and Legislative Councils; on the establishment of Responsible Government in Natal, 1893, became chief engineer P.W.D.; during the war assisted the military engineering and other departments in many directions (C.M.G., despatches several times); Commissioner for Natal at the St. Louis Exposition of 1904; Major on Sup. Staff, 1907; formed Natal Engr. Corps, Feb. 1910; resigned with rank of Major, July 1912; took up dairy farming and wattle planting, 1911; Assessor, Court of Income Tax Appeal, 1915; practising as Consulting Engineer; Member for Ward No. 1, Municipality of Pietermaritzburg, 1911; Hon. Secretary South African Party, Natal Province, 1917-21; Member Natal Mental Hospital Board and Water Court, 1918; Member Rents Board, Natal. *T.:* 821. *Club:* Victoria, Maritzburg. (*Died 24 June 1925.*)

BARNES, Rev. Peter, Vicar of St. Columba's, Wanstead Slip, since 1890; Hon. Canon of Chelmsford, 1919; *b.* 1856; *y. s.* of late Rev. E. B. Barnes, R.N.; *m.* 1919, Ellen Grace, *e. d.* of late Rev. C. Matheson, headmaster, Clergy Orphan School, Canterbury. *Educ.:* Bedford Grammar School; Salisbury Theological Coll. Eleven years with Corrie & Co., colonial brokers; ordained 1883; Assistant Curate of Rampisham, Dorset, 1883; of All Hallows, East India Docks, 1885. *Address:* St. Columba Vicarage, Stratford, E.15. (*Died 15 Dec. 1921.*)

BARNES-LAWRENCE, Herbert Cecil, M.A.; *b.* Bridlington, 9 Dec. 1852;

2nd *s.* of Rev. Canon H. F. Barnes-Lawrence; widower. *Educ.:* King's School, Canterbury; Durham Grammar School; Trinity and Lincoln (Scholar) Colleges, Oxford. Assistant-Master Manchester Grammar School, 1876-81; Giggleswick Grammar School, 1881-83; Headmaster, Perse Grammar School, Cambridge, 1884-1901; Weymouth College, 1902-17. *Recreations:* golf, cycling. *Address:* Melfort House, Crowborough, Sussex. *Club:* National. (*Died 7 June 1921.*)

BARNETT, Harry Villiers; *b.* Bristol, 1 Oct. 1858; *s.* of late Henry N. Barnett, editor of Sunday Times. Virtually self-taught, but was at Newcastle-on-Tyne Grammar School for a year. Assistant Editor, Graphic, 1877-82; then literary and pictorial free-lance; articles and sketches, Graphic, Black and White Magazine of Art, of which last was art critic under W. E. Henley; frequent contributor, St. James's Gazette, and, occasionally, Saturday Review, Athenæum, etc.; founded, 1904, and owns and edits, the Continental Weekly; Riviera Correspondent of the Times since 1920. *Publications:* authorised English versions of the Prince of Monaco's La Carrière d'un Navigateur, 1909, and Massenet's Mes Souvenirs; Portus Heraklis Monoëki: a Vision of the Story of Monaco, 1909 (3rd edition, revised and illustrated); nouvelle version française de Merlin: 1er drame de la Trilogie King Arthur, by Francis Coutts and I. Albeniz, 1914; Les Persans à Monaco; Etude sur l'Origine du Nom de lieu Gaumatá, 1916; Beauvallon and the Pays des Maures; Olivula: a Mystery of the Maritime Alps, 1920; The Revelation of Walter Rummel, 1922. *Recreations:* painting and singing. *Address:* Villa Mer et Mont, Monte Carlo, France, A.M. (*Died 13 May 1928.*)

BARNETT, John Francis, F.R.A.M.; Professor Royal College of Music and Guildhall School of Music; Examiner for the Associated Board; Member of the Philharmonic Society; *b.* London, 16 Oct. 1837; *e. s.* of late Joseph Alfred Barnett and Emma, *d.* of late William Hudson; *m.* Alice Dora Booth, 1875 (*d.* 1882); 2ndly, *m.* Mary Emily Tussaud, 1891. *Educ.:* Royal Academy of Music and Leipsic Conservatoire. Gained King's Scholarship at R.A.M., 1850; performed Concerto D minor Mendelssohn, at New Philharmonic Concert, 1852; played at Gewandhaus Concert, Leipsic, 1861; and at Philharmonic Society, London, 1863; composed Cantata Ancient Mariner for Birmingham Festival, 1867; Paradise and the Peri, produced at Birmingham Festival, 1870; The Raising of Lazarus, Hereford Festival, 1876; The Building of the Ship, Leeds Festival, 1880; The Wishing Bell, Norwich Festival, 1893; The Eve of St. Agnes, London Choral Society, 1914. Works for orchestra: Lay of the Last Minstrel, Liverpool Festival. 1873; Pastoral Suite, Philharmonic Society, 1890; Liebeslied im alten Styl, Crystal Palace Concerts, 1895. *Publications:* The Vocal Scores of the above-mentioned Cantatas; Pianoforte Solos—Home Scenes, Musical Landscapes, Wayside Sketches, The Flowing Tide, Valse Brillante, The Dream Maiden, etc.; songs—A Pair of Sabots, Bird of Happiness, Give me thy Love; book—Musical Reminiscences and Impressions, etc. *Recreation:* sketching from nature. *Address:* St. Ann's Villa, 56 Acacia Road, N.W. (*Died 24 Nov. 1916.*)

BARNETT-CLARKE, Very Rev. Charles William; Dean and Rector of St. George's Cathedral, Cape Town, since 1881. *Educ.:* Worcester College, Oxford. M.A. Ordained 1854; Curate of Lambourn, 1854-58; Vicar of Toot-Oaldon, Oxon, 1858-60; Curate of Fenny Stratford, 1860-64; Vicar of Cadmore End, Bucks, 1868-71. *Address:* Deanery, Cape Town. (*Died 24 Feb. 1916.*)

BARNEWALL, Hon. Reginald Nicholas Francis; *e. s.* and heir of 18th B. Trimlestown; *b.* 24 Sept. 1897; 2nd Lieut. 5th Batt. Leinster Regt. (*Died 24 Mar. 1918.*)

BARNSLEY, Brig.-Gen. Sir John, Kt., *cr.* 1914 ; D.L. ; J.P. ; V.D. ; Governor, King Edward VI. School; Military Member Warwickshire County Association ; *b.* 17 Nov. 1858 ; *m.* 1882, Ellen Rutherford, *d.* of late Robert Davis, J.P. ; three *s.* one *d. Educ. :* King Edward VI.'s School, Birmingham ; Wesleyan. *Recreations :* golf, shooting. *Address :* Earlsfield. Edgbaston, Birmingham. *T. :* Edgbaston, 187, *M. :* LF 4566. *Clubs :* Clef, Liberal, Birmingham.
(*Died 19 Jan. 1926.*)

BARON, Sir Barclay Josiah, Kt., *cr.* 1918 ; M.B., C.M. ; Lord Mayor of Bristol ; Consulting Physician for Diseases of Throat and Nose, Bristol General Hospital. *Educ. :* Edinburgh ; Berlin ; Strasburg ; Vienna. Late Lecturer on Pathology and Morbid Anatomy, Bristol Medical School, and Assistant to Professor of Pathology, Edinburgh University. *Address :* 16 Whiteladies Road, Clifton. Bristol. *T. :* 1445. (*Died 7 June 1919.*)

BARR, Amelia Edith, novelist ; *b.* Ulverston, Lancashire, 29 Mar. 1831 ; *d.* of William Henry Huddleston ; *m.* at 19, Robert Barr, Glasgow, merchant (*s.* of Rev. John Barr) ; left widow, with three daughters, at 35, in Texas ; came to New York ; began writing for Rev. Henry Ward Beecher's paper, and other papers and magazines ; at 50 began novel-writing ; has since published 47 in America and England ; many German and French translations. *Publications :* Jan Vedder's Wife, 1885 ; Bow of Orange Ribbon, 1888 ; Friend Olivia, 1890 ; A Daughter of Fife, 1886 : The Squire of Sandal-Side, 1887 ; A Border Shepherdess, 1887 ; Paul and Christina, 1887 ; The Last of the Macallisters, 1890 ; Between Two Loves, 1886 ; Feet of Clay, 1889 ; Bernicia, A Knight of the Nets, The Lone House, 1894 ; The Hallam Succession, 1885 ; She Loved a Sailor, 1891 ; Love for an Hour is Love Forever, 1892 ; A Sister to Esau, 1891 ; Cluny M'Pherson, 1894 ; Remember the Alamo ; Prisoners of Conscience, 1897 ; I, Thou, and the Other One, Trinity Bells, 1899 ; The Maid of Maiden Lane, 1900 ; The Lion's Whelp ; A Song of a Single Note ; Thyra Varrick ; Black Shilling ; The Measure of a Man, 1915. *Recreations :* music (the organ) and the cultivation of flowers. *Address :* 486 Greenwood Avenue, Richmond Hill, Long Island. New York. (*Died 11 Mar. 1919.*)

BARR, Lieut.-Col. Sir David William Keith, K.C.S.I., *cr.* 1902 ; Indian Army ; *b.* 29 Nov. 1846 ; *e. s.* of late Lt.-Gen. H. J. Barr ; *m.* 1871, Constance, *d.* of late Major-Gen. J. Guillum Scott ; three *s.* one *d. Educ. :* private school ; Royal Military Coll. Sandhurst. Ensign, 44th Regt. 1864 ; served with 33rd (Duke of Wellington's) Regt. Abyssinia, 1868 (medal) ; entered the Political Department, Government of India, 1869 ; First Assist.-Agent, Gov.-Gen. for Central India, 1874 ; Political Agent, Jodhpore, 1880 ; Political Agent and Superintendent, Rewah, 1881-87 ; Resident at Gwalior, 1887-92 ; Resident in Kashmir, 1892-94 ; Agent to the Governor-General in Central India, 1894-1900 ; Resident at Hyderabad, 1900-1905 ; retired 1905 ; member of Council of India, 1905-15. *Address :* 92 Onslow Gardens, S.W. *Club :* United Service. (*Died 22 Nov. 1916.*)

BARR, James (Angus Evan Abbot) ; *b.* Wallacetown, Ontario, Canada, 1862 ; 5th *s.* of. Robert Barr, Windsor, Ontario, Canada, and Jane, *d.* of William Watson, West Glen, Kilmalcolm, Scotland ; *m.* Elizabeth Sabel (*d.* 1909), *d.* of A. C. Wylie, Brook Green, London ; three *s.* three *d. Educ. :* Canadian Public Schools. From 16 to 21 a newspaper man in America ; since then a journalist in London. *Publications :* The Gods Give My Donkey Wings ; The Gods Gave My Donkey Wings ; Under the Eaves of Night ; The Great Frozen North ; The Witchery of the Serpent ; Laughing through a Wilderness ; The Grey Bat ; Jarl Armstrong. *Recreations :* cricket, lacrosse, billiards. *Clubs :* London Sketch, Authors'. (*Died Mar. 1923.*)

BARR, Thomas, M.D., F.F.P.S., Glasgow ; Lecturer on Diseases of the Ear, Glasgow University, since 1895 ; Aural Surgeon, Glasgow Western Infirmary ; Hon. Aurist, Glasgow Sick Children's Hospital ; Senior Surgeon, Glasgow Hospital for Diseases of the Ear, Nose, and Throat : *b.* Elderslie, Renfrewshire, 1846. *Educ. :* University of Glasgow ; Vienna ; London. Graduated M.B., C.M., with highest honours, Glasgow University, 1868 ; M.D., Glasgow, 1870 ; appointed to Glasgow Western Infirmary, 1877 ; Lecturer in Anderson's College, 1879-95 ; President of the Otological Section of the British Medical Association, 1888 ; President of the Glasgow Pathological and Clinical Society. 1899-1900 ; President of the Otological Society of the United Kingdom, 1904-5. *Publications :* Manual of Diseases of the Ear, including those of the Nose and Throat in relation to the Ear (three editions) ; Effects upon the Hearing of those who Work amid Noisy Surroundings ; Investigation into the Hearing of School Children ; Giddiness and Staggering in Ear Diseases ; Traumatic Affections of the Ear ; The Operative Treatment of Intra-Cranial Conditions dependent upon Purulent Diseases of the Ear, etc. *Recreations :* walking and golfing. *Address :* 18 Woodside Place, Charing Cross, Glasgow. *T. :* 1611 Central, Glasgow. (*Died 14 Dec. 1916.*)

BARRATT, Reginald, artist ; R.W.S., F.R.G.S. ; *b.* London, 25 July 1861 ; *s.* of late Dr. J. G. Barratt, F.R.C.S. *Educ. :* King's Coll. and by late Dean Plumptre. Studied architecture under R. Norman Shaw, R.A., and painting under Lefevre and Bouguereau, Paris ; worked for Graphic and Daily Graphic ; exhibits at Royal Academy, Royal Society of Painters in Water Colours ; painted twice for Queen Victoria and King Edward ; travelled in Italy, Spain, Morocco, Algeria, Tunis, Egypt, India, Persia, Asia Minor, etc. ; works chiefly at Oriental life and architecture, such as Abu Simbel for late Khedive, The Mooled Ahmadee, and Courtyard of Ducal Palace, Venice, in Manchester Corporation Gallery ; has published drawings in colour, Venice, Egypt, etc. *T. :* Regent 6400. *Club :* Athenæum.
(*Died 8 Feb. 1917.*)

BARRAUD, Francis ; *s.* of late Henry Barraud, artist ; *nephew* of Arthur Sketchley (George Rose). *Educ. :* Ushaw ; St. Edmund's College, Ware. Studied at the Royal Academy Schools (silver medal for drawing from life) ; Heatherley's, the Beaux Arts, Antwerp ; painter of portraits and genre subjects ; frequent exhibitor at the R.A., Institute of Painters in Oil Colours, and most other art exhibitions. *Works :* An Encore too Many, exhibited at the Walker Art Gallery, Liverpool, 1887, and purchased by the Corporation for the permanent Art-Gallery ; His Master's Voice, purchased by the Gramophone Co. and reproduced as an advertisement ; Portraits : Cardinal Bourne, Admiral the Hon. Sir H. Keppel, Prof. M'Coll of Glasgow, etc. *Recreations :* billiards and walking. *Address :* 28 Finchley Road, N.W.8. *Clubs :* St. John's Wood Arts, Arts.
(*Died 29 Aug. 1924.*)

BARRES, Maurice, Député de Paris ; Member of French Academy ; *b.* Charmessur-Moselle, 17 Aug. 1862 ; studied law, but preferred to devote himself to literature ; elected Deputy, 1889. *Publications :* Sous l'œil des Barbares, 1888 ; Huit jours chez Mons. Renan, 1888 ; Un homme libre, 1889 ; Le Jardin de Berenice ; Les Déracinés ; Lewis Figures ; Au Service de l'Allemagne ; Colette Baudoche ; L'Ennemi des lois ; Du Sang, de la Volupte et de la Mort ; Les Amitiés françaises ; Le Voyage de Sparte ; Amori et Dolori Sacrum (La mort de Venise) ; Trois stations de Psychothérapie ; Toute licence sauf contre l'amour ; Une journée parlementaire (comédie de mœurs en 3 actes) ; La Colline Inspirée ; L'Ame française et la Guerre ; L'Union Sacrée ; Les Saints de la France ; La Croix de Guerre ; L'Amitié des Tranchées ; Les Voyages de Lorraine et d'Artois ; Pour les Mutilés ; Sur le Chemin de l'Asia ; Le Suffrage des Morts ; Pendant le Bataille de Verdun ; Les Familles spirituelles de la France ; Les Traits eternels de la France ; En regardant au fond des crevasses ; L'Appel du Rhin ; La Minute Sacrée ; Un jardin sur l'Oronte, 1922. *Address :* Boul. Maillot 100, Neuilly, Paris. *(Died 4 Dec. 1923.)*

BARRETT, Field Marshal Sir Arthur (Arnold), G.C.B., *cr.* 1918 ; K.C.B., *cr.* 1908 ; G.C.S.I., *cr.* 1920 ; K.C.S.I., *cr.* 1915 ; K.C.V.O. 1912 ; C.B. 1903 ; *b.* 3 June 1857 ; 3rd *s.* of late Rev. Alfred Barrett, D.D. ; *m.* 1st, 1894, Mary *(d.* 1897), *d.* of James Haye of Fowey, Cornwall ; 2nd, 1907, Ella *(d.* 1917), *d.* of H. Lafone, 59 Onslow Square, S.W. Entered army, 1875 ; Captain, 1886 ; Major, 1895 ; Lieutenant-Colonel, 1901 ; Major-General, 1907 ; Lieut.-Gen., 1911 ; General, 1917 ; retired 1920 ; Field Marshal, 1921 ; Brig. Com. Nowshera, 1907-1909 ; Adjt.-Gen. in India, 1909-12 ; Divisional Commander, Poona, 1912-14 ; Northern Command, India, 1916 - 20 ; served Afghan War, 1879 - 1880 ; march to Candahar and battle of Candahar (medal with two clasps, bronze decoration) ; Hazara, 1888 (medal with clasp) ; 2nd Miranzai Expedition, 1891 (clasp) ; Hunza-Nagar Expedition, 1891 (clasp) ; N.W.F. India, 1897 - 98 (despatches, brevet Lt. - Col., medal with two clasps) ; N.W. Frontier, India, 1908 ; Bazar Valley Expedition (despatches) ; Mohmand Expedition (despatches, K.C.B., medal with clasp) ; Mesopotamia, 1914-15 (despatches, K.C.S.I.) ; Afghan War, 1919 (despatches, G.C.S.I.). *Address :* Sharnbrook, Beds. *Club :* United Service. *(Died 20 Oct. 1926.)*

BARRETT, Rev. Daniel William, M.A. ; Rector of Holdenby since 1910 ; Hon. Canon St. Albans since 1905. *Educ. :* Trin. Coll., Dublin. Curate of Waltham, Leicester, 1873-76 ; Chaplain Bishop of Peterbro's railway mission, 1873-79 ; Vicar of Nassington, 1879-87 ; Rural Dean, Oundle, 1881-87 ; Rector of Chipping Barnet, 1887-1910 ; Rural Dean of Barnet, 1898-1910. *Publications :* Life and Work among the Navvies, 4th ed. 1885 ; Sketches of Church Life, 1902 ; Hymns ; Diocesan Charts for Peterborough and St. Albans ; The Royal Prisoner of Holdenby ; King Charles I. at Holmby House. *Address :* The Rectory, Holdenby, Northampton. *(Died 10 Sept. 1925.)*

BARRETT, Francis E. H. Joyce, Musical Editor and Chief Musical Critic of the Morning Post ; *y. s.* of late William Alexander Barrett, Musical Critic of the Morning Post, 1865-91 ; *m.* 1891, Marie Louise Eugénie, *d.* of Louis Pineau Bertin of Paris ; no *c. Educ. :* Dulwich and Durham. Attached to the Morning Post since 1890 ; worked in all branches of journalism since 1887 ; pupil of Manuel Garcia (singing), John Tiplady Carrodus (violin), Edward Howell (violoncello), Henry Gadsby and W. A. Barrett (composition). *Publications :* Daily Criticisms. *Recreations :* Yesterday's Concerts. *Address :* Boitakhana, Endymion Terrace, Finsbury Park, N.4. *T. :* Hornsey 2608. *(Died 19 Jan. 1925.)*

BARRETT, Frank, novelist, inventor, scientist ; *b.* 1848 ; *m.* Joan Barrett, novelist ; one *d.,* artist. Began journalism at eighteen as literary and dramatic critic ; took to pottery ; potter's help, modeller, and then sculptor ; became partner in a pottery ; kiln fell in, destroying the work of two years ; there ended that branch of career ; returned to literature, and so fell into the groove in which he is still running. *Publications :* Fifty-two novels and bound volumes of stories ; contributions to magazines, journals, and other ephemera ; three plays. *Recreations :* modelling, chess, mechanical invention. *Address :* Rocky Close, St. Ives, Cornwall. *(Died 21 May 1926.)*

BARRETT, Rev. George Slatyer, former Pastor of Princes Street Congregational Church, Norwich ; *b.* Jamaica, 16 Sep. 1839 ; father was a missionary ; *m.* 1868, Catharine Lance Bower *(d.* 1910), *y. d.* of late George Lance ; three *d. Educ. :* University College, London ; Independent College, Manchester. B.A. of London University ; D.D. of St. Andrews University ; Chairman of the Congregational Union of England and Wales, 1894. *Publications :* The Temptation of Christ ; The Earliest Christian Hymn ; The Intermediate State ; Religion in Daily Life ; Family Prayers ; The Bible and its Inspiration ; The Seven Words from the Cross ; The Whole Armour of God ; Commentary 1st Epistle of St. John ; Editor of The Congregational Church Hymnal ; The Mission Hymnal ; Sunday School Hymnal. *Recreation :* walking. *Address :* 4 Grove Avenue, Norwich. *T. :* 803 Norwich.
(Died 24 April 1916.)

BARRETT, Sir Wm. Fletcher, Kt., *cr.* 1912 ; F.R.S., Lond., Edin., and Dublin ; M.I.E.E., M.R.I.A., F.P.S.L. ; J.P. Co. Dublin ; *b.* 10 Feb. 1844 ; *s.* of Rev. W. G. Barrett ; *m.* 1916, Dr. Florence Willey *(see* Lady Barrett). *Educ. :* Old Trafford Grammar School Manchester, and private study. Assistant to Professor Tyndall, 1863 ; Science Master, International Coll., 1867 ; Lecturer on Physics, Royal School Naval Architecture, 1869 ; Professor of Physics, Royal College of Science, Dublin, 1875-1910 ; Ex-President of the Society for Psychical Research, of which he was chief founder. *Publications :* Original Investigations published in the Transactions and Proceedings of the Royal Dublin Society, Philosophical Magazine and elsewhere ; editor of Lessons in Science, 1880 ; of Early Chapters in Science, 1899 ; joint author of Introduction to Practical Physics, 1892 ; On the Threshold of a New World of Thought, 1908 ; On Creative Thought, 1910 ; On Swedenborg, 1912 ; On Psychical Research, Home University Library, 1911 ; On the Threshold of the Unseen, 1917 ; Monograph on so-called Divining Rod, vol. i. 1897, vol. ii. 1900 ; Discovery of and Papers on Sensitive Flames, 1807 ; ditto, Recalescence, 1878 *et seq.* ; Shortening of Nickel by Magnetisation, 1882 ; Thought-Transference, 1882 *et seq.* ; Researches on the Electric and Magnetic Properties of Alloys of Iron, 1895 *et seq.,* including the discovery, in 1890, of the remarkable magnetic and electrical properties of the silicon-iron alloy, now known as *Stalloy,* which has been of immense value in electrical engineering for the construction of transformers, dynamos, etc. ; Researches on Entoptic Vision, 1905-7, leading to the invention of the Entoptiscope and a new Optometer. *Recreations :* gardening ; interested in temperance and philanthropic work. *Address :* 31 Devonshire Place, W.1. *T. :* Langham 1691. *(Died 26 May 1925.)*

BARRETT, Sir William Scott, Kt., *cr.* 1918 ; J.P., D.L. Lancs. ; Constable of Lancaster Castle since 1916 ; *b.* 28 Nov. 1843 ; *s.* of late J. C. Barrett of Leeds ; *m.* 1869, Julia L., *d.* of late Rev. A. A. Colvile ; four *s.* three *d.* Alderman and Chairman of Lancashire County Council and of Quarter Sessions. *Address :* Abbotsgate, Blundellsands, Lancs. *(Died 5 June 1921.)*

BARRIE, Sir Charles, Kt., *cr.* 1919 ; J.P., D.L. ; Charles Barrie & Sons, Shipowners ; *b.* 10 Feb. 1840 ; *m.* Jane, *d.* of Alexander Cathro, Arbroath ; two *s.* one *d.* Lord Provost of Dundee, 1902-5. *Address :* Airlie Park, Broughty Ferry. *Clubs :* National Liberal ; Eastern, Dundee. *(Died 28 Feb. 1921.)*

BARRIE, Rt. Hon. Hugh T., P.C. Ireland, 1920 ; M.P. (C.) North Londonderry since 1906 ; D.L., J.P. ; High Sheriff, Derry, 1918 ; Vice-President Department of Agriculture and Technical Education (Ireland) ; *b.* Glasgow, 1860 ; *m.* 1892, Katherine, *e. d.* of Rev. W. H. Quarry. *Address :* The Manor House, Coleraine.

Clubs; Carlton, St. Stephen's, Constitutional; Ulster, Belfast.   *(Died 18 April 1922.)*

BARRINGTON, Hon. Sir (Bernard) Eric (Edward), K.C.B., *cr.* 1902; *b.* London, 5 June 1847; *y. s.* of 6th Viscount Barrington and Jane, *d.* of 1st Baron Ravensworth; *m.* Christina, *y. d.* of late William Graham, 1879. *Educ.:* Eton. Entered Foreign Office, 1867; Private Secretary to Parliamentary Under-Secretaries of State for Foreign Affairs (A. J. Otway and Viscount Enfield), 1869-74; précis writer to Foreign Secretary (Earl of Derby), 1874-78; to Marquis of Salisbury, 1878-1880; Private Secretary to Earl of Iddesleigh, 1885-86; to Marquis of Salisbury, 1887-92, and 1895-1900; to Marquis of Lansdowne, 1900-1905; Assistant Under Secretary of State for Foreign Affairs, 1906; retired from Foreign Office, 1907; attached to Special Mission to Berlin, 1878. *Address:* The Old Lodge, Wimbledon Common, S.W. *T.:* Wimbledon 780. *T.A.:* Esoteric, London. *Club:* Travellers'.
    (Died 24 Feb. 1918.)

BARRINGTON, Hon. Sir William Augustus Curzon, K.C.M.G., *cr.* 1901; *b.* Beckett, Shrivenham, Berks, 28 Jan. 1842; 3rd *s.* of 6th Viscount Barrington and Jane Elizabeth, *d.* of 1st Baron Ravensworth; unmarried. *Educ.:* private schools at Cheam and Woolwich; Mannheim and Bonn, Germany. Entered Diplomatic Service, 1860; Secretary of Legation, Buenos Aires, 1883; Acting Chargé d'Affaires and Consul-General, Lima, 1884; Consul-General, Hungary, Budapest, 1885; Chargé d'Affaires, Belgrade, 1886; Secretary of Embassy, Madrid, 1888; Vienna, 1892; Envoy to the Argentine Republic and Minister in Paraguay, 1896-1902. H.M.'s Envoy Extraordinary and Minister Plenipotentiary to Sweden and Norway, 1902-4; Councillor for Borough of St. Marylebone (Ward 5) since 1912. *Address:* 17a Great Cumberland Place, W. *T.A.:* Linnet Phone, London. *T.:* Paddington 2215. *Clubs:* Bachelors', St. James's, Turf, Pratt's, Travellers', Prince's, Lord's.   *(Died 23 Feb. 1922.)*

BARRINGTON-FLEET, George Rutland, actor; *b.* Penge, 15 Jan. 1853; 4th *s.* of John George and Esther Faithfull Fleet; *nephew* of Emily Faithfull; married. *Educ.:* Private tutor; Merchant Taylors' School. From age of 14 to 21 in the City; then made first appearance on stage at Olympic Theatre under Henry Neville; later joined the Gilbert-Sullivan-Carte management, and played in all their operas except Yeoman of the Guard, during run of which took a lease of St. James's Theatre; relinquished management and returned to Savoy for a time. *Publications:* Thirty-Five Years on the Stage, 1908; produced one play and numerous short pieces and duologues, magazine articles and songs, and at one time a regular contributor to Punch; adapted Kingsley's Water-Babies for the stage (Garrick Theatre) Xmas 1902. *Recreations:* golf, painting.   *(Died 31 May 1922.)*

BARRINGTON-KENNETT, Lieut.-Col. Brackley Herbert Barrington, J.P.; Royal Bodyguard since 1895; *b.* 1846; 2nd *s.* of late Captain Vincent F. Kennett, Manor House, Dorchester-on-Thame, and Arabella Henrietta, last surv. *d.* of Sir J. Barrington, K.C., Judge of Admiralty, and widow of Edward, Baron Calabella; *m.* 1884, Ellinor Frances, *d.* of F. L. Austen of Brightwell Park, Oxfordshire; *g. d.* of Sir H. Austen, D.L., of Shalford Park, Surrey; one *s. Educ.:* Rugby; Trinity College, Cambridge (B.A.). Served with British National Aid to wounded in Franco-German War (2 French orders), 1871, also Carlist War in Spain; Affridi Campaign, 1877 (medal); Afghan War, 1878 (despatches, medal, wounded); Afghan War, 1879-80; Lieut.-Col.; 1885. *Address:* 19 Cheyne Gardens, Chelsea Embankment, S.W.3.

Clubs: Army and Navy, Leander.
    (Died 12 Mar. 1919.)

BARRINGTON-WARD, Rev. Mark James, M.A., S.C.L., D.D., F.L.S.; Rector of Duloe, Cornwall, since 1909; Hon. Canon of Truro Cathedral, 1921; *b.* Belfast; *m.* 1879 Caroline Pearson; five *s.* four *d. Educ.:* Royal Belfast Academical Institution; Royal School, Dungannon; Queen's College, Belfast; Worcester and Hertford (Scholar) Colleges, Oxford; 1st class, Natural Science, 1869; B.A., S.C.L., 1869; M.A., 1872; B.D. and D.D., 1919, Oxford. Assistant Master, Clifton College, 1869-72; H.M. Inspector of Schools, 1872-1907; ordained, 1907; curate of The Tything, Worcester, 1907-9. *Publications:* several geographical works. *Recreations:* gardening and botany. *Address:* The Rectory, Duloe S.O., Cornwall. *M.:* LY 6770. *Club:* United University.
    (Died 1 Feb. 1924.)

BARRON, Major-General Sir Harry, K.C.M.G., *cr.* 1909; C.V.O. 1907; Knight of Grace St. John of Jerusalem; *b.* 11 Aug. 1847; *s.* of Charles Barron, Denmark Hill, Surrey; *m.* 1877, Clara Emily, *d.* of Major-Gen. T. Conyngham Kelly, C.B.; one *d. Educ.:* Rev. W. Foster, Stubbington; Rev. R. Fowler, Tonbridge Wells; Woolwich. Lieut. Royal Artillery, 1867; Capt. 1879: Major, 1884; Lieut.-Col. 1894; Col. 1898; Maj.-Gen. 1904; Adjutant 1st Forfar Artillery Volunteers, 1880-84; Chief Instructor School of Gunnery, Shoeburyness, 1897-1900; Commanding R.A., Thames District, 1900-4; Malta, 1904-8; retired, 1909; Governor of Tasmania, 1909-13; Governor of Western Australia, 1913-17; Col. Commandant, Royal Artillery, 1920. *Address:* Swiss Cottage, Weybridge. *T.:* Weybridge 31. *Club:* Naval and Military.
    (Died 27 Mar. 1921.)

BARRON, James, editor and proprietor of Inverness Courier; *b.* Corshelloch, Edinkillie, Forres, 1847; *m.* 1875, Isabella (*d.* 1912), *d.* of late Evan Macleod, Inverness; one *s.* two *d. Educ.:* Relugas and Rafford Schools. Served business apprenticeship in Nairn, where he had opportunities of private study; joined staff of Inverness Courier in his nineteenth year; J.P.; Hon. Sheriff-Substitute; F.S.A. Scot.; member Inverness Gaelic Society and Inverness Scientific Society and Field Club; twice president of latter society, and has edited seven volumes of its transactions; is engaged on a work illustrating the history of the Northern Highlands in 19th century, of which he has published three volumes. *Address:* Ravelrig, Abertarff Road, Inverness. *T.A.:* Courier, Inverness. *T.:* 59 Inverness. *Club:* Highland, Inverness.   *(Died 13 Feb. 1919.)*

BARROW, Alderman Sir Alfred, Kt., *cr.* 1922; O.B.E., D.L.; *b.* 1850. Mayor of Barrow-in-Furness, 1913-19. *Address:* Ulverscroft, Barrow-in-Furness. *(Died 3 Feb. 1928.)*

BARROW, Sir Reuben Vincent, J.P., Kt., *cr.* 1912; F.R.G.S.; *b.* 27 April 1838; *s.* of John Barrow, Grange, Bermondsey, S.E.; *m.* 1859, Mary (*d.* 1917), *d.* of Edward Aggett, Adelaide; one *d.* M.P. (L) Bermondsey Division of Southwark, 1892-95; an Alderman of Croydon, Mayor 1885. *Address:* Engadine, 9 Park Hill Road, Croydon. *T.:* Croydon 250. *Club:* Reform.   *(Died 13 Feb. 1918.)*

BARRY, Charles David, K.C., 2nd *s.* of late Rt. Hon. C. R. Barry. *Educ.:* Bassett's; Dublin University (Moderatorship and Prizeman). Served Local Government Board; Arbitrator Board of Trade (Tramways and Railways Act); Ministry of Labour (Trade Boards). *Recreations:* Captain University Eleven; won Rackets Cup three years; won Irish Lawn Tennis Championship; rode winner Point to Point Barristers v. Solicitors, 1888; scratch Royal Dublin and Royal Portrush Golf Clubs.

Clubs: Athenæum ; Royal Irish Yacht, Kingstown. (*Died Feb. 1928.*)

BARRY, Sir John Wolfe Wolfe-, K.C.B., *cr.* 1897; LL.D., F.R.S., V.D.; Colonel Engineer and Rly. Volunteer Staff Corps ; D.L. County of London ; late member of Senate of University of London ; Governor of Imperial College of Science and Technology ; Chairman of Delegacy City and Guilds Engineering College, South Kensington ; Past President, Institution of Civil Engineers ; Vice-President of Institution of Mechanical Engineers ; late Chairman Society of Arts ; Chairman Executive Committee City and Guilds of London Technical Institute and British Engineering Standards Committee ; Member of Executive Committee of National Physical Laboratory ; late Representative of Great Britain on International Technical Commission for Suez Canal ; member of the Army Railway Council ; Chairman of Westminster Hospital ; Member of Council, King's College, London ; Chairman of the Eastern and Eastern Extension and Western Telegraph Companies; *b.* London, 7 Dec. 1836 ; *y. s.* of Sir Charles Barry, R.A. [Assumed additional name of Wolfe by Royal license in 1898.] *m.* Rosalind Grace, *y.d.* of Rev. E. E. Rowsell, Rector of Hambledon, Surrey, 1874; four *s.* three *d. Educ.:* Trin. Coll. Glenalmond ; King's Coll. London. Consulting Engineer to following Companies : —Caledonian ; London, Chatham, and Dover ; Lanarkshire and Ayrshire and Barry Railway Companies ; and to the Underground Electric Railways Co. of London; Consulting Engineer to Bridge House Estates Committee of Corporation of London, to Commissioners of River Tyne, to the Surrey Commercial Docks, to the Alexandra Dock, Newport Company, to the Regent Canal and Dock Co., to Bengal Nagpur Rly. to Bombay Port Trust, and to the Kowloon Railway for the Government of Hong-Kong, and to the Shanghai and Nankin, and other Chinese Railways ; Engineer of Tower Bridge, Blackfriars railway arched bridge, Barry Dock and Railways, Kew Bridge, Grangemouth Dock, Surrey Commercial Dock, Middlesborough Dock Extension, Hull Joint Dock, Immingham Dock; New Alexandra Docks, Newport, Natal Harbour, and other important works ; Royal Commissioner, Irish Public Works, Government Commissions, 1886-90; Highlands and Islands of Scotland, 1889-90 ; Estuary of Ribble, 1889-91, and Lower Thames Navigation, 1894-96 ; National Physical Laboratory, 1897-98 ; Royal Commissioner on Accidents to Railway Servants, 1899-1900 ; Vibration on Tube Railways, 1901-2 ; Royal Commissioner on the Port of London, 1900-2 ; Royal Commissioner on London Traffic, 1903-5 ; Member of Court of Arbitration under the Metropolis Water Act, 1902. *Publications :* Railway Appliances, 1874-92 ; Lectures on Railways and Locomotives, 1882 ; The Tower Bridge, 1894 ; Barry Genealogy in England and Wales. *Recreations:* riding, fishing. *Address:* Delahay House, 15 Chelsea Embankment, S.W. *T.A.:* Chelbank, Sloane, London. *T.:* Kensington 201. *M.:* LC 8103. *Clubs:* Athenæum, Reform. (*Died 22 Jan. 1918.*)

BARRY, Hon. Lieut.-Col. James, C.M.G. 1918; Remount Service; served Zulu Campaign, 1879 (medal and clasp); South African War, 1899-1902 (Queen's medal, three clasps; King's medal, two clasps). (*Died 12 June 1920.*)

BARRY, Sir John Edmond, Kt., *cr.* 1899; *e. s.* of late John Barry, merchant, of Middle Abbey Street, Dublin, and Catharine, *d.* of late Thos. Browne of Wexford; *b.* 6 Feb. 1828 ; *m.* 1849, Teresa (*d.* 1909), *d.* of late John Keefe of Iffernock, Co. Meath. *Educ.:* private schools, Dublin and Wexford. President Dublin Chamber of Commerce, 1897-99 ; Member of Dublin Port and Docks Board, 1867-97 ; re-elected, 1899 ; retired, 1903 ; Ex-Chairman of Board of Super-

intendence of Dublin Hospitals ; ex-Governor of Royal Hibernian Military School. *Address :* 12 Mountjoy Square, Dublin. (*Died 12 Mar. 1919.*)

BARRY, Ralph Brereton, K.C. ; County Court Judge of the counties of Kildare, Carlow, Wicklow, and Wexford; *b.* 7 June 1856 ; *e. s.* of James Barry, Solicitor, Limerick, and Elizabeth, *d.* of Ralph Westropp Brereton of Ballyadams, Queen's Co ; *m.* 1884, Claire, *y. d.* of William Roche, Crown Solicitor for City and County of Limerick, 72 Harcourt Street, Dublin ; three *s. Educ.:* Baylis House, Slough ; Clongoweswood Coll. ; Univ., T.C.D. B.A. ; Senior Moderator and gold medallist, 1878 ; first Senior Scholar, Middle Temple, London, Common and Criminal Law, 1879 ; called to Irish Bar, Michaelmas Term, 1880 ; joined the Munster Circuit, 1881 ; appointed Professor of Law, Queen's College, Cork, 1884 ; Professor of Real Property, Incorporated Law Society of Ireland, 1891-96 ; Professor of Equity and Practice, King's Inns, Dublin, 1895-98 ; sometime Examiner in Law at the Royal University of Ireland. *Address:* Langara, Glenageary, Co. Dublin. *Club:* Royal St. George, Kingstown. (*Died 16 Mar. 1920.*)

BARRY, Rt. Rev. Thomas Francis, D.D. ; Bishop of Chatham since 1902 ; *b.* Poke Mouche, N.B., 3 Mar. 1841. *Educ.:* St. John Coll. ; Montreal Coll. ; Grand Seminary, Montreal. Was Rector of Cathedral, Chatham ; Pastor of St. Basil ; of Caraquae, and of Bathurst ; Coadjutor Bishop, 1900. *Address:* Bishop's Palace, Chatham, New Brunswick. (*Died 19 Jan. 1920.*)

BARRYMORE, 1st Baron (*cr.* 1902), Arthur Hugh Smith-Barry, P.C., J.P., D.L. ; *b.* 17 Jan. 1843 ; *m.* 1st, Lady Mary Frances Wyndham - Quin, *d.* of 3rd Earl of Dunraven, 1868 (*d.* 1884) ; 2nd, Elizabeth, widow of Arthur Post, of New York, *d.* of Gen. Wadsworth, Geneseo, U.S.A., 1889 ; two *d. Educ.:* Eton ; Christ Church, Oxford. M.P. Co. Cork, 1867-1874 ; Vice-Pres. of Irish Landowners Convention ; M.P. (C.) South Huntingdonshire, 1886-1900. *Recreation:* Admiral, Royal Cork Yacht Club. *Heir:* none. *Address:* 20 Hill Street, Berkeley Square, W.1 ; *T.:* Grosvenor 2667; Fota Island, Co. Cork; Marbury Hall, Northwich, Cheshire. *Clubs:* Carlton, Travellers'; Royal Yacht Squadron, Cowes. (*Died 22 Feb. 1925.*)

BARTER, Sir Richard, J.P., Kt., *cr.* 1911 ; *e. s.* of late Dr. Richard Barter; *b.* 19 Nov. 1837 ; *m.* 1873, Anna Madeline Jameson. *Educ.:* Flynn's, Hartcourt Street, Dublin. Farming, stock breeding, especially Kerry cattle ; pedigree large York pigs ; Chairman Cork Muskerry Railway Co. ; also was Chairman, Agricultural Section, Cork Exhibition, Co. Cork Agricultural Society. *Publications:* several papers on Agricultural subjects. *Recreations:* yachting, hunting, fishing, shooting. *Address:* St. Ann's Hill, Cork. *Clubs:* Cork, Royal Cork. (*Died 16 Aug. 1916.*)

BARTHOLOME, Albert; peintre et sculpteur; Hon. R.A. 1921 ; Commandeur de la Légion d'Honneur; President de la Société Nationale des Beaux-Arts ; Grande Croix d'Isabella la Catholique; Grand Officier de Leopold de Belgique et du Trésor Sacré du Japon; engagé volontaire de 1870; membre des Académies des Beaux-Arts d'Ecosse, d'Angleterre, de Belgique, de Saxe, de Milan, de Madrid; *b.* Thiverval 29 août 1848 ; *m.* Florence Letessier. *Educ.:* Lycée de Versailles. *Œuvres dans les Musées:* Pau près des blés pastel ; Luxembourg, Paris, Tête de paysanne, pastel; Petite fille pleurant, bronze; Buste de Mme. Bartholomé, marbre; Femme pleurant appuyé sur une stele, marbre ; Dresde, Jeune fille se coiffant, marbre; Moulage du monument aux morts, plâtre ; Arts decoratifs Paris, Petite

BARRY, Edward. See page xv.

BARRY, Richard Fitzwilliam. See page xv.

fontaine, marbre; Bruxelles, L'adieu, pierre; Vienne, Femme sortant du bain, pierre; Krefeld, Le baiser, marbre; Mulhouse, Jeune fille pleurant, pierre; Aix-la-Chapelle, Baigneuse, plâtre; Budapest, Moulage du Monument aux morts, plâtre; Copenhague, Petite fille en pleurs, pierre; Au bord de l'eau, pierre; Santiago du Chili, Jeune fille à sa toilette, bronze; Rome, L'union dans l'au delà, marbre; Reims, Baigneuse, marbre; etc., etc. *Grands Monuments*: Le tombeau du cimetière de Bouillant; Le monument aux morts au Père-Lachaise, Paris; Le tombeau Pam et le tombeau Meilhac, cimetière Montmartre; Le tombeau Dubufe, cimetière du Père-Lachaise; Le monument aux victimes du Pluviôse; Le Chénois, Belfort; Le tombeau de J.-J. Rousseau au Panthéon, Paris; Le monument de Sardou pour Paris; Le monument aux auteurs et compositeurs dramatiques morts pour la patrie; Le monument du sénateur aviateur Reymond à Montbrison, Le Monument à Paris 1914-18 place du Carrousel; Aux avocats morts pour la patrie, palais de Justice; and 1874, embrasse l'epée de 1918 à Cognac. *Recreation*: Les voyages. *Address*: 1 rue Raffet, Paris.   (*Died Oct. 1928.*)

BARTHOLOMEW, John George, LL.D. (Edin.), F.R.G.S., F.R.S.E., etc.; geographer and cartographer to the King; head of the Edinburgh Geographical Institute; b. Edinburgh, 22 March 1860; s. of John Bartholomew, cartographer; m. 1889, Jennie, d. of late A. Sinclair Macdonald of Cyder Hall, Dornoch; two s. two d. *Educ.*: Edinburgh High School and University. One of founders of Royal Scottish Geographical Society, and Hon. Secretary since its foundation in 1884; Secretary of Section E, British Association, 1892; Victoria Research Gold Medallist Royal Geographical Society, 1905; Council of Royal Society, Edinburgh, 1909-12; introduced layer system of contour colouring for topographical maps; Hon. Member of Geographical Societies of Paris, St. Petersburg and Chicago. *Publications*: Survey Atlas of Scotland, 1895-1912; Citizen's Atlas, 1898-1912; Atlas of Meteorology, 1899; Survey Gazetteer of British Isles, 1904; Survey Atlas of England and Wales, 1903; Atlas of World's Commerce, 1907; Imperial Indian Gazetteer Atlas, 1908; Atlas of Zoogeography, 1911; numerous educational atlases and special maps. *Recreations*: fishing and travel. *Address*: The Geographical Institute, Edinburgh. *T.A.*: Bartholomew, Edinburgh. *T.*: 2787 Central. *M.*: S 1058. *Club*: Royal Societies.   (*Died 16 April 1920.*)

BARTLEET, Rev. Samuel Edwin, M.A.; Hon. Canon of Gloucester. 1907; F.S.A., 1890; Vice-President Bristol and Gloucestershire Archæological Society; b. 24 Feb. 1835; s. of Edwin Bartleet, of Birmingham, and Henrietta, d. of Samuel Hiron, of Chipping Campden; m. 1874, Henrietta (d. 1915), d. of Henry Gurney, Torquay. *Educ.*: King Edward's School, Birmingham; Trinity College, Cambridge. Curate of Hallow, Worcestershire, 1858-60; Prestwich, Lancs, 1861-66; Vicar of Crompton (or Shaw), 1866-75, and 1877-1878; Perpetual Curate of Ringley, 1875-77; Vicar of Brockworth, Glos. 1878-85; S. Mark's, Gloucester, 1885-89; Rector of Dursley, 1899-1910; Rural Dean of Dursley, 1907-10. *Publications*: History of the Manor and Advowson of Brockworth; History of the Borough and Manor of Chipping Campden; The Leper Hospital of S. Margaret, Gloucester; The Priory of St. Guthlac, Hereford, in Transactions of Bristol and Gloucestershire Archæological Society; History of the Priory of S. Mary, Bromfield, in Gloucester Cathedral Records. *Recreations*: The Study of Archæology. *Address*: Glenmore Lodge, Pittville, Cheltenham. *T.A.*: Cheltenham. (*Died 27 Oct. 1924.*)

BARTLEMAN, Maj.-Gen. Woodburn Francis, Indian Army; b. 26 April 1840. Entered army, 1857; Maj.-General, 1893; Unemployed Supernumerary List, 1895; served Indian Mutiny, 1858 (medal); Cossyah and Jyntiah Hills Campaign, 1862-68. *Address*: 19 Belmont Drive, Newnham Park, Liverpool.   (*Died 13 July 1924.*)

BARTLETT, Ven. Arthur Robert, Archdeacon of Goulburn, and Canon and Precentor of St. Saviour's Cathedral since 1902; Incumbent of St. Saviour's Cathedral Parish since 1904; b. London, 1851; s. of John and Harriet Huddlestone Bartlett; m. 1887, Mary, 3rd d. of Charles H. Humphrey, J.P., of Luscombe, Burwood, N.S.W. *Educ.*: Merchant Taylors' School; Wadham College, Oxford. Matriculated at Wadham Coll., Oxford, 1870; Death's Exhibitioner at School and College, also Goodridge Exhibitioner at College; took Honours in the Theological School, 1874; B.A. 1874; M.A. 1880; Deacon, 1874; Priest, 1875; served as Curate of Great Risington, Berkeley, West Hackney; appointed Minor Canon of Sydney; Examining Chaplain to the Bishop of Bathurst; Vicar of St. Paul's, Burwood, for nine years; made Hon. Canon of Brisbane and Rural Dean and Rector of Ipswich. *Publications*: tracts; sermons; Story of the Temptation; Story of the Incarnation; Story of the Ascension (in verse). *Recreations*: chess (President of Ipswich club), cricket. *Address*: St. Saviour's Cathedral, Goulburn, New South Wales. *Club*: Broughton, Sydney.   (*Died 14 April 1923.*)

BARTLETT, Sir Herbert Fogelstrom, Kt., cr. 1911; I.S.O.; a Commissioner of Inland Revenue, 1909-13; s. of E. T. Bartlett, Plymouth; b. 24 Nov. 1847; m. 1876, Frances, d. of R. Linwood, Bath. Assistant Secretary to Board of Inland Revenue, 1897-1908; Controller of Stamps and Registrar of Joint Stock Companies, 1903-9. *Address*: 49 Salisbury Road, Southsea. *Club*: Royal Albert Yacht, Southsea.   (*Died Nov. 1923.*)

BARTLETT, Sir Herbert Henry, 1st Bt., cr. 1913; partner in Perry and Co., Contractors; b. 30 April 1842; s. of late Robert Bartlett, of Hardington, Somerset, and Anne Guppy; m. 1874, Ada Charlotte, d. of Joseph Barr; four s. three d. *Heir*: g.s. Basil Hardington, b. 1905. *Address*: 54 Cornwall Gardens, S.W. *T.*: Western 2480. *Clubs*: St. Stephen's, City Carlton, Constitutional, Royal London Yacht (Commodore), Royal Thames Yacht, Royal Temple Yacht.   (*Died 23 June 1921.*)

BARTLETT, Paul Wayland; sculptor; b. New Haven 1865; s. of Truman Howe and Mary Ann White. *Educ.*: New Haven and Boston; began sculpture under the instruction of Frémiet; exhibited in Salon at the age of 14; entered Ecole des Beaux Arts, 1880; received recompense at Salon for the groupe. The Bear Tamer (now in Met. Mus. of New York), 1887; represented U.S. on International Jury of Awards for Sculpture, Paris Exposition, 1900; Chevalier Legion of Honour, France, 1895; officer, 1908. *Principal Works*: Statue of Gen. Joseph Warren, Boston; equestrian statue of Lafayette in the Square of the Louvre, Paris (gift to France from the school children of the U.S.); statues of Columbus and Michelangelo; six statues on the front of the New York Public Library; pediment over House wing of the Capitol, Washington, D.C.; statue of Benjamin Franklin. *Address*: 229 E. 20th Street. New York.   (*Died Sept. 1925.*)

BARTON, Major Charles Gerard, D.S.O. 1900; the King's Own (retired); b. 26 April 1860; s. of Rev. J. Barton; m. Mabel Eleanour, widow of Captain Maurice W. Kirk. *Educ.*: Tonbridge School; Sherborne. Entered army, 1881; Capt. 1889; Maj. 1900; served South Africa, 1899-1902; Relief of Ladysmith (despatches, Queen's medal with two clasps, King's medal, D.S.O.) *Recreation:* has played cricket for Hampshire. *Address:* Hatfield Bury, Witham, Essex. (*Died 3 Nov. 1919.*)

BARTON, Edwin Henry, D.Sc., F.R.S., F.R.S.E., F.P.S.L., F.Inst.P.; Professor of Experimental Physics, University College, Nottingham, since 1905; *b.* 23 Oct. 1858; 3rd *s.* of John Barton, Nottingham, and Eliza Lake, Nottingham; *m.* 1894, Mary, 6th *d.* of late Wm. Stafford, Newark; two *s. Educ.:* People's College and University College, Nottingham; The Imperial College of Science, London; The University of Bonn. Engaged for a number of years in engineering works at Nottingham as draughtsman and in other positions; joined the staff of the physical department of University College, Nottingham, 1893; senior lecturer and demonstrator, 1895. *Publications:* A Text-Book of Sound, 1908 (revised reprints, 1914, 1919, and 1922); Analytical Mechanics, 1911 (2nd ed. 1924); An Introduction to the Mechanics of Fluids, 1915; jointly with late Capt. T. P. Black, M.Sc., Ph.D., Practical Physics for Colleges and Schools, 1912 (revises, 1918 and 1919); sole or joint author of over forty papers giving the results of original researches in magnetism, electrical waves, acoustics, etc., published in the Philosophical Magazine, Physical Society's Proceedings, and Royal Societies of London and Edinburgh, 1894-1924; contributor to Physical Abstracts and Science Abstracts since 1894; author of article on Sound in the Dictionary of Applied Physics, vol. iv., 1923. *Recreations:* cycling, boating, mountaineering, gardening. *Address:* University College, Nottingham. *T.:* 776. (*Died 23 Sept. 1925.*)

BARTON, Maj.-Gen. Sir Geoffry, K.C.V.O.; *cr.* 1906; C.B. 1889; C.M.G. 1900; Col. Royal Fusiliers; J.P. Dumfriesshire; Knight of Grace of the Order of St. John of Jerusalem; *b.* 22 Feb. 1844; *s.* of late C. C. Barton of Rownhams, Hants; *m.* 1890, Beryl, *d.* of Col. Mackenzie, of Auchenskeoch, Kirkcudbrightshire; one *s.* one *d. Educ.:* Eton. Entered army, 1862; Major-General, 1898; served Ashanti War, 1873-74 (wounded, despatches, promoted Captain, medal with clasp); A.D.C. Aldershot, 1874-77; Zulu War, 1879 (despatches, brevet of Major, medal with clasp); Deputy Assistant Adjutant-General with Expeditionary Force to Egypt, 1882; present at Kassassin and Tel-el-Kebir (despatches, medal with clasp, 4th class Osmanieh, Khedive's star, brevet of Lieut.-Col.); Assist. Mil. Sec. China, 1884-85; Military Secretary Expeditionary Force to Suakin, 1885 (clasp); A.A.G. Thames District, 1895-97; A.A.G. North-West District, 1895-98; commanded Fusilier Brigade, South Africa Field Force, 1899 (wounded Ladysmith, despatches twice); later commanded Krugersdorp and Pretoria Districts till end of war, 1902 (despatches). *Address:* Craigs, Dumfries, N.B. *Clubs:* United Service, Wellington; Dumfries and Galloway. (*Died 6 July 1922.*)

BARTON, George Alexander Heaton, M.D., L.R.C.P., M.R.C.S., L.S.A.; Anæsthetist, Hampstead General, Royal National Orthopædic Hospitals; *b.* Hongkong, 1865; *s.* of Z. Barton, merchant; *m.* 1889, Mary Matilda, *d.* of Francis Goold, Madras army; four *s.* one *d. Educ.:* De Aston School. Matriculated London University (1st. div.), 1882; St. Mary's Hospital (Prizeman Prosector and Clinical Assistant to Out-patients); qualified, 1886; Surgeon in Royal Mail and Blue Funnel Lines, and practised in Devonshire till 1901; Fellow, Royal Society of Medicine; Member, British Medical Association and Harveian Society (late Hon. Secretary and Vice-President); formerly Anæsthetist to the Throat Hospital, Golden Square, the Female Lock Hospital, the National Dental Hospital, King George Hospital, and (acting) St. Mary's Hospital. *Publications:* A Guide to the Administra-

tion of Ethyl Chloride; Backwaters of Lethe; Prolonged Anæsthesia by Ethyl Chloride in Operations on the Nose and Throat (Lancet); the C.E.-Ethyl Chloride-Chloroform Sequence (Pract.); The Open Method of Ether Administration with some modifications (Pract.); alkaloids in Anæsthesia (Pract.); the Eye in Anæsthesia (Clin. Jour.); Ether, some simple Methods and Musings (Clin. Jour.). *Address:* 15 Talbot Road, W.2; *T.:* Park 953; 7 Devonshire Street, W.1. *T.:* Langham 1916. (*Died 13 Jan. 1924.*)

BARTON, Richard, I.S.O. 1911; late Superintendent of Demands, Stationery Office (retired, 1913); *e. s.* of Alfred Barton, of Winslow, Bucks; *b.* 25 May 1850; *m.* 1884, Frances, 3rd *d.* of John J. Youlin, M.D., Jersey City, U.S.A. *Educ.:* Cowley School, Oxford. *Address:* Old Rectory, Pitchcott, Aylesbury, Bucks. (*Died 1 Sept. 1927.*)

BARTON, William Henry; pioneer of the popular journalism and the penny Press in Burma (retired, 1927); *b.* 6 May 1869; *e. s.* of late Daniel Barton, of Downend, Isle of Wight, and Southampton; *m.* Jane Caroline (*dec.*), *y. d.* of late Alex. Ritchie, of Aberdeen and London; two *d. Educ.:* British School, Southampton; King's College, London. Editor Queenstown Free Press (South Africa), 1890; proprietor and editor London Associated Press, 1900; editor Rangoon Daily Times, 1905; sole proprietor and editor-in-chief since 1908 of Burma Pictorial Press, Daily Times of Burma, Moulmein Daily News, Weekly Times of Burma, and Burma Sunday Times. *Publications:* Thirty Days in the Jungle; Wild Life in Beautiful Burma; Modern Politics in Ancient India; The Indian Reforms and Diarchy; The Parish and District Councils Act; Holidays; The Book of the Home. *Address:* Park View, Tovil, Maidstone. (*Died 29 Sept. 1928.*)

BARTRAM, Sir Robert Appleby, Kt. *cr.* 1922; J.P.; *b.* 23 March 1835 *e s.* of late George Bartram of South Hylton, near Sunderland, and Margaret Appleby. of Newcastle-on-Tyne; *m.* 1859, Ann, *d.* of William Naizby, of South Hylton. *Educ.:* privately. Chairman of Bartram & Sons, Ltd., Shipbuilders, Sunderland; Chairman of Samuel Tyzack & Co., Ltd., Steel Manufacturers, Sunderland; Director of Sunderland and South Shields Water Co., Ltd. Has always taken a great interest in education; was ten years President Sunderland Chamber of Commerce, three times chosen Chairman of the Sunderland School Board. *Address:* Thornhill Park, Sunderland. *T. A.:* Bartram, Sunderland. *T.:* National 308. (*Died 8 Aug. 1925.*)

BARTTELOT, Major Sir Walter Balfour, 3rd Bt., *cr.* 1875; D.S.O. 1916; Coldstream Guards; *b.* 22 March 1880; *s.* of 2nd Bt. and Georgiana Mary, *d.* of George E. Balfour, of Sidmouth Manor, Devon; *m.* 1908, Gladys St. Aubyn, *y. d.* of W. C. Angove; two *s. Educ.:* Eton; Sandhurst. Contested (U.) Saffron Walden Division of Essex, 1906; served South Africa, 1899-1902 (Queen's medal, 6 clasps: King's medal, 2 clasps); France, 1914 (wounded); Gallipoli, 1915; G.S.O. 3 (Croix de Guerre); Mesopotamia Brigade, 1916-17; Major 13th Division (despatches, D.S.O.). Military Secretary to Lord Denman, Gov.-General of Australia, 1911-14; *Heir: s.* Walter de Stopham, *b.* 27 Oct. 1904. *Address:* Stopham House, Pulborough, Sussex. *Clubs:* Guards', Carlton, Boodle's. (*Died 23 Oct. 1918.*)

BARZELLOTTI, Giacomo, Dottore in Lettere e Filosofia; Decorato di Ordini cavallereschi italiani e Cav. della Legione d'Onore di Francia, Professore ordinario di Storia della Filosofia nella Regia Università di Roma; Senatore del Regno; *b.* Firenze, 7 Luglio 1844; *s.* of Gaspero Barzellotti, medico, and Teresa Benvenuti, *d.* of Pietro Benvenuti, insigne

BARTON, Rt. Hon. Sir Edmund, G.C.M.G. See page xv.

pittore di Arezzo; *m.* Antonietta Tabarrini, *d.* of Marco, Presidente del Consiglio di Stato e Senatore del Regno; two *s.* *Educ.*: Firenze. Prese la doppia Laurea di Dottore in Lettere e in Filosofia all' Università di Pisa nell' anno 1866; Professore di Filosofia nel R. Liceo Dante in Firenze, 1867-77; Libero docente all' Università di Roma nell' anno scolastico 1879-80; vinse il concorso per professore ordinario alla cattedra di Filosofia morale nelle R. Università di Pavia, ove insegnò 1881-83; dopo una rinunzia volontaria all' insegnamento (anni 1884-85), fu incaricato dell' insegnamento della Filosofia della Storia nell' Università di Roma (1886); chiamato dalla Facoltà di Lettere e di Filosofia dell' Università di Napoli, vi riprese l' insegnamento della Filosofia morale, 1887; per voto favorevole della Facoltà di Filosofia e Lettere dell' Università di Roma assunse, nel 1897, in questa Università l' insegnamento della Storia della Filosofia, che tiene tuttora; Membro Nazionale della R. Accademia dei Lincei di Roma. *Publications:* Delle dottrine filosofiche nei libri di Cicerone, 1867; La Morale nella Filosofia positiva, 1871, tradotto in inglese col titolo The Ethics of Positivism, 1878; David Lazzaretti di Arcidosso, detto il Santo, i suoi seguaci, la sua leggenda, 1885; Santi, Solitari e Filosofi, 1886; Studi e Ritratti, 1893; Ippolito Taine; La Philosophie de H. Taine, traduzione francese e seconda ediz. della stessa opera, 1900; Dal Rinascimento al Risorgimento (con un discorso su G. Carducci), 2nd. ed., 1909; Monte Amiata e il suo Profeta (David Lazzaretti), terza e nuova edizione dell' opera sopra citata, con introduzione, aggiunte e illustrazioni, 1910. *Address:* Roma, Via Borgognona, 12.
(Died 18 Sept. 1917.)

BASHFORD, Ernest Francis, M.D., late R.A.M.C., T.C.; *b.* Bowdon, Cheshire, 1873; *e. s.* of Wm. Taylor Bashford and Elizabeth Booth; *m.* 1902, Elisabeth, *e. d.* of Felix Alfermann, Frankfurt-on-Main; one *d.* *Educ.*: Universities of Edinburgh and Berlin, Frankfurt-on-Main, M.B., Ch.B.Edin., 1899; M.D. (Gold Medal), 1902; Vans Dunlop Scholar in Anatomy, Chemistry, Zoology, and Botany; Mackenzie Bursar in Practical Anatomy; Prosector to Sir Wm. Turner; Whitman Prizeman Clinical Medicine; Houldsworth Research Scholarship in Experimental Pharmacology; Stark Scholarship in Clinical Medicine and Pathology; Pattison Prizeman Clinical Surgery; on graduating was awarded the M'Cosh Graduate's Scholarship for Study and Research in the Medical Schools of Europe, and proceeded to Germany; studied bacteriology and pharmacology in the University of Berlin; and later worked with Ehrlich at the Royal Prussian Institute for Experimental Therapeutics, Frankfurt-on-Main; and also studied there under Weigert-Grocers Research Scholar, 1900-1902; Milner Fothergill Gold Medal in Therapeutics University Edinburgh, 1901; Assistant to Director Pharmacological Institut, Berlin, 1901; Assistant to Professor of Materia Medica, Pharmacology and Clin. Med. Univ. of Edin., 1902; founded the modern experimental investigation of cancer in this country, and placed the statistical and biological investigation of cancer on a comparative basis; Honorary President First International Cancer Congress, Heidelberg, 1906; awarded 1911 the Walker Prize for the quinquennial period, 1905-10; Ingleby Lecturer Univ. of Birmingham, 1911; Middleton Goldschmidt Lecturer, New York, 1912; Von Leyden Memorial Lecturer, Berlin, 1912; General Superintendent of Research, 1902-14, and Director of the Laboratories of the Imperial Cancer Research Fund, 1903-14. Served M.E.F. 1915-16, B.E.F. 1916-19, Germany, 1919 (despatches, O.B.E.). *Publications:* Editor and part author of Scientific Reports on the Investigations of the Imperial Cancer Research Fund,

i-v.; numerous papers on pharmacology, immunity, biochemistry, cancer, and pathology of wounds; successfully opposed from 1906 the efforts of the German Cancer Committee, Berlin, to gather all Cancer Research under its control. *Recreation:* fishing. *Address:* c/o Holt & Co., Whitehall Place, S.W.1.
(Died 23 Aug. 1923.)

BASHFORD, James W., D.D., LL.D., Ph.D.; Bishop, Methodist Episcopal Church since 1904; *b.* Fayette, Wisconsin, 29 May 1849; *s.* of Rev. Samuel Bashford and Mary Ann M'Kee; *m.* Jane M. of Madison, Wis., *d.* of Hon. W. W. Field, 1878. *Educ.*: Classical course University of Wisconsin, A.B. 1873; theological course at Boston University, S.T.B. 1876; School of Oratory, Boston University, 1878; course in all sciences of Boston University; Ph.D., 1881; pastor of Methodist Episcopal Churches in Boston, Mass., Newton, Mass., Portland, Me., and Buffalo, N.Y., 1878-89; President Ohio Wesleyan University, 1889-1904; visited Europe, 1881; again, and especially the German Universities, 1887; Italy, Greece, Egypt, Palestine, etc., 1896-97; revisited England, 1907, 1910; in former year visiting also India; and in latter year re-visiting Germany and Russia; Representative M.E. Church on World Commission on Faith and Order, and on Continuation Committee for China; D.D., *pro honore*, from North-Western University, Evanston, Ill., 1890: LL.D. Wesleyan University of Middletown, Conn., 1903; University of Wisconsin, 1912; Ohio Wesleyan University, 1912. *Publications:* Outlines of the Science of Religion, for class use; Wesley and Goethe, 1903; The Awakening of China; China and Methodism, 1906; God's Missionary Plan for the World, 1907. *Address:* Peking, China. *(Died 18 Mar. 1919.)*

BASHFORD, Major Lindsay, O.B.E.; *b.* London, 6 Feb. 1881; *s.* of late Frederick Bashford; *m.* 1919, Catherine, *y. d.* of late Joseph W. Lovibond, J.P., Lake House, Wilts. *Educ.*: Bedford; Germany; Edinburgh University; the College of Political Science, Paris. Lecturer in English Literature at the University of Bordeaux, 1902-1903; Private Sec. to Hon. Joseph Pulitzer, proprietor of the New York World, 1908; London Evening News, 1906; Literary Editor of The Daily Mail, 1908; took a commission in the Army Ordnance Department, 1914; served in Gallipoli, Egypt, and Palestine, 1915-19 (despatches thrice); special correspondent of the Daily Mail in France, Germany, Poland, and on the Baltic, 1919-20; contributor on political subjects to reviews. *Publications:* Everybody's Boy, 1912; Splendrum, 1914; Cupid in the Car, 1914. *Recreations:* music, yachting. *Club:* Devonshire.
(Died 20 Aug. 1921.)

BASING, 2nd Baron (cr. 1887), **George Limbrey Sclater-Booth,** C.B. 1902; D.L., J.P., C.C.; Col. in army; *b.* 1 Jan. 1860; *S.* father 1894; *m.* Mary (*d.* 1904), *d.* of John Hargreaves, Maiden Erlegh, Berks, and Whalley Abbey, Lancashire, 1889; one *s.* two *d.* *Educ.*: Eton; Balliol Coll. Oxford. Late Lieut.-Col. 1st Dragoons. Served South Africa, 1899-1901 (despatches, Brevet Lieut.-Col.); retired, 1906. *Heir:* *s.* Hon. J. L. R. Sclater-Booth. *Address:* Hoddington House, Upton Grey, Hants. *Clubs:* Arthur's, Naval and Military.
(Died 8 April 1919.)

BASKERVILLE, Rev. C. G., M.A.; Hon. Canon of Rochester; Surrogate; *b.* 20 Oct. 1830; *m.* 1858, Ellen Spencer Parsons (*d.* 1919); two *s.* two *d.* *Educ.*: Bishops' College, Clifton. Curate of Bath Abbey; Curate of St. Thomas', Wells; Vicar of St. Silas, Lozells, Birmingham, Vicar of St. Stephen, Walthamstow, and Vicar of Tonbridge. *Publications:* Abba Father; Sidelights on Ephesians and on Philippians; Hints to Sunday School Teachers. *Address:* 3 Park Road, Southborough, Kent. *(Died 28 Feb. 1921.)*

BASKERVILLE, Ralph Hopton, J.P.; *s.* of late Walter Thomas Mynors Baskerville, and Bertha Maria, *o. c.* and heiress of late John Hopton, of Canon-ffrome Court, Co. Hereford, and of Kemerton Court, Gloucestershire; *b.* 13 Feb. 1883. Late Lieutenant 1st Royal Dragoons. *Address:* Clyro Court, Hay, Co. Radnor.   (*Died 9 April 1918.*)

BASSETT, John Spencer, Ph.D.; LL.D.; Professor of American History, Smith College, Mass., since 1906; Head of History Department 1914-21; *b.* Tarborough, N.C. (U.S.A.), 10 Sep. 1867; *s.* of Richard Baxter Bassett and Mary J. Wilson; *m.* 1892, Jessie Lewellin; one *s.* one *d.* *Educ.:* Trinity Coll. (N.C.), A.B. 1888; Johns Hopkins Univ., Ph.D. 1894. Teacher in Durham (N.C.) Public School, 1888-90; Headmaster of High School in connection with Trinity College (N.C.), 1890-91; Student in History and Economics at Johns Hopkins Univ. 1891-94; Fellow in History at Johns Hopkins Univ. 1893-94; founded the South Atlantic Quarterly at Durham (N.C.), 1902, and continued its editor till 1905; Professor of History, Trinity Coll. North Carolina, 1893-1906. Lecturer in History, Yale University, 1907; N.Y. University, 1908-10; Columbia University, 1909-13; Secretary American Historical Society since 1919; Fellow of the Royal Historical Society; Member of the American Historical Association, the Massachusetts Historical Society, the American Antiquarian Society (Worcester, Mass.), and the American Academy for Arts and Sciences (Boston), National Institute of Arts and Letters. *Publications:* Constitutional Beginnings of North Carolina; Slavery and Servitude in North Carolina; Anti-Slavery Leaders of North Carolina; Slavery in the State of North Carolina; The Regulators of North Carolina; The Federalist System, 1789-1801; The Life of Andrew Jackson, 1911; A Short History of the United States, 1913; The Plain Story of American History, 1915; The Middle Group of American Historians, 1917; The Lost Fruits of Waterloo, 1918, revised edition, 1919; Our War with Germany, 1919; The Plantation Overseer as Shown in his Letters, 1925; Expansion and Reform, 1926; The State of History Writing (in Jusserand, Report on the Writing of History), 1926; Martin Van Buren (in Lives of the Secretaries of State), 1926; edited new edition of the writings of Colonel William. Byrd of Westover; The Correspondence of Andrew Jackson, vol. i., 1926; Joint Editor of the Smith College Studies in History, 1915-25. *Recreation:* gardening. *Address:* Northampton, Mass., U.S.A. *Clubs:* English-Speaking Union; Century, New York; Cosmos, Washington: Northampton.   (*Died 27 Jan. 1928.*)

BASSETT-SMITH, Surgeon-Rear-Admiral Sir Percy W., K.C.B., *cr.* 1921; C.B. 1911; C.M.G. 1918; F.R.C.S. Eng.; F.R.C.P. Lond.; D.T.M. and H. Camb.; President Royal Society Tropical Medicine and Hygiene; *b.* St. Albans, 1861; *s.* of William Bassett-Smith; *m.* Constance Brightman, M.B.E. (*d.* 1925), *d.* of Rev. F. Hastings; two *d.* *Educ.:* St. John's College, Hurstpierpoint. House Physician, Middlesex Hospital, London; entered Royal Navy, 1883; served Egyptian Expedition (medal and Khedive star, special promotion to Fleet Surgeon); Gilbert Blane Gold Medal; London School Trop. Medicine, 1899; Cragg's Prze, 1906; Lecturer on Tropical Medicine and Bacteriology, R.N. Medical School, Haslar, 1900-12; late Professor of Pathology and Lecturer Tropical Medicine, Medical School, R.N. College, Greenwich; Physician to Out-Patients Disease of Chest Hospital, Victoria Park, and St. John's Hospital, Lewisham; Consultant Tropical Diseases, 23 Harley Street, W.1. *Publications:* Snake Bites and Poisonous Fishes, Ency. Med. vol. xi.; many

medical scientific papers on undulant fever, typhoid, syphilis, etc.; sub-editor Tropical Disease Bulletins. *Recreations:* golf, natural history. *Address:* 3 Aberdeen Terrace, Blackheath, S.E.3. *T.:* Lee Green 368. *Club:* Royal Societies   (*Died 29 Dec. 1927.*)

BASU, Bhupendra Nath, M.A., B.L.; Member, Council of Secretary of State for India, 1917-23; Member of Executive Council of Governor of Bengal since 1924; Vice-Chancellor, Calcutta University; *b.* Calcutta, Jan. 1859. *Educ.:* Presidency College, Calcutta. Was member Bengal Legislative Council, also Viceroy's Legislative Council; President of the Indian National Congress held in Madras, 1914; Representative of the Government of India at the International Labour Conference at Geneva, 1922; Member Royal Commission on Indian Public Services, 1923. *Address:* Temple Chambers, Calcutta. *Clubs:* National Liberal; Calcutta, Calcutta.   (*Died 16 Sept. 1924.*)

BATCHELOR, Ferdinand Campion, Professor of Surgery, Otago University; Lt.-Col. Expeditionary Force of New Zealand. *Educ.:* Guy's Hospital. *Address:* Otago University. New Zealand.   (*Died 31 Aug. 1916.*)

BATE, Col. Albert Louis Frederick, C.M.G. 1916; L.R.C.S.I., L. and L.M.K.Q.C.P.I., L.M., Rotunda Hospital, Fellow Royal Institute of Public Health, London; F.R.G.S., F.R.C.I.; *b.* 5 Oct. 1862 *s.* of Henry Alexander Bate, Dublin; *m.* 1896, Emily Florence Wilson, *d.* of Henry West, Hampton on Thames; four *s.* *Educ.:* Methodist College, Belfast; Wesley College, Dublin. Royal Army Medical Corps, 1886; Major, 1898; Lt.-Col., 1906; Col., 1915; served Sikkim Expedition, 1888; South African War, 1899-1902, as S.M.O. Zululand, Secretary and Registrar P.M.O., Maritzburg, Natal, and later O.C. No. 21 Stationary Hospital, Machadodorp, Transvaal (Queen's medal, 2 clasps, King's medal, 2 clasps); European War, 1914-19 (despatches twice, C.M.G., Mons star and clasp, Victory medal and General Service medal, with 2 laurel leaves); started and organised a Convalescent Hospital; has materially assisted in the efficient organisation of similar smaller establishments at every divisional headquarters; holds French Médaille d'Honneur de l'Assistance Publique. *Address:* c/o Holt & Co., 3 Whitehall Place, S.W.   (*Died 20 Feb. 1924.*)

BATE, Sir Henry Newel, Kt., *cr.* 1910; Chairman of the Ottawa Improvement Commission; *b.* Truro, 9 April 1828; *m.* 1853, Catherine (*d.* 1906), *d.* of Allan Cameron; four *s.* *Educ.:* St. Catharine's, Ontario, Canada. Has resided in Ottawa since 1854; first Chairman of the Ottawa Improvement Commission on its formation, 1899; President of the Beechwood Cemetery, Ottawa and Aylmer Road Company, the Russell Company, Limited; Director of the Bank of Ottawa, etc. *Recreations:* Member of the Hunt Club, St. Patrick's Golf Club, Green Lake Fish and Game Club. *Address:* Treuwick House, Chapel Street, Ottawa, Canada. *Clubs:* Rideau. Country. Ottawa. (*Died 8 April 1917.*)

BATE, John Pawley, J.P., Barrister-at-Law; Reader to Inns of Court in Roman and International Law since 1897; has been Examiner in these subjects in the Univ. of Oxford and London; *b.* 1857; *s.* *s.* of late Rev. George Osborn Bate; *m.* Mary, widow of Sir Charles Wathen of Cook's Folly, Clifton: one *d.* *Educ.:* Woodhouse Grove School; Peterhouse, Camb. Obtained Members' Prize for English Essay, 1884; LL.D. 1898; for some years Fellow and Law Lecturer of Trinity Hall; Professor of Jurisprudence in Univ. Coll. London, 1894-1901; has contributed articles on International Law to the Quarterly Review; British legal representative on the staff of the League of Nations, 1919-20. *Publication:* Notes on the Doctrine of Renvoi; Declaration of London; Translations of works on International Law by Ayala, Victoria, Rachel, Textor, etc. *Address*: Lambpark, Honiton; 8 Stone Buildings, Lincoln's Inn, W.C. *T.*: Honiton 26. *Club*: Athenæum.   (*Died 10 Feb. 1921.*)

BATEMAN, Alys; soprano singer; *d.* of late Robert Bateman and Marian Moore, relative of Hannah Moore; *m.* 1st, Malcolm Colin, *s.* of Francis Simon Dring, of Simonstown, Co. Cork; 2nd, John Starkie Gardner. *Educ.*: Bodleian College; Trinity College of Music. Début concert in England at St. James' Hall, 1903; initiated Union Jack Club Concerts: toured Canada twice, 1906 and 1907; sang to King and Queen of Spain at Welbeck; organised Requiem Concert in aid of Prince Francis of Teck Memorial Fund, 1911; gave first recitals ever held in London of Russian music, 1914 and 1915; toured England, 1913, with Sapelnikoff; organised five concerts of Russian music, Grand Duke Michael's Fund, 1915; concerts for Belgian Relief Fund, Polish Victims' Relief Fund, Red Cross Fund, and Polish Flag Day, 1915; eight concerts of Russian music, Oct. 1915-June 1916; raised fund for Berkshire room, Star and Garter; gave concert in Queen's Hall for Queen Charlotte's Hospital, 1917; proprietor of the metal works of J. Starkie Gardner. *Recreations*: riding, punting, and gardening. *Address*: 20 Elvaston Place, S.W.7; *T.*: Kensington 7315; 2a Merivale Road, Putney, S.W.15. *Club*: Ladies' Athenæum.
    (*Died 7 Nov. 1924.*)

BATEMAN, Francis John Harvey, J.P. County of London, M.A. (Camb.), M.D., C.M. (Edin.), F.Z.S.; Civil Surgeon, Lewisham Military Hospital; Senior Medical Officer, Blackheath and Charlton Hospital; Hon. Medical Officer, Belmont Home for Ladies, Lewisham; Hon. Medical Officer, Dartmouth Home for Crippled Boys, Blackheath; Hon. Medical Officer, St. Dunstan's Annexe for Blinded Soldiers, Blackheath; Medical Adviser, Blackheath High School; *b.* Norwich; *s.* of late Sir Frederic Bateman, M.D., LL.D., F.R.C.P., and Emma Brownfield, *d.* of John Gooderson of Heigham Fields, Norwich; *m.* 1902, Bertha Isabel, *d.* of late Hugh Roberts, Llanrwst, N. Wales; three *s. Educ.*: Norwich School; Pembroke Coll. Cambridge; medical schools of Edinburgh, Dublin, and Paris; Prizeman in Public Health Edinburgh School of Medicine. After graduating M.B., C.M., was appointed Resident Physician to the Royal Infirmary, Edinburgh, and Resident Surgeon to the Leith Hospital; after holding the post of Assistant Medical Officer to the West Riding Asylum, Wakefield, went to Paris as Resident Medical Officer to the Hertford British Hospital, 1900; worked at the Pasteur Institute and at the French Hospitals; Vice-President of Medical Society, London, and Fellow of Obstetrical Society, Edinburgh; Member d'Alliance Franco Brittanique; has contributed to medical journals. *Recreations*: golf, fishing, shooting. *Address*: Heath End, Blackheath. *T.*: Lee Green 294. *M.*: LK 8664. *Clubs*: Oxford and Cambridge; Magistrates'.   (*Died 2 Aug. 1920.*)

BATEMAN, Rev. William Fairbairn La Trobe-, M.A.; *b.* 8 Jan. 1845; *s.* of late John Frederic La Trobe-Bateman, F.R.S., of Moor Park, Surrey, and Anne, *o. d.* of Sir William Fairbairn, 1st Bart.; *m.* 1870, Mildred Jane (*d.* 1878), 2nd *d.* of Rev. Robert Sumner, and *g.d.* of Bishop Sumner of Winchester; one *s.* two *d. Educ.*: Cheam; Harrow; Trinity College, Cambridge. Deacon, 1868; Priest, 1870; Curate of Alverstoke, 1868-89; Castle Rising, 1869-71; Christ Church, St. Pancras, 1871-74; Vicar of St. John Evangelist, Norwood, 1875-1900; Rector of Ascot, 1900-17; Diocesan Chaplain to Bishop of Oxford, 1917-1919; Hon. Canon of Christ Church Cathedral, Oxford, 1922. *Publications*: Our Companion by the Way; The Pattern Life; Problems and

Issues of the Spiritual Life, 1915. *Address*: Streatley, nr. Reading. *Club*: Athenæum.
    (*Died 3 Oct. 1926.*)

BATEMAN, Rev. William Henry Fraser, Canon of York, 1912-21; Surrogate, 1901-21; Proctor in Convocation, 1913-19; Synodal Secretary of Convocation of York 1917-21; *b.* Manchester, 1855; *s.* of R. D. Bateman, Manchester; *m.* 1883, Jane Thomas (*d.* 1911), Glam., South Wales; one *s.* one *d. Educ.*: Chorlton High School, Manchester; Christ's College, Cambridge (M.A.). Curate St. Lawrence's, York, 1883-90; Rector Holy Trinity, York, 1890-95; Vicar of Mexborough, 1895-1914; Vicar of Wistow, 1914-21. *Publications*: Editor Parish Register, Holy Trinity, Micklegate, York, 1903. *Recreation*: cycling. *Address*: Cartref, Clifton Park Road, Caversham, Oxon.   (*Died 6 Aug. 1923.*)

BATEMAN-HANBURY, Rev. Hon. Arthur Allen, Rector of Shobdon; Prebendary of Hereford; *b.* 13 March 1829; *e. surv. s.* of 1st Baron Bateman; *m.* 1858, Mary Ward (*d.* 1895), *e. d.* of John Davenport of Foxley, Herefords; one *s.* four *d. Educ.*: Eton; Christ Church, Oxford. Ordained 1853. *Address*: Shobdon Rectory, Kingsland, Herefordshire.
    (*Died 5 Mar. 1919.*)

BATES, Arlo, S.B., A.B., A.M., Lit.D., Φ.B.K.; Professor of English, Massachusetts Institute of Technology, Boston, Mass., U.S.A., 1893-1915; *s.* of Dr. Niran Bates and Susan Thaxter Bates; *b.* East Machias, Maine, Dec. 16, 1850; *m.* 1882, Harriet L. Vose; one *s. Educ.*: Washington Academy; Bowdoin College, class 1876. Editor Broadside, 1878-79; Boston Courier, 1880-93; correspondent Providence Journal, Chicago Tribune, Book Buyer, etc.; lecturer on literary subjects before societies, clubs, etc.; member Phi Beta Kappa, American Academy Arts and Sciences, National Institute of Arts and Letters, etc. *Publications*: Patty's Perversities; The Pagans; The Philistines; The Puritans; Mr. Jacobs; F. Seymour Hayden and Engraving; Albrecht; A Lad's Love; Book of Nine Tales; In the Bundle of Time; Talks on Writing English, First and Second Series; Talks on the Study of Literature; Love in a Cloud; The Diary of a Saint; Talks on Teaching Literature; The Intoxicated Ghost and Other Stories; Counsels of a Worldly Godmother (anon.); With Mrs. Bates; Prince Vance. *Poems*: Berries of the Brier; Sonnets in Shadow; The Poet and His Self; The Torchbearers; Told in the Gate; Under the Beech-Tree. *Recreations*: yachting, whist, digging in Indian shell-middens, collecting book-plates. *Address*: 4 Otis Place, Boston, Mass., U.S.A. *Club*: Tavern, Boston.   (*Died Sept. 1918.*)

BATES, Henry Montague; late Principal Clerk, Public Health Department, Corporation of London; *b.* 17 March 1849; *s.* of Robert M. Bates and Charlotte Emily Taylor; *m. o. d.* of Colonel Francis Chancellor Rybot, 1st Bombay Lancers, and *widow* of Lt.-Col. A. Gammell, 12th Lancers; one *s. Educ.*: Bell Burrows and Johnson's Naval Establishment, Southsea., etc. Private Secretary to Rt. Hon. Edward Horsman, M.P., for four years; Assistant Clerk to Commissioners of Sewers of City of London, 1875; Clerk of the Commission, 1895; Commission amalgamated with Corporation of London, 1898, by the City of London Sewers Act, 1897, and the municipal work of the City carried on by the Public Health Department created for the purpose; P.G. Steward, Grand Lodge, Freemasons; twice Master of Lodge of Regularity; Member of Council of London Cart Horse Parade Society; Director of Kent and East Sussex Railway Company, The Selsey Tramway Company, and Snailbeach District Railways; Chairman of North Devon and Cornwall Junction Light Railway Company; Chairman, Committee of Control of Eccentric Club Hostels for Limbless Sailors and Soldiers; Liveryman, Spectacle-Makers' Company; King's Coronation Medal, 1911. *Publication:* Origin, Statutory Powers, and Duties of the Commissioners of Sewers of the City of London. *Address:* 33 Colville Square Mansions, Bayswater, W.; Manaccan, St. Martin R.S.O., Cornwall. *Club:* Eccentric.   (*Died 30 Dec. 1928.*)

BATES, Oric, M.A., F.R.G.S., Curator of African Archaeology and Ethnology, Peabody Museum (Harvard University); Editor of Harvard African Studies; *b.* Boston, Mass., 5 Dec. 1883; *s.* of Arlo Bates;   *m.* 1913, Natica, *d.* of John Chester Inches, Boston; two *s.* *Educ.:* Private School; Harvard University; Berlin University. Assistant in charge Egypt. Department Museum of Fine Arts, Boston, 1906-7; Berlin University, 1907-8; Nubian Archaeological Survey, 1908-9; Harvard Palestinian Expedition; Harvard Univ.-Museum of Fine Arts Egypt. Expedition; Exploration in Cyrenaica, 1909-10; Exploration in Libyan Desert; studied in Cairo, 1910-11; Excavation in Anglo-Egyptian Sudan, 1911-12; Excavation in Marmarica, 1913-14; Excavation in Anglo-Egyptian Sudan, 1915; National Service U.S. Shipping Board, 1917-18. *Publications:* contributions to Harvard African Studies and to various scientific journals; The Eastern Libyans, 1914. *Recreation:* shooting. *Address:* 37 Chestnut Street, Boston, Mass., U.S.A.   (*Died 10 Oct. 1918.*)

BATESON, William, M.A., F.R.S., Hon. D.Sc. Sheffield; Director John Innes Horticultural Institution, Merton Park, Surrey, since 1910; Trustee of the British Museum since 1922; Fullerian Prof. of Physiology, Royal Institution, 1912-14; Hon. Fellow of St. John's College, Cambridge; Silliman Lecturer, Yale University, 1907; Professor of Biology, Cambridge, 1908-9; President British Association for Advancement in Science, Australia, 1914; Foreign Member, National Academy of Science, Washington; Royal Danish Academy; Royal Academy, Belgium; N.Y. Academy of Science; Academy of Sciences, Leningrad; Soc. Helv. Sci. Nat.; Videnskabs Selskabet Christiania, etc.; *b.* Whitby, 1861; *s.* of Rev. W. H. Bateson, D.D., Master of St. John's College; *m.* 1896, Beatrice, *d.* of late Arthur Durham, Senior Surgeon to Guy's Hospital; one *s.* *Educ.:* Rugby School; St. John's College, Cambridge. Balfour Student, 1887-90; Darwin Medal Royal Society, 1904; Royal Medal, 1920. *Publications:* Materials for the Study of Variation, 1894; Mendel's Principles of Heredity, 1902; Problems of Genetics, 1913; various papers on biological subjects. *Address:* The Manor House, Merton, S.W.20. *T.:* Wimbledon 972. *Clubs:* Athenæum, Burlington Fine Arts.   (*Died 8 Feb. 1926.*)

BATH, Engineer - Rear - Admiral George Clark, R.N., M.V.O. 1908; Retired; *b.* 19 Sep. 1862; *m.* 1889, Maria, *o. d.* of late Hector John Davidson, Devonport. Assistant Engineer, 1883; Chief Engineer, 1896; Engineer-Commander, 1900; Engineer-Captain, 1912. *Address:* 14 Whitwell Road, Southsea, Hants.   (*Died 5 May 1925.*)

BATTEN, Adm. Alexander William Chisholm, M.V.O.; D.S.O. 1917; J.P., Mid-Lothian; 2nd *s.* of E. Chisholm Batten, Thornfalcon, Somerset; *b.* 28 Sep. 1851; *m.* Brittie Ellen Wood; one *s.* two *d.* *Educ.:* Eagle House. Joined R.N. 1865; Member War Office Committees Coast Defence; employed suppression slave trade; present Bangkok during French Blockade; Ordnance Department Admiralty; in conjunction with Sir N. Lockyer read paper before Royal Society on Solar Eclipse Expedition; A.D.C. to King, 1905; retired, 1907; served afloat as Captain R.N.R. 1915-17 (D.S.O.). *Address:* Thorncote, Murrayfield Gardens, Edinburgh. *Club:* Caledonian United Service, Edinburgh. (*Died 2 Nov. 1925.*)

66

BATTEN, Frederick Eustace, M.D.; Physician to the National Hospital for the Paralysed and Epileptic, Queen Square, and to the Children's Hospital, Great Ormond Street; *b.* Plymouth, 1865; 3rd *s.* of late John Winterbotham Batten, K.C., and Sarah, *d.* of Samuel Derry, M.R.C.S.; *m.* Jean Evelyn, *d.* of John J. Stevenson. *Educ.:* Westminster; Trinity College, Cambridge; St. Bartholomew's Hospital. Fellow Royal College of Physicians. *Publications:* Scientific papers on the nervous system. *Address:* 22 Harley Street, W. *T.:* Mayfair. 769.   (*Died 27 July 1918.*)

BATTEN, Col. Herbert Cary George, O.B.E., B.A., J.P., D.L., Hon. Col. 3rd Batt. Dorset Regt.; Director of Westminster Bank, Ltd.; 3rd *s.* of John Batten of Aldon, Somerset, F.S.A., D.L., J.P. (*d.* 1900); *b.* 1849; *m.* 1st, 1878, Frances Eleanor, *d.* of John Beardmore, of Uplands, Fareham, Hants; 2nd, 1898, Isabel Frances, *d.* of late Gen. Sir Robert Bright, G.C.B.; two *s.* one *d.* *Educ.:* Cheltenham College; Trinity Hall, Cambridge. Called to Bar, Inner Temple, 1874; practised for some years on the Western Circuit; Lt.-Col. commanding 3rd Batt. Dorset Regt., 1901-9. *Recreations:* hunting, shooting. *Address:* Keyford, Yeovil. *M.:* Y 709. *Club:* New University.   (*Died 26 Nov. 1926.*)

BATTEN, Col. John Mount, C.B. 1903 H.M. Lieut. Dorset and Poole; J.P., Somerset and Dorset; late The King's (Liverpool Regt.); *e. s.* of late John Batten, J.P., F.S.A., of Aldon, Somerset, and Grace Eleanor, *d.* of John White of Upcerne; *b.* 7 Apr. 1843; *m.* 1st, 1873 Margaret Annie (*d.* 1893), *e. d.* of Rev. John Brooks; 2nd, 1895, Mary Edith, *e.d.* of J. Sant R.A., and *widow* of H. F. Naider; one *s.* four *d.* *Educ.:* Winchester. High Sheriff of Dorset, 1903, and Alderman of C.C. of Dorset Patron of two livings. *Address:* Mornington Lodge, West Kensington, W.; Upcerne, Cerne Abbas, Dorset. *Club:* Army and Navy.
      (*Died 5 Mar. 1916.*)

BATTERSBY, Major - General John Prevost; retired; *b.* 16 Oct. 1826; *s.* of Lt.-Colonel Francis Battersby, C.B., and Eliza Jane Rotheram; *m.* Louisa Wilhelmina, *d.* of Sir W. Dillon, 4th Bt.; one *s.* two *d.* *Educ.* Portora Royal School, Enniskillen. Joined the 1st Batt. 60th King's Royal Rifles, 1844; served as A.D.C. to Brig.-Gen. Lord Melville and to Sir Arthur Lawrence, Inspector - General of Infantry; Brigade Major, Dover; Assistant Adjutant-General, Secunderabad; Commandant Royal Military Asylum, Chelsea; Assistant Director of Military Education, War Office *Recreations:* tennis and hockey. *Address:* Lyncroft, Weybridge.   (*Died 12 Jan. 1917*)

BATTISCOMBE, Rear - Admiral Albert H. W.; retired; *b.* 14 April 1831 2nd *s.* of late Rev. Richard Battiscombe of Hacton, Essex; *m.* Lucy, *d.* of late Sir Henry Robinson, D.L., J.P., of Knapton House Norfolk; formerly Lieut. Commanding H.M Body Guard of Gentlemen-at-Arms; one one *d.* *Educ.:* Stoke Poges; Eton College Cadet, Royal Navy, 1846; appointed to the Ringdove and took part in the operation against Bruni Borneo, 1846; midshipman Medea, 1850, which in that year captured fleet of piratical junks in Miro Bay, Cochin China; Sub.-Lieut. 1852; Lieut. 1854; appointed to the Hecla and was present at the bombardment of Bomarsund, and subsequently at the capture of this fortress; as a lieutenant in the Cornwallis was engaged at the bombardment of Sveaborg (Battle Medal); as Gunnery and 1st Lieut. in the Naval Brigade in 1857 in New Zealand under Commodore Beauchamp Seymour in 1860, part of the time acted Assistant Engineer under Colonel Commanding Royal Engineers (despatches, promoted Commander, 1861); served as Commander the Snipe on the West Coast of Africa, and subsequently in the Coastguard; as Commander of the Victory, 1868, and Royal Naval Reserve ship at Bristol; Captain, 1870; retired 1878; Rear-Admiral, retired list, 1887. *Address:* Eastwood, Weston-super-Mare.

(*Died 16 Sept. 1918.*)

BATTISTINI, Mattia, Barone di Poggio Casalino Kamessinger e decorazioni di quasi tutte le nazioni; decorazioni altissime; *b.* Rome, 27 Feb. 1858; Vedovo della nobile donna Dolores Figuera della famiglia del Conte di Romanones, Duca di Cosa e Duca di Villamejor di Spagne. *Educ.:* Roma; Nobile Collegio Bandinello. Dal 1879 la piu gloriose delle carriere artistiche Russia, Italia, Spagna Portogallo, Germania, Austria Ungheria, Polonia, Londres, Boemia, Francia, America del Sud. *Publications:* Qualche romanze di salone e marcia. *Address:* Contigliano, Italia Sabina. (*Died Nov. 1928.*)

BATTY, Herbert (The Hon. Mr. Justice Batty), M.A., Christ's College, Camb.; Barrister-at-law, Lincoln's Inn; *b.* 1849. Entered I.C.S. 1868; Prof. of Logic and Moral Philosophy, Deccan College, Poona, 1872-75, and Assistant Judge and Sessions Judge; Under-Secretary to Government, Bombay, 1885; Remembrancer of Legal Affairs, 1892; Acting Chief Secretary to Government Political Departments, 1896; Acting Judicial Commissioner in Sind, 1899; Acting Judge, High Court, Bombay, 1900; Judicial Commissioner, Sind, 1901; Judge of High Court of Judicature, Bombay, 1902-8. (*Died Mar. 1923.*)

BATTYE, Lt.-Col. Clinton Wynyard, D.S.O. 1900; 85th King's Light Infantry; Lt.-Col. of the 1/4th East Lancashire Regiment in France; *b.* 24 May 1874; 3rd *s.* of late Major Montagu Battye, H.M.'s Hon. Corps of Gentlemen-at-Arms. *Educ.:* Wellington College. Entered army, 1894; served South Africa, 1899-1902, with 1st Batt. Mounted Infantry (Queen's medal, 4 clasps, King's medal, 2 clasps, despatches); Mohmand operations, 1908 (medal and clasp); European War, 1914-17 (wounded). *Club:* Army and Navy. (*Died 25 Nov. 1917.*)

BAUGH, Captain George Johnstone, D.S.O. 1917; R.I.M.; Marine Superintendent and Harbour Master, London & North-Western Railway, Fleetwood, since 1907; *b.* 1862; *s.* of Henry Bempde Baugh, Colonel, Bengal Staff Corps, of Barnstaple, Devon; *m.* 1903, Grace Geraldine, *e. d.* of Edward Franks, India Office, Whitehall; two *s. Educ.:* Westward Ho! College. Entered R.I.M. 1882; Lieut. 1884; Commander, 1894; Captain, 1920; Appointments held: Transport Officer, Upper Burmah; Staff Officer Government Dock Yards, Bombay; Officiating Assistant Director R.I.M., Conservator Port of Madras, and Presidency Port Officer, Madras (retired 1907); served Burmah Campaign, 1885-88 (two clasps), South Africa, China and Somaliland; Royal Humane Society's bronze medal, 1891; posted to Liverpool, 1914, as Divisional Sea Transport Officer under Railway Executive Committee; granted temporary commission as Major, Jan. 1915, and posted to War Office as Deputy Assistant Director of Movements, responsible for the organisation and supervision of building of self-propelled craft in Britain for the inland Water Transport, Royal Engineers, for service on the canals of France and Belgium; service in France as Assistant Director and Deputy Director, Inland Water Transport, R.E., 1915-17 with rank of Colonel (despatches twice). *Recreations:* shooting, fishing, golf. *Address:* Warrenhurst Park, Fleetwood, Lancs. *T.:* 41. *Club:* Sports.

(*Died 3 May 1924.*)

BATTY-SMITH, Henry; late Proprietor and Editor of The Sportsman newspaper; retired, 1924; *m.* Lilian, *d.* of late G. Kent of Farnborough; three *s.* one *d. Educ.:* privately

and abroad (France and Germany). Is well known in the world of sport, having taken an active part in nearly all sports and games. *Recreations:* now golf, shooting, and racing; formerly cricket, football, rowing, tennis, etc. *Address:* Shinfield Grove, Berks. *T.:* Reading 1693. *Clubs:* Sports, M.C.C.; Sunningdale Golf; Thames Rowing, etc. (*Died 21 May 1927.*)

BAX, Ernest Belfort, Barrister-at Law, Middle Temple; author; *b.* Leamington, 23 July 1854; *m.* 1st, 1877(*d.* 1893); 2nd, 1897; four *s.* two *d. Educ.:* privately in London; Germany. Studied music, especially theory and composition; also later, philosophy, more particularly the German movement from Kant to Hegel; practised journalism as foreign correspondent, 1880-81; returning to England, was one of the founders of the English Socialist movement. In 1885 helped to start the Socialist League in conjunction with late William Morris, and for some time co-edited with him the weekly journal Commonweal; subsequently resigned from League, and again became connected with the Social Democratic Federation, co-operating on, and for a time editing, its organ Justice; delegate of the S.D.F. to various international congresses. *Publications:* Jean-Paul Marat, 1878; Kant's Prolegomena, etc., with Biography and Introduction, 1882; Handbook to the History of Philosophy, 1884; Religion of Socialism, 1886; Ethics of Socialism, 1889; French Revolution, 1890; Outlooks from the New Standpoint, 1891; The Problem of Reality, 1893; German Society at the Close of the Middle Ages, 1894; Socialism, its Growth and Outcome (in conjunction with the late William Morris), 1894; Outspoken Essays on Social Subjects, 1897; The Peasants' War in Germany, 1899, etc.; a new Life of Marat (2nd ed.), 1901; Rise and Fall of the Anabaptists, 1903; Essays in Socialism, New and Old, 1906; The Roots of Reality, 1907; The Last Episode of the French Revolution, 1911; Problems of Men, Mind, and Morals, 1912; German Culture, Past and Present, 1915; Reminiscences and Reflections, 1918; The Real, The Rational, and the Alogical, 1920; contributed to Professor Muirhead's Contemporary British Philosophy, 1925; also edited the monthlies Time and To-day. *Recreations:* no special sports. *Clubs:* National Liberal, Authors'. (*Died 26 Nov. 1926.*)

BAXTER, Sir George Washington, 1st Bt.; *cr.* 1918; Kt., *cr.* 1904; *b.* 20 Nov. 1853; *y. s.* of late Rt. Hon. W. E. Baxter of Kincaldrum, Forfarshire, and Janet, *d.* of John Home Scott; *m.* 1889, Edith, O.B.E., *e. d.* of Major-General J. L. Fagan. *Educ.:* High School, Dundee; St. Andrews and Edinburgh Universities. Hon. LL.D. St. Andrews; Chairman of Dundee and District Liberal Unionist Association, 1886-1910; Chairman of Dundee Unionist Association, 1910-19; President Scottish Unionist Association, 1919; President of University College, Dundee; Chairman of Territorial Force Association, Dundee, for some years; contested Montrose Burghs, 1895; Dundee, 1908, and Dec. 1910, D.L., J.P. Dundee; J.P. Forfarshire. *Heir:* none. *Address:* Invereighty, Forfarshire. *T.A.:* Invereighty, Kincaldrum. *Clubs:* Carlton; Eastern, Dundee. (*Died 26 Nov. 1926.*)

BAXTER, Sir William James, Kt., *cr.* 1907; J.P., D.L., Co. Londonderry; *b.* Tattykeel, Cookstown, Co. Tyrone, 1845; *s.* of Samuel Baxter and Sarah, *e. d.* of John Beatty, Mullinahunch House, Co. Tyrone; *m.* 1892, Mary, 2nd *d.* of Rev. Robert Wallace, Beresford Villas, Coleraine; three *d. Educ.:* Ballymena Academy; Carmichael College, Dublin. First place in two examinations of Pharmaceutical Society of Ireland; elected by co-option on Council of this Society; has been 20 years on the Council; President, 1910-11-12-13; Chairman Coleraine Town Commissioners, 1897, 1898 and

1899; being last Chairman of old Commissioners and first Chairman of new Urban Council ; President of Coleraine Agricultural and Industrial Association ; President Coleraine Savings Bank ; Vice-President Congress of Health, Dublin, 1898. Contested (L.) North Antrim, 1910. *Address :* Avondale, Coleraine. *T.A. :* Baxter, Chemist, Coleraine. *T. :* 27. *(Died 19 Dec. 1918.)*

BAXTER, Wynne Edwin, F.G.S., F.R.M.S., J.P., D.L ; Coroner for East London and the Tower of London ; clerk to two of the City Guilds ; Treas. of the Royal Microscopical Soc. ; *b.* 1844 ; *e. s.* of William Edwin Baxter of Lewes (*d.* 1871) ; *m.* 1868, Kate Bliss (*d.* 1915), *d.* of F. H. Parker (Mayor of Northampton, 1849-1851) ; three *s.* one *d. Educ. :* Lewes Grammar School ; Rev. P. Frost, Sussex Square, Brighton. Admitted a solicitor, 1867 ; Under-Sheriff of London and Middlesex, 1876-79, 1885-86 ; High Constable of Lewes, 1877-81 ; first Mayor of Lewes, 1881-82 ; Coroner for Sussex, 1879-87 ; Vice-President of the Provincial Newspaper Society, 1871-76. *Publications :* Baxter's Judicature Acts and Rules (5th ed.) ; Doomsday Book of Sussex, Surrey, Kent, and Middlesex ; Van Heurck's Microscope ; The Diatomaceæ. *Recreations :* the Diatomaceæ, Bibliography, Miltoniana. *Address :* 170 Church Street, Stoke Newington, W. ; The Granvilles, Stroud, Gloucestershire. *T.A. :* Inquest, London. *T. :* 550 Dalston ; 17 Eastern ; 93 Lewes ; 68 Stroud ; 642 Bank. *Club :* Constitutional. *(Died 1 Oct. 1920.)*

BAYARD, Brig.-Gen. Reginald, D.S.O. 1902 ; late the Buffs ; retired pay ; *b.* 11 Sept. 1860 ; *s.* of Robertson Bayard, B.L. of St. Louis, New Brunswick ; *m.* Edith (*d.* 1916), *d.* of late John Quain, J.P. Co. Dublin ; one *d. Educ. :* privately. Entered service, 1881 ; Captain, 1893 ; Major, 1900 ; served S. Africa, 1899-1902 (despatches twice, medal, D.S.O.); Southern Arabia, 1903-4 ; Lieut.-Colonel, 1907. *Recreations :* hunting, polo, cricket, golf, skating. *(Died 23 July 1925.)*

BAYFIELD, Rev. Matthew Albert, M.A. ; Rector of Hertingfordbury, Hertford ; *b.* Edgbaston, Birmingham, 17 June 1852 ; *s.* of L. A. Bayfield, chartered accountant, Birmingham; *m.* Helen Campbell, *d.* of late John Boyes; one *s.* one *d. Educ. :* King Edward's School, Birmingham ; Clare Coll. Camb. (Scholar). 1st class Classical Tripos, 1875. Assistant Master, Blackheath School, 1875-79 ; Marlborough Coll. 1879-81 ; Headmaster's Assistant, Malvern Coll. 1881-90 ; Headmaster, Christ Coll. Brecon, 1890-1895 ; Headmaster, Eastbourne College, 1895-1900; Member of Council of Society for Psychical Research. *Publications :* editor of Ion, Alcestis, and Medea of Euripides ; Electra and Antigone of Sophocles ; Septem contra Thebas (with Dr. Verrall) ; Iliad (with Dr. Leaf); Latin Prose for Lower Forms ; Memoir of A. W. Verrall, 1913 ; Our Traditional Prosody and an Alternative (in Modern Language Review, 1918) ; The Measures of the Poets : a new system of English Prosody, 1919 ; Shakespeare's Versification with an inquiry into the Trustworthiness of the Early Texts, 1920 ; articles on Shakespeare's Versification and Handwriting, Spenser's Versification, etc., in Times Literary Supplement ; various contributions to Proceedings of S.P.R. *Address :* The Rectory, Hertingfordbury. *T. :* Hertford 113. *Club :* Alpine.(*Died 2 Aug. 1922.*)

BAYFORD, Robert Augustus, K.C. ; J.P. for Hants ; retired from the Bar ; Bencher of the Hon. Society of Inner Temple ; Treasurer, 1912 ; *b.* Albury, Surrey, 13 March 1838 ; *o. s.* of late A. F. Bayford, LL.D., formerly Chancellor of the Diocese of Manchester and Principal Registrar of H.M. Ct. of Probate, and Julia, *d.* of late Robert Ballard ; *m.* 1868, Emily Jane (*d.* 1922), *d.* of late John Deverell of Purbrook Park, Hants. *Educ. :* Kensington School ; Trin. Hall Camb. (scholar) ; Kensington exhibitioner ; Wrangler ;

1st class Law Tripos ; Law student Trinity Hall. Rowed head of the river, 1859 ; University Eleven, 1857-59; captain, 1859 ; Barr. 1868 ; Q.C. 1885 ; Bencher, 1891 ; retired, 1897. *Address :* Netley Hill, Botley, Hants. *Club :* Oxford and Cambridge. *(Died 24 Aug. 1922.)*

BAYLEY, Charles Butterworth, C.V.O. 1912 ; M.V.O. 1906 ; Govt. of Bengal, P.W.D. (retired) ; *b.* 7 Sep. 1876 ; 4th *s.* of late Sir Steuart C. Bayley, G.C.S.I. ; *m.* 1918, Violet, *d.* of late Digby Templeton Brett. *Address :* 83 Middle Road, Barrackpore, India. *Clubs :* Junior Carlton ; Bengal, Calcutta. *(Died 30 Sept. 1926.)*

BAYLEY, Charles Clive, H.B.M. Consul-General at New York since 1915 ; *b.* 20 Nov. 1864 ; *s.* of late Sir Edward Clive Bayley, K.C.S.I., C.I.E.; *m.* 1910, Constance Evelina, *d.* of Francis Ricardo of The Friary, Old Windsor. *Educ. :* Harrow ; Trinity College, Cambridge. Colonial Audit Department, 1838-93 ; Treasurer Niger Coast Protectorate, 1894-97 ; served Benin Campaign, 1897 ; H.M.'s Consul New York, 1899-1908 ; Warsaw, 1908-13 ; Visiting Consular Officer for Russia ; Consul-General at Moscow, 1913-15. *Address :* British Consulate General, New York. *Clubs :* Athenæum, Wellington. *(Died 20 Jan. 1923.)*

BAYLEY, Lt.-Col. Edward Charles, C.I.E., 1911 ; O.B.E., 1919 ; Indian Army, retired ; 4th *s.* of late George Bayley, W.S., Edinburgh ; *b.* 13 Dec. 1867 ; unmarried. *Educ. :* Private ; Sandhurst. Joined 2nd Batt. Scottish Rifles, 1887 ; transferred to 15th Lancers (Cureton's Multanis), 1890 ; was Private Secretary to the Lieutenant-Governor North-West Provinces and Oudh, 1899-1901 ; and to the Lieut.-Governor, Punjab, 1907-20 ; served with the Somaliland Field Force, 1903-4 ; retired 1920 ; received Kaisar-i-Hind Medal, 1910. *Recreations :* shooting, golf. *Club :* United Service. *(Died 26 April 1924.)*

BAYLEY, Sir Steuart Colvin, G.C.S.I., *cr.* 1911 ; K.C.S.I., *cr.* 1878 ; C.I.E. ; *b.* 26 Nov. 1886 ; *m.* Anna, *d.* of R. N. Farquharson, Bengal C.S., 1860 ; four *s.* three *d. Educ. :* Eton ; Haileybury. Commissioner of Patna, 1873-74 ; Secretary to Government of Bengal, 1877 ; Lieut.-Gov. of Bengal, 1887-90; Secretary, Political Department, India Office, 1890-1905; member of Indian Council, 1895-1905. *Address :* 2 Cathcart Road, S.W.10. *T. :* Kensington 4024. *Club :* Athenæum. *(Died 3 June 1925.)*

BAYLISS, Sir William Maddock, Kt., *cr.* 1922 ; F.R.S. 1903 ; M.A., D.Sc. (Oxon.) ; LL.D. (Hon.) Aberdeen and St. Andrews ; Professor of General Physiology in University College, London ; Member of Council, Royal Society, 1913-15; President Physiological Section, British Association, 1915 ; Treasurer of the Physiological Society, Editor of Physiological Abstracts and (with Professor Harden) of the Biochemical Journal ; Fellow of University College, London ; Hon. Fellow, Wadham College, Oxford ; Croonian Lecturer, Royal Society, 1904 ; Royal Medal, 1911 ; Copley Medal, 1919 ; Acting Professor of Physiology in University College, 1910-11 ; Baly Medal, Royal College of Physicians, 1917 ; Oliver-Sharpey Lecturer, 1918 ; Silvanus Thompson Lecturer, 1919 ; Herter Lecturer, 1922 ; Chairman, Shock Committee of Medical Research Council, and of Committee on the Biological Action of Light ; Member of Chemical Warfare Medical Committee and of Research Committee of Food Investigation Board ; Corresponding Member of Soc. de Biologie, Paris ; Assoc. Member of Royal Society of Brussels and Belgian Society of Biology ; Foreign Member Danish Acad. Sci. ; *b.* 2 May 1860 ; *s.* of Moses Bayliss, manufacturer ; *m.* 1893, Gertrude E., *d.* of Matthew Henry Starling, late Clerk of the Crown, Bombay ; three *s.* one *d. Educ. :* private school in Wolverhampton ; University College,

London ; Wadham College, Oxford. *Publica-tions :* Principles of General Physiology, 3rd ed. 1920 ; The Nature of Enzyme Action, 1908, 4th ed. 1919 ; The Physiology of Food and of Economy in Diet, 1917 ; Intravenous Injection in Wound-Shock, 1919 ; Introduction to General Physiology ; and others ; numerous articles in the Journal of Physiology and elsewhere, chiefly on the Vasomotor Nervous System and on Secre-tion ; Physical Chemistry of Enzyme-action ; Properties of Colloidal Systems. *Recreations :* lawn-tennis, music, and photography. *Address :* St. Cuthbert's, West Heath Road, N.W.3. *T.A. :* Child's Hill, N.W. *T. :* Speedwell 2267. *Club :* Athenæum.   (*Died 27 Aug. 1924.*)

BAYLY, Major-General Sir Alfred William Lambart, K.C.B., *cr.* 1911 ; K.C.M.G., *cr.* 1917 ; C.B. 1900 ; C.S.I. 1909 ; D.S.O. 1887 ; *b.* Paisley, 18 Feb. 1856 ; *y. s.* of late Major George Bayly, and Eliza, *d.* of Lieut.-Gen. Savage, R.E. ; *m.* 1st, Ada Margaret, *d.* of late Maj.-Gen. S. Thacker, Bombay Staff Corps, 1877 (*d.* 1880) ; 2nd, Eva, *d.* of late John Naylor, Leighton Hall, Montgomeryshire, 1889 ; one *s. Educ. :* Wellington College. Joined 108th Regt. 1874 ; Bombay Staff Corps, 1879 ; passed through Staff College, 1893 ; officiat-ing D.A.Q.M.G. Bombay, 1885-86 ; D.A.A. and Q.M.G. Burma Expedition, 1886-87 ; D.A.A.G. Mhow District, 1887-92 ; commanded 26th Bombay (Baluchistan Regt.), Infantry, 1896 ; Afghan War, 1880-81 ; defence and battle of Kandahar, 1880 (medal and clasp) ; Soudan, 1885 ; Suakin (medal and clasp, bronze star) ; Burma, 1886-87 (despatches, medal and two clasps, D.S.O.) ; South Africa, 1899-1900, as D.A.A.G. (despatches, medal and five clasps, C.B.) ; A.D.C. to the King, 1902-6 ; A.A.G., Dis-trict, India, 1896-1903 ; A.Q.M.G., Headquarters, India, 1903-4 ; D.A.G., Northern Command, 1904-5 ; Commandant, Indian Staff College, 1905-6 ; Col. 126th Baluchistan Infantry, now 2/10th Baluch Regt. ; Secretary to the Govern-ment of India, Army Department, 1906-9 ; retired, 1912 ; special duty War Office, 1914-18 ; Inspector of Temporary Non-Effectives, 1915-18 (despatches, K.C.M.G.). *Address :* c/o Thomas Cook & Sons, Berkeley Street, W.1. *Club :* United Service.   (*Died 27 June 1928.*)

BAYNE, William ; Lecturer in English, Training College, Dundee, since 1906. *Educ. :* Madras College and University, St. Andrews. Rector's Prize for an English Essay, Chancellor's Prize and two Gray Prizes for distinction in theological subjects ; literary work in London, 1885-92, contributed many articles to the literary supplement of the Daily Chronicle ; occupied in literary work in Edinburgh, 1892-1900 ; assistant to the Professor of English Literature, 1900-6, and Lecturer in German in St. Andrew's University, 1900-1902 ; Examiner in English, St. Andrew's Univer-sity, 1914-18. *Publications :* A Summary of the Legends in the Early South English Legendary, published by the Early English Text Society ; library, college, and school editions of Stor-month's Etymological English Dictionary ; James Thomson in the Famous Scots Series, an edition of Poems by James Thomson (Canterbury Poets), Sir David Wilkie, R.A. (Makers of British Art), etc. *Recreations :* walking, cycling, golf. *Address :* Radernie, Cupar-Fife.   (*Died 10 Nov. 1922.*)

BAYNES, Frederick, J.P., D.L. ; *b.* 1848 ; *m.* Anna Adelaide, 3rd *d.* of Thomas Simpson of Church. *Educ. :* Rugby ; Cambridge. High Sheriff of Lancashire, 1900 ; Director L. & N.W. Railway Co. ; Member of Tariff Commission ; Chairman of Cotton Trade Tariff Reform As-sociation. *Address :* Summerhill, Kidderminster. *Clubs :* Junior Carlton, Constitutional.
    (*Died 12 Nov. 1917.*)

BAYNES, Hon. Joseph, C.M.G. 1902 ; Ex-M.L.C. ; J.P. ; owner of Nel's Rust, near

Pietermaritzburg, where he has resided and farmed since 1862 ; senior member for the Ixopo since 1890 ; chairman (1902) of the Indian Immigration Trust Board, and member of the Board, 1887-1904 ; Fellow of the Royal Colonial Institute since 1885 ; and J.P. for the County of Pietermaritzburg ; *b.* near Settle, Yorkshire, England, 2 March 1842 ; *s.* of Richard Baynes ; *m.* 1st, 1874, Maria H., 2nd *d.* of Paul Hermanus Zietsman ; 2nd, Sarah A., *d.* of late Edward Tomlinson of Maritzburg. Minister of Lands and Works, 1903-4. *Address :* 289 Chapel Street, Pietermaritzburg, Natal, S.A. *Club :* Victoria, Pietermaritzburg.   (*Died July 1925.*)

BAYNES, Robert Edward ; student and tutor of Christ Church, Oxford, and Dr. Lee's Reader in Physics ; *b.* Blackburn, Lancashire, 27 Sep. 1849 ; 5th *s.* of John Baynes, J.P., D.L., Co. Lancaster, and Major in 5th Lancashire Artillery Volunteers, of Claremont, Blackburn ; *m.* 1887, Thomasine Anne, *e. d.* of Thomas Hutton of Ormskirk, Lancs. ; one *s. Educ. :* Rugby ; Wadham College, Oxford (Scholar) ; 1st class Mathematical Mods., 1870 ; 1st class Final Mathematics, 1871 ; 1st class Natural Science, 1872 ; student of Christ Church, 1873 ; censor of Christ Church, 1884-87 ; steward of Christ Church, 1895-1902 ; junior proctor, 1886 ; ex-aminer in Natural Science Honours at Oxford, 1878-79, 1881-82, 1891-92, 1897-98, 1912-14, 1916-18 ; examiner in Electricity and Magnetism at South Kensington, 1893-1900 ; Deputy Provincial Grand Master of Oxfordshire Freemasons, 1915 ; formerly Captain in the 3rd Lancashire Artillery Volunteers. *Publications :* The Book of Heat, 1878 ; Lessons on Thermodynamics, Clarendon, 1878. *Recreations :* boating and masonry. *Ad-dress :* 2 Norham Gardens, and Christ Church, Oxford.   (*Died 9 Sept. 1921.*)

BAZELEY, Rev. William, M.A., Cantab., Rector of Matson, Gloucestershire, 1875-1925 ; Hon. Canon of Gloucester Cathedral, 1901 ; *b.* St. Ives, Cornwall, 1843 ; *s.* of William Bazeley ; *m.* Henrietta, *d.* of late Rev. E. J. Selwyn, Rector of Pluckley, Kent, 1879 ; three *s.* three *d. Educ. :* Cheltenham College ; Christ's College, Cambridge. Assistant Master, Chelten-ham Coll., 1864-68 ; deacon, 1867 ; priest, 1868 ; Curate of Charlton Kings, 1867-70 ; Hornsey, 1870-75 ; Bristol and Gloucestershire Archæo-logical Society, Hon. Gen. Sec., 1879-1906 ; President, 1908-9 ; President of Council, 1908-17 ; Hon. Sec., Gloucester Diocesan Con-ference, 1892-1907 ; Hon. Local Sec., Society of Antiquaries of London ; Hon. Librarian of Gloucester Cathedral. *Publications :* Records of Matson and the Selwyns ; Matson in Tudor and Early Stuart Times ; The Bibliographer's Manual of Gloucestershire Literature (Joint Author) ; Battle of Tewkesbury, and many contributions to the Transactions of B. and G. A. S. *Recreations :* rifle shooting, shot in University V.R. match, 1868 ; Queen's Sixty, Wimbledon, 1863 ; travel, archæological re-search, numismatics, philately, mediæval stained glass, autographs, etc. *Address :* Gowan Lea, Charlton Kings, Cheltenham.
    (*Died 12 July 1925.*)

BAZLEY, Sir Thomas Sebastian, 2nd Bt., *cr.* 1869 ; M.A. Trinity College, Cambridge, J.P., D.L. ; *b.* 30 April 1829 ; *S. father* 1885 ; *m.* 1855, Elizabeth (*d.* 1890), *d.* of Robert Gardner of Chaseley, Manchester ; five *d. Heir : g. s.* Thomas Stafford, *b.* 5 Oct. 1907. *Publications :* Charts of the Stars ; books on Geo-metric Turning. *Address :* Kilmorie, Torquay.
    (*Died 6 Jan. 1919.*)

BAZLEY-WHITE, John, J.P., D.L., Kent ; *b.* 1847 ; *e. surv. s.* of J. Bazley-White, J.P., of Swanscombe, Kent, and Mary, *d.* of late William Leedham [assumed additional surname of Bazley, 1887] ; *m.* 1876, Lady Grace, *y. d.* of Countess of Rothes and Capt. Haworth-Leslie, late 60th Rifles ; two *s.* five *d.*

M.P. Gravesend, 1885-92; late Hon. Colonel 3rd Volunteer Brigade, Cinque Ports Division, R.A. *Clubs:* Carlton, Arthur's, Constitutional.
(Died 9 Feb. 1927.)

BEACHCROFT, Sir Charles Porten; Kt., *cr.* 1922; *b.* 13 March 1871; 4th *s.* of late Francis Porten Beachcroft, Bengal Civil Service; *m.* Elizabeth, *d.* of late A. E. Ryles. *Educ.:* Rugby; Clare College, Cambridge. Passed Indian Civil Service, 1890; Assistant Magistrate and Collector, Bengal, 1892; Officiating District and Sessions Judge, 1900; District and Sessions Judge, 1906; Officiating Judge, High Court, Calcutta, 1912; Additional Judge, 1913-15; Puisne Judge, High Court, Calcutta, 1915-21; retired, 1921. *Recreation:* golf. *Address:* Montjoie, Camberley. *T.:* Camberley 80. *Club:* East India United Service. *(Died 15 May 1927.)*

BEACHCROFT, Sir (Richard) Melvill, Kt., *cr.* 1904; *b.* 22 Jan. 1846; *e. s.* of Richard Beachcroft and Henrietta, *e. d.* of late Sir James Cosmo Melvill, K.C.B.; *m.* 1877, Charlotte, *d.* of late Robert M. Bonnor-Maurice, Bodynfoel Hall, Montgomeryshire. *Educ.:* Harrow. Admitted Solicitor, London, 1868; partner in Beachcroft, Thompson, & Co., 29 Bedford Square, W.C.; Solicitor to Christ's Hospital since 1873; Master of the Clothworkers' Co., 1913-14, with which Co. his name has been associated for six generations, his ancestor, Sir Robt. Beachcroft, Lord Mayor of London in 1711, having been a member and master of the Guild; an original member of the L.C.C., representing North Paddington in 1st Council; South Paddington, 1907; Alderman, 1892; Deputy Chairman, 1896; Vice-Chairman, 1897; Chairman, 1909-10; first Chairman Metropolitan Water Board, 1903-8; an old member of the Alpine Club, having served on its committee. *Address:* Littlemount, Cookham Dean; 29 Bedford Square, W.C.1. *Club:* Conservative. *(Died 11 Jan. 1926.)*

BEADON, Bt. Col. Lancelot Richmond, D.S.O. 1918; C.M.G. 1919; Assistant Director of Transport, War Office; *b.* 1875; *y. s.* of late Sir Cecil Beadon, K.C.S.I.; *m.* 1904, Hilda Marian, *o. d.* of late Maj.-Gen. A. G. Raper, C.V.O.; one *d. Educ.:* Winchester; Sandhurst. Served West Africa, 1897-8 (clasp); Sierra Leone, 1898-9 (clasp); First Commission West India Regt., 1896; Garrison Adjutant, Jamaica, 1901; Transferred to Royal Army Service Corps, 1902; A.D.C. to Major-Gen. Inf. Brigade, Gibraltar, 1903; Instructor R.M.C. Sandhurst, 1910; Commdt. Training Establishment, R.A.S.C., 1914; A.Q.M.G., G.H.Q., Dardanelles, 1915; A.Q.M.G. Northern Army Home Defence, 1916; A.Q.M.G., G.H.Q., France, 1917; Deputy Director of Transport, War Office, 1919; European War, 1914-18 (despatches thrice, D.S.O., Legion of Honour). *Address:* Mayfield, Addlestone, Surrey. *(Died 31 July 1922.)*

BEAL, Charles, F.Z.S.; late Senior Registrar, Supreme Court (Chancery Division); retired, 1912; *b.* 16 Sep. 1841; *s.* of Henry Ridley Beal, Solicitor, London. *Educ.:* King's College School. Admitted a Solicitor, 1863; appointed to Chancery Registrars' Office, 1864. *Recreations:* shooting and fishing. *Address:* 14 Pall Mall, S.W. *Clubs:* Junior Carlton, Garrick, Thatched House. *(Died 23 Jan. 1921.)*

BEALE, Sir William Phipson, 1st Bart., *cr.* 1912; K.C., F.G.S., F.C.S.; M.P. (L.) S. Ayrshire, 1906-18; *b.* 29 Oct. 1839; *e. s.* of William John Beale, Bryntirion, Merionethshire; *m.* 1869, Mary, *e. d.* of William Thompson, late of Sydney, New South Wales. *Educ.:* Heidelberg and Paris. Bar, Lincoln's Inn, 1867; Bencher, 1892. *Heir:* none. *Address:* 6 Stone Buildings, Lincoln Inn, W.C.; Drumlamford, Barrhill, Ayrshire. *Clubs:* Savile. Reform, Albemarle. *(Died 13 April 1922.)*

BEALL, Captain George, I.S.O. 1903; F.R.G.S.; *s* of late George Beall(Inland Revenue), Kingston-on-Thames; *b.* 17 Nov. 1840; *m.* 1866,

Annie Robinson Grace (*d.* 1915); went to sea, East India service, 1857; joined John Bibby & Co.; first command, 1865; several years Examiner in Navigation and Nautical Astronomy to H.M.'s training ship Conway; inventor of Deviascope for magnetic work (Gold Medal and Diploma, Liverpool International Exhibition, 1886); Younger Brother of Trinity House; late Principal Examiner of Masters and Mates to Board of Trade; retired 1908. *Publication:* Handbook to Deviascope, with short treatise on magnetism. *Recreations:* golf, croquet, etc. *Address:* London County and Westminster Bank, Ltd., Eastbourne, Sussex.
(Died 28 June 1918.)

BEAMAN, Sir Frank (Clement Offley), Kt., *cr.* 1917; philosophical writer; *b.* 27 Nov. 1858; *s.* of late Surg.-Gen. A. H. Beaman; *m.* 1st, 1881, Caroline Emily Banks; one *s.* two *d.;* 2nd, 1926, Mrs Wilson-Dickson. *Educ.:* Bedford Grammar School; Queen's College, Oxford. Entered I.C.S. 1879; Assist. Judge, 1885; Special Settlement Officer, Baroda, 1886, 1887; Judicial Assist. to Political Agent, Kathia, war, 1891; Judge and Sessions Judge, 1896; Judicial Commissioner and Judge of Sadar Court in Sind, 1904-6; a Puisne Judge High Court, Bombay, 1906-18. *Address:* 18 Palace Gardens Terrace, Kensington, W.8. *T.:* Park 6062. *Club:* Savile. *(Died 12 Aug. 1928.)*

BEAN, Alderman Sir George, Kt., *cr.* 1919; Chairman of Birmingham and Midland Hospital; Trustee for R.U. Dudley's Homes for the Poor of Dudley; *b.* 27 April 1855; *m. d.* of John Harper, Dudley; one *s.* two *d.* Has been three times Mayor of Dudley; Alderman of the Town Council; Chairman of A. Harper, Son & Bean, Dudley, Motor Manufacturers, also Allen Everitt & Sons, Smethwick, and Manning, Wardle & Co., Ltd., Locomotive Manufacturers, Leeds. *Address:* Oakham Lodge, Dudley.
(Died 23 Jan. 1924.)

BEANLANDS, Rev. Arthur John, M.A., F.S.A.; *s.* of Arthur Beanlands, M.A., J.P., late Treasurer of Durham University; *b.* 1857: *m.* 1st 1884, Laura Maud, *e. d.* of Walter A. Hills, M.A., barrister; 2nd 1905, Sophia Theresa (artist and exhibitor), 2nd *d.* of Joseph Despard Pemberton, M.A., 1st surveyor-general of Vancouver Island; one *s.* two *d. Educ.:* Durham School and University. After serving curacies in the Durham and Oxford dioceses was appointed Sub-Dean Christ Church Cathedral, Victoria, B.C., 1884; instrumental in establishing the Provincial Museum, and Natural History Society of B.C., of which he served as President, also the Yorkshire Society of B.C.; wrote several pamphlets for the Government on the condition and prospects of the Province, and addressed the R.C. Institute, 1892, on the same. Instrumental in the passing of the Habitual Drunkards Bill, one of the earliest efforts of legislation in that direction; Rector of the Cathedral, 1892; Canon Residentiary, 1891; Hon. Canon 1909; Hon. Chap. Govern.-Gen. of the Dominion 1895; was a member of the Diocesan Synod; elected continuously 1884-1909; a member of the 1st, 2nd, and 3rd General Synods of the C. of E. in Canada. Resigned and returned to England 1909. *Recreations:* archæology, heraldry and genealogy. *Address:* Wickhurst Manor, Weald, Sevenoaks. *T.A.:* Weald. *T:* Sevenoaks, 247.
(Died 26 Sept. 1917.)

BEARD, Charles Thomas, C.B. 1917; I.S.O. 1903; Secretary to the Irish Land Commission, Dublin; *b.* 18 Oct. 1858; *s.* of late C. T. Beard, Horfield, Glos.; *m.* 1st, Alice C. (*d.* 1886), *d.* of J. Mackay; 2nd, Gertrude A. M., *d.* of E. J. Figgis, J.P. *Educ.:* privately; Trinity College, Dublin; B.A., 1st Senior Moderator and Gold Medallist, Wray Prizeman, etc. Entered Civil Service, 1877; has been Private Secretary to the Chief Secretary and to successive Under Secretaries

for Ireland, and Chief Clerk at the Irish Office, Westminster, S.W. *Recreation:* golf. *Address:* Falmore, Shankill, Co. Dublin. *Clubs:* Royal Societies; University, Dublin.
(*Died 26 May 1918.*)

BEARD, Lt.-Col. George John Allen, D.S.O. 1916; Union Defence Force, S. Africa; *b.* Gloucester, England; *m.* E. M. Myers, Potchefstroom, Transvaal; one *s.* one *d. Educ.:* Sir Thos. Rich's School, Gloucester (winner of open scholarship); Borough Road College, London. Matriculated London University, 1898; served S.A. Rebellion as Captain 11th Mounted Regiment, Oct. 1914; Major and D.A.Q.M.G. 4th Mounted Brigade in German South-West Africa campaign; Lt.-Col. and A.A. and Q.M.G. 2nd Division in German East Africa campaign (D.S.O., despatches). *Recreations:* all-round sportsman, played in representative football and cricket, keen oarsman, President Potchefstroom Rugby F.C., winner several home boxing competitions. *Address:* Cymry, Maré St., Potchefstroom. *T.:* Potchefstroom 102. *Club:* Potchefstroom. (*Died 16 Aug. 1922.*)

BEARÉ, John Isaac, M.A., Fellow and Senior Tutor, Trinity College, Dublin; late Regius Professor of Greek (sometime Professor of Moral Philosophy) University of Dublin. *Publications:* Editor of Select Satires of Horace, 2nd ed., 1887; articles in newer edition of Smith's Dictionary of Classical Antiquities; articles and reviews in Mind and the International Journal of Ethics on philosophical subjects; papers in the Classical Review and in Hermathena on subjects of classical and philosophical criticism; Greek Theories of Elementary Cognition, from Alcmæon to Aristotle, 1906; and a translation (with notes) of Aristotle de Sensu, de Memoria, de Somno, de Somniis, and de Divinatione per Somnum, 1908. *Address:* Carisbrooke, 14 Bushy Park Road, Dublin. *Club:* University, Dublin. (*Died 13 Nov. 1918.*)

BEARNE, Catherine Mary; *e. d.* of late Thomas Broughton Charlton of Chilwell Hall, Notts; *m.* 1882, E. H. Bearne (*decd.*). *Publications:* Lives of the Early Valois Queens; Pictures of the Old French Court; The Cross of Pearls; A Leader of Society at Napoleon's Court; A Queen of Napoleon's Court; Heroines of French Society; A Sister of Marie Antoinette; A Royal Quartette; Four Fascinating Frenchwomen; A Court Painter and his Circle. *Address:* 26 The Parks, Minehead, Somerset. (*Died 9 May 1923.*)

BEARSTED, 1st Viscount, *cr.* 1925, of Maidstone; Baron, *cr.* 1921; **Marcus Samuel,** 1st Bt., *cr.* 1903; Kt., *cr.* 1898; LL.D. Sheffield, 1924; LL.D. Cambridge (Hon.), 1925; D.L. of City; Justice of the Peace for Kent; *b.* 5 Nov. 1853; 2nd *s.* of late Marcus Samuel; *m.* 1881, Fanny Elizabeth, *o. d.* of late Benjamin Benjamin; one *s.* two *d. Educ.:* privately. Travelled widely in Far East and Japan; introduced transport of petroleum in bulk through Suez Canal; knighted for services rendered to H.M.S. "Victorious," 1898; Alderman of City of London, 1891-1902; Lord Mayor of London, 1902-3; Sheriff, 1894-95; developed large oilfields in the Far East and received official vote of thanks from Lord Commissioner of the Admiralty in May 1915, for "services of the utmost importance to the fighting forces at the present time"; Peerage bestowed for eminent public and national services; Lord of Manor Mote; Commander of Order of Leopold of Belgium; Grand Officer, Legion of Honour; Freeman of city of Sheffield and town of Maidstone; Knight Commander Order of Rising Sun, Japan; 2nd Class Sacred Treasure, Japan. Owns about 2000 acres. *Recreations:* fishing, literature. *Heir: s.* Capt. Hon. Walter Horace Samuel. *Address:* 3 Hamilton Place, W.1; *T.:* Grosvenor 2652; The Mote, Kent; *T.:* Maidstone 411. *Club:* Carlton. (*Died 17 Jan. 1927.*)

BEATTIE, Rt. Hon. Sir Andrew, Kt., *cr.* 1920; P.C. Ireland, 1921; D.L., J.P., F.I.D.; a Senator of Southern Ireland; *b.* Rathfriland, Co. Down; *m.* Rachel, M.B.E., J.P., *d.* of late Thomas Brien, Lanistown House, Co. Dublin; four *s. Educ.:* privately. Civic and Social Worker; contested seat for Parliament on three occasions (West Down, Ireland); member of the Governing Body, University College, Dublin; Commissioner of National Education, Ireland; High Sheriff of Dublin, 1918; member of the College of Nursing, Royal Dublin Society; Royal Zoological Society of Ireland; member of the General Council of County Councils of Ireland; member of the Board of Agriculture and Technical Instruction, Ireland; member of the Corporation of Dublin for over 25 years; as Alderman and Councillor has been Chairman of most of the important Committees; member of the Statistical and Social Inquiry Society of Ireland. *Recreations:* riding, driving, and motoring. *Address:* 46 Fitzwilliam Square, Dublin. *T.A.:* Beattie, Dublin. *T.:* Dublin 162. *Club:* National Liberal. (*Died 1923.*)

BEATTY, Major Charles Harold Longfield, D.S.O. 1900; Staff, 1st Canadian Division; late 6th Batt. Royal Warwickshire Regt.; *b.* 16 Jan. 1870; *e. s.* of Capt. D. L. Beatty (late 4th Hussars) of Borodale, Co. Wexford, Ireland; *m.* 1905, Lucy Alice, *widow* of J. S. Langlands, Major 43rd Light Infantry; one *s.* Served South Africa (despatches twice, medal, 5 clasps); European War, 1914-15 (despatches). *Address:* Oakfield Atherstone, Borodale, Co. Wexford. *Club:* Junior United Service.
(*Died 17 May 1917.*)

BEATTY, Haslitt Michael, C.M.G. 1902; Ex-Chief Locomotive Superintendent, Cape Government Railways, South Africa. *Address:* Rosclare, Rouwkoop Road, Rondebosch, Cape Town. *Club:* Senior Civil Service, Cape Town. (*Died 13 June 1916.*)

BEATTY, Wallace, M.D. Univ. Dub.; F.R.C.P.I.; Physician to the Adelaide Hospital, Dublin; Hon. Professor of Dermatology, Trinity College, Dublin; *b.* Halifax, Nova Scotia, 13 Nov. 1853; *s.* of James Beatty (*d.* 1856), Engineer-in-Chief of the Balaklava Railway during the Crimean War, and Sarah Jane (*d.* 1888), *d.* of Rev. Henry Anthony Burke; *m.* Frances Eleanor (*d.* 1908), *d.* of late Samuel Edge, M.D., Grantstown, Queen's Co.; three *s. Educ.:* Royal School, Dungannon; Trinity College, Dublin (Royal Scholarship, 1872; Classical Scholarship, 1875; Medical Scholarship, 1877). B.A. 1876; M.B., B.Ch. 1879; M.D. 1886; F.R.C.P.I. 1887. *Publications:* Lectures on Diseases of the Skin, 1922; various articles in medical journals, the majority on dermatological subjects. *Recreations:* no special recreations; when a student in Trinity College was a footballer. *Address:* 38 Merrion Square, Dublin. *T.:* Dublin 1273. (*Died 8 Nov. 1923.*)

BEAUCHAMP, Sir Edward, 1st Bt., *cr.* 1911; M.P. (L.) Lowestoft, Northern Division of Suffolk, 1906-10, and 1910-22; *b.* 12 Apr. 1849; *s.* of late Rev. Wm. Henry Beauchamp, Rector of Chedgrave, Norfolk, and *g.s.* of Admiral Sir William Beauchamp-Proctor, 3rd Bart.; *m.* 1st, 1875, Frances Mary (*d.* 1886), *d.* of His Hon. Judge Stephen, LL.D., Newport House, Lincoln; 2nd, 1890, Betty Campbell, *d.* of late Archibald Woods, Columbus, Ohio, U.S.A.; one *s. Educ.:* privately, and in Royal Navy. Served as midshipman in Royal Navy; retired, 1867; member of Lloyds since 1873; Deputy-Chairman, 1900; Chairman, 1905 and 1913. *Heir: s.* Brograve Campbell [*b.* 5 May 1897; *m.* 1923, Lady Evelyn Leonora Almina Herbert, *e. d.* of 5th Earl of Carnarvon]. *Address:* 26 Grosvenor Place, S.W.1. *T.:* Victoria 3899.
(*Died 1 Feb. 1925.*)

BEAUCHAMP, Sir Sydney, Kt., *cr.* 1920; M.B., B.C., Camb.; M.A.; Physician; *b.* 18 May 1861; *s.* of late Henry Herron Beauchamp of Bexley, Kent; *m.*; one *s.* one *d.* *Educ.*: Lausanne; University College School; Caius College, Cambridge. Medical Officer-in-charge West Park Military Hospital, 1914-16; Physician to Officers' Families' Fund Lying-in Hospital; Resident Medical Officer to British Delegation during Peace Conference in Paris; Visiteur medical des Hôpitaux Croix Rouge Française. *Address*: 8 William Street, Lowndes Square, S.W.1; Salter's Meadow, Penn, Bucks. *T.*: Kensington 514. *Club*: United University.
(*Died 22 Nov. 1921.*)

BEAUFORT, 9th Duke of (*cr.* 1682), **Henry Adelbert Wellington FitzRoy Somerset**; Baron Botetourt, 1305, confirmed, 1803; Baron Herbert of Raglan, Chepstow, and Gower, 1506; Earl of Worcester, 1514; Marquess of Worcester, 1642; J.P., D.L.; Hon. Col. Royal Glos. Hussars; M.F.H. Badminton Hunt; *b.* 19 May 1847; *e. s.* of 8th Duke and Lady Georgiana Charlotte Curzon, *d.* of 1st Earl Howe; S. father, 1899; *m.* Louise Emily, *d.* of William H. Harford of Oldown, Almondsbury, Gloucestershire, and *widow* of Baron Carlo de Tuyll, 1895; one *s.* two *d.* Captain Royal Horse Guards, 1865-78. Owns about 52,000 acres. *Heir*: *s.* Marquess of Worcester. *Address*: Badminton, R.S.O. Gloucestershire. *T.A.*: Badminton. *T.*: P.O. Badminton. *M.*: AD 195. (*Died 27 Nov. 1924.*)

BEAUFORT, Sir Leicester Paul, Kt., *cr.* 1919; M.A., B.C.L., barrister-at-law; *b.* Warburton, Cheshire, 13 Dec. 1853; 2nd *s.* of late Rev. D. A. Beanfort and Emily Nowell, *d.* of Sir John F. Davis, 1st Bart., K.C.B., D.C.L.; *m.* 1888, Edith M., *d.* of late Rev. C. H. Griffith, B.A., F.R.M.S., of Strathfield Turgis, Hants. *Educ.*: Westminster; Oxford. Barrister Inner Temple, 1879; member of the London School Board, 1888; Gov. Sec. and Judicial Commissioner, B.N.B., 1889; received the Jubilee Medal; Gov. and Commander-in-Chief of the Colony of Labuan, and of the State of N. Borneo, 1895-1900; Chief Justice, Northern Rhodesia, 1901-18; retired. *Recreations*: shooting, fishing, golf. *Address*: Sandown, Wynberg, C.C., Africa.
(*Died 12 Aug. 1926.*)

BEAUFOY, Mark Hanbury, J.P.; *b.* 1854; *o. s.* of late Geo. Beaufoy; *m.* 1884, Mildred Scott, *d.* of Robert Tait; three *s.* one *d.* *Educ.*: Eton; Trinity Hall, Cambridge. M.P. Kennington, 1889-95. *Address*: Coombe House, Shaftesbury. *Clubs*: Kennel, New University.
(*Died 10 Nov. 1922.*)

BEAUMONT, Hon. Hubert; *b.* 6 Apr. 1864; 3rd *s.* of 1st Baron Allendale, *m.* 1900, Elisa Mercedes (*d.* 1917); *e. d.* of M. P. Grace; one *s.* *duc.*: Eton; Cheltenham; Balliol College, Oxford. Contested King's Lynn, 1895; North Bucks, 1900; Barnard Castle, 1908; M.P. (R.) Eastbourne Division of Sussex, 1906-1910. *Address*: 16 Dorset Square, N.W.1; *T.*: Paddington 5496; Wotton House, Aylesbury; *T.*: Aylesbury 130. *Clubs*: Brooks's, Garrick, Reform. (*Died 14 Aug. 1922.*)

BEAUMONT, Admiral Sir Lewis Anthony, G.C.B., *cr.* 1911; K.C.B., *cr.* 1904; K.C.M.G., *cr.* 1901; F.R.G.S.; Grand Officer, Legion of Honour; *b.* 19 May 1847; *m.* 1889, Mary Eleanor (*d.* 1907), *d.* of Charles C. Perkins of Boston, U.S.A. Entered R.N. 1860; Rear-Admiral, 1897; served Arctic Expedition, 1875-76 (promoted, Arctic medal); Naval Attaché for Europe, 1882; Private Secretary to the Earl of Northbrook, 1883-85, as First Lord of Admiralty and High Commissioner to Egypt, 1894; Director of Naval Intelligence, 1894-99; A.D.C. to Queen, 1895-97; Commander-in-Chief, Pacific, 1899-1900; Commander-in-Chief, Australia, 1901-3; Commissioner on the Paris Court of Enquiry, 1904; Admiral, 1906; Commander-in-Chief, Devonport, 1905-8; First and Principal Naval A.D.C. to the King, 1911; retired, 1912. *Address*: St. Georges, Hurstpierpoint, Sussex. *Club*: United Service.
(*Died 19 June 1922.*)

BEAUMONT, Roberts, M.Sc.,M.I.Mech.E.; Prof. of Textile Industries, Leeds Univ., 1889-1913; founder of the Departments of Woollen and Worsted Yarn Manufacture (English and Continental Systems), of the Clothworkers' Museums, and of the Textile Research and Analytical Laboratories, also reorganiser of the Departments of Textile Design, Manufacture, and Fabric Finishing; *b.* 1862; 3rd *s.* of late Prof. John Beaumont; *m.* Annie, 2nd *d.* of late E. J. Rawlins, principal of the firm of the Leeds Colour Works: two *s.* Inspector of Textile Insts. City and Guilds of London Inst. 1892-1916; Vice-Pres. of the International Jury on Textile Machinery, Paris Exhibition, 1900; holds silver medal of Society of Arts; special medal awarded by City and Guilds of London Institute for services as Examiner in Woollen and Worsted Weaving and Designing, 1892-1906. *Publications*: Woollen and Worsted; Colour in Woven Design; Wool Manufacture (Fabrication pratique des lainages); Standard Cloths: Structure and Manufacture; Finishing of Textile Fabrics (Apprêt des tissus); Union Textile Fabrication; Woven Fabrics at the World's Fair, Chicago; articles on Woollen and Worsted Manufacturing and Textiles in Chambers's Encyclopedia, and Newnes' Technological and Scientific Dictionary; on Textile Educational Preparedness; British Dyes—Technical Research, etc.; Director of the Expert and Advisory Department, Textile Interests, Ltd. *Address*: 1 Grosvenor Terrace, Headingley, Leeds; 5 Cheapside, Bradford.

BEAUMONT, Somerset Archibald, D.L.; *b.* 1836; 3rd *s.* of late T. Wentworth Beaumont, M.P., of Bretton, Yorks. *Educ.*: Harrow; Trinity College, Cambridge. M.P., Newcastle, 1860-65; Wakefield, 1868-74; promoted Commercial Treaty by inquiring into Austrian Tariff, 1865; one of the founders (with Messrs. Glyn and Co.) of the Anglo-Austrian Bank. *Address*: Skere, Guildford. *Clubs*: Travellers', St. James's, Burlington Fine Arts.
(*Died 8 Dec. 1921.*)

BEAZLEY, Patrick Langford, editor of the Catholic Times since 1884; *b.* 1859; *s.* of James Beazley, Aghadoe, Killarney; *m.* 1880, Nannie H., *d.* of P. E. Hickey, Newcastle West, Co. Limerick; two *s.* *Educ.*: St. Brendan's Seminary, Killarney; Paris. A journalist for thirty-five years. *Publications*: stories, biographies, poems, etc. *Recreations*: walking and boating. *Address*: Glengariff, Rudgrave Square, Egremont, Cheshire. (*Died 30 Nov. 1923.*)

BECK, Col. Hon. Sir Adam, K.B., *cr.* 1914; LL.D.; Member Legislative Assembly 1905-1919; Chairman of the Hydro-Electric Power Commission since 1906; President London Health Association since 1910; gazetted Colonel of the Canadian Militia, 1912; M.F.H. of the London Hunt: London, Ontario; *s.* of Jacob Beck, and Charlotte, *d.* of George Hespeler; *b.* Baden, Ontario, 20 June 1857; *m.* 1898, Lilian (*d.* 1921), *o. c.* of late C. J. Ottaway; one *d.* *Educ.*: Gait. Mayor of London, Ont., 1902, 1903, and 1904; Episcopalian; manufacturer. *Address*: Headley, London, Ontario, Canada. *Clubs*: Albany, Toronto; London.
(*Died Aug. 1925.*)

BECK, Edward Anthony; Master of Trinity Hall, Cambridge, since 1902; *b.* 21 March 1848; *s.* of late John Redin Beck, of Castle Rising, Norfolk; *m.* 1874, E. M., *d.* of late Jas. Clark, of Winchmore Hill; two *s.* three *d.* *Educ.*: Bishop Stortford Grammar School, Trinity Hall, Cambridge (Scholar, 1867; 1st Class in Classical Tripos, 1871; Fellow, 1871). Chancellor's English Medallist, 1868 and 1870;

72

Seatonian Prizeman, 1874; Assistant Tutor, 1875; Deputy Esquire Bedell, 1876.; Junior Tutor, 1885; Senior Tutor, 1887; served as one of the Proctors or Pro-Proctors for six years between 1881 and 1888; eight years member Council of Senate; Vice-Chancellor, 1904-5 and 1905-6. *Publication:* edited Euripides' Heracleidæ, 1881. *Address:* The Lodge, Trinity Hall, Cambridge.
(Died 12 April 1916.)

BECK, Rev. Edward Josselyn; Hon. Canon of Southwark Cathedral; *b.* 1832; *s.* of Henry Beck of Needham Market, Suffolk; *m.* 1865, Mary Coleridge, *d.* of Charles Bradshaw Stutfield, J.P. *Educ.:* Ipswich School. Formerly Curate of Christ Church, St. Pancras, N.W.; Fellow and Dean of Clare College, Cambridge; Rector of Rotherhithe, S.E., 1867-1907. *Publication:* History of the Parish of St. Mary, Rotherhithe, 1907. *Address:* 4 Scroope Terrace, Cambridge. *(Died 17 Oct. 1924.)*

BECK, Rev. Frederick John; Prebendary of Llandaff. *Address:* Honiton.
(Died 10 June 1922.)

BECK, Hon. Sir Johannes Henricus Meiring, Kt., *cr.* 1911; M.D., F.R.S.E., J.P.; Minister of Posts and Telegraphs, Union of S. Africa, since 1916; Senator since 1910, and Chairman of Committees of Senate; *b.* Worcester, Cape Province, 1855; *s.* of late C. Beck, J.P., of Worcester (Cape); *m.* 1855, Mary Emily, *d.* of W. C. Kuijs of Napier (Cape); three *d. Educ.:* Worcester Public School; S. African College; University of Edinburgh; Berlin, and Vienna. Graduated in medicine, Edinburgh University, 1879 (First Cl. Honours and Beavey Scholarship); M.L.A. Worcester (Cape), 1898-10; one of the delegates from Cape of Good Hope to S. African National Convention; Member of Council, University, Cape of Good Hope, 1888-1912; ex-President, Cape Medical Council. *Publications:* Numerous contributions on hygienic and medical subjects to British and S. African medical and scientific journals. *Recreations:* Horticultural farming, music. *Address:* De Oude' Brostdii, Tulbagh, S. Africa. *Club:* Civil Service, Capetown. *(Died May 1919.)*

BECK, Hon. Nicholas Du Bois Dominic, Puisne Judge of the Supreme Court of Alberta since 1907; one of the Justices of the Appellate Division since 1921; *b.* Cobourg, Ontario, 4 May 1857; *s.* of Rev. J.·W. R. Beck, M.A., for many years Anglican Rector of Peterborough, Ontraio, and Georgina Boulton; *m.* 1st, Mary Ethel Lloyd; two *s.* two *d.*; 2nd, Louisa Teefy. *Educ.:* private schools; Peterborough Collegiate Institute; LL.B. University of Toronto. Admitted to Ontario Bar, 1879; Manitoba, 1883; Bar of North-West Territories, 1889; Q.C., Dominion, 1893; Member and Chairman of the Territorial Educational Council till the formation of the Provinces of Alberta and Saskatchewan, 1905, and since then of Educational Council of Alberta; Member of the Senate and Vice-Chancellor of the University of Alberta; Editor of the Territorial Law Reports, published by the Territorial Law Society, which has now ceased to exist; one of the Board of Management of the Catholic Extension Society of Canada; a member of the Board of Governors of St. Joseph s (Catholic) College, affiliated to the University of Alberta; became a Catholic, 1889. *Publications:* Edited for some years the Catholic North-West Review. *Recreations:* reading, bridge, golf. *Address:* Edmonton, Alberta, Canada. *T.:* 82349. *Clubs:* Edmonton, Edmonton Golf and Country.
(Died 14 May 1928.)

BECKER, Sir Walter (Frederick), K.B.E., *cr.* 1918; Consul-General, Province of Piemonte, for the King of Siam; Chairman of Board of Governors of the British Institute of Florence; Knight Commander of the Order of the Crown of Siam; *b.* 9 March 1855; *s.* of late Frederick Becker; *m.* 1895, Delphine Thérèse, *d.* of late Alphonse de Martelly; no *c. Educ.:* Falmouth Classical and Grammar School. Engaged in ship-owning in various countries, since 1880 in Sicily and Italy; founded, maintained, and acted as Chairman of Maternity and Rescue Home, Turin; founded, maintained, and directed a hospital in Turin for British Expeditionary Force in Italy; war work of various kinds for British sailors and soldiers; local war propaganda work. *Recreations:* study, golf, tennis, sailing, motoring. *Address:* Val Salice, nr. Turin; Villa Delphine, Roquebrune, Cap·Martin, France. *Clubs:* Royal Automobile; Royal Cornwall Yacht; Royal Automobile of Italy, Union, Rome. *(Died 1 May 1927.)*

BECKETT, Brig.·Gen. Charles Edward, C.B. 1898; J.P., Dorset; *b.* 11 June 1849; *s.* of late Chas. Wm. Beckett of Thorne, Yorks; *m.* 1st, Louisa Augusta (d. 1900), *y. d.* of late Field-Marshal Sir J. Michel, G.C.B.; one *d.*; 2nd, Mary Philippa, *d.* of late J. A. Farrell, D.L., J.P., Moynalty, Co. Meath, and *widow* of M. Kenneth Angelo, Culachy, Fort Augustus. *Educ.:* privately. Joined 7th Dragoon Guards, 1869; Adjutant, 1872-77; Brigade-Major, Egypt, 1882-83; Asst. Military Secretary, Ireland, 1886-1888; D.A.A.G. Ireland, 1888-91; commanded 2nd Dragoon Guards, 1892-95; commanded 3rd Hussars, 1895-98; A.D.GO., War Office, 1898-99; A.A.G., Natal, 1899-1901; A.Q.M.G., War Office, 1901-3; served in Egyptian Campaign, 1882; Nile Expedition, 1884-85; South Africa, 1899-1900 (wounded Dundee, despatches); Chief Staff Officer, Malta, 1904-6; Br.-General in charge Administration, Malta, 1905-6; retired 1906; Command of 2nd S.W. Mounted Brigade, 1908-1912, and of 2/1st East Lancashire Division, 1914-15. *Recreations:* hunting, shooting. *Address:* Culachy, Fort Augustus.
(Died 17 Sept. 1925.)

BECKETT, Lt.-Col. John Douglas Mortimer, D.S.O. 1915; 1st Batt. Hants Regt.; *b.* 12 May 1881; *s.* of late Col. Beckett, Royal Fusiliers; *m.* 1915, Wilmet Rose, *d.* of Col. Lumley Peyton, Rosslyn, Winchester. Entered army, 1901; Lieut. Hants Regiment, 1903; Captain, 1907; Major, 1916; Lt.-Col., 1916; served South Africa, ·1901-2 (Queen's medal, 5 clasps); European War, 1914-17 (D.S.O., Bt. Lt.-Col.). *Address:* Bramerton, Norfolk.
(Died 9 Feb. 1918.)

BECKETT, Colonel Stephen, C.B. 1885; retired I.S C.; *b.* 1840; 5th *s.* of late Captain J. O. Beckett, H.E.I.C.S.; *m.* 1st, Cecilia, *d.* of P. Griffith (d. 1889); 2nd, Ida Maud, *d.* of John Macfarlane, 1894; two *s. Educ.:* Private School and Edinburgh Academy. Ensign H.E.I.C.S. 1857; attached 54th Regt. 1857-58; Punjab Frontier Force, 1858-69; Asst. Political Agent and Supdt., Bahawalpur, 1869-79; Commissariat Dept., 1879-81; 31st Punjab Infry., 1881-82; Commissariat and Transport Dept., 1882-87; commanded 38th Bengal Infry., 1887-1889; served in Indian Mutiny (despatches, dangerously wounded, medal); Umbeylah campaign, 1868-64 (despatches twice, medal with clasp); commanded Bahawalpur contingent on Dera Ghazi Khan Frontier during 1st Kabul campaign, 1879; Suakin, 1885, as Director of Indian Transport with British troops (despatches, medal with clasp, Khedive's star, C.B.). *(Died 19 Nov. 1921.)*

BECKETT, Walter Ralph Durie, C.M.G. 1909; F.R.G.S.; Consul-General, Dutch East Indies, since 1913; *b.* Agra, N.W.P., India, 24 Aug. 1864; *s.* of Col. W. H. Beckett; *m.* 1911, Ivy Nina, *d.* of H. R. Goring. *Educ.:* Tonbridge School. Passed a competitive examination, 1886; student interpreter, Siam, 1886; 2nd Assistant, 1888; 1st Assist. 1891; H.M. Vice-Con. at Bangkok, 1893; Acting Con. 11 April to 22 Oct. 1894; acted as Chargé d'Affaires, 23 Oct. to 6 Nov.

1894; Acting Consul, 1894-95, when he was again in charge of the Legation; H.M. Consul for territories of Chiengmai, Lampun, Lakhon, Phré, Nan, etc. (Northern Siam), 1897; H.M. Consul at Bangkok, 1903, and granted local rank of First Secretary 1904: Chargé d'Affaires during 1904, 1906, 1907, 1908, 1909, 1910, 1911, 1912, and 1913; H.B.M. Consul-General, Bangkok, Siam, 1913. *Recreations:* cricket, polo, tennis, golf, etc. *Address:* H.B.M. Consulate-General, Batavia, Java. *Clubs:* Oriental, Queen's.
(Died 18 Sept. 1917.)

BECTIVE, Countess of, Lady Alice; *d.* of 4th Marquess of Downshire; *m.* 1867, Thomas, Earl of Bective, *er. s.* of 3rd Marquess of Headfort. *Address:* 29 Eaton Place, S.W.; Lunefield, Kirkby Lonsdale, Westmorland.
(Died 25 Feb. 1928.)

BEDALE, Rev. Frederick; Vicar of St. Mary's, Nuneaton, since 1903; Canon of Coventry Cathedral, 1920; *s.* of late John Bedale, Streatham; *m.* Mary, *d.* of Staff Commander R. A. Burstal, R.N.; two *s.* four *d.* *Educ.:* Worcester College, Oxford. Curate of Christ Church, Luton, 1891-96; Vicar of Pirton, Herts, 1896-1903. *Address:* St. Mary's Vicarage, Nuneaton, Warwickshire. *(Died 8 Nov. 1924.)*

BEDDARD, Frank Evers, M.A., D.Sc., F.R.S. 1892; formerly Prosector of Zoological Society, 1884-1915 and Lecturer on Biology at Guy's Hospital; has been Examiner in Zoology and Comparative Anatomy, University of London, and of Morphology at Oxford, and in the University of New Zealand; *b.* Dudley, 19 June 1858; *s.* of late John Beddard. *Educ.:* Harrow; New College Oxford. Naturalist to "Challenger" Expedition Commission, 1882-84. *Publications:* Animal Coloration, 1892; Text-book of Zoogeography, 1895; A Monograph of the Oligochæta, 1895; Structure and Classification of Birds, 1898; many papers in the Transactions of Royal Societies of London and Edinburgh, of the Zoological Society, and the Quarterly Journal of Microscopic Science, etc. *Recreation:* conversation at clubs. *Address:* Zoological Society's Gardens, Regent's Park, N.W. *Clubs:* United University, Royal Societies.
(Died 14 July 1925.)

BEDFORD, Maj.-Gen. Sir Walter George Augustus, K.C.M.G., *cr.* 1918; C.B. 1916; C.M.G. 1900; (Hon.) D.C.L. Durh.; M.B.; *b.* 24 Oct. 1858; *s.* of Vice-Admiral G. A. Bedford; *m.* 1880, Harriette Adelaide, *d.* of Rev. D. J. Drakeford, M.A.; one *d.* *Educ.:* St. Bartholomew's Hospital; University of Durham. Headquarters, War Office, 1894-99; Staff Officer to the Surgeon-General, Army Headquarters, S. African Field Force, 1899-1901 (despatches, C.M.G.); P.M.O., South China, 1908-11; Deputy-Director of Medical Services, London District, 1912; Deputy-Director of Medical Services, South Africa, 1914; Deputy Director of Medical Services, Southern Command, 1914-1915; Director of Medical Services, Mediterranean, and Egyptian Expeditionary Forces, 1915-16 (despatches, C.B.); Deputy Director of Medical Services, Northern Command, 1916-1919. *Address:* The Holt, Eynsham, Oxon. *Club:* Junior United Service. *(Died 8 Jan. 1922.)*

BEDFORD, Rev. William Campbell Riland, M.A.; *b.* May 29, 1852; *s.* of late Rev. W. K. Riland Bedford, late Rector of Sutton Coldfield; *m.* 1877, Eleanor Phœbe, *d.* of Sir James T. Chance, 1st Bart.; one *s.* three *d.* *Educ.:* Westminster; Clare College, Cambridge. Curate of St. Michael's, Coventry, 1875-77; All Saints, Leamington, 1878; Vicar of Little Aston, 1878-81; Curate of Sutton Coldfield, 1882-87; Vicar of Knowle, Warwickshire, 1889-92; late Rural Dean of Sutton Coldfield; Hon. Canon of Birmingham; Rector of Sutton Coldfield, Warwickshire, 1892-1908; Grand Chaplain of England (Masonic), 1902; P.P.S.W.,

Warwickshire; P.M., Warden Lodge, 794. *Recreation:* archery. *Address:* Cotswold, Leamington. *T.:* 487. *(Died 15 Aug. 1922.)*

BEDWELL, Rev. Francis, B.D.; late Hon. Canon of Llandaff. *Educ.:* Corpus Christi College, Oxford. Curate of St. Woolos, Newport, Mon., 1861-72; Rector of Holy Trinity, Pillgwenlly, 1872-85; Vicar of Caerleon, Mon., 1885-1906; Rector of Down Hatherley, 1907-12. *Address:* Oakdene, Churchdown, Gloucester.
(Died 18 Aug. 1925.)

BEECHAM, Sir Joseph, 1st Bt., *cr.* 1914; Kt., *cr.* 1911; J.P.; manufacturer and philanthropist; *b.* 1848; *m.* 1873, Josephine, *d.* of William Burnett, London; two *s.* five *d.* Mayor of St. Helens, 1899-1900, 1910-1911 and 1911-12; proprietor of Aldwych Theatre; Knight of the Order of St. Stanislaus (Russia). *Heir: s.* Sir Thomas. *Address:* 9 Arkwright Road, Hampstead, N.W.; *T.:* Hampstead 1653; Ewanville, Huyton, Liverpool. *Club:* Devonshire.
(Died 23 Oct. 1916.)

BEECHING, Maj.-Gen. Frank: Indian Army; *b.* 23 July 1839; *m.* 1870, Marianne, *d.* of P. Mathews. Entered army, 1857; Maj.-Gen. 1894; Unemployed Super. List, 1894. *Address:* 13 Highland Road, Norwood, S.E.
(Died 1 Sept. 1916.)

BEECHING, Very Rev. Henry Charles, D.D., Hon. D.Litt. Durham; Dean of Norwich since 1911; Canon of Westminster Abbey, 1902-11; Preacher to the Hon. Society of Lincoln's Inn, 1904-12; Examining Chaplain to the Bishop of Carlisle, 1905-11; *b.* 15 May 1859; 2nd *s.* of late James P. G. Beeching, of Bexhill, Sussex, and Harriet Skaife; *m.* 1891, Mary, *e. d.* of late Rev. A. J. Plow: three *d.* *Educ.:* City of London School; Balliol College, Oxford (Classical Exhibitioner). Curate of Mossley Hill Church, Liverpool, 1882-85; Rector of Yattendon, Berks, 1885-1900. Oxford Sacred Poem, 1896; Select Preacher Oxford University, 1896-97, 1912-13; Cambridge, 1903-9-12; Dublin, 1905; Clark Lecturer at Trinity Coll. Camb. 1900; Prof. of Pastoral Theology, King's Coll. London, 1900-3; Chaplain of Lincoln's Inn, 1900-3. *Publications:* Faith (eleven sermons with a Preface), 1892; Seven Sermons to Schoolboys, 1894; In a Garden, and other poems, 1895; Pages from a Private Diary, 1898; Conferences on Books and Men, 1900; Two Lectures on Poetry; Inns of Court Sermons, 1901; Religio Laici, 1902; The Apostles' Creed; The Grace of Episcopacy, 1906; Provincial Letters; Lectures on the Atonement, 1907; Lectures on the Doctrine of Sacraments, 1908; Francis Atterbury, 1909; Revision of the Prayer Book, 1910; Inspiration, 1914; The Library of the Cathedral Church of Norwich, 1915. Editor of A Paradise of English Poetry, 1892; Lyra Sacra, 1894; Milton's Poetical Works, 1900; Shakespeare's Sonnets, 1904; Ainger's Lectures and Sermons, 1906; Essays and Studies by Members of the English Association, vol. ii., 1911; Herbert's Country Parson, Vaughan's Poems, Tennyson's In Memoriam, Shakespeare's Julius Cæsar Poems of Daniel and Drayton, Lyra Apostolica, etc. *Address:* The Deanery, Norwich. *T.:* 1090 Norwich. *Club:* Athenæum.
(Died 25 Feb. 1919.)

BEER, Col. James Henry Elias; C.I.E.; 1909; V.D.; Commandant Mussoorie Rifles; *b.* 1848. *Address:* Mussoorie, India.
(Died 1 Nov. 1925.)

BEER BIKRAM SINGH, Rajkumar, Hon. Lt.-Col.; C.I.E. 1898; A.D.C. to Viceroy, 1906; Officer commanding Sirmour Imperial Service Sappers and Miners; also attached to 1st P.W.O. Sappers and Miners. Served in command of his corps in the Tirah expedition, 1897-98; was Acting A.D.C. to Field-Marshal Earl Roberts during the Coronation and rode in procession, August 1902; also rode on the staff of the Prince of Wales at the march past at

Rawal Pindi. *Address:* Sirmour State, Punjab.
(Died 13 Aug. 1923.)

BEESTON, Col. the Hon. Joseph Livesley, C.M.G. 1915; M.D.; Army Medical Corps, Australian Imperial Force; *b.* 19 Sep. 1859; *s.* of late J. L. Beeston; *m.* 1882, Anna Maria, *d.* of William Read. Served Dardanelles, 1914-15 (despatches. C.M.G.). *Address:* New Lambton, New South Wales. *(Died Mar. 1921.)*

BEET, Rev. Joseph Agar, D.D.; Theological Writer and Lecturer; *b.* Sheffield, 27 Sep. 1840; *s.* of W. J. Beet, manufacturer; *m.* Sarah Elizabeth, *d.* of S. T. Baugh, J.P., Wrexham; three *s.* one *d.* *Educ.:* Wesley College, Sheffield; Wesleyan College, Richmond. Theological Tutor Wesleyan College, Richmond, 1885-1905; one of the original Members of the Faculty of Theology, University of London; hon. D.D. of the Univ. of Glasgow; Fernley Lecturer, 1889; Lecturer at University of Chicago and at Chautauqua and Ocean Grove (U.S.A.) Summer Schools, 1896. *Publications:* Commentaries on St. Paul's Epistles; Credentials of the Gospel, 1889; The Last Things, 1897; A Manual of Theology, 1906; Church, Churches, and Sacraments, 1907; Shorter Manual of Theology, 1908; The New Testament, its Authorship, Date, and Worth, 1909; Holiness, Symbolic and Real, 1910; The Old Testament, its Contents, Truth, and Worth, 1912; A Theologian's Workshop, Tools, and Method, 1914. *Address:* 11 Dynevor Road, Richmond, Surrey. *(Died 25 May 1924.)*

BEEVOR, Lt.-Col. Walter Calverley, C.B. 1916; C.M.G. 1900; *b.* 8 Oct. 1858; *m.* 1890, Ella Beatrice, *e. d.* of late Charles Taylor, D.L., J.P., Horton Manor, Slough; one *s.* one *d.* *Educ.:* Edinburgh University. Served Soudan Campaign, 1885 (medal with clasp, Khedive's star); Ashantee, 1895-96 (despatches, promoted Surgeon-Major, Star); North-West Frontier, India, 1897-98 (despatches, medal with two clasps); South Africa, 1899-1902 (despatches, medal with six clasps, King's medal); European War, 1914-19 (despatches, C.B.); served on Personal Staff of Duke of Connaught to Durbar, Nov. 1902 to April 1903; on Personal Staff of Lord Northcote, Governor-General of Bombay, 1903. *Clubs:* Guards', Naval and Military. *(Died 6 Feb. 1927.)*

BEGBIE, Colonel Francis Warburton, C.B.E. 1919; Army Medical Service; Knight of Grace, Order of St. John of Jerusalem; *s.* of James Warburton Begbie, M.D., LL.D., late of Edinburgh; *m.* Mary, *d.* of Walter Reynolds, J.P., late High Sheriff of Herts. Served Indian Frontier Chitral Campaign (medal with clasp); South African War, 1899-1902 (Queen's medal with six clasps, King's medal with two clasps, despatches twice); European War, 1914-19, O.C. Base Hospital, Mesopotamia Field Forces, Commandant R.A.M.C.-Training Battalion, O.C. No. VI. General Hospital, Rouen, A.D.M.S. Le Trepat, Dieppe and Dunkerque (despatches four times, 1915 star, War medal, Victory medal, C.B.E.). *Address:* Holt & Co., 3 Whitehall Place, S.W.1. *Club:* Junior Naval and Military. *(Died 25 April 1922.)*

BEGG, Col. Charles Mackie, C.B. 1918; C.M.G. 1915; M.D.; F.R.C.P., F.R.C.S., Ed.; N.Z. Army Medical Service; Hon. Physician Wellington Hospital; Hon. Surgeon Wellington Children's Hospital. Served Dardanelles, 1914-1918 (despatches, C.M.G., C.B.). *Publications:* Medical Papers. *Address:* 148 Willis Street, Wellington, N.Z. *(Died Feb. 1919.)*

BEGG, Ferdinand Faithfull, F.R.S.E.; *b.* Edinburgh, 27 Dec. 1847; *s.* of late Rev. James Begg, D.D., and Maria, *d.* of Rev. Ferdinand Faithfull, Rector of Headley, Epsom; *m.* 1873, Jessie Maria (*d.* 1925), *d.* of F. A. Cargill, Dunedin, New Zealand. *Educ.:* privately. Emigrated to New Zealand, 1863; returned to Scotland, 1872; became a stock-broker, and was chairman of the Edinburgh Stock Exchange, 1885; established himself on the London Stock Exchange, 1887; retired, 1913; contested Kennington Division of Lambeth, 1892; M.P. for St. Rollox Division of Glasgow, 1895-1900; chairman of London Chamber of Commerce, 1912-15. *Recreations:* golf, yachting, heraldry. *Address:* 46 St. Aubyns, Hove, Sussex. *Club:* Union, Brighton.
(Died 4 Dec. 1926.)

BEGIN, H.E. Most Rev. Louis Nazaire, D.D.; R.C. Archbishop of Quebec since 1898; *b.* Levis, Quebec, 10 Jan. 1840; *s.* of Charles Begin, a farmer, and Luce Paradis. *Educ.:* Levis Model School; Commercial College, St. Michel; Seminary of Quebec, 1857-62, B.A. at Laval, and Prince of Wales Prize; Grand Seminary of Quebec; Professor at Laval; left for Rome, 1863; ordained, 1865; Professor, Faculty of Theology, Laval University, 1868-84; Principal of the Normal School until Oct. 1888; Bishop of Chicoutimi, 1888; Coadjutor of Cardinal Taschereau, 1891; Administrator, Archdiocese of Quebec, 1894; Cardinal, 1914. *Publications:* La primauté et l'infaillibilité des souverains pontifes; La sainte écriture et la règle de foi, 1874; Le culte catholique, 1875; Aide-mémoire, ou chronologie de l'histoire du Canada, 1886; Chronologie de l'Histoire des Etats-Unis d'Amérique, 1895; Catéchisme de Controverse, 1902. *Address:* Archbishop's Palace, Quebec. *T.:* 989. *(Died 19 July 1925.)*

BEHR, Fritz Bernhard; Associate Inst. C.E.; Engineer to the Manchester and Liverpool Electric Express Railway; Consulting Engineer Railway Co. (Tampico-Panuco Valley), and several important oil companies in Mexico and elsewhere; *b.* Berlin, 9 Oct. 1842; *s.* of Dr. Bernhard Behr of the University of Berlin. *Educ.:* Paris; afterwards pupil to Mr. Wentworth Shields and Sir John Fowler; employed on a great many railway works in England and abroad; went through the Franco-German War, 1870-71, administering a portion of the conquered territory for the German Government; became a naturalised Englishman, 1876, and has devoted himself specially to the development of mono-rail lines since 1885; invented practically the mono-rail, now known as the High-Speed Mono-Rail System, and obtained two Acts of Parliament for the construction of the Manchester and Liverpool Electric Express Railway in 1901 and 1902, which is to be worked at an average speed of 110 miles an hour; has published a number of pamphlets and lectures in English, French, and German on high-speed mono-rails, the principal one published in 1893, entitled Lightning Express Railway Service, 120 to 150 Miles an Hour. Was decorated during the German War. *Recreation:* motoring. *Address:* 3 Alexandra Court, 171 Queen's Gate, S.W.7; Villa Violet, Roquebrune, A.M., France. *T.A.:* Syndigef, London. *T.:* Kensington 5844. *Club:* Orleans.
(Died 25 Feb. 1927.)

BEHRENS, Sir Charles, Kt., cr. 1912; J.P.; Member of Sir Jacob Behrens & Sons, of Manchester, Bradford, Glasgow, London and Calcutta; *b.* 5 Aug. 1848; *s.* of late Sir Jacob Behrens, Bradford; *m.* 1883, Emily Milnes, *d.* of late Samuel Shaw, J.P., of Brooklands, near Halifax; three *d.* *Educ.:* Bradford Grammar School and High School. Lord Mayor of Manchester, 1909-10 and 1910-11; Director of Manchester Ship Canal Co.; Local Director of Commercial Union Assurance Co., also of the Ocean Accident and Guarantee Corporation, Ltd.; Governor of the Manchester Grammar School; Member of Court of Victoria University, Manchester; of Board of Manchester Royal Infirmary, and of many other philanthropic institutions. *Address:* Holm-Acre, Altrincham, Cheshire. *Clubs:* Reform; Clarendon, Reform, Manchester. *(Died 25 Sept. 1925.)*

75

BEHRENS, Walter, Knight of Legion of Honour; *s.* of late Louis Behrens, of West Hill, Bowdon, Cheshire; *b.* Manchester, 1856; *m.* 1st, 1894, Evelyn (*d.* 1910), *d.* of S. H. Beddington, 21 Hyde Park Square, W.; two *s.*; 2nd, 1914, Mme. Gomez-Vaëz, Paris. *Educ.:* Grammar School and Owens College, Manchester; Polytechnic Institute, Carlsruhe. Engineer; has taken an active part in the movement for Anglo-French Postal and Telegraphic Reform, and the reciprocal protection of British and French merchandise marks; is an advocate of the Channel Tunnel scheme between England and France, and has written many articles on the subject in the daily papers; has been instrumental in promoting the use of British machinery in France, especially the linotype machine, and the locomotives of the North British Locomotive Co.; President, British Chamber of Commerce, Paris, 1908-9; is the official agent of the Commercial Committee of the House of Commons in Paris. *Recreations:* golf, musical composition, violin. *Address:* 48 Avenue Henri-Martin, Paris. *T.:* Passy 42.00. *T.A.:* Walbe, Paris. *Clubs:* Reform, Royal Automobile, Isthmian; Automobile, Aero, Interallié, Bois de Boulogne, Paris. (*Died 27 April 1922.*)

BEILBY, Sir George Thomas, Kt., *cr.* 1916; J.P., F.R.S., LL.D. Glasgow and Birmingham, D.Sc. Durham, F.I.C., F.C.S., Assoc. Inst. C.E.; Member of Advisory Council on Scientific and Industrial Research; Chairman of the Royal Technical College, Glasgow, 1907-23; *b.* 17 Nov. 1850; *s.* of G. T. Beilby, M.D., of Edinburgh; *m.* 1877, Emma Clarke, *e. d.* of Rev. S. Newnam: one *s.* one *d.* *Educ.:* private schools; University of Edinburgh. Inventor of processes which are in use in several departments of industry, specially studied fuel economy and smoke prevention in connection with the coal consumption of Great Britain, and reported to the Royal Commission on Coal Supplies, 1903; Member of the Royal Commission on Fuel and Engines for the Navy, 1912; Director of Fuel Research, 1917-23; President of Society of Chemical Industry, 1899; of Chemical Section of British Association at S. African meeting, 1905; of Institute of Chemistry, 1909-12; and of the Inst. of Metals, 1916-18; has devoted much time to chemical and microscopical research. *Publications:* Aggregation and Flow of Solids, 1921; Scientific and technical papers in Proceedings of Royal Society, Proceedings of Chemical Society, B.A. Reports, Soc. Chem. Ind. J., and Phil. Mag., etc. *Address:* 29 Kidderpore Avenue, Hampstead, N.W.3. *Club:* Athenæum.
(*Died 1 Aug. 1924.*)

BEITH, Hon. Robert; *b.* Fairfield Farm, Darlington, Durham, Ontario, 17 May 1843; unmarried. Senator since 1907; stock-breeder and importer; M.P. (L.), W. Durham, 1891-96 and 1902. *Address:* Waverley Farm, Bowmanville, Ontario. (*Died Jan. 1922.*)

BELCHER, Lt.-Col. Harold Thomas, D.S.O. 1900; *b.* 17 March 1875; *s.* of Rev. T. H. Belcher. Entered R.A. 1895; served South Africa (severely wounded, medal with five clasps); European War, 1914-16 (despatches, wounded); Lt.-Col., 1915. *Address:* Bramley Rectory, Basingstoke. (*Died 8 July 1917.*)

BELCHER, Major Robert, C.M.G., 1900; *b.* 28 April 1849; *s.* of Robert Tovey Belcher and Elizabeth Bounford; *m.* 1880, Maggie, *d.* of Donald M'Leod; three *s.* four *d.* *Educ.:* Byron House, Ealing. 9th Lancers, 1868-73; North-West Mounted Police of Canada, 1873-1908; through North-West Rebellion, 1885; served in Yukon, 1897-99; attended the Queen's Diamond Jubilee with N.W.M.P., 1897; served South Africa, 1900-1 with Strathcona's Horse (despatches, C.M.G.). *Address:* Edmonton, Alberta, Canada. (*Died 13 Feb. 1919.*)

BELFIELD, Sir Henry Conway, K.C.M.G., *cr.* 1914; C.M.G. 1909; *b.* 29 Nov.

1855; *e. s.* of late John Belfield, J.P., of Primley Hill, South Devon, and Eliza Conway, *o. d.* of Captain George Bridges, R.N.; *m.* 1884, Florence, C.B.E., 4th *d.* of late Rev. James Rathborne; one *s.* two *d.* *Educ.:* Rugby; Oriel College, Oxford, B.A. Barrister-at-law, Inner Temple, 1880, and practised on the Western Circuit and at the Devon and Exeter Sessions; entered Selangor Civil Service as Magistrate, 1884; Chief Magistrate, Selangor, 1888; Senior Magistrate, Perak, 1892; on the federation of the Malay States in 1896 was appointed to be the First Commissioner of Lands and Mines; also chief examiner in the Malay language; acted as British Resident-Selangor, on frequent occasions, 1897-1901; British Resident, Negri Sembilan, 1901; British Resident of Selangor, Federated Malay States, 1902-12; Acting British Resident, Perak, 1904; special mission to Labuan and Brunei, 1905; Acting Resident-General, Federated Malay States, May 1908; British Resident, Perak, 1911; Special Mission to Gold Coast and Ashanti to report on Land Tenure, 1912; Governor of East Africa Protectorate, 1912; also High Commissioner of Zanzibar, 1914; retired, 1918; J.P. Devonshire. *Publication:* The Handbook of the Federated Malay States. *Recreations:* shooting, fishing, reading. *Address:* 4 Roxburghe Mansion, Kensington Court, W.8. *T.:* Western 3565. *Clubs:* Junior Carlton, Bachelors', Ranelagh. (*Died 8 Jan. 1923.*)

BELHAVEN and STENTON, 10th Baron (*cr.* 1647), **Alexander Charles Hamilton,** Scottish Representative Peer, 1900; J.P., D.L.; *b.* Tunbridge Wells, 3 July 1840; *S.* his kinsman, James, 9th Lord, 1893; *m.* Georgiana, *d.* of Legh Richmond, 1880. *Educ.:* Woolwich. Church of England. Conservative. Entered R.E. 1857; served in Zulu War, 1879; retired 1888, with rank of Colonel; commanded Surrey Vol. Brigade, 1888-1902; Territorial Decoration. *Recreations:* on Council Royal Geographical Society. Owns 2200 acres in Lanarkshire. *Heir: n.* Lt.-Col. Robert Edward Archibald Hamilton. *Address:* Wishaw House, Wishaw, N.B.; 41 Lennox Gardens, S.W. *Club:* United Service. (*Died 31 Oct. 1920.*)

BELHAVEN, Master of, Hon. Ralph Gerard Alexander Hamilton, Major, Royal Field Artillery (formerly 3rd Hussars); *b.* 22 Feb. 1883; *e. s.* of 10th Baron Belhaven and Stenton; *m.* 1904, Lady Grizel Cochrane, *d.* of 12th Earl of Dundonald. *Educ.:* Eton; R.M. College, Sandhurst. Hon. Attaché to British Legation at Darmstadt, 1913 and 1914. *Address:* 1 St. James's Terrace, Regent's Park, N.W.; Wishaw House, Wishaw, N.B. *Club:* United Service. (*Died 31 Mar. 1918.*)

BELL, Capt. Adolphus Edmund, C.B.E. 1919; *b.* 1850; an Elder Brother of the Trinity House. *Address:* 23 Down Street, W.1. *T.:* Mayfair 4947. *Club:* Junior Athenæum.
(*Died 11 Sept. 1927.*)

BELL, Alexander Graham, LL.D., Ph.D., D.Sc., M.D.; *b.* Edinburgh, 3 March 1847; *s.* of late Alexander Melville Bell and Eliza Grace, *d.* of Dr. Samuel Symonds, Surgeon, R.N.; *m.* 1877, Mabel Gardiner, *d.* of G. G. Hubbard; two *d.* *Educ.:* Royal High School, Edinburgh; Edinburgh University; University College, London; Matriculated London University, 1867. Went to Canada, 1870; became Professor of Vocal Physiology, Boston Univ.; patented invention of telephone, 1876; invented also photophone, induction balance, and telephone probe, and (with C. A. Bell and Sumner Tainter) graphophone; has investigated laws of flight and studied education of the deaf; founder and endower and late President, American Association to Promote Teaching of Speech to the Deaf; late President National Geographic Society; Regent Smithsonian Institution since 1898; received freedom of city of Edinburgh, 1920; awarded Volta Prix

BELFIELD, Major William Seymour, C.M.G. See page xv.

by French Govt., 1881 ; officier of French Legion of Honour ; Prince Albert Medal (London Society of Fine Arts), 1902 ; Hughes Medal of Royal Society, 1913 ; Founder and endower Volta Bureau ; Member National Academy of Sciences ; and many foreign and American Societies. *Publications:* many scientific monographs, including Memoir on the formation of Deaf Variety in the Human Race ; Census Report on the Deaf of the United States, 1906 ; Lectures on the Mechanism of Speech, 1906 ; many scientific and educational monographs. *Address:* 1331 Connecticut Avenue, Washington, D.C., U.S.A. *T.:* Franklin 58 ; Beinn Bhreagh, nr. Baddeck, Nova Scotia. *Club:* Cosmos.

(*Died 2 Aug. 1922.*)

BELL, Arthur George, R.I., R.O.I. ; *b.* parish of St. Dunstan's, City of London ; *s.* of George Bell, publisher ; *m.* Nancy Meugens two *s.* one *d. Educ.:* Slade School ; Ecole des Beaux Arts, Paris, under Gerôme. *Publications:* Nuremberg ; Picturesque Brittany ; Skirts of the Great City ; The Royal Manor of Richmond ; From Harbour to Harbour ; etc. *Address:* York House, Portugal Street, W.C. ; Eastgarth, Southbourne-on-Sea, Hants.

(*Died 24 Sept. 1916.*)

BELL, Edward, M.A., F.S.A. ; Chairman of G. Bell & Sons, Ltd., publishers ; *e. s.* of late George Bell ; *b.* 1844 ; *m.* 1873, Alice (*d.* 1917), 2nd *d.* of Rev. J. W. van Rees Hoets, M.A., formerly Vicar of Mowbray, Cape Colony ; one *s.* three *d. Educ.:* St. Paul's School ; Trinity Coll., Cambridge. President Publishers Association, 1906-1909 ; a Commissioner of Income and Land Tax. *Publications:* Translator and editor of Goethe's Early Letters, Wilhelm Meister's Travels, and the Nibelungenlied ; author of Architecture of Ancient Egypt ; Prehellenic Architecture in the Ægean ; Hellenic Architecture, Architecture of Western Asia, and of various papers on literature and art. *Recreations:* sketching and photography. *Address:* The Mount, Hampstead, N.W. ; York House, Portugal Street, W.C. *Clubs:* New University, Bath.

(*Died 8 Nov. 1926.*)

BELL, Francis Jeffrey, Emeritus Professor and Fellow of King's College, London ; Assist., British Museum, 1878-1919 ; since when he has been working for unemployed ex-officers ; M.A. Magdalen College, Oxford ; Corr. Member Linnean Soc., New South Wales. *Publications:* Manual of Comparative Anatomy and Physiology ; Catalogue of British Echinoderms in British Museum ; editor of Catalogue of Madreporaria in British Museum, and of Natural History Reports of Voyage of the Discovery ; Memoirs in Trans. and Proc. Zool. Soc., Journal Linnean Society, etc. *Club:* Athenæum.

(*Died 1 April 1924.*)

BELL, Hon. George Alexander; late Provincial Treasurer and Minister of Telephones in the Government of Saskatchewan ; *b.* Brant County, Ont., 3 Aug. 1856 ; 2nd *s.* of David and Agnes Bell (Scotch) ; *m.* 1883, Elizabeth Smith ; four *s.* three *d. Educ.:* Public School No. 1, Colborne Township, Huron County, Ontario. On farm till 20 years of age ; blacksmith for 12 years ; in the farm implement business ; Clerk of County Court. Dominion Homestead Inspector ; elected to Legislative Assembly, 1908 ; re-elected, 1912 and 1917 ; sworn in a member of the Executive Council of Saskatchewan, 1912 ; resigned seat in Leg. Assembly and Executive Council, June 1918 ; Chairman Local Government Board, June 1918 ; left Ontario for Western Canada, 1880. *Recreation:* golf. *Address:* Regina, Saskatchewan, Canada. *T.:* 3021. *Club:* Regina Golf.

(*Died Sept. 1927.*)

BELL, Gertrude Margaret Lowthian, C.B.E. 1917 ; Oriental Secretary to the High Commissioner of the Iraq, Baghdad, since 1920 ; *e. d.* of Sir Hugh Bell, 2nd Bt. *Educ.:* Queen's College, London ; Lady

Margaret Hall, Oxford. 1st Class History (1887) ; F.R.G.S. ; Founder's Medal, 1918 ; attached to Military Intelligence Depart., Cairo, 1915 ; liaison officer of Arab bureau in Iraq, 1916 ; Assistant Political Officer, Baghdad, 1917 (despatches four times). *Publications:* Safar Nameh, 1894 ; Poems from the Divan of Hafiz, 1897 ; The Desert and the Sown, 1907 ; The Thousand and One Churches, 1909 (in collaboration with Sir William M. Ramsay) ; Amurath to Amurath, 1911 ; Palace and Mosque at Ukhaider, 1914 ; Review of the Civil Administration of Mesopotamia, 1921. *Address:* Rounton Grange, Northallerton ; 95 Sloane Street, S.W.1 ; Baghdad.

(*Died 12 July 1926.*)

BELL, Rev. Henry, Hon. Canon of Carlisle ; retired ; *b.* 1838 ; *s.* of John Bell, Vicar of Rothwell, Yorkshire, Hon. Canon of Ripon, and Isabella Elizabeth, *d.* of Sir Charles Loraine, Kirkharle, Northumberland ; *m.* 1873, Katherine, *d.* of Sir Peter Fitzgerald, Knight of Kerry, 1st Bart.; three *s.* three *d. Educ.:* Marlborough College ; University College, Durham. Deacon, 1861 ; Priest, 1864 ; Hon. Canon of Carlisle, 1883 ; Proctor in Convocation, 1896 ; Assistant Master in Marlborough College, 1861-73 ; Vicar of Muncaster, Cumberland, 1873-1907 ; Chaplain to Lord Muncaster, 1873-1907 ; Rural Dean of Gosforth, 1878-1907, and Surrogate. *Recreations:* in the eleven which played the first match *v.* Rugby at Lord's in 1855, was captain of eleven in 1856. *Address:* Eskilenca, St. Jean de Luz, Basses-Pyrenees, France. (*Died 11 June 1919.*)

BELL, Major-General Sir James Alexander, K.C.V.O., *cr.* 1911 ; *s.* of late Col. James Giberne Bell ; *b.* 28 Jan. 1856 ; *m.* 1880, Edith, *d.* of late Colonel James Elphinston Robertson, 21st R.S. Fusiliers and R. Warwicks : two *s.* one *d. Educ.:* Harrow. Joined 44th E. Essex Regt. 1875 ; Indian Army, 1879 ; Commandant 42nd Deoli Regiment, 1889-99 ; Assistant Adjutant General Poona Division, 1899-1902 ; Bombay Command, 1902 ; Commandant School of Musketry, Satara, 1906-8 ; general officer commanding Belgaum and Lucknow Brigades, 1908-10 ; General Officer Commanding and Political Resident, Aden, 1910-1919 ; retired, April 1919. *Recreations:* racquets, fishing, shooting. *Address:* The Wilderness, Sherborne, Dorsetshire. *M.:* 6472.

(*Died 10 Nov. 1926.*)

BELL, Rev. James, M.A. ; Canon of Lincoln ; *m.* Eliza Mary, *d.* of late Henry Peake. *Educ.:* Corpus Christi College, Cambridge. Curate of New Sleaford, 1831-83 ; Dorrington, Lincs., 1883-85 ; Vicar of N. Somercotes, Lincs., 1885-98 ; Rector of Kettlethorpe, 1898-1910 ; Rector of Risholme, 1913-15. *Address:* The Grove, Lincoln. (*Died 3 April 1918.*)

BELL, Alderman Sir John Charles, 1st Bart., *cr.* 1908 ; Kt., *cr.* 1902 ; High Sheriff County of Bucks ; Sheriff of the City of London, 1902 ; Lord Mayor, 1907-8 ; *b.* 1844 ; *m.* 1st, 1868, Caroline Elizabeth (*d.* 1912), *e. d.* of Thomas Clare, Enfield ; one *d.* ; 2nd, 1914, Ellen, *d.* of late John James, Burgess Hill, Sussex. Joined the Court of Common Council as a representative of the ward of Coleman Street, 1882 ; elected by the ward of Coleman Street to represent them in the Court of Aldermen, 1894 ; on the court of the Haberdashers Company ; Master of Haberdashers, 1912-13 ; a past-master of Glovers' and Fanmakers' Companies, and on livery of Innholders', Loriners', and Spectacle-makers' Companies ; J.P., Bucks ; Chairman of E. Section of Commissioner for Income Tax for City ; one of H.M.'s Lieutenants for the City of London ; Grand Officer of Legion of Honour ; Commander of Prussian Order of Red Eagle (2nd class with star) ; received Coronation Medal, 1902 ; member of the No. 1 Grand Master's Lodge, and also a member of the Grand Master Chapter in Royal Archmasonry ; Past

Grand Warden of Freemasons. *Heir:* none. *Address:* Framewood, Stoke Poges, Bucks; 165-167 Moorgate, E.C. *Clubs:* City Carlton, Junior Carlton. (*Died 2 Feb. 1924.*)

BELL, John Keble (pen-name "Keble Howard"), writer; *b.* 8 June 1875; 3rd *s.* of Rev. G. E. Bell, late Vicar of Henley-in-Arden, Warwickshire. *Educ.:* Worcester Coll., Oxford. Joined Sketch as assistant editor, 1899; editor of The Sketch, 1902-4; dramatic critic Daily Mail, 1904-8; founded Croydon Repertory Theatre, 1913; temporary commission in Royal Air Force, 1917; seconded to Ministry of Information, 1918. *Plays:* Compromising Martha, 1906; Martha Plays the Fairy, 1907; Charles, His Friend, 1907; The Dramatist at Home, 1909; Come Michaelmas, 1909; The Girl who couldn't Lie, 1911; The Embarrassed Butler, 1912; Dropping the Pilot, 1913; The Cheerful Knave, 1914; The Green Flag, 1915; The Test Kiss, 1918; Lazy Lubin (America), 1920; Sweet William, 1921; The Smiths of Surbiton, 1922; Puss in the Corner, 1923; An Order to View, 1923; All in Train, 1924; Lord Babs, 1925. *Publications:* The Chicot Papers, 1901; Letters to Dolly, 1902; Love and a Cottage, 1903; The God in the Garden, 1904; Love in June, 1905; The Smiths of Surbiton, 1906; The Whip Hand, 1906; The Bachelor Girls, 1907; Miss Charity, 1908; The Smiths of Valley View, 1909; Potted Brains, 1909; The Cheerful Knave, 1910; The Happy Vanners, 1911; Chicot in America, 1911; One of the Family, 1911; London Voices, 1913; Lord London, 1913; So the World Wags, 1914; Merry-Andrew, 1915; Forked Lightning, 1916; Chin Music; The Gay Life, 1917; The Smiths in War-Time, 1918; The Adorable Lad, 1918; The Comedy of It; Take one at Night; An Author in Wonderland; The Peculiar Major, 1919; Puck and Mr. Purley, 1920; The Purleys of Wimbledon; King of the Castle, 1922; The Fast Lady, 1925; Chicot Calling, 1925; The Chicot Club; Paradise Island, 1926; Lord Babs; My Motley Life, 1927. *Address:* 2 Brunswick Place, Hove. *T.:* Hove 3256; Little Quay, Potter, Heigham, Norfolk. *M.:* PM 5198. *Clubs:* Constitutional; Sussex County Cricket; Royal Norfolk and Suffolk Yacht; Yarmouth Yacht. (*Died 29 Mar. 1928.*)

BELL, Lieut.-Col. John William, V.D., C.M.G. 1900; J.P.; *b.* Edinburgh, 1 Oct. 1844; *s.* of William Bell, native of Dumfries, Scotland (Bells of Blacket House), late of Grahamstown, South Africa, advocate; *m.* 1873, Eliza Jane Bradfield, 4th *d.* of Edward Mortimer Turvey, one of British settlers of 1820; two *s.* two *d.* *Educ.:* High School, Edinburgh. Solicitor, practised at Queenstown, South Africa; mem. of Queenstown Rifle Volunteers since formation of corps in 1873; in command since 1881; holds S. African war medal, 1877-78; was granted long service medal, 1898; holds volunteer officer's decoration (20 years' commissioned service); South African Campaign, 1899-1900 (despatches, medal and three clasps); Master of the Supreme Court of the Transvaal, 1901-6. *Address:* Nairobi, British East Africa. (*Died 27 May 1928.*)

BELL, Louis, Ph.D., Consulting Engineer; M.A.I.E.E.; *b.* New Hampshire, 1864; *s.* of late Gen. Louis Bell, U.S.V. *Educ.:* Dartmouth Coll.; Johns Hopkins University. Past Manager, A.I.E.E.; Fellow and Member Rumford Committee, American Academy of Arts and Sciences; Past Pres., Illuminating Engineering Society; Member, National Electric Light Association, American Astronomical Society, National Geographical Society, American Association for the Advancement of Science; President, Massachusetts Rifle Association; Technical Officer, Volunteer Electrical Corps, 1898; Lecturer, Mass. Institute of Technology, 1895-1905; Lecturer, Harvard Univ., 1914-18; International Electrotechnical Commission;

78

International Illumination Commission, Advisory Commission Council of National Defence. *Publications:* The Elements of Practical Electricity; Power Distribution for Electric Railroads; Electrical Power Transmission; The Art of Illumination; The Telescope. *Address:* 120 Boylston Street, Boston, Mass.; 32 Sylvan Avenue, West Newton, Mass. *Clubs:* Examiner, Engineers', Boston. (*Died 14 June 1923.*)

BELL, Lieut.-Col. Matthew Gerald Edward; Lt.-Col. Special Reserve, 6th Batt. Rifle Brigade; *b.* 24 July 1871; *s.* of Captain M. J. Bell, *e. s.* of Matthew Bell of Bourne Park and Kathleen Matilda, *d.* of John Reilly and Augusta, *d.* of 1st Lord St. Leonards; *m.* Hon. Mary (Maid of Honour to Queen Alexandra), *d.* of Rt. Hon. Sir William H. Dyke; one *s.* *Educ.:* Eton. Joined Rifle Brigade, 1893; served Indian Frontier, Tochi Valley, Signalling Officer 1st Brigade (medal and clasp); Somaliland Field Force (despatches, medal and clasp); retired from regular army, 1909; Staff, Aug. 1914-Sep. 1919. *Recreations:* shooting, fishing, tennis, golf. *Address:* Bourne Park, Canterbury, Kent. *T.:* Bridge 11. *T.A.:* Bridge. *Clubs:* Marlborough, Princes Racquet; St. Georges, Sandwich. (*Died 8 May 1926*)

BELL, Robert, I.S.O. 1903; D.Sc. (Cantab. and M'Gill); M.D., C.M. (M'Gill); LL.D. (Queen's); F.G.S. (L. and A.), F.R.S.C., F.R.S., 1897; late Director and Chief Geologist Geological Survey of Canada; *s.* of late Rev. Andrew Bell and *g. s.* of late Rev. William Bell, both of Church of Scotland; *b.* Toronto, 3 June 1841; *m.* Agnes, *d.* of late Alex. Smith of Westbourne Glasgow, and Auchentroig, Stirlingshire; one *s.* three *d.* *Educ.:* Grammar School of the county of Prescott; M'Gill and Edinburgh Universities; F.C.S., 1865; member of American Institute of Mining Engineers, 1881; hon. member Medico-Chirurgical Society, Montreal, and of Ottawa; Fellow Am.A.A.Sci.; one of foundation Fellows of Royal Society of Canada; Member of Government Geographical Board. Joined Geological Survey of Canada, 1857; has made very extensive topographical and geological surveys in nearly all parts of the Dominion since 1857. The Bell River or W. branch of the Nottaway, which he surveyed in 1895, is officially named after him; was medical officer, naturalist, and geologist of "Neptune" expedition in 1884, and of "Alert" expedition in 1885 to Hudson's Strait and Bay; was also geologist on the "Diana" expedition in 1897, when he surveyed the south coast of Baffinland and penetrated to the great lakes of its interior; among the rivers he has surveyed are the Athabasca, Slave, Beaver, Churchill, Nelson, Hayes and branches, the Winnipeg, English, Albany, Kenogami, Nipigon, Moose and its numerous branches, the Harricanaw, Broadback, Nottaway and its branches, the upper Gatineau and most of the rivers of northern Ontario; also the first surveys of some of largest lakes of Canada, including Great Slave, Nipigon, Seul, Osnaburgh, Timagarni, and parts of Athabasca, Winnipeg, and Lake of the Woods; delegate from the Dominion Government and the Royal Society of Canada to the Intl. Geol. Congress, Vienna, 1903; has been Canadian cor. of the Royal Scottish Geographical Socy. ever since its foundation; Canadian cor. of la Société de Géographie; Fellow of the Royal Ast. Socy. of Canada; was a Royal Commr. on the Mineral Resources of Ontario, 1888-89; has published over 200 reports and papers, mostly on geology, biology, geography, and folk-lore; Professor of Chemistry and Natural Science in Queen's Univ. Kingston, 1863-67; Hon. Chief of Algonquin Indians of Grand Lake; Pres. International Congress of Americanists. 1906; King's or Patron's gold medal of the Royal Geographical Society of London, 1906; Cullum gold medal of the Am. Geographical Society, 1906. *Recreations:* study of the forests and mammals of

BELL, Ven. John White. See page xvi.

Canada, and folk-lore and archæology of the North American Indians. *Address:* 186 Maclaren Street, Ottawa, Canada. *T.A.:* Geologist, Ottawa. *T.:* Queen 2139. *Club:* Rideau, Ottawa.
(*Died 20 June 1917.*)

BELL, Robert, M.D., M.B., F.R.F.P.S., etc.; Consulting Physician, Vice-President of International Cancer Research Society; Superintendent of Cancer Research, Battersea Hospital; *b.* 6 Jan. 1845; *s.* of William Bell, Alnwick, and Annie Turnbull, Alnwick; *m.* Clara Ellen, *d.* of late George Sims; one *s.* two *d. Educ.:* Alnwick Grammar School; Glasgow University; Paris. Commenced practice in Glasgow, 1868; Senior Physician to Glasgow Hospital for Women, 1876-97; Consulting Physician, which ceased on departing to take up consulting work in London, 1904. *Publications:* Cancer, its Cause and Treatment without Operation; Prevention of Cancer; Conquest of Cancer; Reminiscences of an Old Physician; several brochures on Dietetics; contributions to Lancet, British Med. Jour. and Med. Times, also to American Medical Journals. *Recreations:* fishing and shooting. *Address:* 15 Half Moon Street, W.1.; 10 Thorney Court, W.8. *T.A.:* Bell, Thorneydom, London. *T.:* Grosvenor 1201, Kensington 6491. *Club:* Devonshire.
(*Died 20 Jan. 1926.*)

BELL, Robert Stanley Warren, author; *e. s.* of Rev. G. E. Bell, late Vicar of Henley-in-Arden, Warwickshire; *b.* 1871; *m.* 1905, Edithe M. Barry. *Educ.:* St. John's, Leatherhead. Editor of The Captain, 1899-1910. *Publications:* The Cub in Love, 1897; The Papa Papers, 1898; Bachelorland, 1899; Tales of Greyhouse; Love the Laggard, 1901; J. O. Jones, 1903; Jim Mortimer, 1904; The Duffer, 1905; Cox's Cough-Drops, 1906; Green at Greyhouse, 1908; Company for @George, 1911; Black Evans, 1912; Mystery of Markham, 1913; Dormitory Eight, 1914; The Secret Seven, Smith's Week, 1915; Young Couples, The Three Prefects, Greyhouse Days, 1918; Happy Beginnings, 1919; Comedy Company for George (Kingsway Theatre), 1919. *Address:* 4 Cranley Avenue, Westcliff-on-Sea. *Club:* Press.
(*Died 26 Sept. 1921.*)

BELL, Very Rev. Thomas; Dean of Guernsey since 1892; Hon. Canon of Winchester; Rector of the Vale, Guernsey, 1859-1914; *b.* 1820; *m. Educ.:* Exeter Coll. Oxford (M.A.). Ordained, 1845; Curate of Finstock, Oxford, 1845-48; St. Mathew, City Road, 1848-1851; Burston, Norfolk, 1851-53; The Vale, Guernsey, 1853-59; Vice-Dean of Guernsey, 1880-92. *Address:* Guernsey.
(*Died 31 Oct. 1917.*)

BELL, Rev. William; Vicar of Cranbrook, Kent, since 1898; Hon. Canon of Canterbury Cathedral since 1904; Rural Dean of West Charing, 1901; *s.* of William Bell, Highberries, Cumberland; widower; one *s.* one *d. Educ.:* St. Bees' School; Christ's College, Cambridge (Scholar); Second Class Classical Tripos, 1866. Assistant Master, Royal Grammar School, and Curate of Christ Church, Lancaster, 1866-71; first Head Master of Dover College, 1871 Vicar of Parish Church, Sittingbourne, 1892-98; Rural Dean of Sittingbourne, 1897-98; Assessor under Clergy Discipline Act, 1906; Hon. Secretary of Diocesan Board of Education, 1899-1913. *Address:* Cranbrook Vicarage, Kent. *T.A.:* Cranbrook.
(*Died 10 Dec. 1918.*)

BELL, William Abraham; *o. s.* of late William Bell, M.D., and Margaret, *d.* of Abraham Grubb, of Merlin, Clonmel; *b.* 26 April 1841; *m.* 1872, Cara Georgina Whitmore, *d.* and *co-heir* of Whitmore Scovell, of Waddon, Surrey; one *s.* three *d. Educ.:* Ipswich Grammar School; Trinity Hall, Cambridge (M.A., 1865; M.B., 1866). *Heir: s.* Major William A. G. Bell [*m.* 1916, *e. d.* of late Canon Ottley. *Educ.:* Trinity Hall, Cambridge.] *Address:* Pendell

Court Blechingley; 8 Park Street. W.
(*Died 6 June 1920.*)

BELL-IRVING, John, J.P.; *b.* 2 Feb. 1846; *e. s.* of late John Bell-Irving and Mary, *d.* of David Jardine of Muirhousehead, Dumfries; *m.* 1884, Isabella, *d.* of Henry Thornton; one *s.* two *d.* Late M.L.C. Hong-Kong; formerly a partner in the firm of Jardine Matheson and Co., of Hong Kong and China. *Address:* White Hill, Lockerbie; Milkbank, Lockerbie. *T.A.:* Kettleholm. *M.:* GA 818, GA 5999. *Club:* Dumfries and Galloway, Dumfries.
(*Died 30 July 1925.*)

BELL-SMITH, Frederic Marlett, R.C.A.; Artist; Member of Council of the Royal Canadian Academy of Arts; Life Member Ontario Society of Artists, 1904-8; *b.* London, 26 Sep. 1846; *s.* of late John Bell Smith, Artist; *m.* 1871, Annie Myra Dyde; one *s. Educ:* London. Studied drawing at South Kensington; went to Canada, 1867; charter member Society of Canadian Artists, 1867; Member Royal British Colonial Society of Artists, London, since its formation; served in Volunteers in suppressing Fenian invasion, 1870 (has medal); Director of Fine Arts, Alma College, since 1881; teacher of drawing, public schools, London, Ontario, 1882-89; Director Toronto Art School, 1889-91; lecturer and writer on Art subjects. *Principal pictures:* Queen Victoria's Tribute to Canada (for which Her Majesty gave personal sittings); Landing of the Blenheim, National Collection, Ottawa; Whitehead, Diploma work, Nat. Coll.; Lights of a City Street, Ontario Collection; has exhibited at Royal Academy and other principal exhibitions. *Recreations:* annually visits Rocky Mountains of Canada, and has made some ascents; member of Canadian Alpine Club. *Address:* 336 Jarvis Street, Toronto, Ontario, Canada. *Clubs:* Arts and Letters, Palette, Canadian, Toronto. (*Died 23 June 1923.*)

BELL-SMYTH, Brig.-Gen. John Ambard, C.B., 1919; C.M.G., 1916; late 1st Dragoon Guards; *b.* 1868; *m.* 1921, Dorothy, *d.* of late Dr. Charles Sharp Smith, Canford Cliffs, Bournemouth. *Educ.:* Oratory School. Served S. Africa, 1899-1900 (despatches, Bt. Major, Queen's medal, 6 clasps); European War, 1914-18 (despatches, C.B., C.M.G., Bt. Col.) retired, 1920. (*Died 24 Mar. 1922.*)

BELLAMY, Sir Joseph Arthur, Kt., *cr.* 1904, J.P.; Mayor of Plymouth, 1901-2; *b.* 6 Sep. 1845; *m.* 1868, Susan Mill (*d.* 1908), *d.* of William Saul Wills of Plymouth; one *s.* two *d.* Past Chairman, Chamber of Commerce; Chairman, Plymouth Gas Co. and Sutton Harbour Co. *Address:* Yalta, Mannamead, Plymouth.
(*Died 1 Mar. 1918.*)

BELLAMY, Lt.-Col. Robert, D.S.O. 1900; late Royal Sussex Regt.; *b.* 29 Nov. 1871; *s.* of late Col. P. L. Bellamy, Border Regiment; *m.* 1903, Constance Gwendoline, *e. d.* of late Col. Alfred Borton, Welsh Regt.; two *s.* Entered Army, 1894; Adjutant, 1900; Captain, 1902; Lt.-Col. 1920; served South Africa, 1899-1902; European War, 1914-18; retired pay, 1925.
(*Died 29 April 1927.*)

BELLASIS, Edward, J.P.; Lancaster Herald. 1882; *b.* 1852; 2nd *s.* of Mr. Serjeant Bellasis, and Eliza Jane, *d.* of William Garnett of Quernmore Park, Lancashire. *Educ.:* Oratory School, Edgbaston. Barr-at-law, 1873; Bluemantle Pursuivant, 1873; Secretary to the Garter Missions to Spain, 1881; Saxony, 1882; Registrar of College of Arms, 1894-99; Unionist; Catholic. *Publications:* Cherubini: Memorials Illustrative of his Life, 1874-1912; Laws of Arms, Chiefly in Connection with Changes of Name, 1879; Westmorland Church Notes (2 vols.), 1888-89; Memorials of Mr. Serjeant Bellasis, 1893-95; Money Jar of Plautus, 1885; New Terence, etc.; Facsimile ed. Gerontius Coram Cardinali, 1917. *Recreations:* music, church history, cycling. *Address:* 90 Hagley Road, Edgbaston. (*Died 17 Mar. 1922.*)

BELLINGHAM, Sir Henry, 4th Bt. (2nd creation); *cr.* 1796; M.A.. S.C.L. Oxford, LL.D. Dublin; J.P.; H.M.'s Lieut., Louth; *b.* 23 Aug. 1846; *S.* father 1889; *m.* 1st, 1874, Lady Constance Julia Eleanor Georgiana Noel (*d.* 1891), *d.* of 2nd Earl of Gainsborough; two *s.* two *d.*; 2nd, 1895, Hon. Lelgarde Clifton, *d.* of 23rd Baroness Grey de Ruthyn. *Educ.:* Harrow; Exeter College, Oxford. Barrister, 1876; Captain, 5th Battalion Royal Irish Rifles; Commissioner of National Education, Ireland; M.P. Co. Louth, 1880; Private Chamberlain, Pius IX., Leo XIII. and Pius X.; Senator of the Royal University. *Publication:* Social Aspects: Catholicism v. Protestantism. 1878; articles in Dublin Review, Month, Catholic World, and C.T.S. *Recreation:* gardening. Owns about 6000 acres. *Heir:* s. Brig.-Gen. Edward H. C. P. Bellingham. *Address:* Castle Bellingham, Co. Louth, Ireland. *Clubs:* United University, Junior Travellers'; United Service, Dublin. (*Died 9 June 1921.*)

BELLOT, Hugh Hale Leigh, M.A., D.C.L.; Barrister-at-law; Membre de l'Institut de Droit International; *b.* 19 Oct. 1860; *o. surv. s.* of William Henry Bellot, M.D., F.R.C.S.Eng., 3rd Batt. Cheshire Regiment, and Frances Leigh, *d.* of John Egerton Killer, late of Millgate Hall, Stockport; *m.* 1888, Beatrice Violette (*d.* 1927), *y. d.* of Charles Clarke, late of Chorlton-cum-Hardy; one *s. Educ.:* Leamington Coll.; Trin. Coll., Oxford; called to Bar, Inner Temple, 1890; Hon. Sec. International Law Association and Grotius Society; formerly Acting Professor of Constitutional Law, University of London; Secretary Breaches of the Laws of War Committee. *Publications:* Ireland and Canada; Unconscionable Bargains with Moneylenders; The Inner and Middle Temple; The Miner's Guide: Bargains with Moneylenders; Commerce in War; Law of Children and Young Persons; The Pharmacy Acts; Pitt Cobbett's Leading Cases on Int. Law, 4th ed.; Permanent Court of Int. Justice; The Temple; Foote's Private Int. Law, 5th ed.; Gray's Inn and Lincoln's Inn; La Théorie Anglo-Saxonne des conflits de lois; Thomas's Leading Cases in Constitutional Law, 6th ed.; contributor to Reviews, etc. *Address:* 10 Gray's Inn Place, W.C.; The Mill, High Ham, Somerset; 2 King's Bench Walk, Temple, E.C. *T.:* City 1066. *T.A.:* Temple 41.

(*Died 11 Aug. 1928.*)

BELMONT, August, banker; *b.* New York, 18 Feb. 1853; *s.* of late August Belmont; *m.* 1910, Eleanor Robson. *Educ.:* Harvard. Head of August Belmont & Co. *Address:* 45 Cedar Street, New York. (*Died 10 Dec. 1924.*)

BELSHAW, Edward, I.S.O.; *m.* 1st, Mary Ann (*d.* 1909), *e. d.* of late James Couchman of Kensington; 2nd, Gertrude, widow of Rev. M. B. O'Connor of Fulneck, Leeds. Late Chief Clerk, Board of Education, South Kensington. *Address:* 49 Lee Terrace, Blackheath, S.E. *T.:* 1249 Lee Green. (*Died 29 Jan. 1916.*)

BENBOW, Sir Henry, K.C.B. *cr.* 1902; D.S.O., 1891; Chief Inspector of Machinery, R.N.; retired 1898; *b.* 5 Sept. 1888; 5th *s.* of late James Benbow, of Thornton Heath, Surrey, and Caroline, *d.* of late Benjamin Parrey; *m.* 1892, Elizabeth Jean, *o. d.* of late Henry Bird, Uxbridge, Middlesex; one *d. Educ.:* private school. Entered R.N. as Assist.Engineer in 1861; became Chief Engineer, 1879; promoted (for gallantry in action) to Inspector of Machinery, 1885; and Chief Inspector Machinery, 1888; served with Naval Brigade in Nile Expedition, 1884-85 (medal, bronze star), and repaired under heavy fire from the enemy the boiler of the "Safia," when disabled from a shot from Fort Wad Habeshi; specially mentioned in despatches. *Decorated* for services with Nile Expedition.

Address: Osborne House, Eastbourne.
(*Died 20 Oct. 1916.*)

BENCKENDORFF, Count de (Alexandre), Russian Ambassador in London since 1903; *b.* Berlin, 1 Aug. 1849; *s.* of Constantin, Comte de Benckendorff, and Louise, Princesse de Croÿ-Dülmen; *m.* 1879, Sophie, Comtesse Schouvaloff; one *s.* one *d. Educ.:* France; Germany. Entered diplomatic service, 1869; hon. attaché Rome and Vienna; left diplomatic service, 1876; re-entered it as 1st Secretary at Vienna, 1886; Russian Minister at Copenhagen, 1897-1903. *Address:* Chesham House, Chesham Place, S.W. *Clubs:* Turf, St. James's, Marlborough, Travellers', Beefsteak. (*Died 11 Jan. 1917.*)

BENDALL, Ernest Alfred, M.V.O. 1917; late Joint Examiner of Plays, St. James's Palace, 1912-20; *b.* 31 Aug. 1846; *s.* of late Alfred Bendall of Shortlands, Kent; *m.* 1868, Agnes (*d.* 1918), *d.* of late William Chatterley; no *c. Educ.:* Edinburgh Academy; City of London School. Clerk in Paymaster-General's Office, 1866; retired 1896; began journalism on London Figaro when in succession to Clement Scott and as predecessor to William Archer he wrote as Almaviva about the theatres, till in 1874, Edward Dicey, C.B., made him Dramatic Critic of the Observer. This position, together with a similar one on the Daily Mail, he was holding till he resigned both on his appointment in February 1912 as Joint-Examiner of Plays in the Lord Chamberlain's Office. He was Dramatic Critic to the St. James's Gazette during the whole of late Frederick Greenwood's editorship, has from time to time done similar work for the Morning Post, the Standard and the Daily News, and may be regarded, if any one regards dramatic critics, as having been the *doyen* of his craft. *Recreations:* billiards, travel. *Address* Queen Anne's Mansions. S.W. (*Died 12 July 1924.*)

BENEDITE, Leonce, Conservator Musee du Luxembourg, et du Musée Rodin, Paris; President, Société des Peintres Graveurs des Lithographes et des Peintres Orientalistes. Hon. Member The Senefelder Club; Officier de la Légion d'honneur. Many publications of modern art. (*Died May 1925.*)

BENGOUGH, Major-Gen. Sir Harcourt Mortimer, K.C.B., *cr.* 1908; C.B. 1886; *b.* 25 Nov. 1837; *s.* of George Bengough of The Ridge, Gloucester; *m.* Christina, *d.* of H. Maybery, 1876. *Educ.:* Rugby. Entered 77th Regt. 1855; Maj.-Gen., 1894; retired, 1898; served Crimea, 1855; the Zulu Campaign, 1878-1879 (despatches, medal with clasp, Brevet Lt.-Col.); Burma expedition, 1885-86 (despatches, medal with clasp); A.A.G., Madras, 1882-86; commanded 2nd class district, Madras, 1886-91; troops in Jamaica, 1893-94; 1st Infantry Brigade, Aldershot, 1894-97. *Publications:* Preparatory Battle Formations, 2nd ed. 1900; Notes on Boer War, 1901; Night Fighting, from the Russian; Memories of a Soldier's Life, 1913. *Address:* Hyde Brae. Chalford. Gloucester. (*Died 30 Mar. 1922.*)

BENN, Alfred William, B.A. London; Member of the Society for the Promotion of Hellenic Studies; *b.* Moylescar Rectory, Westmeath, Ireland, 1843; *y. s.* of late Rev. Wm. Benn, B.D., and Mary, *d.* of the Rev. Wm. Dunn, 1886, Edith Maude, B.A. London; *y. d.* of late Edward Thomson of Tunbridge Wells. *Educ.:* chiefly at home. 1st class Classical Honours, and 3rd class Honours in Logic and Moral Philosophy at the second B.A. Examination, University of London. Matriculated at the University of London, 1864; graduated B.A. 1865; left England, 1866, and has lived abroad ever since, chiefly in Italy and Switzerland; on the staff of the Academy, 1885-97; Represented London University at the Philosophical Congress, Bologna, 1911. *Publications:* The Greek Philosophers, 2 vols. 1882. 2nd ed. revised and partly rewritten, 1914; The Philosophy of Greece,

1898; The History of English Rationalism in the Nineteenth Century, 2 vols., 1906; Modern England, 2 vols., 1908; A Primer of Early Greek Philosophy, 1908; Revaluations, 1909; History of Ancient Philosophy; History of Modern Philosophy (History of Science Series), 1912. *Recreations*: astronomy, book-collecting, cycling. *Address*: Il Cillegio, Via del Palmerino, Florence, Italy. *Clubs*: Royal Societies, Authors', London University.
(Died 16 Sept. 1916.)

BENN, Sir Joan (Williams), 1st Bt., cr. 1914; Kt. cr. 1906; J.P. D.L.; Chairman, L.C.C., 1904; b. Hyde, Cheshire, 13 Nov. 1850; e. s. of Rev. Julius Benn, and Ann, d. of William Taylor of Gerrards, Cheshire; m. Lily, 4th d. of late John Pickstone of Silver Hill, Hyde, Cheshire; four s. two d. M.P. (L.) St. George's, E., 1892-95; contested Deptford, 1897; Bermondsey, 1900; member of L.C.C. since its creation 1889; chairman, 1904-5; M.P. (L.) Devonport, 1904-10; contested Clapham, 1910; late chairman of the General Purposes and of the Highways Committee. *Recreations*: sketching, golf. *Heir*: s. Ernest John [b. 25 June 1875; m. 1903, Gwendoline Dorothy, y. d. of Frederick M. Andrews, of Edgbaston]. *Address*: Stone Wall, Limpsfield, Surrey. *T.*: Oxted 161.
(Died 10 April 1922.)

BENNETT, Alfred Rosling, M.I.E.E.; Past Vice-Pres. Institution of Locomotive Engineers; b. London, 1850; unmarried. *Educ.*: Bellevue Academy. General Manager and Chief Engineer for Scotland and North of England to the National Telephone Co., 1883-90; subsequently General Manager and Chief Engineer to the Mutual Telephone Co. and the New Telephone Co.; Engineer to the Municipal Telephone Exchange systems at Glasgow, Guernsey, Portsmouth, Hull, Brighton, and Swansea; Vice-Chairman Executive Council, Edinburgh International Exhibition, 1890; Inventor of the Telephonic Translator, 1880; the Caustic Alkali and Iron Battery, 1881; and Convection Mill, 1896. *Publications*: A Cheap Form of Voltaic Battery, 1882; An Electrical Parcels Exchange, 1892; Telephone Systems of Continental Europe, 1895; A Convection-Scope and Calorimeter, 1897; Proposals for London Improvements, 1904; Historic Locomotives, 1906; The First Railway in London, 1912; A Saga of Guernsey, 1918; London and Londoners in the 1850's and 1860's, 1924; and numerous pamphlets on telephonic subjects and papers contributed to scientific societies. *Recreations*: travel and research. *Club*: Engineers.
(Died 24 May 1928.)

BENNETT, George Lovett, M.A., Cambridge; Headmaster of Sutton Valence School 1883-1910; b. 28 March 1846; s. of late Edmund Bennett of Florence, 3rd s. of late George Bennett, Q.C., of Grange, King's County, and Merrion Square, Dublin; m. 1874, Emma Lucretia, d. of Joseph Sheridan Le Fanu, of Merrion Square, Dublin; two d. *Educ.*: Rugby School; St. John's Coll., Cambridge (Scholar). Second Class Classical Tripos, 1869; Assistant Master Rugby School, 1875; Headmaster Plymouth College, 1877. *Publications*: Easy Latin Stories; First and Second Latin Writers; Second Latin Reader; Viri Illustres; Selections from Cæsar; Selections from Virgil. *Recreations*: riding, cycling, shooting, fishing. *Address*: East Sutton, nr. Maidstone. *Club*: Constitutional.
(Died 30 Nov. 1916.)

BENNETT, George Wheatley, I.S.O. 1903; b. 22 Aug. 1845; s. of Richard Wheatley Bennett, Demerara and London; m. 1875, Kathleen, d. of Charles Glenton; one s. Entered the Civil Service as a clerk in the Customs, 1863; Accountant and Comptroller-General of Customs, 1902; retired 1906. *Recreations*: mainly literary. *Address*: 82 Milton

Park, Highgate, N.6. *Club*: Constitutional.
(Died 12 Nov. 1921.)

BENNETT, James Gordon, Proprietor of the New York Herald; b. 10 May 1841; m. 1914, Baroness de Reuter; commissioned the late Hon. H. M. Stanley "to find Livingstone." Owns yacht "Namouna." *Address*: 28 West 21st Street, New York; 120 Avenue des Champs Elysées, Paris. *T.*: 524, 49. *Clubs*: Automobile, Polo. Yacht.
(Died 14 May 1918.)

BENNETT, Engineer Rear-Admiral James Martin Cameron, M.V.O., 1902; Assist. Engineer, 1871; Chief Engineer, 1887; Engineer Captain, 1892; served Perak Expedition, 1885-86 (medal and clasp); Engineer Captain H.M. Yacht Victoria and Albert, 1908. *Address*: Boldrewood, Winn Road, Southampton.
(Died 1922.)

BENNETT, Sir Thomas Jewell, Kt., cr. 1921; C.I.E. 1903; M.P. (U.) Sevenoaks Division of Kent, 1918-23; J.P., Kent; Principal Proprietor of the Times of India; b. 1852; s. of late J. T. Bennett, of Wisbech, Cambridgeshire; m. 1917, Elena, 2nd d. of late Thomas Brooke-Jones. Took to journalism early in life; was for some years assistant editor of the Western Daily Press at Bristol; joined the leader-writing staff of the Standard; proceeded to Bombay, 1884; for eight years associate-editor of the Bombay Gazette; succeeded to the editorship and the principal proprietary interest in the Times of India; when he left India in 1901, he was presented by 3000 of the agriculturists of Guzerat with an address thanking him for the successful persistency with which he had brought the grievances of the cultivating class to the notice of Government; awarded the silver medal of the Society of Arts for a paper on the British connection with the Persian Gulf, 1902; nominated by the Bombay Government a Fellow of the Bombay Univ.; contested Brigg Div. of Lincolnshire 1910; a representative of Rochester Diocese in the National Assembly of the Church of England. *Address*: 38 Hans Place, S.W. *T.*: Kensington 306; Harwarton House, Speldhurst, Tunbridge Wells. *T.*: Tunbridge Wells 779. *Clubs*: Carlton, Oriental; Byculla, Royal Yacht, Bombay. *(Died 16 Jan. 1925.)*

BENNETT, William Hart, C.M.G. 1909; F.R.C.I.; Governor of British Honduras since 1918; b. 4 June 1861; s. of Hart Bennett, C.E.; m. Ella Mary (d. 1914), y. d. of late Charles Tuck, J.P. of Norwich; no c. Entered Colonial Office, 1878; chief clerk, Chief Secretary's Office, Cyprus, 1884-1900; Acting Comsr., Papho, 1894; Asst.-Secretary to Govt., 1895; Colonial Secretary, Falklands, 1900-5; acted as Governor of the Falklands and Bahamas on many occasions; Member of the West India Committee; Colonial Secretary, Bahamas, 1905-17. *Address*: Government House, British Honduras. *Club*: Royal Societies. *(Died 4 Sept. 1918.)*

BENNETT, Sir William Henry, K.C.V.O.; cr. 1901; F.R.C.S. Eng.; F.Z.S.; Knight of Grace of the Order of St. John of Jerusalem; Comm. of the Roy. Order of the Redeemer of Greece; H.M. Inspector of Anatomy; Member of Consulting Staff of Osborne; Consulting Surgeon to St. George's Hospital and to Hospital of St. John and St. Elizabeth; Consulting Surg. to Seamen's Hospital, Greenwich; late Member of Court of Examiners, Royal College of Surgeons of England; Chairman Convalescent Homes Committee, King Edward VII. Hospital Fund; b. 1852; s. of William Francis Bennett of Chilmark; m. 1st, 1882, Isabel (d. 1911), d. of Thomas Dickinson; 2nd, 1914, Gladys Florence Stewart, d. of Rev. Allen S. Hartigan of St. Leonards-on-Sea, and formerly of Monkstown, Co. Dublin. A Wiltshireman, and Fellow of several learned Societies; was for some time Examiner in Surgery at Cambridge University; has been Lecturer on Anatomy and on Surgery at St. George's Hospital, is Surgeon-in-Chief St. John's Ambulance Brigade; Vice-President Seamen's Hospital Socy.; Chairman Invalid Children's Aid Association; Chairman Star and Garter Home, Richmond and Sandgate; President Institute of Hygiene; President Illuminating Engineers Soc. *Decorated* for services rendered to sick and wounded returning from South Africa, Boer War, 1900-2, for which he was publicly thanked by Lord Roberts. Relinquished all private at.airs during the War 1914-19 to take up work with British Red Cross and Order of St. John. *Publications:* various surgical treatises and communications. *Address:* 3 Hyde Park Place, W. *T.:* Pad. 1060. *M.:* LB 8044. *Clubs:* Athenaeum, Junior Carlton. (*Died 27 Aug. 1920.*)

BENNETT, William H., K.C., Senator, Canada, Nov. 1917; *b.* Barrie, 23 Dec. 1859; *m.* 1905, Margaret A., *d.* of Henry Cargill, M.P. *Educ.:* Barrie High School. M.P. for East Simcoe, 1892-1917. *Address:* Midland, Ontario. Canada. (*Died 15 Mar. 1925.*)

BENNETT-GOLDNEY, Francis, F.S.A.; M.P. (C.), and Mayor of the City and County of Canterbury; 2nd *s.* of late Sebastian Evans, M.A., LL.D., author, artist, and journalist, and nephew of late Sir John Evans, K.C.B., F.R.S.; *b.* Moseley, near Birmingham, 1865. *Educ.:* privately Bournemouth, Paris; assumed mother's name of Goldney, 1892. Post of, Hon. Director of the Royal Museum at Canterbury; Hon. Freeman and Alderman of the City; Governor of the Kent and Canterbury Hospital, and of the Simon Langton Schools; formerly Captain 6th Militia Batt. the Middlesex Regiment; Member Territorial Association for the County of Kent. *Recreations:* writing, riding, fencing, and swimming. *Address:* Abbott Barton, Canterbury; Devonshire Terrace, Sandgate. (*Died 27 July 1918.*)

BENNING, Captain Charles Stuart, R.N., D.S.O. 1916; *b.* 28 Nov. 1884; 2nd *s.* of Crichton S. Benning, The Limes, Dunstable, Beds; *m.* 1908, Effie, 2nd *d.* of R. Byrth Rowson, Warrington; two *d.* one *s.* *Educ.:* Dunstable. Joined H.M.S. Britannia, 1899; passed out as Midshipman; passed examination for Lieutenant with five firsts, receiving Admiralty prize for meritorious examination; Lieut., 1905; joined submarine service, 1905; appointed E5, 1914; present at Battle of Heligoland Bight, 28 Aug. (despatches); Commander, June 1915; Captain, 1920; awarded D.S.O. for services in submarines in enemy's waters, Oct. 1916; in command of British Submarines in the Mediterranean, 1918 (despatches, Order of Crown of Italy). *Address:* c/o Admiralty, S.W.1. (*Died 7 Mar. 1924.*)

BENSON, Arthur Christopher, Master of Magdalene College, Cambridge, since 1915; C.V.O. 1907; LL.D. (Hon.) Cambridge, 1915; M.A., F.R.Hist.S., F.R.S.L.; Member of the Academic Committee; Member of the Court of the Fishmongers' Company; Governor of Gresham's School, Holt; *b.* 24 Apr. 1862; *s.* of late Archbishop of Canterbury; unmarried. *Educ.:* Eton; King's College, Cambridge (Scholar). First class Classics, 1884; Master at Eton College, 1885-1903; Fellow of Magdalene College, Cambridge, 1904-15. *Publications:* Memoirs of Arthur Hamilton, 1886; Archbishop Laud: a Study, 1887; Men of Might (with Mr. H. F. W. Tatham), 1890; Poems, 1893; Lyrics, 1895; Essays, 1896; Lord Vyet and other Poems, 1896; Fasti Etonenses (a Biographical History of Eton College), 1899; Life of Archbishop Benson, 1899; The Professor, and other poems, 1900; The Schoolmaster, 1902; The House of Quiet, 1903; Tennyson (Little Biographies Series); Selections from Whittier, 1903; The Hill of Trouble, 1903; The Isles of Sunset, 1904; Rossetti, English Men of Letters Series, 1904; Peace and other

Poems, 1905; Edward FitzGerald, English Men of Letters Series, 1905; The Upton Letters, 1905; The Thread of Gold, 1906; Walter Pater, English Men of Letters Series, 1906; From a College Window, 1906; The Gate of Death, 1906; Beside Still Waters, 1907; The Altar Fire, 1907; Selections from the Correspondence of Queen Victoria (edited, with Viscount Esher), 1907; At Large, 1908; Poems (Collected), 1909; The Silent Isle, 1910; Ruskin: a Study in Personality, 1911; The Leaves of the Tree, 1911; The Child of the Dawn, 1912; Thy Rod and Thy Staff, 1912; Along the Road; Joyous Gard; Watersprings, 1913; Where No Fear Was; The Orchard Pavilion, 1914; Hugh: Memoirs of a Brother; Escape and Other Essays, 1915; Father Payne, 1916; Life and Letters of Maggie Benson, 1917; The Reed of Pan, Selections from Ruskin, A Little History of Magdalene College, The Trefoil, 1923; Memories and Friends, 1924. *Recreations:* football till 1889; Alpine Club, 1894; bicycling, etc. *Address:* The Old Lodge, Magdalene College, Cambridge; Lamb House, Rye. *Clubs:* Alpine, Royal Societies, Athenæum. (*Died 17 June 1925.*)

BENSON, Major-General Sir Frederick William, K.C.B. cr. 1910, C.B. 1901; retired; Colonel, 21st Lancers; Hon. Colonel, 19th St. Catharine's Regt. Canadian Militia; *b.* St. Catharine's, Canada, 2 August 1849; 3rd *s.* of late Hon. J. R. Benson, of the Canadian Senate, and Marianne, *d.* of late Charles Ingersoll, of Ingersoll, Canada; *m.* Caroline, *e. d.* of late Sir G. E. Couper, 2nd Bart., K.C.S.I. *Educ.:* Upper Canada College, Toronto; R.M.C., Sandhurst. Served as Volunteer during Fenian raids in Canada, 1866 (medal with clasp); joined 21st Hussars, 1869; exchanged to 12th Royal Lancers, 1876; passed Staff College 1880; Captain, 5th Dragoon Guards, 1880; exchanged to 17th Lancers, 1881; A.D.C. to Lieut.-Governor, North-West Provinces, India, 1877; Brigade-Major, Poona, 1882-84; Garrison Instructor, Bengal, 1884-90; commanded Egyptian cavalry, 1892-94; D.A.A.G. (Instruction) Dublin, 1895-98; Assistant Adjutant-General, Chief Staff Officer, South-Eastern District, 1898-1900; special service S. Africa, A.A.G. 6th division S.A. Field Force, 1900-1 (despatches, medal, three clasps, C.B.); Headquarters, 1901-3; Inspector-General of Remounts, 1903-4; Director of Transport and Remounts, 1904-7; Maj.-Gen. in charge of Administration, 1907-9. *Address:* Dahinda, 5 Hartfield Road, Eastbourne. *Club:* Army and Navy. (*Died 19 Aug. 1916.*)

BENSON, Sir Ralph (Sillery), Kt., cr. 1906; I.C.S., retired; *b.* 1851; *s.* of Charles Benson, President, Royal College of Surgeons, Dublin, and Maria, *d.* of Maunsell Andrews, J.P.; *m.* 1876, Fanny Catharine Alice (holds Kaiser-i-Hind gold medal), *d.* of Rev. W. Gilbert-Cooper, M.A., formerly of the Indian Ecclesiastical Establishment; one *s.* *Educ.:* Trinity College, Dublin (M.A., LL.B.). Entered I.C.S. 1873; Barrister, Middle Temple, 1887; Registrar, High Court, Madras, 1885; Under-Secretary to Government, Madras, 1887; Secretary to Board of Revenue, 1888; District and Sessions Judge, 1888-95; Puisne Judge, High Court, Madras, 1896-1913 (twice Acting Chief Justice); Vice-Chancellor, Madras University, 1905. *Recreations:* travel, shooting, golf. *Address:* Roebuck Grove, Donnybrook, Dublin. *T.:* Ballsbridge 296. *Club:* University, Dublin. (*Died 19 Oct. 1920.*)

BENSON, Vice-Adm. Robert Edmund Ross, R.N., C.B. 1916; *m.* Williama Margaret (*d.* 1924). Served as midshipman at Bombardment of Alexandria, 1882; Egyptian War (medal, clasp, bronze star); European War, 1914-16 (C.B.); Inspecting Captain of Mechanical Training Establishments, 1912-14, Rear-Adm. retired, 1918; Vice-Adm. 1923.

Address : Snail Creep, Houghton, Stockbridge, Hants.   (*Died 3 Feb. 1927.*)

BENSON, Ven. Archdeacon Thomas M. ; Archdeacon of Connor since 1914 ; Rector of Ballymoney since 1880 ; Rural Dean of Coleraine since 1898 ; member of Diocesan Council since 1898 ; member of General Synod of the Church of Ireland since 1903 ; *s.* of late George Benson, Mus. Bac. Cantab, Professor Royal Academy of Music, Lay Vicar of Westminster Abbey, and Gentleman of Her Majesty's Chapel Royal ; *b.* London ; *m.* 1871, Jane Gardner, *s. d.* of Rev. James Orr, Newmills, co. Down ; five *s.* four *d.*   *Educ. :* King's College School, London ; private tuition in South of France.   Deacon, 1874 ; Priest, 1875 ; Curate of Donaghcloney, Diocese of Dromore, 1874-78 ; Vicar of Scarva, 1878-80 ; Chaplain of Ballymoney Union ; Rural Dean of Ballymena, 1893-98 ; Prebendary of Cairncastle, 1898-1903 ; Chancellor of Connor, 1908.   *Address :* The Rectory, Ballymoney, Co. Antrim.
         (*Died 16 Nov. 1921.*)

BENSON, William Arthur Smith, Architect and Designer in Metal-Work ; *b.* 1854 ; *s.* of William Benson, J.P., of Alresford, Hants ; *m.* 1886, Venetia, *d.* of Alfred W. Hunt, R.W.S. *Educ. :* Winchester ; New College, Oxford. Was a pupil of Basil Champneys ; started the business which bears his name, 1880 ; was one of the originators of the Arts and Crafts Exhibition Society, and of the Home Arts and Industries Association ; has lectured on decorative design for the University Extension. *Publication :* Elements of Handicraft and Design, 1893.   *Address :* 18 Hereford Square, S.W.7.   *Clubs :* Royal Societies, Burlington Fine Arts.   (*Died 5 July 1924.*)

BENSON, His Honour Judge William Denman, LL.D., J.P. Glamorganshire ; Judge of County Courts, Circuit 13, since 1907 ; *b.* 21 March 1848 ; 2nd *s.* of Gen. Henry Roxly Benson, C.B., and Mary Henrietta, *d.* of late Mr. Justice Wightman ; *m.* 1876, Jane, 2nd *d.* of late Thos. Penrice, D.L., of Kilvrough, Glamorganshire ; two *s.* one *d.*   *Educ. :* Eton ; Balliol College, Oxford. Called to Bar, 1874 ; joined South Wales and Chester Circuit ; Revising Barrister and Counsel to the Post Office.   *Recreation :* shooting ; Pres. O.U.B.C. 1870-71 ; rowed Oxford and Cambridge Boat Race, 1868, -69, -70.   *Address :* 10 William Street, Lowndes Square, S.W.   *Clubs :* Reform, National Liberal, M.C.C., Leander ; Sheffield.
         (*Died 19 Feb. 1919.*)

BENTLEY, Alfred, R.E., A.R.C.A. Lond. ; artist ; *y. s.* of late Capt. W. E. Bentley, F.R.G.S. ; unmarried. *Educ. :* Royal College of Art, London. Exhibited in all the principal Galleries in England and abroad ; joined Artists' Rifles, April 1915 ; gazetted to Norfolk Regt. and served in France (M.C.).   *Recreation :* music. *Address :* 15 Radcliffe Square, S.W.
         (*Died 18 Feb. 1923.*)

BENTON, Sir John, K.C.I.E. *cr.* 1911 ; C.I.E. 1902 ; late India Public Works Department ; Chief Engineer and Secretary to Government, Panjab Irrigation Branch ; *b.* 5 Aug. 1850 ; *s.* of late John Benton of Sherrifhaugh ; *m.* 1885, Margaret Forsyth, *d.* of Provost Dick of Rothes, N.B. ; two *d.*   *Educ. :* Aberdeen University, Edinburgh University, Royal Indian Engineering College, Coopers Hill (Fellow). Appointed Assistant Engineer, 1873 ; Executive Engineer, 1881 ; Superintending Engineer, 1897 ; Chief Engineer, 1900 ; Inspector-General of Irrigation, 1905 ; retired, 1912.   *Address :* Westcroft, Silverdale Road, Eastbourne.   *T. :* Eastbourne 1386.   (*Died 29 Aug. 1927.*)

BERENS, Alexander Augustus, country gentleman ; J.P. Northamptonshire ; *o. s.* of Otto Berens, Raleigh Hall Brixton ; *b.* 1842 ; *m.* 1st, 1865, Mary Shaw Hellier ; 2nd, 1866, Louise Winifred, *d.* of Rev. Edward Stewart ; one *s.*

three *d.*   *Educ. :* Trinity Hall, Cambridge (B.A., M.A.) ; Major (retired) 3rd Batt. Northamptonshire Regiment.   *Address :* 30 Chester Square, S.W.1.   *T. :* Victoria 1648.
         (*Died 31 May 1926.*)

BERESFORD, 1st Baron, *cr.* 1916, of Metemmeh and of Curraghmore ; **Admiral Charles William de la Poer Beresford,** G.C.B., *cr.* 1911 ; K.C.B., *cr.* 1903 ; G.C.V.O., *cr.* 1906 ; *b.* Ireland, 10 Feb. 1846 ; 2nd *s.* of Rev. John, 4th Marquess of Waterford ; *m.* 1878, Mina, *d.* of late Richard Gardner, M.P. Leicester ; two *d.*   *Educ. :* Bayford School ; Rev. Mr. Foster's, Stubbington, Fareham, Hants. Entered "Britannia" as cadet, 1859 ; Sub-Lieut. 1866 ; Lieut. 1868 ; Commander, 1875 ; Capt. 1882 ; Rear-Admiral, 1897 ; Naval A.D.C. to H.M. the Queen, 1896-97 ; Naval A.D.C. to H.R.H. Prince of Wales on his visit to India, 1875-76 ; M.P. (C.) Waterford, 1874-80 ; East Division of Marylebone, 1885-89 ; M.P. York, 1897-1900 ; commanded "Condor," bombardment Alexandria, 1882 (medal with clasp, bronze star, 3rd class Medjidieh, and specially mentioned in despatches for gallantry) ; landed at Alexandria after bombardment and instituted regular police system ; served on Lord Wolseley's staff, Nile Expedition, 1884-85 : and subsequently in command of naval brigade at battles of Abu Klea, Abu Kru, and Metemmeh (mentioned for gallantry) ; in command of expedition which rescued Sir Charles Wilson's party in "Safia," when boiler was repaired under fire ; specially mentioned in despatches for gallantry, and in the speeches of both Houses in the vote of thanks for operations in the Soudan ; a Lord Commissioner of the Admiralty, 1886 ; resigned 1888, on question of strength of fleet ; while Capt. of "Undaunted" rendered assistance on the occasion of the grounding of the "Seignalay," for which received thanks of French Government ; in command of steam reserve at Chatham, 1893-96 ; visited China on a special mission, at request of Associated Chambers of Commerce of Great Britain, 1898-99 ; Rear-Admiral, Mediterranean, 1900-2 ; M.P. (C.) Woolwich, 1902 ; Commanded Channel Squadron, 1903-1905 ; Admiral, 1906 ; Commander-in-Chief, Mediterranean Fleet, 1905-7 ; Channel Fleet, 1907-9 ; retired 1911 ; M.P. (U.) Portsmouth, 1910-16. Three medals for saving life. *Publications :* Nelson and his Times ; numerous essays and articles on naval matters and Egypt ; The Break-up of China, 1899 ; The Betrayal, 1912 ; Memories, 1914.   *Recreations :* turning, carpentering, cycling, hunting, or any sport. *Heir :* none.   *Address :* 1 Great Cumberland Place, W.   *Clubs :* Athenæum, Carlton, Turf, United Service, Savage, Marlborough.   (*Died 6 Sept. 1919.*)

BERESFORD, Col. Charles Edward de la Poer ; *b.* Corfu, 23 Oct. 1850 ; *m.* 1882, Solita Henrietta, *d.* and *co-heiress* of H. C. M. Ximénes de Cisneros. *Educ. :* Versailles ; Rev. Mr. Foster's, Stubbington, Fareham ; R.M.C., Sandhurst. p.s.c. Interpreter, French, etc. Entered H.M. 46th Regt. 1869 as Ensign, without purchase ; D.A.A.G. Jamaica, 1890 ; Chief Staff Officer Jamaica, 1891 ; D.A.A.G. Western District, 1893 ; Lieut.-Colonel, 1898 ; Military Attaché, British Embassy, St. Petersburg, 1898-1903 ; Colonel, 1902 ; Knight Commander of Order of St. Anne of Russia, 1903 ; retired 1904 ; rejoined for Active Service, 1914 ; appointed Commandant School of Instruction, N. District ; retired for age, March 1916 ; King's Badge, June 1916.   *Publications :* The Conquest of Oran ; A Historical Account of the Beresford Family, etc. ; contributor to various periodicals ; corresp. The Times, siege of Port Arthur, 1903.   *Recreation :* change.   *Address :* Old Place, Boveney, Windsor.   (*Died 22 Aug. 1921.*)

BERESFORD, Rev. John, M.A. ; Vicar of Wells, 1870-1916 ; Prebendary of Combe, the 9th in Wells Cathedral since 1883 ; *b.* 1839 ; *m.*

1865, Maria Emelia (d. 1918), o. d. of Quintin Jamieson, M.D., late Madras Horse Artillery; six s. two d. Educ.: Priory School, Norwich; Emmanuel Coll., Cambridge. B.A., 1861; M.A., 1865; Curate of St. Margaret's, Ipswich, 1862-64; senior Curate of Walcot, Bath, 1864-70; Curate of St. Stephen, Lansdown, Bath, 1870; Rural Dean of Shepton Mallet, 1898-1916. Publication: Sermons, 1863. Recreation: riding. Address: 6 St. Ann Street, Salisbury. (Died Dec. 1918.)

BERESFORD, Maj.-Gen. John Beresford, retired; Bengal Staff Corps; b. Oct. 1828; m. 1866, Emma E. A., 3rd d. of Rev. B. Savile; five s. five d.. Educ.: Lucan School, Co. Dublin. Entered E. I. Company's service by director's nomination, 1845; posted to 29th Regt. Bengal Infantry; passed Interpreter's Exam. and served as Interpreter and Quartermaster, 1850-56; served in second Punjab campaign (medal) and on Punjab Frontier during Mutiny, 1857-58, passed as Interpreter in Punjabi language; two years British Resident in Cashmere; retired on colonel's pension, 1877, with hon. rank of Major-General. Address: Craig Dhu Varren House, Portrush; Glenamoyle Lodge, Co. Londonderry. M.: 1W 64.

BERESFORD, John Stuart, C.I.E. 1900; b. 11 Feb. 1845; s. of late Thomas Beresford; m. 1872, Elizabeth (d. 1919), d. of late William Quinton; three d. Appointed to Public Works Department, India, 1867; Chief Engineer and Secretary to Government N.W. Provinces and Oudh, 1892; Chief Engineer and Sec. to Chief Commissioner, Central Provinces, 1893-96; Chief Engineer and Secretary to Government of Punjab, Irrigation Branch, 1896-1900; Member of Punjab Legislative Council, 1897-1900; Secretary to the Government of India and Inspector General of Irrigation, 1898; retired from the Indian Service, 1900; M.E. Queen's University, Ireland; Member of the Institution of Civil Engineers; Fellow of Allahabad University. Publications: several monographs and reports on engineering subjects. Address: Maythorne, Ealing, W. T.: Ealing 768. Club: East India United Service. (Died 1 May 1926.)

BERESFORD, Lord Marcus de la Poer, K.C.V.O., cr. 1918; Extra Equerry and Manager of H.M.'s thoroughbreds; b. Christmas Day, 1848; s. of 4th Marquis of Waterford; m. 1895, Louisa Catherine (d. 1920), e. d. of late Maj.-Gen. C. W. Ridley, C.B. Educ.: Harrow. Entered 7th Hussars; A.D.C. to Lord Lieut. of Ireland, 1874-76; starter for Jockey Club, 1885-90; manages Sandringham Stud; member of Royal Victorian Order. (Died 16 Dec. 1922.)

BERESFORD, Hon. Seton Robert de la Poer Horsley, Shipper (Managing Director of two Shipping Associations); b. 25 July 1868; 3rd s. of 3rd Baron Decies; m. 1st, 1899, Delia Dorothy (who obtained a divorce, 1909), d. of late Daniel John O'Sullivan of the Grange, Killarney, Co. Kerry; 2nd, 1915, Rosemary, e. d. of Rear-Admiral Sir Charles Graves Sawle, M.V.O., of Penrice, Cornwall. Educ.: Eton; Camb. Acted for Central News, S.A. Campaign; first to enter Kimberley, 4 hours ahead of Gen. French; notified Cecil Rhodes of approach of relief force; associated with The Tribune during its 3 years' life; went into business in U.S. 1909; carried through negotiations with Peruvian Govt. whereby the Peruvian Irrigation and Colonisation Scheme was sanctioned by Pres. Beuvenides; joined Archer H. Brown, New York, 1914; organised assembly and despatch of 25,000 horses to France and formulated a co-operative shipping plan now in operation between N. and S. America; an authority on the relationship between Capital and Labour, on which subject he has written articles especially dealing with profit-sharing plans and co-partnership between employers and employed. Recreations: shooting, fishing, hunting, skating, boxing, cricket,

etc.; played cricket for Middlesex; played for Old Niagara ice hockey, unbeaten team, and also for All England Team, 1897-98; held the World's Championship, Monte Carlo (trap shooting), 1901-4; won (representing Ireland) International Championship, San Sebastian, Spain; swam Cap Martin to Monaco Bay, 3 hrs. 7 mins.; won Atherstone Hunt, point-to-point steeplechase. Address: 2 Wall Street, New York. T.A.: Bereschili, New York. Club: Wellington. (Died 28 May 1928.)

BERESFORD - PEIRSE, Sir Henry Monson de la Poer, 8rd Bt.; cr. 1814; b. 25 Sep. 1850; S. uncle, 1873; m. 1st, 1873, Lady Adelaide Bernard, d. of 3rd Earl of Bandon (d. 1884); five s.; 2nd, 1886, Henrietta, O.B.E., o. d. of Sir Matthew Smith-Dodsworth, 4th Bt.; one d. Educ.: Eton; Trin. Coll., Camb. Owns over 3000 acres. Heir: s. Henry. Address: The Hall, Bedale, Yorkshire. Club: Carlton.
(Died 8 July 1926.)

BERGH, Rt. Rev. Frederick Thomas; Benedictine Abbot; visitor of certain Benedictine Monasteries in England; Chaplain to nuns; b. Brixham, Devon, 9 Oct. 1840, of Danish family settled in England in eighteenth century. Educ.: England and France; university course in Rome. Priest, 1869; Teacher of Philosophy and Mathematics in Rome; Superior of Ramsgate Monastery, 1877; appointed Abbot by Papal Decree, 1896. Publications: compiling and editing liturgical books, articles in Catholic periodicals. Address: The Convent, Carshalton House, Carshalton. T.: Sutton 287. (Died 12 Aug. 1924.)

BERGHOLT, Ernest George Binckes, M.A., author and journalist; Indoor Pastimes Editor of the Queen since 1908; Cards Editor of Field since 1915; Member of Council and Fellow of Chartered Institute of Secretaries, 1904-21; b. Worcester, 14 Feb. 1856; m. 1892, Florence Woodland. Educ.: Christ's Hospital; Cambridge. Senior Optime, Mathematical Tripos, 1879; entered Civil Service, First Class, by competitive Examination; Chief Modern Side Master, Bradfield College, 1880-81; Army Coach, 1882-86; on staff of Dramatic Review, 1886; on Court and Society Review and Editor of Musical Standard, 1888; at invitation of Cavendish contributed regularly to Field on Whist, etc., 1898; Bridge Editor of Onlooker, 1901-7, when he first introduced journalistic Bridge Tournaments; organized Daily Mirror Bridge Competition, 1903-4; wrote the Auction Bridge Column (under name of Yarborough) in Sunday Times, 1915-24; specialist on all indoor games. Publications: Principles and Practice of Whist, 1902; Double Dummy Bridge Problems, 1905; edited Hoyle's Games Modernized, 1909; First and Second New Book of Patience Games, 1914; Royal Auction Bridge, 1917; Rover Bridge; Outlaw Bridge; Compendium of Poker; Compendium of Dominoes; Contract Bridge; Translations into Latin Elegiac Verse, 1918; Complete Handbook of Solitaire, 1920; Bergholt's Modern Auction, 1925. Recreations: music, private theatricals. Address: Wethermel, Letchworth Garden City. (Died 18 Nov. 1925.)

BERINGER, Oscar, Director of Philharmonic Society; Examiner Royal Academy of Music; Royal Coll. of Music; b. Baden, Germany, 14 July 1844. Educ.: Conservatoire, Leipzig; Tausig's School, Berlin. First appearance, Saturday Concerts, Crystal Palace, 1860. Recreations: no time to indulge in hobbies. Address: 40 Wigmore Street, W. Club: Arts.
(Died 21 Feb. 1922.)

BERKELEY, Sir Henry Spencer, Kt., K.C.; cr. 1896; J.P.; b. 6 Sep. 1851; m. 1878, Katharine, d. of F. S. Cassin, of Antigua, West Indies; two s. three d. Barr. Inner Temple, 1878; Solicitor-General, Leeward Islands, 1878; Attorney-General, Fiji, 1885-89; Chief-Justice, 1889-1902; Attorney-General, Hong-Kong, 1902

1906 ; K.C., Hong-Kong, 1906 ; administered the Government of Fiji and acted as High Commissioner for the Western Pacific on several occasions while Chief Justice of Fiji ; Member of West Suffolk County Council, 1913 ; J.P., West Suffolk, 1916. *Address:* Bures, Suffolk. *Club:* Junior Carlton.   (*Died 30 Sept.* 1918.)

BERKELEY, Maj.-Gen. James Cavan, C.I.E., 1888 ; *b.* Clifton, 23 Jan. 1839 ; *s.* of late General Sackville Hamilton Berkeley ; *m.* 1st, Anna Sophia (*d.* 1886), *d.* of Capt. G. Middlecoat, Madras Art. ; 2nd, Maud, *y. d.* of W. Tomlinson, F.R.A.S., of York and Sandown, Isle of Wight ; three *s.* five *d.* *Educ.:* King's Coll., London, Fellow. Joined Indian Army, 1857 ; entered Political Service under Government of India, 1862 ; and, after holding many minor posts, was successively British Resident at Gwalior, Kashmir and Nipal Courts, and Agent to the Governor-General at Baroda. *Decorated* for political services in India. *Address:* 12 Rosemount Road, Bournemouth, W.   (*Died 12 Oct.* 1926.)

BERNAL, Frederic, C.M.G., 1891 ; retired ; *b.* London, 8 Feb. 1828 ; *y. s.* of late Ralph Bernal (Chairman of Committee of the House of Commons) ; *m.* 1850, Charlotte Augusta (*d.* 1903), *d.* of J. Brewster Cozens, Woodham Mortimer Lodge, Maldon, Essex : one *s.* one *d.* *Educ.:* Eton. Supernumerary Committee Clerk of the House of Commons, 1847-48 ; H.M.'s Consul at Madrid, 1854 ; Carthagena (New Granada), 1858 ; Baltimore, 1861 ; Havre, 1866 ; Consul-General, Havre, 1883. *Decorated* for his services under the Foreign Office, 1891. *Address:* 94 Cheriton Road, Folkestone. *Club:* Royal Yacht Squadron, Cowes (Hon. Mem.).   (*Died 10 June 1924.*)

BERNAL, Lt.-Col. Greville Hugh Woodlee, D.S.O. 1900 ; 4th Batt., Nottinghamshire and Derbyshire Regt. ; *o. s.* of Augustus Woodley Bernal ; *m.* 1905, Florence Mary Fyers, *d.* of late David Kent. *Educ.:* Marlborough. Served S. Africa, 1899-1900 (despatches, Queen's medal, three clasps, King's medal, two clasps, D.S.O.).   (*Died 6 Mar. 1922.*)

BERNARD, Rev. Edward Russell, Canon of Salisbury Cathedral ; Chaplain in Ordinary to the King ; *b.* 12 July 1842 ; *e. s.* of Rev. T. D. Bernard, Chancellor and Canon of Wells Cathedral ; *m.* Ellen, *e. d.* of William Nicholson, of Basing Park, Hants, 4 Sept. 1878 ; three *d.* *Educ.:* Harrow ; Exeter Coll., Oxford ; Hertford University Scholar, 1863 ; Craven University Scholar, 1866. Fellow of Magdalen Coll., Oxford, 1866-76 ; Vicar of Selborne, 1876-89 ; Canon Residentiary of Salisbury, 1889 - 1909. *Address:* High Hall, Wimborne. *T.:* Wimborne 42.   (*Died 22 April 1921.*)

BERNARD, Most Rev. and Rt. Hon. John Henry, D.D., Provost of Trinity College, Dublin, since 1919 ; *b.* India, 27 July 1860 ; *e. s.* of late W. F. Bernard, C.E. ; *m.* 1885, Maud, 2nd *d.* of late Robert Bernard, M.D., R.N., Deputy Inspector-General of Hospitals and Fleets ; one *s.* two *d.* *Educ.:* private school ; Trinity College, Dublin (Scholar), 1879 ; Senior Moderator in Mathematics and in Philosophy, 1880 ; Wray prize, 1880 ; M'Cullagh prize, 1883 ; Madden prize, 1883 ; M.A. 1883 ; B.D. 1888 ; D.D. 1892. Fellow and Tutor, Trinity College, 1884 : ordained 1886 ; chaplain to Lord Lieut. of Ireland, 1886-1902 ; Abp. King's Lecturer in Divinity (Dublin), 1888-1911 ; Treasurer of St. Patrick's Cathedral, 1897-1902 ; Dean of St. Patrick's, 1902-11 ; Bishop of Ossory, Ferns, and Leighlin, 1911-15 ; Archbishop of Dublin, 1915-19 ; Examining Chaplain to Bishop (Reeves) of Down, 1889 ; member of University Council, 1892 ; select preacher, Oxford, 1893-95, 1912, 1919-20 ; Cambridge, 1898, 1901, 1904, 1917, 1923 ; Warden, Alexandra College, Dublin, for higher education of women, 1909-11 ; President of Royal Irish Academy, 1916-21 ; member of General Synod

of Church of Ireland, 1894 ; Representative Church Body, 1897 ; Commissioner of National Education, Ireland, 1897-1903 ; Commissioner of Intermediate Education, Ireland, 1917 ; sometime Visitor of Queen's College, Galway ; Hon. D.C.L. (Oxford) 1920 and (Durham), 1905 ; Hon. D.D. (Aberdeen), 1906 ; Privy Councillor, Ireland, 1919 ; Hon. Fellow of Queen's College, Oxford, 1919 ; Hon. Fellow Royal College of Physicians (Ireland), 1921. *Publications:* editor (in conjunction with Professor Mahaffy) Kant's Critical Philosophy for English Readers, 2 vols. 1889 ; translator Kant's Critique of Judgment, 1892, 2nd ed. 1915 ; author From Faith to Faith, University Sermons, 1895 ; Via Domini, Cathedral Sermons, 1898 ; The Prayer of the Kingdom, 1904 ; St. Patrick's Cathedral, a Handbook and a History, 1904 ; Archbishop Benson in Ireland, 1896 ; (in conjunction with Prof. Atkinson) The Irish Liber Hymnorum, 2 vols. 1898 ; editor The Pilgrimage of St. Silvia of Aquitania, 1893 ; The Pastoral Epistles of St. Paul, 1899 ; The Second Epistle to the Corinthians, 1903 ; The Works of Bishop Butler, 2 vols., 1900 ; the Psalter in Latin and English, 1911 ; The Odes of Solomon, 1912 ; Christmas Thoughts, 1913 ; Verba Crucis 1915 ; Easter Hope, 1916 ; Studia Sacra, 1917 ; In War Time, 1917 ; author of various memoirs in the Transactions of the Royal Irish Academy, etc. *Address:* Provost's House, Trinity College, Dublin. *T.A.:* Provost, Trinity, Dublin. *Clubs:* Athenæum ; University, Dublin. (*Died 29 Aug. 1927.*)

BERNARD, Lt. - Col. Ronald Percy Hamilton ; *c.* and *heir pres.* to 4th Earl of Bandon ;   *b.* 18 March 1875 ; *m.* 1904, Lettice Mina, *y. d.* of Gerald C. S. Paget ; two *s.* one *d.* Captain, late Rifle Brigade. *Address:* Bury Greens, Cheshunt, Herts.
               (*Died 2 Feb. 1921.*)

BERNAYS, Acting-Commander Leopold Arthur, R.N., C.M.G., 1916 ; D.S.O. 1917. Served European War, 1914-17 (C.M.G., D.S.O.) ; 4th class Order of St. Vladimir, with swords, 1915.   (*Died Nov. 1917.*)

BERNERS, 8th Baron, *cr.* 1455 ; **Raymond Robert Tyrwhitt-Wilson** ; Bt., *cr.* 1808 [assumed additional name of Wilson, 1892] ; *b.* 22 July 1855 ; *e. s.* of 7th Baroness Berners and Sir Henry Tyrwhitt, 3rd Bt. ; *S.* father 1894, and mother 1917. *Educ.:* Trinity College, Cambridge. Owns about 12,000 acres. *Heir:* *n.* Gerald Hugh Tyrwhitt, *b.* 18 Sep. 1883. *Address:* 4 Down Street, W. ; Stanley Hall, Bridgnorth ; Ashwellthorpe, Norwich.
               (*Died 5 Sept. 1918.*)

BERNERS, Baroness (*cr.* 1455), **Emma Harriet Tyrwhitt** ; *b.* 18 Nov. 1835, *o. surv. child* of late Hon. Rev. Robert Wilson, *o. b.* of 6th Baron Berners ; *S. uncle* 1871 ; *m.* Sir Henry Tyrwhitt, Bt., 1853 (*d.* 1894). Distinctly Protestant ; nine *c.* *Heir:* *s.* Sir Raymond Tyrwhitt Wilson, Bt. *Address:* Ashwell, Thorpe, Norwich. *T.A.:* Tacolneston
               (*Died 18 Aug. 1917.*)

BERNHARDT, Sarah, French actress and manager of the Théâtre Sarah Bernhardt in Paris ; *b.* Paris, 23 Oct. 1845, widow of M. Jacques Damala. *Educ.:* Grandchamp Catholic convent near Paris. Prize of the Conservatory of Paris, 1862 ; entrée à la Comédie Française—partie de la Comedie Française : entrée à l'Odéon puis de nouveau à la Comédie Française en 1872 : quitte la Comédie Française en 1880, et fait de nombreux voyages en Amérique, en Europe, devient directrice du Théâtre de la Renaissance en 1893 ; et fonde le Théâtre Sarah Bernhardt en 1899 ; Cross of Legion of Honour, 1913 ; Officier, 1921. *Sculpture:* many busts, groups, marbles ; bronzes, Exhibition, 1900, silver medal. *Painting:* several tableaux, some prized in Paris Salon. *Publications:* several books and plays, represented in Paris ; novels in divers papers. *Recreations:* sculpture, painting, etc. ; in sun-mer, at her country house, fishing, boating, lawn-tennis, etc. *Address:* 56 Boulevard Pereire, and Théâtre Sarah Bernhardt, Paris; Manoir de Pen Hoët, Belle-Ile en Mer, Sauzon, Morbihan, France. (*Died 26 Mar. 1923.*)

BERNIER, Hon. Michel Esdras, P.C. Canada; Dep. Chief Commissioner of Railways, Canada, since 1904; Member for St. Hyacinthe since 1882; *b.* 27 Sept. 1841; *s.* of Etienne Bernier, farmer, and Julie Lussier; *m.* 1865, Alida Marchesseault. *Educ.:* St. Hyacinthe Seminary. Notary by profession, also engaged in farming, manufactures, and financial institutions; represented County of St. Hyacinthe, 1882-1904: Minister of Inland Revenue, Canada, 1900-4. *Club:* Garrison, Quebec.
(*Died 30 July 1921.*)

BERRANGÉ, Major Christian Anthony Lawson, C.M.G. 1902; J.P.; Cape Police; *b.* 28 Oct. 1864; *s.* of late Christian Berrangé, of Graaff Reinet, Cape Colony; *m.* 1897, *d.* of John M. Lang. Served Bechuanaland, 1896-7 (despatches several times); South African War (despatches frequently, C.M.G.). (*Died 3 Aug. 1922.*)

BERRIDGE, Sir Thomas Henry Devereux. Kt., *cr.* 1912; K.B.E., *cr.* 1920; *b.* 6 July 1857; *s.* of Rev. W. Berridge, formerly Headmaster of Upholland Grammar School, Lancashire, and Vicar of Lowton St. Mary's, Lancashire; *m.* 1887, Agnes (*d.* 1909), *d.* of Frederick Campion of Frenches, Redhill; one *s.* one *d. Educ.:* Upholland Grammar School; privately. Articled to Maskell Peace of Wigan, Solicitor to Mining Association of Great Britain; admitted Solicitor, 1878; member of firm of Burn and Berridge, Solicitors to Government of Newfoundland, 1882; Past-master City of London Solicitors' Company; M.P. (L.) Warwick and Leamington, 1906-10; contested same Division, 1910; Chairman Executive Committee Royal Flying Corps Voluntary Hospitals, 1916-19. *Recreations:* golf, farming. *Addresses:* 6 Austin Friars, E.C.; *T.:* London Wall 1475; 11 and 12 Southampton Street, Bloomsbury, W.C.; *T.:* Museum 5298; 29 Elm Park Gardens, S.W.10; *T.:* Kensington 4263; Greenwood, Alkham, nr. Dover; *T.:* Kearsney 5Y3. *T.A.:* Bees, London. *Clubs:* Reform, Royal Automobile, National Liberal, Eighty.
(*Died 24 Oct. 1924.*)

BERROW, William Lewis, O.B.E. 1918; I.S.O. 1911; an Assistant in Librarians Dept., Foreign Office, since 1920; *b.* 12 Dec. 1862; *s.* of late John Berrow of Newport, Salop, and Worcester; *m.* Henrietta Adeline (*d.* 1911), *d.* of late Henry Alexander Scott; one *s.* two *d. Educ.:* Newport (Salop) Grammar School. Registrar, Foreign Office, 1906-20; Joint-Editor of Hertslet's Commercial Treaties since 1914. *Address:* Foreign Office, S.W.1. *Club:* North Surrey Golf. (*Died 13 Feb. 1928.*)

BERRY, Henry Fitz-Patrick, I.S.O. 1903; M.A., M.R.I.A.; Barrister-at-Law; Assistant Keeper of the Public Records in Ireland since 1899; *b.* 12 May 1847; *e. s.* of Parsons Berry, M.B., Mallow, Co. Cork; *m.* 1895, S. Elizabeth Letitia, *d.* of Hastings Twiss, J.P., Birdhill House, Co. Tipperary. *Educ.:* privately; Trinity College, Dublin; Honourman in Classics; First Honourman History and English Literature; First Junior Moderator in History, Political Science, English Literature, and Law. Entered the Public Record Office, 1868; a Vice-President, Royal Irish Academy; Fellow Royal Society Antiquaries of Ireland, and member of Council of that Society. *Publications:* edited Early Statutes and Ordinances of Ireland, John to Hen. V. (Irish Record Office Series), 1907, and for Royal Society of Antiquaries of Ireland a Register of Wills and Inventories, Dio. Dublin, 1457-83, from a MS. in the Library, Trinity College, Dublin. Author of The Water Supply of Ancient Dublin; Histories of some of the

old Dublin City Guilds, and numerous other papers in the Journal R.S.A.I.; also Notes on an Unpublished MS. Inquisition, A.D. 1258, as to the Dublin City Water-course and History of St. Anne's Religious Guild, Dublin, 1430-1740, in the Proceedings Royal Irish Academy. *Address:* 51 Waterloo Road, Dublin. *Club:* Dublin University.

BERRY, Hon. Sir William Bisset-, Kt., *cr.* 1900; M.A., M.D., LL.D. 1911; *b.* Aberdeen, Scotland, July 1839; *m.* 1864, Marion (*d.* 1884), *d.* of William Beale. *Educ.:* Public Schools and at University, Aberdeen. Member of the Council of University of Cape of Good Hope; settled at Queenstown, Cape of Good Hope, in 1864, and practised medicine there: took keen interest in municipal and educational needs of his town, bringing several important undertakings to successful termination; returned to Parliament for Queenstown, 1894, 1898, and 1904; Speaker of the House of Assembly of Cape of Good Hope, 1898-1907; elected to Parliament of Union, 1910, as M.L.A. for Queenstown. *Publications:* Contributions at various times to medical and other journals. *Address:* Ebden Street, Queenstown, Cape of Good Hope. (*Died June 1922.*)

BERRY, William Grinton, M.A.; Editor of the Sunday at Home since 1909, and of the Tract and Booklet Publications of the Religious Tract Society since 1918; *b.* Edinburgh, 14 Aug. 1873; *m.* Alice Maud, *d.* of late Captain George Morrison, R.E.; one *s.* one *d. Educ.:* George Heriot's School and Edinburgh University. Sub-Editor of Southern Reporter, Selkirk, 1894-95; on the staff of the British Weekly, 1895-98; editor of the publications of the National Council of the Evangelical Free Churches, 1898-1902; on the editorial staff of the Amalgamated Press, 1902-4; on the editorial staff of the R.T.S. since 1904. *Publications:* Scotland's Struggles for Religious Liberty; a monograph on Milton; France since Waterloo; edited the autobiography of Gipsy Smith, Heroes and Pioneers, The Life of Bishop Hannington, Men of Grit, Men of Faith and Daring, etc. *Recreation:* educational lecturing. *Address:* 4 Bouverie Street, E.C.4. *T.A.:* Tracts, London. *T.:* Central 8428-9. *Club:* 9 Vesta Road, Brockley, S.E.4.
(*Died 12 Mar. 1926.*)

BERTIE of Thame, 1st Viscount, *cr.* 1918; **Francis Leveson Bertie;** Baron, *cr.* 1915; G.C.B., *cr.* 1908; G.C.M.G., *cr.* 1904; K.C.B., *cr.* 1902; G.C.V.O., *cr.* 1903; P.C. 1903; *b.* 17 Aug. 1844; 2nd *s.* of 6th Earl of Abingdon; *m.* Lady Feodorowna Cecilia Wellesley, *d.* of 1st Earl Cowley, 1874; one *s. Educ.:* Eton. Entered Foreign Office, 1863; Private Secretary to Hon. R. Bourke. afterwards Lord Connemara (Parliamentary Under-Secretary of State), 1874-80; attached to Special Embassy to Berlin, 1878; Secretary to Duke of Fife's mission to invest King of Saxony with Order of Garter, 1881; Assistant Under-Secretary of State for Foreign Affairs, 1894; Chairman of Uganda Railway Committee, 1896-1903; British Ambassador at Rome, 1903; at Paris, 1905-18. Coronation Medals, 1902 and 1911; Grand Cross Order of St. Maurice and St. Lazarus; Grand Cross Legion of Honour, 1918. *Heir: s.* Hon. Vere F. Bertie. *Address:* 22 Bryanston Square, W.1. *T.:* Paddington 6710. *Clubs:* Turf, Brooks's, St. James's, Travellers'. (*Died 26 Sept. 1919.*)

BERTIE, Rev. Hon. Alberic Edward, M.A.; Rector of Gedling, Notts, 1887-1923; 3rd *s.* of 6th Earl of Abingdon; *b.* 14 Nov. 1846; *m.* 1881, Lady Caroline Elizabeth M'Donnell, *e. d.* of 6th Earl of Antrim; three *s.* three *d. Educ.:* Merton College, Oxford. *Address:* 86 Woodstock Road, Oxford. *Club:* United University. (*Died 20 Mar. 1928.*)

BERTIE, Lieut.-Col. Hon. George Aubrey Vere, late Coldstream Guards; *b.* 2

May 1850 ; 4th *s.* of 6th Earl of Abingdon ; *m.* 1885, Harriet Blanche Elizabeth (*d.* 1923), *d.* of Sir Walter Farquhar, 3rd Bt. ; two *d.* Served Zulu War, 1879 (medal with clasp). *Clubs :* Guards' ; Royal Yacht Squadron, Cowes.
(Died 8 Nov. 1926.)

BERTRAM, Brig. - Gen. Sir Alexander, Kt., *cr.* 1916 ; *b.* Dundas, Ontario, 18 Feb. 1853 ; *m.* 1869, *d.* of Hugh T. Smith ; three *s.* one *d. Educ. :* Dundas High School. Appointed to command 3rd Infantry Brigade, West Ontario Command, 1905 ; Col. 1910 ; commanded Bisley team, 1909 ; Deputy-Chairman, Canadian Imperial Munitions Board. *Address :* Dundas, Ont. ; Canadian Military Institute, Toronto. *(Died April 1926.)*

BESANT, William Henry, M.A., Sc.D., F.R.S., Fellow St. John's Coll. Camb. 1851-59 ; re-elected 1889 ; *b.* Portsmouth, 1 Nov. 1828 ; *s.* of a merchant of Portsmouth ; *b.* of late Sir Walter Besant : *m.* 1861, Margaret Elizabeth (*d.* 1911), *d.* of late Rev. R. Willis, Jacksonian Professor in the University of Cambridge ; two *s.* one *d. Educ. :* Grammar School, Portsea ; a Proprietary School at Southsea ; St. John's Coll. Camb. ; graduated B.A. as Senior Wrangler and 1st Smith's Prizeman, 1850. In 1883 received degree of Doctor of Science, being the first Sc. D. created by the University of Cambridge. Lecturer St. John's Coll. for thirty-five years ; Moderator for Mathematical Tripos 1856 and 1885 ; one of the Examiners for the University of London, 1859-64 ; very active and successful as private tutor ; College Lecturer and Examiner in Cambridge and elsewhere. *Publications :* Treatises on Hydro - Mechanics, Geometrical Conics, Dynamics, Roulettes and Glissettes, and various papers in the Quarterly Journal of Mathematics, the Messenger of Mathematics, and the Educational Times. *Address :* 4 Harvey Road, Cambridge. *(Died 2 June 1917.)*

BESSBOROUGH, 8th Earl of (*cr.* 1739), **Edward Ponsonby,** K.P. ; Baron of Bessborough ; Viscount Duncannon, 1723 ; Baron Ponsonby, 1749 ; Baron Duncannon (U.K.), 1834 ; K.P. 1915 ; C.V.O., C.B. ; J.P. Middlesex and Co. Carlow ; D.L., J.P., and C.C. Co. Kilkenny ; Knight of Grace, St. John of Jerusalem ; Legion of Honour ; *b.* 1 Mar. 1851 ; *e. s.* of 7th Earl of Bessborough and Lady Louisa Susan Cornwallis Eliot, *o. d.* of 3rd Earl of St. Germans ; *S.* father 1906 ; *m.* 1875, Blanche Vere, C.B.E. (*d.* 1919), *d.* of Sir John Guest, 1st Bart. ; two *s.* three *d.* Lieut. R.N. ; retired 1874 ; Barr. 1879 ; Secretary to Speaker of House of Commons (Peel), 1884-95 ; Secretary to the Caledonian Canal Commissioners, 1896 - 99 ; Chairman Brighton and South Coast Railway, and of Guest, Keen and Nettlefold. *Heir :* Viscount Duncannon. *Address :* 17 Cavendish Square, W. ; Bessborough, Piltown, Kilkenny. *Club :* Brooks's. *(Died 1 Dec. 1920.)*

BETHELL, Hon. (Albert) Victor, *b.* 8 Jan. 1864 ; *s.* of 2nd Baron Westbury and Mary Florence, *d.* of Rev. A. Fownes-Luttrell ; *m.* 1918, Eleanor Violet, *d.* of late Stephen Egan, *widow* of Charles Brett, Coldstream Guards. *Educ. :* Eton. *Publications :* Ten Days at Monte Carlo, 1898 ; Monte Carlo Anecdotes, 1901 ; Bridge Reflections, 1908. *Recreations :* shooting, travelling, bridge. *Address :* 4 Knightsbridge Mansions, S.W.3. *T. :* Kensington 738. *Clubs :* Baldwin, M.C.C., Royal Automobile.
(Died 20 July 1927.)

BETHELL, George Richard, Captain R.N. retired ; 2nd *s.* of W. F. Bethell, of Rise, Hull ; *b.* 23 Mar. 1849. *Educ. :* Laleham ; Gosport ; "Britannia." Entered navy, 1862 ; served as Mid. in "Sutlej" ; Sub-Lieut. in Mediterranean and Gulf of Suez surveys ; Lieut. in "Challenger" and "Minotaur"—attached to Sir C. Warren's expedition to Bechuanaland, 1884 ; M.P. (C.) Holderness Div. Yorks, 1885-1900 ; contested same Division, 1910. *Address :* Sigglesthorne,

Hull. *Clubs :* Naval and Military, Arthur's, Yorkshire. *(Died 3 Dec. 1919.)*

BETHELL, William, J.P., D.L. ; *e. s.* of late W. F. Bethell and Elizabeth, 2nd *d.* of Sir Edmund Beckett, Bart. ; *b.* 11 Aug. 1847 ; *m.* 1880, Hon. Maria Myrtle Willoughby (*d.* 1900), 5th *d.* of the 8th Lord Middleton ; one *s.* one *d. Heir :* Adrian Bethell, 2nd Life Guards [*b.* 11 Sep. 1890 ; *m.* 1st, 1915, Clarissa Tennant (whom he div. 1918), *o. d.* of 1st Lord Glenconner (she *m.* 2nd, Hon. L. Tennyson, one *d.* ; 2nd, 1921, Cicely, *d.* of Sir John Cottrell, *Address :* Rise Park, near Hull ; Watton Abbey, near Beverley. *Clubs :* Carlton, Yorkshire. *(Died 13 Aug. 1926.)*

BETJEMANN, Gilbert H., Hon. R.A.M. ; Member of the Royal Philharmonic Society ; Musician in Ordinary to Queen Victoria and King Edward VII. ; Examiner for Royal Academy of Music, Associated Board R.A.M. and R.C.M. ; Licentiate of Music R.A.M. ; Member of the Court of Assistants of the Royal Society of Musicians ; late Conductor of Italian Opera, Her Majesty's Theatre, and English Opera, Covent Garden Theatre ; many years Director of the Operatic Class R.A.M., and Conductor of the Oxford Philharmonic Society ; Conductor of the Highbury Philharmonic Society (London) 1884-1907 ; Director of Ensemble-playing, Oxford University Musical Union, 1886-1911 ; *b.* London, 17 Nov. 1840. Violinist at Italian Opera, Covent Garden, 1858 ; First Violin and Répétiteur with Pyne and Harrison Co. at Covent Garden, 1860 ; Conductor of the Ballet and Leader of the Second Violins at the Opera until the death of Mr. Carrodus, then became principal First Violin ; resigned this appointment in 1898 ; many years Conductor and Stage Director with the Carl Rosa Opera Co. ; Principal and Solo Violin Norwich Musical Festival. *Recreations :* painting, making working models of engines, billiards. *Address :* Ivy Bank, 14 Hillmarton Road, Camden Road, N.7. *T. :* North 2674. *(Died 26 Nov. 1921.)*

BEVAN, Francis Augustus, late Chairman, Barclay and Company ; *b.* 17 Jan. 1840 ; 2nd *s.* of late Robert Cooper Lee Bevan of Fosbury and of Trent Park, and 1st wife, Lady Agneta Elizabeth, *s.* of 4th Earl of Hardwicke ; *m.* 1st, 1862, Elizabeth Marianne (*d.* 1863), *d.* of Lord Charles James Fox Russell : one *s.* ; 2nd, 1866, Constance (*d.* 1872), *d.* of Sir James Weir Hogg, 1st Bart. ; five *s.* ; 3rd, 1876, Maria (*d.* 1903), *d.* of late John Trotter of Dyrham Park, Barnet ; three *d. Educ. :* Harrow. A Lieutenant for the City of London ; High Sheriff of Middlesex, 1899. *Address :* 1 Tilney Street, Park Lane, W. *Clubs :* Union, National, City. *(Died 31 Aug. 1919.)*

BEVAN, Captain George Parker, C.M.G. 1918 ; D.S.O. 1916, R.N. ; *b.* 23 June 1878 ; 2nd *s.* of late James Frederick Bevan of Stanwell Moor, Middlesex ; *m.* 1911, Lilian, *y. d.* of J. Williams Daw of Walreddon Manor, South Devon. Served European War, 1914-19 ; Dardanelles, did patrol work and carried out valuable feints at landing in Gulf of Xeros and Suvla ; Commodore 2nd Class, 1917-19 (despatches, D.S.O., Albert Medal, Officier of Legion of Honour, France ; 1914-15 Star ; Order of St. Anne, 2nd class, Russia). *Club :* United Service.
(Died 14 Jan. 1920.)

BEVAN, Major the Rev. Llewelyn David, B.A., LL.B. (London), D.D. (Princeton) ; Principal, Parkin College, Adelaide, since 1910 ; *b.* Llanelly, Caermarthenshire, Sep. 11, 1842 ; *s.* of Hopkin and Eliza Bevan ; *m.* 1870, Louisa Jane, *d.* of John Willett, M.D., Bishops Lavington, Wilts ; three *s.* four *d. Educ. :* University College School ; New and University Colleges, London. Colleague of Rev. T. Binney, King's Weigh House Chapel, London, 1865 ; Minister of Tottenham Court Road Chapel, London, 1869 ; Member of London

87

BERUETE Y. MORET, Aureliano de. See page xvi.

School Board for Marylebone, 1873-6 ; Lecturer on English Language and Literature, New College, London, and Dean of Faculty, 1871-6 ; Member of Council, Working Men's College, Great Ormond Street, London, 1866-76 ; Minister of Old Brick Presbyterian Church, New York, 1876-82 ; Minister of Highbury Quadrant Church, London, 1882-6 ; Minister of Collins Street Independent Church, Melbourne, 1886-1910 ; Professor of Systematic Theology, Congregational College of Victoria ; Chaplain of the Forces, Victoria ; Chairman of Jury on Education of the Melbourne International Exhibition, and was made by the French Government Officier d'Instruction publique de la Republique Française, 1888 ; Vice-President of International Congregational Council, London, 1891 ; Vice-President of International Congregational Council, Boston, 1899 ; President Parliamentary Commission on Inebriety, 1901 ; Chairman Congregational Union of Victoria, 1888 and 1898 ; Chairman of Congregational Union of Australasia, 1910-18 ; Past Grand Chaplain of the Grand Lodge of Victoria. *Publications:* Various Sermons, Lectures, and Addresses, Sermons to Students, 1881-82 ; Christ and the Age, 1885 ; Presidential Addresses, 1888-1889-98 ; Articles, in Magazines etc., 1865-1915. *Recreations:* travel, swimming, boating ; book and curio collecting in later years, " far niente in villéggiatura." *Address:* Parkin Coll., Adelaide.
(*Died 9 Aug.* 1918.)

BEVENOT, Prof. Clovis, M.A. Oxon ; *b.* near Cambrai ; *m.* Flavie Bévenot ; three *s.* one *d. Educ.* : Cambrai ; Universities of Göttingen, Naples and Oxford (Balliol Coll.); Classical Honours, Exhibitioner, Lecturer, and Examiner, Oxford ; for six years on staff of Clifton College ; present or past Examiner in the Romance Languages, including Roumanian, to Cambridge, London, Victoria, Liverpool, St. Andrews, National of Ireland, Birmingham, etc., Universities ; L.C.C. Technical Education Board ; I.C.S. ; Interpreter to the Treasury, etc. ; interim Prof. of German, Lecturer in Spanish and Italian, Professor of French Language, Literature, History, and Philology, University of Birmingham, 1889-1909 ; now pensioned. *Publications:* edited various : Cervantes, French and German Poets, etc. ; collaborated in Moncalm's L'Origine de la pensée et de la parole ; the Spanish Grammar (Parallel Series); Ralph Thomas' Swimming ; Report on Physical Education in English Schools for the Education Congress at the Paris Exhibition, etc. Holds cross and medal, Mentana campaign. *Recreations:* coaching in Russian, Spanish, etc. after-war pioneers to-be. *Address:* St. Florence, Tor Vale, Torquay.
(*Died 21 Feb.* 1925.)

BEVERIDGE, Erskine, LL.D., F.R.S.E., J.P. ; manufacturer ; *b.* Dec. 1851 ; *m. Educ.* : private schools ; Edinburgh University. *Publications:* Churchyard Memorials of Crail, 1893 ; A Bibliography of Dunfermline and West Fife, 1901 ; Coll and Tiree, their Prehistoric Forts and Ecclesiastical Antiquities, 1903 ; North Uist, its Archæology and Topography, 1911 ; The Burgh Records of Dunfermline, 1488-1584 (edited), 1917. *Recreations:* archæology (especially Hebridean), photography, fishing. *Address:* St. Leonard's Hill, Dunfermline ; Vallay, North Uist. *Club:* Scottish Conservative.
(*Died 10 Aug.* 1920.)

BEVES Brig.-Gen. Percival Scott, C.M.G. 1917 ; S.A. Defence Force ; late Capt. Royal Inniskilling Fusiliers ; *b.* 25 Jan. 1868 ; 4th *s.* of late Edward Beves, J.P., Brighton. *Educ.* : Leys School, Cambridge. Served Tirah, 1897-98 ; South Africa, 1899-1902 ; German S.W. Africa, 1914-15 ; German East Africa, 1916-17.
(*Died 26 Sept.* 1924.)

BEVILLE, Lt.-Col. Francis Granville, C.S.I. 1921 ; C.I.E. 1908 ; Agent to the Governor-88

General in Central India ; *b.* 24 March 1867. Lieutenant, N. Staffs Regt., 1886 ; Indian Staff Corps, 1888 ; Capt. Indian Army, 1897 ; Major, 1904 ; Lt.-Col., 1912 ; Acting Consul, Muscat, 1896 ; Consul, 1896-7 ; Political Agent, Bundelkhand, 1900-4 ; Bhopawar, 1905-12 ; Resident, Gwalior, 1914. *Address:* Indore, Central India.
(*Died 21 April* 1923.)

BEWERUNGE. Rev. Henry, Professor Church Music, St. Patrick's College, Maynooth, since 1888 ; *b.* Letmathe, Westphalia, 7 Dec. 1862. *Educ.* : Düsseldorf ; Würzburg ; Eichstätt ; Ratisbon. Ordained priest at Eichstätt, 1885. *Publications:* six five-part motets by Palestrina, arranged for five male voices ; The Vatican Edition of Plain-Chant : A Critical Study, 1906 ; Die vatikanische Choralausgabe, 1906 ; Der vatikanischen Choralausgabe zweiter Teil, 1907 ; articles in the Catholic Encyclopedia and English and German periodicals. *Address:* St. Patrick's College, Maynooth. *T.A.:* Bewerunge, Maynooth.

BEWES, Lt.-Col. Arthur Edward, C.M.G. 1916 ; R.M.L.I. : *b.* 7 Jan. 1871 ; 2nd *s.* of late Capt. F. D. Bewes, Newton Abbot ; *m.* 1898, Ethel, *d.* of Rev. T. S. Treanor, Deal : one *d. Educ.* : Newton College : Blundell's School, Tiverton. Joined the Royal Marines, 1890 ; Capt., 1898 ; Major, 1909 ; served European War, 1914-16 ; present at Antwerp, Kum Kale, and at first landing at Gallipoli (wounded, despatches twice, C.M.G.). *Address:* 6 The Beach, Walmer, Kent. (*Died 17 Jan.* 1922.)

BEWICKE-COPLEY, Brig.-Gen. Sir Robert Calverley Alington Bewicke, K.B.E., *cr.* 1919 ; C.B. 1900 ; D.L., J.P. ; late Commanding West Riding (Yorkshire) Volunteers ; *b.* Shotton Hall, Durham, 8 April 1855 ; *e. s.* of Robert Calverley Bewicke Bewicke, Coulby Manor, Yorkshire ; *m.* 1886, Selina Frances, *e. d.* of Sir Chas. Watson, 3rd Bt. ; one *s.* two *d. Educ.* : Rugby ; Merton Coll. Oxford. Sub-Lieut. Royals, 1876 ; trans. 60th Rifles, 1877 ; A.D.C. to Lieut. Governor, Bengal, 1879 ; D.A.C.G. Nile Expedition, 1885 (medal and Khedive's star); D.A.A.G. Barbados, 1890 ; D.A.A.G. Headquarters, Ireland, 1892 ; Military Attaché, special mission Morocco, 1894 ; Chitral, 1895 (medal); A.M.S. Bengal, 1896 ; D.A.Q.M.G. Intelligence, Kuram-Kohat, 1897 ; A.A.G. 2nd Division, Tirah Expeditionary Force, 1898 (2 clasps, despatches) ; commanding 3rd Batt. King's Royal Rifles, South African War, 1899 ; commanding Mobile Columns South Africa, 1900-2 (despatches, Queen's medal, 6 clasps, King's medal, 2 clasps, C.B.); late Brig.-Gen. Commanding 17th Infantry Brigade, Cork ; late Colonel, General Staff, Northern Command ; retired, 1912. *Address:* Sprotborough Hall, Doncaster. *T.A.:* Sprotbro, Doncaster. *Clubs:* Carlton, Naval and Military ; Yorkshire, York.
(*Died 23 June* 1923.)

BHANDARI, Rai Bahadur Sir Gopal Das, Kt., *cr.* 1923 ; C.I.E. 1921 ; M.B.E. 1919 ; *b.* Amritsar, June 1860. *Educ.* : Govt. College and Law School, Lahore. Pleader, 1880 ; President, Bar Association, Amritsar ; Member, Municipal Council for the last forty years ; Rai Bahadur, 1907 ; Punjabis' Representative to the All India Sanitary Conferences, Madras, Simla, and Lucknow ; Special Delegate, All India Malaria Conference, 1907 ; The Kaiser-i-Hind Medal, 1st Class, 1915 ; specially enrolled Advocate, High Court of Judicature, Lahore, 1917 ; Special Commissioner, Lahore Conspiracy Case, 1917 ; First non-official President, Municipal Council since 1921 ; President, Hindu Sabha ; member of the Punjab Legislative Council, 1923 ; President Board of Directors Punjab National Bank (Amritsar Branch). *Publications:* Malaria ; Milk Supply ; Town Planning ; Insanitary Conditions of Boys' and

Girls' Schools in Cities, etc. *Address:* Amritsar, Punjab.   (*Died Feb.* 1927.)

BHANDARKAR, Sir Ramkrishna Gopal, K.C.I.E., *cr.* 1911; C.I.E. 1889; M.A.; Hon. LL.D., Bombay and Edinburgh; Hon. Ph.D. Göttingen and Calcutta; Professor of Oriental Languages, Deccan College, Poona, 1882-93; *b.* 1887; *m.*; two *s.* one *d. Educ.:* Ratnagiri Government English School; Elphinstone College, Bombay, 1847-58. Headmaster of High Schools, 1864-68; Professor of Sanskrit, Elphinstone College, Bombay, 1869-1881. Fellow, and for two years Vice-Chancellor, Bombay University; Fellow of Calcutta University; nominated to membership of Viceroy's Legislative Council in connection with Lord Curzon's Educational Reforms, 1903; member of Bombay Legislative Council, 1904-8; a leader of Hindu social and religious reform movements; Dakshina Fellow, 1859-64. *Publications:* First and Second Books of Sanskrit; Early History of the Deccan; Sanskrit and the derived Languages; Vaisnavism, Saivism, and minor religious systems. *Address:* Poona, Deccan.   (*Died Aug.* 1925.)

BHAVNAGAR, H.H. Maharaja Sir Bhavsinhji Takhtasinhji, K.C.S.I., **Maharaja of**; Hon. Lt.-Col. in Army; *b.* 26 April 1875; *S.* father (Sir Takhtasinhji Jaswatsinhji, G.C.S.I.), 1896; *m.* 1905, H.H. Maharani Nandkunorrba, C.I.; two *s.* one *d.* The State, which ranks high for the efficiency of its administration — the present Chief having fully maintained his father's progressive policy — has an area of 2860 square miles and a population of 441,367. The State came in close and intimate connection with the British Government in the eighteenth century, when it co-operated with them in the extirpation of piracy from the Kathiawar coast; it was the pioneer of railway enterprise in Kathiawar, maintains a line of about 250 miles, and has large projects of extension in hand; has an excellent and sheltered harbour, which is open to ocean-going steamers; maintains a body of Imperial Service Lancers, the largest in the province. *Recreations:* a keen sportsman and an excellent shot, keeps several hunting cheetahs whom he trains personally. Salute, 15 guns. *Address:* Bhavanagar, Kathiawar.
   (*Died* 11 *July* 1919.)

BHUTAN, Maharajah of, Sir Ugyen Wangchuk, G.C.I.E., *cr.* 1921; K.C.S.I., *cr.* 1911; K.C.I.E., *cr.* 1905; *b.* 1861; has a salute of 15 guns. *Address:* Bhutan. (*Died Aug.* 1926.)

BIAGI, Dott. Comm. Guido; Grande Ufficiale dell' Ordine dei SS. Maurizio e Lazzaro e dell' Ordine della Corona d' Italia; Knight of the Polar Star of Sweden; Officer of the British Empire; formerly Director of the Biblioteca Medicea - Laurenziana, and of the Biblioteca Riccardiana, in Florence, since 1895; Bibliographical Superintendent of Umbria and the Marches; *b.* Florence, 29 Jan. 1855; *s.* of Prof. Luigi Biagi, a painter, and Emilia Costetti, of Bologna, Superintendent of the Town Schools of Florence; *m.* Amelia, *d.* of avv. Piroli, member of the Italian Senate and Vice-President of the State Council; one *s.* one *d. Educ.:* Instituto Superiore di Perfezionamento, Florence. D. Lit. 1878; Assistant Librarian, 1880; Vice-Librarian, 1882; Librarian of the Vittorio Emanuele Library in Rome, and Chief of the Cabinet of the Under-Secretary of Public Education, 1884-86; Librarian of the Marucelliana Library in Florence, 1885; Prefetto of the Mediceo-Laurenziana Library in Florence, 1885; Chief of the Cabinet of the Ministry of Public Instruction, 1892-93; General Inspector of the Ministry of Education, 1893-95; Resident Member of the Academy Della Crusca since 1913; Hon. Treasurer of the Societa Dantesca Italiana since 1899; Member of the History Deputation of Tuscany; representative of the

Italian Government at the International Librarians' Conference of London, 1897, St. Louis, 1904, and Brussels, 1908; member of different academies and of the Royal Society of Literature. *Publications:* The Private Life of the Florentines; Men and Manners of Old Florence; The Last Days of Shelley; Napoleon inconnu; Le Novelle antiche; Vita di Giuseppe Giusti; Aneddoti letterari; Vocabolario italiano di Niccolo Tommaseo compendiato e rifatto; Indice del Mare Magnum di F. Marucelli, etc.; Passatisti (Biographies of leading Italian men); La Divina Commedia nella figurazione artistica e nel secolare commento; Rivista delle biblioteche e degli archivi. *Recreation:* making plans. *Address:* Florence, 18 Via Pier Capponi; in summer, Castiglioncello (Pisa). *T.:* 1360 (Private). *Club:* Soc. Leonardo da Vinci, Firenze.   (*Died 6 Jan.* 1925.)

BIBBY, Frank, C.B.E. 1920; J.P., D.L.; *b.* 4 Jan. 1857; *o. surv. s.* of late James Jenkinson Bibby, and Sarah, *d.* of Thomas Cook, Dewsbury; *m.* 1890, Edith, *e. d.* of Maj.-Gen. Sir Stanley de Astel Calvert Clarke; one *s.* two *d. Educ.:* Eton. High Sheriff Shropshire, 1900; Lord of the Manor of Hadnall. *Address:* 39 Hill Street, W.1.; *T.:* Grosvenor 2165; Hardwicke Grange, Sansaw, near Shrewsbury. *Clubs:* Carlton; Royal Yacht Squadron, Cowes.
   (*Died 12 Feb.* 1923.)

BICE, Hon. Sir John George, K.C.M.G., *cr.* 1923; M.L.C.; Chief Secretary and Minister of Marine since 1919; *b.* Callington, Cornwall, 1853; *s.* of Samuel S. Bice, late of Moonta, Wallaroo, and Port Augusta; *m.* 1875, Elizabeth J., 2nd *d.* of late John Trewenack; one *s.* two *d. Educ.:* village school in Cornwall; night school at Moonta. For some time Mayor of Port Augusta; represented the Northern District in the Legislative Council since 1894; Honorary Minister, 1908-9; Chief Secretary, 1909 - 10, 1912-15. *Address:* Ruthven Lodge, Bishopsplace, Kensington, South Australia. *T.:* Norwood 1582. *Club:* Liberal.   (*Died Nov.* 1923.)

BICKERSTAFFE-DREW, Right Rev. Monsignor Count Francis Browning Drew, C.B.E. 1919; K.H.S.; LL.D.; *b.* Headingly, Leeds, 11 Feb. 1858; *s.* of late Rev. Harry Lloyd Bickerstaffe and Mona Brougham, *d.* of Rev. Pierce William Drew, of Heathfield Towers, Youghal; assumed 1879 additional surname of Drew. *Educ.:* King Edward VI. School, Lichfield; St. Chad's Coll., Denstone (A.S.N.C. 1st Class Honours); Oxford; subsequently at St. Thomas's Seminary, Hammersmith. Ordained Priest, 1884; by Bishop Wethers; Assistant Priest of Pro-Cathedral, Kensington, 1884-86; Acting Chaplain to the Forces, 1886-92; Chaplain to the Forces, Plymouth, 1892-99; Senior R.C. Chaplain, Malta, 1899-1905, and 1909; Salisbury Plain, 1905-9 and 1916; Private Chamberlain of His late Holiness Pope Leo XIII., 1891; decorated with Cross of Leo XIII., Pro Ecclesia et Pontifice, 1901; an Examiner in, and Member of the Special Council of the University of Malta, 1899-1905; a Member of the Pontifical Chamber of Malta since 1900; Private Chamberlain of Pope Pius X., 1903; created Domestic Prelate of His Holiness, 1904; Knight of the Sacred Military Order of the Holy Sepulchre and Count, 1909; also special Jubilee Medal from His Holiness; Protonotary Apostolic, 1912; Foreign Member and Delegate of the Société Archéologique de France, 1913; served European War, 1914 - 15 (despatches twice, and Secretary of State's Special Despatch, Mons Medal, 2 roses, Victory Medal, General Service Medal, C.B.E.); Hon. LL.D. University of Notre Dame, Indiana, and of Marquette University, Wisconsin, 1917; Assistant Principal R.C. Chaplain, 1918; retired, 1919. *Recreations:* books and writing them (*v.* John Ayscough). *Heir: cousin* and adopted *s.* Lieut.

Frank Bickerstaffe Drew, Royal Field Artillery.
(Died 3 July 1923.)

BICKERSTETH, Robert Alexander, M.A., M.B. (Cantab.), F.R.C.S. (England); retired; Consulting Surgeon, late Hon. Surgeon, Liverpool Royal Infirmary; late Lecturer and Examiner in Clinical Surgery in the University of Liverpool; Fellow Royal Society of Medicine; Membre Correspondent de l'Association Française d'Urologie; *b.* 4 Sept. 1862; *s.* of late E. R. Bickersteth, F.R.C.S., Liverpool; *m.* Ellen Constance, *d.* of Charles Bowman Wilson, M.R.C.S., Liverpool; three *s.* two *d. Educ.*: Eton; Trinity College, Cambridge; St. Bartholomew's Hospital. *Publications:* occasional contributions to medical journals. *Recreations:* shooting, fishing. *Address:* Borwick Lodge, Outgate, Hawkshead. *Clubs:* Athenæum, University, Liverpool.
(Died 29 Feb. 1924.)

BICKFORD, Admiral Andrew Kennedy, C.M.G. 1885; *b.* India, 16 July 1844; 2nd *s.* of W. Bickford, of Newport House, South Devon; *m.* 1868, Louisa (*d.* of J. D. Dore, M.D.; four *s.* two *d. Educ.*: South Devon Collegiate School; Foster's, Stubbington. Entered Navy, 1858; served in China as sub-Lieut. during operations in Japan; taking of Forts at Simonosaki, etc.; was senior and gunnery Lieut. of Amethyst during actions with Peruvian Rebel ironclad Huascar; as commander, in charge of naval transport arrangements at Alexandria during war; negotiated release of captured crew of Nisero in Acheen; C.M.G. for this service as Capt. senior officer of combined French and English and German and English squadrons at various operations in South Pacific; at Samoa received surrender of Mactafa and chiefs: putting a stop to civil war on that occasion; received thanks of Government, etc.; commanded Resolution in Channel squadron; Capt. of Fleet Reserve at Portsmouth; Superintendent of Sheerness Dockyard, 1898-99; Commander-in-Chief Pacific, 1901-4; Egyptian medal, Khedive Star, Medjidie 3rd Class, Jubilee Medal; A.D.C. to Queen, 1896-99; J.P. and Land Tax Commissioner for County of Sussex. *Address:* 33 Selborne Road, Hove, Sussex. *Club:* United Service.
(Died 9 Oct. 1927.)

BICKFORD, Major Arthur Louis, C.I.E., 1911; 56th Rifles, Frontier Force, Indian Army; D.A.A.G., 1st (Peshawar) Division, since 1914; *b.* 1870; *s.* of Admiral A. K. Bickford, unmarried. *Educ.*: Stonyhurst; Sandhurst. Entered 2nd Queen's Regiment, 1892; Captain Indian Army, 1901; Brevet Major, 1908; Substantive Major, 1910; served Tirah Expedition, 1897-98 (medal with two clasps); Bazar Valley Expedition, 1908 (despatches, Brevet of Major, medal with one clasp); Commandant Khyber Rifles, 1910-13; Durbar medal, 1911. *Recreations:* tennis, golf. *Address:* c/o H. S. King and Co., 9 Pall Mall, S.W. *M.:* P 3. *Club:* East India United Service. *(Died 18 Mar. 1916.)*

BIDDLE, Major Fred Leslie, D.S.O. 1916; O.C. 4th Battery Australian Field Artillery, A.I.F.; *b.* Melbourne, Australia, 27 Oct. 1885; parents, English born; unmarried. *Educ.*: Hawthorn College, Melbourne. Matriculated, Melbourne University, 1901; Business Career, Wholesale Warehouseman (soft goods); joined Australian Field Artillery (Militia), 1904; joined A.I.F. for service abroad, and seconded from A.F.A. 1914; landing to evacuation, Anzac, 1915; Major, 1916. *Recreations:* football (Australian rules), field artillery. *Address:* 92 Vale Street East, Melbourne, Victoria, Australia. *Clubs:* Naval and Military; United Service Institution, Melbourne.
(Died Aug. 1917.)

BIDDULPH, 1st Baron (cr. 1903), **Michael Biddulph**, D.L., J.P.; partner in the banking firm of Cocks, Biddulph, and Co.; *b.* 1884;

e. s. of Robert Biddulph, Ledbury; *m.* 1st, 1864, Adelaide Georgiana (*d.* 1872), *y. d.* of Rt. Hon. Gen. Peel; two *s.* two *d.*; 2nd, 1877, Lady Elizabeth Yorke, V.A. (*d.* 1916), *d.* of 4th Earl of Hardwicke and widow of Henry Adeane, M.P. [Lady Biddulph was author of Charles Philip Yorke, Fourth Earl of Hardwicke.] *Educ.*: Harrow. M.P. (L.) Herefordshire, 1865-85; South Herefordshire, 1885-86; M.P. (L.U.) Ross Division Herefordshire, 1886-1900. *Heir: s.* Hon. John Michael Gordon Biddulph. *Address:* Ledbury, Herefordshire; Kemble House, Cirencester. *Clubs:* Brooks's, Reform.
(Died 6 April 1923.)

BIDDULPH, Assheton; M.F.H. King's Co. Hunt; *b.* 1850, 2nd *surv. s.* of late Francis Marsh Wellesley Biddulph, J.P., Rathrobin, King's Co.; *m.* 1880, Florence Caroline, *y. d.* of late Rev. Cunningham Boothby, Holwell Vicarage, Oxfordshire; one *s.* four *d.* Entered 57th Regt. an Ensign, 1869; retired, 1873; became M.F.H., 1884; hunting the Ormond and King's County till 1897, when the country was divided, and since 1897 has continued Master of King's Co. Hunt, himself hunting his hounds all the time. *Recreations:* field sports in general; fox-hunting particularly. *Address:* Moneyguyneen, Birr, King's Co. *Club:* Junior United Service.
(Died 17 Jan. 1916.)

BIDDULPH, General Sir Robert, G.C.B., *cr.* 1899; G.C.M.G., *cr.* 1880; *b.* London, 26 Aug. 1835; *s.* of Robert Biddulph, M.P., Ledbury; *m.* 1864, Sophia (*d.* 1905), *d.* of Rev. A. L. Lambert, Rector of Chilbolton, and widow of R. S. Palmer; four *s.* six *d.* Royal Artillery, 1853; Captain, 1860; Major, 1861; Lieut.-Col. 1864; Col. 1872; Maj.-Gen. 1888; Lieut.-Gen. 1887; Gen. 1892; served in Crimean War, 1854-56; Indian Mutiny Campaign, 1857-59; China War, 1860; Assistant Boundary Commissioner for Reform Act, 1867; private secretary to Mr. Cardwell when Secretary of State for War, 1871-73; A.A.G. War Office, 1873-78; H.M. Commissioner, Constantinople, 1879; High Commissioner for Cyprus, 1879-86; Inspector-General of Recruiting, 1886-88; Director-General of Military Education, 1888-93; Quartermaster-Gen. to the Forces, Jan. 1893; Governor and Commander-in-Chief Gibraltar, 1893-1900; retired 1902; Army Purchase Commissioner, 1904; Master Gunner of St. James's Park, 1914. *Publication:* Lord Cardwell at the War Office, 1904. *Address:* 88 Cornwall Gardens, S.W. *Club:* United Service.
(Died 18 Nov. 1918.)

BIDDULPH, Thomas Henry Stillingfleet, C.I.E., 1907; late Accountant-General, India; *s.* of Rev. Francis John Biddulph, formerly of Amroth Castle, Pembrokeshire; *b.* 25 Nov. 1846; *m.* 1878, Lydia Beatrice, *d.* of late Col. S. Becher, Indian Army. *Educ.*: Lancing. Joined Financial Department, Government of India, 1871; Deputy Auditor-General, and latterly Accountant-General; specially deputed to reorganise the finances of the Mysore State, and subsequently Patiala State, in connection with which received the thanks of Government on several occasions; Captain in Indian Volunteers, services specially brought to notice of Government of India by G.O.C. Secunderabad, 1886; P.M. Masonic Lodge; retired 1905. *Address:* Biddulph, Rawlins, and Co., 7 Nicholas Lane, Lombard Street, E.C. *T.:* City 4261. *Club:* East India United Service.
(Died 24 April 1919.)

BIGELOW, Melville Madison, Ph.D., LL.D.; *b.* 2 Aug. 1846; *o. s.* of Rev. Wm. E. and Daphne F. Bigelow; *m.* 1898, Alice Bradford, *d.* of Dr. George S. and Jane G. Woodman. *Educ.*: Univ. of Michigan; Harvard University. Lawyer, author, and teacher of law; Memb. Mass. Historical Soc.; Fellow American Academy of Arts and Sciences; Harvard Chap. Phi Beta Kappa, and other learned societies. *Publications:* Law of Estoppel (6 editions); Leading Cases in Law of Torts; Law of Torts (8 American and 3 English editions); Placita Anglo-Normannica; History of English Procedure; Law of Fraudulent Conveyances (2 editions); Law of Bills, Notes, and Cheques (2 editions); Law of Wills; Chaps. vi. and viii. of Cambridge Modern History, vol. 7; A False Equation—The Problem of the Great Trust; Papers on the Legal History of Government. *Address:* 200 Brattle Street, Cambridge, Mass., U.S.A. *(Died 4 May 1921.)*

BIGGAR, Maj.-Gen. James Lyons, V.D., C.M.G. 1918; *b.* 16 July 1856; 3rd *s.* of James Lyons Biggar, M.P. East Northumberland, and Isabel Hodgins; *m.* 1882, Mary Scott, *e. d.* of R. W. Elliot, Toronto; two *s.* one *d. Educ.:* Upper Canada College, Toronto. Argyll Light Infantry, 1881-1901; Camp Quartermaster District Staff, 1891-1900; on Staff Canadian Contingent Queen Victoria's Diamond Jubilee (Jubilee medal); South Africa, 1899-1901; Staff-Officer for Overseas Colonials at chief Base and Lines of Communication; also acted as Canadian Red Cross Commissioner for seven months (Queen's medal with 4 clasps, Hon. Associate Order St. John of Jerusalem); appointed to Headquarters Staff as D.A.G. for A.S.C. and organised the C.A.S.C.; Staff-Officer for Colonials at King Edward's Coronation, 1902 (Coronation medal); Director General Supplies and Transport, 1904; Quartermaster-General, 1917; retired 1920; Order of St. Saba, 1918; Order of Leopold II., 1918; Officer Legion d'Honneur, 1919. *Publications:* Hints to Quartermasters and A.S.C. Manual. *Recreations:* lawn bowling, curling. *Address:* The Roxborough 49, Ottawa. *T.A.:* Biggar, Ottawa. *Clubs:* Rideau, Country, Ottawa. *(Died 19 Feb. 1922.)*

BIGGE, Sir William Egelric, Kt., *cr.* 1909; M.A., Hon. D.C.L. Durham; Chairman, Associated Board of Royal College and Royal Academy of Music. *Educ.:* New College, Oxford. First Judge of Small Cause Court, Rangoon, 1886; officiating Judge, Moulmein, 1892; officiating Recorder, Rangoon, 1898; Judge Chief Court, Lower Burma, 1900-8. *Address:* Queen Anne's Mansions, S.W. *Clubs:* Oxford and Cambridge, Brooks's; Northern Counties, Newcastle. *(Died 24 Dec. 1916.)*

BIGGS, Sir Arthur Worthington, Kt., *cr.* 1906; Major (retired) VI. Lancashire Artillery Vols.; *b.* 2 March 1846; 4th *s.* of late Wm. Biggs, J.P., of Leicester, formerly M.P. for Newport (Isle of W.); *m.* 1872, Lilian (*d.* 1891), 3rd *d.* of late Charles Holland, J.P., Liscard, Cheshire; five *s.* one *d. Educ.:* privately, and in Paris. Has taken active interest in the Volunteer movement; is an active Liberal; contested South Worcestershire, 1906. *Club:* National Liberal (a Vice-President).
(Died 6 Dec. 1923.)

BIGGS, George Nixon, M.B., B.S., Consulting Aural Surgeon to the Evelina Hospital for Sick Children; Surgeon-in-Charge of the Ear and Throat Dept., Waterloo Hospital for Women and Children; Surgeon in charge Ear and Throat Dept., Dreadnought Hospital, at Greenwich; Surgeon in charge Ear and Throat Dept. Hospital for Paralysis and Epilepsy, Maida Vale; Teacher of Otology, Laryngology, and Rhinology at the London School of Clinical Medicine; Lt.-Col., R.A.M.C. (T.); Lt.-Col. R.A.F.; Late Consulting Aurist and Laryngologist, Boulogne Base, B.E.F.; Late Consulting Aurist and Laryngologist, R.A.F.; *b.* 28 March 1881; *s.* of M. G. Biggs, M.D. *Educ.:* Westminster School; St. Thomas's Hospital. Late House Surgeon, Clinical Assistant, and Senior Clinical Assistant, Royal Ear Hospital; Senior Clinical Assistant and Registrar, Metropolitan Ear, Nose, and Throat Hospital; Surgeon-in-Charge of the Ear and Throat Dept., Evelina Hospital. *Publica-*

tions: A Text-Book of Diseases of the Ear, Nose, and Throat; articles in the various medical journals. *Address:* 31 Wimpole Street, W.1. *T.:* Langham 1872. *(Died 10 Nov. 1922.)*

BIGGS, Colonel Henry Vero, D.S.O. 1898; Royal Engineers; *b.* Belgaum, 9 May 1860; 3rd *s.* of late Col. T. Biggs, R.A., and Mary, *d.* of late Rev. W. Beynon; *m.* 1887, Frances Kate, *e. d.* of late Col. C. H. Ewart, B.S.C.; one *s. Educ.:* Private school at Clifton. Passed into R.M.A., Woolwich, 1877; joined R.E., 1879; embarked for India, 1882, where joined the Bombay S. and M.; spent nearly three years on Afghan frontier (including the 1884 Zhob Valley Expedition); in the 3rd Burmese War, 1885-87 (medal with clasp); joined the Military Works from the S. and M., 1887; promoted Captain, 1889; Adjutant, R.E., Tirah Expeditionary Force 1897-98; operations on North-West Frontier, 1897; operations in the Kurram and on the Samana, the Chagru Kotal; capture of the Sampaga Pass, and operations in the Khyber (despatches, medal with 3 clasps, and D.S.O.); Major, 1898; Lieut.-Col. 1905; Bt.-Col. 1908; Col. 1910; Commanding Royal Engineers, 2nd (Rawalpindi) Division, 1909-12; retired, 1912; re-employed for war, 1914 (despatches); retired, 1919. *Recreations:* shooting, riding, rowing. *Address:* c/o Cox's Branch, 6 Pall Mall, S.W.1. *(Died 28 Feb. 1925.)*

BIGGS, Hermann M., M.D., LL.D., Sc.D. Harvard; Professor of Medicine, University and Bellevue Hospital Medical College; consulting Physician Bellevue, Willard Parker, and St. Vincent's Hospitals; late Chief Medical Officer, Health Department, New York City; Commissoner of Health, and Chairman Public Health Council, New York State; Member of International Health Board and War Relief Commission Rockefeller Foundation and Medical Section—Council of National defence; Knight of the Order Isabella the Catholic of Spain; *b.* Trumansburg, New York, 29 Sept. 1859; *s.* of Joseph H. and Melissa P. Biggs; *m.* 1898, Frances Richardson; one *s.* one *d. Educ.:* Cornell University; Bellevue Hospital Medical College; Universities of Berlin, and Greifswald, Germany. Fellow N.Y. Academy of Medicine, President Association American Physicians, British Medical Association; Member Board of Directors Rockefeller Institute for Medical Research. Established Bacteriological Laboratories of New York Health Department, 1892, the first municipal Bacteriological Laboratories in the world; devised the methods of bacteriological diagnosis in diphtheria, tuberculosis, etc., as applied to municipal laboratories; introduced methods for sanitary supervision of tuberculosis, beginning in 1887; member of Medical Faculty of Bellevue Hospital Med. College and New York University since 1885; Hon. Fellow Sanitary Inst. Great Britain; Hon. Fellow Royal College Physicians, Edinburgh; Medical Director-General, League of Red Cross Societies, Geneva, Switzerland, 1920. *Publications:* numerous contributions to current medical literature. *Address:* 39 West 56th Street, New York. *T.:* Circle 137. *Clubs:* University, Century, Psi Upsilon, Automobile of America. *(Died 28 June 1923.)*

BIGLAND, Percy; artist; *s.* of Edwin and Adelaide Bigland, Birkenhead; *m.* Edith McHanbury Aggs; one *s.* one *d. Educ.:* Sidcot, Somerset. Seven years Art Student in Munich; 1st Medal, Royal Academy, Munich, 1880; Original Member Royal Society of Portrait Painters, London. *Recreations:* golf, motoring. *Address:* Stone Dean, Beaconsfield, Bucks. *T.:* 2Y Chalfont St. Giles. *Clubs:* Arts; Beaconsfield Golf; Berrow Golf.
(Died 8 April 1926.)

BIGWOOD, James, M.A., J.P., D.L.; Middlesex County Alderman, Chairman of its Parliamentary Committee, and represents the

County upon the Thames Conservancy; *s.* of James Bigwood, Clifton, Gloucestershire. *Educ.:* St. John's Coll. Camb. M.P. East Finsbury, 1885-86; Brentford Division, Middlesex, 1886-1906. *Recreations:* golf, cricket, tennis, cycling. *Address:* The Lawn, Twickenham. *Club:* Carlton. (*Died 6 Dec. 1919.*)

BILGRAMI, Syed Hossain, Nawab, Imadul Mulk, Bahadur; C.S.I. 1908; *b.* Gya, 18 Oct. 1842; *s.* of Syed Zainuddin Hossain Khan Bahadur of the Uncovenanted Civil Service, Bengal; *m.* 1st, 1864, wife died 1897; *m.* 2nd, Edith Boardman, L.S.A. (Lond.), M.D.; four *s.* one *d.* *Educ.:* Presidency College, Calcutta. Professor of Arabic, Canning College, Lucknow, 1866-73; Private Secretary to H.E. Sir Salas Jung till his death; Private Secretary to H.H. the Nizam; Director of Public Instruction for H.H. the Nizam's Dominions; Member of the Legislative Council, Member of the Universities Commission, 1901-2; retired on good service pension, 1907; 1st Indian Member of Council of Secretary of State for India, 1907-9; Chief Adviser to the Prime Minister, 1912-13. *Publications:* Life of Sir Salas Jung; Lectures and Addresses; (in collaboration) Historical and Descriptive Sketch of His Highness the Nizam's Dominions, 2 vols. *Club:* Secunderabad, Secunderabad. (*Died June 1926.*)

BILIOTTI, Sir Alfred, K.C.M.G.; *cr.* 1896; C.M.G. 1886; C.B. 1890; *b.* 14 July 1833; *s.* of late Charles Biliotti, Vice-Consul; *m.* 1889. Vice-Consul at Rhodes, 1856-78; at Trebizond, 1878; Consul, 1879; Trebizond and Sivas, 1883-85; Crete, 1885-99; Consul-General, 1899; Consul-General at Salonica; retired 1903. *Address:* Island of Rhodes, Turkey. (*Died 1 Feb. 1915.*)

BILLE, Frank Ernest, G.C.V.O.; Chamberlain to H.M. the King of Denmark; Grand Cross of the Order of Dannebrog; *b.* Copenhagen, 14 Feb. 1832; 2nd *s.* of Vice-Admiral Sten Andersen Bille and Caroline Bülow; *m.* Sarah Augusta, *d.* of O. Zabriskie, Chancellor of the State of New Jersey, U.S. 1869; two *s.* one *d.* *Educ.:* Copenhagen. The Danish Army, 1851-65; Royal Engineers and General Staff (Headquarters) during the Danish-German War, 1864; Diplomatic Service; Peace Negotiations in Vienna, 1864; Secretary of Legation in Paris, 1865-67; Minister resident in Washington, 1868-72; Envoy extraordinary in Stockholm, 1872-90; Delegate to the Hague Peace Conference, 1899; Danish Envoy Extraordinary and Minister Plenipotentiary to the Court of St. James, 1890-1908. *Address:* 24 Pont Street, S.W. *T.:* Kensington 4833. *Clubs:* Travellers', Bachelors'. (*Died 10 June 1918.*)

BILLINGTON, Mary Frances, newspaper special correspondent; *b.* Chalbury Rectory, Wimborne, Dorset; *d.* of late Rev. G. H. Billington, M.A. Cantab., and Frances Anne, *d.* of late Rev. T. Barber, B.D., rector of Houghton Conquest, Beds. *Educ.:* home. began journalistic career on the Echo, going subsequently to the Daily Graphic for some few years; exclusively attached since 1897 to the permanent staff of the Daily Telegraph; an occasional contributor to magazines; President, Society of Women Journalists, 1913-19; represented Society as only overseas woman delegate invited to Imperial Press Conference, Ottawa, 1920; paid two long visits of investigation to India; travelled upon North-West Frontier and in Nepal. *Publications:* Woman in India, 1895; edited Marriage, and A Mule-driver at the Front (by her brother), 1900; Women in Journalism, 1903; The Red Cross in War for Daily Telegraph Series of War Books, 1914; The Roll-Call of Serving Women, 1915. *Recreations:* horses — travel. *Address:* 23 Warwick Square, Belgrave Road, S.W.1. *Club:* Cowdray. (*Died 27 Aug. 1925.*)

BILSLAND, Sir William, 1st Bart., *cr.* 1907; LL.D.; Lord Provost of Glasgow and Lord Lieutenant of County of City of Glasgow, 1905-8; *b.* Ballat, 17 March 1847; *s.* of late James Bilsland, Ballat, Stirlingshire; *m.* 1885, Agnes Anne, 3rd *d.* of late Alexander Steven of Provanside, Glasgow; one *s.* two *d.* *Educ.:* Dalmonach School, Vale of Leven. Bread Manufacturer; Chairman of Bilsland Brothers, Ltd., Glasgow; member of Town Council of Glasgow, 1886-1908; Extraordinary Director, Royal Bank of Scotland; Knight Commander of Royal Norwegian Order of St. Olaf, 1906; Imperial Japanese Order of Sacred Treasure (third class), 1907; Hon. LL.D., Glasgow, 1907; F.S.A. Scot.; D.L. and J.P. Counties of Lanark and City of Glasgow. *Heir:* *s.* Alexander Steven [M.C., Director of Bilsland Bros., Ltd., and a partner of Gray, Dunn & Co., Biscuit Manufacturers; late Captain, 8th Scottish Rifles; *b.* 13 Sept. 1892]. *Address:* 28 Park Circus, Glasgow. *Clubs:* Western, Art, Liberal, Glasgow. (*Died 27 Aug. 1921.*)

BINGHAM, Lionel John; late Dramatic Editor and Critic Standard, Evening Standard and St. James's Gazette; formerly Music Critic of these papers and Daily Express; and musical contributor to Standard of Empire; *b.* Alfreton, Derbyshire, 15 March 1878; *s.* of J. J. Bingham, M.D., and K. L. Robinson; *m.* 1908, Margaret Sarah Clarkson, Highgate, N.; one *s.* one *d.* *Educ.:* home and London. Fond of art and music as a child; studied painting when a boy, music later; came to London at about eighteen years of age and entered the Royal Academy of Music; remained there three years studying pianoforte, violin, organ, and harmony; joined the music and dramatic staffs of the papers above mentioned in 1905. *Publications:* chiefly magazine articles, including Choral Singing in England To-day and Behind the Scenes at the Opera. *Recreations:* art; sailing; London Chamber Concert Society. *Address:* Trent House, Oxford Road, Gunnersbury, W.4. (*Died 30 Oct. 1919.*)

BINGHAM, Rear-Adm. Hon. Richard, R.N.; 2nd *s.* of 3rd Earl of Lucan; *b.* 6 Jan. 1847; *m.* 1st, 1877, Mary Elizabeth (*d.* 1908), *y. d.* of Edward H. Cole of Stoke Lyme; two *d.*; 2nd, 1914, Ida Louisa, *d.* of late Charles Galton, late I.C.S., and Mrs. Galton. *Address:* 5 Palmeira Court, Hove. *Club:* Union, Brighton. (*Died 12 Nov. 1924.*)

BINNEY, Rev. William Hibbert, D.D., Hon. Canon of Chester, 1907-13; Residentiary Canon since 1913; Vicar of Northwich, Cheshire, 1886-1913; Rural Dean; *b.* 21 Jan. 1857; *s.* of Rt. Rev. Hibbert Binney, D.D., Bishop of Nova Scotia, 1851-87; unmarried. *Educ.:* Winchester; New College, Oxford; Leeds Clergy School. B.A. degree, 2nd Class Modern History, 1879; M.A., 1882; Hon. D.D. Windsor, Nova Scotia, 1905; Commissary to Bishops of Nova Scotia since 1885; Rural Dean of Middlewich, 1888; Chaplain 3rd V.B. Cheshire Regt., 1889; 1st Class Chaplain Territorial Force, to 1918; Territorial Decoration, 1911; F.R.G.S.; Member of Education Committee Cheshire County Council since 1903; Proctor in Convocation for Archdeaconry of Chester since 1904; Vice-President Society for the Propagation of the Gospel, 1909. *Address:* Witton House, Northwich. *T.A.:* Northwich. (*Died 4 May 1916.*)

BINNIE, Sir Alex. Richardson, Kt.; *cr.* 1897; Member of Council of Inst.C.E.; F.G.S.; Member Inst.M.E.; F.R.M.S. and M.R.I.; *b.* London, 26 Mar. 1839; *m.* 1865, Mary (*d.* 1901), *d.* of Dr. Eames, Londonderry, Ireland. *Educ.:* private schools. Pupil of late J. F. Bateman, F.R.S., President Inst.C.E.; engaged on Welsh railways, 1862-66; in the Indian Public Works Dept. 1868-74; Chief Engineer L.C.C. 1890-1901; Engineer, City of Bradford, 1875-90;

works constructed — Nagpore Water Works; Blackwall Tunnel, Bradford Water Works; Barking Road Bridge, etc. *Publications:* various papers and reports on professional subjects; lectures on waterworks; papers on rainfall, etc. *Recreations:* scientific. *Address:* 77 Ladbroke Grove, W.   (*Died 18 May 1917.*)

BINNIE, Rev. Alfred Jonathan, M.A.; Vicar of Nuthurst-cum-Hockley Heath; Canon of Cathedral Church, Birmingham, 1913. *Educ.:* King's College School; Bruce Castle, Tottenham; Corpus Christi College, Cambridge. Deacon, 1874; Priest, 1875; Curate of St. Andrew's, Leeds, 1874-77; St. George's, Campden Hill, 1877-78; P.C. St. Silas, Leeds, 1878-1879; Curate of Kenilworth, 1880-82; St. Andrew's, Plymouth, 1882-84; Vicar of Kenilworth, 1884-91; St. Asaph's, Birmingham, 1891-1917. *Address:* The Vicarage, Nuthurst-cum-Hockley Heath.   (*Died 14 Feb. 1926.*)

BINNING, Col. Lord, George Baillie-Hamilton; C.B. 1904; M.V.O. 1902; commanding Lothian and Border Horse since 1905; Lord-Lieut. Co. Berwick; Deputy Governor Bank of Scotland; D.L. Co. Haddington; *b.* 24 Dec. 1856; *e. s.* of 11th Earl of Haddington; *m.* 1892, Katherine Millicent, *o. c.* of W. Severin Salting; two *s.* one *d. Educ.:* Eton; Trinity College, Cambridge, B.A. Joined Royal Horse Guards, 1880; served in Egyptian Campaign, 1882, present at Kassassin, Tel-el-Kebir, and capture of Cairo (medal and clasp); Nile Expedition, 1884-5, present, at Abu Klea, El Gobat, and Metemmeh (two clasps); Hazara Campaign 1889 (despatches, medal, and clasp); commanded Royal Horse Guards, 1899-1903; retired 1907; A.D.C. to Viceroy of India, 1888-89. *Address:* Mellerstain, Gordon, N.B. *Clubs:* Carlton, Turf, Naval and Military; New, Edinburgh.   (*Died 12 Jan. 1917.*)

BINNS, Percy, K.C.; Resident Chief Magistrate, Durban; *s.* of late Sir Henry Binns, Premier of Natal; *m.* 1897, Ethel Laura, *d.* of William Hayes Acutt; two *s.* three *d. Educ.:* Bishop's College, Maritzburg; Diocesan College, Rondebosch. Attorney, Supreme Court, Natal, 1885; Notary, 1888; Advocate, 1898. *Address:* Durban, Natal. *Club:* Durban.   (*Died 8 Jan. 1920.*)

BINNY, Major Steuart Scott, D.S.O. 1902; 19th Hussars; *b.* 1 July 1871; *m.* 1911, Marjorie, 3rd *d.* of Henry Champion, Sibdon Castle, Salop. Entered army, 1894; served South Africa, 1899-1901 (despatches, D.S.O.); retired, 1914.   (*Died 5 Mar. 1916.*)

BINSTEAD, Mary; Hon. Secretary of the Femina Vie Heureuse and Bookman Prizes Committee; *d.* of late J. A. Openshaw, Kendal, Westmorland; *m.* Edward Arthur Binstead. *Educ.:* privately; The Manor House, Brondesbury Park. Hon. Secretary of the Society of Women Journalists, 1917-27. *Publications:* Historic Novels: The Loser Pays; The Cross of Honour; Little Grey Girl; Madame Lucifer; Modern Novels; Laughter Street, London, etc., under the name of Mary Openshaw; contributor to daily and weekly papers. *Recreations:* motoring, reading, the theatre. *Address:* 136 Cromwell Road, S.W.7. *T.:* Western 5282. *Club:* Lyceum.   (*Died 28 Sept. 1928.*)

BIRCH, Henry William; 2nd *s.* of late John William Birch and Julia, *e. d.* of late Joseph Arden, of Rickmansworth Park, Herts; *b.* 1854; *m.* 1897, Kate Hazeltine, *d.* of R. Anson Yates of San Francisco. Inherited Loudwater under will of maternal grandfather, and The Grove, Old Windsor, under will of Miss Thackeray, 1879. *Club:* Garrick.   (*Died 15 Dec. 1927.*)

BIRCH, Rev. John George; Senior Moderator T.C.D.; M.R.I.A.; Canon of Killaloe; Incumbent of Kilfinaghty, Diocese of Killaloe, 1885-1918; *e. surv. s.* of late W. H. Birch, The Hills, Roscrea, Co. Tip.; *b.* 22 Feb. 1839;

Educ.: Trinity College, Dublin. Ordained for curacy of Mullingar, Co. Meath, during incumbency of Rev. Dr. Reichel, afterwards Bishop of Meath; then curate in England for several years. *Publications:* a paper entitled Numerical Factors in the Messenger of Mathematics, etc. *Address:* The Hills, Roscrea, Co. Tipperary.

BIRCH, Walter de Gray; *b.* 1 Jan. 1842; *s.* of Dr. Samuel Birch the Egyptologist, and of Charlotte F. Gray, *sister* of Dr. J. E. Gray; *m.* 1st, Maria Carolina (*d.* 1877), *d.* of Colonel J. A. Figueiroa Freitas de Albuquerque, Madeira; 2nd Florence (*d.* 1920), *d.* of Isaac Brown; four *s.* three *d. Educ.:* Charterhouse; Trinity Coll. Cambridge. Hon. LL.D. Glasgow University; Hon. Corr. Member of the Royal Academies of Seville and Turin; F.S.A. of London; Hon. Member of the Hispanic Society of America; Vice-President of the British Archæological Association and the St. Paul's Ecclesiological Society; for many years Hon. Secretary, Editor, and Treasurer, Brit. Archæological Assoc.; Librarian and Curator to Marquess of Bute, 1902-14. Entered MSS. Department in British Museum, 1864, where he was continuously employed in the study and arrangement of the MSS. charters and seals; Senior Assistant, 1885-1902; makes an especial study of the Anglo-Saxon, mediæval Latin, Portuguese, and Spanish languages; a specialist in matters relating to literary and record research, printing, book-binding, and disputed handwriting. *Publications:* The Commentaries of Afonso d'Albuquerque; the Cartularium Saxonicum; edited the Journal of the British Archæological Association for twenty-two years; author of History of Margam Abbey; History of Neath Abbey; Memorials of the See and Cathedral of Llandaff; The Register of Hyde Abbey, Winchester; The Nunnaminster MS.; Catalogues of the Margam and Penrice MSS.; The History of the Domesday Book; History of Scottish Seals, 2 vols.; Catalogue of the Seals in the Dept. of MSS. British Museum, 6 vols.; Ordinale Conventus Vallis Caulium; Sermones Fratris Adæ, Ordinis Præmonstratensis; The Royal Charters of the City of London; The Royal Charters of the City of Lincoln; Catalogue of Saxon Abbots; Memorials of St. Guthlac. *Address:* Belgrave Lodge, Harvard Road, Chiswick, W.4.   (*Died 8 Mar. 1924.*)

BIRCHAM, Major Humphry Francis William, D.S.O. 1915; K.R.R.C.; *b.* 20 Mar. 1875. Entered army, 1896; Adjutant, 1899; Captain, 1901; Major, 1914; Adjutant T.F. 1908-11; served South Africa, 1901-2 (despatches, Queen's medal 3 clasps); European War, 1914-15 (D.S.O.).   (*Died 21 July 1916.*)

BIRD, Sir Alfred (Frederick), Kt., *cr.* 1920; M.P. (C.) Wolverhampton (West) since 1910; D.L., J.P.; *b.* Birmingham, 27 July 1849; *s.* of Alfred Bird, F.C.S.; *m.* 1875, Eleanor Frances, *e. d.* of Robert Lloyd Evans; four *s.* two *d. Educ.:* King Edward's School, Birmingham. Manufacturer; retired 1905; contested Wednesbury, 1906. *Recreations:* mountaineering —member Alpine Club; all matters pertaining to art; travelling all over the world; cycling and motoring. *Address:* Artillery Mansions, S.W.; Tudor Grange, Solihull, Warwickshire. *T.A.:* Bird, Solihull. *T.:* Solihull 81. *Clubs:* Carlton, Junior Carlton, Royal Automobile; Automobile de France, Paris. (*Died 7 Feb. 1922.*)

BIRD, Hon. Bolton Stafford, C.M.G. 1920; late M.L.C. Huon, Tasmania, and Member Executive Council of the State; *b.* nr. Newcastle, 30 Jan. 1840; *s.* of Thomas Bird and Ann Stafford; *m.* 1867, Helen, *d.* of Robert Chisholm, Hope Park, Auckland, N.Z.; one *s.* two *d. Educ.:* private academy. Went to Australia, 1858; entered Wesleyan Ministry, 1865; Congregational Minister in Victoria, Australia, and in Tasmania, 1867-79; farmer and fruit-grower, 1879-94 and 1904-19; M.H.A. Franklin, 1882-1903, and South Hobart, 1904-9; Treasurer, Postmaster-General, and Minister of Education, 1887-92 and 1899-1903; Speaker, House of Assembly, 1894-96; M.L.C., 1909-24; Chairman of Committees in Legislative Council, 1919-22. *Address:* Bruni Vale, Lunawanua, South Bruny, Tasmania.   *(Died Dec. 1924.)*

BIRD, Christopher John, C.M.G. 1901; *b.* Pietermaritzburg, Natal, 1855; *s.* of late John Bird, C.M.G., of the Natal Civil Service; *m.* 1887, Edith, *d.* of late William Armstrong, M.R.C.S.E.; five *s.* three *d.* *Educ.:* High School, Pietermaritzburg. Entered the Natal Civil Service, 1874, and was appointed to be Principal Under-Secretary of the Colony on the establishment of Responsible Government in Natal in 1893; J.P. for the Colony, and chairman of the Civil Service Board; on the establishment of the Union of the South African Colonies, on 31 May 1910, acted as Under-Secretary for the Interior in Natal up to the date of his retirement on pension, 1 Sep. 1911; served as a member of the Higher Education Commission, 1911. *Address:* Pietermaritzburg.   *(Died 17 Nov. 1922.)*

BIRD, Captain Frederic Godfrey, R.N.; C.M.G. 1918; D.S.O. 1916; Commanding Drifter Patrol, Dover; *b.* 3 Nov. 1868; *s.* of late Colonel Frederic Vincent Godfrey Bird, R.M.L.I., and Anne Narcisse Elise Wood; *m.* 1908, Elizabeth, *d.* of late Charles Evans Whitlock of Richmond, Virginia, U.S.A.; four *s.* one *d.* *Educ.:* Stubbington House, Fareham; H.M.S. Britannia. Midshipman, 1884; Sub-Lieut., 1888; Lieut., 1890; Commander, 1903; Commanded H.M.S. Perseus in operations against Afghan gun-runners (Naval General Service Medal, Persian Gulf Clasp); retired, 1911; County Councillor, Norfolk, 1913 and 1919; mobilised for European War, Aug. 1914 (D.S.O., Commander of Swedish Order of Swords of 2nd Class, 1906, Officier Legion d'Honneur). *Recreations:* cricket, shooting. *Address:* Hethel Hall, Norwich. *Clubs:* United Service, Norfolk, Norwich.   *(Died 29 Dec. 1919.)*

BIRD, Sir James, Kt., *cr.* 1918; Clerk of the London County Council since 1915; *b.* 1st July 1863; *s.* of late George Bird; *m.* 1891, Jane, *d.* of late Henry Riley; no *c.* On staff of Metropolitan Board of Works, 1881; became an officer of London County Council, 1889; Deputy Clerk, 1905. *Address:* County Hall, Spring Gardens, S.W.; Oakfield, Oakcroft Road, Blackheath, S.E. *Club:* National.   *(Died 12 Feb. 1925.)*

BIRD, Rev. James Grant; Vicar of Christ Church, Dukinfield; Hon. Canon of Chester Cathedral; Rural Dean of Mottram; *s.* of Rev. Charles Robinson Bird, Vicar of Castle Eden, Co. Durham, and Rural Dean of Easington; Chaplain (Lt.-Col.) 6th Batt. Cheshire Regt.; P.G. Chaplain Lodge of Cheshire; *g.s.* of Robert Merttius Bird, of Taplow Hill, Maidenhead, and Barton, Warwickshire; *m.* Hannah Broome, *d.* of Thomas Bulloch, Rock House, Macclesfield. *Educ.:* Repton; privately. Ordained, 1875; Assistant Curate of St. George's, Macclesfield, 1875-7; Chairman of the (late) Stalybridge School Board; an Alderman of the Cheshire County Council; Chairman of Cheshire County Higher Education Committee and of County Training College; Chairman of the Ashton-under-Lyne Board of Guardians; a Governor of Ashton-under-Lyne Infirmary; Hon. Governor of the British and Foreign Bible Society; President of the Stalybridge Harmonic Society, of the District Branch of the N.S.P.C.C., and of the District Blind and Deaf and Dumb Societies; a Governor of Manchester Grammar School; a member of the Court of Manchester University, etc. *Recreation:* travel in Europe and the near East. *Address:* Albion House, Stalybridge. *T.:* Ashton-under-Lyne 713.   *(Died 16 Dec. 1920.)*

BIRD, Lieut.-Col. Robert, C.I.E. 1905; M.V.O. 1912; V.H.S. 1916; M.D., M.S. (Lond.), F.R.C.S., D.P.H. (Camb.), I.M.S., Surgeon to the Viceroy, 1904; Professor of Surgery, Medical College, Calcutta, since 1908; *b.* 12 Dec. 1866; *m.* 1909, Harriet Ellen, *d.* of late Lt.-Col. Dewar, Royal Artillery. *Address:* 2 Upper Wood Street, Calcutta; c/o Grindlay & Co., Parliament Street, S.W. *Clubs:* East India United Service; Bengal United Service, Calcutta.   *(Died 30 Mar. 1918.)*

BIRD, Rev. Samuel William Elderfield; Prebendary of Exeter. *Address:* 31 Raleigh Road, Exeter.   *(Died 27 June 1926.)*

BIRD, Col. Spencer Godfrey, D.S.O. 1900; Royal Dublin Fusiliers (retired); *b.* 5 Jan. 1854; *s.* of late Rev. Godfrey Bird; *m.* 1880, Mary Katherine, *e. d.* of late W. C. Macready; one *s.* one *d.* Entered Army, 1874; Captain, 1881; Major, 1892; Lieut.-Colonel, 1902; Brevet-Col. 1905; served South Africa, 1899-1902 (despatches three times, Queen's medal, four clasps, King's medal, two clasps); served as Colonel in Command of 15th Royal Fusiliers (Kitchener's Army), 1914-16. *Address:* c/o Cox & Co., 6 Pall Mall, S.W.1.   *(Died 12 Dec. 1926.)*

BIRD, William Seymour, K.C.; *b.* 22 May 1846; *e. s.* of John James Bird, M.D., F.R.C.S.I., of Banagher, King's Co., and Hannah Maria, *d.* of Garrett Moore, of Annaghbeg, Co. Galway, Capt. 88th (The Connaught Rangers). *Educ.:* Trinity Coll. Dublin; Senior Moderator and Gold Medallist in History and English Literature, B.A., M.A. Called to the Bar, 1870; Q.C., 1889; County Court Judge, and Chairman of Quarter Sessions, Co. Cork (West Riding), 1892-1915; resigned Sept. 1915. *Recreations:* shooting, gardening. *Address:* Churchtown House, Dundrum, Co. Dublin. *Club:* University, Dublin.   *(Died June 1919.)*

BIRDWOOD, Sir George (Christopher Molesworth); *cr.* 1881; M.D. Edin., K.C.I.E., *cr.* 1887; C.S.I., Knight of Grace, St. John of Jerusalem; Officer Legion of Honour; Laureate of French Academy; LL.D. Camb.; *b.* Belgaum, Bombay, 8 Dec. 1832; *s.* of late General Christopher Birdwood and Lydia Juliana, *d.* of Rev. Joseph Taylor, agent of the London Missionary Society, Belgaum; *m.* 1856, Frances Anne, *e. d.* of late Edward Tolcher, R.N., and Mary Brodrick Birdwood, Harewood House, Plympton St. Mary, Devonshire; three *s.* two *d.* *Educ.:* Plymouth New Grammar School; Dollar Academy; Watt Institute [Mechanic], and University, Edinburgh. Bombay Medical Staff, 1854; served in the Persian Expedition, 1856-57; Professor Anatomy and Physiology, and of Materia Medica and Botany, Grant Medical Coll. Bombay; Registrar and Fellow Univ. of Bombay; Curator Government Museum; Secretary Asiatic Society and Agri. Hort. Society, Bombay; in co-operation with Dr. Bhau Daji, and the leading Indians of Western India, established the Victoria and Albert Museum and the Victoria Gardens, Bombay; J.P., and Sheriff of Bombay, 1864; has held leading positions at all the principal exhibitions since 1851, and as a Royal Commissioner for the Indian and Colonial Exhibition, 1886, the Chicago Exhibition, 1893, the Paris Exhibition, 1900; with assistance of late Prof. Chenery, Mr. Demetrius Boulger and others, founded Primrose Day; special service Revenue and Statistics Dept. India Office, 1871-1902. *Publications:* Economic Vegetable Products of the Bombay Presidency, 1868; Handbook, British Indian Section, Paris Exhibition, 1878; The Industrial Arts of India, 1888; The Genus "Boswellia," Transactions Linnæan Society, vol. xxvii.; the article Incense, Ency. Brit.; Report on Old Records of the India Office, 3rd ed. 1890; Report on Cultivation of Spanish Chestnuts, 1892; Report on Cultivation of Carrots in India, 1897-1898; First Letter Book of East India Company,

1895; Appendix on the Aryan Fauna and Flora to Max Müller's Biography of Words, 1888; botanical Foot-notes to Markham's translation of Garcias ab Horto, 1914; Introductions to Sir Lewis Pelly's Miracle Play of Hasan and Hasain; Stevens' Dawn of British Trade to the East; Vincent Robinson's Eastern Carpets; Count Goblet d'Alviella's Migrations of Symbols; Charles Lamb's Adventures of Ulysses, 1899; Mrs. Aynsley's Symbolism of the East and West; and S. M. Mitra's Indian Problems, 1908; Preface to Miss Gabrielle Festing's From the Land of Princes, 1904; The Genealogy of the Naosari Parsi Priests; and Grigg's Relics of the Honourable East India Company, 1909; Appendix to the Life of John Hungerfold Pollen, by Anne Pollen, 1912; Monograph on the Antiquity of Carpets in work on Oriental Carpets, published by Austrian Government; Sva, 1915; numerous contributions to Reviews, etc. *Recreation* : gardening. *Address* : 5 Windsor Road, Ealing, W. *Club* : Northbrook.   (*Died 28 June 1917.*)

BIRKBECK, William John, M.A., J.P., D.L., F.S.A.; landowner; a member of House of Laymen, Province of Canterbury; *b.* 13 Feb. 1859; *o. s.* of late W. Birkbeck, J.P.; *m.* 1883, Rose K., *d.* of Sir Somerville Gurney;   two *s.* one *d.* *Educ.*: Eton; Magdalen College, Oxford. Owns about 4000 acres; High Sheriff, 1910; travelled in various foreign countries, more especially Russia; attended the Bishop of Peterborough, Dr. Creighton, at the Coronation of the Emperor Nicholas II. at Moscow, 1896; the Archbishop of Finland at Queen Victoria's Diamond Jubilee, 1897; member of the Speaker's Anglo-Russian Deputation, 1912; appointed to Ilchester Lectureship, Oxford, 1895; Birkbeck Lectureship in Ecclesiastical History, Trinity College, Cambridge, 1914-16. *Publications*: Russia and the English Church, 1895; various pamphlets, articles, and reviews on ecclesiastical, historical, and musical subjects. *Recreations*: ecclesiastical and historical studies, music, shooting. *Address*: Stratton Strawless Hall, Norwich. *T.A.*: Buxton-Norfolk. *T.*: Coltishall. 6. *M.*: AH 711. *Clubs*: Athenæum, United University, Junior Carlton.   (*Died 9 June 1916.*)

BIRKIN, Sir Thomas Isaac, 1st Bart., *cr.* 1905; J.P., D.L.; *b.* 15 Feb. 1831; 2nd *s.* of late Richard Birkin of Apsley Hall, Notts, and Mary Ann, *d.* of late Thomas Walker of Trowell, Notts; *m.* 1856, Harriet, *d.* of Matthew Tebbutt of Bluntisham; six *s.* three *d.* High Sheriff Notts, 1892. *Heir* : *s.* Thomas Stanley [*b.* 18 Oct. 1857; *m.* 1894, Hon. Margaret Diana Hopetoun, *y. d.* of late Capt. Hon. Henry Weyland Chetwynd, R.N., and *sister* of 8th Viscount Chetwynd; two *s.* one *d.* *Address*: Park House, Nottingham]. *Address*: Ruddington Grange, Nottingham.   (*Died 16 Jan. 1922.*)

BISCOE, Lieut. - General William Walters, C.B. 1896; retired; *b.* Donnington, Hereford, 12 Aug. 1841; 2nd *s.* of late Rev. W. Biscoe. *Educ.*: Winchester College. Joined 1st Bengal European Light Cavalry, 1860; appointed to Fane's Horse (now 19th Lancers), 1862; Assist. Adj. - Gen. Umballa Division, 1882-85; commanded 19th Bengal Lancers, 1885-92; Colonel on Staff, Multan, 1892-1895; commanded Bandelkand District, Agra, during 1895; served in Bezoti Expedition, 1869; throughout Afghan Campaigns of 1878-80 (medal and Brevet of Lieut.-Colonel); commanded Cavalry Brigade in Miranzai Expedition, 1891 (medal, C.B.) *Recreations*: hunting, shooting, polo, cricket, racquets. *Club*: United Service.   (*Died 27 April 1920.*)

BISGOOD, Joseph John; B.A.; J.P.; *b.* Glastonbury, 6 Jan. 1861. *Educ.*: Prior Park, Bath; University of London. Editor and Proprietor Insurance Record; author various works on Insurance; Editor Pitman's Life Assurance Dictionary; contributor various journals on Assurance matters; late Secretary in London-Edinburgh Assurance Company, Ltd.; President, Chartered Institute of Secretaries, 1918-19; Chairman London Safety First Council, 1924-26; Member of Surrey County Council and Surrey Education Committee; Member of Richmond Town Council (Alderman-Mayor, 1912-13); Member Richmond Education Committee; Member of Council, London Chamber of Commerce; President various local societies at Richmond; Director Vauxhall Motors, Ltd., and other public companies. *Recreations*: amateur acting and motoring. *Address*: Lindores, Kew Gardens. *T.*: Richmond 0460. *Club*: Gresham.   (*Died 10 Feb. 1927.*)

BISHOP, Joseph Bucklin, Litt.D.; Secretary Isthmian Canal Commission, 1905-14; *b.* 5 Sep. 1847; *m.* 1872, Harriet Hartwell (*d.* 1917), Providence; one *s.* *Educ.*: Brown University (A.B.); Litt.D. 1923. Member National Institute of Arts and Letters; on Editorial Staff, New York Tribune, 1870-88; Editorial Writer, New York Evening Post, 1888-1900; Chief of Editorial Staff, New York Globe, 1900-5. *Publications*: Cheap Money Experiments, 1892; Our Political Drama, 1904; Issues of a New Epoch, 1904; The Panama Gateway, 1913; Recent Tariff Developments in England; Presidential Nominations and Elections, 1916; A Chronicle of One Hundred and Fifty Years, 1918; Theodore Roosevelt's Letters to his Children, 1919; Theodore Roosevelt and his Time—shown in his Letters (2 vols.), 1920; Life of Charles Joseph Bonaparte, 1922; Life of A. Barton Hepburn, 1923. *Club*: University, New York.   (*Died 13 Dec. 1928.*)

BISPHAM, David, B.A.; LL.D.; Mus. Doc.; Baritone. Royal Opera, Covent Garden; Metropolitan Opera House, New York; *b.* Philadelphia, U.S.A., 5 Jan. 1857; *o. s.* of William D. Bispham and Jane Lippincott Scull; *m.* Caroline. *d.* of late Gen. Charles S. Russell, U.S. army, 1885. *Educ.*: Haverford Coll. near Philadelphia. Début as the Duc de Longueville in The Basoche, Royal English Opera, Nov. 1891; later with the Royal Opera, Covent Garden, and the Metropolitan Opera Co. of New York, singing the principal rôles in German, French, and Italian; founder American Singers; Opera Comique Co., New York, 1917. *Publications*: Autobiography, A Quaker Singer's Recollections; magazine articles. *Recreations*: swimming, cycling. *Clubs*: Players', Century, New York; University, Philadelphia.   (*Died Oct. 1921.*)

BISSET, Colonel Sir William Sinclair Smith, K.C.I.E.; *cr.* 1897; *b.* 13 Nov. 1843; *s.* of late Rev. James Bisset, D.D.; *m.* 1888, Henrietta Mary, *d.* of Lt. - Gen. W. P. La Touche, Indian Army; one *s.* two *d.* Entered Royal Engineers, 1863; Colonel, 1895; served Afghan War, 1878-80 (medal, Bt. Maj.); Deputy Consulting Engineer for Railways, 1872-75; Manager Rajputana Malwa State Railways, 1875-1884; Agent for Bombay, Baroda, and Central India Railway System, 1884-93; Secretary to Government of India in Public Works Department, 1898-97; Government Director of Indian Railways 1897 - 1901. *Address*: Hill House, Stoke Poges. *Club*: United Service.   (*Died 30 July 1916.*)

BISSET - SMITH, George Tulloch, F.S.S., Civil Servant (pen - name "George Bizet"); Registration Examiner; Travelling Officer Department of the Registrar-General for Scotland; Member of Council, Franco-Scottish Society and of League of Nations Union for Scotland; Vice-Chairman, Whitley Departmental Council; Founder of the Bizet Correspondence College of Authorship and Journalism; *b.* Aberdeen, 11 Jan. 1863; *o. c.* of late Captain George Bisset-Smith and Christian, *d.* of Theodore Morison, Bognie, Aberdeenshire; *m.* 1900, Élise, *e. d.* of James Morison, Glasgow; three *d.* *Educ.*: Old Aberdeen Grammar School;

Edinburgh University (Prizeman in English Literature and Composition). Entered Civil Service, 1882; office of Registrar-General for Scotland, 1886; H.M. Registration Examiner for East of Scotland, 1899-1922; Southern District, 1922; Member of Sociological Society, of Society of Scottish Economists, and of the Incorporated Society of Authors. *Publications:* Vital Registration: A Manual of the Law and Practice concerning the Registration of Births, Deaths, and Marriages in Scotland, New Edition, 1922; Some Eminent Scotsmen; Leira: a Love Story; Early Part of an Honest Autobiography; The British Constitution compared with Modern Republics; Marriage and Registration, 4th ed., 1921; An Outline of a Philosophy of Population; The Census, and some of its Uses, 1921; Population, and Problems of Sex, 1922; The Census and Social Progress; Industrial Welfare and the League; Hints to Beginners in Literature, 1923. *Recreations:* literature, lawn tennis, sociology. *Address:* 11 Carlton Terrace, Edinburgh. *T.:* Central 7985. (*Died 21 Oct. 1922.*)

BLACK, Andrew, R.S.W. 1884; *b.* 11 May 1850; *s.* of Andrew Black, merchant, and Isabella Jackson; unmarried. *Educ.:* Glasgow; Paris. In business as designer for 11 years, and became a professional artist, 1877; exhibitor occasionally Royal Academy, Paris Salon, Munich, Prague, Edinburgh, and 42 years in Glasgow. *Recreations:* reading and boating. *Address:* 69 St. Vincent Street, Glasgow. *Club:* Glasgow Art. (*Died 16 July 1916.*)

BLACK, Prof. Ebenezer Charlton, LL.D.; Professor of English Literature, Boston University, U.S.A., since 1900; *b.* United Presbyterian Manse, Liddesdale, Scotland, 18 June 1861; *y. s.* of Rev. John Black and Mary Beattie; *m.* 1892, Agnes Knox; one *s.* one *d.* *Educ.:* Edinburgh University. Medallist in Rhetoric and English Literature; Lecturer on English Literature, Harvard University, 1891-1893; Principal of Language and Literature Department, New England Conservatory of Music, Boston, 1898-1900; Lecturer on Literature, Emerson College, since 1903; New England University Extension Commission since 1910; LL.D., Glasgow University, 1902; Hon. Member Phi Beta Kappa Society, 1905; Member Royal Society of Arts, Scottish Text Society; Pres. New England Association of Teachers of English; Pres. Emerson College Endowment Association; authority and lecturer on educational and literary subjects. *Publications:* Early Songs and Lyrics, 1886; Introduction to Shakespeare, 1913; University Addresses, 1913; contributor to reviews and magazines; editor of the New Hudson Shakespeare (school edition and library edition). *Address:* 50 Kirkland Street, Cambridge, Mass. *Clubs:* Authors'; Twentieth Century, Boston. (*Died 11 July 1927.*)

BLACK, James Watt, M.A., Aberdeen; M.D., Edin.; F.R.C.P., London; Consulting Obstetric Physician to Charing Cross Hospital, London; 2nd *s.* of James Black, J.P., and a Commissioner of Supply for the County of Banff, of Knock, Banffshire, and Margaret, *d.* of John Watt of Ordens, Banffshire; *b.* 1840; *m.* 1869, Mary Wedderburn, *r. d.* of Captain James Cox, 92nd (Gordon) Highlanders, and Mary, *d.* of Major Archibald Douglas. *Educ.:* Aberdeen, Edinburgh, Paris, Vienna, and Berlin. Private Assistant to the late Sir James Y. Simpson, Bt., Edinburgh, 1862-67; Obstetric Physician and Lecturer at Charing Cross Hospital, London, 1869-98; President of the Obstetrical Society of London, 1891-92; has been Examiner in Obstetrics and Gynæcology to the University of Oxford, and to the Royal College of Physicians of London. *Publications:* Editor of Selected Obstetrical and Gynæcological Works of the late Sir James Y. Simpson. *Address:* Crockham

Hill Place, Edenbridge, Kent. *Club:* Athenæum. (*Died 22 Feb. 1918.*)

BLACK, John Sutherland; *b.* Kirkcaldy, N.B., 4 July 1846; *e. s.* of late Rev. James Black, A.M. (Aberd.), minister of the Free Church at Dunnikier, Kirkcaldy. *Educ.:* at home and at Burgh School of Kirkcaldy; Edinburgh University and New College, Edinburgh; Tübingen; Göttingen. M.A. Edin., Hon. LL.D. Edin., F.R.S.E. Assist. editor of ninth edition of Encyclopædia Britannica, 1878-89; joint editor of Encyclopædia Biblica, 1894-1903; joint author and editor of Life and Lectures of William Robertson Smith, 1912. *Address:* 125 St. James' Court, Buckingham Gate, S.W. *Clubs:* Athenæum, Savile. (*Died 20 Feb. 1923.*)

BLACK, Sir Robert James, 1st Bt., *cr.* 1922; Director of the Mercantile Bank of India and other companies; *b.* 19 July 1860; 3rd *s.* of late Robert John Black, London; *m.* 1890, Elen Cecilia, 2nd *d.* of late General W. P. La Touche, Indian Army; one *s.* four *d.* *Educ.:* privately. Went to India 1878: left 1900; retired from Best & Co., Ltd., Madras, 1918; sometime President Bank of Madras and member of Port Trust of Madras, and since connected with the finance and commerce of India and the further East. *Recreations:* hunting, shooting, fishing. *Heir:* s. Robert Andrew Stransham Black. *Address:* Midgham Park, Berks. *T.:* Woolhampton 5. *Clubs:* Oriental, Ranelagh. (*Died 28 Sept. 1925.*)

BLACKADER, Maj.-Gen. Charles Guinand, C.B. 1917; D.S.O. 1900; (temp. Maj.-Gen.) Leicester Regt.; A.D.C. to the King, 1916; *b.* 20 September 1869; *s.* of C. G. Blackader; *m.* 1888, Marian Ethel, *d.* of late George Melbourne; two *d.* Entered army, 1888; Captain, 1895; Major, 1904; Lt.-Col. 1912; served West Africa, 1897-98 (despatches, medal, 2 clasps); South Africa, 1899-1902 (despatches twice, Queen's medal with four clasps, King's medal with two clasps, D.S.O.); European War, 1914-1918 (despatches twice, brevet Colonel, promoted Maj.-Gen.). *Club:* Naval and Military. (*Died 2 April 1921.*)

BLACKBURN, Colonel John Edward, C.B. 1917; (late R.E.), retired pay; *b.* 1851; *s.* of late R. B. Blackburn, Sheriff of Stirlingshire. *Educ.:* Trinity College, Glenalmond; Eton. Entered Army, 1871; Capt. 1883; Major, 1890; Lieut.-Colonel, 1898; Colonel, 1902; retired pay, 1903; served in Egypt, 1882-83 and 1884-85 (medal with 3 clasps and large bronze star, despatches); European War, 1915-16 (C.B.). *Clubs:* United Service; New, Edinburgh. (*Died 29 Sept. 1927.*)

BLACKBURNE, Lt.-Col. Charles Harold, D.S.O. 1902; 5th Dragoon Guards; *b.* 20 May 1876; *s.* of late C. E. Blackburne of Oldham; *m.* 1903, Emily Beatrice, *d.* of Canon H. D. Jones; one *s.* one *d.* *Educ.:* Tonbridge. Served South Africa with 11th Batt. Imperial Yeomanry, 1900-2 (King's and Queen's Medals, despatches, D.S.O.); European War, 1914-17 (wounded, despatches, brevet Major and Lt.-Col.); Assistant Secretary for Transvaal Repatriation Department, 1902; General Manager of Transvaal Government Stud, 1902-6. *Address:* Tyddyn, Mold, N. Wales. *Club:* Cavalry. (*Died 10 Oct. 1918.*)

BLACKBURNE, Joseph Henry, British Chess Champion; *b.* Chorlton-on-Medlock, Manchester, 10 Dec. 1841; *m.*; wife died 1922. *Educ.:* Manchester. *Address:* 45 Sandrock Road, Lewisham, S.E. *Club:* City of London Chess. (*Died 1 Sept. 1924.*)

BLACKWELL, Major Francis Victor, C.B.E., M.C.; publicist and journalist; *s.* of John Blackwell, Shipley, Yorks. *Educ.:* Belle Vue; privately. Studied banking, law, and journalism; served in Duke of Wellington's West Riding Regt. (M.C.); wounded, 1916; invalided home; attached Northumbrian Re-

serve Brigade; sent with British Military Mission to America, Oct. 1917; commanded group of British Officers, Camp Dodge, Iowa; attached British War Mission, Crewe House, and afterwards Canadian Mission in London; Assistant Director of Publicity, Victory Loan, 1919; Press Adviser Russian Famine Relief Fund, 1921; Publicity Adviser Dept. of Overseas Trade, Pageant of Empire, British Empire Exhibition, 1924; Brighter London Campaign, 1922; Director of Publicity, Torchlight and Searchlight Tattoo; also responsible for many political, financial, and industrial campaigns. *Address:* 1 Lancaster Gate, W.2. *T.:* Paddington 3587. *Clubs:* Devonshire, Royal Automobile.
(Died 12 Mar. 1928.)

BLACKWOOD, Lieut.-Col. Albemarle Price, D.S.O. 1918; The Border Regt.; *b.* 4 Nov. 1881; *s.* of Major Price Frederick Blackwood; *m.* 1920, Kyra, *d.* of late Albert Llewellyn Hughes. *Educ.:* Eton; Sandhurst. 2nd Lt. The Border Regt. 1901; served S. African War, 1901-2; European War, 1914-18 (Bt. Lt.-Col., D.S.O., 2nd Class Vladimir, Star of Roumania). *Address:* c/o Cox & Co., 16 Charing Cross, S.W.1. *M.:* LW 5009. *Club:* Naval and Military.
(Died Oct. 1921.)

BLACKWOOD, Lord Basil (Ian Basil Gawaine Temple), Private Secretary to Lord-Lieutenant of Ireland; *b.* Clandeboye, Ireland, 4 Nov. 1870; 3rd *s.* of 1st and *b.* and *heir-pres.* of 2nd Marquess of Dufferin. *Educ.:* Harrow; Balliol Coll. Oxford. Barr. 1896; Dep. Judge Advocate, South Africa, 1900-1901; Assist. Colonial Secretary Orange River Colony to 1907; Colonial Secretary Barbados, 1907-9; Intelligence Corps (attached 9th Lancers), Aug. 1914; Grenadier Guards, June 1915; served European War, 1914-16 (wounded). Illustrated the Bad Child's Book of Beasts, More Beasts, and the Modern Traveller under the initials B.T.B. 1898. *Address:* Clandeboye, Co. Down, Ireland. *Clubs:* White's, Pratt's.
(Died 3 July 1917.)

BLACKWOOD, Sir Francis, 4th Bt.; *cr.* 1814; Capt. R.N.; retired 1886; *b.* Stonehouse, 11 Nov. 1838; *S. b.* 1854; *m.* 1st, 1861, Laura Olivia *(d.* 1865), *d.* of R. S. Palmer of Great Torrington; one *d.*; 2nd, 1874, Dorothy *(d.* 1919), *d.* of Rev. E. H. Quicke, Newton St. Cyres, Devon; two *s.* one *d. Heir: g.-s.* Henry Palmer Temple, *b.* 12 May 1896. *Club:* United Service.
(Died 20 June 1924.)

BLACKWOOD, Captain Frederick Herbert, D.S.O. 1914; Lincolnshire Regt.; Inspector-General of Police and Commandant Local Forces British Guiana since 1924; *b.* 9 Nov. 1885; *m.* 1915, Nora, *d.* of Dr. Ponsonby Widdup; one *s.* one *d.* Entered Army from Militia, 1906; served European War, 1914-1915 (D.S.O.); Bimbashi, 13th Sudanese, Egyptian Army, 1916; Commandant Military School, Khartoum, 1916; Kaimakam, commanding 14th Sudanese, 1920. *Address:* Eve Leary Barracks, Georgetown, Demerara. *(Died Aug. 1926.)*

BLAGDEN, Rev. Henry, Hon. Canon, Christ Church, Oxford, 1892; *b.* 25 Oct. 1832; *m.* 1864; three *s.* four *d. Educ.:* Trinity Coll., Cambridge (Scholar, M.A.). Curate of St. Neots, 1855-57 and 1859-62; St. Mark, Torquay, 1858; Westbury, 1859; Christ Church, St. Leonards, 1862-65; Newbury, 1865-69; Vicar of Hughenden, 1869-98. *Address:* 27 Kensington Court Mansions, S.W.8.
(Died 16 Dec. 1922.)

BLAGROVE, Col. Henry John, C.B. 1900; C.B.E.; retired; *b.* 30 July 1854; *s.* of H. J. Blagrove of Gloucester Place, Hyde Park, and Cardiff Hall and Orange Valley estates in Island of Jamaica; *m.* 1st, 1884, Alice Evelyn, *d.* of late Rev. E. Boothby of Whitwell, Derbyshire; 2nd, 1904, Violet, *d.* of F. Walton, of Cwmllecoediog, Montgomeryshire; three *s.*

Educ.: Eton; Magdalen Coll., Oxford. Entered 13th Hussars, 1875; Capt. 1883; Major, 1890; Lt.-Col. 1896; Bt. Col. 1900; served Afghanistan, 1879-80; Egyptian Exped. 1882; Battles of Kassasin and Tel-el-Kebir, and march to Cairo (medal with clasp and bronze star); S. Africa, 1899-1901 (despatches, C.B.); commanded 13th Hussars, 1896-1901; Commandant, Prisoners of War Camp, Leigh, 1915-17. *Address:* Dowdeswell Court, Glos. *Club:* Cavalry.
(Died 29 Nov. 1925.)

BLAIKIE, Walter Biggar, LL.D., J.P., D.L., F.R.S.E.; Chairman of T. & A. Constable, Ltd., University Press, Edinburgh; *b.* Edinburgh, 1847; 2nd *s.* of late Rev. Prof. William Garden Blaikie, D.D., LL.D., Edinburgh; *m.* 1873, Janet Marshall, *o. d.* of John Macfie, Edinburgh; five *d. Educ.:* Edinburgh Academy; Brussels; Edinburgh University. Went to India in 1870; served in the Department Public Works; retired 1879, when Executive Engineer Military Works; entered his present firm, 1879; Chairman Edinburgh Chamber of Commerce, 1903-6; formerly a Member of Council Scottish History Society and Royal Scottish Geographical Society; a Manager of the Edinburgh Royal Infirmary, 1900-20; Hon. LL.D. University of Edinburgh, 1913. *Publications:* The Itinerary of Prince Charles Edward, 1896; Origins of the 'Forty-five, 1916; Edinburgh at the Time of the Occupation of Prince Charles, 1910; numerous contributions to magazines, etc., dealing with the Jacobite period of Scottish history; Monthly Star Maps, an annual series, 1898-1920. *Address:* Bridgend, Colinton, Midlothian. *T.A.:* Blaikie, Colinton. *T.:* Colinton 45. *Clubs:* Savile, Athenæum; University, United Service, Edinburgh. *(Died 3 May 1928.)*

BLAIR, Colonel James Molesworth, C.M.G., D.S.O.; Military Attaché at Belgrade since 1921 and Belgrade and Prague since 1923; *b.* near Ardrishaig, Argyllshire, 15 July 1880; *s.* of Charles Blair, D.L., J.P., of Glenfoot, Tillicoultry; *m.* 1909, Lilian Louise Archer, *e. d.* of Maj.-Gen. Sir O. R. A. Julian of Broomhill, nr. Ivybridge, S. Devon; one *s. Educ.:* Winchester; Magdalen College, Oxford. Served in S. African War as Lieut., 1st Volunteer Battalion Hampshire Regt. (Queen's medal and 5 clasps); nominated by C.-in-C. S. Africa for Commission as 2nd Lieut. in the Black Watch, 1901; Adjutant of Black Watch in India as Orderly Officer to G.O.C.; served in Mohmand Expedition of 1908 (medal with clasp); Captain in Gordon Highlanders, 1911; passed staff college, 1913; Assistant Military Attaché, Petrograd, Aug. 1914; served during World War in Russia and France (despatches twice, D.S.O., Legion of Honour, 2nd Class Order of Stanislaus, 4th Class Vladimir, both with swords, 1914 Star, General Service and Victory medals); with British Military Mission in Siberia, first as Chief Staff Officer then as Chief Mission, 1918-20 (C.M.G. Czech War Cross, 2nd Class Order of Sacred Treasure); Military Attaché, Belgrade, 1921; Colonel, 1923. *Recreations:* fishing, shooting, and golf. *Address:* British Legation, Belgrade, Yugoslavia.
(Died 8 June 1925.)

BLAIR, Rt. Rev. Laurence Frederick Devaynes, D.D. *Educ.:* Pembroke College, Cambridge; Ridley Hall, Cambridge. Ordained, 1892; Curate of Portman Chapel, 1892-95; Rector of Chalgrave and Vicar of Langley, 1895-1902; Chaplain of Bellary, Madras, 1902-3; Sangor, 1903-4; Army Chaplain in England, 1904-5; Church Parochial Mission Society, 1906-10; Bishop of the Falkland Islands, 1910-14. *Address:* The Church House, Westminster, S.W.1. *(Died 18 Nov. 1925.)*

BLAIR, Very Rev. William, M.A., D.D., F.S.A. Scot., V.D.; minister of Leighton Church, Dunblane; *b.* Cluny, Fifeshire, 13 Jan. 1880; 9th *s.* of George Blair and Elspeth Welch; *m.* Eliza-

5   97

beth Allan (*d.* 1904), 2nd *d.* of David Corsar, flax-spinner, Arbroath, 1858 ; five *s.* four *d.* *Educ.* : Auchterderran Parish School ; Univ. of St. Andrews. 1st class honours in Greek, 1847, 1850 ; M.A. 1850 : D.D. 1879. Ordained, 1856 ; Chaplain to 6th Perthshire Rifle Volunteer Corps, 1864 ; and Acting Chaplain to 4th Perthshire Vol. Batt. The Black Watch (Royal Highlanders), 1892 ; Hon. Chaplain, Territorial Force, 1911 ; Clerk to the U.P. Synod, 1884 ; Chairman of Dunblane School Board, 1885-1909 ; Parish Councillor, 1896 ; Moderator of U.P. Synod, 1898-1899 ; one of principal clerks of United Free Church General Assembly, 1900-7 ; member of Univ. Court, St. Andrews, 1903-11. *Publications:* Chronicles of Aberbrothec ; Rambling Recollections of Scenes Worth Seeing ; History and Principles of the United Presbyterian Church ; Life of Rev. George Jacque ; Life of Archbishop Leighton ; Log of " The Hersilia " ; editor of M'Kelvie's Annals of the United Presbyterian Church ; of Jubilee Memorial Volume ; Robert Leighton ; Kildermoch, etc. *Recreation:* golf. *Address:* Leighton Manse, Dunblane, Perthshire. N.B.   (*Died 11 Aug. 1916.*)

BLAIS, Rt. Rev. Andrew Albert, Bishop of Rimouski since 1891 ; *b.* Quebec, 26 Aug. 1842. *Educ.* : Quebec Seminary. Titular Bishop of Germanicopolis ; Coadjutor of Rimouski with future succession, 1890. *Address:* Bishop's Palace, Rimouski, Canada.

(*Died Jan. 1919.*)

BLAKE, Col. Arthur Maurice, C.B. 1897 ; J.P., D.L. ; Col. 1st V.B. Bedfordshire Regt. ; *b.* Glasgow, 11 Sep. 1852 ; *o. s.* of Col. F. R. Blake, C.B., 33rd D. of Wellington's Regt., and Henrietta, *d.* of G. S. Marten ; *m.* Isabella, 2nd *d.* of J. S. Crawley of Stockwood, Luton, 1881 ; two *s.* *Educ.* : Eton. Joined Grenadier Guards, 1870 ; retired 1877 ; Major, 1st Herts Vol. 1878 ; Lt.-Col. of 1st Vol. Bat. Bed. Regt. 1880. *Recreations:* cricket, shooting. *Clubs:* Arthur's, Junior Carlton.

BLAKE, Sir Ernest Edward, K.C.M.G. ; *cr.* 1901 ; Crown Agent for the Colonies, 1881-1909 ; *b.* 1845 ; *s.* of Rev. Edmund Blake, of Bramerton, Norfolk ; *m.* 1874, Catharine Isabella (*d.* 1902), *d.* of Alfred Blyth ; two *s.* one *d.* Entered Colonial Office 1863 ; Assistant Private Secretary to Earl of Kimberley, 1872, Private Secretary 1874 ; 1st class Clerk and Head of Gen. Dept. 1879. *Address:* Woolcombe St. Mary's, Uplyme, Devon. (*Died 30 Nov. 1920.*)

BLAKE, Sir Henry Arthur, G.C.M.G., *cr.* 1897 ; K.C.M.G., *cr.* 1888 ; C.M.G. 1887 ; F.R.G.S. ; J.P. ; D.L. ; Knight of Justice of Order of St. John of Jerusalem ; F.R.C.I. ; F.I.D. ; Hon. Col. Ceylon Mounted Rifles ; District Grand Master Ceylon Freemasons ; Member of the Council Royal Dublin Society ; Hon. Member Royal Zoological Society, London ; *b.* Limerick, 18 Jan. 1840 ; *s.* of late Peter Blake, County Inspector of Irish Constabulary ; *m.* 1st, 1862, Jeannie (*d.* 1866), *d.* of Andrew Irwin of Ballymore, Boyle ; 2nd, 1874, Edith, *e. d.* and co-heir of Ralph Bernal Osborne of Newtown Anner, Clonmel ; two *s.* one *d.* Cadet Irish Constabulary, 1859 ; Resident Magistrate, 1876 ; Special Resident Magistrate, 1882 ; Governor of Bahamas, 1884-87 ; Newfoundland, 1887-88 ; appointed to Queensland, 1888, but resigned without entering upon the administration ; Capt.-Gen. and Gov.-in-Chief, Jamaica, 1889-97 ; at request of Legislature and public bodies of the Island his term was extended in 1894, and again in 1896 ; Governor of Hong-Kong, 1897-1903 ; Governor of Ceylon, 1903-7. *Publications:* Pictures from Ireland, by Terence M'Grath ; China, 1909. *Recreations:* riding, shooting. *Address:* Myrtle Grove, Youghal, Co. Cork. *Clubs:* Marlborough, Brooks's ; Kildare Street, Dublin.
(*Died 23 Feb. 1918.*)

BLAKE, Capt. Sir (Herbert) Acton, K.C.M.G., *cr.* 1918 ; K.C.V.O., *cr.* 1914 ; J.P. ;

F.R.G.S. ; Deputy Master, Trinity House, E.C. ; *o s.* of John George Blake of Winchester ; *b.* 19 Oct. 1857 ; *m.* 1897, Lucy Grace, *e. d.* of James Thin, London. *Educ.* : privately. Mariner ; some years in command in the British India Steam Navigation Company and the African Royal Mail Company ; Captain (retired) R.N.R. ; Elder Brother of Trinity House, 1901 ; Member of Departmental Committee of Board of Trade on Mercantile Marine, and also on Committee on Tonnage ; Member of Port of London Authority, 1906-7 ; a British Delegate on International Committee for Safety of Life at Sea, 1913 ; Chairman, Advisory Committee of Pilotage to Board of Trade ; Chairman, Dock and Harbour Dues Claims Commission. *Address:* 48 Kensington Mansions, S.W.5 ; Puck's Croft, Rusper, Sussex. *T.:* Western 2251 ; Rusper 16. *Club:* United Service. (*Died 7 Mar. 1926.*)

BLAKE, Col. Maurice Charles Joseph, C.B. 1897 ; retired 1897 ; J.P. Cos. Mayo and Galway ; D.L. Co. Mayo ; *b.* 20 July 1837 ; *e. s.* of late Valentine O. C. Blake and Hon. Margaret, *d.* of Rt. Hon. 3rd Baron Ffrench ; *m.* Jeannette, *d.* of Richard P. O'Reilly of Sans Souci, Booterstown, Co. Dublin, and Castle Wilder, Co. Longford, 1863 ; two *s.* three *d.* *Educ.* : Stonyhurst. Joined North Mayo Militia, 1861, which afterwards became 6th Bat. Connaught Rangers ; Major, 1884 ; Lieut.-Col. commanding, 1885 ; granted Hon. rank of Col. 1886 ; High Sheriff for Co. Mayo, 1864. *Recreations:* shooting, farming, and county gentleman's amusements. *Address:* Tower Hill, Ballyglass, Co. Mayo, Ireland. *Club:* United Service, Dublin.
(*Died 5 Feb. 1917.*)

BLAKE, Major Napoleon Joseph Rodolph, D.S.O. 1900 ; retired, 1901 ; D.C.O. Middlesex Regt. ; *b.* 1858 ; *s.* of late Captain Maurice L. Blake ; *m.* 1888, Alice, *d.* of late R. H. Page-Henderson of Oswaldkirk, Yorks ; one *d.* Entered Army, 1873 ; Captain, 1881 ; Major, 1890 ; served Zulu War, 1879 (medal with clasp) ; South Africa, 1899-1901 (despatches, medal with 7 clasps, D.S.O.). *Address:* Skirsgill, Camberley. *T.:* Camberley 32. (*Died 21 Oct. 1926.*)

BLAKE, Lt.-Col. Terence Joseph Edward, D.S.O. 1918 ; Stock Exchange ; *b.* 1886 ; *m.* 1910, Ethel Maud Moore ; two *s.* *Educ.* : Owens School. Joined 2/1st Queen's Westminster Rifles in the ranks, Aug. 1914 ; Commissioned Dec. 1914, and gazetted to 13th Royal Fusiliers ; served European War, 1914-19 (wounded thrice, despatches thrice, D.S.O.). *Address:* 18 Glenmore Road, Hampstead, N.W.3. *T.:* Hampstead 5825. (*Died 15 Dec. 1921.*)

BLAKE, Sir Thomas Patrick Ulick John Harvey, 15th Bt. ; *cr.* 1622 ; *b.* 18 Mar. 1870 ; *s.* of 14th Bt. and Camilla, *y. d.* of Harvey Combe, late M.C.S. ; *S.* father, 1912 ; *m.* 1903, Evelyn Winifred, *y. d.* of L. G. Stewart, late Lieut., R.E. ; one *s.* J.P. Co. Galway ; late Capt. R.G.A. *Heir:* *s.* Ulick Temple, *b.* 6 Aug. 1904. *Address:* Menlough, Co. Galway. *Clubs:* Junior Carlton ; Co. Galway.
(*Died 15 Dec. 1925.*)

BLAKER, Sir John George, 1st Bt., *cr.* 1919 ; Kt., *cr.* 1897 ; O.B.E. 1918 ; Mayor of Brighton, 1895-98 ; *b.* 1854 ; *s.* of J. G. Blaker ; *m.* Lily, *d.* of Samuel Cowell, 1890. *Educ.* : private schools, Sandgate and Brighton. Elected Councillor, 1886 ; Alderman, 1893. *Heir:* *s.* Reginald, *b.* 1900. *Address:* The Romans, Stanford Avenue, Brighton.
(*Died 11 June 1926.*)

BLAKEWAY, Ven. Charles Edward, D.D., ; Canon of Lichfield since 1914 ; *b.* 1868 ; *s.* of Roger Charles and Emily Brassey Blakeway ; *m.* Ophelia Martha Antisdel, Chicago ; two *s.* one *d.* *Educ.* : Shrewsbury School ; Christ Church, Oxford. Ordained, 1897 ; Assistant Master Malvern College, 1894-1902 ; Curate of Great Malvern, 1900-2 ; Vicar of Dunston, Stafford, 1902-14 ; Prebendary of Lichfield

Cathedral, 1912; Archdeacon of Stafford, 1911; Examining Chaplain to Bishop of Lichfield, 1913. *Publication:* Claims of Modern Thought upon the Clergy. *Address:* The Close, Lichfield.

(Died 7 June 1922.)

BLAKISTON-HOUSTON, John, J.P., D.L.; *b.* 11 Sep. 1829; *e. s.* of late Richard Bayley Blakiston-Houston, and Mary Isabella, *d.* of John Holmes Houston (whose name he assumed by Royal Licence in 1843); *m.* 1859, Marion (*d.* 1890), *d.* of Richard Shuttleworth Streatfeild, of Uckfield, Sussex; five *s.* seven *d.* Held a commission in South Down Militia; High Sheriff of Co. Down, 1860; M.P. (C.) North Down, 1898-1900. *Address:* Orangefield, Belfast, Roddens, Co. Down. *Club:* Carlton.

(Died 27 Feb. 1920.)

BLANC, Edmond; *s.* of Francois Blanc; *b.* 1861; *b.* of Princess Constantine Radziwill and late Princess Roland Bonaparte. Officier de la Legion d'Honneur; Grand Officier de l'Ordre de Saint Stanislas de Russie. Uncle of S.A.R. la Princesse Georges de Grece; Membre du Comité des Courses et du Conseil; Supérieur des Haras au Ministère de l'Agriculture; Late Member of the French Parliament. *Address:* Château de la Chataigneraie, La Celle, St. Cloud; 42 Avenue Gabriel, Paris. *T.:* 572-95.

(Died 12 Dec. 1920.)

BLANC, Hippolyte Jean, R.S.A., 1896; Treasurer (R.S.A.); F.R.I.B.A., 1901; F.S.A. Scot.; J.P.; Architect; *b.* Edinburgh, 18 Aug. 1844; *y. s.* of Victor Blanc, Privas, France, who became a naturalised British subject in 1849, and Sara Banress, of French parentage, Dublin; *m. d.* of Thomas Shield, London; one *s. Educ.:* Edinburgh. A.R.S.A., 1892. Pupil of David Rhind, Architect; National Medallist Science and Art Department School, 1866; Chief Assistant H.M. Office of Works, 1877-78; President Edinburgh Architectural Association, 1871-72, 1872-73, 1888-89, 1889-90, 1906-7, 1907-8; Vice-President Royal Scottish Society of Arts, 1889-1890; President Edinburgh Photographic Society, 1892-96; Hon. President since 1896; Medallist for design, Paris, 1889, and Edinburgh, 1886. Designed and erected, among others, Thomas Coats Memorial Church, Paisley; St. Cuthbert's Church, Edinburgh; extensive restorations of Edinburgh Castle; Architect for the new Edinburgh Village Asylum, Bangour; Gymnasium at Dunfermline and Forfar; a Royal Commissioner for the International Exhibitions at Brussels, Rome, and Turin, 1910-11. *Publications:* numerous contributions upon Architectural Art, and Archæological subjects. *Recreations:* sketching, architectural photography, golfing. *Address:* 25 Rutland Square, and The Neuk, Strathearn Place, Edinburgh. *T. A.:* Blanc, Edinburgh. *T.:* 2497 and 504. *Clubs:* Scottish Conservative, Scottish Arts.

(Died 12 Mar. 1917.)

BLANCHE, Rt. Rev. Gustave, C.J.M., D.D.; Vicar Apostolic of Gulf of St. Lawrence since 1905; *b.* Josselin, Vannes, 1848. Sent to Eudist Missions in Canada, 1890; Superior of the Eudist College, Versailles, 1899-1903; Provincial in Canada, 1903-5; Bishop of Sicca-Veneria, 1905. *Address:* Seven Islands, Saguenay Co., Quebec. *(Died 8 July 1916.)*

BLANE, Commander Sir Charles Rodney, 4th Bt.; *cr.* 1812; R.N.; *s.* of late Captain Arthur Rodney Blane, R.N., 2nd *s.* of 2nd Bt., and Mary Georgina, 2nd *d.* of J. Pitcairn Campbell; *b.* 28 Oct. 1879; *m.* 1912, Amy, *e. d.* of Col. G. F. Leverson; one *d.* S. uncle, 1911. Entered Navy, 1893; Lieut. 1900; Commander, 1912; served Benin Expedition, 1897 (General Africa medal, Benin clasp); received the Italian Order of St. Maurice and St. Lazarus for services rendered at the time of the Messina Earthquake, 1911. *Heir:* *b.* James Pitcairn, *b.* 27 May 1883. *Address:* 44 Montpelier Street, S.W. *Club:* Naval and Military.

(Died 31 May 1916.)

BLANE, Gilbert Gordon, J.P.; *e. surv. s.* of Gilbert James Blane (*d.* 1881), and Harriet Stewart, *d.* of Rev. Gordon Forbes, Dyce, Aberdeen; *b.* 1851; *S.* uncle, Thomas Law Blane, 1885; *m.* 1888, Mabel Augusta, 8th *d.* of late Admiral Hon. Keith Stewart, C.B.; three *d. Educ.:* Eton. Was Captain Scots Guards. *Address:* Alltan Donn, Nairn, Scotland; *T.:* Nairn 45X4. *Club:* Wellington. *(Died 24 Nov. 1928.)*

BLASERNA, Pietro, Hon. LL.D.; Professor of Experimental Physics, University of Rome; Director of the Institute of Physics; Member and Vice-President of the Senat d'Italy. *Publications:* Treatises on the Conservation of Force, the Dynamic Theory of Heat, the Theory of Sound in Relation to Music, etc. *Address:* University, Rome. *(Died 26 Feb. 1918.)*

BLAYLOCK, Colonel Harry Woodburn, C.B.E., D.C.L.; *b.* 1878; *s.* of late Rev. Thos. Blaylock, M.A., Quebec; *m.* 1905, Agnes Georgina, *d.* of Dr. Jas. Mills, Dominion Railway Commissioner, Ottawa; one *s. Educ.:* Bishops' College School, Bishops' University; McGill University (Macdonald Scholarship). Studied International Law at Paris University, 1903-4; engaged in commercial undertakings until outbreak of war; served with Canadian Forces; Assistant Commissioner, Canadian Red Cross Society in France, 1915-18; after that Chief Commissioner Overseas (despatches); is Knight of Grace of the Order of St. John of Jerusalem, Officer of the Legion of Honour, Commander of the Order of the Crown of Italy, Commander of the Order of St. Sava of Serbia, Cross of Regina Maria of Roumania; D.C.L. Hon., Bishops' University. *Address:* Chelsea Place, Montreal. *Clubs:* Junior Carlton; St. James's, Montreal. *(Died Jan. 1928.)*

BLECK, Edward Charles, C.M.G., 1910; *b.* 26 July 1861; Consul-General at Genoa since 1918; *s.* of late Joseph Edward Bleck, sometime of Dulwich, Surrey, and Georgiana Henrietta, *d.* of W. L. Reynolds, late H.M. Colonial and Consular Services; *m.* 1895, Helen Laura Ogilvy, *d.* of late Captain David Steuart Ogilvy of Corrimony, N.B.; two *s.* three *d. Educ.:* Dulwich College. Entered public service, 1883; Chargé d'Affaires at Sofia, 1891 and 1892; Archivist of H.M. Embassy at Constantinople, 1894-1906; Consul for Palestine, 1906-9; Consul-General at Port Said, 1909-14; Librarian and Keeper of the Papers at the Foreign Office, 1914-18. *Address:* British Consulate-General, Genoa; Downe Lodge, Richmond Hill, Surrey. *(Died 2 Mar 1919.)*

BLENCOWE, Rev. Alfred James; Canon Residentiary of Chester Cathedral, 1886, 1927; Proctor in Convocation, 1908-21; 3rd *s.* of John Jackson Blencowe, of Marston House, Marston St. Lawrence, Northants; *m.* Sophia Louisa, *d.* of Rev. John Walcot of Bitterley Court, Shropshire; six *s.* one *d. Educ.:* St. John's College, Oxford. Ordained, 1874; Curate of Applethwaite, 1874-76; Vicar of Witton, Northwich, 1876-86; Christ Church, Chester, 1887-89; Rector of West Kirby, 1889-1920. *Address:* Dee Hills Park, Chester.

(Died 25 Mar. 1928.)

BLENKIN, Very Rev. George Wilfrid, D.D.; Dean of St. Albans since 1914; *b.* 16 Feb. 1861; *s.* of Canon G. B. Blenkin, Vicar of Boston; *m.* Katharine Anne, *d.* of Owen March, Solicitor, Rochdale; two *s.* one *d. Educ.:* Harrow (Scholar); Trinity College, Cambridge (Exhibitioner and Scholar); Bell University Scholar; Bachelor's Carus Greek Testament Prize; 1st Class Classical Tripos. Ordained, 1886; Chaplain of Emmanuel College, Cambridge, 1886-91; Trinity College, 1891-99; Fellow and Junior Dean, 1899-1906; Fellow of Corpus Christi College, 1899; Examining Chaplain to Bishop of Lincoln, 1892-1910; to Bishop of St. Albans since 1915; Prebendary of Lincoln, 1903-14; Vicar of Brading, 1906-13; Hitchin,

1913-14. *Publication :* 1st Epistle S. Peter, Cambridge Greek Test. *Address :* The Deanery, St. Albans. *T. :* 106. *(Died 24 Sept. 1924.)*

BLENNERHASSETT, Col. Blennerhassett Montgomerie, C.M.G. 1896 ; F.R.C.S.I. ; *b.* 18 Nov. 1849 ; *m.* Gertrude Harcourt, *d.* of Captain Willcox, R.N. Entered army, 1872 ; Lt.-Col. 1896 ; Col. 1902 ; served Ashanti Expedition, 1895-96 (C.M.G., Queen's Star, despatches) ; retired, 1906. *Club :* Naval and Military. *(Died 24 May 1926.)*

BLEWETT, Francis Richard, K.C. 1908 ; Practising Law at Stratford, Ont., Canada ; Barrister, Solicitor, Notary Public, etc. ; *b.* Napanee, Ont., Canada, 11 May 1869 ; *s.* of John Blewett and Eliza Getty ; unmarried *Educ. :* Napanee Public and High Schools ; Osgoode Hall, Toronto ; Law School. Called to Ontario Bar, 1891 ; moved to Stratford, 1911, and has been practising alone in said city since ; Vice-President North Perth Liberal-Conservative Association ; Anglican ; Conservative. *Publications :* Articles in Oddfellows Review, St. Paul, Minn. ; The Talisman, Indiannapolis ; and other papers. *Recreations :* long-distance walking, whist, etc. *Address :* Stratford, Ont, Canada. *Club :* Stratford Country and Crescent.

BLIND, Rudolf, Artist and Translator ; *b.* Brussels, 1850 ; *s.* of Karl and Frederica Blind ; *m.* 1871, Sarah Annie Parsoné ; three *s. Educ. :* University College School (all available prizes two years following), and Royal Academy. Assisted with the decorations of the Opera House at Vienna ; enlisted as a volunteer with the German Army in the Franco-German War of 1870-71, and was at the siege of Strasburg in the ambulance service ; has painted many well-known pictures, including The Golden Gates, Christ the Consoler, the World's Desire, Love's Extasy, and the Throne of Grace. *Recreations :* walking, fishing, talking, rowing. *Address :* 20 Queen Anne's Grove, Bedford Park, W. *(Died 3 Feb. 1916.)*

BLISS, 4th Baron, Henry Edward Ernest Victor Bliss, J.P. ; *b.* 16 Feb. 1869 ; *s.* of 3rd Baron ; *S.* father 1890 ; *m.* 1891, Ethel Wolton. *Educ. :* Cheltenham. *Recreations :* fishing and yachting. *Address :* Yacht Sea King, Nassau, N.P., Bahamas. *Club :* Royal Yacht Squadron, Cowes.

(Died 9 Mar. 1926.)

BLISS, Sir Henry (William), K.C.I.E., *cr.* 1897 ; J.P. Co. Berks ; *b.* 1840 ; *s.* of late Rev. J. Bliss, Rector of Manningford Bruce, Wilts, and Mary, *d.* of Rear-Adm. Sir Thomas Fellowes, Kt. ; *m.* 1st, 1863, Mary (*d.* 1876), *d.* of late Edmund Rendle, M.D., Plymouth ; 2nd, 1879, Edith (*d.* 1898), *d.* of late James Wheeler, Great Cumberland Place ; 3rd, 1900, Florence (*d.* 1919), *d.* of Sir Frederick Bramwell, 1st Bt. *Educ. :* Merton Coll. Oxford (M.A.). Entered Indian Civil Service, 1863, and filled various appointments ; Member of Council, Madras, 1893-98 ; L.C.C. Holborn, 1901-7. *Address :* The Abbey, Abingdon.(*Died 28 Oct. 1919.*)

BLISS, Rev. Howard S., D.D. ; President of the Syrian Protestant College, Beyrout, Syria, since 1902 ; *b.* on Mt. Lebanon, 6 Dec. 1860 ; *s.* of Daniel Bliss and Abby Wood Bliss ; *m.* 1889, Amy Blatchford of Chicago ; two *s.* three *d. Educ. :* Amherst College, U.S.A. ; Union Theological Seminary, U.S.A. ; Oxford University ; Göttingen and Berlin Universities. Fitted for college at Beyrout ; entered Amherst College, U.S.A., 1878 ; B.A. 1882 ; taught two years at Washburn College, Topeka, Kansas ; studied theology at Union Theological Seminary, New York City, secured Travelling Fellowship, and studied at Oxford University and Mansfield College, Oxford, 1887-88, Göttingen University and Berlin University, 1888-89 ; Assistant Pastor of Plymouth Church, Brooklyn, 1889-94 ; ordained

100

in the Congregational Ministry, 1890 ; Pastor Christian Union Congregational Church, Upper Montclair, N.J., 1894-1902 ; received degree of D.D. from New York University, 1902 ; from Amherst College, 1902 ; from Princeton University, 1913. *Recreations :* golf, tennis, etc. *Address :* Beyrout, Syria. *T.A. :* Beyrout. *Club :* Century, New York. *(Died May 1920.)*

BLISS, Rev. John Worthington, Rector of Betteshanger with Ham since 1876 ; Hon. Canon, Canterbury, 1888 ; Rural Dean of Sandwich, 1881 ; *b.* Halifax, N.S., 1832 ; *s.* of late Hon. Mr. Justice Bliss, Judge of Supreme Court, N.S. ; *m.* 1858, Maria, *d.* of late Rev. Henry Lindsay, Rector of Sundridge, Kent. *Educ. :* Harrow ; Trinity College, Cambridge. Curate of Ide Hill, 1857-58 ; Speldhurst, 1858-1843 ; Betteshanger, 1865. *Recreations :* travelling and golf. *Address :* Betteshanger, Eastry S.O., Kent. *T.A. :* Eastry. *Club :* Union.

(Died 20 April 1917.)

BLISS, Rev. W. H., M.A. 1870 ; Mus. Bac. Oxon. 1863 ; Hon. Chaplain to the King ; *b.* 1884 ; *m.* 1st, 1864, Sara, 2nd *d.* of T. H. Pyle, M.R.C.S., Earsdon, Northumberland ; 2nd, 1900, Margaret Isabella, *e. d.* of late James Ellison, M.D., Surgeon to H.M. Household, Windsor. *Educ. :* private schools ; Exeter Coll. Oxford. B.A. 1862 ; Deacon, 1862 ; Priest, 1863 ; Assistant Master at King's School, Sherborne, 1864-67 ; Minor Canon of St. George's Chapel, Windsor Castle, 1867-74 ; Rector of West Ilsley, Berks, 1873-81 ; Curate in Charge of Wexham, Bucks, 1882-85 ; Vicar of Kew cum Petersham, 1885-90 ; Hon. Chaplain to Queen Victoria, 1874 ; Chaplain-in-Ordinary, 1876-1901 ; Vicar of Kew, 1885-1915. *Publications :* Sermons, various ; Sacred Music ; Anthems ; Chant Communion Office ; Chant Te Deums, etc. ; Kew Supplement of Hymns and Tunes, 1909. *Address :* Eversleigh, Frances Road, Windsor. *(Died 15 Feb. 1919.)*

BLOMEFIELD, Sir Thomas Wilmot Peregrine, 4th Bt., *cr.* 1807 ; C.B. 1903 ; late Assistant Secretary Finance Department of the Board of Trade ; *b.* Winchester, 31 Dec. 1848 ; *S.* father, 1878 ; *m.* Lilias, *d.* of Maj. the Hon. Charles Napier, Woodlands, Taunton, 1874 ; one *s.* two *d. Educ. :* Repton. *Heir : g.s.* Thomas Edward Peregrine, *b.* 31 May 1907. *Address :* Windmill House, Lichfield, Staffordshire.

(Died 20 July 1928.)

BLOMFIELD, Major-Gen. Charles James, C.B. 1904 ; D.S.O. 1898 ; retired 1917 ; J.P. ; *b.* Bow, Devonshire, 26 May 1855 ; 2nd *s.* of Rev. George J. Blomfield and Isabel, *d.* of late Charles James Blomfield, Bishop of London ; *m.* 1881, Henriette, *d.* of late Major E. Briscoe, 20th Foot ; two *s. Educ. :* Haileybury ; Sandhurst. Sub-Lieut. 20th Foot, 1875 ; Lieut. 1875 ; Captain Lancashire Fusiliers, 1881 ; Major, 1890 ; Lt.-Col. 1898 ; Bt.-Col. 1900 ; Maj.-Gen. 1907 ; Adj. Lanc. Fusiliers, 1880-88 ; Acting Military Secretary to H.E. Commander-in-Chief, Bombay Army, 1891 ; D.A.A.G. Poona, 1892-97 ; A.A.G. Bombay, 1897 ; Soudan Expedition, 1898 ; Battle of Khartoum (despatches, D.S.O., Egyptian medal with clasp, Queen's medal) ; S. African War, 1899-1902 ; with Ladysmith relief force (severely wounded at Spion Kop, despatches twice, brevet of Colonel, Queen's medal four clasps, King's medal two clasps) ; Colonel on Staff to command District, 1900, and in command of columns in S.E. Transvaal and on Zululand border ; commanded Harrismith and Natal Sub-District, 1902-6 ; Wessex Division T.F. 1909-10 ; Mhow Division, India, 1911-12 ; Peshawar Division, India, 1913-1915. *Address :* Frampton Lodge, Frampton-on-Severn, Glos. *Club :* Army and Navy.

(Died 3 Mar. 1928.)

BLOMFIELD, Rear-Admiral Sir Richard Massie, K.C.M.G., *cr.* 1904 ; C.M.G. 1903 ; 3rd *s.* of late Rev. G. B. Blom-

field, Rector of Stevenage, Herts, and Canon of Chester Cathedral ; *b.* 3 March 1835 ; *m.* 1877, Rosamund Selina, *d.* of late Rt. Rev. Charles Graves, L.-Bishop of Limerick ; one *s. Educ. :* Stevenage Grammar School. Served throughout Crimean Campaign as Mid., Mate, and Lieutenant of Agamemnon and Royal Albert, flagships of Sir E. Lyons (Crimean and Turkish medals, 2 clasps) ; Lieut. of H.M.S. Hero conveying His present Majesty to the British American colonies and back, 1860 ; selected as Commander of Admiralty flagship in command of Channel Fleet and Reserve Squadron, 1869 ; Member of Admiralty Confidential Torpedo Committee, 1873-76 ; Comptroller of Port of Alexandria from the institution of that office in 1879 ; present by invitation of Commander-in-Chief on board his flagship during bombardment of Alexandria, 1882 ; received thanks of British Government for services rendered during the war (medal with clasp and Khedive's Star) ; Deputy Controller-General of Egyptian Ports and Lighthouses, 1887 ; Controller-General, 1901 ; Director-General, 1905-7 ; retired, 1908 ; Medjidieh, 1st class, and Osmanieh, 3rd class. *Publications:* papers in Alexandria Archæological Society's Bulletins. *Recreations :* natural history, archæology. *Address :* 35 Holland Park Av., W.
(Died 26 June 1921.)

BLORE, Rev. George John, D.D. ; Hon. Canon of Canterbury since 1887 ; *b.* 5 May 1885 ; *s.* of Edward Blore, D.C.L., F.R.S., F.S.A. ; *m.* Mary, *d.* of T. Allen, Headington, Oxfordshire ; five *s.* one *d. Educ. :* Charterhouse ; Christ Church, Oxford. Senior Student and Tutor of Christ Church, Oxford, 1861 - 67 ; Headmaster of King Edward's School, Bromsgrove, 1868-73 ; Headmaster of King's School, Canterbury, 1873-86 ; Examining Chaplain to the Archbishop of Canterbury, 1894. *Address :* St. Stephen's House, Canterbury.
(Died 6 Feb. 1916.)

BLOUNDELLE - BURTON, John Edward, Novelist ; *m.* Frances (*d.* 1910), 2nd *d.* of late Charles W. Churchman, Philadelphia. *Educ.* for Army ; travelled and lived in Canada, United States, and principal countries of Europe ; was a naval correspondent and special correspondent of The Standard. *Publications :* The Silent Shore, 1886 ; His own Enemy, 1887 ; The Desert Ship, 1890 ; The Hispaniola Plate, 1894 ; A Gentleman Adventurer, 1895 ; In the Day of Adversity, 1896 ; Denounced, 1896 ; The Clash of Arms, 1897 ; Across the Salt Seas, 1898 ; The Scourge of God, 1898 ; Fortune's my Foe ; A Bitter Heritage, 1899 ; The Seafarers ; Servants of Sin, 1900 ; A Vanished Rival, 1901 ; The Year One, 1901 ; The Fate of Valsec, 1902 ; A Branded Name, 1903 ; The Intriguer's Way, 1903 ; A Dead Reckoning, 1904 ; The Land of Bondage, 1904 ; The Sword of Gideon, 1905 ; Traitor and True, 1906 ; Knighthood's Flower, 1906 ; A Woman from the Sea, 1907 ; The Last of her Race, 1908 ; Within Four Walls ; The King's Mignon, 1909 ; A Fair Martyr, 1910 ; The Fate of Henry of Navarre (historical work) ; Under the Salamander, 1911 ; The Right Hand, 1911 ; The Sea Devils, 1912 ; Fortune's Frown, 1913 ; Love lies Bleeding, 1915. *Recreations :* riding, cycling, rowing, sailing. *Address :* 385 Upper Richmond Road, Putney, S.W. *Clubs :* Constitutional, Yorick. *(Died 11 Dec. 1917.)*

BLOXAM, John Astley, F.R.C.S., J.P. ; Consulting Surgeon to Charing Cross Hospital and Lock Hospital. *Address :* The Old Malt House, Bourne End, Bucks.
(Died 14 Jan. 1926.)

BLUMHARDT, J. F., M.A. ; formerly Professor of Hindustani, and Reader of Hindi and Bengali, University College, London ; and Teacher of Bengali at Oxford University. *Publications:* a series of Catalogues of Printed Books and Manuscripts in the North-Indian Languages and Dialects, in the British Museum and India Office Libraries. *Address :* Woodlands, Gerrard's Cross, Bucks.
(Died 10 Dec. 1922.)

BLUNDEN, Sir John, 5th Bt. (*cr.* 1776) ; *b.* 26 Feb. 1880 ; *er. s.* of 4th Bt., and Florence, *d.* of Henry Shuttleworth, of New Zealand ; *S.* father 1923 ; *m.* 1918 Phyllis Dorothy, *d.* of P. C. Creaghe, of Shankill, Co. Dublin ; two *s.* Heir : *s.* William, *b.* 26 April 1919.
(Died 28 Oct. 1923.)

BLUNDEN, Sir William, 4th Bt., *cr.* 1776 ; B.A., B.M. Dublin ; L.R.C.S. Ireland ; L.M.K. and L.K., Q.C.P. Ireland ; *b.* 25 July 1840. *S.* father 1890 ; *m.* Florence, *d.* of Henry Shuttleworth of New Zealand, 1879 ; two *s.* one *d.* Heir : *s.* John, *b.* 26 Feb. 1880. *Address :* Castle Blunden, Kilkenny. *(Died 25 Oct. 1923.)*

BLUNT, Rev. Alexander Colvin, Hon. Canon of Winchester, 1889 ; Rural Dean, Kingsclere, 1890 ; *m.* 1865, Lady Susanna (*d.* 1900), *d.* of 2nd Earl Nelson. *Educ. :* Christ Church, Oxford (M.A.). Curate of Alverstoke, 1855-66 ; Rector of Millbrook, 1866-89 ; Burghclere, 1889-1915 ; Rural Dean, Southampton, 1876-89. *Address :* 9 Kingsgate Street, Winchester.
(Died 1 April 1920.)

BLUNT, Sir John Elijah, Kt., *cr.* 1902 ; C.B., *cr.* 1878 ; *b.* 14 Oct. 1832 ; *s.* of Charles Blunt, late H.M. Consul at Smyrna, and Caroline, *d.* of A. Vitalis, late H.M. Consul at Tinos ; *m.* Fanny Janet, *d.* of Donald Sandison, late H.M. Consul at Brussa, 1858. *Educ. :* Dr. Greig's Private School ; Walthamstow ; Kensington Grammar School. Has been connected with His Majesty's Consular Service since 1850, and after holding various Consular appointments in Turkey, was promoted Consul-General for the Vilayets of Salonica, Cossova, Janina, and Monastir, 1878 ; served as Chief Interpreter to the Cavalry Division under Gen. Lord Lucan in the Crimea, and acted as his Lordship's Secretary ; present at battles of the Alma, Balaclava, and Inkerman ; has also acted temporarily as French Vice-Consul, twice at Volo and twice at Monastir ; as German Consul and twice as Belgian Consul at Salonica ; Her Majesty's Consul-General for Salonica, 1879-99 ; H.B.M. Consul (with rank of Consul-Gen.) at Boston, 1899-1902. *Decorated :* Crimean medal with clasps for Alma, Balaclava, and Inkerman ; Turkish Crimean medal, 1855 ; Turkish Imtiaz medal in silver, 1890, and in gold, 1898 ; Jubilee medal, 1897. Received in 1862 and 1868 the thanks of the President of the United States for services rendered to American citizens in the province of Adrianople, and was nominated in 1868 U.S. Consul for Roumelia, but was not permitted to accept the appointment. *Recreations :* shooting, lawn tennis, cricket, bridge. *Address :* Floriana, Malta. *Club :* Athenæum. *(Died 19 June 1916.)*

BLUNT, Captain Sir John Harvey, 8th Bart., *cr.* 1720 ; late 1st Batt. Royal Dublin Fusiliers, retired ; *b.* 1 Jan. 1839 ; *S.* brother 1902 ; *m.* 1869, Susan (*d.* 1917), *d.* of P. Hoad ; four *s.* one *d.* Served with 1st Batt. Royal Welsh Fusiliers through Indian Mutiny, including taking of Futteghur, operations on the Ramgunga, siege and capture of Lucknow, besides several minor engagements (medal and clasp). Heir : *e. s.* John Harvey [*b.* 30 July 1872 ; *m.* 1906, Maud Julia, *e. d.* of Sir David Lionel Goldsmid-Stern-Salomons, 2nd Bart., of Broomhill, Tunbridge Wells ; two *s.* two *d. Educ. :* Beaumont College, Windsor. Capt. Natal Border Police ; served South African War (three medals, eight clasps) ; European War. *Recreations :* hunting and shooting. *Address :* Huntleys, Tunbridge Wells. *T. :* 966. *Club. :* Royal Automobile.] *Address :* East House, St. George's Terrace, Herne Bay. *(Died 26 Jan. 1922.)*

BLUNT, Wilfrid Scawen ; *b.* Petworth House, 17 Aug. 1840 ; *s.* of F. S. Blunt, of

Crabbet Park; *m.* 1869, Lady Anne Noel (late Baroness Wentworth, *d.* 1917), *d.* of 1st Earl of Lovelace; one *d. S.* to Crabbet estates on death of elder brother, 1872; has issue, one daughter, Judith, *m.* 1899, Major Hon. Neville Lytton. *Educ.:* Stonyhurst; Oscott. Diplomatic Service, 1858-70; travelled in Arabia, Syria, Persia, Mesopotamia, etc., 1877-81; took part in Egyptian National Movement, 1881-82; travelled in India, 1883-84; stood for Camberwell, Tory Home Ruler, 1885; Kidderminster, Liberal Home Ruler, 1886; arrested in Ireland for calling meeting in a proclaimed district, Oct. 1887; imprisoned two months in Galway and Kilmainham Gaols, 1888. *Publications:* Love Sonnets of Proteus, 1880; Future of Islam, 1882; The Wind and the Whirlwind, 1883; Ideas about India, 1885; In Vinculis, 1889; A New Pilgrimage, 1889; Esther, 1892; Stealing of the Mare, 1892; Griselda, 1893; Satan Absolved, 1899; Seven Golden Odes of Pagan Arabia, 1903; Secret History of the English Occupation of Egypt, 1907; India under Ripon, 1909; Gordon at Khartoum, 1911; The Land War in Ireland, 1912; Poetical Works, complete Edition, 1914; My Diaries, 1919; My Diaries, Pt. 2, 1920. *Recreation:* breeder of Arab horses. Owns about 2000 acres. *Address:* Newbuildings, Horsham, Sussex. *Club:* Sussex.
(*Died* 10 *Sept.* 1922.)

BLUNT, Rear-Adm. Wm. Frederick, C.B.E. 1919; D.S.O. 1914; *b.* 3 March 1870; 3rd *s.* of late F. W. Blunt of Culcheth Hall, Teddington; *m.* 1896, Laura, *o. d.* of late Maj.-Gen. Henry Way Mawbey, R.M.A.; two *s.* Was midshipman of H.M.S. Garnet during blockade of Zanzibar coast, 1888-89; Lieut. in command H.M.S. Dragon during operations at Crete, 1897-1898; Lieut. in command H.M.S. Esk, China, 1900-1 (medal); European War, 1914-15, in command of H.M.S. Fearless at the action in Heligoland Bight, 28 Aug. 1914 (D.S.O.); and at the Cuxhaven Raid, Christmas Day, 1914; Captain in command of 1st Destroyer Flotilla, 1913-15; H.M.S. Jupiter, 1915-16; operations at Aden and in Suez Canal; Capt. H.M.S. Gloucester at the Battle of Jutland, 31 May 1916 (despatches, commended); H.M.S. Berwick and H.M.S. Achilles, 1916-19, Atlantic Convoy Service (C.B.E.); retired list, 1921; Rear-Adm. retired, 1922. *Address:* Baharini, Lake Solai, Kenya Colony. *Club:* United Service.
(*Died* 5 *July* 1928.)

BLYTH, 1st Baron, *cr.* 1907, **James Blyth,** Bt., *cr.* 1895; J.P. Essex and Herts; Imperial Order of Leopold; Order of the Medjidie; a Knight Commander and Grand Cross of Civil Order of Merito Agricola of Portugal; The Order of the Sacred Treasure of Japan; Vice-President, British Empire League; Treasurer, Homes for Little Boys, Farningham and Swanley; Treasurer, Empire Parliamentary Association, and Treasurer of the Byron Centenary Commemoration; Vice-President, governor or member of many agricultural and other Societies; Manager of the Royal Institution of Great Britain; governor, or member of; British Dairy Farmers' Association, Shire Horse Soc., Royal Agricultural Soc., English Jersey Soc.; Chairman, Organising Committee Franco-British Exhibition, 1908; Japan-British Exhibition, 1910; director of W. and A. Gilbey, Ltd.; *b.* 10 Sep. 1841; *s.* of James Blyth, Chelmsford, and Caroline, *d.* of Henry Gilbey, Bishop Stortford; *m.* 1865, Eliza (*d.* 1894), *d.* of William Mooney, Clontarf, Co. Dublin; two *s.* four *d.* *Publications:* has written on viticultural and agricultural questions, also on the fiscal and commercial policy of the Empire, cheap postal and telegraphic communication, an Anglo-French Commercial Alliance, etc. *Heir:* s. Hon. Herbert William Blyth. *Address:* 33 Portland Place, W.1; Blythwood, Stansted, Essex. *T.A.:* Brigador, London. *T.:* Langham 2176.

102

Stansted 10. *Clubs:* Athenæum, British Empire, Devonshire. (*Died* 8 *Feb.* 1925.)

BLYTH, Alexander Wynter, Public Analyst for St. Marylebone and County of Devon; Registrar of Sanitary Institute; past President of Incorporated Society of Medical Officers of Health; M.R.C.S. London; Barrister at Law (Lincoln's Inn); Fellow of the Chemical Society, London; Associate King's College, London; Member Soc. Français d'Hygiène and Italian Soc. Hygiene, Milan; *s.* of Alex. Blyth, Surgeon, Woolwich; *m.* Anne Eliz. Morgan (*decd.*), Monmouthshire. *Educ.:* King's College, London. *Publications:* Dictionary of Hygiene and Public Health; Foods, their Composition and Analysis, 3rd ed. 1895; Poisons, their Effects and Detection, 4th ed. 1906; Diet in Relation to Health and Work, 1884; A Manual of Public Health, 1890; Lectures on Sanitary Law, 1893; and numerous scientific communications to the Royal Society, Chemical Society, Sanitary Institute, and the Society of Medical Officers of Health. *Address:* Halfway Manor House, Kintbury, Berks; 3 Upper Gloucester Place, N.W.1. *T.:* Paddington 8146. (*Died* 30 *Mar.* 1921.)

BLYTH, Benjamin Hall, M.A., F.R.S.E.; a civil engineer in Edinburgh; *b.* Edinburgh, 25 May 1849; *s.* of Benjamin Hall Blyth, civil engineer, and Mary Dudgeon Wright; *m.* 1872, Millicent, *y. d.* of Thomas Edward Taylor of Dodworth, Yorkshire, J.P., D.L.; one *d. Educ.:* Merchiston Castle School; Edinburgh University. Consulting engineer to the North British and Great North of Scotland Railway Companies; has constructed many railways, docks, bridges, and other works; contested (U.) East Lothian, Jan. and Dec. 1910, and April 1911; Lieut.-Col. in the Engineer and Railway Staff Corps; member of the Royal Company of Archers, King's Bodyguard for Scotland; president of the Institution of Civil Engineers. *Recreations:* shooting, golfing and curling. *Address:* 17 Palmerston Place, Edinburgh; Kaimend, North Berwick. *Clubs:* Carlton, Conservative; Western, Glasgow; University, Conservative, Edinburgh. (*Died* 12 *May* 1917.)

BLYTH, Lt.-Col. James, C.B.E.; *b.* 1869; *m.* 1896, Ethel, *e. d.* of late C. J. Gibb, M.D., of Sandyford Park, Newcastle-on-Tyne; one *s. Educ.:* Eton. Contested (U.) Barnsley Division of Yorkshire, 1897; is Director of the Law Land Co. and the Warner Estate; commanded the 3rd Bn. Oxford and Buckinghamshire Light Infantry during the war (C.B.E.). *Recreations:* shooting and fishing. *Address:* Iver Grove, Iver, Bucks. *Clubs:* Bachelors', Wellington, Garrick. (*Died* 9 *July* 1925.)

BLYTHSWOOD, 2nd Baron (*cr.* 1892), **Rev. Sholto Douglas Campbell,** M.A.; D.D. (Glasgow); J.P. Lanarks; *b.* 1839; 2nd *s.* of late Archibald Douglas, of Mains, Co. Dumbarton (who assumed surname of Campbell on inheriting Blythswood in 1888), and Caroline Agnes, *d.* of late M. Dick, of Pitkerro, Co. Fife; *S.* brother 1908; *m.* 1889, Violet (*d.* 1908), *d.* of late Lord Alfred Paget. *Educ.:* Cheam; Trin. Coll. Camb.; M.A. Curate Nuneaton, Warwickshire, 1866-67; St. Mary's, Gateshead, 1867-70; Vicar of Nonington, Kent, 1870-72; All Saints, Derby, 1872-79; Rector of All Souls, St. Marylebone, 1879-86; St. Silas, Glasgow, 1887-99. *Publications:* Order of Events in Our Lord's Second Coming; The Anti-Christ. *Heir:* b. Maj.-Gen. Sir B. B. D. Campbell-Douglas. *Address:* Blythswood, Renfrew, N.B.; Balmacara House, Loch Alsh, N.B. *Clubs:* Carlton, National; Conservative, Western, Glasgow; New, Edinburgh.
(*Died* 30 *Sept.* 1916.)

BLYTHSWOOD, 3rd Baron; *cr.* 1892; **Barrington Bulkeley Douglas Campbell - Douglas,** K.C.B., *cr.* 1914; C.B. 1900; C.V.O. 1902; M.V.O. 1897; retired; *b.* 18

Feb. 1845; s. of Archibald Campbell of Blythswood, Renfrewshire, formerly Douglas of Mains, Dumbartonshire; S. brother, 1916; assumed additional name Douglas on succeeding to Douglas Support; m. 1869, Mildred Catherine (d. 1902), d. of Sir Joseph Hawley, 3rd Bart.; three s. Educ.: Eton. Entered army, Scots Guards, 1864; commanded 1st Scots Guards, 1892-96; commanded Scots Guards and South London Brigade, 1896-1898; Major-General, 1898; Egyptian War, 1882 (1st Batt. Scots Guards), including El Magfar, Tel-el-Mahuta, Kassassin, and Tel-el-Kebir (medal with clasp, Khedive's star); commanded 16th Brigade Aldershot and South Africa, Jan. 1900 to July 1902; actions Orange River Colony, including battle Biddulphsberg, Prinsloe's surrender; actions in Transvaal and Natal; commanding Ficksberg, Brandwater, Bethlehem district (Queen's medal, three clasps, King's medal, two clasps, despatches twice); D.L. and J.P. Renfrewshire; D.L. Lanarkshire; Lieut.-Governor and commanding-in-chief Guernsey, 1903-8. Heir: s. Capt. Hon. Archibald Campbell-Douglas [b. 25 April 1870; m. 1895, Evelyn, 3rd d. of late John Fletcher of Saltoun; one d. Educ.: Eton. Late Lieut. Scots Guards. Address: 55 Montagu Square, W. Clubs: Guards', Travellers', Naval and Military; New, Edinburgh.] Address: Blythswood, Renfrew; Douglas Support, Coatbridge, Lanarkshire; T.: Coatbridge 225; 13 Manchester Square, W.; T.: Mayfair 4329. M.: LK 8839. Clubs: Carlton, Turf, Marlborough, Guards'; New, Edinburgh; Conservative, Glasgow. (Died 11 Mar. 1918.)

BOARDMAN, Admiral Frederick Ross, R.N., C.B., 1885; retired; b. 1843; e. s. of late Frederick Boardman, Liverpool; m. 1881, Sophia Almon, d. of Hon. Jas. Cogswell of Halifax, Nova Scotia; one s. two d. Commander of Salamis during Egyptian War, 1882; as captain commanded Nile flotilla, Gordon Relief Expedition 1884-85. Specially mentioned in despatches; Egyptian medal and clasp; Khedive's bronze star; Royal Victorian medal and captain's good service pension for Nile flotilla services. Recreations: boating, fishing, riding, reading. Address: Lansdowne Park Road, Lewes. Club: United Service.
(Died 24 Sept. 1927.)

BOCQUET, Roscoe, C.I.E. 1878; b. 9 Apr. 1839; s. of Frances S. Bocquet of Liverpool; m. 1863, Edith (d. 1902), d. of John Bampton, Engineer on Scinde-Delhi Railway to 1885; Engineer for some time in South America. Address: St. Leonard's, Springvale, Ryde, Isle of Wight. (Died 13 Nov. 1920.)

BODDAM-WHETHAM, Major Sydney A., D.S.O. 1917; M.C.; R.F.A.; b. 4 May 1885; e. surv. s. of late J. W. Boddam-Whetham of Kirklington Hall, Notts; m. 1916, E. Sybil, d. of J. L. Brinkley, Allershaw, Folkestone and Fortlands, Ireland; one s. two d. Educ.: Oundle; R.M.A., Woolwich. Joined R.F.A. 1903; A.D.C. and Private Secretary to Governor of Bahamas, 1907-12; served European War continuously with 7th Division in Belgium, France, and Italy, Oct. 1914-March 1918; then transferred to a Corps (despatches six times, D.S.O., M.C., Belgian Croix de Guerre). Recreations: tennis, football, hockey. Address: R.A. Mess, Nasirabad, Rajputana, India. (Died 9 Dec. 1925.)

BODDINGTON, Rev. Edward Henry, Hon. Canon of Coventry. Address: Honington Vicarage, Shipston-on-Stour.
(Died 28 Feb. 1920.)

BODINGTON, Rev. Charles, Canon Residentiary and Precentor of Lichfield Cathedral; b. 28 Nov. 1836. Educ.: King's Coll. London (Fellow). Publications: Books of Devotion; Devotional Life in the Nineteenth Century; The Life of Grace; Notes on Prayer; Jesus the Christ; Lichfield Cathedral; The Twelve Gates of the Holy City; Devotions for Every Day of the Week, Wesley; Devotion; A Gospel of Miracle; The Doctrine of Confession and Absolution in the Church of England. Address: The Close, Lichfield. (Died 23 Nov. 1918.)

BODLE, Brig.-Gen. William, C.M.G., 1900; b. 5 July 1855; s. of C. Bodle, Alfriston, Sussex. Served Basuto War under Sir F. Carrington (medal and clasp); Matabele War, 1893 (medal); Matabele Rebellion, 1896 (clasp); South African War, 1899-1902 (despatches, Queen's medal three clasps, King's medal two clasps); retired with rank of Colonel, Oct. 1909; European War, 1914-18, Commanded a Brigade. Address: c/o B.S.A. Co., London Wall Buildings, E.C. (Died 9 July 1924.)

BODLEY, John Edward Courtenay, M.A.; b. 6 June 1853; e. s. of late Edward Fisher Bodley, J.P., of Dane Bank House, Cheshire, by his 2nd marriage with Mary, d. of Joseph Ridgway; m. 1st, 1891, Evelyn Frances [whom he div. 1908], e. d. of John Bell, of Rushpool Hall, Yorks; 2nd, 1920, Phyllis Helen, d. of late Rev. H. J. Lomax of Stoke Golding. Educ.: Balliol College, Oxford; B.A. 1877; M.A. 1879. Barr. Inner Temple, 1874; private secretary to President of Local Government Board, 1882-85; Secretary to Royal Commission on Housing of the Working Classes, 1884-85, and was author of the three Reports on England, Scotland, and Ireland; Corresponding Member of the French Institute (Académie des Sciences Morales et Politiques), 1902. Publications: France: Vol. I. The Revolution and Modern France; Vol. II. The Parliamentary System: 1898 (7th Eng. ed. 1907), (French eds. tran. by author, 1901-4); L'Anglomanie et les traditions françaises, Paris, 1899; The Coronation of Edward VII., a Chapter of European and Imperial History (by His Majesty's command), 1903 (2nd ed. 1911); Introduction to English ed. of Emile Boutmy's Psychology of the English People, 1904; The Church in France, 1906; two articles in Ency. Brit. on the History of the Third Republic, 1900 and 1910; Cardinal Manning, and other Essays, 1912; L'Age mécanique et le déclin de l'idéalisme en France (discours prononcé à l'Institut de France), 1913; Introduction to English edition of National History of France, 1916; The Romance of the Battle-line in France, 1920. Address: Hatchlands, Cuckfield, Sussex.
(Died 28 May 1925.)

BOEVEY, Sir Francis (Hyde) Crawley-, 6th Bt.; cr. 1784; J.P.; Verderer of the Forest of Dean; b. 25 Apr. 1868; s. of 5th Bt. and Frances Elizabeth, d. of Rev. Thomas Peters; S. father, 1912; m. 1896, Eliza Barbara, o. d. of Valentine Blake McGrath, late of Hope Hall, Manchester; one s. Educ.: Winchester; Christ Church, Oxford. B.A. 1891. Heir: s. Launcelot Valentine Hyde [b. 26 Apr. 1900; m. 1927, Elizabeth G., d. of Herbert d'Auvergne Innes, Moorend Park Lawn, Cheltenham]. Recreations: painting, shooting, lawn tennis (Capt. of O.U.L.T.C., 1891), etc. Address: Flaxley Abbey, near Newnham, Glos. T.: Westbury on Severn 10. (Died 6 Oct. 1928.)

BOGERT, Ven. James John; Archdeacon of Ottawa since 1897; b. 2 Aug. 1835; s. of John Bogert, Barrister, and Mary Radcliffe; m. 1860; four s. four d. Educ.: Trin. Coll., Toronto (M.A., D.C.L.). Ordained 1858; Priest, 1859; Curate of Brampton, 1858; Prescott, 1859-61; Rector of Napanee, 1862-81; Rector of St. Alban's Church, Ottawa, 1881-1914; Rural Dean, Carleton, Ontario, 1891-97. Address: 196 Asgoode Street, Ottawa, Canada.
(Died 10 Feb. 1920.)

BOGLE-SMITH, Colonel Steuart, C.B. 1902; C.B.E. 1919; late Lieut.-Col. commanding 1st Dragoon Guards; b. 11 July 1859; m.

1895, Julia Katharine, *y. d.* of C. H. Berners, of Woolverstone Park, Ipswich; one *s.* Entered army, 1882; Captain, 1892; Major, 1896; Lieut.-Col. 1902; Col. 1905; A.A.G. Irish Command, 1910-14; served South Africa, 1901-2 (despatches, medal with 5 clasps, C.B.). *Club:* Naval and Military. (*Died 6 Jan. 1921.*)

BOITO, Arrigo, poet, composer, librettist; *b.* Padua, 24 Feb. 1842. *Educ.:* Milan Conservatory; Mus. Doc. Cantab. 1893. *Operas:* Mefistofele, 1868. *Cantatas:* Le 4 Juin, 1860; La Sorella d' Italia; Libretti: Otello; Falstaff; La Gioconda; Amleto; Ero e Leandro; Nero. *Publications:* Libro dei versi, 1877; Re Orso(epic poem); L'Alfier Meno(novel). *Address:* Milan. (*Died 10 June 1918.*)

BOLAND, Harry, M.P. (S. Fein) for N. Roscommon since Dec. 1918. (*Died 1 Aug. 1922.*)

BOLE, Hon. W. Norman; retired; Local Judge of the Supreme Court, New Westminster, B.C.; *b.* Castlebar, 6 Dec. 1846; *e. s.* of late John Bole of Lakefield, Mayo, Ireland, and Elizabeth Jane Campbell; *m.* 1881, Florence Blanchard, *o. d.* of Major John Haning Coulthard, J.P.; two *s.* one *d.* Went to New Westminster, 1877; called to British Columbia Bar, 1877; Q.C. 1887; M.P.P. New Westminster, 1886-89; Captain No. 1 Battery, B.C. Brigade Artillery, 1884-1889; Hon. Colonel First Regiment Imperial Canadian Reserve; Fellow Royal Colonial Institute. *Recreations:* shooting, yachting, magazine writing. *Address:* Ardagh, Royal Avenue, New Westminster, B.C. *T.:* 795. *Clubs:* Westminster, Royal Vancouver Yacht, Vancouver. (*Died 7 April 1923.*)

BOLINGBROKE, Leonard George; solicitor; Registrar of the Diocese of Norwich; Chapter Clerk; *b.* 27 May 1859; *y. s.* of Charles Nathaniel Bolingbroke; *m.* Alice Laura, *d.* of William Thomas Bensly, LL.D., F.S.A.; three *s.* two *d.* *Educ.:* Forest School, Walthamstow. *Recreations:* archæology and yachting. *Address:* Ferryside, Norwich. (*Died 9 Aug. 1927.*)

BOLITHO, Thos. Robins, Banker and Landowner; *b.* 13 Sep. 1840; *s. s.* of Thos. S. Bolitho, of Trengwainton; *m.* 1870, Augusta June, *d.* of R. B. Wilson, of Cliffe Hall, Yorks *Educ.* Harrow; Corpus Christi College, Oxford. Engaged throughout life in banking in the county of Cornwall; formerly Bolitho and Co., now Barclay and Co.; and interested in the industries of the county, mining and agriculture; an original member of County Council; Sheriff of County, 1890. *Recreation:* Joint Master of Western Fox Hounds since 1864. *Address:* Trengwainton, Hea Moor, Cornwall. *T.A.:* Heamoor. *Club:* Athenæum.
(*Died 28 Sept. 1925.*)

BOLITHO, Lt.-Col. William Edward Thomas, D.S.O. 1900; Lt.-Col. commanding 2/1st Royal Devon Yeomanry; M.F.H. Western; *b.* 2 July 1862; *s.* of late William Bolitho of Polwithen; *m.* 1888, Ethel Grace, *d.* of Aeneas Bruce Macleod of Cadboll; one *d.* Served with 7th Battalion Imperial Yeomanry, South Africa; 1899-1900 (wounded, despatches, D.S.O.); European War (Bt. Lt.-Col.). *Address:* York House, Penzance; Hannaford, Ashburton, S. Devon. *Club:* Carlton. (*Died 21 Feb. 1919.*)

BOLLARD, Hon. R. F.; Minister of Internal Affairs, New Zealand. *Address:* Dept. of Internal Affairs, Wellington, New Zealand. (*Died 24 Aug. 1927.*)

BOLSTER, Rev. Canon Robert Crofts; Canon of Cloyne since 1870. *Educ.:* Trinity College, Dublin (M.A.). Ordained 1868; Curate of Castlemartyr, Co. Cork, 1868-70; Incumbent, 1870-1904. *Address:* Bedford. (*Died 9 Feb. 1918.*)

BOLTON, 4th Baron (*cr.* 1797), **William Thomas Orde-Powlett,** J.P., D.L., T.D., Alderman, N.R. Yorkshire; late Hon. Col. Commanding Yorkshire (A.P.W.O.) Hussars Imperial Yeomanry; now Hon. Col. of the Regt.; *b.* 31 Jan. 1845; *S.* father 1895; *m.* 1868,

Lady Algitha Frederica Mary Lumley (*d.* 1919), *d.* of 9th Earl of Scarbrough, one *s.* one *d.* *Educ.:* Eton; Trin. Coll. Camb. *Heir:* *s.* Lt.-Col. Hon. W. G. A. Orde-Powlett. *Address:* Bolton Hall, Leyburn, Yorkshire; Hackwood Park, Basingstoke. *Clubs:* Carlton, Junior Carlton; Yorkshire, York. (*Died 14 Aug. 1922.*)

BOLTON, Rev. Charles Nelson, M.A.; Vicar of St. Mary's, Lichfield, since 1895; Prebendary of Dassett Parva in Lichfield Cathedral; *b.* 7 Nov. 1844; *s.* of Charles Bolton, Commander, Royal Navy; *m.* 1872, Catherine Ann, *d.* of John Norman of Botcherby, Carlisle; two *s.* seven *d.* *Educ.:* Rossall; New College, Oxford. Curate, St. John the Evangelist, Carlisle, 1868-1872; Vicar, All Saints, Darlaston, 1872-81; Vicar, Cannock, 1881-95; Rural Dean of Lichfield. *Address:* St. Mary's Vicarage, Lichfield. (*Died 10 Mar. 1918.*)

BOLTON, Charles Walter, C.S.I. 1897; *b.* 1850; *s.* of Dr. J. Bolton; *m.* 1st, 1882, Alice Emma Wilford (*d.* 1895), *d.* of R. R. Wilford Brett, 2nd Bombay Cavalry; 2nd, 1898, Jessie Laura (*d.* 1905), *d.* of late Maj.-Gen. James Templeton Brett; 3rd, 1909, Violet, *d.* of R. J. Graham of Edmond Castle, Cumberland; retired, 1905; two *s.* *Educ.:* University College School; Royal College, Mauritius; King's College, London. Entered I.C.S. 1872; Under Secretary Government, Bengal, 1879; Magistrate and Collector, 1885; Secretary to Board of Revenue, 1891; Chief Secretary to Government, Bengal, 1896; member, Board of Revenue, Bengal, 1900; additional member, Governor-General's Council, 1900; officiating Chief Commissioner of Assam, 1903; J.P., Eastbourne; Mayor, 1912-15. *Address:* Evenmore, Eastbourne. (*Died 27 Dec. 1919.*)

BOLTON, Sir Frederic, Kt., *cr.* 1908; *b.* 7 March 1851; 2nd *s.* of late William Treacher Bolton; *m.* 1876, Ann Haycroft (*d.* 1915), *e. d.* of late William Pearse of Plymouth; one *s.* two *d.* *Educ.:* privately. Underwriter; sometime Chairman of Lloyds; Insurance Broker; Shipowner. *Address:* Westridge, Prince Arthur Road, Hampstead, N.W.3. *T.:* Hampstead 3385. *Clubs:* Reform, City of London. (*Died 25 Jan. 1920.*)

BOLTON, Gambier; *s.* of late Rev. James Jay Bolton, Kilburn; *m.* Georgiana Maria, 4th *d.* of late Col. Evelegh, C.B. *Educ.:* private schools; Corpus Christi College, Cambridge; Public lecturer and writer on (popular) Natural History. *Publications:* A Book of Beasts and Birds; The Animals of the Bible; Psychic Force; has published a large series of animal photographs from life, collected from most parts of the world; travelled in Europe, America, Canada, Hawaian Islands, Japan, China, Java, Malay Peninsula, Burmah, India, South Africa; accompanied the Duke of Newcastle on his tour round the world, 1893-94. *Recreations:* motoring (car, and motor boat). *Club:* Royal Southampton Yacht. (*Died 29 July 1928.*)

BOLTON, Thomas Henry, a Master in the Supreme Court; Taxing Master in Chancery since January 1896; *b.* 1841; *s.* of Thomas Bolton, Canonbury; *m.* 1861, Elizabeth Ann (*d.* 1907), *d.* of William Wegg. Admitted Solicitor, 1869; M.P. (L.) N. St. Pancras, 1885-86, and (L.U.) 1890-95. *Address:* Royal Courts, Strand, W.C. *Club:* Garrick. (*Died 24 Sept. 1916.*)

BONAPARTE, Hon. Charles Joseph; *b.* Baltimore, 9 June 1851; *s.* of Jerome Napoleon Bonaparte and Susan May Williams; *m.* 1875, Ellen Channing Day, of Newport, R.I. Secretary of the Navy, 1905-6; Attorney-General, 1906-1909. *Address:* Glen Arm, Maryland, U.S.A.; 601 Park Avenue, Baltimore, U.S.A. (*Died 28 June 1921.*)

BONAPARTE, H.I.H. Prince Roland, *b.* Paris, 19 May 1858; *s.* of Prince Pierre-Napoléon, 3rd *s.* of Prince Lucien, *b.* of

104

Napoleon I., and Mlle. Ruffin; *m.* Mlle. Felix Blanc (*d.*); one *d.* Marie, who *m.* 1907, Prince George of Greece. *Educ.:* Lycée St. Louis; St. Cyr; Hon. D.Sc. Upsala and Cambridge. Member of the Institute; twice President of the French Geographical Society; much interested in travel and scientific research. *Publications:* Les Habitants de Suriname, 1883; Le Théâtre javanais, 1885; Premiers Voyages; Derniers Voyages; Récents Voyages des Néerlandais à la Nouvelle Guinée; Les Lapps de Finmarck; Le Fleuve Augusta; Le Golfe Huon; La Pêche à la baleine sur les côtes de Norvège; Une Excursion en Corse; Les Idées géographiques à travers l'histoire; Notes Stéridologiques, Vols. I. à VIII. *Address:* 10 avenue d'Iéna, Paris.
(Died 14 April 1924.)

BONAVIA, Hon. Edgar, C.M.G. 1917; f.S.O. 1926; Permanent Secretary to Head of Ministry under Malta Home Rule Constitution, 1919; *b.* 22 Feb. 1868; *m.* 1st, Camilla, *d.* of late Paolo Vassallo, two *s.*; 2nd, Marie, *d.* of late Robert Casolani; four *s.* one *d. Educ.:* St. Ignatius College and Malta University. Entered Malta Civil Service, 1886; Deputy Assistant Secretary to Government, 1911; Assistant Secretary, 1912; visited Tunis to report on Malta Charities in the Regency, 1912; acted as Lieutenant Governor on several occasions; Assistant Secretary to Government of Malta, with seat as official member in Executive and Legislative Councils, 1914; Commissioner for Malta Baden Powell Boy Scouts, 1916 (Silver Wolf, Jamboree, 1920); Hon. Vice-President St. John's Ambulance Association, Malta Branch, 1916. *Address:* 146 Strada Ittorri, Sliema, Malta.
(Died 2 Mar. 1927.)

BOND, Rev. Charles Watson, V.D.; Canon and Prebendary of Chichester Cathedral since 1903; *b.* 19 June 1839; *s.* of William and Maria Bond, Alrewas, Staffordshire; *m.* 1863, Eliza Vines, of Warwick Gardens, Kensington; four *s.* two *d. Educ.:* private school; Cheltenham College; Christ's College, Cambridge. (Scholar) Bishop Porteus Gold Medallist, 1862; B.A., 1862; M.A., 1866; Deacon, 1862; Priest, 1863; Curate of Waltham Abbey, 1862-65; St. John's, Birkenhead, 1865-69; Perpetual Curate of Hanley, Staffs., 1869-76; Vicar of Haddenham, Cambs., 1876-82; All Souls, Brighton, 1882-88; St. Nicholas, Brighton, 1888-1910; Pevensey, 1910-18; Surrogate, 1888. *Publications:* sundry sermons. *Address:* Lyndhurst, Henfield, Sussex. *T.A.:* Henfield. *(Died 20 Aug. 1922.)*

BOND, Edward, M.A.; Chairman East End Dwellings Co.; *b.* London, Oct. 1844; *e. s.* of late Edward Bond, of Elm Bank, Hampstead; unmarried. *Educ.:* Merchant Taylors' School; St. John's Coll. Oxford. Fellow Queen's Coll. Oxford, 1869. Barr. 1871; Assistant Charity Commissioner, 1884-91; contested West Southwark, 1892; L.C.C., Hampstead, 1895-1901; M.P. (C.) East Nottingham, 1895-1906; Chairman of Governing Body of the Cholmeley School, Highgate, and of the Buss Foundation Schools for Girls. *Recreations:* bridge, book-collecting. *Address:* 43 Thurloe Square, S.W. *T.:* Kensington 6861. *Club:* Albemarle, Athenæum, Burlington Fine Arts. *(Died 18 Aug. 1920.)*

BOND, Francis, M.A., F.G.S., Hon. A.R.I.B.A.; *m. Publications:* Gothic Architecture in England; Cathedrals of England and Wales; Screens and Galleries; Stalls and Tabernacle Work; Misericords; Fonts and Font Covers; Westminster Abbey; Introduction to English Church Architecture; Dedications of English Churches; English Chancel. *Recreation:* golf. *Address:* Stafford House, Croydon.
(Died 1918.)

BOND, Rt. Hon. Sir Robert, P.C. 1902; K.C.M.G., *cr.* 1901; Hon. LL.D. Edin.; descended from an old Devonshire family; his father, the late John Bond, a native of Torquay, for more than half a century conducted an extensive mercantile business in St. John's, Newfoundland, under the style of William Hounsell & Co., a branch of the well-known Bridport (Dorsetshire) firm of that name; *b.* 25 Feb. 1857; *s.* of late John Bond of Torquay; not married. *Educ.:* for the Bar but entered politics before being called thereto. Entered the Legislature, 1882; elected Speaker of the House of Assembly, 1884; an executive councillor, with portfolio of Colonial Secretary, 1889-97; appointed a delegate to Her Majesty's Government by the Government of this colony on the French Treaties question, 1890; in the same year Her Majesty's Government appointed him to assist Lord Pauncefote in negotiating a Reciprocity Treaty with the United States, and he was mainly instrumental in completing what is known as the Bond-Blaine Convention; one of the delegates appointed by the Government to meet Sir John Thompson, Sir Mackenzie Bowell, and Sir Adolph Chapleau at Halifax on the Newfoundland Fisheries question, 1892; appointed chairman of the deputation sent by the Government to the "Ottawa Conference," 1895; Premier and Colonial Secy. Newfoundland, 1900-9; special delegate to Conference on French Treaties in Downing Street, 1901; recipient of the Freedom of the City of Edinburgh, 1902; in the same year was authorised by His Majesty's Government to reopen negotiations with the United States for reciprocal trade between that country and Newfoundland, and succeeded in concluding a treaty with that country known as the Hay-Bond Treaty; assisted in drafting regulations for carrying out Anglo-French Convention, 1904; Freedom of City of London, Bristol, and Manchester, 1907; resigned seat in the House of Assembly, and retired from public life in 1913. *Address:* St. John's, and The Grange, Whitbourne, Newfoundland.
(Died 16 Mar. 1927.)

BOND, Maj.-Gen. William Dunn, C.B. 1886; *b.* 5 Nov. 1836; *s.* of late Robert Bond of Dullerton House, Tyrone. Entered army, 1855; Maj.-Gen. 1890; served Zulu War, 1879 (severely wounded, despatches, brevets of Lieut.-Col. and Col., medal with clasp); Boer War, 1881. *Address:* Dullerton, Londonderry. *T.A.:* Dullerton, Londonderry. *Club:* Army and Navy.
(Died 30 Nov. 1919.)

BONE, Rev. Frederic James; Vicar of Lanhydrock, Cornwall, 1903-15; *b.* 1844; *s.* of Allan Belfield Bone, solicitor, and Jane Anne, *d.* of John Scobell, of Holwell, Tavistock. *Educ.:* Cheltenham Coll.; Trinity Coll. Cambridge (Scholar, B.A., M.A.); 22nd Wrangler. Assistant Curate of Stratton, Cornwall, 1870; Vicar, 1873; St. Newlyn, Cornwall, 1892; Hon. Canon of Truro, 1898-1915. *Address:* Betworth, Exmouth. *(Died 31 Dec. 1917.)*

BONET MAURY, Amy-Gaston, Knight of Legion of Honour; D.D. of Paris, Glasgow, and Aberdeen Univs.; LL.D., St. Andrews; Emeritus Professor of Protestant School of Divinity of Paris, etc.; *b.* 2 Jan. 1842; *s.* of Lieut.-General Bonet, late head of Polytechnical School, Paris; *m.* 1868, Isabelle Maury; two *s.* two *d. Educ.:* Lycée Henry IV., Paris; Schools of Divinity Geneva and Strassburg; served as Presbyterian Minister in the Walloon Churches of Netherland, 1868-72; called back to France after the disasters of his country in 1870-71, he served as Protestant minister at Beauvais, where he erected the first church, and at St. Denis; lecturer in Church history at Protestant School of Divinity of Paris, 1879; for twenty years took a large share in all endeavours made to improve in France primary education as librarian of the Musée Pedagogique, and to advance the knowledge of the history of the Huguenots. French delegate at Congress of Health and Education, London, 1884; the Parliament of Religions, Chicago, 1893; the

Congress of Religious Sciences at Stockholm 1897, and of Free Religious Thinkers at Paris 1900, London 1901, Basel 1903, Boston 1907, Berlin, 1910; corresponding member Institut de France, 1908; contributor to Revue politique et littéraire, du protestantisme français, etc. *Publications:* Revue des deux mondes, Bulletin d'Histoire, Gérard de Groote, 1878; Des origines du Christianisme unitaire chez les Anglais, 1881; Arnauld de Brescia, 1881; G.-A. Bürger ou les Origines anglaises de la ballade littéraire en Allemagne, 1890; Lettres et déclarations de Dœllinger au sujet des décrets du Vatican, 1893; Le Congrès des religions à Chicago en 1893-1895; Histoire de la liberté de conscience depuis l'Edit de Nantes jusqu'à la Séparation de l'Etat et des Eglises, 1905; Les Précurseurs de la Réforme et de la liberté de conscience dans les pays latins du XIIe au XVe siècle, 1904; Edgar Quinet, son œuvre religieuse et son caractère moral, 1903; L'Islamisme et le Christianisme en Afrique, 1906; France, Christianisme et Civilisation, 1907; L'Unité morale des religions, 1913. *Address:* 32 Rue du Bac, Paris, VII ème.
(*Died 20 June 1919.*)

BONHAM, Sir George (Francis), 2nd Bt.; *cr.* 1852; M.A., J.P.; *b.* 28 Aug. 1847; *s.* of Sir S. G. Bonham, 1st Bt., K.C.B., and Ellen E., *d.* of Thomas Barnard, Bombay Civil Service; *S.* father, 1863; *m.* 1871, Louisa (*d.* 1923), 3rd *d.* of Right Honourable Sir Andrew Buchanan, 1st Bt., G.C.B.; one *s.* three *d.* *Educ.:* Eton; Exeter Coll., Oxon. Joined Diplomatic Service, 1869; Attaché at St. Petersburg, 1870; at Vienna, 1872; 3rd Secretary at Vienna, 1873; at Rome, 1875; 2nd Secretary at Lisbon, 1876; at Madrid, 1878; at Paris, 1884; First Secretary at Lisbon, 1886; at Hague, 1890; Secretary of Embassy at Madrid, 1898-97; Secretary of Embassy at Rome, 1897-1900; Minister at Belgrade, 1900-3; Envoy Extraordinary and Minister Plenipotentiary Swiss Confederation, 1905-9; retired from Diplomatic Service, 1909. *Heir:* *s.* Eric Henry. *Address:* Knowle Park, Cranleigh, Surrey. *Club:* Travellers'.
(*Died 31 July 1927.*)

BONHAM, Col. John, C.B. 1906; J.P.; *b.* July 1834; 2nd *s.* of late Rev. John Bonham, J.P., of Ballintaggart, and Barbarina, 3rd *d.* of late John Norris, of Hughenden House, Bucks; *m.* 1870, Mary (*d.* 1891), 2nd *d.* of Philip Wroughton, of Woolley Park, Berks; two *s.* one *d.* *Educ.:* Addiscombe. Col. Royal Artillery; retired. Served Indian Mutiny, 1857, including defence of Lucknow (despatches, three times wounded, medal with clasp, brevet of Major). *Club:* Kildare Street, Dublin.
(*Died 18 May 1928.*)

BONHAM-CARTER, Arthur Thomas, Judge of H.M. High Court of East Africa since 1906; Member of the Court of Appeal for Eastern Africa; *b.* 1869; *s.* of John Bonham-Carter, Adhurst St Mary, Petersfield; unmarried. *Educ.:* Winchester; Trinity College, Cambridge. Called to Bar, Inner Temple, and Western Circuit, 1894; Lieutenant (temporary) The Hampshire Regiment, 1900; served South African War (Queen's Medal and 4 Clasps); Assistant Resident Magistrate, Transvaal, 1902; Magistrate East Africa Protectorate, 1905. *Address:* Mombasa, East Africa Protectorate. *Clubs:* Oxford and Cambridge; Royal Southern Yacht; Mombasa; Nyanza; Jubaland. (*Died 1 July 1916.*)

BONI, Comm. Giacomo, Hon. LL.D. Camb.; Director of the excavations in the Roman Forum and on the Palatine; Member of the Superior Council of Antiquities and Fine Arts; *b.* Venice, 25 April 1859. *Educ.:* Venice; Pisa; Austria; Germany. Student journeys in most of the ancient provinces of the Roman Empire; Royal Academy of Fine Arts, Venice (Sup. School of Architecture); D.Litt. (Oxon); R. Inspector of

Antiquities, Minister of Public Instruction; R. Commissioner for the Monuments of Rome. *Publications:* Aedes Vestae; Fons Tuturnae; Prisco-Latin and Romulean Sepulcretum in the Roman Forum; Methods of Archæological Excavations; Hibernica; Forum Ulpium; Trajanic Legends and Column of Trajan; Dalle Origini; Bimbi Romulei; Porta Capena; Terra Mater; Mura Urbane; Flora Palatina; The Tower of St Mark, Venice, etc. Official Reports published by the R. Academia dei Lincei; illustrated articles by the review Nuova Antologia. *Recreation:* Gardening. *Address:* Rome, Palatino. (*Died 7 July 1925.*)

BONNAT, Leon, Hon. R.A.; President Société des Artistes Français; Grand Cross Legion of Honour; Member of the Institute; Member of Council of Legion of Honour. *Address:* Rue de Bassano 48. VIIIe, Paris.
(*Died 7 Sept. 1922.*)

BONNER, Captain Singleton, D.S.O. 1915; 1st Battalion the South Staffordshire Regiment; *b.* 7 July 1879; *s.* of late John Bonner of Liverpool; *m.* 1904, Sisely Alexander, *o. d.* of late Ebenezer Park of Edinburgh; no *c.* *Educ.:* Harrow. Entered army, 1900; Captain, 1908; Adjutant, 1913; Adjutant Volunteers, 1906; served South Africa, 1899-1902 (Queen's medal, 3 clasps, King's medal, 2 clasps); European War, 1914-15 (D.S.O.). (*Died 1 May 1917.*)

BONNEY, Rev. Thomas George, D.Sc. Cambridge; Hon. LL.D. Montreal; Hon. D.Sc. Dublin and Sheffield; F.R.S.; Emeritus Professor of Geology, University College, London; Hon. Canon of Manchester; Fellow of St. John's College, Cambridge: *b.* Rugeley, 27 July 1833; *e. s.* of late Rev. Thomas Bonney. *Educ.:* Uppingham; St. John's Coll. Camb. Tutor St. John's Coll. Camb. 1868-76; Whitehall Preacher, 1876-78; Hulsean Lecturer (Camb.), 1884; President Geological Society, 1884-86; Boyle Lecturer, 1890-92; Rede Lecturer (Camb.), 1892; Vice-President Royal Society, 1899; President of British Association, 1910-11. *Publications:* Outline Sketches in the High Alps of Dauphiné, 1865; The Alpine Regions, 1868; The Story of our Planet, 1893; Charles Lyell and Modern Geology, 1895; Ice-Work, 1896; Volcanoes, 1898; The Building of the Alps, 1912; The Present Relations of Science and Religion, 1913; Text to Anderson's Volcanic Studies, 1917; Memories of a Long Life, 1922; four volumes of sermons and numerous contributions to scientific periodicals. *Recreations:* Alpine travel; ex-President Alpine Club. *Address:* 9 Scroope Terrace, Cambridge. *Club:* Alpine. (*Died 10 Dec. 1923.*)

BONSALL, Major Hugh Edward, J.P., Cardiganshire and Montgomeryshire; retired Maj., late Cardigan Arty.; 2nd *s.* of John George William Bonsall of Fronfraith, Cardiganshire; *m.* 1896, Gertrude E., *d.* of late J. T. Morgan of Nantcaerio, Cardiganshire, M.B.E., J.P. *Address:* Fronfraith, Aberystwyth. *T.A.:* Galltyllan, Machynlleth. *Club:* Junior Constitutional.
(*Died 18 Mar. 1928.*)

BONSEY, His Honour Henry Dawes, Judge of County Courts No. 2 since 1911; Recorder of Bedford 1910-12; 3rd *s.* of late William Henry Bonsey, Slough, Bucks; *m.* 1898, Helen Jane, *d.* of late Archibald Dymock, Louth. *Educ.:* St. John's College, Cambridge, B.A. Called to Bar, Inner Temple, 1875; went Midland Circuit. *Address:* 9 Windsor Crescent, Newcastle-on-Tyne. *Club:* Oxford and Cambridge. (*Died 12 May 1919.*)

BONUS, Maj.-Gen. Joseph, late Royal Engineers; *b.* 1836; 5th *s.* of John Bonus; *m.* 1st, Frances Mary, *d.* of William Hart, I.C.S.; 2nd, Marion Sophia, *d.* of R. Stuart Poole. British Museum; three *s.* one *d.* *Educ.:* privately; Addiscombe. Served Indian Mutiny (medal and clasp); Afghan War, 1878-80 (medal); Engineer-in-

106

BONSALL, Arthur Charles. See page xvi.

Chief, Scindiah State Railway, Punjab Northern Railway; Joint Secretary to Government of Bombay Railways; retired, 1886; J.P. Middlesex. *Address:* Newlands, Stanstead Abbotts, Herts. *T.:* Stanstead Abbotts 9. *T.A.:* Stanstead Abbotts. *M.:* NK 4736. *Club:* United Service. (*Died 11 June 1926.*)

BOOKEY, Col. John Trench Brownrigg, C.B., 1900; Indian Medical Service; late Surgeon to the Viceroy; retired 1902; *b.* Carnew, Co. Wicklow, Ireland, 10 Dec. 1847; *s.* of Dr. Bookey; *m.* 1892. *Educ.:* Trinity College, Dublin. L.R.C.P. Edin.; L.R.C.S.I. Entered I.M.S., 1872; served with the Punjab Frontier Force from 1873-1900; appointed P.M.O. Presy. Dist., May 1900; Colonel same date; served in the following Expeditions—Jowaki Afridi, 1877-78; Mahsud Waziri, 1881; Burmah, 1886-87 (despatches); Hazara Black Mountain, 1888 (despatches); Miranzai, 1891 (despatches); Mahsud Waziri, 1894-95 (despatches); Malakand Field Force, 1897 (despatches); Tirah, 1897-98; China Expeditionary Force, 1900. *Address:* c/o Grindlay & Co., 54 Parliament Street, S.W. *Club:* East India United Service.
(*Died 19 Nov. 1921.*)

BOON, Quartermaster and Hon. Capt. George, D.S.O. 1900; retired; The Buffs; *b.* 9 Sep. 1846; *s.* of Charles Boon; *m.* 1871, Sarah, *d.* of James T. Easter. Served South Africa, 1899-1900 (despatches, Queen's medal four clasps, King's medal two clasps, D.S.O.).
(*Died 8 Oct. 1927.*)

BOON, John; Knight Commander of the Royal Spanish Order of Isabel the Catholic; F.I.J.; member of the Editorial Staff of The Times; editor of the Exchange Telegraph Co. Ltd., 1894-1914; *b.* Clontarf, Dublin, 8 June 1859; *e. s.* of Andrew Boon, near Coollagh, Co. Dublin, and Sophie Léon. *Educ.:* Lycée de Bordeaux; Sorbonne, Paris; Rome; Madrid. Commenced to contribute to English-French Press, 1880; travelled in Algeria and Egypt; spent 3 years in Rome; joined literary staff of Central News; in 1883 acted as foreign editor and special correspondent; in 1886 became special correspondent of the Exchange Telegraph Co., and representative of that Co. in Lobby of House of Commons during the eventful years of 1885-92; acted as special correspondent throughout the three kingdoms and in most parts of Continent; has twice visited Morocco and seen much adventure in Spain; contributed largely to the old Pall Mall Gazette and the Westminster Gazette; acted as Special Correspondent of The Times in France and Flanders during the early stages of the War, and in 1916 as Special Correspondent in Spain and Portugal. *Recreations:* fencing, riding, and mountaineering. *Address:* 46 Upper Park Road, Hampstead, N. *Club:* National Liberal.
(*Died 26 June 1928.*)

BOORD, Sir (William) Arthur, 2nd Bt.; *cr.* 1896; F.R.G.S.; *b.* 24 May 1862; *e. s.* of 1st Bt. and Margaret D'Almaine, *d.* of Thomas G. Mackinlay, F.S.A.; *S.* father, 1912; unmarried. *Educ.:* Harrow; Germany and France. Has travelled extensively. *Publications:* several books of verse. *Recreations:* photography, travel, chess. *Heir:* *n.* Richard William Boord, *b.* 1907. *Club:* Junior Carlton.
(*Died 26 May 1928.*)

BOOT, William Henry James, R.I.; Vice-President Royal Society of British Artists, 1895-1914; Member Japan Society, etc.; *b.* Nottingham. Studied at Derby School of Art. Contributed drawings to Picturesque Europe, British Battles, Our Village, Our Own Country, British Ballads, Royal River, Rivers of England, Greater London, Picturesque Mediterranean, Art Journal, Magazine of Art, Graphic, Illustrated London News, Strand Magazine, etc., 1869-92; art editor Strand Magazine, 1891-1910. *Exhibitor:* R.A. 1874-84, and at intervals since; also at R.B.A., R.I., and most of the principal exhibitions in the provinces. *Publication:* Trees and How to Paint Them, 1883. *Recreation:* travel. *Address:* 1 Cannon Place, Hampstead, N.W. *Club:* Arts. (*Died 8 Sept. 1918.*)

BOOTH, Rt. Hon. Charles, P.C. 1904; F.R.S.; D.Sc. (hon.), Camb.; D.C.L. (hon.), Oxford; LL.D. Liverpool; Chairman of Alfred Booth & Co., Ltd., Liverpool; Director of Booth S.S. Co.; *b.* Liverpool, 30 Mar. 1840; *m.* Mary, *d.* of Charles Zachary Macaulay, 1871. *Educ.:* Royal Inst. Sch., Liverpool. President Royal Statistical Society, 1892-94; Member of Tariff Commission, 1904. *Publications:* Life and Labour of the People in London (Poverty, 1891; Industry, 1897; The Religious Influences of London, 1903; Summary, 1903); Pauperism: a Picture; and the Endowment of Old Age, 1892; The Aged Poor, Condition, 1894; Old Age Pensions, 1899. *Address:* 28 Campden House Court, Kensington, W. *Clubs:* Reform, Athenæum.
(*Died 23 Nov. 1916.*)

BOOTH, Very Rev. Lancelot Parker; Dean of St. John's, Cape Colony, 1900-1912; *s.* of Lancelot Parker Booth of Bishop Auckland, Co. Durham; *m.* 1st, 1884, Olive, *d.* of Dr. Hugh Stott, Blackheath (*d.* 1888); 2nd, 1894, Annie Sophia, *d.* of J. R. Grimes of St. Leonard's. M.D. Durham Univ.; D.D. Trin. Coll. Tor. Natal Govt. Medical Service and Indian Immigration Dept. 1876-83; ordained, 1883; Diocesan Supt. of Indian Missions and Canon of Maritzburg, Natal, 1889; Natal Indian Ambulance M.O., 1899-1900 (medal, 2 clasps); Vicar-General of St. John's, 1900-1901; Vicar and Sub-Dean of St. George's Cathedral, Capetown, 1912-13; Rector of St. Barnabas', Capetown, 1913; Captain R.A.M.C., B.E.F., France, 1916. *Address:* St. Barnabas' Rectory, Capetown.
(*Died 28 Mar. 1925.*)

BOOTH, Leonard William, C.M.G. 1913; Colonial Secretary Ceylon (Acting); *b.* 10 June 1856; 2nd *s.* of George Booth, Solicitor, and Margaret Emily, *d.* of William Shipton Browning; *m.* 1883, Mary Emily, *d.* of H. R. von Dadelszen, Coffee Planter, Ceylon; two *s.* four *d.* *Educ.:* Lancing College. Cadet Ceylon Civil Service, 1878; Class I. 1906; Police Magistrate; District Judge; Forest Settlement Officer; Government Agent North Central, Sabaragamawa, Uva, North-Western, Southern, Central, and Western Provinces; acted as Principal Collector of Customs, Colonial Treasurer, Controller of Revenue, and Colonial Secretary. *Address:* c/o Crown Agents for the Colonies, Millbank, Westminster, S.W.
(*Died 20 Nov. 1923.*)

BOOTH, S. Lawson, R.C.A., J.P. *Address:* 172 Roe Lane, Southport. (*Died 25 Aug. 1928.*)

BOOTHBY, Sir Charles Francis, 12th Bt., *cr.* 1660; 2nd *s.* of 10th Bt. and Martha Serena, *d.* of Rev. Charles Boothby, Vicar of Sutterton, Lincs; *b.* 22 June 1858; *S. b.* 1913. *Educ.:* Harrow. *Heir:* *b.* Rev. Herbert Cecil Boothby, *b.* 8 Dec. 1863. (*Died 4 April 1926.*)

BOOTHBY, Josiah, C.M.G. 1878; *b.* 1837; *m.* 1861, Susannah, *d.* of W. G. Lawrence, Adelaide. Entered Colonial Secretary's Office, South Australia, 1853; Permanent Under-Secretary South Australia, 1868-80; Commissioner Paris Exhibition, 1878. *Address:* 158 Barnard Street, North Adelaide, South Australia.
(*Died 19 June 1916.*)

BORASTON, Sir John, Kt. *cr.* 1916; J.P.; Principal Unionist Agent since 1912; *b.* 1851; *m.* 1876, one *s.* (Maj. J. H. Boraston, O.B.E.) *Address:* Ringwood, 31 Southend Road, Beckenham; 1 Sanctuary Buildings, Great Smith Street, Westminster, S.W. 1. *Club:* Carlton.
(*Died 18 April 1920.*)

BORDEN, Hon. Sir Frederick William, K.C.M.G., *cr.* 1902; Knight of Grace, Order of St. John of Jerusalem, 1902; B.A., M.D., D.C.L., LL.D.; P.C. (Canada) 1896; Minister of Militia Defence, 1896-

1911; *b.* 14 May 1847; *s.* of Dr. J. and Maria F. Borden; *m.* 1st, 1873, Julia M. Clarke (*d.* 1880); 2nd, 1884, Bessie B. Clarke; two *d. Educ.:* University of King's College, Windsor, Nova Scotia, B.A.; Harvard Medical School, Boston, Mass., M.D. Began practice of medicine, 1868; appointed Assist. Surgeon 68th Batt. "King's County" (Militia) 1869; now Surg. Lt.-Col. and Hon. Col. of Canadian Army Medical Corps; Hon. Surgeon-General in the Imperial Army, 1911; first elected to House of Commons, 1874; since then represented same Riding (King's N. S.) continuously to 1911 except during the years 1883-86, having been elected ten times and defeated once. *Recreations:* walking, fishing, music. *Address:* Canning, Nova Scotia; 17 Blackburn Avenue, Ottawa, Ont. *Clubs:* Rideau, Ottawa; Halifax, Halifax, N.S.   (*Died 6 Jan. 1917.*)

BORRADAILE, Col. George William, C.B. 1882; *b.* Poona, Bombay, 13 June 1838; 3rd *s.* of Harry Borradaile, Bombay C.S.; *m.* 1864, Catherine Cornelia (*d.* 1912); 4th *d.* of late Surgeon-General Charles Doyle Straker, Bombay Medical Service. *Educ.:* private school; Cheltenham College, 1854-55. Passed out of Addiscombe as a Bombay artillery cadet, 1857; transferred to Royal Artillery; served in India, 1858-71; England, 1872-83; India, 1883-94, when retired on pension after 38 years; 3rd Class Order of the Medjidie, medal and clasp for Tel-el-Kebir, Bronze Star, Egypt, 1882 (despatches); J.P. Bucks. *Address:* c/o Lloyds Bank, Ltd., Cox & Co.'s Branch (G. 1. Section), 6 Pall Mall, S.W.1. (*Died 3 Feb. 1927.*)

BORRETT, Major-General Herbert Charles, C.B. 1902; *b.* Great Yarmouth, Norfolk, 23 September 1841; *y. s.* of Thomas Borrett of Cransford Hall, Suffolk; *m.* 1867, Annie, *e. d.* of Major John Bennett, 1st Bombay Fusiliers; four *s.* three *d. Educ.:* Radley College. Ensign 4th Foot, 1858; Adjutant, 1869 and 1870; Colonel, 1885; commanded 49th Royal Berkshire Regimental District, 1890-95; A.A.G. for Recruiting, Headquarters Staff, 1895-98; Major-General, 1898; Inspector-General of Recruiting, Headquarters Staff, 1899-1903; served with the 4th Foot throughout the Abyssinian Expedition, 1867-68; present at action of Arogee and capture of Magdala (medal). *Address:* Lancaster Lodge, Bath Road, Reading, Berks. *Club:* United Service. (*Died 4 April 1919.*)

BORROWES, Lieut.-Col. Sir Kildare Dixon, 10th Bt.; *cr.* 1646; J.P. and D.L.; *b.* 21 Sep. 1852; S. father 1898; *m.* Julia Aline, *d.* of late Wm. Holden of Palace House, Lancashire, 1886. *Educ.:* Cheltenham College. Retired Lt.-Col.; late Major 11th Hussars. High Sheriff, 1902; served in France throughout European War (1914-15 Star, War and Victory Medals); served in the South Irish Horse; formerly A.D.C. to Duke of Marlborough, Lord Lieut. of Ireland. Owns 11,000 acres. *Heir pres.: b.* Eustace [*b.* 31 Dec. 1866; *m.* 1899 (Louisa Margaret) Winifred (Mary), *d.* of John Macdonald Royse. *Address:* 49 Rathdown Road, Dublin]. *Address:* Beechborough Park, nr. Folkestone. *Clubs:* Brooks's, United Service, M.C.C.; Kildare Street, Dublin.
(*Died 21 Oct. 1924.*)

BORTHWICK, William Henry; 3rd *s.* of late John Borthwick and 1st wife, Anne, *e. d.* of late Rt. Hon. Robert Dundas, of Arniston, Midlothian; *b.* 28 Nov. 1832; S. *b.* 1907; *m.* 1864, Rebecca (*d.* 1887), *o. d.* of late Robert Cathcart; three *s. Heir: e. s.* Henry [*b.* 23 July 1868; *m.* 1902, Melena Florence, 4th *d.* of late Comdr. James Thomas Pringle, R.N., of Torwoodlee, Selkirkshire; one *s. Address:* Borthwick Castle, Gorebridge, Midlothian]. *Address:* Crookston House, Heriot, Midlothian.
(*Died 8 Oct. 1928.*)

BORTON, Colonel Charles Edward, C.B. 1902; retired; *b.* 3 June 1857; *y. s.* of late

108

General Sir Arthur Borton, G.C.B., G.C.M.G.; *m.* 1893, Amy Louisa, *y. d.* of late Richard Cotton Lewin, I.C.S.; one *s. Educ.:* Wellington. Entered army, 1878; Capt. 1885; Maj. 1896; Lt.-Col. 1901; served Afghan War, 1879-80 (medal with clasp); Burmese Expedition, 1887-1889 (medal with clasp); South Africa, 1900-1902 (despatches, C.B.); European War, Aug. 1914 to Jan. 1918 (despatches). *Address:* Ruthven, Horley, Surrey. *Club:* Naval and Military.
(*Died 23 Mar. 1924.*)

BORWICK, Leonard, pianist; *b.* 26 Feb. 1868. *Educ.:* Hoch Conservatoire, Frankfort-on-the-Main. Appeared first at Frankfort, 1889; London Philharmonic and Richter Concerts, 1890. *Recreations:* travel, chess. *Address:* 14 Brunswick Square, W.C.1. *T.:* Museum 6386.   (*Died 15 Sept. 1925.*)

BOSANQUET, Bernard, formerly Fellow of Univ. Coll. Oxon.; M.A. Oxon., LL.D. Glasgow, D.C.L. Durham; past Pres. of Aristotelian Soc.; Fellow of British Academy; Gifford Lecturer (Edinburgh), 1911-12; *b.* 1848; *s.* of Rev. R. W. Bosanquet of Rock Hall, Alnwick; *m.* Helen Dendy, 1895. *Educ.:* Harrow; Balliol College, Oxford (scholar). First class in Moderations and Literae Humaniores. Lecturer at Univ. Coll. Oxford, 1871-81; in London occupied with authorship and Univ. Extension lecturing and social work, especially in connection with Charity Organisation Society, 1881-97; then went to live in country; Professor of Moral Philosophy, St. Andrews, 1903-8. *Publications:* Logic, or Morphology of Knowledge; History of Aesthetic; Knowledge and Reality; Essays and Addresses; Civilisation of Christendom; Essentials of Logic; Aspects of Social Problem; Psychology of Moral Self; Companion to Plato's Republic for English Readers; Education of the Young in Plato's Republic; Philosophical Theory of the State; Three Lectures on Aesthetic; Social and Internal Ideals; Implication and Linear Influences, 1919; The Meeting of Extremes in Contemporary Philosophy, 1921. *Address:* The Heath Cottage, Oxshott, Surrey. (*Died 8 Feb. 1923.*)

BOSANQUET, Admiral Sir Day Hort, G.C.M.G., *cr.* 1914; K.C.B., *cr.* 1905; G.C.V.O. 1907; J.P., D.L., Hereford; Governor South Australia, 1909-14; *b.* 22 Mar. 1843; *m.* 1881, Mary, *d.* of late Col. T. Bromhead Butt, Cameron Highlanders; two *d.* Entered R.N. 1857; Commander, 1874; Captain, 1882; Rear-Admiral, 1897; Vice-Admiral, 1902; was Commander-in-Chief, East Indies, 1899-1902; Commander-in-Chief, North America and West Indies, 1904-7; Commander-in-Chief, Portsmouth, 1907-8. *Decoration:* Grand Cross of Swords of Sweden, 1906. *Address:* Old Vicarage, Newbury. *Club:* United Service.
(*Died 28 June 1923.*)

BOSANQUET, Sir (Frederick) Albert, Kt., *cr.* 1907; K.C.; an additional Judge of the Central Criminal Court since 1917; *b.* 8 Feb. 1837; *s.* of S. R. Bosanquet, Dingestow Court, Monmouth; *m.* 1st, 1873, Albinia Mary (*d.* 1882), *d.* of J. Curtis-Hayward; two *s.* two *d.*; 2nd, 1885, Philippa, *d.* of W. Bence Jones; one *s.* one *d. Educ.:* Eton; King's College, Cambridge. 1st Class Classics and Senior Optime, 1860; Fellow of King's Coll. Camb. Barr. 1863; Q.C. 1882; Bencher of Inner Temple, 1889; Recorder of Worcester, 1879; Recorder of Wolverhampton, 1891-1900; Common Serjeant of London, 1900-17; Chairman of E. Sussex Quarter Sessions, 1912-21; Chairman of Council of Law Reporting, 1909-17. *Address:* 12 Grenville Place, S. Kensington, S.W.7. *T.:* Western 3083.   (*Died 2 Nov. 1923.*)

BOSANQUET, Helen, LL.D. St. Andrews; *d.* of Rev. John Dendy; *b.* 10 Feb. 1860; *m.* 1895, Bernard Bosanquet (*d.* 1923); no *c. Educ.:* Newnham College, Cambridge; First Class Honours Moral Sciences Tripos; district

Secretary to the Charity Organisation Society ; University Extension Lecturer ; Member of Royal Commission on Poor Laws, 1905 ; Writer on Social Subjects. *Publications*: Rich and Poor ; The Standard of Life ; The Strength of the People ; The Family ; The Poor Law Report of 1909 (Summary) ; Social Work in London, etc. *Address*: 13 Heathgate, Golders Green. N.W.11.   (*Died 7 April 1925.*)

BOSCAWEN, Major Hon. George Edward, D.S.O. 1914 ; Royal Field Artillery ; *b.* 6 Dec. 1888 ; 2nd *s.* of 7th Viscount Falmouth. Entered army, 1907 ; served European War, 1914-16 (despatches, D.S.O., Bt. Major), for gallantly fighting his section of guns in front of La Bassée. *Address*: Tregothnan, Truro.   (*Died 27 May 1918.*)

BOSE, Sir Kailas Chandra, Rai Bahadur, Kt., *cr.* 1916 ; C.I.E. 1910 ; Kaiser-i-Hind Gold Medal, 1909 ; O.B.E. 1918 ; Fellow Calcutta Univ. ; Vice - Pres. Indian Medical Congress ; Fellow, R. Institute of Public Health ; Member British Medical Association ; Hon. Presidency Magistrate ; Member of Governing Body State Medical Faculty of Bengal ; Presidency Magistrate and Ex-off. J.P. ; Municipal Commissioner, President of Calcutta Medical Club, Member of Plague Commission, Bengal Delegate at All India Sanitary Conference, etc. etc. *Address*: 1 Sukeos Street, Calcutta. *T.*: 1993. *M.*: 741.   (*Died Feb. 1927.*)

BOSTOCK, Henry; Chairman, Lotus, Ltd., boot manufacturers, Stafford ; Vik Heels Ltd., Stafford, and Sutor Ltd., Northampton. *Address*: The Oaklands, Stafford. *T.*: 7.   (*Died 11 Oct. 1923.*)

BOSWELL, Arthur Radcliffe, K.C. ; *b.* Cobourg, Ont., 3 Jan. 1838 ; *s.* of late Judge Boswell and Susan Radcliffe ; *m.* Ella, *d.* of M. D. Cruso, late of Cobourg, Ont. ; no *c.* *Educ.*: Brockville Ont. ; U.C. Coll., Toronto. Alderman of Toronto several years ; Mayor of Toronto, 1883 and 1884 ; Commodore Royal Canadian Yacht Club for 14 years ; President Canadian Association Amateur Oarsman for 9 years ; passed Royal Military School. 1864 ; a Freemason ; an Anglican, and a delegate to Synod for many years. *Recreations*: yachting and golf. *Clubs*: York, Royal Canadian Yacht, M. Golf, Toronto.

BOSWORTH, Colonel William John ; Founder and Principal of the Military College, Roehampton ; *b.* Stoke, Devonport, 1858 ; *m.* (*d.* 1916). *Educ.*: King Edward VI. Grammar School, Birmingham ; Caius and Downing Colleges, Cambridge. Founded the Military College, Roehampton, 1884 ; and transferred it to Earl's Court, 1910 ; during South African Campaign commanded the 2nd Provisional Battalion, Aldershot ; greatly interested in aviation and motoring as applied to military uses ; one of the founders and first Chairman of the Automobile Association ; a founder and Chairman for three years of the Motor Club ; Chairman of the first International Rubber Exhibition and other International Exhibitions. *Publications*: contributions to the military publications on technical subjects. *Recreations*: big game shooting, motoring, golf, and bulldog breeding. *Address*: 65 Earl's Court Square, S.W.5. *T.*: Kensington 217. *Clubs*: Savage ; Royal Temple Yacht.   (*Died 28 Nov 1923.*)

BOTELER, Sir Edgar Collins Boehm, 2nd Bt., *cr.* 1889 ; F.R.G.S. ; *b.* 1 Oct. 1869 ; *o. s.* of Sir Edgar Joseph Boehm, R.A., and Louisa France Boteler of West Derby, Lancs. *Educ.*: Eton. *S.* father, 1890 ; late Lieut. Royal Garrison Artillery. *Publications*: Over the World ; The Persian Gulf and South Sea Isles, 1904. *Recreation*: sport. *Heir*: none. *M.*: L 9046. *Address*: Craufurd, Maidenhead, Berkshire. *Clubs*: Badminton, Royal Automobile, New Oxford and Cambridge. (*Died 23 May 1923.*)

BOTHA, Rt. Hon. Louis, P.C. ; LL.D. Edin. Oxon. and Cantab. ; Premier and Minister of Native Affairs, Union of S. Africa ; Hon. General in British Army ; M.L.A. Losberg ; *b.* Greytown, Natal, 1863. Was a member of first Volksraad of Transvaal, in which he represented Vryheid ; acted as veldt-cornet for that district at the beginning of the Anglo-Boer War ; succeeded General Joubert as Commander-in-Chief of the Boer forces, which he commanded at the battle of Colenso and during the rest of the war ; visited England, 1902, 1907, and 1911 ; Premier of Transvaal, 1907-10 ; commanded the Union Forces in South-West Africa, 1914-15, and achieved complete success, receiving surrender of the German army. *Address*: Pretoria, Transvaal.   (*Died 27 Aug. 1919*)

BOTHAMLEY, Rev. Hilton, M.A. *Educ.*: Harrow ; Trin. Coll. Cambridge. Ordained, 1861 ; Curate of St. John, Weymouth, 1867-73 ; Rector of Peperharow, Surrey, 1873-1879 ; Curate of St. Stephen, Lansdown, Bath, 1880-81 ; Vicar, 1881-1909 ; Prebendary of Wells, 1892-1913 ; Archdeacon of Bath, 1895 - 1909. *Address*: Richmond Lodge, Bath.
    (*Died 1 July 1919.*)

BOTTOMLEY, James Thomson, M.A., D.Sc., Hon. LL.D. (Glasgow), F.R.S. ; Electrical engineer ; *b.* 10 Jan. 1845 ; *s.* of late William Bottomley, J.P., Belfast ; *nephew* of Lord Kelvin ; *m.* 1st, Annie Elizabeth, *d.* of late W. W. Heap, Manchester ; one *s.* ; 2nd, Eliza Jennet (*d.* 1913), *d.* of late Chas. R. Blandy, Madeira. *Educ.*: Queen's College, Belfast ; Trinity Coll. Dublin. Gold medallist at degrees of B.A. and M.A. Assistant to late Professor Thomas Andrews, F.R.S., Belfast ; Demonstrator, 1st, of Chemistry ; 2nd, of Physics, King's Coll., London ; for 29 years occupied the position of Arnott and Thomson Demonstrator in the University of Glasgow, and acted as deputy for Lord Kelvin ; resigned 1899, when Lord Kelvin resigned the Professorship of Natural Philosophy. *Publications*: elementary books on Dynamics and Hydrostatics ; Mathematical Tables ; original papers contributed to Royal Society, etc. *Recreations*: swimming, rowing, climbing, cycling, motoring. *Address*: Netherhall, Largs, Ayrshire ; 13 University Gardens, Glasgow. *T.*: 85 Western, Glasgow. *M.*: G 5007, G 9841. *Clubs*: Athenæum, Royal Automobile ; British Empire League ; Western, Royal Scottish Automobile, Glasgow ; Brooklands.
    (*Died 18 May 1926.*)

BOTTOMLEY, William Beecroft, M.A. (Camb.), Ph.D., F.L.S., F.C.S. ; Fellow, King's College, London ; Professor of Botany, King's College, London, 1893-1921 ; Prof. of Biology, Royal Veterinary Coll. London, since 1891 ; *b.* Apperley Bridge, Leeds, 1863 ; *o. s.* of J. Bottomley, Fern Cliffe, Morecambe ; *m.* 1891. *Educ.*: Royal Grammar School, Lancaster ; King's Coll. Camb. Science Tutor and Lecturer on Biology, St. Mary's Hospital Medical School, 1886-91 ; Camb. University Extension Lecturer, 1891-94 ; interested in Agricultural Co-operation ; founder of South-Eastern Co-operative Agricultural Society ; Hon. Sec. Agricultural Banks Association ; Hon. Sec. English Land Colonisation Society. *Recreations*: photography, cycling. *Address*: Botanical Laboratory. King's College, W.C.   (*Died 24 Mar. 1922.*)

BOUCAUT, Hon. Sir James Penn, K.C.M.G., *cr.* 1898 ; *b.* near Falmouth, 29 Oct. 1831 ; *m.* 1864, Janet, *d.* of Alexander M'Culloch of Yongala, S.A. ; six *s.* one *d.* Went to South Australia, 1846 ; Barr. 1855 ; M.L.A. 1861 ; Attorney - General, 1865 ; Premier, 1866, 1875, 1877 ; Deputy - Governor, 1885 - 86, 1888, 1890 ; Administrator of the Government, 1890 and 1891 ; Judge of the Supreme Court of the State of South Australia, 1878-1905 ; retired. *Publica-*

BOTTOMLEY, Col. Herbert, C.M.G.   See page xvi.

tions : The Arab : the Horse of the Future, 1905 ;
Letters to My Boys, 1906 ; The Arab Horse,
The Thoroughbred, and the Turf, 1912. *Recrea-
tion :* breeding pure Arab horses. *Address :*
Glenelg, South Australia.   (*Died 1 Feb. 1916.*)

BOUCHÉ-LECLERCQ, Auguste; Pro-
fesseur d'Histoire Ancienne à l'Université de
Paris ; *b.* Francières (Oise), 30 Juillet 1842 ; *s.* of
Thomas Bouché et Joséphine Leclercq ; *m.* 1876,
Julie Guillaume ; three *s.* one *d. Educ. :* Petit-
Séminaire de Noyon (Oise). Chargé de cours,
puis professeur à la Faculté des Lettres de
Montpellier, 1873-78 ; professeur suppléant, puis
titulaire 1887, honoraire 1918, à la Faculté
des Lettres de Paris since 1879 ; Membre
de l'Institut (Académie des Inscriptions et
Belles-Lettres), 1898 ; officier de l'Instruction
Publique; officier de la Légion d'Honneur ;
officier de SS. Maurizio e Lazzaro. *Publications :* Les Pontifes de l'ancienne Rome,
1871 ; Placita Graecorum de origine generis
humani, 1871 ; Giacomo Leopardi, sa vie et ses
œuvres, 1874 ; Histoire de la Divination
dans l'antiquité, 4 vols., 1879-82 ; Manuel
des Institutions romaines, 1886 ; L'Astrologie
grecque, 1899 ; Leçons d'Histoire grecque,
1900 ; Histoire des Lagides, 4 vols., 1903-1907,
Leçons d'Histoire romaine, 1909 ; L'Intolér-
ance religieuse et la politique, 1911 ; Histoire
des Séleucides, 2 vols., 1913-14. A publié, de
1880 à 1890, onze volumes de traductions des
ouvrages de E. Curtius, J. G. Droysen, G. F.
Hertzberg, concernant l'histoire de la Grèce,
et un Atlas pour servir à l'Histoire Grecque
de E. Curtius, 1883. *Address :* Nogent-sur-
Marne (Seine), 26 Avenue de la Source.
                                (*Died 17 July 1923.*)

**BOUCHER, Lt.-Col. Benjamin Hamil-
ton,** D.S.O. 1900 ; retired ; *b.* 20 Feb. 1864 ;
e. s. of late B. Boucher, of The Croft, Wiveliscombe, Somerset ; *m.* 1st, 1896, Helen (*d.*
1904), *e. d.* of late C. Boucher, J.P., of
Eaglemont, Klimington, Devon, and of Lamb-
croft, Lincolnshire; three *s.* ; 2nd, 1907, Dorothy
(*d.* 1916), *d.* of late Engledue Prideaux, of Luson,
Wellington, Somerset. *Educ. :* Marlborough.
Entered Army, 1885 ; Captain, 1892 ; Station
Staff Officer, Bengal, 1893-95; Adjutant 1st Batt.
Hampshire Regiment, 1896-1900 ; Adjutant 4th
Vol. Batt. 1900-4 ; served Burmese Expedition
1887-89 (medal with clasp) ; Chitral Relief Force,
1895 ; South Africa, 1899 - 1900 (despatches,
D.S.O., medal with 3 clasps). *Club:* Junior
Army and Navy.   (*Died 8 Jan. 1923.*)

BOUGHEY, Sir Francis, 8th Bt. ; *cr.*
1798 ; *b.* 2 Apr. 1848 ; *s.* of 3rd Bt. and Louisa
Paulina, *y. d.* of Thomas Giffard of Chillington ; *S.* brother, 1921. *Heir : c.* George Menteth, O.B.E., I.C.S. [*b.* 1879; *m.* 1913, Noel
Evelyn. *d.* of late J. G. H. Glass, C.I.E. ; two
s. three *d. Educ. :* Wellington]. *Address :* The
Derwen, Oswestry.   (*Died 6 Mar. 1927.*)

**BOUGHEY, Col. George Fletcher
Ottley,** R.E. ; C.S.I., 1896 ; a Light Railway
Commissioner ; *b.* 23 Jan. 1844 ; *m.* 1872, Harriet
Rose Amy, *d.* of late Lieut.-Col. W. Stuart
Menteth ; one *s.* three *d.* Entered army, 1862 ;
Col. 1895 ; served Bhutan Expedition, 1865-66
(medal with clasp) ; Afghan War, 1878-80
(medal). *Address :* 60 Courtfield Gardens, S.W.
                                (*Died 17 Jan. 1918.*)

BOUGHEY, Rev. Sir Robert, 7th Bt. ;
cr. 1798 ; Vicar of Betley, Crewe, since 1876 ;
b. 21 Mar. 1843 ; *s.* of 3rd Bt. and Louisa
Paulina, *y. d.* of Thomas Giffard of Chillington ; *S.* brother, 1912. *Educ. :* Christ Church,
Oxford (B.A.). Ordained, 1867 ; Curate, Stoke-
on-Trent, 1866-76. *Heir : b.* Francis [*b.* 2
Apr. 1848. *Address :* The Derwen, Oswestry.]
Address : Betley Vicarage, Crewe.
                                (*Died 22 May 1921.*)

BOULDEN, Rev. Alfred William, M.A.,
Hon. Canon of Rochester, 1919 ; Rural Dean of

110

Dartford, 1916 ; Vicar of Christ Church, Erith,
Kent, since 1891 ; *b.* 23 April 1849 ; *e. s.* of
Joseph and Elizabeth Boulden ; unmarried.
Educ. : Dane Hill House, Margate ; Corpus
Christi College, Cambridge (Mawson Scholar).
Manners Scholar and Prizeman in Divinity,
1870 ; Prizeman in Greek Testament, Hebrew,
and English Literature, 1871 ; Deacon, 1872 ;
Priest, 1873 ; Headmaster of Dane Hill House
School, Margate, and Hon. Curate of Holy
Trinity, Margate, 1872-88 ; Curate of St. Paul's,
Cliftonville, Margate, 1888-90. *Address :* Christ
Church Vicarage, Erith, Kent. *T.A. :* Boulden,
Erith.   (*Died 10 Feb. 1920.*)

BOULGER, Demetrius Charles; Cheva-
lier of the Order of Leopold II. ; *b.* 14 July 1853.
Educ. : Kensington Grammar School ; and
private tuition. Has contributed to all the
leading journals on questions connected with
our Indian Empire, China, Egypt, and Turkey
since 1876 ; has also closely studied military
questions, especially those connected with the
French frontiers and the position of Belgium ;
founded, in conjunction with Sir Lepel Griffin,
the Asiatic Quarterly Review, 1885, and edited
it during the first four and a half years of its
existence. *Publications :* Life of Yakoob Beg of
Kashgar, 1878 ; England and Russia in Central
Asia ; Central Asian Portraits ; The History of
China ; General Gordon's Letters from the
Crimea ; Armies of the Native States of India ;
Central Asian Questions; Lord William Ben-
tinck ; Short History of China ; Life of Gordon ;
Story of India ; Life of Sir Stamford Raffles,
1897 ; The Congo State, 1898 ; The Belgians at
Waterloo ; India in the 19th Century, 1901 ;
History of Belgium, Part I., 1902, Part II.,
1909 ; Belgian Life in Town and Country, 1904 ;
The Life of Sir Haliday Macartney, 1908 ; Bel-
gium of the Belgians, 1911 ; The Battle of the
Boyne and the Formation of the Irish Brigade,
1912 ; Holland of the Dutch, 1913 ; England's
Arch-Enemy, 1914 ; Reign of Leopold II., 1925.
Recreation : travelling. *Address :* 12 Blooms-
bury Square, W.C.1.   (*Died 15 Dec. 1928.*)

**BOULGER, Dorothy Henrietta (Theo.
Gift),** novelist ; 2nd *d.* of Thomas Havers of
Thelton Hall, Norfolk, and Ellen, *d.* of late
Rogers Ruding ; *b.* 30 May 1847 ; *m.* 1879,
Professor George S. Boulger (*d.* 1922). *Educ. :*
home. Went to the Falkland Islands, 1854,
her father having received the appointment of
Colonial Manager ; removed to Uruguay, 1861,
and resided in Monte Video, till her father's
death in 1870 brought her and her brothers and
sisters to England ; began to publish, 1871, in
Once a Week, and Cassell's (London), and Galaxy
(New York) ; worked for ten years on All the
Year Round under Charles Dickens, Jun., and for
two on Cassell's under G. Manville Fenn. *Publications:* True to her Trust ; Pretty Miss Bellew ;
Maid Ellice ; A Matter-of-Fact Girl ; Visited on
the Children ; Victims; Lil Lorimer ; An Innocent
Maiden ; A Garden of Girls ; Not for the Night-
time ; Dishonoured ; Wrecked at the Outset ;
An Island Princess ; Women who Work ; Cape
Town Dicky ; The Little Colonists ; Fairy Tales
from the Far East ; The Case of a Man with His
Wife, etc. *Address :* 12 Lancaster Park, Richmond, Surrey.   (*Died 22 July 1923.*)

BOULGER, George Simonds, F.L.S.,
F.G.S., F.R.H.S. ; Vice - President, Selborne
Society, Essex Field Club, South - Eastern
Union of Scientific Societies, etc. ; Lecturer
on Botany and Geology, City of London College,
since 1884 ; Imperial Institute, 1917 ; *b.* Blech-
ingley, Surrey, 5 March 1853 ; *s.* of Edward
Boulger, M.D. ; *m.* Dorothy. *Educ. :*
Wellington and Epsom Colleges ; Middle
Temple. Professor of Natural History, Royal
Agricultural College, Cirencester, 1876 ; Hon.
Professor, 1906. *Publications :* Familiar Trees,
1886-89 : 2nd. ed. 1906 - 7 ; The Uses of Plants,

1889 ; Biographical Index of British and Irish Botanists, with J. Britten, 1893 ; The·Country Month by Month, with J. A. Owen, 1894-95 ; 5th ed. 1914 ; Elementary Geology, 1896 ; Flowers of the Field, 1900 ; 33rd ed. 1911 ; Wood, 1902 ; 2nd ed. 1908 ; Botany, 1912 ; Plant-geography, 1912 ; British Flowering Plants, with Mrs. Henry Perrin, 4 vols., 1914. *Recreation :* ecclesiology. *Address :* 12 Lancaster Park, Richmond, Surrey. (*Died 4 May 1922.*)

BOULTER, Stanley Carr, J.P. for Surrey, Chairman of Law Debenture Corporation, Ltd., and Director of other important financial companies ; Barrister-at-Law ; formerly editor of the Times Law Reports ; contested (U.) Spen Valley Division, West Riding of Yorks, 1886 ; four times Unionist candidate for London County Council ; *b.* 29 May 1852 ; *s.* of late John Boulter ; *m.* 1st, Edith, *d.* of James Anderson ; 2nd, Helen (*d.* 1913), widow of Richard D'Oyly Carte ; three *s.* four *d. Educ. :* Cambridge University. *Address:* 3 Essex Court, Temple, E.C. *Clubs:* Oxford and Cambridge, City of London.
 (*Died 5 Jan. 1917.*)

BOULTON, Major Charles Percy, D.S.O. 1902 ; Member (' Lloyds ; *b.* 1 Sept. 1867 ; *s.* of Charles G. Boulton, J.P. *Educ. :* Haileybury ; Magdalen College, Oxford. B.A. 1890. Gazetted to 4th Bedfordshire Militia, 1888 ; served South African War, 1900-1902 ; commanded Regiment from Nov. 1900 to June 1902 ; Camp Commandant, Mafeking ; operations in Transvaal west of Pretoria to Sept. 1900 ; operations in Cape Colony south of Orange River, 1900 ; operations in Cape Colony north of Orange River ; operations in the Transvaal and Orange River Colony, Sept. 1901 to April 1902 ; temporarily Commandant Bloemhof sub-district ; operations in Cape Colony, Dec. 1900 to Sept. 1901 (despatches, Queen's Medal with three clasps, King's Medal with two clasps). *Recreations :* shooting, fishing, golf. *Address :* Th Cottage, Stanmore. *Clubs :* Junior United Service, Constitutional. (*Died 24 Feb. 1916.*)

BOULTON, Sir Samuel Bagster, 1st Bart., *cr.* 1905 ; Knight of Grace of Order of St. John of Jerusalem in England ; F.R.G.S., A.Inst.C.E. ; Lord of the Manor of Totteridge ; J.P. Hertfordshire, Middlesex, and borough of West Ham ; Chairman of the Barnet Bench ; D.L. Hertfordshire ; *b.* 12 July 1830 ; *m.* 1855, Sophia Louisa (*d.* 1900), *d.* of Thomas Cooper ; two *s.* five *d.* Chairman of Burt, Boulton and Haywood, Ltd., of London, Paris, Riga, Selzaette (Belgium), and Bilbao ; in conjunction with late H. P. Burt established this firm more than fifty years ago ; Chairman of the Dominion Tar and Chemical Company, Ltd., and of the British Australian Timber Company, Ltd. ; has been active in promoting the application of scientific methods to chemical and other industries, and has been a contributor to scientific literature in that connection ; received the Telford Medal of the Institution of Civil Engineers, 1884; Chairman of London Labour Conciliation and Arbitration Board 1889-1913 ; he was instrumental in its foundation in 1889, and has, *inter alia,* presided at settlement of more than 50 cases of labour disputes ; member of Tariff Commission ; in 1898-99 he successfully conducted, on behalf of the London Chamber of Commerce and under the auspices of the British Foreign Office, a series of negotiations with the French Customs Administration with respect to grievances of British importers ; a member of the Council of the London Chamber of Commerce ; Vice-President, 1893-98 ; President of the West Ham Chamber of Commerce, 1893-1902 ; president Federation of Working Men's Social Clubs for two periods of service. *Publications :* The Russian Empire, its Origin and Development ; a contributor to periodical literature, and has written numerous pamphlets, and given lectures on social and economic subjects. *Heir :* s. Harold Edwin. *Address :* Copped Hall, Totteridge, Herts. *T. :* Barnet 142 ; 64 Cannon Street, E.C. *Clubs :* Carlton, Bath, Royal Societies, British Empire. *T.A. :* Boultridge, London. (*Died 27 April 1918.*)

BOURCHIER, Arthur, M.A.; Actor-Manager ; *b.* Speen, Berkshire, 22 June 1864 ; *o. s.* of Capt. Charles John Bourchier, late 8th Hussars ; *m.* 1918, Kyrle Bellew. *Educ. :* Eton ; Christ Church, Oxford. Obtained permission and co-operation of late Professor Jowett—then Vice-Chancellor—to found University Dramatic Society and build theatre at Oxford, where he played Shylock, Hotspur, Falstaff, Brutus, Feste, and Thanatos (in Alcestis) ; member of the Old Stagers and Windsor Strollers ; first professional appearance at Wolverhampton, as Jaques in As You Like It, Sep. 1889 ; played Joseph Surface and Charles Courtly with Charles Wyndham ; joined late Augustus Daly as leading man ; joined Mr. Wyndham in partnership at the Criterion, where they produced His Excellency the Governor, Lady Huntworth's Experiment, The Noble Lord, and Mamma; also at Garrick, The Wedding Guest, The Man who Stole the Castle, and Shockheaded Peter; a revival of Peril, Iris, Pilkerton's Peerage; The Bishop's Move ; My Lady Virtue, Water Babies, Whitewashing Julia, The Golden Silence, The Cricket on the Hearth, The Arm of the Law, The Fairy's Dilemma, A Lesson in Harmony, The Walls of Jericho, Shylock, and The Fascinating Mr. Vanderveldt, a Lancashire Lout in the Third Time of Asking ; the Old Costermonger in Down our Alley, Macbeth, Mr. Sheridan, Father Daniel in The Duel ; and the title-part in Simple Simon, Her Father, John Glayde's Honour, 1908 ; The Outsider, Samson, 1909 ; Making a Gentleman ; The Knife ; The Tenth Man ; Parasites ; Glass Houses ; also King Henry VIII., Brutus, Bottom, Sir Toby Belch, and Ford, 1910-11 ; The Firescreen, Proper Peter, Find the Woman, Trust the People, The Greatest Wish, Crœsus, The Double Mystery, The Green Flag, Mrs. Pretty and the Premier, Stand and Deliver, The Fourth of August, The Sacrament of Judas, Pistols for Two, created Old Bill in the Bairns-father war play, The Better 'Ole, and Stillbottle, the Broker's Man in Tilly of Bloomsbury ; took over long lease of Strand Theatre in 1919, produced The Crimson Alibi, Tiger. Tiger !, At the Villa Rose, The Storm, the Safety Match, and created Long John Silver in James Bernard Fagan's adaptation of Robert Louis Stevenson's Treasure Island. *Publications :* adapter Femmes qui pleurent ; Jean-Marie ; Der Rabenvater ; Monsieur le Directeur (The Chili Widow) ; Mr. Richards ; The Cricket on the Hearth ; La Robe Rouge (The Arm of the Law) ; Down our Alley (Crainquebille) ; The Duel. *Recreations:* driving, golf, tennis, motoring. *Address:* 2 King's Gardens, Hove. *Clubs:* White's, St. James's, Garrick, Beefsteak, Lord's, I Zingari.
 (*Died 14 Sept. 1927.*)

BOURCHIER, James David, M.A., F.R.G.S. ; 4th *s.* of late John Bourchier, J.P. of Bagotstown, Co. Limerick, and Maidenhall, Co. Cork. *Educ. :* Cambridge (Scholar of King's College, and 1st class Classical Tripos) ; previously Scholar and Classical Gold Medallist of Trinity College, Dublin. Was for some years Assistant Master at Eton ; in 1888 acted as special correspondent of the Times in Roumania and Bulgaria, and has subsequently represented that journal in South-Eastern Europe ; in 1895 investigated the atrocities at Dospat in Macedonia, and prepared a report for the British Government ; in 1896 received the thanks of the Cretan Assembly for his services in promoting the arrangement with Turkey in that year ; in 1898 accompanied the Emperor William's pil-
111

BOURCARD, Gustave (Amaury René). See page xvi.

grimage to Jerusalem; 1911-12 played an important part in the foundation of the Balkan League; is Grand Officer of the Order of Prince Danilo of Montenegro and Commander of the Orders of the Saviour of Greece, Crown of Roumania, and Officer of the Order of St. Alexander of Bulgaria. *Publications:* numerous contributions to the Fortnightly and other reviews, and the articles Athens, Albania, Bulgaria, Crete, Greece, Macedonia, Montenegro, etc., in the last edition of the Encyclopædia Britannica. *Recreations:* most outdoor sports and games, music, chess. *Address:* La Rive, Castlecomer, Co. Kilkenny. *Clubs:* Athenæum, St. James's, New University; Athenian, Athens; Union, Sofia.

(*Died 30 Dec. 1920.*)

BOURCHIER, Very Rev. William Chadwick, M.A., Dean of Cashel, since 1916; 5th *s.* of late John Bourchier, J.P., of Bagotstown, Co. Limerick; *m.* 1889, Katharine Christian, *y. d.* of Cathcart Thomson, J.P., Nova Scotia, and *g.d.* of Hon. Joseph Howe, Lt.-Governor of Nova Scotia. *Educ.:* Portora Royal School, Enniskillen; Trinity College, Dublin; Scholar and Silver Medallist in classics. Curate of Wellingborough, 1878; Domestic Chaplain to the Marquess Camden at Bayham Abbey, 1879; Curate of S. Mary the Virgin, Dover, 1883; Chaplain, R.N. 1885-1909; Chaplain of the R.N. Dockyards of Sheerness and Chatham; Rector of Aney, Co. Limerick, 1919. *Address:* The Deanery, Cashel, Co. Tipperary. (*Died 24 June 1924.*)

BOURDILLON, Francis William, M.A.; *b.* 22 Mar. 1852; *s.* of late Rev. F. Bourdillon (author of *Bedside Readings,* etc.); *m.* 1882; Agnes, *y. d.* of late R. Watson Smyth, J.P. of Wadhurst, Sussex; two *s.* one *d.* *Educ.:* Haileybury, under Dr. A. G. Butler and the late Dr. E. H. Bradby; Worcester College, Oxford (Scholar). From 1876 to 1879 resident tutor to the two sons of Their R.H.'s Prince and Princess Christian at Cumberland Lodge; then for some years took private pupils for the universities, at Eastbourne. *Publications:* Among the Flowers and other Poems, 1878; Aucassin and Nicolette (edited and translated), 1887; Ailes d'Alouette, 1890; A Lost God, 1891; Sursum Corda, 1893; Nephelé, 1896; Minuscula, 1897; Through the Gateway, 1902; early editions of the Roman de la Rose, 1906; Preludes and Romances, 1908, etc. *Address:* Buddington, near Midhurst, Sussex. *Clubs:* Athenæum, Alpine. (*Died 13 Jan. 1921.*)

BOURGEOIS, Léon Victor Auguste, President of the Senate, 1920; Délégué de la France au Conseil de la Société des Nations; Ministre d'Etat, 1915; Nobel Peace Prize, 1920; *b.* Paris, 29 May 1851. *Educ.:* L'Institution Massin; Lycée Charlemagne. Faculté de Droit de Paris; Docteur en Droit; Secrétaire de la Conférence des Avocats; Secrétaire Général du département de la Marne, 1877; Sous-Préfet de Reims, 1880; Préfet du Tarn, 1882; Secrétaire Général de la Préfecture de la Seine, 1883; Préfet de la Haute-Garonne, 1885; Directeur des Affaires Communales et Départementales au Ministère de l'Intérieur, 1886; Préfet de Police, 1887; élu Député de la Marne, 1888; Sous-Secrétaire d'Etat au Ministère de l'Intérieur, 1888-89; Ministre de l'Instruction Publique, 1890-92; Ministre de la Justice, 1892-93; Président du Conseil, Ministre de l'Intérieur, 1895-96; Ministre des Affaires Etrangères, 1896; Ministre de l'Instruction Publique, 1898, Premier Délégué de la France à la Conférence de La Haye, 1899; Président de la Chambre des Députés, 1902-3; Membre de la Cour permanente d'arbitrage de La Haye; réélu Député en 1889, 1893, 1898 et en 1902; élu Sénateur, 1905 et 1906; Ministre des Affaires Etrangères, 1906; Premier Délégué de la France à la Conférence de la Haye, 1907;

Ministre du Travail et de la Prévoyance sociale 1912-13, 1917; Président de la Société d'Education sociale; Président de l'Alliance d'Hygiène sociale. *Publications:* Solidarité, 1894; Education de la Démocratie, 1897; Philosophie de la Solidarité, 1902; La Déclaration des Droits, 1903; Pour la Société des Nations, 1910; La Politique de la Prévoyance Sociale, 1914; Le Pacte de 1919 et la Société des Nations, 1920; Le Traité de Versailles, 1920. *Address:* Paris, 3 rue Palatine VIe; et au Palais du Petit Luxembourg. (*Died 29 Sept. 1925.*)

BOURKE, Hon. Algernon Henry, *b.* 31 Dec. 1854; *b.* and *heir-pres.* of 7th Earl of Mayo; *m.* 1887, Gwendoline, *d.* of Hans Sloane Stanley, Paultons, Southampton; one *d.* Formerly Member of Stock Exchange *Address:* 7 Church Row, Fulham, S.W.

(*Died 7 April 1922.*)

BOURKE, Lt.-Col. Henry Beresford, D.S.O. 1894; 3rd Batt. West India Regt., retired; now serving as Draft Conducting Officer; *b.* 12 June 1855; *s.* of Rev. John Bourke, *g. s.* of 3rd Earl of Mayo. *Educ.:* Sherborne School. Entered Army, 1878; served West Coast Africa, 1892; Jambaba Expedition, capture of Jambi (medal and clasp); Sofa Expedition, 1893-94 (despatches, D.S.O., clasp); Sierra Leone Rebellion, 1898-99 (clasp). *Club:* United Service.

(*Died 1 Nov. 1921.*)

BOURKE, Hon. Terence Theobald, O.B.E.; Consul Bizerta since 1917; *b.* 2 April 1865; *b.* and *heir-pres.* of 7th Earl of Mayo; *m.* 1896, Eveline Constance (*d.* 1917), *d.* of late Col. T. W. Haines of Haskerton Manor, Suffolk; two *d.* *Educ.:* Eton. Was Consular Agent at Bizerta, 1891; Vice-Consul, 1898; acted as Representative of the Ministry of Shipping at Bizerta during the war; Director of London and Greenwich Railway. *Address:* H.B.M. Consulate, Bizerta; Pekes, Hellingly, Sussex. *Clubs:* Carlton, White's, Pratt's.

(*Died 13 May 1923.*)

BOURNE, Rev. Charles William, M.A.; Rector of Staplehurst, Kent, 1913-20; Fellow of King's College, London, and Member of Council; Fellow of Physical Society; *b.* Atherstone, 2 June 1846; *m.* Ada, *d.* of the late J. M'Minn, 1875. *Educ.:* Atherstone Grammar School; St. John's Coll., Camb. (Exhibitioner and Foundation Scholar); 26th Wrangler and 2nd class in Classics in 1868. Assist. Master Marlborough College, 1868-74; Headmaster Bedford County School, 1875-80; Headmaster Inverness Coll., 1881-89; ordained Deacon by Bishop of Rochester, 1898; Priest, 1899; Headmaster of King's College School, 1889-1906; Rector of Frating, 1906-13; Rural Dean of West Charing, 1919. *Publications:* Key to Tod-hunter's Conic Sections, and numerous contributions to educational periodicals. *Address:* 15 Ridgway Place, Wimbledon. (*Died 10 Dec. 1927.*)

BOURNE, Rev. George Hugh, D.C.L., Canon and Treasurer of Salisbury. *Address:* The College, Salisbury. (*Died 1 Dec. 1925.*)

BOURNS, Newcome Whitelaw; anæsthetist, retired; *b.* Hatley, Carrick-on-Shannon, Ireland. *Educ.:* private tutor. After hospital career went into general practice. *Publications:* papers on medical subjects in Lancet and Medical Annual. *Recreations:* shooting, fishing, golf. *Address:* Churchfield, Wincanton, Somerset. (*Died 2 Oct. 1927.*)

BOUTROUX, Emile, membre de l'Institut de France, 1898, et de l'Académie française, 1912; Prof. Univ. Paris depuis 1888; Direct. Fondation Thiers depuis 1902; *b.* Montrouge (Seine), 28 July 1845; *s.* of Louis Adrien Boutroux and Suzanne Hortense Blanchard; *m.* Aline Catherine Eugénie, *d.* of Léon Poincaré, Prof. Fac. de Médecine, Nancy; one *s.* two *d.* *Educ.:* Paris, Lycée Henri IV, Ecole Normale supre.; étudiant à l'Université de Heidelberg, 1869-70; Docteur ès Lettres, 1874; Prof. de

Philosophie Univers. de Montpellier, 1874; Nancy, 1876; maitre de Conférences à l'Ecole normale sup^re., 1877; R. Instituto Lombardo di Scienze e Lettere, Milano; Institut géné-vois; R. Accademia dei Lincei, Roma; British Academy; National Education Association, U.S.A.; Académie Royal de Danemark; Académie hongroise, Budapest; Accademia delle Scienze morali et politiche, Napoli; Académie des sciences de Pétrograd. *Publications:* De la contingence des lois de la nature, 1874; Trad. franç. de la 1re partie de Die Philos. der Griechen v. Ed. Zeller, 1877-82; Leibniz, La Monado-logie, 1880; De l'idée de loi naturelle dans la sc. et dans la philos., 1895; Questions de morale et d'éducation, 1895; Du devoir militaire, in L'Armée à travers les âges, 1899; Pascal, 1900 (English 1902); Etudes d'histoire de la philosophie, 1901 (English, 1912); Science et religion dans la philosophie contemporaine, 1908 (English, 1909); William James, 1911 (English, 1912); The Beyond that is Within, 1912; Philosophy and War, 1916. *Address:* Paris, XVI., rond-point Bugeaud 5. *T.:* Passy 58-82.
(Died 22 Nov. 1921.)

BOVILL, Charles Harry, 2nd Lieut. Cold-stream Guards, 1916; author; *b.* Coonoor, India, 1878; *o. s.* of Major Charles Edward Bovill, Royal Inniskilling Fusiliers, and Ellen Marie Lang; *m.* 1907, Ethel Rachel, *d.* of Edwin Kay; two *s.* *Educ.:* Bedford Grammar School. Was in the Civil Service, 1899-1912; author of Empire Revues—Everybody's Doing It (with George Grossmith), All the Winners, The Gay Lothario, Nuts and Wine; of the Alhambra Revues—5064 Gerrard, and Now's the Time (with C. G. Lennox); of the London Pavilion Revues—Honi Soit and Pick-a-dilly; part-author of Mr. Manhattan and Half-Past Eight, and of Drury Lane Pantomime, The Sleeping Beauty. *Publications:* The Spur of Love; numerous short stories in The Strand, The Grand, Pearson's, The London, and other magazines. *Address:* 94 Prince of Wales Mansions, S.W.; The Knowle, Barcombe, Sussex. *T.:* Battersea 1267.
(Died 21 Mar. 1918.)

BOWATER, Sir Frederick William, K.B.E., *cr.* 1920; Paper-maker; *s.* of late William Vansittart Bowater of Bury Hall, Enfield, Middlesex; *b.* 8 June 1867; *m.* 1890, Alice Emily, *d.* of Joseph Sharp, Bognor, Sussex; one *s.* three *d.* *Educ.:* Privately. *Recreation:* Golf. *Address:* 181 Queen's Gate, S.W.7; Copley Dene, Walton Heath, Surrey. *T.:* Kensington 4120, Burgh Heath 368. *Clubs:* Constitutional, Ranelagh; Walton Heath Golf; Chislehurst Golf; Gullane Golf, Luffness.
(Died 16 May 1924.)

BOWDEN, Sir Frank, 1st Bt. *cr.* 1915; J.P. Nottingham; F.R.G.S.; *b.* 30 Jan. 1848; *s.* of late William Bowden, Bristol, manufacturer; *m.* 1879, Amelia Frances, *d.* of late Colonel Alexander Houston of San Francisco. *Educ.:* privately. Founder and sole owner, with only son, of The Raleigh Cycle Co., Ltd., princi-pally engaged since the commencement of the war in making munitions; founder, chairman, managing director and principal owner of Sturmey-Archer Gears, Ltd. *Publications:* Cycling for Health; articles upon his travels and other subjects. *Recreations:* oriental studies, travelling, cycling, etc. *Heir:* s. Harold [*b.* 9 July 1880; *m.* 1908; one *s.* one *d.*; 2nd, 1920, Mrs. Smythe, *d.* of late William Ker-Douglas of Dalry, Ayrshire]. *Address:* Best-wood Lodge, Arnold, Notts. *T.:* Arnold 47.
(Died 25 April 1921.)

BOWDEN, Major George Robert Harland, M.P. (U.) North-East Derbyshire, 1914-18. Major commanding 1st Herts Battery R.F.A. (T.); retired, Feb. 1914; Lt.-Col. com-manding 17th Batt. Royal Fusiliers, 1914-15; Member Institute Mechanical Engineers and Iron and Steel Institute. *Address:* 17 Victoria Street, S.W.1; *T.A.:* Harbowdeco, Vic., London. *T.:* Victoria 5076; Hazeldene, St. Albans. *Clubs:* Carlton, Junior Army and Navy.
(Died 10 Oct. 1927.)

BOWDEN, Walter, R.N.; D.S.O. 1894; Dep. Inspector-General, 1908; *b.* London, 10 June 1859; *s.* of late Wm. Bowden of Hilldrop Crescent, Camden Road, N., and Jane, *d.* of James Beer; *m.* Althea M., 2nd *d.* of James Ogilvie, J.P., The Grove, Rushbrooke, Queens-town, Ireland; two *s.* one *d.* M.R.C.S. Eng., L.R.C.P. Lond. Entered Royal Naval Medical Service, 1887; Staff Surg., 1899; Fleet Surg., 1903; retired, 1908; served River Gambia, 1894 (despatches); bombardment and occupation of Gunjur, 1894 (D.S.O., general Africa Medal, Gambia Clasp). *Address:* Bantry, Kirtleton Avenue, Weymouth, Dorset. *Club:* Junior United Service. *(Died 13 Nov. 1919.)*

BOWDEN-SMITH, Admiral Sir Nathaniel, K.C.B., *cr.* 1897; *b.* Careys, Brockenhurst, Hants, 21 Jan. 1838; *s.* of Nath-aniel Bowden-Smith, Careys, Brockenhurst, and Emily Mary, *d.* of John Richard Ripley, merchant, London; *m.* 1864, Emily Cecilia, *d.* of George Glas Sandeman, Westfield, Hayling Island, Hants; three *d.* Entered R.N. 1852; Commander, 1866; Capt. 1872; Rear-Admiral 1888; Vice-Admiral, 1894; Admiral, 1899; served in Burmah war (medal and Pegu clasp), 1852-58; Baltic, during the Russian War (medal), 1854-1855; China war, 1856-59; boat actions in Escape Creek, and at Fatshan; and at capture of the Ta Ku forts (medal, Fatshan and Ta Ku clasps), severely wounded June 1859; has Royal Humane Society's medal for saving life at sea; served as Flag-Capt. successively in a detached squad-ron and on the Mediterranean and East Indian Stations; Sen. Officer, S.E. Coast of America, and commanded the "Britannia," 1883-86; one of the British representatives at the Inter-national Maritime Conference, Washington, 1889; Commander-in-Chief, Australian Station, 1892-1895; at the Nore, 1899-1900. *Address:* 16 Queen's Gate Terrace, S.W.7. *T.:* Kensington 6111. *Clubs:* United Service, Ranelagh.
(Died 28 April 1921.)

BOWDLER, Colonel Cyril William Bowdler, C.B. 1902; *b.* 28 Sept. 1839; late 8th Hussars. Entered army, 1864; Captain, 1876; Major, 1881; Lt.-Col. 1888; Col. 1887; retired, 1891; Knight of Justice and Hon. Commander Order St. John of Jerusalem. *Club:* Army and Navy. *(Died 7 Nov. 1918.)*

BOWELL, Hon. Sir Mackenzie, K.C.M.G.; *cr.* 1895; Premier of Canadian Par-liament 1894-95; *b.* Rickinghall, Suffolk, 27 Dec. 1823; *m.* 1847, Harriet (d. 1884), *e. d.* of late J. G. Moore. Entered Canadian Parliament, 1867; Minister of Customs, 1878-91; Minister of De-fence, 1891; of Trade and Commerce, 1892-94; President of Privy Council, 1895-96; called to the Senate, 1892. *Address:* Belleville, Ont., Canada. *Clubs:* Rideau, Ottawa; Albany, Toronto.
(Died 11 Dec. 1917.)

BOWEN, Sir Albert, 1st Bt., *cr.* 1921, of Colworth, Beds.; Chairman, Buenos Aires Great Southern Railway Ltd.,; Chairman, Wilson Sons and Co. Ltd., etc.; *b.* Hanley, Staff., 1 Nov. 1858; *e. s.* of Edward Bowen of Hanley; *m.* 1884, Alice Anita, *d.* of Frederick Crowther of Buenos Aires; two *s.* three *d.* *Educ.:* Upper Canada College, Toronto. Merchant in Buenos Aires, 1879-1895; Director of public companies in London since 1896; High Sheriff of Bedford-shire, 1910-11; during the war served on many government committees. *Recreations:* racing, fishing, etc. *Heir: s.* Major Edward C. Bowen, M.C., Inniskilling Dragoons. *Address:* 5 Queen's Gate Place, S.W.7.; Colworth, Beds.; Eskadale, Beauly, Scotland. *T.A.:* Bowenical, London. *T.:* Western 32, Sharnbrook 3, Beauly 13. *M.:* BM 100. *Club:* Junior Carlton.
(Died 19 Sept. 1924.)

113

BOVELL, John Redman. See page xvi.

BOWEN, Lt.-Col. Alfred John Hamilton, D.S.O. 1915; 2nd Batt. the Monmouthshire Regiment, Territorial Force; solicitor; *e. s.* of Alfred E. Bowen, Usk; *b.* 15 Dec. 1885; *m.* 1916, Jean Gertrude, *d.* of Henry Wilton, Winnipeg. *Educ.*: Marlborough College; Merton College, Oxford. Served European War, 1914-16 (D.S.O.).
(*Died 2 Mar. 1917.*)

BOWEN, Hon. Sir Chas. Christopher, Kt., *cr.* 1910; K.C.M.G., *cr.* 1914; M.L.C., F.R.G.S.; late Speaker of Legislative Council, New Zealand; Vice-Chancellor of Senate of New Zealand University; *b.* 29 Aug. 1830; *s.* of Charles Bowen, 3rd *s.* of Christopher Bowen, of Milford, Co. Mayo, Ireland; *m.* 1861, Georgina Elizabeth, *d.* of Rev. David Markham, Canon of Windsor; four *s.* three *d. Educ.*: Rugby; Camb. Left Cambridge after first year to join founders of Canterbury, New Zealand, 1850; Private Secretary to Mr. Godley, agent of Canterbury Association, 1851-52; Provincial Treasurer and Member Provincial Government, 1854-59; went to England, 1859; returned, 1862; Resident Magistrate, Christchurch, 1864-74; Member House of Representatives, 1874; Minister of Justice and Education, 1875-77; carried National Education Act, 1877; Member of Royal Commission on Federation, 1901. *Publications:* Visit to Peru in Notes of Travel, 1860; occasional articles in periodicals. *Address:* Middleton Grange, Upper Riccarton, Christchurch, New Zealand. (*Died 14 Dec. 1917.*)

BOWER, George Spencer, K.C. 1903; Barrister-at-law (Midland Circuit); *b.* 12 Oct. 1854; *s.* of late George Bower, St. Neots, Huntingdonshire; *m.* 1885, Minnie Blanche, *d.* of late Sir Charles Wyndham. *Educ.*: Winchester College (Scholar), 1866-73; Senior Prefect, 1872-73; Goddard Scholar, 1872; Queen's Gold and Silver Medals, 1873; New College, Oxford (Scholar). First Class Honours Moderations, 1874; First Class Honours Greats, 1877; Gaisford (Greek Prose), 1876; Chancellor's (English Essay), 1878; called to Bar, 1880; Bencher of the Inner Temple, 1912. *Publications:* Hartley and James Mill, 1880; A Study of the Prologue and Epilogue in English Literature from Shakespeare to Dryden, 1884; A Code of the Law of Actionable Defamation, 1909; 2nd edition, 1923; The Law of Actionable Misrepresentation, 1911; 2nd edition, 1927; The Law of Actionable Non-Disclosure, and other Breaches of Duty in Relations of Confidence and Influence, 1914; The Law of Estoppel by Representation, 1923; The Doctrine of Res Judicata, 1924. *Address:* 45 Finchley Road, N.W.8; *T.*: Primrose Hill 3534; 2 Hare Court, Temple, E.C.4; *T.*: Central 1777. (*Died 4 Sept. 1928.*)

BOWERLEY, Amelia M., A.R.E. Member Ridley Art Club; Royal Water Colour Art Club; Women's Guild of Arts; *b.* London. *Educ.*: Notting Hill High School and abroad. Studied at South Kensington and Slade School of Art and at Munich and Italy; etching under Sir Frank Short; anatomy at Women's School of Medicine, London. *Publications:* Black and white and other drawings for numerous books and magazines, including the Sphere, Graphic, Windsor Magazine, the Yellow Book; numerous etchings, including A Boy of Teneriffe, Spanish Children, Goblin Market, Orpheus, Pan, The Sphinx; exhibited pictures at Royal Academy; Paris Salon; International Exhibs., Franco-British, St. Louis and Christ Church, etc.; Exhibitions at Dowdeswell Gallery—When the World was Young. *Address:* 59 Craven Park, N.W. *Club:* Ladies' University.
(*Died 5 Feb. 1916.*)

BOWERS, Rt. Rev. John Phillips Allcot, Archdeacon of Lynn since 1903; Canon Residentiary of Norwich, 1910; select Preacher before the University of Cambridge, 1905 and 1911; *b.* 15 May 1854; *e. s.* of J.

Bowers of Glenluie, Southampton; *m.* Mary, *e. d.* of late J. Beaumont, of The Lawn, Coggeshall, and 33 Chancery Lane, London, 1879; one *s.* one *d. Educ.*: Magdalen School; St. John's Coll., Camb. (M.A., D.D. Hon. Causa, 1903). Canon Residentiary and Canon Missioner of the Diocese of Gloucester, 1885-1902; Archdeacon of Gloucester, 1902-1903; examining and domestic chaplain to Bishop of Gloucester, 1882-1903; Rector of North Creake, 1903-10; Provincial Grand Master of Norfolk, 1920; Past Grand Chaplain of England, 1898; Suffragan Bishop of Thetford, 1903-26. *Address:* The Close, Norwich. *T.*: Norwich 969. *Club:* Norfolk County, Norwich. (*Died 6 Jan. 1926.*)

BOWERS, Ven. Percy Harris, Archdeacon of Loughborough since 1921; Warden of the Mission Clergy of the Diocese of Peterborough; *b.* 1856; *yr. s.* of James Bowers, Warren Hall, Flintshire; *m.* Annie, *d.* of A. E. Lloyd, Worsley, Lancashire; one *s.* three *d. Educ.*: The Forest School; St. John's, Cambridge. *Address:* The Rectory, Market Bosworth, Nuneaton. (*Died 15 Nov. 1922.*)

BOWLES, Thomas Gibson; *b.* 1844; *m.* 1876, Jessica (*d.* 1887), *d.* of General Evans Gordon; two *s.* two *d. Educ.*: King's College, London. Was in Inland Revenue Office; M.P. (C.) King's Lynn, 1892-1906; and (L.) 1910; contested same division, 1910; Southern Division, Leicester, 1916. *Publications:* The Defence of Paris; Maritime Warfare, 1878; Flotsam and Jetsam, 1882; Log of the Nereid, 1889; The Declaration of Paris of 1856, 1900; Sea Law and Sea Power, 1910, etc. *Address:* 25 Lowndes Square, S.W.1. *T.*: Victoria 3062. *Club:* Carlton. (*Died 12 Jan. 1922.*)

BOWLING, Paymaster-in-Chief Thomas Henry Lovelace, C.B., 1907; *b.* June 1839; *s.* of Thomas Bowling of Ramsgate; unmarried. *Educ.*: privately. Entered navy, 1855; Assistant Paymaster, 1860; Paymaster, 1866; Fleet Paymaster, 1886; Paymaster-in-Chief (retired), 1898; served China, 1857 (medal); Indian Mutiny, 1857-59 (despatches thrice, medal, promoted); Abyssinia, 1868 (medal); Secretary to various Admirals, 1869-85. *Address:* 47 Central Hill, Upper Norwood. S.E. *Club:* Royal Naval, Portsmouth. (*Died 18 Jan. 1922.*)

BOWMAN, Sir William Paget, 2nd Bt., *cr.* 1884; M.A.; *b.* 25 Sept. 1845; *S.* father 1892; *m.* Emily, *d.* of late Capt. W. Swabey, 1870; two *s.* one *d. Educ.*: Eton; Univ. Coll. Oxford. Barr. 1870. Registrar of the Sons of the Clergy and Treasurer Cholmondeley Charities. *Heir: s.* Rev. Paget Mervyn, Vicar of St. Luke, Woodside, S. Norwood [*b.* 1 Sept. 1873; *m.* 1901, Rachel Katherine, *d.* of late James Hanning of Kilcrone, Co. Cork; one *s.* one *d.*]. *Address:* Corporation House, Bloomsbury Place, W.C.; Joldwynds, Dorking. *Club:* Athenæum.
(*Died 7 Jan. 1917.*)

BOWN, Rev. George Herbert; Priest in charge of S. Albar's, Charles Street, Oxford, since July 1918; *b.* 11 Nov. 1871; *s.* of George Bown, Carlton Villa, Bromsgrove. *Educ.*: Bromsgrove School; Trinity College and S. Stephen's House, Oxford. Deacon, 1895; Priest, 1896; Assistant Curate at S. Andrew's, Taunton, 1895-1903; Principal of S. Stephen's House, Oxford, 1903-17; Assistant Priest at S. Barnabas', Oxford, 1917-18. *Address:* S. Albar's Presbytery, Percy Street, Oxford.
(*Died 21 Nov. 1918.*)

BOWRING, Sir William Benjamin, 1st Bt.; *cr.* 1907; Shipowner; *b.* 13 Feb. 1837; *e. s.* of C. T. Bowring of Liverpool; *m.* 1863, Isabel M'Lean, *d.* of E. L. Jarves, St. John's, Newfoundland; no *c. Heir:* none. Lord Mayor, Liverpool, 1893-94; presented Roby Hall Estate to the City. *Address:* Beechwood, Aigburth, Liverpool.
(*Died 20 Oct. 1916.*)

BOWRON, Sir Edward, Kt., *cr.* 1913; Chairman of Joseph Travers and Sons, Ltd.;

114

BOWEN, Rev. David. See page xvii.

Director Société Privilégiée, Athens b. 5 Sep. 1857 ; s. of John Bowron, Cotherstone; m. 1887, Maude Mary, d. of W. F. Morgan, Sevenoaks. Address: Bramley Oaks, Bramley Hill, Croydon. T.: Croydon 1591. Club: Reform.
(Died 10 Dec. 1923.)

BOWSER, Rev. Sidney W., B.A. ; b. Old Mansion House, Cheapside, London, 2 Oct. 1853 ; s. of late Mr. Alfred T. Bowser, a well-known layman in the Baptist denomination; m. 1883, Mary Edwards, of Hackney ; one s. two d. Educ.: Priory House School, Clapton ; University College, London (prizes and honours, and President of the Debating Society); Regent's Park College. Assistant minister to late Rev. F. Bosworth, M.A., at South Street Baptist Church, Exeter, 1879-80 ; Minister of Grange Road Baptist Church, Birkenhead, 1881-99 ; Principal Midland Baptist Coll., Nottingham, 1899-1913; for many years honorary secretary Lancashire and Cheshire Association of Baptist Churches ; Moderator, 1894 ; President of Birkenhead Free Church Council,1898 ; Founder of Liverpool Guild of Bible Study ; for many years President Birkenhead Working Men's Total Abstinence Society ; President of the Nottingham Peace and Arbitration Society, 1905-13. President of the East Midland Baptist Association, 1909-10 ; Minister of the Baptist Church, Long Buckby, 1914-19 ; Lecturer at the Loughborough College (Literary Department) since 1920. Publications: occasional Addresses, etc. Address: 107 Ashby Road, Loughborough. Club: University of London (Died 19 May 1928.)

BOWSTEAD, Rev. Canon Christopher J. K.; Canon of St. Ninian's Cathedral, 1899 ; Priest in charge of Kilmaveonaig, Blair-Atholl ; resigned 1912 ; b. 1844 ; s. of John Bowstead, Vicar of Messingham, Lincolnshire, and Eliza, e. d. of John Kaye, Bishop of Lincoln. Educ.: Durham University. M.A., Theol. Exhibitioner. Ordained deacon, 1872 ; Priest, 1874 ; Curate of Grantham, 1872 ; Riseholme, 1874 ; St. Andrew's, Croydon, 1875 ; Felpham, 1882 ; Domestic Chaplain to Earl of Strathmore, 1890; Rector of Holy Trinity, Pitlochry, 1891-99. Publication: Facts and Fancies about Kilmaveonaig. Address: St. Gabriel's Bield. Elie. Fife.
(Died 11 May 1924.)

BOXALL, Sir Alleyne Alfred, 1st Bt., cr. 1919 ; b. Belle Vue Hall, Brighton, 11 Oct. 1855 ; s. of William Percival Boxall, J.P. Brighton, and Caroline, d. and co-heir of late William Money ; m. 1881, Mary Elizabeth, e. d. of J. H. Lermitte, J.P., of Knightons ; one s. Heir: s. Lt.-Col. Alleyne Percival, R.F.A. (T.D.), b. 14 Sep. 1882. Educ.: Eton ; University College, Oxford. Address: 14 Cambridge Square, W.2.
(Died 5 May 1927.)

BOYD, Charles Walter; C.M.G. 1904 ; 4th s. of Very Rev. A. K. H. Boyd, St. Andrews (d. 1899), and Margaret, d. of late Captain Kirk, 77th Regiment ; b. 11 Apr. 1869. Educ.: Fettes College, Edinburgh ; Edinburgh University for Scottish Bar. Sometime occupied in journalism ; as, under Mr. Henley on old National Observer ; and Saturday Review, from Editorship of Mr. W. H. Pollock, and subsequently ; an occasional contributor Times, Morning Post, Athenæum, Daily Chronicle, Spectator, etc. ; private secretary successively to Right Hon. George Wyndham, M.P., and Dr., now Sir Starr. Jameson, C.B. ; Political Secretary to late Right Hon. Cecil Rhodes, 1898-1902 ; Joint-Secretary Rhodes Trust, 1902 ; Secretary, 1904-8, when sent to Rhodesia on special service ; member Education Committee Victoria League; etc. Publications: George Wyndham, 1913 ; edited The Nation and the Empire, speeches and addresses of Lord Milner, 1913 ; and Mr. Chamberlain's speeches, 2 vols, 1914 ; occasional contributor reviews, etc. Address: 2 Down Street, Piccadilly, W. Clubs: St. James's, Garrick, Savile,

National, Pilgrims ; New, Edinburgh.
(Died 1 Aug. 1919.)

BOYD, Francis Darby, C.B. 1919 ; M.D., F.R.C.P.Ed. ; C.M.G. 1901 ; Professor of Clinical Medicine, University of Edinburgh ; Physician to the Royal Infirmary, Edinburgh ; Consulting Physician to the Deaconess Hospital, Edinburgh; served as Colonel A.M.S. Consultant to British Army in Egypt (despatches, C.B.); formerly Member of Board of Examiners for Entrance to the Indian Medical Service ; Lecturer on Materia Medica and Therapeutics, School of Medicine of the Royal Colleges, Edinburgh ; b. 19 Oct. 1866 ; s. of John Boyd of Edinburgh ; m. 1904, Clara Constance, e. d. of Alfred J. A. Lepper ; two d. Served as physician with Edinburgh Hospital in South Africa (despatches, C.M.G.). Address: 22 Manor Place, Edinburgh. T.: 2462. Club: University, Edinburgh. (Died 4 April 1922.)

BOYD, Rev. Francis Leith, M.A. ; Vicar of St. Paul's, Knightsbridge, S.W., since 1908; b. 1856 ; e. s. of George John Boyd, Toronto, Canada ; m. 1905, Elizabeth Archdale, o. c. of T. Hastings Harris, formerly of Ashfort, Co. Armagh, Ireland ; one d. Educ.: University College, Toronto (Classical Silver Medal) ; Gonville and Caius College, Cambridge (Scholar), 1876. B.A. 1879 ; M.A. 1884 ; Deacon, 1879 ; Priest, 1880 ; Curate of St. Peter's, Eaton Square, 1879-84 ; Vicar of Teddington, Middlesex, 1884-1908 ; Vicar of the Annunciation, St. Marylebone, 1908 ; Select Preacher at Cambridge, 1885 and 1907; Oxford, 1923 ; Golden Lecturer at St. Margaret's, Lothbury, 1911 and 1917 ; Prebendary of Ealdland in St. Paul's Cathedral, 1914. Publications: Law and Love, 1909 ; Tasks and Visions; articles in Nineteenth Century. Address: St. Paul's Vicarage, Wilton Place, S.W.1. T.: Victoria 3599. Club: Oxford and Cambridge.
(Died 13 Dec. 1927.)

BOYD, Henry, D.D. ; Principal of Hertford Coll. Oxford, since 1877 ; late Fellow ; Vice-Chancellor, 1890-94. Ellerton Essay, 1853 ; Denyer Essay, 1856-57. Address: Hertford College, Oxford. (Died 4 Mar. 1922.)

BOYD, Hon. Sir John Alexander, Kt., cr. 1899 ; K.C.M.G., cr. 1901 ; Chancellor of High Court Province of Ontario ; Governor of M'Master University ; b. Toronto, 23 April 1887 ; s. of J. Boyd, late Principal of Bay St. Acad., Toronto; m. Elizabeth, d. of David Buchan, 1863. Educ.: U.C. Coll. and Toronto Univ.; scholarship, gold medal for modern languages ; M.A. degree. Called to the Bar 1863 ; Master in Chancery ; Q.C., by Dominion patent, 1880 ; Chancellor, 1881 ; President of High Court, 1887 ; Arbitrator for Dominion Government, 1888-89 ; LL.D., hon., of Toronto Univ., 1889 ; Arbitrator for Ontario, 1893. Publication: Summary of Canadian History. Address: 119 Bloor Street, Toronto, Ontario. (Died 23 Nov. 1916.)

BOYD, Maj.-Gen. Julius Middleton, Indian Army ; b. 4 Oct. 1837 ; m. 1867, d. of Captain Blennerhassett, R.N. Entered army, 1854 ; Maj.-Gen. 1894 ; unemployed list, 1896 ; served Indian Mutiny, 1858 ; Abyssinian Expedition, 1868 (despatches, medal); Afghan War, 1879-80 (despatches, medal). Address: Upton Dene, 56 Coombe Road, Croydon.
(Died 12 Dec. 1919.)

BOYD, Ven. Robert Wallace, Archdeacon of Ardagh since 1915 ; Vicar of Kilronan since 1896. Educ.: Queen's University, Belfast; Edinburgh. 1st Class Honours Biological Science ; ordained 1887 ; Curate of Maryborough, 1887-1889 ; Templemichael, 1889-96 ; Registrar, Ardagh, 1891 ; Prebendary and Canon of St. Patrick's Cathedral, 1904. Address: Kilronan Vicarage, Keadue, Carrick-on-Shannon, Ireland.
(Died 10 Nov. 1921.)

BOYD, Rt. Hon. Sir Walter, Bt., cr. 1916 ; P.C. Ire. 1916 ; LL.D., J.P.; a Justice of the High Court of Justice in Ireland, 1897-1916; b. Dublin, 28 Jan. 1833; m. 1862, Annie, d. of M. Anderson, Dublin. Educ.: Portôra, Enniskillen; Trinity College, Dublin. Barr. Ireland, 1856; Q.C. 1877; Queen's Advocate for Ireland, 1878; Judge of Court of Bankruptcy, Ireland, 1885-97. Publication: Law and Practice of the Court of Admiralty in Ireland. Recreations: yachting, shooting, photography. Heir: e. s. Walter Herbert Boyd [barrister; b. 31 March 1867. Address: 13 Upper Mount Street, Dublin]. Address: 66 Merrion Square, Dublin; Howth House, Howth, Co. Dublin. Clubs: Kildare Street, Dublin; Royal St. George Yacht; Royal Alfred Yacht. (Died 25 June 1918.)

BOYD-CARPENTER, Henry John, e. s. of late Right Rev. William Boyd-Carpenter, Bishop of Ripon; b. 1865; m. Ethel, y. d. of Sir Francis Ley, 1st Bart.; one s. one d. Educ.: Westminster; King's College, Cambridge. Called to Bar; H.M.I. Board of Education; Chief Inspector, Ministry of Education, Egypt. Publications: various Educational reports. Recreation: Gardening. Address: Riversea, Kingswear. Clubs: Royal Societies; Royal Dart Yacht. (Died 1 June 1922.)

BOYD CARPENTER, Rt. Reverend William, K.C.V.O., cr. 1912; D.D.; Hon. Fellow of St. Catherine's College, Cambridge; Hon. D.D. Glasgow; Hon. D.C.L. Oxon.; Hon. D.C.L. Durham, and Hon. Member University College; Hon. D.D. Aberdeen; Hon. D.Litt. Leeds; LL.D. M'Gill; F.R.S.L.; Knight of the Order of the Royal Crown, Prussia; Clerk of the Closet since 1903; Sub-Dean and Canon of Westminster since 1911; Hon. Chaplain to the Forces (18th County of London); b. Liverpool, 26 March 1841; s. of Rev. Henry Carpenter, incumbent of St. Michael's, Liverpool, and Hester, d. of Archibald Boyd, Londonderry, Ireland; m. 1st, 1864, Harriet Charlotté, o. d. of Rev. J. W. Peers, of Chislehampton, Oxon.; 2nd, 1883, Annie Maude (d. 1915), d. of W. W. Gardner; four s. six d. Educ.: Royal Institution School, Liverpool; St. Cath. Coll. Camb. (Scholar). Senior Optime, 1864; Hulsean Lecturer, Cambridge, 1878; Bampton Lecturer, Oxford, 1887; Pastoral Lecturer on Theology, Cambridge, 1895; Noble Lecturer (Harvard) 1904 and 1913; Donnellan Lecturer, Dublin, 1914-15 and 1915-16. Curate of All Saints, Maidstone, 1864-66; St. Paul's, Clapham, 1866-67; Holy Trinity Lee, 1867-70; Vicar of St. James's, Holloway, 1870-79; Vicar of Christ Church, Lancaster Gate, 1879-84; Canon of Windsor, 1882-84; hon. chaplain to the Queen, 1879-83; chaplain-in-ordinary, 1883-84; Bishop of Ripon, 1884-1911. Publications: Commentary on Revelation, 1879; Thoughts on Prayer, 1871; Witness of Heart to Christ (Hulsean Lectures), 1879; Permanent Elements of Religion (Bampton Lectures), 1889; Lectures on Preaching, 1895; Christian Reunion, 1895; The Great Charter of Christ, 1895; District Visitors' Companion, 1881; My Bible, 1884; Truth in Tale, 1884; Twilight Dreams, 1894; A Popular History of the Church of England, 1900; The Religious Spirit in the Poets, 1900; The Wisdom of James the Just, 1902; Introduction to Study of the Bible, 1902; Witness to the Influence of Christ, 1905; Some Pages of my Life, 1911; The Spiritual Message of Dante, 1914; The Witness of Religious Experience, 1916; Further Pages of my Life, 1916. Recreation: has a good collection of Dante literature. Address: 6 Little Cloisters, Westminster Abbey, S.W.; Riversea, Kingswear. Clubs: Athenæum, Authors'. (Died 26 Oct 1918.)

BOYER, Hon. Arthur; b. 9 Feb. 1851; m. 1875, Ernestine, d. of P. M. Galarneau, Montreal. Educ.: St. Mary's College. M.P. (L.) Jacques Cartier, 1884-92; member of Cabinet without Portfolio, 1891-92; Senator since 1909.

116

Address: 210 Drummond Street, Montreal. Clubs: National Liberal; Forest and Stream, Montreal; Rideau, Ottawa. (Died 24 Jan. 1922.)

BOYES, Charles Edward, C.B.E. 1919; Deputy Resident Commissioner, Basutoland; b. King William's Town, 1866; s. of late Major James Fichat Boyes; m. 2nd d. of E. J. Turner, Will Brook, Natal; two s. two d. Educ.: Bishops College, Rondebosch; St. Andrew's College, Grahamstown. Joined the Basutoland Service in 1888 in which served since. Recreations: Cricket, polo, tennis, golf. Address: Maseru, Basutoland. (Died 12 July 1920.)

BOYLE, Sir Cavendish, K.C.M.G.; cr. 1897; b. 29 May 1849; y. s. of late Captain Cavendish Spencer Boyle, 72nd Highlanders; m. 1914, Louise, y. d. of late Reuben Sassoon, M.V.O. Educ.: Charterhouse. Magistrate, etc., Leeward Islands, 1879; Colonial Secretary, Bermuda, 1882-88; Gibraltar, 1888-94; Government Secy. British Guiana, 1894-1901, during which period administered the Government on several occasions, and was Chairman of the British Guiana Bank 1896-97; delegate for British Guiana and Bermuda in reciprocity negotiations with the U.S.A., 1899; Governor of Newfoundland 1901-1904; Mauritius, 1904-11; retired on a pension, 1911. C.M.G. 1888; is an Associate of the Institution of Civil Engineers. Author of Newfoundland, adopted as the National Ode of the Island, and other Poems. Address: 6 Third Avenue, Hove, Sussex. Clubs: Marlborough, Badminton, Beefsteak. (Died 17 Sept. 1916.)

BOYLE, Daniel, M.P. (N.) North Mayo, 1910-1918; J.P.; b. Kilcoo, Fermanagh, Jan. 1859; y. s. of late Donal Boyle, farmer; m. 1888, Annie (d. 1921), 2nd d. of late Patrick Gardiner, Sligo; two d. Educ.: National School. Qualified as teacher, 1877; settled in Manchester, 1877, adopting journalism as a profession; elected to Manchester City Council, 1894; Alderman, 1908-1917, then resigned; Chairman Tramways Committee, 1898-1906; member Executive Council United Irish League of Great Britain; and leader of Nationalist Party in Manchester; founded an Irish Friendly Society in Manchester, 1880. Visited U.S.A. with Mr. Redmond, autumn of 1910, on the famous "dollar" mission. (Died 1925.)

BOYLE, Commander Edward Louis Dalrymple, C.M.G. 1917; R.N. (ret.); b. 1864; m. 1st, 1889, Theodosia Isabella (d. 1910), 3rd d. of late E. D. S. Ogilvie, N.S.W.; one s. one d.; 2nd, 1912, Sybil Mary, d. of late Berkeley Paget. Served Egyptian War, 1882 (medal, bronze star); Sudan, 1884 (two clasps); Naval Attaché at Rio de Janeiro, 1914-19. Address: 40 Cranley Gardens, S.W.7. (Died 15 Dec. 1923.)

BOYLE, Colonel Lionel Richard Cavendish, C.M.G. 1918; M.V.O. 1903; b. Nov. 1851; s. of Charles Y. Boyle; m. 1883, Alice Putteney; one s. three d. Entered Royal Navy, 1865; retired, 1875; joined Honourable Artillery Company of London, 1886; retired, 1903; commanded Battalion, 1897-1903; raised and commanded 2nd Batt. H.A.C., Aug. 1914. Recreations: golf, foreign travel. Address: 6 Mulberry Walk, Chelsea, S.W.3. T.: Kens. 5786. Clubs: Army and Navy, Naval and Military. (Died 2 Jan. 1920.)

BOYLE, Vice-Adm. Hon. Robert Francis, M.V.O., R.N.; 3rd s. of 5th (and uncle and heir-pres. to 8th) Earl of Shannon and 1st wife, Lady Blanche Emma Lascelles, 3rd d. of 3rd Earl of Harewood; b. 12 Dec. 1863; m. 1899, Cerise, 2nd d. of Sir C. Champion de Crespigny, 4th Bt.; two s. two d. Entered Navy, 1877; Lieut. 1886; Commander, 1897; Captain, 1903; Vice-Adm. retired, 1919; served Egypt, 1882 (medal, Khedive's bronze star); West Africa, 1894 (wounded, despatches, medal, clasp); European War, 1915-1919. Address:

Fairthorne, Catisfield, Fareham. *T.A.:* Titchfield. *T.:* Titchfield 12. *Club:* Naval and Military. *(Died 11 Sept. 19??.)*

BOYLE, William Lewis, M.P. (U.) Mid-Norfolk since 1910; in Ministry of National Service (unpaid); *s.* of Charles John Boyle and Zacyntha, *d.* of late General Sir Lorenzo Moore; *g.s.* of late Vice-Admiral Hon. Sir Courtenay Boyle, 3rd *s.* of 7th Earl of Cork and Orrery; *b.* 27 May 1859; *m.* 1887, Charlotte Mary, *d.* of late Charles Lloyd Norman; one *s.* one *d.* *Address:* Tuddenham Lodge, Honingham, Norfolk. *Clubs:* Carlton, Constitutional.
(Died 2 Oct. 1918.)

BOYSON, Sir John Alexander, Kt., *cr.* 1914; Director of Binny & Co., Madras; *b.* 1846; *m.* 1885, Mary Josephine, *o. d.* of late Col. C. Bowen, R.E.; two *s.* two *d.* *Educ.:* Harrow. *Address:* 9 Hornton Street, W.8. *T.:* Park 2502. *(Died 15 Mar. 1926.)*

BOYTON, Sir James, Kt., *cr.* 1918; member of firm Elliott, Son and Boyton estate agents, since 1878; *b.* 1855; *m.* 1881, Emma, *d.* of Peter Middleton. Member L.C.C. 1907-10; M.P. (U.) East Marylebone, 1910-18; Fellow of the Surveyors' Institution; Fellow of the Auctioneers' and Estate Agents' Institute (President, 1905-6); J.P. County of London. *Address:* 2 Park Square West, N.W.1. *T.:* Langham 1952. *Clubs:* Carlton, Constitutional.
(Died 16 May 1926.)

BRABAZON, Major-Gen. Sir John Palmer, K.C.B., *cr.* 1911; C.B. 1893, C.V.O. 1901; *b.* 13 Feb. 1843; *s.* of late Major H. Brabazon, Brabazon Park, Co. Mayo, late 15th King's Hussars, and Eleanor Ambrosia, *d.* of late Sir Wm. Henry Palmer, Bt., Kenure Park, Co. Dublin, and Palmerstown, Co. Mayo. Served in Grenadier Guards; 10th Prince of Wales' Own Hussars; commanded 4th Queen's Own Hussars; Colonel of the 18th (Queen Mary's Own) Hussars, 1913; served in Ashanti Campaign, 1873-74; Afghan Campaign, 1878-79; 2nd Afghan Campaign as Brigade Major, Cavalry Division, 1879-80, including march Kabul to Kandahar; Soudan Campaign at Suakim, 1884 (wounded at El Teb); and the Nile Campaign for the relief of Gordon, 1884 1885; commanded 2nd Cavalry Brigade, South Africa Field Force, 1899-1900, and Imperial Yeomanry in South Africa, Feb. to Dec. 1900 (despatches, medal with five clasps); is in receipt of pension for distinguished services in the field; A.D.C. to Viceroy of India, 1878-80; A.D.C. to Queen Victoria, 1889-1901; Gentleman Usher to King Edward VII.; Chevalier (1st class) of the order of the Dannebrog (Denmark); unmarried; has a property in Co. Mayo, and another in Co. Galway. *Address:* 10 Wilton Crescent, S.W.1; Brabazon Park, Swinford, Co. Mayo; Glen Corrib, Headfort, Co. Galway. *Clubs:* Marlborough, Turf, Guards', Pratt's, Carlton. *(Died 20 Sept. 1922.)*

BRACKEN, Clio Hinton, Sculptor; *b.* Rhinebeck, N.Y.; *d.* of Howard Hinton and Lucy Bronson; *m.* 1st, 1892, James Huneker; 2nd, 1900, William Barrie Bracken, both of New York; two *s.* one *d.* Studied at Arts Students' League, N.Y. City, and with St. Gaudens and Macmonnies-Paris. France. Exhibited at Paris Salon, Academy of Design (New York), Panama P. L. Expn., San Francisco, 1915. *Principal Works:* Rubaiat Punch Bowl; portrait of Paderewski, etc. *Address:* 140 East 22nd Street, New York. *T.:* Gramercy 5441.
(Died 12 Feb. 1925.)

BRACKENBURY, Col. Henry Langton, J.P.; *o. s.* of late Major Henry Brackenbury, H.M. Bodyguard; *b.* Colchester, 26 April 1868; *m.* 1898, Florence, *d.* of late Edgar Mills, California; two *s.* three *d.* *Educ.:* Corpus Christi College, Oxford. Called to Bar, Inner Temple, 1902; M.P. (U.) Louth Division, Lincolns, since 1910; High Steward of the Borough of Louth; Captain, 3rd Lincolnshire Regiment. *Address:* Thorpe Hall, Louth, Lincs *Clubs:* Oxford and Cambridge, Carlton.
(Died 28 April 1920.)

BRACKENBURY, Admiral John William, C.M.G. 1879; C.B. 1887; retired; *b.* 1842; *s.* of late W. C. C. Brackenbury; *m.* Frances Mary, *d.* of late Colonel Gilbert Francklyn, 1880. Commanded "Shah's" Naval Brigade Zulu War, 1879; promoted captain for services on West Coast of Africa, 1881; captain of "Thalia," Egypt, 1882; captain of "Turquoise" during operations on East Coast of Africa, 1887-91; Rear-Admiral second in command Channel Squadron, 1898-99. *Address:* 8 Belsize Square, Hampstead, N.W. *Club:* Junior United Service. *(Died 15 Mar. 1918.)*

BRADDELL, Octavius Henry, I.S.O.; late Accountant Board of Public Works, Ireland; *b.* 26 Dec. 1843; *s. s.* of late J. R. Braddell, Raheengrany, Co. Wicklow, and Maria, *née* Donovan; *m.* 1866, Theresa Lonisa (*d.* 1911), 2nd *d.* of Fras Abbott Payn, Le Colombier, Jersey; one *s.* one *d.* *Educ.:* Marlborough College. Entered Board of Works, 1862; retired, 1906. *Address:* Lower Bullingate, Carnew, Co. Wicklow.
(Died 23 Oct. 1921.)

BRADDELL, Sir Thomas de Multon Lee, Kt., *cr.* 1914; Chief Judicial Commissioner, Federated Malay States, 1912; retired 1917; *b.* 25 Nov. 1856; *e. s.* of late Thomas Braddell, C.M.G., F.R.G.S., F.E.S.L. (Attorney-General of the Straits Settlements, 1867-82), of Raheengrany, Co. Wicklow, and Anne Lee; *m.* 1879, Ida Violet Nassau, 2nd *d.* of John Roberts Kirby, J.P., formerly of St. Osyth's Priory, Essex; four *s.* two *d.* *Educ.:* Brighton College; Worcester College, Oxford. Called to Bar, Inner Temple, 1879; proceeded to Singapore, where he practised at the Bar of the Straits Settlements; acted as Attorney-General of the Straits Settlements, 1897 and 1908; a Puisne Judge of the Straits Settlements, 1907; Attorney-General of the Straits Settlements, 1911. *Recreations:* yachting, swimming, and all sports connected with the sea or river. *Address:* 32 Westbourne Gardens, Folkestone. *Club:* Reform. *(Died 31 Jan. 1927.)*

BRADFIELD, William Walter, C.B.E. 1918; Director since 1918, and Joint General Manager since 1919 Marconi Wireless Telegraph Co. Ltd; *b.* London, 18 Mar. 1879; *m.* 1906, Jessica Whitcomb. *Educ.:* Parmiter's School; City and Guilds of London Engineering College. *Address:* 1 St. James's Place, S.W.1. *Clubs:* Junior Constitutional, Royal Automobile.
(Died 17 Mar. 1925.)

BRADFORD, Temp. Lt.-Col. Roland Boys, V.C. 1916; Durham Light Infantry; *b.* 23 Feb. 1892. Joined Durham L.I. 1912; Adjt. T.F. 1915; served European War, 1914-17 (despatches, V.C., M.C.). *(Died Nov. 1917.)*

BRADLEY, Francis Herbert, O.M. 1924; Fellow of Merton Coll., Oxford; writer on philosophy; *b.* 1846; *s.* of Rev. Charles Bradley, Vicar of Glasbury, and *half-b.* of late Dean of Westminster. *Educ.:* Cheltenham; Marlborough. *Publications:* The Presuppositions of Critical History, 1874; Ethical Studies, 1876; The Principles of Logic, 1883; Appearance and Reality, 1893; Essays on Truth and Reality, 1914; The Principles of Logic revised, with Commentary and Terminal Essays, 1922. *Address:* Merton College, Oxford. *(Died 18 Sept. 1924.)*

BRADLEY, Henry, joint-editor of the Oxford English Dictionary since 1889 (now senior editor); *b.* Manchester, 3 Dec. 1845; *s.* of John Bradley and Mary Spencer; *m.* Eleanor Kate Hides, 1872; one *s.* four *d.* *Educ.:* Chesterfield Grammar School. Hon. M.A. Oxford, 1891 (M.A. by decree, 1916); Hon. D.Litt. Oxford, 1914; Hon. Ph.D. Heidelberg, 1903; D. Litt. Durham, 1913; Litt.D. Sheffield 1913; Fellow of Magdalen College, Oxford,

1916; Hon. Member of Netherlands Society of Arts, Science, and Literature, and of the Royal Flemish Academy. In early life engaged in private teaching; afterwards (till 1884) employed as commercial clerk and foreign correspondent at Sheffield; removed to London, 1884; contributor to the Academy, Athenæum, etc.; temporary editor of Academy, 1884-85; President, Philological Society, 1891-93, 1900-3 and 1909-10; President, Oxford Philological Society, 1921; Fellow of the British Academy, 1907. *Publications:* The Story of the Goths, 1888; The Making of English, 1904; articles in the Dictionary of National Biography, Encyclopædia Britannica, Chambers's Encyclopædia, the Cambridge History of English Literature, etc.; Revised Edition of Stratmann's Middle - English Dictionary, 1891; revised editions of Morris's Elementary Lessons in Historical English Grammar and Primer of English Grammar, 1897; editions of Caxton's Dialogues (Early English Text Society) and of Gammer Gurton's Needle (in Professor Gayley's Representative English Comedies); has edited the portions of the Oxford English Dictionary comprising E, F, G, L, M, and S, and is now engaged on W. *Recreations:* walking. *Address:* 173 Woodstock Road, Oxford. (*Died 23 May 1923.*)

BRADLEY, Herbert, C.S.I. 1906; *b.* 29 Jan. 1856; *s.* of R. H. Bradley of Blackheath; *m.* 1891, Lillias Sarah, *d.* of Rev. Dr. M'Culloch. *Educ.:* Winchester. Entered I.C.S. 1876; posted to Madras, 1878; Assistant Collector and Magistrate, special duty, 1885-87; Secretary to the Board of Revenue, 1887; Collector, 1891; Member of the Board of Revenue, 1900; President of the Salt Committee, 1904; Member of the Legislative Council, 1900; Chief Secretary, 1905-8; Temporary Member of Council, 1908; retired, 1909; Barrister, Middle Temple, 1878; J.P. Dorset. *Address:* c/o Grindlay & Co., 54 Parliament Street, S.W.1 *Clubs:* East India United Service; Royal and Ancient Golf, St. Andrews. (*Died 3 June 1923.*)

BRADSHAW, Surg. - Maj. - Gen. Sir A. Frederick, K.C.B., *cr.* 1912; C.B. 1891; M.R.C.P. (Lond.), M.R.C.S. and L.S.A. (Lond.), F.R.G.S., Member Royal Society of Medicine; Hon. Physician to Queen Victoria, King Edward VII., and King George V.; M.A. Oxon. (*hon.,* 1900; by decree, 1910); A.M.S. (retired); *b.* 1834; *m.* 1864, Ellen C., *d.* of Col. R. S. Ewart, Bengal Army; two *s.* five *d. Educ.:* private school, Cambridge; St. Bartholomew's Hospital, London; Worcester College, Oxford, 1897-1900. Entered Army Medical Department, 1857, and appointed to Rifle Brigade; served with 2nd Battalion during Indian Mutiny; present at siege of Lucknow, 1858 (medal and clasp); Garrison and Brigade Surgeon, Delhi, 1863-1864; appointed to Chestnut Troop, Royal Horse Artillery, 1866; on personal staff of three Commanders - in - Chief in India, Sir William Mansfield (afterwards Lord Sandhurst), Lord Napier of Magdala, and Sir Fred. Haines, 1869-81; went with last to Afghanistan, 1879, during the war; principal medical officer of the Quetta District, Baluchistan, 1884-86; of the Zhob Valley Expeditionary Force, 1884 (despatches); of the Frontier Field Force, Assuan, Egypt, 1886-87; of the Northern District, England, 1887; of the Rawal Pindi District, Punjab, 1887-92; of the Hazara (Black Mountain) Field Force, 1891 (despatches, medal and clasp, C.B.); Hon. Surgeon to Viceroys of India, Lords Lansdowne and Elgin, 1891-95; principal medical officer, H.M.'s Forces in India, 1892-95; served 35 years in India; retired, 1895; received King's Coronation Medals, 1902 and 1911; received Reward for Distinguished Service, 1914; Member for five years from Dec. 1907 of the Honorary Consulting Staff of the Queen Alexandra's Military Hospital, London; Hon. Consulting Physician to the Military

118

Hospitals in Oxford and Neighbourhood, 1916-1919. *Publication:* Edited Memoir of Catherine G. Loch, Senior Lady Superintendent, Queen Alexandra's Military Nursing Service for India. *Address:* 111 Banbury Road, Oxford. *Clubs:* United Service; Oxford and County, Oxford.
(*Died 27 Sept. 1923.*)

BRADSHAW, Octavius; *b.* 1845; *e. s.* of late William Bradshaw, Barrister-at-law, and Mary Anne, *d.* of Joseph Horsley; *m.* 1871, Emily Sarah, *d.* of Thomas Ferguson, of Greenville, Co. Down, and *widow* of Hon. F. J. Pellew, Canonteign, Exeter. J.P. and D.L. Devon; High Sheriff, 1884; was Major 1st R. Devon Yeomanry Cavalry. *Club:* Wellington.
(*Died 16 Jan. 1928.*)

BRADSHAW, Thomas R., M.D. Dublin; F.R.C.P. London; Consulting Physician at Liverpool Royal Infirmary; Major à la suite, R.A.M.C. (T.F.); *b.* Leamington, 1857; *s.* of John W. Bradshaw, solicitor, Dublin, and Sarah Houghton Waters; *m.* 1904, Rose Mary, *d.* of Professor T. R. Glynn, M.D., F.R.C.P., Liverpool; no *c. Educ.:* Rathmines School, Dublin; Trinity College, Dublin; University College Hospital, London. Held resident posts in Royal Infirmary and Northern Hospital; then Hon. Physician, Liverpool Stanley Hospital, and Hon. Physician, Royal Infirmary; Physician, Samaritan Hospital for Women; Hon. Examining Physician, Queen Alexandra's Sanatorium, Davos; sometime Examiner in Medicine, University of London; President of the Liverpool Medical Institution, 1910 - 11. *Publications:* various contributions to Medical Transactions and Periodicals. *Recreations:* travel, photography, motoring. *Address:* The Tower, Mold, N. Wales, Flintshire. *T.:* Mold 51. *M.:* DM 1983. *Club:* Athenæum, Liverpool.
(*Died 25 Jan. 1927.*)

BRADSHAW, William, J.P.; *b.* 1844; *s.* of late James E. Bradshaw of Darcy Lever Hall, Lancaster, and Fair Oak Park, Hants; *m.* 1st, 1869, Floretta (*d.* 1889), *o. c.* of John Chandless; 2nd, 1892, Maud Hamilton, 2nd *d.* of late Charles George Barclay of Dura, Cupar, Fife. *Address:* 43 Cadogan Place, S.W. *Clubs:* Boodle's; Royal Yacht Squadron, Cowes.
(*Died 18 Jan. 1927.*)

BRADSTREET, Sir Edward Simon Victor, 7th Bt., *cr.* 1759; *b.* 1856; *s.* of 6th Bt. and Emily Matilda. *d.* of General de Gaja, of Las Courtines, Castelnaudary, France, and *g.d.* of Lord Robert Fitzgerald, *y. s.* of 1st Duke of Leinster; *S.* father, 1905; *m.* 1888, Fortuna Mary, *y. d.* of Felix Fiori de Lerichi of Bougie, Algeria. *Educ.:* Trinity College, Dublin. A Civil Engineer. *Heir:* none. *Address:* St. Jean de Luz. France. (*Died 13 Jan. 1924.*)

BRADY, George Stewardson, M.D., M.R.C.S., D.Sc., LL.D., F.R.S., C.M.Z.S.; Professor (Hon.) Natural History, Armstrong College, Newcastle-on-Tyne; Consulting Physician to Sunderland Infirmary; *b.* Gateshead, 18 Apr. 1832; *e. s.* of Henry Brady, Surgeon; *m.* Ellen, *d.* of Robt. Wright, Chesterfield, 1859; one *s.* three *d. Educ.:* Friends' School, Ackworth; Tulketh Hall, Preston; Univ. of Durham Coll. of Medicine. Practised Medicine in Sunderland since 1857; Prof. Nat. Hist. Armstrong Coll. 1875-1906. *Publications:* Reports on the Ostracoda and Copepoda of the Challenger Expedition; A Monograph of the Free and Semi-parasitic Copepoda of the British Islands (Ray Soc.):—jointly, a Monograph of the Ostracoda of the North Atlantic and North-Western Europe; and numerous other contributions to scientific literature. *Recreations:* gardening, photography. *Address:* Park Hurst, Endcliffe, Sheffield. (*Died 25 Dec. 1921.*)

BRADY, Maj. Sir William Longfield, 4th Bt.; *cr.* 1869; *b.* 16 July 1864; *s.* of late Maziere John Brady, 2nd *s.* of 1st Bt. and Elizabeth, *d.* of Rev. Robert Longfield; *S.*

brother, 1909 ; *m.* 1891, Caroline Florence, *d.* of Alfred M'Clintock, M.D. ; one *d. Heir :* none. *Address :* Glenart Avenue, Blackrock, Co. Dublin.   (*Died 7 April 1921.*)

BRAGGE, Rev. Charles Albert, Vicar of Thorncombe since 1875 ; Canon of Ilfracombe, Salisbury Cathedral. *Educ. :* Trinity College, Cambridge, M.A. Deacon, 1863 ; priest, 1864 ; Curate of Huntspill, 1863-5 ; Burstock, 1865-1870 ; Vicar of Hatton, 1870-75. *Address :* Thorncombe Vicarage, Chard.
    (*Died 16 Dec. 1923.*)

BRAIN, Sir Francis William Thomas, Kt., *cr.* 1913 ; Chairman Chepstow Water Co. and Cinderford Gas Co. ; *b.* 28 Oct. 1855 ; *o. s.* of Cornelius Brain, *s.* of Cornelius Brain of Ruardean, and Ann T., *d.* of Thomas Brain of The Hawthorns, Drybrook ; *m.* 1884 ; two *d. Educ. :* Monmouth Grammar School. Member Institute Civil Engineers and Institute Mining Engineers ; Fellow Surveyors Institution ; Past President Mining Association of Great Britain ; Past President National Association of Colliery Managers ; J.P. Glostershire ; Verderer of the Forest of Dean ; pioneer of Electric Blasting in Mines and of Electricity applied to Mines ; Vice-Chairman of the Board for Mining Examinations under Coal Mines Act. *Publications :* various papers to Mining and other Associations ; paper on Electricity applied to Mining, British Association Meeting at Bath, 1886. *Recreation :* foreign travel. *Address :* Huntworth, Stoke Bishop, Bristol. *T. :* Stoke Bishop 80. *T.A. :* Rockleaze Bristol. *M. :* AE 4604. *Clubs :* Royal Automobile ; County, Gloster.   (*Died 31 Aug 1921.*)

BRAITHWAITE, Robert, M.D., F.L.S., F.R.M.S. ; *b.* Ruswarp, near Whitby, Yorks, 10 May 1824 ; *e. s.* of Robert Braithwaite, Shipowner : *m.* 1869, Charlotte Elizabeth Ward, *d.* of N. B. Ward, F.R.S., of Clapham Rise. Retired from practice, 1899. *Publications :* Sphagnaceæ of Europe ; The British Moss-Flora ; various papers in scientific journals. *Address :* 26 Endymion Road, Brixton Hill, S.W.
    (*Died 20 Oct. 1917.*)

BRAITHWAITE, Wm. Charles, J.P., B.A. LL.B. Barrister-at-law (Lincoln's Inn) ; Local Director, Barclays Bank Limited ; Author ; President, Woodbrooke Settlement, Birmingham ; Chairman, National Council of Adult School Unions ; *b.* 1862 ; 3rd *s.* of J. Bevan Braithwaite, London, and Martha Gillett ; *m.* 1896, Janet, *d.* of Charles C. Morland, Croydon ; three *s.* one *d. Educ. :* Oliver's Mount School, Scarboro' ; University College, London. Practised as a barrister till 1896 ; then became a partner in Gillett & Co., Bankers, Banbury and Oxford, and on their amalgamation in 1919 a Local Director in Barclays Bank Ltd. ; Swarthmore Lecturer, 1909 ; Treasurer of Friends' Ambulance Unit during the war. *Publications:* Red Letter Days; a Verse Calendar, 1907 ; The Beginnings of Quakerism, 1912 ; Foundations of National Greatness, 1915 ; The Second Period of Quakerism, 1919 ; various papers on Education, Biblical criticism, Quaker history and religious subjects. *Address :* Castle House, Banbury.   (*Died 28 Jan. 1922.*)

BRAMELD, Rev. William Arthur, M.A. ; Prebendary of North Kelsey in Lincoln Cathedral since 1888 ; *e. s.* of late Rev. A. J. Brameld, vicar of New Wortley, Leeds ; *m.* 1st, 1882, Mary (*d.* 1920), *e. d.* of Henry John Grieveson, J.P., of Startforth Hall, Barnard Castle ; one *s.* four *d.* ; 2nd, 1921, Margaret Isabel, *y. d.* of Charles E. Bousfield, of Leeds and Ilkley. *Educ. :* Leeds Grammar School ; Keble College, Oxford. Deacon, 1876 ; Priest, 1877 ; was Curate of Kintbury, Berks ; and afterwards of Lee, Kent ; Principal of St.

Paul's Missionary College, Burgh, 1883-90 ; Vicar of Wortley, Leeds, 1890-97 ; Vicar of St. Stephen's, Lewisham, 1897-1904 ; Commissary to the Bishop of St. John's, Kaffraria, 1897-1914 ; Vicar of Chapel Allerton, Leeds, 1904-14. *Publications :* In Type and Shadow, 1892, 2nd ed. ; The Marriage Service, with Notes and Prayers, 1904. *Address :* 11 Marine Parade, Folkestone.   (*Died 16 Nov. 1922.*)

BRAMLEY, Fred, Secretary, British Trades Union Congress since 1923 ; *b.* Peel, near Otley, Yorks, 27 Sep. 1874 ; *s.* of journeyman engineer ; *m.* 1898 ; one *s.* one *d. Educ. :* practically self-educated. Served apprenticeship as cabinet-maker ; became lecturer on Social and Economic Questions ; employed by Clarion newspaper for five years as lecturer ; appointed Organising Secretary, Furnishing Trade Association ; three times elected to Parliamentary Committee, Trades Union Congress ; subsequently appointed Assistant Secretary. *Publications:* special articles on Economic and Social Questions in magazines and newspapers. *Recreations :* no special recreation except walking. *Address :* 32 Eccleston Square, S.W.1. *T. :* Victoria 6410.   (*Died 10 Oct. 1925.*)

BRAMLEY, Rev. Henry Ramsden ; *b.* 4 June 1833 ; unmarried. *Educ. :* Blackheath School ; Oriel and University Colleges, Oxford. Fellow Magdalen Coll. Oxford, 1857 ; Tutor, 1858-68 ; 1871-83 ; Precentor and Canon of Lincoln, 1892-1901. *Recreations :* riding, walking. *Address :* Nettleham Hall, Lincoln. *T.A. :* Nettleham, Lincoln.   (*Died 28 Jan. 1917.*)

BRAMLEY - MOORE, Rev. William, M.A. (Cantab.) ; *e. s.* of John Bramley-Moore, of Langley Lodge, Gerrard's Cross, Bucks, formerly of Aigburth, Liverpool, Chairman of the Liverpool Docks, after whom the Bramley-Moore Dock was named, late M.P. for Maldon and Lincoln, J.P., D.L. (*d.* 1886) ; *b.* 1831 ; *m.* 1865, Ella, 3rd *d.* of Swinfen Jordan, of Clifton ; six *s.* four *d.* Vicar of Gerrard's Cross, 1859-1869. *Publications:* Six Sisters of the Valleys ; Great Oblation ; Marturia ; The Church's Forgotten Hope ; Ancient Tyre and Modern England, etc. ; edited Cassell's Foxe's Book of Martyrs. *Recreations:* travelling, writing, authorship. *Address :* 26 Russell Square, W.C.
    (*Died Oct. 1918.*)

BRAMSTON, Sir John, G.C.M.G., *cr.* 1900 ; K.C.M.G., *cr.* 1897 ; C.B., D.C.L. Oxford ; Assistant Under-Secretary of State for the Colonies, 1876-97 ; *b.* Skreens, Essex, 14 Nov. 1832 ; *s.* of T. W. Bramston [M.P. for S. Essex, 1835-66] and Eliza, *d.* of Admiral Sir Eliab Harvey, G.C.B. [who commanded the "Temeraire" at Trafalgar] ; *m.* 1872, Eliza Isabella (*d.* 1920), *d.* of Rev. Harry Vane Russell. *Educ. :* Winchester ; Balliol College, Oxford. Fellow of All Souls College, Oxford, 1855 ; Barr. Middle Temple, 1857 ; Member Legislative Council, Queensland, 1863-1869 ; Legislative Assembly, 1871-73 ; Executive Council, 1863-66, 1870-73 ; Attorney-Gen. Queensland, 1870-73 ; Hong Kong, 1874-76 ; Royal Commissioner in Newfoundland, 1898. *Address :* 18 Berkeley Place, Wimbledon.
    (*Died 13 Sept. 1921.*)

BRAMWELL, John Milne, M.B., C.M. ; consulting physician ; *b.* Perth, 11 May 1852 ; *y. s.* of late James Paton Bramwell, M.D., of Perth ; *m.* 1st, 1875, Mary, *d.* of late Capt. Reynolds, Indian Army ; two *d.* ; 2nd, 1914, Katharine Mary Chisholm, *widow* of Henry Valantine Corrie. *Educ. :* Perth Grammar School ; Edinburgh University. Took degrees at Edinburgh in 1873 ; travelled for a year, and then settled in private practice at Goole, Yorks ; commenced hypnotic researches in 1889 ; settled in London in 1892. *Publications :* On Imperative Ideas ; James Braid, Surgeon and

Hypnotist; On the Evolution of Hypnotic Theory; Hypnotic Anæsthesia; Hypnotic and Post-hypnotic Appreciation of Time; Secondary and Multiplex Personalities; Suggestion, its Place in Medicine and Scientific Research; Hypnotism in the Treatment of Insanity and Allied Disorders; Dipsomania and its Treatment—by Suggestion; "Hypnotism" in Encyclopædia Medica, 1901; Hypnotism, its History, Practice, and Theory, 1903; Hypnotism and Treatment by Suggestion, 1909, etc. *Recreations:* yachting and fishing. *Address:* The Hove, Torquay, S. Devon. *T.:* Torquay 877. *Club:* Royal Torbay Yacht, Torquay.

(Died 16 Jan. 1925.)

BRANCH, James, J.P.; boot manufacturer, Bethnal Green and Kingsthorpe, Northampton; late Member L.C.C.; *b.* Bethnal Green, 27 Feb. 1845; M.P. (L.) Enfield Div. Middlesex, 1906-1910; contested same division, 1910. *Address:* Canford, 43 Etchingham Park Road, Finchley, N.W.3. *(Died 16 Nov. 1918.)*

BRAND, Hon. Arthur George, J.P., D.L.; *b.* 1853; *s.* of 1st Viscount Hampden and Eliza, *d.* of Gen. Robert Ellice; *m.* Edith (*d.* 1908), *d.* of late Joseph Ingram of Brooklands, Cheshire, 1886; one *s. Educ.:* Rugby. Assistant Clerk in House of Commons; M.P. Wisbech Division of Cambs. 1891-95, and 1900-1906; Treasurer in H.M. Household, 1894-95. *Address:* 101 Mount Street, W. *Clubs:* Turf, Bachelors', Garrick.

(Died 9 Jan. 1917.)

BRAND, Ferdinand, I.S.O. 1902; *b.* 28 March 1846; 4th *s.* of late Captain W. H. Brand, R.N., who as a Midshipman served in H.M.S. "Revenge" at the battle of Trafalgar, and Christina Cecilia, 2nd *d.* of J. Greig, Procurator-Fiscal of Shetland; *m.* 1875, Edith Mary, *d.* of late W. F. Hartley, J.P., of Simpson Hill House, Heywood, Lancashire; one *s.* two *d. Educ.:* Royal Naval School, New Cross. Entered Admiralty, 1867; retired 1908; edited Navy List, 1880-98; Admiralty Librarian, 1898-1908. *Recreations:* natural history, naval history, gardening. *Address:* Heywood Lodge, Cumberland Road, Kew. *(Died 19 April 1922.)*

BRAND, Rear-Admiral Hon. Thomas Seymour, J.P.; Alderman C. C., East Sussex; 2nd *s.* of 1st Viscount Hampden; *b.* 1847; *m.* 1879, Blanche, *y. d.* of late H. L. Gaskell, Kiddington Hall, Woodstock; one *s.* one *d. Educ.:* at sea. Flag-Lieut. to late Lord Alcester, 1874-77; commanded "Bittern," Bombardment of Alexandria, 1882; contested Hastings (L.), 1886; Eastbourne Division of Sussex, 1892, 1895, and 1900. *Address:* Glynde Place, Lewes. *T.A.:* Glynde. *Club:* United Service. *(Died 12 Nov. 1916.)*

BRANDES, George, LL.D. St. Andrews; Athens; *b.* Copenhagen, 4 February 1842. *Educ.:* University of Copenhagen. Lived in France and Italy, 1866-67, 1870-71; Berlin, 1877-82; Poland, Russia, 1886-87; Italy, 1898-1913; France, every year; England, 1913; United States, 1914. Member American Academy of Arts and Sciences, Free Trade Association, Thomas Paine Association, New York, of the Rationalist Press Association, the Royal Society of Literature, the Polyglot Club, the Rationalist Peace Society, the Garrick Club, Institute of British Poetry, London. *Publications:* 33 volumes of history, of literature, and criticism. Principal works: Main Currents of the Literature of the 19th Century, 6 vols.; Ludvig Holberg; Sören Kierkegaard; Danish Poets; Impressions of Poland; Impressions of Russia; Berlin; Ferdinand Lassalle; Lord Beaconsfield; William Shakespeare; Men and Works; Men of the Modern Revival; A Study of Ibsen; Poems, 1896; 120

Complete Works, 21 vols., 1910; Goethe, 2 vols.; Julius Cæsar, 2 vols.; The Jesus Myth, 1925; Hellas, 1925; Petrus, 1926; English: Main Currents, 6 vols.; Shakespeare; Beaconsfield; Poland; Creative Spirits; Ibsen and Björnson; Recollections of my Childhood and Youth; Ferdinand Lassalle; The World at War; Voltaire; Cæsar, 2 vols.; Goethe, 2 vols.; Michel Angelo, 2 vols. *Address:* Copenhagen.

(Died 19 Feb. 1927.)

BRANNER, Prof. John Casper, Ph.D., LL.D.; D.Sc. (Chicago); President Emeritus of Stanford University since 1916; Associate Editor Journal of Geology; *b.* New Market, Tennessee, of American parents, 4 July 1850; *m.* 1883, Susan Kennedy; two *s.* one *d. Educ.:* Cornell University, N.Y. Imperial Geological Commission, Brazil, 1875-77; Agent U.S. Department of Agriculture in Brazil, 1882-83; Geological Survey of Penn., 1883-85; Prof. of Geology, University of Indiana, 1885-91; State Geologist of Arkansas, 1887-93; Prof. of Geology since 1891, and Vice-President of Stanford University, 1899-1913; President, 1913-16; Director of the Branner-Agassiz Expedition to Brazil, 1899; Geologist of the U.S. Geological Survey until 1906; Fellow of Geological Societies of London and Belgium and Société Géologique of France; Pres. Geological Society of America, 1904; Member of the National Academy of Sciences, Washington; Member American Philosophical Society, Instituto Historico do Brasil, Academia Brasileira, etc. *Publications:* numerous works on the geology of Brazil and Arkansas. *Address:* Stanford University, California.

(Died 1 Mar. 1922.)

BRASSEY, 1st Earl, *cr.* 1911; **Thomas Brassey,** Baron Brassey, *cr.* 1886; G.C.B., *cr.* 1906; K.C.B., *cr.* 1881; D.L., J.P., D.C.L. Oxford; LL.D. Dublin; Younger Brother Trinity House; Hon. Col. 2nd Home Counties Brigade, Royal Field Artillery, Territorial Force; Military Member, Sussex Territorial Force Association; Hon. Captain R.N.R., June 1914; holds Board of Trade (yacht-owner's) Master's Certificate, by examination, 1872; Commander of Legion of Honour, 1889; late Lord Warden of Cinque Ports; Grand Cross of Order of Crown of Italy; *b.* 11 Feb. 1836; *e. s.* of late T. Brassey and Maria Farrington, *d.* of T. Harrison; *m.* 1st, 1860, Anna (*d.* 1887), *o. c.* of John Allnutt of Charles Street, W.; one *s.* three *d.*; 2nd, 1890, Sybil de Vere, *d.* of Viscount Malden; one *d. Educ.:* Rugby; University College, Oxford, B.A. Honours History School. Liberal. M.P. (G.L.) Devonport, 1865; Hastings, 1868-85; President Statistical Society, 1879-80; Civil Lord of Admiralty, 1880-84; Secretary to Admiralty, 1884-85; served on Royal Commissions on Unseaworthy Ships, Defence of Coaling Stations, Relief of Aged Poor, Opium (Chairman), Canals and Inland Navigation; Lord-in-Waiting, 1894; President, Institute of Naval Architects 1893-95; Governor of Victoria, 1895-1900. *Publications:* Work and Wages, 1872; British Navy, 5 vols. 1881; Foreign Work and British Wages, 1879; Sixty Years of Progress, 1904; founder and first editor of the Naval Annual. Owned yacht "Sunbeam" (presented to Government of India as hospital-ship, 1916), in which he has covered over 400,000 knots. *Heir: s.* Viscount Hythe. *Address:* 24 Park Lane, W.; *T.:* Mayfair 6803; Chapelwood Manor, Nutley, Sussex. *Clubs:* Athenæum, Brooks's; Royal Yacht Squadron, Cowes. *(Died 23 Feb. 1918.)*

BRASSEY, 2nd Earl, *cr.* 1911; **Thomas Allnutt Brassey,** Baron Brassey, *cr.* 1886; D.C.L., M.A., J.P.; Lieut.-Col. West Kent Yeo.; retired 1 May 1914, with thanks of Army Council for services; raised and commanded

2nd West Kent Yeomanry, Sep. to Dec. 1914; b. 7 March 1868; e.s. of 1st Earl Brassey, and Anna (d. 1887), o. c. of John Allnutt of Charles Street, W.; S. father 1918; m. Lady Idina Nevill, Lady of Justice of Order of St. John of Jerusalem in England, d. of 1st Marquis of Abergavenny, 1889; no c. Educ.: Eton; Balliol College, Oxford; D.C.L., Oxford; Hon. Fellow of Balliol. Editor Naval Annual, since 1890; Assistant Private Secretary to Earl Spencer when First Lord of the Admiralty; Assistant Secretary to Royal Commission on Opium, 1894; contested Epsom Division, Surrey, 1892; Christchurch, 1895 and 1900; Devonport, 1902; raised 69th Sussex Company Imperial Yeomanry; First Acting Civil Commissioner of Pretoria, 1900; initiated Oxford University Endowment Fund; served on Archbishop's Committee on Church Finance, 1910-11; Chairman Executive Central Board of Finance; Managing Director of Mining and Lead Smelting business in Italy and Sardinia; holds Master's certificate for yacht owners; Commander of Crown of Italy; Knight of Grace of Order of St. John of Jerusalem. Publications: Problems of Empire; The Case for Devolution, 1913. Heir: none. Recreations: hunting, deerstalking, shooting. Address: Normanhurst, Battle, Sussex. Clubs: Brooks's; Royal Yacht Squadron, Cowes. (Died 12 Nov. 1919.)

BRASSEY, Albert, M.A., J.P.; Master of Heythrop Hounds since 1873; s. of late Thomas Brassey; b. Rouen, Feb. 22. 1844; m. 1871, Hon. Matilda, d. of 4th Lord Clanmorris; one s. five d. Educ.: Eton; Univ. Coll. Oxford. 14th Hussars, 1867-71; Oxfordshire Yeomanry, 1871-94; High Sheriff of Oxfordshire, 1878; Colonel, 1893-94; M.P. (C.) Banbury Div. Oxon. 1895 - 1906. Recreations: Member Royal Yacht Squadron since 1879. Owns about 5000 acres. Address: Heythrop, Chipping Norton; 29 Berkeley Square, W. T.: Gerrard 2424. Clubs: Carlton, Oxford and Cambridge, Army and Navy, Naval and Military, Cavalry; Royal Yacht squadron, Cowes. (Died 7 Jan. 1918.)

BRASSEY, Capt. Harold Ernest, Royal Horse Guards; b. 29 March 1877; 3rd s. of late Henry Arthur Brassey, of Preston Hall; m. 1906, Lady Norah Hely-Hutchinson, y. d. of 5th Earl of Donoughmore; two d. Address: 40 Hill Street, Berkeley Square, W. (Died July 1916.)

BRAY, His Honour Judge Sir Edward, Kt., cr. 1919; County Court Judge, Bloomsbury and Brentford; b. 19 Aug. 1849; s. of Reginald Bray of Shere, Surrey, and Frances, d. of Thomas N. Longman; m. 1873, Edith Louisa, d. of Rev. Thomas Hubbard, Newbury; three s. one d. Educ.: Westminster School (Captain of); Trinity College, Cambridge. Called to Bar, 1875; South Eastern Circuit; County Court Judge, Birmingham, 1905 - 7; London, 1908-11. Publications: Bray on Discovery; Bray's Digest of Discovery. Recreations: Westminster Cricket Eleven, 1864-68; Cambridge University Cricket Eleven, 1871-72; also played for Surrey; shooting and lawn tennis. Address: 26 Queen's Gate Gardens, S.W.7. T.: Western 2307. Club: United University. (Died 19 June 1926.)

BRAY, Sir Reginald More, Hon. Mr. Justice Bray, Kt. cr. 1904; D.L.; Judge of King's Bench Division since 1904; Recorder of Guildford, 1891; Bencher of the Inner Temple since 1891; b. 26 Sep. 1842; s. of Reginald Bray of Shere, Surrey, and Frances, d. of Thomas N. Longman; m. 1868, Emily Octavia, 4th d. of Arthur Kett Barclay of Bury Hill, Dorking; four s. two d. Educ.: Harrow; Trinity College, Camb. (scholar, 12th wrangler).

Called to the Bar, 1868. Recreation: shooting. Address: The Manor House, Shere, Guildford; 17 The Boltons, S.W.10. T.: Kensington 2823. Club: Athenæum. (Died 22 Mar. 1923.)

BRAY, Brig.-Gen. Robert Napier, C.M.G. 1919; D.S.O. 1916; b. 7 Dec. 1872; s. of Major-General G. F. C. Bray; m. 1907, Ruth Ellinor Boys; two s. Educ.: United Services College, Westward Ho. Gazetted to the 1st Batt. Duke of Wellington's Regt. 1894; served in China; present at the Relief of Pekin, 1900; served in France (D.S.O., C.M.G., Bt. Lt.-Col.). (Died 23 Oct. 1921.)

BRAYE, 5th Baron (cr. 1529), **Alfred Thomas Townshend Verney-Cave,** D.L., J.P.; Hon. Col. in Army, late Lieut.-Col. and Hon. Col. 3rd Batt. (Militia) Leicestershire Regt. (S. African medal and clasp); b. 23 July 1849; s. of Edgell Wyatt-Edgell and Henrietta, Baroness Braye; S. mother. 1879; m. 1873, Cecilia, d. of William Gerard Walmesley, of Westwood House, Wigan; one s. two d. Educ.: Eton; Christ Church, Oxford. Publication: Fewness of My Days: A Life in Two Centuries, 1927. Heir: s. Hon. A. V. Verney-Cave. (Died 1 July 1928.)

BREADALBANE, 1st Marquis of (cr. 1885), **Gavin Campbell,** K.G., P.C., J.P., D.L., C.C. for Perthshire and Argyllshire; Lord Lieut. of Argyllshire since 1914; Keeper of the Privy Seal of Scotland since 1907; Knight of the Order of the Seraphim; awarded silver medal Royal Humane Society; Bt. of Nova Scotia, 1625; Earl of Breadalbane; Earl of Holland; Viscount of Tay and Paintland; Lord Glenorchy, Benederaloch, Ormelie, and Weik, 1677; Baron Breadalbane (U.K.), 1873; Earl of Ormelie, 1885; Knight of Order of St. John of Jerusalem; A.D.C. to the King. Late Col. Highland Cyclist Batt.; Hon. Col. Highland Cyclist Batt.; Brigadier - General Royal Company of Archers; b. 9 Apr. 1851; S. father 1871; m. Lady Alma Imogen Carlotta Leonore Graham, Lady of Grace of the Order of St. John of Jerusalem, y. d. of 4th Duke of Montrose, 1872. Educ.: St. Andrews. Lieut. 4th Batt. Argyll and Sutherland Highlanders, and Captain Shropshire Yeomanry Cavalry, 1873-74; Lord-in-Waiting to the Queen; Treasurer Queen's Household, 1880-85; Lord Steward, 1892-95; Lord High Commissioner General Assembly Church of Scotland, 1893-95. Is a member of Fishery Board for Scotland. Owns about 200,000 acres. Heir to earldom: n. Iain Edward Herbert Campbell, b. 14 June 1885. Address: 68 Ennismore Gardens, S.W.7; Craig Dalmally, Argyllshire. T.A.: Breadalbane, London. T.: Kensington 114. Clubs: Reform, Brooks's, National Liberal; Royal Yacht Squadron, Cowes. (Died 19 Oct. 1922.)

BREADALBANE, 8th Earl of; cr. 1677; **Iain Edward Herbert Campbell,** Earl of Holland; Viscount of Tay and Paintland; Lord Glenorchy, Benederaloch, Ormelie and Weik, 1677; Baronet of Nova Scotia; b. 14 June 1885; s. of Capt. Hon. Ivan Campbell, 2nd s. of 6th Earl; S. uncle, 1st Marquess of Breadalbane, 1922. Heir: cousin Capt. Charles William Campbell, b. 11 June 1889. (Died May 1923.)

BREBNER, Arthur, M.R.C.S., L.R.C.P.; late Lieut. R.A.M.C.; b. 5 June 1870; 3rd s. of late James Brebner, Manager of National Provincial Bank of England, Piccadilly; m. 1905, Alice Rose Ewing, e. d. of Alexander Steven, M.D., of St. Kilda, Melbourne. Educ.: Merchant Taylors' School and University College, London. Has travelled in China, Japan, East Indies, Australia, etc. Publications: Patches and

121

Pomander ; John Saint ; Stories in Temple Bar, Argosy, Royal, London, Queen, Argus, Age, Queenslander, etc. *Address :* 5 S. Kilda Villas, Buckhurst Hill, Essex.   (*Died 28 July 1922.*)

BREBNER, Percy James (Christian Lys); *b.* 24 March 1864 ; *e. s.* of late James Brebner, Manager of National Provincial Bank of England, Piccadilly ; *m.* 1892, Adelaide, *e. d.* of late Rev. R. Taylor, Vicar of St. Faith's, Wandsworth; one *s. Educ. :* King's College School. Formerly in Share and Loan Department of Stock Exchange ; subsequently engaged in editorial work. *Publications :* The Gate of Temptation ; A Gallant Lady ; The Turbulent Duchess : Christopher Quarles ; The Little Grey Shoe ; The White Gauntlet ; The Brown Mask ; A Gentleman of Virginia ; A Royal Ward ; Vayenne ; Princess Maritza ; The Crucible of Circumstance ; Mr. Quixley of the Gate House ; The Mystery of Ladyplace ; The Fortress of Yadasara ; The Hepsworth Millions ; Market Sefton ; The Doctor's Idol ; The Dunthorpes of Westleigh ; Suspicion ; The Black Card, etc.; Christopher Quarles, 1921; special articles on Hospitals and their work. *Recreations :* music, tennis, golf. *Address :* 122 Upper Richmond Road, East Sheen, S.W.14. *Clubs :* Authors', Roehampton.
(*Died 91 July 1922.*)

BREDON, Sir Robert Edward, K.C.M.G. *cr.* 1904; C.M.G. 1903 ; M.A. (Dublin), M.B., C.M.; Deputy Inspector-General Imperial Maritime Customs, China, 1898-1908 ; Acting Inspector - General of Customs with rank of Provincial Lieutenant - Governor, 1908-10 ; 2nd Div. 2nd class Double Dragon of China ; Officer Legion of Honour, France ; Commander 1st Class of St. Olaf, Norway ; 2nd Class Sacred Treasure, Japan ; Grand Cross Order of St. Stanislas, Russia ; 2nd Class Crown of Prussia, with star ; 2nd Class Rising Sun, Japan ; Grand Cross Order of Francis Joseph of Austria ; Commander, First Class, Polar Star of Sweden ; Commander, First Class, Dannebrog of Denmark; Civil rank, First Class, with red button, in China. *b.* Portadown, Ireland, 4 Feb. 1846 ; *e. s.* of late Alexander Bredon, M.D., and Katherine, *d.* of late Joseph Breadon, R.N., Stanstead, Canada ; *m.* Lily Virginia, *y. d.* of Thomas Crane Banks, San Francisco, Cal., U.S.A., 1879 ; one *d. Educ. :* Royal School, Dungannon ; Trinity Coll. Dublin. Honourman in Mathematics and Classics, Passed for Army Medical Staff (1st place), 1867 ; passed out of Netley (1st place), 1867 ; appointed 97th Regiment, 1867 ; retired, 1873 ; joined Chinese Customs Service, 1873 ; retired, 1897, and rejoined same year; appointed to Chinese Board of Customs, 1910, but retired in deference to wishes of British Government; war medal and clasp (Defence of Legations), China, 1900. *Address :* Chuan Pan Hutung, Peking, China. *Club :* Junior United Service.
(*Died 3 July 1918.*)

BREE, Ven. William, D.D.; Rector and Patron of Allesley since 1863 ; *b.* 19 Nov. 1822 ; *o. s.* of Rev. W. T. Bree, M.A., Rector of Allesley; *m.* 1st, 1853, Mary, *d.* of Rev. E. Duke, M.A., F.A.S., F.L.S., of Lake House, Co. Wilts : 2nd, 1889, Sophy Adèle, *d.* of Rev. G. Hesketh Biggs, M.A., Vicar of Ettington, Co. Warwick. Rector of Polebrook, Co. Northampton, 1862 ; Archdeacon of Coventry 1887-1908. *Educ. :* Bridgnorth School ; Merton College, Oxford. *Recreation :* natural history. *Address :* Allesley Rectory, Coventry. *T.A. :* Allesley.
(*Died 29 Jan. 1917.*)

BREEKS, Brig. - Gen. Richard William, C.B. 1918 ; D.L.; R.A. ; *b.* 1863; *s.* of late James Wilkinson Breeks, H.E.I.C.S., and Susan Maria, *e. d.* of Sir W. Y. Denison, K.C.B. ; *m.* 1893, Olive, 2nd *d.* of late Henry Arthur Blyth of Stansted House, Essex. Entered R.A., 1883. Served South African

122

War, 1900 (medal, three clasps) ; European War (C.B.); Col. R.H.A., Mons to Aisne, 1914 ; Brig.-Gen. Gallipoli, 1915 ; D.O.A.G.C., 1916-18; C.O. Woolwich, 1918-19. *Address :* Helbeck Hall, Brough, Westmoreland.   (*Died 2 May 1920.*)

BREMA, Marie, opera singer ; *b.* Liverpool ; first appeared in Popular Concerts, 1891 ; engaged to sing at Covent Garden for Royal Opera, 1892 ; first English singer invited by Wagner to sing at Bayreuth festival ; has also appeared in many other operas and at musical festivals. *Address :* Royal College of Music, Manchester.   (*Died 22 Mar. 1925.*)

BREMER, Professor Walther Erich Emanuel Friedrich, Dr. Phil.; Curator of Irish Antiquities in the National Museum, Dublin, since 1925 ; *b.* Wismar, Mecklenburg, Germany, 8 June 1887; *m.* 1922, Friede Berta Busse; one *d. Educ. :* Wismar, Rostock ; Universities Marburg, München, Rostock, Giessen. Dr. phil. Giessen, 1910. Assist. of the Romano-German Central Museum at Mainz, 1911-12 ; travelled through Central and South Eastern Europe, 1913-14 ; Excavations in Greece; Privatdozent of Prehistoric Archæology in the University of Marburg, 1920 ; Professor extraordinary, Marburg, 1922 ; Corresponding Member of the German Archæological Institute ; M.R.I.A., F.R.S.A.I. *Publications :* Die Haartracht des Mannes in Arch. griech Zeit, 1911 ; Eberstadt, steinzeitl. Dorf der Nordwetterau, 1913. *Address :* 34 Fitzwilliam Square, Dublin.
(*Died Nov. 1926.*)

BRENAN, Byron, C.M.G., 1894 ; F.R.C.I. 1907 ; *b.* France, 27 Dec. 1847 ; *s.* of Col. E. F. Brenan; *m.* 1st, M. S. Brenan (*d.* 1899), *d.* of late General T. C. Kelly, C.B. ; 2nd, 1901, Emily, *d.* of Robert Gore of Raveagh, Co. Tyrone. *Educ. :* private. Student Interpreter, China, 1866 ; 3rd Assistant, 1868 ; Acting Interpreter, Canton, 1871 -'72 ; 2nd Class Assistant, 1872 ; Acting Interpreter, Shanghai, 1873 ; 1st Class Assistant, 1874 ; Acting Interpreter, Hankow, 1875 ; Acting Assistant Chinese Secretary, Pekin, 1875 ; and 1877-78. Acting Chinese Secretary, 1878-80 ; Consul at Wuhu, 1880 ; Acting Consul at Tien-tsin, 1882-1883 ; Chefoo, 1883 ; Tientsin and Pekin, 1885. British Representative on Opium Mixed Commission at Hong Kong, 1886 ; Consul, Canton, 1893 ; was instructed to visit officially the principal Treaty Ports of China, Japan, and Corea, to report on the subject of British Trade, 1895 ; H.E.M. Consul-General, Shanghai, China, 1898-1901. Retired on a pension, 1901. *Address :* 30 Bramham Gardens, S.W.5. *Clubs :* Royal Societies, Hurlingham.
(*Died 28 Feb. 1927.*)

BRENNAN, Very Rev. Nicholas J.; President of Blackrock College, Dublin, 1910-1916; *b.* 1854. *Educ. :* Blackrock College, Dublin; Paris. Ordained Priest, 1879; Professor and Dean, Blackrock, 1880-94 ; President of St. Mary's College, Trinidad, and of Rockwell College, Cashel, 1894-1905 ; Member of Council, Classical Association, Ireland. *Address :* Blackrock College, Dublin. *T.A. :* and *T. :* Blackrock 27.
(*Died 4 Oct. 1928.*)

BRERETON, Alfred, C.S.I. 1903 ; *b.* 1849 ; *s.* of Rev. Charles David Brereton, Rector of Framingham Earl, Norfolk ; *m.* 1st, 1894, Haidée (*d.* 1902), *e. d.* of Col. Shaw of Heathburn Hall, Co. Cork ; 2nd, 1908, Frances, *d.* of late D. Stewart of Ealing; one *s. Educ. :* Norwich Grammar School. Entered railway branch of the Indian Public Works Dept., 1873 ; Executive Engineer, 1880 ; Assistant Director, N.W. Railway, 1887 ; District Traffic Superintendent, 1888 ; Deputy Manager, 1891 ; Officiating Manager, Eastern Bengal State Railway, 1893 ; Manager and Engineer in Chief, East Coast Railway, 1893 ; Director of Railway Traffic and Deputy Secretary to the Government of India (Railway Dept.), 1897 ; Secretary, 1901-

1904; retired, 1904; Govt. Director, Guaranteed Railway Companies, 1905; retired, 1914. *Recreations:* a successful gentleman rider both across country and on the flat; good at most games. *Address:* c/o Grindlay and Co., 54 Parliament Street, S.W.1. *Club:* Oriental.

(Died 1 May 1926.)

BRERETON, Austin, journalist; *b.* Liverpool, 13 July 1862. Writer of Dramatis Personæ in The Observer. Came to London, 1881; dramatic critic of The Stage, editor of Dramatic Notes, assistant editor of The Theatre, etc., 1881-87; dramatic and art critic, Sydney (N.S.W.) Morning Herald, 1889-91; dramatic critic and assistant editor of The Illustrated American (New York), 1893-94; dramatic critic of The Sphere, 1901-1906. *Publications:* Henry Irving, a Biographical Sketch, 1883; Some Famous Hamlets, a Record of all the Chief Actors of Hamlet from Burbage to Fechter, 1884; Dramatic Notes, an Illustrated Critical Record of the London Stage from 1880 to 1886; Shakesperean Scenes and Characters, Descriptive Notes on the Plays and on the Principal Shakesperean Players from Betterton to Irving, 1886; Romeo and Juliet on the Stage, 1890; Sarah Bernhardt, an Illustrated Memoir, 1891; Gallery of Players (New York), 1894; A Short History of the Strand Theatre, 1899; Cheltenham, 1899; A Short History of She Stoops to Conquer, The Rivals, and The School for Scandal, 1900; By the Silent Highway, 1900; The Criterion, Past and Present, 1900; Shakespeare (arranged the illustrations, on a novel plan, for the complete works), 1900; new and extended edition of the same, 1902; Peg Woffington, On and Off the Stage, 1901; The Well of St. Ann (Buxton), 1901; A Ramble in Bath, 1901; The Lyceum and Henry Irving, 1903; Henry Irving, 1905; At Home and Abroad; Ellen Terry, a Biographical Sketch, 1906; The Literary History of the Adelphi and its Neighbourhood, 1907; 2nd ed., 1908; The Life of Henry Irving, 1908; The Story of Old Whitehall; Cyril Maude, a Memoir, 1913; The Story of Drury Lane, 1918; A Walk down Bond Street; Whitehall Court and Scotland, 1921; The Hotel Cecil: A Glimpse of Old London and the New, 1921; H. B. and Laurence Irving. *Address:* 19 York Buildings, Adelphi, W.C.2.

(Died 20 Nov. 1922.)

BRERETON, William Westropp, M.R.C.P.I., M.R.C.S.I.; Professor of Surgery, Queen's College, Galway, since 1888; member of staff, Galway Hospital; *s.* of late William Westropp Brereton, Q.C., of Fitzwilliam Square, Dublin; *b.* Dublin 1845; *m.* 1871, Helen, *y. d.* of J. Doig, Oughterard House, Surgeon, Hon. East India Company; three *s.* one *d. Educ.:* Trinity College and College of Surgeons. Pupil of John Morgan, Professor of Anatomy, College of Surgeons; qualified, 1865; Demonstrator of Anatomy, 1866, under Prof. Clelland in Galway; Medical Officer, Oughterard Union, 1868-88. *Publication:* Local Fixation during Operations. *Address:* University College, Galway, Ireland.

(Died Feb. 1924.)

BRETEUIL, Henri Charles Joseph, Marquis de, G.C.V.O., *cr.* 1912; K.C.V.O., *cr.* 1905; *b.* 17 Sep. 1848; *m.* 1891, Miss Garner, New York; two *s. Educ.:* Paris. Officier de Cavalerie, 5ᵉ huissards démissionnaire, 1876; député des Hautes-Pyrénées, 1877-92; Chevalier de la Légion d'honneur, Chevalier de Malte (hérédité). *Heir: s.* François. *Address:* 2 rue Rude, Paris; Château de Bevilliers, Breteuil (Seine-et-Oise). *Clubs:* Jockey, Cercle de la Rue Royale, du Bois de Boulogne, Paris.

(Died 5 Nov. 1916.)

BRETT, Sir Charles Henry, Kt., *cr.* 1906; LL.D.; solicitor; *b.* Grey Abbey, Co. Down, 16 July 1839; *e. s.* of Rev. Wills Hill Brett; *m.* 1863, Margaret, *d.* of Robert Neill, Belfast;

two *s.* three *d. Educ:* privately. *Recreations:* music, gardening. *Address:* Gretton, Malone, Belfast. *Club:* National Liberal.

(Died 17 July 1926.)

BRETT, Sir Henry, Kt., *cr.* 1926; principal proprietor Auckland Star; *b.* Hastings, England, 1843; arrived in Auckland, 1862; with Mr. McCullough Reed, started the Auckland Star, 1870; started the New Zealand Graphic, 1890; Mayor of Auckland, 1877-78; represented New Zealand as Commissioner at Paris Exhibition, 1889. *Publications:* Early History of New Zealand; Brett's Colonist's Guide; Life and Times of Sir George Grey, etc. *Address:* Promenade, Takapuna, Auckland, New Zealand.

(Died 29 Jan. 1927.)

BREUN, J. E., R.B.A., 1895; Portrait Painter; *b.* 27 Nov. 1862; 2nd *s.* of late John Needham Breun. *Educ.:* Private School, London. Bronze medal, South Kensington, for drawing from the nude figure; 1st silver medal for portrait painting in the Royal Academy Schools, 1881; 1st silver medal for the second best drawing from the nude, R.A. Schools, 1882; 1st prize of £50 for the best set of 6 drawings from the nude figure at the R.A. Schools, 1883; 1st silver medal for the best drawing of a figure from the life, R.A., 1884; extra silver medal for the painting of the nude, R.A., 1884; 1st silver medal for the best copy of an oil painting, R.A., 1881; gold medal for a picture at the Paris Salon, 1892, called Cold Steel. *Principal Portraits:* Princess Victoria of Wales; Adelina Patti; Princess of Pless; Countess of Londesborough; Countess of Carnarvon; Marquise d'Hautpoul; Lady Victoria Plunket; Earl of Carnarvon; Gen. Sir Redvers Buller; Maj.-General Sir E. Hutton; Gen. Sir Percy Feilding; Dr. W. G. Grace; Field-Marshal Lord W. Paulet; Earl of Stamford, etc. *Recreations:* boating, lawn tennis, billiards. *Address:* Studio, 4 Greek Street, Soho Square, W. *Club:* Junior Constitutional. *(Died 8 July 1921.)*

BREWER, Sir (Alfred) Herbert, Kt., *cr.* 1926; Mus.Doc. Cantuar. 1905; Mus.Bac. Dublin, 1897; F.R.C.O. 1897; Hon. R.A.M. 1906; Organist and Master of Choristers, Gloucester Cathedral, since 1896; Conductor Gloucester Festivals, 1898, 1901, 1904, 1907, 1910, 1913, 1922, 1925; *b.* Gloucester, 21 June 1865; *e. s.* of late Alfred Brewer, Gloucester; *m.* Ethel Mary, 2nd *d.* of late H. W. Bruton, Gloucester; two *s.* one *d. Educ.:* Cathedral School, Gloucester; Exeter College, Oxford. Chorister, Gloucester Cathedral, 1877-80; Organist, St. Catharine's Church, Gloucester, 1881; Organist, St. Mary de Crypt, 1881; Organist, St. Giles' Church, Oxford, 1882-85; First Organ Scholar, Royal College of Music, 1883; Organ Scholar of Exeter College, Oxford, 1883; Organist of Bristol Cathedral, 1885; Organist of St. Michael's Church, Coventry, 1886-92; Organist and Music Master, Tonbridge School, 1892-97; Conductor, Bristol Choral Society, Gloucestershire Orchestral Society, Gloucester Choral Society; Examiner in Music, Birmingham University, 1924-1926; Examiner for R.C.O. and Associated Board R.A.M. and R.C.M.; High Sheriff, City of Gloucester, 1922-23. *Publications:* chief compositions—Orchestral Service in C (Gloucester Festival, 1895); 98th Psalm (Gloucester Festival, 1898); Emmaus (Gloucester Festival, 1901); Dedication Ode (Worcester Festival, 1902); The Holy Innocents (Gloucester Festival, 1904); A Song of Eden (Worcester Festival, 1905); Three Elizabethan Pastorals (Hereford Festival, 1906); Sir Patrick Spens (Cardiff Festival, 1907); In Springtime (Leeds Festival, 1907); England, my England (Worcester Festival, 1908); Age and Youth (Promenade Concerts, Queen's Hall, 1908); Summer Sports (Gloucester Festival, 1910); Jillian of Berry, Pastorals (Hereford Festival, 1921); Millers Green (Hereford Festival, 1924); A Sprig of Shamrock

(Gloucester Festival, 1925); For Your Delight (song cycle), Hereford Festival, 1927; Idyl for orchestra. *Recreation:* motoring. *Address:* Millers Green, Gloucester. *T.:* 3283. *M.:* FH 4466. *(Died 1 May. 1928.)*

BREWER, Rev. Edward, M.A.; Vicar of Holy Trinity, Old Hill, 1888-1920; Hon. Canon of Worcester; *m.* Mary Jane *(d.* 1920). *Educ.:* St. John's College, Cambridge. Ordained, 1872; Curate of Broadwater, 1872-74; London Diocesan Home Missionary, St. John's, N., 1874-78; Vicar of St. Thomas, Islington, 1878-88. *Address:* Wilton Lodge, Malvern. *(Died 31 May 1922.)*

BREWER, Rt. Rev. Leigh Richmond, S.T.D.; Bishop of Montana since 1880; *b.* Berkshire, Vermont, Jan. 20, 1839; *m.* 1866, Henrietta W. Foote; one *d. Educ.:* Hobart College; General Theological Seminary, New York. Ordained, 1866; in charge of Grace Church, Carthage, N.Y., 1866-72; Rector Trinity Church, Watertown, 1872-80; D.D., 1881. *Address:* Helena, Montana, U.S.A. *(Died 28 Aug. 1916.)*

BREWILL, Lieut.-Colonel Arthur William, D.S.O. 1916; *b.* 17 May 1861; *s.* of late W. R. Brewill, Nottingham; *m.* 1884, Clementine K. Thornley; three *s.* two *d. Educ.:* University School; private tutor Fellow of the Royal Institute of British Architects, and for 20 years Surveyor to the Diocese of Southwell; Lieutenant in The Robin Hoods, 1881 (now the 7th (Robin Hood) Batt. Sherwood Foresters), taking over the command of the Battalion, 31 July 1915, on the O.C. being wounded; commanded the Battalion at Hooge, 31 July 1915, when they were ordered to dig a new trench, and connect the British trench line where it had been captured by the Germans; commanded the Battalion at the attack on the Hohenzollern Redoubt, 13 Oct. 1915 (despatches, D.S.O.). *Address:* Edwalton Valley, Notts. *(Died 18 Feb. 1923.)*

BREWIS, Nathaniel Thomas, M.B., C.M., F.R.C.S., F.R.C.P., Edinburgh; Gynaecologist to the Royal Infirmary of Edinburgh; Lecturer on Gynaecology, Royal Infirmary, Edinburgh; *b.* Eshott Hall, Northumberland; 2nd *s.* of Thomas Brewis of Eshott; *m.* Annie Eliza, *e. d.* of R. S. Douglas of Acton Hall, Northumberland; one *s.* one *d. Educ.:* Edinburgh Institution and Edinburgh University. President Scottish Rugby Football Union; President Edinburgh Obstetrical Society; Examiner in Gynaecology, Edinburgh University; Obstetrician and Gynaecologist, Edinburgh New Town Dispensary; Gynaecologist in Leith Hospital. *Publications:* Outlines of Gynaecological Diagnosis; A Series of Abdominal Sections; Displacements of the Uterus; Endometritis, etc. *Recreations:* riding, fishing, golf. *Address:* 6 Drumsheugh Gardens, Edinburgh. *T.:* Central, 2248. *Club:* Caledonian United Service, Edinburgh. *(Died 21 Oct. 1924.)*

BRICE, Arthur John Hallam Monteflore, of the Middle Temple and the Oxford Circuit; Barrister-at-law; J.P.; F.R.G.S.; Hon. A.R.I.B.A.; Recorder of Tewkesbury since 1923; *s.* of Rev. Thomas Law Monteflore, M.A., Rector of Catherston, Dorset, and Rural Dean, and Katherine, *o. c.* of Rev. Edward Cowell Brice, M.A., Winterbourne Manor and Newnham, Glos.; *m.* 1st, 1886, Sybil *(d.* 1895), *d.* of E. L. Osbaldeston Mitford of Mitford Castle, Northumberland, and Hunmanby Hall, Yorkshire; 2nd, 1902, Sybil Constance, *e. d.* of late Major H. Reveley Mitford (51st K.O.L.I.); one *s.* Major in the Army, attached Staff, 1914-19; Judicial Officer in Ireland, 1920-22. Travelled in earlier years about Asia, North and South America, Oceania, and the Arctic regions. *Publications:* David Livingstone; Geographical Methods, 1895; The Great Frozen Land (editor), 1895; The Law relating to the Architect; the Law of Misrepresentation; numerous scientific

124

and legal papers. *Recreation:* fly-fishing. *Address:* 2 Hare Court, Temple, E.C.4. *T.A.:* 5 Temple. *T.:* Central 1777. *Club:* Reform. *(Died 6 Jan. 1927.)*

BRIDGE, Brig.-Gen. Sir Charles Henry, K.C.M.G., *cr.* 1916; C.B. 1897; C.M.G. 1900; Inspector Remount Department since 1906; 1st Army Corps, 1903; *b.* 16 June 1852; 4th *s.* of late Archdeacon Bridge, and Sarah Christianna, *d.* of J. Dunscombe; *m.* 1885, Elizabeth Dorcas, *d.* of late Sir Edward Morris, K.C.B.; one *s. Educ.:* Canterbury; Jesus College, Cambridge. Joined Control Department, 1872; Egyptian Campaign, 1882 (medal and star); D.A.Q.M.G. Headquarters War Office, 1886-91; command of A.S.C., Aldershot, 1891-96; campaign in Rhodesia, 1896, on staff of Sir Frederick Carrington (medal and C.B.); brevet of Colonel; Headquarters Staff, Colchester, 1897-99; Director of Transport, South Africa Field Force, 1899-1900; A.A.G. Aldershot, 1900-1902 (medal 3 clasps, despatches, C.M.G.); Director of Transport, 1903; Inspector of Remounts, 1903; Brig.-Gen. 1914; retired, 1918. *Club:* Junior United Service. *(Died 18 July 1926.)*

BRIDGE, Admiral Sir Cyprian Arthur George, G.C.B., *cr.* 1903; K.C.B., *cr.* 1899; *b.* 15 March 1839; *s.* of late Archdeacon Bridge; *m.* 1877, Eleanor, *d.* of G. Thornhill, C.S.I. Entered Navy, 1853; Rear-Admiral, 1892; Vice-Admiral, 1898; Admiral, 1903; served White Sea, 1854; Bay of Bengal during Indian Mutiny; and with Naval Brigade in Burma; member of Committee on Heavy Guns, 1878; of War Office Committee on Explosives, 1879; also on Armour Plates and Projectiles, 1879; of Ordnance Committee, 1881; Director of Naval Intelligence, 1889-94; Commander-in-Chief Australian station, 1895-98; Commander-in-Chief China station, 1901-4; retired 1904; presided, North Sea Enquiry Commission, 1904; Admiralty Representative on Royal Patriotic Fund Corporation, 1906-12; Member of Statutory Mesopotamia Commission, 1916-17. *Publications:* The Art of Naval Warfare; Sea-Power and Other Studies, 1910; Some Recollections, 1918. *Address:* Coombe Pines, Coombe Warren. *T.:* Kingston 1746. *(Died 16 Aug. 1924.)*

BRIDGE, Sir Frederick, Kt., *cr.* 1897; C.V.O. 1911; M.V.O. 1902; King Edward Professor of Music, Lond. Univ. since 1902; M.A.; Mus. Doc. Oxon.; F.R.C.O.; Fellow, Royal College of Music, 1921; Organist Westminster Abbey, 1875-1918; retired with title Emeritus-Organist of Westminster Abbey; Gresham Professor of Music from 1890; Conductor Royal Choral Society, 1896-1922; *b.* Oldbury, Worcestershire, 5 Dec. 1844; *s.* of John Bridge; *m.* 1st, 1872, Constance Ellen, *d.* of S. L. Moore; one *s.* one *d.*; 2nd, 1888, Helen Mary Flora *(d.* 1905), *d.* of E. Amplett; one *d.*; 3rd, 1914, Marjory Wedgwood, *d.* of Reginald N. Wood, of Bignall End, Staffordshire. *Educ.:* Cathedral School, Rochester. Chorister, Rochester Cathedral, 1850-59; Assistant Organist, 1865; Organist Trinity Church, Windsor, 1865-69; Organist Manchester Cathedral, 1869-75. *Publications:* Cantatas; Oratorios; Theoretical Works; Church Music; Shakespeare and Music Birthday Book; Samuel Pepys; Lover of Music, 1904; A Westminster Pilgrim, 1919; Twelve good Musicians, 1920; The Old Cryes of London, 1921, Shakesperean Music (In the Plays and early Operas), 1923, etc. *Recreations:* fishing, shooting. *Address:* Cloisters, Westminster Abbey, S.W.1; *T.:* Victoria 3384; Cairnborrow Lodge, Glass, Scotland. *Club:* Athenæum. *(Died 18 Mar. 1924.)*

BRIDGEMAN, Brig.-Gen. Hon. Francis (Charles); J.P. Salop and Staffordshire; *b.* 4 July 1846; *s.* of 3rd Earl of Bradford; *m.* 1st, 1883, Gertrude *(d.* 1911), *e. d.* of George Hanbury, of Blythewood, Bucks.; four *s.*

one d.; 2nd, 1918, Agnes Florence, d. of late Richard Holt Briscoe. Educ.: Harrow. Entered Scots Guards, 1865 ; Lieut. and Capt. 1869 ; Capt. and Lieut.-Col. 1877 ; Colonel, 1887 ; retired on half-pay, 1889 ; retired from the Army, 1894, on retired pay ; A.D.C. to General Officer commanding Home District, 1875-76 ; appointed to Special Embassy to Madrid to marriage of Alphonso XII. ; Knight of Isabel-la-Catolica of Spain ; served in Soudan campaign of 1885 (medal with clasp and Khedive's star). Contested Stafford, 1874 ; Tamworth, 1878 ; Bolton, 1880. M.P. for Bolton at General Elections 1885, 1886, and 1892 ; Brig.-Gen. commanding Staffordshire Volunteer Infantry Brigade, 1892-99 ; Commanded Central London Vol. Group of Co. of London Vol. Regt., 1915. Address: 59 Ennismore Gardens, S.W. ; T.: Western 3308; The Priory, Beech Hill, Reading. Clubs: Carlton, Wellington.
(Died 14 Sept. 1917.)

BRIDGES, John Henry, M.A., J.P. for Surrey and Co. Aberdeen; b. 26 March 1852; o.s. of late Rev. Alexander Henry Bridges, Hon. Canon of Winchester and Rector of Beddington, Surrey, and Caroline Matilda, d. of C. Hodgson, Treasurer of Queen Anne's Bounty; m. 1st, 1879, Edith Isabella (d. 1907), y. d. of late Henry Tritton, banker, 54 Lombard Street; six s. three d.; 2nd, 1909, Dorothy Mary, e. d. of R. B. Jacomb of 4 Wetherby Gardens, S.W. Educ.: Winchester; Oriel College, Oxford. High Sheriff of Surrey, 1919-20. Breeder of Aberdeen-Angus Cattle; Captain Oxford Univ. Assoc. Football XI., 1874-5; played in winning XI. for Oxford in Association Challenge Cup; Champion Archer, 1905; has represented Surrey in cricket; Member of Royal Company of Archers, King's Bodyguard for Scotland. Recreations: agriculture, shooting, archery. Address: The Court, Eastbourne; T.A.: Court, Eastbourne; T.: Eastbourne 62; Fedderate, Aberdeenshire. Clubs: United University; Sussex, Eastbourne.
(Died 12 Feb. 1925.)

BRIDGES, Rear-Admiral Walter Bogue, F.R.G.S., F.R.C.I.; b. 1843, s. of John William and Harriet Bridges of Birch, Essex, and London; m. 1880, Annie Caroline, d. of John and Anna Wilson of Woodlands, Victoria, Australia; one s. four d. Entered Navy, 1856, as naval cadet on board the Royal Albert, flagship of Admiral Lord Lyons, Commander-in-Chief in the Black Sea and Mediterranean ; afterwards served in the English Channel and North Sea, West Indies, and North America, West Coast of Africa and Australian stations, and Pacific Islands ; captain, 1884 ; Rear-Admiral on the retired list, 1899 ; Fellow Royal United Service Institution. Address: Trawalla, Victoria, Australia. Clubs: United Service, London ; Melbourne Melbourne ; Union, Sydney. (Died 27 Dec. 1917.)

BRIDPORT, 2nd Viscount (cr. 1868), Arthur Wellington Alexander Nelson Hood, C.B. 1892 ; Baron Bridport, 1794 ; Duke of Bronté (in Italy), 1799 ; b. 15 Dec. 1839 ; e. s. of 1st Viscount Bridport and Lady Mary Hill, 2nd d. of 3rd Marquess of Downshire ; m. 1872, Lady Maria Georgiana Julia Fox-Strangways (d. 1922), sister of 5th Earl of Ilchester; two d. M.P. West Somerset, 1868-80 ; formerly Captain 25th Foot; Colonel West Somerset Yeomanry, 1872-95. Heir: g.s. R. A. H. Nelson Hood. Clubs: Naval and Military. (Died 28 Mar. 1924.)

BRIERLEY, Edgar, O.B.E. 1918 ; Stipendiary Magistrate for the City of Manchester since 1908 ; b. 1858 ; 5th s. of James Brierley, Rochdale; m. Catharine, d. of J. H. Lancashire, Rochdale ; one s. one d. Educ.: Rugby School; University College, Oxford. Called to the Bar, 1882 ; Northern Circuit ; Member Royal Commission on Divorce, 1909-12 ; Chairman

Manchester Tribunal 1915-18. Address: Sandfield, Rochdale. (Died 25 Jan. 1927.)

BRIGGS, Hon. Sir Henry, Kt., cr. 1916 ; President Legislative Council Western Australia since 1906 ; b. Kettering, 17 Mar. 1844 ; s. of George Briggs. Educ.: Kettering ; St. Mark's College, Chelsea. Master in Practising School, 1865-67 ; Headmaster of Mottram Grammar School, 1868 ; founded Fremantle Grammar School, 1882 ; Member for West Province, 1896 ; Chairman of Committees, Legislative Council, 1900 ; President, 1906 ; Delegate, Australian Federal Convention, 1897-98 ; P.M. and P.Z. in Freemasonry: Member of W.A. Museum, Library and Art Gallery Boards ; Territorial Magistrate for W.A. Address: Fremantle, W. Australia. Clubs: Freemasons', W.A.

BRIGHT, James Franck, D.D.; b. London, 29 May 1832; s. of Richard Bright, M.D.; m. Emmeline Theresa, d. of Rev. E. D. Wickham, Vicar of Holmwood, 1864 ; four d. Educ.: Rugby; Univ. Coll. Oxford. Master at Marlborough Coll. ; Head of Modern Dept. there for 16 years. Returned to Oxford, 1872, as History Tutor in Balliol New College and University ; Fellow and Dean of University College, 1874 ; Hon. Fellow of Balliol, 1878 ; Master of University College, Oxford, 1881-1906. Publications: History of England to 1900 ; Lives of Maria Theresa and Joseph II., 1897. Recreations: fishing, sketching. Property: Lord of the Manor of Brockbury, Colwall, Hereford. Address: Hollow Hill, Ditchingham, Norfolk. Club: Athenæum.
(Died Oct. 1920.)

BRIGHT, John Albert, b. 1848 ; e. s. of late Rt. Hon. John Bright and late Margt. Elizth., d. of late William Leatham of Heath, Wakefield ; m. 1883, Edith Eckersley, d. of late W. T. Shawcross of Foxholes, Rochdale ; one s. one d. Educ.: Grove House School, Tottenham ; Univ. Coll., London ; M.P.(L.U.)Central Birmingham, 1889-95, and (L.) Oldham, 1906-10. Address: One Ash, Rochdale. T.: Rochdale 541; Bright's Farm, Christian Malford, Wilts. ; Monkshill, Monkton Combe, Somerset. Club: Reform.
(Died 11 Nov. 1924.)

BRIGHT, Sir Joseph, Kt., cr. 1906 ; b. 1849 ; s. of Joseph Bright of Nottingham ; m. 1879, Frances Ellen (d. 1906), d. of Nathaniel Dickinson of Nottingham ; two s. two d. Educ.: Sherwood House School, Nottingham. Solicitor, 1871 ; Sheriff of Nottingham, 1892 ; Mayor, 1894, 1895, and 1904 ; Chairman Nottingham University College, 1895-1911 ; Alderman of the City since 1896 ; J.P. 1896. Recreation: golf. Address: Park, Nottingham. T.: 646. Club: National Liberal. (Died 3 July 1918.)

BRIGHTMORE, A. W., D.Sc., M. Inst. C.E.; Engineering Inspector, Ministry of Health, Whitehall ; b. 9 May 1864 ; s. of late Henry Brightmore of Bowdon; m. 1894, Fanny Alexandra, y. d. of late J. McM. Cannon, of Rock Ferry, Cheshire. Educ.: The Owens College, Manchester. Resident Engineer for late Dr. G. F. Deacon on part of the Liverpool (Vyrnwy) Waterworks; afterwards Resident Engineer for late James Mansergh, F.R.S., on part of the Birmingham (Elan) Water Supply ; Professor of Structural Engineering, Royal Indian Engineering College, Coopers Hill, Staines, 1899-1907. Publications: Waterworks Engineering, with J. H. T. Tudsbery, D.Sc., M.Inst.C.E., 1893 ; Structural Engineering, 1908. Address: Egham Hill, Surrey.
(Died 20 April 1927.)

BRINDLE, Rt. Rev. Robert, D.S.O.; b. 1837. Consecrated March 1899 as Bishop Auxiliary to Cardinal Vaughan ; Provost of R.C. Cathedral, Westminster, since 1901. Retired Army Chaplain ; D.S.O. conferred for services in Egypt and Soudan, including battles of Atbara and Khartoum. Holds many medals and clasps, and many times mentioned in despatches. R.C.

Bishop of Nottingham, 1901-16. *Address:* Bishop's House, Nottingham.

(Died 27 June 1916.)

BRINKLEY, Captain John Turner ; O.B.E. 1925 ; Chief Constable of Warwickshire ; *b.* 1855 ; *e. s.* of late Walter Stephens Brinkley, of Knockmaroon House, Co. Dublin ; *m.* Mary *(d.* 1923), *d.* of late General H. A. Carleton, C.B., of Clare, Co. Tipperary ; one *d. Educ.:* Clifton; Pembroke College, Cambridge. Captain North Staffordshire Regt. *Address:* Wasperton House, nr. Warwick. *Club:* Naval and Military.

(Died 14 Dec. 1928.)

BRINSON, J. Paul, R.B.A. ; landscape painter. Exhibitor at the Royal Academy, International Society, Royal Institute of Painters in Water-Colours, etc. ; Secretary of the British Water-Colour Society. *Address:* West Woodlands, Reading. *(Died 21 Dec. 1927.)*

BRISCO, Sir Hylton Ralph, 5th Bt. ; *cr.* 1782 ; *b.* 24 Sep. 1871 ; *s.* of 4th Bt. and Mary, *d.* of Sir W. H. Feilden, 2nd Bt. ; *m.* 1904, Lilian Mabel (who *div.* him, 1915) *d.* of James King and niece of Lucy, Countess of Egmont; 2nd, 1916, Grace (whom he divorced, 1921), *d.* of late Henry Vaughan ; *S.* father 1909. Owns about 4000 acres. *Heir: c.* Aubrey Hylton, *b.* 11 Dec. 1873. *Address:* Coghurst Hall, Hastings, Sussex. *Clubs:* Junior Carlton, Wellington.

(Died 29 Jan. 1922.)

BRISCOE, Sir Alfred Leigh, 2nd Bt., *cr.* 1910 ; J.P., Barrister ; *b.* 26 Apr. 1870 ; *s.* of 1st Bt. and Ellen *(d.* 1910), *o. d.* of A. Charlton, Oak House, Altrincham ; *m.* 1910, Margaret Mackie, *d.* of late Thomas Sinclair of Conyair, Harray, Orkney ; no *c.* ; *S.* father 1919. *Educ.:* Corpus Christi College, Oxford. *Heir: b.* Dr. John Charlton Briscoe. *Address:* 26 Buckingham Mansions, West Hampstead, N.W. ; 8 Old Square, Lincoln's Inn, W.C.2. *T.:* Holborn 899. *(Died 13 May 1921.)*

BRISCOE, Major Edward William, R.A. (retired) ; *b.* 29 Sep. 1857 ; 2nd and *e. surv. s.* of late Henry Briscoe, M.D., R.A. ; *m.* 1887, Helen Mary, *d.* of late Surg.-Colonel E. G. McDowell, C.B. *Educ.:* Royal Military Academy, Woolwich. Lieut. Royal Artillery, 1877 ; retired as Major, 1895 ; appointed to the Prison Service, 1895 ; and served as Deputy-Governor of Portland Prison, and afterwards as Governor of Lincoln, Borstal, and Portland prisons ; Inspector of Prisons, 1907 ; Commissioner, 1916 ; retired, 1921 ; a Member of the Home Office Committee for the Employment of Conscientious Objectors, 1916-19 ; Member of Advisory Committee to Home Secretary at H.M. Preventive Detention Prison at Camp Hill, I. of W. *Club:* Junior United Service.

(Died 27 Nov. 1928.)

BRISCOE, Sir John James, 1st Bt., *cr.* 1910 ; J.P., D.L. ; *b.* 6 Dec. 1836 ; *m.* 1863, Ellen *(d.* 1910), *o.d.* of A. Charlton, Oak House, Altrincham ; four *s.* three *d.* Sheriff of Cambridgeshire and Hunts, 1888. *Heir: s.* Alfred Leigh [*b.* 26 Apr. 1870 ; J.P., Barrister ; *m.* 1910, Margaret Mackie, *d.* of late Thomas Sinclair of Conyair, Harray, Orkney. *Address:* 26 Buckingham Mansions, West Hampstead, N.W. ; 8 Old Square, Lincoln's Inn]. *Address:* Bourn Hall, Cambridgeshire. *Club:* National.

(Died 1 May 1919.)

BRISCOE, John Potter, F.R.S.L., F.R.H.S., Hon. F.L.A. ; City Librarian of Nottingham, 1869-1916 ; Consulting City Librarian, 1917 ; V.P. of Library Association, 1891-1920, of which he was an original member ; Member of Council of Thoroton Society ; *b.* Lever Bridge, near Bolton, 20 July 1848, *e. s.* of late John Daly Briscoe ; *m.* 1st, Elizabeth Baxter, Bolton ; 2nd, Sophia Wallis, Nottingham ; one *s. Educ.:* Bolton; by father. Engaged in tuition at Bolton, 1862-66 ; Assistant Borough Librarian at Bolton, 1866-69. *Publications:* Curiosities of the Belfry ; Bypaths of Notting-

hamshire History ; Chapters of Nottinghamshire History ; Gleanings from God's Acre ; Nottinghamshire Facts and Fictions, two series ; Sonnets and Songs of Robert Millhouse ; Old Nottinghamshire, 2 vols. ; Stories about the Midlands ; Nottinghamshire and Derbyshire at the Dawn of the 20th Century ; A Great Masonic Writer (Dr. Oliver), and other Masonic publications ; Editor of The Bibelots series, 29 vols. ; Sportsman's Classics, 3 vols. ; Notts and Derbyshire Notes and Queries, 6 vols. ; Tudor and Stuart Love Songs, Mitford's Stories of Village and Town Life ; Antiquarian Editor of Nottinghamshire Guardian for twenty-one years. *Recreations:* literary work, gardening, and snapshotting. *Address:* 38 Addison Street, Nottingham. *(Died 7 Jan. 1926.)*

BRISSON, Adolphe, Président d'honneur de la Critique ; late Dramatic Critic of Le Temps ; Directeur des Annales politiques et Littéraires ; Commandeur Legion of Honour ; *m.* Madeleine Sarcey ; four *c. Educ.:* École Monge ; Lycée Condorcet. *Publications:* Portraits intimes ; Florise Bonheur ; L'Envers de la gloire ; Paris intime ; Coindu Parnasse ; Le Théâtre et les mœurs ; Nos humoristes ; Pointes sèches ; La Comédie littéraire ; Les Prophètes ; Le Théâtre contemporain (9 vols.). *Address:* 5 rue la Bruyère, Paris. *(Died 28 Aug. 1925.)*

BRISTOL, Hon. Edmund, P.C., K.C. 1908; *b.* 4 Sep. 1861 ; *m.* 1889, Dorothy, *d.* of late Hon. Chief Justice Armour. *Educ.:* Toronto University (B.A.). Barrister, 1886 ; Member House of Commons of Canada for Centre Toronto since 1905 ; Director Dubilier Condenser and Radio Corporation ; Associate Counsel with legal firm of Bain Bicknell, Macdonnell & Gordon ; Cabinet Minister of the Government of the Dominion of Canada, without portfolio, and a Privy Councillor, 1921. *Recreations:* yachting, hunting, golf. *Address:* 179 Beverley Street, Toronto. *Clubs:* Constitutional ; York, Toronto, Albany, Toronto, Hunt, Royal Canadian Yacht, Toronto ; Mount Royal, Montreal ; Rideau, Ottawa. *(Died 14 July 1927.)*

BRITTAIN, William Henry, F.R.G.S., F.L.A., J.P. ; *b.* 2 April 1835 ; *s.* of late W. Swann Brittain of Sheffield and Mary, *d.* of Rev. T. Bosher of Brightwell, Berks ; *m.* 1871, Fanny, *o. d.* of late J. J. Mellor of Prestbury, Cheshire ; two *s.* two *d.* Member of the Sheffield City Council since 1871 (the senior member); Chairman of the Town Trustees; Mayor 1883-84 and 1884-85 ; entertained the late Prince Albert Victor at Storth Oaks on his first public visit, 1885 ; The Master Cutler of Sheffield 1878 and 1879 ; President of the Chamber of Commerce, 1892-95 ; British Commissioner to Antwerp Exhibition, 1894 ; and to Brussels Exhibition, 1897 ; Chairman Dore and Chinley Railway Company ; Member of the Archæological Association ; Member of the General Committee of the British Association since 1878 ; Past President of the Museums Association, and of the Public Libraries Association ; P.M. of many lodges ; Past P.G. Warden, W. Yorks, and Past G. S. B. (England); *Recreations:* Literature and music and collecting objects of arts and antiquity. *Address:* Storth Oaks, near Sheffield. *T.A.:* Alma Sheffield. *T.:* Broomhill 16, Sheffield. *M.:* LN 3544. *Clubs:* Royal Societies ; Sheffield.

(Died 29 June 1922.)

BRITTEN, James, K.C.S.G. ; Vice-President Catholic Truth Society (Hon. Secy. 1884-1922); *b.* Chelsea, 3 May 1846. *Educ.:* private schools. Assistant in Kew Herbarium, 1869 ; in Department of Botany, British Museum, 1871-1909 ; created Knight of St. Gregory by Leo XIII., 1897, and Knight Commander, con placca, 1917 ; Fellow of Linnean Society, 1870 ; original member of Folklore, English Dialect, Bibliographical and Catholic Record Societies. *Publications:* Dictionary of English Plant-Names

(with R. Holland), 1878-86; European Ferns, 1879-81; Old Country and Farming Words, 1880; Biographical Dictionary of English and Irish Botanists (with G. S. Boulger), 1893; Protestant Fiction, 1896, 1899; Illustrations of Australian Plants collected by Banks and Solander, 1900-1905; edited Aubrey's Remaines of Gentilisme, 1880; Turner's Names of Herbes, 1881; editor League of Cross Magazine, 1884-1887; Nature Notes, 1890-97; Journal of Botany since 1880; Catholic Book-Notes, 1898-1922; numerous pamphlets and contributions to religious, literary and scientific journals. *Recreations*: editing, music, pictures. *Address*: 41 Boston-Road, Brentford, Middlesex. *Club*: Reform.
(*Died 8 Oct. 1924.*)

BRITTON, Hon. Byron Moffat, K.C.; Justice of the Supreme Court of Judicature, Ontario; Judge of King's Bench Division, High Court of Justice; *b.* 3 Sept. 1833, Gananoque, County of Leeds; *m.* 1863, Mary Eliza, *d.* of late Hon. L. H. Holton; one *s.* six *d. Educ.*: Victoria University. Barrister; K.C.; Mayor of Kingston; Chairman Public School Board; County Crown Attorney; Kingston Bencher of Law Society of Upper Canada; Drainage Referee of Ontario; Member House of Commons for Kingston; Director of National Trust Company. *Address*: Osgoode Hall, Toronto. *Clubs*: Frontenac, Kingston; York, Toronto.
(*Died 14 Jan. 1921.*)

BROADBENT, Benjamin, M.A., J.P.; C.B.E. 1918; LL.D.; Freeman of the Borough of Huddersfield, 1918; Fellow of King's College, London; Hon. Member American Child Welfare Association; *b.* 7 May 1850; 6th *s.* of John Broadbent, Longwood Edge, Huddersfield; *m.* 1880, Louisa Ann, *d.* of William Keighley, Huddersfield; one *s. Educ.*: Huddersfield College; King's College, London; Queen's College, Oxford. Member of Huddersfield Corporation, 1886-1913; Chairman of Health Committee; Mayor of Huddersfield, 1904-5 and 1905-6; succeeded to business of Woollen Merchant established by grandfather before 1796 with younger brother as partner; Mill-owner and Director of Parkwood Mills Co., Ltd.; Longwood Finishing Co., Ltd.; Longwood Engineering Co.,Ltd. *Publications*: various articles and papers connected with Public Health Administration, and in particular with the Prevention of Infantile Mortality and the Promotion of the Welfare of Mothers and Children. *Recreations*: reading, gardening, and walking. *Address*: Gatesgarth, Lindley, Huddersfield. *T.A.*: Gatesgarth, Lindley. *T.*: 1286. *Clubs*: Cavendish, Overseas; Huddersfield.
(*Died 25 June 1925.*)

BROADFOOT, Col. Archibald, C.B. 1894; *b.* 15 Jan. 1843; 2nd *s.* of late Alexander Broadfoot, Amberley, New Zealand. *Educ.*: Royal Academy, Woolwich. Lieut. R.A. 1864; Lieut. R.H.A. 1875; Captain R.A. 1877; Captain R.H.A. 1881; Brevet Major, 1881; Major R.A. 1884; Major R.H.A. 1886; Lieut.-Colonel R.A. 1892; Lieut.-Col. R.H.A. 1893; Colonel, 1896; retired, 1898; served Bhootan, 1865-66 (medal with clasp); Abyssinia, 1868 (medal); Afghanistan, 1878-79-80 (medal with three clasps, Brevet Major). Mahsoud Waziri Expedition, 1881; Annexation of Upper Burmah, 1885-86 (clasp). *Recreations*: riding, fishing, shooting. *Address*: Duncree, Newton Stewart, N.B.
(*Died 15 Mar. 1926.*)

BROADFOOT, Major William, Royal Engineers (retired); *b.* 1841; *e. s.* of the late Alexander Broadfoot, and late Margaret, *d.* of late William Douglas; *m.* 1870, Esther Sutherland, *d.* of late Dr. A. Broadfoot; no *c. Educ.*: privately; Addiscombe College. Lieutenant, R.E., 1860; Captain, 1874; Major, on retirement, 1881; served with the Hazara Field Force (Black Mountain) 1868 (medal and clasp); served in civil capacity in Irrigation Depart-

ment of Punjab, 1864-68; Assistant Secretary to Punjab Government, 1868-78; since retirement engaged chiefly in literary work, scientific geography, the study of small arms, ammunition, and bullet wounds; municipal management and public health; was Councillor, Borough of Paddington, 1902; referee of Royal Geographical Society on Afghanistan, Baluchistan, and India. *Publications*: The Career of Major George Broadfoot, C.B., 1888; Billiards, 1896, revised 1906, in Badminton Library; paper on Parts of the Ghilzi Country, Afghanistan; articles in Quarterly, National, and Historical Reviews; in Blackwood's and Badminton Magazines; in Athenæum, Times, Encyclopædia Britannica, etc. *Recreations*: sport, travel, rowing, landscape painting in water-colour, billiards. *Address*: 103 Gloucester Terrace, W.2. *Club*: Naval and Military.
(*Died 8 April 1922.*)

BROADHURST, Sir Edward Tootal, 1st Bart., *cr.* 1918; D.L., J.P.; *b.* 19 Aug. 1858; 2nd *s.* of Henry Tootal Broadhurst of Woodhill, Prestwich, Manchester; *m.* 1887, Charlotte Jane, *y. d.* of Thomas Ashton of Ford Bank, Didsbury, Manchester; no *c. Educ.*: Dr. Huntingford's Eagle House, Wimbledon; Winchester. In business in Manchester since 1876; President Manchester Athenæum; President Warehousemen and Clerks' Orphan Schools; Chairman Manchester and Liverpool District Bank; Director London and North Western Railway; High Sheriff of Lancs., 1906-7. *Heir*: none. *Address*: The Manor House, North Rode, Congleton. *Clubs*: Conservative, Garrick.
(*Died 2 Feb. 1922.*)

BROADHURST, Mary Adelaide, M.A. (Lond.); President of National Political League; *d.* of late William Broadhurst, C.C., Manchester. *Educ.*: London University; M.A. degree in Mental and Moral Science. One of the first to organise Physical Science Laboratories in Girls' Secondary Schools, and other educational movements; founder of the National Political League in association with Miss Margt. Milne Farquharson, and President since its organisation in 1911; on the outbreak of war in 1914 was the originator of the Women's Land Army, and pioneered its work during the war, when it was the means of sending over 30,000 women as workers on the land, and developing food production centres, etc. As President of the League promoted the formation of the American Women's Land Army; was leader in organising the political work of the National Political League after the war, in particular the National Campaign to rouse the spirit of the nation to an understanding of the Communist forces that menace it, and in defence of its own ideals of national freedom; has organised also the movement in England for the promotion of Anglo-Arab friendship and Arab development; and is taking an active part in work for the protection of British Empire interests and against Bolshevist intrigues in the Middle East. *Address*: Bank Buildings, 16 St. James's Street, S.W.1; 22 Hornton Court, Kensington, W.8. *T.*: Gerard 0334; Regent 2944. (*Died 8 Dec. 1928.*)

BROADLEY, Alexander Meyrick, lawyer, author, journalist, and collector; *b.* 19 July 1847; *e. s.* of late Rev. A. Broadley, Canon of Salisbury, and late Frances Jane, *y. d.* of late Thomas Meyrick, of Bush, Pembrokeshire. *Educ.*: Warminster and Marlborough Grammar Schools; Switzerland. Called to Bar, Lincoln's Inn, 1869; began to practise as an advocate in Tunis, 1873; represented the Bey of Tunis in his differences with the French Republic, 1880-1881; special correspondent of Times in Tunis, 1881, and Egypt, 1882; Senior Counsel of Arabi Pacha and the other state-prisoners at Cairo, Dec. 1882; made an Advocate of French Bar by decree of President of Republic, 1883;

BROADBENT, A. See page xvii.

for many years held the appointment of Standing Counsel to the ex-Khedive Ismail Pacha of Egypt. *Publications:* History of Freemasonry in Malta and Tunis, 1880; Tunis Past and Present, 2 vols. 1882; How we defended Arabi, 1883; (joint) The Three Dorset Captains at Trafalgar, 1906; The Boyhood of a Great King, 1906; The History of Freemasonry in West Dorset, 1907; (joint) Napoleon and the Invasion of England, 1907, 2 vols.; (joint) Nelson's Hardy, 1907; (joint) Dumouriez and the Defence of England against Napoleon, 1908; and (joint) Doctor Johnson and Mrs. Thrale, 1909; (joint) The War in Wexford, 1910; Chats on Autographs, 1910; Napoleon in Caricature, 2 vols., 1910; joint author, Bath Pageant, 1909; West Dorset Pageant, 1911; History of Garrards [1731-1911], 1911; The Royal Miracle, 1912; The Romance of an Elderly Poet (joint); The Beautiful Lady Craven, 2 vols. (joint); The Journal of a British Chaplain in Paris during the Peace Negotiations of 1801-2; The Ship Beautiful, Art and the Aquitania, 1914; contributions to numerous reviews and newspapers, etc. *Recreation:* collections of portraits, prints, medals, and MSS. relating to Napoleon, Nelson, Dorset History, Freemasonry, Bath, the Drama, Caricature, Boscobel, Cricket, Aviation, and many other subjects; has extra-illustrated some fifty volumes. *Address:* The Knapp, Bradpole, Bridport, Dorset. *Club:* Junior Conservative.
(Died 16 April 1916.)

BROADWOOD, Brig.-Gen. Arthur, C.V.O. 1905; *b.* 1849; *s.* of late Henry Broadwood, M.P. for Bridgwater; *m.* 1873, Mary Frances (*d.* 1925), *d.* of the late Edward Richard Meade. *Educ.:* Trinity Hall, Cambridge. Entered Scots Guards, 1869; Captain, 1871; Lieut.-Col., 1881; Col., 1902 (retired, 1906); Hon. Brig.-Gen., 1912; served with Soudan Expedition, 1885 (medal with clasp, bronze star); Commandant at School of Instruction for Auxiliary Forces, Wellington Barracks, 1884-86, and at School of Instruction for Mil. and Vol. there, 1900; in command of Royal Guards Reserve Regt., 1900-1, and of 1st Regt. Dist., 1901-5; Brig.-Gen. commanding Lowland Grouped Regt. Dist., Scottish Command, 1905-1906; in command of a Vol. Infantry Brigade, 1906-8; East Midland T.F. Brigade, 1908-11; specially employed on Home Defence, 1914-16. *Address:* 52 Wilbury Road, Hove. *Club:* Carlton.
(Died 2 Jan. 1928.)

BROADWOOD, Lt.-Gen. Robert George, C.B. 1900; retired; late commanding troops in South China, 1906; Brig.-Gen. commanding Orange River Colony District, 1904-6; A.D.C. to the King; *b.* 14 March 1862; *s.* of late Thomas Broadwood of Holmbush Park, Surrey. Entered army, 12th Lancers, 1881; Lt.-Col. 1897; served Dongola Expeditionary Force, 1896 (despatches, brevet of Lieut.-Col., British medal, Khedive's medal with two clasps); Egyptian War, 1898, including Atbara (despatches) and Khartoum (despatches, brevet of Col., Osmanieh, British medal, three clasps to Khedive's medal). Served South Africa, 1899-1902 (despatches, twice, Queen's medal and six clasps, King's medal and two clasps); commanding troops in Natal, 1903-1904. *Address:* 94 Piccadilly, W.
(Died 21 June 1917.)

BROCK, Sir Thomas, K.C.B., cr. 1911; R.S.A. (hon. 1910), A.R.I.B.A. (hon. 1908), R.A. 1891, A.R.A. 1883; D.C.L. Oxford; sculptor; Membre d'honneur de la Société des Artistes français; *b.* 1847; *s.* of Wm. Brock, Worcester; *m.* 1869, Mary Hannah, *o. c.* of late Richard Sumner of Nottingham. *Educ.:* under Foley. *Works:* The Moment of Peril; The Genius of Poverty; Eve; Edward the Black Prince; busts of Queen Victoria and Lord Leighton; statues of Sir Richard Owen and Dr. Philpott, Bishop of Worcester; sepulchral

128

monument to Lord Leighton in St. Paul's; memorial statues of Queen Victoria; designer and sculptor the Queen Victoria Memorial, Buckingham Palace. *Address:* 30 Osnaburgh Street, Regent's Park, N.W.; Merrieweathers, Mayfield, Sussex. *Club:* Athenæum.
(Died 22 Aug. 1922.)

BROCKLEBANK, Thomas, J.P., D.L.; *b.* 1841; 2nd *s.* of late Ralph Brocklebank, J.P. and D.L., Lancashire, and Eliza Ann, *d.* of Richard Moon of Liverpool; *m.* 1867, Mary Petrena, *d.* of Henry Royds of Elm House, Wavertree, J.P., Lancashire; five *s.* *Educ.:* Sir R. Cholmeley's School, Highgate. High Sheriff, Cheshire, 1901; joint patron of four livings. *Address:* Wateringbury Place, Kent; Villa San Leonardo, Florence, Italy. *M.:* LD 7648. *Clubs:* Conservative, Constitutional, Ranelagh, Burlington Fine Arts.
(Died 16 Feb. 1919.)

BROCKWELL, Rev. Canon John Cornthwaite, M.A.; Vicar of Thorpe Salvin, Worksop, 1917-24; Canon of Sheffield Cathedral, 1914; *b.* 25 March 1843; *s.* of Josiah Brockwell, a London merchant; *m.* 1868, Clara Walter, *d.* of Walter Brodie, and *g.-g.d.* of John Walter; four *s.* three *d.* *Educ.:* University College School, London; Christchurch, Oxford. Formerly Curate to Dr. Llewelyn Davies at Christchurch, St. Marylebone, 1866; also Curate of St. Mary Magdalen's, Paddington, 1867, and of Honiton, Devon, 1868; Vicar of Owston, Yorkshire, 1869. *Recreations:* rowing and cycling. *Address:* Ivy House, Norton, Doncaster.
(Died 25 Nov. 1927.)

BRODEUR, Hon. Louis Philippe, LL.D. Laval; P.C.; a Judge of the Supreme Court of Canada since 1911; *b.* Beloeil, Province of Quebec, 21 Aug. 1862; *s.* of Toussaint Brodeur, a patriot of 1837, and of Justine Lambert; *m.* 1887, Emma, *d.* of J. R. Brillon, Notary, of Beloeil; four *s.* one *d.* *Educ.:* College of St. Hyacinthe and Laval University. Called to Bar, 1884; K.C. 1899; editor of Le Soir, 1896; elected to House of Commons for Rouville, 1891, 1896, 1900, 1904, 1908; Deputy-Speaker of the House of Commons, 1896-1900; Speaker, 1900-1904; Minister of Inland Revenue, 1904-1906; Minister of Marine and Fisheries Dominion Government, 1906-11; introduced a Bill against the American Tobacco Trust, and this legislation had the desired effect of putting an end to the American methods which the Tobacco Company wanted to establish in Canada; a member of the Imperial Conferences of 1907 and 1911, and one of the Ministers who negotiated the Franco-Canadian Treaty of 1907; represented Canada at the Imperial Defence Conference of 1909; author of the first Naval Bill introduced in the Canadian Parliament (1910), and when the Department of the Naval Service was organised he was put of charge of it; Canada's representative at the Washington Conference held in pursuance in the decision of the Hague Tribunal on the North Atlantic fisheries; has taken keen interest in navigation in all Canadian waters, and by establishment of innumerable aids to navigation along the St. Lawrence has made that river navigable under all conditions, whether during night or day or in foggy weather. *Address:* Ottawa, Canada. *Clubs:* Hunt, Rideau, Rivermead, Ottawa; Country, Winchester, Montreal.
(Died 2 Jan. 1924.)

BRODIE, George Bernard, M.D., Physician to Queen Charlotte's Hospital; Consulting Physician Accoucheur, to St. George's Hanover Square Dispensary; *b.* 6 Aug. 1839; *s.* of late Charles George Brodie, Salisbury; *m.* 1893, Mary, *d.* of late James Maxwell, Petrograd; three *s.* one *d.* *Address:* 65 Princes Gate, S.W.; Woodbury, Farley Hill, Reading. *Club:* Athenæum.
(Died 27 May 1919.)

BRODIE, Thomas Gregor, F.R.S. 1904; Professor of Physiology, Toronto University, since 1908; Captain, C.A.M.C., No. 4 Canadian General Hospital; *b.* Northampton, Feb. 8. 1866; 2nd *s.* of late Rev. Alexander Brodie, Vicar of Grandborough; *m.*; three *s.* *Educ.* : King's College School, London; St. John's College, Cambridge; King's College, London. Demonstrator of Physiology, King's College, London, 1890; Senior Demonstrator of Physiology, London Hosp. Med. School, 1894; Lecturer on Physiology, St. Thomas's Hosp. Med. School, 1895; Director of the Research Laboratories of the Royal Colleges of Physicians and Surgeons, London, 1899; Fellow of King's College, London; Professor-Superintendent, Brown Animal Sanatory Institution, University of London, 1903-9; Professor of Physiology, Royal Veterinary Coll. London, 1903-9; Lecturer on Physiology, London School of Medicine for Women, 1899-1909; Croonian Lecturer, Royal Society, 1911; F.R.S. Canada. *Publications:* Essentials of Experimental Physiology; and numerous papers in scientific journals. *Recreation:* golf. *Address:* The University, Toronto. *Club:* Devonshire.

(Died 20 Aug. 1916.)

BRODIE, Brevet Major (Acting Lt.-Col.) Walter Lorrain, V.C. 1914; M.C.; 2nd Batt. Highland Light Infantry; *b.* 28 July 1884. Entered army, 1904; served European War, 1914-17 (V.C., M.C.); Brevet Major, 1918. *Address:* 23 Belgrave Crescent, Edinburgh.

(Died 23 Aug. 1918.)

BRODRICK, Sir Thomas, Kt., *cr.* 1922; Late Secretary and Chief Accountant, Co-operative Wholesale Society, Ltd.; *b.* Scarborough, Yorks, March 1856; *s.* of Patrick Brodrick and Bessie Donlon; *m.* 1884, Margaret Kelly; two *s.* two *d.* *Educ.:* Private School, Scarborough. Commenced with C.W.S. as Junior Clerk, 1872; retired, 1923; Member of Committees on Post Office Wages and Food Prices. *Address:* Woodlands, Victoria Crescent, Eccles. *T.:* Eccles 8   *(Died 26 Oct. 1925.)*

BROMFIELD, Rev. George Henry Worth, M.A.; Vicar, St. Mary, Princes Road, Lambeth, 1878-1919; Rural Dean of Lambeth, 1881-1912; Hon. Canon of Southwark Cathedral; *s.* of Henry Jenkins Bromfield, Causton, Dunchurch, Warwickshire; *b.* 29 May 1842. *Educ.:* Rugby; University Coll. Oxford. Ordained to the curacy of St. Mary, Lambeth, 1867. *Address:* St. Botolph's Road, Worthing.

(Died 4 July 1920.)

BROMFIELD, Major Harry Hickman, D.S.O. 1900; of Newnham Hall, Northamptonshire; Chief Constable Radnorshire; *e. s.* of Henry Bromfield of Newnham Hall (*d.* 1888) and Mary Elizabeth, *e. d.* of late John Colthurst of Chew Court, Somersetshire; *b.* 29 Jan. 1869; *m.* 1906, Ethel Philippa, *e. d.* of Sir Charles Philipps, 1st Bart; one *s.* *Educ.:* Malvern; Hertford College, Oxford. Capt. and Hon. Maj. 3rd-Batt. S. Wales Borderers; served with 2nd S. Wales Borderers in S. Africa, 1900-1 (despatches, D.S.O.); afterwards served with 3rd S. Wales Borderers, 1901-2; rejoined 9th Service Batt. S. Wales Borderers, 1915, and transferred to the 1st Batt. Welsh Guards, 1915. *Address:* The Lee, Knighton; County Constabulary Headquarters, Llandrindod Wells, Radnorshire. *Clubs:* Guards', Junior Carlton.

(Died Sept. 1916.)

BROMHEAD, Col. Charles James, C.B. 1893; *b.* 15 Sept. 1840; *s.* of Sir Edmund de Gonville Bromhead, 3rd Bt.; *m.* Alice Marie, *d.* of late Thomas Freckleton, 1876; one *s.* Served in Ashanti, Zulu, and Burmese Wars; in command of the 24th Regimental District, 1892-97; J.P. Denbighshire. *Address:* Plâs Drâw, Ruthin.

(Died 24 Dec. 1922.)

BROOK, Edward Jonas, J.P., County of Dumfries; *b.* 13 Mar. 1865; *e. s.* of Edward Brook and Emma Brooke; *m.* 1905, Jessie Elizabeth,

y. d. of late John Bell-Irving of White Hill. *Educ.* : Radley; Jesus College, Cambridge. Is a Director Glasgow and South-Western Railway. *Recreations:* hunting, shooting, fishing. *Address:* Hoddom Castle, Ecclefechan, N.B. *Clubs:* Boodle's, Carlton. *(Died 17 July 1924.)*

BROOK, Herbert Arthur, I.S.O. 1905; J.P. *b.* 31 Jan. 1855; *s.* of late Joshua Anderson Brook and Eliza Beresford Wylly; *m.* 1888, Mary Elizabeth Brace; one *s.* *Educ.:* Nassau Grammar School, New Providence, Bahamas. Librarian, Nassau Public Library, 1875-79; Clerk to Police Office, 1879-83; Chief Clerk in Colonial Secretary's Department, Bahamas, Clerk to Board of Public Works, 1883-87; Registrar of Records, Bahamas, 1887-1911; retired 1911; superintended Bahamas Census, 1891 and 1901; some time Army Dist. Paymaster, Bahamas. *Address:* 34 Queen Street, Nassau, New Providence, Bahamas.

(Died 25 Jan. 1925.)

BROOKE, Emma Frances, novelist; *b.* Cheshire; descended from old yeoman family on the mother's side, and on the father's side an old Yorkshire family; unmarried. *Educ.:* Newnham Coll., Cambridge. Came to London, 1879; belonged to the Fabian Society since its beginning and formerly a student of London School of Economics. *Publications:* A Superfluous Woman, 1894; Transition, 1895; Life the Accuser, 1896; The Confession of Stephen Whapshare, 1898; A Tabulation of European Factory Acts, in so far as they relate to the hours of labour, and special regulations for women and children, 1898; The Engrafted Rose, 1900; The Poet's Child; Twins of Skirlaugh Hall, 1903; Susan Wooed and Susan Won, 1905; Sir Elyot of the Woods, 1907; The Story of Hauksgarth Farm, 1909; The House of Robershaye, 1912. *Recreations:* walking, and the study of bird life; sitting over the fire with a friend or a book; hearing clever people talk.

(Died 28 Nov. 1926.)

BROOKE, Rt. Rev. Francis Key, D.D.; Missionary Bishop of Oklahoma since 1893; *b.* Gambier, Ohio, 2 Nov. 1852; *s.* of Rev. J. T. Brooke, D.D., and Louisa R. Hunter; *m.* 1881, Mildred R. Baldwin; four *d.* *Educ.:* Kenyon Coll., Gambier, Ohio, U.S.A. Deacon, 1875; Priest, 1877; Clerical Charges at College Hill, Portsmouth, Piqua and Sandusky in Ohio, also in St. Louis, Mo., and Atchison, Kas. *Publications:* Official Reports, Charges, etc., and a few sermons. *Address:* 427 N. 9th Street, Oklahoma City, Oklahoma, U.S.A.

(Died 22 Oct. 1918.)

BROOKE, Rt. Hon. Frank, P.C., D.L., J.P.; Chairman Dublin and South-Eastern Railway; Chairman Irish Branch of Norwich Union Society, National Bank; Commissioner of Irish Lights; Steward of Turf Club; *b.* 1851; *y. s.* of George Brooke and the Lady A. Brooke of Ashbrooke, Brookbore, Co. Fermanagh; *m.* Alice Mary (*d.* 1909), *d.* of very Rev. W. Ogle Moore, Dean of Clogher; two *s.* one *d.* *Educ.* : private school. Joined Royal Navy, 1865; retired as Lieutenant, 1877; contested S. Fermanagh twice in Unionist interest; Land Agent of Fitzwilliam Estates in Ireland. *Recreations:* shooting and hunting. *Address:* Ardeen, Shillelagh, Co. Wicklow. *Clubs:* Bachelors'; Kildare Street, Dublin; Royal St. George Yacht, Kingstown.

(Died 30 July 1920.)

BROOKE, Temp. Lt.-Col. George Frank, D.S.O. 1917; retired list; late Connaught Rangers; *b.* 30 Oct. 1873; *e. s.* of Rt. Hon. Frank Brooke, R.N., and Alice Mary, *d.* of Very Rev. W. Ogle Moore, Dean of Clogher; *m.* 1907, Theodora Olivia, *d.* of Richard Meredith Jackson, Natal; two *s.* Served S. Africa, 1899-1900 (severely wounded, medal with clasp); European War (despatches thrice, D.S.O.); A.D.C. to G.O.C. Dublin, and to G.O.C. Cape Colony. *Address:* Saxenberg,

6

129

Kuils River, Cape Provence, S. Africa. *Club:* Army and Navy.

BROOKE, Sir George Frederick, 1st Bt., *cr.* 1903; D.L.; *b.* 13 Aug. 1849; *s.* of late Francis R. Brooke of Summerton, and Hon. Henrietta (d. 1911), d. of 3rd Viscount Monck; *m.* 1st, 1875, Annie (d. 1877), d. of Geoffrey J. Shakerley; 2nd, 1881, Emily Alma (d. 1917), d. of Augustine H. Barton; seven *s.* two d. *Educ.:* Eton; Trinity Coll., Camb. D.L. City Dublin; J.P. Co. Wexford; High Sheriff, 1882; J.P. Co. Dublin; High Sheriff, 1898; Director (Governor, 1904-6) of Bank of Ireland since 1891. Protestant (Church of Ireland). Owns 6500 acres. *Heir: s.* Francis Hugh, Capt. South Irish Horse, late 60th K.R. Rifles [*b.* 10 Nov. 1882; *m.* 1915, Mabel, *y.* d. of late Sir John Arnott, 1st Bt., and Lady FitzGerald Arnott]. *Address:* Pickering, Celbridge, Co. Kildare. *Clubs:* Carlton; Kildare Street, Sackville Street, Dublin.   (*Died* 21 Aug. 1926.)

BROOKE, Captain Sir Harry Vesey, K.B.E., *cr.* 1920; J.P., D.L.; 2nd *s.* of late Sir Arthur Brinsley Brooke, 2nd Bart., M.P. of Colebrooke, Co. Fermanagh, Ireland, and Hon. Henrietta Julia Anson, Maid of Honour to H.M. Queen Victoria, 1889-42; *b.* 23 Sep. 1845; *m.* Patricia, *o. c.* of late J. G. Moir Byres of Tonley, Aberdeenshire; one *s.* two d. *Educ.:* Sandhurst. Served in 92nd Gordon Highlanders, 1864-79. *Recreations:* shooting, fishing, golfing, etc. *Address:* Fairley, Countess-walls, Aberdeenshire. *Clubs:* Naval and Military; Royal Northern, Aberdeen.   (*Died* 11 June 1921.)

BROOKE, Rev. James Mark Saurin, M.A., F.R.G.S., F.R.B.S.; Rector of St. Mary Woolnoth, and St. Mary Woolchurch Haw, Lombard Street; *b.* Warrenpoint, 23 April 1842; 2nd *s.* of Canon Brooke and Lucy, d. of Rt. Rev. James Saurin, Bishop of Dromore; *m.* Amy, *o. c.* of John Stanford, Bridge Place, Suffolk; one *s.* four d. *Educ.:* Leicester; Trin. Coll. Dublin. Received 1st class certificate extra at School of Musketry, Fleetwood, 1865. Served in 1st Batt. 17th Foot of which was Assistant and Acting Instructor of Musketry in 1865; took Holy Orders, 1867; has travelled in Europe, Asia Minor, Palestine, Egypt, North of Africa, West Indies, Bahamas, etc.; Fellow of Sion College; Fellow of Royal Botanic Society; patron of one living; Lord of the Manors of Bressingham, Norfolk, of Badingham Hall, Colston Hall, Peasenhall, Southolt, Ufford, Woodbridge, etc., Suffolk; Hon. Chaplain to Worshipful Company of Makers of Playing Cards. *Publications:* Heart be Still, 1879; Transcript of Registers of St. Mary Woolnoth, with History of Church, 1886; Under the Lantern, 1888; Opus Consummavi, 1891; A Stirlingshire Pastoral; Hymns for Special Occasions, 1894; Do we believe? Unity and Wisdom, 1908; numerous articles, reviews, poems. *Recreations:* botany, fishing. *Address:* 20 Gledhow Gardens, S.W. *T.:* Kensington, 1702. *Club:* United Service.
    (*Died* 20 Feb. 1918.)

BROOKE, Sir John Arthur, 1st Bt. *cr.* 1919; J.P. West Riding, Yorks, and Co. Ross; *b.* 1844; 4th *s.* of late Thomas Brooke; *m.* 1873, Blanche, d. of Major Weston, Morvich. *Address:* Fenay Hall, Huddersfield. (*Died* 12 July 1920.)

BROOKE, Ven. Richard; Rector of Kalk Bay since 1901; Canon of St. George's Cathedral, Cape Town, since 1887; Archdeacon of the Cape, 1905; resigned, 1925; made Archdeacon Emeritus. *Educ.:* University of the Cape, B.A. Ordained 1864; Tutor Diocesan College Cape Town, 1861-66; Rector of Phillipolis, 1866-1868; Clanwilliam, 1868-78; Claremont, 1878-87; Warden Diocesan College School, 1886-87; Principal Diocesan College, Rondebosch, 1887-1901; J.P. *Address:* Rondebosch (P.), Cape Town.
    (*Died* 4 April 1926.)

BROOKE, Sir Richard Marcus, 8th Bt.; *cr.* 1662; J.P.; D.L.; *s.* of 7th Bt. and Lady Louisa

Duff, *s.* of 5th Earl of Fife; *b.* 26 Oct. 1850; S. father 1888; *m.* Alice, d. of J. S. Crawley, Stockhood Park, Luton, 1883; one *s. Educ.:* Eton. Formerly Lieut. 1st Life Guards. Owns about 6500 acres. *Heir: s.* Richard Christopher [*b.* 8 Aug. 1888; *m.* 1912 Marian Dorothea, *o. d.* of Arthur Charles Innes of Dromantine, County Down]. *Address:* Norton Priory, Runcorn. *Club:* Travellers'. (*Died* 9 Oct. 1920.)

BROOKE, Rev. Stopford Augustus, M.A., LL.D.; man of letters; *b.* Letterkenny, Donegal, Ireland, 1832; *e. s.* of Richard Sinclair Brooke and Anna, d. of Rev. T. Stopford, D.D.; *m.* Emma Diana, d. of Thomas Wentworth Beaumont, M.P., Bretton Park, Yorkshire, 1858. *Educ.:* Kidderminster; Kingstown; Trin. Coll. Dublin. Downe's Divinity Prize and Vice-Chancellor's Prize for English Verse. Ordained, June 1857; Curate of St. Matthew's, Marylebone, 1857-59; of Kensington Church, 1860-63; chaplain to Princess Royal, Berlin, 1863-65; minister of St. James's Chapel, York Street, 1866-75; Hon. Chaplain to the Queen; minister of Bedford Chapel, 1876-94; seceded from the Church of England, 1880. *Publications:* Life and Letters of the late Frederick W. Robertson, 1865; Freedom in the Church of England, 1871; Sermons, 1868-77; Theology in the English Poets, 1874; Primer of English Literature, 1876; A Fight of Faith, 1877; Riquet of the Tuft, a Love Drama, 1880; Spirit of the Christian Life, 1881; Unity of God and Man, 1886; The Early Life of Jesus, 1887; Poems, 1888; Dove Cottage, 1890; History of Early English Literature, 1892; Short Sermons, 1892; History of English Literature, 1894; Study of Tennyson, 1894; God and Christ, 1894; Jesus and Modern Thought, 1894; Old Testament and Modern Life, 1896; Life and Writings of Milton (Primers of English Literature); The Gospel of Joy, 1898; Poetry of R. Browning, 1902; Ten Plays of Shakespeare, 1905; Studies in Poetry, 1907; Four Poets, 1908. *Address:* The Four Winds, Ewhurst, Surrey. *Club:* Athenæum.
    (*Died* 18 Mar. 1916.)

BROOKE, Sir William Robert, K.C.I.E., *cr.* 1895; *b.* 1842; *s.* of Thomas Britannicus Brooke, E.I.C.S.; *m.* 1870, Evelyn, d. of John Simons. Entered Indian Telegraph Department, 1857; Superintendent Bombay, 1866-69; Punjab, 1869-71; Director 1883; Deputy Director-General, 1886-87; Director-Gen. of Telegraphs in India, 1887; retired 1895. *Address:* Albert Gate Mansions, 219 Knightsbridge, S.W. *Club:* Oriental.
    (*Died* 8 July 1924.)

BROOKE-HITCHING, Sir Thomas Henry, Kt.; *cr.* 1902; *b.* 1858; *s.* of John Walter Hitching, Halifax, Yorks; *m.* 1878, Sarah Kussuth, d. of David Brooke of Stannary; two *s.* Adopted surname of Brooke-Hitching by Royal licence; Sheriff of London, 1902-3; one of His Majesty's Lieutenants for the City of London; ex-Member London County Council; Common Councilman, and ex-Mayor of Marylebone Borough Council. One of the prime movers in the creation of separate municipalities for the Metropolis; contested Elland Division (Yorks), 1906. *Orders:* Coronation Silver Medal; Officer of the Legion of Honour, France; Officer of Leopold II., Belgium; Grand Cross of St. Saba, Servia; Grand Cross Danillo, Montenegro. *Address:* 8 Hereford Gardens, W.1; Corston House, Ryde, Isle of Wight. *T.A.:* Brooke-Hitching, London. *T.:* Mayfair 7029. *Clubs:* Royal Thames Yacht, Pilgrims.
    (*Died* 4 Feb. 1926.)

BROOKMAN, Sir George, K.B.E., *cr.* 1920; J.P.; late Chairman Repatriation Department for South Australia; Member of War Council of South Australia during the War; Chairman War Savings' Council during the War; Member of Royal Red Cross Society, South Australian Division; one of the Founders and Deputy-Chairman of the South Australian

Soldiers' Fund ; elected twice as Member of the Legislative Council ; *b.* Glasgow, 1853 ; *m.* 1878, Eliza Martha, *d.* of Alfred Marshall, Melbourne. Member of Council of University of Adelaide ; Life Governor Children's Hospital ; Chairman of Adelaide Electric Supply Company ; organised the original Syndicate which discovered and proved the famous Golden Mile at Kalgoorlie in 1893 ; Chairman of Bank of Adelaide ; assisted to establish School of Mines in 1898. *Address :* Brookman Buildings, Grenfell Street, Adelaide. *T. :* 497. *T.A. :* Brookman, Adelaide. *Club :* Junior Constitutional.

(*Died 20 June 1927.*)

BROOKS, Herbert, J.P., Surrey ; one of H.M. Lieutenants for the City of London ; Director of Bank of England ; *b.* 1842 ; *m.* Alice, *d.* of Rev. Richard Buller of Lanreath, Cornwall. *Educ. :* Harrow. High Sheriff for the County of London, 1912. *Address :* 17 Princes Gardens, S.W. *T. :* Western 2682. *Clubs :* Carlton, Conservative. (*Died 10 Oct. 1918.*)

BROOME, Viscount, Henry Franklin Chevallier Kitchener, Captain retired, R.N. ; *o. s.* of 2nd Earl Kitchener ; *b.* 17 Oct. 1878 ; *m.* 1916, *c.* Adela Mary Evelyn, *e. d.* of late J. H. Monins, Ringwould House, nr. Dover ; two *s.* one *d.* Specialised in gunnery ; Intelligence Division, Admiralty War Staff, 1912 ; served China, 1900 ; European War, 1914-18. *Heir : s.* Hon. Henry Herbert Kitchener, *b.* 24 Feb. 1919. *Address :* Broome Park, Canterbury.

(*Died 13 June 1928.*)

BROS, James Reader White, J.P. ; Police Magistrate, Clerkenwell, 1888-1921 ; *b.* 1841 ; *s.* of Thomas Bros, barrister ; *m.* 1871, Emily Spearman (*d.* 1921), *d.* of A. Wilkinson, of Coxhoe Hall, Co. Durham. Barr. Inner Temple, 1866. *Address :* 31 Elm Park Gardens, S.W. *Club :* Athenæum. (*Died 2 Oct. 1923.*)

BROUGH, Charles Allan La Touche, LL.B., M.B., B.S., F.R.C.S., Barrister-at-Law J.P. ; Mayor of Suva, Fiji (3 times) ; President Fijian Society ; Corresponding Secretary Royal Colonial Institute ; *s.* of Hon. Secker Brough, Judge of Court of Probate, Toronto, Canada ; and Mary Austwick de Bohun, Midhurst ; *m.* Mary Golightly, Durham ; two *d.* *Educ. :* Upper Canada College ; University of Toronto ; University of Durham. Private Secretary to Sir Oliver Mowat, Premier of Ontario ; Stipendiary Magistrate and Medical Officer, New Guinea, 1898 ; Stipendiary Magistrate, Fiji, 1904 ; Governor's Commissioner and Magistrate, 1907 ; Chief Police Magistrate, Suva, Fiji, 1908 ; Acting Attorney-General, Fiji, 1908 ; Member of the Executive and Legislative Councils of Fiji, 1908 ; served through the Fenian and Red River Expeditions in Canada. *Publications :* Law of Parliamentary Elections ; The Monroe Doctrine ; Anchylostomiasis, and various scientific papers. *Address :* Suva, Fiji. *T.A. :* Brough, Fiji. *T. :* Suva 71 and 94. *Clubs :* Royal Societies, Constitutional, Authors', Corona. (*Died 5 May 1925.*)

BROUGH, Major John, C.M.G. 1916 ; M.V.O. 1911 ; Royal Marine Artillery. Assistant to Professor of Fortification, R.N. College, Greenwich, 1901 ; Officer of Company of Gentleman Cadets, R.M. College, Sandhurst, 1908-7 ; P.S.C. ; Staff-Captain, War Office, 1910 ; Coronation medal, 1911 ; Staff-Officer to Insp.-Gen. W. African Field Force, 1911-14 ; served European War (Cameroons), 1914-16 (despatches, C.M.G.). *Club :* United Service. (*Died 29 July 1917.*)

BROUGH, Joseph, B.A., M.Sc., LL.D. ; External Examiner to University of London, 1919-23 ; *b.* 16 Mar. 1852 ; *s.* of William Brough of Rosemary Hill, near Newcastle-under-Lyme ; unmarried. *Educ. :* Grammar School, Newcastle - under - Lyme ; Wesleyan Collegiate Institution, Taunton ; Downing College, Camb. (1st Class in Moral Sciences Tripos, 1880, and in Law Tripos, 1881 ; Cobden Prize,

1883). Articled to Joseph Knight, solicitor, Newcastle-under-Lyme, 1870 ; admitted as a solicitor, 1875 ; lectured on Logic, Political Economy, and Jurisprudence, 1881-83 ; Professor of Logic and Philosophy, University College of Wales, Aberystwith, 1883-1911 ; Lecturer at Bedford College for Women, London, 1912 ; Emeritus Lecturer, 1922. *Publications :* The Study of Mental Science, 1902 ; articles in Encyclopædias of Religion and Education ; reviews and occasional papers in Mind, Proceedings of Aristotelian Society, and other journals, etc. *Recreations :* music and dramatics. *Address :* 12 Carlingford Road, Hampstead, N.W.3.

(*Died 7 Dec. 1925.*)

BROUGHAM and VAUX, 3rd Baron (*cr.* 1860), **Henry Charles Brougham,** K.C.V.O., *cr.* 1905 ; M.A., D.L., J.P. ; *b.* 2 Sept. 1886 ; *s.* of 2nd Baron and Frances, *d.* of Sir C. W. Taylor ; *S.* father 1886 ; *m.* 1882, Adora Frances Olga, *d.* of Peter Wells, Windsor Forest, and *widow* of Sir R. Musgrave, 11th Bt. ; one *d.* *Educ. :* Eton ; Trin. Coll., Camb. Clerk in House of Lords, 1857-86. Owns about 5000 acres. *Heir : g. s.* Victor Henry Peter Brougham, *b.* 1909. *Address :* 36 Chesham Place, S.W.1. *T. :* Victoria 3953 ; Brougham Hall, Penrith ; Château Eléonore, Cannes. *Clubs :* Marlborough, Arthur's, Brooks's, Bachelors', Garrick.

(*Died 24 May 1927.*)

BROUGHAM, Captain Hon. Henry, Coldstream Guards, S.R. ; *o. s.* and *heir* of 3rd Baron Brougham ; *b.* 26 May 1883 ; *m.* 1st, 1908, Hon. Diana Sturt (who obtained a divorce, 1919), *o. d.* of 2nd Baron Alington ; two *s.* one *d.* ; 2nd, 1923, Baroness Hengelmüller, *d.* of late Austro-Hungarian Ambassador in Washington. Knight of Grace of St. John of Jerusalem. *Heir : s.* Victor Henry Peter, *b.* 23 Oct. 1909. *Clubs :* Carlton, Pratt's, White's, St. James's.

(*Died 4 May 1927.*)

BROUGHAM, James Rigg ; *b.* 1826 ; 4th *s.* of J. W. Brougham, Edinburgh ; *m.* 1854, Isabella Eliza, *d.* of late J. Cropper of Dingle Bank, Liverpool. Registrar in Bankruptcy, 1848-91 ; senior Registrar, 1891 ; retired, 1917. *Address :* Beathwaite, Milnthorpe, Westmorland.

(*Died 5 Mar. 1919.*)

BROUGHTON, Rev. Henry Ellis, M.A. ; Vicar of Hugglescote since 1889 ; Hon. Canon, Peterborough, 1908 ; Rural Dean South Akley, 1893. *Educ. :* Harrow ; Caius College, Cambridge. Curate of Polebrook, Northants, 1872-1875. *Address :* Hugglescote Vicarage, Leicester.

(*Died 29 Dec. 1924.*)

BROUGHTON, Rhoda (Miss), novelist ; *b.* North Wales, 29 Nov. 1840. *Publications :* Cometh up as a Flower, 1867 ; Not Wisely but Too Well, 1867 ; Red as a Rose is She, 1870 ; Goodbye, Sweetheart, Goodbye, 1872 ; Nancy, 1873 ; Joan, 1876 ; Second Thoughts, 1880 ; Belinda, 1883 ; Dr Cupid, 1886 ; Alas, 1890 ; Mrs. Bligh, 1892 ; A Beginner, 1894 ; Scylla or Charybdis ? 1895 ; Dear Faustina, 1897 ; The Game and the Candle, 1899 ; Foes in Law, 1901 ; Lavinia, 1902 ; The Devil and the Deep Sea, 1910 ; Between Two Stools, 1912. (*Died 5 June 1920.*)

BROUN, Sir William, 10th Bt. ; *cr.* 1686 ; *b.* 18 Dec. 1848 ; *S.* 1882 ; *m.* Alice, *d.* of late J. C. Peters, Hope House, Manly Beach, Sydney, 1871 ; four *s.* three *d.* *Heir : s.* James Lionel, *b.* 1875. *Address :* Colstoun, Gunnedah, N.S. Wales ; Coonimbia, Coonamble, N.S. Wales. *T.A. :* Gunnedah and Coonamble. *T. :* Gunnedah 72 ; Coonamble 813. *M. :* 1425.

(*Died 23 Oct. 1918.*)

BROUNGER, Richard Ernest, M.Inst. C.E., late Agent-General for Orange River Colony in London ; *b.* 5 Dec. 1849 ; married ; three *s.* one *d.* *Educ. :* King's College, London. Engaged for about thirty years in the survey, construction, maintenance, and management of railways in South Africa ; constructed the main line of railway across the Orange Free State for the Cape Government, and was Director-General of the Orange Free State Government Railways. *Address*: Eden Lodge, Tilford, nr. Farnham, Surrey. *Club*: National Liberal.

(*Died 19 Jan. 1922*.)

BROUSSON, Louis Maurice, of a Huguenot family, editor and manager of London Citizen newspaper since 1895, writer of the financial article, From Moses Moss to Benjamin Boss, also city editor of provincial daily papers, including the Belfast News Letter, Liverpool Daily Courier, Yorkshire Observer, Sheffield Daily Independent, Bristol Daily Times, and the East Anglian Daily Times ; *m*. 1870, Clara Emily, 2nd *d*. of Robert Mace Habgood, of Perth, Western Australia ; four *s*. For many years connected with financial press. Editor, La Cité, French daily financial paper in London and of The City, 1880-88 ; editor of Invention, 1884-90 ; city editor of Truth, 1888-1902 ; city editor, Financial News, 1890-1904. *Address*: 31 Belsize Avenue, N.W.3 ; 2 Copthall Buildings, E.C. *T.*: Wall 4984 and Hampstead 6800.

(*Died 1 Jan. 1920*.)

BROWN, Adrian John, F.R.S. 1911 ; M.Sc., F.I.C. ; Professor of Biology and Chemistry of Fermentation, and Director of School of Brewing, University of Birmingham, since 1899 ; late Examiner in Biological Chemistry, Institute of Chemistry ; *b*. Burton-on-Trent, 27 April 1852 ; *s*. of Edwin Brown, F.G.S., Burton-on-Trent ; *m*. Helen F., *d*. of John Hutchison, Glasgow ; two *s*. two *d*. *Educ*.: Burton-on-Trent Gram. School ; Roy. School of Mines. Assist. to Dr. Russell, F.R.S., St. Bartholomew's Hosp. ; Chemist to T. Salt and Co., Burton-on-Trent. *Publications*: Laboratory studies for Brewing Students ; numerous papers published in Journal of Chemical Society and other journals. *Recreations*: fishing, geology, botany. *Address*: University, Birmingham ; Rimside, Northfield.

(*Died 2 July 1919*.)

BROWN, Hon. Alexander, M.L.C., J.P., Consul for Italy and Belgium, Managing Director, Dalgety & Co., Ltd. ; *b*. N.S. Wales, 1851 ; *s*. of W. Brown, M.D. ; *m*. 1872. *Educ*.: High School, West Maitland. Studied for the Law ; admitted a Solicitor of the Supreme Court of N. S. Wales in 1873 ; abandoned Law for Commerce ; entered Parliament Popular Branch ; was defeated later on, and afterwards called to the Legislative Council ; created Chevalier del order de Leopold for Consular Service, 1902. *Recreations*: reading and walking. *Address*: Cumberland Hall, East Maitland, N. S. Wales. *Club*: Warrigal, Sydney.

(*Died 28 Mar. 1926*.)

BROWN, Alexander Crum, M.A., M.D., Edinburgh ; D.Sc. London ; F.R.S. ; F.R.S.E. ; F.R.C.P.E ; F.C.S. ; F.I.C. ; LL.D. Aberdeen, Glasgow, Edinburgh, and St. Andrews ; *b*. Edinburgh, 26 Mar. 1838 ; *s*. of Rev. John Brown, D.D. ; *m*. Jane Bailie (*d*. 1910), *d*. of Rev. James Porter, Drumlee, Co. Down. *Educ*.: Royal High School, Edinburgh ; Mill Hill School ; Universities of Edinburgh, Heidelberg, Marburg. Extra-academical Lecturer on Chemistry, Edinburgh, 1863-69 ; President Chemical Society of London, 1892-93 ; Professor of Chemistry, Edinburgh University, 1869-1908. *Address*: 8 Belgrave Crescent, Edinburgh.

(*Died 28 Oct. 1922*.)

BROWN, Sir Alexander Hargreaves, 1st Bt. ; *cr*. 1902 ; *b*. 11 Apr. 1844 ; *g.s*. of Sir Wm. Brown, Liverpool, 1st Bt. ; *m*. 1876, Henrietta Agnes Terrell (*d*. 1921), *d*. of C. R. Blandy, Madeira ; two *s*. two *d*. V.D. ; J.P. Lancashire and Surrey ; late partner in Brown, Shipley and Co., Founders Court, Lothbury, E.C. ; M.P (U.) for Wenlock, 1868-85 ; Wellington Division Shropshire 1885-1906. *Heir*: *g.s*. John Hargreaves, [*b*. 16 Aug. 1913. *Address*: Bearehurst, Holmwood, Surrey]. *Ad-*

dress: Broome Hall, Holmwood, Surrey. *Clubs*: Reform, Brooks's. (*Died 12 Mar. 1922*.)

BROWN, Alexander Kellock, R.S.A., R.B.C. ; R.S.W., R.I. ; landscape painter ; *b*. 11 Feb. 1849 ; *s*. of Robert Brown and Margaret Kellock ; *m*. 1881, Mary Frew ; one *s*. one *d*. *Educ*.: Glasgow Normal Seminary ; Glasgow School of Art ; Heatherley's, London. *Works*: Frost in the Air ; A Dagger Day ; September in Arran ; Winter Morn ; A Spring Day ; Winter Twilight ; 'Twixt March and April ; Autumn at the Clachan. *Recreation*: a little cycling. *Address*: 152 Renfrew Street, Glasgow. *T.*: Douglas 2216. *Club*: Glasgow Art. (*Died 9 May 1922*.)

BROWN, Rev. Archibald Geikie; *b*. 18 July 1844 ; *s*. of late John Wm. Brown, Clapham Park. *Educ*.: C. H. Spurgeon's College. Founded Baptist Church, Bromley, Kent, 1863 ; Pastor at Stepney Green Tabernacle, 1866 ; built East London Tabernacle, opened 1872 ; President of London Baptist Association, 1877 ; withdrew from Baptist Union in company with C. H. Spurgeon, owing to "Down Grade Controversy," 1887 ; Pastor of Baptist Church, Chatsworth Road, West Norwood, S.E., 1897-1907 ; Pastor of Metropolitan Tabernacle, 1907-10. *Publications*: several volumes of sermons, and the protest The Devil's Mission of Amusement. *Recreation*: fishing. *Address*: 45 Endlesham Road, Balham, S.W. (*Died 2 April 1922*.)

BROWN, Major Cecil, M.A., R.B.S. ; *b*. Ayr, 1867. *Educ*.: Harrow ; Oxford. Studied in Florence and Paris ; exhibited at R.A., etc., since 1895 ; designed medal for International Medical Congress, London, 1913 ; enlisted Aug. 1914 ; Major, Sep. 1917 ; demobilised March 1919 ; designed Memorial to Imperial Camel Corps. *Publication*: The Horse in Art and Nature. *Recreations*: hunting, rowing, golf. *Club*: Arts.

BROWN, Rev. Prof. Francis, M.A. 1873 ; Ph.D. 1884 ; D.D. 1884, 1894, 1901, 1908, 1909 ; D.Litt. 1901 ; LL.D. 1901 ; Davenport Professor of Hebrew and the Cognate Languages, Union Theological Seminary, New York, since 1890 ; President of the Faculty, Union Theological Seminary, since 1908 ; *b*. 26 Dec. 1849 ; *s*. of Rev. Prof. Samuel Gilman Brown, D.D., LL.D., and Sarah Van Vechten ; *m*. 1879, Louise F. M. Reiss, Berlin ; one *s*. two *d*. *Educ*.: Phillips Academy, Andover, Mass. ; Dartmouth College, Hanover, New Hampshire ; Union Theological Seminary, New York, U.S.A. ; University of Berlin, Germany. Assist.-Master, Ayers' Latin School, Pittsburg, Pa., 1870-72 ; Tutor in Greek, Dartmouth College, 1872-74 ; Fellow of Union Theological Seminary, 1877-79 ; Instructor in Biblical Philology, Union Theological Seminary, 1879-81 ; Associate Professor of Biblical Philology, Union Theological Seminary, 1881-90. *Publications*: editor of Lenormant's Beginnings of History (English trans. of Les Origines de l'Histoire I.), New York, 1882 ; of The Teaching of the Twelve Apostles (with Rev. Prof. R. D. Hitchcock, D.D.), 1884 ; revised and enlarged edit. 1885 ; author of Assyriology : its Use and Abuse, 1885 ; The Christian Point of View (with Rev. Profs. George Wm. Knox, D.D., and Arthur C. McGiffert, D.D.), 1902 ; A Hebrew and English Lexicon of the Old Testament (with Rev. Profs. S. R. Driver, D.D., and C. A. Briggs, D.D.), thirteen parts, 1891-1906 ; also many articles and reviews. *Recreations*: walking, rowing. *Address*: 80 Claremont Avenue, New York, U.S.A. *T.A.*: Brown, Kissamchar, New York. *T.*: Morningside, 1491 New York. *Club*: Century, New York. (*Died 15 Oct. 1916*.)

BROWN, George, M.R.C.S. Eng. 1874 ; L.S.A. Lond. 1873 ; Hon. Surgeon, Exeter Dispensary ; General Secretary of Imperial Medical Reform Union ; Vice-President, Tariff Reform League ; Chairman, General Apothecaries' Co., Ltd., and Native Guano Co., Ltd. ;

Founder and Editor of Medical Times and Hospital Gazette and Founder of General Practitioner; *b.* Callington, Cornwall, 16 Jan. 1844; *s.* of late Thomas Brown; *m.* 1898, Edith Kate, *o. d.* of Maj.-Gen. Joseph Reay, Bengal Staff Corps; one *s.* *Educ.:* private schools; Charing Cross Hospital School of Medicine, London. Golding Scholar, 1871; Llewellyn Scholar, 1872; Gold Medal, 1873. House Surgeon at Charing Cross Hospital, 1873; Resident Medical Officer at the North-Eastern Hospital for Children, 1874; Prosector of Anatomy at the Royal College of Surgeons of England, 1874; Demonstrator of Anatomy at the Westminster Hospital Medical School, 1873-1874; Advocate of Fiscal Reform; Direct Representative for England and Wales on General Medical Council, 1897-1907. *Publications:* Aids to Anatomy, 1875; Aids to Surgery, 1876; The Fiscal Problem, 1903; contributions to the Times, Lancet, British Medical Journal, General Practitioner, etc. *Recreations:* shooting, bowls, and horticulture. *Address:* Mount Lodge, Silver Valley, Callington, Cornwall; 38 Southernhay East, Exeter. *Club:* Liberal Union.

BROWN, Hon. George William, Second Lieut.-Governor of Province of Saskatchewan since 1910; *b.* Holstein, Ont., 30 May 1860; *m.* 1895, Annie Gardiner, *d.* of James Barr, Norwich, Ont. *Educ.:* Toronto University. Studied law, and was admitted to the Bar of North-West Territories, 1892; member of North West Legislative Assembly, 1894-1905. *Address:* Regina, Sask., Canada. (*Died 17 Feb. 1919.*)

BROWN, Major Harold, D.S.O. 1915; 5th Batt. Yorkshire Regt. (T.F.). Entered army, 1914; late Captain, 4th Vol. Batt. Suffolk Regt.; served European War, 1914-15; (D.S.O., Bt. Major); made successful and daring reconnaissances, especially near Hooge.
(*Died 23 Mar. 1918.*)

BROWN, Horace T., F.R.S., LL.D. (Hon.) Edinburgh; *b.* Burton-on-Trent, 20 July 1848; *m.* 1874, Annie (*d.* 1915), *d.* of Paul J. Fearon; one *s.* two *d.* *Educ.:* Burton-on-Trent and Atherstone Grammar Schools; Royal College of Chemistry. Entered brewing business at Burton-on-Trent, 1866; retired 1893; Longstaff Medal of Chemical Society, 1894; President of Chemical Section of British Association, 1899; Royal Medal of the Royal Society, 1903; Member of Royal Commission on Whiskey, 1908; Copley Medal of the Royal Society, 1920; Governor of the Imperial College of Science and Technology, S. Kensington. *Publications:* numerous papers on Chemical, Biological, and Geological subjects, etc. *Address:* 5 Evelyn Gardens, S.W.7. *T.:* Kensington 5665. *Club:* Athenæum. (*Died 6 Feb. 1925.*)

BROWN, Horatio Robert Forbes, J.P., LL.D.; *b.* Nice, 16 Feb. 1854; *e. s.* of late Hugh Horatio Brown of Newhall and Carlops, and late Gulielmina, *d.* of Colonel Ranaldson Macdonell of Glengarry. *Educ.:* Clifton College; New College, Oxford (Exhibitioner); 2nd class, Classical Greats: Taylorian Lecturer, 1895; Hon. LL.D. Edinburgh, 1900; gold medal of the British Academy Serena Foundation, 1923; Member of the Ateneo Veneto; Honorary Member of the Regio Istituto Veneto di Scienze, Lettere ed Arti; Corresponding Member of the Regie Deputazioni, Veneta e Toscana, di Storia Patria. Has had the following manuscripts burned: Life on the Lagoons, at Kegan Paul's, 1883; A Study in the Venetian Inquisition, by fire in a mail car, Switzerland, 1886; Calendar of State Papers, at Spottiswoode's, 1892; Studies in Archæology, at Mr. Cecil Rhodes' house, Rondebosch, Capetown, 1895. *Publications:* Life on the Lagoons, 1884, 5th edition, 1909; Venetian Studies, 1887; The Venetian Printing Press, 1891; Venice, an

Historical Sketch, 1893, 2nd edition, 1895; John Addington Symonds, a Biography, 1895, 2nd edition, 1903; Calendar of State Papers (Venetian) 1581-1591, 1895; 1592-1603, 1897; 1603-1607, 1900; 1607-1610, 1904; 1610-1613, 1905; Drift; Verses, 1900; Temple Primer, The Venetian Republic, 1902; Cambridge, Modern History, vol. i., chapter on Venice, 1902; vol. iv., chapter on The Valtelline, 1905; In and Around Venice, 1905; Pensieri persi a contribution to die Festschrift des Herren Prälat Schneider, 1906; translation of Molmenti's Venice, vols. i. ii. iii. and iv.; Studies in the History of Venice, 1907; Introduction to the Poems of T. E. Brown, Golden Treasury series; translation of Molmenti's Venice, vols. v. and vi., 1908; Letters and Papers of John Addington Symonds, 1923; Cambridge Medieval History, vol. vi. Chapter xiii., 1923; Dalmatia, 1925. *Address:* 560 Campiello Incurabili, Zattere Venice. *Clubs:* Athenæum; New, Edinburgh. (*Died 19 Aug. 1926.*)

BROWN, James Clifton, J.P.; *b.* 13 Feb. 1841; 2nd *s.* of late Alexander Brown, *e. s.* of 1st Bt. of Beilby Grange, Co. York, and Sarah Benedict, *d.* of James Brown; *m.* 1866, Amelia, *d.* of Charles Rowe; five *s.* four *d.* *Educ.:* Trin. Hall, Camb.; M.A. High Sheriff, Sussex, 1888; patron of one living; Col. late Lancashire Artillery, S. Div. R.A.; formerly Lieut.-Col. 1st Lancashire Artillery Volunteers; M.P. Horsham, 1876-80. *Address:* 32 Ennismore Gardens, S.W.; Holmbush, near Horsham. *Clubs:* Reform, New University. (*Died 5 Jan. 1917.*)

BROWN, Hon. James Drysdale, M.L.C. Nelson Province; Minister of Mines, Forests, and Public Health, Victoria, since 1913; late Attorney-General and Solicitor-General. *Address:* Public Offices, Royal Chambers, Collins Street, Melbourne.

BROWN, Rev. (James) Wilson (Davy), B.A.; Hon. Canon of Ely Cathedral; *b.* 25 Aug. 1839; *s.* of late Rev. Thomas Brown, J.P., Rector of Hemingstone, Suffolk; *m.* 1st, *d.* of late Rev. Charles Bridges, Rector of Hinton Martell, Dorset; 2nd, *e. d.* (*d.* 1918) of late Col. F. Maitland Wilson, M.P., of Stowlangtoft Hall, Suffolk. *Educ.:* The Collegiate School, Leicester; Gonville and Caius College, Cambridge. Ordained, 1862; Curate of All Saints, Northampton, 1862-65; Curate in charge of Hinton Martell, Dorset, 1865-69; Brockworth, Gloucestershire, 1869-70; Stoke-by-Nayland, Suffolk, 1870-77; Vicar of Assington, Suffolk, 1877-98; Rector of Stowlangtoft, Suffolk, 1893-1920. *Address:* St. Mary's Square, Bury St. Edmunds. *Club:* County, Bury St. Edmunds.
(*Died 27 May 1922.*)

BROWN, Sir John, Kt., *cr.* 1920; J.P.; landed proprietor; Member of Kincardineshire County Council; Chairman of the Aberdeen Coal and Shipping Co. Ltd.
(*Died 28 April 1928.*)

BROWN, Very Rev. Dr. John D.D., M.A.; Moderator, General Assembly, Church of Scotland, 1916; Minister of Bellahouston, Glasgow, since 1887; *b.* Irvine, 5 Apr. 1850; *e. s.* of John Brown and Janet Sandilands; *m.* 1882, Margaret Romanes, *e. d.* of Very Rev. John Rankine, D.D., Sorn, Ayrs.; one *s.* three *d.* *Educ.:* Irvine; Edinburgh University. Ordained, 1876, to Parish of Galston, Ayrs. *Publications:* Imperialism and Church Union, 1916, and other addresses and papers. *Recreations:* golf, fishing. *Address:* The Manse, Bellahouston, Glasgow. *T.:* Ibrox 221.
(*Died 20 Feb. 1919.*)

BROWN, Dr. John, B.A., D.D., retired Congregational Minister; *b.* 19 June 1830; *e. s.* of William Brown, Bolton, Lancashire; *m.* 1859, Ada Haydon, 2nd *d.* of Rev. D. E. Ford, of Manchester; three *s.* three *d.* *Educ.:* private school; Owens Coll., Manchester; Lancashire Independent Coll. Manchester. Graduated B.A. at London University, 1853 ; received hon. degree of D.D. from Yale University, U.S.A., 1887 ; Minister of Park Chapel, Manchester, 1855 ; Bunyan Church at Bedford, 1864-1903 ; was Chairman of the Congregational Union of England and Wales, 1891 ; was Congregational Union Lecturer, 1898; Lyman Beecher Lecturer at Yale University, U.S.A., 1899. *Publications:* Lectures on the Book of Revelation, 1866 ; God's Book for Man's Life, 1882 ; John Bunyan, his Life, Times, and Work, 1885 ; The Pilgrim Fathers of New England, 1895 ; Apostolical Succession in the Light of History and Fact, 1898 ; Puritan Preaching in England, etc., 1900 ; From the Restoration to the Revolution, 1904. Commonwealth England, 1904 ; The English Puritans, 1910 ; History of the English Bible, 1911. *Address:* 10 Upper Park Road, Hampstead, N.W.3. *T.:* Hampstead 8562. *(Died 16 Jan. 1922.)*

BROWN, John James Graham, M.D., F.R.C.P.E., F.R.S.Ed. ; late Pres. Royal Coll. of Physicians of Edinburgh ; late Lecturer on Neurology, Edinburgh University ; Lecturer in Clinical Medicine in Edinburgh University and in School of Medicine of the Royal Colleges, Edinburgh ; *s.* of Rev. Thomas Brown, D.D. ; *m.* Jane Pasley Hay Thorburn ; three *s.* one *d.* *Educ.:* Edinburgh Academy ; Universities of Edinburgh, Berlin, Vienna, and Prague. Sometime Senior President of the Royal Medical Society ; House Physician and Surgeon to Royal Infirmary, Edinburgh, and in the Chalmers Hospital, Edinburgh ; in practice as a Physician in Edinburgh since 1880 ; Morison Lecturer to the Royal College of Physicians of Edinburgh, 1912 and 1918. *Publication:* Medical Diagnosis (4th ed. 1897) ; Treatment of Nervous Diseases (1905) ; various contributions to medical journals. *Address:* 3 Chester Street, Edinburgh. *T.:* Central 313. *Clubs:* Royal Societies ; University, Edinburgh.
(Died 28 Feb. 1925.)

BROWN, Sir John McLeavy, Kt., *cr.* 1905 ; C.M.G. 1898 ; LL.D. ; Head of the Customs and Controller of Finance, Korea, 1898-1906 ; *b.* 1842 ; *m.* Marie (*d.* 1911). Student-Interpreter in China, 1861 ; Assist. Chinese Secy., 1864 ; in charge of the Legation, 1867 ; Secretary to Chinese Mission to Europe, 1868 ; Acting Chinese Secretary at Pekin, 1871-72 ; resigned, 1872 ; Commissioner in the Chinese Customs ; holds first-class Sacred Treasure of Japan, and first-class Order of Tai-Kuk, Korea. *Address:* 49 Portland Place, W.1. *(Died 6 April 1926.)*

BROWN, Very Rev. John Pierce, Dean of Down, 1912-24 ; *b.* 23 July 1843 ; *m.* Sarah Price (*d.* 1907), *d.* of Rev. W. Ferrier Jex-Blake ; no *c.* *Educ.:* Trinity College, Dublin, **M.A.** Ordained 1868 ; Curate of Kilmore, 1868-70 ; Rector of Loughinisland, 1870 - 1911 ; Archdeacon of Down, 1899 - 1911. *Address:* Newcastle, Co. Down. *T.A.:* Clough, Down. *M.:* IJ 272. *Club:* Ulster, Belfast.
(Died 15 Mar. 1925.)

BROWN, Sir Joseph, Kt., *cr.* 1914 ; President of the Legislative Council of the Bahamas. *Address:* Nassau, Bahama Islands.
(Died 19 Aug. 1919.)

BROWN, Peter Hume, M.A., LL.D. Edin. and St. Andrews ; D.D. Geneva ; member British Academy ; Historiographer-Royal for Scotland since 1908 ; Professor of Ancient (Scottish) History and Palæography, Edinburgh (Sir William Fraser Chair) since 1901 ; Ford Lecturer, 1913-14 ; author ; *b.* Haddingtonshire, Scotland, 17 Dec. 1850. *Educ.:* various schools in Scotland and England ; Edinburgh University. Originally meant to enter the Church ; but took to teaching instead, and eventually to authorship ; appointed Editor of the Register of the Privy Council of Scotland (1898). *Publications:* George Buchanan, Humanist and Reformer, 1890 ; Early Travellers in

Scotland, 1891 ; Scotland before 1700, from Contemporary Documents, 1893 ; John Knox : a Biography, 1895 ; History of Scotland, vol. i. 1898, vol. ii. 1902, vol. iii. 1909 ; Scotland in the time of Queen Mary — being the Rhind Lectures for 1903, 1904 ; A Short History of Scotland, 1909 ; The Youth of Goethe, 1913 ; Ford Lectures — The Legislative Union of England and Scotland, 1914. *Address:* 20 Corrennie Gardens, Edinburgh.
(Died 30 Nov. 1918.)

BROWN, Sir Robert Charles, Kt., *cr.* 1919 ; M.B., F.R.C.P., F.R.C.S. ; Consulting Medical Officer, Preston Royal Infirmary ; *s.* of late Alderman Brown, F.R.C.S., Preston ; *b.* 27 Winckley Square, Preston, 2 Oct. 1836. *Educ.:* King's College, London ; Edinburgh and Dublin. Admitted a member of the Royal College of Surgeons of England and a Licentiate of the Society of Apothecaries, 1858 ; M.B.Lond., 1861 ; F.R.C.S.Eng., 1862 ; a Fellow of the Royal College of Physicians, 1908 ; Associate of King's College, London ; Esquire of the Order of St. John of Jerusalem ; three times President of the Lancashire and Cheshire Branch of the British Medical Association ; M.A. (hon.), Cambridge, 1912 ; presented with the freedom of the borough of Preston, 1910. *Address:* 27 Winckley Square, Preston. *(Died 23 Nov. 1925.)*

BROWN, Major Sir Robert Hanbury, K.C.M.G., *cr.* 1902 ; late Inspector-General of Irrigation, Egypt ; *b.* Brixton Hill, 13 Jan. 1849 ; 2nd *s.* of the late Robert Brown, surgeon ; *m.* 1878, Marian, M.B.E., *e. d.* of Rev. Edwin Meyrick ; one *s.* one *d.* *Educ.:* Marlborough Coll. ; R.M. Academy, Woolwich. Joined R.E. 1870 ; went to India, 1872 ; Irrigation Department of Public Works, Bengal, 1873 ; served in Afghan War, 1879-80 (despatches, medal) ; Egypt, Irrigation Department, 1884 - 1903. Egyptian decorations : 2nd class Osmanieh and 1st class Medjidie. *Decorated* for service in the Irrigation Dept., Egypt. *Publications:* The Fayum and Lake Moeris ; History of the Barrage ; The Land of Goshen and the Exodus ; The Delta Barrage ; Irrigation. *Recreations:* photography and wireless. *Address:* Newlands, Crawley Down, Sussex. *T.A.:* Hanbury Brown, Copthorne.
(Died 4 May 1926.)

BROWN, Lt.-Col. Robert Tilbury, C.M.G. 1918 ; D.S.O. 1916 ; M.D. ; Royal Army Medical Corps (retired) ; *b.* 26 June 1873 ; *s.* of Surg. Lieut. - Colonel Robert Ross Brown, L.R.C.P., etc., V.D., J.P. of Strood, Kent ; *m.* 1904, Pauline, *d.* of F. Normandy, Barrister-at-law. *Educ.:* King's School, Rochester ; Guy's Hospital ; Durham University Medical School. 1st Kent Artillery Vol., Lieut.- Capt. 1894-1900 ; M.R.C.S., L.R.C.P. Lond. 1896; M.B., B.S. Durh. 1899 ; M.D. (Gold Medal) 1904 ; D.P.H., R.C.P.S.I. 1902 ; Specialist in Bacteriology, R.A.M. Coll. 1908 ; general practice and Deputy M.O.H. Strood, 1896-1900 ; Lieut. Royal Army Medical Corps, 1900 ; Lieut.-Col. 1917 ; Specialist in charge laboratory, Lucknow, 1903-6 ; Sanitary Officer, East. Command and Burma Division, 1906 - 13 ; D.A.D.M.S. (San.), G.H.Q., and officer commanding Ind. San. Sec. the forces in East Africa, 1914-15 ; D.A.D.M.S. G.H.Q. 1916 ; A.D.M.S. 1917-19 (despatches four times, D.S.O., C.M.G., Chevalier Ordre de Léopold) ; Officer Commanding Royal Herbert Hospital, Woolwich, 1919 - 21 ; S.M.O., Ceylon Command, 1922-24 ; S.M.O., Bordon, 1925-26 ; retired pay, 1926. *Publications:* The Bacteriology of Asylum Dysentery, Jl. R.A.M.C., 1903 ; Camp Sanitation, 1b. 1908 ; Exam. of Water on Field Service ; Camping Arrangements for Sanitary Officers, 1b. 1909 ; Sanitary Reports of Manœuvres, Eastern Command and Burma Division, 1b. 1910-12 ; Training and Working of an Indian Sanitary Section, 1b. 1912. *Recrea-*

134

tions: shooting, fishing. *Address:* Lambert, Hatherleigh, N. Devon.   *(Died 21 Jan. 1928.)*

BROWN, T. Austen, A.R.S.A.; *b.* and *Educ.:* Edinburgh; *m.* Elizabeth Christie Macrae. Member of the National Portrait Society, London; Associate of the Société Nationale des Beaux Arts, Paris; Corresponding Member of the Société Royale des Beaux Arts, Brussels; Member of the Royal British Colonial Society of Artists; Hon. Member of South Wales Art Society; Member of Society of Graver Printers in Colour; Represented in the Pinakothek, Munich; National Galleries of Dresden, Budapest, and Corporation Galleries of Aberdeen, Glasgow, Mannheim, Exeter, and Leeds; Santiago, Chili; National Gallery, Brussels; Art Musée, Liége; National Gallery of Canada, Ottawa; Art Museum, Toronto; National Gallery, Wellington, New Zealand; Walker Art Gallery, Liverpool; Corporation Gallery, Bath; Victoria and Albert Museum, South Kensington; medal of the 1st class, Munich, 1896; medals of the 2nd class, Munich, Dresden, and Barcelona, 1911; grand gold medal, Budapest; silver medal, Barcelona. *Address:* 16 Fulham Road, Chelsea, S.W.3.
           (Died 9 June 1924.)

BROWN, Lt.-Col. Walter Henry, C.B. 1916; D.S.O. 1919; late 103rd Mahratta Light Infantry; *b.* 27 Jan. 1867; *s.* of Major Francis Brown, Carabineers; *m.* Edith, *d.* of late Col. D. Stewart, Ceylon Rifles; three *d.* *Educ.:* Lancing College; R.M.C., Sandhurst. Entered R. West Kent Regiment, 1886; Capt., Indian Army, 1897; Major, 1904; Lt.-Col. 1912; Adjutant, Indian Volunteers, 1900-2; served European War, Mesopotamia, 1914-18 (wounded—prisoner, C.B., D.S.O., despatches four times); retired, 1919. *Address:* Trevena, The Down, Bexhill-on-Sea. *T.:* 162.   *(Died 8 Mar. 1928.)*

BROWN, William Henry; late Partner in firm of Messrs. Speyer Bros., American bankers; *b.* Highworth, Wiltshire, 1845; *s.* of Samuel Brown and Jemima, *d.* of Samuel Jones, Stratton St. Margaret's; *m.* Jane, *d.* of late Ralph Thorne, Wanborough, Wiltshire; three *s.* two *d.* *Educ.:* The Grammar School, Highworth. Late Director of Metropolitan District Railway Company and Investment Trust Corporation; Chairman of London Congregational Union, 1901; Chairman of London Congregational Union Missions Committee. *Recreation:* farming. *Address:* Harts, Woodford Green, Essex; Crimplesham Hall, Norfolk. *T.A.:* Harts, Woodford Green. *T.:* 536 Woodford. *Club:* City Reform.
           (Died June 1918.)

BROWN, Very Rev. William H.; Incumbent of Moniva since 1890; Provost of Tuam since 1898. *Educ.:* Trinity Coll., Dublin, M.A. Ordained, 1869; Curate of Ballinrobe, 1867-71; Moniva, 1872-76; Incumbent of Ballyconree, 1876-90. *Address:* Moniva, Athenry, Ireland.

BROWN, His Honour William Herbert, B.Sc. (Lond.), M.A., LL.B. (R.U.I.), K.C. 1911, J.P. (Co. Londonderry); *b.* Limavady, Co. Londonderry; 2nd *s.* of late Rev. N. M. Brown, D.D., LL.D., Ex-Moderator of the Presbyterian Church in Ireland; *m.* 1892, Elizabeth Rose, *d.* of late Captain Sandes, J.P., of Clontarf, Dublin, and Carrigafoyle, Co. Kerry; one *s.* two *d.* *Educ.:* Coleraine Academical Institution; Queen's Colleges, Galway and Belfast; private study. Mathematical; Law; and Natural Philosophy Scholar; and Classical Exhibitioner; Peel Exhibitioner and 1st Honorman (Q.U.I.); 1st Honorman (R.U.I.): King's Inns Exhibitioner, 1886. Called to Bar, 1887; went N.E. Circuit; Crown Counsel, County of Louth, 1896-1903; Crown Counsel, County of Down, 1903-14; Revising Barrister, Borough of Cork, 1896-1905; Borough of Dublin, 1909; County of Dublin, 1910-13; Counsel to the Post Office, N.E. Circuit, 1913-14;

contested (L.) North Derry, Dec. 1910; County Court Judge and Chairman of Quarter Sessions for the Counties of Leitrim and Cavan, 1914; retired 1924, on abolition of office of County Court Judge in the Irish Free State. *Publications:* The Present Position of the Law of Lake and River Fishery (Law Magazine and Review); Town Tenants and Landlords: A Popular Explanation of the Town Tenants (Ireland) Act 1906. *Address:* Glenfern, Blackrock, Co. Dublin. *T.:* Blackrock, 132.
           (Died 7 Feb. 1927.)

BROWN, Col. Sir William James, K.C.B., *cr.* 1897; *b.* 1882; *s.* of late Thomas Brown; *m.* 1856, *y. d.* of late William Silverthorne. Hon. Col. 19th Batt. County of London Territorial Regiment (late North Middlesex Rifles). *Address:* Gloster Lodge, Argyle Road, West Ealing.   *(Died 8 Feb. 1918.)*

BROWN, Sir William Slater, Kt., *cr.* 1911; 2nd *s.* of Henry Raeburn Brown, Edinburgh, and Helen, *d.* of James Clyde, Edinburgh; *b.* Edinburgh, 14 Jan. 1845; *m.* 1865, Margaret (*d.* 1912), *d.* of George Dods, Duns, Berwickshire; four *s.* two *d.* *Educ.:* St. Stephen's School, Edinburgh. J.P. of Co. of the City of Edinburgh; ex-Lord Provost of Edinburgh and Deputy Lord Lieutenant of the County of the City of Edinburgh; head of the firm of W. S. Brown and Sons, furnishers. *Address:* 5 Corrennie Gardens, Edinburgh. *T.:* 6478 Central.
           (Died 19 April 1917.)

BROWNE, Hon. Sir Albert, K.B.E., *cr.* 1920; C.M.G. 1911; C.B.E. 1919; I.S.O. 1903; O.B.E. 1918; *b.* Bury St. Edmunds, 1860; *s.* of · J. C. Browne; *m.* Mabel, *d.* of Dr. Lawrence of Cape Colony. *Educ.:* Guildhall School, Bury St. Edmunds; King's College, London. Clerk Colonial Office, 1877; on duty in Cyprus, 1880-83; Assistant Imperial Secretary and Accountant in South Africa, 1891; Acting Imperial Secretary, January to March 1895, and March to August 1896; Financial Adviser to Military Governor, Bloemfontein, 1900; Auditor-General, 1901; Colonial Treasurer, 1901-7, and member of Executive and Legislative Councils of the Orange River Colony; member of the South African Convention for the formation of Union, 1908; Union Delegate to England, 1909; Joint Hon. Sec. Governor-Generals Fund, 1915-19. *Club:* Civil Service, Cape Town.   *(Died 20 Dec. 1923.)*

BROWNE, Major-General Andrew Smythe Montague, J.P., D.L.; Colonel Royal Scots Greys since 1905; *b.* 12 June 1836; *m.* 1872, Alice Jane, *o. c.* of Col. Fergusson; one *s.* five *d.* *Educ.:* Cheltenham; Sandhurst. Entered army 1853; Major-Gen. 1893; retired, 1897; served Crimea, 1855-56 (medal with clasp, Turkish medal); Colonel 3rd Dragoon Guards, 1903-5; Commanded 49th Berkshire Regimental District; High Sheriff, Co. Down, 1905. *Address:* St. John's Point, Killough, Co. Down. *Club:* Army and Navy.
           (Died 10 Mar. 1916.)

BROWNE, Sir Benjamin Chapman, Kt. *cr.* 1887; D.L., D.C.L., J.P., M.Inst. C. E., M.I.N.A., M.I.M.E.; Director of R. and W. Hawthorn, Leslie, and Co., Newcastle-on-Tyne, engineers and shipbuilders; *b.* 26 Aug. 1839; *s.* of Col. Browne, of Stouts Hill, Gloucestershire; *m.* Annie, *d.* of R. T. Atkinson, C.E., 1861; three *s.* four *d.* *Educ.:* Westminster; King's College, London. Apprenticed as an engineer to Lord Armstrong, Elswick Works, 1856; Mayor of Newcastle, 1885-87. *Recreation:* social economic questions. *Address:* Westacres, Newcastle-on-Tyne. *T.:* National 17.
           (Died 1 Mar. 1917.)

BROWNE, Sir Edmond, Kt., *cr.* 1918; Standing Counsel to a number of Trades Unions; *b.* 1857; *m.* 1907; one *d.* Called to Bar; Middle Temple, 1894. *Address:* 2 Pump Court, Temple, E.C.4. *T.:* City 68. *(Died 9 Mar. 1923.)*

BROWNE, Edward Granville, M.A., M.B., M.R.C.S., M.R.A.S., F.B.A., F.R.C.P.; Lecturer in Persian, 1888-1902; Sir Thomas Adams Professor of Arabic since 1902; Fellow of Pembroke Coll. Camb. since 1887; Fellow of British Academy, 1903; Fellow of Royal College of Physicians, 1911; *b.* Uley, near Dursley, 7 Feb. 1862; *e. s.* of late Sir Benjamin C. Browne, of R. and W. H. Hawthorn, Leslie, and Co., engineers and shipbuilders, Newcastle-on-Tyne; *m.* 1906, Alice Caroline Blackburne Daniell (*d.* 1925); two *s. Educ.:* Glenalmond; Eton; Pembroke College, Cambridge; St. Bartholomew's Hospital. Graduated at Cambridge in Natural Sciences Tripos, 1882; Indian Languages Tripos, 1884; Beatson Scholar Pembroke Coll. Camb. 1884. Studied Medicine and Oriental Languages in Cambridge, 1879-84; London, 1884-87; but never practised as a doctor; travelled in Persia, 1887-88. *Publications:* A Traveller's Narrative, written to illustrate the Episode of the Báb, Persian text and English translation, with notes, 1891; A Year amongst the Persians, 1893; The New History of Mirzá Alí Muhammad the Báb, translated from the Persian, 1893; Catalogue of Persian MSS. in Cambridge University Library, 1896; Hand-list of the Muhammadan MSS. in the same library, 1900; Supplement to same, 1922; critical edition of Dawlatsháh's Tadhkira, 1901; do. of Awfí's Lubábu'l - Albáb, 1903; Literary History of Persia until the time of Firdawsi, 1902; continuation of same until the Mongol Invasion, 1906; continuation of same to rise of Safawi Dynasty, 1920; continuation of same until the present day, 1924; abridged translation of Ibn Isfandiyár's History of Tabaristán; Short Account of Recent Events in Persia, 1909; History of the Persian Revolution (1905-9), 1910; The Press and Poetry in Modern Persia, 1914; Materials for the Study of the Bábí Religion, 1918; Translation of *Chahár Maqála* with notes, 1921; Arabian Medicine, 1921; besides numerous Papers in the Journal of the Royal Asiatic Society since 1889. *Recreation:* fishing, bicycling. *Address:* Pembroke College, Cambridge; Firwood, Cambridge. *T.:* Cambridge 245; Westacres, Benwell, Newcastle-on-Tyne. *M.:* ER 2490. *Club:* Royal Societies.   (*Died 5 Jan. 1926.*)

BROWNE, George, C.M.G. 1917; I.S.O. 1903; Hon. Private Secretary to Governor of Tasmania. Entered Tasmanian Civil Service, 1862; was Clerk of the Peace, Deputy Sheriff, Registrar of Insolvency, and Registrar of the Court of Requests, Launceston; Associate to the Judges of the Supreme Court of Tasmania; Registrar of the Supreme Court in Bankruptcy, Curator of Intestate Estates, etc.; J.P.; Private Secretary to the following Governors: Sir C. Du Cane, Sir F. Weld (and in the Straits Settlements, 1881-84), Sir G. Strahan, Sir Robert Hamilton, Viscount Gormanston, Sir Arthur Havelock, Sir Gerald Strickland, Sir Harry Barron, Rt. Hon. Sir W. G. Ellison-Macartney, and Sir Francis A. Newdegate; also to Sir V. Fleming, Sir F. Smith, and Sir L. Dobson, Administrators of the Government. *Address:* Hobart, Australia. (*Club:* Tasmanian, Hobart.   (*Died 15 Dec. 1919.*)

BROWNE, Rev. George Rickards, M.A. Oxon.; Rector of Iron Acton since 1889; Rural Dean of Bitton since 1910; and Hon. Canon of Bristol since 1912; *b.* 20 Feb. 1854; *s.* of Thomas Briarly Browne, M.A., T.C.D., and Mary Ann Rickards; *m.* 1883, Jessie Frances Pearce; two *s. Educ.:* St. John's Foundation School, Hereford Cathedral School and Brasenose College, Oxford. (Somerset Scholar, Philpott Exhibitioner and Hulme Exhibitioner); First Class in Classical Mods., 1875; B.A. (Second Class in Modern History), 1877; M.A. 1880; Deacon, 1878; Priest, 1879; Curate of East Acklam, Yorks, 1878-80; Chaplain of Christ

136

Church, Oxford, 1879-89; Chaplain of New College, 1880-90. *Publication:* National Service. *Address:* Iron Acton Rectory, Bristol. *T.A.:* Iron Acton.   (*Died Sept. 1921.*)

BROWNE, Harold Carlyon Gore, M.A.; Chancellor Diocese of Winchester to 1914; *b.* Wales, 11 June 1844; *e. s.* of late Bishop of Ely and Winchester. *Educ.:* Rugby; Emmanuel Coll. Camb. Barr. Lincoln's Inn. *Recreations:* golf; member of Alpine Club. *Address:* 15 Kingsgate Street, Winchester. *Clubs:* Athenæum, Savile.   (*Died 22 May 1919.*)

BROWNE, Gen. Henry Ralph, C.B. 1905; Col. Norfolk Regt. since 1908; *b.* 29 Dec. 1828; *m.* 1852, Frances M. A., *o. d.* of late Admiral R. W. Parsons. Entered army, 1846; Lt.-Gen. 1885; retired, 1885; served Crimea, 1854 (despatches, medal with clasp, Knight of Legion of Honour, 5th class Medjidieh, Turkish medal, brevet of Major); Afghanistan, 1879-80 (medal). *Club:* United Service.   (*Died 23 Dec. 1917.*)

BROWNE, Henry William Langley, O.B.E., M.D., B.S., F.R.C.S.E., LL.D.; Consulting Surgeon, West Bromwich Hospital; J.P. Co. Stafford; *b.* Bishop Auckland, Co. Durham, 1848; *e. s.* of Dr. Benjamin S. Browne; *m.* Gertrude, *d.* of Richard Heckels, Sunderland; one *d. Educ.:* Edgbaston; Sydenham College; Birmingham Hospital. Commenced practice at West Bromwich, 1870; retired, 1920; Hon. Surgeon to the West Bromwich and District Hospital, 1871 - 1904; elected to represent the Midland Counties' Branch of the British Medical Association on the London Council, 1898; Chairman, 1906 - 8; President of the Branch, B.M.A., 1894; Midland Medical Society, 1902; Association Factory Surgeon, 1905; at the election of English Representatives in the General Medical Council 1906, was returned at the head of the poll, and again at the next election, 1911; retired 1920; life - member of Court of Governors, Birmingham University; Fellow of the Royal Society of Medicine. *Publications:* many articles in the medical papers. *Address:* 196 Hagley Road, Edgbaston, Birmingham. *T.:* Edgbaston 1356.   (*Died 7 Mar. 1928.*)

BROWNE, Maj.-Gen. James; *b.* 9 Nov. 1840; *m.* Evelyn Elizabeth, *y. d.* of late Archdeacon Badnall, D.D., and *widow* of Major F. L. Northcott. Entered army, 1859; Maj.-Gen. 1896; retired 1898; served Zulu War, 1879-81 (despatches, medal with clasp); Transvaal Campaign, 1881. *Address:* The Wilderness, Worthing, Sussex.   (*Died 13 June 1917.*)

BROWNE, John Hutton Balfour-, K.C. 1885; J.P., D.L.; LL.D.; *b.* Scotland, 13 Sep. 1845; *s.* of Dr. W. A. F. Browne; *m.* 1874, Caroline, *d.* of Lord Justice Lush; two *s.* one *d. Educ.:* Edinburgh University. Barr. 1870; Bencher Middle Temple, 1890; Registrar and Secretary to Railway Commission, 1874; contested Dumfriesshire (C.), 1906; East Bradford, 1910. *Publications:* Medical Jurisprudence of Insanity, 1871; Law of Carriers, 1873; Law of Ratings, 1874; Law of Usages and Customs, 1875; Law of Railways, 1880; Law of Compensation, 1896; South Africa, 1905; Essays, Critical and Political, 1907; War Problems, 1914; Forty Years at the Bar, 1916; Recollections Literary and Political, 1917. Owns 500 acres. *Address:* 28 Eaton Square, S.W.1; *T.:* Victoria 6169; Goldielea, near Dumfries. *Clubs:* Athenæum, Carlton; Dumfries and Galloway, Dumfries.   (*Died 27 Sept. 1921.*)

BROWNE, Sir John Walton, Kt., *cr.* 1921; B.A., M.D., LL.D., Hon. M.R.C.S.Eng.; Consulting Surgeon, Belfast Royal Hospital; Surgeon, Belfast Ophthalmic Hospital; Senator, Queen's Univ. of Belfast; late Medical Officer, Belfast P.-O.; D.L. County of Belfast; *b.* 5 Oct. 1845; *e. s.* of late Dr. S. Browne, R.N., formerly Mayor of Belfast; *m.* 1st, Fanny, *d.* of David Anderson, Strandtown,

Belfast; 2nd, Matilda, d. of Rev. Francis B. Grant, M.A., Barbados; one d. Educ.: Belfast, Dublin, London, and Vienna. Ex-President Ulster Medical Society; Ex-President North of Ireland Branch British Medical Association; Ex-President Ophthalmological Section Annual Meeting British Medical Association; Lecturer Clinical Surgery and Ophthalmology, Belfast Medical School; Member of Ophthalmological Society; Medical Referee Workman's Compensation Act. Publications: various papers to Lancet, British Medical Journal, and Transactions of Ulster Medical Society. Recreation: travelling. Address: Lismore, Windsor Avenue, Belfast. T.: Malone 187. Clubs: Ulster, Royal Ulster Yacht, Belfast.
(Died 19 Dec. 1923.)

BROWNE, William, M.V.O. 1902; I.S.O. 1908; late H.M. Office of Works. Address: Ravenswood 210 Preston Road, Preston, Brighton. (Died 21 Nov. 1924.)

B R O W N E, Rev. (William) Bevil, Prebendary of Exeter; Licensed Preacher in the Diocese; b. Standish Vicarage, nr. Gloucester, 7 June 1845; 5th s. of Rev. T. Murray Browne and Catherine, d. of T. Lloyd Baker of Hardwicke Court, Gloucester; m. 1871, Mary, d. of T. Nelson Waterfield, Indian Office; one s. Educ.: Wellington College; Trinity College, Cambridge. (Died 26 July 1928.)

BROWNE, Surgeon-General William Richard, C.I.E. 1906; M.D.; retired, 1908; b. 23 May 1850; joined the Service, 1873; served on jail duty, Madras; Professor of Pathology, Medical College, 1883-90, of Surgery; 1890; Fellow Madras University, 1892; Principal Medical College, 1901; P.M.O. Madras District, 1903; Hon. Surgeon to Viceroy, 1905; served Rumpa, 1879-80. (Died 16 Sept. 1924.)

BROWNELL, William Crary, L.H.D. (Amherst College, 1896), Litt.D. (Columbia University, 1910), LL.D. (Amherst College, 1916), Member of the American Academy of Arts and Letters. Author, editor, and literary adviser, with Charles Scribner's Sons, publishers, since 1888; b. New York City, 30 Aug. 1851; s. of Isaac Wilbour Brownell and Lucia Emilie Brown; m. 1st, 1878, Virginia Shields Swinburne (d. 1911) of Newport, Rhode Island; no c.; 2nd, 1921, Anna Gertrude Hall of New York. Educ.: Amherst College, Amherst. On staff of The World, 1871-79; The Nation, 1879-81; resided in Paris and travelled in Europe, 1881-84; on staff of The Philadelphia Press, 1885-86; contributor to various literary and art journals since 1875. Publications: French Traits: an Essay in Comparative Criticism, 1889; French Art: Classic and Contemporary Painting and Sculpture, 1892, Newport, 1896; Victorian Prose Masters: Thackeray, Carlyle, George Eliot, Matthew Arnold, Ruskin, George Meredith, 1901; American Prose Masters: Cooper, Hawthorne, Emerson, Poe, Lowell, Henry James, 1909; Criticism, 1914; Standards, 1916; The Genius of Style, 1924. Address: 597 Fifth Avenue, New York. Clubs: Century, Barnard, New York. (Died 22 July 1928.)

BROWNING, Oscar, C.B.E. 1923; M.A.; Fellow King's Coll., Camb., 1859; Univ. Lecturer in History and Principal of Cambridge Univ. Day Training College, 1891-1909; b. London. 17 Jan. 1837; s. of William Shipton Browning and Mariana Margaret Bridge; unmarried. Educ.: Eton; King's College, Cambridge; President of the Union; 4th in Classical Tripos, 1860. Master at Eton, 1860-75; College and University work at Cambridge, 1876-1909; Examiner, University of London, 1899; Officier d'Académie, 1889; Officier de l'Instruction Publique, 1898; Fellow of the Arcadia Academy, Rome, 1918; Trustee and Chairman British Academy of Arts, Rome, 1921; candidate for Parliament, Norwood, 1886; East Worcestershire, 1892; West Derby, 1895. Publications.

Cornelius Nepos, 1868; Modern England, 1879; Modern France, 1880; History of Educational Theories, 1881 (translated into Hungarian and Servian); Political Memoranda of the Duke of Leeds, 1884; Earl Gower's Despatches, 1885; England and Napoleon in 1803 (1887); History of England, in 4 vols. 1890; Life of George Eliot, 1890; Dante: Life and Works, 1891; Goethe: Life and Works, 1891; Aspects of Education, 1888; Milton's Tractate on Education, 1883; True Stories from English History, 1886; The Life of Bartolommeo Colleoni, 1891; The Flight to Varennes and other Historical Essays, 1892; The Citizen: his Rights and Responsibilities, 1893; Guelphs and Ghibellines, 1894; The Age of the Condottieri, 1895; Journal of Sir George Rooke, 1897; Life of Peter the Great, 1898; Charles XII. of Sweden, 1898; Wars of the Nineteenth Century, 1899; Preface to President Woodrow Wilson's book The State; History of Europe, 1814-1843 (1901); Impressions of Indian Travel, 1903; Napoleon: the first phase, 1905; The Fall of Napoleon, 1907; Memories of Sixty Years, 1910; Despatches from Paris, vols. i. and ii. 1784-91, 1911; History of the Modern World, 1815-1910, 2 vols., 1912; popular edition in one vol., 1916; General History of the World, 1913; History of Medieval Italy, 568-1530 (1914); General History of Italy, 1915; Memories of Later Years, 1923; many contributions to Quarterly, Edinburgh, and other Reviews. Recreations: music, mountaineering, cycling, swimming, golf. Address: Palazzo Simonetti, 12 Via Pietro Cavallini, Rome. Clubs: Athenæum, Bath, Alpine; Royal Golf, St. Andrews; Circolo Roma, Rome.
(Died 6 Oct. 1923.)

BROWNING, Sidney, C M.G. Assistant District Commissioner Nyasaland Protectorate, 1894; Assistant District Commissioner, Uganda Protectorate, 1900; District Commissioner, 1904; Provincial Commissioner, 1914; retired, 1921. Club: Sports. (Died 27 Oct. 1928.)

BROWNLOW, 3rd Earl (cr. 1815), Adelbert Wellington Brownlow Cust, P.C. 1887. Bt. 1677; Baron Brownlow, 1776; Viscount Alford, 1815. Lord-Lieut. Lincolnshire, since 1867; Ecclesiastical Commissioner for England; Trustee of the National Gallery, 1897; A.D.C. to the King; Hon. Colonel Lincolns. Imperial Yeomanry; b. London, 19 Aug. 1844. S. b. 1867; m. Lady Adelaide Talbot (d. 1917), d. of 18th Earl of Shrewsbury and Talbot, 1868. Grenadier Guards, 1863-66; M.P. N. Shropshire, 1866-67; Parliamentary Secretary to Local Government Board, 1885-86; Paymaster-General, 1887-89; Under Secretary of State for War, 1889. Owns about 58,400 acres. Heir to Barony: kinsman, Capt. A. S. C. Cust. Address: 8 Carlton House Terrace, S.W.1. T.: Regent 3894; Ashridge Park, Berkhampstead, Herts; Belton House, Grantham, Lincolnshire. Club: Carlton.
(Died 17 Mar. 1921.)

BROWNLOW, 5th Baron, cr. 1776; Bt. 1677, **Major Adelbert Salusbury Cockayne Cust;** b. 14 Sept. 1867; y. and o. surv. s. of late Major Henry Francis Cockayne Cust of Cockayne Hatley, Beds; S. 3rd Earl Brownlow, 1921; m. 1895, Maud, d. of late Capt. S. Buckle, R.E.; one s. one d. Educ.: Eton. Entered Army, 1888; served in Somerset Light Infantry; retired, 1908; served European War, 1914-18, France and Belgium; J.P., D.L., Lincolnshire; Hon. Col. 4th Bn. Lincolnshire Regt.; employed in Board of Agriculture and Fisheries, 1918-20; is a Director Hand in Hand Branch Commercial Insurance Company; was A.D.C and Private Secretary to late Sir Frederick Napier Broome, K.C.M.G., Governor and Commander-in-Chief, Trinidad, W.I., 1894-95; Adj. 2nd Vol. Batt. Lincolnshire Regt. 1899-1904; Mayor of Grantham, 1924-25; was Organising Secretary, Royal National Lifeboat

Institution. *Heir: s.* Hon. Peregrine Francis Adelbert Cust, J.P., Lieut. and Adjutant Grenadier Guards [*b.* 1899. *Educ.:* Eton; Royal Military College, Sandhurst. Served European War, 1918]. *Address:* Belton House, Grantham. *Clubs:* United Service, Royal Automobile.   (*Died 19 April 1927.*)

BROWNLOW, Lieut. - Col. Celadon Charles, C.B. 1900; Indian Staff Corps (retired); *b.* 20 Nov. 1843; *s.* of late Henry B. Brownlow, H.E.I.C.S.; *m.* 1888, Rosalie, *d.* of late Rev. J. R. Munn. Entered army, 1861; Col. 1891; served North-West Frontier, India, and Afghanistan (two medals, despatches, brevet of Col., three clasps). *Address:* Stoatley Copse, Farnham Lane, Haslemere, Surrey.
    (*Died 9 Mar. 1925.*)

BROWNLOW, Field - Marshal Sir Charles Henry, G.C.B., *cr.* 1887; *b.* 12 Dec. 1831; *o. s.* of Col. George A. Brownlow [*bro.* of 1st Lord Lurgan]; *m.* Georgiana (*d.* 1912), *d.* of W. C. King, of Warfield Hall, Berks, 1890. Punjab Campaigns, 1848; medal, Hazara, 1852-53; expedition against Momund tribes, 1854 (severely wounded); Bozdar Expedition, 1857; Eusofzai Expedition, 1858 (medal with clasp); China War, 1860: action of Sinho, Taku Forts, occupation of Pekin (medal with two clasps); Ambeyla Campaign, 1863, C.B.; Hazara Campaign, 1868; commanded column Looshai Expedition, 1871-72; K.C.B.; A.D.C. to the Queen, 1869 - 81; Assistant Military Secretary at Horse Guards, 1879-89. *Recreation:* horse-breeding. *Address:* Warfield Hall, Bracknell, Berks. *Clubs:* United Service, Arthur's.   (*Died 5 April 1916.*)

BROWNLOW, Col. Charles William, C.M.G. 1919; C.B.E. 1919; D.S.O. 1918; *s.* of late Capt. H. R. Brownlow, Royal (late Bengal) Artillery; *b.* 1862; *m.* 1895, Ethel Mary, *y. d.* of late W. H. Preston of Minstead Lodge, Hampshire; one *s.* one *d. Educ.:* Cheltenham College; Royal Military Academy, Woolwich. Served Zhob Valley Expedition, 1890; Burma Expedition, 1891-2 (medal and clasp); N.-W. Frontier of India, 1897-18 (medal and clasp); Tirah Expedition, 1897-8 (clasp); European War, 1914-18 (despatches, D.S.O., C.M.G., C.B.E.); retired from Army 1919. *Address:* Kingston Lodge, Dartmouth.
    (*Died 30 April 1924.*)

BROWNLOW, Maj.-Gen. William Vesey, C.B. 1887; Col. 1st King's Dragoon Guards, 1908; *o. surv. s.* of William and Charlotte Brownlow, Knapton House, Queen's Co.; *b.* 14 June 1841; *m.* 1st, 1881, Lady Anne Henrietta (*d.* 1898), 3rd *d.* of 10th Earl of Stair; 2nd, 1904, Lady Kathleen Bligh, 2nd *d.* of 6th Earl of Darnley. *Educ.:* private school. With 1st Dragoon Guards in Zulu War, 1879 (brevet of Major); in command of a mounted force in Boer War, 1880-81 (brevet of Lt.-Col.); Assistant Commandant cavalry depot, 1882-88; Col. commanding a regimental district, 1889-94; Major - General, 1898; retired, 1901; High Sheriff, Co. Monaghan, 1907; J.P. Hampshire. *Decorated:* 1st Boer War. *Recreations:* hunting, shooting. *Address:* Eveley, Bordon, Hants. *Clubs:* Army and Navy; Kildare Street, Dublin.   (*Died 15 Mar. 1926.*)

BROWNRIGG, Rt. Rev. Abraham; R.C. Bishop of Ossory since 1884; *b.* Kildavin, Co. Carlow, 23 Dec. 1836. *Educ.:* St. Peter's College, Wexford; Maynooth Coll. 1856; read a course of Philosophy, sacred Scripture, and Theology; ordained priest, 1861; appointed Professor at St. Peter's Coll., Wexford, 1861; member of a Diocesan missionary community established at Enniscorthy, Co. Wexford, 1866; Rector of same community, 1871. *Address:* Kilkenny.   (*Died 1 Oct. 1928.*)

BROWNRIGG, Colonel Metcalfe Studholme; J.P. London County; late

138

Commanding Wilts and Dorset Brigade, Regimental District and Oxfordshire Light Infantry; *b.* 1845, 3rd *s.* of General Brownrigg, C.B.; *m.* 1869, Emily, *d.* of Sir Edward Borough, Bt., and Lady Elizabeth Borough; two *d. Educ.:* Eton. Entered army, 1863; was first A.D.C. to Lord-Lieutenant of Ireland; Gold Stick Staff Officer at Coronation; Jubilee and Coronation medals. *Address:* 20 Onslow Square, S.W.7. *T.:* Western 2630. *Clubs:* Travellers', United Service.
    (*Died 28 Feb. 1924.*)

BRUCE, Alexander, K.C. 1885; head of law firm of Bruce, Bruce and Counsell, Hamilton, Ontario; 3rd *s.* of William and Isabella Bruce, Longside, Aberdeenshire, Scotland; *b.* 23 Nov. 1836; *m.* 1863, Agnes, *d.* of Rev. Ralph Robb; two *s.* three *d. Educ.:* Longside Parish School; Grammar School, Aberdeen; Marischal College, Aberdeen, M.A. Student of and for some years partner of the late Chief Justice Sir George Burton; called to the Bar of the Law Society of Upper Canada, 1861; practised profession in Hamilton, Ontario, to 1905, when removed to Toronto; a Bencher of the Law Society of Upper Canada since 1886; a member of the Corporation of Trinity University, Toronto; a Director of the Canada Life Assurance Company and National Trust Company, Limited, both of Toronto; President of Calydor Sanatorium, Ltd. (for Tuberculosis), Gravenhurst, Ontario. *Recreations:* walking and travelling. *Address:* 91 Bedford Road, Toronto; *T.A.:* Bruce, Canlife, Toronto. *T.:* Hillerest 2290. *Clubs:* Toronto, Royal Canadian Yacht, Toronto; Hamilton, Hamilton; Caledon Mountain Trout.
    (*Died 20 Aug. 1920.*)

BRUCE, Sir Alexander Carmichael, Kt.; *cr.* 1903; J.P.; Assistant Commissioner Metropolitan Police, 1884-1914; *b.* 1850; 4th *s.* of late Rev. Canon David Bruce; *m.* 1876, Helen (*d.* 1915), *d.* of John Fletcher, D.L. *Educ.:* Brasenose College, Oxford. Called to Bar, Lincoln's Inn, 1875; went North - Eastern Circuit. *Address:* 25 Egerton Terrace, S.W.3. *T.:* Kensington 3670.   (*Died 23 Oct. 1926.*)

BRUCE, Col. Andrew Macrae, C.B. 1900; *b.* 5 Jan. 1842; *s.* of late William Bruce of Symbister, Shetland, and Agnes Macrae; *m.* 1889, Margaret, *d.* of late Charles Hay, Edinburgh; one *s.* (Lieut. 59th Scind Rifles, Frontier Force; killed in a German trench when in charge of a bombing party at Givenchy near La Bassee, 19 Dec. 1914) one *d.* Joined the Indian Army as Ensign, 1860; served with the 2nd Bengal Fusiliers, 1860-61; with the 1st Gurkhas, 1861-65; with the 4th Regt. Punjab Infantry, Punjab Frontier Force, 1865-1894; British Agent in Gilgit, 1893-94; Colonel on the Staff, Ferozepore, 1896-97; Brig.-General commanding at Bangalore, 1897-98; at Lahore and Rohilkund, 1898; served N.E. Frontier of India, Bhutan, 1865 - 66 (medal and clasp); N.W. Frontier of India. Besoti-Afridi Affair, 1869 (received special thanks of Government of India); N.W. Frontier of India, Miranzi, 1869; N.W. Frontier of India, Jowaki, 1877-87 (clasp); Afghanistan, 1879 - 80 (medal); N.W. Frontier of India, Mahsud Waziri, 1881 (despatches, brought specially to notice of C.-in-C.); N.W. Frontier of India, Tukht-i-Suliman, 1881 (despatches); N.W. Frontier of India, Zhob Valley, 1884; N.W. Frontier of India, Hazara, 1888 (clasp); (1st) Miranzai, 1891; commanded 1st column (despatches); Good Service Pension, 1899. *Address:* La Fontaine, Pontac, Jersey, C.I. *Club:* East India United Service. (*Died 6 April 1920.*)

BRUCE, Sir Charles, G.C.M.G., *cr.* 1901; K.C.M.G., *cr.* 1889; J.P., D.L.; *b.* 1836; *m.* Clara (*d.* 1916), *d.* of J. Lucas, 1868; two *s. Educ.:* Harrow; Yale University; Germany. Professor Sanscrit, King's College, 1865; Rector Royal College, Mauritius, 1868; Director of Public Instruction, Ceylon, 1878; Colonial

Secretary, Mauritius, 1882; Lieut.-Gov. of British Guiana, 1885-93; Governor of the Windward Isles, 1893-97; Governor of Mauritius, 1897-1904. *Publications:* Die Geschichte von Nala (Imperial Academy of Petrograd), 1862; Poems, 1865; The Broad Stone of Empire, 1910; The True Temper of Empire, 1912; Milestones on my Long Journey, 1917; and numerous contributions to English and foreign Reviews. *Address:* Arnot Tower, Leslie, N.B. *Clubs:* Carlton; New, Edinburgh. (*Died 13 Dec.* 1920.)

BRUCE, Sir Hervey Juckes Lloyd, 4th Bt.; *cr.* 1804; late Lieut.-Col. Coldstream Guards; *b.* 5 Oct. 1843; *s.* of 3rd Bt. and Marianne, *d.* of Sir J. G. Juckes Clifton, 8th Bt.; *m.* 1872, Ellen Maud (O.B.E.), *d.* of Percy Ricardo of Bramley Park, Guildford; four *s.*; *S.* father 1907. *Educ.:* Eton College. Entered army, 1862; retired 1878. Owns about 22,000 acres. *Heir: s.* Hervey Ronald, Capt., late Irish Guards [*b.* 9 Dec. 1872; *m.* 1903, Ruth Isabel, 3rd *d.* of late H. C. Okeover]. *Address:* Downhill, Londonderry; Clifton Hall, Nottingham. *T.A.:* Clifton, Nottingham. *T.:* Nottingham 5140. *Clubs:* Turf, Guards'.
(*Died 8 May* 1919.)

BRUCE, Sir Hervey Ronald, 5th Bt.; *cr.* 1804; late Major, Royal Irish Rifles; *b.* 9 Dec. 1872; *s.* of 4th Bt. and Ellen Maud (O.B.E.), *d.* of Percy Ricardo of Bramley Park, Guildford. *S.* father 1919; *m.* 1st, 1903, Ruth Isabel (*d.* 1915), 3rd *d.* of late H. C. Okeover; 2nd, 1916, Margaret Florence, *d.* of Rev. Robert Jackson, Rector of Little Thurlow, Newmarket; two *s.* one *d.* Owns about 22,000 acres. Served S. Africa, 1899-1902 (Queen's Medal and five clasps, King's Medal and two clasps); J.P., D.L., Co. Londonderry. *Heir: s.* Hervey John William, *b.* 29 June 1919. *Address:* Downhill, Londonderry; Clifton Hall, Nottingham. *T.A.:* Clifton, Nottingham. *T.:* Nottingham 5140. *Club:* Guards'. (*Died 18 May* 1924.)

BRUCE, Admiral Sir James Andrew Thomas, K.C.M.G.; *cr.* 1900; *b.* 15 July 1846; *y. s.* of Sir Hervey Bruce, 3rd Bt.; *m.* 1877, Catherine Mary Philippa, *d.* of Col. Edwin Wodehouse, C.B. Entered R.N. 1859; Rear-Admiral, 1898; served Niger River, 1876; A.D.C. to Queen, 1895-98; senior officer, Gibraltar, 1895-98; 2nd in command China Station, 1900-1901; Admiral, 1907. *Address:* 3 Montagu Square, W.1. *T.:* Mayfair 3252. *Club:* United Service. (*Died 25 May* 1921.)

BRUCE, Richard Isaac, C.I.E. 1881; Commissioner, Punjab, Indian Provincial Civil Service; retired 1896; *b.* 1840; *s.* of Jonathan Bruce of Miltown Castle, Co. Cork; *m.* 1871, Lilla (*d.* 1912), *d.* of Rev. J. Beavor Webb, Rector of Dunderrow, Kinsale, Co. Cork. Served Afghanistan, 1878-79 (despatches, medal); North-West Frontier of India; Zhob Valley Expedition, affair at Dowlatzai, 1884; Zhob Valley Expedition, 1890 (despatches); received special thanks and commendation of H.M.'s Secretary of State for India for distinguished services in connection with the opening of the Gomal Pass, 1890; appointed British Commissioner of the Afghan-Waziristan Delimitation Commission, 1894; action at Wano, 1894; Waziristan, 1894-95 (despatches, medal with clasp); received on several occasions thanks of Government of India for distinguished frontier service. *Publications:* A Gazetteer of Dera Ghazi Khan District; A Manual of the Beluchi Language; A History of the Marri-Beluch Tribe; The Forward Policy, and its Results. *Address:* Quetta, Fairfax Road, Teddington. *Club:* East India United Service. (*Died 29 Jan.* 1924.)

BRUCE, William, A.M., M.D., LL.D. (Hon.) Aberdeen Univ.; Medical Officer of Health for the County of Ross and Cromarty; Direct Representative for Scotland in the General Medical Council, 1887-1907; *s.* of Alexander Bruce,

Keig, Aberdeenshire; *m. d.* of William Ironside; two *s.* four *d.* *Educ.:* Aberdeen Grammar School, and King's College and University. After practising twelve years in Aberdeenshire, and holding the post of Examiner in Medicine at Aberdeen University, settled in Dingwall 1870, and practised there and in Strathpeffer till 1890; since then Consulting Physician, Governor of Highlands and Islands Educational Trust, 1900-15; Chairman of Ross-shire Advisory Committee of Aberdeen Agricultural College, and of the Parish Council of Dingwall. *Publications:* Sciatica, a fresh Study; and to the newspapers on educational subjects. *Recreations:* gardening and golfing. *Address:* The Castle, Dingwall, N.B. *T.:* Dingwall Exchange X 1; Strathpeffer 13. (*Died 24 Oct.* 1920.)

BRUCE, Ven. William Conybeare, Rector of Rogiet, near Newport, 1901. *Educ.:* Rugby; Univ. Coll. Oxford (M.A.). Canon of Llandaff, 1885; Rector of St. Nicholas, near Cardiff, 1871-82; Vicar of St. Woolos, Newport, 1882-1901; Archdeacon of Monmouth, 1885-1914. *Address:* Rogiet Rectory, Newport, Monmouthshire; Canonry, Llandaff.
(*Died 12 Feb.* 1919.)

BRUCE, William Ironside, M.D., D.P.H.; Physician in Charge of the X-Ray Departments, Charing Cross Hospital; the Hospital for Sick Children, Great Ormond Street, etc.; *s.* of William Bruce, M.D., of Dingwall, and Agnes Ironside; *m.* Violet, *d.* of late N. Randle of Bombay, India; no *c.* *Educ.:* Edinburgh Academy; Aberdeen University. Served as Civil Surgeon in South Africa, and later returned to Aberdeen, obtaining the degrees of M.D., D.P.H.; began practice in London shortly afterwards at Charing Cross Hospital. *Publications:* A System of Radiography with an Atlas of the Normal; X-Ray Examination; Choyce's System of Surgery; X-Ray Treatment; Churchill's System of Treatment; many papers on subjects connected with X-Rays. *Recreations:* motoring, golf. *Address:* 10 Chandos Street, Cavendish Square, W.1. *T.:* 3985; Mayfair 3984. *M.:* LA 8057. (*Died 21 Mar.* 1921.)

BRUCE, William Speirs, LL.D. Aberdeen, F.R.S.E., etc.; *b.* 1 August 1867; *s.* of Samuel Noble Bruce, of Edinburgh, M.R.C.S.; *m.* 1901, Jessie, *d.* of late Alexander Mackenzie, Nigg, Ross-shire; one *s.* one *d.* *Educ.:* Univ. of Edinburgh. George Heriot Research Fellow, University of Edinburgh, 1900-1901; Director of Scottish Oceanographical Laboratory, Edinburgh; Gold Medallist of the Royal Scottish Geographical Society, 1904; Royal Gold Medal (Patron's) of Royal Geographical Society, 1910; Hon. Member, Gesellschaft für Erdkunde zu Berlin; Neill Prize and Gold Medallist of Royal Society of Edinburgh, 1911-1913; Livingstone Gold Medal of American Geographical Society, 1920; Membre de Comité de Perfectionnement de l'Institut Oceanographique, Paris; Honorary Member New Zealand Institute. Lecturer on Geography, Heriot-Watt College, 1899-1901 and since 1917, and Church of Scotland Training College, Edinburgh, 1899-1901; Assistant in Challenger Expedition Commission; also in Zoology at the School of Medicine of the Royal Colleges, Edinburgh; Naturalist, Scottish Antarctic Expedition, 1892-93; in charge of Ben Nevis Observatory, 1895 and 1896; Zoologist, Jackson-Harmsworth Polar Expedition, 1896 and 1897; Naturalist Major Andrew Coats' Expedition to Novaya Zemlya, Wiche Islands, and Barent's Sea, 1898; Naturalist, H.S.H. the Prince of Monaco's Expedition, Spitsbergen, 1898, 1899, and 1906; Leader of Scottish National Antarctic Expedition (S.Y. "Scotia"), 1902-4; discovered 150 miles of the Coast Line of Antarctica, naming it Coats' Land; bathymetrically surveyed the South Atlantic Ocean and

Weddell Sea to 74° 1′ S. and between 60° W. and 20° E. ; explored and surveyed Prince Charles Foreland and other parts of Spitsbergen, 1906, 1907, 1909, 1912, 1914, 1919, and 1920. *Publications:* Scientific Results of the Voyage of S.Y. "Scotia," 1902-4 ; Polar Exploration ; author and joint author of papers and contributions to the Royal Society of Edinburgh and other learned Societies and Journals. *Recreations :* gardening, walking, photography. *Address:* 22 George Street, Edinburgh. *Club:* Royal Eastern Yacht, Edinburgh. (*Died 31 Oct. 1921.*)

BRUCE-JOY, Albert, sculptor ; R.H.A., F.R.G.S. ; *b.* Dublin ; *e. s.* of Dr. W. Bruce Joy, and *b.* of George W. Joy, painter. *Educ.:* Becker's School, Offenbach ; tutor, Paris ; King's Coll., London ; S. Kensington and R.A. Schools of Art. Pupil of Foley ; studied in Rome three years. Public statues, chiefly colossal : Gladstone (in front Bow Church), Lord Frederick Cavendish (Barrow - in - Furness), John Bright (Manchester), Bright (Birmingham), Harvey Tercentenary Memorial (Folkestone), Ch.-Just. Whiteside (St. Patrick's Cath.), Sir M. Wilson (Skipton), Alexander Balfour (Liverpool), Christopher Bushell (University, Liverpool), Graves (Roy. Coll. Phys. Ire.), Oliver Heywood (Manchester), Laird (Birkenhead), Whitley (Liverpool), Berkeley, Bishop (Cloyne Cath.), Lord Kelvin (Belfast), Hornby (Blackburn), Lord Justice FitzGibbon (St. Patrick's Cathedral), Cranmer Memorial (Cambridge), etc. ; the John Bright statue (House of Commons), The Provost, George Salmon, D.D., Memorial (St. Patrick's Cathedral), the Memorial Dean Farrar (Canterbury Cathedral) ; bust Viscount Morley (India) ; busts King Edward VII.—in University, Manchester, Paris Chamber of Commerce, Norwich Memorial Hospital, Indian Memorial (Mayo Hospital, Lahore), and Belfast Memorial Hospital, etc. ; King George V. (Public Park, Amod, India) ; Queen Victoria (colossal), for Victoria, B.C. ; bust Lord Salisbury (Mansion House), Matthew Arnold (Westminster Abbey), Adams (astronomer) Memorial and Russel Wallace (Westminster Abbey), Archbishop Canterbury (Benson), Lord Farnborough (House of Commons), Codrington Memorial (St. Paul's), Montgomery (St. Paul's), Sir R. Montgomery (India Office), Lord Cairns Memorial (Lincoln's Inn), and bust (Royal Law Courts) ; Mark Firth (Firth Coll. Sheffield), Pratt Memorial (School Chapel, Harrow), Archbishop Benson Memorial (Rugby School Chapel) ; the Maharajah of Nepal ; in America—the Ayer Colossal Lion (Lowell, Boston), Chauncey Depew bust (Lotus Club, New York), Hon. Loudon Snowden (Philadelphia) ; bust Mary Anderson (Stratford-on-Avon) ; ideal works— The Young Apollo, The Forsaken, The First Flight, The Little Visitor, The Fairy Tale, Moses and Brazen Serpent, Faith (Christian Knowledge Society's Building), Thetis and Achilles, The Pets, Beatrice, Sunshine, The Cricketer (C. B. Fry), The Fencer (Seligman), Tennis (E. Miles), The Boy Scout. *Recreations:* boating, riding, skating, music. *Address:* 2 Whitehall Court, S.W.1 ; Chase Lodge, near Hindhead, Haslemere. *Clubs:* Athenæum, Arts, Authors'. (*Died 22 July 1924.*)

BRUNGER, Captain Robert, D.S.O. 1916 ; 4th Suffolk Regt. ; *b.* Framlingham, 25 May 1893 ; *s.* of W. T. Brunger of Framlingham College, Suffolk ; unmarried. *Educ.:* Framlingham College. Second Lieut. 4th Suffolk Regt., 1911 ; proceeded to New Zealand in 1913 and was engaged in sheep-farming, during which time he became attached to the 3rd Auckland Infantry Batt. (allied regiment to the Suffolks) ; recalled to rejoin his regiment in England on the outbreak of war ; Captain, Jan. 1915 ; served in France ; wounded May 1916, and returned to
140

England (despatches, D.S.O.). *Address:* College House, Framlingham, Suffolk.
(*Died 8 Oct. 1918.*)

BRUNNER, Ernst August, J.P. ; Life Member Royal Colonial Institute ; general merchant ; *b.* Oude Wetering, Holland ; *s.* of Rev. E. A. Brun er and M. J. Rademaker ; *m.* 1879, Cornelie Louise Colenbrander ; no *c. Educ.:* Leiden. Arrived in Natal, 1872 ; found employment at sugar and coffee estates, and finally settled down at a small trading station in the Lower Tugela valley where he engaged in trade with the natives and few Europeans in the district, running at the same time a ferry, a butchery, and a bakery ; went through the Zulu War as a volunteer, being a member of the Stanger Mounted Rifles ; attached himself to the Natal Guides under Major Barrow, and connected with his Mounted Infantry with Col. Pearson's column (medal and clasp) ; at termination of war was appointed a magistrate under Chief John Dunn, who sent him home in 1881 to interview authorities in Downing Street with regard to the proposed return of Cetywayo to Zululand ; the mission proved futile, and upon the return of the exiled King settled at what is now the township of Eshowe, of which he was the originator, since he built the first house there, 1883, and the town grew around him ; passed through the rebellion of 1885 and 1888, the last Boer war, and the rebellions of 1906 and 1908 ; represented Zululand in the Natal House of Assembly, 1899 - 1910 ; Colonial Treasurer, 1906-7 ; Union medal, presented at time Union was consummated "to those who rendered special service in connection with the establishment of the Union." *Recreations:* music, crayon drawing. *Address:* Samarang, Eshowe, Zululand. *Clubs:* Victoria, Pietermaritzburg.

BRUNNER, Rt. Hon. Sir John Tomlinson, 1st Bt., *cr.* 1895 ; D.L. ; M.P. (L.) Northwich, 1885-86, and 1887-1909 ; P.C. 1906 ; LL.D. (Hon.) and Pro-Chancellor Liverpool University, 1909 ; Chairman, Brunner, Mond and Co., Ltd., alkali manufacturers ; *b.* Everton, Liverpool, 8 Feb. 1842 ; *s.* of Rev. John Brunner, of Canton Zürich, Switzerland, schoolmaster at Everton ; *m.* 1st, 1864, Salome (*d.* 1874), *d.* of James Davies of Liverpool ; two *s.* three *d.* ; 2nd, 1875, Jane (*d.* 1910), *d.* of Dr. Wyman of Kettering ; two *d. Educ.:* his father's school. Entered mercantile life at Liverpool, 1857 ; served John Hutchinson and Co., alkali manufacturers of Widnes, 1861-72 ; in company with Ludwig Mond, F.R.S., he established (1873) the Alkali Works at Northwich, which became the largest in the world. Presented Northwich with a public library ; Runcorn and Winsford with Guildhalls for the use of Trade Unions, Friendly and other Societies ; benefactor to Liverpool University, (endowed three chairs) Witton Grammar School, and several public libraries ; Member of Royal Commission for Paris Exhibition, 1900 ; Member of Civil List Committee, 1901 ; of Royal Commission on Canals and Waterways, 1906 ; Vice-President Cheshire Football Association. *Publications:* Handbooks on Public Education in Cheshire, 1891 and 1896 ; Eight Hours Question. *Recreations:* Sunningdale and Cannes Golf Clubs. *Heir: s.* John Fowler Leece Brunner. *Address:* Silverlands, Chertsey. *T.:* Chertsey 23. *M.:* LB 7197, P 6845. *Clubs:* Reform, National Liberal, Ranelagh. (*Died 1 July 1919.*)

BRUNNER, Roscoe, D.L. ; J.P. ; 2nd *s.* of late Rt. Hon. Sir J. T. Brunner, 1st Bt. ; *b.* 22 Jan. 1871 ; *m.* 1898, Ethel (author of Celia and her Friends, Celia Once Again, Celia's Fantastic Voyage, etc.), *e. d.* of late Arthur Houston, K.C. ; two *s.* one *d. Educ.:* Cheltenham ; Cambridge. Called to bar, Inner Temple, 1895 ;

Director of Brunner, Mond & Co. Ltd. *Club:* Bath.   (*Died 3 Nov. 1926.*)

BRUNSKILL, Gerald FitzGibbon, K.C. Ireland, 1914 ; *b.* 4 April 1866 ; 2nd *s.* of late Thomas R. Brunskill, 58 Upper Mount Street, Dublin ; *m.* 1896, Annie, *d.* of late Archibald Robinson, Taxing Master in Chancery, High Court of Justice in Ireland ; one *s.* one *d. Educ.:* Trinity College, Dublin, B.A. (1887), M.A. (1891) ; Gold Medallist in Oratory and Composition, University Philosophical Society ; Silver Medallist in Oratory and Composition, College Historical Society ; auditor of College Historical Society, 1889 ; called to Irish Bar, 1888 ; admitted a Solicitor, 1900 ; recalled to Bar, 1901 ; a Director of the City of Dublin Steam Packet Co. ; M.P. (C.), Mid-Tyrone, 1910 ; contested same Division, 1910. *Recreation :* golf. *Address:* 35 Leeson Park, Dublin. *T.:* Ballsbridge 471. *Clubs:* Constitutional ; Dublin University.   (*Died 4 Oct. 1918.*)

BRUNTON, Sir (Thomas) Lauder, 1st Bt., *cr.* 1908 ; Kt., *cr.* 1900 ; M.D., Sc.D., LL.D. (Hon.) (Edin.), LL.D. (Hon.) (Aberd.), M.D.R.U.I. (Hon.), F.R.C.P., F.R.S., V.P.R.S. 1906 ; Consulting Physician to St. Bartholomew's Hospital ; late Surg. Lt.-Col. C.M.O. 1st City of London Cadet Brig. ; *b.* 14 March 1844 ; *s.* of James Brunton of Hiltonshill, Roxburghshire ; *m.* 1879, Louisa Jane (*d.* 1909), *d.* of late Ven. Edward A. Stopford, Archdeacon of Meath ; one *s.* two *d. Publications:* The Bible and Science, 1881 ; Text-Book of Pharmacology, Modern Therapeutics, 1892 ; Lectures on the Action of Medicines, 1897 ; on Disorders of Assimilation, 1901 ; collected papers on Circulation and Respiration, 1st Series, 1907 ; 2nd Series, 1916 ; Therapeutics of the Circulation, 1908. *Heir : s.* Capt. James Stopford Lauder [*b.* 11 Oct. 1884 ; *m.* 1915, Elizabeth, *o. d.* of Prof. J. Bonsall Porter, Instructional Staff, Canadian Army]. *Address:* 1 De Walden Court, New Cavendish Street, W. *T.A.:* Lauder Brunton, Wesdo, London. *T.:* Mayfair 1627. *Club:* Athenæum.   (*Died 16 Sept. 1916.*)

BRUYNE, Pieter Louis de, C.V.O. (hon.) 1904 ; M.V.O. (hon.) 1897 ; retired British Vice-Consul ; *b.* 11 Feb. 1845 ; *m.:* three *s. Address:* Middelburg, Holland. *T.A.:* debruyne, Middelburg. *T.:* 251.

           (*Died 1 April 1917.*)

BRYAN, Prof. George Hartley, Sc.D., F.R.S. ; *b.* Cambridge, 1 Mar. 1864 ; *o. s.* of late Robert Purdie Bryan ; *m.* 1906, Mabel Williams ; one *d. Educ.:* Peterhouse, Cambridge. Fellow, 1889-95; Smith's Prize, 1889 ; Hon. Fellow, 1915 ; Hopkins Prize, 1920 ; Gold Medal Inst. Naval Architects, 1901 ; Gold Medal Royal Aeronautical Society, 1914 (both medals recently stolen); silver medal Prestito Littorio, 1926-1927 ; awarded special grant from Research Department, 1917-20 ; Past-President Cambridge Entomological Society, Postal Microscopical Society, Mathematical Association, Inst. Aeronaut Engineers; Hon. Member Calcutta Mathematical Society. *Publications:* chiefly aeroplane rigid dynamics ; Stability in Aviation ; Reports on Compressible Fluids, Acoustics of Airscrews and Canonical Forms (Aeronautics) ; text books, Briggs and Bryan series ; Thermodynamics ; Mathematical Tables ; illustrations in Things seen in Italian Lakes and Riviera. *Recreations:* natural history, photography, cutting rolls for player piano. *Address:* Le Lucciole, Bordighera, Italy. *T.A.:* Lucciole, Bordighera. *Club:* Touring Club Italiano.   (*Died 13 Oct. 1928.*)

BRYAN, William Jennings; late editor and proprietor of The Commoner ; *b.* Salem, Illinois, 19 Mar. 1860 ; Presbyterian ; *m.* 1884, Mary E. Baird, of Perry, Ill. ; one *s.* two *d. Educ.:* Illinois Coll. ; Union College of Law, Chicago ; degrees from many colleges and

universities. Practised at Jacksonville, Ill., 1883-87 ; afterwards at Lincoln, Neb. ; Editor Omaha World - Herald, 1894 - 96 ; Delegate to National Democratic Convention, 1896 ; nominated for President, 1896, 1900, and 1908 ; advocated free coinage of silver, and opposed Trusts and Imperialism ; made tour round world, 1905-1906 ; Secretary of State, 1913-15. *Publications:* The First Battle ; The Old World and its Ways ; In His Image ; Famous Figures of the Old Testament ; Shall Christianity remain Christian ?; Heart to Heart Appeals : many articles in magazines and newspapers *Address:* Miami Florida, U.S.A.   (*Died 26 July 1925.*)

BRYANT, Frederick Beadon, C.S.I. 1911 ; *b.* 20 Mar. 1858 ; *m.* 1885, Mary, *d.* of Alfred Lund. Assistant Conservator, 1881 ; Deputy Conservator, 1890 ; Conservator, 1901 ; Chief Conservator, Burma, 1905 ; Inspector-General of Forests, Government of India, 1908-1913 ; retired, 1913. *Address:* Ryders, Walton-on-Thames. *Club:* East India United Service.   (*Died 28 Nov. 1922.*)

BRYANT, Sophie (*née* Willock), D.Sc. (Lond.) ; Litt.D. Dublin (hon.) ; *b.* Dublin, 1850 ; *d.* of late Rev. W. A. Willock, D.D. *Educ.:* privately ; Bedford College, London. Graduated with Mathematical and Moral Science honours, 1881 ; took degree of Doctor of Science in the Moral Science branch, 1884, being the first woman to take that degree. Childhood spent chiefly in Co. Fermanagh, Ireland, where her father played a prominent part in the Irish national education movement. After removing to London, she gained an Arnott scholarship at Bedford Coll. ; *m.* at 19, Dr. William Hicks Bryant of Plymouth, and after his death, a year later resumed her work as a student, and became mathematical mistress at the North London Collegiate School for Girls ; succeeded Miss Buss as head mistress of the school, 1895 ; retired, 1918. Appointed to serve upon Royal Commission on Secondary Education, 1894, a member of the Consultative Committee of the Board of Education, 1900-11 ; of the Senate of the University of London, 1900-7 ; and of the London Education Committee, 1908-14, Ex-President Head Mistresses' Association. *Publications:* Educational Ends ; Celtic Ireland ; Studies in Character ; The Teaching of Morality in the Family and the School ; The Teaching of Christ on Life and Conduct ; The Genius of the Gael ; How to read the Bible in the Twentieth Century ; Moral and Religious Education ; Liberty, Order and Law under Native Irish Rule, A Study in the Book of the Ancient Laws of Ireland ; and other educational, philosophical, and scientific articles. *Recreations:* cycling, boating, and mountaineering. *Address:* North London Collegiate School for Girls, Sandall Road, N.W. *Club:* University of London.   (*Died 14 Aug. 1922.*)

BRYCE, 1st Viscount, *cr.* 1914, of Dechmont, Lanarks., **James Bryce,** O.M., G.C.V.O., *cr.* 1917 ; P.C., D.C.L., LL.D., F.R.S. ; *b.* 10 May 1838 ; *e. s.* of James Bryce, LL.D., of Glasgow (*d.* 1877) and Margaret, *e. d.* of James Young, Abbeyville, Co. Antrim ; *m.* 1889, Elizabeth Marion, *d.* of Thomas Ashton, Fordbank, near Manchester. *Educ.:* High School and University of Glasgow ; Scholar of Trin. Coll. Oxford (B.A. 1862, D.C.L. 1870) ; Fellow of Oriel Coll. 1862 ; at Heidelberg University, 1863. Barr. Lincoln's Inn, 1867 ; practised till 1882 ; Regius Professor of Civil Law at Oxford, 1870 ; resigned that office, 1893 ; M.P. for Tower Hamlets, 1880 ; Under-Secretary of State for Foreign Affairs, 1886 ; Chancellor of Duchy of Lancaster (with seat in Cabinet), 1892 ; President of Board of Trade, 1894 ; Chairman of Royal Commission on Secondary Education, 1894 ; member of Senate of London University, 1893 ; corresponding member of Institute of France, 1891 (foreign member, 1904) ; foreign

member of Royal Academies of Turin and Brussels, 1896, of Naples, 1903, St. Petersburg and Stockholm; corresponding member of Società Romana di Storia Patria, 1885; member of Reale Accademia dei Lincei, Rome, 1904; one of the British members of the International Tribunal at the Hague. Hon. LL.D. of Edinburgh University, 1883; of Glasgow University, 1886; Michigan University, 1887; St. Andrews, 1902; Aberdeen, 1906; Doctor of Political Science of Royal Hungarian University of Buda Pest, 1896; Litt.D. Victoria University, 1897; D.C.L. Trinity University, Toronto, 1897, Harvard and Princeton University, 1907; Litt.D. Cambridge University, 1898; Oxford University, 1914; LL.D. University of Jena, 1908; of California and of Leipzig, 1909; of Buenos Aires, 1910; of Adelaide and Brisbane, 1912; LL.D. Belfast Univ., 1919; Litt.D. Trinity Coll., Dublin, 1920; Hon. Fellow of Trinity and Oriel Colleges, Oxford; Pres. of the Alpine Club, 1899-1901; Chief Secretary for Ireland, 1905-7; M.P. (L.) Aberdeen, S., 1885-1907; H.M. Ambassador Extraordinary and Plenipotentiary at Washington, 1907-13; Hon. Member Faculty of Law University of Santiago; ex-Pres. British Academy; a trustee of the National Portrait Gallery; Hon. Fellow of the Royal Geographical Society; one of the British Representatives of the Hague Court. *Publications:* The Flora of the Island of Arran, 1859; The Holy Roman Empire, 1862; Report on the Condition of Education in Lancashire, 1867; The Trade Marks Registration Act, with Introduction and Notes on Trade Mark Law, 1877; Transcaucasia and Ararat, 1877; The American Commonwealth, 1888; Impressions of South Africa, 1897; Studies in History and Jurisprudence, 1901; Studies in Contemporary Biography, 1903; The Hindrances to Good Citizenship, 1909; South America: Observations and Impressions, 1912; University and Historical Addresses, 1913; Essays and Addresses on War, June 1918; Modern Democracies, 1921. *Recreations:* mountain-climbing, angling. Heir: none. *Address:* Hindleap, Forest Row, Sussex; 3 Buckingham Gate, S.W. *Club:* Athenæum.
(*Died 22 Jan. 1922.*)

BRYCE, John Annan, M.P. (L.), Inverness Burghs, 1906-18; J.P. for Island of Bombay; s. of James Bryce, LL.D., of Glasgow, and Margaret, d. of James Young, of Abbeyville, Belfast; b. of Viscount Bryce; m. Violet, d. of Captain Champagné L'Estrange, R.A.; one s. two d. *Educ.:* High School and Univ. of Glasgow (M.A.); Edinburgh Univ.; Balliol College, Oxford (Brackenbury History Scholar), B.A. First Class Hons., Final Classical School; Hons. in History School; was Secretary, Treasurer, and Pres., Oxford Union Society; formerly East India Merchant, was Chairman Rangoon Chamber of Commerce, Member of Legislative Council of Burma; made extensive explorations in unknown parts of Upper Burma before the war, and in Upper Siam; Director, London County and Westminster Bank; English Scottish and Australian Bank; Atlas Assurance Co., Bombay Baroda Railway Co., and Burma Railway Co.; Chairman of British Westinghouse Co.; twice Member of Council of Royal Geographical Society; Member of Royal Commission on Congestion in Ireland, 1906-8. *Address:* 35 Bryanston Square, W.1. *T.:* Paddington 400. *Clubs:* Alpine, Savile.
(*Died 25 June 1923.*)

BRYMER, Ven. Frederick Augustus, M.A.; Archdeacon of Wells since 1899; Rector of Charlton Mackrell, Somerset, since 1876; 3rd *surv. s.* of late John Brymer of Ilsington House, Dorchester; m. 1882, Mary, d. of late Preb. W. F. Neville, of Butleigh Vicarage, Somerset; one s. and one d. *Educ.:* Radley; Christ Church, Oxford. Curate of Wargrave, 1874-6; Assistant Diocesan Inspector of Schools for

142

Cary Deanery, 1880-8; Hon. Secretary, Bath and Wells Diocesan Societies, 1887-1902; Prebendary of Wiveliscombe, 1891; Secretary, Bath and Wells Diocesan School Association, 1897; Proctor in Convocation for Bath and Wells, 1898; Prebendary of Huish and Brent, in right of the Archdeaconry, 1899. *Address:* The Rectory, Charlton Mackrell, Somerset. *T.A.:* Charlton Mackrell. *Club:* Oxford and Cambridge.
(*Died 1 May 1917.*)

BUCHANAN, Lt.-Colonel Arthur Louis Hamilton; late Gordon Highlanders; M.P. (C.U.) Coatbridge Division of Lanarkshire 1918-22; b. 1866; e. s. of D. W. R. Carrick-Buchanan of Drumpellier and Carsewall; m. 1903, Adeline Musgave, e. d. of late Richard Harvey; three s. four d. *Educ.:* Newton College, Devon; served twenty-five years Gordon Highlanders; served South African War (despatches); Commanded a Base Depôt, L. of C., European War, 1914-19 (despatches); J.P. and D.L., Lanarkshire. *Address:* Drumpellier, Coatbridge, Scotland. *Clubs:* Carlton; New, Edinburgh.
(*Died 15 Feb. 1925.*)

BUCHANAN, Sir Eric Alexander, 3rd Bt., cr. 1878; b. 19 Aug. 1848; S. brother, 1901; s. of 1st Bt. and Frances Mellish, d. of the Dean of Hereford; m. 1898, Constance (d. 1914), d. of late Com. Tennant, R.N.; one s. one d. *Educ.:* Wellington. Heir: s. Charles James, Lieut. Highland L.I., b. 16 April 1899.
(*Died 29 July 1928.*)

BUCHANAN, Rt. Hon. Sir George (William), P.C.; G.C.B. cr. 1915; G.C.M.G., cr. 1913; G.C.V.O. and K.C.M.G. cr. 1909; K.C.V.O. 1905; C.B. 1900; C.V.O. 1900; LL.D. Birmingham, 1918; b. Copenhagen, 25 Nov. 1854; s. of Sir Andrew Buchanan, 1st Bt., G.C.B.; m. 1885, Lady Georgiana Bathurst (d. 1922), d. of 6th Earl Bathurst; one d. *Educ.:* Wellington College. Attaché, 1876; 3rd Secretary, Rome, 1878; 2nd Secretary, Tokio, 1879; Vienna, 1882; Berne, 1889, where he acted as Chargé d'Affaires several times; Secretary of Legation, 1893; Chargé d'Affaires, Darmstadt, 1893-1900; British Agent to the Venezuelan Arbitration Tribunal, 1898; Secretary of Embassy at Rome, 1900; Berlin, 1901-3; Minister Plenipotentiary at Sofia, 1903-8; Minister at The Hague, 1908-10; Ambassador to Petrograd, 1910-18; freedom of the City of Moscow, 1916; Hon. Member of the Universities of Moscow and Petrograd, 1917; Ambassador to Rome, 1919-21; retired from the Diplomatic Service, Nov. 1921. *Publication:* My Mission to Russia, and other Diplomatic Memories, 1923. *Address:* 15 Lennox Gardens, S.W.1. *T.:* Kensington 1727. *Club:* Marlborough. (*Died 20 Dec. 1924.*)

BUCHANAN, John Lee, A.M., LL.D.; President of the University of Arkansas, Fayetteville, Arkansas, 1894-1902; b. Smyth County, Virginia, 19 June 1831; 2nd s. of Patrick C. Buchanan and Margaret, d. of Major Samuel Graham; m. 1859, Frances Elizabeth, d. of Dr. E. E. Wiley. *Educ.:* Emory and Henry College, Virginia. Professor in Emory and Henry College, 1856-78; Professor of Latin, Vanderbilt University, 1878-79; President of Emory and Henry College, 1879-80; President Virginia Agricultural and Mechanical College, 1880-82; Joint Principal, Martha Washington College, 1882-86; State Superintendent of Public Instruction of Virginia, 1886-90; Professor Latin, Randolph Macon College, 1890-94. *Publications:* Educational Reports of Virginia from 1886-90. *Recreations:* hunting, fishing, chess. *Address:* Fayetteville, Arkansas. *Clubs:* American Institute of Civics; Southern Educational Association.
(*Died 19 Feb. 1902.*)

BUCHANAN, John Young, M.A., F.R.S.; chemist; b. Scotland, 20 Feb. 1844; s. of John Buchanan of Dowanhill. *Educ.:* Glasgow High School and University; Universities of Marburg, Leipzig, and Bonn; École de Médecine, Paris.

Chemist and Physicist of the "Challenger" Expedition; later, Lecturer in Geography, University of Cambridge; Vice-Président du Conseil de Perfectionnement de l'Institut océanographique de Paris; croix du commandeur de l'Ordre de Saint Charles de Monaco: Hon. Member of the Gesellschaft für Erdkunde, Berlin; and the Société Helvétique des Sciences Naturelles; awarded Keith Medal, Royal Society, Edinburgh, and Gold Medal, Royal Scottish Geographical Society. *Recreation:* travelling. *Club:* Athenæum. *(Died 16 Oct. 1925.)*

BUCHANAN, Robert J. M., M.D., F.R.C.P., M.R.C.S., Capt. R.A.M.C. (T.); Professor of Forensic Medicine, University, Liverpool. *Educ.:* University, Liverpool; Hon. Physician Royal Infirmary, Liverpool; was Hon. Physician, Stanley Hospital, and Assistant Hon. Physician, Hospital for Consumption and Diseases of the Chest, Liverpool; Demonstrator of Pathology, University College, Liverpool. *Publications:* Rabies and Hydrophobia; Textbook of Forensic Medicine and Toxicology; The Blood in Health and Disease, etc. *Recreations:* painting, fishing. *Address:* 6 Rodney Street, Liverpool. *T.:* Royal 2356, Liverpool. *Club:* Athenæum, Liverpool. *(Died April 1925.)*

BUCHANAN, Ven. Thos. Boughton, M.A.; *b.* 1833; *m.* Laura Maria (*d.* 1915), *d.* of late George Richmond, R.A. *Educ.:* Exeter Coll., Oxford (1st Class Mods.); ordained 1857; Curate of Wilton, 1857-59; Chaplain to Lord Herbert of Lea, 1859-60; Rector of Wishford Magna, Wilts, 1863-71; Chaplain to Bishop of Salisbury, 1870-85; Vicar Potterne, Wilts, 1871-91; Rector of Poulshot, 1891-1905; Archdeacon of Wilts 1874-1911; Residentiary Canon of Salisbury, 1895-1915. *Address:* Close, Salisbury.
(Died 28 June 1924.)

BUCHANAN, Hon. Sir Walter Clarke, Kt., *cr.* 1913; M.L.C. since 1915; *b.* Argyllshire, 1838. *Educ.:* Parish School, Greenock. Went to Melbourne, 1857; New Zealand a few years later; one of the founders and a Director of Wellington Meat Export Co.; Member House of Representatives for Wairarapa South, 1881-87; Wairarapa, 1887-91, 1902-5, and 1908-14. *Address:* Alexandra Street, Masterton, N.Z.
(Died 19 July 1924.)

BUCHANAN, Sir Walter James, K.C.I.E., *cr.* 1918; C.I.E. 1913; M.D.; Lt.-Col. Indian Medical Service, retired; Editor of the Indian Medical Gazette, Calcutta, 1899-1919; Inspector-General of Prisons, Bengal Presidency, 1902-19; *b.* Londonderry, 12 Nov. 1861; *e. s.* of late Robert Buchanan of Fintona, County Tyrone; *m.* Lilian Edith (*d.* 1916), *d.* of late E. Simpson-Byrne; one *s.* *Educ.:* Foyle College, Londonderry; Trinity College, Dublin; Vienna. B.A., M.D., B.Ch.; Diplomate in State Medicine, Univ. Dublin; University Travelling Prizeman in Medicine, 1887. Entered I.M.S., 1887; took part in Hazara Expedition, 1888; Lushai Expedition, 1890; Manipur Field Force, 1891 (medal and clasp); entered Civil Medical employ, Bengal, 1892; holds Delhi Durbar coronation medals, 1903 and 1911; as Member Indian Prisons Commission visited U.S.A., Japan, China, etc. *Publications:* Manual of Jail Hygiene (2nd éd. 1900); Tours in Sikkim, 1917. *Recreation:* golf. *Address:* 56 Leeson Park, Dublin. *Clubs:* East India United Service; University, Dublin.
(Died 23 Mar. 1924.)

BUCK, Sir Edward Charles; Kt., *cr* 1886; K.C.S.I., *cr.* 1897; Hon. Fellow of Clare Coll., 1898; *b.* 1838; *s.* of Z. Buck, of Norwich. *Educ.:* Norwich and Oakham Schools; Clare College, Cambridge (L.B.), 1861; LL.D. 1886); Bengal Civil Service. Represented Indian Government at Colonial Exhibition, 1886; Secy. Government of India, 1882-97; now retired. *Club:* East India United Service.
(Died 6 July 1916.)

BUCKELL, Sir Robert, Kt., *cr.* 1907; *b.* 22 Sep. 1841; *m.* 1863, Ann Ellen, *d.* of James Goold of Oxford; one *s.* Hon. M.A. Oxford University; Alderman of City of Oxford and J.P.; six times mayor of the city. *Address:* 4 Staverton Road, Oxford.
(Died 1 June 1925.)

BUCKHAM, Sir George Thomas, Kt., *cr.* 1917; chief Ordnance Designer and a Director, firm of Vickers, Ltd.; Member of the Shipbuilding and Armaments Board; Director of the Electrode Co. of Sheffield; Member of Council of Sheffield Chamber of Commerce; Member of Grand Council of Federation of British Industries; *b.* Newcastle, 1863; *s.* of late John Buckham; *m.* Selina Elizabeth (*d.* 1919), 3rd *d.* of late M. Langley, Newcastle; one *s.* one *d.* *Educ.:* Newcastle. Trained as an Ordnance Engineer at the Elswick Works of Sir W. G. Armstrong, Whitworth & Co. Ltd.; joined staff of Vickers, Ltd., in 1895; member of the Institute of Mechanical Engineers; Third Class of the Order of the Rising Sun (Japan). *Address:* Springhill House, Sandygate, Sheffield. *T.:* Broomhill 236. *Club:* Sheffield.
(Died 9 May 1928.)

BUCKLAND, 1st Baron, *cr.* 1926, of Bwlch; Henry Seymour Berry; J.P., County of Breconshire and Borough of Merthyr Tydfil; *b.* 1877; *e. s.* of late Alderman John Mathias Berry, J.P.; *m.* Gwladys Mary, *e. d.* of Simon Sandbrook, J.P.; five *d.* *Educ.:* privately. Coalowner; Chairman, Guest, Keen & Nettlefolds, Ltd.; closely identified with his native town of Merthyr Tydfil, to which he has given a new wing for the Merthyr General Hospital, Public Swimming Baths, and many other gifts; only living Freeman of the Borough of Merthyr Tydfil. *Address:* Buckland, Bwlch, Breconshire; 3 Whitehall Court, S.W.1. *Club:* Carlton.
(Died 23 May 1928.)

BUCKLE, Commander Archibald Walter, D.S.O. 1918; R.N.V.R.; Headmaster, Rotherhithe New Road Nautical School; *m.* Elsie; two *s.* Served European War, 1914-1918 (wounded thrice, D.S.O. and 3 bars, despatches five times). *Address:* Tower House, Crescent Way, Brockley. *(Died 6 May 1927.)*

BUCKLE, Lt.-Col. Arthur William Bentley-, C.M.G. 1915; Army Pay Dept.; *b.* 13 Aug. 1860; *s.* of late Capt. George Bentley-Buckle, 40th Regt., and *g. s.* of late Archdeacon Buckle; *m.* Mary Bunbury, 2nd *d.* of late Bishop of Limerick; one *s.* two *d.* *Educ.:* Wellington College. Entered army, 1881; Lieut. West Riding Regt. 1881; Adjutant, 1885-89; Captain, 1888; Major, 1902; Lieut.-Col. 1908; Adjutant Militia, 1889-94; Paymaster, 1895-1903; Staff Paymaster, 1903; 1st Class Assist. Accountant, 1905-9; served S. Africa, 1899-1902 (Queen's medal with clasp; King's medal, 2 clasps); European War, 1914-18 (C.M.G., Chevalier Légion d'Honneur). *(Died 21 Jan. 1923.)*

BUCKLE, Maj.-Gen. Charles Randolph; *b.* 29 Oct. 1835. Served thirty years in the Royal Artillery; served in the Garibaldian campaign of 1860; afterwards with the Sardinian Artillery at the siege of Gaeta (wounded); killed the largest elephant ever known in Travancore, which had killed over thirty people. *Recreations:* shooting and travelling. *Clubs:* Army and Navy, United Service.
(Died 14 Nov. 1920.)

BUCKLE, John, J.P.; M.P. (Lab.) Eccles 1922-24; *b.* Leeds.
(Died 8 Nov. 1925.)

BUCKLEY, Sir Edmund, J.P.; 2nd Bt., *cr.* 1868; *b.* 7 May 1861; *s.* of 1st Bt. and Sarah, *e. d.* of W. Rees of Tonn, County Carmarthen; *m.* 1885, Harriet Olivia Louisa, *d.* of Rev. Maurice Lloyd. Owns about 11,300 acres. *Heir:* none. *Address:* The Plas, Dinas Mawddwy, N. Wales; Aberturnant Hall, Bala.

143

Club: New Oxford and Cambridge.

(*Died 20 Jan. 1919.*)

BUCKLEY, Rev. James Monroe, D.D., LL.D.; editor of The Christian Advocate, New York, 1880-1912; *b.* Rahway, New Jersey, 16 Dec. 1836; *s.* of Rev. John Buckley, native of Lancashire, and Abby, *d.* of Judge C. Monroe, Mount Holly, New Jersey. *Educ.:* Pennington Seminary, New Jersey; Wesleyan Univ. Middletown, Connecticut; studied theology, Exeter, New Hampshire. Entered ministry, Methodist Episcopal Church, 1858; spent 1863 in Europe; returning, settled Detroit, Mich.; removed to Brooklyn, N.Y., 1866; continued in ministry till 1880; D.D. Wesleyan University; LL.D. Emory and Henry College, Virginia; L.H.D. Syracuse University; Hon. Member American Medico - Psychological Society. *Publications:* Supposed Miracles; Midnight Sun; Czar and Nihilist; Faith Healing; Christian Science and Kindred Phenomena; Travels in Three Continents; History of Methodism in the United States; Extemporaneous Oratory; The Fundamentals of Religion and their Contrasts; Wrong and Peril of Woman Suffrage; Constitutional and Parliamentary History of the Methodist Episcopal Church. *Recreations:* President Board of Managers, Seney Methodist Episcopal Hospital, Brooklyn, and President of the Board of Managers of the State Hospital for the Insane at Morris Plains, N.J.; Vice-President Society for Prevention of Vice. *Address:* 150 Fifth Avenue, New York.

(*Died 8 Feb. 1920.*)

BUCKLEY, Ven. James Rice, B.D.; Archdeacon of Llandaff since 1913; Vicar of Llandaff, 1878-1913; chaplain to the Lord Bishop of Llandaff since 1905; *b.* 28 Jan. 1849; *m.* Catherine, *d.* of late James Kempthorne, solicitor, Neath; four *s.* three *d. Educ.:* Carmarthen Grammar School; Manilla Hall, Clifton; St. David's College, Lampeter. Graduated in Honours, 1872; Curate of Neath, 1872; Surrogate for the Diocese of Llandaff; Rural Dean of Llandaff; Proctor for the Clergy, 1906; Hon. Canon of St. Cross in Llandaff Cathedral; chairman of the Cardiff Board of Guardians and of the Llandaff Diocesan Branch of the Church in Wales Temperance Society. *Recreations:* No special recreation, chiefly change of work. *Address:* The Vicarage, Llandaff. *T.A.:* Llandaff Post Office.

(*Died 8 Sept. 1924.*)

BUCKLEY, Rev. Jonathan Charles, Hon. Canon, St. Albans, 1895. *Educ.:* Hatfield Hall, Durham. Curate of Rotherham, 1870; Holy Trinity, Brompton, 1872-75; St. James', Newhampton, 1875 - 78; Hackney, 1878-82; Vicar of St. Luke's, Victoria Docks, 1882-1918; Surrogate of S. Alban's Diocese, 1918. *Address:* Thornville, Hemel Hempstead.

(*Died 28 Dec. 1927.*)

BUCKLEY, Robert Burton, C.S.I. 1901; *b.* Brighton, 23 August 1847; *s.* of Rev. John Wall Buckley, Vicar of St. Mary's, Paddington; *m.* Ada Marion, *d.* of late Major B. K. Finnimore, R.A., 1880; one *s.* three *d. Educ.:* Merchant Taylors' School. Whitworth Scholar Mechanical Science, 1869; went to India as an Assistant Engineer in the Public Works Department, 1869; rose through various grades to rank of Chief Engineer, 1st class; Member Inst. of Civil Engineers, 1880; was chiefly connected with works of irrigation. *Publications:* three books on irrigation in India and several pamphlets on engineering subjects. *Address:* 44 Clanricarde Gardens, Bayswater, W.

(*Died 19 Dec. 1927.*)

BUCKNILL, His Hon. Sir John Alexander Strachey, Kt., *cr.* 1916; K.C.; Puisne Judge of the Patna High Court since 1920; *b.* Clifton, 14 Sep. 1873; *m.* 1901, Alice, *y. d.* of Admiral Sir George Richards, K.C.B., F.R.S.; two *d. Educ.:* Charterhouse; Keble College,

144

Oxford. M.A. (Oxon), F.Z.S., M.B.O.U., Barrister-at-law; Inner Temple, 1896; Midland Circuit; Commissioner of Patents, Transvaal, 1902; M.L.C. Transvaal, 1904; Chairman of Committees Legislative Council, Transvaal, 1906; a Legal adviser to Transvaal, 1907; Sole Commissioner to enquire into immorality amongst Chinese labourers in Transvaal, 1906; Member of Legislative and Executive Councils of Cyprus, 1907; acted Chief Secretary, 1908; King's Advocate of Cyprus, 1907-12; Attorney-General of Hong-Kong, 1912-14; Chief Justice, Straits Settlements, 1914-20; Chairman, Singapore Military Service Advisory Committee, 1916; President, Commission of Investigation into Administration of State of Trengganu, 1918; President, Straits Settlements, Kedah and Johore Military Service Tribunals, 1918; President, Malayan Public Services Salaries Commission, 1918-19; President, Raffles Centenary Memorial Committee, 1920; Chairman, Raffles Museum and Library Committee, 1920; President, Children's Aid Society, Singapore, 1920; President, Patna Museum Committee, 1921; President, Patna Law College, 1921; President, Numismatic Society of India, 1923. *Publications:* The Birds of Surrey, 1901; The Ornithology of Cyprus, 1910; The Imperial Ottoman Penal Code, 1914; late editor of the South African Ornithologists' Journal. *Recreations:* ornithology, numismatics, shooting, and fishing. *Address:* King George's Avenue, Patna, India. *Club:* Athenæum.

(*Died 5 Oct. 1926.*)

BUCKNILL, Rt. Hon. Sir Thomas Townsend, Hon. Mr. Justice Bucknill, P.C.; Judge of the Queen's Bench Div. of the High Court of Justice, 1899-1914; *b.* 18 Apr. 1845; 2nd *s.* of Sir J. C. Bucknill, F.R.S., of East Cliff House, Bournemouth, and Maryanne, *o.c.* of Thomas Townsend, Esq., of Hillmorton Hall, Warwicks.; *m.* 1878, Annie Bell, 2nd *d.* of late Henry Bell Ford, of Clifton, Gloucestershire; one *s. Educ.:* Westminster; Geneva. Barr. Inner Temple, 1868; Recorder of Exeter, 1885; M.P. (C.) Surrey, Epsom, 1892-1899. *Publications:* editor of Cunningham's Reports; Abbott on Shipping; Sir S. Cook's Common Pleas Reports. *Address:* Woodcote Lodge, Epsom. *Clubs:* Athenæum, Carlton.

(*Died 4 Oct. 1915.*)

BUCKSTON, Rev. Henry, M.A.; *e. s.* of late Rev. Henry Thomas Buckston and Mary Goodwin, *d.* of late John Goodwin-Johnson; *b.* 1834; *m.* 1875, Eliza Amy, *d.* of William John Marrow; one *s. Educ.:* St. John's College, Cambridge. Lord of the Manors of Mapleton and Ash; patron of one living. *Heir: s.* George Moreton [*b.* 1881; *m.* 1907, Victoria Alexandrina, *y. d.* of late H. C. Okeover; two *s.* one *d. Educ.:* Eton; Trinity College, Cambridge]. *Address:* Sutton-on-the-Hill, Derby; Bradborne Hall, Ashbourne; The Ash, Etwall, Derby; The Callow, Ashbourne.

(*Died 22 Nov. 1916.*)

BUDD, Alfred, M.V.O. 1908; British Vice-Consul San Sebastian, 1907-15; Consul since 1915. *Address:* British Consulate, San Sebastian, Spain.

(*Died June 1927.*)

BUDD, John Wreford, M.A. Cambridge; senior partner of the firm of Budd, Johnson, Jecks & Colclough, solicitors; *b.* 10 Dec. 1838; *e. s.* of John Wreford Budd, Plymouth; *m.* 1866, Lucy Isabella, *y. d.* of Rev. George Skinner, M.A., formerly Fellow and Tutor of Jesus College, Cambridge; three *d. Educ.:* home; Pembroke College, Cambridge (Fellow 1861). Thirteenth Wrangler in the Mathematical Tripos, and 2nd Class Classical Tripos; admitted a Solicitor, 1865; a Member of the Council of the Law Society since 1881; President, 1895-6; now and for many years a member of the Statutory Discipline Committee under the Acts of 1888 and 1919, and Chairman of the Legal Education Committee of the Law Society; Member of the Council of Law Reporting; Member of Senate, University of London; Member of Court of University of Bristol; a Life Governor of the London Hospital. *Recreations:* hunting, fishing, shooting, as opportunity occurs. *Address:* 21 Craven Hill Gardens, Hyde Park, W.2; *T.:* Paddington 3946; Combe Park, Lynton, N. Devon. *Clubs:* New University, City of London. (*Died 18 Dec. 1922.*)

BUDWORTH, Major-Gen. Charles Edward Dutton, C.B. 1916; C.M.G. 1917; M.V.O.; Royal Horse Artillery; 3rd *s.* of late P. J. Budworth, J.P., D.L., of Greensted Hall, Ongar, Essex; *m.* 1st, Winifred (*d.* 1914), *d.* of late Sir Patteson Nickalls; no *c.*; 2nd, 1918, Helen, *o. d.* of Maj.-Gen. W. E. Blewitt; two *s. Educ.:* R.M.A., Woolwich. Joined the Royal Artillery, 1889; served South African War (despatches, Bt. Major); European War, 1914-17 (despatches ten times, C.B., C.M.G., Bt. Col., Major-Gen.); has been Adjutant of the Honourable Artillery Company and Chief Instructor of the Royal Horse and Field School of Gunnery; Commander of the Legion of Honour; Croix de Guerre; Order of St. Stanislaus. *Publications:* various military pamphlets. *Recreations:* shooting, fishing. *M.:* AB 903. *Club:* Army and Navy.
(*Died 15 July 1921.*)

BULLEN, Arthur Henry; *b.* London, 1857; *s.* of late Dr. George Bullen, C.B. *Educ.:* Worcester College, Oxford. *Publications:* edited the works of John Day, 1881; Collection of Old English Plays, 1882-84; Selections from Poems of Michael Drayton, 1883; the Works of Christopher Marlowe, Thomas Middleton, John Marston, George Peele, Thomas Campion; Lyrics from the Song Books of Elizabethan Age, 1886; More Lyrics, 1887; England's Helicon, 1887; established in 1904 The Shakespeare Head Press, Stratford-on-Avon. *Address:* Stratford-on-Avon.
(*Died 29 Feb. 1920.*)

BULLER, Arthur Tremayne; Landowner; J.P. Devon; *b.* 19 March 1850; 5th *s.* of late James Wentworth Buller, D.C.L., of Downes, J.P., D.L., M.P., and Charlotte Juliana Jane, 3rd *d.* of Lord Henry Thomas Molyneux Howard; *m.* Elinor Louisa, *d.* of Francis Leyborne Popham of Littlecote; three *s.* three *d. Educ.:* Harrow; Trinity College, Cambridge. *Address:* Downes, Crediton. *Club:* Arthurs'. (*Died 28 Jan. 1917.*)

BULLER, Charles William Dunbar, *e. s.* of late Rev. William Buller of Pelynt and Trenant, Cornwall; *b.* 2 Oct. 1847; *m.* 1890, Georgiana Anne Elizabeth Dunbar (*d.* 1920), *c. surv. c.* of late George Dunbar, M.P., and sister and heiress of late Capt. John George Dunbar, 1st Life Guards. *Educ.:* Eton; Christ Church, Oxford. Was Fellow of All Souls College, Oxford; D.L., J.P., Co. Down, and D.L. Norfolk; High Sheriff, Co. Down, 1894; patron of the living; contested (U.) South Molton Division of Devonshire, 1891, and South Belfast, 1902; assumed by Royal Licence the surname of Dunbar before that of Buller. *Address:* Woburn, Donaghadee, Co. Down; 15 Upper Grosvenor Street, W. *Clubs:* Brooks's, St. James's; Devon and Exeter, Exeter; Ulster, Belfast. (*Died 29 April 1924.*)

BULLER, Major Herbert Cecil, D.S.O. 1915; Rifle Brigade; attached Princess Patricia's Canadian Light Infantry; *b.* 2 Jan. 1882. Entered army, 1900; Captain, 1910; Adjutant, 1907-10; A.D.C. to Governor-General, Canada, 1911-14; Adjutant Canadian Light Infantry, 1914; served European War, 1914-15 (D.S.O.). *Address:* Erle Hall, Plympton, S. Devon. (*Died 3 June 1916.*)

BULLOCK. Lieut.-Gen. Sir George Mackworth, K.C.B., *cr.* 1911; C.B. 1900; *b.* Warangol, India, 15 August 1851; *s.* of Thomas Henry Bullock, Deputy Com-

missioner, Berar; *m.* 1884, Amy Isabel, O.B.E., *d.* of Colonel J. Thomson, D.L.; one *d. Educ.:* Cheltenham; University College, Oxford; Sandhurst. Entered 1st. Batt. 11th Foot, 1872; passed Staff College, 1880; Brigade Major at Shorncliffe, 1882-87; D.A.A.G. India, 1889-94; won Gold Medal, United Service Institution, India, 1892; in command of 2nd Dev. Regt. South Africa, 1899; Colonel on Staff commanding Volksrust Sub. Dist.; Brig.-General commanding a column (despatches, Brevet Colonel, C.B.); Chief Staff Officer, Egypt, 1902-4; Brigadier-General commanding, Alexandria, 1904-5; Major-General Commanding in Egypt, 1905-8; commanded West Riding Territorial Division, 1910-11; Governor and Commander-in-Chief, Bermuda, 1912-17; Colonel, Devonshire Regiment; retired. *Address:* 3 Carlton Hill, N.W.8. *Club:* Junior United Service.
(*Died 28 Jan. 1926.*)

BULLOCK, Rev. Richard, M.A.; Prebendary of Lincoln, 1875; Member of Convocation for Chapter of Lincoln; *b.* London, 23 May 1889; *s.* of late Edward Bullock, Common Serjeant, City of London, and Katharine, *d.* of J. Cripps, M.P., Cirencester; *m.* Ada, *d.* of T. H. Whipham, barrister-at-law; two *s.* two *d. Educ.:* Oriel Coll. Oxford. Curate of Barton-on-Humber, 1863-66; Vicar and Wray Lect. of Barrow-on-Humber, 1866-78; Rector of Welton-le-Wold, Lincs. 1878-1882; Vicar of Holy Trinity, Leeds, 1882-1900; Rural Dean of W. Elloe, 1900; Vicar of Spalding, Lincolnshire, 1900-13, of Shurdington, Gloucestershire, 1913-17; V.D.; late Dep. Prov. Grand Master of Freemasons, Lincolnshire. *Address:* Park Grange, Charlton Kings, Cheltenham. (*Died 13 Sept. 1918.*)

BULLOCK, Samuel, I.S.O. 1902; late Superintendent for Wrecks and Loss of Life at Sea, Board of Trade; *b.* 1844; *s.* of late Thomas Bullock, Teemore, Fermanagh; *m.* Fanny Sarah, *d.* of Edmund Hartley of Banbury; two *s.* two *d. Educ.:* Portora Royal School, Enniskillen. Secretary of the Committee on the Manning of Merchant Ships, 1904-6, and of other Official Committees. *Recreations:* fishing, billiards, golf. *Address:* Holly Nook, Burwood Park Road, Walton-on-Thames.
(*Died 20 May 1922.*)

BULMAN, Henry Herbert, R.B.A.; *b.* 9 Nov. 1871; *s.* of Jonathan and Elizabeth Bulman, Carlisle; *m.* 1896, Beatrice Elizabeth, *d.* of W. A. Boone, A.R.C.S., Ramsgate; two *s.* one *d. Educ.:* Carlisle; Antwerp; London. Portraits in Home surroundings, landscape, flowers; Drawing in South Kensington Museum; Drawings and paintings in Colonial and various collections. *Address:* 51 Oakhill Road, Putney, S.W. 15. *T.:* Putney 3390. *Club:* Chelsea Arts. (*Died 11 Dec. 1928.*)

BULYEA, His Honour George Hedley Vicars, LL.D.; Chairman of the Board of Public Utilities Commissioners for the Province of Alberta since 1915; *b.* Gagetown, Queen's County, New Brunswick, 17 Feb. 1859; *s.* of James Albert Bulyea of N.E. Loyalist; *m.* 1885, Annie Blanche, 2nd *d.* of R. T. Babbit, Registrar of Queen's Co., N.B. *Educ.:* Grammar School, Queen, N.B.; graduated at University of New Brunswick, 1878. Principal of Sunbury Grammar School, 1878-82; came to Winnipeg, 1882, and to Qu'appelle, 1883; engaged there in general business, which was disposed of in 1898, to accept position as Territorial Commissioner in Yukon Territory; candidate for Territorial Assembly, for Electoral District of South Qu'appelle, 1891, but defeated; elected 1894, 1896, 1898, and 1902; Territorial Secretary and Minister of Agriculture, 1899-1903; Commissioner of Public Works, 1903-5; 1st Lieut.-Governor of the Province of Alberta, 1905-15. *Address:* Edmonton. Alberta. (*Died 23 July 1928.*)

BUN BEHARI KAPUR, Raja, Raja Bahadur, C.S.I. 1903; *b.* 11 Nov. 1853. A

scion of Burdwan family, he was appointed Dewan-i-Raj of the zamindari in 1877; joint manager, 1885; and sole manager, on behalf of his natural son, the present Maharaja of Burdwan, 1891-1903, when Maharaja received full charge; has served on Bengal Legislative Council (three times nominated), and, for many years, as hon. magistrate; Kaiser-i-Hind gold medal, 1914. *Address:* The Bonabas, Burdwan.
(Died 4 June 1924.)

BUNBURY, Major-Gen. Sir Herbert Napier, K.C.B.; *cr.* 1911; C.B. 1906; *b.* 15 Feb. 1851; *s.* of late Capt. R. H. Bunbury, R.N., and *g.s.* of late Sir H. E. Bunbury, Bart.; *m.* 1878, Mary Louisa, *d.* of Major D. P. Campbell, of Ballivcolen, Argyllshire, late 92nd Highlanders; two *s.* *Educ.:* Marlborough. Lieut. R.A. 1871; Captain, 1881; Major, 1887; A.S.C. 1889; Lieut.-Col. 1894; Col. 1901; A.A.G. Cork, 1901-2; Director of Transport, 3rd Army Corps, 1902-3; of Supplies and Transport, Irish Command, 1903; served S. Africa, 1899-1900 (Queen's medal, three clasps); Brig.-Gen. in command of Administration at Gibraltar, 1906; in charge of Administration in Irish Command, 1907-11; retired, 1913; is a Commissioner of Chelsea Hospital. *Address:* 85 St. George's Road, S.W. *Club:* United Service.
(Died 18 Jan. 1922.)

BUNBURY, Major-General William Edwin, C.B. 1911; Indian Army, retired; *b.* Clonfert, 5 April 1858; *s.* of late Bishop of Limerick; *m.* 1893, Eva Mary, *d.* of Francis Gale, Cheltenham; one *s.* *Educ.:* St. Columba's College, Rathfarnham. Entered Army, 1878; Captain I.S.C., 1889; Major, Indian Army 1898; Lieut.-Col. 1904; Col. 1908; Major-General, 1912; passed Staff College; D.A.A.G. Bengal, 1894-97; D.A.Q.M.G. 1897-1900; D.A.G. Northern Army, India, 1908; Brig.-General, General Staff Northern Army, 1909-12; served Afghan War, 1880 (medal); Mahsud-Waziree Expedition, 1881; Isazai Expedition, 1892; Chitral, 1895 (despatches, medal and clasp); Waziristan, 1901, 1902 (despatches, clasp); Commanded 14th P.W.O. Sikhs, 1902-8; Commanded Kohat Brigade, May to Nov. 1912; Quartermaster-General in India, 1912-16; Commanded Rawal Pindi Division, May 1916 to Oct. 1917. *Address:* Chope Barton, Northam, N. Devon. *T.:* Northam 84. *(Died 31 Oct. 1925.)*

BUNDI, H.H. Maharao Raja, Sir Raghubir Singhji Sahib Bahadur, G.C.S.I., *cr.* 1919; K.C.S.I., *cr.* 1897; G.C.I.E., *cr.* 1909; G.C.V.O., *cr.* 1912; *b.* 1869; *S.* 1889; the State has an area of 2220 square miles and a population of 187,068. *Address:* Bundi, Rajputana, India. *(Died 28 July 1927.)*

BUNDY, Edgar, A.R.A. 1915; R.I., R.O.I., R.B.C. *Address:* 3 Acacia Road, St. John's Wood, N.W.8. *T.:* Hampstead 7190.
(Died 10 Jan. 1922.)

BUNE, John; Journalist; Chief of the Parliamentary Staff of The Times; 2nd *s.* of late F. J. Bune, paper manufacturer, Clatford, Andover; *b.* Clatford; *m.* Lucy Catherine, *d.* of Henry Bennett; three *s.* one *d.* Has been on the staffs of the Echo and Daily Telegraph; joined The Times staff in 1883; chief sub-editor, 1890-1908; news editor, 1908-14. *Recreations:* golf, gardening. *Address:* The Nook, Oakhill Road, Beckenham, Kent. *(Died 13 Feb. 1925.)*

BUNTINE, James Robertson; Sheriff-Substitute of Stirlingshire, etc., at Stirling since 1876; resigned 1906, and appointed Hon. Sheriff-Substitute; President of the Sheriff-Substitutes' Association. 1905-6; *b.* 10 Nov. 1841; *e. s.* of William Buntine, H.E.I.C.S., of Ayr; *m.* 1st, 1874, Jane (*d.* 1883), *d.* of David Sandeman of Glasgow; 2nd, Jean, *d.* of Archibald Finnie of Springhill and Grange, Ayrshire. *Educ.:* Ayr and Edinburgh Academies, and Edinburgh University, M.A., 1862. Called to Scotch Bar, 1865. *Recreations:* golf, shooting, etc. *Address:* Torbrex
146

House, Stirling, N.B. *Clubs:* Junior Carlton, Conservative; University, New. Edinburgh.
(Died 10 Aug. 1920.)

BURBANK, Luther; owner and manager of Burbank Experiment Farms; *b.* Lancaster, Mass., 7 Mar. 1849; *s.* of Samuel Walton Burbank of Lancaster, Mass., and Olive Ross of Sterling, Mass.; *m.* 1916, Elizabeth Waters. *Educ.:* Lancaster Academy. Naturalist and originator of new fruits and flowers; always devoted to study of nature, especially plant life; moved to Santa Rosa, Cal., 1875; originator of many improved thornless cacti; Gold, Wickson, Apple, October purple, Santa Rosa, America, Climax, and Beauty plums; Giant, Splendor, and Sugar prunes; Peachblow, Burbank, Santa Rosa and other roses; giant and fragrant callas; and numerous new apples, peaches, nuts, berries, and other valuable trees, fruits, flowers, grasses, grains, and vegetables. Fellow of American Association for Advancement of Science; Hon. Member of American Plant and Animal Breeders Association; Special Lecturer, Stanford University; Hon. Member Californian Academy of Science, Swedish Botanical Society, Royal Agricultural Society of Italy, American Eugenic Society; Fellow Royal Horticultural Society; Doctor of Science, Tufts College, 1905. *Publications:* Training of the Human Plant; New Creations in Fruits and Flowers; Fundamental Principles of Plant Breeding; Luther Burbank: his Methods and Discoveries, 12 vols., 1913; How Plants are Trained to Work for Man, 8 vols., 1921; numerous magazine articles on scientific and humanitarian subjects. *Recreations:* botanizing, music. *Address:* Santa Rosa, Sonoma Co., Cal. *T.A.:* Burbank, Santarosa. *T.:* Main 389. *M.:* 44,286.
(Died 11 April 1926.)

BURBIDGE, Sir Richard, 1st Bt., *cr.* 1916; J.P. for the County of London; Chairman of Committee on Royal Aircraft Factory; Managing Director Harrod's Stores since 1890; Member of Advisory Board of the Ministry of Munitions; Trustee of the Crystal Palace; Pres. Society Wiltshiremen in London; *b.* South Wraxall, Wilts., March 1847; 4th *s.* of George Bishop Burbidge; *m.* 1st, Emily (*d.* 1905), *y. d.* of late J. Woodman of Melksham, Wilts.; two *s.* four *d.*; 2nd, 1910, Lilian, *y. d.* of late J. A. Preece of Bartestree Court, Herefordshire. Sat on the Committee on Post Office Wages; Director Hudson's Bay Co.; Chairman, Dickins & Jones, Ltd.; Hon. Treasurer Tariff Commission; was member of the Garrison and Regimental Institutes Committee dealing with Canteens; was also Member of Board of Control of Regimental Institutes and on the General Purposes Committee of this Board. *Recreations:* hackney breeding, horticulture. *Heir:* *s.* Richard Woodman Burbidge [*b.* 7 Dec. 1872; *m.* Catherine Jemima, *d.* of H. Grant, Sodbury House, Great Clacton, Essex]. *Address:* 51 Hans Mansions, S.W.; Littleton Park, Shepperton, Middlesex; Osborne Cottage, Whippingham, Isle of Wight. *T.:* Western 1; Weybridge 25. *M.:* LC 8560; LB 5388. *(Died 31 May 1917.)*

BURD, Rev. Prebendary John, M.A.; Vicar of Chirbury, Shropshire, 1863-1912; *b.* 1828; *s.* of Henry Edward Burd; unmarried. *Educ.:* Shrewsbury School; Christ Church, Oxford (Fell Exhibitioner); 3rd class Lit. Hum. B.A. 1850; M.A. 1853. Deacon, 1852; priest 1853; Curate of Parham, Hacheston, 1852 Myddle Salop, 1855; Surrogate, Diocese of Hereford; Prebendary in Hereford Cathedral, 1888; Rural Dean of Montgomery, 1906. *Address:* Clawdd-y-dre, Montgomery.
(Died 2 April 1918.)

BURDETT, Sir Henry, K.C.B., *cr.* 1897 K.C.V.O., *cr.* 1908; author and statist; founde and editor of The Hospital; *b.* 18 Mar. 1847; *t.* of Rev. Halford Burdett, M.A., of Gilmorton

Co. Leicester, and Alsina, d. of T. Brailsford, D.L. of Barkwith, and Toft Grange, Lincolnshire; m. 1875, Helen (d. 1919), d. of Gay Shute, F.R.C.S.; two s. two d. Late Superintendent of the Queen's Hospital, Birmingham, and of the Seaman's Hospital, Greenwich; late Secretary Share and Loan Department, London Stock Exchange. Publications: Burdett's Official Intelligence of British, American, and Foreign Securities (17 volumes); The National Debt; The Sinking Funds of the National Debt; National Debts of the World; Local Taxation in England and Wales; London Water Companies; Light Railways; Municipal, County, and Indian Finance; Colonial Loans, Finance, and Development; Seventeen Years of Securities; The Patriotic Fund; The Admiralty and the Country; Hospitals and Asylums of the World (4 volumes and portfolio of plans); Cottage Hospitals; Pay Hospitals of the World; The Relative Mortality of Large and Small Hospitals, Burdett's Hospitals and Charities, a Year-book of Philanthropy; The Uniform System of Accounts for Hospitals and Institutions; Hospitals and the State; Unhealthiness of Public Institutions; Architects, Hospitals, and Asylums; A History of the Hospital Saturday and Sunday Funds; The National Pension Fund for Nurses and Officials; A National Pension Fund for Workers among the Sick in the United States; A Practical Scheme for Old Age Pensions; Nurses' Food, Work, and Recreation; The Registration of Nurses; How to become a Nurse; The Nursing Profession, How and Where to Train; Housing of the Poor; Dwellings of the Middle Classes; Helps in Sickness and to Health; Burdett's Official Nursing Directory; The Future of the Hospitals, A Scheme of Co-operation between the Patients, the Hospitals, and the State. Address: The Lodge, 13 Porchester Square, W.2. T.: Park 873. Clubs: Marlborough, City of London, Ranelagh, Roehampton.

(Died 29 April 1920.)

BURDETT-COUTTS, Rt. Hon. William Lehman Ashmead Bartlett-, P.C. 1921; M.P. (C.) Westminster since 1885; b. U.S.A., 1851; 2nd s. of late Ellis Bartlett of Plymouth, New England, and Sophia, d. of John King Ashmead of Philadelphia; grandparents on both sides British subjects; m. 1881, Angela, Baroness Burdett-Coutts (d. 1906), whose name he assumed. Educ.: privately; Keble Coll. Oxford (Scholar; M.A., 1876). The Baroness Burdett-Coutts having originated the Turkish Compassionate Fund, he volunteered to proceed to the Russo-Turkish war as Special Commissioner, 1877 (Star and 2nd class of the Medjidie); was one of the originators of the Fisheries Exhibition, and has interested himself in the question of the food supply of the poor of London; re-opened Columbia Market for the sale of fish and vegetables, and obtained parliamentary powers for railway access, but was unable to make satisfactory arrangements with the Railway Companies; visited Ireland to assist in organising relief in the distressed districts, 1879-80; subsequently largely developed the Baroness's scheme for benefiting the Irish fishermen; founder and owner of the Brookfield Stud; Trustee of the Baltimore Fishery School; Governor of Christ's Hospital; twice Master of the Turners' Company (1888 and 1889); and one of the founders of the British East African Possessions; Mr. Burdett-Coutts carried the Hampstead Heath Act, 1885 (adding Parliament Hill and 300 acres as public recreation ground), Police Enfranchisement, and Metropolitan Management Amendment Acts, 1887, and also the Advertisement Rating Act, 1889; proceeded to S. Africa as Times Correspondent with regard to the sick and wounded, 1900, and thus led to the appointment of a Royal Commission of Inquiry. After the publication of its Report the Government promised a "drastic reform" of the Army Medical Service (Session 1901), and a complete reform followed; since 1902 has been a prominent advocate of railway reform, including better loading, co-operation, and a fuller system of statistics as a guide to efficient working, and for the information of Parliament; this led to the appointment by the Board of Trade of a Committee of Inquiry, as a result of which the Government introduced the Railway (Accounts and Returns) Bill, 1910. Publications: volume on Russo-Turkish War, Lest we Forget (on S. African Hospitals), many articles, etc. Address: 1 Stratton Street, W.1; Holly Lodge, Highgate, N.6. T.: Gerard 3643; Hornsey 496. Club: Carlton.

(Died 28 July 1921.)

BURGE, Sir Charles Henry, Kt., cr. 1918; F.I.C., J.P.; b. Devon, 4 June 1846; s. of late John Burge; m. 1870, Amelia, d. of late Joseph Woodcock; two s. two d. Educ.: Crediton Grammar School; private tuition; Royal College of Chemistry. Somerset House, 1867; became Deputy Principal of the Government Laboratory, and retired 1907; Surrey County Council, 1913; Kingston-on-Thames Town Councillor, 1907; Mayor, 1912-18; Alderman since 1914; Chairman and Treasurer of War Relief Fund; Chairman of the following—Kingston Branch of Red Cross Society, Food Control and Food Savings Committee, Education Committee; Director of various Industrial Companies. Address: Iddesleigh, Crescent Road, Kingston-on-Thames. *(Died 21 Dec. 1921.)*

BURGE, Rt. Rev. Hubert Murray, M.A., D.D.; b. 9 Aug. 1862; s. of Rev. M. R. Burge, of Fort-William, Calcutta; m. 1898, Evelyn, y. d. of late Rev. Dr. J. F. Bright. Educ.: Bedford Grammar School; Marlborough; University Coll., Oxford (scholar, 1882-86). Hon. Mods. I.; Lit. Hum. II.; Sixth form master at Wellington College, 1887-90; Fellow and Tutor of University College, Oxford, 1890; Dean, 1895; Headmaster of Repton School, 1900; Headmaster of Winchester, 1901-11; Hon. Fellow of University College, Oxford, 1908 Bishop of Southwark, 1911-19; Select Preacher, Oxford, 1899-1902, 1920-21; Chaplain of the Order of St. John of Jerusalem in England, 1909; Sub-Prelate, 1911; Chancellor of the Most Noble Order of the Garter; Clerk to the Closet, 1919. Bishop of Oxford, 1919-25. Publications: contributor to Essays on Secondary Education. Address: Bishop's House, Cuddesdon, Oxford. Clubs: M.C.C., Free Foresters, I Zingari.

(Died 11 June 1925.)

BURGER, Schalk William, formerly a member of the Executive Raad, and Acting President of the South African Republic; b. Lydenburg, East Transvaal. Address: Pretoria, Transvaal. *(Died 18 Dec. 1918.)*

BURGES, Ven. Ernest Travers, Archdeacon of Maritzburg; Vicar of Richmond cum Byrne, Natal; late Superintendent of Native Missions; b. 14 May 1851; s. of Daniel and Eliza Mary Burges; m. Janet, d. of William Webb, Sea View, Verulam, Natal; three s. two d. Educ.: Shrewsbury School; St. John's College, Cambridge (M.A.). For 25 years Vicar of Karkloof Parish, Natal; Representative to Provincial Synod; Chairman of Advisory Board to Native Education Department, Colony of Natal; twice appointed to Special Committees by Government of Natal; has acted as R.M.; formerly Chairman of Hilton College, Natal. Publications: several short stories. Recreations: fishing, shooting, riding, driving. Address: Vicarage, Richmond, Natal. *(Died 10 June 1921.)*

BURGESS, Charles (Cathal Brugha), M.P. (S. Fein) Waterford County since Dec. 1918; a candle manufacturer. Address: 5 Fitz-

william Terrace, Upper Rathmines, Dublin.
(Died 7 July 1922.)

BURGESS, Duncan, M.A., M.B. Cantab.,
F.R.C.P. Lond.; Senior Physician, Sheffield
Royal Hospital; Ex - Professor of Medicine,
Sheffield University; *b.* 1850; unmarried.
Educ.: Aberdeen University; Cambridge. 13th
Wrangler, 1875; Fellow of Corpus Christi College; Lt.-Col. R.A.M.C. (T.). *Recreation:* golf.
Address: 442 Glossop Road, Sheffield. *T.:*
Sheffield 1408. *Club:* Sheffield, Sheffield.
(Died 17 J n. 1917.)

BURGESS, Rt. Rev. Frederick, D.D.;
LL.D. (Cantab.); Bishop of Long Island since
1902; *b.* Providence, 6 Oct. 1853; *m.* 1881,
Caroline *(deceased)*; four *s. Educ.:* Brown
University, Providence; General Theological
Seminary; Europe. Rector, Grace Church,
Amherst, Mass., 1878-83; Christ Church, Pomfret, Conn., 1883-89; Church of St. Asaph,
Bala, 1889-96; Christ Church, Detroit, Mich.,
1896-98; Grace Church, Brooklyn, 1898-1902.
Address: See House, Garden City, Long Island,
New York. *Club:* Hamilton, Brooklyn.
(Died 15 Oct. 1925.)

BURGESS, James, C.I.E. 1885; Hon.
LL.D., Edin. 1881, F.R.S.E., Hon. A.R.I.B.A.,
F.R.G.S.; Hon. M. Imp. Russ. Archæol. Soc.,
Amer. Orient. Soc., and R. Phil. Soc. Glasgow;
Hon. Associate Finno-Ugrian Soc.; H. Corr.
M. Ethnol. Soc. Berlin, and Batavian Soc. Arts
and Sciences; M. Soc. Asiat. Paris, M.R.A.S.;
b. Kirkmahoe, Dumfriesshire, 14 Aug. 1832; *m.*
1855; four *s.* three *d.* Engaged in educational
work in Calcutta, 1856, and Bombay, 1861; Secretary Bombay Geographical Society, 1868-73;
head of Archæological Survey, Western India,
1873, and of S. India, 1881; Director-General of
the Archæological Surveys in India, 1886-89;
Publications: The Temples of Shatrunjaya, 1869;
The Rock Temples of Elephanta, 1871; Temples
of Somanath, Junagadh, and Girnar, 1870;
Scenery and. Architecture in Gujarat and Rajputana, 1873; Notes on Ajanta Paintings, 1879;
The Cave Temples of India (conjointly with
late James Fergusson), 1880; Indian Antiquary,
1872-84; Archæological Survey of W. India, 9
vols., 1874-1905; Buddhist Stupas of Amaravati,
etc., 1887; Antiquities of Dabhoi, 1888; The
Sharqi Architecture of Jaunpur (edited), 1889;
Archæological Research in India, 1890; Epigraphia Indica, 2 vols., 1889-94; On Hindu Astronomy,1893; Constable's Hand-Gazetteer of India,
1898; Hypsometry by Boiling-point, 1858 and
1863; Transliteration of Indian Place-names,
1868, 1891, 1894-95; On the Error-function
Definite Integral, 1898 (awarded the Keith
medal, R.S.E.); The Ancient Monuments,
Temples, and Sculptures of India illustrated in
a series of photographs, 1897-1910; Grünwedel's
Buddhist Art in India (enlarged translation),
1901; The Indian Sect of the Jainas (translated and edited), 1903; Fergusson's Indian
Architecture, enlarged ed., 2 vols., 1910; Chronology of Modern India, 1494 to 1894, 1963;
etc., etc. *Address:* 22 Seton Place, Edinburgh.
(Died 5 Oct. 1916.)

BURGESS, James John Haldane, M.A.;
author and private teacher; blind since 1887;
b. Lerwick, Shetland Isles, 28 May 1862. *Educ.:*
Anderson Institute, Lerwick. Entered Edinburgh University 1886; graduated 1889. *Publications:* A Nicht in Tammy Scolla's But-End
and Laama Deep, 1885; Shetland Sketches and
Poems, 1886; Rasmie's Buddie—Poems in the
Shetlandic, 1891; 2nd ed. 1892; 3rd ed. 1913;
The Viking Path—a Tale of the White Christ,
1894; Lowra Biglan's Mutch, 1896; Tang—A
Shetland Story, 1898; Some Shetland Folk,
1902; The Treasure of Don Andres—A Shetland
Romance of the Spanish Armada, 1903; Dr.
Robertson: Memorial Lines, 1914; Rasmie's
Smaa Murr, 1916; short stories, articles, and
poems, from time to time, in various periodicals.
148

Recreations: free gymnastics, gardening, conversation, and dipping into foreign languages.
Address: Lerwick, Shetland.
(Died 16 Jan. 1927.)

BURGESS, Thomas J. W., M.D.,
F.R.S.C.; late Medical Supt. Protestant
Hospital for Insane; Professor of Mental Diseases, McGill University, Montreal, since 1893;
b. Toronto, Canada, 11 March 1849; *y. s.* of
Thomas Burgess and Jane Rigg, both natives of
Carlisle, Cumberland; *m.* 1875, Jessie, 2nd
d. of late Lieut.-Col. Alex. Macpherson,
of Whitby, Ontario; three *d. Educ.:* Upper
Canada Coll. and Toronto Univ. Graduated
in medicine as Starr gold medallist and
1st Univ. silver medallist, 1870; appointed
surgeon to H.M.'s British North American
Boundary Commission, 1872, and served as
such until the close of the work, being thanked
by H.M.'s Government for the efficient way in
which he had carried out the duties; took up
the study of mental diseases and became
assistant physician of the London Asylum for
Insane, 1875; assistant superintendent of
Hamilton Asylum, 1887; medical superintendent
of the Protestant Hospital for the Insane, Montreal, since 1890; F.R.S. Canada, 1885, and
President of the Geological and Biological
Section, 1898; Fellow of the American Association for the Advancement of Science, 1886;
hon. secretary for the Dominion of Canada
of the Pan-American Medical Congress, Mexico,
1896; President American Medico-Psychological
Association, 1904-5. *Publications:* The Beneficent and Toxic Effects of the Various Species of
Rhus; A Botanical Holiday in Nova Scotia;
Canadian Filicinæ; Recent Additions to
Canadian Filicinæ; How to Study Botany;
Orchids; Notes on the Flora of the 49th
Parallel; The Lake Erie Shore as a Botanising
Ground; Art in the Sick Room; Ophioglossaceae
and Filices; A Historical Sketch of Canadian
Institutions for the Insane; The Insane in
Canada; (Joint) Institutional Care of the
Insane in the United States and Canada, 4
vols.; numerous hospital reports, etc. *Recreations:* botany, golf, cricket, philately. *Address:* Suite 91 Laurentian Apts., 29 Cote
des Neiges Road, Montreal, Quebec, Canada.
T.: Montreal 7403. *Clubs:* Authors'; University, Pen and Pencil, Montreal.
(Died 18 Jan. 1926.)

BURGESS, Hon. William Henry, J.P.,
merchant, Hobart; *b.* Hobart, 1847; *m.* 1869,
y. d, of John Turner, Hobart. *Educ.:* Horton
College. Alderman of Hobart, 1876-81; Mayor
of Hobart, 1879-80; Member of Executive
Council, 1884; entered Tasmanian Parliament,
1881; Treasurer, Minister of Defence, and Postmaster General, 1884-87; represented Tasmania
at Sydney Federation Convention, 1891; holds
commission as Captain in Tasmanian Defence
Force (unattached), late S.T.V. Artillery;
Master Warden, Marine Board; Vice-Consul
for France; Officier d'Académie Français.
T.A.: Burgess, Hobart. *T.:* Private 95;
Business, 166. *Address:* Milliara, Hobart,
Tasmania. *Clubs:* Athenæum, Civic, Hobart.
(Died 1 May 1917.)

BURGH, 5th Baron, *cr.* 1529 (called out
of abeyance, 1916), **Lt.-Col. Alexander
Henry Leith,** J.P., D.L., Aberdeenshire
and Isle of Wight; Lt.-Col. late Comdg.
3rd Batt. Gordon Highlanders; Commanding
Garrison and Coast Defences, Aberdeen, during European War; [in 1912 proved his claim
as senior co-heir to the ancient Baronies of
Burgh and Cobham, and in 1914 to ancient
Barony of Strathbogie as senior co-heir]; *b.*
1866; *e. s.* of late Gen. R. W. Disney Leith
C.B., of Glenkindie and Westhall, Aberdeenshire, and Mary Charlotte Julia, (*d.* 1926) of North
Court, Isle of Wight; *o. c.* of Sir Henry Percy
Gordon, 2nd Bart. (*ext.*), and the Lady Mary

Ashburnham, *d.* of 3rd Earl; *m.* 1st, 1893, Mildred Katherine (*d.* 1894), *d.* of Gen. Stuart James Nicholson, C.B.; one *d.*; 2nd, 1902, Phyllis, *y. d.* of Col. Mark Goldie, C.R.E.; two *s.* one *d.* Late Lieut. the Welsh Regiment; served in Soudan Campaigns, 1888-89. *Recreations:* polo, hunting, golf, tennis, shooting, sailing. *Heir: s.* Hon. Alexander Leigh Henry Leith, *b.* 1906. *Address:* Glenkindie and Freefield, Aberdeenshire; Northcourt, Isle of Wight. *Clubs:* Army and Navy; Royal Victoria Yacht, Cowes. (*Died 19 Aug. 1926.*)

[*By some reckonings he was 7th Baron.*]

BURGHCLERE, 1st Baron (cr. 1895), **Herbert Coulstoun Gardner,** P.C., D.L., M.A.; Director of Peninsular and Oriental Steamship Company; President of Board of Agriculture, 1892-95; an Ecclesiastical Commissioner; Chairman of Royal Commission on Historical Monuments; *b.* 9 June 1846; *m.* 1890, Lady Winifred Henrietta Christina Herbert (author of George Villiers, 2nd Duke of Buckingham; Life of James, First Duke of Ormonde, 1610-1688, 1912), *e.d.* of 4th Earl of Carnarvon, and widow of Capt. Hon. Alfred Byng; four *d. Educ.:* Harrow; Trin. Hall, Camb., Member (L.) for N. Essex, 1885-95. *Publications:* The Georgics of Virgil, translated into English Verse, 1904. *Heir:* none. *Address:* 48 Charles Street, W.1. *T.:* Mayfair 2747. *Clubs:* Athenæum, Brooks's, St. James's. (*Died 6 May 1921.*)

BURGUYNE, Colonel **Sir John Montagu,** 10th Bt., cr. 1641; Grenadier Guards, retired 1861; *b.* 23 Oct. 1832; *s.* of 9th Bt. and Mary Harriet, *e.d.* of William Gore-Langton, M.P.; *S.* father 1858; *m.* 1st, Amy, *d.* of Captain H. N. Smith, R.E., 1856 (*d.* 1895); 2nd, 1903, Kate, *e. d.* of late John Gretton of Stapleford Park, Leicestershire. *Educ.:* Eton. Entered army, 1850. Owns about 2400 acres. *Heir:* none. *Address:* Sutton Park, Sandy, Beds. *Clubs:* Carlton; Royal Yacht Squadron, Cowes. (*Died 19 Mar. 1921.*)

BURKE, Rt. Rev. Mgr. Alfred Edward, P.A., D.D., LL.D.; *b.* Georgetown. Prince Edward Island, 8 Sep. 1862; *s.* of James Burke and Mary Moar. *Educ.:* St. Dunstan's College, Charlottetown; Laval University, Quebec. Priest, 1885; Pastor of Alberton, P.E.I., 1888; called by the Apostolic Delegate Mgr. Sbarretti to found the Catholic Church Extension Society of Canada, 1908; President, 1909-15; Catholic Chaplain in Canadian Contingents with rank of Major; Lieut.-Colonel, 1916; served European War, 1914-17; Mexico, 1919-20, secured return of Bishops and re-opening of churches from Carranza. *Publications:* Editor - in - Chief, Catholic Register Extension; author innumerable monographs, religious and secular. *Recreations:* billiards, English croquet, boating, and swimming. *Address:* 119 Wellington Street W., Toronto, Canada. (*Died 1927.*)

BURKE, Major Charles James, D.S.O. 1915; Royal Irish Regiment; Commandant Central Flying School since 1916; *b.* 9 March 1882; *s.* of Michael Charles Christopher Burke of Ballinahore House, Armagh; *m.* Beatrice Osborn, 3rd *d.* of W. Shakspeare, 42 Prince's Gardens, S.W., and Yateley, Hants. Entered army, 1903; Captain, 1909; Major, 1913; with W. African Frontier Force, 1905-9; at Aeroplanes and Balloon School, 1910-11; Air Batt. 1911-12; Royal Flying Corps, 1912; served S. African War, 1899-1902 (Queen's medal, five clasps); European War, 1914-15 (D.S.O.); injured in aeroplane accidents on Jan. 7, 1911, and Jan. 8, 1912; member Royal United Service Institution and Meteorological Society; Associate Fellow of Aeronautical Society. *Address:* Central Flying School, Upavon, Salisbury Plain. *Clubs:* Army and Navy, Royal Aero. (*Died 9 April 1917.*)

BURKE, Henry Lardner, Solicitor-General for the Cape Colony 1903-11; K.C.,

1898; M.A. (Oxford), LL.B. (Cape); *b.* Dublin, 3 May 1850; *e. s.* of late Rev. John Lardner Burke, LL.D., of Rutland Square, Dublin, and Marian, *y. d.* of late Rev. Henry Tweedy, M.A.; *m.* Frances Charlotte, *e. d.* of Samuel Bain, late of Port Elizabeth, Cape Colony; five *s.* one *d. Educ.:* Lincoln College, Oxford (scholar); 2nd class Classical Mods. 1871; 3rd class Final Classical School, 1873. Admitted as Advocate of Eastern Districts Court, 1880; Crown Prosecutor in High Court of Griqualand, 1897-1902; acted as one of the judges of Supreme Court, Cape Colony, July to Sep. 1904, and Nov. to Dec. 1905. *Recreations:* walking, travel, and literature. *Address:* c/o The Standard Bank of S. Africa, Adderley Street, Cape Town, S. Africa. (*Died Aug. 1927.*)

BURKE, Sir John, Kt., cr. 1921; D.L.; J.P.; ship-broker. *Address:* Ravensdale, Strandtown, Belfast. (*Died 14 Mar. 1922.*)

BURKE, Rt. Rev. Maurice Francis, Roman Catholic Bishop of St. Joseph, Missouri, since 1893; *b.* Ireland, 5 May 1845. *Educ.:* St. Mary's, Chicago; Notre Dame, Indiana; American College, Rome. Went to United States with his parents at the age of four; was educated in lower branches in United States; spent nine years at the American College in Rome, studying for the church, and was ordained there, 1875; curate at St Mary's Church, Chicago two years; Pastor of St. Mary's Church, Joliet, Ill., nine years, where he built a church and two schools; Bishop of Cheyenne, Wyoming, 1887. *Recreations:* Reading Dante and studying the languages. *Address:* 718 North 7th Street, St. Joseph, Missouri, U.S.A. (*Died 17 Mar. 1923.*)

BURLINGAME, Edward Livermore; Editor of Scribner's Magazine, 1886-1914, and since 1879 on the editorial staff of Charles Scribner's Sons, New York; on board of directors since 1904; *b.* Boston, Massachusetts, 30 May 1848; *e. s.* of Anson Burlingame; *m.* 1871, Ella F. Badger. *Educ.:* Harvard (hon. M.A. 1901) and Heidelberg, Ph.D.; hon. Litt.D. Columbia, 1914; on staff New York Tribune, 1871; American Cyclopædia, 1872-6. *Address:* 440 West End Avenue, New York. *Clubs:* Century, Harvard, N.Y. (*Died 15 Nov. 1922.*)

BURLS, Sir Edwin Grant, Kt., cr. 1909; C.S.I. 1902; *b.* 25 Apr. 1844; *e. s.* of late Charles Burls; *m.* 1875, Edith Louisa, *d.* of late James Williams; one *s.* one *d. Educ.:* Denmark Hill Grammar School. Entered India Office, 1863; junior clerk, store dept., 1865; senior clerk, 1875; assistant to director-general of stores, 1891; deputy director-general, 1895; late Major 1st Surrey Artillery Volunteer Corps, having held commission, 1868-82; Director-General of Stores, India Office, 1896-1909; Member of Ordnance Council, 1896-1909; Director of John I. Thornycroft & Co. Ltd., and of Vulcan Foundry, Ltd.; Member of Committees of National Hospital for Paralysed and Epileptic, of Evelina Hospital, the Evangelical Church Schools, and of The Missions to Seamen. *Address:* Shortlands, Kent. *T.A.:* Burls, Shortlands. *T.:* Ravensbourne 0668. *M.:* XN 1964. *Clubs:* East India United Service, St. Stephen's. (*Died 10 Sept. 1926.*)

BURN, Very Rev. Andrew Ewbank, D.D.; Dean of Salisbury since 1920; *b.* Bareilly, India, 17 Jan. 1864; *s.* of late Rev. T. H. Burn, Chaplain at Bareilly; *m.* C. M., *d.* of E. Richardson; one *s.* three *d. Educ.:* Clifton Coll.; Charterhouse; Trin. Coll., Camb. (3rd class Class. Trip., M.A., 1889, B.D., 1898, D.D., 1904). Student with Bishop Lightfoot of Durham at Auckland Castle; curate of St. Cuthbert, Bensham, 1887 - 91; St. Andrew, Auckland, 1891 - 93; rector of Kynnersley, 1893; Rural Dean of Edgmond; Prebendary of Lichfield, 1903; Rector of Handsworth, 1904;

Rural Dean of Handsworth ; Special Preacher, Oxford, 1906 ; Vicar of Halifax, 1909-20 ; Chaplain to the King ; Hon. Canon of Wakefield ; Examining Chaplain to Bishops of Lichfield and Wakefield ; Rural Dean, Halifax, 1914. *Publications:* The Athanasian Creed and its early Commentaries ; An Introduction to the Creeds and the Te Deum ; Niceta of Remesiana, His Life and Works ; The Crown of Thorns ; The Council of Nicaea ; The Te Deum and its Author, 1926. *Address:* The Deanery, Salisbury. *Club:* Authors'.   (*Died 28 Nov. 1927.*)

BURN, Lt.-Col. Charles Pelham Maitland ; Lt.-Col. retired, Seaforth Highlanders ; *b.* 6 Feb. 1889 ; *s.* of late Charles Maitland Pelham Burn and Isabella Romanes, *d.* and *co-heiress* of James Russel of Blackbraes, Stirlingshire ; *m.* 1908, Mabel (*d.* 1912), *d.* of Sir John Arthur Fowler, 2nd Bt., of Braemore : one *s.* *Address:* The Lodge, Craigellachie, Banffshire. *T.:* Craigellachie 11. *Club:* New, Edinburgh.
                              (*Died 15 Aug. 1925.*)

BURNABY, Lieut.-Col. Eustace Beaumont ; *b.* 4 April 1842 ; *s.* of late T. F. A. Burnaby, Brampton Manor, Hunts. ; *m.* 1879, Alice Caroline, *d.* of Beaumont Hotham, late Grenadier Guards. Served nearly 18 years in 2nd Lincoln Regt. ; late Senior Major, Hon. Lieut.-Col., 4th Lincoln Regiment (Militia) ; City Marshal of London, 1886-89 ; Common Cryer and Sergeant-at-Arms, City of London, 1889-1901. Jubilee medals of 1887 and 1897. *Address:* 23 Wellington Square, Chelsea, S.W. *T.:* Kensington 3950. *Club:* United Service.
                              (*Died 20 Oct. 1916.*)

BURNABY, Lt.-Col. Hugo Beaumont, D.S.O. 1902 ; Capt. 15th Durham Light Infantry, 1914 ; Lt.-Col. commanding 11th (S.) Batt. The Queens (Royal West Surrey Regt.), 1915 ; *y.* *s.* of Sherrard Beaumont Burnaby, late Vicar of Hampstead, N.W. ; *b.* 5 May 1874 ; *m.* 1906, Evelyn Violet, *y.* *d.* of late Maj.-Gen. C. H. Smith, C.B., R.H.A. ; one *s.* two *d.* *Educ.:* Uppingham. Engaged ranching in British Columbia, 1893-99 ; served in S. Africa, 1900-2 ; first in the ranks ; commission, March 1901 ; Captain, June 1901, 1st Batt. Imperial Yeomanry (despatches, medal, D.S.O.). *Recreation:* shooting. *Address:* Wendover, Bucks. *T.A.:* Rocketer, Wendover.
                              (*Died 8 Sept. 1916.*)

BURNABY-ATKINS, Thomas Frederick, J.P., D.L., Kent ; *b.* 13 March 1836 : 2nd *s.* of late Thomas Fowke Andrew Burnaby of Brampton Manor, Hunts. and Emily, 11th *d.* of late Rupert Chawner, M.D. ; *m.* 1868, Elizabeth, *d.* of late John Francklin, Gonalston Hall, Notts. ; one *s.* six *d.* *Educ.:* Eton ; Trinity Hall, Cambridge (M.A.). Inherited Halstead Place and estate, 1872, under the will of J. P. Atkins, whose name he assumed in addition to that of Burnaby by Royal Licence ; was on the Roll for High Sheriff of Kent for 1902. *Address:* Hamptons, Tonbridge, Kent. *T.A.:* Hadlow, Kent. *T.:* Plaxtole 14. *Club:* Carlton.   (*Died 28 Sept. 1918.*)

BURNAND, Sir Francis Cowley, Kt. ; *cr.* 1902 ; barrister, Lincoln's Inn ; editor of Punch, 1862-1906 ; dramatic author, light literature ; *b.* 29 Nov. 1836. Descended on father's side from old Savoyard family ; great-great-grandfather was partner in Minet and Co., silk merchants ; mother, Emma Cowley, *d.* of Christian Cowley, direct descendant of Hannah Cowley, authoress ; *m.* 1st, 1860, Cecilia Victoria (*d.* 1870), *d.* of James Ranoe ; 2nd, 1874, Rosina, widow of P. Jones ; six *s.* five *d.* *Educ.:* Eton (where at fifteen he wrote a farce played at Cookesley's house, also at Theatre Royal, Worthing) ; Trinity College, Cambridge. Founded the Amateur Dramatic Club, where his earliest pieces were produced ; studied for English Church at Cuddesdon under Canon Liddon ; became a

150

Roman Catholic ; read for Bar at Bourdillon's Chambers ; called ; practised occasionally ; commenced writing ; introduced by George Meredith to Once a Week ; by Lacy, theatrical bookseller, to Charles Young, actor, who successfully produced Dido at St. James's Theatre under management of Chatterton and Willert ; with Montagu Williams, wrote for Robson ; then alone for Robson, Buckstone, and several theatres ; comedies, burlesques, for Strand. His burlesque Black-Eyed Susan ran 800 nights at Royalty Theatre, Soho, was played for years provincially and in America ; twice revived in London. When about 26, wrote for Fun, but on its proprietor refusing his burlesque novelette, Mokeanna, he brought it to Mark Lemon, who accepted it for Punch ; on its staff from that date, succeeding Mark Lemon, Shirley Brooks, Tom Taylor, as editor, 1880. *Publications:* Happy Thoughts, 1866 ; the Happy Thought Series ; Modern Sandford and Merton, New Light on Darkest Africa, Strapmore, Ride to Khiva ; eccentric Guide to Isle of Thanet, illustrated by Phil May. Written over a hundred and twenty plays, chiefly burlesques and light comedies ; among the latter The Colonel, which satirised the æsthetic craze of that period ; adapted several farcical comedies for Augustine Daly, New York ; written two light operas (Contrabandista and The Chieftain) with Sir Arthur Sullivan, with whom he wrote musical version of Morton's old farce, " Box and Cox," entitled, perversely, "Cox and Box" ; "His Majesty," an opera, with R. C. Lehmann ; A.D.C. Reminiscences, 1880, and Records and Reminiscences, 1904. *Recreations:* riding, sea - boating. *Address:* 18 Royal Crescent, Ramsgate. *Club:* Garrick.
                              (*Died 21 April 1917.*)

BURNE, Brig.-Gen. Rainald Owen, C.B.E. ; *b.* 3. Jan. 1871 ; 5th *s.* of Newdigate Burne, Barrister-at-law, and Hon. Mrs. Burne ; *d.* of 2nd Viscount Sidmouth ; *m.* 1897, Sybil Mary, *d.* of David Owen, Senior Registrar of H.M. Court of Probate ; no *c.* *Educ.:* St. Lawrence College, Ramsgate ; Bedford Grammar School ; Royal Military College, Sandhurst ; 2nd Lieut. Royal Fusiliers, 1891 ; transferred to Royal Army Service Corps, 1895 ; served South African War, 1899-1902 (Queen's medal and 3 clasps, King's medal and 2 clasps) ; on Staff, War Office, 1908-11 ; European War, 1914-18 ; served on Staff ; wounded 1st Battle Ypres (despatches, Brevet of Colonel, C.B.E., 1914 Star, Allies medal and Victory medal) ; Brig.-General and Commandant M.T. Reception and Training Area, R.A.S.C. 1917 ; retired, 1920. *Recreations:* fishing, cricket. *Club:* United Service.   (*Died 4 May 1923.*)

BURNE-JONES, Sir Philip, 2nd Bt., *cr.* 1894 ; painter ; *b.* 2 Oct. 1861 ; *s.* of Sir Edward Coley Burne-Jones, 1st Bt., and Georgiana, *d.* of Rev. George Macdonald ; *s.* father, 1898. *Educ.:* Marlborough College ; University College, Oxford. *Address:* 41 Egerton Terrace, S.W.3. *T.:* 607 Western. *Club:* Bath.
                              (*Died 21 June 1926.*)

BURNET, Rev. Amos ; Secretary, Wesleyan Methodist Missionary Society ; President of Wesleyan Methodist Conference, 1924 ; *b.* Little Steeping, Lincolnshire, 5 Aug. 1857 ; *m.* Esther Ann Dring of Brinkhill, Lincolnshire ; five *d.* *Educ.:* Wesleyan College, Richmond. Spent eleven years as a missionary in Bangalore, South India ; then nine years in Nottingham ; went to South Africa at the end of the Boer War as General Superintendent of Wesleyan Missions in the Transvaal and Swaziland District, and remained in that post for seventeen years ; appointed General Secretary of the Wesleyan Missionary Society in 1919. *Publication:* A Mission to the Transvaal. *Address:* 24 Bishopsgate, E.C.2. *T.A.:* Wesleystock, London.   (*Died 1 Aug. 1926.*)

BURNET, John, M.A. (Oxon); LL.D. Edin.; Hon. Ph.D. Prague; LL.D. California, 1926; St. Andrews, 1927; F.B.A.; Emeritus Professor of Greek, St. Andrews University; Officier de l'Instruction Publique, 1911; Associate of the Royal Academy of Belgium, 1919; Hon. Fellow, Educational Institute of Scotland, 1919; *b.* Edinburgh, 9 Dec. 1863; *s.* of John Burnet, advocate; *m.* Mary, *d.* of late John Farmer; one *d. Educ.*: Royal High School and University, Edinburgh; Balliol College (Scholar). 1st class in Moderations and in Lit. Hum. Oxford; Taylorian Scholar. Master at Harrow, 1888; Fellow of Merton College, Oxford, 1890; Hon. Fellow, 1915; Professor of Greek, St. Andrews, 1892-1926; Examiner in Literæ Humaniores, Oxford, 1901-3, 1911, and 1915, and in Classical Tripos (Part II.), Cambridge, 1908-9; Romanes Lecturer, 1923; Hon. Fellow of Balliol, 1925; Sather Professor in Classical Literature, California, 1925. *Publications:* Early Greek Philosophy, 1892 (2nd ed. 1908; 3rd ed. 1920; German translation, 1913; French translation, 1919); Greek Rudiments, 1897; The Nicomachean Ethics of Aristotle, 1899; Aristotle on Education, 1903; Platonis Opera (5 vols), 1899-1907; Plato's Phaedo, 1911; Euthyphro, Apology and Crito, 1924; Greek Philosophy, Part I., Thales to Plato, 1914; Higher Education and the War, 1917. *Address:* Balfour House, St. Andrews. *Club:* Athenæum.
(*Died 26 May 1928.*)

BURNETT, Sir (Edward) Napier, K.B.E., *cr.* 1919; J.P., M.D. Glas., F.R.C.S., F.R.C.P. Edin.; Consulting Surgeon; Chairman Economical Committee Army Medical Dept. War Office; Director of Hospital Service, British Red Cross Society; a Knight of Grace of the Order of St. John of Jerusalem; *b.* 12 July 1872; *y.s.* of late James Burnett, Fraserburgh; *m.* 1903. *Educ.*: Glasgow University; Edinburgh; Dublin. *Publications:* Lectures on Hospital Administration; various papers in Medical Journals. *Address:* 16 Frognall Lane, Hampstead, N.W.3. *T.:* Hampstead 7073. *Club:* Reform. (*Died 25 Dec. 1923.*)

BURNETT, Mrs. Frances Hodgson, novelist and dramatist; *b.* Manchester, 24 Nov. 1849; went with her parents to Knoxville, Tennessee, U.S.A., 1865; *m.* 1st, 1873, Dr. Burnett, Washington, U.S.A.; obtained a divorce, 1898; 2nd, 1900, Stephen Townesend (*d.* 1914). Began to publish 1867; her name began to be known with That Lass o' Lowrie's, Scribner's Magazine and book form, 1877. *Publications:* Surly Tim and other Stories, 1877; Haworth's, 1879; Louisiana, 1880; A Fair Barbarian, 1881; Through One Administration, 1888; Little Lord Fauntleroy, 1886; Sara Crewe, 1888; Little Saint Elizabeth, 1889; The Pretty Sister of José, A Lady of Quality, 1896; His Grace of Ormonde, 1897; The Captain's Youngest, 1898; In Connection with the De Willoughby Claim, 1899; The Making of a Marchioness, 1901; The Little Unfairy Princess, 1902; The Dawn of a To-morrow, 1907; Tembarom, 1913; The Head of the House of Coombe, 1922; Robin, 1922. Little Lord Fauntleroy, which she dramatised, has brought its author over £20,000. Her other plays are: Phyllis, The Showman's Daughter, The First Gentleman of Europe, Esmeralda (which ran for three years in America), and in collaboration with Mr. Townesend, Nixie and A Lady of Quality. *Recreation:* improving the lot of children. *Address:* Maytham Hall, Rolvenden, Kent. (*Died 29 Oct. 1924.*)

BURNETT, Sir Thomas, of Leys, 12th Bt., *cr.* 1626; late Col. Royal Horse Artillery 1890; Lord Lieutenant; *b.* 27 Nov. 1840; *s.* of 10th Bt., and Lauderdale, *d.* of Sir Alexander Ramsay, Bt., of Balmain, and *widow* of David Duncan of Rosemount, Forfar; *S. half-b.*, 1894; *m.* Mary Elizabeth, *e. d.* of J. Cumine of Rattray, Aberdeenshir.; 1875; two *s.* one *d.* Owns about

12,300 acres. *Heir: s.* Col. J. L. G. Burnett. *Address:* Crathes Castle, Aberdeen.
(*Died 25 Jan. 1926.*)

BURNEY, Rev. Charles Fox, M.A., D.Litt., Hon. D.D. (Durham); Oriel Professor of Interpretation of Holy Scripture, Oxford University, since 1914; Canon of Rochester Cathedral; Fellow, Oriel and St. John's Colleges; Examining Chaplain to the Bishop of Rochester; *b.* 4 Nov. 1868; *o. s.* of Charles George Burney, Paymaster-in-Chief, R.N., and of Eleanor Agnes, *d.* of Rev. William Addington Norton, M.A., rector of Alderton and Eyke, Suffolk; *m.* 1913, Ethel Wordsworth, *e. d.* of Falconer Madan; two *s.* one *d. Educ.*: Merchant Taylors' School; St. John's College, Oxford (Exhibitioner, 1887; Senior Scholar, 1893; Lecturer in Hebrew, 1893; Librarian, 1897-1908; Fellow, 1899; Vice-President, 1900, 1906, 1910, 1911; B.A. 1890; M.A. 1894; D.Litt. 1903). Deacon, 1893; Priest, 1894; Curate of All Saints, Oxford, 1893-95. Obtained the following University distinctions: —1st class in Final Honour School of Theology, 1890; 1st class in Final Honour School of Semitic Studies, 1892; Pusey and Ellerton Scholar, 1887; Junior Kennicott Scholar, 1890; Houghton Syriac Prize, 1891; Hall-Houghton Septuagint Prizes, junior 1892, senior 1894; Denyer and Johnson Scholar, 1893; Senior Kennicott Scholar, 1895; Examiner Final Honour Schools of Theology, 1901-3; Oriental Studies, 1904, 1906, 1907, 1916; Examiner, University of London, 1898-1903; Examining Chaplain to the Bishop of Southwell, 1904-15; Grinfield Lecturer on the Septuagint in the University of Oxford, 1911-15. *Publications:* Outlines of Old Testament Theology, Oxford Church Text-Books, 1899; 3rd ed., 1906; Notes on the Hebrew Text of the Books of Kings, 1903; Israel's Hope of Immortality, 1909; Israel's Settlement in Canaan (Schweich Lectures, 1917), 1918, 3rd ed. 1921; The Book of Judges with Introduction and Notes, 1918, 2nd ed. 1920; The New Lessons explained, Part 1, 1920; The Gospel in the Old Testament, 1920; The Aramaic Origin of the Fourth Gospel, 1922; contributor to Contentio Veritatis, 1902; articles in Hastings' Bible Dictionary, Encyclopædia Biblica, Journal of Theological Studies, etc. *Recreations:* formerly running; now breeding horses, riding, and gardening. *Address:* 34 St. Giles', Oxford; The Precinct, Rochester. (*Died 15 April 1925.*)

BURNHAM, 1st Baron, *cr.* 1903; **Edward Levy Lawson,** and a Bt., *cr.* 1892; K.C.V.O., *cr.* 1904; D.L., J.P., Co. Bucks; principal proprietor of the Daily Telegraph; Lieut. for the City of London; *b.* London, 28 Dec. 1833; *e. s.* of J. M. Levy and Esther, his wife, both deceased. Under the will of his uncle, Mr. Lionel Lawson, Sir Edward assumed the name of Lawson in 1875 by Royal license; *m.* 1862, Harriette Georgiana (*d.* 1897), *o. d.* of B. N. Webster; two *s.* one *d. Educ.*: University College, London; High Sheriff for Bucks, 1886; President Royal Institute of Journalists, 1886; late Alderman, Bucks C.C. *Recreations:* golf, shooting, riding. Owns about 4000 acres. *Heir: s.* Hon. Harry Lawson. *Address:* 20 Norfolk Street, Park Lane, W.; Hall Barn, Beaconsfield, Bucks. *T.:* 12 Bourne End. *Clubs:* Marlborough, Garrick, Beefsteak. (*Died 9 Jan. 1916.*)

BURNLEY, James; author and journalist; *b.* Shipley, Yorkshire. *Educ.:* privately. On staff of Yorkshire Observer, 1871-82; Editor of The Yorkshireman, 1875-1885. *Publications:* Idonia, 1870; Phases of Bradford Life, 1871; West Riding Sketches, 1873; Yorkshire Stories Re-told, 1884; Two Sides of the Atlantic, 1878; Looking for the Dawn, 1880; Sir Titus Salt and George Moore (World's Workers Series), 1885; Fortunes made in Business, 1887; The Romance of Life Preservation, 1888; The

Romance of Modern Industry, 1889; History of Wool and Wool-combing, 1891; Romance of Invention, 1892; Desert London, 1895; Industries and Resources of America, 1896; Colorado's Golden Glories, 1900; Millionaires and Kings of Enterprise, 1901; Summits of Success, 1901; Studies in Millionaires, 1901; The Story of British Trade, 1904; Nets of Gold, 1908; In the Trail of a Crime, 1909; contributor to the Encyclopædia Britannica, Dictionary of National Biography, Chambers's Encyclopædia, etc.; author of several plays-including Fetters, Moneysworth, and The Shadow of the Mill; editor of Pears' Cyclopædia and Pears' Annual. *Address:* The Croft, Chesham, Bucks; 71-75 New Oxford Street, W.C. *Club:* National Liberal. (*Died* 29 *Dec.* 1919.)

BURNS, Col. Hon. Sir James, K.C.M.G., *cr.* 1917; M.L.C. since 1908; Chairman and Managing Director of Burns, Philp & Co.; *b.* nr. Edinburgh, 10 Feb. 1846; *s.* of David Burns, retired Colonial merchant; *m.* twice, now widower; two *s.* three *d. Educ.:* Edinburgh High School. Went to Australia, 1862; engaged in pastoral pursuits four years; began commercial career, 1866: the company has 30 branches in Australasia, Pacific, Java, etc.; owns fleet of steamers trading to Java and Singapore; is also interested in cattle and sheep properties in Queensland; commanded N.S.W. Lancer Regt. 14 years; later Brig.-Col. 1st Australian Mounted Brigade; retired, 1907; Director of 20 Australian Companies and Institutions; President of the Highland Society of New South Wales. *Address:* Gowan Brae. nr. Parramatta, N.S.W. *Clubs:* Union, Australian, Sydney. (*Died* 21 *Aug.* 1923.)

BURNS-BEGG, Col. Robert; *b.* 10 Mar. 1872; *s.* of Robert Burns-Begg, Kinross; *m.* Ethel, *o. d.* of C. H. Tapply, Tregenna, Sutton, Surrey; no *c. Educ.:* privately; Edinburgh University. Called to Scotch Bar, 1895; Bar of Southern Rhodesia, 1898; on active service as Lieut. and Capt. South African Mounted Irregular Forces, 1899-1902 (Queen's Medal, 5 clasps; King's Medal, 2 clasps); temporarily attached to Intelligence Dept., War Office, 1902-1903; Legal Adviser to Transvaal Govt. 1903; called to Transvaal Bar, 1903; commanding Northern Mounted Rifles, 1904-7; K.C. 1906; member of Committee on Re-organisation of Police Forces of the Colony, 1908; Commissioner, Transvaal Police, 1908-10; Commandant General and Resident Commissioner, Northern and Southern Rhodesia, 1911-15; Temp. Col. in the Army, 1915. *Recreations:* golf, shooting. *Address:* Tregenna, Sutton. Surrey. *Club:* Windham. (*Died* 9 *Jan.* 1918.)

BURNSIDE, Helen Marion, artist and poet; *b.* Bromley Hall, 1844; *e. d.* of late John Fullerton Burnside. *Educ.:* at home. Exhibited at Royal Academy, 1863; Columbian Exposition (honourable mention), 1895; Society of Lady Artists, 1897; designer to Royal School of Art Needlework, 1880-89; editor to Messrs. Raphael Tuck and Co. 1889-95. *Publications:* first book of poems, 1864; Driftweed, 1897; has written numberless songs (published with music), magazine poems and tales, card verses, etc.; Her Highland Laddie, 1897: The Little V.C.; The Lost Letter; Tales for Children, 1897; The Deaf Girl next Door, 1899; compiled R. N. Carey Birthday Book; A Girl without a Penny, 1907. *Recreations:* reading, gardening, walking. *Address:* Up Down House, Windlesham, Surrey.
(*Died* 5 *Dec.* 1923.)

BURNSIDE, William, M.A., D.Sc. (Dublin), F.R.S., LL.D. (Edin.); Hon. Fellow of Pembroke Coll., Camb, late Professor at Maths., R. N. Coll., Greenwich; *b.* 2 July 1852; *m.* 1886: two *s.* three *d. Educ.:* Pembroke Coll., Camb.; 2nd Wrangler 1st Smith's Prizeman, 1875. *Publication:* Theory of Groups. *Address:* Cotleigh, West Wickham. (*Died* 21 *Aug.* 1927.)

152

BURNSIDE, William Snow, M.A., D.Sc.; Senior Fellow and Member of Governing Body, Trin. Coll. Dublin; Erasmus Smith's Professor of Mathematics, Dublin University, 1879-1914. *Publication* (with the late A. W. Panton): Theory of Equations; some mathematical papers in the Quarterly Journal of Mathematics with some contributions to Salmon's Conic Sections. *Address:* Trinity College, and 35 Raglan Road, Dublin. *Club:* University, Dublin.

BURNYEAT, William John Dalzell, M.A., J.P.; M.P. (L.), Whitehaven, 1906-10; *b.* 13 Mar. 1874; *e. s.* of William and Sarah Frances Burnyeat, of Millgrove, Moresby, Cumberland; *m.* 1908, Hildegard, *d.* of Col. Retzlaff of Friedenaw, Berlin. *Educ.:* Rugby; Corpus Christi College, Oxford (Exhibitioner). Called to Bar, Inner Temple, 1899; has travelled. *Address:* Moresby House, Moresby, Cumberland. *T.:* Whitehaven 90. *M.:* AO 737. *Club:* Reform. (*Died* 8 *May* 1916.)

BURR, Rear-Adm. John Leslie, C.M.G. 1899; M.V.O. 1904; R.N.; retired; J.P.; Capt. of the Port Holyhead since 1902; *b.* 14 Aug. 1847; *s.* of Charles Burr of Luton House, Luton, Beds. Entered navy, 1861; Capt. 1894; served Ashanti War, 1873-74 (despatches twice, medal); West Coast Africa, 1879 (thanks of Foreign Office, Admiralty, and Government at Sierra Leone); in command of H.M.S. Pioneer, went 700 miles up the Niger with presents for the Emir of Nupi (thanks of Governor of Gold Coast and Secretary of Foreign Office); appointed to take the Commissioners for the Behring Sea Commission, 1894. *Decorated* for distinguished services in Central America by putting an end to the revolutions in Nicaragua and Honduras. *Address:* Government House, Holyhead. *Clubs.* United Service; Naval, Portsmouth.
(*Died* 3 *Nov.* 1917.)

BURRINGTON, Arthur, R.I. *Address.* c/o Cole Bros., 2 Percy Street, W.1.
(*Died* 10 *Oct.* 1924.)

BURROUGHS, John; *b.* Roxbury, N.Y., 3 April 1837; *s.* of C. A. Burroughs, farmer; *m.;* one *s. Educ.:* Ashland and Cooperstown Seminaries. Teacher, clerk in Treasury Department, bank examiner, author, farmer; Doctor of Literature, Yale; Doctor of Humane Letters, Colgate University; Member of American Academy of Arts and Letters. *Publications:* Walt Whitman, Poet and Person, 1867; Wake-Robin, 1871; Winter Sunshine, 1875; Birds and Poets, 1877; Locusts and Wild Honey, 1879; Pepacton, 1881; Fresh Fields, 1884; Signs and Seasons, 1886; Indoor Studies, 1889; Riverby, 1894; Whitman, 1896; The Light of Day, 1900; Literary Values, 1902; Far and Near, 1904; Ways of Nature, 1905; Bird and Bough (Poems), 1906; Camping and Tramping with Roosevelt, 1907; Leaf and Tendril, 1908; Time and Change, 1912; The Summit of the Years, 1913; The Breath of Life, 1915; Under the Apple Trees, 1916. *Recreations:* sauntering, automobiling, fishing. *Address:* West Park, New York.
(*Died* 29 *Mar.* 1921.)

BURROWES, Lieut.-Col. Algernon St. Leger, C.B. 1911; R.M.L.I. (retired); *b.* 1847; 2nd *s.* of late Rev. J. R. Burrowes, formerly Rector of Hutton, Somerset; *m.* Fanny Henrietta, *e. d.* of late W. Barry Hoare, J.P. of Monkstown, Co. Cork; two *d.* Entered Royal Marine Light Infantry, 1866; served H.M.S. Ariadne, 1868-69; Special Service to convey Prince and Princess of Wales to the East; served in H.M.S. Serapis, 1875-76, with Guard of Honour of Royal Marines, during cruise of Prince of Wales to India; served Egyptian Campaign, 1882, as Adjutant of the Batt. R.M.L.I., present at the actions of Tel-el-Mahuta, Masamah, Kassassin (horse shot), and storming of Tel-el-Kebir; served Eastern Soudan, 1884-85, as Adjutant of the Batt.

R.M.L.I. during the defence of Suakin, and afterwards in the Mounted Infantry to the close of the campaign; present at the actions of Handoub, Hasheen, Tamai, Thakeol, and attacks on the convoys (despatches, brevet Major); served in H.M.S. Imperieuse, Flagship on the China Station, 1893-94; served as Recruiting Staff Officer, 1916-18 (special mention). *Address:* Moorside, Budleigh Salterton, Devon.
                                        (Died 18 Dec. 1925.)

BURROWES, William Henry Aglionby, I.S.O. 1911; Commissary of Taxation, British Guiana. *Address:* Georgetown, British Guiana.   *(Died 4 Nov. 1922.)*

BURROWS, Colonel Edmund Augustine, C.M.G. 1900; C.B.E. 1919; R.A. (retired); *b.* 19 March 1855; *s.* of late Canon Burrows of Rochester; *m.* 1891, Mary Claudine, *d.* of late William Coode of Trevarna, St. Austell; one *s.* Entered Army, 1875; Captain, 1884; Major, 1892; Lieut.-Col. 1900; served Burmah, 1885-86 (medal with clasp); South Africa, 1900 (medal with 6 clasps and C.M.G.); re-employed Oct. 1914. J.P. Bucks. *Address:* Manor House, Long Crendon, Thame.   *(Died 19 May 1927.)*

BURROWS, Sir Ernest Pennington, 3rd Bt.; *cr.* 1874; *b.* 11 July 1851; *S.* brother 1904; *s.* of 1st Bt. and Elinor, *d.* of late John Abernethy, F.R.S. *Heir:* none. *Address:* 21 Connaught Square, W. *Club:* Oriental.
                                      (Died 4 Aug. 1917.)

BURROWS, Rev. Francis Henry, M.A.; Hon. Canon of Manchester since 1916; *b.* Atherton, 28 Nov. 1857; *s.* of Abraham Burrows, J.P., C.A., Atherton; *m.* Margaret Nelson, *d.* of Richard Curtis, J.P., Bowdon; three *s.* one *d.* *Educ.:* Christ's College, Cambridge, B.A. 1878, M.A. 1881. Curate of S. Mary, Stoke, Ipswich, 1880-82; Assistant Diocesan Inspector, Manchester, 1882-89; Diocesan Inspector, Manchester, 1889-96; Vicar of Christ Church. Ashton-under-Lyne, 1896-1919; Rural Dean, 1909-19; C.T.F., 1909-1919. *Recreation:* golf. *Address:* The Glen, Linden Chase, Sevenoaks. *T.:* Sevenoaks 168. *Club:* Oxford and Cambridge.
                             (Died 20 July 1928.)

BURROWS, General George Reynolds Scott, Bombay Infantry; *b.* 18 Feb. 1827; *m.* 1st, 1851, Emilie, *d.* of General Goodfellow, R.E.; 2nd, 1871, Dorothea, *d.* of J. J. Ellis, Escrick, Yorks. Entered army, 1844; General, 1890; retired list, 1886; served Afghan War, 1880 (despatches four times, medal with clasp). *Address:* 4 Cavendish Crescent, Bath.
                                (Died July 1917.)

BURROWS, Ronald Montagu; Principal, King's College, London, since 1913; *b.* Rugby, 16 Aug. 1867; *y. s.* of late Rev. L. F. Burrows, and Mary, *d.* of Captain Vicars, R.E.; *m.* 1892, Una Geraldine, *d.* of Right Rev. C. J. Ridgeway, Bishop of Chichester. *Educ.:* Charterhouse; Christ Church, Oxford. Scholar, 1st Class Classical Moderations, 1888; 1st Class Lit. Hum. 1890; D. Litt., Oxford, 1910. Hon. Ph.D. Athens, 1914; Fellow of King's College, London, 1914; Assistant to Professor of Greek, University of Glasgow, 1891-97; Professor of Greek in University Coll. Cardiff, 1898-1908; Professor of Greek in the University of Manchester, 1908-13; Acting Chairman Anglo-Hellenic League; Member of Council, Hellenic Society, Serbian Society, Serbian Relief Fund, United Russia Societies Association, British-Italian League, Anglo-Roumanian Society, Anglo-Spanish Society; Hon. Member of Archæological Society of Athens; Grand Commander Order of King George of Greece; Commander Order of the Saviour; Order of St. Sava (3rd Class). *Publications:* various articles in the classical journals, especially on Pylos Sphacteria, Rhitsóna, and Kothons in the Journal of Hellenic Studies, vols. xvi., xviii., xxviii., xxix., and xxxi., and Delium and Rhitsóna in the Annual of the British School at Athens, vols. xi. and xiv.; (with Prof. W. F. Walters) Florilegium Tironis Graecum, 1904; The Discoveries in Crete, 1907; also articles on Social and Educational Reform and Modern Greece. *Address:* King's College, Strand, W.C. *T.:* Gerrard 207. *Club:* Athenæum.
                             (Died 14 May 1920.)

BURT, Sir John Mowlem, Kt.; *cr.* 1902; J.P.; Lieutenant of the City of London; *b.* 2 Feb. 1845; *e. s.* of late George Burt, Sheriff of the City of London, 1878-79; and *g. n.* of John Mowlem of Swanage, founder of John Mowlem & Co.; *m.* 1st, 1869, Marion (*d.* 1903), *d.* of R. K. Aitchison; 2nd, 1904, Grace Emma, *o. d.* of Joseph Blackstone. *Educ.:* private schools; Marischal Coll. Aberdeen. Entered John Mowlem & Co. 1862; partner. 1875; senior partner, 1888; vice-chairman, Swanage Urban District Council, 1899-1902; represented Swanage in Dorset County Council. *Recreation:* yachting. *Address:* Durlston, Elsworthy Road, N.W.   *(Died 20 Feb. 1918.)*

BURT, Hon. Septimus; K.C.; *b.* St. Kitts, 25 Oct. 1847; 7th *s.* of Sir A. P. Burt; *m.* Louisa Fanny, *d.* of G. E. C. Hare, 1872; four *s.* four *d.* *Educ.:* Shaw House School, Melksham, Wilts, England; Bishop's School, Perth, W.A. Barr. West Australia, 1870; member of Legislative Council, 1874-1900; first acted as Attorney-Gen. 1886; Q.C. 1887; Delegate, Colonial Conference (Lond.), 1887; 1st Attorney-Gen. of West Australia, 1890-97, under responsible Government; Acting Agent-Gen. West Australia in London, 1891; returned to W.A. 1891. *Address:* Strawberry Hill, Perth, West Australia. *T.A.:* Minderoo. *T.:* 4083. *Club:* Weld, Perth.
                             (Died 15 May 1919.)

BURT, Rt. Hon. Thomas, P.C. 1906; D.C.L. Durham University; M.P. (L) Morpeth, 1874-1918; *b.* Northumberland, 12 Nov. 1837; *s.* of Peter Burt, miner; *m.* 1860, Mary, *d.* of Thomas Weatherburn, engineman; three *s.* one *d.* *Educ.:* Village Schools (two years' attendance in all) and by half a century of continuous reading and intercourse with men. Commenced working in the coal mines at ten years of age; continued at various kinds of underground work for eighteen years; Secretary of Northumberland Miners' Mutual Confident Association, 1865-1913; one of British Representatives to Berlin Labour Conference, convened by the Emperor of Germany, 1890; President Trades Union Congress, Newcastle, 1891; has taken part in the International Miners' Conferences; Parliamentary Secretary of Board of Trade from 1892-95. *Publications:* articles for Nineteenth Century, Contemporary, Fortnightly. *Recreations:* walking, cycling. *Address:* 20 Burdon Terrace, Newcastle. *Clubs:* Reform, National Liberal, Eighty   *(Died 13 April 1922.)*

BURTCHAELL, George Dames, K.C., M.A., LL.B., M.R.I.A.; Peerage Counsel; Athlone Pursuivant of Arms, 1908; Registrar of the Office of Arms, Ireland; Deputy Ulster King of Arms, 1910-11 and since 1915; J.P. Cos. Kilkenny and Carlow; *b.* 12 June 1853; *e. s.* of Peter Burtchaell, C.E., and Maria Isabella, *d.* of Lundy Edward Foot, barrister. *Educ.:* Kilkenny College; Trinity College, Dublin. Barr. King's Inns, 1879; K.C. 1918; Fellow Royal Society of Antiquaries of Ireland; Assistant Secretary and Treasurer, 1891-99; Hon. Secretary, 1907-9; Vice-President, 1909-14 and 1919; Inspector of Historical MSS., 1899-1903; member of Council of Royal Irish Academy, 1915-18. *Publications:* Genealogical Memoirs of the Members of Parliament for Kilkenny, 1888; A Complete List of Knights Bachelor dubbed in Ireland, incorporated with The Knights of England, by W. A. Shaw, D.Litt., 1906; numerous papers on genealogical and heraldic subjects published in the Journal of the Royal Society

BURROWES, Thomas Cosby. See page xvii.

of Antiquaries of Ireland and other periodicals. *Recreations:* walking, genealogical research. *Address:* The Office of Arms, Dublin Castle; 44 Morehampton Road, Dublin. *Club:* Royal Societies.   (*Died 18 Aug. 1921.*)

BURTON, Rev. Canon Edwin Hubert, D.D., F.R. Hist. S.; Procurator - Fiscal of R.C. diocese of Westminster; *b.* 12 Aug. 1870; *s.* of Major Edwin Burton, late 4th Batt. Royal Fusiliers, and Sarah Mary, *d.* of Thomas Mosdell Smith, late of Vimeira House, Hammersmith. *Educ.:* St. Edmund's College, Old Hall; St. Mary's College, Oscott. Solicitor, 1893; priest, 1898; Vice - President, St. Edmund's College, Old Hall, 1902-16; President, 1916-18; Canon of Westminster Cathedral, 1917; Treasurer to Westminster Chapter, 1918; Archivist of Westminster Diocese, 1919; Catholic Rector at Hampton Hill, 1920-24. *Publications:* Life and Times of Bishop Challoner, 1909; London Streets and Catholic Memories, 1926; Yesterday Papers, printed privately; joint - editor of Kirk's Biographies of English Catholics, 1909; editor of some volumes of Catholic Record Society; various pamphlets; contributor to Dublin Review, Tablet, Universe, etc. *Recreation:* reading. *Address:* Convent Lodge, Sudbury Hill, Harrow, Middlesex. *Club:* Authors'.   (*Died 15 Dec. 1925.*)

BURTON, Rev. Ernest De Witt, D.D. Professor of New Testament Interpretation (and Head of N. T. Depart.), University of Chicago, U.S.A., since 1892; Acting President, University of Chicago since 1923; *b.* Granville, Ohio, 4 Feb. 1856; *s.* of Rev. Nathan Smith Burton, D.D., and Sarah J. Fairfield; *m.* 1883, Frances Mary Townson; one *d.* *Educ.:* Denison Univ., B.A. 1876 (Granville, Ohio); Rochester Theological Seminary, 1879-82; Univ. of Leipzig, 1887; Univ. of Berlin, 1894. Teacher, public and private schools, 1876-79; Instructor in Rochester Theological Seminary, 1882-83; Assoc.- Prof. 1883-86, Prof. 1886-92, of New Testament Interpretation in the Newton Theological Institution; Assoc.-Editor of the Biblical World, 1892-1906, 1913; Editor-in-Chief, 1906-12; Editor (with others) of the American Journal of Theology 1897 - 1920; Univ. of Chicago Commissioner for Oriental Educational Investigation, 1908-9; Chairman of China Educational Commission, 1921-22. *Publications:* Syntax of the Moods and Tenses in New Testament Greek, 1893; Harmony of the Gospels for Historical Study (with W. A. Stevens), 1894, revised ed. 1904; Records and Letters of the Apostolic Age, 1895; Constructive Studies in the Life of Christ (with S. Mathews), 1901; Principles and Ideals for the Sunday School (with S. Mathews), 1903; A Short Introduction to the Gospels, 1904; Principles of Literary Criticism and their Application to the Synoptic Problem, 1904; Studies in the Gospel of Mark, 1904; Biblical Ideas of Atonement: their History and Significance (with J. M. P. Smith and G. B. Smith), 1909; Harmony of the Synoptic Gospels in English (with E. J. Goodspeed), 1917; Spirit, Soul, and Flesh, 1918; Commentary on the Epistle to the Galatians, 1920; Harmony of the Synoptic Gospels in Greek (with E. J. Goodspeed), 1920; A Source Book for the Study of the Teaching of Jesus in its Historical Relationships, 1923; various essays, chiefly in Amer. Journ. of Theol. *Address:* 5525 Woodlawn Av., Chicago; University of Chicago, Chicago, Ill., U.S.A. *Clubs:* Quadrangle, University, Chicago.   (*Died 26 May 1925.*)

BURTON, Rev. John James, M.A.; Vicar of Inkberrow, Worcestershire, 1896-1924; Hon. Canon of Worcester Cathedral; Rural Dean of Feckenham Deanery, 1901-24; *b.* 3 Jan. 1849; *c. s.* of late John Daniel Burton of Alderley Edge, Cheshire; *m.* 1860, Lilian Maria, 2nd *d.* of late Rev. Thomas Pownall Boultbee, LL.D.,

154

Prebendary of St. Paul's; no *c.* *Educ.:* Trinity College, Cambridge; B.A. 1870; M.A. 1874. Member of Lincoln's Inn, 1870; called to bar, 1873; Deacon, 1875; Priest, 1876; Curate of Holbrook, Suffolk, 1875-80; Vicar of Eridge Green, Sussex, 1880-91; Vicar of Milton Ernest, Beds, 1891-96; Chaplain to the Marquess of Abergavenny. *Address:* Elborough Cottage, Charlton Kings, Cheltenham.   (*Died 14 Feb. 1927.*)

BURWASH, Rev. N.; *b.* Argenteuil, Quebec, 25 July 1839; *s.* of Adam Burwash, U.E.L., descended from Burghersh family, Sussex, England, and Anne Taylor of Killean, Argyllshire; *m.* 1868, Margaret Proctor of Sarnia, Ontario. *Educ.:* Victoria College, Cobourg; Yale University, New Haven; Garrett Biblical Institute. Entered Methodist Ministry, 1860; professor in Victoria College, 1866; Dean of Faculty of Theology, 1873; and President and Chancellor of Victoria University, 1887; resigned official position in Victoria College, 1913; secretary of education for the Methodist Church in Canada, 1874-86; president of Conference, 1889-90; member of the several general conferences since 1874; member of Senate and Council of University of Toronto, and of Council of Education for province of Ontario; F.R.S. Can. 1902. *Publications:* Memorials of Edward and Lydia Jackson, 1874; Wesley's Doctrinal Standards, 1881; Handbook on the Epistle to the Romans, 1887; Inductive Studies in Theology, 1896; Manual of Christian Theology, 1900; Life and Times of Egerton Ryerson, 1902; The Development of the University of Toronto as a Provincial Institution, 1905. *Recreations:* canoeing and fishing in Muskoka. *Address:* 26 Aloin Avenue, Toronto, Canada.   (*Died Mar. 1918.*)

BURY, Francis George, C.B.E. 1918; Hon. Treasurer King George's Club for the Overseas Forces; Barrister; *m.;* three *s.* *Educ.:* Eton; Trinity College, Cambridge. *Address:* 8 Cheniston Gardens, W.8. *T.:* Western 3478. *Club:* United University.   (*Died 3 Jan. 1926.*)

BURY, George Wyman; explorer and naturalist; *b.* 3 Jan. 1874; *s.* of late Henry Charles Bury, Mancetter Manor House, nr. Atherstone; *m.* 1913, Florence Ann Marshall; no *c.* *Educ.:* Atherstone Grammar School; Army Crammers. Commission 3rd Batt. Royal Warwicks, 1894; joined one of the rebel tribes in S. Morocco, 1895; Aden littoral desert, 1896; engaged in archæology, natural history, and intelligence survey among the mountaineers of the Aden hinterland and penetrated into the Great Red Desert, 1897-1901; with the Aden Boundary Commission, 1902; political officer in the Aden Protectorate during military operations of 1903-4; Zoological Expedition in Somaliland, 1905-6; South Arabian Exploration, 1908-1909; Yamen highlands, 1912-13; special service in Egypt, Aug. 1914; intelligence staff on the canal front, Feb.-March 1915; political officer to the Red Sea Northern Patrol with rank of Lieut. R.N.V.R. 1915; took part in naval operations on Arabian coast in first half of 1916, and was closely connected with successful Arab revolt headed by the Sherif of Mecca (now King of Hedjaz) against Turkish rule. *Publications:* The Land of Uz, 1911; Arabia Infelix, 1915; Pan-Islam, 1919. *Recreations:* psychical research and pistol - shooting. Lives abroad.   (*Died 23 Sept. 1920.*)

BURY, John B., M.A.; Hon. Litt.D. of Oxford, Durham, and Dublin, and Hon. LL.D. of Edinburgh, Glasgow, and Aberdeen Universities; Regius Professor of Modern History, Cambridge Univ., since 1902; Fellow King's College, Cambridge; Hon. Fellow Oriel College, Oxford; Fellow of the British Academy; Corresponding Member of the Imperial

BURTON, Maj.-Gen. Benjamin, C.B. See page xvii.

Academy of Sciences of Petrograd, the Hungarian Academy of Science, the Roumanian Academy, the Massachusetts Historical Society, and the Russian Archæological Institute at Constantinople ; Romanes Lecturer, 1911 ; Fellow of Trinity Coll., Dublin, 1885-1903 ; Professor of Modern History in Dublin University, 1893-1902 ; Regius Professor of Greek, 1898 ; *b.* 16 Oct. 1861 ; *s.* of Rev. E. J. Bury, Canon cf Clogher ; *m.* Jane, *d.* of J. C. Bury ; one *s.* *Educ.:* Trin. Coll., Dublin. *Publications:* History of the Later Roman Empire from Arcadius to Irene, 1889 ; Student's History of the Roman Empire from Augustus to Marcus Aurelius, 1893 ; History of Greece to Death of Alexander the Great, 1900 (library edit. in 2 vols. 1902) ; The Science of History (Inaugural lecture), 1903 ; Life of St. Patrick and his place in History, 1905 ; The Ancient Greek Historians (Harvard Lectures), 1908 ; The Constitution of the Later Roman Empire (Creighton Memorial Lecture), 1909 ; Imperial Administration in the Ninth Century, 1911 ; Romances of Chivalry on Greek Soil (Romanes Lecture), 1911 ; History of the Eastern Roman Empire (from 802 to 867), 1912 ; History of Freedom of Thought, 1913 ; The Idea of Progress, 1920 ; History of the Later Roman Empire (395-565), 2 vols. 1922 ; ed. of Pindar's Nemean Odes, 1890 ; Pindar's Isthmian Odes, 1892 ; Freeman's History of Federal Government in Greece and Italy, 1893 ; Gibbon's Decline and Fall, vols. i. and ii. 1896, iii. and iv. 1897, v. and vi. 1898, vii. 1900 ; Freeman's Historical Geography of Europe, 1903. *Address:* King's College, Cambridge ; Limne Cottage, Southwold. *Club :* Athenæum. (*Died 1 June 1927.*)

BURY, Rev. William, M.A. ; Residentiary Canon of Peterborough since 1908 ; Rector of Ickenham, Uxbridge, since 1907 ; *b.* Radcliffe-on-Trent, Notts, 1839 ; *s.* of Rev. W. Bury, then Rector of Radcliffe-on-Trent ; *m.* Eliz. A. Foljambe, *d.* of Geo. Saville Foljambe of Osberton, Notts ; one *d.* *Educ.:* Trinity Coll. Cambridge (sen. op., 1861). In the "Varsity" eleven, played twice against Oxford ; and for two years for his county (Notts). Ordained by Archbishop of York ; 1st Curacy, Tickhill, Yorks ; six months sole charge of Handley, Dorset ; travelled three months ; Rector of Fifehead Neville, Dorset, 1866-67 ; Hazelbeach, Northants, 1867 ; Guardian for Hazelbeach, 1868, and made Poor Law his subject, commencing in 1872 a reform in the union to which he belonged (Brixworth), which resulted in reducing the number of outdoor paupers from 1062 in 1872 to 16 in 1894, without increasing indoor pauperism : his policy upset by Local Government Act, 1894, ceased to be chairman : but in 1899 was elected chairman of the D. C., retired 1905 ; established a co-operative public house in Harleston ; all the grocery and general business of the village is on same principle and under same management ; Rector of Harleston, 1882-1907. *Publications:* pamphlets, Charity and the Poor Law ; Out-door Relief, Or A more Excellent Way ; and a few sermons on kindred subjects. *Address:* Ickenham, Uxbridge.

(*Died 1 April 1920.*)

BUSH, Rev. Thomas Cromwell, of Cheshunt Park, Herts ; *e. s.* of late Paul Bush, rector of Duloe and canon of Truro, and Avarilla Oliveria Cromwell, *o. d.* of Thomas A. Russell of Cheshunt Park, Herts ; *m.* 1st, 1887, Gertrude Julia (*d.* 1888), *d.* of G. Coles of Streatham ; 2nd, 1892, Barbara Christiana (*d.* 1914), *d.* of late David Horndon, D.L., and J.P., of Pencrebar, Cornwall ; two *s.* *Educ.:* Rugby ; Hertford College, Oxford. Represented Oxford in mile ; was Hon. Chaplain to North Somerset Imperial Yeomanry. *Address:* Cheshunt Park, Herts. ; Cample Haye, Tavistock.

M. : FB 376. *Club :* R.W. Yacht.

(*Died 4 Mar. 1919.*)

BUSHBY, Thomas, M.B., C.M. (Edinburgh), M.R.C.P. (London) ; Hon. Physician to the David Lewis Northern Hospital ; Consulting Physician, Liverpool School for the Blind ; *b.* Liverpool ; *m.* Mary Bowring Wimble ; one *s.* one *d.* *Educ.:* Marlborough College ; Edinburgh University. Assistant Physician, Liverpool Consumption Hospital ; Lecturer in Clinical Medicine to the University of Liverpool ; Examiner in Clinical Medicine, University of Liverpool. *Address:* 43 Catharine Street, Liverpool. *T.:* 2404 Royal, Liverpool.

(*Died 1 Jan. 1916.*)

BUSHE, Robert Gervase, C.M.G. 1911 ; Auditor-General Trinidad and Tobago, 1903-23 ; retired, 1923 ; *b.* 1851 ; *s.* of late John Scott Bushe, C.M.G., Colonial Secretary, Trinidad ; *m.* 1880, Violet, *d.* of A. R. Gray, Trinidad. *Educ.:* Clifton College ; Queen's Collegiate School, Trinidad ; King's College, Cambridge (scholar), 27th Wrangler, 1875 ; B.A. ; Master Queen's Royal College, Trinidad, 1878 ; Inspector of Schools, 1891 ; acted as Colonial Secretary, 1906, 1908-9, 1911, 1913, and 1914-15. *Address:* Port of Spain, Trinidad. (*Died 13 July 1927.*)

BUSHE, Seymour Coghill Hort, *b.* 5 April 1853 ; *s.* of late Rev. Charles Bushe of Castlehaven, Co. Cork ; *g. s.* of late Rt. Hon. Chief-Justice Bushe of Kilmurry, Co. Kilkenny ; *m.* Lady Kathleen Maude, *d.* of 1st Earl De Montalt, 1886. *Educ.:* Rathmines School, Dublin ; Trinity College, Dublin (B.A.), scholar (classics) ; senior moderator and Berkeley gold medallist ; gold medallist in Oratory of the College Historical Society. Called to Irish Bar, 1879 ; Q.C., 1892 ; Bencher of King's Inns, 1896 ; senior Crown Prosecutor for county and city of Dublin, 1901 ; called to English Bar, 1899 ; K.C., 1904 ; J.P., Co. Cork ; travelled in Australasia and Central America, etc. *Recreations:* fishing, cycling, travel. *Address:* 49 Drayton Gardens, S.W. *Clubs :* Union ; Dublin University ; Cork County.

(*Died 27 Jan. 1922.*)

BUSHE-FOX, Loftus Henry Kendal, M.A., LL.M. : Fellow, Tutor, and Lecturer, St. John's College, Cambridge ; *b.* Hampstead, 6 Dec. 1863 ; *s.* of Major Luke Loftus Bushe-Fox, and Marian, *d.* of Benjamin Brown : *m.* 1906, Theodora, *y. d.* of late H. W. Willoughby ; one *s.* *Educ.:* Charterhouse ; St. John's Coll. Cambridge, Herschel Prizeman, 1884 ; Twelfth Wrangler, 1885 ; Law Tripos, 1886 ; MacMahon Law Student, 1886 ; called to Bar, Inner Temple, 1890 ; Fellow and Junior Dean of St. John's College, 1903 ; Tutor, 1905. *Recreations:* rowing (Camb. Univ. pairs and trial eights), lawn tennis, shooting, sailing. *Address:* St. John's College, and 15 Madingley Road, Cambridge ; Cordara, Lanesborough, Co. Longford.

(*Died 21 Mar. 1916.*)

BUSHELL, Rev. William Done, M.A., V.D. 1887 ; F.S.A. (Bardic Appellation, Ynyswr Pyr) ; *b.* Bristol, 10 Nov. 1838 ; *s.* of William Done Bushell, Resident Director at Cardiff of the Taff Vale Railway, and *g.-s.* of William Bushell, Bristol Merchant ; *m.* 1866, Mary, *e. d.* of Charles Lestourgeon, M.B., of Howes' Close, Cambridge ; four *s.* four *d.* *Educ.:* Cheltenham College ; St. John's College, Cambridge (Scholar and Fellow). M.A. ; Seventh Wrangler and 2nd Class Classical Tripos ; Deacon, 1864 ; Priest, 1866 ; Fellow of St. John's, 1862 ; Assistant Master Clifton College, 1865-66 ; Assistant Master Harrow School, 1866-1899 ; Hon. Assistant Chaplain, Harrow School, 1899-1917 ; Original member of the Cambridge University Volunteers, 1860 ; Capt., 1861-65 ; Hon. Capt. Harrow School Corps, 1884-91 ; Chaplain local Volunteers, 1870-1908 ; Lord of the Manor of Caldey Island. *Publications:* Church Life on Harrow Hill [767-1600] ; Antiquarian articles

in Archæologia Cambrensis and various other journals; Sermons. *Recreations:* Alpine Club, 1863 onwards, Champion Racquet Player, St. John's College, medal (twice); Golf, Northwood and other Clubs. *Address:* The Hermitage, Harrow-on-the-Hill; Caldey Priory, Tenby. *T.A.:* Harrow. *T.:* 395. *M.:* DE 119. *Clubs:* Athenæum, Alpine; Tenby and County, Tenby.
(*Died 27 Aug. 1917.*)

BUSK, Sir Edward Henry, Kt.; *cr.* 1901; M.A., LL.B.; Commissioner by London University Commission Act, 1898, under University College, London, Transfer Act, 1905, and King's College, London, Transfer Act, 1908; *b.* London, 10 Feb. 1844; *o. s.* of Henry William Busk, barrister, and Mary Anne, *d.* of Rev. Philip Le Breton; *m.* 1880, Marian, *y. d.* of Lewis Balfour. *Educ.:* University College School and University Coll., London. B.A. with 1st class Honours, 1863; M.A., 1864; LL.B. with 1st Class Honours and University Law Scholarship, 1866; Joseph Hume Scholar and Fellow of University College, London; solicitor, 1868 to 1899; Reader in Elementary Law to the Incorporated Law Society, 1879-92; past Vice-Chancellor and Chairman of Convocation of Univ. of London; Fellow of that University, 1892; Major (retired) of the Artists' Corps of Volunteers; Member of the Kent Education Committee, 1903-9; Governor of Dulwich College, and of the Ladies' College, Cheltenham; Chairman of the Governors of Holt School, Norfolk, and of the Central Foundation Schools, London; Member of the Governing Body of the Imperial Coll. of Science and Technology; Chairman of Executive Committee and Vice-President of the City and Guilds Institute; Member of the Court of the Fishmongers' Company; Corresponding Member of the Educational Association of America; President of the National Sea Fisheries Protection Association, and President and Treasurer of the Oyster Merchants' and Planters' Association; Chairman of the London Board of the London and Lancashire Insurance Co. *Address:* Heath End, Checkendon, Oxon. *Clubs:* Athenæum, Albemarle.
(*Died 29 Oct. 1926.*)

BUSONI, Ferruccio Benvenuto, Hon. Member of Royal Academy of Music, Bologna; *b.* Empoli, near Florence, 1 April 1866; father and mother musicians; *m.* 1890, Gerda Sjostrand, *d.* of a Finnish sculptor. *Educ.:* Austria. Eight years before public; has composed much chamber music, orchestral scores, piano; teacher at Helsingfors, 1888-89; Professor at the Moscow Imperial Conservatory, 1890; at the Boston (New England) Conservatory, 1891; first Rubinstein prize, 1890. *Recreations:* walking, smoking, billiards; collecting and reading books; writing about music.
(*Died 27 July 1924.*)

BUSZARD, Marston Clarke, M.A.; LL.M.; K.C. 1877; Leader of Midland Circuit; J.P. and Deputy Chairman, Quarter Sessions, Leicestershire; Recorder of Leicester since 1899; *b.* Lutterworth, 13 July 1837; *s.* of Marston Buszard, M.D.; *m.* 1st, 1864, Louisa, *d.* of John Mayor Threlfall, of Salford (*d.* 1895); 2nd, 1898, Annie Violet, *e. d.* of E. R. Whitwell of The Friarage, Yarm-on-Tees; three *d. Educ.:* Rugby; Trin. Coll. Camb. Chancellor's Gold Medallist for Legal Studies, 1863. Barr. 1862. Bencher Inner Temple, 1880; Treasurer, 1903. Contested Stamford (L.) 1874; M.P. Stamford, 1880-85, when the borough was disfranchised; joined Liberal Unionist Party, and unsuccessfully contested Rugby, 1886; Recorder of Derby, 1890-99. *Address:* 25 Pembridge Square, W.2; 5 Crown Office Row, Temple, E.C.4. *T.A.:* 63 Temple. *T.:* (Temple) 807 Central; 4663 Park. *Clubs:* Reform, Brooks's.
(*Died 11 Sept. 1921.*)

BUTCHER, William Deane, M.R.C.S., F.R.S.; Consulting Surgeon, London Skin

Hospital; formerly Editor Archives of the Röntgen Ray; *b.* 17 Oct. 1846; *s.* of William Butcher of Red House, Rudgwick, and Rachel, *d.* of Isaac Deane of Wainbrook, Somerset; *m.* 1877, Fanny, *d.* of Col. C. Y. Bazett, 9th Bengal Cavalry, H.E.I.C.S.; two *d.* three *s. Educ.:* Grammar School, Maidstone; London University; St. Bartholomew's Hospital. (Senior Scholar); House Surgeon to Sir James Paget, 1868; practised in Port of Calcutta, 1870-74; Reading and Windsor; Surgeon on s.s. "Gothic." 1894; introduced the first Röntgen installation in England for dermatological work at London Skin Hospital, 1898; represented the Electrotherapeutic Society at the Congress of Physiotherapy at Liège, 1905, and at the Berlin Röntgen Congress, 1906; represented the Röntgen Society at the International Congress of Electrology and Radiology, Amsterdam, 1908; represented the Electrotherapeutic Section of Royal Society of Medicine at the Congress of Physiotherapy, Paris, 1910; President of Röntgen Society, 1908-9; President of Electrotherapeutic Section of Royal Society of Medicine, 1909-10; President of the Ealing Scientific and Microscopic Society. *Publications:* Papers and Lectures on Radium, X-rays, Osmotic Growth, and Physical Basis of Education; Translation of Belot's Radiotherapy in Skin Diseases, Guilleninot's Medical Electricity, and Leduc's Mechanism of Life. *Recreations:* science, chess, wood-carving. *Address:* Holyrood, Cleveland Road, Ealing, W.
(*Died 10 Jan. 1919.*)

BUTLER, Rev. Alexander Douglas, Superintendent Minister of Whitefields Central Mission, Tottenham Court Road, since 1925; *b.* Brighton; *m.* 1919, Eva M. Pearce of Woolwich, S.E.; one *s.* one *d. Educ.:* Brighton; Moody Bible College; Chicago Theological Seminary (Chicago University). Minister of Ware Independent Church, 1910-12; Rectory Place Congregational Church, Woolwich, 1912-17; Queen's Park Congregational Church, Paddington, 1917-25; Editor of The London Signal; writer and lecturer on Psychology and related subjects. *Recreations:* golf, trout-fishing, all out-of-door sport. *Address:* 15 Kingswood Avenue, Brondesbury, N.W.6. *T.:* Willesden 4300.
(*Died 27 July 1926.*)

BUTLER, Arthur Gardiner, Ph.D., F.L.S., F.Z.S., F.E.S., M.B.O.U.; C.M.A.O.U.; retired Civil Servant; *b.* Chelsea, 27 June 1844; 3rd *s.* of Thomas Butler, late Assistant Secretary at the British Museum; *m.* Mary, *e. d.* of George Tonge of Sittingbourne, Kent; one *s. Educ.:* St. Paul's School. Entered S. Kensington Art School, 1861; received bronze medal for Outlines from Nature, 1862; entered Zoological branch of the British Museum, 1863; Assistant Keeper with special charge of the Arthropods, 1879; retired 1901. *Publications:* Catalogue of Diurnal Lepidoptera of the family Satyridæ in the British Museum, 1868; Catalogue of Diurnal Lepidoptera described by Fabricius in the British Museum, 1869; Lepidoptera Exotica, 1869; Typical Specimens of Lepidoptera Heterocera in the Collection of the British Museum, 1877-89; British Birds' Eggs, 1886; Foreign Finches in Captivity, 1895-96; the first volumes of British Birds with their Nests and Eggs, 1897-98; Foreign Bird-Keeping, 1899-1900; Birds' Eggs of the British Isles, 1901; Hints on Cage-Birds, British and Foreign, 1903; How to sex Cage-Birds, 1907; Birds of Great Britain and Ireland, Order Passeres, 1907-8; Foreign Birds for Cage and Aviary, 1908 and 1910; monographs and other articles dealing with all Orders of Insects, Spiders, Myriopods, and with Cage-Birds. *Recreations:* aviculture, floriculture, reading, writing, and entertaining friends with an excellent cabinet gramophone. *Address:* 124 Beckenham Road, Beckenham, Kent.
(*Died 28 May 1925.*)

BUTLER, Arthur Stanley, M.A.; Prof. of Natural Philosophy, St. Andrews Univer. 1880-1922; 2nd s. of late George Butler, D.D., Canon of Winchester, and Josephine, d. of John Grey, Dilston, Northumberland; b. 17 May, 1854; m. 1886, Edith, d. of Jasper Bolton, Ballykisteen, Tipperary; one s. one d. Educ.: Cheltenham College; Exeter College, Oxford (1st class Math. Mods.; 1st class Final School). Address: c/o University, St. Andrews. Clubs: Royal Societies; Royal and Ancient Golf, St. Andrews. (Died 2 Mar. 1923.)

BUTLER, Rev. Dugald, M.A., D.D.; b. Glasgow, 1862; m. 1893, Catherine, d. of late Sir James Marwick. Educ.: High School and University of Glasgow. Minister of Abernethy, Perthshire, 1890-1902; Tron Parish, Edinburgh, 1902-7; Galashiels, 1907-19 (retired); Hon. D.D. Glasgow University, 1907. Publications: Ancient Church and Parish of Abernethy, 1897; John Wesley and George Whitefield in Scotland, 1898; Henry Scougal and the Oxford Methodists, 1899; Scottish Cathedrals and Abbeys, 1900; Life and Letters of Archbishop Leighton, 1903; Eternal Elements in the Christian Faith, 1905; The Tron Kirk of Edinburgh, 1906; Thomas à Kempis, a Religious Study, 1908; Gothic Architecture, its Christian Origin and Inspiration, 1910; Archbishop Leighton's Practice of the Presence of God, with introduction, 1911; Unity, Peace, and Charity: a Tercentenary Lecture on Archbishop Leighton, 1912; Woman and the Church in Scottish History, 1912; George Fox in Scotland: an Appreciation of the Society of Friends and its Founders, 1913; Life of St. Cuthbert, 1913; Life of St. Giles, 1914; Lindean and Galashiels, or Abbeys, Church, Manor and Town, 1915; Prayer in Experience, 1922; Jottings of an Invalid, 1924. Address: 16 Dreghorn Loan, Colinton, Midlothian. (Died 9 Jan. 1926.)

BUTLER, Capt. Hon. Francis Almeric; late Hampshire Yeomanry; 3rd s. of 6th Earl of Lanesborough; b. 17 May 1872; m. 1902, Madeline, d. of late Richard Birkett Gibbs; one s. one d. Address: Belmore Cottage, Upham, Hants. Clubs: Cavalry, Royal Automobile, Roehampton. (Died 8 May 1925.)

BUTLER, Frank Hedges, F.R.G.S.; b. 17 Dec. 1855; s. of late James Butler, Hollywood, Wimbledon Park, and Frances, d. of late William Hedges; m. d. (d. 1905) of J. B. Tickle, London and Sydney; one d. Director, Hedges & Butler, Ltd., Regent Street, W.1; Orchestral Member, 1st violin, Handel Festival, 1874; Royal Amateur Orchestral Society, 1875; Wandering Minstrels, 1876; Royal Albert Hall Choral Society, 1877; Founder of the Lyric Club Orchestra, 1889; Founder and Chairman of the Imperial Institute Orchestral Society, 1894; first Hon. Treasurer, Royal Automobile Club, 1897-1902; suggested first motor car run of the Automobile Club, 1898; obtained permission from Sandown Park to allow motor cars on course, Eclipse Stakes, 1898; inaugurated first concert at the Automobile Club, Whitehall Court, 1898; obtained sanction to allow motor cars on Ascot course, 1900; introduced motor car races and gymkana at Ranelagh Club, 1900, and balloon ascents, 1902; proposed the first ball (Durbar) at the Royal Automobile Club, 1911; presented challenge shield to the Royal Automobile Club to form a golfing society, 1910; took part in 1000 miles trial of the Royal Automobile Club, 1900; founder of Royal Aero Club, 1901; winner and pilot of the first three Royal Aero Club balloon races, 1906 and 1907; has made over a hundred free balloon ascents, including record of longest distance in England done alone in a balloon, 1902, and record of the world for the longest cross Channel sea voyage from London to Caen in Normandy, 1905; Commemorative medal Aero Club of France, 1905; pioneer of the dirigible balloon, 1907, and aeroplane, 1908; Life-Fellow Royal Geographical Society in 1877; travelled in India, China, Japan, Korea, Burmah, Russia, Lapland, North and South America, Africa, Asia Minor, South Sea Islands, Falkland Islands. Java, Australia and New Zealand. Publications: Five Thousand Miles in a Balloon, 1907; Across Lapland with Reindeer and Skis, 1917; Fifty Years of Travel by Land, Water, and Air, 1920; Round the World, 1925; Wine and the Wine Lands of the World, 1926. Recreations: big-game shooting, golf, yachting, and music. Address: 1 St. James's Street, S.W.1. T.: Gerrard 6131. Clubs: Royal Thames Yacht, Royal Automobile, Ranelagh, Royal Motor Yacht; Aero Club of France; East Brighton Golf. (Died 27 Nov. 1928.)

BUTLER, Sir George Beresford, Kt., cr. 1921; senior resident magistrate, Ireland, to 1921; b. 31 Jan. 1857; o. s. of Capt. A. S. Butler, C.B., late 7th Dragoon Guards, and May, d. of Rev. George de la Poer Beresford; m. 1896, Georgina Rose Mary, o. d. of Capt. Charles Walker, 21st Fusiliers. Educ.: Marlborough. Address: Tullamore, Ireland. Club: Hibernian United Service, Dublin. (Died 1 Sept 1924.)

BUTLER, Rev. Henry Montagu, D.D.; D.C.L. Oxford; LL.D. Glasgow and St. Andrews; Commendatore della Corona d'Italia, 1871; Master of Trinity College, Cambridge, from 1886; Chaplain in Ordinary to the King, 1912; b. Gayton Rectory, Northants, 2 July 1833; 4th s. of George Butler, D.D. [Senior Wrangler, 1794; Headmaster of Harrow, 1805-1829; Rector of Gayton, 1814-53; Dean of Peterborough, 1842-53] and Sarah Maria, d. of John Gray, of Wembley Park, Middlesex; m. 1st, 1861, Georgina Isabella Elliot, g. d. of Rt. Hon. Hugh Elliot, sometime Minister at Court of Frederick the Great; 2nd, 1888, Agnata Frances Ramsay, d. of Sir James Ramsay of Bamff, 10th Bt.; four s. two d. Educ.: Harrow; Trin. Coll. Camb. Fellow of Trinity, 1855; Priv. Sec. to Rt. Hon. W. F. Cowper (Lord Mount Temple), 1856-57; Headmaster of Harrow, 1859-85; Hon. Chaplain to the Queen, 1875-77; Chaplain in Ordinary, 1877-85; Examining Chaplain to Archbishops Tait and Benson, 1879-83; Select Preacher at Oxford, 1877, 1878, 1882, 1899; at Cambridge, 1879, 1885, 1887, 1889, 1890, 1895, 1896, 1897, 1898, 1903, 1906, 1913; Preb. of Holborn in St. Paul's Cathedral, 1882-85; Dean of Gloucester, 1885-86; Hon. Canon of Ely, 1897; Bell Univ. Scholar, 1852; Battie Univ. Sch. and Greek Ode, 1853; Greek Ode, Camden Medal, Porson Prize, Latin Essay Prize, 1854; Senior Classic, 1855; Vice-Chancellor, 1889, 1890. Publications: Sermons preached in the Chapel of Harrow School, 1861; Second Series, 1866; Belief in Christ and other Sermons, 1898; Words of Good Cheer for the Holy Communion, 1898; University and other Sermons, Historical and Biographical, 1899; Public School Sermons, 1899; Ten Great and Good Men, 1909; Romanes Lecture, Lord Chatham as an Orator, 1912; Presidential Address of Classical Association, 1913; Lift up your Hearts, 1898 and 1914; Some Leisure Hours of a Long Life, 1914. Recreations: Harrow Cricket Eleven, 1851; ascended Monte Rosa, 1856, Parnassus, 1857, Sinai, 1858. Address: Trinity Lodge, Cambridge. (Died 14 Jan. 1918.)

BUTLER, Rev. Hercules Scott, Rector of Mareham le Fen; b. 1850; m.; three s. Educ.: Loretto; Rossall; Brasenose College, Oxford. Curate of Leeds, 1875-83; Vicar of St. Barnabas, Holbeck, 1883-94; Farnworth, 1894-1900; Preston, 1900-20. Address: The Rectory, Mareham le Fen, Boston. T.: Horncastle 20 Y1. T.A.: Mareham le Fen. M.: OM 882. (Died 27 Jan. 1928.)

BUTLER, Capt. John Fitzhardinge Paul, V.C. 1915; K.R.R.C.; attached Pioneer

157

Company, Gold Coast Regt., W.A. Frontier Force; *b.* 20 Dec. 1888. Entered Army, 1907; served with West African Frontier Force, European War, 1914-15 (V.C.)
(*Died 4 Sept. 1916.*)

BUTLER, Hon. Sir Richard, Kt., *cr.* 1913; Speaker of House of Assembly, South Australia, 1921-24; *b.* England, 3 Dec. 1850; *s.* of Richard Butler, Pastoralist, S.A.; *m.* 1st, 1878, Helena Kate, *d.* of Edward Wills Lagton, Sydney; 2nd, 1894, Ethel Pauline, *d.* of late Thomas Dixie Finey; four *s.* seven *d.* *Educ.:* St. Peter's Coll., Adelaide. Went South Australia, 1854; M.H.A., Yatala, 1890-1902; Minister of Education and Agriculture, 1898-99; Treasurer and Minister of Agriculture, 1901-5; Commissioner of Crown Lands and Minister of Mines, 1902-5; Premier and Treasurer, 1905; Treasurer and Minister controlling Northern Territory, 1909-10; Commissioner of Public Works, Minister of Mines, and of Marine, South Australia, 1912-15. *Recreation:* work. *Address:* Northcote Road, Mitintie, nr. Adelaide.
(*Died 28 April 1925.*)

BUTLER, Richard William; *b.* London, 21 May 1844. *Educ.:* City of London School. Proof-reader on Daily Telegraph, 1871-77; sub-editor of The Referee, 1877-91; editor, 1891-1921. Contributor to several other journals; many years dramatic critic; part author of several farces, burlesques, melodramas, and comediettas. *Address:* c/o Referee Office, 17 Tudor Street, E.C.4. (*Died 21 Dec. 1928.*)

BUTLER, Slade; Recorder of Rye since 1911; M.A. of Christ Church, Oxford; Barrister of the Middle Temple and South-Eastern Circuit. *Address:* 2 Middle Temple Lane, Temple, E.C. *Club:* Reform. (*Died 6 Dec. 1923.*)

BUTLIN, Sir Henry Guy Trentham, 2nd Bt.; *cr.* 1911; *b.* 7 Jan. 1893; *s.* of 1st Bt. and Annie, *e. d.* of late Henry Balderson; *S.* father 1912. *Heir:* none. *Educ.:* Harrow; Trinity College, Cambridge. *Address:* 22 Harcourt Terrace, S.W. *T.:* Western 2951.
(*Died 16 Sept. 1916.*)

BUTLIN, Sir William, Kt., *cr.* 1921; B.A. Cantab., Hon. Member Real Sociedad Economica (Madrid); Chairman, Louis Cassier Co., Ltd.; *b.* Northampton, 26 April 1851; *s.* of William Butlin, C.E., of Spratton, Northampton: unmarried. *Educ.:* Abington House School, Northampton; Cambridge University. Studied Chemistry, Geology, Metallurgy under Associate of Royal School of Mines, London, in relation to Iron Smelting at Irthlingborough Iron Works, Wellingborough, Northants; has been Chairman and Managing Director of T. Butlin & Co., Ltd., for 24 years; improved quality of British pig-iron and castings; entertained American Institute of Mining Engineers at Wellingborough, also Royal Geological Society; was Hon. Treasurer of British Iron Trade Association; visited United States with Iron and Steel Institute; speciality, direct castings by scientific method, also for tube railways, etc.; 20 years Spanish Vice-Consul, Northampton; has been Chairman of Banquet Ibero-American Benevolent Society, Member of Committee, and is now a Governor of the Foundation; Cross of Isabel la Catolica of Spain; Member of Imperial Air-Fleet Committee. *Publications:* Evolution or Revolution, by Ironicus; Northampton Iron Ore Industry, Proceedings Iron and Steel Inst., London; Direct Castings, Cassiers' Engineering Magazine; Civil Engineering, Iron Age, New York; Contributions to the Press, some foreign Strikes, Anarchy, International Arbitration, Criminal Law, Powers and Physical Force, etc. *Recreations:* reading, writing, antiques, walking, boating, travel, billiards, etc. *Address:* The Grove, Tiptree, Essex. *T.A.:*

158

Tiptree, Kelvedon, Essex. *M.:* HK 9739. *Club:* Authors'. (*Died 13 May 1923.*)

BUTTER, Archibald Edward, C.M.G. 1903; F.R.G.S., F.Z.S.; sportsman; Captain in Scottish Horse I.Y.: *b.* 29 Mar. 1874; *s.* of Lt.-Col. Butter, who served in Mutiny and Crimea, and Juliet Macpherson, *e. d.* of Brewster Macpherson of Belleville; *g.s.* of Archibald Butter of Faskally, who married Miss Menzies of Castle Menzies; *m.* 1910, Helen Ciceley, 3rd *d.* of late Charles W. R. Kerr; two *s.* *Educ.:* Eton. *Address:* Riddell, Lilliesleaf, Roxburghshire. *Clubs:* Carlton. Turf. (*Died 6 Jan. 1928.*)

BUTTERWORTH, Arthur Reginald, Barrister-at-law; Fellow of the Royal Colonial Institute; Hon. Member of the Institute of Bankers of New South Wales; *b.* 22 July 1850; 3rd *s.* of late Rev. Joseph Henry Butterworth and Mary Eliza Alexandrina, *d.* of late Captain William Atkins Bowen, H.E.I.C.; *m.* Margaret (*d.* 1913), *y. d.* of late John Patterson of Craigdarragh, Belfast; one *s.* *Educ.:* Marlborough College. Travelled in Australia, India, Egypt, and Europe, 1869-74; called to the Bar, Inner Temple, 1877; admitted to the Bar of New South Wales, 1888; practised in Sydney, 1883-1895; one of the Crown Prosecutors for New South Wales, 1887-91; practised in the Privy Council and High Court, 1896-1914; has since then lived abroad; Member of the Western Circuit since 1878. *Publications:* (Joint) Treatise on Maximum Railway Rates and Charges, 1896; Treatise on the Criminal Evidence Act, 1898; The Privy Council and Australian Appeals, 1901; Bankers' Advances on Mercantile Securities, 1902; The Creation of Peers as a Constitutional Question (articles republished from The Times), 1911; joint-editor of Benjamin on the Sale of Personal Property, 5th ed., 1906; many articles and lectures on Constitutional and Banking Law. *Address:* 7 Fig Tree Court, The Temple, E.C. *Club:* Montreux, Territet. (*Died 30 Dec. 1924.*)

BUTTERWORTH, Comdr. Henry, R.N., retd.; Captain Superintendent, Training Ship Indefatigable, Rock Ferry, Birkenhead, since 1911; *b.* Southport, 23 May 1866; *y. c.* of Henry Butterworth and Mary Jane Schofield, of Rochdale; *m.* 1899, Mary, *d.* of Rev. Joseph Channey, of Dromiskin, Ireland; no *c.* *Educ.:* Torquay College; Elizabeth College, Guernsey; H.M.S. Worcester. Midshipman R.N.R. 1883; joined Messrs. Shaw Savill's Clipper Ship, 1884-87; Joined B.I.S.N. Co. 1887; serving in Royal Navy. 1891-93; joined R.N. as Supplementary Lieut. 1895; took part in H.M.S. Arethusa in suppressing Boxer rebellion, 1900; King's Harbour-Master, Hong-Kong, 1906-10; retired with rank of Commander, 1911. *Recreations:* reading, walking, billiards, photography. *Address:* Training Ship Indefatigable, Rock Ferry, Birkenhead. *Club:* Conservative, Liverpool. (*Died 28 May 1926.*)

BUXTON, Alfred St. Clair, F.R.C.S.E.; consulting surgeon, and formerly senior active surgeon to the Western Ophthalmic Hospital, London; *b.* Taden, France, 14 Nov. 1854; 2nd *s.* of late Alfred Isaac Buxton. *Educ.:* Dinan; Guy's Hospital. *Publications:* several contributions on ophthalmic surgery; inventor of the Telechrome test for colour blindness. *Address:* 32 Weymouth Street, W.1. *T.:* Mayfair 1818.
(*Died 19 Dec. 1929.*)

BUXTON, Commander Bernard, D.S.O. 1917; R.N.; *b.* 21 Oct. 1882; *s.* of Geoffrey F. Buxton of Hoveton Hall, Norwich; *m.* Lady Hermione Grimston, *d.* of 3rd Earl of Verulam; three *s.* one *d.* *Educ.:* Cheam School; H.M.S. Britannia. Mediterranean (Crete), 1898; Naval Staff College, 1913; North Sea, 1914 and 1915; Mesopotamia, 1916 and 1917; Admiralty, 1918; Staff College, Camberley, 1921. *Clubs:* Bath; Royal Yacht Squadron, Cowes (Hon.). (*Died 29 Dec. 1923.*)

BUXTON, Edward North, J.P., D.L. ; late Chairman of Quarter Sessions, Essex ; Alderman Essex County Council ; a Director, Truman, Hanbury, Buxton and Co. ; 3rd *s.* of Sir E. N. Buxton, 2nd Bt. ; *b.* 1 Sep. 1840 ; *m.* 1862, 3rd *d.* of Hon. and Rev. R. H. Digby ; two *s.* five *d.*   *Educ.:* Trinity Coll., Cambridge. Engaged in public work as a member, vice-chairman, and chairman of the London School Board, 1871-88 ; as a magistrate, alderman of Essex County Council ; M.P. Walthamstow Division, 1885-86 ; a verderer of Epping Forest for 42 years ; Vice-President of the Commons Preservation Society, member since 1866 : for many years a promoter of public open spaces.   *Publications :* Short Stalks ; Short Stalks, second series ; Two African Trips ; Epping Forest.   *Recreations :* a keen follower of big game in four continents ; but he is fond of travelling for its own sake ; Epping Forest owes much to him.   *Heir :* s. Gerald [*b.* Oct. 30, 1862 ; *m.* 1890, Lucy Ethel, *d.* of Sir Joseph Pease, 1st Bt. ; two *s.* two *d.*   *Educ.:* Cambridge.   *Club :* Brooks's.]   *Address :* Knighton, Buckhurst Hill.   *T.:* Woodford 550.   *Club :* Athenæum.

(*Died 9 Jan.* 1924.)

BUXTON, Sir (Thomas Fowell) Victor, 4th Bt. ; *cr.* 1840 ; M.A., J.P., F.R.G.S., F.Z.S. ; *s.* of 3rd Bt. and Lady Victoria Noel, *d.* of 1st Earl of Gainsborough ; *S.* father 1915 ; *b.* 8 April 1865 ; *m.* 1888, Anne Louisa Matilda, 2nd *d.* of Rev. H. T. O'Rorke ; five *s.* one *d.*   *Educ.:* Harrow ; Trinity College, Cambridge.   High Sheriff of Essex, 1905 ; Member of Essex T.F. Assoc. ; Commandant 1/2nd Batt. Essex Vol. Regt. ; President, Anti-Slavery and Aborigines Protection Society ; Treasurer, C.M.S.   *Publications :* Articles on Christian Industrial Missions, African native questions, etc.   *Recreations :* travel (has travelled extensively in Africa), shooting, fishing.   *Heir :* s. Thomas Fowell, *b.* 1889.   *Address :* Warlies, Waltham Abbey ; Colne House, Cromer.   *T.A.:* Upshire.   *Club :* Athenæum.   (*Died 31 May* 1919.)

BUZACOTT, Charles Hardie ; *b.* 3 Aug. 1835 ; *s.* of James Buzacott, Great Torrington, Devon ; *m.* 1857, Louisa, *d.* of Rev. George Whiteford, Sydney.   *Educ.:* Great Torrington. Arrived Sydney, 1852 ; left for Queensland, 1860 ; started Maryborough Chronicle, Peak Downs Telegram, converted Rockhampton Bulletin into daily ; returned to Legislative Assembly (Brisbane), 1873 ; Postmaster-General 1879-80 ; originated scheme British-India Mail Service (London to Brisbane) 1880, Divisional Boards Acts 1879-81, and signed Proclamation in Government Gazette establishing 74 local authorities ; acquired one-third interest and managed Brisbane Courier and Queenslander, 1880-94 ; started Brisbane Daily Mail, 1903 ; late senior leader - writer.   *Address :* Banca View, Garden Street, Stanthorpe, Queensland.   *T.:* Stanthorpe 61.   (*Died 19 July* 1918.)

BUZZARD, Thomas, M.D., F.R.C.P., (retired) Consulting physician National Hospital for the Paralysed and Epileptic, Queen Square ; Fellow Royal Society of Medicine ; late representative of King's College on senate University of London ; *b.* London, 24 Aug. 1831 ; *s.* of late G. Buzzard, solicitor ; *m.* Isabel (*d.* 1901), *d.* of late Joseph Wass, The Green, Lea, Derbyshire ; four *s.* two *d.*   *Educ.:* King's College School, and College, London. University Medical Scholar and Gold Medal (University London) ; Fellow King's College, London ; Vice - President, King's College Hospital. During Crimean War surgeon British Medical Staff, Ottoman Army, attached to headquarters of H.H. Omer Pasha ; was present at the siege of Sebastopol ; with the second expedition to Kertch ; and at the battle of the Tchernaia ; after the fall of Sebastopol accompanied the Turkish army to the Caucasus, and took part in the establishment

and conduct of a base hospital at Trebizonde in Asia Minor ; Crimean medal (clasp for Sebastopol), Order of Medjidie, Turkish war medal. Ex - president Clinical, Neurological, and Harveian Societies ; Foreign Corresponding Member, Société de Neurolgie, Paris.   *Publications :* numerous works on diseases of the nervous system, and contributions to medical and other journals ; With the Turkish Army in the Crimea and Asia Minor, 1915.   *Recreations :* sketching, reading.   *Address :* 74 Grosvenor Street, W.   *T.:* 64 Mayfair.   *Clubs :* Athenæum, Arts.   (*Died 1 Jan.* 1919.)

BYERS, Sir John William, Kt., *cr.* 1906 ; M.A., M.D., M.A.O. (hon. causa), R.U.I. ; Professor of Midwifery and of Diseases of Women and Children, The Queen's University of Belfast ; Consulting Physician for Diseases of Women to the Royal Victoria Hospital, Belfast, and Chairman (1915-18) of the Medical Staff ; Physician to the Belfast Maternity Hospital ; Consulting Physician to the Belfast Hospital for Sick Children ; to the Belfast Hospital for Nervous Diseases, and to the Hilden Convalescent Hospital, Belfast ; ex-Examiner in Obstetric Medicine to Royal University of Ireland ; Member of Central Midwives Board for Ireland (elected by medical practitioners resident in Ireland) ; Member of Medical Advisory Board, Babies of the Empire Society ; Member of Executive Committee of the National Association for Prevention of Infant Mortality ; *b.* Shanghai, China ; *o. c.* of late Rev. John Byres, M.A. (Glas.), missionary to China, and Margaret Byers, LL.D. University, Dublin, Founder and late Principal of Victoria College, Belfast ; *d.* of Andrew Morrow, Windsor Hill, Rathfriland ; *m.* Fanny, *d.* of Mrs. Reid, Netherleigh, Belfast ; three *s.*   *Educ.:* Royal Academical Institution ; Queen's College, Belfast (Senior Scholar in Natural Science and Senior Scholar in Medicine, Midwifery, and Medical Jurisprudence) ; Dublin ; London ; Gold Medallist and 1st of 1st class Honours at B.A. and M.A. degrees of Queen's University of Ireland ; Honours at M.D., Honorary. M.A.O. (Master of Obstetrics) of Royal Univ. of Ireland. Beginning practice in Belfast 1879, was first appointed to the Children's Hosp. ; in 1882 organised the department for Diseases of Women at the Royal Victoria Hosp. ; Hon. President of International Congress of Obstetrics and Gynecology, 1896 ; Vice-President Obstetrical Society of London, 1899-1901 ; President Ulster Medical Society, 1893-94 ; North of Ireland Branch of British Medical Association, 1900-1901 ; Belfast Branch of Irish Medical Association, 1903-9 ; Section of Obstetric Medicine and Gynecology, British Med. Assoc. Cheltenham, 1901 ; Section of Physical Education and Training in Personal Hygiene, International Congress on School Hygiene, London, 1907 ; President Belfast Literary Society, 1885-86 and 1915-16 ; Belfast Natural History and Philosophical Society, 1908-1911 ; Conference on Hygiene of Childhood, Royal Sanitary Congress, Belfast, 1911 ; President. Belfast County Borough Medical Committee, 1912-13 ; Member of Council of British Medical Association, 1902-6 ; Fellow Royal Society of Medicine ; Governor and Vice-Chairman of Campbell College, Belfast.   *Publications :* Antiseptic Midwifery ; The Prevention of Puerperal Fever in Private Practice ; A Plea for the Early Recognition and Treatment of Puerperal Fever ; Puerperal Fever, its Nature, Prevention, and Treatment ; Puerperal Eclampsia ; The Tendon-Reflex Phenomenon ; The Jaundice of Infants ; The Relationship of Chorea to Rheumatism ; Rötheln (German Measles), its Symptoms and Nosological Position ; The Prevention and Treatment of Post-Partum-Hæmorrhage ; Nineteenth - Century Progress in Obstetrics and Gynæcology ; The Early Treatment of Acute Puerperal Infection ; The Address in

Obstetric Medicine, Belfast Meeting of British Medical Association, 1909; The Evolution of Obstetric Medicine, 1912; Tetragenus Septicæmia (with Dr. Houston), 1913; on The Dialect and Folk lore of Ulster; numerous other papers. *Recreations:* literature, folk-lore. *Address:* Dreenagh House, Lower Crescent, Belfast. *T.:* 1340. *M.:* OI 1800.

(Died 20 Sept. 1920.)

BYLES, William Hounsom, late Lieut. (Horse Transport) Army Service Corps; *b.* 19 Feb. 1872. *Educ.:* St. John's Wood Art School; Royal Academy. Gained the medal for figure painting, and the second prize in the Armitage Sketching Competition at R.A. Schools, 1893; first exhibited at Royal Academy, 1894; New Gallery, 1896; has done black-and-white work for most of the London magazines and illustrated papers; had an exhibition of sketches of Morocco, Teneriffe, and Madeira at Messrs. Clifford's, 1901; paints chiefly figure pictures, horses, and portraits; photogravures of his works have been published; went to New Zealand, 1906; returned to England, 1910; joined 2nd Batt. Artists' Rifles; served in France and N. Russia. *Address:* The Cottage, Westerton, Sussex. *Club:* Langham Sketching. *(Died 12 Feb. 1925.)*

BYLES, Sir William Pollard, Kt., *cr.* 1911; M.P. (R.) N. Salford since 1906; *b.* Bradford, 13 Feb. 1839; *s.* of William Byles, founder of Bradford Observer; *m.* Sarah Anne, *o. d.* of late Stephen Unwin, Colchester, 1865. *Educ.:* private schools. M.P. Yorkshire (Shipley Division) 1892-95; strong Radical and Social Reformer. *Address:* 8 Chalcot Gardens, Hampstead, N.W. *Clubs:* National Liberal; Reform, Manchester. *(Died 15 Oct. 1917.)*

BYNG, Col. Hon. Charles Cavendish George; Colonel, retired pay; J.P. Cornwall, Devon, Hants.; *b.* 9 Feb. 1849; *s.* of 2nd Earl of Strafford; unmarried. *Educ.:* Eton. 1st Life Guards, 1867-93; retired pay, 1898; A.D.C. to G.O.C. Southern District, 1878-82; served in Sudan Expedition, 1884-85 (despatches; Brevet Lt.-Col.); Cornwall C.C. 1898-1904; Cornwall C.A. 1904-10. *Club:* Cavalry.

(Died 16 May 1918.)

BYNG, Hon. Sydney; *b.* 9 April 1844; *s.* of late Major Hon. Robert Barlow Palmer Byng (3rd *s.* of 6th Viscount Torrington), and Elizabeth Maria Lowther, *d.* of Col. J. Gwatkin; *uncle* and *heir-pres.* of 9th Viscount Torrington; *m.* 1871, Annie, *d.* of late Henry Chellingworth of Park Attwood, Worcester; three *s.* four *d.* *Address:* Branksome, Hampton Hill, Middlesex.

(Died 27 Feb. 1920.)

BYRDE, Ven Louis; Archdeacon of Kwangsi (Diocese of Kwangsi and Hunan, China), since 1914; *s.* of late Rev. F. L. Byrde, chaplain of Brislington House, Brislington, Bristol; *g.s.* of Col. Henry Byrde, J.P., of Goytrey House, Pontypool; *m.* Emma Constance, *d.* of Major George Croft; one *s.* three *d.* *Educ.:* De Aston School, Market Rasen; Bedford Grammar School; Corpus Christi College, Cambridge (Spencer scholar); Ridley Hall, Cambridge. B.A. Ordained, 1893; curate of St. Peter's, Islington, 1893-94; S.P.G. missionary, Kohala, Hawaii, 1894-98; C.M.S. missionary, diocese Victoria, S. China, 1898-1907; to Chinese students at Tokio, 1907-9; Yungchow, 1909-13; at Siangtan, 1913-14; at Yungchow since 1914. *Publication:* Editor of The Newsletter of the Kwangsi and Hunan Mission (quarterly). *Recreations:* photography, carpentry, gardening. *Address:* Yungchow, Hunan, China; 10 Oakland Road. Bedford. *(Died 11 Dec. 1917.)*

BYRNE, Donn (Brian Oswald Donn-Byrne), Irish novelist; *b.* 20 Nov. 1889; *s.* of Thomas and Jane McFarland Donn-Byrne, of Forkhill, Co. Armagh; *m.* Dorothea Mary, *o. d.* of Anthony Cadogan, Waterford; two *s.* two *d.* *Educ.:* privately; Dublin and Leipsic. Pub-

160

lications: Stories without Women; The Strangers' Banquet; The Foolish Matrons; Messer Marco Polo; The Wind Bloweth; Blind Raftery; An Untitled Story (in America as O'Malley of Shanganagh); Changeling; Hangman's House; Brother Saul. *Recreations:* racing, hunting, golf. *Address:* Coolmain Castle, Co. Cork. *Clubs:* Badminton, Savage; Worplesdon Golf; Sandown Park.

(Died 18 June 1928.)

BYRNE, Right Rev. Monsignor Frederick, Vicar-General of Adelaide, S.A., since 1874; *b.* Dublin, 22 Feb. 1834. *Educ.:* Subiaco, Italy; Jesuit College, Sevenhill, S.A. Went to Italy at the age of eighteen, and entered the Benedictine monastery at Subiaco with the intention of becoming a monk; failure of health after two years obliged him to return home; stayed a short time in Dublin, and went to West Australia, where he conducted the Catholic School of Perth; from West he went to South Australia, and entered the Jesuit College at Sevenhill; ordained Adelaide, 1860; for four years did parochial duty in that city, and was then sent to do pioneer work in the outlying districts; S.T.D. by Brief, 1880; became Administrator of the Archdiocese, 1893; created Urban Prelate by Brief, 1902. *Publications:* Wrote history of Catholic Church in South Australia from landing of first emigrants in 1836 to death of second bishop in 1864; intends to continue work; translated Vera Sapientia, a work of Thomas à Kempis. *Address:* Goodwood, South Australia.

BYRNE, Lieut.-Col. John Dillon, D.S.O. 1917; R.A.; *b.* 1875; *s.* of late W. H. Byrne, Dublin; *m.* 1919, Lena, widow of Capt. C. J. C. Barrett, Royal Scots Fusiliers. *Educ.:* Beaumont College, Windsor. Entered Army, 1900; served India, 1901-14; saw service on Indian Frontier, 1908 (Frontier medal with clasp); went to France with Brigade of Artillery from India, 1914; present at battles Neuve Chapelle, Aubers Ridge, Festubert, Loos, Somme, and Paschendaele; operations in Egypt, 1915; and Palestine, 1918 (wounded at Festubert, Loos, and Ypres); on Staff, Aug. 1915 to March 1917 (despatches three times, Bt. Lt.-Col., D.S.O., Russian Order of St. Stanislas with Swords). *Address:* 77 Cadogan Place, S.W. *Club:* United Service. *(Died 17 Feb. 1925.)*

BYRNE, Louis Campbell, D.S.O. 1919; M.C.; Lieut. The Royal Dublin Fusiliers; *s.* of Dr. B. Byrne, Rocquaine, New Malden, Surrey; unmarried. *Educ.:* Mount St. Mary's College, Chesterfield; Sandhurst. Served with the 2nd Battalion The Royal Dublin Fusiliers in France from May 1915 until the cessation of hostilities in November 1918 (despatches, D.S.O., M.C. and bar). *Recreations:* hockey, golf, tennis, swimming, the drama. *Address:* Rocquaine, New Malden, Surrey. *T.:* Malden 109. *Clubs:* Junior Army and Navy, Carlyle.

(Died 27 June 1923.)

BYRNE, Rev. Peter; C.M., LL.D.; *b.* 1840, *s.* of William Byrne, J.P., Glenconnor, Clonmel. *Educ.:* Castleknock, Dublin; Jesuit College, Rue des Postes, Paris. Vice-President of Castleknock College, 1869-82; Principal St. Patrick's Training College, Drumcondra, Dublin, 1883-1911; Hon. LL.D., R.U.I., 1909, for his educational services in Ireland; Commissioner of Education, Ireland, Endowed Schools. *Publications:* articles in the press. *Address:* St. Patrick's Training Coll., Drumcondra, Dublin.

BYRON, 9th Baron (cr. 1643), George Frederick William Byron; *b.* 27 Dec. 1855; *s.* of Frederick Byron, 2nd *s.* of 7th Baron, and Mary Jane, *d.* of Rev. W. Wescombe, Rector of Langford, Essex; *S.* uncle 1870; *m.* 1901, Lucy, *d.* of late Thomas Radmall, formerly married to Sir Theodore Brinckman, whom she divorced. *Educ.:* Harrow; Christ Church,

Oxon. Late Lieut. West Essex Militia. *Heir:* b. Rev. Hon. Frederick Ernest Charles Byron. · *Address:* Langford Grove, Maldon, Essex; Byron Cottage, Hampstead Heath, N.W. *T.:* Hampstead 584. *Clubs:* Carlton, Bachelors'.

(Died 30 Mar. 1917.)

BYRON, Edmund, J.P. for Surrey; *b.* 5 Oct. 1843; *e. s.* of Thomas and Julia Byron; *m.* Charlotte Emily, *o. d.* of late Gen. E. R. Jeffreys, of Seafield House, Ryde, I. of W. *Educ.:* Eton; Christ Church, Oxford. *Address:* Coulsdon Court, Surrey. *Club:* United University.

(Died 30 April 1921.)

C

CABLE, 1st Baron, *cr.* 1921, of Ideford, Devon; **Ernest Cable,** Kt., *cr.* 1906; senior partner Bird & Co., Calcutta, and Bird & Co., London, and F. W. Heilgers & Co., Calcutta, and F. W. Heilgers & Co., London; *b.* 1 Dec. 1859; *s.* of late G. H. Cable and Emily Pickersgill; *m.* 1888, Lilian S. Sparkes; two *d. Educ.:* privately. Career mercantile; ex-Sheriff of Calcutta; former member Viceroy's Council; ex-President Bengal Chamber of Commerce; ex-High Sheriff of Devonshire; Member The Indian Finance and Currency Commission. *Heir:* none. *Address:* 44 Grosvenor Square, W.1; *T.:* Mayfair 5528; Lindridge, Bishopsteignton, S. Devon. *T.A.:* Cablesque. *Clubs:* Carlton, Brooks's, Wellington, Ranelagh, City of London; Bengal, Calcutta.

(Died 28 Mar. 1927.)

CABLE, George Washington, author; *b.* New Orleans, La., 12 Oct. 1844; *s.* of George W. Cable, a Virginian, and Rebecca Boardman, Indiana; *m.* 1st, Louise S. Bartlett, 1869; six *d.*; 2nd, 1906, Eva C. Stevenson. *Educ.:* New Orleans Public Schools. A.M. (hon.), Doctor in Letters (hon.) Yale Univ.; Doctor in Letters (hon.) Washington and Lee University (Virginia) and Bowdoin Coll. (Maine). Member American Academy of Arts and Letters. At the age of fourteen was required, by the death of his father, to assist in the support of the family; went into commercial employment; at nineteen (1863) he entered the Confederate Army in Gen. Wirt Adams' Brigade, 4th Mississippi Cavalry, where he served until the close of the Civil War, 1865; he returned to New Orleans, re-entered counting-room employment, and with the exception of one summer spent with a State surveying party, and one season's work on the reportorial staff of the New Orleans Picayune, remained in it continuously for fourteen years, serving as accountant and cashier of a firm of cotton factors, and acting at the same time as secretary of the Finance Committee of the New Orleans Cotton Exchange; he was writing in the meantime, and in 1879 formally entered upon a literary career; in 1884 removed to New England. *Publications:* Old Creole Days, 1879; The Grandissimes, 1880; Madame Delphine, 1881; The Creoles of Louisiana, 1883; Dr. Sevier, 1884; The Silent South, 1884; Bonaventure, 1888; The Negro Question, 1888; Strange True Stories of Louisiana, 1888; John March, 1894; Strong Hearts, 1899; The Cavalier, 1901; Bylow Hill, 1902; Kincaid's Battery, 1908; Gideon's Band, 1914; The Amateur Garden, 1914; The Flower of the Chapdelaines, 1918; Lovers of Louisiana, 1918. *Recreations:* landscape gardening; chief interest outside of profession, The Northampton People's Institute, founded by him in 1887. *Address:* Northampton, Massachusetts, U.S.A. *T.A.:* Northampton. *T.:* 1200. *Clubs:* Authors, New York. *(Died 31 Jan. 1925.)*

CABORNE, Capt. Warren Frederick, C.B., 1897; R.D.; R.N.R.; *o. s.* of late Warren Caborne; *b.* 5 July 1849; *m.* 1897, Mary Lilian, *e. d.* of Sir (Thomas) William Boord, 1st Bt.;

one *s. Educ.:* private schools. Entered Mercantile Marine, 1865; joined Royal Naval Reserve as Sub-Lieut. 1879; Lieut. 1882; retired with rank of Commander, 1894; Captain (ret.) for War Services, 1918; commanded a transport during the Burmah Expedition of 1885-86; was subsequently in the Egyptian Coast Guard Service; Assessor for Formal Investigations into Shipping Casualties, 1898-1914; Inspector to Board of Trade for Marine Inquiries; Nautical Assessor to H.M. Court of Appeal, Supreme Court of Judicature, 1903-8; Nautical Assessor to H.M. Privy Council; British Nautical Assessor to Canadian Royal Commission of Inquiry into loss of Empress of Ireland, 1914; Member of Council of Royal United Service Institution since 1900, and Chairman of its Museum Committee; Deputy Chairman of Shipwrecked Mariners' Soc. 1906-20; Hon. Treasurer of St. Andrew's Waterside Church Mission to Sailors; Member of Council of the Curates' Augmentation Fund; Director of the Sailors' Home, London Docks; Hon. Commandant, British Red Cross, V.A.D., London 35; Fellow of Royal Astronomical and Royal Geographical Societies, and Fellow, ex-Secretary, and ex-Vice-President of Royal Meteorological Society. Served Naval Ordnance Department during the War. *Publications:* lectures and magazine articles upon naval reserve, mercantile marine, historical, and other subjects. *Address:* Loppington Hall, nr. Wem, Salop; The Royal United Service Institution, Whitehall, S.W.1. *Club:* Malta Union.

(Died 14 June 1924.)

CADBURY, George, J.P.; Chairman of Cadbury Brothers, Limited; Founder of Bournville Model Village; *b.* Edgbaston, 1839; father and mother both of the Society of Friends; *m.* 1st, 1871, Mary (d. 1887), *d.* of Charles Tylor, London; 2nd, Elsie Mary, *d.* of John Taylor, London. *Address:* Manor House, Northfield, Birmingham; Winds Point, Malvern. *T.A.:* Manorial, Birmingham.

(Died 24 Oct. 1922.)

CADELL, Alan, C.S.I. 1895; Indian Civil Service (retired); *b.* Edinburgh, 25 July 1841; *y. s.* of late John Cadell of Tranent, East Lothian; *m.* 1872, Florence Margaret (d. 1917), *d.* of late W. J. Wallace of Bally Courcy, Co. Wexford; two *s.* three *d. Educ.:* Edin. Academy and Univ.; (B.A.) Germany. Passed into Bengal Civil Service and went to India 1862; was successively Assistant and Joint Magistrate, Assistant Settlement Officer, Settlement Officer, Magistrate and Collector; officiated as Commissioner of Excise, and as Opium Agent; was Commissioner of Agra and Rohilkhand; member of the Board of Revenue, United Provinces; member of the Legislative Council, U.P.; acted as Lieut.-Governor, U.P., from Jan. to Nov. 1895; member of the Council of H.E. the Viceroy from Feb. to May 1896; was member of the Legislative Council of the Viceroy for two years prior to retirement in Oct. 1897. *Address:* 36 Rosary Gardens, S.W.7. *T.:* Kensington 4166. *Club:* East India United Service.

(Died 14 June 1921.)

CADELL, Colonel Thomas, C.B. 1906; V.C., Indian Army; *b.* 5 Sept. 1835; *y. s.* of late H. F. Cadell, Cockenzie, Haddingtonshire; *m.* Anna Catherine, *d.* of late P. C. Dalmahoy, Boorhouse, Haddingtonshire; two *s.* two *d. Educ.:* Edin. Academy; Grange, Sunderland; abroad. Served with 2nd European Bengal Fusiliers (now Royal Munster Fusiliers) at siege of Delhi and subsequent operations, and with 3rd Bengal Cavalry in the Oude Campaign (mentioned in despatches); commanded a Flying Column in Bundelkhand, for which received thanks of Governor-Gen. in Council; entered the Political Department, and held various political appointments in Central India and Rajputana; was Governor of the Andaman and Nicobar Islands from 1879 to 1892. V.C. for saving life on two occasions at the siege of Delhi, 1857; and C.B. for services during the Indian Mutiny. *Address:* Cockenzie House, Prestonpans, N.B. *T.A.:* Cockenzie. *Clubs:* New, United Service, Edinburgh. (*Died 6 April 1919.*)

CADENHEAD, James, R.S.A. 1921; A.R.S.A. 1902, R.S.W.; F.S.A. Scot.; artist; *b.* 1858; *s.* of late George Cadenhead, advocate in Aberdeen; *m.* 1891, Wilhelmina, *d.* of late John Wilson, South Bantaskine, Falkirk. *Educ.:* Aberdeen Grammar School and University. National Gold Medallist, 1879; student of Royal Scottish Academy, and of M. Carolus-Duran, in Paris; exhibitor of landscape, and occasionally of portraits, chiefly in Scottish Exhibitions; member Society of Scottish Artists and of Royal Scottish Society of Painters in Water-colours. *Address:* 15 Inverleith Terrace, Edinburgh. *Club:* Scottish Arts.
(*Died 22 Jan. 1927.*)

CAFE, T. Watt, R.B.A 1896, F.P.S. 1890, F.R.G.S. 1901; artist; *b.* London, 1856; *e. s.* of T. Cafe and Euphemia, *e. d.* of J. B. Watt, S.S.C., of Edinburgh. *Educ.:* King's College, London; student of Royal Academy. First exhibited at R.A. 1876; has since exhibited Wreaths of Welcome, Nydia, The Favourite, Summer Idleness, The Gift, Laurels for the Victor, An Eastern Singer (water colour), Theonoe (water colour), Hence thou Lingering Light, The Valley of the Shadow, besides other works; for some time a member of the Dudley and Cabinet Picture Society; takes great interest in all philanthropic work; holds St. John's Ambulance medallion; takes active part in boys' clubs and associations; and is a Licensed Lay Reader in the Diocese of London. *Publications:* occasional articles on art subjects in daily press. *Address:* 46 Clifton Hill, St. John's Wood, N.W. *Club:* Arts.
(*Died April 1925.*)

CAFFYN, Kathleen Mannington, novelist; (pseudonym Iota); *b.* Waterloo House, Co. Tipperary; *d.* of William de Vere Hunt and Louisa Going; *m.* late Stephen Mannington Caffyn, surgeon, writer, and inventor; one *s.* *Educ.:* at home by English and German governesses. Lived in country until about twenty. Then was trained at St. Thomas's Hospital for a year for National and Metropolitan Nursing Association; after marriage went to Australia; lived there several years and wrote occasionally for papers. *Publications:* A Yellow Aster, 1894; Children of Circumstances, 1894; A Comedy in Spasms, 1895; A Quaker Grandmother, 1896; Poor Max, 1898; Anne Mauleverer, 1899; The Minx, 1900; The Happiness of Jill, 1901; He for God Only, 1903; Patricia; a Mother, 1905; Smoke in the Flame, 1907; The Magic of May, 1908; Whoso breaketh an Hedge, 1909; Mary Mirrielees, 1916; some short stories. *Recreations:* riding, hunting, watching polo matches.
(*Died 6 Feb. 1926.*)

CAIN, Georges; homme de lettres; directeur du Musée Carnavalet et des Collections historiques de la ville de Paris; officier de la Légion d'honneur. *Educ.:* Lycée Louis le Grand, Paris. Anciennement artiste-peintre (hors concours). *Publications:* Promenades dans Paris; Les Pierres de Paris,etc.; Chroniques au Figaro, au Temps, au Journal. *Recreation:* automobile. *Address:* 15 Quai Voltaire, Paris. *Club:* Union artistique, Paris.
(*Died 4 Mar. 1919.*)

CAIN, John Cannell, D.Sc. (Manchester), D.Sc. (Tübingen), F.I.C., Editor of Chemical Society's publications since 1906; *b.* 28 Sep. 1871; *e. s.* of Rev. Thomas Cain of Stubbins, Lancashire. *Educ.:* Owens College, Manchester; Tübingen and Heidelberg Universities. Chemist to Levinstein, Limited, Manchester, 1895-1901; head of Chemistry and Physics Department, Municipal Technical School, Bury, Lancashire, 1901-4; manager and head chemist to Brooke,

Simpson, and Spiller, Ltd., London, 1904-6; Chief Chemist to British Dyes, Limited, Dalton Works, Huddersfield, 1916-17; *Publications:* (Joint) The Synthetic Dyestuffs and the Intermediate Products from which they are derived, 1905 (4th ed. 1918); Joint Editor of Jubilee of the Discovery of Mauve and of the Foundation of the Coal-Tar Colour Industry by Sir W. H. Perkin; The Chemistry and Technology of the Diazo-Compounds, 1908 (2nd ed. 1920); The Manufacture of Intermediate Products for Dyes, 1918 (2nd ed. 1919); numerous scientific papers. *Address:* 24 Aylestone Avenue, Brondesbury Park, N.W.6. *T.:* Willesden 931. *M.:* LP 4111. *Club:* Royal Societies. (*Died 31 Jan. 1921.*)

CAIN, Sir William, 1st Bt., *cr.* 1920; Kt., *cr.* 1917; J.P., Berks; *b.* 3 May 1864; *e. surv. s.* of late Robert Cain; *m.* 1886; one *s.* one *d.* *Educ.:* Winwick Priory. *Recreations:* yachting, motoring. *Heir:* *s.* Ernest, *b.* 25 Sep. 1891. *Address:* Wargrave Manor, Wargrave, Berks. *T.A.:* Wargrave, Berks. *T.:* Wargrave 44. *Clubs:* Carlton, Constitutional, Royal Thames Yacht, Royal Automobile.
(*Died 5 May 1924.*)

CAINE, William; *b.* Liverpool, 28 Aug. 1873; *s.* of William Sproston Caine and Alice, *d.* of Rev. Hugh Stowell Brown; *m.* Gordon, *d.* of Farmer R. Walker of Boston, Mass., U.S.A.; no *c.* *Educ.:* Manor House School, Clapham; Westminster School; St. Andrews University; Balliol College, Oxford. Called to Bar on leaving Oxford; abandoned it for writing after seven years. *Publications:* Pilkington; The Confectioners (with John Fairbairn); The Pursuit of the President; the Victim and the Votery; Boom; A Prisoner in Spain; The Revolt at Roskelly's; Old Enough to Know Better; The Devil in Solution; Save us from Our Friends; An Angler at Large; The New Foresters; Hoffman's Chance; The Irresistible Intruder; But She Meant Well; Bildad the Quill-Driver; Great Snakes; The Fan and other Stories; Drones; The Wife who came Alive; The Strangeness of Noel Carton; Mendoza and a Little Lady; The Author of Trixie; The Brave Little Tailor (with George Calderon); Lady Sheba's Last Stunt. *Recreations:* trout-fishing, sketching. *Address:* 16 The Pryors, East Heath Road, N.W.3. *T.:* Hampstead 5221. *Club:* Reform.
(*Died 1 Sept. 1925.*)

CAIRD, Francis M., LL.D., M.B., F.R.C.S.Ed.; Emeritus Professor of Clinical Surgery, Edinburgh; Consulting Surgeon to the Royal Infirmary. *Educ.:* Edinburgh; Strasburg, etc. Late Consulting Surgeon-Col. A.M.S., B.E.F. *Publications:* (with Mr. Cathcart) Student's Atlas of Bones and Ligaments; and a surgical handbook; contributions to medical journals. *Address:* 39 Royal Terrace, Edinburgh. *T.:* 2128.
(*Died 1 Nov. 1926.*)

CAIRD, Sir James Key, 1st Bt., *cr.* 1918; F.Z.S., LL.D. (St. Andrews); *b.* 7 Jan. 1837; *m.* 1873, Sophie (*d.* 1882), *d.* of George Gray, Perth. *Heir:* none. *Address:* 8 Roseangle, Dundee; Belmont Castle, Meigle, Perthshire. *Club:* Royal Thames Yacht. (*Died 9 Mar. 1916.*)

CAIRNES, William Plunket, Chairman Great Northern Railway (Ireland); Director of the Bank of Ireland; *b.* 1857; *s.* of late Thomas Plunket Cairnes; *m.* 1886; two *s.* *Educ.:* Cheltenham College; Trinity Hall, Cambridge. *Address:* Stameen, Drogheda. *Club:* Kildare Street, Dublin.
(*Died 13 Dec. 1925.*)

CAIRNS, John, O.B.E. 1918; M.P. (Lab.), Morpeth, since Dec. 1918; Financial Secretary of the Northumberland Miners' Association; Secretary of the Men's side of the Joint Committee in the Northumberland Coal Trade, and President of the Northumberland Aged Mine-Workers' Homes Association; Primitive Methodist; *b.* 1859; *m.* 1901, Annie Dixon. *Publications:* Money; Economics of Industry, etc. *Address:* The Drive, Gosforth, Newcastle-on-Tyne.   *(Died 23 May 1923.)*

CALDECOTT, Lt.-Col. Ernest Lawrence, D.S.O. 1916; R.G.A.; retired; *b.* 31 Aug. 1874; unmarried. *Educ.:* Rugby; Oriel College, Oxford. Entered army, 1900; Captain, 1913; Major, 1915; A.D.C. and subsequently Private Secretary to Lt.-Governor of Burma, 1907-12; served Tibet, 1908-4 (medal); European War, 1914-19 (despatches four times, D.S.O.). *Club:* Junior Naval and Military.
    (Died 17 Jan. 1927.)

CALDECOTT, Major-General Francis James, C.B. 1894; retired list Royal Artillery; *b.* 29 Apr. 1842; *s.* of late C. M. Caldecott, J.P. and D.L., of Holbrook Grange, Warwickshire; *m.* 1st, 1866, Georgina (*d.* 1901), *d.* of Hugh Watson of Keillor, Perthshire; 2nd, 1906, Jennie Beatrice (*d.* 1920), *d.* of late R. G. Clarke, formerly of Coldharbour, Wallingford. *Educ.:* Cheltenham Coll. Lieut. Bombay Artillery, 1860; Capt. Royal Artillery, 1872; Major, 1880; Brevet Lt.-Col. 1881; Col. 1885; Maj.-Gen. 1894; retired, 1897. Served Abyssinian Expedition, 1867-68 (despatches, medal); Afghan War, 1879-80 (despatches, medal with clasp, Brevet Lieut.-Col.); many years superintendent of Indian Government Gunpowder and Experimental Explosives Factory at Kirkee, and the inventor of many improvements in the manufacture of gunpowder and its ingredients. *Recreations:* cricketer and Rugby footballer in England in the sixties, since then a leading cricketer in India for many years, also sculler. *Address:* c/o Lloyd's Bank, Ltd., 6 Pall Mall, S.W.1.
    (Died 30 Jan. 1926.)

CALDER, Ven. William, Archdeacon of Auckland, N.Z., since 1901; *b.* 1848; *s.* of Rev. F. Calder, late Headmaster Chesterfield Grammar School; *m.* Lucy, 3rd *d.* of Thomas Shipton. *Educ.:* Chesterfield Grammar School; private coach. Missionary, Honolulu, 1873; Incumbent, Hamilton, Waikato, 1875; Thames, 1881; Vicar, All Saints, Auckland, 1883-1918; Canon, 1894; Bishop's Commissary, 1902-16; Commissary for Melanesia, 1904. *Recreation:* travelling. *Address:* 17 Wairer Road, Auckland, N.Z.   *(Died 10 Aug. 1923.)*

CALDWELL, Rt. Hon. James, P.C., M.P. (G.L.) Lanarkshire, Mid. 1894-1910; J.P.; Deputy Chairman Ways and Means, and Deputy Speaker, 1906-10; *b.* 1839; *s.* of F. Caldwell, Glasgow. *Educ.:* Glasgow and Edinburgh Universities. M.P., Glasgow (St. Rollox Division), 1886-92; Member of the Faculty of Procurators, Glasgow. *Address:* 12 Grosvenor Terrace, Glasgow; 107 Holland Road, Kensington, W. *Clubs:* Reform, National Liberal. *(Died 25 April 1925.)*

CALLAGHAN, Admiral of the Fleet Sir George Astley, G.C.B., *cr.* 1916; K.C.B., *cr.* 1910; G.C.V.O., *cr.* 1912; K.C.V.O., *cr.* 1909; C.V.O. 1907; C.B. 1900; First and Principal Naval A.D.C. to the King since 1914; *b.* 21 Dec. 1852; *s.* of late Frederic M. Callaghan, J.P., Co. Cork; *m.* 1876, Edith Saumarez, *d.* of Rev. Frederick Grosvenor; one *s.* three *d.* Captain, 1894; Adm. of the Fleet, 1917; commanded Hermione, Endymion, Edgar, Cæsar, Prince of Wales; commanded Naval Brigade, China, for relief of Legations, Peking, 1900; was a Naval A.D.C. to King Edward VII.; Naval Adviser to Insp.-Gen. of Fortifications, 1894-97; Rear-Admiral Channel Fleet, 1906; commanded 5th Cruiser Squadron, 1907-8; 2nd in command Mediterranean Fleet, 1908-10; commanded 2nd Division Home Fleet, 1910-11; commander-in-chief Home Fleet, 1911-14; the Nore, 1915-18; is a grand officer of the Crown of Italy; Grand Officer of the Legion of Honour. Bath King of Arms, 1919. *Address:* Avonstone House, Bathampton, Somerset. *Club:* United Service.
    (Died 23 Nov. 1920.)

CALLANDER, George Frederick William, J.P., D.L.; *e. s.* of James Henry Callander (*d.* 1851) and 2nd wife, Charlotte Edith Eleanora, *o. d.* of John George Campbell, *y. s.* of Campbell of Islay; *b.* 28 July 1848; *m.* 1876, Alice Louisa, *e. d.* and *heiress* of Col. J. C. Craigie Halkett (*d.* 1912) of Cramond, Midlothian, and Harthill, Lanarkshire. *Educ.:* Eton. Formerly Lieut. 78th Seaforth Highlanders. *Address:* Ardkinglas, Inveraray, Argyllshire; Cramond House, Midlothian; 24 Ovington Square, S.W. *T.:* Kensington 1938.   *(Died 20 Nov. 1916.)*

CALLCOTT, F. T., R.B.S.; 17 Woodstock Road, Golder's Green, N.W. *(Died May 1923.)*

CALLWELL, Major-Gen. Sir Charles Edward, K.C.B., *cr.* 1917; C.B. 1907; *b.* London, 2 Apr. 1859; *s.* of Henry Callwell of Lismeyne, Co. Antrim, and Maud, *d.* of James Martin of Ross, Co. Galway. *Educ.:* Haileybury College; Royal Military Academy; joined the Royal Artillery, 1878; Passed Staff College, 1886; Colonel, 1904; has held appointments of Staff Captain, D.A.A.G., D.A.Q.M.G., and Colonel of General Staff at Headquarters, and of Brigade Major; served Afghan War, 1880 (medal); Boer War, 1881; South African War, 1899-1902, actions of Vaal Krantz, Pieters Hill, Relief of Ladysmith, Laing's Nek, and Bergendal, commanded a mobile column in 1901-2 (two medals eight clasps, despatches twice, brevet of lieut.-colonel); was with Greek forces in Turko-Greek war, 1897; gold medallist and Chesney Memorial Medallist Royal United Service Institution; retired, 1909; Director of Military Operations at the War Office, with temporary rank of Major-General, during the first seventeen months of European War, afterwards on special service in connection with the Allies (K.C.B., Commander of the Legion of Honour, of the Italian and Belgian Orders of the Crown, and of the Redeemer, Order of the Rising Sun, 2nd Class, Order of the White Eagle, 2nd Class, Grand Officer of the Crown of Roumania, Grand Cross of St. Stanislas); Hon. Major-General, 1916. *Publications:* Small Wars; Tactics of To-day; Military Operations and Maritime Preponderance; The Tactics of Home Defence; Tirah, 1897; Service Yarns and Memories; The Dardanelles; The Life of Sir Stanley Maude, 1920; The Experiences of a Dug-Out, 1920; Stray Recollections, 1923; Contributions to Encyclopædia Britannica, etc. *Recreations:* fishing, golf. *Address:* 24 Campden House Chambers, Campden Hill, W. *Club:* United Service.   *(Died 16 May 1928.)*

CALTHROP, Sir Calthrop Guy Spencer, 1st Bt., *cr.* 1918; General Manager L. & N.W. Railway since 1914; Coal Controller of Coal Mines since 1917; *b.* Uppingham, 26 March 1870; *y. s.* of late Everard Calthrop of The Grange, Sutton, Isle of Ely; *m.* Gertrude Margaret, *d.* of late James Morten. Joined L. & N.W. Rly. 1886; Assistant to General Manager, 1901; General Supt. Caledonian Rly. 1902; General Manager, 1908; General Manager of Buenos Ayres and Pacific Rly. 1910; Lieut.-Col. Railway and Engineer Staff Corps; Lieut. of the City of London; J.P. for the County of Lanark. *Recreation:* golf. *Heir:* none. *Address:* Croxley House, Croxley Green, Herts. *Clubs:* Conservative; Royal and Ancient, St. Andrews; Jockey, Buenos Aires.
    (Died 23 Feb. 1919.)

CALVERT, Mrs. Charles; *b.* Loughborough, 1836; *d.* of James Biddles, actor; *m.* 1856, Charles A. Calvert; four *s.* two *d.* Played as a child actress at the age of seven with Mr. and Mrs. Chas. Kean; was leading lady at Theatre Royal, Southampton, in 1854, then two years' engagement at the Boston Theatre, United States; during her husband's twelve years' management of The Prince's Theatre, Man-

chester, she appeared in his fine Shakespearean productions as Miranda, Cleopatra, Hermione, Katharine of Arragon (with Mr. Phelps as Wolsey), The Queen in Richard the Third, and Chorus in Henry the Fifth; after the death of her husband she toured with Madame Ristori and Mrs. Langtry, and was then engaged for an American tour with Edwin Booth; other American tours were with Mrs. Langtry and Mary Anderson; in 1894 she appeared at the Avenue in Bernard Shaw's Arms and the Man, and then in the following 16 years fulfilled the following engagements: The Comedy (8), Haymarket (7), Garrick (2), Criterion (2), Royalty (2), Court (1), His Majesty's (2); her final appearance was as an old lady in Sir Herbert Tree's magnificent production of Henry the Eighth, 13 July 1911. *Publications:* Sixty-eight Years on the Stage; various contributions to the Daily Mail, Sporting and Dramatic, etc. *Address:* 22 York Mansions, Battersea Park, S.W.
(*Died 20 Sept. 1921.*)

CAMBAGE, Richard Hind, C.B.E. 1925; F.L.S; retired; *s.* of late J. F. Cambage; *b.* Milton, N.S.W., 1859; *m.* 1881, Fanny (*d.* 1897), *d.* of late Henry Skillman, of Booral, N.S.W.; two *s.* two *d.* *Educ.:* Public and private schools. Passed the examination for Licensed Surveyors, 1882; was a Mining Surveyor in N.S.W., 1885-1902; Chief Mining Surveyor, 1902-15; Under Secretary for Mines, N.S.W., 1916-24; President Institution Surveyors, N.S.W., 1907-9; President of Royal Society, N.S.W., 1912 and 1923, and Hon. Sec. for twelve years; President Linnean Society, N.S.W., 1924; President Australian National Research Council, Australasian Association Advancement of Science, Queen Victoria Homes for Consumptives, and Trustee Australian Museum, Sydney. *Publications:* Captain Cook's Pigeon House and Early South Coast Exploration, Sydney, 1916; Exploration beyond the Upper Nepean, Sydney, 1920; Exploration between the Wingecarribee, Shoalhaven, Macquarie and Murrumbidgee Rivers, Sydney, 1921; has contributed about fifty botanical papers to scientific societies dealing largely with the native flora and the geological formation upon which it grows, also on Acacia seedlings. *Recreations:* botanical and historical investigations. *Address:* 49 Park Road, Burwood, Sydney, N.S.W. *T.:* UJ 4355.
(*Died 28 Nov. 1928.*)

CAMBER-WILLIAMS, Rev. Robert, M.A.; Vicar of Lampeter, 1908; Canon Residentiary of St. David's Cathedral, 1899; Examining Chaplain to Bishop of St. David's, 1897; *b.* 30 Mar. 1860; *s.* of late John Williams, Madryn Villa, Chwilog, Carnarvonshire; *m.* 1888, Catherine, *d.* of late Isaiah Davies of Llandudno. *Educ.:* Keble College, Oxford (B.A.), First Class Hon. School of Theology, 1884; Ely Theological College, 1884-85. Deacon, 1885; priest, 1886; Curate of Bangor, 1885-86; Llandudno, 1886-87; Vicar of Dolwyddelan, 1887-96; Diocesan Lecturer in Church History, 1890-91; Lecturer in Theology and Parochialia at St. David's College, Lampeter, 1896-99; St. David's Diocesan Missioner, 1899-1908. *Publications:* History of the Church in Wales; sermons and pamphlets. *Recreation:* climbing.
(*Died 13 Mar. 1924.*)

CAMBON, Paul, D.C.L., LL.D. Camb., Oxon., Edin.; G.C.B., *cr.* 1917; G.C.V.O., *cr.* 1903; French Ambassador to Court of St. James's, 1898-1920; *b.* 20 Jan. 1843. Private Sec. to M. Jules Ferry; Sec. of Prefecture, Alpes-Maritimes, and Bouches-du-Rhône; Prefect of the Aube; Prefect of the Doubs; Prefect of the Nord; Minister Plenipotentiary; Resident-General to Tunis; Ambassador at Madrid and at Constantinople; Grand Cross of the Legion d'Honneur; Member of Institut Académie des sciences, morales et politiques.
164

Address: 146 Boulevard Haussmann, Paris.
(*Died 29 May 1924.*)

CAMBRIDGE, Marquess of, *cr.* 1917; **Lt.-Col. Adolphus Charles Alexander Albert Edward George Philip Louis Ladislaus Cambridge,** Earl of Eltham, *cr.* 1917; Viscount Northallerton, *cr.* 1917; G.C.B., *cr.* 1911; G.C.V.O., *cr.* 1901; K.C.V.O., *cr.* 1897; C.M.G. 1909; Personal A.D.C. to the King, 1910; Governor and Constable of Windsor Castle since 1914; *b.* Kensington Palace, 13 Aug. 1868; *e. s.* of late Duke of Teck and Princess Mary Adelaide (*d.* 1897), *d.* of 1st Duke of Cambridge; *S.* father, 1900; *m.* Lady Margaret Evelyn Grosvenor, 3rd *d.* of 1st Duke of Westminster, 1894; two *s.* two *d.* *Educ.:* Wellington; R.M.C., Sandhurst. Joined 17th (D.C.O.) Lancers, 1888; Captain 1st Life Guards, 1895; Major, 1906; Lt.-Col. 1910; Commanding with B.E.F., 1914-15; Transport Officer of Household Cavalry Regiment in South Africa, 1899-1900 (Brevet Major, Queen's medal 6 clasps); Military Attaché, Vienna, 1904-9; Assistant Military Secretary War Office, 1915. Military Secretary G.H.Q. early part of 1916; Commandeur Legion of Honour and Grand Cordon of Leopold. D.L., J.P. Salop. *Heir: s.* Earl of Eltham, *Address:* Shotton Hall, Shrewsbury. *Clubs:* Guards', Bachelors'.
(*Died 24 Oct. 1927.*)

CAMBRIDGE, Ada (Mrs. George Frederick Cross), novelist; *b.* Wiggenhall St. Germains, Norfolk, 21 Nov. 1844; *m.* 1870, Rev. G. F. Cross (*d.* 1917). *Educ.:* home. Lived in Norfolk and Cambridgeshire until her marriage, when she sailed for Australia with her husband, after which she resided in colony of Victoria, mainly in bush districts; resided in Williamstown, a port of Melbourne, 1893-1912; one *s.* one *d.* *Publications:* My Guardian, 1877; In Two Years' Time, 1879; A Mere Chance, 1882; A Marked Man, 1891; The Three Miss Kings, 1891; Not All in Vain, 1892; A Little Minx, 1893; A Marriage Ceremony, 1894; Fidelis, 1895; A Humble Enterprise, 1896; At Midnight, 1897; Materfamilias, 1898; Path and Goal, 1900; The Devastators, 1901; Thirty Years in Australia, 1903; Sisters, 1904; A Platonic Friendship, 1905; A Happy Marriage, 1906; The Eternal Feminine, 1907; The Retrospect, 1912; The Hand in the Dark, 1913. *Recreations:* chiefly reading. *Club:* Lyceum, Melbourne.
(*Died 20 July 1926.*)

CAMERON, Major Cecil Aylmer, C.B.E. 1920; D.S.O. 1916; Royal Field Artillery; *b.* 17 Sep. 1883; *s.* of Colonel Aylmer Cameron, V.C., C.B., late 72nd Highlanders, *g.s.* of Colonel William Neville Cameron, Knight of Hanover, late Grenadier Guards, and Arabella Piercy, *d.* of Piercy Henderson of Perthshire; *m.* 1909, Ruby Mary, *d.* of J. E. Shawe, late Manager Imperial Bank of India; one *s.* *Educ.:* Eastman's R.N. Academy; Bath College; R.N. Academy, Woolwich. Commission in Royal Field Artillery, 1901; was a General Staff Officer, France, 1914-18 (C.B.E., D.S.O., Chevalier de la Legion d'Honneur, Chevalier de Leopold, officer of Rising Sun, despatches four times); at War Office, 1918; served as G.S.O. Chief Intelligence Officer with General Knox's military mission to Siberia, to assist Admiral Koltchak, 1918-20); General Staff Officer at War Office, military operations Directorate, 1920; served under Irish Office. *Publication:* Articles and Reviews on Russian Affairs, etc., of which language he is a 1st Class Interpreter. *Recreations:* hunting, shooting, games, travelling. *Address:* 7 St. James Court, Buckingham Gate, S.W.1. *T.:* Victoria 2360. *Club:* Union.
(*Died 19 Aug. 1924.*)

CAMERON, Sir Charles, 1st Bt.; *cr.* 1893; M.D., M.A., LL.D.; J.P. Glasgow, Lanarkshire and Renfrewshire; *b.* Dublin, 1841; *s.* of John Cameron, newspaper proprietor, Glasgow and Dublin; *m.* 1st, 1869,

Frances Caroline (d. 1899), d. of William Mac-auley, M.D.; 2nd, 1900, Blanche, d. of late Arthur Perman; one s. one d. Educ.: Madras Coll., St. Andrews: Trin. Coll., Dublin; Medical Schools, Pa·is, Berlin, and Vienna. 1st Senior Moderator and Gold Medallist, 1862; M.B. (1st place-man), and C.M. (1st place-man), 1862. Edited N.B. Daily Mail, 1864 - 74; M.P. (R.) Glasgow, 1874-85; Coll. Div., Glasgow, 1885-95; Bridgeton Division Glasgow, 1897-1900; carried in House of Commons a resolution which led to adoption of six-penny telegrams; introduced and carried the Inebriates Acts; Acts abolishing imprisonment for debt in Scotland; conferring the Municipal Franchise on women in Scotland; securing various reforms of the Scottish Liquor Licensing Laws; Chairman of Departmental Committee on Transit of Cattle Coastwise, 1893; Chairman of Departmental Committee on Habitual Offenders, etc. (Scotland), 1894; member of Royal Commission on Liquor Licensing Laws, 1895. Publications: pamphlets on medical, social, and political subjects. Recreations: travelling, motoring. Heir: s. John Cameron, b. 26 Nov. 1903. Address: Brae-side, Englefield Green, Surrey. T.: 173 Egham. M.: P 171. Club: National Liberal.
(Died 2 Oct. 1924.)

CAMERON, Sir Charles Alexander; Kt., cr. 1885; C.B. 1899; M.D., F.R.C.P.I., D.P.H. (Camb.), Ph.D.; ex-President and Professor of Hygiene and Chemistry, R.C.S.I.; Past President, Irish Medical Graduates and Schools Association; the Royal Institute of Public Health, the Society of Public Analysts, Leinster Branch, B.M.A.; Irish Medical Association, Engineering and Scientific Association, Vice-Pres. R.D.S.; Chief Medical Officer of Health and Public Analyst, Dublin; Hon. Member of many foreign societies; Harben Gold Medallist (1902); b. Dublin, 16 July 1830; s. of Captain Ewen Cameron, Lochaber; m. 1862, Lucie (d. 1888), d. of late John Macnamara; one s. two d. Educ.: Dublin; Guernsey; Germany. Publications: Chemistry of Agriculture, 1857; Stockfeeders' Manual, 1868; Handy Book on Health, 1870; Lectures on Public Health, 1868; Handy Book on Food and Diet, 1871; Manual of Hygiene, 1874; Poems translated from the German, 1876; History of the Royal College of Surgeons, Ireland, and of Irish Medical Institutions, 1886 and 1916; Elementary Chemistry and Geology, 1896 and 1898; Reminiscences, 1913. Recreations: spends holidays attending medical and other congresses, and few leisure hours in reading light literature, and attendance at musical and Masonic dinners; is President of the Corinthian Club, which resembles the London Savage Club. Address: 27 Raglan Road, Dublin. Clubs: Savage; Friendly Brothers', Dublin. T.: 254.
(Died 27 Feb. 1921.)

CAMERON, Major-General Donald Roderick, C.M.G. 1877: late Lieut.-Col. R.A.; b. 25 Apr. 1834; m. 1869, Emma, d. of Rt. Hon. Sir Charles Tupper, 1st Bt. Entered army, 1856; Major-General, 1887; retired; Bhootan Expedition, 1864-66 (despatches, medal with clasp); owns bronze medal of Royal Humane Society for having swum out to a canoe in the canal at Ottawa, and righted it, thus saving the life of its occupant, 1871; superintended Boundary Commission Rocky Mountains, 1872-76. Address: Beaufort Cottage, Dingwall, Ross-shire.
(Died 28 Dec. 1921.)

CAMERON, His Honour Sir Douglas Colin, K.C.M.G., cr. 1914; Lt.-Governor of Manitoba since 1911; b. Hawkesbury, Ontario, 11 June 1854; s. of Colin Cameron and Annie McLaurin; m. 1880 Margaret, d. of Wm. Fergusson and Janet Candlish; two s. one d. Educ.: High School, Vanleek, Ontario; Ottawa Business College. Represented Rainy River in Ontario Legislature, 1902-8; now President Rat Portage Lumber Company, Maple Leaf Milling Company, and 11 other companies. Recreation: Horses. Address: Government House, Winnipeg. T.: Main 707. M.: Manitoba 1004. Clubs: Manitoba, Toronto, Winnipeg Hunt, St. Charles, Winnipeg. (Died 28 Nov. 1921.)

CAMERON, Sir Hector Clare, Kt., cr. 1900; C.B.E. 1918; Emeritus Professor of Clinical Surgery in the University of Glasgow; Dean of Faculties in the University of Glasgow, 1921; b. Demerara, 30 Sep. 1843; s. of Donald Cameron, Plantation Zeelugt, Demerara, sugar-planter; m. 1872, Frances (d. 1879), d. of William Hamilton Macdonald; two s. one d. Educ.: St. Andrews, Edinburgh, and Glasgow Universities, M.B. C.M. Glasgow, 1866; M.D. 1868; LL.D. St. Andrews, 1911, Glasgow, 1912; formerly President of the Faculty of Physicians and Surgeons of Glasgow, and Representative of the Faculty at the General Medical Council. Address: 18 Woodside Crescent, Glasgow.
(Died 22 Nov. 1928.)

CAMERON, Hugh, R.S.A. 1869; R.S.W. 1878; painter of Figure Subjects and Portraits; b. Edinburgh, 1835; s. of John Cameron and Isabel Armstrong; m. Jessie (d. 1895), d. of late Alexander Anderson, manufacturer, Glasgow, and widow of Alexander Allan, jun., shipowner, Glasgow; one s. three d. Studied art at Trustees' Academy under Robert Scott Lauder, A.R.S.A., 1860. Pictures: Maternal Care, Age and Infancy, A Lonely Life, The Village Well, Rummaging, Crossing the Burn, Haymakers Resting, Children of the Riviera, Funeral of a Little Girl on the Riviera, The Rivals, Pleasures of the Sea, The Timid Bather. Recreation: golf. Address: 45 George Square, Edinburgh. Clubs: Scottish Conservative, Scottish Arts, Edinburgh. (Died 15 July 1918.)

CAMERON, James Spottiswoode, M.D., C.M., B.Sc.Ed., M.R.C.S.Eng.; Medical Officer of Health, City of Leeds, 1889 - 1915; Professor of Public Health, University of Leeds; Consulting Physician, Huddersfield Infirmary; b. Dumfries, where father a Congregational minister, mother daughter of late William Spottiswoode of Glenfernate; m. Ruth, 2nd d. of William Nield, Leeds; two s. one d. Educ.: Huddersfield College; Edinburgh University. On graduating held resident appointments at Children's Hospital and Royal Infirmary, Edinburgh, and Bradford Infirmary; practised in Huddersfield; became Physician to the Infirmary; Medical Officer of Health, 1877, and Physician to Fever Hospital; President Royal Medical Society of Edinburgh; President of Literary and Scientific Society five years in Huddersfield; Secretary and President of Huddersfield Medical Society; President Leeds and West Riding Medico-chirurgical Society; of Yorks Branch of British Medical Association; President Yorks Branch of Society of M.O.H.S., later (1902) President of whole Society. Publications: Such Stuff as Dreams are made of; Is my House Healthy?; Editor of Leeds Health Manuals; Various Reports on the Health of Huddersfield and Leeds, and articles in Medical and Sanitary journals. Address: 25 Regent Park Terrace, Headingley, Leeds. (Died 30 Jan. 1918.)

CAMERON, Hon. John Donald, Judge of the Court of Appeal since 1910; b. 18 Sep. 1858; unmarried. Educ.: Woodstock College; Toronto University. Barrister, 1882; M.P. (L.), S. Winnipeg, 1892-99; Provincial Secretary, 1892-96; Attorney-General, 1896; Judge of the King's Bench, 1908. Address: Winnipeg. Club: Manitoba, Winnipeg. (Died 26 Mar. 1923.)

CAMERON, Mrs. Lovett (Emily), novelist; b. Walthamstow; m. H. Lovett Cameron; two s. Educ.: Paris; boarding-school at Putney. Publications: Juliet's Guardian, 1877; Deceivers Ever, 1878; Vera

Nevill, 1880 ; Pure Gold ; A North Country Maid ; In a Grass Country, 1885 ; Jack's Secret ; A Sister's Sin ; A Bad Lot ; A Soul Astray ; The Craze of Christina ; Bitter Fruit ; A Passing Fancy ; Midsummer Madness, etc. ; besides numerous serials and contributions to magazines and illustrated periodicals. *Recreations :* motoring, devoted to dogs. *Address :* Millbrook House, Shepperton. *T. :* Weybridge 303. *Club :* Sesame. *M. :* BL 2476.   (*Died 4 Aug. 1921.*)

CAMERON, Malcolm Graeme, K.C. 1902 ; *b.* Goderich, Ontario, 24 Feb. 1857 ; *s.* of M. C. Cameron, Lt.-Governor, N.W. Territories ; *m.* Flora, *d.* of A. B. McLean, Smiths Falls, Ontario ; one *d. Educ. :* Goderich Grammar School ; Galt Collegiate Inst. Pres. of Goderich Board of Trade for three years, and an unsuccessful candidate for the House of Commons for West Huron at the General Election of 1911. Called to Ontario Bar, 1879 ; elected to Ontario Legislature for West Huron, 1902-4 ; Mayor of Goderich for several years. *Publication :* A Treatise on the Law of Dower. *Address :* Goderich, Ontario, Canada. *T. :* 27. *Club :* Ontario Reform Club.(*Died 10 Aug. 1925.*)

CAMERON - HEAD, James, Deputy-Chairman Union Castle Line ; Director of Royal Mail Steam Packet Co., Pacific Steam Navigation Co., and Nelson Lines ; 4th *s.* of Sir Francis Somerville Head, 2nd Bart. (*d.* 1887) ; and *g. s.* of Rt. Hon. Sir Francis Bond Head, Bart., K.C.H., P.C., formerly Governor of Upper Canada; *b.* 25 April 1851; *m.* 1888, Christian Helen Jane, *e. d.* and *heiress* of Duncan Cameron of Inverailort, Inverness-shire, Black Watch (*d.* 1874) ; and *g. d.* of Sir Alex. Cameron, K.C.B., K.C.H., Rifle Brigade of Inverailort ; one *s.* one *d.* Assumed additional name of Cameron by Royal Licence, 1910 ; J.P. Inverness-shire. *Educ. :* Marlborough College. Formerly Captain Middlesex Yeomanry Cavalry and also Captain 3rd Battalion "Buffs." *Recreations :* stalking, fishing, golf, shooting. *Address :* Inverailort Castle, Inverness -shire ; 40 Lowndes Square, S.W.1 ; *T. :* 3078 Gerrard ; *M. :* LH 3288. *Club :* Carlton.

(*Died 10 Dec. 1922.*)

CAMILLERI, Rt. Rev. Giovanni M., O.S.A. Adviser to the Sacred Congregation of Bishops and Regulars (Rome) ; gia Vescovo di Gozo, ora Titolare di Modena, Prelato Domestico, Assistente al Soglio Pont. Conte ; *b.* Valetta, Malta, 15 Mar. 1843. *Educ. :* Government Elementary Schools, private tuition, and Lyceum, Valetta. Entered the Augustinian Order, 1861 ; elevated to sacerdotal dignity, 1867 ; Lecturer and subsequently Regent of Studies ; Doctor in Theology ; Provincial at Malta and Gozo, 1880 ; recalled to Rome to teach Theology at the International College of the Order, 1883. *Publications :* Giudizi dello storico Rohrbacher sopra alcuni punti della dottrina di S. Agostino ; 8-vol. di emilie (in Maltese) nelle feste dell' Epifania, di Pasqua, di Pentecoste, della Visitazione di M.SS., del, Assunz. di M.SS. ; di tutti i Santi, del Natale di N.S.Q.C., ecc. ; 1st Diocesan Synod, 1904. *Address :* Conv. di S. Agostino, Notabile, Malta.

CAMPBELL, Sir Archibald Augustus Ava, 4th Bt., *cr.* 1831 ; *s.* of 3rd Bt. and Henrietta Ellen, *d.* of Rev. E. H. Uthwatt ; *b.* 5 Dec. 1879 ; *S.* father, 1913. *Heir : b.* William Andrewes Ava ; *b.* 11 Dec. 1880. *Address :* Gibliston, Colinsburgh, Fife.

(*Died 10 May 1916.*)

CAMPBELL, Right Hon. Lady Archibald (of Argyll) ; *d.* of late James Callander of Ardkinglas and Craigforth, and of late Hon. Mrs. Callander (whose portrait hangs in the King of Bavaria's Gallery of Beauty at Munich) ; ward of George, 8th Duke of Argyll ; *m.* 1869, Lord Archibald Campbell (*d.* 1913),

166

2nd *s.* of 8th Duke ; one *s.* (10th Duke), one *d.* Originator of Pastoral Plays in Europe —As You Like It, 1884-1885 (played part of Orlando) ; Faithful Shepherdesse, 1885 (played Shepherd Perigot) ; produced 1886, Fair Rosamund, specially adapted for her from Becket by the late E. W. Godwin, F.S.A. (played Rosamund) ; 1887, played Oberon to Miss Kate Vaughan's Titania (Midsummer Night's Dream) in garden of Pope's villa, Twickenham ; played the Pierrot in Le Baiser of Théodore de Banville, set as a pastoral by herself, 1889 ; author and manager of Tam Lin, Scottish Ballad play, produced at Theatre Royal, Edinburgh, 1899, appearing herself in title-rôle ; dramatised Cap and Bells, Poem by W. B. Yeats, staged it and played it as a monologue at Berkeley Theatre, Glasgow, in aid of the Highland Fair, Oct. 1907. *Publications :* Rainbow Music, treating of philosophy of harmony in colour - grouping : and several articles in leading periodicals on the Drama, West Highland Lore and Occultism, etc. *Recreations :* bicycling, skating. *Address :* Coombe Hill Farm, Norbiton, Kingston-on-Thames. *T. :* Kingston 538.   (*Died July 1925.*)

CAMPBELL, Maj. - Gen. Archibald Edwards, Indian Army ; *b.* 18 Mar. 1834 ; *m.* 1860, Lucy (*d.* 1915), *d.* of Capt. Cardew, R.E. Entered army, 1851 ; Maj.-Gen., 1892 ; retired list, 1892 ; served Sonthal Rebellion, 1855-56 ; Indian Mutiny, 1857 - 58 (severely wounded, medal with clasp). *Address :* Poltair, Seymour Avenue, Mannamead, Plymouth.

(*Died 9 April 1921.*)

CAMPBELL, Rt. Rev. Archibald Ean, D.D. ; Bishop of Glasgow and Galloway since 1904 ; *b.* 1 June 1856 ; *s.* of Col. Walter Campbell of Skipness, Argyll (author of The Old Forest Ranger), and Anna Henrietta, *d.* of Col. Robert Loring ; *m.* 1885, Hon. Helen Anna, *d.* of 8th Viscount Midleton ; one *s.* three *d. Educ. :* King William's Coll., Isle of Man ; Clare Coll., Camb. (Foundation Scholar); sen. optime Mathematical Tripos; B.A. 1880; M.A. 1883; D.D. 1904; D.C.L. 1910; Cuddesdon Coll. 1880-81 ; Curate of Aberdare, South Wales, 1881-85 ; Rector of Castle Rising, Norfolk, 1885-91 ; Vicar of All Souls (Hook Memorial), Leeds, 1891 - 1901 ; Acting Chaplain, Leeds Rifles ; Provost of St. Ninian's Cathedral, Perth, 1901-1904. Commissary to Bishop, St. John's, Kaffraria, 1902-4 ; Mission of Help to South Africa, 1903 ; Select Preacher, Cambridge, 1908 ; Church Commissioner to South Africa, 1919. *Address :* Bishop's House, Woodside Terrace, Glasgow. *T. :* Charing 2. (*Died 18 April 1921.*)

CAMPBELL, Lt.-Col. Charles Lionel Kirwan, C.M.G. 1917 ; 16th Lancers ; Brig.-General Commanding 5th Cavalry Brigade since Oct. 1915; *b.* 1 Nov. 1873. *Educ. :* Cheam School ; Eton ; Cheltenham College ; Sandhurst. Entered Army, 1895 ; Capt. 1900 ; Major, 1909. N.W. Frontier, India, 1897-98 (medal with clasp) ; Tirah, 1897-98 (clasp) ; S. Africa, 1900-1 (despatches, Queen's medal, 4 clasps) ; served European War, 1914-17 (despatches twice, Bt. Lt.-Col., C.M.G.) *Recreations :* hunting, shooting, fishing, polo. *Clubs :* Cavalry, United Service.   (*Died 31 Mar. 1918.*)

CAMPBELL, Lt.-Col. Charles Ferguson, C.I.E. 1906 ; O.B.E. 1920 ; 11th King Edward's Own Lancers, Probyn's Horse ; *s.* of J. Scarlett Campbell ; *m.* 1908, Mrs. Muirhead Gould of Bredisholm, Lanarkshire, *d.* of R. P. Steuart-Muirhead and *widow* of Colonel Arthur Gould (Queen's Bays). *Educ. :* Haileybury; Sandhurst. Served N.W. Frontier of India, 1897-1898 ; operations on the Samana, in the Kurram Valley, 1898 (medal with two clasps) ; Tirah, 1897-98 ; operations against the Khani-Khel Chamkannis (clasp) ; with Indian officers' escort, Diamond Jubilee ; A.D.C. to Prince of Wales during Indian tour, 1905 - 6 ; Extra Equerry to Prince of Wales, 1906 ; Extra

Equerry to the King, 1910 ; Member of The Honourable Corps of Gentlemen-at-Arms, 1912 ; Clerk of the Cheque and Adjutant, 1923. *Address:* Littlebourne, Twyford, Winchester, Hants ; *T.:* Twyford 18 ; 24 St. Edmund's Terrace, N.W.8 ; *T.:* Hampstead 9042 ; Engine Court, St. James's Palace, S.W.1 ; *T.:* Gerrard 4739. *Club:* Naval and Military.

(*Died 1 Aug. 1925.*)

CAMPBELL, Sir Charles Ralph, 11th Bt.; *cr.* 1628; *b.* 24 Sept. 1850; *s.* of 8th Bt. and Charlotte, *d.* of Louis Henry Ferrier; *S. bro.,* 1901 ; *m.* 1878, Sara, *d.* of Hon. William Robinson, of Cheviot Hills, N.Z.; three *s. Educ.:* Edinburgh Academy. Went to New Zealand, 1874 ; engaged in sheep-farming. *Heir : s.* Captain Charles Ralph Campbell, Lieut. 2nd Life Guards [*b.* 14 Dec. 1881 ; *m.* 1915, Nancy Sarah, *o. d.* of late Edward Chapman, Canterbury, New Zealand]. *Address:* Cheviot Hills, New Zealand. *Clubs:* Conservative, Bath.

(*Died 4 Oct. 1919.*)

CAMPBELL, Charles William, C.M.G. 1901 ; F.R.Stat.S. ; F.R.G.S. ; *b.* 21 Oct. 1861 ; *m.* 1903, Violet Gertrude, *y. d.* of Mrs. Coutts of Well House, Banstead ; one *s.* five *d.* Student Interpreter, China, 1884 ; 2nd Class Assistant, 1891 ; 1st Class, 1897 ; H.M.'s Vice-Consul, Shanghai, 1899 - 1900 ; attached to Admiral Seymour's force in China (despatches) ; Acting Consul - General, Tientsin, 1900 - 1 ; Acting Chinese Secretary, Pekin, 1901-2, and 1905-6 ; Acting Consul-General, Canton, 1903-4 ; Cheng-Tu, 1905 ; Consul at Wuchow, 1900-6 ; Chinese Secretary, Pekin, 1906-11. *Club:* Oriental.

(*Died 27 May 1927.*)

CAMPBELL, Capt. Claude Henry, D.S.O. 1915 ; Queen's Own Cameron Highlanders ; *b.* 4 Dec. 1878. Entered army, 1899 ; Captain, 1907 ; Adjutant Volunteers, 1908 ; T.F. 1908 ; served European War, 1914-15 (D.S.O.).

(*Died 15 Mar. 1916.*)

CAMPBELL, Ven. Colin Arthur Fitzgerald, M.A. ; Archdeacon of Wisbech since 1915 ; Rector of Feltwell, Norfolk, since 1912 ; *b.* Woolwich, 17 June 1863 ; 6th *s.* of Col. Sir Edward Campbell, 2nd Bart., and Georgiana Charlotte Theophila, 2nd *d.* of Sir Theophilus Metcalfe, 4th Bart. *Educ. :* Ashbocking, Tonbridge School ; Clare College, Cambridge. Read theology at Llandaff with Dean Vaughan ; Assistant - master, Spondon School, 1885-9 ; Private Secretary to Governor of South Australia (Earl of Kintore), 1889-1902 ; Clerk of the Executive Council, South Australia, 1890-1902 ; Senior Domestic Chaplain to Archbishop (Benson) of Canterbury, 1894 ; Private Chaplain to Lord Henniker, Governor of the Isle of Man, 1896 ; Curate of Hartlebury, Worcester, 1893-4 ; Rector of Thornham, Magnacum-Parva, 1895-1902 ; Street, Somerset, 1902-8 ; Worlingworth, 1908-12 ; Rural Dean of Hoxne, 1909-12. *Recreations :* cricket and music. *Address :* The Rectory, Feltwell, Norfolk. *Club:* Royal Societies. (*Died 6 Jan. 1916.*)

CAMPBELL, C. S., K.C. *Address:* 205 St. James Street, Montreal. (*Died 12 June 1923.*)

CAMPBELL, Douglas Graham, C.M.G. 1912 ; British Adviser to Government of Johore ; *y. s.* of late John Campbell ; *b.* 1867 ; *m.* 1st, Ethel Mary (*d.* 1903), *d.* of late Villiars Taylor, I.C.S. ; 2nd, Mary Abinda, *d.* of late C. E. Spooner, C.M.G. ; two *d.* Joined Malay States Government Service, 1883 ; Land Officer, 1885 ; District Officer, 1890 ; secretary to Resident, 1901 ; Resident of Negri Sembilan, 1904 ; Special Mission to Brunei, 1905 ; General Adviser, Johore, 1910. *Recreation:* motoring. *Address:* Johore, *via* Singapore. *Clubs:* Junior Carlton, Sports. (*Died 25 June 1918.*)

CAMPBELL (of Barcaldine), **Sir Duncan Alexander Dundas,** 3rd Bt. *cr.* 1831 ; C.V.O. 1909 ; J.P. ; F.S.A. Scot., F.R.G.S. ;

Hereditary Keeper of Barcaldine Castle, which ancient Baronial Castle he has restored ; also the Parish Church of Bowers Gifford and its ancient bells, 1399-1413 ; *b.* 4 Dec. 1856 ; *S.* father, 1880. Gentleman Usher of the Green Rod, 1884-95 ; Secretary to the Order of the Thistle, 1895 ; revised and reprinted the Statutes of the Order of the Thistle, 1905 ; and additional Statutes, 1914 ; assisted Dr. Shaw in his The Knights of England, 2 vols. 1905 ; Carrick Pursuivant of Arms, 1909. Formerly Capt. 3rd Batt. Black Watch ; 3rd and 4th Batts. Highland Light Infantry ; retired as Hon. Major ; member of Royal Company of Archers, King's Bodyguard of Scotland ; Queen Victoria's Diamond Jubilee Medal, 1897 ; walked officially in Procession in Westminster Abbey at Coronation of King Edward VII. and Queen Alexandra, 9 Aug. 1902 ; silver Coronation Medal ; also at the Coronation of King George V. and Queen Mary, 22 June 1911 ; silver Coronation Medal. *Publications:* The Clan Campbell, Extracts relating to Campbells in Sheriff Court Books of Argyll at Inveraray, 1689-1784, 1913 ; Abstracts relating to Clan Campbell in Sheriff Court Books of Perthshire, vol. ii. of Series, 1914 ; Abstracts relating to Campbells in Sheriff Court Books of Argyll, vol. iii. of Series, 1915 ; vol. iv., 1916 ; Ducal House of Argyll, Houses, Cadets, etc. vol. v., 1917 ; Unprinted Records of Ayrshire, relating to Clan Campbell, vol. vi., 1918 ; vol. vii., 1920 ; Campbells in some Parish Registers of Counties Argyll and Perth ; vol. viii. Books of Council and Session Acts and Decrets, 1500-1650, 1922 ; vol. ix., Records of Clan Campbell in the Military Service of the H.E.I.C.S., 1600-1858, 1924. *Recreations:* visiting scenes of historical and antiquarian interest, churches, etc. *Heir :* first cousin, Alexander William Dennistoun, Lieut.-Col. (retired) Indian Staff Corps, *b.* 8 Sep. 1848. *Address:* 16 Ridgway Place, Wimbledon, S.W. *Clubs:* Junior United Service ; Royal Highland Yacht. Oban. (*Died 27 May 1926.*)

CAMPBELL, Capt. Duncan Frederick, D.S.O. 1900 ; Lancashire Fusiliers ; transferred to Black Watch, 1908 ; retired, 1910 ; Capt. 3rd Batt. (Reserve) Black Watch since 1910 ; M.P. (U.) North Ayr, since 1911 ; *b.* 28 April 1876. Served South Africa, 1899-1901 (wounded, despatches, Queen's medal, six clasps, D.S.O.) ; European War, 1914 - 15 (despatches). Contested (C.) Paisley, 1910 ; North Ayrshire, Dec. 1910. *Address:* Wardhead House, Stewarton, Ayrshire. (*Died 4 Sept. 1916.*)

CAMPBELL, Capt. Duncan Lorn, D.S.O. 1901 ; late 3rd Batt. Welsh Regt. ; *b.* 12 June 1881 ; *s.* of late Maj.-General Lorn Campbell, C.B. *Educ. :* United Services College, Westward Ho ! Served South Africa, 1900-1 (despatches, D.S.O.). *Decorated* for defence of train at Alkmaar with four men against fifty Boers at close quarters ; served European War, 1914-17. (*Died 1 Feb. 1923.*)

CAMPBELL, Major Hon. Eric Octavius, D.S.O. 1915 ; Seaforth Highlanders (Ross-shire Buffs) ; Brigade Major ; *b.* 3 Dec. 1885 ; 6th *s.* of 3rd Earl Cawdor and Edith Georgiana, *e. d.* of Christopher Turnor of Stoke Rochford ; unmarried. *Educ. :* Eton. Entered army, 1905 ; Captain, 1914 ; served European War, 1914-15 (wounded ; Bt.-Major, D.S.O.). *Address:* c/o Edith, Lady Cawdor, Golden Grove, Carmarthenshire, R.S.O.

(*Died 4 June 1918.*)

CAMPBELL, Colonel Frederick, C.B. 1902 ; V.D. ; J.P. ; late Col. and Hon. Col. 1st Argyll and Bute Royal Garrison Artillery (Volunteers) ; *b.* 15 June 1843 ; 4th *s.* of Sir John Campbell, 8th Bt. ; *m.* 1869, Emilie, *e. d.* of late Donald Maclaine of Lochbuie, N.B. ; six *s.* two *d.* Served New Zealand (medal and clasp). *Address:* Airds, Sydenham Hill, S.E. *Club:* Naval and Military. (*Died 13 Sept. 1926.*)

CAMPBELL, Brigadier-Gen. George Polding, C.I.E., C.B.E. (late Royal Engrs.); retired list; *b.* 1864; *s.* of late Edward Campbell, J.P., of Wanstead and Granbalang, N.S. Wales; *m.* 1891. Frances Georgina, *d.* of Rev. C. B. Fendall of Woodcote House, Windlesham, Surrey; four *s.* four *d. Educ.:* Sydney University (B.A.); S.M.E., Chatham. Lieut. R.E., 1886; Capt., 1896; Major, 1904; Lieut-Col., 1913; Brevet. Col., 1916; Substantive-Colonel, 1918; retired as Brig.-Gen., 1921; served N.W.F., India, 1897-98 (medal and clasp); European War, 1914-19 (despatches 3 times, Brevet-Col., C.B.E.); Afghan War, 1919; Waziristan Expedition, 1919-20 (despatches, C.I.E.). *Publications:* The Engineer's Share in the Bacteriological Treatment of Sewage; many articles in newspapers, etc. *Recreations:* lawn-tennis and golf. *Address:* Home Cottage, Old Farnham Lane, Farnham. *T.:* Farnham 390. *Club:* Junior Army and Navy. *(Died 8 Sept. 1928.)*

CAMPBELL, General Gunning Morehead, C.B. 1919; Commandant Royal Marine Artillery; *s.* of Capt. George John Gunning Campbell, Madras Horse Artillery; *m.* 1887, Charlotte Sophia, *y. d.* of Rev. G. P. Viner; one *s. Educ.:* Wellington; Royal Naval College, Greenwich. Joined R.M. Artillery, 1880; Captain, 1891; Major, 1898; Lt.-Col., 1905; 2nd Commandant, 1914; Colonel Commandant, 1917; Adjutant, R.M.A., 1889-94; Forfar and Kincardine Artillery, 1897-1901; Inspector R.N. and R.M. Recruiting, 1914-17; served Soudan, 1884 (medal and clasp and Khedive's Bronze Star, King Edward VII. Coronation medal); served Ostend and Dunkirk, 1914 (1914 Star, Victory and Allied medals); Brig.-Gen., May 1916; A.D.C. to the King, Sep. 1917; G.S.P., 1917. *Recreation:* shooting. *Address:* Whitehaugh, Bishopstoke, Hants. *Club:* Caledonian. *(Died 29 Nov. 1920.)*

CAMPBELL, Lt.-Col. Harry La Trobe, D.S.O. 1916; M.I.M.E.; C.R.E. of a Division; Hon. Lieut. in Army; *b.* July 1881; *s.* of late Henry Hunter Campbell, St. Helen's; *m.* 1906, Daisy Louise, *d.* of late Samuel Iles (Councillor), Cotham Lawn, Bristol; one *s.* two *d. Educ.:* Chester. Served South African War in R.E. 1901-2 (Queen's medal, 4 clasps); joined 2nd Lancs. (Vols.) R.E. 1899; Adjutant to West Lancs. Div. R.E. 1913-14; served European War, 1914-18 (despatches, D.S.O., Bt. Lt.-Col.); Mining Engineer and Surveyor; senior partner in firm of Campbell & Son, 11 Old Hall Street, Liverpool. *Address:* Cotham, Huyton, Nr. Liverpool.

CAMPBELL, Sir Henry, Kt.; *cr.* 1921; Town Clerk of Dublin; *b.* 1856; *m.* 1st, 1879, Jenny (*d.* 1906), *d.* of R. Brewis; 2nd, Alice Harbottle, *d.* of late R. Fogan. *Address:* Greenwood Park, Newry, Co. Down.

(Died 6 Mar. 1924.)

CAMPBELL, Hon. Capt. Hon. Ivan, D.L.; General Staff Officer, 3rd grade; 2nd *s.* of 6th Earl and *heir pres.* to 1st Marquess of Breadalbane; *b.* 17 Nov. 1859; *m.* Lady Margaret Elizabeth Diana Agar, *d.* of 3rd Earl of Normanton; one *s. Educ.:* Eton. Late 3rd Batt. Royal Scots and Queen's Own Cameron Highlanders; served Egypt, 1882, including Tel-el-Kebir; S. Africa, 1900-1; one of H.M.'s Hon. Corps of Gentlemen-at-Arms. *Clubs:* Naval and Military, Wellington; Royal Dorset Yacht. *(Died 16 Mar. 1917.)*

CAMPBELL, Sir James, Kt., *cr.* 1918; J.P., D.L., LL.D. (Aberdeen), 1903; a Governor of Technical College, Aberdeen; Member of Aberdeen Provincial Committee for Training of Teachers; Member of General Committee of Church of Scotland; *b.* 21 Apr. 1842; *y. s.* of Donald Campbell and Catherine M'Laren; *m.* 1st, 1873, Charlotte Rose (*d.* 1898), *y. d.* of Capt. Alex. Robertson, 33rd Regiment; 2nd, 1906, Grace Campbell, *y.d.* of Ewan Camp-

bell Cameron of Garrows, Perthshire. *Educ.:* Perth Academy; Edinburgh. Trained a civil engineer; appointed land agent for Sir John Heron Maxwell of Springkell, 1873; for H. G. Murray Stewart of Cally and Broughton, 1877; and for Seafield Estates at Cullen House, 1888; gave £4000 to build Infectious Diseases Hosp. at Portsoy, 1903; £1000 to provide Parish Home for Poor of Cullen, 1912; and £3000 to establish Agricultural Bursaries at University of Aberdeen, 1914; Convener of the County of Banff, 1896-1913; Chairman of the County of Banff Road Board, 1890-1913; of County Finance Committee, 1896-1913; Chairman of North of Scotland College of Agriculture, 1911-23; Governor of the Dick Bequest Trust for Higher Education in the Counties of Aberdeen, Banff, and Moray, 1892-1923; holds Coronation medals, 1902 and 1911; Freeman of Royal Burgh of Cullen, 1912. *Recreations:* travelling, shooting, curling. *Address:* 14 Douglas Crescent, Edinburgh; *T.:* Central, Edinburgh, 4848; Garrows, Dunkeld. *Clubs:* Conservative, Edinburgh; University, Aberdeen.

(Died 14 Jan. 1925.)

CAMPBELL, Lieut.-Col. John, D.L.; J.P.; 8th Argyll and Sutherland Highlanders (T.F.), retired; granted rank, on retirement from T.F. Reserve, 1922, of Lt.-Col. Regular Army Reserve; *e. s.* of late John Campbell and Margaret, *o. d.* of late Thomas Lloyd, Leghorn, Italy; *b.* 1872; *m.* 1913, Marion Isabel, *e. d.* of Lt.-Col. Sir Edward Durand, Bart., C.B.; one *d. Educ.:* Harrow; Sandhurst. Capt. retired, late Argyll and Sutherland Highlanders. *Address:* Kilberry, Argyllshire. *Clubs:* Naval and Military; New, Edinburgh.

(Died 7 Feb. 1928.)

CAMPBELL, John Edward, M.A., F.R.S.; Hon. D.Sc. Queen's University of Belfast; Fellow and Tutor Hertford College; Lecturer, Merton College; *b.* 1862; *s.* of late John Campbell, M.D., of Lisburn, Co. Antrim; *m.* Sarah, *d.* of Joseph Hardman. *Educ.:* Methodist College, Belfast; Queen's College, Belfast; Hertford College, Oxford. *Publications:* Introductory Treatise on Lie's Theory of Continuous Groups; various contributions to mathematical journals and societies. *Address:* Hertford College, Oxford. *(Died 1 Oct. 1924.)*

CAMPBELL, Brig.-Gen. John Hasluck, C.V.O. 1909. *Educ.:* Trinity College, Glenalmond; Edinburgh University; Sandhurst. Joined 93rd Sutherland Highlanders, 1876; served N.W. Frontier of India, 1897-1898 (medal with clasp); commanded 2nd Battalion Argyll and Sutherland Highlanders, 1809-1903; commanded Eastern Co.'s Grouped Regimental District, 1906, and the East Anglian Division Territorial Force from 1908, with the rank of Brigadier-General; retired from the Army, 1910. *Address:* Inverardoch, Doune, Perthshire. *Clubs:* Naval and Military, Wellington; New, Edinburgh.

(Died 29 Jan. 1921.)

CAMPBELL, Sir John (Stratheden), K.C.S.I., *cr.* 1918; C.S.I. 1909; C.I.E. 1907; *b.* 1863; *m.* 1st, 1884, Honor (*d.* 1922), *o. d.* of late Maj.-Gen. Sir Oliver R. Newmarch, K.C.S.I.; 2nd, 1923, Helen Colquhoun, *widow* of C. T. B. King. *Educ.:* Rugby; Balliol Coll., Oxford. Entered I.C.S., 1881; Joint Magistrate, 1890; Deputy Commissioner, 1896; Magistrate and Collector, 1898; Commissioner United Provinces, India, 1906; Board of Revenue, U.P., 1913; retired, 1918. *Address:* 92 Regent's Park Road, N.W.1. *Club:* Oriental. *(Died 16 Aug. 1928.)*

CAMPBELL, Senator Hon. Sir Marshall, Kt., *cr.* 1916; J.P.; Natal Senator Union Parliament; *b.* 10 July 1849; *s.* of late William Campbell (sugar planter), Muckle Neuk, Victoria County, Natal; *m.* Ellen, *d.* of John C. Blamey, Mt. Prospect, Natal; two *s.* two *d. Educ.:* privately, Natal.

Sugar planter; managing director of Natal Estates Co., Ltd., etc., and director of many other companies; was M.L.C. when Natal was Crown Colony; nominated Legislative Council under Responsible Government; appointed Natal Commissioner in the Natal-Transvaal Boundary Delimitation Commission after Boer War; one of two Natal Commissioners on Lord Milner South African Native Affairs Commission. *Recreations:* shooting, fishing, and travel. *Address:* Muckle Neuk, Marriott Road, Berea, Durban. *Clubs:* Durban, Natal; Royal Yacht. *(Died 9 Dec. 1918.)*

CAMPBELL, Lieut.-Col. Montagu Douglas, D.S.O. 1901; J.P. County Renfrew; 4th Batt. Argyll and Sutherland Highlanders; *b.* 16 Oct. 1852; *y. s.* of Archibald Campbell of Mains and Blythswood. Served South Africa (despatches, Queen's medal, four clasps, D.S.O.). *Address:* 34 Abercromby Place, Edinburgh. *Clubs:* Boodle's, Bachelors': New, Edinburgh. *(Died 12 Feb. 1916.)*

CAMPBELL, Richard Hamilton, C.I.E. 1912; late Indian Civil Service; Lt.-Col. Bangalore Rifle Volunteers; Private Secretary to H.H. the Maharajah of Mysore, 1909-13; *s.* of late Major-General J. P. W. Campbell, Indian Staff Corps; *g. s.* of late Sir Duncan Campbell, Baronet of Barcaldine, Glenorchy; *m.* 1889; Ellen Emily Harington, *d.* of Henry Gomperz, Madras; two *s.* one *d. Educ.:* Cheltenham College. Assistant Collector and Magistrate, 1885-90; Under Secretary to the Government of Madras, 1891-92; Joint Magistrate, 1893-96; Private Secretary to the Governor of Madras, 1902; District Magistrate, 1896-1909; retired, 1913. *Recreations:* cricket, racquets, lawn tennis, riding, volunteering. *Clubs:* East India United Service; Madras.
(Died 19 Mar. 1923.)

CAMPBELL, Maj.-Gen. Robert Dallas, Indian Army; *b.* 27 June 1832. Entered army, 1850; Maj.-Gen., 1891; unemployed list, 1890; served Sonthal Rebellion, 1855-56; Indian Mutiny, 1857 (medal); Bhootan Expedition, 1865-66 (medal with clasp); Afghan War, 1879-80 (despatches, medal); Mahsud Waziri Expedition, 1881 (despatches). *(Died 12 Feb. 1916.)*

CAMPBELL, Colonel Sir Robert Neil, K.C.M.G., *cr.* 1917; C.B. 1912; C.I.E. 1909; M.B.; Indian Medical Service, retired; Kaiser-i-Hind Gold Medal, 1900; Knight of Grace of St. John of Jerusalem, 1914; Inspector-General Civil Hospitals and Prisons, Assam, 1912-14; retired, 1914; *b.* 24 Sep. 1854; *m.* 1881, Ethel Bensley; two *d. Educ.:* Edinburgh Institution; Edin. University. Served Naga Hills Expedition, 1879-80 (despatches, medal with clasp); Akha, 1883-84 (despatches); Officer Commanding Pavilion Military Hospital, and York Place Hospital, Brighton. *Address:* 29 Medina Villas, Hove, Sussex. *(Died 18 Feb. 1928.)*

CAMPBELL, Samuel George, C.M.G. 1924; J.P.; *b.* 1841; *s.* of late William Campbell, Carndonagh, Donegal; *m.* Margaret Wylie, *d.* of late James Dunnachie, Glenboig, Scotland. *Educ.:* Bishop's College, Natal; Edinburgh University. M.D., C.M., Honours; M.R.C.S., F.R.C.S.E.; D.P.H. Berlin and Vienna Universities. Medical Officer of Health Durban, 1891-99; President of South African Medical Conference, 1919; served S. Africa, 1899-1902; Zululand Native Rebellion, 1906 (despatches). *Address:* 28 Musgrave Road, Durban, S. Africa. *Club:* Durban.
(Died 13 Mar. 1926.)

CAMPBELL, Rev. Canon Stephen; Canon Residentiary Jerusalem since 1909. *Educ.:* Trinity College, Dublin. Ordained, 1867; Curate of Scissett, Yorks, 1867-69; St. Paul, Clapham, 1869-73; Rector of All Saints, Eglantine, Lisburne, 1873-82; Minor Canon of Down, 1882-85; Prebendary of Dunsford, 1885-89;

Rector of Hollymount, 1882-89; Vicar of St. John, Enfield, 1889-91. *Address:* Maydore Mattock Lâne. Ealing, W. *(Died 31 Mar. 1918.)*

CAMPBELL, Capt. Sir Walter Douglas Somerset, K.C.V.O., *cr.* 1910; C.V.O. 1901; late Deputy Ranger, Windsor Park, resigned 1916; Groom-in-Waiting to the King since 1901; *b.* 1853; *s.* of Walter Frederick Campbell of Islay; *m.* 1881, Marie Louise, *d.* of J. Guild; one *s.* one *d. Educ.:* Charterhouse. Groom-in-Waiting to Queen Victoria, 1880-1901; to King Edward, 1901-10; and to King George V., 1910. Holds Grand Cross Order of Franz Josef. *Address:* 64 Belgrave Road, S.W. *Clubs:* Naval and Military, 'Travellers'. *(Died 17 April 1919.)*

CAMPBELL, Col. William Kentigern Hamilton, D.S.O. 1902; late O.C. 6th I.Y. South Africa, 1900-2; *b.* 30 Sep. 1865; *e. s.* of late C. V. Hamilton-Campbell, and Mary, *o. d.* of Samuel Randall, of Orford, Suffolk; *m.* 1908, Edith Agnes, *d.* of Robert Angus, Ladykirk, Markton, Ayrshire; one *s.* two *d.* Lt.-Col. commanding Ayrshire Yeo.; Hon. Lt.-Col. in the army; J.P. and D.L. for Ayrshire; C.C. for Mauchline. *Address:* Netherplace, Mauchline, N.B. *(Died 22 Nov. 1917.)*

CAMPBELL, General Sir William, K.C.B., *cr.* 1911; C.B. 1904; *b.* 7 Feb. 1847; *m.* Frances Maria, *e. d.* of Capt. W. Butler Fellowes, 1887; two *s.* one *d.* Ashanti War, 1873-74 (medal); Egyptian War, 1882 (medal, clasp, Khedive's star, despatches, Bt.-Maj.); Jubilee medal, 1897; Coronation medal, 1901; A.D.C. to Queen Victoria, 1893-1901; to King Edward VII., 1901-4; Col. Comdt. Royal Marine Artillery, 1902; Provincial Grand Master of Freemasonry, Worcestershire; J.P. *Address:* Marchwood, Malvern. *Club:* United Service.
(Died 5 July 1918.)

CAMPBELL, Rev. William, D.D. of Knox College, Toronto; admitted to the Order of the Rising Sun and the Order of the Sacred Treasure (appointments confirmed by His Britannic Majesty); F.R.G.S., M.R.A.S.; Cor. Mem. of the Japan Society; For. Mem. of the Royal Institute for study of the Languages, Topography, and Folklore of Netherlands-India; *b.* 17 Apr. 1841; *m.* 1880, Janet H. Alston, *g. d.* of John Alston (who produced the first complete version of the Bible in any language for blind people); one *s.* two *d. Educ.:* University and Free Church College, Glasgow; ordained missionary to Formosa by the Presbyterian Church of England, 19 July 1871; arrived there 10 Dec.; did some research work during first furlough (1879) when travelling alone through Gilead and from Beersheba to Damascus; withdrew from office in the Mission owing to failing health, 1918. *Publications:* Formosa under the Dutch, with a Bibliography; Handbook of the South Formosa Mission; Dictionary of the Amoy vernacular spoken in Formosa; Sketches from Formosa; revised edition of several 17th-century volumes in the Malay aboriginal dialects of the island. Began work among the Chinese blind fully thirty years ago and continues to use his alphabetic adaptation of Braille for printing Christian literature on both sides of every sheet from movable types. *Address:* 50 St. Michael's Road, Bournemouth. *(Died 7 Sept. 1921.)*

CAMPBELL, Brig.-Gen. William MacLaren, C.B.E. 1919; M.V.O. 1906; *b.* 6 March 1864; *s.* of late Archibald Campbell of Glendaruel, Argyllshire; *m.* 1914, Dorothy Clothilda, *d.* of Rev. R. Lang, Vicar of Old Warden, and widow of Col. F. Shuttleworth of Old Warden Park. Joined Black Watch, 1885; Captain, 1893; Major, 1903; Lt.-Col. commanding 2nd Black Watch, 1911-15; Colonel, 1914; Brig.-Gen. 1916; served Burmah War, 1890-92; South African War with Scottish Horse, 1902; European War. *Clubs:* Naval

and Military : New, Edinburgh.
(*Died 7 June 1924.*)

CAMPBELL, William Middleton, of Colgrain, Dumbartonshire; J.P., D.L. of Dumbartonshire, and on the Commission of Lieutenancy for the City of London; Deputy-Governor Bank of England, 1905-7; Governor, 1907-9; Director since 1886; Director, Commercial Union Assurance Co. Ltd.; member Curtis, Campbell, and Co., Rood Lane, E.C.; *b.* 15 Aug. 1849; *m.* 1873, Edith Agneta, *d.* of R. C. L. Bevan, of Fosbury and Trent Park; four *s.* one *d. Address:* Fen Place, Turner's Hill, Sussex. *Clubs:* Oriental; Western, Glasgow.
(*Died 18 May 1919.*)

CAMPBELL-COLQUHOUN, William Erskine; *b.* 1866; *s.* of late Rev. J. E. Campbell-Colquhoun, M.A., D.L., J.P., of Garscadden, and Killermont, Dumbartonshire, and Chartwell, Westerham, Kent; unmarried. *Educ.:* Harrow; Trinity College, Oxford. *Heir:* *b.* Capt. Archibald John Campbell Colquhoun [late Cameron Highlanders; *m* 1907; two *s.* three *d.*]. *Address:* Knockearn, Crieff, Perthshire. *Club:* Western, Glasgow. (*Died 15 June 1922.*)

CAMPERDOWN, 3rd Earl of, *cr.* 1831; **Robert Adam Philips Haldane-Duncan,** LL.D., St. Andrews; D.L., J.P., B.A. Viscount and Baron Duncan, 1797; *b.* London, 28 May 1841; *S.* father 1867. *Educ.:* Eton; Balliol Coll. Oxon. 1st class in Classics, 1861; Lord-in-Waiting, 1868-70; Lord of the Admiralty, 1870-74. Owns about 14,000 acres. *Publication:* Admiral Duncan, 1898. *Heir:* *b.* Hon. G. A. P. Haldane-Duncan. *Address:* 39 Charles Street, W.; Camperdown, Dundee; Gleneagles House, Perth. *Club:* Brooks's.
(*Died 5 June 1918.*)

CAMPION, George; Sheriff-Substitute Dumfries and Galloway 1890-1925; *b.* 1846; *m.* Mary Janet, *d.* of Thomas Lorimer of Larkfield, Dumfries. *Educ.:* Edinburgh Academy; Oxford. **Advocate,** 1872; Sheriff-Substitute of Argyllshire at Inveraray, 1880. *Recreation:* golf. *Address:* Larkfield, Dumfries. *Clubs:* University, Edinburgh; Dumfries and Galloway, Dumfries. (*Died 1 Nov. 1926.*)

CAMPION, Col. William Henry, C.B. 1902; J.P.; Lieut.-Col. and Hon. Col. 2nd Vol. Batt. Royal Sussex Regiment; *e. s.* of W. J. Campion and Harriet, *d.* of late T. R. Kemp; *b.* 1 Apr. 1836; *m.* 1869, Hon. Gertrude Brand, 2nd *d.* of 1st Viscount Hampden; two *s.* three *d. Educ.:* Eton. 72nd Highlanders, 1854-61; 53rd Regiment, 1861-63; served Crimea and Indian Mutiny with 72nd, now Seaforth Highlanders. *Address:* Danny Park, Hassocks, Sussex. *Club:* Arthur's. (*Died 3 Dec. 1923.*)

CANDLER, Edmund, C.B.E. 1920; author and traveller; *b.* 27 Jan. 1874; *s.* of John Candler, M.R.C.S., and Anne Candler, Harleston, Norfolk; *m.* 1902, Olive Mary Tooth; one *s.* one *d. Educ.:* Repton; Emmanuel College, Cambridge (B.A. 1895). Travelled widely in the East; Special Correspondent of the Daily Mail, Tibet Expedition, 1904 (severely wounded in engagement at Tuna); Correspondent in France for The Times and Daily Mail, 1914-15; Official Eye-witness, Mesopotamia, 1915-18 (despatches); Times Correspondent Middle East, 1918-19; Director of Publicity, Punjab Government, 1920-21. *Publications:* A Vagabond in Asia, 1899; The Unveiling of Lhasa, 1905; The Paraphrase of Poetry, 1905; The Mantle of the East, 1910; The General Plan, 1911; Siri Ram Revolutionist, 1912; The Year of Chivalry, 1916; The Long Road to Baghdad, 1919; On the Edge of the World, 1919; The Sepoy, 1919; Abdication, 1922; Youth and the East, 1924. *Recreations:* riding, travel, etc. *Address:* Villa Ichas Mendy, Hendaye, Basses Pyrénées, France. *Club:* Savage.
(*Died 4 Jan. 1926.*)

CANE, Lucy Mary (Mrs. Arthur Beresford Cane), C.B.E. 1919; 2nd *d.* of late E. W. O'Brien of Cahirmoyle, Co. Limerick; *m.* 1894, Arthur Beresford Cane, C.B.E., Barrister; two *d. Educ.:* at home. Member of a Voluntary Aid Detachment for four years before the war; on the Headquarters of the V.A.D. Department at Devonshire House, 1914-17; Assistant-Director, Women's Royal Naval Service, 1917-19. *Address:* 66 Elm Park Gardens, S.W.10. *T.:* Kensington 667. (*Died 23 April 1926.*)

CANNAN, Charles, M.A., secretary to the Delegates of the University Press, Oxford, since 1898; sometime Fellow and Tutor of Trinity College, Oxford; *b.* 1858; *m.* 1891, Mary Wedderburn, *d.* of late A. Wedderburn Maxwell, of Glenlair, N.B.; three *d. Educ.:* Clifton College; Corpus Christi College, Oxford (Scholar). *Address:* Magdalen Gate House, Oxford. *T.:* Oxford 348. *Club:* Alpine. (*Died 15 Dec. 1919.*)

CANNING, Hon. Albert Stratford George, D.L. and J.P. for Co.'s Down and Derry; 2nd *s.* of 1st Baron Garvagh; *b.* 24 Aug. 1832. *Publications:* Christian Toleration, 1874; Intolerance among Christians, 1876; Political Progress of Christianity, 1877; Religious Strife in British History, 1878; Philosophy of the Waverley Novels, 1879; Philosophy of Charles Dickens, 1880; Baldearg O'Donnell, 1881; Macaulay, Essayist and Historian, 1882, enlarged and revised ed., 1913; Thoughts on Shakespeare's Historical Plays, 1884; Revolted Ireland, 1886; The Divided Irish, 1888; Literary Influence in British History, 1889; Thoughts on Religious History, 1891; Words on Existing Religions, 1893; Religious Development, 1896; History in Fact and Fiction, 1897; British Rule and Modern Politics, 1898; British Power and Thought, 1901; Shakespeare studied in eight Plays, 1903; History in Scott's Novels, 1905; History in Scott's Novels, 2nd edition, 1908; Shakespeare studied in Six Plays, 1906; British Writers on Classic Lands, 1907; Shakespeare studied in Three Plays, 1908; Sir Walter Scott studied in Eight Novels, 1910; Dickens and Thackeray studied in Three Novels, 1911; Dickens studied in Six Novels, 1912; Thoughts on Christian History, 1914. Owns about 4000 acres. *Recreations:* acclimatising foreign birds and animals, and reading. *Address:* The Lodge, Rostrevor, Co. Down. *Club:* Carlton.
(*Died 22 April 1916.*)

CANNING, Hon. Conway Stratford George; *b.* 1854; 2nd *s.* of 2nd Baron Garvagh. Unmarried. Entered army (King's Royal Rifle corps), 1875; retired, 1894; served Egyptian Expedition, 1884, battles of Teb and Tamai (medal with clasp, bronze star); Hazara Expedition, 1891 (medal with clasp); Miranzai, 1891 (clasp); Isazai Expedition, 1892; South Africa, 1902 (medal with 2 clasps); is now Major (retired pay). *Recreations:* formerly polo and rifle-shooting, now golf, fishing, and reading. *Address:* 2 Ryder Street, St. James's, S.W. *Clubs:* Army and Navy, Royal Automobile. (*Died 19 Feb. 1926.*)

CANNING, Hugh, Professor of Comparative Philology, Dublin. *Address:* The University, Dublin. (*Died 23 Dec. 1927.*)

CANNON, Hon. Lawrence John, Puisne Justice Superior Court, Province of Quebec, since 1905; *b.* Quebec, 18 Nov. 1852; *s.* of L. A. Cannon, City Clerk of Quebec; *m.* 1876, Aurelie Dumoulin; five *s.* three *d. Educ.:* Quebec Seminary and Laval University; LL.B. and LL.L. Quebec. Admitted to the Bar of the Province of Quebec, 1874; practised law at Arthabaskaville, P.Q., 1875-91; Assistant Attorney-Gen. and Law Clerk, Quebec, 1891; Liberal candidate for Drummond and Arthabaska at general elections of 1882 for Dominion Parliament; Q.C. 1897; acted as Counsel for the Province of Quebec in the Fisheries Case before

the Judicial Committee of the Privy Council, 1897. *Address:* 5 Collins Street, Quebec.
          (*Died 30 Jan. 1921.*)

CANTAN, Major Henry Thomas, C.M.G. 1915; Duke of Cornwall's Light Infantry; *b.* 11 Jan. 1868. Served six years in ranks; Lieut. army, 1892; Captain, 1900; Major, 1908; Superintendent of Gymnasia, Dublin, 1896-9; Curragh, 1902-6; South Africa, 1910-14; employed with S.A. Constabulary, 1900-2; served S. Africa, 1899-1902 (Queen's medal, 4 clasps; King's medal, 2 clasps); European War, 1914-15 (C.M.G.). *Address:* Tullow Lodge, Tullow, Co. Carlow, Ireland.   (*Died 20 April 1916.*)

CANTERBURY, 5th Viscount, *cr.* 1835; **Henry Frederick Walpole Manners-Sutton,** D.L.; Baron Bottesford, 1835; *s.* of 4th Viscount and Amy, o. *d.* of Hon. Frederick Walpole, M.P.; *b.* 8 Apr. 1879; *S.* father 1914. Owns about 5200 acres. *Heir:* c. Capt. Charles Graham Manners-Sutton. *Club:* St. James's.
          (*Died 22 Oct. 1918.*)

CANTLIE, Sir Jas., K.B.E., *cr.* 1918; Consulting Surgeon, Seamen's Hospital Society; Founder and President (1921-22-23) Royal Society Tropical Medicine and Hygiene; Founder and co-Editor Journal Tropical Medicine; *b.* Keithmore, Dufftown, Banffshire, Scotland, 17 Jan. 1851; *s.* of Wm. Cantlie, banker and farmer; *m.* 1884, Mabel Barclay, O.B.E. (*d.* 1921), *d.* of Robert Barclay Brown; four *s. Educ.:* Milne's Institution, Fochabers; Aberdeen University; Charing Cross Hospital. M.A. Aberdeen, Natural Science Honours; M.B., C.M., Honours in Surgery; F.R.C.S. England; D.P.H. London; LL.D. Aberdeen, 1919; Knight of Grace, Order of St. John of Jerusalem; Imperial Order Osmanieh (4th class). Came to London to finish medical education, 1871; Demonstrator of Anatomy at Charing Cross Hospital, 1872-87; Assistant Surgeon, 1877; Surgeon, 1887; Examiner, Univ. of Aberdeen; went to Egypt, cholera expedition, 1883; Surgeon-Commandant V.M.S.C., London, 1885-88; went to China, 1887; Dean of College of Medicine for Chinese, 1889-96; Plague Officer for London County Council; Consulting Surgeon in London, North Eastern Railway Co.; President Caledonian Society, London, 1902-3; Honorary Colonel, R.A.M.C. (T.) 1st London Division; Comdt., No. 1 V.A.D., London, 1909-22; Member of Council, Red Cross Society. *Publications:* Naked Eye Anatomy, text-book; Ulcers, Veins, etc.; Quain's Dictionary; Ligature of Arteries, etc.; Heath's Dictionary; Gunshot Injuries, etc.; Treves' Surgery; author of Beri-beri; Tropical Surgery, Gould and Warren's Surgery; Tropical Diseases, Allchin's Medicine; Plague; Degeneration amongst Londoners, 1885; Physical Efficiency, 1906. *Recreations:* farming, fishing, and shooting; travel; from China went to India, visited medical schools and places of interest, 1891; Japan, Annam, Pekin, Great Wall, Corea, Vladivostock, United States and Canada. *Address:* 37 Harley Street, W.1; The Kennels, Cottered, Buntingford, Herts. *T.:* Langham 1519.   (*Died 28 May 1926.*)

CANTON, William; *b.* Isle of Chusan, 27 Oct. 1845. *Educ.:* France. For many years sub-editor and leader-writer on the Glasgow Herald; sub-editor of the Contemporary Review, and manager of Isbister & Co., Ltd., 1891-1901. *Publications:* A Lost Epic and other Poems, 1887; The Invisible Playmate, 1894; W. V., Her Book; and Various Verses, 1896; The Invisible Playmate, and W. V., Her Book (with final chapter), 1897; A Child's Book of Saints, 1898; Children's Sayings, 1900; In Memory of W. V., 1901; The Comrades, Poems Old and New, 1902; The History of the British and Foreign Bible Society, vols. i. ii. 1903, vols. iii.-v. 1910; The Story of the Bible Society, 1904; A Child's Book of Warriors, 1912; The Story of St. Elizabeth

of Hungary, 1912; The Bible and the Anglo-Saxon People, 1914; The Bible Story, 1915; Dawn in Palestine, 1918; The Five Colours, 1924. *Address:* Inglewood, 119 Audley Road, Hendon, N.W.4.   (*Died 2 May 1926.*)

CAPELLINI, Prof. Giovanni, Professor of Geology and Paleontology, Bologna University, since 1860; Senatore del Regno; *b.* Spezia, 23 Aug. 1833; *m.* Marchioness Niccolini Beatrix; two *s. Educ.:* Collegio, Spezia; University of Pisa. Was Professor in the College of Genoa, and Rector of the University of Bologna. *Address:* Bologna, Italy.

CAPES, Bernard. *Publications:* The Lake of Wine, 1898; The Adventures of the Comte de la Muette, 1898; Our Lady of Darkness; At a Winter's Fire, 1899; From Door to Door, 1900; Joan Brotherhood, 1900; Love like a Gipsy, 1901; A Castle in Spain, 1903; The Secret in the Hill, 1903; The Extraordinary Confessions of Diana Please, 1904; A Jay of Italy, 1905; The Story of Lohengrin, 1905; A Rogue's Tragedy, 1906; The Green Parrot, 1908; Amaranthus, a Book of Little Songs, 1908; The Love Story of St. Bel, 1909; Jemmy Abercraw, 1910; Historical Vignettes, 1910; The House of Many Voices, 1911; Jessie Bazley, 1912; The Pot of Basil, 1913; The Story of Fifine, 1914; The Fabulists, 1915; Moll Davis, 1916; If Age Could, 1916; Where England sets her Feet, 1918. *Address:* 1 Southgate Road, Winchester.
          (*Died 2 Nov. 1918.*)

CAPPEL, Sir Albert James Leppoc, K.C.I.E., *cr.* 1887; *b.* 1836; *m.* 1873, Fanny Gibbon (*d.* 1907), *d.* of Gen. Sir F. Turner, K.C.B., R.A.; one *s.* two *d.* Served Crimea, 1855-56; entered Indian Telegraph Service, 1857; Director-Gen. of Indian Telegraphs, 1883-89. *Address:* 27 Kensington Court Gardens, W.8. *T.:* Western 855.   (*Died 20 April 1924.*)

CAPPER, Alfred Octavius, demonstrator of thought transmission and other mysterious phenomena; *s.* of late Octavius Capper of Southampton; *m.* 1913, Bettina Maud, *d.* of late W. B. Partridge, J.P., and widow of late H. R. Trafford, J.P., of Michaelchurch Court, Herefordshire. *Educ.:* Springhill School, Southampton. For last 30 years has presented his drawing-room entertainment and thought-reading séance in most towns of the United Kingdom, also in France, Switzerland, and Italy; has appeared by royal command at Windsor Castle and Marlborough House, and has personally "experimented" in thought-reading with King George V. and Duke of Connaught, also with Madame Sarah Bernhardt at her residence in Paris; has also appeared at 500 public and preparatory schools; his various performances have yielded over £60,000 to charitable institutions. During 1912 travelled 50,000 miles and gave 200 séances throughout India, Burma, Malaya, and Ceylon; His entertainment realised £5000 for War Charities and was witnessed by 600,000 soldiers in England, France, and Germany. *Publication:* A Rambler's Recollections and Reflections. *Recreations:* sport generally. *Address:* 15 Egerton Gardens, S.W.; Michaelchurch Court, Hereford.   (*Died 11 Mar. 1921.*)

CAPPER, David Sing, M.A., M.Inst.C.E., M.I.Mech.E.; Professor of Engineering, Univ. of London, King's College, 1902-21; and Member of Senate, 1905-7; Fellow, King's College, London, 1907; one of the Governors of Sir Roger Cholmeley's School, Highgate, 1905-20; member of governing body of Imperial College of Science and Technology, South Kensington, 1908-9; Member of Delegacy of University of London, King's College, 1910-14; Lt.-Col. Commanding University of London Contingent of Officers' Training Corps to 1915; Major, 2/5 Royal Warwicks, B.E.F.; *y. s.* of late Jasper John Capper (*d.* 1895); *m.* 1893, Lillian Grace, *y. d.* of late Dr. A. R.

Shaw, St. Leonards-on-Sea (d. 1899); one s. Educ.: Royal High School, Edinburgh; Edinburgh University; University College, London; Messrs. R. & W. Hawthorns; Messrs. Humphrys, Tennant and Co., Deptford. Assist. to Mr. R. Humphrys, 1888-90. Publications: various professional papers in Proceedings of Engineering Institutions, Royal Agricultural Society, etc. Recreations: gardening, philately. Address: 38 West Heath Drive, Hampstead, N.W.3. T.: Hampstead 2350. Clubs: Athenæum: St. Stephen's. (Died 12 Feb. 1926.)

CAPPER, Stewart Henbest, M.A. (Edin. and Manc.); A.R.I.B.A. 1891; A.R.C.A. 1897; R.C.A. 1899; F.S.A.; Temporary Egyptian Government Official; b. 15 Dec. 1859; 3rd s. of late Jasper John Capper, Upper Clapton, and Harriet Millington Jackson, Douglas, Isle of Man; unmarried. Educ.: Royal High School, and University, Edinburgh; Heidelberg University; Ecole des Beaux Arts, Paris. Medallist and "Dux," Royal High School, 1875; M.A. with first class honours (classics), 1880; private tutor and (for part of the time) acting private secretary in household of the late Sir R. B. D. Morier, Lisbon and Madrid, 1879-83; examiner in Art History and Archæology, Edinburgh University, 1895 and 1904; Macdonald Professor of Architecture, McGill University, Montreal, 1896-1903; Professor of Architecture, Victoria University, Manchester, 1903-12; late Capt. and Bt. Major, 1/6th Batt. Manchester Regt., which he accompanied to Egypt on active service; Military Censor, Port Said, 1914-16, Alexandria, 1916-17, Cairo, 1917-18; Intelligence Corps, E.E.F., 1918; G.S.O., E.E.F., 1919 (despatches twice, T.D.); Chief Press Censor, Ministry of the Interior, Cairo, 1920-21; Major (local), commanding Manchester University Contingent Officers' Training Corps, 1908-12; formerly Captain Canadian Field Artillery (3rd Field Battery, Montreal). Publications: occasional papers. Recreations: member Royal St. Lawrence Yacht Club; R.N.S.Y.C. Address: European Dept., Ministry of the Interior, Cairo; St. Michael's, Reigate, Surrey. Club: Athenæum. (Died 8 Jan. 1925.)

CAPUS (Vincent Marie), Alfred, man of letters; Officer Legion of Honour; Member French Academy; b. 25 Nov. 1858; widower. Educ.: Aix-en-Provence; Lycée Condorcet, Paris. Late Editor Figaro. Publications: Qui perd gagne; Monsieur Veut rire; Années d'aventures; Notre époque et le théâtre. Plays: La Veine; Tout s'arrange; L'Institut de Beauté; etc. Address: Vernon sur Brenne, Indre et Loire, France. T.: 220-82. (Died 1 Nov. 1922.)

CARBONELL, Canon Francis Rohde, M.A.; Vicar of Fairford, 1888-1918, and Rural Dean, 1900-18; Hon. Canon of Gloucester Cathedral since 1911; Proctor in Convocation since 1910; Subwarden Society of Sacred Study, since 1904; b. Manor House, Westbourne Green, 4 June 1849; s. of William Charles and Sarah Mary Carbonell; m. 1874, Katharine Dorinda, d. of Rev. Arthur Rainey Ludlow of Dimlands Castle, Cowbridge; two d. Educ.: Kidderminster Grammar School; Merton College, Oxford (First Class, Natural Science School). Deacon 1873; Priest 1875; Curate of Kinver, Staffs., 1873-76; Rector of Littleton on Severn, Glos., 1876-84; Curate of Tewkesbury (Abbey), 1884-87; Vicar of Kingston, Somerset, 1887-88; Publications: pamphlets. Recreations: violoncello, and music generally; fishing. Address: Worcester House, Pittville, Circus Road, Cheltenham. (Died 27 May 1919.)

CARDEW, Colonel Sir Frederic, K.C.M.G., cr. 1897; Consul for Republic of Liberia since 1896; b. 27 Sept. 1839; m. 1st, Clara, d. of J. D. Newton, West Hoe, Plymouth, 1865 (d. 1881); 2nd, Katharine, d. of late J. Savill and widow of Col. Kent Jones, 1887; three s. Educ.: Sandhurst.

172

Entered Bengal Army, 1858, 104th and 82nd Regts.; Colonel, 1887; retired 1890; served N.W. Frontier of India, 1863 (despatches); Zulu War, 1879-81 (despatches), Brevet-Major; Transvaal, 1880-81; A.A. and Q.M.G. Natal Field Force; D.A.Q.M.G. Aldershot, 1873-78; South Africa 1879-80; Assistant Military Secretary, China, 1882-83; A.A.G. South Africa, 1890; Sub-Commissioner, Zululand, 1884-86; Resident Commissioner, 1890; C.M.G. 1894; Governor and Commander-in-Chief of Sierra Leone, 1894-1900. Address: Tudor Cottage, Whitchurch, Oxon. T.A.: Whitchurch, Oxon. Club: United Service. (Died 6 July 1921.)

CARDIN, James Joseph, C.B. 1897; b. 1839; s. of late Joseph Cardin, of Lincoln's Inn; m. 1870, Mary (d. 1875), d. of late Herbert Smith of Baverstock. Receiver and Accountant-General, General Post Office, 1886-97; Comptroller and Accountant-General, 1897-1901; late Lt.-Col. Prince of Wales's Own 12th Middlesex R.V. Address: 28 Tierney Road, Streatham Hill, S.W. Club: Junior Athenæum. (Died 3 May 1917.)

CARDOT, Rt. Rev. Alexander, Bishop of Limyra and Vicar Apostolic of the Mission of Southern Burma since 1894; b. Fresse, Haute-Saône, France, 10 Jan. 1857. Educ.: Luxeuil, Vesoul, and Paris. Priest, 1879; sent to Southern Burma, 1879; Coadjutor Bishop to Bishop Bigandes, 1893; has built in Rangoon a cathedral; attended the Eucharistic Congress in London, 1908. Address: Rangoon. T.A.: Adexteros. (Died 18 Oct. 1925.)

CARDWELL, Rev. John Henry, M.A.; Prebendary of St. Paul's since 1911; b. Sheffield, 20 June 1842; s. of William Cardwell, colliery owner; m. Elizabeth Barnes, d. of John Barnes, J.P., Reedley Hall, Lancashire, 1869; four s. three d. Educ.: Burnley Grammar School; Lindow Grove School; Caius College, Cambridge. Ordained 1865; Incumbent, St. Andrew's, Fulham, 1868-91; Rector, St. Anne's, Soho, 1891-1914. During twenty-three years in Fulham chiefly engaged in Church Building, and forming new ecclesiastical districts. Three churches (St. Andrew's, St. Peter's, St. Clement's) built during incumbency, and eight churches, school churches, and mission rooms. Has carried out the restoration of St. Anne's Church, and remodelling of the parochial schools. Built new Parish Hall and Clergy House for St. Anne's, 1911. Progressive in municipal politics; led the way in strong measures against disorderly houses in St. Anne's, brought about through the Strand Board of Works, conversion of. St. Anne's churchyard into a public garden. Publications: Story of a Charity School; joint author Two Centuries of Soho: its Institutions, Firms, and Amusements; Men and Women of Soho, Famous and Infamous; Twenty Years in Soho, 1891-1911. Recreations: cycling, walking. Address: Chapel House, Ealing, W.5. T.: Ealing 682. (Died 17 April 1921.)

CAREW, 3rd Baron (U.K.) (cr. 1838), **Robert Shapland George Julian Carew**, D.L.; Baron Carew (Ireland), 1834; b. 15 June 1860; s. of 2nd Baron and Emily, d. of Sir George Richard Philips, Bt.; S. father 1881; m. Julia, d. of the late Albert Lethbridge, and g. d. of Sir John Lethbridge, Bt., Sandhill Park, Taunton, 1888. Educ.: Trinity College, Cambridge (B.A.). Heir: b. Hon. George P. J. Carew. Address: 28 Belgrave Square, S.W.1. T.: Victoria 709. Clubs: Bachelors', Brooks's.(Died 29 April 1923.)

CAREW, 4th Baron (U.K.) (cr. 1838), **George Patrick John Carew**; Baron Carew (Ireland), 1834; s. of 2nd Baron and Emily, d. of Sir George Richard Philips, Bt.; b. 1st Feb. 1863; S. brother, 1923; m. 1888, Maud Beatrice, d. of late J. Ramsay. Educ.: Eton; Magdalen College, Cambridge. Recreation: philately. Heir: c. Gerald Shapland Carew, b. 1860.

Address: Rostrevor, 6 Grassington Road, East-bourne. *Club:* Badminton.
(*Died 21 April 1926.*)

CAREW, 5th Baron (U.K.) (*cr.* 1838), **Gerald Shapland Carew;** Baron Carew (Ireland), 1834; *b.* 26 Apr. 1860; *s.* of late Hon. Shapland F. Carew, *s.* of 1st Baron, and Lady Hester Georgiana Browne, *d.* of 2nd Marquess of Sligo; *S.* cousin, 1926; *m.* 1904, Catherine, *o. d.* of late Thomas Conolly, M.P.; three *s. Educ.:* Eton; abroad. *Heir: s.* William Francis, D.C.L. Infantry, India, *b.* 23 April 1905. *Address:* 18 Tedworth Square, S.W.
(*Died 3 Oct. 1927.*)

CAREW, Lt.-Gen. Sir Reginald Pole, K.C.B., *cr.* 1900; C.V.O., D.L.; J.P. of Antony; *b.* Antony, Cornwall, 1 May 1849; *e. s.* of late W. H. Pole Carew, of Antony, and Frances Anne, *d.* of John Buller, of Morval; *m.* 1901, Lady Beatrice Butler, *e. d.* of 3rd Marquess of Ormonde; two *s.* two *d. Educ.:* Eton; Christ Church, Oxford. Served in Coldstream Guards, 1869-99; private secretary to Sir Hercules Robinson, Governor New South Wales, 1876-77; A.D.C. to Lord Lytton, Viceroy of India, 1878-79; to Sir Frederick Roberts, Afghan War, 1879-80; to Sir Frederick Roberts, South Africa, 1881; to Duke of Connaught, Egypt, 1882; Mil. Sec. to Sir Frederick Roberts, Madras, 1884-85; Mil. Sec. to Sir Frederick Roberts, com.-in-chief, India, 1885-90; commanded 2nd Batt. Coldstream Guards, 1895-99. Commanded consecutively 9th Brigade and Guards' Brigade, and 11th Division South Africa (despatches twice, promoted Major-General, K.C.B.); contested Pembroke Boroughs (C.), 1906; Bodmin Division, 1910. *Decorated:* Afghan War, 1879-80, three clasps; march to Kandahar; Egypt, 1882 (Medjidie, 4th class, Khedive's star); Burma, 1886: C.B.; Jubilee medal, 1897; S. Africa, five clasps; K.C.B., C.V.O.; Coronation medal, 1902; Commanding 8th Division 3rd Army Corps, 1903-5; retired, with rank of Lieut.-General, 1906; M.P. (U.) Bodmin Division, Cornwall, 1910-16; Inspector-General of Territorials, 1914. *Recreations:* hunting, shooting, etc. *Heir: s.* John Gawen, *b.* 4 March 1902. *Address:* Antony, Cornwall. *Clubs:* Guards', Turf, Travellers'. Pratt's.
(*Died 10 Sept. 1924.*)

CAREW-HUNT, Major Thomas Edward, D.S.O. 1916; Royal Berks Regt.; *b.* 27 Nov. 1874; *s.* of Henry Thomas Carew-Hunt; *m.* 1898, Ethel Emily, *d.* of C. Lindsay Nicholson; one *d.* Joined Royal Berkshire Regt. from Militia, 1897; Lieut. 1900; Captain 1904; Major, 1915; Adjutant 1st V.B. Royal Berkshire Regt. 1904-1907; Brigade Major, March 1915; G.S.O. 3, April 1916; G.S.O. 2, Aug. 1916; G.S.O. 1, April 1918; served European War, 1914-18 (despatches twice; D.S.O., O.B.E., 1914 Star); G.S.O. 2, War Office, Sep. 1919-March 1920; District Commissioner Klagenfurt Plebiscite Commission, April 1920-Dec. 1920; Military Inter-Allied Commission of Control, Berlin, Jan 1921; D.A.A.G., Aug. 1921-Dec. 1921; G.S.O. 2, Jan. 1922. *Address:* M.I.A.C.C., Berlin. *Club:* United Service.
(*Died 19 Aug. 1923.*)

CAREY, Sir Bertram Sausmarez, K.C.I.E., *cr.* 1918; C.S.I. 1914; C.I.E. 1898; V.D.; Commissioner, of a District, Burma, since 1909; *b.* 1864; *s.* of late Rev. Alfred H. Carey; *m.* Mary, *e. d.* of late I. D. Chepmell. *Educ.:* Bedford Grammar School. Appointed to Burma Police, 1886; to the Burma Commission, 1887; Political Officer in Chin Hills, 1889-95; Deputy Commissioner, 1900. *Address:* Rangoon, Burma. (*Died 11 July 1919.*)

CAREY, Frank Stanton, M.A., late Professor of Mathematics in the Univ. of Liverpool; *b.* Easton-in-Gordano, Somersetshire, 14 June 1860; *m.* 1894, Jessie Mein; two *s.* two *d. Educ.:*

The Grammar School, Bristol; Trinity Coll., Cambridge. Third Wrangler, 1882, and placed in Division I., Part II., of the Mathematical Tripos, 1882; elected to a Fellowship at Trinity College, Camb. 1884; to a Professorship at University College, Liverpool, 1886. *Publications:* Solid Geometry; Infinitesimal Calculus; Papers on Mathematics; (with J. Proudman) Elements of Mechanics, 1925. *Address:* c/o The University, Liverpool.
(*Died 26 July 1928.*)

CARINGTON, Herbert Hanbury Smith-, J.P.; *e. s.* of late R. Smith-Carington, of Ashby Folville Manor, Leicestershire; *b.* Worcester, 1851; *m.* 1876, Elizabeth P., 2nd *d.* of Josiah Stallard, of The Blanquettes, Worcs; three *s.* one *d. Educ.:* Worcester; King's College, London. Lord of the Manor of Ashby Folville; High Sheriff for Leicestershire, 1910; Director of Sir W. G. Armstrong, Whitworth, and Co., Ltd.; the Norwich Union Life Insurance Soc.; Deputy Chairman of St. Mary's Hospitals; on the Board of the Manchester Royal Infirmary; Member of the Court of Governors and of the Council of the Victoria University of Manchester, of Council of the Manchester Royal College of Music; Governor of the Manchester Whitworth Institute; Fellow of the Royal Historical Society; Member of the Committee of Manchester Steam Users Association, of Council and Past President of the Shire Horse Society; Knight of the Royal Order of the Northern Star (Sweden); Member of the 4th class of the Order of the Rising Sun (Japan); Patron and Trustee of 2 livings. *Recreations:* shooting, farming, and shire horse-breeding. *Address:* Grangethorpe Rusholme, Manchester; Ashby Folville, Melton Mowbray. *T.:* 5 Rusholme. *Clubs:* Carlton, National, Constitutional; Union, Manchester; County, Leicester.
(*Died 4 Mar. 1917.*)

CARLETON, Hon. Brig.-Gen. Frank Robert Crofton, C.B. 1916; retired; late Director of Organisation, War Office; *b.* 8 Sep. 1856. Served S. Africa, 1899-1902 (Queen's medal, 4 clasps, King's medal, 2 clasps).
(*Died 9 June 1924.*)

CARLETON, Brig.-Gen. Frederick Montgomerie, D.S.O 1900; *b.* 21 July 1867; *y. s.* of late Gen. Hy. Carleton, C.B., Royal Artillery; *m.* 1899, Gwendolen, *e. d.* of late S. Lloyd of the Priory, Warwick, and Dolobran, Montgomeryshire; two *s.* one *d. Educ.:* Military Coll. Oxford. Joined King's Own Regt. 1888; served with Dongola Expedition, 1896 (medal and two clasps); Nile Expedition, 1897 (medal); with Mendiland, Karene, and Protectorate Expeditions, Sierra Leone, 1898-99 (medal, clasp, D.S.O., and despatch); A.D.C. S. Africa, 1899-1902 (despatches thrice, Brevet-Major, medal and six clasps, King's medal and two clasps); passed Staff College, 1902; retired, 1909. *Recreations:* hunting, shooting, polo. *Address:* 6 Broad Street Place, E.C.3. *Club:* United Service.
(*Died 15 May 1922.*)

CARLETON, Rev. James George, D.D.; Treasurer of St. Patrick's Cathedral, Dublin, since 1913; Deputy for the Regius Professor of Divinity, University of Dublin, since 1916; *b.* Blackrock, Co. Dublin, 1848, *s.* of late Cornelius Carleton of Dublin and Lisburn; *m.* 1872, Margaret, *d.* of late George Dundas, Manager, Head Office Belfast Banking Company; two *s.* one *d. Educ:* Rathmines School; Trinity College, Dublin; Scholar, 1868; Senior Moderator in Classics, 1869; Ecclesiastical History Prize (1st) and Abp. King's Divinity Prize (2nd), 1870; Theological Exhibition (1st), 1871; Elrington Theological Prize, 1872; B.D., 1877; D.D., 1902; Ordained, 1870, for curacy of St. John's, Limerick; Curate of Kilmallock, 1875; of Holy Trinity, Rathmines, 1877; of St. Peter's, Dublin, 1883; of St. Stephen's, Dublin, 1897; Lecturer in

Divinity, University of Dublin, 1888; Prebendary of Rathmichael and Canon of St. Patrick's Cathedral, Dublin, 1904. *Publications:* The Bible of our Lord and His Apostles; The LXX considered in relation to the Gospel, etc., 1888; The Part of Rheims in the making of the English Bible, 1902; the Prayer Book Psalter, with introduction and marginal notes, 1909; Articles in the Encyclopaedia of Religion and Ethics. *Address :* 17 Harrington Street, Dublin.
(Died 1918.)

CARLILE, Sir Edward, Kt., cr. 1913; K.C., J.P.; b. London, 26 April 1845; s. of John Carlile of Houston, Scotland; m. 1878, Isabella Sophia, y. d. of Robert Hunter Young, W.S., Edinburgh: two s. three d. *Educ. :* private schools; University of Melbourne (Law Gold Medallist, 1868). Entered public service, Victoria, 1861; Registrar-General's Office, 1862; Crown Law Offices, 1865; called to Bar, 1871; Parliamentary and Professional Assistant to Crown Law Offices, 1873; Parliamentary Draughtsman, 1881, retired 1910; Q.C., 1900; is a Trustee and Treasurer of the National Gallery, Museums, and Public Library of Victoria; Government Representative on the Faculty of Veterinary Science of the University of Melbourne; on Committee of Management of Melbourne Hospital. *Address :* South Yarra, Melbourne. *(Died 15 Nov. 1917.)*

CARLIN, Gaston, Swiss Envoy Extraordinary and Minister Plenipotentiary at The Hague since 1920; Member of the Permanent Court of Arbitration; b. Delémont, Berne; m. 1887. *Educ. :* Delémont, Berne (gymnasium and university, doctor juris.); Leipzig; Paris. Attaché, Rome, 1882; Secretary, Vienna, 1884; Councillor, 1887; Secretary Political Division, Foreign Office, Berne, 1891; Envoy Extraordinary and Minister Plenipotentiary, Rome, 1895-1902; London, 1902-20; first Swiss Delegate, Venice International Sanitary Conference, 1897; Rome International Anti-Anarchic Conference, 1898; Second International Peace Conference, The Hague, 1907; Conferences on Bills of Exchange, The Hague, 1910 and 1912; 3rd Opium Conference, The Hague, 1914; Conference between Switzerland, the Scandinavian States and the Netherlands for the elaboration of a uniform scheme for the International Court of Justice, The Hague, 1920; and Communications and Transit Conference, Barcelona, 1921. *Publications:* In French or German—On the Possession and Property of Personal Estate; On the Acquisition and Loss of the Swiss Nationality; On the Transitory Dispositions of the Swiss Federal Code of Obligations; Biography of his Father; Travelling Notes, etc. *Recreations:* climbing, shooting, collecting (china, majolica, old silver, Swiss stained-glass panels, tapestries). *Address:* Swiss Legation, The Hague.
(Died 13 June 1922.)

CARLINE, George, R.B.A.; Painter in Oil and Water-Colour — chiefly portraits; b. Lincoln, 1855; s. of Richard Carline, Solicitor; m. 1884, Annie, d. of late John Smith of Buckhurst Hill; three s. one d. *Educ.:* privately; Lincoln Grammar School; studied at Heatherlies, London, Antwerp, and Paris. First picture, Spelling out the List, on the line at Royal Academy, 1886; among subsequent works, In the Garden of Hollyhocks, Faith, The Harvest Moon, The Blind Sister, The View of London from Hampstead Heath, Portraits of Mrs. Duff, Lady Mary Stewart, Mrs. Duigan, Mrs. Eccles Williams, Beauchamp Tyrwhitt, Nat Gould, Presentation portrait of Colonel Dimmock, M.D., Miss Heberden, sister of the Principal of Brasenose College, Daughters of Sir William Schlich, Children of Rev. E. H. Alington, Dr. Collier, Professor Vinogradoff, Professor Sir Charles Oman, M.P., etc.; an Exhibition at The Dowdeswell Galleries, Bond Street, in 1896 of 59 works entitled The Home of our English

Wild Flowers. *Publications:* Illustrations to Maud Müller, 1886; Aquarelle graveur of Snowdrop, 1895; Water-colour illustrations to Andrew Lang's Oxford, 1915; a coloured reproduction of a water-colour of King's College Chapel, Cambridge, 1920. *Address:* 47 Downshire Hill, Hampstead, N.W. *(Died Dec. 1920.)*

CARLISLE, Rt. Hon. Alexander Montgomery, P.C. 1907; b. Ballymena, Co. Antrim, 8 July 1854; e. s. of late John Carlisle, M.A., Headmaster of Royal Academical Institution, Belfast; m. Edith Wooster of San Francisco; one s. two d. *Educ.:* Royal Academical Institution, Belfast. Career business, shipbuilder and engineer, having joined Harland and Wolff, where apprenticeship was served in 1870; rose to be General Manager and Chairman of Managing Directors; retired, 1910; Member of Departmental Committee on Accidents in Factories and Workshops, 1908; contested West Belfast as Independent, 1906; one of the Merchant Shipping Advisory Committee in making report to the Board of Trade on Life-Saving Appliances, 1911; gave evidence at the Admiralty before Committee appointed to report on the organisation of the Royal Corps of Constructors and other cognate questions; on 9 August 1920, when Coercion Bill on Ireland was just going to be passed, he made a protest from the throne of thirteen words (My Lords, if you pass this Bill you may kill England, not Ireland). *Address:* 7 Orme Square, W.2. *M. :* LH 3997. *Clubs:* Royal Thames Yacht, Phyllis Court, Henley-on-Thames. *(Died 5 May 1926.)*

CARMICHAEL, 1st Baron of Skirling, cr. 1912, **Thomas David Gibson-Carmichael,** 14th Bart.; cr. 1628; G.C.S.I., cr. 1917; G.C.I.E., cr. 1911; K.C.M.G., cr. 1908; M.A., D.L.; b. Edinburgh, 18 Mar. 1859; e. s. of 13th Bt. and Eleanora Anne, d. of David Anderson, St. Germains, N.B.; S. father, 1891; m. 1886, Mary Helen Elizabeth, d. of late Albert Nugent; no c. *Educ.:* St. John's College, Cambridge. Private Secretary to Sir George Trevelyan and Lord Dalhousie, when Secretaries for Scotland; Chairman, Scottish Board of Lunacy, 1894-97; contested Peebles and Selkirk, 1892; M.P. (L.) Midlothian, 1895-1900, succeeding Mr. Gladstone; a Trustee of the National Portrait Gallery, 1904-8, and of National Gallery, 1906-8, and since 1923; Governor of Victoria, Australia, 1908-11; Madras, 1911-12; Bengal, 1912-17; Lord Lieutenant of Peebles-shire. *Heir* (to baronetcy): c. Sir Henry Gibson-Craig, Bt. *Address:* Skirling House, Biggar; 13 Portman Street, W.1. *T.:* Mayfair 6462. *Clubs:* Brooks's; New, Edinburgh. *(Died 16 Jan. 1926.)*

CARMICHAEL, Sir Duncan, Kt., cr. 1917; M.L.C.; partner in firm of Mackinnon, Mackenzie & Co., Calcutta, Bombay, and Karachee; a director Anderson, Green & Co., Ltd.; b. 1866; s. of Dugald Carmichael, Greenock. *Address:* 122 Leadenhall Street, E.C.3. *(Died 22 June 1925.)*

CARMICHAEL, Rev. Frederic Falkiner, LL.D.; Chancellor of the Cathedral of Christ Church, Dublin; Chaplain to His Excellency the Lord Lieutenant of Ireland; member of the council of the Royal Dublin Society and of the council of the Alexandra College; b. 1831; e. s. of late James Carmichael, Clerk of the Crown of the County of Tipperary, and Elizabeth Murray, d. of Singleton Maynard Walker and Anne Kennedy Thorpe; m. 1855, Elizabeth Turton Cotton, d. of Francis Bulkeley Turton Cotton of Allenton, County Dublin, and Susan Lucas, d. of Minchin Lucas of Woodtown, County Dublin; one s. two d. *Educ.:* Private tuition. A.B., T.C.D. and Div. Test, 1857; M.A., 1868; LL.B. and LL.D. Stip. Con., 1877; select preacher, T.C.D., 1875, '78, '81; select preacher, Cambridge, 1877; Donnellan Lecturer

T.C.D., 1875-76, and 1890-91; Deacon, 1857; Priest, 1858; Curate, S. Werburgh, Dublin, 1857; S. Bride's, 1860; Chaplain of the Magdalen, 1865; Canon of Christ Church, 1886; Professor of History, Alexandra College, 1880. *Publications:* Jesus Christ, the Way, the Truth, and the Life; Donnellan Lectures, T.C.D., 1876; The Responsibilities of God, and other sermons, 2nd ed.; The Ghost of Samuel, and other sermons on different subjects; Honour the King, a sermon, 6th ed.; The War, a sermon, 5th ed.; All Men shall at length be Saved, 2nd ed.; sermons on different subjects. *Recreation:* heraldry. *Address:* 10 Sallymount Avenue, Leeson Park, Dublin.

(Died 1 Aug. 1919.)

CARMICHAEL, James, J.P.; *e. s.* of late James Drummond of Ailly-sur-Somme, France, and Helen, *d.* of Robert Stewart, and *n.* of late Peter Carmichael of Arthurstone, whom he succeeded in 1902; *b.* 1846; *m.* 1874, Margaret, *d.* of Alexander Geekie, of Baldowrie, Co. Forfar. *Address:* Arthurstone, Meigle, Perthshire. *Club:* New, Edinburgh.

(Died 14 April 1927.)

CARMICHAEL - FERRALL, John, J.P., D.L. Co. Tyrone; *b.* 8 Nov. 1855; *o. s.* of Captain Carmichael-Ferrall, R.N., and Margaret, 6th *d.* of Sir John Nugent Humble, 1st Bt. of Clonkoscoran, Co. Waterford; *m.* 1899, Elizabeth Emily, 3rd *d.* of late Rev. David Henry Elrington, Vicar of Swords, and Matilda Rowena, *d.* of late Rev. Pierce Wm. Drew, Rector of Youghal. *Educ.:* Harrow; Trinity College, Dublin. Barrister - at - law; succeeded his father, 1904; High Sheriff, County Tyrone, 1907; Member of Council, Royal Ulster Agricultural Society. *Publications:* A Reply to Mr. Hine's Identification of the British Nation with the Lost Tribes of Israel; Ireland and the Irish; The Principality of Orange and its Protestant Exiles. *Address:* Augher Castle, Augher. *T.A.:* Augher, Co. Tyrone. *M.:* OI 4350. *Club:* Tyrone County. *(Died 13 May 1923.)*

CARNARVON, 5th Earl of (*cr.* 1793), **George Edward Stanhope Molyneux Herbert,** D.L., J.P.; Baron Porchester, 1780; High Steward of Newbury; *b.* 26 June 1866; *s.* of 4th Earl and Evelyn, *d.* of 6th Earl of Chesterfield; *S.* father 1890; *m.* Almina, *d.* of late Frederick C. Wombwell, 1895. one *s.* one *d. Educ.:* Eton; Trin. Coll. Camb. Owns about 36,000 acres. *Heir:* s. Lord Porchester. *Address:* 1 Seamore Place, W.1; *T.:* Gerrard 3609; Highclere Castle, Newbury; Bretby Park, Burton-on-Trent; Pixton Park, Dulverton, Somersetshire. *Clubs:* Bachelors', St. James's; Royal Yacht Squadron, Cowes.

(Died 5 April 1923.)

CARNEGIE, Andrew, philanthropist; manufacturer; *b.* Dunfermline, 15 Nov. 1885; *m.* 1887, Louise Whitfield of New York; one *d.* Went with family to America (Pittsburgh), 1848; first work was as weaver's assistant in cotton factory, Allegheny, Pa.; became telegraph messenger boy in Pittsburgh office of Ohio Telegraph Co., 1851; learned telegraphy, entered employ Pennsylvania Railroad Co., and became telegraph operator, advancing by promotions until he became Supt., Pittsburgh Div., Pa. System; joined Mr. Woodruff, inventor of the sleeping car, in organising Woodruff Sleeping Car Co., gaining through it nucleus of his fortune; careful investments in oil lands increased his means. During Civil War served as Supt. Mil. Rlys. and Govt. Telegraph lines in the East; after war developed ironworks of various kinds, and established at Pittsburgh Keystone Bridge Works and Union Ironworks, introduced Bessemer process of making steel, 1868; was principal owner a few years later of Homestead and Edgar Thomson Steel Works, and other large plants, as head of firms of Carnegie, Phipps, and Co., and Carnegie Bros. and Co.; interests were consolidated, 1889, in the

Carnegie Steel Co., which in 1901 was merged in the United States Steel Corporation, when he retired from business; has given libraries to many towns and cities in the U.S. and Great Britain, and large sums in other benefactions; he is a life trustee of Carnegie Corporation of New York foundation to carry on various works in which he has been engaged; Hon. Mem. A.I.A.; Mem. Exec. Com. Nat. Civic Federation; Mem. Am. Philos. Soc.; Life Mem. Lotos Club; Mem. Indian Harbour Yacht Club; Mem. Riding Club; Life Mem. St. Andrews Club; Mem. Chamber of Commerce, etc. Condr. Legion of Honour, France, 1907; Grand Cross, Order of Orange Nassau; Grand Cross, Order of Danebrog; has received the freedom of fifty-three cities in Great Britain and Ireland; Lord Rector St. Andrews University, 1903-7; Aberdeen University, 1912-14. *Publications:* An American Four - in - Hand in Britain, 1883; Round the World, 1884; Triumphant Democracy, 1886 (new edition 1893); The Gospel of Wealth, 1900; The Empire of Business, 1902 (translated into eight languages); Life of James Watt, 1906; Problems of To-day, 1908. *Address:* 2 East 91st Street, New York; Skibo Castle, Sutherland, N.B. *T.A.:* Clashmore, Sutherland.

(Died 11 Aug. 1919.)

CARNEGY, Col. Charles Gilbert, M.V.O. 1911; *b.* 29 June 1864; *s.* of late General Alexander Carnegy, C.B., cadet of family of Northesk; *m.* 1892, Evelyn Mary, *d.* of late Charles John Collins Prichard, of Pwllywrach, Co. Glamorganshire; one *s. Educ.:* Clifton College; Sandhurst. Gazetted as Lieut. to 2nd E. York Regiment, 1884; joined Indian Army, 1886; served in Burmah Campaign, 1886-87 (medal and two clasps); King George V. Coronation Durbar at Delhi (medal); European War, 1914-18 (Bt.-Col., medal); 2nd Class Order of St. Stanislas; A.D.C. to Gen. Sir Stanley Edwardes, K.C.B., 1887-89; Captain, 1895; Major, 1902; Lt.-Col., 1909; Bt. Col., 1917. *Recreation:* golf. *Address:* The Grove, Stutton, near Ipswich, Suffolk. *(Died 23 April 1923.)*

CARNEGY, Maj.-Gen. Sir Philip Mainwaring, K.C.B. *cr.* 1921; C.B. 1911; *b.* 12 Dec. 1858; *s.* of late Maj.-Gen. P. A. Carnegy and Catherine Chitty; *m.* 1897, Jessie Pyne, *d.* of late Maj.-Gen. J. S. Rawlins, Indian Army; no *c. Educ.:* Dollar Academy; Cheltenham College; Royal Military College, Sandhurst. Entered Army, 67th Regt. 1878; Capt. I.S.C. 1889; Major Indian Army, 1898; Lieut.-Col. 1904; Col. 1907; Maj.-Gen. 1912; A.A.G. and A.Q.M.G. India, 1909-10; Brigade Commander, Abbottabad Brigade, 1910-12; Jullundur Brigade, 1912-1915; Indian Army, 1915; Indian Army, Retired List, 1919; served Afghan War, 1878-80 (despatches, medal with two clasps); Burma, 1885-86 (severely wounded, despatches, medal with clasp); Chin-Lushai Expedition, 1888-90 (clasp); Burma, 1889 (clasp); Manipur, 1891 (severely wounded, despatches, clasp); Chitral, 1895 (medal with clasp); Tirah, 1897-98 (despatches, clasps); China, 1900 (medal); European War, 1914-15 (despatches, Bronze Star 1914 with clasp); British G.S. and Victory Medals; Delhi Durbar Medal, 1911. *Recreation:* sport in moderation. *Address:* New Court, Tenbury, Worcestershire. *T.:* Tenbury 34.

(Died 8 Dec. 1937.)

CARNOCK, 1st Baron, *cr.* 1916, of Carnock; **Arthur Nicolson;** 11th Bt., *cr.* 1687; P.C.; G.C.B., *cr.* 1907; G.C.M.G., *cr.* 1906; G.C.V.O., *cr.* 1905; K.C.B., *cr.* 1901; K.C.I.E., *cr.* 1888; K.C.V.O., *cr.* 1903; Permanent Under-Secretary for Foreign Affairs, 1910; retired, 1916; *b.* 19 Sep. 1849; *s.* of 10th Bt. and Mary, *d.* of James Loch of Drylaw; *S.* father, 1899; *m.* 1882, Mary Katherine, *d.* of Capt. Arch. Rowan Hamilton Killyleagh Castle, Co. Down; three *s.* one *d. Educ.:* Rugby; Brasenose College, Oxford; left before taking degree. Foreign Office, 1870-74; Assistant Private Secretary to Earl Granville, 1872-74; 3rd Sec. Embassy at Berlin, 1874-76; 2nd Sec. Legation at Pekin, 1876-78; Berlin, 1878-79; 2nd Sec. at Constantinople, 1879-84; Chargé d'Affaires, Athens, 1884-85; 1st Sec. and Chargé d'Affaires, Teheran, 1885-88; C.M.G. 1886; Consul-Gen. Budapest, 1888-93; Sec. of Embassy, Constantinople, 1894; Agent in Bulgaria, 1894-95; Minister in Morocco, 1895-1904; H.M.'s Ambassador Extraordinary and Plenipotentiary at Madrid, 1904-5; Ambassador to Russia, 1905-10; Grand Cross, Legion of Honour; Grand Cross, Carlos III. of Spain; Grand Cross, Alexander Nevsky; Hon. Fellow Brasenose College. *Publication:* History of the German Constitution, 1873. *Recreations:* riding, tennis, sailing. *Heir:* s. Hon. Frederick Archibald Nicolson. *Address:* 53 Cadogan Gardens, S.W.3. *T.:* Victoria 4141. *Club:* Travellers'. *(Died 5 Nov. 1928.)*

CAROLUS-DURAN, Emile Auguste, painter; b. Lille, 1838; m. Pauline Marie Croizette, herself an artist; one s. two d. Studied under Souchon. *Educ.:* Academie de Lille, Paris. Gained Wicar travelling scholarship and went to Italy. Resided in Spain. Works—La Prière du Soir, 1863; L'Assassine, 1866; St. Francis of Assisi, 1868; The Lady with the Glove. Portraits of Emile Gerardin, Mlle. Sophia Croizette, Queen Maria Pia of Portugal, Countess de Pourtales, Countess of Warwick, Countess de Vandal, Princess de Wagram, Duchess of Marlborough. Commander of the Legion of Honour, 1889; Commandeur of Order of Leopold; Grand Officier de la Légion d'Honneur; Grand Officier de St. Maurice et Lazare; Grand Croix d'Isabelle la Catholique (Espagne); Commandeur Charles III. (Espagne); Commandeur Christ de Portugal; Medaille de Sauvetage, etc.; Président d'Honneur de la Société Nationale des Beaux-Arts; Membre de l'Institut; Directeur honoraire de l'Académie de France a Rome (Villa Médicis). *Address:* 11 Passage Stanislas, Paris. *(Died 18 Feb. 1917.)*

CARPENTER, Capt. Alfred, R.N., A.M., D.S.O. 1887; F.R.Met.Soc., F.Z.S.; retired; b. Brighton, 2 Aug. 1847; s. of Commander Charles Carpenter, R.N.; m. 1st, 1879, Henrietta, d. of G. A. F. Shadwell; one s. one d.; 2nd, 1891, Etheldreda, d. of Judge Homersham Cox of Tonbridge. *Educ.:* Brighton College. Entered Royal Navy, 1861; Lieut. 1870; Commander, 1883; retired Capt. 1895; served in "Challenger" Scientific Expedition (Albert medal 2nd class for saving life); Soudan Expedition, 1884, in command of "Myrmidon" (medal and thanks of Admiralty); and whilst in charge of Marine Survey of India piloted the war flotilla under fire to Mandalay and Bhamo, 1885 (specially mentioned in despatches, Burma medal and D.S.O.); nine years in command of surveying vessels; last service, H.M. Coast-guard at Cowes. *Publication:* Nature Notes for Ocean Voyagers. *Recreations:* billiards, golf; interested in collections of corals, and in astronomy. *Address:* The Red House, Sanderstead, Surrey. *T.A.:* Sanderstead. *Club:* Authors'. *(Died 30 April 1925.)*

CARPENTER, Rev. J. Estlin, Hon. D.D. Glasg., D.Theol. Jena and Geneva; b. 1844; 2nd s. of Wm. B. Carpenter, C.B., M.D., F.R.S.; m. 1878. *Educ.:* University College School, London; University and Manchester New Colleges. M.A. Lond., D.Litt. and D.D. Oxford. Minister Oakfield Road Church, Clifton, 1866-69; Mill Hill Chapel, Leeds, 1869-75; Lecturer in Manchester College London and Oxford, 1875-1906; Principal, 1906-15; Wilde Lecturer, Oxford, 1914. *Publications:* Editor of Ewald's History of Israel, vols. iii.-v.; translator of Tiele's Outlines of the History of Religion; author of the Life and Work of Mary Carpenter;

Life in Palestine; The First Three Gospels, their Origin and Relations; The Bible in the Nineteenth Century; James Martineau, Theologian and Teacher; Phases of Early Christianity; Theism in Medieval India, 1921; joint-editor with Prof. Rhys Davids of the Digha Nikãya, and the Sumangala Vilãsinĩ; Buddhism and Christianity, 1923; joint-editor with Rev. G. Harford - Battersby of The Hexateuch according to the Revised Version; joint-author (with Rev. P. H. Wicksteed) of Studies in Theology; and other works. *Address:* 11 Marston Ferry Road, Oxford.
(Died 2 June 1927.)

CARPENTER-GARNIER, John; b. 28 Feb. 1839; o. s. of late John Carpenter, of Mount Tavy, Tavistock, Devon (d. 1842), and Lucy, d. of Rev. William and Lady Harriett Garnier, of Rookesbury Park, Fareham, Hants. Succeeded to Devon property on coming of age, 1860; and to Rookesbury Park on the death of his uncle, William Garnier; under whose will he assumed the name of Garnier in addition to Carpenter; m. 1868, Hon. Mary Louisa (d. 1903), 2nd d. of 19th Baron Clinton; three s. three d. *Educ.:* Harrow; Christ Church, Oxford. B.A. 1860; M.A. 1863 (was in the Harrow and Oxford Cricket Elevens). Contested South Hants as a Conservative, 1868; M.P. South Devon, 1873-1884; Sheriff for Hants, 1890-91; J.P. and D.L. for Hants and Devon. *Heir:* e. surv. s. George William; b. 1877. *Address:* Rookesbury Park, Fareham, Hants. *T.A.:* Wickham, Hants.
(Died 5 Oct. 1926.)

CARR, David; artist; b. London, 1847; m. Helen, d. of James Wrigley of Netherton, Yorks; one d. *Educ.:* Bruce Castle School, Tottenham. Applied Science Dep. of King's Coll., London. Was articled as a pupil to W. H. Barlow, C.E., Consulting Engineer to the Midland Rly., and for a time followed the profession of a Civil Engineer; relinquishing this, entered as an art student for three years at the Slade Schools, London University, under Prof. Legros, going later to Paris for further study; has been a continuous exhibitor at the Grosvenor Gallery from its commencement and afterwards at the New Gallery; also at the Royal Academy Institute, Munich, Melbourne, Sydney, etc.; has written and illustrated articles in the Pall Mall Gazette and Illustrated Magazines, and having added the profession of architecture to that of painting, is designing country houses, including houses at Beer, Budleigh Salterton, Crewkerne, Exmouth, Frimley and London, etc. *Recreations:* fly-fishing and boating. *Address:* Beer Haven, Beer, S. Devon. *T.A.:* Bear, Devon.
(Died 25 Dec. 1920.)

CARR, Rev. Edmund; inherited from his cousin, the late Sir T. W. Evans, Bart., of Allestree Hall, Derbyshire, his estates in Holbrooke, Derbyshire, and at Boscobel, Shropshire; o. surv. s. of Rev. J. E. Carr of The Outwoods, Derbyshire; b. 1 June 1826; m. 1st, 1858, Emma Anne, y. d. of late R. Stileman of The Friars, Winchelsea, Sussex; 2nd, 1873, Mary Fanny, o. d. of late Lt.-Col. Thomas Salkeld of Holm Hill, Cumberland; 3rd, 1881, Mary (d. 1904), e. surv. d. of late Rev. William Leeke, Vicar of Holbrooke, Derbyshire; three s. two d. *Educ.:* King's Coll., London; St. John's Coll., Camb. B.A. (32nd Wrangler) 1848; M.A. 1851. Ordained Deacon, 1849; Priest, 1850; Curate of Barford St. Martin, Wilts, 1849-56; Rector of Bonchurch, Isle of Wight, 1856-61; Perpetual Curate of Casterton, Westmoreland, 1861-66; Vicar of Dalston, Cumberland, 1866-83; Vicar of Holbrooke, Derbyshire, 1883-1907; Hon. Canon of Carlisle since 1867; Examining Chaplain to the late Bishop (Waldegrave) of Carlisle, 1868-69; Proctor in York Convocation for the Archdeaconry of Carlisle, 1874-86; Rural Dean of Wigton, Cumberland, 1880-83; Rural Dean of Duffield, Derbyshire, 1894-1900. *Address:* Holbrooke

Hall, near Derby. *T.A.:* Holbrooke, Derbyshire.
(*Died 12 May* 1916.)

CARR, Col. Edward Elliott, C.B. 1900;
C.B.E. 1919; Col. in charge of Records, Lowland Group of Regimental Districts, Scotland;
retired, 1909; *b.* 31 May 1854; *s.* of Dep. Surg.-
Gen. J. K. Carr, M.D., R.A.; *m.* 1883, Rosa
Elizabeth, *e. d.* of Rev. A. Hall; one *s. Educ.:*
tutors. Entered Army, 1878; Captain, 1883;
Major, 1891; Lt.-Col. 1898; employed on Staff
N.E. District, 1893-96; served in Tirah Campaign,
1897 (medal with two clasps); S. A. Campaign,
1899-1901 (wounded, clasp), despatches, Queen's
medal four clasps, King's medal two clasps);
A Staff Lowland Division, 1914; Inspector L.
of C. Home, 1914-15; Commanding Base Depot,
France, 1915-16; Reinforcements, 1916-18 (despatches twice, C.B.E.). *Recreations:* hunting,
cricket. *Address:* Hilton, Sidmouth, Devon.
Clubs: Army and Navy, Bath.
(*Died 18 May* 1926.)

CARR, J. W. Comyns, critic and dramatist;
b. 1 Mar. 1849; *m.* Miss Strettell. *Educ.:*
London Univ. Barr. Inner Temple, 1869; Art
Critic on the Pall Mall *Gazette*; English editor
of L'Art, 1875; Director and one of the founders
of the New Gallery. *Publications:* Drawings by
the Old Masters, 1877; The Abbey Church of St.
Albans, 1878; Examples of Contemporary Art
1878; Essays on Art; Papers on Art; Founder and
late Editor of The English Illustrated Magazine;
Joint author of Called Back, Dark Days, Boys
Together, In the Days of the Duke, and The
Beauty Stone; Author of A Fireside Hamlet,
The United Pair, The Naturalist, The Friar,
Forgiveness, King Arthur, Oliver Twist and
Tristram and Iseult; Some Eminent Victorians;
Coasting Bohemia, 1914. *Address:* 12 Northwick Terrace, St. John's Wood, N.W. *Club:*
Garrick. (*Died 12 Dec.* 1916.)

CARR, Most Rev. Thomas Joseph,
D.D., R.C. Archbishop of Melbourne and Metropolitan of Victoria since 1886; *b.* Co. Galway,
1839. *Educ.:* St. Jarlath's, Tuam; Maynooth.
Priest, 1866; parish work at Westport; Professor at St. Jarlath, Tuam; was Professor of
Theology, Dean and Vice-President of Maynooth;
Editor Irish Ecclesiastical Record, 1880-83;
Bishop of Galway and Kilmacduagh, and Apostolic Administrator of Kilfenora, 1883 - 86.
Publications: A Commentary on the Constitution; Apostolicae Sedis Moderationi, 1879;
a series of Lectures and Replies in connection
with a polemical attack by the Anglican Bishops
of Melbourne and Ballarat, 1895; The Blessed
Eucharist; Belief of the Early English Church,
1912. *Address:* Melbourne, Australia.
(*Died 6 May* 1917.)

CARR, Sir William St. John, Kt., *cr.*
1905; *b.* 21 Feb. 1848; *s.* of Captain John Carr
of The Lodge, Clonmel, Ireland; *m.* 1878, Sarah,
d. of E. Slater of Port Elizabeth; one *s.* one *d.
Educ.:* privately; French College, Blackrock;
matriculated at Catholic University of Dublin.
Commenced life as midshipman in mercantile
service, visiting New Zealand, Australia, China,
Cochin China, Japan, Siam, etc.; subsequently
in 1869 went to India, and was on the Great
Indian Peninsula Railway till 1874; then went
to South Africa and entered the service of the
Cape Government Railways; in 1887 went to
Johannesburg, where he was after some experience of the early days of the goldfields eventually a director of some mining and other
companies, and was first Chairman of the
Hospital Board; was a prominent member of
the National Union, a political organisation
started in the Transvaal about 1891; later was
a member of the Reform Committee, and was
imprisoned at Pretoria at the time of the
Jameson Raid, being one of those sentenced to
two years' imprisonment; at the commencement of the Boer War joined the Imperial Light

Horse, was in the siege of Ladysmith, and
served with his regiment till appointed deputy-
Chairman of the Town Council of Johannesburg
in May 1901; was thereafter acting Chairman
till his election as first Mayor of Johannesburg
in 1903; Chairman of the Rand Water Board,
1904-7; created Knight of Saint Gregory by
Pius X., 1907; J.P. *Club:* Rand, Johannesburg.
(*Died 23 June* 1928.)

CARR-GOMM, Francis Culling, V.D.;
2nd *s.* of late Rev. T. W. Carr of Southboro',
Kent; *b.* 1834; *m.* 1st, Jeanie (*d.* 1869), *d.* of
Maj. E. Francklyn; three *s.* one *d.*; 2nd, 1876,
Emily Blanche (*d.* 1909), *d.* of late A. Morton
Carr, Barrister-at-law, and niece of F.-M. Sir W.
M. Gomm, G.C.B., Constable of the Tower of
London; two *s.* one *d. Educ.:* Cheam School;
H.E.I.C.'s College, Haileybury. Liberal. Madras
C.S., retired; for many years District Judge
of Tinnevelly, South India; Barrister, Inner
Temple, 1869; J.P., D.L., Bucks; High Sheriff,
1894; late chairman London Hospital; late
Hon. Col. 3rd V.B. The Queen's R. W. Surrey.
Mrs. Carr-Gomm was Lady of the Manor of
Rotherhithe. They assumed by Royal Licence
the surname and arms of Gomm, 1878. *Publications:* Life of Sir William Gomm; Handbook
of Administrations of Nineteenth Century;
Records of the Parish of Farnham Royal.
Heir: H. W. C. Carr-Gomm. *Address:*
The Chase, Farnham Royal, Bucks. *T.A.:*
Carr-Gomm, Farnham-Common. *T.:* 37 Farnham Common. *Club:* East India United Service.
(*Died 12 Jan.* 1919.)

**CARRICK-BUCHANAN, David Wm.
Ramsay,** of Drumpellier, etc.; *b.* 9 March,
1834; *e. s.* of Andrew Buchanan (2nd *s.* of D.
Carrick-Buchanan, of Drumpellier) and Bethia,
d. of late William Ramsay; *m.* 1863, Lady
Kathleen Alicia Hely-Hutchinson (*d.* 1892), *e. d.*
of 3rd Earl of Donoughmore, K.P.; one *s.*
two *d. Educ.:* Rugby; Edinburgh University.
Was Captain 2nd R. Lanark Regiment, and Sec.
of Commissions in the Court of Chancery.
Address: Corsewall, Stranraer, N.B. *T.A.:*
Kirkcolm. *Clubs:* Junior Carlton; New,
Edinburgh. (*Died 4 May* 1925.)

CARROLL, Hon. Sir James, K.C.M.G.,
cr. 1911; M.L.C. since 1921; Native Minister
and Commissioner of Stamp Duties, 1900-12;
Member of House of Representatives for Waiapu,
1893-1908, and for Gisborne, 1908-19; *b.* Wairoa,
Hawkes Bay, N.Z., 20 Aug. 1857; *m.* Heni
Materoa, O.B.E. Native Interpreter to the
House of Representatives, 1879-83; Member of
the House of Representatives for the Eastern
Maori Electoral Dist. 1887-93; became a member
of the Executive Council representing the native
race in the Ballance Govt. 1892, and continued to
hold same office in Seddon Govt.; became Commissioner of Stamp Duties, 1896; assumed the
portfolio of Native Minister, 1900 (the first of
his race to hold that position); was acting
Premier of N.Z. on occasion of Coronation of
King George V. *Address:* Kahutia Road,
Gisborne, N.Z. (*Died 18 Oct.* 1926.)

**CARROLL, Brig.-Gen. John William
Vincent,** C.M.G. 1916; D.S.O. 1919; *b.* 12 July
1869; *e. s.* of late Frederick Maxwell Carroll, J.P.,
of Moone Abbey, Co. Kildare; *m.* 1901, Barbara
Mary, *y. d.* of late James Tisdall Woodroffe,
C.S.I.; two *s.* two *d. Educ.:* Woburn; Oratory
School. 2nd Lieut. Norfolk Regt. 1891; served
in W. Africa, Northern Nigeria, 1895-99 (2
medals and 6 clasps, despatches, Bt.-Major);
served in S. African War in Mounted Infantry,
1899-1901 (Queen's medal and 3 clasps); Commandant Mounted Infantry, Egypt, 1909; Lt.-
Col. Commanding Mounted Infantry, South
Africa, 1910; Lt.-Col. Commanding 7th (Service)
Batt. Norfolk Reg. 1914-15; served European
War (despatches, C.M.G.); Commanded the
Russian Force at Morjegorskaia, Mar. 1919

(D.S.O., St. George's Cross, 4th Class, St. Vladimir 4th Class). *Recreations*: steeplechase riding, polo, cricket, hunting. *Club*: Naval and Military.
(Died 16 Jan. 1927.)

CARRUTHERS, William, Ph.D., F.R.S., F.L.S., F.G.S.; *b.* Moffat, 1830; *s.* of Samuel Carruthers, Merchant; *m.* 1865, Jeanie, *e. d.* of Wm. Moffatt, Architect, Edinburgh; one *s. Educ.*: Edin. Univ. and New Coll. Late Keeper of the Botanical Department, British Museum; Pres. Linn. Soc. 1886-90; Pres. Royal Micros. Soc., 1900-1; Consulting Botanist, Royal Agricultural Society, England, 1871-1910; Member of the Lawes Agricultural Trust Committee; author of many papers on Systematic, Palæontological, and Agricultural Botany; pursues as a by-study the history and literature of Puritan England and has formed a considerable collection of works thereon; and published a facsimile edition of the Shorter Catechism, with full bibliography; editor of the Annals and Magazine of Natural History and of Children's Messenger, Presbyterian Church of England. *Address*: 44 Central Hill, Norwood, S.E. *T.*: 117 Sydenham. *(Died 2 June 1922.)*

CARSON, Maj. - General Sir John Wallace, Kt. *cr.* 1917; C.B. 1916; Reserve of Officers, Canadian Militia Force: Canadian Expeditionary Force; Director, Union Bank of Canada; Vice-President, Crown Trust Company; Director, Crown Reserve Mining Co. and Associated Co.; Lake of the Woods Milling Co.; *b.* 13 Oct. 1864; *s.* of late William and Mary Johnston Carson; *m.* 1885, Mary A. R., *d.* of late Henry Corran of St. John's, P.Q., two *d. Educ.*: Public and High Schools, Montreal. Served in Canadian Militia for a total period of 39 years; served European War, 1914-18 (despatches, C.B., Order of St. Stanislas of Russia). *Address*: 4113 Sherbrooke Street, Westmount, Montreal. *(Died 13 Oct. 1922.)*

CARSON, Murray, actor - dramatist; *b.* 17 Mar. 1865; *m.* Mary Eleanor Stirling, *y.d.* of J. S. Donald, late of Australia. Made first appearance on stage, 1882; visited America, 1906. *Plays* produced in collaboration: David Gudgeons: The Blue Boar; Spell-bound Garden; Rosemary; Change Alley; The Jest; The Fly on the Wheel; A Man Himself; When a Man's Married; The Trifler; The Bishop's Move; Simple Simon, etc. *Recreations*: golf, billiards, travelling. *Address*: 7 Cowley Street, Westminster Abbey, S.W. *T.*: 3598 Westminster. *Clubs*: National Liberal, Royal Automobile.
(Died 20 April 1917.)

CARSON, Thomas Henry, K.C. 1901; *s.* of Rev. Joseph Carson, D.D., late Vice-Provost of Trinity College, Dublin; *b.* 24 Nov. 1843; *m.* 1st, 1876, Mary Sophia, 3rd *d.* of late Rev. Comyns Tucker; 2nd, 1887, Marie Louise Emma, *d.* of Albert Bernouilli Barlow of Le Havre, France; one *s. Educ.*: Marlborough Coll.; Trinity College, Dublin. Scholar, 1863; Berkeley Medallist; Wray Prize; B.A. 1866, as first Gold Medallist in classics, first Gold Medallist in philosophy, and obtaining a Univ. studentship; M.A. 1867. Barr. Lincoln's Inn, 1869. Bencher of Lincoln's Inn, 1907. *Publications*: Lectures on Prescription and Custom; joint-editor of Carson's Real Property Statutes; Tudor's Leading Cases in Real Property and Conveyancing; and of the Equity articles in Lord Halsbury's Laws of England; editor of Gale on Easements, 9th ed. *Recreations*: member of the Alpine Club and of English and French cycling clubs. *Address*: 4 Vicarage Gardens, W.; 6 New Square, Lincoln's Inn, W.C. *T.*: 1360 Park, 8251 City. *Club*: Athenæum. *(Died 30 June 1917.)*

CARTER, Alfred Henry, M.D.; M.Sc., F.R.C.P.; Consulting Physician (retired); *s.* of C. H. Carter, F.R.C.S.; *b.* Pewsey, Wilts, 1849; *m.* 1st, 1885, Constance Mary, *d.* of Albert C. Goode, The Glebe, Moseley, Birm.; one *s.*;

2nd, 1890, Elizabeth Marian, *d.* of W. H. King, Solicitor, Pedmore House, Stourbridge; one *s.* one *d. Educ.*: Epsom College; University College, London. Emeritus Professor of Medicine, Birmingham University, 1892-1913; Consulting Physician, Queen's Hospital, Birmingham; Emeritus Professor of Physiology, Queen's College, Birmingham; late Examiner in Medicine for London University; J.P., Worcester. *Publications*: Elements of Practical Medicine, 10th ed., 1906; Text-Book of Physical Exercises for Elementary Schools, 1896; and various contributions to Medical Journals. *Address*: The Lindens, Abingdon, Berks. *Club*: Oxford and County. *(Died 4 April 1918.)*

CARTER, Hon. Arthur John, Member of Legislative Council of Queensland since 1901; merchant; Consul for Norway; Consular Agent for France; *b.* St. Ives, Hunts., 27 Sep. 1847; *s.* of Rev. Charles and Margaret Carter. *Educ.*: Woodhouse Grove (Yorks.); Harpur Schools, Bedford; King's College, London. Entered Lloyd's Underwriting Room, London, 1868; left England for Queensland, 1870; since followed mercantile pursuits; Pres. Chamber Commerce, Brisbane, 1898, 1899, 1901, 1902, 1906; nominated Marine Board, 1899; Chairman of Queensland Board of Directors, Atlas Assurance Co., Ltd., London; and of Directors, Queensland Trustees, Ltd., Millaquin Sugar Co., Ltd., E. Rich & Co., Ltd., John Hicks & Co., Ltd.; Director of Dath Henderson & Co., Ltd., and Jacques Leutenegger, Ltd.; Officier d'Académie (France); Chevalier de 1ere classe de l'ordre de St. Olav (Norway). *Publications*: journalistic contributions to local press on Russo-Turkish war, bimetalism, and Australian national defences. *Recreations*: fishing, literature. *Address*: Queen Street and Nunnington, Main Street, Brisbane. *Clubs*: Queensland, Johnsonian. *(Died 4 Nov. 1917.)*

CARTER, Maj.-Gen. Beresford Cecil Molyneux, C.B. 1916; C.M.G. 1915; late Commanding South African Military Command, Capetown, S.A.; *b.* 12 Aug. 1872; *s.* of late Col. H. M. Carter, C.B.; *m.* Bertha Isabel Ada, *e. d.* of late Col. E. Baines; three *s.* two *d. Educ.*: Marlborough College; Gold Medallist United Service Institute (India), 1912. Entered Lancashire Fusiliers, 1891; Captain, 1898; Major, 1904; Liverpool Regt. 1908; Lt.-Col. 1914; employed with Egyptian army, 1900-7; served Nile Expedition, 1898 (Egyptian medal with clasp; medal); Sudan, 1905 (despatches, Egyptian medal with clasp, 4th class Osmanieh); European War, 1914-18 (C.B., C.M.G., Bt. Col.); retired pay, 1922. *Recreations*: big game shooting (fine collection of heads); fishing. *Address*: Ganderbal, Newbury, Berks. *T.*: Newbury 244. *Club*: Junior United Service.
(Died 23 July 1923.)

CARTER, Franklin, Ph.D., LL.D.; President Clarke School for the Deaf 1896-1917; *b.* Waterbury, Conn. 30 Sept. 1837; *s.* of Preserve W. Carter, manufacturer, and Ruth Holmes Carter; *m.* 1st, Sarah L. (*d.* 1905), *d.* of Chas. D. Kingsbury, Waterbury, 1863; three *s.* one *d.*; 2nd, 1908, Mrs. Frederic Leake, *d.* of late H. L. Sabin, M.D., of Williamstown, Mass. *Educ.*: Phillips Academy, Andover, Mass.; Yale and Williams Coll.; Berlin Univ. Professor in Williams College, 1865-72; in Yale University, 1872-81; President of Williams College, 1881-1901; Member of Massachusetts State Board of Education, 1897-1901. *Publications*: Goethe's Iphigenie, 1877; Life of Mark Hopkins, 1892; various addresses and magazine articles. *Recreations*: riding, fishing, golf. *Address*: Williams College, Williamstown, Mass. *Clubs*: Williams, New York. *(Died 22 Nov. 1919.)*

CARTER, Sir George (John), K.B.E., *cr.* 1917; J.P., M.I.C.E., M.I.N.A., M.I.M.E.; Managing Director of Cammell Laird and Co.

Limited, Birkenhead; Director of Coventry Ordnance Works, Ltd.; President of the Shipbuilding Employers' Federation; was Chairman of the Merchant Shipbuilding Advisory Committee to the Controller of Shipping, and later a Member of the Shipbuilding Council; Member of Council of Institute of Naval Architects, Federation of British Industries; Member of Committee, Lloyd's Register; Member of the Mersey Docks and Harbour Board; Deputy Chairman of Liverpool Munitions Committee; *b.* 1860; *m.* 1894, Edith Harriet, *d.* of late J. S. Vaux, Sunderland; two *s. Educ.:* privately. *Recreation:* motoring. *Address:* Brackenwood, Hr. Bebington, Cheshire. *T.:* Rock Ferry 38; Dinbren Hall, Llangollen, North Wales. *T.:* Llangollen 56. *Clubs:* Constitutional, Royal Societies, Royal Automobile.

(Died 9 Feb. 1922.)

CARTER, Capt. Herbert Augustine, V.C. 1904; The 101st Grenadiers; *b.* 26 May 1874; *s.* of Rev. C. R. D. Carter; *m.* 1911, Helen Lilian, *d.* of Rev. Canon Wilmot-Ware; served North-West Frontier, India, 1897-98 (medal with 2 clasps); Somaliland, 1902-4 (despatches, medal with 2 clasps); Somaliland, 1908-10 (despatches, clasp). *Clubs:* United Service, Sports, Royal Aero. *(Died 13 Jan. 1916.)*

CARTER, Hugh Hoyles, K.C. 1904; *e. surv.* s. of late Hon. Sir Frederic B. F. Carter, K.C.M.G., Chief Justice of Newfoundland. *Educ.:* Bishop Field College. Clerk to Legislative Council, Newfoundland, since 1875; called to Bar, Newfoundland, 1876; Bencher of Law Society, 1902. *Recreations:* fishing and shooting. *Address:* St. John's, Newfoundland.

CARTER, John Corrie; Barrister, Inner Temple; Recorder of Stamford, 1891-1912; Chairman of Quarter Sessions for Radnorshire, 1895-1913; *b.* 1839; *s.* of late S. Carter, M.P.; *m.* Amy Josephine Lonsdale. *Educ.:* Trinity College, Cambridge. Went Midland Circuit; Director of Midland Railway, 1896-1910. *Publications:* editor of three editions of Rogers on Elections, and of 19th edition of Ronald's Fly Fisher's Entomology. *Recreations:* fishing, shooting, golf; steered winning boat of the four chief races at Henley in 1862, 1st Trinity, Cambridge. *Address:* 65 Sussex Gardens, W.2; Cefnfaes, Rhayader, Radnorshire. *Club:* Albemarle. *(Died 5 June 1927.)*

CARTER, John Hilton, M.V.O.; in Masonry—Past Grand Deacon of England (P.G.D.); Manager and Secretary of the Royal Albert Hall since 1901; *s.* of late James Carter of Mansfield, Notts; *m.* Alice Ann, *d.* of late Samuel Robinson of Daybrook, Notts, and *niece* of Sir John Robinson of Worksop Manor, Notts; one *s.* one *d. Educ.:* Nottingham High School. A commercial education in Nottingham, afterwards Secretary respectively of the Hampstead Conservatoire, the London Organ School, the Guildhall School of Music; founder of the London Nottinghamshire Society; originator and a founder of the Royal Albert Hall Lodge (No. 2986); holder of the Coronation medals of late King Edward VII. and King George V. *Recreations:* music, gardening, freemasonry. *Address:* Corona, 43 Mapesbury Road, Brondesbury, N.W.2. *T.:* Willesden 425. *(Died 9 April 1926.)*

CARTER, Robert Brudenell, F.R.C.S. England; consulting Ophthalmic Surgeon, St. George's Hospital, 1893-1903; [11th in descent from Thomas Carter, a gentleman bearing arms, who was settled at Higham, Co. Bed., in the reign of Edward IV.]; *b.* Little Wittenham, Berks, 2 Oct. 1828; *s.* of Thomas Carter, Maj. R.M., and 2nd wife, Louisa, *d.* of Richard Jeffrys of Basingstoke and Silchester; *m.* 1st, Helen Ann Beauchamp, *d.* of John Becher; 2nd, Rachel Elizabeth, *d.* of Stephen Hallpike, and

widow of late Walter Browne; four *s. Educ.:* London Hospital. Staff-Surgeon during Crimean War (English and Turkish medals); settled in London as Ophthalmic Surgeon, 1868; Ophthalmic Surgeon to St. George's Hospital, 1870; member General Medical Council, 1887-1900; Hunterian Professor of Pathology and Surgery, Royal College of Surgeons, 1881-82; Lumleian lecturer, Orator, Past Pres., and Hon. Fellow Med. Soc. of London; Knight of Justice and Hon. Commander Order of St. John of Jerusalem. *Publications:* books on Hysteria, Education, Diseases of the Eye; articles on Eye Disease in Quain's Dictionary of Medicine and Holmes's System of Surgery; Doctors and their Work, 1903; translator of Zander on the Ophthalmoscope and of Scheffler's Optical Defects of the Eye. *Address:* 76 South Side, Clapham Common, S.W.

(Died 24 Oct. 1918.)

CARTER-CAMPBELL, Colonel George Tupper Campbell, C.B. 1919; D.S.O. 1915; 2nd Batt. Cameronians; *b.* 2 April 1869; *o. surv. s.* of late Col. Carter Campbell, Possil, Lanarks; Ardrishaig, Argyllshire; *m.* 1908, Frances Elizabeth, *d.* of late Col. David Ward, R.E.; one *s.* one *d.* Entered army, 1889; Captain, 1897; Adjutant, 1899-1903; Major, 1907; Adjutant Volunteers, 1901-7; served South Africa, 1899-1902 (despatches twice; Bt. Major; Queen's medal, 4 clasps; King's medal, 2 clasps); European War, 1914-17 (Bt. Lt.-Col. and Col., D.S.O., C.B.); Temp. Brig.-Gen., Sept. 1915; Temp. Major-General, March 1918. *Club:* Army and Navy. *(Died 19 Dec. 1921.)*

CARTER-COTTON, Baron Francis; LL.D.; First Chancellor of the University of British Columbia; Chairman of Vancouver Harbour Commission; *b.* 1847; *m.* Maria Emily, *d.* of late Thomas Little; two *s.* one *d.* Member of Legislature of British Columbia, 1890-1900, 1903-16; Finance Minister, 1898-1900; President of Council, 1904-10. *Clubs:* Vancouver, Vancouver; Union, Victoria.

CARTMELL, Sir Harry, Kt., *cr.* 1920; J.P. Lancashire; Mayor of Preston, 1913-19; Chairman, Preston Education Committee. *Address:* 9 Victoria Road, St. Annes-on-Sea. *T.:* 221. *(Died 11 May 1923.)*

CARTMELL, James Austen-, Barrister-at-Law, Lincoln's Inn; Junior Equity Counsel to Treasury and Board of Trade since 1913; *b.* 12 Aug. 1862; *o. s.* of late Rev. James Cartmell, D.D., formerly Master of Christ's College, Cambridge, and Chaplain in Ordinary to Her late Majesty, and Frances Eliza, *o. d.* of late Rev. John Thomas Austen, formerly Rector of West Wickham and Honorary Canon of Canterbury; *m.* 1st, 1886, Mary Affleck (*d.* 1906), *y. d.* of late W. H. Peacock of Greatford Hall, Stamford; one *d.*; 2nd, 1919, Constance, *d.* of late James Petrie of Dufftown, Scotland. *Educ.:* Rugby; Christ's College, Cambridge (Scholar, 1881-1885; First Class Classical Tripos, Part I., 1884; Second Class Classical Tripos, Part II., 1885). Called to Bar, Lincoln's Inn, 1889; has throughout practised at the Chancery Bar; Junior Equity Counsel to Board of Inland Revenue, and other Government Departments, 1908-13; Bencher, Lincoln's Inn, 1913. *Publications:* Abstract of Trade Mark Cases, 1892; Finance Act, 1894 (Death Duties, England), 1st ed. 1894, 5th ed. 1912. *Address:* 27 Campden House Court, Campden Hill, W.S. *T.:* Park 5336. *M.:* LC 412. *Clubs:* Athenæum, Brooks's, United University.

(Died 28 May 1921.)

CARTON, R. C., dramatist; *s.* of late George Critchett, F.R.C.S.; *m.* Miss Compton; one *d. Publications:* Sunlight and Shadow, Liberty Hall, Robin Goodfellow, The Home Secretary, A White Elephant, The Tree of

Knowledge, Lord and Lady Algy, Wheels within Wheels, Lady Huntworth's Experiment, The Undercurrent, A Clean Slate, The Rich Mrs. Repton, Mr. Hopkinson, Public Opinion, Mr. Preedy and the Countess; Lorrimer Sabiston, Dramatist; Eccentric Lord Comberdene; The Bear-Leaders; A Busy Day; The Off-Chance; Other People's Worries, One too Many, 1922. *Address:* The Red Lodge, Acton, W.3. *T.:* Chiswick 1200. *(Died 1 April 1928.)*

CARTWRIGHT, Rt. Hon. Sir Fairfax (Leighton), P.C. 1908; G.C.M.G., *cr.* 1914; G.C.V.O., *cr.* 1909; K.C.M.G., *cr.* 1908; M.V.O. 1903; J.P. Oxfordshire; *b.* 20 July 1857; *o. surv. s.* of late William Cornwallis Cartwright of Aynho; *m.* 1898, Maria, *d.* of Marchese Chigi-Zondodari; one *s.* Attaché, 1881; 3rd Sec. 1883; 2nd Sec. 1887; has served at Berlin, Stockholm, Teheran, Madrid, Vienna, Rome; First Secretary, Mexico, 1899-1902; Lisbon, 1902-6; Minister-Resident at Munich, 1906-8; Ambassador to Austro-Hungary, 1908-13; retired, 1913. *Publication:* The Mystic Rose from the Garden of the King, 1925. *Address:* Aynho Park, Banbury.
(Died 9 Jan. 1928.)

CARTWRIGHT, Brig.-Gen. Garnier Norton, C.M.G. 1917; D.S.O.1915; late R.F.A.; *b.* 7 May 1868; *s.* of R. N. Cartwright, Ixworth Abbey, Suffolk; *m.* 1909, Isabel, *d.* of late T. J. Masters, Llanelly Hall, Llantrisant. Entered army, 1888; Captain, 1898; Major, 1903; Lt.-Col., 1914; served European War, 1914-17 (despatches, D.S.O., C.M.G.); retired pay, 1922. *Club:* Naval and Military. *(Died 9 April 1924.)*

CARTWRIGHT, J. R., K.C.; Deputy Attorney-General, Ontario. *Educ.:* Rugby; Queen's College, Oxford; B.A. 1866. *Address:* Toronto, Ontario. *(Died 11 Sept. 1919.)*

CARTWRIGHT, Thomas Robert Brook Leslie-Melville, J.P., D.L.; 2nd *s.* of late Sir Thomas Cartwright, G.C.H., of Aynhoe, Co. Northampton, and Marie Elizabeth Augusta, *d.* of Count Von Sandizell, of Bavaria; *b.* 1830; *m.* 1858, Lady Elizabeth Jane (*d.* 1892), *e. d.* of 8th Earl of Leven and 7th Earl of Melville; four *d.* *Educ.:* Merton College, Oxford. *Address:* Newbottle Manor, Banbury. *Club:* Carlton. *(Died 23 Jan. 1921.)*

CARUS, Dr. Paul; editor of the Monist and the Open Court; *b.* Ilsenburg, Germany, 18 July 1852; *s.* of Gustave Carus, Superintendent-General of Prussian State Church of Eastern and Western Prussia; *m.* 1888, Mary Hegeler; four *s.* two *d.* *Educ.:* Stettin Gymnasium; Universities of Strasburg and Tübingen. *Publications:* The Ethical Problem; Fundamental Problems; The Soul of Man; Primer of Philosophy; Truth in Fiction; Monism and Meliorism; The Religion of Science; The Philosophy of the Tool; Our Need of Philosophy; Science, a Religious Revelation; The Gospel of Buddha; Karma; Nirvana; Lao-tze's Tao Teh King; Homilies of Science; The Idea of God; Buddhism and its Christian Critics; The History of the Devil; Whence and Whither; Eros and Psyche; Goethe and Schiller's Xenions; The Crown of Thorns; The Chief's Daughter; Godward; Sacred Tunes for the Consecration of Life; Kant's Prolegomena; Our Children; Das Evangelium Buddhas; The Surd of Metaphysics; La Conscience du Moi; The Nature of the State; The Dawn of a New Era; Friedrich Schiller; Kan Ying P'ien; Yin Chih Wen; Chinese Life and Customs; Chinese Thought; The Rise of Man; The Story of Samson; The Bride of Christ; God An Enquiry and a Solution; The Foundations of Mathematics; Angelus Silesius; Edward's Dream (Busch); Christianity as the Pleroma; The Philosopher's Martyrdom; Truth on Trial; Personality; The Oracle of Yahveh; The Philosophy of Form; The Buddha (a drama); Buddhist Hymns; The Principle of Relativity; The Mechanistic Principle and the Non-Mechanical; Nietzsche; Truth and other

Poems; Goethe: the Man and his Philosophy; K'ung Fu Tze, a dramatic poem on the life of Confucius; The Venus of Milo; The New Morn (a dramatic poem); The Canon of Reason and Virtue (rev. ed. of Tao Teh King). *Recreation:* photography. *Address:* La Salle, Illinois, U.S.A. *T.A.:* Carus. *T.:* 106. *Clubs:* Authors', New York; Press, University, Cliff-dwellers', Deutsche Studenten, Chicago.
(Died 11 Feb. 1919.)

CARUSO, Enrico, M.V.O. 1907; *b.* Naples, 25 Feb. 1873; *m.* 2nd, 1918, Dorothy, *d.* of Park Benjamin, patent lawyer, New York. No special musical education. *Principal rôles:* Edgardo in Lucia; Des Grieux in Manon Lescaut; Pagliaccia; the Duke in Rigoletto; Lohengrin, etc. *Address:* Villa alle Panche, Porta San Gallo, Florence. *(Died 2 Aug. 1921.)*

CARVILL, Patrick George Hamilton, J.P.; late Member of the Court of Referees in the House of Commons; *b.* 1839; *s.* of late Francis Carvill of Newry and Rosstrevor, Co. Down. Matriculated London University. English Barr. 1888 (Northern Circuit); J.P. Cos. Down and Armagh; Sheriff Co. Armagh, 1878; M.P. (N.) Newry, 1892-1906. *Address:* 5 King's Bench Walk, Temple, E.C.; 105 Pall Mall, S.W.; Ballyvourney, Co. Cork. *Clubs:* Reform, Ranelagh. *(Died 10 Jan. 1924.)*

CARYLL, Ivan; was musical director, Gaiety and Lyric Theatres; *b.* Liege; *m.* Maud Hill. *Educ.:* Liege Conservatoire; Paris. Came to England, 1882. Composer of a large number of musical comedies, including The Earl and the Girl, The Circus Girl, The Toreador, The Spring Chicken, Our Miss Gibbs, The Lucky Star, The Duchess of Dantzic, The Little Cherub, The New Aladdin, Nelly Neil, The Girls of Gottenburg, The Pink Lady. *Address:* c/o Chappell & Co., Ltd., 50 New Bond Street, W.1.
(Died 29 Nov. 1921.)

CASARTELLI, Rt. Rev. Louis Charles, R.C. Bishop of Salford since 1903; Professor of Zend and Pehlevi, Louvain, 1900-1903; Lecturer on Iranian Languages, University of Manchester, 1903-20; *b.* Manchester, 14 Nov. 1852; *s.* of Jos. L. Casartelli native of Como, Italy. *Educ.:* Ushaw Coll., Durham; University of Louvain, Belgium. M.A., London, 1873; Dr. of Oriental Literature, Louvain, 1884; Hon. D.D. Louvain, 1909. Ordained priest (by late Cardinal Vaughan) 1876; Master at St. Bede's College, Manchester, 1877-91; Rector of St. Bede's College, 1891-1903. President Manchester Statistical Society, 1898-1900; Officer of the Order of Leopold (Belgium), 1903, Commander of the Order of Leopold II. (Belgium), 1919; President of the Manchester Dante Society since 1906; Member of the Court of Manchester University, 1907-20; Pres. of Manchester Egyptian Assoc. 1909-11; President of Manchester Egyptian and Oriental Society, 1917-18; Chairman of Universities Catholic Education Board, 1915-23. *Publications:* Lectures on Commercial Geography, 1884; La Philosophie religieuse du Mazdéisme sous les Sassanides, Louvain, 1884; Traité de médecine Mazdéenne, traduit du Pehlevi, Louv. 1886; Sketches in History, chiefly Ecclesiastical, 1906; Moods and Tenses (verses), 1906; Leaves from my Eastern Garden (translations from Sanskrit and Avestan), 1908; The Popes in the Divina Commedia of Dante, 1921; articles, chiefly on Oriental subjects, in Le Muséon, Babylonian and Oriental Record, Dublin Review, American Catholic Encyclopædia, Hastings' Encyclopædia of Religion and Ethics, and proceedings of various Congresses of Orientalists; also in proceedings of the Manchester Statistical and Geographical Societies. *Address:* St. Bede's College, Manchester, S.W. *T.:* Chorlton 241.
(Died 18 Jan. 1925.)

CASE, Thomas, M.A., President of Corpus Christi College, Oxford, 1904-24 ; *m.* 1870, Elizabeth Donn, *o. d.* of late Sir William Sterndale Bennett; one *s. Educ.:* Rugby ; Balliol College, Oxford. Formerly Fellow of Brasenose, Tutor of Balliol, Lecturer at Christ Church, Fellow and Tutor of Corpus Christi College, Oxford ; Fellow of Magdalen College and Waynflete Professor of Moral and Metaphysical Philosophy, Oxford, 1889-1910 ; Hon. Fellow, Magdalen College. *Publications:* Materials for History of Athenian Democracy from Solon to Pericles, 1874 ; Realism in Morals, 1877 ; Physical Realism, 1888 ; St. Mary's Clusters, 1893 ; articles on Aristotle, Logic, and Metaphysics in the Encyclopædia Britannica, 1902, 1910 ; contributor to Lectures on the Method of Science, 1906 ; Preface to Bacon's Advancement of Learning, 1907 ; Twelve Songs, 1918 ; Three Songs, 1924. *Recreations:* Oxford Univ. Eleven, 1864-67. *Address:* Corpus Christi College, Oxford. *Club:* M.C.C.

(*Died 31 Oct. 1925.*)

CASGRAIN, Rt. Hon. Thomas Chase, P.C., K.C., LL.D. ; Postmaster-General of Canada since 1914 ; *b.* Detroit, 28 July 1852 ; *s.* of Hon. Charles Eugene Casgrain, M.D., C.M. ; *m.* 1st, 1878, Marie Louise (*d.* 1914), *d.* of late Alexander Le Moine, Quebec, one *s.* ; 2nd, Madame René Masson, Paris. *Educ.:* Quebec Seminary ; Laval University. Called to Bar, 1877 ; Professor of Criminal Law, Laval University, 1883 ; junior Counsel for the Crown at trial of Louis Riel ; elected to Legislative Assembly, 1886 ; Attorney General, Province of Quebec, 1891-96 ; Member of House of Commons, 1896-1904 ; Batonnier General of Quebec Bar, 1903-5. *Address:* Ottawa. *Clubs:* Constitutional ; Mount Royal, St. James, St. Denis, Montreal, Forest and Stream, Jockey, Montreal ; Rideau, Ottawa ; Garrison, Quebec.

(*Died 29 Dec. 1916.*)

CASHIN, Hon. Sir Michael Patrick, K.B.E., *cr.* 1918 ; Member House of Assembly for Ferryland District since 1893, being longest unbroken record in history of Colony ; *b.* Cape Broyle, 29 Sep. 1864 ; *s.* of Richard Cashin ; *m.* 1888, Gertrude C., *d.* of Capt. P. Mullowney, of Witless Bay ; four *s.* one *d. Educ.:* St. Bonaventure's College, St. John's, N.F. Trained for mercantile career at St. John's ; engaged in business of a fishery merchant at Cape Broyle, 1885, on attaining his majority ; has continued same since ; entered political life in Colonial General Election, 1893 ; joined Liberal party in 1895 ; remained with said party until 1905, when broke from Liberal ranks ; led Independent party in Assembly until 1908, when joined with Sir Edward Morris ; Minister of Finance and Customs of Newfoundland, 1909-19 ; Prime Minister, 1919 ; Leader Opposition, 1920-23 ; represented colony before Imperial Royal Commission on West India trade at Jamaica, Jan. 1910 ; Acting Prime Minister, Acting Minister of Militia, Acting Minister of Shipping, 1918 ; as Minister of Finance raised the first successful Victory Loan in the Colony in 1917-18 ; active war worker, having been Vice-Chairman of Newfoundland Patriotic Fund, and War Finance Committee ; member various Committees of Patriotic Association which conducted all Colony's war activities (K.B.E.). *Address:* Sea View, Cape Broyle, Newfoundland ; Cambroil, Circular Road, St. John's, Newfoundland. *T.A.:* Cashin, St. John's. (*Died 30 Aug. 1926.*)

CASSAL, Colonel Charles Edward, V.D., F.I.C., F.C.S., F.R. San. Inst. ; Public Analyst for St. George's, Hanover Square, 1886-1901, for the City of Westminster since 1901, the Royal Borough of Kensington since 1885, the Metropolitan Borough of Battersea since 1888, and the County of Lincoln (Administrative Counties of Kesteven and Holland) since 1890 ;

Editor of The British Food Journal, 1899-1914 ; late Lt.-Col. (Hon. Col.) Commanding The London Brigade, R.G.A. (T.F.), 1908-14 ; *b.* London, 6 Aug. 1858 ; *e. s.* of late Professor Charles Cassal, LL.D., of University College, London, and the Royal Naval College, Greenwich ; *m.* 1880, Mary Louisa (*d.* 1884), *o. d.* of late F. B. Pearse, F.R.C.S. ; one *s.* one *d. Educ.:* University College School and University College, London (Medallist in Chemistry and in Practical Chemistry, Univ. Coll., Honours in Chemistry, University of London). Chief Demonstrator, Laboratory of Dept. of Hygiene and Public Health, Univ. Coll., 1879-88 ; Censor, Institute of Chemistry of Gt. Brit. and Ireland, 1892-93 ; joined the late 1st London Royal Engineers (Vols.), 1885 ; Lt.-Col. Commanding, 1902-8 ; P. S. School of Military Engineering, Chatham, 1886-87 ; President, Institution of Chemical Technologists, 1914-18. *Publications:* various scientific contributions and official and other Reports relating to Water-supply, Sewage Treatment and Disposal, and to the Analysis of Food and Water : The Hygienic Examination of Drinking Water (Address as Hon. President, Section VII. International Congress of Hygiene, Budapest, 1894) ; Records of Water Enquiries ; etc. *Recreations:* riding, cycling. *Address:* 56 Oxford Gardens, Kensington, W.10. *T.:* Park 3815.

(*Died 22 Dec. 1921.*)

CASSAR DE SAIN, 9th Marquess, **Richard George Eugene Rhenier de Branchefort Cassar De Sain ;** *b.* 27 Jan. 1880 ; *S.* 1906 ; *m.* 1905, Mary, *d.* of late James Turnbull ; two *s.* one *d. Educ.:* St. Ignatius College, Malta. Hereditary Knight of the Holy Roman Empire ; Hon. Secretary to Committee of Privileges, Maltese Nobility. *Address:* 137 Strada Forni, Valetta, Malta ; Bowyer House, Tarxien, Malta ; St. Paul's Bay, Malta.

(*Died 1927.*)

CASSEL, Right Hon. Sir Ernest, G.C.B., *cr.* 1909 ; G.C.M.G., *cr.* 1905 ; G.C.V.O., *cr.* 1906 ; P.C., 1902 ; *b.* Cologne, 3 March 1852 ; *s.* of Jacob Cassel, banker, Cologne ; *m.* Annette, *d.* of R. T. Maxwell, 1878 (*d.* 1881). *Educ.:* Cologne. Commander of the Légion d'Honneur ; Commander of Royal Order of Wasa of Sweden ; Grand Cordon of Polar Star of Sweden ; Grand Cordon Osmanieh ; Order of the Rising Sun of Japan (1st Class). *Recreations:* racing and shooting. *Address:* Brook House, Park Lane, W.1 ; Moulton Paddocks, Newmarket ; Branksome Dene, Bournemouth. *T.A.:* Ploughboy, London. *T.:* Mayfair 3690. *Clubs:* Carlton, Conservative, Garrick.

(*Died 21 Sept. 1921.*)

CASSELS, Hon. Sir Walter ; Kt. *cr.* 1917 ; Judge of the Exchequer Court of Canada since 1908 ; *b.* Quebec City, 14 Aug. 1845 ; *s.* of Robert Cassels, General Manager Bank Upper Canada ; *m.* Susan, *d.* of Robert Hamilton, Hamwood, Quebec. *Educ.:* Quebec High School ; University of Toronto (B.A.). Was a member of the firm of Blake, Lash, and Cassels, Toronto ; called to Bar of Ontario, 1872 ; Q.C. 1883. *Address:* Ottawa. *Clubs:* Toronto, Toronto Golf, Toronto ; Rideau, Ottawa Country, Golf, Ottawa ; Halifax ; Matane Fishing.

(*Died 1 Mar. 1923.*)

CASSELS, Rt. Rev. William Wharton, Bishop of Western China since 1895 ; *b.* Oporto, Portugal, 11 March 1858 ; *s.* of late John Cassels ; *m.* 1887 ; two *s.* four *d. Educ.:* Repton School ; St. John's Coll., Camb. (B.A. 1882). Ordained 1881 ; Curate of All Saints, S. Lambeth, 1882-85 ; missionary to China, 1885. *Address:* Paoning, *via* Wanhsien, Western China. *T.A.:* Cassels, Pao-ning, China.

(*Died 7 Nov. 1925.*)

CASTENSKIOLD, H. Grevenkop ; Hon. G.C.V.O., *cr.* 1913 ; Danish envoy ex-

181

traordinary and minister plenipotentiary for
the Court of St. James since 1912; Chamberlain to H.M. the King of Denmark; *b.*
28 Aug. 1862; 3rd *s.* of late J. M. Grevenkop
Castenskiold, of Hoerby, Denmark, and Thecla
Mathilde Hochschild; *m.* 1st, 1910, Anne Margrethe (Daisy) (*d.* 1917), 3rd *d.* of Count Frijs of
Frijsenborg, Denmark; 2nd, Elisabeth Ahlefeldt
Laurvig, 2nd *d.* of Count W. Ahlefeldt Laurvig,
of Eriksholm, Denmark. *Educ.*: Roskilde and
Copenhagen. Entered diplomatic service,
1888; secretary of Legation, St. Petersburg,
1890-91; and again 1893-94; Berlin, 1894-1900;
London, 1901-1905; Envoy extraordinary and
Minister plenipotentiary Christiania, 1905-1910;
Vienna and Rome, 1910-1912. *Address:* 1 Cadogan
Square, S.W.1. *T.A.:* Legadane, London. *T.:*
Kensington 4834. *Clubs:* Travellers', Turf,
Bachelors'.   (*Died 28 Aug. 1921.*)

CASTLE, Agnes, Author; *d.* of Michael
Sweetman, Lamberton Park, Queen's Co.,
Ireland; *m.* Egerton Castle (*d.* 1920); one
d. Publications: My Little Lady Anne, 1896;
many others in collaboration with late Egerton
Castle. *Address:* Anthony Place, Hindhead,
Surrey; 49 Sloane Gardens, S.W.1.
                                    (*Died April 1922.*)

CASTLE, Egerton, M.A., F.S.A.; author;
late Chairman Egerton Smith and Co. (the
Liverpool Mercury); and, since amalgamation
with Daily Post, a Director of Liverpool Daily
Post, Mercury, and Echo, Ltd.; was on staff of
Saturday Review, 1885-94; member of the
Council and, until 1901, of the Managing Committee of the Society of Authors; a Vice-President of the Navy League; *b.* 12 March
1858; *o. s.* of M. A. Castle, 2 Chapel
Street (now Aldford Street), Park Lane,
London; *g. s.* of Egerton Smith, founder
of the Liverpool Mercury; *m.* Agnes, *y. d.* of
Michael Sweetman, Lamberton Park, Queen's
Co. Ireland; one *d. Educ.:* Universities of Paris
and Glasgow; Exhibitioner, Trin. Coll. Camb.
(Nat. Science Trip.); Inner Temple; Sandhurst.
Lieut. 2nd W. India Regt.; Capt. Royal Engineer
Militia (Portsmouth Div. Submarine Miners);
passed through all courses of submarine mining
at Chatham and Gosport. *Publications and
plays:* Schools and Masters of Fence, 1884;
Bibliotheca Dimicatoria, 1891; The Story of
Swordsmanship, an illustrated lecture, first
delivered at the Lyceum Theatre by request of
Henry Irving, and repeated, by command, for
the Prince of Wales, 1891; Consequences, a
Novel, 1891; La Bella and Others, 1892;
English Book-Plates, 1892; Saviolo, a play
written for Sir Henry Irving (with W. H. Pollock), 1893; The Light of Scarthey, a Romance,
1895; Le Roman du Prince Othon, a rendering
in French of R. L. Stevenson's Prince Otto,
1896; The Jerningham Letters, 1896; The
Pride of Jennico, 1898, the same, dramatised
and first produced at Lyceum Theatre, New
York; The Bath Comedy, the same, dramatised
with David Belasco as Sweet Kitty Bellairs
(these last two novels with Agnes Castle),
1899; Desperate Remedies, a play written for
Richard Mansfield, of New York; Young April,
a romance, 1899; Marshfield the Observer;
The Secret Orchard, 1900; the same dramatised
for Mr. and Mrs. Kendal, 1901; The House of
Romance, re-collected short stories, 1901 (published in America only); The Star-Dreamer,
1903; Incomparable Bellairs, 1904; Rose of
the World, 1904; French Nan, 1904; If Youth
but Knew, 1905; My Merry Rockhurst,
1907; Flower o' the Orange, 1908; Wroth,
1908; Diamond Cut Paste, 1909; Panther's
Cub, 1910; The Lost Iphigenia, 1911; Love
Guilds the Scene and Women Guide the Plot;
The Grip of Life, 1912; Chance the Piper;
The Golden Barrier, 1913; The Ways of Miss
Barbara, 1914; Our Sentimental Garden, 1914;
Forlorn Adventurers, 1915; The Hope of the

House, 1915; A Little House in War Time,
1915; Wind's Will, 1916; Count Raven, 1916;
The Black Office, 1917; Wolf Lure, 1917; The
Third Year in the Little House; Minniglen,
1918; The Chartered Adventurer; New Wine,
1919 (the greater number with Agnes Castle);
etc. *Recreations:* swordsmanship (was captain
of the British epée and sabre teams at the
Olympic Games, 1908); rifle and pistol shooting, cycling, rambling in country scenery and
old towns. *Address:* Anthony Place, Hindhead, Surrey; 49 Sloane Gardens, S.W.1. *T.:*
Victoria 1536. *Clubs:* Athenæum, Garrick,
London Fencing, Authors.' (*Died 16 Sept. 1920.*)

CASTLE, Marcellus Purnell, M.V.O.
1911; J.P.; *b.* 28 Oct. 1849; *s.* of late H. Castle
of Southfields, Surrey; *m.* 1st, 1873, Florence
(*d.* 1878), *d.* of S. Mason, J.P.; 2nd, 1906,
Helene, *d.* of Jean Kübler, Geneva. *Address:*
Oakhill House, Sevenoaks. *Club:* Conservative.
                                    (*Died 21 Mar. 1917.*)

CASTLE, Walter Frances Raphael,
D.S.C.; M.D. Cambridge, M.R.C.P. London;
Physician in charge of skin departments,
Queen's Hospital for Children, West End
Hospital for nervous diseases, Kensington,
Chelsea and Fulham General Hospital; *b.*
London, 1892; *s.* of L. R. Castle; *m.* 1921,
Kathleen, *d.* of C. D. Seligman; one *s.* one *d.
Educ.:* Wellington College; Trinity College,
Cambridge; London Hospital. Honours,
Natural Sciences, Cambridge; temp. Surgeon,
Royal Navy, 1914-19; Archangel Expedition,
1919. *Publications:* many scientific medical
papers, including The Ætiology of Scleroderma
Epidermolysis bullosa, Erythomélie. *Recreations:* golf, cricket, fishing, ice hockey.
Address: 10 Upper Berkeley Street, W.1.; 43
Queen Anne Street, W.1. *T.:* Paddington 303.
M.: XY 5996.   (*Died 1 July 1926.*)

**CASTLESTEWART, 6th Earl (*cr.* 1800)
Andrew John Stuart;** Viscount Stuart
1798; Barony, 1619; Baronetcy, 1628; *b.* 21 Dec.
1841; *s.* of late Rev. the Hon. Andrew G. Stuart
and Hon. Catherine Ann Wingfield, *d.* of 5th
Viscount Powerscourt; *S.* cousin, 1914; *m.*
Emma Georgiana, *d.* of General Arthur Stevens,
1876; two *s.* one *d.* Late Madras Civil Service.
Owns 36,000 acres. *Heir: s.* Viscount Stuart.
       Address: Stuart Hall, Stewartstown, S.O.,
Co. Tyrone.   (*Died 1 Nov. 1921.*)

**CATHCART, 5th Earl (*cr.* 1814), George
Cathcart,** Viscount Cathcart, 1807; Baron
Greenock (United Kingdom), and 14th Baron
Cathcart (Scotland), 1447; *b.* 26 June 1862; 3rd
s. of 3rd Earl Cathcart and Elizabeth Mary (*d.*
1902), *e. d.* and heir of Sir Samuel Crompton,
Bt. (extinct); *S.* brother, 1911; *m.* 1919, Vera
(whom he divorced, 1922), *d.* of late John
Fraser, of Cape Town, and *widow* of Captain de
Grey Warter, 4th Dragoon Guards; one *s.* Late
Lieut. 4th Batt. P.W.O. Yorks Regt. *Heir: s.*,
Lord Greenock. *Address:* 39 Bryanston
Square, W.1. *Clubs:* Bachelors', Carlton.
                                    (*Died 19 Nov. 1927.*)

**CATHCART, Sir Reginald Archibald
Edward,** 6th Bt.; *cr.* 1703; D.L.; Capt. Coldstream Guards, 1868 (retired); *b.* 1838; *S.* father
1878; *m.* 1880, Emily, *d.* of John Robert Pringle,
and *g.-d.* of Sir John Pringle, Bt., of Stichill,
and widow of late John Gordon of Cluny, Aberdeenshire. *Educ.:* Harrow. Owns about
18,000 acres. *Heir:* none. *Address:* 43 Brook
Street, W.; Titness Park, Sunninghill; Killochan, Maybole, N.B. *Clubs:* Carlton, Guards'.
                                    (*Died 14 May 1916.*)

**CATHELS, The Right Reverend
David,** M.A., D.D. (Edin.); Minister of
parish of Hawick since 1892; Moderator of
the General Assembly of the Church of
Scotland, 1924-25; *b.* Arbroath, Forfarshire,
1853; *m.* 1st, Mildred Margaret, *d.* of Peter
Gardner of Grange Academy, Edinburgh; 2nd,
Margaret Agnes, *d.* of John Hewat, Bank of

Scotland, Edinburgh; two *s.* three *d.* *Educ.:* Edinburgh University. Minister of Kirkton, Roxburghshire, 1882-92; Delegate from Foreign Mission Committee of Church of Scotland to Missions in China, especially in Yangtse Valley, 1913-14; Officiating minister to the troops throughout World War; widely interested in educational and social matters throughout the Borders; Associate of Society for Psychical Research. *Publications:* Pamphlets and numerous articles on educational and social subjects. *Recreations:* cycling and golf. *Address:* The Manse, Hawick, Roxburghshire. *T.:* Hawick 217.   *(Died 16 June 1925.)*

CATLING, Thomas; ex-President British International Association of Journalists; *b.* Cambridge, 23 Sept. 1838; 3rd *s.* of Edward Catling, florist; *m.* 1860; four *s.* five *d.* *Educ.:* private schools in Cambridge; Working Men's Coll. London. Worked for twelve years in the composing-room of Lloyd's Weekly London News; news editor, 1866; editor, 1884; retired, 1907. Travelled through America to the Pacific and Canada, 1893; Holy Land and Syria, 1898; up the Nile to Khartoum, 1900; Algeria and Kabylia, 1901; Egyptian Desert and Spain, 1903; Corsica, 1904; Cairo, 1905; Austria, 1906; Dalmatia, Bosnia, and Herzegovina, 1907; Delegate to Conference of the International Association of Journalists at Berlin, 1903; North Cape for Midnight Sun, 1909; Portugal, 1910; Southern France, 1911; Helouan, 1912; France in time of war. *Publications:* mainly journalistic—had sole charge of literary reviews for Daily Chronicle, 1878-90. Edited The Press Album in aid of Journalists' Orphan Fund, 1909; Autobiography, 1910. *Recreation:* travel. *Address:* Heronville, St. James's Road, Brixton, S.W. *Clubs:* Savage, Whitefriars.
    (Died 25 Dec. 1920.)

CATON, Richard, C.B.E. 1920; M.D., LL.D. Edin., Padua, and Liverpool; F.R.C.P., J.P.; Ex-Pro-Chancellor and Emeritus Professor in University of Liverpool; ex-President and Consulting Physician Liverpool Royal Infirmary; ex-Lord Mayor of Liverpool. Family came from Heysham and Caton, Lancashire; *m.* Annie, *d.* of William Ivory, of St. Roque, Edinburgh; two *d.* *Educ.:* Scarborough Grammar School; Univ. of Edinburgh. Member General Medical Council since 1904; Harveian Orator, and late Member Council Royal College of Physicians; Vice-Chairman Liverpool Cathedral Executive Committee; late Chairman of Liverpool Committee for Housing of Poor; late Chairman Secondary Education Committee; ex-Vice-Pres. of University Council; late Chairman Liverpool branch of Classical Association; Member of Hellenic Society, and Vice-Chairman of Liverpool School of Tropical Medicine; late President Liverpool Medical Institution; late Hon. Col. West Lanc. Div., R.A.M.C. (Territorials); Chairman West Lancashire Territorial Nursing Service Committee. *Publications:* Temples and Ritual of Asklepios; Prevention of Valvular Disease of the Heart; Iemhotep and Ancient Egyptian Medicine; How to Live; etc. *Recreations:* travel, mountain climbing, sketching. *Address:* 7 Sunnyside, Princes Park, Liverpool. *T.:* Royal 5168. *M.:* S 7008. *Clubs:* Athenæum, University, Liverpool.
    (Died 2 Jan. 1926.)

CATOR, Rev. William Lumley Bartie, Hon. Canon of Southwell. *Address:* Eakring, Newark.   *(Died 1918.)*

CAULFEILD, Colonel Gordon Napier, D.S.O., Indian army, retired; *b.* 27 Jan. 1862; *s.* of late Col. Robert Caulfeild; *m.* 1902, Mildred, *y. d.* of Philip O'Reilly, D.L.; two *d.* Served Burmese Expedition, 1885-87, 1887-89 (medal with two clasps); Wontho Expedition, 1891 (clasp); Northern Chin Hills, 1892-93 (D.S.O. clasp); Commanded 17th (Reserve) Batt. Durham Light Infantry, 1914. *(Died 17 Mar. 1922.)*

CAULFEILD, Brigadier-General James Edward Wilmot Smyth, C.M.G. 1917; *b.* 4 Sep. 1850; *s.* of Rev. Wm. Caulfeild; *m.* 1876, Sophia Morley, *d.* of W. A. Parker, formerly Chief Justice of British Honduras; two *s.* four *d.* *Educ.:* Trinity College, Dublin, B.A. 1872. 2nd Lieut. 2nd West India Regiment, 1873; served Ashanti campaign, 1873-4 (medal and clasp); commanded Battalion, 1892-8; West Africa (clasp, 1898); Brev.-Col., 1896; commanding Troops, West Africa, 1895-8; Colonel on Staff, West Africa, 1899-1902; Brig.-Gen. commanding, Jamaica District, 1902-6; retired, 1907; recalled, 1914; commanding 96th Infantry Brigade, 1914; commanding 8th Reserve Infantry Brigade, 1915-16 (medal). *Publication:* One Hundred Years History, 2nd West India Regiment. *Address:* 2 Douro Terrace, Jersey. *Clubs:* United Service; Victoria, Jersey.   *(Died 19 Sept. 1925.)*

CAVAYE, Major-Gen. William Frederick, L.C.C.; twice Mayor, Royal Borough of Kensington; *e. s.* of late Gen. W. Cavaye; *m.* Ada Mary, *y. d.* of late Col. The Right Hon. Sir Walter Barttelot, 1st Bart., P.C. M.P., of Stopham, Pulborough, Sussex. *Educ.:* Edin. Acad.; Old Charlton, Kent; R.M.C., Sandhurst. Commanded 2nd Royal Sussex Regt.; Mil. Sec. to General H.R.H. the Duke of Connaught, K.G., when Commander-in-Chief, Bombay, etc.; A.A. General and Chief of Staff, Southern District England; commanded 35th Regimental District, Sussex; specially employed in Zulu War, 1879 (medal and clasp); and during the South African War, 1900-1-2 (medal with clasp, King's medal with two clasps); commanding 2nd East Anglian Division; Special Service, B.E.F. France, 1917-19 (two war medals, despatches). *Address:* 6 Neville Terrace, S.W.7; Birchen bridge, Horsham, Sussex. *T.:* 6086 Kensington. *Clubs:* United Service; Conservative, Edinburgh.
    (Died 30 Jan. 1926.)

CAVE, 1st Viscount, *cr.* 1918; **George Cave,** G.C.M.G. *cr.* 1920; P.C. 1915; Kt., *cr.* 1915; J.P. for Surrey, 1891; D.L. 1897; Chancellor of Oxford University since 1925; Lord Chancellor, 1922-24 and since Nov. 1924; *b.* London, 23 Feb. 1856; 2nd *s.* of late Thomas Cave, M.P., and Elizabeth (*d.* 1925), *d.* of Jasper Shallcrass, Banstead, Surrey; *m.* 1885, Estella Penfold, *d.* of late Wm. W. Mathews, of North Cadbury and Crewkerne, Somerset. *Educ.:* Merchant Taylors' School; St. John's College, Oxford (Scholar; Hon. Fellow, 1916). Taylorian Exhibitioner; first class in Moderations and the Final Classical School; B.A. 1878; M.A. 1912; Hon. D.C.L. 1924; Inner Temple Scholar in Real Property Law; Barrister Inner Temple, 1880; K.C. 1904; Master of the Bench, 1913; practised at Chancery Bar; special, 1913; C.C. for Surrey, 1889; County Alderman, 1892; Deputy-chairman of Quarter Sessions, 1893; Chairman of Quarter Sessions, 1894-1910; Recorder of Guildford, 1904-15; Standing Counsel to Oxford University, 1913-1915; Attorney-General to Prince of Wales, 1914-15; Hon. Lt.-Col.; was Hon. Commandant of 2nd V.B., East Surrey Regt.; Member of Royal Commission on Land Transfer, 1908-9; Chairman of Southern Rhodesia Commission, 1919-20; Chairman of Munitions Enquiry Tribunal, 1921; Chairman of Committee on Voluntary Hospitals, 1921; Chairman of Committee on Trade Boards, 1921-22; Chairman of British Empire Cancer Campaign, 1924; Chairman of Home Office Advisory Committee on Cruelty to Animals Acts, 1924; M.P. (U.) Kingston Div. of Surrey, 1906-18; Solicitor-General, 1915-16; Home Secretary, 1916-19; a Lord of Appeal, 1919-22. *Publications:* editor of some legal treatises. *Recreations:* riding, rowing, golf. *Heir:* none. *Address:* House of Lords, S.W.1; Wardrobe Court, Richmond, Surrey; St. Ann's, Burnham,

Somerset. *T.*: Richmond 159. *Clubs:* Athenæum, Carlton.   (*Died 29 Mar. 1928.*)

CAVE, Sir Charles Daniel, 1st Bt., *cr.* 1896; J.P., D.L., Gloucestershire and Devonshire; Local Director of Union Bank of London; *b.* 17 Sep. 1832; 3rd *s.* of Daniel Cave, Sidbury Manor, Devonshire, and Cleve Hill. Gloucestershire; *m.* Edith Harriet (*d.* 1912), *d* of John Addington Symonds, M.D., of Clifton, 1859; three *s.* one *d. Educ.:* Exeter College. Oxford (M.A.). High Sheriff of Bristol, 1863; High Sheriff of Devonshire, 1898. *Heir:* s. Charles Henry Cave. *Address:* Stoneleigh House, Clifton Park, Bristol.   (*Died 26 Oct. 1922.*)

CAVE-BROWNE-CAVE, Sir Thomas, Kt., *cr.* 1911; C.B. 1907; Special Commissioner, Royal Hospital, Chelsea, since 1899; *b.* 1835; 3rd *s.* of late Thomas Cave-Browne-Cave of Cliff Hall, Warwickshire; *m.* 1870, Blanche M. M. A., *d.* of late Sir John Milton; two *s.* three *d. Educ.:* Repton. Entered War Office, 1853; retired as Deputy Accountant-General of the Army, 1900. *Address:* Burnage, Streatham Common, S.W.16.   (*Died 9 Dec. 1924.*)

CAWLEY, George; Consulting Engineer to the Japanese Imperial Railways for twenty years, covering rapid extension; *b.* Sankey, Lancashire, 29 July 1848; *s. s.* of Thomas Cawley of Aston Grange, Cheshire. In Japanese Government service, as one of the original staff of the Imperial College of Engineering, Tokyo, 1873-78; travelled in United States to visit leading mining centres, 1878; engaged in work connected with gas and hydraulic engineering, the promotion of steam engine economy, and the insurance of work-people, 1879-85; editor-in-chief of Industries, 1886-93; in general consulting practice since 1893. *Address:* Nippon, Cedar Road, Sutton, Surrey. *T.:* Sutton 692. *Club:* Savage.   (*Died 3 Mar. 1927.*)

CAWLEY, Hon. Oswald; M.P. Prestwich Division of Lancashire since Feb. 1918; *b.* 1882; 2nd *s.* of 1st Baron Cawley. *Educ.:* Rugby. Lieut. Yeomanry; served European War. *Address:* Brooklands, Prestwich.   (*Died 22 Aug. 1918.*)

CAWSTON, Sir John Westerman, K.C.B., *cr.* 1919; C.B., 1912; Deputy Master and Comptroller of the Royal Mint, 1917; retired 1921; *b.* 1859; *e. s.* of late Rev. J. Cawston, D.D., R.N., Chaplain of the Fleet, and Hon. Chaplain to Queen Victoria; *m.* 1888, Beatrice F. L., *d.* of late Rev. J. Montague, of Wimbish; two *d. Educ.:* Clifton College (head of school); New College, Oxford (open scholar); 1st class Classical Mods.; 2nd class Final Classical Schools, 1882. Entered War Office, 1883; transferred to Treasury, 1889; Private Secretary to Parliamentary Secretary, 1895-1902; Principal Clerk, 1904-11; Assistant Comptroller and Auditor of the Exchequer, 1911-17. *Recreations:* golf; has also illustrated a few books. *Address:* Gulpher, Felixstowe, Suffolk. *T.:* Felixstowe 68.   (*Died 21 April 1927.*)

CAYLEY, Sir George Everard Arthur, 9th Bt.; *cr.* 1661; J.P., D.L.; *b.* 1861; *S.* father 1895; *e. s.* of 8th Bt. and Catherine Louisa, 2nd *d.* of Sir William Worsley, 1st Bt.; *m.* 1884, Lady Mary Susan, *d.* of Hon. F. D. Montagu-Stuart-Wortley, and *sis.* of 2nd Earl of Wharncliffe; one *s.* three *d.* Late Capt. 3rd Batt. Royal Welsh Fusiliers. *Heir:* s. Kenelm Henry Ernest, *b.* 24 Sep. 1896. Lieut. 3rd Batt. Suffolk Regt. *Address:* Tempe, Woodbridge, Suffolk. *Club:* Junior Carlton.   (*Died 15 Nov. 1917.*)

CAYLEY, William, M.D., F.R.C.P.; Consulting Physician Middlesex Hospital; North-Eastern Hospital for Children; London Fever Hospital; *b.* 1836. *Educ.:* King's Coll. London; Vienna. *Publication:* Croonian Lectures on Typhoid Fever; editor of 3rd edition of Murchison on Continued Fever. *Address:* 120

184

Queen's Road, Richmond, Surrey.   (*Died 17 Dec. 1916.*)

CAYZER, Sir Charles, 1st Bt.; *cr.* 1904; Kt.; *cr.* 1897; J.P.; shipowner; *b.* London, 15 July 1843. Head of the firm of Cayzer, Irvine and Co., Ltd., Steamship Owners, London, Liverpool, Manchester, and Glasgow; Hon. Colonel 3rd Lowland Brigade, R.F.A.; *m.* 1868, Agnes Elizabeth, *o. d.* of William Trickey of Clifton, Bristol; four *s.* three *d.* M.P. Barrow-in-Furness, 1892-1906; first Conservative elected for Barrow; contested Monmouth District (C.), 1910. *Heir: e. s.* C. W. Cayzer. *Address:* St. Lawrence Hall, Isle of Wight; Gartmore, Perthshire; Kinpurnie Castle, Forfarshire. *Clubs:* Carlton, City of London.   (*Died 28 Sept. 1916.*)

CAYZER, Charles William; *b.* Bombay, 19 July 1869; *e. s.* of Sir Charles Cayzer, Bart.; *m.* 1893, Annie Mabel, *d.* of late Thomas Jennings White, Frogmore Lodge, St. Albans; one *s.* four *d. Educ.:* Rugby; Christ Church, Oxford (M.A.). A partner in the firm of Cayzer, Irvine and Co.; Director of the Clan Line Steamers, Ltd., 1890-1911; retired 1911. *Publications:* Ad Astra, 1900; Songs and Lyrics, 1900; David and Bathsheba, 1903; Songs of Summer, 1904; For Greater Britain, 1904; Donna Marina, 1905; Poems and Plays, 1905; The Skaith of Guillardun, 1907; Undine, 1908; By the Way of the Gate, 1911. *Address:* 22 Lewes Crescent, Brighton. *T.A.:* Cayzer, Brighton. *T.:* Kemp Town 6912, Brighton. *Clubs:* Constitutional, Authors', City of London.   (*Died 20 July 1917.*)

CAZALET, Edward Alexander, Founder and President of the Anglo-Russian Literary Society; linguist; examiner in Russian, etc., for the Civil Service Commissioners and War Office; *s.* of Alexander Cazalet and Baroness Charlotte de Bode; descendant of Huguenot family which settled in England at the Revocation of the Edict of Nantes; *m.* Mary Emma, *d.* of late Gen. E. A. B. Travers of Indian Army and Secretary for Indian Affairs to late Duke of Cambridge; one *s.* two *d. Educ.:* private tutors; Windlesham House, Brighton; High Commercial School, Petrograd (first medal). Late of A. Cazalet and Sons at Petrograd, and of the Russian Steam Navigation and Trading Co. at Odessa, 1864-68; travelled repeatedly in Russia, Transcaucasia, Persia, Turkey, etc. *Publications:* John Howard, the Prison Reformer, written in Russian with the object of creating better Anglo-Russian relations (received medal from Jury of the Prison Congress at Petrograd). *Address:* Imperial Institute, S.W.; Neva, Westgate-on-Sea.   (*Died 13 Dec. 1923.*)

CECIL, Colonel Lord Edward (Herbert), K.C.M.G. *cr.* 1913; D.S.O.; Financial Adviser to the Egyptian Government since 1912; *b.* 12 July 1867; 4th *s.* of 3rd Marquis of Salisbury; *m.* 1894, Violet Georgina, *d.* of late Admiral Maxse; one *d. Educ.:* Eton. Entered Grenadier Guards, 1887; Major, 1898; served Dongola Expeditionary Force, 1896 (despatches, bt. Major, 4th class Medjidie; British medal; Khedive's medal, two clasps); accompanied special mission to King Menelik of Abyssinia, 1897; Egyptian campaign, 1898, including Atbara (despatches); Khartoûm (despatches, D.S.O. and two clasps); South Africa, 1899-1901 (despatches, Brevet Lieut. - Col., Queen's medal, two clasps); Agent - General Sudan Government and Director of Intelligence, Cairo; subsequently appointed Under Secretary of War and Under Secretary of Finance; Grand Cordon, Order of the Nile, 1915. *Address:* Ghezireh, Cairo.   (*Died 13 Dec. 1918.*)

CECIL, Lord Eustace Brownlow Henry; J.P. Middlesex, Essex, and Dorset; County Alderman, Dorset; Chairman of Foreign and Colonial, American, Foreign and General, and Alliance Trust Companies; Director Great Eastern Railway; *b.* 1834; 2nd *s.* of 2nd Marquess of Salisbury; *m.* 1860, Lady Gertrude Louisa Scott (*d.* 1919), 4th *d.* of 2nd Earl of Eldon; two *s.* one *d.* *Educ.:* Harrow; Sandhurst. Served with 43rd Light Infantry at the Cape and in India; was nine months in the Crimean War with Coldstream Guards; Captain and Lt.-Col. Coldstream Guards, 1861; retired, 1863; Surveyor-General of the Ordnance, 1874-80; M.P. South Essex, 1865-68; West Essex, 1868-85. *Address:* Lytchett Heath, Poole, Dorset; 111 Eaton Square, W. *Clubs:* Athenæum, Carlton. (*Died 3 July 1921.*)

CHADWICK, Edward Marion; Barrister-at-Law; K.C.; Major, retired from 2nd Regiment the Queen's Own Rifles of Canada; amateur Armorist and Genealogist; *b.* 22 Sep. 1840; *s.* of John Craven Chadwick, of Guelph, Canada, and *g.s.* of John Craven Chadwick of Ballinard; Tipperary, Ireland: *m.* 1st, Ellen Byrne (*d.* 1865), *d.* of James Beatty; 2nd, Maria Martha, *d.* of Alexander Fisher; five *s.* one *d.* Lay Canon and Treasurer of St. Alban's Cathedral, Toronto; Hon. Genealogist to the United Empire Loyalists' Association; is by adoption of the Chiefs in Council an honorary Chief of the Six Nations, of the Anowara or Turtle Clan of the Kanienga or Mohawks, by the name of Shagotyohgwisaks. *Publications:* Ontarian Families; The People of the Longhouse; articles on heraldic subjects to magazines, etc. *Address:* 107 Howland Avenue, Toronto. (*Died 15 Dec. 1921.*)

CHADWICK, Rt. Rev. George Alexander, D.D.; *b.* 10 Oct. 1840; *m.* 1st, 1864, Emma, *d.* of J. F. Browning, Ealing, 2nd, 1911, Helen, *sis.* of Rev. Canon E. T. Crozier. *Educ.:* Trinity College, Dublin. Ordained 1868; Rector of Armagh, 1872-96; Dean of Armagh, 1886-96; Bishop of Derry and Raphoe, 1896-1915. *Publications:* Christ bearing Witness to Himself (Donnellan Lectures), 1879; As He that Serveth, 1880; My Devotional Life, 1882; Exodus and St. Mark in the Expositor's Bible; Pilate's Gift and other Sermons, 1899; Poems, Chiefly Sacred, 1900; The Intellect and the Heart, and other Sermons, 1905. *Address:* 37 St. Mary's Road, Dublin.
(*Died Dec. 1923.*)

CHADWICK, Rev. Canon Robert; Rector of Caldecote, near Nuneaton, since 1922; Hon. Canon Worcester, 1915; *m.* 1887 Emily (*d.* 1924). *Educ.:* St. John's College, Cambridge. Ordained, 1882; Curate of St. Matthew, Brixton, 1882-86; Middle Claydon, Bucks, 1886-87; Vicar of Chilvers-Coton, 1887-1914; Rural Dean of Atherstone, 1907-14; Vicar of Christ Church, Malvern, 1914-22. *Address:* Caldecote Rectory, near Nuneaton. (*Died 15 Feb. 1927.*)

CHADWYCK-HEALEY, Sir Charles Edward Heley, 1st Bt., *cr.* 1919; K.C.B., *cr.* 1909; K.C.; C.B. 1905; Chancellor of Diocese of Exeter; formerly Chancellor of the Dioceses of Salisbury and Bath and Wells; *b.* 26 Aug. 1845; *o.* *s.* of E. C. Healey, of Wyphurst, Cranley, Surrey; *m.* 1st, 1872, Rosa (*d.* 1880), *d.* of John Close; 2nd, 1884, Frances Katharine (*d.* 1909), *d.* of W. K. Wait, formerly M.P. Gloucester. Called to Bar, Lincoln's Inn, 1872; Commander (Hon.) Royal Naval Reserve; Captain, 1914; Chairman of the Admiralty Volunteer Committee, 1903-14; Admiralty Transport Arbitration Board, 1914-18; commanding Hospital Ship No. 15, Queen Alexandra, 1915-18; Fellow of the Society of Antiquaries; Bencher of Lincoln's Inn; D.L.; County Alderman and Chairman, Quarter Sessions, Somerset; High Sheriff of Somerset, 1911-12; J.P. Surrey and Somerset; served on Royal Commission on Care and Control of the Feeble-minded, 1905-9. *Heir:* Gerald Edward,

Lieut. R.N.V.R. *Address:* Wyphurst, Cranleigh, Surrey; New Place, Porlock, Taunton. *Clubs:* Athenæum, Carlton, Savile, Garrick.
(*Died 5 Oct. 1919.*)

CHAFFEY, Colonel Ralph Anderson, C.B.E. 1918; V.D.; Retired List, N.Z. Forces; *b.* Keinton Mandeville, Somerset, 1856; *s.* of late Major E. Chaffey, 25th Somerset R. Vol., and Isabella Anderson, Dalhousie Grange, near Edinburgh; *m.* 1st, 1887, Emilie Lecren (*d.* 1889), Timaru, N.Z.; 2nd, 1897, Agnes Rosa, *d.* of late Dr. Webster of Balruddery, N.Z., Army Medical; three *s.* one *d.* *Educ.:* Sherborne. Educated for Army; owing to health came to N.Z. 1878; sheep farming; managed Taipo and Kauroo Estates for late W. H. Teschemaker, 1881-97; Highfield Estate for late Hy. Wharton, 1897-1903; farming own account since 1903; joined Otepopo Rifles as Lieut. 1882; raised and commanded as Capt., North Otago Hussars, 1887-97; raised and commanded Amuri Mt. Rifles, 1900; Major 2nd Batt. North Canterbury Mt. Rifles, 1901; Lt.-Col. 1905; Colonel, 1911; Brigadier commanding Canterbury Mt. Rifle Brigade, 1911-14; attached to N.Z. Staff Corps and commanded Canterbury Military District, 1914-19. *Recreations:* cricket, 1st XI. Sherborne, West Kent and Oamaru (N.Z.) C.C.; football, 1st XV. Sherborne and North Canterbury, N.Z. *Address:* Keintoncombe, Waiau, Amuri, N.Z. *T.A.:* Waiau. *T.:* 38M Waiau. *M.:* 3601. *Club:* Christchurch, Christchurch. (*Died 8 Nov. 1925.*)

CHAINE, Lt.-Col. William, M.V.O. 1901; *b.* 1 Jan. 1888. Entered Army, 1856; Captain, 1864; retired, 1881; was Marshal and Assistant Master of Ceremonies to Queen Victoria. *Address:* Kensington Palace, W.
(*Died 3 July 1916.*)

CHALMERS, Albert John, M.D., F.R.C.S., D.P.H., F.I.S., F.Z.S., F.R.G.S.; Director Wellcome Tropical Research Laboratories, Khartoum; Member Sudan Government Sleeping Sickness Commission; Central Sanitary Board; and Archaeological Committee; *b.* Manchester, 28 March 1870; *s.* of late Rev. James Chalmers, M.A., Aberdeen, and Mary, *d.* of late Captain Martin, Peterhead, N.B.; *m.* 1898, Alice, 2nd *d.* of late Edwin Cannington, J.P., Waterloo, Lancashire; no *c.* *Educ.:* Manchester Grammar School; University Colleges, Liverpool and London. M.D.; Gold Medal, West African and Ceylon services, 1897-1911; Pellagra Field Commission, 1911-12; late Major Ceylon Volunteer Medical Corps; served Ashanti Field Force (despatches, medal and clasp); Ceylon Coronation Contingent (medal, Order of the Nile, 3rd Class); Membre Correspondant Société de Pathologie Exotique, Paris; collaborating Editor Journal of Tropical Medicine and Hygiene. *Publications:* joint-author Castellani and Chalmers' Manual of Tropical Medicine; works, First-Aid, Physiological Chemistry, Simple Medical Directions; papers connected with Tropical Medicine, Hygiene, and Parasitology. *Recreations:* travel, shooting. *Address:* Balfour House, Khartoum. *T.A.:* Maamal, Khartoum. *Clubs:* Savile, National; Sudan, Khartoum.
(*Died 5 April 1920.*)

CHALMERS, Sir Charles, Kt., *cr.* 1918; J.P., V.D., D.L., M.A. Edinburgh; Convener of County Council of West Lothian; *b.* 17 Feb. 1861; *e.* *s.* of late Thomas Chalmers, of Longcroft, and Jean Menzies, *e.* *d.* of late Charles Cowan, of Loganhouse; *m.* 1900, Elizabeth, 2nd *d.* of John Graham; one *d.* *Educ.:* Merchiston Castle, and University, Edinburgh. Chairman of Directors of the Royal Scottish Institution, Larbert. *Address:* Cathlaw, Bathgate. *T.:* Bathgate 69. *Club:* New, Edinburgh.
(*Died 27 Aug. 1924.*)

CHALMERS, Sir Mackenzie Dalzell, K.C.B., *cr.* 1906; C.S.I. 1899; C.B. 1904; M.A., J.P.; Barr.-at-law; *b.* 7 Feb. 1847; *s.* of

Rev. F. Chalmers, D.D., and Matilda, d. of Rev.
W. Marsh, D.D., Hon. Canon of Worcester.
Educ.: King's College, London and Trinity
College, Oxford. Indian Civil Service, 1869-72;
barr. 1869; revising barrister, 1881; counsel to
Board of Trade, 1882; judge of County Courts,
1884; acting Chief Justice, Gibraltar, 1893;
Commissioner of Assize, 1895; law member of
the Viceroy's Council in India; retired, 1899;
Assist. Parliamentary Counsel, 1899; First
Parliamentary Counsel to Treasury, 1902-3; Perm.
Under-Secretary of State for Home Department,
1903-8; member of the Statute Law Committee,
Royal Commission on Vivisection, and of Royal
Commission on the affairs of Malta; member
of Royal Commission on the Rebellion in Ireland;
Chairman, South Nigeria Liquor Inquiry;
Home Office Committee on Coroners and Deaths
under Anæsthetics; a British Delegate the
Hague Conferences on Unification of Law of
Bills of Exchange, etc.; member of the Sleeping
Sickness Committee, of the Lord Chancellor's
Committees on Criminal Law, and of the Ad-
visory Committee on Egyptian Laws; Vice-
President London Fever Hospital; Chairman of
Belgian Commission in England on Violation
of Laws of War; member of War Risks In-
surance Committees (marine and aircraft),
Aerial Transport Committee; Chairman of the
Committee on Standardization of Biological
Drugs, and member of Council of Royal Aero-
nautical Society; Knight of Grace and member
of the Council and Chapter of the Order of St.
John, and Joint Committee of Red Cross and St.
John; Commander of the Order of the Crown
(Belgium). Publications: contributions to Dic-
tionary of Political Economy and Encyclopædia
Britannica; Digest of the Law of Bills of Ex-
change; Digest of the Law of Sale, etc. Re-
creation: golf. Address: 5 Lauriston Road,
Wimbledon, S.W.19. Clubs: Athenæum, Ranelagh, M.C.C. (Died 22 Dec. 1927.)

CHALMERS, P. MacGregor, Hon.
LL.D. Glas.; F.S.A. Scot.; b. Glasgow; s. of
George Chalmers and Jane M'Gregor; m.
Barbara Greig Steel. Educ.: Secular School,
Glasgow. Began business as architect, 1887;
has carried out church work at Cardonald,
Jedburgh, Crailing, Partick, Govan, Glasgow,
Kilmun, Carnoustie, Ardwell, Leven, Steps,
St. Andrews, Dunfermline, Edinburgh, Elgin,
Ardrossan, Kirn, Carriden, Newlands, Cor-
storphine; has carried out restorations at
Whithorn, Glenluce Abbey, Inverkeithing,
South Queensferry, St. Monans, Town Church St.
Andrews, Melrose Abbey, and Iona Cathedral,
and is now restoring the Abbey of Paisley,
Dalmeny Church, and Symington Church,
Ayrshire; architect for the restoration of St.
Salvator's Chapel, St. Andrews University,
and for the Cathedral Church of St. Anne,
Belfast; was architect for the Marine Biologi-
cal Station, Millport, the Glasgow Golf Club,
Dargavel House, Renfrewshire, Kinnaird House,
Perthshire, and other domestic work; past-
President, Glasgow Architectural Association,
and the Architectural Section of the Royal
Philosophical Society. Publications: St. Ninian's
Candida Casa; a Scots Mediæval Architect;
Art in Our City, Glasgow; Glasgow Cathedral,
a Historical Sketch; The Govan Sarcophagus,
The Shrine of St. Constantine; The Shrines
of St. Margaret and St. Kentigern; Dalmeny
Kirk; the History of Glasgow Cathedral. Re-
creations: the study of ecclesiastical antiquities,
sketching, and photography. Address: 95 Bath
Street, Glasgow.

**CHAMBA, H.H. Raja Sir Bhuri
Singh, Raja of;** K.C.S.I., cr. 1906; K.C.I.E.,
cr. 1918; C.I.E. 1901; b. 1869; widower; two
s. two d. Situated in the Himalayas, on the
frontiers of Kashmir, the State is 3216 square
miles in extent, and has a population of 135,989,
186

H.H. receiving a salute of 11 guns; S. b.
1904 on abdication through ill health; Prime
Minister 1897-1904. He is a Rajput, whose
family has ruled there from very remote times.
Address: Chamba, Punjab. (Died 6 Oct. 1919.)

CHAMBERLAIN, Houston Stewart;
b. Southsea, 9 Sept. 1855; s. of late Rear-
Admiral William Charles Chamberlain and
Eliza Jane, d. of Capt. Basil Hall, R.N.; m.
1908, Eva Wagner, o. d. of the poet and composer, Richard Wagner; no c. Educ.: Lycée
Imperial, Versailles; Cheltenham College;
private tutor. Intended to enter British
Army; much troubled by illness during childhood and youth; incapable of standing English
climate; studied Natural Sciences at University of Geneva, 1879-84; Bachelier ès
Sciences physiques et naturelles; moved to
Dresden, 1885; studied music, philosophy,
history; lived in Vienna, 1889-1908; began
writing, 1892; has continued doing so since
then. Publications: Das Drama Richard Wag-
ners, 1892; Richard Wagner, 1896; Recherches
sur la sève ascendante, 1897; Die Grundlagen
des XIX. Jahrhunderts, 1899; Parsifal-Märchen,
1900; Worte Christi, 1901; Drei Bühnendich-
tungen, 1902; Arische Weltanschauung, 1911;
Immanuel Kant, 1909; Goethe, 1912. Address:
Haus Wahnfried, Bayreuth, Bavaria.
(Died 9 Jan. 1927.)

CHAMBERLAIN, Ven. Thomas, Archdeacon of Kokstad since 1891; Priest in charge
of Clydesdale, Kaffraria, since 1894; b. 21 April
1854; s. of Theodore and Margaret Chamberlain; m. 1882, Edith, y. d. of late Rev. J. F.
May; three s. three d. Educ.: Diocesan Grammar School, King William's Town; Christ's
College, Cambridge (M.A.); Cape University.
Ordained 1880; Curate of Harrow Green, Essex,
1880-81; of Weston, Herts, 1881-82; Rector of
Alice, 1882-83; Rector and Chaplain of Wolesley
Settlement, St. John, East London, 1885-91;
Canon of St. John's Cathedral, Umtata, 1893.
Recreations: astronomy and photography. Ad-
dress: Kaffraria, South Africa.

CHAMBERLAYNE, Tankerville, J.P.;
Lord of the Manors of Hound, North Baddesley,
Woolston and Barton Peveril, Hants, and East
Norton, Leicestershire; Patron of three livings;
b. 9 Aug. 1843; o.-surv. s. of Thomas Chamber-
layne of Cranbury Park; m. 1886, Edith, d. of
late S. J. Ashley; one s. four d. Educ.: Eton;
Magdalen College, Oxford. B.A. 1865; M.P. (C.)
Southampton, 1892-96, 1900-6; Hon. Lt. R.N.R.
Recreations: a well-known yachtsman and pat-
ron of cricket and all athletic sports. Ad-
dress: Cranbury Park, near Winchester;
Baddesley Manor, Romsey. Clubs: Carlton,
Junior Carlton, St. Stephen's, Royal Thames
Yacht, Primrose. (Died 17 May 1924.)

CHAMBERLIN, Arthur George, I.S.O.
1903; late Senior District Auditor Local Government Board. Address: Glen House, Highfield
Street, Leicester. (Died 19 Feb. 1925.)

CHAMBERLIN, Edson J., President
Grand Trunk and Grand Trunk Pacific Railways
1912-17; for twenty years General Manager
of the Canada Atlantic Railway. Address:
333 Metcalfe Street, Ottawa, Ontario.
(Died 27 Aug. 1924.)

CHAMBERLIN, Sir George, Kt., cr.
1919; D.L., Norfolk; J.P., Norwich; Mayor of
Norwich, 1891; Lord Mayor, 1916 and 1918;
High Sheriff of Norfolk. 1926-27; b. 16 Feb.
1846; m. 1876, Emily Mary (d. 1923), d. of A.
F. C. Bolingbroke, Norwich. Recreation:
shooting. Address: St. Catherine's Close,
Norwich. Clubs: Carlton; Norfolk County,
Norwich. (Died 12 Aug. 1928.)

CHAMBERS, Rev. Arthur, Vicar of
Brockenhurst, Hants, since 1899. Curate of
Bow, Middlesex, 1888-89; Holy Trinity, Step-
ney, 1890-92; St. Mark's, Battersea, 1892-99.

Publications: Our Life after Death ; Man and the Spiritual World ; Thoughts of the Spiritual ; Problems of the Spiritual. *Address:* The Vicarage, Brockenhurst, Hants. (*Died* 16 *Mar.* 1918.)

CHAMBERS, Charles Haddon, playwright ; *b.* Stanmore, Sydney, N.S.W., 22 Apr. 1860 ; *s.* of John Ritchie Chambers, N.S.W. Civil Service, formerly of Ulster, and Frances, *e. d.* of William Kellett, Waterford, Ireland. *Educ.:* Marrickville and Fort Street Public Schools, Sydney, and privately. Entered N.S.W. Civil Service, 1875 ; two years later became stockrider, etc., in the Bush ; visited England and Ireland, 1880 ; returned to England, 1882 ; became journalist, story writer, and subsequently dramatic author. *Publications:* Captain Swift ; The Idler ; The Honourable Herbert ; The Old Lady ; John a Dreams ; The Tyranny of Tears ; The Awakening ; The Golden Silence ; Sir Anthony ; Passers-by ; The Impossible Woman ; The Saving Grace ; part-author of The Fatal Card, Boys Together, and The Days of the Duke. *Recreations:* swimming, boat-sailing, riding, driving, shooting, boxing, fencing. *Address:* 4 Aldford Street, Park Lane, W.1. *T.:* Mayfair 2206. *Clubs:* Bath, Green Room, National, Dramatists ; Travellers', Paris. (*Died* 28 *Mar.* 1921.)

CHAMBERS, James, K.C. Ireland ; M.P. (U.) South Belfast since 1910. *Address:* Grove House, Foxrock, Co. Dublin. *Club:* Constitutional. (*Died* 11 *June* 1917.)

CHAMBERS, Julius, F.R.G.S. ; Author, newspaper man ; *b.* Bellefontaine, Ohio, 21 Nov. 1850 ; *s.* of Joseph and Sarabella Chambers ; *m.* 1899, Margaret Belvin. *Educ.:* Ohio Wesleyan University: Cornell University (Phi Beta Kappa and Delta Kappa Epsilon). Entered service of N.Y. Tribune ; joined staff N.Y. Herald, 1873 ; City Editor, 1876-77 ; fitted out expedition to headwaters of Mississippi, 1872 ; discovered Elk Lake, Minn., June 9, now recognised as source of great river ; served N.Y. Herald over fifteen years in London, Paris, Havana, Madrid, and Washington ; Managing Editor, 1886-89 ; started Paris edition of Herald, 1887 ; managing editor N.Y. World, 1889-91 ; since then engaged in literature and travel. *Publications:* A Mad World ; On a Margin, a Wall Street Story ; Lovers Four and Maidens Five ; Missing, a Romance of the Sargasso Sea ; The Rascal Club ; The Destiny of Doris ; The Mississippi River and its Wonderful Valley ; Forty Years' Recollections of New York Journalism ; The Joy of Living ; Jack Sturgeon of Fishkill ; edited an edition of Balzac ; author of a farce produced in N.Y., 1903, and of a comedy produced in N.Y., 1904 ; published 200 short stories and numerous travel books ; writer of Walks and Talks, a daily letter since 1904. *Recreations:* work and travel. *Clubs:* Lotos, Authors', American Dramatists', New York. (*Died* 12 *Feb.* 1920.)

CHAMBERS, Sir Newman Pitts-, Kt., *cr.* 1897 ; J.P., D.L., Donegal ; knighted for services during his official career in Londonderry ; 2nd *s.* of late Thomas Chambers, Aberfoyle, Londonderry, and Mary Anna, *d.* of late Captain Robert Newman, H.M. 56th Regt. ; *m.* 1880, Inez Alexa (*d.* 1914), *y. d.* of late Alex. T. Young, Coolkuragh House, Co. Londonderry, and Drumkeen, Co. Donegal ; one *s.*, Brooke Winsley [*m.* 1917, Marie, *e. d.* of late W. Rermond, Doubly, Neufchatel], one *d.* *Address:* Carrig Cnoc, Co. Donegal ; Lough Ash House, Co. Tyrone. *Clubs:* Constitutional ; Northern Counties, Londonderry.
(*Died* 18 *Aug.* 1922.)

CHAMBERS, Major-General Robert Macdonald, Bombay Infantry ; *b.* 7 June 1833 ; *m.* 1867, Lucy Edith, 3rd *d.* of A. Baird, M.D., Dover ; six *d.* Entered army, 1858 ; Maj.-Gen., 1891 ; retired, 1891 ; served Indian Mutiny, 1860 ; China War (medal) ; Afghan War,

1880 (medal). *Address:* Springfield, Guildford.
(*Died* 1924.)

CHAMIER, Major - General Francis Edward Archibald, C.B. 1907 ; C.I.E., 1902 ; Supernumerary List, Indian Staff Corps ; *b.* 18 May 1833 ; *s.* of late Henry Chamier, Madras Civil Service ; *m.* 1st, Annie Maria Caroline, *d.* of late Dr. James Johnstone, I.M.S. ; 2nd, Amy Macdonell, *d.* of late W. C. Capper, B.C.S. ; nine *s.* three *d.* *Educ.:* Cheltenham. Interpreter 34, B.N.I. ; Adjutant Calcutta Volunteers, 1857 ; A.D.C. and Persian Interpreter to Gen. Sir James Outram, Bart., in first relief, defence, siege, and capture of Lucknow (despatches, medal and two clasps, Brevet majority) ; in command of H.H. Raja of Kapurthala's contingent during its service in Oudh, 1858. *Address:* 55 Warwick Road, S.W.5.
(*Died* 3 *May* 1923.)

CHAMIER, Brig. - Gen. George Daniel, C.M.G. 1900 ; R.A. ; Inspector R.G.A. and Coast Defences in India ; *b.* 24 Sept. 1860 ; *s.* of late Lt.-Gen. S. Chamier, C.B. ; *m.* 1903, Amy St. Leger, *widow* of Hon. James Buchanan ; two *d.* *Educ.:* Cheltenham ; Woolwich. Has served in Royal Horse Artillery, Royal Field Artillery, and Royal Garrison Artillery ; Boer War, 1899-1902 ; commanded the artillery during the defence of Kimberley (despatches) ; Schweizer Renike during its investment, 1900 ; a mobile column in the operations against De Wet, 1901 (despatches) ; commandant and special commissioner, Bloemhof District, 1902 (South African War medal with three clasps, King's medal with two clasps). *Recreations:* hunting, cricket, golf. *Address:* Brook House, Camberley. Surrey. *Club:* United Service.
(*Died* 3 *May* 1920.)

CHAMPION, Henry Hyde ; *e. s.* of Maj.-Gen. J. H. Champion and Henrietta, *d.* of Beauchamp Colclough Urquhart, of Meldrum and Byth ; *b.* 22 Jan. 1859 ; *m.* Elsie Belle, *d.* of Lt.-Col. Goldstein. *Educ.:* Marlborough College ; R.M.A., Woolwich. Served as R.A. during the Afghan War (medal), and as Adjutant at Portsmouth ; resigned to become first Hon. Secretary of Social Democratic Federation ; published first editions of Ibsen, Bernard Shaw, etc. ; tried for sedition after Trafalgar Square riots in 1886 ; defended himself and was acquitted ; won the London Dock Strike in 1889 ; foretold failure of Australasian Strike in 1890 ; Assistant Editor, Nineteenth Century, for two years ; first Independent Labour Candidate (Aberdeen, 996 votes) ; went to Melbourne again in 1893 for good ; leader writer on The Age ; founded Book-Lovers' Library and Australasian Authors Agency. *Address:* 239 Collins Street, Melbourne. *T. A.:* Litaribus, Melbourne.
(*Died* 30 *April* 1928.)

CHAMPNESS, Henry Robert, M.V.O. 1902 ; *b.* 18 June 1852 ; *e. s.* of late Henry Champness, Admiralty timber inspector ; *m.* 1880, Susan Augusta, *e. d.* of late Charles Rowett Quiller and Mary Augusta Quiller of Chelsea ; three *s.* two *d.* *Educ.:* Old Brompton, Kent ; Chatham Dockyard School ; School of Naval Architecture, South Kensington ; Royal Naval College, Greenwich. Passed out R.N. College, 1874 ; Chatham Dockyard until 1875, when ordered to Admiralty ; returning to Chatham, 1875 ; Admiralty, 1877-85 ; 2nd class Assist. Constructor, 1883, on establishment of the Royal Corps of Naval Constructors ; overseer of Admiralty Shipbuilding at Barrow-in-Furness, 1885 ; Portsmouth yard, 1886 ; 1st class Assist. Constructor at Portsmouth, 1887 ; Constructor, 1889. Chief Constructor, Malta, 1895 ; Chief Constructor, Devonport Dockyard, 1897-1902 ; Assist-Director Naval Construction, Admiralty, 1903 ; 1913 ; Member of Royal Corps of Naval Constructors ; several times received thanks of Lords Commissioners of the Admiralty. *Publication:* a paper, The Launch of a Battleship.

Address: 16 Evelyn Mansions, Carlisle Place, Westminster, S.W.   (*Died 22 Feb. 1923.*)

CHAMPTALOUP, Sydney Taylor; Professor of Bacteriology and Public Health, Otago University, since 1911; Government Bacteriologist, Dunedin, since 1910; *b.* Auckland, 10 Aug. 1880; *m.* 1909; two *d. Educ.:* Auckland; Edinburgh University. M.B., Ch.B. 1906, with 1st class honours; B.Sc. in Public Health, 1909 (Edin.); D.P.H, (ad eundem) (N.Z.), 1914; House Physician, Cardiff Infirmary; Chalmers' Hospital, Edinburgh; Junior Assistant Surgical Department, University, Edinburgh; Assistant Medical Waiting Room, Royal Infirmary, Edinburgh; Assistant to Professor Public Health, University, Edinburgh, and Pathologist, Chalmers' Hospital, Edinburgh; Lecturer, Bacteriology and Public Health, Otago University, and Government Medical Officer of Health, New Zealand. *Publications:* various, in N.Z. Medical Journal, British Medical Journal, 1910-16, etc. *Address:* Dunedin, New Zealand. *Club:* Fernhill, Dunedin.
      (*Died 11 Dec. 1921.*)

CHANCE, Sir Arthur, Kt., *cr.* 1905; F.R.C.S.I., F.R.C.P.I. (Hon.), F.R.C.S. Edin. (Hon.), etc.; President Royal Academy of Medicine in Ireland, 1921-24; Member of Council Roy. College of Surgeons, Ireland; Surgeon Mater Misericordiæ Hospital, 1886-1926; Consulting Surgeon Doctor Steevens Hospital, Orthopædic Hospital of Ireland, Dental Hospital of Ireland, and St. Michael's Hospital; Hon. Consulting Surgeon in Orthopædic Surgery, Ministry of Pensions in Ireland, south region; Member of General Medical Council; Medical Visitor in Lunacy under the High Court; *b.* 15 June 1859; *s.* of Albert Chance and Elizabeth Fleming; *m.* 1st, 1886, Martha (*d.* 1891), *d.* of late Daniel Rooney, Belfast; 2nd, 1900, Eileen, *d.* of late William Murphy, Dartry; eight *s.* five *d. Educ.:* University College, Dublin. President Royal College of Surgeons in Ireland, 1904-6; Surgeon to Jervis Street Hospital, 1884-86; Examiner in Surgery, R.C.S.I., 1893-95, 1896-99; Surgeon in Ordinary to the Lord Lieutenant of Ireland, 1892-95 and 1906-15; President Dublin Division British Medical Association, 1903-4; Univ. Examiner in Clinical Surgery Dublin Univ., 1905 and 1906; Member Senate of National University of Ireland, 1914; Col. A.M.S.; Inspector Special Military Surgical Hospitals, Irish Command, 1917-20; Chairman Irish Nursing Board; Member first General Nursing Council for Ireland, 1919-24. *Publications:* Operative Treatment of Enlarged Prostate; The Surgical Treatment of Empyema; Trans. R.A.M.I.; Choledochotomy, Dublin Medical Journ.; etc. etc. *Address:* 42 Merrion Square E., Dublin.   (*Died 26 July 1928.*)

CHANDAVARKAR, Sir Narayen Ganesh, Kt., *cr.* 1910; B.A., LL.B.; President of the Bombay Legislature since 1921; *b.* 1855. *Educ.:* Elphinstone College, Bombay, being appointed junior Dakshina Fellow. Became pleader of Bombay High Court, and for a time English editor of Indu Prakash; General Secretary of the Indian National Social Conferences; Vice-Chancellor University of Bombay, 1909-12; officiated as Chief-Justice, June 1909 and June 1912; Judge of the Bombay High Court, 1901-1913; Chief Minister to H.H. the Maharajah Holkar, Indore, Central India, 1913-14. *Address:* Pedder Road, Bombay.   (*Died 14 May 1923.*)

CHANDLER, Alfred, C.B.E.; *b.* 11 Nov. 1853; 3rd *s.* of Captain James Henry Chandler; *m.* 1880, Kate, 2nd *d.* of late Robert Williams, Liverpool; three *s.* two *d. Educ.:* Liverpool Institute. Assistant-Secretary, Mersey Docks and Harbour Board for about 20 years; General Manager and Secretary for about 9 years; now retired. *Recreations:* shooting and golf. *Address:* Broadlands, Alexandra Drive, Liverpool. *T.:* Lark Lane Liverpool 545. *Club:* Exchange, Liverpool.   (*Died 7 Mar. 1923.*)

188

CHANNELL, Rt. Hon. Sir Arthur (Moseley), Kt., *cr.* 1897; P.C. 1914; *b.* London, 13 Nov. 1838; *s.* of late Sir W. F. Channell, Baron of Exchequer; *m.* 1st, 1865, Beatrice Ernestine (*d.* 1871), *d.* of late A. W. Wyndham of West Lodge, Blandford; 2nd, 1877, Constance Helena, *o. d.* of Walter B. Trevelyan; three *s.* one *d. Educ.:* Harrow; Trinity College, Cambridge. Wrangler and 2nd class Classical Tripos, 1861; Barrister, 1863; Q.C. 1885; Vice-Chairman of General Council of the Bar, 1895; Recorder of Rochester, 1888-97; Judge of the Queen's Bench Division of the High Courts of Justice, 1897-1914; sat as a member of the Judicial Committee of the Privy Council on Prize Court Appeals, 1916-21; sat as a temporary Judge of the King's Bench Division, 1921. *Recreations:* rowing (winner of Colquhoun Sculls, 1860; University Pair Oars, 1861; Henley Grand Challenge and Ladies' Plate (in First Trinity Crew), 1861); yachting (yacht owner since 1876). *Address:* Hillside, Falmouth. *Clubs:* Athenæum, and several yacht clubs.   (*Died 4 Oct. 1928.*)

CHANNER, Col. Bernard, D.S.O. 1886; Indian Army; retired; *b.* 20 Sept. 1846. Served Afghanistan, 1879-80 (medal); Burmah, 1885-87 (despatches, medal with clasp, D.S.O.); Lushai, 1889 (clasp); N.W. Frontier, 1897-98 (medal with clasp).   (*Died 4 Dec. 1916.*)

CHANNING OF WELLINGBOROUGH, 1st Baron (U.K.) *cr.* 1912; **Francis Allston Channing,** Bart.; *cr.* 1906; M.A.; J.P.; *b.* United States, 21 March 1841; *s.* of Rev. W. H. Channing; *m.* 1869, Elizabeth, *d.* of Henry Bryant of Boston; two *d. Educ.:* Exeter College, Oxford. Has taken active part in promoting agricultural, educational, and labour reforms; Member of Royal Commission on Agricultural Depression, 1893-96; Chairman of Central and Associated Chambers of Agriculture, 1894; Member of the Rural Education Conference under the Boards of Agriculture and Education, and of the Rural Education Sub-Committee of the County Councils Association; M.P. (L.) E. Northamptonshire, 1885-1910. Sometime Fellow, Tutor, and Lecturer in Philosophy, University College, Oxford; Barrister, Lincoln's Inn; J.P. Northamptonshire. *Publications:* Instinct; The Greek Orators as Historical Authorities; The Second Ballot; The Truth about Agricultural Depression; Memories of Midland Politics, 1917, etc. *Recreations:* fishing, hunting, cycling. *Heir:* none. *Address:* 40 Eaton Place, S.W.1. *T.:* Victoria 4274. *Clubs:* Oxford and Cambridge, Reform, National Liberal. (*Died 20 Feb. 1926.*)

CHANT, Mrs. Laura Ormiston, preacher (undenominational), lecturer, composer, and writer; *b.* Chepstow, 1848; *d.* of F. W. Dibbin, C.E., and Sophia Ormiston; *m.* 1876, Thomas Chant, M.R.C.S. (*d.* 1913); one *s.* three *d. Educ.:* at home, in Kensington, W. Associate of Arts, Apothecaries' Hall. Has taught in schools; nursed in hospitals; was Sister Sophia in London Hospital; assistant manager of private lunatic asylum; married, and took up public advocacy of Women's Suffrage, Temperance, Purity, and Liberal Politics: became lecturer on literary and social subjects; led crusade against Empire Music Hall; took relief to Armenian refugees in Bulgaria; took out nurses to Greek frontier and Crete, for which she received the Red Cross from Queen Victoria on behalf of the then King and Queen of Greece. *Publications:* Sellouts' Manager (novel); The Prodigal (sermonettes); Verona and other Poems; Short Stories; various pamphlets on temperance, poor law, politics, and purity; many hymns; a song, Ode to Skylark (words by Shelley); Golden Boat Action Songs; Sea-shell Songs; Toddlekins' Songs; May-time Action Songs; Daisies and Breezes Action Songs; Thistledown Action Songs; To and Fro Action

Songs; Galloping Horses Action Songs; Under One Sky, Action Songs; The Dragonfly Action Songs; The Wise Owl Action Songs. *Recreations:* games, especially billiards. *Address:* The Homestead, Pinvin, Pershore. *Clubs:* hon. member of New England Women's; Women's, Chicago. *(Died 16 Feb. 1923.)*

CHAPIN, Capt. Sidney H., D.S.O. 1900; Lieut., Special Reserve, 4th (R. Irish) Dragoon Guards, since 1914; late Assistant Commissioner of Police to the Gold Coast, West Africa; *b.* 23 Feb. 1875. Served with Col. Plumer in Matabeleland, 1896 (medal); Boer War with South African Light Horse (D.S.O. medal, six clasps, King's medal, two clasps); attached to the C.I.D. of the South African Government R.R.'s, 1902-4; Director-General of Hygiene to the Republic of Guatemala, 1904-6. *(Died 25 Sept. 1918.)*

CHAPLEAU, Samuel Edmour St. Onge, ex-Capt. and Brevet-Major U.S. Army; *b.* Syracuse, State of New York, 1839; *m.* Caroline K., 3rd *d.* of Lt.-Col. Geo. W. Patten, U.S. Army; one *s.* *Educ.:* College of Terrebonne. Went to U.S. 1860; entered regular army, 1861. Received brevet rank of Capt. for gallant and meritorious services at battle of Murfreesboro, Tenn., and that of Brevet-Major for gallant services during Atlanta campaign and at battle of Jonesboro', Ga.; was also at battle of Shiloh, Tenn., the siege of Corinth, Miss., and battles of Chickamauga and Chattanooga, Tenn.; sent to Memphis during the riots in that city, 1866; in command of the troops at Augusta, Ga., during the riots, 1868. Retired from U.S. Army, 1871; entered Civil Service of Canada, 1873; was successively Secretary of Department of Public Works, Sheriff of North-west Territories, Clerk of the Crown in Chancery, and Clerk of the Senate and of the Parliament of Canada; retired from active service, 1917. *Address:* Hotel del Coronado, California, United States.
(Died Jan. 1921.)

CHAPLIN, 1st Viscount. See Addenda, page xvii.

CHAPLIN, Col. John Worthy, C.B. 1887, V.C.; *b.* 23 July 1840; *s.* of late W. J. Chaplin. *Educ.:* Harrow. Entered army, 1858; Col., 1883; served Chinese campaign, 1860 (medal with two clasps, V.C.); Afghan War, 1879-80 (medal). *Decorated* for distinguished gallantry North Taku Fort, China. *Address:* 7 Southwick Crescent, Hyde Park, W 2.
(Died 19 Aug. 1920.)

CHAPMAN, Sir Arthur, Kt., *cr.* 1909; H.B.M. Consul-General, Rio de Janeiro, 1901-1909; *b.* 26 Aug. 1851. Vice-Consul Valparaiso, 1875; Bogota, 1882; Guatemala, 1885; Vera Cruz, 1891; several times Acting Consul-General; was twice in charge of the Legation in Bogota, and acted as Chargé d'Affaires in Guatemala. *Address:* 6 Hilltop Road, West Hampstead, N.W. *(Died 13 Oct. 1918.)*

CHAPMAN, Sir Arthur Wakefield, Kt.; *cr.* 1915; Chairman Surrey County Council, 1911-17; J.P., D.L. Surrey; *b.* 8 Aug. 1849; *s.* of Henry Chapman of Wanstead, Essex; *m.* 1876, Agnes (*d.* 1906), *d.* of late Capt. Mangles, Poyle Park, Tongham, Surrey; two *s.* *Educ.:* Tonbridge School; private tutors. Partner in Pigott, Chapman & Co., Calcutta, 1875-1902; contested (L.) Guildford Division, 1900; Alderman of Surrey C.C., 1903; Chairman of Surrey

Educational Committee, 1904-11; Chairman of Surrey C.C., 1911-17; nominated Licensing Commissioner by Liberal Government under Bill of 1908; Chairman County Council Association. *Recreations:* golf, hunting. *Address:* 3 Palmer Street, St. James's Park, S.W.1. *T.:* Victoria 2500. *Club:* Reform.
(Died 25 Mar. 1926.)

CHAPMAN, Hon. Sir Austin, K.C.M.G., *cr.* 1924; M.P.; Minister for Trade and Customs, Australia, 1907-8 and 1923-24, also for Health, 1923-24; Member for Eden Monaro House of Representatives since 1901; *b.* Bowral, N.S. Wales, 10 July 1864; *s.* of Richard Chapman; *m.* Catherine Josephine, *d.* of James O'Brien, Bellevue Station, Braidwood; two *s.* two *d.* *Educ.:* Marulan. M.L.A., Braidwood, in N.S. Wales Parliament, 1891-1901; was Member N.S.W. Commission for the World's Columbian Exposition, Chicago, 1893; J.P. N.S. Wales, 1894; was first Government Whip in Federal Parliament; attended by invitation the Coronation King Edward VII., 1902; was Minister for Defence, 1903-4; was Chairman of Federal Royal Commission on Old Age Pensions, 1905-6; Postmaster-General of Australia, 1905-7; represented Australia, New Zealand, and Fiji at the Postal Union Convention held in Rome, 1906, advocating voting for universal penny post; proposed universal penny postage in Australian Parliament, 1906; introduced penny and toll telephone system in Australia and bush telephone scheme, 1906; also uniform telegraph rates and postal orders throughout the Commonwealth, 1906; was Member Commission New Zealand Exhibition, 1906-7. Introduced the "Chapman Wheat Sack" in Australia. *Recreations:* general athletics, reading. *Address:* The Outlook, Woollahra Point, Sydney Australia. *(Died Jan. 1926.)*

CHAPMAN, Rev. C., M.A., LL.D; Principal Emeritus Western Coll. Bristol, since 1910; *b.* St. Neot's, Hunts, 1828; *s.* of late Thomas Chapman, brewer; *m.* Mary Isabella, *d.* of late Rev. Richard Knill, formerly of St. Petersburg, Russia; five *s.* *Educ.:* private school, St. Neot's. Entered Western College (Congregational), late of Plymouth, now of Bristol, 1851; graduated London University M.A. 1856; Pastor of Church at Chester, 1857-64; Pastor of Percy Church, Bath, till 1871; Pastor of Church and Professor of Congregational College, Montreal, 1871-76; received Diploma of LL.D. at the University in Montreal; Principal Western College, 1876-1910; President of the Devon Association of Science, 1881, and of the Plymouth Institution, 1883-89. *Publications:* Life of Matthew Henry; The Monodologie of Leibnitz; Homiletics of Books of Samuel, Pulpit Commentary, 2 vols.; Pre-Organic Evolution and the Biblical Idea of God; The Emergence of Life and Consciousness. *Recreation:* travelling. *Address:* Crofton, Bronshill Road, Torquay. *(Died July 1922.)*

CHAPMAN, General Sir Edward Francis, K.C.B., *cr.* 1905; R.A.; Colonel Commandant Royal Regiment Artillery; Master Gunner, St. James' Park; *b.* 14 Nov. 1840; *m.* 1886, Georgiana, 3rd *d.* of Sir Edward Clive Bayley, K.C.S.I. Entered army, 1858; General, 1896; served Abyssinia, 1867-68 (despatches, medal); Afghan War, 1878-1880 (despatches twice, brevet of Lieut.-Col., C.B., medal with two clasps, bronze decoration); A.D.C. to the Queen, 1881; brevet of Col. 1881; Burmese Expedition, 1885-86 (medal with clasp); Quartermaster-General in India, 1885-89; Director of Military Intelligence, 1891-96; commanded Scottish District 1896-1901. Was Secretary to Sir Douglas Forsyth's Mission to Yarkand, 1874; a Fellow of the Royal Geographical Society, and an Esquire of the Order of St. John of Jerusalem. *Address:* Strathmore, Limpsfield, Surrey.
(Died 12 May 1926.)

CHAPMAN, Rev. Edward William, M.A., Hon. Canon of Carlisle, assisting at Dean Vaughan Memorial Church, St. Martin's, Kensal Rise, N.W.; *b.* 1841 ; *s.* of William Greenwood Chapman of Pauls Cray Hill ; *m.* 1872, Hon. Theodosia Spring Rice, *s.* of 2nd Lord Monteagle; one *s.* three *d.* *Educ.:* Eton ; Trinity College, Cambridge. Vicar of Lanercost, Cumberland, 1873-79 ; Penrith, Cumberland, 1879-88. *Address:* Pauls Cray Hill, St. Pauls Cray, Kent. *T.A.:* Canon Chapman, St. Mary Cray. *T.:* Cray 5-7. (*Died 1 Feb. 1919.*)

CHAPMAN, Ven. Frank Robert, M.A. *Educ.:* Exeter Coll. Oxford. Vicar of St. James's, Bury St. Edmunds. 1865-73 ; Rector of Stow-Langtoft, Suffolk, 1878-81 ; Archdeacon of Sudbury, 1869-1900 ; Canon of Ely, 1879-1909. *Address:* Coombe Nevile, Warren Road, Kingston, Surrey. (*Died 18 Mar. 1924.*)

CHAPMAN, Colonel Frederic Hamilton, M.V.O. 1910 ; late commanding 2nd Bn. Duke of Cornwall's Light Infantry ; *b.* Chertsey, 9 Feb. 1863 ; *s.* of late Frederic Chapman, publisher ; *m.* 1894, Violet Campbell, *d.* of late Capt. Pearson Campbell Johnstone, R.N. ; two *d.* *Educ.:* Radley ; Sandhurst. Gazetted, 1884 ; served N.W. Frontier of India, 1897-98 (medal with 2 clasps) ; S. African War, 1899-1902 (despatches, Brev. Lieut.-Col., Queen's medal with 3 clasps) ; France, 1914-18 ; Brevet Colonel, 1908 ; medal of Union of S. Africa, 1910 ; twice acted as Administrator to Colony of Bermuda ; served in Malta, India, Burma, Gibraltar, Bermuda, and S. Africa ; was Editor of Gibraltar Chronicle, 1906. *Recreations:* natural history, growing roses and apples ; goats, poultry, rabbits, Japanese art. *Address:* Burston, Diss, Norfolk. (*Died 5 Dec. 1925.*)

CHAPMAN, Maj.-Gen. Hamilton, Hon. Colonel 8th Cavalry, Indian Army, since 1903 ; *b.* 11 Oct. 1835 ; *m.* Adeline (*d.* 1923); one *s.* two *d.* (by second wife, who died 1904). Entered army, 1856 ; Maj.-Gen., 1893 ; unemployed list, 1895 ; served Indian Mutiny, 1857-59 (despatches, medal) ; Afghan War, 1878-80 (despatches, medal, brevet Lieut.-Col.). *Address:* 25 Wilbury Road, Hove, Sussex. (*Died 6 Oct. 1926.*)

CHAPMAN, Hon. Mr. Justice Edmund Pelly ; *b.* Calcutta, 16 August 1867 ; *s.* of R. B. Chapman, C.S.I., formerly Secretary Finance Department Government of India ; *m.* Mary Tupper, *d.* of late Major General D. R. Cameron, C.M.G. ; one *s.* two *d.* *Educ.:* Clifton College ; Emmanuel College, Cambridge. (Exhibitioner and Scholar), 1st Class, Indian Language Tripos ; served in Bengal ; Assistant Secretary Foreign Department Govt. of India ; Registrar High Court, Calcutta ; Superintendent Legal Affairs and Secretary Judicial Department Government of Bengal ; Judge High Court, Calcutta, 1914-15 ; Patna, 1915-19. *Recreation:* golf. *Club:* United Service, Calcutta. (*Died 31 Jan. 1923.*)

CHAPMAN, Martin, K.C. ; Senior King's Counsel for New Zealand ; *b.* Karori, near Wellington, 26 Mar. 1846 ; 3rd *s.* of late Mr. Justice Henry Samuel Chapman, of the Supreme Court of New Zealand ; unmarried. *Educ.:* Church of England Grammar School, Melbourne. Called to Bar, Inner Temple, 1871 ; New Zealand Bar, 1875 ; practised in Wellington during his whole career ; now retired ; was Secretary to the Judicature Commission which produced in 1882 the Code of Civil Procedure now in force; for many years editor of the New Zealand Law Reports and a member, and for a time President, of the Law Society ; has also, as a member of the Council, taken an active part in the proceedings of the New Zealand Institute, having several times had the office of President, and has been interested in other scientific bodies ; an advanced mathematician ; as a young man

he took a leading and scientific part in yachting and other forms of recreation. *Address:* 28 Golders Hill, Wellington, New Zealand. *Clubs:* Wellington ; Dunedin. (*Died 1924.*)

CHAPMAN, Thomas Algernon, M.D. (Hon.) Glas., F.R.S. 1918 ; F.E.S., F.Z.S. ; *b.* 2 June 1842. *Educ.:* Glasgow University. Late Superintendent Hereford C. and C. Asylum. *Publications:* Papers in Journal of Mental Science ; Transactions Entomological Society, and various societies, magazines, etc. *Recreation:* natural history, especially entomology. *Address:* Betula, Reigate. (*Died 17 Dec. 1921.*)

CHAPMAN ; Sir Thomas Robert Tighe, 7th Bt. ; *cr.* 1782 ; J.P. ; *b.* 6 Nov. 1846 ; *s.* of late William Chapman, *s.* of 2nd Bt., and Louisa, *d.* of Col. Vansittart, of Shottesbrook ; S. cousin, 1914 ; *m.* 1873, Edith Sarah Hamilton, *d.* of G. A. Rochfort-Boyd, J.P., D.L., Middleton Park, Westmeath ; four *d.* *Heir:* none. (*Died 8 April 1919.*)

CHAPMAN, William Arthur, I.S.O., 1902 ; Clerk, Admiralty ; *b.* 1849 ; *s.* of late Samuel Chapman, Deputy-Marshal of the Queen's Bench Prison ; *m.* Florence Juliet (*d.* 1914), *d.* of late William Kerrison ; one *d.* *Educ.:* St. Omer, France ; Sydney College, Bath. Entered the Admiralty, 1867 ; appointed Head of the Record Office, 1899. *Publications:* Plays and Lyrics. *Address:* 62 Lancaster Gate, W. *Club:* Authors'. (*Died 15 Feb. 1917.*)

CHAPPEL, Rev. William Haighton, M.A. ; Sub Dean and Vicar of S. Michael's Cathedral Church of Coventry : Rural Dean of Coventry and Vicar of Stivichale (in plurality), 1919; Examining Chaplain to Bishop of Coventry and Commissary, 1921 ; Head Master, King's School, Worcester, 1896-1918 ; Hon. Canon of Worcester Cathedral since 1907 ; Proctor Convocation, 1921 ; *b.* 22 May 1860 ; *s.* of late Canon Chappel, Rector of Camborne, Cornwall; *m.* 1892, M. G. Carnsew, Flexbury, Cornwall; two *s.* four *d.* *Educ.:* Marlborough Coll. (Foundation Scholar) ; Worcester College, Oxford (Classical Scholar). First Class Classical Moderations, 1881 ; Second Class Classical Greats, 1883, B.A. ; First Class Honour Theology, 1884 ; M.A., 1887 ; Assistant Master, Marlborough College, 1884-96 ; Chaplain to the Household, 1892-96 ; Hon. Captain O.C.M.C. Cadet Corps, 1890-94 ; Examining Chaplain to the Bishop of Worcester, 1902-5 ; to the Bishop of Birmingham, 1905-9. *Publication:* Progress in the Future Life, Pamphlet, 1907. *Recreations:* golf and cycling. *Address:* The Sub-Deanery, Coventry.

(*Died 11 July 1922.*)

CHAPPLE, Frederic, B.A., B.Sc., London University ; C.M.G. 1915 ; Headmaster of Prince Alfred College, Adelaide, 1876-1915 ; Warden of the Senate of the University since 1883 ; *b.* London, 12 Oct. 1845 ; *s.* of John and Louisa Chapple ; *m.* Elizabeth Sarah Hunter of Hackney ; four *s.* four *d.* *Educ.:* Westminster Training College ; King's College, London ; Royal Science School, South Kensington. Tutor, Westminster Training College, 1870-75 ; Member of Council of University of Adelaide since 1897 ; President Y.M.C.A., Adelaide. *Publication:* The Boys' Own Grammar. *Recreations:* tennis and walking. *Address:* 26 Parade, Norwood, South Australia. *T.:* Central 2840. *Clubs:* Overseas ; Commonwealth.

(*Died 29 Feb. 1924.*)

CHAPPLE, Paymaster Rear-Adm. Sir John Henry George, K.C.B., *cr.* 1918 ; C.B. 1911 ; C.V.O. 1916 ; M.V.O. 1901 ; Deputy Keeper of the Privy Purse since 1922 ; Assistant Treasurer to the King, 1920 ; Secretary H.M. Privy Purse, 1918-22 ; served on H.M. Yacht Victoria and Albert ; *b.* 4 Dec. 1859 ; *m.* 1893, Edith Blanche, *d.* of Rev. William Dyson. Clerk of Shah during engagement with Peruvian turret-ship Huascar, 1877 ; served Zulu War,

1879 (medal and clasp); Egyptian War, 1882 (medal, clasp, Khedive's bronze star, 5th class Medjidie); Souakim, 1884 (clasp); European War, 1914-17 (K.C.B.). *Club*: Army and Navy.
(*Died 5 Mar. 1925.*)

CHARBONNEAU, Hon. Napoleon, Puisne Judge, Quebec, since 1903; *b.* 12 Feb. 1858; *m.* 2nd, Mlle. Lemieux. *Educ.*: Montreal College. Advocate, 1879; K.C., 1899; M.P. (L.), Jacques Cartier, 1895. *Address*: 36 Simpson Street, Montreal. (*Died 31 Aug. 1916.*)

CHARLES, Rt. Hon. Sir Arthur, Kt., *cr.* 1887; P.C. 1903; *b.* 1839; *y. s.* of Robert Charles, London and Carisbrooke: *m.* Rachel Christian, *d.* of T. D. Newton, Plymouth, 1866: three *s.* one *d. Educ.*: Univ. Coll. School and Univ. Coll. London. Matriculated Univ. of London, 1855; B.A. with Mathematical honours, 1858. Hon. M.A. Cantuar. 1884; Hon. D.C.L. Durham, 1884. Barr. (1st class certificate of honour) Inner Temple, Jan. 1862; Q.C. 1877; Bencher, 1880; Recorder of Bath, 1878-87; Chancellor of Southwell Diocese, 1884-87; Commissary of Westminster, 1884-87; Chief Commissioner of Canterbury Election Commission, 1880; Royal Commissioner to inquire into constitution of Ecclesiastical Courts, 1881-83; formerly for many years member of Councils of Law Reporting, of Legal Education, and of Univ. Coll. London; examiner in Common Law at Lond. Univ. 1877-82; President of Senate of Univ. Coll. 1889-96; contested Lond. Univ. (C.), 1880; Judge of High Court of Justice, Queen's Bench Division 1887-97, and of the Arches Court of Canterbury and Chancery Court of York, 1899-1903. *Address*: Woodlands, Sevenoaks, Kent. *Club*: Athenæum.
(*Died 20 Nov. 1921.*)

CHARLES, Commodore Sir James Thomas Walter, K.B.E., *cr.* 1920; C.B. 1911; C.B.E. 1919; R.D., R.N.R., commanding the Cunard Line R.M.S. Aquitania; Commodore of the Cunard Co.'s Fleet since 1921; *b.* Hursley, 2 Aug. 1865; 2nd *s.* of late James Charles; *m.* 1893, Eleanor Mary, *e. d.* of Rev. T. Macfarlane, of Clyro Vicarage, Radnorshire; no *c. Educ.*: privately. Went to sea in Mercantile Marine, 1880; Sub-Lieut. R.N.R., 1891; Lieut. 1895; Commander, 1907; Capt. 1914; Commodore, retired, 1921; Member Departmental Committee on Boats and Davits, 1912-13; Nautical Adviser to the British Delegation, International Conference on Safety of Life at Sea, 1913-14. *Address*: 21 Winn Road, Southampton.
(*Died 15 July 1928.*)

CHARLESWORTH, Colonel Henry, C.M.G. 1902; M.R.C.S. (Eng.), L.M. (Lond.), etc.: R.A.M.C., retired 1902; *b.* 6 July 1851; *s.* of M. Charlesworth, Heath House, Longnor, Staffordshire; *m.* 1st, 1890, Lilian (*d.* 1897), *o. d.* of W. Armstrong, York; 2nd, 1921, Constance Katherine, *d.* of late George Bennett, 44 Holland Park, and Barnes. *Educ.*: Ockbrook College, Derby. Entered the Army Medical Service, 1875; served Afghan War, 1879-1880 (medal); accompanied as medical officer British mission to Sultan of Morocco, 1885, and again, 1890-91, under Sir Kirby Green, K.C.M.G.; served European War, 1914 (mentioned and thanked, Bt. Col.). *Recreations*: all out-door amusements. *Address*: c/o Holt & Co., 3 Whitehall Place, S.W.1. *Club*: Constitutional.
(*Died 5 June 1926.*)

CHARLTON, John, R.O.I., R.P.S., R.B.C., artist; *b.* Bamborough, Northumberland; *e. s.* of late Samuel Charlton; *m.* 1882, Kate (*d.* 1893), *d.* of Thomas Vaughan, J.P., D.L., Ugthorp Lodge, Cleveland. *Educ.*: Newcastle-on-Tyne; studied at Newcastle School of Arts and S. Kensington; exhibited at R.A. 1870, and regularly since. *Paintings*: A Winter's Day; The Hall Fire; Rescue; Huntsman Courtship; Gone Away; Stag at Bay; British Artillery entering Enemy's Lines at Tel-el-Kebir; Ulundi; Reynard's

Requiem; Bad News from the Front; Incident in the Charge of the Light Brigade, etc.; the Procession of Royal Princes passing through Trafalgar Square to Westminster Abbey, 1887, painted for the Queen; also by command of H.M. the Queen the official picture of the thanksgiving service in front of St. Paul's Cathedral on the occasion of the Royal Diamond Jubilee, entitled " God Save the Queen"; and The Funeral of Queen Victoria; also a great many military, sporting, and other subjects to Graphic. *Address*: 6 William Street, Albert Gate, S.W.; Newcastle-on-Tyne, Northumberland. *Club*: Arts.
(*Died 5 Nov. 1917.*)

CHARLTON-MEYRICK, Colonel Sir Thomas, 1st Bt., *cr.* 1880; K.C.B., *cr.* 1910; C.B. 1897; J.P., D.L.; *b.* 14 Mar. 1887; 2nd *s.* of late St. J. C. Charlton, Apley Castle, Salop, and Jane, *o. d.* and heiress of late Thomas Meyrick, of Bush; *m.* Mary Rhoda, *d.* of Col. F. Hill, and niece of 2nd Viscount Hill, 1860; three *s.* four *d. Educ.*: Eton. Col. and Hon. Col. 3rd Batt. Shropshire Regt.; M.P. Pembroke, 1868-74. *Heir*: *s.* Brig.-Gen. F. Charlton-Meyrick. *Address*: Bush, Pembroke; Apley Castle, Shropshire. *Clubs*: Boodle's, Windham.
(*Died 31 July 1921.*)

CHARMES, Francis; Manager since 1907, and Editor since 1893, of the Revue des Deux Mondes; Officer Legion of Honour; Senator; Member of French Academy; *b.* Aurillac, 21 April 1848. *Educ.*: College d'Aurillac; Lycées of Clermont-Ferrand and Poitiers. Editor Journal des Débats, 1872-80 and 1889-1907; Deputy for Cantal, 1881-85 and 1891-98. *Publications*: many literary and political articles. *Address*: 17 Rue Bonaparte, Paris.
(*Died 4 Jan. 1916.*)

CHARRINGTON, Captain Eric, D.S.O. 1900; R.N. retired; *b.* 30 April 1872; *y. s.* of late Spencer Charrington, M.P.; *m.* 1905, Rose Evelyn, *y. d.* of Lt.-Col. St. J. Daubeney; one *s. Educ.*: Brighton; Portsmouth. Obtained 4 First Classes at College as Sub-Lieut. Entered Navy, 1885; served Zanzibar, 1896; Benin, 1897 (medal, clasp); China, 1900 (medal, D.S.O.); with storming party, capture of Taku Forts; relief of and operations round Tientsin. *Decorated* for services in attack and capture of Taku Forts. *Address*: Wormstall, Newbury. *T.A.*: Wickham, Berks. *Club*: Junior United Service.
(*Died 15 Sept. 1927.*)

CHARRINGTON, Lieut.-Col. and Hon. Col. Francis, C.M.G., 1900; *b.* 17 Nov. 1858: *s.* of late Spencer Charrington, M.P.; *m.* 1885, Alice Maud, *d.* of late Walter Leith, J.P., one *s.* three *d. Educ.*: Winchester. Commanded 4th South Staffordshire Regt. in S. Africa, 1900-1; present at actions Warrenton, Lindley, Bethlehem, and Winburg (despatches, medal with three clasps, C.M.G.). *Address*: Pishiobury, Sawbridgeworth, Herts. (*Died 3 July 1921.*)

CHART, Edwin, M.V.O. 1913; late H.M. Civil Service; *b.* 11 May 1848; *e. s.* of Edwin Chart of Clarendon House, Mitcham, Surrey; *m.* 1871, Martha, *e. d.* of William Godson of Addiscombe Road, Croydon; two *s.* three *d. Educ.*: Dr. Fontaine's Private School, Sutton, Surrey. Entered H.M. Office of Works, 1866; Resident Architect, Hampton Court Palace and District, 1877; retired, 1913. *Address*: Banavie, Brambletye Park, Redhill, Surrey
(*Died 10 Sept. 1926.*)

CHASE, Rt. Rev. Frederic H., D.D., *b.* 21 Feb. 1853; *s.* of late Rev. C. F. Chase, M.A., Rector of St. Andrew by the Wardrobe and St. Anne, Blackfriars; *m.* 1877, Charlotte Elizabeth, *e. d.* of late Rev. G. Armitage, Vicar of St. Luke's, Gloucester; three *s.* one *d. Educ.*: King's College School, London; Christ's College, Camb. Scholar; Powis Medal (Latin verse), 1875; B.A. Classical Tripos (8th in First Class), 1876; Kaye Prize, 1884; M.A. 1879; B.D. 1891; D.D. 1894; Hulsean

Lecturer, 1900 ; Hon. Fellow of Christ's Coll.,
1904 ; Hon. Fellow of Queens' Coll., 1906 ;
Curate of Sherborne, Dorset, 1876-79 ; Curate
of St. Michael's, Cambridge, 1879-84 ; Lecturer in Theology, Pemb. College, Cambridge,
1881-90 ; Lecturer in Theology, Christ's Coll.
Camb. 1898-1901 ; Tutor of Clergy Training
School, Cambridge, 1884-87 ; Principal of same,
1887-1901 ; Examining Chaplain to Archbishop
of York, 1894-1905 ; President of Queens' College, Camb., 1901-6 ; Norrisian Prof. of Divinity,
Cambridge, 1901-1905 ; Bishop of Ely, 1905-
1924. *Publications :* Chrysostom, 1887 ; The
Lord's Prayer in the Early Church (Texts
and Studies, I. iii.) 1891 ; Old Syriac Element
in Codex Bezae, 1895 ; Syro-Latin Text of
the Gospels, 1897 ; Clement of Alexandria (a
lecture), 1897 ; Articles on St. Peter and I.
Peter and II. Peter in Hastings' Dict. of Bible,
1900 ; Credibility of the Book of the Acts, 1901 ;
Essay on the Gospels in the Light of Historical
Criticism in Cambridge Theological Essays,
1905, republished separately with Preface, 1914 ;
Confirmation in the Apostolic Age, 1909 ;
Belief and Creed. 1918 ; The Creed and the New
Testament, 1920 ; What did Christ teach about
Divorce ? 1921 ; Edited Commentary on 1
Peter by the late Rev. F. J. A. Hort, D.D.
Address : St. Etheldreda's, 5 Constitution Hill,
Woking, Surrey.   (*Died 23 Sept. 1925.*)

CHATER, Sir Catchick Paul, Kt., *cr.*
1902 ; C.M.G. 1897 ; J.P. ; Member of Executive
Council, Hong-Kong ; *b.* 1846 ; *s.* of Chater
Paul Chater of Calcutta. M.L.A. 1887-1906.
Address : Marble Hall, Conduit Road, Hong-
Kong. *Club :* Hong-Kong.   (*Died 27 May 1926.*)

CHATER, Colonel Vernor, M.V.O. 1919 ;
retired pay ; *b.* 1842 ; *s.* of George Chater, of Langley, Bucks ; *m.* 1902, Edith Mary (*d.* 1928), *d.* of
John Oliver Hanson. *Educ. :* privately ; Rugby.
Joined the 91st Highlanders, now 1st Batt. Argyll
and Sutherland Highlanders, 1864 ; served in that
Regt. for 29 years ; was Adjutant and Lt.-Col. ;
served in 2nd Batt. 93rd for a short time ;
A.D.C. to General Officer in Scotland, 1877, and
later to the Marquis of Lorne, Governor-General
of Canada ; commanded 25th Regimental District,
King's Own Scottish Borderers, 1895-99 ; retired
for age ; served in India, Canada, South Africa
(Zulu Campaign, despatches, medal and clasp),
Ceylon and China ; European War, served (at
home) on Travelling Medical Board, 1915-17 ;
later as acting Equerry to Princess Louise,
Duchess of Argyll. *Recreations:* fishing, yachting,
and manly exercise. *Address :* 24 Walton Street,
S.W.3. *T. :* Western 4595. *Clubs :* Naval and
Military, Garrick, Beefsteak, M.C.C. ; R.
Southern Yacht.   (*Died 3 Oct. 1928.*)

CHATFEILD-CLARKE, Sir Edgar,
Kt., *cr.* 1913 ; D.L. ; M.P. (L.) Isle of
Wight, 1922-23, retiring owing to ill-health ;
s. of Thomas Chatfeild-Clarke, F.R.I.B.A.,
F.S.I. ; *cousin* of late Rt. Hon. J. Chamberlain,
M.P. ; *b.* 1863 ; unmarried. *Educ. :* King's
College School ; Dresden. Member of the Isle
of Wight County Council since 1900 ; J.P. ;
member of I.W. Education Committee ; member
of I.W. Advisory Committee *re* appointment of
Magistrates. *Recreations :* yachting and Conti-
nental travel. *Address :* Wootton, Isle of Wight.
T. : Wootton 9. *Clubs :* Reform ; Isle of Wight
County.   (*Died 16 April 1925.*)

CHATTERJI, Sir Protul Chandra,
Kt., *cr.* 1909 ; M.A., D.L., LL.D., Rai Bahadur,
C.I.E. ; retired Judge Chief Court, Punjab ;
Advocate Chief Court ; *b.* 8 Oct. 1848 ; *s.* of
Nabo Chandra Chatterji ; *m.* 1st, Nitumbini
Devi, *d.* of Woomachasan Banerji, Calcutta ;
2nd, Basant Kumari Devi, *d.* of Srinath
Mukerji, landholder, Kanchrapora, Bengal ;
five *s.* three *d. Educ. :* General Assembly's
College, Calcutta ; Presidency Coll., Calcutta,
Law Department ; enrolled as a vakil High
Court, Calcutta, 1870 ; removed to Lahore,

192

1870 ; Municipal Commr., Lahore, 1887-95 ;
Offg. Judge Chief Court, 1889 ; Judge Chief
Court, 1894-1908 ; Vice-Chancellor Punjab
University, 1904 and 1907-9 ; President Public
Library, Lahore. *Address :* 168 Cornwallis
Street, Calcutta ; Chatterji Road, Lahore.
Clubs : India, Calcutta ; Punjab Association,
Lahore.   (*Died 17 Aug. 1917.*)

**CHATTERTON, Colonel Frank
William,** C.I.E. 1894 ; unemployed list,
India ; *b.* 1 June 1839 ; 3rd *s.* of John Balsir Chat-
terton, harpist to Queen Victoria ; *m.* 1863,
Susie (*d.* 1923), *e. d.* of Major-Gen. J. F. Richard-
son, C.B. *Educ. :* Christ's Hospital, Mill Hill.
Entered Indian Army, 1859 ; Adjutant 14th
Sikhs ; Umbeyla campaign, 1863 (frontier
medal) ; Adjutant 29th Punjab Infantry ;
Bhootan campaign, 1865 (wounded, clasp) ;
commanded Calcutta Volunteers, 1886-1897 ;
Chief Commissioner Andaman Islands, 1897.
Recreations : cycling. *Address :* Central Lodge,
Norwood, S.E 19. *T. :* Sydenham 1839. *Club :*
Junior Constitutional.   (*Died 4 Mar. 1924.*)

**CHAUDHURI, Hon. Mr. Justice
Asutosh,** Kt., *cr.* 1917 ; B.A. (Cantab.), M.A.
(Calcutta University), Barrister-at-Law ; Judge
of the Calcutta High Court ; *b.* Bengali, Bramhin,
1860 ; *e. s.* of Durgadas Chaudhuri Zemindar of
Rajshye, a member of one of the oldest families
of that district, the title "Chaudhuri" having
been bestowed upon them by the Emperors of
Delhi ; *m.* Prativa Devi, of the Tagore family of
Calcutta, *g.d.* by son of Maharashi Devendra-
nath Tagore ; four *s.* one *d. Educ. :* St. John's
College, Cambridge ; Presidency College, Calcutta. After graduating in Calcutta went to
Cambridge and studied mathematics, taking
3rd Class Honours in the Mathematical Tripos,
1884 ; admitted as an Advocate of the Calcutta
High Court, 1886 ; President of the Bengal
National Conference ; founded the Bengal Landholders' Association in Calcutta, of which he
was the Honorary Secretary for years ; was one
of the founders of the Calcutta National College,
and has always taken a prominent part in reform
movements in Bengal ; first time a Hindu
member of the Calcutta Bar has been appointed
Judge of the Court ; now the Senior Judge on
the original side of the Calcutta High Court ;
was President of the Bengal Literary Conference, and is President of the Calcutta Club.
Publications : Elements of Trigonometry ; some
other works for school use. *Recreation :*
walking. *Address :* 47 Old Ballygunge, Calcutta. *T.A. :* Baratlaw, Calcutta. *Clubs :*
National Liberal ; Calcutta, Calcutta.
                (*Died May 1924.*)

**CHAVASSE, Rt. Rev. Francis
James ;** *b.* 27 Sep. 1846 ; *s.* of Thomas
Chavasse, F.R.C.S., Wylde Green House, Sutton
Coldfield ; *m.* 1881, Edith (*d.* 1927), *y. d.* of Canon
Maude, Vicar of Chirk ; four *s.* three *d. Educ. :*
Oxford ; first-class law and history ; M.A.,
1872 ; D.D., 1900 ; hon. LL.D. Camb. 1908 ; Hon.
LL.D. Liverpool, 1920 ; Curate, St. Paul's,
Preston, 1870-73 ; Vicar, St. Paul's, Upper
Holloway, 1873-78 ; Rector, St. Peter-le-Bailey,
Oxford, 1878-89 ; Principal of Wycliffe Hall,
Oxford, 1889-1900 ; Bishop of Liverpool, 1900-23.
Address : St. Peter's House, Oxford.
                (*Died 11 Mar. 1928.*)

**CHEAPE, Lt.-Col. Hugh Annesley
Gray-,** D.S.O. 1917 ; J.P. Co. Worcester ;
Commissioner of Supply for Forfarshire ;
joint-master and huntsman of the Berwick-
shire Foxhounds ; *b.* 15 Nov. 1878 ; *e. s.*
of late Col. George Clerk Cheape of
Wellfield, Fife, and Mrs. Cheape of Bentley
Manor, Worcestershire ; *m.* 1906, Carsina
Gordon, *o. d.* of late Charles William Gray
of Carse Gray, Forfarshire ; one *s.* three *d.
Educ. :* Gleualmond ; Mulgrave Castle ; Trinity
Hall, Cambridge. Joined Queen's Own Wor-
cestershire Hussars (Yeomanry), 1897 ; com-

manded Worcester Squadron Imperial Yeomanry in S. Africa, 1901-2 ; retired with rank of Hon. Capt. in army ; joined 4th Argyll and Sutherland Highlanders with rank of Capt. 1903 ; retired with rank of Hon. Major, 1912 ; while at Cambridge hunted the Cambridgeshire Harriers, and afterwards his mother's harriers in Worcestershire ; on marriage took additional name and arms of Gray ; joined Queen's Own Worcestershire Hussars, with rank of Major, 1914 ; served European War, 1915-17 (D.S.O.) ; Lt.-Col. Warwickshire Yeomanry, 1916. *Recreation*: hunting. *Address*: Carse Gray, Forfar. *T.*: Forfar 82. *M.*: SR 199. *Clubs*: Cavalry ; New, Edinburgh.   (*Died June 1918.*)

CHECKLEY, Frank S., I.S.O. 1911 ; Comptroller, School Lands Branch, Dept. of Interior, Canada. *Address*: 2 Cloverdale Road, Rockcliffe Park, Ottawa, Canada.
      (*Died 31 Mar. 1918.*)

CHEETHAM, Right Hon. John Frederick ; P.C. 1911 ; *b.* 1885 ; *e. s.* of late John Cheetham of Eastwood, Cheshire (M.P. South Lancashire, 1852 - 59 ; Salford 1865-68) ; *m.* 1887, Beatrice Emma, *y. d.* of late Francis Dukinfield Palmer Astley, D.L., of Dukinfield, Cheshire, and Arisaig, Invernessshire. *Educ.*: University College, London ; graduate B.A. in honours, University of London. M.P. (N.) Derbyshire, 1880 - 85 ; Staleybridge, 1905-9 ; contested High Peak Div. 1885 and 1892 ; Bury (Lanc.), 1895 ; Staleybridge, 1900 ; J.P. Cos. Chester and Lancaster ; Alderman of the Cheshire County Council ; Governor of the Victoria University of Manchester ; Director Manchester and Liverpool District Bank ; received honorary freedom of Staleybridge, 1897, on presenting that borough with Jubilee Memorial gift of a Public Free Library. *Address*: Eastwood, Staleybridge. *Clubs*: Athenæum, Brooks's, Alpine.   (*Died 25 Feb. 1916.*)

CHENEY, E. John, C.B. 1915 ; M.A. (Cantab.), M.R.A.C., Haygarth Gold Medallist, F.S.I. ; Joint Secretary, H.M. Office of Woods, Forests and Land Revenues, 1919 ; *b.* 1862 ; *s.* of late E. Cheney, Brooks Hall, Ipswich ; *m.* Lilla Norman, *d.* of late Rev. Frederick Lawson Hayward, Tunstall Rectory, Suffolk ; one *s.* one *d.* *Educ.*: privately ; Jesus College, Cambridge ; Royal Agricultural College, Cirencester ; Assistant Secretary Board of Agriculture and Fisheries, 1911-14 ; Chief Agricultural Adviser, 1914-18. *Address*: Heather Lodge, Sunningdale. *T.*: Ascot 144. *Club*: Union.
      (*Died 12 Oct. 1921.*)

CHERRY, Rt. Hon. Richard Robert, K.C., LL.D. ; P.C. (Ireland) 1905 ; *b.* near Waterford, 19 March 1859 ; *y. s.* of Robert W. Cherry, Solicitor, and Susan, *d.* of John Briscoe, M.D. ; *m.* 1886, Mary Wilhelmina, *d.* of Robert Cooper of Collinstown House, Leixlip. *Educ.*: Trin. Coll., Dublin ; B.A. 1879 ; Double Gold Medallist in Mental Science and History, and Political Science ; Student in Jurisprudence and Roman Law at Inns of Court examination, London, 1880 ; First Scholar in International Law, Middle Temple, London. Called to Irish Bar, 1881 ; Q.C. 1896 ; Examiner in Political Economy for Indian Civil Service, 1885-89 ; Professor of Constitutional and Criminal Law in University of Dublin, 1889 - 94 ; contested Kirkdale Division of Liverpool (L.) 1900 ; Attorney-General for Ireland, 1905-9 ; M.P. (L.) Exchange Div., Liverpool, 1906-9 ; a Lord Justice of Appeal for Ireland, 1909-14 ; Lord Chief Justice of Ireland, 1914 - 1916. *Publications*: The Irish Land Law and Land Purchase Acts, 1888 (3rd ed., 1903) ; Lectures on the Growth of Criminal Law in Early Communities, 1890 ; An Outline of Criminal Law, 1892. *Address*: 92 St. Stephen's Green, Dublin ; Killincarrig House, Greystones, Co. Wicklow.
      (*Died 10 Feb. 1923.*)

8

CHESNEY, Col. Harold Frank, C.M.G. 1918 ; retired pay R.E. ; *b.* 7 March 1859. Entered Army, 1878 ; retired 1911, having been C.R.E. India ; served Hazara Expedition, 1888 (despatches, medal and clasp) ; N.W. Frontier, Tochi Field Force, 1897 (medal and clasp).
      (*Died 21 Mar. 1920.*)

CHESTER-MASTER, Lt. - Col. (Temp.) Richard ; D.S.O. 1917 ; Chief Constable, Gloucestershire, since 1910 ; *b.* 29 Aug. 1870 ; *e. s.* of late Col. T. W. Chester-Master, J.P., of The Abbey, Cirencester, and Knole Park, Almondsbury, Gloucestershire ; *m.* 1901, Geraldine M. R., *e. d.* of late John H. Arkwright of Hampton Court, Herefordshire ; two *s.* *Educ.*: Harrow ; Christ Church, Oxford. Captain and Brevet-Major, King's Royal Rifle Corps ; retired pay, 1910 ; A.D.C. to Viscount Milner (High Commissioner for South Africa), 1898-1901 ; served South African War, 1899 - 1902 (despatches, Queen's medal and 6 clasps, King's medal and 2 clasps) ; Commandant - General British South Africa Police (with local rank Lieut.-Col.), Rhodesia, 1901-5 ; Resident Commissioner and Commandant-General Southern Rhodesia, 1905-8 ; served European War, commanding 13th Batt. King's Royal Rifle Corps, 1915 (despatches, D.S.O. and Bar). *Recreations*: all field sports. *Address*: St. Clair, The Park, Cheltenham. *T.A.*: Cheltenham. *T.*: Cheltenham 790. *Clubs*: Army and Navy, Carlton.   (*Died 30 Aug. 1917.*)

CHESTERTON, Cecil Edward, Highland Light Infantry ; *b.* Kensington, 12 Nov. 1879 ; *s.* of Edward and Marie Louise Chesterton ; *m.* 1917, A. E. Jones (John Keith Prothero). *Educ.*: St. Paul's School. Entered journalism, 1901, writing first for the Outlook, and afterwards for a large number of journals and magazines ; Member of the Executive of the Fabian Society, 1906 - 7 ; abandoned Fabian Socialism and began to attack the Party System, 1910 ; sub-editor of the Eyewitness, 1911-12 ; editor, 1912 ; founder and editor of the New Witness, 1912 ; commenced the attack on the Marconi Contract, August 1912 ; his energies are mainly devoted to the exposure of the corruption of professional politics ; lectured in America during the winter of 1914-15 ; editor of the New Witness, 1912-16 ; served European War, 1917. *Publications*: Gladstonian Ghosts, 1905 ; the People's Drink, 1909 ; Party and People, 1910 ; The Party System (with Mr. Belloc), 1911 ; Nell Gwynne, 1911 ; The Prussian hath said in his Heart, 1914 ; The Perils of Peace, 1916. *Recreation*: smoking. *Address*: 11 Warwick Gardens, Kensington, W. ; 21 Essex Street, Strand, W.C. *T.A.*: New Witness, Estrand, London. *T.*: City 1978. *Club*: Savage. (*Died 7 Dec. 1918.*)

CHETWYND, Sir George, 4th Bt. ; *cr.* 1795 ; *b.* 31 May 1849 ; *s.* of 3rd Bt. and Lady Charlotte Augusta Hill, *e. d.* of 3rd Marquess of Downshire ; *S.* father 1869 ; *m.* Lady Florence Cecilia Paget (*d.* 1907), *y. d.* of 2nd Marquess of Anglesey, and widow of 4th Marquess of Hastings, 1870 ; one *s.* two *d.* High Sheriff, Warwickshire, 1870. Owns about 6700 acres. *Heir*: *s.* George Guy [*b.* 6 Dec. 1874 ; *m.* Rosamund, who divorced him, 1909, *y. d.* of late Charles Secor, U.S.A. ; one *s.*]. *Address*: 23 Cork Street, W. *Club*: Turf. (*Died 10 Mar. 1917.*)

CHETWYND-STAPYLTON, Rev. William, M.A. ; Hon. Canon of Rochester ; *b.* 15 May 1825 ; *s.* of Major Chetwynd-Stapylton, 10th Hussars, and *sis.* of late Lord Hammond ; his grandfather, *s.* of 4th Viscount Chetwynd, *m.* the heiress of Wighill, Yorkshire, and by royal licence took name of Chetwynd-Stapylton ; descended from Sir Brian Stapilton, one of the first Knights of the Garter, who purchased Wighill in the 14th century ; *m.* 1st, 1852, Elizabeth Biscoe (*d.* 1898), *d.* of Rev. R. B. Tritton ; two *s.* one *d.* ; 2nd, 1898, Mary-

193

Elizabeth, *o. d.* of late Fred. Johnson. *Educ.*: Eton. 2nd Captain of Boats, won sculling, double-sculling, and pair-oar races, the latter 3 times; Merton College, Oxford (Scholar); Fellow, 1847; won gold challenge cups for eights and for fours both at Thames and Henley Regattas, 1844. Rector of Old Malden, Surrey, 1850-94; Hallaton, Leicestershire, 1894-1907. *Address*: 21 Ferndale, Tunbridge Wells.

(Died 4 Mar. 1919.)

CHEVALIER, Albert, comedian; *b.* 21 March 1861; has Italian, French, and Welsh blood in his veins. First appearance in public as a child eight years old; as an actor on the legitimate stage was for many years associated with Mr. and Mrs. Kendal, John Hare, A. W. Pinero, T. W. Robertson, Mr. and Mrs. Bancroft, John Clayton, etc.; was for four years connected with music-halls; has since toured with his own entertainment in England and America, and has given 1000 Chevalier recitals at Queen's Hall, London; author of over 100 sketches, monologues, plays. *Publication*: Before I Forget, 1901. *Address*: 38 Woodberry Down, N.4. *T.*: Dalston 743.

(Died 10 July 1923.)

CHEYLESMORE, 3rd Baron (U.K.), *cr.* 1887; **Herbert Francis Eaton,** K.C.M.G., *cr.* 1919; K.C.V.O. 1909; Major-General; retired Chairman National Rifle Association; Chairman L.C.C.; *b.* 25 Jan. 1848; 3rd *s.* of 1st Lord Cheylesmore; *S. b.* 1902; *m.* 1892, Elizabeth Richardson, *d.* of late F. O. French, of New York; two *s. Educ.*: Eton; passed into army direct from there. Joined Gren. Guards 1867; commanded 2nd Batt. Gren. Guards when sent to Bermuda, 1890; and the Regiment, 1899; contested Coventry, 1887, on elevation of his father to the Peerage, beaten by 16 votes. *Publication*: Naval and Military Medals of Great Britain. *Recreations*: rowing, shooting, rifle-shooting, coaching, etc. Owns Manor of Cheylesmore, Coventry, formerly possessed by Edward the Black Prince; White's Club. *Heir*: *s.* Hon. Francis Ormond Henry Eaton. *Address*: 16 Princes Gate, S.W.7. *T.*: Western 715. *Clubs*: Guards', Travellers', Carlton, Marlborough, Turf, Bachelors', Pratt's, Beefsteak, United Service, Four-in-Hand.

(Died 29 July 1925.)

CHICHESTER, 6th Earl (*cr.* 1801), **Jocelyn Brudenell Pelham,** Bt. 1611; Baron Pelham of Stanmer, 1762; O.B.E. 1918; D.L., J.P. Sussex; Public Works Loan Commissioner; late Bt. Lieut.-Col. Royal Sussex Regt.; *b.* 21 May 1871; *e. s.* of 5th Earl of Chichester and Hon. Alice Carr Glyn, *d.* of 1st Baron Wolverton; *m.* 1898, Ruth, *e. d.* of late F. W. Buxton; two *s.* two *d. Heir*: *s.* Lord Pelham. *Address*: Stanmer, Lewes, Sussex. *Clubs*: Brooks's, Bath, Beefsteak.

(Died 14 Nov. 1926.)

CHICHESTER, 7th Earl of, *cr.* 1801; **Francis Godolphin Henry Pelham,** Bt. 1611; Baron Pelham of Stanmer, 1762; *e. s.* of 6th Earl; *b.* 23 March 1905; *S.* father 1926. *Educ.*: Eton; Trinity College, Oxford. *Recreation*: shooting. *Heir*: *b.* Hon. John Buxton Pelham, *b.* 12 June 1912. *Address*: Stanmer, Lewes, Sussex. *T.*: Preston, Brighton 74.

(Died 22 Nov. 1926.)

CHICHESTER, Rev. Edward Arthur, M.A.; Hon. Canon of Winchester, 1906; Rural Dean, 1891-1920; Vicar of Dorking 1885-1921; *b.* 23 Feb. 1849; *s.* of late Rev. George Vaughan Chichester; *y. b.* of 1st Baron O'Neill, Vicar of Wotton, Surrey, and Harriett, *d.* of Hugh Lyle, of Co. Antrim; *m.* 1884, Hon. Mary Agnes Cubitt, 2nd *d.* of 1st Baron Ashcombe; one *s.* two *d. Educ.*: Cambridge (M.A.). Curate, Farncombe, Surrey, 1875-77; Vicar of Okewood, 1877-85. *Publications*: Ad Clerium, Foreword by Bishop Talbot, 1914: Solemn Reminder.

Address: Ashleigh, Dorking. *T.*: Dorking 210. *Club*: Royal Societies. *(Died 30 Sept. 1925.)*

CHICHESTER, Lord Henry Fitzwarrine; *b.* 11 Sep. 1834; 2nd *s.* of 4th Marquess of Donegall; *m.* 1860, Elizabeth Julia (*d.* 1902), *o. c.* and *heiress* of Samuel Amy Severne of Poslingford, and *g.-d.* of T. A. Severne, of Wollop, Shropshire, and Thenford, Banbury, Northamptonshire; two *s.* four *d. Clubs*: Carlton, Isthmian, Prince's, Hurlingham, Thatched House; Sandown. *(Died 7 Nov. 1928.)*

CHICHESTER, Colonel R. P. D. S.; late commanding 14th Service Batt. Royal Irish Rifles; late Captain Irish Guards; *e. s.* of late Rt. Hon. Lord A. J. Spencer Chichester of Moyola Park, Castledawson, Co. Londonderry, and Droish, Co. Donegal; *m.* 1901, Dehra, *o. c.* and *heiress* of late James Ker-Fisher of the Manor House, Kilrea, Co. Londonderry, and of Chicago, U.S.A.; one *s.* one *d.* Served in Central Africa, 1897-99 (medals and clasps), with Central African Rifles, now King's African Regt.; an Assist. Commissioner and in command of the combined escorts to the Anglo-German Boundary Commission, Nyassa and Tanjanika, 1908; served South Africa, 1899 and 1900; commanded 6th Batt. (The Duke of Cambridge's Own) Middlesex Regt., 1904-13; D.L. Co. Londonderry; J.P. Cos. Antrim, Donegal, and Londonderry; High Sheriff Co. Londonderry, 1904-5; Co. Antrim, 1907. *Recreations*: Master of the Killultagh, Old Rock, and Chichester Harriers since 1905; fishing, shooting, and coursing (a Waterloo Cup nominator), cricket. *Address*: Moyola Park, Castledawson, Co. Londonderry; Eden Lodge, Dungiven, Co. Londonderry. *Clubs*: Guards', White's, Junior United Service; Ulster, Belfast; Union, Brighton. *(Died 10 Dec. 1921.)*

CHIENE, John, C.B.; 1900; LL.D., D.Sc., M.D., F.R.C.S., F.R.S. (Edin.); member Royal Medical and Surgical Society, Edin.; Hon. Fellow Surg. Assoc. America, Paris, and Finland; *b.* 25 Feb. 1843; *s.* of George Todd Chiene of Edinburgh; *m.* 1869, Elizabeth Mary, *d.* of David Lyall of Calcutta; two *s.* one *d. Educ.*: Edinburgh; Paris. Late President Royal Medical Society and College of Surgeons, Edinburgh; late Consulting Surgeon to H.M.'s Forces in South Africa, 1900 (despatches, medal, C.B.). Professor of Surgery, Edinburgh University, 1882-1909 *Publications*: Lectures on Surgical Anatomy, 1878; Principles of Surgery, 1882. *Recreations*: golf, fishing. *Address*: Aithernie, Davidson's Mains. *T.*: Davidson's Mains 42. *Club*: University, Edinburgh. *(Died 29 May 1923.)*

CHILDE-PEMBERTON, William Shakespear; *b.* Millichope, 1859; *s.* of late C. O. Childe-Pemberton, D.L., of Millichope Park, Shropshire; *m.* 1894, Lady Constance, *y. d.* of 6th Earl of Darnley; one *s. Educ.*: Harrow. Became representative of the family of Childe (of Kinlet) on the death of his elder brother, Major Childe, killed in the action of Bastion Hill, Natal, Jan. 1900; is hereditary governor of Childe's Coll. Cleobury Mortimer (founded by Sir Lacon Childe); co-heir to several baronies derived from Plantagenets. *Publications*: Elizabeth Blount and Henry VIII.; The Romance of Princess Amelia; Life of Lord Norton; Memoirs of Baroness de Bode, 1775-1803. *Recreations*: musical composition, sketching, travelling. *Address*: 12 Portman Street, W. *Club*: Bachelors'.

(Died 5 Jan. 1924.)

CHILDERS, Col. Edmund Spencer Eardley, C.B. 1900; *s.* of late Rt. Hon. Hugh Childers, M.P.; *b.* 11 Jan. 1854; *m.* 1883, Florence, 3rd *d.* of late William Leslie, M.P., Warthill, Aberdeenshire; two *s.* one *d. Educ.*: Eton; Cheltenham; R.M.A., Woolwich. Entered Royal Engineers, 1873;

served Afghan War, 1878-80; advance on Candahar, 1878; the operations round Cabul, 1879; march from Cabul to the relief of Candahar under Sir Frederick Roberts in 1880; assistant private secretary to the Secretary of State for War, 1880-81; A.D.C. to the Inspector-General of Fortifications, 1888-84; served in Egyptian Expedition of 1882 as A.D.C. to Sir Garnet Wolseley; present at Tel-el-Kebir, and in the Nile Expedition of 1884-85 in a similar capacity; was Military Secretary in Ireland to Field-Marshal Viscount Wolseley, 1890-95; served on a special commission to inquire into and report on the organisation of the local forces in Cape Colony, 1897; Commanding Royal Engineer, Weymouth, 1900-5; Chief Engineer, London District, 1906-10; Deputy Chief Engineer, Southern Command, 1914-17. *Publication:* The Life and Correspondence of Rt. Hon. Hugh Culling Eardley Childers, 1901. *Club:* Brooks's.   (*Died 18 Mar. 1919.*)

CHILDERS, Lt.-Comdr. Erskine, R.N.V.R.; *b.* 1870. *Educ.:* Haileybury; Trinity College, Cambridge. Served European War with R.N.A.S. Jan.-May 1916 (D.S.C.). *Publications:* In the Ranks of the C.I.V.; The Riddle of the Sands; Vol. V. of the Times History of the South African War; War and the Arme Blanche; German Influence on British Cavalry; The Framework of Home Rule.   (*Died 24 Nov. 1922.*)

CHILSTON, 1st Viscount, *cr.* 1911, of Boughton Malherbe; **Aretas Akers-Douglas,** Baron Douglas, *cr.* 1911; G.B.E., *cr.* 1920; P.C., D.L.; M.P. (C.) for St. Augustine's Division of Kent, 1880-1911; *b.* 21 Oct. 1851; *o. s.* of Aretas Akers, Malling Abbey, Kent; *m.* Adeline, *e. d.* of H. Austen Smith, Hayes Court, Kent, 1875; two *s.* five *d.* *Educ.:* Eton; Univ. Coll., Oxford. Barr. Inner Temple, 1875; late Capt. E. Kent, Yeomanry Cavalry; Whip to Conservative Party, 1883-95; Parliamentary Secretary to Treasury, 1885-86, 1886-92, and for short time, 1895; First Commissioner of Works, with seat in Cabinet, 1895-1902; Secretary of State, Home Department, 1902-6. *Heir: s.* Hon. Aretas Akers-Douglas. *Address:* Chilston Park, Maidstone; 34 Lower Belgrave Street, W. *Clubs:* Carlton, Junior Carlton.   (*Died 15 Jan. 1926.*)

CHISHOLM, Rt. Rev. Æneas, R.C. Bishop of Aberdeen since 1899; *b.* Inverness, 26 June 1836; 4th *s.* of Colin Chisholm, solicitor. *Educ.:* St. Mary's College, Blairs, Aberdeen; Gregorian University, Rome. LL.D., Aberdeen University. Served as priest in Aberdeen Diocese from 1860 in Glenlivet, Beauly, Aberdeen, Glengairn, Banff; appointed Rector of Blairs College, 1890; made a Domestic Prelate to His Holiness, 1898. *Address:* 19 Golden Square, Aberdeen, N.B. *Club:* University, Aberdeen.
    (*Died 15 Jan. 1918.*)

CHISHOLM, Hugh; Editor of the Encyclopædia Britannica (10th, 11th and 12th editions); *b.* London, 22 Feb. 1866; *o. s.* of late H.W. Chisholm, Warden of the Standards, formerly Chief Clerk of H.M.'s Exchequer; *m.* E. Beatrix, *d.* of late Henry Harrison, Holywood House, and Ardkeen, Co. Down, 1893; three *s.* *Educ.:* Felsted School (exhibitioner); Corpus Christi College, Oxford (scholar). 1st class Classical Mods. 1886; 1st class Lit. Hum. 1888; M.A. Barr. Middle Temple, 1892; assistant-editor (1892-97), and editor (1897-1900) of the St. James's Gazette; leader-writer for Standard (1900) and subsequently The Times; co-editor (with Sir D. M. Wallace and President Hadley of Yale) of the supplementary vols. (10th edition, 1902) of the Encyclopædia Britannica (for The Times), 1900-3; editor-in-chief of the 11th edition (Cambridge), 1911, and the New Vols., 1922, forming with it the 12th Edition; director of The

Times Publishing Co., 1913-16; Financial Editor of The Times, 1913-20. *Publications:* articles on public finance, politics, and literature in Encyclopædia Britannica, Fortnightly Review, National Review, etc. *Recreations:* golf, music, bridge, billiards. *Address:* 3 Ellerdale Road, Hampstead, N.W.3; *T.:* Hampstead 2706. *Clubs:* Athenæum, Constitutional, United, Cecil; Crowborough Beacon Golf; Lotos, New York.   (*Died 29 Sept. 1924.*)

CHISHOLM, Sir Samuel, 1st. Bart., *cr.* 1902; J.P., D.L. County of City of Glasgow and County of Lanark, LL.D. Glasgow, 1901; Lord Provost of Glasgow, Lord Lieutenant of the County of the City of Glasgow, chairman of the Clyde Navigation Trustees, member of the Carnegie Education Trust, 1899-1902; chairman of the Executive Council of the Glasgow International Exhibition 1901; Chairman of Housing Commission; Hon. Pres. of Glasgow Foundry Boys Religious Society; Chairman of Glasgow and West of Scotland College of Domestic Science; *b.* Dalkeith, 23 Sept. 1836; *s.* of John Chisholm; *m.* 1st, 1866, Charlotte (*d.* 1900), *d.* of Rev. J. B. Thompson, Holywell; 2nd, 1903, Agnes Gibson (*d.* 1921), *d.* of Andrew Carnduff, The Anchorage, Cathcart, and widow of Thomas Henderson, founder of the Anchor Line of steamships. *Educ.:* Dalkeith. Entered Town Council of Glasgow, 1888; Bailie of the Burgh, 1892-97; Senior Magistrate, 1897; Convener of City Improvement Trust, 1892-1902; was a member of the Government Commission on Glanders, and of Royal Commission on Registration of Title in Scotland; contested Camlachie Division of Glasgow, 1897; member, Natural History Society of Glasgow, Royal Philosophical Society of Glasgow, and Glasgow Art Club. *Recreations:* walking, swimming, motoring. *Heir:* none. *Address:* 20 Belhaven Terrace, Glasgow. *T.:* P.O. 2401. *Clubs:* Liberal, Scottish Automobile, Glasgow; Scottish Liberal, Edinburgh.   (*Died 27 Sept. 1923.*)

CHOATE, Joseph Hodges, a trustee of the Metropolitan Museum of Art and of the American Museum of Natural History since the foundation of each; a Governor of New York Hospital since 1877; a member (and chairman of its Committee of Elections) of the original Committee of Seventy, which in 1871 overthrew the Tweed Ring and expelled from the Bench its corrupt judges; Hon. Bencher Middle Temple; *b.* Salem, Mass. 24 Jan. 1832; *m.* 1861, Caroline, *d.* of Frederick A. Sterling of Cleveland, Ohio; two *s.* one *d.* *Educ.:* Harvard and Harvard Law School. LL.D. Amherst, 1887; Harvard, 1888; Edinburgh and Cambridge, 1900; Yale, 1901; St. Andrews, 1902; Glasgow, 1904; Williams, 1905; Univ. of Pennsylvania, 1908; Union, 1909; McGill, 1913; Toronto, 1915; Columbia, 1916; D.C.L. Oxford, 1902; Bar (Mass.), 1855; New York, 1856; for many years president of Union League Club, Harvard Club, and New England Society of New York; also of New York City Bar Association, New York State Bar Association, American Bar Association, and Harvard Law School Association; President New York State Constitutional Convention, 1894; trustee and chairman of the Peabody Education Fund, and president of the New York Association for the Blind; engaged for more than 30 years in many of the most important causes in the Courts of New York, and in the Supreme Court of the United States; United States Ambassador to Great Britain, 1899-1905; member, American Philosophical Society, 1906; Foreign Hon. Fellow Royal Society of Literature; Ambassador and First Delegate of the United States to the International Peace Conference at The Hague, 1907. *Publications:* The Two Hague Conferences; Abraham Lincoln, 1910; American Addresses, 1911; Admiral Farragut, Rufus Choate, The Supreme Court of the U.S., and many other subjects. *Address:* 60 Wall Street, New York; Stockbridge, Mass. U.S.A. (*Died 14 May* 1917.)

CHOLMONDELEY, 4th Marquess of (*cr.* 1815), **George Henry Hugh Cholmondeley,** D.L. Bt. 1611; Viscount Cholmondeley, 1661; Baron Cholmondeley (Eng.), 1689; Earl of Cholmondeley, Viscount Malpas, 1706; Baron Newburgh (Ire.), 1715; Baron Newburgh (Gt. Brit.), 1716; late Lord Great Chamberlain of England; *b.* 3 July 1858; *s.* of Charles George, *e.s.* of 3rd Marquess, and Susan Caroline, *d.* of Sir George Dashwood, 4th Bt.; *S.* grandfather 1884; *m.* Winifred Ida, O.B.E., *y. d.* of late Col. Sir Nigel Kingscote, K.C.B., and *g. d.* of 1st Earl Howe; two *s.* one *d.* Owns about 34,000 acres. *Heir:* s. Earl of Rocksavage. *Address:* Cholmondeley Castle, Malpas, Cheshire. *Club:* Turf. (*Died 15 Mar. 1923.*)

CHOLMONDELEY, Mary; *e. d.* of late Rev. R. H. Cholmondeley, late Rector of Hodnet, and formerly of Condover Hall, Shropshire, and Emily, *s.* of H. R. Beaumont of Whitley Beaumont, Yorks. [Grandmother was Mary Heber, *s.* of Bishop Heber, the hymn-writer.] *Publications:* The Danvers Jewels; Sir Charles Danvers; Diana Tempest; A Devotee; Red Pottage; and Moth and Rust, 1902; Prisoners, 1906; The Lowest Rung, 1908; Notwithstanding, 1913; Under one Roof, 1918; The Romance of his Life, 1921. *Address:* 4 Argyll Road, Kensington, W.8; The Cottage, Ufford, Suffolk. (*Died 15 July 1925.*)

CHOUINARD, Honore Julien Jean Baptiste, C.M.G. 1908; City Clerk Quebec since 1889; *s.* of late Honoré Julien Chouinard, Barrister, Quebec; *b.* 1850; *m.* 1884, Marie Louise Juchereau Duchesnay, *y. d.* of Hon. Elzear H. Juchereau Duchesnay, Senator of Canada; two *s.* one *d.* *Educ.:* St. Ann's College, Quebec Seminary (L.B.); Laval University (LL.B.). Called to Bar, Quebec, 1873; has been President of l'Institut Canadien of Quebec (literary); of Quebec Geographical Society; twice of National French-Canadian St. Jean Baptiste Society; of Cartier Club (political), 1882; Past Director and Vice-President of Quebec and Lake St. John Railway; sat as alderman in Quebec City Council, 1880-1889; contested County of l'Islet, general elections, 1882; elected for County of Dorchester in 1887; sat in Canadian Commons, 1888-1890; was one of the chief promoters of the Quebec Tercentenary Celebration (C.M.G.); F.R.S. Can. 1917; L.D. Laval University. *Publications:* several literary and historical works (including Annals of St. Jean Baptiste Society). *Address:* Quebec. (*Died 27 Nov. 1928.*)

CHOWN, Maj.-Gen. Ernest Edward, C.B. 1917; late R.M.L.I.; *b.* 14 Feb. 1864. Lt. R.M. 1883; Capt. 1893; Major, 1900; Lt.-Col. 1908; Col. 1914; Superintendent Gymnasium, Malta, 1909-14; retired, 1917. (*Died 24 Sept. 1922.*)

CHOWN, John, *b.* Bradford; *s.* of Rev. J. P. Chown, Baptist Minister; *m.* Emma Emily, *d.* of Rev. Thos. Rees; three *s.* one *d.* *Educ.:* private school at Bradford. Spent six years in Bradford Warehouse; came to London as Agent; afterwards becoming a member of the Stock Exchange; President of the Baptist Union, 1922-3; Vice-President of the British and Foreign Bible Society; President of the Willesden Liberal Association. *Recreations:* music, cycling. *Address:* 17 Brondesbury Park, N.W.6. *T.:* Willesden 51. *Club:* National Liberal. (*Died 11 Aug. 1922.*)

CHREE, Charles, M.A., Sc.D. (Cambridge) 1896; LL.D. (Aberdeen), 1898; F.R.S. 1897; *b.* Lintrathen, Forfarshire, 5 May 1860; 2nd *s.* of Rev. Charles Chree, D.D., and Agnes, *d.* of W. Bain; unmarried. *Educ.:* Grammar School, Old Aberdeen; Universities of Aberdeen and Cambridge. Graduated Aberdeen, 1879; obtaining

gold medal awarded to the most distinguished graduate in Arts of the year; graduated Cambridge, 1883; 6th Wrangler, 1883; 1st division Mathematical Tripos, Part III.; 1st class Natural Sciences Tripos, Part II.; Fellow of King's College, 1885; re-elected as "Research" Fellow, 1890; Superintendent Kew Observatory, 1893-1925; awarded James Watt Medal, Institution of Civil Engineers. 1905; and Hughes Medal, Royal Society, 1919; Past President Royal Meteorological Society; Past President, Physical Society of London. *Recreations:* fishing, golf, cycling. *Address:* 75 Church Road, Richmond, Surrey. (*Died 12 Aug. 1928.*)

CHRISTIAN, Admiral Arthur Henry, C.B., 1916; M.V.O. 1910; 4th *s.* of late George Christian and Mrs. Christian. 13 Lowndes Square, S.W.; *m.* 1911, Geraldine Diana, *d.* of late Lt.-Col. Bolton Monsell; one *s.* two *d.* *Educ.:* H.M.S. Britannia. Midshipman, H.M.S. Bacchante, 1879-82; Lieut. 1885; specially promoted to commander, 1896, for services on East and West Coast of Africa; commander of H.M.S. Blake and Excellent; Captain, 1901; Vice-Admiral, 1917; served H.M.S. Highflyer as Flag-Capt. to Admiral Sir Charles Drury, East Indies, 1902, and in command of H.M S. Juno and Duke of Edinburgh, R.N. College, Osborne, and H.M.S. Temeraire; commanded 3rd Division Home Fleet, 1912-14; served European War, 1914; hoisted flag on Euryalus, Aug. 1914, in command of a special force of cruisers, destroyers, and submarines operating in southern part of North Sea; took part in action off Heligoland, 28 Aug. 1914; Rear-Admiral in Eastern Mediterranean, 1915-17; took part in operations at the Dardanelles, commanded Naval Forces at landing at Suvla Bay, and subsequent operations up to and including evacuation of Gallipoli; wounded at Suvla Bay (despatches, C.B.); Adm. retired, 1919. *Recreations:* golf, riding, and shooting. *Address:* 3 Sloane Gardens, S.W.1. *Club:* United Service. (*Died 20 Aug. 1926.*)

CHRISTIAN, Admiral Henry, M.V.O. 1909; Chief Constable of Gloucestershire, 1865-1910; *b.* 1828; *s.* of Samuel Christian, Malta; *m.* 1865, *d.* of James Moore, Liverpool. Entered Navy, 1841; Lieut. 1849; Commander, 1858; Captain, 1863; retired Captain, 1870; retired Rear-Admiral, 1878; Vice-Admiral, 1884; Admiral, 1889; served in suppression of slave trade; Commander of H.M.S. Euryalus, 1858-61; Commander of Royal Yacht Victoria and Albert, 1861-63. *Address:* Heighthorne, The Park, Cheltenham. *Club:* Army and Navy. (*Died 10 June 1916.*)

CHRISTIE, Herbert Bertram, D.S.O. 1900; N.S.W. Bushmen Contingent; *b.* 1868; *s.* of late Marshall Christie. Served South Africa, 1900 (despatches, D.S.O.). *Address:* Braemar, Casino, New South Wales. (*Died 9 Dec. 1916.*)

CHRISTIE, Sir William Henry Mahoney, K.C.B., *cr.* 1904; M.A., C.B., F.R.S., F.R.A.S., Hon. D.Sc. Oxon.; Astronomer-Royal 1881-1910; *b.* 1845; *s.* of late Professor Christie, F.R.S.; *m.* 1881, Violette Mary (*d.* 1888), *d.* of late Sir Alfred Hickman, 1st Bt.; one *s.* *Educ.:* King's Coll. School, London; Trinity Coll. Cambridge (Fellow). Chief Assistant Royal Observatory, Greenwich, 1870. *Publications:* Manual of Elementary Astronomy, 1875; and various scientific papers. *Address:* The Tower House, Downe, Kent. *Club:* Savile. (*Died 22 Jan. 1922.*)

CHRISTISON, Sir Alexander, 2nd Bt., *cr.* 1871; M.D.; Sur.-Gen. I.M.S. (retired); *b.* 26 Aug. 1828; *S.* father 1882; *m.* 1st, 1854, Jemima Anne (*d.* 1876), *d.* of James Cowley Brown, B.C.S.; one *s.* three *d.*; 2nd, 1892, Florence, *d.* of F. T. Elworthy, Foxdown, Wellington, Somerset; one *s.* three *d.* *Educ.:* Edin. Univ. Served in 2nd Burmese War and

Indian Mutiny. *Heir: s.* Major Robert Alexander [R.G.A. (militia); retired; *b.* 23 Feb. 1870; *m.* 1900, Mary Russell, *d.* of A. R. Gilzean]. *Address:* 40 Moray Place, Edinburgh.
(*Died 14 Oct. 1918.*)

CHRISTMAS, E. W., R.B.A. 1909, *b.* South Australia; *s.* of late John J. Christmas, J.P.; unmarried. *Educ.:* Adelaide; artistically, Adelaide, Sydney, and London. Exhibited Royal Glasgow Institute, 1901; exhibited, 1909, Royal Institute, Royal Oil Institute, London, Leeds Art Gallery, and Hull by special invitation; two pictures hung in Royal Academy, 1910; same year exhibited Royal Oil Institute; two pictures hung in Royal Academy, 1911; also R.B.A. and Corporation galleries of provinces; went to South America, 1910, to paint the Andes and mountains from Argentine to Chile; went Southern Andes, 1911, and painted lakes and mountains of that interior of the far south; represented in seven National and Corporation Galleries of the Colonies of Australasia. *Club:* Langham Sketch. (*Died 30 July 1918.*)

CHRISTOPHER, Maj.-Gen. Leonard William, C.B. 1898; *b.* 22 Jan. 1848; *e. s.* of Maj.-Gen. L. R. Christopher; *m.* 1878, Florence, 4th *d.* of Maj.-Gen. Charles Stuart Lane, C.B.; one *s.* Entered 75th Regt. (present 1st Gordon Highlanders), 1867; Col. Bengal Staff Corps, 1897; Maj.-Gen., 1902; served Afghan War, 1878-80 (despatches, medal); Egyptian Expedition, 1882 (medal, bronze star); Tirah Expedition, 1897-98 (despatches, C.B.); Director-General of Supply and Transport, India, 1900-5; retired, 1908. (*Died 25 Aug. 1927.*)

CHURCH, Robert William, C.I.E., 1921; *b.* April 2, 1882; *e. s.* of W. J. Church, Durham City; *m.* 1919, Winifred Florence, *e. d.* of G. E. Platt, Hungerford, Berks; two *d.* *Educ.:* privately; Armstrong College, Newcastle-on-Tyne. B.Sc. University of Durham, F.G.S. 1907, M.Inst. M.E. 1907. In charge Bokero-Ramgur Coalfield Survey, 1908-10; Mining Engineer Railway Board Government of India, 1910-21. *Club:* Oriental. (*Died 16 Nov. 1923.*)

CHURCH, Maj.-Gen. Thomas Ross, C.I.E. 1888; unemployed list Indian Staff Corps; *b.* 5 Jan. 1881; 2nd *s.* of late Thomas Church, B.C.S.; *m.* 1854, Florence, 4th *d.* of late Capt. Frederick Marryat, R.N., C.B. *Educ.:* privately; Addiscombe Coll. Served in various staff appointments in India, and commanded the Madras Volunteer Guards for 14 years. *Recreations:* shooting, fishing.

(*Died 29 Oct. 1926.*)

CHURCH, Sir William Selby, 1st Bt., *cr.* 1901; K.C.B., *cr.* 1902; M.D., D.Sc. Oxon; LL.D. Glasgow, Sc.D. Victoria, D.C.L. Durham Universities; late President Royal Society of Medicine; President Royal College of Physicians, 1899-1905; Consulting Physician St. Bartholomew's Hospital, the City of London Hospital for Diseases of the Chest, and the Royal General Dispensary; Hon. Fellow University College, Oxford; J.P. Herts; *b.* 4 Dec. 1837; *o. surv. s.* of John Church, of Woodside, Hatfield, Herts, and Isabella, *d.* of George Selby, of Twizell House, Northumberland; *m.* 1875, Sybil Constance (*d.* 1913), *d.* of C. J. Bigge, of Linden, Northumberland; one *s.* one *d.* *Educ.:* Harrow; University Coll., Oxford, 1st Class Natural Science School, 1860; representative for University in General Medical Council, 1889-99. Formerly Lee's Reader in Anatomy at Christ Church, Oxford; Lecturer on Comparative Anatomy, St. Bartholomew's Medical School; member of Royal Commission on the Care and Treatment of the Sick and Wounded during the South African Campaign, 1900, and of the Royal Commission on Arsenical Poisoning, 1901, and of the Royal Commission on Vivisection, 1906; Trustee of Hunterian Museum, Royal Coll. of Surgeons of England. *Heir: s.* Geoffrey Selby [*b.* 11 Jan. 1887; *m.* 1st, 1913, Doris Louise Cleghorn (*d.* 1917), *d.* of Sir William Somerville; *m.* 2nd, 1920, Helene Trayner. *Educ.:* Winchester]. *Publications:* Papers in St. Bartholomew's Hospital Reports; Allbutt's System of Medicine, and various Medical Journals, etc. *Recreations:* outdoor sports. *Address:* Woodside, Hatfield, Herts. *T.A.:* Bell Bar. *T.:* Hatfield 44. *M.:* NK 3870. *Club:* Athenæum. (*Died 27 April 1928.*)

CHURCHILL, Surg.-Gen. Alexander Ferrier, M.B., L.R.C.S.I.; *b.* 1839; *m.* 1869, Ellen Louisa Phayre; one *s.* one *d.* *Educ.:* Trinity College; Royal College of Surgeons, Dublin. Entered Army, 1862; retired, 1899; served Soudan Expedition, 1884-85 (medal with clasp, bronze star). *Address:* Tirley, Brentwood, Essex. *T.:* 329. (*Died 10 Oct. 1928.*)

CHURCHILL, Harry Lionel, C.M.G. 1915; F.R.G.S., H.B.M. Consul-Gen. for Compartimenti of Liguria and Emilia, with the exception of Provinces of Ferrara, Bologna, Ravenna, and Forti, to reside at Genoa, since 1922; *b.* 12 Sep. 1860; *s.* of H. A. Churchill, C.B., Diplomatic and Consular Services; *m.* 1892, *d.* of late Sir Joseph Tholozau, K.C.M.G., who was for 40 years Physician-in-Chief to late Nasr ed Din, Shah of Persia; two *s.* three *d.* *Educ.:* privately. Acting Consul at Resht, Persia, 1878; employed in British Legation on probation, 1880-88; Translator and Clerk, 1883; passed examination, 1883; Vice-Consul, Tehran, 1883; Vice-Consul in the dominions of the Sultan of Zanzibar, 1885; was in attendance on Special Envoy sent by the Shah of Persia on the occasion of Queen Victoria's Jubilee, 1887 (Jubilee medal); Consul at Resht, Persia, 1891; was in attendance on the Special Envoy sent by the Shah of Persia on the occasion of Queen Victoria's Diamond Jubilee (clasp of the Jubilee medal), 1897; transferred to Trieste, 1899; Lisbon, 1905; Havre, 1907. *Address:* 1 Via Marcello, Durazzo, Genoa. *T.A.:* British Consul, Genoa. *Clubs:* Royal Societies, Junior Constitutional; Union, Genoa.

(*Died 5 Nov. 1924.*)

CHURCHILL, Lady Randolph Spencer (Jennie), C.I., R.R.C. 1885; Lady of Grace of St. John of Jerusalem, 1901; Royal Red Cross, 1902; was proprietor and Editor of the Anglo-Saxon Review; *d.* of late Leonard Jerome, New York; *m.* 1st, 1874, Rt. Hon. Lord Randolph Henry Spencer Churchill, 3rd *s.* of 7th Duke of Marlborough (*d.* 1895), two *s.*; 2nd, 1900, George Cornwallis-West (whom she divorced 1913); 3rd, 1918, Montagu Porch. Had charge of hospital-ship Maine, South Africa. *Publications:* The Reminiscences of Lady Randolph Churchill, 1908; (Play) His Borrowed Plumes, 1909; (Play) The Bill, 1912; (Essays) Small Talks on Big Subjects, 1916. *Address:* 8 Westbourne Street, Hyde Park, W.2. *Clubs:* Ladies' Athenæum, Ladies' Automobile.
(*Died 29 June 1921.*)

CHURCHILL, Sidney John Alexander, M.V.O. 1906; Consul-General Campania, Basilicata and the Calabric since 1912; *b.* 1 Mar. 1862; *s.* of late Henry Adrian Churchill, C.B.; *m.* 1908, Stella, *y. d.* of George Myers; one *s.* one *d.* *Educ.:* privately. Entered service of the Government of India, 1880, in the Persian Telegraph Dept. of the Indian Govt. Telegraph; Oriental 2nd Sec. Legation of Teheran, 1886; in attendance on the Shah of Persia during H.M.'s visit to England, 1889; Consul for Dutch Guiana and also for French Guiana, 1894; transferred to Palermo for the Island of Sicily, 1898; in charge of the Consulate of Naples, 1 July-6 Oct. 1900. *Publications:* Monograph on the Present Condition of the Persian Carpet Industry in the great Oriental Carpet Book, published by the Austrian Govt. Ministry of Commerce and Public Instruction; various monographs in the Royal Asiatic Society's Journal; Biblio-

197

grafia Celliniana (Florence Olschki, 1907), 2nd edition, 1909, in Cust's Life of Cellini; The Goldsmiths of Rome under the Papal Authority (in Papers of the British School at Rome, 1907); Bibliografia Vasariana (Florence, 1912), and other publications on art. *Recreations:* from 1880-94 collected Persian, Arabic, Turkish, and Hebrew MSS. for the British Museum, vol. iv. of the Persian Catalogue of MSS. being almost entirely devoted to the Churchill MSS.; under the late Gen. Sir R. M. Smith, R.E., K.C.M.G., collected art objects for the South Kensington Museum in Persia; is now engaged on researches for a history of gold and silver work in Italy. *Address:* Palazzo Capomazza, Arco Mirelli, Naples. *T.A.:* British Consul, Naples.
(Died 11 Jan. 1921.)

CHURCHWARD, Percy Albert, C.I.E. 1917; K.I.H.; Managing Director, Bank of Rangoon, Ltd., Burma; *b.* 27 May 1862; *s.* of late Benjamin Hannaford Churchward; *m.* 1895, Margaret Helena Madden, Balbriggan, Ireland; no *c. Educ.:* Royal Naval School, New Cross, S.E. Banker since 1877. *Club:* Pegu, Rangoon. *(Died 17 May 1924.)*

CHURCHWARD, William Brown; *b.* 24 Dec. 1844; 2nd *s.* of J. G. Churchward, formerly of Kearsney Manor, Dover; *m.* 1889, Mary Lees, 2nd *d.* of late Wm. Nassau Peyton, Inspector-Gen. H.M. Customs. *Educ.:* private schools in England; Lycée Impériale, Paris. Entered 14th Regiment, 1863; served through Maori war; left army in 1872; after interim of diamond digging in South Africa, and sheep farming in Tasmania, was acting Consul at Samoa and Deputy Commissioner for the Western Pacific, 1882-85; Vice-Consul at Kustendji, Roumania, 1889; removed to Ibraila, 1890; Consul, Porto Rico, U.S.A., 1899-1912; retired, 1912; holds New Zealand and Coronation Medals. *Publications:* Jim Peterkin's Daughter; Blackbirding; My Consulate in Samoa; stories, sketches, etc., in magazines, English and foreign. *Recreations:* all English sports. *Club:* Junior United Service.
(Died 26 Sept. 1920.)

CLANCY, John Joseph, M.A.; *b.* Galway, 15 July 1847; *s.* of William Clancy, Carragh Lodge, Clare-Galway, Co. Galway; *m.* Margaret Louise, *d.* of P. J. Hickie of Newcastle West; three *s.* three *d. Educ.:* Summer Hill Coll., Athlone; Queen's Coll. Galway; M.A. Queen's (now National), University of Ireland, with Honours in Ancient Classics. Classical Master, Holy Cross School, Tralee, 1867-70; assistant-editor of The Nation (Dublin), 1870-85; editor of the Irish Press Agency in England, 1886-90; member of editorial staff of Irish Daily Independent, 1891-1902; Irish Bar, 1887; K.C. 1906; M.P. North Dublin, 1885-1918. *Publications:* various political pamphlets and addresses and legal publications; essays in Nineteenth Century, Fortnightly Review, Contemporary Review, etc. *Address:* Holmleigh, Kenilworth Park, Dublin.
(Died 25 Nov. 1928.)

CLANMORRIS, 5th Baron (Ireland) *(cr.* 1800), **John George Barry Bingham,** D.L., J.P.; *b.* Seamount, Galway, 27 August 1852; *s.* of 4th Baron and Sarah Selina, 4th *d.* of Burton Persse of Moyode Castle, Galway; *S.* father 1876; *m.* Matilda, *o. c.* and heiress of late Robert Edward Ward, Bangor Castle, Co. Down, 1878; five *s.* three *d.* Protestant. Conservative. *Educ.:* Eton. Lieut. 1st Batt. Rifle Brigade, 1874-78; A.D.C. to Duke of Marlborough, Viceroy of Ireland, 1876-78; Master of Co. Galway Foxhounds (the Blazers), 1891-95. Owns 18,000 acres; salmon fisheries, shootings; pictures of ancestors and predecessors by old masters; also original oil painting of Sir Richard Bingham, three-quarter-life size. *Recreations:* hunting, yachting, shooting, fishing. *Heir: s.* Hon. Arthur Maurice Robert Bingham. *Address:* Creg Clare,

198

Ardrahan, Co. Galway; Bangor Castle, Belfast. *T.A.:* Bangor, Down. *Clubs:* Carlton; Kildare Street, Dublin; Co. Galway, Galway; Ulster, Belfast; Royal Ulster Yacht, Bangor.
(Died 4 Nov. 1916.)

CLANRICARDE, 2nd Marquis of *(cr.* 1825), **Hubert George de Burgh Canning,** Earl of Clanricarde, Baron Dunkellin, 1543; Viscount Burke, 1629; Marquis of Clanricarde, 1825; Baron Somerhill (U.K.), 1826; *b.* 30 Nov. 1832; *s.* of 1st Marquis and Harriet, only sister of 1st Earl Canning; *S.* father 1874. *Educ.:* Harrow. Attaché, Turin, 1852; 2nd Secretary there, 1862; M.P. for Co. Galway, 1867-71. Owns about 57,000 acres. *Heir:* (to Earldom of Clanricarde), Marquis of Sligo. *Address:* 13 Hanover Square, W.C.; Portumna Castle, Galway. *Clubs:* Travellers', Reform.
(Died 13 April 1916.)

CLARE, Sir Harcourt E., Kt., *cr.* 1916; Clerk of the Peace for Lancashire, Clerk of the County Council, etc.; *b.* 1854; *s.* of late William Harcourt Clare of Twycross, Leicestershire; *m.* Clara Theodora (*d.* 1918), *y. d.* of late Thomas Bateman of Middleton Hall, Youlgreave, Derbyshire; one *d. Educ.:* Repton. Formerly Town Clerk of Liverpool and has been a member of several Royal Commissions. *Address:* Bank Hall, Tarleton, Preston; County Offices, Preston, Lancs. *T.:* 1 Longton, Preston. *(Died 1 Mar. 1922.)*

CLARE, Henry Lewis, M.D., B.Ch. Dublin, D.P.H. Ireland; Surgeon-General and Chief Medical Officer of Health, Trinidad and Tobago, 1907-17; *b.* Dublin, 1858; *o. s.* of late Lewis Clare, solicitor, Dublin; *m.* 1883, Lucy, 4th *d.* of Robert Hampson, Stockport, Cheshire; one *s. Educ.:* Rathmines School; Trinity College, Dublin. Jun. Resident Medical Officer, Public Hospital, Kingston, Jamaica, 1881; various appointments in Jamaica Medical Service; District Medical Officer, Kingston, 1896; Member Central Board of Health; Pres. Jamaica Branch British Medical Association; Acting Superintending Medical Officer, Jamaica, 1906; representative of Trinidad at Conference on Quarantine, Barbados, 1908 and 1912; President First West Indian Inter-Colonial Conference on Tuberculosis, Trinidad, 1913; Delegate from Trinidad to International Congress on Infant Mortality, London, 1913; F. R. San. Inst., F. R. Inst. Public Health. *Publications:* various reports. *Recreations:* gardening, walking, bridge. *Address:* c/o London Co. Westminster, and Parr's Bank, Blackheath, S.E. *Clubs:* West Indian, Royal Societies. *(Died 24 Jan. 1920.)*

CLARINA, 5th Baron, *cr.* 1800; **Lionel Edward Massey,** D.L. for Co. Limerick; late Lieut.-Col. Scots Guards (retired 1870); *b.* 20 April 1837; 3rd *s.* of 3rd Baron and Susan, *y. d.* of Hugh Barton of Straffan; *S. bro.* 1897; *m.* 1st, 1877, Elizabeth Ellen, *d.* of Alexander Bannatyne, Woodstown, Co. Limerick; 2nd, 1887, Sophia Mary (*d.* 1912), *d.* of James Butler, D.L., of Castle Crine, Co. Clare; one *s.* five *d.* Served in 4th West York Militia; 82nd Regiment; Scots Fusilier Guards; High Sheriff, 1896. Owns about 2000 acres. *Heir: s.* Hon. Eyre Massey. *Address:* Elm Park, Clarina, Limerick. *T.A.:* Clarina. *(Died 13 Oct. 1922.)*

CLARK, Rt. Rev. Bernard T., Vicar Apostolic of Seychelles. *Address:* Seychelles Islands. *(Died 1916.)*

CLARK, Vice-Admiral Sir Bouverie Francis, K.C.B., *cr.* 1900; *b.* 19 Mar. 1842; *s.* of late Rear-Admiral William Clark; *m.* 1868, Catherine Colburn (*d.* 1902), *d.* of Capt. Wm. Colburn Mayne, late 5th Fusiliers. Entered navy, 1854; Lieut. 1862; Commander, 1875; Capt. 1884; retired, 1897; Rear-Adm. (retired), 1899. Director of Transports, the Admiralty, 1896-1901. *Decorated:* Baltic, 1855; New Zealand, 1863-65; Italian medal, Al Valor di Marina, 1891; 2nd class, Saxe Ernestine Order, 1893. *Address:*

CHURCHILL, William. See page xvii.

Victoria Lodge, Francis Street, S.W. *Clubs:* United Service, Naval and Military.
(*Died 20 Nov.* 1922.)

CLARK, Edwin Charles, Barr., LL.D., F.S.A.; Regius Professor of Civil Law, Cambridge, 1872-1914; *b.* 5 Nov. 1835; *s.* of Edwin Clark, Ellinthorp Hall, Boroughbridge, Yorkshire. *Educ.:* Richmond (Yorks); Shrewsbury School; Trinity College, Cambridge. Seventh Senior Optime Mathematical Tripos, Camb.; Senior Classic and 1st Chancellor's Medallist, 1858; Browne Medallist for Epigrams; formerly Scholar and Fellow of Trinity; late Professorial Fellow of St. John's. Practised for a short time as a conveyancer in London. *Publications:* Early Roman Law: Regal Period, 1872; Analysis of Criminal Liability, 1880; Practical Jurisprudence: a Comment on Austin, 1883; Cambridge Legal Studies, 1888; History of Roman Private Law, Part I. Sources, 1906, Part II. Jurisprudence. *Recreations:* coin collecting, study of archæology and architecture. *Address:* Newnham House, Cambridge. *Club:* Royal Societies. (*Died 20 July* 1917.)

CLARK, Rev. Francis E., A.B., A.M., D.D., LL.D.; President World's Christian Endeavour Union since 1895; President, United Society of Christian Endeavour, 1887-1925; now President Emeritus; editor in chief of the Christian Endeavour World, 1886-1921, now hon. editor; *b.* Aylmer, Province Quebec, Canada; *m.* Harriet E. Abbott, Andover, Mass., U.S.A., 1876; three *s.* one *d. Educ.:* Kimball Union Academy; Dartmouth College, N.H., U.S.A.; Andover Theolog. Seminary; A.B. at Graduation, 1873; A.M. in course; D.D. Dartmouth College, 1887; LL.D. Iowa College. Graduated at Dartmouth Coll. 1873; at Andover Theol. Sem. 1876; Pastor of Williston Church, Portland, Me., 1876; Founded Christian Endeavour Soc. 1881; Pastor of Phillips Church, Boston, 1888; five times around the world, etc.; Preacher at Cornell and other universities; Trustee of Church Peace Union; Director or Vice-President of several national organizations. *Publications:* The Holy Land of Asia Minor; Following Christ through His Own Country; The Charm of Scandinavia (with Sydney A. Clark); Old Homes of New Americans; Similes and Figures from Alexander Maclaren; Continent of Opportunity; Christian Endeavour in All Lands; Ways and Means; The Children and the Church; Young People's Prayer Meetings; Our Journey Around the World; World-Wide Christian Endeavour; The Great Secret; Fellow Travellers; A New Way around an Old World; Old Lanterns for New Paths; Training the Church of the Future; Christian Endeavour Manual; The Gospel in Latin Lands (jointly with Mrs. Clark) Christ and the Young People; In the Footsteps of St. Paul; Our Italian Fellow - Citizens; The Gospel of Out of Doors; Memories of Many Men in Many Lands, an Autobiography. *Recreations:* fishing and farming. *Address:* Christian Endeavour House, 41 Mt. Vernon Street, Boston, Mass., U.S.A.; Sagamore Beach, Mass., U.S.A. *T.A.:* Endeavour, Boston. *T.:* Haymarket, Boston, 264. *Clubs:* Boston Authors, Twentieth Century, Winthrop, Monday, Boston City, Boston.
(*Died May* 1927.)

CLARK, George Ernest, F.R.G.S.; Founder and Governing Director of Clark's Civil Service and Commercial College, Chancery Lane, W.C.2; Hon. Director of Commercial Instruction, Queen Mary's Convalescent Auxiliary Hospitals for Wounded Soldiers, 1916; Freeman of the City of London; Member of Guild of Freeman of City of London; Member of Horner's Company. *Address:* The Beeches, Bromley, Kent; Willoughby, Sidmouth, Devon. *Clubs:* Constitutional, Eccentric, Aldwych. (*Died 1 Nov.* 1919.)

CLARK, James Robert, C.B., 1902; Chief Naval Instructor, R.N. (retired); *b.* 1844; *s.* of James Richard Clark of Anderton, Cornwall. Served Egypt, 1882 (medal, Khedive's star). *Address:* 1 Chesham Terrace, Brighton.
(*Died 30 Dec.* 1919.)

CLARK, James William, K.C. 1904; *b.* 30 May 1851; *e. s.* of late James Clark, formerly Secretary of the Colonial Bank, London unmarried. *Educ.:* Brentwood Grammar School, Essex; Trinity Hall, Camb. B.A. 1st class in Classical Tripos; Fellow, 1874; Classical Lecturer, 1874-76; M.A. 1877. Barr. Lincoln's Inn, 1879; was Conveyancing Counsel to H.M. Office of Woods and Forests, 1894-95; Counsel to the Attorney-Gen. in charity matters, 1894-95; Legal Adviser to the Board of Agriculture and Fisheries, 1895-1915. *Publications:* joint-author of Elphinstone, Norton, and Clark on Interpretation of Deeds, and of Elphinstone and Clark on Searches; joint-editor of 3rd and 4th editions of Goodeve's Real Property and 2nd ed. of Goodeve's Personal Property, and of Elphinstone's Introduction to Conveyancing; author of Student's Conveyancing Precedents. *Recreations:* rowed in Trinity Hall boats, and was in Trin. Hall cricket eleven; cycling. *Address:* High Croft, Winchmore Hill, N. *Club:* Reform. (*Died 21 July* 1921.)

CLARK, Sir John Maurice, 2nd Bart., *cr.* 1886; M.B.E., V.D., D.L.; head of the publishing firm of T. & T. Clark, Edinburgh; Deputy Lieutenant for the County of Midlothian; J.P. for the County of the City of Edinburgh; Colonel, formerly commanding officer, 7th Batt. Royal Scots (the Royal Regiment); Vice-Chairman Midlothian County Association Territorial Force; National Service Representative for the County of Midlothian; late Master of the Edinburgh Merchant Company; Extraordinary Director of the British Linen Bank; Chairman of the Scottish Life Assurance Company; *b.* 7 Mar. 1859; *s.* of 1st Bt. and Eliza Maule, *d.* of Rev. G. R. Davidson, D.D.; *S.* father, 1900; *m.* 1885, Helen, *d.* of Rev. H. M. Douglas; three *s.* one *d. Educ.:* Edinburgh Academy and University. *Recreations:* riding, motoring, and fishing. *Heir:* *s.* Thomas [*b.* 30 Mar. 1886; *m.* 1914, Ellen Mercy, *o. d.* of late Francis Drake]. *Address:* 17 Rothesay Terrace, Edinburgh. *T.A.:* Dictionary, Edinburgh. *T.:* Central, Edinburgh, 6870. *Club:* University, Edinburgh.
(*Died 27 May* 1924.)

CLARK, Joseph, Member of Institute of Oil Painters; *b.* Cerne Abbas, Dorsetshire, 4 July 1834; *m.* 1868, *d.* of John Jones, Winchester; one *s.* three *d. Educ.:* Dorchester, by Rev. William Barnes, "The Dorset Poet." Came to London at the age of 18; commenced study at gallery of late J. M. Leigh in Newman Street; then became a student at Royal Academy; first picture at R.A. was The Sick Child, 1857; has exhibited at Academy with few exceptions since 1857; several of his pictures have been engraved —The Return of the Runaway, Three Little Kittens, Hagar and Ishmael, etc.; two pictures bought by Chantrey Bequest and now in Tate Gallery; hon. member of the Royal Oil Institute; liberal in politics; a member of the New Church, known as the Swedenborgian religion. *Recreations:* formerly cricket and tennis, now gardening. *Address:* 95 Hereson Road, Ramsgate. (*Died 4 July* 1926.)

CLARK, William Andrews; *b.* near Connellsville, Pa., 8 Jan. 1839; *m.* 1st, 1869, Kate L. Stauffer (*d.* 1893); two *s.* two *d.*; 2nd, 1901, Anna E. La-Chapelle; one *d. Educ.:* Laurel Hill Academy; studied law Mount Pleasant, Ia., University. Taught school, Mo., 1859-60; went to Colorado, 1862; Montana, 1863; owns railways of Butte, the Miner newspaper; President, United Verde Copper Co. of Arizona; State Orator, representing Montana at Centennial Exposition, 1876 ; Grand Master Masons, Mont., 1877 ; Major Butte Battalion, leading it in Nez Perce campaign, 1878 ; President Constitutional Conventions, 1884 and 1889 ; Commissioner from Mont. to New Orleans Exposition, 1884 ; Democrat candidate for delegate in Congress, 1888 ; United States Senator, 1901-1907. *Address :* Butte, Montana ; 111 Broadway, New York.

(Died 2 Mar. 1925.)

CLARK, Sir William Mortimer, Kt., *cr.* 1907 ; W.S., K.C., LL.D.; Lieutenant-Governor of Ontario, 1903-1908 ; Chairman, Knox College, Toronto, since 1880 ; *b.* Aberdeen, Scotland, 24 May 1886 ; *s.* of John Clark, manager, Aberdeen Insurance Company; *m.* 1866, Helen, *d.* of Gilbert Gordon, Caithness ; two *d.* *Educ. :* Grammar School, and Marischal Coll. Aberdeen; Univ. of Edinburgh ; Life Member of General Council of Jatter University. Admitted W.S., 1859 ; settled in Toronto, Ontario, same year ; called to Bar of Ontario, 1869 ; Q.C., 1890 ; for fifteen years Senator of University of Toronto ; LL.D. Toronto, 1902, Queen's University, Kingston, 1903 ; President Toronto Mortgage Company ; Director Gas Company, Canadian General Electric Company, Toronto General Trust Company, and Norwich United Insurance Company; solicitor for various public companies and charities ; President, St. Andrew's Society, for two years ; for five years Secretary, Canadian Institute ; for two years President, County of York Law Association. *Publications :* numerous contributions to Toronto press on public, educational, and literary questions. *Recreations:* travelled largely on American Continent, in Africa, Asia, and almost every country in Europe. *Address :* 28 Avenue Road, Toronto. *(Died 11 Aug. 1917.)*

CLARK, Rt. Rev. William Reid, Bishop of Niagara since 1911. *Educ. :* Trinity College, Toronto (M.A.). Deacon, 1874 ; Priest, 1876 ; Missioner at Eganville, 1874-75 ; Principal, High School, Uxbridge, 1875-76 ; Incumbent, Palmerston, 1877-78 ; Curate of St. Luke, Burlington, 1878-79 ; Vicar of St. John, Ancaster, 1879-93 ; Rector of Barton, 1893-96 ; Rector, Ancaster, Ont., 1896-1902; Secretary-Treasurer of the Diocese since 1903 ; Registrar of the Diocese since 1902 ; Secretary of Lower House of the Provincial Synod of Canada, 1901-4, and of the General Synod of Canada, 1908-11 ; D.D. Bishop's College, Lennoxville, and D.C.L. Trinity College, Toronto ; Archdeacon of Niagara, 1902-11. *Address :* See House, Hamilton, Ont., Canada.

(Died April 1925.)

CLARKE, Lt.-Col. Albert Edward Stanley, D.S.O., M.V.O. ; Lt.-Col., Reserve of Officers ; *b.* 1879 ; *o. s.* of late Maj.-Gen. Sir S. de A. C. Clarke ; *m.* 1907, Evelyn, *e. d.* of Sir Alexander Baird, 1st Bt. ; two *c. Educ. :* Eton ; Sandhurst. Page of Honour to Queen Victoria; Scots Guards, 1898 - 1910 ; served S. Africa at Belmont, Graspan, Modder River, Magersfontein ; served under F.O. in Macedonian gendarmerie, 1904-7 ; Private Secretary to Gen. Sir John French, 1907-10 ; contested (C.) S.W. Norfolk, 1910 ; served European War, 1914-18 (D.S.O.). *Address :* 28 Draycott Place, S.W.3. *T. :* Kensington 5663. *Clubs :* Carlton, Marlborough.

(Died 8 June 1926.)

CLARKE, Vice-Adm. Arthur Calvert, R.N.; C.B.E. 1919 ; C.M.G. 1902; D.S.O. 1917; *b.* 9 Aug. 1848 ; *m.* 1895, Margaret Macgregor, *d.* of J. L. Adams, U.S.A. Entered Navy, 1861; Lieut., 1872 ; Commander, 1883 ; Captain, 1891 ; Rear-Admiral, 1904 ; retired, 1903 ; Vice-Admiral, 1908 ; served Abyssinia 1868 (medal); China, 1901 (medal, C.M.G.); commanded for over 3 years an armed yacht in European War (medals); Officer of Legion of

Honour. *Club :* United Service.

(Died 9 Nov. 1926.)

CLARKE, Bt.-Col. (Charles Henry Geoffrey) Mansfield, M.V.O. 1907 ; *b.* 26 Mar. 1873 ; *e. s.* of Sir Charles Mansfield Clarke; *m.* 1915, Linda Blanche Douglas-Pennant, *e. d.* of 3rd Baron Penrhyn ; one *d.* Entered Army, 1893 ; Captain, 1900 ; retired, 1908 ; served Nile Expedition, 1898 (Egyptian medal, medal) ; S. Africa, 1900 (Queen's medal, 3 clasps). *Address :* 33 Lennox Gardens, S.W. *Clubs :* Marlborough, Army and Navy.

(Died 27 July 1919.)

CLARKE, Charles Kirk, M.D., LL.D. ; Dean of Medical Faculty, University of Toronto, 1907-20 ; Professor of Psychiatry, University of Toronto ; Superintendent Toronto General Hospital, 1911 ; Medical Director of Canadian National Committee for Mental Hygiene since 1918 ; *b.* Canada ; *s.* of Hon. Charles Clarke and Emma Kent; *m.* 1st, Emma De Veber Andrews, *d.* 1902; 2nd, Theresa Gallagher ; four *s.* two *d.* *Educ. :* Grammar School, Elora ; University of Toronto. Began medical career under the tutelage of Joseph Workman, M.D.; became Assistant Superintendent of Hamilton and Rockwood Hospitals for Insane, then Superintendent of Rockwood Hospital for Insane, and eventually Superintendent of Toronto Hospital for Insane until 1911 ; has done a great deal of medico-legal work in Canada, and is one of the authorities on psychiatric matters in the Dominion. *Publications :* many brochures on psychiatric and medico-legal subjects ; also many articles on ornithology ; editor of The University of Toronto Medical Bulletin ; one of the editors of the Journal of Insanity, Johns Hopkins Press, Baltimore, also of the Canadian Journal of Mental Hygiene. *Recreations :* golf, music, etc. *Clubs :* York, Toronto ; Rosedale Golf, and Western Golf. *(Died Jan. 1924.)*

CLARKE, Hon. Sir Charles Pitcher, Kt., *cr.* 1922 ; K.C.; *b.* 26 June 1857 ; *m.* Theresa Matilda, *d.* of late Albert Kohl. London ; one *s.* Member, House of Assembly, since 1893 ; Solicitor-General, 1907 ; Attorney-General, Barbados, 1913. *Address :* Blythswood, Worthing, Barbados. *(Died 16 Dec. 1926.)*

CLARKE, Edith, M.B.E. ; Principal of the National Training School of Cookery and Domestic Subjects, 1875-1919 ; *b.* Shrewsbury House, Shooters Hill, Kent, 27 Oct. 1844 ; *d.* of Lt. Edward Nicolls, R.N. ; *e. s.* of General Sir Edward Nicolls, K.C.B., R.M.L.I., and *g.d.* of Thomas Love Peacock, Chief Examiner East India Company ; *m.* 1876, Charles Clarke, Civil Servant, India Office ; three *d. Educ. :* At home and at private school ; has been the pioneer of Domestic Subjects Training. Church of England. *Publications :* Plain and High-Class Cookery Book; Workhouse Cookery ; Life of her grandfather, Thomas Love Peacock. *Address :* 6 Kensington Mansions, Earl's Court, S.W.5. *(Died 20 Aug. 1926.)*

CLARKE, Lt.-Col. Sir Edward Henry St. Lawrence, 4th Bart. ; *cr.* 1804 ; C.M.G. 1919 ; D.S.O. 1917 ; late Worcestershire Regiment ; *b.* 17 April 1857 ; *s.* of late Rev. John William Clarke and Elizabeth, *d.* of Edward Smyth of Macclesfield ; *S.* cousin 1905 ; *m.* 1884, Susan Douglas (*d.* 1913), *d.* of Charles Langton of Barkhill, Liverpool ; one *d.* Served European War, 1914-18 (D.S.O., C.M.G.). *Heir :* none. *Address :* The Hyde, Bridport.

(Died 7 May 1926.)

CLARKE, Edward Lionel Alexander, B.A. ; Master of the Supreme Court (Chancery Division), 1880-1912 ; *b.* Great Yeldham, Essex, 21 Apr. 1837 ; *o. s.* of late Rev. Edward William Clarke, Rector of Great Yeldham; *m.* 1867, Lorina Alice (*d.* 1911), 2nd *d.* of Rev. William Fletcher, D.D. ; two *s.* *Educ. :* Wimborne Gram-

mar School ; Pembroke College, Cambridge (Scholar). B.A. 1860 (3rd Senr. Op.); solicitor, 1863-80. *Address:* 5 Ladbroke Square, W. ; Lewens, Wimborne, Dorset. *T.:* 1753 Park.
(*Died 10 Dec. 1917.*)

CLARKE, Sir Ernest, Kt. ; *cr.* 1898 ; *b.* Bury St. Edmunds, 21 Feb. 1856 ; *e. s.* of late J. J. Clarke, Bury St. Edmunds ; *m.* 1880, Marguerite (*d.* 1918), 2nd *d.* of late James Prevost, Leghorn. Clerk in Medical Department Local Government Board, 1872-81 ; Assistant Secretary, Share and Loan Department, Stock Exchange, 1881-87 ; Secretary of Royal Agricultural Society of England, 1887-1905 ; Hon. M.A. Cambridge, 1894 (St. John's College). First Lecturer on Agricultural History at Cambridge University, 1896-99. Fellow Society Antiquaries; Vice-President of Council of Bibliographical and other Societies ; Chevalier of French Order of Mérite Agricole, 1889 ; Hon. member of Académie d'Agriculture de France, and of the National Agricultural Societies of England, Scotland, Italy, Moravia, and the Argentine ; President of Sette of Odd Volumes, 1898-99, and Treasurer, 1908-19 ; Chairman Committee London Society of East Anglians, 1899-1900 ; Master of the Worshipful Company of Glovers, 1904-5 ; Member of Court of Worshipful Company of Musicians; Chairman of Committee, Folk Song Society ; President, Chartered Institute of Secretaries, 1910-11. *Publications:* edited The Chronicle of Jocelin of Brakelond, 1903, 3rd ed. 1907 ; Bury Chronicles of the Thirteenth Century, 1905; articles in Dictionary of National Biography, Nineteenth Century and other publications. *Recreations:* books, music. *Address:* 31 Tavistock Square, W.C.1. *T.:* Museum 6619.
(*Died 4 Mar. 1923.*)

CLARKE, His Honour Sir Fielding, Kt., *cr.* 1894; LL.B., F.R.G.S. ; J.P. ; *b.* 23 Feb. 1851 ; *m.* Mary Milward, *d.* of J. Timbrell Pierce, D.L., of Frettons, Danbury, 1888. *Educ.:* King's Coll., London. Barr. Middle Temple, 1876 ; Chief Justice of Fiji, 1881 ; Judge, Hong-Kong, 1889 ; Chief Justice, 1892-95 ; Chief Justice of Jamaica, 1895-1911. *Address:* Coppid Hall, Stifford, Grays, Essex. *Club:* Oriental. (*Died 30 July 1928.*)

CLARKE, Sir Frederick William Alfred, Kt., *cr.* 1917; C.B. 1922; late Accountant and Comptroller-General, H.M. Customs and Excise; *b.* 12 May 1857 ; *s.* of F. W. Clarke, H.M. Civil Service; *m.* 1893, Josephine Fitzgerald Moylan ; two *s. Educ.:* private schools. Entered Civil Service, 1874 ; appointed to Exchequer and Audit Department ; went on official tour of inspection to Hong Kong, Bermuda, etc., 1908. *Recreation:* golf. *Address:* Beverley, The Park, Sidcup, Kent. *T.:* Sidcup 488. *Club:* Royal Automobile.
(*Died 18 Feb. 1927.*)

CLARKE, George Johnson, K.C. 1907 ; LL.D.; Premier and Minister of Lands and Mines of the Province of New Brunswick ; *b.* St. Andrews, New Brunswick ; *s.* of Nelson and Mary Clarke ; *m.* Bessie C., *d.* of Rev. Hezekiah and Elizabeth McKeown ; two *d. Educ.:* St. Andrews and Fredericton, N.B. Admitted to Bar of New Brunswick, 1886 ; practised law in St. Stephen from time of admission to bar; contested Canadian House of Commons, 1891, and Legislative Assembly of Province of New Brunswick, 1899 ; Mayor of the town of St. Stephen, 1898 and 1899 ; Warden of the Municipality of Charlotte, 1899 ; elected to Legislative Assembly, 1903 ; re-elected 1908 and 1912 ; Speaker of the Assembly, 1909 ; Attorney-General of Province, Jan.-Dec. 1914. *Address:* St. Stephen, N.B. *T.:* 160. *M.:* 950. *Club:* Union, St. John. (*Died 26 Feb. 1917.*)

CLARKE, Most Rev. Henry Lowther, D.D., D.C.L. ; *b.* 23 Nov. 1850 ; *s.* of late Rev. W. Clarke, M.A., of Firbank, Westmorland ; *m.* 1876, Alice Lovell (*d.* 1918), *d.* of Rev. Canon Kemp ; two *s.* one *d. Educ.:* Sedbergh ; St. John's College, Cambridge (scholar, 7th wrangler). Episcopal Canon of St. George's, Jerusalem. Ordained, 1874 ; Curate St. John's, Hull ; Vicar of Hedon, Yorks, 1876-83 ; Assistant Master St. Peter's School, York, 1883-84 ; Vicar of St. Martin's, Coney Street, York, 1884-90 ; Chaplain to North Riding Asylum, 1885-90 ; Vicar of Dewsbury, 1890-1901 ; Hon. Canon Wakefield Cathedral, 1893-1902 ; Rural Dean Dewsbury, 1898-1901 ; of Huddersfield, 1901-2 ; Vicar of Huddersfield, 1901-2 ; Proctor in York Convocation, 1902 ; Bishop of Melbourne, 1902-1905 ; Archbishop, 1905-20. *Publications:* Addresses to Men ; Addresses delivered in England and Australia ; Synod Addresses (18) ; Synodical Government, 1920 ; Studies in the English Reformation, 1912 ; Constitutional Church Government in the Dominions beyond the Seas, 1924 ; History of Sedbergh School, 1925 ; Death and the Hereafter, 1925. *Recreation:* literary work. *Address:* Melbourne House, Lymington, Hants. *Clubs:* Royal Societies, Authors' (*Died 23 June 1926.*)

CLARKE, Herbert, J.P. Surrey ; editor and proprietor of The Christian World ; *b.* 16 Jan. 1863 ; *y. s.* of the late James Clarke, editor and proprietor of The Christian World ; *m.* Sarah, *e. d.* of John Durrant of Stowmarket. *Educ.:* Mill Hill School. *Recreations:* turning, carpentry. *Address:* 13-14 Fleet Street, E.C. ; Northfield, Caterham. *T.:* Central 646. *Club:* National Liberal. (*Died 22 Jan. 1925.*)

CLARKE, Rev. John, Vicar of Killead since 1882 ; Canon of Conner. *Educ.:* Queen's University, Ireland (scholar). Ordained 1873 ; Curate of Billy, 1872-75 ; Drumtullah, 1875-82 ; Rural Dean of Antrim, 1902. *Address:* Killead Rectory, British, Co. Antrim.
(*Died June 1923.*)

CLARKE, Rev. John Erskine, M.A.; Hon. Canon of Southwark, 1905 ; Hon. Chaplain to the King, 1901 ; founder of Bolingbroke Hospital, Wandsworth Common, 1880 ; *b.* 1827. *Educ.:* Wadham College, Oxford. 3rd class Lit. Hum. 1850 ; holder of Oxford Univ. sculls, 1849-50. Curate, St. Mary, Low Harrogate, 1851 ; St. Mary, Lichfield, 1856 ; Vicar St. Michael, Derby, 1856-66 ; of St. Andrew, Litchurch, Derby, 1866-72 ; Prebendary of Lichfield, 1869-72 ; Vicar of Battersea, 1872-1909 ; Rural Dean, 1879-1913 ; Vicar of St. Luke, Battersea, 1901-14 ; Chaplain-in-Ordinary to Queen Victoria, 1895-1901 ; to King Edward VII., 1901-10 ; to King George V., 1910 ; Hon. Canon of Winchester, 1875-1905 ; Proctor in Convocation for the Diocese of Rochester, 1888-1905. *Publications:* Heart Music, 1857; Commonlife Sermons, 1861 ; originator of Parish Magazines, and Editor of the Parish Magazine, 1859-95 ; editor of Chatterbox from 1867 to 1901 ; editor of Church Bells, 1871-96. *Address:* St. Luke's Vicarage, Ramsden Road, Balham.
(*Died 3 Feb. 1920.*)

CLARKE, John Mason, Ph.D., Sc.D., LL.D.; State Geologist of New York since 1904 ; Director Department of Science and State Museum ; Professor of Geology, Rensselaer Polytechnic Institute ; *b.* 15 April 1857 ; *s.* of Noah Turner Clarke and Laura Mason Merrill ; *m.* 1887 ; one *s. Educ.:* Amherst ; Goettingen. After teaching in the schools of New York and colleges of Massachusetts, came to Albany, N.Y., 1886, as assistant to the State Geologist ; in the execution of this work has issued a large number of reports and special scientific papers and has also done much scientific work in the Province of Quebec ; has made extensive reports to the Geological Service of Brazil, and of Argentina and written on the geology of the Falkland Islands ; is a member of the National Academy (ex-Chairman of the geology section) and of about forty scientific and historical societies in America and Europe; President of the Albany Institute (founded 1791); Vice-President National Parks Association; Member National Council Boy Scouts; Past President Geological Society of America and of the Paleontological Society; Chairman War Committee on Geology, National Research Council; Foreign Member, Geological Society, London; received the Hayden gold medal of the Philadelphia Academy, the gold medal of the Wild Life Protection Fund, and the Spindiaroff prize of the International Geological Congress. *Publications*: Heart of Gaspé; The Magdalen Islands; The Origin of Disease, etc.; L'Ile Percée. *Recreations*: collection and study of early English lustres, Local Histories of Canada. *Address*: Albany, N.Y. 　　　(*Died May 1925.*)

CLARKE, Col. Lancelot Fox, D.S.O. 1901; commanding 91st Infantry (Tasmanian Rangers), Commonwealth Military Forces; *b.* 15 June 1858; *m.* 1889, Marion (*d.* 1906), *d.* of John Young, and *widow* of Arthur Gilbert. Served S. Africa, 1900-2 with Victorian Imperial Regiment (despatches twice, Queen's medal 4 clasps, King's medal 2 clasps, D.S.O.). *Decorated* for able command in operations against De Wet. *Address*: Devonport, Tasmania.
　　　　　　　　(*Died 25 April 1925.*)

CLARKE. His Honour Lionel H., Lieut.-Governor of the Province of Ontario, Canada, since 1919; *b.* Guelph, 1859; *s.* of Dr. Clarke, T.C.D.; *m.* Miss Small, Kincardine, Ont.; three *s.* one *d.* *Educ.*: privately; Trinity College, Port Hope, Ont., Edinburgh. Early in life entered business and became heavily interested in the grain trade; Pres. of the Canadian Malting Co. Ltd., and a director of Financial and Commercial Companies; was a member of the Broad of Grain Supervisors; President of the Toronto Board of Trade; a member of the York Highways Commission; of the Queen Victoria Niagara Falls Parks Commission; Chairman of the Toronto Harbour Commission under Statute. *Recreations*: golf, riding, driving, fishing, and shooting: a keen patron of outdoor sports. *Address*: Government House, Toronto, Canada. *Clubs*: York, Toronto, Hunt, Toronto.
　　　　　　　　(*Died 20 Aug. 1922.*)

CLARKE, Sir Rupert (Turner Havelock), 2nd Bt.; *cr.* 1882; late Member Legislative Council, Victoria; *b.* 16 March 1865; *s.* of Hon. Sir William John Clarke, 1st Bt., and Mary, *d.* of late Hon. John Walker, M.L.C., Tasmania; *S.* 1897; *m.* 1st, 1886, Aimée Mary (who divorced him, 1909; she *m.* 2nd, 1910, Sir Philip Grey-Egerton), *d.* of Hon. Thomas Cumming; two *d.*; 2nd, 1918, Elsie Florence, *d.* of James Partridge Tucker of Marrickville, Sydney, late of Devonshire; two *s.* one *d.* *Heir*: *s.* Rupert William John, *b.* 5 Nov. 1919. *Club*: Melbourne, Melbourne.　(*Died 25 Dec. 1926.*)

CLARKE, Somers, F.S.A., Architect retired, resident in Egypt; *b.* 22 July 1841; *o. s.* of Somers Clarke, Solicitor, Brighton. *Educ.*: privately. After five years' unwilling servitude in the law, entered Sir G. Gilbert Scott's office, 1864; repaired many ancient churches in connection with his partner, Mr. J. T. Micklethwaite; amongst the largest of his churches is St. Martin's, Brighton; St. John the Divine, Gainsborough, Lincolnshire; doubled the size of Parish Church, Brighton; elected Surveyor to the Fabric, St. Paul's Cathedral, London, 1897; designed electric lighting, gift of Mr. J. Pierpont Morgan; co-operated with Sir W. B. Richmond in internal decorations; suggested in The Times and effected the removal of Alfred Stevens' Monument to the Duke of Wellington from S.-W. Chapel to the place in the Cathedral it was designed to fill; designed the stalls in the S.-W. Chapel for the order of SS. Michael and George; architect to the Dean and Chapter of Chichester

202

Cathedral, 1900; retired, 1922; Fellow of Society of Antiquaries, 1881; served on the Council; Hon. Member of the Comité de Conservation des Monuments de l'Art Arabe, Cairo; assisted in repairs of several ancient temples in Egypt. *Publications*: Christian Antiquities in the Nile Valley; Contributions to Proceedings, Soc. Antiquaries, Journal of Egyptian Archæology, etc. *Recreations*: music, walking, and sketching. *Address*: Helmia, Zeitun, Egypt. *Club*: Burlington Fine Arts.
　　　　　　　　(*Died 31 Aug. 1926.*)

CLARKE, William, I.S.O.; Governor, Duke Street Prison, Glasgow, 1903-8; native of Perthshire; *b.* 1842; *m.* Helen, *d.* of late James Craik, Castle Douglas, Kirkcudbrightshire; one *s.* two *d.* *Educ.*: Perth. Entered Prison Service, 1862, and has been Governor of the prisons of Greenock, Dundee, Perth General. *Recreations*: reading and walking. *Address*: Magdalen Bank, Craigie, Perth.
　　　　　　　　(*Died 27 Jan. 1918.*)

CLAUGHTON, Sir Gilbert Henry, 1st Bt., *cr.* 1912; J.P.; Chairman of London and North Western Railway; *b.* 21 Feb. 1856; *s.* of late Bishop of St. Albans and Julia Sussannah, sister of 1st Earl of Dudley; unmarried. *Educ.*: Eton. For twenty years chief mineral agent to the Earl of Dudley; Director of Barclay's Bank, Ltd.; North British and Mercantile Insurance Company; South Staffordshire Water Works Company; South Staffordshire Mond Gas Company; Alderman of Staffordshire County Council. *Heir*: none. *Address*: The Priory, Dudley; 5 Lygon Place, S.W.1. *T.A.*: Priory, Dudley; Technique, London; Chairman, Euston. *T.*: 20 Tipton; Victoria 1851; Museum 2826. *Clubs*: Carlton, Windham.　　　(*Died 27 June 1921.*)

CLAUS, Emile; *b.* Vive St. Eloi, Belgique, 27 Sep. 1849. *Educ.*: Académie Royale d'Anvers. Représenté dans les musees à Bruxelles, Anvers, Gand, Liège, Dresde, Berlin, au Luxembourg à Paris, à Venise, Namur, Port Adelaide; Officier de l'Ordre de Leopold et Chevalier de la Legion d'Honneur; member of the Senefelder Club. *Publications*: articles in The Studio and The Artist. (*Died 6 June 1924.*)

CLAUSON, Major Sir John Eugene, K.C.M.G., *cr.* 1913; C.V.O. 1912; C.M.G. 1904; late R.E.; High Commissioner and Commander-in-Chief, Cyprus, since 1914; *b.* 18 Nov. 1866; *e. s.* of C. Clauson and Julia, *d.* of Rev. J. W. Buckley; *m.* 1890, Mary Elisabeth, *e. d.* of Sir W. T. Makins, 1st Bt.; three *s.* *Educ.*: Merchant Taylors' School; Clifton College; R.M.A. Woolwich. Entered R.E., 1885; B.A. (hons.) London, 1887; designed army pontoon, 1889; passed Staff College (1st place), 1893; Army Headquarters Staff, 1895-1900; admitted Inner Temple, 1897; Secretary Army Railway Council, 1897; Secretary Mobilisation Committee, 1898; Sec. Col. Defence Com. and Assistant Secretary Committee of Imperial Defence, 1900-6; Chief Sec. to Govt. of Cyprus, 1906-11; Lieut.-Governor, Malta, 1911-14. *Address*: Government House, Cyprus. *Clubs*: Athenæum, Army and Navy, Savage.
　　　　　　　　(*Died 31 Dec. 1918.*)

CLAY, Sir Arthur Temple Felix, 4th Bt., *cr.* 1841; artist; *b.* London, 9 Dec. 1842; 3rd *s.* of 1st Bt.; *S.* brother, 1878; *m.* 1869, Margaret (*d.* 1915), 5th *d.* of A. K. Barclay of Bury Hill, Dorking; one *s.* *Educ.*: Trin. Coll., Camb.; B.A. For years exhibited regularly at the Royal Academy, New Gallery, and other Exhibitions. *Works*: The Court of Criminal Appeal at the Law Courts, The Royal Bodyguard at the War Office, The Yeoman of the Guard at the London Museum, Portraits in several public buildings. *Publications*: Abridgment of Collectivism, by P. Leroy-Beaulieu, 1908; Syndicalism and Labour, 1911; and various pamphlets and contributions to magazines on

social subjects. *Recreations:* fishing, shooting. *Heir: s.* G. F. N. Clay.   *Address:* 19 Hyde Park Gate, S.W.7.   *T.:* 209 Western.
(Died 18 Mar. 1928.)

CLAY, Rev. John Harden, M.A., Hon. Canon of Bristol since 1913; *s.* of Rev. John Clay, Vicar of Stapenhill, and Jessie Harden; *m.* 1873, Alice Spencer, *d.* of Maj.-Gen. M. E. Bagnold, H.E.I.C.'s Service; three *s.* seven *d.* *Educ.:* Repton; Trinity College, Cambridge (Scholar). Curate of Maidstone, 1872-75; Vicar of All Saint's, Child's Hill, N.W., 1875-93; Rector of St. Michael, Bristol, 1898-1918. *Address:* Miller Bridge, Ambleside.
(Died 31 Oct. 1923.)

CLAY, William Henry, Barrister-at-Law; Recorder of Stoke-on-Trent since 1910; *b.* Uxbridge, 1841; *o. s.* of late William Clay, Skinner Street, E.C., and afterwards of West Ford, Droitwich, and Ellen, 5th *d.* of late Joseph Rutter, Hillingdon Heath; *m.* 1875, Charlotte, 2nd *d.* of James Christy, Boynton Hall, Roxwall. *Educ.:* Cheltenham Grammar School. Called to Bar, Middle Temple, 1868; (Bencher, 1907) and joined the Oxford Circuit; Recorder of Hanley, 1900-10. *Address:* 4 Whitehall Court, S.W. *Club:* Reform.   *(Died 4 June 1921.)*

CLAY, Rev. William Leslie, B.A.; D.D.; Minister St. Andrew's Church, Presbyterian Church in Canada, Victoria, B.C., since 1894; *b.* Bedeque, Prince Edward Island, 14 Nov. 1863; *s.* of John Clay, Provincial Land Surveyor, and Jane Townsend Cousins; *m.* 1890, Florence Nightingale Leitch, Stanhope, P.E.I.; one *s.* four *d.* *Educ.:* Public and High Schools, Summerside; Prince of Wales College, Charlottetown, P.E.I.; McGill University and Presbyterian College, Montreal. Minister at Moose Jaw, N.W.T., 1890-94; Director Protestants' Orphan Home, Children's Aid Society; Member Victoria Library Board and Chairman for three years; President Canadian Club, Victoria, two years; Convener of Presbytery's Committee on Home Missions for over thirty years, and of Synod's Committee for over twenty years; Chairman of Commission appointed by the Government of British Columbia to adjust property interests between the United Church of Canada and the Presbyterian Church in Canada, under the United Church of Canada Act; twice Moderator of the Synod of B.C.; Moderator of the General Assembly of the Presbyterian Church in Canada, 1927-28. *Publications:* occasional articles in newspapers and magazines. *Recreations:* golf and summering with family by a mountain lake. *Address:* 821 Linden Avenue, Victoria, B.C., Canada. *T.:* Home 863, Church 1943. *Clubs:* Canadian, Victoria Golf, Victoria.   *(Died 3 Feb. 1928.)*

CLAYTON, Major Edward Francis, 2nd *s.* of late Nathaniel George Clayton and Isabel, 4th *d.* of late Rev. Edward Chaloner Ogle, of Kirkley Hall, Northumberland; *b.* 1864; S. brother, 1900; *m.* 1900, *o. d.* of Baron de Fougeres; one *s.* *Educ.:* Harrow. Formerly a Major, Scots Guards; Lord of the Manor of Charlwood, Surrey; member of the Jockey Club, 1919. *Address:* Chesters, near Humshaugh, Northumberland. *Clubs:* Guards', Turf.
(Died 19 April 1922.)

CLAYTON, Major Sir Edward Gilbert, Kt., *cr.* 1908; C.B. 1905; R.E.; formerly Inspector of Prisons and Secretary to the Prison Commission; *b.* 16 July 1841; *e. s.* of late Major-General Henry Clayton and Jean Henrietta, *d.* of Sir Robert Blair; *m.* 1864, Georgine Elizabeth Sykes, *d.* and heiress of late Sykes Clayton of the Manor House, Rufforth, Yorks; two *s.* four *d.* *Educ.:* Brighton College; East India Military College, Addiscombe. Formerly in Royal Engineers; Captain, 1872; retired with hon. rank of Major,

1880; J.P. Surrey. *Address:* Kingswood, Woking.   *(Died 5 Mar. 1917.)*

CLAYTON, Rev. Horace Evelyn, M.A., Vicar of St. Mary Magdalen, Oxford, since 1884; Rural Dean of Oxford, 1914; Hon. Canon of Christ Church, Oxford, since 1903; Fellows' Chaplain of Magdalen College, Oxford, since 1887; *b.* Farnborough Rectory, 3 April 1853; *y. s.* of late Rev. John Henry Clayton, M.A., sometime Rector of Farnborough; unmarried. *Educ.:* Marlborough Grammar School; Brasenose College, Oxford. Somerset Scholar, 1871; Hulme Exhibitioner, 1876: 3rd Class Mods. (Classical); 2nd Class Theological School, 1875; B.A. 1875; M.A. 1878; Senior Hall Greek Testament Prize, 1877; Denyer and Johnson Scholar, 1878; Deacon, 1876; Priest, 1877; Curate of St. Mary Magdalen, Oxford, 1876-80; Chaplain of New College, Oxford, 1879-1885; Magdalen Coll., 1879; Lecturer in Divinity, 1884-93; Member of the Oxford School Board, 1888-1903; Member of the Oxford City Education Committee since 1907. *Recreations:* music, foreign travel, architecture. *Address:* Magdalen College, Oxford.   *(Died 5 Nov. 1916.)*

CLAYTON, Rt. Rev. Lewis, D.D.; Assistant Bishop to Bishop of Peterborough since 1912; *b.* London, 8 June 1838; *s.* of late John Clayton, solicitor; *m.* Katharine, *d.* of Thomas Hare of Gosbury Hill, Hook, Surrey, 1872; three *s.* one *d.* *Educ.:* King's College School; Emmanuel Coll. Cambridge (M.A.). Ord. 1861; Vicar of St. James's, Dallington, 1873-75; of St. Margaret's, Leicester, 1875-88; Rural Dean, 1884-88; Proctor in Convocation for Chapter of Peterborough, 1892; Canon of Peterborough, 1887; Bishop of Leicester, 1903-13. *Address:* Canonry House, Peterborough.   *(Died 25 June 1917.)*

CLAYTON - GREENE, W. H., C.B.E. 1919; M.B., B.C. (Cantab.), F.R.C.S. (Eng.); Surg. to St. Mary's Hospital, and King Edward VII. Hospital for Officers; *m.* 1915, May, *o. d.* of Captain W. H. Guy, R.N.R. *Educ.:* Oundle; Rossall; Cambridge. University and Kerslake Scholar at St. Mary's Medical School; late lecturer on anatomy, and Dean of the Medical School; Examiner to the Conjoint Board and Society of Apothecaries; late Surgeon to the Hampstead General Hospital and King George Hospital; Chevalier de la Légion d'Honneur; examiner in surgery to the University of Cambridge and in anatomy for the Fellowship of the College of Surgeons of England; Consulting Surgeon to the Richmond Hospital. *Publications:* Pye's Surgical Handicraft; Articles in Cassel's Surgery, Wright's Index of Treatment, etc. *Recreation:* golf. *Address:* 86 Brook Street, W.1. *T.:* Mayfair 5000. *M.:* LD 762. *Clubs:* Devonshire; Deal.
(Died 29 June 1926.)

CLEARY, Ven. Robert: Rector of Galbally since 1879; Archdeacon of Emly since 1904. *Educ.:* Trinity College, Dublin. Ordained 1874; Curate of Cappoquin, 1874-76; Acting Incumbent, 1876-79; Canon of Cashel, 1898-1904; Rural Dean of Duntryleague, 1892-1912. *Publication:* Analysis of Locke's Essay, 1870. *Address:* Galbally Rectory, Tipperary.
(Died 1919.)

CLEAVE, John, I.S.O.; *b.* 9 Nov. 1837; *s.* of Alderman Thomas Cleave of New Windsor, Berks; *m.* Martha (*d.* 1919), *d.* of Mr. Benjamin Wyld, Curzon Street, Mayfair; three *s.* one *d.* *Educ.:* private schools. Clerk in H.M. Customs, 1854; supplementary clerk in Treasury (after competition), 1856; 1st class Assistant in the British Museum, 1858; subsequently designated Accountant there, and retained office till close of 1904; Speaker of first Battersea Local Parliament. *Address:* 28 Vardens Road, New Wandsworth, S.W.11.
(Died 8 April 1928.)

CLEEVE, Major-General William Frederick, C.B. 1916; late R.A.; J.P.; b. 1853; s. of late Charles Ker Cleeve; m. 1894, Gladys Elizabeth, e. d. of F. J. Mitchell, J.P., D.L., of Llanfrechfa Grange, Monmouthshire; four s. one d. Educ.: R.M.A., Woolwich. Lieut. R.A., 1873; Colonel, 1904; retired, 1910; Brig.-Gen. 1914; Maj.-Gen. (Hon.), 1918; service—home, India, and South Africa; Afghan War, 1880 (medal); was a Chief Instructor in Gunnery, 1901-4; Commandant Royal Military Academy, Woolwich, 1914-18. Address: Llanfrechfa, Mon. Club: Naval and Military.
(Died 31 Jan. 1922.)

CLEGHORN, Isabel, L.L.A., M.A. hon. causa, Welsh University and Sheffield University; late Head Mistress of Heeley Bank Council School, Sheffield; b. Rochester, Kent, but has lived for many years in Sheffield. Educ.: Elementary School, North Shields (Scotch Church); pupil teacher in Elementary School, South Shields; Stockwell Training College. Late President Sheffield Teachers' Association, and Sheffield Head Teachers' Association; for three years Chairman Page Hall Orphanage House Committee; for 24 years on Executive of National Union of Teachers, and President of the N.U.T., 1911-12; on Consultative Committee, Board of Education; on Teachers' Registration Council; member of Council of the National Council of Women; member of Sheffield Education Committee since 1903; member of Ecclesall, Sheffield, Board of Guardians, 1922. Address: 89 Meersbrook Park Road, Sheffield. (Died 5 Dec. 1922.)

CLEGHORN, Surg.-Gen. James, Indian Medical Service (retired, 1898); C.S.I. 1897; Hon. Surgeon to King; Fellow of Allahabad University; b. Wick 1841; 3rd s. of John Cleghorn; m. 2nd d. of Gen. de S. Barrow, 1877. Educ.: local school; Edinburgh Univ.; Royal College of Surgeons, Edinburgh. M.D. St. Andrews; L.R.C.S. Edinburgh. Entered Indian Medical Service, 1865; appointed Director General, Indian Medical Service, and Sanitary Commissioner with Government of India, 1895; Government of India delegate to Venice Plague Conference, 1897; Bhotan Campaign, 1865 (medal). Publications: various papers to medical journals. Recreations: fishing, etc. Address: Weysprings, Haslemere, Surrey. (Died 14 June 1920.)

CLELAND, John, M.D., L.R.C.S.E., LL.D. (St. Andrews, Edinburgh, and Glasgow), D.Sc., F.R.S.; b. Perth, 15 June 1835; m. Ada Marion Spottiswoode (d. 1918) d. of late Dr. Balfour, Professor of Botany, Edinburgh, 1888; one s. Educ.: High School and University of Edinburgh. Professor of Anatomy and Physiology Queen's Coll., Galway, 1863-77; Regius Professor of Anatomy, University of Glasgow, 1877-1909. Publications: numerous memoirs, Anatomical and other; The Mechanism of the Gubernaculum, 1856; Animal Physiology, 1874; Directory for Dissection, 1876; volume of essays entitled, Evolution, Expression, and Sensation, Cell Life and Pathology, 1881; Scala Naturae and other Poems, 1887; joint-editor of 7th ed. of Quain's Anatomy, 1867; joint-author of Memoirs and Memoranda in Anatomy, 1889 and of Cleland and Mackay's Human Anatomy, 1896; lectures, addresses, etc. Recreation: sketching from nature. Address: Drumclog, Crewkerne, Somerset. (Died 5 Mar. 1924.)

CLERK, Col. John, C.V.O. 1896; C.S.I. 1889; s. of late Sir George Russell Clerk, G.C.S.I. Served Crimea, with Rifle Brigade, 1854-55 (medal with two clasps, Turkish medal); subsequently exchanging into 4th Dragoon Guards; was guardian to H.H. the Nizam, 1874-76; was Extra Equerry to Queen Victoria and late Duke of Saxe-Coburg; Comptroller and Treasurer to Princess Henry of Battenberg, 1885-99. Address: 33 Elm Park Gardens, S.W. Club: Carlton. (Died Mar. 1919.)
204

CLERMONT-GANNEAU, Charles Simon; b. Paris, 19 Feb. 1846. Educ.: École des Langues Orientales. Was dragoman to Consulate at Jerusalem and Embassy at Constantinople; discovered the Stele of Mesha and the Stele of the Temple, 1870; employed by British Government to take charge of archæological expedition to Palestine, 1874; by French Government to Syria, Tripolitana, Cyrenaica, Elephantina, and Red Sea; Chevalier of the Légion of Honour, 1875; Vice-Consul, Jaffa, 1880; Premier Secrétaire-Interprète for Oriental Languages, Paris, 1882; Consul of the First Class, 1886; Consul General, 1896; Minister Plenipotentiary, 1906; Director at the École des Hautes Etudes and Professor of Semitic epigraphy and antiquities at the Collège de France; elected Member of the Académie des Inscriptions et Belles-Lettres, 1889; LL.D., F.R.S.L.; Member correspondent de l'Académie Impériale de Petrograd; was principally instrumental in exposing the forgeries of the Moabite pottery, of Shapira's manuscripts, and of the tiara of Saitapharnes. Publications: Palestine Inconnue, 1886; Etudes d'Archéologie Orientale, 1880; Les Fraudes Archéologiques, 1885; Recueil d'Archéologie Orientale, 1885-1905, seven volumes; Archæological Researches in Palestine, 1896-99; Album d'Antiquités Orientales, 1897, etc. Address: 1 Av. George V. Paris.

CLERY, Lieut.-Gen. Sir Francis, K.C.M.G., cr. 1900; K.C.B., cr. 1899; C.B. 1884; b. 13 Feb. 1838. Entered army 1858; Maj.-Gen. 1894; retired, 1901; Professor of Tactics, R.M. Coll. Sandhurst, 1872-75; Dep.-Assist.-Adjt.-Gen. Headquarters, Ireland, 1875-77; Aldershot, 1877-78; Chief Staff Officer Flying Column Zulu War, 1878-79 (despatches, brevet of Lieut.-Colonel, medal with clasp); Egyptian War, 1882 (medal and Khedive's star); Chief of Staff, Suakim Expedition, 1884 (despatches twice, brevet of Col., C.B., two clasps); Deputy Adjt.-Gen. Nile Expedition, 1884-85 (clasp); Chief of Staff, Egypt, 1886-1888; Commandant of Staff College, 1888-93; commanded 3rd Infantry Brigade, Aldershot, 1895-96; Deputy Adjt.-Gen. to the Forces 1896-1900; Commanded 2nd Division, South African Field Force, 1899-1900 (despatches). Publication: Minor Tactics, 1875. Address: 4 Whitehall Court, S.W. Club: United Service.
(Died 25 June 1926.)

CLERY, Surg.-Gen. James Albert, M.B., C.B. 1900; R.A.M.C.; retired 1906; Surgeon-General, South Africa; b. 21 Dec. 1846; s. of late Thomas Clery of Ballinahinch, Limerick; m. 1890, Isabel, d. of W. E. Kirby, Newcastle-on-Tyne; one s. Educ.: Stonyhurst College; Trinity College, Dublin. Entered army, 1871; Colonel, 1899; served Nile Expedition, 1884-85 (medal with clasp, Khedive's star); Soudan, 1898 (despatches, British medal, Khedive's medal); South Africa, 1899-1902 (despatches twice, Queen's medal, 6 clasps, King's medal, 2 clasps). Address: 13 St. John's Park, Blackheath, S.E. Club: Junior Constitutional.
(Died 10 Feb. 1920.)

CLEVELAND, Adm. Henry Forster, retired; b. 28 Apr. 1834; s. of Rev. H. Cleveland, Rector of Romaldkirk, Darlington; m. 1863; no c. Educ.: Grantham College. Entered Royal Navy, 1848; retired, 1895. Address: 37 Carlisle Road, Eastbourne. (Died 26 Jan. 1924.)

CLEVERLY, Charles F. M., J.P.; b. Hong Kong, China; father Memb. of Council there, and for over 20 years held the Government appointment of Surveyor-General; m. May, e. d. of J. B. Somers; two s. two d. Educ.: Clifton Coll.; Jesus Coll. Camb. (B.A.). Articled to G. Aitchison, R.A., and afterwards worked in the office of G. Bodley, R.A.; took up church painting and decorative work generally; decorated the chancel of Bexley Church (Kent); the chapel of the Seamen's

Hospital, Greenwich; St. Paul's, Avenue Road, N.W., etc.; several altar-pieces, among them the triptych, Great Massingham Church. *Address:* Dunsborough House, Ripley, Surrey. *Clubs:* Arts; County, Guildford.

(*Died 9 Mar. 1921.*)

CLIFFE, Anthony Loftus, J.P., D.L.; *b.* 4 June 1861; *e. s.* of late Anthony John Cliffe, and Amy, *d.* of Sir John Howley; *m.* 1904, Frances Emma, *d.* of Capt. Segrave of Cabra and widow of Sir John Talbot Power, 3rd Bart.; no *c.* Late Capt. 3rd Batt. Royal Irish Regt.; High Sheriff Co., Wexford, 1897. *Address:* Bellevue, Wexford. *Clubs:* Carlton, Boodle's; Sackville Street, Dublin.

(*Died Jan. 1922.*)

CLIFFORD of Chudleigh, 9th Baron (*cr.* 1672), **Lewis Henry Hugh Clifford,** B.A., D.L.; Barrister; A.D.C.; Count of the Holy Roman Empire; *b.* 24 Aug. 1851; *s.* of 8th Baron and Hon. Agnes Catherine, *y. d.* of 11th Baron Petre; *S.* father 1880; *m.* Mabel, *d.* of Col. John Towneley of Towneley, Lancashire, 1890. *Educ.:* Stonyhurst. Owns about 8000 acres. *Heir: b.* Hon. William H. Clifford. *Address:* Ugbrooke Park, Chudleigh; Court House, Cannington, Somersetshire. *Clubs:* Bachelors', Brooks's. (*Died 19 July 1916.*)

CLIFFORD, Brig. - Gen. Henry Frederick Hugh, D.S.O. 1915; the Suffolk Regiment; *b.* 18 Aug. 1867; 2nd *s.* of late Maj.-Gen. Hon. Sir Henry Clifford, V.C., K.C.M.G., C.B. Entered army, 1888; Captain, 1897; Major, 1910; Lt.-Col. 1914; A.D.C. to Lt.-Gen. Sir William Butler, K.C.B., 1899 and 1902-5; served S. African War, 1899-1902 (Queen's medal, 3 clasps; King's medal, 2 clasps); European War, 1914-1915 (D.S.O., prom. Col.). *Club:* Naval and Military. (*Died 16 Sept. 1916.*)

CLIFFORD, Rev. John, C.H. 1921; M.A., D.D., B.Sc.; *b.* Sawley, Derbyshire, 16 Oct. 1836; *m.* 1862, Rebecca (*d.* 1919), *d.* of Dr. Carter of Newbury, Berks. *Educ.:* Baptist College, Nottingham; University College, London; Royal School of Mines. M.A. 1864; LL.B. with honours, 1866; B.Sc., with honours, 1862, London; D.D. Hon. University of Chicago, etc.; LL.D. Colgate University New York, 1906; LL.D. Macmaster University, Canada, 1910; President, London Baptist Association, 1879; Baptist Union, 1888 and 1899; General Baptist Association, 1872 and 1891; National Council of Free Evangelical Churches, 1898-99; British Chautauqua, 1899-1900; Baptist World Alliance, 1905-11; Baptist European Congress, 1913; Minister of Praed Street and Westbourne Park Church, 1858-1915; President, Baptist World Alliance, 1905-1911; made tour round the world, 1897; President, National Brotherhood Council, 1916-19; President World Federation of Brotherhoods, 1919-1920. *Publications:* editor, General Baptist Magazine, 1870-83; Familiar Talks with the Young, 1872; George Mostyn, 1874; Is Life Worth Living? 1880; Daily Strength for Daily Living, 1885; The Dawn of Manhood, 1886; co-editor, Review of the Churches, 1891; The Inspiration and Authority of the Bible, 1892; The Christian Certainties, 1893; Typical Christian Leaders, 1898; Social Worship an Everlasting Necessity; God's Greater Britain, 1899; The Fight for Education: what is at stake; Clericalism in British Politics, 1902; the Secret of Jesus, 1904; The Ultimate Problems of Christianity, 1906; The Carey Lecture, 1912; The Gospel of Gladness, 1912; Temperance Reform and the Ideal State: Lees and Raper Memorial Lecture, 1913; Brotherhood in Ideal and in Action, 1916; State Education after the War, 1916; The Spirit of Man in 1916, 1917; Our Fight for Belgium and what it means, 1918; Saving the Soul of The World in 1917, 1918; The League of Free

Nations; Facing the Facts, 1919; Darkness and Dawn in 1918, 1919; The Emergence of the International Mind in 1919, 1920; World Brotherhood according to Jesus, the John Clifford Lecture, 1920. *Address:* 18 Waldeck Road, West Ealing, W.13. *Clubs:* National Liberal, Eighty. (*Died 20 Nov. 1923.*)

CLIFFORD, Julian; General Entertainments Manager and Musical Director, Hastings Corporation; Musical Director, Harrogate Corporation; Conductor of the London Symphony Orchestra for the London Ballad Concerts Season, 1921-22; Conductor, Solo Pianist, and Composer; *b.* 28 Sep. 1877; *s.* of late Thomas Clifford, of Dryhill Park, Tonbridge, Kent; *m.* 1902, Alice Margaret, *e. d.* of 5th Lord Henniker; one *s.* one *d. Educ.:* Ardingley College; Tonbridge School; Leipzig Conservatorium; Royal College'of Music. Organist and Choirmaster, English Church, Leipzig, 1892; King Charles the Martyr, Tunbridge Wells, 1894; has played as Solo Pianist at the Queen's Hall Promenade Concerts, Chappell Ballad Concerts, Scottish Orchestra, Norwich Philharmonic, and all principal London and Provincial Concerts; has conducted the following orchestras—The London Symphony, The Hallé, The Leeds Symphony, Bradford Permanent, Birmingham Symphony, The Harrogate Municipal (16 years), Hastings Municipal; conducted British Musical Festival at the Liège Exhibition, 1906; founded the Yorkshire Permanent Orchestra, 1909; late conductor of the Westminster Orchestral Society, West London Choral, Leeds Philharmonic; has conducted his own compositions throughout England and Belgium, and has done much to further the interests of British Music. *Compositions:* Concerto for Piano and Orchestra in E Minor; Ode to the New Year for Solo Quartette, Chorus and Orchestra; Orchestral Ballad in D; Suite de Concert; Tone Poem Lights Out; Song Cycle The Dream of Flowers, and numerous pianoforte solos, songs, etc. *Recreations:* golf, billiards, church bell-ringing. *Address:* The Royal Hall, Harrogate. *T.A.:* Clifford, Harrogate. *T.:* 49. *Clubs:* Royal Automobile; Harrogate Conservative. (*Died 27 Dec. 1921.*)

CLIFFORD, Major Wigram, D.S.O. 1900; Northumberland Fusiliers; *b.* 20 Feb. 1876; *o. s.* of late Maj.-Gen. R. M. Clifford; *m.* 1903, Eva, *y. d.* of late Major T. G. Miles. *Educ.:* U.S. College, Westward Ho! R.M.C. Sandhurst. Joined Loyal North Lancashire Regiment; served in South Africa, 1899-1901 (slightly wounded, despatches, D.S.O.); served N.-W. Frontier, India, 1908; Mohmand Expedition (medal with clasp); European War, 1914-16.

(*Died 20 May 1917.*)

CLIFT, Hon. James Augustus, C.B.E. 1918; K.C. 1904; a Pension Commissioner for Newfoundland; *b.* 1857; married. Bar, Newfoundland, 1884; Parliament, 1889; retired, 1919. *Address:* St. Johns, Newfoundland.

(*Died 8 Feb. 1923.*)

CLIFTON, John Talbot, F.R.G.S., F.Z.S.; *b.* 1 Dec. 1868; *e. s.* of late Thomas Henry Clifton, M.P., and Madeline Diana Elizabeth, *e. d.* of Sir Andrew Noel Agnew, 8th Bart.; *m.* 1907, Violet Mary (authoress of Pilgrims to the Isles of Penance and The Islands of Queen Wilhelmina); *d.* of late W. Nelthorpe Beauclerk, British Minister Plenipotentiary and Extraordinary in Peru, Ecuador, and Bolivia; two *s.* three *d. Educ.:* Eton; Magdalene College, Cambridge. Explored in Africa, discovering new route between Ujiji and Victoria Nyanza; first Englishman on Lena River, Siberia, and discovered on Arctic Ocean new species of wild sheep named in British Museum Ovis Cliftonii; lived alone among Esquimaux far north of Hudson's Bay; in early part of the war carried despatches to the King of the Belgians, and

afterwards served as Lieut. R.N.V.R. Owns 12,500 acres in Lancashire, some by grant of William Rufus, and 17,000 acres in the Isle of Islay; Lord of the Manor of Lytham. *Publication*: Fortune Telling by Japanese Swords. *Recreations*: music, golf, sport. *Address*: Lytham Hall, Lytham, Lancs; Kildalton Castle, Port Ellen, Islay, Scotland. *Clubs*: Carlton, Pratt's.
(*Died 23 Mar. 1928.*)

CLIFTON, Robert Bellamy, M.A., F.R.S., Hon. Fellow of Wadham College; formerly Fellow of Merton College, Oxford, and of St. John's College, Cambridge; *b.* 1836; *m.* 1862, Catherine Elizabeth Butler (*d.* 1917). *Educ.*: Univ. Coll. London; St. John's Coll. Camb. (B.A.) 6th Wrangler, 1859; 2nd Smith's Prizeman; Professor of Natural Philosophy, Owens Coll. Manchester, 1860-65; Professor of Experimental Philosophy, Oxford, 1865-1915; member of Royal Commission on Accidents in Mines, 1879-86; President of Physical Society, 1882-84. *Recreation*: work. *Address*: 3 Bardwell Road, Banbury Road, Oxford. *Club*: Athenæum.
(*Died 22 Feb. 1921.*)

CLINCH, George, F.G.S., F.S.A.Scot.; Librarian to the Society of Antiquaries of London; Vice-President of the Association of Men of Kent and Kentish Men; *b.* Borden, Kent, 1860; two *d.* *Educ.*: Privately. *Publications*: Antiquarian Jottings relating to Bromley, Hayes, Keston, and West Wickham, in Kent, 1889; Bloomsbury and St. Giles's: Past and Present, 1890; Marylebone and St. Pancras: their History, Celebrities, Buildings, and Institutions, 1890; Mayfair and Belgravia: being an Historical Account of the Parish of St. George, Hanover Square, 1892; Bromley and the Bromley District, 1902; Little Guide to Kent, 1903; Little Guide to the Isle of Wight, 1904; Little Guide to St. Paul's Cathedral, 1906; Old English Churches, 1st edition, 1900; 2nd edition, 1903; Handbook of English Antiquities, 1905; English Costume, 1909; Little Guide to London, 1912; English Coast Defences, 1915; editor of Dr. E. F. Rimbault's Soho and its Associations, 1895, etc. *Recreations*: walking and photography. *Address*: 3 Meadowcroft, Sutton, Surrey.
(*Died 2 Feb. 1921.*)

CLINTON, Ven. Thomas William; Rector of Donaghpatrick since 1917. *Educ.*: Trinity College, Dublin. M.A. 1894; Divinity Testimonium, 1900; ordained 1890; Curate of Muckno, Co. Monaghan, 1890; Incumbent of Augher, 1893-94; Rector of Aghavea, Fermanagh, 1894-1901; Moka, Mauritius, 1901-4; Moka cum Quatre Bornes since 1904; Principal, Theological College, Mauritius, 1901-7; Archdeacon and Hon. Canon, Mauritius, 1907-12. *Address*: Donaghpatrick Rectory, Navan, Co. Meath.
(*Died 18 Mar. 1926.*)

CLIPPERTON, Sir Charles (Bell Child), K.B.E., *cr.* 1924; C.M.G. 1916; *b.* 1864, Kertch (Crimea); *s.* of late Capt. R. C. Clipperton, H.M.'s Consul; *m.* 1896, Ella E., *d.* of late M. Ehret of Philadelphia, U.S.A. *Educ.*: Wellington College. Vice-Consul at Baltimore, 1892; Philadelphia, 1894; was in charge of the Consulate at Boston in 1902; transferred to Rouen, 1904; given the personal rank of Consul-General and also charged with the duties of a Visiting Consular Officer, 1913; appointed a Sub-Commissioner of the Joint British Red Cross and Order of St. John Commission in France, 1915-16 (despatches); an Hon. Associate of the Order of the Hospital of St. John of Jerusalem in England, 1918; employed in the Foreign Office since 26 Mar. 1918; Inspector-General of Consulates and given the rank of Acting Counsellor of Embassy in H.M. Diplomatic Service while so employed, 26 Nov. 1918; in charge of the Consulate-General at Antwerp, 16 Dec. 1918-3 Feb. 1919. *Recrea-*

206

tion: motoring. *Address*: c/o Foreign Office S.W.1. *Club*: Royal Automobile.
(*Died 18 June 1927.*)

CLISSOLD, Major Harry, M.A., D.S.O. 1916; R.E., T.F.; Assistant Master in Clifton College; Major, South Midland Field Company R.E. (T.); *e. s.* of late W. G. Clissold, J.P., of Chestnut Hill, Nailsworth, Glos.; unmarried. *Educ.*: Clifton College; Trinity College, Cambridge (Scholar), 1890; B.A. Mathematics (Aegrotat), 1892; 1st Class Science Tripos, 1903; Assistant Physics Master at Marlborough College, 1893-94; Clifton, 1894-1914; House Master, 1912; Commanded Cadet Corps, 1906-1912; served European War, 1914-16 (D.S.O.). *Recreations*: fives and tennis. *Address*: Clifton College, Bristol. *T.*: 3443 (*Died 28 Sept. 1917.*)

CLIVE, Viscount; Percy Robert Herbert; *b.* 2 Dec. 1892; *e. s.* of 4th Earl of Powis. *Educ.*: Eton. Entered army, Scots Guards, 1914; Lieut. Welsh Guards, 1915; served European War, 1914-15. (*Died 13 Oct. 1916.*)

CLIVE, Gen. Edward Henry; *b.* 23 Sept. 1837; *s.* of G. Clive, Perrystone Court, Herefordshire; *m.* 1867, Isabel, *e. d.* of Daniel Hale Webb, Wykham Park, Oxon; four *s.* four *d.* *Educ.*: Harrow. Joined Grenadier Guards, 1854; served Crimea, 1856; Lieut.-Col. commanding Regt., 1880-85; Commandant, St. College, 1885-88; Governor, R. M. College, 1888-93; retired, 1898; Colonel 8th King's Liverpool Regiment, 1907; M.P. Hereford City, 1869-71; J.P. Herefordshire and Mayo; D.L. Co. Mayo. *Heir*: *s.* Major George Sidney Clive, Grenadier Guards [*m.* 1901, Madeline, 2nd *d.* of late F. W. Buxton, M.P.] *Address*: 25 Ennismore Gardens, S.W.; Perrystone Court, Ross; Ballycroy, Co. Mayo. *Clubs*: United Service, Travellers'.
(*Died 1 Mar. 1916.*)

CLIVE, Capt. Percy Archer; M.P. (U.) South Hereford since 1908; *b.* 1873; *e. s.* of C. M. B. Clive and Lady Katherine Fielding, *y. d.* of 7th Earl of Denbigh; *m.* 1905, Alice Muriel, *y. d.* of late Col. G. F. Dallas; two *s.* three *d.* Entered Grenadier Guards, 1891; Captain, 1899; served W. Africa, 1898; South Africa, 1899-1901; M.P. (L.U.) South Herefordshire, 1900-1906; late Parliamentary Private Sec. (hon.) to Mr. Austen Chamberlain when Chancellor of Exchequer; rejoined Grenadier Guards on outbreak of War; commanded 7th Batt. E. York Regt. since May 1916 (despatches, Legion of Honour, twice wounded). *Address*: Whitfield, Allensmore, Herefordshire. *T.*: Wormbridge 2. *Clubs*: Guards', Travellers', Carlton. (*Died 5 April 1918.*)

CLOETE, Hendrik, C.M.G. 1897; barrister-at-law; *b.* 10 Aug. 1851; *e. surv. s.* of late Dirk Cloete of Alphen, Cape Colony; *m.* 1898, *e. d.* of late Rev. Van Warmelo. *Educ.*: private school and Diocesan College, Rondebosch, Cape Colony. Barr. Inner Temple, 1877; advocate to Supreme Court Bar of the Cape Colony, 1878, and to High Court, Transvaal Bar, 1879; served as lieut. and adjutant of volunteers, and was present at the various engagements around Pretoria in the Transvaal War, 1880-81; British agent in the S. African Republic after the Jameson raid, succeeding Sir Jacobus de Wet, during 1896. *Decorated* for service as H.M. acting agent in the S. A. Republic. *Recreations*: cricket, tennis, rowing, shooting. *Address*: Alphen, Wynberg, Cape Colony. *Clubs*: Civil Service, Cape Town; Pretoria, Rand, Transvaal. (*Died 18 May 1920.*)

CLONBROCK, 4th Baron (*cr.* 1790), **Luke Gerald Dillon,** P.C., K.P., J.P.; Representative Peer for Ireland since 1895; H.M.'s Lieutenant Galway since 1892; *b.* 10 Mar. 1834; *s.* of 3rd Baron and Caroline, *d.* of 1st Lord Churchill; *S.* father 1893; *m.* Augusta, *o. d.* of 2nd Lord Crofton, 1866; one *s.* three *d.* *Educ.*: Eton; Balliol College, Oxon. 2nd class Law and Modern History, 1855. Church of

Ireland. Conservative. Attaché, Berlin, 1856 ; Paid Attaché, Vienna, 1859 ; 2nd Secretary at Vienna, 1862 ; Private Secretary to Lord-Lieutenant of Ireland, 1866 - 68 and 1874-76. Owns 28,246 acres. *Heir* : *s.* Hon. Robert Edward Dillon. *Address* : Clonbrock, Ahascragh, Co. Galway. *Clubs* : Travellers', Kildare Street, Dublin ; County, Galway.
(*Died 12 May 1917.*)

CLONBROCK, 5th Baron, *cr.* 1790; **Robert Edward Dillon,** D.L. Co. Galway ; *s.* of 4th Baron and Augusta, *o. d.* of 2nd Baron Crofton : *S.* father 1917 ; *b.* 21 May 1869. *Educ.* : Eton ; University of Neuchatel ; University of Göttingen. Elected member of the Royal Irish Academy, Member of Royal Society of Antiquaries of Ireland, 1916. *Heir* : none. *Recreations* : natural history and science and forestry, gardening, reading, fishing, and shooting. *Address* : Clonbrock, Ahascragh, Co. Galway. *Clubs* : Wellington, M.C.C. ; Kildare Street, Dublin ; County, Galway. (*Died 1 Nov. 1926.*)

CLONCURRY, 4th Baron (*cr.* 1789), **Valentine Frederick Lawless,** Baron (U.K.) 1831 ; Bt. 1776 ; *b.* Lyons, Co. Kildare, 2 Nov. 1840 ; *S.* father, 1869 ; *m.* Hon. Laura Winn (*d.* 1891), *e. d.* of 1st Baron St. Oswald, 1883 ; one *d.* Protestant. Conservative. *Educ.* : Eton ; Balliol Coll., Oxford (B.A.). Owns 12,000 acres. *Heir* : *b.* Hon. Frederick Lawless. *Address* : Lyons, Co. Kildare. *Clubs* : Carlton, Constitutional ; Royal St. George Yacht, Kingstown ; Kildare Street, Dublin.
(*Died 12 Feb. 1928.*)

CLONMELL, 7th Earl of (*cr.* 1793), **Rupert Charles Scott.** Baron Earlsfort, 1793 ; Viscount Clonmell, 1789 ; Captain, Warwickshire R.H.A. (T.F.) (1914 decoration) ; *b.* 1877 ; *o. c.* of 6th Earl and Lucy Maria, *d.* of Anthony Willson, M.P., Rauceby Hall,Sleaford ; *S.* father, 1898 ; *m.* 1901, Rachel Estelle, *d.* of Samuel Berridge, Toft Hill, Rugby ; two *d.* Contested (L.) Rugby, 1910. *Heir* : *u.* Hon. Dudley Scott. *Address* : 20 Hertford Street, W.1 ; *T.* : Mayfair 3944 ; Eathorpe Hall, Leamington ; The Little House, Mermaid Street, Rye. *Clubs* : White's, Garrick, National Liberal, Bath ; Kildare Street, Dublin ; Royal St. George's Yacht, Kingstown. (*Died 18 Nov. 1928.*)

CLORAN, Hon. Henry Joseph, B.C.L., K.C. ; *s.* of Joseph Cloran and Ann Kennedy, both natives of Ireland ; *b.* Montreal, 8 May, 1855 ; *m.* 1st, 1882, Agnes M. Donovan (*d.* 1896), 2nd, 1906, N. Inez, *d.* of George Goodwin. Ottawa ; three *s.* two *d.* *Educ.* : Montreal College, St. Sulpice Seminary, Paris ; McGill and Laval University, Montreal. (B.C.L.) Contested Montreal Centre 1887, and Prescott Co., Ont., 1896 and 1900 ; editor of Montreal Post and True Witness, 1882-87 ; was President Press Association of Province of Quebec ; Crown Prosecutor, 1890-92 ; Attorney of Provincial Revenue, 1897-1908 ; Reeve and Mayor of Hawkesbury, 1894-1901 ; called to Senate, 1903 ; Roman Catholic Liberal. *Address* : Montreal, Quebec. (*Died 8 Feb. 1928.*)

CLOSE, Admiral Francis Arden ; Late High Sheriff of Bristol ; *b.* 1829 ; *s.* of Dean Close, Carlisle Deanery ; *m.* 1st, 1851, M. H. Hebden of Gothenburg, Sweden ; 2nd, Paulina Krantler of Strasburg ; no *c.* *Educ.* : Cheltenham College. Entered R.N., 1842 ; promoted Lieutenant for exemplary examinations at Naval College, 1850 ; Commander for service at Bomarsund, Baltic, Russian War, 1854 ; Captain for service on W. Coast Africa, 1861. *Address* : Trafalgar, Clifton Down, Bristol. *Club* : United Service. (*Died 25 Aug. 1918.*)

CLOSE, Colonel Lewis Henry, C.M.G. 1916; Royal Engineers; Chief Engineer, Western Command, India (Quetta); *b.* 4 Sep. 1869 ; *s.* of late Maj. - Gen. Frederick Close, R.A. ; *m.* 1910, Alys Dora, 3rd *d.* of late Maj.-Gen-

William Creagh, Bombay Staff Corps ; no *c.* *Educ.* : United Services College, Westward Ho ! Commission R.E., 1888 ; ordered to India, 1890; served Miranzai Expedition, 1891, as Asst. Field Engineer, and Waziristan Expedition, 1895, as Company Officer, No. 2 Coy. Bengal Sappers and Miners ; thanked by Government of Bengal for services on famine work in Behar, 1896 ; reverted to Imperial Establishment, 1900 ; Division Officer for Reconstruction, South Aldershot, 1900-5 ; in the Military Works Services in India, 1905-14 ; Assistant Director of Works, Mediterranean Expeditionary Force, Feb. 1915 ; served at Mudros and in Egypt (despatches four times, C.M.G., 3rd Class Order of the Nile); Secretary in the P.W.D. to the Hon. the A.G.G. in Baluchistan. *Recreations* : polo, racquets, tennis, small and big-game shooting. *Address* : c/o Cox's Branch, 6 Pall Mall, S.W.1. *Club* : Junior Army and Navy. (*Died 11 Nov. 1924.*)

CLOSE, S. P., A.R.H.A. *Address* : Fodeen, Eden Road, Carrickfergus.

CLOUGH, Sir John, Kt., *cr.* 1914 ; J.P. ; *b.* 1836 ; *s.* of John Clough ; *m.* 1862, Thamar, *d.* of Prince Smith, Keighley. *Address* : Haincliffe, Ingrow, Keighley, Yorks ; 25 Royal Crescent, Bath. (*Died 31 May 1922.*)

CLOUGH, Walter Owen, J.P. for Middlesex ; one of H.M.'s Lieutenants of the City of London ; Arbitrator of the London Chamber of Arbitration ; Fellow of Institute of Chartered Accountants ; M.P. (L.) Portsmouth, 1892-1900 ; C. C. Corporation of London, 1891-1905 ; *b.* 15 Sep. 1846 ; *s.* of late John Clough, Huddersfield ; *m.* 1871, Hannah (*d.* 1917), *d.* of George Marshall, of Newark ; three *s.* *Educ.* : Huddersfield. Practised as a Chartered Accountant, London. *Address* : 54 Gresham Street, E.C.2. *T.* : Central 5924.
(*Died 17 April 1922.*)

CLOWES, Frank, D.Sc. Lond. ; F.I.C. ; F.C.S. ; M.R.I. ; Emeritus Prof. of Chemistry and Metallurgy, Univ. College, Nottingham ; Governor of Dulwich College ; Expert Adviser in Gas Supply to the Corporation of London ; *b.* 1848, Bradford, Yorkshire ; *s.* of Francis Clowes, Norfolk, and Mary Low, London ; *m.* Mabel H. Waters, 1877. *Educ.* : City of London School ; Royal School of Mines, London ; Royal Coll. of Science, Dublin ; University of Würzburg ; Lecturer on Chemistry and Physics with laboratory, Queenwood College, Hants ; Professor of Chemistry, Univ. Coll., Nottingham, 1881-97, and first Principal ; Chemical Adviser to the London County Council, and Director of the Council's Chemical Staff and Laboratories, 1897-1913; President of the Society of Chemical Industry, 1897-1898 ; member of the Senate, University of London, 1901-3 ; Vice-President of the Institute of Chemistry, 1901-3, 1911-13 ; Vice-President of Chemical Section Brit.Assoc.,1893, 1914; Forrest Lecturer, Institution of Civil Engineers, 1901 ; visitor to the Royal Inst., 1903-4 and 1919-20 ; Pres. of Sec. III. Congress of Sanitary Institute, Glasgow, 1904 ; Hon. Member of the Midland Counties Institution of Engineers, and of the Chester (Kingsley) Society of Science. *Publications* : Text-book of Qualitative Analysis, 1874 (9th ed.); Text - book of Quantitative Analysis, 1891 (12th ed.) ; Elementary Practical Chemistry, 1896, Part I. (7th ed.); Part II. (9th ed.) ; The Detection and Estimation of Inflammable Gases and Vapours in the Air, 1896 ; Experimental Bacterial Treatment of London Sewage, 1904 ; and many original papers to the Royal Society, the Chemical Society, the Society of Chemical Industry, the Federated Institution of Mining Engineers, and Roy. Inst. of Brit. Architects. *Recreation* : golf. *Address* : The Grange, College Road, Dulwich, S.E.21. *T.* : 1457 Sydenham. *Club* : Athenæum.
(*Died 18 Dec. 1923.*)

CLOWES, Lieut.-Col. Peter Legh, C.B. 1900; J.P., D.L. Herefordshire; *b.* 30 Aug. 1853; *e. s.* of late John Clowes; *m.* 1895, Edith, *y. d.* of G. Warren. *Educ.:* Eton; Trinity Coll., Camb. Joined 8th Hussars, 1875; served with the regt. in India (Afghanistan, 1879-1880, medal); Major, 1885; commanded 8th Hussars, 1897-1901; served South Africa, 1900-1 (medal 6 clasps); High Sheriff, Herefordshire, 1921. *Address:* Burton Court, Leominster, Herefordshire. *T.:* Eardisland 3. *T.A.:* Eardisland. *Clubs:* Arthur's, Naval and Military.
(Died 23 Feb. 1925.)

CLOWES, Samuel; J.P.; M.P. (Lab.) Hanley Division of Stoke-on-Trent since 1924; General Secretary, National Society of Pottery Workers; member Stoke-on-Trent Town Council; *b.* 1864. President of the National Pottery Council. *Address:* 5 Hill Street, Hanley.
(Died 25 Mar. 1928.)

CLUTE, Hon. Roger Conger, Judge, High Court of Justice, Ontario, since 1905; *b.* 18 Aug. 1848; *m.* 1873, Rosa, *d.* of late Henry Corby, Belleville, Ont.; one *s.* one *d.* *Educ.:* Grammar School, Stirling; Albert College, Belleville. Barrister, 1873; K.C. 1890; Royal Commissioner to enquire into Labour troubles in British Columbia, 1899; Chairman of Royal Commission on Oriental immigration into Canada, 1900-1901. *Address:* 19 Walmer Road, Toronto. *Club:* Toronto. *(Died 12 Sept. 1921.)*

CLUTTON-BROCK, Arthur, B.A.; Art Critic of the Times; *b.* 1868; *s.* of J. A. Clutton-Brock of Oakfield, Weybridge, and Mary Alice Clutton-Brock; *m.* 1903, Evelyn Alice Vernon-Harcourt; three *s.* *Educ.:* Eton; New College, Oxford. Called to Bar, 1893; practised as a Barrister until 1903; became a journalist; Literary Editor of the Speaker, 1904-6; Art Critic of the Tribune during its existence; then, for a short time, of the Morning Post; has been on the staff of the Times since 1908. *Publications:* Shelley, the Man and the Poet, 1909; William Morris (Home University Series), 1914; Thoughts on the War, 1914; More Thoughts on the War, 1915; Simpson's Choice, an Essay on the Future Life, 1916; The Ultimate Belief, 1916; Studies in Christianity, 1918; What is the Kingdom of Heaven? 1919; Essays on Art, 1919; Essays on Books, 1920; 2nd series, 1921; Shakespeare's Hamlet, 1922. *Recreation:* gardening. *Address:* The Red House, Godalming. *T.:* Godalming 87. *Clubs:* Reform, Burlington Fine Arts. *(Died 8 Jan. 1924.)*

COAPE-SMITH, Maj.-General Henry, Indian Army; *b.* 24 Sept. 1829. Entered army, 1848; Maj.-Gen. 1890; unemployed list, 1887; served N.W. Frontier of India Campaign, 1854-1855 (despatches, medal with clasp).
(Died 13 Dec. 1921.)

COATES, Abraham George, M.V.O. 1906; *b.* 6 April 1861; Vice-Consul Havana, 1890-91; Philadelphia, 1892; Baltimore, 1893; Messina, 1905; Consul for Iceland and Faroe Islands, 1907-16; for Faroe Islands, 1916-19; H.M.'s Consul-General for the States of Maryland, Virginia, and West Virginia 1919-21; retired, 1921. *(Died 17 Aug. 1923.)*

COATES, Major Sir Edward (Feetham), 1st Bt., *cr.* 1911; D.L., J.P.; M.P. (C.) Lewisham, 1903; (Coal. U.) since 1918; Member of Coates, Son, and Co., Stockbrokers; County Alderman for Surrey; Chairman Surrey C.C. 1904-9; Member of the Surrey Territorial Force Association Council; one of the Trustees of the Crystal Palace; *e. s.* of late James Coates, J.P. and D.L., North Riding, Yorks, of Helperby Hall, York, and Elizabeth, *o. d.* of W. Sayer, of Yarm, York; *b.* 28 Feb. 1853; *m.* 1878, Edith, *e. d.* of Captain Philip Woolley of Gravenhurst, Sussex; one *s.* one *d.* *Educ.:* Marlborough. Late 3rd Batt. Duke of Wellington's (West Riding Regiment); one of H.M.'s Lieutenants,

208

1900, City of London; D.L., J.P. Surrey and North Riding of Yorkshire; contested Elland Division, York, 1900; on Roll for High Sheriff, Surrey, 1906; Patron of one Living. *Heir:* *o. s.* Capt. Edward Clive Coates, 15th Hussars, Military Secretary to the Lord-Lieut. of Ireland; *b.* 21 May 1879; *m.* 1906, Lady Celia Crewe Milnes, 2nd *d.* of 1st Marquis of Crewe, two *s.* two *d.*]. *Address:* Tayle's Hill, Ewell, Surrey; Queen Anne's Lodge, Queen Anne's Gate, S.W.1; Helperby Hall, York. *Clubs:* Carlton, Junior United Service; Yorkshire, York; Royal Yacht Squadron, Cowes.
(Died 14 Aug. 1921.)

COATES, Florence Earle; Author; *b.* Philadelphia; *d.* of George H. Earle and Ellen Frances van Leer; *m.* 1879, Edward Hornor Coates, President Pennsylvania Academy of the Fine Arts; one *d.* *Educ.:* private school in New England; Convent of Sacred Heart, France; President Browning Society of Philadelphia, 1895-1903 and 1907-8; a founder of the Contemporary Club, 1886, and of the Trans-atlantic Society of America; Member Society of Mayflower Descendants and Colonial Dames of America; President of the Contemporary Club, 1918-19; chosen poet laureate of Pennsylvania by State Federation of Women's Clubs, 1919. *Publications:* Matthew Arnold, an Essay, 1894; Poems: Poems, 1898; Mine and Thine, 1904; Lyrics of Life, 1909; Ode on the Coronation of George V., 1911; The Unconquered Air, 1912; Poems, 2 vols., 1916; Pro Patria, 1917; Contributor to Harper's Magazine, Scribner's, Atlantic Monthly, Century, and The Athenæum, London. *Recreations:* music, dramatic recitation, walking, and canoeing. *Address:* 2024 Spruce Street, Philadelphia, U.S.A. *Clubs:* Lyceum; Women's Literary, Baltimore (Hon.); New Century (Hon.); Society of Arts and Letters (Hon.), Philadelphia.
(Died 16 April 1927.)

COATES, Rev. Percy, M.A. (Oxon); Canon of Bradford; Rector of Bentham since 1893; Rural Dean of Ewecross; County and District Councillor; Governor of the Royal Infirmary, Lancaster; Member of the Lunesdale Fishery Board; *b.* Willow House, Raskelf; *o. s.* of Richard Coates of Helperby; uncle of Maj. Sir Edward F. Coates, Bt., M.P.; *m.* Margaret, *d.* of James Dey, Aberdeen; five *s.* one *d.* *Educ.:* St. Edward's School and St. John's College, Oxford. Ordained to St. Paul's, Leamington, 1888-89; Senior Curate of Kegworth, Leicestershire, 1889-93; Chaplain to the High Sheriff of Durham, 1913; President of the Royal Lancaster Infirmary, 1923. *Publications:* War-songs and other Poems. *Recreations:* all-round sportsman, golf, fishing, shooting, riding, rowing, football, cricket. *Address:* Bentham Rectory, near Lancaster.
(Died 18 Nov. 1925.)

COATS, Colonel George Henry Brook, C.B. 1909; *s.* of late Colonel John Wilson Coats, M.S.C.; *b.* 30 Sep. 1852; *m.* 1887, May Stella (*d.* 1910), *d.* of Alexander Chisholm; one *s.* two *d.* Entered army, 1871; Captain, I.S.C. (now Indian Army) 1883; Major, 1891; Lt.-Col. 1897; Bt.-Col. 1901; District Staff Officer and D.A.A.G. Bengal, 1886-91; served Afghan War, 1878-80; present at actions of Taif-u-din, battle of Ahmed Khel, action of Urzu, march from Kabul to Kandahar and battle of Kandahar (medal, 2 clasps, bronze star); Isazai Expedition, 1892; Relief of Chitral, 1895 (medal with clasp); Tochi Expedition, 1897-98 (despatches, clasp). *Address:* 5 Powis Square, Brighton. *(Died 18 May 1919.)*

COATS, Rev. Jervis, M.A., D.D.; Principal of the Baptist Theological College of Scotland since 1914, retaining position of Minister Emeritus of the Govan Church; *b.* 7 June 1844; *s.* of William and Mary Coats, Paisley; *m.* 1880, Marion Wark Wyllie (*d.* 1906); two *s.*

two d. *Educ.*: Paisley; Glasgow and Göttingen Universities. Entered, when a lad, the Union Bank of Scotland, continuing there for eight years; in 1867 matriculated at Glasgow University, where obtained a high position in the classes; graduated M.A. 1872; called to a church which was being formed at Govan, Glasgow, 1872; Minister of Govan Baptist Church, 1872-1914; President of Baptist Theological College of Scotland, 1903; engaged for many years in the training of students for the Christian ministry; received the hon. degree of D.D. from University of Glasgow, 1898. *Publications*: The Master's Watchward—an essay recalling attention to some fundamental principles of the Christian religion, 1897; lectures and magazine articles. *Recreations*: golf, music. *Address*: 8 Dalkeith Avenue, Dumbreck, Glasgow. *T.*: Ibrox 189, Glasgow. *Clubs*: Liberal, Glasgow Golf.   (*Died* 15 *Nov.* 1921.)

COATS, William Hodge, D.L. and J.P. County of Renfrew; J.P. County of Glasgow; Chairman J. and P. Coats, Ltd.; *b.* March 1866; *s.* of Archibald Coats and Elizabeth Hodge; *m.* Mrs. B. E. M. Kerr; no c. *Educ.*: Marlborough College; Continent. *Recreations*; shooting, fishing, golf, and yachting, etc. *Address*: Woodside, Paisley. *Clubs*: Carlton; Western, Glasgow.   (*Died* 21 *Aug.* 1928.)

COBBETT, Pitt, M.A., D.C.L. (Oxon.); emeritus Professor of Law in the University of Sydney, N.S.W.; *e. s.* of late Rev. Pitt Cobbett, formerly Vicar of Crofton, Hants. *Educ.*: Dulwich College; University College, Oxford. *Publications*: Cases and Opinions on International Law, 3rd ed. *Address*: Holebrook, Holebrook Place, Hobart, Tasmania; 44 The Temple, E.C. *Club*: Tasmanian, Hobart.   (*Died* 15 *Nov.* 1919.)

COBBETT, Sir William, Kt., *cr.* 1909; a Solicitor; *b.* 20 May 1846; *e. s.* of Richard Baverstock Brown Cobbett, Solicitor, of Oversley, Wilmslow, Cheshire, *y. s.* of William Cobbett, M.P. for Oldham, 1832-35, author of the Political Register and other works; *m.* 1868, Fanny Constantia (d. 1923), *e. d.* of George Fox, late of Elmshurst Hall, Lichfield, High Sheriff, Staffs., J.P., D.L.; four *s.* four *d. Educ.*: Hawthorn Hall School, Wilmslow. Admitted a Solicitor, 1868; President, Manchester Law Society, 1891 and 1906; Under-Sheriff for Staffs., 1887-88 and 1890-91; member Lord Chancellor's Judicature Committee, 1907-8; Chairman Board of Management Manchester Royal Infirmary since 1904. *Recreations*: hunting and shooting. *Address*: Woodlands, Wilmslow, Cheshire; 49 Spring Gardens, Manchester. *T.A.*: Cobbetts, Manchester. *T.*: City 5235. *Club*: Union, Manchester.   (*Died* 26 *Nov.* 1926.)

COBHAM, 8th Viscount, *cr.* 1718; **Charles George Lyttelton**; Baron Lyttelton, 1756 (renewed 1794); Baron Westcote, 1776; Bt. 1618; Chairman, Royal Commission on agricultural depression, 1896-97; Member Royal Commission on London Traffic, 1903-1905; Fellow of Eton, 1891-1918; late Trustee, National Portrait Gallery; *b.* 1842; *S.* father as Baron Lyttelton, 1876, and Duke of Buckingham as Viscount, 1889; *m.* Hon. Mary Susan Caroline Cavendish, *d.* of 2nd Baron Chesham, 1878; four *s.* two *d.* Liberal M.P. E. Worcestershire, 1868-74; Land Commissioner, 1881-89; Deputy Chairman G.W. Railway, 1890-1891; Railway Commissioner, 1891-1905. *Educ.*: Eton; Trin. Coll. Camb. 2nd class in Classical Tripos; 1st class in Law Tripos. Owns about 6000 acres. Hagley Hall Picture Gallery. Pictures by Vandyck, Mirevelt, Lely, Van Somer, Reynolds, etc. *Recreations*: a well-known cricketer to 1866; played in all Gentlemen and Players' matches, 1861-66. *Heir*: *s.* Hon. John Cavendish Lyt-

telton.   *Address*: Hagley Hall, Stourbridge. *Club*: Brooks's.   (*Died* 9 *June* 1922.)

COCHIN, Henry Denys Benoit Marie; *b.* Paris, 81 Jan. 1854; *s.* of Augustin Cochin, membre de l'Institut, d'une ancienne famille parisienne et Adeline, fille du Comte Benoist d'Azy; *m.* 1883, Mlle. Arnaud-Jeanti; one *s.* two *d. Educ.*: Lycée Louis-le-Grand, Paris. Licencié ès lettres et Licencié en droit; engagé volontaire au 17e. bataillon de la Garde nationale (Guerre 1870-1871); Attaché au Ministère de l'Intérieur 1877; Elu député 1893, et sans cesse réélu depuis, s'est retiré en 1914 en faveur de son fils; Conseiller Général du Nord pendant quatre ans. *Publications*: Giulietta et Roméo, 1878; Le Manuscrit de M. Larsonnier (roman), 1880; Boccace, 1890; Un Ami de Pétrarque, 1892; Chronologie du Canzonière de Pétrarqie, 1898; Le Frère de Pétrarque, 1903; Le bienheureux Fra Angelico de Fiesole, 1906; sixième édition en 1920; La Vita Nuova de Dante traduite et commentée, 1908, 2e édition en 1916; Tableaux flamands, 1909; Jubilés d'Italie, 1910; Lamartine et la Flandre, 1912; Les deux Guerres, 1916; L'Œuvre de guerre du peintre Albert Besnard, 1918; François Pétrarque (collection Les cent Chefs-œuvre étrangers) 1920. *Address*: Château de Mousseau, Evry Petit Bourg (Seine-et-Oise), France.   (*Died* 24 *Mar.* 1922.)

COCHRANE, Vice-Admiral Basil Edward; *b.* 1841; *m.* 1873, Cornelia, *y. d.* of Captain John J. Robinson Owen, R.N., of Campbellbello and Windlesham House, Surrey. Entered Navy, 1854; Commander, 1872; Captain, 1884; Rear-Adm. retired, 1899; Vice-Adm. retired, 1904; served Russian War, 1854 (Baltic medal); E. Soudan, 1884 (despatches, Egyptian medal, bronze star). *Address*: Windlesham House, Windlesham, Surrey. *Club*: United Service.   (*Died* 4 *May* 1922.)

COCHRANE, Hon. Francis; Minister of Railways and Canals, Canada; *b.* Clarenceville, Quebec, 18 Nov. 1852; *m.* 1882, Alice Levina Dunlop; one *s.* one *d.* Minister of Lands and Mines, 1905; M.P. Sudbury, 1908. *Address*: 15 Maple Avenue, Rosedale, Toronto. *Club*: National, Toronto.   (*Died* 22 *Sept.* 1919.)

COCHRANE, Col. William Francis Dundonald C.B. 1898; retired; late Chief Staff Officer, Belfast District; *b.* Cosham, Wilts, 7 Aug. 1847; *s.* of late Col. W. M. Cochrane, who was nephew of Admiral 10th Earl of Dundonald; *m.* 1893, Maria Carola, *d.* of Henrique Theodora Müller of Valparaiso, Chili. *Educ.*: Kensington School; Military Coll. Sandhurst. Served in 32nd Light Infantry (D.C.L.I.), 1866-93, being adjutant for nine years; Chief Staff-Officer Cape Colony Colonial Forces, 1879-1882, during Basuto War; D.A.A. and Q.M.G. China and Straits Settlements, 1883-87; Headquarters Staff in Ireland, 1887-88; Assist.-Military Secretary in South Africa, 1890-92; commanded infantry brigade in Egyptian army, 1893-96; on lines of communication in Dongola and Soudan Expedition, 1896-98. *Decorations*: Zulu War, Egypt, 1882, Soudan 1896-98 (5 war medals, 3rd class Medjidie, C.B.). *Recreations*: shooting, hunting, fishing, golf. *Club*: Naval and Military.   (*Died* 23 *Oct.* 1928.)

COCK, Henry, M.V.O., retired Chief Constructor from H.M. Dockyard, Pembroke Dock; *s.* of Thomas Cock, of Torpoint, Cornwall; eight *s.* one *d. Educ.*: private; Devonport Dockyard School. Shipwright apprentice, and subsequently Draughtsman; Foreman of the yard; Constructor, and Chief Constructor; retired, 1902. *Address*: 48 Durnford Street, Stonehouse, Plymouth.   (*Died* 19 *Aug.* 1922.)

COCKBURN, Col. George, C.B.E. 1919; D.S.O. 1898; Rifle Brigade; retired 1905; late commanding 3rd Batt. Rifle Brigade; *b.* Jan.

1856 ; s. of Admiral J. H. Cockburn ; m. 1905, Alice Lindsay, d. of Hasell Rodwell of Tower House, Ipswich, and widow of Charles Reginald Orde, Rifle Brigade. *Educ.:* Eton. Joined Rifle Brigade, 1876 ; Adjutant, 1884-89 ; Major, 1894 ; served in India, 1889-94 ; Staff, Eastern Command, 1896-97 ; Soudan, 1898, including Khartoum (despatches, D.S.O., British medal, Khedive's medal with clasp) ; Crete, 1898-99 ; Transvaal, 1899-1901 (despatches, medal, 4 clasps, Brevet Lieut.-Col.) ; Col. 1904 ; A.A. and Q.M.G., 1st London Territorial Division on Mobilization, 1914 ; Brigadier General commanding 43rd Brigade, 14th Division, Oct. 1914 ; France, 1915 ; 18th Reserve Brigade, 1915-16 ; Commanded Ripon Camp and Tay Defences, 1916 ; retired Nov. 1916 ; N.A.C.B. 1917-20 ; Hon. Brigadier-General, 1917. *Recreations:* cricket, racquets, shooting, etc. *Club:* Naval and Military. *(Died 9 Dec. 1925.)*

COCKBURN, Sir George Jack, Kt., cr. 1910 ; J.P. ; b. 2 Sep. 1848 ; 2nd s. of late John Cockburn, Stirlingshire, and Margaret Jack, Aberdeenshire ; m. 1st, 1871, Emily, e. d. of D. I. Roebuck, Leeds ; 2nd, 1886, Clara, 3rd d. of Wm. Nield, Huddersfield and Leeds ; three s. four d. *Educ.:* Private schools. Was an East India merchant, but retired many years ago and became exclusively engaged in varied forms of public service ; several years Chairman Leeds Poor Law Board, and founder of the Yorkshire Annual Poor Law Conferences ; for 21 years, up to extinction of School Boards, was leader and Chairman Leeds School Board and Vice-President School Board Association of England and Wales ; was pioneer of Higher Grade Board School system ; Royal Commissioner on Secondary Education in England and Wales, 1893-95 ; Education Commissioner to Canada and United States, 1903 ; member of West Riding Education Committee ; member Court and Council University of Leeds ; formerly member National Liberal Federation Executive ; President North Leeds Liberal Association. *Recreation:* golf. *Address:* North Grange Road, Headingley, Leeds. *T.A.:* Headingley, Leeds. *T.:* Headingley 128. *Club:* Leeds and County Liberal, Leeds. *(Died 1 Jan. 1927.)*

COCKBURN, Henry, C.B. 1899 ; b. 2 Mar. 1859 ; s. of late F. J. Cockburn, B.C.S. ; m. 1899, Elizabeth Gordon, d. of Colonel Stevenson. *Educ.:* Edinburgh. Entered consular service, China, 1880 ; Chinese Secretary to the British Legation at Pekin, 1896-1906 ; H.B.M. Consul-General. Korea, 1906-9 ; retired, 1909. *Club:* Caledonian. *(Died 19 Mar. 1927.)*

COCKBURN, General Henry Alexander, J.P. Midlothian ; b. 1831 ; s. of John Cockburn ; m. 1862, Lucy (d. 1916), d. of General Auchmuty Tucker, C.B., Bengal Cavalry ; one s. one d. *Educ.:* Edinburgh Academy ; Edinburgh Military Academy ; Addiscombe College. Joined 58rd Bengal Native Infantry, 1851 ; Adjutant 1st Cavalry Gwalior Contingent Force, 1854 ; commanded in several minor engagements in the Doab in May and June 1857, and present at the actions near Agra in July and October 1857 ; Second in Command of Meade's (Central India) Horse, November 1857 ; commanded that regiment and the Sipri Field Force, 1859-61 ; held various appointments under the Government of India from 1862 ; was thanked by the Government N.W. Provinces on four occasions, and mentioned in despatches ; twice wounded—once severely. One horse killed and one wounded ; medal and clasp for Central India. *Recreations:* painting, riding, etc. *Address:* Eskgrove, Inveresk, Midlothian. *T.A.:* Eskgrove, Musselburgh. *Clubs:* Cavalry ; New, Edinburgh. *(Died 20 Aug. 1922.)*

COCKBURN, Nathaniel Clayton, J.P., D.L., F.R.G.S. ; Major ; M.F.H. Blankney Hounds, 1895-1904 ; b. 1866 ; s. of W. Y. Cock-

210

burn, D.L., J.P. *Educ.:* Eton ; Christ Church, Oxford. Served with Lincolnshire Yeomanry in Egypt and Palestine, 1916-17. *Address:* Harmston Hall, Lincoln. *Club:* Cavalry. *(Died 2 Jan. 1924.)*

COCKIN, Ven. John Irwin Browne, M.A. : Vicar of Milton Lilbourne since 1908 ; b. 20 May 1850 ; s. of late Rev. Canon Cockin ; m. Frances Charlotte, d. of J. B. Moxon ; one d. *Educ.:* King Edward's School, Birmingham ; Richmond School, Yorks ; Queen's College, Oxford ; 2nd Class Theological Curate, Brigg ; St. Mary's, Nottingham ; Vicar, Esholt ; Rector, St. Martin's, Colchester ; Chaplain, Howrah, Dacca, Saugor, Lucknow, Ranikhet, Meerut, Cathedral Allahabad, Mussoorie, Naini Tal ; Archdeacon of Lucknow, 1902-1905 ; Examining Chaplain to the Bishop of Lucknow ; Chaplain on H.M. Bengal Establishment 1880 1905 ; Rector, Barnwell, 1905-1908. *Publication:* The Church of England in the True Church. *Address:* Milton Lilbourne Vicarage, Marlborough, Wilts. *(Died 14 April 1924.)*

COCKRAN, William Bourke, lawyer ; b. Ireland, 28 Feb. 1854 ; m. 1906, d. of Hon. Henry C. Ide, formerly Governor-General or the Philippine Islands and Chief Justice of Samoa. *Educ.:* Ireland and France. Went to United States, 1871 ; taught in private academy ; later principal of a public school in Westchester Co., New York ; admitted to Bar, 1876 ; elected to Congress, 1886 ; became prominent in New York City politics ; Member of Congress, 1891-1895 and 1904-9 ; Democrat ; became advocate of the gold standard and campaigned for M'Kinley, 1896 ; in Dec. 1896 delivered first speech by any American public man favouring intervention by the U.S. to end barbarities in Cuba, but strongly opposed annexation of the Philippines, delivering first speech in opposition to it at the Academy of Music in 1898. *Address:* 100 Broadway, New York City. *(Died 1 Mar. 1923.)*

COCOTO, Spiridon George, C.M.G. 1913 ; M.V.O. 1906 ; s. of George Cocoto ; b. 1843 ; m. 1869, Elizabeth, d. of late James Duff. Pro-Consul at Brindisi, 1878 ; Vice-Consul, 1889 ; Consul there for the Province of Lecce, 1889 ; Consul for the Provinces of Apulia, 1912 ; resigned, 1913 ; *Address:* Palazzo Cocoto, Brindisi, Italy. *(Died 14 Oct. 1916.)*

CODDINGTON, Sir William, 1st Bt., cr. 1896 ; J.P., D.L. ; cotton spinner and manufacturer ; Director of Midland Railway ; b. 12 Dec. 1830 ; s. of late W. D. Coddington ; m. 1st, 1864, Sarah (d. 1911), d. of late W. T. Hall ; one d.; 2nd, 1913, Aimée Josephine, d. of W. J. S. Barber-Starkey, of Darley Dale, Derbyshire. M.P. (C.) Blackburn, 1880-1906. *Heir:* none. *Address:* Wycollar, Blackburn ; 143 Piccadilly, W. *Club:* Carlton. *(Died 15 Feb. 1918.)*

CODRINGTON, Rev. Robert Henry, D.D. ; Prebendary of Wightring in Chichester Cathedral 1895-1921, and Theological Lecturer until 1921 ; b. Wroughton, Wilts, 15 Sep. 1830 ; s. of Rev. T. S. Codrington. *Educ.:* Charterhouse ; Wadham College, Oxford. Scholar, 1849; Fellow, 1855 ; 3rd class Litt. Hum. 1852 ; B.A. 1852 ; Deacon, 1855 ; Priest, 1857 ; Nelson, N.Z., 1860 ; Melanesian Mission, 1866 ; head of the Mission, 1871-77 ; D.D. Oxford, *honoris causa,* 1885 ; Vicar of Wadhurst, Sussex, 1888-93 ; Prebendary of Sidlesham, 1888 ; Examining Chaplain to Bishop of Chichester, 1894-1901. *Publications:* The Melanesian Languages, 1855 ; The Melanesians, etc., 1891 ; Dictionary of the Mota Language 1896 ; translations of great part of the Bible into Mota. *Address:* St. Richard's Walk, Chichester. *(Died 11 Sept. 1922.)*

COFFEY, George, M.R.I.A. : Keeper of Irish Antiquities, National Museum, Dublin, 1896-1914 ; b. Dublin, 1857 ; o. surv. s. of late James Charles Coffey, Co. Court Judge of Co.

Londonderry; *m.* Jane Sophia Frances, *d.* of Sir George L'Estrange; one *s.* *Educ.*: Trinity College, Dublin, A.I.B., B.L. For short time practised at the Irish Bar; was for some time one of the secretaries of the Irish National League; is Hon. Member of the Royal Hibernian Academy. *Publications*: Celtic Antiquities of the Christian Period, 1st edition 1909; 2nd edition 1910; New Grange, influence of Crete and Ægean in West of Europe; The Bronze Age in Ireland; numerous papers on Archæological subjects. *Address*: 5 Harcourt Terrace, Dublin.   (*Died 29 Aug. 1916.*)

COFFIN, Walter Harris, F.C.S., Fellow Royal Society of Medicine; late Editor (13 years), British Dental Journal; *b.* Portland, Maine, U.S.A., 1853; *e. s.* of late Dr. C. R. Coffin, South Kensington; *m.* Sophia Lydia, *e. d.* of late T. R. Carey Walters of Hereford; (authoress of A Dreamer's Sketch Book, Lostara, etc.). *Educ.*: Royal College of Science (Medallist); University College and St. Thomas's Hospital. Student at Royal School of Mines and Royal Dental Hospital; Fellow Physical Society of London; Life Member of Committee British Association; Past President Metropolitan Branch British Dental Association; late Lecturer and Examiner National Dental Hospital; Editor Transactions Odontological Society; Original Member and Founder of Society for Psychical Research; Fabian Society; Stage Society, etc., and Hon. and Corresponding Member of several American and foreign scientific bodies; Inventor and Patentee of Electric Endoscopic Surgical Lamps. *Publications*: Papers to Trans. International Medical Congress, 1881, on A Generalized Treatment of Irregularities, The Use of Peroxide of Hydrogen; Gutta Percha Impressions in Orthodontia, etc.; to Nature, Chemical News, etc., on Primary Batteries; Contributor to American Journal of Science; Journal of the Franklin Institute; Transactions of the Anthropological Institute, etc. *Recreations*: music, books, sociology. *Address*: 30 York Street, Portman Square, W. *T.*: 4624 Padd. *Club*: National Liberal.
(*Died 10 April 1916.*)

COGHILL, Douglas Harry, M.A.; Barr. Inner Temple; *b.* Newcastle-under-Lyme, 6 Aug. 1855; *s.* of Harry Coghill, J.P.; *m.* 1890, Catherine Edith, 2nd *d.* of Charles Orton, M.D., Newcastle-under-Lyme. *Educ.*: Cheltenham; Corpus Christi Coll. Oxford. M.P. for Newcastle-under-Lyme, 1886-92; defeated, 1892; M.P. (C.) Stoke-on-Trent, 1895-1906. *Address*: 14 Stanhope Gardens, S.W.7; *T.*: Kens. 3686; Crowham Manor, Battle. *Club*: Carlton.
(*Died 13 Dec. 1928.*)

COGHILL, Sir Egerton Bushe, 5th Bt., *cr.* 1778; *b.* 7 Feb. 1853; 2nd *s.* of Sir John Joscelyn Coghill, 4th Bt., and Katherine, 2nd *d.* of 3rd Baron Plunket (*d.* 1881); *S.* father, 1905; *m.* 1893, Elizabeth Hildegarde Augusta, *d.* of late Col. Thomas Henry Somerville of Drishane, Skibbereen; three *s.* one *d.* *Educ.*: Haileybury; studied art Düsseldorf and Paris. *Heir*: *s.* Marmaduke Nevill Patrick Somerville, *b.* 17 Mar. 1896. *Recreations*: yachting, painting. *Address*: Glen Barrahane, Castletownshend, Co. Cork. *T.A.*: Castletownshend.
(*Died 9 Oct. 1921.*)

COGHILL, Colonel Kendal, C.B. 1882; J.P.; *b.* nr. Dublin, 21 Aug. 1832; *s.* of Adm. Sir J. Coghill, 3rd Bt., and Anna Maria, *d.* of Rt. Hon. Chief-Justice C.K. Bushe. *Educ.*: Cheltenham Coll. Joined 2nd European Bengal Fusiliers, India, 1851; served Burmah, 1853-55; Adjutant of Regt. during Indian Mutiny, 1857-58; present at Battle of Badlee-ka-Serai, and storming heights of Delhi, 8 June 1857; throughout siege of Delhi, and at all the actions in front of the city; was with the storming column over the breach in Cashmere bastion, and during final

capture of city and palace from 14 to 21 Sept.; served with General Shower's pursuing column, 1857-58; present at taking the forts of Rewarrie, Jujjher, Kanoude, Furrucknugger, Bullubghur, and storming heights of Sonah; Brigade-Major of Cawnpore and Barrackpore; Station Interpreter; Assistant Adjut. - Gen. Lucknow and Calcutta; Assist. Q.M.G. Presidency Division, 1861 - 70; exchanged to 19th Hussars, 1863; which commanded in Egyptian Campaign, 1882; present at battles of Mahuta, Kassassin, and storming of Tel - el - Kebir and taking of Cairo (despatches; medals for India, and bar for Delhi; medal for Egypt, and bar for Tel-el-Kebir; 3rd class order of Medjidie; Khedivial bronze star). *Recreations*: hunting, shooting, sailing. *Address*: Castle Townshend, near Skibbereen, Co. Cork. *Clubs*: Cavalry, Hurlingham, Cork County. (*Died 15 July 1919.*)

COGHLAN, Colonel Charles, C.B. 1909; V.D. 1894; D.L.; J.P.; late Col. 1st W.R.B. R.F.A. (T.F.); Ironmaster; Chairman of the Coghlan Steel & Iron Co. Ltd., Hunslet Forge, Leeds; *b.* 21 Feb. 1852; *s.* of late Wm. Austen Coghlan of Grosvenor House, Leeds; *m.* 1887, Josephine Mary, *y. d.* of Rev. J. Kenworthy, Rector of Ackworth, Yorkshire; two *s.* three *d.* *Educ.*: Ratcliffe College, near Leicester; Maison de Melle lez Gand, Belgique. Joined the 1st W.R.B.V. Artillery, 1874; was given the command, 1896, and has had five extensions; appointed to the Hon. Colonelcy of the Brigade, 1914; Member of the Iron and Steel Institute; a Roman Catholic and Life Member of the Catholic Union of Great Britain and Ireland. *Recreations*: nothing special, unless being a keen Territorial soldier can be deemed a recreation. *Address*: Ashfield, Headingley Hill, Leeds, Yorkshire. *T.A.*: Coghlan, Leeds. *T.*: 211 Headingley, Leeds. *M.*: 664 U. *Clubs*: Junior Army and Navy; Leeds, County Conservative, Leeds.   (*Died 14 Oct. 1921.*)

COGHLAN, Hon. Sir Charles Patrick John, Kt., *cr.* 1910; K.C.M.G., *cr.* 1925; solicitor; M.L.A. Southern Rhodesia; First Premier and Minister of Native Affairs of Southern Rhodesia since 1923; *b.* Cape Colony, 24 June 1863; *m.* 1899, Gertrude, *d.* of late Col. Schermbrucker, M.L.A.; one *c.* *Educ.*: St. Aidan's College, Grahamstown; S. African College, Cape Town. Served as Captain in Kimberley Town Guard (medal and clasp). *Address*: 22 Agency Buildings, Buluwayo.
(*Died 28 Aug. 1927.*)

COGHLAN, Hon. Sir Timothy Augustine, Kt., *cr.* 1914; K.C.M.G., *cr.* 1918; I.S.O. 1903; Agent-General for New South Wales, 1905-15, 1916-17, and 1920-25; Representative of Commonwealth of Australia on the Pacific Cable Board; *b.* 1857; 2nd *s.* of late Thomas Coghlan; *m.* 1897, Helen, 3rd *d.* of D. C. Donnelly, M.L.A., N.S. Wales; one *s.* one *d.* *Educ.*: Sydney Grammar School. Assist. Engineer, Harbours and Rivers, 1884; Government Statistician, New South Wales,1886-1905; Registrar of Friendly Societies, 1892-1905; Chairman Board of Old Age Pensions, 1901-1905; Member of Public Service Board, 1896-1900; Royal Commissioner to divide N.S.W. into electoral districts; Royal Commissioner to divide N.S.W. local government areas; Member various other Royal Commissions; supervised N.S.W. Censuses of 1891 and 1901; Hon. Fellow of Royal Statistical Society, 1893; President of Conference of Australian and New Zealand Statisticians to determine number of Representatives in each State in Federal Parliament, and arrange for uniformity in Census of 1901; President of Australasian Association for the Advancement of Science (Section G, Economics and Statistics), 1902; Member of Actuarial Soc. of New South Wales, 1902; Corresponding Member of Royal Society, Tasmania, 1902; Member of Council of

211

Royal Statistical Society; Member International Institute of Statistics; Order St. Sava, Serbia, 1919. *Publications:* Wealth and Progress of New South Wales; Picturesque New South Wales; The Seven Colonies of Australasia; Discharge of Streams in Relation to Rainfall; Childbirth: A Study in Statistics; Notes on the Financial Aspect of Federation; Report on the Eleventh Census of New South Wales; Deaths of Women in Childbirth; Child Measurement; Decline in the Birthrate of Australia and New Zealand; Statistical Account of Australia and New Zealand; A History of Labour and Industry in Australia, 4 vols. *Address:* 21 Lennox Gardens, S.W.1.
(*Died 30 April 1926.*)

COGSWELL, Rev. Canon William H. L., M.A. Oxon.; Hon. D.D., Windsor, N.S.; Rector of Wallasey since 1896; Rural Dean of Wallasey since 1906; Canon Residentiary of Chester since 1914; *b.* Halifax, Nova Scotia, 11 Dec. 1845; *s.* of Rev. Wm. Cogswell and Eleanor Belcher; *m.* 1868, Alicia Heriot, *d.* of Andrew Mitchell-Uniacke, of Clarges Street, Mayfair, London; one *s.* two *d. Educ.:* King's Coll., Windsor; Wadham College, Oxford. Curate of Stevenage, 1868-71; Vicar of S. Hinksey with Wootton, Berks, 1871-79; Chaplain of Magdalen College, 1873-1879; Vicar of S. Oswald's, Chester, 1879-90; Warden, Special Service Clergy; Organising Secretary C.E.T.S. and Diocesan Missioner, 1890-95; Rural Dean of Birkenhead, 1900-5. *Publications:* Explanatory Readings on the Visitation of the Sick. *Recreations:* canoeing, fishing, sketching, lawn tennis, cricket, golf. *Address:* The Residence, Chester; Riverscote, Boughton, Chester. *T.:* 423. *Club:* Wallasey Golf.
(*Died 28 May 1917.*)

COHEN, Mrs. Nathaniel Louis; President of the Union of Jewish Women; *d.* of Professor Waley, M.A., Conveyancing Council to the Court of Chancery; *widow* of late Nathaniel Louis Cohen, L.C.C.; three *s.* two *d. Educ.:* Queen's College, London. Social and Educational worker. *Publications:* Children's Psalm Book; Infant Bible Reader. *Address:* 10 Sussex Square, W. *T.:* 790 Paddington.
(*Died Dec. 1917.*)

COKE, Brig.-Gen. Edward Beresford, C.V.O. 1904; retired; *y. s.* of late Colonel Edward Thomas Coke, J.P. and D.L., of Trusley Manor, Derbyshire, and Debdale Hall, Notts; *b.* 5 May 1850; *m.* Ada Beatrice, 7th *d.* of W. H. Dawes of The Hall, Kenilworth. *Educ.:* Royal Naval Academy, Gosport; Royal Military Academy, Woolwich. Received H.M.'s Commission, 1870; served on the Staff, Afghan War, 1879-80 (medal); commanded the Royal Horse Artillery at Ipswich and Aldershot, 1896-1901; Commandant of the practice camp, Trawsfynydd, Wales, 1903; Colonel on the Staff Royal Artillery at Woolwich, 1903; commanded Woolwich District, 1903-7; Inspector of Remounts, 1915-16. *Address:* Villa St. Agnes, Mentone, France. *Club:* United Service. (*Died 30 Dec. 1924.*)

COKE, Hon. Henry John, J.P.; 3rd *s.* of 1st Earl of Leicester and 2nd wife, Lady Anne Amelia, *d.* of 4th Earl of Albemarle; *b.* 1827; *m.* 1861, Lady Katharine Grey Egerton, *d.* of 2nd Earl of Wilton, a Lady in Waiting to late Duchess of Teck, and Woman of the Bedchamber to H.M. the Queen; one *s.* one *d.* Was in Royal Navy; served China War, 1840-42. *Publications:* A Ride over the Rocky Mountains; Creeds of the Day; Tracks of a Rolling Stone, 1905; The Domain of Belief, 1910. *Address:* 64 Victoria Street, S.W.; Longford Hall, Derby. *Club:* Athenæum.
(*Died 12 Nov. 1916.*)

COKE, Mrs. Talbot; *b.* 1843; *e. d.* of late Major FitzGerald, Maperton, Somerset; *m.* 1867, late Major-General J. Talbot Coke. Began to write on Home Decoration and other artistic

subjects in the Queen paper, 1887, and in the Ladies Field. *Publications:* The Gentlewoman at Home, Holy Matrimony, The Mills of God, and other stories. *Address:* Craven Lodge, Horsham, Sussex. (*Died Aug. 1922.*)

COLBORNE, Col. Hon. Francis (Lionel Lydstone); M.V.O. 1913; D.L., Suffolk; Major (retired) Royal Irish Rifles; *b.* 29 July 1855; 2nd *s.* of late Maj.-Gen. Lord Seaton and Charlotte, *d.* of late General Lord Downes, *heir-pres.* to the Barony of Seaton; *m.* 1906, Alice Matilda, *d.* of late Capt. W. R. G. Farmer (formerly Grenadier Guards), J.P., D.L. of Nonsuch and Lagham, Surrey, and Denham, Suffolk. *Educ.:* Winchester; Oxford; Sandhurst. Served on the Scinde Frontier, 1878; relief of Kandahar in Afghan Campaign, 1880; with Natal Field Force in South African Campaign, 1881; in the Nile Expedition for relief of Khartoum, 1884-85 (despatches, Brevet of Maj.); Soudan Frontier Field Force, 1886; on the Staff of North Irish District, 1887; South-Eastern District, 1888; served Boer War in South Africa, 1900; European War, 1914-17; Administrative Commandant in III. Army Area; Commandant 8th Batt. City of London Regiment, 1901-10; Hon. Col. 1908; order Merito Militar of Spain and Royal Victorian; Exon, King's Body Guard, since 1892; Equerry-in-Waiting to Princess Beatrice since 1898; Director of the Royal Insurance Company (West End Branch); Member of Lloyd's; *Address:* Nonsuch Park, Surrey; Denham, Suffolk. *Clubs:* Carlton, Bachelors', Wellington.
(*Died 8 Sept. 1924.*)

COLCHESTER, 3rd Baron (cr. 1817), Reginald Charles Edward Abbot, M.A., F.S.A., F.R.G.S., D.L., J.P.; barrister; *b.* London 13 Feb. 1842; *s.* of 2nd Baron and *d.* of 1st Lord Ellenborough; *S.* father 1867; *m.* 1869, Lady Isabella Grace (Maude), *e. d.* of 1st Earl de Montalt. *Educ.:* Eton; Christ Church, Oxon. 1st class Classics, Law and Modern History, 1863; Stanhope Historical Essay Prize, 1861; Fellow of All Souls, 1864; Examiner in Law and History, Oxford; 1869. Church of England and Conservative. Contested E. Sussex, 1865; Devonport, 1866; Member of Standards Commission, 1868-70; Charity Commissioner, 1880-83; London School Board, 1891-94. *Publications:* edited Political Diaries of Lord Ellenborough in 1828-30, and Letters relating to Indian Administration of Lord Ellenborough. *Heir:* none. *Address:* Forest Row, E. Grinstead. *Clubs:* Carlton, Constitutional, Athenæum. (*Died 26 Feb. 1919.*)

COLDRIDGE, Ward, K.C. 1912; *b.* 1864; *o. s.* of C. S. Coldridge; *m.* Amy, *o. d.* of late John Norwood, of Beckenham. *Educ.:* Exeter Grammar School; Emmanuel College, Cambridge; Natural Science Tripos, Parts I. and II.; Bencher, Lincoln's Inn, 1917. *Publication:* Law of Gambling (joint). *Address:* 2 New Square, Lincoln's Inn, W.C.2; 18 Lansdowne Road, Holland Park, W.11. *T.:* Park 2045.
(*Died 3 April 1926.*)

COLDWELL, Hon. George Robson, K.C.; late Minister of Education, Manitoba; *b.* Township Clarke, Co. Durham, Ontario, 4 July 1858; *s.* of William Edward Coldwell and Mary Robson; *m.* Ann Anderson; four *s.* one *d. Educ.:* Clinton Grammar School; Trinity College School, Port Hope; Trinity College, Toronto. Has practised law in Brandon since 1883. *Address:* 122 Eighteenth Street, Brandon Manitoba. (*Died Jan. 1924.*)

COLE, Alfred Clayton, M.A.; Director of the Bank of England; Governor, 1911; Lieut. for the City of London; *b.* London, 17 Dec. 1854; *y. s.* of late William Henry Cole, Pulham, Norfolk, and West Woodhay, Berks; *m.* 1907, *d.* of Col. Arthur T. H. Williams, Canada, and widow of Herbert Chamberlain. *Educ.:* Eton; Trin. Coll. Camb. Captain of Oppidans at Eton, 1874; after leaving Cambridge, spent some time abroad; Barr. 1880. Owns about 4500 acres in Norfolk and Berkshire. *Recreations:* shooting, tennis, golf. *Address:* 64 Portland Place, W.1; *T.:* Gerrard 5342; West Woodhay House, Newbury, Berks. *Clubs:* Athenæum, Carlton, St. James's, Beefsteak.

(*Died 5 June 1920.*)

COLE, Rev. Edward Pattinson, M.A.; Hon. Canon of Bristol Cathedral; *s.* of Thomas Bulman Cole, Somerset; *m.* 1873, Edith Rhoda (*d.* 1925), *d.* of Col. G. E. Thorold, Black Watch; two *s. Educ.:* Exeter College, Oxford. Curate formerly of St. John's, Brighton; St. Paul's, Brighton; Old Shoreham, Sussex; and Midhurst, Sussex; Rector of Christ Church with S. Ewen's, Bristol; Patron of two livings. *Address:* 23 Gt. George Street, Park Street, Bristol. (*Died 26 Oct. 1926.*)

COLE, Grenville Arthur James, F.R.S. 1917; Professor of Geology, Royal Coll. of Science for Ireland, since 1890; Director of the Geological Survey of Ireland since 1905; *b.* London, 21 Oct. 1859; *s.* of J. J. Cole, Architect; *m.* Blanche, *d.* of J. E. Vernon; one *s. Educ.:* City of London School; Royal School of Mines. *Publications:* Aids in Practical Geology, 1891; 7th ed. 1918; The Gypsy Road, 1894; Open-air Studies, 1895; 2nd ed., 1902; The Changeful Earth, 1911; Rocks and their Origins, 1912; 2nd ed., 1922; Outlines of Mineralogy for Geological Students, 1913; The Growth of Europe, 1914; Ireland, the Land and the Landscape, 1915; section on Europe, in The World we Live in, 1917; Ireland the Outpost, 1919; Common Stones, 1921; Memoir and Map of Irish mineral localities (Geol. Survey), 1922; with Blanche Cole, As We Ride, 1902; and scientific papers. Has examined at London, Cambridge, Oxford, and other Universities; Murchison Medal, Geological Society, 1909; President, Geological Section, British Association, 1915; President Geographical Association, 1919; and of Irish Geographical Association, 1919 - 22. *Recreation:* formerly cycling, especially as a means of travel. *Address:* Orahova, Carrickmines, Co. Dublin. *T.:* Foxrock 85. (*Died 20 April 1924.*)

COLE, Rev. John Francis, Head-master French school since 1885; Canon of Kildare since 1908; Incumbent of Portarlington since 1885. *Educ.:* St. Bees. Ordained 1880; Curate Mountrath, 1880-83; Arklow, 1883-85; Rural Dean, 1907; Member of General Synod, 1907; Diocesan Representative of Glebes; Director of Irish Land Finance Co., Limt.; Director of Portarlington Electric Lighting and Power Co., Ltd. *Address:* Portarlington.

COLE, Rev. Robert Eden George, M.A., J.P.; Canon and Prebendary of Lincoln Cathedral; *e. s.* of Lieut.-Col. Robert Cole of the 85th and 48th Regts., and of Mary Eden, *d.* of Col. G. R. P. Jarvis of Doddington Hall, Co. Lincoln; *m.* 1858, Frances Elizabeth Christiana, *e. d.* of James Dawn, 2nd Dragoon Guards. *Educ.:* Rugby; University College, Oxford. Rector of Doddington, Lincoln, 1861-1909; Chairman of Branston District Council since 1898. *Publications:* History of Doddington, Glossary of South - West Lincolnshire, etc. *Address:* 3 Pottergate, Lincoln.

(*Died 9 Jan. 1921.*)

COLE, Robert Henry, M.D. (Lond.); F.R.C.P. (Lond.); Physician for Mental Diseases to St. Mary's Hospital; Lecturer on Mental Diseases at St. Mary's Hospital Medical School and at Bethlem Royal Hospital; Examiner. in Mental Diseases and Psychology, University of London; Home Office Visitor to the State Inebriate Reformatory, Aylesbury; Visitor to the Institutions for the Mentally Deficient, Middlesex; *b.* 13 Nov. 1866; *e. s.* of late R. C. Cole of Ealing; *m.* Mabel Effie, *e. d.* of late N. Randle of Bombay, and widow of A. T. White, M.R.C.S., of Egypt; one *s.* one *d. Educ.:*

Ealing; St. Mary's Hospital. Was a clerk in the India Office before entering the medical profession; Chairman of the Parliamentary Committee of the Medico - Psychological Association; Vice - President of the Section of Psychiatry of the Royal Society of Medicine; late Resident Physician Moorcroft Asylum. *Publication:* Mental Diseases, a Textbook of Psychiatry. *Address:* 25 Upper Berkeley Street, Portman Square, W.1. *T.:* Paddington 4270. *M.:* XA 1849. *Club:* Oriental.

(*Died 10 Aug. 1926.*)

COLE, Robert Langton, F.R.I.B.A.; Architect to Royal Albert Hall since 1907; National Hospital, Queen Square, since 1892; Metropolitan Association for Improving Dwellings, since 1893; *b.* 11 Jan. 1858; *s.* of John Jenkins Cole (Architect to the Stock Exchange) and Josephine, *d.* of Joseph Smith of Kempsey, Worcester; *m.* 1885, Edith (*d.* 1925), *d.* of John Shepherd; five *d. Educ.:* City of London School under Dr. E. A. Abbott. Apprenticed to J. J. Cole and entered his office, 1874; partnership E. Perrott, 1888-90; Architect to the Stock Exchange, 1890-1925; Works: Convalescent Home, Finchley, 1897; Acland Home, Oxford, 1904 - 26; Royal Albert Hall alterations; Warneford Place, Wilts, 1904; S. Ex-Rifle Club, 1904; Radley College extensions, 1909; Dartford Hospital, 1904; alterations and extensions to Stock Exchange, 1893-1925; 26 Austin Friars, 1901; residences in Sutton, Dorking, Sherborne, Oxford, etc.; factory extensions for Stafford, Allen & Co.; Rubber Exchange, 1924 and 1927. *Publications:* Reviews on Architecture and Engineering for Stationer's Almanac, 1893-95; Articles in R.I.B.A. Journal on Hospital Construction. *Recreation:* rifle shooting; member N.R.A. *Address:* Loughrigg, Sutton, Surrey; Abbey House, S.W. *T.:* Victoria 6678.

(*Died 27 May 1928.*)

COLEMAN, Lieut.-Colonel George Burdett, D.S.O. 1917; Royal Army Service Corps; *b.* Hampstead; *s.* of late F. W. S. Coleman of Bitteswell Hall, Leicestershire; *m.* 1908, Claire, *d.* of E. Donajowski, London; one *s. Educ.:* Tutor. Through South African War with Scottish Horse and 3rd Batt. King's Own Royal Lancaster Regt. 1899 - 1902 (Queen's and King's medals); appointed to Royal Garrison Regt. 1902; transferred to Royal Army Service Corps, 1906; Adjutant of Territorial Royal Army Service Corps, 1912-14; Instructor and Adjutant at Royal Army Service Corps Training Establishment, Aldershot, 1914-15; D.A.Q.M.G. of an Infantry Division of New Army, and proceeded to France, 1915; A.Q.M.G. of an Army Corps, 1917 (D.S.O.); Mesopotamian Campaign, 1919-21; Bronze Medal of the Order of St. John of Jerusalem; Bt. Lt.-Col. 1918; 1914-15 Star; L'Ordre de la Couronne (Officier) and Croix de Guerre (Belgian): Croix de Guerre (avec palme) (French). *Recreations:* riding and gardening. *Club:* Army and Navy.

(*Died 3 July 1923.*)

COLENBRANDER, Col. Johann William, C.B., 1902; *b.* Pinetown, Natal, 1859; of Dutch extraction; *m.* 1st, Maria (*d.* 1901), 2nd *d.* of John Mullins; 2nd, 1902, Yvonne Winifred (*d.* 1904), *y. d.* of Capt. Loftus Nunn, late 99th Lanark Rgt.; 3rd, Kathleen, 2nd *d.* of James Gloster of Clonmelan, Co. Kerry. Interpreter to Matabele Envoys in England, 1889; has seen service with Natal Guides and in thick of battle of Enyamadhloon; one of the best Zulu linguists in South Africa; friend of Lo Bengula; accompanied his envoys to England, 1890; held several responsible positions under Chartered Co. 1895; selected by Cecil Rhodes to remain with Lo Bengula while Pioneer Force of Chartered Company passed through Matabeleland; organised and officered

213

"Colenbrander's Boys," 1896; raised and took command of Kitchener's Fighting Scouts in 1901 (despatches, C.B.). *Address:* Box 123, Buluwayo, Rhodesia, South Africa.
(*Died 8 Feb. 1918.*)

COLERIDGE, 2nd Baron (cr. 1873), **Bernard John Seymour Coleridge,** Judge of High Court of Justice (King's Bench Division), 1907 - 23; Commissioner of Assize, Midland Circuit, 1907 - 8; *b.* 1851; *S.* father, 1894; *m.* Mary, *e. d.* of late John F. Mackarness, D.D. Bishop of Oxford, 1876; one *s.* one *d. Educ:* Eton; Trin. Coll., Oxford (Hon. Fellow). K.C. 1892; Bencher of Middle Temple, 1894; Treasurer, 1919; J.P. and Chairman Devon Quarter Sessions; M.P. (G.L.) Sheffield (Attercliffe), 1885-94; Chairman of the Coal Conciliation Board of the Federated Trades, 1912-18; Fellow of the Royal Society of Literature, 1916. *Publications:* The Story of a Devonshire House, 1905; This for Remembrance, 1925. *Heir: s.* Hon. Geoffrey D. Coleridge. *Address:* The Chanter's House, Ottery St. Mary, Devon. *T.:* Ottery St. Mary 5. *Club:* Athenæum. (*Died 4 Sept. 1927.*)

COLERIDGE, Christabel Rose, Editor of Friendly Leaves; novelist; *b.* Chelsea, 1843; *d.* of Rev. Derwent Coleridge. *Publications:* Lady Betty, 1869; Hanbury Mills, 1872; Hugh Crichton's Romance, 1873; The Face of Carlyon, and other stories, 1875; The Constant Prince, 1878; Kingsworth, 1881; An English Squire, 1881; The Girls of Flaxby,1882; A Near Relation, 1886; A Plunge into Troubled Waters, 1888; Waynflete, 1893; The Tender Mercies of the Good, 1895; The Main Chance, 1897; The Thought Rope, 1898; Tricks and Trials, 1899; The Winds of Cathrigg, 1901; Charlotte Mary Yonge, 1903; Miss Brent of Mead: Miss Lucy. *Address:* Cheyne, Torquay. (*Died 14 Nov. 1921.*)

COLERIDGE, Ernest Hartley; *b.* 8 Dec. 1846; *s.* of Rev. Derwent Coleridge, first Principal St. Mark's College, Chelsea, and Mary Simpson, *d.* of John Drake Pridham, Plymouth, banker; *m.* 1876, Sarah Mary (*d.* 1917), *d.* of William Bradford, Newton Abbot; two *s.* two *d. Educ.:* Sherborne School, 1862-66; Balliol College, Oxford, 1866-70; M.A.; Hon. Fellow, Royal Society of Literature; Tutor, 1872-93; secretary to the Lord Chief Justice of England, Jan. to June. 1894. *Publications:* edited Letters of Samuel Taylor Coleridge, 2 vols., 1895; edited Anima Poetae, selections from unpublished notebooks of Samuel Taylor Coleridge, 1895; edited Poetical Works of Lord Byron, vols. i. ii. iii. iv. v. vi. vii., 1898-1903; Life and Correspondence of John Duke, Lord Coleridge, 2 vols., 1904; Poetical Works of Lord Byron, 1905; Christabel, by S. T. Coleridge, 1907; Poems of Coleridge, illustrated by G. Metcalfe, 1907; Poets' Country, ed. by A. Lang; Complete Poetical Works of S. T. Coleridge, 1912. *Address:* Rickford's Hill, Aylesbury. (*Died 19 Feb. 1920.*)

COLERIDGE, Lt.-Col. Hugh Fortescue, C.B.E. 1919; D.S.O. 1900; late commdg. 1st Batt. Loyal North Lancs Regt.; *s.* of Rev. F. J. Coleridge of Cadbury, Thorverton; *b.* 11 Jan. 1859; *m.* 1906, Kathleen, *e. d.* of late Rear-Adm. J. H. Bainbridge and of Mrs. Bainbridge of Elfordleigh, Plympton; five *s.* Entered army, 1879; Captain, 1887; Major, 1899; served South Africa, 1899-1902 (despatches, Queen's medal 4 clasps, King's medal 2 clasps); European War, 1914-18; J.P. Devon. *Address:* Langstone, Tavistock. (*Died 17 April 1928.*)

COLES, Charles, Pasha, C.M.G. 1900; Director-General of Egyptian Prisons, 1897-1915; *b.* 17 Nov. 1853; *s.* of late Maj.-Gen. Gordon Coles of Bath; *m.* 1881, Mary Emma Isabelle, *d.* of late Crewe Alston, of Odell, Beds; two *s.* two *d.,* India Police Dept., 1873; lent to Egyptian Government, 1883; Deputy Inspector-General

214

Police, 1884. *Publication:* Recollections and Reflections, 1919; Occupational Franchise, 1922; Indian Principalities and other Problems, 1922. *Clubs:* County,Taunton; British, Biarritz.
(*Died 12 Nov. 1926.*)

COLES, John, J.P.; Chairman, Clerical, Medical, and General Life Assurance Society, *Address:* 4 Kensington Park Gardens. W.11 *T. :* Park 406. (*Died 18 Oct. 1919.*)

COLEY, Frederic Collins, M.D., M.R.C.S., J.P.; Visiting Physician to the Sanatorium at Barrasford; Physician to the Northern Counties Hospital for Diseases of the Chest; Consulting Physician to the Hospital for Sick Children, Newcastle. *Educ.:* Guy's Hospital. *Publications:* The Turkish Bath: its History and Uses; Article, published in English Review for March 1927, on Trade Unionism, Old and New. *Address:* 21 Eldon Square, Newcastle. *T. :* 2066. *M. :* X 7737.
(*Died 13 Dec. 1928.*)

COLLARD, Allan Ovenden, F.R.I.B.A.; *b.* 24 Jan. 1861; 6th *s.* of John Collard, Herne Bay; *m.* 1892, Lilian Clara Brockelbank; one *s.* two *d. Educ.:* Rock House School, Ramsgate; Queen Elizabeth's Grammar School, Faversham. Articled pupil to Thomas Blashill, F.R.I.B.A., 1878; assistant to Geo. Vulliamy, F.R.I.B.A., Metropolitan Board of Works, 1882; private practice, 1887; Architect to Earl's Court Exhibition, 1894-1925; past Chairman, Vice-President, and Hon. Secretary of the Association of Men of Kent and Kentish Men; Officer in Metropolitan Special Constabulary, 1914-21; Member of Selection Board, The Treasury, Whitehall; Member of Kent Migration Committee. *Publications:* The Oyster and Dredgers of Whitstable. *Address:* 1 Rutland Road, Hammersmith, W.6. *T. :* Riverside 2466. (*Died 1 July 1928.*)

COLLARD, Sir George, Kt.; cr. 1903; *b.* 3 July 1840; *s.* of G. Plomer Collard of Canterbury, H.E.I.C.S.; *m.* 1874, Ann (*d.* 1905), *d.* of Thomas Ash. Has been two times Mayor of Canterbury. *Address:* The Gables, Barton Fields, Canterbury. (*Died 19 June 1921.*)

COLLCUTT, Thomas Edward, F.R.I.B.A.; *b.* 16 March 1840; widower; one *s.* two *d. Educ.:* Oxford Diocesan School, Cowley. Articled to R. W. Armstrong, London; afterwards with G. E. Street, R.A., as assistant; President of Royal Institute of British Architects, 1906-8; Hon. Member of Société Centrale d'Architecture de Belgique; Corresponding Member of the Société des Artistes Français; Grand Prix for Architecture, Paris Exhibition, 1889; King's Gold Medal of the Royal Institute of British Architects, 1902; Member of the British Legion. *Professional work:* Architect of Wakefield Town Hall, the Imperial Institute, Savoy Hotel, Lloyd's Registry, etc. *Publication:* The Future of London. *Recreation:* honorary work. *Address:* Totteridge, Herts. *Club:* Arts. (*Died 7 Oct. 1924.*)

COLLES, Ramsay, J.P., Dublin, Author, F.R.Hist.S.; *b.* Gyah, India, 1862; *s.* of late Richard Colles, C.E., India Civil Service; *m.* Annie, *e. d.* Rev. P. F. Sweeny, M.A., Rector of Annascaul, Co. Kerry; one *s. Educ.:* Bective College and Wesley College, Dublin; private tutors. Proprietor and Editor for four years of Irish Figaro; founded and edited Irish Masonry Illustrated; editor Chic, 1904; Madame, 1905-11. *Publications:* A Forgotten Poet: Ebenezer Jones; A Study of Swinburne: Nature as Interpreted in Poems of George Meredith; Edgar Saltus: Publicist: In Castle and Court House, 1911; History of Ulster, 1914; edited, with Introductions, the Poetical Works of Beddoes, Darley, Hartley Coleridge. Member Royal Irish Academy; F.R.S.A., Ireland. *Address:* c/o Blighty, 40

Fleet Street, E.C.4. *Club:* Conservative, Dublin. *(Died 1919.)*

COLLES, William Morris, B.A., F.R.G.S., F.G.S.; *o. s.* of late Rev. William Morris Colles, D.D., S.T.P., Vicar of Melton Mowbray. *Educ.:* Oakham; Emmanuel College, Cambridge. Barrister Inner Temple, 1880; Founder and Managing Director of Authors' Syndicate, 1890; member of Council, Society of Authors, 1890, and of Copyright Association. *Publications:* Literature and the Pension List; The State's Eminent Domain; Playright and Copyright in all Countries (part author); Success in Literature (part author). *Recreations:* golf, fishing. *Address:* 8-7 Southampton Street, Strand, W.C.2. *T.A.:* Another, Rand, London. *T.:* Gerrard 44. *Clubs:* Royal Societies, Savage. *(Died 11 Oct. 1926.)*

COLLETTE, Charles; *b.* London, 29 July 1842; *m.* Blanche Wilton, sister of Lady Bancroft. Served with 3rd Dragoon Guards, 1861-68; first appearance on the stage at Prince of Wales Theatre under the Bancrofts, 1868; has also been an entertainer, and appeared at music halls. *Club:* Savage. *(Died 10 Feb. 1924.)*

COLLIER, Frederick Wm., I.S.O. 1907; retired; *b.* 6 March 1851; *s.* of Henry Collier, Abingdon, Berks, and Georgetown, Br. Guiana; *m.* 1st, 1884, Susan Georgina (d. 1913), 2nd *d.* of late Geo. Fetherstonhaugh, Westmeath, Ireland; three *s.*: 2nd, 1915, Marion Emily, 4th *d.* of the same. *Educ.:* Richmond House School, Reading. Entered Service of Govt., British Guiana, 1869; served in Govt. Secretariat as clerk, Assist. Govt. Secy., Secy. Quarantine Board; Postmaster-General, 1888; established P.O. Savings Banks and considerably extended postal and electrical services in Colony; served also as Comptroller of Customs and Official Member of Legislature. *Recreation:* gardening. *Address:* 457 Lansdowne Avenue, Westmount, Prov. Quebec, Canada. *T.:* 0139 Westmount. *(Died 27 Feb. 1925.)*

COLLIER, Rev. Samuel Francis; Superintendent of Manchester and Salford Wesleyan Mission since 1886; *b.* Runcorn, 3 Oct. 1855; *e. s.* of Samuel and Mary Collier, of Runcorn; *m.* Ettie Collin, of Manchester; four *s. Educ.:* Bickerton House School, Southport. Entered Wesleyan Ministry, 1877; Didsbury College, 1877-81; Kent and London Circuits, 1881-85; began ministry in Manchester, 1885; inaugurated the first of the great Wesleyan City Missions, and still in charge of twelve centres of evangelistic and social work; organised a system of rescue, relief, and preventive work; extended property of Mission to estimated value of £300,000; elected member of Wesleyan Methodist "Legal Hundred," 1902; British Representative to the Canadian Conference, 1906; British Representative to Australian Methodist Church, 1920; President of the Wesleyan Methodist Conference for 1913-14. *Address:* The Olives, Anson Road, Victoria Park, Manchester. *T.:* Rusholme 149, Manchester. *(Died 2 June 1921.)*

COLLINGRIDGE, William, M.A., M.D., LL.M., D.P.H. Camb.; M.R.C.S.: Barrister-at-law; Gray's Inn; J.P.; *b.* Islington, 1854; *s.* of late W. H. Collingridge, City Press; *m.* Ada Thornsett. *Educ.:* Clewer House, Windsor; Christ's College, Cambridge; St. Bartholomew's Hospital. Formerly Examiner in State Medicine, University of Cambridge; Examiner State Medicine, London University; Milroy Lecturer Royal College of Physicians, 1897; served as Volunteer Surgeon in Servian Army during Turko-Servian War, 1875; private practice two years; Medical Officer of Health, Port of London, 1880-1901; Medical Officer of Health, City of London, 1901-18; Delegate University of Cambridge at International Congress of Hygiene, Paris, 1900; Knight of Grace of the Order of St. John of Jerusalem in England. *Publications:* Hæmorrhage in Typhoid Fever; Scurvy in Mercantile Marine; Water and Filtration; Quarantine in England; Plague Prevention; Sanitary Reports, Port of London; Health Reports, City of London. *Recreations:* 10 years Honourable Artillery Co., F Battery; 4 years Cambridge Univ. Rifle Corps; 7 years in Volunteer Medical Staff Corps; 8 years in command of Militia Medical Staff Corps (Lieut.-Col.); Hon. Colonel R.A.M.C. (Vol.) Woolwich Division; Lieut.-Col. Territorial Force; M.O i/c Auxiliary Military Hospital 122 Kent 1914-1919. *Address:* Yarrell Croft, Pennington, Lymington, Hants. *(Died 29 April 1927.)*

COLLINGS, Rt. Hon. Jesse, P.C.; M.P. (U.) Bordesley (Birmingham), 1886; retired, 1918; *b.* 1881; *s.* of Thomas Collings, Littleham-cum-Exmouth, Devon; *m.* Emily, *d.* of Edward Oxenbould, 1859; one *d.* Was Head of Collings and Wallis, merchants, Birmingham; retired 1879; Mayor of Birmingham, 1878-79; M.P. Ipswich, 1880-86; Parliamentary Secretary Local Government Board, 1886; magistrate for Birmingham; founder and president of the Rural League: was chairman Free Libraries Commission, and governor of King Edward's Grammar School; one of the founders and Hon. Sec. of the National Education League; and one of the founders of the Devon and Exeter Boys Industrial School; moved and carried the Small Holdings Amendment to the address which caused the resignation of Lord Salisbury's Government, Jan. 1886; Under-Secretary of State for Home Office, 1895-1902. *Publications:* Land Reform; The Colonization of Rural Britain, 1914; The Great War: its Lessons and its Warnings. *Address:* Edgbaston, Birmingham. *(Died 20 Nov. 1920.)*

COLLINGWOOD, George Trevor, C.B. 1919; M.V.O. 1910; L.R.C.P. Lond., M.R.C.S. Eng., 1886; Surgeon Rear-Admiral, retired; *b.* 22 Sep. 1863. *Educ.:* London Hospital. Entered Navy, 1887; Surgeon of Widgeon; served in three expeditions on west coast of Africa, Gambia River, 1894 (despatches); Benin River, 1894; Brass River, 1895 (landed as senior medical officer in charge), (general Africa medal and three clasps); served at Dardanelles in Naval Hospital Ship Soudan, 1915; Fellow of the Society of Tropical Medicine and Hygiene; awarded Sir Gilbert Blane Gold Medal, 1909. *Publications:* papers on The Mosquito and Naval Recruits. *(Died 2 Sept. 1922.)*

COLLINGWOOD, Sir William, K.B.E., *cr.* 1917; J.P., M.I.C.E.; Managing Director, The Vulcan Foundry, Limited, since 1892; *b.* London, 18 Aug. 1855; *e. s.* of late George Collingwood, H.E.I.C. Home Establishment; *m.* 1887, Maria Elizabeth, *d.* of Rev. Gerald Thomson Lermit, LL.D.; two *s.* three *d. Educ.:* Dedham Grammar School. District Locomotive Superintendent East Indian Railway, 1880-92; Member Lancashire County Council, 1911-13; Member Engineering Standards Committee; President Manchester Engineering Employers' Federation, 1913; Chairman Manchester and District Armament Output Committee, 1914-18. *Address:* Dedham Grove, nr. Colchester. *T.A.:* Collingwood, Dedham. *T.:* Dedham 4. *M.:* YF 9941; NO 7407; PU 7968. *Clubs:* St. Stephen's, Constitutional. *(Died 2 Nov. 1928.)*

COLLINS, Arthur Ernest, C.M.G. 1911; *b.* 11 June 1871; 7th *s.* of late Samuel Collins, Salisbury; unmarried. *Educ.:* City of London School; Trinity College, Cambridge (Scholar). First Class Classical Tripos, 1893; B.A. 1893; M.A. 1899; clerk, Colonial Office, 1894: Private Secretary to Sir E. Wingfield, Permanent Under-Secretary of State, 1897; Assistant Private Secretary to Mr. Chamberlain, Secretary of State, 1898; 1st Class Clerk, 1898; Principal Clerk, 1907;

COLLIER, James. See page xvii.

Assistant Secretary, 1920; Secretary to Straits Settlements Currency Committee, 1902-3; Head of West Indian Department, 1907-9; Eastern Department, 1909-19; Far Eastern Department, 1920; Member of West African Currency Board in London. *Publications:* Joint Editor of Colonial Office List since 1898. *Recreations:* music, walking, billiards. *Address:* Colonial Office, S.W. (*Died 5 Feb. 1926.*)

COLLINS, Charles, A.R.C.A. *Address:* 20 Horsham Road, Dorking.
(*Died 28 Sept. 1921.*)

COLLINS, Hon. George Thomas, C.M.G. 1919; *b.* 10 May 1839; *s.* of William and Martha Matilda Collins; *m.* Ursula Flora, *d.* of late Captain Robert M'Eachern; three *s.* four *d. Educ.:* Launceston Church Grammar School. Barrister, etc.; Chief Secretary and Minister of Agriculture, Tasmania, 1899-1903; Minister of Defence prior to Federation, 1899-1903; Colonel, V.D. (reserve); late Commanding Officer Launceston Artillery, and late Senior Commanding Officer, Northern Division of Tasmania; for over thirty-five years Chairman Launceston General Hospital Board of Management; President of Central Board of Health, 1900-3; Member for Tamar, 1895-1919; first Chairman Technical School Board, Launceston; member of the firm of Douglas & Collins, barristers and solicitors, Launceston; Chairman Northern Division, Tasmania Branch British Red Cross Society, 1914-23. *Recreations:* yachting, bowling, music. *Address:* Ila House, Launceston, Tasmania. *T.:* No. 11. *Clubs:* Tasmanian, Hobart; Launceston, Launceston.
(*Died 25 Aug. 1926.*)

COLLINS, Michael, M.P. (Sinn Fein) South Division, Co. Cork, since Dec. 1918.
(*Died 22 Aug. 1922.*)

COLLINS, Rt. Rev. Richard, R.C. Bishop of Hexham and Newcastle; *b.* Newbury, Berks, 1857. *Educ.:* St. Cuthbert's College, Ushaw. Priest at Wolsingham, Co. Durham; St. Andrew's, Newcastle-on-Tyne; Canon of St. Mary's Cathedral, Newcastle-on-Tyne. *Address:* St. Mary's Cathedral, Newcastle-on-Tyne. (*Died 9 Feb. 1924.*)

COLLINS, Col. Robert Joseph, C.M.G. 1911; I.S.O. 1909; V.D. 1902; J.P.; *b.* Cavan, County Cavan, Ireland, 28 July 1848; *s.* of late Captain Robert Collins, New Zealand Militia, formerly 57th Regt.; *m.* Annie, *d.* of Richard and Eleanor Cock of New Plymouth, N.Z.; three *s.* one *d. Educ.:* Ireland; India; New Zealand. Served in Taranaki Volunteer Militia, 1863-65; joined New Zealand Government service as clerk at New Plymouth, 1865; Sub-storekeeper Public Works, 1867; transferred to Store Audit, Wellington, 1877; clerk in the Treasury Department, 1878; First Clerk, Paymaster-General's Branch, 1879; took over charge of combined offices of Pay and Revenue as Clerk-in-Charge, 1885; Accountant to the Treasury, 1890; Assistant Secretary, 1903; Secretary to the Treasury, Receiver-General, and Paymaster-General, 1906; Controller and Auditor-General of New Zealand, 1910-21; finance member of Council of Defence, 1906; Member War Pensions Board, New Zealand, 1916; officer commanding 1st Batt. Wellington Rifles, 1898; Lt.-Col. New Zealand Militia, for services rendered in connection with the enrolment and training of the contingents sent to South Africa from Wellington, 1902; Colonel, 1907, on retirement from command of Wellington Rifle Battalion after thirty-four years' service; A.D.C. to Governor-General of N.Z., 1911-21; has been actively identified with rifle-shooting in the Dominion since 1867; elected to Council of N.Z. Rifle Association, 1879; Statistical Officer, 1886; Chief Executive Officer of Dominion Rifle Association, 1904-21, now President National Rifle Association of New Zealand; had command of the team sent to the Commonwealth meeting at Sydney in 1901, and

216

Commandant of the New Zealand Rifle team to Bisley in 1904 (winners of the Kolapore Cup); Colonial medal for long service, 1893; voluntarily retired after being over fifty-six years in the New Zealand public service. *Recreations:* bowling and shooting. *Address:* Collina, Park Terrace, Wellington, N.Z. *Club:* Wellington, Wellington, N.Z. (*Died 1 Dec. 1924.*)

COLLINS, Sir Robert Muirhead, Kt., *cr.* 1919; C.M.G. 1904, Official Secretary for Commonwealth of Australia to 1918; retired Lieutenant-Commander R.N., and retired Captain Australian Naval Forces; Secretary of the Department of Defence, Commonwealth of Australia, 1900-6; *b.* 20 Sep. 1852; *s.* of Charles H. Collins, Chew Magna, Somerset; *m.* 1886; Elizabeth, *d.* of Samuel Brush, Pastoralist, Australia; one *s. Educ.:* Taunton; H.M.S. Britannia. Entered Royal Navy, 1866; Lt. 1876; retired, 1877; engaged by Government of Victoria for employment in Victorian Naval Forces; sent to England to assist in bringing out gunboats, and took command of gunboat Albert for voyage to Australia; Commander, 1884; Secretary for Defence for Victoria, 1886, and placed on retired list with rank of Captain; Secretary for Defence Commonwealth of Australia on establishment of that Government temporarily represented the Commonwealth of Australia in London, 1906-10, when he was appointed official Secretary in Great Britain of Commonwealth of Australia; acted Member of Royal Commission on Shipping Rings; Delegate for the Commonwealth Government at International Conference Life-Saving at Sea, London, 1913. *Recreations:* tennis, shooting. *Address:* 10 Sydney Place, Bath.
(*Died 19 April 1927.*)

COLLINS, Sir Stephen, Kt., *cr.* 1913; M.P. (L.) Kennington Division Lambeth, 1906-1918; J.P. County of London; *b.* 9 Oct. 1847; *s.* of William Collins of Swanage, Dorset; *m.* 1st, 1863, Frances Ann Webber (*decd.*), 2nd, 1901, Jane, *d.* of William Russell of Marsworth, Herts. *Educ.:* Swanage. Was a County Councillor for Kennington Division of Lambeth; has been a member of Wandsworth District Board, and afterwards Alderman of Lambeth; a Congregationalist and a life abstainer; a member of Committee of the National Temperance League, a Good Templar and member of the Rechabite Order, and greatly interested in the Band of Hope movement and the cause of temperance generally. *Recreations:* reading and walking. *Address:* Elm House, Tring, Herts. *Club:* National Liberal.
(*Died 12 Mar. 1925.*)

COLLINS, Most Rev. Thomas Gibson George, D.D.; Bishop of Meath since 1926; *b.* Dublin, 2nd April 1873; *e. s.* of Rev. T. R. S. Collins, B.D.; *m.* 1920, Kathleen Lily Bell, *d.* of John Hollwey, Cabinteely House, Co. Dublin; two *s. Educ.:* Rathmines School; Trinity College, Dublin. Ordained for Curacy of Maralin, 1896; Rector of Rathfriland and Ballyrony, 1902; Rector of Warrenpoint, 1904; Rector of S. James' Parish, Belfast, 1910; Vicar of Belfast and Dean of S. Anne's Cathedral, 1919. *Recreations:* golf and motoring. *Address:* Bishopscourt, Navan, Co. Meath. *T.:* Navan 46. *M.:* IR 1050. *Clubs:* Ulster, Belfast; University, Dublin. (*Died 3 July 1927.*)

COLLINSON, Alfred Howe, C.B.E. 1917; Officer Legion of Honour, 1919; M.Inst.C.E.; late Director-General of Inspection of Munitions of War; *b.* 1866; *m.* 1891, Isabel Douglas Creighton; two *s.* one *d. Address:* 1 Down Street, W.1; Westfield Lodge, Hayling Island, Hants. *Clubs:* Junior Athenæum; Shanghai, Shanghai; Bengal, Calcutta (*Died 28 June 1927.*)

COLLINSON, Thomas Henry, Mus.B. Oxon; Hon. F.R.C.O.; Organist and Choirmaster of St. Mary's Cathedral, Edinburgh, since 1878; *b.* Alnwick, 24 April 1858; 3rd *s.* of Thos.

Collinson, late Master of Duke of Northumberland's School; *m.* 1891, Annie Wyness Scott; three *s.* one *d.* *Educ.:* Duke's School, Alnwick. Articled Pupil of the late Professor Armes, Organist of Durham Cathedral. Organist of St. Oswald's Parish Church, Durham, 1876; Lecturer in Church Music to the Theological College of Scots Episcopal Church; Conductor of Edinburgh Royal Choral Union, 1883-1913; Conductor of the Edinburgh Amateur Orchestral Society 1900-19; received a Cathedral and Diocesan Presentation of £250 on completion of 25th year of Organistship; also a presentation and address at the Jubilee of the Royal Choral Union in 1908, and an Hon. Director's badge in gold at resignation in 1913. *Publications:* Te Deum in F, Anthems, Responses, etc. *Recreations:* golf and sketching. *Address:* 17 Torphichen Street, Edinburgh.   (*Died 18 Feb. 1928.*)

COLLISON, Ven. William Henry; Archdeacon of Caledonia, British Columbia; Commissary to the Bishop of Caledonia, and C.M.S. Missionary to Nishka, Zimshean, and Haida tribes of Indians, N.W. Coast and Islands, B. Columbia; *b.* 12 Nov. 1847; *s.* of J. and M. Maxwell Collison, Armagh, Ireland; *m.* 1873, Marion M. Goodwin; five *s.* three *d.* *Educ.:* Church of Ireland Normal College; Church Missionary College, Islington. Superintendent of Industrial School, Cork; Missionary to Zimshean Indians, 1873; volunteered as first Missionary to the Haidas of Queen Charlotte's Islands, who were known then as the "Pirates of the North Pacific Coast," being the finest and fiercest of the Coast Indians, 1876; opened the Inland Mission to Gitikshans, 1880; Secretary to the North British Columbia Mission of the Ch. Miss. Society, and Bishop's Commissary, 1893-94. *Publications:* translated Prayers, Hymns, etc. into Zimshean, Haida, and Nishka languages; History of the British Columbian Mission; In the Wake of the War Canoe. *Address:* Kincolith, North-West Coast, British Columbia.
(*Died Jan. 1922.*)

COLLISSON, Rev. William Alexander Houston; *b.* Dublin, 20 May 1865; *s.* of William Houston Collisson and Elizabeth O'Callaghan. *Educ.:* Trinity College, Dublin. Mus. B. 1884; Mus. D. 1890; B.A 1897; M.A. 1911. Licentiate in Music, Trinity Coll. Lond.; Organist and Master of the Choir, St. Patrick's, Trim, 1881; then held appointments at Bray, Rathfarnham, Tallaght, St. George's, Dublin; started Dublin Popular Concerts, 1885; also Belfast and London Popular Concerts; ordained, 1898; Assistant Priest, St. Tudy's, Cornwall, 1899-1901; St. Saviour's, Walton Street, 1901-6; St. Mary's, Seymour Street, N.W., 1907-8; St. Stephen's, E. Twickenham, 1908-10; Christ Church, Chelsea, 1911; All Saints, Twickenham, 1912; St. Alban's, Teddington, 1914; St. Andrew's, West Kensington, W.14, 1916; St. John's, Great Marlborough Street, W., 1919. *Compositions:* Comedy Operas—The Knight of the Road; Strongbow; Midsummer Madness; Cantatas—St. Patrick; The Game of Chess; Samhain; Irish Suite—Rosaleen; Operetta—Noah's Ark; Songs—The Mountains of Mourne, The Pride of Petravore, Are ye right there, Michael? Maguire's Motor-bike, etc. *Publication:* Dr. Collisson in and on Ireland. *Recreation:* singing humorous songs. *Address:* 63 Tregunter Road, S.W.10. *T.:* Kensington 3136.   (*Died 1 Feb. 1920.*)

COLLYER, Ven. Daniel; retired; *b.* 1848; *s.* of John Collyer, Barrister, of Hackford Hall, Norfolk, and Georgina, *d.* of Sir Wm. Johnson of that ilk, 7th Bt.; *m.* Helen Augusta Preston (*d.* 1924). *Educ.:* Rugby; Clare College, Cambridge. Formerly Vicar of Wymondham, Norfolk; Chaplain of Christ Church, Cannes; Archdeacon of Malta, 1903-5. *Address:* Octagon House, Dedham, Essex.   (*Died 25 July 1924.*)

COLLYER, William Robert, I.S.O. 1908; *b.* 11 Jan. 1842; 2nd *s.* of John Collyer of Hackford Hall, Norfolk, and Georgina Frances Amy, *e. d.* of late Sir William Johnston of that ilk, Bt. *Educ.:* Rugby; Caius Coll. Camb. (Scholar, 1861). 2nd Class Classical Tripos, 1865; Assistant Master at Clifton College, 1865-67; called to the Bar, Inner Temple, 1869; went first Norfolk, and afterwards Midland Circuit; Acting Chief-Justice, Sierra Leone, 1879; Acting Puisne Judge, Gold Coast Colony, 1880; Acting Attorney-General, Gold Coast, 1880; Queen's Advocate, Cyprus, 1881; Puisne Judge, Straits Settlements, 1892; Attorney-General, 1903; retired, 1906; J.P. Co. Norfolk. *Address:* Hackford Hall, Norwich.   (*Died 27 Oct. 1928.*)

COLMORE, Thomas Milnes, J.P., Recorder of Warwick since 1882; Deputy-Chairman of Warwickshire Quarter Sessions since 1907; *b.* Sheldon House, Warwickshire, 13 Jan. 1845; *e. s.* of late Thomas Colmore; *m.* 1878, Clara, 2nd *d.* of John Dugdale of 9 Hyde Park Gardens, W. *Educ.:* Rugby School; Brasenose College, Oxford. Barr. 1869; Midland Circuit; Stipendiary Magistrate City of Birmingham, 1888-1905. *Recreations:* hunting, shooting. *Address:* The Warren, Knowle, Warwickshire. *Club:* Windham.
(*Died 25 April 1916.*)

COLQUHOUN, Ven. William. *Educ.:* Trinity College, Dublin (M.A., B.D.). Curate of Desertmartin, 1868-72; Incumbent of Drumanl, 1872-82; Curate of St. James's, Bristol, 1882; Incumbent, Aghadoey, 1883-93; Archdeacon of Derry, 1897; Incumbent of Glendermot, 1898; retired 1914. *Address:* 69 Lansdowne Road. Dublin.   (*Died 1920.*)

COLTHURST, Sir George St. John, 6th Bt., *cr.* 1744; *b.* 1850; *S.* father, 1878; *m.* Edith, *d.* of late Captain (The Royals) J. Morris, Dunkettle, Co. Cork, 1881; two *s.* *Educ.:* Harrow. Late Lieut. 43rd Foot. Owns about 31,300 acres. *Heir:* *s.* George Oliver, late Capt. South Irish Horse, *b.* 1882. *Recreation:* golf. *Address:* Blarney Castle, near Cork. *T.A.:* Blarney. *T.:* Blarney 1. *Clubs:* Carlton, Naval and Military.   (*Died 25 Dec. 1925.*)

COLTON, William Robert, R.A. 1919; A.R.A. 1903; Sculptor; Member of Standing Committee of Advice for Education in Art, Board of Education; Principal Examiner for the Board of Education in modelling and sculpture; *b.* Paris, 1867; *m.* 1902, Mignon, *d.* of George Kroll de Laporte; two *d.* *Educ.:* Paris and London. Commenced a sculptor's career at the age of 20; studied at Lambeth, S. Kensington, and Royal Academy Art Schools; also in Paris; exhibited at Royal Academy Exhibition and at Salon at the age of 22; bought by Chantrey Fund, 1899 and 1903; silver medal and mention honorable, Paris; executed statues of King Edward at King's Lynn, war memorial at Worcester, drinking fountain, Hyde Park, Tangye Memorial, Birmingham, Selous Memorial Natural History Museum, and Royal Artillery war memorial in the Mall, St. James's Park, several statues in India, and Angas Memorial, Adelaide; Professor of Sculpture, Royal Academy, 1907-10, 1911-12; formerly Visitor in Sculpture, Royal College of Art; President Royal Society of British Sculptors. *Address:* 5 St. Mary Abbotts Place, Kensington, W. *T.:* Western 6563. *Clubs:* Royal Academy, Arts.   (*Died 13 Nov. 1921.*)

COLVILE, Lieut.-Gen. Sir Fiennes Middleton, K.C.B., *cr.* 1906; C.B.; retired; *b.* 4 April 1832; *s.* of F. C. A. Colvile and Mary, sister of 1st Baron Leigh; *m.* 1862, Helen (*d.* 1910), *d.* of Major Hugh Stafford Northcote; two *s.* two *d.* *Educ.:* Sandhurst. Joined 43rd L.I. 1850; served Indian Mutiny (medal); New Zealand War, 1863-66 (very severely wounded, Bt. Lt.-Col., C.B., medal); commanded Shrewsbury Regt. District, 1876-81; Welsh Border

217

Brigade, 1886-91 ; Colonel of Oxfordshire and Bucks Light Infantry. *Recreations :* shooting, gardening. *Address :* S. Mildred's, Guildford. *Club :* United Service. (*Died 29 March 1917.*)

COLVILLE, 2nd Viscount (*cr.* 1902) **of Culross, Charles Robert William Colville,** 12th Baron (Scot.), *cr.* 1604 ; 2nd Baron (U.K.) *cr.* 1885; *s.* of 1st Viscount and Hon. Cecile Catherine Mary Carington, *e. d.* of 2nd Lord Carington; *S.* father, 1903; *b.* 26 Apr. 1854; *m.* Ruby, *d.* of late Col. Henry D. Streatfeild, Chiddingstone, Kent, 1885; two *s.* two *d. Educ.:* Harrow. Late Maj. Grenadier Guards; served in Zulu War, 1879 (despatches) ; A.D.C. to Commander-in-Chief, Bombay, 1881-83 ; Military Secretary to Gov.-Gen. of Canada, 1888-92 ; Lt.-Col. Territorial Force Reserve, 1915, attached to Staff of London District Command. *Heir :* The Master of Colville. *Address :* Danegate House, Eridge Green, Sussex. (*Died 25 Mar. 1928.*)

COLVIN, Sir Sidney, Kt., *cr.* 1911 ; M.A. ; D.Litt. Hon. Oxon ; LL.D. Hon. St. Andrews ; Corresponding Member of the Institute of France and the Royal Academy of Belgium ; Hon. Fellow Royal Society of Painter-Etchers ; Vice-Pres. of the Library Assoc. ; Member of Council Hellenic Society, School of Athens, National Trust, National Art Collections Fund ; President Art for Schools Association, Vasari Society ; *b.* Norwood, 18 June 1845 ; 3rd *s.* of Bazett David Colvin [of Crawford, Colvin, & Co., and of The Grove, Little Bealings, Suffolk] and Mary Steuart, *d.* of late William Butterworth Bayley ; *m.* 1903, Frances (*d.* 1924), *d.* of late Cuthbert Fetherstonhaugh, and *widow* of late Rev. A. H. Sitwell. *Educ. :* home, Trinity College, Cambridge (Fellow 1868); Slade Professor of Fine Art, Camb. 1873-85 ; Director, Fitzwilliam Museum, 1876-84 ; Keeper of the Prints and Drawings, British Museum, 1884-1912. *Publications :* numerous contributions, chiefly on history and criticism of Fine Art, to periodical literature, especially Pall Mall Gazette, 1868-73, Fortnightly Review, Portfolio, Cornhill Magazine, Nineteenth Century, Edinburgh Review, Encyclopædia Britannica, Dictionary of National Biography, etc.; Lives of Landor (1881) and Keats (1887) in Morley's English Men of Letters Series ; A Florentine Picture-Chronicle, 1898 ; Early Engraving and Engravers in England, 1906 ; Drawings by Old Masters at Oxford, 1902-8 ; John Keats, His Life and Poetry, etc., 1917 ; Memories and Notes, 1921 ; has edited Selections from Landor in Golden Treasury Series, 1882 ; Letters of Keats in Eversley Series, 1887 ; Edinburgh edition of R. L. Stevenson's works, 1894-97, and Letters of R. L. Stevenson, 1899 and 1911. *Address :* 35 Palace Gardens Terrace, Kensington, W.8. *T. :* Park 4675. *Clubs :* Athenæum, Savile, Burlington Fine Arts. (*Died 11 May 1927.*)

COMBE, Maj.-Gen. Boyce Albert, C.B. 1889 ; Colonel 14th Hussars since 1904 ; *b.* 28 August 1841 ; *m.* 1871, Helen Edith (*d.* 1882), *d.* of Maj.-Gen. L. Barrow, C.B. Entered army, 1860 ; Maj.-Gen. 1896 ; served Abyssinian Campaign (medal) ; Afghan War, 1878-80 (despatches frequently, brevets of Major and Lieut.-Col., medal with four clasps, bronze decoration) ; commanded Sind District, Bombay, 1888-94 ; Cavalry Brigade at Aldershot, 1895-96 ; Curragh District, 1896-99 ; Rawal Pindi District, 1899-1903. *Club :* Naval and Military.
(*Died 3 June 1920.*)

COMBE, Charles, J.P., D.L., Surrey ; *b.* 13 Nov. 1836; *e. s.* of Charles James Fox Combe ; *m.* 1st, 1861, Marianne (*d.* 1900), *o. d.* of Captain Inglis, R.N. ; eighs. six *d.* ; 2nd, 1906, Ethel, widow of A. Cushny, Pains Hill, Cobham, *o. d.* of J. W. Leonard, C.M.G. High Sheriff for Surrey, 1885 ; formerly in Bombay Cavalry; served in Persia and Indian Mutiny. *Address :*
218

Pains Hill, Cobham, Surrey, *Club :* Royal Yacht Squadron, Cowes. (*Died 28 June 1920.*)

COMBE, Harvey Trewythen Brabazon, F.R.G.S., J.P. Sussex and Co. Mayo ; *b.* 1852 ; *e. s.* of late Boyce Harvey Combe and Anne, *o. d.* of late Hercules Sharpe of Oaklands, Sedlescombe, Battle, Sussex, and Ann Mary, *e. d.* of Sir Anthony Brabazon, Bart. of Brabazon Park, Swinford, Co. Mayo ; *m.* 1882, Florence Amy, *d.* of Alexander Lambert, J.P., D.L., of Brook Hill, Claremorris, Co. Mayo ; one *s.* Was Captain and Hon. Major late 3rd Batt. Royal Sussex Regt. *Address :* Oaklands, Sedlescombe, Battle, Sussex. *T.A. :* Sedlescombe. *T. :* Battle, 1 × 6. *Club :* White's.
(*Died 18 Dec. 1923.*)

COMBES, Emile, G.C.V.O. ; *cr.* 1908 ; *b.* Roquecourbe, Tarn, 6 Sept. 1839. Docteur-ès-lettres. docteur en médecine ; Président du Conseil Général de la Charente-Inférieure ; élu Senateur, 1885 ; Vice-Président du Senat, 1893-1895 ; Ministre de l'Instruction publique, des Beaux-Arts et des Cultes, 1891-96 ; President du Conseil des Ministres, 1902-5 ; Ministre d'Etat, 1915-16. *Publication :* Psychology of Thomas Aquinas. *Address :* Rue Claude Bernard, 45 Ve, Paris. (*Died May 1921.*)

COMINS, Ven.. Richard Blundell, D.D. ; Corresponding Secretary of the Melanesian Mission since 1912. *Educ. :* Hatfield Hall, Durham. Ordained 1873 ; Curate of Grantham, 1873-76 ; Missionary, Solomon Islands, 1876-94 ; Head of St. Luke's, Siota, 1894-1901 ; Priest in Charge, Florida, Solomon Islands, 1901-3 : Archdeacon of Northern Melanesia, 1900-10 ; Chaplain of Norfolk Islands, 1904-12. *Address :* 31 Woodside Road, Mt. Eden. Auckland, N.Z.
(*Died 11 Mar. 1919.*)

COMMINS, Andrew, A.M., LL.D. Lond. ; *b.* 1829 ; *s.* of late John Commins ; *m.* Jane, *d.* of J. Neville, 1885. *Educ. :* Queen s Univ. Ireland, A.E. (R.U.I.); London Univ. Barr. Lincoln's Inn, 1860 ; Northern Circuit; M.P. Roscommon (N.), 1880-85; South Div. 1885-92; M.P. (N.) Co. Cork, S.E. 1892-1900. *Address :* The Grange, W. Derby ; Eldon Chambers, Liverpool.
(*Died 7 Jan. 1916.*)

COMPARETTI, Professor Domenico, Hon. D.C.L. Oxon ; Senator of the Kingdom of Italy ; Member of the Academy of the Lincei ; Corresponding Fellow of the British Academy ; *b.* Rome, 1835. *Publications :* Virgilio nel medio evo, 1873, 2nd ed. 1896 ; Text and Translation of the Gothic War of Procopius, 1895 ; The Traditional Poetry of the Finns, English translation, 1898 ; Le Leggi di Gortyna, 1893 ; papers on papyri, inscriptions, etc. *Address :* Via Lamarmora, Florence.

COMPTON-RICKETT, Right Hon. Sir Joseph, Kt., *cr.* 1907 ; P.C. 1911 ; D.L.; Paymaster-General since 1916 ; Charity Commissioner, 1917 ; M.P. (L.) Osgoldcross Division, Yorks, since 1906 ; assumed by Royal licence additional surname of Compton, 1908 ; *b.* London, 13 Feb. 1847 ; *e. s.* of late Joseph Rickett, East Hoathly ; *m.* 1868, Catharine Sarah, *d.* of late Rev. Henry John Gamble of Upper Clapton ; four *s.* four *d. Educ. :* King Edward VI. School, Bath ; privately. M.P. (L.) Scarborough, 1895-1906 ; interested in various commercial undertakings ; retired from the chairmanship of several companies in the coal trade, 1902 ; President of the National Council of Evangelical Free Churches, 1915 ; Chairman, Congregational Union of England and Wales, 1907. *Publications :* The Christ that is to be, a latter-day romance ; The Quickening of Caliban, a modern story of evolution ; Origins and Faith ; and other works ; frequently contributes to current journalism. *Address :* Wingfield, Bournemouth. *T.A. :* Compton-Rickett, Wingfield, Bournemouth.

T: Bournemouth 657. *Clubs*: Reform. National Liberal.   (*Died 30 July 1919.*)

CONCANON, Colonel Henry, O.B.E. ; T.D.; J.P.; Director Oceanic Steam Navigation Co. Ltd.; International Navigation Co. Ltd. ; George Thompson & Co. Ltd., and Liverpool Overhead Railway Company ; Joint-Manager Oceanic Steam Navigation Co. (White Star Line) and International Navigation Co. Member of the Mersey Docks and Harbour Board ; Member of Liverpool Committee, Lloyd's Register of Shipping ; Chairman Liverpool Steamship Owners' Association, 1920-21 ; *b.* 1861 ; *m.* Isabel, *d.* of Joseph Ion Wharton of Soulby. Formerly commanded 7th Batt. King's Liverpool Regiment ; retired with rank of Colonel in the T.F.R. ; has the British Empire, Territorial, Coronation (King Edward), Italian Merit, and Messina decorations. *Address*: Beechside, Allerton, Liverpool. *Clubs*: Junior Constitutional; Exchange, Racquet, Liverpool.   (*Died Sept. 1926.*)

CONGDON, Colonel Arthur Edward Osmond, C.M.G. 1918 ; late commanding 1st Royal Munster Fusiliers, retired ; *s.* of T. O. B. Congdon of Clifton and Glen Ridge, New Jersey, U.S.A. ; *m.* 1905, Ann B. G., *d.* of Rev. I. H. Sutton Moxly, C.F. of the Royal Hospital, Chelsea ; one *s.* one *d.* *Educ.* : Clifton College. Entered Army, 1882 ; served Burmah Expedition, 1885-88 ; S. African War, 1901-2 (Queen's medal and four clasps) ; N.W. Frontier, India, 1908 (medal and clasp ; European War, 1914-18 (despatches twice, C.M.G., Officer Legion of Honour). *Recreations*: fishing, painting. *Address*: 60 Brompton Square, S.W.3. *T.*: Kensington, 761. *Club*: Army and Navy.
   (*Died 17 Sept. 1924.*)

CONGREVE, General Sir Walter Norris, V.C., K.C.B., *cr.* 1917 ; C.B. 1911, D.L. ; M.V.O. 1903 ; Governor and Commander-in-Chief, Malta, since 1924 ; *b.* 20 Nov. 1862 ; *s.* of late Wm. Congreve, J.P., D.L., of Congreve, Staffs., and Burton Hall, Cheshire, and Fanny Emma, *d.* of Lee Porcher Townshend of Wincham Hall, Chester ; *m.* 1890, Celia, *d.* of late Captain C. B. La Touche ; two *s.* *Educ.* : Harrow. Entered Rifle Brigade, 1885 ; Captain, 1893 ; Major, 1901 ; Lt.-Col. 1901 ; Col. 1908 ; Maj.-Gen. 1915 ; Lt.-Gen. 1918 ; General 1922 ; served South Africa, 1899-1902 (wounded, despatches twice, V.C., Queen's medal 7 clasps, King's medal 2 clasps, Brevet Lt. - Col.) ; European War, 1914-18 (despatches, K.C.B., Lt.-Gen.) ; Com. School of Musketry, Hythe ; G.O.C. Trops in Egypt and Palestine ; Commander-in-Chief, Southern Command, 1923-24 ; Commander, Legion of Honour ; 1st Class St. Anne of Russia and Crown of Rumania. *Address*: Chartley Castle, Staffordshire.
   (*Died 28 Feb. 1927.*)

CONLAY, William Lance, C.B.E. 1924 ; Deputy Agent, Federated Malay States Government Agency, E.C.4 ; *b.* 21 June 1869 ; *m.* 1902, Georgiana Maud, *y. d.* of Ralph Skene Archbold, Shortlands, Kent. Malay States Civil Service, 1893-1924 ; British Agent, Trengganu, 1909-10 ; Commissioner of Police, Federated Malay States, 1916-24. *Address*: Red House, Hythe, Kent. *Clubs*: Authors'; Sports.   (*Died 2 Jan. 1927.*)

CONNELL, Rev. Alexander, M.A., B.D. ; Minister of Sefton Park Presbyterian Church, Liverpool, since 1906 ; *b.* Portappin, 1866 ; *m.* 1902, Jessie Murdoch, *d.* of late Sir Henry Robson ; two *s.* one *d.* *Educ.* : Edinburgh University ; Theological College of Free Church of Scotland. Ordained, 1891 ; Convener of Foreign Missions, 1897 ; went mission tour, 1898 ; Minister of Regent Square Church, 1893-1906 ; President National Free Church Council, 1913-14. *Publication*: The Endless Quest, vol. of sermons. *Address*: Sefton Park Church, Liverpool. *T.*: 256 Lark Lane. *Club*: University, Liverpool.   (*Died 1? Nov. 1920.*)

CONNER, Henry Daniel, K.C., M.A., J.P. Co. Cork ; Circuit Court Judge for Dublin City and County since 1924 ; *b.* 1859 ; *o. s.* of Daniel Conner of Manch, Co. Cork, and Patience, *d.* of Henry Longfield of Waterloo, Co. Cork ; *m.* 1st, 1881, Anne (*d.* 1917), *d.* of Rev. Goodwin Purcell of Charlesworth, Derbyshire ; two *s.* one *d.* ; 2nd, 1918, Mary Leonora, *widow* of Richard Dowse. *Educ.* : Stratford-on-Avon ; Trinity College, Dublin (Senior Exhibitioner and Gold Medallist). Barrister, 1882 ; Q.C., 1899 ; Bencher King's Inns, 1910 ; contested (U.) St. Stephen's Green Division of Dublin, 1910. *Publications*: The Fishery Laws of Ireland, 1892 ; 2nd ed. 1907 ; Joint Editor for Ireland of The English and Empire Digest. *Recreations*: shooting, fishing. *Address*: 16 Fitzwilliam Place, Dublin ; Manch House, Ballineen, Co. Cork. *T.*: 1594 Dublin. *Clubs*: University, Dublin ; Cork County.   (*Died 24 July 1925.*)

CONNOLLY, Col. Benjamin Bloomfield, C.B. 1900 ; physician ; *b.* 10 Sep. 1845 ; *s.* of Rev. J. C. Connolly, late chaplain, R.N., and Vicar of Brook, Norwich ; *m.* 1881, Olivia Frances, 2nd *d.* of late William Potts, J.P., of New Court, Athlone ; two *s.* two *d.* *Educ.* : Merchant Taylors' School ; Gonville and Caius College, Cambridge (B.A., M.A., M.D., formerly Tancred Student in Physic) ; Guy's Hospital, London. F.R.C.S.; Colonel, Army Medical Staff ; served Franco - German War, 1870-71 (German war medal) ; against Jowaki Afreedees, 1877-78 (medal and clasp) ; Zulu War (medal) ; Egyptian War, Tel-el-Kebir (medal and clasp, promoted) ; Eastern Soudan, El Teb, Tamai (despatches, clasp, 4th class Osmanieh) ; Nile Expedition, 1884-85, Commander of Camel Bearer Company, and present attack on wounded convoy (despatches twice, clasp) ; promoted Colonel for services rendered during operations in South Africa, 1899-1902 ; European War, A.D.M.S. Sussex. *Recreation*: won 100 yards, Cambridge University, 1866. *Address*: Kingsclere, Harrington Road, Brighton. *Clubs*: New Oxford and Cambridge ; Union, Brighton.
   (*Died 20 June 1924.*)

CONRAD, Joseph, author ; Master in the Merchant Service ; *b.* 6 Dec. 1857, of Polish parentage ; married ; two *s.* *Publications*: Almayer's Folly, 1895 ; An Outcast of the Islands, 1896 ; The Nigger or the Narcissus, 1897 ; Tales of Unrest, 1898 ; Lord Jim, 1900 ; Youth, and other tales, 1902 ; Typhoon, 1903 ; The Inheritors, 1901, and Romance, 1903 (with F. M. Hueffer) ; Nostromo, A tale of the Seaboard, 1904 ; One Day More (Play), 1905 ; The Mirror of the Sea, 1906 ; The Secret Agent, 1907 (dramatised, 1922) ; A Set of Six, 1908 ; Under Western Eyes, 1911 ; Some Reminiscences, 1912 ; Twixt Land and Sea, Tales, 1912 ; Chance, 1914 ; Within the Tides, 1915 ; Victory, 1915 ; The Shadow-Line, 1917 ; The Arrow of Gold, 1919 ; Rescue, 1920 ; Notes on Life and Letters, 1921 ; The Rover, 1923. *Address*: c/o J. B. Pinker & Son, Talbot House, Arundel Street, W.C.2. *Club*: Athenæum.   (*Died 3 Aug. 1924.*)

CONSTABLE, Hon. Lord, Andrew Henderson Briggs Constable, C.B.E. 1920 ; K.C. 1908 ; LL.D. (Edin.), F.R.S.E.: one of the Senators of the College of Justice in Scotland since 1922 ; Member University Court of Edinburgh University ; Assessor to the Lord Rector ; Vice-Chairman, Edinburgh Council of Social Service ; Chairman of Executive, Association for the Preservation of Rural Scotland ; *b.* 3 Mar. 1865 ; *y. s.* of late W. Briggs Constable of Benarty, Fife ; *m.* 1895, Elizabeth, *y. d.* of late James Simpson of Mawcarse, Kinross ; two *s.* *Educ.* : Dollar ; Edinburgh University ; Vans Dunlop Scholar in Political Economy. Advocate, 1889 ; Sheriff of Caithness, etc., 1917-20 ; Adviser to the Scottish Office in connection

with Military Tribunals in Scotland, 1917-18; Sheriff of Argyll, Feb.-May 1920; Dean of the Faculty of Advocates, 1920-22; Solicitor-General for Scotland, Mar.-June 1922; contested (U.) E. Fife, 1900; Kirkcaldy Burghs, 1905; Montrose Burghs, 1908; Blackfriars Glasgow, 1910. *Publications:* Treatise on Provisional Orders, 1900. *Address:* 23 Royal Circus, Edinburgh. *Clubs:* Wellington; New University, Edinburgh
(*Died 4 Nov. 1928.*)

CONYBEARE, Charles Augustus Vansittart, B.A.; Barrister; *b.* Kew, 1 June 1853; *e. s.* of late John Charles Conybeare; *m.* 1896, Florence Annie (died 1916), *e. d.* of Gustave Strauss, 2 West Bolton Gardens, S.W. *Educ.:* Tonbridge; Christ Church, Oxford; 1st class Classical Moderations, 1874; 3rd Litt. Hum. 1876; Lothian Prizeman (English Essay), 1877. M.P. Camborne or N.W. Division of Cornwall, 1885-95; imprisoned for three months in 1889 in Derry Gaol under the Coercion Act, 1887, for assisting the tenantry on the Olphert Estate at Falcarragh, Donegal; member London School Board (Finsbury), 1888-90; member of Geographical Society, Lisbon, 1895. *Publications:* Treatises on Married Women's Property Act, 2nd ed. 1883; the Corrupt and Illegal Practices Acts, 2nd ed. 1892. *Recreations:* boating, cycling. *Address:* Bradbourne House, Bexley, Kent. *Clubs:* National Liberal, Eighty, International Women's Franchise.
(*Died 18 Feb. 1919.*)

CONYBEARE, Charles Frederick Pringle, K.C.; Barrister; *b.* Little Sutton, Middlesex, 19 May 1860; *s.* of Henry Conybeare, the eminent engineer; *g.s.* of Dean William Daniel Conybeare, the geologist; *m.* 1890, Ida, *d.* of Lieut.-Col. P H. Attwood, Canadian Militia; one *s.* two *d. Educ.:* Westminster. Entered merchant service as midshipman, 1875; retired 1880, and went to Canada, where he commenced study of Law in Winnipeg, Manitoba; called to Bar, 1885; removed to Lethbridge, Alberta, and commenced practice on his own account; Crown Prosecutor for Southern Alberta, 1888-1900; Q.C., 1894; on the formation of the Law Society of the North-West Territories in 1897, elected one of the Benchers; Vice-President Alberta Law Society, 1907; President, 1926; Chancellor of the Diocese of Calgary, 1904; D.C.L. Bishop's College, Lennoxville, 1907; University of Alberta, 1908; elected on the Council of Dominion Bar Association, 1914; elected President of the Alberta Moderation League, 1919; re-elected 1923, and led the fight on the plebiscite taken in that year which resulted in a sweeping victory for the Moderationists and the repeal of existing Prohibition legislation. *Publications:* Vahnfried, a poetical romance; Lyrics from the West. *Address:* Riverview, Lethbridge, Alberta. *T.A.:* Lethbridge, Canada. *T.:* 3711 and 2201. (*Died 13 July 1927.*)

CONYBEARE, Frederick Cornwallis; *b.* 1856; 3rd *s.* of John Charles Conybeare and Mary Catharine (Vansittart); *m.* 1st, 1883, Mary Emily Max Müller (*d.* 1886); 2nd, 1888, Jane MacDowell; one *s.* one *d. Educ.:* Tonbridge School; University College, Oxford. Scholar, 1875; Fellow and Praelector, 1881; Hon. Fellow, 1913; M.A. Oxon, 1888; Fellow of the British Academy, 1903; Officier d'Académie, 1906; Hon. Doctor Theologiae, Giessen, 1907; Hon. LL.D. St. Andrews, 1913; Member of the Armenian Academy of Venice. *Publications:* The Ancient Armenian Texts of Aristotle, 1892; Philo about the Contemplative Life, 1895; The Apology and Acts of Apollonius, 1894; Key of Truth, a Manual of the Paulician Church of Armenia, 1898; The Dialogues of Athanasius, etc., 1898; The Story of Ahikar, (with J. Rendel Harris and Mrs. Lewis), 1898, 2nd ed. 1913; The Dreyfus Case, 1898; The Roman Catholic Church in International Politics, 1901; Rituale Armenorum, 1905;
220

Letters and Exercises of the Elizabethan Schoolmaster, John Conybeare, 1905; Old Armenian Texts of Revelation, 1906; Myth, Magic, and Morals, 1909; The Ring of Pope Xystus, 1910; A History of N.T. criticism, 1910; Catalogue of the Armenian MSS. of the British Museum, 1912, of those in Bodleian Library, 1918; English Translations of Philostratus, Life of Apollonius, 1912, ot Heliodorus, Ethiopica and of other Greek Romances; The Historicity of Christ, 1914; History of Russian Dissent, 1921; Old Armenian Liturgies, in Patrologia Orientalis, 1922; contributor to the learned journal of England, America, France, and Germany. *Recreation:* travel. *Address:* University College, Oxford; 21 Trinity Gardens, Folkestone. (*Died 9 Jan. 1924.*)

COOCH, Colonel Charles; M.V.O. 1911; *b.* 1829; *e. s.* of late Charles Cooch of Woodlands, near Ryde; *m.* 1858, Charlotte Hyacinth, *e. d.* of late Lieut.-Col. A. H. Kirwan of Cheltenham. Served Crimea, 1854-56; Town Major in Sebastopol, 1855-56; late Major 62nd Foot; Knight Legion of Honour; 5th Class Medjidie; one of H.M.'s Hon. Corps of Gentlemen-at-Arms since 1877. *Address:* St. James's Palace, S.W.; 1 Cambridge Villas, Cheltenham. *Club:* New, Cheltenham. (*Died 30 April 1917.*)

COOCH BEHAR, Maharaja Bhup Bahadur of, Sir Jitendra; K.C.S.I., *cr.* 1917; *b.* 20 Dec. 1886; *s.* of Maharaja Nripendra and Maharani Sunity Deire (*née* Sen); *S.* brother 1913; *m.* 1913, *d.* of Gaekwar of Baroda; two *s.* two *d. Educ.:* Eton; Imperial Cadet Corps. Area of State is 1307 square miles. The Maharaja is entitled to a salute of 13 guns. *Recreations:* sport, games of all kinds. *Address:* Cooch Behar, Bengal. *Clubs:* Princes', Royal Automobile, Automobile Association, Motor; Calcutta, Orient, Royal Calcutta Turf, Calcutta; etc.
(*Died 20 Dec. 1922.*)

COOK, Albert Stanburrough, M.A., Ph.D., Litt. D., LL.D.; Professor of the English Language and Literature, Yale University, since 1889, Emeritus since 1921; *b.* Montville, New Jersey, U.S.A., 6 Mar. 1853; *s.* of Frederick Weissenfels and Sarah Cook; *m.* 1st, 1886, Emily Chamberlain, of Berkeley, California; 2nd, 1911, Elizabeth Merrill, of Cincinnati.Ohio; one *s.* one *d. Educ.:* Rutgers College, New Brunswick, New Jersey; Göttingen; Leipsic; London (with Henry Sweet); Jena (Ph.D., 1882). Tutor in mathematics, Rutgers College, 1872-73; teacher in Freehold (New Jersey) Institute, 1873-77; Associate in English, Johns Hopkins University, 1879-81; Professor of the English Language and Literature, University of California, 1882-89; President of the Modern Language Association of America, 1897; Founder of the Concordance Society, 1906, and President ever since; Member of the Netherlandish Society of Letters (Leyden); Fellow of the Mediæval Academy of America. *Publications:* Translation of Sievers' Old English Grammar, 1885; edition of the Old English Judith, 1888, 1904; edition of Sidney's Defense of Poesy, 1890; The Art of Poetry, 1892; First Book in Old English, 1894; Glossary of the Old Northumbrian Gospels, 1894; The Artistic Ordering of Life, 1898; Biblical Quotations in Old English Prose Writers, 1898, 1903; edition of Cynewulf's Christ, 1900; Select Translations from Old English Poetry (with C. B. Tinker), 1902; edition of The Dream of the Rood, 1905; The Higher Study of English, 1906; The Authorised Version of the Bible and its Influence, 1910; Concordance to Beowulf, 1911; The Date of the Ruthwell and Bewcastle Crosses, 1912; Some Accounts of the Bewcastle Cross, 1914; A Literary Middle English Reader, 1915; The Historical Background of Chaucer's Knight, 1916; The Last Months of Chaucer's Earliest Patron, 1916; edition of Elene, Phœnix, and Physiologus, 1919; Theodore of Tarsus and Gislenus of Athens, 1923; Beowulfian and Odyssean Voyages, 1926, etc. ; editor of Yale Studies in English (73 volumes). *Recreations:* reading, walking. *Address:* 219 Bishop Street, New Haven, Conn.; Greensboro, Vermont, U.S.A. *T.:* 514. *Clubs:* Phi Beta Kappa, Pioneer. *(Died 1 Sept. 1927.)*

COOK, Arthur Kemball; *b.* 1851 ; 3rd *s.* of S. Kemball Cook ; *m.* 1884, Lucy Frances Richardson ; one *d. Educ.:* Winchester College ; New College, Oxford. Assistant Master of Winchester College, 1875-1911. *Publications:* About Winchester College, 1917 ; a Commentary on the Ring and the Book, 1920. *Address:* Colebrook House, Winchester ; Emerald Bank, Stair, Keswick. *M.:* XU 1298.
(Died 21 Nov. 1928.)

COOK, Sir Edward Tyas, M.A., Kt., *cr.* 1912 ; K.B.E. *cr.* 1917 ; *b.* Brighton, 12 May 1857 ; *y. s.* of late S. Kemball Cook ; *m.* 1884, Emily (*d.* 1903), *d.* of late John Forster Baird, Bowmont Hill, Northumberland. *Educ.:* Winchester ; New Coll. Oxford. President of the Union and Palmerston Clubs, Oxford. Graduated (1st Class Classics), 1880 ; Secretary London Society for Extension of University Teaching, 1882-85 ; contributed to Pall Mall Gazette under Mr. Morley's editorship ; succeeded Mr. (now Lord) Milner as assistant editor to Mr. Stead ; on Mr. Stead's resignation became editor, 1890-1892 ; on sale of paper to Mr. Astor, resigned ; invited by Mr. (Sir G.) Newnes to edit Westminster Gazette ; editor thereof, 1893-1896 ; editor of the Daily News, 1896-1901 ; Fellow of Winchester College, 1903 ; Vice-Chairman, Advisory Council. Victoria and Albert Museum, 1913 ; Joint Director, Official Press Bureau, 1915 ; Deputy President, Victoria League, 1917. *Publications:* Popular Handbook to the National Gallery, 8th edition, 1912 ; Studies in Ruskin, 2nd edition, 1891 ; Popular Handbook to the Tate Gallery, 1898 ; The Rights and Wrongs of the Transvaal War, 4th ed. 1902 ; Popular Handbook to the Greek and Roman Antiquities in the British Museum, 1903 ; editor of Ruskin's Works, 1903-11 ; Memoir of Edmund Garrett, 1909 ; Life of Ruskin, 1911 ; Homes and Haunts of John Ruskin, 1912 ; The Life of Florence Nightingale, 1913 ; Catalogue of Dulwich Picture Gallery, 1914 ; Delane, of the Times, 1915 ; Literary Recreations, 1918. *Address:* Southstoke, Oxon. *Clubs:* Athenæum, National Liberal.
(Died 30 Sept. 1919.)

COOK, Sir Frederick Lucas, 2nd Bt., *cr.* 1886 ; Viscount Monserrate in Portugal ; D.L. ; Lieut. for City of London ; head of Cook, Son and Co., warehousemen, St. Paul's ; *b.* London, 21 Nov. 1844 ; *e. s.* of 1st Bt. and Emily, *d.* of late Robert Lucas, of Lisbon ; *S.* father, 1901 ; *m.* Mary (*d.*1913), *d.* of Richard Payne Cotton, M.D., 1868 ; one *s.* two *d. Educ.:* Harrow. M.P. (C.) Kennington, 1895 - 1906 ; *Recreations:* member of committee Coaching Club, golf, tennis. *Heir:* s. Herbert Frederick. *Address:* Doughty House, Richmond, Surrey ; Monserrate, Cintra, Portugal. *Clubs:* Carlton, Prince's, Queen's, Hurlingham, Ranelagh, Sandown. *(Died 21 May 1920.)*

COOK, Lt. - Col. George Trevor-Roper, D.S.O. 1915 ; 20th Hussars ; *b.* 11 Aug. 1877 ; *s.* of George Ward Cook, of Hoylake ; *m.* 1902, Alice, *y. d.* of A. J. Dorman, J.P., of Nunthorpe, Yorkshire ; one *s.* four *d.* Entered army (3rd Dragoon Guards), 1897 ; Captain, 1900 ; Major, 1911 ; Major, 20th Hussars, 1913 ; Lt.-Col. 1915 ; Adjutant, T.F., 1908-11 ; served S. African War, 1899 - 1902 (Queen's medal, 4 clasps) ; European War, 1914-15 (despatches twice, D.S.O.). *Address:* Greenham, Hoylake, Cheshire. *Club:* Cavalry.
(Died Mar. 1918.)

COOK, Sir Henry, Kt., *cr.* 1904 ; senior partner of the firm of W. & J. Cook, Writers

to the Signet, Edinburgh ; Secretary of the King's Bodyguard for Scotland (Royal Company of Archers) ; *b.* 28 July 1848 ; *e. surv. s.* of late John Cook, W.S., Edinburgh ; *m.* 1879, Margaret (*d.* 1905), *e. d.* of late John Patten, Edinburgh ; three *s.* one *d. Educ.:* Edinburgh Academy ; St. Andrews University, M.A., 1866 ; passed as Writer to the Signet, and partner in the firm of W. & J. Cook, 1871 ; appointed Joint Secretary of the King's Bodyguard for Scotland (Royal Company of Archers), 1879 ; D.L. of the City of Edinburgh ; a Director Royal Bank of Scotland and Scottish Widows' Fund Life Assurance Society. *Recreations:* golf, shooting, fishing. *Address:* 22 Eglinton Crescent, Edinburgh. *Clubs:* Caledonian ; University, Edinburgh. *(Died 9 Mar. 1928.)*

COOK, Ven. Henry Lucas, M.A. ; Archdeacon of Craven since 1913 ; Rector of Skipton 1890-1922 ; Hon. Canon of Bradford ; *s.* of R. Lumley Cook of Hull ; *m.* Eleanor Gertrude, *d.* of Welbury Kendall of Skipton. *Educ.:* King's School, Canterbury ; Brasenose College, Oxford. Curate of All Saints, Bradford, 1877-1881 ; Vicar of St. Mark's, Low Moor, 1881-89. *Recreations:* fond of cricket and tennis. *Address:* Woodlands, Crosshills, Keighley. *T.:* Crosshills 111. *T.A.:* Crosshills. *Club:* Union, Bradford.
(Died 16 May 1928.)

COOK, Maj.-Gen. James, C.B. 1899 ; retired, 1900 ; *b.* 22 Mar. 1844. Entered army (I.S.C.), 1861 ; served North-West Frontier, 1863 (medal with clasp) ; Afghan War, 1878-80 (despatches, brevet of Major, medal with clasp) ; Soudan, 1885 (despatches, brevet of Lieut.-Col., medal with two clasps, Khedive's star). *Address:* 59 St. Mary's Mansions, W.2.
(Died 18 Feb. 1928.)

COOK, Mrs. (Mabel Collins) ; widow ; *b.* Guernsey, 1851 ; *o. c.* of Mortimer Collins ; *m.* 1871, Keningale Cook. *Educ.:* at home, according to her father's special ideas about education. *Publications:* Light on the Path ; The Idyll of the White Lotus ; Through the Gates of Gold ; The Crucible: Our Glorious Future ; many other works on occult subjects. *Address:* Cintra Lawn, Cheltenham.
(Died 31 Mar. 1927.)

COOK, Sir Theodore Andrea, Kt., *cr.* 1916 ; Editor-in-Chief of the Field since 1910 ; *b.* Exmouth, Devonshire, 28 Mar. 1867 ; *s.* of Henry Cook and Jane Elizabeth Robins ; *m.* 1898, Elizabeth Wilhelmina Link. *Educ.:* King Alfred's Grammar School, Wantage ; Carr's School, Exmouth ; Radley (Sewell entrance scholarship, head of the school and captain of football and boats) ; Wadham Coll., Oxford (open classical scholar, 2nd class in Honour Moderations and Classical Greats) ; rowed 3 in Oxford crew of 1889 ; Captain, English Fencing Team, Paris, 1903, and Athens, 1906 ; Member of Board of Trade Committee for the Vienna Exhibition, 1910 ; Editor of St. James's Gazette, 1900 ; joined staff of Daily Telegraph, 1901. *Publications:* Old Touraine ; Rouen ; A History of the English Turf ; An Anthology of Humorous Verse ; Turner's Water - Colours in the National Gallery ; Old Provence ; Eclipse and O'Kelly ; Thomas Doggett, Deceased (Part I.) ; Henley Races ; The Curves of Life ; Twenty-five Great Houses of France ; The Mark of the Beast ; The Art and Science of the Oar ; Leonardo da Vinci, Sculptor ; The Sunlit Hours, an Autobiography, 1926 ; Character and Sportsmanship, 1927 ; contributor to Quarterly Review, Nineteenth Century, etc. *Recreations:* writing on Sport. *Address:* 54 Oakley Street, Chelsea, S.W.3. *Clubs:* Oxford and Cambridge, Savile, Leander. *(Died 16 Sept. 1928.)*

COOK, Thomas Reginald Hague, J.P. ; *s.* of late Thomas Hague Cook, of Hall Croft, Mirfield, Yorks ; *b.* 1866 ; *m.* 1893, Sarah Taylor, *e. d.* of late Sir George Elliot, 2nd Bt. *Clubs:*

221

Boodle's, White's; Royal Yacht Squadron, Cowes. (*Died 7 Aug. 1925.*)

COOK, Rt. Rev. Thomas William, M.A. Oxon; Suffragan Bishop of Lewes since 1926. Archdeacon of Hastings since 1922; *b.* 2 Dec. 1866; *s.* of Thomas Cook, Solicitor, Wellingborough; *m.* 1895, Fanny (*d.* 1927), *d.* of John Best, Aldborough, Yorks; two *d. Educ.*: Lancing College, Sussex; Hertford College, Oxford (Exhibitioner of); Cuddesdon College. Curate of Parish Church, Warrington, 1890-94; Vice-Principal and Assistant-Chaplain, Diocesan Training College, Chester, 1894-95; Second House Master, 1895-1911, Chaplain, 1902-11, Lancing College, Sussex; Vicar of Holy Trinity, Hastings, 1911-26; Rural Dean of Hastings, 1913-22; Examining Chaplain to Bishop of Chichester, 1915; Canon and Prebendary of Bracklesham in Chichester Cathedral, 1917; Proctor in Convocation for Archdeaconries of Lewes and Hastings, 1919; Canon and Prebendary of Wittering in Chichester Cathedral, 1921; Proctor for Diocese of Chichester, 1922. *Recreations:* Capt. of School Football, Cricket, Fives. Victor Ludorum, 1885; O.U.A.F.C., 1886-89; Corinthians F.C. *Address:* The White House. Bexhill. *T.:* Bexhill 163. (*Died 16 Oct. 1928.*)

COOKE, Charles John Bowen, C.B.E. 1918; J.P. and C.C. Cheshire; M.Inst.C.E., M.Inst.M.E.; Major, Engineer and Railway Staff Corps; Chief Mechanical Engineer, London and North Western Railway Company; *b.* Orton Longueville, Huntingdonshire, 11 Jan. 1859; *s.* of late Rev. C. J. R. Cooke, M.A. Exhibitioner, Oriel College, Oxford, and *y. d.* of Capt. T. Bowen of Johnstone, Pembrokeshire; *m.* Annie, *d.* of late W. Smith, Nuneaton; one *s.* four *d. Educ.:* Cheltenham College Preparatory School; King's College School, London; on the Continent. Apprentice and pupil, Crewe Works, under late F. W. Webb, M.Inst.C.E.; on completion of pupilage appointed Assistant Running Superintendent of the Southern Division of the L. & N.W. Rly., afterwards Assistant to Geo. Whale, the Chief Mechanical Engineer. *Publications:* British Locomotives; Locomotive Development; various papers. *Recreations:* golf, yachting, campanology. *Address:* Chester Place, Crewe, Cheshire; St. Mawes, Cornwall. *T.A.:* Bowen Cooke, Crewe. *T.:* Crewe 122. *M.:* M 7655; M 5713. *Club:* St. Stephen's. (*Died 18 Oct. 1920.*)

COOKE, Conrad William, M.Inst., E.E.; Officier de l'Instruction Publique; was head of Whieldon & Cooke, Engineers, Lambeth; *b.* Barnes, Surrey, 23 Dec. 1843; *s.* of late E. W. Cooke, R.A., F.R.S., F.S.A., and Jane, *d.* of late George Loddiges, the botanist; *m.* 1st, 1871, Fanny (*d.* 1906), *d.* of late Rev. R. F. B. Rickards, Vicar of Constantine, Cornwall; five *s.* one *d.*; 2nd, 1912, Sophie Augusta, *d.* of August C. B. Bonnevie, late Chief Advocate of the Norwegian Supreme Court, Christiania, Norway. Pupil in the works of John Penn & Sons, marine engineers, Greenwich; surveyed and laid out the first Isle of Wight Railway; assistant to late Sir Joseph Whitworth, Manchester, 1871; removed to London, 1872; introduced the Gramme Electrical Machine (Dynamo), 1883; installed the signal light on Clock Tower of House of Commons; a pioneer of electricity and incandescent gas lighting; a member of the juries of nearly all the International Exhibitions; with late Silvanus Thompson founded the Gilbert Club, 1889; acted as special Astronomical Correspondent for the Morning Post in the Total Solar Eclipse Expeditions of 1896, Norway; 1900, Algeria; and 1905, Spain. *Publications:* Hot Air Engines, 1873; The Loud Speaking Telephone (Society of Arts), 1897; Electric Illumination, 2 vols. 1882 and 1885; Electrical Industries, 1901; Automata Old and New

(issued by the Sette of Odd Volumes), 1893; contributions to many scientific societies and magazines. *Recreations:* travelling, angling, experimental physics, and collecting of books and instruments, illustration of the history and development of physical and mechanical science. *Address:* The Pines, Langland Gardens, Hampstead, N.W.3. *T.:* Hampstead 7030. *Clubs:* Athenæum, Savage (Trustee), Sette of Odd Volumes, Wigwam (Trustee). (*Died 9 Jan. 1926.*)

COOKE, Isaac, landscape painter; *b.* Warrington, 1846; *m.* 1st, 1873; two *s.* one *d.*; 2nd, 1902. The Liverpool Corporation purchased his water-colour of Passing Showers over Langdale Pikes from Blea Tarn, and in 1884 they purchased an oil painting, Golden Moments; has been twice on the Hanging Committee of the Walker Art Gallery Autumn Exhibitions, and was for 7 years Hon. Treasurer of the Liverpool Water-Colour Society; member of Liverpool Academy, 1884; has exhibited in Royal Academy since 1879, and Royal Institute of Painters in Water-Colours since 1881; a member of the R.B.A., 1896-1915. *Recreations:* Natural History, collections of Entomology, Botany, and Oology, etc.; golf. *Address:* 19 Glebe Road, Wallasey, Cheshire. *Club:* Liverpool Artists'. (*Died 22 April 1922.*)

COOKE, Temple, J.P. for Surrey; Barrister; Recorder of Southampton 1899-1924; *b.* 14 Nov. 1851; *e. s.* of William Major Cooke, Metropolitan Police Magistrate; *m.* Margaretta, *o. d.* of late George Beaufoy, R.N. *Educ.:* Cheltenham Coll. Called to Bar, 1874; Western Circuit; Counsel to Admiralty on circuit, 1889. *Recreations:* all outdoor sports. *Address:* Edmondscote, Frimley, Surrey; 2 Dr. Johnson's Buildings, Temple, E.C. *Clubs:* Reform; Hampshire County. (*Died 13 Oct. 1925.*)

COOKE, William Henry, B.A.; Sec. of the Chamber of Shipping of the United Kingdom and of the General Shipowners' Society, London, 1880-1910; of the Shipowners' Parliamentary Committee, 1893-1910, and of the Advisory Committee to the Board of Trade upon New Lighthouse Works, 1900-10; *b.* 18 Jan. 1848; *y. s.* of late Rev. John Hall Cooke of Gomersal; *m.* 1873, Emily Amelia, *d.* of late D. Davison, of the Woodlands, Maldon, Essex; one *s.* three *d. Educ.:* Royal Grammar School and Dr. Bruce's School, Newcastle-on-Tyne; B.A. University of London, 1866; called to Bar, Middle Temple, 1867; went the Northern Circuit, 1867-71; joint-author with late Sir Wemyss Reid of Briefs and Papers: Sketches of the Bar and the Press by Two Idle Apprentices, 1872. Has contributed largely to newspapers and magazines. Was London Correspondent of the Indian Daily News, Calcutta, 1870-93; and is an original Member of the Institute of Journalists. Has visited Japan, China, India, Australia, New Zealand, Ceylon, West Indies (twice), U.S.A., Canada, N. and S. Africa, S. America, Egypt, Palestine (twice), Syria, Iceland, and nearly every country in Europe. Went round the world in 1914 outwards by Cape of Good Hope to Australia and homewards from New Zealand by Cape Horn. *Recreations:* reading, travel. *Address:* Burnmoor, Sutton, Surrey. *Clubs:* Savile, University of London. (*Died 5 Jan. 1921.*)

COOKE-TAYLOR, Richard Whately, F.S.S., F.R.Hist.S., J.P.; *b.* 1842; *s.* of William Cooke-Taylor, LL.D.; *m.* 1880, Mary, *d.* of John Haslam, J.P. of Bolton; one *s. Educ.:* Kilkenny College; Trinity College, Dublin. Entered Office of Paymaster of Civil Services, Dublin Castle, 1859; Paymaster-General's Office, London, 1861; H.M. Inspector of Factories, 1869; H.M. Superintending Inspector for Scotland and Ireland, 1895; H.M. Senior Superintending Inspector, London, 1902; retired, 1905. *Publications:* Introduction to a History of the Factory System, 1886; the Modern

Factory System, 1891; the Factory System and the Factory Acts, 1894; contributor to the Westminster, Fortnightly, and Contemporary Reviews, Temple Bar Magazine, and many other periodicals; also to Dictionary of Political Economy, the Transactions of the British Association, and many other learned societies; has written plays. *Recreations:* fishing, walking. *Address:* High Trees, Chepstow. *Clubs:* Albemarle, National Liberal. *(Died 12 Aug. 1918.)*

COOKSON, Charles Lisle Stirling, J.P.; *b.* 1855; *o. s.* of late Charles Edward Cookson of Hermitage, Co. Durham, and Sarah Turnbull, *e. d.* of late Capt. Robert Lisle Coulson, R.N., Houndwood; *m.* 1st, 1885, Mary Eleanor (*d.* 1898), *e. d.* of Sir Samuel Home Stirling, 7th Bart. of Glorat and Renton; 2nd, 1902, May Elizabeth, *o. d.* of late John Napier of Merchiston, Renfrewshire. Formerly Capt. 2nd Brigade Scottish Div. R.A. *Address:* Renton House, Grantshouse, Berwickshire. *Club:* New, Edinburgh. *(Died 17 Oct. 1919.)*

COOKSON, Colonel Philip Blencowe, C.M.G. 1915; O.B.E. 1919; late Northumberland (Hussars) Yeomanry (Territorial Force); High Sheriff, Northumberland, 1924-25; *b.* 30 Oct. 1871; *s.* of late Col. John Blencowe Cookson and Constance Jane, 2nd *d.* of late George Fenwick; *m.* 1902, Gwendoline, 5th *d.* of late H. A. Brassey; two *s.* one *d.* *Educ.:* Eton. Entered Army, 1st Life Guards, 1894; Major, 1909; retired, 1911; served N.W. Frontier of India, 1897-8; S. African War, 1899-1900; European War, 1914-17 (despatches, C.M.G.). *Address:* Meldon Park, Morpeth. *T.:* Hartburn 3. *Club:* White's. *(Died 27 Feb. 1928.)*

COOLIDGE, Archibald Cary; Professor of History at Harvard University since 1908, and Director of the University Library since 1911; A.B. (Harvard) 1887, Ph.D. (Freiburg, Germany) 1892; LL.D. (hon.) Harvard, 1916; *b.* Boston, 6 March 1866; *s.* of Joseph Randolph Coolidge and Julia, *d.* of John Lowell Gardner; unmarried. *Educ.:* Harvard; University of Berlin; Ecole des Science Politiques, Paris; Freiburg University; foreign travel. Acting secretary, Legation, St. Petersburg, 1890-91; private secretary to Minister to France, 1892; secretary, Legation, Vienna, 1893; instructor history, Harvard, 1893; assist. prof. 1899; Lowell Lecturer (Boston), 1902-3, 1914-15, and 1919-20; lecturer at the Sorbonne and other French Universities, 1906-7; exchange professor University of Berlin, 1913-14; Inquiry Commission to prepare for Peace Conference, 1917-18; special assistant of Dept. of State and War Trade Board, Sweden and North Russia, 1918; Chief of American Mission to Vienna, 1919; special representative of American Commission to negotiate peace, Paris, 1919; with American Relief Administration in Moscow, winter of 1921-22; Editor of Foreign Affairs, an American Quarterly Review, 1922; Mem. Mass. Hist. Soc., Va. Hist. Soc., Am. Acad. Polit. and Social Science, Amer. Ant. Soc., Royal Geog. Soc., Marseilles Geog. Soc. (hon.). *Publications:* The United States as a World Power, 1908; The Origins of the Triple Alliance, 1917, second edition, 1926; editor of English edition of The Secret Treaties of Austria-Hungary, 1879-1914, by Alfred Franzis Pribram, 1920; Ten Years of War and Peace, 1927; contributions American Historical Review, Foreign Affairs, etc. *Address:* Harvard University, Cambridge, U.S.A. *Clubs:* Somerset, etc., Boston; Century, Harvard, New York. *(Died Jan. 1928.)*

COOLIDGE, William Augustus Brevoort; Life Fellow of Magdalen College, Oxford, since 1875; *b.* 28 Aug. 1850, near New York; *e. s.* of Frederic William Skinner Coolidge and Elisabeth Neville Brevoort. Unmarried (as Fellowship dates from before 1881). *Educ.:* St. Paul's School,

Concord, New Hampshire (U.S.A.); Elizabeth Coll., Guernsey; Exeter Coll. Oxford (Taylorian University Scholar for French, 1871; 1st class Modern History, 1873; 2nd class Jurisprudence, 1874; B.A., 1874; M.A., 1876). Hon. Dr. Philos. (University of Bern), 1908. Deacon, 1882; Priest, 1883; Prof. English History, St. David's College, Lampeter, 1880-81; Modern History Tutor Magdalen Coll. Oxford, 1881-85; hon. curate of S. Hinksey, 1883-95; F.R.G.S. 1890-1913; member English Alpine Club, 1870-99, hon. member, 1904-10; Swiss Alpine Club, 1895-1905; hon. member of the French and the Italian Alpine Clubs, 1898; of American Alpine Club, 1911; corresponding member of the Swiss Hist. Society, 1891, hon. member 1908; hon. member Bernese Historical Society, 1905; silver medallist Paris Geographical Society, 1905; hon. member Maurienne Historical Society, 1905; hon. member Lyons Section. French Alpine Club, 1910-17, and Grindelwald Section, Swiss Alpine Club, 1912; Co-founder and Hon. Member of the Société d'Histoire du Valais Romand, 1916. *Publications:* Climbers' Guide to the Bernese Oberland, new edition of vol. i., 2 Parts, 1909-10, and vol. ii. 1904; Josias Simler et les Origines de l'Alpinisme jusqu'en 1600, 1904; The Alps in Nature and History, 1908; Die Petronella-Kapelle in Grindelwald, 1911; A List of my Writings (1868-1912) relating to the Alps or Switzerland, 1912; Alpine Studies, 1912; Die älteste Schutzhütte im Berner Oberland, 1915; Johann Madutz, 1917. Editor, Alpine Journal, 1880-89; The late Aubrey Moore's Lectures and Papers on the History of the Reformation, 1890; Murray's Handbook for Switzerland, 18th ed. 1891. and 19th ed. 1904; Editor of A Pioneer in the High Alps, Alpine Diaries and Letters of F. F. Tuckett, 1856-1894 (1920). *Recreations:* Swiss history, history of the Alps, (formerly) mountaineering. *Address:* Chalet Montana, Grindelwald, Switzerland; Magdalen College, Oxford. *(Died 8 May 1926.)*

COOMBES, Very Rev. George Frederick; Dean of Rupertsland, and Professor of Ecclesiastical History, St. John's College, Manitoba, since 1905; Professor of Classics, University of Manitoba, since 1915; *b.* 1856; 2nd *s.* of late Rev. J. Coombes, Vicar of Portwood, Cheshire; *m.* 1885, Mary Elizabeth, *d.* of Henry Eagles, of Walsall; three *s.* one *d.* *Educ.:* Manchester Grammar School; St. John's Coll. Cambridge (Foundation Scholar, Classical Tripos, M.A.); D.D. (*honoris causa*), Manitoba University. Ordained 1880; Curate of Portwood, Cheshire, and Classical Master Manchester Grammar School, 1880-83; Canon of St. John's Cathedral, Winnipeg, 1883-1905. *Recreations:* golf, etc. *Address:* The Deanery, Winnipeg. *Club:* Manitoba, Winnipeg. *(Died 22 Sept. 1922.)*

COOP, Rev. James Ogden, D.S.O. 1918; M.A.; T.D.; Chaplain to the King, 1926; Hon. Canon of Liverpool, 1920; Sen. Chaplain to the Forces, W. Command, 1923; Proctor in Convocation; Member of National Assembly, 1921; Member of Governing Body, St. Chad's College, Durham, 1925; Vicar of St. Margaret's, Anfield, Liverpool, since 1920; *b.* Ashton-under-Lyne, 1869; *e. s.* of John Hague and Sarah Coop, Albemarle, Ashton-under-Lyne; *m.* Ethel, *d.* of late C. J. Wolstenholme, Headingley, Leeds; five *d.* *Educ.:* Manchester Grammar School; Exeter College, Oxford. 3rd class Modern History; Fellow of the Royal Historical Society, 1892. Ordained 1892; Curate of All Hallows, Leeds, 1892-95, West Derby (Liverpool), 1895-1901, St. Agnes, with charge of St. Pancras, Sefton Park, Liverpool, 1901-5; Vicar of St. Catherine's, Abercromby Square, Liverpool, 1905-20; Chaplain 1st class T.F., 1913; Senior Chaplain C/E, 55th (West Lancashire) Division, 1914-19 (despatches twice, D.S.O.). *Publications:* The Story of the 55th Division; Guide to the Battlefields, 1920; various articles in the Prayer Book Dictionary, 1912. *Recreations:* riding, rowing, etc. *Address:* St. Margaret's Vicarage, Anfield, Liverpool. *T.:* Anfield 108.

(*Died 2 June 1928.*)

COOPE, Edward Jesser, J.P.; *o. s.* of late O. E. Coope, M.P., of Rochetts and Berechurch Hall, Essex; *b.* 1849; *m.* 1872, Pleasance S., *e. d.* of Rev. T. L. Fellowes. Formerly Captain Suffolk Yeomanry. *Club:* Royal Yacht Squadron, Cowes. (*Died 26 Nov. 1918.*)

COOPER, Sir Alfred, Kt., *cr.* 1901; J.P. Surrey; Chairman, Ridgways, Ltd.; *b.* 1846; *s.* of late Henry Cooper of London; *m.* 1st, 1873, Margaret (*d.* 1874), *d.* of James Gilmore Winn; 2nd, 1883, Marion, *d.* of late Charles Nicholson of Dublin. *Educ.:* King's Coll. London. Knighted in recognition of services during S. African war in maintaining a private military hospital at Surbiton as an adjunct to the Princess of Wales's hospital ship. *Recreations:* yachting, motoring. *Address:* Ossemsley Manor, near Christchurch, Hants.

(*Died 21 Jan. 1916.*)

COOPER, Rev. Alfred William Francis; Rector of Killanne since 1898; Canon of Ferns since 1908. *Educ.:* Trinity College, Dublin; Hon. D.D. Univ. of Manitoba. Ordained 1873; Curate of Stradbally, 1873-77; Tipperary, 1877-78; Booterstown, 1878-80; Rector of Glenely, 1880-85; Priest (S.P.G.), N.W. Canada, 1885-87; Rector of Pro-Cathedral of the Redeemer, Calgary, 1887-98; Archdeacon of Calgary, 1895-98. *Address:* Killanne Rectory, Enniscorthy. (*Died 14 Nov. 1920.*)

COOPER, Alice J., tutor and lecturer in education, Oxford, 1897-1914; Occasional Inspector of Secondary Schools under the Board of Education, 1901; 5th *d.* of late Rev. J. T. Cooper, Diss. *Educ.:* private tuition. Assistant mistress, Notting hill High School; head mistress, Edgbaston High School for girls, 1876-95; vice-president Head Mistresses' Association, 1887-95; has sat on many educational and other committees. *Publications:* lectures, addresses, and occasional papers, mostly on educational subjects. *Address:* Steyning, Beaconsfield, Bucks. *Club:* Lyceum. (*Died 17 June 1917.*)

COOPER, Charles Alfred, F.R.S.E.; Hon. LL.D., Edin.; editor of the Scotsman, 1876-1906; *b.* Hull, 16 Sept. 1829; *e. s.* of Charles Cooper, architect; *m.* Susannah, *e. d.* of Thomas Towers, Hull, 1852 (*d.* 1887); one *s.* *Educ.:* Hull Grammar School. Sub-editor and manager Hull Advertiser; went to London to be reporter in Gallery of House of Commons for Morning Star, 1861; sub-editor, 1862; left London in 1868 to become assistant to Alexander Russel, editor of Scotsman; shortly after his death became editor of that paper; retired, 1906. *Publications:* Letters on Egypt with title of Seeking the Sun, 1891; Letters on South Africa, 1895; An Editor's Retrospect, 1896. *Recreation:* books. *Address:* 41 Drumsheugh Gardens, Edinburgh.(*Died 15 April 1916.*)

COOPER, Sir Edward Ernest, 1st Bt., *cr.* 1920; Kt., *cr.* 1913; Head of James Hartley Cooper & Co., Underwriters, Jerusalem Chambers; *b.* Windsor, 1848; *m.* Leonora, D.B.E., *d.* of Thomas Crampton. Sheriff of London, 1912-13; Lord Mayor, 1919-20; Lieutenant of City of London; Grand Officer Legion of Honour; Officer Order of the Crown of Belgium; Order of St. Sava 1st class; Chairman of Committee of Royal Academy of Music. *Address:* Berrydown Court, Overton, Hampshire. *Clubs:* Garrick, Oriental, Junior Carlton; Royal Thames Yacht. (*Died 12 Feb. 1922.*)

COOPER, Col. Harry, C.M.G. 1900; C.B.E. 1919; retired; J.P., D.L. Essex; *b.* London, 14 Apr. 1847; *e. s.* of Henry Cooper and Catherine,

224

d. of late S. Lovegrove; *m.* Emily C. E., *d.* of late Commodore Henry Caldwell, C.B., A.D.C., R.N., 1894; one *s.* one *d.* *Educ.:* Brentwood Grammar School; Blackheath Proprietary School; Royal Military College, Sandhurst; Staff College. Ensign 98th Foot, 1865; 47th Foot, 1866; served in Canada, West Indies, Ireland, England, and East Indies; Special Service, Ashanti, 1873-74; Vice-Consul in Bosnia, 1877-78; in Asia Minor, 1879-80; with Mounted Infantry in South Africa in 1881; A.D.C. to Viceroy, India, 1884-88; Chief Staff Officer, Army of Occupation. Egypt, 1896-98; A.D.C. to the Sovereign, 1898-1904; Assistant-Adjutant-General, Western District, 1899; Colonel on Staff, Cape Colony, 1899-1902; Col. Commanding Essex Volunteer and Territorial Infantry Brigade, 1906-11; Vice-Chairman Essex Territorial Force Association, 1908-14; served Canada, 1866 (medal with clasp); Ashanti, 1873-74 (medal); Burma, 1885-86 (medal with clasp); Sudan, 1896 (medal); South Africa, 1899-1902 (Queen's medal and clasp, King's medal and 2 clasps); G.H.Q. Expeditionary Force, France, 1914-15 (Star, 2 medals); Commanding No. 3 District, 1915-17. *Address:* Pakenham Lodge, Bury St. Edmunds. *Club:* United Service.

(*Died 8 Oct. 1928.*)

COOPER, Rt. Rev. Henry Edward, D.D.; Bishop of Armidale since 1914; *b.* 15 Oct. 1845; *m. d.* of Dr. Holthouse, Ballarat, 1879. *Educ.:* Trin. Coll. Dublin (M.A. 1876). Ordained 1872; Archdeacon and Vicar of Hamilton, Victoria, 1884-93; Archdeacon of Ballarat, 1894-95; Bishop Coadjutor of Ballarat, 1895; Bishop of Grafton and Armidale, 1901-14. *Address:* Bishopscourt, Armidale, New South Wales. (*Died 1 July 1916.*)

COOPER, Henry St. John; novelist; *b.* London, 3rd Nov. 1869; *s.* of Charles Frederick Cooper, and *g.s.* of Henry Russell, composer of Cheer, Boys, Cheer, etc.; *m.* 1st, Laura Ethel Thwaites (*d.* 1924); 2nd, 1925, Anne S. McGlashan; three *s.* *Educ.:* privately, in France and England. Educated originally as an artist, but gave art up for literature; for some years was employed in an editorial and sub-editorial capacity in weekly journalism; has written a vast number of serial stories, a great many of which have been published in book form under the names of Henry St. John Cooper and Mabel St. John; several are being produced in film form. *Publications:* Life of Henry Russell (Cheer, Boys, Cheer); The Voyage of the Avenger; Sunny Ducrow; James Bevanwood; Garden of Memories; The Imaginary Marriage; Carniss & Co.; The Fortunes of Sally Luck; The Golconda Necklace; The Gallant Lover; five books on the British Bulldog. *Recreations:* painting, photography, making model reproductions of antique ships and furniture, judging English and Dutch paintings, inventing mechanical devices, breeding and judging bulldogs. *Address:* The Ivy House, Sunbury-on-Thames. *T.A.:* St. John Cooper, Sunbury. *T.:* Sunbury 33. *M.:* AP 1929. *Clubs:* National Liberal, Press.

(*Died 9 Sept. 1926.*)

COOPER, Very Rev. James, D.D.; Professor of Church History, University of Glasgow, 1898-1922; *b.* Elgin,13 Feb.1846; *e. s.* of late John Alexander Cooper, Spynie, Elgin, and Ann *d.* of late James Stephen, Old Keith; *m.* 1912, Margaret, *e. d.* of late George Williamson, Shempston. *Educ.:* Elgin Academy; Univ. of Aberdeen. M.A.; D.D. Aberdeen, 1892; Oxford, 1920; Litt. D. (Hon.), Trinity College, Dublin, 1909; D.C.L. Durham, 1910; Serbian Order of St. Sava, 4th Class; Olaus Petri Lecturer, University of Upsala; Member of the Ancient Monuments Board, Scotland, 1919; Minister of St. Stephen's, Broughty Ferry, 1873-81; of East Parish of St. Nicholas, Aberdeen, 1881-98; Joint-Secretary, Scottish Church Society;

Founder of the Scottish Ecclesiological Society, and President 1903, 1911, 1916, and 1921; deeply interested in reunion of the Church; V.D., 1899; to Glasgow University Officers' Training Corps, 1909; Moderator of the General Assembly, Church of Scotland, 1917. *Publications:* Cartularium Ecclesiæ S. Nicolai Aberdonensis (2 vols.); Bethlehem, a volume of Advent Sermons; Soldiers of the Bible; Our Sacred Heritage (Closing Address as Moderator), 1917; Reunion, A Voice from Scotland, 1918; has edited Scottish Liturgy of 1637, and, in conjunction with the Rt. Rev. Bishop MacLean, an English translation of Testamentum Domini; etc. *Address:* Brae, Moriston, Elgin.
(Died 27 Dec. 1922.)

COOPER, Margaret; *m.* Capt. Arthur Maughan Humble - Crofts (*d.* 1918), 4th *s.* of Prebendary Humble-Crofts, Waldron, Sussex. *Address:* Framba, 103 Dartmouth Road, Willesden Green, N.W.2. *T.:* Willesden 1283.
(Died 28 Dec. 1922.)

COOPER, Hon. Sir Pope (Alexander), Kt., *cr.* 1904; K.C.M.G., *cr.* 1908; Chief Justice, Queensland, 1903-22; *b.* Willeroo, Lake George, 12 May 1848; 5th *s.* of late Francis Cooper; *m.* 1878, Alice Frener (*d.* 1900), *d.* of late James Cooper; one *s.* two *d. Educ.:* Sydney University; London University. Called to Bar, Middle Temple, 1872; returned to Australia, 1874; M.L.A., Bowen, 1880-83; Attorney-General, 1883; Judge of Supreme Court, N. District, 1880-83. *Address:* Hawstead, Brisbane, Queensland. *Clubs:* Junior Carlton, Union, Sports; Queensland, Brisbane.
(Died Aug. 1923.)

COOPER, Hon. Sir Theo.; Kt., *cr.* 1921; one of the Judges of the Supreme Court of New Zealand, and of the Court of Appeal of New Zealand, 1901-21; *b.* London, 15 November 1850; *s.* of late Theophilus Cooper and Susanna Bugby; *m.* 1878, Bessie, *y. d.* of A. A. Alexander of Auckland; two *s.* (and one killed in action in France, June 1916) three *d. Educ.:* privately. Emigrated to New Zealand with parents as one of the party of Nonconformists who established the Albertland Settlements in the North of Auckland, 1862; was there for 3 years and then returned to the city of Auckland; was employed for some years in the Daily Southern Cross Newspaper Office, Auckland, and then read for the Bar; admitted to New Zealand Bar, 1878; was leader of the Auckland Bar and one of the leaders of the New Zealand Bar for some years; for three years President of the Court of Arbitration of New Zealand; was for nearly 20 years a member of the Board of Education, and a Governor of the Auckland College and Grammar School, and for 15 years as honorary Inspector of Lunatic Asylums in New Zealand. *Recreation:* farming. *Address:* Eltham, Taranaki, New Zealand. *Clubs:* Northern, Auckland; Dunedin, Dunedin. *(Died May 1925.)*

COOPER, Rev. Vincent King, M.A.; Rector of St. Mary le Bow, Durham, since 1910; *b.* 19 April 1849; 6th *s.* of Edward Miles Cooper, of Pendleton, Manchester; four *s.* one *d. Educ.:* Bradfield; Brasenose College, Oxford. Assistant Master, Bradfield College, 1873-75; Head Master, St. Michaels College, Tenbury, 1875; Curate of St. Oswalds, Durham, 1876 - 87; Minor Canon of Durham, 1876-1910; Sacrist, 1885-87; Precentor, 1887-1905; Hon. Fellow S. Michael's College, Tenbury, 1887; Assistant Diocesan Inspector of Schools, Durham, 1887; Hon. Secretary and Treasurer, Durham County Hospital, 1884-1902; Hon. Canon of Durham, 910; Rural Dean of Durham, 1910-17; Censor of Unattached Students in University of Durham, 1912-17. *Publication:* Tales from Euripides. *Address:* 16 South Bailey, Durham. *T.A.:* Durham.
(Died 18 May 1922.)

9

COOPER, Sir William Charles, 3rd Bt., *cr.* 1863; 2nd *s.* of 1st Bt.; *S.* brother, 1909; *b.* 22 Oct. 1851; *m.* 1876, Alice Helen, 3rd *d.* of George Hill of Surrey Hills, Sydney, N.S.W.; three *s.* one *d.* Heir: *s.* William George Daniel [*b.* 14 Dec. 1877; *m.* 1904, Lettice Margaret, *y. d.* of 1st Viscount Long; two *s.* one *d.*; late Lieut. 7th Hussars. *Address:* 15 Ennismore Gardens, S.W. *Clubs:* Orleans, Bachelors']. *Address:* 18 Park Street, W.1. *T.:* Mayfair 2499. *Clubs:* Turf, Orleans.
(Died 2 Sept. 1925.)

COOPER, Lt.-Col. Sir William Earnshaw, Kt., *cr.* 1903; C.I.E., 1897; Hon. Col. Cawnpore Volunteer Rifle Corps; Chairman, Cooper, Allen and Co., Ltd., Cawnpore, India; *b.* 1843; *m.* 1911, Gleadowe, widow of Walter de Castro; two *d.* Commanded 5th Administrative Batt. N.W.P. Volunteers for several years; President Upper India Chamber of Commerce, 1889-99; Member of the Legislative Council, N.W.P. and Oudh, 1893-1900. *Publications:* The Murder of Agriculture; Socialism and its Perils, 1908; Britain for the Briton, 1909; England's Need, 1910; Spiritual Science, 1911; England's Fatal Land Policy; The Blood-Guiltiness of Christendom, 1922, etc. *Address:* Hume Towers, Bournemouth.
(Died 2 July 1924.)

COOPER, William Ranson; Consulting Engineer; Editor of Science Abstracts 1899-1901, and again since 1922; Editor of the Electrician, 1906-19; *b.* 1868; *s.* of late William Cooper and Jane Susanna, *d.* of late Major Cross; two *s.* one *d. Educ.:* privately; Central Technical College and King's College, London. M.A., B.Sc., National University of Ireland; Fellow of City and Guilds of London Institute; Fellow of the Institute of Physics; Associate of Institute of Chemistry; joined staff of Mr. James Swinburne in his consulting practice, 1895; was a member of Advisory Panel, Ministry of Munitions; member of the Electro-Culture Committee of the Board of Agriculture; has served on the Councils of the Institution of Electrical Engineers, of the Institute of Physics, and of the Faraday Society; Hon. Treasurer and for 12 years one of the Honorary Secretaries of the Physical Society; Member of the Board of Studies in Electrical Engineering of the University of London. *Publications:* Primary Batteries; Electro - Chemistry related to Engineering; The Claims of Labour and of Capital; edited 2nd ed. of the Electrician Primers; revised 4th ed. of Macmillan's Electro-Metallurgy; *Papers*—Various, including Electric Traction (Inst. Mining Engineers, 1902); Electric Traction on Tramways (Inst. Civil Engineers, 1902, Telford Premium awarded); Problems of Electric Railways (with J. Swinburne, F.R.S., Inst. Electrical Engineers, 1902); Alternate Current Electrolysis (Faraday Society, 1905); Electricity Supply (Inst. E.E. 1908); Dust Prevention (Automobile Club, 1905, 1909); Heat Tests of Electrical Machines (British Association, 1913); Electric Cooking (Inst. Electrical Engineers, 1915); Electro-chemical Effects by Superimposing Alternating Currents (Faraday Society, 1922). *Recreations:* tennis, photography. *Address:* 82 Victoria Street, S.W.1; 113 Tulse Hill, S.W.2. *T.:* Vic. 1225, Brixton 615. *Clubs:* Athenæum, Royal Automobile. *(Died 15 March 1926.)*

COOTE, Sir Algernon (Charles Plumptre), 12th Bt.; *cr.* 1621; Premier Bt. of Ireland; H.M. Lieut., Queen's Co. since 1900; *b.* 14 Dec. 1847; *s.* of 11th Bt. and Cecilia, *o. d.* of J. P. Plumptre, Fredville, Kent; *S.* father 1899; *m.* 1st, Jean (*d.* 1880), *d.* of Capt. Trotter; 2nd, 1882, Ellen Melesina, *d.* of Philip Chenevix-Trench of Botley Hill, Hants; six *s.* two *d. Educ.:* Eton; Cambridge; M.A. 1875. Owns about 45,000 acres. *Recreations:* golf, farming.

225

Heir : s. Ralph Algernon [*b.* 22 Sept. 1874, late Capt. 17th Lancers; *m.* 1904, Alice, *y. d.* of late Thomas Webber of Kellyville, Queen's Co.; two *s.*]. *Address :* Ballyfin, Mountrath, Ireland. *T.A. :* Ballyfin. *M. :* CI 29. *Clubs :* National, Church Imperial ; Kildare Street, Dublin.
(Died 22 Oct. 1920.)

COOTE, Sir Eyre, Kt., *cr.* 1903 ; J.P., D.L. ; Sheriff for the Queen's County in 1887, for Co. Dublin, 1903 ; *b.* 31 Dec. 1857 ; *s.* of Eyre Coote of West Park, Hants, and *d.* of Lieut.-General Lechmere - Worrall, and *g.-g.s.* of General Sir Eyre Coote, G.C.B. (kinsman of Sir Charles Coote of Ballyfin) ; *m.* 1902, Evelyn Mary, *d.* of Rev. E. Cadogan, Rector of Wicken, Northamptonshire. *Educ. :* Eton. Owns about 11,000 acres. *Recreations :* shooting, estate work, travel. *Address :* West Park, Damerham, Salisbury. *Clubs :* Carlton, Windham, Bath ; Kildare Street, Dublin.
(Died 6 May 1925.)

COOTE, Wm. ; M.P. (U.) South Tyrone, 1916-1922 ; *b.* 10 Dec. 1863 ; *s.* of Wm. Coote, Killevalley, Ballyjamesduff, Co. Cavan, and Sarah Wilson, Ahikist, Ballybay, Co. Monaghan ; *m.* 1889, Letitia A. Allen (*d.* 1923), of Castleblayney, Co. Monaghan ; four *s.* one *d. Educ. :* local primary school and local private classical academy. Apprenticed to the provision trade : at twenty years started and successfully carried on a business in his native district ; removed to Newry, Co. Down, 1891 ; and from thence to Clogher, Co. Tyrone, 1893, where he built up a business as auctioneer and stock-owner ; rented a large mill premises at Ballygawley idle for 35 years, where he started and developed the manufacture of woollen yarns, 1900, subsequently forming this into a private limited Coy. of which he is the Managing Director ; removed business to Clogher, Co. Tyrone, 1918 ; J.P., Co. Tyrone, 1901 ; a County Councillor, Co. Tyrone, 1903. *Recreation :* gardening. *Address :* Carrick House, Clogher, Co. Tyrone. *T.A. :* Coote, Clogher, Tyrone. *Clubs :* Constitutional ; Ulster Reform, Belfast.
(Died 14 Dec. 1924.)

COOTE, William Alexander ; O.B.E. 1918; Secretary of National Vigilance Association since 1885 ; *b.* 24 Dec. 1842 ; 27th *c.* of W. Coote, Queen's County. *Educ. :* private. Apprenticed to a compositor ; deeply interested in labour questions, and in 1870 led movement for shorter hours ; official delegate to five Trade Union Congresses ; Labour Candidate for North Camberwell, 1883 ; for many years Member of Camberwell Vestry and Borough Council ; organised the Municipal Employés Union (7000 members from the unskilled labourers of London Vestries obtained shorter hours and higher wages) ; has organised National Committees for Suppression of White Slave Traffic in all the European capitals, in Egypt, Canada, the United States, South America, and South Africa ; in recognition of his National Vigilance Association work, Chevalier of the Legion of Honour of France, and the Royal and Most Distinguished Order of Charles III. of Spain. *Publications :* A Vision and its Fulfilment ; pamphlets on Social Purity ; A Romance of Philanthropy ; Commercialised Vice. *Address :* 2 Grosvenor Mansions, 76 Victoria Street, S.W.
(Died 26 Oct. 1919.)

COPE, Sir Thomas, 1st Bart., *cr.* 1918 ; M.A., D.L., J.P. ; for 26 years Chairman of Leicestershire County Council, of Leicestershire Quarter Session, and of the Leicestershire Appeal Tribunal ; *b.* 22 Aug. 1840 ; *e. s.* of Thomas Cope of Osbaston Hall ; *m.* 1879, Alice Kate (*d.* 1916), *d.* of George Walker, Walthamstow ; one *s.* one *d. Educ. :* Rugby ; Trinity College, Cambridge. Called to Bar, Lincoln's Inn, 1866 ; practised at the Chancery Bar till 1879 ; has been actively engaged in County work ; contested (U.) Bosworth Division, 1895. *Recreations :* joined the Cam-

bridge University Volunteers and shot in their team against Oxford at the first Wimbledon meeting ; cricket, shooting, and fishing. *Heir :* Lt.-Col. T. G. Cope. *Address :* Osbaston Hall, Nuneaton. *M. :* 8050. *Club :* New University.
(Died 17 Oct. 1924.)

COPLAND, William Wallace, M.V.O., 1912; Civil Engineer, M.I.C.E., Gibraltar ; *b.* 1858 ; *s.* of James Copland of Dumfries ; *m.* 1st, Mary (*d.* 1887), *d.* of Joseph Pritchard ; 2nd, Caroline, *d.* of Joseph R. Brett. *Address :* Gibraltar. *Clubs :* Junior Constitutional ; Mediterranean, Gibraltar. *(Died 9 June 1922.)*

COPLAND-SPARKES, Rear-Admiral Robert, R.N. ; C.M.G. 1901 ; 2nd *s.* of late John Sparkes, of Green Place, Wonersh, Surrey ; *b.* 20 Nov. 1851 ; *m.* 1902, Alice Maud, 2nd *d.* of late Charles Jackson, of Newcastle-on-Tyne. Served Egypt, 1882 (medal, Khedive's star) ; Borneo Expedition, 1898 ; Gambia Expedition, 1900 ; Boer War, 1901-1902. *Address :* Woodhill, Shamley Green, Surrey. *Club :* Naval and Military. *(Died 10 July 1924.)*

COPLESTON, Most Rev. Reginald Stephen, M.A., Hon.D.D. Oxon; Hon.D.Litt. Oxon ; Hon. D.C.L. Durham ; Hon. LL.D. Camb ; Hon. Fellow of St. John's Coll. Oxon ; lately Canon of St. George in Jerusalem ; *b.* 26 Dec. 1845 ; *s.* of Rev. R. E. Copleston ; *m.* Edith, *d.* of Archbishop Trench, Dublin, 1882 ; one *s.* two *d. Educ. :* Merchant Taylors' ; Merton Coll., Oxford. 2nd Class Lit. Hum. 1869 ; Fellow and Tutor St. John's Coll. Oxford, 1869-75 ; Bishop of Colombo, 1875-1902 ; of Calcutta, and Metropolitan of India, 1902-13. *Publications :* Buddhism : Primitive and Present, 1894 ; etc. *Address :* 25 St. John's Road, Putney, S.W.
(Died 19 April 1925.)

COPLEY, Very Rev. John Robert, Dean since 1886, and Incumbent of Kilfenora since 1873. Ordained, 1870 ; Curate of Kilnaboy, 1870 - 73 ; Precentor of Kilfenora, 1884 - 86. *Address :* Worthing.

CORBAN, Maj.-Gen. William Watts ; *b.* 26 Nov. 1829 ; *e. s.* of W. Corban, of Grange, Francestown, Co. Cork ; *m.* Alice, *d.* of H. H. Peard, of Coole Abbey, Co. Cork. Entered army, 1850 ; Lieut.-Col., 1878 ; retired, 1883 ; served Crimea, 1854-55 (mentioned in general orders, medal, 3 clasps, Turkish medal) ; Egyptian Expedition, 1882 (medal, bronze star, 3rd class Medjidieh) ; Distinguished Service Reward, 1905. *Address :* Bettyville, Fermoy, Co. Cork.
(Died 29 Jan. 1916.)

CORBET, Maj.-Gen. Arthur Domville, C.B. 1894 ; Royal Marine Light Infantry ; retired ; *b.* West Felton, Shropshire, 7 Feb. 1847, *y. s.* of late V. R. Corbet, J.P. for Salop, and Maria, *d.* of late P. Humberston, The Friars, Chester ; *m.* 1888, Louisa Marie, *d.* of late H. Huish, of Park Lodge, Stoke Damerel, and widow of R. Rundle ; two *d. Educ. :* Leamington College. Joined Royal Marines, 1865 ; expeditionary force, Egypt, 1882 ; Gambia Expedition, 1894 (despatches, medal with clasp, promoted Lieut. - Colonel, C.B.). *Decorated* for operations against Fodi Silah on Gambia, 1894 (meritorious service in the field). *Recreations :* fishing, archæology. *Club :* United Service. *(Died 26 May 1918.)*

CORBET, Eustace Kynaston, C.M.G. 1905 ; 7th and *y. s.* of late Rev. Andrew Corbett, (2nd *s.* of William Thompson Corbett, of Darnhall, Cheshire, and Elsham, Lincs ; of a younger branch of the Corbets of Acton Reynold) and Marianne, 3rd *d.* of Sir M. W. Ridley, 3rd Bt., of Blagdon, Northumberland ; *b.* South Willingham Rectory, Lincolnshire, 22 June 1854; unmarried. *Educ. :* Cheltenham ; Balliol College, Oxford. English Secretary to late Khedive Tewfik, 1885-91 ; Judge in Native Court of Appeal, Cairo, 1891-97 ; Procureur-Général, Native Courts, Egypt, 1897-1908 ; Director of the Egyptian Educational Mission in England, 1908-13 ; has Grand Cordon of Medjidieh, and second class Osmanieh. *Publication :* verse translation of Lessing's Nathan der Weise, with introductory essay, 1883. *Address :* Rock House, Boughton Monchelsea, Kent. *Club :* New University. *(Died 21 Mar. 1920.)*

CORBET, Hon. Frederick Hugh Mackenzie ; H.M.'s Advocate-General for the Presidency of Madras since 1912; *b.* Barcelona, 17 July 1862 ; 2nd *s.* of Reginald John Corbet, J.P., M.L.C., Ceylon; and *g.-s.* of Sir Andrew Corbet, 2nd Bt., of Moreton-Corbet ; *m.* Eila, *e. d.* of Sir George W. R. Campbell, K.C.M.G.; one *d. Educ. :* Ceylon ; privately; special attention to law and modern languages. Was granted Letters Patent of Venia Ætatis, 1879 ; Private Secretary to Hon. Mr. Justice Lawrie, 1885, 1886, and 1888 ; Librarian of Colombo Museum, 1886-93 ; Acting Secretary of Central Irrigation Board, Ceylon, 1890-91; resigned salaried Government employment (services acknowledged by Secretary of State for the Colonies), ·1893 ; Hon. Executive Officer and Home Agent of the Government of Ceylon at the Imperial Institute, 1893-1904 ; Secretary of the Royal Commission on the Church of·England and other Religious Bodies in Wales and Monmouthshire, 1909-11 ; Hon. Secretary of Ceylon General Committee for Paris Exposition, 1889 ; Member of Council, and successively Hon. Sec. and Hon. Treas. of Ceylon Branch, Royal Asiatic Society, 1887-1893 ; Delegate to International Congress of Orientalists, London, 1891 ; Barrister-at-Law, Gray's Inn, 1897 ; practised in England, mainly before the Privy Council, until 1912 ; Chairman and Director of several South African and other Companies, 1895-1912 ; Member of Committee or Council of several Societies ; President of Hardwicke Society, 1902-3 ; Jubilee Gold Medal of Ceylon, 1897. *Publications :* various official Reports, etc. ; Introduction to Ceylon portion of The Golden Book of India, 1900 ; The Laws of the Empire, 1901. *Address :* College Bridge House, Egmore, Madras ; 5 Pump Court, Temple, E.C. *T. :* City 8870. *(Died 1 Dec. 1916.)*

CORBETT, Edward, J.P., *e. s.* of late Lieut.-Col. Edward Corbett, of Longnor Bank and of Aldershaw, Staffordshire, and Elizabeth Ann Teresa, *d.* of late Robert Scholl ; *b.* 1843 ; *m.* 1871, Louisa Mary, *e. d.* of Sir Charles Isham, 10th Bart. ; one *s. Educ. :* Cheltenham ; R.M.C., Sandhurst ; formerly Lieut. 17th Lancers, and Captain, Shropshire Y.C. ; Patron of 1 living. *Address :* Longnor Bank, Shrewsbury. *Club :* Junior Carlton. *(Died 1918.)*

CORBETT, Rev. Frederick St. John, M.A., F.R.S.L. ; Rector of St. George in the East and Vicar of St. Matthew's, Pell Street, since 1903 ; Founder of Church of England Guild of Sponsors, 1911 ; *b.* Dublin, 1862 ; 2nd *s.* of John Corbett, M.A., LL.D., member of the Senate of Trinity College, Dublin, and Susanna Jane, *d.* of William Richard Manderson of Dublin ; *m.* Elsie Lucy Victoire, *e. d.* of Rev. Edmund A. Askew, M.A., Trinity College, Cambridge, Rector of Greystoke, Cumberland, and Hon. Canon of Carlisle Cathedral ; two *s.* two *d. Educ. :* Trinity College, Dublin ; B.A. 1884 ; M.A. 1887. Deacon, 1885 ; Priest, 1887 ; Curate of Hunslet, Leeds, 1885-91 ; Chaplain to the Leeds Rifles, 1886-93 ; Curate of St. Michael's, Chester Square, 1891-96 ; Rector of Long Marton, 1896-1903 ; Chaplain to the High Sheriff of Westmorland, 1901 ; Dean of Sion College and Lord of the Manor of Bradwell in Essex, 1917 ; a Freemason—nominated Assistant Grand Chaplain of Cumberland and Westmorland, 1908 ; Governor East London Hospital for Children, 1905 ; Chairman of Managers, L.C.C. Schools (St. George's Group), 1905-9 ; Representative Manager for Church Schools and Member of Advisory Committee, 1916; Surrogate

for the Diocese of London, and the Master of the Faculties, and the Vicar-General of the Province of Canterbury, 1909 ; Chaplain to the Territorial Force, 1911 (Hon. Lt.-Col. 1917); Commissary in England to the Bishop of the Falkland Isles, 1913-15 ; Pioneer of Church Finance Reform. Fellow of the Royal Society of Literature, 1903 ; Member· of the Council, 1904-10 ; Fellow of the Royal Historical Society, 1904-13. *Publications :* The Preacher's Year ; Sermon Outlines ; Echoes of the Sanctuary ; The Problem of Life, Led by a Little Child, 1906 ; Two Men and a Girl ; A Thousand Things to Say in Sermons, 1906 ; Life : from a Parson's Point of View ; A History of British Poetry from the Earliest Times to the Beginning of the Twentieth Century ; The Communicants' Little Book ; The Poet of the Church of England : a Tribute to George Herbert ; Church Finance Reform, Its Need and Possibilities ; A Thousand Thoughts for Practical Preachers ; Editor : The Service of Perfect Freedom, etc. *Recreations :* cycling, boating, swimming. *Address :* The Rectory, St. George in the East, E.1 ; Elm Grove, Ruislip. *T.A. :* Rector, Cannon Street Road. *(Died Mar. 1919.)*

CORBETT, Rev. John Reginald, Rector of Wanstead, Essex, since 1907 ; Hon. Canon of S. Albans since 1897, of Chelmsford, 1914; *b.* 1844, New Ross, Co. Wexford ; *s.* of Rev. John Corbett, M.A., Dublin. *Educ. :* King's School, Canterbury ; Magdalen Hall, Oxford (Scholar). Curate of Barking, Essex ; Vicar of St. Botolph's, Colchester, 1870-1907 ; Rural Dean of Colchester, 1897-1907 ; Rural Dean of Wanstead and Woodford, 1919. *Address :* The Rectory, Wanstead, E.11. *T. :* Wanstead 417.

(Died 28 Nov. 1920.)

CORBETT, Sir Julian Stafford, Kt. *cr.* 1917; LL.M., F.S.A. ; Barrister-at-law ; Hon. Fellow of Trinity College, Cambridge ; Director of Historical Section, Committee of Imperial Defence ; *b.* 12 Nov. 1854 ; 2nd *s.* of late Chas. J. Corbett, F.R.A.S., Imber Court, Surrey ; *m.* 1899, Edith, *o. d.* of George Alexander ; one *s.* one *d. Educ. :* Marlborough ; Trinity College, Cambridge. 1st class Law Tripos, 1876 ; Barr. (Middle Temple), 1877 ; practised till 1882 ; special correspondent to Pall Mall Gazette, Dongola Expedition, 1896 ; Ford Lecturer in English History (Oxford), 1903 ; Lecturer in History to the Naval War College ; Chesney Gold Medal, 1914. *Publications :* Romances—The Fall of Asgard ; For God and Gold ; Kophetua XIII. ; A Business in Great Waters, etc. : monographs on Monk and Drake (English Men of Action) : Drake and the Tudor Navy ; The Successors of Drake ; England in the Mediterranean ; Fighting Instructions, 1530-1816 ; England in the Seven Years' War ; Signals and Instructions, 1778-94 ; The Campaign of Trafalgar, 1910 ; Some Principles of Maritime Strategy, 1911 ; The Spencer Papers (1794-1801), 1913-14 ; Official History of the Great War Naval Operations, 1920. *Recreations :* sport and travel. *Address :* 3 Hans Crescent, S.W. *T. :* Victoria 42. *Clubs :* Athenæum, Ranelagh.

(Died 21 Sept. 1922.)

CORBY, Henry, B.A., M.D. ; Professor of Obstetrics and Gynæcology, University College, Cork ; Member of Council British Medical Association ; Consulting Physician, Cork Maternity Hospital ; Surgeon, South Infirmary and County Hospital. *Educ. :* Queen's College, Cork. High Sheriff, Cork, 1904 ; ex-President Incorporated Medical Practitioners' Assoc., and Cork Medical and Surgical Society ; ex-Vice-President Cork Scientific Society ; ex-Member of Council Cork Literary and Scientific Society ; ex-Vice-President School Section Royal Institute of Public Health. *Publications :* Some Experiences of a House Surgeon ; Healthy Homes ; Industry and Ability ; Technical Education ; Bacteria the Foes and

Friends of Man; Some Medical Aspects of School Life. *Address:* 19 St. Patrick's Place, Cork. *T.A.:* Cork. *T.:* X 26.
(Died April 1917.)

CORDER, Lt.-Col. Arthur Annerley, C.M.G. 1916; O.B.E.; attached R.A.O.C; served European War, 1914-18 (despatches four times, C.M.G., B.E.). *Address:* Glendoon, Havant, Hants. *(Died 4 April 1923.)*

CORELLI, Marie, novelist; of mingled Italian and Scotch (Highland) parentage and connections; adopted in infancy by Charles Mackay, the well-known song-writer and *littérateur*, and brought up during childhood in England. Afterwards sent to France and educated in a convent, where she received, with other instruction, a first-class musical training. Her first book, A Romance of Two Worlds, was an instant success, and from that time she has devoted herself entirely to literature. Her favourite recreations are reading and music. *Publications:* A Romance of Two Worlds, 1886; Vendetta, 1886; Thelma, 1887; Ardath, 1889; Soul of Lilith, 1892; Barabbas, 1893; The Sorrows of Satan, 1895; Mighty Atom, 1896; The Murder of Delicia, 1896; Ziska: the Problem of a Wicked Soul, 1897; Jane, 1897; Boy, 1900; The Master Christian, 1900; Temporal Power, A Study in Supremacy, 1902; God's Good Man, 1904; Free Opinions, 1905; The Treasure of Heaven, 1906; Holy Orders, 1908; The Devil's Motor, 1910; The Life Everlasting, 1911; Innocent, Her Fancy and His Fact, 1914; The Young Diana, 1917; My Little Bit, a Record of War Work, 1919; The Love of Long Ago, 1920; The Secret Power, 1921. *Address:* Mason Croft, Stratford-on-Avon.
(Died 21 April 1924.)

CORFE, Rt. Rev. Charles John, D.D.; *b.* 1848; unmarried; *s.* of C. W. Corfe, Mus. Doc. Oxford. *Educ.:* All Souls Coll. Oxford (M.A. 1869). Ordained 1866; Chaplain R.N. 1867-89; Bishop of Church of England in Corea, 1889-1904; resigned, 1904. Served H.M.S. "Victor Emanuel," Ashanti War, 1874 (medal). *Address:* Church House, Westminster, S.W.
(Died 30 June 1921.)

CORFIELD, Rev. Claud Evelyn Lacey, M.A.; Rector of Heanor, 1886-1911; Prebendary of Wells Cathedral, 1919; Vicar of Taunton since 1911; *s.* of Rev. Frederick Corfield, J.P., Domestic Chaplain to Lord Claremont; *m.* 1916, Hon. Mary Hay Burns, 3rd *d.* of 1st Baron Inverclyde, *widow* of the Rev. E. Murray Robinson, and patroness of Merton, Surrey; one *d. Educ.:* Trent College, Derbyshire; St. Catherine's College, Cambridge (B.A. 1877; 1st Class Theology, M.A., 1881). Ordained, 1880; Curate at Parish Church, Plymouth; Senior Curate, Rotherham Parish Church; Vicar of Shirley, Derbyshire, 1883. Hon. Canon of Southwell, 1910-11; Proctor in Convocation for Diocese of Bath and Wells, 1925. *Address:* The Vicarage, Taunton.
(Died 3 June 1926.)

CORK and ORRERY, 10th Earl of (*cr.* 1620), **Charles Spencer Canning Boyle,** Baron Boyle of Youghall, 1616; Viscount Dungarvan, 1620; Viscount Kinalmeaky, Baron Broghill and Bandon Bridge (Ireland), 1628; Earl of Orrery, 1660; Baron Boyle of Marston, 1711; D.L.; *b.* 24 Nov. 1861; *e. s.* of 9th Earl of Cork and Emily, 2nd *d.* of 1st Marquis of Clanricarde; *m.* 1918, Rosalie, *d.* of late William Waterman de Villiers of Romsey, Hants. Protestant. Unionist. Lt.-Col. North Somerset Yeomanry; served South Africa, 1900-1901. Possesses the historical Orrery Jewel, connected with the accession of James I. *Heir:* s. Hon. Robert Lascelles Boyle. *Address:* 56 Pont Street, S.W.1. *T.:* Kensington 3891. *Clubs:* White's, Garrick, Beefsteak; Royal Yacht Squadron, Cowes.*(Died 25 Mar 1925.)*
228

CORKE, Sir John Henry, Kt., *cr.* 1916; K.L.H., J.P., four times Mayor of Portsmouth. Took an active part in recruiting, and raised three battalions for the Hampshire Regt. *Address:* 6 Alhambra Road, Southsea.
(Died 3 Jan. 1927.)

CORKRAN, Alice, journalist, etc.; *b.* Paris; *d.* of J. Frazer Corkran, journalist and man of letters. *Educ.:* home, especially in Paris. *Publications:* Bessie Lang; Latheby Towers; Down the Snow Stairs; Marjery Merton's Girlhood; Mag's Friend; Young Philistine; Life of Lord Leighton; The Romance of Woman's Influence; The National Gallery; The Dawn of British History; etc. *Recreation:* chess, and sketching from nature. *Address:* 47 Walpole Road, Boscombe, Hants.
(Died 2 Feb. 1916.)

CORNABY, Rev. William Arthur; China Missionary; *b.* 1860; *m.* 1st, Margaret (*d.* 1915), *d.* of late George Baker; three *s.* one *d.*; 2nd, Emma, *d.* of late G. Foggitt; one *s. Educ.:* Sydenham Grammar School; School of Mines, S.W.; Wesleyan Coll., Richmond. Assistant teacher of chemistry, Clifton Coll., 1881-1883; Wesleyan Mission, Hankow, 1885-1903; on the editorial staff of the Christian Literature Society since 1899; resident in Shanghai, 1904-1911; founding and editing the Ta Tung Pao magazine for Chinese officials and scholars; Wesleyan Mission, Hupeh, 1912. *Publications:* A String of Chinese Peach-Stones, 1898; China under the Searchlight, 1901; In Touch with Reality, 1905; China and its People (Madras), Let us Pray, The Call of Cathay, 1910; Prayer and the Human Problem, 1912; Chinese Letter-writing (Shanghai), 1914; also ten works in Chinese. *Recreations:* music, photography, drawing, and gardening. *Address:* Hanyang, China. *(Died 11 Mar. 1921.)*

CORNEY, Bolton Glanvill, I.S.O. 1904, M.R.C.S. (Eng.), F.R.G.S.; late Member Legislative Council and Chief Medical Officer, Fiji; *b.* Barnes, Surrey, 1851; *s.* of Bolton Corney, M.R.S.L., and Henrietta Mary, *d.* of Vice-Admiral Pridham, R.N. *Educ.:* privately, in France, England, and Germany; St. Thomas's Hospital. Fellow of the Royal Society of Medicine and Royal Colonial Institute; Member of Council of the Royal Geographical Society, that of the Hakluyt Society; and that of the Society for Nautical Research; Surgeon Superintendent of Melanesian immigrants, Fiji, 1876; Colonial Surgeon, Fiji, 1877; Acting Chief Medical Officer, 1882-83; appointed Official Delegate from Fiji on Australasian Sanitary Conference, Sydney, 1884; Acting Agent-General of Immigration, 1885-87; Member Native Regulation Board, Member Legislative Council, 1885; Chief Medical Officer, 1887; Superintendent Public Lunatic Asylum, 1887-1903; Acting Receiver-General, 1892, and Member Executive Council; a Commissioner to inquire into decrease of native population; Chairman of same Commission, and joint author of Report, 1893; Commissioner to investigate misgovernment of Tailevu province by native Chief, 1895; a Commissioner of Customs; Pres. of Board of Health (Fiji); Governor's Deputy to visit the Leper Asylum; retired, 1908. *Publications:* Hakluyt Society's vols. xiii., xxxii., xxxvi., xliii. (Series II.); in Transactions of the Epidemiological Society of London—On Epidemic Diseases in Polynesia, 1884; On Epidemic Cerebro-Spinal Meningitis; On Dengue; Folk Lore Society—On Leprosy Stones, 1896; contributions to the Lancet, Geographical Journal, etc. *Address:* c/o Coutts & Co., 440 Strand, W.C.2.
(Died 29 Sept. 1924.)

CORNFORD, Leslie Cope; *s.* of Rev. James Cornford and Emily, *d.* of C. W. Cope, R.A.; *m.* Christabel, 7th *d.* of Philip Henry Lawrence; two *s. Educ.:* privately.

Naval Correspondent to the Morning Post during European War. *Publications:* R. L. Stevenson, 1899; English Composition, 1900; Essay-writing for Schools, 1903; Parson Brand, 1906; Troubled Waters, 1911; W. E. Henley, 1913; editor Memoirs Admiral Lord Charles Beresford, 1914; Echoes from the Fleet; Lord High Admiral, 1915; Secret of Consolation, 1915; The Merchant Seaman in War, 1918; The British Navy: the Navy Vigilant, 1918; The Paravane Adventure, 1919; Interpretations, 1926. *Address:* 9 Stone Buildings, Lincoln's Inn, W.C.   (*Died 4 Aug. 1927.*)

CORNISH, Rev. Ebenezer Darrel, President of the United Methodist Free Churches, 1898; Chapel Secretary, United Methodist Church, 1910; *b.* Exeter, 7 Mar. 1849; *s.* of John Lawrence Cornish of Launceston; *m.* Charlotte Screen, Exeter; three *d. Educ.:* Hele's School, Exeter. Assistant Master Hele's School; then engaged in business in London; entered the Ministry, 1869; Secretary of Conference, 1895-98; elected President, 1898; elected Chapel Secretary, 1902. *Publications:* sundry articles in various magazines. *Recreation:* chess. *Address:* 7 Northumberland Street, Higher Broughton, Manchester.
    (*Died 26 Oct. 1922.*)

CORNISH, Francis Warre, M.A.; Vice-Provost of Eton College, 1893-1916; *b.* 8 May 1839; *s.* of Rev. H. K. Cornish, Fellow of Exeter Coll. Oxford, Vicar of Bakewell, and Louisa, *d.* of Rev. F. Warre, D.C.L., Rector of Cheddon Fitzpaine, Somerset, and Hemyock, Devon; *m.* Blanche, *d.* of late Hon. W. Ritchie, Legal Member of Council in India, 1866. *Educ.:* Foundation, Eton College; King's College, Cambridge (Fellow). Battie University Scholarship; 3rd in 1st class of Classical Tripos, 1861; assist. master at Eton College, 1861-93. *Publications:* Life of Oliver Cromwell; Sunningwell; Darwell Stories; Dr. Ashford, etc.; Chivalry; articles in periodicals. *Address:* Cloisters, Eton College. *Club:* Athenæum.
    (*Died 28 Aug. 1916.*)

CORNISH, Rt. Rev. John Rundle, D.D.; Bishop of St. Germans since 1905 (Suffragan to Truro); Archdeacon of Cornwall, 1888-1916; *b.* Tavistock, 7 Oct. 1837; *m.* 1874, Constance Eliza, *d.* of C. Barham, M.D., of Truro; one *s.* one *d. Educ.:* Bideford Grammar School; Sidney Sussex College, Cambridge; Fellow, Dean, and Taylor Lecturer of Sidney Sussex College; 14th Wrangler in 1859. Vicar of St. John's, Kenwyn, of Veryan, and of Kenwyn; Principal Truro Training College; Examining Chaplain to Bishops Benson, Wilkinson, Gott, Stubbs, and Burrows; Select Preacher at Cambridge, 1894-1907; Vicar of Kenwyn, 1883-1916. *Address:* Truro. *T.A.:* Truro.
    (*Died 20 April 1918.*)

CORRIE, Major Alfred Wynne, J.P., D.L.; 4th *s.* of late John Malcolm Corrie, of Itchen Abbas, Hants, and Fanny, *d.* of late William Wynne of Itchen Abbas; *b.* 1856; *m.* 1st 1886, Charlotte Anne (*d.* 1913), *o. d.* and heiress of late Jacob Fletcher-Fletcher, of Peel Hall, Lancashire; 2nd 1916, Mary Constance, *e. d.* of George Butler Lloyd; one. *s. Educ.:* Charterhouse. High Sheriff, Shropshire, 1909; Major, Assistant Commandant, Royal Defence Corps, Western Command; Major Shropshire Imperial Yeomanry, 1901; Mayor of Oswestry, 1889-93 (freedom of Borough). *Address:* Park Hall, Oswestry; Swan Hill House, Shrewsbury. *Clubs:* Marlborough, Carlton.   (*Died 4 April 1919.*)

CORRY, Sir William, 2nd Bt.; *cr.* 1885; Director Cunard Line, and Commonwealth and Dominion-Line, Ltd.; *b.* 20 Mar. 1859; *S.* father 1891; *m.* Charlotte, *d.* of late J. Collins, 1889 (*d.* 1896); two *s.* one *d. Heir:* *s.* James Perowne Ivo Myles [*b.* 10 June 1892; *m.* 1921,

Molly Irene, *y. d.* of Major O. J. Bell. *Educ.:* Eton; Trinity Coll., Cambridge]. *Recreations:* yachting, billiards, golf. *Address:* 118 Eaton Square, S.W.1; *T.:* Victoria 6297; Claremont, Esher. *Club:* Junior Carlton.
    (*Died 9 June 1926.*)

CORSTORPHINE, George Steuart; *b.* 1868; *e. s.* of John Corstorphine, Edinburgh; *m.* 1896, Clara Ursula, 2nd *d.* of George Hoffmann, Munich; one *d. Educ.:* Universities of Edinburgh and Munich. Baxter Scholar in Natural Science, Edinburgh University, 1892; Falconer Fellow in Geology and Palæontology, 1892-95; Assistant to Dr. James Geikie, Murchisonian Professor of Geology, Edinburgh, 1892-1894; appointed Professor of Geology and Mineralogy, South African College, and Keeper of Geological Department, South African Museum, Cape Town, 1895; Director Geological Survey of the Cape Colony, 1896-1902; Consulting Geologist, Consolidated Gold Fields of South Africa, Ltd., 1902-8; in private practice, 1908-12; Principal, South African School of Mines and Technology, 1913; President, Geological Society of South Africa, 1906, Hon. Sec., 1910-15. *Publications:* Dissertation; Die Massengesteine des südlichen Teiles der Insel Arran, Wien, 1895; Annual Reports of Geological Survey of Cape Colony for 1896-1901; Papers in Trans. Geol. Society South Africa; also in Rep. South African Association Advancement of Science, 1904; co author with Dr. F. H. Hatch of The Geology of South Africa, 1905. *Address:* Box 1758 and Ravensworth, Yeo Street, Johannesburg. *T.A.:* University. *T.:* (Office) 2318; (Residence) Yeoville 1096. *Club:* Rand, Johannesburg.
    (*Died 25 Jan. 1919.*)

CORTIE, Rev. Father Aloysius Laurence, S.J., F.R.A.S., F.Inst.P.; Doc. Univ. Padua; F.R. Met. S.; Director of the Stonyhurst College Observatory; *b.* London, 22 April 1859. *Educ.:* Stonyhurst Coll.; St. Beuno's Coll., N. Wales. Entered novitiate S.J. 1878; priest, 1892; studied astronomy under the late Father Perry, S.J., F.R.S., and attached to Stonyhurst Observatory since 1881; F.R.A.S. 1891, and served for many years on the Council; Director of the Solar Section British Astronomical Association, 1900-10; President Manchester Astronomical Society since 1911; directed an expedition to observe total solar eclipse at Vinaroz, Spain, 1905; and the Government expeditions to the Tonga Islands, S. Pacific, 1911, and to Hernösand, Sweden, 1914; distinguished in solar and stellar physics and in terrestrial magnetism; taught physics and mathematics at Stonyhurst for twenty-seven years, and director of music for nineteen years; a Gilchrist lecturer. *Publications:* numerous memoirs and papers on astrophysics and terrestrial magnetism; Memoirs and Monthly Notices R.A.S., the Astrophysical Journal; Memoirs and Journal, B.A.A., Reports of British Association. *Recreations:* music, golf. *Address:* Stonyhurst College, Blackburn. *T.A.:* Stonyhurst.
    (*Died 16 May 1925.*)

CORYNDON, Sir Robert (Thorne), K.C.M.G., *cr.* 1919; C.M.G. 1911; Governor and Commander-in-Chief, Kenya, and High Commissioner of Zanzibar since 1922; *b.* Queenstown, Cape Colony, 2 Apr. 1870; *s.* of Selby Coryndon of Plymouth; *m.* 1909, Phyllis Mary, *d.* of late J. C. Worthington; three *s.* one *d. Educ.:* Cheltenham College. Joined Bechuanaland Border Police, under B.S.A. Co., 9 Nov. 1889, and the Pioneer force for the occupation of Mashonaland, June 1890-91; private Secretary to the Rt. Hon. C. J. Rhodes, 1896-97, and during Parliamentary Inquiry into Jameson Raid; served in Matabele War, 1893, and Matabele rebellion, 1896 (medal and clasp); British Resident with Lewanika, and B.S.A. Co.'s

229

representative in Barotseland, June 1897 ; took expedn. to Lealui ; Upper Zambesi river, 1897 ; Administrator of North-Western Rhodesia, Sept. 1900 ; Resident Commissioner for Swaziland 1907-16 ; Basutoland, 1916 ; Governor and Comdr.-in-Chief, Uganda, 1917-22 ; Chairman of the S. Rhodesia Native Reserves Commission, 1914-15 ; Commander, Crown of Belgium. *Address :* Government House, Nairobi, Kenya. *Clubs :* Travellers', Athenæum.
(*Died 10 Feb. 1925.*)

CORYTON, Frederick, J.P. and M.F.H. ; Joint-Master of the Hampshire pack, 1888-1909 ; Lord of the Manor of Greatham ; *b.* 1 Mar. 1850 ; *s.* of late George Edward Coryton, J.P., of Liss Place, Hants ; *m.* 1888, Augusta, *d.* of late Richard Manders of Shanganagh, Co. Dublin ; one *s.* two *d. Educ. :* Harrow. *Address :* The Manor House, Greatham, Liss, Hants.   (*Died 12 Nov. 1924.*)

CORYTON. William, country gentleman, landowner; J.P., D.L., Cornwall; Master of Dartmoor Foxhounds, 1889-1916 ; Sheriff of Cornwall, 1902 ; *b.* Hampshire, 30 Oct. 1847 ; *e. s.* of George Edward Coryton of Liss Place, Hants (*d.* 1886), and of Mary Louisa Phillott, *d.* of Rev. Phillott (*d.* 1884) ; *m.* 1887, E. A. Parker, *d.* of Admiral Parker, Delamore, South Devon ; three *s.* three *d. Educ. :* private school and tutors. S. uncle 1891 ; paid much attention to farming ; has a very large dairy farm ; took his pack of beagles from Hampshire to Cornwall in 1868 ; substituted harriers and eventually foxhounds in 1875, hunting the E. Cornwall country at his own expense for fourteen years. *Heir :* Capt. John Tillie Coryton [Rifle Brigade ; *b.* 25 Aug. 1888 ; *m.* 1911, Dorothy, *y. d.* of T. S. Parker-Jervis of Footherley Hall, Lichfield]. *Address :* Pentillie Castle, St. Mellion, R.S.O., E. Cornwall. *M. :* AF 460 and 912. *Clubs :* Boodle's, Royal Western Yacht.   (*Died 27 Aug. 1919.*)

COSBY, Dudley Sydney Ashworth, D.L.; F.R.A.S. ; *b.* 12 Jan. 1862 ; *o. surv. s.* of late Col. R. A. G. Cosby and Alice Sophia Elizabeth (*d.* 1878). *o. d.* of Sir George Edward Pocock, 2nd Bart. ; *m.* 1895, Emily Mabel (*d.* 1918), *o. c.* of Lt.-Gen. James Gubbins, C.B.; three *s.* two *d. Educ. :* Eton. Late Lieut. the Rifle Brigade, and Capt. 4th Scottish Rifles ; served European War on the Cable Censorship—Military Intelligence Department, 13 March 1916-22 May 1918. *Publications :* The Irish Land Problem, and How to Solve it, 1901 ; The Menace of Socialism (two editions) ; Why England needs an Upper Chamber : A Defence of the House of Lords, 1908 ; Fair Trade v. Free Trade : Cobden's Unrealised Ideal, 1909 ; King Edward VII. : the Passing of a Great Ruler, 1910 ; The Governance of Empire : Forward but Not Too Fast, 1911 ; German Kultur : What Is It? ; Towards Universal Peace, 1915 ; many articles to reviews and letters to the Press. *Address :* Stradbally Hall, Queen's Co. ; Westcliff Lodge, West Bournemouth. *Club :* Naval and Military.
(*Died 23 Dec. 1923.*)

COSBY, Col. Robert Ashworth Godolphin, J.P., D.L.; head of Cosby family; *b.* 1887; *o. s.* of late Sydney Cosby, and Emily, *d.* of late Robert Ashworth; *m.* 1st, 1859, Alice Sophia Elizabeth (*d.* 1878), *o. d.* of Sir George Edward Pocock, 2nd Bart. ; 2nd, 1885, Eliza (*d.* 1920), *d.* of Rev. Capel Molyneux, and widow of Sir Charles Goring, 11th Bart. *Educ. :* Eton. Vice-Lieut. of Queen's Co. ; High Sheriff, 1863 ; Hon. Col. 3rd Batt. Leinster Regt. ; late Lieut. 6th Dragoons. *Heir : s.* Dudley.   *Address :* Stradbally Hall, Queen's Co. *Clubs :* Wellington, Army and Navy ; Kildare Street, Dublin.
(*Died 29 Aug. 1920.*)

COSGRAVE, MacDowel, M.D. Dub. ; M.R.I.A. ; late Physician in Ordinary to Lord Lieutenant of Ireland ; Knight of Grace, Order of St. John of Jerusalem ; Professor of Bi-

ology, Royal College of Surgeons ; Physician to Drumcondra and Simpson's Hospitals ; *s.* of late Wm. A. Cosgrave, Corrstown House, Co. Dublin, Clerk of the Peace for County Longford ; *m.* Anna (*d.* 1920), *d.* of late Rev. Wm. Crofts Bullen, Ballythomas, Co. Cork ; she was author of " Life Studies in Palmistry " and of papers on Poor Law Reform). *Educ. :* Kingstown School ; Dublin University. Practised first at Huddersfield, then at Colchester, where founded a branch of the S.I.I. Ambulance Association ; returning to Dublin joined the College of Physicians, being President 1914-16, during which time was one of founders of Dublin Castle Red Cross Hospital and Chairman of Irish Medical War Committee ; was Hon. Sec. to Dublin Sanitary Association, and member of Council, Royal Society of Antiquaries of Ireland, of which was elected Fellow in 1908 ; was for eight years Hon. Treasurer Royal Zoological Society of Ireland ; founded the Georgian Society, 1909-13, and acted as Hon. Secretary and member of Editorial Committee. *Publications :* Hints and Helps for Home Nursing and Hygiene ; The Student's Botany ; Photography and Architecture ; The Illustrated Dictionary of Dublin ; Dublin and the Co. Dublin in the Nineteenth Century ; Catalogue of Engravings of Dublin ; Alcohol and Longevity ; The Role of Alcohol ; Book-plates of Irish Medical Men ; edited Commonsense, 1893-1901. *Recreations :* photography ; collecting Dublin prints and book-plates. *Address :* 5 Gardiner Row, Dublin. *T. :* Dublin 2191. *M. :* RI 8850.   (*Died 16 Feb. 1925.*)

COSTIGAN, Capt. Charles Telford, D.S.O. 1915 ; 10th Batt. Canadian 1st Division ; *s.* of Thomas John Costigan ; unmarried. *Educ. :* Halbrake College. Came over to Europe with 1st Canadian Division, 1914 ; Field Cashier ; Transferred to 10th Batt., 1915 ; 64th Regt. Canadian Militia : served European War, 1914-1916 (despatches, D.S.O.), led a bombing party at Messines. *Address :* Calgary, Alberta, Canada.
(*Died Nov. 1917.*)

COSTIGAN, Senator Hon. John, M.P., P.C. ; *b.* St. Nicholas, Province of Quebec, 1 Feb. 1835, of Irish parentage ; *m.* 1855, Harriet S. Ryan of Victoria, N.B. ; one *s.* two *d. Educ. :* provincial schools ; St. Anne's College, Province of Quebec. Appointed Registrar of Deeds and Wills for Victoria County, New Brunswick, 1858 ; resigned 1861, to accept the candidature for that county in the general elections for the Legislature of New Brunswick ; was elected and continued to represent Victoria in the N.B. Legislature until the election just previous to the Confederation, when, though duly elected by a majority, he authorised the Returning Officer to declare his opponent elected, to prevent a grave and serious riot ; in 1867, at the first general election for the Federal House of Commons was elected to represent the said County of Victoria, N.B., and has been elected at every general election since, and is the only member of the House of Commons that has held his seat continuously since confederation : Minister of Inland Revenue, 1882-1892 ; Secretary of State, 1892-94 ; Minister of Marine and Fisheries, 1894-96 ; called to the Senate, 1907. *Recreations :* for the last forty-eight years has spent from four to ten weeks each year in the Canadian forests, which has contributed to his good health and enabled him to acquire valuable information regarding the interior of Canada. *Address :* 152 Carling Ave., Ottawa, Ontario.   (*Died 1 Oct. 1916.*)

COTES, Mrs. Everard; *b.* Brantford, Canada; *d.* of Charles Duncan, merchant ; *m.* Everard Cotes. *Educ. :* Brantford chiefly. Began literary work as a correspondent, and later joined the editorial staff of the Washington Post ; afterwards became attached to the Toronto Globe and Week, and later to the Montreal Star as writer of special articles, which included the letters from Japan and the East, afterwards rewritten for A Social Departure. *Publications*: A Social Departure; An American Girl in London; The Simple Adventures of a Memsahib; Vernon's Aunt; The Story of Sonny Sahib; A Daughter of To-Day; His Honour and a Lady; A Voyage of Consolation, 1898; The Path of a Star, 1899; On the Other Side of the Latch, 1901; Those Delightful Americans, 1902; The Pool in the Desert, 1903; The Imperialist, 1904; Set in Authority, 1906; Cinderella of Canada, 1908; The Burnt Offering, 1909; The Consort, 1912; His Royal Happiness, 1915. *Address*: 17 Paultons Square, Chelsea, S.W.3. *Club*: Ladies' Empire.

(Died 22 July 1922.)

COTES, Sir Merton Russell, Kt.; *cr.* 1909; J.P., F.R.G.S.; art connoisseur and collector; *b.* Tettenhall, near Wolverhampton, 8 May 1835; *m.* 1860, Annie Nelson (*d.* 1920), *d.* of John King Clark, W.S., Glasgow; one *s. Educ.*: Old College, High Street, Glasgow. Resided in Bournemouth since 1876, and has taken an active part in developing the town, mainly responsible for the construction of the Undercliff Drive and Promenade, the Sanitary Hospital, etc.; projected the idea of the direct line between Christchurch and Brockenhurst on the L. and S.W. Railway; Member of the local Board of Improvement Commissioners prior to the incorporation of Bournemouth, 1890, when he presented the mace—a replica of that presented to Wolverhampton by Queen Elizabeth; invited to fill the Mayoral Chair in 1892 and 1893, but declined on account of ill-health; Mayor of Bournemouth, 1894-95; during his Mayoralty the Meyrick Park was opened, also two free libraries, and the two first schools of art in the borough; for upwards of thirty-five years his loan collection of about 250 pictures was exhibited in the Corporation Art Galleries of Liverpool, Leeds, Sheffield, Bradford, Nottingham, Derby, Glasgow, Bath, Oldham, Burnley, and other cities, and many of his pictures have been borrowed for exhibition in Chicago Exhibition, the Guildhall (London), the People's Palace (Whitechapel), the Grafton Gallery, etc., etc.; through Mr. Choate (when American Ambassador to England) he presented to the American people an original black basalt bust of Washington made by Josiah Wedgwood, which is now in the Congressional Library, Washington; has travelled with his wife in many parts of the world, including South America, Australia, New Zealand, Canada, United States of America, South and North Africa, West Indies, China, Japan, Egypt, Palestine, Syria, Turkey, Russia, Sweden and Norway, Finland, Spain, and generally the European continent; explored and wrote a paper on the volcano of Mauna Loa and the great crater of Kilauea, Hawaii; explored the Pink and White Terraces, etc., New Zealand; in conjunction with his wife has given to the Borough of Bournemouth their residence East Cliff Hall and its art treasures, to become the Russell-Cotes Art Gallery and Museum, in recognition of which they were presented with the honorary freedom of the borough, 15 July 1908. *Recreations*: art, music, foreign travel, exploration. *Address*: East Cliff Hall, Bournemouth. *Clubs*: United Empire, Constitutional.

(Died 27 Jan. 1921.)

COTMAN, Frederic George, R.I.; *b.* 14 Aug. 1850; *s.* of Henry Cotman, *y. b.* of John Sell Cotman; *m. d.* of late B. Grahame of Morphie, Kincardineshire, 1875; three *s.* three *d. Educ.*: Ipswich; admitted student Royal Academy, 1868; gold medal for historical painting, 1873. *Recreation*: boating. *Address*: Whitegates, Felixstowe. *(Died 16 July 1920.)*

COTTELL, Col. Reginald James Cope, C.B.E., 1919; late R.A.M.C.; *b.* 1858; 4th *s.* of late Major James W. Cottell, H.E.I.C.S., and Elizabeth Ann, *e. d.* of late Rev. Edward Warren Caulfeild, M.A.; *m.* 1899, Edith Clementina, *d.* of James Ruthven; three *d.* Entered Army, 1886; Major, 1898; Lt.-Col. 1906; retired 1913; served in Gibraltar, 1888-94; S. Africa, 1897-1902; during the S. African War was in medical charge of the 2nd Royal Berkshire Regt. and secondly of the Medical Division of No. 7 General Hospital, Pretoria (Queen's medal three clasps, King's medal two clasps, officially thanked for war services by the Commander-in-Chief); subsequently was medical officer to the Royal Military Academy, Woolwich, and afterwards was physician and surgeon for seven years to the Royal Hospital, Chelsea; volunteered for service and rejoined Army 5 Aug. 1914; was officer commanding the King George Hospital, Stamford Street, S.E., Aug. 1915-Sept. 1919 (mentioned for valuable medical services 1917; promoted Brevet-Colonel, 1918, C.B.E.); a Knight of Grace of the Order of St. John of Jerusalem. *Address*: 7 Phillimore Terrace, Kensington, W.8. *(Died 7 Aug. 1924.)*

COTTENHAM, 4th Earl of (*cr.* 1850), **Kenelm Charles Edward Pepys;** Bt. 1784 and 1801; Baron Cottenham (U.K.), 1836; Viscount Crowhurst, 1850; late M.F.H. Bicester and Warden Hill; *b.* 18 May 1874; *s.* of 3rd Earl and Theodosia Selina, *o. d.* of Sir Robert E. Dallas, 2nd Bt.; S. father, 1881; *m.* 1st, 1899, Lady Rose Nevill (*d.* 1913), *d.* of 1st Marquess of Abergavenny; three *s.*; 2nd, 1916, Patricia, *d.* of late John Humphrev Burke, California. *Educ.*: Eton; Oxford. Owns about 6000 acres. *Heir*: *s.* Viscount Crowhurst. *Address*: Clare Priory, Suffolk. *Clubs*: Carlton, Marlborough.

(Died 22 April 1919.)

COTTER, Maj.-Gen. Francis Gibson; *b.* 12 June 1857; *s.* of late Maj. J. Cotter; *m.* 1891, Rose, *d.* of Rev. Anson Cartwright; one *d.* Entered Royal Marines, 1876; Captain, 1885; Major, 1893; Lt.-Col. 1900; Col. 1908; served Soudan, 1884-85. *(Died 24 Sept. 1928.)*

COTTER, Lt.-Col. Harry John, C.I.E. 1918; D.S.O. 1916; R.A.; *b.* 10 Sep. 1871; *s.* of Major John Cotter, the Buffs; *m.* Alice Elizabeth, *d.* of Rev. G. Armitage; one *s. Educ.*: Kelly College, Tavistock; R.M.A. Woolwich. Served Isazai Expedition, 1892; Chitral, 1895 (medal and clasp); China, 1900 (medal); European War (C.I.E., D.S.O.); Serbian Order of the White Eagle, 4th class. *(Died July 1921.)*

COTTER, Sir James Laurence, 5th Bt.; *cr.* 1763; F.R.H.S., F.N.C.S., N.R.S.; *b.* 11 July 1887; *s.* of late James Lombard Cotter, 2nd *s.* of 4th Bt., and Clara Mary, *d.* of late Capt. Thomas Segrave. [She married 2ndly, John Francis O'Connor.] S. grandfather 1902; *m.* 1908, Ethel Lucy (who obtained a divorce, 1924), *d.* of Alfred Wheeler, 98 Buckingham Gate, S.W.; two *s.* one *d. Educ.*: Bradfield College, Berks. Author, journalist and artist; has published various works on agricultural and horticultural matters. *Heir*: *s.* Delaval James Alfred, *b.* 29 April 1911. *Address*: c/o Cox's R.A. Branch, 6 Pall Mall, S.W.1. *(Died 22 Aug. 1924.)*

COTTERILL, James Henry, M.A. Camb. 1866, F.R.S. 1878; Hon. V.P. of the Institution of Naval Architects, 1905; *b.* Norfolk, 2 Nov. 1836; *y. s.* of late Rev. Joseph Cotterill, Blakeney; unmarried. *Educ.*: Brighton Coll.; apprenticed to Messrs. Fairbairn and Co., engineers; subsequently at St. John's Coll. Camb. Lecturer (1866) and Vice-Principal (1870) of the former Royal School of Naval Architecture, South Kensington; Professor of Applied Mechanics at Royal Naval Coll. Greenwich, 1873; retired Sep. 1897. *Publications*: Steam Engine considered as a Thermodynamic Machine, 1878, 2nd ed. 1890, 3rd ed. 1895; Applied Mechanics, 1884, 5th ed. 1900, reprinted, 1909. *Address*: Hill Crest, Parkstone, Dorset. *(Died 8 Jan. 1922.)*

COTTESLOE, 2nd Baron (U.K.) (*cr.* 1874), **Thomas Francis Fremantle,** M.A., D.L., J.P.; Bt. 1821; Baron of Austrian Empire, *cr.* 1816; Director London, Brighton and South Coast Railway Co.; *b.* 30 Jan, 1830; *s.* of 1st Baron and *d.* of Sir George Nugent; *S.* father 1890; *m.* Lady Augusta Henrietta Scott (*d.* 1906), 2nd *d.* of 2nd Earl of Eldon, 1859; four *s.* one *d. Educ.:* Eton; Balliol Coll. Oxford. B.A. 1st class Classics, 1852; M.P. Bucks, 1876-85. Owns about 3000 acres. *Heir: s.* Hon. Thomas Fremantle. *Address:* 43 Eaton Square, S.W.; Swanbourne, Winslow, Bucks. *Clubs:* Carlton, Travellers'. (*Died 13 April 1918.*)

COTTET, Charles; Artiste - peintre; sociétaire de la Société Nationale des Beaux-Arts, Paris; soc. des orientalistes français, des peintres graveurs, des peintres lithographes, de la Société Nouvelle; de l'International Society of Painters, Gravers, and Sculptors, London; Secessions, Vienne, Berlin; *b.* Puy, Hte.-Loire. *Educ.:* Evian-les-bains. Peintre et graveur. Principaux ouvrages: série au Pays de la Mer, consacré à la Bretagne, les côtes et ses habitants; série de tableaux Egyptiens, vénitiens, algériens, espagnols; vues de montagnes de la Savoie; quelques portraits nus et nature morte; quelques paysages d'Islande. Principaux tableaux dans les musées de Paris, Luxembourg, "et ville de Paris," Bordeaux, Lille, Saint - Etienne, Trieste, Rome, Padoue, Barcelone, Dusseldorf, Münich, Venise, Carlsruhe, Moscou, Helsingfors, Gothensburg, Vienne, Strasbourg, Buenos Ayres, Philadelphie, Cincinnati, Buffalo, Providence. Officier de la Légion d'Honneur; médaille d'or Exposition Universelle, Paris, 1900; Venise, Münich, Dresden, Barcelone. *Address:* 10 rue Cassini, Paris. (*Died Sept. 1925.*)

COTTIER, Sir Charles Edward, Kt., *cr.* 1924; Solicitor; Hon. Treasurer of Empire Industries Association; *b.* 13 Jan. 1869; *s.* of late Francis Cottier, Co. Cork, and Plymouth; *m.* 1889, Lydia Jane Avent, Plymouth; two *s.* two *d. Address:* Swyncombe, Oxfordshire. *Clubs:* Carlton, American. (*Died 22 Aug. 1928.*)

COTTON, Lt.-Col. Arthur Egerton, D.S.O. 1917; late Rifle Brigade; *b.* 1876; 3rd *s.* (twin) of late C. C. Cotton; *m.* 1909, Beryl Marie, *d.* of late H. J. Cumming; three *d.* Served European War, 1914-19 (wounded twice, despatches thrice, D.S.O., 1914-15 star). *Address:* 7 Seymour Place, W.1. *T.:* Paddington 4530. *Clubs:* Wellington, Royal Automobile. (*Died 10 June 1922.*)

COTTON, Rev. Henry Aldrich, Priest in Ordinary to the King; *b.* Ellesmere, Salop, 12 July 1835; *e. s.* of William Aldrich Cotton. *Educ.:* Bedford Grammar School; Exeter College, Oxford. B.A. 1858; M.A. 1860. Curate of Holy Trinity, Bedford, 1859; Curate of St. Michael's, Tenbury, 1861; 2nd master of Eagle House School, Wimbledon, 1862-69; Vicar of Haynes, Beds, 1869-78; Minor Canon of Westminster, 1876-92; Priest in Ordinary to Queen Victoria, 1878-1901; Vicar of Stanford-in-the-Vale, 1892-15. *Address:* Stanford-in-the-Vale, Faringdon, Berks. *Club:* Junior Conservative. (*Died 3 Feb. 1927.*)

COTTON, James Sutherland, M.A.; editor revised edition Imperial Gazetteer of India; Hon. Secretary Egypt Exploration Fund; late editor of The Academy; *b.* Coonoor, Madras, 17 July 1847; *s.* of J. J. Cotton, H.E.I.C.S.; *m.* Isabella, *d.* of John Carter, Clifton, Bristol, 1873. *Educ.:* Magdalen Coll. School; Brighton Coll.; Winchester Coll.; Trin. Coll. Oxford. Scholar of Trin. Coll.; Fellow and Lecturer of Queen's Coll. Oxford; 1st class Classical Moderations; 1st class Final Classical School. Barr. *Publications:* Decennial Report on the Moral and Material Progress of India, 1885; India, Citizen Series, 1883; Elphinstone, Rulers of India Series, 1892; Quinquennial Report on Educa-

tion in India, 1898; editor of Paterson's Practical Statutes. *Address:* 13 Warwick Mansions, Cromwell Crescent, S.W. *Club:* Savile. (*Died 9 July 1918.*)

COTTON, William Francis, D.L., P., M.P. (Nat.) Dublin Co. South since 1911; Alderman; First Secretary and Chairman Alliance Gas Co., Dublin; *b.* Dublin, 1847. Sheriff of Dublin City, 1901. *Address:* Hollywood, Roebuck, Dundrum, Co. Dublin. (*Died 8 June 1917.*)

COTTON - JODRELL, Colonel Sir Edward Thomas Davenant, K.C.B., *cr.* 1911; C.B., 1902; D.L.; County Director, Cheshire Branch, British Red Cross Society, since Aug. 1914; J.P.; *b.* Rugby, 29 June 1847; *s.* of G. E. L. Cotton, late Bishop of Calcutta; *m.* Mary, *d.* of W. R. Coleridge, Salston, Ottery St. Mary, 1878; two *d. Educ.:* Rugby; Marlborough. Passed first in Artillery Commissions in June 1868, from Woolwich; entered R.A. 1868; retired 1881; M.P. (C.) Wirral Div. Cheshire, 1885-1900; Lt.-Col. and Hon. Col. 2nd Cheshire R.E. (Railway Vols.), 1888-1908; Deputy Assistant-Director, Headquarters Staff, 1906-12. *Address:* Reasebeath Hall, Nantwich, Cheshire; Shallcros-Manor, 'Whaley Bridge; 2 Portman Square, W. *T.:* Paddington 748; Nantwich 36. *T.A.:* Jantu, Baker, London. *Clubs:* Carlton, Army and Navy. (*Died 13 Oct. 1917.*)

COTTRELL, Lieut.-Colonel Reginald Foulkes, D.S.O. 1918; late R.F.A.; *b.* 1885; *s.* of Major W. F. Cottrell, R.E.; *m.* 1920, Margaret (*d.* 1921), *d.* of late Robert English. *Educ.:* privately; Royal Military Academy, Woolwich. Entered Royal Artillery, 1903; resigned, 1909; engaged in business for six years; rejoined Army, 5 Aug. 1914; served European War, 1914-18, (D.S.O., Bt. Lt.-Col., Mons Star, Order of the Redeemer, Greek Medal for Military Merit, despatches twice); Assistant-Director, War Office, 1919-21; resigned commission, 1922; has travelled extensively in America, Mexico, India, Europe, etc. *Clubs:* Wellington, New Oxford and Cambridge, Royal Automobile. (*Died 9 Nov. 1924.*)

COTTRELL, William Henry, C.M.G. 1915; O.B.E. 1919; Capt. R.N.V.R., Eastern Mediterranean Squadron; *b.* 17 Aug. 1863; *s.* of late Major W. F. Cottrell, R.E.; *m.* 1889, Louise Baglietto, Gibraltar; two *s.* three *d. Educ.:* S.M.E., Chatham. Started in the Eastern Telegraph Co., 1878; joined the staff afloat, 1881; took part in the bombardment of Alexandria, 1882; appointed Chief Electrician and served in the Mediterranean, Red Sea, India, E. and W. coasts of Africa, etc., till 1892, when rejoined shore staff on appointment as Superintendent and H.M.'s Consul at Syra, Greece, till 1909, being then appointed Divisional Superintendent at Athens; joined the Rear-Admiral's Staff at Mudros, Feb. 1915; took part in the Gallipoli Campaign with the rank of Commander, R.N.V.R. (despatches, C.M.G.); Officer of Communications and Chief Censor at Mudros; acting Capt., 1918 (despatches, O.B.E.); Divisional Manager E.T. Co. of the Levant, Feb. 1919, and Chairman of British Chamber of Commerce for Greece and the British Club, Athens; retired, 1922; Officer French Legion of Honour and Commander Order George 1st (Greek), 1920. *Publications:* written various articles on electrical and kindred subjects. *Recreations:* music, photography, shooting, fishing, and most sports. *Address:* c/o Royal Colonial Institute, 18 Northumberland Avenue, W.C.2. *Club:* Overseas. (*Died 18 Nov. 1926.*)

COUE, Emile, Professeur de psychologie appliquée; *b.* Troyes, France, de parents occupant une situation très modeste; *m.* Mlle. Lemoine, fille de V. Lemoine de Nancy, qui fut considéré comme l'un des plus grands horticulteurs du monde; sans enfants. *Educ.:*

petit collège de Nogent-sur-Seine; lycée de Troyes. A été pharmacien à Troyes pendant 30 ans après avoir étudié la pharmacie à Paris où il fut interne des hôpitaux pendant deux ans. *Publications:* N'a jamais publié que quelques articles parus dans les Bulletins de la Société lorraine de Psychologie appliquée dont il est le président, et La Maîtrise de soi-même par l'autosuggestion consciente qui a été traduite en anglais sous le nom "Selfmastery by Conscious Autosuggestion," dans laquelle il a exposé ses théories d'une façon, aussi claire et aussi brève que possible; La Maîtrise de Soi-même per l'autosuggestion Consciente; Ce que j'ai fait (Jugements portés sur mon œuvre). *Recreations:* Travaillait autrefois dans son jardin, mais n'a plus le temps de prendre la moindre distraction. *Adresse:* rue Jeanne d'Arc 186, Nancy, France. *(Died 2 July 1926.)*

COUGHLAN, Cornelius, V.C.; pensioner; *b.* June 1828; *s.* of Edward and Catherine Coughlan; *m.* 1856; three *s.* one *d.* *Educ.:* Eyrecourt, County Galway. Served in the 75th Regiment for 21 years; Indian Mutiny medal for 1857-58, with two clasps for Delhi and relief of Lucknow; wounded on left knee, 8 June 1857; served 13 years in India; 4 years as sergeant-major, 10 years as colour-sergeant, 2 years as sergeant, 3 years as corporal, and 2 as private; also served as sergeant-major for 21 years in 3rd Connaught Rangers permanent staff. Decorated, 1857, for gallantly venturing under a heavy fire with three others into a serai occupied by the enemy in great numbers, and removing Private Corbett, 75th Regt., who lay severely wounded amongst a number of mutilated men; also for cheering and encouraging a party which hesitated to charge down a lane in SubzeeMunday, Delhi, lined on each side with huts and raked by a cross fire, then entering with party into an enclosure filled with the enemy and destroying every man; for having also on the same occasion returned under a cross fire to collect dhoolies and carry off the wounded, a service which was successfully performed. *Recreation:* angling. *Address:* Altamount Street, Westport, Co. Mayo, Ireland.

COULCHER, Mary Caroline, C.B.E., 1919; O.B.E., 1918; *b.* 1852; *d.* of Rev. George Coulcher, Rector of Wattisfield, Suffolk. *Educ.:* Lymington House School, Clapham. Lady of Grace of the Order of St. John of Jerusalem; Coronation medal, 1911; Long Service medal with two bars, St. J. A. Brigade; Vice-President for Ipswich of British Red Cross Society, Suffolk Branch. Hon. Secretary and Treasurer Ipswich Centre St. John Ambulance Association, 1879-1919; late Lady Superintendent Ipswich Nursing Division and late Lady District Superintendent to X district St. J. A. Brigade; Town Councillor Ipswich, 1910-12. *Recreation:* music. *Address:* Beechholme, Ipswich. *T.:* Ipswich 719. *Clubs:* V.A.D., St. Andrew's House. *(Died 15 June 1925.)*

COULING, Samuel; *b.* 1859; for 25 years a Missionary in Shantung, China. *Publication:* Encyclopædia Sinica; awarded the Prix Stanislas Julien, by the Académie des Inscriptions et Belles Lettres, 1918. Editor and Proprietor of New China Review. *Address:* New China Review, Shanghai, China. *(Died 15 June 1922.)*

COULL, Hon. William, Registrar-General, Escheator-General, District Magistrate and Coroner (Roseau), and Member of Executive and Legislative Councils, Dominica, Colony of Leeward Islands; *b.* 1857; *o. surv s.* of late Hon. William A. Coull, President of General Legislative Council of Leeward Islands, of Coral Hall, Antigua, and Joyce, 2nd *d.* of late Dr. Musgrave of Antigua, and sister of late Sir Anthony Musgrave, G.C.M.G., Governor of Queensland, Australia; unmarried. *Educ.:*

The Antigua Grammar School; private tuition. Enrolled law student, Leeward Is., 1875; Clerk Colonial Secretary's Office, Leeward Is., 1878; acted on several occasions as Chief Clerk and Clerk of the Antigua and Federal Executive and Legislative Councils; Dep. Coroner for Dist. A, 1880; Acting Magistrate, Dist. B, Antigua, 1882; Magistrate and Coroner for Dist. E, Roseau, and Registrar-General of births, marriages, and deaths, Dominica, 1882; Member of the Board of Poor Law Guardians; a visiting justice of the gaol, and nominated M.L.A. 1883; Escheator-General, 1885; Member Executive Council, 1895; Official Member Legislative Council, 1895; in charge of out-door poor relief, 1898; Chairman of Quarantine Board under new (Convention) Act, 1906; retired on pension, Dec. 1911. *Address:* Eversleigh House, Roseau, Dominica, B.W.I. *(Died 5 Aug. 1918.)*

COULSON, Frederick Raymond; Author and Journalist; Vexatus and Democritus of the Sunday Chronicle; *b.* London, 16 April 1864; *m.* 1888, Ada, *d.* of Joseph Emery, Berwick; one *s.* (2nd *s.* Leslie, killed in action). Forsook commercial life for journalism, 1894; before and since has contributed articles, short stories, and much verse to magazines and periodicals; has written many songs and monologues; associated since 1895 with the Sunday Chronicle and allied publications as Member of Literary Staff. *Publications:* A Jester's Jingles, 1899; The Social Scale, 1908; This Funny World, 1911. *Recreations:* reading, travel, gardening. *Address:* 68 Corringham Road, Golders Green, N.W.4. *Club:* Whitefriars. *(Died 4 Mar. 1922.)*

COULTER, Robert Millar, C.M.G. 1907; M.D.; Deputy Postmaster General, Canada, 1897-1924; *b.* 9 Sep. 1857; *m.* 1887, Emma, *d.* of late J. P. Wells. *Educ.:* Toronto University; Victoria University. Began practising medicine at Aurora, Ontario. *Address:* 190 Cooper Street, Ottawa, Canada. *Club:* Rideau, Ottawa. *(Died Feb. 1927.)*

COUPER, John, M.D., F.R.C.S; Consulting Surgeon, London Hospital, Royal London Ophthalmic Hospital, and Scottish Hospital. *Educ.:* Glasgow and Berlin. Was Lecturer in Surgery, London Hospital Medical College. *Address:* 80 Grosvenor Street, W.; Ellesborough House, Butlerscross, Bucks. *M.:* BH 77. *(Died 30 April 1918.)*

COUPERUS, Louis, Officer of the Order of Orange-Nassau, 1896; novelist; *b.* the Hague, 10 June 1863; 4th *s.* of John Ricus Couperus and Jonkvrouwe Geertruida Johanna Reynst; *m.* 1891, Elizabeth Johanna Wilhelmina Elizabeth, *d.* of Ricus Baud. *Educ.:* Batavia; the Hague. *Publications* (in England): Eline Vere, 1890; The Footsteps of Fate, 1891; Ecstasy, 1892; Majesty, 1894; Psyche, 1906; Small Souls, 1914; The Later Life, 1915; The Twilight of the Souls, 1917; Dr. Adriaan, 1918; Old People and the Things that Pass, 1919; The Tour, 1920; The Law Inevitable, 1921. *Recreation:* travelling. *Address:* c/o A. Teixeira de Mattos, 9 Cheltenham Terrace, S.W.3.
(Died 16 July 1923.)

COURROUX, George Augustus, C.V.O.; *b.* 29 Jan. 1852; *s.* of A. F. Courroux, formerly Chief Clerk of the Board of Green Cloth (*d.* 1895); *m.* 1886, Jane, *d.* of late P. T. Renaud, Chief Clerk, Duchy of Lancaster Office. J.P. 1898, County London, Middlesex, Surrey, Berks; Chief Clerk, Board of Green Cloth, 1888 - 98; Secretary, 1898; retired, 1 Jan. 1903. *Address:* 17 Chesham Road, Brighton. *(Died 5 Jan. 1923.)*

COURTENAY, Colonel Arthur Henry, C.B. 1900; Hon. Lieut.-Colonel in Army; late Master of the High Court of Justice in Ireland (King's Bench Division); retired, 1918; *b.* 16 Oct. 1852; *s.* of late Thomas Lefroy Courtenay, J.P., of Grange, Co. Antrim, and 14 Fitzwilliam Square, Dublin, and Jane Caroline, *e. d.* of late

Martin Morris, J.P. of Spiddal, Co. Galway; *m.* 1875, Mary Ellen Mildmay, *d.* of David Fullerton, J.P. of Pennington, Hants; two *d. Educ.:* privately; Trinity College, Dublin. Called to Irish Bar; Master of the Common Pleas in Ireland, 1888; Lieutenant 2nd Royal Lanark Militia, 1871; Lieut.-Colonel and Hon. Colonel 4th Batt. the Cameronians (Scottish Rifles), 1891; Col. Commandant 3rd and 4th Batts. Scottish Rifles, 1895; served with 4th Batt. Scottish Rifles in South African Campaign, 1900-1 (C.B.); Commandant of Boshof, Orange River Colony, 1900-1 (despatches, medal and three clasps, C.B.); on Headquarters Staff, Northern Command, York, 1915-17; attached to Ministry of National Service, 1917-18; Assistant Competent Military Authority London District, 1919-22; D.L. Lanarkshire; J.P., D.L. Co. Galway; High Sheriff, 1887 and 1909. *Recreations:* shooting, hunting. *Address:* Heathbourne, Lansdown Road, Wimbledon, S.W.20. *T.:* Wimbledon 1186. *Clubs:* Junior Carlton; United Service, Dublin; County, Galway; Royal St. George Yacht, Kingstown.
(Died 19 May 1927.)

COURTENAY, Brig.-Gen. Edward Reginald, C.B. 1905; C.M.G. 1917; D.A.G., 2nd Army Central Force; on the General Staff; *b.* 1853; *e. s.* of Major G. H. Courtenay of Southtown House, Kenton, Devon, and *g.-s.* of Rt. Hon. T. P. Courtenay, *b.* of 10th Earl of Devon; *m.* 1891, Mary Emily (May), *d.* of Major-Gen. F. Hammersley of Ash Grange, Surrey; one *d. Educ.:* Charterhouse. Lieut. 20th Hussars, 1873; Adj. 20th Hussars, 1881-86; Capt. 20th Hussars, 1881; Major 11th Hussars, 1889; Lieut.-Col. commanding 11th Hussars, 1896-1900; Colonel, 1900; commanded 10th Regimental District, 1900; Assistant Adjutant-General and Chief Staff Officer, N.W. district, 1900-1905; Colonel General Staff Welsh and Midland command, 1905; Inspector of Yeomanry and in Charge of Hussar Records, 1907-10; passed Staff College; served in Zulu War, 1878-79 (despatches, medal and clasp); Nile Expedition with Camel Corps, 1884 (medal and clasps and Khedive's star); Egyptian Frontier Expedition, 1885 (despatches); Tirah campaign, N.W. Frontier of India, 1897 (medal and clasp); European War, 1914-17 (despatches, C.M.G.). *Address:* 7 Eaton Terrace, S.W. *Club:* Cavalry.
(Died 29 Mar. 1919.)

COURTENAY, Henry, I.S.O. 1903; late Assistant Secretary, Irish Local Government Board; J.P., Co. Dublin; a member of several religious and benevolent societies in the City of Dublin; *m.* 1916, Victorine Charlotte (Ena), *e. d.* of Rt. Hon. Sir Robert Matheson. *Address:* Rosslyn, Monkstown, Co. Dublin.
(Died July 1921.)

COURTHOPE, William John, C.B., 1895; M.A.; Civil Service Commissioner, 1887; First Civil Service Commissioner, 1892; retired, 1907; Hon. Fellow New College, Oxford, 1896; Hon. D.Litt. Durham, 1895; Hon. LL.D. Edinburgh, 1898; Fellow of the British Academy of Letters, 1906; Fellow, Royal Society of Literature, 1907; *b.* 17 July 1842; *e. s.* of Rev. William Courthope, Rector of S. Malling, Sussex; *m.* 1870, Mary, *e. d.* of John Scott, H.M. Inspector-General of Hospitals, Bombay; four *s.* two *d. Educ.:* Harrow; New Coll. Oxford. 1st Class Classical Moderations, 1863; 1st class Lit. Hum. 1865; Newdigate Prize Poem, 1864; Chancellor's Prize for English Essay, 1868; Professor of Poetry, University of Oxford, 1895-1901. *Publications:* Ludibria Lunae, 1869; The Paradise of Birds, 1870; Life of Addison (Men of Letters Series), 1882; History of English Poetry vol. i. 1895, vol. ii. 1897, vols. iii. and iv. 1903, vol. v. 1905; vol. vi. 1909; Life in Poetry, Law in Taste, 1901,

234

etc.; editor of Pope's Works, and author of his Life. *Address:* The Lodge, Wadhurst, Sussex. *Club:* Athenæum. *(Died 10 April 1917.)*

COURTNEY of Penwith, 1st Baron, *cr.* 1906, **Rt. Hon. Leonard Henry Courtney,** P.C., M.A.; *b.* Penzance, 6 July 1832; *e. s.* of John Sampson Courtney, Alverton House, Penzance, and Sarah, *d.* of John Mortimer; *m.* Catherine, *d.* of Richard Potter of Lancashire and Gloucestershire, Apr. 1883. *Educ.:* St. John's Coll. Camb. (2nd Wrangler, 1855); equal as Smith's Prizeman, 1855; Barr. Lincoln's Inn, 1858; Bencher, 1889; Prof. of Political Economy, Univ. Coll. London, 1872-75; Under-Sec. of State for Home Dept. 1880-81; Colonial Office, 1881-82; appointed Financial Sec. to the Treasury; resigned this office in 1884; Chairman of Committees and Deputy Speaker, 1886-92; since this date out of office. Hon. Fellow of St. John's Coll. Camb.; Hon. LL.D. Camb., 1898; M.P. Liskeard, 1876-85; M.P. (U.) for Bodmin Division Cornwall, 1885-1900. *Publications:* The Working Constitution of the United Kingdom and its Outgrowths, 1901; has been a large contributor to the Times and Nineteenth Century. *Heir:* none. *Recreations:* takes considerable interest in literature and art. *Address:* 15 Cheyne Walk, Chelsea, S.W. *Clubs:* Athenæum. Reform. *(Died 11 May 1918.)*

COURTNEY, Colonel Edward Arthur Waldegrave, C.M.G. 1915; C.B.E. 1918; late R.A.S.C.; *b.* 10 Oct., 1868; *e. s.* of late Maj.-Gen. Edward H. Courtney C.V.O., and Mary Dorothy Saunder, *g.-m.* of 7th Earl Waldegrave; *m.* 1894, Hilda Maria, *y. d.* of T. E. Chapman, Silksworth Hall, Co. Durham; three *s.* one *d.* Entered army (Lancashire Fusiliers) 1889; R.A.S.C. 1898; Captain, 1896; Major, 1903; Lt.-Col. 1912; served South African War,1899-1901 (Queen's medal, 6 clasps); European War, 1914-18 (despatches, C.M.G., C.B.E.; Croix d'officier Légion d'Honueur, Croix d'officier L'ordre de Léopold, Croix de Guerre); Staff Captain, Cork District, 1902-3; Deputy Assistant Director of Supplies and Transport, Eastern Command, Sep. 1906-Sep. 1910; Assistant Director of Supplies, 5 Aug. 1914-31 Dec. 1914; Assistant-Director of Requisition Services, 1 Jan. 1915-6 June 1915; Deputy Director of Requisition Services, 1915-16; Director of Requisition Services, 1916-18; Liaison Officer with Army Headquarters, June 1915-May 1918; Assistant Director of Supplies and Transport, Northern Command, 1918-19; Assistant Director of Supplies and Transport, Southern Command, 1919-22; retired pay, 1922. *Club:* United Service.
(Died 18 June 1926.)

COURTNEY, Rt. Rev. Frederick, D.D.; Rector of St. James's Church, New York, 1904-15; Rector-emeritus since 1915; *b.* Plymouth, 1837; *s.* of Rev. S. Courtney, Vicar of Charles, Plymouth; *m.* Caroline (*d.* 1909), *d.* of Philip Nairn, Waren House, Northumberland, 1865; four *s.* one *d. Educ.:* King's College, London. Ordained, 1864; Curate of Hadlow, Kent, 1864-66; Incumbent of Charles's Chapel, Plymouth, 1865-70; St. Jude's, Glasgow, 1870-1876; Assistant, St. Thomas's, New York, 1876-1880; Rector of St. James's, Chicago, 1880-82; of St. Paul's, Boston, 1882-88; Bishop of Nova Scotia, 1888-1904. *Address:* St. James's Church, 71st Street, and Madison Avenue, New York. *T.:* 2185-79th. *Club:* Overseas.
(Died Dec. 1918.)

COURTNEY, John Mortimer, C.M.G. 1897; I.S.O. 1903; Knight of Grace, St. John of Jerusalem; Deputy Minister of Finance and Receiver-Gen., and Sec. of the Treasury Board of Canada 1878-1906; *b.* Penzance, Cornwall, 22 July 1838; 2nd *s.* of John Sampson Courtney of Alverton House, Penzance, and Sarah, *d.* of John Mortimer; *m.* 1870, Mary Elisabeth Sophia, 2nd *d.* of late Fennings Taylor, Clerk Assistant of the Senate of Canada ; one *s. Educ.* : Penzance. Several years banking, Chief Clerk of the Treasury, Canada, 1869 ; served on several Commissions ; Hon. Treasurer in Canada for the Indian Famine Fund; also of Canadian Patriotic Fund and Association for Prevention of Tuberculosis ; President of the Victorian Order of Nurses, Canada. *Recreation* : reading. *Address* : 638 Rideau Street, Ottawa. *Clubs* : Rideau, Royal Ottawa Golf, Ottawa.   (*Died 8 Oct. 1920.*)

COURTNEY, Col. Richard Edmond, C.B. 1915 ; Acting Comdt. 5th Military District (W.A.) ; *b.* 1870 ; *s.* of Capt. T. Wilson Courtney ; unmarried. *Educ.* : Melbourne University.' Barrister and Solicitor, Victoria, 1897. Served European War (Dardanelles), 1914-15 (despatches, C.B.). *Club* : Naval and Military, Melbourne.   (*Died 22 Oct. 1919.*)

COURTNEY, William Leonard, M.A., LL.D. St. Andrews ; Fellow New College, Oxford ; editor of the *Fortnightly Review,* 1894 ; formerly on editorial staff of the *Daily Telegraph* ; retired ; director of Chapman & Hall, Ltd.; *b.* Poona, 5 Jan. 1850 ; *y. s.* of William Courtney, late of I.C.S., and Anne Edwardes Scott ; *m.* 1st, 1874, Cordelia Blanche (*d.* 1907), *d.* of Lionel Place, Commander R.N. ; 2nd, 1911, Janet Elizabeth Hogarth (*see* J. E. Courtney). *Educ.* : Somersetshire College, Bath ; Univ. Coll., Oxford (Scholar, 1868). 1st class First Public Examination, 1870 ; 1st class Greats, 1872 ; Fellow Merton College, 1872 ; Headmaster Somersetshire College, Bath, 1873 ; Fellow New College, Oxford, 1876 ; many years Treasurer O.U.B.C. London 1890 ; editor of *Murray's Magazine,* 1891. *Publications* : *The Metaphysics of John Stuart Mill,* 1879 *Studies on Philosophy,* 1882 ; *Constructive Ethics,* 1886 ; *Studies New and Old,* 1888 ; *Life of John Stuart Mill,* 1889 ; *Kit Marlowe* (produced at St James's Theatre), 1893 ; *The Idea of Tragedy,* 1900 ; *Undine,* 1902 ; *The Development of Maeterlinck,* 1904 ; *The Feminine Note in Fiction,* 1904 ; *The Literary Man's Bible,* 1907 ; *Rosemary's Letter Book,* 1909 ; *In Search of Egeria,* 1911 ; *The Soul of a Suffragette,* 1913 ; *The Literary Man's New Testament,* 1915 ; *Old Saws and Modern Instances,* 1918 ; *The Passing Hour,* 1925 ; *The Bedside Bible,* 1926. *Address* : 2 Luxborough House, Northumberland Street, W.1. *T.* : Mayfair 4009. *Clubs* : Garrick, Beefsteak, Authors'.(*Died 1 Nov. 1928.*)

COUSINS, John Ratcliffe, Metropolitan Police Magistrate sitting at Greenwich and Woolwich, 1922; at West London Police Court since 1925 ; *b.* 22 Aug. 1863 ; *s.* of Edward Ratcliffe Cousins, F.R.C.S. ; *m.* 1887, Eleanor Fanny, *d.* of Rev. J. E. Law, Rector of Little Shelford, Cambridge; one *s.* two *d. Educ.* : University College, London ; St. John's College, Cambridge. Honours, Natural Science Tripos, 1884, and LL.B. ; called to Bar, Inner Temple, 1887 ; Western Circuit ; Member for Dulwich, London County Council, 1898-1903 ; Organiser of the Tariff Reform League from its formation until 1906 ; Stipendiary Police Magistrate of the Borough of West Ham, 1917-22 ; Ex-Chairman of the Estates Governors of Dulwich College. *Recreations* : golf, bicycling, etc. *Address* : 3 College Gardens, Dulwich, S.E. *Club* : Devonshire.   (*Died 12 Mar. 1928.*)

COUSINS, William Henry, C.B., 1887 ; retired civil servant and country gentleman ; *b.* Chelsea, 30 Dec. 1833 ; bachelor ; *e. s.* of Captain Cousins. *Educ.* : private tutor ; King's Coll. London. Served in Exhibition of 1851 under late Lord Playfair ; appointed to the Inland Revenue, 1853 ; and became Controller of Stamps and Registrar of Joint Stock Companies, 1871-83 ; and then Secretary of Inland Revenue to 1896; when retired on pension. *Decorated* for Inland Revenue and Stamp Reforms. *Publications* : editor of the *Law List,* 1870-82. *Recreations* : collecting old china and

curios. *Address* : Vaughan Lodge, Long Ditton, Surrey. *Club* Constitutional.   (*Died 7 Sept. 1917.*)

COUZENS, Sir George Edwin, J.P., Kt., *cr.* 1905 ; *b.* 29 Sep. 1851 ; *s.* of George Couzens, Portsmouth ; *m.* 1885, Mary Ellen (*d.* 1908), *d.* of James Haming, R.N. ; one *s.* one *d.* Mayor of Portsmouth, 1897, 1904-5, 1905-6 ; Officer Legion of Honour ; Order of Holy Redeemer of Greece, member of Board of Guardians ; Vice-President, Royal Agricultural Society. *Address* : Glenthorne, Kingston Crescent, Portsmouth.   (*Died 17 Aug. 1925.*)

COVENTRY, Henry Arthur ; *b.* Melton Mowbray, 7 Dec. 1852 ; *y. s.* of late Hon. Henry Coventry. Formerly starter to the Jockey Club ; a well-known amateur rider ; won National Hunt Steeplechase, 1879. *Club* : Turf.   (*Died 22 Aug. 1925.*)

COVENTRY, Rev. Henry William, M.A., Rural Dean of Bredon ; Rector of Severn-Stoke since 1869 ; J.P. Worcestershire. *Educ.* : Winchester; Pembroke College, Oxford. Rector of Woolston, 1864-69 ; Rector of Hill-Croome, 1899-1905. *Address* : Severn-Stoke Rectory, Worcester.   (*Died 10 April 1920.*)

COWAN, Rev. David Galloway, Prebendary of St. Paul's Cathedral, 1917. *Educ.* : King's College School ; St. Edmund Hall, Oxford. Curate of Holy Trinity, Dalston, 1882-89 ; St. John, Isle of Dogs, 1889-92 ; Vicar, 1892-1902; Vicar of St. John Evangelist, Holborn, 1902. *Address* : St. John's Clergy House, Red Lion Square, W.C.1.   (*Died 15 Sept. 1921.*)

COWAN, Colonel Henry Vivian : C.V.O. 1904, C.B. 1908 ; A.D.C. to the King 1901-11 ; *b.* 10 Nov. 1854 ; *s.* of late Richard Cowan, J.P. for Midlothian, of St. Kilda, Sidmouth ; *m.* Mabel Talbot, *d.* of late Sir James Laing, Thornhill, Sunderland, and Etal Manor, Cornhill-on-Tweed ; three *d. Educ.* : Winchester College ; R.M.A., Woolwich. Joined Royal Artillery, 1873 ; served Afghan War, 1878-80 (despatches, medal and 3 clasps); Egypt, 1882 (severely wounded, despatches, Brevet Major, medal and clasp, 5th Class Mejidie, Khedive's star) ; S. Africa, 1899-1900 (despatches twice, Queen's medal and 6 clasps, A.D.C. to King, Brevet Colonel) ; recently Commandant R.M.A., Woolwich ; A. A. G. Irish Command, 1914-17. *Address* : Ford House, Bideford, N. Devon. *Clubs* : United Service, United Sports.   (*Died 25 Jan. 1918.*)

COWAN, John, K.C. 1898 ; of Cowan, Towers & Cowan, Barristers and Solicitors ; President Industrial Mortgage and Savings Co. ; Director Canada Trust Co. ; *b.* on board vessel on Atlantic Ocean, 8 July 1849 ; *s.* of John Cowan and Catherine Sudin ; *m.* 1881, Eliza A., *d.* of John M'Intyre, four *s.* four *d. Educ.* : common schools ; Osgoode Hall. Read law with John Idington, now Mr. Justice Idington ; called to Ontario Bar, 1879 ; practised Watford, 1879-83 ; came to Sarnia and practised, in partnership with late Mr. Justice Lister, 1883-98 ; formed present partnership, 1898 ; City Solicitor, also Solicitor, County Lambton, townships of Moore, Dawn, Brooks, Warwick and Bosanquet, and villages of Watford and Wyoming; Bencher, Law Society of Upper Canada ; Liberal ; Presbyterian. *Recreations* : horseback riding, gardening. *Address* : Sarnia, Ontario. *Club* : Ontario, Toronto.   (*Died June 1926.*)

COWAN, Hon. John, Member of Executive Council and Minister of Finance and Customs, Newfoundland, 1900-06 ; *b.* St. John's, Newfoundland, 12 Nov. 1847 ; parents from Moffat, Dumfriesshire, Scotland ; *m.* 1874, Eliza Julia Earle, whose parents were from Devonshire. *Educ.* : General Protestant Academy, St. John's, Newfoundland. At the age of 14 left school ; served his apprenticeship to the dry goods business ; from that gravitated to office work, for which he was more suited ; held the position of book-keeper in two of the principal business houses in St. John's for some 17 years, and in 1890 was appointed assistant manager for J. & W. Stewart, a large supplying firm; after the bank crash of 1894, went into the commission business on his own account and built up a considerable business; was elected for the District of Bona-vesta Bay, 1897. *Recreations:* enthusiastic curler. *Address:* Harbor View, 37 Queen's Road, St. John's, Newfoundland. *Club:* Masonic.

(*Died Mar. 1927*.)

COWAN, Thomas William, F.L.S.,F.G.S., F.R.M.S., F.R.H.S., D.Sc., Ph.D.; Chairman of Council British Bee-keepers' Association since 1874; President since 1922; Chairman Board of Examiners B.B.K.A.; President Somerset Bee-keepers' Association; hon. member Victoria Natural History Society; hon. member of several Bee Associations in Europe, Canada, and United States; Chairman of Committee on the Bee-keeping Industry and Foul Brood in the United Kingdom, 1895; Chairman Joint Committee of B.B.K.A. and County Councils to promote legislation against Bee-pest, 1895; lecturer at University of California Farmers' Institutes on fruit-growing and relation of bees to horticulture; steward and judge at shows of the Royal Agricultural Society; also judge at shows of Bath and West of England, Royal Counties, Lancashire, Lincolnshire, and other agricultural societies; member of international juries at shows in France, Germany, and Switzerland; *b.* 1840. *Educ.:* private schools; School of Mines. Has travelled and studied bees, and lectured in many countries of Europe, in Africa, Canada, and the United States of America; editor of the British Bee Journal (weekly) and Bee-keepers' Record (monthly). *Publications:* The Honey Bee, its Natural History, Anatomy, and Physiology (2nd edition), 1904, translated into French, German, Norwegian, Bulgarian, and Russian; British Bee-keepers' Guide Book, 25th edition, 100th thousand, 1924, translated into French (2 editions), German, Danish, Swedish, Russian (4 editions), Spanish (2 editions), and Dutch; Wax Craft: all about beeswax, its history, production, adulteration, and commercial value, 1908, translated into French and Russian (2 editions); Foul Brood and its Treatment; British Bee-keepers' Note Book (3rd edition); Bees and their Management; Wintering Bees (3 editions); How to make an Extractor and Bellows Smoker; Beneficial Results from the Fertilisation of Fruit Blossoms by Bees, 1909, translated into French and Dutch; also author of numerous articles, pamphlets, and lectures on bees in connection with horticulture and agriculture. *Recreations:* natural history, horticulture, wood carving, travelling. *Address:* Sutherland House, Clevedon, Somerset; 23 Bedford Street, Strand, W.C. *T.A.:* Clevedon. (*Died 23 May 1926*.)

COWANS, General Sir John Steven, G.C.B., *cr.* 1919; G.C.M.G., *cr.* 1918; K.C.B., *cr.* 1913; G.B. 1911; M.V.O. 1902; Knight of Grace of the Order of St. John of Jerusalem, 1918; F.Z.S.; *b.* 11 March 1862; *s.* of late John Cowans of Carlisle and Hartlands, Cranford, Middlesex; *m.* 1884, Eva May, *d.* of Rev. J. E. Coulson, vicar of Long Preston, Yorkshire. Joined Rifle Brigade (Prince Consort's Own), 1881; Captain, 1890; *p.s.c.* 1891; Major, 1898; Lieutenant-Colonel, 1900; Colonel, 1903; Brig.-Gen. 1908; Lt.-Gen. 1915; General, 1919; Staff-Captain, Headquarters of Army, 1893-94; Brigade Major, Aldershot, 1894-97; D.A.Q.M.G., Headquarters of Army, 1898-1903; A.Q.M.G., 2nd Division, Aldershot, 1903-6; Director-General Military Education, Indian Army, 1906; Director of Staff Duties and Training, Army Headquarters, India, 1907-8; commanded Presidency Brigade, Calcutta, 1908-10; Director-General of

236

the Territorial Forces, 1910-12; Quartermaster-General of the Forces, War Office, 1912-19; member of H.M.'s Army Council, European War, 1914-19; Grand Officer of the Legion of Honour, Crown of Belgium, Crown of Italy, Sacred Treasure of Japan, Holy Redeemer, Greece, and Chia Ho (Ta Shou) of China. *Address:* 72 Curzon Street, W.1. *T.:* Mayfair 3967. *Clubs:* Beefsteak, Naval and Military; United Service, Simla; Turf, United Service, Calcutta.

(*Died 16 April 1921*.)

COWDRAY, of Cowdray, 1st Viscount, *cr.* 1916; **Weetman Dickinson Pearson,** Bt., *cr.* 1894; Baron, *cr.* 1910; P.C.; G.C.V.O., *cr.* 1925; D.L. Aberdeenshire; Rector University of Aberdeen, 1918-21; President of the Air Board, 1917; Head of the firm of S. Pearson & Son, Ltd.; *b.* 1856; *e. s.* of late George Pearson, Brickendonbury, Hertford, and Sarah, *d.* of Weetman Dickinson, High Hoyland, Yorkshire; *m.* Annie, *d.* of late Sir John Cass, Bradford, Yorks, 1881; two *s.* one *d.* *Educ.:* privately at Harrogate. Contested Colchester, 1892. M.P. (L.) Colchester, 1895-1910; High Steward of Colchester. *Heir: s.* Hon. Weetman Harold Pearson. *Address:* 16 Carlton House Terrace, S.W.1; Paddockhurst, Worth, Sussex; Dunecht House, Aberdeenshire. *Clubs:* Reform, Marlborough.

(*Died 1 May 1927*.)

COWELL, George, F.R.C.S.; Vice-President and Consulting Surgeon to the Westminster and Royal Westminster Ophthalmic Hospitals; Consulting Surgeon to the Victoria and East London Hospitals for Children; *b.* Ipswich, 1 June 1836; *e. s.* of late George Kersey Cowell, surgeon of that town, and Martha, *d.* of George Notcutt Conder; *m.* 1892, Mary Margaret Elizabeth (*d.* 1925), *widow* of W. Hamilton Roe, M.B. Oxon., and *d.* of late John Laurie, M.P. for Barnstaple. *Educ.:* Ipswich, Birmingham, London, and Paris. Surgeon to the Victoria Hospital for Children, 1866-85; Surgeon to Westminster and Royal Westminster Ophthalmic Hospitals, 1869-96; Lecturer on Surgery, 1873-93; took an active part in bringing about the complete rebuilding of the Medical School and the Outpatient Department and Chapel of the Westminster Hospital; has filled various offices in the Medical Societies. *Publications:* Lectures on Cataract, and articles and lectures in the medical journals: The Life and Letters of Prof. Cowell. *Recreations:* fishing and golf. *Club:* Athenæum. (*Died 18 Nov. 1927*.)

COWELL, Rev. Maurice Byles, M.A.; Canon of Norwich since 1911; Vicar of Ash-Bocking since 1862. *Educ.:* Wadham College, Oxford. Ordained, 1858; R.D. Claydon, 1895; Curate of Coseley, Staffs, 1858-60. *Address:* Ash-Bocking Vicarage, Ipswich.

(*Died 8 Jan. 1919*.)

COWEN, Richard John; Consulting Surgeon; *b.* 1871; *s.* of John Cowen, M.D.; *m.* Margaret Isabella, *d.* of Captain George Stavers. *Educ.:* Dublin University. Diplomate R.C.S.I. and R.C.P.I.; Gold Medallist in Surgery; Gold Medallist, Académie Parisienne; late Senior Surgeon, Kensington and Fulham General Hospital; late Captain, 4th Middlx.; served in Egyptian War (wounded, medal and star); working in Cancer Research; Captain Westminster Division National Reserve; rejoined Army, 1914, as Captain, Rifle Brigade; service in Dardanelles and Salonika. *Publications:* What is Life? Electricity in Gynæcology; X-Rays in the Treatment of Cancer and other Diseases; The Social Grindstone; Half-an-hour in a Doctor's Study; The Ideal Trajectory for Conical Bullets; A New Treatment for Leucocythæmia; numerous articles in lay and professional journals. *Recreations:* golf, tennis, shooting. *Address:* 4 Chandos Street, W.1. *T.:* Langham 2665. *Club:* Devonshire.

(*Died 16 Feb. 1928*.)

COWIE, William Patrick, C.I.E., 1920; Indian Civil Service; *s.* of George Cowie; *b.* Dunedin, New Zealand; *m.* Margaret Burne, of Loynton Hall, Newport, Salop; one *d. Educ.:* Malvern Coll.: Corpus Christi Coll., Oxford. Passed into I.C.S. 1908; Bombay Political Department, 1912-17; 28th Light Cavalry, 1917-18; Private Sec. to the Governor of Bombay, 1918-20; Collector, Belgaum District. *Recreations:* shooting and all games. *Address:* c/o Grindlay & Co., 54 Parliament Street, S.W.1. *Club:* East India United Service.
(Died 1 Aug. 1924.)

COWLEY, 3rd Earl (cr. 1857), Henry Arthur Mornington Wellesley, J.P.; Baron Cowley (U.K.), 1828; Viscount Dangan, 1857; served with Imperial Yeomanry in South Africa; late Captain 3rd Battalion Wiltshire Regiment; *b.* 14 Jan. 1866; S. father 1895; *m.* 1st, 1889, Lady Violet Neville (*d.* 1910), *d.* of 1st Marquis of Abergavenny (by whom he was divorced, 1897); one *s.*; 2nd, 1905, Millicent Florence Eleanor, *d.* of 1st Baron Nunburnholme (by whom he was divorced, 1913); one *s.* [She married 1st Sir C. Hartopp, by whom she was divorced; and 3rd, 1914, Major G. William Duberly, Grenadier Guards, Gaynes Hall, St. Neots]; 3rd, 1914, Clare (Mrs. Buxton), *o. c.* of Sir Francis Stapleton, 8th Bt.; one *d. Educ.:* Eton. Owns about 4000 acres. *Heir: s.* Viscount Dangan. *Address:* Draycott House, Chippenham, Wilts. *Clubs:* Carlton. Marlborough, Turf, White's.
(Died 15 Jan. 1919.)

COWLEY, Hon. Sir Alfred Sandlings Cowley, Kt., *cr.* 1904. Chairman, Bank of North Queensland; Member of the Australian Mutual Provident Society; Speaker of Legislative Assembly, Queensland, 1893-99 and 1903-7; *b.* Fairford, Glos., 24 Apr. 1848; *s.* of Isaac Cowley, late of Durban; *m.* 1880, Marie, *d.* of late W. Campbell. Went to Natal: went to N.S.W., 1871; M.L.A. Herbert, 1888-1907; Member Royal Commissions on Sugar Industry, 1888-89; and on Laws relating to Intoxicating Liquors, 1900-1901; Minister Lands and Agriculture 1890-93. *Address:* Silky Oaks, Toowong, Queensland.
(Died 1 Dec. 1926.)

COWLEY-BROWN, Rev. George James, M.A.; Canon of Edinburgh Cathedral (retired); Chancellor, 1907-11; Rector of St. John the Evangelist, Edinburgh, 1883-1909; *b.* Juanpur, India, 1832; *s.* of G. F. Brown of the Indian Civil Service, and *g. s.* of Rev. David Brown, scholar of Magdalene Coll. Cambridge, Provost of the College of Fort William; *m.* 1868, Isabel, *d.* of Charles Tottenham of Ballycurry, many years M.P. for New Ross; adopted in 1874 by legal deed the name of his great-grandmother, Mrs. Cowley, authoress of The Belle's Stratagem, etc. *Educ.:* Christ Church, Oxford. Ordained, 1855, by Bishop Wilberforce of Oxford; Rector of Shipton-on-Cherwell, 1867-74; Buckhorn Weston, 1874-77; St. Edmund, Salisbury, 1877-83. *Publications:* Daily Lessons on the Life of Our Lord on Earth, 1880; Prayers for a Household from Old Divines, 3rd ed. 1908: Some Reasons for believing Christianity to be True, 1897; Verselets and Versions; articles in Blackwood's Magazine, the National Review, and other periodicals. *Address:* 6 Learmonth Grove, Edinburgh. *T.:* Central 7150. *(Died 17 Dec. 1924.)*

COWPER, Cecil, J.P. Surrey; Editor of The Academy; *b.* 24 Oct. 1856; *s.* of Major Francis Baynton Cowper, 86th Regiment; *m.* 1st, Kate, *d.* of R. Nevill, 61st Regiment; 2nd, May, *d.* of Donald H. Waddell. Barrister, Inner Temple, 1881. *Address:* Cammeray, Burghley Road, Wimbledon Common, S.W. (*Died 27 April 1916.*)

COWPER, Sydney, C.M.G. 1901; *b.* Kensington, 1854; *s.* of late Charles Cowper, C.E.; *m.* 1883, Mary Louisa, *d.* of late Richard Cockerton, F.R.C.S. *Educ.:* King's College School. Office of Commissioners for Exhibition of 1851, 1871; Technical Assistant, South Kensington Museum, 1875; Cape Civil Service, 1879; in charge of Cape Section, Colonial and Indian Exhibition, 1886; Secretary to Prime Minister, Cape Colony, 1887-91; Principal Clerk, Department of Agriculture, 1892; permanent head of Prime Minister's Department, Cape Town, 1896; retired 1904; O.C. 4th Batt. Cape Peninsula Regt. 1902; Major, and B.C. Cape Field Artillery, 1903; Trustee of Art Gallery; Pres., Western Province Agricultural Society, 1915-17; M.P.C. and J.P.; Fellow Royal Colonial Institute; Mayor of Wynberg, 1912-14 and 1918-1921; Deputy-Mayor, 1915-17. *Address:* Wynberg, near Cape Town. *Club:* Civil Service, Cape Town. *(Died 5 Sept. 1922.)*

COX, Arthur Frederick, C.S.I. 1901; Indian Civil Service; retired; *b.* Kurnool, Madras Presidency, 14 March 1849; 4th *s.* of late Major E. T. Cox, M.N.I. (of Ham Common, Surrey); *m.* Flora (*d.* 1923), *d.* of late Alexander Ranken of Hampstead; two *s.* three *d. Educ.:* Great Ealing School; King's College School and King's College, London. Appointed to the Madras Presidency, 1871; served there in the Revenue and Magisterial Department until 1882, when he joined the Finance Department of the Government of India; returned to Madras as District and Session Judge, 1887-89; reappointed to the Financial Department as Accountant-General, Bombay; transferred to Calcutta, 1894, to officiate as Comptroller and Auditor-General; confirmed as such in 1898; Kaiser-i-Hind Gold Medal for public service in India, 1900; retired, 1906. *Publication:* The District Manual of North Arcot, Madras Presidency, 1880. *Address:* Cumballa, St. John's Road, Meads, Eastbourne. *T.:* Eastbourne 1193.
(Died 8 Feb. 1925.)

COX, A. W.; *b.* 1857, *s.* of A. R. Cox of Hafod Elwy, North Wales; no occupation; mostly travelling; collector of art, etc.; one of original syndicate Broken Hill Mine; won first race, 1888; won One Thousand Guineas with Galeottia, 1895; St. Leger with Bayardo, 1909; Derby with Lemberg, 1910; Gold Cup (Ascot), Bayardo, 1910; Chester Cup and Ascot Gold Cup with Aleppo, 1914; Triple Crown Horse, Gay Crusader, 1917; The Oaks with My Dear, 1918. *Address:* 30 St. James's Place, S.W.1. *T.:* Regent 1897; The Old Barn, Harrow Weald, Middlesex. *Clubs:* Carlton, Boodle's, Portland's. *(Died 4 May 1919.)*

COX, Colonel Edgar William, D.S.O. 1915; R.E.; G.S.O. 1st Grade; *b.* May 1882. Entered army, 1900; Captain, 1910; employed on Sierra Leone and Siberia Boundary Commission, 1902-3; Anglo-Portuguese Boundary Commission, Africa, 1904-6; survey duty East Africa Protectorate, 1906-9; General Staff Officer, War Office, 1912-14: served European War, 1914-18 (D.S.O., despatches, bt. Major and bt. Lieut.-Col. and Col.); Chevalier, Legion of Honour, 1915. *(Died 26 Aug. 1918.)*

COX, Lt.-Col. Edward Henry, D.S.O. 1902; late Royal Fus.; *b.* 21 May 1863; *s.* of late Arthur Zachariah Cox of Harwood Hall, Essex. Entered army, 1884; Capt., 1892; Maj., 1900; served South Africa, 1899-1902 (despatches, 1900, Queen's medal with 5 clasps, King's medal with 2 clasps). *(Died 23 July 1925.)*

COX, Francis Albert, Founder and Secretary of The National Equine Defence League; 4th and *y. s.* of late George James and Caroline Wintle Cox; *b.* 24 June 1862; *m.* 1886, Augusta Elizabeth, *e. d.* of late J. Wildsmith; one *s.* two *d.* For 29 years held a post, for the last 12 as Assistant to the Chief Engineer, in the Civil Engineers Department of the Great Northern Railway; a life-long worker on behalf of animals, he was impelled to start a public agitation respecting the treatment and conditions of pit ponies, 1908, which work eventually led to his founding the above-mentioned League; this, and his representations to the Government, led to the matter being considered by a Royal Commission, with the result that stringent legislation respecting animals was included in the Mines Act, 1911; eventually resigned his position in order to devote himself entirely to the extended work of the League; is at present engaged in endeavouring to secure just—not kind or merciful—treatment of horses generally, to obtain the total abolition of animal labour in mines, and the use of the Bearing and Hame Reins; has promoted in Parliament, 1913-14, a Bill to Prohibit the Docking of Horses; as Assistant Hon. Sec. of the Government Commission for obtaining employment for Belgian refugees (1915), he organised all the work of the Commission in the Metropolitan area. *Publications:* The Tragedy of the Pit Pony; The Pit Pony; Three and eightpence a day; The Unnecessary Whip, A Dog's Life, and other pamphlets; What do *you* know about a horse; devotes most of his literary efforts to press letters. *Recreations:* reading, particularly Napoleonic literature as a guide to his efforts. "Impossible! a word found only in the dictionary of fools"; loves listening to music; any form of manual labour productive of material results. Has never played a game. *Address:* Beaconsfield Road, New Southgate, N.11. *T.:* Finchley 1086. *Club:* National Liberal. *(Died 25 May 1920.)*

COX, George Henry, J.P.; Chairman, Salt Union, Ltd., Mersey Power Co., Ltd., and Weston & Westall, Limited; Director North-Eastern Salt Co.; *b.* Liverpool, 1848; *e. s.* of late Geo. Frederick Cox and Emma Thirkell, both of Liverpool; *m.* 1878, Isabella, *d.* of James Richardson, Edinburgh, and *g.d.* of Adam Black, publisher, Edinburgh; two *s.* one *d. Educ.:* Castle Howell Private School, Lancaster; privately, in Liverpool. Engaged in commerce, mainly in relation to sugar, cotton, etc., for about thirty years; subsequently actively engaged in the production and distribution of salt and electricity; was Vice-President and Chairman of Council of Liverpool Chamber of Commerce for many years; and Member, Executive Committee of Association Chambers of Commerce; was also Member of the Advisory Committee of Board of Trade on Commercial Intelligence; was also Trustee of the Weaver Navigation; Chairman, Liverpool Reform Club, 1898; Chairman, Birkenhead Liberal Association. *Recreations:* angling, gardening, reading. *Address:* Underfell, Bowness on Windermere. *T.:* Windermere 209. *Clubs:* National Liberal, Reform, Atheneum, Liverpool. *(Died 26 Jan. 1927.)*

COX, Gen. Sir H. Vaughan, G.C.B., *cr.* 1921; K.C.B., *cr.* 1918; K.C.M.G., *cr.* 1915; C.B. 1912; C.S.I. 1911; *b.* Watford, Herts., 12 July 1860; *e. s.* of late Rev. F. Cox, Rector of Upper Chelsea; *m.* 1894, Violet O'Bryen Horsford; one *s.* one *d. Educ.:* Charterhouse; Sandhurst. Second Lieut. K.O.S.B. 1880; joined Indian Army, 1883; Adjutant S.I.R.V.C. 1891; D.A.A.G.M. 1892; D.A.A.G.M. and Inspecting-Officer, Imperial S. Troops, 1894-1902; Officer Commanding 69th Punjabis, 1902-7; A.Q.M.G. Mobilization Headquarters, 1907; D.Q.M.G. Headquarters, 1908-1911; Military Member, Durbar Committee, 1911; G.O.C. 4th Infantry Brigade, R. Pindi, 1912-14; commanded 2nd (Nowshera) Infantry Brigade, Indian Army, 1914; served Afghan War, 1879-80; Khyber Line Force (medal); Burmese War, 1885-89; taking of Minhla Fort, and Mandalay and subsequent operations (despatches, medal, and two clasps); North-West Frontier, 1897; Mohmund Expedition (despatches, medal, and clasp); Tirah, 1907-8 (clasp), Buner (clasp); China, 1901-2 (medal and clasp); European War, 1914-15, command of 238

Gurkha Brigade, in Arabia, Egypt, and Gallipoli (despatches twice, K.C.M.G., wounded, 2nd class order of White Eagle, Serbia); commanded 4th Australian Division, Egypt and France, 1916-1917 (despatches); Secretary Military Department, India Office, 1917-21 (K.C.B. and G.C.B.); member Esher Committee, 1919-20; retired Indian Army, 1921. *Address:* Woodhayes, Camberley, Surrey. *Club:* United Service. *(Died 8 Oct. 1923.)*

COX, Irwin Edward Bainbridge, J.P., D.L.; barrister-at-law; chairman Petty Sessional Division of Gore, Middlesex; High Sheriff, Middlesex, 1898-99; *b.* Taunton, Somerset, 9 July 1838; *e. s.* of late Mr. Serjeant E. W. Cox, Moat Mount, Mill Hill, Middlesex, and Sophia, 2nd *d.* of the late W. Harris, M.D., R.H.A.; *m.* 1865, Katharine, *d.* of late Rev. Bartholomew Nicols, vicar Mill Hill, Middlesex (*d.* 1898). *Educ.:* Magdalene Coll. Camb. (B.A.). Barr. 1864; elected to Middlesex C.C. 1889, alderman 1901; elected chairman Gore Petty Sessional Division, 1894; M.P. (C.) Harrow Division of Middlesex, 1899-1906; president Harrow Central Conservative Association; Lord of the Manor of Taunton. *Publications:* Anglers' Diary; Hints on Fishing and Shooting; Country House. *Recreations:* fishing, shooting. Owns about 2000 acres. *Address:* Moat Mount, Mill Hill, Middlesex. *Clubs:* Carlton, 1900, New Oxford and Cambridge. *(Died 27 Aug. 1922.)*

COX, John Charles, LL.D., F.S.A.; late Rector of Barton le Street and Holdenby; admitted into the Roman Catholic Church, 1917; *b.* 1848; 2nd *s.* of Rev. Edward Cox, Rector of Luccombe; *m.* 1867, Marian, *d.* of E. W. Smith, of Tickton Hall, East Riding, Yorks; seven *s.* three *d. Educ.:* Repton; Som College, Bath; Queen's College, Oxford. J.P., Derbyshire; Member of Royal Archæological Institute and British Archæological Association; Council Member of Canterbury and York Society and British Numismatic Society; Hon. Mem. Derbyshire and East Riding Archæological Societies; formerly Editor of Reliquary, Antiquary, and Derbyshire Archæological Journal; now Editor of series of Antiquary's Books; on Advisory Council of Victoria Counties Histories Scheme, and writer therein; contributor to Times, Athenæum, Academy, Country Life, Builder, Guardian, Church Times. *Publications:* Churches of Derbyshire (4 vols.), 1876-79; Chronicles of All Saints, Derby, 1881; How to Write History of a Parish, 5th ed., 1910; Lichfield Capitular Monuments,1886; Three Centuries of Derbyshire Annals (2 vols.), 1888; The Sober, Righteous, and Godly Life, 1890; The Gardens of Scripture, 1893; Northampton Borough Records, 1897; Church of St. Sepulchre's, Northampton, 1898; Quarter Session Records of Derbyshire, 1899; Strutt's Sports and Pastimes, edited and enlarged, 1901; Little Guide to Derbyshire, 1902; English Monasteries, 1904; Little Guide to Hants, 1904; Royal Forests of England, 1905; History of Canterbury, 1905; Memorials of Old Derbyshire, English Church Furniture (joint), 1907; The Cathedral Church and See of Essex, 1908; Little Guide to Essex, 1909; Parish Registers of England, 1909; Little Guide to Surrey, 1910; Rambles in Surrey, 1910; Churches of Norfolk (2 vols.), 1910; Churches of Isle of Wight, 1911; Sanctuaries, 1911; Churches of Cornwall; Churches of Notts, 1912; Memorials of Old Surrey, 1912; Rambles in Kent, 1913; Churchwardens' Accounts, 1913; Churches of Cumberland and Westmorland, 1913; Little Guide to Cambs, 1914; Little Guide to Warwickshire, 1914; The English Parish Church, 1914; Little Guide to Gloucestershire, 1914; Little Guide to Kent, 1915; Pulpits, Lecterns, and Organs, 1915; Bench Ends of English Churches, 1916; contributor to The Tablet and Universe. *Recreation:* archæological research. *Address:* St. Albans, Sydenham, S.E. *(Died 23 Feb. 1919.)*

COX, John Hugh, C.I.E. 1912; C.B.E. 1919; Excise Commissioner, Central India, since 1906; b. 1870; s. of Surg.-Gen. Charles Lindsay Cox, H.E.I.C.S.; m. 1895, Augusta Edith, d. of E. C. R. Warner, Barrister-at-law. Educ.: Clifton College; Balliol College, Oxford. Entered I.C.S. 1888; Joint-Magistrate, 1896; Assist. Commissioner, 1899; Deputy Commissioner, 1903; Joint Secretary, Board of Revenue, 1904. Address: Indore, Central India.
(Died 30 Dec. 1922.)

COX, Rt. Hon. Michael Francis, P.C., M.D., F.R.C.P.I., M.R.I.A., Physician St. Vincent's Hosp., Dublin; Consulting Physician Children's Hospital, Temple Street; Linden Convalescent Home; and Our Lady's Hospice; Member of Senate and Chairman of Convocation, National University of Ireland; b. 20 Sep. 1852; s. of Hugh Cox and. Anne, d. of Richard Kelly, Co. Roscommon; m. 1886, Elizabeth, d. of William Nolan, Co. Kildare; one s. Educ.: St. Mel's College, Longford; Catholic University of Ireland; London University. When qualified engaged in medical teaching, afterwards in private practice, and as physician and clinical teacher to Hospital; interested in Science, in Literature, and in public affairs, especially educational. Publications: The Country and Kindred of Oliver Goldsmith; Notes on the History of the Irish Horse. Recreation: golf. Address: 26 Merrion Square, Dublin. T.: Dublin 1421. Clubs: Royal Golf, Dollymount; Leopardstown Dublin.
(Died 20 Feb. 1926.)

COX, Palmer, author and artist; b. Granby, Province of Quebec, Canada, 28 April 1840; 5th s. of Michael Cox, farmer, and pensioner of the English army; unmarried. Educ.: Granby Academy. Went to California, 1863; followed railroading, contracting, etc.; wrote for newspapers; came to New York, 1875; took up writing and illustrating for children's magazines, and also humorous books. Publications: Squibs of Everyday Life, 1874; Hans Von Pelter's trip to Gotham, 1878; How Columbus found America, 1878; That Stanley, 1878; The Brownies, their Book, 1887; Queer People with Wings and Stings, 1888; Comic Yarns (revision of Squibs), 1888; Another Brownies' Book, 1890; Brownies at Home, 1893; Brownies around the World, 1894; Palmer Cox's Brownies, a spectacular play in three acts, 1894; The Brownies in Fairyland, a musical cantata, 1894; Brownies through the Union, 1895; Brownies Abroad, 1899; Brownies in the Philippines, 1904; Palmer Cox's Brownie Primer, 1906. Recreations: rifle target shooting, fishing, cycling. Address: Granby, Province of Quebec, Canada.
(Died 24 July 1924.)

COX, Sir Reginald Henry, 1st Bart., cr. 1921; D.L.; J.P.; Berks.; 2nd surv. s. of late Frederick Cox, D.L., J.P., of Hillingdon House, and Harefield Place, Uxbridge; m. 1890, Sybil, y. d. of late T. M. Weguelin, M.P. Educ.: Eton. Senior partner of Cox & Co., Bankers and Army Agents, 16 Charing Cross, S.W.1. Address: 4 Cavendish Square, W.1.; T.: Mayfair 6173; Manor Cottage, Old Windsor. Clubs: St. James', Boodle's
(Died 27 Mar. 1922.)

COX, Prof. S. Herbert; Emeritus Professor of Mining, Royal School of Mines, South Kensington, S.W. Address: Vicars Hill Lodge, Boldre, nr. Lymington, Hants.
(Died 11 April 1920.)

COX, Hon. Sir (William Henry) Lionel, Kt. cr. 1896; b. 1864; 2nd s. of Geo. Cox, M.D., of Mauritius; m. 2nd, 1903, Elizabeth Cushing, d. of late Lewis Pughe of Seranton, Pennsylvania. Educ.: Mauritius. Barrister, Middle Temple, 1866; Substitute-Procureur and Advocate-General Mauritius, 1880; Puisne Judge of the Supreme Court, 1881-87; Advocate-General, 1889-93; Chief Justice Straits Settlements, 1893-1906. Address: 13 Midvale

Road, Jersey. Clubs: Athenæum, Sports.
(Died 1 Nov. 1921.)

COX-EDWARDS, Rev. John Cox, Chaplain to the King; widower; three d. Educ.: Emmanuel Coll., Cambridge. Ordained, 1863; Chaplain and Naval Instructor, R.N. 1871; retired 1899; present at bombardment of Alexandria (medal with clasp, and Khedive's medal); Chaplain of the Fleet and Inspector of Naval Schools, 1888-99. Rector of Ectou, Northants, 1900-1908. Address: 11 St. David's Road, Southsea, Hants.
(Died 25 Mar. 1926.)

COXE, Rev. Seymour Richard, M.A.; Hon. Canon of Newcastle; b. 23 Jan. 1842; s. of Ven. Richard C. Coxe, M.A., Archdeacon of Lindisfarne; m. 1872, Fanny, e. d. of Philip S. Coxe; one s. one d. Educ.: Durham School; Brasenose College, Oxford; 2nd class mods., B.A., M.A. Deacon 1866; Priest, 1867; Vicar of Brompton, Yorks, 1873-81; Rector of Baconsthorpe, Norfolk, 1881-85; Vicar of Stamfordham, Northumberland, 1885-95; Rural Dean of Corbridge; Exam. Chaplain to Bishop (Wilberforce) of Newcastle; Proctor in Convocation for Northumberland; Rector of Stoke Bruerne, 1895-1912. Publication: The Psalms of Penitence, 1916. Recreations: formerly rowing (Captain B.N.C. boat, head of river); Treasurer O.U.B.C. Address: The Precincts, Canterbury.
(Died 2 Aug. 1922.)

COZENS-HARDY, 1st Baron (cr. 1914) of Letheringsett, **Rt. Hon. Herbert Hardy Cozens-Hardy;** P.C., 1901; Chairman of Hist. MSS. Commission since 1907; Master of Rolls, 1907-18; b. Letheringsett, Norfolk, 22 Nov. 1888; 2nd s. of late William Hardy Cozens-Hardy; m. 1866, Maria (d. 1886), d. of Thomas Hepburn. Educ.: Amersham School; Univ. College, London (Fellow). A Bencher of Lincoln's Inn; M.P. (L.) N. Norfolk, 1885-1899; Chairman, General Council of the Bar, to 1899; Judge of the Chancery Division of the High Court of Justice, 1899-1901; Lord Justice of Appeal 1901-7. Heir: s. Hon. W. H. Cozens-Hardy. Address: 50 Ladbroke Grove, W.11.; T.: Park 596; Letheringsett Hall, Holt, Norfolk. Club: Athenæum.
(Died 18 June 1920.)

COZENS-HARDY, 2nd Baron, cr. 1914, of Letheringsett; **William Hepburn Cozens-Hardy;** K.C. 1912; J.P. Norfolk; M.P. (L.) Norfolk, 1918-20; b. 25 March 1868; e. s. of 1st Baron and Maria, d. of Thos. Hepburn; S. father, 1920; m. 1895, Constance Gertrude Lilian, e. d. of Colonel Sir William Everett, K.C.M.G.; one d. Educ.: New College, Oxford. Called to Bar, Lincoln's Inn, 1893; Commander R.N.V.R., 1914-18; Bencher of Lincoln's Inn, 1916. Heir: b. Hon. Edward Herbert Cozens-Hardy. Address: Gunthorpe Hall, Norfolk; 1 Halkin Place, Belgrave Square, S.W.1, 7 New Square, W.C.2. Clubs: Travellers', Athenæum.
(Died 25 May 1924.)

CRADOCK, Major Sheldon William Keith, D.S.O. 1900; b. 1 Oct. 1858; e. s. of Christopher Cradock of Hartforth, Yorks, and Georgiana, 3rd d. of Major Duff. Formerly Captain 5th Dragoon Guards; served Egyptian Campaign, 1882 (medal with clasp, Khedive's star); with Imperial Yeomanry, South Africa (despatches, Queen's medal, 5 clasps, D.S.O.); European War, 1914-16, with 2nd King Edward's Horse (despatches). Address: Hartforth, Richmond, Yorks. T.A.: Gilling, West. Clubs: Cavalry, Boodle's.
(Died 5 July 1922.)

CRAFTS, Wilbur Fisk, minister, author, editor, lecturer, traveller, reformer; b. Fryburg, Maine, 12 Jan. 1850; s. of Rev. Frederick A. Crafts, a Methodist preacher, of Puritan stock; m. 1874, Sara J. Timanus, Sunday School writer and speaker; graduated at Wesleyan University, Middletown, Ct.; 1869, B.A.; 1871, A.M.; also from Boston University School of Theology,

239

CRADDOCK, Charles Robert; See Murfree, Mary Noailles.

1871, B.D. (Ph.D., Marietta College, 1896);
Methodist minister, 1867-79; Congregationalist,
1880-83; Presbyterian since; was pastor of
prominent churches in Stoneham, Haverhill,
New Bedford, all Mass., Dover, N.H., Chicago,
Brooklyn, and New York. Since 1871 has been
active in Sunday School work, and has participated in scores of Sunday School assemblies,
known as Chautauquas, and in countless conventions; founded the American Sabbath Union,
now National Lord's Day Alliance, 1889;
lectured in all parts of the United States as
its Field Secretary, 1889-90; founded The International Reform Bureau, 1895; Superintendent
of same down to date; author of 18 laws
of Congress, on temperance, gambling, prize
fights, impurity, and Sunday; chief editor
Christian Statesman, 1901-3; 20th Century
Quarterly since 1896; has travelled extensively;
Chairman of U.S. Government delegates to
12th International Congress on Alcoholism,
London, 1909. Member of National Prohibition
Amendment Commission, 1915. *Publications*:
Through the Eye of the Heart, 1873; Wagons
for Eye Gate, Trophies of Song, 1874; Childhood, the Text-Book of the Age, 1875; The
Ideal Sunday School, 1876; Fireside Talks
on Genesis, Song Victories, 1877; the Bible and
the Sunday School, The Two Chains, 1878;
The Coming Man is the Present Child, Illustrations of the International Sunday School
Lessons, Symbols and System in Bible Reading, Normal Outlines, 1879; Rescue of Child-
soul, 1880; Normal Half-hours, Plain Uses of
the Blackboard, 1881; Talks to Boys and Girls
about Jesus, Teacher's Edition of the Revised
Testament, Successful Men of To-day, 1883;
Must the Old Testament Go? Talks and Stories
of Heroes and Holidays, The Sabbath for Man,
Rhetoric made Racy, 1884; The Temperance
Century, 1885; Reading the Bible with Relish,
1887; The Civil Sabbath, 1890; Practical
Christian Sociology, 1895; Social Progress,
1896; Before the Lost Arts, Intoxicating
Drinks and Drugs in All Times and Lands,
1900; The March of Christ down the Centuries,
1902; A Primer of Internationalism (editions
in Japanese and Arabic); World Book of Temperance, 1908; National Perils and Hopes,
1910; Quarter Century of Moral Legislation,
1911; Bible in Schools Plans of Many Lands,
1914; Illustrated Bible Readings, 1915; Why
Dry? Briefs for Prohibition, 1919; Made in
Mayflower Land, 1920; Short History of Prohibition, 1921. *Address*: 206 Pennsylvania
Avenue, S.E. Washington, D.C. *T.A.*: Inrefbu.
(*Died 27 Dec. 1922.*)

CRAGGS, Sir John (George), Kt., *cr.* 1903;
b. 1856; *s.* of late James Craggs; *m.* 1884, Helen
Lewins (*d.* 1916), *d.* of late Andrew Millar;
one *s.* six *d.* A Chartered Accountant, admitted
1880; Member of the Council of the Institute
of Chartered Accountants; Hon. Sec. of King
Edward's Hospital Fund, 1897-1906; a member
of its Council; received Jubilee Medal, 1897;
M.V.O. 1902. *Publications*: Rate-supported *v.*
Voluntary Hospitals; and a technical work on the
Agreement of Trial Balances. *Recreation*: golf.
Address: Redland, Chesham Bois, Bucks. *Clubs*:
City Carlton, Ranelagh, Royal Automobile.
(*Died 2 May 1928.*)

CRAIG, Sir Archibald, Kt., *cr.* 1924;
M.A., LL.B., LL.D., J.P.; solicitor, Glasgow;
s. of Andrew Craig, calico printer, Barrhead.
Educ.: High School and University of Glasgow.
Clerk of the General Council of the University
of Glasgow; Secretary, Glasgow Centre of
Franco-Scottish Society; Corresponding Mem-
ber, Institut d'Etudes Françaises de Touraine;
Officier d'Académie; Officier de l'Instruction
Publique; Médaille de la Reconnaissance
Française; Chevalier de la Légion d'Honneur;
Freeman of London; Member of Court of
Worshipful Company of Plumbers; Member

240

of Merchants' House, Glasgow; Chairman,
Glasgow Unionist Association; Convener (1923)
Western Divisional Council. Scottish Unionist
Association; Member of Council, Faculty of Pro-
curators, Glasgow; Member of Glasgow Coun-
cil Scottish Ecclesiological Society. *Publica-
tions*: Two volumes as to Elder Park, Govan.
Recreations: foreign travel. *Address*: 174 West
George Street, Glasgow. *T.A.*: Instrument,
Glasgow. *T.*: Douglas 480. *Clubs*: Glasgow
Conservative, Cercle Français, Glasgow.
(*Died 24 Dec. 1927.*)

CRAIG, Frank, artist; painter; Member of
the National Portrait Society; Hors Concours
Société des Artistes Français (Paris Salon); *b.*
27 Feb. 1874; 5th *s.* of late Hugh Brown Craig
and Helen Beet Lloyd Smith; *m.* 1898, Katharine,
d. of late R. J. Moser; two *s. Educ.*: Merchant
Taylors' School. Studied at Cook's life class,
Fitzroy Street, the Lambeth School of Art, and
Royal Academy Schools. Illustrations in the
Graphic, Pall Mall, and Nash's Magazine in
England, and in Scribner's Magazine, Harper's
Magazine, Cosmopolitan, and Hearst's Magazine
in America; following pictures in permanent
public collections: Communion on the Velt,
Boer War, 1900, in Durban Corporation Gallery;
Henley, in National Art Gallery, Sydney; The
Heretic, in the National Gallery of British Art
(Tate Gallery), London; The Maid, purchased
by the French Government for the National
Collection, Paris; Goblin Market, purchased by
New Zealand Academy of Fine Arts for the
proposed National Gallery; and paintings in
Government Buildings, Ottawa, and City Hall,
Cardiff; medal of 3rd class, Paris Salon, 1908;
medal of 2nd class, Paris Salon, 1910; medal
of 2nd class, Barcelona International Exhibi-
tion, 1911; medal of 2nd class and award £200,
Carnegie Institute, Pittsburg, 1911. *Address*:
Shottermill, Surrey. *Club*: Arts.
(*Died July 1918.*)

CRAIG, Colonel John Francis, C.M.G.
1918; J.P. Dorset; *b.* 1856; *s.* of R. M. Craig
of Garrane, Co. Tipperary, and *g.s.* of John Craig
of Preston Home, Midlothian, and of Thomas
de Quincey; *m.* Florence Mary, *d.* of James
Lyall of Arrat, Forfarshire; two *d. Educ.*:
Shrewsbury; R.M.A. Woolwich. Joined Royal
Artillery, 1876; A.D.C. and Private Secretary
to Governor of Mauritius, 1879-81; served in
S. Africa during Boer War, 1881, and in Egypt,
1882 (medal with clasp for Tel-el-Kebir and
Khedive's star); served in Chestnut Troop,
R.H.A. 1883-85; . Adjutant, Clare Artillery
Militia, 1887-92; commanded Auxiliary
Artillery, Western District, 1902-7; promoted
Colonel, 1905, and retired, 1910; volunteered
for service, 1914; trained 109th Brigade, R.F.A.,
and commanded it at Battle of Loos; took
command of D.A.C. of 12th Division, 1916, and
served with it until March, 1919 (C.M.G.,
despatches 3 times, 1914-15 Star, Victory and
Allies medal). *Recreations*: hunting, fishing,
bridge. *Address*: Rosehill, Weymouth. *Club*:
Royal Dorset Yacht, Weymouth.
(*Died 8 April 1927.*)

CRAIG, His Hon. Sir (John) Walker,
Kt., *cr.* 1920; K.C.; Recorder of Belfast
and County Court Judge of Antrim, 1911-
1919; *b.* Strabane, Co. Tyrone, 1847; *y. s.* of
late Thomas Craig, of Ardcoen, Strabane; *m.*
Elsie Oakman, *y. d.* of late George A. Hume,
M.D., Crumlin, Co. Antrim. *Educ.*: Raphoe
Royal School; Queen's Coll., Belfast. 1st
classical Scholar, Peel Prizeman, and Senior
Scholar in Classics, Queen's Coll., Belfast; gold
medallist, Queen's University in Ireland. Irish
Barr. 1871; Crown Prosecutor, Co. Louth,
1883-97; Senior Crown Prosecutor, Co. Monaghan, 1892-97; Inner Barr. 1889; Senior Counsel
for Belfast Corporation and for Belfast
Water Commissioners, 1892-97; contested South
Down (L.U.), 1892; County Court Judge of the

counties of Monaghan and Fermanagh, 1897-1911; for many years a Commissioner of Education in Ireland and of Intermediate Education. *Recreation:* motoring. *Address:* 54 The Drive, Hove, Sussex. *Club:* Hove, Hove.
(*Died 21 July 1926.*)

CRAIG, Lt.-Comdr. Norman(Carlyle), K.C. 1909; R.N.V.R.; M.P. (U.) Isle of Thanet Div., Kent, since 1910; *b.* 15 Nov. 1868; *s.* of William Simpson Craig, M.D., and Frances Margaret Morrison; *m.* 1918, Dorothy, *d.* of E. Storrock Eccles, J.P., Hoylake, and widow of Lieut. Arthur W. Stone, R.N.V.R. *Educ.:* Bedford; Peterhouse, Cambridge: Classical Scholar; M.A. Classical Tripos, 1890. *Recreations:* yachting and motoring and all outdoor sports. *Address:* 10 King's Bench Walk, E.C.4; 1 Harley Street, W.1.; Fairfield House, St. Peter's, Thanet. *T.:* Mayfair 3958. Central 2143, Broadstairs 16. *T.A.:* 50 Temple. *Clubs:* Carlton, St. Stephen's, Ranelagh, Prince's, Royal Thames Yacht; Royal Temple Yacht.
(*Died 14 Oct. 1919.*)

CRAIG-BROWN, Thomas, of Craigend, Midlothian, J.P., F.S.A.S.; retired manufacturer; *b.* 30 July 1844. Accompanied British Commission for negotiating Treaty of Commerce with France, to Paris, 1880; President South of Scotland Chamber of Commerce, 1882; Member Executive Council, Associated Chambers of Commerce of U.K., 1883-86, 1896 and 1907; Vice-President, 1904; Member Advisory Committee, Intelligence Branch, Board of Trade, 1900-17; Provost of Selkirk, 1889-94; Member Royal Commission on Exhibitions, 1909, and on International Exhibitions, 1910; Member of Textiles Committee on Trade after War, 1916; Sub-Commissioner, National Serv. Dept. 1917; when provincial prisons closed, purchased from Crown the old prison of Selkirk (originally erected at instance of Sheriff Sir Walter Scott), fitted it as public library, and presented it to town. *Publications:* History of Selkirkshire, 2 vols. 4to, 1886; Effect of Foreign Tariffs on British Commerce (pamphlet), 1886; Letters of Mrs. Cockburn, 1900. *Recreations:* antiquarian research, travel, curling. *Address:* Woodburn, Selkirk. *T.A.:* Selkirk. *T.:* Selkirk 60. *Club:* Royal Societies. (*Died 7 April 1922.*)

CRAIGIE, Rev. Charles Edward; 2nd *s.* of late Admiral Robert Craigie; *m.* 1888, Margaret Jane, *d.* of late John Dent Goodman; three *s.* three *d. Educ.:* Winchester College; Keble College, Oxford; Wells Theological College. Curate of Woolston, Southampton, 1881; St. George's, Edgbaston, 1883; Vicar of Kington, 1888-1913; Rural Dean, 1892-1913; Prebendary of Norton in Hereford Cathedral, 1904-22; Rector of Weston-under-Penyard, Ross, Herefordshire, 1913-20; Royal Humane Society Testimonial, 1874. *Address:* Kington, Herefordshire. *Club:* County, Hereford.
(*Died 30 Aug. 1922.*)

CRAIGIE, John, K.C. 1905; Sheriff-Substitute at Glasgow, 1910; *b.* 1857. *Educ.:* Blairgowrie; Perth Academy; Edinburgh University (M.A., LL.B.). Called to Scottish Bar, 1884. *Publications:* Heritable Rights (3rd ed.); Moveable Rights (2nd ed.); Elements of Conveyancing; and Conveyancing Statutes. *Recreations:* golf, riding. *Address:* 3 Montague Terrace, Kelvinside, Glasgow.
(*Died 19 Oct. 1919.*)

CRAIK, Rt. Hon. Sir Henry, P.C. 1918; 1st Bt. *cr.* 1926; K.C.B., *cr.* 1897; M.A. (Oxon.), LL.D. (Glasgow and St. Andrews); M.P. (C.) Glasgow and Aberdeen Universities since 1906; and one of the Members for the Scottish Universities since 1918; Principal, Queen's College, Harley Street, 1911-14; *b.* Glasgow, 18 Oct. 1846; *s.* of Rev. James Craik, D.D. [Moderator of General Assembly, Church of Scotland]; *m.* 1873, Fanny Esther (*d.* 1923),

d. of late Charles Duffield, Manchester; two *s. Educ.:* High School, Glasgow; Glasgow University; Balliol Coll., Oxford. Honours in Classics and History, 1869. Examiner in Education Department in 1870; Senior Examiner, 1878; C.B. 1887; Sec. Scotch Education Department, Whitehall, 1885-1904. *Publications:* Life of Swift, 1882; The State and Education, 1883; Selections from Swift, 1893; English Prose Selections, 1892-96; A Century of Scottish History, 1901; Impressions of India, 1908; Life of Edward. First Earl of Clarendon, 1911. *Address:* 5A Dean's Yard, S.W.1. *T.:* Victoria 0256. *Club:* Athenæum. (*Died 16 Mar. 1927.*)

CRAMP, Sir William Dawkins, Kt., *cr.* 1908; I.S.O. 1903; *b.* Leamington, 29 Dec. 1840; *s.* of late James Cramp of Leamington; unmarried. *Educ.:* privately. Assistant Master Guilsborough Grammar School, 1860; Clerk in Examiner's Office, H.M. Customs, London, 1861; H.M. Inspector of Factories, 1868, in charge successively of North Ireland, Mid-Lancashire, North Staffordshire, and South Midland Districts to 1891; H.M. Superintending Inspector of Factories, Birmingham, 1891-99; London, 1899-1902; Deputy Chief Inspector, 1902-7. *Address:* Kirkland, Hersham, Walton-on-Thames.
(*Died 21 Sept. 1927.*)

CRANE, Robert Newton, K.C. 1921; M.A.; *b.* 1848; *o. s.* of late Rev. John Newton Crane, New Jersey, U.S.; *m.* 1873, *e. d.* of late Gerard B. Allen, St. Louis, U.S.; three *s.* one *d. Educ.:* Wesleyan University, Middleton, Connecticut. Founder, with Richard Watson Gilder, Newark (N.J.) Morning Register, 1869; Editor St. Louis Globe-Democrat, 1873; Consul at Manchester, 1874-80; Member U.S. Supreme Court Bar, 1881; Chancellor Diocese of Missouri, 1882; Barrister Middle Temple, 1894; Chairman American Society in London, 1898; Representative of U.S. Government in South African Deportation Claims Commission, 1901; Agent U.S. Government in Samoan Arbitration Award, 1903-4; U.S. Government Despatch Agent since 1904; Member Ex. Com. Society of Comparative Legislation, 1908; Grand Deacon of Freemasons; Chairman London Branch American Navy League; Bencher of the Middle Temple, 1919; Doctor Civil Law, Wesleyan University, 1921; contributor to legal and other periodical literatures. *Address:* Sheldon Cottage, Sheldon Avenue, N.6; *T.:* Mountview 3677; 4 Temple Gardens, E.C.4; *T.:* Central 1083. *Clubs:* Arts, Albemarle, American, Whitefriars.
(*Died 6 May 1927.*)

CRANSTON, Brig.-Gen. Sir Robert, Kt., *cr.* 1903; K.C.V.O., *cr.* 1905; C.B. 1909; C.B.E. 1918; LL.D., D.L., J.P., V.D., T.D.; Officer, Legion of Honour, France, 1904; Knight Commander of St. Olaf, Norway, 1906; Col. commanded Lothian Brigade; Member of Advisory Committee, War Office; *b.* Edinburgh, 2 June 1843; *m.* 1868, Elizabeth, *d.* of James S. Gilbert, of Edinburgh; two *s.* two *d. Educ.:* Edinburgh; Tillicoultry; Wilmslow; Paris. Entered The Queen's, 1870; subsequently Lt.-Col. 2nd Batt.; Fellow of Educational Institute of Scotland and of Royal Scottish Society of Arts; Treasurer of City of Edinburgh, 1899-1908; Lord Provost, 1903-6; contested (C.) Leith, 1910. *Address:* Corehouse, 19 Merchiston Avenue, Edinburgh. *T.:* Central 823. *Clubs:* Junior Constitutional; Conservative, Edinburgh. (*Died 22 Oct. 1923.*)

CRAUFURD, Rev. Alexander Henry, M.A.; *b.* 1843; *s.* of late Rev. C. H. Craufurd, and *g.s.* of General Robert Craufurd, who commanded the Light Division under Wellington. *Educ.:* Oriel Coll. Oxford (Exhibitioner). Life spent chiefly in reading; has held few charges, on account of weak health and Broad Church views; preached every autumn in St. Peter's, Vere Street, London, 1879-86; has spent much time in voluntarily helping to minister to

241

CRAIGHEAD, Edwin Boone, LL.D., D.C.L. See page xvii.

soldiers. *Publications:* General Craufurd and his Light Division; The Unknown God; Enigmas of the Spiritual Life; Christian Instincts and Modern Doubt; Recollections of James Martineau, 1903; The Religion of H. G. Wells and other Essays, 1909. Religion and Ethics of Tolstoy, 1912. *Recreation:* walking. *Club:* Union.
(Died 22 Sept. 1917.)

CRAVEN, 4th Earl of (or. 1801), William George Robert Craven; Viscount Uffington, 1801; Baron Craven, 1665. Capt. Royal Berks Yeomanry; D.L.; late A.D.C. to Lord Zetland, Lord Lieutenant of Ireland; H.M. Lieut. Co. Warwick; *s.* of 3rd Earl and Hon. Evelyn Laura Barrington, *d.* of 7th Viscount Barrington; *b.* 16 Dec. 1868; *S.* father 1883; *m.* 1893, Cornelia, *d.* of late Bradley Martin; one *s. Educ.:* Eton. Owns 40,000 acres. Coombe Pictures; Elizabeth, Queen of Bohemia's collection, left by her to Lord Craven at her death, whom she had previously married. *Heir: s.* Viscount Uffington. *Address:* Coombe Abbey, Coventry; Ashdown Park, Hampstead Marshall, Newbury, Berks. *Clubs:* Turf, Bachelors', White's; Royal Yacht Squadron, Cowes. *(Died 9 July 1921.)*

CRAVEN, Arthur Scott (Capt. Arthur Keedwell Harvey James), Author and Actor; *b.* 17 May 1875; *s.* of late Stephen Harvey James, Secretary for Law to the Government of India, and Secretary to the Viceroy of India's Council; *m.* Lucie, *d.* of Colonel Milner, late Royal Irish Regiment; one *s.* one *d. Educ.:* Cheltenham Junior School; Eton. Formerly special correspondent in India; represented various newspapers in Simla and Calcutta as special correspondent with the Government of India, 1894-97; entered dramatic profession, and assumed the name of Scott Craven; has played large number of parts at most of the London Theatres; is a frequent contributor to current English and American magazines, and author of several plays. Received commission in the Buffs, 1914; Captain commanding Company, 1915; formerly in the Artists' Rifles, also saw service in India; served European War, Officiating Assistant Provost-Marshal, 15th Div. B.E.F.; Assistant Provost-Marshal, 9th (Scottish) Division B.E.F., France, Nov. 1915. *Publications:* Poems in Divers Keys; Alarums and Excursions; The Last of the English, a play; The Fool's Tragedy; The Phœnix, etc. *Recreations:* cycling, cricket. *Address:* Hereward House, Westward Ho! Devonshire. *Clubs:* Garrick, Savage. *(Died 14 April 1917.)*

CRAVEN, Ven. James Brown, Archdeacon of Orkney since 1913; Rector of St. Olaf, Kirkwall, 1875-1914; *b.* 1850; *s.* of Rev. J. E. Craven; unmarried. Hon. D.D. Aberdeen; ordained 1875; Curate of St. Andrew, Aberdeen, 1875. *Publications:* History of Church in Orkney, 1883; 2nd edition, 1912; Journals of Bishop R. Forbes and History of Church in Ross, 1886; The Holy Eucharist (four Sermons), 1889; History of the Church in Moray, 1889; History of the Church in Orkney (1662-88), 1893; (1558-62), 1896; Scots Worthies (1560-1662), 1894; Prayers, etc. from Old Scottish Sources, 1894; Scotch Communion Office with Historical Note, 1897; Descriptive Catalogue of Bibliothek of Kirkwall (1683), 1897; Kirkwall Masonic Scroll, 1897; History of the Church in Orkney prior to 1558, 1901; Blazon of Episcopacy in Orkney, 1901; Dr. Robert Fludd, the English Rosicrucian, 1902; Ancient Earls of Caithness, 1904; Records of Dioceses of Argyll and The Isles, 1907; History of Church in Caithness, 1908; Count Michael Maier, 1910; Family of Cravie or Craven in Scotland, 1910; Church in South Ronaldshay and Burray, 1911; Sir John Arnot and Arnots in South Ronaldshay, 1913; David, Lord Balcarres, 1913; Esoteric Studies of Archbishop

242

Leighton, 1918. *Address:* Kirkwall, Orkney.
(Died 17 April 1924.)

CRAVEN, Hon. Osbert William; J.P.; late commanding Berkshire Yeomanry; *b.* 1848; 3rd *s.* of 2nd Earl of Craven. *Address:* Ashdown Park, Shrivenham. *M.:* BL 817. *Clubs:* Turf, Royal Automobile. *(Died 5 Mar. 1923.)*

CRAVEN, Lt.-Col. Waldemar Sigismund Dacre, D.S.O. 1917; late R.F.A.; *b.* 8 Aug. 1880; *s.* of late Rev. Dacre Craven and Florence Lees; *m.* 1913, Margaret Celia, *d.* of late Sir Frederick Mirrielees, *g.d.* of Sir Donald Currie, K.C.M.G.; one *s.* two *d. Educ.:* Haileybury; R.M.A., Woolwich. 2nd Lieut. R.F.A. 1898; served South Africa, 1899-1902 (despatches twice); India, 1907-10; France in B.E.F. Aug. 1914, Nov. 1914, and 1915-17 (severely wounded at battle of Ypres, Nov. 1914, despatches four times, D.S.O.); retired pay, 1920; Captain of Blackheath Rugby Football Club, 1911-13, and of Kent R.F.C. 1912 and 1913; Member for Kent on Rugby Union Committee; heavy-weight champion, Army and Navy, 1905 and 1906, and of Western India, 1907. *Recreations:* football, fishing, shooting, big-game shooting, and boxing. *Address:* Middleham, Ringmer, Sussex. *M.:* P9006, T3128. *Club:* Army and Navy. ·
(Died 11 Dec. 1923.)

CRAWFORD, Donald, K.C.; late Sheriff of Aberdeen, Kincardine, and Banff; D.L. cos. of Aberdeen and Banff; *b.* 1837; *s.* of Alexander Crawford of Aros, Argyllshire, and Sibella, *d.* of Donald Maclean of Kiniochscridan, Writer to the Signet; *m.* 1914, Hon. Lilian Mary Susan Moncreiff, 2nd *d.* of 3rd Baron Moncreiff. *Educ.:* Edinburgh Academy; University of Glasgow; Balliol Coll. Oxford; Heidelberg University. Fellow of Lincoln Coll. Oxford, 1861-81; Advocate at Scottish Bar, 1862; Legal Secretary to Lord Advocate, 1880-85; Parliamentary Boundary Commissioner, 1885; M.P. (L.) Lanarkshire N.E. Division, 1885-95; Member of Scottish University Commission, 1889-97; Sheriff, 1895; Deputy Chairman of Fishery Board for Scotland, 1897; Hon. LL.D. Aberdeen, 1909. *Address:* 35 Chester Street, Edinburgh. *Clubs:* Brooks's, Oxford and Cambridge; New, Edinburgh.
(Died 1 Jan. 1919.)

CRAWFORD, Very Rev. John, Canon of Clonfert, 1898; Provost of Kilmacduagh and Canon of Kilconnell; was Member of General Synod, Dublin; Hon. Sec. for many years to Dio. Board of Education; Member of Senate T.C.D.; *m.* Mary S., *d.* of Rev. Thomas Moore, M.A., authoress of Rolf the Imprudent, etc. *Educ.:* Portora Royal School, Enniskillen; Trinity College, Dublin (M.A., D.D.). Ordained 1856; Curate of Clontarf, 1856-61 and 1864-70; Kildrought, 1861-64; Curate of Duncavey, 1870-72; Finnes, 1872-77; Woodford, 1877-78; Lickmolassy, 1878-93. *Recreations:* books and nature. *Address:* Clonmoylan Abbey, Portumna, Co. Galway.

CRAWFORD, Capt. Lawrence Hugh, C.B. 1895; R.D., R.N.R.; Elder Brother of Trinity House since 1914; *e. s.* of late Lieut. Wm. Crawford, R.N., formerly Police Magistrate, Williamstown, Victoria (*s.* of Gen. Robert Crawford, R.A.), and Marianne Winthorp, *d.* of late Admiral Sir Lawrence Halsted, G.C.B.: unmarried. Is a Commander (retired) Royal Naval Reserve. *Decorated* on recommendation of 1st Lord of the Admiralty. *Recreations:* shooting and golf. *Address:* Holmwood, Claygate, Surrev. *Club:* Junior Constitutional.
(Died 19 Oct. 1918.)

CRAWFORD, Col. Raymund, C.B. 1918; retired pay; *b.* Paris, 1858; *o. s.* of Mervyn Archdale Nott Crawford, late of Millwood, Co. Fermanagh, and Emily, *e. d.* of late Hans Busk; *m.* 1st, Evelyn Violet Kempe, *g.d.* of Robert Bristow, Broxmore Park,

Romsey; one *s.*; 2nd, Cecilia Grant, *e. d.* of Wm. Grant Henry of Edinburgh and Riga. *Educ.*: Stonyhurst; joined the Royal Irish Regt. 1880; transferred permanently to Ordnance Dept. 1890; retired as Colonel, 1918. *Club*: Naval and Military.   (*Died 3 July 1927.*)

CRAWFORD, Sir Richard Frederick, K.C.M.G. 1911; K.B.E., *cr.* 1917; Minister Plenipotentiary in H.M.'s Diplomatic Service; a Commissioner of Customs, 1904-11; Adviser to Turkish Minister of Finance since 1911; *b.* 18 June 1863; *m.* 1894, Augusta, *o. d.* of late Lieut.-Col. A. A. D. Lestrange. *Club*: National.   (*Died 6 Aug. 1919.*)

CRAWFORD, Susan Fletcher, A.R.E., artist; *b.* Glasgow; *d.* of James R. Crawford, manufacturer in Glasgow. *Educ.*: private school; under W. Francis H. Newbery, Glasgow School of Art. Spent most of her life since leaving school at art work in the School of Art and in her own studio; exhibited in most of the principal towns in Europe, Paris, Old and New Salons, the Royal Academy, Royal Scottish Academy, Glasgow Royal Institute of the Fine Arts, Liverpool, Manchester, Leeds, Dundee, and other places, and in Munich, Prague, Vienna and Toronto. *Recreations:* walking, boating and rowing, motoring. *Address:* 10 Lansdowne Crescent, Glasgow, W.; Mountgreenan, Tyndrum, Perthshire; (Studio) 58 Renfield Street, Glasgow. *T.*: 1127 Charing, Glasgow. *Clubs:* Society of Lady Artists: Glasgow Literary, Glasgow.
  (*Died 23 April 1919.*)

CRAWFORD, Sir William, Kt., *cr.* 1906; J.P., City of Belfast; Chairman of the York Street Flax Spinning Company, Ltd.; *b.* 1840; *y. s.* of the late Rev. Alexander Crawford, Presbyterian Minister, Randalstown; *m.* 1866, Annie Coulson, *d.* of late Rev. James Glasgow, D.D., Missionary to India, Fellow of the University of Bombay; four *s.* one *d.* Served his apprenticeship with the York Street Flax Spinning Co.; went to Paris, 1862; there for 25 years, represented first the old Company and afterwards the Limited Company; twice President of the Paris British Chamber of Commerce; has been residing in Belfast since 1888; an ex-President of the Belfast Chamber of Commerce and of the Linen Merchants' Association; has taken an active interest in the Irish Presbyterian Church and in local charities. *Address:* Mount Randal, Belfast. *T.*: Malone 119. *M.*: OI 2282. *Clubs:* Ulster, Ulster Reform, Belfast.   (*Died 12 May 1922.*)

CRAWLEY, Alfred Ernest; an authority on social anthropology, and skating, golf, lawn tennis, etc.; *b.* 1869; *s.* of Rev. S. Crawley, Rector of Oddington, nr. Oxford. *Educ.*: Sedbergh; Emmanuel College, Cambridge. Scholar; Classical Tripos, 1st Class (2nd div.). Part ii., 1st class; Sudbury Hardyman Prize; M.A. *Publications:* Omar Khayyam in Greek Elegiacs, 1902; The Mystic Rose, a Study of Primitive-Marriage, 1902; The Tree of Life, a Study of Religion, 1905; The Idea of the Soul, 1909; The Book of the Ball, 1913; Lawn Tennis, 1919; Lawn Tennis Do's and Dont's, 1922. *Recreations:* Lawn tennis, figure-skating, fives, revolver-shooting. *Address:* 78 Redcliffe Square, S.W.10.   (*Died 21 Oct. 1924.*)

CRAWLEY, William John Chetwode; LL.D., D.C.L., F.R.G.S., F.G.S., F.R.Hist.S., F.R.S.S.A.; Member of Council of University of Dublin; *b.* 15 Nov. 1844; *s.* of William Crawley, of Mansfieldtown, Beds., and Margaret Brown Crawley, of Friars' Croft, Irvine, N.B.; *m.* Ellen M., *d.* of John M'Carthy, formerly of Desert Serges, Co. Cork; four *s. Educ.*: Trinity College, Dublin. For many years Director of the Dublin Military Classes; Member of the Academic Body elected to assist the Board of Trinity College in the

government of the University of Dublin; sometime Chairman of Dublin Council of Teachers' Guild of Great Britain and Ireland, Council of Classical Association, of Dublin Sanitary Association, and of various local societies; Freemason, for many years Grand Officer of the Freemasons of Ireland. *Publications:* The Handbook of Competitive Examinations (ten editions); Manual of Historical Geography; Caementaria Hibernica, Fasiculus I., 1895, II., 1896, III., 1900; and of numerous Archæological papers, and articles on the History of Freemasonry and kindred subjects; editor and joint author of The Latin Handbook and The French Handbook in the Open Competition Series. *Recreations:* formerly athlete and cricketer. *Address:* Mertonpark, Sandford, Dublin. *Clubs:* New Oxford and Cambridge; University, Dublin; Royal Irish Yacht, Kingstown.   (*Died 13 Mar. 1916.*)

CREAGH, Charles Vandeleur, C.M.G. 1892; Barrister at Law (Middle Temple); *b.* 1842; *e. surv. s.* of late Capt. James Creagh, R.N., Cahirbane, Clare, and Grace Emily, *d.* of the O'Moore of Cloghan Castle, King's Co.; *m.* 1882, Blanche Frances, *e. d.* of late Captain F. A. Edwardes, 30th Regiment, of Rhydgors, Carmarthenshire; two *s.* one *d. Educ.:* Royal Naval School, New Cross; Eastman's, Southsea. In 1866, when Assistant District Superintendent Punjab Police, was selected to raise and organise the Sikh Police for the Hong Kong Government; served for sixteen years in the latter colony in magisterial, police, and other appointments; received the thanks of Government for services during the typhoon of 1874; Chief Assistant to Sir Hugh Low, British Resident, Perak, and appointed Judge and Member of Council of that State, 1889; Governor and Chief Judicial Officer, North Borneo, 1888; Governor and Commander-in-Chief of Labuan, 1891 - 95. *Decorated* for distinguished services. *Address:* 82 Charlton Road, Blackheath, S.E.   (*Died 18 Sept. 1917.*)

CREAGH, General Sir O'Moore, V.C.; G.C.B., *cr.* 1909; G.C.S.I., *cr.* 1911; Rising Sun of Japan, 2nd class, 1903; K.C.B., *cr.* 1903; C.B. 1902; *b.* Cahirbane, Co. Clare, 2 April 1848; 7th *s.* of Captain Creagh, R.N., of Cahirbane, Co. Clare; *m.* 1st, 1874, Mary Letitia Longfield (*d.* 1876), *d.* of John Brereton; 2nd, 1890, Elizabeth, *d.* of late E. Reade; one *s.* one *d. Educ.:* private school; Royal Military College, Sandhurst. Ensign, 95th Foot, 1866; Indian Army, 1870; Commanded Merwara Batt. 1882; Commanded 2nd Baluchis, Colonel 129th Duke of Connaught's Own Baluchis, 1912; Assist. Quartermaster-General Bombay Command, 1895; Political Resident and General Officer Commanding Aden, 1898-1900; served Afghan War, 1879 - 80 (despatches, medal, Brevet Major, V.C.); Zhob Valley Expedition, 1890 (despatches); China Expedition, 1900 (despatches); commanding 1st Class District India, 1903-1906; Secretary of Military Department of India Office, 1907-9; Commander-in-Chief, India, 1909-14; retired from the army, May 1914. *Address:* 65 Albert Hall Mansions, Kensington Gore, S.W.7. *Club*: United Service.
  (*Died 9 Aug. 1923.*)

CREAK, Capt. Ettrick William, R.N.; C.B. 1901; F.R.S.; *b.* 28 May 1835; *s.* of late Commander W. Creak, R.N.; *m.* 1867, Grace Mary, *d.* of W. B. Brodie; three *s.* one *d.*; late Superintendent of Compasses, Hydrographic Department, Admiralty. *Address:* 9 Hervey Road, Blackheath, S.E.   (*Died 3 April 1920.*)

CREAN, Major Thomas Joseph, D.S.O. 1915; V.C. 1901; retired Captain R.A.M.C. and 1st Imperial Light Horse; L.R.C.P. and S.I.; Hon. F.R.C.S. Ire.; L.M. Rotunda Hospital, Dublin; late Assistant Master Lying-in-Hospital, Dublin; Arnott Memorial Gold Medal, 1902; Royal Humane Society Testimonial for saving life at sea, 1891; Member of Council Irish Graduate Society, 1908 ; *b.* Dublin, 1873 ; 2nd *s.* of late Michael Theobald Crean, barrister ; *m.* 1905, Victoria, *o. d.* of Señor don Tomas Heredia, Malaga ; one *s.* one *d. Educ.:* Clongowes. Served S. Africa and West Africa (wounded Elandslaagte twice dangerously Tygerskloof) ; European War, with 1st Cavalry Brigade, 1914-15 (despatches, D.S.O.) ; officer commanding 44th Field Ambulance, B.E.F. France, 1916 ; Medical Officer in charge, Hosp., Roy. Enclosure, Ascot ; Clin. Assist. Samaritan Hosp. for Women, Lond. ; Member of the Irish Twenty Club. *Decorated* for Tygerskloof, South Africa. *Recreations :* Irish International Rugby XV., 1894-6 ; English team in South Africa, 1896. *Address :* 13 Queen Street, Mayfair, W.1. *T.A. :* Masinto Lond. *T. :* 9382 Gerrard. *Clubs :* Army and Navy, Bucks. *M. :* LM 9850.

                                (*Died 25 Mar. 1923.*)

CREASY, Leonard, I.S.O. 1905 ; M.Inst.C.E. ; 3rd *s.* of late Sir Edward Creasy, Chief Justice of Ceylon ; *b.* 1854 ; *m.* 1890, Ellen Maud, *d.* of late Sir George Elvey, Mus. Doc. Windsor. *Educ. :* University College School, London. Served in Public Works Department, Ceylon, 1874-1905. *Address :* Hurstleigh, Windsor Forest
                                (*Died 9 May 1922.*)

CREIGHTON, Charles, M.D. ; *b.* Peterhead, 22 Nov. 1847. *Educ. :* The Gymnasium, Old Aberdeen : Aberdeen University (M.A., 1867). Studied medicine at Aberdeen Edinburgh, Vienna, and Berlin ; occupied with research on cancer for Med. Dep. L.G.B. four years ; thereafter Demonstrator of Anatomy at Cambridge for five years (M.A. King's Coll.) ; formerly resided in London, occupied with original work in pathology, epidemiology, and microscopic anatomy. *Publications :* Physiology and Pathology of the Breast ; Researches on Cancers, etc., of the Breast ; Bovine Tuberculosis in Man ; Natural History of Cowpox ; Jenner and Vaccination ; History of Epidemics in Britain ; Microscopic Researches on Glycogen, 2 parts ; Some Conclusions on Cancer ; Shakespeare's Story of his Life ; Allegories of Othello and King Lear ; Monographs on the second sense in Macbeth, Antony and Cleopatra, Cymbeline, and The Winter's Tale ; Plague in India—conclusions from a visit in 1904-5. *Address :* The Yews, Upper Boddington, Byfield, Northants. (*Died 18 July 1927.*)

CREMIEU-JAVAL, Paul ; Consul-General of Monaco for the United Kingdom ; Member of the Order of Mercy ; Knight of the Order of the Crown of Italy ; Grand Officer Order of St. Sava, Servia ; Commander of the Order of Danilo I. of Montenegro ; Knight Commander Order of the Redemption, Liberia ; Gold Medal of Merit with Ribbon of St. Anne, Russia ; Officer of the Order of St. Charles, Monaco ; J.P., A.C.A. ; *b.* 1857 ; *m.* 1893, *d.* of Col. Bradshaw, J.P., of Carrick-on-Shannon. Chairman of Executive of Exhibitions at Earl's Court, 1894-1909. *Recreation :* hunting. *Address :* 39 Ennismore Gardens, S.W.7. *T. :* Western 4095.   *Club :* Royal Automobile.
                            (*Died 11 April 1927.*)

CRESSWELL, Colonel George Francis Addison, C.V.O. 1906 ; M.V.O. 1901 ; V.D. ; commanding 5th Batt. Norfolk Regt., 1904-14 ; *b.* 1852 ; *m.* 1882, Harriet Eva, *d.* of Rev. W. H. Gurney, Rector of N. Runckton, Norfolk. *Address :* King Street, King's Lynn ; Garden House, Hunstanton. *Club :* Royal Thames Yacht.
                            (*Died 5 July 1926.*)

CRESSWELL, Herbert Osborn, F.R.I.B.A. 1895 ; architect ; *b.* Twickenham, 13 June 1860 ; *s.* of late Charles Neve Cresswell, Barrister at Law, of 1 Hare Court Temple and Ashtead, Surrey ; *m.* 1911, Mollie, *d.* of late Richard Adams, County Court Judge of Limerick. *Educ. :* Ewell ; private tuition. Articled to Trench and Murray, Surveyors, 1876 ; in office of Sir Aston Webb, R.A., 1879-

1884 ; studied in the schools of the R.A. and the Architectural Association, and travelled abroad ; was for a short time in the design branch of the War Office, and started in independent practice in 1885 ; A.R.I.B.A., 1886 ; has served on the Council of the Institute ; President of the Architectural Association, 1892-93 ; during the period of the War was appointed expert adviser to the War Office on questions of Dilapidations and Damage to Buildings in Military Occupation, and made a Captain on the Staff. *Recreations :* water-colour drawing, sketching, and photography, mountain climbing, golf, tennis, and other games. *Address :* 12 Charles Street, Knightsbridge, S.W. *T. :* Western 6644. *Clubs :* Constitutional, Arts.
                          (*Died 11 June 1919.*)

CRESWELL, John Edwards, C.B.E., M.B., B.C. (Cantab.) ; retired ; *b.* 12 March 1864 ; *s.* of late Edmund Creswell of Gibraltar ; *m.* Catherine Burleigh, *d.* of Mathew Towgood, Ceylon. *Educ. :* Bruce Castle School ; Cavendish College, Cambridge ; University College Hospital, London. Served in Egyptian Public Health as P.M.O. at Suez, 1892-1920. *Address :* Charmouth House, Charmouth, Dorset.
                          (*Died 25 Oct. 1928.*)

CRESWICK, Colonel Sir Nathaniel, K.C.B., *cr.* 1909 ; C.B., 1896 ; V.D., J.P. for Derbyshire ; solicitor ; *b.* Sheffield, 31 July 1831 ; *e. s.* of Nathaniel Creswick, late of Easthill, Sheffield ; *m.* 1866, Sarah Ann, *o. d.* of John Walker of York : one *s.* one *d. Educ. :* Sheffield Collegiate School. Received H.M. Humane Society's Medal, 1861 ; commanded 4th West York Vol. Artillery (Western Division R.A.), 1861-97. *Address :* Norton, near Sheffield. *T. :* 3028 Sheffield ; 127 Beauchief.
                          (*Died 20 Oct. 1917.*)

CREWDSON, Rev. George, Hon. Canon Carlisle ; late Rural Dean ; *b.* Kendal, 18 Aug. 1840 ; *s.* of G. B. Crewdson ; *m.* 1870, M. S. H. Sweet-Escott (*d.* 1910) ; two *s.* two *d. Educ. :* Windermere College ; Trinity College, Cambridge. Curate of All Saints', Mile End, New Town, London, 1864-67 ; St. Andrew's, Clifton, Bristol, 1867-68 ; St. Ann's, Nottingham, 1869-71 ; Rector of Scaleby, Carlisle, 1871-74 ; Vicar of St. George's, Kendal, 1875-93 ; Vicar of St. Mary's, Windermere, 1893-1911. *Address :* Whitstead, Barton Road, Cambridge. *T. :* Cambridge 474. (*Died 18 Feb. 1920.*)

CREWDSON, Wilson ; J.P., M.A., F.S.A. ; Chevalier Order of Rising Sun, Japan ; Vice-President and Member of Council, Japan Society ; Hon. Treasurer Royal Asiatic Society ; Hon. Secretary the New East ; *b.* 13 April 1856 ; *e. s.* of Wilson Crewdson, manufacturer, Manchester, and Ellen Waterhouse; *m.* Mary Frances Adelaide, *d.* of William Bevan of London. *Educ. :* Grove House, Tottenham ; King's College, Cambridge (Exhibitioner). Joint Hon. Secretary Japan Society, 1904-7; Chairman, 1907-11; S.G.D. English Freemasons, 1914. *Publications :* Japan, Our Ally, 1915 ; various articles in Nineteenth Century and other Reviews. *Address :* Southside, St. Leonards-on-Sea ; Queen Anne's Mansions, S.W. *T :* 491. *T.A. :* Crewdson Hastings. *Clubs :* Savage, Oriental, Burlington Fine Arts.   (*Died May 1918.*)

CREWE, Sir Vauncey Harpur, 10th Bt. ; *cr.* 1626 ; J.P., D.L. ; *s.* of 9th Bt. and *d.* of Vice-Adm. W. S. Lovell ; *b.* 14 Oct. 1846 ; *S.* father 1886 ; *m.* Hon. Isabel Adderley, *y. d.* of 1st Lord Norton, 1876 ; four *d.* High Sheriff Derbyshire, 1900. Owns about 28,000 acres. *Heir :* none. *Address :* Calke Abbey, Derby ; Warslow Hall, Ashbourne. *Club :* Carlton.
                          (*Died 13 Dec. 1924.*)

CRICHTON, Lt.-Col. Hon. Charles (Frederick), J.P., D.L. ; *b.* 5 Nov. 1841 ; 2nd *s.* of 3rd Earl of Erne ; *m.* 1873, Madeline Taylour, *e. d.* of 3rd Marquis of Headfort ; one *s.* one *d. Educ. :* St. Columba's College, Ireland

Exeter College, Oxford. B.A., 1861; joined 1st Batt. Grenadier Guards, 1861; served in Canada, 1861 and 1864; leaving the Grenadiers as Captain and Lieut.-Colonel in 1876. *Recreations:* hunting and yachting. *Address:* Mullaboden, Ballymore-Eustace, Ireland. *M.:* 4799. *Clubs:* Bachelors'; Kildare Street, Dublin; St. George's Yacht, Kingstown.

(Died 20 Aug. 1918.)

CRICHTON, Colonel Hon. Sir Henry (George Louis), K.C.B., *cr.* 1911; A.D.C.; D.L., J.P., Hants; Alderman Hants County Council; Director L. and S.-W. Ry.; Chairman Territorial Association of Hampshire; County Commissioner Boy Scout Association; *b.* 7 Apr. 1844; 3rd *s.* of 3rd Earl of Erne; *m.* 1st, *d.* (*d.* 1888) of Maj. A. W. Cole Hamilton; 2nd, 1890, Lady Jane Emma Baring, C.I., C.B.E. 1920, *o. d.* of 1st Earl of Northbrook; three *s.* one *d. Educ.:* Radley Coll.; Christ Church, Oxford. Served in 10th Royal Hussars, 1863-74; 21st Hussars, 1874-84; Lieut.-Col. commanding Hampshire Yeomanry Carabiniers, 1884-95; commanding Hampshire Brigade, 1895-1910; A.D.C. to the King; Hon. Col. 5th Territorial Batt. Hampshire Regt.; Hon. Colonel Hampshire Carabiniers Yeomanry; Commandant Hampshire Volunteer Regiment. *Address:* Netley Castle, Netley Abbey, Hants. *Clubs:* Army and Navy, Cavalry; Royal Yacht Squadron, Cowes; Royal Southern Yacht.

(Died 10 May 1922.)

CRILLY, Daniel, journalist, reviewer; *b.* 14 Dec. 1857; *s.* of late Daniel Crilly, Rostrevor, Co. Down; *m.* Mary Ellen Colclough, Dublin, 1887. *Educ.:* Catholic Institute, Hope Street, Liverpool; Sedgley Park College, Staffordshire. Served his full apprenticeship to a cotton broker in Liverpool; became a journalist; edited the United Irishman, Liverpool, 1876; joined the editorial staff of The Nation, Dublin, 1880; after extension of franchise was selected as National candidate for North Mayo, 1885; stood his trial before a jury in Dublin, 1887, for alleged connection with Plan of Campaign; jury disagreeing, prosecution was abandoned; was Hon. Sec. Home Rule Confederation 1875-77 and Irish National League of Great Britain; M.P. (A.P., H.R.) North Mayo, 1885-1900. *Publications:* In the Bye-ways with Young Ireland,1888; The "Felon" Literature of Ireland, 1889; The Celt at Westminster, 1892; Pencillings on Parnassus, 1892; In the Footsteps of John Mitchel, 1900-1. *Recreations:* cricket, cycling. *(Died Dec. 1923.)*

CRIPPS, W. Harrison, F.R.C.S.; late Senior Surgeon to St. Bartholomew's Hospital; Council Royal College of Surgeons; Chairman Metropolitan Electric Supply Company; *s.* of H.W.Cripps,Q.C.; *m.* 1st, Blanche, *d.* of Richard Potter of Standish House, Gloucestershire; four *s.* one *d.*; 2nd, Giulia, *d.* of Sig. M. N. Ravogli of Rome. *Publications:* Ovariotomy and Abdominal Surgery; Cancer of Rectum. *Recreations:* shooting and fishing. *Address:* Glendaruel, Argyllshire; 19 Bentinck Street, W.1. *T.:* Mayfair 3514. *Club:* Conservative. *(Died 8 Nov. 1923.)*

CRISP, Sir Frank, 1st Bt., *cr.* 1913; Kt., *cr.* 1907; senior partner in firm of Ashurst, Morris, Crisp & Co., solicitors, Throgmorton Avenue, London; *b.* 1848; *o. c.* of John Shalders Crisp and Harriet, *o. d.* of John Childs of Bungay, Suffolk, opponent of Church Rates and Queen's Printers' Bible Monopoly; *m.* 1867, Catherine, *o. d.* of George D. Howes; four *s.* two *d. Educ.:* privately and University College School; LL.B. and B.A. of University of London; admitted Solicitor (Honours), 1869; J.P. Oxon.; Hon. Secretary, Royal Microscopical Society, 1878-89; V.P. and Treasurer Linnean Society of London, Burlington House, 1881-1906; Member of Board of Trade Committee for Amendment of Companies Act. *Recreations:* Company Law, Horticulture, Microscopy. *Heir:* *s.* Frank Morris, *b.* 13 March 1872. *Address:*

17 Throgmorton Avenue, E.C.; 5 Lansdowne Road, Holland Park Avenue, W.; Friar Park, Henley-on-Thames. *Clubs:* Reform, National Liberal. *(Died 29 April 1919.)*

CRISP, Frederick Arthur, J.P., *b.* Walworth, Surrey, 27 June 1851; *s.* of late Frederick Augustus Crisp, of The Hall, Playford, Suffolk, and Sarah, *d.* of John Steedman, of Walworth; *m.* 1880, Gertrude, *d.* of John South, of Stutton, Suffolk; six *d.* Lord of the Manor of Godalming; Patron and Lay Rector of Capel, Surrey. *Publications:* Visitation of England and Wales; Visitation of Ireland; Fragmenta Genealogica; and other genealogical works. *Address:* The Manor House, Godalming, Surrey; Little Wenham Hall, Suffolk. *T.:* 7 Godalming. *T.A.:* Crisp, Godalming. *Clubs:* Royal Societies, Burlington Fine Arts, Royal Automobile. *(Died 25 April 1922.)*

CRITCHELL, James Troubridge, J.P.; late London correspondent of Pastoralists' Review, Sydney Morning Herald, North Queensland Register, and Queensland Sugar Journal; *s.* of John Critchell of Yeovil; *b.* 22 April 1850. *Educ.:* Wootton-under-Edge Grammar School. *Publications:* History of the Frozen Meat Trade, 1912; Polynesian Labour in Queensland, 1892; Preliminary Inquiry into the Markets of the European Continent, 1895; Guide to Queensland; contributor to the Encyclopædia Britannica. *Address:* 22 Basinghall Street, E.C.; Queensland Cottage, Billericay, Essex. *Club:* Australasian. *(Died 8 Nov. 1917.)*

CRITCHETT, Sir George Anderson, 1st Bt., *cr.* 1908; Kt., *cr.* 1901; C.V.O.; M.A., F.R.C.S.E.; K.C.V.O., *cr.*1919; Surgeon Oculist to the King since 1901; Knight of Grace Order of St. John; Consulting Ophthalmic Surgeon to St. Mary's Hospital, London; 1st President Council of British Ophthalmologists; *e. s.* of late George Critchett, F.R.C.S.; *m.* 1883, Agnes, *d.* of late C. J. Dunphie; one *s.* two *d. Educ.:* Harrow; Caius College, Cambridge. Ex-President of Ophthalmological Society of United Kingdom; President Ophthalmic Section International Medical Congress, 1913; Master of the Oxford Ophthalmological Congress. *Publications:* Eclecticism in Operations for Cataract, 1883; Nature's Speculum in Cataract Extraction, 1886; Conical Cornea, its Surgical Evolution, 1895. *Recreations:* cricket, lawn-tennis. *Heir:* *s.* George Montague [*b.* 7 June 1884; *m.* 1914, Innes, 3rd *d.* of Colonel Wiehe, Littlebourne Lodge, Sandgate. Late Lieut. 3rd Batt. Oxfordshire and Bucks L.I.; Captain 9th London Regiment]. *Address:* 21 Harley Street, W.1. *T.:* Langham 1065. *Clubs:* Athenæum, Ranelagh, Garrick. *(Died 9 Feb. 1925.)*

CROCKER, George, C.B. 1902; J.P. Falmouth; *b.* 27 May 1846; *s.* of J. W. Crocker; *m.* 1st, 1870, Sarah (*decd.*), *d.* of J. A. Dodd; 2nd, 1894, Alice, *d.* of W. J. Barratt; one *d. Educ.:* privately; Devonport Dockyard; obtained Queen's Scholarship, 1864. Employed at Admiralty and Portsmouth Dockyard till 1884; Naval Constructor, Bombay and Calcutta, 1884-87; Chatham, 1887-89; Inspector of Admiralty Overseers, 1890-92; Chief Constructor, Devonport, 1892-95; Chatham, 1895-1897; Civil Technical Assistant to Adm. Supt. at Devonport, 1897-1905; Manager at Devonport, 1906; retired, 1906. *Address:* Coningsby, Mannamead, Plymouth. *T.A.:* Coningsby, Plymouth.

(Died 21 Feb. 1923.)

CROCKET, Henry Edgar, R.W.S. *Educ.:* the Royal College of Art; Julian's, Paris. *Recreation:* concerted music. *Address:* Salterns, Bradford Road, Lewes, Sussex.

(Died 13 Mar. 1926.)

CROFT, Sir Alfred Woodley, K.C.I.E., *cr.* 1887; J.P. Devon; *b.* 1841; *s.* of C. W. Croft, Plymouth. *Educ.:* Mannamead School, Plymouth; Exeter College Oxford; B.A. 1863,

245

M.A. 1870. Sometime Lecturer, Exeter Coll. Oxford; entered Bengal Educational Department, 1866; Director Public Instruction, Bengal, 1877-97; retired 1897; M.L.C. Bengal, 1887-92; President, Asiatic Society of Bengal, 1892-93; Trustee, Indian Museum, 1894-96; Vice-Chancellor Calcutta University, 1894-96; Hon. LL.D. 1897. *Address:* Rumleigh, Bere Alston, S. Devon. *T.:* Bere Alston 13. *T.A.:* Bere Alston.   (*Died 29 Oct. 1925.*)

CROFT, Henry Herbert Stephen, barrister-at-law; Recorder of Tenterden since 1891; *b.* Ipswich, 22 Feb. 1842; *e. s.* of Rev. Stephen Croft, Rector of St. Mary, Stoke, Ipswich, Rural Dean; *m.* 1876, Emma (*d.* 1914), *d.* of Mr. Kearse, New Brighton; one *s.* one *d. Educ.:* Eton; Trin. Coll. Camb. Junior optime, third class Classical Tripos; M.A. Appointed Registrar of Courts for trial of Municipal Election Petitions, 1875, 1883-1891. *Publications:* editor of Sir Thomas Elyot's Boke named the Governour; joint-editor of Archbold's Quarter Sessions Practice, 4th ed.; joint-editor of the Election Manual, 1874. *Address:* 11 King's Bench Walk, E.C.; 27 Holland Villas Road, W.14. *T.:* Park 3319.   (*Died 8 June 1923.*)

CROFTON, Sir Malby, 3rd Bt.; *cr.* 1838; J.P., D.L.; *b.* 20 Aug. 1857; *e. s.* of H. B. Crofton; S. grandfather 1872; *m.* Louisa, *d.* of R. J. Verschoyle, Tanrego, Co. Sligo, 1880; one *s.* two *d. Educ.:* Univ. Coll., Oxford. *Heir:* s. Major M. R. H. Crofton. *Address:* Longford House, Ballisodare, Co. Sligo. *T.A.:* Beltra.   (*Died 17 Sept. 1926.*)

CROFTON, Col. Morgan, C.B. 1899; D.S.O. 1886; *b.* 2 Jan. 1850; *s.* of late Rev. Morgan Crofton; *m.* 1894, Ruperta, *d.* of late Col. Charles Edward Gostling Murray and widow of W. H. Willats of Denton Court, Kent. *Educ.:* Cheltenham College. Joined army, 1868; served on staff in South Africa, Zulu war, 1879-80; A.D.C. to Gen. commanding Scotland, 1881-85; served Nile Expedition, 1884-86; Chief Staff Officer South Africa, 1894-99. *Address:* 5 Brunswick Terrace, Brighton. *Clubs:* Pratt's, Army and Navy.   (*Died 9 Jan. 1916.*)

CROFTS, Major Richard, D.S.O. 1900; R.A.M.C.; late Senior Medical Officer, Sierra Leone; retired; *b.* 11 Aug. 1859. Served against the Jebus, Lagos, 1892 (despatches, medal with clasp).   (*Died 16 Jan. 1916.*)

CROISET, Alfred, Dean of the Faculty of Letters, Paris; Member of the Academy of Inscriptions and Belles-Lettres; Hon. D.Litt., Oxford, 1903; Corresponding Fellow of the British Academy; *b.* 1845. *Publications:* La Poesie de Pindare; Histoire de la Litterature grecque, 5 vols. (with Maurice Croiset); Les Democraties antiques. *Address:* 13 rue Cassette, Paris.   (*Died 7 June 1923.*)

CROKER, Mrs. B. M.; novelist; *o. d.* of late Rev. William Sheppard, Rector of Kilgefin, Co. Roscommon; wife of Lieut.-Col. John Croker, late Royal Scots and Royal Munster Fusiliers; one *d. Educ.:* Rockferry, Cheshire. Tours. Spent 14 years in the East (India and Burmah). *Publications:* Pretty Miss Neville, 1883; A Bird of Passage, 1886; Diana Barrington, 1888; Interference 1891; A Family Likeness, 1892; Mr. Jervis, 1894; The Real Lady Hilda, 1895; Beyond the Pale, 1897; Peggy of the Bartons, 1898; Terence (dramatised in the U.S.A.); Infatuation, 1899; The Happy Valley; Angel, 1901; The Cat's Paw; Her Own People; The Spanish Necklace, 1907; Katherine the Arrogant, 1910; In Old Madras, 1913; Lismoyle, 1914; Given in Marriage, 1916; The Road to Mandalay, 1917; Odds and Ends, 1919. *Recreations:* reading, travelling, theatre. *Address:* 5 Radnor Cliff, Folkestone. *Clubs:* Writers', Sesame.   (*Died 20 Oct. 1920.*)

CROKER, Richard, Leader of Tammany Hall, 1884-1903; *b.* Clonakilty, Co. Cork, 23

Nov. 1841; *m.* 1st, 1873, Elizabeth, *d.* of Samuel Fraser, New York; one *s.* one *d.* ; 2nd, 1914, Bula Benton Edmondson. *Educ.:* New York. Alderman, New York, 1868-70; Coroner, 1873; served term, 1876; re-elected, served 1879; Fire Commissioner, 1883; City Chamberlain, 1889-90; Freeman of Dublin, 1908. *Recreations:* horse-racing; won the Derby, Irish Derby, Curragh, and Baldoyle Derby with Orby, 1907; also won the English Guineas with Rhodora, Orby's half-sister, 1908. *Address:* Glencairn, Co. Dublin; The Wigwam, Palm Beach, U.S.A. *Club:* Democratic, New York.   (*Died 29 April 1922.*)

CROLE, Charles Stewart, C.I.E., 1898; late I.C.S.: retired, 1898; *m.* 1st, Katharine (*d.* 1913); 2nd, 1913, Mary, *e. d.* of late Walter de Voil. *Educ.:* High School and Univ., Edinburgh. Entered service, 1862; District and Sessions Judge, Kistna, 1881; Collector and Magistrate, 1882; Member of Board of Revenue, 1890; Legislative Board, 1893; contested Enfield (L.), 1900. *Publication:* Chinglepat District Manual. *Address:* 28 Queen's Mansions, Victoria Street, S.W.   (*Died 4 May 1916.*)

CROLE, Gerard Lake, Advocate, K.C.; Sheriff of Lothian and Peebles since 1918; *b.* 22 Nov. 1855, *y. s.* of late David Crole, Solicitor of Inland Revenue for Scotland, 1893; *m.* Elizabeth Ann, *widow* of late Patrick Turnbull, C.A., Edinburgh, and 2nd *d.* of late George Carrick Coats, Aberdeen; one *s. Educ.:* The Royal High School and University, Edinburgh. M.A. 1876; LL.B., 1880; called to Scottish Bar, 1881; K.C. 1904; LL.D., 1919; Principal Clerk of Justiciary, 1892-1918; elder, United Free Church. *Recreations:* golf, fishing. *Address:* 1 Royal Circus, Edinburgh. *T.:* Central Edinburgh 21572. *Club:* Northern, Edinburgh.   (*Died 26 Oct. 1927.*)

CROLY, Very Rev. Daniel George Hayes, Dean of Killala, 1911-15; Incumbent of St. Patrick's, 1904-15. *Educ.:* Trinity College, Dublin (M.A.). Ordained 1870; Curate of Kilcommon, 1870-71; Pulathomas, 1871-77; Perpetual Curate of Kilaraught, 1877-78; Vicar of St. Anne, Easky, 1878-1904; Examining Chaplain to Bishop of Tuam. *Address:* Hill House, Killala, Ballina.   (*Died 14 Oct. 1916.*)

CROMER, 1st Earl of (*cr.* 1901), **Evelyn Baring,** Viscount (*cr.* 1898), Baron (*cr.* 1892), P.C., G.C.B., O.M., G.C.M.G., K.C.S.I., C.I.E., F.R.S., LL.D. (hon.), Oxf. and Camb.; Hon. F.B.A.; Minister Plenipotentiary in the Diplomatic Service; *b.* Cromer Hall, Norfolk, 26 Feb. 1841; *s.* of Henry Baring, M.P., and Cecilia Anne, *d.* of Vice-Admiral William Windham, Felbrigg Hall, Norfolk; *m.* 1st, Ethel Stanley (*d.* 1898), *d.* of Sir Rowland Stanley Errington, Bt., 1876; two *s.*; 2nd, 1901, Lady Katherine Georgiana Louisa Thynne, 2nd *d.* of 4th Marquess of Bath; one *s. Educ.:* Ordnance School, Carshalton; R.M.A., Woolwich. Hon. D.C.L. Oxford and Cambridge. Protestant. Entered Royal Artillery, 1858; Capt. 1870; Major, 1876; A.D.C. to Sir Henry Storks in Ionian Islands, 1861, and Secretary, 1865, during inquiry into outbreak in Jamaica; Private Secretary to Earl of Northbrook, Viceroy of India, 1872-76; Commissioner Egyptian Public Debt, 1877-79; Controller-General in Egypt, 1879; Financial Member of Council of Governor-Gen. of India, 1880; Financial Assistant at Conference in London on Egyptian Finance, 1884; Agent and Consul-Gen. in Egypt, 1883-1907; holds Albert Medal, Society of Arts. *Publications:* Staff College Essays; Paraphrases and translations from the Greek; The War Game; and other military works; Modern Egypt, 2 vols., 1908; Ancient and Modern Imperialism, 1910; Political and Literary Essays, 1908-13; 3rd Series, 1916; Abbas II., 1915. *Recreations:* shooting, fishing. *Heir:* s. Viscount Errington.   *Address:* 36

Wimpole Street, W. *T :* Mayfair 478. *Club :* Turf. *(Died 29 Jan. 1917.)*

CROMIE, Com. Francis Newton Allen, D.S.O. 1916 ; Kt. of St. George, Chevalier Légion d'Honneur ; commanding E19 and English flotilla in the Baltic since 1916 ; *b.* Duncannon Fort, Ireland, 30 Jan. 1882 ; *s.* of late Capt. F. C. Cromie, Hants Regt., Consul-General, Dakar, and Mrs. Lennard, *d.* of T. I. Webb Bowen, late Chief of Police, Pembrokeshire. *Educ. :* Haverfordwest Grammar School ; Britannia. Joined Repulse 1898 ; midshipman, 1898 ; with Barfleure brigade in Seymour's Expedition, 1900 (China medal, Pekin clasp, despatches) ; Sub.-Lt. 1901 ; Lt. 1903 : entered submarine service, 1903 ; Humane Society's medal (bronze) trying to save a man overboard from A3, 1906 ; commanded H.M.S. Onyx and III. flotilla submarines, 1911-12 ; Rosario and China flotilla submarines, 1913-14 ; commissioned E19, August 1915 ; forced passage into Baltic, 10 Sep. 1915 (4th class St. Vladimir with swords) ; entirely suspended German traffic in Baltic for one week, Oct. 1915 (St. Anne, 2nd class) ; sank German cruiser Undine, 7 Nov. 1915 (St. George's Cross, prom. Commander, D.S.O.). *Recreations :* out - door sports and sailing. *Address :* Cromore, Dovercourt, Essex. *(Died 31 Aug. 1918.)*

CROMIE, Rev. William Patrick, M.A., Rector of Stoke Newington since 1918 ; Prebendary of St. Paul's since 1917 ; Rural Dean of Hackney and Stoke Newington, 1919 ; Proctor in Convocation for Diocese of London, 1921 ; *m.* 1893, Harriette, 2nd *d.* of late John Jones, The Hollies, Oswestry, Shropshire ; one *s.* two *d.* *Educ. :* Corpus Christi College, Cambridge ; Deacon, 1891 ; Priest, 1892 ; Curate of St. Philip, Kingston-on-Hull, 1891-94 ; St. Stephen, Kingston-on-Hull, 1894-96 ; Curate-in-charge of the Abbey Church (St. Andrew the Less), Camb., 1896-1900 ; Vicar of Harlesden (All Souls) with St. Luke's and St. Mark's, 1900-18 ; Surrogate to Master of F*a*culties, 1902 ; Chaplain to Willesden Union, 1907-18 ; Assessor under Clergy Discipline Act, 1912 ; Chaplain to the Forces, 1914-18 ; Rural Dean of Willesden, 1914-1918. *Recreation :* fishing. *Address :* The Rectory, Stoke Newington, N.16.*(Died 3 Aug. 1927.)*

CROMPTON, James Shaw, R.I., A.R.B.C. ; *b.* Bootle, near Liverpool, 7 March 1853 ; *s.* of Robert Crompton, author and editor ; *m.* 1886 ; two *d.* *Educ. :* under John Finnie, Liverpool ; Liverpool Academy ; Heatherley's School of Art. Member of the Selborne Society (Vice-President and Council) ; Langham Sketching Club (past-Chairman) ; Royal Drawing Society ; Hampstead Art Society. (Council) ; has exhibited at New Gallery, R.A., R.I., and the Provinces ; Picture purchased by the Council for Permanent Collection, Liverpool ; has done much book illustration. *Recreations :* walking, gardening. *Address :* 1 England's Lane, Haverstock Hill, N.W. *Club :* Langham Sketching.

(Died 22 July 1916.)

CROMPTON, John Gilbert Frederic, J.P. ; *b.* 1869 ; *o. s.* of late John Gilbert Crompton and 2nd wife Caroline Georgiana, *o. d.* of late Frederick Chaplin of Tathwell Hall, Lincolnshire. High Sheriff Derbyshire, 1917. *Address :* Flower Lilies, Windley, Derby. *Club :* Boodle's. *(Died 31 Mar. 1919.)*

CRONSHAW, Rev. Christopher, Hon. Canon of Manchester. *Address :* 63 Cambridge Road, Southport, Lancs. *(Died 3 Jan. 1921.)*

CRONSHAW, Rev. George Bernard, M.A. ; Principal of St. Edmund Hall, Oxford, since 1928 ; late Fellow and Bursar, Queen's College, Oxford ; *m.* 1926, Dorothy, *d.* of Bernard Wardle, of Scarthwaite, near Lancaster. *Address :* St. Edmund Hall, Oxford.

(Died 20 Dec. 1928.)

CROOK, Charles W., B.A., B.Sc. (Lond.) ; M.P. (U.) East Ham (North), 1922-23, and since 1924 ; Member of Senate, London University ; *b.* 4 Mar. 1862 ; *o. surv. s.* of William Crook and Mary Williamson, Preston, Lancs ; *m.* 1900, Grace, *e. d.* of Benjamin and Grace Swinfen, Hackney ; one *s.* one *d.* *Educ. :* St. James's National School, Barrow-in-Furness ; Alston College, near Preston ; St. John's College, Battersea. Member of the Executive N.U.T. fourteen years ; Member of the B. and O. Council, N.U.T., fifteen years ; Member of Board of Teachers' Provident Society ; Treasurer of the War Aid Fund, N.U.T. ; President of the N.U.T., 1916-17 ; former Member of the Burnham Committees on Salaries in Primary, Secondary, and Technical Schools ; Hon. Secretary Conservative Teachers' Advisory Committee, and of the National Savings Committee. *Recreation :* walking. *Address :* 15 Manor Road, Sidcup. *T.A. :* Curriculum, Kincross, London. *T. :* Museum 1570 and 1571. *Club :* Constitutional. *(Died 29 Mar. 1926.)*

CROOKE, William, C.I.E. 1919 ; Hon. D.Sc. (Oxon.) 1919 ; Hon. Litt.D., Dublin, 1920 ; retired Indian Civil Service ; *b.* 6 Aug. 1848 ; *m.* 1884, Alice, *y. d.* of Lieut.-Col. George Carr, 2nd Madras Native Infantry ; two *s.* *Educ. :* Trinity College, Dublin. Entered Indian Civil Service, 1871 ; served as Assistant Magistrate and Collector, and District Magistrate and Collector in the United Provinces of Agra and Oudh ; Manager of the Awa Estate, Court of Wards ; President Anthropological Section British Association, 1910 ; President Folklore Society, 1911-12. *Publications :* The Tribes and Castes of the North-Western Provinces, 1896 ; Popular Religion and Folklore of Northern India, 1896 ; Things Indian, 1906 ; Anglo-Indian Glossary, 1903 ; edited Fryer's New Account of of East India and Persia, Hakluyt Society,'1909 ; Observations on the Mussalmans of India, 1916 ; Annals of Rajasthan, 1920 ; Islam in India, 1922 ; numerous articles in Hastings' Encyclopædia of Religion and Ethics, 1908-18, and numerous papers in Journal Royal Anthropological Institute, Folklore Society Journal, etc. *Address :* Langton House, Charlton Kings, Cheltenham. *Club :* New, Cheltenham.

(Died 25 Oct. 1923.)

CROOKES, Professor Sir William, Kt., *cr.* 1897 ; O.M., 1910 ; Pres. R.S. ; LL.D. Birmingham ; D.Sc. (Oxon., Camb., Ireland, Cape of Good Hope, Sheffield, Durham) ; Foreign Secretary, Royal Society, 1908 - 12 ; Past President Chemical Society, Brit. Assoc., Inst. Elect. Eng., Soc. Chem. Industry ; Hon. Mem. Roy. Phil. Soc. Glasgow, Roy. Soc. N.S.W., Pharm. Soc., Chem. Metall. and Mining Soc. of South Africa, Amer. Chem. Soc., Amer. Philos. Soc., Roy. Soc. Sci. Upsala, Deutsch Chem. Gesell. Berlin, Psychol. Soc. Paris, Antonio Alzate Sci. Soc. Mexico, Sci. Soc. Bucharest, Reg. Accad. Zelanti ; Foreign Mem. Accad. Lincei, Rome ; Corresp. Inst. de France (Acad. Sci.), Corresp. Mem. Bataafsch Genoots., Rotterdam, Soc. d'Encouragement pour l'Indust. Paris ; For. Assoc. National Acad. Sciences, Washington ; Foreign Member of the Royal Swedish Academy of Sciences ; Royal medallist, Davy medallist, Copley medallist, and three times Bakerian Lecturer of the Royal Society ; proprietor and editor of Chemical News ; *b.* 17 June 1832 ; *m.* 1856, Ellen (*d.* 1916), *d.* of W. Humphrey of Darlington ; four *s.* one *d.* *Educ. :* Royal Coll. of Chemistry ; Professor of Chemistry, Training Coll., Chester, 1855. Discoverer of— the Selenocyanides ; Thallium, a new element, 1861 ; Repulsion resulting from Radiation, 1873 ; the Radiometer, 1875 ; Illumination of Lines of Molecular Pressure, 1878 ; Radiant Matter, 1879, an ultra-gaseous, fourth state, of matter ; Radiant Matter Spectroscopy, 1881 ; New Elements in Gadolinite, etc., 1886 ; Genesis of Elements, 1887 ; Some Possibilities of Electricity, Wireless Telegraphy, 1892 ; Fixation of Atmospheric Nitrogen, 1898 ; the Spintharis-cope, 1903 ; Eye-Preserving Glass for Spectacles, 1913. International Exhibition, 1862, medal ; Académie des Sciences, 1880, gold medal and prize of 3000 frs. ; Electrical Exhibition, Paris, 1881, medal ; Society of Arts, 1885, Fergusson Gold Medal ; Exposition Universelle, Paris, 1889, medal ; Society of Arts, 1899, Albert Gold Medal ; Franklin Institute, Philadelphia, 1912, Elliott Cresson Gold Medal ; Soc. Chem. Industry, 1912, gold medal. *Publications:* Select Methods in Chemical Analysis, 4th edition, 1905 ; Manufacture of Beetroot-Sugar in England, 1870 ; Handbook of Dyeing and Calico-Printing, 1874 ; Dyeing and Tissue Printing, 1882 ; Kerl's Treatise on Metallurgy, 1868, with Ernst Rohrig ; Wagner's Chemical Technology ; Auerbach's Anthracen and its Derivatives, 2nd edition, 1890 ; Ville's Artificial Manures, 3rd edition, 1909 ; A Solution of the Sewage Question ; The Profitable Disposal of Sewage ; The Wheat Problem, 1899, 3rd ed. 1917 ; Diamonds, 1909. *Address:* 7 Kensington Park Gardens, W. *T.A.:* Crookes, Nottarcll, London. *T.:* 1601 Park. *Clubs:* Athenæum, Royal Societies, Carlyle. *(Died 4 April 1919.)*

CROOKS, Rt. Hon. William ; P.C. 1916; M.P. (Lab.) Woolwich, 1903-10, and since Dec. 1910 ; *b.* 6 April 1852 ; *m.* 1st, 1871, Matilda South (*d.* 1892); 2nd, 1893, Elizabeth Coulter ; two *s.* four *d.* Apprenticed to a cooper, 1866 ; member of L.C.C. (P.) since 1892 ; Mayor of Poplar, 1901 ; Chairman Poplar Board of Guardians, 1898-1906. *Address:* 81 Gough Street, Poplar, E. *(Died 5 June 1921.)*

CROOM, Sir (J.) Halliday, Kt., *cr.* 1902; LL.D., M.D.; F.R.C.S.; F.R.C.P.; F.R.S.E.; Hon. M.D., Dublin ; Emeritus Professor of Midwifery, Edinburgh University, late President Royal College of Surgeons, Edinburgh, and British Gynaecological Soc.; three times President of Edinburgh Obstetrical Society ; Hon. Fellow American Soc. of Gynaecologists, and Société Gynecologie, Belgium ; *b.* Sanquhar, Dumfries, 15 Jan. 1847 ; *s.* of Rev. D. M. Croom of Lauriston Place U.P. Church, Edinburgh ; *m.* 1875, Anna Isabella, *d.* of Daniel Walker, H.M. Inspector of Factories for Scotland ; one *s.* three *d.* *Educ.:* Royal High School, Edinburgh ; University of Edinburgh ; afterwards studied in London and Paris. Was for several years assistant to Professor of Gynaecology and Obstetrics in the University of Edinburgh ; formerly Lecturer on Obstetrics and Gynaecology in the Edinburgh School of Medicine, Minto House ; Chairman Central Midwives Board for Scotland ; Phys. Roy. Maternity Hosp. Edinb. ; Consulting Gynaecologist Royal Infirmary ; was on the active staff for twenty years ; was for fifteen years prior to 1901 in charge of Gynaecological wards at the Royal Infirmary, Edinburgh. *Publications:* Minor Gynaecological Operations and Appliances, 2nd edition, 1883 ; The Bladder during Parturition, 1883 ; Collection of Clinical Papers, 1901 ; numerous contributions to Scientific and Medical journals. *Address:* 8 Morningside Place, Edinburgh. *T.:* Edinburgh 2284.
(Died 27 Sept. 1923.)

CROPPER, Charles James, J.P., D.L.; chairman of James Cropper and Co., Ltd.; late Director of L. and N.-W. Railway, and of Cockermouth, Keswick, and Penrith Railway; *b.* 1852 ; *s.* of James Cropper, late M.P. for Kendal ; *m.* 1876, Hon. Edith Emily Holland (*d.* 1923), *e. d.* of 1st Viscount Knutsford ; one *s.* four *d.* *Educ.:* Rugby ; Trinity Coll., Cambridge. High Sheriff, 1905. *Heir:* *s.* Maj. James Winstanley, J.P.; [*b.* 1879 ; *m.* 1910, Marjorie Constance, 2nd *d.* of late Lt.-Col. J. F. Bagot of Levens Hall, Westmorland. *Educ.:* Eton : Trinity College,

Cambridge. *Address:* Tolson Hall, Kendall. *Address:* Ellergreen, Kendal. *T.A.:* Burneside. *T.:* Kendal 385 D. *Club:* Brooks's.
(Died 6 Oct. 1924.)

CROSBIE, Lieut.-Gen. Adolphus Brett. Royal Marines ; *e. surv. s.* of late Capt. W. A. Crosbie of the Rifle Brig.de ; *m.* 1884, Anne Geraldine, *o. d.* of late Capt. Thomas Lloyd of Prospect, Co. Limerick, and Huntington Ct., Herefordshire. Entered Army, 1864 ; Maj.-Gen. 1900 ; Lieut.-Gen. 1903 : served China, 1867-69 (despatches) ; Ashanti in command of Royal Marines (despatches, medal with clasp) ; commanded Royal Marines, Congo, 1875 (despatches) ; commanded Royal Marines, Niger, 1876 (despatches), brevet of Major ; A.D.C. to Queen Victoria, 1895-1900. *Address:* Harestock House, W. Winchester. *Club:* Army and Navy.
(Died 15 Dec. 1916.)

CROSBIE, Henry, C.B. 1911 ; (late) Colonel Commanding 3rd Battalion the Manchester Regiment ; 4th *s.* of Captain W. A. Crosbie, late Rifle Brigade ; *b.* 8 Aug. 1852 ; *m.* 1880 ; divorced, 1910 ; two *d.* *Educ.:* Royal Military College, Sandhurst. Joined 81st Regiment as Sub-Lieutenant, 1872 ; Lieutenant, 1874 ; Captain, 1882 ; Major 1st Sherwood Foresters, 1894 ; Reserve of Officers, 1896 ; Lt.-Colonel 5th Manchesters, 1900 ; granted hon. rank of Colonel, 1901 ; served E. Indies, 1874-88 ; Afghan War, 1878-79 (medal with clasp) ; S. Africa, 1901-2 (medal with 4 clasps) ; commanded 5th Bn. Manchester Regt. (now 3rd Battalion) during the war in S. Africa (despatches) ; Coronation medal for King George V., 1911. *Recreations:* travelling and boating. *Club:* Naval and Military. *(Died 19 Dec. 1923.)*

CROSBY, Sir Thomas Boor, Kt., *cr.* 1907 ; *b.* 1830; Lord Mayor of London, 1911-1912; Sheriff, 1906-7 ; M.D., LL.D., Dublin and St. Andrews, F.R.C.S. ; member, late President Hunterian Society ; Medical Officer to the Scottish Amicable, Scottish Provident, and Yorkshire Life Offices ; formerly Demonstrator of Anatomy and House Surgeon, St. Thomas's Hospital. Legion of Honour (Officier), France ; Crown, Germany ; St. Olaf, Norway ; Danebrog, Denmark ; Rising Sun, Japan. *Address:* 19 Gordon Square, W.C. ; 136 Fenchurch Street, E.C. *Club:* Constitutional. *(Died 7 April 1916.)*

CROSLAND, T. W. H.; *s.* of William Crosland of Leeds ; *b.* 21 July 1868 ; *m.* Annie, *d.* of Edward Thomas Moore, Solicitor, Oxford. *Educ.:* privately. Contributed to the Leeds Mercury supplement, Yorkshire Weekly Post, Black and White, Outlook, Academy, Saturday Review, The Gentlewoman, Public Opinion, Evening Standard, etc. ; Assistant Editor of the Outlook, 1899-1902 ; Editor of The English Review, 1905; Assistant Editor of the Academy, 1908-11. *Publications:* Literary Parables; Other People's Wings ; The Finer Spirit (verse) ; English Songs and Ballads ; The Unspeakable Scot, 1902 ; Lovely Woman, 1903 ; The Lord of Creation, 1904 ; The Enemy, 1904 ; The Wild Irishman, 1905 ; The Suburbans, 1905 ; Red Rose (verse), 1905 ; The Country Life, 1906 ; The Beautiful Teetotaller, 1907 ; Sonnets, 1912 ; Taffy was a Welshman, 1912 ; The First Stone, 1912 ; The Chant of Affection, 1915 ; The Showmen, 1915 ; The Soul of a Crown Prince, 1915 ; War Poems by X, 1911 ; Collected Poems, 1911; The English Sonnet, 1916 ; Pop Goes the Weasel, 1924 ; The Laureate's Job (verse) 1924. *Address:* Mitcham House, Mitcham Street, Marylebone, N.W. *T.:* Padd. 1354.
(Died 23 Dec. 1924.)

CROSS, Hon. Alexander George, B.A., B.C.L., Puisne Judge, Quebec, since 1907 ; Professor of Commercial Law, McGill University ; *b.* 1858 ; *m.* 1907, Laura M., *d.* of late J. J. Buchanan, Dundee, P.Q. *Educ.:* McGill University. Advocate, 1881 ; K.C. 1899 ; Mayor of Westmount, 1903-4. *Address:* 369 Metcalf

Avenue, Westmount, Montreal.
(Died 19 Aug. 1919.)

CROSS, Hon. Charles Wilson, late Attorney-General of Alberta; *b.* Madoc, Ontario, Canada; *s.* of Thomas and Marie Cross; married; one *s.* two *d.* *Educ.:* Upper Canada College; Toronto University, and Osgoode Hall, Toronto. Barrister at Edmonton, Alberta. *Address:* Edmonton, Alberta. *Club:* Edmonton. *(Died 2 June 1928.)*

ROSS, Hon. John Edward; Land Agent; J.P. Cheshire; Member of Council of the Royal Agricultural Society, England, and of Council of the Land Agents Society; Director of the Manchester Branch of the Atlas Assurance Co.; Member of District Council and Board of Guardians; *b.* 6 Sep. 1858; *e. surv. s.* of 1st Viscount Cross; *m.* 1st, Katherine Ellen, *d.* of late Rev. F. Haden Cope; one *d.* ; 2nd, Sophy K. M., *d.* of late H. R. Sandbach, D.L., J.P. of Hafodunos, Denbighshire; two *d.* *Educ.:* Wellington; Pembroke College, Cambridge. Served in the 1st Royal Lancashire Militia and the Princess Charlotte of Wales Royal Berks Volunteers; acted as private secretary to late Lord Wantage; member of the Cheshire County Council, 1904-7. *Address:* The West Hall, High Legh, Knutsford; *T.A.:* Highlegh. *T.:* 74 Lymm, Warrington District. *M.:* M 3746. *Clubs:* Carlton, Wellington; Union, Manchester. *(Died 26 June 1921.)*

CROSSE, Lieut.-Col. Charles Robert, C.M.G. 1917; M.V.O. 1909; late Royal West Kent Regt.; Secretary, National Rifle Association since 1899; *b.* India, 1851; 2nd *s.* of late Robert Crosse, 73rd B.N.I.; *m.* Catherine, *o. d.* of late Major-General Whitworth Porter, R.E. *Educ.:* Paris, private tutor; R. M. College, Sandhurst. Served 20 years in the army, retiring with the rank of Lieut.-Col. 1892; was Secretary of the United Service College, Westward Ho; also Brigade-Major of the Hampshire Vol. Infantry Brigade. *Address:* The Secretary's Lodge, Bisley Camp, Surrey. *Club:* Junior United Service. *(Died 15 Feb. 1921.)*

CROSSING, William, author; *b.* Plymouth, 14 Nov. 1847; *s.* of Joseph Crossing; *m.* 1872, Emma (*d.* 1921), *d.* of Richard Witheridge, Ivybridge; no *c.* *Educ.:* South Devon. Collegiate School; Mannamead School. The Dartmoor country among earliest recollections; went to sea on leaving school; afterwards settled down on the edge of Dartmoor; Free Churchman; gave much attention to antiquarian investigations; for eight years contributed West-country People and Places to the Western Weekly News; great lover of animals. *Publications:* The Ancient Stone Crosses of Dartmoor; Amid Devonia's Alps; Tales of the Pixies; A Hundred Years on Dartmoor; From a Dartmoor Cot; Gems in a Granite Setting; Guide to Dartmoor; Folk Rhymes of Devon; Echoes of an Ancient Forest; Oranmere and other Poems, 1927, etc. *Recreation:* reading. *Address:* Cross Park House, Hartley, Plymouth. *(Died Sept. 1928.)*

CROSSLEY, Arthur William, C.M.G. 1917; C.B.E. 1919; D.Sc. (Vict.), Ph.D. (Wurzburg), Hon. LL.D. (St. And.), F.R.S., Past-President C.S., F.I.C.; Lieut.-Colonel, late R.E.; Officier de la Legion d'Honneur; Director British Cotton Industry Research Association; *b.* 25 Feb. 1869; *s.* of late Richard Crossley, of Accrington, Lancashire; *m.* Muriel, *d.* of Ralph Lamb, of Liverpool; one *s.* one *d.* *Educ.:* Mill Hill School; Victoria University of Manchester; Würzburg and Berlin Universities; Longstaff Medallist of the Chemical Soc., 1918. Late Berkeley Fellow of the Owens College; late Lecturer on Chemistry at St. Thomas's Hospital; late Professor of Chemistry to the Pharmaceutical Society of Great Britain; late University Professor of Chemistry in University of London, King's College. *Publica-*

tions: Contributions to the Journals of the Chemical Societies of London and Berlin. *Recreations:* fishing, billiards. *Address:* Shirley Institute, Didsbury, Manchester; Thorngrove, Alderley Edge, Cheshire. *Club:* Devonshire.
(Died 5 Mar. 1927.)

CROSSLEY, Rt. Rev. Owen Thomas Lloyd, D.D.; Assistant Bishop to Bishop of Llandaff, 1914-20; Chief Missioner and Superintendent of Special Service Work, Diocese of Llandaff, 1914-21; *b.* 30 April 1860; *m.* 1896, Grace Mary, *e. d.* of Robert Joy, J.P. *Educ.:* Trinity College, Dublin (M.A.). Ordained 1884; Curate of Sea Patrick, Co. Down, 1884-88; St. John, Birkenhead, 1888-92; Vicar of Egremont, 1892-1900; Almondbury, 1901-5; Select Preacher, University of Dublin; Lecturer St. Aidan's, Birkenhead, 1900; at Lichfield Theological College, 1908-4; Fellow Australian College of Theology; Lecturer St. John's College, Melbourne; Chairman of Governors, Geelong Grammar School; Archdeacon of Geelong, 1905-1911; Incumbent of All Saints, St. Kilda, 1905-1911; Bishop of Auckland, N.Z., 1911-13; Chaplain to the Archbishop of Melbourne; Rector of S. Andrew's Major, Dinas Powis, Cardiff, 1914-17. *Address:* Wheelers, Bramshott, Liphook, Hants.
(Died 3 Mar. 1926.)

CROSSLEY, Thomas Hastings Henry, M.A. Dubl., Hon. Litt.D. Queen's University, M.A., and late Fellow Royal University of Ireland; *b.* 1 Aug. 1846; 3rd *s.* of Major Fras. Crossley, H.E.I.C.S., of Glenburn, Co. Antrim, and Elizabeth Helen, 2nd *d.* of late William Irwin, J.P., Mount Irwin, Tynan, Co. Armagh; *m.* Emily Agnes, *y. d.* of Col. F. C. Irwin, Commandant of the Troops and sometime Governor, Western Australia; one *s.* *Educ.:* Bonn; Royal School, Dungannon; Trinity College, Dublin. Honours in Classics, 1st gold meal, Philosophy, 2nd gold medal, Senior Moderatorship, both in 1868; Royal Exhibitioner, University Scholarship in first year, Vice-Chancellor's Prize for Greek Verse; Berkeley gold medal, 1866 for Greek, M.A. stip. condonato, honoris causa. Senior Classical Master Trinity College, Glenalmond, 1873; deputy Professor of Latin, Queen's College, Belfast, 1875-76; Chair of Classics and Ancient History University College, Bristol, 1876-79; Professor of Greek, Queen's College, Belfast, 1879-90; Classical Examiner to Queen's University and Royal University for twelve years; Examiner to Civil Service Commission; has lectured on Ancient History and Literature at Bristol, Belfast, Bridgewater, Eastbourne, Bordighera; studied music with H. Stiehl & Berthold Tours. *Publications:* numerous contributions to Kottabos and Dublin Translations into Greek and Latin Verse; articles in Hermathena on Theocritus, and the Corresp. of Fronto and M. Aurelius; The Fourth Book of M. Aurelius with revised text, trans. and Appendices, 1882; Golden Thoughts of Epictetus, with the Hymn of Cleanthes, Golden Treasury, 1902; Contributor to Thackeray and Stone's Anthology of Latin Verse; Style and Composition (National Home Reading Union pamphlet). *Recreations:* sketching, music, photography, gardening. *Address:* Casa del Vallone, Bordighera, Italy. *T. A.:* Crossley, Bordighera.
(Died 23 Mar. 1926.)

CROSTHWAITE, Rt. Rev. Robert Jarratt, D.D.; *b.* Wellington, Somerset, 13 Oct. 1837; 3rd *s.* of Rev. Canon Benjamin Crosthwaite; *m.* 1st, 1867, Eleanor F. (*d.* 1885), *d.* of Rev. Philip Simpson; 2nd, 1887, Anne Elizabeth (*d.* 1921), *d.* of Rev. William Moore Crosthwaite, Prebendary of Cork Cathedral; three *s.* three *d.* *Educ.:* Leeds Grammar School; Trinity College, Cambridge (Fellow, 1862-67); 8th Wrangler, 1860; Curate, North Cave, Yorkshire, 1862-66; Private Secretary and Domestic Chaplain to Archbishop of York (Thomson), 1866-69; Vicar of Waghen, 1869-73; Vicar of

Brayton, 1873-83 ; Vicar of St. Lawrence with St. Nicholas, York, 1883-85 ; Rector of Bolton Percy, 1885-1923 ; Prebendary of Grindal in Cathedral of York, 1884 ; Archdeacon of York, 1884 - 1923 ; Bishop of Beverley, 1889 - 1923. *Publication :* The Gospels of the New Testament, their Genuineness and Authenticity, 1887. *Address :* Oliver House, Bolton Percy, Yorkshire. *T.A. :* Bolton Percy.

(*Died 9 Sept. 1925.*)

CROSTHWAITE, Sir Robert Joseph, K.C.S.I., *cr.* 1897 ; *b.* 17 Jan. 1841 ; 3rd *s.* of Rev. John Clarke Crosthwaite, Rector of St. Mary at Hill, London ; *m.* 1st, 1868, Charlotte Frances, *d.* of W. W. T. Baldwin, Stede Hill, Kent ; 2nd, 1877, Mary, *d.* of S. Harvey James, St. Just, Cornwall ; five *s.* one *d.* *Educ. :* Merchant Taylors' School ; Brasenose College, Oxford (B.A.). Entered Indian Civil Service, 1863 ; was Judicial Commissioner of Burmah and of Central Provinces ; late Additional Member of Legislative Council, India ; Agent to the Gov.-Gen. for Central India ; and Agent to the Gov.-Gen. in Rajputana ; Barr. Middle Temple, 1868. *Address :* Lakenham, Northam, N. Devon. *T.A. :* Northam. (*Died 2 July 1917.*)

CROTHERS, Hon. Thomas Wilson, B.A., K.C., Minister of Labour, Canada, 1911-1919 ; *b.* Northport, 1 Jan. 1850 ; *m.* Mary E. Burns. *Educ. :* Victoria College. Headmaster High School, Wardsville, Ont. ; contested (C.) West Elgin, Canada, 1879 ; elected, 1908, 1911, and 1917 ; practised law at St. Thomas, 1880-1911. *Address :* Ottawa, Ontario.

(*Died 11 Dec. 1921.*)

CROWE, Sir Eyre, G.C.B., *cr.* 1928 ; K.C.B., *cr.* 1917 ; G.C.M.G., *cr.* 1920 ; K.C.M.G., *cr.* 1911 ; C.B. 1907 ; Permanent Under-Secretary of State for Foreign Affairs since 1920 ; *b.* 30 July 1864 ; 3rd *s.* of late Sir Joseph Archer Crowe, K.C.M.G., C.B., and Asta, *e. d.* of G. von Barby ; *m.* 1903, Clema von Bonin, *e. d.* of late Professor Gerhardt. Clerk in Foreign Office, 1885 ; Senior Clerk, 1906 ; Counsellor of Embassy, 1907 ; Assistant Under-Secretary of State, 1912 ; Minister Plenipotentiary, 1919. *Address :* 74 Elm Park Road, Chelsea, S.W. *Club :* Travellers'. (*Died 28 April 1925.*)

CROWE, Maj.-Gen. Thomas Carlisle, late R.H.A. ; *e. s.* of Captain John Crowe, 98rd Sutherland Highlanders ; *b.* 1830 ; *m.* 1859, Ellen, *d.* of Rev. M. B. Clarke, F.R.S. ; one *s.* Entered army, 1847 ; Lt.-Col. 1872 ; Bt. Col. 1877 ; served Persia, 1857 (medal with clasp) ; Indian Mutiny, 1857 - 58 (medal with clasp) ; Canada, 1866 ; retired, 1878. *Address :* 71 Bouverie Road West, Folkestone. *Club :* United Service. (*Died 18 Jan. 1917.*)

CROWE, William Henry, *b.* 1844 ; *s.* of late Edward F. Crowe of Ravenscourt Park, Hammersmith ; *m.* Violet Mary, 5th *d.* of late Col. Charles Caldwell Grantham, of 9th and 89th Regts. ; one *d.* *Educ. :* Godolphin School, Hammersmith ; King's Coll. London. Barrister-at-law, Lincoln's Inn ; Fellow of the Bombay University. Entered the Indian Civil Service, 1867 ; Judge and Sessions Judge of Poona and agent for the Sardars in the Deccan, 1881 ; member of the Legislative Council, Bombay, 1893 ; Judicial Commissioner and Judge of the Sadar Court in Sind, 1894 ; additional member of the Legislative Council, Bombay, 1896 ; Judge of H.M.'s High Court of Judicature, Bombay, 1899-1904. *Address :* 99 Sloane Street, S.W.1 ; *T. :* 2663 Victoria ; Tythe Barn, Cookham Dene, Berks. *Clubs :* East India United Service, Ranelagh, Royal Automobile ; Byculla, Royal Bombay Yacht, Bombay.

(*Died 4 July 1925.*)

CROWEST, Frederick J. ; General Manager and Editor of The Walter Scott Publishing Company, Limited, 1901-17 ; *b.* London (City), 30 Nov. 1860. *Educ. :* London and in

Italy. Served early life with Messrs. Cassell, Petter and Galpin ; joined their Editorial staff in 1886 ; assistant - editor and editor of Work, 1889-93 ; general editor and reader, 1898-1900 ; projector and editor of The Year's Music ; editor and originator of The Master Musicians Series ; projector and editor of The Music-Story Series ; London correspondent of Church's Musical Visitor ; winner of the Thomas Hughes Prize Essay, The Newspaper Press ; contributor to Blackwood, National Review, Westminster and Anglo-Saxon Reviews, and general press ; for many years engaged in East London educational and polytechnic work ; President Newcastle and Gateshead Master Printers' Association, 1907 ; re-elected, 1908 ; President Jarrow Division Tariff Reform League. *Publications :* The Great Tone-Poets, 1874 ; a Book of Musical Anecdote, 2 vols., 1877 ; Phases of Musical England, 1881 ; Advice to Singers, 1878 ; Musical History and Biography, 1883 ; Cherubini (Great Musicians Series), 1890 ; Musical Groundwork, 1890 ; Dictionary of British Musicians, 1895 ; The Story of British Music, 1895 ; Verdi: Man and Musician, 1897 ; Beethoven (Master Musicians Series), 1899 ; The Story of Music, 1902 ; Musicians' Wit, Humour, and Anecdote, 1902. *Address :* Hill House, Fladbury, Worcestershire.

(*Died 14 June 1927.*)

CROWFOOT, Rev. John Henchman, Prebendary of Milton Manor, Lincoln Cathedral, 1913 ; *b.* 16 Oct. 1841 ; 2nd *s.* of W. E. Crowfoot, M.D., of Beccles, Suffolk ; *m.* 1872, Mary Elizabeth, *e. d.* of Robert Bayly, Barr. of Inner Temple ; one *s.* two *d.* *Educ. :* Rugby School, 1854-60 ; Trinity Coll. Oxford, 1860-64 (scholar). 1st class Mods. ; 1st class Lit. Hum. ; B.A. 1864 ; M.A. 1867 ; Fellowship at Jesus Coll., 1866-72. Ordained Deacon, 1866 ; Priest, 1867 ; Ox. S.P.G. Missionary at Delhi, 1867-71 ; Rector of Wigginton, Oxon, 1872 - 75 ; Vice-Chancellor of Lincoln Cathedral, 1874-98 ; Prebendary of Buckden in Lincoln Cathedral, 1874-98 ; Commissary of Bishop of Likoma, 1896 ; Chancellor of Lincoln Cathedral, 1898-1913. *Address :* Ravenscourt, West Worthing.

(*Died 29 Mar. 1926.*)

CROWLY, Joseph Patrick, C.B. 1911 ; Commissioner of Inland Revenue since 1908 ; *b.* 1 Nov. 1859 ; *s.* of John Crowly of Bandon, Co. Cork ; *m.* 1893, Margaret Caecilia, *d.* of A. J. Fox of Hunmanby, Yorkshire ; one *d.* *Educ. :* St. Stanislaus' College (S.J.), Tullamore. Appointed a Class I. clerk in the Admiralty, 1881 ; transferred to Treasury, 1884 ; private secretary to Sir Reginald (now Lord) Welby, 1891-94 ; to Sir Francis Mowatt, 1894-97. *Recreations :* travel and anything else that may turn up. *Address :* 17 Leinster Gardens, W.

(*Died 18 July 1917.*)

CROZIER, Most Rev. John Baptist, D.D. ; Archbishop of Armagh and Primate of all Ireland (Church of Ireland) since 1911 ; *b.* 8 April 1853 ; *e. s.* of Rev. Baptist Barton Crozier, B.A., Rockview, Ballyhaise, Co Cavan, and Kate, *o. d.* of John Bolland Yorkshire ; *m.* Alice, *d.* of Rev. John W. Hackett, M.A., and Jane Monck Mason, *g. d.* of Sir Robert Langrishe, Bt., Co. Kilkenny, 1877 ; two *s.* one *d.* *Educ. :* Trinity Coll. Dublin. Honours and Prizes in Classics, Logics, Ethics, Hebrew, and Irish ; Moderator and Medallist in Logics and Ethics ; Downes Divinity Prize (first) ; 1st class Divinity Testimonium ; B.A. 1872 ; M.A. 1875 ; B.D. and D.D. 1888 ; Member of the University Senate. Fellow R.S. Antiquaries (Ireland), M.R.I.A. ; President Univ. Philosophical Society, 1874 ; Auditor Coll. Theological Society, 1875 ; ordained 1876 ; Vicar of Holywood, Co. Down, 1880-97 ; Chaplain Bishop of Down, 1885-97 ; to Archbishop of Armagh, 1886 ; Canon of Down Cathedral, 1887 ;

Chaplain to Lord-Lieutenant of Ireland 1893-1897; Canon of St. Patrick's National Cathedral, 1896; Hon. Sec. General Synod of the Church of Ireland, 1896; Bishop of Ossory, Ferns, and Leighlin, 1897-1907; of Down, Connor, and Dromore, 1907-11. *Recreations:* one of the earliest members of the Wanderers Football Club (Rugby), Dublin; Vice-President of the Holywood Cricket Club and Rugby Football Club; a keen horseman. *Address:* The Palace, Armagh. *Clubs:* Royal Societies; University, Dublin; Ulster, Belfast. (*Died 12 April 1920.*)

CROZIER, John Beattie, LL.D., philosopher, historian, and political economist; *b.* Canada, 1849; *m.* 1877, Katharine Augusta (*d.* 1918), *niece* of late Colonel William Anderson, Mount Aboo; two *d.* *Educ.:* Galt Grammar School and Toronto Univ. Univ. medallist and Starr medallist in Medicine, 1872; LL.D. (honoris causa) Univ. of Toronto, 1899. *Publications:* The Religion of the Future, 1880; Civilisation and Progress, 1885 (translated into Japanese, 1903); Lord Randolph Churchill: a Study of English Democracy, 1887; History of Intellectual Development, vol. i. 1897; vol. iii. 1901; My Inner Life, being a Chapter in Personal Evolution and Autobiography, 1898; The Wheel of Wealth, 1906; First Principles of Investment, 1910; Sociology applied to Practical Politics, 1911; Last Words on Great Issues, 1917; articles in Fortnightly Review. *Recreation:* formerly, boxing, skating, and step-dancing; now (with failing eyesight), music, conversation, and being read to. *Address:* 9 Elgin Avenue, W.
(*Died 8 Jan. 1921.*)

CRUDDAS, Lt.-Col. Hugh Wilson, D.S.O. 1915; 41st Dogras; *b.* 2 Feb. 1868; *s.* of John Cruddas of Newcastle-on-Tyne and Bombay; *m.* 1909, Alice, *d.* of late J. Medhurst; no *c.* *Educ.:* Newton Abbot. Entered army, 1889; Captain Indian army, 1900; Major, 1907; served China, 1900 (medal); European War, 1914-15 (D.S.O.). (*Died 20 Jan. 1916.*)

CRUICKSHANK, Alexander Walmsley, C.S.I. 1898; late Indian Civil Service; *b.* 24 July 1851; *y. s.* of late Major John James Farquharson Cruickshank, H.E.I.C.S., Bombay Engineers; *m.* 1881, Fanny Nina, *d.* of late Claremont Daniell; two *s.* two *d.* *Educ.:* Wimbledon School. Passed 4th into Woolwich, but entered I.C.S. 1872; Barr. Middle Temple, 1883; became Junior Secretary to Board of Revenue, N.W. Provinces, 1878; Under-Secy. to Government, 1886; Settlement Officer, 1886; Deputy Commissioner, 1890; Magistrate and Collector, 1891; Commissioner of the Allahabad Division, 1897; and Commissioner of Rohilkhand Division, 1897; placed on special duty from 9 to 25 Nov. 1897; and reverted to appointment of Commr. Rohilkhand Division on 26 Feb. 1898 on return from privilege leave; commanded Rohilkhand Vol. Rifle Corps, 1898-1903, with the rank of Major. *Decorated* for services in the Indian Famine, 1897, when Commr. Allahabad Division; additional member Governor-General's Council, 1903; reappointed member of Council of Lieut.-Governor, United Provinces, 1903; Commissioner of Rohilkhand Division, N.W.P., India, 1898-1905; member Board of Revenue, United Provinces, 1905-8. *Publications:* Settlement Report of Gorakpur District, U.P. *Recreations:* shooting, riding, ordinary field sports and games. *Address:* c/o Grindlay & Co., 54 Parliament Street, S.W.1.
(*Died 14 April 1925.*)

CRUICKSHANK, Rev. Alfred Hamilton, M.A. Oxon, Hon. D.Lit⁺. Durham; Canon of Durham; Professor of Greek and Classical Literature in the University of Durham; *b.* 18 March 1862; *s.* of George Cruickshank and Eliza Septima, *d.* of Sir Thomas Howell, Kt.; *m.* 1898, Ethel Mary, *d.* of Rev. H. J. Wickham; no *c.* *Educ.:* Winchester; New College, Oxford; 1st Class Classical Moderations, 1883; Hertford University Scholar, 1883; 1st Class Final Classical School, 1886; Fellow of New College, and Tutor, 1885; ordained, 1891; Composition Master at Harrow, 1891-93; Assistant Master at Winchester, 1894-1910; Chaplain, 1896. *Publications:* Bacchae of Euripides; Fair Copies; Philip Massinger, 1920. *Address:* The College, Durham.
(*Died 13 May 1927.*)

CRUM, Sir Walter Erskine, Kt., *cr.* 1920; O.B.E.; partner in Graham & Co., Glasgow; *b.* 2 Sept. 1874; *s.* of late Ewing Crum and Sara Margaret Tinne; *m.* Violet Mary, *d.* of late C. H. B. Forbes; two *s.* two *d.* *Educ.:* Eton; New College, Oxford. Captain of Boats, Eton, 1892-3; President O.U.B.C. 1895-7; President Bengal Chamber of Commerce, 1919-1920; Member Imperial Legislative Council, India, 1919-20. *Address:* c/o William Graham & Co., Sackville Street, Manchester.
(*Died 10 Oct. 1923.*)

CRUMLY, Patrick, M.P. (N.) South Fermanagh, 1911-18; J.P.; was Vice-Chairman, Enniskillen Board of Guardians. *Address:* Town Hall Street, Enniskillen.

CRUMP, Rev. John Herbert, M.A.; *b.* 1849; 2nd *s.* of late Rev. Wm. Crump, Vicar of Rowley Regis, Staffs; married. *Educ.:* St. Edmund's School, Canterbury; Jesus Coll. Camb. Curate of St. Matthew's, Smethwick, 1879-80; St. Stephen's, 1881-84; Vicar of Holy Trinity, Smethwick, 1884-92; Rector of Stoke-on-Trent, 1892-97; Vicar of Longdon, 1898-1905; Archdeacon of Stoke-on-Trent, 1905-8; Prebendary of Lichfield, 1901-12. *Address:* Greycourt, Old Colwyn, N. Wales. *T.:* Old Colwyn 15. *T.A.:* Old Colwyn. (*Died 12 June 1924.*)

CRUMP, Sir William John, Kt., *cr.* 1902; solicitor; ex-High Sheriff, D.L., and J.P. Middlesex; past Chairman National Unionist Association; *b.* 1850; *e. s.* of late Wm. Alex. Crump; *m.* 1872, Anna Maria (*d.* 1921), *d.* of late Charles Buttery, 173 Piccadilly, W.; three *s.* four *d.* *Educ.:* privately. Has a large maritime, mercantile, and company practice in the City of London; was a Member of second Hornsey School Board, and of Hornsey Urban District Council; Past-Master Worshipful Company of Upholders; Past-Master of the City of London Solicitors' Company; past Chairman Metropolitan Division of the National Unionist Association; Chairman of North Islington Unionist Association, 1884-1919, now President; a Member of Council and Executive Committee of City of London Conservative Association; Chairman of the Hendon Division of Middlesex Central Conservative and Unionist Association; a Member of the Middlesex Licensing Committee and a Member of the Territorial Force Association for the County of Middlesex; Member of the Council of the Imperial Society of Knights; has taken an active part in obtaining open spaces for the people in Hornsey; one of the promoters and an original Director of the Crouch End Playing Fields; a Member of the Committee for the acquisition of the Queen's Wood, Highgate, and the Alexandra Palace; first Mayor of Islington, 1900; re-elected, 1901; Vice-Chairman, 1900-1902, of the Metropolitan Mayors and ex-Mayors Association; received Coronation Medals from King Edward and King George; Freemasonry, P.M. of several lodges; is P.A.G.D.C. (Eng.), and P.P.G.W. (Essex). *Recreations:* golf and motoring. *Address:* 17 Leadenhall Street, E.C.; Glenthorne, Harrow Weald, Middlesex. *T.A.:* Legal, London; Crump, Bushey Heath. *T.:* Avenue 1149; Bushey Heath 291. *Clubs:* Junior Carlton, Royal Automobile, City Carlton, Canada. (*Died 8 Jan. 1923.*)

CRUTCHLEY, Maj.-Gen. Sir Charles, K.C.B. *cr.* 1917; K.C.V.O., *cr.* 1913; Lieut.-Governor and Secretary Royal Hospital, Chelsea, 1909-18; *b.* 10 Dec. 1856; 2nd *s.* of late Gen. Charles Crutchley; *m.* Sybil Mary, *o. d.* of Hon. Henry and Lady Katharine Coke of Longford, Derbyshire; one *s. Educ.:* Harrow; Sandhurst. Entered army, 1874; Capt. Scots Guards, 1887; Major, 1895; Lt.-Col. 1897; Col. 1900; Staff Captain for Recruiting, 1886-89; D.A.A.G. for recruiting, Headquarters of Army, 1889-1900; A.A.G., recruiting, Headquarters of Army, 1900-8; Director of Recruiting, 1908-9; served Egypt, 1882 (medal with clasp, bronze star, 5th class Medjidie, Bt. Major); Soudan, 1884-85 (severely wounded, two clasps). *Address:* 3 Durham Place, Chelsea, S.W.3; *T.:* Kensington 3828.   *(Died 1 Dec. 1920.)*

CRUTCHLEY, William Caius, Commander R.N.R., R.D., F.R.G.S.; *y. b.* Trinity House; late Secretary to the Navy League; *b.* 1848; *s.* of William Crutchley, architect, Wolverhampton; *m.* 1st, 1876, Elizabeth, *d.* of John Symon, Southampton; 2nd, 1882, Edith, *o. d.* of Felton Matthew, Cape Town; two *s.* one *d. Educ.:* private school, Margate. Thirty-one years' sea service, of which seventeen were spent in command of first-class mail steamers; has served in H.M. ships; retired from the sea, 1894; has given considerable attention to matters of maritime interest. *Publications :* My Life at Sea, 1912; has contributed (by papers at the R. U.S.I. and otherwise) towards the solution of the problem "How to protect the Mercantile Marine in war time"; has been a journalist; made contributions to Meteorology and Nautical Science generally. *Address:* 23 Argyll Mansions, Addison Bridge, W. *Club:* Yorick.   *(Died 22 Nov. 1923.)*

CULLEN, Commander Percy, R.N.R.; C.M.G. 1902; late Commanding Naval Forces in Brit. Central Africa; *b.* 10 Mar. 1861; *s.* of late W. H. Cullen; *m.* 1895, Ethel Mary, *d.* of F. J. Collart. Served Lake Nyasa, 1895; Mepesu Expedition, 1898 (despatches, medal and clasp).   *(Died 15 Nov. 1918.)*

CULLUM, George Gery Milner-Gibson, F.S.A., F.Z.S., J.P., D.L.; *b.* 1857; 5th and *o. surv. s.* of late Rt. Hon: T. Milner-Gibson, M.P., of Theberton House, Suffolk, and Arethusa Susanna, *o. d.* of Rev. Sir Thomas Gery Cullum, 8th Bart. (*ext.*) of Hardwick. *Educ.:* Trinity Coll. Cambridge (M.A.) Inherited Hardwick in 1875, on death of grandmother, Lady Cullum, whose name he assumed; High Sheriff, Suffolk, 1888; admitted to the freedom of Bury St. Edmunds, 1911; Hon. Curator of Moyses Hall Museum, 1912; Mayor of Bury St. Edmunds, 1913-14; Fellow of the Society of Genealogists, 1916; Hon. Member New England Historic Genea Society, 1918; patron of one living. *Publications :* Pedigree of Middleton or Myddleton of Chirk Castle, 1897; Pedigree of Ray of Denston in Suffolk, 1903; Pedigree of Wittewronge of Ghent in Flanders, and other Families from them descended, 1905; Inscriptions in the Old British Cemetery at Leghorn, 1907; Pedigree of the Family of Corsellis of Essex, 1914; Mary Beale; Suffolk Artist, 1919; contributions to genealogical and archæological publications. *Address:* Hardwick House, Bury St. Edmunds; 4 Sterling Street, Montpelier Square, S.W. *Clubs:* Athenæum. St. James's, Bachelors'.

      (Died 21 Nov. 1921.)

CUMBERBATCH, Henry Alfred, C.M.G., 1896; H.M. Consul-General for the Vilayet of Beirut, Syria, and for the Lebanon 1908-14; was also British Post Office Agent; has been employed at the Foreign Office since Nov. 1914; *b.* Berdiansk (Russia), 27 June 1858; *s.* of late R. W. Cumberbatch of H.M.'s Consular Service; *m.* Hélène Gertrude, *d.* of late

252

T. B. Rees of Smyrna, 1891; three *s.* two *d. Educ.:* Christ College, Finchley. Student Dragoman, Constantinople, 1876; employed at Belgrade, 1876-78; appointed H.M.'s Vice-Con. Bucharest, 1879; H.M.'s Vice-Con. Soulina (Roumania), 1881; Con. Adrianople, 1888; Acting Consul-General, Philippopolis (Bulgaria), 1888 and 1890; Acting Consul-General, Salonica, 1891; Acting Con.-Gen., Smyrna 1892; transferred to Angora, 1893; was at Erzeroum (Kurdistan) during the massacres of Armenians at that place, 1895; Consul for Kurdistan, 1895-1896. Consul at Smyrna, 1896-1900; was also British Post Office Agent; Consul-General, 1900-8. *Decorated* for services rendered in Asia Minor, etc. *Recreation:* golf. *Address:* Foreign Office. S.W. *Club:* St. James's.

      (Died 3 Dec. 1918.)

CUMBERLAND, Maj.-Gen. Charles Edward, C.B. 1881; J.P. Kent; *b.* 1830; *s.* of R. E. Cumberland; *m.* 1st, Elizabeth Anne (*d.* 1891), *d.* of late Rev. W. Moss King, 1883; 2nd, 1907, Adelaide, *d.* of late Philip H. Crampton, of Fassaro, Co. Wicklow. *Educ.:* R.M. Academy, Woolwich. Entered Royal Engineers, 1847; Brevet Maj. 1860; Col. 1877; retired Maj.-Gen. 1887; served in Crimean Campaign, 1855-56 (medal and Turkish medal); Indian Mutiny, 1857-59 (medal and clasp). *Recreations:* cricket, chess. *Address:* Manor House, Maidstone.   *(Died July 1920.)*

CUMBERLAND, Major Charles Sperling; retired; *b.* Dec. 1847; *s.* of Major G. B. Cumberland, late 42nd Highlanders. *Educ.:* Repton School. Joined 39th Regiment, 1867; and served with that regiment until 1882, when he exchanged into the 30th E. Lancashire; served Afghanistan, 1878-79; retired 1887; since then has travelled for the purpose of big game hunting and exploration in Asia, Africa, Canada, and New Zealand. *Publications :* Sport in the Pamir Steppes; also wrote for Country Life Library of Sport, The Big Game of Asia, and also for Great and Small Game of India. *Recreations:* fishing, shooting, golf. *Address:* County Club, Dorchester. *Club:* Naval and Military.   *(Died 6 Dec. 1922.)*

CUMBERLAND, Gerald, dramatic and musical critic, and dramatic author; *b.* Manchester, 7 May 1879; *m.* Esther Innes Luffman. *Educ.:* Victoria University, Manchester. Musical and Dramatic Critic of the Manchester Courier, 1908-13; Critic of the Daily Citizen, 1913. *Publications :* Imaginary Interviews with Great Composers; Set Down in Malice, 1918; Play, The Chivalry of Dreams, 1911; The Poisoner, 1921; Striving Fire, 1924. *Recreation :* swimming. *Club:* Press.   *(Died 2 June 1926.)*

CUMMING, Capt. Sir Mansfield, R.N., K.C.M.G. *cr.* 1919; C.B. 1914; retired; *b.* 1 April 1859; *m.* 1st, 1885, Dora, *d.* of T. Cloete of Constantia, S.A.; 2nd, 1889, Leslie Valiant, *d.* of Capt. V. Cumming of Logie, Morayshire. A.D.C. during expedition against Malays, Straits of Malacca, 1875-76 (medal and clasp); served Egypt, 1888 (medal and Khedive's Star); Officer Legion of Honour, St. Stanislaus, St. Leopold, and St. Vladimir; Crown of Italy, 1914 Star, General Service Medal, Victory Medal. *Address:* 1 Melbury Road, W.14; Bursledon, Hants. *Clubs:* Naval and Military, Royal Automobile, Garrick, Royal Motor Yacht; Royal Yacht Squadron.

      (Died 14 June 1923.)

CUMMINS, Henry Ashley Travers, C.B.E.1919; Hon. Paymaster Rr.-Adm.(retired), R.N.; Director of Petersen & Co., Lond. American Maritime S.S. Co., and Thompson Steamship Co.; *b.* Cork, 25 Jan. 1847; *m.* Frances Wathan Hill (*d.* 1923), *d.* of late Commander Hugh Price, Royal Navy; one *d. Educ.:* Chester College; Eastman's Royal Naval Establishment, Southsea. Entered Royal Navy,

1864; joined Fisgard; Assistant Paymaster, 1868; Octavia, Commodore's ship, East Indies, 1865-69; served in the Abyssinian Expedition (medal); Minotaur, Flagship Channel Fleet; took passage in Megaera for Clio in Australia, 1871; was wrecked on St. Paul's Island during the voyage; was on Australian Station, 1872-75; lent to Pearl for duty as Assist. Secretary to the Commissioners for the annexation of Fiji; served in Warrior, Channel Fleet, 1875-78, and Flora, Cape of Good Hope Station, 1878-81; during the Boer War of 1881 was Accountant Officer of Flora and Secretary at the Cape Yard; received the special thanks of the Commodore in command of the Station and of the Flag Officer in command of the Detached Squadron; retired list, 1882; Cashier, Royal Naval Hospital, Great Yarmouth, 1882; came to the aid of the Medical Officer in charge, when attacked by a lunatic; received thanks of the Admiralty; Paymaster of Contingencies, Admiralty, 1890-1915; 51 years continuous Naval Service; Coronation Medal, 1911; General Service Medal, 1918; Paymaster-in-Chief, 1914. *Recreation*: golf. *Address*: 86 Oakwood Court, W.14. *T.*: Park 3890. *Club*: Constitutional.
(Died 10 Dec. 1926.)

CUMMINS, (Wm. Edward) Ashley, M.D.; Professor of Practice of Medicine, University College, Cork; Examiner in Medicine, National University, Ireland; Senior Surgeon, Victoria Hospital, Cork; Senior Medical Officer, Cork District Hospital; Consulting Physician, Lying-in Hospital, Cork; also of Cork Eye, Ear, and Throat Hospital; Consulting Physician, Southern Command; *m.*; four *s*. *Educ.*: University College, Cork. *Address*: 17 St. Patrick's Place, Cork; Woodville, Glanmire, Co. Cork. *T.A.*: Ashley Cummins, Cork. *T.*: 6; 10 Glanmire. *(Died 18 Oct. 1923.)*

CUNARD, Sir Bache, 3rd Bt., *cr.* 1859; J.P.; *s.* of 2nd Bt. and Mary, *d.* of Bache M'Evers of New York; *b.* 15 May 1851; *S.* father 1869; *m.* Maud Alice, *d.* of late E. F. Burke, New York, 1895; one *d.* (she *m.* S. Fairbairn, Grenadier Guards). *Educ.*: Rugby; Trinity College, Cambridge. *Heir*: *b.* Gordon [*b.* 22 May 1857; *m.* 1889, Edith Mary, *d.* of late Col. John Stanley Howard of Ballina Park, Co. Wicklow; three *s.* *Address*: Shantock Hall, Bovingdon, Herts. *Club*: Arthur's]. *Address*: The Haycock, Wansford, Peterborough. *Club*: Turf *(Died 3 Nov. 1925.)*

CUNARD, Ernest Haliburton; *b.* 1862; 2nd *s.* of late William Cunard of Orleans House, Twickenham; *m.* Florence, *d.* of late I. M'Pheeters, Baltimore, U.S.A., and widow of Edward Padelford. *Educ.*: Eton. Was a Director of the Cunard Steam Ship Co. (of which Sir Samuel Cunard (1st Bart.) was the original founder); Great Western Railway Co.; Peninsular and Oriental Steam Navigation Co.; The London County and Westminster Bank; The Royal Exchange Assurance Corporation; British India Steam Co. *(Died 6 Nov. 1926.)*

CUNEO, Cyrus Cincinatto, R.O.I.; *b.* San Francisco, California; Italian parentage. *Educ.*: San Francisco. Studied art in Paris under Girado, Prenet, and Whistler. *Address*: 215 Uxbridge Road, W. *T.*: 1558 Hammersmith. *Club*: Langham Sketching.
(Died 23 July 1916.)

CUNINGHAM, Maj.-Gen. Charles Alexander, Indian Army, and Col. 127th (Queen Mary's Own) Beluch Light Infantry; *b.* 29 Jan. 1842; 2nd *s.* of late Alexander Cuningham, Sec. to Northern Lighthouse Board, and Caroline, *d.* of General A. D. Faunce, C.B.; *m.* 1st, Annie, *e. d.* of J. M. Balfour, of Pilrig; 2nd, Innes, 3rd *d.* of Sir R. Playre, G.C.B.; one *s.* two *d.* *Educ.*: Edinburgh Academy and privately. Entered Army, 1858; Maj.-Gen. 1899; served Afghan War, 1880 (medal); held

various Staff appointments, including Secretary to Govt. of Bombay Military Department, and G.O.C. and Political Resident, Aden. *Recreations*: golf, etc. *Address*: 16 Lypiatt Terrace, Cheltenham. *Club*: New, Cheltenham.
(Died 24 Feb. 1925.)

CUNINGHAM, Granville Carlyle, M. Inst. C.E.; M. Can. Soc. C.E.; Consulting Engineer; *b.* Edinburgh, 27 April 1847; 5th *s.* of late Alexander Cuningham, W.S., Sec. to Commrs. of Northern Lighthouses, and Caroline, *d.* of Gen. Alured D. Faunce, C.B.; *m.* 1873, Frances Bethune, 3rd *d.* of late Robert Pilkington Crooks, Barrister, Toronto, Canada; one *s.* *Educ.*: Edinburgh Academy and University. Honduras, Central America, surveying for railway, 1870-1; Ontario, various railway works, 1871-74; preliminary surveys for Canadian Pacific Railway, 1874-75; Engineer-in-charge of Prince Edward Island Railway and of Harbours in the Island, 1875-79; Canada Southern Railway, 1879-81; Chief Engineer, 1881-1883. General Assist. to Manager of Construction of Rocky Mountain Div. Canadian Pacific Railway, 1884-86; Railway Contractor, Lower Canada, 1886-89; Assistant City Engineer and City Engineer of Toronto, 1889-92; General Manager and Chief Engineer, Montreal (Electric) Street Railway, 1892-97; Managing Director, City of Birmingham Tramways, 1897-99; General Manager, Central London (Tube) Railway, 1899-1911. *Publications*: Imperial Federation, 1895; Bacon's Secret Disclosed, 1911: Wake up, England! 1919. *Address*: Bedwyn Cottage, Farnham Common, Bucks. *Club*: Constitutional.
(Died 18 Dec. 1927.)

CUNINGHAME, Col. John Anstruther Smith, D.L., late 2nd Life Guards; *b.* 15 Nov. 1852; *m.* 1887, Violet Mary (*d.* 1917), *e. d.* of Sir Alfred Slade, 3rd Bart.; one *s*. *Address*: Caprington Castle, Kilmarnock, Ayrshire. *Club*: Marlborough. *(Died 17 Dec. 1921.)*

CUNINGHAME, J. C., D.L., J.P., Renfrew and Inverness, etc.; *b.* 29 May 1851; *s.* of Alexander Cuninghame of Craigends; *m.* his cousin, Alison, *d.* of late Alexander L. Pearson, and *g.-d.* of Commander Hugh Pearson, R.N.; no *c.* *Educ.*: Harrow; Cambridge. *Recreations*: shooting, billiards, racing. *Address*: Craigends, Johnstone, N.B.; Dunragit, Wigtonshire; 25 Hill Street, Mayfair, W. *T.*: 3316 Mayfair. *Clubs*: Carlton, Turf; New, Edinburgh.
(Died 30 Jan. 1917.)

CUNLIFFE, 1st Baron, of Headley, *cr.* 1914; **Walter Cunliffe**, G.B.E., *cr.* 1917; Lieut., City of London; Director of the Bank of England, 1895; Deputy Governor, 1911; Governor since 1913; Director North Eastern Railway Co.; Member of Cunliffe Brothers, White Lion Court, Cornhill, E.C.; *b.* 1855; *s.* of Roger Cunliffe and Anne Edge; *m.* 1st, Mary Agnes (*d.* 1893), *d.* of Robert Henderson of Randalls Park, Leatherhead; 2nd, 1896, Edith, *d.* of Col. R. T. Boothby, St. Andrews, Fife; two *s.* three *d.* *Educ.*: Harrow; Trinity Coll. Cambridge (M.A.); patron of the living of Headley, Surrey. 1st Class, Order of St. Anne (Russia), 1915; Grand Cross, Order of the Crown of Italy, 1916. *Heir*: *s.* Hon. Rolf Cunliffe, *b.* 13 May 1899. *Address*: Headley Court, Epsom. *T.A.*: Cunliffe, London. *Club*: New University. *(Died 6 Jan. 1919.)*

CUNLIFFE, Sir Foster Hugh Egerton, 6th Bt.; *cr.* 1759; *b.* 17 Aug. 1875; *s.* of 5th Bt. and Eleanor (*d.* 1898), *o. d.* of Major Egerton Leigh, West Hall, Cheshire; *S.* father 1905. *Educ.*: Eton; New College, Oxford (M.A.); Fellow of All Souls. *Heir*: *b.* Robert Nevill Henry, *b.* 8 Feb. 1884. *Address*: Acton Park, Wrexham. *(Died 19 July 1916.)*

CUNLIFFE, Sir (Robert) Ellis, Kt., *cr.* 1910; *b.* 30 Jan. 1858; 2nd *s.* of Robert Cunliffe (*d.* 1908) and Laetitia (*d.* 1899), 3rd *d.* of late Ven. John Williams, Archdeacon of

Cardigan; *m.* 1885, Clementina, 3rd *d.* of late Richard Cockerton; two *s.* three *d.* Formerly member of Cunliffes and Davenport, Chancery Lane. *Educ.:* Bradfield; Corpus Christi Coll., Oxford (M.A.). Admitted to Roll of Solicitors, 1884; Solicitor to Board of Trade, 1900-20; Member of the Council of Bradfield College, 1914; Chairman of London Society for Teaching and Training the Blind, Swiss Cottage, N.W.; Chairman of the Kensington, Fulham and Chelsea General Hospital. *Address:* 34 The Grove, The Boltons, S.W.10. *T.:* Ken. 5617. *M.:* XE 3999.   (*Died 18 Aug. 1927.*)

CUNNINGHAM, Alfred, M.J.L.; member Imperial Japanese Order of Rising Sun; *b.* Paddington, London, 31 Dec. 1870; 2nd *s.* of F. Cunningham, London, journalist; *m.* 1893, Cecilia Helen, 3rd *d.* of John Colledge, of Singapore; one *s. Educ.:* privately. General London and provincial experience; filled editorial appointments, Singapore, Shanghai, Hong Kong, and Cairo; served in Chino-Japanese War (for Central News) as special correspondent; special correspondent for the New York Journal with Spanish forces in Philippines, Spanish-American War; special correspondent at Chinese Rebellion at Tset Tze Lin, and in 1905 for Daily Mail and New York Sun at Camrang Bay with the Baltic Fleet, Russo-Japanese war; special correspondent for South China for the New York Sun; Special Correspondent, Berlin, 1912; Gold Medallist of Hanoi Exposition, Tonkin, of 1902; founded and edited the South China Morning Post, 1903; founded and edited the *Review of* the Far East. *Publications:* Special articles on Siberia, 1899; History of the Szechuen Riots; The French in Tonkin and South China; The Chinese Soldier and other Sketches; Scrutator's Letters on the Insanitary Condition of Hong Kong; To-Day in Egypt, 1912; acted as Mediator in the Coal Claim Dispute between Viceroy of Canton and the Bank of China, 1906 (thanked by Governor of Hong Kong in despatches); delegate Overseas Press Conference, London, 1901. *Recreations:* tennis, sketching, music, travel. *Address:* Altwood Bailey, Maidenhead, Berks. *Club:* Authors'.   (*Died 14 May 1918.*)

CUNNINGHAM, Sir Henry (Stewart), K.C.I.E.; *cr.* 1889; *b.* 1832; *s.* of late Rev. J. W. Cunningham, Vicar of Harrow, and Mary, *d.* of late Sir H. Calvert; *m.* Hon. Harriett Emily, (*d.* 1918), *d.* of John, 1st Lord Lawrence, 1877; one *d, Educ.:* Harrow; Trinity College, Oxford. Barr. 1859; Advocate-General, Madras, 1872; Judge of High Court, Bengal, 1877-87. *Address:* 83 Eaton Place, S.W.1. *T.:* 2205 Kensington. *Club:* Athenæum.
     (*Died 3 Sept. 1920.*)

CUNNINGHAM, Ven. William, F.B.A., D.D. Camb.; D.Sc. and Hon. LL.D. Edinb.; Fellow Trinity Coll. 1891; Archdeacon of Ely, 1907; Hon. Fellow Caius College; *b.* Edinburgh, 29 Dec. 1849; 3rd *s.* of James Cunningham, W.S., and Elizabeth Boyle, *d.* of Alexander Dunlop of Keppoch; *m.* Adèle Rebecca, *d.* of A. A. Dunlop, Dublin, 1876; one *d. Educ.:* Edin. Acad. and Univ. Jun. Greek Med., 1866; Caius Coll. and Trin. Coll. (scholar) Camb.; 1st class Moral Science Tripos, 1873; Hulsean, Maitland, and Kaye Prizes, Camb. University Extension Lecturer, 1874-78; University Lecturer on History, 1884-91; Deputy to Knightbridge Professor, 1880; Professor of Economics, King's Coll. London, 1891-97; Lecturer on Economic History, Harvard University, U.S.A., 1899; ordained by Bishop of Ely, 1873; Curate at Horningsea and St. Saviour's, Everton; Chaplain of Trin. Coll. 1880-91; Hulsean Lecturer, 1885; Vicar of Great St. Mary's, Cambridge, 1887-1908; also of St. Michael's, Cambridge, 1907-8; Examining Chaplain to the Bishop of Peterborough, 1911. *Publications:* Growth of English Industry and Commerce, 2 vols. 4th edition; Outlines of English Industrial History (part); Western Civilisation; Modern Civilisation; Use and Abuse of Money; Alien Immigrants; also S. Austin, Path towards Knowledge; Gospel of Work; Rise and Decline of Free Trade; Cure of Souls; Christianity and Social Questions; Case against Free Trade; Efficiency in the Church of England; Christianity and Economic Science; Christianity and Politics; English Influence on the United States; Progress of Capitalism; Increase of True Religion. *Address:* Trinity College, Cambridge. *Clubs:* Oxford and Cambridge, Albemarle.   (*Died 10 June 1919.*)

CUNNINGHAME GRAHAM, Com. Charles Elphinstone Fleeming, M.V.O., R.N.; Commander on the Emergency List, R.N.; Groom-in-Waiting to H.M. the King; *b.* 1 Jan. 1854; 2nd *s.* of William Cunninghame Graham Bontine, of Ardoch and Gartmore, and Hon. Anne Elizabeth, 4th *d.* of Admiral the Hon. Charles Elphinstone Fleeming of Cumbernauld, and *sister* of 14th Baron Elphinstone; *m.* 1882, Mildred Emily Barbara, *d.* of Rev. C. W. Bagot; one *s.* one *d. Educ.:* Harrow; H.M.S. Britannia. Served in Royal Navy, 1867-86, when he resigned his commission and took service in Royal National Lifeboat Institution, in which he served for 23 years; during his time of service he assisted on various occasions in saving life, and wrote many technical articles on lifeboat matters; invited by Admiralty to join Emergency List, and commission restored to him, 1901; commander, 1903; has Humane Society's silver medal for saving life; Knight Commander of Royal Danish Order of the Dannebrog; 2nd class of Red Eagle of Prussia; Commander of Polar Star of Sweden, and St. Stanislas of Russia; 2nd class of White Eagle of Serbia. *Address:* 60 Warwick Square, S.W. *Clubs:* Marlborough, Naval and Military; Royal Yacht Squadron (Naval Hon. Member), Cowes.   (*Died 8 June 1917.*)

CUNYNGHAM, Sir William Stewart-Dick-, 10th Bt., *cr.* 1669; C.B.E. 1919; of Prestonfield and Lamburghtoun, a Gentleman-at-Arms, 1920; Brigade-Major, Lowland Mounted Brigade, Ayr, N.B.; Major Scottish Horse I.Y.; late Capt. 1st Batt. Black Watch (Royal Highlanders); *b.* 20 Feb. 1871; *s.* of 9th Bt. and Sarah Mary, *o. d.* of W. Hetherington S. father; 1897; *m.* 1903, Evelyn Eleanora, *e. d.* of Arthur Fraser. *Educ.:* Harrow; Sandhurst. A.D.C. to Gen. Sir E. F. Chapman, K.C.B., Scottish Dist., 1898-1900; Assistant Private Secretary to Gen. Hon. Sir Neville Lyttelton, 1905-7; served South Africa (despatches); European War, commanded 10th Black Watch in France and the Balkans (despatches, C.B.E.); served with Italian Expeditionary Force as Commandant G.H.Q. Reinforcement Camp. *Heir: n.* Colin Keith, *b.* 3 March 1908. *Address:* Prestonfield, Edinburgh. *Clubs:* Army and Navy; New, Edinburgh.
     (*Died 25 Mar. 1922.*)

CURE, Sir Edward Capel, Kt., *cr.* 1919 Commercial Counsellor of Embassy, for Italy, 1918-22; *b.* 1866; *e. s.* of late Rev. Edward Capel Cure, Canon of Windsor and Chaplain in Ordinary to Queen Victoria, and Gertrude, 2nd *d.* of Sir John Thomas Selwin, 6th Bart., and sister of 7th Bart. and 1st Baron Rookwood; *m.* 1889, Muriel, *e. d.* of Sir Percy Oxenden, 10th Bart.; one *d. Educ.:* Winchester; New College, Oxford (in honours history). Italian Correspondent for the Engineer, 1906-14; Temporary Italian Correspondent of the Times, 1914; Assistant Commercial Attaché H.B.M. Embassy, Rome, 1914, was on the Anglo-Italian Financial Conference, Nice, 1915, on the British Delegation at the Economic Conference of the Allies, Paris, 1916; and was British Representative on the Servian Revictualling Commission, 1916; accompanied

CUNNINGHAM, Rt. Rev. John F., D.D. See page xvii.

Mr. Runciman's Special Mission to Pallanza, Aug. 1916, and the Italian Ministers of the Treasury and the Interior on their Missions to London, 1916-19; Grand Officer of the Order of S. Maurice and Lazarus; Commendatore of the Crown of Italy; Serbian Order of the White Eagle. *Publications*: Italian author Risveglio, Sul Meriggio, etc., and articles in Reviews (British and Italian). *Recreation*: driving. *Address*: Villa Della Quercia, Pallanza, Lago Maggiore, Italy. *Club*: Travellers'.

(*Died 30 Dec. 1923.*)

CURRAN, His Honour Judge John Adye; *b.* 1837; *s.* of late John Adye Curran, Barrister, Dublin. B.A. Trinity College, Dublin; called to Irish Bar, 1860; K.C. 1882; J.P. Co. Dublin; Divisional Magistrate for Dublin, 1881-83; chairman of Quarter Sessions and County Court Judge for King's, Longford, Meath and Westmeath Cos., 1883-86, and 1891-1914; Co. Kerry, 1886-91. *Publication*: Recollections of an Irish K.C.; Reminiscences, 1916. *Address*: 58 Palmerston Road, Dublin.

(*Died 16 Mar. 1919.*)

CURRE, John Mathew; M.F.H. Radnors and West Herefords, 1910-19; *s.* of late E. M. Curre, of Itton Court, Chepstow; *b.* 1859; *m.* 1901, Mrs. Palmer Jenkins, Beachley, Chepstow. *Address*: Titley, Hereford.

(*Died 24 Oct. 1919.*)

CURRIE, Very Rev. Edward Reid, D.D., V.D.; Dean of the Peculiar of Battle, and Vicar since 1882; R.D. of Hastings, 1905-18; b. Calcutta, 16 Feb. 1844; *s.* of late Edward Currie, B.C.S.; *m.* 1st, Geraldine Dowdeswell, o. c. of late Richard Tyrrell; one *s.*; 2nd, 1889, Hon. Frances Emma (*d.* 1920), o. d. of late Rev. W. F. Hotham, Rector of Buckland, Surrey. *Educ.*: Cheltenham; Wadham College, Oxford. Curate of Christ Church, Eastbourne, 1868; Senior Curate of Battle, 1869-74; Vicar of St. Bartholomew, Chichester. 1874-82; Acting Chaplain to the Forces, Chichester, 1878-82; Acting Chaplain, 1st Cinque Ports R. Vo. 1884-1908; Chaplain, 1st Class, Territorial Force, 1908-9. *Address*: Deanery, Battle, Sussex. *Clubs*: Junior Constitutional, Junior Army and Navy. (*Died 4 Feb. 1921.*)

CURRIE, Maj.-Gen. Fendall, Bengal Cavalry; *b.* 24 Nov. 1841; 6th *s.* of Sir Frederick Currie, 1st Bart.; *m.* 1st, 1866, Susan (*d.* 1868), y. d. of Rev. J. R. Pears, Woodcote House, Windlesham; one *s.* one *d.*; 2nd, 1869, Julia (*d.* 1920), d. of F. P. Buller; one *s.* four *d.* Entered army, 1858; Maj.-Gen. 1898; Commissioner in Oudh, U.P., India, 1888-96.

(*Died 4 Dec. 1920.*)

CURRIE, Lieut.-Col. Ivor Bertram Fendall, D.S.O. 1919; late R.G.A.; e. s. of Maj.-Gen. Fendall Currie, and 2nd wife; *b.* 1872; *m.* 1906, May Constance, d. of late Field Marshal Sir George White; two *d.* *Educ.*: Clifton College; Royal Military Academy, Woolwich. Served European War 1914-19 (despatches, D.S.O.); retired pay, 1921. *Address*: c/o Lloyd's Bank, Ltd., Charing Cross, S. W.1. *Club*: Army and Navy.

(*Died 1 April 1924.*)

CURRIE, Col. (Temp. Brig.-Gen.) Ryves Alexander Mark, C.M.G. 1919; D.S.O. 1917; *b.* 18 June 1875; *s.* of late Lt.-Col. F. A. Currie, Norfolk Regt.; *m.* 1908, Ida M., d. of J. H. Hatchell, M.D., no c. *Educ.*: Wellington College. Joined 1st Batt. Somerset Light Infantry, 1896; Adjutant, 1904; passed Staff College, 1911; Brigade-Major, 18th Infantry Brigade, 1912; served N.W. Frontier, India, 1897; European War, 1914-18 (despatches, Bt. Maj., Bt. Lieut.-Col., Bt. Col., D.S.O., C.M.G., Legion d'Honneur). *Address*: Merton, Camberley. *Clubs*: United Service, M.C.C.; I. Zingari. (*Died 30 Mar. 1920.*)

CURTEIS, Brig.-General Francis Algernon, C.B. 1911; C.M.G. 1917; retired, 1912; *b.* June 1856; *s.* of Capt. H. J. Curteis, late 37th Regt.; *m.* 1894, Jeannie H. M., d. of late Philip Myburgh, Q.C.; one *d.* *Educ.*: Malvern College. Entered Royal Artillery, 1876; served Soudan, 1885-86; S. Africa, 1900-1902; Brig.-Gen. commanding Western Coast Defences, 1908-12. *Address*: 4 The Croft, Tenby.

(*Died 1 May 1928.*)

CURTEIS, Maj.-Gen. Reginald Lawrence Herbert J.P.; *b.* 3 Jan. 1848. Entered army, 1860; Maj.-Gen. 1900; retired, 1908. *Address*: Glan-yr-afon, Crickhowell.

(*Died 17 Dec. 1919.*)

CURTIS, Colonel Edward George, C.M.G. 1916; *b.* 1868; 3rd *s.* of late Maj.-Gen. Reginald Curtis, R.A.; *m.* 1903, Ethel, d. of late Walter Coote, F.R.G.S.; one *s.* *Educ.*: Westminster School; Cheltenham College; R.M.C. Sandhurst. Bedfordshire Regiment, 1888-1909; served with the Chitral Relief Force, 1895 (medal with clasp); commanded 4th Northamptonshire Regt., and served with it in Gallipoli (despatches), and in Egypt, B.E.F., 1916-19 (despatches); an Organising Secretary of the National Service League, 1909-14. *Recreation*: football; Hon. Secretary, Army Football Association, 1900-1907; several years' a member of the Consultative Committee, F.A.

(*Died Mar. 1923.*)

CURTIS, Major-Gen. Sir Reginald Salmond, K.C.M.G., *cr.* 1917; C.B. 1915; D.S.O. 1909; C.M.G. 1908; *b.* 21 Nov. 1868; e. s. of Maj.-Gen. Reginald Curtis, R.A.; *m.* 1894, Hon. Hilda Margaret, y. d. of 9th Viscount Barrington; three *d.* *Educ.*: Cheltenham Coll.; R.M.A. Woolwich. Commissioned in Royal Engineers, 1888; served Egyptian Army, 1890-93; in campaign, Eastern Soudan, 1891, including capture of Tokar (bronze star with clasp, 4th class Medjidie); served in Ashanti expedition, 1895-96, as director of telegraphs (star, brevet of Maj., despatches); special service under Admiralty, Falkland Islands, 1899; served South African war, 1899-1902, as A.D.C. to Engineer-in-Chief, also as Assistant Director of Telegraphs, and with South African Constabulary (D.S.O., Queen's medal with five clasps, King's medal with two clasps, Brevet Lieut.-Colonel, despatches); Chief Staff Officer, S.A. Constabulary, 1903-5; Inspector General, S.A. Constabulary, 1905-8; Member of the Intercolonial Council of the Transvaal and Orange River Colony, 1904-8; Commandant Army Signal School, 1912-13; Assistant Adjutant-General, War Office, 1913-17; commanded Cromarty Defences, 1917; in charge of Administration Aldershot Command, 1917-19; retired, 1920; Major-General and K.C.M.G. for valuable services rendered in connection with the European War, 1914-17. *Address*: The Croft, West Farleigh, Maidstone. *Club*: Army and Navy. (*Died 11 Jan. 1922.*)

CURTIS, Sir William Michael, 4th Bt., *cr.* 1802; *b.* Knole, 11 Nov. 1859; S. grandfather 1870; *m.* 1st, 1887, Mabel (d. 1888), 4th d. of Sir S. A. Gurney of North Runcton Hall, King's Lynn; one d.; 2nd, 1895, Georgina, d. of Col. J. S. Howard, and widow of Capt. A. B. Mesham; three d. *Recreation*: Master of Ludlow Fox-hounds, 1886-1907. *Heir*: c. Edgar Francis Egerton [b. 18 Dec. 1875; *m.* 1903, Madeline, 3rd d. of late C. W. Alexander, I.C.S.]. *Address*: Cavnham Court, Ludlow, Salop.

(*Died 19 Dec. 1916.*)

CURWEN, Eldred Vincent Morris, J.P.; *b.* 1842; 3rd *s.* of late Edward Stanley Curwen, of Workington, and Frances Margaret, d. of late Edward Jesse; *m.* 1st, 1865, Hebe Emily (d. 1889), o. d. of Sir Chaloner Ogle, 3rd Bart., of Withdeane Court; 2nd, 1913, Evelyn, y. d. of General Sir Edmund Ogle, 6th Bart., of San Remo, Italy. *Clubs*: Arthur's, Conservative; Royal Yacht Squadron, Cowes.

(*Died 16 Feb. 1927.*)

CURWEN, John Spencer; *e. s.* of John Curwen, originator of the Tonic Sol-Fa System ; editor of the Musical Herald since 1866 ; *b.* Plaistow, Essex, 30 Sept. 1847 ; *m.* 1877, Annie Jessy, *d.* of J. C. Gregg of Dublin (*see* Annie J. Curwen); one *s.* two *d. Educ.:* City of London School ; R. Acad. of Music under G. A. Macfarren, Sullivan, and Prout. A.R.A.M. 1879 ; F.R.A.M. 1885 ; Associate Philharmonic Society, 1882 ; Welsh Bard (ap Derwent Pencerdd), 1896 ; F.Z.S. President Tonic Sol-Fa College on death of his father, 1880 ; has travelled much in Europe and America investigating the organisation of music in schools and among the masses of the people ; President Tonic Sol-Fa Association. *Publications:* Studies in Worship Music ; Memorials of John Curwen ; The Boy's Voice ; School Music Abroad ; Music at the Queen's Accession. *Recreations:* pedestrianism, tennis, dogs ; social questions. *Address:* 6 Portland Court, Great Portland Street, W. *T.:* 2191 Mayfair.
(*Died 6 Aug.* 1916.)

CURWOOD, James Oliver; author ; *b.* Owosso, Michigan, U.S.A., 12 June 1879 ; *s.* of James Moran Curwood and Abigail Griffin, descendant on father's side of Captain Marryat, the novelist ; *m. Educ.:* University of Michigan. In newspaper work seven years ; assistant editor and editor, News - Tribune, Detroit ; resigned to take up literary work exclusively, 1907 ; former member Troop B., Michigan State Cavalry ; Republican ; one of the foremost North American naturalists ; spends several months each year in Canadian wildernesses, travelling as far north as Arctic coast ; the only American ever employed by the Canadian Government as an exploratory and descriptive writer ; has one of the largest collections of great game photographs (taken by himself) in America. *Publications:* God's Country—the Trail to Happiness ; Baree, Son of Kazan ; The Courage of Captain Plum ; The Courage of Marge O'Doone ; The Danger Trail ; Flower of the North ; God's Country—and the Woman ; The Gold Hunters ; The Golden Snare ; The Great Lakes ; The Grizzly King ; The Honor of the Big Snows ; The Hunted Woman ; Isobel ; Kazan ; Nomads of the North ; Philip Steele ; The Wolf Hunters ; The River's End ; The Valley of Silent Men ; The Flaming Forest ; The Country Beyond ; Swift Lightning ; The Last Frontier ; The Alaskan ; A Gentleman of Courage ; The Ancient Highway ; The Black Hunter ; The Glory of Living, an autobiography ; The Plains of Abraham. *Address:* Owosso, Michigan, U.S.A. (*Died 13 Aug.* 1927.)

CURZON of Kedleston, 1st Marquess, *cr.* 1921 ; **George Nathaniel Curzon,** K.G., G.C.S.I., G.C.I.E., M.A., P.C., F.R.S., D.C.L., LL.D., J.P., D.L. ; Baron Scarsdale, 1761 ; Baron (Ireland), 1898 ; Viscount Scarsdale, 1911 ; Baron Ravensdale, 1911 ; Earl Curzon of Kedleston, 1911 ; Earl of Kedleston, 1921 ; Irish Representative Peer since 1908 ; Secretary of State for Foreign Affairs 1919-24 ; Leader of the House of Lords 1916-24 ; Fellow of British Academy, 1908 ; Member of Imperial War Cabinet, 1916 ; Trustee of the British Museum, 1920 ; *b.* Kedleston, 11 Jan. 1859 ; *e. s.* of Rev. Alfred Nathaniel Holden Curzon, 4th Baron Scarsdale, and Blanche, *d.* of Joseph Pocklington Senhouse, Netherhall ; *m.* 1st, 1895, Mary Victoria, C.I. (*d.* 1906), *d.* of L. Z. Leiter, Washington, U.S.A.; three *d.*; 2nd, 1917, Grace Elvina, G.B.E. *cr.* 1922, *d.* of late J. Monroe Hinds, U.S.A. Minister, Brazil, and widow of Alfred Duggan, Buenos Ayres. *Educ.:* Eton ; Balliol Coll. Oxford. President of the Union, 1880 ; Assistant Private Secretary to Marquis of Salisbury, 1885 ; contested S. Derbyshire, 1885 ; Under-Secretary of State for India. 1891-92 ; Under-Secretary of State for Foreign Affairs, 1895-98 ;

Lord Privy Seal, 1915-16 ; President of the Air Board, 1916 ; Lord President of the Council, 1916-19 ; has travelled extensively in Central Asia, Persia, Afghanistan, the Pamirs, Siam, Indo-China, and Korea ; received the Gold Medal of Royal Geographical Society, 1895. Lothian Essay Prize, Oxford, 1883 ; Arnold Essay Prize, 1884 ; Fellow All Souls' Coll. Oxford, 1883 ; Hon. D.C.L. (Oxford), 1904 ; Hon. LL.D. (Cambridge), 1907 ; Hon. LL.D. (Manchester), 1908 ; Hon. LL.D. (Glasgow), 1911 ; Hon. D.C.L. (Durham), 1913 ; Romanes Lecturer, Oxford, 1907 ; Chancellor of Oxford University, 1907 ; Lord Rector, Glasgow University, 1908 ; Hon. Fellow, Balliol College, 1907 ; Rede Lecturer, Cambridge, 1913 ; M.P. (C.) Southport Division S.W. Lancashire, 1886-98 ; Viceroy and Gov.-Gen. of India, 1899-1905 ; Lord Warden of the Cinque Ports, 1904-5 ; President of the Royal Geographical Society, 1911-14 ; Trustee of the National Gallery, 1911. *Publications:* Russia in Central Asia, 1889 ; Persia and the Persian Question, 1892 ; Problems of the Far East, 1894 ; Lord Curzon in India, 1906 ; Principles and Methods of University Reform, 1909 ; Modern Parliamentary Eloquence, 1913 ; War Poems and Other Translations, 1915 ; Subjects of the Day, 1915 ; Tales of Travel, 1923. *Heir (to Viscounty):* n. Richard N. Curzon (*to Barony*) *e. d.* Lady Mary Irene Curzon, *b.* 20 Jan. 1896 ; (*to Marquisate*) none. *Address:* 1 Carlton House Terrace, S.W.1 : *T.:* Regent 1628 ; Hackwood, Basingstoke ; Kedleston, Derby ; Montacute House, Somerset. *Clubs:* Carlton, Athenæum, Bachelors'. (*Died 20 Mar.* 1925.)

CURZON, Hon. Alfred Nathaniel; 2nd *s.* of 4th Baron Scarsdale ; *b.* 12 Mar. 1860 ; *m.* 1891, Henrietta Mary, *d.* of Hon. Spencer D. Montagu ; one *s.* two *d. Address:* Weston Underwood, nr. Derby. *Club:* Wellington.
(*Died 20 Sept.* 1920.)

CURZON, Frank; Theatrical Manager and Racehorse Owner; Lessee and Manager, The Playhouse and Wyndham's Theatre ; *b.* Wavertree, Liverpool, 17 Sep. 1868 ; *s.* of W. Clark Deeley, Curzon Park, Chester, and Elizabeth, *d.* of J. Mallaby of Loxley Hall, Staffordshire ; *m.* Isabel Jay. *Educ.:* privately. Joined the theatrical profession and played with several provincial companies, afterwards touring Cos. on his own account ; took the Avenue Theatre (now the Playhouse) in 1899, and there in conjunction with Mr. Charles Hawtrey produced A Message from Mars ; following this took the Strand and Globe (both now demolished), and at one time had no less than nine West-End Theatres under his management ; produced A Chinese Honeymoon ; Miss Hook of Holland ; An Englishman's Home, and numerous other plays. *Recreations:* racing, hunting, golfing, fishing. *Address:* 37 Bury Street, St. James's, S.W.1 ; *T.:* Gerrard 2229 ; Primrose House, Newmarket. *Clubs:* Bucks; Union, Brighton. (*Died 2 July* 1927.)

CUSACK-SMITH, Sir William, 4th Bt., *cr.* 1799 ; 4th Roy. Wurtemberg Lancers (retired) ; *b.* 1822 ; *S.* father 1859. *Heir:* cousin, Sir Berry Cusack-Smith. *Address:* Hope Villa, Southsea. (*Died 15 April* 1919.)

CUSHNY, Arthur Robertson, M.A., M.D., LL.D., F.R.S. 1907 ; Professor of Materia Medica and Pharmacology, University of Edinburgh, since 1918 ; *b.* 1866 ; 4th *s.* of late Rev. John Cushny, Speymouth, Morayshire ; *m.* 1896, Sarah, *d.* of Ralph Firbank ; one *d. Educ.:* University of. Aberdeen ; Berne ; Strassburg. Entered University of Aberdeen, 1882 ; graduated in Arts and Medicine, 1889 ; Thompson Fellow, 1889 ; Assistant to Professor of Pharmacology Strassburg, 1892-93 ; Professor of Pharmacology in the University of Michigan, Ann Arbor, U.S.A., 1893-1905 ; Professor of Pharmacology and Materia Medica in University

of London, University College, 1905-18 ; member Royal Commission on Whisky and other Potable Spirits, 1908. *Publications :* Textbook of Pharmacology and Therapeutics, 8th ed. 1924 ; The Secretion of the Urine, 1917 ; The Action and Uses in Medicine of Digitalis and its Allies, 1924. *Recreations :* walking, golf. *Address :* University, Edinburgh. *Club :* Athenæum.⌐
        (Died 25 Feb. 1926.)

CUST, Very Rev. Arthur Perceval Purey-, D.D., F.S.A. ; J.P. for Bucks ; Dean of York since 1880 ; *b.* 1828 ; *s.* of late Hon. William Cust and Sophia, *d.* of Thos. Newnham, Southborough ; *m.* 1854, Lady Emma Bess Bligh, *d.* of 5th Earl of Darnley. *Educ.:* Proprietary School, Lee Kent ; Brasenose Coll. Oxford. Fellow of All Souls' Coll. 1850-54 ; M.A. 1854 ; D.D. 1880. Curate of Northchurch, Herts, 1851-1853 ; Rector of Cheddington, Bucks, and Rural Dean, 1853-62 ; Vicar of St. Mary's, Reading, and Rural Dean, 1862-75 ; Hon. Canon of Christ Church, Oxford ; Vicar of Aylesbury, 1875-76 ; Archdeacon of Buckingham, 1875-80 ; Chaplain to the Archbishop of Canterbury, 1868. *Publications :* sermons, lectures, papers at Church Congresses ; Archidiaconal Charges ; magazine articles ; The Heraldry of York Minster, 4to, 1st series, 1890, 2nd series, 1896 ; Picturesque Old York, 1896 ; York Minster, 1897. *Recreations :* archæology, history, music, etc. *Address :* Deanery, York. *Clubs :* United University ; Yorkshire, York.   *(Died 23 Dec. 1916.)*

CUST, Henry John Cockayne, D.L., J.P. ; heir to Barony of Brownlow ; *b.* 10 Oct. 1861 ; *s.* of Major H. F. Cockayne Cust, Cockayne Hatley, and Sarah Jane, *d.* of late Isaac Cookson, and widow of Major Sidney R. Streatfeild ; *m.* Emmeline M. E., *o. d.* of Sir William Welby-Gregory, 4th Bt., 1893. *Educ.:* Eton ; Trinity College, Cambridge (Scholar). M.P. Stamford, 1890-95 ; M.P. (C.) Bermondsey, 1900-1906 ; editor of the Pall Mall Gazette, 1902-6 ; member of the French Bar. *Address :* Chancellor's House, 17 Hyde Park Gate, S.W. ; Belton House, Grantham. *Clubs :* Carlton, Travellers', Beefsteak.   *(Died 2 Mar. 1917.)*

CUSTANCE, Colonel Frederic Hambleton, C.B. ; Hon. Colonel 3rd Batt. Norfolk Regt. ; *e. s.* of late Colonel Sir H. F. Custance, K.C.B. ; *b.* 2 Dec. 1844 ; *m.* 1871, Eleanor (*d.* 1908), *d.* of late Capt. Hylton Jolliffe, *e. s.* of 1st Lord Hylton ; two *d.* Served South Africa 1900-1901 (despatches, Queen's medal 3 clasps, C.B.) ; Lieut.-Col. late Grenadier Guards. *Address :* Weston Hall, Norwich. *T.A.:* Great Witchingham. *M.:* AH 46. *Club :* Carlton.
        (Died 29 Sept. 1925.)

CUTLER, Edward, J.P. ; K.C. 1884 ; *b.* 4 May 1831 ; *s.* of Edward Cutler, Surgeon to St.George's Hospital, and Marianne, *d.* of Sir Thomas Plumer, Master of the Rolls ; *m.* Ellen Mona, *d.* of late Major Larkins (murdered at Cawnpore) ; one *s.* two *d.* *Educ.:* Eton ; Paris ; Dresden ; Balliol Coll. Oxford ; graduated with Classical Honours. Barr. 1857 ; Grand Organist, English Freemasons, 1892, 1893 ; on the Imperial Commission for Copyright, 1909 ; employed in revising International Copyright Bill, 1910. *Publications :* The Teacher's Legal Guide (co-author with H. Lynn) ; A Treatise on Musical and Dramatic Copyright (co-author with Eustace Smith and Fred. E. Weatherly) ; A Manual of Musical Copyright Law, 1906 ; pamphlets in the French language on Les grades Universitaires, and on other subjects ; Golden Years, a song published about 1890, and numerous other songs and pieces for full orchestra, organ, and pianoforte. *Recreations :* London Skating Club ; gives frequent organ recitals in public. *Address :* 32 Eaton Place, S.W. *Clubs :* Junior Carlton, Skating.   *(Died 22 Dec. 1916.)*

CUTLER, John, K.C., M.A. ; Emeritus Professor of Law, King's College, University of London ; formerly Editor, Reports of Patent

Design and Trade Mark Cases, published by H.M. Patent Office, *b.* Dorchester, 9 Jan. 1839 ; *m.* Edith Ruth, *d.* of late Thomas Hayes, 1884. *Educ.:* King's Coll. School, London ; Exeter Coll. Oxford ; Edinburgh University. Barr. 1863 ; Queen's Counsel, 1897 ; Bencher, Lincoln's Inn. *Publications :* Treatise on Law of Naturalisation, 1871 ; Treatise on Passing Off, 1904 ; A Brace of Humbugs, Her Début at Court, Dora's Dream, and other dramatic works. *Recreations :* music and the drama. *Address :* 7 Addison Court Gardens, Blythe Road, W.14 ; 4 New Square, Lincoln's Inn, W.C.2. *T.:* Hammersmith 1669.
        (Died 19 Mar. 1924.)

CUYLER, Sir Charles, 4th Bt.; *cr.* 1814 ; O.B.E. 1918 ; reserve of officers since 9 Mar. 1919 ; Lieut.-Colonel commanding Depot Oxford and Bucks Light Infantry and 43rd Recruiting Area, 6 Aug. 1914-9 Mar. 1919 ; *b.* Oakleaze, Gloucestershire, 15 Aug. 1867 ; *S.* father 1885 ; *m.* 1897, Maud Geraldine, *d.* of late A. H. Jenney. *Educ.:* Clifton College ; R.M.C. Sandhurst. *Recreations :* cricket, golf, shooting, fishing, etc. *Heir : b.* George Hallifax [*b.* 23 Apr. 1876 ; *m.* 1913, Amy, *d.* of late Frederick Gordon, of the Briery, Sunderland, and *widow* of Gordon M'Kenzie]. *Address :* Kingswood, Medmenham, Bucks. *T.A :* Medmenham. *(Died 1 Oct. 1919.)*

CZAPLICKA, Marie Antoinette, F.R.A.I. ; F.R.G.S. ; author, lecturer and traveller ; *b.* near Warsaw, Poland ; *d.* of Felix Lubicz de Czaplicki and Sophie de Zawisza. *Educ.:* in Poland and Russia. Came to England with Mianowski Research Scholarship(Warsaw), 1910 ; studied in London and Oxford (Somerville College) ; took Diploma in Anthropology in Oxford, 1912 ; Anthropological Expedition to the Yenisei Valley in Siberia, under the auspices of the Oxford University Committee for Anthropology and as Mary Ewart Travelling Scholar, Somerville College, 1914-15 ; hon. member of Lady Margaret Hall, Oxford, since 1916 ; Mary Ewart Lecturer in Ethnology to the Oxford School of Anthropology, 1916-19 ; Murchison Grant, R.G.S., 1920. *Publications :* Aboriginal Siberia, 1914 ; My Siberian Year, 1916 ; The Turks of Central Asia, 1918 ; essays on East European and North-Central Asiatic subjects in the Hasting's Encyclopædia of Religion and Ethics ; various pamphlets and articles on anthropology in English, Polish and Russian. *Recreations :* walking and fencing. *Address :* Lady Margaret Hall, Oxford. *Club :* Lyceum.
        (Died 27 May 1921.)

D

D'AETH, John, M. Inst. C.E. ; I.S.O., 1910 ; *b.* 10 Aug. 1853 ; *e. surv. s.* of James Death, Waltham Abbey, Essex, and Cheshunt, Herts ; *m.* 1885, Anna Marie, *d.* of Thomas Oughton, Solicitor and Advocate, and Clerk to the Legislative Council of Jamaica ; one *s.* *Educ.:* High School, Bishop's Stortford ; King's College, London. Selected from King's College, London, and appointed Assistant Draughtsman, P.W. Department, Jamaica, 1873, subsequently Chief Draughtsman, District Engineer, N.W. District, 1883 ; Kingston District, 1886 ; Eastern District, 1889 ; Southern District, 1892 ; Eastern District, 1894 ; in charge of construction of mountain roads. Selected by Sec. of State and seconded 1901 to take charge of alteration and construction of Imperial Road, Dominica, in consequence of wasteful expenditure thereon ; invalided home, 1901 ; acted as Director Public Works, 1902, 1903, 1905, 1907, 1908-9, 1912-13 ; mentioned in despatches in connection with service rendered on the Relief Works after the severe hurricane of Aug. 1903 ; Assistant Director Public Works, Jamaica, 1902-14. *Publica-*

tions: Paper to Institution of Civil Engineers on the Engineering Enterprises of the Victorian Age. *Recreations:* none. *Address:* c/o Lloyd's Bank, Torquay.   (*Died 21 Nov. 1922.*)

DA FANO, Corrado Donato, M.D.; F.L.S.; F.R.M.S.; Reader in Histology, King's College, University of London, since 1922; *b.* Urbino, Italy, 1 June 1879; 3rd *s.* of Comm. Alessandro and late Adele Maroni; *m.* 1915, Dorothea Landau.   *Educ.:* Milan. Pupil in Golgi's Institute of Histology and General Pathology, University of Pavia, 1902-5; degree of M.D., University of Pavia, 1905; awarded the Fossati Prize by the Istituto Lombardo di Scienze e Lettere, 1906; Resident Physician of the Cernusco Department, Hospital of Milan, 1908: awarded the Sangalli Travelling Scholarship by the Hospital of Milan, 1908; Honorary Assistant in Ziehen's Neurological Klinik, University of Berlin, 1908; Honorary Assistant at the Imperial Cancer Research Fund, London, 1909; 1st Assistant and Prosektor of the Pathological Institute, University of Groningen, 1910; degree of L.D. (Libero Docente) in Morbid Anatomy at the University of Pavia, 1912; Vice-Director of the Pathological Institute of Milan, 1912-15; Captain, Italian R.A.M.C., in command of a Field Ambulance at the Italian Front, 1915-18 (bronze medal, Benemeriti della Salute Pubblica); Lecturer on Histology, University of London, 1918; Member of the Real Sociedad Espanola de Historia Natural; Member of the Council of the Royal Microscopical Society; Correspondent Member of the Società Medica-Chirurgica di Bologna; Co-editor of Physiological Abstracts. *Publications:* Over sixty papers on Histological, Histopathological and Histophysiological subjects published in various scientific periodicals. *Address:* Hypatia Lodge, Sheffield Terrace, W.8.   (*Died 14 Mar. 1927.*)

DAGA, Sir Dewan Bahadur Kasturchand, Rai Bahadur, K.C.I.E., *cr.* 1911; C.I.E. 1909; banker, land-owner, mill-owner, etc.; *b.* 17 Nov. 1855; *s.* of Abirchand Daga Rai Bahadur; *m.* five times; four *s.* five *d. Educ.:* home. Title of Rai Bahadur from the Bikaner State, 1880; title of Rai Bahadur from the British Government, 1887; title of Dewan Bahadur, 1903; Kaiser-i-Hind Silver Medal, 1898; Coronation Delhi Durbar Medal, 1903; Coronation Delhi Durbar Medal, 1911; Hon. Magistrate with 2nd class powers in Kamptee, C.P., 1885; 1st class powers, 1887; Chairman Nagpur Electric Light and Power Co., Ltd.; Member of Cantonment Committee, Kamptee; is a Life Member of the Central Committee of the Imperial Institute in India and a Life Councillor of the Dufferin Fund; is exempt from the Arms Act and from personal attendance in Civil Courts, also from payment of Custom duty in the Bikaner State; helped in famine works; constructed a number of tanks, wells, market and pavilion, and did good many other philanthropic works of general utility and public convenience, costing nearly 2 lacs in the British Territory and 1½ lacs in the Bikaner State. *Address:* Bikaner, Rajputana.   (*Died Jan. 1917.*)

DAGLISH, Hon. Henry; *b.* 18 Nov. 1866; *m.* 1894, Edith, *d.* of late Charles Bishop, Smythesdale, Victoria. *Educ.:* South Geelong School; Melbourne University. M.L.A. Subiaco, 1901; Premier, Western Australia, 1904-5. *Address:* Subiaco, Western Australia.   (*Died 16 Aug. 1920.*)

DALBIAC, Philip Hugh; C.B. 1911; a Director George Allen and Unwin, publishers, since 1914; *b.* 1855; 3rd *s.* of H. E. A. Dalbiac, Durrington, and Mary, *d.* of Sir H. E. A. Mainwaring, 1st Bt.; *m.* Lilian, 4th *d.* of Sir Charles Seely, 1st Bt., 1888; one *s.* four *d. Educ.:* Winchester. Joined 70th Regt. 1875; exchanged

to 45th Foot, 1875; retired as Major, 1890; M.P. (C.) North Camberwell, 1895-1900; Col. Commanding 18th Middlesex R.V. 1896-1908; raised and commanded Transport and Supply Column, 2nd Lond. Div. Territorial Forces, 1908-12; raised and commanded 60th Div. Train, 1914-17; served in France and Salonika, 1916-17 (despatches). *Publications:* Dictionary of Quotations (English), 1896; French and Italian, 1900; History of the 45th Regiment, 1902; History of the Chancellorsville and Gettysburg Campaign. *Recreations:* taken leading part in cricket, as player and organiser; was good runner and athlete generally. *Address:* Heathfield, Freshwater, Isle of Wight.   (*Died 28 April 1927.*)

DALBY, Sir William Bartlett; Kt. *cr.* 1886; Consulting Aural Surgeon St. George's Hospital; *b.* Ashby-de-la-Zouche, 10 Dec. 1840; *s.* of late Charles Allsopp Dalby and Sarah, *d.* of William Bartlett, Lymington; *m.* Hyacinthe, *d.* of late Maj. Edward Wellesley, 73rd Regiment, 1873; one *s.* three *d. Educ.:* Sidney Sussex Coll. Camb. President Medical Society, 1894-95; President of the Otological Society of the United Kingdom. *Publications:* Lectures on Diseases and Injuries of Ear; article on same subject in Holmes's System of Surgery, Quain's Dictionary of Medicine. *Recreation:* shooting. *Address:* 14 Montagu Place, Portman Square, W. *Clubs:* Athenæum, Garrick, Carlton.   (*Died 29 Dec. 1918.*)

DALDY, Frederick Francis; Barrister-at-law; Master of the Supreme Court, 1916-26; *b.* 18 Aug. 1857; *s.* of late Frederic Richard Daldy: *m.* Elizabeth Violet Frances, *d.* of late Judge Melville; two *d. Educ.:* Charterhouse; Pembroke Coll., Cambridge (M.A.). Called to the Bar, Inner Temple, 1881; joined the South-Eastern Circuit; devilled for Sir Richard E. Webster (Lord Alverstone), 1884-90; Junior Counsel to H.M. Customs and Excise, 1900; for many years in practice at the Common Law Bar; was Assistant Executive Officer to the National Rifle Association at Wimbledon and Bisley. *Address:* 12 Pembroke Road, Kensington, W.   (*Died 11 July 1928.*)

DALE, Admiral Alfred Taylor; retired; *b.* 26 Sep. 1840; *s.* of Clement Dale. Entered Navy, 1854; Captain, 1876; Rear-Adm. 1891; Vice-Adm. 1897; Admiral, 1903; served China, 1858. *Address:* 28 Sloane Court, S.W.   (*Died 14 Nov. 1925.*)

DALE, Sir Alfred (William Winterslow), Kt., *cr.* 1911; M.A. (Cantab.); LL.D. (Aberdeen, Bristol); *b.* 2 Dec. 1855; *s.* of R. W. Dale, LL.D., Birmingham; *m.* 1882, May, 2nd *d.* of William Jeeves; three *d. Educ.:* King Edward's School, Birmingham; Trinity College and Trinity Hall, Cambridge. Chancellor's medal for English poem, 1876 and 1878; Members' Prize, 1880: Hulsean Prize, 1881; Seatonian Prize, 1885, 1920. 8th Classic, 1879; Fellow of Trinity Hall, 1881; Lecturer, Bursar, and Tutor of the College, 1879-1899; Examiner in the Classical Tripos, 1883-84; Member of the Council of the Senate, and Secretary of the General Board of Studies; a university representative in the Municipal Council, Cambridge. Principal of University College, Liverpool, 1899; Vice-Chancellor University of Liverpool, 1903-19; Chairman of the Board of Studies of Victoria University, 1902-4; of Northern Universities Joint Matriculation Board, 1905-16; of Council and Board of Education, Mansfield College, Oxford; Member of the Examinations Council for Secondary Schools, 1918-9; Chairman, 1921. *Publications:* The Synod of Elvira, 1882; The Origenistic Controversies, in Smith's Dictionary of Christian Biography, 1887; Life of R. W. Dale, 1898; completed and edited History of English Congregationalism, 1907; edited Warren's Book: documents and collections relating to the foundation and history of Trinity Hall, Cambridge, 1911. *Address:* Red Lodge, Cold Ash, Newbury. *Club:* Athenæum.

(*Died 13 Aug. 1921.*)

DALE, Frank Harry, C.B. 1913 ; Chief Inspector for Elementary Schools, Board of Education, since 1911 ; *b.* 1871 ; *s.* of H. J. Dale, manufacturing electrician; *m.* Lucy, *d.* of C. H. Hanson and sister of P. Hanson. *Educ.:* St. Paul's School, London ; Balliol College, Oxford. Fellow of Merton College, Oxford, 1895 ; Junior Examiner in Board of Education, 1897 ; H.M. Inspector of Schools, 1900. *Address:* 33 Clarendon Road, Holland Park, W. ; Board of Education, Whitehall, S.W. *Club:* Royal Societies. (*Died 3 Nov. 1918.*)

DALE, Henry Sheppard, A.R.E. 1909 ; Water-Colour Painter ; *b.* 13 Nov. 1852 ; *s.* of B. H. Dale, Bank Manager, Sheffield ; *m.* 1887, Emily, *d.* of S K. Pollard, Taunton. No *c.* *Educ.:* Sheffield Grammar School. After short time at Cary's Art School, entered the Slade on its opening, 1871 ; studied in Italy, 1874-7 ; engraved aquatint plates for the coloured numbers of the Graphic, 1879-81 ; has done architectural illustrations for several books. *Publications:* portfolios of Etchings of Venice, 1881 ; Glastonbury, 1885 ; Wells, 1886 ; Salisbury, 1887 ; Exeter, 1888 ; numerous etchings. *Address:* Green Cliff Studio, Rye.

(*Died 24 Nov. 1921.*)

DALE, John Gilbert, F.R.G.S., F.Z.S. ; *s.* of James Dale and Sarah Gilbert ; *b.* Hanley, Staffs., 1869 ; *m.* Jessie May, *d.* of Bernard Collett ; two *s.* two *d.* *Educ.:* Hanley, Staffs ; Congleton, Cheshire. Contested Kennington for L.C.C. 1910 and 1913 ; Parliamentary Candidate North St. Pancras, 1918 and 1922 in Labour interest ; Labour Parliamentary Candidate for Walthamstow, East, 1923 ; First Chairman and one of Founders of National Union of Police and Prison Officers ; First President of Prison Officers Federation ; Member Society Psychical Research ; Member of Council of Industrial Christian Fellowship, also of Council of Union of Democratic Control ; Wesleyan Lay Preacher for over thirty years ; Member of Fabian Society, Independent Labour Party, etc. *Publications:* Epilepsy : its Causes, Symptoms and Treatment ; various articles Medical, Religious, Political. *Recreations:* reading, motoring, foreign travel. *Address:* 68 Holland Park, W.11. *T.:* Park 3027. *M.:* XL 4510. *Club:* Royal Societies. (*Died 6 Mar. 1926.*)

DALE, Rev. Thomas F. ; M.A., Queen's College, Oxon.; Senior Chaplain, retired, Bengal Ecclesiastical Establishment. Writes in The Field as Stoneclink ; contributor on sport and travel to various journals in England, America, and India ; Steward (resigned 1920 after 18 years' service), appointed Hon. Member of the Council of the National Pony Society ; appointed (1912) by President of Board of Agriculture and Fisheries Member of Departmental Committee on Mountain and Moorland Ponies ; acts as Official Judge for distribution Ministry of Agriculture Premiums to Mountain and Moorland Stallions in New Forest ; Joint-Sec. to Burley and District Society for Improvement of Ponies, Cattle, and Pigs since 1914 ; Chairman of Mountain and Moorland Pony Committee, 1918. *Publications:* The Game of Polo, 1897 ; Two Fortunes and Old Patch (with Slaughter), 1898; History of the Belvoir Hunt, 1899; Riding, Driving, and Kindred Sports, 1899 ; edited Polo in Badminton Series ; The 8th Duke of Beaufort and the Badminton Hunt: The Riding and Polo Pony ; Fox Hunting in The Shires, 1902 ; Polo Past and Present, 1905 ; The Fox (Fur, Fin, and Feather Series), 1906 ; The Stable Handbook, 1906 ; Arab and Colonial Horses in Sir H. de Trafford's Horses of the British Empire; editor and part author Polo at Home and Abroad.

Recreations: hunting, natural history, and reading. *Address:* Brush End, Burley, Hants. *Clubs:* Ranelagh, United University.

(*Died 15 Oct. 1923.*)

DALE, Rev. William, Secretary of Foreign Missions Committee, 1898-1915, and first Editor and then Joint-Editor of Messenger of Presbyterian Church of England, 1893-1915 ; *b.* Glasgow, 9 Oct. 1841 ; *m.* Mary Blackhall, Edinburgh, 1881 ; two *s.* three *d.* *Educ.:* Free Normal School, Glasgow ; Glasgow Univ. ; Free Church Coll., Glasgow. 2nd prize, Senior Logic Class ; 1st prize, Sen. Mathematics ; twenty guineas for essay on Intellectual Advantages of Sabbath Observance ; silver medal for essay on Hobbes ; scholarships, etc., in Free Church College. Minister of Free Church, Gordon, Berwickshire, 1868-71 ; minister of Presbyterian Church, Singapore, 1871-75 ; minister of New Barnet Presbyterian Church, 1877-1... *Publications:* Sermons (occasional) ; The Story of our Missions in the Far East ; Presbyterian Missions and the Bible Society ; The Opened Door ; Foreign Mission Reports. *Address:* New Barnet, Herts. (*Died 15 Feb. 1924.*)

DALGETY, Major Frederick John, D.L., J.P. county of Southampton ; *b.* 19 Nov. 1866 ; *s.* of late F. G. Dalgety of Lockerley Hall, Hants ; *m.* 1897, Hon. Pauline Caroline M'Clintock Bunbury, *d.* of 2nd Baron Rathdonnell ; three *s.* one *d.* *Educ.:* Eton. Late Capt. 15th Hussars ; served commencement of South African War as Adjutant Imperial Yeomanry ; served in 14th Reserve Cavalry Regt. and 3rd Reserve Hussars, 1914-19 ; *Address:* Lockerley Hall, Romsey, Hants. *T.:* Lockerley 3. *T.A.:* Lockerley. *Clubs:* Naval and Military, Wellington.

(*Died 23 May 1926.*)

DALGLIESH, Richard, C.B. 1918, J.P., D.L., Chairman, Leicesters T.F. Association ; Deputy Chairman, Quarter Sessions ; Chairman Leicestershire County Council ; *b.* 1844 ; *s.* of D. Dalgliesh, Carsethorne, Dumfries ; *m.* 1867, Mary, *d.* of late John Pearson, High Sheriff, 1907. *Address:* Asfordby Place, Melton Mowbray. (*Died 16 Oct. 1927.*)

DALHOUSIE, 14th Earl of (cr. 1633), Arthur George Maule Ramsay, D.L.; Baron Ramsay, 1619 ; Lord Ramsay, 1633 ; Baron Ramsay (U.K.), 1875 ; Lieut. Reserve of Officers ; *b.* 4 Sep. 1878 ; *s.* of 13th Earl and Ida, *d.* of 6th Earl of Tankerville ; *S.* father, 1887 ; *m.* 1903, Lady Mary Adelaide Heathcote Drummond Willoughby, *d.* of 1st Earl of Ancaster ; two *s.* two *d.* Late Forfar and Kincardine Artillery Militia ; late Capt. Scots Guards ; served S. Africa, 1901-2 ; European War. Owns about 138,000 acres. *Heir: s.* Lord Ramsay. *Address:* Brechin Castle, also Panmure House, Carnoustie, Forfarshire ; Dalhousie Castle, Bonnyrigg, Midlothian ; 82 Eaton Square, S.W.1. (*Died 23 Dec. 1928.*)

DALLAS, Hon. Francis Henry, late Member of Council of Rajah of Sarawak, and Treasurer of independent State of Sarawak ; *b.* Heworth. nr. York, 1865 ; *y. s.* of William Sweetland Dallas, F.L.S., C.M.Z.S., writer on Zoological subjects, and Frances Esther, *y. d.* of Liscombe Price, Solicitor, London and Abergavenny ; *m.* 1889, Ethel Jane, *y. d.* of Charles Santley, and Gertrude, *e. d.* of John Mitchell Kemble. Formerly editor of Sarawak Gazette. *Address:* The Borneo Co. Ltd., 79 Fenchurch Street, E.C. 3. *Club:* Sports.

(*Died 10 Mar. 1920.*)

DALLAS, Sir George Edward, 3rd Bt.; *cr.* 1798 ; late Chief Clerk of the Foreign Office ; *b.* London, 9 Oct. 1842 ; *e. s.* of 2nd Bt. and Frances, *d.* of 1st Baron Ellenborough ; *m.* Felicia, *d.* of Rev. Canon Welby, Bar. by, Grantham, 1884 ; *S.* father 1874. *Educ.:* Eton ; Heidelberg ; Dresden ; Paris.

Appointed Clerk in Foreign Office, 1863. *Heir :* none. *Address :* 36 Eaton Square, S.W. *Clubs :* Travellers', Wellington.   (*Died 27 Nov. 1918.*)

DALMAHOY, Maj.-Gen. Patrick Carfrae, Bengal Infantry ; *b.* 7 Sep. 1840 ; *m.* 1868, Emily (*d.* 1925), *d.* of Edward Wylly ; one *s.*   Entered Army, 1856 ; Major-General, 1890 ; unemployed supernumerary list, 1890 ; served Indian Mutiny (siege of Delhi), 1857-59 (medal with clasp), and Campaign in Bundelkund, 1858-60. *Address :* 13 Buckingham Terrace, Edinburgh. *Clubs :* New, Edinburgh ; Royal and Ancient, St. Andrews.
(*Died 24 Dec. 1926.*)

DALMAHOY, Patrick Carfrae, D.S.O. 1902 ; Magistrate ; *b.* 31 Oct. 1872 ; *s.* of late Maj.-Gen. Patrick Carfrae Dalmahoy ; *m.* Mabel Houstoun, *d.* of late W. H. Rogers of Johannesburg ; one *s.* four *d..* *Educ. :* Haileybury ; Edinburgh University. Writer to the Signet, Edinburgh, 1896 ; served with C.I.V. (M.I.) in South Africa ; gazetted to 1st Batt. The Royal Scots, 1900, and served with them till the end of the war (twice wounded, despatches, D.S.O.); resigned commission, 1903. *Recreation :* golf. *Address :* Magistrate, Benoni, Transvaal, S.A. ; 13 Buckingham Terrace Edinburgh. *Clubs :* University, Edinburgh ; Royal and Ancient, St. Andrews ; Rand, Johannesburg.
(*Died 11 Nov. 1928.*)

DALRYMPLE, Rt. Hon. Sir Charles, 1st Bt., *cr.* 1887 ; P.C. 1905 ; M.A., D.L., LL.D. (hon.); *b.* Kilkerran, Ayrshire, 15 Oct. 1839 ; 2nd *s.* of Sir Charles Dalrymple Fergusson, 5th Bt., and Helen, *d.* of Rt. Hon. D. Boyle, Lord Just.-Gen. of Scotland ; *m.* Alice Mary, 2nd *d.* of Sir E. Hunter-Blair, 4th Bt. (*d.* 1884) ; one *s.* two *d.* *Educ. :* Harrow ; Trin. Coll. Camb. Barr. 1865 ; M.P. Bute, 1868-85 ; opposed Mr. Gladstone in Mid-lothian, 1885 ; M.P. (C.) Ipswich, 1886-1906 ; member Cathedral Establishments Commission, 1879-85 ; Reformatories and Industrial Schools Commission, 1882-83 ; Vaccination Commission, 1890-96 ; Scottish Univs. Commission, 1889-96 ; Grand Master Mason of Scotland, 1893-96. *Heir :* *s.* David Charles Herbert, late Lieut. R.N. [*b.* 29 Mar. 1879 ; *m.* 1906, Margaret Anna, *d.* of Sir M. Mactaggart Stewart, Bt. ;   one *d.*]. *Address :* Newhailes, Musselburgh, N.B. *T.A. :* Fisherrow. *Clubs :* Athenæum ; New, Edinburgh ; Western, Glasgow, etc.
(*Died 20 June 1916.*)

DALRYMPLE, Hon. David Hay, Member of Senate, Queensland Univ., since 1910 ; *b.* Newbury, Dec. 1840. *Educ. :* Independent College, Taunton ; Bristol Medical School. Went Australia, 1862 ; M.L.A., Mackay, 1888-1904 ; Secretary for Public Instruction, 1895-99, and 1902-3 ; Public Works, 1896-98 ; Public Lands, 1899 ; member of Executive Council, 1899-1901 ; Sec. for Agriculture, 1901-3. *Address :* Dalry, Crescent Road, Hamilton, Brisbane.
(*Died 31 Aug. 1912.*)

DALRYMPLE, Sir Walter Hamilton-, 8th Bt.; *cr.* 1697 ; J.P., D.L. ; *b.* 6 Jan. 1854 ; *S.* father 1888 ; *m.* 1882, Alice, *d.* of Maj.-Gen. Hon. Sir H. H. Clifford, V.C. ; one *s.* three *d.* Owns about 8100 acres. *Heir :* *s.* Hew Clifford [*b.* 11 Aug. 1888 ; *m.* 1919, Dorothea Dyce Nicol, *y. d.* of late Augustus Thorne]. *Seat :* Luchie, North Berwick. *Address :* Villa della Pergola, Alassio, Italy. *Club :* New, Edinburgh.
(*Died 29 Nov. 1920.*)

DALTON, Sir Cornelius Neale, K.C.M.G., *cr.* 1908 ; C.B. ; hon. D.C.L., Oxford ; *b.* 9 March 1842 ; 3rd *s.* of late Rev. John Neale Dalton, M.A., Rector of Milton Keynes, Bucks ; *m.* Margaret, *d.* of late Frederick Gaskell, Chelsea, 1873. *Educ. :* Blackheath Proprietary School ; Trin. Coll. Camb. Scholar, 2nd class Classics. Barr. Inner Temple, 1871 ; entered Civil Service, 1873 ; became Assist.-Sec. to the Local Govt. Board, 1882 : was a member of the Royal Commissions
260

on Tithe Redemption (1891-92), Agriculture (1893-97), and Local Taxation (1896-1901); British Delegate to the International Conference at Brussels for protection of industrial property, 1897 and 1900 ; Comptroller-General of Patents, Designs, and Trade Marks 1897-1909 ; Chairman of the East London College Council. *Publications :* The Real Captain Kidd, 1911 ; The Life of Thomas Pitt, 1915. *Address :* 57 Belsize Avenue, N.W.3. *T. :* Hampstead 3055.
(*Died 19 Oct. 1920.*)

DALTON, Frederick Thomas, M.. *b.* 29 Oct. 1855 ; *s.* of late Rev. Chart.. Browne Dalton, vicar of Highgate, and Mary Frances, *d.* of Charles James Blomfield, Bishop of London ; *m.* 1st, 1895, Mary Edna (*d.* 1922), *d.* of late Rev. H. G. Evans, headmaster of King Edward VI.'s School, Stratford-on-Avon ; 2nd, 1924, Mary Davenport, *d.* of late Rev. C. H. Rice, Rector of Cheam. *Educ. :* Highgate School ; Corpus Christi College, Oxford (Scholar): 1st class Classical Mods. 1876 ; 2nd class Lit. Hum. 1878 ; Ellerton Prize, 1879 ; Chancellor's English Essay, 1880. Assistant master Radley College, 1879-86 ; kept terms as student at Lincoln's Inn, and subsequently qualified for admission as a solicitor ; joined the staff of The Times, 1893 ; retired, 1923 ; assistant editor of Literature, 1897 ; editor of Literature, 1900-1. *Recreations :* drawing and sketching from Nature. *Address :* Sunningwell, Sandfield Road, Headington. *Club :* Athenæum.
(*Died 11 Nov. 1927.*)

DALTON, Rev. Herbert Andrew, D.D.; *b.* Lambeth Rectory, 18 May 1852 ; *s.* of late Rev. Charles Browne Dalton, Vicar of Highgate, Prebendary of St. Paul's, and Mary Frances, *d.* of Charles James Blomfield, Bishop of London ; *m.* Mabel Selina, *d.* of Capt. Charles Simeon, 1879 ; four *d.* *Educ. :* Highgate School ; Corpus Christi Coll., Oxford. Scholar C.C.C. Oxford, 1871 ; 1st class Classical Mods. 1873 ; 1st class Final School of Lit. Hum. 1875. Senior Student, Christ Church, Oxford, 1875-78 ; Headmaster St. Edward's School, Oxford, 1877-84 ; Assistant Master Winchester College, 1884-90 ; Member Essex Education Committee representing Oxford University, 1903-6 ; Headmaster Felsted School, 1890-1906 ; Headmaster Harrison Coll., Barbados, 1906-22 ; Canon of Barbados Cathedral, 1918-22. *Publications :* editor Select Epodes and Ars Poetica of Horace, 1884 ; Helps to Self-Examination for Boys in Public Schools, 1892 ; essay on Education in Church Problems, 1900. *Recreation :* croquet. *Address :* 37 Milner Road, Merton, S.W.19. *Club :* Oxford and Cambridge.
(*Died 18 May 1928.*)

DALTON, Norman, M.D., F.R.C.P.; Fellow King's College, London ; Senior Physician to King's College Hospital; late Professor of Pathological Anatomy in King's College, London; Lecturer on Medicine, King's College Medical School ; late Examiner in Medicine, University of London ; Physician to the National Provident Institution ; Medical Officer to the London branch of the Scottish Union and National Insurance Company ; Lt.-Col. R.A.M.C. (T.) ; *s.* of E. T. E. Dalton, of Demerara, British Guiana. *Educ. :* Queen's Coll., British Guiana ; Christ's College, Finchley ; King's Coll., London. *Publications :* A Method of ascertaining the Position and Size of the Stomach by means of the X-rays and a tube filled with Subnitrate of Bismuth ; Influenza in relation to the Digestive Organs ; Transactions Clinical Society, 1905. *Address :* 35 Nottingham Place, W.1. *T. :* Mayfair 3976.
(*Died 9 Mar. 1923.*)

D'ALVIELLA, Count Goblet, LL.D. ; Philos. D. : Belgian Minister of State ; Member and late Vice-President, Belgian Senate ; Member of the Belgian Cabinet during the War ; Professor, University of Brussels ; Grand Officer Ordre de Léopold ; Grand-Cordon Order of

Medjidie; and Order of the Crown of Italy; Grand Cross of the Belgian Order of the Crown; Grand Cordon of the French Legion of Honour; war medal of King Albert; *b.* Brussels, 10 August 1846; *m.* 1879, Margaret Alice Packard, Albany, New York; one *s.* one *d. Educ.:* Brussels and Paris. Member of the Belgian Bar since 1870; Member and late President Royal Academy of Belgium; Member of the Royal Asiatic Society of Great Britain; hon. member of the Oxford Soc. of Historical Theology; Hon. LL.D. Univ. of Glasgow and of Aberdeen; former M.P. for Brussels. Late Rector of Brussels Univ.; Hibbert Lecturer at Oxford, 1891; late Envoy-Extraordinary to Constantinople and to Rome; long time director of the Revue de Belgique. *Publications:* Sahara and Lapland, 1874; Inde et Himalaya, 1877, 2nd ed. 1880; Contemporary Evolution of Religious Thought in England, America, and India, 1885; Hibbert Lectures, 1892; The Migration of Symbols, 1894; Ce que l'Inde doit à la Grèce, 1897; Eleusinia : de quelques problèmes relatifs aux Mystères d'Eleusis, 1903; A travers le Far West, souvenirs des Etats-Unis 1906; l'Université de Bruxelles pendant son troisième quart de siècle, 1909; Croyances, Rites, Institutions (3 vols.), 1911; The True and the False Pacifism, 1917; publications in French. *Address:* 10 rue Faider, Brussels. *(Died 8 Sept. 1925.)*

DALY, Ven. Henry Varian, M.A.; Rector of Gort since 1874; Archdeacon of Clonfert since 1881; Archdeacon of Kilmacduagh since 1891; Member of General Synod since 1882; Member of Committee of Patronage since 1882; Secretary of Diocesan Council since 1869; Member of Representative Church Body, 1915; *b.* 20 July 1838; *e. s.* of late Joseph Daly of The Altar, Co. Cork; *m.* 1st, 1865, Anne Mary, *e. d.* of late Robert James Burkitt, A.M., M.B., of Waterford; three *s.* two *d.*; 2nd, 1879, Elizabeth Alice, *d.* of Rev. W. St. George, late Rector of Bryansford, Co. Down; two *s.* three *d. Educ.:* Diocesan College, Rosscarbery, Co. Cork; Trinity College, Dublin (M.A.). Ordained 1861; Curate of St. Patrick's, Waterford, 1861-65; Ballinasloe, 1866-72; Killinane, 1872-74; Canon of Clonfert, 1872-81. *Recreations:* chess and reading. *Address:* Deanery, Gort, Co. Galway. *T.A.:* Gort. *(Died 3 June 1925.)*

DALY, Hon. Sir Malachy Bowes, K.C.M.G., *cr.* 1900; Lieut.-Gov. of the Province of Nova Scotia, Canada, 1890-1900; *b.* Quebec, 6 Feb. 1836; *s.* of late Sir Dominick Daly of County Galway, Ireland, and Caroline Maria, *d.* of Colonel Ralph Gore of Banowmount, Co. Kilkenny, Ireland; *m.* Joanna, 2nd *d.* of late Sir Edward Kenny; one *d. Educ.:* St. Mary's College. Oscott (R.C.), near Birmingham, England. Barrister-at-law; Private Secretary to Sir D. Daly, Lieut.-Gov. of Prince Edward Island, and to Sir R. G. Macdonnell and Sir W. Fenwick Williams, while Governors of Nova Scotia; M.P. (Canada), Halifax, N.S., 1878-86; Deputy Speaker, House of Commons, Canada, 1882-86. *Recreations:* cricket, salmon fishing. *Address:* Halifax, Nova Scotia. *Club:* Halifax. *(Died 26 April 1920.)*

DALY, Col. Thomas, C.M.G. 1917; R.A.M.C., L.R.C.P.I. and L.M., L.R.C.S.I.; served N.W. Frontier, India, 1897-8 (medal with clasp); S. Africa, 1899-1902 (Queen's and King's medals, 5 clasps); European War, 1914-17 (C.M.G.) *Address:* c/o Holt & Co., 3 Whitehall Place, S.W. *(Died 15 April 1917.)*

DALYELL, Lt.-Gen. John Thomas, Colonel Royal Scots Fusiliers; *b.* 22 July 1827; *m.* Constance Louisa (*d.* 1913), *d.* of Rt. Rev. Thomas Parry, Bishop of Barbados. Entered army, 1847; Major-General, 1883; retired, 1886, served Crimea, 1854-55 (medal with three clasps Turkish medal, 5th class Medjidie, brevet Major), *Address:* 10 Merchiston Crescent, Edinburgh. *(Died July 1919.)*

DALZELL, Reginald Alexander, C.B. 1924; C.B.E.: Director of Telegraphs and Telephones, 1922-27; retired; *b.* Poona, Bombay, 1865; *s.* of late N. A. Dalzell, M.A., Conservator of Woods and Forests; *m.* Katherine Ann, *d.* of late James Livingston, Edinburgh; one *d. Educ.:* Dulwich College. Entered Telephone service, 1881; Provincial Superintendent for the West of England under the National Telephone, 1906-12; Chief Inspector, Telegraph and Telephone Traffic, General Post Office, 1916-22. *Recreation:* golf. *Address:* 1 Cleveland Road, Ealing W. 13. *T.:* Ealing 1512. *(Died 27 Nov. 1928.)*

DALZIEL, 1st Baron, *cr.* 1927; of Wooler; **Davison Dalziel,** Bt., *cr.* 1919; M.P. (C.), Brixton Division, Lambeth, 1910-23, 1924-27; Chairman Pullman Car Company; President Board of Directors and Managing Committee International Sleeping Car Co.; Officier Legion of Honour; Commander Crown of Italy; first introduced motor cabs into London; *b.* 1854; *m.* 1876, Harriet, *d.* of J. Godfrey Dunning. *Recreation:* yachting. *Heir:* none.
(Died 18 April 1928.)

DALZIEL, Sir Kennedy, Kt., *cr.* 1917; J.P., M.B., C.M.; F.R.F.P.S. Glas.; Lt.-Col. late R.A.M.C.(T.); Surgeon; Surg. to Western Infirmary and Consult. Surg. to Glasgow and S.W. Railway; *b.* Merkland, Penpont, Dumfriesshire, 25 Oct. 1861; *m.* Margaret, *d.* of John Waddell of Inch, Bathgate; two *s.* three *d. Educ.:* Dumfries Private School; Edinburgh University; Berlin; Vienna. House Surgeon to Glasgow Royal Infirmary; joined Staff of Western Infirmary in 1899, and Royal Hospital for Sick Children, 1891; Senior Surgeon of latter institution, and retired 1914; Casualty Surgeon in Central Division of Glasgow, 1885-1894; Late Professor of Medical Jurisprudence and Public Health, and also of Surgery in Anderson's College; Lecturer on Anatomy in Western Medical School; late Examiner in Final Examination, Glasgow University, and Royal Faculty of Physicians and Surgeons. *Publications:* numerous contributions to medical literature. *Recreations:* shooting, fishing, golf. *Address:* 196 Bath Street, Glasgow; Nether Kinnedder, Oakley, Fife. *Clubs:* Art, Automobile, Glasgow.
(Died 10 Feb. 1924.)

DAMANT, Lt.-Col. Frederick Hugh, C.B. 1902; D.S.O. 1901; Resident Magistrate for District of Lydenburg, Transvaal; *b.* District of King Williamstown, S. Africa, 1864; *y. s.* of Hugh Atherstone Damant. Served S. Africa, 1899-1902; commanded Rimington's Scouts; promoted Lieut.-Col.; in a desperate struggle with 800 Boers he received five bullet wounds, but succeeded in saving the guns entrusted to his charge (D.S.O.); later he took part in operations in Western Transvaal until the cessation of hostilities. *Address:* Lydenburg, Transvaal.
(Died 13 Oct. 1926.)

DANBY, Frank (Mrs. Julia Frankau); *b.* 30 July 1864; father an artist; *m.* 1883, Arthur Frankau (*d.* 1904), merchant; three *s.* one *d. Educ.:* at home by Mme. Paul Lafargue, *e. d.* of Karl Marx. Began work with dilettante journalism; wrote for Saturday Review, etc. *Publications:* Dr. Phillips, a Maida Vale Idyll, 1887; A Babe in Bohemia, 1889; abandoned novel writing for a few years in favour of studying engraving; after 10 years wrote Eighteenth Century Colour Prints, 1900; Life of John Raphæl Smith, 1902; The Lives of James and William Ward, 1904; relapsed into novel writing and published Pigs in Clover, 1902; Baccarat, 1904; The Sphinx's Lawyer, 1906; A Coquette in Crape, 1907; The Heart of a Child, 1908; An Incomplete Etonian, 1909; Let the Roof Fall In, 1910; The Story of Emma, Lady Hamilton, 1910; Joseph in Jeopardy, 1912; Concert Pitch, 1913; Full Swing, 1914; Nelson's Legacy, 1915; The Story behind the Verdict, 1915. Re-

261

DALY, John Archer Blake-, J.P., D.L.   See page xxxii.

creations · needlework, bridge. *Address:* 64 Grosvenor Street, W. *(Died 17 Mar. 1916.)*

DANE, Lt.-Col. James Auchinleck, D.S.O. 1917; 84th East Anglian Field Brig., R.F.A.; D.L.; *b.* 18 May 1883; *s.* of late Judge Richard Martin Dane, K.C.; *m.* 1909, Elgiva Mary Kathorn Wentworth Fitz-william; two *s.* one *d. Educ.:* Portora Royal School, Enniskillen; Trinity College, Dublin; R.M Academy. Joined R.A., 1902; Special Reserve, 1910; served with B.E.F. France, Aug. 1914-May 1918; (wounded, April 1918; despatches thrice; D.S.O.). *Recreation* hunting. *Address:* Harpley Lodge, King's Lynn, Norfolk. *T.:* Great Massingham 10. *T.A.:* Dane, Houghton - Norfolk. *Club:* Royal Automobile. *(Died 20 Jan. 1927.)*

DANGAR, Rev. James George, V.D., D.D.; Rector of Washfield, Tiverton; Hon. Chaplain in the Terr. Force; Officier d'Académie (France); late Principal of the Exeter Diocesan Train. Coll. 1869-1906; Prebend. of Exeter Cathedral; *b.* London, 20 Nov. 1841; *s.* of late Jas. Dangar; *m.* Elizabeth, *d.* of Daniel Shilson of Launceston, Cornwall; one *s.* one *d. Educ.:* St. John's Coll., Oxford. (School Exhibitioner and Lord Camden's Mathematical medallist); Latin Prose Prizeman; Double Honorary 4th, 1864. Ordained to Curacy of Stoke Climsland, Cornwall, 1864; Vicar of Boyton, Cornwall, 1866-69; Formerly Bodleian Lecturer in Exeter, and University Examiner for the Oxford Local Examination; Vice-President Exeter Diocesan Board of Education; *Publications:* Hon. Editor of the Exeter Diocesan Calendar; Notes on the Metric System; Text-book on Mental Arithmetic. *Address:* Washfield Rectory, Tiverton. *(Died 31 July 1917.)*

DANIEL, Rev. Charles Henry Olive, D.D.; Provost of Worcester College, Oxford; late Fellow Bursar, and Chaplain; formerly Tutor; Fellow of King's College, London; Alderman; *e. s.* of Rev. Alfred Daniel and Eliza Anne, *d.* of Clement Wilson Cruttwell; *m.* Emily, 3rd *d.* of Edmund Crabb Oliva. *Educ.:* King's College, London; Worcester College, Oxford. 2nd class Mod.; 1st class Lit. Hum. 1858; Classical Moderator, 1864-65; Classical Examiner, 1876-77; Proctor, 1873. Classical Lecturer and Censor of King's College, 1859-63. *Publication:* History of Worcester College. *Recreation:* private press. *Address:* Worcester College, Oxford. *(Died 6 Sept. 1919.)*

DANIEL, Rev. Wilson Eustace, Prebendary and Sub-Dean of Wells Cathedral; *b.* 1841; 3rd *s.* of Rev. Alfred Daniel, Frome; *m.* 1st, O. Gertrude Godfrey of Stow Bedon; 2nd, Mary Nevins Martin, Summit, New Jersey; two *s.* three *d. Educ.:* King's College, London; Worcester College, Oxford. 2nd class Lit. Hum. 1864, Denyer and Johnson Scholar, 1866; Grinfield Lecturer on Septuagint, 1880-1903; Chaplain of Worcester College, 1865; Curate, St. Mark's, Whitechapel, 1866; All Saints', Oxford, 1868; Vicar, Holy Trinity, Frome, 1875; East Pennard, 1890; Horsington, Somerset, 1897-1922; Merston, 1911-16. *Publication:* Parish Register of Horsington. *Address:* Ansford Lodge, Castle Cary, Somerset. *(Died 15 Feb. 1924.)*

DANIELL, Major Francis Edward Lloyd, D.S.O. 1915; Seaforth Highlanders; *b.* 19 Dec. 1874. Entered army, 1895; Captain, 1901; Adjutant, 1902-6; Major, 1913; Brigade-Major. India, 1909-11; General Staff Officer, 2nd grade, India, 1911-13; served Nile Expedition, 1898 (despatches); S. African War, 1899-1901 (Queen's medal, 4 clasps); N.W. Frontier, India, 1908 (medal with clasp); European War. 1914-15 (D.S.O.). *(Died 4 Mar. 1916.)*

DANIELS, Charles Wilberforce, M.B. Camb.; F.R.C.P.; *s.* of late Rev. T. Daniels, Manchester. *Educ.:* Manchester Grammar

262

School; Trinity College, Cambridge; London Hospital. Formerly Medical Services, Fiji, British Guiana; Member of Royal Society Malaria Commission, India and Central Africa; Director Institute Medical Research, Kuala Lumpur, Federated Malay States; Director London School of Tropical Medicine; Consulting Physician to Albert Dock Hospital, E.; Lecturer on Tropical Diseases, London School of Tropical Medicine, London Hospital, London School of Medicine for Women, St. George's Hospital; retired. *Publications:* Laboratory Studies in Tropical Medicine; Tropical Medicine and Hygiene; various reports. *Recreations:* golf, fishing. *Address:* 283 Wanstead Park Road, Ilford. *(Died 6 Aug. 1927.)*

DANKS, Sir Aaron Turner, Kt., *cr.* 1925; Managing Director John Danks & Son Pty. Ltd.; *b.* South Melbourne, 1861; *s.* of late John Danks, Melbourne; *m.* 1887 *d.* of F. G. Miles, late Town Clerk of South Melbourne. *Educ.:* Wesley College; Horton College, Tasmania. President Melbourne Hospital since 1918; a Past President of the Melbourne Metropolitan Hospital Association, and Chairman of the Walter and Eliza Hall Research Institute. *Address:* Hazeldene, Balwyn Road, Canterbury, Victoria, Australia. *(Died 4 June 1928.)*

DANKS, Ven. William, M.A., Canon of Canterbury, 1907; Archdeacon of Richmond, 1894; *b.* Nottingham, 3 Sept. 1845; *y. s.* of Thomas Danks, Sherwood Rise, and Mary Anne Wheatcroft, Wingfield Park, Derbyshire; *m.* Helena, *y. d.* of Thomas Manlove, The Park, Nottingham, 1869; one *s.* two *d. Educ.:* Queen's Coll. Oxford. Ordained to New Basford Curacy, Nottingham, 1868; Vicar St. Margaret's, Ilkley, 1884; Rural Dean of South Craven, 1886; Select Preacher at Cambridge, 1888; Rector of Richmond, Yorkshire, and Rural Dean of Richmond West, 1890; Hon. Canon of Ripon, 1891; Canon, 1896-1907; Select Preacher at Oxford, 1909. *Publications:* The Church on the Moor, Sermons, 1886; Canterbury described, 1910; Memorials of the Cathedral and Priory of Christ in Canterbury, 1912. *Address:* Canterbury. *(Died 4 April 1916.)*

DANSON, Sir Francis Chatillon, Kt., *cr.* 1920; J.P., F.S.A., F.S.S.; senior partner of F. C. Danson and Co., of Liverpool and London, average adjusters; Representative of the Board of Trade on the Liverpool and London War Risks Insurance Association, Ltd., since the outbreak of the War; Member of Admiralty Transport Arbitration Board since 1914; Member of the Mersey Docks and Harbour Board; Chairman of Liverpool Institute Schools; Governor of Sedbergh School, 1909-14; Chairman of Liverpool School of Tropical Medicine, and Chairman of Liverpool Shipwreck and Humane Society; Member of Council of Liverpool Chamber of Commerce and Institute of Archaeology; Member of the International Law Assoc.; Member of the Tidal Institute; *b.* Barnston, Cheshire, 1855; *s.* of John Towne Danson, barrister-at-law; *m.* 1888, Edith, *o. d.* of William Norman Rudolf, of Liverpool, shipowner; one *s.* one *d. Educ.:* Liverpool College; Paris. Pres. of the Liverpool Chamber of Commerce, 1896-99; Chairman of the Conservative Party in Birkenhead, 1899-1904; Chairman of the Association of Average Adjusters of Great Britain, 1892; High Sheriff of Westmorland, 1914-15; President Liverpool Philomathic Society, 1913-14; member of Council of University of Liverpool, 1903-18. *Recreations:* motoring and collecting books and antiquities. *Address:* Rosewarne, Bidston Road, Birkenhead; *T.:* Birkenhead 616; Dry Close, Grasmere, Westmorland. *M.:* CM 4868, FY 1030. *Clubs:* Burlington Fine Arts, British Empire; University, Conservative, Exchange, Liverpool. *(Died 3 July 1926.)*

DARBISHIRE, Charles William; M.P. (L.) Westbury Division of Wiltshire since

1922; *b.* London, 17 June 1875; *s.* of Col. C. H. Darbishire, J.P., D.L., of Plas Mawr, Penmaenmawr, and Mary Lilian, *d.* of late William Eckersley; *m.* 1905, Frances Middleton, *d.* of late Sheriff Davidson, Fort-William. *Educ.:* Giggleswick. East India Merchant; one of the Managing Directors of Paterson, Simons & Co., Ltd., of London, Straits Settlements, and Federated Malay States; Member Municipal Commission of Singapore, 1908-10; Unofficial Member of Legislative Council of the St. aits Settlements, 1910-19; Member Singapore Harbour Board, 1910-19; Chairman Singapore Chamber of Commerce, 1914-19; Artists' Rifles, 1897-99; Lieut. Royal Welch Fusiliers (T.F.), 1905-8; O.C. (Temp. Major) Singapore Volunteer Rifles, 1914-19; Singapore Mutiny operations, Feb. - March, 1915; President, Association of British Malaya, 1921-22. *Publication:* article on Commerce and Currency in One Hundred Years of Singapore, 1919. *Recreations:* lawn tennis, golf, shooting. *Address:* Elms Cross, Bradford-on-Avon; Queen Anne's Mansions, S.W.1. *Clubs:* Reform, National Liberal, City of London, Queen's; West Wilts Golf.   (*Died 5 June 1925.*)

DARBOUX, Jean Gaston. Secrétaire perpétuel de l'Académie des Sciences, Paris; Membre du Bureau des Longitudes; Professeur de Géométrie supérieure à l'Université; *b.* Nîmes, 13 Aug. 1842; *m.*; one *s.* one *d.* *Educ.:* Lycée de Nîmes; l'Ecole Normale Supérieure de Paris. Maître de Conférences à l'Ecole Normale Supérieure; professeur à la Sorbonne; membre de l'Académie des Sciences, 1884; membre étranger des Sociétiés Royales de Londres, Edimbourg et Dublin, de la Royal Institution; correspondant des Académies de Berlin, Petrograd, Rome, Washington, Vienne, etc. *Publications:* nombreux mémoires d'analyse mathématique; 6 à 7 volumes sur la Géométrie infinitésimile. *Address:* 3 rue Mazarine, Palais de l'Institut, Paris.   (*Died Feb. 1917.*)

DARBY, Very Rev. John Lionel, D.D., Dean of Chester since 1886; *b.* Ireland, 20 Nov. 1831; *y. s.* of Rev. Christopher Darby; *m.* Cecilia C., *d.* of Rev. Canon and Lady Ellinor Hopwood, 1871; three *s.* two *d.* *Educ.:* St. Columba's Coll.; Trin. Coll. Dublin. Assistant Curate, Winwick, Lancashire, 1856; Assistant Curate, Mells, Somerset, 1858; Incumbent of Newburgh, Lancashire, 1859-68; Assistant Curate, Kells, Ireland, 1868-70; Assistant Curate, Southam, 1870; Diocesan Inspector for Diocese of Chester, 1871-75; Archbishop's Inspector of Training Colleges, 1875-95; Rector of St. Bridget's, Chester, 1875-86; Archdeacon of Chester, 1877-86; Hon. Canon, 1873-85; Canon Residentiary, 1885-86. *Recreations:* microscope; telescope. *Address:* The Deanery, Chester.   (*Died 5 Nov. 1919.*)

DARBY, William Evans, B.D., S.T.D., LL.D., D.D., Vice-President Peace Society, Secretary, 1888-1915; *b.* Laugharne, Carmarthenshire, 1844; *e. s.* of Evan Darby, Saundersfoot; *m.* 1868, Sarah, *y. d.* of Joseph, Marshall, Hertford; three *s.* *d.* *Educ.:* Tenby; New College, Hampstead; London University. Ordained as Congregational Minister, 1869; Secretary, Preacher, Lecturer, Writer; Vice-President of the International Law Association; **Manager of the London Institution; Member** of the International Peace Bureau, Berne; of the Grotius Society, etc; Joint Secretary of the Universal Peace Congresses at London, 1890; Chicago, 1893; Glasgow and London, 1908. *Publications:* Fiction; Out of the Depths; Walter Vaughan; Worth the Winning, etc.; Sermon Notes on Peace Topics; International Tribunals, Modern Pacific Settlements; Proved Practicability of International Arbitration; Numerous Papers and Publications on International Law, Arbitration, and the

Peace Question generally; The Christ Method of Peace-making; History of Hague Peace Conferences, etc. *Address:* Jesmond, Norfolk Road, Seven Kings, Essex. *Club:* National Liberal.   (*Died Nov. 1922.*)

D'ARCY, William Knox; *b.* 11 Oct. 1849; *s.* of William Francis of Newton Abbott, Devon, and Elizabeth Baker, *d.* of late Rev. Robert Bradford of Wolborough, Devon; *m.* 1st, 1872, Elena (*d.* 1897), *d.* of S. B. Birkbeck of Glenmore Queensland; 2nd, Nina, *d.* of A. L. Boucicault of Queensland. *Educ.:* Westminster School. In Queensland, Australia, where he followed legal, pastoral, and mining pursuits, 1866-1889; returned to England, 1889. *Recreations:* shooting and golf. *Address:* 42 Grosvenor Square, W.; Stanmore Hall, Middlesex; Bylaugh Park, East Dereham, Norfolk   *Clubs:* Carlton, Garrick, Wellington.   (*Died 1 May 1917.*)

DARE, Adm. Sir Charles Holcombe, K.C.M.G., *cr.* 1919; C.B. 1917; M.V.O. 1904; *b.* 9 Nov. 1854. Entered Navy, 1868; Commander, 1894; Captain, 1900; retired, 1915; Adm. retired, 1918. *Address:* Hill House, Erwarton, Ipswich.   (*Died 6 Aug. 1924.*)

DARELL, Sir Lionel Edward, 5th Bt. of Richmond Hill, Surrey; *cr.* 1795; J.P., D.L., C.C.; late Capt. Roy. Gloucestershire Y.C.; Pres. Gloucester Conservative Club and Gloucester Club; High Sheriff, 1887-88; *b.* 6 Sept. 1845; *S.* father 1883; *m.* Helen Frances, *o. c.* of late Edward Marsland, Henbury Park, Cheshire 1870; three *s.* five *d.* *Educ.:* Christ Church, Oxford. Late President Conservative Club. *Recreations:* hunting, shooting, etc. *Heir: s.* Lionel Edward Hamilton Marmaduke [*b.* 2 Apr. 1876; Capt. 1st Life Guards; *m.* 1903, Eleanor, *d.* of Capt. J. H. Edwards-Heathcote of Apedale, Staffs; two *d.* *Educ.:* Eton; Christ Church, Oxford.] *Address:* 39 Upper Grosvenor Street, W.; Fretherne Court, Gloucestershire. *T.:* 2 Saul. *M.:* AD 155   *Clubs:* Carlton, Junior Carlton, Orleans.   (*Died 17 Feb. 1919.*)

DARLEY, Cecil West, I.S.O., M.inst.C.E.; late Inspecting and Consulting Engineer to New South Wales Government; *b.* 1842; 4th *s.* of late Henry Darley, Wingfield, Co. Wicklow; *m.* 1st, 1877, Rosanne (*d.* 1878), *d.* of late E. C. Close, Merpeth, N.S.W.; 2nd, 1885, Leila, *d.* of late Hon. Alex. Campbell, M.L.C., Rosemount, Sydney; two *s.* one *d.* *Educ.:* King William's Coll., Isle of Man; privately. Resident Engineer, Harbour Works, Newcastle, N.S.W., 1867; Principal Assist. Engineer, Harbour and River Dept., 1881; Engineer-in-Chief for Harbours and Rivers, 1889; Engineer-in-Chief for Public Works, N.S.W., 1896; President of the Metropolitan W.S. and S. Board, 1892. *Address:* Longheath, Bookham, Surrey. *T.:* 27 Bookham. *Clubs:* Overseas; Australian (Hon. Life Member), Sydney   (*Died 18 Oct. 1928.*)

DARLING, Frank, LL.D. (Hon.), University of Toronto, 1916; Dalhousie University, 1922; F.R.I.B.A.; Senior Member of the firm of Darling and Pearson, Architects, 2 Leader Lane, Toronto; *b.* Canada, 17 Feb. 1850; *e. s.* of late Rev. W. S. Darling, Rector of Holy Trinity, Toronto; unmarried. *Educ.:* Upper Canada College; Trinity College School; worked under Street and Sir Arthur Blomfield. Began practice in Toronto, 1875; Member Royal Canadian Academy; Royal Gold Medal for architecture, R. Inst. British Architects, 1915. *Address:* 11 Walmer Road, Toronto. *Clubs:* York, Toronto, Golf and Hunt, Toronto; Mont Royal, Montreal; Manitoba, Winnipeg; City, New York; Country, Ottawa.   (*Died June 1923.*)

DARLINGTON, Edwin, C.I.E. 1897; *b.* 1839; *s.* of James Darlington of St. Austell; *m.* 1881, Mary (*d.* 1924), *d.* of David Ring of Templemore. Assist. and Junior Sec. to Chief Commissioner, Burma, 1868-72 and 1875-77; Collector of Customs, Akyab, 1872-75; Collector of

Customs, Rangoon, 1877-80 ; Chief Collector of Customs, Burma, 1880 - 96 ; Vice - Chairman of Rangoon Port Commissioners, 1881 - 96. *Address:* 153 St. James's Court, Buckingham Gate, S.W. *Club:* East India United Service.
(*Died 5 Mar. 1928.*)

DARLOW, Rev. Thomas Herbert ; *b.* Ramsey, Hunts, 26 Apr. 1858 ; *e. s.* of late Thomas Darlow ; *m.* Ellen Frances, *e. d.* of late John Stephen Arthur, Liverpool, 1889 ; two *s.* one *d. Educ. :* Clare College, Cambridge (Minor and Foundation Scholar : M.A.) ; Lancs Coll., Manchester ; Leipzig Univ. Mathematical Master, Royal Institution School, Liverpool, 1881 ; Minister of Crosby Congregational Church, Liverpool, 1885 ; Warden of Browning Hall, Walworth, 1891 ; Minister of New College Chapel, Hampstead, 1892 ; Literary Superintendent of the British and Foreign Bible Society, 1898 1923. *Publications :* Christmas Poems ; The Print of the Nails ; The Upward Calling ; Via Sacra ; Holy Ground ; God's Image in Ebony ; At Home in the Bible ; Historical Catalogue of Printed Editions of Holy Scripture (with H. F. Moule) ; Letters of George Borrow to the Bible Society ; William Robertson Nicoll : Life and Letters ; The Love of God. *Recreations :* gardening, reading, smoking. *Address :* Beauleigh, Northwood, Middlesex. *T.A. :* Northwood. *T. :* Northwood 160. *Club :* Authors'. (*Died 23 Oct. 1927.*)

DARNLEY, 8th Earl of (*cr.* 1725), Ivo Francis Walter Bligh, D.L. ; late Hon. Col. 4th Batt. Volunteer R. W. K. Regt. ; Baron Clifton, 1721 ; Viscount Darnley, 1723 ; Earl of Darnley, 1725 ; Irish Representative Peer ; County Alderman for Kent ; *b.* 13 Mar. 1859 ; *s.* of 6th Earl and Harriet, *e. d.* of 3rd Earl of Chichester ; *S.* brother, 1900 ; *m.* 1884, Florence Rose, D.B.E., *d.* of late John Stephen Morphy of Beechworth, Victoria ; two *s.* one *d. Educ. :* Eton ; Trin. Coll., Camb. *Recreations :* golf and shooting ; Eton XI. 1876-77, Cambridge XI. 1878-81, Captain 1881 ; Captain English XI. in Australia 1882-83 ; represented Cambridge v. Oxford tennis and racquets. *Heir : s.* Esme Ivo, Lord Clifton of Rathmore. *Address :* Puckle Hill, Cobham, Kent. *T. :* Cobham, Kent 14. *Club :* Carlton. (*Died 10 April 1927.*)

DARROCH, Alexander, Professor of Education Edinburgh University, since 1903 ; *b.* Greenock, 20 Jan. 1862 ; *m.* 1905, Mabel (*d.* 1922), *d.* of George Hood, Redcar ; one *d. Educ. :* E.C. Training College, Glasgow ; Edinburgh University : M.A. with First Class Honours in Philosophy ; Rhind Phil. Scholarship, 1896 ; Heriot Research Fellow, 1899 ; Assistant Lecturer in Educ. University College of N. Wales, Bangor, 1900-1901 ; Lecturer in Psychology and Educ. in E.C. Training College, Edinburgh, 1901-3 ; also assistant to Professor of Education in Edin. Univ. 1901-3 ; Chairman of the Edinburgh Committee for the training of Teachers, since 1909 ; appointed First Chairman of the National Committee for the Training of Teachers in Scotland ; Chairman of Edinburgh Education Authority, 1920. *Publications :* Herbart and the Herbartian Theory of Education, 1903 ; The Reform of the Scottish Universities Arts Curriculum, 1904 ; The Children, 1906 ; The Place of Psychology in the Training of the Teacher, 1911 ; A History of Educational Thought (cf. Teachers' Encyclopædia, vol. VII.), 1912 ; Education and the New Utilitarianism, 1914 ; Articles in Hibbert Journal and in Journals devoted to Education. *Address :* 12 Abbotsford Park, Edinburgh. *T. :* 6663 Edinburgh. *Club :* Northern, Edinburgh.
(*Died Sept. 1924.*)

DARTREY, 2nd Earl of (*cr.* 1866), Vesey Dawson ; Baron Cremorne, 1797 ; Baron Dartrey, 1847 ; *b.* 22 April 1842 ; *m.* Julia, *d.* of Sir George Orby Wombwell, 4th Bt., 1882 ; two
2b4

d. ; S. father 1897. Formerly Capt. and Lt.-Col. Coldstream Guards ; retired from army, 1876 ; M.P. Monaghan (L.), 1865-68 ; High Sheriff, 1878. Owns about 25,000 acres. *Heir : b.* Hon. Edward S. Dawson. *Address :* 3 Eaton Place, S.W.1 ; *T. :* Victoria 536 ; Dartrey, Co. Monaghan. *Clubs :* Travellers' ; Kildare Street, Dublin. (*Died 14 June 1920.*)

DARWIN, Colonel Charles Waring, D.L., J.P., C.B. 1911 ; late Lt.-Col. and Hon. Col. 3rd Batt. Durham Light Infantry ; 2nd surv. *s.* of late Francis Darwin, of Creskeld Arthington, Yorks ; *b.* 23 Aug. 1855 ; *m.* 1894, Mary Dorothea, *o. c.* of late Rt. Hon. J. L. Wharton ; three *s. Educ. :* Winchester. Entered Army, 1872 ; Lt.-Col. 1894 ; retired, 1895 ; served S. Africa 1902 (medal 3 clasps) ; Chairman Durham County Territorial Association, 1908-18. *Address :* Elston Hall, Newark. *Club :* Arthur's
(*Died 1 Aug. 1928.*)

DARWIN, Sir Francis, Kt., *cr.* 1913 ; D.Sc., M.B., F.R.S. ; Hon. Fellow, Christ's College, Cambridge ; President, British Assoc., 1908 ; *b.* Down, Kent, 16 Aug. 1848 ; 3rd *s.* of Charles Robert Darwin and Emma Wedgwood, *g. d.* of Josiah Wedgwood ; *m.* 1st, 1874, Amy Ruck (*d.* 1876) ; one *s.* ; 2nd, 1883, Ellen (*d.* 1903), *d.* of John Crofts ; one *d.* ; 3rd, 1913, Mrs. Maitland (*d.* 1920), Brookthorpe, Gloucester. *Educ. :* Trinity College, Cambridge ; St. George's Hospital, London. Did not practise medicine, but became assistant to his father at Down ; after the latter's death settled at Cambridge. *Publications :* Life and Letters of Charles Darwin, 1887 ; Charles Darwin, 1892 ; various papers on physiological botany from 1876 onwards ; Practical Physiology of Plants (with late E. H. Acton) 1894 ; Elements of Botany, 1895 ; More Letters of Charles Darwin (with A. C. Seward), 1903 ; Foundations of the Origin of Species, 1909 ; Rustic Sounds, 1917 ; Springtime, 1920. *Address :* 10 Madingley Road, Cambridge. *Club :* Athenæum. (*Died 19 Sept. 1925.*)

DARWIN, Sir Horace, K.B.E., *cr.* 1918 ; M.A., F.R.S. ; Assoc. M. Inst.C.E. ; Chairman of the Cambridge Instrument Company, Ltd. ; *b.* 13 May 1851 ; *s.* of Charles Robert Darwin, author of the Origin of Species, etc., of Down, Kent ; *m.* 1880, Hon. Emma Cecilia Farrer, *d.* of 1st Lord Farrer ; two *d. Educ. :* Trin. Coll., Camb. Mayor of Cambridge, 1896-97. *Address :* The Orchard, Cambridge. *T.A. :* Horace Darwin, Cambridge. *T. :* Cambridge 17.
(*Died 22 Sept. 1928.*)

DAS, Hon. Satish Ranjan, Barrister-at-law ; Member Governor-General's Executive Council since 1925 ; *b.* 29 Feb. 1872 ; 2nd *s.* of Durga Mohun Das ; *m.* 1905, Bonolata, *d.* of Behari Lal Gupta, I.C.S., C.S.I. ; two *s. Educ. :* Univ. Coll. School, London ; Grammar School, Manchester. Called to Bar, Middle Temple, 1894 ; Advocate, Calcutta High Court, 1894 ; Standing Counsel, Govt. of India, 1917 ; Advocate-General Bengal, 1922. *Publications :* A Letter to my Son ; A New Policy for India, etc. *Recreation :* tennis. *Address :* Simla, India.
(*Died 26 Oct. 1928.*)

DASHWOOD, Arthur George Frederick ; 2nd *s.* of late Capt. G. A. C. Dashwood, 71st Highlanders, and Hon. Harriet Anne, *e. d.* of 1st Lord Bateman ; *b.* 1860 ; *m.* 1st, 1882, Caroline Isabella (*d.* 1920), *y. d.* of late Capt. A. O. Lord, 72nd Highlanders ; one *d.* ; 2nd, 1921, Alice, twin *d.* of Hon. Mrs. Kane and late Lt. - Col. Henry Green - Wilkinson, Scots Guards. *Address :* Thurlow House, Folkestone. *Clubs :* Arthur's ; Royal Yacht Squadron, Cowes. (*Died Feb. 1922.*)

DASHWOOD, Charles James, K.C. 1906 ; Crown Solicitor, South Australia, since 1905 ; *b.* 17 July 1843 ; unmarried. *Educ. :* St. Peter's Coll., Adelaide ; University of Ghent. M.H.A. Noarlunga, 1887-92 ; Government Resident and Judge in Northern Territory, 1892-1905. *Address*: Adelaide.

DAUNT, Lt.-Col. Richard Algernon Craigie, D.S.O., 1900; late 1st. Batt. Royal Irish Rifles; *b.* 1 Oct. 1872; *s.* of late Lt.-Col. Richard Daunt, County Cork; *m.* 1903, Feroze, *d.* of late Capt. H. J. Cooper; one *s.* one *d.* *Educ.*: Haileybury College. Joined, 1894; served with 2nd R. I. Rifles, Malta, India, Ireland, and South Africa; appointed Divisional Signalling Officer 3rd Division S.A.F. Force, 1900 (despatches, Queen's medal 3 clasps, King's medal 2 clasps, D.S.O.); served European War, 1914-16; commanded 1st Batt. Royal Irish Rifles, 1915-19; retired, Aug. 1919; Fellow Royal Astronomical Society. *Address*: Lanston, Pentire, Newquay, Cornwall.
(*Died 4 July 1928.*)

DAUNT, Ven. William, Archdeacon of Cloyne since 1909; *b.* 23 Dec. 1841; *s.* of late Achilles Daunt, J.P., Tracton Abbey, Co. Cork; *m.* Rosamond Anne, *y. d.* of late Sir G. King, Bt., Charlestown, Co. Leitrim. *Educ.*: Trinity Coll., Dublin (M.A.). Ordained 1865; Curate of Kincurran, 1865-67; Kinsale, 1867; St. Matthias, Dublin, 1868-70; Incumbent of St. Barnabas, 1870-72; Rector of Kinsale, 1872-81; Clonmel, 1881-1918. *Address*: Ardcæin, St. Ann's Hill, Co. Cork. (*Died Sept. 1919.*)

DAVAR, Hon. Justice Sir Dinsha Dhurjibhai, Kt., *cr.* 1911; one of the Judges of His Majesty's High Court of Judicature, Bombay; *b.* Bombay, 6 Nov. 1856; *o. s.* of Dhurjibhai Dinsha Davar, Parsi-Zoroastrian; one *s.* two *d.* *Educ.*: Proprietary School; Elphinstone College. Joined Middle Temple, 1877; called to Bar, 1880; practised at Bombay; was Law Professor and later Principal of the Government Law School; raised to the Bench, 1906. *Recreations*: spends most of his annual summer vacations in London. *Address*: Goolshun, Pedder Road, Bombay. *Clubs*: Orient, Elphinstone, Bombay.
(*Died 29 July 1916.*)

DAVERIN, John; *b.* Limerick, 1851; *m.* 1895, Clotilde Maud Mary, *d.* of John E. D'Alton, J.P. of Ballygriffin, Co. Tipperary. *Educ.*: Grey Institute, Port Elizabeth. Went to S. Africa, 1859; founded John Daverin & Co. 1876. *Address*: Knockfierna, Park Drive, Port Elizabeth, S. Africa. (*Died 27 Oct. 1922.*)

DAVEY, Henry, M.I.C.E., etc.; *b.* 1843; *s.* of Jonathan and Mary Davey, Lewtrenchard, Devon; *m.* Elizabeth Barbenson, *d.* of Pierre Barbenson Le Ber, J.P., of Alderney, Channel Islands; one *s.* *Educ.*: Tavistock. Inventor of the Differential pumping engine, and of various improvements in hydraulic machinery; founder of the firm of Hathorn, Davey & Co., Hydraulic Engineers, Leeds, established in 1871; Consulting Engineer in London, 1887; now retired. *Publications*: Textbook, The Principles and Construction of Pumping Machinery; papers in Transactions of Institution of Civil Engineers (Watt medal and Telford premium); Papers in Transactions of Inst. of Mechanical and other Engineering Societies; The British Association, etc.; author of various papers on scientific subjects. *Recreations*: sketching in water-colour, etc. *Address*: Bedford Hotel, Tavistock. (*Died 11 April 1928.*)

DAVEY, Very Rev. William Harrison, M.A.; Dean of Llandaff, 1897-1913; *b.* Thorpe, Norwich, 28 July 1825; *e. s.* of William Davey. *Educ.*: Charterhouse; Lincoln Coll. Oxford (Scholar). 2nd class Lit. Hum.; 2nd class Mathematics, 1847. Denyer Theological Prize, Oxford, 1851. Master at Marlborough, 1848-49; Vice-Principal of Chichester Theological Coll. 1852-59; Cuddesdon Coll. 1859-64; St. David's Coll. Lampeter, 1872-96; 3rd Cursal Prebendary, St. David's, 1876-95; Examining Chaplain to Bishop of Llandaff, 1895; Canon and Chancellor of St. David's, 1895-97. *Publications*: Articuli

Ecclesiae Anglicanae, 1861; The Books of Deuteronomy and Joshua in the Commentary on the Old Testament, 1876, etc., S.P.C.K. *Address*: The Green, Llandaff. (*Died 26 Mar. 1917.*)

DAVID, Hon. Laurent Olivier, Senator, 1903; City Clerk, Montreal, since 1892; *b.* 24 Mar. 1840; *m.* 1st, Albina Chenet; one *s.* nine *d.*; 2nd, Ludivine Garceau. *Educ.*: Ste. Thérèse College. Admitted to Bar, 1864; practised in partnership with Hon. I. A. Mousseau up to 1873; left profession then to be a journalist; one of the founders of L'Opinion Publique; established Le Bien Public with M. Beausoleil, 1874; returned to his profession and founded La Tribune; elected in Montreal for local House, 1886. *Publications*: Portraits et Biographies; Les Patriotes de 1837-38; Les Deux Papineau; Le Clergé Canadien; Mes Contemporains; L'Union des deux Canadas; Histoire du Canada depuis la Confédération; Souvenirs et Esquisses biographiques; Biographies de Mgr. Bourget et de Mgr. Tachet; drama entitled Le Drapeau de Carillon; Laurier et son temps, Mélanges historiques et littéraires, Gerbes Canadiennes. *Address*: Outremont, Canada.
(*Died 24 Aug. 1926.*)

DAVID, Sir Sassoon, 1st Bart., *cr.* 1911; K.C.S.I., *cr.* 1922; Kt., *cr.* 1905; J.P.; Member of Viceroy's Council, 1909; head and founder of the firm of Sassoon J. David & Co., Ltd.; communal worker; *b.* Bombay, 11 Dec. 1849; *s.* of J. David, prominent member of the Jewish community and one of the first to come to Bombay; *m.* 1876, Hannah (*d.* 1921), *d.* of Elias David Sassoon, *n.* of late Sir Albert Sassoon, 1st Bart.; one *s.* one *d.* *Educ.*: Bombay. Joined firm of E. D. Sassoon and Co., doing business with China; spent some years in China and was partner in the firm for several years in China and Bombay. In 1885 he started his own firm and became agent of the David and Standard Mills and the leading cotton yarn merchant of Bombay; Chairman of the Millowners' Association, 1904-5; Sheriff of Bombay, 1905; was for several years a Government nominee on the Bombay Municipal Corporation and the Standing Committee; Pres. of the Bombay Municipal Corporation, 1921-22; Director of several public companies and on the committee of several charitable associations; has firms in China, headquarters Bombay. *Heir*: *s.* Percival Victor [*b.* 21 July 1892; *m.* 1913, *c.* Vere Mozelle, *d.* of Aubrey David; one *d.* *Educ.*: Elphinstone College; Bombay University, B.A. Member of Inner Temple. *Club*: Royal Automobile]. *Address*: Bombay. *T.A.*: (firm) Psalmist; (private) Sanhedrim. *Clubs*: Orient, Willingdon Sports, Bombay.
(*Died 27 Sept. 1926.*)

DAVID, Bt.-Col. Thomas Jenkins, D.S.O. 1918; O.B.E. 1924; T.D. 1919; *b.* Margam, South Wales, 1881; *s.* of late Lt.-Col. D. R. David, J.P.; *m.* 1912, Nita, *d.* of late Pendrill Charles, Neath, S. Wales; one *s.* one *d.* *Educ.*: Malvern; Christ College, Brecon. Solicitor and Notary Public (Honours), 1904; commissioned 1900; commanding 81st Welsh Brigade R.F.A.; served European War, 1914-1918 (despatches, D.S.O.); Brevet Colonel 1924. *Recreations*: golf, riding. *Address*: Prysowen, Pyle, Glam. *Clubs*: Junior Army and Navy; Royal Porthcawl Golf. (*Died 6 Nov. 1926.*)

DAVIDS, T. W. Rhys, LL.D., Ph.D., D.Sc., Professor of Comparative Religion, Manchester, 1904-15; Professor of Pali and Buddhist Literature, University Coll., London, 1882-1912; President of the Pali Text Society and India Society; late President Manchester Oriental Society; Fellow of the British Academy; Sec. and Librarian of the Royal Asiatic Society, 1885-1904; took part in founding the British Academy, 1902; founded Pali Text Society, 1882; Oriental Translations Fund, 1895; and Indian Text Series, 1900; *b.* Colchester, 12

May 1843; *s.* of Rev. T. W. Davids; *m.* 1894, Caroline Augusta [D.Litt., Author of Buddhist Psychological Ethics, 1900; Vibhanga, 1904; Patthāna, 1906; Visuddhi Magga, 1920; Psalms of the Early Buddhists, 1909-13; Buddhism, 1912; Buddhist Psychology, 1914; Kindred Sayings, 1917, 1922; joint-author of Dialogues of the Buddha, II. 1910, 111. 1921; Compendium of Philosophy, 1910; Points of Controversy, 1915; the Expositor, 1920], *d.* of Rev. J. Foley, B.D., Fellow of Wadham Coll. Oxford, late Vicar, Wadhurst, Sussex; one *s.* two *d. Educ.:* Brighton School; Breslau University. Entered Ceylon Civil Service, 1866; Barr. Middle Temple, 1877; delivered Hibbert Lectures, 1881. *Publications:* Buddhism, 1878 (23rd ed. 1914); Buddhist Birth Stories, vol. i. 1880; Ancient Coins and Measures of Ceylon, 1877; Buddhist Suttas from the Pali, 1881; Questions of King Milinda, 1890-94; Hibbert Lectures, 1881; American Lectures, 1896; joint-author of Vinaya Texts, 1881-1885; Digha Nikāya, 1890 and 1902; Sumangala Vilāsinī, 1886; Sacred Books of the Buddhists; Dialogues of the Buddha, 1899, 1910, 1921; Pali-English Dictionary, 1921, etc.; Buddhist India, 1903 (2nd ed. 1905); Early Buddhism, 1908. *Recreation:* Chipstead Golf Club. *Address:* Chipstead, Surrey. *T.A.:* Rhys Davids, Chipstead, Surrey. (*Died 27 Dec. 1922.*)

DAVIDSON, Col. Sir Arthur, K.C.B., *cr.* 1910; G.C.V.O., *cr.* 1921; K.C.V.O., *cr.* 1906; C.B. 1902; Extra Equerry to the King and Equerry to Queen Alexandra; *b.* 12 November 1856; *s.* of W. Davidson, Welwyn, Herts. and Louisa, *d.* of J. Barnard Hankey, Fetcham Park, Surrey. *Educ.:* private tutor; Petersham. Joined 60th Rifles, 1876; served with 2nd Batt. in Afghan War, 1878-80; occupation of Candahar and Kelati-Ghilzie; engagements of Ahmed Khel (mentioned in despatches), and Urzoo near Ghuznee; A.D.C. to Sir Donald Stewart at Cabul; accompanied Sir F. Roberts's Cabul-Candahar March as A.D.C. to Sir John Ross; battle of Candahar (mentioned in despatches, brevet of Major, medal with 2 clasps, bronze decoration); served in Marri Expedition under Gen. MacGregor; in Boer War of 1881 with Natal Field Force; in Egyptian War, 1882; was present battle of Tel-el-Kebir (medal with clasp, 5th class Medjidie, Khedive's star); served in Bechuanaland Expedition of 1884-1885 under Sir Charles Warren (mentioned in despatches); A.D.C. to H.R.H. the Duke of Cambridge, K.G., 1890-95; Groom-in-Waiting to Queen Victoria, 1895-96, and Equerry-in-Waiting, 1896-1901; Equerry and Assistant Keeper of the Privy Purse, and Assistant Private Secretary to King Edward, 1901-10. Has received the Orders of the Dannebrög, the Rising Sun, the Sacred Treasure, and the Redeemer. *Recreations:* shooting, riding. *Address:* Red House, Warnham, Sussex. *T.A.:* Warnham. *Clubs:* United Service, Naval and Military.
(*Died 16 Oct. 1922.*)

DAVIDSON, Sir Charles, Kt., *cr.* 1919; is a Member of the London Stock Exchange; *s.* of late John Henry Davidson, Glasgow; *b.* 1 Jan. 1878; *m.* 1919, Agnes Clare, *d.* of late Frederick James Chard. Chairman Statistical Committee, Department of Surveyor-General of Supply, War Office, 1917-18; Deputy Chairman of Establishment, Ministry of Munitions, 1918-21. *Address:* 22 Suffolk Street, S.W.1. *T.:* Regent 4705. *M.:* R 4592. *Clubs:* Constitutional, Gresham, Royal Automobile, Ranelagh.
(*Died 27 Feb. 1927.*)

DAVIDSON, Duncan, of Tulloch; J.P.; D.L. Ross and Cromarty; Chief of Qlan Dhai; Landed Proprietor; *b.* 8 Oct. 1865; *s.* of late Duncan H. C. R. Davidson of Tulloch (*d.* 1889); *m.* Gwendoline, *e. d.* of William Dalziel Mackenzie of Fawley Court, Bucks. ' *Educ.:* The College, Inverness; Stubbington House,

266

Fareham; private tutors. Was brought up for a Commercial career, and after being in the City for 14 years left it on his health breaking down; now lives on his property; takes a great interest in County business, and among other things is Hon. Sheriff-Substitute, County Com. of the Boy Scouts, member of the County Com. of Secondary Education, Chairman of the Dingwall Academy, etc; a very keen sportsman and horticulturalist; Tulloch is an old Barony held direct from the Crown, and is one of the few families in which the head member has the real right of signing "of" Tulloch. *Recreations:* farming, gardening, shooting, fishing, and all games, such as cricket, croquet, and billiards. *Address:* Tulloch Castle, Dingwall, N.B. *T.:* Inverness District, 8. *T.A.:* Tulloch, Dingwall. *M.:* JS 369. *Clubs:* Caledonian; Highland, Inverness. (*Died 11 Nov. 1917.*)

DAVIDSON, George, C.B.E. 1927; Divisional General Manager, North Eastern Area, London and North-Eastern Railway Company, York; formerly General Manager Great North of Scotland Railway and Solicitor (Scotland) for London and North-Eastern Railway Company, Lt.-Col. Engineer and Railway Staff Corps R.E. (T.A.). *Address:* Clifton Lodge, York. *T.:* York 2027. (*Died 18 Aug. 1928.*)

DAVIDSON, Major George Harry, D.S.O. 1900; The Royal Scots; *b.* 16 Sep. 1866; *s.* of late Archibald Davidson; *m.* 1891, Ethel Maud, *d.* of J. A. Fairbairn of Ledgerwood, Claremont, Cape of Good Hope; two *d.* Entered Army, 1887; Adjutant 1st Batt. 1894-1898; Captain, 1896; Major, 1904; Adjutant 3rd Batt. 1898-1903; served in operations in Zululand with Mounted Infantry, 1888-91; South African War, 1900-2 (despatches, medal with three clasps, King's medal with two clasps, Coronation medal); Reserve of Officers. *Club:* New, Edinburgh. (*Died 17 April 1927.*)

DAVIDSON, Sir James Mackenzie, Kt., *cr.* 1912; M.B., C.M. University Aberdeen; Consulting Surgeon to Röntgen Ray Department, Charing Cross Hospital, Consulting Surgeon in charge of X-ray Department of Royal London Ophthalmic Hospital (Moorfields), Consulting Radiologist to the Military Hospitals of the London district; Member of Royal Institution, Royal Photographic Society; Past President Röntgen Society; President Radiology Section 17th International Medical Congress, 1913; Fellow of Physical Society; *b.* 6 Dec. 1856; *s.* of John Davidson, Estancia, Santo Domingo, Buenos Ayres; *m.* 1886, Georgiana, *d.* of William Henderson, Aberdeen. *Educ.:* Scotch School, Buenos Ayres; tutors in London; studied medicine in Edinburgh, Aberdeen, and London. After graduation at Aberdeen in 1882, became assistant to Professor of Surgery; subsequently Lecturer on Ophthalmology to the University of Aberdeen, and Ophthalmic Surgeon to the Royal Infirmary, Royal Sick Children's Hospital; Physician to Blind Asylum, etc.; came to London, 1897, and then devoted attention to X-ray work; invented a precise method of localisation by means of X-rays for foreign bodies in eye and orbit, and for bullets, etc.; also a mercury rotary break for coils. *Publications:* The Electric Light applied to the Ophthalmoscope, Lancet, 1886; Röntgen Rays and Localisation, British Medical Journal, 1898; Stereoscopic Skiagraphy, British Medical Journal, 1898; Localisation of Foreign Bodies in Eyeball and Orbit, Trans. IX. International Ophth. Congress, Utrecht; and various articles in the Trans. of the Ophthalmological Society of the United Kingdom; Notes of cases treated by Radium Bromide Rays, British Medical Journal, 1904. *Recreations:* photography, golf, motoring. *Address:* 26 Park Crescent, Portland Place, W. *T.:* Mayfair 1187. *M.:* A 8699 and LC 1794. *Clubs :* Royal Automobile, Empire, Argentine, Savage.(*Died 31 Mar. 1919.*)

DAVIDSON, Colonel John, C.B., 1902; unemployed super. list, Indian Army; *b.* 28 Aug. 1845; *y. s.* of late Alexander Davidson, M.D., Deputy Inspector - General, B.M.S. ; *m.* 1877, Anna, *e. d.* of Thomas Elliott, of Dolhaidd, Caer-marthenshire. *Educ. :* Winchester College. 21st R.N.B. Fusiliers, 1863 ; 3rd Punjab Cavalry, 1866 ; Assistant-Adjutant-General, Punjab Fron-tier Force,1875; served Jowaki Afridi Expedition, 1877-78 ; D.A.Q.M.G. Afghan Campaign, 1878-79 ; Waziri Expedition, 1880, as A.Q.M.G.; Military Secretary, Punjab Government, 1885-86; Colonel on Staff, Chitral, 1896-98, *Publication :* Notes on Bashgali Kafir Language, 1902. *Address :* 3 Talbot Houses, Blackheath, S.E.
(Died 9 Sept. 1917.)

DAVIDSON, Major Leslie Evan Outram, D.S.O. 1915 ; late R.F.A. ; *b.* 23 Sep. 1882 ; *s.* of late Duncan Davidson of Inchmarlo ; *m.* 1914, Matilda Rome, *d.* of Lionel Maitland-Kirwan, R.N., of Gelston, Castle Douglas; two *d.* *Educ. :* Marlborough. Entered army, 1902; Captain, 1914 ; Major, 1916 ; served European War, 1914-15 (despatches twice, D.S.O.).
(Died 26 Feb. 1925.)

DAVIDSON, Lt.-Col. Peers, K.C. ; *b.* Montreal, 7 Nov. 1870 ; *s.* of Hon. Sir Charles Peers Davidson, Kt. ; *m.* 1897, Louise, *d.* of late Rt. Hon. Sir W. V. Whiteway, K.C., K.C.M.G., P.C., formerly Prime Minister, New-foundland ; two *s.* one *d.* *Educ. :* McGill Uni-versity, Montreal (B.C.L., M.A.). Barrister ; Lt.-Col., late O.C. 73rd Batt. Royal High-landers of Canada, Canadian Overseas Forces. *Address :* Transportation Building, Montreal. *T.A. :* Sreep, Montreal. *Clubs :* Junior Army and Navy ; Mount Royal, St. James, Forest and Stream, Royal St. Lawrence Yacht, Mon-treal ; University, New York.
(Died 19 July 1920.)

DAVIDSON, Sir Samuel C., K.B.E., *cr.* 1921; Inventor of wind fans for H.M. ships. *Address :* Sea Court, Princetown Road, Bangor, Co. Down. *(Died 18 Aug. 1921.)*

DAVIDSON, Thomas, editor with W. and R. Chambers, Edinburgh, for 17 years ; Presby-terian Chaplain at Vienna, Brussels, Karlsbad from 1898 to the outbreak of the war ; Minister at Afton, New Cumnock, since Dec. 1914 ; *b.* Leswalt, near Stranraer, 27 April 1856 ; 2nd *s.* of John Davidson and Anna Pringle; unmarried. *Educ. :* Edinburgh Univ. and New College, Edin-burgh. Assistant-editor of Globe Encyclopædia, 1876-79, and of Chambers's Encyclopædia, 1888-1892. *Publications :* annotated editions, in Chambers's series of English Classics, of parts of Chaucer, Milton, Macaulay, Byron, Scott, Wordsworth, etc. ; Chambers's English Dic-tionary, 1898 ; Chambers's Twentieth Century Dictionary, 1901 ; contributions to Scots' Ob-server, Gypsy Lore Journal, Dr. Hastings' Encyclopædia of Religion and Ethics, etc. ; is preparing an elaborate study of the history of Jeanne d'Arc; a book on Austrian folk-tales ; and a novel of cosmopolitan life. *Recreations :* walking, hill climbing ; telling stories to children ; the study of folk-lore, especially folk-tales, and the problem of their diffusion. *Ad-dress :* Afton Manse, New Cumnock, Ayrshire. *Clubs :* Scottish Arts, Edinburgh ; Anglo-American, Vienna. *(Died 16 June 1923.)*

DAVIDSON, Sir Walter Edward, K.C.M.G., *cr.* 1914 ; C.M.G. 1902 ; Governor of New South Wales since 1918; *b.* 20 Apr. 1859; *s.* of late Jas. Davidson of Killyleagh, Co. Down ; *m.* 1st, 1882, *d.* of John Baber, M.D., of 34 Thurloe Square, S.W. ; one *s.* ; 2nd, 1907, Margaret Agnes, D.B.E., Lady of Grace of St. John of Jerusalem, *y. d.* of late Gen. Hon. Sir Percy Feilding; two *d.* Scholar of Christ's College, Cambridge. Entered the Ceylon Civil Service, 1880 ; Secretary to Ceylon Commission, Colonial and Indian Ex-hibition, 1886 ; Chairman of Municipal Council and Mayor of Colombo, April 1898 ; Ceylon Commissioner at Paris Exhibition, 1900 ; Officier d'Instruction Publique ; Col. Sec., Administra-tion, Transvaal, 1902-4 ; Governor of Seychelles Islands, 1904-12; Newfoundland, 1913-17; Knight of Grace of St. John of Jerusalem. *Publica-tions :* two books on Ceylon and its resources : in 1886 for the Colonial and Indian Exhibition, and in 1900 for the Paris Exhibition ; in 1909 a volume of Archives of Seychelles prior to 1810. *Address :* Government House, Sydney, New South Wales. *Club :* Savile *(Died Sept. 1923.)*

DAVIDSON, Sir (William) Edward, M.A. ; K.C.M.G., *cr.* 1907 ; C.B. 1897 ; K.C. ; Legal Adviser to Foreign Office, 1886-1918 ; holds a Commission as Acting Coun-cillor of Embassy in H.M.'s Diplomatic Service ; *b.* 17 April 1853 ; *s.* of late William Davidson, Mount House, Braintree, Essex ; unmarried. *Educ. :* Balliol College, Oxford. Barr. Inner Temple, 1879 ; Bencher, 1901 ; assisted Law Officers of Crown in their official work, 1881-86 ; one of the Counsel to Board of Trade in Bankruptcy matters, 1884 ; and in Shipping matters, 1885 ; Private Secre-tary and Secretary of Commissions of the Peace to Lord Chancellor, 1886 ; Q.C. 1892. *Recrea-tions :* mountaineering and other outdoor sports; tennis, etc. ; Hon. Sec. Alpine Club, 1880-85 ; President, 1911-14 ; President of the Association of Clan Dhai (Davidson), 1909 and 1910; Member of the Society of Dilettanti. *Address :* 12 Lower Sloane Street, S.W.1; 4 Temple Gardens, Temple, E.C.4. *T. :* Victoria 581. *Clubs :* Athenæum, Brooks's, Oxford and Cambridge.
(Died 12 July 1923.)

DAVIE, Major Arthur Francis Ferguson-, C.I.E., 1906 ; D.S.O., 1898 ; *b.* 11 July 1867 ; 3rd *s.* of Sir W. A. F. Davie, 3rd Bt. ; *m.* 1906, Eleanor Blanche Daphne, *e. d.* of C. T. Naylor of Dean House, Kelmeston, Hants ; two *s.* *Educ. :* Marlborough. Entered army, 1888 ; Captain, 1899 ; served Waziristan De-limitation Escort, present at action at Wana, 1894 ; Waziristan Expedition, 1894-95 (medal with clasp); Chitral Relief Expedition, 1895 (medal and clasp); Tirah Campaign, 1897 - 98 (despatches, D.S.O., two clasps) ; Mahsud Waziri Expedition, 1901-2 (despatches, clasp); Operations against Darwesh Khel Waziris, 1902 ; Bayar Valley Field Force, 1908 (medal and clasp) ; Major, 1906. *Address :* Nowshera, N.W.F.P., India. *Club :* Naval and Military.
(Died 11 April 1916.)

DAVIES, Hon. Charles Ellis, M.L.C., J.P. ; managing proprietor of The Mercury, Hobart, since 1885 : *b.* New South Wales, 13 May 1848 ; *m.* 1st, 1870, Sophia M. Wilson, Belfast (*d.* 1906); 2nd, 1909, Nellie Grace Collins, of Evandale of Tasmania ; one *s.* one *d.* *Educ. :* High School, Hobart (obtained Associate of Arts Degree, Tasmania, 1865). Joined the Victorian Railways, Melbourne, 1866 ; joined father, proprietor of The Mercury, 1870 ; president and founder of the Southern Tasmanian Agricultural and Pastoral Society, 1874 ; Member Legislative Council, Cambridge, since 1897 ; Grand Master of the Tasmanian Masonic Grand Lodge, 1896-1914 ; Pro. G. Master, 1914-16 ;, Re-elected G.M., 1917 ; District G.M. of M. Masons G.L.E. ; Representative of Tasmanian Press at the Imperial Press Conference in London, 1909. *Publications :* Our Trip to Europe; Impressions on a Trip to Japan. *Recreations :* steward, Tasmania Racing Club ; specially interested in all outdoor sports, and president and vice-president of several racing, cricket, and foot-ball clubs ; one of the principal horse-owners —*nom de course,* S. M. Wilson. *Address :* Lynd-hurst, Hobart, Tasmania. *(Died 1921.)*

DAVIES, Charles Llewelyn, C.B.E. 1918;
M.A.; Assistant Paymaster-General, 1910-24;
b. London, 29 June 1860; e. s. of late Rev. John
Llewelyn Davies and Mary (d. 1895), d. of late
Mr. Justice Crompton. Educ.: Marlborough
College; Trinity College, Cambridge (Scholar);
Fellow, 1883; First Class in Classical Tripos,
1882; and Bell University Scholar. Clerk in
Local Government Board, 1884; transferred to
Treasury, 1888. Address: 10 Lupus Street,
Pimlico, S.W.   (Died 30 Nov. 1927.)

DAVIES, Rt. Rev. Daniel, D.D.; Bishop
of Bangor since 1925; Canon Residentiary
of St. Asaph, 1910-25; Vicar of Bodel-
wyddan, near Rhyl, 1923-25; b. 7 Nov.
1863; s. of Evan Davies, Llanddewi,
Cardigan; m. Frances Hester Mary, o. d. of
Major R. C. Dobbs Ellis, late 1st Batt. 22nd
Regiment and Royal Inniskilling Fusiliers;
four s. two d. Educ.: Ystrad Meurig School;
St. John's College, Cambridge; 2nd Class
Theol. Tripos, Part I., 1886, and B.A.; 2nd Class
Theol. Tripos, Part II., 1887. Curate of
Conway, 1887; Bangor, 1889; Vicar Choral of
St. Asaph Cathedral, 1890; Vicar of Brymbo,
1893; Rector of Denbigh, 1897; Rural Dean of
Denbigh, 1904; Proctor in Convocation for St.
Asaph Diocese, 1906; Vicar and Rural Dean
of Wrexham, 1907; Chairman of the Executive
Committee of the National Eisteddfod of
Wales, 1912. Address: Bishopscourt, Bangor.
M.: DM 3634.   (Died 23 Aug. 1928.)

DAVIES, Edward, R.I. Address: 131
Narborough Road, Leicester. (Died Aug. 1920.)

DAVIES, Colonel Edward Campbell,
I.S.O. 1910; V.D.; Public Works Department,
Ceylon; retired Aug. 1911 after 33 years'
service. Address: 129 King's Road, Brighton.
                        (Died 5 May 1919.)

DAVIES, Canon Evan Thomas; Canon
Residentiary, Bangor Cathedral, since 1906;
m. Anne Catherine (d. 1923). Educ.: Lam-
peter, B.A. Curate of Llanwonno, 1870-71;
Ferndale, 1871-72; Bettws, 1872-75; Perpetual
Curate of St. David's, Liverpool. 1875-82; Vicar
of Aberdovey, 1882-90; Canon and Preb. of
Llanfair, 1897-1906; Vicar of Denio, 1890-
1906; Rural Dean, Lleyn, 1897-1906; Rector of
Llanfihangel-ysceifiog, 1906-13. Publications:
Cydymaith y Cymro, 1884; Pregethau ac Aner-
chiadau, 1894. Address: Hafodunos, Bangor.
                        (Died 1927.)

DAVIES, Frederick William Samuel,
M.R.C.S., L.R.C.P.; Senior Anæsthetist to
King Edward VII. Hospital, Cardiff; M.O.
Llwynarthan Auxiliary Hospital; Acting M.O.
H.M. Priory, Cardiff; Hon. Medical Attendant
Queen's Nurses in Cardiff; Medical Officer St.
Margaret's House of Mercy and Children's
Home; Physician French Consulate, Cardiff;
late Clinical Assistant Evelina Hospital for Sick
Children; Medical Officer and Anæsthetist
Glamorgan and Monmouth Hospital for French
wounded, Berckplage. Educ.: Guy's Hospital.

DAVIES, Rev. Gerald Stanley, M.A.;
The Master of Charterhouse since 1908; b. Banff
Castle, 1845; s. of Admiral George Davies and
Julia Hume; m. 1874, Constance Mary Hilliard
(d. 1922); five d. Educ.: Charterhouse; Nominated to Foundation by Edward VII., then Prince
of Wales; Christ's College, Cambridge (Scholar).
Curate of Shefford and Campton, Beds.; Assistant Master, Charterhouse, Godalming, 1873,
1905. Publications: St. Paul in Greece: Gaud-
entius; Julian's Dream; Franz Hals; Holbein;
Ghirlandaio; Michelangelo; Renaissance Tombs
of Rome; History of Charterhouse. Address:
The Master's Lodge, Charterhouse, E.C.
                        (Died 12 Feb. 1927.)

DAVIES, Lieut.-Col. Henry, C.M.G.
1917; late Army Service Corps; b. London, 13
July 1867; s. of late Henry Davies and Ellen
Shuttleworth; m. 1895, Clara Maud, e. d. of late

Henry Moore; one s. one d. Educ.: Cheltenham
College, Sandhurst. Joined 1st S. Lanc. Regt.
1887; transferred to A.S.C. 1891; Captain, 1894;
Major, 1902; Lt.-Col. 1914; served S. African
War, 1899-1902 (Queen's medal, 6 clasps, King's
medal, 2 clasps); European War, 1914-18 (despatches thrice, C.M.G.); commanded 6
Divisional Train and Guards Train; retired
pay, 1919. Recreations: riding, cycling.
                        (Died 4 Nov. 1923.)

DAVIES, Hubert Henry, Dramatist; b.
Woodley, Cheshire. Educ.: private schools.
Went to San Francisco, 1893, where he became
a journalist and produced several vaudeville
sketches; returned to England, 1901. Publica-
tions: Plays—Mrs. Gorringe's Necklace; Cousin
Kate, 1903; Cynthia, 1904; Captain Drew on
Leave, 1905: The Mollusc, 1907; Lady Epping's
Lawsuit, 1908; Bevis, 1909; A Single Man,
1910; Doormats, 1912; Outcast, 1914. Address:
Park Lodge, Park Place, Knightsbridge, S.W.
Clubs: Garrick, Beefsteak.   (Died Aug. 1917.)

DAVIES, Sir John Cecil, Kt., cr. 1922;
C.B.E.; J.P.; Legion of Honour; Vice-
Chairman of Baldwins, Ltd.; a director of
many companies; b. 23 Sep. 1864; s. of Thomas
Davies, Swansea; m. 1893, Emma Jane, d. of late
J. Edmunds of Coed-y-Paen, Monmouthshire;
four s. one d. Chairman of the South Wales
Siemens Steel Association; Chairman of the
Welsh Plate and Sheet Manufacturers Associa-
tion, Member the Executive Com. of the Nat.
Federation of Iron and Steel Manufacturers;
a Member of the Council of the University
College of Swansea; has served for many years
on the Llanelly Board of Guardians, the Swan-
sea Rural District Council, and the Gowerton
Council; one of the founders of the Swansea
National Shell Factory, and acted throughout
as Chairman of the Board of Management;
Member of the Executive Committee appointed
by the Ministry of Munitions to control shell
factories; represented the Ministry in the allo-
cation of steel supplies in South Wales; was a
member of the South Wales and Monmouthshire
Railway Transport Joint Committee. Heir: s.
Captain Leighton Davies, Director of Baldwins,
Ltd. Address: Stelvio, Newport, Mon. T.:
Newport 2251. Clubs: Conservative, Royal
Automobile, British Empire.
                        (Died 29 Aug. 1927.)

DAVIES, John Humphreys; s. of late
R. J. Davies of Cwrt Mawr, Llangeitho, Cardigan-
shire; unmarried. Educ.: University College
School; Lincoln College, Oxford (M.A.).
Barrister-at-law (Lincoln's Inn); Principal of
the University College of Wales, Aberystwyth;
Vice-Chancellor of the University of Wales,
1923-25; late Fellow of Jesus College, Oxford;
Member of the Council of the University of
Wales; Ex-Chairman of the Cardiganshire
County Council; High Sheriff of Cardigan-
shire, 1912. Publications: Letters of Lewis
Morris and his Brothers; Bibliography of
Welsh 18th Century Ballads; The Works of
Morgan Llwyd. Address: Cwrt Mawr, Llan-
geitho, Cardiganshire; Cwm, Aberystwyth.
                        (Died 10 Aug. 1926.)

DAVIES, Rev. John Llewelyn, M.A.;
Hon. D.D. (Durham); Hon. Litt.D. (Victoria);
Hon.Chap. to the King; Vicar of Kirkby Lonsdale,
1889-1908; b. Chichester, 26 Feb. 1826; s. of
Rev. J. Davies, D.D.; m. 1859, Mary (d. 1895), d.
of late Mr. Justice Crompton; four s. one d.
Educ.: Repton; Trinity Coll., Cambridge (Bell
Scholar, 1845; 1st class in Classics, 1848).
Fellow Trin. Coll. Camb. 1851-59; Curate of St.
Ann's, Limehouse, 1851-52; Vicar of St. Mark's,
Whitechapel, 1852-56; Rector of Christ Church,
St. Marylebone, 1856-89. Publications: Trans-
lation of the Republic of Plato (jointly with
D. J. Vaughan); Commentary on the Ephesians,
Colossians, and Philemon; Social Questions;
Order and Growth; Spiritual Apprehension.

Recreation: original member of Alpine Club; made first ascents of the Dom and the Täschhorn. *Address:* 11 Hampstead Square, N.W.
(Died 18 May 1916.)

DAVIES, Hon. Sir John Mark, K.C.M.G., *cr.* 1918; President Legislative Council, Victoria, since 1910; Solicitor, 1863; M.L.C., South Yarra, 1889; Melbourne, 1899; Minister for Justice, 1890-2; Solicitor-General, 1899-1900 and 1902-3; Minister of Public Instruction, 1903; Attorney-General and Solicitor-General, Victoria, 1903. *Address:* Valentines, Burke Road, Malvern, Australia.
(Died 14 Sept. 1919.)

DAVIES, Rt. Hon. Sir Louis Henry, P.C. 1919; K.C.; K.C.M.G. *cr.* 1897; Chief Justice of the Supreme Court of Canada (Appeal) since 1918; Kt. of Grace Order of St. John of Jerusalem, 1913; Deputy Governor-General of Canada since 1918; LL.D. McGill University, 1922; *b.* Prince Edward Island, Canada, 4 May 1845; *s.* of Hon. Benjamin Davies; *m.* Susan, *d.* of Rev. Dr. Wiggins, 1872; one *s.* three *d. Educ.:* Prince of Wales Coll. Barr. Prince Edward 'Island, 1867; Solicitor-General, 1869 and 1871-72; Leader of the Opposition, 1873-76; Premier and Attorney-General, Prince Edward Island, 1876-79; Q.C. 1880; elected to Dominion House of Commons, 1882, and re-elected continuously until his appointment to Appeal Court; Counsel for Great Britain before the International Fisheries Arbitration at Halifax in 1877 between Great Britain and United States of America; P.C., Canada, 1896; Joint Delegate to Washington with Sir Wilfrid Laurier, 1897, on Behring Sea seal question; one of Joint High Commissioners on part of Great Britain in 1898 for settlement of all differences with U.S.A. in respect of Canada; Minister of Marine and Fisheries, Canada, 1896-1901. *Address:* Ottawa, Canada. *T.A.:* Ottawa. *T.:* 533. *Club:* Rideau, Ottawa : City, Charlottetown.
(Died 1 May 1924.)

DAVIES, Bt. Col. Owen Stanley, D.S.O. 1918; *yr. s.* of Sir William Howell Davies; *m.* 1923, Ruth Winsome, *o. d.* of Stanley Gange of Sneyd Park, Bristol. Served European War, 1914-18 (despatches, D.S.O.).
(Died 19 Dec. 1926.)

DAVIES, Rev. Philip Latimer; Vicar of Dalton Parbold, nr. Wigan, since 1921; Hon. Canon in Liverpool Cathedral; Hon. Secretary, Liverpool Council of Education; *b.* Swansea, 1864; unmarried. *Educ.:* Swansea Grammar School; Royal University of Ireland; B.A. Mathematical Master, Liverpool College, until 1907; Vicar of St. James', Toxteth, Liverpool, 1907-12; Vicar of St. Thomas', Wavertree, Liverpool, 1912-21. *Address:* Dalton Parbold Vicarage, near Wigan. *T.:* Parbold 41. *Clubs:* Athenæum; University, Liverpool.
(Died 18 Sept. 1928.)

DAVIES, Col. Richard Hutton, C.B. 1900; N.Z. Staff Corps; Brigade Commander 6th Infantry Brigade since 1910; N.Z. Mounted Rifles; served South Africa, 1900 (despatches, C.B.); European War, 1914-15 (despatches).
(Died 9 May 1918.)

DAVIES, Robert Gwyneddon; *b.* 1870; *s.* of John Davies, Gwyneddon; *m.* Grace, *d.* of Lewis Roberts, Liverpool. *Educ.:* University College, Bangor. Solicitor (retired, 1918); Mayor of Carnarvon, 1908; High Sheriff of Carnarvonshire, 1924; Chairman of County Council, 1927; member of Council of University College of North Wales and of Court of University of Wales. *Publication:* Visions of the Sleeping Bard (translated from Welsh). *Address:* Llanwnda, Carnarvon. *T.:* Llanwnda 3. *(Died 17 April 1928.)*

DAVIES, Sarah Emily, Hon. LL.D. Glasgow; late Hon. Sec. Girton College, Cambridge; *b.* Southampton, 22 April 1830; *d.* of Rev.

J. Davies, D.D., Rector of Gateshead. *Educ.:* home. Hon. Secretary to Committee for obtaining admission of women to University Examinations, 1862-69; Hon. Sec. of Committee of Proposed New College for Women, 1867; Member School Board of London, 1870-78; Life-Governor of Univ. College, London; late Governor of Grammar School, Hitchin. *Publications:* The Higher Education of Women, 1866; Thoughts on some Questions relating to Women, 1860-1908, 1910. *Address:* 17 Glenmore Road, Belsize Park, N.W. *(Died 13 July 1921.)*

DAVIES, Rev. Sidney Edmund, Rector of Wyke Regis since 1899; Canon of Sarum since 1896; Surrogate. *Educ.:* Worcester College, Oxford, M.A. Ordained 1873; Curate of St. Martin, Sarum, 1873-79; Vicar of Shipton, Bellinger, Hants, 1879-85; Vicar of Broad Windsor, 1885-91; Gillingham, 1891-99; Rural Dean of Shaftesbury, 1891-99. *Address:* Wyke Regis Rectory, Weymouth. *(Died 10 July 1918.)*

DAVIES, T. Witton, B.A. (Lond.); Ph.D. (Leipzic), D.Th. (Geneva); D.D. (Durham); M.R.A.S.; F.R.A. Inst.; Emeritus Professor of Semitic Languages, University College of North Wales, Bangor; *b.* Nantyglo, Monmouthshire, 1851; *s.* of late Edmund Davies, Witton Park, Durham; *m.* 1st, 1880, Mary Anne (*d.* 1910), *o. d.* of late Henry Moore of Ainger Road, London, and of Great Yarmouth; one *d.*; 2nd, 1911, Hilda Mabel, *y. d.* of late Frederic Everett, Homewood, Swaffham, Norfolk; one *s.* one *d. Educ.:* Witton Park; Baptist Colleges, Pontypool and Regent's Park; Univ. Coll., London; 1st Prize in Logic and Philosophy at University College; also 1st class prize Hebrew, etc., Examination, University of London; Universities of Berlin, Leipzig, and Strasburg, Pastor of High Street Baptist Church, Merthyr-Tydfil, 1878-80; Professor of Classics, Hebrew, and Mathematics, Baptist College, Haverfordwest, 1880-91; Principal Midland Baptist College, Nottingham, 1892-99; Lecturer in Arabic and Syriac, University College, Nottingham, 1897-1899; Professor of Hebrew and Old Testament Literature, Baptist College, Bangor, 1899-1906. *Publications:* Oriental Studies in Great Britain, 1892; Magic, Divination and Demonology among the Hebrews and their Neighbours, 1898; The Scriptures of the Old Testament, 1900; Heinrich Ewald, Orientalist and Theologian, 1905; Century Bible, Psalms, vol. ii. 1906; and also Ezra, Nehemiah, and Esther, 1909 (Introduction and Commentary); The Survival of the Evangelical Faith, a Lesson and a Warning (Essays for the Times), 1907; (joint) Welsh Political and Educational Leaders, 1907, and Wales To-day and To-morrow, 1907; Outstanding Literary and Human Factors in my Life, 1911 (reprint); Bel and the Dragon, Introduction and Commentary in the Oxford Apocrypha, 1913; contributor to Review of Theology and Philosophy, Biblical World; Expositor, Journal of the Apocrypha, etc. *Recreations:* walking, foreign travel, music, and book-hunting. *Address:* Bryn Haul, Victoria Drive, Bangor, North Wales. *Club:* University. *(Died 12 May 1923.)*

DAVIES-EVANS, Herbert, Lord-Lieut. of Cardiganshire, resigned; *o. s.* of Capt. Delmé Seymour Davies, Scots Guards, Penlan, Carmarthenshire, and Mary Anne, *o. d.* of Capt. Watkin Evans, R.N., Highmead and Dolgadfan, Montgomeryshire; *m.* 1869, Mary Eleanor Geraldine (*d.* 1926), *e. d.* of David Jones, M.P., Pantglas, Carmarthenshire; three *s.* one *d.* Joined R.N. 1856; and 10th Hussars, 1860. *Heir: e. s.* Herbert, Major, Royal Field Artillery; *b.* 1870. *Address:* Highmead. Llanybyther, S. Wales. R.S.O. *T.A.:* Llanybyther. *M.:* EJ 5. *(Died 4 June 1928.)*

DAVIS, Colonel Charles Herbert, C.B.E. 1919; D.S.O. 1917; V.D.; merchant; *b.* Kilmore, Victoria, 4 June 1872; *s.* of William

Davis, Manager of the Colonial Bank of Australasia, and Ellen Mary Hayes; *m.* 1907, Emily Beatrice Deloitte; two *s.* one *d.* *Educ.:* St. Andrew's College, Bendigo; University of Melbourne. A barrister and solicitor at Bendigo, 1895; continued in practice there till the outbreak of war; joined the Militia Forces of Victoria as a Lieut. Dec. 1897, and was at the time of the outbreak of war a Lieut.-Col. in the Commonwealth Forces; appointed Censor, Melbourne, Aug. 1914, and continued in that office till gazetted to a command in the A.I.F. 1916; organised and commanded the 38th Batt. A.I.F. which left Australia June 1916; served with his batt. in France till 1 June 1918, when appointed Commandant to Australian Base Depots at Le Havre, which appointment he retained till demobilisation (despatches, C.B.E., D.S.O.). *Address:* 81 Clarence Street, Sydney, N.S.W. *(Died Dec. 1922.)*

DAVIS, Very Rev. Evans, Rector of St. James, London, since 1874; Dean of Huron Cathedral since 1904; *b.* 20 May 1848; *m.* 1882, Louisa Victoria Greenwood, St. Catharine's, Ontario. *Educ.:* Western University; D.D. Ordained, 1871; Incumbent, Bayfield, 1871-74; Canon of Huron, 1888; Archdeacon of Huron, 1894; member of the General Synod and of the General Board of Missions of the Canadian Church. *Address:* The Deanery, London, Ontario. *(Died Mar. 1918.)*

DAVIS, F. W.; R.I.; *b.* Handsworth, Birmingham. *Educ.:* Birmingham Municipal School of Art; Antwerp Academy; L'Ecole des Beaux-Arts (Anatomy course), Paris. *Works:* Yule-Tide Festival exhibited at National Eisteddfod of Wales Exhibition, Swansea (gold medal); Sword and Pen, Paris Exhibition, 1900; A Forgotten Craft, St. Louis Exhibition, 1904; The Love Philtre, New Zealand Exhibition, 1906; Six Large Frescoes for Wootton-Wawen Hall; two large decorative panels for presentation to the Shakespeare Memorial Museum, Stratford-on-Avon; Triptych for St. Andrew's Church, Handsworth, 1909, etc.; a panel for Reredos, St. Patrick's, Earlswood Lakes, 1911; four panels for Triptych, St. Stephen's Church, Birmingham, 1912. *Publications:* The Butterfly; A Picture on his Head; His Latest Acquisition. *Address:* Oakley Villa, Corbett Avenue, Droitwich. *Died Dec. 1919.)*

DAVIS, Lt.-Col. Gronow John, D.S.O. 1916; Military Secretary to the Chief Commissioner N.W.F.P., India; *b.* 9 Nov. 1869; *s.* of late Major-General Gronow Davis, V.C.; *m.* Evelyn Mary, *d.* of W. C. Beloe, J.P.; three *s.* one *d.* *Educ.:* Clifton College; Sandhurst. Joined Scottish Rifles, 1890; Indian Army (22nd Punjabis), 1892; served N.W. Frontier, India, 1897-98, including Relief of Malakhand (medal, 2 clasps); Tirah, 1897-1898 (clasp); N.W. Frontier, 1898-99; East Africa, 1902-4 (medal, 2 clasps); European War, 1914-16 (despatches twice, D.S.O.). *Address:* Harley Cottage, Clifton Down, Bristol. *Club:* Junior Army and Navy. *(Died 20 June 1919.)*

DAVIS, Henry William Carless, C.B.E. 1918; Director Dictionary National Biography since 1902; Regius Professor of Modern History, Oxford, since 1925; *b.* 1874; *s.* of H. F. A. Davis, of Ebley, Stroud; *m.* 1912, Rosa Jennie, *o. d.* of Walter G. Lindup; three *s.* *Educ.:* Weymouth College; Balliol College, Oxford (Scholar, 1891-95). Fellow of All Souls, Oxford, 1895-1902; Fellow of Balliol, 1902-21; War Trade Intelligence Department, 1915; Ford's Lecturer, Oxford, 1924; War Trade Advisory Committee, 1916; Professor of Modern History, University of Manchester, 1921-25. *Publications:* History of Balliol College, 1899; Charlemagne, 1900; England under the Normans and Angevins, 1905; Mediæval Europe, 1911; Regesta Regum Anglo-Normanuorum, vol. i. 1913; new ed. of Stubbs' Select

Charters, 1913; Political Thought of Treitschke, 1914; England, 1815-1846, in Story of British Nation, 1923; (joint) Why We are at War, 1914; editor of Oxford Pamphlets, 1914-15; contributions to the English Historical Review, The Quarterly Review, Cambridge Modern History, Helmolt's History of the World (English edition); Encyclopædia Britannica (1910 and 1922); Mowbray's Dictionary of Church History, 1912; History of Peace Conference (ed. Temperley, 1920); etc. *Address:* The Old Vicarage, Summertown, Oxford. *Club:* National. *(Died 28 June 1928.)*

DAVIS, John Samuel Champion, C.B.E. 1918; D.L., J.P., M.A., V.D.; *b.* 21 Feb. 1859; 2nd *s.* of Rev. S. Davis, Vicar of Burrington, North Devon; *m.* 1880, Minna Sophia, *d.* of William Butt of Axmouth; one *d.* *Educ.:* Rossall; Balliol College, Oxford. Entered Indian Civil Service, United Provinces, 1880; Junior Secretary and Joint Secretary, Board of Revenue, 1886-91; Settlement Officer, 1893-97; Deputy Commissioner, 1900-2; Commissioner, 1903-6; special duty with Viceroy, 1903; retired, 1906; held commission in various Indian Volunteer Corps from 1888; Captain United Provinces Light Horse, 1900-1907; retired with rank of Major, 1907; County Director, British Red Cross Society, Devonshire Branch; Member of Council of British Red Cross Society; Member of Devon County Council, and Devon Territorial Army Association; Treasurer University College of the South-West, Exeter. *Publications:* Settlement Reports of the Hardoi District, Oudh, 1894-97; Handbook of the Devonshire Voluntary Aid Organisation, 1910; 4th edition, 1912. *Address:* Kingford, Burrington, Umberleigh, N. Devon. *Clubs:* National; Devon and Exeter, Exeter.
(Died 12 Feb. 1926.)

DAVIS, Sir Mortimer (Barnett), Kt., *cr.* 1917; Director of several Industrial Corporations; *b.* Montreal, 1866; *m.* 1st, 1898, Henriette Marie Meyer; 2nd, 1924, Countess Morini. *Educ.:* High School, Montreal. *Address:* Villa Glaieuls, Gulfe Juan, France.
(Died 22 Mar. 1928.)

DAVIS, Richard Harding, F.R.G.S.; American novelist and playwright; Times war correspondent in Greek-Turkish war, Spanish-American war, and for the New York Herald in South African war, also in Russian-Japanese war, Spanish Cuban revolution, Matos revolution in Venezuela, American occupation of Vera Cruz, and representing Daily Chronicle with the allied armies in Belgium and France; *b.* 1864; *s.* of Rebecca Harding Davis, American novelist, and L. Clarke Davis, editor of the Philadelphia Public Ledger; *m.* 1899, Cecil Clark, Chicago; 1912, Bessie McCoy; one *d.* *Educ.:* Lehigh and Johns Hopkins Universities. *Publications:* Soldiers of Fortune; Gallegher and Other Stories; The Princess Aline; Cuba in War Time; Three Gringoes in Venezuela and Central America; The Cuban and Porto Rican Campaigns, 1898; With Both Armies in South Africa, 1900; In the Fog, 1901; Ranson's Folly; Captain Macklin, 1902; Farces, Real Soldiers of Fortune, 1906; The Congo and Coasts of Africa, 1907; The Scarlet Car, 1908; Vera, the Medium, 1908; The White Mice, 1909; Once Upon a Time, 1910; Man who could not lose, 1911; The Red Cross Girl, 1912; The Lost Road, 1913; With the Allies, 1915; Somewhere in France, 1915. *Plays:* The Taming of Helen, 1902; Ranson's Folly, 1903; The Dictator, 1904; The Galloper, 1905; A Yankee Tourist, 1906; Vera, the Medium, 1908; Blackmail, 1912; Who's Who?, 1913. *Address:* The Cross-roads, Mount Kisco, New York, U.S.A. *Club:* The Brook, New York.
(Died 11 April 1916.)

DAVIS, R. Bramwell, K.C.; *b.* London, 1849; *s.* of late Richard Powell Davis of Bedwellty House, Tredegar, Mon. ; *m.* 1st, Margaret Adelaide Salmond ; 2nd, Elaine Beatrice Vaughan; two *s.* one *d.* *Educ. :* privately ; Trin. Hall, Camb. Called to Bar, 1873 ; Q.C. 1896 ; practised in the Chancery Courts at first before Mr. Justice Kekewich, subsequently before Mr. Justice Farwell, Mr. Justice Neville, and Mr. Justice P. O. Lawrence. *Recreations :* golf, etc. *Address :* 15 Old Square, Lincoln's Inn, W.C. *T. :* Holborn 4899. *Club :* New University.

(Died 25 Aug. 1923.)

DAVISON, John Emanuel, M.P. (Lab.) Smethwick since Dec. 1918 ; a Labour Whip since 1924 ; *b.* Smethwick, 28 Nov. 1870 ; *s.* of John Davison, Sheffield. *Educ. :* Sheffield Elementary School. An Official of the Ironfounders' Society ; Vice-Chamberlain of the King's Household, 1924. *Address :* 32 Cottingham Street, Attercliffe, Sheffield. *(Died 2 Mar. 1927.)*

DAVY, Sir Henry, K.B.E., *cr.* 1919 ; C.B. 1917 ; M.D. (London University), F.R.C.P. (London), Honorary D.Sc., Sheffield ; Consulting Physician Royal Devon and Exeter Hospital ; Colonel A.M.S. ; Consulting Physician Southern Command ; *b.* 1855 ; *y. s.* of Henry Davy, Solicitor, Ottery St. Mary, Devon ; *m.* 1st, 1885, Beatrice Mary (*d.* 1905), *d.* of J. T. Tucker, Solicitor, Chard, Somerset ; one *d.* ; 2nd, 1920, A. I. Mary, *d.* of late Samuel Octavius Gray and widow of Dr. John Mortimer. *Educ. :* Honiton Grammar School ; Guy's Hospital ; M.D. University of London. Took 1st prize for 1st year's students and Gurney Hoare prize for Clinical Medicine at Guy's Hospital ; President of the British Medical Association at their Meeting at Exeter, 1907 ; Vice-President of Association. *Publications :* Papers in "Pathological Transactions," "Guy's Hospital Reports," "Lancet," and "British Medical Journal." *Address :* Southernhay House, Exeter. *T. :* Exeter 209. *M. :* T 1806. *Club :* Devon and Exeter, Exeter.

(Died 10 May 1922.)

DAVY, Richard, F.R.C.S. Eng., F.R.S.E. ; land-owner ; *b.* 1888 ; 2nd *surv. s.* of John Croote Davy, of Chulmleigh, Devon, and Elisabeth, *d.* of late John Sweet, of Burstone Manor ; *m.* Edith, *d.* of George Cutcliffe, of Coombe House, Witheridge, Devon ; three *d.* *Educ. :* Univ. of Edinburgh (M.B. 1862). Practised for 30 years as a consulting surgeon in London ; and is one of the consulting surgeons to the Westminster Hospital. *Publications :* Surgical Lectures, 1880. *Recreations :* superintendence of farm and land improvements. *Address :* Burstone Manor, Bow, North Devon. *(Died 25 Sept. 1920.)*

DAWBARN, Charles ; *b.* 22 Nov. 1871 ; *s.* of Robert Dawbarn, Solicitor, March, Cambs. ; *m.* 1914, Nora Payne, Durban, S. Africa. *Educ. :* Edinburgh University. Edited Midland Daily Telegraph ; joined Pall Mall Gazette under Sir Douglas Straight ; Paris Correspondent, 1900 ; acted as its special correspondent in Russia 1905, and in America and Canada, 1908 ; became Observer Correspondent in Paris ; joined Paris Staff of The Times, 1914 ; was in charge of Paris Bureau at battle of Marne ; sent special correspondence from Paris and neutral centres to Times, 1915-16 ; Diplomatic Correspondent, Daily Chronicle, 1917 ; represented that journal at Peace Conference ; likewise in long tour in South and Central Africa, 1920-21 ; toured Italy for British and American Journals, 1922. *Publications :* France and the French ; Makers of New France ; France at Bay ; Joffre and his Army ; My South African Year, 1921 ; innumerable articles, mostly on French subjects in Nineteenth Century, Fortnightly Contemporary, Atlantic Monthly, Saturday Review, etc. *Address :* Mitchell's Bureau, 23 Fleet Street. E.C. *(Died 16 Sept. 1925.)*

DAWES, James Arthur, M.P. (L.) Southwark, S.E. (formerly Walworth), since 1910; *b.* 16 June 1866 ; *s.* of Richard Dawes, of Castle Hill, Ealing ; *m.* 1920. Violet Maud Garner, *yr. d.*

of Mr. and Mrs. Pridmore, Penge. *Educ. :* Harrow ; University College, Oxford (M.A., B.C.L.). Admitted a Solicitor, 1891 ; chairman, Vestry of Newington, 1897-1900; first Mayor of Southwark, 1900-1 ; re-elected, 1913-1914, 1914-15 ; member of Metropolitan Water Board, 1904 ; member of London County Council, 1906 ; re-elected, 1907, 1910, and 1913 ; Chairman of the London Insurance Committee, 1912-14 ; J.P., Co. of London ; Sub.-Lieut. R.N.R. 1914 ; Lieut.-Commander, R.N.V.R. 1915 ; Commander (acting), 1918. *Recreation :* yachting. *Address :* 71 Kennington Park Road, S.E. 11; Ravensbury, Dartmouth, S. Devon. *T. :* Hop 1175. *Club :* Oxford and Cambridge. *(Died 14 Nov. 1921.)*

DAWES, William Charles, J.P.; M.F.H. Tickham ; *e. s.* of Sir Edwyn Sandys Dawes K.C.M.G. (*d.* 1903) of Mount Ephraim, Faversham, Kent, and Lucy Emily, *e. d.* of late William Bagnall, of Hamstead Hall, Staffordshire ; *b.* 20 Sep. 1865 ; *m.* 1893, Jane Margaret, *d.* of late James Simpson, J.P., of Inverboyndie, Banffshire ; two *s.* one *d.* *Educ. :* Winchester. Director Commercial Union Assurance Co., Ltd. *Address :* Queen Anne's Mansions, S.W. ; Mount Ephraim, near Faversham ; Swordanes, Banff. *Clubs :* Gresham, Royal Thames Yacht. *(Died 20 July 1920.)*

DAWKINS, Maj.-Gen. Sir Charles Tyrwhitt, K.C.M.G. *cr.* 1918 ; C.B. 1915; C.M.G. 1897 ; A.Q.M.G. Eastern Command 1910-14 ; *b.* 22 Nov. 1858 ; *s.* of late Rev. James Annesley Dawkins ; *m.* 1887, Hon. Nersdah Leeta Robinson, *d.* of 1st Baron Rosmead, one *s.* Entered King's (Shrops.) Light Infantry, 1878 ; Capt. 1886 ; Col. 1907 ; served Afghan War, 1879-1880 (medal) ; S. Africa, 1899-1901 (severely wounded, despatches, 1900, 1902 ; Queen's medal, 4 clasps ; King's medal, 2 clasps : brevet of Lt.-Colonel) ; European War, 1914-18 at D.Q.M.G. at G.H.Q. (despatches 5 times, C.B., K.C.M.G.). *Address :* 21 Emperor's Gate, S.W.

(Died 4 Oct. 1919.)

DAWNAY, Sir Archibald Davis, Kt., *cr.* 1918 ; J.P., C.E. ; for ten years Mayor of Wandsworth. *Address :* Sheviocke, Cedars Road, Clapham. S.W.4. *T.A. :* Yanwad, Clapcom, London. *T. :* Battersea 796, 125. *Clubs :* St. Stephen's, Junior Constitutional, British Empire. *(Died 23 April 1919.)*

DAWSON, Hon. Edward Stanley ; *heir-pres.* of 2nd Earl of Dartrey ; *b.* 16 Aug. 1843 ; *m.* 1898, Lady Elizabeth Meade, *e. d.* of 4th Earl of Clanwilliam ; one *d.* Retired Captain, R.N.; High Sheriff Co. Monaghan, 1899 ; *Address :* 30 Cadogan Square, S.W.1. *T. :* 1654 Victoria. Cannon Hill, Maidenhead. *T. :* 62 Maidenhead. *Clubs :* Turf, Travellers', Bachelors'.

(Died 24 Oct. 1919.)

DAWSON, Rev. Edwin Collas, Canon of St. Mary's Cathedral and Synod Clerk of the Diocese of Edinburgh since 1906 ; *e. s.* of Rev. John Dawson, M.A., late Vicar of Holy Trinity, Weston-super-Mare, and Mary Le Mesurier, *d.* of Capt. Peter Collas. R.N. of Hauteville, Guernsey ; *m.* 1875, Lucy, *d.* of Lt.-Col. Robert Wyllie, J.P., of Ellerslie, N. Devon, Mil. Secretary to Govt. of India, and Catherine, *d.* of Humphrey Herbert-Jones, D.L., J.P., M.F.H., of Llynon Hall, Anglesea, and Tynewdd, Carnarvons. ; one *s.* one *d.* *Educ. :* Marlborough ; Tonbridge ; St. Mary Hall, Oxford. B.A. 1872 ; M.A. 1876 ; Deacon, 1873 ; Priest, 1874 ; Curate of Hale, 1873 ; Sandgate, 1875 ; Incumbent of St. Thomas's, Edinburgh, 1878-90 ; Rector of St. Peter's, Edinburgh, 1890-1921 ; Clerical Secretary F.M. Board Edinburgh Diocese, 1905 ; Convener of Publication Committee of F.M. Board of Scottish Church, and Editor of the F.M. Chronicle of the Scottish Episcopal Church (now discontinued) ; Member of every Provincial Synod of the Scottish Church since 1890. *Publications :* The Life and Work of James

271

DAVIS, Major William Hathaway, D.S.O. See page xviii.

DAWNAY, Hon. Eustace (Henry). See page xviii.

Hannington, first Bishop of E. Equatorial Africa, 1886; Lion-hearted; The Last Journals of Bishop Hannington; Our Work Overseas; In and Out of Chanda; Success to You! Talks with Boys; Comrades; In the Days of the Dragons; The Life of Dr. Stern; Heroines of Missionary Endeavour, 1908; The Book of Honour, 1910; articles in various magazines, etc. *Recreations*: fishing and chess. *Address*: University Hall, 9 Ramsay Garden, Edinburgh.
(*Died Mar. 1925.*)

DAWSON, Lt.-Col. (Brig.-Gen.) Frederick Stewart, C.M.G. 1916; D.S.O. 1918; A.D.C. to H.M. 1917; 1st S. A. Infantry; *m.*; one *s.* Served European War, 1914-18 (despatches, C.M.G., D.S.O.). *Adress*: Intwood, Farnham Royal, Slough. (*Died 26 Oct. 1920.*)

DAWSON, Col. Harry Leonard, C.V.O. 1902; C.B. 1900; I.S.C.: late Col. on Staff Commanding Madras Brigade; *b.* 5 Dec. 1854; *s.* of late Major-Gen. John Dawson, I.S.C.; *m.* 1904, Ada Marion, *e. d.* of late H. Binny Webster, B.C.S. *Educ.*: Cheltenham College. Entered army, 1873; Lieut.-Col. 1899; served Soudan, 1885; present at actions of Hasheen and Tamai (medal with clasp, Khedive's Star); Chitral Relief Force, 1895 (medal with clasp); Tirah, 1897-98 (two clasps); South Africa, 1899-1900 (despatches, C.B., medal with six clasps); commanded Indian Coronation Contingent, 1902 (C.V.O., Coronation medal). *Address*: Rosemead, Horley, Surrey. (*Died 27 June 1920.*)

DAWSON, M. Damer, O.B.E. 1918; Chief Officer of the Women Police Service; *b.* Sussex, 1875; *d.* of Richard Dawson, formerly R.A. *Educ.*: privately. Studied music under Benno Schönberger and Herbert Sharpe; gold medal and diploma London Academy of Music; worked for the protection of animals in England and on the Continent, 1903-14; Organising Secretary of Congress of International Animal Protection Societies held in London, 1906; holds silver medal given by King of Denmark for animal protection work; silver medal of Finnish Society for Protection of Animals; founded the Women Police Service, Feb. 1915; was Co-Founder of the Women Police Volunteers, Sep. 1914; Agent to the Minister of Munitions for the training, supplying, and controlling of a force of police-women in H.M. Munition Factories, 1915. *Recreations*: riding, Alpine climbing, motor cycling. *Address*: Danehill Lodge, Lympne, Kent. *Club*: International Suffrage. (*Died 18 May 1920.*)

DAWSON, Sidney Stanley, O.B.E. 1920; M. Com., F.C.A., J.P.; Professor of Accounting, Birmingham University, 1907-10; Mayor of the County Borough of Wallasey, 1915-16; head of firm of Dawson, Graves & Co., chartered accountants, Liverpool. *Publications*: The Accountants' Compendium, and other professional works. *Address*: 51 North John Street, Liverpool; Windermere House, Liverpool. *T.A.*: Problem, Liverpool. *T.*: Bank 4163, Royal 546, Liverpool. (*Died 19 May 1926.*)

DAWSON, Rev. William James; Emeritus Pastor of the Old First Presbyterian Church, Newark, N.J.; *b.* Towcester, Northamptonshire, 21 Nov. 1854; *e. s.* of Rev. W. J. Dawson, Wesleyan minister; *m.* Jane, *d.* of late William Powell, merchant, Lowestoft, 1879; three *s.* three *d.* *Educ.*: Kingswood School, Bath; Didsbury College, Manchester. Entered Wesleyan Ministry, 1875, holding various appointments at Wesley's Chapel, City Road, London, Glasgow, and Southport, until 1892, when he resigned his position as a Wesleyan minister; Minister of Highbury Quadrant Congregational Church, London, N., to 1906. During these years lectured widely on literature and historical subjects. Visited America, 1891, as a delegate of the Methodist Œcumenical Council, held at Washington, and lectured in various cities. *Publications*: A

272

Vision of Souls (poems), 1884; Quest and Vision, Essays on Life and Literature, 1886 (republished with additions, 1892); The Threshold of Manhood, 1889; The Makers of Modern Poetry, 1890; The Redemption of Edward Strahan, A Social Story, 1891; Poems and Lyrics, 1893; London Idylls, 1895; The Comrade-Christ (Sermons), 1894; The Story of Hannah, 1896; The House of Dreams, 1897; Through Lattice Windows, 1897; Table Talk with Young Men, 1898; Judith Boldero, a Tragic Romance, 1898; Makers of Modern Prose, 1899; Savonarola, a Drama, 1900; The Man Christ Jesus, 1901; The Quest of the Simple Life, 1903; The Evangelistic Note, 1905; The Book of Courage, 1911; The American Hymnal, 1913; America, and other Poems, 1914; Robert Shenstone: a Novel, 1917; The Autobiography of a Mind, 1925. *Address*: 583 Mount Prospect Avenue, Newark, N.J., U.S.A. (*Died 23 Aug. 1928.*)

DAWSON, Major (Temp. Lt.-Col.) William Robert Aufrère, D.S.O. 1916; Bar, 1917; commanding 6th Batt. R. West Kent Regt; *b.* 23 June 1891; *s.* of Wm. Dawson, M.A., Oxon. and Lincoln's Inn. *Educ.*: Bradfield; Oriel College, Oxford. Joined the R.F.A. (S.R.), 1911; regular commission in 1st Batt. Queen's Own (Royal West Kent Regt.), 1914; served with 6th Batt. R.W.K.R. till March 1916 (twice wounded that month in the Hohenzollern Redoubt, D.S.O., severely wounded at Monchy le Preux, May 1917, bar to D.S.O., 30 Nov. 1917; wounded near Cambrai, 30 Nov. 1917; wounded near Albert, 29 March 1918 (2nd bar to D.S.O.). *Recreations*: fishing, motoring, riding. *Address*: Cold Ash, near Newbury, Berks. *T.*: Thatcham 7. *Club*: Army and Navy. (*Died 3 Dec. 1918.*)

DAWSON-SCOTT, General Robert Nicholl, R.E.; J.P.; Colonel Commandant R.E. since 1905; *b.* 4 Feb. 1836; *e. s.* of Col. Dawson, R.E., C.B., of Lee Grove, Blackheath; *m.* 1870, Grace M., *d.* of J. W. Nicholl Carne of S. Donat's Castle, Glamorganshire. Assumed name Scott, 1872. Entered army, 1854; General, 1897; retired, 1898; Commandant, School of Military Engineering, Chatham, 1888-93. *Address*: Brent House, Penrith.
(*Died 31 Mar. 1922.*)

DAY, Rev. Charles V. P., C.B.E., T.D., M.A., Vicar of Glastonbury, Somerset, since 1912; Commissary to the Bishop of North Queensland; *b.* East Hall, Feltwell, Norfolk, 1864; 4th *s.* of Rev. T. H. C. Day, Limpenhoe Rectory, Norfolk; *m.* Helen Constance, 4th *d.* of Mark Lambert of Whitley Hall, Northumberland. *Educ.*: Oundle, Durham; Cuddesdon College, Oxon. Priest and Deacon, 1888; served as Curate to St. George's, Cullercoats, St. Paul's, Beckenham; Chaplain (domestic) to the Bishop of Brisbane and Rector of Christ Church, Milton, 1899; Chaplain to the R.A.A. and Q.D.F. Australia; to the Imperial troops in South African War (Queen's Medal and King's Medal with 5 clasps); Sub-dean and Canon of Townsville Cathedral, Archdeacon of Mackay, 1903; Returned to England, 1906; Rector of Limpenhoe with Southwood, Norfolk, and Principal of Abbey School, Beckenham, 1907; Rector of Wookey, Somerset, 1910; Chaplain to Somerset R.H.A., 1914; to S.W.M.B., Dardanelles, 1915; Egypt, 1916; Senior Chaplain, Baghdad, and 3rd Corps H.Q., Mesopotamia, 1917 (despatches); returned to England, 1919. *Address*: The Abbey House, Glastonbury.(*Died 19 Aug. 1922.*)

DAY, James Roscoe, S.T.D., D.C.L., LL.D., L.H.D.; Chancellor, Syracuse University; *b.* Whitneyville, Maine, U.S.A.; *s.* of Thomas Day and Mary Plummer Hillman; *m.* Anna E. Richards; one *d.* *Educ.*: Maine Wesleyan Seminary and Bowdoin College. Clergyman of Methodist Episcopal Church; pastorates in Portland, Boston, and New York City; Chancellor of Syracuse University since 1893;

elected Bishop of Methodist Episcopal Church, 1904, but resigned to continue in present position. *Publications*: The Raid on Prosperity; My Neighbour; The Working-Man; magazine articles, sermons, etc. *Address*: Syracuse University, Syracuse, New York. *T.*: 973.
(Died 13 Mar. 1923.)

DAY, Right Rev. Maurice, D.D.: Bishop of Clogher since 1908; *b.* Valentia Island, Co. Kerry, 2 Sept. 1843; *s.* of Very Rev. John Godfrey Day, Dean of Ardfert; *m.* 1873, Charlotte Frances Mary Forbes Ottley; three *s.* one *d.* *Educ.*: Queen's College, Cork (Scholar); Trinity College, Dublin. First Honourman in Mathematics, Trinity; Junior Moderator and Medallist and B.A., 1865; Deacon, 1866; Priest, 1867; Curate of St. Luke's, Cork, till 1870; Curate of St. Matthias's, Dublin, till 1873; Vicar of Greystones, Co. Wicklow, till 1876; Rector of Killiney, Co. Dublin, till 1894; Incumbent of St. Matthias's, Dublin, till 1905; Dean of Ossory; Dean of St. Canice's Cathedral and Rector of St. Mary's, Kilkenny, 1905-8; Commissioner of National Board of Education in Ireland since 1911. *Address*: Bishopscourt, Clones, Ireland. *T.A.*: Bishopscourt, Clones. *Club*: University, Dublin. *(Died 27 May 1923.)*

DAY, Very Rev. Maurice William, Dean of Waterford and Rector of Holy Trinity with St. Olaf, Waterford, since 1913; *b.* 23 April 1858; *s.* of Rev. M. F. Day, sometime Bishop of Cashel; *m.* 1887, Catherine L. F. Garfit; three *s.* one *d.* *Educ.*: Repton School; Trinity College, Dublin. Ordained 1882; Curate of Queenstown, 1882-86; of Holy Trinity, Waterford, 1886-93; Rector of St. John, Newport, Co. Tipperary, 1893-1904; Rector of Kilbrogan, Co. Cork, 1904-8; Dean of Cashel, 1908-13. *Address*: The Deanery, Waterford.
(Died 29 Aug. 1916.)

DAY, W. Cave, R.B.A. 1903; *s.* of Parker Day of Dewsbury; *b.* Dewsbury, 1862; *m.* Kathleen G. Maclellan, 2nd *d.* of late G. W. Smales of Whitby; one *s.* one *d.* *Educ.*: privately. Always desired art as a career, and studied in leisure time from seventeen years of age; followed landscape under various masters; in 1890 devoted himself entirely to art, and exhibited same year at Royal Academy Gossips in St. Ives; since then frequent exhibitor at Royal Academy, Royal Society of British Artists, Liverpool Walker Art Gallery, Manchester City Art Gallery, etc.; studied in Paris under Benjamin Constant, Jules Lefebvre for painting, and M. Chapu for modelling, and was two years at the Herkomer School, Bushey; painter of Her Own Plot, One O'Clock Two O'Clock, Passing, A Lady in White, etc.; works principally at portraits and figure subjects in oils, and fond of water-colour for landscape work. *Recreation*: violin. *Address*: Hilbree, Godrevy Terrace, St. Ives, Cornwall.
(Died April 1924.)

DAYRELL, Elphinstone, F.R.G.S., F.R.A.I.; District Officer, Southern Nigeria; *b.* 16 Dec. 1869; *s.* of late Edmund Marmaduke Dayrell, Captain, R.N., and Bella Elphinstone Holloway. *Educ.*: Cheltenham College; Germany. Solicitor; served in South African War, 1900-1, with 1st Bucks. Yeomanry (Queen's medal and four clasps and commission as temporary 2nd Lieut. in Army); Transport Officer and Political on Ebegga Expedition, 1903; Political Officer, Cross River Expedition, 1904; Political Officer, Anglo-German Boundary Commission, 1903-1909 (African General Service medal and three clasps). *Publications*: Folk Stories from S. Nigeria; Ikom Folk Stories. *Recreations*: shooting, fishing and golf. *Clubs*: Junior Army and Navy; Golfers'; Royal Ashdown Forest Golf.

DEADMAN, H. E., C.B. 1904; F.R.S.N.A.; M. Inst. N.A.; *b.* London, 7 March 1843;

s. of late John Deadman, of Brockley, S.E.; *m.* 1870, Susannah *(d.* 1890), *d.* of late Captain Robert Duffill, of Rochester, Kent; one *s.* one *d.* *Educ.*: private schools; Royal Dockyard Technical Schools; Royal School of Naval Architecture, S. Kensington. After completing professional education as above and obtaining diploma of Fellow of the Royal School of Naval Architecture (F.R.S.N.A.), has been employed by Admiralty as follows:— Assistant and principal overseer of war-ships building in private yards, also foreman of the yard, H.M. Dockyard, Devonport, 1867-80; constructor in charge of shipbuilding and engineering departments of the Indian Government Dockyard, Bombay, 1880-88; in this capacity was very highly commended in Government of India despatches for work in connection with the transport of the Indian contingent of the Egypt Expeditionary Force of 1882; constructor, H.M. Dockyard, Chatham, 1883-86; chief constructor, H.M. Dockyard, Portsmouth, 1886-92; Admiralty, 1892-1902; Assistant Director of Naval Construction, Admiralty, 1902-6; has served as Member of several Admiralty Departmental Committees, and been selected to give evidence before other Departmental and House of Commons Committees on subjects connected with naval architecture and dockyard management; has several times received the thanks of the Board of Admiralty for services rendered; sometime Director of Cammell, Laird & Co., Ltd.; the Fairfield Shipbuilding and Engineering Co., Ltd., and Holzapfels, Ltd. *Address*: 10 Bolingbroke Grove, S.W. *(Died 20 Mar. 1925.)*

DEAKIN, Hon. Alfred, M.P.; Barrister-at-Law; late member for Ballarat in the House of Representatives; formerly several times member of Federal Council of Australia, and of the Parliament of Victoria continuously for twenty years; Chairman of Committee of Public Accounts, Victoria; Chairman of Executive of Victorian Federation League; member of the three Nat. Australian Federal Conventions; *b.* Melbourne, 3 Aug. 1856; *s.* of William Deakin, accountant, Melbourne *(d.* 1892); *m.* Pattie, *e. d.* of H. J. Browne, J.P. Melbourne; three *d.* *Educ.*: Church of England Grammar School, Melbourne; Melbourne University. Elected West Bourke, 1879; Essendon and Flemington, 1889; Minister of Public Works and Water-Supply, 1883-86; Solicitor-Gen., 1885; Pres. Royal Comm. on Water-Supply, 1884; Chief Sec., 1886-90; senior representative Imperial Conference in London, 1887; member of Federal Council, 1889-95-97-99; member of Federation Conference, Melbourne, 1890; of National Australian Convention, 1891; of National Australian Federal Convention, 1897-98; Australian delegate from Victoria to London to secure passing of the Commonwealth Bill, 1900: first Attorney-General of the Commonwealth of Australia, 1901-3; Prime Minister Commonwealth of Australia, 1903-4, 1905-8, 1909-10; Leader Federal Opposition, 1910-13; represented Australia Imperial Conference, 1907; Bencher of Gray's Inn; received freedom of London, Edinburgh and Manchester; President of the Australian Commonwealth Commission to the San Francisco Exposition, 1915, and LL.D. of the Berkeley University of California. *Publications*: Irrigation in Western America, 1885; Irrigation in Egypt and Italy, 1887; Irrigated India, 1892; Irrigation in Australia, 1893; Temple and Tomb, 1894. *Recreations*: reading; a book-lover. *Address*: Llanarth, South Yarra, Melbourne.
(Died 6 Oct. 1919.)

DEAN, Bashford, A.M., Ph.D., Curator of Armour, Metropolitan Museum of Art; Hon. Curator Fishes and Reptiles, American Museum of Natural History; Prof. Vertebrate Zoology,

273

DEACON, Col. William Thomas, C.B. See page xviii.

Columbia University; Prof. Fine Arts, N.Y. University; b. 1867, Puritan-Huguenot stock; m. Mary Alice Dyckman. *Educ.*: Columbia University; Munich; Col. City, N.Y. Has held appointments U.S. Fishes Commission; organiser of Cold Spring Harbour Biological Laboratory; Advisory Committee N.Y. Aquarium; Major, Ordnance, U.S.A., 1917-18; Chevalier Legion d'Honneur, member, fellow and correspondent of a number of European scientific societies. *Publications:* Over two hundred brochures, memoirs, books, dealing with Fishes (anatomy, embryology, fossil), evolution (orthogenesis), and a hundred dealing with Armour ancient and modern. *Address:* Riverdale on Hudson, N.Y. *Club:* Century, N.Y. *(Died 6 Dec. 1928.)*

DEANE, Canon Arthur Mackreth, M.A.; F.R.A.S.; Canon Residentiary, 1897-1923, and Prebendary of Middleton since 1888, in Chichester Cathedral; Vicar of Ferring, 1888-1918; Rural Dean of Storrington (Worthing division), 1904-6; Proctor in Convocation, 1906; b. 1837; s. of late Richard T. Deane, of Knutsford, Cheshire; m. 1883, Mary Jane, d. of C. Lennox Teesdale, J.P., of Whyke House, Chichester; two s. five d. *Educ.*: Sedbergh School; Emmanuel College, Cambridge. Foundation scholar, 8th senior optime, 1859; ordained, 1860, and served curacies in Dioceses of Canterbury, Lichfield, and Manchester; Rector of East Marden, near Chichester, 1871-1888; formerly secretary of the Diocesan Conference, the Diocesan Association, and Bishop of Chichester's Fund, and was secretary of the Brighton Church Congress, 1901; represented the Diocese on Central Council of Diocesan Conferences, and the Committees of S.P.G. and National Society; gave evidence before the Royal Commissions on Education and Redemption of Tithe Rent Charge; served on Joint-Committee of Upper and Lower Houses of Convocation on Letters of Business, and on Committee of Lower House on Prayer Book Revision. *Publications:* was editor of the Chichester Diocesan Kalendar, and Gazette. *Recreations:* is known as a composer of chess problems. *Address:* Apuldram, Chichester. *T.:* Chichester 286. *M.:* BP 8044. *(Died 4 July 1926.)*

DEANE, Augustus Henry, V.D., C.I.E. 1918; b. Geneva, 5 Nov. 1851; 3rd s. of Rev. Barry O'Meara Deane, M.A., Trinity College, Dublin; m. Eugénie Amelia Frederica, d. of John Frederic Galiffe, late H.E.I.C.'s service, and g.d. of Lt.-Col. J. P. Galiffe, C.B.; one s. four d. *Educ.*: Geneva. Officer Volunteer Forces of India, 1885-1912; attended Coronation King Edward VII. 1902 (medal); Hon. A.D.C. to Viceroy of India, 1905-10; commanded Volunteer dismounted troops at King George V. Delhi Durbar (medal); Consul for Belgium in Madras, 1904-13; Consul Pondicherry and Karikal, 1913-20; Member of La Société Académique d'Histoire Internationale, Paris, and of L'Académie latine des Sciences, Arts and Belles-Lettres, Paris. *Recreations:* riding, shooting, tennis. *Address:* c/o Mercantile Bank of India, Madras, India. *Club:* Madras, Madras; United Service, Bangalore. *(Died 25 Mar. 1928.)*

DEANE, Sir Henry Bargrave, Rt. Hon. Mr. Justice Deane, P.C. 1917; Kt., cr. 1905; K.C.; Judge of Probate and Admiralty Div. High Court of Justice, 1905-17; o. surv. s. of late Sir J. P. Deane; b. 28 April 1846; m. 1875, Edith Mary, e. d. of late J. Lindsay Scott, Mollance, Kirkcudbrightshire; one s., Captain, Scots Guards. *Educ.*: Winchester; Balliol College, Oxford. International Law Essay Prize, 1870; Barr. Inner Temple, 1870; South-Eastern Circuit; Secretary of Royal Commission on Wellington College, 1879-80; Recorder of Margate, 1885-1905; Bencher of Inner Temple, 1895; Treasurer, 1917; Q.C. 1896. *Publication:* A Treatise on the Law of Blockade. *Address:* 2 King's Bench Walk,

Temple. E.C.; 52 Eaton Place, S.W. *(Died 21 April 1919.)*

DEANE, Hermann Frederick Williams, M.A., F.S.A.; Librarian and Chapter Clerk to the Dean and Canons of St. George's Chapel, Windsor Castle; publisher and editor; Chairman H. F. W. Deane & Sons, The Year Book Press; b. Cork, 1858; y. s. of late Sir Thomas Deane, P.R.H.A., of Dundanion Castle, Co. Cork, and Harriet, d. of Major Williams; m. Frances Gertrude Emily, d. of late Rev. W. H. Cartwright; two s. one d. *Educ.*: Repton; Trinity College, Cambridge; B.A. 1881. *Publications:* Editor, Public Schools Year Book, Schoolmasters' Year Book, etc. *Recreations:* fishing, golf, philately. *Address:* Gower Lodge, Windsor. *T.:* Windsor 135.
(Died 21 Dec. 1921.)

de BLAQUIERE, 6th Baron (cr. 1800), **William de Blaquiere,** J.P.; Bt. 1784; Great Almager of Ireland; b. 5 Sept. 1856; S. cousin 1889; m. Marie Lucienne Henriette Adine, O.B.E., d. of M. George Desbarats, Montreal; one d. *Heir:* none. *Address:* 3 The Circus, Bath. *Club:* White's.
(Died 28 July 1920.)

de BURGH, Colonel Ulick George Campbell, C.B. 1902; Knight of Grace of the Order of St. John; b. 19 July 1855; 2nd s. of Thomas de Burgh of Oldtown (d. 1872); m. 1883, Blanche (d. 1915), o. c. of Charles Augustus Francis, s. of Lord William Paget; one s. *Educ.*: Trinity Coll., Dublin (B.A.). Entered 7th Dragoon Guards, 1876; Capt. 1881; Maj. 1890; Lt.-Col. 1897; Col. 1900; served as Adjutant 7th Dragoon Guards, Egypt, 1882 (medal with clasp, bronze star); commanded 3rd Dragoon Guards, 1897; special service, 1900; Assistant Director, War Office, 1902; Staff, Gibraltar, 1906; retired 1908; recalled to Army Service, 1914. *Club:* Army and Navy. *(Died 17 Nov. 1922.)*

DEBUSSY, Claude Achille, Chevalier Legion of Honour; b. St. Germain-en-Laye, 22 Aug. 1862. *Educ.*: Paris Conservatoire. Gained Grand Prix de Rome, 1884. *Works:* Pelléas et Mélisande; Ariettes oubliées; cinq Poèmes de Baudelaire; Fêtes Galantes; Trois Chansons de France; Trois Chansons de Charles d'Orléans; Quatuor à cordes; Petites Suites; La Damoiselle élue; Prélude à l'après-midi d'un faune; Trois nocturnes; La Mer; Images; Printemps; Ronde de Printemps; Gigue; Iberia; Le Martyre de Saint Sébastien; Ballades de Villon; Jeux; La Boite à joujoux; Douze Etudes—En Blanc et noir; Children's Corner; 3 Poèmes de S. Mallarmé; Sonate pour Piano et Violoncelle; Sonate pour Harpe, Flute, et Alto; etc. *Address:* 24 Square du Bois de Boulogne, Paris.
(Died 26 Mar. 1918.)

DECARIE, Hon. Jeremie L.; Chief Justice of the Court of Sessions of the Peace, Montreal, since 1919; b. Aug. 1870; m. 1st, 1898, Rose Alba (d. 1902), d. of A. C. Decary; 2nd, 1907, Juliette, e. d. of Hon. H. B. Rainville. *Educ.*: Montreal College; St. Mary's College; Laval University, now Université de Montreal. Advocate, 1896; K.C. 1906; M.P. (P.), Hochelaga, since 1904; Maisonneuve since 1912; Minister of Agriculture, 1909; Provincial Secretary, Quebec, 1909; Life Governor of Notre Dame Hospital, Montreal; Hon. Lieutenant-Colonel, 85th Regiment, Montreal. *Address:* 857 Dorchester Street, West, Montreal. *Clubs:* Canadian, St. Denis, Montreal Jockey, Montreal Hunt, Royal Montreal Golf, Montreal; Laval sur le Lac Golfe.
(Died 5 Nov. 1927.)

DE CELLES, Alfred Duclos, C.M.G. 1907; Chevalier de la Legion d'Honneur; F.R.S.C., LL.D.; General Librarian of Parliament, 1880 (now superannuated); b. 15 Aug. 1844; father, French Canadian; mother, American; m. Eugenie Dorion. *Educ.*: Laval

University, Quebec. Lawyer; Editor of Le Journal de Quebec; La Minerve, Montreal; L'Opinion Publique, Montreal.' *Publications:* La Crise du regime parlementaire; A la conquête de la liberté en France et au Canada; Les Etats Unis; Papineau (Political History of Canada); Papineau and Cartier (in English); La Fontaine, Cartier (in French); The Province of Quebec from 1867 to date; The Habitant in Canada; The Constitutions of Canada. *Address:* 49 Wilton Crescent, Ottawa, Canada.
(Died Oct. 1925.)

DE COLYAR, Henry Anselm, K.C., 1905; *o. surv. s.* of late Augustine de Colyar, F.R.S.E. [direct descendant of Robert Collier, who came to England from France, temp. Henry VI.; *m. o. d.* and heiress of Sir John de Doddington and settled at Darlaston, Staffs]; and Anne, *d.* of Alexander Park; unmarried. *Educ.:* The Oratory School, Edgbaston. Barr. Middle Temple, 1871; Bencher of the Middle Temple, 1914; Gold Staff Officer at Coronation of King Edward VII. (silver coronation medal), and at the Coronation of King George V. (silver Coronation medal); member of English deputation from Catholic Union to Pope Leo XIII., 1903; a National Service Representative on Military Service Committees, 1918; member of the Court of Assistants of the Poulters' Livery Company, of which Company he has been Renter Warden, Upper Warden, and Master. *Publications:* The Law of Guarantees and of Principal and Surety, 3rd edition; County Court-Cases; contributor to Encyclopædia Britannica, the Laws of England, Encyclopedia of the Laws of England, Encyclopædia of Forms, Encyclopædia of Accounting, Journal of Comparative Legislation, Great Jurists of the World, the Life of Colbert, etc. *Recreations:* travelling, golf. *Address:* 24 Palace Gardens Terrace, W.; 1 Elm Court Temple, E.C. *Club:* Athenæum.
(Died 31 Jan. 1925.)

DECOPPET, Camille; *b.* Canton of Vaud, 1862. Member of the Federal Council, 1912; later head of the War Department; President of the Federal Council of Switzerland for 1916; Directeur du Bureau International de l'union postale universelle, 1920; Radical Democrat. *Address:* Berne. *(Died 14 Jan. 1925.)*

DE CUREL, Viscomte Francois, dramatic author; Member of the French Academy, 1918; Officer Legion of Honour; *b.* Metz, 10 June 1854. *Educ.:* Ecole Centrale. *Publication:* l'Amour brode; l'Envers d'une Sainte; la Figurante; les Fossiles; l'Invitée; le Repas du Lion; la Nouvelle idole; la Fille sauvage; le Coup d'aile; la Danse devant le miroir; l'Âme en folie, Terre inhumaine, édit. Crès. *Address:* 5 rue de Solférino, Paris; *T.:* Elysée 6728; Château de Ketzing, Gondrexange, Lorraine. *(Died 26 April 1928.)*

DEED, Rev. Canon John George, M.A., D.D.; Vicar of Nuneaton and Canon of Coventry, since 1908; *b.* 18 Sep. 1842; *s.* of John Simpkin Deed and Elizabeth, *d.* of John Cornell; *m.* 1868, Elizabeth (*d.* 1922), *d.* of William Snowdon Gard; five *s.* three *d. Educ.:* University College School; New College, London; Trinity College, Dublin. Deacon, 1867; Priest, 1858; Curate of Paddock, Huddersfield, 1867-69; Hemel Hempsted, 1869-72; Clapham, 1872-73; Blakedown, in the Parish of Hagley, 1873-75; Organising Secretary National Society, 1875-83, also Hon. Secretary Church School Managers and Teachers Association; Secretary of A.C.S., 1883-93; also Hon. Secretary Ordination Candidates Exhibition Fund; Parochial Missions to the Jews Fund; Incumbents Sustentation Fund; Vicar of Nuneaton (Patron the Crown) since 1893; Rural Dean of Atherstone, 1914; Chairman of the Governors of the King Edward VIth Grammar School, Nuneaton, since

1893; Chairman of the Nuneaton Higher Education Committee; Commissary of the Lord Archbishop of Perth, W.A.; Vice-President of the Additional Curates' Society. *Publications:* Sermons; Continuity of the Church of England, etc. *Recreations:* reading and change of work. *Address:* Nuneaton Vicarage, Warwickshire. *T.A.:* Deed, Nuneaton. *T.:* Nuneaton 52. *Club:* Royal Societies.
(Died 18 Jan. 1923.)

DEEDES, Rev. Arthur Gordon, Vicar of S. John the Divine, Kennington, 1911; Hon. Canon of Southwark Cathedral, 1911; *b.* 4 Feb. 1861; *s.* of Rev. Canon Gordon F. Deedes, Vicar of Heydour, Grantham. *Educ.:* Haileybury College; Oriel College, Oxford; Cuddesdon Theological College. Ordained, 1884; Assistant Curate of S. John the Divine, Kennington, 1884-1911; Warden of the Community of Reparation, Southwark, 1892; Commissary to Bishop Trollope of Corea, 1911. *Address:* 125 Vassall Road, S.W. *T.:* Brixton, 1491. *Club:* New Oxford and Cambridge.*(Died 29 Nov. 1916.)*

DEEDES, Ven. Brook; Rector of St. Vedast, Foster Lane, 1913-21; *b.* 1847; *y. s.* of William Deedes of Sandling Park, Kent, M.P. for East Kent; *m.* 1889, Mary Caroline, *d.* of Hon. Mr. Justice Brodhurst. *Educ.:* Harrow; Christ Church, Oxford. Ordained, 1871; Curate of St. Mary, Charterhouse, 1871-75; Vicar of St. Crispin, Bermondsey, 1875-76; Domestic Chaplain to Bishop of Calcutta, 1877-85; Chaplain at Allahabad, 1885-95; Archdeacon of Lucknow, 1892-97; Naini Tal, 1895-96; Moradabad, 1896-1897; Fellow of Allahabad University; Vicar of Hawkhurst, 1897-1900; Vicar of Hampstead, 1900-1913; Archdeacon of Hampstead, 1912-20. *Address:* 8 Victoria Park, Dover.
(Died 28 Oct. 1922.)

DEEDES, Rev. Cecil, M.A., F.R. Hist.S.; Prebendary of "Exceit" in Chichester Cathedral, 1903; *b.* 1845; *s.* of late Rev. Lewis Deedes, M.A., Rector of Bramfield, Herts; unmarried. *Educ.:* Winchester; Brasenose College, Oxford; 2nd class Law and History School, 1866. Curate of St. Philip and St. James, Oxford, 1867-72; Chaplain of Christ Church, Oxford, 1868-72; Vicar of St. Mary Magd. Oxford, 1872-76; Organising Sec. of Central African Mission, 1876-77; Canon of Maritzburg, Natal, 1877-80; Curate of Horspath, Oxford, 1881-82; Rector of Wickham St. Paul's, Halstead, Essex, 1882-89; Curate of Brighton, in charge of St. Stephen's Chapel-of-ease, 1889-1902; Prebendary of "Hova Ecclesia," Chichester, 1902-3; Rector of Saints Martin and Olave, Chichester, 1910-20. *Publications:* Articles in Smith's Dictionary of Christian Biography, 1877; Wase's Electra in Stuart Series, 1903; Editor Bishop Praty's Register, 1905, Bishop Rede's Register, 2 vols. 1908 and 1910, both for Sussex Record Society; Consecration form of St. Bartholomew's Hospital, Chichester, 1909; Church Bells of Essex (jointly with H. B. Walters), 1909; The Muniments of the Bishopric of Winchester, 1912; The Register of John de Pontissara, Bishop of Winchester (part i.), for Canterbury and York Society, 1913; (part ii.) 1914; (part iv. with Introduction), 1916; contributions to Essex Review, 1917-18; Editor of Chichester Diocesan Gazette, 1905-14. *Address:* Frensham, Farnham, Surrey. *Club:* Authors'.
(Died 30 Dec. 1920.)

DEERHURST, Viscount, George William Reginald Victor Coventry; *b.* 10 Sep. 1900; *g.s.* of 9th Earl of Coventry; *s.* of late Viscount Deerhurst and Virginia, *step-d.* of late Charles W. Bonynge; *m.* 1921, Nesta Donne, *e. d.* of 1st Baron Kylsant; two *d. Educ.:* Eton. *Address:* Amroth Castle, Amroth, Pembs. *Clubs:* Carlton, Bachelors'.
(Died 8 Aug. 1927.)

DEERING, William Henry, I.S.O. 1906 ; F.I.C. ; late Chemist, War Department ; b. 1848. *Address :* Glanmire, Bronshill Road, Torquay, Devon. (*Died 5 Sept. 1925.*)

DE FREYCINET, C. L.; Séni;teur ; Minister of State since 1915 ; Membre de l'Académie des Sciences et de l'Académie Française. Ancien élève de l'Ecole Polytechnique et de l'Ecole des Mines ; Ingénieur des Mines, puis Inspecteur Général des Mines ; Délégué au Ministère de la Guerre, 1870-71 ; Ministre des Travaux Publics, 1877-79 ; Ministre des Affaires Etrangères et Président du Conseil des Ministres, 1880, 1882, 1885 et 1886 ; Président du Conseil et Ministre de la Guerre, 1888-93 ; Ministre de la Guerre, 1898-99. *Publications :* Traité de Mécanique Rationnelle ; Analyse Infinitésimale ; Rapport sur l'Assainissement en Europe ; La Guerre en Province, 1870-71 ; Essai sur la Philosophie des Sciences ; Sur les planètes télescopiques ; Principes de la Mécanique Rationnelle ; De l'Expérience en Géométrie ; La Question d'Egypte ; Souvenirs, etc. *Address :* rue de la Faisanderie, 123, XVIe, Paris
(*Died 15 May 1923.*)

DEGAS, Hilaire Germain Edgard ; b. Paris, 19 July 1834. *Educ. :* Ecole des Beaux-Arts. *Works :* War in the Middle Ages, Salon, 1865 ; Steeplechase, 1866 ; Family Portraits, 1867 ; Ballet of La Source, 1868 ; Portraits of Criminals, 1880 ; Races, 1884 ; Interior of a Cotton - Broker's Office at New Orleans, and The Rehearsal, 1900. *Address :* Rue Victor Massy, 37, IXe, Paris. (*Died 26 Sept. 1917.*)

DE GEX, Colonel (temporary **Brig.-Gen.**) **Francis J.,** C.B. 1914 ; C.M.G. 1915 ; b. 5 July 1861 ; Deputy Inspector Gen. of Communication since 1915 ; s. of late George F. de Gex, M.A. ; m. 1905, Edith Hope, d. of C. J. Miller, Oughtrington House, Lymm, Cheshire ; one s. one d. *Educ. :* Reading ; Sandhurst. Lieut., West Riding Regiment, 1882 ; Capt., 1888 ; Major, 1900 ; Bt.-Lt.-Col., 1900 ; Bt.-Col., 1907 ; Col., 1913 ; D.A.A.G., South Africa, 1901-3 ; D.A.Q.M.G., Third Division, 1st Army Corps, D.A.A. and Q.M.G., 3rd Division, Aldershot Army Corps, D.A.A. and Q.M.G., Aldershot Command, 1903-7 ; A.A.G. Irish Command, 1914 ; Expeditionary Force, Nov. 1914. Served S. Africa, 1899-1902 (despatches, Queen's medal 3 clasps, King's medal 2 clasps, Bt. Lt.-Col.); European War, 1914-15 (despatches, C.M.G.). *Address :* Highfield House, Rathgar, Dublin. *Clubs :* Army and Navy ; Royal Western Yacht.
(*Died April 1917.*)

DE HORSEY, Admiral Sir Algernon (Frederick Rous), K.C.B., cr.1903 ; Deputy-Governor (Joint) Isle of Wight since 1913 ; b. 25 July 1827 ; s. of late Spencer de Horsey of Great Glemham, Suffolk, M.P., and d. of 1st Earl of Stradbroke ; m. 1861, Caroline, d. of Admiral Drew ; one s. two d. Served on coast of Syria, 1840 ; senior naval officer during Jamaica insurrection, 1865, and Fenian raids on Lakes of Canada, 1866 ; A.D.C. to Queen Victoria, 1871-75 ; Commodore in W. Indies, 1872-75 ; Commander-in-Chief, Pacific, 1876-79 ; in the flagship Shah engaged Peruvian rebel iron-clad Huascar, forcing her to surrender to Peruvian authorities ; the Admiral's action being questioned in Parliament, Sir J. Holker, Attorney-General, said, "Huascar having committed acts which made her an enemy of Great Britain, de Horsey was justified in what he did" ; commanded Channel Squadron, 1884-85 ; retired list, 1892 ; J.P. Hants ; Chairman Isle of Wight Bench to 1918. *Publications :* Draysonia ; African Pilot ; Rule of the Road at Sea ; Letters to the Press. *Recreations :* county administration, yachting, astronomy, and mechanic's work. *Address :* Melcombe House, Cowes. *Club :* United Service.
(*Died 22 Oct. 1922.*)

276

DEIGHTON, Frederick, M.A., M.B. Cantab. ; Consulting Surgeon to Addenbrooke's Hospital ; b. 20 April 1854 ; s. of late John Deighton, Surgeon, Cambridge ; m. Louisa Ellen, d. of late Francis Fisher, Crown Solicitor, Sydney, N.S.W. ; two s. three d. *Educ. :* St. Peter's College, Cambridge ; St. George's Hospital. Ex-President of the Cambridge Medical Society ; Ex-President of the Cambs and Hunts branch of the British Medical Association ; Lt.-Colonel R.A.M.C.(T.). *Publications :* With the late Prof. Balfour, A renewed Study of the Germinal Layers of the Chick, Quarterly Journal of Microscopic Science ; various papers in the Transactions of the Cambridge Medical Society. *Recreations :* travel, golf, and chess. *Address :* St. Bernard's Hills Road, Cambridge. *T. :* Cambridge 80. *M. :* ER 825. *Club :* Royal Automobile. (*Died 29 Sept. 1924.*)

DE KANTZOW, Commander Arthur Henry, D.S.O. 1918 ; R.N (retired) ; s. of late Capt. Walter Sidney de Kantzow, R.N. ; m. ; three d. Southern Nigerian Civil Service, 1906-1913. *Address :* 3 Addison Court Gardens, Kensington, W.14. *T. :* Riverside 1453.
(*Died 6 Mar. 1928.*)

DE LA BERE, Captain Richard Norman, D.S.O. 1902 ; late Captain and Hon. Major 3rd Batt. King's Own Royal Lancaster Regiment ; b. 1869 ; s. of late Major Charles R. de la Bere, R.M.L.I. Served S. Africa, 1900-2 (despatches twice, Queen's medal, 2 clasps, King's medal, 2 clasps). *Club :* Junior United Service. (*Died 20 Sept. 1922.*)

DELAFAYE, Hon. Sir Louis Victor, K.C. ; Chief Judge of the Supreme Court of the Colony of Mauritius since Dec. 1898 ; b. 10 March 1842 ; m. 1865, Marie Lucia, o. d. of late Theodore Cloarec, D.M.P. Called to Bar, Middle Temple, 1863 ; Municipal Councillor, St. Louis, 1870 ; Member Prison Board, 1884 ; Member Civil Service Commission, 1884-95 ; Acting Puisne Judge, 1884-85, and 1890-92 ; Q.C. 1892 ; Puisne Judge, 1894 ; Acting Chief-Justice, 1898. *Address :* Port Louis, Mauritius.
(*Died 1920.*)

DELAGE, Yves ; Professeur de Zoologie à la Faculté des Sciences de Paris ; Directeur de la Station Biologique de Roscoff ; b. Avignon, 13 Mai 1854 ; m. ; one s. one d. *Educ. :* divers collèges et lycées de province. Aspirant répétiteur au Lycée de La Rochelle, 1874 ; Préparateur de Zoologie (Hautes Etudes), 1878 ; Chargé de Conférences de Zoologie à la Sorbonne, 1880 ; Préparateur à la Faculté des Sciences de Paris, 1881 ; Maître de Conférences, 1882 ; Chargé de Cours à la Faculté des Sciences de Caen et Directeur de la Station Zoologique de Luc-sur-Mer, 1883 ; Professeur titulaire du même cours et Directeur titulaire de la station, 1884 ; Chargé du Cours de Zoologie, Anatomie, et Physiologie comparées à la Faculté des Sciences de Paris, 1885 ; Professeur titulaire du même cours, 1886 ; Directeur-adjoint du Laboratoire de Recherches de Zoologie expérimentale, 1889 ; Directeur de la Station Zoologique de Roscoff, 1901 ; Membre de l'Institut (Académie des Sciences), 1901 ; holds Darwin Medal of Royal Society, 1916. *Publications :* L'Appareil circulatoire des crustacés édriophhalmes(thèse), 1881 ; Evolution de la sacculine, 1884 ; Fonction des canaux demicirculaires et otocystes des invertébrés, 1887 ; Embryogénie des éponges 1892 ; L'Hérédité et les grands problèmes de la biologie générale, 1895 ; L'Année biologique (23 vols., 1897-1918) ; Traité de zoologie concrète (6 vols., parus 1896-1903) ; Nombreux Travaux sur la parthénogénèse expérimentale 1900-1908 ; Les théories de l'évolution, 1 vol. Bibl. scient. internat., 1909 ; La Parthénogénèse naturelle et expérimentale, 1 vol. ibid 1913 ; Divers travaux d'Océanographie publié dans les Annales et le Bulletin de Monaco

Address: 14 .rue du Docteur Berger, Sceaux (Seine), France. *T.:* 16.   (*Died 3 Oct. 1920.*)

DE LANGE, Daniel, Director Conservatorium since 1895 ; *b.* 11 July 1841 ; *m.* 1st, A. M. H. van Oordt (*d.* 1910); 2nd, A. M. Gouda ; two *s.* three *d.*   *Educ.:* Rotterdam and Brussels.   Virtuose - Violoncellist first at Vienna, afterwards Hungary, Galicia, Roumania, then a short time in Holland (Rotterdam); Paris, 1865-70; established himself in Amsterdam, 1870 ; was conductor of several choirs and teacher at the music school of the Maatsch. t. Bev. d. Toonkunst; General Secretary of the Society for Music, 1879 ; erected the Conservatory for Music, 1885 ; he made a journey with the Amsterdam à Cappella Choir to Vienna, Berlin, Leipzig, Dresden, Koningsberg, Brussels, Paris, London, etc., 1892-93. *Publications:* Symphonie ; pieces for fortepiano ; Songs ; Cantata for Choir and Orchestra; Dramatic Scenes ; a Theory of Music ; etc. *Address:* Point Loma, California, U.S.A.
(*Died 30 Jan. 1918.*)

DELANY, Mgr. Patrick, D.D. ; R.C. Archbishop of Hobart since 1908 ; *b.* near Ballinamore, Co. Galway, Ireland, 1 Feb. 1853. *Educ.:* St. Ignatius' College, Galway, by the Jesuits ; read philosophy and theology at All Hallows' College, Dublin ; and higher philosophy and theology at the Catholic Institute or University, Paris. Graduated there B.D. in 1879 ; his teachers included Duchesne, Martin, Bayonne, and Joven ; took the Chair of Civil History at All Hallows' College immediately after his elevation to the priesthood, 1879 ; proceeded to Australia on a commission from the College, 1885 ; elected to accept the position of Chancellor offered by the Bishop of Ballarat, 1887 ; Bishop of Laranda and acting coadjutor to Archbishop of Hobart, with right of succession to See of Hobart, 1893-1908. *Publications:* has written much on religious and economico-social questions in various publications, the Austral Light, the Ecclesiastical Record, etc., chiefly organs of the Roman Catholic Church in Australia. *Address:* Archbishop's House, Hobart.
(*Died 7 May 1926.*)

DELANY, Rev. William, S.J., LL.D. ; *b.* 1835. *Educ.:* Carlow College ; Maynooth College ; Gregorian University, Rome. Entered the Society of Jesus at St. Acheul, near Amiens, 1856 ; taught classics and mathematics in Clongowes and Tullabeg Colleges, 1858-65 ; studied in Rome, 1865-68 ; Priest, 1866 ; Chaplain to Irish Zouaves in Rome, 1867 ; returned to Tullabeg College, 1868 ; Prefect of Studies, Tullabeg, 1868-70 ; Rector, 1870-80 ; travelled in Canada and the United States, 1881 ; Rector St. Ignatius' College, Dublin, 1882-83 ; President, Catholic University College, Dublin, 1883-88 ; Missionary Work in Jesuit Church, Dublin, 1888-97 ; again President of University College, Dublin, 1897-1909 ; Provincial in Ireland, 1909-1912 ; Senator of the Royal University, 1885-1909 ; Senator of the National University, 1909-1919 ; and Member of the Governing Body of the Dublin University College, 1908 ; gave evidence before the Royal Commissions on University Education in Ireland. *Publications:* Lectures on Christian Reunion, 1897 ; pamphlets and letters on Irish University Education. *Recreation:* reading. *Address:* 35 Lower Leeson Street, Dublin. *T.:* Dublin 532.
(*Died 1924.*)

DELANY, William P., M.P. (N.) Ossory Div. Queen's Co. since 1900 ; farmer ; *b.* 1855 ; *s.* of Denis Delany, Roskeen ; unmarried. Landholder in King's and Queen's Counties. *Address:* Tullamore, Ireland ; House of Commons, S.W. *T.A.:* Commons, London. *T.:* 800-801 Victoria ; 172, 293, 757 Western.   (*Died 7 Mar. 1916.*)

DE LA RUE, Stuart Andros; 3rd *s.* of Sir Andros la de Rue, 1st Bart. ; *b.* 29 May 1883 ; *m.* 1912, Margaret Griselda, *o. d.* of Alexander Wedderburn, K.C.;   four *s.* one *d. Educ.:* Eton ; Magdalen College, Oxford. J.P. Hertfordshire. *Address:* The Hoo, Willingdon, Sussex. *Address:* Willingdon, Sussex. *T.:* Hampden Park 28. *Clubs:* Junior Carlton, Bath, Royal Automobile.   (*Died 26 Oct. 1927.*)

DE LA RUE, Warren Wm., J.P. ; *b.* 27 Feb. 1847 ; *e. s.* of Warren de la Rue, D.C.L., F.R.S. ; *m.* 1916, Lilla Livingstone, *d.* of late W. Forster Smithe, and widow of Sir Henry Thobie Prinsep, K.C.I.E. (*d.* 1914). *Educ.:* private tutors. Entered the family business of Thos. de la Rue & Co. at the age of 22 ; very soon assumed the entire management and developed it fourfold ; retired at the age of 42 and then took to racing and shooting ; held over 10,000 acres of shooting at Chippenham near Newmarket, and kept a large stud of racehorses ; his horse Thayles established a record by winning the Ascot Gold Cup, the Alexandra Plate, and the Goodwood Cup, all in 1889. *Address:* 3 Holland Park, W.11 ; *T.:* Park 2049 ; Thayles, Tenby, S. Wales. *Club:* White's.
(*Died 15 April 1921.*)

DELAVOYE, Col. Alexander Marin, C.B. 1902 ; *b.* 12 May 1845 ; *m.* ; one *s.* Entered army, 1864 ; Captain, 1878 ; Major, 1882 ; Lieut.-Col. 1888 ; Col. 1891 ; Assistant Military Secretary for Education, 1898-1903 ; retired, 1903.
(*Died 26 April 1917.*)

DELCASSE, Théophile; *b.* Pamiers, Ariège, 1 Mar. 1852; *m.* Mdlle. Wallet; joined staff of journal La République Française, and wrote articles on foreign politics ; Conseiller-Général, Ariège, 1888 ; elected Deputy of Foix, 1889 ; Under Sec. for Colonies, 1893 ; Colonial Minister, 1894-95 ; Foreign Minister, 1898-1905 ; Minister of Marine, 1905-13 ; French Ambassador to St. Petersburg, 1913-14 ; acted as mediator between United States and Spain, 1899 ; received decoration of Legion of Honour, 1887 ; Order of St. Andrew, Russia, 1914 ; Minister of Foreign Affairs, 1914-15. *Address:* Boul de Clichy, 11, IXe, Paris ; Les Cascatelles, Ax-les-Thermes, Ariège, France.   (*Died 21 Feb. 1923.*)

DELEPINE, Sheridan, M.B., C.M., M.Sc.; Professor of Public Health and Bacteriology (formerly Professor of Pathology), University of Manchester, since 1891 ; Director of Public Health Laboratories, University of Manchester, since 1901 ; Hon. Fellow, Incorporated Society Medical Officers of Health : *b.* 1 Jan. 1855 ; *s.* of Antoine Delépine of Paris and Henriette Mennet, Canton de Vaud, Switzerland ; *m.* Florence, *d.* of Frederick Rose of London ; one *d. Educ.:* Collège Charlemagne, Paris ; Académie de Lausanne ; Université de Genève ; Edinburgh University. 1st class Honours M.B. C.M. Examinations ; Lecturer in Physiology and Lecturer in Pathology, St. George's Hospital Medical School, London, etc., B.Sc. with distinction, Lausanne, 1872 ; medical studies, 1877-82 ; Demonstrator of Anatomy and Pathology, 1881 and 1882. *Publications:* contributions to Anatomy, Physiology, and Pathology in the Journal of Anatomy and Physiology, Journal of Physiology, Proceedings of the Royal Society, Transactions of the Pathological Society, London, Practitioner, British Medical Journal, Lancet, Medical Chronicle, Journal of Comparative Pathology and Therapeutics, Journal of State Medicine, Public Health, Journal of Hygiene, Encyclopædia Medica, Quain's Dictionary, etc., between the years 1883 and 1921. *Address:* 41 Palatine Road, Withington, Manchester ; *T.:* Didsbury 229 ; Public Health Laboratory, York Place, Manchester ; *T.A.:* Laboratory, Manchester ; *T.:* Rusholme 8. *Club:* Authors'.
(*Died 13 Nov. 1921.*)

DE LISLE, Edwin Joseph Lisle March Phillipps, F.S.A., D.L. ; *b.* Gracedieu Manor, 13 June 1852 ; 7th *s.* and 13th *child* of Ambrose

277

DE LEMOS, Charles Herman.   See page xviii.

Lisle March Phillipps de Lisle of Garendon Park and Gracedieu Manor, Leicestershire, and Laura Mary Clifford, *g. d.* of 4th Lord Clifford of Chudleigh ; *m.* 1889, Agnes Henriette Ida, *e. d.* of Adrian Elias Hope and Lady Ida Duff, *sister* of 1st Duke of Fife ; four *s.* three *d.* *Educ.* : Oscott College ; Universities of Münster, in Westphalia, and Innsbruck, in Tyrol. Private Secretary to Sir Frederick Weld, G.C.M.G., Governor of the Straits Settlements, 1881-82, and to Lord John Manners, late Duke of Rutland, when Postmaster-General, 1885-86 ; M.P. (C.) Mid-Leicestershire, 1886-92 ; *Publications :* The Majesty of London ; Centenary Studies on Luther and Wyclif ; The Parliamentary Oath ; The Royal Declaration Amended ; The Evolutionary Hypothesis ; and joint author with Edmund Sheridan Purcell of Life and Letters of Ambrose Phillipps de Lisle. *Club :* Carlton. (*Died 5 May 1920.*)

DE L'ISLE and DUDLEY, 3rd Baron (*cr.* 1835), **Philip Sidney** ; J.P. ; Bt. 1818 ; Major (late), Rifle Brigade ; Hereditary Visitor of Sidney Sussex Coll. Camb. ; *b.* 14 May 1853 ; *s.* of 2nd Baron and Mary, *d.* of Sir William Foulis, Bt. ; *S.* father 1898 ; *m.* 1902, Hon. Elizabeth Maria Astell, *d.* of 4th Viscount Gort, and widow of late W. H. Astell, of Woodbury Hall, Sandy. *Educ.* : Eton ; Trin. Coll. Camb. Owns about 10,000 acres. *Heir :* b. Colonel Hon. Algernon Sidney, R.F.A. *Address :* Penshurst Place, Kent ; Ingleby Manor, Great Ayton. Yorkshire. *Club :* Carlton.
(*Died 24 Dec. 1922.*)

DELMEGE, Alfred Gideon, M.V.O. 1898 ; M.D., L.R.C.S.I. ; Hon. Surgeon to the King ; Deputy Inspector-General of Hospitals and Fleets (extra) ; *b.* 1846 ; *s.* of Julius Delmege of Rathkeale, Co.Limerick; *m.*1884, Mary Elizabeth, *d.* of late Rt. Hon. James Anthony Lawson ; two *s.* Entered Royal Navy, 1869 ; served with Royal Marines during Ashantee War, 1873 (received thanks of the Admiralty) ; on board H.M.S. Bacchante during cruise round world of T.R.H. Princes Albert Victor and George of Wales, 1879-82 ; in Royal Yacht Osborne, 1887-1899 ; Hon. Physician to Prince of Wales, 1899 ; Hon. Surgeon to King Edward VII. *Address :* 33 Westcombe Park Road, Blackheath, S.E.
(*Died 2 Feb. 1923.*)

DE MAULEY, 3rd Baron, U.K., *cr.* 1838, **William Ashley Webb Ponsonby**, J.P. ; *b.* 2 March 1843 ; *s.* of 2nd Baron and Mary, *d.* of 4th Earl of Bessborough. *S.* father 1896. Formerly Lieut. Rifle Brigade and A.D.C. to Gov.-Gen. of Canada. Owns about 4000 acres. *Heir :* b. Hon. Maurice Ponsonby. *Address :* Langford House, Lechlade, Oxfordshire.
(*Died 13 April 1918.*)

DE MOLEYNS, Maj.-Gen. Townsend Aremberg ; retired list, 1886 ; late the Royal Artillery ; *b.* Dublin, 20 June 1838 ; *o. surv. s.* of late Thomas de Moleyns, Q.C. ; *m.* 1866, Selina Harriet, *o. d.* of Henry Sneyd French ; one *s.* one *d. Educ.* : Royal Military Academy, Woolwich. Served at siege and fall of Sebastopol, and Fenian Raid Canada. *Address :* 5 Brechin Place, South Kensington, S.W.7. *T.* : 2860 Kensington. *Club :* Army and Navy.
(*Died 13 Nov. 1926.*)

DE MONTMORENCY, Ven. Waller ; J.P. Kilkenny ; Archdeacon of Ossory since 1911 ; *b.* 1841 ; *m.* 1872, Mary, 3rd *d.* of late Bishop O'Brien of Ossory, Ferns, and Leighlin ; two *s. Educ.* : Trinity College, Cambridge (M.A.). Ordained, 1865; Treasurer of Kilkenny Cathedral, 1883-91 ; Chancellor, 1891-1911. *Address :* Castle Morris, Knocktopher, Co. Kilkenny.
(*Died 25 Oct. 1924.*)

DE MORGAN, William Frend; author ; *b.* 16 Nov. 1839, 69 Gower Street; *s.* of Augustus De Morgan, at the time Professor of Mathematics in University College, London, and
278

Sophia Elizabeth, *d.* of William Frend, expelled from Cambridge University for heretical opinions. *Educ.* : University College School, and College, Gower Street ; *m.* 1888, Evelyn Pickering, *d.* of Perceval Andree Pickering, Q.C. Was student at Royal Academy, 1859, having adopted Art as a profession ; in the years following 1864 was chiefly engaged in stained glass - work ; in 1870 turned his attention to ceramic work, when his experiments in lustre, at that time not much known in England, attracted some attention among artists ; in 1905 he commenced as a writer of fiction. *Publications :* Joseph Vance : An Ill-written Autobiography, 1906 ; Alice - for - Short : a Dichronism, 1907 ; Somehow Good, 1908 ; It Never Can Happen Again, 1909 ; An Affair of Dishonour, 1910 ; A Likely Story, 1912 ; When Ghost Meets Ghost, 1914. *Address :* 127 Church Street, Chelsea, S.W.
(*Died 15 Jan. 1917.*)

DE MORLEY, 21st Baron in elder line by Writ (Eng. *cr.* 1299), **James Thorne Parker Roe de Morley**, title brought in by marriages ; Barony of Marshal (*cr.* 1309), also the ancient Baronies of Hingham and Rie ; claimed at Court of Claims for their Majesties Coronation, 1902, the office of Hereditary Royal Standard Bearer of England and the Marshalship of Ireland—having proved pedigree of blood descent in 1897-98 to the satisfaction of her late Majesty's Attorney - General, by royal command ; *b.* St. Martin's-in-the-fields, Middlesex, 17 Feb. 1844 ; *e. s.* of Freeman Roe, Hydraulic Engineer, late of Bridgefield Hall, Manor of Duntsford, Wandsworth, and Susan, *d.* of Timothy Thorne, late of Westminster ; *m.* Emily Martha, *d.* of Wm. Passmore, late of Truro, Cornwall. *Educ.* : College House, Southgate. Commenced business life with Jackson and Graham of Oxford Street ; managed Duntshill Flock Mills for his father ; was the leaseholder and proprietor of Ravensbury Wool Mills, Surrey, 1868 ; became an inventive engineer ; took diploma of honourable mention, London International Universal Exhibition, London, 1884, and medals and diploma of special merit 1885 and 1886 ; travelled in South America, 1899. *Publications :* words to Jubilee Anthem ; book of poems on Doré pictures ; Bobs' Call recruiting poem set to music. *Recreations :* various ; also sketching and painting ; founder of the Spencer Cricket Club, Surrey, and an early member of the West London Rowing Club ; Staff Captain, Volunteer Civil Force, and Chairman of the Ways and Means Committee, Ruskin House, Westminster, 1914 - 15 ; engaged making War munitions, Vickers, Ltd., June 1915 ; Inspector in their Maxim gun department, Jan. 1916 ; machinery distribution staff, 1917. *Address :* Falcon Lodge, Oppidans Road, Primrose Hill, N.W.
(*Died June 1918.*)

DEMPSEY, Sir Alexander, M.D. ; Kt., *cr.* 1911 ; F.R.C.S.I. ; Consulting Physician Mater Infirmorium Hospital ; Clinical Lecturer in Gynæcology, Queen's University, Belfast ; Member of Senate, National Univ. ; Member governing body, University College, Dublin ; External Examiner, National University ; Fellow Royal Society of Medicine ; *b.* Coldugh, Ballymoney, 15 Feb. 1852 ; *s.* of Bernard Dempsey ; *m.* 1876 (wife died 1905) ; three *s.* four *d. Educ.* : St. Malachy's College, Belfast ; Catholic University Medical School, Dublin ; Queen's College, Galway. *Publications :* papers in medical journals. *Recreations :* golf, motoring. *Address :* 36 Clifton Street, Belfast ; Coldugh, Fortwilliam Park, Belfast. *T. :* 214 ; 2270.
(*Died 18 July 1920.*)

DENDY, Professor Arthur, D.Sc., F.R.S., F.L.S., F.Z.S. ; Hon. Member New Zealand Institute ; Corresponding Member Royal Societies of Victoria and Tasmania ;

Professor of Zoology, King's College, Univ. of London since 1905 ; *b.* 1865 ; *s.* of Rev. John Dendy, B.A. ; *m.* Ada Margaret, *d.* of late Louis Courtauld, Barrister ; one *s.* two *d.* *Educ.* : Manchester Grammar School ; Owens Coll-Manchester. Assist. in the Zoological Department, British Museum (Natural History), 1887 ; Demonstrator and Assistant Lecturer in Biology in the University of Melbourne, 1888-94 ; Professor of Biology in the Canterbury College, University of New Zealand, 1894-1903 ; Professor of Zoology in the South African College, Cape Town, 1903-5. *Publications* : Outlines of Evolutionary Biology, 1912 (3rd ed. 1923); The Biological Foundations of Society, 1924 ; numerous memoirs on systematic zoology, comparative anatomy, etc. *Address* : King's College, Strand, W.C. ; 113 Corringham Road, N.W.11. *T.* : Speedwell 1288. *Club* : Savile.
(Died 24 Mar. 1925.)

DE NEUFLIZE, Baron Jean, Officer Legion of Honour ; Head of Neuflize and Co. ; Regent of the Bank of France ; Président de la Compagnie d'Assurances Générales ; Vice-Président de la Compagnie des Chemins de Fer, P.L.M. ; Président de la Régie de Tabac Ottoman, etc. ; *b.* Paris, 21 August 1850 ; *m.* Miss Dolfus-Davillier (*d.* 1926). *Educ.* : Lycées St. Louis et Buonaparte. *Address* : 7 rue Alfred de Vigny, Paris ; *T.* : 508-88 ; Chateau de Tilles, par Caye, Oise. *Clubs* : Rue Royale, l'Union Artistique, ois de Boulogne, l'Ile des Pateaux, Paris. *(Died 20 Sept. 1928.)*

DENHAM, Harold Arthur, D.S.O. 1919 ; M.A. ; Headmaster of the Harvey Grammar School, Folkestone, since 1920 ; *b.* 20 Mar. 1878 ; *s.* of Arthur Denham, now of Harrogate, formerly of Ilford, Essex ; *m.* Phyllis Janet, *d.* of John Tyrrell, Heaton Moor, Stockport ; two *d.* *Educ.* : St. John's College, Cambridge. (Foundation Scholar and Prizeman) 1st Class Nat. Sci. Trip. 1901 ; Senior Science Master, High School, South Shields, 1903-5 ; Senior Physics Master, Hymers College, Hull, 1905-1920 ; Commissioned in 2nd East Riding of Yorkshire Volunteer R.G.A. 1907, and in the East Riding R.G.A. (T.F.) 1908 ; Captain, 1912 ; Major, 1916; served in France as Major commanding various Siege Batteries, 1916-17 and 1918 (D.S.O., despatches). *Recreations* : Geology and Photography. *Address* : The Harvey Grammar School, Folkestone. *(Died July 1921.)*

DENHAM, Sir James, Kt., *cr.* 1921 ; *s. surv. s.* of J. Denham-Smith (*g.s.* of John Denham of Danescourt), of Bellevue and Vesey Place, Ireland, and York Terrace, London ; *m.* Grace, *d.* of Colonel Hector Stewart Vandeleur of Kilrush and Cahircon and Cadogan Square, London, Lord Lieutenant of County Clare, and Charlotte, *d.* of William Orme Foster, M.P., of Apley Park, Shropshire, Stourton Castle, Worcestershire, Spratton Grange, Northampton, and Belgrave Square, London. *Educ.* : Christ Church, Oxford (B.A., M.A.). Has raised considerable sums for charities by his rendering of selections from the English Classics, and has addressed large audiences throughout the country on the Social and Political problems of the day. *Publications* : My Ladye and Others ; Beauty at a Dinner-party ; the Loves of Vandyck; the Log o' the Norseman ; Serbelloni; The Roadways of London and sixty miles round; The Cradle of the Hapsburgs ; the Byeways of Byron ; The Prayer of a Peasant (Oberammergau Passion Play) ; Queen Mary o' Scots ; The Love of Annie Lee ; Wake up, England ; The Gates of Dream ; Songs from Beyond the Night ; The Divine Desert ; The Holy Shrine ; Memoirs of the Memorable—(autobiography); Ode to December ; The Passing of Christ; Sowing the Sunrise, etc. *Recreations* : hunting, fishing, cycling (has cycled 60,000 miles in twelve different countries), photography ; has

bred and exhibited black spaniels, Clumbers and St. Bernards, for which he is a Crystal Palace prize winner. *Club* : White's.
(Died 3 Oct. 1927.)

DENIKER, Joseph, D.Sc. (Paris); Librarian of the Museum d'Histoire Naturelle, Paris ; Anthropologist and Ethnographer; *b.* Astrakhan, Russia, of French parents, 6 March 1852 ; *m.* ; three *s.* one *d.* *Educ.* : Technological Institute, Petrograd ; Faculté des Sciences, Paris. Travelled in Caucasus and Persia, in Italy, Germany, Austria, etc., specially for ethnological research ; Chevalier de la Légion d'Honneur ; President or Secretary of many International Congresses; late President of Société d'Anthropologie de Paris ; Hon. Fellow of Royal Anthropological Institute of Great Britain ; late President of Association des Bibliothécaires français; LL.D.(Hon.) Aberdeen; Delegate (for France) to International Catalogue of Scientific Literature ; Vice-President of Société pour la Propagation des Langues étrangères en France ; member of the Comité des travaux historiques et scientifiques; Laureat of the Institut de France. *Publications:* Anatomie et Embryologie des Singes anthropoides, 1886 ; Anthropologie et Ethnographie de la Mission du Cap Horn, 1892 (with Dr. Hyades) ; Les Races de l'Europe, 1896-1908 ; Bibliographie des Sociétés savantes de la France, 1889-95 ; The Races of Man, London, 1900 ; Les six Races de l'Europe (Huxley Memorial Lecture), 1904 ; Les Races et les Peuples de la terre (2nd ed.), 1916. *Recreation:* fond of collecting ethnographical photographs. *Address* : 36, rue Geoffroy Saint-Hilaire, Paris. *(Died 18 Mar. 1918.)*

DENISON, Colonel George Taylor, Hon. Colonel Governor-General's Bodyguard ; *b.* Toronto, 31 Aug. 1839 ; *s.* of late Col. George T. Denison ; *m.* 1st, 1868, Caroline (*d.* 1885), *d.* of late Oliver Macklem : 2nd, 1887, Helen, *d.* of late James Mair, of Perth, Ontario ; three *s.* four *d.* *Educ.* : Upper Canada Coll., Toronto ; University of Toronto. LL.B. ; ex-President of the Royal Soc. of Canada, 1903. Served 44 years in the Canadian Militia ; commanded the Governor-General's Bodyguard in the Fenian Raid on Fort Erie, 1866 (medal and clasp); and in the North-West Rebellion, 1885 (medal) ; President of the Imperial Federation League in Canada in 1893-95 ; President of the British Empire League in Canada since 1896 ; Vice-President Royal Colonial Institute, 1911. *Publications:* Manual of Outpost Duties, 1866 ; The Fenian Raid on Fort Erie, 1866 ; Modern Cavalry, 1868 ; History of Cavalry, 1877 ; Soldiering in Canada, 1900 ; The Struggle for Imperial Unity, 1909 ; Recollections of a Police Magistrate, 1920; also magazine articles in the Nineteenth Century, Westminster Review, and Canadian magazines. *Address* : Heydon Villa, Toronto, Canada. *Club:* National, Toronto.
(Died 6 June 1925.)

DENISON, William Evelyn, J.P. and D.L. for Notts ; *b.* 25 Feb. 1843 ; *s.* of late Sir W. T. Denison, K.C.B. ; *m.* 1877, the Lady Eliner Amherst, *d.* of 3rd Earl Amherst. *Educ.* : Eton, Woolwich. Served in Royal Artillery ; retired as Captain in 1878 ; M.P. Nottingham, 1874-80. *Recreations* : President M.C.C., 1892, and of Cricketers' Fund Friendly Society. *Address* : Ossington Hall, Newark. *Clubs* : Carlton, Junior United Service.
(Died 24 Sept. 1916.)

DENNE, Major William Henry, D.S.O. 1915 ; 2nd Battalion, The Bedfordshire Regiment ; *b.* 15 July 1876. Entered army, 1897; Adjutant, 1905-9 ; Captain, 1906 ; Major, 1914 ; Staff Captain number 9 District, Eastern Command, 1909-14 ; served South Africa, 1899-1902 (despatches; Queen's medal, 3 clasps; King's medal, 2 clasps) ; European War, 1914-1915 (despatches, wounded, D.S.O. for Neuve

Chapelle). *Address:* Ingrave Cottage, Brent-wood; Essex.   *(Died 21 Feb. 1917.)*

DENNETT, Richard Edward, F.R.A.I., F.Z.S.; *b.* Valparaiso, 1857; *s.* of Rev. R. Dennett, D.C.L. *Educ.:* Marlborough, 1869-74. Served Thomas Wilson, Sons, and Co., 1875-79; left for Africa in the employ of Hatton and Cookson, 1879; drew attention to irregularities in Congo Free State, 1886; edited manuscript newspaper called Congo Mirror, and accused Congo officials of murders and atrocities; with help he carried on the agitation until the Congo Reform Association was formed; in a series of letters to the African Mail entitled the Lower Congo he pointed out the injustice of the French rule and the concessionaire system in Congo Français; joined the Nigerian Forest Service, 1902; retired on pension, 1918. *Publications:* Seven Years among the Fjort (Fiote); Notes on the Folk-lore of the Fjort (with Preface by the late Mary Kingsley); At the Back of the Black Man's Mind; Nigerian Studies; West African Categories; British and German Trade in Nigeria; My Yoruba Alphabet; The African Table of Periodic Law. *Recreations:* study of the natives, golf. *Address:* c/o H. S. King and Co., 9 Pall Mall, S.W.1. *Club:* Royal Societies.   *(Died 28 May 1921.)*

DENNEY, Rev. James, D.D.; Principal and since 1897 Professor of New Testament Language, Literature, and Theology, United Free Church Coll. Glasgow; *b.* Paisley, 5 Feb. 1856. *Educ.:* Highlanders'Academy,Greenock; Glasgow Univ. and Free Church Coll. M.A., B.D., and D.D. (Glasgow); D.D. (Chicago Theological Seminary); D.D. (Princeton University and Aberdeen). Minister of East Free Church, Broughty Ferry, 1886-97. *Publications:* The Epistles to the Thessalonians, 1892, and The Second Epistle to the Corinthians, 1894 (Expositor's Bible); Studies in Theology, 1895; The Epistle to the Romans (Expositor's Greek Testament), 1900; The Death of Christ, 1902; The Atonement and the Modern Mind, 1903; Jesus and the Gospel, 1908; The Way Everlasting, 1911. *Address:* 15 Lilybank Gardens, Glasgow.   *(Died 12 June 1917.)*

DENNIS, Ven. Thomas John; Archdeacon of Onitsha, S. Nigeria, since 1905; Commissary and Examining Chaplain to the Rt. Rev. the Bishop in W. Eq. Africa; C.M.S. Missionary in W. Africa since 1893; *b.* 1869; *m.* 1897; three *s.* two *d.* *Educ.:* C.M. College, Islington; Durham Univ. (M.A.). Ordained, 1893; C.M.S. Missionary, Sierra Leone, 1893-94; Onitsha, R. Niger, W. Africa, 1894-1906; Ebu, Owerri District, S. Nigeria, 1906; 1906-13 mainly occupied in making a new translation of the Bible into the Ibo language for the British and Foreign Bible Society. *Address:* C.M.S., Ebu, Owerri, Southern Nigeria.   *(Died July 1917.)*

DENNIS, Senator William; President of the Halifax Herald; *b.* Cornwall, 4 Mar. 1856; *m.* 1877, Agnes Miller; two *s.* five *d.* Went to Canada, 1873; reporter, Halifax Herald, 1875; called to Senate, 1912. *Address:* Cobourg Road, Halifax, Nova Scotia. *Clubs:* Halifax, R.N.S. Yacht, Golf, Halifax; Rideau, Ottawa.   *(Died 11 July 1920.)*

DENNISS, Charles Sherwood; Lt.-Col. Engineer and Railway Staff Corps; General Manager, Cardiff Railway, Bute Docks, Cardiff, 1910-17; *b.* 1860; *s.* of late Henry Denniss, Goods Manager, North Eastern Railway Co., Hull; *m.* 1st, 1891, Ethel, *d.* of Henry Burnet; one *d.*; 2nd, 1899, Edith, *d.* of late Rev. Henry J. Pope, D.D. *Educ.:* Hull and East Riding College, Hull. General Manager, Cambrian Railways, 1895; previously District Superintendent, North Eastern Railway, Darlington; Assistant Docks and District Goods Manager, North Eastern Railway, Hull; formerly in the service of Great Western Railway at Shrewsbury and Reading; Member of the Advisory Trade Com-

280

mittee for South Wales under the Labour Exchange Act, 1909; Member of the Glamorgan County Territorial Association; Member of the Order of St. John of Jerusalem (St. John Ambulance Assoc.). *Recreations:* golf and cycling. *Address:* South Cliff, Penarth, Glam. *T.A.:* Denniss, Cardiff. *T.:* Penarth, 411.
(Died 8 Dec. 1917.)

DENNISTON, Hon. Sir John Edward Kt., *cr.* 1917; *b.* Scotland, 20 June 1845; *m.* 1877, Helen, *d.* of late Hon. John Bathgate, New Zealand. *Educ.:* Greenock Academy; Blair Lodge; Glasgow University. Went to New Zealand, 1862; called to bar, 1874; Puisne Judge, Supreme Court, New Zealand, 1889-1917. *Address:* Canterbury, New Zealand.
(Died 22 July 1919.)

DENNY, Captain Sir Cecil Edward, 6th Bt. of Tralee Castle, Co. Kerry; *cr.* 1782; Archivist to the Government of Alberta; *b.* 14 Dec. 1850; 2nd *s.* of late Rev. Robert Day Denny, Vicar of Shedfield, Hants, 2nd *s.* of 3rd Bt. and 2nd wife, Frances (who *m.* 2nd, Very Rev. A. H. Boyd, Dean of Exeter), *d.* of Thomas Waller of Ospringe, Kent; S. half-brother, 1921; unmarried. *Educ.:* Cheltenham Coll.; France and Germany. Sub-Inspector and Superintendent of the Royal North-West Mounted Police of Canada at its original formation in 1874, afterwards Captain and Inspector; was subsequently an official of the Indian Department (in charge of the Western Plain Indians during the Riel Rebellion, 1885), and a Police Magistrate. *Publication:* The Riders of the Plains. *Heir: c.* Rev. H. L. L. Denny. *Address:* The Library, Parliament Buildings, Edmonton, Alberta, Canada.
(Died 24 July 1928.)

DENNY, John M'Ausland, C.B. 1917; D.L., J.P.; Chairman of William Denny and Brothers, Ltd., shipbuilders and engineers, Dumbarton; Director of Caledonian Railway Co.; Hon. Col. 9th (Dumbartonshire) A. & S. H.; *b.* 1858; *s.* of P. Denny, Dumbarton; *m.* Janet, *d.* of J. Tulloch, 1885; four *d.* *Educ.:* Dumbarton; Lausanne. M.P. (C.) Kilmarnock District, 1895-1906. *Address:* Helenslee, Dumbarton. *T.A.:* Denny, Dumbarton; Rowlocks, London. *T.:* Dumbarton 201; (London) Avenue 538. *M.:* SN 302. *Clubs:* Oriental; Conservative, Glasgow.   *(Died 9 Dec. 1922.)*

DENNY, Sir Robert Arthur, 5th Bt.; *cr.* 1782; late Lieut. 22nd Foot; *b.* 23 July 1838; *e. s.* of Rev. R. D. Denny, 2nd *s.* of 3rd Bt., and Sarah, *d.* of G. Grant of Soberton, Hants; *S. u.* 1889; *m.* Jane, *d.* of T. Kirton, Exeter, 1872. *Educ.:* Harrow. *Heir: half-b.* Cecil Edward, *b.* 14 Dec. 1850. *Club:* Naval and Military.   *(Died 24 Nov. 1921.)*

DENNYS, Colonel George William Patrick, I.M.S., C.I.E. 1915; M.R.C.S.(Eng.), L.R.C.P. (Lond.). Inspector-General of Civil Hospitals, Central Provinces, India, 1911; retired from service, 1917; *b.* 28 April 1857; *s.* of General J. B. Dennys, Bengal Staff Corps; *m.* 1885, Alice Isobel, *d.* of Colonel Gordon Young, Bengal Staff Corps; one *s.* three *d.* *Educ.:* Bedford Grammar School; St. Bartholomew's Hospital and School, London. Joined I.M.S. 1879; entered civil employment, Punjab, 1882; held appointments as Civil Surgeon successively at Karnal, Amritsar, Kangra, Sialkot, Jullundur, Rawal Pindi, Amballa, Delhi, and Peshawar; Administrative Medical Officer, N.-W.F. Province, 1908; Colonel, 1910; Principal Medical Officer Aden Brigade, 1910; Derajat and Bannu Brigades, 1910; served Afghanistan, 1880 (medal); Delhi Durbar medal, 1911. *Publications:* articles in Lancet and other medical papers on Litholapaxy, with special reference to the operation on male children; Indian Snakes, how they are caught and handled, Cornhill Magazine. *Recreations:* lawn-tennis, golf, and billiards, modelling in clay. *Address:* South Lea, Milford-on-Sea, Hants. *(Died 30 July 1924.)*

DENNEHY, William Francis. See page xviii.

DENNYS, Lt.-Colonel Sir Hector Travers, K.B.E., *cr.* 1919 ; C.I.E. 1915 ; Indian army ; *b.* 9 Mar. 1864 ; *s.* of General Julius Bentall Dennys, late B.S.C. ; *m.* 1888, Lucy Maud Massy, *d.* of General George Wheeler, late I.S.C. ; one *s. Educ. :* Cheltenham, Sandhurst. Entered army, Manchester Regt., 1885 ; Captain Indian army, 1896 ; Major, 1903 ; Lt.-Col. 1911 ; served in Q.O. Corps of Guides and 28th Punjabis ; joined Punjab Police, 1888 ; Superintendent of Police, 1891 ; Deputy Inspector-General Police, 1906 ; Inspector - General of Police, 1914 ; retired, 1919. *Recreations :* most games. *M. :* P 47. *Club :* East India United Service.
(Died 2 April 1922.)

DENT, Sir Alfred, K.C.M.G., *cr.* 1888 ; J.P. Sussex ; High Sheriff, 1908-9 ; merchant ; *b.* 1844 ; 3rd *s.* of Thos. Dent ; *m.* Margaret, *d.* of Charles Aird, 1896 ; one *s. Educ. :* Eton. Engaged in business in China, Ceylon, etc., since 1864 ; obtained the Royal charter for British North Borneo Co., 1881 ; a member of the Indian Silver Currency (1898) Commission. *Recreations :* hunting, shooting, rowing, tennis, etc. *Clubs :* Oriental, City of London. *(Died 23 Nov. 1927.)*

DENT, Lt.-Col. H. F., J.P., N. and E. R. Yorks. ; Master of the Bedale Hounds, 1878-84, and 1896-98 ; *b.* Ribston Hall, Yorkshire, 1839 ; *m.* Isabella (*d.* 1908), *o. c.* of Rev. J. Tomkyns, Greenford Rectory, 1870. *Educ. :* Eton ; Trinity College, Cambridge. Entered Army, 1859, 17th Foot ; exchanged into 3rd Hussars ; Major in 7th Dragoon Guards ; employed on Remount Department in Canada during Boer War, 1900-2, and given rank of Lt. - Col. *Address :* Menethorpe, near Malton. *Club :* Yorkshire, York.
(Died 23 Nov. 1916.)

DENT, Maj. Joseph Leslie, D.S.O. 1914 ; S. Staffordshire Regt. ; *y. s.* of late J. H. and Mrs. Dent, Merivale, Edgbaston ; *b.* 10 Apr. 1889 ; *m.* 1915, Isabel Doris, *e. d.* of Arthur T. Keen, Harborne Park, Harborne. Entered army, 1909 ; Captain, 1915 ; served European War, 1914-15 (despatches, D.S.O.).
(Died 11 April 1917.)

DENT, Joseph Mallaby ; *b.* Darlington, 1849 ; *s.* of George Dent (musician) and Isabella, *d.* of Hugh Railton, of Staindrop, Co. Durham ; *m.* 1st, Hannah (*d.* 1887), *d.* of George Wiggins, London ; 2nd, Alexandra Campbell, *d.* of Thomas Main, London ; three *s.* four *d. Educ. :* Elementary Schools. Left Darlington for London at the age of 17 to finish apprenticeship in book-binding and printing ; began business as book-binder, 1872 ; commenced publishing in 1888, and has had great delight in the production of the Temple Shakespeare, Temple Classics, Everyman's Library, the Collection Gallia, the King's Treasuries, complete editions of the Works of W. H. Hudson and Joseph Conrad, etc. *Recreations :* photography, archæology and travel ; Member of British Archæological Society. *Address :* Crohamleigh, Harewood Road, South Croydon. *T. :* Croydon 2588. *(Died 9 May 1926.)*

DENTON, Sir George Chardin, K.C.M.G. ; *cr.* 1900 ; C.M.G. 1891 ; F.R.G.S., F.Z.S. ; Governor of Gambia 1900-11 ; *b.* 22 June 1851 ; *y.* and *o. surv. s.* of Rev. R. A. Denton, Rector of Stower Provost, Dorset, and Mary, *d.* of George Wroughton, Adwick Hall, Doncaster ; *m.* 1879, Jean Margaret Alan (*d.* 1900), *e. d.* of Alan Stevenson, F.R.S., Edinburgh ; one *d. Educ. :* Rugby ; private tutors. Entered 57th Regiment, 1869 ; Lieut. 1871 ; Capt. 1878 ; joined Colonial Service as Chief of Police, St. Vincent, 1880 ; Col. Sec. Lagos, 1888 ; administered the Govt. of St. Vincent, 1885-88 ; of Lagos, 1889-91 ; 1893-1900. *Decorated* for service in West Africa ; retired 1911. *Recreations :* hunting, shooting, fishing. *Address :* Fairlight, Chigwell Row,

Essex. *T.A. :* Chigwell Row. *T. :* Chigwell 73. *Clubs :* Windham, Naval and Military.
(Died 9 Jan. 1928.)

DENYS - BURTON, Sir Francis (Charles Edward), 3rd Baronet, *cr.* 1813 ; J.P. N. Riding of Yorkshire and Carlow ; 2nd *s.* of 2nd Baronet and Catherine Eliza, *e. d.* of M. H. Perceval, M.L.C., of Spenser Wood, Quebec ; *b.* 15 Mar. 1849 ; *S.* father 1881 ; *m.* 1890, Grace Ellen, *d.* of late Col. A. W. D. Burton, C.B., and *heiress* of Sir Chas. W. Cuffe Burton ; one *s.* four *d. Educ. :* Harrow ; Paris. Entered Diplomatic Service, 1871 ; became 3rd Sec., 1873 ; 2nd Sec., 1878 ; 1st Sec. of Legation, 1887 ; served at Athens, Brussels, Washington, Copenhagen, Mexico, Berlin, and Rome ; Chargé d'Affaires at Brussels, Mexico, and Copenhagen ; retired 1896. Assumed by royal licence surname and arms of Burton under will of late Sir Charles W. Cuffe Burton, 5th Bart. ; High Sheriff, Co. Carlow, 1906. *Heir : s.* Charles Peter, *b.* 27 May 1899. *Address :* Draycott Hall, Richmond, Yorkshire ; Pollacton, Carlow, Ireland. *T.A. :* Reeth. *Club :* Arthur's. *(Died 19 Nov. 1922.)*

DENZA, Luigi, Chevalier de l'ordre de la Couronne d'Italie ; Chevalier de l'ordre de Charles III. d'Espagne ; a Director of the London Academy of Music ; Professor of Singing at the Royal Academy of Music : *b.* Castellamare di Stabia, Italy, 24 Feb. 1846 ; 2nd *s.* of Giuseppe Denza, Palermo (*d.* 1864) ; *m.* Mlle. Dufour, 1890 ; one *s. Educ. :* Naples Conservatoire of Music (Diploma) ; under the celebrated composer Saverio Mercadante, Paolo Serrao, and Carlo Costa (brother of Sir Michael Costa). Scholarship at Naples Conservatoire, 1862 ; Under-Professor, 1866 ; opera, Wallenstein, produced Theatre del Fondo, Naples, 1876 ; travelled through Italy, Russia, France, and England, giving recitals of his songs and singing lessons ; first visit to England, 1879 ; settled in London since 1883. *Publications :* over six hundred songs, the most popular are : Funiculì Funiculà ; Si tu m'aimais ; Come to me ; Call me back ; Fettered ; A May Morning, 'Tis June. *Recreations :* walking, shooting, fishing. *Address :* 9 Clifton Hill, N.W. *(Died 26 Jan. 1922.)*

DE PARAVICINI, Percy J., C.V.O. 1921 ; M.V.O. 1908 ; J.P., Bucks ; *b.* 15 July 1862 ; 3rd *s.* of Baron Prior de Paravicini ; *m.* 1891, Lady Marcia (Charlotte Sophia) Cholmondeley, 3rd sister of 4th Marquis of Cholmondeley. *Educ. :* Eton ; Trinity College, Cambridge. *Address :* Hillfield, Pangbourne. *T. :* Pangbourne 47. *(Died 11 Oct. 1921.)*

DEPEW, Chauncey Mitchell, LL.D. ; Chairman Board of Directors New York Central R.R. Company, and Director in many other railroad companies ; *b.* Peekskill, New York, 23 April 1834 ; *s.* of Isaac Depew and Martha Mitchell, *g.d.* of Rev. Josiah Sherman, *bro.* of Roger Sherman, one of the signers of the Declaration of Independence ; *m.* 1st, 1871, Elise Hegeman (*d.* 1893) ; 2nd, 1902, May Palmer ; one *s. Educ. :* Yale. Barr. 1858 ; member Legislature, State of New York, 1861, 1862 ; Secretary of State of New York, 1863 ; Attorney for New York and Harlem Railroad Company, 1866 ; U.S. Minister in Japan, 1866, and resigned ; General Counsel for Vanderbilt System, 1875 ; Regent of the University of the State of New York, 1874-1904 ; Member of Corporation of Yale University, 1893-1905 ; Boundary Commissioner, 1875 ; declined United States Senator, 1885 ; candidate for Presidency, 1888 ; declined appointment of Secretary of State, 1892 ; United States Senator, State of New York, 1899, 1905-11 ; delegate at large to National Republican Conventions to nominate President of 1888, 1892, 1896, 1900, 1904, 1908 ; delegate, 1912, 1916, 1920,

1924; chosen as orator at unveiling of Statue of Liberty in New York Harbour; at Centennial of inauguration of George Washington as first President; at opening of World's Fair at Chicago; at Centennial Celebration of organisation of Legislature of State of New York, and on other occasions; Hereditary Member Society of the Cincinnati; Officer of the Legion of Honour. *Publications:* Orations and Addresses, eight volumes, 1911; Speeches and Addresses at 80, one volume; Addresses and Literary Contributions at 82, one volume, 1916; also one volume at 86, 1920; My Memories of Eighty Years, 1922; Miscellaneous Speeches at 92, one volume, 1925. *Address:* 27 W. 54th Street, New York.

(Died 5 April 1928.)

DE RAMSEY, 2nd Baron (cr. 1887), **William Henry,** J.P., D.L. for Hunts; Custos Rotulorum, Isle of Ely; b. 1848; s. of 1st Baron and Mary, d. of 4th Lord Sondes; S. father, 1887; m. 1877, Lady Rosamond Jane Frances Spencer-Churchill (d. 1920), d. of 7th Duke of Marlborough, K.G.; one s. four d. *Educ.:* Eton. Conservative. 1st Life Guards, 1867-77; Huntingdonshire Light Horse till regiment disbanded; Hon. Col. Hunts Volunteers, 1901; Lord-in-Waiting to Queen Victoria; M.P. Huntingdonshire, 1880-85; N. Hunts, 1885-87. *Heir:* g.s. Ailwyn Edward Fellowes. *Address:* Ramsey Abbey, Huntingdonshire; 3 Belgrave Square, S.W.1; T.: Vic. 19; Haveringland Hall, Norwich. *(Died 8 May 1925.)*

DERHAM, Hon. Frederick Thomas; b. England, 8 Jan. 1844; m. 1st, 1864, Ada M. Anderson; 2nd, 1878, Frances D. Swallow. Went to Victoria, 1856; M.L.A. Sandridge, 1883-92; Postmaster-General, 1884-90. *Address:* Harptree, Sir William Street, Kew, Australia.

(Died 12 Mar. 1922.)

DE ROBECK, Admiral of the Fleet Sir John Michael, 1st Bt., cr. 1919; G.C.B., cr. 1921; G.C.M.G., cr. 1919; G.C.V.O., cr. 1924; K.C.B., cr. 1916; Commander-in-Chief Atlantic Fleet, 1922-24; Mediterranean, 1919-1922; late High Commissioner, Constantinople; b. 10 June 1862; 2nd s. of 4th Baron de Robeck of Gowran Grange, Naas, Ireland; m. 1922, Hilda, widow of Col. Sir Simon Macdonald Lockhart, Bt. *Educ.:* H.M.S. Britannia. Entered R.N. as Cadet, 1875; Lieut., 1885; Comdr., 1897; Captain, 1902; Rear-Admiral, 1911; Vice-Admiral, 1917; Admiral of the Fleet, 1925; Late Inspector of Boys' Training Establishments; Admiral of Patrols, 1912-14; Commanded Naval Force in Dardanelles during the time the Expeditionary Force was landed, 1915 (despatches); Legion of Honour; 1st Class Sacred Treasure, Japan; Grand Cross Order Crown of Italy. *Recreations:* hunting and shooting. *Heir:* none. *Address:* 5 Southwick Crescent, W.2. *T.:* Paddington 1754. *Club:* Army and Navy.

(Died 20 Jan. 1928.)

DERRY, Ven. Percy A., Archdeacon of Auckland since 1914; Residentiary Canon of Durham Cathedral since 1922; b. 5 Oct. 1859; 4th s. of late Wm. Derry, of Houndiscombe, Plymouth; m. 1889, Blanche Mary, d. of Robert R. Broad, Falmouth; three d. *Educ.:* Harrow; Trinity College, Oxford. Studied for holy orders under Bishop Lightfoot at Auckland Castle; deacon, 1882; priest, 1883; first curacy at Holy Trinity, Stockton-on-Tees; curacy later at Sunderland; vicar of Rawtenstall, Lancs, 1894-98; vicar of Norbiton, 1898-1904; Rector of Gateshead, 1904-14; of Sedgefield, 1914-22; Rural Dean of Gateshead; Hon. Canon of Durham Cathedral. *Recreations:* walking, golf, reading. *Address:* The College, Durham. *Club:* County, Durham.

(Died 13 Oct. 1928.)

DERWENT, 1st Baron (cr. 1881), **Harcourt Vanden Bempde Johnstone,** J.P., D.L.; Bt. 1795; Lieut. 2nd Life Guards (retired); b. 3 Jan. 1829; s. of Sir John Vanden-Bempde-Johnstone, 2nd Bart., and Louisa, 2nd d. of Edward Harcourt, Archbishop of York; S. father (Btcy.) 1869; m. 1850 (d. 1903), Charlotte, sister of 1st Lord Hillingdon; five s. one d. *Educ.:* Eton. M.P. Scarborough, 1869-80. Owns about 12,800 acres. *Heir:* s. Hon. Francis Johnstone. *Address:* Hackness Hall, Scarborough. *Club:* Brooks's. *(Died 1 Mar. 1916.)*

DE SALES LA TERRIÈRE, Colonel Fenwick Bulmer, J.P. Hants and Oxon; the King's Body Guard of the Yeomen of the Guard; b. 1856; o. s. of late Fenwick de Sales La Terrière, of Alstone, Gloucestershire, and Mary Gurney; m. 1888, Agneta, d. of late Charles Hambro, of Milton Abbey, Dorset; one s. *Educ.:* Eton; Magdalen College, Oxford. Late 18th Hussars, retired 1888; served first Egyptian War (medal and clasp and Khedive's star); Nile Expedition (medal and clasp); Order of the Medjidie. *Publication:* Days that are gone. *Recreations:* shooting, fishing, and racing. *Address:* Friary Court, St. James's Palace, S.W.; Solent Cottage, Fawley, Hants. *Clubs:* Bath, Boodle's, Pratt's, Naval and Military.

(Died 21 June 1925.)

de SARAM, John Henricus, C.M.G. 1901; b. 1 Sep. 1844; s. of Frederick John de Saram of Colombo; m. 1867, Amelia Caroline (d. 1891), 2nd d. of Sir Richard F. Morgan, Kt., Queen's Advocate of Ceylon; three s. one d. *Educ.:* Colombo Academy (now the Royal College); S. Thomas's College, Colombo; King's College School, London. A member of Ceylon Civil Service; became District Judge of Badulla, 1867; District Judge of Kurunegala, 1875; of Kalutara, 1883; Fiscal and Registrar-General, Colombo, 1886; District Judge of Jaffna, 1891; of Galle, 1891; of Kandy, Ceylon, 1893; Acting Treasurer of the Colony, 1902; retired on pension, 1906; acted as Commissioner of Assize in Colombo, 1908. *Address:* Hillside, Kandy, Ceylon. *(Died 19 Dec. 1920.)*

DESBOROUGH, Maj.-Gen. John, C.B., 1873; retired Col., Royal Artillery; b. 24 Jan. 1824; 2nd s. of late Henry Desborough of Pilton, N. Devon; m. 1857, Eliza Mary (d. 1891), y. d. of late Gen. Sir Peregrine Maitland, G.C.B., and Lady Sarah Maitland; three s. four d. Employed as assist. Royal Engineer in Canada during disputed boundary question, 1845-46; commanded the R.A. attached to 1st Div. of Expeditionary Force, China, 1860-61 (medal and clasps); brevet of Lieut.-Col. and C.B.; served in Canada, the Mediterranean, East and West Indies, and China; Governor, Oxford Military Coll., 1876-83. *Decorated* for China war, 1860-61. *Recreations:* fishing and inlaid wood-work. *Address:* Cross House, Northam, R.S.O., N. Devon. *Club:* National. *(Died 14 Jan. 1918.)*

DESCHANEL, Paul Eugène Louis, Membre de l'Académie Française et de l'Académie des Sciences morales et politiques; b. 1856; m. Germaine, d. de René Brice, député. *Educ.:* Collège St-Barbe; Lycée Condorcet. Licencié ès lettres et en droit; Sous-préfet de Dreux, 1878; Secrétaire général de Seine-et-Marne, Sous-préfet de Brest, 1879; de Meaux, 1881; député d'Eure-et-Loir, 1885; Vice-Président de la Chambre des Députés, 1896; Président, 1898-1902; Président de la Commission des Affaires Extérieures et Coloniales, 1905-12; Rapporteur du Budget des Affaires étrangères, 1906-12; Président de la Chambre des Députés, 1912; President of the French Republic, 1920. *Publications:* La Question du Tonkin, 1883; La Politique française en Océanie, 1884; Les Intérêts français dans l'océan Pacifique, 1885; Orateurs et Hommes d'Etat, 1888; Figures de femmes, 1889; Figures litté-

raires, 1890; Questions actuelles, 1891; La Décentralisation, 1895; La Question sociale, 1898; La République nouvelle, 1898; Quatre ans de présidence, 1902; L'Idée de Patrie, 1905; Politique intérieure et étrangère, 1906; A l'Institut, 1907; L'organisation de la Démocratie, 1910; Hors des frontières, 1910; Paroles françaises, 1911; Segrais, Madame de Sévigné, 1911; Lamartine, 1913; Gambetta, 1920. *Address:* Palais Bourbon, Paris.
　　　　　　　　　　　(Died 28 April 1922.)

DESHON, Edward, C.M.G. 1902; *b.* Belgaum, Bombay Presidency, 3 Jan. 1836; *s.* of Lieut.-Col. C. J. Deshon, 17th Regiment; *m.* 1863, Emily, *d.* of late J. Sawyer. *Educ.:* Bath Grammar School. Served in Crimea with 68th Light Infantry, 1854-55 (medal and clasp for Sebastopol, and Turkish medal): passed competitive examination for Staff College, 1861, but retired from service in October of that year; came to Queensland: managed the Cabulture Cotton Company; joined Public Service of Queensland, having amongst other positions filled that of Under-Secretary Public Lands, member of Land Boards, and Auditor-General for twelve years; retired from Public Service of Queensland, 1901; Trustee Agricultural Bank. *Address:* Kemendine, Coorparoo, Queensland. *Club:* Queensland. *(Died 4 Sept. 1924.)*

DESHON, H. F.; F.R.G.S.; *b.* West Ashton, Wilts, 24 April 1858; *s.* of Rev. H. C. Deshon, M.D., late vicar of East Teignmouth, Devon; *m.* 1889, Nora, *y. d.* of late George Bird, Madras Civil Service. *Educ.:* Sidney College, Bath. Entered the Sarawak Service, 1876, as cadet; appointed Assist. Resident in charge of Batang Lupar District, 1881; promoted to Resident of the same district, 1883, which post he held till 1891, when he was promoted to Divisional Resident of the 4th Division; Feb. 1894 to Aug. 1896, Acting Resident of the 1st Division; Personal Aide-de-Camp to His Highness the Rajah, G.C.M.G., in which capacity he accompanied His Highness to England in 1888 and in August 1901; in June 1902 commanded a large punitive force sent to punish some turbulent head-hunters in the interior of Batang Lupar; Resident 1st Division March 1903; administered Government during absence of H.H. the Rajah, 1903-4; retired, 1904; Member Sarawak State Advisory Council, 1913. *Address:* Southfield, Combe Down, Bath. *Clubs:* Sports, Royal Automobile; Bath and County, Bath.
　　　　　　　　　　　(Died 30 June 1924.)

DESIKA-CHARRY, Sir Vembakkam C., Kt., *cr.* 1906; B.A., B.L., F.M.U.; Judge of the Court of Small Causes, Madras, 1908-18; *b.* 29 Dec. 1861; *s.* of late V. Rajagopala Charlu. *Educ.:* Presidency College, Madras. Member Corporation of Madras, 1896-1908; Lecturer in Law College, 1896-1900; additional Member Madras Legislative Council, 1904-8; High Court Vakil, Madras, 1887-1908; Fellow Madras Univ. since 1903; elected Life Trustee of the Victoria Memorial Fund and Member of the Council of the Victoria Technical Institute, Madras; Hon. Treasurer Madras Agri-Horticultural · Society; sometime Vice - President Madras Collegiate Athletic Association, and Vice-President National Indian Association, Madras. *Address:* Padma Vilas, Luz, Mylapore, Madras. *T.:* 390. *Clubs:* Cosmopolitan, Madras.

DESJARDINS, Hon. Alphonse, Membre du Conseil Privé pour le Canada; *b.* 6 mai 1841; *s.* of Ed. Desjardins et Josephine Panneton; *m.* Hortense Barsalon; five *s.* eight *d. Educ.:* Collèges Masson and Nicolet. Avocat, journaliste, député, 1874-93; Senateur, 1893-96; Maire de Montreal, 1893-94; Minister de la Milice, 1896; Ministre des travaux publics, même année Industrie et finance. *Publication:* écrits sur diverses questions d'économie sociale

and politique. *Recreations:* Culture de jardin, etc. *Address:* Terrebonne, Chateau, Que.; *T.:* 64; (Office) R. 23, Board of Trade, Montreal; *T.* 3378. *Clubs:* Canadian, Lafontaine, Montreal.

DE SMIDT, Henry, C.M.G. 1901; J.P., F.S.S.; late Permanent Head of the Treasury, Accountant - General, Receiver - General, and Paymaster-General of the Colony of the Cape of Good Hope; *b.* 6 October 1845; *m.* 1878, Jessie, *d.* of late Dr. J. Z. Herman, Cape Town. *Educ.:* South African College. B.A. Cape University; certificate in Trigonometrical Surveying; elected a Fellow of the Royal Statistical Society, 1892. Entered Cape Civil Service, Colonial Office, 1865; served continuously in that office until 1898; promoted Under Colonial Secretary, 1891; has also held the offices of Permanent Head of Convict Stations and Prisons Department, Inspector of Immigrant Coolie Ships and Controller of Printing; was specially charged with duties of Director of Census of 1891 (congratulations of the Government); Member of Civil Service Commission, 1913. *Publications:* Result of a Census of the Cape on the 5th April 1891; also various reports on convicts, prisons, etc. *Address:* The Cottage, Gordon Road, Kenilworth, Cape Town Suburb. *(Died 13 Feb. 1919.)*

DE SOLA, Rev. Meldola, Rabbi of the Spanish and Portuguese Synagogue, Montreal; 1st Vice-President of the Union of Orthodox Jewish Congregations of the U.S. and Canada; *b.* 22 May 1853; *s.* of Rev. Prof. Abraham de Sola, LL.D., Prof. of Hebrew and Oriental Literature at M'Gill University, Montreal, and Esther Joseph; *m.* 1887, Katherine, *d.* of Rev. Isaac Samuel, late Senior Minister of the Bayswater Synagogue; one *s.* one *d.* Received his theological education under direction of his father; entered ministry, 1882; one of three rabbis who formulated Declaration of Principles at first orthodox Jewish convention, New York, 1898; 1st Vice-President of the Union of Orthodox Synagogues of the United States and Canada; has preached in England and the United States. *Publications:* numerous pamphlets and contributions to the press on Orthodox and Reform Judaism. *Recreation:* music. *Address:* 35 MacGregor Street, Montreal.
　　　　　　　　　　　(Died 29 April 1918.)

DE SOVERAL, Marquess (Sir), G.C.M.G. (Hon.), *cr.* 1897; G.C.V.O., *cr.* 1903; Councillor of State; Portuguese Envoy Extraordinary and Minister Plenipotentiary to the Court of St. James's, 1897-1910; formerly Attaché and Secretary of Legation at Vienna, Berlin, and Madrid; Ambassador Extraordinary to the late Peace Conference at the Hague; Ambassador Extraordinary to the King's Coronation; first Secretary, London, 1885; Minister, 1891; Secretary of State for Foreign Affairs, Portugal, 1895-97. *Address:* 6 Granville Place, W.1. *T.:* Mayfair 5337. *(Died 5 Oct. 1922.)*

D'ESTOURNELLES DE CONSTANT, Baron (Paul Henri Benjamin), Member of the French Senate; *b.* La Flèche, Sarthe, 22 Nov. 1852; *m.* Miss Sedgwick-Berend; two *s.* three *d. Educ.:* France; Diplomat eight years French Embassy, London. Member of French Parliament; Member of the two Hague Conferences; Member of the Hague Court. *Publications:* many on politics, economic science, arbitration, limitation of armaments, organisation of peace; Pygmalion; La Vie de Province en Grèce; La politique Française en Tunisie (couronné pas l'académie Française); Les Etats Unis d'Amérique. *Address:* 34ter rue Molitor, Paris, 16ème; Château de Créans—Clemont - Créans (Sarthe). *T.:* Auteuil 05. 77. *(Died May 1924.)*

DEUCHAR, William, M.V.O. 1918; J.P. (Aberdeen); Passenger Superintendent, Great North of Scotland Railway, 1900-18; retired,

1918; *b.* 1849; *m.* 1881, Charlotte, *d.* of late Charles William Sharpe, Line Engraver, Burnham, Bucks; two *s.* one *d. Educ.:* Auchterless, Aberdeen. Local Chairman, St. Andrew's Ambulance Association; Member of Aberdeen Education Authority; Governor of the North of Scotland College of Agriculture. *Recreations:* gardening, mechanics. *Address:* 189 Great Western Road, Aberdeen. (*Died 23 May 1925.*)

DE VEBER, Hon. Leverett George, Senator since 1906; *b.* 10 Feb. 1849; *m.* 1885, Rachel Frances Ryan; one *s. Educ.:* King's College, Windsor; St. Bartholomew's Hospital; M.P. 1898-1906. *Address:* Lethbridge, Alta, Canada. (*Died 9 July 1925.*)

DEVENISH, Very Rev. Robert Jones Sylvester, Dean of Cashel since 1913. *Educ.:* Trinity College, Dublin (M.A.). Ordained, 1873; Curate of St. Patrick, Waterford, 1874-1881; Prebendary in Waterford Cathedral, 1883-1886; Archdeacon of Waterford, 1886-1913; Vicar of Cahir, 1881-1913. *Address:* The Deanery, Cashel. (*Died 16 Sept. 1916.*)

DEVITT, Sir Thomas Lane, 1st Bt., *cr.* 1916; Senior Partner in the firm of Devitt & Moore; late Chairman of Lloyd's Register of Shipping; late President, Equitable Life Assurance Society; *b.* 28 Mar. 1839; *e. s.* of Thomas H. Devitt; *m.* Fanny Theodora (*d.* 1917), *d.* of late Ebenezer Pye-Smith; three *s.* three *d. Educ.:* Madras House Grammar School, Hackney. Has been twice Master of the Skinners' Company; President of the U.K. Chamber of Shipping, 1890; Chairman of the General Shipowner's Society, 1893, and for one year of the London Missionary Society; President, Institute of Marine Engineers, 1913-14. *Recreations:* travelling and a lover of art. *Heir: g. s.* Thomas Gordon, *b.* 1902. *Address:* 6 Buckingham Gate, S.W.1. *T.:* Victoria 1749. *Clubs:* City of London, Burlington Fine Arts, Arts, Oriental.
(*Died 8 Dec. 1923.*)

DEVLIN, Emmanuel, K.C. 1906; M.P. (L.) since 1905; *b.* 1872; *m.* 1907, Cecile, *d.* of late Hon. L. R. Masson, Lieut.-Governor of Quebec. *Educ.:* St. Mary's College, Montreal; Mount St. Mary's; B.A. Laval University; M.A. Canisius College, Buffalo; B.C.L. M'Gill University. *Address:* 523 Besserer Street, Ottawa; Aylmer P.Q., Canada. (*Died 30 Aug. 1921.*)

DEVON, 14th Earl of (*cr.* 1553), Charles Pepys Courtenay, Bt. 1644; *e. s.* of Lord Courtenay (*d.* 1898), *e. s.* of 13th Earl of Devon and Lady Evelyn Pepys, *d.* of 1st Earl of Cottenham; *b.* 14 July 1870. *S.* grandfather, 1904; Major, 3rd Batt. The Prince Albert's (Somersetshire Light Infantry); Temp. Major, 1914-15. Inspector Board of Agriculture, 1895-1904. Owns about 10,000 acres. *Heir: b.* Rev. Hon. Henry Hugh Courtenay. *Address:* Powderham Castle, Exeter; Walreddon Manor, Tavistock; Ford House, Newton Abbot. *Clubs:* Carlton, Boodle's, Isthmian. (*Died 4 Feb. 1927.*)

DEWAR, Lord; Arthur Dewar; Senator of College of Justice, Scotland, since 1910; K.C. Scotland; 4th *s.* of John Dewar, distiller; *m.* 1892, Lettie Dalrymple, *d.* of late Robert Bell of Clifton Hall, Midlothian; one *d. Educ.:* Edinburgh University; M.A. In practice at Scotch Bar since 1885; M.P. South Edinburgh, 1899-1900 and 1906-10; Solicitor-General, Scotland, 1909-10. *Address:* 8 Drumsheugh Gardens, Edinburgh. *Clubs:* Reform; University, Edinburgh. (*Died 14 June 1917.*)

DEWAR, Sir James, Kt., *cr.* 1904; F.R.S., M.A., Hon. LL.D. Glasgow, St. Andrews, Edin., Aberdeen; D.Sc. Victoria, Oxford, and Dublin; Ph.D. (Christiania, Freiburg); Corr. Member of the French Academy of Sciences; Hon. Member of Institution of Civil Engineers and of many Foreign Societies; F.R.S.E., F.I.C., F.C.S.; late President of the Chemical Society and the Society of Chemical Industry;

President of the British Association, 1902; Professorial Fellow of St. Peter's College, Cambridge; Jacksonian Professor of Experimental Philosophy, University, Cambridge; Fullerian Professor of Chemistry, Royal Institution, London; Director of the Davy-Faraday Research Laboratory; co-inventor with Sir Frederick Abel of cordite, the smokeless powder used by H.M. Govt.; introduced into Science and Industry the Silvered Vacuum Vessels known as Dewar Flasks, or popularly as Thermos Flasks, for keeping cold or hot liquids or solids for long periods of time; *b.* Kincardine-on-Forth, 20 Sep. 1842; *m.* 1871, Helen Rose, *d.* of William Banks, Edinburgh. *Educ.:* Dollar Academy; Edinburgh Univ. Assistant to Lord Playfair when Professor of Chemistry, Edinburgh University; late member of the Government Explosives Committee; Hon. Ph.D. (Christiania, Freiburg); Foreign Member, Nat. Acad. Sci. U.S.A.; R. Acad. dei Lincei, Rome, Deutsch, Chem. Gesell. Berlin; Acad. Roy. Sci., Belg.; received Gold Medals from the following Scientific Societies: England—Rumford, Davy, Copley (Royal Society); Albert (Royal Society of Arts); (Society of Chemical Industry). America—First Hodgkins (Smithsonian Institution, Washington); Franklin (Franklin Institute, Philadelphia). France — First English Award Lavoisier (French Academy of Science). Italy—First Award Matteuci (Società Italiana delle Scienze); also recipient of the Gunning Victoria Jubilee Prize of the Royal Society of Edinburgh, 1893; Delivered the Bakerian Lecture of 1901 to the Royal Society on the Nadir of Temperature and Allied Problems; investigations include the following: Hydrogenium, Pyridine, and Chinoline Bases; Physiological Action of Light; Problems of Spectroscopy; Liquefaction of Gases; the scientific use of Liquid Oxygen, Air, Fluorine, Hydrogen. By evaporating liquid hydrogen under diminished pressure, a temperature of 13° absolute or 470° F. of frost was attained. At this temperature hydrogen became a frozen foam-like mass, air a rigid inert solid; only helium of known gases remained uncondensed. Pure metals cooled to this temperature became almost perfect conductors of electricity. By the use of charcoal as an absorbing agent for gases at low temperature the highest vacuum can be rapidly obtained, and gases like hydrogen, helium, and neon separated from air. Problems of capillarity; soap films of the greatest tenuity like the black of Newton's rings, which is about a hundred-thousandth of a millimetre thick, were shown to be exceedingly stable and long-lived, when made in a cryophorus vacuum; soap bubbles when blown in perfectly pure air can be preserved for a period of two months or more, and can reach a thinness when the bubbles are uniformly black, having lost all colour; photographs taken in natural colours of bubbles, 42 cent. diameter (17 inches), in various stages of development, were exhibited at the Royal Society, 22 June 1916; a gold loving cup was presented to Sir James and Lady Dewar on their golden wedding by the Members of the Royal Institution, 17 June 1921. *Publications:* Collected Papers on Spectroscopy (with G. D. Liveing), 1915; numerous papers contributed to the Proceedings of the Royal Societies of London and Edinburgh, the Royal Institution, the British Association, the Chemical Society, etc. *Address:* 21 Albemarle Street, W.1; 1 Scroope Terrace, Cambridge. *T.A.:* Royal Institution, London. *T.:* Regent 669. *Clubs:* Athenæum, Garrick. (*Died 27 Mar. 1923.*)

DE WEND-FENTON, West Fenton, Sole Proprietor and Controlling Editor of the World; *b.* Oldbury, in Shropshire, 23 Oct. 1881; *e. s.* of William Fenton de Wend-Fenton,

of Underbank Hall, Yorkshire (*d.* 1899). *Educ.:* Shrewsbury ; Christ Church, Oxford (Classical scholar). Represented Oxford *versus* Cambridge in the Inter-University Steeplechase, 1900 ; whip to the Oxford University Drag Hounds, 1900-1 ; member of the Bullingdon Club ; hunted four days a week at Oxford and kept a string of racehorses, which he rode himself in public ; took honours in the final school of history ; owner of Vedas, winner of the Two Thousand guineas in 1905 and many other races ; rode Mark Time in the first hurdle race he won, and rode many other winners ; Founder and Editor of the Looking Glass, which is now incorporated with the Sporting Times ; late Editor and Managing Director of the Sporting Times. *Publications:* The Primrose Path ; Realities. *Recreations:* hunting, racing, and theatre-going. *Address:* 15 Park Square, N.W. *T.A.:* Fentonlike, London. *T.:* Gerrard 3807.
(Died 6 April 1920.)

DE WET, Gen. Hon. Christian Rudolf ; Minister for Agriculture, Orange River Colony, 1907-15 ; late M.L.A. Vredefort ; *b.* Smithfield District, 7 Oct. 1854 ; *s.* of Jacobus De Wet of De Wetsdorp ; *m.* 1873, Cornelia Margaretta Kruger, Bloemfontein ; ten *c. Educ.:* privately. Field Cornet Heidelburg District, 1881 ; served Boer War, 1881 ; Representative Lydenburg in Transvaal Volksraad, 1885 ; Member O.F.S. Volksraad, 1885-97 ; General and Commander-in-Chief of the Free State Forces during S. African War ; rebelled during European War, 1914 ; was defeated and taken prisoner ; condemned to six years' imprisonment and a fine of £2000. *Publication:* Three Years' War. *Address:* Bloemfontein, O.R.C. *Club:* Bloemfontein.*(Died 3 Feb. 1922.)*

DEWEY, George, Admiral of the Navy ; *b.* Montpelier, Vt., 26 Dec. 1887 ; *m.* 1st, 1867, Susan B. Goodwin (*d.* 1872), *d.* of Governor Ichabod Goodwin, of New Hampshire ; one *s.* ; *m.* 2nd, 1899, widow of General Hazen. *Educ.:* Naval Academy, 1854 - 58. Entered United States Navy, 1858 ; Commander, 1872 ; Captain, 1884 ; Commodore, 1896 ; Admiral of the Navy, 1899 ; served in Mississippi River in Farragut's squadron, 1861 - 63 ; in command of Asiatic squadron, 1898, when he destroyed Spanish fleet in Manila Bay on May 1. *Publication:* Autobiography, 1913. *Address:* Navy Department, Washington. *(Died 16 Jan. 1917.)*

DEWEY, Sir Thomas Charles, 1st Bt., *cr.* 1917 ; J.P., President Prudential Assurance Co. ; Hon. Colonel 4th London (Howitzer) Brigade, R.F.A., Territorial Force ; *b.* 1840 ; *s.* of Charles Dewey of Cheshunt, Herts. ; *m.* 1866, Clara, *d.* of Thomas Daws of Pyrford Place, Surrey ; one *s.* four *d. Educ.:* Broxbourne, Herts. General Manager Prudential Assurance Company for thirty years, subsequently Chairman of the Company ; Charter Mayor at the Incorporation of Bromley, 1903 ; Member of the Executive and Trust Fund Committee of King's College for Women, University of London ; Deputy Chairman Royal National Pension Fund for Nurses ; Member of War Office Expenditure Committee, 1916. *Heir:* s. Rev. Stanley Dewey, M.A. [Rector of Moretonhampstead ; *b* 12 Aug. 1867 ; *m.* 1891, Emily Rose, *d.* of late Rev. H. L. Pryce. *Educ.:* Dulwich College ; Pembroke College, Cambridge]. *Address:* South Hill Wood, Bromley, Kent ; Peak House, Sidmouth, Devon. *T.:* Bromley 455 ; Sidmouth 036. *M.:* LM 3191. *Club:* Constitutional.
(Died 13 July 1926.)

DE YOUNG, Michel Harry, proprietor and editor San Francisco Chronicle since 1865 ; *b.* St. Louis, 1849 ; mother's maiden name Morange, *d.* nobleman of France ; *m.* 1880 ; one *s.* four *d. Educ.:* San Francisco. Delegate Republican National Conventions, 1888, 1892, 1908 ; twice member Republican National Committee, and vice-chairman one term ; commissioner from

California to Paris Exposition, 1889 ; Vice-President Columbian International Exposition, and originator of its classification plan, 1893 ; President International League of Press Clubs, 1893 ; organiser and director - general of California Mid - winter International Exposition, 1894 ; organiser Mid - winter Fair Memorial Museum, 1894 ; commissioner - general for California at Omaha Transmississippi Exposition, 1898 ; President United States Commission at the Paris Exposition, 1900 ; member French Legion of Honour ; director Associated Press since 1882 ; Vice-President of the Panama Pacific International Exposition. *Recreations:* bicycling, golf, tennis. *Address:* 1919 California Street, San Francisco ; Tuckerway, Burlingame, Cal. *T.A.:* Chronicle, San Francisco. *T.:* Chronicle Exchange 432, 25, and 7119. *Clubs:* Lotus, Manhattan, Press, New York ; Union League, Commonwealth, Merchants', Olympic, Golf, San Francisco. *(Died 15 Feb. 1925.)*

DHAR, Lt.-Col. H.H. Maharaja Sir Udaji Rao Puar Major, Bahadur ; K.C.S.I., *cr.* 1911 ; K.C.V.O., *cr.* 1922 ; K.B.E., *cr.* 1918 ; *cr.* Maharajah, 1918 ; *b.* 1886 ; *m.* eldest Princess of Sawantwadi State (Kaiser - i - Hind gold medal) ; five *c. Educ.:* Daly College, Indore. Salute, 15 guns. Area of State, 1783 square miles. Population, 230,333. Has 8 motor cars. Principal organiser and contributor toward fleet of six motor ambulances in European War, 1915 ; also a second Ambulance Corps ; and other war contributions. *Publication:* Driving in India ; With Horses in India ; With Rifles and Guns in Dhar State ; Training of Vicious Horses. *Recreations:* shooting, polo, cricket. *Address:* Dhar, Central India. *(Died 30 July 1926.)*

DHARAMPUR, H.H. Maharana Shri Mohandevji Narandevji, Maharana of ; is a Sisodia Rajput ; *b.* 1863 ; one *s.* His State is 704 square miles in extent, and has a population of 114,995. Salute, 9 guns. Gross revenue, 9¼ lacs of rupees. *Address:* Dharampur, Western India. *(Died April 1921.)*

DIAZ, Maresciallo d'Italia Armando, Duca della Vittoria ; Collar of the S.S. Annunziata ; Senator of the Kingdom ; Vice-Presidente del Comitato deliberativo della Commissione Suprema di Difesa ; *b.* Naples, 5 Dec. 1861 ; *s.* of Ludovico Diaz and Baroness Irene Cecconi ; *m.* 1896, Sara de Rosa ; one *s.* two *d. Educ.:* Military Academy, Turin. Served Libyan War, 1912 ; European War ; Commander-in-Chief of the Italian Armies, 1917. *Address:* Via G. Battista Vico 11, Rome. *T.:* 20870. *M.:*55-14323. *(Died 29 Feb. 1928.)*

DIBBS, Sir Thomas Allwright, Kt., *cr.* 1917 ; General Manager of Commercial Banking Co. of Sydney, Ltd., since 1867 ; *b.* Sydney, 31 Oct. 1832 ; *s.* of Captain John Dibbs, St. Andrews ; *m.* 1857, Tryphena Gaden ; one *s.* seven *d. Educ.:* Australian College, Sydney. Joined the Banking Co. 1847. *Address:* Graythwaite, Point Piper, Edgecliff, Sydney.
(Died 18 Mar. 1923.)

DIBDIN, William Joseph, Analytical and Consulting Chemist ; *b.* London, 1850 ; *y. s.* of Thomas Colman Dibdin ; *m.* 1878, Marian, 2nd *d.* of Augustine Aglio ; three *s.* five *d. Educ.:* privately. Formerly Chief of Chemical and Gas Department, Metropolitan Board of Works and London County Council, 1882-97 ; Fellow of Institute of Chemistry, Chemical Society, Royal Sanitary Institute, Royal Microscopical Society ; Past President of Institute of Sanitary Engineers and of Association of Managers of Sewage Disposal Works ; Past Vice-President of Society of Public Analysts ; Inventions, etc. ; utilisation of micro-organisms for purification of sewage in contact and slate beds ; Board of Trade standard pentane argand ; radial photometer ; Dibdin's hand photometer. In private practice since 1897. *Publications:* Practical Photometry ;

Purification of Sewage and Water; Lime, Mortar, and Cement; Public Lighting; editor and part author vol. iv. Churchill's Chemical Technology; Composition and Strength of Mortars (research for and published by Royal Institute of British Architects); Papers (48), including Purification of Thames (1897 Journal Inst. C.E.), London Water Supply (Journal Soc. Chem. Ind., 1897), Recent Improvements in Biological Treatment of Sewage (*ibid.* 1906). *Recreations:* golf, photography. *Address:* 31 Idmiston Road, West Norwood, S.E.27. *T.:* Streatham 140. (*Died 9 June 1925.*)

DICCONSON, Hon. Robert Joseph Gerard-: Master of Mr. Gerard's Staghounds; *b.* 8 Aug. 1857; *y. s.* of 1st Lord Gerard and Harriet, *d.* of Edward Clifton; *m.* 1888, Eleanor, 2nd *d.* of Mrs. Bankes, of Winstanley Hall, Lancashire; one *s.* two *d.* Formerly Capt. 3rd Batt. K.O. Lancaster Regiment; assumed surname of Dicconson by royal licence, 1896. *Address:* Wrightington Hall, near Wigan; 11 Chesterfield Street, W. *Clubs:* Boodle's, Marlborough, Turf. (*Died 16 Sept. 1918.*)

DICEY, Albert Venn, M.A., Hon. D.C.L. Oxford, LL.D. (Hon.) Cambridge, Glasgow, and Edinburgh; K.C.; Fellow of All Souls'; *b.* 1835; *m.* 1872, Elinor Mary, *d.* of John Bonham Carter, M.P. *Educ.:* Balliol College, Oxford; late Official Fellow; now Hon. Fellow of Trinity Coll., Oxford. Barr. Inner Temple, 1863; Vinerian Professor of English Law, 1882-1909. *Publications:* The Privy Council (Arnold Essay), 1860; Treatise on Rules for Selection of Parties, 1870; The Law of Domicil, 1879; Law of the Constitution, 1885; England's Case against Home Rule, 1886; Treatise on the Conflict of Laws, 1896; Lectures on the Relation between Law and Public Opinion in England during the 19th Century, 1905; (with Prof. Rait) Thoughts on the Union between England and Scotland, 1920. *Address:* All Souls' College, Oxford; The Orchard, Oxford. *Club:* Athenæum. (*Died 7 April 1922.*)

DICK, Brig.-Gen. Archibald Campbell Douglas, C.B. 1900; C.M.G. 1917; late 4th Batt. Argyll and Sutherland Highlanders; *s.* of late William Douglas Dick and Jane Hay, *d.* of Sir Francis Walker Drummond, 2nd Bt. of Hawthornden; *b.* 1847; *m.* 1883, Isabella, *d.* of late John Parrott of San Francisco; six *d.* *Educ.:* Stonyhurst. Served South Africa, 1900-1 (despatches, Queen's medal 3 clasps, C.B.). *Address:* Pitkerro, by Dundee. *T.:* Broughty Ferry 151. *M.:* SR 131. *Clubs:* Wellington; New, Edinburgh. (*Died 5 Sept. 1927.*)

DICK, Sir James (Nicholas), K.C.B. *cr.* 1895; Hon. Surgeon to the King; *b.* 1832; *m.* 1868, Elizabeth, *d.* of Robert Beveridge. Served in Crimean and Abyssinian Wars; Director-Gen. of Medical Department of the Navy, 1888-98. *Address:* 37 Upper Park Fields, Putney, S.W.; Sea Wood, Bembridge, Isle of Wight. *Club:* United Service.
(*Died 12 July 1920.*)

DICK, Captain Quintin, D.L., Co.Wicklow; *b.* 1847; 2nd *s.* of late Rev. Quintin Dick Hume [assumed by Royal Licence surname of Dick, 1892]; *m.* 1908, Lorna Katherine, *o. d.* of Major Penn Curzon. Late Captain Derbyshire Yeomanry and Royal Antrim Rifles; High Sheriff, Co. Wicklow, 1898. *Recreations:* shooting, fishing, driving, stalking. *Address:* 12 Grosvenor Crescent, S.W.1; *T.:* Vic. 6057; Carantrila, Co. Galway. *Clubs:* Carlton, Bachelors', Arthur's; Kildare Street, Dublin. (*Died 9 Dec. 1923.*)

DICKIE, William; Editor, Dumfries and Galloway Standard; *b.* 1856; 2nd *s.* of late George Dickie, Dumfries; *m.* 1884, Jane, *d.* of R. B. Paterson, Dumfries (*d.* 1917); one *s.* three *d.* *Educ.:* Moniaive; Newcastle-on-Tyne. Ex-Chairman Parish Council; Chairman of Books Committee of Public Library; Vice-President, Dumfries and Galloway Natural History and

Antiquarian Society; Member of Carlyle's House (Chelsea and Ecclefechan) Trust; ex-President, Dumfries Burns Club; President, Y.M.C.A. Social Centre; Trustee of Foresters' Friendly Society. *Publications:* Dumfries and Round About; sundry political and archæological pamphlets; papers in Transactions of Dumfries and Galloway Antiquarian Society, relating chiefly to Scottish burghal life, and in various reviews. *Recreations:* rural rambles and unscientific observations in natural history. *Address:* Merlewood, Dumfries. *T.:* Dumfries 268. (*Died 12 Aug. 1919.*)

DICKINS, Rev. Henry Compton, M.A.; Vicar of S. John's, Winchester, since 1871; Fellow of New College, Oxford; *b.* 2 Oct. 1888; *s.* of William Dickins of Cherrington, Warwickshire; unmarried. *Educ.:* Winchester; New College, Oxford. A Master of Winchester College, 1861-68. *Publication:* The Moral Lessons of the French Revolution, in 8 Lectures. *Recreations:* reading, riding, and driving. *Address:* S. John's Vicarage, Winchester.

DICKINS, Col. Spencer William Scrase-, C.B. 1916; Brig.-General; *b.* 27 Sep. 1862; 2nd *s.* of late C. Spencer Scrase-Dickins, Coolhurst, Sussex. Served Egypt, 1882 (medal with clasp, bronze star); N.W. Frontier, India, 1897-8 (medal with clasp); European War, 1914-1918 (despatches, C.B.). (*Died 23 Oct. 1919.*)

DICKINS, Rev. Thomas Bourne, Doctor of Laws; *b.* 7 Jan. 1832; *s.* of Richard T. Dickins, surgeon of King's Norton, Worcestershire, and Amelia, *d.* of Thomas Bourne of Highgate; *m.* 1858, *o. d.* of Isaac Trow of Balsall Heath, Birmingham; two *s.* one *d.* *Educ.:* Shrewsbury School; Jesus College, Cambridge. Ordained, 1855; Curate of Thurstaston, Cheshire, 1855; St. Nicholas, Warwick, 1857; Vicar of All Saints, Emscote, Warwick, 1861-1914; Rural Dean of Warwick, 1890-1911; Canon of St. Michael's Collegiate Church, Coventry, 1908. *Address:* Royston, Kenilworth Road, Leamington Spa. (*Died 30 Jan. 1919.*)

DICKINS, Ven. William Arthur; Vicar of Over-Stowey, Bridgwater, since 1918. *Educ.:* Lincoln College, Oxford; Lichfield College. Deacon, 1886; Priest, 1888; Curate of Penn. Staff. 1886-91; Chaplain, Bombay Ecclesiastical Establishment, 1891; Ahmedabad, 1891; Nasirabad, 1891-94; Aden, 1894; Kirkee, 1895; Nasirabad, 1896; Malabar Hill, 1896; Domestic Chaplain to the Bishop, 1897 and 1900; Chaplain of Kirkee, 1897; Senior Chaplain, 1901; Ahmednagar, 1903-05; Acting Archdeacon, 1905; Bombay Cathedral, 1905; Hon. Chaplain to the Bombay Rifle Vols. 1906. Archdeacon of Bombay, 1907, and Commissary. *Address:* The Vicarage, Over-Stowey, nr. Bridgwater. *Club:* Westminster.
(*Died 21 June 1921.*)

DICKINSON, Frederic William; Director and Chief Editor of Reuter's, Ltd. since 1902; *b.* Lee, Kent, 1856; *s.* of Henry Dickinson; *m.*; two *s.* two *d.* *Educ.:* Tonbridge School. For 43 years on Editorial Staff at Reuter's. *Address:* Sherwell, Blackheath, S.E.10. *T.:* Greenwich 1036. *M.:* LK 4544. *Clubs:* Savage; Point House, Blackheath. (*Died 2 Sept. 1922.*)

DICKINSON, Lieut.-Col. William, C.S.I. 1869; retired; *b.* 1881; *m.* Laura (*d.* 1905). Entered army, 1848; Lieut.-Col. 1876; served Punjab, 1848-49 (medal with two clasps); Sind Irregular Horse, 1857 (medal with clasp); Rajpootana, 1859 (thanked by Gov.-Gen.); Abyssinia, 1867-68 (medal). *Address:* The Old Bear House, Bisley, Gloucesters.
(*Died 9 June 1917.*)

DICKINSON, Col. William Vicris, C.M.G. 1916; retired; A.A.G.; *b.* 28 Apr. 1856; *s.* of Douglas J. Dickinson, Glanhonddar, Brecon; *m.* 1885, Mary Joyce, *d.* of Jonathan Ambrose. Served European War, 1914-16 (despatches twice, C.M.G.). (*Died 23 Oct. 1917.*)

DICKSEE, Sir Francis Bernard (Frank), K.C.V.O., *cr.* 1927; Kt., *cr.* 1925; D.C.L. Oxford, 1926; R.A., 1891; A.R.A. 1881; President of the Royal Academy since 1924; *b.* London, 27 Nov. 1853; *e. s.* of late Thos. F. Dicksee. *Educ.:* Rev. G. Henslow's School, London. First exhibited at Academy, 1876; since then has painted Harmony, Evangeline, The House Builders, The Symbol, The Love Story, Too Late, Romeo and Juliet, Chivalry, Memories, The Passing of Arthur, The Redemption of Tannhäuser, Mountain of the Winds, The Crisis, Startled, Funeral of a Viking, The Magic Crystal, A Reverie, Paolo and Francesca, The Mirror, The Confession, Dawn, An Offering, The Two Crowns, Yseult, La Belle Dame sans Merci, A Duet, The Ideal, The Shadowed Face, The End of the Quest, The Light Incarnate, The Moon Maiden, This for Remembrance, Daughters of Eve, and Portraits of Lady Aird, The Duchess of Buckingham, The Duchess of Westminster, The Marchioness Camden, The Hon. Mrs. Ernest Guinness, Mrs. Frank Shuttleworth, etc. *Address:* Greville House, Greville Place, N.W.6. *T.:* Maida Vale 2642. *Clubs:* Athenæum, Arts.
(*Died 17 Oct. 1928.*)

DICKSON, Right Hon. Lord (Scott Dickson), P.C., M.A., K.C., J.P., D.L.; LL.D. Glasgow and Aberdeen; Lord Justice Clerk, Scotland, since 1915; *b.* Glasgow, 13 Sep. 1850; 2nd *s.* of J. R. Dickson, M.D.; *m.* 1888, Hester Bagot, *d.* of W. Banks, Edinburgh; two *s. Educ.:* Glas. and Edin. Univs. Practised as law-agent in Glasgow, 1875-76; Advocate, 1877; Advocate Depute, 1892, 1895; Solicitor-General, 1896-1903; Lord-Advocate, 1903-6; Dean of the Faculty of Advocates, 1908-15; M.P. (C.) Bridgeton Division, Glasgow, 1900-1906; M.P. (U.) Central Division, Glasgow, 1909-15. *Address:* 22 Moray Place, Edinburgh. *T.:* Central, Edinburgh 5454. *M.:* S 1799. *Clubs:* Carlton; New, Edinburgh; Western, Glasgow. (*Died 5 Aug. 1922.*)

DICKSON, Rev. Canon Daniel Eccles Lucas, Vicar of Killeedy 1872-1916; Canon of Limerick since 1905. *Educ.:* Trinity College, Dublin, Ordained 1862; Curate of Aghalurcher, 1862-67; Incumbent of Garvary, 1867-72. *Address:* Hollybank, Lisnaskea, Co. Fermanagh.

DICKSON, Lt.-Col. George Arthur Hamilton, M.V.O. 1910; Major 5th Worcestershire Regt., Special Reserve; seconded to the Egyptian Army, 1915; *s.* of late Rev. G. Dickson, M.A., Vicar of St. James the Less, Westminster; *m.* Nanne, *d.* of Consul Wiborg of Norway. Formerly in the Derby Regt.; served through the South African War with B.M.I. (2 medals, 8 clasps); and was O.C. Regiment the S.A. Defence Forces; served on Staff in Egypt and France, 1916. *Club:* Junior Carlton.
(*Died 16 Feb. 1918.*)

DICKSON, Henry Newton, C.B.E. 1918; Assistant Editor of the Encyclopædia Britannica; *b.* Edinburgh, 24 June 1866; *m.* 1891, Margaret, *d.* of Richard Stephenson; one *s.* one *d. Educ.:* Edinburgh University; M.A., D.Sc. Oxon; Professor of Geography at University College, Reading, 1906-20; President Royal Meteorological Society, 1911-12; President Section E, British Association, 1913; Head of Geographical Section Intelligence Department, Admiralty, 1915-19; F.R.S.E. *Publications:* Elementary Meteorology, 1893; Climate and Weather, 1912; Maps and Map Reading, 1912; papers and articles on Meteorology and Oceanography in Philosophical Transactions, Proceedings of the Royal Society of Edinburgh, Encyclopædia Britannica, Geographical Journal, Journal of the Royal Meteorological Society, Reports of Fishery Board for Scotland, etc. *Club:* Royal Societies. (*Died 2 April 1922.*)

DICKSON, Maj.-Gen. John Baillie Ballantyne, C.B., 1893; C.M.G., 1901; retired; *b.* London, 24 Oct. 1842; *s.* of late S. Dickson, M.D., and Eliza, *d.* of late D. Johnstone, Overton, N.B.; *m.* 1st, 1871, Marion (*d.* 1876), *d.* of late C. F.-Huth; 2nd, 1889, Kathleen, *d.* of late W. J. Browne, Buckland Filleigh, N. Devon. Cornet Bengal Cavalry, 1860; Adj. Lahore Light Horse; Adj. 18th Bengal Lancers; exchanged to Royal Dragoons; special service Zulu War, 1879 (despatches, Zulu medal and clasp); Nile Expedition, 1884-85; D.A.A.G. and D.A.Q.M.G. (severely wounded Abu Klea, despatches, medal with two clasps, bronze star); promoted Lieut.-Col. 5th Dragoon Guards; commanded Regt. till 1893; commanded 49th Regimental District, 1895-97; Jubilee medal; commanded 4th Cavalry Brigade, 1897-99; commanded troops Straits Settlements, 1899-1900; commanded 4th Cavalry Brig., S. Africa, 1900 (despatches, medal with five clasps); Lord of the Manor of Keevil; J.P. *Address:* Keevil Manor, Trowbridge, Wilts. *Clubs:* United Service. Junior United Service, Cavalry. (*Died 15 Aug. 1925.*)

DIGAN, Lt.-Col. Augustine J., D.S.O. 1899; late 3rd Batt. (Reserve) Connaught Rangers; *b.* 1878; *m.* 1914, Helen, *d.* of Angus Macgregor. Entered Mid-Ulster Artillery, 1897; served Nigeria 1898 (despatches, medal with clasp, D.S.O.); European War (wounded, despatches); resigned commission, 1922.
(*Died 4 June 1926.*)

DIGBY, 10th Baron (Great Brit.); *cr.* 1765. **Edward Henry Trafalgar Digby,** J.P., Baron (Ireland), 1620; Col. Coldstream Guards; retired 1889; Hon. Col. Dorset Garrison Artillery, T.F.; *b.* 21 Oct. 1846; *s.* of 9th Baron and Theresa, *d.* of 3rd Earl of Ilchester; *m.* Emily, *d.* of Hon. Albert Hood, 1893; three *s.* three *d.* Lt. and Capt. Coldstream Guards, 1868; Instructor of Musketry, 1869-72; Adj. 1874-76; Regimental Adj. 1881; served in Suakim Expedition, 1885. M.P. (C.) Dorset, 1876-85. *Heir: s.,* Capt. Hon. E. K. Digby. *Address:* 16 Grosvenor Place, S.W.1; *T.:* Victoria 3145; Minterne House, Cerne Abbas, Dorsetshire; Geashill Castle, Tullamore. *Clubs:* Carlton, Travellers'.
(*Died 11 May 1920.*)

DIGBY, Sir Kenelm Edward, G.C.B., *cr.* 1906; K.C.B., *cr.* 1898; K.C. 1904; M.A.; *n.* of 9th Baron Digby; *b.* 9 Sept. 1836; *m.* 1870, Caroline, *d.* of 1st Baron Belper; two *s.* two *d.* Barr. Lincoln's Inn, 1865; Bencher, 1891; Vinerian Law Reader at Oxford, 1868-74; County Court Judge, 1892-94; Permanent Under-Secretary of State at Home Office, 1895-1903. *Address:* King's Ford, Colchester. *Club:* Athenæum.
(*Died 21 April 1916.*)

DIGBY, Samuel, C.I.E. 1907; *s.* of late William Digby of New Walsoken, Norfolk. Has been for many years connected with the English Press in India; formerly Assist. Editor of the Times of India; secretary of Indian Section of Royal Society of Arts since 1890, and of Dominions and Colonies Section since 1898; member of Organising Committee and Hon. Secretary for India of Seventh International Congress of Hygiene and Demography (London, 1891), and Hon. Secretary for India of Eighth Congress (Budapest, 1894); assisted in movement which led to appointment of a Select Committee of House of Commons to consider the grievances of the Uncovenanted Services of India (1890). *Recreation:* country walks. *Address:* 1 Whitehall Court, S.W.1; Royal Society of Arts, John Street, Adelphi, W.C.2.
(*Died 22 Sept. 1925.*)

DIGGLE, Rt. Rev. John William, D.D.; Bishop of Carlisle since 1905; *b.* Strawberry Hill, Pendleton, 2 Mar. 1847; *e. s.* of W. Diggle, 19 Cornwall Terrace, Regent's Park, N.W.; *m.* 1st, 1874, Cicely Jane, *y. d.*

287

of John Butterfield, Broughton, Manchester;
2nd, Edith Moss, *y. d.* of Gilbert Winter Moss,
The Beach, Aigburth, Liverpool, 1884 ; four *s.*
one *d. Educ.* : Manchester Grammar School ;
Merton Coll. Oxford. Math. Postmaster Merton Coll. 1866 ; 1st class Law and History,
1870 ; Lect. Merton and C.C.C. Colleges, Oxford,
1871 ; B.A., M.A. in same Class List of Final
Honours School with Rt. Hon. A. D. Acland,
M.P., and late Lord Randolph Churchill,
M.P. Ordained, 1871 ; Curate Whalley Range,
1871 ; All Saints', Liverpool, 1872 ; St. John's,
Walton, 1874 ; Vicar of Mossley Hill, 1875-97,
Surrogate ; Rural Dean of Childwall, 1882 ;
Hon. Canon of Liverpool, 1887 ; President of
Liverpool Council of Education, 1891 ; Select
Preacher, University of Oxford, 1899 ; Canon of
Carlisle and Archdeacon of Westmorland, 1896-
1902 ; Examining Chaplain to Bishop of Carlisle,
1896-1902 ; Archdeacon of Birmingham, 1903-4 ;
Rector, Birmingham, 1902-5, and Rural Dean,
1903-4 ; late Examining Chaplain to Bishop of
Worcester. *Publications :* Godliness and Manliness ; True Religion ; Bishop Fraser's University
and Parochial Sermons ; Bishop Fraser's Lancashire Life ; Rainbows ; Religious Doubt ;
Short Studies in Holiness ; Quiet Hours with the
Ordinal ; Home Life ; The Ministry of the Word
and Sacraments ; The Foundations of Duty ;
Death and the After-Life. *Recreation :* fishing. *Address :* Rose Castle, Carlisle. *Club :*
Athenæum. (*Died 24 Mar. 1920.*)

DIGGLE, Joseph Robert, M.A.; J.P.;
b. 12 May 1849; *y. s.* of William Diggle, Park
House, Astley; *m.* Janie Wrigley, *d.* of
J. W. Macrae, Aigburth, Liverpool, 1878;
two *s.* two *d. Educ. :* Manchester Grammar School ; Wadham College, Oxford. 1st
class Modern History. Chairman London
School Board, 1885-94. Curate, St. Mary's,
Bryanston Square, W., 1876-79 ; resigned to
devote himself to public work ; was nominated
at General Election (1885) for West Marylebone
to test eligibility of clergy to be nominated ;
received 101 votes ; removed, under the Clerical
Disabilities Act, his ineligibility to sit in Parliament in 1889 ; Member London School Board
(Marylebone Div.), 1879-97 ; member of Kent
County Council, 1898 ; Chairman of Elementary
Schools Education Committee, Kent, 1903 ;
Mayor of Tentenden, 1896-99 ; Chairman of the
Council of the Royal Botanic Society, 1907 ;
Chairman of the Council of the Ragged School
Union and Shaftesbury Society, 1906-8 ;
Hon. Fellow of British Institute of Public
Health ; Corresponding Member of Société
Royale de Médecine Publique de Belgique,
1891 ; President of Sec. V. International Congress of Hygiene and Demography, London,
1892 ; and of Sec. VI. at Buda Pesth, 1894 ; contested Camberwell (U.) 1900. *Publications :* Pleas
for Better Administration upon the London
School Board, 1881 and 1885. *Recreations :*
tennis, out-door games. *Address :* St. Michael's
Grange, Tenterden, Kent ; 24 Merton Street,
Oxford. (*Died 16 June 1917.*)

DILKE, Sir Charles Wentworth, 3rd
Bt. ; *cr.* 1862 ; *b.* 19 Sept. 1874 ; *e. s.* of 2nd Bt.
and Katherine, *o. d.* of late Capt. Arthur Gore
Sheil ; *S.* father 1911 ; *m.* 1915, Miss Faithfull
of N.S.W. *Educ. :* Rugby ; Trinity Hall, Cambridge. *Recreations :* travel, riding, rowing,
swimming, golf. *Heir : c.* Fisher Wentworth
Dilke ; [*b.* 5 Jan. 1877. *Address :* 53 Sussex
Gardens, W.]. (*Died 7 Dec. 1918.*)

DILL, Sir Samuel, Kt., *cr.* 1909; M.A., Hon.
Litt.D. Dublin ; Hon. LL.D. Edinburgh and St.
Andrews ; Hon. Fellow of C.C.C. Oxford ; Prof.
of Greek, Queen's College, Belfast, since 1890 ; *b.*
26 March 1844 ; *e. s.* of Rev. S. M. Dill, D.D.
Educ. : Royal Academical Institution, Belfast ;
Queen's College, Belfast ; Lincoln College,
Oxford. First-class Moderations, 1867 ; first
class final Classical Schools, 1869 ; Lecturer
288

Lincoln College, 1869 ; Fellow, Dean, and
Tutor, Corpus Christi College, 1869-77 ; High
Master of Manchester Grammar School, 1877-
1888 ; Governor of Owens Coll. Manchester,
and of Victoria Univ. 1880-89 ; Chairman
of Intermediate Board, Ireland ; Member of
Belfast University Commission, and Pro-Chancellor of Queen's University ; Chairman of
Vice-Regal Committee on Primary Education,
Ireland, 1913. *Publications :* Roman Society in
the last Century of the Western Empire, 3rd ed. ;
Roman Society from Nero to Marcus Aurelius,
2nd ed. *Address :* Montpelier, Malone Road,
Belfast. *Clubs :* Athenæum ; Ulster, Belfast.
(*Died 26 May 1924.*)

DILL, Very Rev. S. Marcus, M.A.,
D.D. ; Minister of Alloway Parish, Ayrshire ; resigned, 1918 ; Ex-Moderator of Church
of Scotland ; *b.* Belfast, 1843 ; *s.* of late
Professor Robert Foster Dill, M.D., Belfast ; *m.*
1878, Agnes Graham, *d.* of late John James
Rowe of Dinglefield, Liverpool ; two *s.* four *d.*
Educ. : Royal Belfast Institution ; Queen's
College, Belfast (scholar) ; Assembly's Theological College, Belfast ; Theological College,
Geneva ; graduated M.A. Queen's University,
Ireland (first-class Honours and a gold medal).
Early Ministry spent in the Parishes of Lower
Cumber, Co. Londonderry, and Ballymena, Co.
Antrim ; a prominent member of Church
Courts, taking an active interest in many
Church enterprises, and specially in augmentation of Small Livings. *Publications :* sermons ;
contributed occasionally to Theological and
Literary magazines. *Address :* 23 Greenhill
Gardens, Edinburgh. *T. :* Edinburgh 3351.
Club : Scottish Conservative, Edinburgh.
(*Died 23 Jan. 1924.*)

DILLON, Captain Constantine Theobald Francis, D.S.O. 1902 ; late 4th Batt.
Worcestershire Regiment ; *b.* 9 Sept. 1873 ; *e. s.* of
Lt.-Col. H. B. C. Dillon of Redhurst, Cranleigh.
Entered army, 1899 ; Captain, 1902 ; served
South Africa, 1899-1900 (dangerously wounded,
despatches, Queen's medal, three clasps, D.S.O.).
(*Died 27 April 1920.*)

DILLON, Major Henry Mountford,
D.S.O. 1915 ; Oxfords and Bucks Light Infantry ; *b.* 20 Jan. 1881 ; *s.* of late H. B. C.
Dillon. Entered army, 1900 ; Captain, 1910 ;
Major, 1915 ; employed with West Africa
Frontier Force, 1905-13 ; served South Africa,
1900 (medal) ; West Africa, 1906 (medal with
clasp) ; European War,1914-16 (despatches twice,
D.S.O.). (*Died 13 Jan. 1918.*)

DILLON, John ; M.P. (N.) Co. Mayo E.,
1885-1918 ; *b.* 1851 ; *s.* of late J. B. Dillon ; *m.*
1895, Elizabeth (*d.* 1907), *d.* of late Rt. Hon. Sir
J. C. Mathew. *Educ. :* Catholic Univ., Dublin.
Member of Royal Coll. of Surgeons, Ireland ;
M.P. Co. Tipperary, 1880-83 ; Chairman of
Irish Nationalist Party, 1918. *Address :* 2 North
Great George Street, Dublin. (*Died 4 Aug. 1927.*)

DILLON, Sir John Fox, 7th Bt. ; *cr.* 1801 ;
J.P., D.L. ; Baron of the Holy Roman Empire,
1782 ; *b.* 1843 ; *S.* father 1875 ; *m.* Marion Louisa,
d. of late R. S. Dykes, 1879 ; one *d. Educ. :*
Magdalene College, Cambridge. Late Major
5th Batt. Prince of Wales' Leinster Regt. Owns
about 3300 acres. *Heir : c.* Robert Arthur.
Address : Lismullen, Navan ; *T.A. :* Tara ; Longworth Hall, Hereford. *Club :* Kildare Street,
Dublin. (*Died 1 Nov. 1925.*)

DILWORTH, W. J., Secretary to Board
of National Education, Ireland, since 1903 ; *b.*
1863 ; *m.* 1895 ; Mary Tempe Kildahl ; two *s.*
three *d. Educ. :* Santry School, Dublin ; Trinity
College, Dublin. Graduated with First Class
Honours in Mathematics in Dublin University,
1886 ; M.A. 1890 ; Professor in the Training
College of the Commissioners of National Education, 1894 ; Principal of the College, 1901.
Publications : New Sequel to Euclid. *Recreations :* lawn tennis and golf. *Address :* Tyrone

House, Dublin. *Club:* University, Dublin.
(Died 10 Dec. 1922.)

DIMMER, Lieut.-Col. John Henry Stephen, V.C. 1914; Brig.-Major 92nd Infantry Brigade; Lieut. K.R.R.C.; *b.* 1 June 1884. Was with West Africa Regiment; promoted 2nd Lieut. K.R.R.C. 1908; served European War (V.C.); served his machine gun at Klein Zillebecke until he was wounded five times and the gun destroyed ; was for four years in the office of a firm of civil engineers in Westminster.
(Died 21 Mar. 1918.)

DIMSDALE, 7th Baron of the Russian Empire, **Charles Robert Southwell,** D.L., J.P.; *b.* 4 June 1856 ; *m.* 1st, 1882, Alice (*d.* 1886), *d.* of C. J. Monk, M.P. for Gloucester; one *s.*; 2nd, 1891, Mabel Sophia, *d.* of Sir Brydges Henniker, 4th Bt., and *widow* of Col. Hastings, C.B.; two *d.*; *S.* father, 1898. *Educ.:* Eton; Trin. Coll. Camb. Called to the Bar of the Inner Temple. *Heir: g.s.* Thomas, *b.* 1911 [*s.* of Edward Charles (*d.* 1915), Capt. Rifle Brigade, and Katharine, *d.* of Edward Barclay]. *Address:* Meesden Manor, Buntingford, Herts. *Club:* Carlton.
(Died 6 Dec. 1928.)

DIMSDALE, Sir John Holdsworth ; 2nd Bt., *cr.* 1902 ; *s.* of 1st Bart. and Beatrice, *d.* of R. H. Holdsworth ; *b.* 10 Feb. 1874 ; *m.* 1st, 1901, Edith Kate (*d.* 1911), *d.* of late John Connacher; three *s.*; 2nd, 1912, Elizabeth Grace, *d.* of late William John Harling. *Educ.:* Eton. *Heir : s.* John Holdsworth, *b.* 31 Dec. 1901. *Club :* Carlton.   *(Died 10 April 1923.)*

DINAJPUR, Maharaja Sir Girijanath Ray, Bahadur of, K.C.I.E. ; *b.* 1860 ; *s.* by adoption to Maharaja Taraknath Ray and Maharani Shyammohini of Dinajpur ; *m.* 1876. *Educ.:* Queen's College, Benares. Member, Eastern Bengal and Assam Legislative Council, 1906-11 ; Hon. magistrate, Dinajpur ; Vice-President British Indian Association, Calcutta ; former President East Bengal Landholders Association ; Chairman Dinajpur Municipality ; former Vice-Chairman Dinajpur District Board ; President Dinajpur Landholders' Association ; Member East India Association, London ; Asiatic Society, Bengal ; Calcutta Literary Society ; Bangiya Sahitya Parisat. *Recreations:* sports, music. *Heir :* Maharaja Kumar Jagadishnath Ray, *m.* 1916. *Address:* Dinajpur Rajbati, Dinajpur, Bengal, India ; 43 Wellesley Street, Calcutta. *Clubs:* India, Calcutta, Indian Sangita Samaj.
(Died 22 Dec. 1919.)

DINES, William Henry, F.R.S. 1905 ; B.A. Cambridge ; F.R.Met.Soc. ; Hon. Fellow R. Aeronautical Society; F.Inst.P.; *b.* 1855 ; *s.* of G. Dines of Hersham, Walton-on-Thames, and Grosvenor Road. *Educ.:* Woodcote House School, Windlesham ; Corpus Christi Coll. Cambridge. *Publications :* papers in Proceedings of R.S. and Quarterly Journal of the Royal Meteorological Society, Journals of Sanitary Institute and R. Aeronautical Society, and in publications of the Meteorological Office and elsewhere. *Address:* Benson, Wallingford, Berks.
(Died 24 Dec. 1927.)

DIONNE, Narcisse-Eutrope, LL.D., M.D., F.R.S.C. ; Officier de l'Instruction Publique de France ; Professeur d'archéologie à l'Université Laval, Québec ; Librarian of the Legislature of the Province of Quebec, 1892-1913; *b.* 18 May 1848 ; *m.* 1st, 1873, Laure Bouchard ; 2nd, 1896, Emma Bidégaré ; four *s.* one *d. Educ. :* St. Ann's College ; Laval University. Practised medicine at Quebec, 1873-80 ; Chief Editor of Le Courrier du Canada, 1880-84 ; Chief Inspector of federal licences, 1884-86 ; Chief Editor of Le Journal de Québec, 1886 ; Permanent Secretary of the Quebec Conservative Club, 1886-92. *Publications* (in French): Life of Jacques Cartier, discoverer of Canada ; La Nouvelle France, 1540-1603 ; Life of Samuel

Champlain, founder of Quebec ; Life of C. F. Painchaud, founder of St. Ann's College ; Serviteurs et servantes de Dieu au Canada ; Les Ecclésiastiques et les royalistes français réfugiés au Canada à l'époque de la Révolution ; Inventaire chronologique des livres, brochures, journaux et revues publiés en langue française dans la Province de Québec depuis l'établissement de l'imprimerie jusqu'à nos jours (1764-1905) ; Québec et Nouvelle France ; Bibliographie, inventaire chronologique des ouvrages publiés à l'étranger en diverses langues, depuis la découverte du Canada jusqu'à nos jours (1534-1906) ; Inventaire chronologique des livres, brochures, journaux et revues publiés en langue anglaise, 1764-1908; Inventaire chronologique des cartes, etc., 1508-1908 ; Supplément à l'Inventaire chronologique, 1904-12 ; Life of Champlain (in English) ; Le Parler populaire des Canadiens français, ou Lexique des Canadianismes, etc., et Galerie historique ; Pierre Bédard et ses fils ; Les Trois Comédies du Statu Quo ; Historique de la paroisse de Ste-Anne de la Pocatière ; L'Œuvre de Mgr. de Forbin-Janson, évêque de Nancy, en Canada ; Chouart et Radisson, ou Odyssée de deux Canadiens-français au XVIIe siècle ; L'Abbé Gabriel Richard, Sulpicien, second fondateur de la ville de Détroit, Michigan ; Les Abbés J. Demers et Thos. Maguire—Dispute grammaticale ; La Petite Hermine de Jacques Cartier, Etude archéologique ; Origine et étymologie des noms de famille canadiens-français, de 1608 à 1908 ; and fifteen other smaller publications. *Address:* Quebec, Canada.   *T. :* 1828.
(Died Mar. 1917.)

DIÓSY, Arthur, F.R.G.S.; writer and lecturer ; Knight Commander of Rising Sun of Japan and of Medjidieh ; Kt. of Christ of Portugal ; Officier de l'Instruction Publique, France ; *b.* London, 6 June 1856 ; *s.* of Hungarian patriot, Martin Diósy; *m.* 1882, Florence, *d.* of late George W. Hill, of Denton Hall, Lancs; one *d. Educ.:* in England and Germany. Advocated, for many years, the Anglo-Japanese Alliance ; founded, 1891, the Japan Society ; chairman, 1901-4, now Vice-President ; hon. member Paris Ethnographical Society and Société Franco-Japonaise ; member of Council China Society ; Interpreter of the Sette of Odd Volumes (President, 1903-4) ; member Navy League ; Siver Medallist Ligue Maritime Française, 1920 ; served in Royal Naval Artillery Volunteers, 1875-82 ; Lecturer for Prince of Wales's National Relief Fund, 1914-15 ; delivered many Recruiting Lectures, 1914-16 ; served as Staff-Lecturer, Y.M.C.A., with British Expeditionary Forces in Mediterranean War Area, Jan. to June 1917 ; visited Italian Front, Sep. 1917 ; attached to First Army, B.E.F., France, 1918 ; G.H.Q. Lecturer, British Army of Occupation, Belgium and Germany, Feb. and March 1919, and British Army of the Rhine, May 1919. *Publications:* The New Far East, 1898 ; 8th ed. 1904 ; History of New Japan in Harmsworth's History of the World, 1907 ; edited vols. i. and ii. of Transactions and Proceedings of the Japan Society, *Recreations :* foreign travel: Europe, Asia, Africa, America ; visited ruined Maya cities of Yucatán, 1910. *T. :* Gerrard 2927. *Clubs :* Savage, Royal Automobile, London Sketch.   *(Died 2 Jan. 1923.)*

DISNEY, Henry William, Barrister-at-Law ; Metropolitan Police Magistrate since 1918 ; Thames Court since 1922 ; formerly Revising Barrister on Midland Circuit, Lecturer, London School of Economics, and Legal Correspondent of the Department of Labour Statistics, Ministry of Labour ; Member of General Council of the Bar ; *b.* 1858 ; *e. s.* of late Rev. W. H. Disney, Rector of Winwick, Rugby ; *m.* 1892, Isabel Wemyss, *d.* of late Rev. P. B.

Power; two *s.* one *d.* *Educ.:* Christ's College, Finchley; Hertford College, Oxford (Mathematical Scholar). 2nd Math. Mods., 3rd Math. Greats, B.A., 1880; rowed in Oxford University Eight, 1879; called to Bar, Lincoln's Inn, 1884, and joined Midland Circuit; Recorder of Great Grimsby, 1914-18. *Publications:* The Law of Carriage by Railway, 6th ed., 1923; The Elements of Commercial Law, 3rd ed., 1922; Railways and Canals and other matter in Lord Halsbury's Laws of England. *Address:* 8 West Hill Road, S.W.18. *T.:* Putney 403. *Club:* New University.   (*Died 16 Jan. 1925.*)

DISTANT, William Lucas; *b.* 12 Nov. 1845; *o. surv. s.* of late Capt. Alex. Distant; *m.* 1874, Edith Blanche de Rubien (*d.* 1914); three *s.* three *d.* *Educ.:* privately. Director and Hon. Sec. Anthropological Institute, 1878-81; Sec. Entomological Society, 1878-80; Vice-President, 1881 and 1900; Editor of the Zoologist, 1897-1915; travelled and made natural history collections in the Malay Peninsula and in the Transvaal. *Publications:* Rhopalocera Malayana; Monograph of the Oriental Cicadidæ; A Naturalist in the Transvaal; Rhynchota, vol. i. in Godman and Salvin's Biologia Centrali Americana; Faun. Brit. India, Rhynchota, vols. i.-vii.; Insecta Transvaaliensia (in parts); numerous scattered publications on Lepidoptera, Rhynchota, and Coleoptera, and a few on anthropological subjects. *Recreation:* angling. *Address:* Glenside, Birchanger Road, South Norwood, Surrey.   (*Died 4 Feb. 1922.*)

DISTURNAL, William Josiah, K.C., 1913; *e. s.* of Thomas Disturnal, late of Walsall and Wednesbury; *m.* Charlotte Elizabeth, 2nd *d.* of Thomas Southern, late of Walsall and Wednesbury; one *d.* *Educ.:* The Leys School; Trinity Hall, Cambridge (Scholar and Prizeman). Law Tripos (Cambridge), 1884; M.A. and LL.B.; called to Bar, Inner Temple, 1885; Bencher, 1921; Oxford Circuit; 1st Recorder of Dudley, 1908. *Address:* 48 Cheyne Walk, Chelsea, S.W.3. *T.:* Kensington 2360; 2 Temple Gardens, Temple, E.C.4. *T.A.:* 71 Temple, E.C. *T.:* 2470 Central. *Club:* United University.   (*Died 2 Mar. 1923.*)

DIXEY, Sir Harry Edward, Kt., *cr.* 1925; M.D. Aberdeen; D.L., J.P. Worcestershire; Sheriff, 1921; *b.* 26 Aug. 1853; *s.* of Charles Anderson Dixey, Highgate; *m.* Ellen Mary, *d.* of J. Dyson Perrins, Malvern. Alderman Worcestershire County Council; Chairman Worcester City and County Nursing Association; Chairman King Edward VII. Memorial Sanatorium, Worcestershire; Chairman St. John Brine Bath Hospital, Droitwich. *Address:* Woodgate, Malvern. *T.:* Malvern 108. *Club:* Junior Carlton.   (*Died 6 Jan. 1927.*)

DIXIE, Sir Alexander Beaumont Churchill, 11th Bt., *cr.* 1660; *b.* 22 Dec. 1851; *o. s.* of 10th Bt. and Maria, *d.* of Rev. Charles Walters, Rector of Bramdean, Hants; *m.* 1st, 1875, Lady Florence Caroline Douglas (*d.* 1905), *y. d.* of 7th Marquess of Queensberry and Caroline, *d.* of Gen. Sir William Robert Clayton, 5th Bt.; two *s.*; 2nd, 1906, Alice, widow of Edward John Ewart. *Heir: s.* George Douglas [*b.* 1876; *m.* 1900, Margaret, *d.* of Sir A. Jardine, 8th Bart.; one *s.* two *d.*; was a midshipman R.N., and late Lieut. 3rd Batt. K.O.S.B.].   (*Died 21 Aug. 1924.*)

DIXON, Sir Alfred Herbert, 1st Bt., *cr.* 1918; Chairman of the Cotton Control Board; Fine Cotton Spinners' and Doublers' Association, Ltd.; Great Leven Spinning Co., Ltd.; Manchester Royal Exchange, Ltd. *Address:* Temple Chambers, St. James's Square, Manchester.   (*Died 10 Dec. 1920.*)

DIXON, Amzi Clarence, B.A., D.D.; Pastor, University Baptist Church, Baltimore; *b.* North Carolina, U.S.A., 6 July 1854; *s.* of Thomas Dixon and Amanda M'Afee; *m.*

Mary Faison; one *s.* three *d.* *Educ.:* Wake Forest College, N.C., U.S.A.; Southern Baptist Theological Seminary. Began to preach at 19 years of age; ordained at Bear Marsh Church, Duplin Co., N.C., U.S.A.; Pastor three years of Baptist Church at Chapel Hill, N.C.; three and a half years of Baptist Church in Asheville, N.C.; eight years Pastor of Emmanuel Baptist Church in Baltimore, Md.; ten years Pastor of Hanson Place Baptist Church, Brooklyn, N.Y.; five and a half years Pastor of Ruggles Street Baptist Church, Boston, Mass.; five and a half years Pastor of Moody Church, Chicago, Ill.; eight years Pastor of Metropolitan Tabernacle, London; held many evangelistic missions in many places. *Publications:* Heaven on Earth; Evangelism Old and New; Young Convert's Problems; Lights and Shadows; Present-Day Life and Religion; Milk and Meat; The Christian Science Delusion; Back to the Bible; The Bright Side of Life; The Bright Side of Death; Through Night to Morning; The Glories of the Cross; Christian Character; Speaking with Tongues; The Prophet Jonah; The Touches of God; Reconstruction; Why I am a Christian; Victory: Why I am an Evangelical Christian and not a Modernist; many single Sermons. *Address:* University Baptist Church, Baltimore, Md., U.S.A.   (*Died 15 June 1925.*)

DIXON, Charles, naturalist, author, journalist, and lecturer; *b.* London, 20 July 1858; *e. s.* of late Charles Thomas Dixon, landscape painter and engraver; *m.* Mary, *o. c.* of John Knight, Torquay, 1886. *Educ.:* various public schools. Boyhood passed near Sheffield; London, 1880-91; Devonshire, 1891-1900; has devoted his whole life to the study of Natural History; in pursuing this study he has visited most parts of the British Islands from the English Channel to St. Kilda, where he discovered the wren peculiar to that locality; he has also travelled in North Africa, where a new species and many rarities were obtained by him; for five years he was associated with the late Henry Seebohm, writing in collaboration with him a work on British Birds; of late years he has made the migration of birds and the geographical distribution of species his special study, promulgating several new theories, and suggesting an entirely new law, bearing upon these questions. *Publications:* Rural Bird Life, 1880; Evolution without Natural Selection, 1885; Our Rarer Birds, 1888; Stray Feathers from Many Birds, 1890; Annals of Bird Life, 1890; Idle Hours with Nature, 1891; The Birds of our Rambles, 1891; The Migration of Birds, 1892 (Russian ed. 1895; amended English edition, 1897); Jottings about Birds, 1893; The Game Birds and Wild Fowl of the British Islands, 1893; The Nests and Eggs of British Birds, 1893 (illustrated ed. 1894); The Nests and Eggs of Non-indigenous British Birds, 1894; The Migration of British Birds, 1895; British Sea Birds, 1896; Curiosities of Bird Life, 1897; Our Favourite Song Birds, 1897; Lost and Vanishing Birds, 1898; Bird-life in a Southern County, 1899; new and enlarged edition of The Game Birds and Wild Fowl of the British Islands, with 40 coloured plates, 1899; Among the Birds in Northern Shires, 1900; The Story of the Birds, 1900; Birds' Nests: An Introduction to the science of Caliology, 1902; Open Air Studies in Bird Life: Sketches of British Birds in their Homes, 1903; new and popular edition of The Migration of British Birds, 1904; The Bird-Life of London, 1909, etc. *Address:* 50 Crown Hill Road, N.W.10. *T.:* Willesden 848.   (*Died 17 June 1926.*)

DIXON, Charles Harvey, M.P. (U.) Rutland and Stamford Division since 1922; *b.* 1862; *m.* 1896, *d.* of late J. P. Robinson, Esher; one *s.* three *d.* M.P. (C.) Boston, 1910-18. *Address:* Gunthorpe, Oakham, Rutland. *Club:* Carlton.   (*Died 22 Sept. 1923.*)

DIXON, Maj.-Gen. Edward George,
Madras Infantry; *b.* 15 Dec. 1887. Entered
army, 1857; Maj.-Gen. 1891; retired, 1893.
(Died 27 Feb. 1918.)

DIXON, Lt.-Col. Frederick Alfred,
C.M.G. 1919; D.S.O. 1917; late R.F.A.; *b.* Man-
chester, 27 March 1880; *s.* of late John P. Dixon,
J.P., The Mount, Marton, Lancs.; *m.* 1908,
Ethel Howard Coulston; one *s.* three *d.*
Educ.: Rossall. Commissioned Lancs. Vol.
Artillery, 1899; Tipperary Militia Artillery,
1900; R.H. and R.F.A. 1901; served 8 years
in India in both R.H. and R.F.A.; Lt.-Col.
1915, to command 150th Brigade, R.F.A. which
was raised by him; served European War
(C.M.G., D.S.O.). *Recreations:* big and small
game shooting, and polo. *Address:* Bramley
Meade, Whalley, Lancs. *T.:* Whalley 2. *M.:*
LE 7001. *Club:* Junior Army and Navy.
(Died 18 Jan. 1925.)

DIXON, Colonel Sir George, 1st
Bart., *cr.* 1919; late Chairman Cheshire County
Council, etc; *b.* 23 May 1842; *s.* of John
Dixon, of Astle Hall; *m.* 1885, Emily
Katherine, 2nd *d.* of G. Beacham Cole, of
Twickenham; one *s.* one *d.* *Educ.:* Eton.
Joined the King's Own Borderers (the 25th
Foot), 1860; took part in the campaign against
the Fenians in Canada, 1866 (Canadian medal);
in 1873 left the Borderers and entered the 5th
Battalion Cheshire Rifle Vols. as Major; re-
tired, after serving thirteen years, with the
rank of Lt.-Col.; Colonel Commandant
Cheshire Volunteer Training Corps; Vice-
Lieutenant for County of Cheshire; J.P.
Cheshire; High Sheriff, 1881; a D.L. and
Chairman of the Cheshire County Council, 1893-
1922; was a Councillor since 1889, when C.
Councils were formed. *Recreations:* travelling,
shooting, and fishing. *Heir: s.* John [*b.* 13
June 1886; *m.* 1910, Gwendolen Anna, *d.* of Sir
J. L. E. Spearman, 2nd Bt.; two *s.* one *d.*].
Address: Astle Hall, Chelford, Cheshire. *T.A.:*
Chelford. *M.:* M 4686. *Club:* Arthur's.
(Died 1 April 1924.)

DIXON, Capt. Kennet, C.B.E. 1919;
R.N., retired list; *m.* Evelyn, *d.* of late General
Cadwallader Adams. Served European War
(C.B.E.). *Address:* Cogreshall, Essex.
(Died 13 April 1927.)

DIXON, William Gray, M.A. Glasg. et
Melb.; D.D.Edin.; Minister Emeritus of the
Presbyterian Church of New Zealand; *b.*
Paisley, Scotland, 21 May 1854; *e. s.* of Rev.
James Main Dixon, Minister of Free Martyrs'
Church, and Jane Gray Dixon, Ayr; *m.* 1900,
Elizabeth Aitken, 4th *d.* of John Glen of
Crosshill, Glasgow. *Educ.:* Ayr Academy
(Dux); Glasgow University, M.A.; New
College, Edinburgh. Professor of English in
the Imperial College of Engineering, Tokyo,
Japan, 1876-80; Recording Secretary and Life
Member of the Asiatic Society of Japan;
Assistant Minister of Scots Church, Melbourne,
1886; Minister of Fitzroy, Melbourne, 1887-89;
of St. John's, Warrnambool, Victoria, 1889-
1900; of St. David's, Auckland, N.Z., 1900-10;
of Roslyn Presbyterian Church, Dunedin, N.Z.,
1910-21; Examiner in Theology Ormond
College, Melbourne, and Knox College, Dunedin;
Theological Tutor; Moderator of the Presbyterian Church of New Zealand, 1919; retired,
1921; Official Delegate of the Presbyterian
Church of New Zealand to the World Conference on Faith and Order, Lausanne, Aug.
1927, and to the Alliance of the Reformed
Churches holding the Presbyterian System,
Budapest, Sep. 1927. *Publications:* The Land
of the Morning, 1882; The Romance of the
Catholic Presbyterian Church, 1918; revised
and enlarged edition, 1928; numerous
magazine articles, chiefly descriptive and
theological; Acting Editor of various
magazines. *Recreations:* mountaineering,

bowling, golf. *Address:* Glenfruin, St.
Leonards, Dunedin, New Zealand. *T.:* 18-760.
(Died 4 Sept. 1928.)

**DIXON-WRIGHT, Rev. Henry
Dixon,** M.V.O., Chaplain R.N. College, Dart-
mouth; *b.* 25 April 1870; *m.* 1904, Annie Louisa,
d. of late Major J. Paton Lawrie, 2nd Queen's
Regt.; two *s.* *Educ.:* Highgate School; Cor-
pus Christi College, Cambridge; 3rd class
Classical Tripos, 1892; Ordained, 1893; Curate
of St. Stephen, S. Lambeth, 1893-94; St. James',
Paddington, 1894-97; Stoke-Next-Guildford,
1897-98; Chaplain R.N. 1899; served in
H.M.S. Resolution, 1899-1900; Ramillies,
1900-3; Bedford, 1903-6; R.N. Hospital,
Malta, 1906-7; R.N. College, Dartmouth, 1907;
H.M.S. Medina, 1911-12. *Address:* Royal
Naval College, Dartmouth. *(Died 31 May 1916.)*

DIXSON, Sir Hugh, Kt., *cr.* 1921; Retired,
Director Chm. (local) of Alliance Assurance Co.,
Ltd., London, Royal Prince Alfred Hospital,
Dixson Trust, Ltd., &c.; *b.* 29 Jan. 1841; *s.* of Hugh
Dixson and Helen Craig, both Edinburgh; *m.*
1866, Emma Elizabeth Shaw (*d.* 1922); two *s.*
four *d.* *Educ.:* Cape's Academy, Darlinghurst,
Sydney. Tobacco manufacturer; Director and
Chairman City Bank, Sydney; Contributor
Religious, Imperial and Charitable Institutions;
Ex-President Baptist Union, N.S.W. *Recrea-
tion:* gardening. *Address:* Abergeldie, Summer
Hill, Sydney, N.S.W. *T.A.:* Aberdix, Sydney.
T.: V 1013. *M.:* 62. *Club:* British Empire.
(Died 11 May 1926.)

DOBB, His Honour Harry, Judge of
County Court, Circuit No. 20, 1921-25;
of Birmingham County Court, 1925-27; of
Lambeth since 1927; Magistrate for county of
Leicester and City of Leicester and for City
of Birmingham; *b.* 15 Aug. 1867; *e. s.* of
Henry and Emily Dobb of Arnmore, Frognal,
N.W., and Richard Dobb, Felixstowe, Suffolk;
m. 1st, Florence (*d.* 1907), *d.* of W. J. Willats
of Lansdowne Crescent, Kensington; 2nd,
Kathleen Mildred, *e. d.* of late Henry
Caldwell Lipsett, of Ballyshannon, Co.
Donegal, and Wickford, Essex; two *s.*
Educ.: Dawlish; Merchant Taylors' School;
Pembroke College, Cambridge. B.A. 1888.
Called to Bar, Lincoln's Inn, 1891. *Address:*
5 Essex Court, Temple, E.C.; The Shrubbery,
Stoneygate, Leicester. *Club:* United Univer-
sity. *(Died 23 Mar. 1923.)*

DOBBIE, Sir James (Johnston), Kt., *cr.*
1915; F.R.S. 1904, LL.D. Glasgow, M.A.,
D.Sc.; *b.* 4 Aug. 1852; 2nd *s.* of Alexander
Dobbie, Glasgow; *m.* 1887, Violet, *d.* of Thomas
Chilton, J.P., of Liverpool and Gresford; one
s. two *d.* *Educ.:* High School, Glasgow; Universities of Glasgow (George A. Clark Scholar in
Natural Science), Edinburgh, and Leipzig. As-
sistant to the Professor of Chemistry, University
of Glasgow, 1881-84; Professor of Chemistry,
Univ. Coll. of North Wales, Bangor, 1884-1908;
Director Royal Scottish Museum, Edinburgh,
1903-9; Principal of the Government Labora-
tories, London, 1909-20; Past President of the
Institute of Chemistry, 1915-18; President of
the Chemical Society, 1919-21; Member of the
Royal Commission on Awards to Inventors;
Member of the University Grants Committee.
Publications: Numerous papers on the chemical
constitution of alkaloids, and the relation
between chemical constitution and absorption
spectra of organic compounds. *Address:* The
Cottage, Fairlie, Ayrshire. *Club:* Athenæum.
(Died June 1924.)

DOBBIE, Brig.-Gen. William Hugh,
C.B. 1912; late Mandalay Brigade, Burma; *b.*
9 May 1859; *s.* of Lt.-Col. Robert Shedden
Dobbie. Entered army, 1879; Captain, I.S.C.
1890; Major, Indian army, 1899; Lt.-Col.,
1904; Bt.-Col., 1907; A.Q.M.G. India; served
Burmese Expedition, 1885-87 (despatches thrice,
medal with clasp); Manipur, 1891 (clasp); S.

African War, 1899-1900 ; retired 1920.
(*Died 25 Nov. 1922.*)

DOBBIN, Lt.-Col. William James Knowles, C.B.E.; Indian Army, retired, 1905; *b.* 1 June 1856; *s.* of Rev. W. P. H. Dobbin and Fanny *d.* of Sheridan Knowles the Dramatist; *m.* 1st, 1886, Ethel (d. 1906), *d.* of Major R. Callwell Smith, R.A.; two *d.*; 2nd, 1910, Edith, *d.* of Major Octavius Lowry, 96 Regt. and Galway Militia. *Educ.:* Rathmines School ; Trinity College, Dublin. Joined Militia, 1874 ; Army, 1877 ; Bengal Staff Corps, 1880 ; served in six Indian Expeditions, and at the Relief of the Peking Legations, 1900 ; European War, 1915-19, at Mudros, in Egypt, and the Egyptian Expeditionary Force ; commanded 19 Battn., the Rifle Brigade, 1917-19 (despatches twice, C.B.E., Order of the Nile). *Recreations:* golf, tennis, croquet. *Address:* Charleville, Rostrevor, Co. Down.
(*Died 27 June 1926.*)

DOBSON, Henry Austin, LL.D.; *b.* Plymouth, 18 Jan. 1840; *e. s.* of George Clarisse Dobson, C.E.; *m.* Frances Mary, *d.* of Nathaniel Beardmore, C.E., of Broxbourne, Herts ; five *s.* five *d. Educ.:* Beaumaris Grammar School ; private school, Coventry ; Gymnase, Strasbourg. Entered Board of Trade, 1856 ; First-class Clerk, 1874-84 ; Principal, 1884-1901 ; retired, 1901 ; Hon. LL.D., Edinburgh, 1902 ; Committee of London Library ; Council of Society of Authors ; Council of Royal Literary Fund. *Publications:* Poems : Vignettes in Rhyme, 1873 ; Proverbs in Porcelain, 1877 ; Old-World Idylls, 1883 ; At the Sign of the Lyre, 1885 ; Collected Poems, 1 vol. 1897, ninth ed. 1913. Prose : Thomas Bewick and his Pupils, 1884 ; Lives of Fielding, 1883, Steele, 1886, Goldsmith, 1888, Horace Walpole, 1890-1910, William Hogarth, 1891, 1897, 1907, Richardson, 1902 ; Fanny Burney, 1903 ; Four Frenchwomen, 1890 ; Eighteenth Century Vignettes, three series, 1892, 1894, 1896 ; A Paladin of Philanthropy, 1899 ; Side-Walk Studies, 1902 ; De Libris, 1908 ; Old Kensington Palace, 1910 ; At Prior Park, 1912 ; Rosalba's Journal, 1915 ; Bookman's Budget, 1917 ; Later Essays (1917-20), 1921 ; contributions to the Encyclopædia Britannica, Chambers's Encyclopædia, Chambers's Cyclopædia of English Literature, and Dictionary of National Biography ; has also—besides editing Mme. D'Arblay's Diary, 1904-5, and Evelyn's Diary, 1906— edited several books for Clarendon Press, World's Classics, etc., and written for many of the more important magazines and reviews. *Address:* 75 Eaton Rise, Ealing, W. *Club:* Athenæum. (*Died 2 Sept. 1921.*)

DOBSON, Henry John, R.C.A. 1920; A.R.C.A. 1907, R.S.W. 1890; native of Innerleithen, Peeblesshire; *b.* 1858; *e. s.* of Thomas and Rebecca Dobson; *m.* 1890, Jeanie Charlotte Hannah Cowan; three *s.* one *d. Educ.:* Innerleithen ; Edinburgh. Painter of Scottish character and interiors; studied at School of Design, and Royal Scottish Academy, Edinburgh ; Exhibitor at Royal Academy, London, and leading provincial Exhibitions ; winner of £100 Prize, London, with R.A. picture The New Toy, open competition best oil picture, 1897 ; his picture A Scottish Sacrament purchased by Bradford Corporation, 1893 ; other best-known pictures are The Little Minister, Burns's Grace, The Last Request, The Hand that Rocks the Cradle, The New Arrival, Auld Lang Syne, Burns and Highland Mary, Her Dochter's Bairn, etc.; invited to visit America and Canada, 1911, to read paper on Scottish Art at Convention held at Red Oak, Iowa, and presented with Gold Medal in recognition of his work ; Newcastle Corporation in 1913 purchased his picture The Sabbath Hat. *Publications:* Scottish Life and Character ; Scottish Art. *Recreations:* golf and walking. *Address:* 5 Merchiston Place, Edinburgh. (*Died July 1928.*)

DOCKRELL, Benjamin Morgan, Senior Physician, St. John's Hospital for Diseases of Skin, London ; Chesterfield Lecturer on Dermatology ; *b.* 2 Feb. 1860 ; *s.* of late Thomas Dockrell, J.P., Monkstown, Co. Dublin, and Anne Morgan Brooks ; *m.* 1882, Emily, *o. d.* of late Alexander Oldfield of Cahir, Tipperary ; one *s.* two *d. Educ.:* Cheltenham College ; University of Dublin ; Royal College of Surgeons ; Steevens and Adelaide Hospitals ; M.A., M.D. (2nd place at M.B.) ; B.Ch.; M.O.Sc. (1st place) University of Dublin. In practice as a specialist in skin diseases since 1888 ; President of the London Dermatological Society, 1912 ; President of the West Kent Medico-Chirurgical Society, 1898 ; Vice-President (for life) of the Balneological Section of the Royal Society of Medicine ; President of the United Hospitals London Swimming Association, 1903-12 ; for twenty-five years Physician to St. John's Hospital; Chesterfield Lecturer on Dermatology since 1895, and Medallist in Dermatology ; Fellow of the Medical Society of London, Royal Society of Medicine, and of London Dermatology Society ; formerly Physician to the out-patient department Millar Hospital and Royal Kent Dispensary ; Dermatologist to the National Society for Prevention of Cruelty to Children ; Pathologist and Director of Laboratory the Hospital for Diseases of Skin, Leicester Square ; Lecturer and Demonstrator in the London School of Dermatology. *Publications:* Hydronaphthol as a Specific in the Treatment of Ringworm, 1889 ; The Skin and how to Keep it Healthy, 1893 ; Research into the alleged Parasitic Nature of Eczema (Proc. Internat. Congress of Dermatol. Paris, 1900) ; Lichen from a Histological Point of View, 1901 ; Atlas of Dermatology, Clinical and Microscopical, 1904 ; many papers on Syphilis and Diseases of Skin. *Recreations :* research work, golf, swimming, tennis, and croquet. *Address:* 9 Cavendish Square, W. *T.:* 898 Paddington. (*Died 15 Mar. 1920.*)

DODD, Henry Work, F.R.C.S. Eng., L.R.C.P., L.S.A. Ophthalmic Surgeon ; *b.* Victoria, Vancouver Island, B.C. ; *s.* of late Charles Dodd, H.B.C. ; *m.* Agnes, *y. d.* of James Legasick Shuter ; one *d.* two *s. Educ.:* Norwich School under Rev. Augustus Jessop, D.D.; St. Bartholomew's Hospital ; Ophthalmic Surgeon to, and Clinical Lecturer on Ophthalmic Medicine and Surgery at the Royal Free Hospital ; Surgeon to the Royal Westminster Ophthalmic Hospital ; Ophthalmic Surgeon to the Hospital for Nervous Diseases, Welbeck Street, W., etc.; Major (retired) R.A.M.C. Vols. *Publications:* Has contributed various papers on ophthalmic subjects. *Address:* 136 Harley Street, W.1 ; *T.:* 7468 Paddington. *Clubs:* Reform, Savage.
(*Died 28 June 1921.*)

DODDS, Rev. Canon Matthew Archbold, Vicar of Chilvers Coton, Nuneaton (the Shepperton of George Eliot's Scenes), since 1914 ; *b.* Galway, 5 June 1864 ; *e. s.* of late Jackson and Maria Dodds, Stroud Green, N. ; *m.* Bertha (d. 1909), *e. d.* of late Robert Blackman ; three *s.* two *d. Educ.:* The Magnus School, Newark ; The London College of Divinity. Deacon, 1887 ; Priest, 1888 ; Curate of St. Andrew and St. Philip, N. Kensington, 1887-90 ; St. Chad's, Derby, 1890-92 ; Missionary West Africa, 1892-93 ; Curate of Boulton, Derby, 1893-96 ; Chaplain, Newstead Colliery, 1897-1902 ; Vicar of St. Philip's, Nottingham, and Chaplain of Plumtre Hospital, 1902-14 ; Canon of Coventry, 1922 ; Rural Dean of Atherstone, 1923. *Publications:* Sundry papers on missionary and temperance matters. *Address:* Chilvers Coton Vicarage, Nuneaton. *M.:* NX 9984. (*Died 9 Jan. 1928.*)

DODGE, Grenville Mellen, Maj.-Gen. U.S.V. ; President Society Army of the Tennessee, 1892 ; Vice-President Abilene and Southern Ry.; Commd. M.O.L.L.; President

292

of Commission to investigate conduct of the War Dept. in war with Spain, 1898 ; *b.* Danvers, Mass., 12 April 1831 ; *s.* of Sylvanus Dodge, and Julia T. Phillips. *Educ. :* Norwich University, Vt. ; C.E., A.M., and LL.D. Civil engineer ; Maj.-Gen. war rebellion ; Commander Regt. Brigade, Div. Corps and Army and Department ; Chief Eng. U. Pac. Ry. and built that and numerous other railways in the U.S. ; member 89th Congress ; Hon. Member American Society Civil Engineers. *Address :* Baldwin Block, Council Bluffs, Iowa, U.S.A. *Clubs :* Union League, Army and Navy, Republican, New York. (*Died 3 Jan.* 1916.)

DOLGOROUKI, Princess Alexis (Frances) ; widow of late Prince Alexis Dolgorouki (*d.* 1915) ; *o. c.* and heir of Fleetwood Pellew Wilson of Wappenham Manor, Northants, D.L., J.P. *Address :* 46 Upper Grosvenor Street, W. ; Nashdom, Taplow, Bucks ; Wappenham Manor, Northants ; Braemar Castle, N.B. *T. :* Mayfair 1260. (*Died 23 Aug.* 1919.)

DOLMAN, Frederick, F.J.I., Editor of the Art Trade Journal ; contributor to the Strand, Pearson's and other Magazines ; *b.* London, 1867 ; *m.* ; one *s.* Entered journalism at age of 18—London Echo, Scarborough Evening News, National Press Agency, etc. ; travelled round the world, 1897 ; L.C.C. (Brixton) 1901-07 ; Member of the London War Pensions Committee. *Publication :* Municipalities at Work, 1895. *Recreations :* chess, playgoing, motoring, rambles. *Address :* 9 King's Bench Walk, Temple, E.C. 4 ; *T. :* City 334 ; 18 Buckingham Street, Strand, W.C. 2 ; *T. :* Regent 3473 ; The Dell Cottage, Englefield Green, Surrey ; *T. :* Egham 214. *M. :* XC 4961. *Club :* National Liberal.

DOMINGUEZ, Don Vicente J., Envoy Extraordinary and Minister Plenipotentiary of the Argentine Republic to Great Britain since 1911 ; *b.* and *educ. :* Buenos Aires ; *s.* of Don Luis L. Dominguez, former Argentine Ministers in London ; *m.* Helen, *d.* of Daniel T. Murphy, New York ; one *s.* Private Secretary to the Argentine Minister in Peru, 1876 ; in Brazil, 1878 ; in the United States, 1882 ; in England, 1886 ; First Secretary of Legation in Madrid, 1891 ; in Washington, 1895 ; in Paris, 1896 ; in London, 1899 ; represented the Argentine Government at the celebrations of the 400th anniversary of the Discovery of America at Huelva and Seville, Spain, 1892 ; Special Envoy from the Argentine President at the Coronation of King George V. 1911. *Address :* 7 Tilney Street, Park Lane, W. ; 2 Palace Gate, W. *Clubs :* Argentine, Marlborough, Royal Automobile, St. James's. (*Died 28 June* 1916.)

DOMVILE, Sir Compton Edward, G.C.B., *cr.* 1904 ; K.C.B., *cr.* 1898 ; G.C.V.O. 1903 ; *b.* Worcestershire, 10 Oct. 1842 ; 2nd *s.* of late Henry Barry Domvile ; *m.* 1876, Isabella, *d.* of Capt. Edmund Peel, late 85th Regt. ; two *s.* three *d. Educ. :* Royal Academy, Gosport. Entered Navy, 1856 ; appointed to Royal yacht, 1862 ; Lieut. 1862 ; promoted Commander for service against pirates, 1868 ; Captain, 1876 ; Captain of the "Dido," 1879-83 ; W. Africa and Cape during the Boer War ; Acting Commodore, Jamaica, 1882 ; Captain of "Téméraire," 1884-1886 ; Captain H.M.S. "Excellent"—Gunnery School, Portsmouth, 1886-90 ; Ordnance Committee, 1890-91 ; Director of Naval Ordnance, 1891-94 ; second in command Mediterranean, 1894-96 ; Adm. 1902 ; Adm. Supt. of Naval Reserves, 1897-1902 ; Commander-in-Chief Mediterranean Station, 1902 - 5. *Address :* 7 San Remo, Hove, Sussex. (*Died 19 Nov.* 1924.)

DOMVILLE, Sir James Henry, 5th Bt. ; *cr.* 1814 ; Lieut., R.N. ; commanding destroyer P. 19 ; *b.* 10 Dec. 1889 ; S. father 1904 ; *s.* of 4th Bt. and Moselle, *d.* of H. M. Ames, Linden,

Northumberland ; *m.* 1912, Kathleen, *d.* of B. A. Charlesworth of Gunton Hall, Lowestoft ; two *d.* Served European War, 1914-15. *Heir :* *b.* Cecil Lionel, *b.* 14 Sep. 1892. *Club :* United Service. (*Died 13 Sept.* 1919.)

DOMVILLE, Lieut. - Colonel Hon. James, F.R.G.S., M.I.M.E. F.R.C.I., M.Inst.C.E. ; S.G.I.G. 33° ; Senator since 1903 ; Chairman Select Standing Committee of Senate on Mineral Resources of Canada ; Hon. Col. 8th Princess Louise's New Brunswick Hussars ; *s.* of late Lieut.-Gen. J. W. Domville and Frances, *d.* of late Hon. W. Usher ; *b.* 29 Nov. 1842 ; *m.* 1867, Isabella, *d.* of W. H. Scovil. *Educ. :* Woolwich. Has travelled a great deal ; built and sailed the first British steamer on the Yukon ; organised the 8th Hussars and commanded it for twenty years (decorations, Long Service, Fenian Medal, Queen's Diamond Jubilee Medal) ; regiment volunteered for the Soudan, 1884-96 ; and for South Africa (received the thanks of the Home Authorities) ; sat as an Alderman, City of St. John, N.B., and Chairman Finance Committee ; M.P. 1873 ; was for four years Chairman of the Select Standing Committee of the House of Commons on Banking and Commerce ; founded the St. John Free Library. *Address :* Rothesay, New Brunswick, Canada. *Clubs :* Rideau, Ottawa ; Union, St. John ; Liberal, Montreal ; Moncton, Moncton. (*Died 30 July* 1921.)

DON, Sir William, K.B.E., *cr.* 1918 ; Deputy-Lieutenant of the County of the City of Dundee ; ex-Lord Provost of Dundee ; a partner of the firm of Don & Duncan, Ltd., Jute Spinners and Manufacturers ; *b.* 1861 ; *s.* of late James Don, Dundee ; *m.* 1894, Martha Nicoll, *d.* of J. H. Lindsay ; two *s.* three *d. Educ. :* Dundee High School. Seventeen years a member of the Town Council of Dundee. *Recreation :* bowling. *Address :* Ardarroch, Dundee. *T. :* Dundee 2709. *Club :* Eastern, Dundee. (*Died 20 Oct.* 1926.)

DON, Surg.-Gen. William Gerard, M.D. ; Deputy Surgeon-General, Army Medical Service ; retired on the Non-Effective List Army Medical Service, 1885 ; *b.* Stracathro, Forfarshire, 10 Jan. 1836 ; *y. s.* of Alexander Don, Ballownie ; *m.* 1st, 1866, Louisa Jane Elliott ; three *s.* two *d.* ; 2nd, 1889, Jean Ann Fairweather ; two *s.* two *d. Educ. :* Locally, Aberdeen, Edinburgh. Doctor of Medicine, Edinburgh University, 1857 ; served medical volunteer in Flagship Duke of Wellington, Baltic Fleet, 1855, and at bombardment of Sweaborg, August (medal) ; entered army, 1858 ; served in Mutiny, Central India, in actions with Tantia Topee at Rajpore, and Beilkaira, Nov. 1858 (despatches, medal) ; served in 28th Regt. Royal Engineers, and Royal Artillery, on Staff, and in Medical Branch, War Office ; employed in fitting out hospital ships for Egyptian Expedition, 1882 ; and re-writing and editing the Army Medical Regulations of 1885 ; as Senior Medical Officer, London Recruiting Staff, for seventeen years ; President of the Caledonian Society of London ; Life Governor, Royal Scottish Corporation, and connected with Scottish Societies in London. *Publications :* privately, Recollections of the Baltic Fleet of 1855 ; several Family Genealogies ; publicly, Archæological Notes on Early Scotland, 1899 ; numerous contributions to current medical and other literature. *Recreations :* literature, gardening, fishing, shooting. *Address :* 52 Canfield Gardens. W. Hampstead. N.W.6. (*Died 27 July* 1920.)

DONALDSON, Sir George, Kt., *cr.* 1904 ; *b.* 25 May 1845 ; *s.* of late A. Donaldson, of Edinburgh ; *m.* 1872, Alice (*d.* 1907), *d.* of John Stronach, Edinburgh ; three *s.* four *d.* Created and equipped the series of Historic Music Rooms at the Inventions Exhibition of 1885 ; Vice-President International Jury, Paris Exhibitions, 1889 and 1900 ; Chevalier Legion of Honour ; Member of Royal

Commission, St. Louis Exhibition, 1904; presented the Donaldson Museum to Royal College of Music, 1894, and a collection of furniture to the Victoria and Albert Museum, 1900: is a Director of the Royal Academy of Music and a Member of the Royal Institution; it was solely on his initiative that the fine new building of the Royal Academy of Music in the Marylebone Road came into existence. *Address:* 1 Grand Avenue, Hove. (*Died 19 Mar. 1925.*)

DONALDSON, Sir Hay Frederick, K.C.B., *cr.* 1911; C.B. 1909; Technical Adviser to Minister of Munitions since 1915; *b.* 7 July 1856; 2nd *s.* of late Sir Stuart Alexander Donaldson, first Premier of New South Wales, and Amelia, *d.* of the late Frederick Cowper of Carleton Hall, Penrith, and Unthank, Cumberland; *m.* Selina, *y. d.* of late Col. F. M. Beresford, sometime M.P. for Southwark; one *s.* two *d. Educ.:* Eton; Trinity College, Cambridge; Edinburgh; Zurich; L. and N.W.R. Works, Crewe; Past President, Institution of Mechanical Engineers; Member of Council of Institution of Civil Engineers; Member of Iron and Steel Institute, etc.; on the Board and Executive Committee of the National Physical Laboratory; Chairman of Sectional Committee on Screw Threads and Limit Gauges of the Engineering Standards Committee; Civil and Mechanical Engineer; employed at Goa, India, 1884-7, Railway and Harbour construction; 1887-1891, on the Manchester Ship Canal; 1892-97, Chief Engineer, London India Docks Joint Committee; 1898-99, Deputy Director General of Ordnance Factories; Chief Mechanical Engineer of Ordnance Factories, 1899-1903; Chief Superintendent since 1903. *Recreations:* shooting and fishing. *Address:* Wood Lodge, Shooters' Hill, Kent. *Clubs:* Athenæum, St. Stephen's, Ranelagh. (*Died 5 June 1916.*)

DONALDSON, William, C.B., 1900; *b.* 13 Mar. 1838; *s.* of George Donaldson, merchant, Edinburgh; *m.* 1870, Mary, *d.* of the late P. Ross of Leiffie, Meigle, N.B. *Educ.:* High School; University, Edin. Was in the public service for 43 years; began official career in the office of the Law Agent of the late General Board of Directors of Prisons for Scotland; in 1868 acted as Deputy Governor of Perth General Prison, but a year later returned to Edinburgh to assist the late Dr. J. H. Burton in organising the Department of Judicial Statistics and arranging for an Annual Blue-Book on the subject; Secretary of the Prison Commission and Superintendent of the Scottish Department of Judicial Statistics, 1877-1900; gave much assistance in carrying out the provisions of the Prisons Act of 1877; and among other services acted as a member of and Secretary to a Departmental Commission, appointed by Lord Balfour in 1896, to consider in what way the Judicial Statistics could be made of more value to Statisticians and Criminologists; edited the Revised Statistics for the years 1897 and 1898. *Address:* 4 Ravelston Park, Edinburgh. (*Died 22 July 1924.*)

DONCASTER, Leonard, M.A., Sc.D.; F.R.S. 1915; Professor of Zoology, University of Liverpool; Fellow of King's College, Cambridge; *b.* Sheffield, 31 Dec. 1877; *s.* of Samuel Doncaster, Sheffield; *m.* 1908, Dora, 2nd *d.* of Walter Priestman, Birmingham; one *s.* two *d. Educ.:* Leighton Park School, Reading; King's College, Cambridge (Scholar). 1st class Natural Sciences Tripos Part I. 1898, Part II. (distinction in Zoology) 1900; Walsingham Medallist, 1902; Mackinnon Student of Royal Society, 1904-6; Lecturer on Zoology, Birmingham University, 1906-10; Special Lecturer on Variation and Heredity; 1909; Fellow of King's College, Cambridge, 1910; Trail Medal of Linnæan Society, 1915. *Publications:* Papers on Zoological Subjects in Quarterly Journal Microscopical Science, Transactions and Proceedings

Royal Society, etc.; Heredity in the Light of Recent Research, 1910; The Determination of Sex, 1914. *Address:* University, Liverpool. (*Died 28 May 1920.*)

DONELAN, Capt. Anthony J., M.P. (N.) Co. Cork, E., 1892; unseated on petition, 1911; M.P. (N.) Wicklow unopposed, 1911-18; *b.* 1846; *s.* of late Col. Donelan, 48th Regt. *Educ.:* Sandhurst. Was in army. *Address:* Ballymona, Midleton, Co. Cork. (*Died Sept. 1924.*)

DONELAN, James; M.B., M.Ch., etc.; Chevalier of the Crown of Italy, 1909; Officer 1918; Fellow Royal Society of Medicine; Surgeon Throat Dept., Italian Hospital, London, and to Royal Society of Musicians of Great Britain and Ireland; Lecturer, Diseases Nose and Throat, Medical Graduates College, London; Pres. of the Section of Laryngology, Royal Socy. of Medicine, 1918-19; Permanent Organiser of Surgical Staff, Hôpital Régional, Villeneuve-sur-Lot, 1914-18; *e. s.* of late John Donnellan of Mount Kennett House, Limerick; (adopted present form of spelling name 1886); *m.* 1889, Sophia Annie, 2nd *d.* of late Maj.-Gen. James M'Killop Taylor; one *s.* one *d. Educ.:* privately; Trinity Coll., Dublin. Honours in Surgery and Medicine Royal University of Ireland, 1886; Member of the Royal Italian Military Medical Commission for recruiting, 1915-18; Surgeon in temporary charge of the Ambulance Hospital at Crépy-en-Valois (Oise) during the first battle of the Aisne, Sep. 1914; appointed Medical Referee to the London Committee of the Croix Rouge Française; organised short service system by which over 300 British and Colonial surgeons gave voluntary service to the French wounded, 1914-16; Hon. Laryngologist to Royal Society of Musicians, established and developed the Throat Dept. of the Italian Hospital; formerly Hon. Secretary and Member of Council of the Laryngological Society of London now merged in the Royal Society of Medicine. *Publications:* Many communications to societies and medical journals on his specialty, as well as on subjects of wider interest. *Address:* 6 Manchester Square, W.1; Bruntsfield, Harrow-on-the-Hill. *T.:* Pad. 269; Harrow 24. (*Died 25 Aug. 1922.*)

DONINGTON, 3rd Baron (*cr.* 1880) **Gilbert Theophilus Clifton-Hastings-Campbell;** *b.* 29 May 1859; 3rd *s.* of late Countess of Loudoun and Lord Donington; *m.* 1894, Maud Kemble, *o. c* of Sir C. E. Hamilton, 1st Bart.; two *d.;* S. *b.* 1920. *Address:* 47 Eaton Square, S.W.1; *T.:* Victoria 5781; Glenlee Park, New Galloway, Kirkcudbrightshire. *Clubs:* Bachelors', Carlton, Ranelagh. (*Died 31 May 1927.*)

DONKIN, Sir (Horatio) Bryan, Kt., *cr.* 1911; M.D. Oxon., F.R.C.P. London; Member of Prisons Board, and a Director of Convict Prisons; Consulting Physician to Westminster Hospital, and East London Hospital for Children, King George Hospital, 1915, etc.; Hon. Member of the Royal Medico-Psychological Association; Member of Advisory Committee to Home Secretary at H.M. Preventive Detention Prison at Camp Hill, I.W.; Member of Society for the Prevention of Venereal Disease; *b.* Blackheath, Kent, 1 Feb. 1845; *e. s.* of late Bryan Donkin, C.E.; *m.* 1st, 1888, Auguste Margaretha Elisabeth (*d.* 1919), *d.* of late Count di Langhi of Cracow; 2nd, 1923, Marie Louise, widow of Isaac Bates, Belfast, and *d.* of late William Reston, Wilmington, North Carolina, U.S.A. *Educ.:* Blackheath Proprietary School; Queen's College, Oxford; Open Scholar; 1st class in Greats (classical). Formerly Physician and Lecturer on Medicine at Westminster Hospital; Physician to East London Hospital for Children; Lecturer on Medicine at London School of Medicine for Women; Examiner in Medicine for Royal College of Physicians on Examining Board for England; H.M. Commissioner of

Prisons; Medical Adviser to the Prison Commission; Member of Visiting Committees at the Borstal institutions; Harveian Orator, Royal Coll. Physicians, on the Inheritance of Mental Characters, 1910; member of Royal Commission on Control of the Feeble-minded, 1904-8, and of several Departmental Committees appointed by Home Office, etc. *Publications:* Diseases of Childhood; Lectures at the Maudsley Hospital on Mental Defect and Criminal Conduct, Lancet, Nov. 1920; many articles in medical journals, and in Reviews: some relating to mental pathology, crime, psychical researches, medium - craft, the medical prevention of venereal diseases, the fallacies of psychoanalysis, etc. *Address:* 28 Hyde Park Street, W.2. *T.:* Padd. 5705. *Clubs:* Savile, Athenæum.
(*Died 26 July 1927.*)

DONKIN, Richard Sims, J.P., D.L.; director of Suez Canal Co.; *b.* 1836; *s.* of late James Donkin, Tynemouth; M.P. (C.) Tynemouth, 1885 - 1900. *Clubs:* Carlton, Junior Carlton; Travellers', Paris. (*Died 5 Feb. 1919.*)

DONNELLY, Rt. Rev. Nicholas, R.C. Bishop of Dublin (auxiliary) since 1883; Bishop of Canea and Vicar-General of Dublin; Parish Priest of St. Mary's, Haddington Road, Dublin, since 1904; *b.* 23 Nov. 1837; *e. s.* of John Donnelly of Dublin, merchant. *Educ.:* St Vincent's Coll., Castleknock; Irish Coll. Rome. Appointed Curate, 1861, to St. Nicholas, Francis St.; transferred to Pro-Cathedral, Marlborough St., 1864; appointed Administrator St. Andrews, 1879; Parish Priest, Rathgar, 1882; Parish Priest of Bray, 1894. *Publications:* English translation of Haberl's Magister Choralis; Magazine and Newspaper articles. *Recreations:* Music and travel. *Address:* St. Mary's, Haddington Road, Dublin. *Club:* Royal Societies. (*Died 28 Mar. 1920.*)

DONOHOE, Martin Henry, F.J.I.; journalist and war correspondent; Paris correspondent, London Daily Chronicle; *b.* Galway, Ireland, 10 Nov. 1869; *m.* 1900, Madge Tilley of Sydney. *Educ.:* National and Marist Brothers' Schools; Sorbonne et Ecole des langues Orientales. Began journalistic career, Courrier Australien, Sydney, 1892; subsequently staffs Evening News and Town and Country Journal, Sydney; traced De Rougemont; became war correspondent, London Daily Chronicle, 1899; in the Boer war; with Methuen from the Orange River to Magersfontein; acted as assistant galloper to Hector M'Donald in the fight at Koodoesberg Drift; accompanied Lord Roberts on march from Enslin; present at Paardeberg; subsequently captured; released on fall of Pretoria; in Russo-Japanese war; attached first Japanese army with Kuroki through Korea and Manchuria; battles of the Yalu, Motien Pass, Towan, Liaoyang, and the Shaho; travelled in America, Australia, China, Japan, Korea, and South Sea Islands; in Turkish Revolution, 1909; witnessed taking Constantinople, Young Turks; first journalist to interview new Sultan; in Portuguese Revolution, 1910; escaped Lisbon with first detailed account fighting, 1911; Italian-Turkish War, with General Caneva in Tripoli; Balkan War (Abdullah Pasha's retreat, Rodosta, Chatalja, etc.), 1912-13; in European War was Officer British Intelligence Corps, served Greece, Roumania, Russia; Special Service Officer North Persian Expedition, 1918 - 19. *Publications:* various. *Recreations:* rowing, cycling, swimming, and golf. *Address:* 24 Boulevard des Capucines, Paris.
(*Died 19 Jan. 1927.*)

DONOVAN, John Thomas, M.P.(N.), West Wicklow, 1914 - 18; Barrister; *b.* Belfast, 1878; Hon. Secretary, National Volunteers, Ireland; *m.* 1915, Alda, *d.* of W. J. Ralph, Auckland, New Zealand; one *s.* Visited Australia and New Zealand as Envoy of Irish Party, 1906 - 7, 1912 - 13. *Address:* Dunloe, Terenure Road, Dublin. (*Died 17 Jan. 1922*)

DOOLETTE, Sir George Philip, Kt., *cr.* 1916; J.P.; *b.* Dublin, 24 Jan. 1840; *m.* 1st, Mary (*d.* 1889), *e. d.* of George M'Ewin of Glen Ewin, South Australia; 2nd, 1895, Lillie (*d.* 1910), *d.* of late Dr. R. W. Dale, Birmingham; one *s.* one *d.* *Educ.:* Private tutor. One of the principal pioneers of the Western Australian Goldfields; Director Great Boulder Proprietary, etc.; Fellow Royal Geographical Society, Royal Colonial Institute, etc. *Address:* Merlebank, Caterham Valley, Surrey. *T.A.:* Doolettian, London. *T.:* Caterham 29. *M.:* 6641. *Clubs:* City Liberal, Australian, Royal Automobile, British Empire. (*Died 19 Jan. 1924.*)

DOONER, Lt.-Col. William Dundas, C.M.G. 1918; O.B.E. 1919; B.A.; p.a.c.; late Royal Army Ordnance Corps and formerly Royal Irish Fusiliers; *b.* 20 March 1876; *s.* of late Col. William Toke Dooner, O.B.E.; *g.s.* of late John Dooner of Barton, Rathfarnham, Co. Dublin; *m.* 1914, Marion Emily, *e. d.* of late Walter Wilson, Belvoir Park, Belfast. *Educ.:* private tutor; Bradfield College. Entered Army from Militia as 2nd Lieut. Royal Irish Fusiliers, 1895; Capt. 1902; Major 1913; Brev. Lt.-Col. 1915; served South African War, 1899-1900 (severely wounded); transferred to Army Ordnance Department, 1912; retired, 1922. *Address:* Greenan, Dunmurry, Co. Antrim. (*Died 28 Aug. 1927.*)

DOONER, Colonel William Toke, C.B.E. 1922; J.P., Co. Kent and Rochester; 2nd *s.* of John Dooner of Barton Lodge, Rathfarnham, Dublin, and Sarah Georgina, *e. d.* of Major Lawrence Dundas (*d.* 1867), formerly of the 5th Fus.; *m.* 1875, Augusta, 5th *d.* of W. P. Metchim of Petersham Lodge, Surrey; one *s.* one *d.* (two sons killed in War). *Educ.* Aldenham School, Elstree; Trinity College, Dublin; Staff College, Camberley. Entered Army, 1868 (8th King's Liverpool Regt.); transferred to Royal Inniskilling Fus. as Capt. 1875; Brig.-Maj. Gibraltar, Aldershot, and Curragh, 1877-83; D.A.A.G. Dublin, 1883-88; Commanded 1st Batt. Royal Inniskilling Fusiliers, 1888-93; 87th Regimental District, 1894-99; Assistant Adjutant-General, 1899-1902; served Ashantee Expedition, 1873-74 (medal with clasp, despatches); retired from Army, 1902; Mayor of Rochester, 1905-6. *Publications:* To Coomassie and Back, 1874; Map of Gibraltar and the Country near, 1878; The Infantry of our Army and Mr. Arnold Forster's Proposals, 1903; has lectured on military subjects at Royal United Service Institution. *Recreations:* cricket and all games; school eleven. *Address:* Ditton Place, near Maidstone, Kent. *Club:* United Service.
(*Died 9 Nov. 1926.*)

DOPPING - HEPENSTAL, Major Lambert John; O.B.E. 1920; D.L.; J.P. Co. Longford; *b.* 1859; *s.* of late Col. R. A. Dopping-Hepenstal, D.L., of Derrycassan, and Diana, *d.* and *heiress* of late Rev. L. W. Hepenstal of Altadore Castle, Delgany; *m.* 1920, Amy Maude, *d.* of late Maj. C. R. W. Tottenham, D.L., of Woodstock, Co. Wicklow, and Plas Berwyn, Llangollen; one *s.* one *d.* *Educ.:* Harrow. Commissioned R.E., 1879; retired list as Major, 1907; served European War; High Sheriff Co. Wicklow, 1909, and Longford, 1910; inventor of the direct engine-room telegraph for steamers, modified railway points, etc. *Address:* Derrycassan, Granard, Co. Longford; 73 Harcourt Street, Dublin; 1 Albany Road, Bedford. *T.:* Bedford 2352. *M.:* TM 657. *Club:* Kildare Street, Dublin. (*Died 5 Dec. 1928.*)

DORAN, Alban Henry Griffiths; President of the Obstetrical Society of London, 1899-1900; Consulting Surgeon, Samaritan Free Hospital; *b.* London, 1849; *s.* of Dr. Doran, F.S.A., author of Annals of the Stage, Lives of the Queens

of the House of Hanover, etc. *Educ.:* Nassau School, Barnes, Surrey; St. Bartholomew's Hospital. F.R.C.S. England; Hon. Fellow of Obstetrical* and Gynæcological Societies of Bordeaux, and of Buenos Aires, and American Gynæcological Society; Fellow of Royal Society of Medicine. For 8 years was attached to the museum of the Royal College of Surgeons under Sir William Flower; compiler (with Sir James Paget and Sir James Goodhart) of the second edition of the Catalogues of the Pathological Series in that museum; was on the surgical staff of the Samaritan Free Hospital 1877-1909; practising the operative surgery of the abdomen; lastly, prepared a descriptive Catalogue of Surgical Instruments, Mus. R.C.S., Eng. 1912-25. *Publications:* The Morphology of the Mammalian Ossicula Auditûs, Trans. Linn. Soc. 1878; Tumours of the Ovary, 1884; Handbook of Gynæcological Operations, 1887; Shakespeare and the Medical Society (annual oration, Medical Society, 1899); Chapter XIV. Medicine in Shakespeare's England, 1916; Burton (Dr. Slop), his Forceps and his Foes, Journal of Obstet. etc. of British Empire, vol. 23. *Recreations:* Literary pursuits, especially Shakespeare, English and French history. *Address:* 3 Lisgar Terrace, Kensington, W.14.
(Died 23 Aug. 1927.)

DORAN, Edward Anthony, C.I.E. 1907; *m.* Joined service, 1880; Postmaster-General, Madras, 1904; Bengal, 1904; Bombay, 1906.
(Died 11 May 1922.)

DORAN, Sir Henry Francis, Kt., *cr.* 1915; J.P. Cos. Mayo and Roscommon; *b.* 15 April 1856; *s.* of late Henry Doran of Ardagh, Killarney, Co. Kerry; *m.* 1885, Margaret Caroline, *d.* of late Thomas Cox of Bunreagh, Croghan, Co. Roscommon; three *s. Educ.:* St. Brendan's Seminary, Killarney; The Albert Agricultural College, Glasnevin, Dublin. Assistant to Superintendent of Agricultural Education in Ireland, 1875-77; Estate Surveyor and Valuer for various estates in counties of Roscommon, Mayo and Sligo, 1879-90; Assistant Land Commissioner, 1890-91; Inspector Congested Districts Board for Ireland, 1892; Chief Land Inspector, 1903; Permanent Member of the Congested Districts Board for Ireland, 1910. *Address:* Redcroft, Seaford, Sussex.
(Died 23 June 1923.)

DORCHESTER, Baroness, *cr.* 1899; **Henrietta Anne Leir-Carleton;** *b.* 1846; *d.* and co-heiress of 3rd and *cousin* of 4th and last Baron Dorchester (*d.* 1897, when title, *cr.* 1786, became extinct, but was revived in her favour); *m.* 1st, 1864, Capt. Francis Paynton Pigott, 16th Lancers, of Banbury, Oxon. (who assumed the additional name of Carleton (*d* 1888); one *s.* one *d.*; 2nd, 1887, Maj.-Gen. Richard Langford Leir, of Ditcheat, Somerset (who assumed additional name of Carleton). *Heir: s.* Hon. Dudley Massey Carleton. *Address:* Greywell Hill, Winchfield; Ditcheat Priory, Evercreech, Somerset. *T.A.:* Greywell.
(Died 2 Mar. 1925.)

DORIS, William; *b.* 13 April 1860; *s.* of Robert and Margaret Doris, Westport; *m.* 1910, Sara, *d.* of Luke Cannon Westport. *Educ.:* Christian Brothers' Schools, Westport. J.P., Westport; late Chm., Westport Urban Council, and Vice-Chairman, Castlebar District Asylum; Harbour Commissioner for Westport; Vice-Chairman, Mayo County Council, 1900-08; Acting Secretary of Irish Land League when no rent manifesto issued, 1881; arrested as suspect in Land League Office, Dublin, on suppression of the League, 1881, and imprisoned in Dundalk Jail for six months; first Secretary of United Irish League; M.P. (N.) Mayo West, 1910. *Address:* 37 North Side, Clapham Common, S.W.; Westport, Co. Mayo. *T.A.:* W. Doris, Westport.
(Died 13 Sept. 1926.)

296

DORLING, Colonel Lionel, O.B. 1916; C.M.G. 1919; D.S.O. 1902; late Army Pay Department; *b.* 7 Aug. 1860; *s.* of Henry Dorling of Epsom; *m.* 1888, Constance, *y. d.* of W. H. Price of Karachi. Formerly Captain Yorks Light Infantry; entered army, 1879; served South Africa, 1800-1902 (despatches, Queen's medal, five clasps; King's medal, two clasps; D.S.O.); European War (Dardanelles), 1915 (despatches); Egypt, 1916. *Club:* Naval and Military.
(Died 11 July 1925.)

DORMER, 13th Baron (*cr.* 1615), **Roland John Dormer,** Bt. 1615; J.P. and D.L.; late Sub-director Egypt. Fin. Min.; Commander of Imperial Order of the Medjidie; *b.* St. Leonards-on-Sea, 24 Nov. 1862; *e. s.* of late Lieut.-Gen. Hon. Sir James Dormer, K.C.B. *S.* uncle 1900; *m.* Marie Hanem, *d.* of late F. Eywaz of Cairo, 1897; one *d. Educ.:* Oscott College. Owns about 5000 acres. *Heir: b.* Hon. Capt. C. J. T. Dormer. *Recreations:* shooting, gardening. *Address:* Maderno, Italy. *(Died 9 Feb. 1920.)*

DORMER, 14th Baron (*cr.* 1615), **Charles Joseph Thaddeus Dormer,** Bt. 1615; Captain R.N.; C.B.E. 1919; Gentleman Usher to H.M., 1919; *b.* 24 Feb. 1864; *s.* of Lt.-Gen. Hon. Sir James Dormer, K.C.B.; *S.* brother 1920; *m.* 1908, May, *y. d.* of late Col. Sir Spencer Clifford; two *s.* three *d. Educ.:* Oscott College. Joined Britannia as naval cadet, 1877; sub-Lieut. 1883; Lieut. 1887; Commander, 1899; retired, 1908; Capt. retired list, 1914; served as Flag-Lieut. to Admiral Lord Walter Kerr in Mediterranean, 1890-92; to Vice-Admiral Sir H. Fairfax in Channel Squadron, 1893-95; Naval Attaché, Tokio, 1906-8. *Heir: s.* Hon. Charles Walter James Dormer, *b.* 20 Dec. 1903. *Address:* Grove Park, Warwick. *Club:* Naval and Military.
(Died 4 May 1922.)

DORNHORST, Frederick, K.C.; *b.* Ceylon, 26 April 1849; *s.* of Frederick Dornhorst, Notary Public, Trincomalee; *m.* Lydia, *d.* of E. G. Sisouw, Proctor. Supreme Court; four *s.* one *d. Educ.:* Colombo Academy (now Royal College). Master, Royal College, 1868-73; called to Ceylon Bar, 1874; English Bar, 1901; Member Ceylon Council of Legal Education. *Address:* Calverley House, Colombo, Ceylon. *Club:* Orient, Colombo. *(Died 24 April 1927.)*

DORRIEN-SMITH, Thomas Algernon, J.P., D.L.; *b.* Berkhamsted, 7 Feb. 1846; *e. s.* of late Col. Smith-Dorrien, and Mary Ann, *heiress* of Thomas Dorrien, Haresfoot, Gt. Berkhamsted; *m.* 1875, Edith Anna Maria (*d.* 1892), *d.* of Mr. and Lady Sophia Tower; two *s.* five *d. Educ.:* Harrow. Served in 10th Hussars, 1864-74; retired as Lieut.; afterwards Herts Yeomanry. *Address:* Tresco Abbey, Isles of Scilly; Ashlyns Hall, Herts. *Clubs:* Carlton, Cavalry. *(Died 6 Aug. 1918.)*

DORRITY, Rev. David, B.D.; Rector of St. Ann's, Manchester, since 1895; Hon. Canon of Manchester since 1917; *s.* of James and Susan Dorrity, Liverpool; *m.* 1891, Mabel Rosa, *y. d.* of Henry Raine Marriott, Whalley Range, Manchester; one *d. Educ.:* Liverpool; Dublin University. Ordained, 1888; Curate of Waterhead, Oldham, of Whalley Range, and Chaplain to the Blind at Old Trafford successively. *Recreations:* golf, trout-fishing, chess. *Address:* 62 Platt Lane, Manchester. *T.:* Rusholme 205.
(Died 1 June 1926.)

DOUDNEY, Sarah, novelist; *b.* Portsmouth, 15 Jan. 1843; *y. c.* of G. E. Doudney. *Educ.:* by Mrs. Kendall, Southsea. Began to write very young, contributing to many magazines. *Publications:* A Woman's Glory, 1885; The Missing Rubies, 1886; When We Two Parted, 1887; Strangers Yet, Stepping Stones, etc., between 1886 and 1896; also several novels for girls: Where the Dew falls in London, 1890; Through Pain to Peace, 1892; A Romance of Lincoln's Inn, 1894; Katherine's Keys, 1895;

DOREZ, Léon Louis Marie. See page xviii.

DOTTIN, Henri Georges. See page xviii.

Pilgrims of the Night, 1896 ; A Cluster of Roses, etc. ; Lady Dye's Reparation, 1899 ; Silent Strings, 1900 ; One of the Few, 1904 ; Shadow and Shine, 1906. *Recreations:* walking, antiquarianism.
(Died 15 Dec. 1926.)

DOUGALL, Lily, theological writer and novelist ; *b.* Montreal, 16 Apr. 1858 ; *y. d.* of John Dougall and Elizabeth Redpath. *Educ. :* privately ; Edinburgh University Classes for Women. L.L.A. St. Andrews. *Publications:* Beggars All, 1891 ; What Necessity Knows, 1898 ; The Mermaid, 1895 ; Zeitgeist, 1895 ; Question of Faith, 1895 ; The Madonna of a Day 1896 ; A Dozen Ways of Love, 1897 ; The Mormon Prophet, 1898 ; The Earthly Purgatory, 1904 ; The Spanish Dowry, 1906 ; Paths of the Righteous, 1908 ; (anonymously) Pro Christo et Ecclesia, 1900 ; Christus Futurus, 1907 ; Absente Reo, 1910 ; Voluntas Dei, 1912 ; The Practice of Christianity, 1914 ; The Christian Doctrine of Health, 1916 ; part author of Concerning Prayer, 1916, Immortality, 1917, The Spirit, 1919, God and the Struggle for Existence, 1919, Arcades Ambo (poems), 1919, The Lord of Thought, 1922. *Address :* Cutts End, Cumnor, near Oxford. *T.A. :* Cumnor. *Club:* University Women's.
(Died 9 Oct. 1923.)

DOUGHTY, Charles Montagu, M.A. ; Honorary Fellow of Gonville and Caius College, Cambridge ; Hon. D.Litt. Oxford ; Hon. Litt.D. Cambridge, *b.* 1843 ; *y. s.* of late Rev. Charles Montagu Doughty, of Theberton Hall, Suffolk, and Frederica, *d.* of late Hon. and Rev. Frederick Hotham, Prebendary of Rochester and Rector of Dennington, Suffolk ; *m.* 1886, Caroline Amelia, *d.* of late General Sir Montagu McMurdo, G.C.B. ; two *d. Educ. :* Naval School at Portsmouth ; Caius College, Cambridge. Royal Founder's medal, Royal Geographical Society, 1912 ; Hon. Member British Academy. *Publications :* Travels in Arabia Deserta, 2 vols. 1888 ; Documents Epigraphiques (pub. 1884 par la Commission du Corpus Inscr. Semiticarum) ; The Dawn in Britain, 6 vols., 1906 ; Adam Cast Forth, 1908 ; The Cliffs, 1909 ; The Clouds, 1912 ; Mansoul, or the Riddle of the World, 1920 *Address:* Sissinghurst, Kent.
(Died 21 Jan. 1926.)

DOUGHTY, Rear-Adm. Henry Montagu, R.N. ; C.B. 1918 ; C.M.G. 1919 ; Rear-Adm. 1st Battle Squadron, Atlantic Fleet ; *b.* 1870 ; *s.* of H. M. Doughty, Theberton Hall, Suffolk ; *m.* 1907, Gwendoline, *d.* of Lieut.-Col. C. E. G. Burr. Went as Lieut. of H.M. Theseus to observe eclipse of the sun at Santa Pola, 17 May 1900 ; Captain of Gunnery School, Devonport, 1914 ; served European War in command H.M.S. Royal Sovereign 1st Battle Squadron (C.M.G.). *Address:* Spencer Place, Bishops Waltham, Hants. *Club:* Naval and Military.
(Died 1 May 1921.)

DOUGLAS, Arthur, M.D., L.S.A. (graduated University of Ghent, Belgium) ; physician ; *b.* 1850 ; *s.* of Dr. George Douglas (Friarshaw) ; *m.* three *s. Educ. :* private tuition ; Queen's College (Divinity and Medicine). Visited Straits Settlements and China (studying for Navy) ; also India, Ceylon, Madeira, Canada, Norway, Germany ; employed by Colonial Government for some years, also by War Office at the Royal Arsenal, Woolwich, and Royal Small Arms Factory, Enfield Lock ; served through Boer War, Staff Surgeon attached R.A.M.C. ; in charge of several large depots and the insane (two metals, 5 clasps). *Publications:* various articles on Psychology and Hypnotism as a curative agent in certain mental conditions ; articles published in the Press on kindred subjects ; an exhaustive dissertation on Tabes Dorsalis, embracing Treatment by Suspension, with sketches ; an article on Phthisis, copied into French and German medical Press ; notes on interesting cases in South Africa ; various minor articles. *Recreations:* heavy athletics,

walking, riding, cycling. *Address:* 57 Devonshire Street, Portland Place, W.1. *T.A. :* Medicato, London. *T. :* Paddington 1488. *Club:* Junior Army and Navy.
(Died 22 Dec. 1920.)

DOUGLAS, Arthur Henry Johnstone-, D.L., J.P. ; *e. s.* of late Robert Johnstone-Douglas of Lockerbie, and Lady Jane Mary Margaret Douglas, 5th *d.* of 5th Marquis of Queensberry ; *b.* 1846 ; *m.* 1869, Jane Maitland, *d.* of the late Stair Hathorn Stewart of Physgill. Late Lieut. Dumfries Militia ; was in 42nd Highlanders. *Address:* 9 Doune Terrace, Edinburgh.
(Died 26 Mar. 1923.)

DOUGLAS, Cecil George, Chief Clerk, Mansion House Justice Room, London, since 1887 ; *b.* 1 April 1854 ; *s.* of late George Douglas, a Superintendent of the General Register Office, Somerset House ; *m.* 1885, Sophia Pitt, *d.* of late Surgeon-Major Nicolson ; two *d. Educ. :* University College School, London. Served two years in General Register Office ; three years in Board of Trade ; five years Bow Street Police Court ; two and a half years as Assistant Clerk Mansion House Justice Room ; four and; a half years as Chief Clerk Guildhall Justice Room. *Address:* Wathla, Surbiton Hill Park.
(Died 8 Jan. 1919.)

DOUGLAS, Charles Mackinnon, C.B. 1918 ; J.P., D.L. ; Officier de l'ordre de la Couronne, Belgium, 1920 ; *b.* Edinburgh, 2 Oct. 1865 ; *s.* of A. Halliday Douglas, M.D., and Jessie, *d.* of Kenneth Mackinnon, M.D. ; *m.* Anne Isabel, *d.* of Robert Tod, Clerwood, Corstorphine, 1895. *Educ.:* Edinburgh Academy ; Universities of Edinburgh and Freiburg ; M.A., D.Sc.; first-class Honours in Philosophy, Univ. of Edinburgh ; Vans Dunlop Scholar ; Hamilton Fellow ; Ferguson Scholar, Scottish Universities ; seven years Lecturer in Moral Philosophy, University of Edinburgh ; M.P.N.W. Division of Lanarkshire, 1899-1906 ; contested (L.U.) South Lanarkshire Division, 1910 ; Chairman, Lanarkshire Territorial Force Association ; six years Chairman of Directors of the Highland and Agricultural Society of Scotland ; President of the Scottish Agricultural Organisation Society ; Ex-Chairman of the Scottish Council of Agriculture ; Ex-President of the Scottish Chamber of Agriculture. *Publications :* John Stuart Mill, a study of his Philosophy, 1895 ; Ethics of John Stuart Mill, 1898 ; minor philosophical writings. Owns about 400 acres. *Address:* Auchlochan, Lesmahagow. *T. :* Lesmahagow 2. *Clubs:* Brooks's ; New, Edinburgh ; Western, Glasgow.
(Died 3 Feb. 1924.)

DOUGLAS, David, F.R.S.E. ; publisher in Edinburgh ; *b.* Stranraer, Wigtownshire, 1823. Business training received in the house of Blackwood, first in Edinburgh and then in London, 1839-47. Bookseller in Edinburgh, 1847 ; first publication, 1854 ; editor of North British Review, 1868-69 ; also Scott's Journal and Familiar Letters, etc., 1890-92 ; Fellow of the Royal Society of Edinburgh since 1866, and of the Antiquaries since 1861 ; Treasurer to that body, 1871-83. *Address:* 9 Castle Street, Edinburgh.
(Died 5 April 1916.)

DOUGLAS, Brig.-Gen. Douglas Campbell, C.B. 1917 ; *b.* 19 Aug. 1864 ; *s.* of A. H. Campbell, J.P., D.L., and Agnes, *d.* of J. C. Douglas of Mains, Dumbartonshire ; *m.* 1899, Hon. Violet Averil Margaret Vivian, *e. d.* of 1st Baron Swansea ; one *s.* two *d. Educ. :* Eton ; R.M.C., Sandhurst. Assumed the surname of Douglas in lieu of Campbell on succeeding to Mains, 1925 ; served Hazara Expedition, 1888 ; Chitral Relief Force, 1895 ; European War in France, 1915-17 (despatches, C.B.) ; Lieut.-Col. commanding 2nd Battn. Seaforth Highlanders, 1909-13 ; Colonel, 1913 ; Brigade Commander, 1914-19; retired pay, 1919. *Address:* Mains, Milngavie, Scotland. *T. :*

Milngavie 29. *Clubs:* Naval and Military; New, Edinburgh. (*Died 17 June 1927.*)

DOUGLAS, Rev. Evelyn Keith, M.A., Rector of Cheveley, Cambs., since 1895; Hon. Canon of Ely, 1913; Rural Dean of Cheveley; *b.* 27 July 1859; *s.* of Stewart Douglas and Catherine, *d.* of Robert Wright Wood; unmarried. *Educ.:* Eton; New College, Oxford. Curate of Newcastle Cathedral, 1884-85; Weybridge, 1885-89; East London Missionary in charge of Eton Mission, Hackney Wick, 1889-90; Curate of Alverstoke, 1891-95; Rural Dean of Thurlow, 1903-14; Fordham, 1914-17; Secretary of Ely Diocesan S. School Council, 1907-14; Ely Diocesan Fund, 1912-13; Member of Diocesan Board of Finance, 1913-16; Secretary of Ely Diocesan Conference, 1915. *Recreations:* cricket (Eton XI., 1878); golf. *Address:* Cheveley Rectory, Newmarket. *T.:* Cheveley, Newmarket. *Clubs:* New Oxford and Cambridge. (*Died 6 Dec. 1920.*)

DOUGLAS, James, LL.D., B.A.; Member and Vice-President, American Institute Mining Engineers, New York; *b.* Quebec, Canada, 1837; *s.* of James Douglas, M.D., and Elizabeth Ferguson; *m.* 1860, Naomi Douglas; two *s.* two *d.* *Educ.:* Queen's Univ., Kingston, Canada; Edin. Univ. Mem. of the Iron and Steel Inst. of Great Britain; the North of England Society of M. E.; the American Geographical Society, N.Y.; the Philosophical Society, Phil.; the Society of Arts, London; Member and Gold Medallist of the Institution of Mining and Metallurgy, London; formerly Professor of Chemistry, Morrin College, Quebec; president of Phelps, Dodge & Co., the Copper Queen Mining Company, Detroit Copper Company and others in Arizona, and of the Moctezuma Copper Company, Mexico; president of the El Paso and S.W.R.R., and the Nacozari R.R. Companies; twice president of the American Institute of Mining Engineers; president of the Can. Society of New York; representative of the U.S. at the Mining Congress in Paris, 1900. *Publications:* Old France in the New World; New England and New France; Biography of Dr. T. Sterry Hunt, F.R.S.; Canadian Independence; Imperial Federation and Annexation; Untechnical Addresses on Technical Subjects; a Cantor Lecturer, Society of Arts, and writer on various subjects in American and English journals. *Recreation:* fishing. *Address:* 99 John Street, New York; Spuyten Duyvil, New York. *Clubs:* Century Association, Engineers, City, Adirondack League; Montmorency, Quebec.
(*Died 26 June 1918.*)

DOUGLAS, Hon. James Moffat, Senator since 1906; *b.* Scotland, 26 May 1839; *m.* 1861, Jane, *d.* of George Smith, Darlington, Ontario. *Educ.:* Toronto University; Knox College, Toronto; Princeton Seminary. Ordained Presbyterian Church, 1865; Chaplain to troops at Mhow, 1876-82; M.P. E. Assiniboia, 1896-1904. *Address:* Tantallon, Sask., Canada.
(*Died 19 Aug. 1921.*)

DOUGLAS, Lt.-Col. Robert Jeffray, C.M.G. 1915; 5th Battalion the Cameronians (Scottish Rifles) (Territorial Force); *b.* 4 Oct. 1869; unmarried. *Educ.:* Bellahouston Academy; Blairlodge School, Polmont. Served S. African War, 1901-2; European War, 1914-15 (C.M.G.). *Address:* Ashlea, Bellahouston, Glasgow. *Clubs:* Conservative, New, Glasgow. (*Died 3 July 1916.*)

DOUGLAS, Major (Bt.Lt.-Col.) Robert Vaughan, C.B.E.; R.G.A.; *b.* 29 June 1881; *s.* of late C. P. Douglas, Solicitor, Chester; *m.* 1917, Gladys Mary, *o. d.* of Col. J. Lewes, J.P., late R.A. of Llanllyr, Cardiganshire. *Educ.:* Cheltenham College; R.M.A. Woolwich. Served European War, 1914-19 (C.B.E.). *Address:* c/o Cox and Co., 16 Charing Cross, S.W.1. *Club:* Army and Navy. (*Died 30 Sept. 1922.*)

298

DOUGLAS, Maj.-Gen. Sir William, K.C.M.G., *cr.* 1915; *;* C.B. 1908; D.S.O. 1900; Royal Scots; Brig.-Gen. commanding 14th Infantry Brigade, 1909-13; commanding a Division since 1913; *b.* Cranborne Lodge, Dorset, 13 August 1858; *s.* of William Douglas, late East India Civil Service; *m.* 1885, Ellen Lytcott, *d.* of S. Taylor, Crown Solicitor, Barbados. *Educ.:* Bath. Joined 1st Batt. The Royal Scots, 1878; served as Adjutant, 1st Batt. 1880-87; Captain, 1885; Adjutant, 3rd Royal Scots, 1888-93; Adjutant, 1st Royal Scots, 1893-94; Major, 1895; Staff College, 1896-97; Lieut.-Col. 1900; served with Bechuanaland expedition, 1884-85; South Africa, 1900-1902 (despatches, Queen's medal, three clasps; King's medal, two clasps; D.S.O.); Dardanelles, 1914-1915 (K.C.M.G.); appointed to command a mobile column; Brevet-Colonel, 1904; Colonel, General Staff, 6th Division, 1906. *Club:* Naval and Military. (*Died 2 Nov. 1920.*)

DOUGLAS, William Douglas Robinson-, F.L.S., F.R.G.S., J.P., D.L.; *o. s.* of late Rev. George Robinson-Douglas and Jane Eleanor, *o. d.* of late Boyd Miller, of Colliers Wood, Surrey; *b.* 1851; *m.* 1st, 1879, Frances Mary (*d.* 1881), *e. d.* of late Col. William Burnett-Ramsay, of Banchory Lodge, Co. Kincardine; 2nd, 1889, Constance, *d.* of Sir Thomas Proctor-Beauchamp, 4th Bart. *Educ.:* Christ Church, Oxford, M.A. *Address:* Orchardton, Castle Douglas, Kirkcudbrightshire. *T.A.:* Auchencairn. *M.:* SB 18. *Club:* United University. (*Died 3 Oct. 1921.*)

DOUGLAS, Comdr. William Ramsay Binny, C.I.E. 1917; R.I.M.; Senior Military Transport Officer, Bombay. *Address:* Senior Transport Officer, Bombay. (*Died 28 June 1919.*)

DOUGLAS-SCOTT-MONTAGU, Hon. Robert Henry, *b.* and *heir-pres.* to Baron Montagu of Beaulieu; *b.* 30 July 1867; *m.* 1904, Alice, widow of Oscar Davies. Formerly Lieut. Lothian Regt. (*Died 10 Feb. 1916.*)

DOVER, Rev. Thomas Birkett, Hon. Canon of Southwark; *s.* of Thomas Dover, late Mayor of Liverpool; *b.* 7 Nov. 1846; *m.* 1876, Fenella Smith, *d.* of Andrew Low, shipowner; three *s.* three *d.* *Educ.:* Royal Institution, Liverpool; Exeter College, Oxford; Cuddesdon College. Ordained 1870; Curate at St. John the Divine, Kennington, for three years; Chaplain, Stockwell Small-Pox Hospital; Vicar of St. Agnes, Kennington Park, 1874-94; Old Malden, 1894-1914; Rector of Shenley, 1917-20; Member London School Board, 1891-94; Domestic Chaplain to the Earl of Home, K.T., 1914-15. *Publications:* Some Quiet Lenten Thoughts; The Hidden Word; The Ministry of Mercy. *Address:* 20 Holywell, Oxford. *Clubs:* Oxford and County, Oxford Union, Oxford. (*Died 23 Dec. 1926.*)

DOVERDALE, 1st Baron, *cr.* 1916; **Edward Partington,** Kt., *cr.* 1912; J.P., D.L. Derbyshire; Director of the Manchester and Liverpool District Bank; has Officer's Cross of Order of Francis Joseph of Austria; presented a Convalescent Home to the Borough of Glossop; Freeman of the Borough of Glossop; *b.* 1836; *s.* of Edward Partington; *m.* Sarah (*d.* 1917), *d.* of Thomas H. Haworth; one *s.* two *d.* Formerly (1874) Captain 23rd Derbyshire (Volunteer) Rifle Corps. Owns about 5000 acres. *Heir: s.* Hon. Oswald Partington. *Address:* Easton, Glossop; Westwood Park, Droitwich; 10 Ennismore Gardens, S.W. (*Died 5 Jan. 1925.*)

DOW, Thomas Millie, R.S.W.; *b.* Dysart, Fifeshire; *s.* of Thomas Dow, town-clerk and solicitor, and Margaret Millie; *m.* Florence Ellen, *d.* of William Cox of Snaigow, Perthshire, Scotland. *Educ.:* home; Edinburgh. Served law apprenticeship; studied in the Ecole de Beaux-Arts, Paris, under Gérome, and·with Carolus Duran. *Address:* Talland, St. Ives, Cornwall.   (*Died July 1919.*)

DOWDING, General Townley Ward; *s.* of late Rev. Townley W. Dowding, M.A., St. Peter's, Marlborough, and Elizabeth, *d.* of J. Eamonson of Beale, Yorkshire; *b.* 11 April 1847; *m.* 1886, Florence Mary, *d.* of Hon. Walter Lamb, M.L.C., Sydney, N.S.W.; one *s.* Entered Royal Marines, 1865; Captain, 1879; Major, 1885; Lieut.-Col. 1893; Colonel, 1899; Major-Gen. 1902; Lieut.-Gen. 1910; Gen. 1910; retired, 1912. Inspector of Marine Recruiting, 1898-1900; served S. Africa, 1877-79 (despatches, medal with clasp, prom. Captain, brevet Major); Jubilee medal, 1897. *Address:* Singleton, Alverstoke, Hants. *Club:* United Service.
(*Died 4 Sept. 1927.*)

DOWLING, Rev. Theodore Edward, D.D.; late Archdeacon in Syria, and Canon of St. George's Collegiate Church, Jerusalem; Commissary for Eastern Church Intercourse within the Anglican Bishopric in Jerusalem; Chaplain of St. Luke's Church, Haifa-under-Mount-Carmel, Palestine; *b.* 15 Oct. 1837; *s.* of late Rev. John Goulter Dowling, M.A., Rector of St. Mary de Crypt, Gloucester. *Educ.:* St. Augustine's College, Canterbury. Twenty-seven years in the Diocese of Fredericton, New Brunswick, Canada; in Turkey since 1890; 3½ years Chaplain of the Crimean Memorial Church, Constantinople, and 22 years in Jerusalem and Haifa, Galilee; visited the United States of America, Mexico, France, Germany, Austria, Hungary, Ceylon, India, Australasia, Denmark, Sweden, Russia, Mount Athos, Damascus, Egypt, The Soudan, Asia Minor, Mount Lebanon, Damascus, Aintab, Petra, Greece. *Publications:* The Orthodox Greek Patriarchate of Jerusalem, 3rd edition; Sketches of Georgian Church History; Gaza: a City of Many Battles; The Armenian Church; The Egyptian Church; The Abyssinian Church; The City of Safed: A Refuge of Judaism; Hellenism in England. *Recreations:* the study of Eastern Churches; numismatics: Jewish, Syrian, and Phœnician coinage. *Address:* 47 Anerley Park, S.E.   (*Died 12 Jan. 1921.*)

DOWLING, Rt. Rev. Thomas Joseph; R.C. Bishop of Hamilton since 1889; *b.* 28 Feb. 1840; went to Canada, 1851. *Educ.:* Hamilton; St. Michael's College, Toronto; Grand Seminary, Montreal Ordained, 1864; Vicar-general, Hamilton, 1881; Bishop of Peterborough, Kingston, Canada, 1887-89. *Address:* King Street West, Hamilton, Toronto, Canada.
(*Died 7 Aug. 1924.*)

DOWN, Lieut.-Commander Sir Charles Edward, R.N.R.; K.B.E., *cr.* 1920; O.B.E. 1919; Marine Superintendent, Royal Mail Steam Packet Company, 1917-24; *b.* 13 July 1857; *s.* of late Rev. Chas. J Down, who was *s.* of Rear-Admiral Edward Augustus Down, R.N.; *m.* 1892, Gertrude Louisa, *d.* of Dean May of Demerara, British Guiana; one *s.* one *d. Educ.:* Marlborough College; Switzerland. Went to sea, 1876; joined the R.M.S.P. Co. as Fifth Officer, 1881; worked up through the various grades, and was promoted to Commander, 1896; commanded the following ships of the said company — Essequibo, Orinoco, Magdalena, Thames, Trent, Aragon, Avon, Arlanza, Desna, Amazon, Descado; was in command of Arlanza when captured by the German armed merchant cruiser Kaiser Wilhelm der Grosse in the early days of the War. *Address:* 15 Whitewell Road, Southsea.   (*Died 20 Aug. 1927.*)

DOWNE, 8th Viscount (*cr.* 1680), **Major-General Hugh Richard Dawnay;** C.B. 1900; K.C.V.O. 1903; C.I.E., M.A.; Bt. 1642; Baron Dawnay of Danby (U.K.), *cr.* 1897; late Steward of Jockey Club; *b.* London, 20 July 1844; *s.* of 7th Viscount and *d.* of Bishop of Bath and Wells (Bagot); *S.* father

1857; *m.* 1st, 1869, Lady Cecilia Maria Charlotte Molyneux, V.A. (*d.* 1910), *d.* of 3rd Earl of Sefton; one *s.* three *d;* 2nd, 1911, Faith, *d.* of Rev. Henry Dening. Protestant. Conservative. *Educ.:* Eton; Christ Church, Oxford. Cornet and sub-Lieutenant, 2nd Life Guards, 1865; Lieutenant, 1869; Captain, 1873; Major, 1879; Lieut.-Col. 10th Royal Hussars, 1886; Col. 1912; commanded 10th R.H. 1887-92; served Zulu War, 1879; A.D.C. to Duke of Connaught, Com. Meerut Div. 1883-85; A.D.C. to Duke of Cambridge, 1892-95; Col. Com. Cavalry Brigade at the Curragh, 1897-99; served S. Africa, 1899-1900 (despatches twice), and 1901-2; Special Envoy to Shah of Persia, 1903; Brig.-Gen. 1901; retired; Officer of the Legion of Honour. *Heir:* *s.* Hon. John Dawnay. *Address:* Dingley, Market Harborough; Danby Lodge, Grosmont, York. *Clubs:* United Service, Turf. (*Died 21 Jan. 1924.*)

DOWNES, Maj.-Gen. Major Francis, C.M.G. 1885; *b.* Dedham, Essex, 1834; *y. s.* of W. Downes of Dedham; *m.* 1858, Helen (*d.* 1903), *d.* of R. Chamberlin of Catton House, Catton, Norwich; three *s.* one *d. Educ.:* R.M.A. Woolwich. Entered Royal Artillery, 1852; Col. 1882; retired as Hon. Maj.-Gen. 1884; Maj.-Gen. South Australia, 1888; Maj.-Gen. Victoria, 1899; served in Crimean Campaign, 1855-56 (medal, clasp, and Turkish medal); Commandant, South Australia, 1877-85; also 1888-1893; Secretary for Defence, Victoria, 1885-1888; Comm., Victoria, 1899-1902; prepared five contingents for the war in South Africa. *Decorated* for service in South Australia. *Recreations:* reading, out-of-door amusements. *Address:* Brighton, Melbourne.   (*Died Oct. 1923.*)

DOWNES, Sir Joseph, Kt., *cr.* 1900; *b.* 1848; *s.* of Christopher Downes of Kiltele, Trim, Ireland; *m.* 1st, 1884, Teresa, *d.* of Dennis Carton; 2nd, Johanna, *widow* of Alderman Hennessy, Dublin, and *d.* of Thomas Davy, Newtown, Tipperary; knighthood bestowed in honour of Queen Victoria's visit to Ireland, 1900; High Sheriff of City of Dublin, 1900. *Address:* 40 Eccles Street, Dublin.
(*Died 22 Sept. 1925.*)

DOWNES, Rev. Robert Percival, LL.D.; Wesleyan minister; *b.* Ripon, 22 Apr. 1842; *s.* of Christopher Downes; *m.* 1869, Clara Elizabeth (*d.* 1921), *d.* of T. W. Trouncer, J.P., Shrewsbury; two *s.* two *d. Educ.:* Ripon Grammar School; private tutors. Entered Wesleyan ministry, 1865; started Great Thoughts for the purpose of presenting to the masses something of the best which has been said and written; retired from pastoral work of the ministry for the editorship of the paper, 1885; resigned 1914. *Publications:* John Ruskin; Pillars of Our Faith; Pure Pleasures; Woman: her Charm and Power; The Art of Noble Living; Man's Immortality and Destiny; Seven Supreme Poets; Hours with the Immortals (British Poets); (Foreign Poets); Thoughts on Living Subjects; Cities which Fascinate; Our Fallen Heroes and their Destiny, 1915; Hildebrand, an Historical Play in Blank Verse, 1919, etc. *Recreations:* reading and walking. *Address:* 13 Vallance Road, Hove, Sussex.
(*Died 20 April 1924.*)

DOWNHAM, 1st Baron, *cr.* 1919, of Fulham; **William Hayes Fisher,** P.C. 1911; Chairman L.C.C. since 1919; a director of the Suez Canal since 1919; *b.* Downham, 1853; *e. s.* of late Frederick Fisher, Rector of Downham, Isle of Ely, and Mary, *d.* of late William Hayes; *m.* 1895, his *c.* Florence Fisher; one *d. Educ.:* Haileybury; University College, Oxford. Graduated in Classical and Legal Honours Schools, Oxford, 1876 (M.A.). Barr. Inner Temple, 1879; Hon. Private Secretary to Sir Michael Hicks-Beach, 1886-87, and Rt. Hon. A. J. Balfour, 1887-92; Junior Lord of the Treasury, and a Ministerial Whip, 1895-1902;

Financial Secretary to Treasury, 1902-1903; Royal Patriotic Commissioner (Chairman), 1904; Alderman L.C.C. 1907-13; M.P. (C.) Fulham, 1885-1906, and 1910; Parliamentary Secretary to Local Government Board, 1915-17, and President, 1917-18; Chancellor of the Duchy of Lancaster, Nov. 1918-Jan. 1919; Knight of the Order of St. John of Jerusalem. *Recreations:* President National Skating Association; Leander Rowing Club; Hayling Island and Sandwich Golf Clubs. *Heir:* none. *Address:* 13 Buckingham Palace Gardens, S.W.1. *T.:* Victoria 3365. *Club:* Carlton.

(*Died 2 July 1920.*)

DOWNHAM, Rev. Isaac, Hon. Canon of Manchester. *Address:* Baxendin, Accrington.

(*Died 10 Mar. 1923.*)

DOWNIE, Capt. John, D.S.O. 1916; M.B.; R.A.M.C., T.F. Served European War, 1914-16 (Order of St. Anne, D.S.O.). *Address:* Maybush, Bellevue, Wakefield.

(*Died June 1921.*)

DOWNIE, Walker, M.B., C.M., F.R.F.P. and S. Glasgow; Lecturer on Diseases of the Throat and Nose, University of Glasgow; Surgeon, Throat and Nose Department, Western Infirmary; Aurist and Laryngologist to the Royal Hospital for Sick Children, Glasgow; Hon. President Glasgow University Medico-Chirurgical Society; Ex-President, Scottish Otological and Laryngological Society; 2nd *surv. s.* of late James Downie of Bertrohill; *m.* Elsie, *y. d.* of late John Maitland, Lauderdale, Liverpool; one *d. Educ.:* High School and University, Glasgow; London Hospitals. Formerly House Surgeon, Glasgow Western Infirmary; House Physician, Glasgow Royal Infirmary; Assistant Surgeon, Lock Hospital; Clinical Assistant, Central London Throat and Ear Hospital; Vice-President, British Laryngologicaland Rhinological Association; Lecturer on Diseases of the Throat and Nose, Western Medical School; ex-President, Glasgow Royal Medico-Chirurgical Society; Fellow of the Royal Society of Medicine, London; Fellow of the Royal Philosophical Society, Glasgow; Member of the Medical Consultative Committee, Consumption Sanatoria for Scotland; Examiner for Fellowship, and late Visitor, Royal Faculty of Physicians and Surgeons, Glasgow, etc. *Publications:* Clinical Manual for Study of Diseases of the Throat, 2nd edit., 1909; History of Med.-Chir. Society of Glasgow, 1908; many papers to Scientific Journals. *Address:* 4 Woodside Crescent, Glasgow. *T.:* Charing Cross 520; Cragmohr, Shandon. *Clubs:* Royal Societies; Literary, Glasgow. *M.:* G 4218. (*Died 21 July 1921.*)

DOWNING, Arthur Matthew Weld, M.A., D.Sc. (Dubl.), F.R.S., F.R.A.S.; formerly Superintendent of the Nautical Almanac; *b.* Ireland, 13 Apr. 1850; *y. s.* of late Arthur Matthew Downing. *Educ.:* Trin. Coll. Dublin. *Publications:* many papers on Astronomical subjects; Nautical Almanac, 1896-1912 inclusive. *Address:* 12 Oakcroft Road, Blackheath, S.E. *Club:* Royal Societies.

(*Died 8 Dec. 1917.*)

DOWNING, Col. Cameron Macartney Harwood, C.M.G. 1900; J.P. County of Suffolk; *b.* 8 Dec. 1845; *s.* of late Gen. David Downing of The Grange, Plaxtol, Kent; *m.* 1877, Adela (*d.* 1919), *widow* of Surg.-Major Cavendish Johnson, and *d.* of Harbut Ward of Carshalton; one *d.* Entered R.A., 1866; Lt.-Col., 1894; retired, 1902; served Abyssinia, 1867-68 (medal); Afghan War, 1878-79 (medal); Chief Instructor, Horse and Field Artillery, School of Gunnery, and Comm. of Okehampton, 1897-99; Colonel on Staff commanding R.A. Natal Field Force, 1899-1900; Defence of Ladysmith, 1899-1900; Commanded the Drakensburg Defence Force, South Africa, with local rank of Maj.-Gen., May to November 1900, when that Force

300

was broken up (despatches twice, medal with 3 clasps); reward for distinguished military services, 1908. *Address:* Thurleston, Whitton, Ipswich, Suffolk. *Club:* United Service.

(*Died 7 June 1926.*)

DOWNSHIRE, 6th Marquess of (*cr.* 1789), **Arthur Wills John Wellington Blundell Trumbull Hill.** Viscount Hillsborough, Baron Hill, 1717; Earl of Hillsborough, Viscount Kilwarlin, 1751; Baron Harwich (Great Brit.), 1756; Earl of Hillsborough and Viscount Fairford, 1772; Hereditary Constable of Hillsborough Fort; Derbyshire Regt.; Capt. Berks Yeomanry Cavalry; *b.* 2 July 1871; *s.* of 5th Marquess and Georgiana, *d.* of John Balfour; *S.* father 1874; *m.* 1st, 1893, Katherine (from whom he obtained a divorce, 1902), 2nd *d.* of Hon. Hugh Hare Forest House, Bracknell, Berks, and *g. d.* of 2nd Earl of Listowel; two *s.* one *d.*; 2nd, 1907, Kathleen Grace May, *d.* of E. Benson Foster, Clewer Manor, Windsor. *Educ.:* Private tutors; Eton. Owns about 120,000 acres. *Heir: s.* Earl of Hillsborough. *Address:* 43 Charles Street, Berkeley Square, W.; East Hampstead Park, Wokingham, Berks; Hillsborough Castle, also Murlough House, Dundrum, Co. Down. *Clubs:* Carlton, Cavalry, Bachelors'.

(*Died 29 May 1918.*)

DOXFORD, Sir William Theodore, Kt.; *cr.* 1900; J.P., D.L.; Director of William Doxford and Sons, Ltd., shipbuilders; *b.* 1 Feb. 1841; *s.* of late William Doxford, Sunderland; *m.* 1863, Margaret (*d.* 1916), *d.* of R. Williamson; one *s.* five *d. Educ.:* Bramham College. M.P. (C.) Sunderland, 1895-1906. *Address:* Grindon Hall, Sunderland. *Clubs:* Carlton, Constitutional, City of London. (*Died 1 Oct. 1916.*)

DOYEN, Dr. E.; claims to have discovered the cancer microbe; *b.* 16 Dec. 1859. *Publications:* Traitement de Cancer, 1904; Le Malade et le Médecin, 1906; Traité de Thérapeutique chirurgicale et de Technique opératoire, 1907; Le Cancer, 1909. *Address:* rue Piccini 6, Paris. *T.:* 698-13. *T.A.:* Clidoyen, Paris.

(*Died 22 Nov. 1916.*)

DOYLE, His Honour Charles Francis, K.C.; Judge of East Circuit Court, Irish Free State, since 1924; County Court Judge and Chairman of Quarter Sessions for the County of Mayo, 1910 till abolition of office, 1924; now Circuit Judge of Eastern Circuit Saorstat Eireann; formerly Professor of the Law of Property and Contracts, University College, Dublin; *b.* Limerick, 1866; 2nd *s.* of late D. Doyle, solicitor; *m.* Florence Mary, *y. d.* of late James Haran, J.P., Manager National Bank, Limerick; two *s. Educ.:* Jesuits' College, Limerick; Trinity College, Dublin; M.A. (Dublin), Ex-Scholar and Senior Moderator, Berkeley and Vice-Chancellor's Gold Med. T.C.D., Ex-Aud. College Historical Society T.C.D.; Society's three medals; M.A., and sometime Fellow in Ancient Classics (R.U.I.). Irish Bar, 1888; Inner Bar, 1906; English Bar (Middle Temple), 1902.

(*Died 30 Sept. 1928.*)

DOYLE, Major Ignatius Purcell, D.S.O., Indian Medical Service (retired); *b.* 1 June 1863; *s.* of Surg.-Maj. William Doyle, I.M.S. Served Burmah, 1888-89 (twice wounded, despatches, D.S.O., medal and clasp); Chin-Lushai Expedition, 1889-90 (clasp); Chin Hills, 1891-93 (clasp); Lushai Expedition, 1892 (clasp); Somaliland Field Force, 1903 (medal and clasp).

DOYLE, Lt.-Col. John Francis Innes Hay, C.M.G. 1918; D.S.O. 1916; Royal Field Artillery; *s.* of late Charles Altamont Doyle, Edinburgh, and *b.* of Sir Arthur Conan Doyle; *b.* 31 March 1873; *m.* 1911, Clara, *d.* of Reinhold Schwensen, Copenhagen; two *s. Educ.:* Richmond, Yorkshire; R.M.A., Woolwich. Entered R.A., 1893; served China, 1900; South Africa, 1902; passed Staff College, 1909; employed on

Staff in European War (despatches four times, D.S.O., C.M.G., Lt.-Col., 1915; Temp. Brig.-Gen., 1917). *Clubs:* Army and Navy, M.C.C.
(*Died 19 Feb. 1919.*)

DOYLE, Very Rev. Thomas, Canon of Westminster since 1918; *b.* 1853. *Educ.:* Sedgley Park; St. Edmunds; Hammersmith Seminary. Priest, 1880; Chaplain, Manor Park Industrial School; Curate, Saints Mary and Joseph, Poplar, 1880; Rector of Grays and Tilbury, 1887; Our Lady and St. Catherine, Bow, 1897; Rector and Parish Priest, Saints Mary and Joseph, Poplar, 1902; Missionary Rector of Saints Mary and Joseph, Poplar, 1003-20; resigned Poplar; Chaplain, Convent Waltham Cross, 1920; retired, 1922. *Address:* 24 Golden Square, W.1.   (*Died Dec. 1926.*)

D'OYLY, Sir Warren Hastings, 10th Bart.; *cr.* 1663; *b.* 6 April 1838; *s.* of 8th Bart. and Mary, *e. d.* of Hon. John Fendall; *s.* half brother, 1900; *m.* 1st, 1859, Henrietta Mary (*d.* 1904), *d.* of Sir Frederick Halliday, K.C.B.; four *s.* six *d.*; 2nd, 1909, Amy, Lady Cotton, *d.* of J. G. White, Indian Civil Service. *Educ.:* Haileybury. Entered B.C.S. 1858; retired 1891; Inspector-General of Jails, 1876; magistrate and collector, 1st grade; officiating opium agent, Behar, and officiating commissioner, Bhagalpur. *Heir: s.* Hastings Hadley, Deputy Commissioner, Andaman Islands; [*b.* 28 July 1864; *m.* 1st, 1897, Beatrice Alice, *d.* of F. B. Clerk, Mysore; two *s.* one *d.*; 2nd, 1910, Evelyn Maude, *d.* of G. Taverner Miller]. *Publications:* Report on the Cultivation of Flax in India; article on the Ganja Tract, published in the Statistical Reporter, Calcutta; illustrated article on The Heart of Queen Anne Boleyn, Jan. 1902 Antiquary. *Recreations:* hunting, pig-sticking in India; cricket, Haileybury and county Dorset Elevens, 1863-69; Calcutta Cricket Club, 1858-68; painting in watercolours.   (*Died 16 Feb. 1921.*)

DOYNE, Chas. Mervyn, J.P., D.L.; *b.* 27 Sep. 1889; *e. s.* of late Robert Stephen Doyne, J.P., D.L. Wells, and Sarah Emily, *d.* of Col. Joseph Pratt, of Cabra Castle, Co. Cavan; *m.* 1867, Lady Frances Mary Wentworth-Fitzwilliam, *e. d.* of 6th Earl Fitzwilliam; two *s.* three *d. Educ.:* Magdalene College, Cambridge, B.A. 1862, M.A. 1864; J.P. and D.L. Co. Wexford; High Sheriff, 1878; High Sheriff, Co. Carlow, 1875. *Heir: s.* Robert Wentworth, J.P., D.L. [*b.* 30 Dec. 1868; *m.* 1898, Lady Mary Diana Lascelles, *y. d.* of 4th Earl of Harewood; one *s.* Late Captain 4th Batt. Oxfords. L.I.]. *Address:* Wells, Gorey, Co. Wexford. *T.A.:* Kilmuckridge. *Club:* Kildare Street, Dublin.
(*Died 24 Aug. 1924.*)

DOYNE, Robert Walter, M.A. Oxon.; F.R.C.S.; *b.* 15 May 1857; 2nd *s.* of late Rev. P. W. Doyne; *m.* Gertrude Irene Hope, *y. d.* of late John Hollings; two *s. Educ.:* Marlborough; Keble Coll., Oxford. After qualifying, travelled; then entered navy, which he left on marriage; founded Oxford Eye Hospital; Consulting Ophthalmic Surgeon, Radcliffe Infirmary, 1900-15; Reader in Ophthalmology, University of Oxford, 1902-13; late Senior Surgeon Oxford Eye Hosp.; Surgeon Royal Eye Hospital, London; Ophthalmic Surgeon S. John's Hospital, Cowley. *Publication:* The More Common Diseases of the Eye; Retinal Extract on the Treatment of Atrophic Retinae; several papers. *Recreation:* fencing. *Address:* 121 Woodstock Road, Oxford.
(*Died 30 Aug. 1916.*)

DRAGO, Luis Maria, LL.D.; Member of the Permanent Court of Arbitration at The Hague, and of House of Representatives at Buenos Ayres; *b.* Buenos Ayres, 6 May 1859; *s.* of Dr. Luis M. Drago, Physician, and Estela, *d.* of Col. Modesto Sanches; *m.*; three *s.* six *d. Educ.:* University of Buenos Ayres. After practising law for some time, became a judge in Buenos Ayres; afterwards elected for Congress; Minister for Foreign Affairs under the Presidency of General Roca; while holding this office he sent to the Argentine Minister in Washington the instructions known as the Drago Doctrine, 1902; one of the Argentine Delegates to the Second Peace Conference; was one of the arbitrators nominated by agreement between Great Britain and the United States for the hearing of the differences regarding fisheries on the North Atlantic coast; Nominated Member of Commission encharged with preparation of Project for Permanent International Court of Justice under the League of Nations; Doctor *honoris causa,* Columbia Univ.). *Publications:* La Literatura del Slang; La Idea del Derecho (with D. Matienzo); Coleccion de Fallos en Materia Civil y Comercial; Los Hombres de Presa (The Men of Prey) (translated into Italian with introduction by Professor Lombroso); Cobro Coercitivo de Deudas Publicas; La Republica Argentina y el caso de Venezuela; Les Emprunts d'etat et leur relations avec la politique internationale; El Abitrage de las Pesquerias del Atlantico Norte. *Address:* Buenos Ayres, Junin 52. *Clubs:* Jockey, Circulo de Armas, Buenos Ayres.   (*Died 9 June 1921.*)

DRAKE, Sir Francis George Augustus Fuller-Eliott-, 2nd Bt.; *cr.* 1821; *b.* 24 Dec. 1837; *o. s.* of late Capt. Rose Henry Fuller, R.N. and Margaret, *d.* of late Sir Robert Sheffield, 3rd Bt.; *S. u.* 1870; *m.* Elizabeth, *d.* of Sir R. A. Douglas, 2nd Bt., of Glenbervie, 1861; one *d.* Edited Lady Knight's Letters from France and Italy, 1776-95, 1905; joined Royal Horse Guards, 1858; retired (Captain) 1870. [The founder of this family was the celebrated Admiral Sir Francis Drake, 1545-96; 1st Bt. served under Sir John Moore in Peninsular War, 1808-1814.] Owns about 7700 acres. *Heir:* none. *Address:* Nutwell Court, Exeter; Buckland Abbey, Plymouth; Sheafhayne House, Devon. *Club:* Carlton.   (*Died 25 July 1916.*)

DRAKE, Maurice, Glass Painter and Novelist; *b.* 31 May 1875; *e. s.* of Frederick Drake, Glass Painter, of Exeter; *m.* 1897, Alice, *d.* of late George Wilson, of Powderham; one *d. Educ.:* St. James' Grammar School, Teignmouth. *Publications:* Novels: The Salving of a Derelict, 1906; Lethbridge of the Moor, 1908; Wrack, 1910; WO₂, 1913; The Ocean Sleuth, 1915; The Doom Window, 1923; On Glass Painting: The Heraldic Glass at Ashton, 1905; The Great East Window of Exeter Cathedral, 1907; A History of English Glass Painting, 1912; Saints and their Emblems, 1915; The Costessey Collection of Stained Glass, 1919. *Address:* 4 The Close, Exeter. *T.:* Exeter. 876. *Club:* Savage.   (*Died 29 April 1923.*)

DRAKE, Robert James, K.C. 1914; 3rd *s.* of late John Drake formerly of Dromore; *m.* 1897, Edith, *o. d.* of late W. J. Cooke formerly of Hereford. *Educ.:* privately; Trinity College, Dublin. B.A.; L.L.B.; King's Inn, Dublin; called to Bar, Middle Temple, 1887; Member Midland Circuit. *Address:* 131 Victoria Street, Westminster, S.W.; 1 Essex Court Temple, E.C. *Club:* Royal Automobile. *T.:* 1973 Central.
(*Died 8 July 1916.*)

DRAKE, Capt. Thomas Oakley, I.S.O. 1911; *b.* 1863; *s.* of late T. W. Drake; *m.* 1887, Kathleen Maud, *y. d.* of late Lieut. W. Devine; three *s.* two *d.* Enlisted, 1878; served in second phase of Afghan Wars of 1878-79-80 (medal), and Mahsud-Waziri Expedition of 1881; retired from the Army with the rank of Commissary (Hon. Captain), 1905; Registrar, Department of Commerce and Industry, Government of India, 1905-16. *Address:* Toongabbie, N.S.W., Australia.   (*Died 28 July 1928.*)

DRAKE, William James, I.S.O. 1912; Assistant Secretary to the Govt. of India Public Works Dept.; *b.* 26 Dec. 1872; *s.* of Conolly Pakenham Drake, Tyrone Co., Ireland; *m.* 1902, *d.*

of William Maddocks, Bishop Stortford. *Address:* Simla. *Club:* Junior Conservative.

DRAKE, William Wyckham Tyr-whitt, J.P., M.F.H. ; Squire of Shardeloes ; *b.* 27 Sep. 1851 ; *s.* of Thomas T. Drake ; *m.* Augusta, *d.* of late Rev. H. Peel, Thornton, Bucks ; one *s.* two *d.* *Educ.:* Eton. Studied farming in Hampshire and Shropshire ; was given a small farm on the estate by his father until his marriage, when he took a house and some land in Oxfordshire and broke and made hunters ; on coming into the property of Shardeloes in 1900 he took the Old Berkeley West hounds for a season ; hunted for three years with the Bicester and then took the Old Berkshire hounds for four seasons, 1905-9 ; Master of them again for two seasons, 1913-14. *Recreations:* hunting and farming. *Address:* Shardeloes, Amersham, Bucks. (*Died 29 July 1919.*)

DRAPER, Herbert James, R.B.C., *b.* London ; *m.* Ida, *y. d.* of W. Walton Williams, J.P. ; one *d.* *Educ.:* Bruce Castle. Studied art R.A. Schools, and at Paris and Rome ; awarded Royal Academy Gold Medal and Travelling Studentship, 1889 ; spent 1890 in travel ; settled in London 1891, painting subject pictures and portraits ; has exhibited each year at R.A. since 1890 ; Lament for Icarus was bought by the Chantry Trustees for the National Gallery of Brit. Art, 1898 ; awarded medal at the International Exhibition in Paris, 1900 ; principal pictures : The Sea Maiden, The Vintage Morn, The Lament for Icarus, The Golden Fleece, Tristram and Yseult, Calypso's Isle, The Foam Sprite, The Dawn Star, Ulysses and the Sirens, etc., etc. Pictures of his have been bought for the permanent collections of the following public galleries : Liverpool, Manchester, Bradford, Preston, Truro, Hull ; Durban and Pietermaritzburg, S. Africa ; The Government of Adelaide, Australia ; chief decorative painting, the ceiling of the Livery Hall of the Drapers Company, City of London principal portraits, late Duchess of Abercorn, Lord and Lady Inchiquin, Viscountess Ennismore, Hon. Maude Stanley of Alderley, Lord Ninian Crichton-Stuart, Capt. G. A. Boyd-Rochfort, V.C., H. Cosmo Bonsor, the children of the Earl of Jersey, etc. *Address:* 15 Abbey Road, N.W.8. *T.:* Hampstead 3949. *Club:* Arts. (*Died 22 Sept. 1920.*)

DRAYTON, Edward Rawle, C.M.G. 1902 ; *b.* 2 Apr. 1859 ; *s.* of late Rev. John Drayton ; *m.* 1882, Edith, *y. d.* of F. G. Browne, M.D., of Barbados ; four *s.* three *d.* *Educ.:* Harrison College, Barbados. Entered Colonial service, 1878 ; Chief Clerk to Gov. of Windward Islands, 1882 ; Provost-Marshal, Grenada, 1885 ; Registrar, 1886 ; member, Legislative Council, 1887 ; Inspector of Prisons, 1888 ; member, Executive Council, 1888 ; Chairman, Special Commission Police and Prisons, St. Lucia, 1888 ; Treasurer of Grenada, 1890 ; Colonial Secretary of Grenada, 1892-1914 ; administered Government of Grenada whenever Governor absent between 1890 and 1914 ; of St. Vincent, June 1893, Feb. to Sep. 1897, Feb. 1900 to April 1901 ; of Windward Islands, Jan. 1897, Oct. 1907, and Sep. 1913. Delegate to West Indian Quarantine Conferences, 1904 and 1910, and to Canadian Trade Conference, 1908 ; President, Legislative Council, and Chairman, Harbour Improvement Committee, Grenada, 1912 ; Administrator, Dominica, 1914 ; retired on pension, 1915 ; Chairman, Barbados S.P.C.A., 1916-25. *Publications:* The Grenada Handbook, annually from 1896 to 1914 ; The Advantages of St. George's, Grenada, as a Port of Call for Steamers ; West Indian Hurricanes and other Storms. *Address:* Frankfort Villa, Hastings, Barbados. (*Died 31 May 1927.*)

DREAPER, Surgeon Rear-Admiral George Albert, C.B. 1920 ; *b.* 7 July 1863 ; *s.* of late Richard Henry Dreaper, Finsboro'

House, Castlecomer, Co. Kilkenny ; *m.* 1910, Constance Amy, *d.* of late Henry de Blaquiere, J.P., of Fiddane, Gort, Co. Galway ; no *c.* *Educ.:* Dublin. Surgeon, Royal Navy, 1884 ; Staff-Surgeon, 1896 ; served Boer War, 1899 ; Jubaland Expedition, 1901 ; Somaliland Expedition, 1904 ; Fleet-Surgeon, 1904 ; in charge of the Surgical Wards, Chatham Naval Hospital, 1908-10 ; Deputy Surgeon-General, 1913 ; in charge of the Surgical Wards, Plymouth Naval Hospital, 1914-16 ; in charge of Royal Naval Hospital, Hong-Kong, 1916-19 ; Surgeon Rear-Admiral, 1919 ; retired list, 1923. *Recreations:* shooting, fishing, golf, tennis, walking. (*Died 28 June 1927.*)

DREW, Clifford Luxmoore, Barrister-at-Law ; His Majesty's Coroner for the Western Division of London ; 2nd *s.* of late Charles Drew, H.E.I.C.'s 3rd Extra Madras Regt. ; *m.* Augusta, *y. d.* of late William Yeo, Richmond House, N. Devon. *Educ.:* private tutor and Aberdeen, of which University he is a graduate. Was in India with his parents during a part of the Indian Mutiny ; Past President of the Coroners' Society of England and Wales ; formerly held a Captain's commission in the 6th Brigade South Irish Division R.A. and Argyll and Bute Artillery Militia ; is now a Captain in the National Reserve ; called to bar, 1890 ; is a member of the Middle Temple, Western Circuit, and the Central Criminal Court. *Recreations:* salmon fishing, shooting. *Address:* 15 Pembridge Villas, Kensington, W. *Clubs:* Savage, M.C.C. (*Died 26 May 1919.*)

DREW, Mary, *b.* Nov. 1847 ; *d.* of Rt. Hon. W. E. Gladstone ; *m.* 1886, Rev. Harry Drew, Rector of Hawarden, Canon of St. Asaph ; one *d.* [Dorothy, *m.* 1912, Col. Francis Parish, M.C., D.S.O., K.R.R.C.; died of war wounds 1921]. *Educ.:* Home. Was secretary to her father and to her mother until they died, as she lived with them both unmarried and married. *Publications:* The Mothers' Union ; Some Hawarden Letters ; Catherine Gladstone ; Acton, Gladstone and others ; Forty Years' Friendship. *Address:* 2 The Boltons, S.W.10. *T.:* Kensington 4530 ; Hawarden, Chester. (*Died 1 Jan. 1927.*)

DREW, William Wilson, *s.* of Rev. William Henry Drew, Professor of Mathematics, King's College, London ; *m.* 1st, 1894, Mary Louisa, *d.* of Rev. S. F. F. Auchmuty ; 2nd, 1905, Gertrude Caroline, *d.* of George Bowles, 6 Hall Road, N.W. ; one *s.* two *d.* *Educ.:* Charterhouse ; King's College, Cambridge. Indian Civil Service, 1878 ; served as Assistant Commissioner in the Punjab until 1882 ; then transferred to Bombay Presidency ; Census Superintendent, 1890-92 ; member of Anglo-Portuguese Commission, 1892 ; Commissioner, Southern Division, 1904 ; Member of the Legislative Council of the Governor-General, 1907-9 ; Commissioner of Customs, Salt, Opium, and Abkari, Bombay, 1908-11. *Address:* 53 Hamilton Terrace, St. John's Wood, N.W.8. *Club:* East India United Service. (*Died 1 Nov. 1923.*)

DREWRY, Lieut. George Leslie, R.N.R., V.C. 1915 ; *b.* 3 Nov. 1894. *Educ.:* Merchant Taylors' School. Entered Mercantile Marine, 1909 ; was wrecked on desert island near Cape Horn, 1912 ; 4th Officer P. & O. S.N. Co., Ltd., 1912 ; joined R.N.R., 1913 ; served Dardanelles, 1914-15 (V.C.) ; promoted to Sub.-Lieut. and appointed Act. Lieut. 2 Sep. 1916. *Address:* 58 Claremont Road, Forest Gate, Essex. (*Died 2 Aug. 1918.*)

DREYER, John Louis Emil, Ph.D., Hon. M.A. (Oxon) ; Hon. D.Sc. (Belfast) ; *b.* Copenhagen, 13 Feb. 1852 ; 3rd *s.* of Lieut.-Gen. F. Dreyer ; *m.* Katherine Hannah (*d.* 1923), *d.* of John Tuthill, formerly of Kilmore, Co. Limerick ; three *s.* one *d.* *Educ.:* Copenhagen Univ. Astronomer at Earl of Rosse's Observatory, 1874-78 ; Assist. Astronomer at

Dublin Univ. Observatory, 1878-82; Director Armagh Observatory, 1882-1916; Member Royal Danish Academy of Sciences; Knight of the Dannebrog; awarded Gold Medal of Royal Astronomical Society, 1916; President R.A.S., 1923-25. *Publications:* Second Armagh Catalogue of 3300 Stars, 1886; New General Catalogue of Nebulae and Clusters of Stars, 1888; Supplements, 1895 and 1908; Tycho Brahe: a Picture of Scientific Life and Work in the 16th Century, 1890; Planetary Systems from Thales to Kepler, 1906; Copernicus: an International Journal of Astronomy, 1881-84 (jointly with Prof. Copeland); editor of W. Herschel's Scientific Papers, 1912, and of Tycho Brahe's Opera Omnia from 1913. *Recreation:* reading. *Address:* 14 Staverton Road, Oxford.   *(Died 14 Sept. 1926.)*

DRISCOLL, Very Rev. James, D.D.; Canon of Westminster Cathedral; first Headmaster of the Cardinal Vaughan School; *b.* London, 20 Mar. 1870. *Educ.:* St. Edmund's College, Ware; Seminario Romano, Rome. M.A. of London University; D.D. of Apollinare University, Rome; Assistant Master for nine years at St. Edmund's College, Ware: Headmaster of Westminster Cathedral Choir School, 1903-14; Member of the Catholic Education Council; Hon. Secretary of the Conference of Catholic Colleges. *Address:* Cardinal Vaughan School, Addison Road, W.14. *T.:* Park 3145.
      (Died 29 Dec. 1927.)

DROMGOOLE, His Honour Charles, M.A., LL.D., K.C. 1910; Circuit Judge for the City and County of Dublin; County Court Judge, Kerry, 1913-20, Carlow, Kildare, Wexford, and Wicklow, 1920-24; *o. surv. s.* of late Charles Dromgoole, Newry; *b.* Newry, Co. Armagh; *m.* Gertrude, *d.* of late John George Fleming, Ph.D., Head Inspector of National Schools; three *d. Educ.:* St. Colman's College, Newry; Blackrock College; University College, Blackrock, Dublin. Called to Irish Bar, 1894, and went the North-East Circuit. *Clubs:* St. Stephen's Green, Royal Dublin Golf, Dublin.
      (Died Jan. 1927.)

DROUGHT, Rev. Charles Edward, M.A.; Rector of S. John's, Toorak, since 1900; Canon of S. Paul's Cathedral, Melbourne; *b.* Rectory Aghancon, King's Co., Ireland, 3 Oct. 1847; *s.* of Rev. A. T. Drought, of Balliver Estate, King's Co., Ireland; *m.* Mary Lillias, *d.* of Frederic Race Godfrey; one *s. Educ.:* Trinity College, Cambridge. Curate of Hanley Castle and Alvechurch; 3½ years Chaplain of Linares in Spain. *Publications:* Dangers and Duties of the Spiritual Life; The Music of the Cross; Our Church's Standards; My Rectors; My Curates; etc. *Address:* S. John's, Toorak, Melbourne.   *(Died 8 Dec. 1917.)*

DRUITT, Right Rev. Cecil Henry, Bishop of Grafton since 1914; *b.* 1874. *Educ.:* Corpus Christi College, Cambridge (M.A., D.D.); Ridley Hall, Cambridge. Ordained, 1898; Curate of Christ Church, Torquay, 1898-1900; Theological and Hebrew Lecturer, C.M. College, Islington, 1900-2; Rector of St. Bride, Stretford, 1902-10; Vicar of St. Mary, Overchurch, Birkenhead, 1910-11; Lecturer at St. Aidan's College, Birkenhead, 1910-11; Coadjutor Bishop of Grafton and Armidale, 1911-14. *Publications:* The Obligation of Prayer; The Missionary Message of St. John's Gospel. *Address:* Bishop's Lodge, Grafton, New South Wales. *(Died July 1921.)*

DRUMMOND, Rev. Arthur Hislop, M.A., Hon. Canon of Christ Church, Oxford; Proctor in Convocation, 1907-17; Vicar of All Saints, Boyne Hill, Maidenhead, 1876-1917; *b.* 5 Apr. 1843; *s.* of Rev. Arthur Drummond, Rector of Charlton, Kent, and Margaretta Maria, *d.* of Sir Thomas M. Wilson, Bt.; *m.* 1st, 1868, Armynel Mary, *d.* of Rev. C. Baylay; 2nd, Anna Harriet (*d.* 1915), *d.* of Wm. Dodsworth; one *s. Educ.:* Marlborough; Christ Church,

Oxford; Cuddesdon Theological Coll. Formerly Curate of Hungerford, Berks, and Long Compton, Warwickshire; presented to Vicarage of Kempley, Glos, by Earl Beauchamp, 1871; was a Guardian of the Poor, and on the Technical Instruction and Education Committees for the borough of Maidenhead. *Address:* 9 Elm Park Gardens, S.W.10. *T.:* Kensington 4361.
      (Died 19 Feb. 1925.)

DRUMMOND, Maj.-General Sir Francis Henry Rutherford, K.C.I.E., 1912; C.B. 1908; *b.* 9 Sept. 1857; *e. surv. s.* of late Maj.-Gen. Henry Drummond; *m.* Violet Fraser, *o. d.* of Col. F. J. Home, C.S.I. *Educ.:* Wellington College. Entered army, 1875: Brevet Major, 1887; Major, 1895; Lieut.-Col. 1901; Brevet Col. 1904; Substantive Colonel and Brig.-General, 1907; Maj.-Gen. 1909; served Afghan War, 1878-80 (despatches twice, medal with clasp). Served with Afghan Boundary Commission, 1884-86 (Bt. Majority); Afghan Order of Honour; was lately Inspector-General of Imperial Service Troops; is an Esquire of the Order of St. John of Jerusalem in England. *Address:* Aveland House, Crieff, Perthshire. *T.A.:* Crieff. *Club:* Cavalry.
      (Died 27 Mar. 1919.)

DRUMMOND, Capt. George Robinson Bridge, M.V.O. 1904; retired, Chief Constable of West Sussex; *b.* 1845. Late 26th Regt. Bombay N.I. *Address:* 14 The Drive, Hove, Sussex. *(Died 27 April 1917.)*

DRUMMOND, Brig.-General Sir Hugh Henry John, 1st Bt., *cr.* 1922; C.M.G. 1918; J.P. Devonshire; Chairman, The Southern Railway Co.; Director of National Provincial and Union Bank of England; Dep. Chairman, Alliance Assurance Co.; Member, Royal Bodyguard of Scotland; *b.* Clovelly Court, Devonshire, 29 Nov. 1859; 3rd *s.* of Sir James Hamlyn Williams Drummond, 3rd Bart. of Hawthornden, Midlothian, and Edwinsford, Llandilo; *m.* 1889, Gertrude Emily, *e. d.* of late Hon. Mark G. K. Rolle of Bicton and Stevenston, Devonshire; one *d. Educ.:* privately. Joined 1st Devon Militia, 1878; Rifle Brigade, 1879; contested (C.) West Carmarthenshire, 1889; in 1895 became a partner in Sanders & Co., Exeter Bank, which was amalgamated in 1894 with Messrs. Snow & Co. and Prescott Dimsdale & Co. and later with the Union of London & Smith's Bank; a Director of the London and South Western Railway Co., 1900; Deputy Chairman, 1904; joined Royal North Devon Hussars (Yeomanry) as Captain, afterwards becoming Lieut.-Col. commanding; on outbreak of war raised second Regiment of Yeomanry, and in Jan. 1915 was given command of the 2nd South Western Mounted Brigade; Hon. Brig.-General, Aug. 1917. *Recreations:* shooting, fishing, golf, yachting. *Address:* 98 Eaton Place, S.W.1. *Clubs:* Carlton, Travellers', Naval and Military; Royal Yacht Squadron, Cowes.   *(Died 1 Aug. 1924.)*

DRUMMOND, Rev. James, M.A., LL.D.; Principal Manchester Coll. Oxford, 1885-1906; *b.* Dublin, 14 May 1885; *s.* of Rev. William Hamilton Drummond, D.D.; *m.* Frances, *d.* of John Classon, Dublin, 1861; two *s.* six *d. Educ.:* Trinity College, Dublin; Manchester New College, London. B.A. with 1st classical gold medal, Trin. Coll. Dub., 1855; LL.D. (T.C.D.), 1882; Litt.D. (Hon. T.C.D.), 1892; M.A. Oxon. 1889; D.D. (Tufts), 1905. Colleague of Rev. William Gaskell, Cross Street Chapel, Manchester, 1859-69; Professor of Theology in Manchester New Coll. London, 1870; succeeded Dr. Martineau as Principal, 1885; removed with the College to Oxford, 1889; retired, 1906. *Publications:* Spiritual Religion: Sermons on Christian Faith and Life, 1870; The Jewish Messiah: A Critical History of the Messianic Idea among the Jews, 1877; Introduction to the Study of Theology, 1884; Philo-Judæus: or the Jewish - Alexandrian Philosophy in its Development and Completion, 2 vols. 1888 ; The Epistle of St. Paul to the Galatians, 1898 ; Via, Veritas, Vita (the Hibbert Lectures for 1894, on Christianity in its most simple and intelligible form), 1894 ; The Pauline Benediction (three sermons), 1897 ; International Handbooks to the New Testament, ed. by Orello Cone, D.D., vol. ii., The Epistles of Paul the Apostle to the Thessalonians, etc. 1899 ; Some Thoughts on Christology (Essex Hall Lecture), 1902 ; Life and Letters of Dr. Martineau (in union with Prof. Upton), 1902 ; The Character and Authorship of the Fourth Gospel, 1904 ; Studies in Christian Doctrine, 1908 ; The Transmission of the Text of the New Testament (a little manual for teachers), 1909 ; Johannine Thoughts, 1909 ; Lectures on the Composition and Delivery of Sermons, 1910 ; Paul ; his Life and Teaching, 1911 ; several articles on theological subjects ; College addresses ; and sermons. *Recreations :* carpentering, cycling. *Address :* 18 Rawlinson Road, Oxford. (*Died 13 June 1918.*)

DRUMMOND, Lister Maurice ; Metropolitan Police Magistrate since 1913 ; *o. s. of* late Maurice Drummond, C.B., and Hon. Adelaide Lister, *e. d. of* 2nd Baron Ribblesdale ; *b.* 23 Aug. 1856. *Educ. :* Privately. Called to Bar, Inner Temple, 1879 ; Revising barrister on South-Eastern Circuit, 1887-1913 ; Secretary to the Evicted Tenants Commission, Dublin, 1892-3 ; Commissioner to try the Municipal Election Petition at Grimsby, 1904 ; and that at Gloucester, 1907 ; Secretary to Worcester Royal Commission, 1906 ; A Knight of the Papal Order of St. Gregory the Great, 1901. *Recreations :* fencing, swimming, and cycling. *Address :* 10 Hampstead Square, N.W. *Club :* London Fencing. (*Died 27 Feb. 1916.*)

DRUMMOND, Malcolm, of Megginch and Kilspindie ; *o. s. of* John Drummond of Megginch, late Grenadier Guards (*d.* 1889), and Frances, *d. of* late Gen. Sir John Oswald, G.C.B., of Dunnikier ; *b.* 2 Mar. 1856 ; *m.* 1890, Geraldine, *d. of* 1st Baron Amherst of Hackney ; ones. three *d. Educ. :* Eton. Served in Northumberland Militia, 1873-76 ; in Grenadier Guards, 1876-90 ; A.D.C. and private secretary to Governor of Newfoundland, 1881 ; served with 3rd Battalion Grenadier Guards, Soudan campaign, 1885 ; Guards' Mounted Infantry (medal and clasp and Khedive's Star) ; Capt. Grenadier Guards, 1885 ; retired 1890 ; Groom of Privy Chamber to Queen Victoria, 1890 ; groom-in-waiting, 1893-1901 ; J.P. and D.L. Perthshire. *Address :* Megginch Castle, Errol, Perthshire. *Club :* Guards'. (*Died 28 May 1924.*)

DRURY, Rev. John Frederick William ; Vicar of Saddleworth since 1918 ; Secretary of the Manchester Diocesan Societies 1891-1918 ; *b.* 18 Oct. 1858 ; *m.* 1900, Charlotte, *d.* of Mrs. Humphreys of Wyberslegh Hall, Cheshire ; two *d. Educ. :* Christ Church, Oxford (B.A. and M.A.). Curate of St. Mary's Cathedral, Glasgow, 1887 - 89 ; Morecambe, Lancs, 1889-91 ; Chaplain to the Hon. Lady Leighton-Warren, Tabley House, Knutsford, 1898-1912 ; Hon. Canon of Manchester Cathedral, 1911. *Publications :* Manual of Education, 1902 ; editor of Manchester Diocesan Directory, 1906. *Recreations :* golf, chess, gardening. *Address :* The Vicarage, Saddleworth, Yorks. *T. :* Saddleworth 69. *Club :* Old Rectory, Manchester.

DRURY, Rt. Rev. Thomas Wortley, D.D., M.A. ; Master of St. Catharine's College, Cambridge, since 1920 ; *b.* 12 Sep. 1847 ; *m.* 1871, Catharine Beatrice (*d.* 1914), *d. of* Captain Dumergue, Madras Army ; two s. four *d. Educ. :* King William's College, Isle of Man ; Christ's College Camb. (25th Wrangler, 3rd class Classical Tripos and 1st class Theological Honours). Ordained 1871 ; Curate of Kirk Braddan, 1871-73 ; Mathematical Master of King

William's College, 1873 - 76 ; Rector of Holy Trinity, Chesterfield, 1876 - 82 ; Principal, Church Missionary College, Islington, 1882-1899 ; select preacher, Cambridge, 1891, 1899, 1905, 1907, etc. ; Member of the Fulham Conference on Confession and Absolution, 1900-1901 ; and of the Royal Commission on Ecclesiastical Discipline, 1904-6 ; Principal of Ridley Hall, Cambridge, 1899-1907 ; Dean of St. German's Cathedral, 1908 ; Bishop of Sodor and Man, 1907-11 ; Bishop of Ripon, 1911-20 ; War Office Committee on Chaplains, 1915 ; Sub-Prelate of the Order of St. John of Jerusalem, 1918. *Publications :* Confession and Absolution ; How we got our Prayer Book ; Two Studies in the Prayer Book ; Elevation in the Eucharist, its History and Rationale : A Prison Ministry ; The Ministry of Our Lord. *Recreations :* fishing (river and sea). *Address :* The Master's Lodge, St. Catharine's College, Cambridge. (*Died 12 Feb. 1926.*)

DRURY, William D., F.E.S., F.R.H.S. ; Editor of the Bazaar, Exchange and Mart, 1884 - 1926 ; *o.* Oxford, 1857 ; *m.* 1881 ; one *s.* two *d. Educ. :* Nixon's Grammar School, Oxford. Apprenticed to Jas. Parker & Son, book and classical printers, passing afterwards to the Oxford University Press (Classical Side) ; acted as Press Corrector to The Bazaar, Iron, and to Clowes & Sons, Beccles ; spent five years on Editorial staff of Nicholson's Dictionary of Gardening. *Publications :* The Collie, Popular Dog Keeping, British Dogs, Popular Toy Dogs, Fruit Culture, Garden Animals, Home Gardening, The Book of Gardening, Hardy Perennials, English and Welsh Terriers, Scotch and Irish Terriers, The Fox Terrier, and The Greyhound ; edited numerous books for the Collector, gardening and dogs. *Recreation :* gardening, entomology and curio-collecting. *Address :* Stepaside, 50 St. Helen's Park Road, Hastings. (*Died 30 Mar. 1923.*)

DRYSDALE, Hon. Arthur, K.C. ; *b.* Nova Scotia, 5 Sep. 1857 ; *s.* of George Drysdale, of Scottish descent ; *m.* Carrie, *d.* of late George P. Mitchell, Halifax. A Judge of the Supreme Court of Nova Scotia, formerly Attorney-General of the Province, and represented Hants County in Provincial Legislature for 16 years. Liberal. *Address :* Halifax, Nova Scotia. *Club :* Halifax.

DRYSDALE, Rev. A. H., M.A., D.D. (Edin.) ; ex-Moderator, English Presbyterian Synod ; Hon. President of its Historical Society ; Governor of Edward VI. Roy. Grammar School, Morpeth ; *b.* Bridge of Allan, 1837 ; *m.* 1867 ; two *s.* one *d. Educ. :* Stirling High School ; Edinburgh Univ. ; won the Gray Prize (Essay) ; Theological training in the United Presbyterian Hall. First charge, Maisondieu, Brechin, 1861 ; Trinity Church, Rochdale, 1867 ; St. George's, Morpeth, 1883 ; now Emeritus. *Publications :* Philemon (Epistle to), for English Readers, 1879 ; Early Hebrew Songs (Bible Bypaths Series), 1890 ; History of the Presbyterians in England, 1889 ; Ditto, as handbook, 1891 ; A Moderator's Year, 1904 ; Christ Invisible Our Gain, 1909 ; and much current literature. *Recreations :* rambling and ruminating. *Address :* The Stanners, Morpeth.
(*Died 2 Jan. 1924.*)

DRYSDALE, Lt.-Col. William, D.S.O. 1915 ; Royal Scots ; *b.* 4 Nov. 1876 ; *s.* of William Drysdale, Kilrie, Kirkcaldy ; *m.* 1904, Mary Louisa, *d.* of Sir John Muir Mackenzie, K.C.S.I. ; three *s.* Entered army, 1893 ; Captain, 1902 ; Brigade - Major 15th Brigade, Irish Command, 1912 ; served European War, 1914-16 (despatches, prom. Bt. Lt.-Col., D.S.O.). *Address :* Kilrie, Kirkcaldy, Fife.
(*Died 29 Sept. 1916.*)

DUBOIS, Théodore, Directeur honoraire du Conservatoire National de musique et de déclamation ; Compositeur de musique ; Membre

DRUMMOND, His Honour Judge Michael, K.C. See page xviii.

de l'Institut. *Educ.*: Conservatoire de Paris. Entré au Conservatoire, 1854 ; obtint les prix d'harmonie, d'accompagnement, de fugue, d'orgue, et enfin le grand prix de Rome, 1861 ; Maître de chapelle de Ste. Clotilde, 1863-68, après en a voir été organiste accompagnateur ; Maître de chapelle de la Madeleine, 1868-76, puis organiste du gd. orgue de cette église jusqu'en 1896, succédant à C. Saint-Saens ; Professeur d'harmonie au Conservatoire, 1871 ; de Composition, 1891 ; Directeur du Conservatoire, 1896-1905 ; Inspecteur de l'Enseignement musical, 1884-96 ; élu Membre de l'Académie des Beaux-Arts, 1894. *Publications:* Sept Paroles du Christ ; Le Paradis Perdu ; Messes, Motets ; La Guzla de l'Emir, opéra comique ; Le Pain Bis, op. comique ; La Farandole, ballet de l'opéra ; Aben-Hamet, grand opéra ; Xavière, Idylle dramatique ; Plusieurs Suites d'Orchestre ; Concertos de Piano, de Violon ; Ouverture de Frithioff et autres ouvertures, Diverses scènes lyriques ; L'Enlèvement de Proserpine, Hylas, Le Baptême de Clovis ; Notre Dame de la Mer ; Prière de France ; recueils de pièces de piano, d'orgue, de mélodies sonate pour piano et violon ; trios pour piano, violon, et violoncelle ; chœurs divers ; notes et études d'harmonie ; traité de Contrepoint et de Fugue ; Petit Manuel d'Harmonie ; quintette pour piano, violon, hautbois, alto et violoncelle ; sonate pour violoncelle et piano ; Fantaisie de Harpe ; Quatuor avec piano ; 12 Etudes de concert pour le piano, Dixtuor pour double quintette à cordes et à veut ; Symphonie française ; In Memoriam Mortuorum, pour orchestre ; 2e Symphonie ; Exquisses Orchestrales ; Fantaisie-Stuck pour violoncelle et orchestre ; Fantasietta pour flute, violon, trompette, cor, violoncelle, harpe, timbales et orchestre à cordes ; Quatuor à cordes ; Poëmes Sylvestres, Virgiliens, Alpestres pour le piano ; Sonate pour le piano ; traité d'harmonie 2e quatuor à cordes ; nombreuses pièces diverses pour piano, organ, chant, instruments, etc. *Address:* Boulevard Pereire 201, Paris ; Rosnay, Marne.   (*Died 11 June 1924.*)

DUBOSE, William Porcher, S.T.D., D.C.L.; Dean since 1894 and Professor Emeritus, Theological Department, University of the South, Sewanee, Tennessee, U.S.A. ; *b.* 11 April 1836 ; *s.* of Theodore Marion and Jane Porcher Dubose, in Winnsboro', South Carolina ; *m.* 1st, 1863, Anne Barnwell Peronneau ; 2nd, 1878, Maria Louisa Yorger ; one *s.* two *d. Educ.*: Military Academy of South Carolina ; University of Virginia. While a student for the ministry of the Church, entered the military service of the Southern Confederacy, 1861 ; served as an officer through war (several times wounded and once a prisoner) ; priest in the Protestant Episcopal Church, 1865 ; served in S.C. until became Chaplain and Professor, Univ. of South, 1871 ; S.T.D. Columbia Univ., N.Y., 1874 ; D.C.L. Univ. of South, 1907. D.D. General Theological Seminary, N.Y., 1908 ; after continuous service in the University of the South for over thirty-six years, resigned active duties in summer of 1908 and elected Dean and Professor Emeritus. *Publications:* Soteriology of the New Testament, 1892 ; The Ecumenical Councils, 1896 ; The Gospel in the Gospels, 1906 ; The Gospel according to St. Paul, 1907 ; High Priesthood and Sacrifice, 1908. *Recreations:* for many years has spent winter vacations in Florida, and done there the writing for which duties at Sewanee allowed no leisure. *Address:* Monteagle, Tennessee, U.S.A.   (*Died 18 Aug. 1918.*)

DUBOST, Antonin, President of the French Senate since 1906 ; *b.* l'Arbresle, Rhone, 6 Apl. 1844 ; Member Chamber of Deputies, 1880-97 ; Minister of Justice, 1893-94 ; Senator since 1897 ; President of the Senate, 1906. *Address:* Présidence du Sénat, Paris.   (*Died 15 April 1921.*)

DU BOULAY, Ven. Henry Houssemayne, M.A. ; Hon. Canon of Truro, 1882 ; *b.* Lawhitton, 25 Jan. 1840 ; *s.* of late Rev. Francis Du Boulay, Rector of Lawhitton, and Sybella, *d.* of Bishop Phillpotts, Exeter ; *m.* 1870, Emily Henrietta (*d.* 1924), *d.* of Rev. Richard Stephens, Vicar of Dunsford and Sub-Dean of Exeter ; three *d. Educ.*: Exmouth; Harrow; Exeter Coll., Oxford ; Theological Coll., Exeter. Domestic Chaplain and Secretary to the Bishop (Phillpotts) of Exeter, 1864-66 ; Rural Dean of Kerrier, 1877-80 ; Proctor in Convocation for the Chapter of Truro, 1887-92 ; Editor Truro Diocesan Kalendar, 1877-1902 ; Vicar of S. Sithney, 1869-1880 ; Vicar of Newlyn, 1880-92 ; Archdeacon of Bodmin, 1892-1923 ; Rector of Lawhitton, 1892-1923. *Address:* Chy-an-dour, Falmouth.
    (*Died 6 April 1925.*)

DU CANE, Colonel Hubert John, C.B. 1913 ; M.V.O. 1905 ; *b.* 22 July 1859 ; 2nd and *o. surv. s.* of late Major-General Sir Edmund Du Cane, K.C.B., formerly Chairman of Commissioners of H.M. Prisons, etc., and late Mary Dorothea, *d.* of Captain John Molloy, late Rifle Brigade ; unmarried. Served Hazara Expedition, 1888 (despatches, medal with clasp) ; South African War, 1899-1902 (despatches, Bt. Lt.-Col., Queen's Medal with clasp, King's Medal with two clasps). *T.A.*: 94 Piccadilly. *Clubs:* Naval and Military, Travellers', Garrick. (*Died 15 June 1916.*)

DUCAT, Ven. William Methven Gordon, M.A. ; Archdeacon of Berkshire since 1903 ; Hon. Canon, Christ Church, Oxford, 1894. *Educ.*: Balliol College, Oxford (Snell Exhibitioner, 2nd class Mods., 2nd class Lit. Hum.). Ordained, 1873 ; Curate of All Souls, Langham Place, 1873-76 ; Chaplain of Cuddesdon College, 1877 ; Rector of Lamplugh, 1877-1880 ; Principal, Leeds Clergy School, 1880-83 ; Principal, Cuddesdon College and Vicar of Cuddesdon, 1883-94 ; Rural Dean, Cuddesdon, 1890-1894 ; Vicar of St. Giles's, Reading, 1894-1903 ; Rural Dean, Reading, 1899-1903. *Publication:* Hints to those who are preparing for Holy Orders, 1909. *Address:* 5 Bath Road, Reading.
    (*Died 17 Mar. 1922.*)

DUCHESNE, Mgr. Louis Marie Olivier ; Hon. D.C.L. Cantab. and Oxon. ; Archæologist ; Member of the Institute of France (French Academy and Academy of Inscriptions and Belles Lettres) and of British Academy ; Director of the Ecole Française of Rome ; *b.* St. Servan, 13 Sep. 1843. *Address:* passage Stanislas, 2, Paris.   (*Died 21 April 1922.*)

DUCIE, 3rd Earl of (*cr.* 1837), **Henry John Moreton,** P.C., D.L., F.R.S., G.C.V.O. ; Baron Ducie, 1763 ; Baron Moreton, 1837 ; Lord-Lieutenant Gloucestershire, 1857-1911 ; *b.* 25 June 1827 ; *s.* of 2nd Earl and *d.* of 2nd Lord Sherborne ; *S.* father, 1853 ; *m.* 1849, first cousin, Julia (*d.* 1895), *d.* of James Haughton Langston, M.P., Sarsden, Oxfordshire ; one *s.* one *d.* M.P. for Stroud, 1852-53 ; Captain of the Yeomen of the Guard, 1859-66 ; Lord Warden of the Stanneries, 1888-1908 Owns about 14,000 acres. *Heir: b.* Hon. Berkley B. Moreton. *Address:* Tortworth Court, Falfield, Gloucestershire. *Clubs:* Athenæum, Brooks's, Travellers'; Royal Yacht Squadron, Cowes.
    (*Died 28 Oct. 1921.*)

DUCIE, 4th Earl of (*cr.* 1837), **Berkeley Basil Moreton,** Baron Ducie, 1763 ; Baron Moreton, 1837 ; *b.* 18 July 1834 ; 4th *s.* of 2nd Earl and *d.* of 2nd Lord Sherborne ; *S.* brother 1921 ; *m.* 1862, Emily Eleanor Kent (*d.* 1921) ; two *s.* seven *d. Educ.*: Rugby ; Magdalen Coll., Oxford ; R.A.C. Cirencester. Went to Australia, 1855 ; M.L.A. Burnet, 1870 ; Maryborough, 1878 ; Burnet, 1883 ; late M.L.C. ; P.M.G., 1885 ; Colonial Secretary and Minister of Public Instruction, Queensland, 1886-8. Owns about 14,000 acres. *Heir: s.* Lord Moreton. *Address:*

Tortworth Court, Falfield, Gloucestershire.
(Died 7 Aug. 1924.)

DUCKWORTH, Sir Dyce, 1st Bart., *cr.* 1909; Kt., *cr.* 1886; Consulting Physician St. Bartholomew's Hospital; Consulting Physician Seamen's Hospital Greenwich; Medical Referee to Treasury, 1904-10; Member of Court, University of Liverpool; *b.* Liverpool, 24 Nov. 1840; *y. s.* of Robinson Duckworth and Elizabeth Forbes, *d.* of William Nicol, M.D., Stonehaven, N.B.; *m.* 1st, 1870, Annie Alicia (*d.* 1886), *relict* of John Smith, of Mickleham Hall, Dorking; 2nd, Ada, *y. d.* of G. Arthur Fuller, of the Rookery, Dorking, 1890; three *s. Educ.:* Royal Institution School, Liverpool; Edinburgh University; St. Bartholomew's Hospital. M.D. Edin. 1868 (gold medallist); F.R.C.P. Lond. 1870; Hon. M.D. Cincinnati, 1879; Hon. M.D. Roy. Univ. Ireland, 1887; M.D. Member Convocation, Queen's University, Belfast; Hon. F.R.C.P. Ireland, 1887; Hon. LL.D. Edin. 1890; Knight of Justice, Order of St. John of Jerusalem. Assistant Surgeon, R.N., 1864 - 65; Senior Censor, 1903-4; Representative of Roy. Coll. Phys. in Gen. Med. Council, 1886-91; late President Clinical Soc.; late Hon. Physician to King Edward VII. when Prince of Wales; Mem. Correspondt. Acad. de Méd., Paris. *Publications:* Views on some Social Subjects, 1915; numerous contributions to medical literature, addresses, etc. *Heir: s.* Edward Dyce. *Address:* 28 Grosvenor Place, S.W.1. *T.,* Gerrard 4745. *(Died 20 Jan. 1928.)*

DUCKWORTH, Rev. William Arthur, M.A.; J.P. Somerset; *b.* 17 March 1829; *e. surv. s.* of William Duckworth of Orchardleigh Park, Frome, and Hester Emily, *d.* of Robert Philips of the Park, Manchester; *m.* 1859, Hon. Edina, *y. d.* of John, Lord Campbell, then Lord Chancellor; two *s.* four *d. Educ.:* Eton, 1842-46; Trin. Coll. Camb, 1849-52. Ordained, 1854; Curate of Ashbourne, Derbyshire. 1854-59; Rector of Puttenham, Surrey, 1859-77; lord of the manors of Frome, Orchardleigh, Lullington, and Buckland Dinham in Somerset; President of the Victoria Hospital, Frome, 1903. *Address:* Orchardleigh Park, Frome. *Clubs:* United University, Athenæum. *M.:* LC 6653, Y 1624.
(Died 6 Dec. 1917.)

DU CROS, William Harvey, M.P. (C.) Hastings, 1906-8; *b.* 19 June 1846; *s.* of Edouard Pierre du Cros (the family being of noble Huguenot descent, driven from Montpelier in the Hérault and settled in Dublin, 1702), of the Rectory Moone, Co. Kildare, and Maria, *d.* of late John Molloy of Dublin; *m.* 1st, 1866, Annie (*d.* 1899), *d.* of late John Roy of Durrow, Queen's Co.; 2nd, Florence, *d.* of William Gibbings of Walston, Bow, N. Devon. *Educ.:* The King's Hospital, Dublin. J.P. Sussex; Chevalier of the Legion d'Honneur; Knight of the Order of Isabella la Católica; founded the pneumatic tyre industry, and now largely interested in the development of the automobile industry. *Recreations:* has been a noted athlete in Irish amateur circles; now an ardent motorist. *Address:* Howbery Park, Wallingford, Berks; Inniscorrig, Dalkey, Co Dublin; Wildcroft, Putney Heath, S.W. *T.:* Putney 1753. *Clubs:* Carlton, St. Stephen's, Royal Automobile.
(Died 21 Dec. 1918.)

DUDDELL, W., F.R.S., Consulting Engineer; Past President of the Rontgen Society and of the Institution of Electrical Engineers, and Hon. Treasurer of the Physical Society; *b.* London, 1872; unmarried. *Educ.:* private school; College Stanislaus, Cannes. Served apprenticeship with Davey, Paxman & Company, Colchester, 1890-93; attended courses in engineering and physics, and carried out research work at Central Technical College, London, 1893-1900; obtained a Whitworth Exhibition 1896, and Whitworth

Scholarship 1897; read, in conjunction with Dr. E. W. Marchant, a paper on Experiments on Alternate Current Arcs by Aid of Oscillographs before the Institution of Electrical Engineers, 1898; read a paper on Rapid Variations of Current through the Direct Current Arc, 1900; also read papers on Resistance and E.M.F.'s of the Electric Arc, before Royal Society, 1901; and on Oscillographs, British Association meeting, 1897; in conjunction with Dr. Marchant, contributed to The Electrician an article entitled Experiments on Periodic Variations Occurring in the Exciting Current of an Inductor Alternator, 1901; received a gold medal for oscillographs at Paris Exhibition of 1900; and at St. Louis, 1904; was hon. sec. to delegates to International Electrical Congress at St. Louis, U.S.A., 1904, and to the International Conference on Electrical Units and Standards, 1908; received the Hughes medal of the Royal Society, 1912. Member of Admiralty Board of Invention and Research, and the Advisory Council for Industrial Research. *Address:* 56 Victoria Street, S.W. *T.:* Victoria 5753. *(Died 4 Nov. 1917.)*

DUDDING, Rear - Admiral Horatio Nelson; retired; *b.* 1849; *s.* of late Rev. H. N. Dudding, Vicar of St. Peter's, St. Albans; *m.* 1882, Florence Louisa, 3rd *d.* of Jas. J. Gape, of St. Michael's Manor, St. Albans, J.P.; two *s.* one *d. Educ.:* H.M.S. Britannia. With Eastern Soudan Field Force, 1891; 3rd Class Mejidie; Egyptian medal, 1892; Capt. 1893-1902; retired, 1905. *Address:* Ashley Mead, St. Albans. *T.A.:* London, Colney.

(Died 1917.)

DUDGEON, Sir Charles John, Kt., *cr.* 1903; *b.* 3 Sep. 1855; *s.* of late Patrick Dudgeon of Cargen, Dumfries; *m.* 1884, Isabelle Annie, *d.* of late Maj.-Gen. W. C. O'Shaughnessy; one *d. Educ.:* Repton; College Hall, St. Andrews University. Assistant British Commissioner for Revision of Commercial Treaties with China, 1901-12; President, The China Association, 1911. *Recreations:* fishing, shooting, golf. *Clubs:* Conservative, Thatched House, Bath. *(Died 23 Jan. 1928.)*

DUFF, General Sir Beauchamp, G.C.S.I., *cr.* 1916; G.C.B., *cr.* 1911; K.C.B., *cr.* 1907; K.C.V.O., *cr.* 1906; K.C.S.I., *cr.* 1910; C.B. 1901; C.I.E. 1897; A.D.C. General to the King; 1914; Commander-in-Chief, India, 1913-16; *b.* 17 Feb. 1855; 2nd *s.* of late Garden William Duff of Hatton Castle, Aberdeenshire, and Douglas Maria, *d.* of late Beauchamp Urquhart of Meldrum; *m.* Grace, *d.* of late Oswald Wood, 1877; one *s. Educ.:* Trinity College, Glenalmond; Royal Military Academy, Woolwich. Commissioned as Lieut. R.A., 1874; Afghan War, 1878-80; transferred to Indian Staff Corps, 1881; Capt., 1886; passed through Staff College, 1888-89; D.A.A.G. Indian Army Headquarters, 1891-95; Brigade Major Isazai Expedition, 1892; Major, 1894; D.A.A.G. Waziristan Expedition, 1894-95 (despatches twice, brevet of Lieut.-Col.); Military Secretary to Commander-in-Chief in India, 1895-99; Substantive Col., 1898; Assistant Military Secretary War Office (for Indian affairs), 1899; South Africa, 1899-1901 (despatches twice, medal with five clasps, C.B.); D.A.G. Indian Army Headquarters, 1901-2; Brig.-Gen. commanding Allahabad District; Maj.-Gen. 1903; Adjutant-General in India, 1903-1906; Sec. Military Department India Office, 1910; Chief of the Staff in India, 1906-9. *Recreations:* shooting, fishing. *Address:* c/o Railway Mail Service, India. *Clubs:* United Service, Caledonian.

(Died 20 Jan. 1918.)

DUFF, Lieut.-Col. Benjamin Michael, I.S.O. 1903; V.D.; *b.* 1840; *s.* of late Captain Benjamin Duff, Edinburgh; *m.* 1865, Jane, *d.* of late Edward Jones, Port Elizabeth. Entered

Civil Service, Cape Colony, 1868; Chief Clerk Postal Department, and Superintendent of Telegraphs, 1886; Secretary, Posts and Telegraphs, 1892; acted General Manager of Telegraphs, and Postmaster-General for various periods from 1888 to 1904; served as lieutenant, "Cape Field Artillery," in Transkei campaign, 1880-81, S.A. (medal and clasp); Lieut.-Colonel commanding Cape Town Highlanders, 1895, and Boer War, 1899-1900 (medal and clasp); is a M.I.E.E. and a J.P. for the Colony. *Address:* Green Point, near Cape Town, Cape of Good Hope.
(Died 15 Nov. 1926.)

DUFF, Edward Gordon, M.A. Oxon; librarian of the John Rylands Library, Manchester, 1893-1900; *b.* 16 Feb. 1863; *y. s.* of late Robert Duff. *Educ.:* Cheltenham College; Wadham College, Oxford. Sandars Reader in Bibliography in the Univ. of Cambridge,1898-99, 1903-4, 1910-11; President of the Edinburgh Bibliographical Society, 1899-1900. *Publications:* Early Printed Books, 1893; Early English Printing, 1896; The Printers, Stationers, and Bookbinders of London, 1899; William Caxton, 1903; A Century of the English Book Trade, 1905; Editor of The Dialogue of Salamon and Marcolphus, 1892; Information for Pilgrims, 1893; writer of many reviews and articles in literary and sporting periodicals. *Recreations:* fishing, swimming, tattooing, book-collecting. *Address:* 293 Woodstock Road, Oxford.
(Died 28 Sept. 1924.)

DUFF, Hon. James Stoddart, Minister of Agriculture since 1908; *b.* 20 June 1856; *m.* Jane Bell, *d.* of late John E. Stoddart. M.P. West Simcoe since 1898. *Address:* Cookstown, Ontario, Canada. *(Died 19 Nov. 1916.)*

DUFF, John, I.S.O. 1912; H.B.M. Consul for the West and South coasts of Sweden, 1881-1919; *b.* 18 Jan. 1850; 2nd *s.* of Fredrik William Duff, late H.B.M. Consul at Gothenburg; unmarried. *Educ.:* Gothenburg. After five years commercial studies, entered the Consular Service as Secretary to H.B.M. Consul at Gothenburg, 1874; Vice-Consul, 1880; Coronation Medal, 1911. *Recreations:* shooting, rowing and sailing. *Address:* 16 Nordhemsgatan, Gothenburg. *T.A.:* Duff, Gothenburg. *T.:* 722. *(Died 14 Feb. 1921.)*

DUFF, Thomas Duff Gordon, C.B.E., J.P., D.L., Vice-Lieut. Banffshire; *b.* 1848; *s.* of late Major Lachlan G. Duff and Jane Ellen. *d.* of late Thomas Butterfield, Chief Justice of Bermuda; *m.* 1st, Pauline (*d.* 1880), *d.* of late Sir Charles Tennant of The Glen; 2nd, Mildred, *d.* of late E. C. Walker, Chester; three *s.* four *d. Educ.:* Harrow; Trinity College, Oxford. For 20 years member of County Council and other local bodies; during the war Chairman of County Territorial Force Association and Agricultural Executive Committee. *Address:* Drummuir, Keith, Scotland. *Club:* Royal Automobile. *(Died 27 Mar. 1923.)*

DUFFERIN and AVA, 2nd Marquess of, **Terence Temple-Blackwood,** *cr.* 1888; Baron Clandeboye, 1800; Earl of Dufferin; Viscount Clandeboye, 1871; Earl of Ava, 1888, and a Bt.; formerly 2nd Secy. H.M. Diplomatic Service; *b.* 16 March 1866; 2nd *s.* of 1st Marquess of Dufferin and Ava, and Hariot (see Marchioness of Dufferin); *S.* father 1902; *m.* Florence, *d.* of John H. Davis of New York, 1893; three *d. Educ.:* Harrow. Entered Diplomatic Service 1891; served at Constantinople, Paris, and Stockholm; in Foreign Office since 1896; D.L., J.P., Co. Down. *Heir: b.* Lord Basil Blackwood. *Address:* North House, Putney Hill, S.W. *T.:* 223, Putney. *Club:* Travellers'. *(Died 6 Feb. 1918.)*

DUFFIELD, William Bartleet; *s.* of W. W. Duffield, Browning's, Chelmsford. *Educ.:* Harrow; abroad; Trinity Hall, Cambridge. Scholar; M.A. 1890; 1st Class Historical Tripos. Barr. Inner Temple, 1887; has acted as Examiner

at various times for Woolwich, Sandhurst, the Diplomatic and Civil Services, etc.; Secretary to Royal Commission on Canals and Waterways, 1906-10. *Publications:* has contributed to most of the leading reviews (Edinburgh, Nineteenth Century, Fortnightly Saturday Review, Spectator, etc.) many articles, principally on history, foreign affairs, and current politics; contributor to the Encyclopedia Britannica, 11th edition, and the Dictionary of Nat. Biography. *Recreation:* travel. *Address:* 4 Whitehall Court, S.W. *Clubs:* Athenæum, Reform. *(Died 5 June 1918.)*

DUGAS, Hon. Mr. Justice Calixter Aimé, a Judge of the Supreme Court of the Yukon Territory; *b.* 1845. *Educ.:* St. Sulpice College, Montreal. Judge of Sessions, Montreal, 1878-98. *Address:* Dawson City, Yukon Territory, Canada. *(Died 24 June 1918.)*

DUGDALE, Colonel Frank, C.V.O., T.D., D.L., J.P. Warwickshire; Equerry-in-Waiting to the Queen; Extra Equerry to the King; *b.* 5 Apr. 1857; 2nd *s.* of late James Dugdale, Wroxall Abbey, Warwickshire; *m.* 1895, Lady Eva Sarah Louisa Greville (Woman of the Bedchamber to the Queen), *o. d.* of 4th Earl of Warwick; two *s.* one *d. Educ.:* Harrow; Brasenose College, Oxon. Commanded Warwickshire Yeomanry, 1911-16; Hon. Colonel since 1924. Has received the Order of the Redeemer of Greece, and Order of St. Anne of Russia; Territorial Decoration, 1909. *Address:* Royal Lodge, Windsor Great Park. *T.:* Egham 76. *Clubs:* Turf, Marlborough.
(Died 26 Nov. 1925.)

DUGDALE, James Broughton, J.P., D.L.; *b.* 19 Sep. 1855; *e. s.* of late James Dugdale, of Wroxall, and Mary Louisa, *d.* of John Plummer; *m.* 1878, Laura Jane, *e. d.* of J. T. Arkwright, of Hatton House, Co. Warwick. *Educ.:* Harrow; Trinity College, Oxford. Captain and Hon. Major late Warwickshire Yeomanry Cavalry; Alderman Warwickshire County Council; High Sheriff Warwickshire, 1907. *Address:* Wroxall Abbey, Warwick. *T.:* Haseley Knob 20. *Clubs:* Carlton, Cavalry.
(Died 15 Jan. 1927.)

DUGDALE, John Stratford, K.C. 1882; Recorder of Birmingham since 1877, and Chancellor since 1905; Chancellor of Diocese of Worcester; Chancellor of Diocese of Coventry; Chairman of Warwickshire Quarter Sessions since 1888; Chairman of Warwickshire County Council from its commencement till 1919; *b.* 30 July 1835; 2nd *s.* of W. S. Dugdale of Merevale Hall, Warwicks; *m.* 1890, Alice, *d.* of Gen. Henry Alexander Carlton, C.B., R.A., of Clare, Co. Tipperary; one *d. Educ.:* Eton; Merton Coll. Oxford (M.A.). Barr. Inner Temple, 1862; Recorder of Grantham, 1874; M.P. Nuneaton, 1886-92. *Address:* Avonside, Barford, Warwick; 1 Paper Buildings, Temple, E.C. *Clubs:* Carlton, Oxford and Cambridge.
(Died 27 Oct. 1920.)

DUGMORE, Rev. Ernest Edward; Canon and Prebendary of Salisbury Cathedral since 1890, and Succentor, 1909; Hon. Chaplain to the Bishop, 1917-21; *b.* 1843; 4th *s.* of William Dugmore, Q.C., Bencher of Lincoln's Inn, of Swaffham, Norfolk, and Mary Louisa; *m.* 1883, Lady Elizabeth (*d.* 1902), *d.* of 10th Earl of Kinnoull, and widow of Colonel Sir Frederick Arthur, Bart. *Educ.:* Bruce Castle School, Tottenham; Wadham College, Oxford. B.A. 1867; M.A. 1869; ordained deacon, 1867; priest, 1870; assistant-curate, St. Peter's, Vauxhall, 1867-71; Vicar of Parkstone, 1872-1910. *Publications:* Sunday Readings on the Collects; From the Mountains of the East, a dramatic poem, 1882; Gospel Idylls and other Sacred Verses, 1884; Some Principles of the Holy Catholic Church, 1898; Hymns of Adoration, 1900; The Church's Prayer Meeting, 1912. *Recreation:* reading. *Address:* 9 The Close, Salisbury. *(Died 10 Mar. 1925.)*

DUGAS, Hon. Francois Octave, K.C. See page xix.

DUGMORE, Lt.-Col. William Francis Brougham Radclyffe, D.S.O. 1899; 2nd in command 72nd Highlanders (Canada); late Capt. North Stafford Regt.; *b.* 1 Oct. 1868; *e. s.* of late Capt. Francis Dugmore, 64th Regt., and Hon. Evelyn Mary, *d.* of 2nd Baron Brougham and Vaux; *m.* 1910, Phyllis, *d.* of J. Wilson Usher. *Educ.*: The Oratory, Edgbaston; St. Mary's Coll., Oscott. Entered Prince of Wales's (North Staffs.) Regt. 1894; served East Africa Arab War, Mzrui Expedition, 1895-96 (medal); Unyoro, 1896-97 (medal); Uganda Mutiny, 1897-1898 (medal with 2 clasps, despatches, D.S.O.); South Africa, 1901 - 2, with Mounted Infantry and Colonial Forces (medal with 5 clasps); Somaliland, 1902-3-4 (medal with clasp); retired 1909; served European War, 1914-15 (despatches). *Recreation:* sport. *Address:* Willhayne, Colyton, Devon. *Club:* East India United Service.   (*Died 12 June 1917.*)

DUGUID, Charles; writer on finance and cognate subjects; Founder and Managing Director of General Publicity Agency, Ltd.; *b.* London, 22 Feb. 1864; *m.* 1888, Laura, *e. d.* of N. Nixon of Brampton, Cumberland; three *s.* three *d. Educ.:* Gordon's Coll. Aberdeen. Asst. editor Economist, 1890-1892; previously on editorial staff of the Stock Exchange and the Mining Journal; city editor Pall Mall Gazette, 1893-97; Westminster Gazette, 1897-1902; Morning Post, 1902-6; World, 1901-9; Observer, 1906-11; Financial Editor of the Daily Mail, Evening News, and associated newspapers, London, Provincial, and Continental, 1906-20; consulting editor of the financial section of The Times, 1911-20; Director of Associated Newspapers, Ltd., 1912-20; organised the Daily Mail Exchange in 1912; signal officer to Hertfordshire Volunteer Regt. 1916-20; presented with sword by City of London National Guard; advisory officer, volunteer signals, Eastern Command, 1918-20; retains rank Hon. Captain. *Publications:* History of the Stock Exchange, 1900; How to Read the Money Article; The Feeding of Finance; The Story of the Stock Exchange, 1901; The Stock Exchange and its Machinery (Lectures), 1902; The Stock Exchange (Books on Business), 1904; Money, Stocks, and Insurance, 1911; The Money Article (Bankers' Institute Lectures), 1914. *Recreation:* golf. *Address:* Park Lodge, New Barnet, Herts. *T.:* Barnet 84.
               (*Died 13 Dec. 1923.*)

DUHM, Bernhard Laward, Doctor der Theologie; ordentl. Professor der Theol. für die alttestamentl. Wissenschaft an der Universität; Lehrer der hebräischen Sprache am Gymnasium zu Basel; *b.* Bingum in Ostfriesland, Provinz Hannover, 10 Oct. 1847; *s.* of Johannes Duhm und Friederike Knopf; *m.* 1877, Helene Bunjes (*d.* 1884), drei Söhne, sämtlich Theologen. *Educ.:* Bingum (Dorfschule); Aurich (Gymnasium); Göttingen. (Universität, 1867 - 70). Candidat der Theologie, 1870; Repetent am theolog. Stift zu Göttingen, 1871-72; lic. der Theolog., 1873; Privatdocent für das alte Testament zu Göttingen, 1873-77; ausserordentl. Professor der Theologie zu Göttingen, 1877-89; als ordentlicher Prof. der Theol. nach Basel berufen, 1889. *Publications:* Pauli apostoli de lege judicia dijudicata, 1873; Theologie der Propheten, 1875; Ueber Ziel und Methode der theol. Wissenschaft, 1889-1921; Kosmologie und Religion, 1892; Erklärung des Buches Iesaia, 1892-1902 - 1913 - 1922; Erklärung des Buches Hiob, 1897; Das Geheimnis in der Religion, 1896; Die Entstehung des alten Testaments, 1897-1906; Uebersetzung des Buches Hiob, 1897; Erklärung der Psalmen, 1899-1922; Uebersetzung der Psalmen, 1899; Erklärung des Buches Jeremia, 1901; Uebersetzung des B. Jeremia, 1903; Die Gottgeweihten in Israel, 1905; Buch Habakuk, Text, Übersetzung, Erklärung, 1906; Das kommende Reich Gottes, 1909 (englisch

durch Prof. A. Duff, 1911); Die zwölf Propheten, 1910 (englisch durch Prof. Duff, 1912); Anmerkungen zu den zwölf Propheten, 1911; Israels Propheten, 1916; 2 Aufl. 1922. *Address:* Basel, Johannrheinweg, 101. (*Died Sept. 1928.*)

DUKE, Sir [Frederick] William, G.C.I.E., *cr.* 1918; K.C.S.I., *cr.* 1915; K.C.I.E, *cr.* 1911; C.S.I. 1910; Permanent Under Secretary of State for India since 1919; *b.* 8 Dec. 1863; *s.* of Rev. William Duke, D.D.; *m.* 1889, Mary Eliza, *d.* of James Addison-Scott, of Wooden, Roxburghshire; two *s.* one *d. Educ.:* Arbroath High School; University College, London. Entered I.C.S. 1882; Magistrate and Collector, 1900; Commissioner of Orissa, 1905-8; Chief Secretary to Government of Bengal, 1908; Member Executive Council, Bengal, 1910; last Lieutenant-Governor of Bengal, 1911; Member and Vice-President of the Council of the Presidency of Fort William from its creation, 1912 to 1914; Member of Council of India, 1914-19. *Address:* Peel Street Cottage, Campden Hill Road, W.S. *T.:* Park 3127. *Clubs:* Athenæum, East India United Service. (*Died 11 June 1924.*)

DUKE, James Buchanan, late President American Tobacco Co., Continental Tobacco Co., and Consolidated Tobacco Co.; Chairman of Directors British-American Tobacco Co., Ltd.; Director American Cigar Co., etc; *b.* nr. Durham, N.C., 1857: *m.* 2nd, 1907, Nannie Lee Inman, Atlanta, Ga. *Address:* Somerville, New Jersey. (*Died 10 Oct. 1925.*)

DULEEP SINGH, Prince Frederick, M.V.O. 1901; T.F.; F.S.A.; *b.* London, 23 Jan. 1868; 2nd and *o. surv. s.* of late Maharajah Duleep Singh of Lahore, G.C.S.I. *Educ.:* Eton; Magdalene College, Cambridge. M.A. (History Tripos) 1890; Lieut. Suffolk Yeomanry, 1893; Captain, 1898; Major, Norfolk Yeomanry, 1901; resigned, 1909; Gazetted to 2/1 Norfolk Yeomanry, Oct. 1914; served in France, 1917-19. *Publications:* Articles in the Proceedings of Norfolk Archæological Society; Suffolk Institution of Archæology; Connoisseur; Burlington Magazine, etc. *Recreations:* archæology, music, gardening, and shooting. *Address:* Blo'Norton Hall, Diss, Norfolk. *Clubs:* White's, Carlton. (*Died 15 Aug. 1926.*)

DULEEP SINGH, Prince Victor Albert Jay; *b.* London, 10 July 1866; *e. s.* of late Maharajah Duleep Singh, Lahore, G.C.S.I., etc., and Bamba, *d.* of L. Müller, Alexandria, Egypt; *m.* 1898, Lady Anne, *y. d.* of 9th Earl of Coventry. *Educ.:* Eton; Trinity and Downing Colleges, Cambridge. Gazetted 1st Royal Dragoons, Feb. 1888; Hon. A.D.C. to Lieut.-Gen. Ross, K.C.B., General commanding at Halifax, Nova Scotia, 1888-90. Captain Royal Dragoons, 1894-8. *Recreations:* shooting, music. *Address:* 40 Avenue du Trocadéro, Paris. *Club:* Carlton.
               (*Died 7 June 1918.*)

DUMARESQ, Rear-Adm. John Saumarez, C.B. 1916; C.V.O. 1920; M.V.O. 1908; Commodore 1st Class, commanding the Australian Fleet since 1919; Naval A.D.C. to the King since 1920; *s.* of late William Alexander Dumaresq, M.A., Ferruckabad, Glen Innes, N.S.W., and Edith Helen, *d.* of late Capt. John Neilson Gladstone, R.N., M.P.; *b.* 1873; *m.* 1907, Christian Elizabeth Louisa, *d.* late Rt. Hon. Sir Charles Dalrymple, 1st Bart.; two *s.* two *d.* Entered Navy, 1886; Lieut. 1894; Commander, 1904; Captain, 1910; Rear-Adm., 1921; served European War, 1914-18 (C.B.). *Address:* Monckton Croft, Alverstoke, Hants. *T.A.:* Alverstoke, Hants. *T.:* 55 Alverstoke. *Club:* United Service.
               (*Died 22 July 1922.*)

DUMBLETON, General Charles, Bengal Cavalry; *b.* 13 May 1824; *m.* 1856, Elizabeth Frances J. (*d.* 1910), *e. d.* of Sir Thomas Reed, K.C.B. Entered army, 1840; General, 1890; retired list, 1884; served Gwalior Campaign,

1848 (bronze star); Indian Mutiny, 1857 (medal). *Address:* Wyke Lodge, Winchester.

(*Died 15 Mar. 1916.*)

DUN, William Gibb, M.D., F.R.F.P.S. Glasgow; ex - President, Royal Faculty of Physicians and Surgeons of Glasgow; ex-President, Glasg. Royal Medico - Chirurgical Society; Hon. Physician, Royal Scottish Society for Prevention of Cruelty to Children; Physician Glasgow City Mission; *s.* of Thomas Dun, banker; *m.* Margaret Gibb; one *s.* three *d. Educ.:* Glasgow High School and University; Vienna University. Assistant Physician, Western Infirmary; Resident Physician, Royal and Western Infirmaries; Medical Tutor, Glasgow University. *Publications:* Blood Letting in Treatment of Disease, and other papers in Medical Press. *Address:* 15 Royal Crescent, Glasgow, C.3. *T.:* Douglas 4343.

DUNALLEY, 4th Baron (*cr.* 1800), **Henry O'Callaghan Prittie,** D.L., J.P.; Representative Peer for Ireland since 1891; Lieut. Co. Tipperary; *b.* 21 Mar. 1851; *s.* of 3rd Baron and Anne, *o. d.* of 1st Viscount Lismore; *S.* father, 1885; *m.* Mary Frances, M. B.E., *o.d.* of Maj.-Gen. Onslow Farmer, R.A., Aspley Guise, Bedfordshire, 1876; one *s. Educ.:* Harrow; Trin. Coll., Camb. (B.A.). Late Lieut. Rifle Brigade. *Heir: s.* Hon. Henry Cornelius O'Callagan Prittie. *Address:* Kilboy, Nenagh, Co. Tipperary. (*Died 5 Aug. 1927.*)

DUNBAR, (Rev.) Sir Charles Gordon-Cumming, 8th Bt., Scot. *cr.* 1700; *b.* 14 Feb. 1844; *s.* of 6th Bt., and his 2nd wife, Sophia, *d.* of Geo. Orred, of Tranmere Hall, Cheshire; *S.* half-brother, 7th Bt., 1910; *m.* 1872, Edith (*d.* 1891), *d.* of W. C. Wentworth, Pres. Legislative Council, Sydney, N.S.W.; one *d. Educ.:* Winchester; abroad. Deacon, 1867; Chaplain to Bishop of Colombo, 1867-71; Priest, 1868; Chaplain to H.M. Forces, Ceylon, 1868-72 (on leave of absence to Europe, 1869-72); appointed Senior Chaplain, 1871; Curate, All Saints', Lambeth, 1869-71; Chaplain to Bishop Claughton, London, 1871-75; D.D. Jena, 1873; accepted Vicarage, Nether Exe, Exeter, 1875; released from Nether Exe to accept Archdeaconry and First Bishop of Pretoria, 1875; released from that acceptance to take Archdeaconry, Rural Deanery, and Rectorship of St. John's and of St. Mark's, Grenada, 1875; offered the Episcopate for 2nd time, 1876, but declined; Archdeacon of Grenada, W.I., 1875-77; incumbent of St. James's, Little Heath, Essex, 1887-90; took charge Parish Church, Walthamstow, 1890-92. *Heir-pres.: c.* Archibald Edward Dunbar, *b.* 1889. *Recreations:* speaking in public, antiquarian subjects, science, music, art, horticulture, and forestry. *Address:* Elmina, Albion Road, East Cliff, Ramsgate. *Club:* Royal Societies.

(*Died 8 Jan. 1916.*)

DUNBAR, Lieut. - Comdr. Kenneth James Duff-, R.N., D.S.O. 1916; commanding one of H.M. Submarines; *b.* 16 Oct. 1886; *s.* of late Garden Duff-Dunbar of Hempriggs, and Jane Louisa Duff-Dunbar; *b.* of Sir George D. S. Dunbar, 6th Bt. of Hempriggs; *m.* 1914, Katharine Isabel, *d.* of late William Adams Daw. *Educ.:* Stubbington House, Fareham. Joined H.M.S. Britannia as naval cadet; Midshipman H.M.S. Good Hope, 1902: Sub-Lieut., 1905; Lieut., 1907; joined submarine service, 1907; appointed in command of submarine, Nov. 1909; appointed H.M.S. Princess Royal, 1912; rejoined submarine service for command, April 1915; served European War, 1914-16 (D.S.O.). *Address:* Ackergill Tower, Wick, Caithness, N.B. *Clubs:* United Service; Royal Naval, Portsmouth. (*Died Aug. 1916.*)

DUNBAR, Robert Haig; Editor of Derbyshire Printing Company's papers, 1910-15; *b.* Galashiels, N.B.; 2nd and *e. surv. s.* of late

Adam Dunbar, J.P., Provost of Huntly, N.B.; *m.* Maria, *y. d.* of late William Atkinson, retired manufacturer, Sheffield; three *s. Educ.:* Gala School, Galashiels; privately. Edited Huntly Express (his father's paper) for several years up to 1869, when left north to edit the Sheffield Evening Star (now Yorkshire Telegraph and Star), which he combined with the editorship of the Sheffield Times; joined the staff of Sheffield Daily Telegraph as Chief of Reporting Staff and occasional leader and descriptive writer, 1875; Assistant Editor and Acting Editor; Editor of Sheffield Daily Telegraph, 1902 - 1906; original Member Institute of Journalists (Fellow, 1898), and of Original Society the National Association of Journalists; Member of the Sheffield Chamber of Commerce; Hon. Life Member of the Caledonian Society of Sheffield. *Publications:* several small pamphlets descriptive of enterprises engaged in and travels, the latest of which was Notes in Norway. *Recreations:* golf; cricket (spectator only now); travel, more especially on the moors and hills of Derbyshire. *Address:* Aldersyde, 27 Crescent Road, Sharrow, Sheffield. *Club:* Athenæum, Sheffield. (*Died 10 Sept. 1919.*)

DUNCAN, Alexander Robert, J.P.; *s.* of John Duncan (*d.* 1905), and Catherine, *d.* of late Robert F. Gourlay; *b.* 1844; *m.* 1873, Frances Euphemia (*d.* 1921), *d.* of Sir William Edmonstone, 4th Bart.; three *s.* two *d. Educ.:* Cheltenham; Trinity College, Cambridge; admitted a Member of the Scottish Faculty of Advocates, 1869. *Address:* Parkhill, Arbroath Forfarshire. (*Died 13 April 1927.*)

DUNCAN, Sir David, Kt., *cr.* 1919; J.P.; County of Glamorgan and City of Cardiff; *s.* of late David Duncan of Penarth, J.P.; *m.* Elizabeth Beverley, *d.* of late Christopher Marshall, Gosport; one *s. Address:* Bronyglyn, Penarth, Glamorganshire. *Clubs:* Reform, National Liberal. (*Died 23 Oct. 1923.*)

DUNCAN, David, M.A., D.Sc., LL.D.; *b.* 5 Nov. 1839; *s.* of David Duncan, Aberdeen; *m.* Janet, *d.* of Rev. Joseph Morison, Millseat, Aberdeenshire; two *s.* one *d. Educ.:* Grammar School, Aberdeen; Universities of Edinburgh, Aberdeen, and Berlin. Private secretary to Mr. Herbert Spencer, 1867-70; entered Madras Educational Service, 1870, as Professor of Logic and Moral Philosophy in the Presidency College; Registrar of the Madras University, 1875-79 and 1881-86; Fellow of the University, 1877; Principal and Professor, Presidency College, 1884; Member of the University Syndicate; Director of Public Instruction and Commissioner for Government Examinations, 1892; Member of the Legislative Council, 1894; Vice - Chancellor of the University, 1899; retired from the service, 1899. *Publications:* Compiled, under the direction of Mr. Herbert Spencer, the four volumes of Descriptive Sociology dealing with uncivilized races; author of The Life and Letters of Herbert Spencer; one of the trustees of the Herbert Spencer Trust. *Recreations:* tennis, golf, cycling. *Address:* 14 Rubislaw Den North, Aberdeen. *Club:* Athenæum.

(*Died 18 May 1923.*)

DUNCAN, Edmondstoune; Composer and Writer on Musical Subjects; *b.* Sale, Cheshire, 22 Apr. 1866. *Chief Compositions:* 50 English Songs in Prose and Verse, 1918-20; Perseus (opera); Tone-poem (op. 108) for Orchestra; Declamatory Songs (op. 115); Editor of 100 Folk-dances of all Countries; Minstrelsy of England, 2 vols.; Traditional Nursery Rhymes; Art of Piano-playing. *Literary Works:* Modern Interpreters; Life of Schubert; Story of the Carol; History of Music; History of the Dance; English Lyrical Poems; Professor of Musical Composition in the Leeds College of Music, 1918. Correspondent of the Musical Standard, Musical Times, Musical Record, Musical Opinion, the Musician (Boston,

U.S.A.), and the New Music Review (NewYork, U.S.A.). *Recreations*: swimming, chess; cycling. *Address*: Alexandra Road, Sale, nr. Manchester.
(*Died 28 June 1920.*)

DUNCAN, Sir James, Kt., *cr.* 1922; Managing Director of Steel Bros. and Co. Ltd., East India Merchants; Chairman Royal Insurance Co., Ltd., London Board; Deputy Chairman British and Foreign Marine Insurance Co. Ltd., London Board *Address*: Steel Bros. & Co. Ltd., 6 Fenchurch Avenue, E.C.3.
(*Died 4 May 1926.*)

DUNCAN, Sir (James) Hastings, Kt., *cr.* 1914; M.P. (R.) West Riding, Otley Division of Yorkshire, 1900-1918; member William Ackroyd & Co., Otley, worsted spinners; *b.* March 1855; *m.* 1879, Janette, *d.* of Thomas Hunter, Newall Close; one *s.* one *d. Educ.*: privately. *Address*: Kineholm, Otley, Yorks. *Club*: National Liberal. (*Died 31 July 1928.*)

DUNCAN, John Murray, I.S.O. 1902; was Receiver-General of the Land Revenues of the Crown, now retired; *e. surv. s.* of Robert Duncan of Newton Stewart, Wigtownshire; *m.* Janet, *y. d.* of Daniel Kemp of Edinburgh. *Educ.*: Douglas Academy; Edinburgh University. Entered the Civil Service (Woods and Forests Department), 1874; has been called to the Bar at Lincoln's Inn, but does not practise. *Address*: Usborne House, Wallington, Surrey. (*Died 20 Aug. 1922.*)

DUNCAN, Leland Lewis, M.V.O. 1902; O.B.E. 1918; F.S.A.; *b.* 24 Aug. 1862; *s.* of late Leland Crosthwait Duncan of H.M. Customs, and Caroline Ellen, *d.* of late Frederick Lewis of the Paymaster-General's Office. *Educ.*: Lewisham Grammar School (Colfe's). Entered War Office, 1882; retired 1922; is a member of the Kent Archæological Society. *Publications*: Histories of the Borough of Lewisham, of St. Mary's Parish Church, and of Colfe's Grammar School, Lewisham; The Churches of West Kent, their Altars, Images, and Lights; and various contributions to Archæologia Cantiana and St. Paul's Ecclesiological Society, Folk Lore Society, etc. *Recreation*: medieval history, ecclesiology, and custom. *Address*: Rosslair, Lingards Road, Lewisham.
(*Died 26 Dec. 1923.*)

DUNCAN, Norman; author; Adjunct Professor of English Literature, the University of Kansas, 1907-9; *b.* Brantford, Ont., 1871. *Educ.*: Toronto University; Litt.D. Univ. Pittsburg, 1913. Staff of New York Evening Post, 1896-1901; Professor of Rhetoric, Washington and Jefferson Coll., 1902-6; for McClure's Magazine, Newfoundland and Labrador; for Harper's Magazine, Syria, Palestine, and Arabian Desert; for Harper's Magazine, Australia, Papua, and Dutch East Indies. *Publications*: The Way of the Sea; Dr. Luke; The Mother; Dr. Grenfell's Parish; The Soul of the Street; The Adventures of Billy Topsail; The Cruise of the Shining Light; Every Man for Himself; The Suitable Child; Billy, Topsail, & Company; Going down from Jerusalem; The Measure of a Man; The Best of a Bad Job; A God in Israel; Australian Byways. *Address*: Fredonia, N.Y. *Club*: City, New York.
(*Died 18 Oct. 1916.*)

DUNCAN, Hon. Thomas Young, Minister of Lands and Agriculture and Commissioner of State Forests for New Zealand, 1900-1907; *b.* Eden, Plumbridge, Tyrone, Ireland; married; one *s.* three *d. Educ.*: National School, Castledamph. Left for Victoria in July 1858, in the Eastern City (Captain Johnston), from Liverpool for Melbourne, which caught fire and was burned at sea; a merchantman with troops for India took the passengers off the burning vessel, and put them ashore at Cape of Good Hope; on arrival at Melbourne he went to the Victorian goldfields, and came to 310

New Zealand in 1862, where he put in two years on the Otago goldfields; he engaged in farming pursuits in the Oamaru district, which he has continued ever since; first elected to represent Waitaki, 1881; represented Waitaki for three successive Parliaments, and when the electorates were reduced in 1890, he left Waitaki and was elected for Oamaru; has represented that constituency up to the present time. *Address*: Pukauri, Oamaru, New Zealand.

DUNCOMBE, Alfred Charles; J.P. for Staffordshire and Derbyshire; Member of Staffordshire County Council; *b.* 5 June 1843; *s.* of Very Rev. and Hon. Augustus Duncombe, Dean of York, and Lady Harriet Duncombe; *m.* Lady Florence Montagu, 2nd *d.* of 7th Earl of Sandwich. *Educ.*: Eton. Late Capt. 1st Life Guards and Hon. Major Staffordshire Yeomanry; High Sheriff for Staffords, 1883. *Address*: Calwich Abbey, Ashbourne. *Clubs*: Guards', Arthur's.
(*Died 22 Feb. 1925.*)

DUNCOMBE, Hon. Hubert Ernest Valentine, D.S.O. 1900; Hon. Lieut.-Col. in Army, 1900; *b.* 14 Feb. 1862; *s.* of 1st Earl of Feversham. *Educ.*: Harrow; R.M.A. Woolwich; Magdalene Coll. Camb. M.P. (C.) Egremont Div. Cumberland, 1895-1900; served South Africa, 1900 (despatches). *Address*: Duncombe Park, Helmsley, York; Clairville, S. Norwood. *T.*: 540 Croydon.
(*Died 21 Oct. 1918.*)

DUNCOMBE, Walter Henry Octavius, J.P.; *e. s.* of late Col. Hon. Octavius Duncombe, M.P., and Lady Emily Caroline, *e. d.* of 1st Earl Cawdor; *b.* 1846. Formerly Captain 1st Life Guards; High Sheriff, Cambridge and Hunts, 1899. *Address*: Waresley Park, Sandy, Beds; Westerdale, Yarm, Yorks. *Clubs*: Carlton; Royal Yacht Squadron, Cowes.
(*Died 6 Jan. 1917.*)

DUNCOMBE, Rev. William Duncombe Van der Horst, Prebendary of Hereford since 1916. *Address*: The College, Hereford. (*Died 4 Oct. 1925.*)

DUNDAS OF DUNDAS, Admiral Sir Charles; K.C.M.G., *cr.* 1917; *b.* 9 Aug. 1859; *m.* 1897, Helen, *d.* of E. B. Watson; three *s.* three *d. Educ.*: Clifton Bank, St. Andrews. Joined H.M.S. Audacious, China flagship, as Naval Cadet, 1874; Lieutenant, 1883; Commander, 1896; served in Cape Squadron during Boer War, and took part in Delagoa Bay operations (medal, and promoted Captain); served in command of H.M.S. Forte, 1904-5, on the East African Station, and received approval of Admiralty for his prompt action in reference to Russian auxiliary cruisers; presented with order of Brilliant Star by Sultan of Zanzibar; received thanks of French Government for services rendered on East African Station; commanded H.M.S. Ocean, Channel Fleet, 1905-8; Naval Attaché, Tokio, 1908-10; received 2nd class Order of Rising Sun; A.D.C. to King George V., 1920; Rear-Admiral, 1910; attached to suite of Prince H. Fushimi of Japan at Coronation of King George V.; attached to personal staff of Admiral-Count Togo during his visit to England, July 1911; Rear-Admiral on the staff at Sheerness, 1911; 2nd in command of 7th Battle Squadron at manœuvres of 1912; Vice-Admiral, 1916; Admiral, 1919; Principal Naval Transport Officer, France, 1915-17; Commandeur Legion d'Honneur, 1917; Commander Order of Redeemer of Greece, 1909. Succeeded his father as 28th chief of Dundas, 6 March 1904. *Publication*: An Admiral's Yarns, 1922. *Address*: Inchgarvie House, South Queensferry, Scotland. *Club*: New, Edinburgh.
(*Died 1 July 1924.*)

DUNDAS, David (the Hon. Lord Dundas); one of the Senators of the College of Justice in Scotland (under above judicial title), 1905; D.L. for County of City of

Edinburgh; LL.D. (Edin. Univ. 1909); member University Court of Edinburgh University as assessor to Rt. Hon. A. J. Balfour, M.P., Chancellor of the University; b. Edinburgh, 8 June 1854; y. s. of late George Dundas, one of the Senators of the Coll. of Justice in Scotland, and of late Elizabeth, d. of Colin Mackenzie, Portmore, Peeblesshire; m. 1885, Helen, d. of David B. Wauchope (d. 1897). Educ.: Edinburgh Academy, 1864-71; Balliol College, Oxford, 1872-76 (B.A. Oxon.); Edinburgh University, 1876-78. Scottish Bar, 1878; was an Advocate Depute, 1890-92; Interim Sheriff of Argyllshire, 1896-98; Q.C. 1897; Solicitor-General for Scotland, 1903-1905; contested Linlithgowshire (C.), General Election, 1900. Address: 11 Drumsheugh Gardens, Edinburgh. Clubs: Wellington; New, Edinburgh. (Died 14 Feb. 1922.)

DUNDAS, Colonel Sir Lorenzo George, K.C.B. cr. 1907; C.B. 1896; Late Commanding 6th Battalion the Royal Fusiliers; b. 6 April 1837; e. s. of late I. Dundas, J.P., Clobemon Hall, Wexford; m. Lily, d. of late R. Adams, 6 Kensington Park Gardens, London, 1868; three s. two d. Educ.: Trinity Coll. Dublin. Joined 62nd Regt. Jan. 1855; served with it in the trenches before Sebastopol and formed one of the stormers at the attack on the Redan, 8 Sept.; retired from Army, 1873, and joined the Militia force; commanded the 17th Brigade on Jubilee day, 1887; and 8th Provisional Batt. Belfast, 1901-2; Hon. Colonel 6th Royal Fusiliers 29 May 1905. Decorated for Crimean War (Crimean medal and clasps, Turkish medal); C.B.; Jubilee medal. Recreations: riding, shooting, boating. Address: Gloucester Lodge, East Molesey.

(Died 10 Dec. 1917.)

DUNDAS, William John, LL.D. (Edin.); Writer to the Signet; Crown Agent for Scotland, 1895-1905, and 1916-19; b. 16 March 1849; s. of late George Dundas, a Senator of the College of Justice. Educ.: Edinburgh Academy and University. Address: 11 Drumsheugh Gardens, Edinburgh. Club: New, Edinburgh.

(Died 9 July 1921.)

DUNFEE, Col. Vickers, C.B.E., V.D., J.P.; b. 30 April 1861; m. 1893, Lilla (d. 1922), y. d. of W. N. Froy; four s. Educ.: King's College School and College. Served in City of London Militia; joined Hamlet's Rifle Brigade, 4th V.B. Royal Fusiliers; commanded 2/4th Batt. City of London Regt. (Royal Fusiliers) during European War; served Egypt, Gallipoli, Senussi Campaign, Southern Force and France (despatches twice); Commandant City of London Police Reserve. Recreations: general. Address: 53 St. John's Road, Putney, S.W.15. Club: Royal Automobile. (Died 17 Feb. 1927.)

DUNHAM, E. K., M.D.; Emeritus Prof. of Pathology, the University and Bellevue Hospital Medical College, New York City; b. 1 Sept. 1860; s. of Carroll and Harriet E. Kellogg, Dunham; m. 1903, Mary Dows; one s. one d. Educ.: Columbia College; School of Mines; Harvard Medical School. Address: 35 East 68th Street, New York. (Died 15 April 1922.)

DUNKERLEY, Ven. William Herbert Cecil; Rector of Leybourne, Kent, since 1920; s. of late Rev. William Dunkerley, M.A., LL.D., and Annie Swann; m. 1886, Mary Beatrice Taylor; six c. Educ.: Denstone Coll.; Pembroke Coll., Oxford (M.A.); Cuddesdon (Organ Studentship); Ordained deacon, 1885; priest, 1886; Curate of St. Thomas', Toxteth Park, Liverpool, 1885-86; Sigglesthorne, Yorks, 1886-89; Cuddesdon, Oxon., 1889-91; Colonial Chaplain of Malacca, 1891-1897; Penang, 1897-1901; Singapore, 1901; J.P., Visiting Justice, and Licensing Justice, Malacca, 1892; Acting Headmaster, Govt. High School, Malacca, 1893; Assistant Examiner for Government Clerkships, Malacca, 1894-95; passed final Civil Service Malay Examination, 1894; Hon.

Chaplain and Captain Penang Volunteer Corps, 1898; Hon. Chaplain and Captain Singapore Volunteer Corps, 1901; Acting Chaplain to the Forces, 1902; Diocesan Surrogate, 1892; Ecclesiastical Registrar, 1902; Archdeacon of Singapore, 1902-5; Vicar of Castle Morton, 1906-9; Vicar of St. Mark's, Bush Hill Park, N., and Surrogate, 1909-10; Chaplain of St. Paul's, Cannes, 1910-13; Vicar of St. John's, Sevenoaks, 1913-20. Address: Leybourne Rectory, West Malling. (Died 21 Aug. 1922.)

DUNLOP, Alexander Johnstone, C.I.E. 1901; b. 7 April 1848; s. of late Henry Dunlop of Craigton House, Lanark; m. 1873, Constance Susan Mary, d. of late W. R. Myers, of Jamaica. Entered Service, 1869; Director-General of Revenue His Highness Nizam's Government, 1885; retired 1914; holds Kaisar-i-Hind Medal. Address: Crescent Lodge, Largs, Ayrshire.

(Died 25 Oct. 1921.)

DUNLOP, Col. James William, C.B. 1902; C.M.G. 1916; late R.H.A.; b. 16 Oct. 1854; s. of Colin Robert Dunlop (d. 1896) of Torwood Hill, Row, Dumbartonshire. Educ.: Cheltenham College; Royal Military Academy, Woolwich. Entered army, 1875; Captain, 1884; Major, 1892; Lt.-Col. 1900; Colonel, 1904; served Afghan War, 1879-80 (despatches, medal); Burmese Expedition, 1886-87 (medal with clasp); South Africa, 1901-2 (despatches, Queen's medal with five clasps, C.B.); retired 1908; served European War, 1914-18 (1914 Star, despatches, C.M.G., British War Medal, Victory Medal). Recreations: hunting and shooting. Address: Struan, St. Boswells, Roxburghshire. Clubs: Army and Navy; New, Edinburgh.

(Died 20 Nov. 1923.)

DUNLOP, Hon. John, D.C.L.; Puisne Judge of Superior Court of Province of Quebec since 1904, and Admiralty Judge Exchequer Court of Canada since 1906; b. 1837; 3rd s. of late Alexander Dunlop of Clober, Stirlingshire, Scotland; m. 1863, Eleanor, d. of late David Bellhouse; two s. three d. Educ.: Edinburgh Academy and University; McGill University, Montreal. Emigrated to Canada, 1857; B.C.L. 1860; D.C.L. 1910; admitted to Bar, Province of Quebec, 1861; K.C. 1889; Treasurer Bar of Montreal, 1888-91; Batonnier Bar of Montreal, 1891-93. Address: 299 Peel Street, Montreal, Canada. T.A.: Magdala, Montreal. T.: Up Town, 2028. Clubs: Mount Royal, Montreal.

(Died 7 Nov. 1916.)

DUNLOP, Sir Nathaniel, Kt. cr. 1907; LL.D. (Glasgow), B.A., J.P.; retired shipowner; formerly Chairman Allan Line Steamship Company and of James and Alexander Allan, Glasgow, the founders and former managing directors of the line; b. 1830; s. of Archibald Dunlop, Campbeltown; widower; one d. Educ.: Grammar School, Campbeltown. Publications: various pamphlets on Trade and Commerce; magazine articles. Recreation: country life. Address: 21 Bothwell Street, Glasgow; Shieldhill, Biggar, Lanarkshire. Clubs: Constitutional; New, Glasgow. (Died 17 Nov. 1919.)

DUNLOP, Col. Samuel, C.M.G. 1884; late R.A.; b. 8 Mar. 1838; m. 1864, Martha, d. of Robt. Potts of Belfast. Entered R.A. 1856; retired 1882; Acting Commissioner of Police, Straits Settlements, 1870; Inspector-General, 1875; served Perak, 1875; retired 1890. Address: 74 Cromwell Avenue, Highgate, N.

(Died 28 June 1917.)

DUNLOP, Major William Hugh, D.L.; Chief Constable of the East Riding of Yorkshire since 1899; b. 1857; s. of Colin Robert Dunlop (d. 1896) of Torwood Hill, Row, Dumbartonshire; m. 1st, 1882, Clara Helena (d. 1887), d. of Hon. H. F. Colthirst, Jamaica; no c.; 2nd, 1893, Elizabeth Georgina, d. of William Donald of Lisle House, Cheltenham; one s. one d. Educ.: Cheltenham College; Royal Military College, Sandhurst. Joined the

2nd Royal Lanark Militia, 1877 ; joined the army as 2nd Lieut., 1879 ; Captain, 1887 ; Major, 1898 ; retired from the Royal Irish Rifles, 1899 ; served as Adjutant of the 4th Batt. and Depot Royal Irish Rifles, 1893-97 ; on the Recruiting Staff of the Army, 1897-99 ; accompanied the Expedition under General Olive Justice to quell a rising of the Ashantis in 1881. *Recreations:* shooting, fishing, golf. *Address:* Beverley, Yorkshire. *T.A.:* Dunlop, Beverley. *T.:* 23 Beverley. *M.:* CC 89. *Clubs:* Boodle's, Junior Athenæum.

(*Died 28 Nov. 1924.*)

DUNN, Captain Arthur Edward, C.B.E. 1919 ; R.D., A.D.C., R.N.R.; *s.* of Robert Lowthorpe Dunn; *b.* 1876 ; *m.* Grace Adeline, *d.* of George Glover, Oriental Bay, Wellington, New Zealand. *Educ.:* Newark Grammar School ; H.M.S. Worcester. Joined R.N.R. as Midshipman, 1893 ; Commander, King's Birthday Honours, 1914 ; Captain, 1920 ; Marine Superintendent The New Zealand Shipping Company, Limited, Federal Steam Navigation Company, Limited, and the Irish Counties Section of the Union Steamship Company of New Zealand, Limited ; a Younger Brother of Trinity House, London, and Freeman of the City of London : served European War, 1914 (eleven clasps), Commanding H.M. ships and latterly Organising Officer of Convoys ; despatches for services at evacuation of Serbian troops from Durazzo ; Officer of the Order of Redeemer of Greece ; rendered services as Commodore of Convoys and on Staff of British Senior Naval Officer, New York ; A.D.C. to H.M. ; a selected member of the Royal Naval Reserve Advisory Committee, and a member of the Promotions Board. *Address:* Wakefield, Albion Hill, Loughton. *T.:* Loughton 325. *Club:* Junior Athenæum. (*Died 6 Jan. 1927.*)

DUNN, James Nicol, London Editor Glasgow News since 1914 ; *b.* Kincardineshire, N.B., 12 Oct. 1856 ; *e. s.* of Joseph Dunn and Margaret Macleod. *Educ.:* Aberdeen. Destined for the law, but wrote for journals and magazines while still a student, and speedily devoted himself to press work ; joined staff of the Dundee Advertiser and then that of the Scotsman ; when the National Observer was started became managing editor ; resigned that position to go on staff of the Pall Mall Gazette ; editor of Black and White, 1895-97, and of the Ludgate for the same period ; editor of Morning Post 1897-1905 ; President of the Institute of Journalists, 1904 ; Editor of Manchester Courier, 1905-10 ; Star, Johannesburg, 1911-14. *Recreations:* golf, chess. *Address:* Craigallion, Champion Hill, S.E. *Clubs:* Press, Yorick, Cecil, Savage. (*Died 30 June 1919.*)

DUNN, Louis Albert, M.S., M.B., F.R.C.S.; Surgeon, Guy's Hospital ; Consulting Surgeon to the East London Children's Hosp. ; Consulting Surgeon Children's Hosp. Plaistow ; Member of Court of Examiners, Royal Coll. of Surgeons ; Examiner in Surgery at Cambridge University ; *b.* 1858 ; *y. s.* of late J. Roberts Dunn, J.P., D.L., of Stone House, Warbleton, Sussex. *Educ.:* Guy's Hospital. *Address:* Dunholme, North Park, Gerrard's Cross, Bucks.

(*Died 7 June 1918.*)

DUNN, Thomas Smith, I.S.O. 1903 ; late head of Stock and Coupon Department of the Crown Agents for the Colonies ; *b.* 1836. *Address:* Hazelwood, Brunswick Road, Sutton, Surrey. (*Died 16 Dec. 1916.*)

DUNN, Sir William (Henry), 1st Bt., *cr.* 1917 ; Kt., *cr.* 1907 ; *y. s.* of late John Quinn Dunn, Clitheroe, and Susannah Scarf ; *b.* Clitheroe, 1856 ; *m.* 1885, Ellen, *d.* of John Pawle ; one *s.* one *d.* *Educ.:* privately. Late Hon. Col. 1st London Div. Transport and Supply Column ; Fellow of Surveyors' Institution ; Magistrate for the County of London ; Alder-

312

man of City of London, 1909-28 (Sheriff, 1906-7) ; Lieutenant of the City of London ; Chairman of the Royal Botanic Society ; Trustee and Treasurer Lord Mayor Treloar Cripples Hospital and College ; Liveryman of Shipwrights' and other City Companies, being on the Court of several ; has the Orders of the Legion of Honour (France), the Crown (Italy), the Dannebrog (Denmark), St. Olaf (Norway), and the Rising Sun (Japan), 4th class ; Knight Commander of the Order of St. Gregory and Grand Officer of the Order of the Saviour (Greece) ; M.P. (U.) West Southwark, 1910 ; Lord Mayor of London, 1916-17. *Heir:* s. John Henry, *b.* 12 Dec. 1890. *Address:* 9 Gloucester Gate, N.W.1. *T.:* Museum 5674. *Clubs:* Carlton, Junior Carlton, Hurlingham.

(*Died 12 June 1926.*)

DUNNE, Right Rev. John, D.D. ; First Bishop of Wilcannia since 1887 ; *b.* Rhode, King's Co., Ireland, 21 Sept. 1846. *Educ.:* Carlow College, Ireland. Ordained, 1870 ; Priest in Diocese of Goulburn, 1871-87 ; stationed in charge of Burrowa and Vicar at Aldbury, 1880-87. *Address:* Bishop's House, Broken Hill, Australia. (*Died 13 Jan. 1917.*)

DUNNE, General Sir John Hart, K.C.B., *cr.* 1906 ; Grand Cordon Order of Medjidie, 1907 ; retired ; Colonel Duke of Edinburgh's Wilts Regt. ; *b.* 11 Dec. 1835 ; *s.* of John Dunne of Cartron, Co. Roscommon, and Marianne, *d.* of Colonel Hart ; *m.* Julia, *d.* of W. R. Chapman of Whitby, 1870 ; two *s.* one *d.* *Educ.:* Private schools. Ensign, Wilts Regt., 1852 ; Lieut., R. Scots Fusiliers, 1854 ; Maj.- Gen. 1881 ; Gen. 1898 ; served through Crimean campaign, 1854-55, in battles of Alma, Balaclava, Inkerman, and siege of Sevastopol ; served throughout the China War of 1860 ; carried and hoisted the Union Jack at the capture of the Inner North Taku Fort ; was with the advance guard at the action of Changiawhan and Poliatchan and capture of Pekin ; commanded 2nd Infantry Brigade, Aldershot, 1885-86 ; Thames District, Chatham, 1887-90 ; Lieut. Tower of London, 1894-97. Holds 1st Class Medjidie. *Publication:* From Calcutta to Pekin. *Address:* Fortfield, Sidmouth.

(*Died 20 April 1924.*)

DUNNE, Rt. Rev. John Mary, Bishop of Bathurst since 1901 ; *b.* Ireland, 1843. *Educ.:* Mount Melleray Seminary ; All Hallows'. Went to Australia, 1871. *Address:* Bathurst, New South Wales. (*Died 22 Aug. 1919.*)

DUNNING, Albert Elijah, D.D. Beloit College, 1887 ; Editor-in-Chief, The Congregationalist, Boston, since 1889 ; *b.* Conn, 5 Jan. 1844 ; *m.* 1870, Harriet W. Westbrook, Kingston, N.Y. *Educ.:* Yale University ; Andover Theological Seminary. Pastor Highland Church, Boston, 1870-81 ; General Secretary for Congregational Churches, 1881-89 ; Editor-in-chief of The Congregationalist and Christian World, 1889-1911 ; Lecturer Andover Theological Seminary, 1915-16 ; Member of Massachusetts Pilgrim Tercentenary Commission, 1915-16. *Publications:* The Sunday School Library, 1888 ; Bible Studies, 1886 ; Congregationalists in America, 1894 ; The Making of the Bible, 1911. *Address:* 43 Druce Road, Brookline, Mass.

(*Died 14 Nov. 1923.*)

DUNNING, Sir Edwin Harris, Kt., *cr.* 1904 ; C.C. Devons. ; J.P. County Devon ; J.P. Borough Tiverton ; *b.* 8 Apr. 1858 ; *s.* of Richard Dunning of Exeter ; *m.* 1881, Hannah Louise (*d.* 1914), *d.* of Richard Freeman of Hereford ; three *s.* two *d.* Patron or Rectory of Washfield. *Address:* Jacques Hall, Bradfield, Essex. *Club:* Carlton. (*Died 14 Dec. 1923.*)

DUNNING, William Archibald, Ph.D., LL.D.; Litt.D.; Lieber Professor of History and Political Philosophy, Columbia University, New York ; *b.* Plainfield, New Jersey ; *s.* of John H. and Catharine D. Dunning ; *m.* 1888,

Charlotte E. Loomis (*d.* 1917), Brooklyn, New York. *Educ.* : Columbia University. After completing university study with doctor's degree in 1885, began work of instruction in Columbia in history and political science, and rose through various grades to professorship in 1891 ; entered the editorial board of the Political Science Quarterly in 1889, and was managing editor, 1895-1903 ; President American Historical Association, 1913 ; has contributed extensively to the Quarterly, American Historical Review, Yale Review, Atlantic Monthly, etc. *Publications* : Essays on the Civil War and Reconstruction, 1898 ; A History of Political Theories, 3 vols., 1902-20 ; Reconstruction, Political and Economic, 1907 ; The British Empire and the United States, 1914. *Address* : Columbia University, New York. *Club* : Century, New York.

(*Died 25 Aug.* 1922.)

DUNRAVEN and MOUNT-EARL, 4th Earl of, cr. 1822, **Windham Thomas Wyndham-Quin**, K.P. ; C.M.G. 1902 ; P.C. (Ireland), 1899 ; O.B.E. ; Baron Adare, 1800 ; Viscount Mountearl, 1816 ; Viscount Adare, 1822. Baron Kenry (U.K.), 1866 ; Senator Irish Free State ; *b.* 12 Feb. 1841 ; *o. s.* of 3rd Earl and 1st wife, Augusta, *d.* of Thomas Goold ; *S.* father, 1871 ; *m.* Florence Elizabeth (*d.* 1916), *d.* of Lord Charles Lennox Kerr, 1869 ; one *d.* *Educ.* : Christ Church, Oxford. Lieut. 4th Oxford Univ. Rifles, 1860-61 ; late Lieut. 1st Life Guards ; Hon. Col. Glamorgan Artillery Militia ; Hon. Col. 5th Batt. Royal Munster Fusiliers (disbanded 1922) ; War Correspondent to Daily Telegraph in Abyssinia, 1867, and in Franco-Prussian War and siege of Paris ; A.D.C. to Lord-Lieut. of Ireland, 1868 ; Under-Secretary to Colonies, 1885-86, 1886-87 ; Chairman of the House of Lords Committee on Sweating, 1888-90 ; H.M.'s Lieut. County Limerick, 1894 ; Chairman Irish Horse-Breeding Commission, 1896 ; Chairman Irish Land Conference, 1902-3 ; President Irish Reform Association ; served South Africa, Capt. 18th Batt. Imperial Yeomanry Sharpshooters (Queen's medal with two clasps) ; Hon. Colonel 5th County of London Armoured Car Company (Sharpshooters) ; has twice built a yacht for the sailing competitions with the United States. Owner of motor yacht Sona ; holds Board of Trade's Extra-master certificate ; purchased and fitted out as hospital transport carrier S.Y. Grianaig, 1914 (O.B.E.) ; Hon. Capt. R.N.R. *Publications* : The Great Divide, the Upper Yellowstone, 1874 ; Irish Question, 1880 ; Self-Instruction in the Theory and Practice of Navigation, 1900 ; The Legacy of Past Years, 1911 ; Canadian Nights, 1914 ; Past Times and Pastimes, 1922. Owns about 39,800 acres. *Heir* : *cousin*, W. H. Wyndham-Quin. *Address* : 22 Norfolk Street, Park Lane, W.1 ; *T.* : Mayfair 4978 ; Kenry House, Putney Vale, S.W.1 ; *T.* : Kingston 465 : Dunraven Castle, Bridgend, Glamorgan ; Adare Manor, Adare, Limerick. *Clubs* : Athenæum, Carlton, Bachelor's, Turf, Jockey, Royal Automobile ; Kildare Street, Dublin ; Royal Yacht Squadron, Cowes.

(*Died 14 June 1926*.)

DUNSMUIR, Hon. James, Lieutenant-Governor, British Columbia, 1906-10 ; late Premier and Pres. of Executive Council, British Columbia ; *b.* 8 July 1851 ; *m.* Laura, *d.* of W. B. Surles of Fayetteville, North Carolina ; one *s.* eight *d.* Was owner of Esquimalt and Nanaimo Railway, which was sold to the C.P.R. with a million and a half acres of land ; Director of C.P.R. ; late owner of the Wellington Colliery Company. *Recreations* : yachting, shooting, fishing, and croquet. *Address* : Hatley Park, Victoria, British Columbia. *T.A.* : Dunsmuir, Victoria, B.C. *T.* : 531. (*Died 6 June 1921*.)

DUNSTAN, Ven. Ephraim, Rector of Mudgee since 1903 ; Archdeacon of Bathurst since 1910. *Educ.* : St. Paul's College ; and

University, Sydney ; Moore College, N.S.W. Ordained, 1872 ; Incumbent of Forbes, 1892-1902 ; Archdeacon of Mudgee, 1908-10. *Address* : Mudgee, N.S.W.

DUNTZE, Sir George Alexander, 4th Bt., cr. 1774 ; *b.* 27 Jan. 1889 ; *s.* of late Rev. Samuel Henry Duntze and *d.* of Very Rev. Dr. Palmer, Dean of Cashel ; *S. cousin* 1884 ; *m.* Harriet (*d.* 1908), *e. d.* of Lloyd Thomas, 1869 ; one *s.* two *d.* *Heir* : *s.* George Puxley [*b.* 6 Dec. 1873 ; *m.* 1908, Violet May, *d.* of Henry M. Sanderson ; one *s.* two *d.*]. *Address* : Club Anglais, Dinard, France. (*Died 2 May 1923*.)

DUPUY, Charles Alexander ; Sénateur de le Haute-Loire since 1900 ; Ancien President de la Chambre de Députés et du Conseil des Ministres ; *b.* Puy le 5 Nov. 1851. *Educ.* : Le Puy (Haute-Loire). Professeur Agrégé de Philosophie, 1879 ; Inspecteur de Académie, 1880 ; Vice-Recteur de la Corve, 1883 ; Député de la Haute-Loire, 1889. *Decorations* : plusieurs grands cordons. *Address* : Quai de Bethune, 18, IVe, Paris. (*Died 23 July 1923*.)

DUPUY, Jean, Sénateur des Hautes-Pyrénées depuis 1891 ; *b.* Saint-Palais (Gironde), Directeur du journal Le Petit Parisien depuis 1888 ; Président du Comité Général des Associations de la Presse Française depuis 1899 ; Ministre de l'Agriculture, 1899-1902 ; Ministre du Commerce et de l'Industrie, 1909-11 ; Ministre des Travaux Publics, des Postes et des Télégraphes, 1912-13. *Address* : 9 rue Scribe, Paris. (*Died 31 Dec.* 1919.)

DUPUY, Paul, Sénateur des Hautes Pyrénées ; Directeur du Petit Parisien depuis 1908 ; Directeur d'Excelsior depuis 1917 ; *b.* Paris ; *m.* Miss Browne ; two *s.* one *d.* Ancien Député des Hautes-Pyrénées. *Address* : 29 rue Octave Feuillet, Paris. (*Died 10 July 1927*.)

DURAND, Colonel Algernon George Arnold, C.B. 1892, C.I.E. 1897 ; Gentleman-at-Arms ; *b.* 31 March 1854 ; *s.* of Maj.-Gen. Sir Henry Marion Durand, R.E. (*d.* 1871) ; *m.* 1895, Elizabeth Marjorie, *d.* of late Hon. T. C. Bruce, M.P. ; two *s.* A.D.C. to Lord Ripon, Viceroy of India, 1881-82 ; British Agent at Gilgit, 1889-93 ; commanded troops in Hunza Nagar Expedition, 1891 ; Military Secretary to Viceroy of India, 1894-99. *Publication* : The Making of a Frontier, 1899. *Address* : 47 Egerton Gardens, S.W.3. *T.* : Kensington, 6481. *Club* : Travellers'. (*Died 7 Oct. 1923*.)

DURAND, Sir Edward (Law), 1st Bt., cr. 1892 ; C.B. ; *b.* 5 June 1845 ; *s.* of late Sir H. Durand, R.E. ; *m.* 1880, Maude Ellen, *d.* of late A. Hebar-Percy ; three *s.* three *d.* *Educ.* : Bath ; Repton ; Guildford. Entered 96th Regt. 1865 ; B.S.C. 1868 ; Assistant Commissioner Afghan Boundary, 1884-86 ; Resident in Nepaul, 1888 ; retired 1893 (Lieut.-Col.). *Publications* : Cyrus the Great King, 1906 ; Rifle, Rod, and Spear in the East. *Heir* : *s.* Edward Percy Marion [*b.* 11 July 1884 ; *m.* 1918, Vera Helen, *d.* of Sir R. L. Lucas-Tooth, 1st Bt. ; Lieut. Indian Army]. *Address* : 35 Ennismore Gardens, S.W.7. *T.* : Kens. 5013. *Club* : Sports. (*Died 1 July 1920*.)

DURAND, Rt. Hon. Sir (**Henry**) **Mortimer**, G.C.M.G., cr. 1900 ; K.C.S.I., cr. 1894 ; K.C.I.E., cr. 1889 ; P.C. 1901 ; *b.* 14 Feb. 1850 ; *s.* of late Major-General Sir H. Durand, R.E., and Anne, *d.* of Sir J. M'Caskill, K.C.B. ; *m.* 1875, Ella (*d.* 1913), *d.* of T. Sandys ; one *s.* one *d.* *Educ.* : Blackheath School ; Eton House, Tonbridge. Barr. Lincoln's Inn, 1872 ; entered Bengal Civil Service, 1873 ; Political Secretary to Sir F., afterwards Earl, Roberts during Kabul Campaign, 1879 ; Foreign Secretary in India, 1884-94 ; conducted Mission to Ameer of Afghanistan, 1893 ; Minister at Teheran, 1894-1900 ; Ambassador and Consul-Gen. at Madrid, 1900-3 ; Ambassador at Washington, 1903-6 ; Contested Plymouth (C.), 1910. *Publications* : edited Sir Henry Durand's

History of the first Afghan War, 1879; Life of Sir Henry Durand, 1883; Helen Treveryan, 1891; Nadir Shah, 1908; A Holiday in S. Africa, 1911; Life of Rt. Hon. Sir Alfred Comyn Lyall, P.C., 1913; Life of Field-Marshal Sir George White, V.C., 1915; The 13th Hussars in the Great War, 1921. *Address:* Penmayne House, Rock, Wadebridge, Cornwall. *Clubs:* Athenæum, Ranelagh.   (*Died 8 June 1924.*)

DURELL, Henry E. Le Vavasseur dit; Attorney General, Jersey, since 1912; *b.* St. Helier, Jersey; *m.* 1914, Winifred Mary, *d.* of late Surg.-Major Lucas G. Hooper, 10th Hussars. *Educ.:* Victoria College, Jersey; Caen, Normandy. Called to Bar (Middle Temple), 1868; since practised continuously at Jersey Bar; leader of local Bar, 1896-99; represented St. Helier in the Jersey States Assembly, 1874-96, having been elected on eight consecutive occasions; Mayor of St. Helier, 1896-99; Solicitor General, Jersey, 1899-1911. *Address:* The Anchorage, St. Luke's, Jersey.
(*Died July 1921.*)

DURET, Rt. Rev. Augustin, General Superior of the Society of African Missions since 1914; *b.* 1846. Ordained priest, 1870; titular Bishop of Bubastis and Vicar Apostolic of the Nile Delta, Egypt, 1910-14. *Address:* Lyons, Cours Gambetta 150, France.
(*Died 29 Aug. 1920.*)

DURHAM, 3rd Earl of (cr. 1833), John George Lambton; G.C.V.O., cr. 1912; P.C. 1912; K.G. 1909; Baron Durham, 1828; Viscount Lambton, 1833; Lord Lieut. of Durham, 1884-1928; *b.* 19 June 1855; *s.* of 2nd E. and Beatrix, *d.* of 1st D. of Abercorn; *S.* father, 1879; *m.* Ethel, 2nd *d.* of Henry B. M. Milner, West Retford House, Notts, 2nd *s.* of Sir Henry, 4th Bt., 1882. Chancellor University of Durham; Lieut. Coldstream Guards, 1877-79. Owns about 30,500 acres. *Heir:* twin *b.* Hon. Frederick Lambton. *Address:* 39 Grosvenor Square, W.1; *T.:* Mayfair 875; Lambton Castle, Fence Houses, Durham; Harraton House, Exning, Newmarket. *Clubs:* Marlborough, Turf.
(*Died 18 Sept. 1928.*)

DURHAM, Rev. William Edward, M.A.; Rector of Trusham, nr. Chudleigh, Devon, since 1919; Prebendary of Exeter Cathedral, 1912; *b.* 15 Aug. 1857; *s.* of W. J. Durham; *m.* 1880, Priscilla Evelyn, *d.* of Rev. T. F. Arthur, Eastdown Rectory, N. Devon; one *d.* *Educ.:* Cheltenham College; Trinity College, Cambridge. Ordained, 1881; Curate of Tavistock, 1881; Rector of Eastdown, N. Devon, 1882; Vicar of St. Matthew's, Burnley, 1888; Rector of Wolborough with Newton-Abbot, 1896; Rural Dean of Morton, 1904. *Publication:* Summer Holidays in the Alps. *Recreation:* Mountaineering. *Address:* Trusham Rectory, nr. Chudleigh, S. Devon. *T.A.:* Lower Ashton. *Club:* Alpine.   (*Died 16 May 1921.*)

DURNFORD, Robert Chichester, D.S.O., 1917; 2nd Lieutenant 1/4th Hampshire Regt.; *b.* 19 Oct. 1895; *y. s.* of Richard Durnford, C.B.; unmarried. *Educ.:* Eton. Scholar elect of King's College, Cambridge, 1913; Newcastle select, 1914; commissioned 4th Hampshire Regt. (T.F.), 1 Oct. 1914; Temp. Lieut. Nov. 1914; went to India with 2/4th Hampshire Regt. Dec. 1914; Quetta, 1915-16; Temp. Captain, Oct. 1915; proceeded to Mesopotamia and joined 1/4th Hampshire Regt. Oct. 1916; reverted to Temp. Lieut. (wounded, D.S.O.); invalided, March 1917. *Recreations:* cricket, football, etc. *Address:* Hartley Wespall House, Basingstoke, Hants.
(*Died 21 June 1918.*)

DURNFORD, Sir Walter, LL.D., G.B.E., cr. 1919; J.P., V.D.; Provost of King's College, Cambridge, since 1918, and Fellow of Eton College; *b.* 21 Feb. 1847; *s.* of Richard Durnford, Bishop of Chichester, 1870-95. *Educ.:*
314

Eton; King's College, Cambridge; 4th in the First Class Classical Tripos, 1869. Scholar and Fellow of King's College, Cambridge, 1865, 1869; Assistant Master, Eton, 1870-99; commanded 2nd Bucks (Eton College) R.V.; Member of Governing Body of Eton College, 1909; Vice-Provost King's College, 1909-18. *Address:* The Lodge, King's College, Cambridge. *Club:* United University.   (*Died 7 April 1926.*)

DURST, Rev. William; Hon. Canon of Winchester since 1885; Proctor in Convocation for the archdeaconries of Winchester and Isle of Wight, 1896-1917; *b.* 1838; 2nd *s.* of late John Durst of Tunbridge Wells and Walmer; *m.* Edith Harriet (*d.* 1922), *d.* of late Rev. W. Gibson, Rector of Fawley, Hants; three *s.* six *d.* *Educ.:* King's College School; Emmanuel College, Cambridge (M.A.). Ordained Deacon, 1861; Priest, 1862, by the Bishop of Worcester; served in curacies at St. John's, Ladywood, Birmingham, St. John's, Worcester, and Penshurst, Kent; Curate in charge of Crondall, Hants; Vicar of Alton, Hants, 1874; Rural Dean of Alton, 1879; Rector and Rural Dean of Alverstoke, 1881; Canon Residentiary of Winchester, 1887; Rector of St. Mary's and Rural Dean of Southampton, 1894-1912. *Address:* S. Giles House, Fareham, Hants.   (*Died 27 Aug. 1922.*)

DURSTON, Sir Albert John, K.C.B., cr. 1897; R.N.; Engineer-in-Chief R.N., 1889-1907; *b.* Devonport, 25 Oct. 1846; *m.* Agnes Mary, *d.* of C. R. B. Wilkinson, 1869 (*d.* 1887); two *s.* four *d.* *Educ.:* privately; Portsmouth Dockyard and Royal School of Naval Architecture, South Kensington, of which he is a Fellow. Entered Royal Navy, 1866; Chief Engineer, 1877; Chief Inspector of Machinery, 1893; Chief Engineer, Sheerness and Portsmouth Dockyards, 1881-88; Engineer Vice-Admiral, retired 1906; C.B. 1895; M.Inst.C.E.; M.Inst.Mech.E.; Past President Inst. of Marine Engineers; Vice-President Inst. of Naval Architects, Association of Engineers-in-Charge; Royal Naval Benevolent Society; Hon. Mem. Society of Engineers, Inst. of Engineers and Shipbuilders of Scotland, and of Junior Engineers, London. *Address:* St. Andrews, Westcombe Park Road, Blackheath, S.E. *T.:* Greenwich 487. *Clubs:* United Service; Royal Blackheath Golf.
(*Died 18 April 1917.*)

DUSE, Signora Eleonora; *b.* Venice, 1861; father and grandfather actors. Appeared New York, 1893; London, 1893-94 and 1923; appeared before Queen Victoria, Windsor, 1894.
(*Died 21 April 1924.*)

DUTHIE, Sir John, K.B.E., cr. 1918; Senior Assistant Director-General of Voluntary Organisations; *b.* 15 July 1858; *s.* of late William Duthie of Cairnbulg, Aberdeenshire, Shipowner, and Martha, *d.* of late James Birnie of Aberdeen; *m.* 1890, Lesley, *d.* of late John Fyfe, D.L., J.P., Aberdeen; four *s.* two *d.* *Educ.:* privately; Aberdeen University. Barrister-at-Law, Lincoln's Inn; represented London County Council on Board of Port of London Authority for seven years; J.P. Aberdeenshire. *Address:* 22 Hyde Park Street, W.2; Cairnbulg Castle, Aberdeenshire; Kempsons, Whitchurch, Bucks. *Clubs:* Oriental; Royal Northern, Aberdeen.   (*Died 19 June 1922.*)

DU VERNET, Most Rev. Frederick Herbert, Archbishop of Caledonia since 1915; Metropolitan of British Columbia since 1915; President, Anglican Theological College of B.C., 1912; *b.* 1860; *s.* of Rev. Canon Du Vernet and Frances Ellegood; *m.* 1885; one *s.* one *d.*; Visitor Wycliffe College since 1904. *Educ.:* Wycliffe College, Toronto. Ordained 1883; Curate St. James the Apostle, Montreal, 1883-84; Diocesan Missioner, Montreal, 1884-1885; Professor of Practical Theology, Wycliffe College, 1885-95; Rector of St. John, Toronto, 1895-1904; B.D., 1893; D.D., 1904; Bishop of

Caledonia, 1904. *Address:* Prince Rupert, British Columbia. *T. :* 255. (*Died 22 Oct. 1924.*)

DWIGHT, Rev. Timothy, D.D., LL.D. ; President of Yale University, New Haven, Connecticut, 1886-99 ; *b.* Norwich, Connecticut, 16 Nov. 1828 ; *s.* of James Dwight, *s.* of Rev. Timothy Dwight, D.D., LL.D., President of Yale College, 1795-1817, who was *g. s.* of Jonathan Edwards, the eminent divine, and Susan Breed Dwight, *d.* of John M'Laren Breed, whose grandfather was Rev. John M'Laren, of Edinburgh, Scotland ; *m.* Jane Wakeman Skinner, *d.* of Roger Sherman Skinner, *g. s.* of Hon. Roger Sherman, one of the signers of the Declaration of Independence of the United States, and Mary Lockwood De Forest Skinner, *d.* of Lockwood De Forest, of New York, 1866 ; one *s.* one *d. Educ.:* Yale Coll. B.A., 1849 ; studied Theology in the Divinity School of Yale Coll. ; Tutor in the College, 1851-55 ; studied at the Universities of Bonn and Berlin, 1856-58. Professor of New Testament Greek and Exegesis, Yale Divinity School, 1858-86. *Publications:* Translated and edited with additional notes the American edition of Godet's Commentary on St. John's Gospel ; Edited with additional notes several volumes of the American edition of Meyer's Commentary on the New Testament ; volume of sermons entitled Thoughts of and for the Inner Life ; Memories of Yale Life and Men ; a considerable number of articles on Theological and Educational subjects. A member of the American Committee for the Revision of the English Version of the Scriptures, which was published in 1881-85. *Address:* New Haven, Connecticut, U.S.A. (*Died May 1916.*)

DWYER, Edward, V.C. 1915 ; commission in Northumberland Fusiliers, 1915.
(*Died Sept. 1916.*)

DYCE, Col. George Hugh Coles, C.B. 1896 ; I.S.C., late commanding at Mooltan ; retired ; *b.* 19 Feb. 1846 ; *m.* 1876, Marion, *d.* of late Matthew Hamilton of Ardmore, Dunoon ; two *s. Educ.:* Cheltenham College. Entered army, 1864 ; Colonel, 1894 ; Colonel on the Staff at Ferozepore, 1897-98 ; Multan, 1898 ; Tochi Valley, 1898 - 99 ; Tochi Valley and Bannu, 1899-1900 ; temporary Brigadier-General, Allahabad, 1900 ; temporary Deputy-Adjutant-General with rank of Brigadier-General, Bengal command, Naini Tal, 1900-1901 ; served Hazara Campaign, 1868 (medal with clasp) ; Afghan War, 1878-80 (despatches, medal) ; Mahsood-Wuzeeree Expedition, 1881 ; Burmese, 1886-87 (despatches, clasp) ; Waziristan Expedition, 1894-95 (clasp) ; Chitral Relief, 1895 (despatches, C.B., medal with clasp). *Address:* Grindlay & Co., 54 Parliament Street, S.W.1.
(*Died 2 Jan. 1921.*)

DYER, Henry, C.E., M.A., D.Sc., Hon. LL.D. Glasgow, Kogaku-Hakushi (D. Eng.), Japan ; Order of Sacred Treasure (2nd Class) ; Order of Rising Sun, Japan (3rd Class) ; Emeritus Professor University of Tokyo, Japan ; J.P. County and City of Glasgow. *b.* 1848 ; *s.* of John Dyer ; *m.* 1874, Marie Aquart, *d.* of D. Ferguson, Glasgow ; three *s.* one *d. Educ.:* Anderson's College, and University, Glasgow. Served apprenticeship as engineer under Alex. C. Kirk, LL.D. ; Whitworth Scholar, 1870 ; attended Glasgow Univ. for five years ; appointed first Principal of the Imperial College of Engineering, Tokyo, Japan, and Professor of Civil and Mechanical Engineering, 1873 ; in addition, became director of large engineering works ; remained in Japan ten years, and was appointed Hon. Principal of College on retirement, and Hon. Member of the Institutions of Civil Engineers, Mechanical Engineers, and Naval Architects, Japan. Since return to Britain, has taken an active part in engineering, educational, and social work. Is a Life Governor of the Glasgow and West of Scotland Technical College, a Governor of the West of Scotland Agricultural College, of the West of Scotland College for Domestic Science, and of the Glasgow School of Art ; Chairman School Board of Glasgow, and Convener of the Continuation Classes Committee ; Vice-President of the Board of Conciliation and Arbitration of the Manufactured Steel Trade of the West of Scotland, 1894-1916, etc. *Publications:* Dai Nippon; The Britain of the East; Japan in World Politics ; The Evolution of Industry ; Science Teaching in Schools ; Education and National Life ; Education and Industrial Training; Education and Citizenship ; numerous papers and articles on engineering, educational, literary, and social subjects. *Address:* 8 Highburgh Terrace, Dowanhill, Glasgow. *Club:* Liberal, Glasgow.
(*Died 4 Sept. 1918.*)

DYER, Captain Sir John Swinnerton, 12th Bart. ; *cr.* 1678 ; Scots Guards ; *b.* 27 May 1891 ; *S.* father 1907 ; *s.* of 11th Bart. and Dona Edith, *d.* of Sir C. R. M'Grigor, 2nd Bart. ; *m.* 1912, Maude, *d.* of W. H. Turner, Western Australia ; one *s. Educ.:* Eton. Entered army 1910 ; Capt. 1915 ; served European War, 1914-15 (wounded). *Heir :* s. John Lodovicke Swinnerton ; *b.* 20 Jan. 1914. *Address:* 7 Park Lane, W. *T.:* Mayfair 777. *Clubs:* Guards', Boodle's, Pratt's.
(*Died 31 July 1917.*)

DYER, Ven. Joseph Perry, M.A.; late Rector of Datchworth, Stevenage; late Archdeacon of Rangoon ; Examining Chaplain and Commissary to the Bishop of Rangoon; Senior Chaplain H.M. Bengal (Rangoon) Establishment; *b.* 19 Oct. 1855 ; *m.* 1909, Mina, *e. d.* of late Maj.-Gen. C. J. Tyler, R.A. *Educ.:* Godolphin School ; Bishop Hatfield Hall, Durham University. Curate St. Jude's, Leeds, 1882 ; appointed Chaplain on the Bengal Establishment, May 1885 ; Burma Expeditionary Force (Base), 1886-87 ; services lent to Punjab Government, 1890 ; Member of the Governing Council, Royal Army Temperance Association ; Chaplain Rangoon Cantonments, 1896 ; Senior Chaplain Rangoon Cathedral, 1899 ; Commissary in charge of the Diocese, 1901-2 ; Lecturer Army Education Scheme. *Recreation:* golf. *Address:* 2 Templeton Place, S.W.5. *Club:* Overseas. (*Died 30 Aug. 1926.*)

DYER, Brig.-Gen. Reginald Edward Harry, C.B. 1917 ; Indian Army, retired ; *b.* 9 Oct. 1864 ; *s.* of E. Dyer, Simla ; *m.* ; two *s. Educ.:* Middleton College, Co. Cork. Commanded 45th Infantry Brigade ; retired, 1920. *Publication:* The Raiders of the Sarhad, 1921. *Address:* Ashton Keynes, Swindon, Wilts ; St. Martin's, Long Ashton, nr. Bristol.
(*Died 23 July 1927.*)

DYER, Major Stewart Barton Bythesea, D.S.O. 1903 ; Hon. Attaché, British Embassy, Madrid, since 1916 ; *b.* 26 Nov. 1875 ; *s.* of Captain Stewart Dyer of Westcroft Park, Surrey ; *m.* 1906, Mai, *o. c.* of late Captain S. L. Osborne, R. N. ; one *s.* 2nd Life Guards ; entered army, 1899 ; served with the Kaduna Expedition, 1900 (despatches, medal and clasp) ; Bornu Expedition, and operations in Warkun Hills and Bussama country, 1902 (wounded, despatches, medal and clasp) ; Kano-Sokoto Expedition, 1903 (twice wounded, despatches twice, clasp, D.S.O.) ; Dakakerri Expedition, in command, 1904 (despatches and clasp) ; General Staff Officer, 1914 ; relinquished commission, 1916, on account of ill-health. *Address:* British Embassy, Madrid. *Clubs:* White's, Brooks's, Cavalry, Ranelagh.
(*Died 26 Jan. 1917.*)

DYKE, Rev. Edwin Francis, M.A.; Rector of Mersham, Kent, 1896-1916; Hon. Canon of Canterbury ; Rural Dean of North Lympne ; *b.* 27 Sept. 1842 ; *s.* of Francis Hart Dyke, Queen's Proctor, and Charlotte Lascelles, *d.* of Sir Herbert Jenner; *m.* 1870, Katharine Louisa (*d.* 1914), 3rd *d.* of

Sir Frederick Currie, 1st Bt. *Educ.*: Eton; Trinity Hall, Cambridge. Deacon, 1866; Priest, 1867; Curate of Crayford, 1866-68; West Wickham, Kent, 1868-76; Vicar of Orpington, Kent, 1877-83; Maidstone, 1888-96; Rural Dean of Sutton, 1889-96. *Recreations:* cricket, rowing, tennis, fishing, shooting. *Address:* Normanton, Maidstone. (*Died 26 Aug. 1919.*)

DYKE, Lt.-Col. John Samuel, O.B.E. 1919; M.V.O. 1908; *b.* 14 Aug. 1859; *s.* of late Samuel Dyke of Warwick; *m.* 1st, Anna Elizabetha Bergner, 1894 (*d.* 1907); no *c.*; 2nd, 1912, Harriet, *widow* of Lt.-Col. William Wellington Lake. Formerly in Queen's Royal Regt.; served Burma Expedition, 1886-88 (medal and two clasps); South African War, 1900-2 (despatches twice, Queen's medal with two clasps, King's medal with two clasps). *Address:* 41 Kingsnorth Gardens, Folkestone. *T.:* Folkestone 644. (*Died 5 Feb. 1927.*)

DYKES, William Rickatson, M.A., L.-ès-L.; Secretary, Royal Horticultural Society; *b.* 4 Nov. 1877; 2nd *s.* of late Alfred Dykes; *m.* 1924, Elsie Katherine Kaye. *Educ.*: City of London School; Wadham College, Oxford; Sorbonne, Paris. Assistant Master at Charterhouse, 1903-19. *Publications:* Irises, 1911; The Genus Iris, 1913; Handbook of Garden Irises, 1924; The Lorette System of Pruning, 1925. *Address:* Royal Horticultural Society, Vincent Square, Westminster, S.W. *T.A.:* Hortensia, Sowest, London. *T.:* Victoria 5363.
(*Died 1 Dec. 1926.*)

DYMOTT, Rev. Sidney Edward, Hon. Canon of Liverpool. *Address:* The Vicarage, Glazebury, nr. Manchester.(*Died 11 April 1924.*)

DYSON, William, B.A., M.D., M.R.C.S., J.P.; *b.* Thurgoland, Sheffield, 15 July 1849; *s.* of John Dyson, J.P.; *m.* E. J., *d.* of Thomas Andrews of Wortley Iron Works. *Educ.*: Wesley College, Sheffield; University College, London; London University. Consulting Physician to Sheffield Royal Hospital; Consulting Physician to Sheffield Royal Infirmary; Emeritus Professor of Medicine University of Sheffield. *Address:* 35 Westbourne Road, Sheffield. *T.:* 1817 Central, Sheffield. *Club:* Sheffield. (*Died 9 July 1928.*)

E

EADIE, Dennis, actor-manager; *b.* Glasgow, 14 Jan. 1875; first appearance in London, 1900. Manager of Royalty Theatre with J. E. Vedrenne, 1911; appeared in Milestones, 1912; My Lady's Dress, 1913; The Man who Stayed at Home, 1915; Billeted, 1917. *Address:* 8 Dorset Square, N.W. 1. *T.:* Padd. 3366.
(*Died 10 June 1928.*)

EAGLES, General Henry Cecil; R.M.L.I.; 3rd *s.* of late Rev. C. L. Eagles, Longtown, Herefordshire; *b.* 25 Feb. 1855; *m.* 1885, Amy, *y. d.* of T. W. Fox, Hoe House, Plymouth; one *d. Educ.*: Marlborough College. Entered Royal Marines, 1873; Capt. 1885; Major, 1892; Lt.-Col. 1899; Col. 1902; Maj.-Gen. 1909; Lt.-Gen. 1910; Gen. 1912. *Address:* Summerlesze, Yelverton, Devon. *T.:* Yelverton 57. (*Died 3 Aug. 1927.*)

EALES, Herbert, C.S.I. 1911; M.A. Hon. Oxon. 1916; *b.* 20 Aug. 1857; *s.* of Charles Eales and Frances Lindstedt Eales of Kingston, Devon; *m.* 1889, Mary, *d.* of Joseph Eales, Devon; one *s.* four *d. Educ.*: Dulwich College; Balliol College, Oxford. Joined India Civil Service as Assistant Commissioner, Burma, 1879; Political Officer with Field Force during Burmese War, 1885-88; despatches; received thanks of Viceroy; medal with two clasps; received thanks of Lieut.-Gen. Sir H. Prendergast, commanding forces in

Burma, for conduct in a brush with rebels at Magyigon, 16 Feb. 1886; officiated as Secretary to the Chief Commissioner of Burma, 1890; Superintendent of Census, Burma; President of Rangoon Municipality, 1896; Commissioner of Pegu and Member of Legislative Council, 1907; officiated as Financial Commissioner, 1910; Member of Imperial Legislative Council, India, 1912; retired, 1914; joined Catholic Church, 1911. *Publication:* Report on the Census of Burma, 1891. *Recreations:* riding, motoring, and billiards. *Address:* Harberton House, Headington Hill, Oxford.
(*Died 2 Jan. 1927.*)

EAMES, Alfred Edward, I.S.O. 1910; late Controller Central Telegraph Office G.P.O. *Address:* 54 Alleyn Road, Dulwich, S.E.
(*Died 15 Nov. 1924.*)

EAMES, James Bromley; Barrister-at-Law; Recorder of Bath since 1914; *b.* Bath, 8 Dec. 1872; 3rd *s.* of Frederick Eames; *m.* 1910, Ellen Lois, *d.* of C. H. Price, Worcester; no *c. Educ.*: King Edward's School, Bath; Worcester College, Oxford (Exhibitioner; B.A. 1895; M.A., B.C.L. 1898). Professor of Law Imperial Tientsin University, 1898-1900; served in Boxer Campaign, 1900, with Tientsin Volunteers (medal and clasp, Relief of Legations); Legal Adviser to Tientsin Provisional Government, 1900-1; returned to England, 1901; joined Western Circuit, 1902. *Publications:* The English in China, 1908; joint editor of Odgers on the Law of Libel and Slander, 4th and 5th editions. *Address:* 9 Campden Hill Gardens, W.; 4 Paper Buildings, Temple, E.C. *T.:* 924 Park. *Clubs:* Reform, Eighty. (*Died 1 July 1916.*)

EARDLEY-RUSSELL, Lt.-Col. Edmund Stuart Eardley Wilmot, M.V.O., 1909; R.F.A.; *b.* 15 June 1869; *e. s.* of late Capt. T. Stuart Russell, D.L., Chief Constable of West Riding of Yorkshire, and Louisa (now of Woodthorpe, Farncombe), *d.* of late Rev. Sir Thomas Eardley Wilmot Blomefield, Bart.; *m.* 1903, Aurea Louisa Harriett, *d.* of late C. Alfred W. Rycroft of Everlands, Sevenoaks, and late Edith Maud (of Freston Lodge, Sevenoaks), *d.* of late Capt. Hugh Berners, R.N., of Woolverstone Park, Ipswich; one *s.* two *d.*; assumed by Deed Poll the additional surname of Eardley, 1904. *Educ.*: Charterhouse; R. M. A., Woolwich. Joined R.F.A. 1888; appointed R.H.A. 1893; Adjutant, R.H.A., Aldershot, 1896-98; Captain, 1898; qualified as interpreter in German, 1899; and in French, 1900; passed in Russian, 1902; graduated at Staff College, 1900; Instructor at School of Gunnery, H. and F.A., 1901-4; Staff-Capt. Headquarters of Army, 1904-6; Major, 1904; D.A.Q.M.G. Headquarters of Army, 1906; General Staff, Headquarters of Army, 1907-9; Military Attaché Vienna and Cettinjé, 1909-12; Bucharest, 1909-11, with temporary rank of Lieut.-Col.; commanded 39th Battery, R.F.A. (4th Division), in Expeditionary Force to France, 1914; Lieut.-Colonel, 1914; G.S.O. 1st Grade, War Office, 1914-16; Military Attaché, Stockholm, 1916-17; served on staff in S. African War (including actions of Rietfontein and Lombard's Kop and defence of Ladysmith), 1899-1900 (despatches, medal and 2 clasps); China War, 1900-1 (medal); European War, 1914; in attendance upon Prince Albert of Schleswig-Holstein at the Coronation of King Edward VII. (Coronation medal), and upon the Archduke Karl Franz Josef at the Coronation of King George V. (Coronation medal); Commander, 2nd class, of Danebrog Order (Denmark), 1905; Commander of the Order of the Crown of Roumania, 1910; Commander of the Austrian Imperial Order of the Iron Crown, 2nd Class, 1912. *Address:* The Park Farm, Berechurch, Colchester. *T.:* Colchester 212. *M.:* AA 6074. *Club:* United Service.
(*Died 29 Mar. 1918.*)

EARDLEY-WILMOT, Captain Cecil F.; Commissioner of Prisons since 1909; *b.*

4 Aug. 1855; *m.* 1888, Alice Maule, *d.* of late Edmund Scott, San Francisco. 2nd Lieut. the Cheshire Regt., 1877; retired as Captain, 1890; Deputy Governor Wandsworth Prison, 1890; subsequently Governor of Lincoln and Canterbury Prisons, and of Borstal and Parkhurst Convict Prisons; appointed an Inspector of Prisons, 1904; Secretary to Departmental Committee on Education of Prisoners, 1896; Member of Departmental Committee on Vagrancy, 1904-6. *Address:* 35 Tedworth Square, Chelsea, S.W. *Club:* Junior United Service.
(Died 14 July 1916.)

EARDLEY-WILMOT, His Honour Judge Hugh Eden; *b.* 7 Nov. 1850; 6th *s.* of Sir John Eardley-Wilmot, 2nd Bt.; *m.* 1879, Ellen Elizabeth (*d.* 1923), *d.* of John Williams, S. Wales; one *s. Educ.:* Charterhouse. Bar, Lincoln's Inn, 1871. Was Counsel to Mint at Central Criminal Court. Judge of County Courts (Circuit 33), 1891 - 1920. *Address:* 2 The Avenue, Colchester.
(Died 10 Mar. 1926.)

EARDLEY-WILMOT, Major-General Revell, C.B. 1896; *b.* 29 Aug. 1842; 2nd *s.* of late Sir John Eardley Eardley-Wilmot, 2nd Bt., of Berkswell Hall, M.P. for South Warwickshire; *m.* 1906, Elizabeth, *d.* of J. W. Toone Smith, M.D. *Educ.:* Winchester Coll. Founder's Kin. Late 14th Bengal Lancers and A. A.-G. Meerut Div.; entered Army 1860; Brevet Lt.-Col. 1881; Maj. - Gen. 1895; Bhotan Expedition, 1864-66 (wounded; despatches, medal with clasp); Jowaki Expedition as A.D.C. (despatches, clasp); Kabul War of 1878-79-1880; attack on Ali Musjid Charasiak, capture of Kabul and all operations around Kabul city, 1879 (despatches, medal, three clasps, Bt. Lt.-Col.); in receipt of distinguished service pension. *Decorated* for military services. *Recreations:* polo, cricket, shooting, fishing, pigsticking, tent-pegging. *Address:* The Cottage, Lowther Road, Bournemouth.
(Died 14 June 1922.)

EARLE, Rt. Rev. Alfred, D.D.; Bishop of Marlborough; Dean of Exeter, 1900-1918; *b.* 1827; *s.* of Henry Earle, F.R.C.S., Surgeon in Ordinary to Queen Victoria; *m.* 1866, Frances Anne (*d.* 1911), *e. d.* of Wm. Roope Ilbert of Bowringsleigh, Devon; one *s.* two. *d. Educ.:* Eton; Hertford Coll. Oxford (Lusby Scholar). Ordained, 1858; Curate of St. Edmund's, Salisbury; Rector of Monkton-Farleigh, Wilts, 1863-1865; Vicar of West Alvington, South Huish, South Milton, Marlborough; joint Vicarage, Devon, 1865-87; Rural Dean; Archdeacon of Totnes, 1872 - 87; Prebendary of Exeter Cathedral; Examining Chaplain to Bishops Temple and Bickersteth; Canon Residentiary of Exeter Cathedral, 1886 - 88; Rector of St. Michael's, Cornhill, 1888-95; Rector of St. Botolph's, Bishopsgate, and Prebendary of St. Paul's Cathedral, 1895 - 1900; Suffragan Bishop of W. and N.W. London, with the title of Bishop of Marlborough, 1888 - 1900. *Publications:* charges printed at request of clergy on Church Reform; The Reform of Patronage; Reform of Episcopal Visitations; Our Duty to the Nonconformists; Our Duty to the Masses; Some Pressing Duties of Churchwardens and Clergy, 1874; On Consecutive and Systematic Church Education, Exeter, 1873; Work in West and North-West London, 1897. *Address:* Torquay.
(Died 28 Dec. 1918.)

EARLE, Arthur, J.P., Lancashire; F.R.G.S.; *b.* 14 Dec. 1838; *y. s.* of Sir Hardman Earle, 1st Bart.; *m.* Ida E. B. (*d.* 1903), *e. d.* of H.E. Sir George Buckley-Matthew, K.C.M.G., H.M. Minister in Brazil; four *s.* one *d. Educ.:* Harrow. Merchant; Vice-Chairman of The Liverpool Cathedral Committee; Director, Bank of Liverpool, Liverpool, London, and Globe Insurance Co.; contested Scotland Division, Liverpool, 1885. *Recreations:* has

visited most of the world, and explored the interior of Brasil with the late Sir F. Burton; hunting, motoring. *Address:* Childwall Lodge, Wavertree, near Liverpool; Earles Court, Camberley. *T.:* 123 Wavertree. *M.:* AE 900 and AE 2200. *Clubs:* Windham, Racquet.
(Died 5 Dec. 1919.)

EARLE, Mrs. C. W. (Maria Theresa Villiers); *b.* 8 June 1836: *m.* 1864, late Capt. Charles William Earle, Rifle Brigade; two *s. Publications:* Pot-pourri from a Surrey Garden; More Pot-pourri; A Third Pot-pourri, 1903; Letters to Young and Old, 1906; Memoirs and Memories, 1911; Gardening for the Ignorant, 1912; Pot - pourri mixed by Two (with Ethel Case). *Address:* Woodlands, Cobham, Surrey.
(Died 27 Feb. 1925.)

EARNSHAW, Albert, Puisne Judge, Supreme Court, Straits Settlements, since 1914; *b.* Netherton, Huddersfield, 31 Oct. 1865; *o. s.* of David Earnshaw; *m.* 1898, Sarah Maude, *o. d.* of William Haley. *Educ.:* Huddersfield College; University Coll.; Durham University; Pembroke College, Oxford. M.A., Durham; B.A., Oxford; Open Classical Scholar and took 1st Class Honours in Classics at both Universities; Fellow of Durham University, 1889-1897; called to Bar, 1893; North - Eastern Circuit, 1893-1904; Magistrate, Grenada, 1904-1907; British Guiana, 1907-9; Puisne Judge, Gold Coast, 1909-12; British Guiana, 1912-14. *Address:* Supreme Court, Singapore, Straits Settlements. *(Died Mar. 1920.)*

EAST, Sir George Frederick Lancelot Clayton-, 4th Bt. *cr.* 1838; 8th Bt. *cr.* 1782; O.B.E. 1919; Major late R.A.; *b.* 3 Sept. 1872; 2nd *s.* of 3rd Bt. and Eleanor Theresa, *d.* of Maj.-Gen. A. R. Fraser; S. father 1925; *m.* 1906, Frances Louise Helen, *yr. d.* of late Lieut.-Col. James Colquhoun, D.L.; one *s.* two *d.* Served European War, 1914-18 (despatches). *Heir: s.* Robert Alan, *b.* 1908. *Address:* Hall Place, Maidenhead. *(Died 27 April 1926.)*

EAST, Sir Gilbert Augustus Clayton, 3rd Bt., *cr.* 1838; 7th Bt., *cr.* 1731; J.P.; *b.* 25 April 1846; *e. s.* of 2nd Bt. and *e. d.* of Sebastian Smith; S. father, 1866 and *c.* 1914; *m.* 1867, Eleanor Theresa (*d.* 1924), *d.* of Maj.-General Fraser; one *s.* one *d. Educ.:* Eton; Magdalene Coll., Cambridge. Owns about 1500 acres. *Heir: s.* George Frederick Lancelot, O.B.E., *b.* 1872. *Address:* Hall Place, Maidenhead. *(Died 26 Sept. 1925.)*

EAST, Col. Lionel William Pellew, C.M.G. 1916; D.S.O. 1895; R.A.; General Staff Officer 2nd Grade West since 1909; *b.* 27 July 1866; *m.* 1897; one *s. Educ.:* R.M.A. Woolwich. Entered R.A. 1885; Captain, 1896; served Hazara and 2nd Miranzai expeditions, 1891 (despatches); N.E. Frontier, Assam, 1894 (severely wounded, D.S.O.); European War, 1914-18 (C.M.G., Bt. Col.). *Address:* Cox & Co., 16 Charing Cross, S.W.1.
(Died 6 Sept. 1918.)

EASTERBROOK, James, M.A.; *b.* Dean Prior, Devonshire, 1851; *m.* Edith Montague Hamilton. *Educ.:* St. Mark's; University College, London. B.A., Honours in Logic; M.A. 1878; Master St. Mark's College Schools, 1872 - 75; Mathematical Tutor St. Mark's College, 1875-80; Headmaster Owen's School, Islington, 1881 - 1909; Life Governor University College, London; Vice - President Incorporated Association of Headmasters; Treasurer, 1899-1905; President, 1906; Member L.C.C. Technical Education Board, 1893 - 98. Chairman Federal Council of Secondary School Associations, 1909-12; Member Consultative Committee, Board of Education, 1910-16. *Club:* Constitutional. *(Died 1 Feb. 1923.)*

EATON, Sir John Craig, Kt., *cr.* 1915; President of the T. Eaton Co. Ltd., Toronto and Winnipeg; *b.* Toronto, 28 April 1876; *s.* of

late Timothy Eaton and Margaret Wilson Beattie; *m.* 1901, Florence M'Crea, Omemee, Ontario; four *s.* one *d. Educ.:* Toronto Public Schools; Upper Canada College. Director of the Dominion Bank; Director of the Canadian Pacific Railway; Hon. Director Canadian National Exhibition; member of Senate, Victoria College; Hon. Governor and member of Board of Trustees, Toronto General Hospital; Member of the Board of Governors of Toronto University. *Recreations:* yachting, automobilism. *Address:* Ardwold, Toronto; Kawandag, Lake Russian, Muskaka. *Clubs:* York, National, Lambton Golf, Caledon Mountain Trout, Royal Canadian Yacht, Toronto; Manitoba, Winnipeg.
(Died 29 Mar. 1922.)

EAYRS, Rev. George, Ph.D., F.R.Hist.S.; Minister London, Newington Circuit United Methodist Church; on Executive of Committee for Union of Wesleyan, Primitive, and United Methodist Churches; essayist, at Ecumenical Conference, London; *b.* Leicester, 18 Nov. 1864; *s.* of Warren and Sarah Burrows Eayrs; *m.* Clara Wagg, *d.* of Councillor C. Smithurst, Harrogate; two *s.* one *d. Educ.:* Wesleyan School; Manchester and Leeds Universities; Research Student, Durham, Ph.D.; Junior law clerk and cashier; entered ministry, 1887; Circuits in Nottingham, Eccles, Huddersfield, Bradford (Superintendent), Batley, Bristol, Downham, Newcastle; District Chairman, Bristol and S. Wales, Lincoln, Norwich and London; Conference Journal Secretary, Hanley, 1912; British Secretary world-wide Methodist Historical Union, founded Toronto Conference, 1911; lectured on Methodist History and Wesley in Canada and United States, 1914, and frequently in England; Member of National Free Church Council Committee for many years, and President Leeds Federation, Bristol Council, etc.; Continental Chaplain, Grindelwald, 1902; member of the Aristotelian Society, London; Member League of Nations and Council of Christian Churches. *Publications:* A Son of Issachar—Times of Wesley and Kilham; Alfred to Victoria: Connected Historical Studies; Richard Baxter: Wesley and Kingswood and its Free Churches; co-editor of Free Methodist (1904-7) and United Methodist weekly journals; proposed, edited, and contributed largely to A New History of Methodism in all countries (2 vols.); edited Letters of John Wesley: Important and New Letters with Introductions and Biographical Notes; British Methodism as it is, as it was, as it will be: A Methodist Union Handbook and History; Programme and Working Philosophy of Jesus Christ; Wesley, Christian Philosopher and Church Founder. *Recreations:* historical study, great pictures and Wesley relics. *Address:* 74 Sisters Avenue, Clapham Common, North Side, S.W.11.
(Died 25 Oct. 1926.)

EBERTS, Hon. David MacEwen, K.C.; late Attorney-General, British Columbia; 3rd *s.* of W. D. MacEwen and Mary Bell; *b.* 22 April 1850; *m.* 1884, Mabel Hope, *e. d.* of William Charles. *Educ.:* Chatham Grammar School, Ontario; called to bar, 1882; K.C., 1892; in British Columbia Legislature since 1890; Speaker, 1907. *Address:* Victoria, B.C. *Clubs:* Union. Victoria; Vancouver, Vancouver.
(Died May 1924.)

EBRAHIM, Sir Currimbhoy, 1st Bt., *cr.* 1910; Kt., *cr.* 1905; C.B.E. 1918; J.P.; *b.* 21 Oct. 1840; *y. s.* of late Ebrahim Pabaney, shipowner; married; family belongs to Cutch; *m.* 1st, 1854, Foolbai (decd.), *d.* of Asoobhai Gangji 2nd, 1876, Foolbai, *d.* of Vishram Sajan; seven *s.* ten *d. Heir: s.* Mahomedbhoy Currimbhoy [*b.* Bombay, 11 Sep. 1867; *m.* 1882, Sakinabai, *d.* of Jairajbhoy Peerbhoy; one *s.*]. Is a leading member of the Khoja community; Past President of the Anjuman-i-Islam; of the Mahomedan Educational Conference in Bombay, and an opium, yarn, cotton, silk, tea, sugar, and cloth merchant of Bombay, Hong-kong, Kobe, Singapore, Shanghai, and Calcutta; owns the Currimbhoy Mills, the Mahomedbhoy Mills, the Ebrahimbhoy Pabaney Mills, the Fazulbhoy Mills, the Crescent Mills, the Indore Malwa United Mills, and many other factories (ginning and pressing) and the Indian Bleaching, Dying, and Printing Works; has established a girls' school, a Madressa at Mandvi; the Currimbhoy Ebrahim Khoja Orphanage in Bombay; dharamsalas at Mandir and Bhuj; gave large donations to Bombay New Museum fund; interested in many charitable institutions. *Address:* Pabaney Villa, Warden Road, and 13 Esplanade Road, Bombay.
(Died 26 Sept. 1924.)

EBRAHIM, Sir Mahomedbhoy Currimbhoy, 2nd Bt., *cr.* 1910; Kt., *cr.* 1924; J.P.; partner in Currimbhoy Ebrahim & Sons; *b.* 11 Sep. 1867; *e. s.* of Sir Currimbhoy Ebrahim, 1st Bt.; *m.* Bai Sakinabai, *d.* of Jairazbhoy Pirbhoy; one *s. Educ.:* Bombay (privately). Trustee of the Port of Bombay, 1908-23; a member of the Haj Committee since its creation (Gold medal of the Kaiser-i-Hind); was a member of the Labour Commission; Sheriff of Bombay, 1921-22; a Trustee of the Currimbhoy Ebrahim Khoja Orphanage; a Director of the Alexandra School for Girls; a Treasurer of the Islam Gymkhana. *Heir: s.* Huseinali, *b.* 1903. *Address:* Belvedere, Warden Road, Bombay, India. *Clubs:* Willingdon Sports, Orient, Radio, Bombay.
(Died 3 Mar. 1928.)

EBURY, 2nd Baron (*cr.* 1857), **Robert Wellesley Grosvenor,** D.L.; Capt. 1st Life Guards, retired 1866; *b.* 25 Jan. 1834; *s.* of 1st Baron and Charlotte, *d.* of 1st Lord Cowley; *S.* father 1893; *m.* Hon. Emilie Beaujolais White, *d.* of 1st Lord Annaly, 1867; two *s.* two *d. Educ.:* Harrow; King's Coll. London. Entered 1st Life Guards, 1858; M.P. (L.) Westminster, 1865-74. *Heir: s.* Hon. Robert V. Grosvenor. *Address:* Moor Park, Rickmansworth, Herts. *Clubs:* Turf, Travellers'. *(Died 13 Nov. 1918.)*

EBURY, 3rd Baron (*cr.* 1857), **Robert Victor Grosvenor,** *s.* of 2nd Baron and Hon. Emilie Beaujolais White, *d.* of 1st Lord Annaly; *b.* 28 June 1868; *S.* father, 1918; *m.* 1908, Florence, *d.* of Edward Padelford, of Savannah, Georgia, U.S.A. Late Captain 13th Middlesex Rifle Volunteers: served South Africa, 1900-1901 (Queen's medal 3 clasps). *Heir: b.* Capt. Hon. F. E. Grosvenor. *Address:* 79 Gloucester Place, W.1; *T.:* Mayfair 4599; Moor Park, Rickmansworth, Herts.
(Died 5 Nov. 1921.)

ECCLES, Lt.-Col. Cuthbert John, D.S.O. 1915; retired pay; District Remount Officer; *b.* 2 Feb. 1870; *s.* of Major-General Eccles. 2nd Lt. 16th Lancers, 1894; Captain, 1899; Major, 1909; Lt.-Col. 1914; served S. African War, 1900-1902 (Queen's medal, 4 clasps, King's medal, 2 clasps, wounded); European War, 1914-17 (wounded twice, despatches twice, D.S.O.). *Address:* Cowley House, Headington Hill, Oxford. *Club:* Cavalry. *(Died 10 Jan. 1922.)*

ECCLES, Rev. Canon John Charles, Vicar Holy Trinity Church, Woodville, 1892-1919; Canon of Waiapu, 1903; *b.* 6 March 1845; *m.* 1880, Emma Beilby Rabone; four *s.* one *d. Educ.:* St. John's College, Auckland. Ordained, 1874; Curate of Waipawa, 1874; Incumbent, 1877; served as Chaplain in the Maori War, 1864 and 1865. *Address:* 4 Alma Street, Newmarket, Auckland, New Zealand.

ECHEGARAY, José; *b.* Madrid, March 1833. *Educ.:* Grammar School, Murchia; Escuela de Caminos, Madrid. Professor of Mathematics at Engineering College, Madrid, 1888; member of Academy of Sciences, 1866; member of Cortes, 1868; Minister of Commerce, of Education and of Finance 1867-1874; · Minister of Finance, Spain, 1905. *Publications:* La Esposa del Vengadar, 1874; El Libro talonario, 1874; La Ultima Noche, 1875; El Gran Galeoto, 1881; Dos Fanatismos, 1887; Mariana, 1892; El hijo de San Juan, 1892; El Loco Dios, 1900; Mancha qua limpia, 1895. *Address:* Madrid.

(Died 15 Sept. 1916.)

ECHLIN, Sir Henry Frederick, 8th Bt.; cr. 1721; b. 14 Aug. 1846; s. of 6th Bt. and Mary, o. d. of William Cavanagh of Grange Beg, Westmeath; S. brother 1906; m. 1890, Mary Dennis (d. 1913); one d. *Heir:* b. John Fenton -[b. 1847; m. 1869, Harriet, d. of late George Kennedy of Westport, Co. Mayo; three s. five d.]. *Address:* Haddenham, Thame, Oxon.

(Died 8 Nov. 1923.)

EDEN, Rev. Frederick Nugent, M.A., Hon. Canon of Rochester; b. 3 Sep. 1857; 5th s. of late Canon I. P. Eden, Rector of Sedgefield; m. 1919, Katherine Mary, e. d. of late Bryan Holme Holme, Paull Holme, Holderness, Yorks. *Educ.:* Reading School; Pembroke College, Cambridge. Assistant Curate of Sedgefield, 1880-85; St. James', West Hartlepool, 1885-86; Curate-in-Charge of Norton, Durham, 1886; Vicar of St. James', West Hartlepool, 1886-90; Missionary (C.M.S.) on River Niger, W. Africa, 1890-91; Vicar of All Saints, Belvedere, Kent, 1892-1904; of St. Paul's, Rusthall, 1904-18; Rector of North Cray, 1918-22. *Address:* Verno, Horeham Road, E. Sussex.

(Died 11 June 1926.)

EDEN, Hon. George, Partner in Mullens, Marshall & Co., 13 George Street, E.C., Stockbrokers; 2nd s. of 4th Lord Auckland; b. 29 May 1861; m. Amy Violet Powlett, 3rd d. of late Col. Hon. C. R. Hay Drummond; two s. one d. *Educ.:* Eton. *Address:* 6 Cromwell Place, S.W.7. *T.:* Western 522. *Clubs:* Wellington, Royal Automobile. *(Died 14 June 1924.)*

EDEN, Brig.-Gen. William Rushbrooke, C.M.G. 1917; D.S.O. 1900; R.H.A.; b. Bath. 11 Oct. 1873; s. of Lieut.-Col. A. D. Eden (late "The Cameronians"); m. 1911, Marjorie, d. of Major Lyon Campbell, 74th Highlanders; one s. one d. *Educ.:* Haileybury College; R.M.A. Woolwich. 2nd Lieut. Royal Artillery, 1893; Lieut., 1896; served in South African War, 1900 (despatches, Queen's medal, 6 clasps, D.S.O.), with A Battery R.H.A.; Capt. 1900; Major, 1910; Lt.-Col. 1915; European War, 1914-17 (C.M.G.); Brig.-Gen. 1916; Officier Legion d'Honneur, 1917. *Address:* 8 Manson Place, Queen's Gate, S.W. *Club:* Army and Navy.

(Died 11 July 1920.)

EDGAR, George, Journalist and writer of fiction; b. Warrington, 11 June 1877; e. s. of Peter Edgar, Warrington; m. Jeannie, y. d. of Thomas D. Howard, Dewsbury; one s. three d. *Educ.:* privately. Connected with provincial press many years, and later with London journals; edited Modern Business, 1909; Ed. Careers, 1910-11; Associate Editor, Advertisers' Weekly; contributes to many daily and weekly journals, stories, sketches, articles, and essays; writes on subjects relating to journalism. *Publications:* The Blue Bird's Eye, 1912; Martin Harvey, 1912; Swift Nick of the York Road, 1913; The Red Colonel, 1913; The Pride of the Fancy, 1914; Kent, the Fighting Man, 1916; Honours of War, 1916. *Recreations:* golf, angling. *Address:* 2 Chartham Terrace, Ramsgate. *Clubs:* Savage, Aldwych.

(Died April 1918.)

EDGAR, Prof. John; M.A. Glas.; B.A. Oxon.; Bell Prof. of Education, St. Andrews University, since 1902; m. y. d. of Rev. Thomas Bowman, Catrine; one s. two d. *Educ.:* Dumfries Academy; Glasgow University (1st Class Honours, Classics; Snell Exhibition); Balliol College (Honours in Classical Modera-

tions, and Honours in Final School Lit. Hum.). Formerly Master Royal High School, Edinburgh, and Secretary of the Secondary Schoolmasters in Scotland; Examiner in Classics, University of Glasgow, 1897-1901; Examiner in Education, University of Manchester, 1909-11. *Publications:* History of Early Scottish Education; Translation of Homeric Hymns, etc. *Recreations:* golf, angling, photography. *Address:* East Scores, St. Andrews, Fifeshire.

(Died 5 May 1922.)

EDGE, His Honour Judge James Broughton, J.P.; Judge of Metropolitan Co. Courts, 1898-1911; o. s. of Adam Edge, Bolton, and Mary, d. of Thomas Broughton, Preston; m. Alice Ann, d. of John Whittle, Bolton, 1859; two s. *Educ.:* privately. Admitted solicitor, 1858; Barr. Middle Temple, 1871; Coroner for Lancashire, 1869-88; Counsel to the Mint for Lancashire, 1872-88; was Judge of Circuit No. 58 (Devonshire), 1888-1898, and Chairman of Quarter Sessions for Devon; is J.P. for the county of Devon, and Hon. Capt. and Q.-M. (retired) 5th Batt. Loyal North Lancashire Regt. *Address:* Lynton Lodge, Rickmansworth, Herts.

(Died 23 Oct. 1926.)

EDGE, Rt. Hon. Sir John; Kt., cr. 1886; K.C. 1886; P.C. 1908; b. 28 July 1841; o. s. of late Benjamin Booker Edge of Clonbrock, Queen's Co.; m. 1867, Laura, d. of T. Loughborough; three d. *Educ.:* Trinity College, Dublin. Irish Barr. 1864; English Barr. Middle Temple, 1866 (elected Bencher, 1898); Chief Justice of High Court of Judicature, North-Western Provinces. India, 1886-98; Member of Council of India, 1898-1908; Member of Judicial Committee, Privy Council, 1909. *Address:* 123 Oakwood Court, W.14. *T.:* Park 0957. *Club:* Junior Carlton. *(Died 30 July 1926.)*

EDGE, John Henry, M.A., K.C., Ex-Legal Assist. Land Commissioner, Ireland; b. 11 June 1841; o. surv. c. of late John Dallas Edge, Barrister-at-Law. *Educ.:* Trinity College, Dublin. *Publications:* Forms of Leases, 2nd edit. 1884; An Irish Utopia, 1906; The Quicksands of Life, 1908. *Address:* 16 Clyde Road, Dublin. *Club:* Dublin University.

(Died 22 Sept. 1916.)

EDGEWORTH, Francis Ysidro, M.A. (Oxon.), D.C.L. (Durham); Emeritus Professor of Political Economy, University of Oxford; Fellow of All Souls College, Oxford; Fellow of King's College, London; Fellow of the British Academy; sometime President of the Royal Statistical Society; joint editor of the Economic Journal; b. Edgeworthstown, Ireland, 8 Feb. 1845; s. of Francis Beaufort Edgeworth; n. of Maria Edgeworth. *Educ.:* at home; Trinity College, Dublin; Balliol College, Oxford. 1st class Lit. Hum. Oxford; Lecturer on Logic, afterwards Tooke Professor of Political Economy at King's College, London, to 1891. *Publications:* Mathematical Psychics, 1881; Papers relating to Political Economy, 1925; article on Probability in the Encyclopædia Britannica (11th edition), 1911; articles on Probabilities, Statistics, and Economics in the Philosophical Magazine, Journal of the Statistical Society, Economic Journal, and other periodicals. *Recreations:* boating and golf. *Address:* All Souls' College, Oxford. *Clubs:* Athenæum, Savile

(Died 13 Feb. 1926.)

EDGHILL, Rev. John Cox, M.A., D.D.; Chaplain Tower of London, 1887-1902; Fellow of King's Coll. London; m.: one s. Ordained, 1858; Curate of St. Mark, Whitechapel, 1858-60; served at Halifax, N.S.; Gibraltar; Aldershot, 1881-82; Portsmouth, 1882-85; Chaplain-Gen. to Forces, 1885-1901; Hon. Chaplain to the King; Prebendary of Wells, 1908. *Address:* Soulby, Clarence Park, Weston-super-Mare.

(Died 20 Nov. 1917.)

E D I S, Sir Robert William, K.B.E., cr. 1919 ; C.B. 1902 ; architect since 1862 ; D.L., J.P. Norfolk ; Colonel, V.D. Artists R.V.; b. Huntingdon, 13 June 1839 ; m. 1862, Elsie Jane (d. 1897), d. of late James Anton of Abingdon Street ; five d. Educ.: Huntingdon Grammar School ; Brewers' Company School at Aldenham. President of Architectural Association for two years ; late Fellow and Member of Council of the Royal Institute of British Architects ; Architect of the Constitutional, Junior Constitutional, and Badminton Clubs, London ; Conservative Club, Glasgow ; Great Central Hotel, London ; Ball - room and additions, Sandringham ; alterations and additions, York Cottage ; mansions at Cheveley Park, Rangemoor, for Lord Burton ; School Board additions ; Inner Temple Library, etc., etc. ; largely engaged in building and altering various mansions in England and Scotland ; has travelled much abroad, and published sketches of old buildings in France, Italy, and Germany ; has written and lectured on domestic art and house sanitation, and published various works on these subjects, including Decoration and Furniture of London Houses, Handbook on Healthy Furniture for the Council of the International Health Exhibition ; a keen sportsman and Volunteer ; has shot big game in North America ; joined the "Artists" Volunteers in 1860, and has commanded them for 20 years, after retirement of late Lord Leighton, and is now Hon. Col., of the Regiment ; was aide-de-camp to late Earl of Albemarle in the French and German War ; in Paris during last days of the Commune, and wrote a paper on Fireproof Materials as the result of his observations during the Paris fires, which was read before the Royal Institute of British architects. Address: The Old Hall, Great Ormesby, Norfolk. T.A.: Ormesby Norfolk. T.: Ormesby 11. Clubs: Junior Constitutional ; The Norfolk, Norwich.
(Died 23 June 1927.)

E D M E A D E S, Lt.-Col. James Frederick, M.V.O. 1905 ; J.P. ; b. 1843 ; 4th s. of Rev. William Henry Edmeades, Nurstead Court, Kent ; m. 1883, Mary Erskine, e. d. of late Frederick James Isacke of Wood View, Booterstown, Co. Dublin. Educ.: Harrow. Major West Kent Imperial Yeomanry, 1901-7. Address: Hazells, nr. Gravesend.
(Died 6 Feb. 1917.)

EDMONDES, Ven. Frederic William, M.A.; Archdeacon of Llandaff, 1897-1913 ; b Llanblethian, near Cowbridge, 1840 ; 2nd s. of Thomas Edmondes, M.A., Hon. Canon of Llandaff ; m. Constance Sarah, 3rd d. of Rev. Edward Doddridge Knight, of Nottage Court, Glams, 1868 (d. 1889); one d. Educ.: Cowbridge Grammar School ; Jesus College, Oxford. Assistant-master at Trinity Coll. Glenalmond, 1863-64 ; Curate of Newcastle, 1864-67 ; Rector of Michaelston, with St. Bride's-super-Ely, 1867-73 ; Rural Dean, 1876-1897 ; Surrogate ; Proctor for Clergy, 1892-97 ; Rector of Coity, 1873-1901. Address: Nolton Court, Bridgend, Glams.
(Died 10 Nov. 1918.)

EDRIDGE, Sir Frederick Thomas, Kt., cr. 1897 ; J.P. Surrey ; D.L.; b. 22 Jan. 1848 ; s. of Sir Thomas R. Edridge ; m. 1867, Elizabeth Sara, d. of J. M. Eastty of Wellesley House, Croydon. Educ.: Marlborough. Five times Mayor of Croydon ; High Sheriff of Surrey, 1909 ; Hon. Col. 4th Queen's. Address: Bramley Croft, Croydon. T.: Croydon 1677.
(Died 3 Oct. 1921.)

EDSALL, Rt. Rev. Samuel Cook, D.D. ; Bishop of Minnesota (Episcopal Church) since 1901 ; b. Dixon, Illinois, U.S.A., 4 March 1860 ; s. of James Kirtland Edsall and Caroline Florella More ; m. 1883, Grace Harmon ; two s. one d. Educ.: Racine College, Wisconsin ; Western Theological Seminary, Chicago. Early years spent in Dixon, Ill. ; from 1870 a good 320

deal of time spent at Springfield, Ill., the State capital, where his father was State senator and attorney-general ; studied law under his father in Chicago, and admitted to Bar, 1882 ; interested in Church work as a layman ; candidate for Orders, 1886 ; Deacon, 1888 ; founded St. Peter's, now largest parish in Chicago, 1887 ; became Rector thereof on ordination; Missionary Bishop of North Dakota, 1898 ; resided in Fargo, N.D., three years ; Bishop Coadjutor of Minnesota, 1901. Address: 2642 Portland Avenue, Minneapolis, Minn. Clubs: Minikahda, Church.
(Died Feb. 1917.)

EDWARDES, General Sir Stanley de Burgh, K.C.B. ; cr. 1898 ; b. 29 Mar. 1840 ; s. of late Capt. George Harris Edwardes, Bengal Army; m. Adelaide Jane, d. of Gen. George Alexander Leckie, I.S.C., 1861 ; three s. three d. Educ.: Mount Radford School, Exeter. Entered Bombay Army as Ensign, 1857 ; Lieut. 1858 ; Capt. 1864 ; Major, 1869 ; Lieut.-Col. 1871 ; Col. 1876 ; Maj.-Gen. 1885 ; Lieut.-Gen. 1889 ; Gen. 1896 ; Col. 102nd (K.E.O.) Grenadiers, 1904 ; served during Indian Mutiny in pursuit of Tantia Topee, 1858; D.A.Q.M.G. Abyssinian Expedition, 1868 (medal) ; Ch. Director of Transport, Afghan Campaign, 1879-80 (medal and clasp, C.B. Mil.); commanded Quetta District, 1881-84 ; Northern Division, Bombay Army, 1887-89. Recreations: cricket, riding, shooting, carpentering and turning, gardening and bee-keeping. Address: Sandhurst, Hawkhurst, Kent. Clubs: East India United Service, M.C.C.
(Died 24 Jan. 1918.)

EDWARDES, Stephen Meredyth, C.V.O. 1912 ; C.S.I. 1915 ; I.C.S. ; b. 1873 ; s. of late Rev. Stephen Edwardes, Fellow of Merton College, Oxford ; m. 1895, Celia, d. of Arthur Darker of Nottingham ; two s. one d. Educ.: Eton ; Christ Church, Oxford. Entered Indian Civil Service, 1895 ; served as Assistant Collector and Magistrate, Under Secretary to Govt., Assistant Collector of Customs, Special Collector ; Deputy Secretary to Govt. Compiler and Editor of the Bombay City Gazetteer; Commissioner of Police, 1909-16 ; Municipal Commissioner for the City of Bombay, 1916-18 ; Fellow of the Bombay University ; Ex-President of the Anthropological Society, Bombay ; retired from the service, 1918 ; represented India at International Conference on Traffic in Women and Children at Geneva, 1921 ; Joint Editor, Indian Antiquary, 1923. Publications: The Rise of Bombay—a Retrospect, 1902 ; The Ruling Princes of India—a historical and statistical Account of Junagadh and Bhavnagar, 1906; The Gazetteer of Bombay City and Island, 1909 ; By-ways of Bombay, 1912 ; and other works on Indian history ; Crime in India, 1925 ; Memoirs of Sir D. Petit and K. R. Cama. Address: c/o Grindlays, 54 Parliament Street, S.W.1. Clubs: East India United Service ; Orient, Bombay.
(Died 1 Jan. 1927.)

EDWARDS, Canon Allen; b. 1844 ; e. s. of Rev. Allen Edwards of Alleyndale, Cambridge Park, Twickenham. Educ.: Corpus Christi College, Cambridge (M.A.). Vicar of All Saints and St. Augustine's, South Lambeth, 1874 ; Member of the School Board for London, 1891 ; Rural Dean of Kennington, 1891 ; Canon of the Collegiate Church, Southwark, 1897-1905 ; Proctor in Convocation for the Diocese of Rochester, 1900 - 5 ; Canon Residentiary of Southwark, 1905 ; Proctor in Convocation for the Diocese of Southwark, 1905. Address: 248 South Lambeth Road, S.W. (Died 7 June 1917.)

EDWARDS, Charles Lewis, C.B.E. ; Chief Accountant, London and North-Eastern Railway Co. ; o. surv. s. of late Charles Edwards, Winchester; b. 19 March 1865 ; m. Alice, e. d. of late H. Mundy, Marlborough ; one s. five d. Accountant, North - West Argentine Railway, 1890-95 ; Buenos Ayres and Rosario Railway, 1895-1902. and re-appointed upon amalgamation with Central Argentine Railway, to 1903 ; Chief Accountant Great Northern Railway, 1903-22 ; Fellow of Chartered Institute of Secretaries, Incorporated Society of Accountants and Auditors, Royal Horticultural Society, and of Royal Geographical Society ; Liveryman of W. Company of Turners ; Past Grand Deacon of G. L. of Freemasons of England. *Publications:* various Masonic publications. *Address:* Santa Caterina, Loudwater, Bucks. *T.:* Penn 59. *Club:* Constitutional. (*Died 11 May 1923.*)

EDWARDS, D.; Editor and Managing Director, Nottingham Daily Express and Evening News since 1908 ; J.P. County Borough of Nottingham ; *b.* 11 April 1858 ; *m.* 1888, Annie, *e. d.* of late G. Lloyd, Carnarvon. Served apprenticeship at Herald Office, Carnarvon ; left for Liverpool and engaged on Liverpool Daily Post ; returned to Carnarvon ; General Manager, North Wales Observer Series, 1864-91 ; managing editor, Nottingham Daily Express and Nottingham Evening News, 1891-1897 ; assistant-manager Daily News, 1897-1901. editor and manager, 1901-1902. *Address:* 10 Ebury Road, Nottingham. *T.:* 392 Nottingham.
(*Died 22 Feb. 1916.*)

EDWARDS, Sir Francis ; 1st Bart., *cr.* 1907 ; M.P. (R.) Radnorshire, 1892-95, 1900-10, and 1910-18 ; D.L., J.P. ; *b.* 28 Apr. 1852 ; *m.* 1880, Catherine (*d.* 1915), *d.* of David Davis, Aberdare ; one *d. Educ.:* Shrewsbury ; Jesus College, Oxford. Sheriff of Radnorshire, 1898. *Heir:* none. *Address:* The Cottage, Knighton, Radnorshire. *Club:* Reform.
(*Died 10 May 1927.*)

EDWARDS, G. Spencer ; journalist and dramatic critic ; *s.* of late Henry Francis Edwards, a popular preacher in connection with the Wesleyan body, and *n.* of late Rev. William Spencer Edwards, an eminent Congregationalist divine. Joined staff of the Era under the late Frederic Ledger, 1870 ; became chief of editorial staff, and so remained for more than twenty years ; was the original "Carados" of the Referee, and wrote over that signature for thirty-four years ; author of numerous short stories, and, with G. H. Snazelle, of Snazelleparilla, a book of foreign travels, adventures, and laughable stories ; and contributed to the once popular periodical Funny Folks under the editorship of late William Sawyer ; for six years a regular contributor to the Illustrated Sporting and Dramatic News, and for a considerable time dramatic critic to Lloyds' Newspaper. *Recreations:* an ardent cyclist. *Address:* 147 Clapham Road, S.W. (*Died 1 Aug. 1916.*)

EDWARDS, Lt. - Comdr. Harington Douty, R.N., D.S.O. 1915 ; Served European War, 1914-15, landing naval guns in Belgium (D.S.O.). (*Died 11 Mar. 1916.*)

EDWARDS, Henry John, C.B. 1911 ; C.B.E. 1919 ; O.B.E. 1918 ; M.A. ; Fellow and Lecturer of Peterhouse, Cambridge ; *b.* 8 Sep. 1869 ; *e. s.* of Major Henry Charles Edwards, V.D., of Woodbridge, Suffolk, and Sarah Jane, *d.* of H. L. Freeman, M.R.C.S., of Saxmundham, Suffolk ; *m.* 1905, Margaret Ethel, *e. d.* of Rev. Arthur Ashton, B.D., Rector of Uggeshall, Suffolk ; one *s. Educ.:* Woodbridge School ; Bath College ; Trinity College, Cambridge. Scholar ; Browne Medal (Latin Epigram), 1890 ; B.A. (1st class, 1st division, Classical Tripos, Part i.), 1891 ; 1st class (Classics and History) Classical Tripos, Part ii., 1892 ; Jeremie Prize, 1892 ; Classical Lecturer and Dean of Selwyn College, 1895-99 ; Fellow and Classical Lecturer of Peterhouse, 1899 ; Assistant Tutor and Dean, 1900 ; Tutor, 1907-20 ; Examiner, Classical Tripos Part i., 1902, 1903, 1907, 1919, 1920, 1921; Part ii., 1906, 1908, 1909, 1912, 1913 ; C.U.R.V., 1891-1908 ; Lieut.-Colonel commanding, 1901-8 ; "Q" Club gold medal, 1904 ; Secretary, Board of Military Studies, Cambridge, 1904-20 ; Colonel Commanding Cambridge University Contingent,

Officers' Training Corps, 1908-19 ; T.D. 1911 ; Commandant, Cambridge University School of Instruction, 1914-16 ; Commanding Officer, Cadet Battalion, 1916-18. *Publications:* Edition of Livy I. (Pitt Press) ; Translation of Caesar's Gallic War (Loeb Classical Library) ; Articles and reviews on classical and military subjects. *Recreations:* music, sketching, rifle-shooting. *Address:* Peterhouse, Cambridge. *Club:* United University. (*Died 26 June 1923.*)

EDWARDS, Captain Hugh, R.N., D.S.O. 1915 ; H.M.S. President. Served European War, 1914-15 (D.S.O. for services in a patrol cruiser). *Address:* Fair Oak, Eastleigh.
(*Died 5 Dec. 1916.*)

EDWARDS, Lt.-Gen. Sir James Bevan, K.C.M.G., *cr.* 1891 ; C.B. 1877 ; K.C.B., *cr.* 1912 ; retired ; *b.* 5 Nov. 1834 ; *m.* 1st, 1868, Alice (*d.* 1899), *d.* of late R. Brocklebank ; 2nd, 1901, Nina (*d.* 1916), *d.* of late John Balfour, of Steephurst, Peterfield, and widow of Sir R. Dalrymple Elphinstone. 3rd Bt. ; 3rd, 1918, Amy Ann, *d.* of late J. N. Harding of Buzzacott, North Devon. *Educ.:* Woolwich. Entered Royal Engineers, 1852 ; Lieut.-Gen. 1891 ; Col. Commandant, 1908 ; served in Crimean War (medal, Turkish medal), Indian Mutiny (despatches thrice, medal with clasp, Brevet-Major, C.B.); China, 1864 (gold medal) ; Suakim Expedition, 1885 (despatches, medal with clasp, bronze star) ; Commandant of School of Military Engineering, 1885-88 ; commanded the troops in China, 1889-90 ; M.P. (C.) Hythe, 1895-99 ; Chairman, Royal Colonial Institute, 1909-15. *Address:* 48 Egerton Crescent, S.W.3. *T.:* Kensington 1444. *Clubs:* United Service, Travellers'.
(*Died 8 July 1922.*)

EDWARDS, Sir John Bryn, 1st Bt., *cr.* 1921 ; M.A., LL.B.; *b.* 12 Jan. 1889; *s.* of late William Henry Edwards, J.P., and late Margaret Hannah Edwards; *m.* 1911, Kathleen Ermyntrude, *d.* of late John Corfield, J.P. ; one *s.* one *d. Educ.:* Winchester College ; Trinity Hall, Cambridge. Member of Swansea Town Council ; Director of English Crown Spelter Co. *Heir:* *s.* John Clive Leighton Edwards. *Address:* Hendrefoilan, Sketty, Glamorganshire. *T.:* Sketty 88. *Clubs:* Swansea and Counties; Bristol Channel Yacht. (*Died 22 Aug. 1922.*)

EDWARDS, Lady (Laura Selina), 2nd *d.* of J. C. Clark, Bridgefoot House, Iver, Bucks ; *m.* as his second wife Sir Henry Coster Lea Edwards, 2nd Bt. (*d.* 1896). *Address:* Ashbrittle, Wellington, Somerset ; 17 Wordsworth Road, Worthing. *Clubs:* Caravan, Ladies' Parkside. (*Died 24 Mar. 1919.*)

EDWARDS, Matilda Betham-, poet, novelist, and writer on French rural life; *b.* Suffolk; *d.* of Edward Edwards and Barbara, *née* Betham ; niece of Sir William Betham, Ulster King-at-Arms, and Matilda Betham, friend of Charles and Mary Lamb. *Educ.:* at home ; by herself. Purely literary. Officier de l'Instruction Publique de France, 1891. *Publications:* The White House by the Sea ; Kitty ; Dr. Jacob ; John and I ; France of To-Day ; Poems ; The Golden Bee (ballads), 1896 ; Reminiscences ; A Romance of Dijon ; The Lord of the Harvest ; Anglo-French Reminiscences, 1899 ; A Suffolk Courtship, 1900 ; Mock Beggars' Hall, 1901 ; East of Paris, 1902 ; Barham Brocklebank, M.D., 1904 ; Home Life in France, 1905 ; Literary Rambles in France, 1907 ; Poems, 1907 ; French Men, Women, and Books, 1910 ; In French Africa, 1913 ; Hearts of Alsace, 1916. *Recreations:* music, botany, French travel. *Address:* Villa Julia, Hastings.
(*Died 4 Jan. 1919.*)

EDWARDS, Sir Owen Morgan, Kt., *cr.* 1916 ; H.M. Chief Inspector of Education for Wales since 1907 ; Fellow of Lincoln College, Oxford, and Modern History Lecturer, 1889-1907 ; Hon. Fellow of Lincoln College ; *b.* 25 Dec. 1858 ; *s* of late Owen Edwards, Coedypry,

Llanuwchllyn; *m.* Ellen [*d.* 1919], *d.* of late Evan Davies, Prys Mawr, Llanuwchllyn. *Educ.:* Bala Grammar School; University College of Wales; Balliol College, Oxford. B.A., London University; B.A. and M.A., Oxford University; Stanhope Essay; Lothian Prize. M.P. for Merioneth, 1899-1900. *Publications:* Tro yn yr Eidal, Tro yn Llydaw, Er Mwyn Iesu, Cartref Cymru, Story of Wales, etc.; editor of works of Dafydd ab Gwilym, Goronwy Owen, Ceiriog, Islwyn, etc.; editor and proprietor of Cymru till 1907. *Address:* Neuadd Wen, Llanuwchllyn, Bala; Board of Education, Whitehall, S.W.
(Died May 1920.)

EDWARDS, Rev. Thomas; Rector of Aber, Wales; Hon. Canon Bangor Cathedral. *Address:* The Rectory, Aber, Wales.

EDWARDS, Hon. William Cameron, Member Canadian Senate since 1903; *b.* Clarence, Ontario, 7 May 1844; *s* of William Edwards, Portsmouth, England and Ann Cameron, Fort William, Scotland; *m.* 1885, Catherine Margret Wilson, Cumberland, Ontario. *Educ.:* Ottawa Collegiate Institute. Entered employ of Cameron and Edwards, lumber manufacturers, 1863; established firm of W. C. Edwards and Co., lumber manufacturers. at Rockland, Ontario, 1868; elected to House of Commons for Co. of Russell, 1887, and again at subsequent elections; largely interested in agriculture and growing of good live stock; President of Russell Agricultural Society for over thirty years; President of W. C. Edwards and Co., Limited, Canada Cement Co., Bathurst Lumber Co., Cascapedia Manufacturing and Trading Co., Ottawa; and Hull Power and Manufacturing Co., and several minor companies; Director of Canadian Bank of Commerce and Toronto General Trusts Corporation. *Recreations:* regular sleep and constant work, also careful diet. *Address:* 80 Sussex Street, Ottawa. *T.:* Rideau 340. *M.:* Ontario 4199. *Clubs:* Rideau, Country, Golf and Hunt, Ottawa; Mount Royal, St. James's, Montreal; Toronto, York, Toronto; Garrison, Quebec. *(Died 17 Sept. 1921.)*

EDWARDS, Colonel William Egerton, late R.F.A.; C.M.G. 1918; Superintendent of Design, Ordnance Factories, Royal Arsenal, Woolwich, since 1920; *b.* 25 June 1875; *s.* of late C. F. Edwards, Registrar-General, Mauritius; *m.* 1901, Jessie Maud, *d.* of late Lt.-Col. T. G. Thomson, Indian Army; one *s.* one *d. Educ.:* Royal Military Academy, Woolwich. Joined R.A. 1894; employed with West African Frontier Force, 1899-1901; operations in Ashanti, 1900 (severely wounded, despatches, brev. of maj., medal); operations in Southern Nigeria, 1901 (dangerously wounded, medal with clasp); Secretary Explosives Committee and Ordnance Research Board, 1904-7; Staff Capt. H.Q. of Army, 1905-7; Deputy Assistant Director H.Q. of Army, 1907-9; Inspector Inspection Staff, 1910-14 and 1914-16; Assistant Deputy Director-General, Ministry of Munitions, 1916; Director of Inspection of Munitions, Canada, 1916-19; (temp. Col. Oct. 1916; temp. Brig.-Gen. Oct. 1918; Col. 1920). *Publications:* Article, Armour Plates, Encyclopædia Britannica, 11th Edition; Sundry papers, R.A. Journal. *Club:* Junior United Service. *(Died 25 July 1921.)*

EDWARDS, Hon. Maj.-Gen. Sir William Rice, K.C.B., *cr.* 1923; K.C.I.E., *cr.* 1921; C.B. 1914; C.M.G. 1900; King's Hon. Physician, 1917; M.D., F.R.C.S.E., M.R.C.S.; *b.* 17 May 1862; *s.* of Rev. Canon Howell Powell Edwards, Monmouthshire, and Elizabeth Evans, Lovesgrove, Cardiganshire; *m.* 1st, 1896, Anne Vaughan (*d.* 1911), *y. d.* of late W. H. Darby of Leap Castle, King's County; 2nd, 1919, Nellie, *d.* of late Lt.-Col. R. Dewar and Mrs. R. Dewar, 31 Beaufort Gardens, S.W., widow of Lieut.-Colonel R. Bird, C.I.E., M.V.O. *Educ.:* Magdalen College School, Oxford; Clifton College; London Hospital. Was House-Surg.

and House-Physician London Hospital; entered the Indian Medical Service, 1886; served on Lord Roberts' staff, 1890, services lent to War Office, 1900; joined Lord Roberts in S. Africa as Surgeon to Headquarters staff (despatches, Queen's medal, 5 clasps, C.M.G.); Superintending Surgeon Kashmir State Hospitals, 1901; Chief Medical Officer of North-West Frontier Provinces, India, 1910; Assistant Director Medical Services Derajat and Bannu Brigades, 1914-15 (British war medal); Surgeon-General, Bengal, 1915; Director-General Indian Medical Service, 1918-22; Member Legislative Assembly Bengal, 1915-18; Govt. of India, 1918-1920; Council of State for India, 1920-22. *Recreations:* shooting, golf, etc. *Clubs:* Naval and Military, Royal Automobile; United Service, Simla. *(Died 13 Oct. 1923.)*

EDWARDS, Hon. Sir (Worley) Bassett, Kt., *cr.* 1919; Puisne Judge, Supreme Court, New Zealand, 1896-1920; *b.* London, 5 Sep. 1850; *s.* of Charles S. Wilson Edwards; *m.* 1886, Mary A. Cutten. Went to New Zealand, 1855. *Address:* Auckland, New Zealand. *(Died 2 June 1927.)*

EFFINGHAM, 4th Earl of, *cr.* 1837, **Henry Alexander Gordon Howard,** D.L. for West Riding of Yorkshire; 14th Baron Howard of Effingham, *cr.* 1554; *b.* 15 Aug. 1866; *s.* of Henry, 3rd Earl, and Victoria Francisca, *d.* of Monsieur Alexandre Boyer of Paris; unmarried; *S.* father, 1898. *Educ.:* privately. Patron of 6 livings. *Decorated:* gold star for services to athletics and cycling in North Oxon. since 1892. Owns 8018 acres in Yorkshire, 2776 in Oxfordshire, and 910 in Northamptonshire. *Heir-pres.:* *c.* Gordon Frederick Henry Charles Howard [*b.* 18 May 1873; *m.* 1904, Rosamond Margaret, who obtained a divorce, 1914, *d.* of late E. H. Hudson; two *s.*] *Recreation:* motoring. *Address:* Tusmore Park, Bicester, Oxon.; Thundercliffe Grange, Rotherham, Yorkshire. *T.A.:* Tusmore Hethe-Oxon.
(Died 6 May 1927.)

EGAN, Sir Henry Kelly, Kt., *cr.* 1914; Managing Director Hawkesbury Lumber Company, Bank of Ottawa, Ottawa Stock Exchange, etc.; *b.* Aylmer, P.Q., 15 Jan. 1848; *y. s.* of late John Egan, M.P. Canada, Lisswane, Co. Galway, and Anne Margaret, *d.* of late Captain Gibson, R.N.; *m.* 1878, Harriet Augusta, *y. d.* of late W. A. Himsworth. *Educ.:* Montreal High School; Conservative. Anglican. *Address:* 30 Cartier Street, Ottawa. *Clubs:* Jockey, Mount Royal, Montreal; Rideau, Golf, Country, Hunt, Ottawa. *(Died 19 Oct. 1925.)*

EGAN, Hon. Maurice Francis; American Minister to Denmark, 1907-18; *b.* Philadelphia, 1852; *m.* 1880, Katharine Mullin (*d.* 1921), Philadelphia; one *s.* two *d. Educ.:* Las Salle College; A.B., Georgetown University. LL.D. (Columbia University, N.Y.), J.U.D. (Ottawa University, Canada), Ph.D. (Villanova College, Pa.). Professor of English Literature, University of Notre Dame, Indiana, 1888; Catholic University, Washington, 1895; Member of the American Academy of Arts, President of the Dante League of New York; President of the International Institute of Arts and Letters; Commander of the Danish Order of the Dannebrog; Officer of the Order of King Leopold of Belgium, Holder of the Laslare Medal for poetry. *Publications:* Songs and Sonnets; John Longworthy; Preludes; The Life Around Us; Lectures on English Literature; Studies in Literature; The Wiles of Sexton Maginnis; The Ghost in Hamlet and other Essays in Comparative Literature; Everybody's St. Francis. *Address:* 2308 19th Street, Washington, D.C. *Club:* Century, Players', New York. *(Died Jan. 1924.)*

EGERTON, Field-Marshal Sir Charles (Comyn), G.C.B., *cr.* 1904; K.C.B., *cr.* 1908; C.B. 1895; D.S.O. 1891; Col. 23rd Cavalry

Frontier Force, India ; A.D.C. to Queen Victoria and King Edward VII. ; *b.* 10 Nov. 1848 ; *m.* 1877, Anna Wellwood (*d.* 1890), *d.* of late J. L. Hill, W.S., Edinburgh ; one *s.* *Educ.:* Rossall ; Sandhurst. Entered army, 1867 ; Col. 1895 ; served Afghan War, 1879-80, including battle of Candahar (despatches, medal with clasp, bronze decoration) ; Murree Expedition, 1880 ; Black Mountain Expedition, 1888 (despatches, medal) ; 1st and 2nd Miranzai Expeditions (severely wounded, despatches, Bt. Lt.-Col., D.S.O., clasp) ; Waziristan Field Force, 1894-95 (despatches, C.B., clasp) ; Dongola Expedition, commanded Indian contingent (despatches, British and Khedive's medals) ; commanded 1st Brigade, Tochi Force, 1897-98 (despatches, medal with clasp) ; Waziristan, 1901-2, in command (thanks of Government, clasp) ; commanded Expedition against Darwesh Khel Waziris, 1902-3 ; commanded Somaliland Field Force, 1903-4 ; action of Jidballi (medal, two clasps) ; commanding troops Madras, 1904-7 ; General, 1906 ; retired, 1907 ; Field-Marshal, 1917 ; Member of the Council of India, 1907-17. *Address:* The Staithe, Christchurch, Hants. *Club:* United Service.   (*Died 20 Feb. 1921.*)

EGERTON, Rt. Hon. Sir Edwin Henry, P.C. 1904 ; K.C.B., *cr.* 1897 ; G.C.M.G., *cr.* 1902 ; *b.* 8 Nov. 1841 ; *m.* 1895, Olga, widow of M. Michel Katkoff, and *d.* of Prince Nicholas Lobanow Rostowski ; one *s.* Entered Diplomatic Service, 1859 ; Secretary of Legation, Buenos Ayres, 1879 ; Athens, 1881 ; Consul-General, Egypt, 1884 ; Secretary of Embassy, Constantinople. 1885 ; Paris, 1885 ; C.B. 1886 ; Envoy Extraordinary and Minister Plenipotentiary to the King of the Hellenes, 1892-1904 ; H.M.'s Ambassador to the Court of Italy, 1904-8. *Club:* Travellers'.   (*Died 8 July 1916.*)

EGERTON, Hugh Edward, Beit Professor of Colonial History, 1905-20 ; Fellow of All Souls College, Oxford ; *b.* 19 Apr. 1855 ; 2nd *s.* of late E. C. Egerton, M.P. ; *m.* 1886, Margaret Alice, *d.* of Alexander Trotter of Dreghorn, Midlothian. *Educ.:* Rugby ; Corpus Christi College, Oxford ; 1st class in Literæ Humaniores. Assistant Private Secretary to late Hon. E. Stanhope, M.P., 1885 ; Member of Managing Committee of Emigrants Information Office since its foundation in 1886 till 1906 ; Member of L'Institut Colonial International, 1923. *Publications:* A Short History of British Colonial Policy, 1897, 6th ed., 1920 ; Sir Stamford Raffles, 1900 ; Origin and Growth of the English Colonies, 1902, 3rd ed., 1920 ; Canada under British Rule, in Sir Charles Lucas's series on the History and Geography of the British Colonies, 1908, 3rd ed., 1922 ; Canadian Constitutional Development, 1907 (with Prof. W. L. Grant) ; Federations and Unions within the British Empire, 2nd ed. 1924 ; British Foreign Policy in Europe, 1917 ; British Colonial Policy in the 20th Century, 1922 ; Causes and Character of the American Revolution, 1923 ; edited Sir W. Molesworth's Speeches, 1903, and The Royal Commission on Loyalists' Claims, 1783-85, 1915, for Roxburghe Club ; contributed to Palgrave's Dictionary of Political Economy ; Poole's Historical Atlas of Modern Europe ; Cambridge Modern History, vols. iv. and ix. ; The Oxford Survey of the British Empire ; The (American) Cyclopædia of Government ; Supplement to Encyclopædia Britannica ; Supplement to Dictionary of National Biography ; English Historical Review, and other publications. *Address:* 14 St. Giles, Oxford. *Club:* Athenæum. (*Died 21 May 1927.*)

EGERTON, Lady Mabelle, C.B.E., Lady of Justice of St. John of Jerusalem ; mentioned in despatches, 1917 ; *b.* 1865 ; *d.* of 1st Earl Brassey, G.C.B. ; *b.* 1865 ; *m.* 1888, Charles A. Egerton of Mountfield Court ; four *s.* three *d.* *Address:* 32 Ashley Gardens, S.W.1. *T.:* Victoria 4470. (*Died 18 Feb. 1927.*)

EGGELING, Professor H. Julius, Ph.D. ; Professor of Sanskrit and Comparative Philology, Edinburgh University, 1875-1914 ; *b.* Germany, 12 July 1842 ; *s.* of late H. S. Eggeling, country gentleman ; *m.* 1871, Marie, *d.* of W. Homann. *Educ.:* Bernburg Gymnasium ; Breslau and Berlin Universities. Came to England 1867 to work at Sanskrit MSS. in India Office and Royal Asiatic Society's Libraries ; Assistant to Professor F. Max Müller, Oxford, 1867-69 ; Secretary and Librarian of Royal Asiatic Society, 1869-75 ; Professor of Sanskrit at University College, London, 1872-1875. *Publications:* edition of Kâtantra Grammar with Commentary (Calcutta), 1874-78 ; edition of Vardhamâna's Ganaratnamahodadhi, 1879-80 ; Translation of Satapatha Brâhmana, vols. i.-v. in Sacred Books of the East ; Catalogue of Sanskrit Manuscripts in Library of India Office, 1887-99 ; articles on Brahmanism, Hinduism, and Sanskrit Language and Literature, in Encyclopædia Britannica, 1876-86 ; and on Veda, and Sanskrit, in Chambers's Encyclopædia ; with E. B. Cowell) Catalogue of Buddhist Sanskrit Manuscripts in the possession of the Royal Asiatic Society, 1875. *Recreation:* gardening. *Address:* Brunstane House, near Joppa, Edinburgh.   (*Died 3 Mar. 1918.*)

EGLINGTON, Rev. Canon Arthur, M.A., Vicar of St. Anne's, Wandsworth, since 1920 ; Rural Dean of Wandsworth since 1924 ; *s.* of William Eglington of Southbro) Surbiton ; unmarried ; *b.* 13 Feb. 1871. *Educ.:* Sherborne ; Lincoln College, Oxford ; Salisbury Theological College. Curate Woolwich Parish Church, 1894-1901 ; Vicar of St. John's, East Dulwich, 1901-9 ; St. Paul's, Lorrimore Square, 1909-20 ; Chaplain Springfield Mental Hospital, 1920 ; Hon. Canon of Southwark, 1923 ; Chaplain Wandsworth Intermediate Schools, 1920 ; Proctor in Convocation, Diocese of Southwark, 1924. *Address:* St. Anne's Vicarage, Wandsworth. *T.A.:* St. Anne's, S.W.18. *T.:* Latchmere 4673. *Club:* New University.
   (*Died 31 Aug. 1925.*)

EGLINTON and WINTON, 15th Earl of (*cr.* 1507), **George Arnulph Montgomerie,** D.L. Lord Montgomerie, Baron Setop and Tranent, 1448 ; E. of Winton, 1600 ; Baron Kilwinning, 1615 : Baron Ardrossan (U.K.), 1806. E. of Winton (U.K.), 1859 ; Hereditary Sheriff of Renfrewshire ; Lieut. Grenadier Guards (retired) ; President Territorial Association ; Lord-Lieutenant Co. Ayr, 1897 ; M.F.H. (Eglinton) ; *b.* 23 Feb. 1848 ; *s.* of 18th Earl and his 1st wife, *d.* of C. Newcomen ; *S. b.* 1892 ; *m.* Janet, *d.* of B. A. Cunninghame, 1873 ; two *s.* two *d.* *Educ.:* Eton. Master of Foxhounds. Owns about 30,200 acres. *Heir: s.* Lord Montgomerie. *Address:* Eglinton Castle, also Redburn, Irvine, N.B. ; Skelmorlie Castle, Largs, N.B. *T.:* Irvine 38. *M.:* S.D. 206, S.D. 263. *Club :* Carlton.   (*Died 10 Aug. 1919.*)

EIFFEL, Alexandre Gustave, engineer ; *b.* Dijon, 15 Dec. 1832 ; *m.* Marguerite Gaudelet (decd.) ; four *c.* *Educ.:* Colleges of Dijon and Sainte-Barbe ; Central School of Arts and Manufacture ; late President of Civil Engineers of France Society ; Honorary Member of the Mechanical Engineers' Institution of London. Built Eiffel Tower, Paris, 1889 ; bridge over the Douro, Portugal ; Viaduct of Garabit, Cantal ; Aerodynamic Laboratory at Auteuil ; Officer Legion of Honour ; Knight of Iron Crown of Austria ; Commander of the Order of Conception, Portugal ; of Isabella of Spain ; of Crown of Italy ; of St. Anne of Russia. *Address:* 1 rue Rabelais, Paris ; Château des Bruyères, Sèvres, France.   (*Died Dec. 1923.*)

EINTHOVEN, Willem, Medic. and Philosoph. Dr. Utrecht, LL.D., Aberdeen ; Professor of Physiology at the University of Leyden since 1886 ; *b.* Samarang, Java, 21 May 1860 ; *m.* 1886 ; four *c.* *Educ.:* Utrecht. Student at the

University of Utrecht, Scholar of Donders, Koster and Snellen, Assistant of Donders and Snellen, 1879: promotion to medic. doctor, 1885; M.D. Edin. 1928; Nobel Prize for Medicine, 1924. *Publications:* several papers in scientific journals; also a chapter in Heyman's Handbuch der Laryngologie und Rhinologie, and one in Bethe's Handbook der normalen und pathologischen Physiologie; editor of Onderzoekingen Physiol. Laborat., Leyden. *Address:* Leyden, Holland.

(*Died 29 Sept. 1927.*)

ELDER, John Munro, B.A., M.D., C.M.G. 1918; Col. A.M.S. (R.O.); Assist. Prof. Surgery, McGill University since 1905; Surgeon, Montreal General Hospital since 1905; *b.* Huntingdon, P.Q., Canada, 29 Oct. 1860; *e. s.* of George Elder and Catherine Munro; *m.* 1886, Grace Whitehead Hendrie; two *s.* *Educ.:* McGill University, Montreal, 1st Rank Honours and Prince of Wales Gold Medal; 1st Rank Honours and Sutherland Gold Medal; Surgeon-Major, Com. Heavy Artillery in North-West Rebellion, Canada, 1885 (medal and clasp); Colonial Officers' Long Service Decoration, 1906; Demonstrator of Anatomy, 1890; Lecturer in Surgery, McGill University, 1900; Examiner in Surgery, Dominion Medical Council, Canada, 1912; Lieut.-Col. i/c Surgery, No. 3 Casualty Clearing Hospital, B.E.F., France, 1915; O.C. of same Hospital (despatches four times, C.M.G.) 1917; Consulting Surgeon, British Armies in France (stationed at Rouen), 1918. *Publications:* numerous articles in Medical Journals; Surgery of Neck in Buck's System Surgery. *Recreation:* golf. *Address:* 781 Sherbrooke Street, Montreal, Canada. *T.A.:* Eldersurg, Montreal. *T.:* Uptown 9654. *Clubs:* Mount Royal, Hunt, University, Montreal. (*Died 5 Feb. 1922.*)

ELDON, 3rd Earl of (*cr.* 1821), **John Scott,** D.L., J.P.; Baron Eldon, 1799; Viscount Encombe, 1821; *b.* London, 8 Nov. 1845; *s.* of 2nd Earl and *d.* of 1st Lord Feversham; *S.* father 1854; *m.* 1869, Henrietta, *d.* of Captain Henry Martin Turnor; four *s.* two *d.* *Educ.:* Eton; Christ Church, Oxford. Owns about 25,800 acres. *Heir: g.-s.* Viscount Encombe. *Address:* Encombe, Corfe Castle, Dorset; 43 Portman Square, W.1. *Club:* Carlton.

(*Died 10 Aug. 1926.*)

ELGEE, Captain Cyril Hammond, F.R.G.S.; British Resident at Ibadan since 1903; *b.* 1871; *e. s.* of late Rev. W. F. Elgee, Otterbourne, Hants; unmarried. *Educ.:* Lancing; France; Sandhurst. First Commission, 16th Foot, 1892; Captain, 1899; served Chitral, 1895 (medal with clasp); Ashanti Campaign, Relief of Kumasi, 1900 (medal); A.D.C. and Private Secy. to Sir William Macgregor, Governor of Lagos, 1900-2; resigned commission, 1904; Member of Court of Enquiry into importation of Liquor into W. Africa, 1909; has travelled in India, Europe, America, Newfoundland, Labrador, Canada, Africa, Denmark, Sweden, Bohemia, Germany, and Austria. *Publication:* Memorandum on Negro Education, for which received thanks of Secy. of State, 1906. *Clubs:* United Service, Baldwin, Royal Automobile, Queen's.

(*Died 17 Aug. 1917.*)

ELGIN and KINCARDINE, 9th Earl of (*cr.* 1633), **Victor Alexander Bruce,** K.G., *cr.* 1899; G.C.S.I., G.C.I.E., P.C., LL.D., D.C.L.; Baron Bruce, 1603; Earl of Kincardine and Baron Bruce of Torry, 1647; Baron Elgin (U.K.), 1849; *b.* Monklands, near Montreal, 16 May 1849; *s.* of 8th Earl and his 2nd wife, 4th *d.* of 1st Earl of Durham (*d.* 1898); *S.* father 1863; *m.* 1st, 1876, Constance (*d* 1909), 2nd *d.* of 9th Earl of Southesk, K.T.; six *s.* four *d.* ; 2nd, 1913, Gertrude, *d.* of Commander W. Sherbrooke, R.N., and widow of Capt. F. Ogilvy, R.N. *Educ.:* Eton; Balliol Coll. Oxford (M.A.). Lord Lieut. of Fifeshire since 1886; Treasurer

324

of Household and First Commissioner of Works, 1886; Viceroy of India, 1894-99; Secretary of State for the Colonies, 1905-8; Chancellor of Aberdeen University, 1914. *Heir: s.* Lord Bruce. *Address:* Broomhall, Dunfermline, Fifeshire. *Clubs:* Brooks's, Travellers'.

(*Died 18 Jan. 1917.*)

ELHORST, Hendrik Jan; Professor of Hebraic and Aramaic Language, antiquities, and literature University of Amsterdam since 1906; *b.* Wisch (Guelderland), 21 Oct. 1861; *s.* of W. F. G. L. Elhorst and J. van der Ploeg; *m.* Hermine Maes; two *d.* *Educ.:* University of Amsterdam. Minister of the Mennonites at Irnsum (Friesland), 1887; Arnhem, 1888; The Hague, 1898; Harlem, 1900; Member of Teyler's Theological Society, 1901; Theol. Dr. University of Amsterdam, 1891; D.D. University of St. Andrews, 1911; Kt. Dutch Lion. *Publications:* De profetie van Micha (a critical introduction to the book of Micah with translation and commentary), 1891; De profetie van Amos (a critical introduction to the book of Amos with translation and commentary), 1899; Israel in het licht der jongste onderzoekingen (Israel in the light of the latest investigations), 1906; the rites of mourning among the Israelites (Festschrift zum 70. Geburtstage Wellhausens); several articles in Dutch and foreign periodicals, *e.g.* on the ephod ; Deut. 21: 1-9 (Zeitschrift für die alttestamentliche Wissenschaft); the books of the Maccabees; the Messiah of the Samaritans; the Hexateuch (Teyler's Theologisch Tydschrift); The Elephantine-papyri; the book of the Wisdom of Solomon (Nieuw Theologisch Tydschrift), etc.; editor of Nieuw Theologisch Tydschrift (formerly Teyler's Theologisch Tydschrift). *Address:* P.C. Hooftstraat 170, Amsterdam.

ELIBANK, 1st Viscount (*cr.* 1911) **Montolieu Fox Oliphant Murray,** D.L., J.P.; Bt. 1628; 10th Baron (*cr.* 1643); Lord-Lieut. of Peeblesshire, 1896-1908; Commander R.N., retired 1870; *b.* Edinburgh, 27 April 1840; *e. s.* of 9th Baron and Emily, *o. d.* of Archibald Montgomery, niece of Sir James Montgomery; *S.* father, 1871; *m.* Blanche, *e. d.* of Edward John Scott, Portland Lodge, Southsea, Hants; two *s.* five *d.* *Educ.:* privately. Conservative. Entered Navy, 1854; served in China War, H.M.S. "Cambrian" (medal and Taku clasp), 1860; served in H.M.S. "Wolverine," Jamaica Rebellion, 1865. *Heir: s.* Master of Elibank. *Address:* Darn Hall, Eddleston, Peeblesshire; Elibank, Selkirkshire; *Club:* New, Edinburgh. (*Died 20 Feb. 1927.*)

ELIOT, Charles William, LL.D.; *b.* Boston, Mass., 20 March 1834; *s.* of Samuel Atkins Eliot and Mary Lyman ; *m.* 1st, 1858, Ellen Derby Peabody (*d.* 1869); 2nd, 1877, Grace Mellen Hopkinson; one *s.* *Educ.:* Boston Public Latin School; Harvard. Studied Chemistry and investigated Educational Methods in Europe, 1863-65. Tutor in Mathematics, Harvard, 1854-58; Assistant Professor of Mathematics and Chemistry, 1858-61; Chemistry, 1861-63; Prof. of Chemistry in Mass. Inst. of Technology, 1865-69; President of the National Educational Association, 1902-3; President of Harvard University, 1869-1909; President Emeritus, 1909. *Publications:* (with F. H. Storer) Manual of Inorganic Chemistry, 1866, and Manual of Qualitative Chemical Analysis, 1869; American Contributions to Civilisation, and other Essays and Addresses, 1897; Educational Reform, 1898; Charles Eliot, Landscape Architect (biography), 1902; More Money for the Public Schools, 1903; Four American Leaders, 1906; The Durable Satisfactions of Life, 1910; The Road toward Peace, 1915; numerous addresses on Education; Annual Reports as President of Harvard, 1869-1909. *Address:* Cambridge, Mass.

(*Died 22 Aug. 1926.*)

ELIOT, Laurence Stirling, C.M.G. 1914; J.P., I.S.O. 1903; Under-Treasurer of State of

Western Australia since 1891; *b.* 20 Nov. 1845; *e. s.* of late George Eliot, Government Resident, Geraldton, W.A.: *m.* 1871, Eliza Ernestine von Bibra, *d.* of late Francis von Bibra of Tasmania; three *s.* one *d.* *Educ.:* Bishop's College, Perth, W.A. Clerk to Magistrates, W.A.; Landing and Tide Waiter at Bunbury, 1863; also Postmaster and Assistant District Registrar; Clerk in Colonial Secretary's Office, 1872; Secretary to Central Board of Education, and Assistant Clerk in Legislative Council, 1873; Registrar General, Registrar of Deeds, and Registrar of Brands, 1876; Acting Chief Clerk, Colonial Secretary's Department, 1878-80; First Clerk and Registrar General, Colonial Secretary's Department, 1880; Chief Clerk and Accountant, Treasury, 1881; Appointed to take the Census, and to superintend its compilation, 1881; Acting Assistant, Colonial Secretary, 1889; Paymaster of Imperial Pensions, Jan. 1891; Commonwealth Officer, July 1902; retired 1914. *Address:* Belmont, near Perth, W. Australia.

(*Died 22 Feb. 1922.*)

E L I O T, Very Rev. Philip Frank, K.C.V.O., *cr.* 1909; D.D.; Dean of Windsor; Domestic Chaplain to His Majesty; Registrar of the Most Noble Order of the Garter since 1891; *b.* Weymouth, Dorset, 21 Dec. 1835; 3rd *s.* of William Eliot, J.P. and D.L., and Lydia, *d.* of John Ffoliott, M.P. for Sligo; *m.* 1st, Mary Anna Marriott, *d.* of Rev. Frank Smith, Rector of Rushton, Dorset, 1859; 2nd, 1883, Mary Emma Pitt, *d.* of 4th Lord Rivers (*d.* 1900); four *s.* four *d.* *Educ.:* Bath Grammar School; Trinity College, Oxford (Exhibitioner). 2nd class Mods. 1855; 2nd class Lit. Hum. 1857. Curate of St. Michael's, Winchester, 1858-60; Chaplain at Cally, Gatehouse, N.B.; Curate of Walcot, Bath, 1864-67; Vicar of Holy Trinity, Bournemouth, 1867-90; Hon. Canon, Winchester Cathedral, 1881; Canon of Windsor, 1886; Domestic Chaplain to Queen Victoria, 1891-1901; to King Edward VII., 1901-10; Prolocutor of the Lower House of the Convocation of Canterbury, 1904-1913. *Address:* Deanery, Windsor Castle. *T.A.:* Windsor. *Club:* Constitutional.

(*Died 1 Nov. 1917.*)

ELIOT, Sir Whately, Kt., *cr.* 1907; M.Inst. C.E.; *b.* 22 Nov. 1841; *s.* of late William Eliot, of Weymouth; *m.* Jessy Dingwall Fordyce, *d.* of Patrick Jamieson, of Peterhead; one *s.* one *d.* *Educ.:* Windlesham School; Queenwood Coll. Pupil of Sir J. Coode, C.E., at Portland Breakwater; has been engaged on dock and harbour works at Sunderland, Tynemouth, and Isle of Man; conducted survey for harbour works in New Zealand; designed and carried out works for Peterhead Harbour Board and Scarborough Corporation; resident engineer of harbour works for Cape Government, and of Eastham Section Manchester Ship Canal; Admiralty Superintending Civil Engineer in charge of Keyham Dockyard Extension, 1894-1906. *Address:* 10 Inglewood Road, West Hampstead, N.W. (*Died 12 Mar. 1927.*)

ELIOT, Sir Arthur Boswell; 9th Bt: of Stobs, *cr.* 1666; Chief of ancient family of Eliott; *b.* 13 July 1856; *s.* and *o. c.* of Alexander Boswell Eliott, 2nd *s.* of 7th Bt., and Katherine, *d.* of William Craigie; *S.* uncle, 1910; *m.* 1884, Lilla, *d.* of John Burbank; one *s.* two *d.* Heir: *s.* Gilbert Alexander Boswell [*b.* 5 May 1885; *m.* 1912, Flournoy Adams, *o. d.* of late Alexander Hopkins, Atlanta, U.S.A.; two *s.* two *d.*]. *Address:* 25 Montague Street, Portman Square, W.1. *T.:* Paddington 3026.(*Died 15 Jan. 1926.*)

ELIOTT, Lt.-Col. Francis Hardinge, C.S.I. 1915; Indian Army; *b.* 1 April 1862; *s.* of late Edward Frederick Eliott, I.C.S.; *m.* Mary Agnes Wardrop. *Educ.:* Harrow. Entered army, 1881; joined Indian Army, 1885; Burma Commission, 1888; Lt.-Col. 1907; served Burma, 1888-9 (medal, 2 clasps); Com-

missioner Irrawaddy Division, Burma, 1911; retired, 1917. *Club:* Naval and Military.

(*Died 26 Dec. 1928.*)

ELKAN, John, M.V.O. 1920; Governing Director of John Elkan, Ltd., Goldsmiths and Jewellers; *b.* 11 Dec. 1849; *s.* of late Isaac Elkan; *m.* Harriet, *d.* of Henry Samuel; three *s.* two *d.* *Educ.:* privately. Member of the Corporation of London since 1907; Past Master of the Turners' Company. *Recreation:* amateur artist. *Address:* 40 Hanover Gate Mansions, Regent's Park, N.W.1. *T.:* Paddington 5726.

(*Died 24 July 1927.*)

ELKINGTON, John Simeon, M.A., LL.B.; late Professor of History and Political Economy, University of Melbourne; *b.* England, 22 Nov. 1841; *m.* 1867, Helen Mary Guilfoyle. *Educ.:* Grammar School; University, Melbourne. *Address:* c/o The University, Melbourne.

ELLERTON, Rev. Arthur John Bicknell, M.A., Hon. Canon of Southwell; Rector of North Wingfield, Derbyshire, since 1918; Proctor in Convocation, 1920-22; Warden of Community of St. Lawrence, Belper; *b.* 25 Dec. 1865; 3rd *s.* of late Rev. Canon John Ellerton; *m.* 1896, Evelyn Constance (*d.* 1925), 2nd *d.* of late Col. W. M. Barnard, 96th Regiment and Grenadier Guards, and *g.d.* of late Sir Henry Barnard, K.C.B.; five *d.* *Educ.:* Merchant Taylors' School; St. John's College, Oxford. Curate of Halifax Parish Church, 1890-93; Elland, Yorks, 1893-95; Senior Curate of Nantwich, Cheshire, 1895-96; London Diocesan Home Missionary for Merchant Taylors' School Mission, 1896-1902; Vicar of Chaddesden, Derbyshire, 1902-6; Southwell Diocesan Missioner, 1906-14; Rector of Nuthall, Notts, 1914-18. *Address:* North Wingfield Rectory, Chesterfield. *T.:* Clay Cross 64. *M.:* NU 7782.

(*Died 21 Mar. 1928.*)

ELLICOTT, Rosalind, A.R.A.M. 1896; *d.* of late Bishop of Gloucester. *Educ.:* Royal Academy of Music, under Frederick Westlake and Thomas Wingham. *Works:* overture (Gloucester Festival), 1886; part-song, Bring the Bright Garlands; choral ballad, Henry of Navarre, 1894; fantasie for piano and orchestra. *Address:* Tresco, Birchington-on-Sea.

(*Died 5 April 1924.*)

ELLIOT, Hon. Arthur Ralph Douglas; *b.* 17 Dec. 1846; 2nd *s.* of 3rd and heir-pres. of 5th Earl of Minto; *m.* 1888, Madeleine (*d.* 1906), *d.* of late Sir Charles Lister Ryan, K.C.B.; one *s.* [Hubert William Arthur; *b.* 1891; *m.* Mary, *d.* of Hon. Mr. Justice Owen, Sydney, N.S.W. *Educ.:* Eton; Cambridge University, B.A. Capt. 4th Batt. Wilts Regt.] *Educ.:* Edinburgh Univ.; Trinity Coll. Camb. (M.A.); Hon. D.C.L. Durham, 1903. Barr. 1880, and practised on the Northern Circuit; (M.P. L.) Roxburghshire, 1880-86; (L.U.) 1886-92, when he was defeated by Hon. Mark Napier; stood in for City of Durham 1895, when he was defeated by one vote; Financial Secretary to Treasury, 1903; M.P. (L.U.) City of Durham, 1898-1906; Editor of the Edinburgh Review, 1895-1912. *Publications:* Criminal Procedure in England and Scotland, 1878; The State and the Church, 1881; 2nd ed. 1899; Life of the First Viscount Goschen, 1911; Traditions of British Statesmanship, 1919. *Address:* Dimbola, Freshwater Bay, Isle of Wight. *Clubs:* Brook's, Athenæum; New, Edinburgh. (*Died 12 Feb. 1923.*)

ELLIOT, Major Sir Edmund Halbert, Kt., *cr.* 1911; M.V.O. Ensign of the King's Bodyguard of Yeomen of Guard since 1908; *b.* 1854; *s.* of late Lieut.-Col. E. J. Elliot, 79th Highlanders, and *d.* of Charles Craigie-Halkett-Inglis of Cramond; *m.* 1898, Isabella, *d.* of late James C. H. Colquhoun, and *widow* of 3rd Earl of Limerick, K.P. *Educ.:* Cheltenham; R.M. Academy, Woolwich. Lieut. Royal Artillery, 1874; South Africa, 1879; Zulu War: Battle of Ulundi (medal and clasp, despatches); Capt. Royal Artillery, 1883; Adjutant 3rd Middlesex Artillery Volunteers, 1885-91; Major Royal Artillery, 1891; retired, 1892: appointed one of the Exons of H.M.'s Royal Body-Guard of the Yeomen of the Guard, 1892; Clerk of the Cheque and Adjutant, 1901. *Recreations:* golf, hunting, shooting, etc., etc. *Address:* 40 Queen's Gate Gardens, S.W.7; Friary Court, St. James's Palace, S.W. *T.:* Kens. 6176. *Clubs:* Carlton, Naval and Military.

(*Died 20 Sept. 1926.*)

ELLIOT, Rev. Frederick Roberts, M.V.O. 1906; *b.* 15 June 1840. *Educ.:* Exeter Coll., Oxford. M.A.; ordained, 1864; Curate of Tormohen, 1865-69; perpetual curate of the Lodge, Salop, 1870-75; Chaplain at Kadikeui, Asia Minor, 1875-77; curate of St. John the Evangelist, Kingston-on-Thames, 1881-89; Chaplain to H.M. Legation Athens, 1891-98; was tutor to Prince Christopher of Greece. *Address:* Tregie, Paignton, Devon. (*Died 25 Dec. 1918.*)

ELLIOT, Canon George Edward; retired, on Colonial pension; *b.* Tobago, B.W.I., 29 Jan. 1851; *s.* of John L. Elliot, M.D. (Glasgow), and Rosa Eliza Thomas; *m.* 1876, Flora Jane Hutson; three *s.* five *d.* *Educ.:* England; Codrington College, Barbados. Ordained, 1874; Curate of St. John, Antigua, 1874-77; Rector of St. George, Dominica, 1877-79; Curate of St. Luke, Barbados, 1879-85; Vicar of St. Martin, 1885-96; of Holy Trinity, 1896-97; Rector of St. Andrew, 1897-98; of St. Peter, 1898; Rural Dean of St. Peter, 1905; Canon (St. Basil), 1906-9; Assistant Priest at S. Lawrence 1913. *Recreations:* walking, reading. *Address:* 9th Avenue, Belle Ville, Barbados, B.W.I. (*Died 7 Jan. 1916.*)

ELLIOT, Maj.-Gen. Henry Riversdale; *b.* 11 Dec. 1836; *s.* of William Elliot, Madras Civil Service; *m.* 1866, Carmina Macintire; three *s.* one *d.* *Educ.:* Cheltenham College; Military Academy, Edinburgh. Joined Madras 42nd Infantry, 1855; served with Madras Sappers and Miners, Abyssinian Campaign, present at assault and capture of Magdala, 1867-68; Brigade-Major; Assistant Quartermaster-Gen. Madras Presidency and Burmah; commanded 11th M.N.I.; returned to England on Colonel's allowances, 1886. *Address:* 1 Fauconberg Villas, Cheltenham. *Club:* New, Cheltenham.

(*Died 11 Dec. 1921.*)

ELLIOTT, His Honour Judge Adshead, M.A.; Judge of County Courts on Circuit 13 since 1919; J.P. Sheffield and West Riding of Yorkshire; *b.* 1869; 5th *s.* of late John Matthews Elliott, Manchester; *m.* 1904, Florence, *o. d.* of late Joseph Fulton, Paisley. *Educ.:* Manchester Grammar School; Oriel College, Oxford. Called to Bar, Inner Temple, 1894; joined Northern Circuit and practised in Manchester; President of Pensions Appeal Tribunal, 1918-19. *Publications:* Treatise on Workmen's Compensation Acts (seven editions). *Address:* Dunluce, Ranmoor, Sheffield. *Club:* The Club, Sheffield. (*Died 7 Sept. 1922.*)

ELLIOTT, Maj.-Gen. Edward Draper; Col.-Commandant, Royal Artillery (late Bengal), since 1900; *b.* 30 Sept. 1838; *o. surv. s.* of late Maj.-Gen. W. E. A. Elliott, H.E.I.C.S.; *m.* 1899, Maria, 2nd *d.* of late Charles Jecks Dixon, Blackheath. *Educ.:* Rugby; Addiscombe College. Entered army, 1857; served at the end of Indian Mutiny; Col. on Staff Commanding R.A. Thames District. 1890-95; Maj.-Gen. 1895; retired, 1900. *Clubs:* Naval and Military, M.C.C., Sandown Park.

(*Died 30 Sept. 1918.*)

ELLIOTT, George, K.C.; *b.* Luton, Bedfordshire, 24 Oct. 1860; *e. s.* of George Elliott, Buxton Lodge, Luton; *m.* 1889, Charlotte, *y. d.* of Frederick Farr, Surgeon; two *s.* three *d.* *Educ.:* Mill Hill School. Member of Inner and Middle Temple; called to Bar, 1882; Surrey Sessions and South-Eastern Circuit; pupil of Sir Edward Clarke; engaged in following cases:

326

Edmund Lawrence Levy perjury case, the Great Pearl Case, the Walnut Case, Diamond Jubilee Syndicate Frauds, the Lupton Companies Fraud, and the trials of Chapman the poisoner; Dougal, the Moat Farm murderer; Devereux, the trunk case; Rayner, the murderer of Mr. Whiteley; the Stoddart Coupon Case, D. S. Windell Fraud, Lody the German Spy, etc.; contested (U.) South Bedfordshire, 1900 and 1910. *Publications:* The Law of Newspaper Libel, 1883; assisted the late Walter Shirley in the preparation of his work on Leading Cases in the Common Law; Fifth Edition—Illustrations in Advocacy by Harris. *Recreations:* golf, swimming. *Address:* 1 Garden Court, Temple, E.C. *T.:* Holborn 660; 29 Clarges Street, Mayfair, W. *T.:* Mayfair 6987. *Clubs:* Garrick, United. (*Died 27 Oct. 1916.*)

ELLIOTT, Sir George (Samuel), Kt., *cr.* 1917; M.P. (C.U.) West Islington, 1918-1922; Refreshment Contractor; *m.* Elizabeth Frances, *d.* of Robert Hellier, Upottery, Devonshire; three *s.* three *d.* *Educ.:* privately; City of London School. Entered municipal life as a member of the Islington Vestry, 1875; for 38 years a member of the Islington Board of Guardians, of which body he was Chairman for 20 years and Vice-Chairman for 9 years; Churchwarden twice; Mayor of Islington, 1902-3, 1906-9, 1910-18; Vice-Chairman of the Metropolitan Water Board; member of the Metropolitan Asylums Board; original member of the London County Council, served 18 years; has taken an active interest in the acquisition of open spaces; raised the memorial to Islingtonians who fell in the Boer War; greatly interested in Free Masonry; P.M. of 11 lodges; P.A.G.D.C. (England) and P.P.G.S4.B. Hertford; P.P.G.D.C. Middlesex; raiser of the 21st (S.) Battalion Middlesex Regiment (Islington); Chairman of the Islington Local Tribunal. *Address:* 14 Upper Street, Islington, N.1; The Chalkpit, Maidenhead, Berks.

(*Died 4 May 1925.*)

ELLIOTT, Sir Thomas Henry, 1st Bt., *cr.* 1917; K.C.B., *cr.* 1902; C.B. 1897; British Delegate to the International Institute of Agriculture, and Counsellor of Embassy, Rome; *b.* London, 7 Sep. 1854; *o. s.* of late Thomas Henry Elliott of Rue Ruhmkorff, Paris; *m.* Ellen, *d.* of late James Rowe, 1880; pne s. one *d.* *Educ.:* privately. Entered Inland Revenue Department by open competition, 1872; a Principal Clerk, 1887; Private Secretary to Rt. Hon. C. T. Ritchie, President of Local Government Board, 1889-92; Sec. to Board of Agriculture and Fisheries, 1892-1913; Deputy-Master and Comptroller of the Mint, 1913-17; Member of the Royal Commission on Local Taxation, 1896-1902; Hon. Member Royal Agricultural Society of England, 1903, and Highland and Agricultural Society, Scotland, 1905; Vice-President of the Land Agents' Society, 1906; Hon. Member Surveyors' Institution, 1906, and of the Society of Agriculturists of Spain, 1911; Hon. Associate Royal College of Veterinary Surgeons, 1914; a Delegate to the International Agricultural Conference, Rome, 1905; a Public Works Loans Commissioner, 1914-19; a Boundary Commissioner, and a Commissioner for the Experimental Application of Proportional Representation, 1917-18; Chairman of the Air Raid Compensation Board, 1917-19; Commander of the French Order du Mérite Agricole and of the Orders of the Crown of Belgium and S. Maurizio and S. Lazaro, Italy; Officier de l'Instruction Publique, France. *Heir: s.* Ivo D'Oyly, *b.* 1882. *Address:* 12 Queen Anne's Gate, S.W.; 173 Woodstock Road, Oxford; Institut International d'Agriculture, Rome. *Club:* National.

(*Died 4 June 1926.*)

ELLIS, Arthur; *b.* Holloway, 1 Sept. 1855; *s.* of late Edward and Catherine Ellis of 33 Lansdowne Crescent, Notting Hill, W.; *m.* Lydia C. L.,

d. of late Basil John Charles Pringle. *Educ.*: The King's School, Peterborough. Began life in the City, but after some years left it to follow painting; entered the Royal Academy Schools, 1882; Paris, 1886; exhibitor in chief London and provincial exhibitions; member of the Royal Drawing Society, and on the Board of Examiners. *Address*: 4 Queen's Park Gardens, Seaford. *Club*: Chelsea Arts.
(Died 4 April 1918.)

ELLIS, Lieut.-Commdr. Bernard Henry, D.S.O. 1916, R.N.V.R.; Commanding Hawke Battalion, R.N. Division, B.E.F.; *s.* of Henry Ellis of Potters Bar and Lyme Regis, and Margaret Morley, *b.* Hampstead, 26 May 1885; *m.* 1915, Marjorie, *d.* of Lieut.-Col. J. L. Blumfeld, 9th Middlesex Regt. T.F. *Educ.*: University College School, London. Articled to Lieut.-Col. C. F. T. Blyth; admitted Solicitor, 1908; partner in the firm of Peters & Ellis, Guildhall Chambers, Basinghall Street, E.C.; served in ranks of R.N.V.R., London, 27 Jan. 1904, till outbreak of war; was mobilised then having rank of C.P.O.; served with R.N. Divn. Benbow Battalion at Antwerp, Oct. 1914 (despatches, D.S.M.); landed in Gallipoli with Benbow Battalion end of May 1915, and served there and at Suvla till the evacuation; commissioned as T. Sub-Lieut. R.N.V.R. Oct. 1915; promoted T. Lieut. and Adjt. Nov. 1915; T. Lieut.-Commdr. Oct. 1916, served at Stavros Feb. to April 1916; in France May 1916 to present time, with Anson Battalion from June 1915 to Apr. 1917 (4 months in command), Hood Batt. 21 to 30 Apr. 1917, Hawke Batt. since, in command (D.S.O. after action near Beaumont Hamel, R.N.V.R. long service medal Jan. 1916). *Address*: 2A Guildhall Chambers, Basinghall Street, E.C. *Club*: Swiss Alpine. *(Died 21 April 1918.)*

ELLIS, Col. Charles Conyngham, C.B., 1908; C.B.E. 1919; *b.* 2 March 1852. Lieut. R.E., 1872; Captain, 1884; Major, 1891; Lieut.-Col. 1899; Col. 1903; served Chitral, 1899 (medal with clasp); retired, 1909. *Club*: Army and Navy. *(Died 7 Dec. 1921.)*

ELLIS, Sir Evelyn (Campbell), Kt., *cr.* 1914; *b.* London, 8 Dec. 1865; *s.* of late Robert Ellis, M.R.C.S.; *m.* 1st, 1900, Margaret (*d.* 1918), *d.* of George E. Craig, Manchester; one *d.*; 2nd, 1920, Kathleen Rose (head sister of St. Bartholomew's Hospital for 14 years), widow of W. H. P. Jenkins, D.L. J.P., Frenchay Park, Bristol, *d.* of late Henry John Abernethy. *Educ.*: privately; Solicitor, England, 1891; Advocate and Solicitor of the Straits Settlements, 1896; Acting Attorney-General, Straits Settlements, 1912-13; Member Statute Law Revision Commission Straits Settlements, 1912-16; Unofficial Member, Legislative Council, Straits Settlements, 1908-1916. *Recreations*: golf, billiards, motoring. *Address*: Farncombe Hall, Godalming. *Clubs*: Carlton, Sports.
(Died 1 Sept. 1920.)

ELLIS, Sir Joseph Baxter, Kt., *cr.* 1906; J.P.; Principal of the firm of Hindhaugh's, millers and merchants; *b.* Bramley, near Leeds; *s.* of Mark Ellis; *nephew* of the preacher and controversialist, Joseph Barker; *m.* 1st, 1867, Frances (*d.* 1886), *d.* of William Laidler, Newcastle; four *s.* one *d.*; 2nd, 1892, Mary Sharp, *d.* of late John Taylor, N. Shields; two *s.* two *d.* *Educ.*: East Keswick, near Leeds. Came to Newcastle, 1865; entered the business founded over a century ago by his uncle, J. Hindhaugh; Sheriff of Newcastle, 1887-88; Mayor, 1890-91, and 1904-5; created first Lord Mayor by King Edward VII., July 1906; is an Alderman of, and has served thirty-seven years on, the Newcastle Council; was the pioneer of wood paving in Newcastle; Chairman of the Tramways Committee; Chairman of the Parks Committee, and a River Tyne Commissioner; Vice-Chairman of Trade and Commerce Com-

mittee; entertained Mr. Gladstone when the historic Newcastle Programme was launched. *Address*: North Ashfield, Newcastle.
(Died 28 Dec. 1918.)

ELLIS, Robert Powley, M.V.O. 1907; late Superintendent of the Line, Great Eastern Railway; *b.* 20 July, 1845; *s.* of John Erskine Ellis of Bentley, Suffolk; *m.* Emily Ann, *d.* of William Rose of Bentley, Suffolk; three *s.* one *d.* *Educ.*: Ipswich. Officer of the Great Eastern Railway for 43 years, 17 of which he was District Goods Manager at Norwich and London, and the last 14 years of his connection with the Company was first Assistant Superintendent and then Superintendent of the Line. In recognition of the large number of Royal journeys so satisfactorily arranged and accompanied, his late Majesty King Edward VII. conferred upon him the Royal Victorian Order. *Address*: Rosecroft, Woodford Road, South Woodford, Essex. *T.*: Wanstead 125. *(Died 16 June 1918.)*

ELLIS, Tristram, A.R.E., A.K.C., artist; *b.* Great Malvern, 1844; *s.* of Alexander J. Ellis, F.R.S., Lit.D., etc.; *m.*: one *s.* two *d.* *Educ.*: Queenwood College; King's College, London. Took all scholarships in applied Science Department; articled to Partner of Sir John Fowler, M.I.C.E., etc., 1861; worked on District and Metropolitan Railways till 1868; became A.I.C.E.; carried out several minor engineering works; entered Mons. Bonnat's Studio in Paris, 1874; travelled through Cyprus directly after its occupation, 1878; travelled in Syria, Asia Minor, and Mesopotamia and Great Syrian Desert 1879-80; Egypt 1881-1882; Portugal, 1883, 1884; Greece and Constantinople, 1885, 1886; Spitzbergen, 1894. *Publications*: On a Raft and Through the Desert, illustrated with 38 etchings on copper by the author, 1881; Sketching from Nature. *Address*: 15 Gerard Road, Barnes, S.W.
(Died 25 July 1922.)

ELLIS, T. Mullett; poet and novelist; founder and editor of The Thrush, a periodical for original poetry; *b.* 29 Dec. 1850; 2nd *s.* of Rev. R. S. Ellis; *m.* Gwendoline, *d.* of Wm. Hayhurst of Billington; one *s.* one *d.* Educated as architect. First prize in Architecture, Nottingham; A.R.I.B.A. After 15 years' practice as architect engaged in literature; founded the War Emergency Committee, 1899; assisted to found The Evening News, the first halfpenny Conservative newspaper in England; one of the earliest members of the Primrose League; travelled in Malta, Sicily, Italy, Austria, Hungary, Sweden, Morocco, and Algeria. *Publications*: The Earl's Nose, a book of humour in verse, with illustrations by the author; Bone et Fidelis (a poem); Elegy on the Death of Lord Beaconsfield, 1884; Reveries of World History, 1893; Seven Sonnets (illustrated). Novels—The Beauty of Boscastle, 1894; Zalma, 1895; Tales of the Klondyke; God is Love, 1898; The Three Cats'-Eye Rings; Kitty, a story of the Transvaal War; What can a Woman do for the Empire? 1915; also several poems and short stories in Illustrated London News, Sketch, To-Day, etc. *Recreations*: caricaturing, boating, gardening. *Address*: Creek House, Shepperton-on-Thames. *T.A.*: Shepperton; *Club*: Savage. *(Died 20 Aug. 1919.)*

ELLIS, William, F.R.S., F.R.A.S., M.I.E.E.; late Superintendent of the Magnetical and Meteorological Department, Royal Observatory, Greenwich; *b.* Greenwich, 20 Feb. 1828; *m.* 1st, 1869, Sarah Elizabeth (*d.* 1906); *c. d.* of late Edward Campion; 2nd 1908, Margaret Anne, *e. d.* of late Francis Ellis of Settle. Joined the Royal Observatory, 1841; attached to the Astronomical Department until 1874, having during the preceding 18 years had charge of the chronometric and electric branch; was transferred to and had charge of the Magnetical and Meteorological Department, 1875-93;

from March 1852 to May 1853 had charge of the University Observatory, Durham. *Recreation:* music. *Address:* 78 Coleraine Road, Blackheath, S.E. (*Died 13 Dec. 1916.*)

ELLIS, Rev. Hon. William Charles; Rector of Bothal, Morpeth; *b.* 22 July 1835; 2nd *s.* of 6th Lord Howard de Walden; *m.* 1873, Henrietta Elizabeth (*d.* 1915), *d.* of Henry Metcalf Ames of Linden; four *s.* two *d. Educ.* · Oxford University (M.A.). *Address:* Bothalhaugh, Morpeth. *Club:* Athenæum.
(*Died 20 June 1923.*)

ELLIS, William Hodgson, M.A., M.B., F.R.S., Can.; LL.D. Toronto; LL.D. McGill; Dean of Faculty of Applied Science, Toronto University; *b.* 1845; *s.* of John Eimeo Ellis, M.R.C.S., Bakewell, Derbyshire, and Eliza Hodgson; *m.* Ellen Maude Mickle; two *s.* one *d. Educ.:* Toronto University. *Address:* 86 Woodiam Avenue East, Toronto, Canada. *Club:* York, Toronto. (*Died 23 Aug. 1921.*)

ELLISON, William Augustine, M.V.O. 1901; V.D.; Surgeon to H.M.'s Household at Windsor Castle; Consulting Physician King Edward VII. Hospital, Windsor; Lt.-Col. and Hon. Col.; retired 1st Vol. Batt. 4th Royal Berks Regt.; Major and Hon. Lt.-Col. T.F. Reserve; Lt.-Col. Commanding 4th (Reserve) Batt. Royal Berks Regt. 1915-16 (mentioned for war services); *b.* 28 Aug. 1855; *s.* of James Ellison, M.D.; *m.* 1894, Catharine May Murray, *g.-d.* of late Rev. H. Headley, of Ashley, Arnewood, Hants; one *s. Educ.:* Eton; University Coll. Oxford; B.A. (Honours) 1878, M.A. 1881, M.B. 1884, M.D. 1895; Surgeon to Queen Victoria's Household at Windsor Castle, 1888; to King Edward VII. Household, 1901; Acting Resident Physician to Queen Victoria at Balmoral, 1894, '95, '97, '98. *Publications:* contributions to Lancet. *Recreations:* yachting, gardening, boating, music; Rowed Eight, 1873-4; "Wall" Football Eleven, 1873; rowed in Head of the River Crew, Oxford, 1875, '77, '78; in Winning Trial Eight, 1875, '76, '77; Gymnastic Medallist, 1877; rowed in University Boat Race, 1878; won O.U.B.C. "pairs," 1878; also Visitors' Cup, 1876; Silver Goblets, 1878; and Grand Challenge Cup (stroke of Leander Eight) at Henley Regatta, 1880. *Address:* Eton, Bucks. *T.:* Windsor 262. *M.:* BL 3477. *Clubs:* New University, Leander, Royal Harwich Yacht, Royal Cruising.
(*Died 1 Nov. 1917.*)

ELLISTON, Col. George Sampson, C.B. 1911; V.D.; M.R.C.S.; *s.* of late Dr. Wm. Elliston of Ipswich; *b.* 1844. Administrative Medical Officer, East Anglian Division, 1908-12; retired; Knight of Grace, Order of St. John of Jerusalem; Commissioner in charge of Eastern District, St. John Ambulance Brigade; Member of Suffolk Territorial Association. *Address:* St. Edmunds, Felixstowe. (*Died 20 Nov. 1921.*)

ELLISTON, Guy, Secretary British Medical Association since 1902; Assistant Secretary 1898; *b.* Ipswich, 1872; 3rd *s.* of late W. A. Elliston, M.D.; *m.* Clare, *y. d.* of late Benjamin Warner, Wanstead, Essex, and Newgate Street, E.C.; four *d. Educ.:* Ipswich School. Commenced business career Liverpool, 1888; interested in initiating direct steamship service, Manchester and Paris; joined Weekly Sun, 1897; Manager, Naval and Military Magazine and Public Health Magazine, 1898; joined 1st Lancashire Artillery/Volunteers, 1891; retired senior captain, 1897. *Recreations:* golf, tennis, gardening. *Address:* 429 Strand, W.C.; Belstead, Northwood. *T.:* Gerrard 2630. *Clubs:* Savage; Arts; Felixstowe and Northwood Golf.
(*Died 13 April 1918.*)

ELMHIRST, Capt. Edward Pennell; late 9th Norfolk Regt.; *b.* 7 Jan. 1845; *e. s.* of late Rev. Edward Elmhirst, Shawell Rectory, Leicestershire; *m.* Laura M., *d.* of late Stephen P. Kennard, 1873. *Educ.:* Rugby, Sandhurst.

Served in China and Japan with 9th Foot, 1864-68; Musketry Instructor to same, 1871-74; A.D.C. to General C. Elmhirst at Malta and Bangalore, 1874-78; Adj. of Artists' Volunteer Corps, 1878-82; Master and Huntsman Neilgherry Hounds, 1875-77; Woodland-Pytchley Hounds, 1880-81; served in South Africa, 1899-1900 (medal with two clasps). *Publications:* Our Life in Japan, 1869; The Hunting Counties of Great Britain, 1882; The Cream of Leicestershire, 1883; The Best Season on Record, 1884; Foxhound, Forest, and Prairie, 1892; The Best of the Fun, 1903. *Recreations:* hunting correspondent of the Field as "Brooksby" since 1870; has done much big game shooting in Malay Peninsula, India, and the Rocky Mountains of America. *Address:* Blisworth House, Blisworth, Northamptonshire. *Club:* Naval and Military.
(*Died 2 Dec. 1916.*)

ELPHINSTONE, Sir Howard Warburton, M.A.; 3rd Bt., *cr.* 1816; *b.* London, 26 July 1880; *e. s.* of 2nd Bt. and Elizabeth, *d.* of E. J. Curteis, M.P.; *S.* father 1893; *m.* Constance, *d.* of J. A. Hankey, Balcombe Place, Sussex, 1860; three *s.* five *d. Educ.:* Eton; Trinity College, Cambridge (Scholar). 17th Wrangler, 1854. Librarian, Trin. Coll. Camb.; Barr. Lincoln's Inn, 1862; Lecturer to Incorporated Law Society, 1869-71; Professor of Real Property Law to the Inns of Court, 1889-92; Reader on the Law of Real Property, Inns of Court, 1892-96; Conveyancing Counsel to the Court, 1895-1914. *Publications:* Introduction to Conveyancing, 1871; Patterns for Turning, 1872; joint-author of Key and Elphinstone's Precedents of Conveyancing, 1878; On the Interpretation of Deeds, 1886; On Searches, 1887; joint editor of Goodeve's Real Property, 1897, and Goodeve's Personal Property, 1892. *Recreation:* photography. *Heir: g. s.* Howard Graham, *b.* 28 Dec. 1898. *Address:* Struan, Wimbledon Park. *T.A.:* Struan, Southfields. *T.:* 446 P.O. Wimbledon. *Club:* Athenæum.
(*Died 3 Jan. 1917.*)

ELSTOB, Rev. John George, Hon. Canon of Chester, 1911; *m.* Rural Dean of Macclesfield, 1904-12. *Address:* Fanshawe, Chelford, Cheshire. (*Died 6 Oct. 1926.*)

ELSTOB, Lieut.-Colonel Wilfrith, V.C. 1919; D.S.O., M.C., 16th Manchester Regiment; *s.* of Rev. J. G. Elstob. Served European War. *Address:* Fanshawe, Chelford, Cheshire.
(*Died 21 Mar. 1918.*)

ELTON, Sir Edmund Harry, 8th Bt.; *cr.* 1717; J.P.; *b.* 8 May 1846; *S. u.* 1883; *m.* Agnes, *d.* of Sir A. H. Elton, 7th Bt., 1868; two *s.* three *d. Educ.:* Bradfield; Jesus Coll. Cambridge. Hon. Col. 1st Gloster Artillery Vol.; County Councillor Somerset; High Sheriff, 1894-95; originator and designer of Elton Ware Pottery; has received ten gold and two silver medals in International and other Exhibitions. Owns about 4200 acres. *Heir: s.* Ambrose [*b.* 1869; *m.* 1901, Dorothy, *o. d.* of Arthur Wiggin of Oddington Estate, Ceylon; two *s. Educ.:* Lancing Coll.; Jesus College, Cambridge; B.A.; Barr. 1895]. *Address:* Clevedon Court, Somerset.
(*Died 17 July 1920.*)

ELTON, Col. Frederick Coulthurst, C.B. 1882; R.A.; retired; *b.* 15 July 1836; *m.* 1866, Olivia, *d.* of late Major Power. Entered army, 1854; Col. 1885; served Crimea, 1855 (medal with clasp, Knight of Legion of Honour, Turkish medal); Egyptian War, 1882 (despatches, C.B., medal with clasp, 3rd class Medjidie, Khedive's star). *Club:* Army and Navy. (*Died 12 Jan. 1920.*)

ELWES, Gervase Henry, J.P., D.L. Lincs.; J.P. Northants; Professional Musician; Knight of Malta, 1917; *b.* Billing, Northants, 15 Nov. 1866; *e. s.* of V. D. H. Cary-Elwes, of Billing, Northants, and Roxby and

ELWELL, Col. Francis Edwin, Sc. See page xix.

Brigg, Lincs, and Alice, d. of Hon. and Rev. Henry Ward, b. of 3rd Viscount Bangor; m. 1889, Lady Winefride Feilding, 3rd d. of 8th Earl of Denbigh; six s. two d. Educ.: Oratory School, Birmingham; Woburn School; Christ Church, Oxford; Munich; Paris. Served in H.M. Diplomatic Service, 1891-95; entered musical profession, 1903; High Sheriff, Northamptonshire, 1917. Recreations: shooting and games. Address: Billing Hall, Northampton; Roxby, Lincolnshire. T.: Cogenhoe 6. Clubs: Carlton, Savile, Oxford and Cambridge Musical. (Died 12 Jan. 1921.)

ELWES, Henry John, F.R.S., landowner; b. 16 May 1846; e. s. of late J. H. Elwes, of Colesborne, and Mary, d. of late Sir R. Bromley, Bt., of Stoke, Notts; m. Margaret, d. of late W. C. Lowndes, of Brightwell Park, Oxon. Educ.: Eton, and abroad. Served five years in Scots Guards; travelled in Turkey, Asia Minor, Tibet, and in India four times; in N. America and Mexico, three times; in Chile; in Russia and Siberia, three times; in Formosa, China, and Japan twice; in Nepal and Sikkim; has been Vice-President of Royal Horticultural Society, and is Victoria Medallist of the same; Past President of Royal English Arboricultural Society and of the Royal Entomological Society of London; scientific member of Indian Embassy to Tibet, 1886; represented Great Britain officially at Botanical and Horticultural Congresses at Petrograd and Amsterdam. Publications: A Monograph of the Genus Lilium; The Trees of Great Britain and Ireland; many papers in the Transactions and Proceedings of the Zoological, Linnean, Entomological, Horticultural, and Royal Agricultural Societies between 1869 and 1899. Recreations: big game shooting, horticulture, hunting. Address: Colesborne Park, near Cheltenham. Club: Athenæum.
(Died 26 Nov. 1922.)

ELWOOD, Hon. Edward Lindsey; A Judge of Appeal for Saskatchewan since 1918; b. Goderich, Ont., 13 Feb. 1868; s. of John Yeats and Marion W. Elwood; m. 1895, Cara A. Slack, Goderich, Ont.; four s. one d. Educ.: Goderich Collegiate Institute; Osgood Hall, Toronto. Practised Law at South Bend, Washington State, 1890-92; Oxbow, Sask., 1892-97; Moosomin, Sask., 1897-1912; Regina, Sask., 1912-13; public appointment one of the Benchers of Law Society of Saskatchewan, and had been a Bencher of the Law Society of North West Territories; Mayor of Moosomin, 1909 and 1910; Chancellor of the Diocese of Qu'Appelle until 1915; Judge of the Supreme Court of Saskatchewan, 1913-18. Recreation: golf. Address: 2249 Rae St., Regina, Canada. T.: 2717. M.: 21. Clubs: Assiniboia, Wascana Country, Regina.

ELY, 5th Marquess of; cr. 1800; **John Henry Loftus**, Bt. 1780; Baron Loftus, 1785; Viscount Loftus, 1789; Earl of Ely, 1794; Baron Loftus (U.K.), 1801; b. 6 Mar. 1851; s. of Rev. Lord Adam Loftus, 3rd s. of 2nd Marquis and Margaret, d. of Robert Finnin, Dublin; S. cousin, 1889; m. 1895, Margaret, d. of Frederick A. Clark, Lynton Court, Sussex, and Gracefield Park, Bucks. Heir: b. Lord George H. Loftus. Owns about 49,000 acres. Address: Ely Lodge, Enniskillen; Loftus Hall, Wexford; Rathfarnam Lodge, Brighton; Long Loftus, Yorkshire. Clubs: Royal Automobile; Royal St. George's, Kingstown; Kildare Street, Dublin. (Died 18 Dec. 1925.)

EMANUEL, Samuel Henry, K.C. 1919; LL.D.; Barrister; Recorder of the City of Winchester since 1915; Master of the Bench of the Inner Temple; s. of late Henry Herschel and Julia Emanuel of Southampton; m. Ethel Gertrude, d. of late A. L. Lazarus of the Metal Exchange, London; two s. one d. Educ.: University College School, London; Trinity Hall, Cambridge. Called to Bar. Inner Temple,

1886; Member of the Western Circuit. Address: 1 Temple Gardens, Temple, E.C.4; 48 Holland Park, W.11. T.A.: 70 Temple. T.: Central 4257. Clubs: Athenæum; Hants County; Royal Southampton Yacht; Dorset County. (Died 15 May 1925.)

EMARD, Most Rev. Mgr. Joseph Médard, R.C. Archbishop of Ottawa since 1922; b. 1853. Priest, 1876; Bishop of Valleyfield, 1892-1922. Address: Archbishop's Palace, Ottawa. (Died 28 Mar. 1927.)

EMERSON, Hon. Charles H., K.C.; M.H.A. Newfoundland since 1900; Member of Executive Council without Portfolio since 1899; b. 1864. Address: St. John's, Newfoundland.
(Died 18 Feb. 1919.)

EMERSON, Ven. Edward Robert, D.D.; Archdeacon of Cork; Rector of Ballymodan since 1890; b. 1838; s. of Rev. George Emerson; m. Annie, d. of William Roberts. Abbeyville Park, Dublin. Educ.: Bandon Grammar School; Trinity College, Dublin. Ordained, 1861; Curate of Fanlobus, 1861-65; Rector of St. Edmund's, Cork, 1865-90; Canon of Cork, 1884; Chaplain to the Lord Lieutenant of Ireland; Chaplain to Earl of Bandon; formerly Select Preacher to University of Dublin; Diocesan Nominator, Governor Diocesan Education Board; Clerical Member of Diocesan Court. Address: Ballymodan, Bandon, Co. Cork. (Died 30 Nov. 1926.)

EMERSON, Hon. George Henry; Judge Supreme Court of Newfoundland since 1896; b. 1853; m. Katherine, o. d. of Edward and Jane Maher. Educ.: Grammar School, Harbor Grace. Barrister, 1876; Bencher, 1888; Q.C. 1890; elected Member of Colonial Legislature (Placentia District), 1885; re-elected, 1889 and 1893; appointed Official Delegate to England on Fisheries Question, 1890, and again on same subject, 1891; Official Delegate to Ottawa to discuss with Dominion Government terms of Union between Canada and Newfoundland, 1895; Commissioner for Consolidation and Revision of Statute Law of Colony, 1888-96; Speaker of Newfoundland Assembly (being twice unanimously elected by House), 1890-94; M.E.C. and M.L.C. 1895-96; Delegate London Conference, Imperial Court of Appeal, 1901. Address: Calvert House, St. John's, Newfoundland; Virginia Water, St. John's, Newfoundland.
(Died 5 Mar. 1913.)

EMERSON, Maj. Norman Zeal, D.S.O. 1900; b. 4 Oct. 1872; m. 1919. Entered army, 1895; Capt. 1900; Maj. 1914; served North-West Frontier, India, 1897 (medal with two clasps); S. Africa, 1899-1902 (despatches, Queen's medal 3 clasps, King's medal 2 clasps); retired, 1911; rejoined for active service, 1914; served in France and Salonica (British War Medal, Victory Medal, 1914-15 Star). Address: Crown Point. Ealing, W. (Died 28 April 1928.)

EMERSON, Sir William, Kt., cr. 1902; President R.I.B.A. 1899-1900, 1900-1, 1901-2; b. 1843; s. of William Emerson of Whetstone, Middlesex; m. 1872, Jenny, d. of Coutts Stone of Prince's Square, Bayswater. Educ.: King's Coll. Pupil of William Burges, A.R.A.; went to India when 21 years of age; erected there the Bombay markets, several churches, and other buildings; on returning home designed for the Govt. of India the Allahabad University, carried out by the Royal Engineers; also designed the Cathedral for the Lucknow Diocese and the Bhoununggur Hospital; was architect of St. Mary's Church, Brighton; the Clarence Memorial Wing, St. Mary's Hospital; his design was placed first in the competition for Liverpool Cathedral, and Hamilton House, Victoria Embankment, and the New Royal Caledonian Asylum are his work; besides these he is carrying out the Victoria Memorial for India in Calcutta, and has designed a large palace for the late Maharajah of Bhoununggur.

Publications: several papers read before the Royal Institute of Architects. *Recreations:* golf, billiards. *Address:* Carlton Chambers, 4 Regent Street, S.W. *Clubs:* Arts, St. Stephen's.
(*Died 26 Dec. 1924.*)

EMERY, Henry Crosby; *b.* 21 Dec. 1872; *s.* of Justice L. A. Emery of the Supreme Court of Maine; *m.* 1917, Susanne Carey Allinson. *Educ.:* Bowdoin Coll.; Harvard and Columbia Univs. Taught political economy at Bowdoin College, 1894-1900; Professor of Political Economy, Yale University, 1900-16; Chairman U.S. Tariff Board, 1909-12; Foreign representative of Guaranty Trust Company; while in Petrograd Commissioned as Major in U.S. Army to work with American Military Mission in connection with the Mickleson Commission; captured by the Germans, 1918; with Guaranty Trust Company of New York in home office from the Armistice until the spring of 1920, when he became manager of the Asia Banking Corporation, Peking. *Publications:* Speculation on the Stock and Produce Exchanges of the United States, 1896. *Address:* Asia Banking Corporation, Peking, China. (*Died 6 Feb. 1924.*)

EMERY, Walter d'Este, M.D., B.Sc. (Lond.), M.R.C.S., M.R.C.P.; Capt. R.A.M.C. (T.F.); formerly Director of Laboratories and Lecturer on Pathology and Bacteriology to King's College Hospital; late Pathologist Children's Hospital, Paddington Green; late Hunterian Professor Royal College Surgeons; Scholar and Gold Medallist, University, London. *Publications:* Immunity and Specific Therapy; Clinical Bacteriology and Hæmatology (6 editions); Tumours, Their Nature and Causation; articles in Quarterly Review, Practitioner, etc. *Address:* Old Manor House, Shirehampton, Bristol. *Club:* Savage.
(*Died 19 June 1923.*)

EMERY, Winifred (Isabel Winifred Maud Emery Maude), actress; *b.* Manchester; *o. d.* of Samuel Anderson Emery, actor; grand-daughter of John Emery, actor; *m.* 1888, Cyril Francis Maude, Chapel Royal, Savoy; one *s.* two *d. Educ.:* London, private school. Made first appearance on the stage at Liverpool at the age of eight years; as a child-actress, Princess Theatre, London, 1875; first appearance in London, 1879, Imperial Theatre, Westminster; at Court Theatre under Wilson Barrett; went to the Lyceum under Henry Irving, 1881; twice to America and Canada with his company, and has played at all the principal theatres in London; played at the Haymarket Theatre, 1896-1905. *Recreations:* gardening, reading. *Address:* The Corner, Little Common, Sussex. *T.:* Cooden 56. *Club:* Bath.
(*Died 15 July 1924.*)

EMMET, Rev. Cyril William, M.A., B.D.; Chaplain and Fellow University College, Oxford; Theological Lecturer, Hertford College; Vice-Principal of Ripon Hall, Oxford; *b.* 24 March 1875; *s.* of Rev. W. E. Emmet; *m.* Gertrude Julia, *d.* of James Weir; one *s.* two *d. Educ.:* St. Paul's School; Corpus Christi College, Oxford. Classical Scholar, 1894; 1st Class Mods., 1896; 2nd Class Lit. Hum., 1898. Ordained 1898 to Curacy of St. Mary's, Plaistow; Curate of St. James', Norlands, 1901-06; Vicar of West Hendred, Berks, 1906-20; Select Preacher, Oxford, 1918-20, and Cambridge, 1920; Examining Chaplain to Bishop of Oxford, 1919. *Publications:* The Eschatological Question in the Gospels, 1911; Galatians (Readers' Commentary), 1912; The Third and Fourth Books of Maccabees, 1918; Conscience, Creeds and Critics, 1918; contributor to Oxford Corpus of Apocrypha, Hastings' Dictionaries, Faith and the War, Immortality, The Spirit; articles in Nineteenth Century and theological periodicals. *Recreations:* lawn tennis, golf. *Address:* University College, Oxford; 14 Lathbury Road, Oxford. (*Died 22 July 1923.*)

530

EMMOTT, 1st Baron, of Oldham, *cr.* 1911; **Alfred Emmott,** P.C., G.C.M.G., *cr.* 1914; G.B.E., *cr.* 1917; *b.* 1858; *e. surv. s.* of late Thomas Emmott of Brookfield, Oldham, and Anchorsholme, Poulton-le-Fylde; *m.* 1887, Mary Gertrude, *d.* of late John William Lees; two *d. Educ.:* Grove House, Tottenham. B.A., London; M.P. (L.) Oldham, 1899-1911; Chairman of Ways and Means, 1906-11; Under-Secretary of State for the Colonies, 1911-14; First Commissioner of Works, 1914-15; Director of the War Trade Department, 1915-19. *Recreations:* shooting, etc. *Heir:* none. *Address:* 30 Ennismore Gardens, S.W.7. *T.:* Kensington 1542. *Clubs:* Brooks's, Reform, Ranelagh. (*Died 13 Dec. 1926.*)

EMMOTT, George Henry, M.A., LL.M.; Queen Victoria Professor of Law, University of Liverpool, since 1896, and Dean of the Faculty of Law since 1903; Barr. Inner Temple; *b.* 28 Sept. 1855; *e. s.* of late Thomas Emmott, J.P., of Brookfield, Oldham, and Anchorsholme, Poulton-le-Fylde; *m.* 1881, Elizabeth, 4th *d.* of late Joseph Bevan Braithwaite, Barrister-at-Law; three *d. Educ.:* The Owens Coll. Manchester; Trinity Hall, Cambridge (Foundation Scholar and twice Law Prizeman); 1st Class Law Tripos, 1878; Barrister-at-Law, 1879; Lecturer in Roman and English Law at the Owens Coll., Manchester, 1880-85; Associate Professor of Logic and Ethics and lecturer in Roman Law at The Johns Hopkins University, Baltimore, 1885-92; hon. sec. to the Board of University Studies, 1887-96; Prof. of Roman Law and Comparative Jurisprudence 1892-96; lecturer on Civil Law, Columbian University, Washington, D.C., 1892-96; Secretary Departmental Board of Law, Victoria University, 1901-8; representative of Faculty of Law on Council of University of Liverpool, 1903-5, and 1907-13. *Address:* The University, and 10 Cook Street, Liverpool; 64 Park Road West, Birkenhead. *T.:* 4866 Bank.
(*Died 8 Mar. 1916.*)

EMRYS-ROBERTS, Edward, M.D.; Professor of Pathology and Bacteriology, Welsh National School of Medicine; Hon. Pathologist and Bacteriologist to King Edward VII.'s. Hospital, Cardiff; *b.* 14 May 1878; *e. s.* of E. S. Roberts, Brookdale, Dawlish, Devon, and Mary, *y. d.* of Emrys Evans, Cotton Hall, Denbigh; *m.* 1910, Rosamond, *y. d.* of J. Wynne Paynter, Bryntirion, Amlwch, Anglesey; three *s.* two *d. Educ.:* Liverpool College, Upper School, and University of Liverpool. While a student of Medicine served with the Welsh Hospital, South African Field Force, 1900 (medal and 3 clasps); held a Research Fellowship in Pathology at the University of Liverpool, 1903-6, and was subsequently appointed Sub-Curator of the Pathological Museum; Demonstrator of Pathology, University of Bristol, and Pathologist to the Bristol General Hospital, 1908-10; O.C. Welsh Mobile Bact. Lab., B.E.F., France, 1915-18; Local Secretary of the Cambrian Archæological Association, and Local Correspondent of the Ancient Monuments Board for Wales. *Publications:* papers in Medical and Scientific journals. *Recreations:* ethnology, archæology, music, fishing. *Address:* Romarys, Penarth, Glamorgan. (*Died 15 Jan. 1924.*)

ENGELBACH, Alfred H. H., I.S.O. 1902; *b.* 1850. Clerk in the Accounts Branch, Office of Secretary of State for Colonies, 1868; First Class Assistant Clerk, 1879; Book-keeper and Senior Assistant to Financial Clerk, 1884; Accountant in Colonial Office, 1896; retired, 1915. *Address:* 36 Stockwell Park Road, S.W.
(*Died 22 April 1928.*)

ENGLEHEART, Sir John Gardner Dillman, K.C.B.; *cr.* 1897; M.A. Oxon.; *b.* 2 Feb. 1823; *s.* of J. C. D. Engleheart, Tunbridge Wells; *m.* Emily (*d.* 1911), *d.* of Maj. J. A. Willows, I.C.S., 1859. *Educ.:* Rugby; Christ Church, Oxford. Barr. Lincoln's Inn, 1849; Private

Secy. to Duke of Newcastle, Secy. of State for Colonies, and accompanied him in suite of Prince of Wales on visit to Canada and U.S. 1859-64 ; Comptroller of the Household of the Prince and Princess Christian, 1866-69 ; Clerk of the Council, Duchy of Lancaster, 1872-99 ; Member of the Duchy Council, 1901-12. *Address :* 28 Curzon Street, Mayfair, W.1. *Club :* Athenæum.
(*Died 10 April 1923.*)

ENNIS, John Matthew, Mus. Doc. ; Professor of Music in the University of Adelaide since 1901. *Address :* The University, Adelaide.

ENNISKILLEN, 4th Earl of (*cr.* 1789), **Lowry Egerton Cole**, K.P. 1902 ; D.L., J.P. ; M.F.H. (North Cheshire) ; Baron Mountflorence, 1760 ; Viscount Enniskillen, 1776 ; Baron Grinstead (U.K.), 1815 ; *b.* London, 21 Dec. 1845 ; 2nd *s.* of 3rd Earl and Jane, *e. d.* of J. A. Cassamajor ; *S.* father 1886 ; *m.* Charlotte, *d.* of Douglas Baird, Closeburn, Dumfriesshire, 1869 ; three *s.* two *d.* *Educ. :* Eton. Formerly in Rifle Brigade ; Hon. Col. 3rd Batt. Royal Inniskilling Fusiliers since 1887 ; M.P. (C.) Enniskillen, 1880-85. Owns about 30,300 acres. *Heir : s.* Viscount Cole. *Address :* Florence Court, Enniskillen, Co. Fermanagh. *Clubs :* Turf, Orleans ; Kildare Street, Dublin. (*Died 28 April 1924.*)

EPPSTEIN, Rev. William Charles ; *b.* Bagdad, 8 Feb. 1864 ; *s.* of Rev. J. M. Eppstein, missionary and British chaplain ; *m. d.* of Rev. A. C. H. Bolton, Rector of Shimpling, Suffolk ; one *s.* two *d.* *Educ. :* Corpus Christi College, Cambridge. M.A. Cambridge and D.D. Oxford (incorporated St. John's College) ; Mathematical Honours, F.R.A.S. ; College First Boat, Cricket XI., Football XV. ; Curate, St. Mary's, Spital Square, 1887 ; Curate of Stowmarket, 1889 ; Assistant Master, St. Lawrence's College, Ramsgate, 1892-94 ; Bradfield College, Berks, 1894 ; Headmaster of Reading School, 1894-1914 ; Rector of Lambourne, Essex, since 1916 ; Select Preacher at Cambridge, 1922. *Publication :* Editor of Gray's Poems. *Recreation :* reading. *Address :* Lambourne Rectory, Romford. *T. A. :* Abridge. *T. :* Loughton 346.
(*Died 30 Aug. 1923.*)

ERNST, Harold Clarence, A.M., M.D. ; Professor of Bacteriology in Harvard University ; Visiting Bacteriologist to Children's Hospital, and Chairman of the Visiting Staff ; late Major, M.R.C., U.S.A. ; In command of Laboratory of North Eastern Depart. ; Ex-President of Boston Society of Medical Sciences ; Secretary and Ex-President of A merican Association of Pathologists and Bacteriologists ; Editor of the Journal of Medical Research, etc. ; *b.* Cincinnati, Ohio ; *s.* of Andrew H. and Sarah (Otis) Ernst ; *m.* Ellen Lunt Frothingham of Boston. *Educ. :* private schools ; Harvard University (Academic and Medical Departments) ; Paris and Berlin. Professor and Teacher in Harvard University ; student and editor. *Publications :* many articles in medical journals ; special monographs on Infectiousness of Milk, Infection and Immunity, Phagocytosis, Tuberculine ; Ultra-Violet Photomicrography. *Recreations :* all outdoor sports ; of late years the saddle, sailing, golf. *Address :* The Medical School of Harvard University ; in summer—The Cedar-Bushes, Manomet, Plymouth Co., Mass. *T. :* Jamaica 108. *Clubs :* St. Botolph, Country ; Harvard, Boston ; Old Colony, Plymouth.
(*Died 7 Sept. 1922.*)

ERNST, Oswald Herbert, Maj.-Gen. U.S. Army, retired ; *b.* near Cincinnati, 27. June 1842 ; *s.* of Andrew H. and Sarah Otis Ernst ; *m.* Elizabeth Amory Lee, 1866 ; two *d.* *Educ. :* Harvard College ; U.S. Military Academy at West Point. Commissioned First Lieut., Corps of Engineers, 1864 ; served as Assist. Chief Engineer, Army of the Tennessee, to close of Atlanta campaign ; as astronomer with the Commission sent by U.S. Government to Spain to observe solar eclipse of Dec. 1870 ; as instructor of practical military engineering and military signalling and telegraphy at U.S. Military Academy, 1871-78 ; in charge of improvement of Mississippi river and other western rivers, 1878-86 ; also of harbour at Galveston, and other harbours on Texas coast, 1886-89 ; aide-de-camp to President Harrison, 1889-93, superintendent, U.S. Military Academy, 1893-1898 ; in command of 1st Brigade, 1st Div., 1st Corps in the war with Spain ; Inspector-General of Cuba, 1898-99 ; member of Commission to investigate the Isthmus connecting North and South America, with a view to the construction of an inter-oceanic canal, 1899-1903 ; Division Engineer N.-West Division, 1901-5 ; President Mississippi River Commission, 1903-6 ; Member of the Isthmian Canal Commission, 1905-6 ; member of International Commission to investigate the condition of the waters adjacent to the boundary lines between the U.S. and Canada, 1905-14 ; member of numerous Boards of Engineers, 1880-1906. *Publication :* Manual of Practical Military Engineering, 1873. *Recreations :* golf, bridge. *Address :* 1524 18th Street, Washington, D.C. *Clubs :* Metropolitan, Chevy Chase, Washington. (*Died 21 Mar. 1926.*)

ERRINGTON, Sir George, 1st Bt., *cr.* 1885, for services rendered at Rome ; J.P. for Cos. Longford, Tipperary, and Wexford ; *b.* 1839 ; *e. s.* of late M. Errington, Clintz, Yorks, and Rosanna, *d.* of late A. M. O'Ferrall, Balyna, Co. Kildare ; *m.* Frances, *d.* of H. R. de Ricci, and widow of Capt. Shuldham, Moy, Co. Longford, 1892. *Educ. :* Ushaw Coll. Durham ; Roman Catholic University, Ireland. M.P. Co. Longford, 1874-85 ; High Sheriff, Tipperary, 1888 ; Wexford, 1901. *Heir :* none. *Address :* Ramsfort, Co. Wexford ; Rathcline, Hampton Court. *Clubs :* Reform, Brooks's, Bachelors' ; Kildare Street, Dublin. (*Died 19 Mar. 1920.*)

ERROLL, 19th Earl of, *cr.* 1458, **Charles Gore Hay**, C.B. 1901 ; K.T. 1901 ; J.P. ; LL.D., Aberdeen ; D.L., J.P. ; 23rd Hereditary Lord High Constable of Scotland, created 1315 ; Baron Hay, 1543 ; Baron Kilmarnock, with seat in House of Lords ; *b.* Kingston, Canada West, 7 Feb. 1852 ; *s.* of 18th Earl and Eliza, *d.* of Gen. Hon. Sir Charles Gore, K.C.B., *g.d.* of 2nd Earl of Arran ; *S.* father, 1891 ; *m.* 1875, Mary, *d.* of Edmund and Lady Harriett l'Estrange ; three *s.* *Educ. :* Harrow. Cornet Royal Horse Guards, 1869 ; Lieut.-Col. commanding, 1891-95 ; Colonel, 1895 ; late Brig.-Gen. on staff commanding Yeomanry Brigade, S. Africa ; retired, 1907 ; A.A.G. Cavalry Division, S.A. Field Force ; late Col. comm. Royal Horse Guards ; late A.D.C. to Field-Marshal Lord Wolseley, Commander-in-Chief ; Assistant Adjutant-General for Cavalry ; Hon. Colonel 3rd Batt. Gordon Highlanders, 1892 ; Hon. Major-General, 1917 ; late Lord-in-Waiting to King Edward VII. ; Commanded 65th (Lowland) Division, April 1915-Feb. 1916 ; county Commandant for Cumberland, and member of Central Vol. Association ; served on Staff in France, July 15, 1917-Sep. 6, 1918. *Heir :* Lord Kilmarnock. *Address :* 34 Sussex Gardens, W.2. *T. :* Paddington 3998. *Clubs :* Marlborough, Pratt's. (*Died 8 July 1927.*)

ERROLL, 20th Earl of, *cr.* 1453, **Victor Alexander Sereld Hay**, K.C.M.G., *cr.* 1924 ; C.M.G. 1919 ; 24th Hereditary Lord High Constable of Scotland, *cr.* 1315 ; Baron Hay, 1543 ; Baron Kilmarnock, with seat in House of Lords, 1881 ; British High Commissioner, Inter-Allied Rhineland High Commission, since 1921 ; *b.* 17 Oct. 1876 ; *e. s.* of 19th Earl and Mary, *d.* of Edmund and Lady Harriett l'Estrange ; *S.* father, 1927 ; *m.* 1900, Mary Lucy Victoria, *o. d.* of Sir Allan Mackenzie, 2nd Bt., of Glen Muick, Aberdeenshire ; two *s.* one *d.* Attaché, 1900 ; 3rd Secretary,

1902; 2nd Secretary, 1906; 1st Secretary, 1913; Counsellor, 1919; 1st Secretary, Copenhagen, 1918-19; Chargé d'Affaires, Berlin, on resumption of diplomatic relations with Germany, 1920, till arrival of Ambassador; subsequently Counsellor till Nov. 1921. *Publication:* Ferelith, 1903. *Plays:* The Dream Kiss, produced Wimbledon Theatre, 1924; The Anonymous Letter, produced Q. Theatre, 1927. *Heir:* Lord Kilmarnock. *Address:* Inter-Allied Rhineland High Commission, Coblenz, Germany. *Club:* St. James's. (*Died 20 Feb. 1928.*)

ERSKINE, David, D.L., J.P.; s. of James Erskine of Linlathen. *Educ.:* Harrow; France and Germany. Secretary to Governor-General of Canada, 1897-98; M.P. for West Perthshire, 1906-10; Parliamentary Secretary to Secretary for Scotland, 1906-10; Chairman of the Board of the Trustees for the National Galleries of Scotland since 1908. *Address:* Linlathen, Broughty Ferry, Forfarshire; 33 Brompton Square, S.W.3. *Clubs:* Brooks's, Burlington Fine Arts; New, Edinburgh.
(*Died 26 May 1922.*)

ERSKINE, Sir Henry (David), K.C.V.O., cr. 1911; C.V.O. 1901; J.P., D.L., Serjeant-at-Arms in House of Commons, 1885-1915; Gentleman Usher to the Robes, 1901-19; b. 5 Jan. 1838; s. of James Erskine, Cardross, and Mary, d. of Major-General Fagan; m. 1861, Lady Horatia Seymour, d. of 5th Marquess of Hertford; six s. one d. *Educ.:* Harrow. Served in 30th Regiment and the Scots Fusilier Guards from 1854-61; in Crimea, 1856; became Lieut. and Capt. 1859; Groom of the Robes to H.M. 1870-1901. *Address:* Cardross, Port of Menteith, Perthshire, N.B.; 26 Burton Court, S.W.3.
(*Died 7 Sept. 1921.*)

ERSKINE, Colonel Thomas Harry, V.D., J.P., D.L.; served on Staff in France, 1917-18; Master of Fife Foxhounds since 1907; b. 12 May 1860; 2nd s. of Sir Thomas Erskine, 2nd Bart. of Cambo, Fife; m. 1913, Kathleen, d. of Colonel James Crosbie of Ballyheigue Castle, Co. Kerry. *Educ.:* Eton. Served in Fife Light Horse, and Fife and Forfar Yeomanry from 1881; commanded the latter, 1905-11; rejoined 1914 on outbreak of war; is Hon. Colonel of Fife and Forfar Yeomanry. *Recreations:* hunting, shooting. *Address:* Grangemuir, Pittenweem, Fife. *T.:* Pittenweem 13. *M.:* SP 401; SP 593. *Clubs:* Boodle's, Wellington; New, Edinburgh. (*Died 6 May 1924.*)

ESCOTT, Thomas Hay Sweet, M.A.; e. s. of Rev. Hay Sweet-Escott; m. 1st, 1865, Kate (d. 1899), 2nd d. of Colonel Charles Liardet, of the English branch of an old Austrian family ennobled under Maria Theresa for State service; 2nd, Edith, widow of Chas. Rawnsley Hilton; one s. one d. *Educ.:* Somersetshire College (now by amalgamation with Sidney Coll. become Bath Coll.); Queen's Coll. Oxford. Lecturer in Logic, King's Coll. Strand; Dep. Prof. in Classical Literature, 1866-73; leading-article writer for the Standard since 1866; succeeded Mr. John Morley as editor of the Fortnightly Review; since 1865 actively connected with London daily and weekly journalism. *Publications:* England: Its People, Polity, and Pursuits, 1879; editor of Juvenal and Persius, 1867; Politics and Letters,.1886; Lord Randolph Churchill: a Monograph, 1895; Platform, Press, Politics, and Play, 1895; Social Transformations of the Victorian Age, 1897, being a sequel to England, etc.; Personal Forces of the Period, 1898; A Trip to Paradoxia, 1899; Gentlemen of the House of Commons, 1902; Sovereigns of the Nineteenth Century, 1902; King Edward VII. and his Court, 1903; Society in the Country House, 1906; The Story of British Diplomacy: its Makers and Movements, 1908; Edward Bulwer: First Baron
332

Lytton of Knebworth, 1910; Masters of English Journalism, 1911; Anthony Trollope, His Work and Originals, 1913; Club Makers and Club Members, 1914; Great Victorians, 1916; City Characters in Several Reigns, 1922; National and International Links, 1922. *Address:* 33 Sackville Road, Hove, Brighton.
(*Died 14 June 1924.*)

ESCREET, Ven. Charles Ernest; Archdeacon of Lewisham since 1906; Canon of Southwark since 1900; b. 20 Feb. 1852; m. 1892, Adelaide, d. of Charles J. F. Stuart of Harrow Weald. *Educ.:* Tonbridge School; Wadham College, Oxford (Smythe Exhibitioner). Ordained Assist. Curate, Barham, near Canterbury, 1875; Battersea Parish Church under Canon Erskine Clarke, 1878; Vicar of St. Andrew's, Stockwell, 1882-92; Rector of Woolwich, 1892-1909; Vicar of the Church of the Ascension, Blackheath, 1909-17. *Recreations:* cricket, climbing. *Address:* 96 Grove Lane, Camberwell, S.E.5. (*Died Mar. 1919.*)

ESLER, Erminda Rentoul, novelist; b. Ireland; d. of Rev. Alexander Rentoul, M.D., D.D., Manor Cunningham, Co. Donegal; m. Robert Esler, M.D., London and Marlow House, Ballymena, Ireland, 1883; two s. *Educ.:* privately and at schools in Nîmes and Berlin. Awarded First Honour Certificate by Royal University, Ireland, 1879. *Publications:* The Way of Transgressors, 1890; The Way they Loved at Grimpat, 1894; A Maid of The Manse, 1895; 'Mid Green Pastures, 1895; The Wardlaws, 1896; Youth at the Prow, 1898; The Awakening of Helena Thorpe, 1901; The Trackless Way, 1904. *Recreations:* walking, reading, conversation with people of individual mind. *Address:* Petherton, Bexley, Kent. *Club:* Lyceum.

ESMOND, Henry V., actor and dramatic author; b. Hampton Court; 4th s. of R. G. Jack, M.D.; m. Eva Moore, 1891; one s. one d. *Educ.:* by private tutors. Went on stage 1885. *Plays:* produced Rest, Bogey and The Divided Way, One Summer's Day, 1897; Grierson's Way, 1899; The Wilderness, 1901; When we were Twenty-one, 1901; The Sentimentalist; My Lady Virtue, 1902; Billy's Little Love Affair, 1903; The O'Grindles, 1907; Under the Greenwood Tree, 1907; A Young Man's Fancy, 1912; Eliza Comes to Stay, 1913; The Dangerous Age, 1914; A Kiss or Two, 1917; The Law Divine, 1918; Birds of a Feather, 1920. *Recreations:* tennis, golf, cycling. *Address:* 21 Whiteheads Grove, Chelsea, S.W.3. *T.:* Kensington 146. *M.:* A 1294. *Club:* Green Room. (*Died 17 April 1922.*)

ESPINAS, Professor Alfred, Doyen honoraire, Docteur ès Lettres, LL.D. Victoria University; membre de l'Académie des Sciences Morales et Politiques; né le 23 mai 1844, à St. Florentin, Yonne. *Educ.:* Lycées de Sens et de Paris; École Normale supérieure, 1864-67. Professeur de Philosophie aux Lycées de Bastia (Corse), de Chaumont, du Hâvre, de Dijon; Professeur de Philosophie aux Universités de Douai, Lille, et Bordeaux; Doyen de la Faculté des Lettres de Bordeaux, 1887-90; Professeur d'Histoire de l'Economie sociale (fondation de Chambrun) à la Faculté des Lettres de l'Université de Paris, 1894-1912. *Publications:* Psychologie de Spencer, traduction en collaboration avec T. Ribot, 1874; Des Sociétés animales, 1877 et 1878; La Philosophie expérimentale en Italie, 1880; République de Platon, livres VIII. et VI., édition classique, 1886, avec une introduction sur la polit. Platonicienne; Histoire des Doctrines économiques, 1893; Les Origines de la Technologie, 1897; La Philosophie sociale du XVIIIe Siècle et la Révolution (étude sur le Babouvisme), 1898; Dans la Revue Philosophique: Collaboration active dès la fondation; chargé pendant 4 ans de

la recension des ouvrages Italiens ; Le Sens de la Couleur, son origine et son développement : étude critique du livre de Grant Allen sur le même sujet, 1880 ; La Philosophie en Ecosse depuis le commencement du XVIIIe Siècle, 1881; Les Etudes sociologiques en France, 1882 ; Etre ou ne pas être, ou du.postulat de la Sociologie, 1901. Dans les Annales de la Faculté des Lettres de Bordeaux : Essai sur l'Esthétique de Pascal, 1881 ; Le Sens de l'Espace et les Canaux semi-circulaires, 1882. Dans la Revue Internationale de l'Enseignement : L' "Extension" des Universités en Angleterre et aux Etats-Unis, 1892. Le "Système" de Jean-Jacques Rousseau, 1895. *Address :* 84, rue du Ranelagh, Paris.
(*Died Feb. 1922.*)

ESSEX, 7th Earl of (*cr.* 1661), **George Devereux de Vere Capell,** J.P. ; Baron Capel, 1641; Viscount Malden, 1661 ; *b.* 24 Oct. 1857 ; *s.* of Viscount Malden and Emma, *d.* of Sir H. Meux ; *S.* grandfather 1892 ; *m.* 1st, 1882, Ellen Harriet Maria (*d.* 1885), *d.* of W. H. Harford of Oldown House, Almondsbury ; one *s.* ; 2nd, 1893, Adela, *d.* of Beach Grant, New York ; two *d.* Entered Grenadier Guards, 1877 ; retired 1882 ; served with Imperial Yeomanry in South Africa, 1900 ; Col. Herts Imperial Yeomanry, 1901. Owns about 15,000 acres. *Heir :* s. Viscount Malden. *Address :* Bowdon House, Davies Street, W. ; Cassiobury Park, Watford. *Clubs :* Carlton, Turf.
(*Died 24 Sept. 1916.*)

ESSLEMONT, George Birnie, J.P. ; *b.* 1860 ; *e. s.* of late Peter Esslemont, D.L., merchant, Aberdeen ; *m.* 1890, Clementina, *d.* of late Ranald Macdonald ; two *s.* four *d.* *Educ. :* Privately ; Aberdeen Grammar School. Entered business, 1876 ; served on numerous local Boards, and was Senior Magistrate of the city, 1905-6 ; Chairman Parliamentary Committee of National Sea Fisheries Protection Association since 1910 ; M.P. (L.) South Aberdeen 1907-17. *Address :* King's Acre, Aberdeen. *T.A. :* Esslemont, Aberdeen. *T. :* 1699. *Clubs :* Reform, National Liberal ; Scottish Liberal, Edinburgh. (*Died 2 Oct. 1917.*)

ESSON, William, M.A., F.R.S. ; Savilian Professor of Geometry, 1897 ; Deputy Savilian Professor of Geometry, Oxford, 1894-97 ; Fellow of New College ; Fellow of Merton, 1860-97 ; Bursar of Merton ; Curator of University Chest; *b.* 1838. *Educ. :* Inverness Royal Academy ; Cheltenham Grammar School ; St. John's Coll. Oxford (Junior and Senior Mathematical Scholar, M.A.). *Publications :* The Laws of Connexion between the Conditions of Chemical Change and its Amount, Transactions Royal Society, 1864, 1866, 1895 ; Notes on Synthetic Geometry, Proceedings of the London Mathematical Society, 1897 ; Variation with temperature of rate of chemical change, Transactions Royal Society, 1912 ; The Characters of Plane Curves, a law of connexion between two phenomena which influence each other, International Congress of Mathematicians, 1912. *Address :* Merton College, Oxford. (*Died 25 Aug. 1916.*)

ESTALL, Thomas, J.P. ; late Sen. General Manager, National Provincial Bank of England, Ltd. ; Past Master of the Worshipful Company Turners ; *b.* 1848. *Address :* 51 Evelyn Gardens, S.W.7. *T. :* Kens. 1380. *Clubs :* Junior Athenæum, County of Loudon Magistrates.
(*Died 30 July 1920.*)

ESTELL, Hon. John; *b.* Minmi, N.S.W., 14 Oct. 1861 ; *s.* of Robert Estell ; *m.* 1885, Alicia Jane Kirk ; two *s.* *Educ. :* Public Schools, Rydal and Bathurst. Worked as a coal miner ; Minister for Labour and Industry, New South Wales, 1914-16 ; Minister for Works and Secretary for Railways, New South Wales, 1920-22. *Address :* Wallsend, N.S.W.
(*Died 18 Oct. 1928.*)

ETCHELLS, Ernest Fiander, Hon. A.R.I.B.A., M.I.Struct.E., A.M.Inst.C.E.,

A.M.I.Mech.E., M.Math.Assoc., F.Inst.Phys. ; Fellow of the Physical Society of London ; Membre de la Société des Ingénieurs Civils de France ; Hon. Member British Engineering Standards Association ; Hon. Member Junior Institution of Engineers ; Fellow of King's College Engineering Society ; Structural Engineer in the department of the Superintending Architect of Metropolitan Buildings ; *b.* 1876 ; *o. s.* of Ernest Fiander Etchells, Romiley ; *m.* 1901, Mary, *y. d.* of late George Breakwell, Cleobury Mortimer *Educ. :* Old Andersonian College, Glasgow ; Royal Technical College, Glasgow ; University of London, King's College ; University of London, University College. Pupil of Francis Lawrence Lane, Civil Engineer ; afterwards Chief Assistant in the office of John Strain, Chartered Civil Engineer ; has been engaged on the design of Rolling Stock for the Pretoria and Pietermaritzburg Railway, Aerial Ropeways for Bolivia, Nitrate Plants for Taltal Chili ; was in charge of the structural steelwork for the reconstruction of Lanarkshire Steelworks ; was engaged on the Clyde Valley Electric Power Scheme, and the City of Mexico Electricity Supply Scheme ; has been engaged on structural work in all materials, including structural steelwork and reinforced concrete ; since 1902 has been engaged principally on the duties of an engineer and surveyor under the London Buildings Acts ; President of the Concrete Institute, 1920-21, 1921-22 ; President of the Institution of Structural Engineers, 1922-23 ; President of the Société des Ingénieurs Civils de France (Section Britannique), 1926-27 ; President of the Association of Architects, Surveyors and Technical Assistants, 1925-26 ; Hon. President of the Association of Floor Constructors, 1926 ; Advisory Member of the Board of Architectural Education, 1922 ; Superintending Examiner of the Institution of Structural Engineers, 1923 ; Member of the Grand Committee for the International Congress on Architectural Education, 1924 ; Member of Council of the London Society. *Publications :* Standard Mathematical Notation ; Chapters on Steelwork in Rivingtons Notes on Building Construction ; Foreword on Standard Mathematical Notation for Engineering Formulæ in Twelvetrees' Treatise on Reinforced Concrete, and Foreword on Standard Notation in Harrington-Hudson's Handbook on Reinforced Concrete ; Foreword on Standard Notation in Travers Morgan's Tables for Reinforced Concrete ; Evolution of Engineering Institutions ; also papers on structural engineering in various transactions and journals ; also editor of technical transactions. *Address :* Architects' Department, County Hall, Westminster Bridge, S.E.1. (*Died 5 Jan. 1927.*)

ETHE, C. Hermann, Ph.D. ; Hon. M.A. Oxford ; *b.* Stralsund, 13 Feb. 1844 ; *g. s.* of Kar-Lappe. *Educ. :* Stralsund Gymnasium ; Greifswald and Leipsic Univs. ; Lecturer in Oriental Languages in the Univ. of Munich, 1867-71. Called to Oxford beginning of 1872, to continue and complete Catalogue of Persian, Turkish, Hindústáni, and Pushtû MSS. in Bodleian Library, and compile supplementary Cat. of Arabic MSS. ; entrusted same year by Secretary for India with Cat. of Persian MSS. in India Office Library ; public examiner for Honours School of Oriental Studies, Oxford, 1887-89, and since 1893 ; Professor of German and Oriental Languages, Univ. Coll. Aberystwyth, 1875-1915. *Publications :* Catalogue of Persian, Turkish, Hindústáni, and Pushtû MSS. in the Bodleian Library, vol. i. 1889 ; Catalogue of the Persian MSS. in the Library of the India Office, vol. i. 1903 ; Yûsuf and Zalîkhâ, by Firdausi of Tûs, critical edition, fasciculus primus (Anecdota Oxoniensia, Aryan Series, part vi.), Oxford, 1908 ; numerous publications in Germany ; a series of articles on Persian literature in the Encyclopaedia Britannica. *Address:* 29 Royal York Crescent, Clifton, Bristol.

(Died 7 June 1917.)

ETHERINGTON-SMITH, John Henry, F.S.A. ; *b.* 1841 ; *e. s.* of Henry Etherington Smith of Norris Hill, Ashby de la Zouch; *m.* 1873, Margaret, *d.* of General Sir Thomas Pears, K.C.B. ; one *s.* three *d. Educ.:* Repton ; University College, Oxford (1st Class Moderations ; 2nd Lit. Hum. ; B.A. 1863 ; M.A. 1867). Called at the Inner Temple, 1866 ; Midland Circuit, 1867 ; Revising Barrister, 1877 ; Recorder of Newark, 1884-99 ; Derby, 1899-1913 ; a Governor of Repton School ; Leicestershire Yeomanry, 1863 - 88, when retired as Major; one of the Wordsworth (Dove Cottage) Trustees ; Member Royal United Service Institution and Royal Archæological Institute ; Bencher of the Inner Temple, 1900. *Recreations:* travel, rowing, sketching, archæology. *Address:* East Ella, Putney, S.W.15 ; *T.:* Putney 801 ; Butharlyp How, Grasmere. *Clubs:* New University, Leander, Skating.

(Died 15 April 1923.)

ETTLES, William James M'Culloch, M.D., M.S., F.R.C.S.E. ; Ophthalmic Surgeon ; *b.* Brighton, 16 Feb. 1869 ; *m.* Helen Edith, *d.* of John Sell Cotman, M.R.C.P. ; two *s. Educ.:* Aberdeen, Edinburgh, and Paris Universities. Highest Academical Honours ; M.D. degree, 1896 ; late President Optical Society of London ; Treasurer (late President) Hunterian Society ; Consulting Oculist to the Eastern Public Dispensary and London Spectacle Mission ; Foreign Member of the Spanish Red Cross ; Knight Hospitaller of the Order of St. John the Baptist of Spain ; Honorary Fellow and Medallist (1st Class) Italian Physical Academy ; Member of the Court of Assistants of the Worshipful Company of Gold and Silver Wyre Drawers ; Liveryman of the Worshipful Company of Spectaclemakers ; Vice-President and Hon. Medical Officer, London Morayshire Club ; late Pathologist, Royal Eye Hospital ; Consulting Oculist, Shipping Federation, Recuperative Hostels for Sailors and Soldiers, etc. ; Lecturer on Physiology of Vision, Northampton Institute, and Society of Illuminating Engineers ; Vice-President of the Institute of Ophthalmic Opticians ; silver medal (Paris, 1900) ; gold medal (London, 1903) for ambulance work ; Special Lecturer, London College of Ambulance. *Publications:* Hunterian Oration, 1907 ; numerous articles on diseases of eye in various medical journals. *Recreations:* cruising (Rear-Commodore, Chichester Harbour Yacht Club) ; wild - fowling (National Wild - fowling Association); astronomy; violoncello. *Address:* 114A Harley Street, W. *T.:* 3245 Mayfair ; The Ingle Nook, West Wittering, Sussex. *M.:* BP 2713. *Club:* Junior Constitutional.

(Died 9 July 1918.)

EUCKEN, Rudolf; *b.* Aurich, Ostfriesland, 5 Jan. 1846. *Educ.:* Göttingen (Dr. Phil.); Berlin. War einige Jahre Lehrer an gelehrten Schulen, wurde 1871 Professor der Philosophie in Basel und wirkt seit 1874 als solcher in Jena, seit 1920 im Ruhestand; seine Schriften waren zuerst mehr der Geschichte der Philosophie zugewandt, später überwiegend der systematischen Philosophie ; er sucht einen neuen Idealismus zu begründen, der bei voller Anerkennung der Tatsachen und Aufgaben der Gegenwart die Überlegenheit des Geisteslebens behauptet und im besonderen den Konflikt zwischen Religion und moderner Kultur überwinden möchte ; 1903 wurde er von der Universität Giessen, und 1910 von der Universität Glasgow zum D.D. ernannt ; seit 1908 ist er auswärtiges Mitglied der Königl. Schwedischen Akademie der Wissenschaften, seit 1911 der Finnländischen Societät der Wissenschaften ; 1913 wurde er Dr. of Letters (Columbia Univer-
334

sity), Dr. of Humane Letters (Syracuse University), LL.D. (New York University); 1914 auswärtiges Mitglied der Accademia dei Lincei (Rom) ; Senator der Deutschen Academie (München); won Nobel Prize for Literature, 1908. *Publications:* Grundbegriffe der Gegenwart, 1878 ; (später Geistige Strömungen), 6. Aufl, 1920 ; Die Einheit des Geisteslebens, 1888, 2. Aufl. 1925; Die Lebensanschauungen der grossen Denker, 1890, 18. Aufl. 1922 ; Der Kampf um einen geistigen Lebensinhalt, 5. Aufl. 1925 ; Der Wahrheitsgehalt der Religion, 1901, 4. Aufl. 1920 ; Grundlinien einer neuen Lebensanschauung, 1907, 2. Aufl. 1913 ; Hauptprobleme der Religionsphilosophie der Gegenwart, 1907, 4. u. 5. Aufl. 1912 ; Der Sinn und Wert des Lebens, 1908, 9. Aufl. 1923 ; Einführung in die Hauptfragen der Philosophie, 1908, 4. Aufl. 1925 ; Können wir noch Christen sein ? 1912 ; Erkennen und Leben, 1911, 2. Aufl. 1923 ; Zur Sammlung der Geister, 1913 ; Present-day Ethics, 1913 ; Mensch und Welt, 1918, 3. Aufl. 1923 ; der Sozialismus und seine Lebensgestaltung, 1920, 2 Aufl. 1926 ; Lebenserinnerungen, 1920, 2. Aufl. 1922 ; das Lebensproblem in China und in Europa, 1921 ; Der Kampf um die Religion in der Gegenwart, 1923, 3-4 Aufl. ; Ethik als Grundlage des Staatsbürglichen Lebens, 1924. *Address:* Jena, Botzstr. 5.

(Died 14 Sept. 1926.)

EUGENIE, Empress (Marie Eugenie de Guzman y de Porto-Carrero, Condesa de Teba, Marquesa de Moya); *b.* Granada, 5 May 1826 ; *d.* of Cyprien, conde Montijo, duque de Penerauda, and Marie Manuela Kirkpatrick of Closeburn, Scotland ; *m.* at Paris, 29 January 1858, Napoleon III., Emperor of the French. *Address:* Farnborough Hill, Farnborough, Hants. *(Died 11 July 1920.)*

EUSTACE, Major-Gen. Sir Francis John William, K.C.B., *cr.* 1913 ; C.B. 1900 ; *b.* 17 Sept. 1849 ; *s.* of late A. T. Eustace-Malpas of Rochestown, Co. Dublin ; *m.* 1882, Marina, 2nd *d.* of late Field - Marshal Sir Donald Stewart, 1st Bart., G.C.B. ; one *s. Educ.:* Somersetshire College, Bath ; R.M. Academy, Woolwich. Joined R.A. 1870 ; Captain, 1880 ; Major, 1885 ; Lieut.-Col. 1896 ; Col. 1900 ; Maj.-Gen. 1904; was present in the autumn of 1877 at the Schipka Pass and passage of the Balkans during the Russo-Turkish war, and received the Turkish war medal from the Sultan of Turkey for Red Cross services ; served throughout the Afghan war, 1878-80 (medal) ; Boer war, as A.A.G. for R.H.A. on the staff of Lieut.-Gen. Sir J. P. French, K.C.B., from Nov. 1899 to Nov. 1900 (medal with six clasps, despatches several times, C.B.); was A.D.C. to Sir D. M. Stewart, Commander-in-Chief in India, 1882 - 83 ; commanded R.H.A. Aldershot, 1896-99 ; Commandant, School of Gunnery for Royal Horse and Field Artillery, 1901-4 ; Major-General on Staff commanding R.A., Aldershot, 1904-7 ; retired ; Colonel Commandant Royal Artillery, 1919. *Address:* Doric House. Bath. *T.:* Bath 854.

(Died 7 Dec. 1925.)

EUSTACE, Lieut. - Col. Henry Montague, D.S.O. 1900 ; J.P. Co. Wexford ; late Middlesex Regt. ; *b.* 28 Nov. 1863 ; *e. surv. s.* of late Rev. R. H. Eustace of Sampford Grange, Essex ; *m.* 1903, Monica Alice, *d.* of Col. John Thomas Eustace, Wynberg, S. Africa ; two *s.* one *d. Educ.:* Harrow. Entered army, 1885 ; Captain, 1895 ; Major, 1902 ; served South Africa, 1899 - 1903 (despatches, Queen's medal six clasps, King's medal two clasps ; D.S.O.) ; European War, 1915 ; commanded 6th Batt. York and Lancaster Regt. in Dardanelles (very severely wounded, despatches). *Address:* Vellore, St. Marychurch, Torquay. *Club:* Torquay Yacht.

(Died 27 Feb. 1926.)

EVAN-JONES, Rev. Canon Richard, M.A.; Vicar of Llanllwchaiarn, since 1884; Rural Dean of Cedewain, 1901; Precentor and Prebendary of Vaenol in St. Asaph Cathedral, 1916; *e. s.* of late Reverend J. Evan-Jones; *b.* Lynesack Vicarage, Durham, Nov. 1849; *m.* Hannah Rose, 2nd *d.* of late Edward Evans, Bronwylfa, Wrexham; one *s. Educ.:* Ruthin School; Merton Coll. Oxford. Deacon, 1873; Priest, 1874; Curate of Pont Bleiddyn, nr. Mold, 1873-76; Llanrhaiadr, nr. Denbigh, 1876-77; Gresford, nr. Wrexham, 1877-84; Member of the Governing Body of the Church in Wales. *Publication:* A Few Plain Words to Working Men on Holy Communion, 1887. *Recreation:* walking. *Address:* Llanllwchaiarn Vicarage, Newtown, North Wales.
(*Died 30 Sept. 1925.*)

EVAN-THOMAS, Admiral Sir Hugh, G.C.B., *cr.* 1924; K.C.B., *cr.* 1916; K.C.M.G., *cr.* 1919; C.B. 1916; M.V.O. 1906; LL.D.; *b.* 27 Oct. 1862; *s.* of late Charles Evan-Thomas of Gnoll, Glamorganshire; *m.* 1894, Hilda, *d.* of late Thomas Barnard. Entered Navy, 1875; Commander, 1896; Captain, 1902; Rear-Admiral, 1912; Rear-Adm. First Battle Squadron, 1913-1914; commanded Fifth Battle Squadron, battle of Jutland Bank, 1916 (despatches, C.B. and K.C.B.); Vice-Adm. 1917; Admiral, 1920; Commander-in-Chief the Nore, 1921-24; retired list, 1924; Commander Legion of Honour; Croix de Guerre with palms, Rising Sun, Japan, Order Crown of Italy, St. Annes, Russia. *Address:* Charlton House, Shaftesbury. *Club:* Travellers'. (*Died 30 Aug. 1928.*)

EVANS, Rev. Arthur Robertson, M.A.; Hon. Canon Ely, 1881. *Educ.:* Oriel College, Oxford; Cuddesdon College. Curate of Clifton-Hampden, 1865-67; Kempsford, 1867-68; Leeds, 1868-73; Rector of Newton-in-the-Isle, 1885-1907; Domestic Chaplain to Bishop Woodford (Ely), 1874-85; Chaplain to Bishop Compton (Ely), 1886-1905. *Address:* St. Mary Street, Ely.
(*Died 20 Dec. 1923.*)

EVANS, Bernard Walter, R.I. 1887; R.B.A. 1880; landscape painter; *b.* Birmingham, 26 Dec. 1843; 2nd *s.* of late Walter Evans, who was associated with Pugin in the revival of mediæval architecture; is a cousin of George Eliot; *m.* 1870, Marian (*d.* 1902), *d.* of late Samuel Hollyer. Studied painting from 7 years of age under Samuel Lines of Birmingham; studied under late Edward Watson, 1865; came to London at the age of 21; exhibited regularly at Royal Academy from 1870 until his election to Royal Institute of Painters in Water Colours; selected to represent English art in the Paris Exhibition; also St. Louis, 1903-1904; originated City of London Society of Artists; has pictures in the permanent collection at South Kensington, the Sydney Art Gallery, and the Melbourne Art Gallery; also in Cartwright Hall, Bradford. *Recreation:* smoking. *Club:* Savage. (*Died 26 Feb. 1922.*)

EVANS, Captain Bertram Sutton, R.N., M.V.O. 1910. Entered Navy, 1886; Commander, 1905; Captain, 1913; commanded armed cruiser Macedonia in action of Falkland Islands, 1914 (despatches). *Address:* Little Orchard, St. Helen's, Isle of Wight. (*Died 2 Mar. 1919.*)

EVANS, Charles Barnard, C.M.G., 1914; Commissioner for Railways, Queensland. *Address:* Dept. of Railways, Brisbane.
(*Died 31 Dec. 1920.*)

EVANS, Sir David William, Kt. *cr.* 1925; Director and Legal Adviser to the King Edward VII. Welsh National Memorial Association since 1913; *b.* 4. Nov. 1866; *s.* of late Thomas Evans, Dowlais; *m.* Clare, *d.* of late Rees Jones, J.P., Porthkerry, Glam.; two *s.* two *d. Educ.:* Llandovery School; Jesus College, Oxford. Solicitor; interested in all things pertaining to Wales, particularly matters of health, education, and music; member of the Council of the Cardiff Royal Infirmary, the Prince of Wales' Hospital, the Nursing Association, the National Eisteddfod Association, the National Council of Music, the Ministry of Health Consultative Council (Wales). *Publications:* Reports of the Memorial Association. *Recreations:* golf; formerly Rugby football; Oxford, 1886-87-88; Welsh International, 1889-90-91. *Address:* 199 Newport Road, Cardiff. *T.A.:* Memorial, Cardiff. *T.:* Cardiff 4728 and 32. *Club:* Cardiff and County, Cardiff.
(*Died 17 Mar. 1926.*)

EVANS, Sir Edward, Kt., *cr.* 1906; J.P.; *b.* 1846; 3rd *s.* of late Edward Evans, D.L., J.P., of Bronwylfa, Denbighshire; *m.* 1869, Martha, *d.* of W. Nevett of Marton, Salop; two *s.* three *d. Educ.:* Wallace Hall, Dumfriesshire; privately. *Recreation:* golf. *Address:* Spital Old Hall, Bromborough, Cheshire. *T.:* 20 Bromborough. *Clubs:* Reform, National Liberal; Liverpool Reform; Glasgow Liberal. (*Died 10 Oct. 1917.*)

EVANS, Col. Edward Stokes, C.B. 1900; commanded Royal Munster Fusiliers; retired; *b.* 31 July 1855; *s.* of late W. Evans, M.D., unmarried. The Royal Munster Fusiliers; served South Africa, 1899-1900 (despatches, Queen's medal with clasp, C.B.). *Address:* Brancaston, King's Lynn. (*Died 27 Aug. 1926.*)

EVANS, Sir Edwin, Kt. *cr.* 1927; J.P.; Fellow of the Auctioneers and Estate Agents Institute; *s.* of late John Evans, London; *m.* 1880, Elizabeth, *d.* of late John Perry, South Street, Manchester Square; three *s. Educ.:* various schools. Travelled in South Africa, 1874-76; articled to a local surveyor, 1877; started in business and founded the present firm of Edwin Evans & Sons of Lavender Hill, Clapham Junction, Auctioneers, Surveyors and Land Agents, 1880; member of the London County Council for twelve years, first Wandsworth, later South Battersea; for some time Vice-Chairman of the Housing of the Working Classes Committee; a Director of Arding & Hobbs (Ltd.), Clapham Junction; Chairman of the Housing and Land Development Corporation; Director of several building societies. *Recreations:* motoring and work. *Address:* 9 Ashley Gardens, Westminster, S.W.1. *T.:* Victoria 3884. *Club:* Constitutional.
(*Died 4 April 1928.*)

EVANS, Evan William, J.P. Merionethshire; *b.* 7 Dec. 1860; *s.* of David and Jane Evans, Cae Einion, Dolgelley; *m.* 1888, *o. d.* of Joseph Roberts, Dolgelley; two *s. Educ.:* Dolgelley Grammar School. Editor of the Goleuad, 1879-1914; of the Cymro (Welshman) since 1914; publisher of the Lladmerydd, Gymraes, &c. *Publications:* Travels in the East; With Dr. Parker in Switzerland; Egypt; numerous articles on travels through Egypt, Palestine, and Germany. *Recreation:* motoring. *Address:* Frondirion, Dolgelley; Isfryn, Fairbourne. *T.:* Dolgelley 23, Fairbourne 2. *T.A.:* Cymro, Dolgelley; Cymro, Fairbourne. *M.:* HF 103. (*Died 28 Oct. 1925.*)

EVANS, Rev. Frederic Rawlins, M.A.; Rector of Bedworth since 1876; Hon. Canon of Worcester since 1905; *b.* 1 June 1842; *s.* of Isaac P. Evans, of Griff, Nuneaton, who was brother of George Eliot; *m.* 1888, Charlotte, *d.* of John Rotherham, Coventry; one *d. Educ.:* Rugby; Exeter College, Oxford. Curate Hagley, Worcestershire, 1866-68; St. George's, Kidderminster, 1868-72; Vicar, St. George's, Kidderminster, 1872-76; Rural Dean of Monks Kirby, 1886-1924. *Publications:* single sermons. *Recreation:* Oxford University Eleven, 1863-4-5; Gents *v.* Players, 1865. *Address:* Bedworth Rectory, Nuneaton. *T.A.:* Rector, Bedworth. *T.:* Bedworth, S. Midland 7. *M.:* DU 5335.
(*Died 4 Mar. 1927.*)

EVANS, Rev. Henry, D.D., M.R.I.A.; Commissioner of National Education in Ireland, 1890-1921, now retired; Member of the Board

335

of Technical Instruction. Was Examiner for Board of Intermediate Education for many years; was Departmental Commissioner of Income Tax for National Board; represented the Commissioners of National Education at International Congresses connected with Education; was Representative of Board of National Education at the British Association, Dublin, 1908, and was Vice-President of Education Section; was a Member of the Royal Commission on Manual and Practical Instruction, 1897; Member of Advisory Committee of Standard Dictionary. *Publications:* articles in quarterly reviews, magazines, weeklies, etc.; editions of books for primary and secondary schools. Wrote the articles on The English Versions of the Bible; on Archaic, Obsolete, and Obscure Words in English Bible; and on Biblical Antiquities, Customs, etc., in Aids to Biblical Study for Students. *Address:* St. Helens, Blackrock, Co. Dublin. *T.:* Blackrock, Dublin, 242.

(*Died 2 Sept. 1924.*)

EVANS, General Sir Horace Moule, K.C.B., *cr.* 1911; C.B. 1894; Hon. Col. 2nd Batt. 8th Ghurkha Rifles, Indian Army; *b.* 8 Dec. 1841; *m.* 1866, Elizabeth Anne, *d.* of late Surg.-Gen. J. T. Tresidder, I.M.S.; five *s.* three *d.* Served in Dufla expedition, 1874-75 (despatches); Naga expedition, 1879-80 (despatches, medal with clasp, brevet Lt.-Col.); Manipore operations, 1891 (despatches, clasp). *Address:* Edgecombe, Steyning, Sussex.

(*Died 28 July 1923.*)

EVANS, Maj.-Gen. Leopold Exxel; Bengal Infantry; *b.* 13 March 1837; *m.* Mary, *d.* of F. C. Armstrong, Penged Hill, Carmarthenshire. Entered army, 1856; Maj.-Gen. 1891; retired, 1893; served Indian Mutiny, 1857-59 (medal).

(*Died 8 Oct. 1916.*)

EVANS, Richardson; *b.* Cork, 5 April 1846; *s.* of late William Evans; *m.* 1879, Amy Laura, *d.* of late John Frederick Feeney, Edgbaston, Birmingham; one *s.* five *d.* *Educ.:* Queen's Coll. Cork; Wadham College, Oxford. M.A. Royal University of Ireland; Barrister, Middle Temple; Member of Civil Service of India (N.W.P.), 1867-1876; leader-writer Pall Mall Gazette and St. James's Gazette during the editorship of Mr. Frederick Greenwood; leader-writer Standard, 1881-1906; interested in preserving scenery from disfigurement; for many years a Conservator of Wimbledon Common; Chairman of Committee of the Scapa Society; Founder of the John Evelyn Club for Wimbledon; Hon. Sec. of Wimbledon and Putney Commons Extension Fund, 1905-21, and of the Memorial Garden Fund; Hon. Secretary and Treasurer of Wimbledon and Merton Belgian Refugees' Fund, Sept. 1914-18; Hon. Burgess of the Borough of Wimbledon; First Hon. Freeman of the Borough of Wimbledon. *Publications:* The Age of Disfigurement, 1893; (with Mrs. Richmond Ritchie) Lord Amherst (Rulers of India Series), 1894; A Beautiful World, Nos. i-xi, 1893-1909; Ireland in the Realm: Ulster in Ireland, 1917; Conditions of Social Well-being considered in the Light of the War, 1918; An Account of the Scapa Society, 1925. *Address:* Holly House, Dorking. *Club:* Savile.

(*Died 10 May 1928.*)

EVANS, Rt. Hon. Sir Samuel Thomas, G.C.B., *cr.* 1916; P.C. 1910; K.C. 1901; President Probate, Divorce and Admiralty Courts since 1910; President of the British Prize Court since the outbreak of the War; *b.* 1859; *s.* of John Evans, Skewen, Neath; *m.* 1st, 1887, Rachel (*d.* 1889), *d.* of Wm. Thomas of Skewen; 2nd, 1905, Blanche, *y. d.* of late Charles Rule, Cincinnati, U.S.A.; one *s.* one *d.* J.P. Glamorganshire, Pembrokeshire, and Breconshire; Hon. Freeman of County Borough of Swansea, and of Borough of Neath; Hon. Fellow of Jesus Coll., Oxford; Hon. LL.D. Univ. of Wales; Barr.

336

Middle Temple; the last Q.C. appointed, 1901; Bencher and Trustee of the Middle Temple, 1908; Recorder of Swansea, 1906-8; Solicitor-General, 1908-10; M.P. (L.L.) Glamorganshire (Mid. Div.) 1890-1910. *Address:* 11 Lancaster Gate, W.; 9 Sussex Square, Brighton. *Clubs:* Athenæum, United Service, Reform, Garrick.

(*Died 13 Sept. 1918.*)

EVANS, Very Rev. Thomas Frye Lewis, M.A., D.D., D.C.L.; Dean of Montreal since 1902; Rector of St. Stephen's Church since 1874; *b.* St. John's Rectory, Simcoe, Ontario, 17 Dec. 1845; *s.* of Rev. Francis Evans, D.C.L., Rector of Woodhouse, and Maria Sophia Lewis; *m.* 1st, 1874, Maria Stuart (*d.* 1903), *e. d.* of Strachan Bethune, K.C., Chancellor of the Diocese of Montreal; 2nd, 1908, Emily Elizabeth, *d.* of late Robert H. Bethune of Toronto. *Educ.:* Upper Canada College, and Trinity University, Toronto. 4th Foundation Scholarship, 1863; B.A. 1866; M.A. 1871; Hon. D.C.L. 1894; D.D. 1902; D.D. jure dignitatis, Bishop's College, Lennoxville, 1902. Deacon, 1869; Priest, 1870 (Huron); Missionary at Norwich, Ontario, 1869-71; Assistant, Christ Church Cathedral, 1871-74; Hon. Canon, Christ Church Cathedral 1874; Archdeacon of Iberville, 1882; Archdeacon of Montreal, 1886. *Address:* 1 Weredale Park, Westmount, Province of Quebec.

(*Died Oct. 1920.*)

EVANS, Rev. Thomas Jones, M.A.; Vicar of S. John Baptist, Knutsford, since 1916; Rural Dean of Bowdon, 1917; *b.* April 1856; *s.* of late Rev. David Evans, Rector of Llansantffraid, G.D., Merionethshire; two *s.* one *d.* *Educ.:* Ruthin School; Jesus College, Oxford (Scholar). Powis Scholar; 2nd Class Honours in Classical Moderations; 3rd Class Lit. Hum; Deacon, 1880; Priest, 1881; Assistant Master King's School, Chester, 1880-1884; Curate of Eccleston, Chester, 1882-87; Vicar of Hargrave, Chester, 1887-96; Tarvin, 1896-1904; Rock Ferry, 1904-16; Co-opted Member of Cheshire County Education Committee, 1903; Hon. Canon of Chester, 1914; Member of Sub-Committee for Higher, Elementary, and Agricultural Education; Member of Bucklow Union Board of Guardians, etc. *Recreations:* bee-keeping; lecturer on Apiculture to County Education Committee, etc.; Chairman of Cheshire Beekeeper's Association. *Address:* The Vicarage, Knutsford, Cheshire.

(*Died 25 Oct. 1921.*)

EVANS, Maj.-Gen. Thomas Julian Penrhys, C.B. 1903; R.M.L.I.; retired; *b.* 21 Dec. 1854; *s.* of late Col. H. W. Evans; *m.* 1891, Florence Albina, *o. d.* of Col. H. G. Rogers; one *d.* Served South Africa (Queen's medal and clasp, despatches); European War, Dec. 1914-19 (despatches). *Educ.:* Tonbridge School. Entered army, 1873; Captain, 1884; Major, 1891; Lieut.-Col. 1898; Colonel, 1902. *Club:* Junior United Service.

(*Died 20 May 1921.*)

EVANS, Walter Jenkin, M.A., J.P.; Principal Presbyterian College, Carmarthen, since 1888; *b.* 1 April 1856; *e. s.* of Rev. Titus Evans, Carmarthen, and Rachel, *d.* of Rev. John Jeremy of Lampeter, Cardigan; *m.* Annie Wright, *o. c.* of S. S. Curtis of Upper Clapton and Leadenhall St., E.C., 1888; one *s.* two *d.* *Educ.:* Grammar School and Presbyterian College, Carmarthen; Jesus College, Oxford (Scholar). M.A. 1880; 2nd class Honours in Classical Moderations, 1875; assistant-master in Stirlingshire, 1877-78; Brighton, 1879-83; London, 1883-84; Classical Professor at Presbyterian College, Carmarthen, since 1884; Chairman of Carmarthen School Board, 1892-98; President of Carmarthen Literary and Scientific Institute, 1893-96; Chairman of Carmarthen County Governing Body, 1897-1900; President of Carmarthen Liberal Association, 1896-1904;

EVANS, Maurice Smethurst, C.M.G. See page xix.

Governor of Bristol, Cardiff, and Aberystwyth University Colleges, and in the last (until 1922) Member of Council ; Member of Court of University of Wales and formerly of Executive Committee ; President of the Theological Board, University of Wales, 1915-19 ; Dean of Divinity in the University of Wales, 1910-13. *Publications*: Allitteratio Latina, 1921 ; Articles and Addresses, chiefly on educational subjects. *Address*: Green Hill, Carmarthen. *T.A.*: Principal Evans, Carmarthen.   (*Died 10 Feb. 1927.*)

EVANS, His Hon. Judge William, B.A. Oxon. ; Judge of County Courts, Mid Wales, since 1897 ; *b.* Merthyr Tydfil, 27 Dec. 1847 ; 3rd *s.* of the late James Evans and Mary his wife ; *m.* 1897, Frances Louisa, *o. d.* of late George Cheatle, 117 Harley Street, W. *Educ.*: Jesus College, Oxford. Honours in Classics and Law, Oxford. Inner Temple, 1870 ; and the South Wales and Chester Circuit, 1874 ; Assistant Revising Barrister, 1890 ; went on Commissions to France and Spain, 1879 ; Australia, 1893 ; and Griqualand, S. Africa, 1894 ; Deputy County Court Judge, 1895. *Publications*; The Law of Principal and Agent ; The Remuneration of Commission Agents ; A Fair Reward ; Cæsar Borgia and other Poems ; Ballads of Wales. *Recreation*: gardening. *Address*: 2 Cambridge Terrace, Hyde Park, W. ; Ilmington Manor, nr. Shipston-on-Stour. *Club*: Reform.
(*Died 15 Feb. 1918.*)

EVANS, William, C.B. 1908; *b.* 1841; 2nd *s.* of Daniel Evans, schoolmaster at Dolgelly and Holyhead ; *m.* 1st, *o. sis.* (*d.* 1878) of J. Kerfoot Evans, J.P., Greenfield, Flintshire ; 2nd, Caroline, *e. d.* of Charles Hughes, J.P. of Wrexham ; two *s.* one *d.* Bank Manager at Holywell and Chester, 1870-84 ; Official Receiver in Bankruptcy for Chester and North Wales District, 1884-89 ; First Inspector of Official Receivers for England and Wales, Board of Trade, 1889-1905 ; Inspector-General, 1906-7. *Address*: 14 Meadway, Golders Green, N.W.4. *T.*: Finchley 1862. *Club*: National Liberal.   (*Died 7 Dec. 1919.*)

EVATT, Major-General Sir George (Joseph Hamilton), K.C.B., *cr.* 1919 ; C.B. 1903 ; M.D., R.A.M.C. ; retired ; Member Council Brit. Med. Assoc., 1904 ; *b.* 11 Nov. 1843 ; *s.* of Capt. George Evatt, 70th Foot ; *m.* 1877, Sophie Mary Frances, *d.* of William Walter Raleigh Kerr, Treasurer of Mauritius, and *g.d.* of Lord Robert Kerr ; one *d.* *Educ.*: Royal Coll. of Surgeons, and Trinity Coll. Dublin. Entered Army Medical Service, 1865 ; joined 25th (K.O.S.B.) Regt. 1866 ; Surg.-Maj. 1877 ; Lt.-Col. R.A.M.C. 1885 ; Col. 1896 ; Surg.-Gen. 1899 ; served Perak Expedition with Sir H. Ross's Bengal Column, 1876 (medal and clasp) ; Afghan War, 1878-80 ; capture of Ali Musjid (despatches) ; action in Bazaar Valley, with Gen. Tytler's Column (despatches) ; advance on Gundamak, and return in "Death March," 1879 (specially thanked in General Orders by Viceroy of India in Council and Commander-in-Chief in India for services) ; commanded Field Hospital in second campaign, including advance to relief of Cabul under General Sir Charles Gough, 1879 ; action on the Ghuzni Road ; return to India, 1880 (medal and two clasps) ; Suakin Expedition, 1885, including actions at Handoub, Tamai, and removal of wounded from MacNeill's Zareba (despatches, medal and clasp, Khedive's Star) ; Zhob Valley Expedition, 1890 ; commanded a Field Hospital (despatches) ; Medical Officer, Royal Military Academy, Woolwich, 1880-96 ; Senior Medical Officer, Quetta Garrison, Baluchistan, 1887-91 ; Sanitary Officer, Woolwich Garrison, 1892-94 ; Sec. Royal Victoria Hospital, Netley, 1894-96 ; P.M.O. China, 1896-99 ; P.M.O. Western District, 1899-1902 ; Surg.-Gen. 2nd Army Corps, Salisbury, 1902-3 ; raised with Sir James Cantlie R.A.M.C. Volunteers, 1888 ; founded 1884, Medical Officers of Schools Assoc. London ; and 1886, drew up

scheme for Army Nursing Service Reserve ; Member Committee International Health Exhibition, 1884 : Vice-President, British Medical Temperance Association ; Member of Council Royal Army Temperance Association, 1903 ; President Poor Law Medical Officers' Association ; President Travelling Medical Board, Western Command, 1915-16 ; contested (L.) Woolwich, 1886, Fareham Division, Hampshire, 1906, and Brighton, 1910 ; Hon. Col. Home Counties Division, R.A.M.C., Territorial Force, 1908 ; received Distinguished Service Reward, 1910. *Publications*: Travels in the Euphrates Valley and Mesopotamia, 1873 ; and many publications on military and medical subjects. *Address*: 33 Earl's Court Square, S.W.5 ; Wayside, Camberley, Surrey. *Club*: Junior United Service.   (*Died 5 Nov. 1921.*)

EVE, Sir Frederic Samuel, Kt., *cr.* 1911 ; F.R.C.S. Eng. ; Consulting Surgeon to London Hospital and to Evelina Hospital ; Member of Council and Vice-President Royal College of Surgeons ; Lt.-Col. R.A.M.C. (Temp.), Consulting Surgeon to the Eastern Command ; *s.* of late Wm. Eve, N. Ockendon, Essex ; *m.* Ella, *d.* of Hon. H. E. Cox, Claremont, Jamaica ; one *s.* one *d.* *Educ.*: St. Bartholomew's Hospital ; Leipsic. Pathological Curator at Royal College of Surgeons, England, 1881-90 ; Erasmus Wilson Lecturer (on Pathology of Tumours), R.C.S. 1882-84 ; late member of Court of Examiners, Royal College of Surgeons. *Publications*: Monographs on Surgery of Abdomen and Pathological Anatomy. *Address*: 61 Harley Street, W. *T.A.*: Event, Westdo, London. *T.*: Paddington 183. *Club*: Arts.
(*Died 15 Dec. 1916.*)

EVELYN, John Harcourt Chichester, J.P. ; *b.* 11 August 1876 ; *o. s.* of late W. J. Evelyn and Frances Harriet, *e. d.* of Rev. G. V. Chichester ; *m.* 1902, Frances Edith, *d.* of late Gen. and Hon. Mrs. Ives of Moyns Park ; two *s.* one *d.* *Educ.*: Eton ; Christ Church, Oxford. Heir : *s.* Cecil John Alvin Evelyn. *Address*: Wotton House, Dorking. *Clubs*: Arthur's, Carlton.   (*Died 2 Jan. 1922.*)

EVEN, Col. George Eusebe, C.B. 1909 ; late 127th Queen Mary's Own Baluch L.I. ; *b.* 12 Aug. 1855 ; *s.* of late Count Rene Even de la Tremblais, Cholet, Brittany ; *m.* 1885, Susan Ellen, *d.* of late Colonel Southey, Madras S.C. ; two *d.* *Educ.*: Cheltenham College. Entered army, 1874 ; Capt. I.S.C. 1886 ; Major, 1895 ; Lt.-Col., Indian Army, 1901 ; Bt.-Col. 1904 ; Adjutant, G.I.P. Railway Volunteers, 1883-87 ; served Afghan War, 1879-80 (medal) ; Chin-Lushai Expedition, 1889-90 (medal with clasp) ; operations in Mekran, 1898 (despatches) ; Indian Army, retired ; served European War (England, Egypt, France), 1914-19. *Address*: c/o Thos. Cook & Son, Ludgate Circus, E.C. *Club*: Junior Army and Navy.
(*Died 29 June 1924.*)

EVERETT, Colonel Edward, C.B. 1907 ; D.S.O. 1886 ; late Cameron Highlanders ; *b.* 4 June 1837. *Educ.*: Marlborough. Entered army, 1855 ; Colonel, 1899 ; served Indian Mutiny, 1858-59 (despatches, medal with clasp) ; Nile Expedition, 1884-85 (despatches, Brevet Lieut.-Col., medal with clasp, Khedive's star) ; Soudan, 1885-86 (despatches, 3rd class Medjidie, D.S.O.).   (*Died 2 April 1920.*)

EVERETT, Robert Lacey, M.P. (L.) S.E. Suffolk, 1906-10 ; J.P. Suffolk ; retired yeoman farmer ; *b.* 1833 ; *s.* of Joseph David and Elizabeth Everett of Rushmere, Ipswich ; *m.* 1863, *d.* of O. Nussey, J.P. of Leeds ; four *s.* four *d.* *Educ.*: private school, Ipswich. Hon. Sec. Ipswich Farmers' Club and E. Suffolk Chamber of Agriculture ; member of Ipswich School Board from commencement, and Town Council nine years ; Alderman E. Suffolk County Council from commencement ; former candidate for E. Suffolk, 1880 ; M.P. Woodbridge Division, E. Suffolk,

EVERARD, Captain Andrew Robert Guy.   See page xix.

371

1885 - 86, 1892 - 95, 1906 - 1909; then retired. *Publications:* prize essay on Repeal of the Malt Tax; special report on Cause of Agricultural Depression, written for Royal Commission which sat 1895-97; prize essay on the Silver Question for Bimetallic League. *Address:* Rushmere, Ipswich. *(Died 21 Oct. 1916.)*

EVERINGHAM, Ven. William, B.D.; Archdeacon of Suffolk since 1917; Diocesan Missioner; late Hon. Canon of Bristol Cathedral; Examining Chaplain to the Bishop; *b.* 1856; *m.* 1896, Clara Isabella, *sis.* of Sir E. R. P. Edgcumbe. *Educ.:* Lincoln Theological College (1st class Camb. Prelim. Theo. Exam.). Ordained Deacon, 1879; Priest, 1880; Curate of Beeston and Diss, Norfolk; Chaplain to the Forces at Singapore, 1881; Acting Col. Chaplain of Hong Kong, 1884; Col. Chaplain of Malacca for five years; Missioner of the Society of St. Andrew, Salisbury, 1890-96; commissioned by Archbishop Benson to visit the Armenian Church in Asia Minor, 1892; Special Missioner for Diocese of Salisbury, 1897-1900; Vice-President C.E.T.S. *Publications:* pamphlet on Parochial Missions; series of five mission tracts. *Recreations:* travel, sketching, and gardening. *Address:* Waveney House, Henley Road, Ipswich. *(Died 14 Sept. 1919.)*

EVERSHED, Arthur, Hon. Fellow, Royal Society Painter - Etchers; M.R.C.P. London; M.R.C.S. and L.S.A.; Physician (retired); *b.* Billingshurst, Sussex, 1836; 4th *s.* of Peter Evershed, a country doctor; *m.* 1864, Mary Hester Field (a direct lineal descendant of Oliver Cromwell); four *s.* three *d. Educ.:* private school; Alfred Clint's Studio and Leigh's School of Art; Guy's Hospital. Studied Art, 1852-59; exhibited at R.A. 1857; and since then has exhibited several works in oil, water colour and etching; commenced the regular study of medicine, 1859; qualified, 1863; for ten years was in general practice at Ampthill, Beds.; subsequently qualified as a physician, and spent twenty years at Hampstead; Senior Physician, Mount Vernon Hospital; Physician to the Artists' Fund; Consulting Medical Adviser to North London Railway; his health failing, retired from practice, 1894, and lived in the country; subsequently spent two years in Italy, where he did several etchings. *Publications:* An Etcher's Rambles—The Thames, 1879-81; contributions on Medicine, Art, and various subjects to daily and other periodicals. *Recreations:* The observation of Nature, and study of Shakespeare. *Address:* Eversfield, Fishbourne, Chichester. *(Died 17 Nov. 1919.)*

EVERSLEY, 1st Baron, *cr.* 1906; **George John Shaw - Lefevre,** P.C., L.C.C.; *b.* 12 June 1831; *o. s.* of Sir George Shaw-Lefevre, K.C.B., and Rachel Enid, *d.* of Ichabod Wright, Mopperley Hall, Nottingham; *m.* 1874, Constance Moreton, *d.* of 3rd Earl of Ducie. *Educ.:* Eton; Trinity College, Camb. (M.A.). Barr. 1855; contested Winchester, 1859; member of Sea Fisheries Commission, 1862; M.P. Reading, 1863-85, when defeated by Charles T. Murdoch; Civil Lord of the Admiralty, 1856; Commissioner to negotiate a Convention on Fisheries with French Government, 1858; carried vote in House of Commons for arbitration of the Alabama claims, 1868; Secretary Board of Trade under Mr. Bright, 1869-71; carried the General Tramways Act; Under-Secretary, Home Office, 1871; Secretary to Admiralty, 1871-74; First Commissioner of Works, 1881-88; Bencher of Inner Temple, 1882; Postmaster - General, 1883-84; carried Act establishing 6d. telegrams; M.P. Central Bradford, 1885-95; Chairman of Royal Commission on Loss of Life at Sea, 1885; was again First Commissioner of Works and a member of Mr. Gladstone's Cabinet in 1892-93; President of Local Government Board, 1894-95; carried Equalisation of Rates of London Act;

founded (1866) the Commons Preservation Soc., of which chairman with short intervals till present time; Chairman Royal Commission on Agricultural Depression, 1893-96 (resigned); elected Member of L.C.C. Feb. 1897, as Progressive for the Haggerston Div. in place of Mr. E. R. Turton (resigned); Chairman important Committees in House of Commons—Married Woman's Property Act 1868, the Bright Clauses of Irish Land Act 1877-78, the London Parochial Charities Act 1879, the Agricultural Holdings Act 1879, Railway Charges 1891-92; President Statistical Society, 1878-79. *Heir:* none. *Publications:* English and Irish Land Questions; Incidents of Coercion; Peel and O'Connell; Agrarian Tenures; English Commons and Forests; Gladstone and Ireland, 1912; The Partitions of Poland, 1915; The Turkish Empire, its Growth and Decay, 1917. *Recreations:* cycling, fishing. *Address:* Abbotsworthy House, Kingsworthy, Winchester. *Clubs:* Athenæum, Reform, National Liberal. *(Died 19 April 1928.)*

EVERSLEY, William Pinder, Barrister-at-law; Recorder of Sudbury, Suffolk, since 1897; *b.* Barbados, West Indies, 23 April 1850; *e. s.* of William Eversley of Barbados. *Educ.:* Somersetshire College, Bath; Queen's College, Oxford. M.A.; B.C.L. Called to Bar, 1877; joined South-Eastern Circuit same year; appointed Revising Barrister for South-Eastern Circuit, 1898. *Publications:* The Law of the Domestic Relations, 1885 and 1896; Midnight Tales, 1892. *Recreations:* walking, cricket. *Address:* 13 Upper King Street, Norwich. *Clubs:* Oxford and Cambridge, West Indian; Norfolk County, Norwich. *(Died 23 Jan. 1918.)*

EWART, Admiral Arthur Wartensleben; *b.* 23 Dec. 1862; 2nd *s.* of late General Sir John Ewart, G.C.B.; *m.* Violet Louisa, 3rd *d.* of late Colonel B. B. Haworth - Booth of Hullbank and Rolsto.. Halls, Yorkshire; no *c. Educ.:* H.M.S. Britannia. Entered Navy, 1875; Commander, 1895; Captain, 1901; Rear-Admiral, 1911; retired through ill-health, 1911; Naval Attaché Maritime Courts, in Germany and Scandinavia, 1900-3; Knight Commander of the Dannebrog; Spanish Naval Order of Merit; French Legion of Honour. *Recreation:* naval history. *Address:* Laneside, Dumfries, Scotland. *M.:* SW 164. *(Died 18 Nov. 1922.)*

EWART, David, I.S.O. 1903; Chief Architect, Department of Public Works, Canada; *b.* 1841. Entered Civil Service, Canada, 1871; Dominion Consulting Architect, 1914. *Address:* Public Works Department, Ottawa.
(Died June 1921.)

EWART, Maj.-Gen. Sir Henry (Peter), 1st Bt., *cr.* 1910; K.C.B., *cr.* 1885; G.C.V.O., *cr.* 1902; Colonel 7th Dragoon Guards since 1900; Crown Equerry, 1894-1910; *b.* 20 Aug. 1838; *s.* of late Rev. P. Ewart, Kirklington, Yorkshire; *m.* 1888, Lady Evelyn Clementina Heathcote-Drummond Willoughby (*d.* 1924), *d.* of 1st Earl of Ancaster. *Educ.:* Eton; Oxford. Joined 2nd Life Guards, 1858; commanded the regiment, 1878; commanded Household Cavalry in Egypt, 1882 (despatches, C.B.); commanded Cavalry Brigade in Soudan Campaign, 1885 (K.C.B.); Equerry to Queen Victoria, 1884 - 94. *Heir:* none. *Address:* The White House, Hythe, Southampton. *Clubs:* Carlton, Marlborough.
(Died 16 April 1928.)

EWART, Maj. - Gen. Sir Richard (Henry), K.C.M.G., *cr.* 1918; C.B. 1915; C.I.E. 1912; D.S.O. 1895; A.D.C. to the King, 1911-16; *b.* 26 Dec. 1864; *s.* of late Col. C. H. Ewart, I.S.C.; *m.* 1st, 1889, Charlotte Frewen Laurie; two *d.*; 2nd, 1899, Marion Annie (*d.* 1920), *d.* of Lt.-Gen. Norris Baker, Redholme, Folkestone, and *widow* of J. R. Thomas; one *d.*; 3rd, Ethel Mary, *er. d.* of the late Sir John Boraston, Beckenham, Kent. Entered army, 1883; Captain, 1894; Major, 1901; Lieut.-Col. 1906; Bt.-Col. 1910; served

with the Hampshire Regiment, 1883-86, then joined 31st Punjabis, Indian Army, afterwards transferring to the Supply and Transport Corps; A.Q.M.G., Army Headquarters, Simla, 1905; Director of Military Farming Operations in India, 1906-12; Hazara Expedition, 1891 (medal with clasp); Isazai Expedition, 1892; Waziristan Field Force, 1894-95 (despatches, D.S.O., clasp); France as D.D.S. and T., Indian Corps, 1914-15 (despatches, C.B., 1914 Star); D.A. and Q.M.G., East African Expeditionary Force, 1915-18 (despatches 4 times, prom. Maj.-Gen. for distinguished services in the field, K.C.M.G., General Service and Victory Medals); worked for Central Prisoner of War Committee, first in London and then as Director of Red Cross Depot in Berne, Switzerland; proceeded to Berlin on signature of Armistice as Red Cross Commissioner to repatriate British prisoners of war; Chief of the British Military Mission, Berlin, and President, Inter-Allied Commission for Repatriation of Russian Prisoners of War, Jan.-May 1919; Colonel Commandant Indian Army Service Corps, 1925; American Distinguished Service Medal, Commander of the Orders of the Legion of Honour (France), Saint Maurice and Saint Lazarus (Italy) and Leopold (Belgium); Order of Saint Stanislaus, 2nd Class, with Swords (Russia), White Eagle, 2nd Class, with Swords (Serbia). *Address:* Glinton, Farnborough, Kent. *T.:* Farnborough (Kent) 202. *Club:* Junior United Service.
(Died 27 May 1928.)

EWART, Sir William Quartus, 2nd Bt., *cr.* 1887; M.A. T.C.D.; J.P. Co. Down; D.L. Belfast; High Sheriff, Co. Antrim, 1897; Chairman of William Ewart and Son, Ltd., linen manufacturers, Belfast; *b.* 14 June 1844; *e. s.* of Sir Wm. Ewart, 1st Bart., M.P. (C.) N. Belfast; *S.* father 1889; *m.* 1876, Mary, *d.* of R. Heard, of Pallastown, Kinsale; two *s.* three *d. Educ.:* Trinity College, Dublin. A Knight of Grace of the Order of St. John of Jerusalem. *Heir:* s. Robert Heard, *b.* 5 Nov. 1879. *Address:* Glenmachan, Strandtown, Belfast. *Club:* Ulster, Belfast. *(Died 17 Oct. 1919.)*

EWING, Rev. J. C. R., Hon. K.C.I.E. 1923; C.I.E. 1915; M.A., D.D., LL.D., Litt.D., Secretary India Council Presbyterian Church (U.S.A.) in India; Principal Forman Christian College, Lahore, 1888-1918; Vice-Chancellor Panjab University, 1910-1917; *b.* Pennsylvania, U.S.A., 23 June 1854; *m.* 1879, two *s.* three *d. Educ.:* Washington and Jefferson, U.S.A. Went to India, 1879; Work, that of an Educational Missionary; Kaiser-i-Hind Gold Medal, 1906. *Publication:* Numerous Magazine articles, addresses, A Prince of the Church in India, etc. *Address:* Lahore, India.
(Died 20 Aug. 1925.)

EWING, Hon. Norman Kirkwood, K.C. 1914; *s.* of Rev. T. C. Ewing, Wolligong, New South Wales; *b.* 1870; *m.* 1897, Maude Louisa, *d.* of late Hon. Sir Edward Albert Stone, K.C.M.G., Chief Justice and Lt.-Gov. of Western Australia. Admitted a solicitor, N.S.W., 1895; Barrister and Solicitor, Western Australia, 1897; of High Court, Australia, 1903; Supreme Court, Tasmania, 1907; M.L.A. for W. Australia, 1898-1901; Federal Senator for W. Australia, 1901-3; member of House of Assembly, Tasmania, 1909-15; Leader of the Opposition, 1914-15; a Puisne Judge of the Supreme Court, Tasmania, 1915; Acting Administrator of Tasmania, 1923-24. *Address:* Hobart, Tasmania. *(Died 11 July 1923.)*

EWING, Hon. Sir Thomas Thomson, K.C.M.G., *cr.* 1908; M.P. Richmond, N.S.W., since 1901; Acting Postmaster-General, 1906; Minister for Home Affairs, 1906-7; *b.* Pitt Town, Hawkesbury River, N.S.W.; *s.* of Rev. Thomas Campbell Ewing, R.D.; Member of Legislative Assembly of N.S.W. for Richmond, 1885-94;

Lismore, 1894-1901; Minister for Defence, Commonwealth of Australia, 1907-8; Vice-President of the Executive Council, 1905-6; Chairman of Parliamentary Public Works Committee of N.S.W.; Chairman of Royal Commission with reference to extension of Railway System of N.S.W. into the city of Sydney; was Staff Surveyor for State of N.S.W. *Publications:* (with T. A. Coghlan), Progress of Australia during the 19th Century; various publications on Australasian subjects. *Address:* Musgrave Street, Mosman, Sydney, N.S.W.
(Died 15 Sept. 1920.)

EXHAM, Col. Simeon Hardy, C.B. 1911; C.B.E. 1919; *b.* 5 July 1850; *s.* of late Thomas Exham, Monkstown, and Frances, *d.* of Simeon Hardy; *m.* 1873, Emily, *d.* of late Rev. Godfrey Clarke Smith of St. Olans, Coachford, Cork. Entered Royal Engineers, 1871; Lt.-Col. 1896; retired, 1901; rejoined 1914; served Afghan War, 1878-79 (medal with clasp); Superintending Engineer, Portsmouth and Rosyth Dockyards, 1895-1911; retired, 1911. *Address:* Walton House, Walton, Suffolk. *(Died 26 Nov. 1926.)*

EXMOUTH, 5th Viscount *(cr.* 1816), **Edward Addington Hargreaves Pellew,** Bt. 1796; Baron, 1814; *b.* 12 Nov. 1890; *s.* of 4th Viscount and Edith, 3rd *d.* of Thomas Hargreaves, Arborfield Hall, Reading, Berks. *S.* father, 1899. *Educ.:* Eton; Trinity College, Cambridge. *Heir:* c. Henry Edward Pellew, *b.* 1828. *Address:* Canonteign House, Lower-Ashton, nr. Exeter. *(Died 16 Aug. 1922.)*

EXMOUTH, 6th Viscount *(cr.* 1816); **Henry Edward Pellew,** Bt. 1796; Baron, 1814; *b.* 26 Apr. 1828; *o. s.* of Very Rev. the Hon. George Pellew, 3rd *s.* of 1st Viscount and Hon. Frances Addington, 2nd *d.* of 1st Viscount Sidmouth; *S.* cousin 1922; *m.* (first) 1858, Eliza (*d.* 1869), *d.* of Hon. Judge William Jay, of New York; one *s.*; (second) 1873, Augusta, *y. d.* of Hon. Judge William Jay; one *d. Educ.:* Trinity College, Cambridge, M.A. *Heir:* s. Hon. Charles Ernest Pellew, *b.* 11 March 1863. *Address:* Washington, D.C., U.S.A. *(Died 4 Feb. 1923.)*

EYLES, Sir George Lancelot, K.C.M.G., *cr.* 1914; C.M.G. 1902; Lieut.-Colonel Engineers and Railway Staff Corps; Consulting Engineer for railways to the Crown Agents for the Colonies for Government railways in Ceylon, the Federated Malay States, Straits Settlements, Trinidad, Nyasaland, etc., and for other railways abroad; *b.* 15 Feb. 1849; *s.* of late George Eyles. *Address:* 12 Dean's Yard, Westminster, S.W. *Clubs:* Junior Carlton, St. Stephen's, Garrick.
(Died 12 Mar. 1919.)

EYRE, Ven. Christopher Benson; Archdeacon of Yaoland and Priest-in-charge of Mtonya, Portuguese Nyasaland; Canon of St. John the Divine, Likoma Cathedral, 1922; *b.* 1849; 2nd *s.* of Rev. G. H. Eyre, sometime Fellow of Pembroke College, Cambridge. No education to speak of. Ordained, 1894; Curate of Lwynypia, 1894; Missionary, Universities' Mission to Central Africa, 1896. *Address:* Universities' Mission. Mponda's, Fort Johnston, Nyasaland. *(Died 28 June 1928.)*

EYRE, Colonel Edmund Henry, C.B. 1894; I.S.C.; *b.* 26 Nov. 1838; *m.* 1862, Louisa, *d.* of late Maj.-Gen. C. Pooley, Ind. Army. Entered army, 1858; Colonel, 1887; served Zhob Valley Expedition, 1884; Burmah, 1885-86 (despatches, brevet of Col., medal with clasp); Q.M.G. Madras, 1890-95. *Address:* Redfield, Newbury, Berks. *(Died 4 Dec. 1919)*

EYRE, Rev. Edward Vincent, M.A.; *b.* 29 March 1851; *s.* of Rev. Edward Eyre, Rector of Larling, Norfolk. *Educ.:* Harrow; Corpus Christi College, Oxford. Deacon, 1876; Priest, 1877; Curate at S. Philip's, Clerkenwell, 1876-1882; appointed Minister of new parish, 1882; first Vicar of the Church of the Holy Redeemer, Clerkenwell, 1888-1904; resigned, 1904; Vicar of Chollerton, Northumberland, 1905-21; Rural Dean of Bellingham, 1917-21; Hon. Canon of Newcastle Cathedral, 1919-21. *Address:* 10 West Cliff Gardens, Folkestone.

(*Died 4 Feb. 1925.*)

EYRE, John, R.I.; A.R.C.A; *b.* Staffordshire; one *s.* two *d.* *Educ.:* Staffordshire. Studied art in the South Kensington schools; in early days designed for pottery, and became a painter in water-colours and enamels; exhibits in the Royal Academy, Royal Institute, French Salon, etc.; also book illustrator. *Publications:* illustrations to the English Poets, etc. *Recreations:* fishing, walking. *Address:* Laurel Cottage, The Common, Cranleigh, Surrey.

(*Died 13 Sept. 1927.*)

EYSTON, John Joseph, J.P.; 2nd *s.* of Charles John Eyston (*d.* 1883) and Agnes Mary, 5th *d.* of late Michael Henry Blount of Maple-durham, Oxfordshire; *b.* 1867; *S. b.* 1889; *m.* 1890, Elizabeth, *o. d.* of late George Dunn of Bath House, Newcastle-on-Tyne; one *s.* three *d.* High Sheriff of Berkshire, 1915. *Address:* Hendred House, near Steventon, Berkshire. *Club:* Junior Carlton. (*Died 7 June 1916.*)

F

FABER, 1st Baron (*cr.* 1905) of Butterwick, **Edmund Beckett Faber,** senior partner in Beckett's Bank, Leeds and York; director, Yorkshire Post; director, L. & N.W. Railway and Sun Insurance Company, and London County Westminster and Parr's Bank; J.P. and D.L. for W. R. of Yorks; *b.* 9 Feb. 1847; *e. s.* of Charles Wilson Faber of Northaw, Herts, J.P. and D.L. for Herts, and Mary Beckett Faber, *d.* of Sir E. Beckett, Bart., and sister of 1st Baron Grimthorpe. *Educ.:* Eton; Trinity College, Cambridge. Contested Pudsey Div., Yorkshire, 1900; M.P. (C.) Andover Div., Hants, 1901 - 5. *Heir:* none. *Recreation:* shooting. *Address:* Belvedere, Harrogate; 19 Park Street, W.1. *T.:* Mayfair 3377. *Clubs:* Carlton, Junior Carlton, Yorkshire.

(*Died 17 Sept. 1920.*)

FABER, Lt.-Col. Walter (Vavasour), Dep.-Lieutenant Hants; partner in Strong's Brewery, Romsey; *b.* 1857; 5th *s.* of Charles Wilson Faber of Northaw, Herts., D.L. for Hants, and Mary Beckett Faber, *e. d.* of Sir E. Beckett, 4th Bart., and *sister* of 1st Baron Grimthorpe; *m.* 1915, Mrs. Arthur Byass of Bosworth House, Husband's Bosworth, *d.* of S. Laing. *Educ.:* Cheam; Malvern; Royal Military Academy. Entered Royal Artillery, 1877; Royal Horse Artillery, 1884; Captain, 1885; Major, 1914; Lt.-Col. 1915; A.D.C. to Sir Albert Williams, 1888-90; retired, 1890; volunteered during S. African War, 1900; entered Wilts Yeomanry, 1901; retired, 1903; M.P. (C.) Andover Division of Hants, 1906-18. *Recreations:* hunting and shooting. *Address:* Welford Grange, near Rugby. *T.:* Welford 8. *Club:* Naval and Military. (*Died 2 April 1928.*)

FAGAN, Charles Edward, C.B.E. 1920; I.S.O.; F.R.G.S.; Secretary, British Museum (Natural History) since 1919; *b.* 25 Dec. 1855; *y. s.* of late George Fagan, Minister Resident, Caracas; *m.*; one *s.* *Educ.:* private. Entered the British Museum, 1873; 1st Class Assistant, 1887; Assistant Secretary, 1889-1919; Hon. Treasurer International Ornithological Congress, 1905; British Scientific Expedition to Mt. Ruwenzori, 1905 - 6; British Ornithologists Union's Expedition to Dutch New Guinea, 1910-12; Society for the Promotion of Nature Reserves; Selous National Memorial; Goodman Exploration Fund; Organised British Section International Sports Exhibition, Vienna, 1910; Member Colonial Office Committee for

340

Ghent International Exhibition, 1913; Member of Colonial Office Conference on the Protection of Plumage Birds; British Representative on the International Committee for the Protection of Nature, 1913; President of the Vesey Club, Sutton Coldfield, 1912-13; Council Royal Geographical Society; Member of the Executive Committee of the National Trust; Corresponding Member Lisbon Geographical Society; Knight Order of the Crown, Belgium; Order of St. Sava, Serbia. *Recreations:* football (Rugby), now as a spectator; country walks. *Address:* 50 FitzGeorge Avenue, West Kensington, W.14; *T.:* Hammersmith 125; Natural History Museum, Cromwell Road, S.W. *Clubs:* Savile, Arts, Savage. (*Died 30 Jan. 1921.*)

FAGAN, Maj. - Gen. James Lawtie, Indian Army; *b.* 4 Feb. 1843. Entered army, 1859; Maj. - Gen. 1899; retired list, 1902; served Afghan War, 1879-80 (despatches, medal). *Address:* 32 Porchester Terrace, W.2. *T.:* Paddington 8579. *Clubs:* East India United Service, M.C.C. (*Died 12 Mar. 1919.*)

FAGUET, Emile, Professeur de Littérature Française à la Faculté des Lettres de Paris; *b.* 17 Dec. 1847 à La Roche sur Yon (Vendée); *s.* de Victor Faguet, Professeur et Homme de Lettres; unmarried. *Educ.:* Lycée de Poitiers; Lycée Charlemagne, Paris. Elève de l'Ecole normale en 1867; Professeur dans différents lycées de province, 1869-83; Professeur dans différents lycées de Paris, 1883-90; Professeur à la Faculté des Lettres de Paris, 1890; élu de l'Académie Française en 1900. *Publications:* XVIme Siècle, XVIIme Siècle, XVIIIme Siècle, XIXme Siècle Etudes littéraires (4 vols.); Les Moralistes du XIXme siècle (3 vols.); Le Libéralisme (1 vol.); Le Socialisme (1 vol.); L'Anti-cléricalisme (1 vol.); En lisant Nietzsche (1 vol.); Pour qu'on lise Platon (1 vol.); etc. etc. *Address:* Paris, 59 Rue Monge; Poitiers, 39 Rue Carnot. (*Died 7 June 1916.*)

FAHEY, Rt. Rev. Mgr. Jerome, D.D., Vicar General of Galway and Kilmacduagh; *b.* 1843. *Educ.:* Maynooth. *Address:* Gort, Co. Galway. (*Died 12 Mar. 1920.*)

FAIRBANKS, Charles Warren, LL.D.; Vice-President of the United States, 1905-9; *b.* Unionville Center, Ohio, 11 May 1852; *s.* of Loriston Monroe and Mary Adelaide Smith Fairbanks; *m.* 1874, Cornelia Cole (*d.* 1913); four *s.* one *d.* *Educ.:* Ohio Wesleyan University, Delaware, Ohio. Admitted to bar by Supreme Court of Ohio, 1874; removed to Indianapolis, 1874; elected a trustee of Ohio Wesleyan University, 1885; chairman of Indiana Republican State Conventions, 1892, 1898, and 1914; elected to United States Senate, 1897; re-elected, 1903; resigned, 1905; appointed a member of United States and British Joint High Commission which met in Quebec in 1898 for the adjustment of Canadian questions, and was chairman of United States High Commissioners; was a delegate at large to Republican National Convention at St. Louis in 1896, and was temporary chairman of the convention; was a delegate at large to Republican National Convention at Philadelphia in 1900, and as chairman of the committee on resolutions reported the platform; delegate at large to Republican National Conventions at Chicago, 1904 and 1912; chairman Indiana delegation; Vice-President, U.S.A., 1905; representative of U.S.A., Tercentenary Celebration Quebec, 1908; travelled round the world, 1909-10; Republican; Regent Smithsonian Institution, Washington, D.C.; unanimously nominated for Vice-President, U.S.A. by Republican National Convention at Chicago, June 1916. *Address:* Indianapolis, Ind., U.S.A. (*Died 15 June 1918.*)

FAIRBROTHER, William Henry, M.A.; Lecturer in Philosophy, Lincoln College, Oxford, since 1889; Tutor to the Non-Collegiate Students since 1900; Major (retired) The

Royal Warwickshire Regt.; *b.* Pendleton, nr. Manchester, 9 Dec. 1859; *m.* 1887, Jeanie Prentice Dunlop, of Southport. *Educ.:* Owens College, Manchester (prizeman); Keble College, Oxford. 2d class Classical Moderations, 1882; 1st class in Literis Humanioribus, 1885; B.A. 1885; M.A. 1888; Lecturer at Keble College, 1886-89. *Publications:* Several articles and reviews in Mind, in the International Journal of Ethics, and in the Transactions of the Aristotelian Society, London; Philosophy of Thomas Hill Green. *Recreations:* rowing and golf; late Captain in the Oxford University Volunteers. *Address:* Lincoln College, Oxford; Freshwater, I.W. *Clubs:* United Service Institution; Union Society, Oxford.
(*Died 20 July 1927.*)

FAIRBROTHER, Col. William Tomes, C.B. 1909; F.R.G.S.; Indian Army; *b.* 19 July 1856; *e. s.* of late Geo. Berford Fairbrother, Clonsilla, Co. Dublin; *m.* 1901, Marie B. L., *e. d.* of late Rev. W. Lamb. Entered army, 11th Foot, 1875; Captain, I.S.C., 1886; Major, 1895; Lt.-Col., Indian Army, 1901; Brevet-Col. 1904; served Afghan War, 1878-80 (despatches, medal); Sikkim Expedition, 1888 (medal with clasp); N.W. Frontier, Assam, 1894; Chitral, 1895 (medal with clasp); Waziristan, 1901-2 (clasp); was Commandant 13th Rajputs, 1898-1905. *Recreations:* big game shooting, fishing, sketching. *Address:* Bareilly, India; Srinagar, Kashmir. *M.:* IF 167.
(*Died 16 June 1924.*)

FAIRFAX, Sir James Oswald, K.B.E., *cr.* 1926; C.B.E. 1918; a Director of The Sydney Morning Herald and Sydney Mail; *b.* Sydney, 1863; *s.* of Sir James Reading Fairfax and Lucy Armstrong; *m.* Mabel, *d.* of Captain Hixson, R.N.; one *s.* *Educ.:* Sydney Grammar School; Balliol Coll. Oxford. Called to Bar, Inner Temple, 1886; Chairman of Australian Section of the Empire Press Union; Chairman of the N.S.W. Division of the Australian Red Cross Society, 1915-21; M.A. Oxford and Sydney. *Recreations:* yachting, golf. *Address:* Herald Office, Sydney. *Clubs:* Oriental; Union, Sydney. (*Died July 1928.*)

FAIRFAX, Sir James Reading, Kt.; *cr.* 1898; senior proprietor of the Sydney Morning Herald and the Sydney Mail; *b.* Leamington, 17 Oct. 1834; 2nd *s.* of late Hon. John Fairfax, Member of the Legislative Council of New South Wales, and Sarah, *d.* of James Reading, Warwick; *m.* Lucy, *d.* of John Armstrong, Sydney; five *s.* one *d.* *Educ.:* private schools (Rev. Dr. Woolls and Rev. Henry Cary, M.A.), Paramatta and Sydney, N.S.W. Engaged in newspaper work early in life, and has continued so up to present time; Trustee, Royal Naval House; Director Royal Prince Alfred Hospital; Trustee, Queen Victoria Homes for Consumptives; President, Nat. Art Gallery of New South Wales; Trustee, National Shipwreck Relief and Humane Society of N.S.W., Australia; held commission as captain in the Sydney Brigade, Volunteer Rifles; Hon. Treasurer Sydney Boys' Brigade. *Recreation:* yachting; President Royal Sydney Golf Club. *Address:* Ginahgulla, Belle Vue Hill, near Sydney; Woodside, Moss Vale, N.S.W. *Cable A.:* Heralding, Sydney. *T.:* Edgecliffe 9, Sydney. *M.:* 445; 1806. *Clubs:* Oriental; Union, Sydney; Melbourne, Melbourne.
(*Died 29 Mar. 1919.*)

FAIRHOLME, Brig.-Gen. William Ernest, C.B. 1919; C.M.G. 1890; M.V.O. 1903; late R.A.; *b.* Leamington, 5 Feb. 1860; *s.* of late George K. E. Fairholme of Old Melrose, Co. Roxburgh, and Baroness Poellnitz-Frankenberg of Bavaria; unmarried. *Educ.:* Harrow; R.M.A. Woolwich; F.R.G.S. Joined Royal Artillery, 1879; Staff-Captain, Intelligence Department, War Office, 1893-1894; D.A.A.G. same department, 1894-98; British Delegate on International Commission for rectification of Turco-Greek Frontier, 1898; Assistant British Military Commissioner in Crete, 1898-99; British Civil Commissioner in Crete from 18th June 1899 till 24 July 1899; served South Africa, 1899-1900, as A.A.G.; Military Secretary, Gibraltar, 1900-1902; Military Attaché, Vienna, Bucharest, Belgrade, and Cettinje, 1902-1904; British Staff Officer for the reorganisation of the gendarmerie in Macedonia, 1904-6; Military Attaché, Paris, Madrid, and Lisbon, 1909-12; Brig.-General Commanding Artillery 3rd Division, 1912-13; British Delegate for delimitation of Turco-Bulgarian frontier, 1913; Military Attaché, Brussels, The Hague, Copenhagen, and Christiania, 1914-15; specially employed at Dunkerque under G.H.Q. in France, 1915; G.S.O.1 (Chief Liaison Officer), British Salonika Force, 1915-16; Military Attaché, Athens, 1916-19; Officer of Legion of Honour; Commander Order of Leopold; Grand Commander Order of the Redeemer; Greek War Cross, 2nd Class; 1915 Star; S. African War medal with 2 clasps. *Clubs:* Army and Navy, St. James's.
(*Died 7 Aug. 1920.*)

FAIRLIE, James Ogilvy Reginald, J.P. Co. Fife; *b.* 28 Dec. 1848; 3rd *s.* of late James Ogilvy Fairlie, J.P., D.L., 2nd Life Guards, of Coodham, Ayrshire, and Elizabeth Constance, *o. surv. d.* of William Houison Craufurd of Craufurdland, Ayrshire, and Braehead, Midlothian; *m.* 1880, Jane Mary, 3rd *d.* of John Buchanan of Downhill; three *s.* one *d.* *Educ.:* Glenalmond; Christ Church, Oxford; B.A. 1873. Resided for some time in Rome; for twenty-five years a Privy Chamberlain to H.H. Leo XIII.; appointment confirmed by H.H. Pius X. 1904, and by H.H. Benedict XV., 1915; for some years a member of the Catholic Education Council; Captain of the Royal and Ancient Golf Club of St. Andrews, 1893; Preses of the Fife Hunt, 1907; Chairman of the Pontifical Court Club, 1910; served for many years on the Rules of Golf Committee. *Recreations:* golf, painting, heraldry. *Address:* Myres Castle, Auchtermuchty, Fife. *Club:* New, Edinburgh.
(*Died 20 Sept. 1916.*)

FAIRTLOUGH, Major Edward Charles D'Heillemer, C.M.G. 1900, D.S.O. 1897; late R. Dublin Fusiliers; *b.* 1869; *m.* 1901, Gertrude, *d.* of Thomas Murray of Milmount House, Westmeath; two *d.* Sierra Leone Frontier Force, 1894; Commanded Expedition against Bandi Tribes, 1896; against Gizehs 1897; appointed District Commissioner, Ronietta, Sierra Leone, 1898; in military charge of operations in Ronietta and Pangoma during Sierra Leone Rebellion, 1898-99; commanded Expedition for relief of Pangoma Fort, June and July 1898, successful after 29 days' bush-fighting; Official Member Legislative Council, Sierra Leone.
(*Died 24 April 1925.*)

FAIRWEATHER, Lt.-Col. James McIntyre, D.S.O. 1902; Commanding Rand Light Infantry, Johannesburg; *b.* Dundee, 13 Oct. 1876. Served South Africa, 1899-1902 (despatches, Queen's medal, 4 clasps, King's medal, 2 clasps, D.S.O.). *Club:* Athenæum, Johannesburg. (*Died 18 Feb. 1917.*)

FAIYAZ ALI KHAN, Nawab, Sir Mumtazud-Dowlah, Mahomed, of Pahasu, K.C.V.O., *cr.* Delhi, 1911; K.C.I.E., *cr.* 1907; C.S.I. 1903; C.B.E. 1919; family traces origin to Rama, King of Ayodhya; hereditary head of Lalkhani clan of Rajputs; Prime Minister at Jaipur; *b.* 1851; *s.* of late Nawab Sir Faiz Ali Khan Bahadur; married; one *s.* one *d.* Served for fourteen consecutive terms on Provincial Legislative Council of United Provinces, and for two years on Viceregal Imperial Council. Represented United Provinces, as guest of nation, at King Edward's Coronation

341

1902, and at Delhi Durbar 1902; Hon. Magistrate and Munsif of Pahasu; President of Board of Trustees, M.A.O. College, Aligarh; trustee, Government College, Agra, Lady Dufferin Fund, etc. *Address:* Nawab's House, Jaipur, Rajputana; Pahasu, Bulundshahr, U.P., India.
(*Died 26 Mar. 1922.*)

FALCONBRIDGE, Hon. Sir Glenholme, Kt., *cr.* 1908; M.A.; Chief Justice of the King's Bench, Ontario, since 1900; a Judge of the Supreme Court of Judicature for Ontario and senior puisne Judge of the King's Bench Division of the High Court of Justice since 1887; President of High Court Division of Supreme Court since 1916; *e. s.* of late John Kennedy Falconbridge, J.P., of Richmond Hill, Co. York, Ontario; *b.* 12 May 1846; *m.* Mary Phœbe, *y. d.* of late Hon. Mr. Justice Sullivan, 1873; one *s.* four *d. Educ.:* Model Grammar School for Upper Canada; University of Toronto. Scholarship at matriculation, 1862; prizes and scholarships in every year of course; gold medal at grad. 1866; B.A. 1866; M.A. 1870. Lecturer in Univ. Coll., Toronto, 1867-68; called to Bar, 1871; bencher of Law Society, U.C., 1883; Q.C. 1885; wrote the Introduction to the Canadian Edition de Luxe of Burke's works, 1901; member of several important Royal Commissions, 1897-1902; a Vice-President of the Imperial Maritime League; an Honorary Colonel in the Canadian Militia; President of the Ontario Branch of the Secours National de France; Member of Board of Governors of Upper Canada College. *Recreation:* angling; President of the Ontario Forest, Fish and Game Protective Association; President of Toronto Club. *Address:* Osgoode Hall, Toronto, Ontario, Canada. *Clubs:* Toronto, Royal Canadian Yacht, Toronto. (*Died 8 Feb. 1920.*)

FALCONER, J. B., K.C. Ireland; LL.D. Dublin University. *Address:* 27 Fitzwilliam Square, Dublin. (*Died 31 Aug. 1924.*)

FALCONIO, His Eminence Cardinal Diomed; *b.* Pescocostanzo, Monte Casino, Italy, 20 Sep. 1842. Entered Franciscan Order, 1860; sent as Missionary to U.S.A., 1865; Priest, 1866; Professor of Philosophy and Vice-Pres. of St. Bonaventure's College, Alleghany, 1866; President, 1868; Secretary and Chancellor to R.C. Bishop of Newfoundland, 1871-82; Provincial of the Franciscans in the Abrizzi, 1884; Procurator-General of the Franciscan Order, 1889; Bishop of Lacedonia, 1892; Apostolic Delegate to Canada, 1899; to the United States, 1902; Cardinal, 1911; Cardinal Bishop of Velletri, 1914; Prefect of the Sacred Congregation of Religious, 1916. *Address:* 17 Piazza Cavour, Rome.
(*Died 7 Feb. 1917.*)

FALKINER, Sir Leslie Edmond Percy Riggs, 7th Bt. of Annmount, Cork; *cr.* 1777; *b.* 2 Oct. 1866; *S.* father 1893; *m.* 1st, 1894, Elaine (*d.* 1900), *d.* of W. M. Farmer of Maynardville, Cape of Good Hope; 2nd, 1902, Kathleen, *e. d.* of Hon. Henry Robert Orde-Powlett, 2nd *s.* of 3rd Baron Bolton; three *s.* one *d. Educ.:* in France; Marlborough; H.M.S. Worcester. *Recreations:* shooting, hunting, fishing. Owns about 6500 acres. *Heir: s.* Terence Edmond Patrick, *b.* 17 March 1903. *Address:* Burghley Park, Stamford, Lincs. *Clubs:* Junior Carlton; County Cork. (*Died 17 Jan. 1917.*)

FALKLAND, 12th Viscount and 12th Lord Cary (*cr.* 1620), **Byron Plantagenet Cary,** Representative Peer for Scotland; late commanding 4th Batt. Yorkshire Regt.; *b.* 3 Apr. 1845; *s.* of Capt. Hon. Byron-C.-F.-P.-Cary, R.N., and Selina, *d.* of Rev. Francis Fox, of Foxhall, Co. Longford; *m.* 1879, Mary (*d.* 1920), *d.* of Robert Reade, New York; one *s.* three *d.*; *S. u.* 1886. Church of England. Moderate Conservative. *Educ.:* privately; Cheltenham; Sandhurst. Entered 49th

342

Regt. 1863; served in 49th Regt. and 35th Regt., 1863-83; retired on a pension with honorary rank of Lieut.-Col. A small property in the City worth about £25,000; has no gallery, but owns a few good pictures by Vansommer, Cornelius Jansen, Sir Joshua Reynolds, Sir Peter Lely, Sir Godfrey Kneller, John Riley, and Romney. *Recreations:* boating, fishing, shooting; has no hobbies. *Heir: s.* Master of Falkland. *Address:* 26 Upper Grosvenor Street, W.1. *T.:* Mayfair 416. *Clubs:* Carlton; Royal Yacht Squadron, Cowes.
(*Died 10 Jan. 1922.*)

FALKNER, Rev. Thomas Felton, M.A., D.S.O. 1900; *b.* 17 July 1847; *s.* of Thomas Falkner of Bath; *m.* 1877, Maria Louisa, *d.* of Rev. James Bacon, B.D.: two *s.* two *d. Educ.:* Christ's College, Cambridge. B.A. 1870; M.A. 1875. Sub-Warden St. Thomas's College, Colombo, 1872-79; Domestic Chaplain to Bishop of Colombo, 1873; Acting Colonial Chaplain and Chaplain to Forces at Colombo, 1874-75; Priest-in-charge of Woolland, Dorset, 1879-81; Chaplain to the Forces, 1881; served at Aldershot, Bermuda, Guards' Depot, Chatham, Aldershot, Portsmouth, with the S. African Field Force, 1899-1900 (despatches, D.S.O., promoted 1st class), and as Senior Chaplain 1st Army Corps, Aldershot, 1901-1903; retired list, 1904; Rector of Burnham Westgate, with Burnham Norton, King's Lynn, 1902-23. *Address:* Oakley Lodge, Claverton Down, Bath.(*Died Aug. 1924.*)

FALMOUTH, 7th Viscount, *cr.* 1720; **Evelyn Edward Thomas Boscawen,** C.B., K.C.V.O., D.L., J.P.; Baron Le Despencer, 1264; Baron Boscawen-Rose, 1720; late Col. commanding Coldstream Guards and a regimental district; Osmanieh (4th class) and Khedive orders 1882; member Jockey Club since 1898; *b.* 24 July 1847; *s.* of 6th Viscount and 23rd Baroness Le Despencer; *S.* father 1889, and mother 1891; *m.* Kathleen, *d.* of 2nd Lord Penrhyn, 1886; two *s.* one *d. Educ.:* Eton. Ensign and Lieut. Coldstream Guards, 1866; served Egypt, present at Tel-el-Kebir, 1882; Nile Expedition (despatches); present at Abu Klea and Abu Kru, and commanded at Metemmeh, 1884-85; Assistant Military Sec. to Commander-in-Chief, Ireland; retired, 1902. *Heir: s.* Hon. Evelyn H. Boscawen. *Address:* Tregothnan, Truro; Mereworth Castle, Maidstone; 2 St. James's Square, S.W. *T.:* Regent 566. *Clubs:* Guards', Bachelors', Travellers'. (*Died 1 Oct. 1918.*)

FANCOURT, Colonel Sir John Fancourt Michell, C.B. 1904; J.P. Suffolk; *b.* 1847; *m.* 1897, Ethel Malins, *y. d.* of Sir Henry Wiggin, Bt. Cornet 5th Lancers, 1869; Major 1st Duke of York's Lancers, 1889; Brevet Lt.-Col.1891; Brevet Col. 1895; General Officer commanding, Assam, etc., 1898-1901. *Address:* Danecroft, Stowmarket, Suffolk. *Club:* United Service. (*Died 11 June 1917.*)

FANCOURT, Ven. Thomas, Archdeacon of Wellington since 1888; Diocesan Secretary, Bishop's Commissary, and Examining Chaplain; *b.* 22 Jan. 1840; *s.* of Rev. W. J. Fancourt; *m.* 1865, Elizabeth Emma, *d.* of W. Robinson, Knostrop, Leeds; one *s.* three *d. Educ.:* Lancing; St. Augustine's College, Canterbury. Ordained, 1865; Perpetual Curate of Porirua and Karori, 1865-70; Incumbent of Lower Hutt, 1870-84; Perpetual Curate of Johnsonville, 1886-1896; Editor Church Chronicle, Wellington Diocese 1884-1903. *Address:* Diocesan Office, Mulgrave Street, Wellington, N.Z.
(*Died 1 Feb. 1919.*)

FANE, Capt. Octavius Edward, D.S.O. 1917; M.C.; R.G.A.; *b.* 15 Oct. 1886; 8th *s.* of Capt. Henry George Fane and Blanche Louisa, *o. d.* of Col. Hon. R. C. H. Spencer. Served European War (M.C., despatches, D.S.O.) *Address:* Bicester House, Bicester. *Club:* United Service. (*Died 17 Sept. 1918.*)

FANE, Maj.-Gen. Sir Vere (Bonamy), K.C.B., *cr.* 1921; K.C.I.E., *cr.* 1918; C.B. 1914; C.I.E. 1915; Indian Army; commanding Burma Independent District; Col. of the Manchester Regt.; F.R.G.S.; *b.* 16 June 1863; *o. s.* of Capt. H. J. Fane, late 54th Regt.; *m.* 1892, Kathleen Emily, 2nd *d.* of late James Barratt of Hanslop, Bucks; no *c.* *Educ.*: Privately; Woolwich. Entered army from Militia, 1884; joined Manchester Regiment and served with that regiment till 1888; then joined 1st Punjab Cavalry, serving with it till 1908; promoted as 2nd in command of 20th Brownlow's Punjabis; appointed to command 21st Punjabis, 1909; served as orderly officer to Gen. Penn Symons, Waziristan, 1894-95 (medal and clasp); Tochi Field Force, 1897-98; D.A.A.G. 1st Brigade (medal and clasp); China, 1900; D.A.Q.M.G. Cavalry Brigade (despatches, medal); China, 1901-2, Chief of Police (despatches, brevet Lt.-Colonel); N.W.F. India, 1908; Mohmand, actions of Matta and Kargha (despatches, medal and clasp); commanded at action near Dirdoni, Tochi, 26 March 1915 (despatches, C.I.E.). European War, 1914-18 (despatches six times; promoted Major-General for distinguished service in the field; K.C.I.E., Croix de Guerre (2nd Class), Order of Nile). *Recreations*: golf, tennis. *Clubs*: East India United Service, Junior Army and Navy. (*Died 23 May 1924.*)

FANING, Joseph Eaton, Mus.Doc. Cantab. 1900; F.R.A.M.; Member of Associated Board of R.A.M. and R.C.M. 1901-23; of the Royal Philharmonic Society; Council of the Royal College of Music; Board of Studies in Music, University of London; Director of the British Columbia Land and Investment Agency, Ltd.; Director of the Western Canadian Ranching Co., Ltd.; Director of the London and Canadian Investment Co., Ltd.; *b.* Helston, Cornwall, 20 May 1850; *s.* of Roger and Caroline Faning of Helston; *m.* 1882, Caroline Pare, 3rd *d.* of Thomas Dixon and Emma Amelia Galpin of Bristol House, Roehampton; one *s.* three *d.* *Educ.*: privately. Played violin at a very early age and studied privately until he entered the Royal Academy of Music, 1870, when he studied pianoforte, harmony and composition, organ, singing and violoncello. and obtained many prizes; Professor of Pianoforte at R.A.M., 1878; Guildhall School of Music, 1881; Professor and Conductor of the Choral Class at the National Training School of Music; Conductor of several Choral Societies including Eaton Faning's Select Choir at the Boosey Ballad Concerts, St. James' Hall and Queen's Hall; Professor Pianoforte, Harmony, and Conductor of the Choral Class at the Royal College of Music, 1883; Director of the Music at Harrow School, 1885-1901; Examiner for Musical Degrees, Cambridge University, 1904-1909, and 1919; Mus. Bac., 1894; P.G.O. Grand Lodge of Freemasons; travelled in France, Spain, Portugal, Belgium, Holland, Italy, Switzerland, Germany, Austria, Norway, Denmark, South Africa, China, and Japan. *Publications:* Festival Magnificat and Nunc Dimittis; Te Deum; Benedictus and Jubilate; Anthems; Cantata, Buttercups and Daisies; Operetta, Mock Turtles; various pieces for Pianoforte, Part-songs, Choruses, Odes, Songs; Harrow School Songs. *Recreation*: trout-fishing. *Address*: 19 Preston Park Avenue, Brighton. *Club*: Arts. (*Died 28 Oct. 1927.*)

FANNING, Sir Roland Francis Nichol, Kt., *cr.* 1886; J.P.; *b.* 1829; *m.* Mary (*d.* 1901), *d.* of late Thos. Stanton. Late Deputy-Inspector-Gen. Royal Irish Constabulary. *Address*: Rosslyn, Bray, Co. Wicklow. *Clubs*: Hibernian United Service, Dublin; Royal St. George Yacht. (*Died 20 Feb. 1919.*)

FANSHAWE, Rev. Gerald Charles; Rector of St. Maurice and St. Lawrence, Winchester, since 1922; Hon. Canon of Winchester, 1922; *b.* 16 Nov. 1870; *s.* of late General Charles Fanshawe, R.E.; *m.* 1904, Morforwyn, *d.* of late Col. Lloyd-Verney; one *s.* one *d.* *Educ.*: Westminster School; Trinity College, Cambridge; M.A. Deacon, 1893; Priest, 1894; Curate of St. Thomas, Portman Square, 1893-1900; Domestic Chaplain to Bishop (Ryle) of Exeter, 1900, and Bishop (Ryle) of Winchester on his translation; Hon. Chaplain to Bishop of Winchester, 1904-11; Vicar and Rural Dean of Godalming, 1904. *Address*: St. Maurice Rectory, Winchester. *T.*: Winchester 555.
(*Died 15 April 1924.*)

FANSHAWE, Herbert Charles, C.S.I. 1900; *b.* 28 March 1852; *s.* of Rev. John Faithfull Fanshawe; *m.* 1906, Harriot Wollaston, widow of William Ramsay, Bombay Civil Service. *Educ.*: Tonbridge; Repton. Entered I.C.S., 1873; Settlement officer, Rohtak; Under, Junior, Revenue, and Chief Secretary, Punjab Govt.; Commissioner (Delhi), Punjab; Member Legislative Council, Punjab, 1898-1901; Additional Member of Legislative Council, Governor-General of India, 1900; retired 1901; F.R.A.S., F.R.G.S., F.R.H.S. *Publications*: Rohtak Settlement Report; Delhi, Past and Present, 1902; Murray's Handbook of India, 1904, 1909, and 1911; Memoirs of Lady Fanshawe, 1907. *Address*: 72 Philbeach Gardens, Earl's Court, S.W.5. *T.*: Western 3121. *Club*: East India United Service. (*Died 26 Mar. 1923.*)

FARDELL, Sir [Thomas] George, Kt., *cr.* 1897; J.P.; late Chairman Quarter Sessions, Isle of Ely; M.P. (C.) S. Paddington, 1895-1910; *b.* 26 Oct. 1833; *y. s.* of late Rev-Henry Fardell, Canon of Ely and Vicar of Wisbech, and Eliza, *e. d.* of late Rt. Rev. B. E. Sparke, Bishop of Ely; *m.* Letitia Anne (*d.* 1905), *o. d.* of late Henry Swahn Oldfield, B.C.S., 1862; two *s.* two *d.* *Educ.*: Eton; Christ Church, Oxford. B.A. 1856. Barr. Lincoln's Inn, 1862, Norfolk Circuit; appointed Registrar in Bankruptcy, Manchester, 1868; been engaged in Municipal work since 1877; represented Paddington in Metropolitan Board of Works from 1884, and instrumental in obtaining Royal Commission thereon in 1888; and subsequently in passing into law the Public Bodies' Corrupt Practices Act, 1889; and L.C.C., S. Paddington, 1889-98; was twice put forward for the post of Deputy-Chairman of the L.C.C., and was six years Chairman of the Licensing Committee; travelled in America and Canada; Chairman, 1896-1912; Metropolitan Division National Union Conservative Associations. *Recreation*; shooting. *Address*: 2 South Eaton Place, S.W. *T.*: Victoria 3080. *Club*: Conservative.
(*Died 12 Mar. 1917.*)

FARIDOONJI JAMSHEDJI, Nawab Sir Faridoon Jung, Faridoon Daula Faridoon Mulk Bahadur, K.C.I.E., *cr.* 1915; C.S.I. 1911; C.I.E. 1908; C.B.E. 1918; Extraordinary Member the Nizam's Executive Council; *b.* Sep. 1849; widower; one *s.* Decorated for good services rendered to the Hyderabad State. *Recreation*: used to be big game shooting. *Address*: Saifabad, Hyderabad, Deccan.
(*Died 26 Nov. 1928.*)

FARLEY, His Eminence Cardinal John; 4th Archbishop of New York since 1902; *b.* Newton Hamilton, co. Armagh, Ireland, 20 April 1842; *s.* of Philip Farley and Catherine Murphy. *Educ.*: St Macartan's College, Monaghan; St. John's College, Fordham, N.Y. City; St. Joseph's Seminary, Troy, N.Y.; North American College, Rome, Italy. Priest, 1870; returned to U.S. 1870; Assistant Pastor, St. Peter's Church, New Brighton, Staten Island, 1870-72; Secretary to Archbishop M'Closkey, 1872-84; Private Chamberlain to Pope Leo XIII, with title of Monsignore, 1884; Vicar-General, Archdiocese of New York, 1891; Domestic Prelate to Pope Leo XIII., 1892; Protonotary Apostolic, 1895; Auxiliary Bishop of New York, with titular See of Zeugma, 1895; Admin-

istrator of New York, 1902; made Assistant to the Pontifical Throne, 1904; created Cardinal Priest Consistory, 1911. *Publications:* Life of Cardinal M'Closkey, 1900; Neither Generous nor Just (reply to Bishop Potter), Catholic World, 1889; Why Church Property should not be taxed, Forum, 1893; St Patrick's Cathedral, New York, 1908. *Recreation:* walking. *Address:* 452 Madison Avenue, New York City, U.S.A.
(*Died 17 Sept. 1918.*)

FARMER, Sir Francis Mark, Kt., *cr.* 1916; Dental Surgeon and Lecturer on Dental Surgery and Pathology at London Hospital Medical College; L.D.S., R.C.S. Eng.; Recipient of Presentation from Secretary of State for War, 1902; Member British Dental Assoc. and British Society for Study of Orthodontics; Fellow Royal Soc. of Medicine. *Publications:* Restoration of Chin after Gunshot Wound, and various articles. *Address:* 53 Wimpole Street, W.1. *T.:* Padd, 184.
(*Died 24 Dec. 1922.*)

FARMER, Colonel George Devey, C.B.E. 1919; Canadian A.M.C.; *b.* 6 July 1866; *m.* 1895, Eleanour Shelton, *d.* of Richard Devey and Margaret Farmer, of Ancaster, Canada; two *s.* two *d.* *Educ.:* private school; Hamilton College Institute, and Trinity College University, Toronto. Mobilised 5th Canadian Field Ambulance, Nov. 1914; commanded it on the Kemmel, Ypres, and Somme fronts till Nov. 1916; commanded No. 2 Stationary Hospital at Boulogne, till Dec. 1917; since then in command of No. 5 General Hospital, Canadian, Liverpool (despatches). *Address:* Ancaster, Ontario, Canada. *T.:* Ancaster 152.
(*Died 7 May 1928.*)

FARNALL, Edmund Waterton, C.B., 1912; Assistant Secretary to G.P.O. since 1906; *b.* 1855; *m.* 1894, Helen Frances, *d.* of late Leonard Bidwell, Blackheath. British Delegate to the International Conferences at Paris on White Slave Traffic Convention and Suppression of Obscene Publications, 1910; British Plenipotentiary to International Wireless Telegraph Conference, London, 1912. *Address:* 2 Morden Road, Blackheath, S.E. *T.:* Lee Green 501. *Club:* British Empire.
(*Died 14 April 1918.*)

FARQUHAR, 1st Earl, *cr.* 1922; of St. Marylebone; **Horace Brand Farquhar**; Viscount, *cr.* 1917; Baron, *cr.* 1898; Bt. *cr.* 1892; G.C.B. *cr.* 1922; G.C.V.O. 1902; K.C.V.O. 1901; P.C., J.P., D.L.; Lord Steward, 1915-22; late Master of the Household of King Edward VII.; *heir-pres.* to Sir R. Townsend-Farquhar; *b.* 19 May 1844; *m.* Emily (*d.* 1922), *d.* of Col. H. Packe, Grenadier Guards, Hurleston, Northamptonshire, and Twyford Hall, Norfolk, and widow of Sir E. H. Scott, 5th Bt., 1895. M.P. Marylebone, W., 1895-98; L.C.C. Marylebone West, 1889-1901; Grand Officer Legion of Honour. *Heir:* none. *Address:* 7 Grosvenor Square, W.1. *T.:* Mayfair 5476; Castle Rising, Norfolk. *Clubs:* Marlborough, Turf.
(*Died 30 Aug. 1923.*)

FARQUHAR, Alfred; *b.* 25 April 1852; *e. s.* of late Harvic Morton Farquhar and Hon. Louisa Harriet Ridley Colborne, *d.* and *co-heir* of Lord Colborne. *Address:* 11 Belgrave Square, S.W.1. *T.:* Victoria 3465. *Clubs:* Carlton, St. James', Arthurs', Bachelors'. White's.
(*Died 28 Dec. 1928.*)

FARQUHAR, Very Rev. George Taylor Shillito, D.D. St. Andrews, 1922; Dean of St. Andrews, Dunkeld, and Dunblane, since 1910; Canon of St. Ninian's Cathedral 1885-1926. *Educ.:* Keble College, Oxford (M.A. 1882); D.D. (Hon.) St. Andrews, 1922. Ordained 1881; Precentor of Cathedral, 1885-1926; Diocesan Inspector of Schools, 1895-1900; Synod Clerk, 1900-10. *Publications:* The Episcopal History of Perth, 1894; Our Ancient Scottish Cathedrals, 1897; The Church's Year, 1904; Musicians, 1908; The History of the Lay Claims

under the Scottish Bishops, 1911; Three Bishops of Dunkeld, 1915; A Scottish Twelvemonth and Other Poems, 1923. *Address:* Castlegate, St. Andrews, Scotland.
(*Died 30 July 1927.*)

FARQUHAR, Gilbert; *b.* 1 Feb. 1850; *y. s.* of Sir Minto Farquhar, 2nd Bart., *b.* of Sir Robert Farquhar, 6th Bart., and Lord Farquhar, P.C. *Educ.:* Eton. An actor, 1883-1906. *Publications:* stories and articles. *Clubs:* Bachelors', Beefsteak, Garrick.
(*Died 1 April 1920.*)

FARQUHAR, Sir Henry Thomas, of Gilmilnscroft, 4th Bart., *cr.* 1796; D.L.; *b.* 18 Sept. 1838; *s.* of 3rd Bart. and Lady Mary, *d.* of 6th Duke of Beaufort; *m.* Hon. Alice Brand, *d.* of 1st Viscount Hampden; one *s.* one *d.* *Educ.:* Harrow. *Recreations:* hunting, shooting, fencing. *Heir:* *n.* Walter Randolph Fitzroy [*b.* 31 May 1878: *m.* 1903, Violet, *d.* of Col. C. S. Corkran, late Grenadier Guards; three *s.* one *d.* *Address:* 3 Eaton Square, S.W.]. *Address:* 22 Bryanston Square, W.; Gilmilnscroft, Mauchline, N.B. *Clubs:* Carlton, Travellers', Turf.
(*Died 15 Jan. 1916.*)

FARQUHAR, Sir Robert Townsend-, 6th Bt.; *cr.* 1821; artist; *b.* Goldings, 26 Sep. 1841; 4th *s.* of Sir Minto W. Townsend-Farquhar, M.P., and Erica, *d.* of 7th Lord Reay; *S. b.* 1877; unmarried. *Educ.:* R.M.A. Woolwich. Seven years Royal Artillery, retiring 1866; afterwards on Stock Exchange and Lloyd's; active supporter of the Conservative party in Westmoreland; 20 years member of the committee which organised "The Grasmere and Lake District Athletic Sports." *Publications:* 2 vols. verse, 1870, 1892; pamphlet on Thirlmere Water Scheme, 1878; musical compositions—three songs (words and music); march commemorating Queen's jubilee. Exhibitor at R.S.A., Dudley Gallery, Liverpool Autumn Exhibition, etc. *Recreations:* angling; shooting. *Heir:* *b.* Earl Farquhar. *Address:* 5 Oriental Place, Brighton. *Clubs:* Junior United Service (hon.); New, Brighton.
(*Died 30 June 1924.*)

FARQUHAR, Sir Walter Randolph Fitzroy, 5th Bart., *cr.* 1796; *b.* 31 May 1878; *s.* of Walter Randolph Farquhar, 2nd *s.* of 3rd Bt., and Hon. Kathleen Mary, *d.* of 1st Lord Deramore; *S.* uncle, 1916; *m.* 1903, Violet, *d.* of Col. Charles Seymour Corkran, late Grenadier Guards; three *s.* one *d.* *Heir:* *s.* Peter Walter, *b.* 8 Oct. 1904. *Address:* 3 Eaton Square, S.W. *Clubs:* Turf, Arthur's.
(*Died 15 Oct. 1918.*)

FARQUHARSON, Rt. Hon. Robert, P.C. 1906; M.D., LL.D.; J.P., D.L.; *b.* Edinburgh, 1836; 2nd *s.* of Francis Farquharson, Finzean. *Educ.:* Edinburgh Academy and University; Medical Schools of Paris, Berlin, and Vienna. Assistant Surgeon in Coldstream Guards, 1859-68; Medical Officer to Rugby School, and Assistant Physician to St. Mary's Hospital; Lecturer on Materia Medica; M.P. West Aberdeenshire, 1880-1906. *Publications:* Guide to Therapeutics, 5th ed.; School Hygiene; The House of Commons from Within, 1912; In and Out of Parliament. Owns about 16,900 acres. *Recreation:* shooting. *Address:* Finzean, Aboyne, N.B.; Migvie Lodge, Porchester Gardens, W. *Clubs:* Reform, Junior United Service; Royal Northern, Aberdeen; Scottish Liberal, Edinburgh.
(*Died 8 June 1918.*)

FARR, William Edward, C.B.E., J.P.; Solicitor, member of Booth, Wade, Farr Lomas-Walker and Foster; Alderman of Leeds City Council; Vice-Chairman Leeds Education Committee; Chairman, Leeds Higher Education Committee; Hon. Sec. Leeds Luncheon Club; member of Council of Leeds University; *b.* Weston, Herts, 1872; *e. s.* of Albert Hart and Louisa Farr; *m.* Hilda Lomas-Walker, Harrogate; one *s.* *Educ.:* privately. Past Pres. Leeds Incorporated Law Society; Chairman, Leeds Military Advisory Committee, 1916-18; Chairman, Leeds Employment Committee, 1918-20;

member of Executive of National Liberal Federation, 1907-19 ; Hon. Secretary, Leeds Liberal Federation, 1902-22. *Address :* 1 Central Bank Chambers, Leeds ; South Gables, Langcliffe Avenue, Harrogate. *T.A.:* Wafer, Leeds. *T. :* 20787, Leeds. *Clubs:* Leeds, Leeds Liberal, Leeds. *(Died 2 Oct. 1923.)*

FARRAN, Major George Lambert, D.S.O. 1917 ; O.B.E., M.C. ; 2nd Lancers, Indian Army ; *s.* of late Sir Charles F. Farran and Lady Farran of Brackendale House, Camberley ; *m.* 1909, Myrtle Keatinge ; one *s.* one *d. Educ. :* Rugby ; Cheltenham ; Sandhurst. Entered Army, 1900 ; served Waziristan operations, 1901-2 (medal and clasp) ; European War, France, 1914-15 ; Egypt, 1915 ; Mesopotamia, 1915-16 ; S. Persia, 1916-19 (despatches, D.S.O., O.B.E., M.C.) ; Afghan War, 1919 (medal and clasp) ; graduated Staff College, Quetta, 1920. *Recreation :* polo. *Address :* 2nd Lancers, Poona, India. *(Died 21 Dec. 1925.)*

FARRAR, Rt. Rev. Walter, D.D. ; Vicar of Bognor since 1915 ; *b.* British Guiana, 1865 ; Assistant Bishop, West Indies, 1912-13 ; *s.* of late Very Rev. F. W. Farrar, D.D., Dean of Canterbury ; *m.* Alice, *e. d.* of W. F. Bridges, J.P., Administrator-General of British Guiana. *Educ. :* Queen's College, Guiana ; Keble College, Oxford. Has held, besides various posts of importance in Guiana, the Rectory of Hawkchurch, Dorset ; has been Acting Warden of the Jamaica Church Theological College, and Commissary in England of the Bishop of Guiana ; he was in Jamaica when the call to Antigua came ; Bishop of Antigua, 1905-10 ; resigned, 1910 ; late Assistant Bishop of Queensland ; Assist. Bishop in the Diocese of York, and Commissary to the Archbishop of York, 1910 ; Assistant Bishop of Quebec, and later Archdeacon of St. Francis, Canada ; on return to England acted for a term as Principal of Bishop's College, Cheshunt ; he was then asked to go to Honduras on a special mission ; Bishop of British Honduras, 1913-15. *Publications :* besides many reviews, etc., a work on the Cultus of the Sacred Heart, co-author of Notes on the History of the Church in Guiana. *Address :* The Vicarage, Bognor, Sussex. *(Died 6 Dec. 1916.)*

FARRELL, James Patrick; M.P. (N.) North Longford, 1900-18 ; *b.* Longford, 18 May 1865 ; *s.* of Patrick Farrell and Anne, *e. d.* of late John Lynam, Strokestown, Co. Roscommon ; *m.* 1888, Bride, *d.* of late M. Fitzgerald, Co. Longford ; five *s.* two *d. Educ.:* St. Mels Coll. Longford. Became a journalist early, Roscommon Herald ; always actively engaged in politics in Land League and National League periods ; imprisoned two months 1889 for a speech ; contested Kilkenny City, 1895 ; M.P. (A.P.) West Cavan, 1895-1900. *Publications :* Fireside Talks about Co. Longford ; Historical Notes and Stories of Co. Longford ; a large Illustrated History of Co. Longford. *Address :* Market Square, Longford ; 10 Gloucester Street, S.W.
(Died 11 Dec. 1921.)

FARRER, Reginald, J.P., F.R.H.S. ; Clerk in the Foreign Office ; *b.* 17 Feb. 1880. ; *e. s.* of James Farrer of Ingleborough, Yorkshire, and Elizabeth Reynell-Pack. *Educ. :* privately ; Balliol College, Oxford. Second in Mods., third in Greats, 1902 ; travelled in Japan, China, Korea, Canada, 1903 ; yearly journeys of botanical exploration in the Eastern and Western Alps of Europe ever since ; Ceylon, 1907 ; Athens and Constantinople, 1912 ; contested Ashford Division (L.), 1911 ; Yorkshire County Council ; from Feb. 1914 to April 1916 was across Northern China and over the Tibetan Border ; was rejected for military purposes on returning, and has since been employed at the Foreign Office ; Gill Memorial R.G.S., 1920. *Publications:* Novels—The House of Shadows ; The Sundered Streams ; The Ways of Rebel-

lion ; The Anne-Queen's Chronicle ; Through the Ivory Gate (censored). *Horticulture and Travel*—My Rock-Garden ; Alpines and Bog-Plants ; In a Yorkshire Garden ; Among the Hills ; King Laurin's Garden (the Dolomites); The Garden of Asia ; In Old Ceylon ; On the Eaves of the World, 1917. *Drama*—The Dowager of Jerusalem ; Vasanta the Beautiful ; Jane Austen's Memorial Article, Quarterly Review, July 1917 ; The Void of War ; The English Rock-Garden. *Recreations :* gardening, being on mountains, talking (without music), indulging in drama. *Address :* Ingleborough, Yorkshire, *via* Lancaster ; 50 Ennismore Gardens, S.W.7. *T. :* Ken. 2926. *Clubs :* Travellers', Athenæum, Alpine. *(Died 16 Oct. 1920.)*

PARRINGTON, Col. Malcolm Charles, C.B., 1887 ; *b.* 4 June 1835. Entered army 1853 ; Col. 1884 ; retired 1890 ; served Burmah 1886-89 (thanks of Govt. of India, despatches, C.B., medal with two clasps).
(Died 7 July 1925.)

FASKEN, Maj.-Gen. Charles Grant Mansell, C.B. 1904 ; *b.* 24 May 1855 ; *s.* of late General Edward Thomas Fasken ; *m.* 1885, Eveline, *d.* of late Rev. William Pratt, Rector of Harpley, Norfolk ; one *s.* two *d. Educ. :* Marlborough ; Royal Military College, Sandhurst. Entered army, Bedfordshire Regt., 1874 ; B.S.C. (now Indian Army) 1878 ; Brevet-Col. 1904 ; served Afghan War, 1878-80 ; present at battle of Ahmad Khel and action of Arzu, march from Kabul to the relief of Kandahar and battle of Kandahar (medal with 2 clasps and bronze star) ; Aitchakzai Expedition and operations against the Marri tribe, 1880 ; served as a Brigade Major in Black Mountain Expedition of 1888 (despatches, medal with clasp) ; received commendations of Government of India and of Commander-in-Chief for the surprise of village of Maizar, Tochi Valley, N.W. Frontier, India, 1900 ; operations in Somaliland, 1903-4 ; was Brigadier-General commanding 2nd Brigade, action at Jidballi (despatches twice, C.B., medal and 2 clasps) ; Maj.-Gen. 1907 ; Commanded The Southern, Bannu, and Ferozepore Brigades, India, 1906-11 ; Colonel 52nd Sikhs F.F. 1909 ; retired, 1914 ; Divisional Commander, European War, Sep. 1914-June 1916 (1914-15 Star, two medals) ; served in the B.E.F. until invalided. *Address :* c/o Westminster Bank, Wokingham, Berks. *(Died 15 April 1928.)*

FATEH ALI KHAN, Hon. Sir Hajee, Nawab Kizilbash, K.C.I.E. cr. 1921 ; C.I.E. 1903 ; *b.* 1862 ; *S.* to headship of Kizilbashes, 1896. Placed himself and his great clan at disposal of Government for Chitral campaign, and induced many of tribes across the border to adopt an attitude of pacific non-intervention. For this service received 3000 acres of land in Chenab Canal Colony for settlement of his followers ; has served on Punjab Legislative Council ; representative of Punjab at Famine Conference, 1897 ; Life President of Anjumani-Islamia, Lahore, and Imamia Association of Punjab ; a Counsellor of the Aitchison Chiefs' College, Lahore ; Fellow of the Punjab University ; Trustee of the Aligarh College ; represented the province as guest of Great Britain at King Edward's Coronation. *Heir : s.* Nisor Ali Khan, *b.* 1901. *Address :* Aitchison Chiefs Coll., Lahore, India.
(Died 28 Oct. 1923.)

FAUCONBERG and CONYERS, Baroness, Marcia Amelia Mary Pelham, O.B.E. ; *b.* 18 Oct. 1863 ; *S.* father 1892 as 13th Baroness ; *m.* 1886, 4th Earl of Yarborough. Lady of Justice of the Order of St. John of Jerusalem. Owns landed estates in North and West Riding of Yorkshire ; possesses a collection of miniatures and pictures by Drouet, Kneller, and Sir Thomas Lawrence. *Heir : s.* Lord Worsley. *Ad-*

dress: Brocklesby Park, Lincolnshire.
(*Died 17 Nov. 1926.*)

FAUDEL - PHILLIPS, Sir Benjamin Samuel, 2nd Bt.; *cr.* 1897; *s.* of 1st Bt. and Helen (*d.* 1916), *d.* of late J. M. Levy, *sister* of 1st Lord Burnham; *b.* 21 July 1871; *S.* father, 1922. *Heir: b.* Lionel Lawson Faudel.
Address: Balls Park, Hertford. *T.:* Hertford 9.
Club: Reform. (*Died 11 Jan. 1927.*)

FAUDEL-PHILLIPS, Sir George Faudel, 1st Bt.; *cr.* 1897; G.C.I.E.; *cr.* 1897; J.P., D.L.; *b.* 20 July 1840; *2nd s.* of Sir Benjamin S. Phillips, Alderman, Lord Mayor of London, 1865 - 66, and Rachel, *d.* of S. H. Faudel; *m.* Helen, (*d.* 1916), *d.* of late J. M. Levy, *sister* of 1st Lord Burnham, 1867; two *s.* three *d. Educ.:* Univ. Coll. School; Berlin, Paris. Sheriff, London and Middlesex, 1884 - 85; Alderman of Ward of Farringdon Within, 1888 - 1912; Governor of the Honourable the Irish Society, 1894; High Sheriff, Co. of London, 1895; Lord Mayor of London, 1896 - 97; an Almoner of Christ's Hospital; Governor of St. Bartholomew's; Past Master Spectacle-Makers' Company; High Sheriff Hertford, 1900 and 1901; Commander of the Siamese Order of the White Elephant; 2nd class Osmanieh Order; 2nd class Persian Order of Lion and Sun; Commander of the Order of Leopold; Grand Cross of Servian Order of Takova. *Recreations:* shooting, golfing, riding, driving; a true bibliophile, possessor of a valuable and well-selected library. *Heir: s.* Benjamin Samuel, *b.* 21 July 1871. *Address:* Balls Park, Hertford. *T.:* Hertford 9. *Club:* Reform. (*Died 28 Dec. 1922.*)

FAUNTHORPE, Rev. John Pincher, M.A., F.R.G.S.; *b.* Scotter, 7 Aug. 1839; *m.* 1st, C. E. Blackmore, *d.* of late Rev. John Blackmore, M.A.; 2nd, L. J. (*d.* 1917), *d.* of late James Russell, Q.C.; three *s. Educ.:* St. John's College, Battersea. M.A. (Lond.); 1st B.A.; 1st in English Honours; 1st, Holy Scripture Exam. Lond. Univ.; pupil teacher, St. George's School, Ramsgate, 1853-57; student, Battersea College, 1858-59; 2nd on Q. S. list for England at entrance; master in Chester Training College, 1860; St. John's College, Battersea, Geography Lecturer, 1861-62; Secretary and Lecturer, 1863 - 66; Vice-Principal (ordained by Bishop of Winchester), 1867-74; Principal, Whitelands College, Chelsea, S.W., 1874-1907. *Publications:* Standard Reading-books; Household Science; Map - drawing Atlases; Colonial Geography, British; Complete Index to Ruskin's Fors Clavigera; formerly President of London Ruskin Society. *Recreation:* driving. *Address:* Elmfield, Bromley Common, Kent. (*Died 14 May 1924.*)

FAURE, Gabriel, General Inspector of the Fine Arts in France; *b.* Pamiers, 13 May 1845. Studied at School of Sacred Music directed by Niedermeyer under Dietsch and Saint-Saëns. Maître de Chapelle, Church of the Madeleine, 1877; organist, 1896; Directeur du Conservatoire national de Musique et de Declamation, 1905-20. *Works:* The Birth of Venus, etc. *Address:* Conservatoire Nationale, Paris.
(*Died 4 Nov. 1924.*)

FAVELL, Richard, Ch.M., M.R.C.S.; Professor of Midwifery University of Sheffield; Surgeon Jessop Hospital for Women. *Educ.:* St. Bartholomew's Hospital, Sheffield. *Address:* Brunswick House, Glossop Road, Sheffield. *T.:* 2128. (*Died Nov. 1918.*)

FAWCETT, Henry Heath, C.B. 1918; *b.* 7 Dec. 1863; *s.* of Peter Fawcett; *m.* 1892, Colina, *d.* of late John Colin Sharp; one *s.* three *d. Educ.:* Dulwich College; University College, London. Clerk Higher Division, War Office, 1886; Private Secretary to Sir Arthur Haliburton and to Sir Ralph Knox, Permanent Under-Secretaries of State for War, 1896-98; Principal Clerk, 1899; Auditor 1st Army Corps

1902-4; Financial Adviser and ·Auditor, S. Africa, 1904; Chief . Accountant, Aldershot, 1905-9; Assistant Secretary, War Office, 1916-17; Director of Army Contracts, 1917-19; Director of Finance, War Office, 1919-24; graded as Principal Assistant-Secretary with rank of Assistant Under-Secretary of State; retired on pension, 1924; Officer Legion of Honour. *Recreations:* bicycling, sculling. *Address:* Oaken Cottage, Berkhamsted.
(*Died 23 Dec. 1925.*)

FAWKE, Sir Ernest (John), Kt., *m.* 1922; Director of the Central and Western Corporation; *m.* Wemyss Gertrude; one *s.*
(*Died 26 Oct. 1928.*)

FAWKES, Admiral Sir Wilmot Hawksworth, G.C.B., *cr.* 1911; K.C.B., *cr.* 1907; K.C.V.O., *cr.* 1903; LL.D., Cambridge University, 1913; *b.* 22 Dec. 1846; 2nd *s.* of Major Richard Fawkes and Fanny, *d.* of A. Paris; *m.* Juliana (*d.* 1916), *e. d.* of J. W. G. Spicer, Spye Park, Wilts, 1875. *Educ.:* St. John's College, Cambridge. Entered Royal Navy, 1860; Lieut. Nov. 1867; Com. Mar. 1880; Capt. July 1886; Com. Royal yacht Osborne, 1884-86; H.M.S. Raleigh, 1888-90; Mercury, 1893-96; Terrible, 1896; Canopus, 1899-1900; Naval Adviser to Inspector-General of Fortifications, 1891-92; A.D.C. to Queen Victoria, 1899-1901; Private Secretary to First Lord of the Admiralty, 1897-99, and 1900-1902; Rear-Adm. commanding Cruiser Squadron, 1902-4; Commander-in-Chief, Australian station, 1905-8; Plymouth, 1908-11; retired, 1911. *Recreations:* field sports. *Address:* Steel Cross House, Steel Cross, Tunbridge Wells. *T.A.:* Crowborough. *Clubs:* United Service, Arthur's.
(*Died 29 May 1926.*)

FAYOLLE, Emile; Marshal of France, 1921; *b.* Le Puy, Haute Loire, 1852. *Educ.:* Polytechnic School. Sub-Lieut. Ecole d'Application de l'Artillerie et de Genie, 1875; Professor of Applied Artillery Tactics at the Superior School of War; Lieut. - Colonel, 1903; General, 1910; commanded the Artillery Brigade of Vincennes; Commander 70th Division of Infantry, 14 Aug. 1914; Commander of the Legion of Honour, Oct. 1914; Commander 33rd Army Corps, June 1915; 6th Army, Feb. 1916; G.A.C. May 1917; Commandant supérieur des forces françaises en Italie, Nov. 1917; Commander G.A.R. Feb. 1918; Grand Officer of the Legion of Honour, Oct. 1916; Croix de Guerre, Oct. 1916; Grand Croix of the Legion of Honour, July 1918; Médaille Militaire, 1919. *Address:* 18 Avenue de la Bourdonnais, Paris.
(*Died 27 Aug. 1928.*)

FEARNSIDES, Edwin Greaves, M.A., M.D., B.C. (Cantab.), B.Sc. (London), F.R.C.P. (London); Assistant Physician to the Hospital for Nervous Diseases, Maida Vale, W.; Beit Memorial Research Fellow; *b.* Horbury, Yorks, 17 June 1883; *y. s.* of late Joshua and Maria Fearnsides; unmarried. *Educ.:* Wheelwright Grammar School, Dewsbury; Trinity Hall, Cambridge; London Hospital; Universities of Berlin and Munich; West Riding County Major Scholarship, 1900; Scholar of Trinity Hall, 1902-6; Class I. Natural Science Tripos, Part I., 1904; Part II. (Physiology), 1906; 1st Class Honours, London, B.Sc., 1905; Price University Scholar, London Hospital, 1906; after qualification held all the Resident appointments at the London Hospital; Medical Registrar, London Hospital, 1910-14. *Publications:* Various papers dealing with Nervous and General Diseases in Medical Journals. *Recreation:* travel. *Address:* 46 Queen Anne Street, Cavendish Square, W.; *T.:* Mayfair 2562; Highfield, Golders Green Road, N.W.4. *Club:* United University. (*Died 26 June 1919.*)

FEARON, Daniel Robert, C.B. 1894; M.A.; Barrister; *b.* Assington, 1 Dec. 1835; *m.*

FAWCETT, Lieut.-Col. P. H., D.S.O. See page xix.

Margaret (d. 1909), d. of Prof. Bonamy Price (Political Economy, Oxford), 1861. Educ.: Marlborough; Balliol Coll. Oxford. 1st Class Lit. Hum. Oxford. H.M. Inspector of Schools, 1860; Assistant-Com. Schools Inquiry Commission, 1865; Assistant Commissioner Endowed Schools Commission, 1870; Assistant Charity Commissioner, 1874; Secretary Charity Commissioners, 1886-1900; Charity Commissioner, 1900-1903: retired June 1903. Address: Messrs. Bury, 47 Lincoln's Inn Fields, W.C. Club: Athenæum.
(Died 30 Oct. 1919.)

FEARON, Rev. William Andrewes, D.D.; b. Assington Vicarage, 4 Feb. 1841; 3rd s. of Rev. Daniel Rose Fearon and Frances Andrewes; m. Mary, e. d. of late Archdeacon Freeman, Exeter. Educ.: Winchester; New Coll. Oxford (Hon. Fellow, 1901). Double 1st (Classics and Mathematics) in Moderations and again in the Final Schools. Fellow and Tutor of New College from 1864-67; had a tutor's house at Winchester and the mastership of the Junior VI. from 1867-82; Headmaster of Durham School and Examining Chaplain to Bishop of Newcastle, 1882-84; Hon. Canon of Winchester Cathedral, 1889; Headmaster of Winchester College, 1884-1901; Member of Teachers' Registration Council, 1903-4; Examining Chaplain to Bishop of Winchester, 1903-15; Archdeacon of Winchester, 1903-20; Canon of Winchester, 1906-20. Address: 12 Cresswell Gardens, S.W.5. Club: Athenæum.   (Died 29 April 1924.)

FEETHAM, Brig.-Gen. Edward, C.B. 1915; C.M.G. 1917; b. 4 June 1863; m. 1904, Isabel Beatrix, d. of Col. Ewen Grant; one d. Lieut. Royal Berks Regt. 1883; Captain, 1892; Adjutant, 1895-6; Major, 1903; Lt.-Col. 1911; Adjutant, Volunteers, 1896-1901; served Sudan, 1885 (medal, 2 clasps; bronze star); Sudan, 1885-86; South Africa, 1901-2 (despatches, Bt.-Major, Queen's medal, 5 clasps); European War, 1914-1917 (C.B., C.M.G.). Address: Farmwood, Ascot. Club: United Service.
(Died 30 March 1918.)

FEILDEN, Major-General Sir Henry Broome, K.C.B. cr. 1923; C.M.G. 1903; b. 31 July 1834; s. of Rev. Robert M. Feilden. Entered army, 1852; Maj.-Gen. 1890; served Crimea, 1854-55 (severely wounded, despatches, medal with three clasps, Turkish medal); retired, 1893. Address: Wear Giffard, Warwick.
(Died 1 Dec. 1926.)

FEILDEN, Col. Henry Wemyss, C.B. 1900; retired; b. 6 Oct. 1838; 2nd s. of Sir W. H. Feilden, 2nd Bart.; m. 1864, Julia (d. 1920), d. of David MacCord of S. Carolina. Educ.: Cheltenham College. Served Indian Mutiny, 1857-58 (medal with clasp); China, 1860 (medal with clasp). Served in army of Confederate States, with rank of A.A.G. 1862-65; surrendering after last battle of war between the States, with the remnant of army of Tennessee, under Gen. J. E. Johnston, to Gen. Sherman; Naturalist to the British Polar Expedition, 1875-76 (medal); Boer War, 1881; South Africa, Boer War, 1900-1901 (medal with three clasps); F.G.S., F.R.G.S., G.M.Z.S. Has visited Grinnell Land, Ellesmere Land, Greenland, Spitzbergen, Novaya Zemlya, Waigats, Lapland, and Northern Russia for scientific research. Publications: papers in Geological, Biological, and Botanical research. Address: Rampyndene, Burwash, Sussex. Club: Junior United Service.
(Died 18 June 1921)

FELBERMAN, Louis, F.R.Hist.Soc.; late Chairman Francis Joseph Institute; Founder and acting President Hungarian Society for Encouragement of Home Industries; Fellow of the Hungarian Geographical Society; Hungarian Ethnographical Society, and several learned Societies; Knight of the Imperial Order Francis Joseph; Officer of the Royal Orders St. Sava and Takova; b. Hungary, 1861; s. of

a landed proprietor; m. 1901, Isabelle Maud (d. 1918), d. of late Capt. Ross Caldwell, 7th Dragoons, and widow of Col. H. Webber. Came to England 1881, and devoted several years to study of English language and literature. Publications: Hungary and its People; The Puszta; Gypsy Czinka's Prophecy; The Land of the Khedive; The Pyrenees, Auvergne, South Coast of Brittany, Touraine; The Land of the Magyars; Hungary and the Hungarians; Francis Joseph I., The Hungarian Origin of Margaret of Scotland; The House of Teck; edited the Souvenir Album of the Hungarian Millennial Festival; translated Maurice Jokai's In Love with the Czarina; The Blind Poet, Love's Puppets, and numerous other stories. Recreation: fond of travelling in order to study the customs and manners of the different nationalities. Address: The Boltons, 55 Naphegy Utca (Sun Hill), Budapest. Clubs: Authors', Royal Automobile, Albemarle; Radnor, Folkestone.
(Died 1 Nov. 1927.)

FELL, Thomas Edward, C.M.G. 1918; Colonial Secretary, Fiji, since 1919; s. of John Fell, J.P., D.L., Flan How, Ulverston; b. 1873. Educ.: Lancaster Royal Grammar School; Owens College, Manchester; Pembroke College, Cambridge, B.A. 1897. Chief Clerk, Colonial Secretary's Office, Gold Coast, 1897; Inspector of Preventive Services, Gold Coast, 1899; Travelling Commissioner, Gold Coast, 1901; Acting Secretary for Native Affairs, Gold Coast, 1902; District Commissioner, Ashanti, 1905; Provincial Commissioner, 1907; Colonial Secretary, Barbados, 1916; Acting Governor, Barbados, 1918; Acting Governor, Fiji, and Acting High Commissioner, Western Pacific, 1920 and 1921. Recreations: games and sport of all kinds. Address: Suva, Fiji. Club: Sports.   (Died 21 May 1926.)

FELLING, Sir Christian Ludolph Neethling, Kt., cr. 1928; C.M.G. 1922; M. Inst. T.; General Manager Kenya and Uganda Railways since 1923; b. Cape Town, 1880; m.; one s. one d. Educ.: Public School, Stellenbosch. Studied law at South African College, Cape Town. Joined Cape Govt. Railways, 1895; Chief Assist. General Manager, S. African Railways, 1918. Address: Nairobi, Kenya Colony. (Died 19 Aug. 1928.)

FELLOWES, Rear-Admiral Sir Thomas Hounsom Butler, K.C.B., cr. 1911; C.B. 1868; J.P., D.L., Herts; b. 1827; s. of late Sir J. Fellowes, M.D., of Adbury House, Hants; m. 1st, 1857, Constance Fanny (d. 1888), d. of C. S. Hanson of Constantinople; 2nd, 1890, Margaret, d. of Rev. W. Jowitt; two s. Entered navy, 1845; Senior Lieutenant of Mersey frigate at landing of allied forces at Vera Cruz, 1861; Rear-Admiral, 1886; served Crimea, 1854-56 (Baltic medal); Black Sea (Crimean and Turkish medals, Sebastopol clasp); commanded Naval Brigade, Abyssinian War, 1868 (despatches, promoted, C.B., medal); National Lifeboat Institution Medal. Address: Woodfield, Stevenage, Herts. T.A.: Stevenage. (Died 26 Mar. 1923.)

FELLOWS, Col. (Robert) Bruce, C.B. 1895; J.P.; b. 5 Aug. 1830; s. of late Thos. Fellows, Moneyhill, and Mary, d. of late Thos. Howard, Batchworth Heath; m. Emily Ann (d. 1917), d. of John Fellows, Eynsford, Kent, 1867; one s. Educ.: Eton; Christ Coll. Camb. Thirty-seven years in Hertfordshire Militia; commanded it nearly fifteen years; Hon. Col. 4th Bedfordshire and Hertfordshire Regiment (Special Reserve), 1908; entered Privy Council Office, 1858; became Deputy Clerk of the Council and Chief Clerk, 1894; retired 1895. Publication: Historical Records of the Hertfordshire Militia. Recreation: shooting. Address: Stanborough Cottage, Hatfield, Herts. T.A.: Hatfield.   (Died 6 Jan. 1922.)

FELLS, John Manger, C.B.E. 1920; *b.* 1858; *s.* of late William Fells, Deal; *m.* 1897, Henrietta Emily (*d.* 1918), *d.* of William Julian; three *s.* one *d.* *Educ.:* Deal College; privately. Started commercial career in the Accountant's office of a Railway Co.; Accountant and Assistant Secretary of the Anglo-American Brush Electric Light Corporation (now the Brush Electrical Engineering Co., Ltd.); Superintending Accountant, Salt Union Ltd., 1889, and General Manager, 1895; commenced practice as an Accountant, 1900; Fellow, Member of Council, and Examiner of the Society of Incorporated Accountants and Auditors, Fellow of the Institute of Cost and Works Accountants, an original Fellow, Royal Economic Society; Private Secretary to the Surveyor General of Supply, War Office, 1917; member of several War Office Committees including Cost Accounting Committee, 1917-19; Hon. Life Member British Red Cross for work in connection with Red Cross. *Publications:* Factory Accounts, their Principles and Practice, 7th Edition; various Lectures and Addresses on Industrial Economics, and Scientific Accountancy. *Recreation:* walking. *Address:* 128 Goldhurst Terrace, N.W. 6; 7 Union Court, E.C.2. *T.:* Central 4506. *Club:* National Liberal.
                        (Died 7 Dec. 1925.)

FENN, Colonel Ernest Harrold, C.I.E. 1894; Royal Army Medical Corps; retired 1907; *b.* 16 Feb. 1850; *s.* of T. H. Fenn, Nayland, Colchester; *m.* 1886, Bertha, *d.* of Robert Jobson. *Educ.:* Sherborne School. Entered Army Medical Staff, Sept. 1875; served in Afghan War, 1879-80; present at affair at Zaidabad; accompanied force under Lord Roberts to relief of Kandahar; present at Battle of Kandahar (despatches, medal and clasp, bronze star); joined Grenadier Guards, 1881; Soudan Campaign, 1885; Battle of Hasheen and destruction of Temai (medal with clasp and Khedive's star); accompanied Sir Mortimer Durand on his mission to Cabul, 1893 (thanked by Government of India); served on Lord Lansdowne's Staff in India, 1888-94; served on Lord Curzon's Staff in India, 1898-1903 (Durbar medal). *Decorated* for services on Durand Mission. *Recreation:* shooting. *Club:* Naval and Military.   *(Died 24 Nov. 1916.)*

FENN, Frederick, dramatist; *b.* Bishop Stortford, 6 Nov. 1868; *e. s.* of late George Manville Fenn, novelist. *Educ.:* privately. Was Assistant Editor of The Graphic and Dramatic Critic Daily Graphic. *Publications:* Plays: Judged by Appearances (one act); A Married Woman (four acts); The Convict on the Hearth (one act); Amasis (comic opera); and Dame Nature (four acts), adapted from the French of Henry Bataille; (with Richard Pryce) Saturday to Monday (three acts); 'Op 'o me Thumb (one act); etc. *Recreation:* none. *Address:* 12 Gloucester Road, N.W. *Clubs:* Savile, Green Room.   *(Died 2 Jan. 1924.)*

FENN, John Cyril Douglas, C.M.G. 1924; Colonial Secretary of British Guiana, 1925-1926; *b.* 25 Nov. 1879; *y. s.* of late Colonel E. G. Fenn, Shanklin; *m.* 1914, Evelyn Blanche, *y. d.* of late James Lawford, Springvale House, Springvale. *Educ.:* Marlborough. Entered Civil Service, Gold Coast, 1903; retired, 1908; reappointed Cyprus, 1910; Chief Secretary to Government of Cyprus, 1920-25; administered the Government of Cyprus on several occasions. *Address:* Gastelu Zahar, St. Jean-de-Luz, France. *Club:* Badminton.
                        (Died 27 Jan. 1927.)

FENNELLY, Most Rev. Thomas; b. 28 Jan. 1845. *Educ.:* Thurles College; St. Vincent's, Castleknock; Maynooth. Ordained 1870; parish priest, Moycarkey, 1889; R.C. Bishop Coadjutor to Archbishop Croke, 1901-1902; Archbishop of Cashel, 1902-13; retired,

348

1913. *Address:* Moycarkey, Co. Tipperary.
                        (Died 24 Dec. 1927.)

FENTON, Ferrar, M.R.A.S.; author; previously and also a Manufacturer and Financial Organiser; *b.* Waltham Rectory, Lincolnshire, 1832; *s.* of R. C. Fenton, of an old historic family of Norman origin of Fenton-on-Trent, late generations of Pembrokeshire. *Educ.:* by father and private schools and tutors. To 28 a student and man of letters, and acquired a knowledge of 25 or 26 classic, Oriental, and modern languages and dialects. Events threw on own resources; started as an operative in a factory; then manager, overseer, merchant; saw financial opening in 1882 in the collapse of the S.A. Diamond Mines; organised, as originator, and carried through the Diamond Mines Monopoly, called De Beers Co.; made a large fortune, but rascally lawyer bolted with his money, 1893; buckled up and set to work again. *Publications:* Connection of the Welsh and Oriental Languages; Seven Years of an Indian Officer's Life; Plassey, an Ode; Poems from the Persian; Memoirs of G. Tresham Gregg, D.D., the Orientalist, Rector of St. Patrick's, Dublin; When I served with General Gordon; Life of Richard Fenton, K.C., F.A.S., the historian; Life of John Fenton, the archæologist; St. Paul's Epistles in Modern English; The New Testament in Modern English; The Book of Job in Modern English and the Original Metre; The Five Books of Moses, direct from the Hebrew, in Modern English, with Critical Notes; The Six Historical Books of the Bible; The Books of the Prophets in the Original Verse or Prose; The Psalms and Sacred Writers; Complete Holy Bible in Modern English, with Critical Notes; The Bible and Wine. *Recreations:* having an object to accomplish and study for attaining it. *Address:* 8 King's Road, Mitcham.

FENTON, Sir Myles, Kt., *cr.* 1889; J.P.; Consulting Director South-Eastern and Chatham Railway since 1896; Lt.-Col. Engineer and Railway Vol. Staff Corps; Chevalier of Legion of Honour of France; Officer of Order of Leopold of Belgium; *b.* Kendal, 5 Sept. 1830; *s.* of Myles Fenton, Kendal; *m.* Charlotte Jane, *d.* of G. Oakes. *Educ.:* Kendal. Commenced on Kendal and Windermere Railway, 1845; after holding situations on East Lancashire, Great Eastern (then Eastern Counties), London and S.-Western, Manchester, Sheffield, and Lincolnshire (now Great Central) Railways, and Rochdale Canal, became Secretary of East Lancashire Railway, 1856; afterwards Assistant Manager of Lancashire and Yorkshire; General Manager Metropolitan Railway, 1863; South-Eastern Railway, 1880. *Address:* Redstone Hall, Redhill, Surrey.   *(Died 14 Mar. 1918.)*

FENTON, Rt. Rev. Patrick; Auxiliary R.C. Bishop to Cardinal Bourne, and Bishop of Amycla since 1904; *b.* London, 1837; *s.* of Bartholomew Fenton, Cork. *Educ.:* St. Edmund's, Old Hall, Ware; President, 1882-87; ordained, 1866; served successively at Ogle Street, at the Bavarian Chapel, and under Mgr. Gilbert at St. Mary's, Moorfields; Conventual Chaplain of the Order of the Knights of St. John of Jerusalem since 1878; Domestic Prelate to Leo XIII., 1885-87; Rector of St. Thomas, Fulham, 1887; Canon of Westminster, 1895; Titular Bishop of Amycla, and Vicar-General of Westminster; Provost of the Metropolitan Chapter; The First Administrator of the Westminster Cathedral, 1899. *Address:* 30 Morpeth Mansions, Westminster, S.W.1.
                        (Died Aug. 1918.)

FENTON, (Thomas) Charles, I.S.O. 1912; late of the Parliamentary Branch, India Office. Called to Bar, Middle Temple, 1898. *Recreations:* horticulture and antiquities. *Address:* Cranford, Vineyard Hill, Wimbledon Park, S.W.
                        (Died 7 April 1927.)

FENTON, William Hugh, M.D., M.A., M.R.C.S., L.R.C.P.; Senior Surgeon, Chelsea Hospital for Women; Surgeon to Society of Women Journalists; *b.* Shardlow, Derbyshire, 1854; *e. s.* of Michael Thomas Fenton Jones, M.D.; *m.* 1887, Alice Anne, *e. d.* of William Foster, Hornby Castle, Lancaster, J.P., D.L.; no *c. Educ.:* Derby School; Merton College, Oxford (Postmaster in Natural Science); Honours in Natural Science, B.A., 1876; M.A., 1886. Lecturer on Midwifery and Diseases of Women, Zenana Medical Mission; Vice-President and Hon. Secretary, British Gynæcological Society; Gold Medallist in Surgery and Duckworth Nelson Prizeman, London Hospital; Surgeon to Throat Hospital, Golden Square; Surgeon to London Throat Hospital. *Publications:* Contributions to medical journals; also Nineteenth Century. *Recreations:* salmon fishing, shooting, and motoring. *Address:* Litley Court, Hereford. *M.:* LE 3663. *Club:* Royal Automobile. *(Died 5 Oct. 1928.)*

FENWICK, Right Hon. Charles, P.C. 1911; M.P. (G.L.) Northumberland, Wansbeck, since 1885; *b.* Cramlington, Northumberland, 5 May 1850; *s.* of late John Fenwick, Bebside, Northumberland; *m.* 1869, Jane, *d.* of H. Gardner. A working miner, 1860-85; Delegate to Trades Union Congress, 1883; Secretary to Parliamentary Committee on Trades Unions, 1890; Member of Parliamentary Coal-Dust Commission, 1891; served on Royal Commission on Secondary Education, 1894. *Address:* 14 Tankerville Terrace, Newcastle-on-Tyne; 95 Vauxhall Bridge Road, S.W. *(Died 20 April 1918.)*

FENWICK, Hon. Sir (George) Townsend, K.C.M.G., *cr.* 1912; C.M.G. 1904; late senior unofficial member Legislative Council Trinidad and Tobago; *b.* 25 Jan. 1846; *s.* of John Fenwick of Preston House, Northumberland; *m.* 1873, Lucy Frances (*d.* 1916), *d.* of J. T. Bowen of Trinidad; one *d. Educ.:* Stockton; St. Mary's College, Windermere. *Address:* Port of Spain, Trinidad, West Indies. *Clubs:* Wellington, West Indian; Union, Savannah, Trinidad. *(Died 25 Mar. 1927.)*

FERGUSON, Lieut.-Col. George Arthur, J.P., D.L.; *b.* 17 Mar. 1835; *s.* of Rear-Adm. George Ferguson and Hon. Elizabeth Jane Rowley, *d.* of 1st Baron Langford; *m.* 1861, Hon. Nina Maria Hood (*d.* 1928), *e. d.* of 1st Viscount Bridport; three *s.* two *d.* Formerly Grenadier Guards; served Crimea, including Fall of Sebastopol, 1855 (medal and clasp and Turkish medal). *Heir: s.* Lt.-Col. Arthur George Ferguson. *Address:* Pitfour, Mintlaw, Aberdeenshire. *(Died 15 Dec. 1924.)*

FERGUSON, James, of Kinmundy, K.C. 1902; Sheriff of Forfarshire since 1905; D.L. and J.P. Aberdeenshire; *e.* and *o. surv. s.* of Wm. Ferguson of Kinmundy (Aberdeenshire); *b.,* 28 July 1857; *m.* Georgina Anne, *e. d.* of Capt. John de Courcy Agnew, R.N., 1885; one *s. Educ.:* Birkenhead School; Craigmount School; Edin. Univ. M.A. Called to Scots Bar, 1879; appointed Assistant Advocate-Depute, 1888; Advocate-Depute, 1892; reappointed, 1895; Senior Advocate-Depute, 1896-98; was Honorary Secretary, National Union of Conservative Associations for Scotland, Central Office, 1882-92; Lieut.-Col. and Hon. Col. (V.D.) 1st Batt. 9th V.B. (Highlanders) Royal Scots, 1900-4; Lieut.-Col. 2nd Batt., 1914-15, and 3rd Batt. since 1915; Sheriff of Argyllshire, 1898-1905; of Inverness, Elgin, and Nairn, Jan.-May 1905. *Publications: Legal*—Railway Rights and Duties, 1889; Five Years' Railway Cases, 1894; The Law of Railways in Scotland, by F. Deas, revised and extended, 1897; Scottish Railway Statutes, 1898; The Law of Roads, Streets, and Rights of Way in Scotland, 1904; The Law of Water in Scotland, 1907;

Railway Cases and Statutes, 1897-1912, 1913. *General*—Robert Ferguson the Plotter, 1887; Two Scottish Soldiers, 1888; Records of 3rd (the Buchan) Vol. Batt. the Gordon Highlanders, 1894; Records of Clan and Name of Ferguson, etc. (with Rev. J. Menzies Fergusson), 1895 and 1899; Papers illustrating the History of the Scots Brigade in the service of the United Netherlands (Scottish History Society), 1899-1901; Records of 9th Vol. Batt. (Highlanders) the Royal Scots, 1909. *Address:* 10 Wemyss Place, Edinburgh; Kinmundy, Mintlaw, N.B. *Clubs:* Carlton; New, Edinburgh; Royal Northern, Aberdeen. *(Died 25 April 1917.)*

FERGUSON, John, M.A., M.D. (Tor.), L.R.C.P. (Edin.), L.F.P.S. (Glas.); Senior Physician, Toronto Western Hospital; Associate Professor of Medicine, University of Toronto; Editor, The Canada Lancet; President, Ontario Publishing Company; Medical Referee, Excelsior Life Assurance Company; Medical Referee, Dominion of Canada Accident Company; sometime Secretary, Ontario Hospital Association; Grand Medical Examiner of the Sons of Scotland Benevolent Association; *b.* Glasgow, Scotland, 1854; *s.* of Adam Ferguson and Elizabeth Donaldson, both of Glasgow; *m.* 1882, Helen Baird of Toronto. *Educ.:* Walton Village Public School; Clinton Collegiate Institute; University of Toronto; Edinburgh and London. Came to Ontario when very young; was Demonstrator of Anatomy in Medical Department, Toronto University, for eleven years; lectured on nervous diseases, and was for some years Examiner in Anatomy; took an active part in the organisation of the Excelsior Life Insurance Company, of the Ontario Publishing Company, of the Toronto Western Hospital, and of the Ontario Hospital Association; sometime Chairman of the Toronto High School Board; has been in medical practice for 35 years. *Publications:* The Canada Lancet; numerous articles and addresses, as—Diet in Epilepsy, Nerve Path of Taste, Nerve Degeneration in Lead, Arsenic and Alcoholism, Observations on Hemiplegia, The Knee Jerk, Selection of Insurance Risks, The Phrenic Nerve, Reply to Dr. Osler, Capital Punishment, Addresses to Students; Text-Book of Pathology; The Physiology and Pathology of the Internal Secretory Glands; The Relation of Sickness and Accidents in Insurance Work; The Medical Aspects of Septic Peritonitis; Sir William Tennant Gairdner, the Ideal Physician, etc. *Recreations:* boating, curling, violin-playing, natural history. *Address:* 264 College Street, Toronto. *(Died 3 Nov. 1916.)*

FERGUSON, John Macrae, I.S.O. 1911; Collector of Customs and Excise, Edinburgh, since 1907; *b.* 11 Nov. 1849; 3rd *s.* of Alexander Ferguson, farmer and land steward, Burnside of Newhall, parish of Resolis, Ross-shire, and Flora Mackenzie; *m.* 1882, Eliza Jane, *o. d.* of Henry Kellas, farmer, Strathdon, Aberdeenshire; four *s.* two *d. Educ.:* Free Church School, Resolis. Entered the Excise Service 1870; passed through all grades in Department; appointed Collector, 1899; promoted to Manchester, 1st Class, 1906. *Address:* Woodfield, Banchory. *(Died 15 Dec. 1919.)*

FERGUSSON, Sir James Ranken, 2nd Bt., *cr.* 1866; J.P., Vice-Lieutenant: *b.* 10 Aug. 1835; *e. s.* of 1st Bt., and Helen Hamilton, *d.* of William Ranken of Spitalhaugh; *S.* father 1877; *m.* 1st, 1862, Mary Ann (*d.* 1868), *d.* of late Thomas Colyer of Wombwell Hall, Northfleet; one *s.*; 2nd, 1877, Louisa (*d.* 1878), *d.* of late William Forbes; one *s.*; 3rd, 1886, Alice, *d.* of late J. P. Simpson; one *s.* two *d. Educ.:* King's Coll. London; Christ Church, Oxford. Barr. Lincoln's Inn, 1858; F.S.A.Scot.; Member of Royal Archers, King's. Bodyguard for Scotland; County Councillor,

FERGUSON, Hon. William Nassau. See page xix.

Peeblesshire, etc. *Publications:* Poems and Ballads, 1876. *Recreations:* books, fishing, shooting, country life and occupations. *Heir:* s. Thomas Colyer Colyer-Fergusson. *Address:* Spitalhaugh, West Linton, N.B. *Clubs:* Constitutional ; New, Edinburgh.
(Died 28 Oct. 1924.)

FERGUSSON, Lt.-Col. Vivian Moffatt, D.S.O. 1916 ; R.A. ; 3rd *s.* of late James Fergusson, F.R.C.S.E., and Mrs. Fergusson, Lincoln House, Richmond, Surrey ; *m.* 1918, Dulce Alice Mollie D'Ewes, *e. d.* of Percy U. Allen, I.C.S. Served European War, 1914-18 (despatches, D.S.O., Bt. Lieut.-Col.). *Club:* Naval and Military. *(Died 16 Nov. 1926.)*

FERMOY, 2nd Baron (*cr.* 1856), **Edmund Fitz-Edmund Burke Roche,** D.L. ; *b.* 23 May 1850 ; *s.* of 1st Baron and Eliza (*d.* 1897), *e. d.* of J. B. Boothby, Twyford Abbey, Middlesex ; *S.* father 1874 ; *m.* 1877, Hon. Cecilia O'Grady (*d.* 1919), *d.* of 3rd Viscount Guillamore ; one *d.* Owns about 21,400 acres. *Heir: b.* Hon. James B. B. Roche. *Address:* Rockbarton, Bruff, County Limerick. *(Died 1 Sept. 1920.)*

FERMOY, 3rd Baron (*cr.* 1856) ; **James Boothby Burke Roche,** B.A. ; *b.* 28 July 1852 ; 2nd *s.* of 1st Baron Fermoy ; *S.* brother 1920 ; *m.* 1880, Frances, *d.* of F. Work, of New York ;—two *s.* one *d. Educ.:* Trin. Coll. Camb. (M.A.). M.P. (N.) for East Kerry, 1896-1900. *Heir: s.* Hon. Edmund Maurice Roche, *b.* 15 May 1885. *Address:* 60 St. James's Street, S.W. *Clubs:* Brooks's, Hurlingham.
(Died 30 Oct. 1920.)

FERNOW, Prof. Bernhard Eduard, LL.D., Dean, Faculty of Forestry, University of Toronto, 1907-19 (Professor Emeritus) ; *b.* Inowraclaw, Prussia, Jan. 7, 1851 ; *m.* 1879, Olivia Reynolds of Brooklyn, N.Y. ; four *s. Educ.:* Forest Academy, Münden ; University, Königsberg. Six years Prussian Forest Dept. ; ten years variously occupied ; Chief, Division of Forestry, U.S. Dept. of Agriculture, 1886-98 ; Director Forest School, Cornell University, Ithaca, N.Y., 1898-1903 ; private, 1903-6 ; Professor of Forestry, State College, Pennsylvania, 1907. *Publications:* Economics of Forestry ; The Care of Trees ; Short History of Forestry. *Address:* University, Toronto.

FERRERO, Baron Augusto, Assistant Editor of La Tribuna, Rome ; *b.* Turin ; *s.* of Col. F. Ferrero ; *m.* Gina, *e. d.* of Senator Roux. *Educ.:* Turin University. Journalist, formerly at the Stampa of Turin. *Publications:* Nostalgie d'Amore (verses) ; From Florence to Rome, a Political Diary of 1870-71 ; The Cartoons of Teja, a series of humoristic cartoons on recent Italian history ; The Marriage Law. *Recreations:* any kind of sport, from horse-riding and fencing to bicycling. *Address:* Office of La Tribuna, Rome.

FERRIER, Sir David, Kt., *cr.* 1911 ; M.A., M.D., LL.D., D.Sc., F.R.C.P., F.R.S. ; Emeritus Prof. of Neuropathology, King's College, Lond. ; Consulting Physician to King's Coll. Hospital, and to the National Hospital for Paralysed and Epileptic ; *b.* 13 Jan. 1848 ; *m.* Constance, *d.* of late Albert C. Waterlow, 1874 ; one *s.* one *d. Educ.:* Aberdeen, Edinburgh, Heidelberg. Graduated M.A. (Aberdeen), 1863 (1st class Hons.) ; M.D. (Edinburgh), 1870. *Publications:* Functions of the Brain, 1876 ; Cerebral Localisation, 1878, 1890, etc. *Recreations:* various. *Address:* 27 York House, Kensington, W.8. *T.:* Park 4033. *Club:* Athenæum. *(Died 19 Mar. 1928.)*

FESSENDEN, Clementina, Founder of Empire Day ; contributor to the Press on current topics ; *d.* of Marion Ridley and Edward Trenholm, Trenholme, Quebec ; *b.* and *educ.* in that Province ; *m.* E. J. Fessenden, B.A., late Rector of Ancaster ; three *s.* Early identified with national work, she is a member of the National Council of Women ; a representative member of the League of Empire ; Convener
350

Flag Committee, Ontario Historical Society ; Corresponding Secretary, Wentworth Historical Society ; President, Shaftesbury Ragged School Dinner Fund of Hamilton, Ontario. An ardent Imperialist ; member of English Church ; Conservative ; originated the idea of Empire Day, 1897 ; edited the Niagara Letter Leaflet ; author of brochure Our Union Jack ; a member of the Anti-Suffrage League, England ; hon. member, Canadian Women's Historical Society ; hon. Regent, St. Hilda's Chapter, Daughters of the Empire ; hon. Life Member National Chapter of Canada, Imperial Order Daughters of the Empire, 1913. *Address:* Hamilton, Ontario, Canada. *(Died 14 Sept. 1918.)*

FESTING, Gabrielle ; *b.* The Residences, South Kensington Museum ; *d.* of Maj.-Gen. E. Robert Festing, R.E., C.B., F.R.S., and Frances Mary Legrew. *Publications:* John Hookham Frere and His Friends ; Unstoried in History ; On the Distaff Side ; From the Land of Princes ; When Kings Rode to Delhi ; Strangers within the Gates ; Honor Among Thieves ; The Gift of a Son. *Recreations:* music (Member of Bach Choir), cooking, embroidery. *Address:* 56 Queen's Gate Terrace, S.W.
(Died 17 April 1924.)

FESTING, Major Harold England, D.S.O. 1916 ; *b.* 18 Feb. 1886 ; *s.* of late Major-Gen. Sir Francis W. Festing, K.C.M.G., C.B., Royal Marine Artillery, and Selina Eleanor Mary, *d.* of L. W. Carbonell, who *m.* 2nd Col. R. C. Drysdale, R.A. (*d.* 1904). *Educ.:* Cheltenham College ; Sandhurst. Was page of honour to Queen Victoria and King Edward VII., 1897-1902 ; joined 1st Border Regt., 1905 ; Captain, 1914 ; Major, 1922 ; awarded Royal Humane Society's medal in India, 1914 ; served European War (Gallipoli), 1915 (wounded, despatches, D.S.O.) ; France, 1918 (despatches, bar to D.S.O., French Croix de Guerre). *Recreations:* fishing and shooting. *Club:* Junior United Service. *(Died 14 Oct. 1923.)*

FETHERSTON, Rev. Sir George Ralph, 6th Bt., *cr.* 1776 ; Fellow and Vice-President, the Incorporated Guild of Church Musicians, London ; Fellow and Vice-President, the Victoria College of Music, London ; J.P. Co. Longford ; *b.* Dublin, 8 April 1852 ; *o. s.* of 5th Bt., and Sarah, *y. d.* of Harry Alcock, Wilton Castle, Wexford ; *S.* father 1869. *Educ.:* Brighton Coll. ; Theological Coll. Salisbury. Ordained Salisbury Cathedral, 1880 ; Priest, 1883 ; Vicar of Pydeltrenthide, 1887-1893 ; High Sheriff, Co. Longford, 1897 ; Jubilee medal, 1897 ; Hon. Assistant Chaplain, the Queen Alexandra Military Hospital, Millbank, S.W., 1916 ; Licensed Curate of St. Martin's Parish Church, Worcester ; has visited North America, Europe, Africa, Malta, Portugal, South America (Brazil), St. Vincent, Canada, Canary Islands, Egypt, Madeira, Corsica. Owns island Innisclerann, in Lough Ree. *Publications:* The Mystery in Maple Street ; Loyalty in Sorrow ; Interrupted Harmony ; Through Corsica with a Pencil, 1914 ; A Legend of Corpus Christi, 1915 ; An Incident in the Siege of Antwerp (a poem) ; A Garden Eastward, and other Sermons ; A Marriage Address, 1919 ; The Rose of England, 1919 ; The Malvern Hills (a poem) 1921. Composer of 150 hymn tunes, also various chants, songs, and other music. *Recreations:* music, photography, cycling, fishing ; is an ornithologist, entomologist, philatelist, collector of ancient china. *Heir:* none. *Address:* Cleeve Court, Kempsey, Worcester ; Ardagh House, Edgeworthstown, Co. Longford. *M.:* NP. 268. *Clubs:* Authors', Royal Automobile.
(Died 11 Feb. 1923.)

FETHERSTONHAUGH, Godfrey, K.C. 1898 ; M.P. (U.) Fermanagh N. 1906-16 (resigned Oct. 1916) ; *b.* 1858 ; *s.* of Stephen R. Fetherstonhaugh of Milltown, Co. Westmeath, and Rokeby, Co. Dublin. *Educ.:* Chard Grammar

School ; Trin. Coll. Dublin (Scholar in Classics, 1878 ; First Senior Moderator in Classics, 1880 ; M.A. 1883). Called to Irish Bar, 1888 ; called to English Bar, 1895 ; Bencher of King's Inn, 1900 ; J.P. Fermanagh. *Recreations:* fishing, shooting. *Address:* Glenmore, Crossmolina, Co. Mayo. *Clubs:* Junior Constitutional ; University, Dublin. *(Died Sept. 1928.)*

FETHERSTONHAUGH-WHITNEY, Henry Ernest William, J.P., D.L. , *o. surv. s.* of Rev. Sir Thomas Francis Fetherston, 4th Bart., and 2nd wife Anne. *d.* of late Edmund L'Estrange ; *b.* 21 Nov. 1847 ; *m.* 1st, 1876, Jeannie (*d.* 1880), *y. d.* of late Edward Atkinson ; 2nd, 1885, Alice Marion Caroline, *e. d.* of late Col. Robert Caulfeild of Camolin House, Co. Wexford. *Educ.:* Trinity College, Dublin. Assumed name of Fetherstonhaugh-Whitney by Royal license, 1881. High Sheriff, Westmeath, 1887 ; Capt. and Hon. Major late 7th Batt. King's Royal Rifle Corps ; formerly Lieut. 60th Rifles. *Address:* Furry Park, Raheny, Co. Dublin ; Newpass Rathowen, Co. Westmeath. *Club:* Junior United Service.

(Died 3 Sept. 1921.)

FEVERSHAM, 2nd Earl of (*cr.* 1868), **Charles William Reginald Duncombe** ; Baron Feversham (U.K.), 1862 ; Viscount Helmsley, 1868 ; Major, Yorkshire Hussars, Imperial Yeomanry ; M.F.H. Sinnington Hounds since 1904 ; *b.* 8 May 1879 ; *s. s.* of William Reginald Viscount Helmsley, M.P. (*d.* 1881), and Muriel, Viscountess Helmsley. *S.* grandfather, 1st Earl, 1915 ; *m.* 1904, Lady Marjorie Greville, *e. d.* of 5th Earl of Warwick; *two s. one d. Educ.:* Christ Church, Oxford ; M.P. (U.) Thirsk and Malton Div., N.R., Yorks, 1906-15 ; Assistant Private Secretary to 1st Lord of Admiralty (Lord Selborne), 1902-5. *Heir:* s. Viscount Helmsley. *Address:* Duncombe Park, Helmsley, Yorkshire. *Clubs:* Carlton, Turf, Bachelors', Pratt's, Ranelagh ; Yorkshire, York.(*Died 15 Sept. 1916.*)

FFINCH, Rev. Matthew Mortimer, Chaplain of Huggens College, Northfleet, Kent, since 1870 ; Hon. Canon of Rochester, 1908 ; Rural Dean of Gravesend, 1909; *b.* Greenwich, Dec. 1838 ; 2nd *s.* of John Drake Ffinch of Greenwich ; *m.* 1863, Lydia Jane (*d.* 1915), *d.* of late John Jones Dyer of the Admiralty, Whitehall ; four *s. one d. Educ.:* Christ's Hospital ; Oriel College, Oxford. Assistant Curate, Holy Trinity and St. Peter's, Shaftesbury, 1862 ; Donhead St. Mary, Wilts, 1863-70. *Address:* The College, Northfleet. *(Died 8 Feb. 1920.)*

FFRANGCON-DAVIES, David, M.A. Oxon. ; Hon. R.A.M. London ; Vocal Artist, and late Professor at the Royal Academy of Music, London ; *b.* Carnarvonshire, 11 Dec. 1850 ; *s.* of David and Gwen Ffrangcon-Davies ; *m.* Annie Frances, *d.* of late Thomas Rayner, M.D., of Manchester ; two *d. Educ.:* private tutors ; Friars School ; Jesus College, Oxford (Classical Exhibitioner). Educated for and entered the Church ; owing to theological difficulties resigned position, and became vocal student ; has sung in opera at Covent Garden and Drury Lane, and continues to sing in oratorios at all the principal festivals of the world ; has toured 12 seasons in America ; resided 3 years in Berlin, taking his position in the German art world ; his public work is now confined to festivals and great choral societies. *Publication:* The Singing of the Future. *Recreations:* theology and philosophy. *(Died 13 April 1918.)*

FIASCHI, Col. Thomas Henry, D.S.O. 1901 ; N.S.W. A.M.C. ; Surgeon practising in Sydney ; Hon. Consulting Surgeon Sydney Hospital; *b.* Florence, 3 May 1853; *s.* of late Prof. L. Fiaschi of Florence, and Clarissa Fisher ; *m.* 1st, 1886, Katherine Anna, *d.* of James W. Reynolds ; 2nd, Amy Curtis, *d.* of Capt. W. E. Curtis of Bundaberg, Queensland. *Educ.:* Pisa and

Florence Universities. M.D., Ch.D., Pisa and Florence. Came to Australia, 1875 ; practised at first in Windsor, N.S.W.; settled in Sydney, 1883 ; joined the N.S.W. Army Medical Corps, 1891 ; was attached as Medical Officer to New South Wales Lancers ; obtained leave of absence for six months and joined the Italian army in Abyssinia, 1896, marching with them as far as Kassala ; received cross of Cavaliere dei SS. Maurizio e Lazzaro from late King Humbert for special merits during Italo-Abyssinian campaign ; in Oct. 1899 volunteered for active service in South Africa, where he remained till 1900 in command of the New South Wales No. 1 Field Hospital ; specially mentioned by Lord Roberts for services rendered at Paardeberg ; S.M.O. to Gen. Hutton's Brigade ; Col. A.M.C. 1911 ; served with the A.I.F. at Lemnos, O.C. of 3rd Australian General Hospital ; invalided to England; went to Italy and served as Surgeon with Italian Red Cross, 73 Ospedale di Guerre, at Schio. *Publication:* Da Cheren a Cassala, 1896. *Address:* 149 Macquarie Street, Sydney. *Club:* Australian. *(Died 16 April 1927.)*

FIELD, Major Kenneth Douglas, D.S.O. 1917 ; R.G.A. ; on service in France ; *s.* of late Joshua Field, J.P., D.L.; *b.* 12 Aug. 1880 ; *m.* 1913, Elizabeth Mary, *d.* of J. H. Noble, M.A., of Selby House, Ham Common ; two *d. Educ.:* Woolwich ; served in Indian Mountain Artillery, and as Instructor in gunnery ; active service in Waziristan, 1901 ; operations against Darwesh Khels, and Tibet (Indian g.s. medal, medal for Tibet) ; European War (D.S.O.). *Recreations:* reading and travel. *Address:* Selby House, Ham Common, Surrey.

FIELDHOUSE, William John, C.B.E. 1918, F.S.A., J.P. ; *b.* 1858 ; *m.* 1882, Lucy, *d.* of Abraham Wood. *Educ.:* Newport Grammar School. Head of George H. Hughes Ltd., St. Stephen's Wheel Works, Birmingham. *Address:* Austy Manor, Wootton Wawen, Warwickshire. *Club:* Royal Thames Yacht.

(Died 28 Oct. 1928.)

FIELDING-HALL, Harold ; Retired ; *b.* Rathowen, Ireland, 1859 ; *o. s.* of H. B. Hall, D.C.L. ; last representative of the Halls of Birtley and Consett, Co. Durham, from 1407 ; *m.* 1905, Margaret Evelyn, *d.* of J. M. Smith, Ceylon, and Cornwall Gardens.; one *s.* one *d. Educ.:* Leamington College. Went round world in sailing ship, 1878 ; coffee planting in Wynaad, 1879-85 ; in Upper Burma before the war ; entered Government Service, 1886 ; Political Officer, 1887-91 (medal and two clasps) ; visited China and Japan, 1891 ; Famine Officer, 1896-97 ; District Magistrate, 1901 ; organised Rural Banks, 1904-6 ; retired, 1906. *Publications:* The Soul of a People ; The Hearts of Men ; The World Soul ; The Inward Light ; Famine Manual ; A People at School ; The Passing of Empire ; Margaret's Book ; Love's Legend, 1914 ; For England, 1916 ; etc. *Recreations:* shooting, sailing, golf. *Address:* 4 Essex Court, Temple, E.C. *Club:* Savage.

(Died 5 May 1917.)

FIENNES, Gerard Yorke Twisleton-Wykeham, C.B.E. 1920, Chevalier of the Order of Leopold I. of Belgium, 1918 ; *b.* 18 July 1864 ; *e. s.* of late Rev. Hon. Wingfield T. W. Fiennes, 4th *s.* of 14th Baron Saye and Sele, and Alice, *d.* of Very Rev. Hon. Grantham Yorke, Dean of Worcester ; *m.* 1905, Gwendolen, *o. c.* of late Francis Gisborne of Holme Hall, Bakewell ; five *s. Educ.:* Winchester ; New College, Oxon., 3rd class Mod. Hist., B.A. 1888. Tutor to sons of Rajah of Sarawak, 1887 ; visited Sarawak with them; Assistant Editor New Review, 1891-3; member London School Board, 1893-6(Hackney); Secretary, Unionist Association, N. Bucks Division, 1896-1900 ; Assist. Editor, St. James's Gazette, 1901-3 ; Editor, 1903 ; Editor Birmingham Gazette and Express, 1904-5; Assist. Editor Standard, 1905-7; Assist. Editor Pall Mall Gazette, 1912-15; again of Standard, 1915-16; writer on naval matters for Observer, Daily Graphic, etc.; General Editor National War Aims Committee, Oct. 1917-Dec. 1918; Church of England; no Party. *Publications:* The Ocean Empire, 1911; Navy at War, 1916; Sea Power and Freedom (a course of Lectures to L.C.C. Teachers), 1917; and with L. G. Pilkington, Getting our Living, an easy Handbook of Economics for Schools, 1924; articles in Nineteenth Century, Fortnightly, New Review Navy League Annual, etc. *Recreations:* cricket, lawn tennis, rowing till too old. *Address:* Wellwick, Wendover. *T.:* Wendover 68. *Club:* Savile. *(Died 15 Jan. 1926.)*

FIFE, Colonel Sir Aubone, Kt., cr. 1902; C.V.O. 1909; standard-bearer of H.M.'s Bodyguard of Gentlemen-at-Arms; b. 1 Feb. 1846; 3rd s. of late W. H. Fife and g.-s. of late Sir John Fife of Ghortanloisk, Argyll. *Educ.:* Cheltenham College. Entered army, 1866; served Canadian Frontier, 1866; Afghan War, 1879-80 (medal); Burmese Expedition, 1886-87 (medal with clasp); formerly Adjutant and Clerk of the Cheque H.M.'s Bodyguard. *Address:* St. James's Palace, and 42 Jermyn Street, S.W.; Lee.Hall, Wark, Northumberland. *(Died 5 Feb. 1920.)*

FIGG, Captain Donald Whitly, D.S.O. 1915; 24th (County of London) Batt. the London Regiment (the Queen's), T.F. Served European War, 1914-15 (D.S.O.). *Address:* Garlands, Redhill, Surrey. *(Died 5 Mar. 1917.)*

FIGGIS, Rev. J. B., M.A.; Chairman of the Countess of Huntingdon's Trustees; b. Dublin; m. 1862, Harriet Webb Chaffey (d. 1914); two s. *Educ.:* Taunton School; Trinity College, Dublin (M.A.); New College, London (Scholar). Ordained, 1861; Pastor, North Street Church, Brighton, 1861-97; Emmanuel Church, Hove, 1897-1912. *Publications:* Keswick from Within; Agnosticism; Christ and Full Salvation; The Christ Life; Visions, etc. *Address:* 38 Compton Avenue, Brighton.
(Died 4 Sept. 1916.)

FIGGIS, Rev. John Neville, D.D., Litt. D.; Member of Community of Resurrection since 1909; Hon. Fellow, St. Catherine's College, Cambridge; b. Brighton, 2 Oct. 1866; s. of late Rev. John Benjamin Figgis, M.A. *Educ.:* Brighton College; St. Catharine's College, Cambridge (Scholar); Wells Theological College. Senior Optime, 1888, and B.A.; 1st class Hist. Tripos, 1889; Lightfoot Scholarship, 1890; 2nd Whewell Scholarship, 1891; Prince Consort Prize, 1892 M.A.; Curate of Kettering, 1894-95; Great St. Mary's, Cambridge, 1895-98; Lecturer in St. Catharine's College, 1895-1901; Chaplain Pembroke College, 1898-1900; Birkbeck Lecturer in Trinity College, 1900; Rector of Marnhull, Dorset, 1901-7; Examiner to Univ. of Cambridge in Historical Tripos, Lightfoot, etc.; Hulsean Lecturer, 1908-9; Noble Lecturer, Harvard, 1911; Bishop Paddock Lecturer, General Theological Seminary, New York, 1913; Bross Lecturer, Lake Forest, Illinois, 1915. *Publications:* Divine Right of Kings, 1896; Illustrations of English History, 1660-1715, 1902; Christianity and History 1904; From Gerson to Grotius, 1907; The Gospel and Human Needs, 1909; Religion and English Society, 1910; Civilisation at the Cross Roads, 1912; Antichrist, 1913; Churches in the Modern State, 1913; The Fellowship of the Mystery, 1914; Some Defects in English Religion, 1916; The Will to Freedom (lectures on Nietzsche), 1917; contributor to Cambridge Modern History; editor with R. V. Laurence of Lord Acton's Lectures and Essays. *Address:* House of Resurrection, Mirfield. *(Died 13 April 1919.)*

FILDES, Sir Luke, K.C.V.O., cr. 1918; Kt., cr. 1906; R.A., 1887; b. England, 18 Oct. 1843; m.

1874, Fanny, d. of William Woods, Warrington; four s. two d. *Educ.:* private school. Studied South Kensington Art Schools and Royal Academy, London; illustrator of books and magazines for several years; afterwards painted English and Venetian subjects; latterly portraits. *Paintings:* first picture, Fair, Quiet, and Sweet Rest, exhibited R.A. 1872; The Casual Ward, 1874; The Widower, 1876; The Return of the Penitent, 1879; The Village Wedding; Venetian Life; The Al Fresco Toilette; The Doctor, 1892; The State Portrait of the King, 1902; The State Portrait of the Queen, 1905; The State Portrait of the King, 1912. *Address:* 11 Melbury Road, Kensington, W.14. *T.:* Park 4552. *Club:* Athenæum. *(Died 27 Feb. 1927.)*

PILGATE, William de Salis, J.P. and D.L.; High Sheriff, Co. Louth, 1879; b. 2 Dec. 1834; m. 1870, Georgiana Harriet, e. d. of late William John French of Ardsallagh, Co. Meath; two d. *Educ.:* Rugby; Cheltenham College. Louth Rifle Militia, 1855-58; permanent duty, retired as Captain; Master of Louth Hounds since 1860. *Address:* Lissrenny, Ardee, Co. Louth. *Club:* Sackville St., Dublin.
(Died 11 June 1916.)

FILMER, Sir Robert Marcus, 10th Bt., cr. 1674; b. 25 Feb. 1878; s. of 9th Bt. and Mary Georgiana Carolina, e. d. of Lord Arthur Marcus Hill, 4th s. of 2nd Marquess of Downshire, who succeeded his brother as 3rd Baron Sandys, 1880; S. father 1887. Served in Grenadier Guards, 1897-1904; Soudan campaign, 1898; South African War, 1899-1902; Lt. Reserve of Officers, 1904; contested (U) N.W. Durham, 1906; Lincoln, Jan. and Dec. 1910; Lieut. Royal East Kent Mounted Rifles, 1907; Major, 1912; rejoined the Grenadier Guards from the R. East Kent Yeomanry, Feb. 1915, for the duration of the War. Owns about 10,000 acres. *Heir:* none. *Address:* Little Charlton Manor, East Sutton, Maidstone, Kent. *Clubs:* Guards', Turf, Carlton, Beefsteak.
(Died 27 Jan. 1916.)

PILOSE, Lt.-Col. Sir Michael, K.C.I.E., cr. 1911; C.I.E. 1908; Chief Secretary Huzur Durbar, Gwalior since 1894; s. of Major Julien Filose, Gwalior; b. 18 April 1836; m. 1853, Annie Donnery; two s. five d. *Educ.:* London University College. Accompanied Jiageerao Maharaja Scindia on his retreat to Agra during the mutiny of 1857; Major and Director of Public Instruction, Educational Department, 1863; designed and built Jai Vilas Palace, Gwalior, 1872-74; constructed Jal Mahal Moti Mahal, Law Courts, Central Jail, etc.; carried out first revenue survey of the Malwa Praut, 1879-81; Governor of the Province of Malway, 1882; Lt.-Col. 1891; Knight of the Order of St. Sylvester, 1874. *Address:* Gwalior, India. *Clubs:* Aligha, Elgin, Gwalior. *(Died 5 Feb. 1925.)*

PINCK, Henry T., A.B.; on editorial staff, New York Evening Post and Nation, 1881-1924; (specialty, musical criticism); b. Bethel, Shelby Co., Missouri, 22 Sep. 1854; s. of Henry C. Finck and Beatrice; m. 1890, Abbie H. Cushman. *Educ.:* Harvard (1872-76); Heidelberg, Berlin (1878-81); (specialties, psychology, sociology). Harris Fellowship (1878 - 81) of Harvard; highest honours in philosophy. Professor of Musical History at National Conservatory. *Publications:* Anton Seidl, a Memorial; Wagner and his Works; Chopin and other Musical Essays; Songs and Song - Writers; Paderewski and his Art; Grieg and his Music; Development of Musical Instruments; Success in Music; Massenet and his Operas; Romantic Love and Personal Beauty; Primitive Love and Love Stories; Pacific Coast Scenic Tour; Spain and Morocco; Lotos Time in Japan; Food and Flavour; Richard Strauss; Gardening with Brains; Girth Control; Musical Progress; Musical Laughs; My Adventures in the Golden

Age of Music, 1926; magazine articles on woman question, psychology, gastronomy, etc.; Editor of Fifty Master-Songs, Thirty Sterling Songs for High Schools, Fifty Grieg Songs, and Fifty Schubert Songs. *Recreations:* travel, walking, gardening. *Address:* Bethel, Maine, U.S.A. *(Died 1 Oct. 1926.)*

FINDLAY, Alexander, M.A., D.Sc. (Aber.), Ph.D. (Leipzig), F.I.C.; Professor of Chemistry, University of Aberdeen, since 1919; *b.* 24 Sep. 1874; *y. s.* of William Findlay and Catherine Fyfe; *m.* 1914, Alice Mary, *y. d.* of late Herbert de Rougemont of Lloyd's; two *s.* *Educ.:* Grammar School, Aberdeen; Universities of Aberdeen and Leipzig. Interim Lecturer on Organic Chemistry, University of St. Andrews, 1900; Lecturer on Chemistry and Special Lecturer on Physical Chemistry University of Birmingham, 1902-11; Member of Council, Institute of Chemistry, 1915-18; Member of Council, Chemical Society; Thomson Lecturer, United Free Church College, Aberdeen, 1915-16; Professor of Chemistry, University College of Wales, Aberystwyth, 1911-1919; Editor of Monographs on Inorganic and Physical Chemistry. *Publications:* The Phase Rule and its Applications; Physical Chemistry and its Applications in Medical and Biological Science; Practical Physical Chemistry; Osmotic Pressure; Chemistry in the Service of Man; The Treasures of Coal Tar; Translation of Ostwald's Principles of Inorganic Chemistry; a number of memoirs contributed to various scientific journals. *Recreation:* golf. *Address:* Marischal College and Broomhill Park, Aberdeen. *T.:* 2793. *(Died 2 Feb. 1921.)*

FINDLAY, Rev. George Gillanders, B.A., D.D.; Tutor in N.T. Exegesis and Classics at the Headingley Branch of the Wesleyan Theological Institution, 1881-1917, now retired; *b.* 3 Jan. 1849; *s.* of late James Findlay, Wesleyan minister; *m.* 1875; three *s.* four *d.* *Educ.:* Woodhouse Grove School and Wesley College, Sheffield; Richmond Theological College. B.A. Lond. 1867, University Scholar in Classics; D.D.(Hon.) St. Andrews, 1901. Assistant Tutor at Headingley College, 1870-74; Classical Tutor at Richmond, 1874-81; Fernley Lecturer, on "Christian Doctrine and Morals," 1894. *Publications:* several commentaries on St. Paul's Epistles in the Expositor's Bible, Expositor's Greek Testament, Cambridge Greek Testament and Bible for Schools and Colleges; Epistles of Paul, and Books of the Prophets, in Handbooks for Bible Students; vol. of Sermons on The Things Above; Fellowship in the Life Eternal, an Exposition of the Epistles of St. John; Life of Wm. F. Moulton; Wesley's World Parish, etc. *Address:* Headingley College, Leeds. *(Died 2 Nov. 1919.)*

FINDLAY, James Thomas; F.R.Hist.S.; F.S.A. Scot.; author; *b.* Peterhead, Aberdeenshire, 22 July 1875; *e. s.* of late William Findlay, and Isabella, *d.* of James Scott, Peterhead; *m.* 1922, Mary Katherine, *o. d.* of late Alexander Keith of Pitmedden, Aberdeenshire. *Educ.:* Peterhead Academy; Gordon's College, Aberdeen; Edinburgh University; abroad. Editor, Peterhead Sentinel; assistant-editor and leader-writer of Shields Daily Gazette, 1898-1900; acting editor, Ripon Observer, 1903-1905; chief sub-editor, The Shipping World, 1905-19; editor, 1920-27. *Publications:* Socialism in France, a study of contemporary French Socialism; The Secession in the North, and The Ingenious and Learned William Meston, A.M.—two historical studies of the North-East of Scotland; three novels—A Deal with the King, Silent Places, The Chosen. *Recreations:* skating, when there's ice. *Address:* Cairnbrogie, Old Meldrum, Aberdeenshire. *T.:* Udny Green 24. *Club:* Savage. *(Died 31 Oct. 1927.)*

FINDLAY, Surg.-Maj. John, M.B., C.M., C.I.E. 1889; *b.* 29 July 1851. *Educ:* Edinburgh University. Joined Army Medical Staff, 1875; served in Afghan War; Burmah Campaign; on personal staff of Governor of Bombay, 1881-85; and on Viceroy of India's (Marquess of Dufferin), 1885-89; retired 1890. *Recreations:* shooting, golf. *Club:* Junior United Service. *(Died 14 Jan. 1920.)*

FINLAY, David White, B.A., M.D. (Glasg.), LL.D. (Yale and Aberdeen), F.R.C.P. (Lond.), D.P.H. (Camb.); F.R.S. Ed.; Hon. Physician-in-Ordinary to King in Scotland; Emeritus Professor of Practice of Medicine, Aberdeen University; Consulting; late Senior Physician to Aberdeen Royal Infirmary; Member of the General Medical Council, 1901-1911; *b.* Glasgow; *m.* Catherine Mary, *e. d.* of late Stephen Thompson, shipowner, London; two *s.* four *d.* *Educ.:* High School and University, Glasgow; Vienna. Was physician and lecturer at Middlesex Hospital, London; also physician to Royal Hospital for Diseases of the Chest and to Royal Scottish Hospital, and consulting physician to the Caledonian Asylum, London; formerly Inspector of Examinations in Medicine to General Medical Council; recently Hon. Lt.-Col. R.A.M.C.; Commandant, Scottish National Red Cross Hospital, Glasgow. *Publications:* on medical subjects in the medical papers, and in the Transactions of various Medical Societies in London; also Reminiscences of Yacht-Racing and some Racing Yachts, 1910. *Recreations:* yachting (was a member of the first council of Yacht-Racing Association), photography. *Address:* Balgownie, Helensburgh, Dumbartonshire. *T.:* 164. *Clubs:* Royal Clyde Yacht, Conservative, Glasgow. *(Died 4 Nov. 1923.)*

FINLAY, Ian Archibald; late Major North Irish Horse and Lieutenant Royal Scots Greys; *b.* 1878; *s.* of late Major John Finlay of Castle Toward, Argyll, and Mary Marcella, 2nd *d.* of late Thomas Taylor, B.C.S.; *m.* 1904, Elizabeth Muriel, *o. d.* of 1st Baron Glenarthur; two *s.* one *d.* *Educ.:* Eton. Served South African War, 1899-1901 (despatches twice; severely wounded; Queen's medal with 7 clasps); European War, 1914-19 (wounded). *Address:* Temple Hall, Coldingham, Berwickshire. *T.A.:* Coldingham. *Club:* Cavalry. *(Died 9 Nov. 1925.)*

FINLAY, Very Rev. John, M.A.; Dean of Leighlin, 1895-1912; Rector of Carlow, 1890-1912; Rural Dean of Carlow, 1899-1912; *b.* 27 June 1842; 6th *s.* of John Finlay, J.P., Brackley House, Bawnboy, Co. Cavan; *m.* Isabella Anne, *d.* of Very Rev. W. Smyth-King, Dean of Leighlin; no *c.* *Educ.:* Trinity College, Dublin. Ordained, 1867; Curate of Clonenagh, 1867-73; Rector of Lorum, 1873-90; Prebendary of Ullard in Leighlin Cathedral, 1876-1895; Chaplain Lord-Lieutenant, 1902; Dio. Nominator, 1890-1912; Member of Church Representative Body. *Address:* Brackley House, Bawnboy, Co. Cavan. *(Died 11 June 1921.)*

FINLAYSON, Lt.-Col. Walter Taylor, D.S.O. 1917; L.R.C.P. (London); M.R.C.S. (England); *b.* Broughty Ferry, Scotland, 14 July 1877; *s.* of David Finlayson and Kathleen Nina Macarthur; *m.* 1905, Elizabeth Mary Dorothea, 6th *d.* of late Benjamin Neville, Winchester; two *d.* *Educ.:* Haileybury College; Melbourne University; St. Mary's Hospital, London. Qualified in medicine and surgery, 1903; entered the Indian Medical Service, 1904; Captain, 1907; Major, 1915; Lt.-Col. 1923; served European War, 1914-18 (despatches, D.S.O.). *Publications:* Some Effects of Hornet Stings, Indian Medical Gazette; Notes and Observations on the Borstal System as carried out at Borstal, England. *Recreations:* cricket, golf, and lawn tennis. *Address:* c/o

Lloyd's Bank Ltd., Bombay, India. *Club:* East India United Service. *(Died 10 June 1928.)*

FINN, Alexander, F.R.G.S. ; *b.* 5 Nov. 1847 ; *s.* of James Finn, Consul for Palestine ; *m.* 1887, Mary Margaret, *d.* of late Jos. Sanders ; two *d. Educ.:* Royal Institution School, Liverpool ; Royal School, Dungannon ; King's Coll. London. Was some time in Home Civil Service ; Clerk to H.M. Legation, Tehran, 1873 ; Vice-Consul, 1880 ; Consul, Resht, 1883 ; special service on Perso-Afghan Frontier, 1884-5 ; Consul, Malaga, 1887-1904 ; in charge of United States interests during Spanish-American War ; received thanks of German Government for assistance rendered at shipwreck of their training corvette the Gneisenau, Dec. 1901 ; Consul, Chicago, 1904-1907 ; Consul-General, 1907-1909 ; Consul-General, Chile, 1909, and in charge of Turkish Consular affairs at Valparaiso ; retired, 1912. *Recreations:* anything and everything out of doors. *Address:* 2 Park Road, Richmond, Surrey. *Club:* Royal Societies.

(Died 15 Feb. 1919.)

FINN, Brig.-Gen. Harry, C.B., D.C.M., 1907 ; F.R.C.O.; Secretary The Walter and Eliza Hall Trust, Sydney, 1912 ; half-pay, 1907; retired, 1907; *b.* 6 Dec. 1852 ; *y. s.* of late Samuel Finn of Tenterden, Kent ; *m.* 1886, Kate, *e. d.* of late W. Scott, 9 Leeson Park, Dublin ; one *s.* two *d. Educ.:* British School, Tenterden. Enlisted 9th Lancers, 1871 ; 2nd Lt. 21st Hussars, 1881 ; Capt. 1887 ; Major, 21st Hussars, 1894 ; Lieut.-Col. 21st Lancers, 1900; Brevet Col. 1904; Col. 1907 ; Brig.-Gen. 1912 ; D.A.A.G., Madras, 1893-95 ; A.A.G., Madras, 1895-98 ; Commandant, Military Forces, Queensland, 1900-1 ; New South Wales, 1902-4 ; Inspector-General (local Major-General) of Forces, Australia, 1905-6 ; served Afghan War, 1878-80 (despatches, medal for distinguished conduct in the field, medal with clasp); Nile, 1898 (despatches, Brevet Lieut.-Col., two medals and clasps). *Address:* Ashmore, Point Piper, Sydney, New South Wales, Australia. *Clubs:* Junior Constitutional ; Union, Sydney.

(Died 24 June 1924.)

FINNEY, Sir Stephen, Kt., *cr.* 1913 ; C.I.E. 1904 ; Member of the Indian Railway Board ; *s.* of J. D. Finney of Old Charlton, Kent ; *b.* 8 Sep. 1852 ; *m.* 1888, Constance, *d.* of Colonel Pilcher, I.M.S. ; one *s.* one *d. Educ.:* Clifton ; Cooper's Hill. Entered Indian Public Works Dept. 1874 ; served four years as assistant and district engineer ; joined the administrative branch of the railway dept. ; Manager, Eastern Bengal State Railway, 1891-99 ; North-Western Railway, India, 1899-1907. *Publications:* a series of lectures on Railway Construction and Working in Bengal, and papers on subjects connected with railway economics. *Recreations:* plays tennis, was formerly fond of games of all kinds, played for England against Scotland, Rugby, in 1872 and 1873. *Address:* 28 Evelyn Gardens, S.W.7. *T.:* 6220 Kensington. *Club:* Oriental.

(Died 1 Mar. 1924.)

FINNIS, Admiral Frank, C.V.O. 1907 ; retired ; *b.* 8 Nov. 1851 ; *s.* of late Steriker Finnis, Dover ; *m.* 1906, Anna, *d.* of late Prof. John MacRobin, Aberdeen, and *widow* of Herbert Lake. Entered Navy, 1864 ; Lieut., 1874 ; Commander, 1886 ; Capt., 1893 ; Rear-Admiral, 1905 ; late commanding Chatham Division, Home Fleet. *Address:* Lightlands, Frant, Sussex. *Club:* United Service.

(Died 17 Nov. 1918.)

FINNY, John Magee, B.A., M.D., Univ. Dublin ; Fellow and Past President Royal College Physicians, Ireland ; ex-President of Royal Academy of Medicine in Ireland and of Leinster Branch, B.M.A. ; ex-King's Professor of Practice of Medicine Trin. Coll. Dubl.; ex-Physician to Sir Patrick Duns' Hospital ;

Consulting Physician to Sir Patrick Duns Hospital, Mercer's Hospital, Masonic Female Orphan School, Bloomfield Asylum, and Royal Hospital for Incurables, Dublin ; Member of Senate Trinity College, Dublin, and of Board of Superintendence of Dublin Hospitals ; Visitor in Lunacy ; late Examiner in Medicine, R.A.M.C.; *b.* 9 Feb. 1841 ; 3rd *s.* of Rev. T. H. C. Finny, rector of Clondulane, Co. Cork, and Frances, *d.* of William Magee, Archbishop of Dublin ; *m.* 1873, Agnes Anne, *y. d.* of William Watson, Dublin; four *s.* three *d. Educ.:* private school ; Trinity Coll. Dublin (Med. scholar and senior exhibitioner, 1864). President Royal College Physicians, Ireland, 1890-92. *Publications:* on various medical subjects, and contributions to British Medical Journal and other journals. *Address:* Erith Lodge, Sandymount, Dublin. *T.:* Ballsbridge 460. *Club:* University, Dublin. *(Died 7 Dec. 1922.)*

PINOT, Jean ; Directeur de La Revue ; officier de la Légion d'Honneur ; membre de l'Académie des Sciences de Lisbonne ; membre de l'Académie de Rio-de-Janeiro ; membre de l'Institut de Coimbra, Président de l'Alarme ; vice-Président des Amitiés franco-étrangères, etc. ; Commandeur de Maurice et Lazare et de la Couronne d'Italie ; Commandeur du Soleil Levant, etc. ; *b.* 1856 ; *m.* ; one *s. Publications:* Race Prejudice ; Philosophy of Longevity ; Problems of the Sexes ; Science of Happiness ; (ouvrages non traduits en anglais :) Progrès et Bonheur (2 vols.) ; Civilisés contre Allemands ; Anglais et Français. Tous ces ouvrages sont traduites dans beaucoup de langues ; espagnole, allemande, italienne, russe, grecque, polonaise, etc., et plusieurs d'entre eux ont été couronnés par l'Académie française, l'Académie des Sciences Morales, etc. *Address:* La Revue, Paris. *(Died 25 April 1922.)*

FIRBANK, Arthur Annesley Ronald ; 2nd and *o. surv. s.* of late Major Sir Thomas Firbank, M.P., St. Julians, Monmouthshire, and Jane Harriette, 4th *d.* of late Rev. James Perkins Garrett, of Kilgarron, Co. Carlow ; *b.* 1886. *Educ.:* abroad ; Trinity Hall, Cambridge. *Publications:* Odette, 1905 ; Vainglory, 1915 ; Inclinations, 1916 ; Caprice, 1917 ; Valmouth, 1919 ; The Princess Zoubaroff, 1920 ; Santal, 1921 ; The Flower Beneath the Foot, 1922 ; Sorrow in Sunlight, 1924 ; Concerning the Eccentricities of Cardinal Pirelli, 1925. *Recreations:* travelling, literature, and art. *Club:* Junior Carlton. *(Died 21 May 1926.)*

FISH, Ven. Lancelot John, M.A., Archdeacon of Bath ; *b.* 1861 ; *s.* of late Rev. J. D. Fish ; *m.* 1891, Mary, *d.* of Rev. H. Girdlestone ; no *c. Educ.:* Harrow ; Trinity College, Cambridge. Chaplain at Christ Church, Cannes, 1900-1903 ; Vicar of Bathampton, Bath, 1894-1907 ; Diocesan Inspector of Schools, 1899-1902 ; Hon. Sec. Bath and Wells Diocesan Societies, 1902-7 ; Proctor in Convocation, 1906 ; Prebendary of Wells Cathedral, 1906 ; Chaplain at St. Andrew's Church, Biarritz, France, 1907-9 ; Vicar of St. Stephen Lansdown, Bath, 1909-23. *Address:* 12 Lansdown Place East, Bath. *Clubs:* New University, M.C.C.; Bath and County, Bath. *(Died 29 Sept. 1924.)*

FISH, Stuyvesant ; *b.* New York, 24 June 1851 ; *s.* of late Hon. Hamilton Fish, Secy. of State in Grant's Administration ; *m.* Marian G. Anthon. *Educ.:* Columbia College. Clerk in New York office, Illinois Central R.R., 1871 ; Secretary to President, 1872-1874 ; Director since 1877 ; Clerk with Morton, Bliss and Co., New York, and Morton. Rose and Co., London ; Memb. New York Stock Exchange ; Treas. and Agent for purchasing com. New Orleans, Jackson and Great Northern R.R. ; Secretary, 1877-1882, Chicago, St. Louis and New Orleans R.R. ; Vice-President, 1883-84 ; 2nd Vice-President, 1884-87 ; President Illinois Central R.R., 1887-

354

FISET, Hon. Jean Baptiste Romuald, M.D. See page xix.

1906; member, Monetary Commission created by Indianapolis Monetary Conference, 1897; Pres. American Railway Association, 1904-6; Chairman 7th Session International Railway Congress, 1906; Trustee of New York Life Insurance and Trust Co.; for many years Vice-President and Director, National Park Bank, New York, and Director of other fiscal and fiduciary institutions; Trustee of Mutual Life Insurance Company of New York from 1883 until his resignation in 1906, owing to disapproval of "ring" methods then brought to light among certain of his co-trustees and disclosed at that time in the press; Member St. Nicholas Society. *Address:* 52 Wall Street and 25 E. 78th Street, New York. *Clubs:* Union, Metropolitan, Down Town, St. Anthony's. New York.

(*Died 10 April 1923.*)

FISHER, 1st Baron, of Kilverstone, *cr.* 1909, **Admiral of the Fleet John Arbuthnot Fisher,** G.C.B., *cr.* 1902; G.C.V.O., *cr.* 1908; Order of Merit, 1905; Chairman of Inventions Board since 1915; Grand Cordon of Legion of Honour, 1906; Memb. Committee Imperial Defence; *b.* 25 Jan. 1841; *s.* of Capt. William Fisher, 78th Highlanders, and Sophia, *d.* of A. Lambe of New Bond Street, and *g. d.* of Alderman Boydell; *m.* 1866, Frances (*d.* 1918), *d.* of Rev. T. Delves Broughton; one *s.* three *d.* Entered Navy, 1854; Lieut., 1860; took part in capture of Canton and Peiho forts; obtained Beaufort Testimonial; Rr.-Adm. 1890; served Crimean War, 1855; China War, 1859-60; Egyptian War, 1882; in command of the "Inflexible," Bombardment of Alexandria, 1882; Director Naval Ordnance, 1886-91; Admiral Superintendent at Portsmouth Dockyard, 1891; Controller of the Navy; Lord of the Admiralty, 1892-97; Commander-in-Chief on the North American and West Indies Station, 1897-99; Delegate to Peace Conference at the Hague, 1899; Commander-in-Chief, Mediterranean Station, 1899-1902; 2nd Sea Lord of Admiralty, 1902-3; Commander-in-Chief, Portsmouth, 1908-4; First Sea Lord of Admiralty, 1904-10 and 1914-15; Chairman Royal Commission on Oil Fue, 1912. *Heir: s.* Hon. Cecil Vavasseur Fisher. *Club:* Athenæum.

(*Died 10 July 1920.*)

FISHER, Rt. Hon. Andrew; P.C. 1911; *b.* Crosshouse, Kilmarnock, 29 Aug. 1862; *s.* of Robt. Fisher; married; five *s.* one *d. Educ.:* Crosshouse. Went to Queensland, 1885; entered Queensland Parliament, 1893; Minister of Railways in Dawson Ministry; represented Wide Bay in the Commonwealth Parliament for first fifteen years of the Parliament; Minister for Trade and Customs, Commonwealth of Australia, 1904; Leader of Federal Parliamentary Labour Party, 1907-15; Prime Minister, Australia, 1908-9; Leader of Federal Opposition, 1909-10; Prime Minister, 1910-13, and 1914-15; represented Australia at opening of Union Parliament, S. Africa, 1910; at Imperial Conference, 1911, and at Coronation of King George V.; High Commissioner of Australia in England, 1916-21. *Address:* 57 South Hill Park, N.W.3.

(*Died 22 Oct. 1928.*)

FISHER, Rev. Cecil Edward, Prebendary of Lincoln since 1877; *b.* 12 Aug. 1838; *y. s.* of Rev. William Fisher, Rector of Poulshot, Devizes; Canon of Salisbury; *m.* 1862, Agnes, *y. d.* of John Mirehouse of Brownslade. Pembroke, Common Serjeant of London; two *s.* six *d. Educ.:* Westminster School; Christ Church, Oxford (Student). Curate of Bremhill, Wilts, 1864; Rector of Stoke Rochford, Lincs, 1865-78; Vicar of Grantham, 1878-83; Rector of Hagworthingham, Lincs, 1883-90; Rural Dean of Hill, 1885-86; Vicar of St. Peter's, Bournemouth, 1890-1904. *Address:* Ankerwyke, Shirley Warren, Southampton. *T.A.:* Canon Fisher, Shirley, Southampton. (*Died 13 Jun. 1925.*)

FISHER, Frederic Henry, editor of the Literary World, 1888-1915; *b.* London, 13 April 1849; *e. s.* of late Rev. F. W. Fisher; *m.* 1872, Clara (*d.* 1914), 2nd *d.* of late James Clarke, Beech-hanger, Caterham; one *s.* one *d. Educ.:* Boston Grammar School; B.A. London University. Entered Indian Civil Service by open competition, 1868; Officiating Civil and Sessions Judge, Saharanpur, North-Western Provinces, 1881; editor of North-Western Provinces Gazetteer, 1881-83; retired 1885. Barr. Middle Temple, 1885. *Publications:* Cyprus our New Colony and What we Know about it, 1878; Afghanistan and the Central Asian Question, 1878. *Recreation:* chess. *Address:* Westover, Cobham Road, Westcliff-on-Sea, Essex. *Club:* Alexandra Yacht, Southend-on-Sea. (*Died 30 Dec. 1926.*)

FISHER, Rt. Rev. George Carnac, D.D.; *b.* 1844; *s.* of William Fisher, H.M. Madras Civil Service, and Frances Euggles-Brise, *d.* of Rev. C. J. Fisher, Ovington Rectory, Essex; *m.* 1876, Mary Penelope Gwendoline, *o. d.* of late T. C. Thompson, at one time M.P. for Durham, of Sherburn Hall, Durham, and Ashdown Park, Sussex; four *s.* four *d. Educ.:* Harrow; Brasenose Coll. Oxford (M.A.). Vicar of Forest Row, Sussex, 1874-79; St. George, Barrow-in-Furness, 1879-81; St. Mary, Beverley, 1882-89; Croydon, 1889-94; Bishop of Southampton (Suffragan to Bishop of Winchester), 1896-98; Bishop of Ipswich (Suffragan to Bishop of Norwich), 1899-1906; resigned, 1905. *Address:* Burgh House, Fleggburgh, Norfolk.

(*Died 9 April 1921.*)

FISHER, Inspector-Gen. James W., M.D., R.N. *Address:* Failthe, Dover Road, Walmer, Kent. (*Died 3 Feb. 1919.*)

FISHER, Maj.-Gen. John Frederick Lane, Indian Army; *b.* 10 Dec. 1832. Entered army, 1848; Maj.-Gen., 1890; unemployed list, 1890; served Indian Mutiny, 1857-59 (slightly wounded, medal with clasp).

(*Died 20 June 1917.*)

FISHER, Mark, R.A. 1919; A.R.A. 1911; *b.* Boston, U.S.A., of English and Irish parents. *Educ.:* Boston Pub. School. When quite a child showed a marked talent for drawing, his taste and talent developing rapidly in this direction; the opportunities for studying Art at that time being much fewer than now, his earliest instruction was gained at Lowell Institute; his first efforts were portraits and figures, but his love of outdoor subjects and life induced him to take up landscape and animal painting; at the age of twenty he went to Paris, and was for a short time in Gleyre's studio; on his return to Boston he met with scant encouragement, so came to England, married and settled here; represented in the following permanent exhibitions—Dublin, Manchester, Birmingham, Leeds, Bradford, Oldham, Huddersfield, Dudley, Rochdale, Adelaide, Perth (Australia), Johannesberg; Medals—Paris, Chicago, St. Louis. *Address:* Hatfield Heath, Harlow, Essex.

(*Died 30 April 1923.*)

FISHER, Hon. Sydney Arthur, B.A., D.C.L. (hon.) McGill; Minister of Agriculture, Canada, 1896-1911; *b.* Montreal, Canada, 12 June 1850; *s.* of Dr. Arthur Fisher, F.R.C.S., Edinburgh, and Susan Corse, both of Montreal; unmarried; Church of England; Liberal. *Educ.:* High School and McGill Coll., Montreal; Trinity College, Cambridge (B.A.). Farmer by profession, at Knowlton, in Eastern Townships, P.Q.; entered Parliament of Canada as M.P. for County Brome, 1882; re-elected 1887, 1896, 1900, 1904 and 1908; defeated, 1891 and 1911; First Vice-President International Institute of Agriculture, convened at Rome, 1908. *Recreations:* riding and cricket. *Address:* Alva House, Knowlton, P.Q., Canada; 4 Range Road, Ottawa. *Clubs:* University, Reform, Montreal; Rideau, Golf and University, Ottawa. (*Died April 1921.*)

FISHER, Commander Sir Thomas, R.N.; K.B.E., cr. 1920; General Manager, Canadian Pacific Steamships Ltd.; b. Birmingham, 1883; s. of Thomas Fisher, and Margaret, d. of Sir A. Hickman, Bart., Wolverhampton; m. 1912, Aimée, d. of Walter Loveridge of Codsall; one s. one d. Entered R.N., 1897; Served in China (medal), Mediterranean, and Home Fleets; Specialised in Gunnery; Qualified as War Staff Officer; Flag Commander in Reserve Fleet, 1914; Admiralty Trade Division, 1915-17 (C.B.E.); represented Ministry of Shipping in Washington, U.S.A., 1918-19; Retired 1920. Address: 8 Waterloo Place, S.W. T.: Regent 2925; 108 Sloane Street, S.W. T.: Victoria 6972. Clubs: United Service, St. James's. (Died 22 Feb. 1925.)

FISHER, Adm. William Blake, R.N., C.B. 1900; b. 19 Feb. 1853; s. of late Capt. W. E. Fisher, R.N.; m. 1887, Edith Lilian, d. of Francis A'Beckett Chambers of N.S.W.; one s. Entered Navy, 1866; Captain, 1896; Commodore, 1905; commanded punitive expedition, New Hebrides, 1885; Senior Officer commanding Delagoa Bay Blockading Squadron (medal and Natal clasp); commandant of Base Jubaland Expedition, 1901; G. S. East African Medal, Jubaland clasp; Commodore R.N. Barracks, 1905-7; Rear-Admiral, 1906; Rear-Admiral, Second in Command of Atlantic Fleet, 1908; Vice-Admiral, 1911; retired, 1914; commandes H.M. Yacht Medusa, 1915; also served ad Admiralty representative for Munition Supply; Royal Humane Society's medal and clasp for saving life on two occasions. Club: United Service. (Died 8 May 1926.)

FISHER, William James, J.P., London, 1906; Chairman, Holborn Bench of Justices; Member, County Licensing Committee, since 1910; Visiting Justice, Wormwood Scrubs Prison, since 1915; e. surv. s. of late Walter Fisher; m. 1st, Emma, d. of late J. J. Florac; one s. two d.; 2nd, Adrienne Dairolles, 1897. Joined the staff of the Daily Chronicle as foreign editor in 1883; assistant editor, 1894; editor-in-chief, 1899-1904; contested (L.) Canterbury, general elections 1905 and Dec. 1910; Director, Edmond Coignet, Ltd., and other public companies. Recreations: fishing, swimming, golfing. Address: 37 Cathcart Road, S.W.10. T.: Kensington 5567. Clubs: Reform, Mid-Surrey Golf. (Died 28 Feb. 1924.)

FISON, Alfred Henry, D.Sc. Lond.; Secretary to the Gilchrist Educational Trust since 1912; Lecturer on Physics at Guy's Hospital since 1906, and the London Hospital since 1910; b. Hendon, 1857; s. of Rev. Thomas Fison, Congregational Minister; m. 1888, Alice Maud, d. of Alexander W. Williamson, F.R.S., Professor of Chemistry at University College, London; one s. two d. Educ.: Mr. Munro's School, Elstree; Royal School of Mines. Mathematical Master at three private schools, 1879-84; Demonstrator of Physics at University College London, 1884-92; Lecturer to the Oxford University Extension Delegacy, 1892-1912. Publications: Recent Advances in Astronomy, 1898; Article on the Evolution of Double Stars in Lectures on the Methods of Science, 1905; A Text Book of Practical Physics, 1911; re-written, 1922. Address: 147 Dartmouth Road, Cricklewood, N.W.2. T.: 1551 Willesden. Club: Sandy Lodge Golf. (Died 4 Feb. 1923.)

FISON, Sir Frederick William; 1st Bt.; cr. 1905; J.P., D.L.; b. 4 Dec. 1847; o. s. of late William Fison, Greenholme, Burley-in-Wharfedale, Yorkshire, m. Isabella, d. of late Joseph Crossley, Broomfield, Halifax; two s. two d. Educ.: Rugby; Christ Church, Oxford; 1st Class Natural Science. Contested Otley Division 1885, Buckrose Division 1892; M.P. (C.) for Doncaster Div., Yorkshire, 1895-1906. Heir: s. Capt. Francis Geoffrey Fison, M.C.,

356

late K.R.R.C. [b. 12 Mar. 1878. Educ.: Harrow; Christ Church, Oxford (B.A.)]. Address: Boarzell, Hurst Green, Sussex. T.: Hurst Green 7 Clubs: Carlton, United University.
(Died 20 Dec. 1927.)

FITCHETT, Rev. William Henry, LL.D. Toronto University; editor of Life, a monthly magazine; of a weekly paper, The Southern Cross; principal of the Methodist Ladies' College, Hawthorn, Melbourne; b. Lincolns.; married. Educ.: Melbourne University (B.A.). Wesleyan minister (ex-Pres. of the Wesleyan Conference of Victoria and Tasmania); President of the General Conference of the Methodist Church of Australasia; also educationist and journalist, having edited the Melbourne Daily Telegraph at one time. Publications: Deeds that won the Empire, 1897; Fights for the Flag, 1898; The Tale of the Great Mutiny; How England saved Europe, 1899; Wellington's Men, 1901; Nelson and his Captains, 1902; The Commander of the Hirondelle, 1904; The Unrealised Logic of Religion, 1905; Life of Wesley, 1905; Ithuriel's Spear, 1906; The Pawn in the Game, 1907; The Beliefs of Unbelief, 1907; The Great Duke, 1911; The New World of the South, 1913; The Romance of Australian History, 1913. Recreations: golf, takes considerable interest in cricket. Address: Hawthorn, Melbourne.
(Died May 1928.)

FITTON, Col. Hugh Gregory, C.B. 1911; D.S.O. 1896; A.D.C. to the King, 1907; Royal W. Kent Regt.; b. 15 Nov. 1863; m. 1910, May, 6th d. of late Sir Alfred Hickman Entered Royal Berks, 1884; Brevet-Major, 1898; served Eastern Soudan, 1885 (medal with clasp, Khedive's star); Egyptian Frontier Field Force, 1885-86; Dongola Expeditionary Force, 1896 (despatches, D.S.O., Khedive's medal, two clasps); D.A.A.G. 7th Division South Africa, 1900-4 (despatches twice, Bt. Lieut.-Col., Queen's medal, 3 clasps); P.S.C.; Colonel, 1907. Address: 42 Albert Court, S.W. (Died 20 Jan. 1916.)

FITZCLARENCE, Hon. Harold Edward, M.C.; Governor H.M. Prison Manchester since 1919; b. and heir-pres. to 4th Earl of Munster; b. 15 Nov. 1870; m. 1902, Frances Isabel, d. of late Lieut.-Col. William Keppel, of Lexham Hall, Norfolk; one s. one d. Late Lieut. 3rd Batt. Yorkshire Light Infantry; served South Africa with Imperial Yeomanry, 1900-1; Governor of Worcester Gaol, 1909; on active service B.E.F. 1915; Assistant Provost Marshal 31st and 47th Divisions (despatches, M.C.). (Died 28 Aug. 1926.)

FITZGEORGE, Rear - Admiral Sir Adolphus (Augustus Frederick), K.C.V.O., cr. 1904; Deputy Ranger of Richmond Park; s. of late Duke of Cambridge; b. 1846; m. 1st, 1875, Sophia Jane (d. 1920), d. of Thomas Holden, of Winestead Hall, Hull; one d.; 2nd, 1920, Margarita Beatrice, d. of late John Watson of Waresley Hall, Worcestershire. Address: 20 Eccleston Square, S.W.1. Clubs: Carlton, Naval and Military, Marlborough.
(Died 17 Dec. 1922.)

FITZGERALD, Admiral Charles Cooper Penrose; Admiral, 1905; b. Corkbeg, Co. Cork, 30 Apr. 1841; 2nd s. of Robert Fitzgerald and Frances, d. of Rev. Robert Austin; m. Henrietta, d. of late Rev. F. Hewson, 1882; two s. two d. Educ. at sea. Joined the "Victory," 1854; Midshipman of "Colossus" in the Baltic; "Retribution," round the world; Lieut. of "Ariadne"; First Lieut. "Cordelia," "Hercules"; Commander, "Agincourt." "Asia," "Rapid"; Capt. "Inconstant," R.N. College, "Bellerophon," "Inflexible," "Collingwood"; Superintendent, Pembroke Dockyard; second in command of the China Station, 1898-99. Publications: a book on Boat Sailing, 1883; Life of Sir George Tryon, 1897; Memories of the Sea,

1918; From Sail to Steam, 1916. *Address:* 2 Trinity Road, Folkestone.(*Died 11 Aug. 1921.*)

FITZGERALD, Charles Edward, M.D., M.Ch.; Ex-President Royal College of Physicians of Ireland; Hon. Surgeon-Oculist-in-Ordinary to the King in Ireland; Professor of Ophthalmic Surgery, Royal College of Surgeons, Ireland; Consulting Ophthalmic Surgeon, Richmond Hospital; *b.* 9 Feb. 1843; *s.* of F. A. FitzGerald, late Baron of Exchequer, Ireland; *m.* 1st, Isabel, *d.* of late Peter Roe Clarke; four *s.*; 2nd, Edythe, *d.* of late John Overend. *Educ.*: Trin. Coll. Dublin. *Address:* 27 Upper Merrion Street, Dublin.
(*Died 27 May 1916.*)

FITZGERALD, His Honour Judge, K.C. (Hon. David FitzGerald); C.C. Judge, Cos. Waterford, Kilkenny, and Queen's; *b.* 14 Jan. 1847; *s.* of late Rt. Hon. Lord Fitz-Gerald (Lord of Appeal); *m.* 1894, Isabel, *d.* of Luke J. M'Donnell. *Educ.*: Downing College, Cambridge, B.A. Called to bar, Lincoln's Inn, 1871; King's Inns, Dublin, 1872. *Address:* 18 Clyde Road, Dublin. *Clubs:* Reform; University, Kildare Street, Dublin.
(*Died 5 Mar. 1920.*)

FITZGERALD, Capt. Lord Desmond; Captain, Irish Guards; *b.* and *heir-pres.* to 6th Duke of Leinster; *b.* 21 Sep. 1888. *Educ.*: Eton. Served European War, 1914 (despatches, wounded). (*Died 5 Mar. 1916.*)

FITZGERALD, Lt.-Col. Lord Frederick; *b.* 18 Jan. 1857; *s.* of 4th Duke of Leinster. *Educ.*: Eton. Late Major King's Royal Rifle Corps; served Afghan Campaign (medal with 2 clasps and bronze star), 1878-80; South African Campaign, 1881; Egyptian Campaigns, 1882; Nile Expedition (medal with two clasps and bronze star), 1884-85; J.P., Co. Kildare *Address:* Carton, Maynooth. *Clubs:* Junior United Service; Kildare Street, Dublin.
(*Died 8 Mar. 1924.*)

FITZGERALD, Hon. George Parker, M.E.C., Tasmania; Head of firm of G. P. Fitz-Gerald & Co., Merchants, Hobart, Tasmania; *b.* Hobart, 13 Feb. 1843; twice married; four *s.* two *d. Educ.*: Hutchins School, Hobart. Was Minister of the Crown, Tasmania, 1888-91; President of Tasmanian Section at Melbourne International Exhibition; also Chairman of the Board of Technical Education, and succeeded in getting a vote through Parliament for the construction of Technical College at Hobart; appointed chief liquidator of the Bank of Van Diemen's Land, which closed, 1901. *Recreations:* fishing, yachting, rowing. *Address:* Hobart, Tasmania.
(*Died 1917.*)

FITZGERALD, Hon. Gerald, K.C.; *b.* 12 Aug. 1849; 3rd *s.* of late Lord Fitzgerald (Lord of Appeal). *Educ.*: Oscott; Trinity Coll., Dublin. Irish Barr. 1871; County Court Judge, 1886-90; Q.C. 1892; Land Commissioner in Ireland, 1890; Judicial Commissioner, 1903; *Address:* 6 Fitzwilliam Square, Dublin. *Clubs:* Brooks's, Wellington; Kildare Street, University, Dublin; Royal St. George Yacht, Kingstown.
(*Died 30 Oct. 1925.*)

FITZGERALD, Gerald A. R., K.C. 1909; Barrister; *e. s.* of late Rev. A. O. Fitz-Gerald, Archdeacon of Wells; *b.* 1844; *m.* 1875, Alice Caroline Frances (*d.* 1917), *e. d.* of late H. D. Skrine of Warleigh and Claverton Manors, Co. Somerset; two *s. Educ.*: Sherborne; Corpus Christi, Oxford; late Fellow of St. John's Oxford. Called to Bar, 1871; employed in office of the Parliamentary Counsel for 3 or 4 years; then practised as draftsman of private Bills, etc., and before Parliamentary Committees; Light Railway Commissioner (unpaid), 1896-1900; J.P. Wilts. 1904. *Publications:* Editor of two editions of Thring's Companies Acts; Manual of Ballot Act, 1872; The Public Health Act, 1875. *Address:* 9 Parktown, Oxford. (*Died 1 Aug. 1925.*)

FITZGERALD, Brigadier-General Herbert Swayne, C.B. 1900; retired; *b.* 12 Mar. 1856; 2nd *s.* of Major C. M. Fitz-Gerald, Bengal Staff Corps; *m.* 1884, Charlotte, *d.* of J. Baumgartner. Entered 68th Durham Light Infantry, 1875; attached 15th Sikhs, Afghan War, 1880, including Candahar (medal with clasp, bronze decoration); Marri Expedition, 1881; D.A.A.G. for Intelligence Soudan Frontier Field Force, 1885-86 (medal, Khedive's Star); operations on Niger, 1897-98 (despatches, Brevet Lieut.-Col., medal with clasp); commanded 1st Bn. Durham L.I.; South Africa, 1899-1902, including Colenso, Tugela, Vaal Krantz (severely wounded, despatches twice, C.B.); commanded 64th Brigade, 1914-15; 226th, 1915-16. *Club:* Army and Navy. (*Died 2 July 1924.*)

FITZGERALD, Hon. John Donohoe, K.C.; *b.* Dublin, 20 Jan. 1848; 2nd *s.* of late Rt. Hon. Lord FitzGerald and Rose, *d.* of late John Donohoe; *m.* 1881, Emma Ysolda, 2nd *d.* of Sir Thomas Barrett Lennard, 2nd Bart.; one *s.* four *d. Educ.*: Christ's Coll., Camb. LL.B. Cambridge, 1st class Law Tripos, 1870; LL.M. 1873. Barr. Inner Temple, 1872; Q.C. 1896. *Address:* 33 Harrington Gardens, South Kensington; 38 Parliment Street, S.W. *Clubs:* Athenæum, Brooks's, Reform.
(*Died 11 May 1918.*)

FITZGERALD, Sir Maurice, 2nd Bt., *cr.* 1880; 20th Kt. of Kerry; C.V.O. 1905; formerly Equerry to Duke of Connaught; Captain Rifle Brigade, 1875; retired, 1881; D.L., J.P. for Cambridgeshire, Suffolk, and Cos. Kerry and Carlow. [The title Knight of Kerry has been considered prescriptive from early times. The founder of this family, John Fitz Thomas Fitzgerald, Lord of Decies and Desmond, created three of his sons by his second marriage hereditary Knights—The White Knight, The Knight of Glin, and the Knight of Kerry.] *b.* 5 Feb. 1844; *S.* father 1880; *m.* Amelia, *d.* of late H. L. Bischoffsheim, 1882; two *s.* one *d. Educ.*: Harrow. Served in Ashanti War, 1873-74. Owns about 10,000 acres. *Recreations:* owner of yacht "Satanita," owner of race horses. *Heir: s.* John Peter Gerald Maurice, *b.* 14 May 1884 (Capt. Royal Horse Guards). *Address:* Buckland, Berkshire; The Severals, Newmarket; Valencia Island, Co. Kerry. *Clubs:* Travellers', Brooks's; Royal Yacht Squadron, Cowes. (*Died 22 Oct. 1916.*)

FITZGERALD, Maurice F., D.Sc., Professor of Civil Engineering, Queen's College, Belfast, 1881-1910; Prof. Emeritus since 1910. *Educ.*: Trinity Coll., Dublin; Eastons and Anderson, Erith. *Address:* Queen's University, Belfast. (*Died 5 May 1927.*)

FITZGERALD, Michael, C.M.G. 1897; *b.* Dysert, Co. Clare, 1851; 2nd *s.* of George Fitz-gerald, Roughan, Co. Clare; *m.* 1887, Florence, *d.* of Deputy-Inspector-Gen. Daniel Finucane, R.N. *Educ.*: Ennis Coll.; Royal Coll. of Surgeons, Ireland. L.R.C.S.I. 1871; L.M., L.R.C.P.I. 1872. Surgeon in charge of H.M.S. "Magpie," 1874 (officers and men thanked by Admiralty for services in disturbances at Masnaah, Persian Gulf); received thanks of Admiralty for services at Malta Hospital during operations in Egypt, 1882; of Secretary of State for War; of Dutch Government; of United States Government for services to Admiral—then Capt. —Dewey; P.M.O. of hospital ship "Malacca," and of forces landed with Admiral Rawson in punitive naval expedition against King of Benin, 1897 (mentioned in despatches). *Decorated* for this latter service. R.N. Dep. Insp.-Gen. Hospitals and Fleets, 1901-5; retired, 1905, with rank of Insp.-Gen. of Hospitals and Fleets. *Recreations:* cricket, fishing, shooting, boxing, cycling. *Club:* Royal Naval, Portsmouth.
(*Died 13 Mar. 1918.*)

FITZGERALD, Lieut.-Col. Oswald Arthur Gerald, C.M.G. 1915; 18th K.G.O. Lancers; Personal Military Secretary to Secretary of State for War since Aug. 1914; *s.* of late Col. Sir Charles Fitzgerald. *Educ.:* Wellington. Received first commission Indian Staff Corps, 1895; gazetted to 18th K.G.O. Lancers, 1897; served N.-W. Frontier of India, 1897-98 (medal with 2 clasps); A.D.C. to Commander-in-Chief in India, 1904-6; Assistant Military Secretary to Lord Kitchener, Commander-in-Chief in India, 1907-8; Staff Officer to Lord Kitchener on his mission to Japan, Australia, and New Zealand, 1909; Staff College, 1909-10; Military Secretary to Lord Kitchener, commanding troops at Coronation, 1911; General Staff Officer Egypt, 1911-12; Military Attaché Egypt, 1912-14. *Club:* Cavalry. *(Died 5 June 1916.)*

FITZGERALD, Percy Seymour Vesey, C.S.I. 1906. Assistant Political Agent, Kathiawar, 1874; Mahi Kantha, 1875; Kathiawar, 1877; Baroda, 1878; Kathiawar, 1879; Administrator, Gondal State, 1881; Administrator, Sangli State, 1883; Assistant Political Agent, Kolhapur, 1884; Kathiawar, 1885; Aden, 1889; Political Agent, Sawantwadi, 1893; Mahi Kantha, 1894; Cutch, 1895; Palanpur, 1898; Mahi Kantha, 1901; Agent to Governor in Kathiawar, 1906-8; retired 1908. *Club:* Carlton. *(Died 17 Nov. 1924.)*

FITZGERALD, Mrs. Robert; (Marion), C.B.E. 1920; *b.* 1860; *d.* of late Mahony Harte, B.L., of Batterfield House, Co. Kerry; *m.* 1878, Robert Fitzgerald, J.P., D.L., 2nd *s.* of Sir Peter Fitzgerald, Bt., Knight of Kerry; two *s.* President, Soldiers' and Sailors' Families Association for Co. Kerry; Chairman, War Pensions Committee for Co. Kerry; District Head, Soldiers' and Sailors' Help Society for Tralee; President, Tralee Women's National Health Association; Hon. Secretary, Tralee Red Cross Association; Commandant, Kerry 4 V.A.D. during European War. *Address:* 40 Onslow Square, S.W. 3. *T.:* Kens. 2108. *(Died 11 Feb. 1928.)*

FITZGERALD, Sir Robert Uniacke-Penrose-, 1st Bt., *cr.* 1896; D.L., J.P.; *b.* Cork-Beg Island, Co. Cork, 10 July 1839; *e. s.* of Robert Penrose-Fitzgerald and Frances, *d.* of Rev. R. Austen; *m.* Jane, *d.* of General Sir William Codrington, 1867. *Educ.:* Westminster and Trin. Hall, Cambridge. Travelled in India and Thibet, 1863-67; Hon. Col. of North Cork Rifles; contested Youghal, 1874; M.P. (C.) Cambridge, 1885-1906; working member of Committee of Royal National Lifeboat Society; President of the Council of the Yacht-racing Association; director Property Defence Association and Cork Defence Union against Land League. *Recreations:* sailing, shooting, farming, and gardening. Owns about 6000 acres in Co. Cork, of which 1000 are farmed by himself. *Heir to title:* none. *Address:* Cork-Beg Island, Co. Cork: 35 Grosvenor Road, Westminster, S.W. *Clubs:* Carlton; Kildare Street, Dublin; Royal Cork Yacht. *(Died 10 July 1919.)*

FITZGERALD, Hon. Rowan Robert, (Hon.) D.C.L.; Vice-Chancellor, and Judge Supreme Court of the Province, Charlottetown, since 1894; *b.* 1847. *Educ.:* Prince of Wales' College, Prince Edward Isle. Barrister, 1869; Stipendiary Magistrate, 1875; K.C., 1880; Recorder to 1894. *Address:* Charlottetown, P.E.I.

FITZ-GERALD, Shafto Justin Adair; novelist and dramatist; *b.* 9 Nov. 1859; 2nd *s.* of late Captain Thomas Justin Fitz-Gerald; *m.* 1899, Blanche Adeline Cawse. *Educ.:* privately. *Publications:* Sketches from Bohemia, 1890; The Wonders of the Secret Cavern, 1892; Ballads of a Bohemian, 1893; A Book of Words, 1895; The Zankiwank and the Bletherwitch, 1896; The Mighty Toltec, 1897;

A Tragedy of Grub Street, 1897; Stories of Famous Songs, 1897; Fame the Fiddler, 1898; That Fascinating Widow, 1898; The Grand Panjandrum, 1898; The Black Tulip, 1899; Rip Van Winkle, 1900; How to Make Up, 1901; Drink (from L'Assommoir), 1902; The Love Thirst of Elaine, 1903; Prince Conan, 1907; Dickens and the Drama, 1910; Nine One-Act Plays (three volumes), 1914; The Idol of Paris (from the French of Sarah Bernhardt), 1921; The Story of the Savoy Opera, 1924. *Plays:* The Barringtons, 1884; A Lucky Girl, 1889; The Parson, 1891; Two Hearts, 1904; The Bric-à-Brac Will, 1895; A Jealous Mistake, 1899; The Parting, 1899; Waiting for the Train, 1899; Rip Van Winkle, 1899; Cinq Mars, 1900; That Sister of Mine, 1900; The Forgotten Favorite, 1902; Son of a Duke, 1903; Her Answer, 1907; The Lilac Domino (part author), 1918; and several pantomimes and children's plays; for over thirty years one of the chief writers on The Era, and contributor, at one time or another, to nearly every London daily newspaper. *Recreations:* carpentry, music. *Address:* 8 Lancaster Road, Bowes Park, N.11. *Club:* Actors'. *(Died 23 Oct. 1925.)*

FITZGERALD, Lord Walter, J.P. Co. Kildare; *b.* 22 Jan. 1858; 4th *s.* of 4th Duke of Leinster; unmarried. *Educ.:* Cheam, Surrey; Eton; Sandhurst. Gazetted to 4th Battalion 60th Rifles, 1879; served in India; retired as a Captain, 1888; served with the Carlow Militia, 1888-98. *Publications:* papers on archæological subjects in the Journal of the Royal Society of Antiquaries of Ireland, and in the Journal of the County Kildare Archæological Society. *Recreations:* shooting and archæologising. *Address:* Kilkea Castle, Maganey, Co. Kildare, Ireland. *(Died 31 July 1923.)*

FITZGIBBON, John, M.P. (N.) South Mayo since 1911; *b.* 1 June 1849; *m.* Mary A. O'Carroll. *Educ.:* St. Kyran's College, Kilkenny. Chairman Roscommon County Council; a trustee of the Irish Parliamentary Fund; on Congested Districts Board, Ireland (unpaid). *Address:* Castlerea, Co. Roscommon. *(Died 8 Sept. 1919.)*

FITZHARDINGE, 3rd Baron (U.K.) (*cr.* 1861), **Charles Paget Fitzharding** D.L.; M.F.H. (Fitzhardinge); *b.* 19 April 1830; *s.* of 1st Baron; *S.* brother 1896; *m.* 1866, Louisa Elizabeth (*d.* 1902), *o. d.* of H. Lindow-Lindow. M.P. Gloucester, 1862-65. *Heir:* none. *Address:* Berkeley Castle, Berkeley, Gloucestershire; Cranford House, Hounslow. *Club:* Travellers'. *(Died 3 Dec. 1916.)*

FITZHERBERT, Basil Thomas, J.P., D.L.; *e. surv. s.* of late Francis Fitzherbert and Maria Teresa, *d.* of late John Vincent Gandolfi, of East Sheen, Surrey; *b.* 1836; *s.* uncle, 1863; *m.* 1st, 1858, Emily Charlotte (*d.* 1881), *e. d.* of late Hon. Edward Stafford-Jerningham; 2nd, 1887, Emma Eliza, (*d.* 1912) 2nd *d.* of late Frederick Sewallis Gerard, and widow of 9th Lord Stafford. *Educ.:* Oscott. *Address:* Ensleigh, Grayshott, Haslemere. *(Died 13 April 1919.)*

FITZHERBERT - BROCKHOLES, William Joseph, C.B.E. 1918; J.P., D.L., and County Alderman, Lancaster; M.B.O.U.; Lord of the Manors of Claughton and Heaton; *b.* 1851; 2nd *surv. s.* of Francis Fitzherbert of Swynnerton, and Maria Teresa, *d.* of late John Vincent Gandolfi of East Sheen, Surrey; *S.* cousin, 1875; *m.* 1st, 1876, Mary Ida (*d.* 1883), 2nd *d.* of late Robert Berkeley of Spetchley, Co. Worcester; two *d.*; 2nd, 1885, Blanche (*d.* 1918,) 2nd *d.* of late Maj.-Gen. Hon. Sir Henry Hugh Clifford, V.C., K.C.M.G.; three *s.* two *d.* *Educ.:* St. Mary's College, Oscott. Farmed in Staffordshire, 1870-75; on the Council of the Royal Agricultural Society; an active Member of the Central Chamber of Agriculture and other agricultural bodies ; Member of the Lancs. C.Q. since its inception. *Recreations :* shooting, ornithology, formerly hunting. *Heir :* s. Major John William Fitzherbert-Brockholes, M.C. [*b.* 23 May 1889 ; *m.* 1917, Hon. Agnes Eileen French, *y. d.* of 4th Baron de Freyne.] *Address :* Claughton Hall, Garstang, Lancs. *T.A. :* Claughton, Bilsborough. *T. :* Preston, Brock 5. *Clubs :* Junior Carlton, Wellington.

(Died 21 Jan. 1924.)

FITZMAURICE, Sir Maurice, Kt., *cr.* 1912 ; C.M.G. 1902 ; F.R.S. 1919 ; Consulting Engineer ; member of firm of Coode, Fitzmaurice, Wilson. & Mitchell, Consulting Engineers for Harbours to the Crown Agents for the Colonies ; Consulting Engineers for Harbours and Docks at Singapore, Colombo, Hong-Kong, Lagos, and other ports ; Chief Engineers of the National Harbours at Dover and Peterhead ; Consulting Engineers to the Sudan Government for Blue Nile Irrigation Works ; Chief Engineer to the London County Council, 1901-12 ; *b.* 11 May 1861 ; *m.* 1911, Ida, *d.* of late Colonel Edward Dickinson, R.E., of West Lavington Hill, Midhurst, Sussex ; two *d. Educ. :* Trinity College, Dublin. M.A., M.A.I. (Dublin) ; LL.D. (Birmingham). Apprenticed to late Sir Benjamin Baker, K.C.B. ; President Inst.C.E. 1916-17 ; M.Inst. Mech. E. ; Chairman Engineering Joint Council, 1923-24 ; Hon. Member American Society of Civil Engineers ; Hon. Fellow Society of Engineers ; Hon. Member Royal Engineers Institution ; Member Engineering Institute of Canada ; Member of Advisory Council on Scientific and Industrial Research ; Member of International Technical Commission Suez Canal ; Chairman of Admiralty Advisory Committee on Naval Works, 1912-18 ; Chairman Canal Control Committee (Board of Trade), 1917-19 ; Chairman of Committee dealing with Civilian Labour London Defences (War Office), 1914-19 ; Member of War Office Committee on Hutted Camps, 1915-18 ; Chairman Nile Projects Committee (Foreign Office), 1918-19 ; Chairman of Committee on Aerodrome Accounts, etc. (Treasury), 1919 ; Member of Royal Commission on Fire Prevention ; Member of Advisory Council Science Museum, 1915-21 ; Commandant Engineer and Railway Staff Corps ; Engineer of the Rotherhithe Tunnel ; New Vauxhall Bridge ; visited Australia in 1913 at request of Commonwealth Government to advise on Naval Harbours and Works ; visited British Front in Flanders in 1915 at request of War Office to advise on questions of drainage and in 1918 ; also engaged on the Forth Bridge ; Railways and Docks in Canada ; the Blackwall Tunnel ; Nile Reservoir Dam, Assouan, Egypt. Order of Mejidieh, 2nd Class, 1901 ; Telford and Watt gold medals of Institution of Civil Engineers. *Publications :* Plate Girder Railway Bridges ; The Thames and Lea ; London County Bridges ; Main Drainage of London ; and many papers. *Recreations :* shooting, fishing. *Address :* 9 Victoria Street, Westminster, S.W. ; 54 Onslow Square, S.W.7. *T. :* Victoria 47, Kensington 6241 ; West Bay, Bridport, Dorset. *Club :* Reform. *(Died 17 Nov. 1924.)*

FITZ MAURICE, Vice-Admiral Sir Maurice Swynfen, K.C.V.O. *cr.* 1925 ; C.B. 1921 ; C.M.G. 1916 ; Commander-in-Chief, Africa Station, since 1924 ; *b.* 12 Aug. 1870 ; *e. s.* of late J. G. Fitz Maurice, Barrister ; *m.* 1896, Mabel Gertrude, *y. d.* of late S. W. Gray ; one *s.* Served Vitu, East Africa, 1893 (wounded, despatches, medal, clasp) ; River Gambia, 1894 (despatches, clasp) ; Boer War, 1899-1901 (medal 2 clasps) ; European War, 1914-18 (C.M.G.) ; Sacred Treasure of Japan (2nd cl.), 1917 ; Legion of Honour (officer), Royal Order of Redeemer, Greece ; Croix de Guerre, Greece ; Assistant Director of Naval

Intelligence, 1910 ; of Intelligence Division, Admiralty War Staff, 1912-14 ; Senior Officer on the Yangtse, 1914 ; Captain of Triumph, 1914, until torpedoed and sunk May 1915 ; Principal Naval Transport Officer, Dardanelles and Salonika. 1915-16 ; Chief of Staff Eastern Mediterranean, 1916-17 ; Capt. of Dreadnought, 1918 ; S.N.O. Coast of Palestine, 1918 ; Commodore Commanding British Aegean Squadron, 1919 ; Director of Naval Intelligence Admiralty, 1921-24 ; Vice-Admiral, 1926. *Clubs :* White's, United Service, Royal Automobile ; Royal Norfolk and Suffolk Yacht. *(Died 23 Jan. 1927.)*

FITZPATRICK, Rt. Rev. Mgr. Bartholomew, Vicar-General, Dublin, and Dean of the Chapter ; Priest of St. Kevin's, Dublin ; *b.* Dublin, 1847. *Educ. :* Carlow ; Clonliffe ; Irish College, Rome. Priest, 1870 ; Privy Chamberlain to the Pope, 1873 ; Domestic Prelate since 1905. *Address :* St. Kevin's, Heytesbury Street, Dublin.

(Died 16 Feb. 1925.)

FITZPATRICK, Sir Dennis, G.C.S.I., *cr.* 1911 ; K.C.S.I., *cr.* 1890 ; late Lt.-Gov. of Punjab ; and afterwards Member of Council of India, 1897 ; *b.* 1837 ; *s.* of late Thomas Fitzpatrick, M.D., Dublin ; *m.* 1862, Mary, *d.* of Col. H. Buller ; two *s.* two *d. Educ. :* Trinity College, Dublin. Barr. Inner Temple, 1872 ; was Resident at Hyderabad, and Secretary to the Government of India, Judge of the chief Court of the Punjab, and Chief Commissioner of Assam and of the Central Provinces : Member of Public Service Commission ; Acting Resident at Court of Maharajah of Mysore, 1877. *Address :* 2 Queen's Gate Gardens, S.W. *(Club :* Athenæum.

(Died 20 May 1920.)

FITZROY, Lord Frederick (John) ; Magistrate for Sussex and Northamptonshire ; *b.* 4 April 1823 ; *s.* of 5th Duke of Grafton ; *m.* 1853, Catherine Sarah Wilhelmina, *d.* of late Rev. William Wescomb, Rector of Langford ; one *s.* one *d. Educ. :* at sea. Entered the Navy, 1836 ; served in Syria, 1840 ; Grenadier Guards, 1848 ; served in Crimea, 1855 ; Canada, 1861-62 ; retired Lieut.-Col., 1862 ; M.P., Thetford, 1863-65. *Recreations :* shooting and farming. *Address :* 23 Grosvenor Street, W. ; Forest Farm, Balcomb, Hayward's Heath. *Clubs :* Travellers', Wellington. *(Died 13 Feb. 1919.)*

FITZWILLIAM, Captain Hon. Sir (William) Charles Wentworth-, G.C.V.O. *cr.* 1921 ; K.C.V.O. *cr.* 1911 ; C.V.O. 1910 ; D.L. ; Crown Equerry to King George, 1910-24 ; *b.* 31 March 1848 ; *s.* of 6th Earl Fitzwilliam and Lady Frances Harriet, *e. d.* of 19th Earl of Morton ; *m.* 1882, Constance Anne, *d.* of late Henry Brocklehurst ; one *s.* Late Captain Royal Horse Guards ; A.D.C. to Marquess of Ripon, Governor-General of India, 1880-82 ; Extra Equerry and Master of the Stables to the King (when Prince of Wales), 1901-10 ; High Sheriff of Rutland, 1898. *Address :* Barnsdale, Oakham. *Clubs :* Brooks's, Bachelors', Turf.

(Died 17 April 1925.)

FITZWILLIAM, Hon. William Henry Wentworth- ; D.L. Co. Wicklow ; *b.* 26 Dec. 1840 ; 2nd *s.* of 6th Earl Fitzwilliam ; *m.* Lady Mary Grace Louisa Butler, *d.* of 2nd Marquess of Ormonde, 1877 ; three *d. Educ. :* Eton ; Trinity Coll. Cambridge. M.P. (L.) Co. Wicklow, 1868-74 ; W.R Yorks, South Division, 1880-85 ; W.R. Yorks, Doncaster Division (L.U.), 1888-92 ; Member of Jockey Club since 1875. Hon. Lt.-Col. and Commandant 2nd Battalion North Riding of Yorkshire Volunteer Regt. ; Hon. Major 1st West Yorks Yeomanry, 1881. *Address :* Wigganthorpe, York. *T.A. :* Wigganthorpe, Terrington, Yorks. *Clubs :* Turf, Brooks's, Yorkshire. *(Died 10 July 1920.)*

FITZWYGRAM, Sir Frederick Loftus Francis, 5th Bart., *cr.* 1805 ; *b.* 11 Aug. 1884 ; *o. s.* of 4th Bart. and Angela, *d.* of Thomas Nugent Vaughan and Viscountess Forbes. *S.*

father 1904. *Educ.:* Eton; Magdalen College, Oxford (M.A.). Is Captain Scots Guards; served European War, 1914 - 15 (despatches, wounded twice). Owns 2000 acres in Hants. *Heir-pres.:* Edgar Thomas Ainger Wigram, B.A. [b. 23 Nov. 1864. *Educ.:* Trinity Hall, Cambridge. *Address:* Watling House, St. Albans] *Address:* Leigh Park, Havant, Hants. *Clubs:* Guards', Carlton. *(Died 5 May 1920.)*

FLAMMARION, Camille; Astronomer: *b.* Montigny-le-Roi (Haute Marne), 26 Feb. 1842; *m.* 1st 1874; 2nd 1919, Gabrielle Renaudot. *Educ.:* Langres, 1853-56; Paris Observatory under Le Verrier, 1858-62; Sorbonne, under Delaunay, 1862; Bureau des Longitudes, 1862-66. Founded monthly review l'Astronomie, 1882; founded Observatory of Juvisy, 1883; founded Astronomical Society of France, 1887. *Publications:* (translated into English) Marvels of the Heavens, 1870; The Atmosphere, 1873; Urania, 1891; Omega, the Last Days of the World, 1893; Popular Astronomy, 1894; Lumen, 1897; The Unknown, 1900; Astronomy for Amateurs, 1904; Mysterious Psychic Forces, 1907; Death and its Mystery, in three parts, 1920, 1921, 1922; Dreams of an Astronomer, 1923. *Address:* The Observatory, Juvisy, Seine-et-Oise, France.
(Died 4 June 1925.)

FLANAGAN, Rev. J., minister of the Primitive Methodist Church; *b.* Mansfield, 18 December 1851; *s.* of William Patrick Flanagan, Co. Waterford, Ireland; and Elizabeth Robinson, Edwinstowe, Notts; *m.* Mary Jane Richardson of Newark-on-Trent, 1872; four *s.* four *d. Educ.:* became a Christian after marriage; commenced education while toiling as a miner. Called by Providence to be a mission preacher; toiled at this for about 15 years; then pastor of the United Gospel Mission, Albert Hall, Nottingham, 4 years; received into full ministry of Primitive Methodist Church, 1890; sent to London; built up a mission church in the Boro', S.E.; erected St. George's Hall and Schools, Old Kent Road; earned and raised £20,000 in 13 years for the poor of slums; now minister without charge. *Publications:* Romance of Evangelism; Man's Quest in Sermon and Song; Scenes from my Life, both Grave and Gay; Thy Brother's Blood. *Recreations:* preaching, travelling, and lecturing. *Address:* 20 Patrick Road, West Bridgeford, Nottingham.
(Died 30 Mar. 1918.)

FLATHER, James Henry, M.A.; late Secretary for Examinations to the Local Examinations and Lectures Syndicate of the University of Cambridge; *b.* Sheffield, 11 Aug. 1853; *y. s.* of late Rev. John Flather; *m.* Jane, *y. d.* of late Charles Thomas Shaw of Birmingham. *Educ.:* Collegiate School, Sheffield; Emmanuel College, Cambridge. First Class in Classical Tripos, 1876; Lightfoot University Scholar, 1877; Assistant Master at Lancaster Grammar School, 1877; Tutor (1878) and Master (1888-91) of Cavendish College; Assist. Secretary to Local Examinations and Lectures Syndicate, 1892. *Publications:* contributions to Smith's Dictionary of Greek and Roman Antiquities (3rd edit.); editions of works by Scott, etc. *Address:* Lawden Cottage, Newton Road, Cambridge. *T.:* Cambridge 838. *(Died 3 Nov. 1928.)*

FLEET, Vice-Adm. Henry Louis; C.B.E. 1918; *b.* 1 May 1850; 3rd *s.* of J. G. Fleet, late of Roystons, Chiswick, and Esther Faithfull, *d.* of Rev. F. F. Faithfull; *m.* Alice Mary, *d.* of W. F. Elliot of Wilton, Somerset. *Educ.:* St. Paul's School; St. Mary's Hall, Southsea. Entered Royal Navy, 1864; Captain, 1895; commanded Indian Naval Defence, Bombay, 1897-1900; J.P., Bombay; Flag Capt. at Queenstown, 1900-3; Capt. Western District, 1903; Rear-Admiral (retired), 1905; possesses the Canadian Medal, Egyptian Medal, Khedive's

Star, and Coronation Medal; awarded Humane Society's Certificate, 1884; Nautical Assessor to House of Lords, 1910; County Director Auxiliary Hospitals of V.A.D., Berkshire. *Publications:* An Admiral's Yarns; My Life and a Few Yarns, 1922. *Address:* The Camber, Coley Avenue, Reading. *Club:* United Service.
(Died 17 Sept. 1923.)

FLEET, John Faithfull, C.I.E. 1884; *s.* of John George Fleet; *b.* 1847. *Educ.:* Merchant Taylors' School. Was in Indian Civil Service, 1867-97; Commissioner of Central and Southern Divisions of Bombay, 1891-97. *Publications:* Inscriptions of the Early Gupta Kings, vol. iii. of the Corpus Inscriptionum Indicarum, 1888; and numerous other writings on the ancient history and antiquities of India, in the Indian Antiquary, the Epigraphia Indica, the Journal of the Royal Asiatic Society, and elsewhere; holds Triennial Gold Medal, Royal Asiatic Society. *Address:* 8 Leopold Road, Ealing Common, W. *Club:* East India United Service.
(Died 21 Feb. 1917.)

FLEMING, Sir Andrew Fleming Hudleston 1e, 8th Bt.; *cr.* 1705; *b.* Easedale, near Canterbury, New Zealand, 1855; *s.* of 7th Bt. and Mary, *d.* of Capt. Boddie, Russian Navy; *S.* father, 1883; *m.* 1895, Jeannette, *d.* of late Roderick Frazer, Otago. *Educ.:* Christ Coll., Canterbury. *Heir: c.* William Hudleston Le Fleming. *Address:* Woodgrove, Canterbury, N.Z. *(Died 20 Oct. 1925.)*

FLEMING, Major Charles Christie, D.S.O. 1898; late Royal Army Medical Corps; Assistant Director of Medical Services, Highland Division, with rank of Colonel, since 1915; late Secretary (Scottish Branch) British Red Cross Society, Headquarters, Glasgow; *b.* 6 Nov. 1864; 2nd *s.* of late Dep.-Surg.-Gen. A. Fleming and Catherine, *d.* of Capt. Joseph Henry Garner. *Educ.:* Edinburgh University (M.B., C.M.). Entered Army Med. Service, 1892, and became Surg.-Capt. (now Capt. Royal Army Med. Corps), 1895; Major, 1904; served as Senior Med. Officer at Suakim (1896-97), at Kassala (1897-98), and at actions at Gedaref, 1898 (despatches, medal with clasp, Soudan medal (Queen's), D.S.O.); South Africa as M.O. in charge No. 2 Ambulance Train, 1899-1902 (medal with five clasps; King's medal, 2 clasps). *Recreations:* fishing, shooting. *Address:* 8 Napier Road, Edinburgh. *Clubs:* Junior Constitutional; Caledonian United Service, Edinburgh; Western, Glasgow. *(Died 24 Dec. 1917.)*

FLEMING, Rev. David, Hon. Canon of Durham. *Address:* Coxhoe Vicarage, County Durham. *(Died 15 Dec. 1920.)*

FLEMING, Sir Francis, K.C.M.G., *cr.* 1892; J.P.; *b.* 1842; *s.* of late James Fleming, Q.C. and Julia, *d.* of late Maj. John Canning; *m.* Constance Mary, *d.* of M. D. Kavanagh, barrister, and Hon. Mrs. Kavanagh, 1892. *Educ.:* Downside College. Barr. Middle Temple, 1866; Crown Solicitor, Mauritius, 1869; District Magistrate, 1872; District Judge, Jamaica, 1876; Attorney-General, Barbados, 1878; acted as private sec. to Sir G. C. Strahan, K.C.M.G.; Gov. of Cape Colony, 1880; Puisne Judge, British Guiana, 1882; Queen's Advocate, Ceylon, 1883; Col. Sec. Mauritius, 1886; Col. Sec. Hong-Kong, 1889; Act.-Gov. Mauritius, 1886-87; of Hong-Kong, 1890; Gov. Sierra Leone, 1892; Consul for Liberia, 1892; Governor of Leeward Islands, 1895-1901; late Poor Law Guardian for Parish of St. Mary Abbot's, Kensington. *Address:* 9 Sydney Place, S.W.7. *T.:* Kens. 568.
(Died 4 Dec. 1922.)

FLEMING, Frederick, K.C. Ireland. *Address:* 69 Merrion Square, Dublin.

FLEMING, Rev. Herbert James, C.M.G., 1916; M.A.; Chaplain to the Forces, 1st class; *b.* 1 Jan. 1873. *Educ.:* Pembroke College, Oxford (Scholar). Ordained 1897;

Curate of St. Mary, South Shields, 1897-99 ; South Petherton, 1899-1902 ; Chaplain to Forces, Aldershot, 1902-4 ; Ballincollig, 1904-6 ; Woolwich, 1906-7 ; Crete, 1907-9 ; Gibraltar, 1909-11 ; R.M.A., Woolwich, 1911-14 ; served European War, 1914-18 (despatches twice, C.M.G.) ; R.M.A., Woolwich, 1918 - 22 ; Shorncliffe, 1922-23 : Royal Hospital, Chelsea, 1923. *Address :* Royal Hospital, Chelsea, S.W.
(Died 17 Nov. 1926.)

FLEMING, James, I.S.O. 1903 ; late Collector of Customs, London, and Chief Registrar of Shipping ; retired, 1906 ; *b.* Aghadowey, Co. Londonderry, 1841 ; 5th *s.* of late Edward Fleming of Coleraine ; *m.* 1868, Jane, *d.* of late Wm. Hastings of Portstewart ; two *s.* four *d.* Clerk in Customs, London, 1858 ; Surveyor, 1882 ; Inspector, 1894 ; Surveyor-General, 1900 ; witness before Playfair, Ridley, Port of London, and Civil Service Superannuation Royal Commissions ; Chairman of Inter - departmental Committee on Tobacco Drawback, 1904 ; Member of Committee of Civil Service Supply Association, Ltd. *Address :* Hastings Villa, Rudall Crescent, Hampstead Heath, N.W.
(Died 22 Dec. 1923.)

FLEMING, James Alexander, K.C. 1903 ; Sheriff of Fife and Kinross since 1913 ; Vice-Dean of the Faculty of Advocates, 1905-21 ; *b.* 1855 ; *e. surv. s.* of late James Simpson Fleming, Cashier and General Manager of the Royal Bank of Scotland, and Elizabeth, *d.* of Thomas Reid of Hayston, Stirlingshire ; *m.* Helen Mary, *d.* of William Hudson Swire, merchant, London, 1898. *Educ. :* Glasgow Academy ; Uppingham ; Edinburgh University. Apprenticed to mercantile firms of James Finlay & Co., Glasgow and London ; Steel, Macfarlane & Co., Port-Elizabeth, Cape Colony ; served with James Finlay & Co., Liverpool ; Heugh Balfour & Co., and Robert Barclay & Co., Manchester, and Royal Bank of Scotland ; passed as advocate, 1883 ; Scottish Counsel to Statute Law Committee, 1890-98 and 1900 ; Counsel to Post Office in Scotland, 1891-1900 ; Sheriff-Court Depute, 1892 ; and again in 1895 ; Extra Advocate Depute, 1896 ; Advocate Depute, 1898 ; Sheriff of Dumfries and Galloway, 1900-1913. *Address :* 33 Melville Street, Edinburgh. *T. :* Central 2373, Edinburgh. *Clubs :* Junior Carlton ; New, University, Edinburgh ; Western, Glasgow.
(Died 12 April 1926.)

FLEMING, Sir John, Kt., *cr.* 1908 ; J.P., D.L., LL.D. ; *b.* 1847 ; *s.* of John Fleming, Dundee ; *m.* 1870, Elizabeth, *d.* of John Dow, Dundee ; three *s.* four *d.* *Educ. :* Brown Street and High Schools, Dundee. Timber Merchant, Aberdeen ; has been Member of Aberdeen Town Council, Harbour Board, and Chamber of Commerce ; Vice-Chairman Aberdeen Territorial Force ; Lord Provost of Aberdeen, 1898-1902. *Address :* Dulmumzie, Murtle, near Aberdeen.
(Died 25 Feb. 1925.)

FLEMING, His Honour Patrick D., M.A., K.C. ; County Court Judge for King's Co., Longford, Meath, and Westmeath, 1918-24 ; *b.* Sunville, Kilmallock, Co. Limerick, *Educ. :* Trinity College, Dublin (M.A. Senior Moderator and Gold Medallist) ; Middle Temple (Scholar). Called to Irish Bar, 1881 ; Inner Bar, 1904. *Address :* 15 Herbert Street, Dublin. *Club :* Stephen's Green, Dublin. *(Died April 1928.)*

FLEMING, Lt.-Col. Samuel, Metropolitan Police Magistrate, Greenwich and Woolwich, 1921-24 ; Lambeth, since 1924 ; *b.* 1865 ; *s.* of late Fredk. Green Fleming ; *m.* 1892, Elizabeth Knox, *d.* of Col. Wm. Clare Ball, C.B. Bar. Gray's Inn and Middle Temple, 1897 ; legal adviser and Judge Advocate Aldershot Command, and subsequently legal adviser at War Office to Army Medical Dept. during European War, 1914-19 ; Deputy Assistant Director-General, 1917 ; Recorder of Doncaster, 1920-1 ; Member of Bar Council ; J.P. Surrey, 1921.

Address : 315 St. James Court, Buckingham Gate, W.1. *Clubs :* Conservative, Royal Automobile. *(Died 20 Dec. 1925.)*

FLEMING, Valentine, M.P. (C.) South Oxfordshire (Henley Division) since 1910 ; Barrister-at-Law ; Major Oxfordshire Yeomanry ; *e. s.* of Robert Fleming, of Joyce Grove, Nettlebed, and 8 Crosby Square E.C. ; *b.* Newport, Fife, N.B., 1882 ; *m.* Evelyn B. St. C. Rose, *d.* of George A. St. C. Rose, The Red House, Sonning ; four *s.* *Educ. :* Eton ; Magdalen Coll., Oxford ; B.A. (Honours in History), 1905. Rowed in Eton Eight, 1900 ; Magdalen College Eight three years ; won Ladies' Plate at Henley, 1904, and Final of Visitors Cup ; rowed University Trial Eights ; called to Bar, Inner Temple, 1907 ; partner in Robert Fleming and Co., 8 Crosby Square, E.C. ; has travelled in Europe and America ; served European War (despatches). *Recreations :* deerstalking, salmon fishing, fox-hunting, hunts a pack of Basset hounds. *Address :* Arnisdale, Loch Hourn, Invernessshire ; Pitt House, Hampstead Heath, N.W. *Clubs :* Carlton, Travellers', White's, Bath.
(Died 20 May 1917.)

FLEMMING, Hon. James Kidd, LL.D. ; M.P. for Carleton, Victoria, New Brunswick, since 1925 ; *b.* 27 April 1868, of Irish parentage ; *m.* 1890, Helena S. Fleming ; three *s.* two *d.* *Educ. :* common schools and Provincial Normal School. Since 1890 been engaged in commercial pursuits ; contested the provincial election for native county in 1895, and again in 1899 ; in a by-election, Jan. 1900, was successful, and was re-elected 1903, 1908, and 1912 ; Provincial Secretary and Receiver-General in the Hazen Administration, 1908 - 11 ; Premier of New Brunswick, 1911-16 ; President and Manager, Flemming and Gibson Ltd., and engaged in lumbering business. *Address :* Box 297, House of Commons, Ottawa, Ontario ; Juniper, New Brunswick. *T. :* 10-3. *(Died 10 Feb. 1927.)*

FLEMWELL, George Jackson, artist and author ; *b.* The Chesnuts, Mitcham, Surrey, 29 May 1865 ; *e. s.* of John Flemwell and Anne Catherine Lancefield ; *m.* 1912, Grace, *y. d.* of John Priddle, of Muswell Hill. *Educ. :* Thanet College, Margate ; private tutor. Studied four years with W. P. Frith, R.A., afterwards, on the advice and introduction of Sir Alma Tadema, R.A., going to Antwerp and studying with Prof. Rosier ; then to Nuremberg and Munich ; exhibited figure subjects at the Royal Academy for four or five years, but abandoned this branch of work ; settled in Switzerland and devoted himself to painting and studying the Alps and Alpine wild life. *Publications :* Alpine Flowers and Gardens ; The Flower Fields of Alpine Switzerland ; Sur l'Alpe Fleurie ; Beautiful Switzerland ; Lucerne ; Locarno ; Lugano ; Lausanne ; Villars and Champery ; Chamonix ; Zermatt : Known and Little-Known ; Mooning in Paradise ; the plates for H. Stuart Thomson's Sub-Alpine Plants ; essays and illustrations in various English, Continental and American publications. *Recreations :* nature-study, gardening. *Address :* c/o Swiss Office of Tourism, Löwenstrasse, Zurich, Switzerland. *Clubs :* Alpin Suisse ; Alpin Francais. *(Died 5 Mar. 1928.)*

FLERS, Marquis de (Robert de Flers) ; Membre de l'Académie Française 1920 ; Président de la Société des Auteurs et Compositeurs Dramatiques ; Directeur littéraire du Figaro ; *b.* Pont l'Évêque, 25 Nov. 1872 ; petit - fils d'Eugène de Rozière, membre de l'Institut ; arrière-petit-fils de Charles Giraud, membre de l'Institut et ministre de l'Instruction Publique ; *m.* 1901, G., *d.* of Victorien Sardou, de l'Académie Française ; one *s.* *Educ. :* Lycée Condorcet, Paris. Licencié en Droit et ès Lettres, Lauréat de l'Académie Française en 1894 homme de lettres, journaliste et auteur dramatique; plusieurs fois président de la Société des Auteurs et Compositeurs Dramatiques; Officier de la Légion d'Honneur 1913. *Publications:* articles parus dans la Liberté, le Gaulois et dans le Figaro; Vers l'Orient; La Courtisane Taïa et son singe vert; Ilsée, princesse de Tripoli; Entre cœur et chair; Sur les chemins de la Guerre; La Petite Table Théâtre; Le Cœur a ses raisons; La Chance du mari; Les Sentiers de la vertu; La Montansier; L'Ange du foyer; Miquette et sa mère; L'Amour veillé; Les Travaux d'Hercule; Le Sire de Vergy; Paris ou le Bon Juge; Monsieur de la Palisse; Papa; Le Roi; L'Habit vert; L'Âne de Buridan; Le Bois sacré; Monsieur Brotonneau; Primerose; Venise; Le Retour; Fortunio; Béatrice; (Collaborateurs; pour le plupart de ses pièces: G.,A de Caillavet; pour le Retour: F. de Croisset. Musiciens collaborateurs A. Messager; Claude Terrasse). *Address:* 70 boulevard de Courcelles Paris 17. *T.:* Wagram 01-09 (*Died 30 July 1927.*)

FLETCHER, The Honourable Edward Ernest; Judge of the Supreme Court, Calcutta; *m.* Millicent Valentine (*d.* 1917); *e. d.* of Horace Waddington, late H.M.I. of Schools. *Address:* Supreme Court, Calcutta.

FLETCHER, Lt.-Col. Sir Henry Arthur, Kt., *cr.* 1919; C.V.O. 1909; Lieutenant H.M. Bodyguard of the Honourable Corps of Gentlemen-at-Arms since 1922; *b.* 20 Apr. 1843; *s.* of the late Charles William Fletcher, Board of Control, India Office; *m.* 1881, Constance (*d.* 1921), *d.* of E. Headland, 93 Portland Place, W.; no *c.* *Educ.:* Private Schools. Served in Bengal Cavalry, 1860-1889; North-West Frontier of India, 1863-64; affair of Shabkadar, etc. (medal and clasp); Egyptian Campaign, 1882 (medal and bronze star); appointed to the Honourable Corps of Gentlemen-at-Arms, 1892; Clerk of the Cheque and Adjutant, 1900-20; Standard Bearer, 1920-1922. *Address:* 17 Victoria Square, S.W.1; St. James's Palace, S.W. *Clubs:* United Service, Garrick. (*Died 24 Dec. 1925.*)

FLETCHER, Herbert Phillips, F.R.I.B.A., F.S.I., A.M.I.C.E., architect; *b.* 27 Feb. 1872; *s.* of late Professor Banister Fletcher, M.P., J.P., etc.; *m.* Lydia, *o. d.* of late T. T. Lindrea, J.P., Westbury, Glos. *Educ.:* King's College, London. (Gold Medal in the Architectural and Engineering Course.) Has travelled round the world; obtained the highest examination diplomas at the Institute of British Architects, Surveyors' Institute, and the Institution of Civil Engineers; has been called to Bar at Middle Temple; Architect to the Worshipful Company of Carpenters, and Technical Adviser to six of the associated City Companies; is Director of their Trades Training Schools; lately Lecturer on staff of King's College, and acting District Surveyor for Newington; Godwin Bursar, R.I.B.A., 1904; partner in firm of Banister Fletcher and Sons, whose works include King's Coll. School, and numerous banks, schools, churches, city buildings, and country houses; alterations and additions King's College, London, Carpenters' Hall, London Wall, etc. ; was lent to the French Navy as senior military observer for reconnaissance work in seaplanes from Aden to Gallipoli, March 1915–Feb. 1916; awarded Croix de Guerre three times, twice by the French navy and once by the army; afterwards attached to the R.N.A.S. in same capacity when they took over this patrol, and was O.C. of Military Observers' School at Port Said; seconded to the Royal Flying Corps, 1916. *Publications:* The English Home, Architectural Hygiene, Carpentry and Joinery, Arbitrations, Quantities, London Building Acts, Valuations and Compensations, Light and Air, Dilapidations, and other text-books. *Recreations:* hunting; late deputy master and joint-huntsman of the North Bucks Harriers. shooting, sailing,

and golf; major Middlesex Hussars. *Address:* 29 New Bridge Street, E.C.; Park House, Marden, Kent; Cuthbert Villa, Westgate-on-Sea. *T.A.:* Banister, London. *T.:* 741 Holborn *Clubs:* Cavalry, Pegasus; various golf. (*Died Aug. 1917.*)

FLETCHER, James Douglas, J.P., D.L.; *b.* 1857 ; *e. surv. s.* of late James Fletcher, and Frederica Mary, *d.* of John Stephen and *widow* of Alexander Hay, 58th Regt.; *m.* 1000, Lilian, *y. d.* of late Col. Stephen, C.B. *Educ.:* Eton; Balliol College, Oxford. *Address:* Rosehaugh, Avoch, Ross-shire; 26 Curzon Street, W.1. *T.:* Mayfair 1925. *Clubs:* Arthur's, Carlton (*Died 30 Aug. 1927.*)

FLETCHER, Rev. John Charles Ballett, Canon of Chichester. *Address:* North Mundham Vicarage, Chichester. (*Died 6 May 1926.*)

FLETCHER, Sir John Samuel, 1st Bt., *cr.* 1919; J.P.; *b.* 1841; 2nd *s.* of Samuel Fletcher, Manchester; *m.* 1895. Sara, *d.* of late Jonathan Clark of Winchendon, Bucks. *Educ.:* Harrow; Christ Church, Oxford. Chairman, Hampstead Board of Guardians, 1880-1898; Member L.C.C., 1889-1904; Deputy Chairman, 1900;. Bar, Lincoln's Inn, 1868; M.P. (U.) Hampstead, 1905-18. *Heir:* none. *Address:* Bryony Hill, Hambledon, Surrey. *Clubs:* Albemarle, St. Stephen's.

(*Died 20 May 1924.*)

FLETCHER, Sir Lazarus, Kt., *cr.* 1916; M.A. (Oxon.), Hon. LL.D. (St. Andrews), Hon. Ph.D. and A.M. (Berlin), F.R.S.; Hon. Fellow of University College, Oxford, 1910; *b.* Salford, 3 Mar. 1854; *e. s.* of Stewart Fletcher, Manchester; *m.* 1st, Agnes Ward (*d.* 1915), *d.* of Rev. Thomas Holme, Vicar of Moorside, Oldham; one *d.*; 2nd, 1916, Edith, sister of the above. *Educ.:* Manchester Gram. School; Balliol Coll. Oxford (Brakenbury Science Scholar); 1st class Math. Mods.; 1st class Final Mathematical School; 1st class Natural Science School. National Gold Medal (Mechanics) and Bronze Medal (Mathematics) awarded by Science and Art Department, 1872; highly distinguished for the University Junior Mathematical Scholarship, Oxford, 1874; Demonstrator in the Clarendon Laboratory, Oxford, 1875-77; Fellow Univ. Coll. Oxford, 1877-1880; Millard Lecturer in Physics, Trin. Coll. Oxford, 1877-1878; University Senior Mathematical Scholarship, Oxford, 1876; Keeper of Minerals in British Museum (Natural History), 1880-1909; Director of the Natural History Depts. of the British Museum, 1909-19; Public Examiner (Natural Science) Oxford, 1880; Examiner for Natural Sciences Tripos, Camb. 1882-83, 1889-91, 1896-97; Vice-Pres. Royal Soc. 1910-12; Vice-Pres. Geological Society, 1890-92, and Vice-Pres. of Physical Society, 1895-97; Council of Royal Society, 1895-97 and 1910-12; Pres. Mineralogical Society, 1885-88; General Secretary, 1888-1909; Pres. of the Geological Section of the British Association at Oxford, 1894; Wollaston Medallist, Geological Society, 1912; Member of the Boards of Electors to the Professorships of Mineralogy at Oxford and Cambridge; Corresponding Member of the Royal Society of Göttingen, the Academy of Sciences, Munich, and the New York Academy of Sciences. Honorary Member of the Sociedad Cientifica Antonio Alzate, Mexico; Association Scientifique et d'Enseignement Médical complémentaire; Selborne Society; Hertfordshire Natural History Society and Field Club; Ealing Scientific and Microscopical Society; Museums Association. *Publications:* Introduction to the Study of Meteorites, 1881; Introduction to the Study of Minerals, 1884; Introduction to the Study of Rocks, 1895; The Optical Indicatrix, 1892; papers on crystallographical, physical, and mineralogical subjects and on meteorites; article on Meteorites in the Encyclopædia Britannica and on Precious Stones of the Bible in the International Standard Bible Encyclopædia. *Recreation :* gardening. *Address :* The .White House, Ravenstonedale, Westmorland. *Clubs :* Athenæum, Savile. *(Died 6 Jan. 1921.)*

FLETCHER, Rev. Philip, 5th *s.:* of Sir Henry Fletcher, 3rd Bt. ; *b.* Ashley Park, Walton - on - Thames, 30 Oct. 1848. *Educ. :* Exeter College, Oxford (M.A.). For six years curate at St. Bartholomew's 'Church, Brighton ; received into the Catholic Church, 1878 ; Priest, 1882 ; Founder of the Guild of Our Lady of Ransom for the Spread of the Catholic Religion and the organisation of Public Process ons and Pilgrimages ; these have been carried on for 30 years ; has contributed weekly articles to the Catholic Press since 1886 ; Chevalier d' l'Ordre de la Couronne (Belgium, 1919) ; Knight Commander of the Order of the Holy Sepulchre, 1920. *Address :* 29 Portugal Street, Kingsway, W.C. *(Died 13 Jan. 1928.)*

FLETCHER, Rev. Robert, M.A. ; Prebendary of Hereford since 1902. *Address :* Armidale, Roumania Crescent, Llandudno.
(Died 15 April 1921.)

FLETCHER, Ven. Robert Crompton ; Archdeacon of Blackburn since 1901 ; Rector of Chorley, Lancashire, 1907 ; Alderman of Lancashire County Council since 1889 ; Surrogate of diocese of Manchester since 1888 ; *b.* Fremantle, W. Australia, 9 Dec. 1850 ; *e. s.* of late Rev. Matthew Fox Fletcher, Rector of Tarleton, and Louisa Jane Crompton, *d.* of Andrew Todd of Lower Darley Hall ; *m.* 1st, 1878, Nina Helen (*d.* 1904), *e. d.* of Henry Rawcliffe, J.P., of Gillibrand Hall, Lancs ; three *s.* five *d.* ; 2nd, 1909, Jessie, *d.* of late James Knowles, and widow of Rev. J. Tyas. *Educ. :* Rossall ; Sidney-Sussex College, Cambridge (M.A.). Ordained, 1874 ; Assis -Master, King William's College, Isle of Man, 1872-73 ; Curate of Tarleton, 1874-75 ; Rector and Vicar of Tarleton, 1875-1907. *Address :* The Rectory, Chorley, Lancashire. *T.A. :* Archdeacon, Chorley, Lancashire. *T. :* 140 Chorley. *Club :* Royal Societies.
(Died 27 Feb. 1917.)

FLETCHER, Major William Alfred Littledale, D.S.O. 1900 ; Lieut.-Col., 2/6 Rifle Batt. King's Liverpool Regt. ; *b.* Childwall, 25 Aug. 1869 ; *s.* of Alfred Fletcher, J.P., D.L. *Educ. :* Eton ; Christ Church, Oxford. Served South Africa, Lieut., 2nd Batt. Imperial Yeomanry, 1900 (D.S.O.) ; European War, 1914-18 (Bt. Major), now commanding in France (despatches thrice, Legi on of Honour). *Recreations :* rowing (Eton Eight, 1890 ; Oxford Eight, 1890-93), big game shooting and travelling. *Address :* Allerton, Liverpool. *Clubs :* Bath, Sports, Leander. *(Died 14 Feb. 1919.)*

FLETCHER, Ven. William Henry, M.A. ; Archdeacon of Wrexham, 1910-25 ; *s.* of late Rev. Henry Fletcher and Mrs. Fletcher of Ulceby Grange, Lincolns. ; *m.* Agnes (*d.* 1922), *d.* of George Crawford, Thornwood, Lanarkshire ; one *s. Educ. :* Shrewsbury School. Caresswell Scholar of Christ Church, Oxford ; 2nd Class Moderations, 1874 ; B.A. 1876 ; curate of Holy Trinity, Shrewsbury, 1876-78 ; vicar of Criftins by Ellesmere, 1878-82 ; vicar of Holy Trinity, Shrewsbury, 1882-88 ; vicar of Oswestry, 1888-91 ; cursal canon of St. Asaph Cathedral, 1891-97 ; Vicar of Wrexham, 1891-1907 ; Rural Dean of Wrexham, 1891-1907 ; Rector of Marchwiel, Denbighshire, 1907 ; Canon Residentiary, 1897-1910 ; Proctor in Convocation for Cathedral Chapter, 1897 - 1910. *Address :* Marchwiel Rectory, Wrexham. *(Died 2 April 1926.)*

FLINN, D. Edgar, V.D., F.R.C.S., D.P.H., M.R.C.P. ; Medical Member General Prisons Board, Ireland ; H.M. Chief Inspector, Reformatory and Industrial Schools, Ireland, 1910-17 ; *b.* 1850 ; *s.* of late David Edgar Flinn, Buenos

Ayres. *Educ. :* Clongowes, Royal College Surgeons, Ireland ; Univ., Dublin. Served for 25 years in the Volunteer and Territorial Forces, and Army Medical Reserve, retiring with rank of Colonel, 1904 ; Fellow of the Royal Sanitary Institute, London ; Medical Inspector, Local Government Board, Ireland, 1896-1910 : Member of Belfast Vice-Regal Commission, 1907-8 ; Member of Committee of Inquiry as to the causes of Typhoid Fever in Dublin, 1893 ; President State Medicine Section Royal Academy Med., Ireland, 1894 and 1895 ; Editor Health Record, 1890-94 ; Fellow and Member of Council, Royal College Surgeons, Ireland, 1906-11 and 1916-1921 ; formerly M.O.H., East Staffordshire, combined Urban and Rural Districts ; Examiner in Hygiene and Public Health, Royal Colleges Physicians and Surgeons, Ireland. *Publications :* Ireland, its Health Resorts and Watering Places ; Refuse Disposal ; Public Cleansing of Towns ; Rural Water Supplies ; Our Dress and Our Food ; The Administration of the Public Health Acts in Ireland, the Public Health of Dublin, and many Government Reports. *Recreations :* golf, travel, and reading. *Clubs :* Stephen's Green, Dublin. *(Died 18 Aug. 1926.)*

FLINT, Joseph, C.M.G. 1900 ; Formerly Agent-General Niger Co. Ltd. ; *b.* 7 Sep. 1855. Twenty-four years in Nigeria ; transferred the administration Royal Niger Co. Ltd. to the Gov. of Northern Nigeria to Sir Frederick Lugard, C.B., K.C.M.G., and S. Nigeria to Sir Ralph Moor, K.C.M.G., Jan. 1900 ; Agent-Gen. for the Royal Niger Co. Ltd. in conjunction with W. Wallace, C.M.G., from 1886 to time of transfer to Government, Jan. 1900. *Address :* Rosemount, Sanderstead. *(Died 26 Aug. 1925.)*

FLINT, Thomas Barnard, M.A., LL.B., D.C.L. ; Clerk of the House of Commons of Canada since 1902 ; *b.* Yarmouth, Nova Scotia, Canada, 28 April 1847 ; *s.* of late John Flint, Shipowner, and Anne Barnard Flint of Yarmouth, N.S. ; *m.* 1874, Mary Ella, of Yarmouth, *d.* of late Thos. B. Dane. *Educ. :* Mt. Allison University, Sackville, New Brunswick, Canada ; Harvard University, Cambridge, Mass., U.S.A. Admitted to the Supreme Court Bar of Nova Scotia, 1871 ; Commissioner of the Supreme and County Courts and in Admiralty, 1873 ; High Sheriff of the County of Yarmouth, Nova Scotia, 1884 - 87 ; Assistant Clerk of the Provincial Assembly, 1887-91 ; Member (L.) for the County of Yarmouth, House of Commons of Canada, 1891 ; re-elected, 1896 and 1900 ; Chief Government Whip for Maritime Provinces, 1896 - 1900 ; Chairman of the Committee on Standing Orders of the House, 1898-1902 ; Grand Master of the Grand Lodge of Nova Scotia, A.F. and A.M., 1897, 1898, and 1899. *Publications :* editor 3rd and 4th editions Bourinot's Parliamentary Practice a id Procedure. *Recreations :* travel and research. *Address :* House of Commons, Ottawa, Canada. *Club :* Canadian, Ottawa.
(Died 7 Mar. 1919.)

FLOOD, Chevalier William Henry Grattan, Hon. Mus.D., N.U.I. ; K.S.G. ; P.C., Organist of Enniscorthy Cathedral since 1895 ; *b.* Lismore, Co. Waterford, 1 Nov. 1859 ; *e. s.* of William Flood and Catherine, *d.* of Andrew Fitzsimon ; *m.* 1898, Margaret, *e. d.* of Patrick Delaney, Enniscorthy ; two *s.* four *d. Educ. :* Mount Melleray, Catholic University, All Hallows College, and Carlow College. Successively Organist of Belfast pro-Cathedral ; Professor at Tullabeg and Clongowes Wood Colleges ; Organist of Thurles Cathedral ; Professor at St. Wilfrid's, Cotton Hall (Staffs.), and St. Kieran's College, Kilkenny. *Publications :* History of Enniscorthy ; History of Irish Music, 4th ed. 1927 ; Story of the Harp; Story of the Bagpipe; Memoir of W. Vincent Wallace; History of the Diocese of Ferns, 1916; Introductory Sketch of Irish Musical History, 1921; Memoir of John Field, Inventor of the Nocturne, 1921; Early Tudor Composers, 1925; Late Tudor Composers, 1929; two Masses, numerous Motets and Services, songs, part music, hymns, etc. Editor of Moore's Irish Melodies, the Spirit of the Nation, and Selected Airs of O'Carolan; musical editor of the standard Catholic Hymnal for Ireland; decorated by Pope Leo XIII. and by Pius X. and XI.; received the Cross Pro Ecclesia et Pontifice, 1917; Vice-President of the Irish Folk Song Society; Council Member of the Catholic Record Society of Ireland; Foundation Member of the National Academy of Ireland. *Publications:* contributions to the Dictionary of National Biography, Grove's Dictionary of Music and Musicians, 3rd. ed. 1927-8, Catholic Encyclopaedia, home and foreign periodicals, etc. *Recreation:* tracing the sources of old songs and tunes. *Address:* Rosemount, Enniscorthy, Co. Wexford. *(Died 6 Aug. 1928.)*

FLORENCE, Lt.-Col. Henry Louis, V.D.; Past Vice-Pres. Roy. Inst. of Brit. Architects; Fellow of the Geol. Soc.; architect; *b.* 9 June 1843; *e. s.* of late John Henry Florence, Streatham, Surrey. *Educ.:* privately. Articled, 1860; subsequently studied in Atelier Questel, Paris; Soane medallist, R.I.B.A. 1869; travelling student and gold medallist, R.A. 1870; travelled in Italy, 1870; commenced practice as an architect, 1871; for 21 years a Volunteer officer, retiring with rank of Lt.-Col. in 1892, and receiving the Volunteer decoration. *Professional works:* Holborn Viaduct Hotel and Station; Holborn Town Hall; mansion for Edward Lloyd, Delahay St.; Hotel Victoria; Paddington Branch of the London Joint-Stock Bank; new library, pension-room, and class-rooms, Gray's Inn; restoration of Gray's Inn Hall; offices for Edward Lloyd, Ltd., Salisbury Square, E.C.; Coombe House and Coombe Farm, near Croydon; Coburg Hotel; Carlton Hotel; Buildings for Woolland Bros., Lowndes Terrace; new station, St. James's Park, for Met. Dist. Railway; Empire Hotel, Lowestoft; extension of First Avenue Hotel; Queen Victoria Memorial, Kensington; the Institute of Journalists; new Library, Museum, and exit staircase, Freemasons' Hall; alterations and additions to the United Service Club. *Recreations:* travel, music. *Address:* 9 Princes Gate, Hyde Park, S.W.; 16 Royal Crescent, Bath. *Club:* Arts. *(Died 20 Feb. 1916.)*

FLOWER, Benjamin Orange, author; editor Twentieth Century Magazine since 1910; *b.* Albion, Ill., 19 Oct. 1858; *s.* of Rev. Alfred and Elizabeth Orange Flower; *m.* 1885. Hattie Cloud, Evansville, Ind. *Educ.:* public schools of Evansville, Ind.; Ky. University, Lexington, Ky. Editor The American Sentinel, Albion, Ill., until 1880; went to Philadelphia, and later to Boston; established The American Spectator, which subsequently was merged into The Arena, which he founded; remained at its head until the end of 1896, then was for a short time in 1897-98 one of the editors of The New Time, a Chicago magazine; subsequently became editor of The Coming Age, which position he held until that magazine was merged into The Arena; editor till it ceased publication in 1910; extensive contributor to leading magazines and periodicals. *Publications:* Lessons Learned from Other Lives, 1891; Civilisation's Inferno, 1893; The New Time, Essays on Social Problems, 1894; Gerald Massey, Poet, Prophet, and Mystic, 1895; Whittier, Prophet, Seer, and Man, 1895; The Century of Sir Thomas More, 1896; Persons, Places, and Ideas, 1896; How England averted a Revolution of Force, 1901; Progressive Men,

Women, and Movements of the Past Twenty-Five Years. *Address:* 145 Aspinwall Avenue, Brookline, Mass.: 5 Park Square, Boston. *(Died 1918.)*

FLOWER, Sir Ernest (Francis Swan), Kt., *cr.* 1903; *b.* 24 Aug. 1865; *o. surv. s.* of John Flower; Member of the Grand Council of Primrose League; Fellow of the Royal Colonial Institute; member London School Board, 1897; Member of the Committees of the Metropolitan and Royal Orthopaedic Hospitals; one of the founders and hon. secs. of the People's Palace and East London Horticultural Society; has been much engaged in philanthropic work in East London; Hon. Treasurer of Queen Mary's Royal Naval Hospital, Southend-on-Sea; Chairman of the Blue Cross Fund; Hon. Treasurer of Red Cross and St. John Hostel for Nurses; a Governor of St. Bartholomew's Hospital; contested Bradford, 1892; M.P. (C.) Bradford (W. Div.), 1895-1906; contested same Division, 1910; a J.P. Co. of London; one of H.M.'s Lieutenants for the City; a Knight of Grace of the Order of St. John of Jerusalem; decorated by the French Government for services in the Great War; Member of the Council of the Imperial Society of Knights Bachelor. *Address:* 6 Upper Phillimore Gardens, Kensington, W. *T.:* Western 2464. *Clubs:* Carlton, Junior Carlton, Bath, Cecil, 1900, Savage. *(Died 30 April 1926.)*

FLOWER, Major Horace John; D.S.O. 1916; M.C.; 60th Rifles; *b.* The Hyde, Luton, Herts., 6 April 1883; *s.* of late Arthur and Isabel Flower; *m.* 1912, Richenda Louisa, *d.* of H. G. Barclay, M.V.O. of Colney Hall, Norwich; two *d.* *Educ.:* Winchester; Sandhurst; joined 60th Rifles in S. Africa, 1902; served S.A., Cork, Bermuda, Malta, India; Adjt. Queen's Westminsters T.F., 1913; served European War in France Oct. 1914-Sept. 1915 (wounded battle of Loos and now invalided out of the service, D.S.O., M.C.). *Recreations:* hunting, polo, etc. *Address:* Camp House, Gerrard's Cross, Bucks. *Club:* Army and Navy. *(Died 31 Jan. 1919.)*

FLOWER, Major Victor Augustine, D.S.O. 1917; Temp. Lieut.-Col. Commanding 1/22nd Batt. London Regt. (the Queen's); *b.* London, 1875; *y. s.* of late Sir W. H. Flower, K.C.B., F.R.S., and Georgiana Rosetta, *d.* of Admiral W. H. Smyth, F.R.S.; *m.* 1914, Winifride, *d.* of Sir T. Digby Pigott, C.B., J.P.; one *s.* *Educ.:* Winchester. Licentiate, R.I.B.A.; practised in the Straits Settlements, 1900-12; formerly Captain, West London Rifles (1898), and Captain and O.C. Singapore R.E. (V.) (1905); Captain 13th Kensington Batt., London Regt. 1914; Brevet Major, 1916; Major, 1916; Temp. Lieut.-Col. 1915; served European War (D.S.O., despatches twice). *Recreations:* rifle-shooting, walking. *Address:* 42 Earl's Court Square, S.W.5. *(Died 15 Aug. 1917.)*

FLOWERDEW, Herbert, novelist; *b.* York, 14 June 1866. *Educ.:* Nottingham High School. *Publications:* In an Ancient Mirror, 1897; A Celibate's Wife, 1898; The Realist, 1899; Retaliation, 1901; The Woman's View, 1903; The Third Kiss, 1905; Maynard's Wives, 1907; The Ways of Men, 1909; The Second Elopement, 1910; The Third Wife, 1910; The Villa Mystery, 1912; Mrs. Gray's Past, 1913; Love and a Title, 1914; The Seventh Postcard, 1914. *Recreation:* invention of mechanical toys. *Address:* 7 Clarendon Gardens, Ramsgate. *(Died 29 May 1917.)*

FLOWERS, Hon. Frederick, M.L.C.; President of Legislative Council, New South Wales since 1915; *b.* Sandon, March 1864; *s.* of William Flowers, Leamington, Warwickshire; *m.* Annie, *d.* of J. C. Foster, Manchester; one *s.* two *d.* *Educ.:* Church of England Grammar

School, Wolstanton. M.L.C. 1900 ; Vice-President of the Executive Council and Representative of the Government in Legislative Council, 1910-15 ; Secretary for Lands, 1911 ; Acting Chief Secretary, 1910-11 ; Minister for Public Health, 1913-15 ; Minister for Public Instruction, 1911-12. *Address:* Parliament House, Sydney, New South Wales. (*Died 14 Dec. 1928.*)

PLUDYER, Sir Arthur John, 5th Bt. ; J.P. ; *b.* 12 Oct. 1844 ; 2nd *s.* of 4th Bt. and Augusta, *d.* of Sir Richard Borough, 1st Bt. ; *m.* Augusta, 3rd *d.* of Sir Edward Borough, 2nd and last Bt., 1876. Late Lieut.-Col., 3rd Northants Regiment. Owns about 4900 acres. *Heir: b.* Colonel Henry. *Address:* Ayston Hall, Uppingham. *Clubs:* Windham, Carlton.
(*Died 27 Jan. 1922.*)

PLUDYER, Colonel Henry, C.V.O., 1901; Gentleman Usher in Ordinary to His Majesty; *b.* 22 May 1847; 2nd *s.* of Rev. Sir J. H. Fludyer, Bart., and Augusta, *d.* of Sir Richard Borough, 1st Bart. ; *m.* Mary Stuart, *d.* of A. R. Hordern, 1891. Joined Scots Fusilier Guards as Ensign ; Lieutenant, 1866 ; Captain, 1869 ; Lieut.-Colonel Scots Guards, 1877 ; Regtl. Major, 1884 ; Colonel, 1887 ; Lieut.-Col. commanding 2nd Batt. 1892 ; retired on half-pay, 1896 ; served in the Egyptian Campaign, 1882 ; in Suakim Expedition, 1885 (Egyptian medal with clasps for Tel-el-Kebir and Suakim, 1885 ; Khedive's bronze star and Jubilee medal, 1897) ; King Edward's and King George's Coronation medals ; commding Scots Guards and Regimental District, 1898-1903 ; retired ; reappointed Command of Scots Guards, Aug. 1914. *Recreations:* racing, hunting, shooting. *Address:* 62 Warwick Square, S.W.1. *T.:* Victoria 1916. *Clubs:* Turf ; Jockey Club Rooms, Newmarket. (*Died 8 April 1920.*)

PLYNN, The Hon. Edmund James, LL.D., K.C. 1887 ; Judge of the Court of Appeals (Court of King's Bench) since 1920 ; Professor of Law, Laval Univ., since 1874 ; heretofore Dean of Law Faculty ; *s.* of late James Flynn, trader, and late Elizabeth Taudevin (father of Irish descent, mother of Guernsey descent) ; *b.* Percé, Co. Gaspé, P.Q., 16 Nov. 1847 ; *m.* 1st, 1875, Augustine, *d.* of Augustin Côte, J.P. and printer and Editor of Journal de Quebec ; four *c.* ; 2nd, 1912, Cecile Pouliot, *widow* of Eugene Globenski, of Montreal. *Educ.:* Quebec Seminary ; Laval University. Admitted to Bar, 1873 ; Member for Gaspé in Quebec Legislative Assembly, 1878-1900 ; Nicolet, 1900-4 ; contested the County of Quebec, 1891, and Dorchester, 1908, for House of Commons ; Commissioner of Crown Lands, 1879-82 ; Minister of Railways and Solicitor-General, 1884-87 ; Minister of Crown Lands, 1891-96 ; Prime Minister, 1896-97 ; Leader of Quebec Opposition, 1897-1905 ; a Liberal-Conservative ; has been batonnier of Quebec Bar ; has practised his profession with his son Francis as Flynn and Flynn. *Address:* 9 Hamel Street, Quebec City. *T.:* 848. (*Died June 1927.*)

PLYNN, James Christopher, M.P. (N.) Cork Co. N., 1885-1910 ; *b.* London, 1852 ; 2nd *s.* of late Daniel Flynn, Whitechurch, Co. Cork, and Sarah Nicholls, Northampton ; *m.* 1st, Maggie, *d.* of P. Malone, Rathmines, Dublin ; 2nd, Rebecca, widow of J. F. Rice, Co. Kerry. *Educ.:* Christian Brothers' College ; Keogh's Classical Schools, Cork. Secretary Evicted Tenants' Association, 1882, 1886-91 ; imprisoned under Coercion Act, 1888. *Recreations:* cricket, rowing, cycling. *Address:* 4 York Terrace, Cork.
(*Died 15 Nov. 1922.*)

FOGG, Ven. Peter Parry, M.A. Oxon. ; Archdeacon of George, Cape of Good Hope, since 1871 ; *b.* Coppa, Mold, Flintshire, 1832 ; 3rd *s.* of J. Barratt Fogg. *Educ.:* Germany ; Christ College, Tasmania ; Jesus College, Oxford. Third Class Lit. Hum. ; secretary, treasurer, and president of Oxford Union Society ; ordained, 1860 ; curate of St. Mary the Less, Lambeth, St. Michael's, Highgate, All Saints', N. Hill St., and Streatham ; member of the first council of the university of the Cape of Good Hope, 1873 ; vicar-general of St. Helena, 1899. *Address:* George, Cape of Good Hope. (*Died 22 Mar. 1920.*)

FOLEY, 6th Baron (*cr.* 1776), **Fitzalan Charles John Foley** ; J.P. County of London and J.P. and D.L. County of Surrey ; *b.* 1852 ; *s.* of 4th Baron, and *e. d.* of 13th Duke of Norfolk ; *S.* brother, 1905. Late Major, Sherwood Foresters. *Heir: c.* Gerald Henry Foley. *Address:* Ruxley Lodge, Claygate, Surrey. (*Died 14 Feb. 1918.*)

FOLEY, 7th Baron (*cr.* 1776), **Gerald Henry Foley** ; late Flight-Lt. R.A.F. ; *s.* of late Henry St. George Foley and Lady Mary Adelaide Agar, *y. d.* of 3rd Earl of Normanton ; *b.* 15 April 1898 ; *S.* cousin, 1918 ; *m.* 1922, Mrs. Min Barrie, *widow*, and *d.* of H. Greenstone, South Africa ; one *s. Heir: s.* Hon. Adrian Gerald Foley, *b.* 9 Aug. 1923. *Address:* Westbrook, Meads, Eastbourne. *T.:* Eastbourne 1969. *Clubs:* Royal Aero, Bachelors', Royal Automobile. (*Died 3 April 1927.*)

FOLEY, Right Rev. Patrick, D.D. ; R.C. Bishop of Kildare and Leighlin ; consecrated April 1896 ; *b.* Mensal Lodge, Leighlinbridge, Carlow, 8 Mar. 1858 ; 4th *s.* of Patrick Foley and Mary Delaney. *Educ.:* Carlow College. Solus Theological Prizeman, 1881 ; do. S. Scripture Prizeman, 1881 ; B.A. Lond. Ordained Priest, 1881 ; Professor of Mental and Moral Philosophy and S. Scripture, Carlow College, 1885-92 ; President of same institution, 1892-96 ; Commissioner of National Education, 1905 ; Member of Governing Body University College, Dublin, 1908. *Address:* Braganza House, Carlow.
(*Died 24 July 1926.*)

FOLEY, Paul Henry, J.P., D.L. ; *b.* 1857 ; *o. s.* of late Henry John Wentworth Hodgetts-Foley of Prestwood and Hon. Jane Frances Anne (*d.* 1860), 2nd *d.* of 1st Lord Vivian ; *m.* 1904, Dora, *o. c.* of Hamilton W. Langley. *Educ.:* Eton ; Christ Church, Oxford. M.A. ; called to Bar, Inner Temple, 1881 ; Lord of several manors in Herefordshire and Staffordshire ; patron of 3 livings. *Address:* Stoke Edith, Hereford. *Club:* Travellers'.
(*Died 21 Jan. 1928.*)

FOLJAMBE, Rt. Hon. Francis John Savile, P.C., M.A. ; High Steward of Burgh of E. Retford ; *b.* Osberton, 9 Apr. 1830 ; *e. s.* of late George Savile Foljambe ; *m.* Lady Gertrude Emily Acheson, *e. d.* of 3rd Earl of Gosford, 1856 ; two *s. Educ.:* Eton ; Christ Church, Oxford. M.P. E. Retford and Hundred of Bassetlaw, 1857-85, continuously. Owns about 14,500 acres. *Recreations:* field sports. *Address:* Osberton, Worksop. *T.A.:* Worksop. *Club:* Brooks's. (*Died 5 Feb. 1917.*)

FOLJAMBE, George Savile, C.B. 1917 ; V.D., D.L., and J.P. for Notts ; Lieut.-Col. Terr.-Force ; late commanding 8th Sherwood Foresters ; *b.* 30 Oct. 1856 ; *e. s.* of late Rt. Hon. F. J. S. Foljambe and Lady Gertrude F., *e. d.* of late Earl of Gosford ; *m.* Dora M., *e. d.* of late Rev. E. Warre, Provost of Eton ; two *s.* three *d. Educ.:* Eton ; Christ Church, Oxford. Joined the 8th Sherwood Foresters (then the first Administrative Batt., Notts Volunteers), 1875 ; served in the regiment till 1913 ; Lt.-Colonel Commanding, 1908 ; employed at Depôt and in command of 3rd line, Aug. 1914-Dec. 1915 ; since then served with Red Cross in France till Feb. 1917 ; employed on Staff of Northern Command as President of an Area Quartering Committee, 1917-19. *Recreations:* hunting and fishing, and in early days cricket, football, and tennis. *Address:* Osberton, Worksop, Notts.

T.A.: Ranby, Retford. *T.*: **Worksop** 89. *Club*: Brooks's. (*Died 13 Sept.* 1920.)

FOLLETT, Sir Charles John, Kt.; *cr.* 1902; C.B. 1891; *b.* 1838; *s.* of John Follett of Countess Wear, Devon; *m.* 1st, 1863, **Eliza** (*d.* 1895), *e. d.* of William Nation of Rockbeare House, Devon; 2nd, 1897, Blanche, *e. d.* of Lieut.-Col. Henry Green-Wilkinson and the Hon. Mrs. Green-Wilkinson; one *s.* three *d.* Late Fellow of St. John's Coll., Oxford; B.C.L., M.A.; Solicitor of His Majesty's Customs to 1903. *Decorated* for official work. *Address:* Culm Davy, Hemyock, Devon.
(*Died 11 Sept.* 1921.)

FOLLETT, Lt.-Col. Gilbert Burrell Spencer, M.V.O. 1907; D.S.O. 1917; Coldstream Guards; *b.* 31 July 1878; *m.* 1904, Lady Mildred Murray, 3rd *d.* of 7th Earl of Dunmore; one *s.* one *d. Educ.*: Eton; Sandhurst. Entered army, 1899; Captain, 1908; Major, 1915; served S. Africa, 1899-1900 (wounded, Queen's medal, two clasps); European War, 1914-15 (wounded thrice, despatches thrice, D.S.O., Bt. Lt.-Col.). *Clubs*: Guards', Bachelors'.
(*Died 27 Sept.* 1918.)

FOLLETT, Colonel Robert William Webb; *e. s.* of late Sir William Webb Follett, M.P., of Culm Davy, Devon, and Jane Mary, *e. d.* of late Sir Ambrose Hardinge Giffard, Chief-Justice of Ceylon; *b.* 1844; *m.* 1869, Lady Julia Alice Kennedy, *d.* of 2nd Marquis of Ailsa. *Educ.*: Eton; Christ Church, Oxford; 1st Class Law and Modern History. Late Colonel Coldstream Guards; served Egyptian Campaign, 1882; Suakim, 1885. *Address:* Woodside, Old Windsor. *Clubs*: Guards', Travellers', Turf.
(*Died April* 1921.)

FOOTE, John Alderson, K.C.; Recorder of Exeter since 1899; *b.* Plymouth, 15 Dec. 1848; *e. s.* of Capt. John Foote, R.N.; *m.* 1877, Jessie, *d.* of J. A. Eaton, C.E., of The Priory, Shrewsbury; one *d. Educ.*: Charterhouse; St. John's College, Cambridge (Minor Scholarship, 1868; Scholar, 1870); 1st class Classical Tripos, 1872; Chancellor's Legal Medallist, 1873; Sen. Whewell Scholar of International Law, 1873; Senior Studentship (Inns of Court Examination), 1874; Barr. 1875; joined Western Circuit; Revising Barrister, 1892; Counsel to the Post-Office (Western Circuit), 1898; Bencher Lincoln's Inn, 1905; a Commissioner of Assize, N.E. Circuit, 1913; Counsel to Cambridge University, 1915; *Publications:* Treatise on Private International Jurisprudence, 1878, 2nd ed. 1892. *Address:* 8 Albert Hall Mansions, Kensington Gore, S.W.7; *T.*: Kensington 3077; 2 Dr. Johnson's Buildings, Temple, E.C.4; *T.*: City 7081; Beacon Beech, Dormansland, East Grinstead. *T.A.*: 3 Temple, London.
(*Died 26 April* 1922.)

FORBES, 21st Baron (*cr.* 1442 or before), **Atholl Monson;** J.P., D.L.; landed proprietor; *b.* Castle Forbes, Aberdeenshire, 1841; *s.* of 19th Baron and 1st wife, *d.* of Sir John Gregory Shaw, 5th Bt.; *S.* brother 1914; *m.* 1876, Margaret Alice, *d.* of Sir William Hanmer Dick-Cunyngham of Prestonfield, Midlothian, 8th Bart.; one *s.* one *d. Educ.*: Magdalen School, Oxford; private tutor. *Heir*: *s.* Master of Forbes. *Address:* Castle Forbes, Littlewood Park, Aberdeenshire; Brux Lodge, Co. Aberdeen. *Club*: Wellington.
(*Died 31 Jan.* 1916.)

FORBES, Arthur, C.S.I. 1895; late I.C.S.; *b.* 1843; *s.* of late Rev. E. Forbes, D.D., formerly chaplain in Paris; *m.* May Grace, *d.* of late Andrew Cassels, a member of the Indian Council, 1879; one *s. Educ.*: Sedbergh; St. John's College, Cambridge. Exhibitioner; B.A. 1867. Entered I.C.S. 1867; served as Assist. and Joint-Magistrate in different districts and through Behar famine, 1874; Deputy-Commissioner, Assam, 1875; Magistrate-Collector, Dacca, 1879; Junior Secretary, Board of Revenue, Lower Provinces, 1880-84; member and secretary of Opium Commission, 1888 (thanked by Government of India and Secretary of State); subsequently Magistrate-Collector of Sarun, 24 Pergunnahs, Shahabad, and Mózafferpur; acted as Commissioner of Excise, Bengal, 1890, and as Commissioner of Dacca, 1891; Commissioner of Patna Division, 1892-96; of Chutia-Nagpur, Bengal, 1896-1902; retired, 1902. *Recreations:* yachting, Capt. Lymington Cadet Corps 7th Batt. Hants Regt. *Address:* Yaldhurst, Lymington, Hants.
(*Died 5 April* 1919.)

FORBES of Pitsligo, Sir Charles Hay Hepburn, 10th Bt., *cr.* 1626; *b.* 3 June 1371; *S.* father, 1906; *m.* 1896, Ellen, *d.* of Captain Huntley of Picton, Marlborough, N.Z.; five *s.* three *d. Heir*: *s.* Hugh, *b.* 9 Nov. 1896. *Address:* Picton, Marlborough, New Zealand.
(*Died Aug.* 1927.)

FORBES, Sir Charles (Stewart), 5th Bt., *cr.* 1823; J.P., D.L.; *o. s.* of 4th Bt. and Helen (*d.* 1913), 2nd *d.* of Sir Thomas Moncreiffe of Moncreiffe, 7th Bt.; *b.* 19 Jan. 1867; *S.* father 1884; *m.* Emma Theodora, *d.* of Robert Maxwell, 1888; one *s.* four *d.* Owns about 9000 acres in Aberdeenshire. *Heir*: *s.* John Stewart, *b.* 8 Jan. 1901. *Address:* 25 Holland Park, W.; Castle Newe, Strathdon, Aberdeen.
(*Died 12 Dec.* 1927.)

FORBES, Daniel, I.S.O.; *b.* 1 May 1853; *e. s.* of Alexander Forbes, Edinburgh; *m.* Frances Gray, *d.* of George Leitch, Norham-on-Tweed; two *d. Educ.*: Western Institution and Hamilton Place Academy, Edinburgh. Junior clerk, Department of General Board of Lunacy for Scotland, 1875; chief clerk, 1905; retired, 1918. *Recreations:* cycling, golf. *Address:* 19 Cluny Terrace, Edinburgh. *T.*: Central 7425. *Club*: Scottish Conservative, Edinburgh.

FORBES, Lady Helen (Emily), author; *b.* London, 13 Dec. 1874; 2nd but *o. surv. d.* of 3rd Earl of Craven and Evelyn, *d.* of 7th Viscount Barrington; *m.* 1901, Ian Forbes; two *s.* four *d. Educ.*: Ashdown Park. Began writing in 1885. Tory. Roman Catholic. *Publications:* Notes of a Music Lover, 1897; Katharine Cromer, 1897; His Eminence, 1898 (book form, 1904); The Outcast Emperor, 1900; The Provincials, 1905; It's a Way the have in the Army, 1905; Lady Marion and the Plutocrat, 1906; The Bounty of the Gods, 1910; The Polar Star, 1911; The Saga of the Seventh Division, 1920. *Recreations:* hunting, riding, music, very fond of languages, literature, history, heraldry. *Address:* Hill House, Purton, Wilts.; *M.*: MS 358. *Club*: Ladies' Athenæum.
(*Died 13 Oct.* 1926.)

FORBES, James, M.V.O. 1904; late H.M.'s Commissioner at Balmoral. *Address:* Eallabus, Bridgend, Islay, Argyllshire.
(*Died 25 Mar.* 1919.)

FORBES, John Colin, R.C.A., Canadian artist; *b.* Toronto, 3 Jan. 1846; *s.* of late Duncan Forbes, Doune, Perth; *m.* 1888, Laura Gertrude, *d.* of George M. Holbrooke, Ottawa. *Educ.*: U.C. College, Toronto; R.A., and South Kensington Museum. *Principal Works:* Mr. Gladstone; Sir H. Campbell-Bannerman; King Edward VII.; Queen Alexandra (Canadian House of Parliament); Earl of Dufferin; Sir J. Macdonald, etc. *Address:* Sherwood Studio Buildings, 57th and 6th Avenue, New York. *Club*: Salmagundi. (*Died Oct.* 1925.)

FORBES, Hon. Mrs. Walter R.D. (Eveline Louisa Michell); *d.* of late Frederick Cooper Farwell and Louisa Whitbread, *o. c.* of late Admiral Sir Frederick Michell, K.C.B., etc.; *b.* The Lowlands, Tettenhall; *m.* Feb. 1888, Hon. Walter Robert Drummond Forbes, Capt. Gordon Highlanders, *s.* of Walter, 18th Baron Forbes; one *s. Educ.*: at home. *Publications:* Fingers and Fortune, 1896; Her Last

Run, 1888 ; Blight, 1897 ; A Gentleman, 1900 ; Dumb, 1901 ; Unofficial, 1902 ; Leroux, 1908 ; Vane Royal, 1908 ; Nameless, 1910 ; His Alien Enemy, 1918. *Recreations :* riding, theatre, reading. *Address :* 47 Onslow Gardens, S.W.7. *T. :* Kensington 279.   *(Died 18 April 1924.)*

FORBES, Brig.-Gen. Willoughby Edward Gordon, C.B., 1898 ; *b.* 11 Sep. 1851 ; 3rd *s.* of late Gordon Forbes and Charlotte, *d.* of Major Edward Lake ; *m.* Edith, *d.* of late Francis Forbes, I.C.S., 1882 ; three *d. Educ. :* private school. Joined 6th (Royal Warwickshire) Regt., 1869 ; served Afghan Campaign, 1879-80 ; Orderly Officer to Brig.-Gen. Palliser ; present at engagements of Ahmed Khel, Urzoo, and Patkao Shana (despatches, medal with clasp) ; Com. 1st Batt. Royal Warwickshire in Egyptian Soudan Campaign, 1898 ; present at engagements of Atbara and Omdurman (despatches, medal with clasp, C.B.) ; A.A.G. IX. Secunderabad Division, 1902-7 ; retired, 1907 ; com. 2/1 Lothian Inf. Brigade (T.), Jan.-Nov. 1915, and "B" Group Lowland Division, Feb.-July 1916 ; Gazetted Hon. Brig.-Gen. Aug. 1917. *Address :* Shorebank, Bognor, Sussex. *(Died 13 Dec. 1926.)*

FORD, Charles, I.S.O. 1904 ; F.L.S. ; *b.* 1844 ; *m.* 1871 ; was Superintendent Botanical and Afforestation Department in the Colony of Hong-Kong, 1871-1902. *Address :* Lindeth, Stanmore.   *(Died 14 July 1927.)*

FORD, Ernest A. C., F.R.A.M. ; Conductor Royal Amateur Orchestral Society, 1897-1908 ; Professor of Singing at Guildhall School of Music ; *b.* 17 Feb. 1858, of Celtic descent ; *s.* of a Local Government official ; *m.* 1896, Alice, 2nd *d.* of James Philp of East Finchley and Partridge Green, Sussex. *Educ. :* R.A.M., and afterwards in Paris ; pupil of Sir Arthur Sullivan ; was the first holder of the Sir John Goss Scholarship. Visited America, 1887, where his motett Domine Deus, which, with English words, has become a standard work of modern Church music, was the principal work performed at the 250th anniversary of Harvard University ; in 1889 was selected by Sir Arthur Sullivan to conduct Ivanhoe at the Royal English Opera House ; he was subsequently engaged to write the ballets for the Empire. *Publications:* Short History of Music in England ; Cantata, The Eve of the Festa ; much sacred music and many songs ; orchestral works ; Scène Bacchanale, produced by Robert Newman at the Queen's Hall, 1897. *Recreation :* golf. *Address :* 45 Prince of Wales Mansions, Prince of Wales Road, S.W.   *(Died 2 June 1919.)*

FORD, Rev. Gabriel Estwick, B.A. ; Vicar of Bilston since 1909 ; Hon. Canon, Birmingham, 1905-9. *Educ. :* University of London. Curate of Stepney, 1881-85 ; Vicar of Holy Trinity, Bristol, 1885-98 ; Rector All Saints, Birmingham, 1898-1901 ; Rector of St. George's, Birmingham, 1901-9. *Publications:* Gambling : an Analysis ; The New Testament Doctrine of the Holy Communion. *Address :* The Vicarage, Bilston, Staffs.

FORD, John ; *s.* of late Rt. Hon. Sir F. Clare Ford, G.C.B., G.C.M.G., H.M.'s Ambassador at Madrid, Constantinople and Rome, and Anna, *d.* of the Marquis Garofalo ; *m.* Mary Augusta, *d.* of George Cavendish-Bentinck. *Educ. :* Eton. Entered Diplomatic Service, 1892 ; Attaché—Athens and Washington ; 3rd Secretary, 1894, Copenhagen, Rome and Brussels ; 2nd Secretary, 1898, Teheran, Munich and Paris ; 1st Secretary, 1906, Copenhagen, and Rome ; a trustee of National Portrait Gallery. *Club :* St. James's.   *(Died 11 Oct. 1917.)*

FORD, Surgeon-General Sir Richard (William), K.C.M.G., *cr.* 1917 ; C.B. 1916 ; D.S.O. 1900 ; late R.A.M.C. ; *b.* 26 Sep. 1857 ; *m.* 1884. Mary Augusta, *d.* of late Rear-Admiral Wainwright, R.N. Deputy Surgeon, Royal Hospital, Chelsea, 1901-6 ; served European War,

1914-17 (C.B., K.C.M.G.). *Club :* Army and Navy.   *(Died 31 Mar. 1925.)*

FORD, Sir Theodore Thomas, Kt. ; *cr.* 1898 ; *b.* 1829 ; *m.* Ellen, *d.* of George Watson, 1859 ; four *s.* two *d.* Barr. Middle Temple, 1866, Judge in Straits Settlements, 1874 ; Chief Justice, 1886-89. *Address :* Devon House, Harold Road, Upper Norwood, S.E.   *(Died 23 May 1920.)*

FORDE, Col. Lionel, C.M.G. 1917 ; retired pay, late R.A. ; *b.* 18 April 1860 ; 3rd *s.* of late Henry Charles Forde, M.I.C.E. St. Brendan's, Wimbledon ; *m.* 1895, Gertrude Emily Meredith, *d.* of late Frederick Pollen, I.C.S. (Bengal) ; one *s.* two *d. Educ. :* Cheltenham College ; R.M.A. Woolwich. Church of England. Entered Army, 1879 ; Lt.-Col. 1905 ; retired, 1910 ; served Burma, 1885-87 (medal with clasp) ; Chin-Lushai, 1889-90 (clasp) ; N.W. Frontier, India, 1897-98 (medal with clasp) ; European War (France and Flanders), 1915-19 ; (C.M.G. 1914-15 Star, British War Medal, Victory Medal, Oak Leaf). *Publication :* Lord Clive's Righthand Man, 1910. *Recreations :* genealogical research, gardening, lawn tennis. *Address :* St. Mary's, Battle.   *(Died 25 Oct. 1926.)*

FORDHAM, Edward Snow, D.L., J.P., Herts, Cambs, and Beds ; J.P. Kent, Surrey, London, Middlesex, and Essex ; Metropolitan Police Magistrate, North London, 1898-1910 ; West London, 1910 ; retired, 1917 ; Chairman, Quarter Sessions for Cambridgeshire, 1901-12 ; *b.* Ashwell, Herts, 15 Jan. 1858 ; *e. s.* of late Edward King Fordham, J.P., D.L., Ashwell Bury ; *m.* Annie, *d.* of late T. Carr-Jackson, F.R.C.S., 1880 ; three *s.* two *d. Educ. :* Caius Coll., Camb. B.A. 1880 ; M.A., I.L.M. 1888. Barr. Inner Temple, 1883 ; pupil of Mr. Justice Channell ; practised on Midland Circuit. Owns about 450 acres. *Address :* Elbrook House, Ashwell, Herts. *Club :* Brooks's. *M. :* AR 2345.   *(Died 28 Jan. 1919.)*

FOREMAN, Sir Henry, Kt., *cr.* 1921 ; O.B.E. 1918 ; M.P. (U.) North Hammersmith since Dec. 1918 ; *b.* 1852 ; *m.* 1st, 1873, *d.* of W. Howe of Bayswater, W. ; 2nd, 1901, *d.* of A. J. Randall. Mayor of Hammersmith, 1913-20 ; Alderman since 1919 ; Hon. Col. and Founder 20th London Cadet Corps ; Chm. and Hon. Comdt. Hammersmith Div. Red Cross Society ; presented to War Office Ravenscourt Park Hospital for Officers ; raised 140th Heavy Battery R.G.A., and 40th Division Ammunition Column during European War (O.B.E.) ; *Address :* 17 Kensington Court, Kensington, W.8. *T. :* Western 1244. *Clubs:* Carlton, Constitutional, Royal Automobile.   *(Died 11 April 1924.)*

FORESTER, 5th Baron (U.K.) (*cr.* 1821), **Cecil Theodore Weld-Forester,** D.L., J.P. ; *b.* 3 Aug. 1842 ; *S.* father 1894 ; *m.* Emma, *d.* of Sir W. W. Dixie, 8th Bt. 1866 ; five *s.* one *d. Educ. :* Harrow ; Trin. Coll. Camb. M.P. (C.) Wenlock, 1874-85. Owns about 15,700 acres. *Heir : s.* Capt. Hon. G. C. B. Weld-Forester. *Address :* Rose Bank, Birchington ; Willey Park, Broseley, Shropshire. *Clubs :* Carlton, Turf ; Royal Yacht Squadron, Cowes.   *(Died 20 Nov. 1917.)*

FORGET, Sir (Joseph David) Rodolphe, Kt., *cr.* 1912 ; President Quebec and Saguenay Railway and Quebec Railway Light, Heat, and Power Company ; Vice-President Montreal Light, Heat, and Power Co., Ltd. ; *b.* Terrebonne, Quebec, 10 Dec. 1861 ; *s.* of David and Angèle Limoges Forget ; *m.* 1st, 1885, Marie Alexandra, *d.* of late Hon. Louis Tourville, M.L.A. ; 2nd, 1894, Marie Louise Blanche, *d.* of late Robert Macdonald ; three *s.* two *d. Educ. :* Masson College, Terrebonne. Partner L. J. Forget & Co., 1887-97 ; founded Rodolphe Forget, Montreal, 1907 ; M.P., Charlevoie and Montmorency, since 1911 ; Hon. Col. 1914.

Address: 71 Ontario Avenue, Montreal; Gil Mont, St. Irenee les Bains, Quebec. *Clubs:* St. James, Mt. Royal, Canadien, Montreal, Canada, Montreal Hunt, Montreal; Rideau, Ottawa; Garrison, Quebec.

(*Died 19 Feb. 1919.*)

FORMAN, E. Baxter, M.D., M.R.C.P., M.R.C.S.; Member of London County Council 1891-1910; J.P. Co. of London. *Educ.:* privately; Guy's Hospital (scholarship in Medicine). Represented North Hackney on the L.C.C. ten years; Aldermun six years; South Kensington, three years; belongs to Municipal Reform party; has filled many offices on Council; Deputy Chairman of Council; Vice-Chairman of Education Committee; Chairman third time of Public Health Committee and of Midwives Committee; many years Chairman of Hackney Institute. *Publications:* papers on medical and municipal subjects. *Address:* Newmount, Chalfont St. Giles, Bucks. *T.A.:* Chalfont St. Giles. *T.:* 25 Chalfont St. Giles. (*Died 25 Nov. 1925.*)

FORMAN, Harry Buxton, C.B., 1897; late Second Secretary General Post Office, and Controller of Packet Services; *b.* London 1842; *m.* Laura, *d.* of W. C. Selle, 1869; two *s.* one *d. Educ.:* Teignmouth. Entered Civil Service, 1860; retired 1907. *Publications:* Our Living Poets, 1871; The Works of Shelley (ed.), 1876-80; Letters of John Keats to Fanny Brawne, 1878; Poetical Works and other writings of John Keats, 1883; The Shelley Library, 1886; Elizabeth Barrett Browning and her Scarcer Books, 1896; The Books of William Morris, 1897; Letters of Edward John Trelawny, 1910; Note Books of Shelley deciphered, with a Commentary, 1911; Elopement of Shelley and Mary as narrated by Godwin, 1911; Medwin's Life of Shelley, enlarged and fully commented, 1913. *Address:* 46 Marlborough Hill, N.W.

(*Died 15 June 1917.*)

FORRER, Ludwig; *b.* Winterthur, 9 Feb. 1845; Member of Federal Council, 1877-1900; Minister of Commerce and Agriculture, 1902; President of the Swiss Confederation, 1906 and 1912. *Address:* Elfenauweg 88, Berne.

(*Died 29 Sept. 1921.*)

FORREST, 1st Baron; *cr.* 1918; **John Forrest,** P.C. 1897; G.C.M.G. 1901; K.C.M.G. 1918; C.M.G. 1882; LL.D. Camb. 1897; Adelaide, 1902; Perth, 1916; F.L.S., F.R.G.S., F.G.S.; Treasurer, Australia, 1917-18; Hon. Fellow of the Geographical Societies of Rome, Vienna, and St. Petersburg; Knight of Order of Crown of Italy, 1875; *b.* W. Australia, 22 Aug. 1847; 3rd *s.* of William Forrest, Leschenault, near Bunbury; *m.* 1876, Margaret Elvire, *e. d.* of Edward Hamersley, J.P., Pyrton, near Guildford, W. Australia, and *niece* of Hugh Hamersley, J.P., D.L., of Pyrton Manor, Oxon. *Educ.:* Bishop's School, Perth. Entered Survey Department, 1865; commanded exploring expedition into interior in search of Dr. Leichhardt, 1869; exploring expedition Perth to Adelaide, via the head of Great Australian Bight, 1870; exploring expedition from Champion Bay to overland telegraph line between Adelaide and Port Darwin, nearly 2000 miles, through centre of Australia, without aid of camels, with horses only, 1874; received thanks of Governor and Legislative Council, Gold Medal R.G.S. London, 1876; presented by Government with grant of 5000 acres; Deputy Surv.-Gen. W. Australia, 1876; conducted trigonometrical surveys of Murchison District, Nickol Bay District, and Gascoyne and Lyons District, W. Australia, 1876-78-82; Acting Commr. of Crown Lands and Surv.-Gen. 1878-79; Acting Comptroller of Imperial Expenditure, 1880-81; Commissioner of Crown Lands and Surveyor-Gen. W. Australia, with seat in Executive and Legislative Councils, 1883-1900; in 1883 proceeded to Kimberley

district, N.W. Australia, on behalf of Government, to report on its character and capabilities; proceeded to Cambridge Gulf, and selected site of town of Wyndham, 1886; introduced and passed the Land Act, 1887; First Premier and Treasurer of W. Australia under responsible government, 1890-1901; represented Western Australia at the Colonial-Imperial Conferences in London, 1887-97, at National Australian Convention, 1891, and at Federal Convention, 1897-8; President Australian Federal Council, 1897. Introduced system of giving free grant of 160 acres of land to persons willing to reside upon it and make specified improvements, and established the Agricultural Land Bank. During his administration was responsible for the construction of the great harbour at Fremantle and the project of conveying, by pumping through steel pipes, 6,000,000 gallons of water daily to the Coolgardie Goldfields, a distance of 350 miles. Has been a member of the Federal Parliament since 1901. Postmaster-General, 1901; Minister of Defence, 1901-3; Minister of Home Affairs, 1903-4; Treasurer of the Commonwealth, 1905-7, 1909-10, and 1913-14; acting Prime Minister of the Commonwealth from Mar. to June 1907; strongest and most persistent advocate of the East to West Trans-Australian Railway, 1060 miles, now nearly completed; represented Western Australia at Queen Victoria's two Jubilees, 1887 and 1897; attended as a Privy Councillor the coronation of King Edward VII., 1902, and of King George V., 1911. *Publications:* Explorations in Australia, 1875; Notes on Western Australia, 1884-87. *Heir:* none. *Address:* The Bungalow, Perth, Western Australia. *Clubs:* Athenæum; Weld, Perth; Melbourne, Melbourne.

(*Died 3 Sept. 1918.*)

FORREST, Sir Charles, 5th Bart. of Comiston, Midlothian; *cr.* 1838; *b.* Kinross, 5 Jan. 1857; 2nd *s.* of late Sir William Forrest, 3rd Bart.; *S.* brother 1899; *m.* Edith I., *e. d.* of late A. J. T. Morris, Incumbent, St. Columba's, Crieff, 1892. *Educ.:* Glasgow Academy; Merchiston Castle School, Edinburgh. Formerly manager of Imperial Bank of Canada, Fergus, Ontario. *Heir:* none. *Recreations:* golf and boating. *Club:* Caledonian United Service, Edinburgh. (*Died 25 Sept. 1928.*)

FORREST, Rev. David William, M.A., D.D. (Glasgow); Professor of Systematic Theology and Apologetics, United Free Church College, Glasgow, since 1914; *s.* of Rev. David Forrest, St. Rollox United Presbyterian Church, Glasgow. *Educ.:* High School, Glasgow; Universities of Glasgow and Leipzig; United Presbyterian College, Edinburgh. Minister of Saffronhall Church, Hamilton, 1882-87; United Presbyterian Church, Moffat, 1887-94; Wellington Church, Glasgow, 1894-99; United Free Church, Skelmorlie, Wemyss Bay, 1899-1903; North Morningside Church, Edinburgh, 1903-14; Kerr Lecturer at Edinburgh, 1897; was offered, but declined, Professorship of Apologetics in Knox College, Toronto, and also Principalship of United College, Bradford; Special Lecturer at Yale University, U.S.A., 1901. *Publications:* The Christ of History and of Experience (Kerr Lectures), 1897 (Seventh Edition, 1914); The Authority of Christ, 1906 (Fourth Edition, 1914); joint-editor of Letters of Dr. John Brown, 1907; various articles in magazines. *Recreations:* cycling, golf. *Address:* 15 Bute Gardens, Glasgow. *Clubs:* Liberal, Glasgow; Scottish Liberal, Edinburgh. (*Died 3 Mar. 1918.*)

FORREST, Sir George William, Kt. *cr.* 1913; C.I.E. 1899; F.R.G.S.; F.R.H.S.; *b.* Nusseerabad, 8 Jan. 1846; 2nd *s.* of Captain George Forrest, V.C.; *m.* Emma G., *d.* of late Thomas Viner, Broadfield, Crawley, Sussex; one *s.* one *d. Educ.:* private tutor; St. John's College, Camb. (B.A). Fellow of the Bombay Uni-

FORNERET, Ven. George Augustus, D.D. See page xix.

versity, read for Bar, 1870-72; member of Inner Temple; contributed to the Saturday Review and other London journals; appointed by Secretary of State for India to Bombay Educational Department, 1872; acted as Census Commissioner, Bombay, 1882; employed on special duty in connection with Bombay Records, 1884-88; Professor of English History, Elphinstone Coll., 1887; Director of Records, Bombay, 1888; Director of Records Government of India, 1891-1900; Assistant Secretary to the Government of India, 1898; Secretary to the Government of India Patents Branch, 1894-1900; retired, 1900. *Publications:* Selections from the State Papers preserved in the Bombay Secretariat (Home Series); (Mahratta Series); Selections from the State Papers preserved in the Foreign Office Government of India, relating to Warren Hastings; The Administration of Warren Hastings; Selections from the State Papers preserved in the Military Department of the Govt. of India relating to the Mutiny, vol. i. Delhi; vol. ii. Lucknow; The Administration of the Marquis of Lansdowne; Sepoy Generals; Cities of India; History of the Indian Mutiny, vols. i. ii. and iii.; Life of Sir Nevile Chamberlain, 1909; Life of Lord Roberts, K.G., V.C., 1914; Life of Lord Clive, 1918. *Address:* Iffley Turn, Oxford. *Clubs:* Savile, Burlington Fine Arts.   *(Died 28 Jan. 1926.)*

FORREST, Lt.-Col. William, D.S.O. 1900; D.L.; late 3rd Batt. Welsh Regt.; b. 30 Sep. 1868; s. of late Col. Peter Forrest; m. 1898, Hon. Marie Spencer Lewis, d. of 1st Baron Merthyr; one s. Served South Africa, 1900-1902 (despatches, Queen's medal with clasp, King's medal, 2 clasps, D.S.O.). *Address:* Greenwood, St. Fagans, Co. Glamorgan. *M.:* L 9149. *Club:* Junior United Service.
     (Died 1 Nov. 1921.)

FORREST, Sir William (Croft), Kt., cr. 1919; J.P West Riding; Mayor of Pudsey, 1913-19; Chairman of Local Food Control Committee; Chairman War Pensions Association. *Address:* Aldingham, Roundhay, Leeds. *T.:* Roundhay 625.   *(Died 12 April 1928.)*

FORSTER, Lt.-Gen. Bowes Lennox, R.A.; Col. Commandant, R.A., since 1904; b. 9 Oct. 1837; m. 1868, Jessie Kate, 3rd d. of Sir William Mackenzie, K.C.B. Entered army, 1855; Lt.-Gen., 1895; retired, 1900; served New Zealand War, 1860-61 (despatches, medal, brevet Maj.); Commanded R.A., Gibraltar, 1888-92; Thames District, 1892-95. *Address:* Hillsides, Parklands, Surbiton.   *(Died 7 Oct. 1919.)*

FORSTER, Lt.-Col. George Norman Bowes, D.S.O. 1917; Commanding 1st Batt. The Royal Warwickshire Regiment; b. 26 Oct. 1872; 3rd s. of Lieut.-General Bowes Lennox Forster, Commandant Royal Artillery; m. 1902, Margaret (Daisy) Ethel, d. of Brig.-General R. A. Gilchrist, Indian Cavalry; no c. *Educ.:* United Services College, Westward Ho; R.M. College, Sandhurst. Second Lieut. Royal Warwickshire Regiment, 1893; Lieut. 1898; Captain, 1900; Major, 1911; Lieut.-Col. 1916; served Nile Expedition, 1898 (Queen's medal, 1898; Khedive's medal with clasps, Atbara and Khartoum); S. African War, 1899-1902 (despatches, Queen's medal with 5 clasps); European War (despatches thrice, D.S.O., wounded twice); Adjutant of 1st Batt. 1902-4. *Address:* c/o Cox & Co., 16 Charing Cross, S.W. *Club:* Army and Navy.   *(Died 4 April 1918.)*

FORSTER, Robert Henry, M.A., LL.B., author, archæologist; barrister-at-law (not in practice); b. Backworth, near Newcastle-on-Tyne, 10 March 1867; 3rd surv. s. of late George Baker Forster, mining engineer, of Newcastle-on-Tyne, and Hannah Elizabeth, d. of late Rev. Isaac Todd, formerly vicar of Shincliffe, near Durham; m. 1912, Margaret Hope, e. d. of A. G. Payne, Dartmouth. *Educ.:*

Aysgarth School, Harrow; St. John's College, Cambridge. Entrance Scholarship, Harrow, 1881; Leaf Scholarship, 1885; Minor Scholarship, St. John's, 1884; Foundation Scholarship, 1887; M'Mahon Law Student, 1891; 1st Class (3rd Div.) Classical Tripos, 1888; 1st Class (Senior) Law Tripos, 1889; called to the Bar, 1892; was many years captain of the Thames Rowing Club, Putney, and a member of the Committee of the Amateur Rowing Association. *Publications:* The Hand of the Spoiler, 1898; The Amateur Antiquary, 1899; Down by the River, 1900; A Tynedale Comedy, 1902; The Last Foray, 1903; In Steel and Leather, 1904; Strained Allegiance, 1905; The Arrow of the North, 1906; The Mistress of Aydon, 1907; A Jacobite Admiral, 1908; Harry of Athol, 1909; Midsummer Morn, 1911; The Little Maister, 1912; Idylls of the North (verse), 1908; In Old Northumbria (verse), 1905; War Poems of a Northumbrian, 1st series, 1914, 2nd series, 1915; The Double Realm, 1920. *Recreation:* walking. *Address:* Rest Dod, Coombeinteignhead, S. Devon.   *(Died 6 June 1923.)*

FORSYTH, Lt.-Col. James Archibald Charteris, C.M.G. 1919; D.S.O. 1916; R.F.A.; o. s. of late Archibald Forsyth of Culeaze, Wareham, Dorset; m. 1917, Ethel Winifred, twin d. of late Janvrin Robin of Steephill, Jersey, Channel Isles; one d. *Educ.:* Haileybury College; Royal Military Academy, Woolwich. Commissioned Second Lieut. 1897; Lt. 1900; Captain, 1904; Major, 1914; Lieut.-Col. 1916; served South Africa, 1899-1900 (Queen's medal 3 clasps); China, 1900 (medal); European War, 1914-18 (despatches four times, C.M.G., D.S.O., Bt. Lt.-Col. 1917). *Recreations:* hunting, pig-sticking, polo, fishing. *Address:* Culeaze, Wareham, Dorset. *Clubs:* Army and Navy, Bath.   *(Died 21 Nov. 1922.)*

FORSYTH, Maj.-Gen. John Keatly, C.M.G. 1917; b. 1867; s. of late William Forsyth; m. 1897, Kate, d. of John M'Master, M.L.C., Brisbane. *Educ.:* Fortitude Valley State School, Normal School, Brisbane. Served European War, 1914-16 (despatches, C.M.G.); Q.M.G. Australian Forces, 1919-22; sometime member Australian Military Board; retired 1922. *Address:* 6 Hepburn Street, Auburn, Melbourne, Australia.   *(Died 12 Nov. 1928.)*

FORSYTH, Rev. Dr. Peter Taylor, M.A., D.D.; Principal of Hackney Theological College, Hampstead, since 1901; Chairman of Congregational Union of England and Wales, 1905; b. Aberdeen, 1848; twice married; one d. *Educ.:* Grammar School and University Aberdeen (1st class honours Classics); some time Assistant to Professor of Humanity, Aberdeen; Göttingen under Ritschl; New College, Hampstead; also under Dr. Fairbairn. Has held ministries at Shipley, Hackney, Manchester, Leicester, Cambridge; Congregational. *Publications:* Children's Sermons; Religion in Recent Art; The Charter of the Church; The Holy Father and the Living Christ; On Christian Perfection; Rome, Reform, and Reaction; The Taste of Death and the Life of Grace: Positive Preaching and Modern Mind (Yale Lectures, 1907); Missions in State and Church; The Cruciality of the Cross; The Person and Place of Christ (Congregational Lecture, 1909); The Work of Christ; Christ on Parnassus (Lectures on Art, Ethic, and Theology), 1911; Faith, Freedom, and the Future, 1912; The Religion and Ethic of Marriage, 1912; The Principle of Authority, 1913; Theology in Church and State, 1915; The Christian Ethic of War, 1916; The Justification of God, 1916; The Soul of Prayer, 1916; The Church and Sacraments, 1917; This Life and the Next, 1918; articles in the Contemporary Review, London Quarterly, Hibbert Journal, etc. *Recreations:* novels, friends, travel. *Address:* Hackney College, Hampstead. *T.:* P.O. Hampstead 3719.   (*Died 11 Nov. 1921.*)

FORT, Sir Hugh, Kt., *cr.* 1911; 4th *s.* of Richard Fort, M.P. Clitheroe, and Margaret Ellen, *d.* of Major-General Smith, H.E.I.C.S.; unmarried. *Educ.:* Winchester; New College, Oxford. Barrister, Inner Temple, 1887; Advocate and Solicitor of the Straits Settlements, 1898; Acting Unofficial Member of the Legislative Council of the Straits Settlements, 1908; Unofficial Member of the Legislative Council of the Straits Settlements, 1905-8, and 1909-11. *Recreations:* racing, and lawn-tennis. *Address:* 11 Portland Place, W. *Clubs:* United University, Sports.   (*Died 28 May 1919.*)

FORT, Richard, Master of the Meynell Hounds, 1898-1903 and since 1915; *b.* 29 July 1856; *s.* of Richard Fort, M.P. for Clitheroe, and Margaret Ellen, *d.* of Maj.-Gen. Smith, H.E.I.C.S.; *m.* Anna Alice, *d.* of Henry Blundell Leigh, 1882. *Educ.:* Eton; Brasenose College, Oxford. Served in 11th P.A.O. Hussars, 1878-81; M.P. (L.) Clitheroe, 1880-85. *Recreations:* hunting and reading. *Address:* King's Standing, Burton-on-Trent. *T.:* 3 National, Burton-on-Trent. *Clubs:* Arthur's, Brooks's, Boodle's, Naval and Military.
    (*Died 31 Jan. 1918.*)

FORTESCUE, Rev. Adrian, D.D., D.Ph.; *b.* 1874; *s.* of Rev. Edward Bowles Knottesford Fortescue, sometime Provost of St. Ninian's, Perth, and Gertrude M., *d.* of Rev. Sanderson Robins, M.A. *Educ.:* Scots College, Rome; Innsbruck University. Priest, 1898; first resident priest at the Garden City, Letchworth, 1907. *Publications:* The Orthodox Eastern Church; The Greek Fathers; The Liturgy of St. John Chrysostom; The Mass, a Study of the Roman Liturgy; The Lesser Eastern Churches; The Ceremonies of the Roman Rite Described, 1918, etc. *Address:* St. Hugh, Letchworth, Herts.   (*Died 11 Feb. 1923.*)

FORTESCUE, Laurence Knottesford-, C.M.G. 1916; I.S.O. 1905; *b.* 17 Aug. 1845; 3rd *s.* of late Very Rev. E. B. Knottesford-Fortescue of Alveston Manor, Warwickshire; *m.* 1877, Emily Alison, *d.* of late A. J. Russell, Ottawa. *Educ.:* Trinity College, Glenalmond. Joined Royal Marine Light Infantry, 1862; retired on half pay, 1871; entered Royal North West Mounted Police Force of Canada on its organisation, 1873; Assistant Comptroller, 1908-13; Comptroller, 1913-16. *Address:* 11 Polstead Road, Oxford.   (*Died 26 Jan. 1924.*)

FORTESCUE - BRICKDALE, John Matthew, M.A., M.D., Oxon.; M.R.C.P. Lond.; Captain R.A.M.C. (T.F.); Physician to Clifton College, Physician, Bristol Royal Infirmary, Clinical Lecturer, University of Bristol; 2nd *s.* of late M. I. Fortescue-Brickdale, barrister of Lincoln's Inn; *m.* Edith Augusta, 3rd *d.* of late George White; two *s.* *Educ.:* Dulwich College; Christ Church, Oxford; Guy's Hospital. House Physician, Guy's Hospital, 1898-9; Registrar, Assistant-Physician and Physician, Royal Hospital for Sick Children, Bristol, 1903-7; Lecturer on Pharmacology, University of Oxford, 1909-10. *Publications:* Chemical Basis of Pharmacology (jointly); Practical Guide to the Newer Remedies; Numerous Papers in Medical Journals. *Address:* 52 Pembroke Road, Clifton, Bristol. *T.:* Bristol, 1797.   (*Died 2 June 1921.*)

FORTH, Francis Charles, F.R.C.Sc.I.; Principal Municipal Technical Institute, Belfast, and Director of Technical Instruction, Belfast; *m.*; two's. three *d.* *Educ.:* Royal College of Science, Dublin. Now serving as a Captain in the 18th Batt. Royal Irish Rifles, 1915. *Publications:* various, on educational subjects. *Address:* Ravenswood, Belfast. *T.:* 1228 Belfast. *Club:* Ulster Reform, Belfast (*Died 28 Feb. 1919*)

FORTIN, Ven. Octave, B.A., D.D.; *b.* 5 Jan. 1842; *s.* of William and Sophia Fortin of Iberville, Province of Quebec; *m.* 1874, Margaretta Elizabeth, *e. d.* of Edward Stayner Freer of Montreal; two *s.* two *d.* *Educ.:* St. John's, P.Q.; Bishop's Coll., Lennoxville; and M'Gill Univ., Montreal. Ordained deacon, 1865; priest, 1866; his first charge was among the Abenakis Indians of St. Francis, where he built a substantial church and parsonage; after spending a year in England in deputation work for the C. and C.C.S., he became assistant minister at Trinity Church, Montreal, where he remained till 1875; Rector of Holy Trinity, Winnipeg, Man., 1875-1917, and Archdeacon of Winnipeg, 1888-1920; was one of the professors of St. John's College, an examiner in the University of Manitoba, and a member of the Diocesan Provincial and General Synods.   (*Died Oct. 1927.*)

FORWOOD, Sir William Bower; Kt., *cr.* 1883; K.B.E., *cr.* 1918; D.L.; Hon. Freeman of Liverpool; High Sheriff of Lancashire, 1909; *b.* Liverpool, 21 Jan. 1840; 2nd *s.* of late Thomas B. Forwood, Thornton Manor, Cheshire; *m.* 1st, 1862, *d.* of William Miles Moss, Liverpool (*d.* 1896); 2nd, 1898, Elizabeth, *d.* of late General le Fleming, J.P., D.L., Rydal Hall, Westmorland. *Educ.:* Liverpool College. Formerly Merchant and Shipowner, Liverpool; President Liverpool Chamber of Commerce, 1871-77; Pres. Joint Committee on Railway Rates, which led to formation of Railway Commission; one of the founders and the first Chairman, Liverpool Overhead Railway, the first full-gauge Electrical Railway ever built; Member of the City Council 58 years; Mayor of Liverpool, 1880-81; Lord Mayor, 1903; a Founder of the Liverpool Cathedral and raised the funds for its construction, Chairman, 1900-13; Chairman Quarter Sessions, Lancashire, 1890-1910; Chairman Lancashire Magistrates (Kirkdale Division); Chairman Liverpool Public Libraries, Museum, and Art Committee, 1890-1909; President Seaman's Orphanage; Director Cunard Steamship Co.; Bank of Liverpool. *Publications:* sundry pamphlets and papers on economical questions and on literary subjects. *Recreations:* yachting; one of the founders of the Yacht Racing Association, and for many years member of council; has built and sailed many well-known racing yachts. *Address:* Bromborough Hall, Cheshire. *T.:* Bromborough 39. *M.:* M 491.   (*Died 23 Mar. 1928.*)

FOSBERY, Hon. Edmund Walcott, C.M.G. 1902; Member of the Legislative Council of New South Wales; *b.* Wootten, 6 Feb. 1834; *s.* of late Capt. Godfrey Fosbery, R.N. *Educ.:* Royal Naval School. Went to Australia, 1852; Inspector-General, Police Department, N.S.W., 1874-1904. *Address:* Eaton, Bayswater Road, Sydney. *Club:* Union.   (*Died 1 July 1919.*)

FOSTER, Ernest; *b.* Purwell, Herts; *y. s.* of William Foster; *m.* Annie, *d.* of James Belley, 1892. *Educ.:* privately. Editor of Little Folks Magazine, 1880-94; Cassell's Saturday Journal, 1887-1907; Chums, 1894-1907; Family Reader, 1910. *Publications:* An Editor's Chair; Heroes of the Indian Empire; Men of Note: their Boyhood and School Days; Abraham Lincoln; miscellaneous journalistic and other contributions. *Recreations:* cycling, walking, outdoor pursuits. *Address:* 35 Surrey Street, Strand, W.C. 2. *Club:* Constitutional.
    (*Died 11 Jan. 1919.*)

FOSTER, Very Rev. Ernest, M.A.; Dean of Perth, W.A., since 1918; *b.* North Curry, Somerset, 22 April 1867; *s.* of Chas. Millett Foster, solicitor, and Helen Jane Drury; *m.* 1922, Cassie, *o.-c.* of late George Hickman Johns, I.C.S. *Educ.:* King's School, Taunton; New College, Oxford; Wells Theological College; Auckland Castle. 2 Cl. Mod., 1888; 2 Cl. Lit. Hum., 1890; B.A. 1891; M.A. 1893. Deacon,

1892; Priest, 1893; Curate, St. Jude's, South Shields, 1892-96; St. Hilda, South Shields, 1896-99; Vicar of St. Aidan's, Gateshead, 1899-1907; D.L. Dio. Winchester, 1907; Minor Canon, St. George's Cathedral, Perth, W.A., 1908-13; Rector of Guildford, W.A., 1913-18; Chaplain, C.M.F. 4th Class, 1914; Examining Chaplain to the Archbishop of Perth, 1922. *Address:* Deanery, Perth, Western Australia.

(*Died 13 Sept. 1925.*)

FOSTER, George Carey, B.A., LL.D., D.Sc., F.C.S., F.R.S., J.P.; *b.* 1835; *s.* of late George Foster, Sabden, Lancashire; Professor of Physics, Univ. Coll. London, 1865-98; Principal of Univ. Coll. London, 1900-4; *m.* Mary Anne F., *e. d.* of late Andrew Muir, Rosebank, Greenock, 1868; four *s.* four *d. Educ.:* University College, London; Universities of Ghent, Paris, Heidelberg. Pres., Physical Soc., London, 1876-78; Society Telegraphic Engineers (now Institution of Electrical Engineers), 1881; General Treasurer Brit. Association for Advancement of Science, 1898-1904. *Address:* Ladywalk, Rickmansworth. *Clubs:* Athenæum, National Liberal. (*Died 9 Feb. 1919.*)

FOSTER, Rev. Herbert Charles, T.D., *s.* of Prebendary Henry Foster, late Rector and Vicar of Selsey, Chichester, and Augusta Georgiana, *d.* of General Knollys; *m.* 1889, Edith Susan, *d.* of Prebendary Sutton, late Rector of Rype, and Henrietta, *d.* of Thomas Woodward, of Winkenhurst and Highands, Sussex. *Educ.:* Chigwell Grammar School; St. Edmund Hall, Oxford; Gloucester College. Curate of All Saints, Gloucester, 1875-84; Vicar, 1884-1910; Vicar of Groombridge, Sussex, 1910-17; Hon. Canon, Gloucester Cathedral, 1901; Rural Dean, Gloucester, 1904-10. *Recreations:* gardening and books. *Address:* 22 West Hill, St. Leonards-on-Sea. (*Died 13 Nov. 1926.*)

FOSTER, Canon Herbert Henry; *b.* 1864. *Educ.:* Sherborne School; St. Edmund's College, Salisbury; Pembroke College, Oxford, M.A.; Wells College. Ordained 1887; Curate of Rowbarton, 1887-88; St. John's Pro-Cathedral, Umtata, 1888-91; Vice-Principal Burgh Missionary College, 1891-94; Curate of Claremont, Cape Town, 1894-95; Priest in charge Salisbury, Mashonaland, and Chaplain to the Bishop, 1895-1901; Incumbent of Estcourt, 1901-6; Vicar and Sub-Dean of St. Saviour, Pietermaritzburg, 1906-8; Archdeacon of Matabeleland, 1908-13; Rector of Bulawayo, 1910-1913; Principal St. Paul's Miss. College, Burgh, Lincs., 1912-20; Prebend. of Welton Beckhall in Lincoln Cathedral, 1916; Vicar of Orby, Lincs., 1918-20; on special service, N.Z., 1920-23; Commissary Bishop of Auckland, 1923. *Address:* Shiba, Tokyo, Japan.

(*Died June 1927.*)

FOSTER, Rev. James, D.C.L.; Prebendary of Lincoln. *Address:* Tathwell Vicarage, Louth, Lincs. (*Died 17 Dec. 1926.*)

FOSTER, John Watson, International Lawyer; *b.* Indiana, U.S.A., 2 March 1886; *m.* 1859, Mary Parke M'Ferson. *Educ.:* University of Indiana; Harvard. Doctor of Laws, Yale, Princeton, Indiana, and Pennsylvania Universities. Served in Union Army during Civil War, 1861-64; Minister to Mexico, Russia and Spain, 1873-86; Agent of United States before Bering Sea Tribunal of Arbitration, Paris; Secretary of State of the United States, 1892-93; Counsel of Emperor of China in peace negotiations with Japan, 1895; Special Ambassador to Russia, 1897; Member, Anglo-American Commission on Canadian questions, 1898-99; Agent of United States before the Alaskan Boundary Tribunal, 1903; Delegate of Chinese Government to second Hague Conference, 1907. *Publications:* A Century of American Diplomacy; American Diplomacy in the Orient; The Practice of Diplomacy; Arbitration and the Hague

Court; Diplomatic Memoirs; and various diplomatic papers and addresses. *Recreations:* golf, fishing. *Address:* Washington, D.C., U.S.A. *Club:* Cosmos, Washington. (*Died Nov. 1917.*)

FOSTER, Joshua James, F.S.A.; *o. s.* of James Foster; *b.* Dorchester; *m.* 1883, Bertha Woodman, 5th *d.* of George Carter, Stone Hall, Wallingford; one *s.* one *d.* Hon. Sec. Folk-Lore Society 1885-92; Hon. Sec. Folk-Lore Congress, 1891; Member British Committee International Exhibition of Miniatures, Brussels, 1912. *Publications:* British Miniature Painters and their Works, 1898; The Stuarts in 16th, 17th, and 18th Century Art, 2 vols. 1902; Miniature Painters, British and Foreign, 2 vols. 1903; Concerning the True Portraiture of Mary Stuart, 1904; Life of George Morland, 1904; French Art from Watteau to Prudhon, 3 vols. 1905; Chats on Old Miniatures, 1908; Samuel Cooper and English Miniature Painters of the XVII. Century, 1915; Wessex Worthies, 1920; numerous reviews and articles, chiefly on Art subjects. *Address:* Aldwick, Holland Road, Sutton, Surrey. *T.:* Sutton 957.

(*Died 24 Mar. 1923.*)

FOSTER, Sir Norris Tildasley, Kt., *cr.* 1920; C.B.E. 1920; *b.* Bromsgrove, 15 Dec. 1855; *s.* of late Frederick F. Foster; *m.* 1st, 1875, Alice Maud, *e. d.* of late Rev. H. Dewhurst; 2nd, 1905, Eliza, *e. d.* of late Elijah Barnett. *Educ.:* King Edward's School, Birmingham; Oxford University, M.A. Called to Bar, Inner Temple, 1891; joined the Midland Circuit; on the passing of the Military Service Act, 1916, was elected member of Warwickshire County Appeal Tribunal and continued an active member until its close; Chairman (for Ministry of Labour) at Court of Referees, 1919-20; Vice-President of University Graduates Club; Member of General Purposes, Finance and Administration Committee of War Pensions and Citizens Committee, 1914-19; Chairman of Committee of Appeals against decisions from any of the 29 districts of the city; founder and chairman and organiser of Birmingham Streets' Collection Committee, 1915-18; Hon. Treasurer of War Pensions Committee, 1920; for 15 years Chairman of East Birmingham Conservative Association; on formation of Birmingham Unionist Association elected Hon. Secretary; Vice-President of Erdington Parliamentary Division; Hon. Secretary of Midland Unionist Association for 7 years. *Address:* Southfield, Priory Road, Edgbaston, Birmingham. *T.:* South 850.

(*Died 5 Dec. 1925.*)

FOSTER, Robert John, J.P., D.L.; *b.* 1850; 2nd *s.* of late William Foster, J.P., D.L., of Hornby Castle, County Lancaster, and of Harrowins, Queensbury, Yorks., and first wife, Emma Eliza, *d.* of Swithen Anderton, of Ashfield, Yorks; *m.* 1st, 1884, Hon Evelyn Augusta Bateman-Hanbury (*d.* 1907), 2nd *d.* of 2nd Lord Bateman; three *s.* one *d.*; 2nd, Susan R. H., *d.* of late Rev. Frederick Fawkes, Farnley Hall, Yorkshire. High Sheriff, County York, 1898. *Address:* Stockeld Park, Wetherby, Yorkshire. *T.:* Wetherby 3. *Clubs:* Arthur's; Yorkshire, York. (*Died 25 July 1925.*)

FOSTER, Sir Tom Scott, L.D.S., J.P., Kt. *cr.* 1911; *b.* 1845; *s.* of William Foster; *m.* Elise, *d.* of D. Godden; one *s.* three *d. Educ.:* Portsmouth Grammar School. Entered public life, 1876; Mayor of Portsmouth, 1891, 1898, 1911, 1912; Alderman, 1892; Hon. Freeman of Portsmouth; Past Chairman Board of Guardians and Chairman of Governing Body of Grammar School; is President of Portsmouth Hospital; entertained Sanitary Congress, British Medical Association, British Association; presented Freedom to Earl Roberts during office as Mayor; Deputy Chairman of Directors of Portsmouth Water Co.; Director

Gas Co., etc. ; Chairman of Finance Committee of Portsmouth Corporation for 18 years ; governor and trustee of several charities ; King's Coronation Medal, and Volunteer Veterans' Badge ; Member Imperial Society Knights. *Recreation :* motoring. *Address :* Braemar, St. Helen's Parade, Southsea. *T. :* Post Office 4715. *M. :* BK 1 : BK 58. *Club :* Hants Automobile.   (*Died 18 Sept. 1918.*)

FOSTER, Sir Wm. Edward, Kt. *cr.* 1918 ; F.S.A. ; *b.* Manor House, Moulton, Lincolnshire, 1846 ; *o. s.* of late Thomas Foster and Susanna Mary Hunnings ; *m.* 1879, Alexandrina Macpherson, *y. d.* and co-heiress of late Hugh Matheson and Christina Macpherson ; two *s.* *Educ. :* The Grammar School, Moulton. Admitted a solicitor, 1869 ; late head of firm of Foster and Wells, Solicitors, Aldershot ; Coroner for the Aldershot District ; held a number of public appointments ; largely interested in Church work in the Aldershot District—in the Church of England Soldiers' Institute, of which he was Hon. Solicitor, also in hospital work ; is a trustee and a vice-president of the Aldershot Hospital and Hon. Solicitor ; takes great interest in Freemasonry ; a member of several Antiquarian Societies ; and of the Spalding Gents' Society ; for eight years a member of the Council of the Law Society ; a founder and past-president of the Hampshire Law Society. *Publications :* Has written and published a number of works, antiquarian and genealogical, relating to South Lincolnshire and its families. *Address :* Lindum House, Aldershot. *T. :* 345.
     (*Died 7 July 1921.*)

FOSTER, William Henry, J.P., D.L. Shropshire ; High Sheriff, 1903 ; J.P. Northamptonshire ; *b.* 9 Apr. 1846 ; *s.* of late W. O. Foster, Apley Park, Bridgnorth ; *m.* 1874, Henrietta Grace, *d.* of late H. Pakenham Mahon, Strokestown House, Roscommon ; one *s.* three *d.* *Educ. :* Eton ; Christ Church, Oxford. M.P. Bridgnorth, 1870-85. *Heir : s.* Arthur William, M.C., Major, Royal Horse Guards ; *b.* 8 Feb. 1884. *Address :* Apley Park, Bridgnorth, Shropshire ; Spratton Grange, Northampton. *Clubs :* Carlton, Wellington.   (*Died 9 Mar. 1924.*)

FOSTER, Bt. Col. (temp. Col. Comdt.) William James, C.B. 1919 ; C.M.G. 1918 ; D.S.O. 1916 ; commanding 2nd Cavalry Brigade since 1927 ; late Brigade-Major, Staff Australian Imperial Force ; *b.* 8 Dec. 1881. Served European War, including Egypt, 1914-18 (despatches, C.B., C.M.G., D.S.O.) ; Director of Military Operations and Intelligence, Australian Staff. *Address :* Tidworth, Wilts. (*Died 15 Nov. 1927.*)

FOTHERGILL, William Edward, M.A., B.Sc., M.D. (Edin.) ; Hon. Consulting Gynæcological Surgeon, Manchester Royal Infirmary, and Hon. Surg., St. Mary's Hospital ; Professor of Clinical Obstetrics and Gynæcology, Univ. of Manchester ; *b.* 1865 ; *s.* of late Samuel Fothergill of Darlington ; *m.* 1895, Edith A., *d.* of late J. Dillon Woon of Chelsea. *Educ. :* Edinburgh ; Paris ; Jena. Neil Arnott Prize, 1886 ; Essay Prize Edin. Univ. Club of London, 1888 ; M.B., C.M., 1st class honours and Buchanan Scholarship, 1893 ; Gold Medal for M.D. thesis, and Milner-Fothergill Gold Medal, 1897 ; late Resident, Royal Maternity and Royal Infirmary, Edin. ; Consulting Practice in Manchester since 1895 ; former honorary appointments, Northern and Southern Hospitals for Women, and Maternity ; some years Director Clinical Laboratory, Royal Infirmary, Manchester. *Publications :* Manual of Midwifery, 1896 ; 5th ed. 1922 ; Golden Rules of Obstetrics, 1898 (6 editions) ; Handbook for Midwives, 1907 ; 5th ed. 1925 ; Manual of Diseases of Women, 2nd ed. 1922 ; over 60 articles in various medical journals and transactions ; Green's Encyclopædia Medica, Churchill's System of Treatment, and Eden & Lockyer's System of Gynæcology. *Address :*

337 Oxford Road, Manchester ; *T. :* Ardwick 2950 ; 21 Rathen Road, Withington, Manchester ; *T. :* Didsbury 767. (*Died 4 Nov. 1926.*)

POTTRELL, Sir George, K.C.B., *cr.* 1919 ; Clerk of the Crown and Peace, County and City of Dublin ; *b.* 6 Feb. 1849 ; *s.* of late George Drevar Fottrell, Solicitor ; *m.* 1872, Mary, *d.* of William Watson, Dublin ; one *s.* five *d.* *Educ. :* Belvedere College, Dublin ; Catholic University of Ireland. *Address :* 8 North Gt. George's Street, Dublin ; Dunmara, Ballybrack, Co. Dublin. *T. :* Dublin 2363, Killiney-Dublin 23. *Clubs. :* Reform ; Stephen's Green, Dublin ; Royal Irish Yacht, Kingstown.
     (*Died 1 Feb. 1925.*)

FOULIS, Sir William Liston-, 10th Bt. ; *cr.* 1634 ; *e. s.* of 9th Bt. and Sara Helen, *e. d.* of Sir Charles M. Ochterlony, 2nd Bt. ; *b.* 27 Oct. 1869 ; *S.* father 1896. Owns about 2900 acres in Midlothian. *Heir : b.* Charles James Liston Foulis (*b.* 4 Jan. 1873 ; *m.* 1903, Maria, *d.* of Richard Moore ; one *s.*). *Address :* 14 Murrayfield Avenue, Edinburgh ; Millburn Tower and Woodhall, Midlothian. *Club :* Caledonian United Service, Edinburgh. (*Died 16 April 1918.*)

FOWLE, Col. John, C.B. 1911 ; C.M.G. 1918 ; Inspector of Remounts Irish Command ; *b.* 26 May 1862 ; *m.* 1908 ; entered Army, 1881 ; Captain 1887 ; Major, 1898 ; Lieut.-Colonel, 1902 ; Colonel, 1907 ; A.D.C. to Governor Madras and Bombay, 1889-1903 ; Commander S.E. Mounted Brigade, 1908-10. Served Soudan, 1884-5 (medal with clasp, bronze star) ; Nile Expedition, 1898 (despatches, 4th class Osmanieh, Egyptian medal with clasp, medal), South Africa, 1900-1 (Queen's medal, 2 clasps). *Clubs :* Naval and Military, Cavalry.
     (*Died 25 Sept. 1923.*)

FOWLER, James Stewart, M.D., F.R.C.P.Ed. ; Physician, Royal Edinburgh Hospital for Sick Children and Chalmers' Hospital ; University Clinical Lecturer on Diseases of Children ; Editor Edinburgh Medical Journal ; *b.* 22 Oct. 1870 ; *s.* of James Stewart Fowler, M.D., Demerara ; *m.* 1902, Edith (*d.* 1924), *d.* of Philip Sharkey Hudson, C.E., Hyderabad ; one *d.* *Educ. :* Edinburgh Academy ; Universities of Edinburgh and Vienna. *Publications :* contributions on medical subjects in Journals and Treatises. *Recreations :* fishing, photography. *Address :* 55 Northumberland Street, Edinburgh. *T. :* Central 1361. *Club :* University, Edinburgh.   (*Died 24 Aug. 1925.*)

FOWLER, Rev. Joseph Thomas, M.A., Hon. D.C.L. Dunelm., F.S.A., M.R.C.S., L.S.A. ; Vice-Principal of Bishop Hatfield's Hall, Durham, 1870-1917 ; University Hebrew Lecturer, 1872-1917 ; Librarian, 1874-1901 ; Maltby Librarian, 1881-1911 ; Keeper of Bishop Cosin's Library, 1889-1911 ; Hon. Canon of Durham, 1897 ; *b.* Winterton, Co. Lincoln, 9 June 1833 ; *e. s.* of Joseph, *e.s.* of William Fowler, the Antiquary and Engraver, of Winterton, and Elizabeth, *e. d.* of Thomas Fowler, Ownby, near Spital, Co. Lincoln ; unmarried. *Educ. :* at home (by his father) ; West Riding Proprietary School, Wakefield ; St. Thomas's Hosp. London ; Bishop Hatfield's Hall, Durham. Hospital appointments at St. Thomas's ; House Surgeon St. Thomas's, 1856-1857 ; Bradford Infirmary, 1857-58 ; Hebrew Prizes ; Theological, Entrance, and Barry Scholarships at Durham ; Curate of Houghtonle-Spring, Co. Durham, 1861-63, Chaplain and Precentor at St. John's College, Hurstpierpoint, 1864-69 ; Curate of North Kelsey, 1870 ; a Local Sec. for Durham of Society of Antiquaries, *c.* 1873-1917 ; a Vice-President of Surtees Society. *Publications :* editor of Ripon Chapter Acts ; Newminster Cartulary ; Memorials of Ripon, 4 vols. ; Metrical Life of St. Cuthbert (Surtees Society) ; The Coucher Book of Selby, 2 vols. (Yorkshire Record Society) ; Cistercian Statutes (Yorkshire Archæol. Society) ; Adamnani Vita S-

FOWKE, Frank Rede. See page xx.

Columbæ (two eds.), and Translation ; Durham Account-Rolls, 3 vols. ; Memorials of Fountains Abbey, vol. 3, and Rites of Durham (Surtees Society) ; Durham Cathedral ; Life and Letters of Dr. Dykes ; St. Cuthbert, a sermon preached in York Minster ; History of the University of Durham. 904 (College Histories) ; Correspondence of W. Fowler, 1907 (privately printed) ; many articles in various periodicals, 1862-1920. *Recreations :* formerly part-singing, bell - ringing, cycling, photography. *Address :* Winterton. Scunthorpe *T.A. :* Winterton, Lincs.   *(Died 22 Mar. 1924.)*

FOWLER, Robert, R.I. ; artist ; *b.* Anstruther, Fifeshire ; married. *Educ. :* Liverpool Coll. First exhibited at Royal Academy, 1876 ; has exhibited at Grosvenor, Grafton, and New Galleries, London, and Champ de Mars, Paris ; also in Munich, Berlin, Brussels, Venice, Vienna, and other cities of the Continent. *Principal Pictures :* Coming of Apollo, R.A., 1896 ; Some Enchantment Old, R.A., 1897 ; Conway Castle, R.A., 1903 ; After Music, New Gallery, 1896 ; The Enchanted Glade, Grafton, 1895 ; Shy Nymph, now in Magdeburg Museum : Eve, Ariel, and Sleeping Nymphs discovered by a Shepherd, belonging to Corporation of Liverpool ; Light and Shadow in the Gipsy Camp, R.A., 1908 ; Light and Laughter in Kentish Hopfields, R.A., 1909. etc. *(Died 28 Oct. 1926.)*

FOWLER, William Warde, M.A. ; Hon. D.Litt. Manchester ; Hon. LL.D. Edinburgh ; *b.* Somerset, 1847 ; 2nd *s.* of J. Coke Fowler, Stipendiary Magistrate of Swansea ; unmarried. *Educ. :* Marlborough ; Lincoln College, Oxford (Scholar, 1866) ; Fellow, 1872 ; Sub-Rector, 1881-1904 ; Gifford Lecturer Edinburgh Univ. 1909. *Publications :* A Year with the Birds. 1886 ; Tales of the Birds, 1888 ; Life of Julius Cæsar, 1892 ; The City-State of the Greeks and Romans, 1893 ; Summer Studies of Birds and Books, 1895 ; The Roman Festivals of the Republican Period, 1899 ; More Tales of the Birds, 1902 ; An Oxford Correspondence of 1903, 1904 ; Social Life at Rome in the Age of Cicero, 1909 ; The Religious Experience of the Roman People, 1911 ; Kingham Old and New, 1913 ; Roman Ideas of Deity, 1914 ; Virgil's Gathering of the Clans, 1916 ; Essays in Brief for War-Time, 1916 ; Æneas at the Site of Rome, 1917 ; The Death of Turnus, 1919 ; Roman Essays and Interpretations : articles in Zoologist, Classical Review, etc. *Recreations :* observation of bird-life, especially in England and Switzerland ; trout-fishing. *Address :* Lincoln College, Oxford ; Kingham, Oxford. *(Died 14 June 1921.)*

FOWLER, Rev. William Weekes, D.Sc., M.A., Vicar of Earley, Reading, since 1904 ; Prebendary and Canon of Lincoln Cathedral, 1887 ; *s.* of Rev. Hugh Fowler, Barnwood Vicarage, Gloucester ; *b.* Jan. 1849 ; *m.* 1875, Anne Frances, *d.* of B. Bonnor, J.P., Gloucester ; two *s.* two *d.* *Educ. :* Rugby ; Jesus College, Oxford ; Assistant and House Master at Repton, 1873-80 ; Head Master of Lincoln School, 1880-1901 ; President of the Incorporated Association of Head Masters, 1897 ; Rector of Rotherfield Peppard, Oxon., 1901-4 ; President of the Entomological Society of London, 1901-2 ; Vice-President of the Linnean Society, 1906-7 ; Member of the Scientific Committee, Royal Horticultural Society. *Publications :* The Coleoptera of the British Islands (5 vols.) ; the Membracidæ and other groups of Honoptera of Central America (Biologia Centrali Americana) ; Notes on new species of Languriidæ, etc. ; Fauna of British India (India Office) ; Coleoptera, General Introduction : Cicindelidæ and Paussidæ. *Recreations :* Gardening, Natural History. *Address :* Earley Vicarage, Reading. *T.A. :* Earley. *(Died 5 June 1923.)*

FOWLER - BUTLER, Major-Gen. Robert Henry; retired list; *b.* 11 May 1838; *s.* of Richard Fowler-Butler, late Rifle Brigade ; *m.* Agnes, *d.* of Rev. J. de Courcy O'Grady, Knockany, Co. Limerick ; one *s.* *Educ. :* Cheltenham. Served in Royal Fusiliers, 1858 - 87 ; commanded 1st battalion ; Colonel of Chichester district, 1888-93 ; commanded troops, West Indies, 1895-1900 ; Major-General, 1898 ; served Kandahar campaign, 1881. *Address :* The Hall, Barton-under-Needwood, Staffs. *T.A. :* Barton-under-Needwood. *Club :* Naval and Military. *(Died 17 Nov. 1919.)*

FOX, Lt.-Col. Arthur Claude, D.S.O. 1915 ; R.A.M.C. ; *b.* 23 April 1868 ; Captain, 1897 ; Major, 1905 ; Lt.-Col., 1915 ; served European War, 1914-16 (despatches, D.S.O.). *(Died 15 April 1917.)*

FOX, Sir (Charles) Douglas. Kt., *cr.* 1886 ; J.P. London, Kent, and Surrey ; Past President Inst. C.E. ; civil and mechanical engineer ; *b.* 14 May 1840 ; *s.* of late Sir Charles Fox ; *m.* Mary (*d.* 1920), *d.* of Francis Wright of Osmaston Manor, Derby, 1863 ; one *s.* four *d.* *Educ. :* Cholmondeley School ; King's College, London. Fellow of King's College, London. Has practised in London since 1861. *Publications :* several professional papers. *Address :* 27 Campden House Road, Kensington, W.8. *(Died 13 Nov. 1921.)*

FOX, Sir Charles Edmund, Kt., *cr.* 1907 ; K.C.S.I., *cr.* 1917 ; *b.* 1854 ; *s.* of late John Fox of St. John's, Newfoundland ; *m.* Ethel Mary, *e.d.* of Sir Charles Parry Hobhouse, 3rd Bt. *Educ. :* Prior Park College, Bath. Called to Bar, 1877 ; Government Advocate, Burma, 1884-1900 ; Judge of Chief Court, Lower Burma, 1900 ; Chief Judge, 1906-17. *Address :* Bigswear House, St. Briavels, Glos. *Club :* East India United Service. *(Died 9 Oct. 1918.)*

FOX, Major Charles Vincent, D.S.O. 1914 ; late 2nd Batt. Scots Guards ; *b.* 31 Dec. 1877 ; *e. s.* of late Capt. H. C. Fox, King's Dragoon Guards, of Glen-a-gearagh Hall, Co. Dublin. *Educ. :* Clongowes ; Oxford University. Gazetted into Scots Guards, 1900 ; Captain, 1906 ; Major, 1915 ; Second in Command and Commanding Battalion, 1919 ; Lieut.-Col. 1921, on appointment as Deputy Inspector-General. Employed with South Nigeria Regiment, West African Field Force, 1901-7 ; served West Africa, 1901 - 2 ; Aro Expedition (despatches, medal and clasp, wounded) ; again in 1902 ; operations in N. Hibio District (despatches, clasp) ; again in 1904-5 ; Onitsha Hinterland Expedition (despatches) ; again in 1905-6 ; Bende - Onitsha Hinterland Expedition (despatches, clasp) ; attached Egyptian Army, 1908-12 ; Political Inspector, Mongalla Province, Sudan, 1911-13 ; Annak and Bier Patrol Expeditions (despatches, medal and 2 clasps) ; conducted elephant poacher hunt, 1911, and taken prisoner by the Belgians (despatches, Order of the Mejidieh) ; special war correspondent in Turco - Balkan War (Turkish Army), 1912 ; European War, 1914 (despatches twice, D.S.O. for conspicuous gallantry at Kruiseik, in which action he captured five officers and 200 prisoners (thrice wounded, 1914 Star) ; taken prisoner Kruiseik, 26 Oct. 1914 ; escaped from Crefeld ; escaped from Berlin express ; recaptured ; escaped from Schwarmstedt, 1917 (received in special audience by the King, despatches) ; President of the Escapers, 1918 ; Deputy Inspector-General Iraq Levies, 1921-22 ; retired pay, 1923. *Publications :* (serial) various, on war and sport. *Recreations :* Record-holder Oxford University and Wingfield Sculls (Championship Great Britain) ; won Diamond Sculls, 1901 ; also Championships of France and Ireland ; runner-up Army Middle Weight Championship, 1900 ; yachtsman, oar, big game, Rugby, polo, hunting, cricket, golf. *Address :* Brookfield, Milltown, Co. Dublin. *Clubs:* Guards', Army and Navy, Royal Automobile.   (*Died 8 Nov. 1928.*)

FOX, Sir Francis, Kt., *cr.* 1912; J.P.; M.Inst.C.E.; Hon. A.R.I.B.A.; *s.* of late Sir Charles Fox; *b.* 1844; *m.* 1st, 1869, Selina, *d.* of Francis Wright, of Osmaston Manor, Derby; two *s.* three *d.*; 2nd, 1901, Agnes, *d.* of H. King Horne, of Guerres, Normandy. Appointed by the Federal Government of Switzerland, on the nomination of the British Government, as Member of Committee of Three Experts on Tunnelling, for the construction of the Simplon Tunnel. *Publications:* River, Road, and Rail; Sixty-three years of Engineering Science and Social Work; The Mersey Tunnel; The Simplon Tunnel; The Cape and Cairo Railway; The Saving of Winchester Cathedral, etc. *Address:* Alyn Bank, 12 The Downs, Wimbledon, S.W.20. *T.:* 35 P.O. Wimbledon.   (*Died 7 Jan. 1927.*)

FOX, Sir Gilbert Wheaton, 1st Bart., *cr.* 1924; J.P.; *b.* 1 July 1863; *y. s.* of John Palk Fox, shipowner, Liverpool; *m.* 1902, May, *e. d.* of Edward William Jones, Hoylake, Cheshire; one *s.* one *d.* : privately. Sole partner Edward Grey and Co., sugar merchants, of Liverpool and Mincing Lane, London; went to America and Cuba on behalf of the Sugar Commission, 1919-20; Director Colonial Bank and Guardian Insurance Co.; Chairman Reliance Marine Co.; one of the Auditor Commissioners of the Mersey Docks Harbour Board; member of the Executive Committee of the Empire Exhibition at Wembley; Government Representative on the Wallasey Board of Commissioners; Director at Lever Bros., 1916-1920. *Heir: s.* Gifford Wheaton Grey, *b.* Feb. 1903. *Address:* 87 Aigburth Drive, Liverpool; Pinfold, West Kirby, Cheshire. *Clubs:* Portland; Down Town, New York; Travellers', Paris; Racquet, Liverpool.   (*Died 21 Feb. 1925.*)

FOX, H. B. Earle; Secretary of the British Numismatic Society and Editor of the British Numismatic Journal since 1918. *Address:* 43 Bedford Square, W.C.   (*Died 21 Mar 1920.*)

FOX, Rev. Henry Elliott, M.A. ; Prebend of Holborn in St. Paul's Cathedral; *b.* Masulipatam, S. India, 21 Oct. 1841; *e. s.* of late Henry Watson Fox (*d.* 1848) and Elizabeth James (*d.* 1845); *m.* 1st, 1866, Emily Stebbing Sandle, (*d.* 1867); 2nd, 1871, Frances Alice Highton (*d.* 1904); 3rd, 1906, Effie, *d.* of Rev. H. James; one *s.* five *d.* *Educ.:* Harrow; Trinity College, Cambridge. Entered Lincoln's Inn, 1864; ordained to the Curacy of St. Ebbe's, Oxford, 1869; Vicar of Christ Church, Westminster, 1873; Vicar of St. Nicholas', Durham, 1882; Hon. Clerical Secretary Church Missionary Society, 1895-1910. *Publications:* Our Lord and His Bible; Christian Inscriptions in Ancient Rome; occasional sermons, pamphlets, papers. *Address:* The Croft, Putney Hill, S.W.15. *T.:* 484 Putney Post Office. *Club:* National(*Died 12 May 1926*)

FOX, Henry Wilson-; M.P. (U.) North Warwicks., since 1917; *b.* London, 18 Aug. 1863; 2nd *s.* of late Dr. Wilson Fox, F.R.S.; *m.* 1898, Hon. Eleanor Birch Sclater-Booth, C.B.E.; 5th *d.* of 1st Baron Basing; one *s.* *Educ.:* Charterhouse; Marlborough; University College, London; Trinity College, Cambridge (B.A., Scholar). Barrister-at-Law, Lincoln's Inn (Exhibitioner), 1888; Johannesburg, 1889; editor South African Mining Journal, 1892; Public Prosecutor of Rhodesia, 1894; served Matabeleland rebellion, 1896; Director of Transport and Commissariat, Mashonaland, 1897 (despatches, medal with clasp); Manager of the British South Africa Company, 1898; Director, 1913; Vice-President of the Royal Geographical Society; Member Conjoint Board Scientific Societies; Fellow of the Royal Statistical Society; Fellow, Royal Colonial Institute; Member of Committee of the All England

Lawn Tennis and Croquet Club. *Publications:* Articles in Nineteenth Century, etc. *Recreations:* lawn - tennis, golf, fishing. *Address:* 20 Lowndes Square, S.W.1. *T.:* Victoria 462. *Clubs:* Carlton, St. Stephen's, Wellington, Princes.   (*Died 22 Nov. 1921.*)

FOX, John (Junior); *b.* Bourbon, County Kentucky, 1863. *Educ.:* Kentucky (Transylvania University); Harvard; Columbia Law School. Acted as Correspondent of Harper's Weekly in Spanish-American War; and for Scribner's Magazine in Russo-Japanese War. *Publications:* A Mountain Europa; A Cumberland Vendetta; Hell for Sartain; The Kentuckians; Crittenden; Bluegrass and Rhododendron; The Trail of the Lonesome Pine; The Heart of the Hills; Following the Sun-Flag; Christmas Eve on Lonesome; The Little Shepherd of Kingdom Come. *Address:* Bigstone Gap, Virginia.   (*Died 8 July 1919.*)

FOX, His Honour John Scott, K.C.; Judge Leeds Circuit since 1916; *b.* Selby, Yorkshire, 17 January 1852; *s.* of Rev. William Fox; *m.* 1901, Agnes Maria Theresa Hammer; two *s.* one *d.* *Educ.:* Bedford Grammar School; University College, Oxford. Double First in Moderations, 1872; 1st class Classical Greats, 1874; B.A. 1875; M.A. and B.C.L. 1877. Barr. 1877; joined the North-Eastern Circuit, 1881; Examiner to the Court, 1884 - 94; revising barrister on the North-Eastern Circuit, 1885-96; Queen's Counsel, 1898; Solicitor-General, Co. Palatine, Durham, 1901; Bencher Middle Temple, 1905; Chancellor County Palatine of Durham, 1905-15; Recorder of Sheffield, 1903-15. C.C. Judge Circuit 7 (Birkenhead, etc.), 1915-16. *Recreations:* travel, golf. *Address:* Fountain Court, Temple, E.C.; 13 Cornwall Gardens, S.W. *T.A.:* Scott Fox, 86 Temple, E.C. *T.:* Central 1727; Western 1559. *Club:* United University.   (*Died 3 Mar. 1918.*)

FOX, Colonel Sir Malcolm, Kt. *cr.* 1910; *b.* Derby, 4 March 1843; *s.* of Douglas Fox, Derby, and Marian, *d.* of J. Strutt, Green Hall, Belper; *m.* 1st, 1881, Mary Rose, *d.* of Captain Wm. Newall, Gordon Highlanders; one *d.*; 2nd, 1884, Marion Jane, *d.* of John Remington Mills of Tolmers, Hertford; one *d.* Served in 100th Royal Canadians and 42nd Royal Highlanders; served Egyptian Campaign (severely wounded, medal and clasp, Khedive's star); Assistant Inspector of Army Gymnasia, 1883-87; Inspector, 1889-96; Assistant Adjutant General N.E. District, 1897-1900; Inspector of Physical Training to Board of Education, 1903-10; was member of Inter-Departmental Committee which drew up a course of physical training for elementary schools and training colleges; Commander of the Royal Order of the Sword, Sweden. *Address:* 118 Eaton Square, S.W. *Club:* Naval and Military.   (*Died 10 Mar. 1918.*)

FOX, Sir Robert Eyes, Kt., *cr.* 1913; Town Clerk of Leeds since 1904; *s.* of Rev. George Fox; *b.* 22 Oct. 1861; *m.* 1890, Laura Stuart, *d.* of late Edward Pearson; one *s.* one *d.* Solicitor 1883; Deputy Town Clerk, Birkenhead, 1886-88; Town Clerk of Burnley, 1888-92; of Blackburn, 1892-1904. *Address:* Moorlands, Moortown, Leeds. *T.:* Chapeltown, Leeds, 158. *Clubs:* National; Leeds.   (*Died 2 Oct. 1924.*)

FOX, Thomas Colcott, B.A. (Cantab.), M.B. (Lond.), F.R.C.P.; Consulting Physician for Diseases of the Skin to the Westminster Hospital; Consulting Medical Referee to the Mutual Life Insurance Company of New York; *b.* 1849; 8th *s.* of Dr. L. O. Fox of Broughton, Hants; *m.* 1890. Ida Mary, *y. d.* of J S. Hay - Newton of Newton Hall, Gifford, N.B. *Educ.:* Queenwood Coll., Univ. Coll. School and Coll., London; Peterhouse, Cambridge (Natural Science Scholar). Formerly Medical Superintendent of Fulham Smallpox Hospital, Physician to Victoria Hospital for Children,

and for Skin Diseases to the Paddington Green Children's Hospital. *Publications:* numerous medical contributions. chiefly on Diseases of the Skin. *Recreations:* various games and sports; formerly played cricket for Hampshire and Incogniti. *Address:* 10 Walpole Street, Chelsea, S.W. *T.:* 798 Victoria.
(Died 11 April 1916.)

FOXCROFT, Frederick Walter, M.D., C.M. Edin.; Aural Surgeon and Laryngologist to the General Hospital, Birmingham; Clinical Lecturer on Otology and Laryngology to the University of Birmingham; *b.* Broughton, Manchester, 16 Jan. 1858; *y. s.* of late Joseph Foxcroft, Manchester, and Margarette Anne, *o. d.* of late Thomas Slatter, Hope House, Pendleton; *m.* 1904, Mary Lydia, *d.* of late Thomas Cockbain, Liverpool. *Educ.:* private school, Universities of Edinburgh, Berlin, and Vienna. Late Clinical Assistant at the Saughton Hall Lunatic Asylum, Edinburgh; House Surgeon and Resident Medical Officer, General Hospital, Birmingham; Assistant Surgeon to the Birmingham and Midland Ear and Throat Hospital for five years. *Recreations:* cricket, yacht and boat sailing, golf. *Address:* 47 Newhall Street, Birmingham. *T.:* 33 Central. *Clubs:* Royal Societies; Union, Birmingham. *(Died 1916.)*

FOX - DAVIES, Arthur Charles; *b.* Bristol, 28 Feb. 1871; 2nd *s.* of late T. Edmond Fox-Davies of Coalbrookdale, Shropshire, and Maria J., *e. d.* and *co-heiress* of John Fox, J.P., of Coalbrookdale; *m.* 1901, Mary E. B., *e. d.* of Capt. Septimus Wilkinson Crookes of The Wyke, Shifnal; one *s.* one *d. Educ.:* Ackworth, Yorks. Is a Barrister-at-Law, Lincoln's Inn (Surrey and South London Sess., C.C.C., and S.E. Circuit), late Editor of Dod's Peerage and Burke's Landed Gentry; is Editor of Armorial Families; contested Merthyr Tydvil as a Tory, 1910, 1923 and 1924; formerly Member of Holborn Borough Council; Gold Staff Officer at Coronation of King George V.; member of Anti - Aircraft Corps, 1914 - 1916; Naval Law Branch at Admiralty, 1916-1920. *Publications:* The Book of Public Arms; The Art of Heraldry; The Law of Names and Changes of Name; Heraldic Badges; Heraldry Explained; The Complete Guide to Heraldry; Their Majesties' Court; The Dangerville Inheritance; The Average Man; The Mauleverer Murders; The Finances of Sir John Kynnersley; The Sex Triumphant; The Troubles of Colonel Marwood; The Duplicate Death; The Testament of John Hastings; The Ultimate Conclusion; The Book of Public Speaking; and various other works, including printed "cases" for numerous claims of peerage. *Address:* 23 Old Buildings, Lincoln's Inn, W.C.2; 65 Warwick Gardens, Kensington, W.14; Coalbrookdale, R.S.O., Shropshire. *T.:* Holborn 1912; Western 6084. *(Died 19 May 1928.)*

FOX-PITT, Douglas; 5th *s.* of late General Pitt Rivers, F.R.S.; member of The London Group; edited and illustrated Count Sternberg's book, The Barbarians of Morocco, 1908; has a water-colour drawing of British Museum Library in Print Room of British Museum presented by late Lord Avebury; a water-colour drawing, Under the Pier, bought by the Brighton Corporation, 1912; water-colour drawing of Ceylon at the Imperial Institute; water-colour drawing at the Fitzwilliam Museum, Cambridge; oil painting, The Indian Hospital at the Dome, Brighton, purchased for the Imperial War Museum. *Recreations:* travelling and reading. *Address:* The Cottage, Thorpe, Chertsey, Surrey. *(Died 19 Sept. 1922.)*

FOXTON, Col. Hon. Justin Fox Greenlaw, C.M.G. 1903; V.D.; A.D.C. to Governor - General of Australia; *e. s.* of late John Greenlaw Foxton, H.E.I.C.S.

(naval); *b.* 24 Sept.1849; *m.* 1874, Emily Mary, 3rd *d.* of late.Hon. John Panton, M.L.C. Queensland; two *s.* two *d. Educ.:* Melbourne Grammar School and privately. A Solicitor of Supreme Court of Queensland; received commission as Lieut., and afterwards as Captain, in old volunteer force, Queensland, 1879; Captain in Militia (Artillery), 1885; late Brigadier in command of Queensland Field Force (Commonwealth Military Forces); retired, 1912; elected member for district of Carnarvon in Queensland Parliament, 1883; five times re-elected for same constituency, which he represented for 21 years; Minister for Lands in Nelson ministry and Byrnes ministry; Home Secretary in Dickson ministry; Home Secretary and afterwards Minister for Lands in Philp ministry; was a member of Federal Council of Australasia until its abolition on the establishment of the Commonwealth; was member of late Defence Committee for Queensland; member for Brisbane in Commonwealth Parliament, 1906-10; Minister without portfolio, Deakin Ministry, and as such represented Australia at Imperial Conference on Naval and Military defence of Empire, 1909; President Charity Organisation Society, Brisbane; holds medal of Royal Humane Society, having received the Society's award on two occasions for saving life. *Recreations:* cricket (Pres. Queensland Assoc.), yachting, shooting, tennis, golf. *Address:* Bulimba House, Bulimba, nr. Brisbane, Queensland. *T.A.:* Circe, Brisbane. *T.:* 79 and 3127 Brisbane. *Clubs:* Queensland, Johnsonian, United Service Institution of Queensland, Brisbane; Naval and Military, Melbourne.
(Died 23 June 1916.)

FOY, Hon. James Joseph, K.C., LL.D.; Attorney - General of Ontario; *b.* Toronto, Canada, 22 Feb. 1847; *s.* of Patrick Foy; *m.* 1879, Marie Cuvillier (*d.* 1903) of Montreal. *Educ.:* St. Michael's College, Toronto; Ushaw College, Durham, England. Barrister-at-Law, Osgoode Hall, 1871; Bencher of Law Society of Ontario; Q.C. 1888; LL.D. Toronto University; elected Ontario Legislature, 1898, 1902, 1905, 1908, and 1911. *Address:* 90 Isabella Street, Toronto. *Clubs:* Albany, Toronto, Royal Canadian Yacht. York. Granite. Toronto.
(Died 12 June 1916.)

FRAMPTON, E. Reginald, R.O.I., 1904; Painter; Staff of L.C.C. Higher Education Art Section; *s.* of Caroline and Edward Frampton, artist; *m.* Lola, *d.* of Francis Mallard Clark, late of the Admiralty, London. *Educ.:* Brighton; Westminster School; France and Italy. R.B.A., 1894, resigned; Tempera Society, 1907; Art - Workers' Guild, 1910; Exhibitor, International Art Exhibitions at Rome, Ireland, Canada, Brussels, Ghent, etc.; Salon, R.A., New Gallery, Franco-British, Japan, Pittsburg 1922, Liverpool, Glasgow, Birmingham, Manchester, and other Provincial Galleries. Principal pictures painted: Annunciation; St. Cecilia; Navigation; St. Brandan (Mention Honourable Paris Salon); The Kiss of Spring (Silver Medal, Paris Salon 1920); Holy Grail; Jeanne d'Arc; Love and the West Wind; A Madonna of Brittany, bought by Corporation of Bradford; Our Lady of Snows, bought by Corporation of Liverpool; The Sleep of Summer; One Man Show, London, 1914; executed Mural Paintings in All Saints. Hastings; Rushall Church, Mellish Memorial, St. Peter's, Birstall; Batty Memorial, Southampton; Seaforth Church, Waddington Hall, Yorks; Liverpool High School, Smithwick Memorial; Ranmore Church, Lord Ashcombe Memorial. *Publications:* Reproduction and Account of Work, Art Journal, 1907, Studio, 1906 and 1914; Colour-print of the Island of Brechow, Sark, 1923: Illustrations for Poems of William Morris. *Recreations:* chess, sailing, etc. *Address:* 1 Brook Green Studios, Brook Green, W. 14.   (*Died 4 Nov. 1923.*)

FRAMPTON, Sir George James, Kt., *cr.* 1908; R.A. 1902; A.R.A., LL.D., 1894; F.S.A. 1904; an Honorary Life Member of the Oxford Union Society, 1904; Hon. Associate, Royal Institute of British Architects; Member Royal Academy of Fine Arts, Milan; past Master of the Art Workers' Guild; sculptor; President Royal Society British Sculptors, 1911-12; *b.* 1860; *m.* 1893, Christabel Cockerell; one *s.* Studied under W. S. Frith; entered Royal Acad. schools, 1881; Gold Medal and Travelling Studentship, 1887; since then gold and silver medals, and other honours in France; Germany, Belgium, Spain, and America, including Médaille d'Honneur at the Paris Exposition, 1900; Mem. of l'Academie Royale de Belgique, 1926; Member of Corps Académique, Antwerp; Commandeur de l'ordre de Leopold II.; Commandeur de l'Ordre de la Couronne; Master of the Merchant Taylors' Company, 1918-1919; has executed many memorials and statues, including that of H.M. Queen Victoria for Calcutta, Southport, St. Helens, Newcastle-on-Tyne, Winnipeg, and Leeds; Liveryman of the Merchant Taylors' Company and Founders' Company; designed the terra-cotta decoration on the Constitutional Club; the sculpture on the Glasgow Art Galleries; the whole of the sculpture on the exterior of Lloyd's Register, City; the entrance to Electra House, Moorgate Street, City; spandrels at entrance of the Victoria and Albert Museum; Peter Pan, Kensington Gardens; figures on the spire of St. Mary's, Oxford; saints on the shrine of William of Wykeham, Winchester Cathedral; lions at the entrance to the new extension to the British Museum; statues of Queen Mary for Victoria Memorial Hall, Calcutta, and Government House, Delhi; portrait-busts of King George V. and Queen Mary for the Guildhall; the Edith Cavell Memorial, London; has designed and executed works in ivory, silver, enamels, etc.; the C.I.V. medal; many other medals, including Coronation medal. *Address:* 90 Carlton Hill, St. John's Wood, N.W. *Clubs:* Athenæum, Garrick.
          (*Died 21 May 1928.*)

FRANCE (Jacques) Anatole (Thibault), French author; Officer Legion of Honour; Member of French Academy; *b.* Paris, 16 April 1844; *m.* 1920, Emma Leprévotte. *Educ.:* Collège Stanislaus. *Publications:* Alfred de Vigny, 1868; Les Poèmes dorés, 1873; Les Noces corinthiennes, 1876; Jocaste et le Chat maigre, 1879; Le Crime de Sylvestre Bonnard, 1881; Les Désirs de Jean Servien, 1882; Le Livre de mon ami, 1885; Nos enfants, 1886; Balthazar, 1889; Thais, 1890; La Vie littéraire, 1890; L'Étui de Nacre, 1892; L'Elvire de Lamartine, 1893; Les Opinions de Monsieur Jérôme Cogniard, 1893; La Rôtisserie de la Reine Pédauque, 1893; Le Lys Rouge, 1894; Le Puits de Sainte-Claire, 1895; Le Jardin d'Épicure, 1895; Poesies, 1896; Le Mannequin d'osier, 1897; L'Orme du Mail, 1897; L'Anneau d'améthyste, 1899; Clio, 1899; M. Bergeret à Paris, 1901; Le Procurateur de Judée, 1902; Mme de Luzy, 1902; Mémoires d'un volontaire, 1902; Histoire comique, 1903; L'Église et la République, 1905; Sur la pierre blanche, 1905; Le Jongleur de Notre-Dame, 1906; Sainte Euphrosyne, 1906; Histoire de Jeanne d'Arc, 1908; Les Sept Femmes de la Barbe Bleue, 1909; La Révolte des Anges, 1914; La Vie en fleur, 1922. *Address:* Villa Said V (XVIe), Paris.
          (*Died 13 Oct. 1924.*)

FRANCILLON, Robert Edward, LL.M.; novelist, journalist; *b.* in Gloucester, 25 Mar. 1841; *e. s.* of James Francillon, County Court Judge; *m.* Rosamond, *d.* of John Barnett, the musical composer, 1872. *Educ.:* Cheltenham College; Trin. Hall, Camb. Barr. Gray's Inn,

376

1864; on staff Globe newspaper, 1872-94. *Publications:* Earl's Dene; Pearl and Emerald; Olympia; Strange Waters; Zelda's Fortune; A Real Queen; Queen Cophetua; A Dog and his Shadow; King or Knave; Jack Doyle's Daughter; Ropes of Sand: Gods and Heroes; Nine Christmas Numbers of the Gentleman's Magazine; Mid-Victorian Memories, 1913. *Address:* St. Paul's House, Warwick Square, E.C.
          (*Died 11 May 1919.*)

FRANCIS, Augustus Lawrence, M.A.; *b.* Hurley-on-Thames, Berkshire, 16 Jan. 1848; *s.* of late Henry Ralph Francis, formerly Fellow of St. John's College, Cambridge, and Judge, N.S.W., and Beata, *d.* of John Lloyd-Jones of Plasmdoc, N. Wales; *m.* 1874, Emily Constance, *d.* of Major-General Robert Unwin; two *s.* two *d.* *Educ.:* Christ's Hospital; Jesus College, Cambridge, sometime Fellow; First Class Classical Tripos, 1870; Assistant Master at Dulwich College, 1872; Headmaster, Blundell's School, Tiverton, 1874-1917. *Publications:* (Joint) An Advanced Latin Syntax and an English Verse translation of Martial's Epigrams. *Recreations:* golf, shooting, fishing. *Address:* Blundell House, Tiverton. *T:* Tiverton 1Y4.
          (*Died 18 Oct. 1925.*)

FRANCIS, Charles King, Metropolitan Police Magistrate, at Westminster, since 1896; J.P. Home Counties; *b.* 3 Feb. 1851; 2nd *s.* of late Fred. Francis, East Molesey Court, Surrey; *m.* 1881, Edith Rose Alma, *e. d.* of late F. F. Lovell, Hinchelsea, Brockenhurst, Hants, and late Lady Rose Lovell, *sister* of 8th and *d.* of 7th Duke of Beaufort; one *s.* *Educ.:* Rugby; Brasenose Coll. Oxford (B.A.) Barr. 1876; practised in London and S.E. Circuit. *Recreation:* cricket — Rugby Eleven, 1867 - 69; captain in 1869; Oxford Eleven, 1870-73; played for Gentlemen *v.* Players, 1870 - 75, and for Middlesex. *Heir:* Noel Charles Fitzroy Francis, late Capt. R.A.F. [*m.* 1914, Gwendolyne, 2nd *d.* of late Charles van Raalte of Brownsea Island, Dorset]. *Address:* 7 Granville Place, Portman Square, W.1; *T.:* Mayfair 1305; East Molesey Court, Surrey. *Clubs:* Boodle's, Pratt's.
          (*Died 28 Oct. 1925.*)

FRANCIS, Very Rev. Henry, M.A., Dean of the Peculiar of Battle and Vicar since 1920; late Rector of Garboldisham, Thetford. *Address:* Deanery, Battle, Sussex.
          (*Died 27 Jan. 1924.*)

FRANCIS, John Collins; *b.* 11 Sep. 1888; *e. s.* of late John Francis, who from 1881 until his death, 1882, was publisher of The Athenæum, and from 1872 also of Notes and Queries; took leading part in agitation for repeal of fiscal restrictions on the press; *m.* 1868, Louisa Anne Martel. *Educ.:* owing to ill-health mostly private, but for three years went to City of London School. Joined The Athenæum Staff, 1881, and on his father's death took entire management. In 1911 he became proprietor of The Athenæum and Notes and Queries with his nephew, John Edward Francis, who five years previously had joined him in the management. In the same year he became editor of Notes and Queries. He has now retired from both papers in favour of his nephew, in order to devote himself. to continuing the history of The Athenæum till MacColl's death, with memoir of him. *Publications:* John Francis and The Athenæum, being the history of the paper to 1882-1888; Notes by the Way, containing Memoirs of Joseph Knight and the Rev. Joseph Woodfall Ebsworth, 1909. *Address:* Florence House, Christchurch Road, Streatham Hill, S.W.   (*Died 27 Dec. 1916.*)

FRANKFORT DE MONTMORENCY, 4th Viscount, Ireland (*cr.* 1816), **Willoughby John Horace de Montmorency;** Baron Frankfort, 1800; *b.* 3 May 1868; *s.* of 3rd Viscount Frankfort de Montmorency and Rachel

Mary, d. of Field-Marshal Sir John Michel; S. father, 1902; m. 1916, Mabel Augusta Pearson, y. d. of late C. L. Throckmorton and Mrs. Wrench, of Woollahra, Sydney, N.S.W. Educ.: Marlborough. Capt. 1st Batt. Duke of Cornwall's L.I.; with Egyptian army. Entered army, 1888; Capt., 1897; commanded Wuntho Expedition, 1891 (medal with clasp); North-West Frontier India, 1897-98 (medal with two clasps). Owns in Co. Kilkenny 5500 acres, Co. Carlow 1631 acres, and in Co. Cavan 1045 acres; houses in Dublin and environs. Heir: none. Address: 56 Warwick Square, S.W.

(Died 5 July 1917.)

FRANKLEN, Sir Thomas Mansel, Kt., cr. 1921; Clerk of the Peace for Glamorgan since 1878; b. 1840; s. of Richard Franklin of Clemenstone, Glamorgan; m. 1872, Florence, o. d. of late Thomas Allen of Freestone, Co. Pembroke. Address: St. Hilary, Cowbridge, Glamorgan. T.: Cowbridge 40.

(Died 29 Sept. 1928.)

FRANKLIN, Surgeon-General Sir Benjamin, K.C.I.E., cr. 1903; C.I.E., cr. 1896; I.M.S., retired; Hon. Physician to the King; late Director-General Indian Medical Service, and Sanitary Commissioner with the Government of India; Knight of Grace of the Order of St. John of Jerusalem, 1905; Member of Council of British Red Cross Society; b. 1 May 1844; m. 1871, Harriette, d. of John Ferra Watson, of Heigham Hall, Norwich; one s. two d. Educ.: Univ. Coll. London; Paris. Entered I.M. Service, 1869; Civil Surgeon, Lucknow, 1878-80; Civil Surgeon, Simla, 1881-86; Surgeon to H.E. the Viceroy of India (Earl of Elgin), 1894-99; officiated as Inspector-General of Hospitals, Bengal, 1897; Inspector-General of Hospitals, N.W. Province and Oudh, 1899; Inspector-Gen. of Hospitals, Punjab, 1900-1; Hon. Physician to Queen Victoria and to King Edward VII.; a British Delegate to the International Sanitary Conferences at Rome, 1907, and Paris, 1911-12. Address: Westhay, East Sheen, Surrey. Club: United Service. (Died 17 Feb. 1917.)

FRANKLIN, Sir George, Kt., cr. 1916; Litt.D., F.C.A., J.P.; Pro-Chancellor, University of Sheffield; late Chairman and Managing Director, National Telephone Co., Ltd.; b. 19 July 1853; s. of late Alexander Franklin; m. 1876, Ann, d. of George Hawksley, Sheffield. Lord Mayor of Sheffield, 1897-8; Alderman and Councillor, 1881-1909; Senior Partner of Franklin, Wild & Co., London, and Franklin, Greening & Co.. Sheffield; been engaged in important negotiations for sale and purchase of Electric Light and Telephone undertakings; carried through negotiations for transfer of telephones to Post Office, 1911; Member of Departmental Committees on University of London and Employment of Disabled Soldiers and Sailors and Admiralty Expenditure. Address: Tapton Holt, Sheffield; 10 Cavendish Square, W. T.: 218; Gerrard 300. Clubs: Carlton, Bath, Royal Automobile, Constitutional. (Died 23 Sept. 1916.)

FRANKLIN, George Cooper, M.B.E. 1918; F.R.C.S., LL.D. (Hon.), Toronto; J.P.; Consulting Surgeon, Royal Infirmary, Leicester; b. Leicester, 16 April 1846; m. Lucy Hannah Denne; three s. two d. Educ.: Leatherhead, Surrey; St. Thomas's Hospital. Surgeon, Leicester Provident Dispensary, 1875-1880; Hon. Surgeon, Leicester Infirmary, 1886-1906; late Surgeon, Midland and London & North-Western Railway Companies; President, British Medical Association, 1905-6; Vice-President, B.M.A. Publications: Reports and contributions to medical journals. Address: 18 High Street, Fareham. (Died 2 June 1919.)

FRANKS, Lieut.-Colonel George Despard, D.S.O. 1917; Commanding 19th Royal Hussars; 2nd s. of Matthew Henry Franks, D.L., of Garrettstown, Kinsale, and of

Westfield, Mountrath, Ireland; m. 1908, May Geraldine, e. d. of late Lt.-General Sir Gerald de Courcy Morton, K.C.I.E., C.V.O., C.B.; one s. Educ.: Repton School: R.M.C. Sandhurst. Joined 19th Hussars, 1894; served in India, 1894-99; A.D.C. to Governor of Madras, 1898-1899; served South Africa with 19th Hussars, 1899-1900 (despatches); A.D.C. to General Officer Commanding Dublin and Curragh, 1902-1906; Capt. 1904; Major, 1908; Lt.-Col. 1915; served European War in France, 1914-17 (despatches twice, D.S.O.). Address: 3 Halkin Place, S.W. Clubs: Cavalry, White's.

(Died 8 Oct. 1918.)

FRANKS, Sir Kendal, Kt. cr. 1904; C.B. 1900; M.D., F.R.C.S.I.; b. 8 Feb. 1851; s. of late R. F. Franks of Kilkenny, and g. s. of Rt. Hon. Charles Kendal Bushe, Lord Chief-Justice of Ireland; m. 1st, 1879, Charlotte Selira (d. 1883), e. d. of R. J. and Hon. Mrs. Greene; 2nd, 1885, Gertrude (d. 1896), d. of Lieut.-Col. T. B. Butt, 79th Highlanders; three s. one d. Educ.: Trin. College, Dublin; Leipzig. Served S. Africa; Consulting Surgeon to H.M. Forces (despatches thrice, C.B.); Hon. Consulting Surgeon, Johannesburg Hospital; Lt.-Col. S.A. Defence Force (Reserve); President, S.A. Committee, British Medical Association; formerly Surgeon, Adelaide Hospital, Dublin; Vice-President, Royal College of Surgeons; Examiner in Surgery, Univ. Dublin; Surgeon-in-Ordinary to Lord-Lieutenants. Address: Kilmurry, Hospital Hill, Johannesburg. Clubs: Junior Constitutional; Kildare Street, Dublin; Royal St. George Yacht, Kingstown; Rand, Johannesburg. (Died May 1920.)

FRANKS, Captain Norman, C.I.E. 1896; late "The Buffs" Regt.; b. 1843; e. s. of late Robert Fergusson Franks, of Jerpoint, Co. Kilkenny; m. Frances Mary, d. of late Charles Yorke Lucas-Calcraft, J.P., D.L., of Ancaster Hall, Lincolnshire, 1875. Educ.: Marlborough. Entered the army, 1862; became captain, 1871; retired, 1874. Address: 65 Onslow Square, S.W.7. T.: Western 2930. Club: Army and Navy

(Died 5 Feb. 1923.)

FRANKS, William Temple, C.B. 1914; B.C.L.; Comptroller-General of Patents, Designs, and Trade Marks; b. 1863; 2nd s. of late J. F. Franks of Shanghai and Streatham, Surrey, and Catherine Smithwayte Temple. Educ.: Dulwich; Wadham College, Oxford. Classical Scholar, 1883; Hody Greek Prizeman, 1885; 1st Class Honours Literae Humaniores, 1885; B.A., 1887; B.C.L. degree, 1889; Stowell Law Fellow, University College, Oxford, 1888; 1st Class Studentship (Inns of Court), Roman Law, Jurisprudence, and International Law, 1888; Barrister, Inner Temple, 1890; practised at Bar, South Eastern Circuit and Surrey Sessions, 1890-1902; Assistant Librarian House of Commons, 1902-5; Secretary Railway Companies Association, 1905-9; Member of Board of Trade Railway Conference, 1908; Departmental Committee on Railway Amalgamations, 1909; Colonial Conference Copyright, 1910; British Delegate Industrial Property Conference, Washington, 1911; Delegate Peace Conference (Economics Section), 1919; Departmental Committee Merchandise Marks, 1919-20; Royal Commission Awards to Inventors, 1919-20; Lecturer on Railway Law and History, London School of Economics, 1907-8; Lieutenant Inns of Court Mounted Infantry, 1902; Sub.-Lieut. R.N.V.R., 1915-16. Recreations: fishing, shooting, riding. Address: 46 Westminster Mansions, S.W.; H.M. Patent Office, Southampton Buildings, W.C. Clubs: Carlton, Bath, St. Stephen's.

(Died 4 July 1926.)

FRANQUEVILLE, Amable Charles Franquet, Comte de; Member and late President of the Institut de France; LL.D. Cambridge, Dublin, Edinburgh, Glasgow, St. Andrews, etc.; b. Paris, 1840; m. 1903,

Sophia Matilda (d. 1915), 3rd d. of 1st Earl of Selborne. Member of the Council of State, 1860-1879 ; Officer of Legion of Honour, 1878. *Publications:* Les Institutions politiques, judiciaires et administratives de l'Angleterre, 1863 ; Du régime des travaux publics en Angleterre, 4 vols., 1875 ; Le Gouvernement et le Parlement britanniques, 3 vols.,1887 ; Le système judiciaire de l'Angleterre, 2 vols., 1893 ; Le premier Siècle de l'Institut de France, 2 vols., 1895, etc. etc. *Address:* Château de la Muette, Paris, XVIe ; de Bourbilly, par Semur, Côte-d'Or.
(Died Dec. 1919.)

FRASER, Sir Andrew Henderson Leith, K.C.S.I., cr. 1903; M.A.,L.LD., D.Litt.; J.P., Forfarshire ; b. 14 Nov. 1848; e. s. of Rev. A. G. Fraser, D.D., and Joanna, d. of Rev. J. Shaw ; m. 1st, Agnes (d. 1877), d. of R. Archibald, Devonvale, Tillicoultry ; 2nd, 1883, Henrietta, d. of Col. H. I. Lugard, I.S.C.; four s. one d. *Educ.:* Edinburgh Academy, Institution, and University (M.A.). Barrister-at-Law, Middle Temple, 1874; Indian Civil Service, 1871 ; Commissioner of Division, 1888; Member of Hemp Drugs Commission, 1893-94; Officiating Secretary to Government of India Home Department, 1898 - 99 ; Chief Commissioner Central Provinces, 1899; President Police Commission, 1902 ; Lt.-Gov. of Bengal, 1903-8 ; Moderator Indian Presbyterian Church, 1907 ; C.S.I. 1897. *Decorated* for services in India. *Publication:* Among Indian Rajahs and Ryots. *Recreation:* golf. *Address:* Auchenleish, Glenisla, Alyth, N.B. *Club:* University Edinburgh.
(Died 26 Feb. 1919.)

FRASER, Major Arthur Ion, D.S.O. 1917; 9th Hodson's Horse, Indian Army ; b. 28 Dec. 1879 ; e s. of Arthur Matheson Fraser, Barrister-at-law, and Mary Gordon ; unmarried. *Educ.:* Haileybury College ; Sandhurst. Gazetted to Indian Army, 1900 ; Captain, 1909 ; Major, 1915 ; served European War in France, 1914-17 (despatches, D.S.O.). *Club:* United Service.
(Died 30 Nov. 1917.)

FRASER, Mrs. Augusta Zelia (Alice Spinner), writer; e. d. of W. F. Webb; m. Affleck Fraser, of Reelig, Inverness-shire, N.B., 1889 ; one s. two d. *Educ.:* home. Spent some years abroad before her marriage ; in 1892 accompanied her husband to Jamaica, where he held a Government appointment, and on her return wrote the W. Indian stories which first appeared in 1894. They were first written at a friend's suggestion, and without any idea that the public would care for them. *Publications:* A Study in Colour; Lucilla ; A Reluctant Evangelist ; Livingstone and Newstead, 1913 ; and occasional magazine stories. *Address:* Newstead Abbey, Nottingham.
(Died Dec. 1925.)

FRASER, Sir Charles Frederick, Kt. cr. 1915; LL.D. ; Superintendent of the School for the Blind, Halifax, Nova Scotia, 1873-1923 ; b. Windsor, N.S., 4 Jan. 1850; s. of late Dr. B. D. Fraser; m. 1st, 1891, Ella J. (d. 1909), d. of late James Hunter ; 2nd, 1910, Janie C. R., d. of William Stevens; one s. *Educ.:* Windsor ; Perkins School for the Blind. Lost sight at six years of age. Publicly thanked by House of Assembly in Nova Scotia for his forty years' service ; President or Director of a number of public companies. *Address:* Beaufort, Halifax, Nova Scotia.
(Died July 1925.)

FRASER, Sir Edward Cleather, Kt. cr. 1923 ; C.M.G., 1912; Member of Legislative Council of Government, Mauritius, 1909-23 ; s. s. of late James Fraser of Newfield, Blackheath ; b. 1853 ; m. 1st, 1882, Mary (d. 1901), d. of late Thomas Howie; two d. ; 2nd, 1908, Aimée, d. of late John Ferguson. *Educ.:* Blackheath Proprietary School ; Merton College, Oxford. *Recreations:* shooting and golf. *Address:* Port Louis, Mauritius. *Clubs:* Junior Carlton : Norfolk County, Norwich.
(Died 15 Oct. 1927.)

FRASER, Sir Edward Henry, Kt., cr. 1908 ; D.C.L., J.P. ; Solicitor ; admitted 1872 ; b. 15 Feb. 1851 ; m. 1877, Jane, d. of Charles Keightley of Nottingham ; one s. three d. *Educ.:* Sherwood House School, Nottingham. Sheriff for City of Nottingham, 1884 : Mayor, 1896-97, 1897-98, 1898-99, 1910-11 ; Hon. D.C.L. Cantuar, 1897 ; Director of Great Central Railway and other Companies ; contested East Nottingham (L.) 1900 : Kidderminster (L.) 1910. *Address:* Wellington House, Nottingham. *Clubs:* National Liberal ; Notts County, Nottingham.
(Died 10 Nov. 1921.)

FRASER, Sir Everard Duncan Home, K.C.M.G., cr. 1912; C.M.G. 1901; H.M. Consul-General, Shanghai, since 1911 ; b. 27 Feb. 1859; s. of Lt.-Col. R. W. Fraser, B.N.I. ; m. 1899, Constance, d. of A. W. Walkinshaw, of Foochow. *Educ.:* Aberdeen. Vice-Consul, Canton, 1895 - 97 ; Vice-Consul, Pagoda Island, 1897; acting Consul, Foochow, 1897-99 ; Consul, Chinkiang, 1899, but acted as Consul, Hankow, till 1901, when made Consul-General there ; Consul-General, Hankow, 1901-1911 ; Coronation Medal, 1911. *Address:* Shanghai, China. *(Died 20 Mar. 1922.)*

FRASER, Galloway, former editor of Tit-Bits. *Educ.:* St. Andrew's School, Dundee ; Glasgow and Edinburgh Universities. Edited in Edinburgh The Scottish Liberal; came to London as Parliamentary representative of Dundee Courier in Press Gallery and Lobby of House of Commons ; wrote largely for Scottish press ; invited by late Sir George Newnes to join his staff, July 1890; retired 1921; J.P. Middlesex. *Address:* St. Nicholas, Strawberry Hill. *(Died 26 Sept. 1925.)*

FRASER, Gilbert ; b. Inverness, 5 Sep. 1848; y. s. of Gilbert Fraser, shipbuilder ; m. Josephine, d. of Henry A. Kellogg.of Ohio ; one d. *Educ.:* public schools and privately. Trained for the Bar ; second Vice-Consul at New York, 1874 ; first Vice-Consul, 1880 ; Consul, 1891 ; Consul-General, Baltimore, 1913 ; on numerous occasions acted Consul-General at New York ; retired, 1919. *Recreations:* horseback riding, cricket, tennis, golf, cycling. *Clubs:* Century, New York ; Maryland ; Elkridge Fox Hunting ; Baltimore Country ; Baltimore Yacht, Baltimore. *T.:* St. Paul 6096.

FRASER, The Hon. Sir Hugh, Kt., cr. 1917; **The Hon. Mr Justice Fraser,** Judge of the King's Bench Division of the High Court of Justice since 1924 ; M.A., LL.D., J.P. County of Ross and Cromarty ; Honorary Fellow of Trinity Hall, Cambridge ; Arbitrator, Building Trade Dispute, 1923 ; Member, Irish Deportees Compensation Tribunal, 1923-24; Member, Committee for dealing with claims of Police Strikers, 1924 ; called to Bar, 1886 ; Bencher, Inner Temple, 1918 ; e. s. of late Thomas Fraser (y. s. of John Fraser of Gortuleg and Farraline, Inverness - shire) ; m. 1888, Ethel Mary, e. d. of late Rev. James Milne Hamilton, M.A., Vicar of Ridgmount, Bedfordshire; one s. three d. *Educ.:* Charterhouse ; Trinity Hall, Cambridge (Exhibitioner, Scholar, Law Student, Cressingham prizeman) ; Inns of Court Studentship, 1884 ; Proxime Accessit Chancellor's medal for Legal Studies, Cambridge, 1885; Inner Temple Scholarship, 1886 ; Lecturer on Equity to Incorporated Law Society, 1888-91 ; Reader and Examiner in Common Law at the Inns of Court, 1897-1924; sometime Examiner for Honours in Law at the Universities of Oxford, Cambridge, and London. *Publications:* Law of Torts, 11th ed. ; Law of Libel and Slander, 6th ed. ; Law of Parliamentary Elections and Election Petitions, 3rd ed.; Representation of People Act, 1918, 2nd ed. ; Amid the High Hills, 1923. *Recreations:* shooting and fly-fishing. *Address:* 43 Linden Gardens, W.2 ;

T.: Park 3566; Stromeferry, Ross-shire. *Club:* Athenæum. *(Died 8 July 1927.)*

FRASER, Captain Ian Mackenzie, R.N.; D.S.O. 1893 ; *b.* Dundee, 15 Nov. 1854; *e. s.* of late Captain Ian Fraser, 93rd Sutherland Highlanders, of Whitehill, county of Fife, and Charlotte, *d.* of late John Mackenzie of Ness House, Inverness ; *m.* 1887, Effie, *e. d.* of late William P. Edwards, J.P., 17 Belgrave Crescent, Edinburgh, and Broadwell, Perth. Joined Royal Navy, 1868; Lieutenant, 1879; Commander, 1893 ; Captain (retired), 1904 ; in command of H.M.S. Sparrow, and second in command of Naval Brigade at night attack on Fodey Kabba at Marigé, Gambia, 1891 (highly mentioned in despatches, received the thanks of Governor of Gambia, specially commended by him to Secretary of State for Colonies); in command of Sparrow with Gambia Expedition, 1892, resulting in capture of Tambi and Toniataba (medal with clasp, D.S.O.). *Address:* 7 Albert Park, Liverpool. *Club:* Naval and Military.
(Died 2 Dec. 1922.)

FRASER, John, I.S.O.; Auditor-General of Canada since 1905 ; *b.* 18 Dec. 1852 ; *s.* of James Fraser and Isabella M'Donald ; *m.* 1876, Mary Atchison ; six *s.* three *d.* *Educ.:* Loch Garry, Ont., Canada. Entered Civil Service of Canada as clerk in the Department of Finance, 1875 ; chief clerk, 1898. *Recreations:* motor boating, lawn bowling, curling. *Address:* Ottawa, Ont. *T.:* 1101. *Club:* Civil Service.

FRASER, John, M.B., C.M., Edin. ; Lunacy Commissioner for Scotland, 1895, retired, 1910. *Educ.:* Edin. (1st class honours), 1870 ; M.B., C.M., 1882 ; (Edin.), F.R.C.P. (Edin.), 1896 ; F.R.S.E., and Fellow of Royal Botanical Society, Edin. *Recreations:* golf and shooting. *Address:* 54 Great King Street, Edinburgh. *T.:* 2299. *Club:* University, Edinburgh.
(Died 18 Jan. 1925.)

FRASER, Sir John George, Kt., *cr.* 1905 See Addenda, page xx.

FRASER, Lovat; Chief Literary Adviser and Contributor, Sunday Pictorial and Daily Mirror; Editorial Staff of The Times, 1907-1922; *b.* 18 Nov. 1871. Was Editor of the Times of India for several years ; afterwards went on various special missions for The Times (London) to India, China, and the Dominions, and round the world ; attended Imperial Coronation Durbars at Delhi in 1903 and 1912 ; has travelled extensively in many parts of the world, notably the Persian Gulf, the Balkans, the China Seas, Manchuria, Siberia, Egypt, Japan, and most European countries. *Publications:* At Delhi, 1903 ; India under Curzon and After, 1912, etc. *Recreations:* visiting islands, sea-fishing, small-boat sailing. *Address:* Bucklands, Churt, Farnham, Surrey (station Haslemere). *T.:* Hindhead 74. *(Died 20 April 1926.)*

FRASER, Brig.-Gen. Lyons David, C.B. 1918; C.M.G. 1916; R.A.; *s.* of late Colonel Lyons Fraser, Indian Army ; *b.* 15 April 1868 ; unmarried. *Educ.:* Tonbridge ; R.M.A., Woolwich. Commissioned in R.A. 1887 ; Capt. 1896 ; Major, 1906 ; Lt.-Col. 1914 ; Col. 1917 ; temp. Brig.-General, 1916 ; employed with Intelligence Branch, India, 1898-1903 (MacGregor medallist, 1904) ; G.S.O. 3rd grade, Military Operations, 1906-9 ; 2nd grade, 1909-11 ; served European War, 1914-18 (despatches 6 times, Bt. Col., C.B., C.M.G.) ; Commanding Heavy Artillery, Australian Corps (France), 1916-18 ; Brig.-Gen. R.A. Scottish Command,

1919 ; retired, 1921 ; F.R.G.S. 1900. *Club:* United Service. *(Died 4 Feb. 1926.)*

FRASER, Senator Hon. Sir Simon, Kt. *cr.* 1918 ; politician and pastoralist ; *b.* Nova Scotia, 21 Aug. 1832; *s.* of Wm. Fraser, farmer and mill owner ; *m.* twice ; three *s.* one *d.* *Educ.:* West River Seminary, Picton County. Came to Australia, 1852 ; some months gold-digging, afterwards contracting for bridges, etc. ; later with partners built several railways in Victoria, New South Wales, including one in South Australia 200 miles long, first section transcontinental railway ; the Deniliquin and Moama Railway Company, being private line and worked as private company, 45 miles long, in New South Wales ; with exception of three years spent in travelling throughout the world, been in Parliament in Victoria forty years ; Legislative Assembly, Legislative Council of Victoria ; Member of the Convention which framed the Commonwealth Constitution, and Member of Federal Senate from its beginning to the present time, retiring in his eighty-first year ; largely interested as a pastoralist in New South Wales and Queensland. *Recreations:* in early life, hunting and shooting. *Address:* Toorak, Melbourne. *Club:* Australian, Melbourne.
(Died 30 July 1919.)

FRASER, Major-Gen. Sir Thomas, K.C.B., *cr.* 1900; C.B. 1891 ; C.M.G. 1882 ; p.s.c. ; *b.* 15 Nov. 1840 ; *s.* of G. R. Fraser, barrister-at-law, and Elizabeth Allen, *d.* of S. Chichester Smythe; *m.* 1865, Matilda, *d.* of late Jas. Beckford Wildman, M.P., formerly of Chilham Castle, Kent; two *s.* *Educ.:* abroad; R.M. Academy, Woolwich. Entered R.E. 1862 ; Brevet Major, 1878 ; Brevet Lieut.-Col. 1882 ; Brevet Colonel, 1885 ; Local Maj.-Gen. 1896 ; Maj.-Gen. 1898 ; in France after military operations of 1871 ; Paris during Communist Revolution and Siege, 1871 ; on military duty in Turkey, 1876 ; Military Officer with British Naval C.-in-C. Besica Bay, 1877 ; accompanied Turkish C.-in-C. in Russo-Turkish Bulgarian Campaign, 1877 ; Transvaal War, 1881 as D.A.A., and Q.M.G., and as A.Q.M.G. (despatches) ; Political and A.M.S to Sir Evelyn Wood, 1881-82 ; Egyptian Campaign, 1882, on H.Q. Staff, as Brigade Major, R.E. (despatches, bronze star, medal with clasp, Osmanieh) ; A.G. and Q.M.G. Egyptian Army, 1882-85 ; Nile Expedition, 1884-85 (despatches, clasp, Medjidie); Member of Royal Commission on Piers and Roads, Ireland, 1886-88 and 1900; Assistant Inspector-Gen. of Fortifications, 1891-94; Col. on the Staff C.R.E. S. District, 1894-96; Commandant School of Military Engineering, Chatham, 1896-1902 ; Substantive Maj.-Gen. and G.O.C. Thames District, 1898-1902 ; Col. Commandant R.E., 1913. *Publication:* The Military Danger of Home Rule for Ireland, 1912 ; Recollections with Reflections. *Address:* 83 Onslow Square, S.W. *Club:* Athenæum.
(Died 5 May 1922.)

FRASER, Sir Thomas Richard, Kt., *cr.* 1902 ; M.D., Edin., Hon. LL.D., Aberdeen, Glasgow and Edinburgh ; Hon. Sc.D. Camb. ; Hon. M.D. Dublin, F.R.S., F.R.S.E., F.R.C.P.E.; Hon. Physician to King in Scotland ; Pres. of Royal College of Physicians of Edinburgh, 1900-2 ; President Medico-Chirurgical Society of Edinburgh, 1901-1903 ; Laureate of the Institute of France ; Macdougall-Brisbane and Keith Prizeman of the Royal Society of Edinburgh ; Cameron Prizeman in Therapeutics of the University of Edinburgh ; Prof. of Materia Medica, 1877-1918, and of Clinical Medicine, Edinburgh University, since 1878; Emeritus Professor since 1918 ; Medical Adviser to H.M. Prison Commission for Scotland ; Consulting Physician to the Standard Life Assurance Company ; Member of University Court, 1904-13 ; representative of the University on the General Medical Council since 1905 ; President of the

379

FRASER, Mrs. Hugh. See page xx.

Indian Plague Commission, 1898-1901 ; President of the Association of Physicians of Great Britain and Ireland, 1908-9 ; Assist. Physician to Royal Infirmary, ·1869-74 ; Examiner in Materia Medica, 1870-75, and in Public Health, 1876-79, in the Univ. of London ; Member Admiralty Committee on Sir George Nares' Arctic Expedition, 1877 ; Dean of Faculty of Medicine, 1880-1900 ; *b.* Calcutta, 5 Feb. 1841 ; *m.* 1874, Susanna Margaret, *d.* of Rev. R. Duncan ; four *s.* three *d. Educ.:* Public Schools in Scotland ; University, Edinburgh. *Publications;* many papers in practical medicine, on the action and therapeutic uses of medicinal substances and on Serpent's Venom in Transactions Royal Societies of London and Edinburgh, etc. *Recreations:* fishing, shooting, golf, photography. *Address:* 18 Drumsheugh Gardens. Edinburgh ; Druimbeg, Acharacle, Argyllshire, T. : Edinburgh, 2485. *Clubs:* Athenæum, Royal Societies ; University, Edinburgh.

(*Died 4 Jan. 1920.*)

FRASER, Rev. William, Moderator of the Free Church of Scotland, 1912 ; Minister of the Free Church, Strathpeffer ; *b.* Parish of Urquhart, 1851 ;· *s.* of William Fraser, stone mason, builder ; *m.* 1881 ; three *s.* one *d. Educ.:* Beauly Public School ; Glasgow University ; Free Church Divinity College, Edinburgh. Began life as artisan joiner ; after serving apprenticeship and working for a few years, at same time attending classes in Latin and Greek, etc., entered Glasgow University ; finished Arts and Divinity, 1884 ; ordained at Sleat, Isle of Skye, 1886 ; translated to Plockton, 1905 ; Strathpeffer, 1908 ; at the Church crisis 1900, one of the twenty-five who remained faithful and gained the case in the House of Lords. *Publications:* Sketches of Noted Ministers in the Free Church of Scotland ; the Opening and Closing Addresses as Moderator of Assembly. *Recreations:* visiting the sick and preaching. *Address:* Manse, Strathpeffer. (*Died July 1919.*)

FRASER, Hon. Sir William, K.C.V.O., *cr.* 1920 ; Kt., *cr.* 1918 ; Member of Legislative Council since 1920 ; Minister of Mines, New Zealand ; *b.* 1840 ; *s.* of Capt. Hugh Fraser, 5th Madras Light Cavalry of Leadclune, Invernessshire ; *m.* 1874, Ellen Isabel, *d.* of Alfred Edward Chetham Strode of Dunedin, N.Z. ; one *d. Educ. :* Elizabeth College, Guernsey ; Lycée Imperiale de Ste. Brieux and Victoria College, Jersey. Arrived in New Zealand, 1858 ; elected to Otago Provincial Council, 1866 ; to N.Z. Parliament, 1893 ; retired 1919 ; joined Massey Cabinet, 1912, as Minister of Public Works, and the National Cabinet in same capacity, 1915-20 ; resigned Portfolio in 1920, but retained position as Member of Cabinet, and was appointed to Legislative Council. *Clubs:* Wellington, Wellington, N.Z. ; Dunedin ; Christchurch. (*Died 16 July 1923.*)

FRASER, William Henry, Professor of Italian and Spanish, University of Toronto, since 1901 ; *b.* Bond Head, Ontario, Canada, 1853 ; 5th *s.* of late Rev. William Fraser, D.D. ; *m.* 1883, Helene Zahn. *Educ. :* Bradford Grammar School ; University of Toronto. After graduation in 1880, taught as resident master in Upper Canada College for three years ; and was French and German master there, 1884-1887 ; lecturer in Italian and Spanish in the University of Toronto, 1887-92 ; associate-professor, 1892-1901 ; has taken considerable interest in educational affairs, and has held various offices in connection therewith. *Publications:* joint author with Professor Van der Smissen of German Grammars, 1887, 1909, and with Professor Squair of French Grammars, 1891, 1900, 1913 ; has also published various papers on literary and educational subjects. *Address:* York Mills, Ontario. (*Died 1916.*)

FRASER-TYTLER, Edward Grant, of Aldourie, J.P., D.L. ; Lt.-Col. in Lovat's Scouts,

Imperial Yeomanry ; *b.* 19 July 1856 ; *e. surv. s.* of C. E. Fraser-Tytler and Harriet Jane, 2nd *d.* of late Rev. John Pretyman ; *m.* 1st, 1881, Edith Adriana (*d.* 1910), *d.* of late Rt. Hon. Sir Charles J. Selwyn, Lord Justice of Appeal ; one *s.* one *d.* ; 2nd, 1912, Christian, *d.* of late William Scott-Kerr of Chatto and Sunlaws, Roxburghshire, and *widow* of late J. W. Fraser-Tytler of Woodhouselee, Midlothian. *Educ.:* Eton. Was Captain in 3rd Battalion Cameron Highlanders for some years ; Lieutenant in 1st Invernesshire Highland Volunteer Batt. *Recreations:* deer-stalking, hunting, shooting, pig-sticking and tiger-shooting in India and Ceylon ; has travelled in South America, etc. *Address:* Aldourie Castle, Inverness, N.B. *T.A. :* Dores. *Clubs:* Junior Carlton, Bath. (*Died 12 Mar. 1918.*)

FRAYLING, Frederick George, I.S.O. ; Senior First Class Clerk, Department of Director of Public Prosecutions, Whitehall ; *b.* 1846 ; *m.* 1873, Ellen *d.* of late Thomas Cooper, Oxford ; one *s.* two *d. Educ. :* Dulwich College. Entered firm of Maples, Teesdale and Co., City Solicitors, 1864 ; received an appointment in the old Court of Queen's Bench at Westminster, 1866 ; while there received temporary appointments from 14 judges and the three associates ; appointed. one of the 8 clerks in the newly created Office of Director of Public Prosecutions, 1880 ; transferred to the Treasury Solicitor's Department, 1884 ; Senior Representative of the Director of Public Prosecutions at the Central Criminal Court, 1885-1911, when retired ,from Civil Service. *Publications:* Infanticide, Law and Punishment ; Reminiscences of Criminal Courts, and views and observations thereon. *Recreations:* walking and literary pursuits. *Club:* Croydon Constitutional.

FRAZER, Robert Watson, LL.B., C.E. ; Indian Civil Service, retired ; late Principal Librarian and Secretary London Institution, and Lecturer in Tamil and Telugu, School of Oriental Studies ; London Institution, Finsbury Circus, E.C. ; *b.* Dublin, 1854. *Educ. :* Royal College of Science ; Dublin University. I.C.S. ; in charge disturbed tracts during Rumpa rebellion ; invalided in consequence of fever there contracted ; formerly Lecturer, University Extension, on Indian Architecture. *Publications:* Silent Gods and Sun-Steeped Lands, 1895, 2nd ed. 1896 ; British India, Story of Nations Series, 1897, 2nd ed. 1898 ; A Literary History of India, 1898 ; Text-Book Indian History (League of the Empire), 1907 ; Indian Thought, Past and Present, 1915 ; Articles, Encyclopædia of Religion and Ethics, etc. *Address:* The Hollies, Balcombe, Sussex. (*Died 30 Nov. 1921.*)

FREAKE, Sir Thomas George, 2nd Bt., *cr.* 1882 ; Mayor of Dartmouth since 1897 ; *b.* 12 Oct. 1848 ; *S.* father 1884 ; *m.* Frederica, *d.* of Col. F. T. Maitland, Holywich, Sussex, 1868 ; one *s.* two *d. Educ.:* Magdalene Coll. Camb. *Heir:* *s.* Frederick Charles Maitland, [*b.* 7 March 1876 ; *m.* 1902, Alison, *d.* of late Christopher Ussher of Eastwell, Co. Galway ; one *s. Address:* Halford Manor, Shipstone, Warwicks.]. *Address :* 43 Sloane Street, S.W. *T.:* Western 3946. *Clubs:* Conservative, Ranelagh, Hurlingham. (*Died 21 Dec. 1920.*)

FRÉCHETTE, Achille, K.C., I.S.O. 1910 ; formerly Chief of Translation Department, House of Commons, Canada ; *b.* Levis, P.Q., 13 Oct. 1847 ; *s.* of Louis and Marguerite Martineau Fréchette ; *m.* Annie Thomas Howells ; one *s.* one *d. Educ. :* Lévis College ; Quebec Seminary ; Royal Military School, Quebec ; Art Students' League, New York. Barrister ; journalist ; for many years a Director, and also Secretary, Art Association, Ottawa ; exhibited Royal Canadian Academy of Arts ; edited the French papers in Transactions of Royal Society of Canada ; for a time Chairman French Section Separate. School

Board, Ottawa; commissioned by Canadian Government to report upon the organisation of the parliamentary translation services in Belgium and Switzerland. *Publications:* occasional poems and papers; Member Canadian Authors' Association. *Address:* c/o Howells Fréchette, Dept. of Mines, Sussex Street, Ottawa. Canada. *(Died 15 Nov. 1927.)*

FREELING, Sir Clayton Pennington, 8th Bt., *cr.* 1828; *b.* 26 Nov. 1857; *s.* of late Sir Stanford Freeling, K.C.M.G., *b.* of 5th Bt., and Frederica Selina Owen, *d.* of late George James Pennington; *S.* uncle 1916. *Heir: c.* Charles Edward Luard [solicitor; *b.* 1858; *m.* 1913, Ethel Amy, *d.* of late Iltid Nicholl. *Address:* Beenham Lodge, Reading]. *Address:* 57 Hurlingham Court, S.W.6.

(Died 8 July 1927.)

FREELING, Rev. Sir James Robert, 7th Bt., *cr.* 1828; *b.* 3 June 1825; *s.* of John Clayton Freeling, 2nd *s.* of 1st Bt., and Mary Coxe; *S.* nephew, 1914; *m.* 1851, Annabella Elizabeth (*d.* 1903), *e. d.* of Walpole Eyre; one *d.* *Educ.:* Exeter College, Oxford; Durham University. Ordained, 1852; Curate of Farley, Wilts, 1852-55; Shanbrook, 1861-68; Chaplain at Chantilly, 1868-70; Assistant Chaplain, Brussels, 1870-77; Chaplain at Bonn, 1878-82. *Heir: n.* Clayton Pennington, *b.* 26 Nov. 1857. *Address:* 414 Avenue Louise, Brussels.

(Died 30 Oct. 1916.)

FREEMAN, Edward Bothamley, I.S.O. 1903; *b.* London, 5 Jan. 1888; *y. s.* of late Luke Freeman, solicitor, and Henrietta Illingworth; *m.* 1884, Minna, *d.* of Baron Carl Cnobloch; one *d.* *Educ.:* Rev. Edward Wickham's, Brookgreen, Hammersmith; private tutor; Rev. H. A. Box's, Heavitree, Exeter. Assistant Superintendent of the Dardanelles Depot of the Land Transport Corps, 1855-56; Chancelier in the Consulates of Diarbekir and Serajevo, 1858-76; Vice-Consul, Mostar, 1876; Consul, Serajevo, 1879 (Jubilee medal, 1897); Con.-Gen. for Bosnia and the Herzegovina, 1891-1905. *Address:* Clyde Lodge, Cyprus Road, Exmouth. *Club:* Exmouth.

(Died 30 Oct. 1921.)

FREER, Charles L.; *b.* Feb. 1854; unmarried. *Educ.:* public and private schools; Hon. M.A. University of Michigan, and Rutgers College. Ex-railroad supply manufacturer, traveller, art collector; gave collection of Whistler paintings (including the Peacock Room), etchings, lithographs, and drawings, also Oriental collection of paintings, potteries, bronzes, and sculptures, to the National Gallery at Washington, D.C.; special building at Washington to hold and exhibit the collections now being built. *Publications:* Facsimiles of the Washington Biblical Manuscripts. *Recreation:* travel. *Address:* 33 Ferry Avenue, East, Detroit, Michigan, U.S.A. *T.A.:* Freer, Detroit. *(Died 25 Sept. 1919.)*

FREMANTLE, Very Rev. Hon. William Henry, D.D.; Dean of Ripon, 1895-1915; *b* 1831; 2nd *s.* of 1st Lord Cottesloe and Louisa, *d.* of F.-M. Sir George Nugent, 1st Bt.; *m.* 1st, Isabella (*d.* 1901), *d.* of Sir Culling Eardley, 3rd Bt., 1863; three *s.* two *d.*; 2nd, 1903, Sophia Frances, *e. d.* of late Major G. F. Stuart of the 88th and 49th Regts. *Educ.:* Cheam; Eton; Balliol College, Oxford. First class Final Classical Schools; Newcastle Medallist, 1849; English Essay Prize; Fellow of All Souls, 1854-64; of Balliol, and Theological tutor, 1888-94; Select Preacher, 1879-80; Bampton Lecturer, 1883. Ordained, 1855; Vicar of Lewknor, Oxon. 1857-66; chaplain to Bishop of London (Tait), 1861, and to Archbishop of Canterbury (Tait), 1868-82; Rector of St. Mary's, Bryanston Square, 1866-83; Canon of Canterbury, 1882-95. *Publications:* The Influence of Commerce on Christianity (Oxford Prize Essay), 1854; The Ecclesiastical Judgments of the Privy Council

(with Hon. G. C. Brodrick), 1865; Reconciliation to God through Jesus Christ, 1870; Lay Power in Parishes, 1870; The Gospel of the Secular Life (University Sermons), 1882; The World as the Subject of Redemption (Bampton Lectures), 1885; Works of St. Jerome and Rufinus, translated, 1893; Church Reform (Imperial Parliament Series), (with Earl Grey and others), 1887; Christian Ordinances and Social Progress (published in America), 1900; Natural Christianity (Harper's Library of Living Thought), 1911. *Address:* 25 Barkston Gardens, S.W. *(Died 24 Dec. 1916.)*

FRENCH, General Arthur, C.B. 1892; Royal Marine Artillery; retired; *b.* Chester, 20 Aug. 1840; *s.* of Major E. F. French, 82nd and 22nd Regts.; *m.* 1875, Mary Julia Eveleigh, *d.* of Capt. Belson, Royal Engineers; one *s.* *Educ.:* Fairfield, nr. Manchester; Brindley's Collegiate School, Leamington. Joined Royal Marine Artillery, 1858; served in H.M. Ships "Diadem," "Nile," "Valiant," "Revenge," "Zealous," "Lord Warden," "Hercules," and "Minotaur"; served with Egyptian Expedition, 1882 (despatches Brevet Lieut.-Col., medal, bronze star, C.B., and Jubilee medal); was A.D.C. to Her Majesty, 1888-93. *Decorated* for Egyptian Expedition, 1882. *Recreations:* fishing, shooting, otter-hunting, and field sports generally. *Address:* Eastney Lodge, Wilton, Salisbury.

(Died 22 Mar. 1928.)

FRENCH, Hon. Charles, J.P.; *s.* of 3rd Lord de Freyne and Catherine, *d.* of Luke Maree; *b.* 1851; *m.* 1880, Constance, 2nd *d.* of Lt.-Col. Charles Raleigh Chichester of Runnamoat, Co. Roscommon; one *s.* six *d.* *Educ.:* Downside. High Sheriff Co. Roscommon, 1887; M.P. Co. Roscommon, 1873-80. *Address:* Headlands, Dalmeny Road, Southbourne-on-Sea.

(Died 27 Oct. 1925.)

FRENCH, Sir Edward Lee, K.C.V.O., *cr.* 1911; *b.* 22 July 1857; 2nd *s.* of late Rev. F. French, Rector of Worlingworth, Suffolk; *m.* Wilna, *d.* of late David Ross, C.I.E. *Educ.:* Marlborough College. Entered Indian Police, 1879; Deputy Inspector-General, Criminal Investigation Department, Punjab, 1905; Inspector-General, N.W. Frontier Police, 1908; Punjab Police, 1909; in charge of Police arrangements Coronation Durbar, 1911. *Recreations:* cricket, tennis, golf, and billiards. *Address:* c/o H. S. King and Co., 9 Pall Mall, S.W. *Club:* United Empire. *(Died 17 May 1916.)*

FRENCH, Maj.-General Sir George Arthur, K.C.M.G., *cr.* 1902; C.M.G. 1877; Col.-Commandant R.A. since 1912; *b.* Roscommon, Ireland, 19 June 1841; *e. s.* of John French, Mornington Park, Co. Dublin, and Isabella Hamilton, his wife; *m.* 1862, Janet Clarke (*d.* 1917), *d.* of Robert Long Innes, formerly 37th Regiment; two *s.* three *d.* *Educ.:* R.M.C. Sandhurst and R.M.A. Woolwich. Joined Royal Artillery, 1860; Adjutant R.A. Kingston, Canada, 1862-66; Inspector of Artillery, Canada, with rank Lt.-Col., 1870-73; Commissioner North-West Mounted Police, 1873-76; I.W.S. Devonport, 1878-83; Commandant of Forces, Queensland, with rank Colonel, 1883-91; received thanks of both Houses of Parliament; commanding R.A. Dover, 1891-92; Chief Instructor S.G. Shoeburyness, 1892-93; Col.-on-Staff and Brigadier-Gen. R.A. Bombay, 1894-96; Major-General commanding N.S.W. Forces, 1896-1902; retired full pay, Sep. 1902. *Decorated* for services in Canada, and specially with reference to an expedition from Red River to Rocky Mountains in command North-West Mounted Police in 1874; was promoted Colonel for "distinguished services other than in the field," Nov. 1892. *Recreations:* shooting, fishing, sailing. *Club:* Junior Constitutional. *(Died 7 July 1921.)*

FRENCH, Sir John Russell, K.B.E.; *cr.* 1918; General Manager, Bank of New South

Wales ; President of Institute of Bankers ; b. 1847 ; m. d. of late W. L. Hawkins, Christchurch, N.Z. ; two s. one d. Educ. : Cheltenham College. (Died 30 June 1921.)

FRENCH, Percy, B.A., C.E. ; Humorist, Artist, and Poet ; b. 1854 ; 2nd s. of Christopher French, Cloonyquin, Co. Roscommon ; m. 1st, 1890, Ethel Armytage Moore (d. 1891), of Arnmore, Co. Cavan ; 2nd, 1894, Helen May Sheldon, of Burmington, Co. Warwick ; three d. Educ. : Windermere College ; Trinity College, Dublin. After College tried Civil Engineering for six years ; editor of a Dublin humorous journal for two years ; composed music and words of about thirty songs ; took up Art, and painted some Irish scenes for the King ; has united his talents in a combined song, story, and sketching entertainment ; gave a series of recitals in London in 1899. Publications : The First Lord Liftinant, and other Stories ; Phil the Fluter's Ball : The Mountains of Mourne ; Abdallah Bulbul Ameer ; and Come Back Paddy Reilly ; Noah's Ark, a fairy play produced at the Waldorf, 1905. Recreations : cycling, lawn tennis, water - colour sketching, and writing pathetic poems. Address : 27 Clifton Hill, N.W.8. T. : Hampstead 155. Club : St. John's Wood Arts. (Died 24 Jan. 1920.)

FREND, Col. George, C.B. 1919 ; Military Knight of Windsor ; b. 1857 ; s. of Col. George French, Ardsallagh, Fethard, Co. Tipperary. Address : Salisbury Tower, Windsor Castle.
(Died 24 Sept. 1923.)

FRERE, John Tudor, J.P. ; b. 12 Jan. 1843 ; e. s. of George Edward Frere, F.R.S., and Isabella Tudor ; m. 1st, 1869, Constance, d. of Forbes Winslow, M.D., D.C.L. : two d. ; 2nd, 1893, Agatha Mary Gabrielle (d. 1919), d. of Rev. Edmund Thomas Daubeney. Educ. : Trin. Coll. Oxford (B.A. 1866). Entered as student at the Inner Temple, 1863 ; practised as a specia pleader, not at the bar, 1867-80. Address : Roy don Hall, Diss. Clubs : New University, Queen's Norfolk, Norwich. (Died Feb. 1918.)

FREWEN, Colonel Edward, D.L., J.P., C.B. 1911 ; Col. commanding R.E. Kent Yeomanry since 1908 ; b. 25 July 1850 ; m. 1873, Anne Mary, d. of Cs)t. H. Byng, R.N., Quendon Hall, Essex ; two s. Sheriff of Rutland, 1876 ; Major Imp. Yeo. S. Africa, 1900-1. Address : Brickwall, Northiam, Sussex. Club : Carlton.
(Died 13 Jan. 1919.)

FREWEN, Moreton, M.P. North-East Cork, 1910-11 ; J.P. Cos. Galway and Cork ; s. of late Thomas Frewen, M.P. S. Leicestershire ; b. 1853 ; m. Clare, d. of Jerome of New York ; two s. one d. Educ. : Trinity College, Cambridge (B.A.). A Vice-President Imperial Federation League, and a frequent writer in the Reviews on economic problems, Tariff and the Exchanges. Publications : The Economic Crisis, etc. ; Melton Mowbray and other Memories, 1924. Address : Brede Place, Sussex. T.A. : Frewen, London. Club : Carlton.
(Died 2 Sept. 1924.)

FREYER, Sir Peter J., K.C.B., cr. 1917 ; C.B. 1917 ; Lieut.-Col. (retired list) I.M.S. ; Consulting Surgeon ; Surgeon to St. Peter's Hospital, Consulting Surgeon Queen Alexandra's Military Hospital, and to the Eastern Command ; late Examiner in Surgery at the University of Durham ; s. s. of late Samuel Freyer, Selerna, Galway ; widower ; one s. one d. Educ. : Erasmus Smith's Coll. Galway ; Royal Univ. of Ireland ; Steeven's Hospital, Dublin ; and Paris. B.A., R.U.I. (First Class Honours and Gold Medal), 1872 ; M.A. (hon. causa), 1886 ; M.D. (First Class Honours and Gold Medal), M.Ch. and L.M. 1874. Obtained first place at the open competition for Indian Medical Service, 1875 ; after period of military employment, services lent to govt. of N.W. Provinces, India, under which held consecutively the appoint-

ments of Civil Surgeon, Moradabad, Bareilly, Allahabad, Mussoorie, and Benares ; Surgeon to Prince of Wales' Hospital, Benares ; was for some time Medical Officer to the Lt.-Governor, N.W. Provinces and Oudh, and subsequently to His Highness the late Nawab of Rampur ; Delegate from the Indian Govt. to the International Medical and Surgical Congress at Rome, 1894 ; awarded Arnott Memorial Medal, for original surgical work, 1904 ; since retirement from the Indian army practising as consulting surgeon, London. Publications : The Modern Treatment of Stone in the Bladder ; Clinical Lectures on Stricture of the Urethra and Hypertrophy of the Prostate ; Total Enucleation of the Prostate for Enlargement of that Organ ; lectures and articles on surgical subjects. Recreations : big game shooting in India, shooting, golf. Address : 27 Harley Street, Cavendish Square, W.1. T. : Paddington 1704. Clubs : Junior United Service, Reform.
(Died 6 Sept. 1921.)

FRICK, Henry Clay ; b. W. Overton, Pa., 19 Dec. 1849 ; m. 1881, Adela de Howard, d. of late Asa P. Childs. Began business life as a clerk for his grandfather, a flour merchant and distiller ; later embarked in coke business ; founded the H. C. Frick Coke Co. and was its President until it was absorbed by the U.S. Steel Corporation ; was Chairman of the Board of the Carnegie Steel Co. until absorbed by the U.S. Steel Corporation ; is now a Director of the U.S. Steel Corporation, Pennsylvania Railroad Co., Chicago and Northwestern Railway Co., Norfolk and Western Railway Co., Atchison, Topeka and Santa Fe Railroad Co., and a member of the Executive and Finance Committees of those Companies ; also a Director of the Union Trust Co. and Mellon National Bank of Pittsburgh, Pa. Address : Pittsburgh, Pa. ; 1 East 70th Street, New York ; Prides Crossing, Mass. (Died 2 Dec. 1919.)

FRICKER, Edward T., Editor, The Australasian, Melbourne, since 1903 ; s. of Henry R. Fricker, architect, of South Hackney, London ; m. 1883, Emily May, d. of Capt. J. Cousens, of Victoria ; two s. two d. Educ. : London ; Margate. After short commercial experience in London and Adelaide, joined staff of Otago Daily Times, Dunedin, New Zealand, 1881 ; joined The Argus, Melbourne, 1889 ; for several years dramatic critic and leader writer. Recreations : cycling, billiards. Address : Australasian Office, Melbourne, Victoria, Australia. Club : Yorick. (Died 4 April 1917.)

FRIEDERICHS, Hulda (Miss) ; b. Ronsdorf, Rhenish Prussia. Educ. : Ronsdorf ; Cologne ; St. Andrews. Joined the staff of Pall Mall Gazette 1883 (the first woman journalist engaged on exactly the same terms, with regard to work and pay, as male members of the staff) ; left P.M.G. when that paper changed politics 1893, and joined Westminster Gazette. Publications : Translated Poems (into German and English) from Russian, Swedish, Spanish, and French ; Mr. Gladstone in the Evening of his Days, 1895 ; co-author of Half-Holidays at the Zoo, 1895 ; translator of Dr. Martin's The Future of Russia, 1906 ; The Romance of the Salvation Army, 1907 ; editor, Westminster Budget, 1896 - 1905 ; The Life of Sir George Newnes, Bart., 1911. Recreations : reading and writing. Address : Westminster Gazette, 104 Shoe Lane, E.C. T.A. : Lobby, Lud, London. T. : Central 7600-6. (Died 11 Feb. 1927.)

FRISWELL, Sir Charles Hain, Kt., cr. 1909 ; s. of George Friswell ; b. 30 Dec. 1871 ; m. 1915, Edith Kate, d. of William Frewer ; no c. Educ. : privately. Has travelled considerably in India, Africa, Ceylon, Burmah. Recreations : shooting, riding, and sports generally. Address : Woodland, Ewhurst, Surrey.
(Died 15 Dec. 1926.)

FRITH, W. S., R.B S. *Address:* Elgin Studios, Trafalgar Square, Chelsea, S.W.3. *(Died Aug. 1924.)*

FRIZELL, Rev. Charles William, M.A.; Registrar, Secretary and Surrogate for the Diocese of Down and Connor and Dromore; Chaplain to the Bishop of Down and Connor; Member of the General Synod of Church of Ireland; *e. s.* of Charles Frizell, J.P., Castle Kevin, Co. Wicklow; unmarried. *Educ.:* Harcourt Street School, Dublin; Trinity College, Dublin. President of the University Philosophical Society T.C.D. 1872; B.A. 1873; M.A. 1897; Curate of Coleraine, 1873-77; Castlerock, Co. Derry. 1877-79; Rector of Dunluce, Co. Antrim, 1879-93; Diocesan Chaplain and Assistant Diocesan Inspector of Religious Education, 1897-99; Minor Canon of Belfast Cathedral, 1899-1904; Examining Chaplain to the Bishops of Down, 1899-1907. *Address:* Knocknamona, Fortwilliam Park, Belfast. *T.:* Fortwilliam 120. *(Died 13 Jan. 1920.)*

FRIZELLE, Sir Joseph, Kt., *cr.* 1899; *b.* 1841; *m.* 1868, Elizabeth, *d.* of late J. W. Keene. *Educ.:* Royal School, Dungannon; Trinity College, Dublin. Entered Indian Civil Service, 1863; Assistant Magistrate and Collector, N.W.P., 1864; Punjab Commission, 1864-98; Judge of Chief Court, Punjab, 1889-98; Chief Judge, 1898. *Address:* Jersey *(Died 17 Oct. 1921.)*

FROST, Edward Purkis, J.P., D.L. Co. Camb.; A.F.A.S.; Past-President Royal Aeronautical Society of Great Britain, now Vice-President; Vice-President of Tariff Reform League; Commissioner of Income Tax; Chairman of Linton Bench; Member of various Scientific Associations; Member of the Council of the Aerial League of Great Britain; *b.* 1842; *s.* of late Edward Frost, J.P.; unmarried. *Educ.:* Blackheath, Brentwood. and Bishop-Stortford. Joined Cambs. Rifle Volunteers, 1861; served on various County Committees prior to the County Councils; served on County Bench since 1871; Aeronautical since 1868; Agricultural, Horticultural, Scientific, Political Associations. *Publications:* Union of Science and Religion; The Influence of Physiological Discovery on Thought; Safeguards for Peace; National Insurance against War, etc. *Recreations:* shooting, fishing, natural history, science, aviation, art, and music. *Address:* West Wratting Hall, Cambridge. *T.A.:* West Wratting. *M.:* CE 1113. *Clubs:* Constitutional, Royal Aero; Cambridge County. *(Died 26 Jan. 1922.)*

FROST, Hon. Sir John, K.C.M.G., *cr.* 1904; C.M.G. 1879; *b.* 1828; *s.* of Wm. Frost, farmer, Leicestershire. Emigrated to S. Africa, 1849, and farmed for three years in the div. of Graaf Reinet; served with the Somerset Burghers under Commandant Bowker,1850-51, for which service he received a grant of land in the div. of Queenstown, 1857; served under Sir Walter Currie when the Kaffir Chief Kreile was expelled from the territory now known as the Transkei; elected member for House of Assembly for div. of Queenstown, 1874, and has represented that district continuously for 27 years; when the war of 1877-78 broke out he was appointed Commandant of Queenstown Div. and of all the burghers operating in Gaikaland, and in 1890-81 was appointed Chief Commandant of the Burghers and of several bodies of levies in the Transkei; joined Mr. Rhodes' Ministry as Secy. of Native Affairs, 1893; this office was abolished, when he became Minister of Agriculture during the same year; joined Sir Gordon Sprigg, 1900, as minister without portfolio, and represented the Cape Govt. in Australia at the inauguration of the Commonwealth and opening of the Federal Parliament by H.R.H. the Duke of York; appointed Minister of Agriculture on reconstruction of Ministry in June, 1902. *Address:* East-

brooke, Rondebosch, Cape Town; Thibet Park. Cape Colony. *(Died 2 April 1918.)*

FROST, Lieut.-Col. John Meadows, D.S.O. 1918; R.F.A. (T.F.); *e. s.* of Sir J. M. Frost; *b.* 1885; *m.* 1910, Olivia, *e. d.* of Henry Shelmerdine, South Lawn, Southport; three *s.* two *d. Educ.:* Charterhouse; Christ Church, Oxford. Served European War, 1914-1918 (despatches, D.S.O.). *Address:* The Dene, Hoole, Chester. *(Died 15 Aug. 1923.)*

FROUDE, Robert Edmund, C.B. 1911; C.E.; F.R.S.; LL.D.; Superintendent Admiralty Experiment Works, Haslar, Gosport, 1879 [retired, 1919]; *b.* Devonshire, 22. Dec. 1846; 3rd *s.* of William Froude, C.E., F.R.S., *a.* of Hurrell Froude of the Oxford Tract Movement, and James Anthony Froude the historian. *Educ.:* Bradfield College, Berkshire; Oratory School, Edgbaston, Birmingham. Served under his father, Admiralty Experiment Works, then at Torquay, 1871-79; afterwards Superintendent of same; later at Haslar (Gosport); retired, 1919. *Publications:* papers on scientific subjects bearing on Naval Architecture. *Recreations:* cycling, boating, photography. *Address:* North Lodge, Alverstoke, Gosport. *(Died 19 Mar. 1924.)*

FROWDE, Henry, late publisher to the University of Oxford; *b.* 1841. *Address:* 25 The Waldrons, Croydon, Surrey. *T.:* Croydon 726. *(Died 3 Mar. 1927.)*

FRY, Rt. Hon. Sir Edward, G.C.B., *cr.* 1907; P.C., B.A., D.C.L., LL.D., F.R.S., F.S.A., F.L.S.; Kt., *cr.* 1877; Judge of High Court. Chancery Division, 1877-83; Lord Justice of Appeal, 1883-92; *b.* Bristol, 4 Nov. 1827; 2nd *s.* of Joseph Fry, Bristol, and Mary Anne, *d.* of Edward Swaine, Reading; *m.* 1859, Mariabella, *d.* of John Hodgkin, Lewes; two *s.* six *d. Educ.:* Bristol College; University College, London; Fellow University of London; Fellow of the British Academy; Hon. Fellow of Balliol College, Oxford. Formerly a Trustee of the Hunterian Museum, College of Surgeons; a member of Historical MSS. Commission, and formerly of Permanent Court of Arbitration at the Hague (1900-12); formerly Alderman and Chairman of Quarter Sessions County of Somerset; Barrister, 1854; Q.C. and Bencher of Lincoln's Inn, 1869; Treasurer Lincoln's Inn, 1892; presided over the Royal Commission on the Irish Land Acts, 1897-98; Conciliator in the S. Wales Colliery dispute, 1898; Chairman of the Departmental Committee on the Patent Laws, 1900; Arbitrator in the Grimsby Fishery dispute, 1901; was Chairman of the Court of Arbitration under the Metropolis Water Act, 1902; and of University College, London, Transfer Commission, 1906; and was legal assessor to the International Commission on the North Sea incident,1904-6; Arbitrator between the U.S. of America and Mexico in the Pious Funds case, 1902, and between France and Germany on the Casa Blanca incident, 1909; was Chairman of the Royal Commission on Trinity College, Dublin, and on the University of Dublin, 1906-7; Arbitrator between the London and N.W. Rly. Company and their employees, 1908; was Ambassador Extraordinary and First British Plenipotentiary to the Hague Peace Conference in 1907. *Publications:* Essays on the Accordance of Christianity with Nature of Man, 1857; The Doctrine of Election, an Essay, 1864; A Treatise on the Specific Performance of Contracts, edits. 1858, '81, '92, 1903, and 1911; British Mosses, 1892 and 1908; James Hack Tuke, 1899; and The Mycetozoa, 1899, 1915; Studies by the Way, 1900; The Liverworts, 1911. *Address:* Failand House, Failand, near Bristol. *T.A.:* Failand, Abbots-Leigh. *Clubs:* Athenæum; County, Taunton *(Died 18 Oct. 1918*

FRY, Francis James, D.L., J.P.; Lord of the Manor of Cricket St. Thomas, Chard; *b.* 1835; *e. s.* of Francis Fry, F.S.A.; *m.* 1st, 1861, Elizabeth Greer, *d.* of Joseph Rake, Bristol; 2nd, 1885, Elizabeth, *d.* of A. Capper Pass, Bristol; four *s.* one *d. Educ.:* a private school in Bristol. Sheriff, Bristol, 1887; Somersetshire, 1906; spent the greater part of life in Bristol on business and in public matters; was for many years an alderman of the city, and a member of the Council of University College; now a member of the Court of Bristol University. *Recreations:* foreign travel, shooting, art and science. *Address:* Cricket St. Thomas, Chard. *T.A.:* Cricket, Winsham. *T.:* 37 Chard. *Club:* Royal Societies.   *(Died 4 Nov. 1918.)*

FRY, Sir Henry James Wakely, Kt., *cr.* 1916; C.I.E. 1914; Director General of Stores, India Office, 1912-15; *b.* 13 Nov. 1849; 2nd *s.* of William Wakely Fry of Taunton, Somerset; *m.* 1877, Elizabeth, *y. d.* of Charles Parsons of Steepleton Preston, Dorset; five *d. Educ.:* Church College, Taunton; privately. B.A. (honours) London University, 1875; Junior Clerk, India Office, 1873; Senior Clerk, 1896; Deputy Director General of Stores, 1909. *Address:* Holly Cottage, Englefield Green, Surrey.   *(Died 18 Dec. 1920.)*

FRY, Rt. Hon. Lewis, P.C., J.P., D.L., LL.D.; Governor of Clifton College; Pro-Chancellor of University of Bristol; President of Clifton High School for Girls: *b.* 16 April 1832; *s.* of late Joseph Fry, Bristol; *b.* of late Rt. Hon. Sir Edward Fry; *m.* 1859, Elizabeth Pease (*d.* 1870), *o. d.* of late Francis Gibson of Saffron Walden, Essex; one *s.* three *d.* Formerly a Solicitor; member of Bristol Town Council, and Chairman of School Board; M.P. (L.U.) for Bristol, 1878-85; N. Bristol, 1885-92, 1895-1900; Chairman of Parliamentary Committee on Town Holdings, 1886-92; and author of two reports of same. *Address:* Goldney House, Clifton, Bristol. *Club:* Burlington Fine Arts.   *(Died 10 Sept. 1921.)*

FRY, Peter George, C.M.G. 1919; D.S.O. 1916; T.D., F.R.I.B.A.; *s.* of Peter Fry; *b.* 1875; *m.* 1901, Minnie, *d.* of Llewellin Llewellin; one *s.* Served European War, 1914-18 (despatches, D.S.O., Brevet Lieut. Col., C.M.G., White Eagle of Serbia). *Address:* c/o Barclays Bank, Weston-super-Mare. *(Died 23 Oct. 1925.)*

FRYER, Sir Charles (Edward), Kt., *cr.* 1915; I.S.O. 1907; F.L.S., A.A., Oxford; Hon. Member American Fisheries Society; Hon. Member Salmon and Trout Association; *b.* July 1850; *e. s.* of late Charles Biden Fryer of Leamington; *m.*; one *s. Educ.:* privately. Clerk to Inspectors of Fisheries, Home Office, 1869; Inspectors' Assistant, 1883; Inspector, 1886; transferred to Board of Trade, 1886, and to Board of Agriculture and Fisheries (as Superintending Inspector), 1903; Secretary to, or Member of, various Commissions and Committees of Inquiry into Fisheries of England, Wales, and Scotland, 1874-1915; received thanks of Government of New Zealand for services in connection with introduction of trout and efforts to acclimatise salmon in the colony, 1878, 1910-18; awarded silver medal Society of Arts for invention of preserving pilchards as sardines—a new industry in this country—1876; silver medal Royal Cornwall Polytechnic Society, 1875; bronze medal Philadelphia International Exhibition, 1876; first prize for essay on Relations of the State with Fishermen and Fisheries, International Fisheries Exhibition, 1883, and diploma of Royal Commission for services rendered; Official English Delegate and Juror, International Fisheries Exhibition, Bergen; Official English Delegate, Internat. Fish. Congress, Dieppe, 1898; member of Committee, Internat. Fish. Congress, Paris, 1900; Vice-Pres. Washington, 1908; Official English Delegate, Rome, 1911; Official English Delegate and Pres. Maritime Section, Internat. Fish. Congress, Ostend, 1913; Member of Organising Committee for ensuing Internat. Fish. Congress, San Sebastian. *Publications:* Handbook on Salmon Fisheries, 1883; A National Fisheries Society, 1883; Relations of the State with Fishermen and Fisheries, 1883; International Regulation of the Fisheries on the High Seas, 1910; The Management of our Salmon Rivers, 1916; annual and other reports on Fisheries, etc., 1886-1915; editor of The Colonies and India, 1874-90; contributor to various journals and other publications. *Clubs:* Royal Automobile, Fly-Fishers'. *(Died 19 Nov. 1920.)*

FRYER, Sir Frederic William Richards, K.C.S.I., *cr.* 1895; *b.* 1845; *s.* of F. W. Fryer of West Moors, Dorset, and Emily Frances, *d.* of John Richards, M.P.; *m.* 1870, Frances (*d.* 1920), *d.* of W. C. L. Bashford, J.P., D.L.; one *s.* Entered Bengal Civil Service, 1864; Barr. Middle Temple, 1880; Deputy-Commissioner Punjaub, 1877; Commissioner Central Division Upper Burma, 1886; Financial Com. of Burma, 1888; Acting Chief Com. of Burma, 1892-94; Officiating Financial Com. of the Punjaub, and Additional Member of the Viceroy's Council, 1894-95; Chief Com., Burma, 1895-97; Lieut.-Governor, Burma, 1897-1903. *Address:* 23 Elvaston Place, S.W.7. *T.:* 3779 Kensington. *Clubs:* Athenæum, East India United Service.   *(Died 20 Feb. 1922.)*

FRYER, Lt.-Gen. Sir John, K.C.B., *cr.* 1903; C.B. 1881; Colonel 6th Dragoon Guards (The Carabiniers), 1902; *b.* Wimborne Minster, Dorset, 27 June 1838; *e. s.* of late John Fryer (*d.* 1854), and Mary, *d.* of late Christopher Hardinge; *m.* 1862, Catherine (*d.* 1914), *d.* of late George Reed, East Brent Manor, Somerset; one *s.* two *d. Educ.:* Exeter Coll. Oxford. Entered army, 1860, as a cornet 6th Dragoon Guards (The Carabiniers), and passing through every grade, commanded that regiment as Lieut.-Col. from 1877 to 1882; as a Colonel commanded 17th Leicester regimental District, 1883-88; as a Maj.-Gen. commanded the South Irish (Cork) District 1893-98; war service, command of the Carabiniers throughout campaign, Afghanistan, 1879-80; command of 2nd movable column, Khaibar Field Force, etc., etc., 1879-80; Afghan medal; Victoria Jubilee medal; in receipt of Reward for Distinguished Service. *Recreations:* polo (winner of silver cup); rowing (winner of cups); won presentation sword as best swordsman of officers of The Carabiniers, 1872; steeple-chasing (won his regimental cup twice); is on the Councils of the Hunters Improvement Society, Army and Navy Pensioners Employment Society, etc.; hunting, shooting, deer-stalking, golf. *Address:* 42 Evelyn Gardens, S.W. *Clubs:* Army and Navy, Cavalry, Hurlingham, M.C.C.   *(Died 28 Jan. 1917.)*

FUKUSHIMA, Gen. Baron; Hon. K.C.B., *cr.* 1902; Governor-General of Kwantung 1912-17; *b.* Matsumoto, Shinano Province, 1853 (Samurai); married; four *s.* one *d.* Began life as a drummer-boy; studied in Tokio University; entered Judicial Department, 1874; transferred to General Staff Office, 1875; visited Philadelphia Exhibition, 1876; Lieut. in army, 1877; travelled in Mongolia, 1879; Military Attaché, Peking, 1882-84; sent to India, 1886; Military Attaché, Berlin, 1887-1892; travelled on horseback, Berlin to Vladivostock, through Russia, Siberia, Mongolia, Manchuria (9000 miles), 1892-93; General Staff Officer, 5th Division, First Army; then Chief of Administrative Bureau of Territory occupied by Japan during war with China; sent to Egypt, Turkey, Persia, Caucasia, Arabia, Turkestan, India, Burma, Siam, and Annam, 1895-97; in command of Japanese contingent till fall of Tientsin, then attached to General Yamaguchi, then to Field-Marshal Waldersee as General

Staff Officer during Boxer troubles, 1900-1; attended King Edward's Coronation; General Staff Officer, Headquarters, Manchurian Army, Russo - Japanese War, 1904 - 5; Vice - Chief of General Staff of the Army, 1906; Gen. 1914 (retired). *Address:* Tokio, Japan.

(Died 18 Feb. 1919.)

FULFORD, Francis, A.K.C., J.P., Devon; District Councillor St. Thomas's R.D.C.; *b.* 15 Sep. 1861; *e. s.* of Francis Drummond Fulford of Fulford, D.L., J.P.; *m.* 1897, Constance, *d.* of late Edgar Drummond of Cadland, Hants, D.L., J.P., and *d.* of 3rd Baron Muncaster; three *s. Educ.:* Sherborne; King's College, London. Assistant Engineer on Canadian Pacific Railway, 1883-85; Assistant Secretary to Royal Commission on Civil Establishments, 1886-91; Inspector Board of Agriculture, 1891; private secretary to Rt. Hon. Walter Long, 1899; to Rt. Hon. R. W. Hanbury, 1900; Superintending Inspector Ministry of Agriculture and Fisheries, 1901-21. *Address:* Great Fulford, Dunsford, Exeter; *T.A.:* Fulford, Dunsford. *Clubs:* National, M.C.C. *(Died 4 Nov. 1926.)*

FULFORD, Rev. Frederick John, Rector of Fornham All Saints with Westley, 1904-25; Rural Dean of Thingoe, 1917-24; Hon. Canon of St. Edmundsbury and Ipswich; *b.* London, 1860; *y. s.* of William Fulford; *m.* 1890, Emily Constance, *d.* of W. H. Ellis of Ottermouth, Budleigh, Salterton; two *s.* one *d. Educ.:* King's College School, London; Clare College, Cambridge. Vice-Principal of Gloucester Theological College, 1888-90; Vicar of Flaxley, Gloucestershire, 1890-1904; Representative of the Senate of Cambridge University on the West Suffolk Education Committee; Chairman of the Governors of the West Suffolk County School and Pupil Teachers' Centre; Chairman of the Diocesan Education Committee and Member of the Diocesan Board of Finance of St. Edmundsbury and Ipswich; Chm. of the West Suffolk Local War Pensions Committee. *Recreations:* walking, croquet, and poultry-keeping. *Address:* 5 Louisa Terrace, Exmouth. *(Died 3 Jan. 1927.)*

FULLER, George Pargiter, J.P.; *b.* Baynton, Wilts, 8 Jan. 1833; *o. surv. s.* of John Bird Fuller, Neston Park, Wilts, and Sophia, *d.* of John Hanning, Dillington Park, Ilminster, Somerset; *m.* Emily, 2nd *d.* of Sir M. Hicks-Beach, 8th Bt., 1864; five *s.* one *d. Educ.:* Winchester; Christ Church, Oxford (M.A.). M.P. (L.) for West Wilts, 1885-95. *Recreations:* coaching, hunting, cricket. *Address:* Neston Park, Corsham, Wiltshire. *T.A.:* Fuller, Corsham. *T.:* Corsham, 1. *M.:* AM 3247. *Clubs:* United University, National Liberal.

(Died 2 April 1927.)

FULLER, James Franklin, architect, author; F.S.A.; F.R.I.B.A.; Fellow Royal Institute of Architects of Ireland; *b.* 1835; *m.* Helen, *d.* of J. P. Gouvion. Principal professional works: churches of Clane, Arthurstown, Killadease, Rattoo, Kylemore, Syddan, Rathdaire, etc.; Lord Ardilaun's mansions at St. Ann's, Dublin, and Ashford, Co. Galway; Harristoun House, Kildare; Ballyburley House, King's Co.; Mount Falcon, Co. Mayo; Lord Ventry's, Co. Kerry; has been Architect to the Church Representative Body, to the Honourable the Benchers of King's Inns, and to the National Board of Education. *Publications:* John Orlebar; Culmshire Folk; The Young Idea; Doctor Quodlibet; Chronicles of Westerly; Omniana, the Autobiography of an Irish Octogenarian; has been a frequent contributor to genealogical and heraldic periodicals, such as the Miscellanea Genealogica et Heraldica, The Genealogist, and Walford's Antiquarian Magazine. *Recreations:* genealogy and heraldry. *Address:* Glashnacree, Kenmare, Co. Kerry; Lissatier, Eglinton Road, Dublin.

14   *(Died 8 Dec. 1924.)*

FULLERTON, Hugh, J.P.; *b.* 1851, *s.* of Samuel and Mary Fullerton, of Manchester; *m.* 1891. *Educ.:* public school. Working man, then foreman, then master, now retired; taken active part in various educational, social, and political movements; been Guardian of Poor; was Chairman of School Board Progressive Party, Manchester; was Member of a Trades Council; Executive Treasurer, Discharged Prisoners' Aid Society, Manchester; Member of Executive for seven years of National Liberal Federation; Magistrate, City of Manchester and Cumberland; M.P. (L.) Egremont West, Cumberland, 1906-10. *Address:* Brackenhoe, Sale, Cheshire. *Clubs:* National Liberal; Reform, Manchester. *(Died 31 Aug. 1922.)*

FULLERTON, Admiral Sir John Reginald Thomas, G.C.V.O., *cr.* 1901; K.C.V.O., *cr.* 1899; C.B., 1896; Extra-Groom-in-Waiting to the King; *b.* 10 Aug. 1840; *m.* 1874, Ada, *d.* of late Col, E. S. Capell, Lady's Close, Watford, Herts; two *s.* three *d.* Entered Royal Navy, 1853; Commander, 1872; Capt. 1878; Rear-Admiral, 1893; Lieut. of '' Bombay '' when that vessel took fire and blew up off Monte Video, 1864; Order of St. Anne, 1st class; Order of the Prussian Crown, 1st class. *Recreations:* yachting, motoring. *Address:* Hamble, South Hants. *Clubs:* United Service, Royal Automobile. *(Died 29 June 1918.)*

FULTON, Sir Forrest, Kt., *cr.* 1892; K.C.; LL.B.; J.P., Norfolk; Recorder of London, 1900-1922; one of H.M.'s Lieutenants for the City of London; *b.* Ostend, 12 July 1846; *y. s.* of late Lieut.-Col. Fulton, K.H., and Fanny, *d.* of John Sympson Jessopp; *m.* 1875, Sophia Browne, *e. d.* of John B. Nicholson; three *s. Educ.:* Norwich Grammar School, under his uncle the Rev. Augustus Jessopp, D.D.; London University, B.A. 1867; LL.B. 1873; Barr. Middle Temple, 1872; Bencher, 1898; Treasurer, 1921-2; Counsel to Treasury at Middlesex Sessions and Central Criminal Court; Senior Counsel to Post Office; Counsel to Mint, Hertfordshire; Common Serjeant, 1892-1900; M.P. West Ham (North), 1886-92. *Address:* The Cottage, Sheringham, Norfolk. *Club:* Carlton. *(Died 25 June 1925.)*

FULTON, Lt.-Col. Harry Townsend, C.M.G. 1917; D.S.O. 1900; Indian Army; 2nd K.E.O. Gurkhas; *b.* 15 Aug. 1869; 6th *s.* of late Lieut.-Gen. John Fulton, R.A.; *m.* 1905, Ada Hermina, 2nd *d.* of John James Dixon. Entered army, 1892; served N.W. Frontier of India, 1897-98 (medal and clasp); Tirah, 1897-1898 (clasp); S. Africa, 1899-1901 (medal, three clasps, despatches, D.S.O.); European War, 1914-17 (despatches twice, C.M.G., Bt. Lt.-Col., Croix de Guerre). *Address:* Dehra Dun, India.

(Died 29 Mar. 1918.)

FULTON, Robert Burwell, A.M., LL.D., President Miller Technical School since 1906; *b.* Sumter Co., Alabama, 8 April 1849; *s.* of William and Elizabeth K. Fulton; *m.* 1st, 1871, Annie Rose Garland (*d.* 1893); four *s.* one *d.*; 2nd, 1903, Florence Thompson. *Educ.:* private schools; University of Mississippi. A.B. 1869; A.M. 1873; LL.D. University of Nashville, 1893; South Carolina College, 1905; University of Alabama, 1906; University of Mississippi, 1909; taught in high schools, Alabama, 1869-1870; New Orleans, 1870-71; Tutor, University of Mississippi, 1871; Adjunct Professor Physics, 1872; Professor Physics and Astronomy, 1875-1906; Fellow A.A.A.S. since 1888; President Department of Higher Education, National Educational Association, 1898; Pres. Southern Educational Association, 1899; Pres. National Association of State Universities, 1896-1902; Chancellor of the University of Mississippi, 1892-1906; member of the Board of Trustees of the Miller Fund of the University of Virginia since 1910. *Publications:* contributions to Ency. Brit., 1878, and revision 1903; author of various reports and addresses on educational and

scientific topics ; Virginia and the Cession of the North-west Territory, a historical review, 1910. *Address:* Miller School, Albemarle Co., Va. *T.A.:* Charlottesville, Va. *T.:* Charlottesville 915 R. *Club:* Chi Psi.
(*Died 28 May 1918.*)

FULTON, Sir Robert Fulton, Kt., *cr.* 1908 ; M.A., LL.D. : *b.* 1844 ; *m.* 1887, Margaret Edith, *.d.* of Brigade-Surgeon R. G. Mathew : one *d. Educ.:* Edinburgh Academy, and University. Entered Bengal Civil Service, 1864 ; District Judge, 1875-93 ; Barrister-at-law, Inner Temple, 1884 ; Acting Puisne Judge, High Court, Calcutta, 1888, 1889, 1890, 1892 ; Puisne Judge, 1898 ; additional Member of Legislative Council of Viceroy of India, 1902-3 : Acting Chief-Justice of Bengal, 1907, 1908 ; retired, 1908. *Publications:* Commentary on Bengal Tenancy Act ; revised editions of Field's Law of Evidence, Alexander's Law of, Torts, O'Kinealy's Code of Civil Procedure. *Address:* 7 Sloane Gardens, S.W.1. *T.:* Victoria 1582. *Clubs:* East India United Service ; Bengal, Calcutta. (*Died 15 Oct. 1927.*)

FUNSTEN, Rt. Rev. James Bowen, B.L., D.D., Bishop of Idaho since 1907 ; *b.* Clarke, Co. Virginia ; *s.* of Colonel Oliver Ridgeway Funsten, of 11th Virginia Cavalry, U.S.A., and Mary Bowen, of Mirador, Virginia ; *m.* Ida Vivian Pratt of Camden, Virginia ; four *s.* one *d. Educ.:* University High School ; Virginia Military Institute ; University of Virginia ; Virginia Theological Seminary. Till 20 years manager of mother's Plantation (Mirador) in Virginia ; practised law in Baltimore ; deacon at 23 ; missionary in charge of Bristol and Marion, Virginia ; priest ; spent some time in travel abroad, 1884 ; rector of Christ Church, Richmond, 1884-90 ; general missionary, Virginia, 1890-92 ; rector of Trinity Church, Portsmouth, Virginia, 1892-99 ; first Missionary Bishop of Boisé, 1899 ; Bishop in charge of Wyoming, 1907-9 ; Chaplain 2nd Regt. Idaho National Guards, U.S.A. Founder and President of St. Luke's Hospital, Boisé, Idaho. *Publications:* tracts, occasional magazine articles, sermons, monograms. *Recreation:* travelling. *Address:* Boisé, Idaho, U.S.A.

FUNSTON, Brig.-Gen. Frederick ; *b.* New Carlisle, Ohio, 9 Nov. 1865 ; *m.* 1898, Eda Blankart. *Educ.:* Kansas University. Commissioner Department of Agriculture to explore Alaska and report on its flora, 1893 ; Captain Major and Lt.-Col. Cuban Insurgent Army, 1896-1897 ; Col. Commdg. 20th Kansas Infantry, 1898 ; went to Philippines (prom. Brig.-Gen., medal of honour) ; organised and commanded an expedition resulting in capture of Aguinaldo ; Commandant Army Service School, Fort Leavenworth, 1909. *Publication:* Memories of Two Wars, 1912. *Address:* Iola, Kansas, U.S.A.
(*Died 9 Feb. 1917.*)

FURLEY, Sir John, Kt., *cr.* 1899 ; C.B. 1902 ; C.H. 1918 ; late Capt. East Kent Rifle Vol. ; D.L., J.P. ; *b.* Ashford, Kent, 19 March 1836 ; *s.* of Robert Furley, J.P. ; *m.* Maria Turner, (Royal Red Cross, Lady of Justice Order of the Hospital of St. John of Jerusalem, S. African war medal), *d.* of George Baker of Holmfels, Reigate, J.P., 1874. *Educ.:* Harrow. Commissioner of British National Aid Soc., Franco-German War, 1870-71 ; Director of Ambulances Volantes of French Army during War of Commune, 1871 ; Delegate of British Seed Fund Committee for French peasant Farmers (Lord Vernon's Fund), 1871 ; Director of Ambulances in Spain during Carlist War, 1874 ; special Commissioner of Mansion-House Fund for relief of sufferers from inundations in valley of Garonne, 1875 ; Special Commissioner of British National Aid Society to inspect and report on Ambulance arrangements, and to afford necessary assistance to wounded in Montenegro during Russo-Turkish

war, 1876 ; Chief Commissioner Central British Red Cross Committee in S. Africa, 1900 (despatches twice) ; one of original organisers of St. John Ambulance Association, 1877 ; Deputy-Chairman and Director of Ambulance Dept. of Order of St. John of Jerusalem ; member of International Congress of Red Cross Societies, held at Berlin, 1868 ; Hon. Sec. of similar Conference held at Vienna, 1873 ; member of the Conference at Geneva, 1884 ; Hon. Sec. of the Conference at Carlsruhe, 1887 ; Vice-President of the Conference at Rome, 1892 ; Vice-President of Conference at Vienna, 1897 ; Vice-President of Conference at Petrograd, 1902 ; one of the delegates for Great Britain at International Conference for revision of the Convention of Geneva, 1906 ; Vice-Pres. of International Conference, London, 1907 ; Vice-President of 9th International Conference, Washington, 1912 ; Hon. Pres. of first International First-Aid and Life-Saving Congress, Frankfort-on-Main, 1908 ; Knight of Justice and Hon. Bailiff, Order of St. John of Jerusalem ; Jubilee medal, 1887; Jubilee bar, 1897; Coronation medal, 1902; Order of St. John Service medal ; South African War medal and 3 bars ; Knight Commander Royal Order of Wasa ; Knight of the Dannebrog ; Grand Star of Honour and Knight Commander of Isabel the Catholic ; Knight Commander Montenegro ; Officer of Légion d'Honneur ; French Commemoration medal (Decree 1910) for Campaign of 1870-71. *Publications:* War and Charity (translation of La Guerre et la Charité, by MM. Moynier and Appia), 1870 ; Struggles and Experiences of a Neutral Volunteer (2 vols.), 1871 ; In Spain Amongst the Carlists (1 vol.), 1876 ; The Red Cross, its Past and Future (translation of La Croix Rouge son Passé et son Avenir, by M. Gustave Moynier), 1883 ; In Peace and War, 1905. *Address:* 14 Evelyn Gardens, S.W. (*Died 27 Sept. 1919.*)

PURLONG, Hon. L. O'Brien, Manager of the Newfoundland Government Savings Bank ; *b.* 1856 ; *m.* 1885, Helen, *d.* of Inspector-General Carty. *Educ.:* St. Mary's College, Montreal. Elected for St. John's East to House of Assembly, 1893 ; was Minister of Public Works and member of Executive under Sir Jas. Winter's government ; resigned and was appointed Speaker, which position held for ten years. *Address:* City Club, St. John's, Newfoundland.

PURLONG, Robert O'Brien, C.B. 1901 ; Solicitor of Inland Revenue for Ireland ; and Special Commissioner of Income Tax 1880-1907 ; *b.* 1842 ; *s.* of Wm. Croker Furlong ; *m.* 1871, Henrietta (*d.* 1915), *d.* of Henry Courtney ; one *s.* two *d. Educ.:* Trinity College, Dublin (M.A.). Irish Barrister, 1867 ; Secretary, Royal Sanitary Commission, Dublin, 1879-80 ; Counsel, Post Office (Ireland), 1879 ; J.P., Hants. *Address:* Maesbury, Cavendish Road, Bournemouth. *Clubs:* Constitutional ; University, Royal St. George Yacht, Dublin ; Bournemouth.
(*Died 5 July 1917.*)

FURNEAUX, Rev. William Mordaunt, D.D. ; *b.* 29 July 1848 ; *e. s.* of Rev. W. D. Furneaux, Swilly, Devon ; *m.* 1877, Caroline Octavia (*d.* 1904), *d.* of Joseph Mortimer, of Weymouth ; three *d. Educ.:* Marlborough ; Corpus Christi Coll., Oxford. 1st class Classical Moderations, 1870 ; 1st class Lit. Hum. 1872 ; Assistant Master at Clifton, 1873 ; at Marlborough, 1874-1882 ; Headmaster of Repton to 1900 ; late Canon of Southwell ; Dean of Winchester, 1903-19. *Publications:* Commentary on the Acts of the Apostles ; The Book of Psalms ; Introduction to the Lessons of the Lectionary. *Club:* Church Imperial. (*Died 10 April 1928.*)

FURNISS, Harry, caricature artist, author, and lecturer ; *b.* Wexford, 1854 ; *s.* of Mr. Furniss, English engineer, and *d.* of Eneas Mackenzie, Newcastle-on-Tyne. Settled in London at nineteen ; many years contributor to Illustrated London News, The Graphic, Black and White, Illustrated Sporting and Dramatic News, and the principal magazines in England and America ; Punch ; joined Punch staff 1880 ; Humorous Lecturer ; has toured in America, Canada, Australia, etc. ; illustrated Happy Thoughts, Incompleat Angler, Comic Black-stone, Lewis Carroll's Sylvie and Bruno founded Lika Joko, New Budget. *Publications:* Romps, Flying Visits · exhibited Artistic Joke in Bond Street, 1887 ; Royal Academy Antics ; Humours of Parliament, America in a Hurry, 1900 ; illustrated London Letter ; Peace with Humour ; P. and O. Sketches, 1898 ; Confessions of a Caricaturist, 1901 ; Harry Furniss at Home, 1903 ; Poverty Bay, a novel, 1905 ; How to Draw in Pen and Ink, 1905 ; Friends without Faces, a book for children, 1905. Illustrated all the works of Charles Dickens, 1910 ; Illustrated all the works of W. M. Thackeray (the Harry Furniss Centenary Edition), 1911 ; Our Lady Cinema, 1914 ; More about How to draw in Pen and Ink, 1915 ; humorous lectures throughout England, What you are Thinking About, The Frightfulness of Humour ; The Blue Moon, an intermittent publication for concrete objects ; The Cranks No. (Brewers), Peace in War (Salvation Army War Work Fund), and so on, 1917 ; Deceit, a reply to Defeat, 1917 ; My Bohemian Days ; The By-ways and Queer Ways of Boxing, 1919 ; Stiggins, 1920 ; Some Victorian Women (Good, Bad, and Indifferent), 1923 ; Some Victorian Men, 1924. Has written many photo-plays for the cinematograph, produced and acted in them both in the United States and in England, 1912. *Address:* The Mount, High Wickham, Hastings. *Club:* Garrick. *(Died 14 Jan. 1925.)*

FYFE, Thomas Alexander, C.B.E. 1918 ; Sheriff-Substitute of Lanarkshire at Glasgow since 1900 ; *b.* Dundee, 1852. *Educ.:* Perth ; Edinburgh University. Appointed Sheriff-Substitute at Lanark, 1895. *Publications:* The Law and Practice of the Sheriff Court ; The Bankruptcy Code (Scotland) ; Employers and Workmen under the Munitions of War Acts. *Address:* 1 Kingsborough Gardens, Glasgow, W. *T.:* W. 606. *(Died 13 Mar. 1928.)*

FYSH, Hon. Sir Philip Oakley, K.C.M.G., *cr.* 1896 ; Hon. D.C.L. Oxon. ; *b.* 1 Mar. 1835 ; *s.* of John Fysh, Highbury ; *m.* 1856, Esther (*d.* 1912), *e. d.* of William Willis, manufacturer, Luton, Beds. M.L.C. Hobart, 1866 - 69 ; Buckingham, 1870 - 73, 1884, 1887, 1890 ; M.H.A. for East Hobart, 1878 - 78 ; Treasurer in Mr. Kennerly's Ministry, 1873-75, and without portfolio to 1876 ; Leader of the Opposition, July 1877 to Aug. 1877 ; Premier without office, 1877-78 ; held portfolio without office in Mr. Giblin's first Administration, 1878 ; Premier and Chief Secretary, Mar. 1887 to Aug. 1892 ; Leader of the Opposition in Legislative Council, 1892-94 ; member of the Executive Council ; a Magistrate for the Territory ; President of the Central Board of Health ; Chairman of Metropolitan Drainage Board ; Major commanding the Tasmanian Volunteer Rifle Regiment, 1880-84 ; Alderman of Hobart, 1868-69 ; one of the Delegates from Tasmania to the Federal Conventions held in Sydney, Adelaide, and Melbourne, 1891, 1897, 1898 ; one of the Representatives of Tasmania in the Federal Council of Australasia ; Treasurer in Sir E. Braddon's Ministry since 1894 - 99 ; member for North Hobart, 1894-99 ; one of the Australian Delegates to London 1900, in connection with the Commonwealth Bill of Australia ; Postmaster-General, Commonwealth of Australia, 1903-4 ; late Minister without Portfolio ; Agent-General for Tasmania in London, 1899-1900 ; retired from public life, 1910. *Address:* Hobart, Tasmania. *(Died 21 Dec. 1919.)*

FYSON, Rt. Rev. Philip Kemball, D.D. ; *b.* 1846 ; *m.* 1874, Eleanor Furley of Hull ; five *s.* four *d.* *Educ.:* Christ's Coll., Camb. 1st class Classical Tripos, 1870. Ordained 1871 ; missionary, C.M.S. Japan, 1874-96 ; Bishop of Hokkaido, N. Japan, 1896-1908. *Address:* Sutton Valence, Maidstone.
(Died 30 Jan. 1928.)

G

GADOW, Hans Friedrich, Ph.D., Hon. M.A. Cantab. ; F.R.S. 1892 ; Strickland Curator since 1884 and Reader in Morphology of Vertebrates, Cambridge University, *b.* Pomerania 8 Mar. 1855 ; *e. s.* of late M. L. Gadow, Inspector Royal Forests, Prussia ; *m.* Clara Maud, *e. d.* of late Sir George Edward Paget, K.C.B., F.R.S., Regius Professor of Physic, Cambridge. *Educ.:* Frankfurt - on - Oder ; Berlin, Jena and Heidelberg Universities. British Museum, Natural History Department, 1880-82. *Publications:* In Northern Spain, 1897 ; A Classification of Vertebrata, 1898 ; The Last Link by E. Haeckel, 1898 ; Through Southern Mexico, 1908 ; vol. Aves in Bronn's Animal Kingdom ; vol. Amphibia and Reptiles, Camb. Nat. Hist. ; The Wanderings of Animals ; and papers in Royal Society Philosophical Transactions and other scientific periodicals. *Address:* Museum of Zoology, Cambridge ; Cleramendi, Great Shelford. *(Died 16 May 1928.)*

GADSBY, W. H., R.B.A. *Address:* 5 Carleton Road, Tufnell Park, N.
(Died 15 Oct. 1924.)

GADSDEN, Edward Holroyd, I.S.O. 1914 ; *b.* 21 Aug. 1859 ; *s.* of late Maj.-General Frederick Gadsden, Madras Staff Corps ; *m.* 1885, Hester Sinclair, *d.* of George Hamnett, C.D.E., Inspector General of Registration, Madras ; three *s.* two *d.* *Educ.:* Monmouth Grammar School. Joined the Madras Police for special service in Rumpa, 1879 ; Assist. Superintendent Police, 1883-86 ; Services transferred to the Jail Department, 1886 ; Superintendent Central Jail, Coimbatore, 1898-1914 ; Inspector General of Prisons, Madras, 1914 ; retired, 1918 ; awarded Delhi Durbar medal in 1912. *Address:* Commercial Bank of Tasmania, Latrobe, Tas. *(Died 17 Feb. 1920.)*

GAFFNEY, Thomas Burke, C.E., I.S.O. 1903 ; *b.* 23 Jan. 1839 ; *s.* of Edward Gaffney, C.E., late Sub-Commissioner of Valuation in Ireland, and Bridget Burke of Bekan, Co. Mayo ; *m.* 1885, Joan, *d.* of P. O'Donnell, High Constable of Glenquin, Killeedy, Co. Limerick ; six *s.* two *d.* *Educ.:* Catholic University, Dublin. Served his apprenticeship to his father ; began in 1855 and completed his career in the Valuation and Boundary Survey Department (Ireland) ; during the last twelve years of his service was chief of the technical branch of that service ; retired under the 65 rule, 1904. *Address:* 23 Waterloo Road, Dublin. *(Died 1 April 1927.)*

GAGE, Hon. Lyman Judson, President of the United States Trust Company of New York City, 1902 - 6 ; *b.* 28 June 1836 ; *m.* 2nd, 1909, Mrs. Francis Ballon. *Educ.:* common school ; Rome (N.Y.) Academy. LL.D. Beliot College, Wis. ; LL.D. (Hon.) New York University, 1903 ; banker and financier ; in 1858 book-keeper and in 1868 cashier, Merchants' Loan and Trust Co., Chicago ; cashier, 1st National Bank, Chicago, 1868 ; Vice.-Pres. and General Manager, 1882 ; President, 1891 ; Secretary of the Treasury, 1897 - 1902 ; was three times Pres. American Bankers' Association ; first Pres. and organiser of Chicago Clearing-House Association ; first Pres. and organiser of Chicago Civic Federation ; devoted to municipal reform ; first Pres. of World's Columbian Exposition at Chicago. *Publications:* contributor to popular and technical magazines; pamphlets on money questions. *Address:* San Diego, California. (*Died Jan. 1927.*)

GAGE, Sir William James, Kt., *cr.* 1918; publisher; *s.* of Andrew Gage and Mary Jane Grafton; *b.* Peel County, Ontario, 1849; *m.* 1880, Ina, *d.* of David Burnside, F.E.I.S.; four *d. Educ.:* Brampton High School and Toronto Normal School (First-Class Certificate). Taught for several years; entered into partnership with Adam Miller & Co., Publishers, 1874; on death of Mr. Miller, 1876, became head of Firm; later changed to W. J. Gage & Co., Ltd.; President, Educational Book Co. of Toronto, and Kinleith Paper Mills, Ltd., St. Catherines Ont.; Vice-President, Chartered Trust and Executor Company; Chairman, Executive Committee of Toronto Branch, Victorian Order of Nurses; Founder and President of National Sanatorium Association, controlling Muskoka Cottage Sanatorium and Muskoka Free Hospital for Consumptives near Gravenhurst; Chairman of Toronto Free Hospital for Consumptives; also the Queen Mary Hospital for consumptive children; originated and successfully established in 1912 The King Edward Memorial Fund of One Million Dollars for Consumptives; President of the Toronto Board of Trade in 1910; organised and became First President of Associated Boards of Trade of Ontario, 1911; Delegate to 6th Chamber of Commerce in Australia, 1911; Knight of Grace of St. John, 1913; contributed with his wife one hundred thousand dollars for the establishment of The Ina Grafton Homes for the benefit of widows and children of Canadian soldiers, 1916; Hon. Degree of LL.D. was conferred by Mount Allison University for educational and philanthropic work, 1917. *Recreation:* golf. *Address:* Wychwood Park, Toronto, Canada. *Clubs:* National, York, Lambton, Toronto.
(*Died 14 Jan. 1921.*)

GAIMES, John Austin, D.S.O. 1918; *s.* of Henry Austin Gaimes; *b.* 1886. *Educ.:* Tonbridge School; entered H.M.S. Britannia, 1901; Lieut.-Comdr. 1916. *Address:* c/o Admiralty, S.W.1. (*Died 20 Jan. 1921.*)

GAINER, Canon Harry, Canon of the Cathedral, Georgetown, Guiana, since 1908; *b.* 1858; *s.* of late E. J. Gainer of Gloucester; unmarried. *Educ.:* Grammar School, Gloucester; St. Augustine's College, Canterbury. Ordained 1882, curate of the Cathedral, Georgetown, Guiana, 1883; Curate of St. Philip's, Georgetown, 1883-85; perpetual Curate of St. Mary's on the East Coast Demerara, 1885; Vicar of Enmore, 1892, and Rural Dean of Demerara, British Guiana, 1905; Secretary to the Synod of the Diocese for 14 years; retired on pension, 1914. *Publications:* Editor of the Diocesan Magazine for about 10 years, and as Secretary was responsible for Diocesan Synod Report for many years. *Recreations:* ecclesiastical architecture, church music, croquet. *Address:* Greenfield House, Greenfield, East Coast Demerara.
(*Died 2 May 1920.*)

GAINSBOROUGH, 3rd Earl of, *cr.* 1841; **Charles William Francis Noel**, J.P. Cos. of Gloucester and Worcester; J.P., D.L. Co. of Rutland. Bt. 1781; Baron Barham, 1805; Viscount Campden, Baron Noel, 1841. Lt. 10th Hussars, retired 1876; *b.* 20 Oct. 1850; *s.* of Charles George, 2nd Earl and Lady Ida Adelaide Harriet Augusta Hay, *d.* of 17th Earl of Erroll; *S.* father, 1881; *m.* 1st, 1876, Augusta Mary Catherine (*d.* 1877), *e. d.* of late Robert Berkeley, Spetchley; 2nd, 1880, Mary, *d.* of James Arthur Dease, Turbotston, Co. Westmeath; two *s.* two *d. Educ.:* Oscott Roman Catholic Coll. *Heir: s.* Viscount Campden. *Address:* Exton Park, Oakham. *T.:* Oakham 53. *Clubs:* Junior United Service, Marylebone Cricket. (*Died 17 April 1926.*)
388

GAINSBOROUGH, 4th Earl of, *cr.* 1841; **Arthur Edward Joseph Noel**, O.B.E. 1919; T.D. 1919; Bt. 1781; Baron Barham, 1805; Viscount Campden, Baron Noel, 1841; Major, the Gloucestershire Regt. (T.A.R.); J.P. Co. Rutland; *b.* 30 June 1884; *e. s.* of 3rd Earl and Mary, *d.* of James Arthur Dease, Turbotston, Co. Westmeath; *S.* father, 1926; *m.* 1915, Alice Mary, *e. d.* of Edward Eyre, Gloucester House, Park Lane, W.1; one *s.* one *d. Educ.:* Downside; Exeter College, Oxford. Private Chamberlain of Sword and Cape to the late Pope and to Pope Pius XI.; President of the Amateur Gymnastic Association; Vice-President British Olympic Association; Attaché to the British Legations at Christiania and Stockholm, 1908-12, and to the British Embassy at Washington, U.S.A., 1913-14, when he resigned; accompanied Dr. Charles Harriss's Musical Festival throughout the British Empire, 1911; served European War, France, 1915; D.A.M.S. Forces in Great Britain, Horse Guards, 1917-19; mentioned for valuable service during the War; organised, with Dr. Harriss, Imperial Concert of 10,000 voices in Hyde Park on Empire Day, 1919. *Recreations:* hunting, shooting, lawn tennis. *Heir: s.* Viscount Campden. *Address:* Exton Park, Oakham, Rutland; 30 Pont Street, S.W.1. *T.:* Ken. 4534. *Clubs:* White's, Turf, Beefsteak, M.C.C.
(*Died 27 Aug. 1927.*)

GAIRDNER, Rev. Canon W. H. Temple, B.A., Missionary of the Church Missionary Society, Cairo; *b.* Ardrossan, Ayrshire, 31 July 1873; *s.* of late Sir W. T. Gairdner, K.C.B., M.D., LL.D., F.R.S.; *m.* Margaret Dundas, *d.* of late J. O. Mitchell, LL.D., Glasgow; three *s.* two *d. Educ.:* St. Ninian's, Moffat; Rossall; Trinity College, Oxford (Exhibitioner). Missionary at Cairo, Egypt, 1899; Canon-Missioner of the Pro-Cathedral, Cairo. *Publications:* Life of D. M. Thornton; The Rebuke of Islam; Edinburgh, 1910; the Mishkât al Anwâr of al-Ghazzâli, an Introduction and Translation; The Phonetics of Arabic; Egyptian Colloquial Arabic; Arabic Syntax; Bible Dramas (Joseph and his Brothers; Pass-over-night; Saul and Stephen; King Hezekiah, a Tragical Drama). *Recreation:* music. *Address:* C.M.S., Boulac, Cairo. *T.A.:* Jardinier, Cairo. (*Died 22 May 1928.*)

GAISFORD, Brig.-Gen. Richard Boileau, C.B. 1911; C.M.G. 1900; *b.* 14 Dec. 1854; *s.* of late Rev. S. H. Gaisford, Cowthorpe Rectory, Wetherby, Yorkshire, and *g.s.* of late Joseph Yarker, of Ulverston; *m.* Elsy, *d.* of late Major-General A. H. Lindsay, C.B., R.H.A.; one *s.* one *d. Educ.:* Haileybury College; St. John's College Oxford (B.A. Hons. 1876); R.M.C. Sandhurst, 1877; passed Staff College, 1893. Entered 21st Royal Scots Fusiliers, 1878; Adjutant, 1885-1890; Brig.-Maj., Shorncliffe, 1896-99; D.A.A.G. South Africa, 1899; Assistant Adj.-General, Headquarters, South Africa, 1900-1902; selected to command 3rd Battalion Royal Fusiliers, 1903-1907; A.Q.M.G. Scottish Command, 1908-11; was an Inspector of Infantry with temp. rank of Brig.-Gen. 1914-16; Hon. Brig.-Gen., 1917; served Boer War, 1881; Burmese Expedition, 1886-87 (medal with clasp); Boer War, 1899-1902 (despatches, Queen's medal four clasps, King's medal two clasps, C.M.G.); European War, France, 1917 (British Victory and War Medal). *Address:* Conynger Hurst, Ulverston, Lancashire. *Club:* Naval and Military. (*Died 25 Sept. 1924.*)

GAJJUMAL, Rai Sahib, Lala, I.S.O. 1911; *b.* 1857. Descended from a respectable family of Kapur Khatris of Peshawar. Father's name, Lala Jaggan Nath. *Educ.:* C. Mission School, Peshawar. Passed Matriculation Ex., Calcutta University, 1877; entered Govt. Service as Record Keeper Commissioner's Office, 1879;

joined the Khyber Agency as H.C., 1880, and accompanied the Khyber Column during the 2nd Afghan war, 1879-80, and the Tirah Campaign of 1897-98 ; was present in the Fort at Landi Kotal when the Afghans attacked the Fort, and throughout the disturbances of 1908 (medals with clasps); title of Rai Sahib, 1910; coronation medal in 1911 ; retired 1912, on completion of 33 years of active service. *Address:* Peshawar City, India.

GALDOS, Benito Perez, Spanish novelist ; Member of Spanish Academy and Deputy in the Cortes ; *b.* Las Palmas, Canary Islands, 1845. *Educ.:* Madrid. Holds Medal of the Royal Society of Literature, Great Britain, 1917, as "most distinguished living representative of Spanish Literature." *Publications:* (novels, 1st, 2nd, 3rd, and 4th series, Episodios nacionales, 1873-1907) ; La Fontana de Oro, 1871; El Audaz ; Doña Perfecta, 1876 ; Gloria (2 vols.) ; Marianela ; La familia de Léon Roch (12 vols.) ; La Sombra ; La Desheredada, 1881 ; El Doctor Centano ; El Amigo Manso, 1883 ; Tormento ; La de Bringas ; Lo Pronibido ; Fortunana y Jacinta (4 vols.), 1887 ; Miau ; La Incognita ; Realidad ; Angel Guerra (3 vols.), 1890 ; Tristana ; La Loca de la casa ; Torquemada ; Nazarin ; Halma ; Misericordia ; El Abuelo, 1898 ; El Caballero Encantado ; Casandra ; (Plays) Realidad ; La de San Quintin ; Los Condenados ; Voluntad ; La Fiera ; Electra, Marincha, Bárbara; Amor y Ciencia ; Pedro Minio ; Casandra (drama). *Address:* Madrid, Hilarión Eslava 5, hotel.
(Died 4 Jan. 1920.)

GALER, John Maxcey, I.S.O. 1908 ; *b.* Rochester, Kent, 10 June 1839 ; *s.* of late John Galer ; *m.* 1866, Louise Jane, *d.* of late Henry Hughes Allen of H.M. Civil Service ; five *s.* two *d.* *Educ.:* private schools, Rochester. Appointed after competition to a Clerkship in H.M. Stationery Office, 1859 ; Accountant in H.M. Stationery Office, 1892-1904. *Recreations:* music and horticulture. *Address:* 110 Croxted Road, West Dulwich. *(Died 16 Nov. 1919.)*

GALLAGHER, Sir James Michael, Kt., *cr.* 1917 ; *s.* of Patrick Gallagher, of Kilty Clogher, Co. Leitrim ; *b.* 1860; *m.* Annie, *d.* of John O'Brien, Limerick. Lord Mayor of Dublin, 1916. *Address:* 149 Lower Baggott Street, Dublin. *(Died 2 Jan. 1926.)*

GALLAGHER, Rt. Rev. John, D.D., R.C. Bishop of Goulburn since 1900 ; *b.* Castlederg, Co. Tyrone, 4 July 1846. *Educ.* St. Patrick's College, Maynooth. Ordained, 1869 ; arrived at Goulburn, 1870; engaged in missionary work for first four years ; President St. Patrick's College for fourteen years ; Permanent Rector of Wagga Wagga, 1887; Coadjutor Bishop, 1895. *Publications:* Numerous lectures, sermons, addresses, and essays, published in newspapers, magazines, and pamphlets. *Recreations:* incessant travelling by train and coach for official duties in his extensive diocese and to other dioceses and cities for special functions occupy nearly all his time. *Address:* Bishop's House, Goulburn, N.S. Wales. *T.* 16.
(Died 26 Nov. 1923.)

GALLAHER, Thomas, J.P. ; Founder and Head of Gallaher, Limited, tobacco manufacturers ; Member of Tariff Commission ; *b.* 1840. *Address:* Belfast. *T.A.:* Tobacco, Belfast. *T.:* 6646 and 6647. *(Died May 1927.)*

GALLETTI DI CADILHAC, The Countess (Hon. Margaret Isabella Collier); author ; *b.* 1846; *d.* of 1st Baron Monkswell ; *m.* 1873, Count Arturo Galletti di Cadilhac, Colonel in the Reserve, and Deputy in Italian Parliament (*d.* 1912) ; two *s.* one *d.* *Publications:* The Camorristi and Other Tales, 1882 ; Our Home on the Adriatic, 1886 ; Prince Peerless, 1886 ; Babel, 1887 ; Rachel and Maurice, 1892 ; Annals of an Italian Village, 1896. *Address:* 4 Hillside, S. Brent, Devon.
(Died 27 June 1928.)

GALLIENI, Joseph, général de division ; Gouverneur militaire de Paris et Commandant en chef de l'armée de Paris ; *b.* St. Beat, Hautte Garonne, le 24 avril 1849 ; *m.* 1882, Mlle. Savelli ; one *s.* one *d.* *Educ.:* Prytanée militaire de la Flèche, Saint Cyr. Lieutenant pendant la guerre de 1870-71 ; Commandements aux colonies : Soudan, Tonkin, Madagascar ; Gouverneur général de Madagascar, 1896-1905 ; Général commandant le XIVe Corps; Gouverneur militaire de Lyon ; membre du Conseil supérieur de la Guerre ; Grand Croix de la Légion d'honneur ; medaille militaire ; membre correspondant de l'Academie des Sciences ; membre d'honneur de nombreuses Sociétés scientifiques, géographiques ; titulaire de la grande médaille d'or de la Société de Géographie et de nombreuses autres médailles de Sociétés scientifiques et de Chambres de Commerce. *Publications:* Voyage au Soudan Français, 1880-81 ; Deux Campagnes au Soudan Français, 1886-88 ; Trois Colonnes au Tonkin, 1894-95 ; Rapport sur Madagascar, 1896-99 ; Le Guide de l'immigrant, 1898 ; Rapport sur la pacification, l'organisation et l'administration de Madagascar, 1896-1905 ; Neuf ans à Madagascar, 1908. *Recreations:* marche à pied, lectures ; mèmoires et voyages, collection d'objets des colonies. *Address:* La Gabelle, St. Raphael, Var, France. *Club:* Cercle militaire.
(Died 27 May 1916.)

GALLOP, Rev. Edward Jordan, M.A. ; Hon. Canon of St. Albans : *b.* 1850 ; *s.* of John Gallop, of Rio de Janeiro and New York, afterwards of Streatham, Surrey ; *m.* 1874, Julia, *d.* of E. S. Judkins ; three *s.* one *d.* *Educ.:* North America ; Germany ; King's College, London ; Lincoln College, Oxford. Vicar of St. Paul, Hemel Hempstead, 1878-1905 ; Chaplain, St. Margaret's School, Bushey, 1906-17. *Address:* Denford, St. Albans. *T.:* St. Albans 158. *M.:* XN 8288. *Clubs:* Royal Societies, Royal Automobile. *(Died 26 April 1928.)*

GALLOWAY, 11th Earl of, *cr.* 1623 ; **Randolph Henry Stewart**. Lord Garlies, 1607 ; Bt. 1627 ; Baron Stewart of Garlies (Gt. Brit.), 1796 ; *b.* Galloway House, 14 Oct. 1836, *s.* of 9th Earl and Lady Harriet Blanche Somerset, 7th *d.* of 6th Duke of Beaufort ; *S.* brother 1901 ; *m.* 1891, Amy Mary Pauline, *d.* of late Anthony John Cliffe of Bellevue, Co. Wexford ; two *s.* (the 2nd *s.*, Lieut. Hon. Keith Stewart, Black Watch, Royal Highlanders, killed in action at the head of his platoon, at Aubers Ridge, 9 May 1915). Formerly Captain 42nd Royal Highlanders ; served Crimea, 1855 (medal with clasp, for Sebastopol, Turkish medal); Indian Mutiny, 1857-59 (medal with clasp, for Lucknow). Owns about 69,000 acres. *Heir:* *s.* Lord Garlies. *Address:* Cumloden, Newton-Stewart, N.B. ; Garlies Lodge, Bargrennan, N.B. ; Glen Trool Lodge, Bargrennan, N.B. *T.A.:* Randolph, Newton-Stewart, Scotland *M.:* LB 7843. *Clubs:* Army and Navy, Bachelors'. *(Died 7 Feb. 1920.)*

GALLOWAY, Admiral Arthur Archibald Campbell; *b.* Delhi, 30 June 1855 ; *s.* of A. Galloway, Magistrate in Indian Civil Service, who was *s.* of Major-General Sir A. Galloway, Chairman East India Company ; mother was of the Campbells of Melfort ; *m.* Evelyn Royston, 2nd *d.* of Edward Rawson-Walker, late H.M. Consul Philippine Islands ; two *s.* one *d.* *Educ.:* Carshalton House, Carshalton ; Burney's Naval Academy. Joined navy, 1869 ; Lieut. 1876 ; Commander, 1891 ; Captain, 1898 ; Rear-Admiral, 1907 ; Vice-Admiral, 1913 ; Admiral, retired 1916. A.D.C. to King Edward VII., 1906-7 ; served in Egypt, 1882 ; saved lives from drowning in 1873, 1877, 1882, 1885, 1911 (2) ; seen much service in revolutions ; selected to command Portsmouth Barracks after the mutiny, 1906 ; has commanded 11 ships, 2 establishments, and 1 squadron. *Recreations:* formerly boxing, row-

389

ing, football, now cycling, swimming, and rowing. *Address:* Barsham House, Bedford. *Club:* Junior United Service. *(Died 12 Feb. 1918.)*

GALLOWAY, Sir James, K.B.E., *cr.* 1918; C.B. 1917; M.D., LL.D. (1919), F.R.C.P., F.R.C.S.; Colonel A.M.S.; Senior Physician, and Lecturer on Medicine, Charing Cross Hospital; Censor, Royal College of Physicians; Consulting Physician, Metropolitan Asylums Board; Examiner in Medicine, University of London; late Consulting Physician, 1st and 2nd Armies, B.E.F., and Chief Commissioner for Medical Services, Ministry of National Service; Examiner Conjoint Board, Royal Colleges of Physicians and Surgeons, England; Member Examining Board, Royal Navy, Medical Service; *b.* Calcutta, *s.* of James Galloway, Calcutta, and Jeanne Hermina de Villeneuve; *m.* 1898, Jessie Hermina Sawers; two *s.* two *d. Educ.:* Chanonry School, Aberdeen; Aberdeen University. A.M. 1883; M.D. 1892 (Highest Honours). Subsequently became a Fellow of the Royal Colleges of Physicians, and of Surgeons in London, and an Examiner in Medicine in the University of Aberdeen. After a period of study and of teaching at the London Hospital, was appointed to the Medical Staff of Charing Cross Hospital (1894), and engaged in the teaching and practice of medicine. After the South African War, appointed to serve on the Advisory Board for Army Medical Services. Served with 1st and 2nd Armies, B.E.F. *Publications:* Morton Lecture on Cancer, Royal College of Surgeons, England; late editor of the British Journal of Dermatology; numerous papers in Scientific and Medical Journals; Story of Saint Mary Roncevall; Eleanor of Castile; Historical Sketches of Old Charing, 1914. *Recreation:* field studies. *Address:* 54 Harley Street, W.1. *T.:* 1148 Paddington.

(Died 18 Oct. 1922.)

GALLOWAY, Maj.-Gen. John Mawby Clossey, Colonel, 27th Light Cavalry, Indian army; J.P. Co. Southampton; *b.* 19 April 1840; *s.* of Major Thomas Leech Lennox Galloway, 10th Foot, and Isabella Ann Coffin; *m.* Emilie, *d.* of Aylmer G. W. Harris, Mysore and Nagpore Commissions; three *s.* one *d. Educ.:* Cheltenham Coll. Served Indian Mutiny, 1858-59 (medal with clasp); Burmese War, 1886 (medal with clasp); granted the Distinguished Service Reward, 1894. *Address:* Egmore, East Cliffe, Bournemouth. *Clubs:* Bournemouth, Bournemouth Golf

(Died 25 Oct. 1916.)

GALLOWAY, Sir William, Kt., *cr.* 1924; Hon. D.Sc. Wales; F.G.S.; Hon. M.I.M.E.; *s.* of late William Galloway, J.P., of Paisley; *m.* 1st, Christiana Maud Mary, *d.* of late W. F. Gordon, of Milrig, Ayrshire; two *s.*; 2nd, Mary Gwenap Douglas, *d.* of late Captain Wood, R.M.L.I., of Nunlands, Surrey. *Educ.:* private school; University of Giessen; Bergakademie, Freiberg; University College, London. Formerly H.M. Inspector of Mines in the West of Scotland and South Wales Districts; past Professor of Mining in the University College of South Wales and Monmouthshire; Fellow of the Institute of Directors; Past President and Hon. Member S. Wales Institute of Engineers; a member of the Panel of Referees appointed under the Coal Mines Act, 1911; one of the Central Examiners appointed by the Board for Mining Examinations; External Examiner in Mining for the University of Birmingham, the Treforest School of Mines, etc.; author of the coal-dust theory of great colliery explosions; investigated the causes and mode of occurrence of colliery explosions; suggested the use of stone-dust as a means of preventing great colliery explosions, 1896; again suggested in 1908, after which it was universally adopted; made series of experiments with different kinds of explosives fired into mixtures of gas, air, and coaldust for the

Royal Commission on Accidents in Mines; determined the relation between height of firedamp cap and proportion of firedamp in the air of mines; invented the guides for sinking pits; presented with the Shaw gold medal by the Royal Society of Arts, a special gold medal and later an illuminated album by the South Wales Institute of Engineers, the medal of the Institution of Mining Engineers, and his portrait and later a gold watch by the Monmouthshire and South Wales Coalowners' Assoc. in recognition of his researches into the action of Coaldust in Colliery Explosions; described External Capillarity in 1926. *Publications:* twenty-one papers (four in collaboration with R. H. Scott, F.R.S.) on researches as to the causes of colliery explosions, eight of which were read before, and published by the Royal Society; paper on the Flying Fish; nineteen papers, mostly on mining and kindred subjects; course of lectures delivered before, and published by the South Wales Institute of Engineers; four of the subjects in Practical Coal-Mining, etc. *Recreation:* bicycling. *Address:* 17 Park Place, Cardiff. *T.:* 3907 Cardiff. *Club:* Athenæum.

(Died 2 Nov. 1927.)

GALLWEY, Col. Edmond Joseph, C.B. 1900; *b.* 7 Feb. 1850; *s.* of late H. Gallwey, J.P., of Tramore, Co. Waterford; *m.* 1871, Augusta, *d.* of J. Burtchaell, J.P., of Carbally, Co. Clare. Entered 18th Light Infantry, 1870; Capt. 1880; Major, 1886; Lieut.-Col. commanding 2nd Somerset Lt. Infantry, 1898; Col. 13th Regt. Dist. 1902; Zululand, 1877-79, including Kambulu Hill and Ulundi (medal with clasp); S. Africa, 1899-1902 (Queen's medal 5 clasps, King's, 2 clasps); Tugela Heights and Relief of Ladysmith (C.B. despatches 3 times); commanding 13th Regimental District, 1902-5; Col. in charge of Records, Western Counties, 1906; retired, 1907; 11 District, 1915-18 (mentioned). *Recreations:* shooting, stag-hunting, rackets, cricket, golf. *Club:* Junior United Service.

(Died 11 May 1927.)

GALLWEY, Sir Ralph William Frankland Payne-, 3rd Bt., *cr.* 1812; formerly Lt. Rifle Brigade; *b.* 19 Aug. 1848; *e. s.* of 2nd Bt. and Emily Anne, 3rd *d.* of Sir Robert Frankland-Russell, Bt.; *s.* father 1861; *m.* Edith Alice, *d.* of T. M. Usborne, Clifton, Co. Cork, 1877; one *s.* four *d. Educ.:* Eton. *Publications:* The Fowler in Ireland, 1882; The Book of Duck Decoys, 1886; Letters to Young Shooters, 3 vols., 1891-96; The Cross-Bow, 1903; The Mystery of Maria Stella, Lady Newborough, 1907; The History of the George of Charles 1st, 1908; High Pheasants in Theory and in Practice, 1913. *Recreations:* shooting, golf, cricket, fishing, well known as experienced and enthusiastic wild-fowler. *Address:* Thirkleby Park, Thirsk. *Clubs:* Carlton; Yorkshire, York.

(Died 24 Nov. 1916.)

GALLWEY, Capt. William Thomas Frankland Payne-, M.V.O. 1908; Grenadier Guards; *o. s.* of Sir R. W. P. Gallwey, 3rd Bt.; *b.* 5 Mar. 1881; entered Army, 1900; Capt. 1908; served S. Africa 1901-2 (medal, 2 clasps); Coronation medal. *Address:* Thirkleby Park, Thirsk.

(Died 14 Sept. 1914 (Presumed).)

GALPIN, Rev. Arthur John, D.D. Oxford; Hon. Canon of Canterbury Cathedral since 1910; Rector of Saltwood, Hythe, since 1910; Member of Kent Education Committee since 1911; *b.* Dorchester, Dorset, 3 March 1861; *s.* of John Galpin, J.P.; *m.* 1900. Millicent Jane, *d.* of late Rev. F. H. Hichens, Hon. Canon of Canterbury; one *s.* one *d. Educ.:* Sherborne School; Trin. Coll., Oxford (Senior Scholar, 1st Class Classical Mods., 1880, 1st Class Final School of Lit. Hum., 1883); Assistant Private Secretary to Lord Lansdowne, Governor-General of Canada, and Tutor to his sons, 1883-85; Classical Lecturer, Trinity College, Oxford, 1886-87; Assistant

Master, Marlborough College, 1887-96; House-master, 1893-96; Headmaster, King's School, Canterbury, 1896-1910. *Recreations:* music, motoring, archæology. *Address:* Saltwood Rectory, Hythe, Kent. *M.:* KE 7069.
(*Died 2 Oct. 1926.*)

GALSWORTHY, Sir Edwin Henry; Kt., *cr.* 1887; J.P., D.L.; late Chairman of Metropolitan Asylums Board, resigned 1901; *b.* 24 Dec. 1831; *m.* 1st, 1858, Eleanor (*d.* 1872), *d.* of late Charles Pennington, Manchester; 2nd, Laura, *d.* of late John Oakes, Manchester, 1873; five *s.* three *d. Educ.:* City of London School. *Address:* 26 Sussex Place, Regent's Park, N.W.1. *T.:* Paddington 147.
(*Died 21 Dec. 1920.*)

GAMBLE, Admiral Edward Harpur, R.N.; C.B. 1902; *b.* 6 Sep. 1849; *m.* 1904, Charlotte Mainwaring, 3rd *d.* of W. H. Prance. Served Egypt, 1882 (medal, Khedive's star); Gambia, 1894 (despatches, medal with clasp); Brass River, 1895 (medal). *Address:* Rowe House, Vernham Dean, nr. Hungerford.
(*Died 18 Nov. 1925.*)

GAMBLE, Frederick William, D.Sc., 1900; F.R.S., 1907; F.Z.S., Professor of Zoology, University of Birmingham, since 1909; late Assistant-Director of the Zoological Laboratories, and Lecturer in Zoology, University of Manchester; President of Zoology Section, British Association. Toronto, 1924; *b.* Manchester, 13 July 1869; *e. surv. s.* of late William Gamble and late Mrs. Gamble of Brantfell, Arnside, Westmorland; *m.* 1904, Ellen, *d.* of Rev. J. M. Bamford, Aruside. *Educ.:* Manchester Grammar School; Manchester and Leipzig Universities. 1st Class Hons. B.Sc. 1891; Bishop Berkeley Fellowship, 1892; M.Sc., 1893; Junior Lecturer and Demonstrator in Zoology, 1893; Senior Lecturer and Demonstrator, 1895. *Publications:* Animal Life; The Animal World; editor of 5th, 6th, and 7th editions of Practical Zoology, by Marshall and Hurst; author of many papers in the Transactions and Proceedings of the Royal Society, the Quarterly Journal of Microscopical Science, and other scientific journals. *Recreation:* gardening. *Address:* The University, Birmingham.
(*Died 14 Sept. 1926.*)

GAMBLE, James Sykes, C.I.E. 1899; F.R.S., F.L.S.; retired officer of the Indian Forest Service; *b.* London, 2 July 1847; *s.* of late Harpur Gamble, M.D., R.N.; *m.* 1911, Gertrude, *d.* of late Rev. A. S. Latter. *Educ.:* Royal Naval School, New Cross; Magdalen College, Oxford (M.A.); Ecole Nationale des Eaux et Forêts, Nancy, France. Entered Indian Forest Department, 1871; last appointment, Conservator of Forests, School Circle, N.W.P. and Oudh, and Director of the Imperial Forest School, Dehra Dun, India; for some time Fellow of the University of Madras; Jury Medal and Diploma, Paris International Exposition, 1900; Barclay Medal, Asiatic Society of Bengal, 1915; Examiner in Forestry, University of Oxford, at various times and Lecturer on Indian Forest Botany. *Publications:* List of Trees, Shrubs, and Climbers of the Darjeeling District, Bengal (Ed. 1st 1877, 2nd 1895); A Manual of Indian Timbers (1st ed. 1881, 2nd ed. 1902); The Bambuseæ of British India (Ann. R. Bot. Gard., Calcutta, 1895); Materials for a Flora of the Malay Peninsula (with late Sir George King); Flora of the Madras Presidency. *Address:* Highfield, East Liss, Hants; *T.:* East Liss 10; 63 Kew Green, Surrey. *Club:* Athenæum.
(*Died 16 Oct. 1925.*)

GAMLEY, Henry Snell, R.S.A. 1920; A.R.S.A., 1908; R.B.S. 1926; sculptor; *b.* Logie-Pert, Craigo, 1865; *m.* 1898, Margaret, *e. d.* of Alexander Hogg, Carnoustie; one *d.* one *s. Educ.:* James Gillespie's School, Edinburgh; Royal Institution, Edinburgh. National

Gold and Silver Medals. *Works:* Ideal works: The Whisper, A Message to the Sea; Inspiration and Achievement, for Usher Hall, Edinburgh; St. Andrew, for Grand Lodge of Scotland. Statue of His Majesty King Edward, Holyrood Palace; War Memorial, Cupar Fife; War Memorial, Montrose; War Memorial, St. Giles' Cathedral, Edinburgh. Portraits: J. B. Dunlop, Joseph Laing Waugh, John Geddie, Sir William Marris, Charles Murray, LL.D., Medallions: William Murdoch, Alexander Anderson, Surfaceman, Sir Alexander R. Simpson, Lord Salvesen, Medallion, Clarinda. *Recreation:* music. *Address:* The Studio, 7 Hope Street Lane, Edinburgh.
(*Died 24 Oct. 1928.*)

GANGA RAM, Rai Bahadur Sir Lala, Kt., *cr.* 1922; C.I.E. 1903; M.V.O. 1911; Rai Bahadur, M.I.M.E., M.I.C.E.; *b.* May 1851; *m.*; three *s. Educ.:* Thomason College. Entered India Public Works Department, 1873; Executive Engineer, 1883; Superintendent Coronation Durbar Works, Delhi, 1903; retired, 1903; Superintending Engineer Patiala State; retired, 1911; Consulting Engineer, Delhi Durbar, 1911; patentee slide rule, bricks for wells. *Publication:* Pocket-Book of Engineering. *Address:* Lahore. *T.A.:* Ganganivas, Lahore. *M.:* P 340.
(*Died 10 July 1927.*)

GANNON, Hon. James Conley, K.C., M.L.C., New South Wales since 1904; *b.* 1860. Called to Bar, N.S.W., 1887; Attorney-General, 1907. *Address:* 165 Phillip Street, Sydney, N.S.W.
(*Died 1 Oct. 1924.*)

GANT, Hon. Tetley, C.M.G. 1918; M.A. Oxon; President of the Legislative Council of Tasmania, 1907-26; Chancellor of the Univ. of Tasmania, 1914-24; *b.* Bradford, Yorkshire, 19 July 1856; *s.* of James Greaves Tetley Gant; *m.* Frances Amy, *d.* of Lavington Roope, of Hobart; one *d. Educ.:* Rugby;. St. John's College, Oxford. Called to Bar, Inner Temple, 1884; elected to the Legislative Council of Tasmania for Buckingham, 1901; Chairman of Committees of the Council, 1904-7. *Club:* Tasmanian, Hobart.
(*Died 7 Feb. 1928.*)

GARDE, Engineer Captain Robert Boles, R.N (retired); C.B.E. 1919; Marine Engineer Superintendent S.E. & C Railway, Dover; *b.* 1863; 3rd *s.* of Dr. H. W. Garde, M.B., Timoleague, Co. Cork; *m.* 1899, Amy Ethel, *y. d.* of T. Richards, Mutley, Plymouth; no *c. Educ.:* Midleton College, Co. Cork. Joined H.M.S. Marlborough as Naval Engineering Student, 1879; spent the whole of life in Navy up to 1919; during European War was Admiralty Engineer Overseer at J. S. White & Co, Cowes, and later at Sunderland and Hartlepool districts (C.B.E.). *Recreations:* all sports, particularly cricket, shooting, and boat-sailing. *M.:* DL 473. (*Died 29 Oct. 1921.*)

GARDINER, Rev. Frederic Evelyn, Hon. Canon of Truro; Rector of Bishopsbourne, Kent, 1918-23; late Vicar of Holy Trinity, Folkestone. *Address.* 15 Castle Hill Avenue, Folkestone. (*Died 30 May 1928.*)

GARDINER, Frederick William, I.S.O. 1902; Clerk in the office of the Parliamentary Counsel, 1871-1914; *b.* 1849; *s.* of late W. Gardiner, of Tetbury. *Address:* 25 Malwood Road, Balham Hill, S.W. (*Died 24 April 1918.*)

GARDINER, James, M.P. (C.L.) Kinross and Western Perthshire, 1918-22, (N.L.) 1922-1923; *b.* near Crieff, 1860; *s.* of John Gardiner, Eastmill, and Harriet A. B. D. Allan; *m.* 1st, 1887, Elizabeth Maule (*d.* 1921), *d.* of John Christie, Engineer, Ruthvenvale; 2nd, 1922, Elizabeth, *y. d.* of late Daniel Christie, Mokameh, Bengal, and Drummondearnoch, Comrie. *Educ.:* Morrison's Academy, Crieff; privately. Director of Scottish Chamber of Agriculture; Hon. President of Scottish National Farmers' Union; Member of Ministry of Foods, Potato Advisory Committee; Member of Council National Institute of Agricultural Botany; Expert in Agricultural Plant Breeding and raiser of several of the most popular immune varieties of potatoes now in cultivation; J.P. Perthshire; keen on social and temperance reform; authority on practical agriculture in all its advanced branches. *Address:* Dargill, Crieff. *T.:* Crieff 133. *Clubs:* Scottish National Liberal, Edinburgh; Liberal, Glasgow.   *(Died 31 Dec. 1924.)*

GARDINER, Rev. Canon William; Vicar of Southbroom, Wilts, 1907-1918, Canon of Salisbury; Prebendary of Teignton Regis since 1910; Rural Dean of Avebury (Cannings Portion), 1906-19; Acting Chaplain to the Forces at Devizes; *b.* 24 March 1848; *s.* of Rev. R. Gardiner of Wellesford Manor and Bindon House, Somersetshire, and Augusta Elizabeth, *d.* of Robert Jackson of Swallowfield, Wellington, Somerset; *m.* 1873, Jessie, *d.* of Rev. William T. Redfern, Vicar of St. James, Taunton; two *s.* three *d.* *Educ.:* Taunton College School; private tuition; Exeter College, Oxford; B.D. Oxon; ad eundem M.A., T.C.D., and Member of the Senate. Captain Oxford University Volunteers; Grand Chaplain of English Freemasons, 1899; Vicar of St. George's Claines, Worcester, 1873; St. Mary's, Marlborough, 1887; Rural Dean of Marlborough, 1891-97; member of Worcester School Board; Hon. Secretary of Royal City and County of Worcester Nursing Institution, of Savernake Hospital, Wilts. *Publications:* Southbroom Catechisings on the Church Catechism; Benefice Record Book for Deanery of Cannings. *Recreation:* fishing. *Address:* St. Alban's Priory, Wallingford, Berks.   *(Died 10 April 1925.)*

GARDINER, Alice, M.A. Bristol; Associate of Newnham College, Cambridge, since 1893; Reader in Byzantine History in the University of Bristol since 1919; *b.* Hackney, 1854; *y. d.* of late Thomas Gardiner, of the Stock Exchange, and Ann, *d.* of Peter Pearse. *Educ.:* Laleham, Clapham Park, etc.; Newnham College, Cambridge (student, 1876-79). First Class in Historical Tripos; Assistant Mistress in the Girls' High School, Plymouth, 1880-82; Professor of Ancient and Modern History in Bedford College, London, 1883-84; Lecturer in History at Newnham College, Cambridge, 1884-1914; temporary lecturer in the University of Bristol, 1915-19; first Secretary of the University Association of Women Teachers; a Vice-President of the Historical Association; on Council of Royal Historical Society; Member of British Institute of Philosophical Studies. *Publications:* Synesius of Cyrene, Philosopher and Bishop; Friends of the Olden Time (for children); Rome the Middle of the World (a sequel to above); Julian, Emperor and Philosopher; Studies in John the Scot; The Conflict of Duties, and other Essays; Theodore of Studium, his Life and Times; Letters to a Godchild; Supplementary Chapter to English Translation of Professor Hans von Schubert's Church History; The Lascarids of Nicæa; Within our Limits; Chapter in the Faith and the War; article in History on some Episodes in the History of Mediæval Salonika; History of Sacrament in Relation to Thought and Progress; A Short History of Newnham College; various reviews. *Recreations:* country walking. *Address:* 3 Canynge Road, Clifton, Bristol *Clubs:* Ladies' University; Ladies', Clifton.   *(Died 11 Nov. 1927.)*

GARDINER, Sir Ernest, Kt *cr.* 1923; M.P. (C.) Wokingham Div. of Berks, 1901-18; Windsor Division, 1918-22; J.P.; *b.* 1846; *s.* of Joseph Goodwin Gardiner of Havering, Essex; *m.* 1st, 1878, Mary (*d.* 1903), *d.* of Wm. Peto of Cannon Court, Cookham, Berks; 2nd, 1910, Amy Inglis, *y. d.* of Lt.-Gen. Laurie, C.B. *Educ.:* Orsett House, Essex. Successor to Berkshire property of his uncle, John Silvester, Spencers, Maidenhead,

1864; J.P., Maidenhead, 1887; Mayor, Maidenhead, 1892-93; J.P., Berkshire, 1895; County Councillor, 1889; Alderman, 1898; Liveryman Drapers' Company, 1873; member of Court, 1895; Master of Company, 1901-2; yeoman. *Address:* Spencers, Maidenhead.   *(Died 7 Aug. 1925.)*

GARDNER, Ven. George Lawrence Harter; Mus. Bac. Oxon. *Educ.:* Cheltenham College; Corpus Christi, Cambridge (M.A.) Curate of St. Mary's, Nottingham, 1878-84; All Saints, Cheltenham, 1884-1911; Diocesan Chaplain to the Bishop of Birmingham, 1911; Archdeacon of Aston, 1913-20; Archdeacon of Cheltenham, 1920-24; Hon. Canon, Gloucester Cathedral, 1906-11-20; Hon. Canon, Birmingham Cathedral, 1911. *Publications:* Worship and Music; English Catholicism; joint Editor of a Manual of English Church Music. *Address:* The Deanery, Marlow, Bucks. *T.:* Marlow 29. *Club:* Church Imperial.   *(Died 20 Sept. 1925.)*

GARDNER, Rt. Hon. Sir James Tynte Agg, Kt., *cr.* 1916; P.C. 1924; M.P. (U.) Cheltenham since 1918; *b.* Cheltenham, 25 Nov. 1846; *e. s.* of late James Agg Gardner of Cheltenham and Emily Hopkyns Northey of Oving House, Bucks; unmarried. *Educ.:* Harrow; Trinity College, Camb. Barr. Inner Temple; contested Cheltenham, 1868, 1880, and 1906; M.P. (C.) Cheltenham, 1874, 1885, 1886, 1892, 1900, and 1911-18; J.P. Glos.; Lord of the Manor of Cheltenham. *Address:* Queen's Hotel, Cheltenham. *Clubs:* Carlton, St. James's, Garrick, Windham.   *(Died 9 Aug. 1928.)*

GARDNER, Sir Robert, Kt., *cr.* 1905; member of firm of Craig, Gardner, and Co., Chartered Accountants, of Dublin; *b.* 14 Apr. 1838; *s.* of late John Gardner, of Ballymoney, Co. Antrim; *m.* 1895, Norah Kathleen, *d.* of Captain P. L. Peacocke of Villaggio, Dalkey. *Educ.:* Ballynnoney. Is a J.P. for Dublin. *Address:* Ashley, Clyde Road, Dublin. *Clubs:* Royal Irish Yacht, Stephen's Green. Dublin.   *(Died 1920.)*

GARDNER, William, M.D., C.M.: Emeritus Professor of Gynæcology in McGill University, Montreal; Consulting Gynæcologist to the Royal Victoria Hospital; *b.* Province of Quebec, 1845; *e. s.* of William Gardner; *m.* Jane, *d.* of A. Cauth, of Montreal; no *c.* *Educ.:* McGill University, Montreal. Graduated with honours, 1867; general practice for several years, then specialist in Gynæcology; Professor of Medical Jurisprudence, Bishop's Coll., 1870-75; McGill University, 1875-83; Professor of Gynæcology, 1883-1910; Consulting Gynæcologist to the Montreal General Hospital; Past President of the Montreal Medico-Chirurg. Society; Past President and present Member of Council of the Montreal Art Association. *Recreation:* billiards. *Address:* 457 Sherbrooke Street West, Montreal. *T.:* Up 1263. *Clubs:* Mount Royal, University, Montreal.   *(Died 20 Sept. 1926.)*

GARFIT, William, J.P., D.L.; Sheriff Lincolnshire, 1892; Chairman of Holland Division Lincolnshire Quarter Sessions, 1900-14; banker; Director Lloyds Bank; *b.* 9 Nov. 1840; *s.* of late William Garfit, Boston; *m.* Mary, *d.* of C. Norman, 1868; one *d.* *Educ.:* Harrow; Trinity College, Camb.; Capt., 2nd Lincoln R.V., 1874-81; M.P. (C.) Boston, 1895-1906. *Address:* Mortimer House, Egerton Gardens, S.W. *Clubs:* Carlton, New University, Walton. *M.:* DO 94.   *(Died 29 Oct. 1920.)*

GARFORTH, Rear-Admiral Edmund St. John, C.B. 1887; D.L., J.P., Sussex; *b.* 1836; *s.* of late William Garforth, Wiganthorpe, near York, J.P., and Louisa, *d.* of St. John Charlton, Apley Castle, Salop; *m.* 1871, Haidie, *d.* of late E. Cooper, Failand House, near Bristol; one *s.* two *d.* Served in Baltic War, 1854 (medal);

Crimean War, 1854-55; present at siege of Sebastopol (medal with clasp, Turkish medal); New Zealand War (medal), 1859-60; in command of expedition against Masnâah Forts (Persian Gulf), 1874 (thanked by Indian Government); in command of Naval Brigade attached to Larut Field Force, 1875-76 (Perak medal); in Egyptian War, 1882 (medal, bronze star, and 3rd class Order of Osmanie); while in command of Hastings Div. of Coast Guards, 1870, was presented by German Emperor with a silver telescope for assisting in saving lives of German emigrants wrecked off that coast; created C.B. on occasion of H.M. Jubilee, 1887. *Address:* 14 Upper Maze Hill, St. Leonards-on-Sea. *Clubs:* United Service; Honorary member Royal Yacht Squadron, Cowes.

                  (Died 27 Dec. 1920.)

GARFORTH, Sir William Edward, Kt. *cr.* 1914; LL.D.; J.P. Cheshire, 1876, and W.R Yorks., 1892; 2nd *s.* of late William Garforth of Dukinfield, Cheshire, J.P.; *b.* 30 Dec. 1845; *m.* 1882, Mary E., *d.* of late Rev. Canon Eagar, M.A., R.D., Rector of Ashton-under-Lyne. Mem.-Inst.C.E.; Past President Mining Association of Great Britain; President Inst.M.E.; Chairman of Mining Committee, University of Leeds; awarded Fothergill gold medal R.S.A.; First Medal Inst.M.E.; Peake Gold Medal, Mid. Inst.M.E.; Vice-Pres. Jurors Brussels Exhibition, 1910. *Address:* Snydale Hall, near Pontefract. *Club:* Author's. *(Died 1 Oct. 1921.)*

GARLAND, Charles Tuller. *Address:* 26 Grosvenor Street, W.1; *T.:* Mayfair 5540; Avenue House, Newmarket; Moreton Hall, Moreton Morrell, Warwick. *(Died 10 June 1921.)*

GARLAND, Hon. John, K.C., 1912; M.L.C. since 1908; *b.* Cowhythe, Banffshire, 17 Sep. 1868; *s.* of Robert Garland; *m.* 1896, Isabel, *d.* of Edward Chisholm, Sydney; one *d. Educ.:* Fordyce Academy; Aberdeen and Edinburgh Universities. M.A. (Phil. Honours), Aberdeen, 1882; LL.B. (Highest Distinction), Edinburgh, 1886; called to Bar, New South Wales, 1888; Member of the Legislative Assembly for Wollahra, 1898-1901; and for Tamworth, 1903-4; Minister for Justice and Solicitor-General, 1909-10; Minister for Justice and Solicitor-General since 1916; Representative of the Government in the Legislative Council; Procurator of the Presbyterian Church of New South Wales since 1894; of Australia since 1901; Councillor of St. Andrews College; representative of the Legislative Council on Senate of Sydney University since 1915; President, Sydney University Law Society, 1915; Vice President of the National Association of New South Wales. *Recreation:* golf. *Address:* Cairnton, Belle Vue Hill, Sydney, N.S.W. *Clubs:* Australian, University, Royal Sydney Golf, Sydney.

                  (Died Feb. 1921.)

GARNER, Colonel Cathcart, C.M.G. 1919; C.B.E. 1919, Kt. of Grace, Order of St. John of Jerusalem; Officer, Legion of Honour; M.B., B.Ch. Trinity College, Dublin, 1885; A.M.S. Retired Pay; late Under Secretary of State (Health), Ministry of Interior, Egypt; *b.* 9 Aug. 1861; *e. s.* of late Wm. Hastings Garner of St. Grellans, Monkstown, Co. Dublin; *m.* 1900, Annette Jane, *y. d.* of late J. Nadin, M.R.C.S., L.R.C.P., Tipperary; one *s. Educ.:* St. Columba; Trinity College, Dublin. Entered Army Medical Dept. 1886; seconded for Civil Service Egyptian Govt.1896; President International Quarantine Board, Alexandria, 1898; Deputy Director General Public Health Dept. Cairo, 1907; rejoined Army for war service, 8 Aug. 1914; Gallipoli, Egypt and Palestine (despatches three times); A.D.M.S. of Occupied Enemy Territory, Palestine, 1917-19; Commander Order of George I. of Greece; for former services in Egypt, 2nd Class

Medjidia and 3rd Class Osmania; Grand Officer Order of the Nile. *Recreations:* sailing and shooting. *Address:* 19 St. Helen's Parade, Southsea. *Clubs:* Windham, Royal Thames Yacht: Royal Albert Yacht, Southsea.

                  (Died 5 Feb. 1928.)

GARNETT, Frank Walls, C.B.E. 1918; J.P.; Pres. Royal College of Veterinary Surgeons, 1914-19. *Address:* 10 Red Lion Square, W.C.1.; Dalegarth, Windermere.

                  (Died 22 Aug. 1922.)

GARRATT, Brig.-Gen. Sir Francis Sudlow, K.C.M.G., *cr.* 1918; C.B. 1902; C.M.G. 1915; D.S.O. 1900; J.P., Devon; *b.* 18 June 1859; *e. s.* of late Rev. Sudlow Garratt, Merifield, Devonport; *m.* 1st, 1897, Frances Lucy (*d.* 1921), *e. d.* of Colonel Troyte of Huntsham Court, Devon; three *d.* ; 2nd, 1925, Florence Kate, *d.* of late David L. Gooch of Anerley. *Educ.:* Winchester; Sandhurst. Appointed 2nd Lieut 6th Dragoon Guards, 1878; Captain, 1887; Major, 1897; second in command 6th Dragoon Guards, 1900; commanded a column in South Africa with local rank of Colonel; Lieutenant-Colonel 3rd Dragoon Guards, 1903; Lieutenant-Colonel 6th Dragoon Guards, 1904; commanded Jhansi Brigade, 1905-6; Ambala Cavalry Brigade with temporary rank Brigadier-General, 1907-9; 4th Cavalry Brigade, 1909-11; served Afghanistan, 1879-80 (medal); South Africa, 1899-1902 (despatches, Queen's medal 6 clasps, King's medal 2 clasps, C.B., D.S.O.); European War, 1914-18 (despatches five times), C.M.G., K.C.M.G.). *Address:* Ashbury, Devon. *Club:* Naval and Military. *(Died 23 June 1928.)*

GARRATT, Lieut.-Col. John Arthur Thomas, J.P., D.L.; late Lt.-Col. Grenadier Guards, and Captain, 1st Devon Yeo. Cavalry; *b.* 1842; *o. s.* of late John Garratt, and Anne, *d.* of Richard Heming; *m.*1867, Georgina Henrietta, *d.* of John Henry, *s.* of Jerome, Count Fane-De Salis, of Dawley Court; two *s.* two *d. Educ.:* Eton; Christ Church, Oxford. *Address:* Bishop's Court, Exeter. *Clubs:* Guards', Travellers'.

                  (Died 10 June 1919.)

GARRETT, R. W., M.A., M.D., C.M.; late Professor of Obstetrics, Queen's University, Kingston, Canada; *b.* Brock, Ontario, 31 May 1853; father English, and mother Irish; *m.* 1887, M. L., *d.* of A. S. Kirkpatrick, County Crown Attorney; two *s.* one *d. Educ.:* Preliminary Ontario College, Picton; M.A. Trinity College, Toronto; M.D. Queen's University, Kingston, Ontario. Practised profession in Kingston; Professor of Anatomy in the Women's Medical School; Demonstrator of Anatomy Royal College of Physicians and Surgeons; Professor of Anatomy; Senior Surgeon Kingston General Hospital, and Surgeon Major in the 14th Batt. Princess of Wales' Own Rifles. *Publications:* Medical and Surgical Gynæcology; editor, Kingston Medical Quarterly. *Recreations:* boating, fishing, and cycling; also very fond of photography.

GARRETT, Samuel; late Head of firm of Parker Garrett & Co., Solicitors, St. Michael's Rectory, Cornhill, E.C.; J.P. Suffolk; on retirement from business in 1921 elected Hon. Member of Lloyd's and of Institute of London Underwriters and Association of Average Adjusters; *b.* 20 Nov. 1850; 3rd *s.* of late Newson Garrett of Aldeburgh, Suffolk; *m.* 1882, Clara, *d.* of late Col. Thornbury, Bombay Army; three *s.* one *d. Educ.:* Rugby; Peterhouse, Cambridge. 8th in First Class in Classical Tripos; Le Bas Prize; Fellow of Peterhouse, 1875; admitted as solicitor, 1876; entered into partnership with late Sir Henry Parker in 1879, and became head of the firm on the latter's death in 1894; Member of the Council of the Law Society, 1907, and served as President of the Society, 1917-18; has served on Departmental Committees appointed by Lord Chancellor in 1918 on British and Foreign Legal Procedure, and in 1919 on the Public Trustee's Office. *Publications:* Address to the Law Society in 1910 on Codification; Address to the Law Society as President in 1918 on A Ministry of Justice and its Task; Dissenting Report as Member of the Committee on the Public Trustee's Office in 1919, in which radical changes in the organisation of the office were recommended. *Recreations:* yachting and gardening. *Address:* Gower House, Aldeburgh, Suffolk. *Clubs:* City of London, Royal Thames Yacht.   *(Died 22 April 1923.)*

GARRICK, Rev. James Percy, late Rector of Blofield, Norwich; Hon. Canon, Norwich, 1889. *Educ.:* Caius College, Cambridge (M.A., 9th Wrangler, Senior Fellow, and Tutor); Curate of St. Marylebone. *Address:* Merlewood, Old Cotton, Norwich.*(Died 27 Feb. 1919.)*

GARROW, Hon. James Thompson, Justice of the Court of Appeal, Ontario, since 1902; *b.* 1843. Called to Bar, 1869; member of Ontario Legislature, 1890-1902. *Address:* Toronto, Ontario, Canada.

GARSTIN, Sir William Edmund, G.C.M.G., *cr.* 1902; G.B.E., *cr.* 1918; K.C.M.G., *cr.* 1897; Grand Cordon Medjidie and Grand Cordon Osmanie; Chevalier of Legion d'honneur; British Government Director Suez Canal Co. since 1907; engaged on Red Cross work in England during the War; *b.* India, 29 Jan. 1849; 2nd *s.* of late Charles Garstin; *m.* 1888, Mary Isabella, *d.* of late Charles Augustus North, 56 York Terrace, N.W. *Educ.:* Cheltenham College; King's College, London. Entered Indian Public Works Dept. 1872; sent to Egypt 1885 and retired from India 1892; Inspector-General of Irrigation, Egypt, 1892; Under-Secretary of State for Public Works, 1892; Adviser to the Ministry of Public Works in Egypt, 1904-8; C.M.G. 1894. *Address:* 17 Welbeck House, Wigmore Street, W. *Clubs:* Turf, Brooks's. *(Died 8 Jan. 1925.)*

GARTH, Sir William, Kt., *cr.* 1914; K.C. 1919; Barrister, Middle Temple; *b.* 26 Aug. 1854; 3rd *s.* of late Rt. Hon. Sir Richard Garth, P.C. *Educ.:* Eton; Merton College, Oxford (B.A.). Advocate, Calcutta High Court, 1885-1913. *Address:* 132 Oakwood Court, W.14. *T.:* Park 3545. *Clubs:* United University, Oriental.   *(Died 20 Feb. 1923.)*

GARTSIDE-TIPPING, Colonel Robert Francis, C.B. 1900; I.S.C.; J.P. Co. Chester; *b.* 17 Aug. 1852; *s.* of G. Gartside-Tipping of Rossferry, Co. Fermanagh, Ireland, and Jane, *d.* of R. Fowler, of Rahinston, Co. Meath; *m.* 1885, Jane, *d.* of J. Sclater of Newick Park, Sussex; one *d. Educ.:* Oswestry. Entered army, 1872 (51st K.O. Light Infantry); Indian Staff Corps (2nd Bengal Lancers), 1875; 1st Bengal Lancers, 1879; served Afghan War, 1879-80; Zaimukt Expedition, 1880; Takt-i-Suleman Expedition, and Egypt, 1882; Miranzai Expedition, 1890; Isazai Expedition, 1892; China, 1900. *Address:* 30 Redcliffe Gardens, S.W.10. *T.:* Kensington 6227. *Club:* East India United Service. *(Died 16 Dec. 1926.)*

GARVAN, Sir John Joseph, Kt.; *cr.* 1927; *b.* Hill End, New South Wales, 17 Jan. 1873; *s.* of late James P. Garvan. Managing Director of Mutual Life and Citizens Assurance Co. Ltd.; Chairman of Commonwealth Bank, 1924-26. *Address:* Sydney, New South Wales.   *(Died 18 July 1927.)*

GARVICE, Charles, F.R.S.L., novelist, dramatist, and journalist; correspondent for several English and American papers; President of Institute of Lecturers; late President Farmers' and Landowners' Association; C.C. for Northam, Devon; Conservator of Rivers. *Publications:* Eve: Poems. Novels: Nance, Her Heart's Desire, The Outcast of the Family, A Coronet of Shame, Just a Girl, In Cupid's

394

Chains, Love Decides, Linked by Fate, Love the Tyrant, A Girl of Spirit, Diana and Destiny; Where Love Leads; The Gold in the Gutter; In Wolf's Clothing; Queen Kate; The Scribbler's Club; Love in a Snare; Two Maids and a Man; The One Girl in the World, 1915. Plays: The Fisherman's Daughter; A Life's Mistake; part author of A Heritage of Hate and Marigold Comes to Town. *Recreations:* riding, fishing, motoring, amateur farming. *Address:* 4 Maids of Honour Row, Rich mond, Surrey; The Thatch Cottage, Hambleden, Henley-on-Thames. *T.:* Richmond 899. *Clubs:* Garrick, Authors'. *(Died 1 Mar. 1920.)*

GARVICE, Major Chudleigh, O.B.E. 1919; D.S.O. 1900; Royal Dublin Fusiliers; *b.* 12 Jan. 1875; *s.* of Charles Garvice, of Bradworthy, N. Devon; *m.* 1920, Isabel, *d.* of Andrew Ormiston. Entered army, 1896; served South Africa, 1899-1902 (despatches, Queen's medal, 3 clasps, King's medal, 2 clasps, D.S.O.); Sudan medal with clasp; holds 4th Class Osmanieh and 3rd Class Order of the Nile. *Address:* Alexandria City Police, Egypt. *Club:* Naval and Military. *(Died 23 Mar. 1921.)*

GARVIN, Thomas, I.S.O. 1909; formerly Inspector-General of Police, New South Wales; *b.* Sydney, 7 Aug. 1843; *m.* 1865, Harriet, *o. d.* of late Charles Field, Sydney; joined N.S.W. Mounted Police, 1862. *Address:* Carbethon, 69 Edgecliffe Road, Woollahra.

GARY, Elbert Henry, LL.D., Sc.D., LL.B.; Chairman, United States Steel Corporation; *b.* father's farm near Chicago; *s.* of Erastus Gary and Susan A. Vallette Gary; *m.* 1st, Julia E. Graves (*d.* 1902); 2nd, 1905, Emma T. Townsend; two *d. Educ.:* Wheaton Public Schools and Wheaton College; Chicago University; LL.B. 1867; LL.D. M'Kendree College, 1906; Lafayette College, 1915; Lincoln Memorial University, 1919; Trinity College, 1919; Syracuse University, 1921; Northwestern University, 1922; Sc.D., University of Pittsburgh, 1915; D.C.S. New York University, 1925. Practised law in Chicago twenty-five years; County Judge eight years; first Mayor, City of Wheaton; prominently connected with organisation Federal Steel Co., 1898; removed from Chicago to New York to become its President; identified with organisation of the United States Steel Corporation 1901, of which is Chairman Board of Directors, Chairman Finance Committee and Chief Executive Officer; President Chicago Bar Association, 1893-4; President American Iron and Steel Institute since its organisation in 1910; Trustee, North-Western University, Syracuse University; Member U.S. Section International High Commission, 1915-17; Member of Society of Colonial Wars and Sons American Revolution; Grand Cordon of the Order of Leopold II.; Second Class Order of the Sacred Treasure; Officer of the Legion of Honour; Grand Cross Knight of the Crown of Italy; Grand Commander, Morocco; Golden Cross of the Commandership of the Royal Battalion of George I. of Greece. *Publications:* Numerous Addresses: Gary Genealogy. *Recreation:* farming. *Address:* 856 Fifth Avenue, New York City; 71 Broadway, New York City; Jericho, L.I., N.Y. *T.A.:* 71 Broadway, New York City; Jericho, Long Island, New York. *T.:* Syosset 800. *Clubs:* Chicago, Chicago Golf, Union League, Chicago; Metropolitan, Automobile of America, National Golf Links, New York Yacht, Piping Rock, Meadowbrook, Sleeping Hollow Country, New York.*(Died 15 Aug. 1927.)*

GASCOIGNE, John Henry, M.V.O. 1911; Senior Clerk, Scottish Office, 1902-17; *b.* 1856; *m.* 1888, Florence, *d.* of Benjamin Gregory. Scottish official delegate to Diplomatic Conference on International Circulation of Motor Cars, Paris, 1909; Jubilee Medal, 1897; Coronation Medals, 1902 and 1911. *Address:* 14

GARSTIN, John Ribton. See page xx.

Beatrice Avenue, Norbury, S.W.16. *T.:* Streatham 3969. *Club:* North Surrey Golf.
(*Died 2 Oct. 1928.*)

GASCOIGNE, Maj.-Gen. Sir William Julius Gascoigne, K.C.M.G., *cr.* 1901; C.M.G. 1899; late commanding at Hong Kong; *b.* 29 May 1844; *m.* 1875, Helen, *d.* of Martin T. Smith and *widow* of Hon. Arthur F. Egerton. Entered army, 1863; Maj.-Gen. 1895; served Egyptian War, 1882 (medal with clasp, Khedive's star); Soudan, 1885 (clasp). *Address:* Boyton House, Boscombe, Hants. *Clubs:* Travellers', United Service.
(*Died 9 Sept. 1926.*,

GASELEE, Gen. Sir Alfred, G.C.B., *cr.* 1909; G.C.I.E., *cr.* 1901; K.C.B., 1898; Colonel 54th Sikhs (Frontier Force), Indian Army, since 1904; *b.* 3 June 1844; *s.* of Rev. John Gaselee; *m.* 1895, Alice-Margaret, *d.* of late G. Gartside-Tipping of Rossferry, Co. Fermanagh. Entered army, 1863; Capt., 1875; Maj., 1881; Col., 1898; Col.-on-Staff, Cawnpore, 1896; temporary Brig.-General, 1898. N.W. Frontier, 1863 (medal with clasp); Abyssinia, 1868; Bizoti expedition, 1869 (despatches, thanked by Governor-General); Jowaki Afridi expedition, 1877-78 (despatches, clasp); Afghan, 1878-80 (despatches); Candahar (Bt. of Major, medal with two clasps, bronze decoration); Zhob Valley expedition, 1884 (despatches); Hazara expedition, 1891 (despatches, C.B. and clasp); Isazai expedition, 1892; Waziristan Field Force, 1894-95 (despatches, clasp); Tirah Expeditionary Force and Khyber Field Force, commanding 2nd Brigade (K.C.B., despatches, medal, two clasps); officiated Q.M.G. in India, 1898; commanded second class district, India, 1898-1901; commanded British Forces in North China, 1900 (medal and clasp, promoted Maj.-Gen.); Lt.-Gen. 1903; Gen. 1906; commanded Northern Army, India, 1907-8. *Address:* 54th Sikhs, Kohat, India. *Clubs:* United Service; Guildford.
(*Died 29 Mar. 1918.*)

GASKELL, Rt. Hon. Charles George Milnes, P.C., LL.D., M.A., D.L., J.P.; Chairman West Riding County Council, 1898-1910; *b.* 28 Jan. 1842; *e. s.* of J. Milnes Gaskell of Thornes House, Yorks, M.P. (*d.* 1873), and Mary, 2nd *d.* of Rt. Hon. C. W. Williams-Wynn, M.P.; *m.* 1876, Lady Catherine Henrietta, *d.* of 5th Earl of Portsmouth [author of 'Old Shropshire Life]; one *s.* one *d. Educ.:* Eton; Trin. Coll. Camb. Third class classical tripos. Barrister Inner Temple, 1866; M.P. Morley Division, West Riding, Yorks, 1885-92. *Heir: s.* Evelyn [Major Yorks. Dragoons I.Y.; *b.* 19 Oct. 1877; *m.* 1905, Lady Constance Harriet Stuart Knox, *e. d.* of 5th Earl of Ranfurly.] *Address:* Thornes House, Wakefield; Wenlock Abbey, Shropshire. *Club:* Travellers'.
(*Died 9 Jan. 1919.*)

GASKIN, Arthur J., Director of the Jewellers' and Silversmiths' School, Vittoria Street, Birmingham; retired, 1925; *b.* Birmingham, 1862; *s.* of Henry and Harriet Gaskin; *m.* 1894, Georgie Evelyne Cave France; two *d. Educ.:* Wolverhampton Grammar School. Painter and goldsmith; member of London Arts and Crafts, and Royal Birmingham Society of Artists. *Publications:* Various illustrated books, including work for the Kelmscott Press. *Recreation:* golf. *Address:* Chippen Campden. *M.:* D 9034. (*Died 4 June 1928.*)

GATES, Lewis Edwards; *b.* 23 March 1860; *s.* of Seth M. Gates, Member of Congress and abolitionist. *Educ.:* Harvard; studied in France, Germany, England. Assistant Professor of English, Harvard Univ., till 1901, and of Comparative Literature till 1902. *Publications:* Selections from Jeffrey, 1894; Selections from Newman, 1895; Three Studies in Literature, 1899; Studies and Appreciations, 1900. *Address:* The Wareham, 88 Willett Street, Albany, N.Y.
(*Died 1 Oct. 1924.*)

GATHORNE-HARDY, Hon. Alfred Erskine, J.P., D.L.; a Railway Commissioner since 1905, and Chairman of the Light Railway Commission; barrister; formerly Counsel for Woods and Forests, and Commissioner of Works; does not now practise; *b.* London, 27 Feb. 1845; 3rd *s.* of 1st Earl of Cranbrook; *m.* 1875, Isabella Louisa, *o. d.* of late John Malcolm of Poltalloch, Argyllshire; one *s.* one *d. Educ.:* Eton; Balliol Coll., Oxford. First class Honours in History. M.P. Canterbury, 1877; re-elected 1880, but unseated on petition; contested Northern Division Yorkshire, West Riding, 1883, on assassination of Lord Frederick Cavendish; and Doncaster Division, Yorkshire, 1885; M.P. North Sussex, 1886-95; retired, 1895. *Publications:* The Salmon: Fur, Feather, and Fin Series, 1898; Autumns in Argyllshire with Rod and Gun, 1900; Life of Gathorne-Hardy, First Earl of Cranbrook, 1910; My Happy Hunting-Grounds, 1914. *Address:* Donnington Priory, Newbury, Berks. *Clubs:* Carlton, Burlington Fine Arts. (*Died 11 Nov. 1918.*)

GATHORNE-HARDY, Col. Hon. Charles Gathorne; *b.* 11 May 1841; 2nd *s.* of 1st Earl of Cranbrook; *m.* 1872, Lady Cicely Louisa Nevill, *d.* of 1st Marquess of Abergavenny; two *d.* Formerly Lt.-Col. Grenadier Guards. *Address:* 48 Lennox Gardens, Chelsea, S.W. *Clubs:* Turf, Carlton. (*Died 17 Feb. 1919.*)

GATLIFF, General Albert Farrar, D.L. Sussex; *b.* 1857; *s.* of late Henry Gatliff and *g.s.* of Rev. John Gatliff of Brinkworth Hall, York, Canon of Manchester Cathedral; *m.* Rosamund (*d.* 1923), *widow* of Lt.-Col. C. F. Dashwood, late Gordon Highlanders; no *c. Educ.:* Alston College; London University; Royal Naval College, Greenwich. Entered Royal Marine Light Infantry, 1876; Capt. 1885; Major, 1892; Brevet Lt.-Col. 1899; Col. 1903; Maj.-Gen. 1910: Lt.-Gen. 1911; Gen. 1915; served in Mendiland Expedition (West Coast of Africa), 1898 (medal and clasp); Commanded Royal Marines on Cape Station (H.M.S. Doris), 1897-99; special service South African War, 1899-1901; Press Censor Capetown; Assistant Adjutant-General, operations in Orange Free State and Cape Colony; present at Paardeberg (medal and three clasps); Senior Officer Royal Marines for fourteen months during the War; appointed to command 37th Battalion of Imperial Yeomanry; Passed Staff College, 1888; Instructor of Fortifications, Royal Military College, 1890-97; called to Bar, Middle Temple, 1897; Passed first in Common Law and gained J. J. Powell prize; Member of Admiralty Volunteer Committee, 1903-7, and compiled regulations for R.M. Volunteers (received thanks of Admiralty); Times correspondent on various occasions; Specially selected to assist in writing official history of South African War; Colonel Commandant Portsmouth Division, R.M.L.I. 1908-1910; Awarded Good Service Pension, 1909; retired pay, 1922; Member of Council, Royal United Service Institution and British Legion, etc.; in attendance on H.I.H. The Hereditary Prince of Turkey representing the Sultan at the Coronation (medal); a Pall-bearer at Funeral of Unknown Warrior at Westminster Abbey, 11th Nov. 1920; J.P., Cape Colony. *Recreations:* cricket (I Zingari and Free Foresters), golf and shooting. *Address:* 5 Clarendon Mansions, Brighton; Silverstream, Thorpe, Chertsey. *Clubs:* Army and Navy; New, Brighton.
(*Died 28 Sept. 1927.*)

GATT, Hon. Camillo. *Educ.:* Malta University. Private Secretary to Sir Richard Wood, H.M.'s Diplomatic Agent and Consul General, Tunis 1868-71; Superintendent of the Government Printing Office, Malta, 1882; Assistant Secretary to Government, Gozo, 1892; Receiver-General, 1899; Auditor-General, 1902; member of the Executive Council and of the Council of Government, 1903; Pensioned. *Address:* Malta.

GATTIE, Alfred Warwick, Chairman of Gattie Springs, Limited; *b.* London, 21 June 1856; 2nd *s.* of William and Henrietta Warwick Gattie; *m.* Carlotta, *d.* of Walter Elliot. *Educ.:* Brighton Grammar School. Began life as a clerk in the Bank of England; inventor of the Gattie System of Goods Clearing Houses; inventor of Gattie co-ordinating springs for vehicles, aeroplanes, etc. *Publications:* The Transgressor; The Honourable Member; Oh Jackanapes; The Millionairess; and a number of other plays; articles in the Nineteenth Century and Fortnightly Reviews, etc.; a number of lectures on Transport Reform by Road, Rail, and Water. *Recreations:* reading, music, drama, science, and sociology. *Address:* 11 Montague Gardens, Acton, W.3. *T.:* Chiswick 653. (*Died 21 Sept.* 1925.)

GATTY, Sir Stephen Herbert, Kt., *cr.* 1904; K.C.; *b.* 9 Oct. 1849; *s.* of late Rev. Alfred Gatty; *m.* 1st, 1876, Alice Georgina (*d.* 1894), *e. d.* of late Rev. G. Rawlinson; 2nd, 1905, Katharine, *d.* of late Alfred Morrison; two *s.* one *d. Educ.:* Winchester; New Coll. Oxford. Called to Bar Middle Temple, 1874; N.E. Circuit; Attorney-Gen. Leeward Isles, 1883; Acting Chief-Justice Antigua, 1884; Attorney-Gen. Trinidad, 1885; Puisne Judge Straits Settlements 1892; Chief-Justice cf Gibraltar, 1895-1905. *Address:* Ossemsley Manor, Christchurch, Hants. *T.A.:* New Milton. *T.:* New Milton 13. (*Died 20 Mar.* 1922.)

GAUGHRAN, Rt. Rev. Laurence, R.C. Bishop of Meath since 1906; *b.* 1842. *Educ.:* Maynooth. Ordained, 1868; Professor at St. Finian's, 1872-77; at Mullingar, 1877-85; Pastor of Kells, 1885; Vicar-General of Meath, 1894; Domestic Prelate to the Pope, 1895. *Address:* The Palace, Mullingar, Ireland. (*Died 14 June* 1928.)

GAUL, Rt. Rev. William Thomas, D.D.; Hon. Canon Cape Town Cathedral since 1913; *cons.* 1895; resigned, 1907. *Educ.:* Trin. Coll. Dublin (M.A.). Ordained, 1873; Vicar of Bloemfontein, 1875-80; Rector of All Saints, Dutoitspan, 1880-84; of Kimberley, 1884-95; Archdeacon of same, 1887-95; Bishop of Mashonaland, 1895-1907. *Address:* Capetown, S. Africa. (*Died 17 May* 1928.)

GAULT, James, A.K.C.; late Prof. of Commerce and Commercial Law, King's College, London; *b.* Jersey, 21 June 1850; *s.* of D. Gault of Ahoghill, Co. Antrim, Ireland; *m.* 1887, Ellen Sarah, *y. d.* of R. Rixon of Woolwich; two *d. Educ.:* King's Coll., London. Called to the Bar, 1887; appointed by the Council of King's College lecturer in Roman Law; for several years was Dean of the Evening Classes of the College. *Publications:* revised and edited, under the title of Lessons in Commerce, The Law and Customs of British Trade by Prof. Gambaro of Genoa; assisted with J. E. Forster's Registration of Business Names Act; Excess Profits Duty and Corporation Tax. *Recreations:* rowing and music. *Address:* 3 Elm Court, Temple. E.C. *T.:* Central 1234. (*Died 13 Dec.* 1927.)

GAUNT, Percy Reginald, C.B.E.; Mill Manager and a Director of Reuben Gaunt & Sons, Ltd., Broom Mills, Farsley, nr. Leeds; *b.* Farsley, nr. Leeds, 6 Nov. 1875; *s.* of John Wm. Gaunt of Summerfield, Bramley, nr. Leeds; *m.* 1902, Ethel Mary, *d.* of late Abimelech Hainsworth of Farsley, nr. Leeds; two *s.* two *d. Educ.:* Leeds Boys' Modern School; Leeds University. District Commissioner for the Farsley District (West Riding of Yorkshire) B.P. Boy Scouts' Association; Freeman of the City of London; Liveryman of the Worshipful Company of Dyers; President of the Leeds University Textile Association; 396

Member of Council and Research Control Committee, The British Research Assoc. for the Woollen and Worsted Industries, Leeds, etc., Honorary Assistant Director of Wool Textile Production, War Depart., Bradford; Member of the Board of Control of Wool Textile Production, and Chairman of various Sub-Committees in relation thereto; responsible for the following Sections: Costing of Textile Fabrics and Commission. Rates for Textile Processes, Costings in Consultation with Directorate of Costings, Dyewares, Dyeing, *i.e,* Piece-dyeing, Wool-dyeing, and Slubbing-dyeing. *Recreations:* golf, gardening. *Address:* Elmwood, Calverley, nr. Leeds. *T.:* Stanningley, Leeds 111. *Clubs:* National Liberal; Union, Bradford: New Leeds and County Liberal, Leeds. (*Died 3 Dec.* 1926.)

GAUSSEN, Perceval David Campbell, K.C. 1909; *b.* 1862; *m.* 1908, Letitia Elisabeth, *d.* of Rev. J. Wilson, Rector Tyholland, Co. Monaghan; one *d. Educ.:* Trinity College, Dublin. Wray Prizeman in Logics and Ethics; Senior Moderator in Moral and Mental Philosophy; B.A. 1884; ex-President of Dublin University Philosophical Soc. Called to Bar, 1885; Senior Crown Counsel, Co. Cavan; J.P. for Cos. Londonderry, Antrim, and Tyrone. *Address:* Clifton, Monkstown, Co. Dublin; *T.:* 308 Dun Laoghaire, Co. Dublin; Shanemullagh House, Castledawson, Co. Londonderry. (*Died 19 Oct.* 1928.)

GAUTHIER, Most Rev. Charles Hugh, R.C. Archbishop of Ottawa since 1910; *b.* Alexandria, Ont., Canada, 1843. *Educ.:* Regiopolis College, Kingston; later Professor of Rhetoric there. Priest Gananoque, Westport, Williamstown, Glen Nevis, and Brockville; Dean, 1886; Vicar-General, 1891; Archbishop of Kingston, 1898-1910. *Address:* Archbishop's Palace, Ottawa, Canada. (*Died 19 Jan.* 1922.)

GAUTIER, C. Lucien; Honorary Professor of Theology; *b.* Cologny, near Geneva, Switzerland, 17 Aug. 1850; *s.* of late Col. E. A. Emile Gautier, Director of the Observatory of Geneva, and P. E. Victorine, *née* Sarasin; *m.* 1878, Bertha V. Hentsch of Geneva; three *s.* two *d. Educ.:* Geneva, Collège Lecoultre and State Gymnasium. B.Lit. 1867; B.Sc. 1869; B.Theol. 1874; studied evangelical theology and Semitic languages at the Universities of Geneva, Leipzig, and Tübingen; Ph.D. Leipzig, 1877; appointed 1877 to the Professorship of Hebrew and Old Testament Exegesis at the Theological Faculty of the Free Evangelical Church of Canton de Vaud at Lausanne; resigned and was nominated Honorary Professor, 1898; D.D. Hon., Berne, 1906, and Glasgow, 1908; Hon. Professor University of Geneva, 1909; was President of the Synod of the Free Evangelical Church of the Canton de Vaud, 1885, 1886, 1891, 1892, of the Geographical Society of Geneva, 1906-7, of the Christian Evangelical Association of Geneva, 1906-9, of the Société Pastorale Suisse, 1916-17; Chairman of the Association of the International Monument of the Reformation, 1906-17; Central President of the Société Suisse des Vieux-Zofingiens, 1915-19; President of the Board of Delegates of the South African Swiss Mission, 1918-20; Member of the International Committee of the Red Cross since 1919; was one of the editors of the Review La Liberté Chrétienne, Lausanne, 1898-1907; travelled in the Holy Land, 1893-94, and 1899. *Publications:* Le Sacerdoce dans l'A.T., 1874; Ad-Dourra al-Fâkhira, la Perle Precieuse de Ghazâli, Traité d'Eschatologie musulmane, 1878; La Mission du Prophète Ezéchiel, 1891; Au dela du Jourdain, 1896, 2nd ed.; Souvenirs de Terre-Sainte, 1898, 2nd ed.; Vocations de Prophètes, 1922, 2nd ed. (German translation, 1903); Autour de la Mer Morte, 1901; Introduction à l'A.T. (2 vols.), 1914, 2nd ed.; La Loi dans l'ancienne alliance, 1908; l'Evangéliste de l'Exil, 1911; le

Prophète Jérémie, 1916, etc. *Address:* Cologny, Geneva, Switzerland. *T.A.:* Lucien Gautier, Cologny. *T.:* St. 6687. *(Died Feb. 1924.)*

GAUTIER, Judith; *d.* of Théophile Gautier; Member Goncourt Academy; Chevalier de la Légion d'honneur. *Romans:* Le Dragon Impérial (Chinois); Iskender (Persan); La Sœur du Soleil (Japonais); Le Vieux de la Montagne (Croisade); Khou 'N Atonon (Egyptien); L'Inde Ebloule (Hindou); etc. *Théâtre:* La Marchande de Sourires (Odéon); L'Avare Chinois (Odéon); Princesse d'Amour (Vaudeville); etc.; La Fille du Ciel (en collaboration avec Pierre Loti) (New York). *Traductions:* Parsifal, Le Livre de Jade (Poèmes Chinois). *Poésie:* Poèmes de la Libellule (Japon). *Mémoires:* Collier des jours, 3 volumes. *Address:* 30 rue Washington, Paris; Pre' des Oiseaux, Dinard, Ile-et-Vilaine. *(Died Dec. 1917.)*

GAVEY, Sir John, Kt., *cr.* 1907; C.B. 1908; M.I.C.E.; Engineer-in-Chief to the Post Office, 1902-7; Consulting Engineer to Post Office, 1908-13; *b.* Aug. 1842; *o. s.* of J. Gavey, St. Heliers, Jersey; *m.* 1870, Mary de Gruchy; two *s.* three *d. Educ.:* Victoria College, Jersey. Received professional training under Mr., later Sir, W. H. Preece, in the service of Electric International Co.; on the transfer of the telegraphs to the State appointed Superintendent of the South-Eastern Subdivision, 1870; and of the Great-Western Subdivision, 1872; Superintending Engineer, South Wales District, 1878; Chief Technical Officer, General Post Office, 1892; Assistant Engineer-in-Chief, 1897, and Electrician, 1899; has been closely associated with all telegraphic and telephonic developments of the Post Office; Past President of the Institution of Electrical Engineers. *Publications:* papers read before Engineering Institutions, and contributions to technical press. *Recreation:* boating. *Address:* The Croft, Hampton Wick. *T.:* Kingston 1616. *(Died 1 Jan. 1923.)*

GAVIN, Ethel; M.A., Dublin; Head Mistress, Wimbledon Hill School, since 1908; 4th *d.* of late John Gavin of Kandy, Ceylon. *Educ.:* Maida Vale High School; Girton Coll. Classical Tripos, Cambridge, Class II.; Russell Gurney Scholar, Girton College. Assistant Mistress, Maida Vale High School, 1888-93; Head Mistress Shrewsbury High School, 1893-1900; Head Mistress, Notting Hill High School, 1900-8. *Address:* Wimbledon Hill School, S.W. *Club:* Ladies' University. *(Died 2 Mar. 1918.)*

GAVIN, Michael, Jesuit Priest, Member of the Staff attached to Farm Street Church, Berkeley Square, London, W., since 1882; *b.* Limerick, Jan. 1843; *s.* of Capt. Michael Gavin, Limerick, and Eliza Gallwey, Kilkenny. *Educ.:* Castleknock, near Dublin; Stonyhurst College. Taught literature at Beaumont College, Old Windsor, 1869-74; Theology at St. Beuno's College, St. Asaph, 1878-81. *Publications:* The Sacrifice of the Mass; Memoirs of Father P. Gallwey, S.J.; the Decay of Faith; the Devotion to the Sacred Heart; the Salvation of God; and other Sermons. *Address:* 114 Mount Street, W. *(Died 23 June 1919.)*

GAWAN TAYLOR, His Honour Judge Henry, B.A., LL.B. (Cantab.), County Court Judge, on Circuit No. 3, since 1912; J.P. Lancashire, Cumberland, and Westmorland; *b.* 16 Dec. 1855; 2nd *s.* of late William Taylor, Cober Hill, Cloughton, Yorkshire, and of Scarborough; *m.* 1883, Rachel (*d.* 1927), 3rd *d.* of late T. J. Candler of Low Hall, West Ayton, Yorks; one *s.* three *d. Educ.:* Trinity Hall, Cambridge (Law Scholar and Prizeman); Lond. Univ., Honours 1st LL.B.; called to Bar, Lincoln's Inn, 1882; Lincoln's Inn Scholarship in International and Constitutional Law; a Revising Barrister on the North-Eastern Circuit, 1895-1911; Chairman of the Joint Committee of the Durham Coal Trade, 1906-10. *Address:* Croftlands, Heads Nook, Carlisle. *Club:* Cumberland County, Carlisle. *(Died 9 Dec. 1928.)*

GEAKE, Charles, Secretary Liberal Publication Department, and editor Liberal Magazine, Liberal Monthly, and Liberal Year Book since 1894; member Editorial Staff of Westminster Gazette since 1896; *b.* 7 May 1867; *e. s.* of late Joseph Ford and Ellen Geake of Launceston, Cornwall; *m.* 1899, Jessie Margaret, *d.* of late Robert and Jessie Hudson of Lapworth, Warwickshire; one *d. Educ.:* Dunheved College, Launceston; Clare College, Cambridge (Scholar); Eighth Wrangler, 1889; First Class (3rd Div.), Part II., Math. Tripos, 1890; Fellow Clare College, 1891; read in Chambers for Bar, 1892-1894; called at Lincoln's Inn, 1894; Cambridge Editor of the Granta, 1890-2; frequent contributor to Punch, 1891-6 *Publications:* John Bull's Adventures in the Fiscal Wonderland (with Sir F. C. Gould); Appreciations and Addresses by Lord Rosebery (editor). *Address:* Percy Lodge, Campden Hill, W.8. *T.:* Park 3141. *Clubs:* Union, National Liberal, Eighty, Whitefriars, Omar Khayyam. *(Died 29 April 1919.)*

GEARY, Lieut.-Gen. Sir Henry Le Guay, K.C.B., *cr.* 1900; Col. Commandant R.A.; *b.* 29 Apr. 1837; *s.* of late Fred. Augustus Geary, Platt House, Putney, Surrey; *m.* Sophia Mary, *d.* of George Symes, Bridport, Dorset, 1865; one *s.* three *d. Educ.:* R.M.A. Woolwich. Joined R.A., 1855; Crimea, 1855-56 (medal, clasp for Sebastopol, Turkish medal, 5th class Medjidie for distinguished conduct in the field); Indian Mutiny Campaign, 1858-59 (medal); Abyssinian Campaign (medal, despatches, Brevet Major); Brig. Major, and A.A.Gen. R.A. Ireland, 1873-77; D.A.A.G. and A.A.G. Army Headquarters, 1879-84; Assist.-Director of Artillery, War Office, 1885-90; Maj.-Gen. com. R.A. South. Dist. 1890-95; Maj.-Gen. com. Belfast Dist. 1895-99; President of Ordnance Committee, 1899-1902; Governor of Bermuda, 1902-1904; Jubilee medal, 1897. *Recreations:* nothing special. *Address:* Arreton, Camberley. *T.:* 169 Camberley. *Club:* Junior United Service. *(Died 31 July 1918.)*

GEDDES, Brig.-Gen. John Gordon, C.B. 1915; C.M.G. 1918; R.A.; *b.* 4 Nov. 1863; *s.* of Col. John Geddes, Cheltenham; *m.* 1898, Eling Esther, *y. d.* of Brig.-Gen. C. H. Spragge, C.B. Entered army, 1883; Capt., 1892; Maj., 1900; Lt.-Col. 1910; Col., 1913; Brig.-Gen. 1915; D.A.A.G., India, 1897-1900; Instructor, School of Gunnery, 1901-4; D.A.A. and Q.M.G., 3rd Div. Southern Command, 1908-10; served Tirah Expedition, 1897-8 (medal with clasp); European War, 1914-18 (wounded, despatches four times, C.B., C.M.G.). *Address:* 4 Suffolk Square, Cheltenham. *(Died 26 Aug. 1919.)*

GEDDES, Colonel Robert James, C.B. 1915; M.B.; D.S.O. 1900; late A.M.S.; *b.* 18 Aug. 1858; *m.* 1907, Christina Gowans, *d.* of late J. G. Whyte. Entered army, 1884; Maj. 1896; Lt.-Col. 1904; Col. 1913; served Burmah, 1885-88 (medal, 2 clasps); Chin-Lushai, 1889-90 (clasp); Mekran Expedition, 1898; South Africa, 1899-1902 (despatches, Queen's medal four clasps, King's medal two clasps, D.S.O.); European War, 1914-17; D.D.M.S. 4th and 2nd Corps, B.E.F. (despatches twice, C.B.); Inspector Medical Services for Scotland, 1917-19. *Address:* Westcliff, St. Andrews, Fife. *(Died 27 Sept. 1923.)*

GEDGE, Rev. Hugh Somerville, M.A.; Hon. Canon of Peterborough, 1900; *b.* 24 Oct. 1844; *s.* of Rev. Sydney Gedge, M.A., sometime Fellow of St. Catharine's College, Cambridge; some time Second Master of King Edward's School, Birmingham, afterwards Vicar of All Saints', Northampton; *m.* 1882, Georgiana Caroline, *d.* of Lieut.-Col. Clunes, H.E.I. Army.

Educ.: King Edward's School, Birmingham; Marlborough; St. Catharine's College, Cambridge. B.A. 1866 (2nd class Classical Tripos); M.A. 1873; Carus Greek Testament Prize, 1867; 2nd class Theological Hons. 1867; ordained Deacon, 1868; Priest, 1869; Curate of St. Peter's, Sowerby, Halifax, 1868-71; All Saints', Northampton, 1871-77; Perpetual Curate of St. Paul's, Northampton, 1877-82; Vicar of All Saints', Leicester, 1882-91; Rural Dean of Christianity or Leicester, 1908-10; Rector of Aylestone, Leicester, 1891 1019; Proctor in Convocation, 1906-16. *Recreation:* travel. *Publications:* editor of Peterborough Diocesan Calendar, 1902-8-13-20; several Tracts. *Address:* Park House, Stoneygate, Leicester. *T.A.:* Leicester.   (*Died 10 April 1923.*)

GEDGE, Sydney, M.A.; solicitor; head of Gedge, Fiske, and Gedge; Governor and Almoner Christ's Hospital, Gov. Westfield Coll., Ridley Hall, and Wycliffe Hall; Director Henley's Telegraph Works Co.; *b.* 16 Oct. 1829; *e. s.* of Rev. Sydney Gedge; *m.* Augusta, *d.* of R. Herring, 1857. *Educ.:* King Edward's School, Birmingham; Corpus Christi Coll. Cambridge. 1st class Moral Science Tripos, 1854. Contested South Bedfordshire, 1885; M.P. (C.) Stockport, 1886-92; Member House Laymen, Rep. Church Council; Vice-Pres. C.M.S.; Licensed Preacher Dioceses of London and Southwark. M.P. (C.) Walsall, 1895 - 1900; contested Walsall, 1900. *Publications:* Articles in the Churchman on Church subjects. *Address:* Mitcham Hall, Surrey. *T.:* Mitcham 825; 10 Norfolk Street, Strand, W.C. *T.:* Central 4220. *Club:* Junior Constitutional.   (*Died 6 April 1923.*)

GEE, William Winson Haldane, B.Sc. (Lond.), M.Sc.Tech. (Manchester); Professor of Pure and Applied Physics at the College of Technology, Manchester, 1902; retired under superannuation, 1924; *b.* near Bolton, Lancs, 29 June 1857; *s.* of William Gee, formerly of Manchester; *m.* Caroline, *e. d.* of M. M. Rooker, of Sale, Cheshire; one *d.* *Educ.:* Manchester Grammar School; the Royal College of Science; the Owens College. Demonstrator and Assistant Lecturer in Physics at the Owens College, Lecturer of the Victoria Unersity, 1881-91; Chief Lecturer in Physics and Electrical Engineering at the Municipal Technical School, Manchester, 1891-1902; has been largely responsible for the design and equipment of the laboratories, etc., in Physics, Electrical Engineering, and Electro-Chemistry at the College of Technology; Hon. Curator Manchester Literary and Philosophical Society. *Publications:* papers relating to Physics and Electro-Chemistry, etc.; with the late Balfour Stewart, three volumes on Practical Physics; joint translator of Rosenberg's Electrical Engineering. *Address:* Oak Lea, Whalley Avenue, Sale, Cheshire.
              (*Died 3 Mar. 1923.*)

GEER, Ven. George Thomas; *b.* 1844; *s.* of G. T. and Sarah Geer, London, England; *m.* 1870, Davinia Louisa Macdougall. *Educ.:* English Public School; Moore College, Liverpool; New South Wales. Licensed as Reader at Timor, by Bishop of Melbourne, Victoria, 1874; ordained Deacon, by Bishop of Ballarat, Victoria, 1877; Priest, 1879. Incumbent of East Charlton, 1878; Dimboola, 1881; Rector of Condobolin, New South Wales, 1883; Coonamble, 1884; Cowra, 1891; Carcoar, 1896; Bourke, 1898; appointed Canon, All Saints Cathedral, Bathurst, 1891; Archdeacon of the Lachlan, 1895; Rector of Bourke, Archdeacon of Bourke, 1901-6; Rector of Gulgong, 1904-13; late Hon. Archdeacon and Rural Dean; licensed for general work, Diocese of Sydney, 1913. *Recreations:* photography; horticulture (prizetaker), ferns, cut flowers, chrysanthemums; portraits, landscape, lantern slides, buildings, etc. *Address:* Magic Street, Mosman, N.S. Wales.   (*Died 2 Feb. 1918.*)

398

GEIKIE, Sir Archibald; Kt., *cr.* 1891; O.M. 1914; K.C.B., *cr.* 1907; Officier de la Légion d'Honneur; F.R.S., F.G.S.; Hon. M.R.I.A.; President Royal Society, 1908-13; Foreign Associate Institute of France; Member Lincei, Rome, Academies of Berlin, Vienna, Petrograd, Belgium, Stockholm, Turin, Naples, Munich, Christiania, Göttingen, Kais. Leopold. Carol., Philadelphia, New York, National Academy of Sciences of United States, etc.; *b.* Edinburgh, 28 Dec. 1805; *e. s.* of late James Stuart Geikie; *m.* 1871, Alice Gabrielle (*d.* 1916), *y. d.* of late Eugène Pignatel of Lyons; two *d.* *Educ.:* High School and University, Edinburgh; Hon. D.C.L. Oxford; D.Sc. Cambridge and Dublin; LL.D. Edinburgh, Glasgow, Aberdeen, St. Andrews, Durham, Birmingham, Sheffield, Liverpool; Ph.D. Upsala, Leipzig, Prague, Strasbourg. Entered Geological Survey, 1855; Director Geo. Survey of Scotland, 1867; first Murchison Prof. of Geology and Mineralogy, University, Edinburgh, 1871-82; Foreign Secretary Royal Society, 1890-94, and Secretary, 1908-8; President Geological Soc., 1891-92, 1906-8; President British Association, 1892; Director - General Geological Survey of United Kingdom, and Director Museum of Practical Geology, 1882 - 1901; Wollaston medallist and Murchison medallist of Geological Society; twice Macdougal - Brisbane medallist of Royal Society, Edinburgh; Royal medallist, Royal Society; Hayden gold medallist, Philadelphia Academy of Natural Sciences; Livingstone Gold Medallist of Royal Geograph. Soc. Scotland; Gold Med. of Instit. of Mining and Metallurgy; Governor of Harrow School, 1892-1922; Trustee of the British Museum; Member of the Royal Commission for the Exhibition of 1851; Member of Council of the British School at Rome; Chairman of Royal Commission on Trinity College, Dublin, 1920. *Publications:* The Story of a Boulder, or Gleanings from the Notebook of a Field - Geologist, 1858; Memoir of Edward Forbes (with G. Wilson), 1861; Geological Map of Scotland (with Murchison), 1862; The Scenery of Scotland viewed in connection with its Physical Geology, 1865 (3rd ed. 1901); Memoir of James David Forbes, 1869; Life of Sir Roderick I. Murchison, 2 vols. 1875; Geological Sketches at Home and Abroad, 1882; Text-book of Geology, 1882; 4th ed. in two vols. 1903; Class-book of Geology, 6th edit. 1915; Field - Geology, 5th edit. 1900; New Geological Map of Scotland, with descriptive notes, 1892, 2d edit. 1910; Memoir of Sir Andrew Crombie Ramsay, 1895; The Ancient Volcanoes of Britain, 2 vols., 1897; The Founders of Geology, 1897, 2nd ed. 1906; Geological Map of England and Wales, with descriptive notes, 1897; Types of Scenery, and their Influence on Literature (Romanes Lecture), 1898; The Geology of Central and Western Fife and Kinross (Mem. Geol. Surv.), 1901; The Geology of Eastern Fife (Mem. Geol. Surv.), 1902; Scottish Reminiscences, 1904; Landscape in History, 1905; Charles Darwin as Geologist, the Rede Lecture for 1909; The Love of Nature among the Romans, Presidential Address to Classical Association, 1911, expanded into a volume, 1912; The Birds of Shakespeare, 1916; Annals of the Royal Society Club, the Record of a London Dining Club in the Eighteenth and Nineteenth Centuries, 1917; John Michell, M.A., F.R.S., of Queen's College, Cambridge (1724-93), 1918; A Long Life's Work, an Autobiography, 1924; smaller school-books on Physical Geography and Geology, which have been translated into most European languages; many original contributions to science in the journals and transactions of learned societies and in the Memoirs of the Geological Survey, and literary papers in the Quarterly and Edinburgh Reviews, and other periodicals. *Address:* Shepherd's Down,

Haslemere, Surrey. *Club:* Athenæum.
(Died 10 Nov. 1924.)

GEIL, William Edgar, M.A., Litt. D.,
LL.D., F.R.G.S., F.R.A.S., M.R.A.S.; explorer;
b. near Philadelphia; mother Scotch; *m.* L.
Constance Emerson, B.A., *d.* of Hon. E. O.
Emerson. Crossed Africa; penetrated as far as
Mount Douglas in New Guinea; visited the
Dyacks in Borneo; visited the D'Entrecasteaux
Archipelago; crossed China from Shanghai to
Burma; followed the Great Wall of China from
the Yellow Sea to Tibet; visited the Koko Nor;
visited Australia, Friendly Islands, Samoa,
Fiji, Friday Island, New Zealand, Timour,
Japan, Corea, Siberia; visited all the capitals
of China; explored the five sacred mountains of
China, 1919-20. *Publications:* A Yankee on
the Yangtze; A Yankee in Pigmyland; The Isle
Called Patmos; The Men on the Mount; The
Man of Galilee; Ocean and Isle; The Great
Wall of China; Eighteen Capitals of China;
Hunting Pigmies. *Recreation:* golf. *Address:*
The Barrens, Doylestown, Pa., U.S.A.
(Died 11 April 1925.)

GELDART, William Martin, C.B.E. 1917;
M.A., B.C.L.; Vinerian Professor of English
Law, and Fellow of All Souls College, Oxford,
since 1909; *b.* 7 June 1870; *s.* of Rev. Edmund
Martin Geldart; *m.* 1905, Emily Falk. *Educ.:*
Whitgift Grammar School, Croydon; St. Paul's
School; Balliol College, Oxford (Scholar);
Fellow of St. John's College, 1892-99; called to
Bar, Lincoln's Inn, 1897; Official Fellow and
Lecturer in Law at Trinity College, 1901-9;
All Souls Reader in English Law in the Uni-
versity, 1906-9; member of the Hebdomadal
Council since 1905. *Publications:* Joint-Editor
with F. W. Hall of Aristophanes in Oxford
series of Classical Texts; Contributor to A
Digest of English Civil Law, edited by E. Jenks;
Elements of English Law, in Home University
Library. *Recreation:* Entomology. *Address:*
10 Chadlington Road, and All Souls College,
Oxford. *T.:* Oxford 126. *(Died 12 Feb. 1922.)*

GELL, Philip Lyttelton; *b.* 29 Apr. 1852;
s. of Rev. John Philip Gell and Eleanor, sole issue
of Admiral Sir John Franklin, the Arctic explorer; *m.* 1889; J.P. Oxford-
shire and Middlesex; Director, Guardian
Assurance Co.; Director and late President of
British South Africa Company. *Educ.:* King's
Coll., London (Hon. Fellow); Balliol College,
Oxford (Scholar). 1st class Mod. History, 1876;
Arnold Prize Essay on Turkish Races in Europe,
1877. First Chairman of Council Universities
Settlement in East London (Toynbee Hall),
1884-96; Archbishops' Church Finance Com-
mittee, Empire Settlement Committee, 1917.
Address: Hopton Hall, Wirksworth, Derby-
shire; Haven Hill, Kingswear, S. Devon.
Clubs: Brooks's, Athenæum; Derbyshire
County. *(Died 29 May 1926.)*

GEMMILL, James Fairlie, F.R.S.E.,
F.R.S., Professor Natural History, University
College, Dundee, since 1919; *s.* of late Cuth-
bert Gemmill, Hillhead, Mauchline, and Jeanie
Leiper. *Educ.:* Mauchline Public School;
Kilmarnock Academy; Glasgow University;
Cowan Medallist, Blackstone Medallist, Coulter
Prizeman, Bellahouston Medallist; M.A. (Hons.
Classics, 1890); M.D. (Hons. 1900), D.Sc.
(1910); Leipzig and Naples. First Presi-
dent (now Hon. Vice-President) of the
Marine Biological Association of the West of
Scotland (now Scottish Marine Biological Association); F.Z.S.; late Research Fellow in Embryology at Glasgow University, and Lecturer
in Zoology at the Glasgow Provincial Training
College. *Publications:* various on embryo-
logical, zoological, and teratological subjects,
including work on Ovogenesis; Origin of Mül-
lerian Duct; Vitality of Ova and Sperm; Aquarium Aeration; Development of Sun Star (Trans.
Zool. Soc. Lond. 1912); Locomotor Function of

Lantern of Aristotle (Proc. Roy. Soc. Lond.
1912); The Teratology of Fishes, Glasgow, 1912;
Development of Common Crossfish, etc. (Phil.
Trans. Roy. Soc. Lond. 1914, and Quart. Journ.
Micr. Sc. 1915); Development of Sea Anemones
(Phil. Trans. Roy. Soc. Lond. 1920). *Address:*
Hawkhill House, Dundee. *T.: 2412.*
(Died 10 Feb. 1926.)

GEMMILL, Lt.-Col. William, D.S.O.
1915; J.P.; 8th Batt. Royal Scots (T.F.); *b.*
4 Sep. 1878; *s.* of late William Gemmill of
Greendykes. Served South Africa, 1899-1901
(Queen's Medal with 4 clasps); European War,
1914-15 (D.S.O., despatches). *Address:* Greendykes, Gladsmuir, East Lothian, Scotland.
(Died April 1918.)

GENESE, Robert William, M.A.; Professor of Mathematics, Univ. College of Wales,
1879-1919; *b.* Dublin, 8 May 1848; *m.* Margaretta,
d. of Capt. Richards, Aberystwyth. *Educ.:* The
Institute, Liverpool; St. John's College, Camb.
(Local Examinations, Holt Scholar, Liverpool,
Minor and Foundation Scholar, St. John's, Cambridge, 8th Wrangler, 1871); vice-principal of
the Training College, Carmarthen, and minor
appointments; a Vice-President of the Council
of the Association for the Improvement of
Mathematical Teaching; member of the General
Committee of the British Association. *Publications:* problems in the Educational Times;
articles in the Messenger of Mathematics,
Quarterly Journal, and Nouvelles Annales des
Mathématiques; papers in the Proceedings of
the London Mathematical Society, British
Association, Association Francaise, and International Congresses. *Recreations:* wireless,
chess. *Address:* 49 Prospect Road, Southborough, Tunbridge Wells. *(Died 21 Jan. 1928.)*

GENT, His Hon. Judge (John), County
Court Judge, Halifax District, 1906; transferred
to Cornwall, 1911; retired, 1919; *b.* North-
umberland, 19 July 1844; *s.* of William and
Anne Gent; *m.* 1886, Harriet Frankland, *d.* of
Edward Randall of Loders, Dorset; three *s.* two
d. *Educ.:* Durham School; Trinity College,
Oxford. Scholar and Fellow, 1st class Mods.
and Final Classical Schools; Hertford, Ireland,
and Craven scholarships; Arnold History
Essay; Eldon Law Scholar. Called to Bar,
Lincoln's Inn, 1874. *Address:* 8 Crescent
Road, Kingston Hill, Surrey. *(Died 14 Mar. 1927.)*

GENTILI, Most Rev. Dr. Charles,
O.S.F.C.; Archbishop of Agra since 1898; *b.*
Italy, 1842. *Educ.:* Italy. Entered the Order
of Capuchins; Missionary Apostolic in India,
1870; Bishop of Allahabad, 1897. *Address:*
Agra, India.

GEOFFRION, Victor, B.C.L., K.C.,
Canada; *s.* of Felix Geoffrion and Catherine
Brodeur; *b.* St. Simon, Quebec, 23 Oct. 1851;
m. 1884, Francesca, *d.* of late Hon. Senator
Paquet, of St. Cuthbert. *Educ.:* St. Hyacinthe
Seminary; the Guild College, Montreal. Member
Canadian House of Commons since 1900;
Liberal; head of legal firm, Geoffrion, Geoffrion,
and Coussin, Montreal. *Address:* House of
Commons, Ottawa. *(Died 31 May 1923.)*

GEORGE, Sir Ernest, Kt., *cr.* 1911;
R.A. 1917; architect; *b.* London, 13 June
1839; *s.* of late John George of Streatham;
m. 1865, Mary Allan, *d.* of late Robert Burn
of Epsom; three *s.* two *d.* *Educ.:* Brighton;
Reading; R.A. gold medal for Architecture,
1859; Queen's gold medal of the Royal Institute British Architects, 1896. President
R.I.B.A. 1908-9; articled to S. Hewitt; entered
Royal Academy as student; began practice with
T. Vaughan; at Vaughan's death was joined
by Harold Peto, and on Peto's retirement
by A. B. Yeates; A.R.A. 1910. *Professional
work:* Stoodleigh Court, Devon; Rousdon,
Devon; Motcombe, Dorset; Batsford, Gloucester; Edgeworth Manor, Gloucester: Monk
Fryston, Yorks; Poles, Herts; North Mymms,

Herts ; Buchan Hill, Sussex ; Dunley Hill, Surrey ; Welbeck Abbey ; Eynsham Hall, Oxon ; Sedgwick Park, Sussex ; Ruckley Grange, Salop ; Foxcombe, Oxon. ; Putteridge Bury, Herts ; Busbridge Park, Surrey ; Crathorne Hall, Yorks. ; Shiplake Court ; Harrington Gardens ; Mount Street ; 17 Grafton Street ; Collingham Gardens, S. Kensington ; houses in Cadogan Square and Berkeley Square ; Royal Exchange Buildings, E.C. ; The Golder's Green Crematorium ; The Shirpur Palace, India ; Royal Academy of Music ; Ossington, Newark : Church of St. Andrew, Streatham ; St. Pancras, Rousdon, Devon ; the Churches of Samaden and Tarasp in the Engadine ; villa at Antibes, France ; Restorations, Berkeley Castle. *Publications:* as an etcher— Etchings on the Mosel ; Etchings on the Loire ; in Belgium ; in Venice, and Old *Address :* 71 Palace Court, W.2. *T. :* Park 696. *Club :* Arts. (*Died 8 Dec. 1922.*)

GEORGE, W. L.; author ; *b.* of Brit. parents, Paris, 20 March 1882; *m.* 1st, 1908, Helen (*d.* 1914), *d.* of Richard Porter ; 2nd, 1916, Helen Agnes (*d.* 1920), *y. d.* of late Col. Travers Madden, B.S.C. ; two *s.* ; 3rd, 1921, Kathleen, *o. d.* of Herbert Geipel, J.P., the Old Hall, Coxwold, York. *Educ. :* Paris (school and university); Germany. Has contributed to most London publications ; has been special correspondent of various papers in France, Belgium, and Spain : served in the French army ; during the War, Section Officer in the Ministry of Munitions. *Publications :* various political and economic works; novels : A Bed of Roses, 1911 ; The City of Light, 1912 ; Israel Kalisch, 1913 ; The Making of an Englishman, 1914 ; The Second Blooming, 1914 ; The Strangers' Wedding, 1916 ; Blind Alley 1919 ; Caliban, 1920 ; The Confession of Ursula Trent, 1921 ; The Stiff Lip, 1922 ; One of the Guilty, 1923 ; The Triumph of Gallio, 1924 ; Gifts of Sheba, 1926 ; miscellaneous : Woman and To-Morrow, 1913 ; Dramatic Actualities, 1914 ; Anatole France, 1915 ; Olga Nazimov, stories, 1915 ; The Intelligence of Woman, 1917; A Novelist on Novels, 1918; Eddies of the Day, 1919 ; Hail, Columbia ! 1921 ; A London Mosaic, 1921 ; How to Invest your Money, 1924 ; The Story of Woman, 1925. *Recreation :* travel. *Address:* 2 Hyde Park Terrace, W.2. *T. :* Paddington 137. *Club :* Savile. (*Died 30 Jan. 1926.*)

GEPP, Rev. Nicolas Parker, M.A.; Hon. Canon of Ely, 1915 ; Hon. Canon, Norwich, 1899 ; *s.* of Thomas Morgan Gepp, Maynetrees, Chelmsford ; *m.* Alice P. Melvill (*d.* 1915), *y. d.* of Philip Melvill, B.C.S., *e. s.* of Sir James Cosmo Melvill, K.C.B. ; one *s.* two *d. Educ. :* New College, Oxford. Curate of St. George's, Bloomsbury, 1866-69 ; Aspley-Guise, 1870 ; Great and Little Henny, 1870 ; Vicar of Sandon, Herts, 1871-77 ; Rector of St. James's, Colchester, 1877-86 ; Vicar and Rector of Great and Little Witchingham, 1886-1910 ; Rector of Northwold, 1910-19. *Address :* Oakdene, 201 Richmond Road, Kingston-on-Thames. (*Died 6 June 1921.*)

GERALD, William John, I.S.O. 1909 ; *b.* Prescott, Ont., 27 July 1850; *m.* 1869, Elizabeth Hainsworth, *d.* of William Billyard, C.E., of Windsor, Ont. ; two *d. Educ. :* St. Joseph's College, St. Laurent, Montreal. Entered Inland Revenue Department, 1867 ; Collector at Brantford and London ; Chief Inspector and Assistant Commissioner ; late Deputy Minister of Inland Revenue ; retired, 1912 ; now Parliamentary and Departmental Agent. *Recreation:* angling. *Club:* Canadian, Rotary, Ottawa. (*Died 19 Nov. 1923.*)

GERRANS, Henry Tresawna, M.A. ; Fellow, Vice-Provost, and Lecturer, sometime Bursar and Tutor, Worcester College, Oxford ; Secretary to Delegates of Local Examinations since 1887 ; *b.* Plymouth, 23 Aug. 1858 ; *e. s.* of Sampson Tresawna Gerrans and Jane, *d.* of

400

Robert Dunn ; *m.* Anna Elizabeth, 2nd *d.* of late Rev. N. F. English, 1889. *Educ.:* Cheltenham and Bristol Grammar Schools ; Christ Church, Oxford. Junior and Senior Mathematical Scholar ; 1st class in Mathematics, Mods., and Greats ; 2nd class in Natural Science, Junior Student, Christ Church, 1877 ; Fellow, Worcester College, 1882 ; Pro-proctor, 1889 ; Assist.-Commissioner to Mr. Bryce's Royal Commission, 1894 ; Proctor, 1895 ; Member of Hebdomadal Council ; Curator of the Chest ; Member of the Board of Finance ; Curator of Taylor Institution ; Delegate of the Oxford University Press, Museum, Local Examinations, and for Training of Teachers ; F.R.A.S., F.C.S., F.S.A. ; member of the London Mathematical Society, the Mathematical Association, the Physical Society, the American Mathematical Society, the Société mathematique de France, and the Circolo matematico di Palermo ; Member of the Teachers' Registration Council and of the Secondary School Examinations Council. *Address :* 20 St. John Street, Oxford. *Clubs :* Savile, Royal Societies. (*Died 20 June 1921.*)

GERRY, Hon. Elbridge Thomas ; President, New York Society for Prevention of Cruelty to Children, 1876-1901 ; Counsellor at Law ; *b.* New York, 25 Dec. 1837 ; *s.* of Thomas R. Gerry (formerly U.S. Navy) and Hannah G., *y. d.* of Peter P. Goelet ; *g. s.* of Elbridge Gerry, Vice-President U.S.A., and a signer of the Declaration of Independence ; *m.* 1867, Louisa M. (*d.* 1920), *o. d.* of Robert J. Livingston and Louisa M. Storm. *Educ.:* Columbia College, N.Y. A.B. 1857 ; A.M. 1858 ; Nashotah, Ll. D., 1910. Admitted to Bar, 1860 ; Member N.Y. State Constitutional Convention, 1867 ; Vice-President, American Society for Prevention of Cruelty to Animals until 1899 ; Governor of N.Y. Hospital, 1878-1912 ; Commodore N.Y. Yacht Club, 1886-93 ; Chairman, N.Y. State Commission on Capital Punishment (which substituted electricity for hanging), 1886-88 ; Chairman, Executive Committee, Centennial Inauguration of George Washington, 1889 ; President, Annual Conventions, N.Y. Societies for Prevention of Cruelty, 1889-1903 ; Trustee, General Theological Seminary, P.E. Church, 1877-1913 ; Trustee, American Museum of Natural History, 1895-1902 ; Director of Fifth Avenue Trust Co., 1897-1907; Director of Newport Trust Co., 1901-13 ; Director of Industrial Trust Co. of Providence, 1902-10 *Publications:* Manual of Prevention of Cruelty to Children, several editions. The following articles in North American Review, "Cruelty to Children," July 1883 ; "Capital Punishment by Electricity," Sep. 1889 ; "Children of the Stage," July 1890. *Recreations:* Yachting ; private law library of 30,000 volumes. *Address :* Newport, Rhode Island, U.S.A. ; 258 Broadway, New York ; Private Park, Lake Delaware, New York. *Clubs :* Newport Reading Room ; Hope, Providence ; Metropolitan, Knickerbocker, New York Yacht, N.Y. ; Metropolitan, Washington, D.C. (*Died 18 Feb. 1927.*)

GERVIS, Henry, M.D. (Lond.), F.R.C.P., F.S.A., J.P. Middlesex ; Consulting Obstetric Physician to St. Thomas's Hospital ; Consulting Physician to the Grosvenor Hospital and the Royal Maternity Charity. Fellow (late President) of the Obstetrical Society and of the Hunterian Society; Fellow of Royal Society of Medicine ; Fellow of Society of Antiquaries, Huguenot Society of London, British Numismatic Society, London and Middlesex Archæological Society, Somersetshire Archæological Society, and Devonshire Association ; *b.* 1837 ; *e. s.* of late F. S. Gervis, Tiverton ; *m.* Phœbe Louisa Pollard (*d.* 1918) ; one *s.* one *d. Educ.:* St. Thomas's Hospital. Successively Assistant Obstetric Physician, Lecturer on Forensic Medicine,

and Obstetric Physician and Lecturer on Obstetric Medicine at St. Thomas's ; Examiner in Obstetric Medicine at the Universities of Cambridge and London, and at the Royal College of Physicians. *Publications:* contributions to the Transactions of various medical and other societies, and of articles in Quain's Dictionary of Medicine, and Prof. Allbutt's System of Medicine. *Address:* 15 Royal Crescent, Bath. *Club:* Bath and County, Bath.
(Died 25 Sept. 1924.)

GETHIN, Sir Richard Charles Percy, 8th Bt., *cr.* 1665 ; late Major 4th Batt. Suffolk Regt. ; *b.* 20 Nov. 1847 ; *S.* father 1885 ; *m.* Catherine, *d.* of F. E. B. Scott, Ingham Lodge, Cheshire, 1876 ; three *s.* Barr. Inner Temple, 1879. Served South Africa, 1900-1902 (Queen's medal, one clasp, King's medal, two clasps) ; J.P., Hampshire. *Heir : s.* Col. R. W. St. L. Gethin. *Address :* The Grove, Hythe, Hants. *Club :* Junior United Service.
(Died 17 June 1921.)

GHOSE, Sir Chunder Madhub, Kt. ; *cr.* 1906 ; late Senior Puisne Judge, High Court, Calcutta, 1885 - 1906 ; President (Hon.) of the Board of Examiners of Candidates for Professional Pleadership and Mukhlearship, 1898-1906 ; *b.* 26 Feb. 1838 ; *s.* of late Rai Doorga Persad Ghose Bahadoor ; *m.* Srumutty Hemunt Coomary Ghose ; three *s.* two *d. Educ. :* Hindu College ; Presidency College, Calcutta University (Fellow). Began his professional career as a Pleader at Burdwan in 1860, where he held the position of Government Pleader for sixteen months ; was enrolled as Vakel, Sudder Court (now High Court), at Calcutta in 1861 ; Member of the Bengal Legislative Council, 1884 ; President of the Faculty of Law, Calcutta University, for three years ; officiating Chief-Justice at Bengal, 1906 ; took an active part (President, 1905) in the establishment of the Bengal *Kyashi Shobha* (for the amalgamation of the different subsections of the *Kyashts* of Bengal, for the improvement of their social condition and status, and for the curtailment of their extravagant marriage expenses) ; President Indian Social Conference, Dec. 1906 ; retired from office as Judge, 1907. *Address :* Bhowanipore, Calcutta.
(Died 2 Mar. 1918.)

GHOSE, Sir Rashbehary, Kt., *cr.* 1915 ; C.S.I. 1909 ; M.A., D.L., C.I.E. ; Member Viceregal Council ; *b.* 23 Dec. 1845 ; *s.* of Jagabandho Ghose of Torekona, Burdwan, India ; *m.* 1st, 1867, Priambada Dassi (*d.* 1879) ; 2nd, 1880, Matibala Dassi (*d.* 1882) ; no *c. Educ. :* Presidency College, Calcutta. M.A. 1st Class Honours, 1866 ; D.L. 1884 ; Tagore Law Professor, Calcutta University, 1876 ; Fellow, 1879 ; member of Bengal Legislative Council, 1888-91 ; Council of Viceroy of India, 1891-94 ; re-nominated, 1906. *Publication:* Law of Mortgage. *Address:* Sans Souci, Alipore, India. *Clubs:* Landholders, Calcutta, Calcutta.
(Died Mar. 1921.)

GIBB, Sir George Stegmann, Kt., *cr.* 1904 ; LL.B. (London) ; Chairman Oriental Telephone Co., Ltd. ; *b.* Aberdeen, 30 Apr. 1850 ; *y. s.* of late Alexander Gibb, C.E., Willowbank, Aberdeen, and Margaret, *d.* of John Smith, architect, of Aberdeen ; *m.* Dorothea Garrett Smith, 1881 ; four *s.* one *d. Educ. :* Aberdeen Grammar School and University. Entered solicitor's office as articled clerk, 1872 ; Assistant in Great Western Railway Solicitor's Office, 1877 ; practised as Solicitor in Fenchurch Avenue, 1880-82 ; Solicitor to the North-Eastern Railway at York, 1882 ; acted as Arbitrator for the Company in Wages Arbitration before Lord James of Hereford, 1897 ; Member of Committee on War Office Reorganisation, 1901 ; Member of Royal Commission on London Traffic, 1903 ; General Manager, North Eastern Railway, 1891-1906 ; Director, 1906-10 ; Chairman Metropolitan

District Railway Co. and of Tube Railways controlled by Underground Electric Railways Co. of London, Limited, of which company was Managing Director, 1906-10 ; Chairman of the Road Board, 1910-19 ; Member (Chairman, 1918) of Government Arbitration Board (Committee on Production), 1915-18. *Address :* South Corner, Alan Road, Wimbledon, S.W.19. *T. :* Wimbledon 568. *Club:* Reform. *(Died 17 Dec. 1925.)*

GIBBE, James A. T., I.S.O. 1902 ; *b.* 18 Apr. 1842 ; *m.* 1868, Margaret Bridget (*d.* 1912), *e. d.* of William Scott, Lanark. Late Accountant and Registrar of Bonds, Post Office, Edinburgh. *Address :* 7 Dalkeith Street, Joppa, Midlothian.
(Died 5 April 1922.)

GIBBES, Cuthbert Chapman, M.D., M.C. (Aberdeen), D.P.H. (Camb.), M.R.C.P. (London), F.L.S., F.C.S. ; Consulting Physician to the National Hospital for Diseases of the Heart ; *b.* 5 Sep. 1850 ; *s.* of Rector of Bradstone, Devon, and Margaret Murray. *Educ. :* Aberdeen University ; Westminster Hospital. Graduated M.B., M.C., Aberdeen, 1872, and shortly after was appointed R.M.O. to the Public Hospital, Kingston, Jamaica : after returning to England held the following appointments : R.M.O., Tiverton Infirmary ; House Surgeon and Physician, South Devon and East Cornwall Hospital, Plymouth ; Surgeon, Surbiton Cottage Hospital ; Medical Officer, Kingston Rural Sanitary District ; Medical Superintendent, Tolworth Isolation Hospital ; Physician, Western General Dispensary ; Pathologist, National Hospital for Diseases of the Heart. *Publications:* The Effect of Pregnancy on Chronic Heart Disease ; Sleeplessness in Heart Disease and its Treatment ; many other papers in the medical journals of Great Britain and America. *Recreations :* entomology, botany. *Address:* 89 Harley Street, Cavendish Square, W.1. *(Died 25 Aug. 1927.)*

GIBBON, Perceval, novelist and short story writer; *b.* Trelech, Carmarthenshire, 4 Nov. 1879 ; *e. s.* of Rev. J. Morgan Gibbon ; *m.* ; two *d. Educ. :* Moravian School, Königsfeld, Baden. Formerly in merchant service in British, French, and American ships ; as journalist and war-correspondent, travelled in South, Central, and East Africa, America, and Europe ; Major, Royal Marines, 1918-19. *Publications—Verse :* African Items. *Novels :* Souls in Bondage, Salvator, Margaret Harding. *Volumes of Stories :* The Vrouw Grobelaar's Leading Cases, Adventures of Miss Gregory, The Second-class Passenger, Those Who Smiled ; many contributions to all chief English and American magazines. *Recreations :* golf, motoring, shooting. *Address:* c/o J. B. Pinker, Talbot House, Arundel Street, Strand, W.C. *T.A. :* Gibbon, Bookishly, London. *(Died 30 May 1926.)*

GIBBON, Thomas Mitchell, C.I.E. 1878 ; formerly Member of Council of India. *Address :* The Hern, Beddington Lane, Croydon. *T. :* Croydon 657. *(Died May 1921.)*

GIBBON, Sir William Duff, Kt. *cr.* 1912 ; *b.* 22 July 1837 ; *s.* of Rev. Charles Gibbon, D.D., Church of Scotland, Lonmay Parish, Aberdeenshire ; *m.* Katherine (*d.* 1916), *d.* of Andrew Murray of Allathan, Aberdeen ; three *s.* three *d. Educ. :* Banff Academy ; Grammar School and University, Aberdeen. Went to Ceylon when eighteen years of age ; Chairman, Ceylon Planters' Assoc. 1878 ; member Kandy Municipal Council ; J.P., Ceylon ; acting Planting Member Legislative Council, Ceylon ; Fellow of Royal Colonial Institute. *Address:* Hathaway Cottage, Surrey Road, Bournemouth, W. *T. :* Bournemouth Area 1636. *(Died 18 Mar. 1919.)*

GIBBONS, Major Edward Stephen, D.S.O. 1914 ; 1st Batt. Middlesex Regt. ; *b.* 18 June 1883 ; *s.* of Sir William Gibbons ; *m.* 1914, Annie MacGregor, *e. d.* of late John Lyle, Finnart House, Weybridge ; one *s.* one *d.*

401

d. Entered army, 1902 ; Captain, 1912 ; **served** N.W. Frontier of India (Mohmand), 1908 (medal and clasp) ; European War, 1914-18 (despatches, D.S.O.). *Address:* Finnart House, Weybridge.
(Died 19 Sept. 1918.)

GIBBONS, Sir George Christie, Kt., *cr.* 1911 ; K.C. Can. ; President London and Western Trusts Co. ; President City Gas Co. ; Life Bencher Law Society ; *b.* 2 July 1848 ; *m.* 1876, Elizabeth, *d.* of Hugh Craig, Montreal. *Address:* London, Canada. *Clubs:* London, Toronto, York, Toronto ; Rideau, Ottawa ; St. James's, Montreal. *(Died 3 Aug. 1918.)*

GIBBONS, Cardinal (James) ; *b.* Baltimore, 23 July 1834. *Educ.:* St. Charles' Coll. Maryland ; St. Mary's Seminary, Baltimore. Ordained Priest, 1861 ; Vicar Apostolic, North Carolina, 1868 ; Bishop of Richmond, 1872 ; Archbishop of Baltimore, 1877 ; Cardinal, 1886. *Publications:* The Faith of Our Fathers ; Our Christian Heritage ; The Ambassador of Christ. *Address:* 408 N. Charles Street, Baltimore.
(Died Mar. 1921.)

GIBBONS, John Lloyd, J.P. Co. Stafford ; County Councillor N. Bilston, 1891-98 ; *b.* 1887 ; *e. surv. s.* of late Henry Gibbons, agricultural chemist, Wolverhampton. M.P. (U.) S. Wolverhampton, 1898-1900. *Address:* Ellowes Hall, Sedgley, Staffs. *T. A.:* Sedgley, Dudley. *T.:* 43 Sedgley. *(Died 27 April 1919.)*

GIBBS, Sir Charles Henry, Kt., *cr.* 1918 ; Mayor of Lambeth, 1907-8 and 1914-18 ; Leader of the Unionist Party in Lambeth since 1900 ; *b.* 1854. *Address:* 3 St. Saviour's Road, S.W.2. *T.:* Brixton 1976. *Clubs:* Constitutional, City Carlton. *(Died 12 May 1924.)*

GIBNEY, Rt. Rev. Matthew, D.D., R.C. Bishop of Perth, 1887 -1910 ; *b.* 1888. Priest, 1863 ; arrived in Western Australia, 1863 ; attended to Ned Kelly of the Ned Kelly gang after his capture, when he was supposed to be dying, and in the afternoon, whilst the other members of the gang were making their final stand in the burning hotel at Glenrowan, Victoria, in 1880, entered the burning building to endeavour to rescue them, but found Dan Kelly and his comrade, Steve Hart, lying side by side, both dead, with no signs of wounds on either. *Address:* Lourdes, Vincent Street, North Perth, Western Australia.
(Died 22 June 1925.)

GIBSON, Rt. Rev. Alan George Sumner, D.D. ; Gen. Lic. Dio. St. John's, 1911 ; *b.* 1856 ; *y. s.* of Rev. William Gibson, Rector of Fawley, and Louisanna, *d.* of Rt. Rev. Charles Richard Sumner, Bishop of Winchester ; unmarried. *Educ.:* private school (Kineton), 1866-67 ; Haileybury Coll. 1867 -75 ; Oxford, 1875-79. Scholar of Haileybury College, 1869 ; Exhibitioner of Haileybury College, 1875 ; Scholar of Corpus Christi College, Oxford, 1875 ; 1st class Class. Mods. 1876 ; 1st class Lit. Hum. 1879 ; Prox. Acc. Junior Univ. G.T. Prize, 1880 ; Senior Univ. G.T. Prize, 1881 ; M.A. 1882. Deacon, 1879 ; Priest, 1881 ; Vice - Principal Burgh Miss. Coll. 1879-80 ; Curate of Croft, Lincolnshire, 1879 - 82 ; Incumbent of Pro-Cathedral, Umtata, 1882 - 84 ; Missionary at Ncolosi, 1884 - 93 ; Canon of Umtata, 1885 - 94 ; Archdeacon of Kokstad, 1886 - 91 ; Dioc. Sec. 1882-4,1893-4; Rector of Claremont, Cape Colony, 1894-97 ; Coadjutor-Bishop of Cape Town, 1894-1906 ; Canon of St. George's, Cape Town, 1895-1906. *Publications:* Intloko Zentshumayelo (Kaffir Sermon Sketches), 1890 ; Eight Years in Kaffraria, 1891 ; Some Thoughts on Missionary Work and Life, 1894 ; Sermon Sketches for a Year, 1898 ; Between Cape Town and Loanda, 1905 ; joint-author of Translations from the Organon of Aristotle, 1877 ; edited Reminiscences of the Pondomisi War of 1880 (2nd ed., 1900) ; Sketches of Church Work and Life in the Diocese of Cape Town (1900) ; joint editor Hand-boek voor Communicanten. *Recreations:*

football XX. Haileybury, 1878, 1874 ; paperchases, fives, cricket, football, music, literature, swimming, at school ; walking, riding, music, literature, swimming, in manhood. *Address:* Matatiele, Griqualand East, S. Africa.
(Died 20 Oct. 1922.)

GIBSON, Rt. Rev. Edgar Charles Sumner, D.D. ; *b.* Fawley, Southampton, 23 Jan. 1848 ; 4th *s.* of late Rev. William Gibson, Rector of Fawley ; *m.* 1875, Mary Grace, *s. d.* of Rev. R. S. Philpott, M.A., Vicar of Chewton Mendip ; three *s. Educ.:* Charterhouse ; Trinity Coll. Oxford (Hon. Fellow, 1921). Priest, 1872 ; Chaplain of Wells Theological College 1871-74 ; Vice-Principal, 1875 ; Principal of Leeds Clergy School, 1876-80 ; Principal of Wells Theological College, 1880 - 95 ; Lecturer on Pastoral Theology, Cambridge 1893 ; Exam. Chap. to Bishop of Bath and Wells, 1894 - 1904 ; Hon. Chaplain to Queen Victoria, 1901 ; Vicar of Leeds and Rural Dean, 1895-1905 ; Bishop of Gloucester, 1905-22 ; Warburton Lecturer, 1903-1907 ; Member Royal Commission on Ecclesiastical Discipline, 1904 ; a Governor of the Charterhouse ; late Preb. of Wells ; Chaplain-in-Ordinary to King Edward VII. *Publications:* Northumbrian Saints, 1884 ; Commentary on St. James in Pulpit Commentary, 1886 ; translation of the Works of Cassian, in Nicene and Post-Nicene Library, 1894 ; Self-discipline, 1894 ; Commentary on the XXXIX. Articles, 2 vols. 1896-97, 2nd ed. (1 vol.) 1898, 9th ed. 1915. Commentary on the Book of Job, 1898, 2nd ed. 1905 ; John Howard, 1901 ; Messages from the Old Testament, 1904 ; 3rd ed. 1906 ; The Old Testament in the New, 1907 ; The Three Creeds, 1908, 2nd ed. 1909 ; the Revelation of St. John the Divine (Churchman's Bible), 1910 ; The Declaration of Assent, 1918 ; Editor George Herbert's Temple, 1899, 2nd ed. 1906. *Address:* St. Giles' House, Fareham, Hants.
(Died 8 Mar. 1924.)

GIBSON, Hon. Edward Graves Mayne, J.P. ; Barrister ; *b.* and *heir-pres.* to 2nd Baron Ashbourne ; *b.* 28 July 1875 ; *m.* 1st, 1900, Mary Philips (*d.* 1919), *d.* of late H. R. Greg, Lode Hill, Cheshire ; three *s.* three *d.* ; 2nd, 1922, Deloraine Amy Norah, *d.* of C. W. E. Henslowe of Pinewood, Grayshott, Hants. *Educ.:* Wellington ; Trinity College, Cambridge. Barrister-at-law. *Address:* Highlands, Haslemere, Surrey. *T.:* Haslemere 108. *Club:* Carlton. *(Died 26 April 1928.)*

GIBSON, Hope, C.B.E. 1919 ; Argentine landowner and stockbreeder ; Senior partner in the house of Gibson Brothers, produce brokers and export merchants, Buenos Aires ; *b.* 23 May 1859 ; *s.* of late Thomas Gibson, of the estancia, Los Yngleses, and 1 Eglinton Crescent, Edinburgh ; *m.* Agnes Russell, M.B.E., *d.* of late John Waddell, J.P., of The Inch, Bathgate, and 4 Belford Park, Edinburgh ; two *d. Educ.:* England. Civil engineer, engaged on the construction of public works at home and abroad ; joined the house of Gibson Brothers, 1889 ; held office as first Chairman of the British Chamber of Commerce in the Argentine Republic for five years ; and has been re-elected for the current year ; was President of a Committee composed of Chairmen and Representatives of six Allied Chambers of Commerce in Buenos Aires during the war. *Recreations:* shooting and fishing. *Address:* estancia Los Ynglesitos, Province of Buenos Aires ; 1833 Rodriguez Pena, City of Buenos Aires. *Club:* Jockey, Buenos Aires.
(Died 10 Oct. 1923.)

GIBSON, Rev. John Campbell, M.A. (Glasgow), D.D. (Glasgow) ; Missionary of the Presbyterian Church of England, Swatow, South China ; *b.* Kingston, Glasgow ; *s.* of Rev. James Gibson, M.A., D.D., Prof. of Divinity and Church History in Free Church College, Glasgow ; *m.* 1883. Agnes Gillespie Barclay

(d. 1915); one s. one d. *Educ.*: Academy and University of Glasgow; United Free Church Theological College. First holder, along with T. Barclay, Tai-nan, of the Thompson (Lord Kelvin) Experimental Scholarship, University of Glasgow, 1869-72; ordained Missionary of Presbyterian Church of England to China, 1874; arrived Swatow, 1874; Lecturer on Evangelistic Theology in United Free Church Colleges of Edinburgh, Glasgow, and Aberdeen, 1898-99; British Chairman of Protestant Missionary Centenary Conference, Shanghai, 1907; Moderator of Synod of the Presbyterian Church of England, 1909; Hon. Moderator of General Assembly of Presbyterian Church of China, 1918. *Publications:* The Number of Readers in China, 1887; Learning to Read in South China, 1888; A Swatow Index to the Syllabic Dictionary of Chinese, 1886; Mission Problems and Mission Methods in South China; various papers and articles chiefly relating to Missions in China. In collaboration with others; Translations of Books of the Old Testament, and the whole of the New Testament in Swatow Vernacular in Roman Letter; the whole New Testament in Simple Classical Chinese (in Chinese character). In collaboration with T. Barclay (afterwards of Tai-nan), Paper on Measurements of Specific Inductive Capacity of Dielectrics, in Transactions of Royal Society, London. *Address:* Swatow, China; Kirnan, Bearsden, Scotland.

(Died 25 Nov. 1919.)

GIBSON, Rev. John George; First Class Prelim. Theol., 1886; LL.D. (Washington Coll.), 1904; D.D. 1923; Tusculum Coll., D.D. 1924; F.S.A. (Scot.); F.E.I.S.; Rector of Ebchester, Durham, since 1895; District Head, Incorporated Soldiers and Sailors Help Society; *b.* North Shields, 14 February 1859; *o. s.* of late Captain Ralph Coxon-Gibson, R.N., and Margaret, 3rd *d.* of late John Rossiter, of Topsham and Murton; *m.* 1902, Harriette, *y. d.* of late Nathan Meanock (Mannock) of Thorn Mount, Royton, Co. Lancaster. *Educ.:* Albion Street Academy, North Shields; Private Tutors; University Coll., Durham; Heidelberg and U.S.A. Formerly H.M.I.S.; Deacon, 1887; Priest, 1888; Curate of St. Mary, Preston, 1887-1889; Royton, near Oldham, 1889-91; East Rainton, Co. Durham, 1891-93; Vicar of Irchester, Wellingborough, 1893-4; Hartford, near Huntingdon, 1894-5; F.R.G.S., F.R.S.L.; Member British Institute of Philosophical Studies; Freeman and Liveryman, City of London. *Publications:* Series of Primary School Books, 1881-1886; Primary School Arithmetic, 15th ed. 1889; Stepping Stones to Life, 3rd ed. 1893; Divine Song in its Human Echo, or Song and Service, 2nd edition, 1899; History and Folk-lore of Ebchester and District, 1900; The Registers of the Parish of Ebchester, County and Diocese of Durham, 1901; Watching for the Daybreak, 1902; Along the Shadowed Way, 1903; From Blanchland to the Tyne, or in Derwent Dale, 1905, 2nd ed. 1924; Orations of Freemasonry; The King in the East; A Casket of Masonic Verse, 1906; Freemasonry in its Relation to the Social Questions of Modern Times and other Essays, 1906; Illustrated Guide to Whitley Bay, Tynemouth, Cullercoats, Monkseaton, and District, 15th edition 1924; Dermatographs and Criminal Investigtion; Through Fast and Festival in Metre, 1907; Cleveland Watering-Places, 1909; Heroic Northumbria, 1909; The Masonic Problem, 1911; Masonry and Society, 1914, 7th ed. 1924; Masonic Problem, 2nd Series, 1915; War-time Sermons from an Old Norman Church, 1916; Fair Marjorie's Trust; The Metaphysic of Ethics, 1917; The Problem of Origin, 1919; Builders of Man, 1924; The Romance of Ebchester and its Parish Church, 1926. *Recreations:* reading and writing for the Press;

mission work and lecturing; historical research and antiquities; freemasonry, cycling, golfing, photography, and walking. *Address:* The Rectory, Ebchester, Co. Durham; Saint Ebba's, 1 Greenfield Place, Newcastle - on - Tyne; St. George's, Ormonde Avenue, Blackpool, Lancs. *T.A.:* Rector, Ebchester. *T.:* Ebchester 5; Newcastle - on - Tyne 120. *Clubs:* Authors', Canadian; Arts, Manchester.

(Died 2 Mar. 1927.)

GIBSON, Rt. Hon. John George, P.C., Hon. Mr. Justice Gibson, Judge, Queen's Bench Division, High Court of Justice, Ireland, 1888-1921; *b.* Dublin, 18 Feb. 1846; *y. s.* of late William Gibson, Rockforest, Tipperary, and Louisa, *d.* of Joseph Grant; *m.* Anna, *d.* of Rev. John Hare, 1871. *Educ.:* Portora Royal School, Enniskillen; Trin. Coll. Dublin; scholar, double first gold medallist; Vice-Chancellor's prizeman, Trin. Coll. Dublin. Barr. 1870; Q.C. 1880; Serjeant, 1885; Solicitor-General, 1885, 1886-87; Attorney-General, 1887-1888; M.P. for Walton Division of Liverpool, 1885-8. *Address:* 38 Fitzwilliam Place, Dublin. *Clubs:* Athenæum; University, Dublin.

(Died 28 June 1923.)

GIBSON, Rev. John Monro, M.A., D.D., LL.D.; Minister St. John's Wood Presb. Ch. London, since 1880; *b.* Whithorn, Scotland, 24 Apr. 1838; *s.* of Rev. James Gibson, U.P. Minister; *m.* Lucy (d. 1909), *d.* of Rev. Henry Wilkes, D.D., Principal of Theological College of British N. America (Congregational), 1864; two *s.* one *d. Educ.:* Brechin High School; University Coll. and Knox College (Theological), Toronto. Double 1st class Honours, 1862-68. Minister, Erskine Church, Montreal, as colleague to Dr. William Taylor, 1864-74; Lecturer in Greek and Hebrew Exegesis in Montreal Theological Coll., 1868-74; Minister Second Presbyterian Church, Chicago, 1874-80; Moderator Presbyterian Church of England, 1891 and 1915; President Nat. Council of Free Churches, 1897. *Publications:* Ages before Moses, 1879; The Foundations (Lectures on Sources of Christianity, 1880); The Mosaic Era, 1881; Rock versus Sand, 1883; Pomegranates from an English Garden, 1885; Christianity according to Christ, 1888; Gospel of Matthew (in Expositor's Bible) 1890; From the Outpouring of the Spirit to the Death of St. Paul (in the People's Bible History), 1895; Unity and Symmetry of the Bible, 1896; From Fact to Faith, 1898; A Strong City, and other Sermons, 1899; The Glory of Life, 1900; Apocalyptic Sketches, 1901; Protestant Principles, 1901; Devotional Study of Holy Scripture, 1904; The Inspiration and Authority of Holy Scripture, 1908. *Recreations:* music, travel, in old days cricket and chess. *Address:* Linnell Close, Hampstead Garden Suburb, N.W. *T.:* Finchley 1461. *(Died 13 Oct. 1921.)*

GIBSON, Margaret Dunlop, Hon. D.D. Heidelberg; LL.D. St. Andrews; Hon. Litt. D. Dublin; *y. twin d.* of John Smith, solicitor, Irvine, Ayrshire, one of the original Ferguson's trustees, and of Margaret Dunlop; *m.* 1883, Rev. James Young Gibson, translator of Cervantes' poetry; *d.* 1886. *Educ.:* chiefly by private tuition, in classics and Oriental and modern languages by university men. Gold Medallist, Royal Asiatic Society, 1915. Visited Sinai six times. In 1892 assisted her sister, Mrs. Lewis, to photograph the famous Syriac palimpsest of the Gospels; in 1896 they brought to England the first leaf of the Hebrew Ecclesiasticus; they also gave the site for Westminster Theological College, Cambridge, and laid its memorial stone 25 May 1897. *Publications:* How the Codex was found; Studia Sinaitica: Arabic versions of some of St. Paul's epistles, the Acts, and Catholic epistles; Catalogue of Arabic MSS.; Apocrypha Sinaitica; Apocrypha Arabica; Horæ Semiticæ, No. 1; Didascalia

Apostolorum, in Syriac and English; The Gospel Commentaries of Ishodad, in Syriac and English; Commentaries on Acts, 1913; on St. Paul's Epistles, 1916; co-editress of Palestinian Syriac Lectionary of the Gospels, of Pal.-Syr. Fragments, and of 41 facsimiles of dated Christian Arabic MSS. *Recreation:* travel. *Address:* Castlebrae, Chesterton Road, Cambridge. *M.:* CE 2078. *(Died 11 Jan. 1920.)*

GIBSON, Rt. Rev. Robert Atkinson, D.D.; Bishop of Virginia since 1897; *b.* Petersburg, Virginia, 9 July 1840, s. of Rev. Churchill Jones Gibson, D.D., and Lucy FitzHugh Atkinson; *m.* 1872, Susan Baldwin Stuart; two *s.* three *d.* *Educ.:* Hampden, Sidney College, Virginia; Virginia Theological Seminary. Private in the Rockbridge Battery of Virginia Artillery C.S.A., 1864; Assistant Minister St. James' Church, Richmond, Virginia, 1872-78; Rector Trinity Church, Ponkersburg, West Virginia, 1878-88; Rector Christ Church, Cincinnati, Ohio, 1888-97. *Address:* 906 Park Avenue, Richmond, Virginia. *(Died 17 Feb. 1919.)*

GIBSON, Thomas, C.M.G. 1919; D.S.O. 1918; medaille d'Honneur avec Glaives en Vermeil, 1921; barrister-at-law; *b.* 14 June 1875; *s.* of Joseph Gibson and Janet Buchanan; *m.* 1908, Clara Annie, *d.* of F. Sharon; two *s.* three *d.* *Educ.:* Ingersoll Collegiate Institute; Toronto University; Osgoode Hall. Read law with Maclaren, Macdonald, Shepley, and Middleton, Toronto, 1897-1900; called to Ontario Bar, 1900; practised law Ingersoll, 1900-1903; partner, Rowell, Reid, Wilkie, Wood, and Gibson, Toronto, 1908-9; General Counsel for Lake Superior Corporation and Subsidiary Companies since 1909; Head firm, Gibson & Gibson, Barristers, Toronto; Vice-President and General Counsel, Spanish River Pulp and Paper Mills, Ltd.; President and General Counsel Fort William Paper Co. Ltd. Assisted in recruiting and went overseas as second-in-command 168th Batt. Oxford's Own, C.E.F.; upon this Battalion being broken up in England, was appointed Senior Major, 4th Pioneer Batt.; after service in field, later appointed assistant Deputy Minister Overseas Militia Forces, Canada, London. Conservative, Methodist. *Recreations:* golf, gardening. *Address:* 707 Bank of Hamilton Building, Toronto; 88 Roxborough Drive, Toronto, Ont. *T.A.:* Songib. *T.:* M 5780. *M.:* 47,402. *Clubs:* Toronto, Albany, University, Toronto; Rideau, Ottawa; Lawyers, New York. *(Died Feb. 1925.)*

GIBSON, Very Rev. Thos. B., A.M., Dean of Ferns 1908-26; Rector of Kilbride and Ferns, 1896-1925; Canon of Kilrane and Taghmon 1896-1908; Rural Dean of Gorey, 1901-25; member of Diocesan Council, etc.; *s.* of Joseph and Mary Gibson of Stackallan, Co. Meath; *b.* 17 March 1847; *m.* 1st, 1878, Caroline O. Leney; 2nd, 1887, Annie M. Lowry; one *s.* four *d.* *Educ.:* Trinity College, Dublin. Ordained for Curacy of Dunmanway (Fanlobbus), Co. Cork, 1876; Headmaster of King's Hospital, Dublin, 1878-1896; Member of General Synod and Diocesan Nominator. *Publications:* Essays and Reviews in Hibernia and Dublin University Review, etc.; Ferns Cathedral Restorations; Jottings from a Parish Registrar; Sermons, etc. *Recreations:* founded Hockey Union in Ireland and held Presidency for 25 years, Fellow of Antiquarian Society, etc. *Address:* 60 Grosvenor Square, Dublin. *(Died 19 Jan. 1927.)*

GIBSON-CARMICHAEL, John Murray, Lieut. Royal Defence Corps; *b.* of Baron Carmichael, and *heir pres.* to his baronetcy; *b* 27 Dec. 1860; *m.* 1892, Amy Katherine (*d.* 1909), *d.* of Frederick Archdale of Baldock, Herts.; two *d.* *(Died 6 May 1923.)*

GIBSON - CRAIG - CARMICHAEL, Captain Sir Henry Thomas, 5th Bt.

404

cr. 1831; 12th Bt. *cr.* 1702; late 4th Batt. (Extra Reserve) Highland Light Infantry; *s.* of 3rd Bt. and Julia, *o. d.* of Archibald Buchanan, Curriehill, Midlothian; *b.* 5 Jan. 1885. *S.* brother, as 5th Bt., 1914, and kinsman, 1st Baron Carmichael, as 12th Bt., 1926. *Heir:* *c.* Eardley Charles William Gibson-Craig, *b.* 22 Nov. 1887. *Address:* Riccarton, Currie, Midlothian. *(Died 5 Sept. 1926.)*

GIDDENS, George, comedian; *b.* Bedfont, 17 June 1845; his forebears were farmers in Berks and Wilts. *Educ.:* National Schools. Commenced career at Theatre Royal, Edinburgh, and went to America; remained there till 1878, and joined Criterion Theatre; remained there till 1894; has played since at Drury Lane in Derby Winner; Cheer, Boys, Cheer; The Passport; and A Night Out, Never Again, On and Off, and Elixir of Youth, at Vaudeville; Dandy Dick, and Cyrano de Bergerac, at Wyndham's Theatre; Noble Lord, at Criterion; Women are so Serious,. at Court; Are you a Mason?; Sam Gerridge in Caste: *Recreations:* fly-fishing, landscape-painting, gardening. *Clubs:* Garrick, Green-Room, Crichton. Kinsmen. *(Died 11 Nov. 1920.)*

GIDHOUR, Maharajah Sir Ravneswar Prasad Singh, Bahadur of, K.C.I.E., *cr.* 1895; the premier nobleman in the Province of Bihar and Orissa; *b.* 1860; *m.* 1886; one *s.* Member of Bengal Legislative Council, 1898-95 (thanked for services); again elected, 1895-97; 3rd time, 1901-3; 4th time, 1903; has been member of Local Board and District Board; Hon. Magistrate; Life Vice-President B.L. Association; title of Maharajah Bahadur made hereditary, 1877; Hon. Member of the Legislative Council of the new Province of Behar, 1913-22. *Heir:* Gidhour, Maharaj Kumar Chandra Moulesshur Prasad Sing [*b.* 1890; *m.* 1913. Formally installed on the Gudee on the 17th May 1915 for investiture with powers of management over a major portion of the Raj. Member, District Board; Member Legislative Council, Patna; Honorary Magistrate]. *Address:* Gidhour, Monghyr, Behar, India. *(Died 21 Nov. 1923.)*

GIFFARD, Admiral George Augustus, C.M.G. 1902; J.P.; *b.* 20 Feb. 1849; *e. s.* of late Capt. H. W. Giffard, R.N., and Ella Emilia Stephenson; *m.* 1884, Eleanor, *y. d.* of Col. and Mrs. Bruce Brine; one *d.* *Educ.:* sea. Entered Navy, 1862; served on the Canadian Lakes, 1866; Fenian raid (medal); Victoria and Albert, 1870; in H.M.S. Alert, Arctic Expedition, 1875-76 (medal); operations in Egypt, 1882 (medal and bronze star); Commodore and senior officer, Newfoundland fisheries, 1899-1901 (C.M.G.); Admiral-Superintendent of H.M. Dockyards at Chatham, 1907-9; retired, 1913. *Address:* Highfield, Bishops Waltham, Hants. *T.A.:* Bishops Waltham. *T:* 19 Bishops Waltham. *Club:* Royal Naval. Portsmouth. *(Died 23 Sept. 1925.)*

GIFFARD, Major-General Sir Gerald Godfray, K.C.I.E. *cr.* 1923; C.S.I. 1913; M.R.C.P., M.R.C.S.; *b.* 19 Jan. 1867; *m.* 1898, Alice Melicent, *e. d.* of James Grose, C.I.E., I.C.S.; two *s.* two *d.* *Educ.:* St. Bartholomew's Hospital. Lieutenant I.M.S. 1890; Captain, 1893; Major, 1902; Lt.-Col. 1910; Major-General, 1918; Resident Surgeon, General Hospital, Madras, 1897; District Medical and Sanitary Officer, Chingleput, 1899; Professor, Materia Medica, Madras College, 1901; Professor, Surgery, 1903; Professor of Midwifery and Superintendent Government Maternity Hospital, 1906; Commandant Hospital Ship, Madras, 1914-15; A.D.M.S. 6th Poona Div., 1915; Surgeon-General with the Govt. of Madras, 1919-23; retired, 1924. *Address:* c/o Grindlay & Co., 54 Parliament Street, S.W.1. *(Died 5 Jan. 1926.)*

GIFFARD, Sir Henry Alexander, Kt., cr. 1903; K.C.; Bencher of Lincoln's Inn since 1885; b. 1838; e. s. of Col. Henry Giffard, R.G.A., and Elizabeth, d. of James Agnew; m. Helen Agnes (d. 1913), o. d. of Stephen Alers Hankey, 1866; two s. Educ.: Elizabeth College, Guernsey; Corpus Christi College, Oxford (M.A.). Exhibitioner, 1857; Junior Mathematical Scholar, 1858; 1st class Mods. (classics and mathematics), 1859; Taylorian scholar, 1860; 1st class Lit. Hum. and 1st class Math. 1861; Eldon scholar, 1861; Senior student of Christ Church, 1863; called to the Bar, Linc. Inn, 1865; Q.C., 1882; Assistant Commissioner on Schools Inquiry Commission, 1865-66; contested East Cambs. 1892; Reader in Equity to Inns of Court, 1888-91; Bailiff of Guernsey, 1902-8. Recreations: golf, shooting. Address: Braye du Valle, Guernsey. Clubs: New University, Cecil. (Died 1 July 1927.)

GIFFARD, Walter Thos. Courtenay, D.L., J.P. Co. Stafford; b. 11 Jan. 1839; s. of Walter Peter Giffard of Chillington, Co. Stafford, and Henrietta Dorothy, 2nd d. of late Sir John Fenton Boughey, 2nd Bart. of Aqualate, Co. Stafford; m. 1879, Mary Constance, e. d. of Richard Holt Briscoe, Somerford, Co. Stafford; two s. two d. Educ.: Leamington Coll. Heir: s. Thomas Arthur Walter [b. 2 Aug. 1882; m. 1918, Angela Erskine, e. d. of Sir William Trollope. Educ.: Oxford, B.A.]. Address: Chillington, Wolverhampton. T.A.: Codsall. Club: Conservative, Wolverhampton. (Died 31 Oct. 1926.)

GIFFARD, Colonel William Carter, D.S.O. 1900; Welsh Regt.; retired; b. 25 June 1859; s. of late Major E. C. Giffard; m. 1906, Cecile Margaret Stewart, d. of Mrs. Schwabe. Served Suakin, 1888 (despatches, medal with clasp, 4th class Medjidie, Khedive's Star); Gold Coast, 1897-98 (despatches, brevet Lt.-Col., medal with clasp); South Africa, 1899-1902 (wounded, despatches, Queen's medal, 5 clasps, King's medal, 2 clasps, D.S.O.; European War (despatches, Bt. Col.). Address: Skiddaw View, Keswick. (Died 25 April 1921.)

GIFFORD, Charles Edwin, C.B. 1894; Retired Paymaster-in-Chief, Royal Navy; b. Milton Abbott, Devon, 8 Apr. 1848; s. of George Mitchell Gifford, m. Effie (d. 1902), d. of Mark A. Neef, Chicago, U.S.A., 1880; one s. two d. Educ.: King Edward's School, Launceston. Entered R.N. 1861; served as Secretary to Naval Commanders - in - Chief of Channel Squadron, Cape of Good Hope, Portsmouth, The Nore, Mediterranean; Secretary at Portsmouth during Jubilee Naval Review, 1887; Naval Review, 1897; employed at Admiralty on manning and recruiting duties 1897-1908. Publication: (joint) Manual of Naval-Law and Court-Martial Procedure. Address: Chesterton House, West Ewell, Surrey. T.: Epsom 476. (Died 18 Feb. 1923.)

GILBERT, Albert, R.O.I.; Art Master, Leys School, Cambridge; Governing Member of the Artists Society and Langham Sketching Club; b. London. Educ.: Southport. Exhibitor at Royal Academy and other London exhibitions; also the Provincial Galleries; illustrator. Address: 39 Fairfax Road, Bedford Park, W.4. T.: Chiswick 2143. Club: Chelsea Arts. (Died 15 June 1927.)

GILBERT, Rev. Charles Robert, Rector of Seagrave, Leicestershire, since 1906; b. Oxford, 12 July 1851; s. of late Charles Gilbert, C.E.; m. 1877, Edith Mary Walton, 2nd d. of Rev. J. Dawson, Vicar of Holy Trinity, Weston-super-Mare; three d. Educ.: Rugby; Christ's Coll. Camb. (Open Scholar), 19th wrangler, and 2nd class Moral Sciences Tripos; B.A. 1874; M.A. 1877; private coaching at Cambridge after degree till 1875; Mathematical Master, Derby School, 1875-78; Deacon, 1876;

Priest, 1877; Head Master of Weymouth Coll. 1879-85; Master of Modern Side and Senior Mathematical Master, St. Peter's School, York, 1885-90; Head Master of King Henry VIII. School, Coventry, 1890-1905; Select Preacher at Cambridge, 1891; Domestic Chaplain to Lord Leigh at Stoneleigh Abbey, 1891-1905; Chaplain of Ragdale, Leics., 1910-15; Editor of Shakespeare's King Henry V., 1911; You Like It, 1912. Publication: Notes on St. Matthew's Gospel, 1914. Recreations: cycling, bowls, reading, singing. Address: Seagrave Rectory, near Loughborough. T.A.: Gilbert, Seagrave, Sileby. (Died 29 Dec. 1919.)

GILBERT, Lady (Rosa Mulholland), authoress; 2nd d. of Joseph Stevenson Mulholland, M.D., Belfast; b. Belfast; m. 1891, Sir John T. Gilbert, LL.D. (d. 1898). Educ.: home. Publications: Hester's History; The Wild Birds of Killeevy; Marcella Grace; A Fair Emigrant; The Late Miss Hollingford; Banshee Castle; Giannetta; Vagrant Verses; Hetty Gray; Four Little Mischiefs; Puck and Blossom: The Walking Trees; Nanno; Onora; Cynthia's Bonnet Shop; Terry; The Squire's Granddaughters; The Tragedy of Chris; A Girl's Ideal; The Life of Sir John T. Gilbert; Our Sister Maisie; The Return of Mary O'Murrough; Spirit and Dust (poems); Cousin Sara; The O'Shaughnessy Girls; Father Tim; Fair Noreen; Twin Sisters; Old School Friends; The Daughter in Possession; Narcissa's Ring, 1915; etc. Recreations: gardening, reading, seeing friends. Address: Villa Nova, Blackrock, Co. Dublin.
(Died April 1921.)

GILBERT, Rev. Thomas Morrell; Vicar of Heversham, 1866-1921; Hon. Canon Carlisle since 1877; m. Esther Anne Harrison (d. 1917). Educ.: Trinity College, Cambridge (Fellow). Ordained 1861; Curate of Hurstpierpoint, 1861-63; St. Bartholomew's, Chichester, 1863-1864; Incumbent, 1864-66; Vice-Principal Chichester College, 1863-66; R.D. Kirkby Lonsdale, 1888-1912. Address: 21 Warwick Square, S.W.1. (Died 16 Dec. 1923.)

GILBERT-CARTER, Sir Gilbert Thomas, K.C.M.G., cr. 1893; F.Z.S.; F.S.A.; F.Ent.S.; F.R.C.I.; F.R.G.S.; b. 14 Jan. 1848; o. s. of Commander Thomas Gilbert Carter, R.N.; m. 1st, 1874, Susan Laura (d. 1895), 4th d. of Lieut.-Col. Edward Hocker, C.B.; 2nd, 1903, Gertrude Codman, o. c. of late Francis Parker of Boston, U.S.A.; three s. two d. Educ.: Royal Naval School, Greenwich; private tutors. Royal Navy, 1864-75; Private Sec. to Governor Leeward Islands, 1875-79; Treasurer and Collector of Customs, Gold Coast, 1879-82; transferred to Gambia in same capacity, 1882-88; Administrator, 1888-91; Governor and Commander - in - Chief, Lagos, 1891-96; Bahama Islands, 1897-1904; Barbados, 1904-10; transferred temporarily to Trinidad, 1907; retired, 1910; by deed-poll name changed to Gilbert-Carter, 1919. Recreations: lawn tennis, archery, natural history pursuits and gardening. Address: 43 Charing Cross, S.W.; Ilaro Court, Barbados, West Indies. (Died 18 Jan. 1927.)

GILBERTSON, Rev. Lewis, M.A., F.S.A.; Rector of St. Martin's, Ludgate, with St. Gregory by St. Paul, and St. Mary Magdalen, Old Fish St.; Hon. Minor Canon of St. Paul's since 1903; b. 1857; m. 1912, Edith, d. of Sir Brydges Henniker, 4th Bart. Educ.: Magdalen School, and Queen's College, Oxford (honours, Natural Science, 1876). Curate of Fulham, 1880; Minor Canon, St. Paul's Cathedral, 1882; Succentor, 1893-1903; Librarian, 1897-1903. Address: 32 Dorset Square, N.W.1. T.: Paddington 0662. Clubs: Athenæum, Burlington Fine Arts.
(Died 12 June 1923.)

GILBEY, Lt.-Col. Alfred, J.P., V.D.; Director of Barclays Bank and W. & A. Gilbey; b. Jan. 1859: s. of late Alfred Gilbey, one of the founders of W. and A. Gilbey; *m.* 1885, Beatrice Elizabeth (*d.* 1926), *d.* of W. J. Holland of Cadogan Gardens; five *s.* Contested (L.) South Bucks, 1886; member of Tariff Reform Commission; commanded Buckinghamshire Vol., 1900-1906; Master of The Old Berkeley Hunt West Hounds, 1895-1902; High Sheriff, Bucks, 1906; raised and commanded a Bucks Territorial Battalion in 1915-16. *Address:* 78 Upper Berkeley St., W.1. *T.:* Mayfair 7114. *Clubs:* Carlton, Marlborough. (*Died 24 Oct. 1927.*)

GILCHRIST, Douglas Alston, B.Sc. (Agric., Edin.); Hon M.Sc., Durham, F.R.S.E.; F.H.A.S.; Professor of Agriculture, Armstrong College (University of Durham), Newcastle-upon-Tyne; and Director of Northumberland Agricultural Experiment Station at Cockle Park; *s.* of late Wm. Gilchrist, Bothwell, Scotland; *m.* Jessie Kathleen, *d.* of late J. F. Ferguson, Reading. *Educ.:* Hamilton Academy; Technical College, Glasgow; Edinburgh University. Director of the Agricultural Department, University Coll., Reading, 1894-1902; head of Agricultural Department of University College of North Wales, Bangor, 1889-94. *Address:* The Quarries West, Clifton Road, Newcastle-on-Tyne. (*Died 4 April 1927.*)

GILCHRIST, John Dow Fisher, M.A., D.Sc., Ph.D., F.L.S., C.M.Z.S.; Professor of Zoology, University of Cape Town, since 1918; *b.* 1866; 2nd *s.* of late Andrew Gilchrist, Anstruther, Scotland; *m.* Elfreda Ruth, *d.* of late S. H. Raubenheimer, Heimers River, George; one *s.* one *d. Educ.:* Madras College, St. Andrews; Universities of St. Andrews, Edinburgh, Munich, and Zurich. Assistant in Zoological Department, University of Edinburgh, 1893; Marine Biologist to the Government of the Cape of Good Hope, 1895; carried out Marine Biological and Fisheries Survey of Cape Coasts, 1896-1904; discovered trawling ground on Agulhas Bank, 1898; carried out Marine Biological and Fisheries Survey for Natal Government, 1902; President of the S. African Philosophical Society, Cape Town, 1903-4; Hon. Member Soc. Centrale d'Aquiculture; Joint Hon. Secretary S. African Association for the Advancement of Science, 1902-5; Professor of Zoology, South African College, Cape Town, 1905-17; Chairman of Fishery Board of Cape Province, 1908; Marine Biological and Fisheries Adviser for Cape Province, 1912; President of the Royal Society of South Africa, 1918; Hon. Director S. Africa Fishing and Marine Biological Survey, 1920; President S. Africa Association for Advancement of Science, 1922. *Publications:* Annual Reports of Marine Biologist to Cape Government, 1895-1904; editor and part author of Marine Investigations in S. Africa (5 vols.), 1902-8; Joint Editor Science in S. Africa, 1905; South African Zoology, 1911; Marine Biological Reports to Cape Province from 1913; Reports on the Fisheries and Marine Biological Survey of S. Africa, since 1920; papers, chiefly on Fishes, Mollusca, Crustacea, Hemichordata, Temperatures and Currents of S. African Seas, etc., in various scientific publications. *Address:* University of Cape Town. (*Died Oct. 1926.*)

GILCHRIST, Robert Murray; novelist; *b.* Sheffield, 6 Jan. 1868; 2nd *s.* of Robert Murray Gilchrist and Isabella, *d.* of Peter Murray; unmarried. *Educ.:* Sheffield Royal Grammar School; privately. Began to write at an early age; spent many summers in Derbyshire; and afterwards lived for several years in a remote part of the High Peak, studying the country folk; contributed to the National Observer in W. E. Henley's day. *Publications:* Passion the Plaything 1890; Frangipanni, 1893; The Stone Dragon and other Tragical Romances, 1894; Hercules and the Marionettes, 1894; A Peak-

land Faggot, 1897; Willowbrake, 1898; The Rue Bargain, 1898; Nicholas and Mary, 1899; The Courtesy Dame, 1900; The Labyrinth, 1902; Natives of Milton, 1902; Beggar's Manor, 1903; Lords and Ladies, 1903; The Wonderful Adventures, 1905; The Gentle Thespians, 1908; Good-bye to Market, 1908; The Abbey Mystery, 1908; The Two Goodwins, 1909; Pretty Fanny's Way, 1909; The Peak District, 1911; Willowford Woods, 1911; The Firstborn, 1911; The Secret Tontine, 1912; Damosel Croft, 1912; The Dukeries, 1913; Roadknight, 1913; Weird Wedlock, 1913; The Chase, 1913; Ripon and Harrogate, 1914; Scarborough, 1914; Under Cover of Night, 1914; Honeysuckle Rogue, 1916. *Recreations:* long moorland walks, motoring, music. *Address:* Cartledge Hall, Holmesfield, Sheffield. (*Died 4 April 1917.*)

GILDEA, Col. Sir James, Kt., *cr.* 1902; G.B.E., *cr.* 1920; K.C.V.O. *cr.* 1908; C.V.O., 1901; C.B., 1898; F.S.A., F.R.G.S.; Knight of Justice Order of St. John of Jerusalem; Jubilee (Queen Victoria) and Coronation medals, King Edward VII. and King George V.; King Edward and Queen Alexandra Personal Gold Medal; Col. comm. 6th Royal Warwickshire Regt. 1890-1898; Hon. Col. 4th Batt. (Special Reserve) Royal Warwickshire Regt. 1909; *b.* Kilmaine, Co. Mayo, 23 June 1838; 3rd *s.* of late Very Rev. George Robert Gildea, Provost of Tuam; *m.* 1864, Rachel Caroline (*d.* 1888) (a Lady of Justice Order of St. John of Jerusalem), *d.* of Arthur Kett Barclay of Bury Hill, Dorking; one *s.* two. *d. Educ.:* St. Columba's College, Ireland; Pembroke Coll. Cambridge. Served in Franco-German War (Nat. Soc. for Aid to Sick and Wounded in War); mainly instrumental in raising a fund of £12,000 for relief of widows and orphans of those killed during the Zulu War, 1879; raised a similar fund in connection with the Afghan War, 1880; to these funds he acted as Treasurer and Hon. Secretary; Treasurer in England at the same time to the Indian Patriotic and Bombay Military Relief Funds; Organising Secretary of Queen Victoria's Jubilee Institute for Nurses, 1890-95; founded the Soldiers' and Sailors' Families Association, of which he is Chairman, Treasurer, and one of Trustees, 1885; founded also in connection with this the "Officers," "Nursing," and "Clothing" branches, Royal Homes for Officers' Widows and Daughters, Queen Alexandra's Court, Wimbledon, 1899; was instrumental in raising the "Serpent" and "Edgar Boat" Funds, as also the N.W. Frontier Fund, all of which are administered by the Assoc., over one million and a quarter was placed in the hands of and administered by the Assoc. during the South African War, 1899-1902; and two million and a half during the European War, 1914-17; is one of the members of the Royal Patriotic Fund Corporation (1903); has taken an active part (being one of its promoters) in the St. John Ambulance Association, of which he was treasurer, as well as assistant almoner of the Order of St. John of Jerusalem. *Publications:* The Order of St. John of Jerusalem in England; The St. John Ambulance Association; Naval and Military Funds and Institutions; For King and Country, being a Record of Funds and Philanthropic Work in connection with the South African War, 1899-1902; For Remembrance, being memorials erected in memory of those who lost their lives in the same war; Memorials to His late Majesty King Edward VII.; The Gildeas of Port Royal and Clooncormack; Historical Record of the Work of the Soldiers' and Sailors' Families Association from 1885 to 1916; and History of the Royal Homes from 1899 to 1918. *Recreations:* oarsman at Cambridge; cycling. *Address:* 11 Hogarth Road, S.W.5.

(*Died 6 Oct. 1920.*)

GILDEA, Rev. William; Rector of Upwey 1901-22; Canon of Salisbury since 1898; *b.* Dec. 1883; 2nd *s.* of Very Rev. George Robert Gildea, Provost of Tuam, and Esther, *o. d.* of Thomas Green of Green Mount, Enniscorthy; *m.* 1862, Sarah Caroline (*d.* 1924), *e. d.* of N. P. Simes, Strood Park, Horsham; five *s.* four *d. Educ.:* Marlborough; Exeter College, Oxford. B.A. (4th class Lit. Hum.), 1856; M.A. 1858; Deacon, 1856; Priest, 1858; Curate of Compton Valence, Dorset, 1856-61; Vicar of West Lulworth, Dorset, 1862-79; Netherbury, Dorset, 1879-1901; Rural Dean, Beaminster Portion, 1890-1901; Chaplain of Beaminster Union, 1888-1901; Acting Chaplain, Valparaiso, 1897-98. *Publications:* an article in the National Review in answer to the late H. Farquharson, M.P., on Tithe. *Recreations:* wood work, shooting, salmon fishing, yachting. *Address:* Innellan, Verne Road, Rodwell, Weymouth. *T.A.:* Weymouth. *Club:* Royal Dorset Yacht, Weymouth. (*Died 11 Dec. 1925.*)

GILDER, Jeannette Leonard, special literary agent since 1908; *b.* Flushing, New York, 3 Oct. 1849; *d.* of Rev. William H. Gilder. Left school at fourteen to accept clerical position, father having died during Civil War; journalist since 1872, first on New York Tribune; was musical, dramatic, and literary critic on N.Y. Herald seven years; left Herald to start The Critic, later Putnam's Magazine, with J. B. Gilder, in 1881. *Publications:* Taken by Siege, pub. anonymously, 1886, repub. with name, 1897; The Autobiography of a Tomboy, 1900; The Tomboy at Work, 1904; and dramatic versions of Quo Vadis, Folly Corner, Joan of the Sword Hand, and other popular novels; edited Representative Poems of Living Poets, 1888; Pen Portraits of Literary Women, with Helen Gray Cone, 1889; and Authors at Home, with J. B. Gilder, 1888; literary correspondent of Chicago Tribune since 1888; established The Reader, 1911. *Recreation:* loafing in Europe, and among the hill farms of Connecticut. *Address:* 100 East 17th Street, New York. *Club:* Colony. (*Died 17 Jan. 1916.*)

GILDERSLEEVE, Basil Lanneau, Ph.D., LL.D.; Hon. D.Litt. Oxford and Cambridge; Professor of Greek, Johns Hopkins University, Baltimore, 1876-1915; *b.* Charleston, S.C., 23 October 1831; *e. s.* of Rev. Benjamin Gildersleeve and Louisa Lanneau; *m.* Elizabeth Fisher, *e. d.* of Raleigh Colston and Gertrude Powell; one *s.* one *d. Educ.:* Princeton (B.A. 1849, M.A. 1852); Berlin; Göttingen (Ph.D. 1853); Bonn. Professor of Greek, Univ. of Virginia, 1856-76; of Latin, 1861-1866. *Publications:* Latin Grammar, 1867; 3rd ed., with Lodge, 1894; and other Latin school books; joint-editor of Gildersleeve-Lodge Latin Series; Ed. Persius, 1875; Justin Martyr's Apologies, 1877; Pindar's Olympian and Pythian Odes, 1885; Essays and Studies, 1890; Syntax of Classical Greek, First Part, 1901; Second Part, 1911; Problems in Greek Syntax, 1903; Hellas and Hesperia, 1909; Creed of the Old South, 1915; Associate Editor for Greek Literature, Johnson's Cyclopædia; Founder and Editor of the American Journal of Philology, 1880-1919; Corresponding Fellow of British Academy; Member of American Academy of Arts and Letters. *Address:* The Johns Hopkins University, Baltimore, Maryland, U.S.A. *Clubs:* University, Country, Johns Hopkins, Baltimore. (*Died Jan. 1924.*)

GILES, Sub.-Lieut. Alfred Edward Boscawen, R.N., D.S.O. 1915. Served European War, Dardanelles, in H.M.S. Inflexible, 1914-15 (despatches, D.S.O.). (*Died Oct. 1917.*)

GILES, Bertram, C.M.G. 1916; Consul-General, Nanking, since 1924; *b.* Hankow, 24 Sep. 1874; *s.* of Prof. H. A. Giles; *m.* 1903, Violet Jessie, 2nd *d.* of David Gilmour of Shanghai; one *s. Educ.:* Belgium (Liége); Austria (Feldkirch); Scotland (Aberdeen). Student Interpreter, China, 1894; 1st Class Assist. 1902; Assist. in Mixed Court, Shanghai, 1902-4; Vice-Consul at Canton, 1904-5; Hankow, 1910; Acting Consul at Foochow, 1905; Changsha, 1905-7; Tsinan, 1908-10; Consul at Changsha, 1910-13; Nanking, 1914-21; Consul-General, Tsinan, 1922; Senior British Delegate on Joint Commission for Rendition of Wei-hai-wei, 1922-3; Consul-General, Canton, 1923-4. *Recreations:* billiards, croquet, pedestrianism. *Address:* H.B.M. Consulate-General, Nanking, China. *T.A.:* Britain, Nanking. (*Died 26 Mar. 1928.*)

GILES, Peter Broome, C.B. 1911; T.D., V.D., J.P.; *b.* 5 April 1850; *e. s.* of Peter Broome Giles and Caroline, *d.* of late Admiral T. Bennett; *m.* 1879, Florence, *e. d.* of late J. C. Houghton, of the Quinta, Brobury, Hereford, and 20 Devonshire Place, W.; one *s.* one *d. Educ.:* St. Catherine's Hermitage, Bath; University College. J.P. Hereford, Bucks and Kent; High Sheriff, Bucks., 1907; Member of County Council; County Director for the City of London Branch of the British Red Cross Society since 1905; Commandant of the Military Convalescent Hospital, Alnwick, 1915; Commandant of Vol. Ambulance School of Instruction; Commandant of the Military Convalescent Hospital, Ashton-in-Makerfield, 1917; Master of Herefordshire Staghounds. *Publications:* a large number of articles upon Ambulance work, the organisation of Royal Army Medical units, Sanitation. *Recreations:* hunting, shooting, fishing. *Address:* 51 Earls Avenue, Folkestone. *T.:* 187. *Club:* Junior Army and Navy. (*Died 19 Dec. 1928.*)

GILES, Robert, M.A. (Cantab.), C.I.E. 1899; *b.* 27 Sept. 1846; *s.* of late Archdeacon Giles, Precentor of Lincoln and Rector of Willoughby, Lincolnshire; *m.* Isabel, *d.* of General Thom, I.M.S., 1885. *Educ.:* Durham Grammar School; St. John's Coll. Cambridge; Joined the Sind Commission; Collector of Karachi, 1895; acted repeatedly as Commissioner in Sind, 1890-1900, and confirmed in that appointment; retired, 1902; J.P. West Sussex; Member of West Sussex County Tribunal. *Address:* Ash, Stedham, Midhurst, Sussex. *Club:* East India United Service. (*Died 17 Mar. 1928.*)

GILHOOLY, James Peter, J.P.; *b.* 1847; *s.* of late P. Gilhooly, Bantry, Cork; *m.* Mary, *d.* of J. Collins, 1882. Draper, Bantry; member of Poor Law Board; President of Local National League; Chairman of Town Commissioners, Rural District Council, and local branch United Irish League; Representative of Provincial Executive of United Irish League was imprisoned several times under the Coercion régime; M.P. (N.) Co. Cork, W., 1885-1910, and since 1910. *Address:* Bantry, Co. Cork. (*Died 16 Oct. 1916.*)

GILKES, Rev. Arthur Herman, M.A.; Curate St. James's Church, Bermondsey, since 1915; *s.* of William Gilkes, chemist, Leominster, Herefordshire; *m. d.* of B. M. Clarke, Clairville, Sydenham Hill, 1892; four *s. Educ.:* Shrewsbury School; Christ Church, Oxford. 1st class in Mods. and in Final Schools Litteris Humanioribus. Assistant Master at Shrewsbury, 1873-85; Head Master of Dulwich College, 1885-1914; ordained 1915. *Publications:* School lectures on Electra and Macbeth; Boys and Masters; The Thing that Hath Been; Kallistratus; The New Revolution; A Dialogue; A Day at Dulwich; Four Sons. *Recreations:* cycling and cricket. *Address:* St. James's Church, Jamaica Road, Bermondsey, S.E. (*Died 13 Sept. 1922.*)

GILL, Andrew John Mitchell-, F.S.A. (Scot.); has assumed the additional surname of Mitchell; J.P. and Commissioner of Supply for Cos. of Aberdeen and Elgin; *b.* 1 Aug. 1847;

o. surv. s. of late David Gill, J.P., of Blair-ythan and Savock, Aberdeenshire, and Margaret, *d.* of Gilbert Mitchell of Savock ; *m.* 1894, Margaret, 2nd *d.* of late Charles S. Lindsell of Holme, J.P., D.L. Bedfordshire ; three *d. Educ. :* Marischal College and Univ. Aberdeen ; R. A. College, Cirencester. Has travelled extensively in Australia, S. Africa, Morocco, etc. Is an authority in Genealogy and Heraldry, particularly so far as the north country families are concerned. *Publications:* The Houses of Moir and Byres ; many genealogical articles and pamphlets. *Address :* Auchinroath House, Rothes, and Savock House, Newburgh, Aberdeenshire. *Club :* Conservative, Edinburgh.
(Died 1 Mar. 1921.)

GILL, Sir Charles Frederick, Kt., *cr.* 1921 ; K.C. ; Recorder of Chichester 1890-1921 ; *b.* 10 June 1851 ; *s.* of late Charles Gill of Dublin ; *m.* 1878, Ada, 7th *d.* of John Crossley Fielding of Forest Hill, Kent ; one *s.* one *d. Educ. :* Royal School, Dungannon. Barr. Middle Temple, 1874, Bencher 1905, Lent Reader 1919 ; Junior Counsel to Post Office, 1886-87 ; Senior Counsel to Post Office, 1887-89 ; Junior Counsel to Treasury, 1889-92 ; Senior Counsel to Treasury, 1892 - 99 ; Junior Counsel to London Bankers' Association, 1889-98 ; Senior Counsel to London Bankers' Association, 1901 ; Senior Counsel to the Jockey Club, 1908-22 ; Hon. Member of the Jockey Club. *Address :* Tappington, Birchington, Thanet. *T. :* Birchington 10 ; 1 Brick Court, Temple, E.C.4. *Clubs :* Carlton, Garrick, Beefsteak, Turf.
(Died 22 Feb. 1923.)

GILL, L. Upcott, part proprietor of the Bazaar, Exchange and Mart newspaper; formerly Governing Director and Chairman L. Upcott Gill and Son, Ltd., and past Chairman of the Master Printers' Association ; is a Fellow of the Institute of Journalists; *b.* 7 Nov. 1846; 2nd and *e. surv. s.* of Chas. J. Gill and Emma Gill, *sister* of late Serjeant Cox (last of the Serjeants-at-Law) ; *m.* Gertrude Alice, *e. d.* of late Dr. A. Sumner, St. John's Wood, 1874 ; two *s.* four *d. Educ. :* City of London School. Entered Life Assurance Office of which his father was secretary, and subsequently joined staff of The Field and Queen, and when the Exchange and Mart was started, 1868, was appointed manager and editor. Entered for the Bar, Lincoln's Inn, for a time, but subsequently relinquished law to devote himself to journalism. Has edited a large number of technical handbooks. *Recreations :* fly-fishing, gardening. *Address :* The Old Manor House, Feltham, Middlesex.
(Died 9 Mar. 1919.)

GILL, Thomas, C.M.G. 1918 ; I.S.O. 1903 ; Under Treasurer of South Australia, 1894-1920 ; *b.* 23 Feb. 1849; *m.* 1876, Louisa Jane, (*d.* 1915) *d.* of John Bristow. Entered Civil Service, 1865 ; retired 1920; Member of Public Library Board, etc., since 1896; Hon. Treasurer Royal Geographical Soc. of Australasia, S.A. Branch, since 1885 ; Government Member Adelaide Tramways Trust since 1896 ; a Trustee of the State Savings Bank since 1920 ; a S.A. Commissioner of Charitable Funds ; a Governor of the Wyatt Benevolent Institution, and Member of Board Da Costa Charitable Fund. *Publications :* Bibliography of South Australia ; The History of Glen Osmond ; Colonel William Light ; Coinage and Currency of S.A. *Address :* Willalar, Glen Osmond, South Australia. *(Died 22 July 1923.)*

GILLESPIE, Robert Alexander ; Stipendiary Magistrate for the Borough of West Ham ; *b.* 30 March 1848 ; *s.* of Alexander Gillespie, merchant, of London, and Montreal, Canada, and Eliza Greenshields ; *m.* 1896, Helen Duncan, *d.* of John Inglis of 10 Upper Phillimore Gardens, Kensington. *Educ. :* Weybridge School ; St. John's College, Cambridge. B.A. 1869. Barr., Middle Temple, 1871 ; has

practised on the Home and South-Eastern Circuits, and at Surrey and South London Sessions. *Address :* 3 Plowden Buildings, Temple, E.C. *Club :* United University.
(Died 11 April 1917.)

GILLETT, Major William, D.L., Herefordshire ; F.R.G.S., F.Z.S.; *b.* 1839, *o. surv. s.* of late Joseph Ashby Gillett, of Banbury, Oxfordshire, Banker. Unmarried. *Educ. :* private tutors. Originated and carried out clearing of Country Bankers' Cheques, 1859-60, for which he was presented with a testimonial by the Country Bankers of England and Wales. Travelled United States, Canada, West Indies, and in Europe, 1860-61 ; visited Russia, Turkey, Palestine, and North Africa, 1867-68 ; travelled with American Army Commission through Japan, China, and India, 1875-76; visited South America, Mexico, Sandwich Islands, New Zealand, and Australia, 1877-78 ; Middlesex Yeomanry Cavalry, 1869-1881 ; Major 1873 - 81 ; attached to 1st Life Guards, 1870 - 72. In conjunction with the late Colonel Farquharson of Invercauld, and the late Mr. Augustus Savile of Rufford Abbey, established the Bachelors' Club in 1881, of which club he is President and one of the Trustees. *Publications :* A British Zollverein, 1879 ; The Revival of British Industries, 1885 ; Detailed Proposals for a Tariff Bill, 1904 ; House of Lords Reform, 1911 ; Reduction of the National Debt and Decrease of Taxation, 1920. *Recreations :* hunting, shooting, yachting. *Address :* 19 Lowndes Square, S.W.1. *T. :* Victoria 3114. *Clubs :* Carlton, Junior Carlton, Bachelors', Royal Thames Yacht. *(Died 5 Dec. 1925.)*

GILLIES, Hon. William Neal, lay member of Queensland Board of Trade and Arbitration since 1925 ; *b.* 28 Oct. 1868 ; *s.* of Dugald Gillies ; *m.* 1897, Margaret, *d.* of late Shelton Smith, of Queanbeyan, N.S.W. ; one *s.* one *d.* M.L.A. 1912-25 ; Chairman of Public Works Commission, 1916; Minister of Justice, 1918 ; Secretary for Agriculture and Stock, 1919-1925 ; Premier, Vice-President of the Executive Council, Chief Secretary and Treasurer of Queensland, 1925 ; resigned premiership, 1925. *Address :* St. Osyth Street, Toowong, Brisbane, Queensland. *(Died 9 Feb. 1928.)*

GILLMAN, Herbert Francis Webb, C.S.I. 1917 ; I.C.S. ; Ordinary Member of Council of Governor of Madras ; Collector and Magistrate, Madras, since 1907. *Educ. :* Dulwich College ; Emmanuel College, Cambridge. Entered I.C.S. 1886. *Address :* Madras. *Club :* East India United Service. *(Died 23 Nov. 1918.)*

GILLOT, E. Louis, painter, engraver; Official Painter to the French Armies ; Member of Committee of the Société Nationale des Beaux Arts ; Vice-President of the Société des Peinteurs - Graveurs de Paris ; Member of the Committee of Peintres Orientalistes Français ; Hors Concours ; Knight of Legion of Honour ; M.V.O. ; *b.* Paris, 14 April 1867 ; *s.* of August Nicholas Gillot, architect. *Educ. :* Lycée Ste. Barbe, Paris ; Ecole des Beaux Arts. Inventor of the monotype in colours ; chiefly known for paintings representing great industrial works. *Works :* Mines of St. Etienne ; Records of President Loubet's Visits to London and Naples, and an impression of the Thames (gold medal at the Barcelona Exhibition); The Naval Review at Spithead, 1911 (ordered by the French Government for presentation to King George) ; The Coronation of George V. in Westminster Abbey ; Investiture of the Prince of Wales at Carnarvon ; in addition to etchings and engravings, he has also done a number of portraits, among which may be mentioned that of Baron Dard. *Recreations :* fishing, shooting, boating. *Address :* 15 rue Théophile Gautier, Paris. *T. :* 675-47.

GILMAN, Harold John Wilde ; Artist-Painter ; *b.* England, 1878 ; 2nd *s.* of Rev. John

Gilman, Rector of Snargate, Romney Marsh, Kent, and Emily Purcell Gulliver. *Educ.*: Tonbridge School. *Address*: 47 Maple Street, W.
(*Died 12 Feb. 1919.*)

GILMOUR, Sir John, 1st Bart. ; *cr.* 1897; of Lundin and Montrave, Fife, and of South Walton, Renfrewshire; J.P., D.L. Fifeshire; Convener of Commissioners of Supply for Fife. Was Hon. Col. Fife and Forfar Imperial Yeomanry; *b.* 24 July 1845 ; *e. s.* of Allan Gilmour of Lundin and Montrave and of South Walton ; *m.* Henrietta, 2nd *d.* of David Gilmour, Quebec, Canada, 1873 ; two *s.* two *d.* *Educ.*: Glasgow and Edinburgh Academies; Edinburgh University. President of Royal Caledonian Curling Club, 1913. *Recreations*: hunting, stalking, shooting. *Heir*: *s.* Major John Gilmour. *Address*: Montrave, Leven, Fife. *T.A.*: Leven. *Clubs*: Carlton, Junior Carlton ; New, Conservative, Scottish Unionist, Edinburgh ; Conservative, Glasgow. (*Died 20 July 1920.*)

GILMOUR, William Ewing, D.L. ; *b.* 21 May 1854 ; 3rd *s.* of late Allan Gilmour, of Eaglesham, and Isabella Buchanan Ewing ; *m.* 1882, Jessie Gertrude (*d.* 1923), 3rd *d.* of late James Campbell, of Tullichewan ; one *s.* three *d.* *Educ.*: Edinburgh Academy and University. J.P., Dunbarton, Sutherland, and Ross. *Address*: Glencassley Castle, Sutherland. *Clubs*: University, Edinburgh ; Western, Glasgow.
(*Died 31 Jan. 1924.*)

GILPIN, Peter Valentine, J.P. ; *b.* 1858 ; *o. s.* of late Peter Valentine Purcell of Halverstown, Capt. 13th Light Dragoons, and Agnes Maria (she *m.* 2nd, 1866, Col. Henry St. John Le Marchant, R.H.A.), 8th *d.* of Sir John Hesketh Lethbridge, 3rd Bart. ; *m.* 1883, Amy Mary Louisa, *e. d.* of late Capt. Henry Meux-Smith of Hockliffe ; seven *s.* two *d.* *Heir*: *s.* Peter Raleigh Purcell, *b.* 1885. Late Lieut. 5th Lancers ; assumed the name of Gilpin, 1888. *Address*: Clarehaven, Newmarket ; Dollanstown, Kilcock, Ireland. *T.*: 17 Newmarket. *Clubs*: Cavalry, Orleans. (*Died 9 Nov. 1928.*)

GILRAY, Thomas, M.A., F.R.S.E., Hon. LL.D.Edin. ; Professor of English Language and Literature since 1889, and Dean of the Faculty of Arts and Science, Otago University ; *b.* Scotland, 1851 ; *m.* ; four *s.* one *d.* *Educ.*: High School and University, Edinburgh ; Berlin and Heidelberg Universities ; one of the trustees of Carlyle's House, Cheyne Row ; Member of Board of Studies, New Zealand University, and Member of the New Zealand University Senate. *Address*: Ellangowan, Sargood Street, Dunedin, New Zealand. (*Died 3 Feb. 1920.*)

GINGRAS-DALY, Lt.-Col. Ludger Jules Olivier, D.S.O. 1917 ; Commanding 2nd/2nd Quebec Regiment, Canada ; *b.* 11 July 1876 ; *m.* 1899 ; no *c.* *Educ.*: St. Patrick's College, Quebec. Served European War in France, 20 May 1915-Sept. 1917 (wounded at Courcelette with 22nd French-Canadians, D.S.O., despatches). *Recreations*: golf, equitation. *Address*: 122 Arlington Avenue, Westmount, Montreal, Canada. (*Died 20 Feb. 1919.*)

GINNELL, Laurence, B.L. ; M.P. (N.) N. Westmeath, native county, since 1906 ; Barr. Middle Temple and also of King's Inns, Dublin; *b.* 1854 ; 3rd *s.* of Laurence Ginnell : *m.* 1902, Alice, *d.* of J. King, J.P., Kilbride. *Educ.*: self-educated. One of the founders of the Irish Literary Society, London. *Publications*: Brehon Laws, 1894 ; Doubtful grant of Ireland, 1899, and presented personally to Pope Leo XIII.; Land and Liberty, 1908. *Recreations*: literary.
(*Died 17 April 1923.*)

GIOLITTI, Giovanni ; *b.* Mondovi, Piedmont, 27 Oct. 1842. *Educ.*: Turin. Deputy for Dronero (Coni), 1882 ; Minister of the Treasury, 1889-90 ; Premier, 1892-3 ; Interieur, 1901-3 ; Premier, 1903-5, 1906-9, 1911-14, 1920-21. *Publication*: Memoirs of My Life. *Address*: Rome.
(*Died 17 July 1928.*)

GIRARD, Robert George, Uncovenanted Civil Service of India ; I.S.O. 1912 ; *b.* 11 Aug. 1859, *s.* of late Henry Charles Girard, H.E.I.C.S. (Bengal) ; *m.* 1911, Marie, *d.* of late Charles Frederick Pitlar, Solicitor, Calcutta. *Educ.*: Bedford Grammar School. Military Accounts Dept. Govt. of India, 1876-84 ; Revenue Dept. (Stamps and Excise) Govt. of Bengal, 1884-96 ; Collector of Income Tax, Calcutta, since 1896 ; Major, V.D., and Officiating Commandant, Calcutta Volunteer Rifles. *Clubs*: Oriental ; Bengal, Calcutta. (*Died 17 May 1921.*)

GIRAUD, Surg.-Maj.-Gen. Charles Herve. Entered army, 1858 ; retired, 1896 ; served Indian Mutiny, 1858 (medal with clasp); China War, 1860 (medal with clasp) ; Taeping Rebellion, 1863-64 ; South African War, 1879-81.
(*Died 10 May 1918.*)

GIRDLESTONE, Rev. Robert Baker, M.A. ; Hon. Canon of Christ Church, Oxford ; *b.* 1836 ; *s.* of Rev. Charles Girdlestone, formerly Fellow of Balliol ; *m.* 1st, Maude, *d.* of Rev. J. Richey ; 2nd, Mary, *d.* of J. Wood of Thedden Grange ; three *s.* *Educ.*: Charterhouse ; Christ Church, Oxford. Superin. of the Translation Department of the Bible Society, 1866 - 76 ; Principal of Wycliffe Hall, Oxford, 1877-89 ; Minister of St. John's, Downshire Hill, N.W., 1889-1903. *Publications*: Synonyms of the Old Testament ; Students' Deuteronomy ; Foundations of the Bible ; Grammar of Prophecy ; Deuterographs ; How to Study the English Bible ; Age and Trustworthiness of Old Testament ; Doctor Doctorum ; Churchman's Guide ; Why do I Believe in Jesus Christ ; O. T. Theology ; Outlines of Bible Chronology ; Commentary on Galatians ; Building up of Old Testament ; Mission of Christ. *Address*: Saxholme, Wimbledon, S.W.19. *T.*: Wimbledon 550.
(*Died 6 April 1923.*)

GIRDWOOD, Gilbert P., Emeritus Professor of Chemistry, McGill University, since 1902 ; *b.* London, 22 Oct. 1832 ; *s.* of G. F. Girdwood, M.D., Edinburgh, from Polmont, Scotland, and *d.* of Rev. Thos. Bazely, Rector of Lavenham, Suffolk ; *m.* 1862, F. M., *d.* of late T. E. Blackwell, C.E., Managing Director Grand Trunk Railway ; five *s.* three *d.* *Educ.*: private school, and St. George's School of Medicine, London. Passed Coll. of Surgeons, London, 1854 ; House Surgeon Liverpool Infirmary, 1854 ; joined 1st Battalion Grenadier Guards, as Assistant Surgeon, 1854 ; went to Canada with 1st Battalion ; at Trent Affair, 1862 ; stationed in Montreal ; left the service on the regiment returning to England ; joined the Victoria Rifle Volunteer Militia as surgeon ; called out with regiment at Fenian disturbance, 1866 (medal); promoted to Medical Staff Officer of Militia of Canada ; M.D., C.M. M'Gill University, 1865 ; Lecturer in Practical Chemistry in Medical Faculty of M'Gill University, 1869 ; Professor of Practical Chemistry, 1872-94 ; Professor of Chemistry, 1879 - 1902 ; 12 years Surgeon to Montreal Dispensary, and to Montreal General Hospital ; now Consulting Surgeon to both institutions ; Consultant Physician in X - Rays Department, Victoria Hospital, Montreal ; Chief Medical Officer Canadian-Pacific Railway ; ex-President Roentgen Society of America ; Vice-President Canadian Branch Society of Chemical Industry ; Fellow Chemical Society, Chemical Institute of Great Britain, Society of Public Analysts, Society of Chemical Industry, Royal Society of Canada, Natural History Society and Microscopical Society of Montreal. *Publications*: various articles. *Recreations*: won mile race open to all officers in British Army, Aldershot, 1856 ; athletic exercise ; boating. *Address*: 615 University Street, Montreal, Canada. *Club*: St. James's, Montreal. (*Died 2 Oct. 1917.*)

GISBORNE, Lt.-Col. Lionel Guy, C.M.G. 1916 ; late R.F.A., T.F. ; *b.* 1866 ; *s.* of late Hon. William Gisborne, M.L.C., New Zealand,

and Allestree Hall, Derby; *m.*; one *s.* one *d.*
Served S. Africa, 1899-1900 (Queen's medal 3
clasps); European War, 1914-1918 (despatches,
C.M.G.). *Address:* Lingen Hall, Bucknell,
Shropshire; Ros Vean, Mullion, S. Cornwall.
(Died 24 Oct. 1928.)

**GIUFFRIDA - RUGGERI, Dr. Vin-
cenzo,** Professor Ord. of Anthropology and
Director of Anthropological Institute in the
Royal University of Naples since 1907; Professor
of Ethnology at Royal Oriental Institute of
Naples since 1914; *b.* Catania, 1 Feb. 1872; *m.*
1914, Lilian C. Strachan of Newcastle-on-Tyne;
two *s.* Physician at Rome, 1896; later, Libero
Docente of Anthropology; Assistant Professor of
Anthropology, University of Rome, 1900-5; Pro-
fessor of Anthropology at University of Pavia,
1906-7; late Vice-President of Società Italiana
di Antropologia ed Etnologia, and of Società
Romana di Antropologia; Hon. Fellow of the
Royal Anthropological Institute of Great
Britain and Ireland; Corres. Member Anthropological Societies Paris, Vienna, Moscow, Lyons,
Bruxelles, Porto, Liége, Ord. Member of the
R. Accad. delle scienze fis. e matem. di Napoli,
Member of the Institut suisse d'Anthropologie
générale; and the École d'Anthropologie de
Paris. *Publications:* Sullà dignità morfologica
dei segni degenerativi, Roma, 1897; Homo
sapiens, Einleitung zu einem Kurse der Anthropologie, Wien, 1913; L'Uomo attuale, Una
specie collettiva, Roma (Albrighi - Segati),
1913; Antropologia dell' Africa orientale,
Firenze, 1915; A Sketch of the Anthropology
of Italy, Lond. 1918; Antropologia sistematica
dell' Asia, Firenze, 1919. *Address:* Istituto
Antropologico, R. Università, Napoli.

GIVENS, Hon. Thomas, President of the
Commonwealth Senate, 1913-26; Senator for
Queensland since 1903; *b.* Co. Tipperary, Ire-
land, 12 June 1864; *m.* 1901, Katie, *d.* of J.
Allen, Cairns, Queensland. M.L.A. Queensland,
1899-1902. *Address:* Federal Parliament House,
Melbourne. *(Died 9 June 1928.)*

GJELLERUP, Karl; Danish novelist. Nobel
prize for literature, 1917. *Publications:* Anti-
gonos, 1880; Rödtjörn, 1881; Minna, 1889;
Möllen, 1896. *(Died 14 Oct. 1919.)*

GLADSTONE, Helen; *b.* 28 Aug. 1849; *y.
d.* of late Right Hon. W. E. Gladstone. *Educ.:*
home; Newnham College, Cambridge. Vice-
Principal of Newnham College, 1882-96; Warden
of Women's University Settlement, 1901-6,
Address: Sundial, Hawarden, Chester.
(Died 19 Aug. 1925.)

GLADSTONE, Sir John Robert, 3rd
Bt.; *cr.* 1846; D.L.; Capt. Coldstream Guards;
retired; *b.* 26 April 1852; *o. s.* of 2nd Bt. and
Louisa, 2nd *d.* of Robert Fellowes of Shotesham
Park, Norfolk; *S.* father, 1889. *Educ.:* Eton;
Christ Church, Oxford. Served Egyptian Ex-
pedition, 1882; Suakin, 1885. *Heir: c.* J. E.
Gladstone. *Address:* Fasque, Fettercairn,
N.B.; Glendye Lodge, Banchory, Kincardine-
shire. *Clubs:* Guards', Travellers', Carlton.
(Died 25 June 1926.)

GLADSTONE, Robert; J.P. Co. of Lan-
cashire; late Chairman Mersey Docks and
Harbour Board; *b.* 1833; *e. s.* of late Thomas
Steuart Gladstone of Capenoch, Dumfriesshire,
N.B.; *m.* 1860, Mary Ellen (*d.* 1895), *d.* of
Robertson Gladstone of Court Hey, near Liver-
pool; four *s.* five *d.* *Educ.:* Eton; Edinburgh
University. J.P. for Liverpool for 32 years;
Treasurer of University College, Liverpool, for
22 years. LL.D. University of Liverpool, and
Hon. Freeman of Liverpool. *Address:* Woolton
Vale, Liverpool. *T.A.:* Gladstone, Woolton.
T.: Gateacre 59. *Club:* Palatine, Liverpool.
(Died 12 July 1919.)

GLADSTONE, Rev. Stephen Edward,
b. 4 April 1844; 2nd *s.* of late Right Hon. W. E.
Gladstone; *m.* Annie Crosthwaite, *d.* of late
C. B. Wilson, Surgeon, Liverpool; three *s.* two *d.*,

410

Educ.: Eton; Christ Church, Oxford (2nd Mods;
2nd class Lit. Hum.). M.A., 1868; Priest, 1870;
Curate of St. M. Less, Lambeth, 1868-72; Rural
Dean of Mold, 1884-92; Rector of Hawarden,
1872-1904; Rector of Barrowby, Lincs, 1904-11.
Address: Manley Hall, Helsby, Cheshire.
(Died 23 April 1920.)

**GLAISHER, James Whitbread
Lee,** M.A., Sc.D., F.R.S.; Fellow of Trinity
College, Cambridge; *b.* Lewisham, Kent, 5 Nov.
1848; *e. s.* of late James Glaisher, F.R.S., and
Cecilia Belleville; unmarried. *Educ.:* St.
Paul's School, London; Trinity Coll. Camb.
Campden Exhibitioner, St. Paul's School, 1867;
Scholar of Trinity Coll. Camb. 1868; graduated
(2nd Wrangler), 1871; Fellow of Trinity, 1871;
F.R.S. 1875; President of the Cambridge Philo-
sophical Society, 1882-84; of the London Mathe-
matical Society, 1884-86; of the Royal Astro-
nomical Society, 1885-87, 1900-1902; of Section
A of the British Association, 1890; of the Cambridge Antiquarian Society, 1899-1901; Sc.D.
Cambridge, 1887; Dublin, 1892; Victoria University, 1902; Tutor of Trinity, 1883-93;
Lecturer, 1871-1901; De Morgan Medal of
London Mathematical Society, 1908; Sylvester
Medal of Royal Society, 1913. *Publications:*
editor of the Messenger of Mathematics since
1871, and of the Quarterly Journal of Pure and
Applied Mathematics since 1878; numerous
papers on Pure Mathematics. *Recreations:* Pre-
sident Cambridge University Bicycle Club, 1882-
1885; interested in faience and pottery. *Address:*
Trinity College, Cambridge. *Club:* Athenæum.
(Died 7 Dec. 1928.)

GLAISTER, Rev. William, Hon.
Canon of Southwell since 1908; Chancellor
of the Cathedral; *s.* of late Rev. W. Glaister,
Vicar of Beckley, Sussex. *Educ.:* Marlborough;
University Coll. Oxford (M.A., B.C.L.). Vicar
of Grantham, 1888-1905; Rural Dean and Surro-
gate; Hon. Canon Lincoln Cathedral, 1890-
1908. *Publications:* Life of St. Wulfram; Life of
Karl the Great. *Recreations:* cricket, boating
(winner of Grand Challenge, Ladies' Plate, and
Stewards' Cup, Henley, 1863). *Address:* The
Burgage, Southwell. *(Died 7 Feb. 1919.)*

**GLANCEY, Rt. Rev. Mgr. Michael
Francis;** Bishop of Flaviopolis since 1924;
Auxiliary of the Archbishop of Birmingham;
Provost of Birmingham Metropolitan Chapter;
b. Wolverhampton, 25 Oct. 1854. *Educ.:* Sedgley
Park School; Oscott College. Priest, 1877;
Professor at Oscott College, 1877-88; Diocesan
Inspector of Schools, 1888-97; Diocesan Chan-
cellor, 1897-1918; Pastor at Solihull, 1899-
1908; Principal St. Charles', Begbroke, 1908-14;
Canon of Chapter, 1905; Provost of Chapter,
1922; Protonotary Apostolic, 1916; Vicar-
General of Birmingham, 1921-25; Chairman of
Education Committee of Old Birmingham
School Board, 1899-1902. *Publications:* Char-
acteristics from the Writings of Archbishop
Ullathorne; English version of Knecht's
Commentary on Scripture; translation of
Schanz's Christian Apology, 3 vols., 1890;
Editor Birmingham Catholic Directory, 1900-12;
Birmingham Provincial Directory, 1912-16;
Orbis Catholicus: A Directory of the Catholic
World, 1916; The Present Position of the
Education Question: A Course of Lectures,
1896; Catholics and the Education Question,
1902. *Address:* Archbishop's House, 6 Norfolk
Road, Edgbaston, Birmingham. *T.:* Edgbaston
564. *M.:* AC 2877. *(Died 16 Oct. 1925.)*

GLANFIELD, Sir Robert, Kt., *cr.* 1920;
Chairman G. Glanfield & Son, Ltd., London;
b. London, 16 Oct. 1862; 2nd *s.* of George
Glanfield, Hale End, Woodford; *m.* 1888, Mabel,
e. d. of late H. H. C. Baker of King William's
Town, South Africa; two *s.* two *d.* *Educ.:*
Campden Grammar School; Oundle. *Recreation:*
golf. *Address:* 34 Eton Avenue, N.W.3. *T.:*

Hampstead 5689. *Clubs:* Devonshire, Royal Automobile.   (*Died 17 Aug. 1924.*)

GLANUSK, 2nd Baron, *cr.* 1899, **Joseph Henry Russell Bailey,** Bt., *cr.* 1852; C.B.E. 1919; C.B. 1911; Lord - Lieutenant of Brecknock since 1905; D.S.O. 1900; J.P. and D.L. Breconshire; retired; late Major Grenadier Guards; commanded Guards Depot, Caterham, 1901-3; 3rd Batt. S.W.B. 1905-10; Brecknockshire Batt. 1911-16; London Command Depot since 1916; *b.* 26 Oct. 1864; *e. s.* of 1st Baron Glanusk, and Mary, *d.* of Henry Lucas, M.D.; *S.* father 1906; *m.* Editha Elma, C.B.E. 1920, *o. d.* of late Warden Sergison of Cuckfield Park, Sussex, 1890; one *s.* one *d. Educ.:* Eton; R.M.C. Sandhurst. Joined Grenadier Guards, 1885; was adjutant to C.I.V., South Africa. *Recreations:* cricket, football (capt. of Eton Football, 1883), shooting, fishing, hunting, etc. *Heir: s.* Hon. Wilfred Russell Bailey. *Address:* Pwll-y-faedda, Erwood. *Club:* Guards.
    (*Died 2 Jan. 1928.*)

GLASSE, John, M.A., D.D.; Minister Emeritus of Old Greyfriars, Edinburgh; *b.* Auchtermuchty, Fifeshire, 27 Jan. 1848; *m.* 1st, 1878, Jane Scott (*deod.*), *d.* of Provost White, Auchtermuchty; one *s.* one *d.*; 2nd, Louisa Plymer, *d.* of Alexander Gibson, Ceylon. *Educ.:* Free Church School, Auchtermuchty; St. Andrews Univ.; New Coll. Edinburgh. Licensed by Presbytery of Edinburgh, 1876; Assist. in Old Greyfriars and ordained Minister, 1877; intimately associated with public movements and public bodies; Vice-President of Sunday Society; ex-President Edinburgh Burns Club; a prominent advocate of Christian Socialism; an enthusiastic Freemason. *Publications:* John Knox, a Criticism; Pauperism in Scotland, Past and Present; Poor Law Amendment; Modern Christian Socialism; The Relation of the Church to Socialism; Robert Owen and his Life-Work; has written and lectured extensively on Ethical and Social questions. *Recreation:* an occasional game of golf. *Address:* 16 Tantallon Place, Edinburgh; Bayview, Upper Largo, Fifeshire. *Club:* Scottish Liberal, Edinburgh.   (*Died 8 Feb. 1918.*)

GLASSINGTON, Charles William, M.R.C.S., L.D.S.Ed.; Senior Dental Surgeon, Westminster Hospital; Member of the British Dental Association, etc.; *b.* 1857; *m.* 1892; widower; no *c. Educ.:* St. Mark's College, S.W.; Westminster Hospital; National Dental Hospital. House Surgeon; Administrator of Anæsthetics; Assistant Dental Surgeon; Dental Surgeon and Lecturer; formerly Dental Surgeon at the Duke of York's Royal Military School, Chelsea. *Publications:* Dental Materis Medica and Therapeutics, 2nd Edit.; Golden Rules of Dental Surgery, 4th Edit.; contributions to various dental journals. *Recreations:* sea angling, bowls. *Address:* 6 Pelham Crescent, South Kensington, S.W.7. *T.:* 615 Kensington.
    (*Died 7 Feb. 1922.*)

GLAZEBROOK, Rev. Michael George, D.D.; Canon of Ely since 1905; *b.* London, 4 Aug. 1853; *s.* of M. G. Glazebrook; *m.* Ethel, 4th *d.* of Sir B. C. Brodie, 2nd Bart., 1880. *Educ.:* Dulwich College; Balliol Coll. Oxford; double 1st in Mods.; 1st class Lit. Hum. Assist. Master at Harrow, 1878; High Master of Manchester Grammar School, 1888; Hon. Canon of Bristol Cathedral, 1898; Headmaster of Clifton Coll., 1891-1905. *Publications:* editions of the Prometheus and Medea; Lessons from the Old Testament; various educational essays; Sermons; Studies in the Book of Isaiah; The End of the Law; The Layman's Old Testament; The Faith of a Modern Churchman; The Letter and the Spirit; The Apocalypse of St. John. *Recreations:* rowing, golf. *Address:* The College, Ely. *Club:* Athenæum.
    (*Died 1 May 1926.*)

GLAZEBROOK, Philip Kirkland, M.P. (U.) South Manchester since 1912; Major, Cheshire Yeomanry; *b.* 1880; *s.* of John K. Glazebrook; unmarried. *Educ.:* Eton; New College, Oxford. Left Oxford, 1903, and travelled a good deal until 1910; contested S. Manchester, 1910, but owing to a mistake was not nominated. *Recreations:* travelling, shooting. *Address:* Twemlow Hall, Holmes Chapel, Cheshire. *T.A.:* Glazebrook, Goostrey. *M.:* 3515. *Clubs:* Bath, Prince's; Vincent's, Oxford.   (*Died 11 Mar. 1918.*)

GLEADOWE-NEWCOMEN, Colonel Arthur Hills, C.I.E. 1907; V.D., F.R.G.S., F.R.S.A., F.A.G.S.; late Officer Commanding 1st U.P. Horse, and Hon. A.D.C., Lords Curzon, Minto, and Hardinge, Viceroys of India; *b.* 9 Nov. 1858; *o. s.* of Robert Gleadowe-Newcomen of Killester House, Co. Dublin; *m.* 1st, 1876, Clara, *d.* of Capt. J. Masson, I.A.; one *s.* one *d.*; 2nd, 1925, Marye Eveleen, *d.* of Rev. Algernon Clementi Smith; no *c. Educ.:* Ripon and Durham Schools. Has travelled over the greater part of the world, and served 40 years in India. seeing much service, and spent many years exploring; served in Egypt, Soudan, and in South Africa during Boer War; in Japan and China during Russo-Japanese War, also in France and Flanders during European War, 1914-15. *Publication:* Report on the Trade and Commerce of S.W. Persia, of which commission he was in command. *Recreations:* cricket, football, racquets, tennis, polo, pig-sticking, big-game shooting, etc. *Address:* Killester Ranch, Coppice Hill P.O., Ardrossan, Alberta, Canada. *Club:* Junior Army and Navy.
    (*Died 30 May 1928.*)

GLEGG, Edward Maxwell; owner of Backford Hall and Irby Hall, Cheshire; *o. surv. s.* of late Col. Edward Holt Glegg, Rifle Brigade, and Margaret Maxwell, *o. c.* of John Maxwell Logan of Fingalton, N.B.; *b.* 24 June 1849; *m.* 1901, Elizabeth, 2nd *d.* of late Stuart Hawkins of Hayford Hall, Devon; no *c. Educ.:* Harrow. Late Lieut. 32nd Light Infantry. *Address:* Backford Hall, Chester. *Clubs:* Naval and Military, Wellington.   (*Died 6 Feb. 1927.*)

GLEICHEN, Lady Feodora, Sculptor; *b.* London; *d.* of late Admiral Prince Victor of Hohenlohe-Langenburg; unmarried. *Educ.:* Slade School and University College, London, under Professor Legros. Hon. Member Royal Institute of Painters in Water-colours and Royal Society of Painter Etchers. Worked at sculpture in London and Rome; exhibited at the Royal Academy regularly since 1893, and previously at the New Gallery and Grosvenor Gallery; completed life-size group of Queen for Victoria Hospital, Canada, 1895; fountain in Paris, 1961; fountain for Sir W. Palmer, 1902, placed in Hyde Park; external decoration, Foundling Hospital, Cairo, 1904; Panel for exterior of National Art Gallery; King Edward VII. Memorial, Windsor; Florence Nightingale Memorial, Derby; two Busts of Queen Victoria, and several other busts, etc.; bronze medal for Sculpture, Paris Exhibition, 1900. *Recreations:* travelling and country pursuits. *Address:* Engine Court, St. James's Palace, S.W.1. *T.:* Gerrard 7187.   (*Died 22 Feb. 1922.*)

GLENARTHUR, 1st Baron, *cr.* 1918; **Matthew Arthur,** of Carlung, Ayrshire; Bt., *cr.* 1903; *b.* 9 March 1852; *e. s.* of late James Arthur of Carlung, Ayrshire, and Barshaw, Renfrewshire, and Jane, *d.* of Thomas Glen, Thornhill, Co. Renfrew; *m.* 1879, Janet Stevenson Bennett, O.B.E., J.P. Co. Ayr, President Ayrshire Branch British Red Cross Society, *y. d.* of late Alexander Bennett M'Grigor, LL.D., of Cairnoch, Stirlingshire; one *s.* one *d. Educ.:* Glasgow University. J.P. and D.L. Co. Ayr and County of City of Glasgow; LL.D. Glasgow; Member Royal Company of Archers (King's Bodyguard for Scotland);

Chairman of Arthur & Company, Ltd., and of Lochgelly Iron & Coal Company, Ltd. ; President of Scottish Unionist Association ; President of West of Scotland Liberal Unionist Association, 1898-1912; Convener Western Divisional Council Scottish Unionist Association, 1913 ; Member of Executive Committee National Unionist Association, 1912-18 ; Chairman of Western Infirmary, Glasgow, 1904-21 ; Chairman Glasgow and South-Western Railway, 1920-22. *Heir: s.* Hon, J. C. Arthur. *Address.* one *s.* one *d.* Fullarton, Troon, Ayrshire. *T.A.:* Fullarton Troon. *T.:* Troon 21. *Clubs:* Brooks's, Carlton, Boodle's, Windham ; Western, Glasgow ; New, Edinburgh.   *(Died 23 Sept. 1928.)*

GLEN-COATS, Sir Thomas Glen, 1st Bt., *cr.* 1894; C.B. 1911; Chairman, J. & P. Coats, Ltd. ; Lord-Lieut. Renfrewshire, 1908 ; *b.* 19 Feb. 1846 ; *s.* of Thomas Coats, Ferguslie, and Margaret, *d.* of Thomas Glen, Thornhill, Renfrewshire ; *m.* Elise Agnes (*d.* 1910), *d.* of Alexander Walker, Montreal, 1876 ; two *s.* one *d. Educ.:* Queenwood College, Hants. Hon. Colonel (V.D.), 6th Argyll and Sutherland Highlanders ; assumed additional surname of Glen, 1894; contested West Renfrewshire, 1900 ; M.P. (L.) West Renfrewshire, 1906-10. *Recreations:* shooting and yachting. *Heir: s.* Thomas Coats Glen [*b.* 5 May 1878. *Educ.:* Merton College, Oxford. B A.]. *Address:* Ferguslie Park, Paisley. *Clubs:* Reform, National Liberal; Western, Glasgow.   *(Died 12 July 1922.)*

GLENCONNER, 1st Baron, *cr.* 1911; **Edward Priaulx Tennant**; 2nd Bart., *cr.* 1885; Lord High Commissioner to General Assembly of Church of Scotland, 1911-12-13-14; Lord-Lieutenant, Peeblesshire; *b.* 31 May 1859 ; *s. surv. s.* of Sir Charles Tennant, 1st Bt., and Emma, *d.* of Richard Winsloe, Mount Nebo, Taunton ; *S.* father 1906; *m.* 1895, Pamela, *y. d.* of late Hon. Percy Wyndham ; three *s.* one *d.* [Lady Glenconner is author of The White Wallet, The Sayings of the Children, and other books.] *Educ.:* Eton ; Trinity College, Cambridge; M.A. 1885. Inner Temple; travelled extensively in Africa, India, and America ; Assistant Private Secretary to Sir George Trevelyan at the Scottish Office, 1892-95 ; contested Partick Division of Lanarkshire, 1892; united counties of Peebles and Selkirk, 1900 ; M.P. (L.) Salisbury, 1906-10. Owns about 7000 acres. *Heir: s.* Hon. Christopher Grey Tennant, *b.* 14 June 1899. *Address:* Glen, Innerleithen, Peebles ; 34 Queen Anne's Gate, S.W.1 ; Wilsford Manor, Salisbury. *T.:* Victoria 2501. *Club:* Brooks's.
     (Died 21 Nov. 1920.)

GLENDINNING, Rt. Hon. Robert Graham, P.C., Ireland; D.L. of County of City of Belfast, 1914; M.P. (L.) North Antrim, 1906-10; J.P. Belfast ; Linen Merchant ; *b.* 5 April 1844; *s.* of William Bell Glendinning of Brakagh, Co. Tyrone ; *m.* 1st, Elizabeth Harden (*d.* 1882) ; 2nd, 1886, Mary W. Hastings ; four *s.* three *d. Educ.:* privately. *Recreations:* motoring and golf. *Address:* Knock-Dhu, Sans Souci Park, and Murray Street, Belfast. *T.A.:* Eccles, Belfast. *T.:* 474. *Club:* National Liberal.
     (Died 8 June 1928.)

GLENN, Very Rev. Henry Patterson, B.A., T.C.D.; Ex-Moderator of General Assembly of Presbyterian Church in Ireland ; Ex-Senator, Irish Free State ; *b.* Indianapolis, U.S.A., 4 Sep. 1858 ; *s.* of Wm. Glenn, J.P., and Maria Morgan; *m.* 1908, Ida Moncreiff, *d.* of Rev. John Sturrock, Edinburgh ; no *c. Educ.:* Trinity College, Dublin ; Edinburgh University ; New College, Edinburgh ; and Leipzig University. Licensed 1883 ; Assistant Free High Church, Inverness, 1883-84 ; Minister of Tullamore, 1884 ; Minister of Bray since 1892 ;

Synodical Convener of Sustentation Fund, 1890; Assembly Convener of Sustentation Fund, 1912 ; Convener of Committee on Bequests, 1898. *Recreation:* golf. *Address:* The Manse, Bray, Co. Wicklow. *T.:* Bray 46.
     (Died 12 Sept. 1923.)

GLENNIE, Rev. Herbert John, M.A., Canon of Bradford 1921 ; *b.* 22 Jan. 1860 ; *s.* of Rev. John David Glennie, late Vicar of Croxton, Staffs. ; *m.* 1886, Mary Nathalie Katherine, *s. d.* of Rev. Nathaniel Cooper, Vicar of Oxon, Salop ; one *s.* one *d. Educ.:* Marlborough; Keble College, Oxford. Deacon, 1885 ; Priest, 1886 ; Curate of St. Mary's, Shrewsbury, 1885 ; Leeds Parish Church (and Acting Chaplain of Gen. Infirmary), 1889 ; Vicar of Holbeck, 1894 ; Rector of Goldsborough, 1904 ; Ripon Diocesan Inspector of Schools, 1905 ; Vicar of St. Margaret's, Ilkley, 1908-22 ; Chaplain Middleton Sanatorium 1916 ; Vicar of Hawley Green, Hants, 1922-26. *Publications:* A Battalion in Training; Ripon Diocesan Dialogues. *Recreations:* cricket, football, hockey, rowing, tennis, sketching, motoring. *Address:* Redheath, Wokingham, Berks. *M.:* DL 6096.   *(Died 19 Oct. 1926.)*

GLENTANAR, 1st Baron, *cr.* 1916 ; **George Coats;** Director of J. and P. Coats, Limited ; J.P., Ayrshire ; *b.* 11 Feb. 1849; *s.* of late Thomas Coats of Ferguslie ; *m.* 1880, Margaret Lothian Black ; one *s.* two *d. Educ.:* Queenwood College, Hampshire. *Recreations:* hunting, fishing, yacht-racing, and shooting. *Heir: s.* Hon. Thomas Coats, *b.* 1894. *Address:* Forest of Glen Tauar, Aboyne, N.B. ; Belleisle, Ayr, N.B. ; 11 Hill Street, Berkeley Square, W. *T.:* Gerrard 6615. *Clubs:* Carlton ; Royal Yacht Squadron, Cowes ; Western ; Glasgow ; Northern. Aberdeen.
     (Died 25 Nov. 1918.)

GLENTWORTH, Viscount: Edmond William Claude Gerard de Vere; R.F.C.; *b.* 14 Oct. 1894; *e. s.* of 4th Earl of Limerick. *Educ.:* Eton. Lieut. Warwickshire Yeomanry. *Address:* Dromore, Pallaskenry, Limerick.   *(Died 18 May 1918.)*

GLOSSOP, Rev. George Henry Pownall, Hon. Canon of St. Albans Cathedral, 1907 ; *b.* 1858 ; *s.* of F. H. N. Glossop of Silver Hall, Isleworth, J.P., D.L., and Ann, *s. d.* of Henry Pownall, J.P., D.L. ; *m.* 1886, Frances Mary, J.P., *d.* of Maj. Gape, J.P., of St. Michael's Manor, St. Albans ; one *s.* three *d. Educ.:* Harrow ; St. John's College, Oxford ; Wells Theological College. Curate of Uffculme, Devon, 1882-4 ; Curate St. Albans Cathedral, 1884-1905 ; has been Chairman St. Albans Board of Guardians, School Board ; is an Alderman of Herts County Council ; Hon. Secretary, St. Albans Diocesan Conference and of the St. Albans Diocesan Board of Finance ; Chairman Herts Mental Hospital, Hill End ; Chairman Hertfordshire Education Committee; Member of Executive of Poor Law Unions Associations and of Board of Health Advisory Committee for the Blind. *Address:* Romeland House, St. Albans ; Whitechapel Manor, South Molton. *T.:* 64 S. Albans.   *(Died 8 June 1925.)*

GLOSTER, Brig.-Gen. Gerald Meade, C.M.G. 1916 ; retired pay ; *s.* of late Rev. Thomas Gloster, M.A., Castleterra Rectory Co. Cavan: *b.* 8 June 1864; *m;* Wilhelmina Ormonde, *o. c.* of C. Brown, C.I.E. Lieut. Devon Regt. 1884 ; Col. 1914 ; served N.W. Frontier, India, 1897-98 (medal 2 clasps) ; S. Africa, 1899-1900 (Queen's medal and clasp) ; European War, 1914-18 (despatches, C.M.G., 1914 Star, General Service medal, Allied medal). *Address:* Oak Manor, Cheltenham.
     (Died 14 April 1928.)

GLOVER, Lady (Elizabeth Rosetta) ; *widow* of late Captain Sir John Hawley Glover, G.C.M.G., R.N. ; *d.* of late J. W. Butler-Scott, Annegrove Abbey, and Elizabeth Rosetta, *d.* of late John Bolton-Massy of Ballywire,

Tipperary, and Clareville, Co. Dublin; one d. *Publications:* The Life of Sir John Hawley Glover, G.C.M.G., R.N. ; Lest We Forget Them ; Memories of Four Continents ; short stories, and a number of magazine articles in various journals. *Address:* 68 Carlisle Mansions, Victoria Street, S.W.1. *T.:* 3642 Victoria.

(*Died Feb. 1927.*)

GLOVER, George Wright, D.S.O. 1916 ; M.A., Ph.D. ; 2nd Lieut. 1st Batt. The Rifle Brigade ; b. Pretoria, S. Africa, 1 Oct. 1884 ; English parents. *Educ.:* Leigh Grammar School; Manchester, Berlin; Marburg Universities. Graduated 1911, 1st Class Hons. Mod. Langs., Manchester ; Gilchrist travelling studentship to Berlin University; English Lektor at Marburg (Hesse), 1912-14 ; Ph.D. there, 1914 ; instructor in German at Princeton University, N.J., U.S.A., 1914-15 ; Commissioned Spec. Res. 6th Batt. Rifle Brigade, Nov. 1915 ; joined 1st Batt. in France, Apr. 1916 (wounded, D.S.O., despatches); with 1st Batt. again since Nov. 1916. *Address:* Ivy Cottage, Croft, Lancs. (*Died 1 Sept. 1918.*)

GLOVER, Sir John, Kt., cr. 1900; s. of late Alderman Glover of S. Shields; b. 6 Sept. 1829 ; s. of late Terrot Glover of South Shields ; m. 1854, Louisa (d. 1915), d. of Richard Moser of Penge, Surrey; three s. three d. J.P. Middlesex and London ; Ex-Chairman of Liberal Unionist Association of the City of London ; and of Lloyd's Registry of British and Foreign Shipping ; Ex-Chairman of the Mercantile Steamship Company, Limited ; senior partner in the firm of Glover Brothers, ship-brokers, 59 Bishopsgate, E.C.2. *Address:* Highgate Lodge, Highgate. *T.:* Hornsey 148. *Club:* Reform. (*Died 24 Mar. 1920.*)

GLOVER, Dr. Richard, D.D., Edin. ; LL.D., Bristol ; b. South Shields, 1837 ; s. of Terrot Glover, J.P.; m. Anna, d of R. G. Finlay, Glasgow ; one s. two d. *Educ.:* Edin. Univ. ; King's Coll. London ; English Presbyterian College. Educated for Presbyterian Ministry, but joined Baptist Ministry, becoming minister in Glasgow, 1861, and in Bristol, 1869 ; President of the Baptist Union of Great Britain, 1884 ; for many years member of Baptist Missionary Committee and Chairman of China Committee ; visited China in 1890-91 ; retired from ministry, 1911. *Publications:* Teacher's Commentary on St. Mark ; Teacher's Commentary on St. Matthew; Lectures on Lord's Prayer; Lectures on Beatitudes; Lectures on the Ministry to the Young ; The Comforts of God, Lectures on XIV. Chap. of St. John. *Address:* Bristol. *T.A.:* Redland, Bristol. *T.:* 1886. (*Died 26 Mar. 1919.*)

GLUCKSTEIN, Montague; Chairman J. Lyons & Co., Ltd. ; Chairman Salmon & Gluckstein, Ltd. ; Chairman Strand Hotel, Ltd. ; Director A. I. Jones & Co., Ltd., Westminster Electric Light Corporation, St. James Pall Mall Electric Light Corporation and Guardian Eastern Insurance Co.; b. 18 July 1854 ; m. 1884, Matilda Franks ; two s. one d. *Educ.:* Foundation School, St. Mary's, Whitechapel. *Address:* 38 Hyde Park Gate, Kensington, S.W.7. *T.:* Kensington 1186.

(*Died 7 Oct. 1922.*)

GLYN, Hon. Alice Coralie ; Author ; unmarried; d. of late Admiral Hon. Henry Carr-Glyn, and *sister* of 4th Baron Wolverton. Has written and lectured on Industrial Questions, is identified with the movement for better Housing, and is connected with various undertakings for the furtherance of Humanitarian and Progressive Ideals ; Founder of a Sunday Institution which was carried on for the benefit of working women. *Publications:* A Woman of To-morrow ; The Idyll of the Star-Flower, being a study of the mystic interpretations of Norwegian Sagas. *Address:* Ernstein House. Tunbridge Wells.

(*Died 28 Sept. 1928.*)

GLYN, Rt. Rev. Hon. Edward Carr; b. London, 21 Nov. 1843 ; 8th s. of 1st Lord Wolverton and Marion, d. of Pascoe Grenfell, M.P., of Taplow Court; m. Lady Mary Emma Campbell, d. of 8th Duke of Argyll ; one s. two d. *Educ.:* Harrow, University College, Oxford (M.A.). Ordained, 1868 ; curate of Doncaster under Dr. Vaughan ; domestic chaplain to the Archbishop of York, 1871 ; Vicar of St. Mary, Beverley, 1872-75 ; Vicar of Doncaster, 1875-78 ; Vicar of Kensington, 1878-97; hon. chaplain to the Queen, 1881 ; chaplain-in-ordinary, 1884 ; proctor for the clergy of London in Canterbury Convocation, 1891 ; Bishop of Peterborough, 1897-1916. *Publications:* sermons and pamphlets. *Address:* 23 Chester Square, S.W.1. *T.:* Victoria 7867. *Club:* Athenæum.

(*Died 14 Nov. 1928.*)

GLYN, Rev. Frederick Ware, M.A. ; J.P. Co. Durham ; Rector of Brancepeth since 1900; Private Chaplain to Viscount Boyne ; 4th s. of late Rev. Canon Glyn, Rector of Fontmell, Dorset; m. Eleanor, e. d. of late John Bayntun Stanley, Spye Park, Wilts; three d. *Educ.:* Marlborough ; Keble College, Oxford. Spent fifteen months at Auckland Castle with the late Bishop Lightfoot ; Curate of St. Andrew, Auckland, 1880 ; Vicar of Lanchester, 1885 ; Rector of Fontmell Magna and West Orchard, 1893 ; keenly interested in social matters and is an active Magistrate, Guardian, District Councillor, etc. *Publications:* The Bishopric (before the War) ; editor of the Durham Diocesan Calendar since 1901. *Recreations:* driving. *Address:* Brancepeth Rectory, Durham. (*Died 30 Oct. 1918.*)

GLYN, Sir Gervas Powell, 6th Bt. ; cr. 1759 ; b. Ewell, 8 Oct. 1862 ; 2nd s. of 4th Bt. ; S. half-b. 1891 ; m. 1898, Dorothy, d. of late Edmund Charles Hislop of Clapham Park. *Educ.:* Winchester Coll. ; New Coll. Oxford (M.A.) Studied medicine at Univ. Coll. London ; afterwards visited, besides European countries, Ceylon, India, Straits Settlements, China, Japan, British Columbia, Alaska, United States, New Zealand, Australia, Tasmania, Egypt, Syria, Tunis, and Algiers. *Recreations:* violoncellist; collector of foreign and antique musical instruments ; photography. *Heir:* b. Arthur Robert [b. 5 Aug. 1870. *Educ.:* Pembroke College, Cambridge. *Club:* New University]. *Address:* Rectory House, Ewell, Surrey ; The Close, Burcote, Oxon. (*Died 16 July 1921.*)

GLYN, Lewis Edmund, K.C.; b. 1849 2nd s. of late William Glyn, one of the Clerks of the House of Commons ; m. 1875, o. d. of late Rev. Richard Dugdale. Barr. Middle Temple, 1871 ; Bencher, 1907 ; South-Eastern Circuit. *Address:* 3 Essex Court, Temple, E.C. ; Broom-Hills, Bexley, Kent ; Thistlewood, Cumberland. (*Died 27 Feb. 1919.*)

GLYN, Maurice George Carr, J.P.; Partner in Glyn, Mills, Currie, and Co., Bankers ; 2nd s. of Hon. P.C. Glyn ; b. 1872 ; m. 1897; Hon. Maude Grosvenor, e. d. of 2nd Baron Ebury; six s. Sheriff Hertfords, 1912 ; late 2nd Lt. Dorsets Yeomanry. *Address:* 21 Bryanston Square, W.1; *T.:* Padd. 2676; Albury Hall, Hadham, Herts. *Club:* Arthur's. (*Died 20 Aug. 1920.*)

GLYN, Sir Richard George, 3rd Bt. ; cr. 1800 ; J.P., D.L. ; Capt. Royal Dragoons, retired 1859 ; b. London, 22 Nov. 1831 ; s. s. of Robert Glyn and Frederica, d. of Henry Harford, Down Place, Berks; S.u. 1863; m. Frances, d. of Maj. Fitzgerald, Maperton House, Somerset, 1868 ; one s. one d. *Educ.:* Cheam School ; Merton Coll. Oxford. Joined Royal Dragoons, 1852 ; sailed with them to Varna, 1854, present at battles of Balaclava and Inkerman, returned with Regt., 1856 ; made an expedition from Natal to the interior of Africa, was one of first Europeans after Dr. Livingstone to reach the Victoria Falls of River Zambesi, 1863 ; Master Blackmoor Vale Hounds, 1865-84. Owns about 9800 acres. *Heir:* s.

Richard Fitzgerald [b. 13 May 1875 ; late Lieut. Royal Dragoons ; m. 1906, Edith Hilda, e. d. of G. D. Hamilton-Gordon ; two s. one d.]. *Address :* Gaunt's House, Wimborne ; Fontmell-Magna, Shaftesbury. *Club :* Arthur's.
(*Died 9 Aug. 1918.*)

GLYN, Hon. Sidney Carr ; b. 11 Oct. 1835 ; 7th s. of 1st Baron Wolverton ; m. 1868, Fanny (d. 1907), d. of M. Adolphe Marescaux of St. Omer, France ; one s. M.P. (L.) Shaftesbury, 1880-85 ; late Capt. Rifle Brigade. *Address :* 27 Grosvenor Place, S.W. *Clubs :* Army and Navy, Brooke's. (*Died 26 Feb. 1916.*)

GLYN-JONES, Sir William Samuel, Kt., cr. 1919 : J.P. Middlesex ; Chairman of Council of the Proprietary Articles Trade Association, and since 1926 of the Canadian Proprietary Articles Trade Association ; M.P. (L.) Stepney, 1911-18 ; pharmacist ; Secretary to the Pharmaceutical Society of Great Britain, 1918-26 ; b. Worcester, 1869 ; m. 1894, Mary, d. of John Evans of Tower Hill, Llanybyther, Carmarthen ; two s. two d. *Educ.:* Merthyr Tydfil Grammar School. Called to Bar, Middle Temple, 1904. *Publication :* The Law of Poisons and Pharmacy. *Address :* 43 Gordon Square, W.C.1. *T. :* Museum 8885. *Club :* National Liberal. (*Died 9 Sept. 1927.*)

GOAD, Col. Howard, C.S.I. 1907 ; b. 15 Sep. 1857 ; s. of late C. W. Goad, formerly 5th Dragoon Guards, and Sophia, d. of Col. T. B. Thoroton Hildyard, M.P. of Flintham Hall, Newark ; m. 1908, Ethel May, y. d. of late John Groome Howes of Kingscliffe, Northants. *Educ.:* Marlborough. Entered Army, 1875 ; Capt. I.S.C. 1886 ; Major, 1895 ; Lt.-Col. Indian Army, 1901 ; Col. 1904 ; Director Army Remount Dept. 1898-1908 ; Director-General Army Remount Department, India, 1908-1908 served Afghan War, 1879-80 (medal) ; Commandant Swaythling Remount Depot, 1915-18. *Address :* Kennedy, Thurlestone, South Devon. *Club :* Naval and Military. (*Died 18 Dec. 1923.*)

GOBEIL, Antoine, I.S.O. 1904 ; b. St. Jean, Island of Orleans, Quebec, 22 Sep. 1854 ; m. Blanche Gingras ; two s. two d. *Educ. :* Seminary of Quebec ; Laval University. Entered Civil Service, 1872 ; retired, 1908 ; admitted to Bar, Province of Quebec, 1902 ; Law Clerk, Dept. of Public Works, Ottawa, 1880-85 ; Secretary, 1885-91 ; Deputy Minister, 1891-1908 ; resumed practice of Law in Quebec, 1911. *Address :* 81 St. Peter Street, Quebec ; Aux Quatre Vents, St. Laurent, Island of Orleans, Quebec. *Club :* Rideau, Ottawa.

GODDARD, Arabella (Mrs. Davison) ; pianist ; b. St. Servan, Brittany, 12 Jan. 1836 ; parents English ; m. 1859, J. W. Davison, musical critic of the Times. *Educ. :* at 8 years old had lessons from Kalkbrenner in Paris ; afterwards under Mrs. Anderson, Thalberg, and J. W. Davison in England. Played to Chopin as a child of seven, and was caressed by Georges Sand on that occasion ; debut at Grand National Concerts at Her Majesty's Theatre, 1850 ; was the first pianist to play Beethoven's Posthumous Sonatas publicly in England ; travelled in Germany and Italy and gave concerts, 1854-55 played at the Gewandhaus Concert, Leipsic, 1855, receiving an enthusiastic reception ; at the Philharmonic Concert in England, 1856 (gold medal) ; later at the Monday Popular Concerts ; toured through America, Australia India, Java, and China, 1873-76 ; took part in Sir Arthur Sullivan's Concerts, Paris Exhibition, 1878 (medal) ; retired from public life the same year ; Mrs. Davison has played many times before the Queen Victoria, the German Emperor and Empress William, and King Edward and Queen Alexandra ; she was asked to join the professional staff of the Royal College of Music.
(*Died 6 April 1922.*)

GODDARD, Arthur ; b. 1853. One of the originators and subsequently editor of Society ;

joined the editorial staff of the Lady's Pictorial, 1887 ; editor, 1900-14 ; has been a dramatic critic since 1884. *Publications :* Players of the Period, 2 vols., 1891 ; Windsor, the Castle of our Kings, and some Notes on Eton College, 1911. *Recreations :* books and print collecting. *Address :* Redholme, 23 Holmdene Avenue, Herne Hill, S.E.24. *T. :* Brixton 1895. (*Died Aug. 1920.*)

GODDARD, Rt. Hon. Sir Daniel Ford, Kt., cr. 1907 ; P.C. 1916 ; J.P. ; b. 17 Jan. 1850 ; o. s. of late Ebenezer Goddard ; m. 1st, 1074, Lucy, d. of Thomas Harwood, Belstead Hall, Suffolk ; 2nd, Elizabeth, d. of Ebenezer Hitchcock, Bramford ; one d. *Educ. :* privately at Ipswich and Hastings ; articled to Messrs. E. R. and J. Turner, engineers, Ipswich ; Associate member of the Inst. of Civil Engineers ; studied Chemistry in London and Newcastle ; succeeded father as Engineer and Secretary Ipswich Gas Co. 1877-87 ; Mayor of Ipswich, 1891 ; contested Ipswich, 1892 ; M.P. (L.) Ipswich, 1895-1918 ; Chairman of Directors, Ipswich Gas Co. since 1887 ; founded and built Ipswich Social Settlement. *Recreations :* travelling, photography. *Address :* Oak Hill, Ipswich. *T.A. :* Sir Daniel Goddard, Ipswich. *T. :* Ipswich 583. *M. :* DX 520. *Clubs :* National Liberal, Reform. (*Died 6 May 1922.*)

GODFRAY, Brig.-Gen. John William, C.B. 1900 ; C.V.O. 1905 ; C.B.E. 1919 ; A.D.C. to the King, 1911 ; late The King's Own Scottish Borderers ; retired ; b. 20 Oct. 1850 ; m. 1880, Annie Julia, d. of late J. D. Muntz of Baddesley, Clinton, Warwick ; one s. *Educ. :* Cheltenham College. Entered army, 1871 ; Capt., 1879 ; served Chitral, 1895 (despatches, medal and clasp, brevet of Lieut.-Colonel) ; Tirah Campaign, 1897-98 (two clasps, N.W. Frontier and Tirah) ; commanded 1st K.O.S.B., South Africa, 1900, then Chief Staff Officer VII. Division, and afterwards C.S.O. Orange River Colony to end of war (despatches, C.B., Queen's and King's South African medals) ; commanded 25th Regimental District, 1902-5 ; Brig.-Gen. in charge of Administration, Scottish Command, 1905-7 ; A.A.G. Jersey Militia, 1908-14 ; A.A. and Q.M.G. Jersey Defences to 1919. *Address :* 3 Hastings Terrace, Jersey. (*Died 10 Jan. 1921.*)

GODFREY, Charles, M.V.O., 1910 ; M.A. ; Professor of Mathematics at R.N. College, Greenwich ; b. 4 Oct. 1873 ; e. s. of G. H. Godfrey, Birmingham ; m. 1908, Evelyn Patience, d. of J. Armine Willis ; one s. three d. *Educ. :* King Edward's School, Birmingham ; Trinity College, Cambridge. 4th Wrangler, 1895 ; 1st div. 1st class in second part of Mathematical Tripos, 1896 ; Senior Mathematical Master at Winchester College, 1900-5 ; Head Master of the Royal Naval College, Osborne, 1905-21. *Address :* 57 Westcombe Park Road, Blackheath, S.E.3. *T. :* Greenwich 1338. *Club :* Savile. (*Died 4 April 1924.*)

GODFREY, Sir William Cecil, 5th Bt., cr. 1785 ; b. 21 July 1857 ; s. of 4th Bt. and Mary, d. of T. W. Scutt, late of Clapham House, Litlington, Sussex ; S. father, 1900 ; m. 1st, 1835, Adela Maud (d. 1890), d. of F. F. Hamilton ; one d. ; 2nd, 1901, Mary, e. d. of late Richard Leeson-Marshall of Callinafercy, County Kerry. Late Lieut. South Wales Borderers ; served S. Africa, 1879 (medal with clasp). Owns about 6100 acres. *Heir :* b. John Ernest [b. 6 Oct. 1864 ; m. 1897, Eileen Mary, e. d. of S. Curry, M.D., Lismore ; one s. three d.]. *Address :* Kilcoleman Abbey, Milltown, Co. Kerry.
(*Died Nov. 1926.*)

GODLEE, Sir Rickman John, 1st Bart., cr. 1912 ; K.C.V.O., cr. 1914 ; B.A., M.S., F.R.C.S., LL.D., M.D. Dublin ; Hon. Surgeon in Ordinary to the King ; Fellow of University Coll. ; Emeritus Professor of Clinical Surgery, University College, London ; late Surgeon at

414

University College Hospital; *b.* 15 Apr. 1849; *m.* 1891, Juliet Mary, *d.* of Frederic Seebohm, LL.D., of Hitchin, Herts. *Educ.:* University College, London. *Publications:* Lord Lister, 1917;- numerous works on professional subjects. *Heir:* none. *Address:* Coombe End Farm, Whitchurch, Oxon. *T.:* Pangbourne 96. *Clubs:* Athenæum, Burlington Fine Arts, University of London. (*Died 20 April 1925.*)

GODLEY, Alfred Denis, M.A.; O.B.E.; Public Orator, Oxford, since 1910; *b.* Ireland, 1856; *e. s.* of late Rev. James Godley, Carrigalien, Co. Leitrim, and Eliza, *d.* of P. La Touche; *m.* Amy, *d.* of late C. H. Cay, 1894. *Educ.:* Harrow; Balliol Coll. Craven Scholar, 1880; various University prizes, 1874-1879; Classical Moderator, 1887-88, 1895-96, 1906-7; Deputy Public Orator, 1904-6; Assistant Master at Bradfield College, 1879-82; Fellow and Tutor of Magdalen College, 1883-1912; Hon. Fellow of Magdalen College since 1912; Hon. LL.D. Princeton, 1913; Hon. D.Litt. (Oxon), 1919; Lieut.-Col., Oxfordshire Volunteer Corps, 1916-19; Member of the Governing Body of Harrow School; an Alderman in the Oxford City Council. *Publications:* Verses to Order, 1892 and 1903; Aspects of Modern Oxford, 1893; Socrates and Athenian Society, 1895; edition of Tacitus' Histories, 1887 and 1890; translation of the Odes of Horace, 1898; Lyra Frivola, 1899; Nova Anthologia Oxoniensis (edited with Prof. Robinson Ellis), 1899; Fables of Orbilius, 1901 and 1902; Second Strings, 1902; Oxford in the Eighteenth Century, 1908; The Casual Ward, 1912; Translation of Herodotus (Loeb series), 1921-28; Joint editor of the Classical Review, 1910-20; of Horace, Book V., 1920; various magazine articles and introductory essays. *Address:* 27 Norham Road, Oxford. *Club:* Alpine (Vice-Pres. 1924). (*Died 27 June 1925.*)

GODMAN, Frederick Du Cane, D.C.L., F.R.S., M.R.I.; Trustee of the British Museum; *b.* 1834; 3rd *s.* of J. Godman, Park Hatch, Surrey; *m.* 1st, Edith Mary, *d.* of late J. H. Elwes, Colesborne, Gloucestershire (*d.* 1875); 2nd, Alice Mary, *d.* of late Maj. Percy Chaplin, J.P., 60th Rifles. *Publications:* Natural History of the Azores, 1870; Monograph of the Petrels, 1910; Biologia Centrali-Americana, 1916. *Address:* 45 Pont Street, S.W.; South Lodge, Horsham. *Club:* Athenæum. (*Died 19 Feb. 1919.*)

GODMAN, Major Laurence, D.S.O. 1916; Royal Artillery; *b.* 4 Sep. 1880; 3rd *s.* of Colonel A. F. Godman, C.B. *Educ.:* Rugby; R.M.A. Woolwich. Joined Royal Artillery, 1899; Captain, 1908; Major, 1914; served European War (despatches twice, D.S.O.). *Address:* Smeaton Manor, Northallerton. *Club:* Army and Navy. (*Died 30 Sept. 1917.*)

GODSELL, Sir William, Kt., *cr.* 1903 *b.* 23 Feb. 1838; *e. s.* of late Thomas Godsell of King's Caple, Herefords; *m.* 1st, 1864, Georgina Mary (*d.* 1903), *d.* of late Rev. James Buckoll; 2nd, 1908, Emily Helen, *d.* of late George Grimmette. Entered Government Service, 1860; Auditor of Accounts of Secretary of State for India, 1895-1903. *Address:* 15 Grosvenor Avenue, Carshalton, Surrey.(*Died 27 Sept. 1924.*)

GODWIN, Sir Arthur, Kt., *cr.* 1913; *b.* 17 Oct. 1852; *o. s.* of John Venimore Godwin, J.P., Mayor of Bradford (*d.* 1898), and Rachel Catherine, *d.* of late Rev. James Acworth, LL.D.; *m.* 1887, Mary Elizabeth, *d.* of late William Geddes, Liverpool. *Educ.:* Edinburgh University. Taken active part in political, municipal, and philanthropic life of city; J.P. City of Bradford, 1892; entered City Council, 1900; Alderman, 1903; first Lord Mayor of Bradford, 1907; is a Freemason and Senior Grand Deacon of England, 1908. *Recreations:* fishing and sketching. *Address:* Colvend, Grassington, near Skipton. *T.A.:* Godwin, Bradford. *T.:* Grass-

ington 21. *M.:* DU 3631, WR 1690. *Clubs:* Royal Canoe; Bradford. (*Died 29 April 1921.*)

GODWIN-AUSTEN, Henry Haversham, F.R.S.; F.Z.S.; F.R.G.S., etc.; J.P.; Lieut.-Col. retired 1877; *b.* Teignmouth, 6 July 1834; *e. s.* of Robert A. C. Godwin-Austen, F.R.S., a distinguished geologist, and Maria, *d.* of General Godwin, C.B.; *m.* 1st, Pauline, *d.* of Major Chichele Plowden, 1861; one *s.*; 2nd, Jessie (*d.* 1913), *d.* of J. H. Robinson, 1881. *Educ.:* R.M.C. Sandhurst. Gazetted H.M.'s 24th Regt. of Foot, 1851; went to India, 1852; served in 2nd Burmese War (medal and clasp Pegu) and Punjab; appointed Topographical Assistant in Trigonometrical Survey of India, and joined the Kashmir Survey party, 1857; surveyed very large extent of country in Kashmir and Baltistan; in latter country the enormous glaciers at head of Shigar river and Hunza Nagar frontier, which included the Baltoro glacier, which he was the first to discover, coming down in part from the second highest mountain in the Himalayas, since named after him; surveyed the lofty country of Rupshu and Zaskar in Ladakh, 1862; in July and August of that year he made 13 different ascents of a mean height of 17,900 feet, the highest peak, Mata, being 20,607; took up the Changchingmo and carried the topography to the eastern end of the Pang Kong lake, close up to Rudok in Chinese territory, where he was met and stopped by the Lhassan Governor, 1863; in winter of 1863-64 on special duty with last mission to Bhutan, and mapped the country between Darjeeling and Punakha, the capital; 1864-65 on special duty with the Bhutan Field Force, and was present at the capture of Dalingkote and Chamurchi Forts (clasp for Bhutan); 1866-76 in charge of Survey Operations in the Garo, Khasi, Jaintia, North Cachar and Naga Hills, and Manipur, including in 1874 the expedition against the Dafla tribe at base of the Eastern Himalayas, when a large area of new country was mapped and many distant peaks fixed; President of Section E (Geography) British Association, 1883; President Malacological Society, 1897-99; President Conchological Society of Great Britain and Ireland, 1908-9; awarded by the Royal Geographical Society the Founder's medal (1910) for his exploration work. *Publications:* On the Land and Fresh-water Mollusca of India, 1882-1920; (with late Dr. W. T. Blanford, F.R.S.) The Fauna of British India, vol. Mollusca, 1908; 181 papers in the Journals of various Scientific Societies on Geology and Physical Features, Ethnology and Natural History. *Recreations:* shooting, fishing, drawing. *Address:* Nore, Godalming. (*Died 2 Dec. 1923.*)

GOETHALS, George Washington; army engineer; *b.* Brooklyn, 29 June 1858. *Educ.:* College, City of New York; United States Military Academy; LL.D. University of Pennsylvania, 1913; Princeton University, 1915. 2nd Lieut., Engineers, 1880; 1st Lieut., 1882; Capt., 1891; Lieut.-Col., Chief Engineer Volunteers, 1898; hon. discharged from Volunteer service, 1898; Major, Engineer Corps, 1900; graduated Army War College, 1905; Lieut.-Col., Engineers, 1907; Col., 1909; Major-General, 1915; retired, 1916; Instructor in Civil and Military Engineering, U.S. Military Academy; in charge of Mussel Shoals Canal construction on Tennessee River; Chief of Engineers during Spanish-American War; Member Board of Fortifications (coast and harbour defence); Chief Engineer Panama Canal, 1907-14; 1st Civil Governor Panama Canal Zone, 1914-16; Chairman Board appointed to report on Adamson 8-Hour Law, 1916; State Engineer, New Jersey, 1917; General Manager, Emergency Fleet Corporation, 1917 (resigned); Acting Quarter-Master-General U.S.A., 1917; Chief

Division of Storage and Traffic of General Staff, 1918; Chief of Division of Purchase, Storage and Traffic, 1918; Member War Industries Board; relieved from active duty at own request, 1919; received thanks of Congress, 4 Mar. 1915, for distinguished service in constructing Panama Canal; D.S.M. 1918, for especially meritorious and conspicuous service in reorganising O.M. Dept.; Commander Legion of Honour, 1919; medals; Nat. Geog. Soc., Civic Forum, and Nat. Inst. Social Sciences. *Address:* 40 Wall Street, New York.

(*Died 21 Jan. 1928.*)

GOFF, Sir Herbert William Davis, 2nd Bt., *cr.* 1905; *o. c.* of Sir W. G. D. Goff, 1st Bart., and Anna, *d.* of M. D. Hassard; *S.* father 1917; *b.* 20 Oct. 1870; *m.* 1908, Margaret Ainée, *d.* of Rt. Hon. Sir C. S. Scott; three *s.* one *d. Educ.:* Wellington; Trinity College, Cambridge (B.A.). Lieut. Army Motor Reserve; Capt. in command of A.S.C. Co., attached to No. 6 Motor Ambulance Convoy, B.E.F., France, 1914-16. *Heir: s.* Ernest William, *b.* 11 June 1904. *Address:* Maypark, Waterford. *Clubs:* Bath, Royal Automobile; Kildare Street, Dublin.

(*Died 26 June 1923.*)

GOFF, Colonel Robert Charles, late of the Coldstream Guards; retired 1878; *m.* 1899, Clarissa Catherine, *d.* of 8th Baron de Hochepied. Is a Fellow of the Royal Society of Painter Etchers; has been a frequent exhibitor both of water-colours and of etchings in London and abroad, and is an Hon. Member of the Florence and Milan Academies of Arts. *Address:* Wick Studio, Holland Road, Hove, Sussex; Villa dell' Ombrellino, Via della Piazzola, Florence. *Club:* Army and Navy.

(*Died 1 July 1922.*)

GOFF, Sir William Goff Davis-, 1st Bt., *cr.* 1905.; J.P., D.L.; *b.* 12 Sept. 1888; *s.* of late S. Davis Goff and Susan, *d.* of late Arthur Ussher; *m.* 1866, Anna, *d.* of M. D. Hassard; one *s. Educ.:* M.A. Trinity College, Dublin. Formerly cornet, 2nd Dragoon Guards. *Recreations:* yachting, motoring. *Heir: s.* Herbert William Davis Goff. *Address:* Glenville, Waterford. *T.:* 5 Waterford Exchange. *M.:* WI 20, WI 36. *Clubs:* Constitutional, Royal Automobile; Royal St. George Yacht, Royal Mersey; Kildare Street, Dublin. (*Died 23 Nov. 1918.*)

GOLD, Sir Charles, Kt., *cr.* 1906; D.L., J.P.; Director of W. and A. Gilbey; *b.* 1887; *s.* of Mr. Gold, Birmingham; *n.* of Sir J. Allport; *m.* 1859, Fanny Georgina (*d.* 1910), sister of Sir W. Gilbey, 1st Bt.; two *s.* M.P. (G.L.) Saffron-Walden, Essex, 1895-1900. *Address:* The Limes, Birchanger, Essex. *Clubs:* Orleans, Devonshire. (*Died 2 Nov. 1924.*)

GOLDIE, Rt. Hon. Sir George Dashwood Taubman, P.C. 1898; K.C.M.G., *cr.* 1887; D.C.L. (Hon.), Oxford; LL.D.(Hon.),Camb.; F.R.S.; founder of Nigeria; *b.* The Nunnery, Isle of Man, 20 May 1846; *y. s.* of Col. Goldie-Taubman, Scots Guards, and Speaker of the House of Keys; *m.* 1870, Matilda (*d.* 1898), *d.* of John Elliot, Wakefield; one *s.* one *d. Educ.:* Royal Military Academy, Woolwich. Lieut. R.E.; attended Berlin Conference, 1884-85, as expert on Niger questions; Royal Commissions on South African War, 1902-3, and on War Stores, 1905-6; President National Defence Association, 1905-14 and 1915-20. *Clubs:* Naval and Military, Athenæum; Royal Yacht Squadron, Cowes. (*Died 20 Aug. 1925.*)

GOLDNEY, Hon. Sir John Tankerville, Kt., *cr.* 1898; J.P. Wilts; Lay-Rector of Corsham; *b.* 1846; 3rd *s.* of Sir G. Goldney, 1st Bt.; *m.* 1st, 1875, Jane (*d.* 1911), *d.* of J. Laird, M.P.; 2nd, Alice Frances Holbrow, *d.* of Major F. C. Goldney, late 8th Gurkha Rifles. *Educ.:* Harrow; Trin. Coll., Camb. (B.A., LL.B.). Barr. Inner Temple 1869; Acting Chief Justice, Leeward Islands, 1881; Judge of Supreme Court of British Guiana, 1883; Judge

of Straits Settlements, 1887; Chief Justice of Trinidad, 1892-1900; High Sheriff for Wilts, 1910-1911. *Address:* Monks Park, Corsham; Hanover Court, Hanover Square, W. *Clubs:* Junior Carlton, Oxford and Cambridge.

(*Died 11 April 1920.*)

GOLDNEY, Sir Prior, 2nd Bt., *cr.* 1880; C. B. 1902; C.V.O. 1903; D.L., London; J.P., Wilts and Somerset; late Major Royal Wilts Yeo. Cavalry; *b.* 4 Aug. 1843; *s.* of 1st Bt. and Mary, *o. d.* of R. H. Alexander, Corsham, Wilts. *Educ.:* Harrow; Exeter Coll. Oxford. Called to Bar, Inner Temple, 1867; Recorder of Helston, 1876-1870; Poole, 1879-82; Remembrancer of City of London, 1882-1902. *Heir: b.* F. H. Goldney. *Address:* Derriads, Chippenham, Wilts; Manor House, Halse, Somerset. *Club:* Junior Carlton. (*Died 4 May 1925.*)

GOMEZ, Alice; Singer; *b.* Calcutta, of Eurasian parentage; *m.* T. H. Webb, Professor of Music. Made debut in London 1885. Resides in Calcutta. (*Died 1922.*)

GOMME, Sir (George) Laurence, Kt., *cr.* 1911; J.P.; F.S.A.; F.S.S.; Fellow of the Anthropological Institute; formerly President and now Vice-President of the Folklore Society; Hon. Member of the Glasgow Archæological Society; author; original founder and some time secretary of the Folklore Society; Secretary to the Lieutenancy of London; *b.* London, 1853; *m.* 1875, Alice Bertha Merck, author of Traditional Games of Great Britain, 1896-98; seven *s. Educ.:* City of London School. Formerly edited the Antiquary, the Archæological Review, and the Folklore Journal; lecturer at the London School of Economics and University Extension; formerly Statistical Officer and Clerk to the London County Council. *Publications:* Index of Municipal Offices, 1879; Primitive Folk-Moots, 1880; Folklore Relics of Early Village Life, 1883; The Gentleman's Magazine Lib. (ed.), 1883-1906; Chap-Books and Folklore Tracts, 1885; The Literature of Local Institutions, 1886; The London County Council, 1888; The Village Community, 1889; Ethnology in Folklore, 1892; Lectures on the Principles of Local Government, 1898; Editor of the King's Story-Book, 1897; Queen's Story-Book, 1896; Prince's Story-Book, 1899; Princess's Story-Book, 1900; historical novels — Lytton's Harold, Macfarlane's Camp of Refuge and Reading Abbey, and Kingsley's Westward Ho!; Governance of London, 1907; Index of Archæological Papers (edited), 1907; Folklore as an Historical Science, 1908; The Making of London, 1911; London, 1914. *Recreations:* change of work. *Address:* 20 Marlborough Place, N.W.; The Mound, Long Crendon, Bucks. *Clubs:* Royal Societies, Municipal and County. (*Died 24 Feb. 1916.*)

GOMPERS, Samuel; President American Federation of Labour; Editor American Federationist; 1st Vice-President Cigarmakers' International Union; President Pan-American Federation of Labour; *b.* London, England, 27 Jan. 1850; *s.* of Solomon Gompers and Sarah Rood; *m.* 1st, 1867, Sophia Julian (*d.* 1920); three *s.;* 2nd, 1921, Gertrude Gleaves Neuscheler. *Educ.:* from sixth year until little more than ten years of age attended the public schools of London. Cigarmaker by trade; came to U.S.A. 1868; helped develop the Cigarmakers' International Union, of which he has been an officer since 1887; one of the founders of the Federation of Trades and Labour Unions organised in 1881, of which he was president 3 years; one of the founders of the American Federation of Labour organised in 1886, of which he has since been elected president annually, with the exception of the year 1895; member of New York Factory Investigating Committee, 1912; member of Advisory Committee to the Council of National Defence, 1916-19; President of the International Commission on Labor

Legislation of the Paris Peace Conference, 1919; member Advisory Committee to American Delegates in the Conference for the Limitation of Armaments; member President's First Industrial Conference, 1919; member President's Unemployment Conference, 1921; member Sulgrave Institute. *Publications:* Labor in Europe and America; American Labor and the War; Labor and the Common Welfare; Labor and the Employer; Out of Their Own Mouths; and a number of pamphlets on the labour question and the labour movement. *Address:* 318 West 51st Street, New York City; A.F. of L. Building, Washington, D.C. *T.A.:* Afel. *T.:* Main 3871.
(*Died 13 Dec. 1924.*)

GONNER, Prof. Sir Edward Carter Kersey, K.B.E., *cr.* 1921; C.B.E. 1918; M.A. Oxford; Hon. M.A. Sydney; Hon. Litt.D., Manchester; Professor of Economic Science in the University of Liverpool; sometime Economic Adviser to the Ministry of Food; Director of Statistics, Ministry of Food; a Chairman in the Committee on Production; *b.* 1862; *s.* of Peter Kersey and Elizabeth Gonner; *m.* 1890, Nannie Ledlie; one *d.* *Educ.:* Merchant Taylors' School, London; Lincoln Coll. Oxford. Lecturer for the London Extension Society, 1885; Lecturer at University College, Bristol, 1885; Lecturer at University Coll., Liverpool, 1888; Professor at University College, Liverpool, 1891; Rae Lecturer, University College, Bangor, 1911; President of Section F, Economics and Statistics, of the British Association (Toronto), 1897; President of Section F, British Association (Australia), 1914; Vice-President Economic History Sub-section, International Historical Congress, London, 1913; Member of the Royal Commission on Shipping Conferences, 1906-9; Chairman of the Sub-Committee for Elementary Education, County of Chester; Chairman of the War Savings Committee, County of Chester, 1917-18. *Publications:* edited Ricardo's Principles of Political Economy and Taxation; The Socialist State; The Social Philosophy of Rodbertus; Commercial Geography; Interest and Saving; Common Land and Inclosure; The Economic History of Germany in the Nineteenth Century; contributor to Dict. of Nat. Biography, Dict. of Political Economy, Conrad's Handwörterbuch der Staatswissenschaften, etc. *Address:* Red Gables, Headington, Oxford.
(*Died 24 Feb. 1922.*)

GOOCH, Sir Daniel Fulthorpe, 3rd Bt., *cr.* 1866; *b.* 25 May 1869; *S.* father 1897; *m.* 1896, Mary Winifred (*d.* 1921), *d.* of late Edward William Monro; one *s.* two *d.* *Heir: s.* Robert Douglas, *b.* 19 Sep. 1905. *Address:* Tatchbury Mount, Totton, Hampshire. *Club:* Boodle's.
(*Died 22 Dec. 1926.*)

GOODDEN, Rev. Edward Wyndham, Rector of Nether and Over Compton since 1884; Canon and Prebendary of Salisbury since 1904; *b.* 17 Feb. 1847; 2nd *s.* of late John Goodden of Compton House, Sherborne; *m.* 1871, Georgina, *e. d.* of late Rev. J. Frewen Moor of Bradfield, Berks, and Sion Place, Bath. *Educ.:* Harrow; Merton Coll. Oxford. Curate of Limpsfield, Surrey, 1870-72; Nether and Over Compton, 1872-84; Alderman Dorset County Council since 1888; Chairman of Dorset Education Committee since 1903. *Recreations:* fishing, motoring, yachting. *Address:* Nether Compton Rectory, Sherborne, Dorset. *T.:* Yeovil 20. *T.A.:* Nether Compton. *M.:* FX 5810. *Clubs:* Royal Societies; Royal Dorset Yacht.
(*Died 19 May 1924.*)

GOODE, Sir Charles Henry, Kt., *cr.* 1912; Chairman of Goode, Durrant & Co., Limited, Adelaide, Perth, Broken Hill, N.S.W. and 27 Milton Street, E.C.; *b.* 26 May 1827; *m.* 1st, 1856; 2nd, 1890; no *c.* *Educ.:* Docklow Academy, Herefordshire. Left school at 10

15

years of age; apprenticed to draper, 1839; went to London, 1845; went to Adelaide, 1849; started business in a cart; gradually climbed up; has visited London four times, staying 4 years, 12 years, and 2 short visits; has been right round the world twice since he was 70. *Publications:* None of consequence; only Letters to Young People from Japan. *Recreations:* looking after the blind, deaf and dumb, consumptives, state children, etc.; taking carriage drives occasionally. *Address:* North Adelaide, South Australia. (*Died 5 Feb. 1923.*)

GOODEVE, Mrs. Arthur (Florence Everilda), composer of many popular songs; *d.* of Thomas John Knowlys, J.P., of Heysham Tower, Lancashire, and Hollybrook, Hants, niece of Sir Peter Fleetwood-Hesketh, Bt., M.P., of Rossall; *m.* Louis Arthur Goodeve, Advocate, High Court, Calcutta, *s.* of late Joseph Goodeve, Master in Equity, Supreme Court, Bengal. Composer of Fiddle and I; Ah, Well a Day! The Jovial Beggar; Come Again; Litany for the War; Round the Clock, etc. *Address:* 36 Harcourt Terrace, S. Kensington, S.W.; Clayton, Clifton. *Club:* Ladies' Park.
(*Died 15 Jan. 1916.*)

GOODEVE, Hon. Arthur Samuel, Member of Board of Railway Commissioners for Canada since 1912; *b.* Guelph, Ontario, 15 Dec. 1860; *s.* of Arthur Henry Goodeve and Caroline Higginson; *m.* 1884, Ellen Edith Spence; four *s.* two *d.* *Educ.:* Guelph Collegiate Institute. Druggist; Mayor Rossland, B.C., 1889 and 1900; Provincial Secretary, 1902; M.P. Kootenay, B.C., 1908 and 1911. *Recreations:* tennis, bowling. *Address:* Ottawa, Canada. *T.:* Q 8651, Q 3204. *Clubs:* Country, Rideau, Ottawa; Rossland, Rossland.
(*Died Nov. 1920.*)

GOODHART, Comdr. Francis Herbert Heveningham, R.N.; D.S.O. 1916; *b.* Sheffield, 10 July 1884; *s.* of the Vicar of St. Barnabas, Sheffield, later Rector of Lambourne, Essex for 23 years, and *d.* of late C. Warner of Birmingham (*d.* 1885); *m.* 1912, Isabella, *y. d.* of Mrs. Turner of Eastbourne and S. Africa, and *g. d.* of late Thomas Turner of Worksop; two *d.* *Educ.:* Chigwell Grammar School, Essex; H.M.S. Britannia, Dartmouth. Served as midshipman in Mediterranean, H.M.S. Ramillies, 1900-3; passed exams. for Lieutenant, 4 firsts, 1903-4; Lieutenant, 1905; served in Submarine Service since June 1905; also in H.M. ships Magnificent and Agamemnon, 1910-11; serving in H.M.S. Maidstone for command of submarine E 8, Aug. 1914 (despatches) for reconnaissance of Heligoland Bight; Commander, 1915 (D.S.O.) for services in command of a submarine; Order of St. Vladimir, 4th class; Order of St. George, 4th class; Chev. of Legion d'Honneur. *Recreations:* tennis, golf. *Address:* c/o Admiralty, S.W. (*Died 30 Jan. 1917.*)

GOODHART, Sir James Frederic, 1st Bart., *cr.* 1911; M.D., C.M., F.R.C.P., London; Hon. LL.D. Aberdeen, Consulting Physician to Guy's Hospital, the Evelina Hospital for Sick Children, Royal Hospital for Incurables, Putney, Female Orphan Asylum, Beddington, and Spurgeon Orphan Asylum; on Consulting Committee of King Edward VII. Sanatorium, Midhurst; late one of the Hon. Staff of King Edward VII. Hospital for Officers and Osborne Convalescent Home; *b.* London, 24 Oct. 1845; *m.* Emma Sandford (*d.* 1915), *d.* of W. Bennett, J.P., of Ashgrove, Herefordshire; two *s.* Fellow of the Royal Society of Medicine; President Harveian Society, 1898. *Publications:* Common Neuroses; the Diseases of Children, 10th Edition; many medical addresses. *Heir: s.* Ernest Frederick (Barrister; *b.* 12 Aug. 1880; *m.* 1906, Frances Evelyn, *d.* of M. F. Armstrong; one *s.* one *d.* *Educ.:* Merton College, Oxford]. *Address:* 25 Portland Place, W.; Hoitye Corner, Cowden, Kent. *Club:* Conservative. (*Died 28 Mar. 1916.*)

417

GOODIER, Rev. Joseph Hulme, Hon. Canon of Ripon. *Address:* 11 Crescent Parade, Ripon. (*Died Feb.* 1920.)

GOODLIFFE, Francis Foster, C.I.E. 1924; M.L.C.; Managing Director, Barnett Bros., Ltd., Rangoon; *s.* of W. G. Goodliffe, late Accountant-General, India Office; *m.* Alice Hilda, *d.* of W. D'Arcy Porter, Rangoon; two *d. Educ.:* University College School, London. Came to Burma, 1887; Member of the Legislative Council, Burma; Trustee of the Rangoon Development Trust; Commissioner of the Port of Rangoon. *Recreation:* stock-breeding. *Address:* Rangoon, Burma. (*Died 7 Oct.* 1925.)

GOODMAN, Hon. Sir Gerald Aubrey, Kt., *cr.* 1920; Attorney-General of Straits Settlements since 1915; K.C.; J.P.; *b.* 6 Sep. 1862; *s.* of late Flavius Augustus Goodman; *m.* 1885, Gertrude Winifred, *y. d.* of E. J. Cobbett, R.B.A.: three *s. Educ.:* Lodge School and Harrison College, Barbados; University College, London. First Common Law Scholar, Middle Temple, 1885; Called to Bar, Middle Temple, 1885; practised Barbados; acted judge of Petty Debt Court and of Assistant Court of Appeal, 1889; acted Solicitor General in 1890-1-2; appointed Solicitor General, 1896; acted Attorney General, 1891, 1898, 1900-1-2-3-4; Attorney-General, Barbados, 1907-13; Member of the Barbados House of Assembly, 1889-1912; of the Board of Education, 1891-1912; of the Quarantine Board and General Board of Health, 1902-1912; Delegate to Canadian Reciprocity Conference at Barbados, 1908. *Address:* Cahore, Goodwood Hill, Singapore. (*Died 20 Jan.* 1921.)

GOODMAN, Hon. Sir William Meigh, Kt., *cr.* 1902; K.C.; *b.* 1847; *m.* 1st, 1874, Fanny, 2nd *d.* of B. B. Breach of Burwash, Sussex; 2nd, 1892, Katie, *d.* of F. J. Smith. *Educ.:* University College; University of London (B.A. Honours). Called to the Bar, Middle Temple, 1870; went S.E. Circuit; Attorney-General Brit. Honduras, 1883; Chief-Justice, 1886; Attorney-General, Hong-Kong, 1889; Chief-Justice Supreme Court, Hong-Kong, 1902-5; retired, 1905. *Address:* Clavadel, Guildford, Surrey. *Club:* Constitutional. (*Died 3 May* 1928.)

GOODRICH, Dr. A., *b.* 3 March 1840; *s.* of William Goodrich, wholesale furniture manufacturer, Curtain Road, London, and Harriet Gale of Bath; *m.* 1865, Emma Susan, *e. d.* of John Barr, wholesale furniture manufacturer; one *s.* five *d. Educ.:* The Hoxton Acad.; Hackney Coll. Ordained to the Congregational Ministry, 1865; Minister of the Braintree Congregational Church, 1865-76; Elgin Place Congregational Church, Glasgow, 1876-90; Congregational Church, Chorlton Road, Manchester, 1890-1912; Chairman of the Congregational Union of Scotland, 1885; Lecturer in the Congregational Theological Hall; received the degree of Doctor of Divinity from Glasgow University, 1889; Chairman of the Congregational Union of England and Wales, 1904. *Publications:* Primer of Congregationalism; Primer of the Christian Life; Sundry Sermons and Addresses. *Recreation:* golf. *Address:* Candor, Whitehall Road, Colwyn Bay. (*Died 26 Sept.* 1919.)

GOODRICH, Admiral Sir James Edward Clifford, K.C.V.O.; *cr.* 1908; *b.* Maisemoor Court, Gloucester, 23 July 1851; *s.* of James Pitt Goodrich, J.P., of Energlyn, Glamorganshire, and Mary, *o. c.* of Richard Miles Wynne of Eyarth House, Denbighshire; *m.* 1897, Adeline Rose, *d.* of Capt. Frederic John Helbert, Indian Army, and Sarah Magdalene, *d.* of Richard Lane. *Educ.:* H.M.S. Britannia. Commodore 2nd Class of Pacific Squadron, 1903-5; Admiral Superintendent of the Gibraltar Dockyard, and in charge of all His Majesty's Naval Establishments at Gibraltar to 1909; J.P. Gloucestershire. *Address:*

Stinchcombe Manor, Dursley, Gloucestershire. *Club:* United Service. (*Died 21 Dec.* 1925.)

GOODWIN, Harvey, J.P., D.L.; *b.* 3 Feb. 1850; *e. s.* of late Rt. Rev. Harvey Goodwin, D.D., Bishop of Carlisle, and Ellen, *e. d.* of George King of Higher Bebington Hall, Cheshire; *m.* 1879, Ruth, 2nd *d.* of W. H. Wakefield of Sedgwick, Westmorland; two *s.* one *d.* High Sheriff, Westmorland, 1904. *Address:* Ortou Hall, Tebay, Westmorland. *Club:* Carlton. (*Died 25 Oct.* 1917.)

GOODWIN, Nathaniel Carl, actor; *b.* Boston, 25 July 1857; *s.* of Nathaniel C. and Caroline R. Goodwin; *m.* 1st, Eliza Weathersby, actress (*d.* 1887); 2nd, 1898, Maxine Elliott, actress; 4th, 1908, Edna Goodrich, actress. *Educ.:* public and private schools. Made his debut with Stuart Robson, Howard Athenæum, Boston, in The Law in New York, 1878; played comedy parts until 1879; appeared as Modus in The Hunchback and as a grave-digger in Hamlet, Cincinnati, 1883; at Bijou Theatre, New York, 1885; played in A Gold Mine and The Bookmaker, London, and in The Nominee, 1890; starred as Captain Crosstree in Black-Eyed Susan, Evangeline, Hobbies, The Member from Slocum, In Mizzoura, Nathan Hale, The Skating Rink, Cruets, Confusion, Turned Up, A Gilded Fool, David Garrick, The Rivals, An American Citizen, 1896; Nathan Hale, 1898; The Cowboy and the Lady, 1899; When we were Twenty-One, 1900; played Shylock in The Merchant of Venice, 1901; appeared in The Altar of Friendship, 1902; The Usurper, 1903; played Bottom in A Midsummer Night's Dream, 1904; starred in The Beauty and the Barge, 1905; Wolfville, and The Genius, 1906; What Would a Gentleman Do?; The Master Hand; The Easterner, 1908-9; Nat Goodwin's Book, 1915. *Address:* Ocean Park, California. (*Died 31 Jan.* 1919.)

GOODWIN, Shirley, M.A.; Head master of Emanuel School, Wandsworth Common, S.W., since 1914; *b.* 1 Feb. 1880; 2nd *s.* of Alfred Goodwin, Scholar, Tutor, and Fellow of Balliol College, Oxford, M.A., F.S.A., Professor of Latin and Greek at University College, Gower Street, W.C., and Sara, *d.* of Samuel Ford Simmons, Coventry. *Educ.:* University College School; Balliol College, Oxford. Master at Malvern Link Preparatory School, 1905; Loretto School, Musselburgh, 1905-7; Perse School, Cambridge, 1907-9; Rector of the High School, Glasgow, 1909-13. *Recreations:* fishing, golf. *Address:* The Headmaster's House, Emanuel School, S.W.11. (*Died 2 June* 1927.)

GOODYEAR, William Henry, Curator of Fine Arts, Brooklyn Institute Arts and Sciences since January 1899; *b.* New Haven, Conn., 21 April 1846; *s.* of late Charles Goodyear. *Educ.:* Yale; Heidelberg; Berlin. Visited Cyprus, Syria, Greece, and Italy, 1869-70; Curator Metropolitan Museum of Art, 1881-88; visited Egypt for studies of lotus ornaments, 1891; surveyed many cathedrals in Italy and Northern Europe for studies of architectural refinements; founder American Anthropological Association, 1902; M.A. Honorary Member, Royal Academies of Milan and Venice, Architectural Associations of Rome and Edinburgh, Society of Architects, London, Royal Institute of Architects of Ireland; Corresponding member of the American Institute of Architects. *Publications:* Ancient and Modern History, 1883; A History of Art, 1887; The Grammar of the Lotus, 1891; Roman and Mediæval Art, 1893; Renaissance and Modern Art, 1894; Greek Refinements, 1912; contributions to periodical literature. *Address:* 329 Lincoln Place, Brooklyn. *Club:* Elizabethan, New Haven. (*Died 19 Feb.* 1923.)

GOOLD, Sir James Stephen, 4th Bt., *cr.* 1801; *b.* 13 Oct. 1848; *s.* of George Ignatius

Goold, late Resident Magistrate, Waterford, and Clara, *d.* of Maj.-General James Webber Smith, C.B. Went to Australia, 1863. *S. uncle*, 1893; *m.* 1878, Bridget Mary (*d.* 1898), *d.* of Patrick Jordan; three *s.* three *d. Heir: s.* George Patrick [*b.* 9 July 1878; *m.* 1902, Mary, *d.* of Nicholas Browne; two *s.*]. *Address:* Gladstone, Adelaide, South Australia.
(Died 12 Aug. 1926.)

GOOLD-ADAMS, Major Sir Hamilton (John), G.C.M.G., *cr.* 1907; K.C.M.G., *cr.* 1902; Governor of Queensland since 1914; C.M.G. 1894; C.B. 1898; *b.* 27 June 1858; *s.* of late R. W. Goold-Adams; *m.* 1911, Elsie, *y. d.* of Charles Riordan, Montreal; one *s.* one *d.* Lieut. 1878; Captain,1885; Major Royal Scots,1st Batt.,1895; served with Bechuanaland Expedition under Sir Charles Warren, 1884-85; commanded the Field Force against the Matabele, 1893; late Resident Commissioner Bechuanaland Protectorate; served South Africa, 1899-1901 (despatches); Lt.-Gov. Orange River Colony, 1901-7; Governor, 1907-10; High Commissioner, Cyprus, 1911-1914. *Address:* Government House, Brisbane. *Club:* Army and Navy. *(Died 12 April 1920.)*

GOOLD-ADAMS, Ven. John Michael, M.A.; Archdeacon of Derry since 1914; Rector Clonleigh, Lifford, Co. Donegal, since 1914; of Examining Chaplain to the Bishop of Derry and Raphoe; *b.* 7 April 1850; *e. s.* of Michael Goold Adams of Rhincrew Abbey, Co. Waterford; *m.* 1878, Emma, fourth *d.* of Robert M'Clintock, D.L. of Dunmore, Carrigans, C. Donegal; one *d. Educ.:* Midleton College, Co. Cork; Trinity College, Dublin; 1st Prizeman Greek Prose Composition, 1869; 1st Classical Honourman, 1870; awarded by decree of the Board a special Exhibition in lieu of Scholarship, 1873. Ordained, 1875; Curate of Taughboyne, 1876-78; Derry Cathedral, 1878-81; Vicar of Clooney, Londonderry, 1881-1914; Canon of Derry Cathedral, 1893-1914. *Address:* The Rectory, Lifford, Co. Donegal. *Clubs:* Primrose; University, Dublin. *(Died 19 July 1922.)*

GORDON, Lt.-Col. Adrian Charles, D.S.O. 1915; 16th County of London Battery, 6th London Brigade, Royal Field Artillery, Territorial Force; *b.* 4 July 1889; *s.* of Charles Gordon; *m.* 1912; one *s.* twin *d. Educ.:* Bishops Stortford School. Employed in shipping; served European War, 1914-16 (despatches twice, D.S.O.). *Address:* 8 Park Crescent, Finchley, N.3; 36 Lime Street, E.C.3. *T.:* Avenue 1315. *T.A.:* Gordonia, London.
(Died 12 Dec. 1917.)

GORDON, Brig.-Gen. Alister Fraser, C.M.G. 1915; D.S.O. 1900; commanding 2nd Batt. Gordon Highlanders; *b.* 1 Feb. 1872; 3rd *s.* of W. G. Gordon, Drumdevan, Inverness; *m.* 1908, Pilar Mary, *d.* of late C. E. H. Edmondstoune Cranstoun of Corehouse; one *s.* two *d. Educ.:* the College, Inverness; R.M.C. Sandhurst. Served Chitral, 1895; N.W. Frontier, India, 1897-98, including storming of Dargai (despatches); with 2nd British Central Africa Regt., Ashanti, 1900 (D.S.O., despatches); S. Africa, 1901 (Gordon Highlanders), 1901 (Queen's medal, 3 clasps); European War, 1914-16 (despatches thrice, C.M.G.). *Club:* Naval and Military. *(Died 29 June 1917.)*

GORDON, Rev. Hon. Arthur, M.A., D.D.; Chaplain to the Royal Company of Archers (King's Bodyguard for Scotland). Formerly Minister of St. Andrew's Church, Edinburgh, and Monzievaird, Perthshire; *m.* 1893; two *s.* one *d. Publication:* The Life of Archibald Hamilton Charteris, 1912. *Address:* 16 Hermitage Drive, Edinburgh. *Club:* Scottish Conservative. *(Died 11 June 1919.)*

GORDON, Arthur John Lewis, of Ellon, C.M.G. 1876; J.P. and D.L. for Aberdeenshire; landed proprietor; *b.* 19 Mar. 1847; 2nd *s.* of G. T. R. Gordon of Ellon; *m.* Caroline, 2nd *d.* of Gen. Hon. Sir Alexander Hamilton Gordon, K.C.B.,

1885; one *s. Educ.:* Radley Coll. Private Secy. to Governor of Trinidad, 1866-70; Acting Colonial Secretary, 1870; Private Secretary to Governor of Mauritius, 1870; to Governor of Fiji, 1875-80; to Governor-General of Canada (Earl of Aberdeen), 1893. *Decorated* for services connected with the suppression of rebellion of native tribes in Fiji. *Address:* Ellon Castle, Aberdeenshire. *Club:* Caledonian. *(Died 13 Aug. 1918.)*

GORDON, Lt.-Gen. Sir Benjamin Lumsden, K.C.B.; *cr.* 1899; late R.H.A.; *b.* Revack, Inverness-shire, 8 July 1833; *s.* of Captain James Gordon of Revack and Ivybank, and Janet, *d.* of Major Grant of Auchterblair; *m.* 1860, Laura Sophia, *d.* of R. R. Caton of Binbrook; one *s.* three *d. Educ.:* Edin. Military Acad.; Addiscombe. Joined Madras Artill. 1852; served with Horse Artillery in Indian Mutiny, and was present at Relief of Lucknow, battle of Cawnpore, and several minor engagements (medal and clasp); Captain R.H.A. 1863; Major, 1872; Lieut.-Col. 1875; Colonel, 1880; commanded R.A. in Sir F. Roberts's advance on Kabul; present at Charasiah and Kabul (despatches, medal with two clasps, C.B.); commanded a brigade in Madras, 1884-86, and was then appointed as Maj.-General to command in Lower Burmah; in 1889 assumed command of the whole of Burmah (despatches twice, three times thanked by Viceroy of India, medal with two clasps); retired, 1891. *Decorated* for Afghan campaign. *Address:* Moustows Manor, Henfield, Sussex. *T.A.:* Henfield. *(Died 20 Nov. 1916.)*

GORDON, Very Rev. Daniel Miner, C.M.G. 1915; D.D., LL.D.; Vice-Chancellor and Principal of Queen's University, Kingston, Canada, 1902; retired and was appointed Principal Emeritus, 1917; *b.* Pictou, Nova Scotia, 30 Jan. 1845; *s.* of William Gordon, merchant; *m.* 1869, Eliza S. (*d.* 1910), *d.* of Rev. John Maclennan; three *s.* two *d. Educ.:* Pictou Academy; Universities of Glasgow (M.A., B.D.) and Berlin. Ordained a Minister of the Church of Scotland by the Presbytery of Ayr, 1866; Pastor of St. Andrew's Church, Ottawa, 1867-82; Knox Church, Winnipeg, 1882-87; St. Andrew's Church, Halifax, 1888-1894; Professor of Theology in Presbyterian College, Halifax, 1894-1902; D.D. Glasgow University, 1895; LL.D. St. Andrew's University, 1911, and University of Toronto, 1913; Moderator of the General Assembly of the Presbyterian Church in Canada, 1896. *Publication:* Mountain and Prairie, an account of a journey across Northern British Columbia, the Peace River Country, and the Western Canadian Prairies, 1880. *Recreations:* golf, boating, skating. *Address:* 122 University Avenue, Kingston, Ontario, Canada. *T.A.:* Gordon, Kingston, Ontario. *T.:* 623. *Club:* Frontenac, Kingston. *(Died Sept. 1925.)*

GORDON, Major Duncan Forbes, M.V.O. 1906; D.L., Chief Constable, Aberdeen; *b.* 30 May 1849; *m.* 1st, Elizabeth Alexandrina (*d.* 1913); 2nd, 1915, Edith, *widow* of Col. T. S. Gildea. Entered Army, 1867; Major, 1885; retired, 1889; served Afghan War, 1878-79 (severely wounded, despatches, medal, two clasps, brevet Major). *Address:* 19 Queen's Road, Aberdeen. *Club:* Junior United Service.

GORDON, Francis Frederick, J.P., and Hon. Presidency Magistrate; Governing Director of the Advocate of India and Illustrated Sunday Advocate, Bombay; *b.* 1866. Went to India on literary staff of Bombay Gazette, 1890, and has since been closely connected with Indian journalism; purchased the Advocate of India, 1894; pressed and obtained the introduction of the anna nickel coin into the Indian currency; has taken an active part in plague suppression measures; and, through his efforts, succeeded in inducing the Government to abolish the quarantine imposed at Bombay on Mahomedan pilgrims to Mecca, for which he received the thanks of leading Mahomedans of India. *Address:* Advocate of India, Bombay.   *(Died 27 Feb. 1922.)*

GORDON, Lieut.-Colonel Francis Lewis, D.S.O. 1917; *b.* 28 March 1878; *s.* of Francis Fredrick Gordon, *y. s.* of Lord Francis Gordon; unmarried. *Educ.:* Haileybury. 3rd Gordon Highlanders; joined 2nd Gordon Highlanders; served South Africa (Queen's medal, 3 clasps); retired, 1903; Major, Royal Irish Rifles, Sep. 1914; 2nd in Command, 1915; Commanded, 1915-17; Commanded 2/1 Leicester Yeo., Sep. 1917-Feb. 1919; served European War, 1914-19 (D.S.O.). *Recreations:* shooting, hunting, fishing, dog-breaking; a partner in the Hollingbourne Retriever Kennel. *Club:* Bachelors'.   *(Died 30 Jan. 1920.)*

GORDON, Maj.-Gen. Hon. Sir Frederick, K.C.B., *cr.* 1917; C.B. 1915; D.S.O. 1900; late commanding 1st Batt. Gordon Highlanders; retired pay since 1920; 4th *s.* of late Lord Gordon of Drumearn; *b.* 9 Oct. 1861; *m.* 1897, Mabel Rose, *d.* of late J. D. Robinson, M.C.S.; one *s.* one *d.* Served Egypt, 1882-85, including Tel-el-Kebir, El Teb, Tamaai (medal with 3 clasps, and bronze star); Soudan, 1889 (clasp); South Africa, 1899-1902 (despatches four times; Brevet Lt.-Col.; Queen's medal 6 clasps, King's medal 2 clasps; D.S.O.); European War, 1914-17 (despatches 5 times, C.B., specially promoted Maj.-Gen., K.C.B., Order of White Eagle, 2nd Class, Serbia; Grand Officer Crown of Rumania. *Address:* Lloyds Bank, Ltd., 6 Pall Mall, S.W.1.   *(Died 18 Oct. 1927.)*

GORDON, Col. George Grant, C.I.E. 1911; *b.* 20 Mar. 1863; *s.* of late Capt. G. Grant Gordon, Bengal H.A., of Milton, Kilravrock, Nairn; *m.* 1891, Mary, *d.* of late John Fergusson of Kirkcudbright. Late Manager and Proprietor of Tea Estates in Darjeeling District. *Address:* The Elms, 60 Queen's Road, Richmond, Surrey. *T.:* Richmond 578.   *(Died 12 Nov. 1926.)*

GORDON, Rt. Hon. John (Hon. Mr. Justice Gordon), P.C. 1915; Judge of High Court (King's Bench Division), Ireland, since 1916; B.A., LL.D., K.C.; *b.* 23 Nov. 1849; *s.* of Samuel Gordon, Shankhill, Co. Down; *m.* 1887, *d.* of late Robert Keating Clay, Dublin. Called to Bar, King's Inn, Dublin, 1877; M.P. (L.U.) South Londonderry, 1900-16; Attorney-General, Ireland, 1915-16. *Club:* Constitutional.   *(Died 26 Sept. 1922.)*

GORDON, Colonel John Charles Frederick, C.I.E. 1897; *b.* 4 May 1849; *s.* of J. Tomline Gordon, J.P.; *m.* 1879, Grace Hay, *d.* of late Fleetwood Williams, C.S.I. Entered army, 1869; Col. 1899; served Mahsood Wuzeeree Expedition; Egyptian war, 1882 (despatches, medal with clasp, Khedive's Star); North-West Frontier, India, in command of 6th Bengal Cavalry, with Kurram movable column, and afterwards Tirah Expeditionary Force, 1897-98 (despatches, medal with two clasps); S. African War, 1901-2 (medal, 2 clasps); commanded Her late Majesty's Guard of Honour, Diamond Jubilee, 1897; J.P. County Waterford.   *(Died 2 Sept. 1923.)*

GORDON, Hon. Sir John Hannah, Kt., *cr.* 1910; C.M.G. 1908; K.C.; Judge of the Supreme Court, South Australia, since 1904; *b.* Kilmacolm, N.B., 26 July 1850; *s.* of Rev. James Gordon, Presbyterian minister of Gawler, South Australia; *m.* 1876, Ann Wright, *d.* of late William Rogers of Sandergrove. *Educ.:* under private tutors. Admitted to South Australian Bar, 1876; entered Parliament, 1888; Minister of Education in Cockburn Government; Minister of Education in Holder Government; Chief Secretary in Kingston Government; Attorney-General in Holder Government; Attorney-General and Minister of Education in Jenkins Government; Delegate to Federal Convention and Member of the Con-

stitutional Committee of the Convention; Attorney-General for South Australia to 1904. *Address:* Clairmont, Glen Osmond, South Australia.   *(Died Dec. 1923.)*

GORDON, Major-Gen. Lochinvar Alexander Charles, C.B. 1915; C.S.I. 1916; late R.A.; *b.* 26 May 1864; *m.* 1895, Maria, *d.* of J. T. Withers; one *s.* one *d.* Entered army, 1883; retired, 1919; served European War, 1914-18 (C.B., C.S.I., despatches, Order of White Eagle, Serbia, 3rd class. *Address:* Snowhill, Midhurst, Sussex. *(Died 7 Aug. 1927.)*

GORDON, Col. Philip Cecil Harcourt, C.M.G. 1918; Assistant Director Medical Services, Celeis B.E.F.; *b.* London, 17 Jan. 1864; *s.* of Philip Brodie Gordon, solicitor; *m.*; one *s.* two *d.* *Educ.:* Edinburgh. Entered Army Medical Service, 1885; served Burmese War, 1886-87 (medal and two clasps, despatches); South African War, 1901-2 (medal three clasps); European War since Dec. 1914. *Recreations:* shooting, cycling, motoring. *Address:* Sunny Corner, Queen's Road, Jersey, C.I. *Club:* East India United Service.   *(Died 4 May 1920.)*

GORDON, Reginald Hugh Lyall; *b.* 14 July 1863; *e. s.* of late Lewis Gordon of Abergeldie Castle, Aberdeen, and Louisa Isabella, 4th *d.* of William Lyall; *m.* (*d.* 1906); one *d.* *Educ.:* Blackheath School. *Address:* 15 Belmont Park, Lee, Kent. *(Died 17 July 1924.)*

GORDON, Victor, C.M.G. 1926; High Commissioner for Newfoundland in London since 1924; *b.* St. John's, Newfoundland, 28 June 1884; *y. s.* of late James Gordon, merchant; unmarried. *Educ.:* St. John's; Academical Institution, Coleraine. Received early business training in Bank of Montreal; called to Bar, Middle Temple, 1912; served in European War, 1914-18; in Gallipoli Campaign, Egypt and France; temporary Captain King's Own Scottish Borderers; severely wounded at Monchy le Preux, April 1917; secretary, High Commissioner for Newfoundland, 1919; Acting High Commissioner, 1922-24; represented Newfoundland at Imperial Economic Conference 1923 in advisory capacity, and on Imperial Economic Committee, 1925-26; Chairman, London Advisory Committee, Newfoundland Section, British Empire Exhibition. *Publications:* numerous articles on Newfoundland. *Recreation:* golf. *Address:* 58 Victoria Street, S.W.1; *T.:* Victoria 2302. *T.A.:* Rurality. *Clubs:* National, British Empire.   *(Died 6 Oct. 1928.)*

GORDON, General William, C.I.E.; *cr.* 1878; General, unemployed list; *b.* 10 Feb. 1824; *y. s.* of late Adam Gordon of Cairnfield, D.L. Banffshire; *m.* Harriet Elizabeth (*d.* 1908), *e. d.* of Andrew Steuart of Auchlunkart, Banffshire, 1871; five *s.* three *d.* *Educ.:* Addiscombe College; private schools. Ensign, 1841; arrived in India 30 Dec.; joined 49th Bengal N.I. 1842; Lieut. 1845; at siege of Mooltan as Assist. Field Engineer, and with Sappers and Pioneers, 1848-49; present at the surrender of Fort of Chiniout, 1849; battle of Goojerat, in command of 2nd and 6th Companies Pioneers (medal and 2 clasps); throughout the Mutiny as Brigade-Major and Deputy-Assist. Q.M.G. Mooltan (medal); District Inspector of Musketry, 1860-62; Chief Inspector of Musketry, Army Headquarters, 1862-63; twice reappointed, 1868, 1873; Brig.-Gen. 1878; commanded districts Rawal Pindi, Gwalior, and Peshawar; Maj.-Gen. 1882; left India, 1883. *Address:* 9 Tavistock Road, Croydon, Surrey.   *(Died 3 April 1917.)*

GORDON-CUMMING, Miss Constance Frederica; *b.* Altyre, 26 May 1837; 12th child of Sir William Gordon-Cumming, 2nd Bt., Altyre and Gordonstoun, and Eliza, *d.* of John Campbell, Islay. *Educ.:* home; school at Fulham, London. An invitation to spend a year with a married sister in India, 1867, awoke the taste for travel and led to very extensive wanderings extending over twelve years. *Publications:* Memories, Autobiography; At Home in Fiji and New Zealand; A Lady's Cruise in a French Man-of-War among the South Sea Isles; Fire Fountains of Hawaii; Granite Crags of California; Wanderings in China; In the Hebrides; In the Himalayas; *Via* Cornwall to Egypt; Two Happy Years in Ceylon. *Recreations:* water-colour painting, but especially, now, working for the development of the invention of the Numeral-Type for the use of illiterate Chinese, both blind and seeing, in Mandarin-speaking districts of China. *Address:* College House, Crieff, Scotland. *(Died 4 Sept. 1924.)*

GORDON - LENNOX, Colonel Lord Algernon (Charles), Col. on Retired List; *b.* 19 Sep. 1847; 2nd *s.* of 6th Duke of Richmond and Gordon and Frances, *e. d.* of Algernon Frederick Greville (Warwick); *m.* Blanche, D.B.E., *d.* of late Col. Hon. Charles Maynard and Blanche, now Dow. Countess of Rosslyn, 1886; one *d.* *Educ.:* Eton, 1859-61. Served in Royal Navy, 1862-1865; joined 1st Life Guards, 1867; transferred to Grenadier Guards, 1867; served with 2nd Batt. Gren. Guards in Egyptian campaign, 1882 (medal and Khedive star); A.D.C. to Duke of Cambridge, 1883-95; served South Africa, 1900, as Assist. Military Secretary to Sir Alfred Milner, and latterly on the staff of General French (medal and three clasps); Jubilee medal, 1887. *Recreations:* hunting, shooting, yachting, fishing, golf. *Address:* 20 Queen Street, Mayfair, W.1. *T.:* Mayfair 5833. *Clubs:* Guards', Turf; Royal Yacht Squadron, Cowes. *(Died 3 Oct. 1921.)*

GORDON-LENNOX, Cosmo Charles; *b.* 1869; *e. s.* of Lord Alexander Gordon-Lennox and Emily, *d.* of Col. Charles Towneley of Towneley; *m.* 1898, Marie Tempest. *Educ.:* Woburn. *Publication:* Letters of Two People in War Time, 1916. *Plays:* The Impertinence of the Creature, etc. *(Died 31 July 1921.)*

GORDON-LENNOX, Rt. Hon. Lord Walter Charles, P.C.; *b.* London, 29 July 1865; *y. s.* of 6th Duke of Richmond and Gordon; *m.* 1889, Alice, *d.* of late Hon. G. H. Ogilvie-Grant of Grant; one *s.* *Educ.:* Eton; Christ Church, Oxford. Private Secretary to Marquis of Salisbury, 1886; M.P. S.W. Sussex, 1888-94; Treasurer of H.M. Household, 1891-92. *Recreations:* shooting, fishing, golf. *Address:* 19 Palace Court, W. *T.:* Park 1501. *Clubs:* Carlton, Beefsteak. *(Died 21 Oct. 1922.)*

GORDON-SMITH, Richard, F.R.G.S.; *b.* 20 April 1858; *s.* of late John Bridson Smith and Elizabeth Anne, *d.* of late George Lawrence of Moreton Court, Herefordshire, and *g. g. s.* of James Gordon-Smith of the Manor of Poulton-cum-Seacombe, Cheshire; *m.* Ethel, *y. d.* of late William Newcomb, of Montreal, Canada; three *d.* *Educ.:* Cheltenham College. Entered Royal South Lincoln Militia, 1877; resigned, 1879; rest of life spent big game hunting, travel, and sport. Holds 4th Class Order of Rising Sun, Japan. *Publication:* Ancient Tales and Folklore of Japan, 1908. *Clubs:* Arthur's, Hurlingham; Royal Albert Yacht, Southsea. *(Died 8 Nov. 1918.)*

GORE, A. Wentworth; *b.* Lyndhurst, 2 Jan. 1868; 3rd *s.* of Augustus Wentworth Gore, late 7th Hussars, and Emily Ann, *d.* of Hon. Edward Curzon; *m.* 1893, Minnie, *e. d.* of Francis Rutledge Alexander. Captain of the first international lawn tennis team England *v.* America, 1900; International, 1900, 1906, 1907, 1912, 1913; lawn tennis champion of England, 1901, 1908, and 1909 and Doubles, 1909; Scotland, 1892. *Recreations:* lawn tennis and golf. *Address:* 12 Hereford Square, S.W.7. *T.:* Kensington 5847. *(Died 1 Dec. 1928.)*

GORE, Col. Charles Clitherow, M.V.O. 1914; one of H.M.'s Hon. Corps Gentlemen-at-Arms, 1887-1921; *b.* 1839; *m.* 1st, 1875, Maria *(d.* 1881), *d.* of Rev. Thomas and Lady Louisa

Cator; 2nd, 1882, Lavinia *(d.* 1912), *d.* of Francis Charles Fitzroy. Served Indian Mutiny, 1857-59 (medal and clasp); Boer War, 1881. *Address:* 56 Stanhope Gardens, S.W.7. *Club:* Junior United Service. *(Died 13 Aug. 1926.)*

GORE, Lieut. - Col. J. C.; Acting Chief Secretary to the Government of Cyprus several times; *y. s.* of late Lieut.-Col. Henry Ross Gore, C.B.; *b.* 16 Jan. 1852; *m. e. d.* of late Major M. Doorly, Police Magistrate, Sierra Leone; two *s.* four *d.* Auditor-General West African Settlements, 1882-87; appointed to administer the Government of the Gambia, June to November 1894; Colonial Secretary, Sierra Leone, 1894-1901; Receiver-General Cyprus, 1901-1909; served Ashanti War (medal), 1873-74; Expedition against Yonnie Tribes, Sierra Leone, 1887-88 (medal and clasp, despatches). *Address:* c/o Westminster Bank, Jersey. *Club:* Victoria, Jersey.
(Died 11 Nov. 1926.)

GORE, Col. Robert Clements, C.M.G.; Temp. Brig.-Gen.; 2nd Batt. Argyll and Sutherland Highlanders; *b.* 1867; *s.* of Nathaniel Gore; *m.* 3rd *d.* of Llewellyn Saunderson; one *s.* *Educ.:* Haileybury; Sandhurst. Joined 1st Batt. A. & S. Highlanders, 1886; served European War, 1914-17 (despatches, C.M.G., and Bt.-Col.). *Club:* Army and Navy.
(Died 14 April 1918.)

GORE-BOOTH, Eva; 2nd *d.* of Sir Henry Gore-Booth, 5th Bart. of Lissadell, Sligo; Writer. *Publications:* Poems; Unseen Kings; The One and the Many; The Three Resurrections and the Triumph of Maeve; The Egyptian Pillar; The Sorrowful Princess; The Agate Lamp; The Perilous Light; The Death of Fionavar; The Sword of Justice; Broken Glory; articles in Reviews and leaflets.
(Died 30 June 1926.)

GORE - BROWNE, Sir Francis, Kt., *cr.* 1921; M.A. Oxon.; K.C. 1902; Master of the Bench of the Inner Temple, 1911; J.P. Berks.; Chairman Civil Service Arbitration Board, 1918-20; Chairman Rates Advisory Committee, Ministry of Transport, 1919-21; *b.* 1860; *s.* of Col. Sir Thomas Gore-Browne, K.C.M.G., C.B.; *m.* Helenor, *e. d.* of J. A. Shaw Stewart; two *s.* one *d.* *Educ.:* Harrow; New College, Oxford. Called to the Bar, 1888. *Address:* 8 Pont Street, S.W.; *T.:* Kensington 7248; Oakley House, Abingdon; 4 Crown Office Row, Temple, E.C.4. *T.:* Central 758. *Clubs:* Athenæum, Carlton. *(Died 2 Sept. 1922.)*

GORE-BROWNE, Rt. Rev. Wilfred, M.A.; Bishop of Kimberley and Kuruman since 1912; *s.* of late Colonel Sir Thomas Gore-Browne, K.C.M.G. *Educ.:* Harrow; Trin. Coll., Camb., M.A. Ordained, 1882; Curate of Pallion, 1882-83; St. Hilda, South Shields, 1883-87; St. John Evangelist, Darlington, 1887-89; Perpetual Curate St. Hilda's, Darlington, 1889-1902; Rector of Pretoria, 1902-9; Dean of Pretoria, 1909-12. *Address:* Bishopsgarth, Kimberley. *T.:* 330.
(Died 15 Mar. 1928.)

GORELL, 2nd Baron, *cr.* 1909; **Henry Gorell Barnes,** M.A.; *b.* 21 Jan. 1882; *e. s.* of 1st Baron and Mary Humpston, *d.* of T. Mitchell of West Arthurlie; *S.* father 1913. *Educ.:* Winchester; Trinity College, Oxford; Harvard University. Barr. 1906; Secretary to the President of the Probate, Divorce, and Admiralty Division of the High Court of Justice, 1906-10; to County Courts Committee, 1908-9; to Royal Commission on Divorce and Matrimonial Causes, 1909-1912; Chairman Kensington Division Red Cross Society; Member of T.F. Association, County of London; Capt. 19th Battery, 7th London Brigade, R.F.A. (T.F.). *Publication:* The Divorce Commission: The Reports Summarised (with J. E. G. de Montmorency). *Recreations:* travelling, shooting, riding, fishing, golf. *Heir:* *b.* Hon. Ronald

Gorell Barnes [Barrister, *b.* 16 Apr. 1884. *Educ.:* Balliol College, Oxford. *Address:* 6 John Street, W.C. *Club:* Garrick]. *Address:* 14 Kensington Park Gardens, W. *T.:* Park 1424. *Clubs:* Garrick, Ranelagh. (*Died* 16 *Jan.* 1917.)

GORGAS, William Crawford; *b.* Mobile, Ala., 3 Oct. 1854; *s.* of Josiah Gorgas, Brig.-Gen. and Chief of Ordnance in the Confederate States Army, and Amelia, *d.* of Governor Gale of Alabama; *m.* 1885, Marie Cook, *d.* of William Doughty; one *d. Educ.:* University of the South; Bellevue Hospital Medical College, New York. Entered Medical Corps, United States Army; served in Florida, Western Texas, Indian Territory, and the Territory of Dakota; Captain, 1885; Major, 1898; served Santiago, 1898; Chief Sanitary Officer of Havana; Colonel, 1903; Surgeon-General, 1914; Chief Health Officer of the Isthmian Canal Commission, 1904; Member Isthmian Canal Commission, 1907; United States' delegate to first Pan-American Congress at Santiago, 1908; Associate Fellow of Philadelphia College of Physicians and Surgeons; Doctor of Science, University of Pennsylvania, 1903, Harvard University, 1908, Jefferson Medical College and Brown University, 1909, Columbia University, 1913, Oxford, Princetown University, 1914; LL.D. University of Alabama, 1910, Tulane University, 1911, Johns Hopkins University, 1912; Hon. Fellow of New York Academy of Medicine; Associate Member of Société de Pathologie Exotique, Paris, 1908; President, American Medical Association and American Society of Tropical Medicine; Vice-President, Association of Military Surgeons, 1909; was the recipient of the Mary Kingsley medal from the Liverpool School of Tropical Medicine, 1907. *Address:* War Department, Washington, U.S.A. *Clubs:* Army and Navy, Chevy Chase, Cosmos, Washington. (*Died* 3 *July* 1920.)

GORGES, Sir (Edmond) Howard (Lacam), K.C.M.G., *cr.* 1919; C.M.G. 1917; M.V.O. 1911; Chairman, Board of Trade and Industries, Union of S. Africa, 1921; *b.* King William's Town, Cape of Good Hope, 16 Jan. 1872; *s.* of late Col. E. H. Gorges, A.P.D.; *m.* 1901, Dora, *d.* of late Rev. D. P. Faure of Cape Town; two *s. Educ.:* South African College, Cape Town. Cape Civil Service, 1889-1901; Transvaal Civil Service, 1901-10; Chief Clerk Colonial Secretary's Office, 1901; Under-Secretary, 1903; Secretary to the Prime Minister and Clerk of Executive Council, 1907; Assistant Colonial Secretary, 1907; Chairman, Transvaal Public Service Board, 1908-10; on formation of the Union of South Africa appointed Secretary for the Interior; Chairman, Union Public Service Advisory Committee, 1910-12; Deputy Chief Censor (Cablegrams and Radiograms) for South Africa, and Chief Press and Postal Censor for the Union, 1914-15; Seconded on Gen. Botha's personal staff as Chief Civil Secretary to organise the Public Service and establish Civil Government in South-West Africa; Chief Secretary for the Protectorate, July-Oct. 1915; Administrator of the Protectorate, 1915-20; Chairman Board of Control under Union of South Africa Anti-Profiteering Legislation, 1920-22; also a Member of the Transvaal Mining Leases Board. *Clubs:* Pretoria; Civil Service, Cape Town. (*Died Nov.* 1924.)

GORMAN, Ven. William Charles; *b.* 25 Sept. 1826; *o. s.* of Rev. Fortescue Gorman, of Tanaghmore, Co. Antrim, Ireland, and Harriet, *d.* of Sir Jonas Greene, Recorder of Dublin; *m.* 1856, Harriet Pitcairn, *o. d.* of Lieut. H. A. West and Eliza Deane West; one *s.* one *d. Educ.:* Trinity College, Dublin (M.A.). Ordained, 1850; Curate of Kiltegan, 1850-52; Archdeacon's Vicar of Kilkenny Cathedral, 1852-59; Vicar of Kilmocar, 1859-63; Kilsheelan, 1865-69; Rector of Thomastown, 1869-1908;

Archdeacon of Ossory, 1883-1911. *Address:* Mall House, Thomastown, Co. Kilkenny. (*Died 20 May* 1916.)

GORMANSTON, 15th Viscount (*cr.* 1478), **Jenico Edward Joseph Preston**; Baron Loundres, 1478; Baron Gormanston (U.K.), 1868; late Lieut. Reserve of Officers; Lieut. 15th Co. of London Regt., Railway Transport Officer; *b.* 16 July 1879; *s.* of 14th Viscount and Georgina, *d.* of Peter Connellan, Coolmore, County Kilkenny; *S.* father, 1907; *m.* 1911, Eileen, *y. d.* of late Lt.-Gen. Sir W. Butler; three *s.* one *d. Educ.:* Prior Park Coll., Bath. Late Lieut. Manchester Regt. Owns about 11,000 acres. *Heir: s.* Hon Jenico William Richard Preston, *b.* 7 Oct. 1914. *Address:* Gormanston Castle, Co. Meath; Whitewood House, Co. Meath. *Clubs:* Carlton; Sackville Street, Dublin. (*Died 7 Nov.* 1925.)

GORST, Mrs. Harold (Nina Cecilia Francesca), Novelist and Dramatist; *b.* 2 Nov. 1869; *d.* of E. R. Kennedy, whose father and uncles, all senior classics, were known at Cambridge as the four Kennedys; three *s.* one *d. Educ.:* home. *Publications:* Possessed of Devils, 1897; And Afterwards? 1901; This our Sister, 1905; The Light, 1906; The Soul of Milly Green, 1907; The Thief on the Cross, 1908; The Leech, 1911; The Night is Far Spent, an Autobiography, 1919; The Misbegotten, 1921; Ede's Trouble; Timfy's Mother; That Fascinating Foreigner; The Cloche; The Curate and the Columbine; Moll o' the Clothes' Line. *Recreation:* talking. *Address:* 92 Abingdon Road, W. (*Died 19 Oct.* 1926.)

GORST, Rt. Hon. Sir John Eldon, M.A., LL.D., F.R.S., K.C.; *b.* Preston, 24 May 1835; 2nd *s.* of E. C. Lowndes (formerly Gorst) and Elizabeth, *d.* of John D. Nesham, Houghton-le-Spring, Durham; *m.* 1st, 1860, Mary (*d.* 1914), *d.* of Rev. Lorenzo Moore, Christ Church, N.Z.; two *s.* five *d.*; 2nd, Ethel, *d.* of late Edward Johnson. *Educ.:* Preston Grammar School; St. John's College, Camb. Fellow and Hon. Fellow, 1890; 3rd Wrangler, 1857; Barr. Inner Temple, 1865; Civil Commissioner, Waikato, N.Z., 1861-63; Solicitor-General, 1885-86; Under Secretary for India, 1886-91; Financial Secretary to Treasury, 1891-92; M.P. for Cambridge, 1866-68, for Chatham, 1875-1892; Deputy Chairman of Committees, House of Commons, 1888-91; Lord Rector, Glasgow University, 1893-94; Vice-President of Committee of Council on Education, 1895-1902; British Plenipotentiary, Labour Conference, Berlin, 1890; M.P. (C.) Cambridge University, 1892-1906; contested (L.) Preston, 1910. *Publication:* The Children of the Nation, 1907; New Zealand Revisited, 1908. *Address:* Castle Combe, Wilts; 84 Campden Hill Court, W. *Club:* Royal Societies. (*Died 4 April* 1916.)

GOSCHEN, Hon. George Joachim, Lieut. 5th Batt. East Kent Regt.; *e. s.* of 2nd Viscount Goschen; *b.* 18 Nov. 1893. (*Died 19 Jan.* 1916.)

GOSCHEN, Rt. Hon. Sir William Edward, 1st Bt., *cr.* 1916; G.C.B., *cr.* 1911; G.C.M.G., *cr.* 1909; K.C.M.G., *cr.* 1901; G.C.V.O., *cr.* 1904; P.C., 1905; *b.* 18 July 1847; *y. s.* of late W. H. Goschen, Templeton House, Roehampton; *m.* 1874, Harriet Hosta (*d.* 1912), *d.* of Darius Clarke; two *s. Educ.:* Rugby; Oxford. Attaché, 1869; Madrid, 1870; 3rd Sec., 1873; Buenos Aires, same year; Paris, 1875; 2nd Secretary at Rio de Janeiro, 1877; attached to Rt. Hon. G. J. Goschen's special embassy to Constantinople, 1880; 2nd Secretary, Constantinople, 1881; secretary of legation, Pekin, 1885; Copenhagen, 1888; Lisbon, 1890; secretary of Embassy, Washington, 1893; Petrograd, 1894; minister plenipotentiary during absence of ambassador; acted as Chargé d'Affaires at Copenhagen, Lisbon, Washington, and Minister Plenipotentiary at Petrograd during absence of Ambassador; Envoy Extraordinary and Minister Plenipotentiary at Belgrade, 1898-1900; at Copenhagen, 1900-1905; Ambassador, Vienna, 1905-8; Berlin, 1908-14; has the grand crosses of the Danebrog of Denmark, the Leopold Order of Austria, and the Red Eagle of Prussia. *Heir*: *s*. E. H. Goschen. *Address*: Beacon Lodge, Christchurch, Hants. *T.A.*: Highcliffe. *T.*: Highcliffe 15. *Clubs*: Travellers', St. James'. Beefsteak.] (*Died 20 May 1924*.)

GOSFORD, 4th Earl of (*cr.* 1806), Archibald Brabazon Sparrow Acheson, K.P., Bt. of Nova Scotia, 1628; Baron Gosford, 1776; Viscount Gosford, 1785; Baron Worlingham (U.K.), 1835; Baron Acheson (U.K.),1847; Vice-Chamberlain to H.M. Queen Alexandra since 1901; Kt. Grand Cross of the Danebrog; St. Saviour of Greece; The White Eagle of Russia; *b*. 19 Aug. 1841; *s*. of 3rd Earl and *o. d*. of 10th Earl of Meath; *S*. father 1864; *m*. Lady Louise Augusta Beatrice Montagu (Lady of the Bedchamber to H.M. The Queen), 2nd *d*. of 7th Duke of Manchester; two *s*. three *d*. *Educ.*: Harrow. *Heir*: *s*. Viscount Acheson. *Address*: 24 Hyde Park Gardens, W.2. *T.*: Padd. 4002. *Clubs*: Travellers', White's; Royal Yacht Squadron, Cowes. (*Died 11 April 1922*.)

GOSLING, Col. (Temp. Brig.-Gen.) Charles, C.M.G. 1916; K.R.R.C.; *b*. 24 June 1868; Brigade-Commander. Served S. Africa, 1899-1900, and 1902 (Queen's medal with clasp); European War, 1914-16 (despatches, C.M.G.). (*Died 12 April 1917*.)

GOSSE, Sir Edmund, Kt., *cr.* 1925; C.B. 1912; LL.D.; Litt.D.; Librarian, House of Lords, 1904-14; a Trustee of the National Portrait Gallery; *b*. London, 21 Sep. 1849; *o. s*. of late P. H. Gosse, F.R.S., the eminent zoologist; *m*. Ellen, *d*. of late Dr. G. N. Epps; one *s*. two *d*. *Educ.*: privately in Devonshire. Hon. M.A. Trinity College, Cambridge, Hon. LL.D. St. Andrews, 1899; Hon. Litt.D. Cambridge, 1920; Hon. Dr. Strasburg,1920; Hon. Dr.Gothenburg,1923; Hon. Dr.Paris (Sorbonne); Commander Legion of Honour, 1925; Knight of the Royal Norwegian Order of St. Olaf, First Class, 1901; Knight of the Royal Swedish Order of the Polar Star, 1908; Knight of the Royal Danish Order of the Dannebrog, 1912; Member of the Academic Committee; Assistant Librarian British Museum, 1867-75; Translator to Board of Trade, 1875-1904; Clark Lecturer in English Literature Trin. Coll. Camb. 1884-90; Chairman of the Board of Scandinavian Studies, University College, London, since 1917; President of the English Association, 1921. *Publications*: Verse — On Viol and Flute, 1873; King Erik, 1876; New Poems, 1879; Firdausi in Exile, 1885; In Russet and Silver, 1894; Hypolympia, 1901; The Autumn Garden, 1908; Collected Poems, 1911. Prose—Northern Studies, 1879; Life of Gray, 1882; Seventeenth Century Studies, 1883; Life of Congreve, 1888; History of Eighteenth Century Literature, 1889; Life of P. H. Gosse, 1890; Gossip in a Library, 1891; The Secret of Narcisse, 1892; Questions at Issue, 1893; The Jacobean Poets, 1894; Critical Kit-Kats, 1896; History of Modern English Literature, 1897; Life and Letters of Dr. John Donne, Dean of St. Paul's, 1899; Illustrated Record of English Literature, vols. iii. and iv., 1903; Life of Jeremy Taylor, 1904; French Profiles, 1905; Coventry Patmore, 1905; Life of Sir Thomas Browne, 1905; Father and Son, 1907 (crowned by the French Academy, 1913); Henrik Ibsen, 1908; Two Visits to Denmark, 1911; Portraits and Studies, 1912; Collected Essays (5 vols.), 1913; Inter Arma, 1916; The Life of Algernon Charles Swinburne, 1917; Three French Moralists, 1918; Diversions of a Man of Letters, 1919; Malherbe, 1920; Books on the Table, 1921; Aspects and Impressions, 1922; More

Books on the Table, 1923; Silhouettes, 1925. Leaves and Fruit, 1927. *Address*: 17 Hanover Terrace, Regent's Park, N.W.1. *T.*: Paddington 4254. *Clubs*: Marlborough, Savile, National, Grillions. (*Died 16 May 1928*.)

GOSSELIN, Major Sir Nicholas, Kt., *cr.* 1905; D.L.; *b*. 12 Feb. 1839; *s*. of late Nicholas Gosselin, Capt. 46th Regiment; *m*. 1865, Katherine Rebecca, *e. d*. of William Haslett, J.P., Carrownaffe, Moville, Co. Donegal; two *s*. two *d*. Entered Army, 1855; Civil Service, 1882; retiring, 1905, after fifty years of public service. *Address*: Westaria, West Malling, Kent; Lackenagh, Burton Port, County Donegal. (*Died 4 Feb. 1917*.)

GOSSELIN - GRIMSHAWE, Reltter Robert Hadsley, J.P.; *b*. 1849; 2nd *s*. of late Martin Hadsley Gosselin, J.P., of Ware Priory, and Blakesware, Hertfordshire, and Frances, *e. d*. of late Admiral Sir John Marshall, K.C.H., C.B.; *m*. 1902, Mary Ambrose Louisa, *e. d*. of late Samuel Grimshawe of Errwood Hall. High Sheriff Herts, 1906; assumed additional surname of Grimshawe by deed poll, 1902; Mrs. Gosselin-Grimshawe is joint owner, with her sister, the Hon. Mrs. Preston, of Errwood Hall. *Address*: Bengeo Hall, Hertford. (*Died 31 Mar. 1924*.)

GOSSET, Ven. Charles Hilgrove; Archdeacon of Christchurch, 1909 - 18; 4th *s*. of Rev. I. H. Gosset, Vicar of Northam, N. Devon; *m*. Helen L. Morison; four *d*. *Educ.*: Clifton; University of St. Andrews. Late Member of General Synod, also of Standing Committee, Diocese of Christchurch, and Assessor of Bishop's Court. Ordained, 1877; Curate of Masterton, 1877-80; Perpetual Curate of Bank's Peninsula, 1880; Rangiora, 1881-83; Vicar of Woodend, 1883-87; Woodend, Ashley, and Loburn, 1887-91; Heathcote, 1891-1902; Merivale, 1902-15; Archdeacon of Akaroa, 1909. *Publications*: Notes on Charagia Virescens; Transactions of N.Z. Institute. *Recreations*: played rugby football for University, for Kidderminster, England, and for Masterton, New Zealand; represented University in mile, 1st Scotch Inter-University sports; member of golf clubs. *Address*: Christchurch, N.Z. *T.*: Christchurch 2209, N.Z. *Club*: Union, Westward Ho. (*Died 31 Mar. 1923*.)

GOSTLING, Col. Ernest Victor, D.S.O. 1916; M.A.,B.Ch. (Cantab.), M.R.C.S.,L.R.C.P. Lond.; late A.M.S.T.A.; *b*. 6 April 1872; *m*. 1917, Joan Edith, *d*. of Rev. C. Wilton, Beverley, Yorks; one *s*. one *d*. *Educ.*: Cambridge; St. Thomas's Hospital. Late House Physician, Royal Infirmary, Derby, and Senior House Surgeon, Addenbrooke's Hospital, Cambridge; served European War, 1914-16 (D.S.O.); A.D.M.S. East Anglian Div. T.A., 1920. *Address*: Bedingfield House, Needham Market, Suffolk. *T.*: Needham 18. (*Died 30 Dec. 1922*.)

GOUDY, Henry, M.A., D.C.L. (Oxon.), Hon. LL.D. (Edin.); Fellow of All Souls College; *b*. Ireland, 16 Sep. 1848; *s. s*. of late Rev. Alexander P. Goudy, D.D., of Strabane, Co. Tyrone. Unmarried. *Educ.*: private schools; Glasgow, Edinburgh, and Königsberg Universities. Advocate of the Scottish Bar; elected Professor of Civil Law, Edinburgh University, 1889; editor Juridical Review from foundation till 1891; Regius Professor of Civil Law, Oxford, 1893; resigned, received the hon. title of Emeritus Prof. from the University, 1919; Ex-Pres. of the Soc. of Public Teachers of Law and the Grotius Society; Honorary Bencher of Gray's Inn. *Publications*: joint author of Manual of Local Government in Scotland, 1880; a Treatise on the Law of Bankruptcy in Scotland, 1886 (4th ed. 1914); Inaugural Lecture on the Fate of the Roman Law north and south of the Tweed, 1894; edited 2nd ed. of Muirhead's Private Law of Rome, 1898; translated, with notes and additions, Von

Jhering's Jurisprudenz d. täg. Lebens, 1904; Trichotomy in Roman Law, 1910 (translated into German by Prof. E. Ehrlich, 1913); contributor of various articles to the Encyclopædia Britannica, etc. *Recreations:* golf, angling. *Address:* All Souls College, Oxford; Strathmore, West Malvern. *Club:* Reform.

(*Died 3 Mar. 1921.*)

GOUGH, 3rd Viscount (of Goojerat, Punjab, and Limerick), cr. 1849; Hugh Gough, M.A.; K.C.V.O.; Bt. 1842; Baron Gough, 1846; Minister Resident at Coburg and Dresden, 1901-7; *b.* 27 Aug. 1849; *s.* of 2nd Viscount and *d.* of George Arbuthnot, Elderslie, Surrey; *S.* father 1895; *m.* Lady Georgiana Frances Henrietta Pakenham, *e. d.* of 4th Earl of Longford, G.C.B., 1889; one *s.* one *d.* *Educ.:* Eton; Brasenose Coll. Oxford. Entered Diplomatic Service, 1873; Secretary to Legation at Rio de Janeiro, 1887-88; Stockholm, 1888-94; Secretary of Embassy, Washington, 1894-96; Berlin, 1896-1901. *Heir: s.* Hon. H. W. Gough. *Address:* 9 Upper Belgrave Street, S.W.1; *T.:* Victoria 5810; Lough Cutra Castle, Gort, Co. Galway. *Clubs:* Oxford and Cambridge, Travellers'; Kildare Street, Dublin.

(*Died 14 Oct. 1919.*)

GOUGH, Rev. Edwin Spencer, M.A.; Rector of Barningham, Darlington, 1889-1924; Rural Dean, Richmond North, Surrogate; Hon. Canon, Ripon Cathedral; *b.* Feb. 1845; *s.* of Edwin Twizell Gough; *m.* Caroline Lydia Gough (*d.* 1902), *d.* of Augustus Morand of Philadelphia; two *s.* three *d.* *Educ.:* Godolphin Grammar School, Hammersmith; Trinity Coll., Dublin; King's College, London. Curate of St. Paul's, Leeds, 1868; Chaplain of the Leeds General Infirmary, 1870-77; Vicar of Burley, Leeds, 1877-89. *Address:* c/o Ballman Rectory, Darlington. (*Died 14 Feb. 1927.*)

GOUGH, Frederic Harrison, M.A. Oxon; *b.* 1868; *e. s.* of Rev. R. L. H. Gough, Vicar of Chilton Moor, Co. Durham; *m.* 1904, Emma Briscoe, *d.* of John Tompsett, Merefield House, Crewkerne. *Educ.:* Durham School; Oriel College, Oxford. Barrister-at-Law, Inner Temple, 1894; Police Magistrate, Freetown, Sierra Leone, 1903; Solicitor-General, 1903; Solicitor-General, Gold Coast Colony, 1908; Puisne Judge, 1908; Senior Puisne Judge, Gold Coast Colony, 1911. *Publications:* prepared revised edition of The Ordinances of the Gold Coast Colony, Ashanti and Northern Territories. 1910.

GOUGH, Maj.-Gen. Hugh Sutlej, D.L.; C.B. 1899; C.M.G. 1886; J.P. Carnarvonshire; *b.* 4 Feb. 1848; *e. s.* of late General Sir John B. Gough, G.C.B.; *m.* 1886, Beatrice Sophia, Lady of Grace of the Order of St. John of Jerusalem, *d.* of late Richard Hemming, of Bentley Manor; one *s.* *Educ.:* Royal Naval School, Gosport; Emmanuel Coll. Cambridge. Served in R.N. 1862-65; entered 10th Royal Hussars as Cornet, 1868; Capt. 1875; Major, 1881; Bt. Lieut.-Col. 1884; Colonel, 1888; Maj.-Gen. 1900; A.D.C. to Commander-in-Chief, India, 1876-81; served in Afghan war, 1878-79; Egyptian campaign, 1884 (despatches); Bechuanaland expedition, 1884-1885, where he raised and commanded 3rd Mounted Rifles; commanded 18th Hussars, 1889-93; Assist.-Adjt. for Cavalry at Headquarters, 1893-98; Lt.-Governor and Commander of the Troops in Jersey, 1904-10; Col.-in-Chief, 20th Hussars; Hon. Colonel Royal Militia of the Island of Jersey; Distinguished Service Reward, 1905. *Decorated:* Afghan war; Egyptian war; Bechuanaland expedition. *Recreations:* hunting, shooting, etc. *Address:* Caer Rhûn, Tal-y-Cafn, North Wales.

(*Died 30 Mar. 1920.*)

GOULD, Sir Alfred Pearce, K.C.V.O., cr. 1911; C.B.E. 1919; Lieut.-Col. R.A.M.C. (T.F.), Officer-in-Command, 3rd London General Hospital, Wandsworth; late Vice-Chancellor of University of London; President, Boys' Life Brigade; late President of the Clinical Section of the Royal Society of Medicine; late President of Medical Society of London, Master in Surgery, London Univ.; Fellow of Royal College of Surgeons of England; Consulting Surgeon and Emeritus Lecturer on Surgery to Middlesex Hospital; late Lecturer on Surgery to Medical School; late President of Röntgen Society; *b.* Norwich, 1852; 2nd *s.* of Rev. George Gould; *m.* 1885, *y. d.* of late Rt. Hon. Lord Justice Lush; two *s.* four *d.* *Educ.:* Amersham Hall School; University Coll. London. Entered Medical School of University Coll. London, 1869; graduated at University of London, 1874; was appointed Assistant-Surgeon to Westminster Hospital and Lecturer on Anatomy, 1877; in 1882 was elected at Middlesex Hospital. *Publications:* The Elements of Surgical Diagnosis; joint-editor with Dr. Collins Warren of The International Text-Book of Surgery; The Evolution of Surgery; Bradshaw Lecture on Surgery, Royal College of Surgeons of England, 1910; and several papers and contributions to various scientific societies. *Address:* 26 Ferncroft Avenue, Hampstead, N.W.3; *T.:* Hampstead 2829; Ashe, Ashburton, S. Devon. *M.:* LA 7500. *Clubs:* Athenæum, University of London.

(*Died 19 April 1922.*)

GOULD, Edward, I.S.O. 1902; late Deputy Chief Inspector of Factories and Workshops; *b.* 1837. *Educ.:* Eton; Trinity College, Cambridge (B.A.). *Clubs:* St. James's, Carrick.

(*Died 25 July 1922.*)

GOULD, Edward Blencowe, I.S.O. 1903; *b.* Stokeinteignhead, Devon, 9 Aug. 1847; *e. surv. s.* of Rev. John Nutcombe Gould and Katharine, *d.* of General James Grant, C.B.; *m.* Alice Elizabeth, *e. d.* of George Gordon of Ellerslie, Toorak, Melbourne, 1895. *Educ.:* private school. Entered Consular Service in Siam, 1868; 1st Vice-Consul in Siamese Shan States, 1883; Consul at Bangkok, 1885; Chargé d'affaires in Siam, 1886 and 1887-89; Consul, Port Said, 1891; Consul-General, Alexandria, 1897; retired, 1909. *Recreations:* shooting and fishing. *Address:* 7 Alfred Place West, S.W. *Club:* Conservative.

(*Died 16 Nov. 1916.*)

GOULD, Sir Francis Carruthers, Kt., cr. 1906; caricaturist, assist. editor Westminster Gazette; *b.* Barnstaple, 2 Dec. 1844; 2nd *s.* of Richard Davie Gould, architect; *m.* 1869, Emily (*d.* 1920), *d.* of Hugh Ballment, Barnstaple; three *s.* two *d.* *Educ.:* private schools in Barnstaple. Over twenty years a member of the London Stock Exchange; illustrated the Christmas Number of Truth many years, and constant contributor to Pall Mall Gazette, till it passed to Mr. Astor; since then attached Westminster Gazette; has lectured for four years on parliamentary subjects in different parts of England and Scotland; retired Major, London Irish Rifles; J.P. London and Somerset. *Publications:* A large number of Stock Exchange sketches and caricatures for private circulation; Who killed Cock Robin? 1897; Tales told in the Zoo (with one of his sons), 1900; Froissart's Modern Chronicles, 2 vols.; also Westminster cartoons; edits and illustrates Picture Politics. *Recreations:* sketching in Normandy and Brittany; natural history, especially ornithology. *Address:* Upway, Porlock, Somerset. *Clubs:* National Liberal, Eighty, Johnson, Whitefriars', Omar Khayyam.

(*Died 1 Jan. 1925.*)

GOULD, George Jay; President Texas and Pacific Railway since 1893; *b.* New York, 6 Feb. 1864; *s.* of late Jay Gould and Helen Day Miller; *m.* 1st, 1888, Edith M. Kingdon (*d.* 1921); three *s.* four *d.*; 2nd, 1922, Alice Sinclair. *Educ.:* privately. Preferred business to college; became clerk in banking house of W. E. Connor and Co., in which his father was partner; on father's retirement he became member of firm; member of N.Y. Stock Exchange, 1886; entered railway service, 1888, as President Little Rock and Fort Smith Railway; Pres. International and Great Northern R.R. 1893-1911; Manhattan Railway 1888-1913; President and Director Weatherford Railway; Chairman of the Board, St. Louis Iron Mountain and Southern R.R. since 1911; Chairman Missouri Pacific Co.; and Director of numerous railway and other companies. *Recreations:* riding, hunting, polo, yachting, and photography. *Address:* Georgian-court, Lakewood, New Jersey; 857 Fifth Avenue and 165 Broadway, New York. *Clubs:* Royal Thames Yacht; Lawyers, New York, N.Y. Athletic, N.Y. Yacht, New York; Royal Southampton Yacht.   (*Died* 16 *May* 1923.)

GOULD, Rev. George Pearce, M.A., D.D.; President of Regent's Park College, 1896-1920; *b.* 1848; *e. s.* of late Rev. G. Gould, Norwich; unmarried. *Educ.:* Grey Friars' Priory, Norwich; Amersham Hall School; Glasgow University. Hibbert Travelling Fellow, 1874-76, studying at Berlin, Göttingen, Leipzig. Minister of Bournemouth and Boscombe Baptist Church, 1876-80; Cotham Grove Baptist Church, Bristol, 1880-85; Professor of Hebrew and Old Testament Exegesis, Regent's Park College, 1885-96; President of the Baptist Union of Great Britain and Ireland, 1913-14. *Publications:* Memoir of Rev. G. Gould; Editor of Baptist Historical Manuals; sundry articles. *Recreations:* walking, foreign travel. *Address:* 5 Kidderpore Gardens, N.W.3. *T.:* Hampstead 1476.   (*Died* 21 *Mar.* 1921.)

GOULD, Nathaniel, novelist; *b.* Manchester, 21 Dec. 1857; *s.* of late Nathaniel Gould, Manchester, and Pilsbury Grange, Derbyshire; *m.* 1886, Elizabeth Madeline Ruska; three *s.* two *d.* *Educ.:* Strathmore House, Southport. Journalist of wide experience for 25 years in England and Australia; travelled in Queensland, Victoria, N.S. Wales, S. Australia, Tasmania, and elsewhere. *Publications:* The Double Event, 1891; Running It Off, 1892; Jockey Jack, 1892; Harry Dale's Jockey, 1893; Banker and Broker, 1893; Thrown Away, 1894; Stuck Up, 1894; Only a Commoner, 1895; The Miner's Cup, 1896; The Magpie Jacket, 1896; Who Did It? 1896; On and Off the Turf in Australia; Town and Bush, 1896; The Doctor's Double, 1896; A Lad of Mettle, 1897; Horse or Blacksmith (now Hills and Dales), 1897; A Gentleman Rider, 1898; The Pace that Kills, 1899; Sporting Sketches; The Roar of the Ring, 1900; A Stable Mystery, 1901; A Racing Sinner, 1902; Bred in the Bush, 1903; The Rajah's Racer, 1904; The Second String; Charger and Chaser, 1906; The Chance of a Lifetime; The Little Wonder; The Dapple Grey; A Run of Luck, 1907; The Stolen Racer, 1908; A Reckless Owner, 1909; The Magic of Sport; The Roarer; The Lucky Shoe; A Great Coup, 1910; The King's Favourite; Good at the Game; The Phantom Horse; The Cast-Off; The Trainer's Treasure, 1911; A Northern Crack; The Head Lad; Fast as the Wind; At Starting Price; A Fortune at Stake; A Gamble for Love; The Wizard of the Turf; Lost and Won; The Smasher; The White Arab; Never in Doubt; in all about a hundred and thirty novels; short stories and newspaper articles. *Address:* Newhaven, Bedfont, Middlesex. *Club:* Authors'.   (*Died* 25 *July* 1919.)

GOULDING, Rt. Hon. Sir William Joshua, 1st Bt., *cr.* 1904; J.P., D.L.; P.C. 1917; Chairman, Great Southern and Western Railway of Ireland; Deputy-Chairman, Fishguard and Rosslare Harbours and Railway Company; an Irish Lights Commissioner; Chairman Irish Railway Clearing House; Chairman Property Losses Committee (Ireland), 1916; Director National Bank, Ltd.; Chairman W. & H. M. Goulding, Ltd.; Irish Convention, 1917-18; a Senator for Southern Ireland; Member of the Church Representative Body of Ireland; A Steward of the Turf Club of Ireland; *e. s.* of W. Goulding, D.L., M.P., Summerhill House, Co. Cork; *b.* 7 Mar. 1856; *m.* 1881, Ada, *d.* of Charles Lingard Stokes of Pauntley, Worcesters; one *s.* four *d.* *Educ.:* Cambridge (M.A.). High Sheriff, Co. Dublin, 1906; Co. Kildare, 1907. *Heir: s.* William Lingard Amphlett [Capt. Royal Irish Fusiliers; A.D.C.; *b.* 5 Oct. 1883; *m.* 1908, Nesta Violet, *d.* of late Hon. Mr. Justice Wright, and *g.d.* of Sir Croker Barrington, 4th Bt.; two *s.*]. *Recreation:* hunting. *Address:* Luttrellstown, Clonsilla, Co. Dublin; Millicent, Sallins, Co. Kildare. *T.:* Naas 14. *Clubs:* Carlton; University, Kildare Street, Dublin; Royal St. George Yacht.   (*Died* 12 *July* 1925.)

GOURLAY, Charles, B.Sc., F.R.I.B.A., F.S.A.Scot.; Professor of Architecture and Building, the Royal Technical College, Glasgow, since 1895; *b.* Edinburgh; *s.* of Charles Gourlay and Anne Ingram Clark; *m.* 1905, Helen Mary Ramsay (*d.* 1920), Constantinople; one *d.* *Educ.:* Glasgow University. Served apprenticeship as an architect in Glasgow; afterwards began professional practice, and executed several buildings; began teaching architecture and building subjects, 1886; resolved to devote all his time to teaching, 1890; Lecturer, Royal Technical College, Glasgow, 1888. *Publications:* Elementary Building Construction and Drawing for Scottish Students; The Construction of a House; The Italian Orders of Architecture; Rheims Cathedral in The Architect; The Parthenon; Santa Sophia; The Churches of Constantinople; The Churches of Salonica, in the R.I.B.A. Journal; etc. *Recreations:* photography, Hon. Pres. of the Royal Technical College Architectural Craftsmen's Society; archæology pertaining to architecture. *Address:* Coniston, Craigdhu Road, Milngavie, Glasgow.
    (*Died* 30 *June* 1926.)

GOW, Andrew Carrick, R.A. 1891; artist; Keeper of the Royal Academy since 1911; *b.* London, 15 June 1848; *m.* Ethel, *d.* of Fredk. Relfe; one *s.* four *d.* Studied at Heatherley's School of Art; elected R.I. 1868; since 1869 has exhibited continuously at R.A.; elected A.R.A. 1881. *Principal Pictures:* The Relief of Leyden, 1876; No Surrender, 1878; The Last Days of Edward VI., 1880; Cromwell at Dunbar, 1886 (purchased by Chantrey Fund); The Garrison Marching out with the Honours of War, Lille 1705, 1887; Flight of James II. after the Battle of the Boyne, 1888; After Waterloo, 1890; Queen Mary's Farewell to Scotland, 1892; The Queen's Diamond Jubilee at St. Paul's (for the Corporation); Nelson Cartoon in the Royal Exchange, etc.; Cartoon presented by the Royal Academy to the Houses of Parliament. *Address:* Burlington House, Piccadilly, W. *Club:* Athenæum.   (*Died* 1 *Feb.* 1920.)

GOW, Rev. James, Litt.D.; Headmaster of Westminster School, 1901-19; *b.* 1854; *s.* of James Gow, member of Royal Soc. of British Artists; *m.* Gertrude Sydenham, *d.* of the late G.P. and M.A. Everett Green; two *s.* *Educ.:* King's College School; Trinity College, Cambridge (M.A.); 3rd Classic and Chancellor's Classical Medallist, Cambridge, 1875; Fellow of Trinity College, 1876; Fellow of King's College, London, 1876; Litterarum Doctor (Cambridge), 1885. University Extension Lecturer, Cambridge, 1876-78; Barr. Lincoln's Inn, 1879; President of Headmasters' Association, 1900-1902; Chairman of Headmasters' Conference, 1906-8, 1911-12; Master of the High School, Nottingham, 1885-1901. *Publications:* A Short History of Greek Mathematics, 1884; A Companion to School Classics, 1888; A Method of English, 1893; Odes and Epodes of Horace, 1896; Articles in Smith's Dictionary of Antiquities, etc. *Recreation:* walking.

Address : 40 West End Lane, Hampstead, N.W.6. *Club :* Athenæum. (*Died 16 Feb. 1923.*)

GOW, William, Secretary of the British and Foreign Marine Insurance Co., Ltd., Liverpool, since 1908 ; occasional Lecturer on Marine Insurance at University College, Liverpool ; *b.* 1853 ; *e. s.* of John Gow, J.P., banker and worsted spinner, Dalry, Ayrshire ; *m.* 1884, Katharine Mary, 2nd *d.* of late John Thornborrow Manifold, Government Engineer, British Guiana; one *s.* one *d. Educ. :* Glasgow Academy ; Glasgow and St. Andrews Universities and University College, London (M.A. Glasgow) ; afterwards Paris (Conservatoire de Musique, etc.), Berlin, Jena, Heidelberg. Secretary of Union Marine Insurance Company, Liverpool, 1883-92 ; then appointed Liverpool underwriter for the Marine Insurance Company of London ; in 1897 went to New York as American manager of the London Assurance Corporation, marine branch ; returned to Liverpool to be underwriter of Union Marine Insurance Co. there, 1899 ; Secretary of British and Foreign M.I.C.O. 1908 ; *Publications :* Marine Insurance ; British Imperial Customs Union ; Sea Insurance according to British Statute. *Address :* Druid's Lodge, Hoylake, Cheshire. *T.A. :* c/o Elysium, Liverpool. *T. :* Liverpool Central 26 ; Hoylake 426. *Club :* Exchange, Liverpool (*Died 21 Nov. 1919.*)

GOWER, Rt. Hon. Lord Ronald Sutherland-, ex-M.P. Co. Sutherland ; *b.* 1845 ; *y. s.* of 2nd Duke and 20th Earl of Sutherland and Harriet Howard, *d.* of 6th Earl of Carlisle ; uncle and great uncle of the Dukes of Argyll, Sutherland, Leinster, and Westminster, etc. *Educ. :* home ; Eton ; Trinity Coll. Cambridge. A Trustee of the National Portrait Gallery, and of the Birthplace and Shakespeare Memorial Building at Stratford-on-Avon ; Sculptor of statues of Marie Antoinette on her Way to Execution ; The Old Guard at Waterloo ; the Shakespeare Monument at Stratford-on-Avon, consisting of colossal statue of the poet, with four life statues at the base of the Memorial, etc. *Publications :* many on the Fine Arts ; My Reminiscences ; Life of Joan of Arc ; Rupert of the Rhine ; Stafford House Letters ; Bric à Brac ; Last Days of Marie Antoinette ; De Brosses' Letters from Italy ; Life of Sir Thomas Lawrence ; Life of Sir D. Wilkie ; History of the Tower ; Old Diaries ; Life of Michael Angelo ; Life of Thomas Gainsborough ; Records and Reminiscences, 1903 ; Life of George Romney, etc. *Recreations :* literature and art. *Address :* 66 Mount Ephraim, Tunbridge Wells. *Clubs :* Royal Societies, Royal Automobile, Authors'. (*Died 9 Mar. 1916.*)

GOWING, Lionel Francis, journalist ; on staff of Daily Telegraph ; *s.* of late Richard Gowing ; *b.* Ipswich, 1859 ; *m.* Florence, *d.* of William Senior, 1893 ; one *s.* one *d.* On staff of North China Daily News, and Weekly Herald, Shanghai, 1882-87 ; and acted for over thirty years as London correspondent ; published at Shanghai Notes of a Visit to Corea ; travelled with one companion (the late Mr. C. J. Uren) through Siberia in midwinter in a sledge, from Vladivostock to Moscow. *Publication :* Five Thousand Miles in a Sledge : a Mid-Winter Journey across Siberia, with illustrations by Mr. Uren, 1889. *Address :* 11 Thornton Avenue, Streatham Hill, S.W.2. (*Died 2 Dec. 1925.*)

GOWLAND, Professor William, F.R.S., A.R.S.M. ; Chevalier Imperial Order of the Rising Sun ; Emeritus Professor of Metallurgy, Royal School of Mines, London ; late Member of the Governing Body of the Imperial College of Science and Technology ; a Governor of the School of Metalliferous Mining, Camborne ; late Examiner in Metallurgy Board of Education and London University ; *b.* Sunderland, 1842 ; *e. s.* of late George Thompson Gowland ; *m.* 1st, 1890, Joanna (*d.* 1909), *y. d.* of late

4氐

Murdoch Macaulay, J.P., of Linchader, Isle of Lews ; one *d.* ; 2nd, 1910, Maude Margaret, *e. d.* of late D. J. Connacher. *Educ. :* Royal College of Chemistry ; Royal School of Mines. 1st and 2nd years Scholarships ; Murchison and De la Beche Medallist ; Associateship in Mining and Metallurgy ; Chemist and Metallurgist Broughton Copper Co. 1870-72 ; Chemist, Assayer, and Foreign Head of Imperial Japanese Mint, 1872-88 ; sometime Metallurgical Adviser to the War Dept. Japan ; Chief Metallurgist Broughton Copper Company, 1889-91; Past President Institute of Mining and Metallurgy, of Royal Anthropological Institute, and of the Institute of Metals ; gold medallist of the Institute of Mining and Metallurgy ; Fellow or Member of Society of Antiquaries, Institute of Chemistry, Chemical Society, American Institute of Mining and Metallurgical Engineers, Society Chemical Industry, Royal Society Arts, and Royal Institution. *Publications :* The Metallurgy of the Non-Ferrous Metals ; Imperial Mint Technical Reports ; various papers in the Journals of the Institute of Mining and Metallurgy, Chemical Society, Society Chemical Industry, Royal Anthropological Institute, and in Archæologia and Proceedings Society Antiquaries, etc. *Address :* 13 Russell Road, Kensington, W.14 ; Royal School of Mines, S. Kensington, S.W. *T. :* Park 4540. (*Died 10 June 1922.*)

GRAAFF, Senator Hon. Sir Jacobus Arnoldus Combrinck, K.C.M.G., *cr.* 1917 ; Minister without Portfolio, 1913-20 ; Minister of Public Works, Posts and Telegraphs, 1920-21 ; *s.* of late Petrus Novbertus Graaff and Annie Elizabeth de Villiers ; *m.* 1889, Susan Elsebie Maria Theunissen. Director of Messrs. Graaffs' Trust Limited, Cape Town and Pretoria ; is a keen politician, and was for many years Chairman of the Cape Town Branch of the Afrikander Bond ; commenced Parliamentary career in 1903, and at successive elections successfully contested the seat for the North Western Circle in the Legislative Council of the Cape Colony ; Chief Whip of South African Party in Legislative Council, which position he continued to fill in the Union Senate ; an ardent Protectionist. *Address :* Bordeaux, Sea Point, Cape Province. *Clubs :* National Liberal ; City, Royal Automobile of South Africa, Cape Town ; Country, Pretoria. (*Died 5 April 1927.*)

GRACE, Ven. Thomas Samuel ; Archdeacon of Marlborough since 1890 ; Canon of Christchurch Cathedral, Nelson, since 1916 ; Vicar of Church of Nativity, Blenheim, since 1885 ; *b.* at sea, 1850 ; *s.* of Rev. T. S. Grace, C.M.S. Missionary ; *m.* Rhoda Caroline, 2nd *d.* of Capt. Colt ; five *s.* four *d. Educ. :* Church of England Grammar School ; Bishopdale College, Nelson ; University of New Zealand. Ordained, 1878 ; Domestic Chaplain to Bishop of Nelson : Assist. Tutor Bishopdale College; and Perpetual Curate of Suburban North Nelson, 1874-81 ; C.M.S. Missionary, Putiki, 1881-85. *Publications :* Sketches of Church History in Maori ; Outline of Scripture History in Maori ; Superintendent of Maori Mission, Diocese of Nelson, N.Z., since 1890. *Address :* Blenheim, Marlborough, N.Z.

(*Died 1 April 1918.*)

GRACEY, Col. Thomas, C.S.I. 1897 ; late India Public Works Dept. ; *b.* 21 Jan. 1843 ; *s.* of Thomas Gracey, of Ballyhosseth, Co. Down. *Educ. :* Enniskillen Royal School. Entered R.E. 1862 ; Col. 1895 ; 1st assistant engineer, 1867 ; executive engineer, 1870 ; engineer-in-chief, Pindi-Kohat section of Punjab Railway, 1879 ; North-West Provinces and Oudh, 1882 ; secretary to Chief Commissioner, Public Works Department, Burma, 1887 ; superintending engineer, 1888; consulting engineer to Government of India, 1891 ; chief engineer, 1892 ; director-general of railways, 1895 ; secretary to Government of India, railway branch, 1897 ; retired

1898. *Address:* 22 Kidbrooke Grove, Blackheath, S.E.   (*Died 16 June 1921.*)

GRAFTON, 7th Duke of (*cr.* 1675), **Augustus Charles Lennox FitzRoy**, K.G., C.B., D.L., J.P. Baron Arlington, 1664; Earl of Arlington and Euston, Viscount Thetford and Ipswich, Baron Sudbury, 1672. Hon. Equerry to the King; late Coldstream Guards; General, retired 1881; Hereditary Ranger of Whittlebury Forest, Northamptonshire; Equerry to Queen Victoria, 1849-82; Hon. Equerry, since 1882, to late King Edward VII. and to King George V.; *b.* 22 June 1821; *s.* of 5th Duke and Mary, *d.* of Adm. the Hon. Sir George Cranfield Berkeley, G.C.B.; *S.* brother, 1882; *m.* Anna, *y. d.* of late James Balfour, Whittingehame, Haddingtonshire, 1847 (*d.* 1857); one *s. Educ.:* Harrow. Entered 60th Rifles, 1837; Coldstream Guards, 1839; served Crimea (severely wounded at Inkerman). *Heir: s.* Earl of Euston. *Address:* 6 Chesterfield Gardens, W.; Euston Hall, Thetford; Wakefield Lodge, Stony-Stratford. *Clubs:* Travellers', United Service.   (*Died 4 Dec. 1918.*)

GRAHAM, Flight - Lieut. Charles Walter, R.N.A.S., Eastchurch, Kent; D.S.O. 1916; *b.* 12 Nov. 1893; *s.* of Charles Knott Graham and Helena Reutt; unmarried. *Educ.:* Two years college in France; Merchant Taylors' School. Joined the Triumph Engineering Co., Coventry, to study motor engineering; after about 1¾ year went to Germany to the Bosch Magneto Factory at Stuttgart; was in Germany at outbreak of war; got out *via* Switzerland; on arriving in England immediately started to study science of Aviation at Hendon, finally buying an aeroplane and teaching himself to fly; joined R.N.A.S. 12 April 1915; sent to France May 1915; attacked and destroyed a German seaplane off the Belgian coast (with Flight Sub. - Lieut. Ince), Dec. 1915 (D.S.O.); seriously injured at Dunkerque, 8 Feb. 1916. *Recreations:* everything, particularly gymnastics and motoring. *Address:* 9 Kitson Road, Barnes, S.W.   (*Died Sept. 1916.*)

GRAHAM, Sir Claverhouse Frederick Charles, Kt., *cr.* 1905; J.P., Derbyshire; *s.* of Sutherland Graham; *m.* Emily, 2nd *d.* of George Moulson, Hove; Past Grand Master, Parliamentary Secretary, and Trustee of the M.U. Friendly Society; Founder and Past President of the National and State Paid Old Age Pension League, 1890; Past Pres. Licensed Victuallers' Society; Past Prov. Senior Grand Warden Prov. of Staffs; formerly C.C. for Staffs; Founder and Past Pres. of the Pioneer Three Counties Conference. *Publications:* House of Lords, Past, Present, and Future; Friendly and Thrift Progress and Development; Old Age Pensions, a Duty of the State (1st ed. 1884; 10th ed. 1904); State Pensions for all the Thrifty (Address, Church Congress, 1905 at Norwich); Labour, Religion, and Science; The Parliamentary Committee Old Age State Pension Bill. *Address:* Helmsley, Lennox Road South, Southsea.   (*Died 19 May 1924.*)

GRAHAM, E. J., M.P. (I.N.) Tullamore since 1915. *Address:* House of Commons, S.W.   (*Died 26 Mar. 1918.*)

GRAHAM, Capt. (temp. Major) Francis, D.S.O. 1915; M.C. 1916; 71st Brigade R.F.A.; *b.* 29 Mar. 1894. Entered army, 1913; served European War, 1914-17 (despatches, D.S.O., M.C.). *Address:* Forston House, nr. Dorchester, Dorset.
     (*Died 28 Mar. 1918.*)

GRAHAM, Sir Frederick, K.C.B., *cr.* 1907; C.B. 1899; late Assistant Under Secretary of State, Colonial Office; *b.* 1848; *s.* of late Frederick Graham of Cherry Bank, Newhaven, N.B., and Marjory, *d.* of Rev. Alexander Niven, D.D., of Dunkeld. *Educ.:* Edinburgh. Entered Colonial Office, 1870; principal clerk, 1896; retired, 1907. *Address:* Aros, Haslemere, Surrey. *Club:* St. Stephen's.(*Died 21 Feb.1923.*)

GRAHAM, Hon. George, *b.* Scotland, 1838; *m.* 1863, Miss Welch, of Langer, Nottinghamshire. M.L.A. Moira, 1883; Numurkah and Nathalie, 1889; Goulburn Valley, 1894; Minister for Water Supply, 1890-92; Agriculture, 1891-92; Public Works, Water Supply, and Agriculture, 1892-93; Public Works and Agri, culture, 1899-1900; Minister of Water Supply and of Agriculture, 1912-13. *Address:* Wungburn, Australia.

GRAHAM, Rev. Chancellor George R.; Vicar of Lea, 1890-1923; Chancellor of Kildare Cathedral, 1909-23; *b.* 1850, *s.* of Rev. Christopher Graham, rector of Derver, Co. Louth, and Frances Caroline Skelton; *m.* 1876, Emily Mary, *d.* of Capt. F. Page; two *s.* two *d. Educ.:* Dundalk Grammar School; Dublin University. Curate, Irishtown, Dublin, 1873-75; Carbury, Co. Kildare, 1875-79; Vicar, Carnalway, Co. Kildare, 1879-87; Eyrecourt, Co. Galway, 1887-90; 1st Canon of Kildare, 1905. *Address:* Killylea House, Killylea, Co. Armagh.
     (*Died 1927.*)

GRAHAM, John, I.S.O. 1903; late a Chief Clerk, Board of Agriculture and Fisheries; *b.* 1844; *m.* 1880, Louise (*d.* 1913), *d.* of late Rev. George Yenkins, Rector of Manatan, Devon. *Address:* 26 Sandringham Court, Maida Vale, W.
     (*Died 9 Jan. 1918.*)

GRAHAM, Sir John Hatt Noble, 1st Bt., *cr.* 1906; of Larbert and Househill, Stirlingshire; *s.* of John Graham of Lancefield, Glasgow, and Elizabeth Hatt Noble; *b.* 14 Aug. 1887; *m.* 1st, 1862, Jane Brown (*d.* 1890), *d.* of James Graham Adam of Denovan, Stirlingshire; two *s.* five *d.*; 2nd, 1891, Frances Lucy, *d.* of Martin Collingham Clodd, of Bury St. Edmunds. *Educ.:* Merchiston Castle, Edinburgh; Glasgow University. Partner of William Graham & Co., Glasgow, and all its corresponding firms in England, India, Portugal, since 1855; J.P. Lanark, Glasgow, and Stirling Counties. *Recreation:* shooting. *Heir: s.* J. F. N. Graham. *M.:* MS 181. *Club:* Western, Glasgow.   (*Died 25 May 1926.*)

GRAHAM, Sir John (James), K.C.M.G., *cr.* 1905; C.M.G. 1899; Secretary to Law Department, Cape of Good Hope, 1889 - 1908; *b.* Wynberg, 21 Feb. 1847; *e. s.* of Robert Graham of Fintry; *m.* 1873, Annie Julia, *d.* of Hon. J. Murison, M.L.C.; four *s.* one *d. Educ.:* St. Andrew's College, Grahamstown. Clerk to Civil Commissioner and Resident Magistrate, Albany, 1864; to Registrar Eastern Districts Court, 1865; Assistant Registrar Supreme Court, 1872; Registrar and Master Eastern Districts Court, 1875; Chief Clerk to Attorney-General and Clerk of Peace for Cape Town, 1878; Secretary to Law Department, 1882; High Sheriff and Taxing Officer Supreme Court, 1884; reappointed Secretary to Law Dept. with control of convict stations and prisons, 1889; retired, 1908. *Address:* Monorgan, Newlands, Cape Town.   (*Died 17 Dec. 1928.*)

GRAHAM, Michael, J.P.; *b.* Glasgow, 22 Jan. 1847; *m.* 1887; one *s.* one *d. Educ.:* St. Andrew's Parish School, and Andersonian University, Glasgow. Sub-Editor and Leader-Writer, Glasgow Herald, 1872-86; Editor The Evening Times, Glasgow,1886-1919. *Recreations:* books and walking. *Address:* Hillend, Old Cathcart, Glasgow. *T.:* Langside 75.
     (*Died 1925.*)

GRAHAM, Sir Reginald (Henry), 8th Bt. of Norton Conyers; *cr.* 1662; J.P., D.L.; late Capt. Rifle Brigade; *b.* 22 April 1835; *e. s.* of 7th Bt. and 2nd *w.* Harriet, 3rd *d.* of late Rev. R. Cottam; *S.* father 1866; *m.* 1876, Annie Mary (*d.* 1917), *d.* of late T. Shiffner, Westergate House, Sussex; two *s.* Served with 14th Foot in Crimean campaign at Sebastopol, 1854-56 (medal and clasp); Crimean and Turkish medals; Capt. Rifle Brigade, 1856 (retired 1863). *Heir: s.* Reginald Guy. *Publications:* Fox-

427

hunting Recollections, 1907; Poems of the Chase, 1912. *Address*: Norton Conyers, near Ripon, Yorkshire. *Clubs*: Carlton, Jockey; Yorkshire, York; Royal Yacht Squadron, Cowes. (*Died 27 Dec. 1920.*)

GRAHAM, Sir Robert James Stuart, 10th Bt.; *cr.* 1629; *b.* 2 Dec. 1845; *S.* father 1864; *m.* Eliza, *d.* of Charles Burns, Brooklyn, N.Y. 1874; four *s.* *Heir*: *s.* Montrose Stuart, [*b.* 20 May 1875; *m.* 1908 Helen Ursula, *d.* of John Henderson, Lerwick; one *s.* one *d.* *Address*: 563 52nd Street, New York.] *Address*: 629 54th Street, Bay Ridge, Brooklyn, New York, U.S.A. (*Died 12 May 1917.*)

GRAHAM, General Sir (S.) James, K.C.B., *cr.* 1902; C.B. 1882; Royal Marines; retired; *b.* Malta, 1837; *s.* of late Col. J. J. Graham, at one time Military Secretary Turkish Contingent, and *g. s.* of late General Graham, Lieut.-Governor of Stirling Castle; *m.* 1st, Laura Christiana, *d.* of late A. H. Williams, H.E.I.C.S. (*d.* 1874); three *s.*; 2nd, 1879, V. Rosabel, *d.* of late Gen. T. Conyngham Kelly, C.B., of Loughbrown, Co. Kildare, Ireland. Served in Baltic campaign, 1854-55 (medal); served in H.M.S. "Agamemnon" when engaged in laying Atlantic Telegraph Cable; H.M.S. "Black Prince" when towing Floating Dock to Bermuda; commanded a Batt. of Marines sent to Port Said to assist Navy in seizing Suez Canal during insurrection under Arabi Pasha; landed at Ismailia (despatches) present at actions of Tel-el-Mahuta, Mahsemah, Kassassin, and battle of Tel-el-Kebir (despatches twice, medal and clasp, C.B.); selected to receive Egyptian War Medal at hands of H.M. at Windsor; Queen's Jubilee Medal; 4th class of the Order of the Osmanieh. *Address*: 3 Kensington Court Mansions, Palace Gate, S.W. *Club*: United Service. (*Died 11 May 1917.*)

GRAHAM, Peter, R.A. 1881; *m.* *Address*: Westoun, St. Andrews, Scotland. *Club*: Athenæum. (*Died 19 Oct. 1921.*)

GRAHAM, P. Anderson, Editor of Country Life. A Northumbrian, who early in life took to journalism and literature; has edited or helped to edit several journals before coming to Country Life about 1900; has acted as special commissioner to the Standard, Morning Post, and St. James's Gazette at various times. *Publications*: Nature in Books: Seven Studies in Biography; The Rural Exodus; the Problem of the Village and the Town; All the Year with Nature; Country Pastimes for Boys; The Victoria Era; The Red Scaur: A Novel of Manners; edited the Country Life Anthology of Verse, 1916; Highways and Byways in Northumbria, 1919; The Collapse of Homo Sapiens, 1923; Iwerne, Before, During and After the War, 1923 (for private circulation only); editor of the Country Life Increased Productivity Series. *Recreations*: chess, billiards, golf. *Address*: 20 Tavistock Street, W.C. *T.A.*: Countrylife, London. *T.*: Gerrard 2748. *Club*: Constitutional. (*Died 25 Oct. 1925.*)

GRAHAM, Maj.-Gen. Sir Thomas, K.C.B., *cr.* 1908; C.B 1889; late R. Bengal Artillery; *b.* 26 Jan. 1842; *s.* of late Gen. Joseph Graham; *m.* 1869, Elizabeth, *d.* of Maj.-Gen. Bean, B.S.C.; two *s.* (younger killed in action in France, 21 Dec. 1914). Entered army, 1858; Major-General, 1891; retired; served Hazara expedition (medal with clasp); Afghan war, 1878-80 (despatches, Brevet Lieut.-Col., medal, bronze decoration); Burmah (despatches, clasp); Sikkim, 1888-89 (C.B., clasp); Manipur, 1891 (thanks of Government, despatches, clasp). *Address*: Glencoe, Camberley. (*Died 4 Nov. 1925.*)

GRAHAM, Hon. Sir Wallace, Kt., *cr.* 1916; Chief Justice of Nova Scotia since 1915; Governor of Dalhousie College, Halifax, N.S.; *b.* Antigo-

nish, N.S., 15 Jan. 1848; *s.* of David Graham and Mary Elizabeth Bigelow; *m.* Annie Lyons, of Cornwallis, N.S.; one *s.* two *d.* *Educ.*: Acadia Coll. (B.A. 1867). Called to Bar, 1871; Q.C. 1881; Standing Counsel in N.S. for Govt. of Canada 8 years; appointed on Commission to revise Statutes of Canada, 1883; and to revise Statutes of Nova Scotia, 1898; Judge in Equity of Supreme Court and of Court for Divorce in Nova Scotia, 1889. *Address*: 37 South Park Street, Halifax, N.S. *T.A.*: Halifax. *T.*: St. Paul 517. *Club*: Halifax. (*Died 12 Oct. 1917.*)

GRAHAM, William Perceval Gore; one of H.M.'s Inspectors at the Home Office since 1914; 3rd *s.* of late Robert Gore Graham, J.P., of Southmead, Westbury, Gloucestershire; *b.* 1 July 1861; *m.* 1st, Isabel Mary, *d.* of late Sir Thomas Longmore, C.B., of Woolstone, Hants; 2nd, Isabel Margaret, *d.* of Frederick W. Harris, J.P., D.L., of Park Grove. Withyham, Sussex; two *s.* two *d.* *Educ.*: privately; University College School; Caius College, Cambridge; Scholar and Prælector 1st Class Nat. Sci., Tripos. Entered Royal Army Medical Corps, 1887 (Montefiore Prizeman and Medallist in Military Surgery); joined Egyptian Army, 1890; served Tokar Expedition, 1891 (despatches, star and clasp, Osmanieh); transferred to Public Health Department, 1896; Administrator of the International Municipality of Alexandria, 1902-1904; Deputy Director-General Public Health Dept., 1905-7; Director-General Department of Public Health, Egypt, 1907. *Address*: Cheriton House, Alresford, Hants. *Clubs*: Arthur's, Leander, Royal Automobile. (*Died 30 Dec. 1918.*)

GRAHAME, Thomas George; In Charge of British Consulate Canea, Crete, since May 1917; *b.* 10 Jan. 1861; *s.* of Robert Vetch Grahame. *Educ.*: Harrow. Travelled extensively on the Continent and in Far East; resided at Paris for many years; Vice-Consul, Teheran, 1900; Consul, Shiraz, 1903; Consul-General, Ispahan, 1908-16. *Publications*: articles, chiefly on travel and art, to various English and continental periodicals. *Recreations*: travel, riding. *Club*: Royal Societies. (*Died 22 Oct. 1922.*)

GRAMIGNA, Rt. Rev. Fr. Petronius, D.D., O.S.F.C.; Bishop of Allahabad since 1904; *b.* Castel-Bolognese, Italy, 13 Dec. 1844. Admitted into Capuchin branch of Franciscan Order at age of 19; priest, 1868; Missions in East India, 1871; was Principal of Schools, Chaplain to Cathedral, and in charge of troops, Allahabad; was elected Superior of his Order in the Missions; Vicar-General of the Diocese and Administrator Apostolic, 1896. *Recreation*: walking. *Address*: Allahabad, India. (*Died 18 Dec. 1917.*)

GRANET, Col. Edward John, C.B. 1911; Military Attaché, Rome, since 1911; *b.* 2 Aug. 1858; *m.* 1885, Evelyn Pulcherie, *d.* of David Ward Chapman. Lieut. R.A. 1878; Captain, 1886; Major, 1896; Lieut.-Col. 1903; Colonel, 1906; Staff Captain N.E. District, 1892-95; Brigade Major Southern District, 1896-99; D.A.A.G. S. Africa, 1901-2; Headquarters of Army, 1902-5; Assist. Director Remounts, 1906-1910; served European War, 1914-15 (wounded). *Address*: British Embassy, Rome. *Club*: Naval and Military. (*Died 22 Oct. 1918.*)

GRANGER, His Hon. Sir Thomas Colpitts, Kt., *cr.* 1921; J.P.; County Court Judge, Greenwich, Woolwich, and Southwark, since 1911; 3rd *s.* of late T. Colpitts Granger, Q.C., M.P.; *b.* 30 Aug. 1852; *m.* 1st, 1886, Lilian (*d.* 1910), *d.* of James Payn, the novelist; 2nd, 1919, Ellen, *widow* of Godfrey Walker of Northbrook Park, Countess Wear, Devon. Called to Bar, Inner Temple, 1874; County Court Judge, Cornwall, 1891-1911; Joint Chairman of Quarter Sessions, Cornwall, until 1918.

Address: 25 Lower Belgrave Street, S.W.1. *T.:* Victoria 6275. *Club:* Reform.

(*Died 13 Jan. 1927.*)

GRANNUM, Edward Thomas, J.P., C.M.G., 1911 ; Auditor - General, Barbados, 1894 ; retired 1918 ; *b.* 1843 ; *s.* of Henry Grannum ; *m.* 1864, Mary, *d.* of William Jordan ; three *s.* *Educ.:* Codrington Grammar School, Barbados. Member for Bridgetown, Barbados House of Assembly, 1883-95 ; Member of Finance Commission, 1885 ; of Executive Committee, 1885-1889 and 1900-4 ; of General Board of Health, 1885 ; represented Barbados in negotiations at Washington in connection with McKinley Tariff Act, 1891 ; Member of Technical Education Committee, 1892 ; of Emigration Commission, 1893 ; Director of General Hospital, and Member of House Committee, 1906 ; Member of Education Commission, 1894 and 1907 ; Chairman of Conference at Barbados to consider trade relations with Canada, 1908 ; Member Customs Commission, 1908 ; administered government of Barbados for a short time in 1907 ; M.L.C. 1906 ; Acting Colonial Secretary and Member of Executive Council. *Club :* Bridgetown, Barbados. (*Died 6 June 1922.*)

GRANT, Col. Alexander Brown, M.V.O., V.D., D.L., J.P. ; *b.* 20 Oct. 1840 ; *m.* ; three *s.* two *d.* *Educ. :* Irvine Royal Academy. Joined Volunteer Force, 1859 ; retired, 1907 ; gave evidence before many committees at War Office ; Commandant Glasgow National Reserve ; Military Member, Glasgow Territorial Force Association ; Lord Rector's Assessor, Glasgow University ; Hon. Colonel 4th Lowland (H) Brigade R.F.A. (T). *Recreations:* fishing, shooting, and country life. *Address:* Killochan Castle, Ayrshire ; 7 Athole Gardens, Glasgow. *T.A. :* Grant, Glasgow. *T.:* Glasgow 2525 Bell, 796 Hillhead. *Clubs:* National Liberal, Junior Army and Navy ; Liberal, Art, Glasgow. *M.:* LA 8072. (*Died 2 April 1921.*)

GRANT, Sir Arthur Henry, 9th Bt. ; *cr.* 1705 ; J.P., D.L. ; late Lieut. 27th Inniskillings ; Capt. and Hon. Maj. Hampshire Yeomanry (Carabiniers), retired ; Hon. Col. 1st Aberdeenshire R.E. (Vols.) *b.* 1849 ; *S.* cousin 1887 ; *m.* Mary, *d.* of Capt. H. Sholto Douglas, late 42nd Highlanders, 1878 ; two *s.* *Educ.:* Oriel Coll. Oxford. M.A. 1873 ; contested W. Aberdeenshire (U.) 1892, 1895, and 1900. *Heir: s.* Arthur Grant. *Address:* House of Monymusk, Aberdeen, N.B. ; Fairoak Lodge, Bishopstoke, Hants. *Clubs:* Junior Carlton, Carlton, Cavalry. (*Died 1 Mar. 1917.*)

GRANT, Corrie, M.P. (R.) for South-East (Rugby) Division of Warwick since 1900 ; K.C. 1906 ; *b.* 14 Nov. 1850 ; *s.* of James B. Grant, Kettleburgh, Suffolk ; *m.* 1885, Annie Adams. *Educ. :* City of London School. Called to Bar, Middle Temple, 1877 ; contested Woodstock, 1885 ; W. Birmingham, 1892 ; Rugby Div. 1895 ; Harrow Div. 1899. *Address:* 26 The Avenue, Bedford Park, Chiswick. *Club :* National Liberal. (*Died Dec. 1924.*)

GRANT, Rev. Cyril Fletcher, M.A. ; Hon. Canon, Rochester, 1890 ; *m.* 1909, Alicia, *d.* of late Capt. W. P. Salmon, 60th Rifles. *Educ. :* Balliol College, Oxford. Curate of St John's, Chatham, 1871-74 ; St James's, Gravesend 1874-75 ; St Margaret's Lee, 1875 ; Aylesford, 1876-78 ; Vicar. 1878-95 ; Rector of Holy Trinity, Guildford, 1895 - 1907 ; Rural Dean, Guildford, 1905-7 ; Chaplain at Rome, 1909-10. *Publication:* North African Shores of the Mediterranean. *Address :* 1 Sloane Gardens, S.W. (*Died 9 Feb. 1916.*)

GRANT, Lieut.-Col. and Hon. Col. Edward James, C.B. 1900 ; late Royal Scots ; *b.* 31 Aug. 1854 ; *s.* of late Col. A. G. Grant ; *m.* 1882, Mary (*d.* 1926), *y. d.* of Rev. H. Addington of Henlow Grange, Beds. *Educ. :* Cheltenham College. Served Egypt 1882 with

Royal Irish Regiment, Battle of Tel-el-Kebir ; South Africa, 1899-1902, in command of 3rd Royal Scots (despatches, Queen's medal three clasps, King's medal two clasps, C.B.). *Address :* 71 Philbeach Gardens, S.W.5. *Club :* Naval and Military. (*Died 2 Sept. 1928.*)

GRANT, General Sir Henry Fane, K.C.B., *cr.* 1908 ; C.B. 1885 ; G.C.V.O., *cr.* 1909 ; retired ; *b.* 4 May 1848 ; *s.* of late Field-Marshal Sir Patrick Grant, and Hon. Lady Grant, *d.* of 1st Viscount Gough ; *m.* Lily, widow of late Colonel Pemberton, R.A., and *d.* of late E. Sandys, I.C.S. *Educ. :* Eton. Entered army, 1868 ; Col. 1888 ; served Egyptian army, 1884 (Brevet Lt.-Col., 3rd Class Medjidie) ; Nile Expedition, 1884 - 85 (despatches, C.B., medal with two clasps, Khedive star) ; Com. 5th Div. 2nd Army Corps, 1903-7 ; Governor and Commander-in-Chief of Malta, 1907-9 ; Lieut. Tower of London, 1909-13. *Address :* Laggan Lodge, Scaniport, Inverness-shire. *Club :* United Service. (*Died 28 July 1919.*)

GRANT, Colonel Hugh Gough, C.B. 1900 ; late commanding Regimental Districts, Fort - George and Inverness ; retired ; *s.* of late Field - Marshal Sir Patrick Grant, G.C.B., G.C.M.G. ; *b.* 23 July 1845 ; *m.* Isabel, *d.* of Eneas Mackintosh of Balnespick, Inverness-shire, 1885 ; two *s.* one *d.* *Educ. :* Eton ; R.M.C. Sandhurst. Served with Seaforth Highlanders, 1863-95 ; received thanks of Indian Government for special services during Madras Famine, 1877-1878 ; Brigade-Major Kurram Column during Afghan War, 1879-80 (despatches, medal) ; Brig.-Major 2nd Column during Mahsud Waziri Expedition, 1881 (despatches) ; served in Black Mountain Expedition, 1891 (medal) ; was Assistant Adjutant-General Punjab Command, 1895-97. (*Died 19 Aug. 1922.*)

GRANT, Sir James Alexander, K.C.M.G., *cr.* 1887 ; M.D., M.R.C.S. (Eng.), F.R.C.P. (Lond.), F.R.C.S. (Edin.) ; *b.* Inverness, 11 Aug. 1831 ; *m.* 1856, Maria, *d.* of Edward Malloch, M.P. *Educ. :* Queen's Coll. Kingston, Ont. : London ; Edinburgh. M.P. (Canadian) for Co. of Russell, 1865-73 ; Ottawa, 1892-96 ; introduced Pacific Railway Bill to construct the present Trans-continental Railroad, 1872 ; President Tuberculosis Association of Canada, 1901-2 ; President Royal Society of Canada, 1903 ; Ex-President Medical Council, Ontario ; Hon. Member British Medical Association ; awarded gold medal of Palermo, Sicily, for Medical Science ; also Legion of Honour of Italy ; Hon. President Medico - Chirurgical Society, Ottawa ; President International Congress of Hygiene for Canada, 1909 ; and of Canadian Section 4th International Hygienic Congress, Buffalo, 1913 ; Hon. Member Canadian Medical Association, 1912 ; Hon. President Ottawa Valley Graduates, McGill University ; discoverer of serum therapy, 1861 ; Hon. President Medico-Chirurgical Society, Ottawa. *Publications:* Essays on Medical, Surgical, and Scientific Subjects in the Journals of Canada, United States, and England ; Organic Heart Disease (Montreal Med. Mal. Dec. 1897). *Recreations:* chiefly in field of Geology ; has made a large collection Silurian fossils. *Address :* Roxborough Apartments, Ottawa, Canada. *Club:* Rideau, Ottawa. (*Died Feb. 1920.*)

GRANT, John Peter, of Rothiemurchus, D.L. for Cos. Inverness and Banff, J.P. for Co. Inverness ; Sheriff-Substitute of Inverness-shire ; *b.* 1860 ; *s.* of late John Peter Grant, Rothiemurchus ; *m.* 1st, 1882, Edith Mary, *d.* of Lt. - Col. David Macpherson, Belleville, Inverness-shire ; 2nd, 1899, Lady Mary Augusta Pierrepont (*d.* 1917), *d.* of 3rd Earl Manvers ; four *s.* one *d.* *Educ. :* Marlborough ; Trinity Coll., Oxford ; University of Edinburgh. M.A. Oxon (2nd Cl. Hon. History) ; LL.B. Edin. Barrister-at-law (Inner Temple), 1883 ; Advocate (in Scotland), 1888; Sheriff-Substitute of Banffshire, 1890-1900; Major 1st Vol. Batt. Q.O. Cameron Highlanders (retired, 1898). *Address:* The Doune of Rothiemurchus, nr. Aviemore, Inverness-shire. *Clubs:* New, Edinburgh; Highland, Inverness.(*Died 18 Feb. 1927.*)

GRANT, Hon. MacCallum, LL.D., D.C.L.; *b.* Hants County, Province of Nova Scotia, 17 May; *m.* Laura McNeill, *d.* of Hon. D. McN. Parker, M.D.; four *s.* one *d.* *Educ.:* Newport, Hants Co., N.S. Commenced business career 1873; Lieutenant-Governor Province Nova Scotia, 1916-25; Director Bank of Nova Scotia; Vice-President Nova Scotia Loan Society; Chairman Old Ladies' Home; Director Halifax Dispensary, etc. *Recreations:* golf, tennis. *Address:* 114 Young Avenue, Halifax, Nova Scotia, Canada. *Clubs:* Halifax City, Halifax, N.S. (*Died 23 Feb. 1928.*)

GRANT, Rr.-Adm. Noel, R.N.. C.B., 1915; in command of Air Store Depot, White City; *b.* 13 Sep. 1868; *s.* of John Miller Grant; *m.* Mary Annette, *d.* of E. Allen; no *c.* *Educ.:* Burney's School; H.M.S. Britannia. In command of the Carmania at sinking of German cruiser, Cap Trafalgar, 1914. *Club:* United Service. (*Died 6 Mar. 1920.*)

GRANT, Major Robert Francis Sidney, M.V.O. 1911; D.S.O. 1900; late Rifle Brigade; *b.* 18 Sep. 1877; *s.* of late Sir C. Grant, K.C.S.I., and Ellen, *d.* of Rt. Hon. Henry Baillie, of Redcastle, N.B.; *m.* 1917, Vera, *d.* of Lt.-Col. Walter Campbell, The Ivy House, Hampton Court. *Educ.:* Eton. Entered army, 1898; Captain, 1904; Major, 1914; served South Africa, 1899-1902 (despatches, Queen's medal 6 clasps, King's medal 2 clasps, D.S.O.); European War, 1914-15 (despatches twice, severely wounded, Feb. 1915). *Address:* 29 Sussex Square, Brighton. *Clubs:* Travellers', Army and Navy. (*Died 4 Aug. 1927.*)

GRANT, William, C.M.G. 1899; 1st Class Assistant, Sub-Commissioner Uganda Protectorate Service, 1898-1904; *b.* 22 Sept. 1863; *s.* of Alex. Grant and Bella Young of Inverness. *Educ.:* Rhumaharime Public School, Kintyre, Argyllshire, Scotland. Left home, 1883; was variously employed until 1890; in I.B.E.A. Co.'s service, 1890-93; left Mombasa for Uganda, 1890. *Address:* Pennygowan, Campbeltown, Argyllshire. (*Died 28 Oct. 1919.*)

GRANT-DUFF, Sir Evelyn, K.C.M.G., *cr.* 1916; C.M.G. 1911; British Envoy to Nova Confederation, 1913-16; *b.* 9 Oct. 1863; 2nd *s.* of late Rt. Hon. Sir Mountstuart Grant-Duff, G.C.S.I.; *m.* 1900, Edith Florence, C.B.E., a Lady of Grace of the Order of St. John of Jerusalem, *e. d.* of Sir G. F. Bonham, 2nd Bart. Entered Foreign Office, 1888; appointed to Rome, 1889; 3rd Secretary, 1890; Tehran, 1892; 2nd Secretary, 1894; St. Petersburg, 1895; Stockholm, 1896; Berlin, 1897; Stockholm, 1898; employed Foreign Office, 1899-1903; Secretary of Legation, Tehran, 1903-6; Councillor of Embassy, Madrid, 1906-1910; appointed Minister to Venezuela, 1910, but did not proceed; Consul-General for Hungary, 1911-13. *Address:* 14 Marlborough Buildings, Bath. (*Died 19 Sept. 1926.*)

GRAVES, Rev. Charles Edward, M.A., Fellow, 1863-65, and since 1893 of St. John's College, Cambridge; *b.* London, 11 Nov. 1839; *o. surv. s.* of J. J. Graves, partner in H. Graves and Co., silk manufacturers, and Mary, *d.* of J. Barlow, Ardwick, Manchester; *m.* Ann Hughes, *d.* of Rev. Richard Gwatkin, sometime Fellow and Tutor of St. John's Coll. Camb., and afterwards vicar of Barrow-on-Soar, 1865; one *s.* four *d.* *Educ.:* Leamington College; Shrewsbury School; St. John's Coll. Cambridge. Porson Prize, 1861; 2nd in 1st class Classical Tripos, 1862; Naden Divinity Student, 1862. Has mostly lived in Cambridge;

worked as a private tutor for some years; Lecturer at St. John's College, 1866-1901; at Sidney Sussex College, 1871-82; at Jesus College, 1877-90; Tutor St. John's College, 1895-1905; ordained in 1866; Curate of Chesterton, Cambridge, 1866-68; Chaplain of Magdalene Coll. 1886-94; Select Preacher, Camb. 1875, 1886, and 1892. *Publications:* editor of Thucydides, books iv. and v.; Plato's Menexenus and Euthyphro; the Acharnians, Clouds, Wasps, and Peace of Aristophanes. *Address:* St. Martin's, Cambridge. (*Died 21 Oct. 1920.*)

GRAVES, Robert Ernest, C.B.E. 1918; H.M. Chief Inspector of Factories, Home Office, since 1920; Deputy Commissioner for Trade Exemptions, Ministry of National Service, Aug. 1917-Dec. 1918; *b.* Waterford, Ireland, 22 Dec. 1866; *s.* of James Palmer Graves, J.P., Waterford; *m.* Marion Burt, Ventnor, Isle of Wight; one *d.* *Educ.:* Portora Royal School, Enniskillen. H.M. Inspector of Factories, 1890; Superintending Inspector, 1908; Deputy Chairman of Reserved Occupations Committee; Director of Substitution in the National Service Department, Feb.-Aug. 1917. *Recreations:* fishing, sailing, gardening. *Address:* Cowley Cottage, Cowley, Uxbridge. *Club:* Royal Automobile. (*Died 21 May 1922.*)

GRAVES, Rev. Walter Eccleston, Hon. Canon of Truro. *Address:* St. Clement's Vicarage, Truro. (*Died 21 May 1922.*)

GRAY, Baroness (Eveleen Smith Gray), 19th in line; *cr.* 1445; *b.* Dresden, 3 May 1841; *o. d.* of Lady Jane and Capt. Lonsdale Pounden; *m.* James Maclaren Smith, Hazelgreen, Lancs, 1863; one *s.* three *d.*; *S.* to Barony of Gray, 1895; claim established, 1896. *Heir: s.* Master of Gray. *Address:* 14 The Boltons, South Kensington; Brownswood, Enniscorthy, Co. Wexford. (*Died 24 Dec. 1918.*)

GRAY, 20th Baron (*cr.* 1445); **James Maclaren Stuart**, *b.* 4 June 1864. *S.* mother 1918. *Educ.:* Pembroke Coll., Camb. Formerly Captain, 5th Batt. Rifle Brigade. *Address:* Cwmeron, Llanwrtyd Wells, R.S.O., S. Wales. *Club:* Junior Athenæum. (*Died 2 May 1919.*)

GRAY, Sir Albert, K.C.B., *cr.* 1919; C.B. 1916; K.C.; Counsel to the Chairman of Committees in the House of Lords, 1896-1922; *b.* 10 Oct. 1850: 4th *s.* of George Gray of Bowerswell, Perth, N.B.; *m.* 1895, Sophie, *d.* of S. Wells Williams, of the U.S. Legation, Peking, and widow of the Hon. Thos. G. Grosvenor, C.B. *Educ.:* Rugby. Entered the Ceylon Civil Service, 1871; resigned 1875, and was called to the Bar at the Inner Temple, 1879; Bencher, 1914; Chancellor of the Diocese of Ely, 1894-97; President of the Hakluyt Society, 1908; Mayor of Chelsea, 1924-25. *Address:* Catherine Lodge, Trafalgar Square, Chelsea, S.W.3. *T.:* Kensington 0284. *Clubs:* Athenæum, Brooks's. (*Died 27 Feb. 1928.*)

GRAY, Andrew, M.A., D.Sc., LL.D., F.R.S.; Emeritus Professor of Natural Philosophy, University of Glasgow; Professor of Natural Philosophy, 1899-1923; *b.* Scotland, 1847; *e. s.* of John Gray, Lochgelly, Fifeshire; *m.* Annie, *d.* of James Gordon; three *s.* four *d.* *Educ.:* Subscription School, Lochgelly; privately; Glasgow University. Eglinton Fellow in Mathematics, Glasgow University, 1876. Private Secretary and Assistant to Sir W. Thomson (Lord Kelvin), 1875-80; Official Assistant to Prof. of Nat. Phil. in Glasgow University, 1880-84; Professor of Physics University Coll. of North Wales, 1884-99. *Publications:* Absolute Measurements in Electricity and Magnetism, 1888; Theory and Practice of Absolute Measurements in Electricity and Magnetism, vol. i. 1888; vol. ii. (pts. 1 and 2), 1893 (new edition, 1921); A Treatise on Bessel Functions (with late Dr. G. B. Mathews, F.R.S.), 1895, revised edition (with Dr. MacRobert), 1922; Magnetism and Electricity, vol. i. 1898;

Dynamics and Properties of Matter, 1901; the Scientific Work of Lord Kelvin, 1908; A Treatise on Dynamics (with Prof. J. G. Gray), 1911; revised edition, 1920; A Treatise on Gyrostatics and Rotational Motion, 1919; and various scientific papers. *Address:* The University, Glasgow. *(Died 10 Oct. 1925.)*

GRAY, George Buchanan, M.A., D.Litt. (Oxon.); Hon. D.D. Aberd.; M.R.A.S.; Tutor since 1891, and (since 1900) Prof. of Hebrew and O.T. Exegesis in Mansfield College, Oxford; Speaker's Lecturer in Biblical Studies in the University of Oxford, 1914-19; Grinfield Lectures on the Septuagint, 1919-21; *b.* Blandford, Dorset, 13 Jan. 1865; 2nd *s.* of Rev. Benjamin Gray, B.A., and Emma Jane, *d.* of late George Buchanan Kirkman; *m.* Frances Lilian, *o. d.* of Alfred Williams, J.P., F.R.G.S., of Salisbury; one *s.* one *d. Educ.:* private schools; New and Univ. Colls. London; Mansfield Coll. Oxford; Marburg. B.A. London, 1886; Prizeman, 1887; Oxford, 1st class in School of Semitic Studies, 1891; Pusey and Ellerton Scholar, 1889; Junior Septuagint Prizeman, 1890; Junior Kennicott Scholar, 1891; Sen. Kennicott Scholar, 1893; M.A. 1895. Entered Indep. ministry, 1893; Examiner in Oriental Languages in Univ. of Oxford, 1896, 1898-1900, and frequently since; Lecturer on the Old Testament to the Friends Summer School, 1897-99; Follow of the German Oriental Society, 1898. *Publications:* Studies in Hebrew Proper Names, 1896; The Divine Discipline of Israel, 1900; Numbers (Temple Bible), 1902; Numbers, 1903, and Isaiah, i.-xxvii., 1911, and (with the late S. R. Driver) Job, 1921 (International Critical Commentary); A Critical Introduction to the Old Testament, 1913; The Forms of Hebrew Poetry, 1915; Names of Places, and several other articles in Encyclopædia Biblica; contributions, chiefly on Semitic Philology and Old Testament Criticism, to the Academy, Expositor, Jewish Quarterly Review, Contemporary, etc. *Recreations:* lawn-tennis, cycling, climbing. *Address:* 83 Norham Road, Oxford. *(Died 2 Nov. 1922.)*

GRAY, Hon. George Wilkie, M.L.C. Queensland; Chairman of Directors, Quinlan, Gray & Co., Ltd., and Castlemain Brewery; *b.* Sydney, 1844. Minister without Portfolio, 1859, 1899-1908. *Address:* Eldernel, Brisbane, Queensland. *(Died 22 Sept. 1924.)*

GRAY, James Hunter, K.C. 1918; M.A., B.Sc., M.I.E.E.; called to bar, Middle Temple, 1895; *b.* 3 Sep. 1867; *m.* Julie, *d.* of late Professor Dittmar, LL.D., F.R.S. Chiefly engaged in Patent Trade Mark and Technical Litigation. *Address:* 17 Chantrey House, S.W.1. *T.:* Victoria 5581; 5 Fig Tree Court, Temple, E.C.4. *T.:* Central 978. *Clubs:* Garrick, Beefsteak, Royal Automobile. *(Died 1 June 1925.)*

GRAY, Maxwell (M. G. Tuttiett), novelist; general writer; *b.* Newport, Isle of Wight; *o. d.* of late F. B. Tuttiett, M.R.C.S., and Eliza, *d.* of the late Thomas Gleed. *Publications:* The Silence of Dean Maitland, 1886; Reproach of Annesley, 1888; Westminster Chimes and other Poems, 1889; In the Heart of the Storm, 1891; An Innocent Impostor, 1892; The Last Sentence, 1893; A Costly Freak, 1898; Lays of the Dragon-Slayer, 1894; Sweethearts and Friends, 1897; Ribstone Pippins, 1898; The House of Hidden Treasure, 1898; The Forest Chapel and other poems, 1899; The World's Mercy, 1900; Four-Leaved Clover, 1901; Richard Rosny, 1903; The Great Refusal, 1906; The Suspicions of Ermengarde, 1908; England's Son and other Poems, 1910; Unconfessed, 1911; Something Afar, 1913; The Worldmender, 1916; The Diamond Pendant, 1918; A Bit of Blue Stone, 1923; essays, poems, etc. *Address:* 144A Argyle Road, West Ealing, W. *(Died 21 Sept. 1923.)*

GRAY, Sir Walter; Kt., *cr.* 1902; J.P. for the City of Oxford; Alderman of City of Oxford; *b.* 1848; *s.* of late Thomas Gray of Litlington, Cambs; *m.* 1874, Emily Alice, *d.* of late James Savage of Box Hall, Herts; one *s.* two *d. Educ.:* Grammar School, Stevenage, Herts. Has been prominent in municipal life in Oxford since 1875; Mayor four times. *Address:* Oxford. *(Died 17 Mar. 1918.)*

GRAY, Rt. Rev. William Crane, D.D.; Missionary Bishop of the Episcopal Church in Southern Florida since 1892; *b.* Lambertville, New Jersey, 6 Sep. 1835; *e. s.* of Dr. Joseph Gray; *m.* 1st, 1863, Maggie Trent, one *s.*; 2nd, 1877, Fannie Bowers, one *s. Educ.:* Kenyon College and Bexley Hall, Gambier, Ohio. Deacon, 1859; Priest, 1860; spent a year and a half in Missionary work in West Tennessee; Rector St. James' Church, Bolivar, Tenn., 20 years; charge of the Church of the Advent, Nashville, Tenn., 1881; Delegate to General Convention since 1868; has work going on among red men, black men, brown men, and white men. *Publications:* sermons, addresses, and brief treatises on Church subjects. *Recreations:* very few, and coming only in the line of duty; no vacations as such, but councils, conventions, and especially the Lambeth Conference, much enjoyed. *Address:* Bishopstead, Main Street, Orlando, Fla., U.S.A. *T.:* 61. *(Died 14 Nov. 1919.)*

GRAY, Sir William Cresswell, 1st Bt., *cr.* 1917; D.L., J.P.; Chairman of Wm. Gray & Co., Ltd.; late Sheriff of Durham; *o. surv. s.* of late Sir William Gray of Greatham, Durham; *b.* 1 May 1867; *m.* 1891, Kate, *d.* of late C. T. Casebourne, C.E.; one *s.* four *d. Educ.:* Leys School, Cambridge. *Heir: s.* William [Captain Yorkshire Regt., *b.* 1895. *Educ.:* Loretto School, Edinburgh. Served European war, 1915-17 (despatches)]. *Address:* Tunstall Manor, West Hartlepool. *(Died 1 Nov. 1924.)*

GRAY, Col. William Lewis, C.M.G. 1917; M.B., C.M., Glas., B.Sc. Ed.; A.M.S., retired; *b.* 1864; 2nd *s.* of Alexander Gray, M.D., Selby; *m.* 1897, Janet, *d.* of Thomas Orr, Accountant, London; no *c. Educ.:* Universities of Glasgow and Edinburgh. Examiner in Chemistry, Malta University, 1906; served Anglo-Siamese Boundary Commission, 1889-90; Kaingtung-Chiengmai Mission, 1890-91; Chitral, 1895 (medal with clasp); S. Africa, 1899-1901 (despatches, Queen's medal 4 clasps); European War, 1914-17 (C.M.G., despatches). *Address:* North Holt, Hythe, Kent. *Club:* Junior United Service. *(Died 5 Nov. 1924.)*

GRAYFOOT, Col. Blenman Buhot, M.D., C.B., 1916; Indian Medical Service. Served European War, 1914-16 (despatches, C.B.). *(Died Oct. 1916.)*

GREANY, Surg.-Gen. John Philip, M.D., I.M.S. (retired); *b.* 21 July 1851; *m.* 1889, Agnes Norah, *d.* of late Andrew Wingate, Glasgow; one *s.* one *d. Educ.:* Queen's College, Cork. Graduated M.D., M.Ch., L.M. from the Royal University, Ireland, 1874; joined the Indian Medical Service, 1875; Surg.-Gen. with the Government of Bombay, 1905-8. *Address:* 31 Woodville Gardens, Ealing, W.5. *(Died 7 Oct. 1919.)*

GREANY, Capt. John Wingate, D.S.O. 1915; *b.* 1892; *s.* of Surg.-Gen. J. P. Greany, I.M.S. Served European War in Gallipoli, 1915 (despatches, D.S.O.). *Address:* 31 Woodville Gardens, Ealing, W. *(Died April 1916.)*

GREAVES, Gen. Sir George Richards, G.C.B., *cr.* 1896; K.C.M.G., *cr.* 1881; K.C.B., *cr.* 1885; C.B. 1875; General, 1896; retired, 1896; *b.* 9 Nov. 1831; *s.* of late Capt. George Greaves, 60th Rifles, who served in Peninsular War as a Lieut. in the 5th Fusiliers and received the war medal with five clasps; *m.* 1st, Ellen, *d.* of Brig.-Gen. Hutchison, 1859 (*d.* 1880); 2nd, 1908, Julia Rose, *d.* of Rev. E. Morris, Rural Dean, Vicar of Llanelly, and widow of Surg.-Major W. Venour, A.M.S. *Educ.:* Sandhurst. Ensign 70th Foot;

served in Indian Mutiny, 1857-58; Ensotzie Expedition, 1858; New Zealand War, 1860-66; Ashantee campaign, 1874; Soudan, 1885; on the staff at the War Office, 1870-78; Chief Secretary and Commissioner, Cyprus, 1878; Adj.-Gen. in India, 1879; commanded Division in India, 1886; Commander-in-Chief, Bombay, 1890; resigned 1893; Colonel East Surrey Regiment, 1898. *Recreations:* shooting, fishing, yachting. *Address:* Netherwood, Saundersfoot, South Wales. *T.A.:* Saundersfoot.
(*Died 11 April 1922.*)

GREEN, Col. Bernard Charles, C.M.G. 1915; T.D.; D.L.; late Commanding 14th Batt. London Regt. (London Scottish); *b.* 1866; *m.* 1922, Marguerite Mary, *d.* of late Captain Whiteway, R.N.R., and Mrs. Whiteway, 190 Earl's Court Road, S.W. 5. Served with City of London Imperial Volunteers and Gordon Highlanders S. African War, 1900-2 (despatches, Queen's medal 4 clasps, King's medal 2 clasps); European War, 1914-16 (despatches, C.M.G.). *Address:* Warren Grange, Crowborough, Sussex. (*Died 26 Mar. 1925.*)

GREEN, Charles Edward, F.R.S.E., publisher; *b.* Edinburgh 1866; *m.* 1897, *y. d.* of late John Dalrymple, Edinburgh. *Educ.:* Edinburgh University. Founded Juridical Review, 1887; Scots Law Times, 1891; Green's Encyclopædia, 14 vols. 1895; Encyclopædia of English Law, 12 vols. 1896; Scots Revised Reports, 45 vols. 1897; Encyclopædia Medica, 15 vols. 1898; Scots Statutes Revised, 10 vols. 1899; English Reports, 180 vols. 1900; Encyclopædia of Accounting, 8 vols. 1903; Encyclopædia of Agriculture, 4 vols. 1907. *Publications:* Lives in a Lowland Parish; History of East Lothian; The Cancer Problem, 4th ed.; editor, Juridical Review; editor, Encyclopædia of Agriculture. *Address:* Gracemount House, Midlothian; *T.A.:* Viridis, Edinburgh. *T.:* Edinburgh 766 and 968. (*Died 6 Jan. 1920.*)

GREEN, David, R.I. *Publication:* Marine Painting in Water-colours. *Address:* 117 Finchley Road, N.W. *Club:* St. John's Wood Arts. (*Died 6 Mar. 1918.*)

GREEN, Sir Edward, 1st Bt., *cr.* 1886; D.L. J.P.; head of E. Green and Son, Ltd.; M.P. Wakefield, 1874, 1885 - 92; contested Pontefract, 1880; Director of Lancashire and Yorkshire Railway; *b.* Wakefield, 4 Mar. 1831; *e. s.* of Edward Green, Wakefield; *m.* Mary (*d.* 1902), *d.* of W. E. Lycett; two *s.* Owns about 5000 acres. *Recreations:* business, hunting, shooting. *Heir: s.* E. Lycett Green. *Address:* Treasurer's House, York; Ken Hill, Snettisham, Norfolk. *Clubs:* Carlton, Marlborough. (*Died 30 Mar. 1923.*)

GREEN, Everard, Somerset Herald since 1911; formerly Rouge Dragon Pursuivant of Arms; F.S.A.; *b.* 1844; *y. s.* of Charles Green, Holdich House, Spalding, Lincolnshire, and Mary, *d.* and *co-heir* of Henry Everard, Spalding, and Anne, *d.* of George Toynbee, Waddington, Lincolnshire. *Publications:* A Plea for the Resurrection of Heraldry; O Sapientia; The Insignia of an Archbishop; The Westminster Tournament Roll of 1510; Arms of the Popes; Lincolnshire Pedigrees, etc. *Address:* College of Arms, E.C.
(*Died 22 June 1926.*)

GREEN, Sir Frederick, Kt., *cr.* 1912; K.B.E., *cr.* 1918; *b.* Essex, 17 June 1845; *s.* of late Frederick Green of Princes Gardens, Kensington, W.; *m.* 1868, Alice, 2nd *d.* of late Sir Daniel Cooper, 1st Bt.; four *s.* three *d.* *Educ.:* Harrow. J.P. Essex; High Sheriff, 1918; Director, Suez Canal Co., Bank New South Wales; Member of the Council of King Edward's Hospital Fund. *Address:* Oaklawn, Wimbledon Park, Surrey. *Clubs:* City of London; Travellers', Paris. (*Died 18 Feb. 1927.*)

GREEN, Frederick Ernest, author and farmer; *b.* Hongkong, 16 Oct. 1867; *s.* of Thomas Green, Hongkong, and Jane Stuart, Aberdeen; *m.* 1st, Gertrude Beane (*decd.*); one *s.*; 2nd, her sister Constance. *Educ.:* Southampton. After leaving school was perched on a stool in the City to earn a living; hating the regimentation of commercialism and the boredom of suburbanism, after enduring City life for some years flung up his job to seek a living on the land; but it is as a free lance he has chiefly won his way in the republic of letters; aloof from political parties and boldly criticising the agricultural policy or lack of policy of succeeding Governments he has contributed much towards creating the new agricultural atmosphere; Member Royal Commission on Agriculture; Surrey District Wages Committee; Surrey C.C. Small Holdings Committee. *Publications:* The Awakening of England; The Tyranny of the Countryside; The Surrey Hills; A Few Acres and a Cottage; The Small Holding; How I Work my Small Farm; The Settlement of Ex-Service Men; Everyman's Land and Allotment Book; First Advice to Would-be Farmers; History of the Agricultural Labourer, 1870-1920; A New Agricultural Policy; Life of Cobbett. *Recreations:* tramping and tennis. *Address:* Barings Field, Newdigate, Surrey. *T.A.:* Green, Newdigate. (*Died 20 Jan. 1922.*)

GREEN, Sir George, Kt. *cr.* 1911; Inspector for Scotland for Prudential Assurance Company; *b.* Stockport, Dec. 15, 1843; *s.* of Thomas Green and Elizabeth Meadows; *m.* Jane, *d.* of John and Anne Heywood, Stockport; one *s.* six *d.* *Educ.:* St. Thomas's School, Stockport. Been with Prudential Assurance Co. since 1870; risen from the ranks to highest position attainable; been a Methodist lay preacher since 1861; contested Glasgow, 1895; Stockport, 1900; for eighteen years member of Lanarkshire County Council; been Vice-Convener and also Convener of that Council; Chairman of the Scottish Liberal Association, 1905-12; Chairman of Executive Scottish Band of Hope Union; J.P. Lanarkshire; been Vice-President, Primitive Methodist Conference. *Address:* Methven, Balshagray Avenue, Partick, Glasgow. *T.:* 243 Hillhead, Glasgow. *Clubs:* National Liberal; Liberal, Glasgow.
(*Died 8 April 1916.*)

GREEN, Mrs. Hetty (Howland Robinson), financier; *b.* New Bedford, Mass., 21 Nov. 1835; *d.* of late Edward Mott Robinson; *m.* 1867, Edward H. Green (*d.* 1902), New York. *Address:* Bellows Falls, Vermont. U.S.A.
(*Died 2 July 1916.*)

GREEN, John Alfred, B.A. (London), M.A. (Sheffield); Professor of Education, University of Sheffield, since 1906; *b.* 15 October 1867; *m.* Adeliza Norman, *d.* of Alderman J. Johnston, Manchester. *Educ.:* Firth College, Sheffield; Borough Road Training College. Junior Tutor at the Borough Road College, 1882-92; Assistant Master in a London Pupil Teachers' School, 1893-94; Lecturer in Education at Bangor, 1894. Studied educational systems of Germany, Austria, and Switzerland, 1904-5; Professor of Education, Bangor, 1900-6; Member of Central Welsh Board, 1898 - 1906; Member of Executive Council, Teachers' Guild; Recorder (Section L) British Association; Member of Teachers' Registration Council, 1912-16; Secretary of Committee (Sect. L), dealing with research into Mental and Physical Factors involved in Education, and Chairman of Committee appointed to enquire into development of Museums as Educational Institutions; Chairman of Executive Committee, Educational Handwork Association; Secretary of Board of Examinations for Educational Handwork; Member of Sheffield Education Committee. *Publications:* Educational Ideas of Pestalozzi,

1904; (Joint) Primer of Teaching Practice, 1911; Life and Work of Pestalozzi, 1912; (Joint) Introduction to Psychology, 1912; Educational Writings of Pestalozzi, 1912; Editor, Journal Experimental Pedagogy; various Articles. *Address* : The University, Sheffield.

(*Died 12 Mar. 1922.*)

GREEN, Max Sullivan, J.P.; Chairman of the Irish Prison Board since 1912; *b.* 1864; *s.* of late J. S. Green, Air Hill, Co. Cork; *m.* 1913, Johanna, *y. d.* of late John Redmond, M.P. (Mrs. Green is the author of several plays.) *Educ.* : Trinity College, Dublin; R. College of Sciences (Diploma in Civil Engineering); Assoc. M.I.C.E., 1890. Engaged on harbour and railway construction and public works, 1885-97; Engineer to Prison Service, 1897-1906; Inspector Local Government, 1907; Private Secretary to Viceroy of Ireland, 1907-12. *Address* : General Prisons Board, Dublin Castle; Windsor House, Windsor Road, Dublin. (*Died 4 Mar. 1922.*)

GREEN, Rev. Professor Samuel Walter, M.A. (Lond.); Professor of New Testament Exegesis and Criticism, Regent's Park College, New College, and Hackney College (University of London); *b.* Bradford, 1853; *s.* of Rev. S. G. Green, D.D., President of Rawdon College nr. Leeds, and late Editorial Secretary of the Religious Tract Society, London; *m.* 1881, *e. d.* of Charles Hemming, M.D.; one *s.* two *d. Educ.* : University College, London. Graduated M.A. London, 1878; Tutor at Regent's Park College, 1878; Dean of the Faculty of Theology; Representative of the Faculty on the Senate of the University of London. *Publications* : Commentary on St. Mark's Gospel (Westminster New Testament); Lessons in New Testament Greek; The Early Witness to the Four Gospels; minor writings. *Address* : 9 Bellasis Avenue, Streatham Hill, S.W.2. (*Died 12 July 1926.*)

GREEN, Rev. William Spotswood, C.B. 1907; M.A.; J.P. 1917; Govt. Inspector of Irish Fisheries, 1889-1914, and Commissioner of Congested Districts Board for Ireland 1892-1909; *b.* 10 Sep. 1847; *o. c.* of Charles Green of Youghal, Co. Cork, J.P., and Catherine Frances, *d.* of Mr. Fitzsimons; *m.* 1875, *cousin*, Belinda Beatty, *d.* of James Butler of Waterville House, Waterville, Co. Kerry, J.P., and *g.d.* of Roger Green Davis of Dromdiah, Co. Cork, J.P., 1875; one *s.* five *d. Educ.* : Trin. Coll. Dublin; B.A. 1871, M.A. 1874. Ord. 1872; Incumbent Carrigaline, Co. Cork, 1880-89; first to ascend Mount Cook, New Zealand. *Publications* : The High Alps of New Zealand; The Selkirk Glaciers, etc. *Address* : Westcove House, Cahirdaniel, Co. Kerry.

(*Died 22 April 1919.*)

GREENE, Sir (E.) Walter, 1st Bt.; *cr.* 1900; J.P.; D.L.; Hon. Colonel of 3rd Batt. Suffolk Regt.; late Lieut.-Col. (Hon.) Loyal Suffolk Hussars; High Sheriff for Suffolk, 1897; *s.* of Edward Greene, M.P. for Stowmarket Division of Suffolk; 25 years M.P. for Bury St. Edmunds; *b.* 14 Mar. 1842; *m.* 1864, Anne E. (*d.* 1912), *d.* of Rev. C. Royds of Haughton Rectory, Prebendary of Lichfield Cathedral; two *s.* three *d. Educ.* : Rugby. M.P. for Bury St. Edmunds, 1900-6. *Recreations* : hunting; hunted Suffolk Foxhounds, Croome Hounds, and kept harriers and staghounds at own expense; hunted hounds 34 years; shooting, yachting. *Heir* : *s.* Walter Raymond. *Address* : Nether Hall, Bury St. Edmunds. *Clubs* : Carlton, Cavalry; Royal Yacht Squadron, Cowes. (*Died 27 Feb. 1920.*)

GREENE, Gen. Francis Vinton, Major-Gen. U.S. Volunteers in Spanish - American War. *Publications* : The Russian Army and its Campaigns in Turkey; Army Life in Russia; Life of Major - Gen. Nathanael Greene; The Mississippi Campaigns of the Civil War; The Revolutionary War and the Military Policy of the United States; The Present Military Situation in the United States, 1915; Why Europe is at War, 1915; Our First Year in the Great War, 1918; and numerous magazine articles on military and historical subjects. *Address* : 62 East 77th Street, New York City.

(*Died 15 May 1921.*)

GREENE, George Arthur, Litt.D.; F.R.Hist.S.; Author and Lecturer; employed on National work under War Office; *b.* 1853; *e. surv. s.* of late Rev. Henry Greene, and *g.s.* of late Sir Jonas Greene, Recorder of Dublin; *m.* 1885, Mary Dorothea Lucy (*d.* 1914), *d.* of late Rev. Henry Roundell, Vicar of Buckingham; two *s. Educ.* : Florence; Trinity College, Dublin. First in Modern Literature Tripos, with large gold medal; Vice - Chancellor's Prizeman; member of Academic Senate; President and Gold Medallist, University Philosophical Society. Professor of English Literature at Alexandra College, 1877-80; afterwards an Examiner to the Board of Intermediate Education; has been Taylorian Examiner at Oxford; was long Vice-Chairman of the Irish Literary Society. *Publications* : Italian Lyrists of To-day, second edition, 1898; Dantesques, 1903; Songs of the Open Air (verse), 1912; editions of Southey's Life of Nelson, Irving's Life of Columbus; selections from Lamb's Essays of Elia and from Prescott's Peru; editor and part author of the two Books of the Rhymers' Club; has contributed to various miscellanies and periodicals; a novel, The Lost Prima Donna (in collaboration with A. C. Hillier) has appeared in serial form; translated Giacosa's Tristi Amori, acted in America as The Wife of Scarli; The Wartburg, 1907; and several works on art and history from the German. *Recreations* : reading, walking. *Address* : 2 Tanfield Court, Temple, E.C. *Club* : Authors'.

(*Died 12 May 1921.*)

GREENE, H. Barrett ; Editor and Leader-writer Staffordshire Daily and Weekly Sentinel, Stoke - on - Trent, since 1899; *e. s.* of late J. C. Greene, over fifty years on Somerset County Gazette, Taunton; *b.* Bridport, 24 Nov. 1861; married; one *s. Educ.* : Huish's, Taunton; private study and experience. Early training in journalism at Taunton, Wigan, and Sunderland; joined Newcastle Chronicle, 1883; Editor of Newcastle Evening Chronicle for some years; sent many verbatims of W. E. Gladstone, J. Morley, R. Churchill, A. Balfour, and J. Chamberlain to The Times; persistently advocated federation of six Potteries towns into one County Borough (Stoke-on-Trent), leading up to Act of Parliament, 1908, which came into operation March 1910; helped to raise £50,000 for North Staffordshire Infirmary by Sentinel Funds; Hon. Vice-President, North Staffordshire Infirmary; J.P. County Borough of Stoke-on-Trent; Democrat and Imperialist; interested in educational and industrial questions. *Address* : Elmhurst, Wolstanton, Staffs.

(*Died 30 Oct. 1927.*)

GREENFIELD, Brig.-Gen. Richard Menteith, C.B. 1907; Brig.-Gen. General Staff, Ireland; Commander Bombay Brigade, 1905-9; *b.* 27 Dec. 1856; *s.* of James Greenfield of Brynderwen, Monmouth; *m.* 1893, Mary Frances, *d.* of Col. Bateman, I.M.S. *Educ.* : Winchester. Entered army, 1874; Captain R. Inniskilling Fusiliers, 1881; Major, 1890; Lieut.-Col. 1897; Col. 1899; A.A.G. India, 1899-1902; D.A.G. Headquarters, India, 1902-5; served Burma, 1892-93 (despatches, medal with clasp, Brevet Lieut.-Col.); N.W. Frontier, 1897-98 (medal with two clasps). *Address* : Parkgate, Dublin.

(*Died 5 April 1916.*)

GREENFIELD, William Smith, LL.D. Edin.; F.R.S. Edin.; M.D. Lond.; F.R.C.P. Lond. and Edin.; M.R.C.S.; *b.* 9 Jan. 1846.

Educ.: Univ. Coll. London. Emeritus Professor of Pathology and Clinical Medicine, Edinburgh University, 1881-1912 ; Fellow University College, London. *Address:* Muir House, Juniper Green, Midlothian. (*Died 12 Aug. 1919.*)

GREENHILL, Sir George, Kt., *cr.* 1908 ; –M.A. ; *b.* 29 Nov. 1847 ; formerly Professor of Mathematics in the Artillery College, Woolwich. *Publications:* Differential and Integral Calculus with Applications, 1885 ; Applications of the Elliptic Function, 1892 ; Hydrostatics, 1894 ; Notes on Dynamics, 1908 ; Report 19, Theory of a Stream Line with application to an Aeroplane, 1910, 1916 ; Dynamics of Mechanical Flight, 1912 ; Report 146, Gyroscopic Theory, 1914. *Address:* 1 Staple Inn, W.C.1. *Club:* Athenæum. (*Died 10 Feb. 1927.*)

GREENHILL-GARDYNE, Lieut.-Col. Charles ; *b.* 1831 ; *m.* 1858, Hon. Amelia Anne Drummond (*d.* 1912), *d.* of 7th Viscount Strathallan ; two *s.* four *d.* Late Coldstream Guards ; retired, 1868 ; J.P. and D.L. for Argyll and Forfar. *Address:* Finavon, Forfarshire, *T.A.:* Tannadice. *Club:* New, Edinburgh. (*Died 25 Nov. 1923.*)

GREENHOW, William Thomas ; *b.* Newcastle-on-Tyne, 6 Feb. 1831 ; 2nd *s.* of late Thos. Michael Greenhow, M.D., F.R.C.S., of Newcastle-on-Tyne, and subsequently of Leeds ; *m.* Marion, *e. d.* of the late Charles Martineau of London, 1857 ; one *d.* *Educ.:* Proprietary School, Edgbaston ; University College, London (B.A., LL.B.). Barr. 1864 ; joined Northern Circuit and Durham Sessions ; Recorder of Berwick-on-Tweed, 1870-99 ; County Court Judge of Leeds and Wakefield, 1880-1916. *Recreations:* cricket, skating, rowing. *Address:* Warling Dean, Esher, Surrey. *T.:* Esher 154. *T.A.:* Kitcat, Esher. (*Died 30 April 1921.*)

GREENLY, Edward Howorth, J.P., D.L. ; *b.* 1837 ; *o. s.* of Charles Williams Allen (afterwards Greenly) (*d.* 1878), and Frances, *d.* of late Richard Rosser ; *m.* 1869, Sarah Caroline (*d.* 1892), 2nd *d.* of Lt.-Gen. Bowes Forster. *Educ.:* Harrow ; Balliol College, Oxford. M.A. 1863 ; called to Bar, Lincoln's Inn, 1862 ; High Sheriff, Herefordshire, 1881 ; Lord of the Manor of Titley. *Address:* Titley Court, Titley R.S.O., Herefordshire. *Club:* New University. (*Died 1 Mar. 1926.*)

GREENWELL, Sir Walpole Lloyd, 1st Bart. *cr.* 1906 ; J.P. ; *b.* 9 June 1847 ; 2nd *s.* of late Walpole Eyre Greenwell and Eliza Theophila, *d.* and *heiress* of John Morris, Hastings ; *m.* 1873, Kathleen Eugenie, *e. d.* of John Tizard of Radipole, Weymouth ; four *s.* seven *d.* High Sheriff, Surrey, 1903 ; one of H.M. Lieuts., City of London ; Breeder of Pedigree Stock. *Heir:* s. Bernard Eyre [Major Hants Carabineers, Imp. Yeomanry ; *b.* 29 May 1874 ; *m.* 1902, Anna Elizabeth, *e. d.* of Admiral Sir Francis Leopold McClintock, K.C.B. ; one *s.* five *d.* *Educ.:* Harrow ; Trinity Coll. Camb. Served S. African War (Queen's medal, 5 clasps). *Address:* Woodcock Lodge, Little Berkhamsted, Herts. *Club:* Junior Carlton]. *Address:* Marden Park, Godstone, Surrey ; Greenwell, Wolsingham, Co. Durham ; 17 Portman Square, W.1. *T.A.:* Greenwell, Wolsingham. *T.:* Mayfair 1050. *Clubs:* Carlton, Bachelors' ; Royal Yacht Squadron, Cowes. (*Died 24 Oct. 1919.*)

GREENWELL, Rev. Dr. William, M.A. D.C.L., F.R.S., F.S.A., J.P. ; Rector of St. Mary in the South Bailey, Durham ; *b.* Greenwell Ford, Durham, 23 March 1820 ; *e.s.* of late William Thomas Greenwell, J.P., D.L. ; unmarried. *Educ.:* Grammar School and University Coll. Durham. M.A. ; Hon. D.C.L. Durham. Fellow of Univ. Coll. Durham, 1844-54 ; Vicar of Ovingham and Mickley, Northumberland, 1848-50 ; Principal of Neville Hall, Newcastle-on-Tyne, 1852-54 ; Minor Canon of Durham, 1854. *Publications:*

British Barrows, 1877 ; Durham Cathedral 1881 ; Electrum Coinage of Cyzicus, 1887 ; editor of Boldon Buke, 1852 ; Bishop Hatfield's Survey, 1856 ; Wills and Inventories from the Durham Registry, vol. ii. 1859 ; Feodarium Prioratus Dunelmensis, 1872 (all Surtees Society) ; papers in Archæologia, the Journal of the Royal Archæological Institute, the Numismatic Chronicle, Transactions of the Durham and Northumberland Archæological Society, etc. *Recreation:* angling (trout and salmon). *Address:* 27 North Bailey, Durham.
(*Died 27 Jan. 1918.*)

GREENWOOD, Sir G. George, Kt., *cr.* 1916 ; of the Middle Temple ; Barrister-at-law ; M.P. (L.) Peterborough, 1906-Dec. 1918 ; *b.* 3 Jan. 1850 ; 2nd *s.* of late John Greenwood, Q.C., of the Western Circuit, and for many years Solicitor to the Treasury, and late Fanny H. Welch, *d.* of William Collyns of Starcross, Devon ; *m.* 1878, Laurentia Trent, *d.* of the late L.T. Cumberbatch, M.D. ; one *s.* three *d.* *Educ.:* Eton ; Trinity College, Cambridge. Foundation Scholar, 1871 ; first-class in Classical Tripos, 1873 ; called to Bar, 1876 ; joined the Western Circuit ; original member of the Eighty Club previously to the election of 1880 ; contested Peterborough, 1886 ; Central Hull, 1900. *Publications:* The Shakespeare Problem Restated, 1908 ; *In re* Shakespeare, 1909 ; The Vindicators of Shakespeare, 1911 ; Is there a Shakespeare Problem ? 1916 ; Shakespeare's Law, 1920 ; Ben Jonson and Shakespeare, 1921 ; The Shakspere Signatures and Sir Thomas More, 1924 ; The Stratford Bust and the Droeshout Engraving, 1925 ; The Faith of an Agnostic, 1919 ; The Powers and the Turk, 1923. *Address:* 33 Linden Gardens, W.2. *T.:* Park 0237. *Club:* United University. (*Died 27 Oct. 1928.*)

GREENWOOD, Rev. Sydney, Canon of York since 1908. *Educ.:* Magdalene College, Cambridge (Scholar). Priest, 1869 ; Vicar of Wortley, 1880-97. *Address:* The Croft. Kirkby-Wharfe, Tadcaster. (*Died 14 July 1926.*)

GREENWOOD, William, M.P. (U.), Stockport, since 1920 ; Cotton Spinner ; *b.* 1875 ; *s.* of Edmund Greenwood ; *m.* 1900, E. M. (*d.* 1923), *d.* of T. S. Whittaker, Marple, Cheshire. *Address:* House of Commons, S.W. ; 35 Belgrave Road, Oldham. (*Died 12 Aug. 1925.*)

GREER, Rt. Rev. David Hummell, Bishop of New York since 1908 ; *b.* Wheeling, West Virginia, March 20, 1844 ; *s.* of Jacob R. Greer and Elizabeth Armstrong ; *m.* ; two *s.* two *d.* *Educ.:* Washington College, Pennsylvania. In charge of Christ Church, Clarksburg, West Virginia, during Diaconate ; Rector, Trinity Church, Covington, Ky., 1868-71 ; Grace Church, Providence, Rhode Island, 1872-88 ; St. Bartholomew's Church, New York, 1888-1904 ; Bishop-Coadjutor of New York, 1903. *Publications:* The Historic Christ ; Visions ; The Preacher and His Place (Yale Lectures) ; From Things to God. *Address:* Amsterdam Avenue and 110th Street, New York City.
(*Died 13 May 1919.*)

GREER, Sir Francis (Nugent), Kt., *cr.* 1920 ; K.C.B. *cr.* 1923 ; C.B. 1913 ; Third Parliamentary Counsel to the Treasury since 1923 ; *b.* 24 Feb. 1869 ; *s.* of Samuel M'Curdy Greer, County Court Judge, one time M.P. for Co. Londonderry ; *m.* 1897, Mary Elizabeth, *d.* of F. A. Barlow, solicitor ; one *s.* *Educ.:* High School and Trinity College, Dublin. (Scholar, Senior Moderator, Brooke Prizeman) ; Degree, 1891. Auditor College Historical Society, 1893 ; Parliamentary Draftsman, Irish Office, 1908-23 ; called to Bar, Ireland, 1893 ; England, 1912 ; K.C. (Ireland) 1918. *Address:* Arundel House, The Bank, Highgate, N.6. *T.:* Hornsey 876. *Club:* University, Dublin. (*Died 6 Feb. 1925.*)

GREER, Rev. George Samuel, Incumbent of Ballyphilip ; *m.* *Address:* Ballyphilip, Portaferry, Co. Down.

GREER, Joseph, C.M.G. 1900; *b.* Armagh, 6 Aug. 1854; *s.* of late Robert Greer, Armagh; *m.* 1890, Emily, *d.* of late W. Wheeler. *Educ.:* Dundalk; Santry, nr. Dublin. Clerk S.W. Postal District, London, 1878; Chief Officer Sorting Office, S.W.D., London, 1887; Chief Clerk E. District, London, 1889; Chief Clerk S.W. District, London, 1890; Postmaster N. District, London, 1899; Director of Military Postal Services, S. Africa, 1900-1902; Postmaster, E. District, London, 1903-8; Assistant Controller London Postal Service Department, 1908-15. *Decorated* for service in S.A. on postal work. *Recreations:* walking, bowls. *Address:* 41 Dowsett Avenue, Southend-on-Sea.
(Died 16 Jan. 1922.)

GREER, Thomas Macgregor, J.P.; D.L.; retired County Solicitor, Land Agent, etc.; Senator Parliament of Northern Ireland since 1921; *b.* 1853; *s.* of Samuel Macurdy Greer, County Court Judge, one time M.P. for Co. Londonderry, and Marion, *d.* of James McCrone, Crown Agent, Isle of Man; *m.* Margaret Baines, *d.* of Sir Charles Reed, M.P., Chairman London School Board; one *d.* *Educ.:* Coleraine Academical Institution; Trinity College, Dublin, M.A. Admitted Solicitor, 1875; County Solicitor for Antrim, 1900; Delegate for Co. Antrim on Council of Incorporated Law Society of Ireland; Convener of General Assembly's Northern Committee on Tenures and Trusts. *Recreations:* foreign travel; golf. *Address:* Ballycastle, Co. Antrim. *T.:* Ballycastle 31. *M.:* YN 888. *Club:* Ulster, Belfast.
(Died 19 Feb. 1928.)

GREGG, Sir Henry, Kt., *cr.* 1920; *b.* 1859; *m.* 1922, Annie Gladys Samuels. Mayor of Tynemouth, 1913-18; member of Central Organisation for the County. *Address:* Leonie House, Whitley Bay, Northumberland.
(Died 6 Aug. 1928.)

GREGGE-HOPWOOD, Major Edward Byng George, D.S.O. 1915; 1st Batt. Coldstream Guards; *s.* and heir of Edward Robert Gregge-Hopwood; *b.* 24 Dec. 1880. Entered army, 1902; Captain, 1910; served European War, 1914-15 (despatches, Bt. Major, D.S.O.). *Address:* Hopwood Hall, Middleton, Lancs. *(Died July 1917.)*

GREGORIE, Maj.-Gen. Charles Frederick, C.B. 1882; Col. Royal Irish Regiment since 1897; *b.* 25 Nov. 1834; *m.* 1859, Henrietta Amy (*d.* 1904), *d.* of George Lawrence of Moreton, Hereford. Entered army, 1855; Maj.-Gen. 1890; served Indian Mutiny, 1857-58 (medal, two clasps); Egyptian War, 1882 (despatches, C.B., medal, clasp, 3rd class Medjidie, Khedive's star).
(Died 13 April 1918.)

GREGOROWSKI, Hon. Reinhold, Judge of the Supreme Court of South Africa since 1913; *b.* Somerset East, Cape Colony, 1856; *s.* of Rev. R. T. Gregorowski; *m.* Mary Brown; five *c.* *Educ.:* Gill College, Somerset East; Gray's Inn (studentship). Called to Bar, 1878; Advocate, Cape Supreme Court, 1878; Judge of the High Court, Orange Free State, 1881-92; State Attorney, 1892-4; State Attorney and Chief Justice, South African Republic; M.L.A. Pretoria. *Address:* Pretoria. *Club:* Pretoria.
(Died Nov. 1922.)

GREGORY, Hon. Alexander Frederick; *b.* 1843; 4th *s.* of late 3rd Viscount Hood and Mary Isabella, *d.* of late Richard Tibbits; *m.* 1870, Ethel Cecilia (*d.* 1923), *d.* of Algernon C. Heber Percy of Hodnet, Co. Salop; one *s.* two *d.* *Educ.:* Eton. Succeeded his cousin, Major F. Hood Gregory, to Styvechall Estates, 1909, and took the name of Gregory by Royal licence, 1911; Lieut. R.N. and Lieut. 15th Hussars; J.P. E. and W. Ridings, Yorks, and Warwickshire. *Address:* Styvechall Hall, Coventry, Warwickshire. *(Died 20 May 1927.)*

GREGORY, Charles, R.W.S. *Address:* Maisemore, Marlow-on-Thames.
(Died 21 Oct. 1920.)

GREGORY, Rt. Rev. Francis Ambrose, D.D.; *b.* 1848; *s.* of late Very Rev. Robert Gregory, Dean of St. Paul's; *m.* 1924, Mildred, *d.* of late W. H. Peel, Trenant Park, Cornwall. *Educ.:* Corpus Christi College, Oxford, M.A. Ordained, 1873; Curate of Cheam, 1873-74; Warden of St. Paul's College, and S.P.G. Missionary at Ambatoharanana, Madagascar, and Chaplain to Bishop of Madagascar, 1874-1900; Legion of Honour for services with French troops, 1900; Chancellor of Cathedral of St. Laurence, Antananarivo, 1889-1901; Chaplain of St. John's, Mentone, 1901-3; Bishop of Mauritius, 1904-1919. *Publications:* Commentaries and Manuals in Malagasy—Translations. *Address:* Elmside, Northiam, Sussex. *(Died 31 Jan. 1927.)*

GREGORY, Frederick; *b.* near Wakefield, 15 Mar. 1831. *Educ.:* Winterton, Lincolnshire, at the private school of the Vicar. Followed his father and grandfather's occupation, dating two centuries back, as corn merchants at Wakefield, and came to London on his own account in 1854. Late Master of Surrey Staghounds; *Recreation:* golfing. *Address:* Woodlands Road, Earlswood, Surrey. *T.:* Redhill 96. *Clubs:* Overseas; New, Brighton.
(Died Aug. 1919.)

GREGORY, George Frederick, Supreme Court Judge, New Brunswick, since 1900, and Judge of the Court of Divorce and Matrimonial Causes since 1901; *b.* Fredericton, New Brunswick, 31 Aug. 1839; *s.* of John Gregory, originally of Edinburgh, Scotland, clerk assistant Leg. Council of N.B., and Mary, *d.* of Samuel Grosvenor of Fredericton; *m.* 1st, 1860, Marion (*d.* 1871), *d.* of Francis Beverly of Fredericton, stationer; 2nd, 1879, Isabella, widow of C. J. Davis of Fredericton, druggist. *Educ.:* Collegiate School and King's College, Fredericton. Admitted Bar of N.B., 1865; elected and served as Mayor of Fredericton, 1869-73, and 1878-81; Q.C., Bar of Canada, 1891; Presbyterian. *Address:* Fredericton, New Brunswick.

GREGORY, Sir Philip Spencer, Kt., *cr.* 1913; barrister; one of the Conveyancing Counsel to the Supreme Court since 1902; *b.* 2 Feb. 1851; *y. s.* of late John Gregory, Governor of the Bahamas; *m.* 1876, Edith Anne, *d.* of late Rev. Edward James, Rector of Hindringham, Norfolk; one *s.* *Educ.:* Eton; King's College, Cambridge (Scholar). B.A. 1873, 10th Wrangler and 2nd Class Classical Tripos; Fellow of King's College, 1873-77; M.A. 1876; called to Bar, Lincoln's Inn, 1875; Bencher, 1907; Additional Member of the General Council of the Bar; Member of the Royal Commission on the Land Transfer Acts, 1908; Member of the Rule Committee under the Land Transfer Acts. *Address:* 9 Lowndes Square, S.W.; 1 New Square, Lincoln's Inn, E.C. *Club:* Athenæum.
(Died 28 Oct. 1918.)

GREGORY, Reginald Philip; Fellow since 1904 and Tutor since 1912, St. John's College, Cambridge, University Lecturer in Botany since 1907; *b.* 7 June 1879; *s.* of Arthur Gregory of Trowbridge, Wilts; *m.* 1908, Joan Laidlay, *d.* of T. G. Bisdee, Hutton Court, Weston-super-Mare; three *d.* *Educ.:* St. John's College, Cambridge; Walsingham medal, 1904; University Demonstrator in Botany, 1902-7; 2nd. Lieut. the Gloucestershire Regiment. *Publications:* papers on genetics and cytology in various scientific publications. *Recreations:* golf and other games. *Address:* 7 Harvey Road, Cambridge. *T.:* Cambridge 959.
(Died 24 Nov. 1918.)

GREGSON, Ven. Francis Sitwell Knight, M.A. Oxon.; Rector of Steeple Aston, Oxfordshire, since 1918. Ordained, 1888;

Curate of Christ Church, Gateshead, 1888-95; Vicar of All Hallows, Leeds, 1895-1903; Vicar of St. Thomas's, Durban, 1903-14; Archdeacon of Durban and Canon of St. Saviour's Cathedral, Pietermaritzburg, 1908-14; Vicar of All Souls, Leeds, 1914-18. *Address:* Steeple Aston Rectory, Oxford. *(Died 26 May 1926.)*

GREIG, Capt. Ronald Henry, D.S.O. 1900; R.E.; *b.* 4 April 1876; *s.* of Lt.-Col. B. R. Greig, and 2nd *d.* of late Sir J. D. Sibbald Scott, 3rd Bt. of Dunninald; *m.* 1909, Mary Hope Letitia, *d.* of Mr. and Mrs. Clutterbuck of Hardenhuish Park; one *s.* one *d.* Entered army, 1896; served South Africa, 1899-1902 (severely wounded, despatches, Queen's medal, 4 clasps, King's medal, 2 clasps, D.S.O.). *Address:* Woolmer Lodge, E. Liss, Hants.
(Died 27 Aug. 1916.)

GRENFELL, 1st Baron of Kilvey (*cr.* 1902), Francis Wallace Grenfell; P.C., G.C.B., G.C.M.G., F.S.A.; Hon. LL.D., Cambridge and Edinburgh; Field Marshal, 1908; Colonel 1st Life Guards and King's Royal Rifles; *b.* 29 April 1841; *s.* of P. St. L. Grenfell, J.P., and Madelena Du Pré; *m.* 1st, 1887, Evelyn (*d.* 1899), *d.* of General Robert Wood, C.B.; 2nd, 1903, Hon. Aline (*d.* 1911), *o. d.* of late Lewis A. Majendie of Hedingham Castle, Essex; two *s.* one *d.* Entered 60th Rifles, 1859; served in Kaffir War, 1878; Zulu War, 1879; Q.M.G. in Transvaal, 1881-82; Egyptian Expedition, 1882; Nile Expedition, 1884; Sirdar Egyptian Army, 1885-92; commanded Forces, Suakim, 1889; at Toski, 1889; Inspector-General of Auxiliary Forces, War Office, 1894-97; Inspector General of Recruiting, 1896; commanded the forces in Egypt, 1897-98; Governor and Commander-in-Chief of Malta, 1899-1903; commanded 4th Army Corps, 1903-4; Commander-in-Chief in Ireland, 1904-8. *Heir: s.* Hon. Pascoe Christian Victor Francis Grenfell, *b.* 12 Dec. 1905. *Address:* Foresters, Windlesham, Surrey. *Club:* Army and Navy, Travellers'. *(Died 27 Jan. 1925.)*

GRENFELL, Bernard Pyne, D.Litt., M.A.; Hon. Litt.D. (Dublin); Hon. Ph.D. (Koenigsberg); Hon. D. Jur. (Graz); late Fellow of Queen's College, Oxford; Fellow of the British Academy; Drexel Medallist of the University of Pennsylvania, 1903; Socio delle reale Academia dei Lincei, Rome; Corresponding Member of the Munich Academy of Sciences; Professor of Papyrology, Oxford, since 1916; *b.* Birmingham, 16 Dec. 1869; *e. s.* of late John Granville Grenfell, Master at Clifton College. *Educ.:* Clifton College; Queen's College, Oxford. Craven Fellow in the University of Oxford, 1894-95; Fellow of Queen's College, 1894; engaged in the discovery and editing of Greek Papyri since 1894. *Publications:* The Revenue Laws of Ptolemy Philadelphus; An Alexandrian Erotic Fragment and other Greek Papyri; and, in collaboration with A. S. Hunt, New Classical Fragments and other Greek and Latin Papyri; Sayings of Our Lord from an Early Greek Papyrus; New Sayings of Jesus and Fragment of a Lost Gospel; The Geneva Fragment of Menander; The Oxyrhynchus Papyri; The Amherst Papyri; Fayûm Towns and their Papyri; The Tebtunis Papyri; Greek Papyri in the Cairo Museum; Hellenica Oxyrhynchia; The Hibeh Papyri. *Recreation:* travelling. *Address:* Queen's College, Oxford. *Club:* Athenæum.
(Died 17 April 1926.)

GRENFELL, Lt.-Col. Cecil A.; *s.* of Pascoe du Pre Grenfell; *m.* Lady Lilian Spencer-Churchill, sister of 9th Duke of Marlborough; two *d. Educ.:* Eton. Member of Stock Exchange; served as Capt., South African War; Col. of Bucks Yeomanry; Member of Bucks Territorial Association and Political Council City Liberal Club; M.P. (L.) S.E. Cornwall, 1910; served European War (despatches). *Recreations:* hunting, polo, golf, rode Father o' Flynn in

436

Grand National Steeplechase, 1896. *Address:* 4 Great Cumberland Place, W.1. *T.:* Paddington 856. *Clubs:* Turf, Garrick.
(Died 11 Aug. 1924.)

GRENFELL, Charles Seymour, Banker; *b.* Carshalton Park, Surrey, 14 Sept. 1839; *s.* of late Riversdale Grenfell of Ray Lodge, Maidenhead; *m.* 1862, Elizabeth Graham; one *s.* three *d.* Bucks Yeomanry for many years as Captain; for over 30 years a partner in the firm of Pascoe, Grenfell and Sons; is sub-Governor of the Royal Exchange Assurance Corporation, and Director of the London and County Bank. *Recreations:* hunting, shooting, and fishing; now only a bicyclist and golfer. *Heir: s.* Riversdale Grenfell, Welwyn Hall, Herts. *Address:* Elibank, Taplow, Bucks. *Club:* Arthur's.
(Died 11 Jan. 1924.)

GRENIER, Gerard, I.S.O. 1905; Registrar of Superior Court, Ceylon; retired, 1906.
(Died Feb. 1917.)

GRENIER, Gustave, I.S.O., J.P.; Clerk of the Executive Council, Province of Quebec, since 1886; and Deputy Lieutenant-Governor for signing warrants; *b.* Montreal, June 1847; *m.* 1st, 1879, Kate Winifred Heatley of Quebec (*d.* 1880); 2nd, 1889, Helen, *d.* of late Hon. F. A. G. Marchand, Premier of the Province; one *s.* three *d. Educ.:* Toronto and Quebec. Entered Civil Service of Province, 1867, as a junior clerk in the Executive Council Dept. *Address:* 89 Berthelot Street, Quebec. *T.A.:* Quebec, Canada. *T.:* 1022.

GRENIER, Joseph Richard, late a Judge of the Supreme Court of Ceylon, Barrister-at-law, Gray's Inn; *b.* 4 July, 1852; *s.* of F. C. Grenier and Matilda Aldons. French by descent; *m.* Lydia, *d.* of John Drieberg; six *s.* three *d. Educ.:* St. Thomas' College; admitted an Advocate of the Supreme Court, 1873; Commissioner of Assize on several occasions; acted twice as H.M.'s Solicitor-General; permanent District Judge of Colombo, 1903; a Puisne Justice of the Supreme Court, 1910; retired on attaining the age limit of 60, 1912; K.C. 1913; now a leader of the Ceylon Bar; President Y.M.C.A. of Ceylon. *Recreations:* fishing and shooting. *Address:* Meadowsweet, Barnes Place, Colombo. *(Died June 1926.)*

GRENSTED, Rev. Frederic Finnis, Vicar of Melling, nr. Liverpool, since 1912; Diocesan Inspector of Religious Education for Diocese of Liverpool since 1895; Hon. Canon of Liverpool, 1908; *b.* Maidstone, 14 Dec. 1857; *s.* of William and Julia Theresa Grensted; *m.* 1884, Gertrude Ellen, *y. d.* of Alexander Plimpton of Spring House, Merton, Surrey; one *s.* one *d. Educ.:* Maidstone Grammar School (Lubbock Scholar); University College, Oxford (Gunsley Exhibitioner). First-Class Honours in Natural Science; ordained 1883; Curate of St. Nicholas, Blundellsands, 1888-90; Second Master of Merchant Taylors' School, Great Crosby, 1883-95. *Publications:* A few scientific papers, Liverpool Geological Society, etc.; article in Hibbert Journal, Timelessness of the Eternal, Jan. 1907; and in the Interpreter, Rev. xii., Oct. 1911; articles in The Prayer Book Dictionary, 1912, on The Calendar, The Punctuation of the Prayer Book, etc. *Address:* Melling Vicarage, Liverpool. *T.A.:* Melling Maghull.
(Died Feb. 1919.)

GRESLEY, Rear-Adm. Richard Nigel, *b.* 3 Mar. 1850; *e. s.* of late Major F. Gresley; *m.* 1892, Ruth Slingsby (*d.* 1925), *d.* of G. Peirse-Duncombe; one *d.* Retired list, 1902; Rear-Adm. 1905. *Address:* Drakelow, Compton, Winchester. *Club:* Naval and Military.
(Died 11 Sept. 1928.)

GRESSON, Lt.-Col. Thomas Tinning, D.S.O. 1900; York and Lancaster Regiment; *b.* 29 April 1870; *s.* of Major W. H. Gresson. Entered army, 1889; Captain, 1899; Adjutant,

Dec. 1896 to June 1901; special service South Africa, Nov. 1899 to Feb. 1900; rejoined Batt. as Adjutant; Feb. 1900; served with 5th Division M.I. (despatches twice, Queen's medal, 6 clasps, King's medal, 2 clasps, D.S.O.). *Club:* Army and Navy. *(Died 1921.)*

GRESWELL, Rev. William Henry Parr, M.A., F.R.G.S.; Rector of Dodington, Somerset, 1888-1913; *e. s.* of Rev William Parr Greswell, late Fellow of Balliol Coll. Oxford and Rector of Kilve, Somerset; *m.* 1895, Blanche Caroline Annie, *y. d.* of late Coventry Carew of Crowcombe, Somerset. *Educ.:* Somersetshire College, Bath; Brasenose College, Oxford. Classical Scholar and Hulme Exhibitioner; 2nd class Moderations (Classical); 3rd class Greats (Classical). Lecturer of Classics and English Literature under the Higher Education Act of the Cape Legislature, 1876-84; Secretary Coleridge Cottage Fund, 1893-1908. *Publications:* Our South African Empire, 1885; Imperial Federation, 1887; A History of the Canadian Dominion, 1890; A Geography of the Canadian Dominion, 1891; A Geography of Africa South of the Zambesi, 1892; The British Colonies and their Industries, 1893; Outlines of British Colonisation, 1893; The Growth and Administration of the British Colonies, 1897; The Land of Quantock, 1903; The Forests and Deerparks of Somerset, 1905; Chapters on Glastonbury Abbey, 1909. *Recreations:* cricket, ornithology. *Address:* Martlet House, Minehead. *(Died 19 Jan. 1923.)*

GRETTON, Major Frederic, Director of Bass & Co.; *s.* of the late John Gretton; unmarried. *Educ.:* Home. *Recreations:* hunting, racing, shooting, and yachting. *Address:* Egginton Hall, Derby. *Clubs:* Marlborough, Boodle's; Royal Yacht Squadron, Cowes. *(Died 19 July 1928.)*

GREVILLE, Hon. Sir Sidney Robert, C.B. 1899; K.C.V.O., *cr.* 1912; C.V.O. 1901; Groom-in-Waiting to H.M. since 1920; *b.* Warwick Castle, 16 Nov. 1866; 4th *s.* of 4th Earl of Warwick and Lady Ann Charteris, *d.* of 8th Earl of Wemyss and March. *Educ.:* Marlborough. Assistant Private Sec. to Sir John Gorst as Under-Secretary for India, 1887; Private Sec. to Marquess of Salisbury as Prime Minister, 1888-92, 1896-98, 1900-1. Equerry to Prince of Wales, 1898-1901; Groom-in-Waiting to King Edward VII.; Private Sec. to H.M. Queen Alexandra, 1901-10; Paymaster to H.M.'s Household, 1911-15; Comptroller and Treasurer to H.R.H. the Prince of Wales, 1915-20; Groom-in-Waiting to King George V. till 1911 and since 1920. *Address:* St. James's Palace, S.W.1. *T.:* Gerrard 6226. *Clubs:* Carlton, Marlborough, Bachelors'. *(Died 12 June 1927.)*

GREY, 4th Earl (*cr.* 1806), **Rt. Hon. Albert Henry George Grey**, P.C. 1908; G.C.B., *cr.* 1911; G.C.M.G., *cr.* 1904; G.C.V.O., *cr.* 1908; LL.M., J.P.; Bt. 1746; Baron Grey, 1801; Viscount Howick, 1806; *b.* 28 Nov. 1851; *s.* of General Hon. Charles Grey and Caroline, *d.* of Sir Thomas Harvie Farquhar, Bt.; *S. u.* 1894; *m.* Alice, 3rd *d.* of Robert Stayner Holford, M.P., Westonbirt, Gloucestershire, 1877; one *s.* two *d. Educ.:* Harrow; Trin. Coll. Camb. (Senior in Law and History Tripos, 1873); M.P. (L.) S. Northumberland, 1880-85; Administrator of Rhodesia, 1896-97; Director of British South Africa Company, 1898-1904; Governor-General and Commander-in-Chief of Canada, 1904-11; Lord-Lieutenant of Northumberland, 1899-1904; Chancellor of the Order of St. Michael and St. George since 1916. *Publication:* Hubert Hervey, a Memoir, 1899. Owns about 17,600 acres. *Heir:* Viscount Howick. *Address:* 22 South Street, Park Lane, W.; Howick House, Lesbury, Northumberland. *Club:* Brooks's. *(Died 29 Aug. 1917.)*

GREY, Viscountess (Pamela), *y. d.* of late Hon. Percy Wyndham; *m.* 1st, 1895, 1st Baron Glenconner (*d.* 1920); three *s.* one *d.* 2nd, 1922, Viscount Grey. Fellow of the Royal Society of Literature. *Publications:* The Earthen Vessel, The Sayings of the Children; Shepherds' Crowns, 1923; Edward Wyndham Tennant, 4th Grenadier Guards, and other books. *Address:* Mulberry House, 37 Smith Square, S.W.1; *T.:* Victoria 0961; Wilsford Manor, Salisbury; Fallodon Hall, Christen Bank, Northumberland. *(Died 18 Nov. 1928.)*

GREY, Colonel Arthur, C.I.E. 1910; V.D.; *b.* 1855; *s.* of late Col. Francis D. Grey, *g. s.* of late Rt. Rev. Hon. Edward Grey, Bishop of Hereford; *m.* 1907, Teresa Mary, *d.* of Rev. A. Alleyne; four *s.* one *d. Educ.:* Wellington; New College, Oxford. Barrister Inner Temple, 1886; sometime President Punjab Chief Court Bar Association, and practising before the Judicial Committee of the Privy Council; raised the Punjab Light Horse, 1893, which he commanded until retirement, 1912; commanded Volunteer Cavalry at Delhi Durbar, 1902, and at H.M. Coronation, 1911; special appointment War Office, 1915. *Address:* 1 Essex Court, Temple, E.C.4. *T.:* Temple 1304; Richmond 522. *M.:* EK 90. *Clubs:* St. Stephen's, Royal Automobile. *(Died 13 Oct. 1924.)*

GREY, Rev. Harry George, M.A.; *b.* 1 Oct. 1851; 2nd *s.* of Adm. Hon. George Grey and Jane Frances, *d.* of Gen. Hon. Sir Patrick Stuart. *Educ.:* Wadham Coll. Oxford (3rd class Mods., 2nd class Lit. Hum.); ordained 1874; Curate of St. Giles in the Fields, 1874-77; Vicar of Holy Trinity, Oxford, 1877-85; Curate of St. James's, Clapham Park, 1885; C.M.S. Missionary, Quetta, Panjab, India, 1887-1900; Principal of Wycliffe Hall, Oxford, 1900-5; Examining Chaplain to Bishop of Liverpool, 1900-1905; returned to India, 1905-9; Principal Wycliffe Hall, Oxford, 1910-18; Resigned. *Address:* 17 New Inn Hall Street, Oxford. *(Died 22 Jan. 1925.)*

GREY, Colonel Leopold John Herbert, C.S.I. 1877; *b.* 1 July 1840; *s.* of late L. J. H. Grey, and *g.s.* of late Rt. Rev. Hon. Edward Grey, Bishop of Hereford; *m.* 1864, Josephine Catherine, *d.* of General H. C. van Cortlandt, C.B. *Educ.:* Cheltenham College. Served through the Mutiny and on the North-West Frontier, 1857-62; Bhutan Campaign, 1865-66, as political officer with Eastern Column; Superintendent Bahawalpur State, 1871-78, 1877-79, 1899-1903; Commissioner Hissar Division, 1882; retired, 1894. *Publications:* A Manual of the Construction and Management of Canals, 1884; The India of the Future, 1907.

GREY, Major Robin, D.S.O.; 2nd Bn. Grenadier Guards; *b.* 28 June 1874; *s.* of Sir William Grey, K.C.S.I., late Governor of Bengal and Jamaica; unmarried. *Educ.:* Harrow. Was A.D.C. to Sir Trevor Plowden in India; served Mateleland campaign, 1896; Secretary to Lord Beresford, 1898-1900; served South African War; Unionist Candidate for the Bishop Auckland Division, 1911-13; seconded for service with the R.F.C. 1913; flew to France on outbreak of war as 2nd in command 5th Squadron R.F.C.; Chevalier de la Legion d'Honneur at the end of the retreat; later taken prisoner; after the Armistice went to Archangel; became C.R.A.F. in North Russia (D.S.O., despatches twice). *Recreations:* travelled much in America, China, Japan, India, Africa, and Europe. *Clubs:* Guards', Travellers', 1900. *(Died 15 May 1922.)*

GREY-WILSON, Sir William, K.C.M.G., *cr.* 1904; K.B.E., *cr.* 1918; Commander of the Star of Roumania, 1921; *b.* Kent, 7 Apr. 1852; *y. s.* of late Andrew Wilson, Inspector-Gen. of Hosps., H.E.I. Company, and Charlotte, *g. d.* of 1st Earl Grey; *m.* 1884, Margaret, *o. d.* of

437

Robert Glasgow Brown, of Broadstone, Ayrshire; two *s.* one *d.* *Educ.:* Cheltenham Coll.; France. Private Secretary to Sir William Grey, Governor of Jamaica, 1874; to Sir Frederick Barlee, 1877; Clerk of the Executive and Legislative Councils, British Honduras, 1878; Magistrate in command of scouts on Mexican Frontier, 1879; Special Commissioner to take over territory between Sierra Leone and Liberia, West Africa; Assist. Colonial Secretary, Gold Coast, 1884; Colonial Secretary, St. Helena, 1886; Governor, 1887-97; Governor, Falkland Isles, 1897-1904; Governor of the Bahamas, 1904-12; Chairman The Central Committee For National Patriotic Organisations; Chairman Institute of Patentees (incorporated) and Past President. *Address:* 188 Cromwell Road, S.W.5. *Recreations:* riding, mechanics. *Club:* Junior Carlton.
(Died 14 Feb. 1926.)

GRIBBLE, George James, J.P.; *b.* 1846; *s.* of Thomas Gribble; *m.* 1881, Norah (*d.* 1923), *d.* of Rev. F. C. Royds, Rector of Coddington and Hon. Canon of Chester; two *s.* three *d.* *Educ.:* Harrow. High Sheriff of Bedfordshire, 1897. *Recreation:* yachting. *Address:* 34 Eaton Square, S.W.1; Kingston Russell House, Dorset. *T.:* Vict. 7214. *Clubs:* Junior Carlton, Burlington Fine Arts; Royal Yacht Squadron, Cowes. *(Died 16 June 1927.)*

GRICE, Col. Walter Thomas, V.D., F.C.S., C.I.E. 1915; late Colonel Commanding 1st Batt. Calcutta Volunteer Rifles and 5th Battalion Indian Defence Force; Member Legislative Council, Bengal, 1914-16; *b.* 11 Sept. 1868; 3rd *s.* of late William Grice, Yardley, Birmingham; *m.* 1908, Helen, 2nd *d.* of Archibald Symington, J.P., Allanton, Auldgirth, Dumfriesshire; one *s.* *Educ.:* Solihull Grammar School; Mason's College, Birmingham. Hon. A.D.C. to Viceroy of India, 1912-17; to Commander-in-chief, 1918-19. *Address:* The Coppice, Cookham Dean, Maidenhead. *T.:* 1Y3 Marlow. *M.:* SM 1806. *Clubs:* Junior Constitutional, Royal Automobile.
(Died 28 Feb. 1926.)

GRIEP, Louis Monro, R.B.A.; Principal of St. Ives School of Landscape and Marine Painting; *b.* Melbourne, Australia, 1864; *s.* of Dr. Charles Grier and Maria Agnes Monro of Craiglochart. *Educ.:* Upper Canada College, Toronto; King's College School, London. Was a banker in Canada; returned to England to devote himself to Art; has visited many countries and voyaged round the world; has exhibited in principal European Galleries; Medal at Paris Salon for The Night Watch, 1891. *Address:* The Foc'sle, St. Ives, Cornwall. *Club:* St. Ives Arts.
(Died 24 Oct. 1920.)

GRIERSON, Francis; musician and author of books on philosophy, art, and literature; *b.* Birkenhead, Cheshire, 1848. Began musical career in Paris, 1869, under the patronage of Auber, Director of the Conservatoire; gave improvisational piano recitals in all the principal cities and at the Courts of Continental Europe for many years before turning his attention to literature; has made long sojourns in France, Russia, Germany, Austria, and Italy; studied political economy and psychology in Berlin and Paris; made exhaustive art studies in the principal galleries of the world; lectured at leading clubs and universities in the United States; has contributed critical articles to La Nouvelle Revue and La Nouvelle Revue Internationale, of Paris; the English Review, the Nation, Westminster Review, the New Age, Oxford and Cambridge Review, Atlantic Monthly, Century Magazine, Washington Herald, New York Tribune, Philadelphia Ledger. *Publications:* La Revolte Idealiste, Paris, 1889; Modern Mysticism, London, 1899; The Celtic Temperament, 1901; The Valley of Shadows, 1909; Parisian Portraits, 1910; La Vie et les Hommes, Paris, 1911; The Humour of

the Underman, London, 1911; The Invincible Alliance, 1913; Illusions and Realities of the World War, 1918; Abraham Lincoln, 1919. *Recreations:* walking and nature studies. *Address:* Los Angeles, California.
(Died 29 May 1927.)

GRIERSON, James Cullen, J.P.; *e. s.* of late Andrew John Grierson and Alice, *d.* of Herbert John Clifford; *b.* 1863; *m.* 1895, Alice Stanley, *d.* of late Henry Peake of Westholme, Sleaford; three *s.* two *d.* Convener of Shetland; Captain, Shetland Companies, Gordon Highlanders; Member of Committee to enquire into adequacy of Medical Relief in Highlands and Islands of Scotland, 1912. *Address:* Quendale House, Lerwick, N.B.
(Died 1919.)

GRIERSON, Sir Philip James Hamilton-; Kt., *cr.* 1910; LL.D. Edin.; J.P.; Solicitor for Scotland to the Board of Inland Revenue, 1892, till retirement in 1919; *b.* 9 March 1851; *o. s. c.* of late John Hamilton, Chartered Accountant, Edinburgh, took the name of Grierson in 1879 on succeeding to his uncle, James Grierson of Dalgoner, Dumfriesshire; *m.* 1881, Lilias, *d.* of late Deputy Surg.-Gen. James Kirkpatrick; one *s.* two *d.* *Educ.:* Cheltenham College; Oxford University. B.A. 1876. Called to Scots Bar, 1880; Sheriff-Substitute of Aberdeen, Kincardine, and Banff, 1887; removed to Aberdeen, 1890. *Publications:* Has contributed frequently to current literature; has edited and is author of several law books; also The Silent Trade, a contribution to the Early History of Human Intercourse, 1903, and several articles in Hastings' Encyclopedia of Religion and Ethics. *Address:* 7 Palmerston Place, Edinburgh. *Club:* New, Edinburgh. *(Died 25 April 1927.)*

GRIEVE, Hon. Walter Baine, C.B.E. 1918; O.B.E. 1918; M.L.C. Newfoundland; Merchant and Shipowner; *b.* 1850; *s.* of James Johnston Grieve, formerly M.P. for Greenock; *m.* 1880, Helen Marion, *d.* of Henry Stone, Ryde, Isle of Wight; one *s.* *Educ.:* St. Andrew's; Glasgow Univ. Liberal; Church of England. *Recreations:* fishing and golf. *Address:* Musgrave Terrace, St. John's, Newfoundland. *T.A.:* Baine St. John's. *T.:* 43. *M.:* M 363, Motor Association. *Clubs:* Devonshire; City, St. John's; Greenock, Greenock. *(Died 3 Feb. 1921.)*

GRIFFIN, Lieut.-Col. Cecil Pender Griffith, D.S.O. 1900; I.S.C., 1st (D.Y.O.) Lancers; *b.* 22 Jan. 1864; *s.* of late Col. Griffin, commanding 45th Regiment; *m.* 1893, Annie, *o. d.* of E. Janes, Plymouth; one *d.* *Educ.:* Wellington College; R.M.C., Sandhurst. Served Frontier, India, 1898 (medal and 2 clasps); China, 1901 (despatches, D.S.O.); retired, 1912; European War, 1914-16 (wounded). Granted silver medal Royal Humane Society, 1893. *Address:* Berridon Hall, Bradworthy, N. Devon. *Club:* Cavalry. *(Died 2 April 1922.)*

GRIFFIN, Charles Thomas, I.S.O. 1911; late Assistant Principal Civil Medical Officer and Inspector-General of Hospitals, Island or Ceylon; *m.* Katherine Agnes Iago-Lucas (*d.* 1913). *Club:* Badminton. *(Died 15 Dec. 1923.)*

GRIFFIN, Lt.-Gen. Edward Christian, Colonel Commandant, Royal Artillery; *b.* 2 June 1836. Entered army, 1854; Lieut.-General, 1895; unemployed list, 1895; served Indian Mutiny, 1857-58 (despatches twice, medal).
(Died 6 May 1917.)

GRIFFIN, Martin Joseph, LL.D., C.M.G. 1907; Parliamentary Librarian, Ottawa, since 1885; *b.* St. John's, 7 Aug. 1847; *m.* 1872, Harriet, *d.* of late D. Starratt, Liverpool, N.S. *Educ.:* St. Mary's College, Halifax. Called to Bar, 1868; Conservative candidate for Legislature, 1874; Editor of The Express, 1868-74; Secretary and Assistant to Counsel for Fisheries, 1873; Secretary to Civil Service Commission,

1880 ; Editor Toronto Mail, 1878-85 ; Roman Catholic. *Publications* : many articles to magazines. *Address* : 319 Daly Avenue, Ottawa.
(Died Mar. 1921.)

GRIFFIS, Rev. William Elliot, A.M., D.D.; L.H.D.; President of the De Witt Historical Society ; Dudleian Lecturer at Harvard and on Missions at Yale University ; Preacher at Yale, Chicago, Pennsylvania and Cornell University ; *b.* Philadelphia, 17 Sep. 1843 ; 2nd *s.* of late Capt. John L. Griffis ; *m.* 1st, Katharine Lyra (*d.* 1898), *d.* of late Prof. B. I. Stanton, Union College, Schenectady, N.Y.; 2nd, Frances King, *d.* of late Don King of Pulaski, N.Y. ; two *s.* one *d. Educ.* : Philadelphia public schools ; Rutger's College ; Union Theological Seminary. Served in 44th Pennsylvania Volunteer Militia during Gettysburg Campaign, 1863 ; in service of Japanese Government organising schools according to American methods, 1870-74 ; the only white man living who at a daimio's capital saw the feudal system in full operation ; Order of Rising Sun, 1908 ; active pastor in Schenectady, Boston, and Ithaca, 1877-1903 ; has been eleven times in Europe ; has made nine preaching tours in Great Britain. *Publications* : The Mikado's Empire, 1876, 12th ed. 1912 ; Japanese Fairy World, 1880 ; Corea, the Hermit Nation, 1882, 9th ed. 1911 ; Matthew Calbraith Perry, 1887 ; The Lily Among Thorns, 1889 ; Sir William Johnson ; Japan in History, Folk-lore and Art, new ed. 1906 ; Brave Little Holland and What She Taught Us ; The Religions of Japan ; Townsend Harris, First American Envoy in Japan ; The Romance of Discovery ; Motley's Dutch Nation, 2nd ed. 1908 ; Romance of American Colonisation ; The Pilgrims in their Three Homes, 2nd ed. 1910 ; America in the East ; Romance of Conquest ; The American in Holland ; Verbeck of Japan, 1900 ; In the Mikado's Service, 1901 ; A Maker of the New Orient ; Sunny Memories of Three Pastorates, 1903 ; Youth's History of Holland, 1902 ; Dux Christus, 1904 ; Christ the Creator of the New Japan, 1907 ; The Japanese Nation in Evolution, 2nd ed. 1911 ; The Fire-Fly's Lovers and other Fairy Tales of Old Japan, 1908 ; The Story of New Netherland, 1909 ; China's Story, 1911 ; The Unmannerly Tiger and other Korean Fairy Stories, 1911 ; Belgium : The Land of Art ; second edition, revised and enlarged, 1916 ; A Modern Pioneer in Korea ; The Call of Jesus to Joy, 1912 ; Mighty England ; Hepburn of Japan ; The House We Live In, 1914 ; Japan and America : A Chronicle of Friendship, 1914 ; Millard Fillmore, Constructive Statesman, 1915 ; The Mikado, Institution and Person, 1915 ; Bonnie Scotland and What We Owe Her, 1916 ; Dutch Fairy Tales, 1917 ; Belgian Fairy Tales, 1919 ; Swiss Fairy Tales, 1920 ; Young People's History of the Pilgrims, 1920 ; Welsh Fairy Tales, 1921 ; (with H. D. Sawyer) The Pilgrim and Puritan Fathers of New England, 1922 ; (with H. de H. Scheffer) History of the Free Churchmen in the Dutch Republic, 1581-1701, 1922 ; Korean Fairy Tales, 1922 ; Japanese Fairy Tales, 1923 ; The Story of the Walloons, 1923 ; Japanese Proverbs, 1924 ; Jesus : of the International Mind, 1925 ; Things Borrowed from Japan ; Why Americans should visit Holland, 1926 ; The Stripes and Stars, a History of the American Flag, 1926. *Recreations* : lecturing, pedestrianism, Japanese art, collects monographs on Japan, Pilgrim history, Dutch prints of American interest. *Address* : Pulaski, N.Y.
(Died Feb. 1928.)

GRIFFITH, Arthur, M.P. (S. Fein) East Cavan since 1918 ; *b.* Dublin, 1872 ; *s.* of Arthur Griffith, printer. *Educ.* : Christian Brothers School, Dublin. Founder and first editor of Sinn Fein, 1906-15 ; Editor of Nationality since 1916. *Address* : 6 Harcourt Street, Dublin. *(Died 12 Aug. 1922.)*

GRIFFITH, Rev. David, Prebendary of St. David's. *Address* : Clyro Vicarage, Hereford.

GRIFFITH, Rt. Hon. Sir Ellis Jones Ellis-, 1st Bt., *cr.* 1918 ; P.C. 1914 ; K.C. 1910 ; Under-Secretary of State, Home Department, 1912 - 15 ; M.P. (G.L.) Anglesey, 1895 - 1918 ; (L.) Carmarthen Division, 1923-24 ; *b.* 1860 ; *s.* of T. M. Griffith, Anglesey ; *m.* Mary, *d.* of Rev. R. Owen, Mold. *Educ.* : University Coll. of Wales, Aberystwyth ; Downing College Cambridge (late Fellow and now Hon. Fellow). President of the Union, 1886 ; Barr. 1887 ; contested Toxteth Division Liverpool, 1892 ; Recorder of Birkenhead, 1907-1912. *Heir* : *s.* Elis Arundell Ellis-Griffith, *b.* 15 Sep. 1896. *Address* : New Court, Middle Temple, E.C.4 ; (Chambers) 3 (North) King's Bench Walk, Temple, E.C.4 ; *T.* : Central 2552 ; Towyn Capel, Trearddur Bay, Anglesey. *Clubs* . Athenæum, National Liberal. *(Died 30 Nov. 1926.)*

GRIFFITH, Lt.-Col. George Richard, D.S.O. 1896 ; late Principal Vet. Officer, Egypt. army ; *b.* 5 July 1857 ; *m.* 1909, Alice Maud, *e.* *d.* of Rev. G. D. Redpath, of Harbledown. Entered army Veterinary Department 1880 ; Maj. 1900 ; served Egyptian War, 1882 (medal with clasp, Khedive's star) ; Nile Expedition, 1884-85 (clasp) ; Suakim, 1888 (clasp) ; capture of Tokar, 1891 (4th class Osmanie, clasp, Khedive's star) ; Dongola, 1896 (despatches, D.S.O., British medal, Khedive's medal with two clasps) ; Soudan, 1898 (despatches, 2nd class Medjidie, clasp) ; Reserve of Officers.
(Died 21 Mar. 1920.)

GRIFFITH, Rt. Hon. Sir Samuel Walker, G.C.M.G., *cr.* 1895 ; K.C.M.G., *cr.* 1886 ; P.C. 1901 ; hon. F.B.A. ; a member of the Judicial Committee of the Privy Council ; Chief Justice of Australia 1903-19 ; *b.* 21 June 1845 ; *s.* of Rev. Edward Griffith ; *m.* Julia, *d.* of J. Thomson, 1870 ; one *s.* four *d. Educ.* : Univ. of Sydney (B.A. 1863 ; M.A. 1870) ; LL.D. Universities of Queensland and Wales ; Barr. Queensland, 1867, also of N.S.W. and Victoria ; Q.C. 1876 ; Attorney-Gen. of Queensland, 1874-78, 1890-1893 ; Sec. for Public Instruction, 1876-79, 1883-1884 ; Sec. for Public Works, 1878-79 ; Premier of Queensland, 1888-88, 1890-93 ; Colonial Treas., 1887-88 ; President of Federal Council of Australasia, 1888, 1891, 1893 ; Chief Justice of Queensland, 1893-1903 ; Lt.-Governor of Queensland, 1899-1903. *Publications* : The Queensland Criminal Code ; translator of Dante's Divina Commedia. *Address* : Sydney, N.S.W.
(Died 9 Aug. 1920.)

GRIFFITHS, Rev. Charles ; Vicar, St. Paul's Church, Bedminster, Bristol, 1888-1914 ; *b.* London, 19 April 1847 ; *s.* of Thomas Griffiths of Kirkby Wharf, Tadcaster, Yorkshire ; *m.* Fanny Pote, *d.* of Rev. Frederic Williams, B.A., Vicar of Saltley, Warwickshire ; one *s. Educ.* : priv. ; Gloucester Theo. Coll. ; Oxford Univ. Ordained, 1877 ; first curacy, St. Peter's, Clifton Wood, Bristol ; appointed Missions to Seamen ; Chaplain to the Port of Bristol, 1879 ; Bristol Seamen's Church and Institute built 1881 ; place found so suitable to the wants of seamen that same kind of erection is now placed in many ports at home and abroad ; restoration and enlargement of Parish Church, 1892 ; Hon. Canon of Bristol Cathedral, 1900 ; Proctor in Convocation, 1900-19 ; member of the Bristol Board of Guardians, 1898-1914 ; Governor of Bristol General Hospital, 1889 ; Governor of Queen Victoria Convalescent Home, 1901 ; selected Speaker Cardiff Church Congress. *Publications* : Numerical Decline of British Seamen ; Haddon, a Child's Doctor ; A Short Record of the Life of Melville Charles Griffiths, First Vicar of All Saints', Fishponds, Bristol. *Recreation* : chess. *Address* : Hazelwood, Stoke Bishop, Bristol. *T.* : 107 Stoke Bishop, Bristol. *Club* : Authors'.
(Died 9 May 1924.)

GRIFFITHS, Ven. David Henry, M.A., Archdeacon of Monmouth since 1922; *b.* 1864; *s.* of late Thomas Griffiths, J.P., Aberystwyth; *m.* 1901, Jennie Isabella Wailes, Cardiff; three *s.* two *d. Educ.:* The Grammar School, Aberystwyth; Christ College, Brecon; Corpus Christi College, Cambridge. Deacon, 1888; priest, 1889; Vicar of Aberavon, 1901-8; St. Woolos, Newport, 1908; Rural Dean of Newport, 1915-1922; Grand Chaplain of Grand Lodge of England, 1924. *Address:* St. Woolos Vicarage, Newport, Mon. *(Died 27 Aug. 1926.)*

GRIFFITHS, John G., C.V.O. 1917; M.V.O. 1916; Fellow and late President of Institute of Chartered Accountants, *b.* 1845; *s.* of George Griffiths; *m.* 1874, Emily Wilhelmina (*d.* 1918), *d.* of E. W. Dubois. *Educ.:* Private Schools in England and under tutors in France. Appointed to an Ensigncy in the 100th Foot, 1865; shortly afterwards entered the office of Deloitte and Co., Accountants in the City of London, of which firm he was for some years the senior partner, and retired in 1902; was engaged, on behalf of the Electric and International Telegraph Co., when the Govt. took over the Electric Telegraph business in Great Britain, and, on behalf of the Khedive, during the inquiry into the financial condition of Egypt in 1875-6 by the Rt. Hon. Stephen Cave, M.P., and again, in 1876-77, during the investigation by Lord Goschen and Mr. Joubert; has acted as advising accountant or auditor to most of the Telegraph Cable Companies and of the English Railway Companies in the Argentine Republic, as well as to the Great Western Railway Co., the London Joint Stock Bank, and many other of the larger English business enterprises; an original member of the council of the Institute of Chartered Accountants, of which he was president during the two years from June 1897 to June 1899; a Director of the Western Telegraph Company, and Great Western Railway. *Address:* 4 Hyde Park Gardens, W.2. *T.:* Paddington 5394. *Clubs:* Arts, Burlington Fine Arts, Ranelagh. *(Died 16 Nov. 1922.)*

GRIFFITHS, Vincent, C.B. 1897; a Magistrate for Middlesex; *b.* 27 Oct. 1831; *y. s.* of late Thos. Griffiths; *m.* late Louisa Emily Caroline, *d.* of Edmund Bechinoe Ashford of Westbury, Sherborne, 1869; two *s.* two *d.* Entered Poor Law Commission, 1845; private secretary to Parliamentary Sec., Poor Law Board, 1852; Principal of Poor Law Audit Department, 1860; H.M. Treasury Inspector and Valuer, 1869-99. *Decorated* for official services. *Address:* Yelverton Lodge, Twickenham.
(Died 9 May 1917.)

GRIGGS, Sir (William) Peter, Kt., *cr.* 1916; M.P. (U.) Ilford since 1918; Alderman for County Council, Essex; J.P. Essex; *s.* of late John Griggs; *b.* 1854; *m.* Georgina, *d.* of Thomas Hodges of Kensington; no *c. Educ.:* private school. Had to make his own way in the world, his father dying when he was seven years old; apprenticed himself to the water, but left it to find a path not quite so rough and on firm ground; Ilford Councillor, since 1899; Chairman, Ilford District Council, 1910; Essex County Councillor, since 1901; Governing Director of W. P. Griggs & Co. Ltd. and of the South Essex Recorders, Ltd. *Address:* The Drive, Ilford. *(Died 11 Aug. 1920.)*

GRIMBLE, Augustus; *s.* of late William Grimble of The Distillery, Albany Street, Regent's Park; *b.* 1840; *m.* 1880, Alice, *e. d.* of late Edward Mathew Ward, R.A.; served in 25th and 41st Regiments. *Publications:* Deerstalking; Shooting and Salmon-fishing; Highland Sport; The Deer Forests of Scotland; Leaves from a Game Book; The Salmon Rivers of Scotland. *Recreations:* all outdoor sports. *Address:* 44 Duke Street, S.W.1.
(Died 1 Feb. 1925.)

GRIMES, Mary Katharine, Hon. Sec. of Church Emigration Soc. since 1901; member Emigration Committee Church of England Waifs and Strays Society since 1904; Associate Royal Colonial Institute, 1910, and Member of R.C.I. Standing Committee on Emigration; F.R.Hort.S.; *b.* Funchal, Madeira, 26 Sept. 1861; *e. d.* of John Ralph Grimes and Mary Ann, *o. d.* of George Lund, M.D., etc., of Edinburgh, Scarborough, and Madeira. *Educ.:* at home. Voluntary worker, Battersea parish, Hon. Sec. and Librarian, parochial library; Poor-law Infirmary Visitor, and Visitor for Metropolitan Association for Befriending Young Servants, Wandsworth and Battersea, 1885-94; Hon. Secretary, Clapham and East Battersea Committee of Charity Organisation Society, 1894-97; Representative at Council for Brixton Committee Charity Organisation Society, 1898-1899; Poor-law Infirmary Visitor, and Visitor for Metropolitan Association for Befriending Young Servants for Lambeth, 1897-1901; Visitor for Ministry of Pensions, 1918; Member National Union of Womens' Suffrage Societies, and of Conservative and Unionist Women's Franchise Society; visited Canada, British Columbia, and Vancouver Island, 1905; South Africa, 1914. *Recreations:* music, photography, travelling. *Address:* Church House, Dean's Yard, Westminster, S.W.; 312a Vauxhall Bridge Road, S.W. *T.A.:* Emigration. *T.:* Victoria 1298. *(Died 10 Jan. 1921.)*

GRIMSTON, Rev. Hon. Robert; Vicar of St. Michael's, St. Albans, since 1915; Hon. Canon of St. Albans, 1914; Member of Industrial Christian Fellowship; *b.* of 3rd Earl of Verulam; *b.* 1860; *m.* 1896, Gertrude Mary Amelia, *d.* of late Rev. Charles Villiers, two *s.* two *d. Educ.:* Harrow; Trinity Coll., Camb., M.A. *Address:* Darrowfield, St. Albans. *T.:* St. Albans 232. *(Died 8 July 1927.)*

GRIMSTON, Brig.-Gen. Sir Rollo Estouteville, K.C.V.O., *cr.* 1911; C.I.E. 1906; Inspector-General Imperial Service Troops, India; *b.* 26 Oct. 1861; *s.* of Col. O. J. A. Grimston of the Lodge, Itchen, Hants. *Educ.:* United Services College. Entered army, 1881; Captain, Indian Cavalry, 1892; Major, 1901; Lieutenant-Colonel, 1907; Brig.-Gen., 1911; A.D.C. to Viceroy, 1893-98; A.D.C. to Prince of Wales during tour in India, 1905-6; extra Equerry-in-Waiting to H.R.H., 1906; extra Equerry-in-Waiting to King George V., 1910; Military Secretary to King George V. during tour in India; served N.-W. Frontier, India, 1897-98 (despatches, medal with clasp); Tirah, 1897-98 (despatches, clasp). *Clubs:* Cavalry, Hurlingham. *(Died 29 Jan. 1916.)*

GRIMSTON, Brig.-Gen. Sylvester Bertram, C.M.G. 1916; 18th Lancers, Indian Army; *b.* 27 Nov. 1864; *s.* of Col. Oswald Augustus Grimston and Frances Campbell; *m.* 1904, Nina, *d.* of late Colonel G. W. Macauley; one *s.* one *d. Educ.:* U.S. College, Westward Ho! Joined King's Liverpool Regiment, 1884; 2nd Queen's Own B.L.I. (Indian Army), 1886; 18th Lancers, 1887; was on Staff as D.A.A.G. China F. Force, 1901-2; D.A.A.G. Div. Staff, India, 1904-8; A.Q.M.G. Divisional Staff, India, 1916; commanded Brigade, India, Dehra Dun, 1917, March-Nov. 1918; Delhi, Dec. 1918-Feb. 1919; retired 1919; served Burma, 1885-1887 (medal and clasp); N.W. Frontier, India, and Tirah, 1897-98 (medal and 3 clasps); China, 1900 (medal); European War in France, 1914-1916 (4th Class Legion of Honour, C.M.G., despatches, 1914-15 Star, Medal 1914-18, Victory Medal 1914-19). *Address:* The White House, Willingdon, Sussex. *Club:* United Service.
(Died 24 Mar. 1928.)

GRIMTHORPE, 2nd Baron (*cr.* 1886); **Ernest William Beckett;** Hon. Col. Yorkshire Hussars; *b.* 1856; *s.* of William Beckett-Denison, Nun Appleton, Yorkshire,

GRIGGS, Hon. John William. See page xx.

M.P., *b.* of 1st Baron Grimthorpe, and Helen, *d.* of 2nd Baron Feversham; *m.* Lucy Tracy Lee, New York, 1883 (*d.* 1891); one *s.* one *d.*; *S.* uncle 1905. *Educ.:* Eton; Cambridge. M.P. (C.) Whitby Div. Yorkshire, 1885-1905; formerly partner in Beckett and Co., Bankers, Leeds; D.A.G. Imperial Yeomanry, 1900; late Lt.-Col. Yorkshire Hussars. *Heir:* *s.* Hon. Ralph William Ernest Beckett. *Recreations:* shooting, golf, travelling, amateur and collector of works of Art. *Address:* 27 Welbeck Street, W. *T.:* Mayfair 3864. *Clubs:* Brooks's, Turf, Marlborough, St. James'. (*Died 9 May 1917.*)

GRISDALE, Rt. Rev. John, D.D., D.C.L.; *b.* 25 June 1845; *m.* Anne, *d.* of J. Chaplin, Hinckley, Leicestershire, 1871. *Educ.:* Missionary College, Islington. Ordained, St. Paul's Cathedral, 1870; Lambeth B.D. 1876; Professor of Systematic Theology, St. John's College, Winnipeg, and Canon of St. John's Cathedral, 1878-82; Dean of Rupert's Land and Professor of Pastoral Theology, 1882-96; Hon. D.C.L. Trinity, Toronto, 1893; Bishop of Qu'Appelle, 1896-1911. *Address:* 341 Redwood Avenue, Winnipeg.

GROGAN, Col. Sir Edward Ion Beresford, 2nd Bt., *cr.* 1859; C.M.G. 1920; D.S.O. 1917; late Rifle Brigade; *b.* 29 Nov. 1873; *o. s.* of 1st Bt. and Katherine Charlotte, *e. d.* of Sir B. B. McMahon, 2nd Bt.; *m.* 1907, Ellinor, *d.* of R. Bosworth Smith, and *widow* of Sir H. Langhorne Thompson, K.C.M.G.; *S.* father, 1891. Served South Africa, 1899-1900 (despatches, Queen's medal 5 clasps); p.s.c.; at War Office, 1904-6; served in Imperial Ottoman Gendarmerie, 1906-8; Military Attaché, South America, 1911-14; served European War, 1914-19 (despatches, D.S.O., Bt. Col.); retired pay, 1924. *Heir:* none. *Address:* Shropham Hall, Norwich, Norfolk. *Club:* United Service.
(*Died 11 July 1927.*)

GROOME, Admiral Robert Leonard, R.N.; C.V.O. 1905; *b.* 10 September 1848. Entered navy, 1861; Commander, 1890; Rear-Admiral, 1903; Vice-Admiral, 1907; commanded S.E. Coast of America; Reserve Division Portsmouth, 1905; Rear - Admiral, Channel Fleet, 1905-6; Director of Transports, 1907-11; retired, 1911. *Address:* St. James's Court, S.W. (*Died 22 Nov. 1917.*)

GROSS, Edward John, M.A.; Senior Fellow since 1878 and President since 1923 of Caius College, Cambridge; *b.* Alderton, Suffolk, 3 Feb. 1844; *s.* of Samuel Chilton Gross; *m.* 1st, 1877, Maria Isabella Chance of Malvern; 2nd, 1896, Constance Bertha King of Wimbledon; one *s.* five *d.* *Educ.:* Ipswich School; Caius College, Cambridge (Scholar). 8th Wrangler, 1866; Fellow, 1866; Bursar, 1876-86; Secretary to the Board of Examinations, 1874-1921; Secretary to the Oxford and Cambridge Schools Examination Board, 1875-1915. *Publications:* Treatise on Algebra, 1874; Treatise on Kinematics and Kinetics, 1876; Chronicle of the Estates of Gonville and Caius College, 1912. *Address:* Gonville Lodge, Cambridge.
(*Died 30 Aug. 1923.*)

GROSSMITH, Weedon, artist, actor and author; *s.* of late George Grossmith, lecturer and journalist; *m.* May Lever, *y. d.* of late Dr. James Palfrey, 1895; one *d.* *Educ.:* Simpson's School, Hampstead; Slade School; London University; R.A. Schools. First picture in Academy three-length portrait of his father; exhibited many times at the R.A. and Grosvenor Gallery. First appearance on stage at old Prince of Wales Theatre, Liverpool, as Specklebury in Time Will Tell, 1885; and in New York same year; first appearance in London as Woodcock in Woodcock's Little Game (Gaiety), 1887; started management at Terry's Theatre, 1894; lessee and manager of Vaudeville Theatre, 1894-96; lessee of Avenue Theatre, 1901; produced The Lady of Ostend at Terry's Theatre, 1900. *Principal parts* (out of numerous others): appeared in The M'Haggis, The Noble Lord, and The Duke of Killiecrankie; at the Haymarket Theatre, 1906 and 1907, in The Man from Blankley's and Lady Huntworth's Experiment, and at His Majesty's Theatre in The Vandyk, 1907; Mrs. Ponderbury's Past; The Worm; Sir Anthony, 1908; produced under own management at Criterion Theatre Mr. Preedy and the Countess, 1909; went to Canada and America, 1910; at the command performance, Drury Lane, 1911, played Frantz in Money; at the Gala performance, His Majesty's, 1911, played Jones in David Garrick; appeared with Miss Marie Tempest in a revival of The Duke of Killiecrankie at the Playhouse, June 1914. *Publication:* The Diary of a Nobody (with George Grossmith); written articles for Punch and Art Journal. *Plays:* A Commission; The Night of the Party; The Cure; The Duffer, 1905; The Mystery of Redwood Grange; Billy's Bargain, 1910; From Studio to Stage, 1912. *Recreations:* shooting, fishing, books, old furniture, antiquities, etc. *Address:* 1 Bedford Square, W.C. *Clubs:* Beefsteak, Savage, Garrick.
(*Died 14 June 1919.*)

GROSVENOR, Capt. Lord Hugh (William), 1st Life Guards; *b.* 6 April 1884; 4th *s.* of 1st Duke of Westminster; *m.* 1906, Lady Mary Florence Mabel Crichton, *d.* of 4th Earl of Erne; two *s.* Entered Army, 1903; Captain, 1908; served European War, 1914-15 (despatches). *Address:* 9 Southwick Crescent, W. *T.:* Paddington 1382.
(*Died 30 Oct. 1914.*)

GROSVENOR, Hon. Richard Cecil, *y. s.* of 1st Baron Ebury; *b.* 1848; *m.* 1898, Jessie Amelia, *d.* of late Rev. Charles Clarke Esher. Director-General Life Assurance Company. *Address:* Morrisburne House, Woking.
(*Died 29 Oct. 1919.*)

GROUT, Rev George W. G., M.A.; Clerical Secretary since 1901, and Registrar since 1903, Diocese of Ontario; Senior Canon, St. George's Cathedral, Kingston; *b.* 12 June 1837; *s.* of Rev. G. R. F. Grout, Rector of Grimsby, and Eliza Walker; *m.* 1863, C. E., *d.* of Rev. F. J. Lundy, D.C.L., Rector of Grimsby; four *s.* *Educ.:* Trinity College, Toronto. Diocese of Ontario, North Gower, 1860-63; Loughboro, 1863-65; Stirling, 1865-72; Carleton Place, 1872 - 81; Elizabethtown, 1881 - 1901; Rural Dean of Lanark and Renfrew, 1881-88; Leeds, 1888-98. *Publications:* compilation and publication of the Journal of Synod, 1901-11, etc. *Address:* St. George's Hall, Wellington Street, Kingston, Ontario. (*Died 14 Feb. 1917.*)

GROVE, Lady (Agnes); *b.* 25 July 1864; *d.* of Maj.-Gen. and Hon. Mrs. Pitt Rivers; *m.* 1882, Sir Walter J. Grove, 2nd Bart.; two *s.* two *d.* *Educ.:* home and Oxford. First essay appeared in Oxford High School Magazine when aged 15; has written many articles for magazines, Nineteenth Century, Fortnightly, Cornhill, etc.; has travelled since marriage in Europe, America, and Africa; in Morocco crossed the Atlas Mountains and made the acquaintance of the then reigning Sultan Abdul-Aziz; has visited Spain, Italy, France, Germany, Switzerland; was Member of Executive Committee of Women's Liberal Federation, Anti-Vivisection Society, and President of the Forward Suffrage Union; also member of National Union of Women Suffrage Societies, and is Pres. of National Anti-Vaccination League, etc.; speaks at public meetings; represented Berwick St. John, in Wiltshire, on District Council, 1898-1903. *Publications:* Seventy-one Days' Camping in Morocco, 1902; The Social Fetich, 1907; The Human Woman, 1908; On Fads, 1910. *Recreations:* reading, motoring, entertaining friends; chief interest and pleasure her home and children and grandchildren. *Ad-*

441

dress : Sedgehill Manor, Shaftesbury, Wiltshire.
(*Died 7 Dec. 1926.*)

GROVE, Maj.-General Sir Coleridge,
K.C.B., *cr.* 1898 ; Colonel East Yorks Regiment since 1901 ; *b.* Wandsworth 26 Sept. 1839 ; 2nd *s.* of late Rt. Hon. Sir W. R. Grove (*d.* 1896), and Emma, *d.* of late John Powles. *Educ.:* private school ; Balliol Coll. Oxford (B.A., exhibitioner ; first class in Mathematics, Moderations and Greats). Joined 15th Regiment, 1863 ; passed through Staff College, 1879 ; Private Secretary to three successive war ministers, viz. Mr. Campbell-Bannerman, Mr. W. H. Smith, and Mr. Stanhope ; A.D.C. to Lieut.-Gen. and Gen. Gov. of Ireland, 1882 ; D.A.A. and Q.M.G. Exped. Force, Egypt, 1882 ; D.A.A.G., H.Q. of Army, 1883-84 ; Spec. Serv. Egypt, 1884-85 ; Mil. Sec. to G.O. Comm.-in-Chief, Egypt, 1885 ; A.A. and Q.M.G., Gibraltar, 1885-86 ; Priv. Sec. to S. of S. for War, 1886-88 ; A.A.G., H.Q. of Army, 1888-94 ; Mil. Sec. War Office, 1896-1901 ; Col. East Yorks Regt., 1901 ; war services, Egyptian Expedition, 1882 ; D.A.A.G., H.Q. (despatches, medal with clasp, bronze star, Brev. of Lt.-Col., 4th class Osmanieh) ; Soudan Expedition, 1884-85 ; Nile and Suakin ; as A.A.G. for Boat Service, Commandant at Gemai, and A.A.G. and Acting Military Secretary at Headquarters (despatches, 2 clasps, promoted Colonel). *Address :* 7 Wellington Court, Knightsbridge, S.W.1. *T.:* Western 4481. *Clubs:* Oxford and Cambridge, Army and Navy.(*Died 17 May 1920.*)

GROVE (Thomas Newcomen), Archibald, J.P. for Bucks and Essex ; M.P. (L.) Northants S. since 1906 ; 2nd *s.* of late Capt. Edward Grove and Elizabeth, *d.* of Colonel Ponsonby Watts ; *m.* Kate Sara, *d.* of Henry James Sibley, 1889 ; one *s. Educ.:* private tutors ; Oriel College, Oxford ; double Honours. Educated for Barrister ; ate dinners and passed all examinations at the Inner Temple ; founded New Review and edited it from commencement till 1894 ; contested Winchester, 1886 ; M.P. West Ham (North), 1892-95 ; travelled extensively on Continent, Asia, and in Africa. *Publications:* Co-operation or Spoliation ; The Big Black Hog ; and many political and social articles. *Recreations:* fishing, shooting, golf. *Address:* Pollards Park, Chalfont St. Giles, Bucks. *T.A.:* Chalfont St. Giles. *T.:* Amersham Common 18. *Clubs:* White's, Eighty.
(*Died 4 June 1920.*)

GROVE-HILLS, Col. Edmond Herbert, D.Sc., F.R.S. 1911 ; C.M.G. 1902 ; C.B.E. 1919 ; R.E. ; Pres. Royal Astronomical Society, 1913-15 ; *b.* 1 Aug. 1864 ; *s.* of late Herbert A. Hills of High Head Castle, Cumberland ; *m.* 1892, Juliet, *d.* of late James Spencer-Bell, M.P. ; assumed name Grove-Hills, 1920. *Educ.:* Winchester ; Woolwich. Entered army, 1884 ; Captain, 1893 ; Major, 1901 ; Assistant-Instructor, School of Military Engineering, 1898-99 ; rejoined, Aug. 1914 ; Col. 1914 ; Brig.-Gen. 1918 ; D.A.A.G. Headquarters, 1899-1905 ; contested (C) Portsmouth, 1906. *Publications:* many papers on astronomical and allied subjects. *Address :* 1 Campden Hill, W.8. *T.:* Park 4655. *Club:* Athenæum.
(*Died 2 Oct. 1922.*)

GROZIER, Edwin Atkins, editor and publisher, Boston Post ; *b.* San Francisco, 12 Sep. 1859, New England parentage ; *m.* 1885, Alice G. Goodell of Salem. *Educ.:* Brown University, Providence, R.I. ; Boston University, Ph.B. Reporter, 1882 ; private secy. to Governor of Massachusetts, 1884-85 ; editorial and business positions on New York World, 1886-91 ; controlling owner of Boston Post, 1891-1922. *Publications:* chiefly newspaper and magazine work ; Editor, One Hundred Best Novels — Condensed. *Address:* 168 Brattle Street, Cambridge, U.S.A. *Clubs:* Algonquin, Boston Athletic, Oakly, Country, Press, Boston

Chess, Belfry, Economic, Bostonian Society, Mass. Society of Mayflower Descendants.
(*Died 9 May 1924.*)

GRUBBE, Walter John, Stipendiary Magistrate for the Borough of East Ham, 1906-25 ; 2nd *s.* of late John Eustace Grubbe, Barrister Inner Temple and Parliamentary Agent, and Julia Catharine, *d.* of Rev. George Wm. Hall, D.D., Master of Pembroke College, Oxford ; *m.* 1912, Dora, *d.* of late Rev. William Jowitt, Rector of Stevenage, Herts, and widow of Charles Arnold Edgell. *Educ.:* Cheltenham College ; Pembroke College, Oxford (M.A.); Barrister Inner Temple, 1874 ; South-eastern Circuit ; Herts and Essex Sessions. *Address:* 1 Dr. Johnson's Buildings, Temple, E.C. ; Southlands, Margaretting, Essex ; Southwold, Suffolk. *Club:* New University.
(*Died 16 Mar. 1926.*)

GRUEBER, Herbert Appold, F.S.A., Keeper of Department of Coins and Medals, British Museum, 1906-12 ; *b.* 1846 ; *s.* of Rev. C. S. Grueber, Hambridge, Somerset ; *m.* Alice Emily (*d.* 1926), *d.* of W. H. Hewitt of Lancaster Gate, Hyde Park. *Educ.:* private tuition. Assistant, British Museum, 1866 ; Assistant Keeper, Coins and Medals, 1893-1906 ; Hon. Sec. and Vice-President of Royal Numismatic Society, 1874-1912 ; Hon. Treasurer of Egypt Exploration Fund, 1883-1912 ; barrister Middle Temple, 1872 ; Hon. Member of French, Austrian, Italian, and American Numismatic Societies. *Publications:* Joint editor of the Numismatic Chronicle ; edited Medallic Illustrations of the History of Great Britain and Ireland, and Thorburn's Guide to the Coins of Great Britain and Ireland ; Roman Medallions in the British Museum ; Guide to English Medals exhibited in the British Museum ; Catalogue of Anglo-Saxon Coins in the British Museum, vol. ii. ; Handbook of the Coins of Great Britain and Ireland (British Museum); Roman Republican Coins in the British Museum ; Illustrated Edition of the Medallic Illustrations of British History ; numerous articles on Numismatics. *Address :* Bembridge, Isle of Wight.   (*Died 21 Nov. 1927.*)

GRUNING, John Frederick, C.I.E. 1915 ; I.C.S. ; Member of the Board of Revenue since 1921 ; *b.* 1 Oct. 1870 ; *s.* of late Henry Gruning ; *m.* Mabel, *d.* of E. B. Baker, late Deputy-Inspector-General Bengal Police ; three *s.* two *d. Educ.:* Eastbourne College ; St. John's College, Cambridge. Entered I.C.S., 1892 ; Magistrate and Collector, 1906 ; Secretary to Government, Revenue and Gen. Departments, 1911 ; Magistrate and Collector, Shahabad ; Magistrate Collector, Patna ; Additional Commissioner, Patna, Bihar and Orissa ; Commissioner of the Orissa Division, 1917-21. *Publications:* a Gazetteer ; pamphlet on emigration to Assam. *Recreations:* any available game— tennis, polo, racquets. *Address:* Patna, E.I.R., India. *Clubs:* East India United Service ; United Service, Calcutta and Simla.
(*Died 3 Oct. 1922.*)

GUARD, Lieut.-Col. Frederic Henry Wickham, C.M.G. 1919 ; C.B.E. 1922 ; D.S.O. 1918 ; late Royal Scots ; Squadron Leader, R.A.F., since 1922. Served European War, 1914-18 (despatches, D.S.O.). *Address:* c/o Air Ministry, W.C.   (*Died 17 June 1927.*)

GUBBINS, Lieut.-Col. Richard Rolls, D.S.O. 1900 ; King's Shropshire Light Infantry ; Reserve of Officers, employed on Staff as A.A. and Q.M.G., B.E.F. ; J.P. Cumberland ; *b.* 14 Dec. 1868 ; *e. s.* of late Rev. Richard Shard Gubbins, Rector of Upham, Hants, and Ellen Rolls, *sister* of 1st Baron Llangattock ; *m.* 1902, Agnes Edith, *e. d.* of late G. W. Mounsey Heysham of Castletown, Carlisle ; two *s.* Entered army, 1890 ; Captain, 1899 ; Major, 1908 ; retired, 1912 ; served South Africa,

1899-1902 (despatches, Queen's medal, 3 clasps, King's medal, 2 clasps, D.S.O.) ; European War, 1914-17 (despatches). *Address :* The Old Hall, Rocliffe, Carlisle. *Club :* Army and Navy.
(Died 24 Jan. 1918.)

GUBBINS, Lieut.-General Sir W. Launcelotte, K.C.B., *cr.* 1911 ; C.B. 1905 ; M.V.O. 1902 ; K.H.S. 1909 ; M.B. ; J.P. (Surrey) ; late Director-General A.M.S. ; *s.* of late Rev. George G. Gubbins, M.A., Prebendary and Chancellor of Limerick, and Dora, *d.* of Edward Purdon, J.P., Lisnabin, Killucan Westmeath ; *b.* 26 July 1849 ; *m.* 1885, Florence Margaret, 2nd *d.* of Rev. H. Tripp (formerly fellow of Worcester College, Oxford) of Huntspill and Winford, Somerset ; one *d. Educ. :* Trinity College, Dublin ; Erasmus Smith Scholar. Entered Army Medical Service, 1873 ; served Afghan War, 1878-79, with 5th Fusiliers, and subs. on Staff of Lt.-General Sir F. Maude, V.C., was present at numerous engagements in Khyber Pass ; again in Afghanistan in 1879-80, as Sanitary Officer on Staff of Lt.-General Sir R. Bright, present with Expeditions against Mohmunds and Gilzais (despatches) ; with Egyptian Expedition, 1882 ; with Burmah Expedition, 1886, and in S. Africa 1899-1901, as Principal Medical Officer ; 6th Division ; present at relief of Kimberley ; battles of Paardeberg and Driefontein ; occupation of Bloemfontein, and subsequently as Principal Medical Officer, Pretoria and Pietersburg Districts (despatches, promoted Colonel) ; filled also various posts during Great War ; was Assistant Director, Army Medical Service, War Office, 1894-99 ; Principal Medical Officer Home District, 1902-3 ; since when in a similar post in Western and Eastern Commands and Army Headquarters, India ; is a Commissioner Royal Hospital, Chelsea. *Recreations :* hunting, golf, cycling. *Address :* Belvedere Drive, Wimbledon. *Club :* United Service.
(Died 8 July 1925.)

GUEST WILLIAMS, Rev. Samuel Blackwell, Vicar of Pittington since 1895 ; Rural Dean of Easington, 1905 ; Hon. Canon of Durham, 1913 ; *b.* 1851 ; *s.* of late Mr. Guest Williams, formerly of Manchester ; *m.* 1884, Catherine, *d.* of late William Gray, formerly of York ; three *s.* one *d. Educ. :* Shrewsbury School ; Exeter College, Oxford. (Scholar) first-class Moderations ; Assistant Master at Hereford and Marlborough College ; Second Master at Durham Grammar School, 1877-95 ; ordained, 1878. *Publications :* Reviews and magazine articles. *Recreations :* cycling, golf, photography. *Address :* Prior's Hallgarth, Durham. *T.A. :* Littletown. *Club :* Constitutional, Durham. *(Died 11 Dec. 1920.)*

GUILLAMORE, 5th Viscount (*cr.* 1831), **Hardress Standish O'Grady,** Baron O'Grady, 1831 ; Major R.A. Madras (retired) ; *b.* 20 Oct. 1841 ; 4th *s.* of 2nd Viscount and *d.* of Hon. Berkeley Paget ; *S. b.* 1877. *Educ.* Addiscombe. *Heir : b.* Hon. Frederick S. O'Grady.
Address : Cahir Guillamore, Kilmallock, Co. Limerick. *T.A. :* Bruff. *(Died 6 Feb. 1918.)*

GUILLAMORE, 6th Viscount ; **Frederick Standish O'Grady,** Baron O'Grady of Rockbarton, *cr.* 1831 ; F.Z.S. ; *b.* Cahir Guillamore, Co. Limerick, and *s.* of 2nd Viscount Guillamore, and Gertrude Jane, *d.* of Hon. Berkeley Pagèt ; *S.* brother, 1918 ; *m.* 1st, 1881, Mary Theresa Burdett (*d.* 1910), *d.* of late Hon. William James Coventry ; 2nd, Gertrude Lily, *y. d.* of J. Langford of Draycott ; one *d. Educ. :* Charterhouse ; St. John's College, Oxford. Winner of High Jump, Inter-Varsity Sports, 1868. Formerly Lieut. Isle of Wight Artillery ; travelled and resided in New Zealand, Hawaii, etc. *Recreation :* fishing and fish culture. *Heir : c.* Hugh H. M. O'Grady. *Address :* Ingleside, Holt, Trowbridge, Wilts ; Cahir Guillamore, Co. Limerick. *T.A. :* Holt-Wilts. *M. :* CH 567. *(Died 11 Oct. 1927.)*

GUINEY, Louise Imogen ; *b.* Boston, Mass. ; *o. c.* of Gen. P. R. Guiney and Janet Margaret Doyle. *Educ. :* Elmhurst Academy, Providence ; and private tutors. *Publications :* Goosequill Papers, 1885 ; The White Sail and other Poems, 1887 ; Monsieur Henri, a Footnote to French History, 1892 ; A Roadside Harp (poems), 1893 ; A Little English Gallery, 1894 ; Patrins (essays), 1897 ; "England and Yesterday " (poems), 1898 ; The Martyrs' Idyl and shorter Poems, 1899 ; Robert Emmet : his Rebellion and his Romance, 1904 ; Hurrell Froude : Memoranda and Comments, 1905 ; Blessed Edmund Campion (in St. Nicholas Series), 1908 ; Happy Ending (collected poems), 1910 ; edited Selected Poems of James Clarence Mangan, Matthew Arnold, The Matchless Orinda, and Thomas Stanley : Dr. T. W. Parsons' translation of Divina Commedia, 1893 ; Henry Vaughan's Mount of Olives, 1902 ; has contributed to various magazines since 1885. *Recreations :* walking, canoeing. *Address :* Grangeleigh, Amberley, Glos.(*Died 2 Nov. 1920.*)

GUINNESS, Lieut. Eric Cecil, D.S.O. 1918 ; Adjutant, 2nd Irish Regt. since 1920 ; *b.* 30 Aug. 1894 ; *s.* of Robert Cecil Day Guinness and Madeline Ride Guinness, of Bury House, Baldock, Herts ; *m.* 1916, Hannah Mary, *d.* of late Robert Marlborough Pryor of Western Park, Stevenage, Herts ; one *s.* one *d.* Served European War, 1914-18 (despatches, D.S.O.). *Club :* Junior Army and Navy. *(Died 11 Sept. 1920.)*

GUINNESS, Col. Henry William Newton, C.B. 1900 ; late A.A.G. 5th Division ; *b.* 5 Aug. 1854 ; *s.* of late Rev. W. N. Guinness, Collooney, Co. Sligo ; *m.* 1893, Frances Helen, *d.* of late Henry West, Q.C., Loughlinstown House, Co. Dublin ; one *s. Educ. :* Newton Abbot College. Joined 18th Regt., 1873 ; Captain Royal Irish Regt., 1881 ; Brevet Major, 1885 ; Lieut.-Col., 1889 ; served in Afghan War, 1880 (medal) ; Nile Expedition, 1884-85 (despatches, medal and clasp, Khedive's Star, Brevet Major) ; S. Africa 1900-1 (despatches, C.B., medal and three clasps, King's medal and two clasps). *(Died 5 Aug. 1925.)*

GUISE, Sir William Francis George, 5th Bt., *cr.* 1783 ; J.P., D.L. ; Hon. Colonel 3rd Batt. Gloucestershire Regt. ; 2nd *s.* of 4th Bt. and Margaret Anna Maria, *e. d.* of Rev. D. H. Lee-Warner of Tyberton Court, Herefords., and Walsingham Abbey, Norfolk ; *b.* 14 Dec. 1851 ; *S.* father, 1887 ; *m.* Ada Caroline, *d.* of late O. E. Coope, M.P., Rochetts, Brentwood, 1887 ; one *s.* one *d. Educ. :* Eton. Patron of two livings ; High Sheriff, 1898. Owns about 2100 acres. *Heir : s.* Anselm William Edward, *b.* 18 Sep. 1888. *Address :* Elmore Court, Gloucester. *Clubs :* Brooks's, Wellington. *(Died 17 Jan. 1920.)*

GUITRY, Lucien, actor ; *b.* Paris, 1860 ; *m.* 1882. Spent nine years in Russia, Théatre Michael, Petrograd ; Manager of Porte St. Martin ; Director of Renaissance Theatre, Principal parts : L'Assommoir ; La Veine ; L'Adversaire ; Le Mannequin d'osier ; La Griffe ; Le Voleur ; Sampson ; L'Emigré ; Chantecler.
(Died 1 June 1925.)

GULL, Cyril Arthur Edward Ranger ; *b.* 1876 ; *e. s.* of Rev. J. E. Gull, Rector of Rushall. *Educ. :* Denstone ; Oxford University. Member Literary Staff, Saturday Review, 1897-1898 ; also Bookman, and Academy ; Editor, London Life, 1899 ; then joined Editorial Staff, Daily Mail, afterwards Daily Express ; gave up journalism for novel writing. *Publications :* The Hypocrite, 1898 ; Miss Malevolent, 1899 ; From the Book Beautiful, 1900 ; Back to Lilacland, 1901 ; The Cigarette Smoker, 1901 ; The Serf, 1902 ; His Grace's Grace, 1903 ; Portalone, 1904 ; The Harvest of Love, 1905 ; The Soul Stealer, 1906 ; When Satan Ruled, 1911 ; under name of Guy Thorne has published When It Was Dark (500th thousand) ; A Lost Cause ;

First It Was Ordained; Made In His Image; The Charioteer, 1907; I Believe, 1907; The Angel, 1908; The Socialist, 1909; Not in Israel, 1913; The Drunkard, 1912; Love and the Freemason, The Secret Service Submarine, The Cruiser on Wheels, The Secret Seaplane, 1914-15. *Recreations:* shooting, especially wild fowling, French literature, travelling. *Clubs:* Primrose. Cocoa Tree.   (*Died 9 Jan. 1923.*)

GULL, Sir (William) Cameron, 2nd Bt., *cr.* 1872; O.B.E. 1918; J.P.; Alderman, County Council, Berks; *b.* 6 Jan. 1860; *S.* father 1890; *m.* 1st, 1886, Hon. Annie Clayton Lindley (*d.* 1908), *d.* of Rt. Hon. Lord Lindley; one *s.* three *d.*; 2nd, 1910, Evelyn Louisa (*d.* 1914), *d.* of late His Hon. Sir Thomas Snagge; one *s.* one *d.* *Educ.:* Eton; Christ Church, Oxford. 1st Class Law and Vinerian Scholar; Barr. Lincoln's Inn, 1886. Contested (L.U.) Moray and Nairn, 1892; London School Board, 1891-94; M.P. (U.) Barnstaple Div. Devon, 1895-1900; High Sheriff of Berks 1908. *Heir: s.* Richard Cameron, Rifle Brigade [*b.* 18 Mar. 1894; *m.* 1917, Dora, *d.* of late Sir T. Dyer, Bt. *Educ.:* Eton; Christ Church, Oxford; Sandhurst. Served European War, 1914-16 (despatches, wounded)]. *Address:* Frilsham House, Yattendon. Berks. *Club:* Athenæum.   (*Died 15 Dec. 1922.*)

GULLAND, Rt. Hon. John William, P.C. 1917; M.P. (L.) Dumfries Burghs, 1906-1918; *b.* Edinburgh, 1864; *s.* of late John Gulland, Magistrate of City of Edinburgh; *m.* 1912, Edith Mary, *d.* of late Walker Allen of Whitefield. *Educ.:* Edinburgh High School and University. Was a corn merchant; director of Edinburgh Chamber of Commerce; lecturer on Practice of Commerce in Heriot-Watt College, 1898-99; member Edinburgh School Board, 1900-6; Edinburgh Town Council, 1904-1906; J.P., County of City of Edinburgh; on Advisory Committee of United Free Church; Hon. Treas. of Scottish Liberal Association; late Hon. President Young Scots Society; Secretary to Scottish Liberal Committee in House of Commons, 1906-9; Junior Lord of the Treasury and Scottish Whip, 1909-15; Joint Parliamentary Secretary to Treasury, 1915-1917. *Publications:* numerous pamphlets, leaflets, and magazine articles. *Recreations:* cycling, golf, angling. *Address:* 23 Sumner Place, S.W.7. *T.:* Kensington 5895. *Clubs:* Reform, National Liberal; Scottish Liberal, Edinburgh; Glasgow Liberal.
                         (*Died 26 Jan. 1920.*)

GUNDRY, Richard Simpson, C.B. 1904; *b.* 1838; *s.* of Richard Hickley Gundry of Hillworth Cottage, Devizes. *Educ.:* privately; Brussels. Editor of the North China Herald and correspondent of the Times in China, 1865-1878; Hon. Sec. to the China Association in London from its formation in 1889 to 1901; President, 1905-8; a frequent contributor to the principal reviews. *Publications:* China and Her Neighbours; China Present and Past, etc. *Address:* Hillworth Cottage, Devizes. *Club:* Conservative   (*Died 13 Mar. 1924.*)

GUNN, Sir John, Kt., *cr.* 1898; *b.* 28 Oct. 1837; *s.* of Donald Gunn of Achalybster, Caithness; *m.* 1st, 1871, Sarah Jane (*d.* 1874), *o. d.* of Thomas Hill of Cardiff; 2nd, 1877, Harriette (*d.* 1914), *d.* of James Boyle of Ballymacrea, Co. Antrim. *Address:* Ty-to-Maen, St. Mellons, nr. Cardiff; Mountstewart Square, Cardiff. *Clubs:* Reform; County Cardiff.   (*Died 20 Jan. 1918.*)

GUNNING, Col. Orlando George, C.M.G. 1915; D.S.O. 1917; 3rd Batt. (Reserve) Manchester Regt.; late Indian Army; *b.* 31 July 1867; *m.* 1902, Margaret Cecilia, *d.* of late Clinton Dawkins; one *s.* two *d.* Joined Manchester Regt. 1888; Captain Indian army, 1899; Major, 1906; Lt.-Col. 1914; served Miranzai Expedition, 1891 (medal with clasp); Expedition to Dongola, 1896; (Egyptian medal, medal); N.W. Frontier, India, 1897-8 (severely wounded;

despatches twice, medal with clasp); European War, 1914-15 (C.M.G., Bt. Col.); Mesopotamia, 1916-17 (despatches, D.S.O.). *Club:* East India United Service.   (*Died 15 Nov. 1917.*)

GUNSAULUS, Frank Wakeley, D.D., LL.D.; President of Armour Institute of Technology since 1892; Lyman Beecher Lecturer on Preaching at Yale Divinity School, 1911; *b.* Chesterville, Ohio, 1 Jan. 1856; *s.* of Hon. Joseph Gunsaulus, of Spanish extraction, and Mary J. Hawley, of English extraction; *m.* 1875, Anna Long of West Virginia; one *s.* four *d.* *Educ.:* Delaware Wesleyan Coll. Ohio. Began preaching in the M.E. Church at 19 years; Columbus, Ohio, first important church; left M.E. Church for Congregational, 1881; called to Newtonville, Massachusetts; Baltimore, Maryland, and Chicago, Illinois; Divinity Lecturer at Yale University, 1890; Professorial Lecturer at University of Chicago, 1896; Lecturer Chicago Theological Seminary, 1905; D.D. Beloit College, 1889; LL.D. Ohio Wesleyan University, 1905; Miami University, Oxford, LL.D., 1908. *Publications:* November at Eastwood; Transfiguration of Christ; Sermons, 1881-86; Monk and Knight, historical romance; Phidias and other Poems, 1891; Loose Leaves of Song, 1893; Songs of Night and Day, 1895; Gladstone, the Man and His Times, 1898; Man of Galilee, 1899. Sermons—Paths to Power, 1905; Paths to the City of God, 1906. Essays—The Higher Ministries of Recent English Poetry, 1907; The Minister and the Spiritual Life, 1911; Lecturing—Savonarola; John Hampden; Oliver Cromwell; Washington; Wendell Phillips; Five Points of American Statesmanship. *Address:* Armour Institute of Technology, Chicago, Ill. *Clubs:* Union League, Congregational, Mayflower. Colonial Wars, Society, University.
                         (*Died 17 Mar. 1921.*)

GUNTER, Colonel Sir Robert Benyon Nevill, 2nd Bt., *cr.* 1901; J.P.; 3rd Batt. Yorkshire Regiment; *b.* 4 Aug. 1871, *e. s.* of Sir Robert Gunter, 1st Bart., M.P., and Jane Marguerite, *d.* of Thomas Benyon, of Gledhow Hall, Yorkshire; *m.* 1902, Clara Lydia, widow of John Pritchard-Barrett; one *s.* Served S. African War, 1900-2 (despatches, Queen's medal with two clasps, King's medal with two clasps). *Heir: s.* Ronald Vernon; *b.* 8 Mar. 1904. *Address:* Wetherby Grange, Wetherby, Yorkshire. *Clubs:* Carlton, Hurlingham; Yorkshire, York.   (*Died 20 Aug. 1917.*)

GUNTHER, Venerable William James, M.A.: Canon of St. Andrew's Cathedral, Sydney; Archdeacon of Camden; Administrator of the Diocese, 1910; *b.* Wellington, N.S.W., 28 May 1839; *s.* of Archdeacon Günther; *m.* 1868, Mary Jane Willis; three *s.* two *d.* *Educ.:* The King's School, Parramatta; Queen's College, Oxon. Ordained Deacon, 1863; Priest, 1864; Curate of Stapenhill, Derbyshire, 1863-1865; St. Philip's, Sydney, 1866-68; Fellow of St. Paul's Coll. University of Sydney, 1884; Commissary, 1902-9; Vicar-General diocese of Sydney, 1902; Rector of St. John's, Parramatta, 1867-1910. *Publications:* Sermons, and Lecture, The Church of England in Australia; various papers. *Address:* 259 Walker Street, North Sydney. N.S.W.   (*Died 1918.*)

GUPPY, Henry Brougham, F.R.S. 1918; F.R.S.E., F.L.S., M.B., C.M.Edin. 1876; Gold Medallist, Linnæan Society, 1917; *b.* Dec. 1854; *s.* of T. S. Guppy, M.D., Falmouth; *m.* 1st, 1887, Annie, *d.* of J. Jordon; 2nd, 1900, Letitia, *d.* of A. J. Warde, Yalding, Kent; no *c.* *Educ.:* King's School, Sherborne; Queen's College, Birmingham; St. Bartholomew's Hospital, London; Edinburgh University. Served in the Medical Service of the Royal Navy, 1876-85, being Surgeon of H.M.S. Hornet on the China and Japan station, 1877-80, and of H.M.S. Lark, a surveying schooner in the Western Pacific, 1881-84; investigated coral-reef formation and plant-dispersal in the Keeling Islands and West Java, 1887-88; botanical and geological exploration in the Hawaiian and Fijian Islands, 1896-1900; investigating the littoral flora of the Pacific side of South America from the Straits of Magellan to Panama, 1903-4; after a short visit to Teneriffe, 1905, spent the winters of 1907-11 in the West Indies in botanical work; made a detailed examination of the flora of Mount Pico in the Azores, 1913-14. *Publications:* two volumes on the Solomon Islands, 1887; one volume on the Homes of Family Names, 1890; two volumes on his observations in the Pacific in Hawaii and Fiji, 1903-6; one volume on Studies in Seeds and Fruits, 1912; and one volume dealing with results obtained in the West Indies and Azores, 1917. *Recreations:* walking and boating. *Address:* Red House, Fowey.   (*Died 23 April 1926.*)

GUPTA, Bihari Lal, C.S.I. 1914; retired Indian Civil Service Pensioner; *b.* Calcutta, of Hindu parents of high caste, 26 Oct. 1849; *m.* 1872; now widower; three *s.* four *d. Educ.:* Calcutta; London University. Passed I.C.S. open competitive examination, 1869; called to Bar, Middle Temple, 1871; joined the Civil Service in India (Bengal); served in various districts; was Presidency Magistrate and Coroner of Calcutta for 5 years, and then District and Sessions Judge; was Remembrancer and Superintendent of Legal Affairs, Bengal, and member Bengal Council; raised to the Bench of the Calcutta High Court whence he retired, 1907; Minister of Law and Justice in the Baroda State, 1909; chief minister, 1912; retired 1914 to travel in Europe with H.H. the Maharaja Gaekwar; holds Degrees of Honour in Sanskrit and Persian; Delhi Durbar medals of 1908 and 1912. *Address:* 9 Lower Rawdon Street, Calcutta. *Club:* Calcutta.
    (*Died 20 Nov. 1916.*)

GUPTA, Sir Krishna Govinda, K.C.S.I., *cr.* 1911; C.S.I. 1909; Barrister-at-law, Middle Temple, 1878; late I.C.S.; *b.* Bhatpara, Dacca, 28 Feb. 1851; *e. s.* of Kali Narayan Gupta; *m.* 1866, Prasannatara, *d.* of Nabin Chandra Das (*d.* 1908); three *s.* five *d. Educ.:* Mymensing Government School; Dacca Coll.; London University College. Joined Indian Civil Service, 1873 (2nd at the final examination); passed through all the grades in Bengal; Secretary, Board of Revenue, 1887; Commissioner of Excise, 1893; Divisional Commissioner, 1901; Member Board of Revenue, 1904, being the first Indian to hold that appointment; Member Indian Excise Committee, 1905; on special duty in connection with the Fisheries of Bengal, 1906; deputed to Europe and America in 1907 to carry on fishery investigation, as a result of which a new department has been organised to conserve and develop the provincial fisheries; nominated to the Indian Council, 1907, being one of the two Indians who were for the first time raised to that position; retired from India Office on completion of term, March 1915; Member, Lord Esher's Army in India Committee, 1920. *Clubs:* National Liberal; Calcutta.   (*Died Mar. 1926.*)

GURDON, Maj.-Gen. Evelyn Pulteney, Indian Army; *b.* 4 June 1838; *e. s.* of late Rev. Philip Gurdon, M.A., J.P., of Cranworth, Norfolk, and Henrietta Laura, *e. d.* of late J. Pulteney of Northerwood House, Lyndhurst, Hants; *m.* 1858, Mary, 2nd *d.* of late Maj.-Gen. R. T. Sandeman, Indian Army, and *sis.* of late Col. Sir Robert Sandeman, K.C.S.I.; three *s.* one *d.* Entered army, 1852; Maj.-General, 1892; Punjab Commission, 1860-90; Commissioner and Divisional Judge and J.P. Punjab; served Indian Mutiny, 1857 (despatches, medal). *Address:* 12 Norton Road, Hove, Brighton. *Club:* Hove.   (*Died 5 Feb. 1921.*)

GURNEY, Sir Eustace, Kt., *cr.* 1911, J.P.; Lord Mayor of Norwich, 1910-11; *b.* 4 Oct. 1876; 2nd *s.* of late John Gurney, Sprowston Hall, Norfolk, and Isabel, Lady Talbot de Malahide; *m.* 1904, Anne Agatha, *d.* of late John Lee-Warner; three *s.* four *d. Educ.:* Eton; New College, Oxford. *Address:* Walsingham Abbey, Norfolk. *Clubs:* Athenæum, New University.   (*Died 3 Dec. 1927.*)

GURNEY, John Henry, J.P., D.L.; *b.* 31 July 1848; *m.* Margaret Jane, *d.* of Henry Edmund Gurney; one *s.* three *d. Educ.:* Harrow. Elected member of the Zoological Society, 1868, of the British Ornithologists Union, 1870, and of the Linnæan Society, 1885. *Publications:* works on Ornithology. *Address:* Keswick Hall, Norfolk. *Club:* Athenæum.
    (*Died 8 Nov. 1922.*)

GURNEY, Sir Somerville Arthur, K.C.V.O., *cr.* 1909; J.P., D.L.; Director of Barclay and Co., Ltd.; *b.* 21 Oct. 1885; *y. s.* of late Daniel Gurney and Lady Harriet Jemima, 4th *d.* of 16th Earl of Erroll; *m.* 1857, Katharine, *d.* of A. Hamond of Westacre, Norfolk; two *s.* four *d. Heir: s.* Walter Somerville [*b.* 1858; *m.* 1893, Violet, 2nd *d.* of Sir Thomas St. Vincent Hope Cochrane Troubridge, 2nd Bt.; one *s.* two *d.*]. *Address:* North Runcton Hall, Lynn. *Club:* White's.   (*Died 17 May 1917.*)

GURNEY, Sir Walter Edwin, Kt., *cr.* 1919; Auditor-General, Union of South Africa, since 1910. *Address:* Cape Town, South Africa.
    (*Died 8 Jan. 1924.*)

GURNHILL, Rev. James, B.A.; Canon of Lincoln; Member of the Aristotelian Society. *Educ.:* Emmanuel College, Cambridge. *Publication:* Through Creative Evolution to Incarnation and the Goal of Humanity, 1926. *Address:* The Priory, Minster Yard, Lincoln.
    (*Died 5 Feb. 1928.*)

GUTHRIE, Lord, Charles John Guthrie; M.A.; K.C. 1897; F.R.S.E.; F.S.A. (Scot.); Hon. LL.D. Edin.; Senator of the College of Justice in Scotland since 1907; Sheriff of Ross, Cromarty, and Sutherland, and one of the Commis. of Northern Lights, 1900-7; *b.* Edinburgh, 1849; *s.* of late Rev. Thomas Guthrie, D.D., Edinburgh, one of the founders of Ragged Schools, and first editor of The Sunday Magazine; *m.* Anne, *d.* of Rev. J. C. Burns, D.D., Kirkliston, 1876; two *s.* three *d. Educ.:* High School and Univ. of Edin. Admitted Advocate at the Scotch Bar 1875; mem. Edin. School Board, 1879-81; Legal Adviser of Free Church of Scotland, 1881-1900, and of United Free Church, 1900-2; Chairman, Houseletting Commission, 1906-7; Member of the Royal Commission on Historical Monuments in Scotland, 1908; Member of the Royal Commission on Divorce, 1910; chairman of Early Scottish Text Society, 1910; President of the Boys' Brigade of Great Britain and Ireland, 1910-19; President of Royal Scottish Geographical Society, 1917-19; member of Councils of Antiquarian and Scottish History Societies. *Publications:* joint-author of Memoir of Thomas Guthrie, D.D., 1875; John Knox and his House, 1898; editor of The History of the Reformation in Scotland, by John Knox, 1898; Cummy, R. L. Stevenson's nurse, an Appreciation, 1914. *Recreations:* travel, antiquities, music. *Address:* 13 Royal Circus, Edinburgh; Swanston Cottage, Midlothian. *T.:* Edinburgh 2049. *Clubs:* Royal Societies; University, Edinburgh.
    (*Died 28 April 1920.*)

GUTHRIE, David Charles; *b.* 25 July 1861; *e. s.* of late James Alexander Guthrie and Ellinor, 2nd *d.* of late Admiral Sir James Stirling (*m.* 2nd, 1879, Forster Fitzgerald Arbuthnot); *m.* 1891, Mary, *d.* of late Andrew Low, of Savannah, U.S.A.; one *s.* two *d.* M.P. Northamptonshire (S. Div.), 1892-95.

Address: Craigie, Dundee ; East Haddon Hall, Northampton.   *(Died 12 Jan. 1918.)*

GUTHRIE, John Douglas Maude, J.P., D.L. ; only *s.* of John Guthrie *(d.* 1877) and Harriet *(d.* 1879), *e. d.* of late Barnabas Maude ; *b.* 1856 ; *m.* 1884, Mary Macpherson (Myra), *d.* of late Duncan Davidson, of Tulloch, Ross-shire ; four *s.* one *d. Educ.:* Harrow. Captain, retired, late 19th Hussars ; served Egypt, 1882 (medals, Tel-el-Kebir and Khedive's Star) ; Lord of the Barony of Guthrie. *Recreations:* hunting, coaching, fishing, shooting. *Heir : s.* Ivan Douglas, M.C. [*b.* 6 Aug. 1886 ; *m.* 1921, Kathleen Mona, *yr. d.* of late Col. Hon. G. H. Gough, C.B., and Hon. Mrs Gough, 13 Grosvenor Place, S.W.]. *Address:* Guthrie Castle, Guthrie, Scotland. *Club:* Junior United Service.   *(Died 27 Jan. 1928.)*

GUTHRIE, Leonard George, M.A., M.D. Oxon., F.R.C.P. Lond. ; Senior Physician Children's Hospital, Paddington Green ; Physician Hosp. for Epilepsy and Paralysis, Maida Vale, W. ; Consulting Physician Home of Rest for the Dying, Clapham, and Potter's Bar Cottage Hospital ; *b.* 7 Feb. 1858 ; 2nd *s.* of late Thomas Anstey and Augusta Guthrie, of Kensington ; unmarried. *Educ.:* King's College School ; Magdalen College, Oxford University ; St. Bartholomew's Hospital, London. *Publications:* Various contributions to medical journals and societies. *Recreation:* study of antiquities of all sorts. *Address:* 15 Upper Berkeley Street, Portman Square, W. *T.:* 1623 Pad. *Club:* United University.   *(Died 28 Dec. 1918.)*

GUTTERY, Rev. Arthur Thomas, D.D. ; Minister, Princes Avenue Primitive Methodist Church,. Liverpool ; President National Free Church Council ; *b.* Birmingham, 15 June 1862 ; *s.* of Rev. Thos. Guttery, *m. d.* of Rev. E. Alford ; three *s.* three *d. Educ.:* Elinfield College, York ; London University. Entered Ministry, 1883 ; General Secretary Primitive Methodist Missionary Society, 1905-1913 ; President, Primitive Methodist Conference, 1916 ; Hartley Lecturer, 1920. *Publications:* constant writer in weekly and daily press both in England and America. *Recreations:* golf and chess. *Address:* Elmfield, Hartington Road, Sefton Park, Liverpool. *T.:* Wavertree 420, Liverpool. *Club:* Liverpool Reform.   *(Died 17 Dec. 1920.)*

GUY, John Crawford, M.A., LL.B. ; Advocate ; Sheriff-Substitute of the Lothians and Peebles at Edinburgh, 1904-21 ; *b.* Shawlands, Renfrewshire, 10 March 1861 ; *s.* of John Guy, solicitor, Glasgow ; *m.* 1891, Jessie, *d.* of John Morrison, Ruadhsgeir, Pollokshields, Glasgow ; two *s. Educ.:* Church of Scotland Training College, and University, Glasgow. Advocate, 1886 ; appointed Counsel for the Crown in *ultimus hæres* cases, 1895 ; Sheriff Court Depute, 1899 ; Extra Advocate Depute, 1899 ; Advocate Depute, 1901. *Address:* Carsaig House, North Knapdale, Argyllshire.   *(Died 18 Jan. 1928.)*

GUY, Lt.-Col. Robert Francis, C.M.G. 1919 ; D.S.O. 1916 ; Duke of Edinburgh's (Wiltshire) Regt. ; *b.* 1878 ; *e. s.* of late R. J. Guy ; *m.* 1915, Mrs. M. A. Dolphin (*née* de Blaquière) of Turoe, Loughrea, Co. Galway. *Educ.:* Monkton Combe School, nr. Bath. Joined the Wiltshire Regt. in South Africa, from the 9th K. Royal Rifle Corps, 1900 ; served S. African War, 1900-2 (Queen's medal with 3 clasps, King's medal with 2 clasps) ; Railway Staff Officer, 1901-2, at railhead, N. Transvaal ; Adjutant, 1st Batt. Wiltshire Regt. in India, 1905-8 ; Brigade-Major to York and Durham Infantry Brigade (T.F.), 1912-16 ; served European War, 1915-19, as a General Staff Officer (despatches 8 times, D.S.O., C.M.G., Bt. Lt.-Col.). *Address:* The Barracks, Devizes, Wilts.   *(Died 2 Oct. 1927.)*

446

GWALIOR, H.H. Maharajah Sindhia of, Hon. Lieut.-Gen. H.H. Mukhtar-ul-Mulk Azim-ul-Iktidar Raflush Shan Wala Shikoh Mohtasham-i-Dauran Umdat-ul-Umara Maharajadhiraja Alijah Hisam-us-Saltanat Maharaja Sir Madho Rao Scindhia Bahadur Srinath Mansur-i-Zaman Fidvi-i-Hazrat-i-Malika-i-Muazzam-i.Raff-ud-Darja-i-Inglistan, G.B.E. *cr.* 1917 ; Hon. Lt.-Gen. in the Army ; G.C.V.O., *cr.* 1902 ; G.C.S.I., *cr.* 1895 ; Hon. LL.D., Cambridge ; D.C.L.Oxon. ; Hon. and Extra A.D.C. to the King ; Hon. Col. 1st Duke of York's Own Lancers, 1906 ; *b.* 20 Oct. 1876 ; *S.* 1886. Made Hon. Col. British Army, 1898 ; Maj.-Gen. ; went to China as Orderly officer to General Gaselee, 1901 (medal) ; provided the expedition with a hospital ship ; organised the hospital ship Loyalty in 1914 and financed it for the duration of the war ; his troops fought with distinction in France, East Africa, Egypt, and Mesopotamia ; granted salute of 21 guns at 1911 Durbar ; salute made hereditary in 1917 ; Kaiser-i-Hind medal, 1900 ; London Coronation medals 1902 and 1911 ; Delhi Coronation medals, 1903 and 1911. *Heir : s.* George Jivaji Rao, *b.* 26 June 1916 (to whom the King stood sponsor). *Address:* Gwalior, Central India ; Shivpuri, Central India. *Club:* Marlborough.   *(Died 5 June 1925.)*

GWATKIN, Rev. Henry Melvill, M.A. ; Dixie Professor of Ecclesiastical History, Cambridge University and Fellow of Emmanuel College since 1891 ; Gifford Lecturer, Edinburgh University, 1903-5 ; Hon. D.D. Edinb. ; *y. s.* of Rev. R. Gwatkin, formerly Tutor of St. John's College, Cambridge ; *m.* Lucy de L., *d.* of Rev. Thos. Brock, vicar of St. John's, Guernsey, 1874 ; one *s.* one *d. Educ.:* Shrewsbury School ; St. John's College, Cambridge ; Fellow, 1868-74 ; Theological Lecturer, 1874-91. 1st Class Honours Mathem., Classics, Moral Science, Theology ; Carus Greek Test Prize, 1865 and 1869 ; Crosse Scholar, 1869 ; Tyrwhitt Hebrew Scholar, 1870. *Publications:* Studies of Arianism, 1882 ; The Arian Controversy, 1889 ; Selections from Early Christian Writers, 1893 ; Editor of the Church Past and Present 1899 ; The Eye for Spiritual Things (Sermons) ; The Knowledge of God (Gifford Lectures, 1906) ; Early Church History, 1909 ; Joint Editor of Cambridge Medieval History since 1911. *Address:* 8 Scrope Terrace, and Emmanuel College, Cambridge.   *(Died 14 Nov. 1916.)*

GWATKIN, Major-General Sir Willoughby Garnons, K.C.M.G., *cr.* 1920 ; C.B. 1916 ; C.M.G. 1918 ; LL.D. Toronto ; Hon. Major-General (retired) ; Major-General and Hon. Lieut.-General Canadian Militia ; *b.* 11 Aug. 1859 ; 4th *s.* of late Frederick Gwatkin of 9 New Square, Lincoln's Inn, and Grove House, Twickenham. *Educ.:* Shrewsbury ; King's College, Cambridge ; Sandhurst. Appointed to Manchester Regiment, 1882, and Colonel of it since 1924 ; Grand Officer of the Order of St. Sava ; Commander of the Legion of Honour ; Commander of the Crown of Belgium. *Clubs:* United Service, Garrick, Sports.   *(Died 2 Feb. 1925.)*

GWILLIM, John Cole, B.Sc., Professor of Mining, Queen's University, Kingston, since 1902 ; *b.* England ; *m.* 1900, Jane Birch, Vanconver, B.C. *Address:* Queen's University, Kingston, Ontario. *Club:* Frontenac, Kingston.

GWYNNE, Major-General Nadolig Ximenes, Hon. Major-General (retired) ; *b.* Glanbràn, Carmarthenshire, 25 Dec. 1832 ; *m.* Mary Shee Jackson, *d.* of Major G. C. Jackson, 16th Lancers. *Educ.:* Cheltenham ; Llandovery. Received Commission in 41st The Welch Regt. 1855 ; served on the Staff in India and in the Afghan Expeditions of 1878-80 ; commanded the 85th, 2nd King's Shropshire Light Infantry ; half pay, 1887 ; P.S.C. ; raised 5th Batt. Devon

GWYNN, Rev. John, D.D., D.C.L. See page xx.

Volunteers, 1914. *Address:* Brockendean, Bournemouth.   (*Died 9 May 1920.*)

GWYNNE, Rupert Sackville, M.P. (C.), Eastbourne or Southern Division of Sussex since Jan. 1910; Financial Secretary War Office, 1923-1924; *b.* 2 Aug. 1873; *s.* of late James Eglinton Anderson Gwynne, of Folkington Manor, Sussex; *m.* 1905, Hon. Stella Ridley, *d.* of 1st Viscount Ridley; four *d. Educ.:* Shrewsbury; Pembroke College, Cambridge (B.A. 1895). Called to Bar, Inner Temple, 1898. *Address:* Wootton Manor, Polegate, Sussex; 47 Catherine Street, S.W., T.: Victoria 5335. *Clubs:* Bachelors', Carlton.   (*Died 12 Oct. 1924.*)

GWYNNE-EVANS, Sir William, 1st Bt., *cr.* 1913; Director of the Real Estate Corporation of South Africa; *b.* 3 Feb. 1845: *m.* 1st, 1886, Mary Anna (*d.* 1902), *d.* of Evan Williams; one *s.* five *d.*; 2nd, 1909, Blanche Sophia, *d.* of Rev. J. C. E. Besant, Vicar of Lydney; one *s.* one *d.* Gave to the nation the Arthur Morrison collection of Chinese and Japanese Paintings now at the British Museum. *Heir:* *s.* Evan Gwynne [*b.* 4 May 1877; *m.* 1908, Ada, *d.* of W. S. Andrews, New York; two *s. Address:* Oaklands Park, Newnham, Co. Gloucester]. *Address:* 93 Queen's Gate, S.W.1; *T.:* Western 4096; Penlan Hall, Fordham, Essex. *Clubs:* Queen's; Rand, Johannesburg.
    (*Died 23 Jan. 1927.*)

GWYTHER, Ven. Arthur, Archdeacon of Demerara, 1896-1910; Canon of St. George's Cathedral, Georgetown, 1894-1910; Incumbent of St. Philip's, Georgetown, 1896-1910. *Educ.:* St. John's College, Cambridge (M.A.). Ordained, 1874; Curate of Weybridge, 1874-75; Headmaster, Queen's College Grammar School, Georgetown, 1875-77; Vicar of St. Pauls, Wakenaam, 1877-80; missionary, Demerara River, 1880-88; Chaplain, H.M. Penal Settlement, Mazaruni, 1888-90; Rector of Holy Trinity, Essequibo, 1890-96; Clerical Assessor, 1896-1910; Vicar-General, 1897, 1899, 1902, 1904-1910; Administrator of Diocese, 1900; Chaplain, Georgetown Gaol (unpaid), 1897-1910 (retired 1910); Licensed Preacher, Diocese Lincoln, 1912-15. *Address:* Rawnsley, Capstone Road, Bournemouth.   (*Died 21 Feb. 1917.*)

GWYTHER, Frank Edwin, C.I.E. 1914; Secretary to Government, Punjab, since 1912. *Educ.:* Thomasson College. Entered Public Works Department, India, 1881; Executive Engineer, 1895; Under Secretary to Government, 1904; Superintending Engineer, 1908. *Address:* Public Works Department, Lahore, Punjab.   (*Died 6 Sept. 1918.*)

GYE, His Honour Judge Percy, County Court Judge for Hampshire since 1896; 4th *s.* of late Frederick Gye; *b.* 25 Nov. 1845; *m.* Constance, 3rd *d.* of James Sant, R.A., 1880; two *s.* one *d. Educ.:* privately. Called to Bar, Inner Temple, 1872. *Address:* Piper's Field, Winchester, Hants. *T.A.:* Gye, Winchester. *Club:* Hampshire County. (*Died 13 June 1916.*)

H

HABBERTON, John; author; *b.* 24 Feb. 1842; father, English; mother, American; *m.* 1868; two *s.* two *d. Educ.:* various schools, no college. Printer, soldier, merchant, journalist, author. *Publications:* Helen's Babies; All He Knew; Life of George Washington; Brueton's Bayou; Caleb Wright; Some Boys' Doings; The Tiger and the Insect, and other books; his only play, Deacon Crankett, had a two years' run. *Recreations:* sailing and gardening. *Address:* Montclair, New Jersey, U.S.A.   (*Died 25 Feb. 1921.*)

HACKER, Arthur, R.A. 1910; A.R.A. 1894; R.I., 1918; figure painter; *b.* London, 25 Sept.

1858; 2nd *s.* of Edward Hacker, line engraver; *m.* 1907, Lilian, 3rd *d.* of late Edward Price-Edwards. *Educ.:* London, Paris. Student Royal Academy, 1876; studied Atelier Bonnat, Paris, 1880-81; travelled in Morocco, Algeria, Spain, Italy, etc. *Pictures:* Her Daughter's Legacy, 1880; The Mother; Children's Prayer, and other domestic subjects; Pelagia and Philammon, 1887; Via Victis; Christ and the Magdalen; Annunciation; The Cloud; Vale; Studies of London, etc.; also many portraits. *Recreations:* river, billiards. *Address:* 178 Cromwell Road, S.W. *Club:* Arts.   (*Died 12 Nov. 1919.*)

HACKETT, Hon. Sir John Winthrop, Kt., *cr.* 1911; K.C.M.G., *cr.* 1913; J.P., M.L.C., M.A.; Hon. LL.D. Dublin, 1902; Member Legislative Council, W. Australia, 1890, now Senior Member; *b.* Ireland, 1848; *s.* of late Rev. J. W. Hackett, M.A., and Jane, *d.* of late H. Monck Mason, LL.D., Librarian, King's Inns; *m.* 1905, Deborah, *d.* of Frederick Slade Drake-Brockman, Perth; one *s.* four *d. Educ.:* Trinity College, Dublin. Editor and Proprietor of the West Australian and Western Mail, Perth; member of Irish, N.S.W., W.A., and Victorian Bars; late member Federal Council of Australasia. Offered Knighthood 1902, but declined; Delegate National Australasian Federal Convention, 1891, and Federal Convention, 1897-98; P. Grand Master Freemasons, West Australian Grand Lodge; President Zoological Gardens, West Australian Museum, Library, and National Gallery, etc.; Registrar of diocese of Perth, and Chancellor of Cathedral; Chairman of Royal Commission on the establishment of a State University in W.A.; First Chancellor of the University, 1912; First Hon. degree in University of LL.D.; founded first Chair, that of Agriculture, in University. *Address:* St. George's Terrace, Perth, Western Australia. *Clubs:* National Liberal; Weld, Perth, W.A.; South-Western, Bunbury; Albany, Albany, W.A.   (*Died 19 Feb. 1916.*)

HACKETT. Colonel Robert Isaac Dalby, C.B.E., M.A., M.D. with honours; retired pay; *b.* 31 March 1857; *s.* of Thomas Hackett, J.P., Castletown, King's County; *m.* 1895, Evelyn Mary Wynne Jones; one *s.* one *d. Educ.:* Chesterfield School; Queen's University, Ireland. Entered Army Medical Service, 1881; served in Cyprus and Egypt, 1882; Sudan, 1885; in Nova Scotia, 1886-7; South Africa, 1888-94, in Denizulu Rebellion; South African War, 1899-1902; South Africa, 1902-6 and 1910-11; in India as Administrative Officer, Sialkote and Abbotabad Brigades, 1911-1912; retired, 1912; rejoined for European War. *Address:* Ocala, Eldorado Road, Cheltenham. *Club:* New, Cheltenham.   (*Died 15 Feb. 1925.*)

HACKETT, Very Rev. T. Aylmer P., D.D., Dean of Limerick since 1913; Chaplain to Forces; *b.* 5 December 1854; *e. s.* of Thomas Hackett, J.P., Castletown, King's Co.; *m.* 1st, 1880, Helen, *d.* of James Whiteside, M.D., Ballyarton, Coleraine; two *s.* one *d.*; 2nd, Ella T., *d.* of Col. T. H. Maginniss. *Educ.:* Chesterfield College; Trinity College, Dublin. Graduated 1877 as Senior Moderator in Mental and Moral Philosophy, after taking honours in several subjects; B.D. 1889, D.D. 1890; Curate of Coleraine, 1877-80; Curate in Charge of Newcastle West, 1880-81; Rector of Kilmallock, 1881-1910; Chancellor, 1904; Archdeacon of Limerick, 1912-13; Rector of St. Michael's, Limerick, 1910-13; Canon of St. Patrick's, 1907; Member of Board of Patronage, Diocesan Court; Church Representative Body, Diocesan Council; Board of Education and Board of Missions. *Publications:* The Intermediate State; Papal Infallibility and Supremacy; The Parson and Priest. *Recreations:* In College days cricket, fond of athletics. *Address:* The Deanery, Limerick. *Clubs:* Dublin University; Limerick County. (*Died 4 Dec. 1923.*)

HACKETT, William Henry, F.J.I.; Writer on Finance and Allied Subjects; *s.* of late T. Sandys Hackett; *b.* Leicester, 11 June 1853; *m.* Helen Louisa, *d.* of late Thomas Whitehead, Liverpool; two *s.* two *d.* *Educ.:* Grammar School, Manchester. Apprenticed to, and sub sequently foreign correspondent in, a Manchester shipping firm; began contributing to Manchester Guardian, 1881, and accepted appointment on London staff, 1883; City Editor, Yorkshire Post, 1890-1920; for ten years chief subeditor of Statist; commercial contributor to Glasgow Herald, 1894-1907; financial correspondent and leader writer for the Scotsman, 1909-19; relinquished all journalistic work in 1920 owing to failing health. *Recreations:* gardening and billiards. *Address:* Sandhills, Wethersfield, nr. Braintree, Essex.
(Died 19 Oct. 1926.)

HADDEN, Sir Charles Frederick, K.C.B., *cr.* 1908 : C.B. 1902 ; Major-General, R.A. retired ; J.P.: D.L. ; Sheriff for Herts, 1919; Member Herts County Council ; *b.* Nottingham, 2 June 1854 ; *o. s.* of late Charles Stanton Hadden, Ingleside, Sunningdale ; *m.* 1885, Frances Mabel, 3rd *d.* of late Col. Clement Strong, Coldstream Guards. *Educ.:* Elstree School; Cheltenham College. R.M.A. Passed out of R.M.A. first for Royal Engineers, but selected Royal Artillery; commissioned Lieut. 1873 ; assistant to superintendent Royal Laboratory, 1885 ; Inspector of laboratory stores, 1888 ; Chief Inspector, Royal Arsenal, Woolwich, 1893 ; Member of the Ordnance Committee, and Associate Member of the Explosives Committee, 1901 ; Commandant Ordnance College, 1904 ; Director of Artillery, Headquarters, 1904-7; Master-General of the Ordnance and Member of the Army Council, 1907-13 ; President Ordnance Board and Royal Artillery Committee, 1913-15. *Recreations:* shooting, fishing, motoring. *Address:* Rossway, Berkhampstead, Herts. *T.A.:* Northchurch. *Club:* United Service. *(Died 13 Sept. 1924.)*

HADDINGTON, 11th Earl of (*cr.* 1619), **George Baillie-Hamilton Arden,** K.T. 1902 ; A.D.C., V.L., J.P. ; Baron Binning, 1613 ; Representative Peer for Scotland since 1874 ; Lord-Lieutenant Haddingtonshire since 1876 ; A.D.C. to the King ; Hon. Colonel Lothians and Berwickshire Yeomanry ; *b.* 26 July 1827 ; *s.* of 10th Earl and Georgina, *d.* of Archdeacon Robert Markham ; *S.* father 1870 ; *m.* Helen, *d.* of Sir John Warrender, Bt., and Frances, *d.* of Lord Chief Justice Alvanley, 1854 (*d.* 1889); two *s.* three *d.* Owns about 34,100 acres. *Heir:* *s.* Lord Binning. *Address:* Tyninghame, Prestonkirk, Haddington ; Arderne Hall, Tarporley, Cheshire. *Clubs:* Carlton, Hurlingham, New, Edinburgh. *(Died 11 June 1917.)*

HADDOCK, Edgar Augustus, Principal of the Leeds College of Music ; *b.* Leeds, 23 Nov. 1859; *y. s.* of G. Haddock ; *m.* 1896, Hilda, *d.* of Joseph Sykes, Harrogate and Morley; one *s.* *Educ.:* private schools in Leeds. Made debut at Crystal Palace, 1883 ; given many Concerts of Programmes entirely of British Music, Recitals devoted to Schumann, Brahms, the complete Sonatas for Pianoforte and Violin of Beethoven in chronological order, Historical Recitals, etc., 1884 ; he began his series of Musical Evenings at Leeds, 1885 ; played with Joachim one of the unaccompanied duets of Spohr at a Huddersfield Subscription Concert, 1890 ; founded the Leeds College of Music in 1894, the Leeds Orchestra in 1899; instituted in 1923 the Leeds Competitive Musical Festival. *Publications:* Violin music: Practical Violin School; The Student's Series of Violin Solos; Scale Manual; The Complete Soloist for Violinists. Orchestral music: Ballade Norvegienne for Violin and Orchestra; Triumphal March. Church music:

448

Jesu, my Lord; Lord God Almighty; numbers of fugitive instrumental and vocal pieces. Literature: Music in Yorkshire ; A Retrospect: Then—and Now; Pages from a Music-Lover's Note-book ; The Art of Clear Speech, etc. *Recreations:* chess, collecting curios. *Address:* 37 University Road, Leeds ; Kearby, via Wetherby, Yorkshire. *T.A.:* Haddock, Leeds. *T.:* Leeds, Central 24641 and 27924. *M.:* NW 2913. *(Died 9 Aug. 1926.)*

HADEN, Francis Seymour, C.M.G. ; *b.* 7 Mar. 1850 ; *e. s.* of late Sir Francis S. Haden ; *m.* 1885, Ethel, *d.* of Lt.-Col. Branfill (late 10th Hussars), Upminster Hall, Essex ; one *d.* *Educ.:* Westminster School; Christchurch, Oxford (B.A. with honours, 1873). Assist. private secretary, 1876, and private secretary, 1877, to Sir Henry E. G. Bulwer, G.C.M.G., Lt.-Gov. of Natal; Chief Clerk, Colonial Secretary's Office, Natal, 1880 ; Assist. Colonial Secretary, 1881 ; Acting Colonial Treasurer, 1885, and Acting Colonial Secretary in same year ; Colonial Secretary, 1887, and on several occasions Deputy-Governor of Natal and Zululand ; in 1892 was granted a Dormant Commission, under which he twice administered the Governments of Natal and Zululand ; a member of the Executive and Legislative Councils of the Colony from 1885 ; was President of the Natal Trade Commission in 1885 ; and on various occasions a delegate to the Governments of the Cape Colony and the South African Republic on customs and railway matters; retired in 1893 on the adoption by Natal of responsible government. *Decorated,* 1890, for services in connection with proposed Customs and Railway Union between the Orange Free State, Cape Colony, and Natal. *Recreations:* golf, shooting, and fishing—especially the last-named. *Club:* Whites'. *(Died 21 Mar. 1918.)*

HADLEY, William Sheldon; LL.D., Master of Pembroke Coll., Cambridge, since 1912 ; Lecturer in Classics and in Modern History; Fellow of Pembroke College, 1882; Treasurer, 1887 ; Assistant Tutor, 1891 ; President and Tutor, 1902 ; *m.* 1894, Edith Jane, *d.* of late Rev. R. Foster, formerly Chaplain of Royal Hibernian Military School, Phœnix Park, Dublin, and Vicar of Upavon, Wilts ; one *surv. s.* *Address:* Master's Lodge, Pembroke College, Cambridge ; Shallcross, Heacham, Norfolk. *Club:* Junior Carlton.
(Died 25 Dec. 1927.)

HADOW, Col. Reginald Campbell, D.S.O. ; retired ; late Commanding 15th Sikhs, I.S.C. ; *s.* of late Patrick Douglas Hadow, J.P. (chairman of P. & O. Steam Navigation Co.) of the Priory, Sudbury, Middlesex ; *b.* 6 July 1851 ; *m.* 1876, Annie Sophia Erskine (*d.* 1912), *d.* of late Gen. David Pott, C.B., of Borthwickshiel, Hawick, N.B. *Educ.:* Cheltenham. Entered 55th Regt., 1870; B.S.C., 1876; Capt. (15th Sikhs) B.S.C. (now I.S.C.) 1882 ; Major, 1890 ; Lt.-Col. 1896; Brevet Colonel, 1902 ; served Afghan War, 1878-80 ; present at actions of Ahmed Khel and Urzoo; march from Kabul to Khandahar, and battle of Khandahar (medal with 2 clasps, bronze star) ; Soudan Expedition, 1885 ; present at actions of Tofrek and Tamai (medal with 2 clasps, bronze star) ; Miranzai Expedition (medal with clasp), 1891 ; Chitral relief force, 1895 ; present at storming of Malakand Pass, and forcing passage of Swat River (despatches, medal with clasp, D.S.O.) ; Tirah Expedition, 1897 ; present at actions of Dargai and operations in Khanki Valley (very severely wounded, 3 clasps). *Recreations:* cricket, golf, and shooting. *Address:* The Ferns, Spencer Road, Eastbourne. *Clubs:* United Service: Sussex, Eastbourne.
(Died 10 Oct. 1919.)

HAGGARD, Lieut.-Col. Andrew Charles Parker, D.S.O. 1886; author, novelist, historian, poet; *b.* Bradenham Hall, Norfolk, 7 Feb. 1854; 5th *s.* of late William Meybohm Rider Haggard and Ella, *d.* and co-heiress of late Bazett Doveton, K.I.C.S.; *m.* 1906, Ethel Fowler, widow of late Edward Fowler. *Educ.*: Westminster School. Joined 25th Regt. (King's Own Borderers), 1873; served in India, Aden; also on Staff, Egypt, 1882; joined Egyptian Army, 1883; on special service on the Red Sea Littoral (special naval despatches), 1884; present at battle of Tamai (despatches), 1884; investment of Suakin by Osman Digna, in command of 1st Batt. Egypt. Army (4th Class Osmanieh), 1884-85; reconnaissance to Hasheen, 1885; operations at Suakin, 1885; Special Recruiting Commission with Brig.-Gen. Yusuf Pasha Schudi to investigate abuses of the conscription, 1885; commanded 1st Batt. Egypt. Army in operations on the Nile, including the battle of Ginness, 1885-86; commanded Egypt. troops on the frontier (despatches, medal and star, several clasps, D.S.O., 3rd class Medjidie), 1886; co-founder Veterans' Club of British Columbia, 1915. *Publications*: Ada Triscott, written 1881, published 1890; articles on sport and travel, in Blackwood and the Field, constantly from 1884; Polyglot Poems, 1887; Dodo and I, 1889; Leslie's Fate, 1889; A Strange Tale of a Scarabaeus, 1891; Tempest-Torn, 1894; Under Crescent and Star, 1896; Hannibal's Daughter, 1898; Love rules the Camp, 1901; Sporting Yarns, 1903; Sidelights on the Court of France, 1903; A Canadian Girl, 1904; Louis XIV. in Court and Camp, 1904; A Bond of Sympathy, published in America under name of Silver Bells, 1905; The Regent of the Roués, 1905; The Real Louis XV., 1906; A Persian Roseleaf, 1906; Louis XVI. and Marie Antoinette, 1909; Two Great Rivals, 1910; The Amours of Henri de Navarre and of Marguerite de Valois, 1910; The France of Joan of Arc, 1911; Two Worlds, a Romance, 1911; The Romance of Bayard, 1912; Louis XI. and Charles the Bold, 1913; Remarkable Women of France (1431-1749), 1914; Women of the Revolutionary Era, 1914; Thérèse of the Revolution, 1921; Madame de Staël, Her Trials and Triumphs, 1922. *Recreations*: fishing, shooting, especially in connection with exploration of little-known rivers, forests, and mountain ranges in Canada. *Address*: Camp Haggard, Vancouver Island. *Club*: Fly Fishers'.

(Died 13 May 1925.)

HAGGARD, Major Edward Arthur (pseudonym, Arthur Amyand), author; *b.* Bradenham Hall, Norfolk, 5 Nov. 1860; *y. s.* of late William Meybohm Rider Haggard, Bradenham Hall; *m.* Emily, *d.* of late Edmund Calvert of Walton-le-Dale, Lancashire, 1887; one *s.* one *d. Educ.*: Shrewsbury; Pembroke Coll. Camb.(B.A.); Royal Military Coll. Joined 1st Batt. King's Shropshire Light Infantry, 1884; appointed to Army Service Corps, 1889; retired and joined 3rd Batt. Bedfordshire Regt. (Militia), 1892; retired May 1904; served in Suakin Campaign, including march to Tamai, 1885, and throughout British occupation until May 1886 (Egyptian medal with clasp and star); on special service attached to A.S.C., South Africa, March 1900 till May 1901 (medal, four clasps); First Secretary, Union Jack Club, 1902-7; Founder and Chairman Veterans' Club, 1907; Founder of the Veterans' Corps, 1908; Joint-Founder (with Mr. J. A. Malcolm) of the Veterans' Association, 1915. *Publications*: Only a Drummer Boy, 1894; With Rank and File, or Sidelights on Soldier Life, 1895; Comrades in Arms, 1895; The Kiss of Isis, 1900; The Social Status of the Soldier in connection with Recruiting, 1906; Malcolm the Patriot, 1907. *Recreations*: hunting, fishing, shooting, travelling. *Address*: 27J Bramham Gardens, S. Kensington, S.W.5. *T.*: Kensington 8727. *Clubs*: Army and Navy, Junior Naval and Military. *(Died 19 Jan. 1925.)*

HAGGARD, Sir (Henry) Rider, Kt., *cr.* 1912; K.B.E., *cr.* 1919; J.P. for Norfolk and Suffolk; Chairman of Justices Petty Sessional Division of Bungay; barrister-at-law; is an Authority on Empire Migration and on Imperial, Agricultural, and Social Conditions; author; *b.* Bradenham, Norfolk, 22 June 1856; 6th *s.* of William Meybohm Rider Haggard, Bradenham Hall; *m.* Mariana Louisa, *o. c.* of late Major Margitson, Ditchingham, Norfolk, 1880; three *d.* Secretary to Sir Henry Bulwer, Governor of Natal, 1875; on the staff of Sir Theophilus Shepstone, special commissioner to the Transvaal, 1877; with late Gen. Brooke, R.E., formally hoisted the British flag over the South African Republic at Pretoria, on the Queen's Birthday, 1877; Secretary to Secocoeni Commission; Master High Court of the Transvaal, 1878; Lieutenant and Adjutant Pretoria Horse, 1879; Barr. Lincoln's Inn, 1884; Chairman of Committee, Society of Authors, 1896-98; journeyed through England investigating condition of agriculture and of the rural population, 1901 and 1902; appointed British Government Special Commissioner to Report on Salvation Army Settlements U.S.A., etc., 1905; Chairman Reclamation and Unemployed Labour Committee of the Royal Commission on Coast Erosion and Afforestation, 1906-11; travelled round the world as Member Dominions Royal Commission, 1912-17; visited all the Oversea Dominions as Honorary Representative of the Royal Colonial Institute in connection with the After-War Settlement of Ex-Service Men, 1916; nominated Hon. Life Fellow of R. Colonial Institute, and presented with inscribed address of thanks signed by President and Council of the Institute, in recognition of "conspicuous service to the British Empire," 1916; elected a Vice-President R. Colonial Institute, 1917; Member Empire Settlement Committee, 1917; Member East Africa Committee, 1924; Member of Council of Imperial Society of Knights; has travelled much throughout the world. *Publications*: Cetywayo and his White Neighbours, 1882; Dawn, 1884; The Witch's Head, 1885; King Solomon's Mines, 1885; She, 1887; Jess, 1887; Allan Quatermain, 1887; Maiwa's Revenge, 1888; Mr. Meeson's Will, 1888; Colonel Quaritch, V.C., 1888; Cleopatra, 1889; Allan's Wife, 1889; Beatrice, 1890; Eric Brighteyes, 1891; Nada the Lily, 1892; Montezuma's Daughter, 1894; The People of the Mist, 1894; Joan Haste, 1895; Heart of the World, 1896; Dr. Therne, 1898; Swallow, a Story of the Great Trek, 1899; A Farmer's Year, 1899; Black Heart and White Heart, 1900; Lysbeth, a Tale of the Dutch, 1901; A Winter Pilgrimage, 1901; Rural England (2 vols.), 1902; Pearl Maiden, 1903; Stella Fregelius, 1903; The Brethren, 1904; A Gardener's Year, 1905; Ayesha, or The Return of She, 1905; Report to British Government on Salvation Army Colonies, U.S.A., and at Hadleigh, England, with Scheme of National Land Settlement, 1905; The Poor and the Land, 1905; The Way of the Spirit, 1906; Benita, 1906; Fair Margaret, 1907; The Ghost Kings, 1908; The Yellow God, 1909; Morning Star, 1910; Queen Sheba's Ring, 1910; Regeneration (Report on Social Work of Salvation Army), 1910; Rural Denmark and its Lessons, 1911; The Mahatma and the Hare, 1911; Red Eve, 1911; Marie, 1912; Child of Storm, 1913; The Wanderer's Necklace, 1914; The Holy Flower, 1915; The Ivory Child, 1916; Report to Royal Colonial Institute, 1916; Finished, 1917; Love Eternal, 1918; Moon of Israel, 1918; When the World Shook, 1919; The Ancient Allan, 1920; Smith and the Pharaohs, and other stories, 1920; She and Allan, 1921; The Virgin of the Sun, 1922; Wisdom's Daughter, 1923; Heu-Heu: or The Monster, 1924; The World's Desire (with Andrew Lang), 1891. *Address*: Ditchingham

House, Norfolk. *T.A.:* Haggard, Ditchingham. *Clubs:* Athenæum, National, Cecil.
(*Died 14 May 1925.*)

HAGGARD, Sir William Henry (Doveton), K.C.M.G., *cr.* 1908 ; C.B. 1903 ; J.P. ; *b.* 25 June 1846 ; *e. s.* of William Meybohm Rider Haggard, Bradenham Hall, Norfolk, and Ella, *d.* of Bazett Doveton ; *m.* 1887, Emily Margaret (Nitie) (*d.* 1924), *d.* of Joseph Hancox ; one *s.* two *d. Educ.:* Tonbridge School ; Winchester ; Magdalen College, Oxford. Entered Diplomatic Service, 1869 ; Secretary of Legation, Rio de Janeiro, 1885 ; Athens, 1887 ; Minister Resident at Quito, 1890 ; Consul-General at Tunis, 1894 ; Minister Resident at Caracas, 1897-1902 ; Envoy Extraordinary and Minister Plenipotentiary at Buenos Aires and Asuncion, 1902-6 ; Brazil, 1906-14 ; retired, 1913 ; has Diamond Jubilee and Coronation Medals of King Edward VII. and King George V. ; is a Fellow of the Royal Geographical and Royal Asiatic Societies. *Publications:* (with Mr. Guy Le Strange) The Vazir of Lenkuran—a standard book for the study of modern Persian. *Recreation:* fond of all sports, specially of hunting. *Address:* Hartlip House, Sittingbourne. *Club:* National.
(*Died 22 Jan. 1926.*)

HAGGERSTON of Haggerston, Sir John de Marie ; 9th Bt. ; *cr.* 1643 ; *b.* Axminster, Devonshire, 27 Nov. 1852 ; *e. s.* of 8th Bt. and Sarah, *d.* of Henry Knight, Axminster ; *S.* father 1858 ; *m.* Marguerite, *d.* of Lewis Eyre, 1887., *Educ.:* Ushaw. *Recreations:* shooting, hunting. Owns about 15,000 acres in Northumberland. *Heir:* b. Edward Charlton de Marie [b. 8 Feb. 1857 ; *m.* 1904, Florence, 3rd *d.* of W. H. Perrin ; two *s.* two *d. Club:* Junior Carlton]. *Address:* Ellingham Hall, Chathill, R.S.O.
(*Died 29 Nov. 1918.*)

HAGGERSTON of Haggerston, Sir Edward Charlton de Marie ; 10th Bt., *cr.* 1643 ; J.P. ; *b.* Teignmouth, Devonshire, 8 Feb. 1857 ; *s.* of 8th Bt. and Sarah, *d.* of Henry Knight, Axminster ; *S.* brother, 1918 ; *m.* 1904, Florence, 3rd *d.* of W. H. Perrin ; two *s.* two *d. Educ.:* Ushaw ; Prior Park. Passed exams. for Solicitor, but never practised ; a Member of Belford Guardians and R.D.C. for 30 years ; served on the Northumberland Military Appeal Tribunal (Berwick Panel) during the War. Owns about 13,000 acres in Northumberland. *Heir: s.* Hugh Carnaby de Marie, *b.* 7 Mar. 1906. *Address:* Ellingham Hall, Chathill, R.S.O., Northumberland. *T.:* Chathill 4. *Club:* Junior Carlton. (*Died 1 April 1925.*)

HAGUE, Anderson, R.I. *Address:* Vardre, Deganwy, Llandudno(*Died 24 Dec. 1916.*)

MAGUE, Arnold, D.Sci. Columbia, 1901 ; LL.D. Aberdeen, 1906 ; Geologist, U.S. Geological Survey, since 1880 ; *b.* Boston, 3 Dec. 1840 ; *s.* of Rev. Dr. William Hague and Mary Bowditch Moriarty ; *g. s.* of James Hague, Yorkshire. *Educ.:* Yale ; Göttingen ; Heidelberg. Geologist, U.S. Geological Exploration of 40th Parallel, 1867-78 ; Geologist in the service of Chinese Government, 1878-79 ; Field service in Rocky Mountains and for several years in Yellowstone National Park and adjacent country ; Secretary, National Academy of Sciences, since 1901 ; President Geological Society of America ; member of many scientific societies. *Publications:* Descriptive Geology, vol. ii., U.S. ; Geological Exploration of 40th Parallel, 1877 ; Geology of the Eureka District, 1892 ; Geology, Yellowstone National Park, 1899 ; Tertiary Volcanoes of the Absaroka Range, 1898 ; Geological Atlas of Yellowstone Park, 1904. *Recreations:* mountain climbing, sailing, fishing. *Address:* Washington, U.S.A.
(*Died 15 May 1918.*)

HAIG, 1st Earl, *cr.* 1919 ; **Douglas Haig ;** Viscount Dawick, *cr.* 1919 ; Baron Haig and

29th Laird of Bemersyde ; O.M. 1919 ; K.T. 1917 ; G.C.B., *cr.* 1915 ; K.C.B., *cr.* 1913 ; K.C.I.E., *cr.* 1911 ; G.C.V.O., *cr.* 1916 : K.C.V.O. 1909 ; C.B. 1900 ; A.D.C. Gen. to H.M. 1914-1917 ; Colonel of R.H.G., 17th Lancers, K.O.S.B., and London Scottish ; Chairman of Council of the United Services Fund since 1921 ; *b.* 19 June 1861 ; *y. s.* of John Haig, J.P., of Cameronbridge, Fife, and Rachael, 4th *d.* and co-heiress of Hugh Veitch of Stewartfield, Midlothian ; *m.* 1905, Hon. Dorothy Vivian, *d.* of 3rd Lord Vivian ; one *s.* three *d. Educ.:* Clifton ; Brasenose College, Oxford (Hon. Fellow, 1915). Joined 7th Hussars, 1885 ; P.S.C. ; served Soudan, 1898, including Atbara and Khartoum (despatches, Bt.-Major, British medal, Khedive's medal with two clasps) ; South Africa, 1899 ; D.A.A.G. for Cavalry, Natal ; C.S.O. to General French during the Colesberg operations ; A.A.G. Cavalry Division, 1900 ; Commanded group of columns, 1901-2 (despatches, A.D.C. to King, Brevet-Colonel, C.B., Queen's medal with seven clasps, King's medal) ; Lt.-Col. Com. 17th Lancers, 1901-3 ; Inspector-Gen. Cavalry, India, 1903 - 6 ; Major-General, 1904 ; Lieut.-General, 1910 ; General, 1914, for distinguished service ; Field-Marshal, 1917, for distinguished service ; Director of Military Training, 1906-7 ; Director of Staff Duties at Army Headquarters, 1907-9 ; Chief of Staff, India, 1909-12 ; General Officer Commanding, Aldershot, 1912-14 ; Commanding 1st Army, 1914-15 ; Commander-in-Chief of the Expeditionary Forces in France and Flanders, 1915-1919 ; Field-Marshal Commander-in-Chief the Forces in Great Britain, 1919-20 ; Lord Rector, St. Andrews Univ., 1916-19 ; Chancellor of St. Andrews Univ., 1922 ; served European War, 1914-18 (despatches five times, prom.: Gen., Field-Marshal, G.C.B., G.C.V.O., K.T.) ; Grand Cordon Legion of Honour ; Medaille Militaire ; Grand Cross Order of Leopold ; Grand Cross St. Maurice and St. Lazarus ; Obolitch Gold Medal (Montenegro) and 1st Class Order of Danilo, 1917 ; 4th Class of St. George (Russia). *Publication:* Cavalry Studies, 1907. *Heir: s.* Viscount Dawick. *Address:* Bemersyde, St. Boswells, Roxburghshire. *Clubs:* Cavalry, Marlborough, United Service.
(*Died 29 Jan. 1928.*)

HAIG, Alexander, M.A., M.D. (Oxon.); F.R.C.P. (Lond.); Consulting Physician to Metropolitan Hospital ; Consulting Physician Royal Hospital for Children and Women ; *b.* 1853 ; *o. s.* of late George Andrew Haig, formerly of Maulesden, Brechin, Forfarshire ; *m.* 1878, Gertrude Mary, *d.* of late James Haig, Barrister, Lincoln's Inn ; one *s.* one *d. Educ.:* Harrow ; Exeter College, Oxford. Second Class Honours in the School of Natural Science, Oxford, 1876. Practised as a physician in London since 1882 ; spare time spent in physiological researches. *Publications:* Uric Acid as a Factor in the Causation of Disease, 1892, 7th ed. 1908 ; Diet and Food, 1898, 6th ed. 1906 ; Uric Acid, an Epitome of the Subject, 2nd ed. 1906 ; Uric Acid in the Clinic, 1910. *Recreations:* cycling and the natural sciences. *Address:* 57 Inverness Terrace, W.2.
(*Died 6 April 1924.*)

HAIG, Lieut. - Colonel Arthur Balfour, of Bemersyde ; C.M.G. 1880 ; C.V.O. 1902 ; J.P. Co. Berwick ; R.E. ; Extra Equerry to the King ; Principal Conservative Agent, 1905-1906 ; *b.* 10 July 1840 ; *s.* of late Robert Haig and Magdalene Murray ; *m.* 1874, Hon. Frances Charlotte Harris, *o. d.* of 3rd Baron Harris ; one *s. Educ.:* Rugby ; Royal Academy, Woolwich. Entered R.E. 1859 ; Equerry to Duke of Edinburgh, 1864-80 ; Extra Equerry to King Edward VII., 1902 ; Companion of Ernestine Order of Saxe-Coburg and Gotha ; Companion of Imperial

Russian Order of St. Vladimir; Jubilee Medal and clasp; Coronation Medal. *Decorated* for services rendered in Colonies when in attendance upon H.R.H. 1867-71, and in Russia and Coburg. *Recreations:* salmon fishing, shooting. *Address:* 75 Elm Park Gardens, S.W.10. *T.:* Kensington 1841. *Club:* Marlborough.
(Died 15 April 1925.)

HAIG, Axel Herman, R.E.; Member of the Royal Swedish Academy, Stockholm; Knight Commander of the Swedish Order of the Wasa, and Knight of the Order of Nordstjernan (northern star); *b.* Katthamra, island of Gotland, in the Baltic, 1835; *m.*; one *s.* *Educ.:* Wisby, the town of Gotland. In early life studied naval architecture at the Swedish Naval Dockyard, Carlskrona, and had a diploma as Naval Architect; came to Scotland and worked under Laurence Hill, shipbuilder, at Port-Glasgow; drifted by degrees into other architecture, came to London and worked under Evan Christian, architect to the Ecclesiastical Commissioners; worked for William Burges, A.R.A., and other architects; did numerous water-colour drawings, lithographs, etc.; designs for churches and mural decorations in Sweden, and has during the last thirty years mostly devoted himself to etching, finding many subjects abroad and in England; has lived and worked at Haslemere, Surrey, and has exhibited at the Royal Academy, Fine Art Society, and many other English exhibitions, as well as at various places abroad; Gold Medal at the Paris Salon, 1882; Medal and First Order of Merit at the Adelaide Intern. Exhibition, 1887; Diploma Chicago Exhibition, 1891; Gold Medal, 1st Class, Paris International, 1889; Gold Medal, Munich, 1890; Diploma, Berlin, 1891; Gold Medal, 1st Class, Paris International, 1900, and has every year since been an exhibitor in London, Paris, and various places abroad. *Publications:* over 400 etchings, among them The Vesper Bell; The Quiet Hour; The Morning of the Festival; Burgos Cathedral, Spain; Chartres Cathedral; San Marco, Venice; Toledo Cathedral, Seville; Notre Dame, Paris; Tarragona; Capella Palatina, Palermo; Reims, etc. *Recreations:* travelling, and going over to Sweden every year to visit relatives and friends. *Address:* Grayshurst, Haslemere, Surrey. *Club:* Savage.
(Died 23 Aug. 1921.)

HAIG, Brig.-Gen. Neil Wolseley, C.B. 1919; C.M.G. 1917; late Inniskilling Dragoons; *b.* 30 Oct. 1868; 2nd *s.* of late Henry Haig and Annie, *d.* of Edward Meyer, East Sheen; *m.* 1913, Gerard Fitz-Gerald, *o. c.* of late Major-Gen. Fitz-Gerald Creagh, of Co. Clare, Ireland. Served S. Africa, 1899-1900 (Queen's medal 3 clasps); European War, 1914-18 (C.M.G., C.B.), retired, 1922. *Address:* The Dale House, Hassocks, Sussex, *Clubs:* Boodle's, Cavalry.
(Died 18 April 1926.)

HAIGH, Rev. Henry, D.D.; ex-President of the Wesleyan Methodist Conference; Secretary of Wesleyan Methodist Missionary Society; *b.* Ossett, Yorks, 26 June 1853; *s.* of John Haigh; *m.* Miss Shillington, Portadown, Ireland; one *s.* three *d. Educ.:* privately; Richmond College. For 27 years a missionary in the Mysore, South India; founder of a very large missionary printing - press; founder and editor of a Kanarese newspaper and Missionary Magazine; since returning to England, Chairman for nine years of the Wesleyan Synod of the Newcastle-on-Tyne District; member of Edinburgh Continuation Committee; has travelled extensively in Asia, Australasia, United States, Canada, and West Indies. *Publications:* many theological works and commentaries in the Kanarese language; chief reviser of Kanarese New Testament; Fernley Lecture, Some Leading Ideas of Hinduism. *Recreations:* formerly riding, tennis,

cricket, and golf. *Address:* 24 Bishopsgate, E.C. *T.A.:* Wesley Led, London. *T.:* London Wall 421.
(Died 14 July 1917.)

HAIN, Sir Edward, Kt., *cr.* 1910; member of Edward Hain and Son, St. Ives; Foster, Hain, and Co., Cardiff; Foster, Hain, and Read, London, steamship owners; J.P. Cornwall and St. Ives; *o. s.* of late Edward Hain of St. Ives; *b.* 1851; *m.* 1882, Catherine, *d.* of James Hughes of Whitehaven, Cumberland; one *s.* one *d.* M.P. (L.U.) West (St. Ives) Cornwall, 1900-1906; President of the Chamber of Shipping of the United Kingdom, 1910-11; member St. Ives Town Council over 20 years, six times Mayor; 12 years member Cornwall County Council; Sheriff of Cornwall, 1912. *Address:* Exchange Chambers, St. Mary Axe, E.C.; Treloyhan, St. Ives, Cornwall. *T.A.:* Trelawny, London. *T.:* 13 and 14 St. Ives, Cornwall, and 182 London Wall. *Clubs:* Reform, City of London, Royal Automobile, Ranelagh.
(Died 20 Sept. 1917.)

HAITE, George Charles, F.L.S., R.B.A., R.I., R.O.I., R.B.C., Decorative Artist, Designer, Painter, and Illustrator; Writer and Lecturer on art; President Institute of Decorative Designers; Examiner to Board of Education in Principles of Ornament; Pres. Langham Sketching Club, 1883-87 and 1908; late Pres. London Sketch Club; President Nicholson Institute, 1897; past-pres. Artists' Society; vice-pres. South Wales Art Society; vice-pres. and member of Council since 1881; Society Encouragement of Fine Arts; member of Royal Colonial Art Society; member of Royal Institute of Oil Painters; elected Life Member of the National Association of House Painters and Decorators of England and Wales; *b.* 8 June 1855; *e. s.* of George Haite, designer. *Educ.:* Mitcham College. Absolutely self - taught in art; commenced work before 16, owing to father's sudden death; came to London, 1873; early part of career devoted to design; exhibited at R.A. since 1883; exhibited oil and water colours at all leading galleries; has worked in black and white illustrations in all leading magazines;—designed the covers to the Strand Magazine and the Strand Musical Magazine, etc. *Publications:* Haite's Plant Studies, Lectures, etc. *Recreations:* football, cricket, running, boxing, of the past; cycling, golf, shooting, present. *Address:* Ormsby Lodge, The Avenue, Bedford Park, W. *Clubs:* Arts, Sette of Odd Volumes (past president).
(Died 31 Mar. 1924.)

HAJIBHOY, Sir Mahomedbhoy, Kt., *cr.* 1925; merchant. *Address:* Bombay.
(Died 24 Feb. 1926.)

HALAHAN, Very Rev. John; Dean of Ross since 1905; married. *Educ.:* Trinity College, Dublin (M.A.). Ordained, 1846; Curate of Berehaven, 1846-62; Rector, 1862-1918. *Address:* Black Rock Terrace, Bantry, Ireland.
(Died 28 Sept. 1920.)

HALDANE, 1st Viscount, of Cloan, *cr.* 1911; **Rt. Hon. Richard Burdon Haldane,** F.R.S.; K.T.; O.M.; Member of Judicial Committee of Privy Council; P.C., LL.D.; Rector of Edinburgh University, 1905-8; Chancellor, University of Bristol; Chancellor St. Andrews University, 1928; *b.* 30 July 1856; 4th *s.* of late Robert Haldane, Cloanden, W.S., and late Mary Elizabeth Burdon Sanderson. *Educ.:* Edinburgh Academy; Edinburgh and Göttingen Universities. M.A. 1st Class Honours in Philosophy, Edinburgh University; Gray Scholar and Ferguson Scholar in Philosophy of four Scottish Univs., 1876; Gifford Lecturer in St. Andrews University, 1902-4; M.P. (L.) Haddingtonshire, 1885-1911; Secretary of State for War, 1905-12; Lord High Chancellor of Great Britain, 1912-15 and 1924; Barr. 1879; Q.C. 1890; Hon. D.C.L. (Oxon.).

Publications: Essays in Philosophical Criticism (with Prof. Seth); Life of Adam Smith; translator (with Mr. Kemp) of Schopenhauer's World as Will and Idea, 3 vols.; Education and Empire, 1902; The Pathway to Reality, 1903; The Reign of Relativity, 1921; The Philosophy of Humanism, 1922; Human Experience: a Study of its Structure, 1926. *Heir:* none. *Address:* 28 Queen Anne's Gate, S.W.1; *T.:* Victoria 5193; Cloan, Auchterarder, Perthshire. *Clubs:* Brooks's, Athenæum, National Liberal; New, Edinburgh. (*Died 19 Aug. 1928.*)

HALE, Col. Charles Henry, C.M.G. 1916; D.S.O. 1896; Army Medical Service; *b.* Eastbourne, 9 Mar. 1863; 2nd *s.* of G. W. Hale, M.A., Trin. Coll. Camb.; *m.* 1889, Elsie Innes MacGeorge Brown (whom he *div.* 1904); one *d. Educ.:* Plymouth Grammar School. Decorated for Matabele Campaign, 1896; served S. Africa, 1890-1897 (despatches, D.S.O.); S. Africa, 1901-1903 (Queen's medal with clasp); European War, 1914-16 (despatches, C.M.G.); retired on retired pay owing to heart trouble, 1917. *Recreations:* various. *Address:* c/o Holt and Co., 3 Whitehall Place, S.W.1. (*Died 20 July 1921.*)

HALE, Col. E. Matthew, V.D.; late Lt.-Col. 24th Middlesex Post-Office Rifle Vols.; Member of Royal Institute of Painters in Oil. Served as special artist to Illustrated London News during Russo-Turkish War, 1877-78. *Address:* Shackleford, Godalming. *Club:* Savile. (*Died 24 Jan. 1924.*)

HALE, Sarah J., Principal, Edge Hill Training College for Teachers in Elementary Schools, since 1890; *y. d.* of late John Hale of Burton Latimer, Northants. *Educ.:* Wellingborough, Northants. Prepared for the profession of a Teacher in Elementary Schools, at Freeman's Endowed School, Wellingborough, and at Whiteland's College, Chelsea; took charge successively of the Derby Girls' School, Great Windmill St., W.; of Park St. Girls' School, Wellingborough, and of Holy Trinity School, Leicester; was appointed to the New Training College of St. Katharine's, Tottenham, 1878, leaving it for Newnham College, Cambridge, 1885; after the Cambridge course (Moral Science Hons.) some few months were spent as Mistress of Method at St. Mary's Hall, Cheltenham; one of a select committee appointed to inquire into the conditions of the training of pupil teachers, 1908. *Publications:* The Teaching of Infants; Diagram Sheets for the Teaching of Needlework. *Recreations:* travelling, cycling, walking, etc., reading, and the drama. *Address:* Edge Hill College, Liverpool. *T.:* 791 Royal. (*Died 1 April 1920.*)

HALKETT, George Roland, artist and writer on art; *b.* Edinburgh, 11 Mar. 1855; *m.* 1891, Lucy Marion, *d.* of Joseph Lees, J.P. of Minnickfold, Holmwood; two *d. Educ.:* privately. Studied art in Paris; became a regular contributor to journalism and the art magazines; art critic, Edinburgh Evening News, 1876; joint-compiler and artist of the New Gleanings from Gladstone and Gladstone Almanack; and author and artist of The Irish Green Book (1887), which had an enormous circulation during the first Home Rule controversy; joined the Pall Mall Gazette, 1892, as political cartoonist and writer on art; contributed many drawings and caricatures to Punch; became art editor of the Pall Mall Magazine, 1897; editor of the Pall Mall Magazine, 1900-5; has travelled extensively in the Colonies and in the East; finds his chief recreation in politics and motoring. *Address:* 6 Aubrey Road, Campden Hill, W. *T.:* Park. 1993. *Club:* Garrick. (*Died Dec. 1918.*)

HALL, Alexander Cross, landowner and J.P. in Cambs. and Oxon.; late Captain and Hon. Major 3rd Batt. Suffolk Regt.; *b.* 16 Sept. 1869; *s.* of late William Henry (Bullock) Hall (who changed his name to Hall in 1872 to succeed his uncle, the late Gen. John

452

Hall, 1st Life Guards), and 1st wife, Elizabeth Dennistoun, *d.* of William Cross; *m.* 1899, Favell Helen, *y. d.* of late Lt.-Col. H. C. Jones-Mortimer of Plas Newydd, Denbigh; two *s.* one *d. Educ.:* Marlborough; Trinity College, Cambridge; B.A. 1893; M.A. 1899. While at Cambridge hunted the Trinity Beagles, 1889-91; on leaving Cambridge studied agriculture and land management with late W. T. Scarth at Raby Castle and at Downton Agricultural College; travelled and hunted big game in Canada and U.S.A. in 1896; and in India and Kashmir in 1898; breeder of pedigree shorthorns; Southdown sheep. *Recreations:* hunting, shooting, fishing, golf. *Address:* The Manor, Great Rollright, Oxon. *Club:* Brooks's. (*Died 2 Oct. 1920.*)

HALL, Alexander William, J.P., D.L.; *b.* 1838; *e. s.* of late Henry Hall and Hon. Catherine Louisa, 4th *d.* of 2nd Lord Bridport; *m.* 1863, Emma Gertrude, 2nd *surv. d.* of late Edward Jowitt of Eltofts, Co. York. *Educ.:* Eton; Exeter College, Oxford; High Sheriff, Oxfordshire, 1867; M.P. Oxford, 1874-1880, 1885-92. *Address:* Barton Abbey, Steeple Aston, Oxfordshire. (*Died 29 April 1919.*)

HALL, Sir Douglas Bernard, 1st Bt., cr. 1919; *b.* 1866; *y. s.* of Bernard Hall, J.P. (*d.* 1890), and Margaret, *d.* of William Calrow, D.L., J.P.; *m.* 1890, Caroline, *o. d.* of T. Y. Montgomery, of Larchmont Manor, New York State, U.S.A.; one *s. Educ.:* Charterhouse; Christ Church, Oxford. On outbreak of War employed with his yacht on patrol work on the Solent and in the Channel, assisting in the transport of the original British Expeditionary Force; later on he went out to the Seine and assisted in conveying wounded officers on that river; started the first Hospital Barge Flotilla of 200 beds, under the title of British Water Ambulance Fund, of which he was President (special thanks of the Army Council); taken over by the War Office as No. 1 Ambulance Flotilla, which he commanded; relinquished his command for a post in the High Explosives Department, Ministry of Munitions; M.P. (U.), Isle of Wight, since 1910; J.P. Sussex, High Sheriff, 1907; 1st Lieut. R.N.R. (retired); Capt. R.E.; Lord of the Manors of Barlavington, Burton, and Crouch. *Heir: s.* Capt. D. M. B. Hall. *Recreations:* shooting, golf. *Address:* 10 Cadogan Gardens, S.W.3; Castle Priory, Berks. *T.:* Victoria 2170. *Clubs:* Carlton, White's, Boodle's. (*Died 30 June 1923.*)

HALL, Edwin Thomas, a Fellow and Past Vice-President of the R.I.B.A.; Fellow and Member of Council of Royal Sanitary Institute; Past - Chairman Estates Governors of Dulwich College; a Governor of Dulwich College; Chairman of the Dulwich Picture Gallery; a Vice-President of the London Society; was President of Section of Architecture and Engineering at Sanitary Congress at Bristol, 1906; Architect to the British Home and Hospital for Incurables, and the City of Westminster Union; *b.* Suffolk, 1851; *m.* 1878, Florence, *e. d.* of Julian Byrne; three *s.* four *d. Educ.:* South Kensington School of Art; office of late J. Fogerty. Commenced practice, 1876. *Professional work:* churches, mission halls, mansions, public buildings, hospitals, &c., including St. Ermin's Hotel, Westminster, Park Hospital, Hither Green, S.E., Plaistow Hospital, St. George's Children's Home, Chelsea; Library, Dulwich College; head offices of the Metropolitan Asylums Board, Victoria Embankment; National Press Agency building; Seacroft and Killingbeck Hospitals, City of Leeds; Camberwell Infirmary and Guardians' Offices; Sanatorium, Frimley; New Royal Infirmary, Manchester, in conjunction with a Manchester colleague; the new wing and Nurses' Home for the London Homœopathic Hospital; the

Barnato Memorial additions to the Middlesex Hospital; the South-Wales Sanatorium and Meadowslea Hospital, Cheshire, for the King Edward VII. Memorial; Liberty's, Regent Street, London; the King George Hospital for wounded in London; the Welsh War Hospital at Netley (in conjunction with E. Stanley Hall); Sanatoria for London at Godalming and East Grinstead, etc.; Consulting Architect to King Edward VII. Sanatorium, Midhurst, to the Leeds General Infirmary, and to St. Bartholomew's Hospital, London; designed several houses in Cadogan Square and Pont Street, and in the country. *Literary work:* Victoria, the Last Progress; Architecture and the other Arts; Art Museums and Picture Galleries; Modern Hospitals; Sanatoria for Consumptives; Flats and Apartment Houses on the Continent, etc. etc. *Recreation:* golf. *Address:* 54 Bedford Square, W.C.1; Hillcote, Dulwich, S.E.21. *T.:* 37 Museum; 1388 Brixton. *Clubs:* Arts; Dulwich.(*Died 15 April 1923.*)

HALL, Brig.-Gen. Francis Henry, C.B. 1900; C.V.O. 1907; retired 1909; *b.* 21 March 1852; *s.* of Rev. F. H. Hall of Drum-Cullen, Co. Down. Served Afghan War, 1878-80 (despatches medal); South Africa, 1899-1900 (despatches twice, C.B.); Brig.-Gen. in charge of Administration, Malta,1906-7, Scottish Command,1908-9. (*Died 19 Nov. 1919.*)

HALL, Granville Stanley; President Clark University; retired, 1920; *b.* Ashfield, Mass., Feb. 1, 1846; *s.* of Granville Bascom Hall and Abigail Beals; married. *Educ.:* Williams, A.B. 1867; A.M. 1870; Ph.D. Harvard, 1878; LL.D. University of Michigan, 1888; Williams Coll., 1889; Johns Hopkins, 1902. Professor Psychology, Antioch (Ohio) Coll. 1872-6; studied in Berlin, Bonn, Heidelberg and Leipzig; Lecturer on Psychology in Harvard and Williams, 1880-1; Professor Psychology, Johns Hopkins, 1881-8. *Publications:* Aspects of German Culture; Hints toward a Select and Descriptive Bibliography of Education (with John M. Mansfield); Adolescence (2 vols.); Youth: its Education, Regimen, and Hygiene, 1907; Aspects of Child Life and Education, 1907; Educational Problems, 1911; Founders of Modern Psychology, 1912; Jesus, the Christ, in the Light of Psychology (2 vols.), 1917; Morale: The Supreme Standard of Life and Conduct, 1920; Recreations of a Psychologist, 1920; Senescence, 1922; Life and Confessions of a Pyschologist, 1923; has contributed largely to periodical literature in the fields of experimental psychology, genetic psychology, psychology of religion and education. Founder of the American Journal of Psychology, Editor of The Pedagogical Seminary, and Founder of Journal of Applied Psychology. *Recreations:* walking, farming. *Address:* 156 Woodland Street, Worcester, Mass., U.S.A. *T.:* Cedar 4125. (*Died 24 April 1924.*)

HALL, Sir Henry, Kt., *cr.* 1919; *s.* of late Henry Thomas Hall, of Oxford, and Jemima, *d.* of Thomas Gill, of Middlesex. *Educ.:* privately. Chairman of Stephen Smith & Co., Ltd., London, Adelaide, and Toronto; Organiser of the Fertiliser Section in the Ministry of Munitions, 1917. *Address:* Gloverswood, Charlwood, Surrey; *T.:* Norwood Hill 12. *Clubs:* Constitutional, Royal Automobile. [*Died 30 March 1928.*

HALL, Ven. Henry Armstrong, C.B.E. 1919; B.D.; Archdeacon of Richmond; Chaplain to the King; Rector of Methley; Chaplain to the Forces, 1st Class, and Deputy Assistant Chaplain General (Northern Command), 1915-19; *b.* Parkhurst, I. of Wight, June 2, 1853; *s.* of George Hall, late 2nd Light Infantry, and Julia, *d.* of Col. Geo. Gawler, K.H.; *m.* 1878. Catherine Gertrude, *d.* of John Ross Hutchinson, H.E.I.C.S.; one *d. Educ.:* Christ's Hospital; Vevey; King's College, London. Curate of Holy Trinity, Lee, Kent, and has been successively incumbent of St. George's, Douglas, I. of Man; Holy Trinity, Bristol; Swindon, Wilts; St. Mary's, Spring Grove, Isleworth; St. John's, Perth, N.B.; and Methley, Yorks.; has conducted parochial missions in all parts of the country during the last thirty years. *Recreations:* golf and fishing. *Address:* Methley Rectory, Leeds. (*Died 12 May 1921.*)

HALL, Col. Henry Samuel, C.B. 1902; late Captain 6th Dragoon Guards and late Lieut.-Col. and Hon. Col. 2nd Vol. Battalion Oxford Light Infantry; 2nd *s.* of late Henry Hall of Barton Abbey, Oxon., and Hon. Catherine Louisa Hood, 4th *d.* of 2nd Baron Bridport; *m.* 1874, Eleanor, *d.* of late Gen. Edward Boxer, R.A., F.R.S. Served in Indian Mutiny. *Address:* 25 Longride Road, S.W. *Club:* Army and Navy. (*Died 24 May 1923.*)

HALL, Rev. Herbert, M.A. & S.C.L.; Rector of Glemsford, Suffolk, since 1887; Hon. Canon, Diocese St. Edmundsbury and Ipswich; *b.* 11 July 1845; *s.* of late Charles Ranken Hall, Rector of Shirenewton, Mon., and Harriett, *d.* of John Baker of Aldwick Court, Somerset and Weston-super-Mare; unmarried. *Educ.:* Cheltenham and Marlborough Colleges; B.N.C., Oxford. Curate of St. James's, Bury St. Edmunds, 1869-76; Vicar of Linton, Cambridgeshire, and Chaplain of the Union until 1887. *Address:* The Rectory, Glemsford, Suffolk. *T.A.:* Glemsford. (*Died 16 Feb. 1921.*)

HALL, John Basil, M.A., M.C. (Camb.), F.R.C.S. (Eng. and Edin.); Hon. Consulting Surgeon, Bradford Royal Infirmary; J.P., Bradford; *b.* 1866; *s.* of William Hall of Leeds; *m.* Lisbeth, *d.* of late Thomas Mackenzie, J.P., of Achnaaird, Scotland; one *d. Educ.:* King's School, Canterbury; Cambridge University; St. Thomas's Hospital; Leeds and Vienna. Qualified in 1890; held several appointments at the Leeds General Infirmary; Hon. Surgeon, Bradford Royal Infirmary, 1900. *Publications:* various papers in medical journals. *Recreations:* fishing, motoring, and outdoor sports. *Address:* Eldon Place, and North Park Road, Bradford. *T.:* Bradford 1358. *M.:* AK 1358. *Club:* Bradford. (*Died 12 Jan. 1926.*)

HALL, John Carey, C.M.G. 1912; I.S.O. 1902; *b.* Coleraine, Co. Londonderry, 22 Jan. 1844; *s.* of John Hall of Coleraine and Portrush, Co. Antrim; *m.* 1876, Agnes, *d.* of Charles Wyclif Goodwin, Assistant Judge of British Supreme Court for China and Japan; two *s.* four *d. Educ.:* Coleraine Academical Institution; Queen's Coll. Belfast. Entered Consular Service, Japan, 1868; Acting Vice-Consul at Yedo (Tokio), 1869-70; services lent to Japanese Commission for Prison Reforms, 1871; called to Bar, Middle Temple, 1881; Assistant Japanese Secretary to Legation at Tokio, 1882; Acting Japanese Secretary, 1884-86; Acting Assistant Judge Supreme Court for China and Japan at Shanghai, 1888-89; H.M.'s Consul-General for Yokohama, 1902-14; has acted or officiated as Consul at all the open ports of Japan; one of the founders of the China Society, London; Coronation medal, 1911; President Asiatic Society of Japan, Tokio, 1913. *Publications:* General View of Chinese. Civilisation; The Positive Science of Morals, both translated from the French of Pierre Laffitte, &c.; Papers on Japanese Feudal Law and other subjects in the Trans. of the Japan Asiatic Soc.; occasionally contributes to Positivist Review. *Recreation:* reading. *Club:* Royal Societies. (*Died 21 Oct. 1921.*)

HALL, Col. Sir John (Richard), 9th Bt., cr. 1687 ; C.B.E. 1919 ; late Major 3rd (Reserve) Batt. Irish Guards ; late Coldstream Guards ; b. 14 Nov. 1865 ; s. of late Lt.-Gen. Julian Hamilton Hall, 5th s. of 5th Bt., and Augusta Wilhelmina Louisa, d. of late Col. John Fremantle ; S. uncle, 1913 ; m. 1903, Sophia, d. of H. Duncan and widow of Captain S. A. Olliver, D.S.O. *Publications:* The Bourbon Restoration ; England and the Orleans Monarchy ; General Pichegru's Treason, 1915 ; Four Famous Mysteries, 1922 ; The Bravo Mystery, and other Cases, 1923. *Heir:* b. M. J. Hall. *Address:* 6 Chichester Terrace, Brighton. *T.:* Kemp Town 7248. *Clubs:* Turf, Beefsteak, Guards', Carlton.   (*Died 15 Feb. 1928.*)

HALL, Joseph, M.A., D.Litt. ; b. Portadown, Ireland, 23 April 1854 ; e. surv. s. of William Hall of Portadown, Ireland ; unmarried. *Educ.:* Coleraine Institution ; Queen's College, Belfast. B.A. with honours in classics, Queen's University, 1875 ; Peel Prize for English Essay, 1878 ; M.A. 1882 ; Hon. D.Litt. Durham University, 1904 ; representative of secondary schoolmasters on Lancashire Education Committee, 1904-6 ; Assistant Master, Manchester Grammar School, 1877-87 ; Headmaster of the Hulme Grammar School, Manchester, 1887-1913. *Publications:* Poems of Laurence Minot, 1887, third edition, 1914 ; King Horn, 1901 ; Selections from Early Middle English, 1920 ; Selections from Layamon, 1924 ; has collaborated with late Professor Kölbing and others in Middle English and other books, and contributed to Englische Studien and other periodicals. *Recreation:* gardening. *Address:* Woodstock, Oxfordshire.   (*Died 8 Nov. 1927.*)

HALL, Brig.-Gen. Lewis Montgomery Murray, C.B. 1907 ; retired 1910 ; b. 10 Sep. 1855 ; s. of Maj.-Gen. Lewis Hall, R.A. ; m. Blanche, d. of Captain Symons, Royal Navy ; three s. one d. Entered R. Mar. Art. 1873 ; Captain I.S.C. 1885 ; Major, 1893 ; Lieut.-Col. Indian Army, 1899 ; Bt.-Col. 1903 ; Col. 1906 ; Brig.-Gen. 1907 ; served Chin-Lushai, 1899-90 (despatches, medal with clasp) ; N.W. Frontier, 1897-98 (medal with clasp) ; commanded a Brigade in India, 1906-10 ; Aviator's Certificate, 1915. *Address:* 12 Kent Gardens, Ealing, W. *Club:* Junior Army and Navy.
    (*Died 14 April 1928.*)

HALL, Lt.-Col. Montagu Heath, D.S.O. 1900 ; late commanding 3rd Batt. South Lancashire Regt. ; b. 26 Dec. 1856 ; s. of late Isaac Hall of Upton Bank, Macclesfield, and Castleton, Derbyshire. *Educ.:* Repton ; Trinity Hall, Camb. Joined 4th Royal Lancashire Militia, 1876 ; served South Africa, 1900-1 (despatches twice, medal and 3 clasps). *Address:* The Cottage, Cranleigh, Surrey. (*Died 22 June 1928.*)

HALL, Sydney Prior, M.A. ; M.V.O. 1901 ; painter ; b. 18 Oct. 1842 ; e. s. of late Harry Hall, painter, of Newmarket ; m. 1st, Emma Holland (d. 1894) ; 2nd, Mary, d. of late James Gow. *Educ.:* Merchant Taylors' ; Pembroke College, Oxford. 1st Class Lit. Hum. (Greats), 1865 ; M.A. 1871 ; special artist of The Graphic during Franco-German War, 1870-71 ; member of the suite of King Edward VII. on his voyage to India in 1875-6 ; member of the suite of the Marquess of Lorne and H.R.H. Princess Louise on going out to Canada as Governor-General, 1879 ; accompanied the Marquess of Lorne on his journey in the North-West Territories, 1881 ; member of the suite of T.R.H. the Duke and Duchess of York, and special artist of The Graphic on board H.M.S. Ophir, 1901. *Address:* 36 Grove End Road, N.W.   (*Died 15 Dec. 1922.*)

HALL-DEMPSTER, Colonel Reginald Hawkins, D.S.O. 1900 : b. 14 March 1854 ; e. s. of late Capt. Henry Hall, formerly of 1st Madras Light Cavalry ; m. 1894, Edith Gertrude Dickson, e. d. of late Rev. Francis Home Atkinson of Morland Hall, Westmorland ; one d. *Educ.:* Wellington College. Entered 82nd Regt. 1873 ; Capt. 1883 : Major, 1893 ; Lt.-Col. 1st Bn. South Lancashire Regt. 1900 ; Bt.-Colonel, 1904 ; retired, 1904 ; served Boer War, 1899-1903, and was at Spionkop and Relief of Ladysmith (despatches 4 times, D.S.O., Queen's Medal 5 clasps, King's Medal 2 clasps) ; S. his cousin, Miss Helen Hawkins-Dempster of Dunnichen in 1918 and assumed additional name of Dempster under Deed of Entail ; J.P. Co. Forfar. *Recreations:* shooting and golf. *Address:* Dunnichen, Forfar. *Club:* Naval and Military.   (*Died 17 May 1922.*)

HALL-EDWARDS, John Francis, L.R.C.P., L.M. (Edin.), D.M.R. and E. (Cantab.), F.R.S. (Edin.), Hon. F.R.P.S. ; Major, R.A.M.C. 1914 ; Councillor for the City of Birmingham ; Vice-Chairman of the Birmingham and Sutton Coldfield War Pensions Committee, and Vice-Chairman of the Birmingham King's Roll Committee ; Hon. Life Member of the Roentgen Society, of the Electro-Therapeutic Section of the Royal Medical Society, of the British Institute of Radiology, of the American Roentgen-Ray Society, of the American Electro-Therapeutic Society, and of the Birmingham Natural History and Philosophical Society ; late Vice-President of the Roentgen Society ; Vice-President of the Midland Institute ; Hon. Member of the American Roentgen Ray Society ; Hon. Fellow of the American Electro-Therapeutic Society ; b. 19 Dec. 1858 ; e. s. of John Edwards, M.D., M.R.C.S. *Educ.:* King Edward's School and Queen's College, Birmingham. Late Consulting Radiographer to 1st Southern General Hospital ; Radiographer to 1st Birmingham War Hospital, Rubery ; Military Orthopædic Hospital, Hollymoor ; Monyhull Military Hospital ; Consulting Radiographer to the Guest Hospital, Dudley ; Surgeon Radiographer to the Royal Orthopædic, and Dental Hospitals, Birmingham ; Fellow of the Royal Society of Medicine ; late Vice-President Birmingham Photographic Society ; President Birmingham and Midland Institute Scientific Society ; Editor of Archives of Roentgen Ray, and President British Electro-Therapeutic Society ; British Correspondent to the American X-Ray Society ; served as surgeon X-ray expert to the Imperial Yeomanry Hospitals in South Africa, 1900-1 (medal and four clasps) ; a pioneer in X-ray investigation, during which lost both hands as the result of burns ; awarded Civil List Pension, 1908, in recognition of services rendered to the country by the application of the X-rays to medicine and surgery ; mentioned for valuable services rendered during the war, 1916 ; mentioned for valuable medical services, 1917 ; lecturer on scientific subjects ; awarded the Carnegie Hero Trust Medallion, Jan. 1922. *Publications:* Bullets and their Billets, or Experiences with the X-Rays in South Africa ; X-Ray Dermatitis—its Cause, Cure, and Prevention ; Carbon-dioxide Snow : its Therapeutic Uses ; The Radiography of Metals ; The Metal Industry ; numerous papers on the application of Electricity, Photography, X-Rays, and Radium to Medicine and Surgery. *Address:* 141 Gt. Charles Street, Birmingham ; *T.:* Central 6807 ; 112 Gough Road, Edgbaston, Birmingham. *T.:* Midland 2173. *Clubs:* Conservative, Press, Birmingham.
    (*Died 15 Aug. 1926.*)

HALLAS, Eldred, M.P. (Lab.), Duddeston Division of Birmingham, 1918-22 ; b. 1870 ; s. of Edward Hallas ; m. 1892, d. of Arthur Bottomley. Lecturer at the Ethical Church, 1906 ; City Council, 1911 ; District President of the National Union General Workers.
    (*Died 13 June 1926.*)

HALLE, Charles E., late Director of New Gallery; *b.* Paris, 1846; *s.* of late Sir Charles Hallé; unmarried. Learnt drawing from Baron Marochetti and Victor Mottez. Exhibited four pictures at Royal Academy, 1866; practised portrait-painting for several years; assisted Sir Coutts Lindsay in founding the Grosvenor Gallery, 1876; resigned directorship of Grosvenor, 1887, and built the New Gallery, which still continues under his management; besides organising and arranging the many exhibitions of the Grosvenor and New Galleries, has painted about 100 portraits and many subject pictures, which have passed into well-known collections here and abroad; his principal works are: Madonna and Child with attendant Angels; Sic transit Gloria Mundi; Buondelmonte and the Donati; Paolo and Francesca; The March of the Seasons; The Wishing Well; Fleeting Beauty; An Invocation; and The Rock of the Sirens; besides single figures, generally life size half length, of beautiful women and children, in which he has made study of expression his principal aim. *Publication:* Notes from a Painter's Life, 1909. *Address:* 585G Campo Sta Maria Formosa, Venice. *Club:* Burlington Fine Arts.
(Died 31 Jan. 1919.)

HALLIDAY, Lieut.-Gen. George Thomas, Bengal Cavalry; *b.* 1841; *y. s.* of late Sir Frederick James Halliday, K.C.B.; *m.* Minnie, *d.* of late General G. W. Bishop, Indian Army. Entered army, 1858; Lieut.-Gen. 1900; Brigade-Major and Deputy Assist. Adjutant-General, India, 1874; Commandant 16th Bengal Cavalry, 1889; Colonel on the Staff, 1894; Commanding Oudh District (Officiating), 1895; Colonel, 16th Cavalry, Indian Army; Lt.-General, 1900; Hazara expedition, 1888 (medal with clasp). *Address:* 75 Redcliffe Gardens, S.W.10. *T.:* Kensington 294.
(Died 15 Sept. 1922.)

HALLIDAY, General John Gustavus; unemployed supernumerary list; *b.* May 1822; 3rd *s.* of Thomas Halliday of Ewell, Surrey; *m.* 1845, Lucy (*d.* 1888), *d.* of W. M. Cotton of Petrograd; one *s.* three *d. Educ.:* Switzerland. Appointed to the Indian Army, Madras Establishment, 1838; appointed by Lord Dalhousie to the Mysore Commission under Sir Mark Cubbon, K.C.B., in which served for several years, leaving it on promotion; Vice-President, Victoria Institute. *Address:* 5 Church Terrace, Blackheath, S.E.
(Died 4 Feb. 1917.)

HALLINAN, Most Rev. Denis; Bishop of Limerick since 1918; *b.* Coolcappa, Co. Limerick, 1849. *Educ.:* Irish College, Rome. Priest, 1874; Curate, Newcastle West, 1875-86; St. Michael's, Limerick,1886-94; Parish Priest of St. Mary's, Limerick, 1894-98; Newcastle West, 1898-1918; Domestic Prelate to the Pope, 1900; Chancellor, Cathedral Chapter, 1912. *Address:* Bishop's House, Corbally, Limerick
(Died 2 July 1923.)

HALLOWES, Major-Gen. Henry Jardine; *s.* of Admiral John Hallowes; *b.* 13 Nov. 1838; *m.* Charlotte Elizabeth Ormonde (*d.* 1916), *d.* of Hon. J. Hamilton Gray, D.C.L.; one *d. Educ.:* privately. Served in army since 1855; Adjutant, 15th Foot; Adjutant-General, New Brunswick Militia; Adjt. School for Officers of Reserve Forces; A.D.C. to Hon. A. Gordon, Gov. of Trinidad, etc.; Inspector Gymnasia, India; A.A.G. of Division, India; Commanded 15th Regimental District; General Officer commanding the troops, Jamaica; commands a Brigade of National Reserve, London Division; Colonel-in-Chief the West India Regt.; European War 1914-19 (medal); war medals, etc.— Canada medal and clasp, 1866; Afghan medal and clasp, despatches; Jubilee decoration and Coronation medal; Collar of Commandeur de la Legion d'honneur; Croix de Guerre avec Palmes. *Publications:* The Drill and Working

of the Three Arms; Thirteen Lectures on Tactics with regard to Fortification. *Recreations:* all outdoor games; riding, golf, cycling. *Address:* Inwoodbarn, by Tongham, Surrey. *Club:* Naval and Military. *(Died 28 June 1926.)*

HALSBURY, 1st Earl of (cr. 1898); Hardinge Stanley Giffard, F.R.S., M.A., P.C., J.P., V.P.L.S.L., K.B. 1875; Baron Halsbury, 1885; Viscount Tiverton, 1898; President Royal Society of Literature; Senior Grand Warden of English Freemasons; High Steward of University of Oxford since 1896; Hon. Fellow, Merton; *b.* London, 3 Sep. 1823; *s.* of Stanley Lees Giffard, LL.D., and Susanna, *d.* of late Frank Moran; *m.* 1st, Caroline (*d.* 1873), *d.* of C. O. Humphreys, 1852; 2nd, Wilhelmina, *d.* of late Henry Woodfall, 1874; one *s.* one *d. Educ.:* Merton Coll. Oxford; B.A. 1855; Barr. Inner Temple, 1850; Q.C. 1865; treasurer of Inner Temple, 1881; Solicitor-General, 1875-80; M.P. (C.) Launceston, 1877-85; Lord Chancellor, 1895-1905. *Heir: s.* Viscount Tiverton. *Address:* 4 Ennismore Gardens, S.W.7; *T.:* Kensington 1557; Pendruccombe, Launceston. *Clubs:* Athenæum, Carlton, Junior Carlton, St. Stephen's. *(Died 11 Dec. 1921.)*

HALSEY, Rt. Hon. Sir (Thomas) Frederick, 1st Bt., *cr.* 1920; P.C.; J.P.; Deputy Grand Master, England, 1903-26; Provincial Grand Master, Herts, 1873-1923; *b.* 9 Dec. 1839; *s.* of late T. P. Halsey, M.P.; *m.* 1865, Mary Julia (*d.* 1922), *d.* of late F. O. Wells; six *s.* two *d. Educ.:* Eton; Christ Church, Oxford (M.A.); rowed in 'Varsity Boat Race. M.P. (C.) Herts., Watford Division, 1874-1906; Maj., hon. Lt.-Col. (retired), Herts Yeo. Cavalry. *Heir: s.* Lt.-Col. Walter Johnston. *Address:* Gaddesden, Hemel Hempstead. *Club:* Carlton. *(Died 12 Feb. 1927.)*

HALTON, Herbert Welch, LL.D.; Vice-President of Court of Appeal, Cairo, since Oct. 1916; British Red Cross Commissioner in Cairo; *b.* London, 26 July 1863; *e. surv. s.* of late Walter Fox Halton of the Home Civil Service; unmarried. *Educ.:* University College School, London. Studied law in London and Paris; Barrister-at-law Middle Temple, 1890; LL.D. University of Paris, 1898; formerly an Inspector attached to the Committee of Judicial Control at the Ministry of Justice, Cairo; one of the pioneers of the English section of the School of Law, Cairo (Lecturer, 1900-4); a judge of the Native Court of Appeal, Cairo, 1897, transferred to the Mixed Tribunal, Cairo, 1909; President, 1914-16; Mixed (International) Court of Appeal, Alexandria, March 1916. *Decorations:* 2nd Class Medjieh, 3rd Class Osmanieh, Grand Officer of the Order of the Nile. *Publications:* (English) An Elementary Treatise on the Egyptian Civil Codes, 2 vols.; (French) Étude sur la Procédure Criminelle en France et en Angleterre. *Recreations:* modest golf and a dilettante pleasure in visiting places of historic interest. *Address:* Court of Appeal. Cairo. *Clubs:* Royal Societies, Royal Automobile; Turf, Cairo. *(Died 8 Sept. 1919.)*

HAMBIDGE, Jay, Lecturer and writer on Fine Art; *b.* Simcoe, Elgin Co., Ontario, Canada, 13 Jan. 1867; Artist and investigator of design principles. *Publications:* Dynamic Symmetry, The Greek Vase, The Diagonal, The Parthenon and its Plan, The Erechtheum and its Plan, The Nike Temple and its Plan, Greek Bronzes, Classic Surveyors and Classic Designers. *Recreations:* golf. *Address:* Department of Fine Arts, Yale University, New Haven, Conn., U.S.A. *(Died 20 Jan. 1924.)*

HAMBLEDEN, 2nd Viscount, *cr.* 1891; **William Frederick Danvers Smith,** D.L., J.P.; partner in W. H. Smith and Son; *b.* 1868; *o. s.* of Rt. Hon. William Henry Smith, P.C., M.P., and 1st Viscountess Hambleden, *d.* of Frederick Dawes Danvers, formerly Clerk of Council, Duchy of Lancaster; *S.* mother, 1913; *m.* Lady Esther (Caroline Georgiana) Gore, 3rd *d.* of 5th Earl of Arran, 1894; three *s.* two *d. Educ.*: Eton; New College, Oxford; late Lt.-Col. Royal 1st Devon Yeomanry; M.P. (C.) Strand, 1891-1910; served European War, Gallipoli and Egypt, 1915-16 (despatches). *Heir*: *s.* Hon. William Henry Smith, *b.* 25 July 1903. *Address*: 3 Grosvenor Place, S.W.1; *T.*: Kensington 2200; Greenlands, Henley-on-Thames; The Manor House, North Bovey, Moretonhampstead. *Clubs*: Carlton, Wellington, Travellers'. (*Died 16 June 1923*.)

HAMBRO, Sir Everard Alexander, K.C.V.O., *cr.* 1908; J.P., D.L.; Director of Bank of England; *b.* 11 April 1842; *s.* of Baron Hambro, Milton Abbey, Dorset, and Caroline Gostenhofer; *m.* 1st, 1866, Gertrude Mary (*d.* 1905), *d.* of late Henry Stuart; four *s.* one *d.*; 2nd, 1911, Ebba, *y. d.* of C. Beresford Whyte, of Hatley Manor, Co. Leitrim. *Educ.*: Trin. Coll. Camb. *Address*: Hayes Place, Kent; *T.*: Bromley 135; Milton Abbey, Dorset. *Club*: Travellers'. (*Died 26 Feb. 1925*.)

HAMBURGER, H. J., Sc.D., M.D., LL.D. (Aberdeen and St. Andrews), F.R.S. (Netherlands, Copenhagen, and Turin); Professor of Physiology in the University of Groningen since 1901; *b.* March 9, 1859; *s.* one *d. Educ.*: Alkmaar; University of Utrecht. Assistant to late Professor Donders at the Physiological Laboratory at Utrecht, 1882-88; Professor in the Royal Veterinary School in Utrecht, 1888-1901; introduced the application of physical chemistry in the medical sciences, 1888; and published a work containing the researches of himself and others on this subject: Osmotischer Druck und Ionenlehre in den medicinischen Wissenschaften, 1902-4; on 4th June 1908, date of commemoration of his first 25-years doctorship (chemistry), the merits of his scientific work were celebrated by the publication of an international jub. w-book, containing a great number of biochemical contributions of medical and chemical scientists of the old and the new world; President ix. International Physiological Congress, Groningen, 1913; First Charles E. Dolme Lecturer, Johns Hopkins University, Baltimore, 1922; Herter Lecturer, New York, 1922. *Address*: Praediniussingel 2, Groningen. *T.*: 939. (*Died 5 Jan. 1924*.)

HAMEL, A. C., F.R.S. (Can.), M.D.; Professor of Histology and Bacteriology. *Address*: Laval University, Quebec, Canada.

HAMEL, Gustav, M.V.O. 1901, M.D.; *b.* 12 Sep. 1861. *Educ.*: Sweden; Switzerland; St. Bartholomew's Hospital. *Address*: 1 Stratford Place, W.1; *T.*: Paddington 5656; Westfield House, Portsmouth Road, Surbiton; *T.*: Kingston 1182. (*Died 3 May 1922*.)

HAMILL, Rev. Thomas Macafee, M.A., D.D., Professor of Systematic Theology, Assembly's College, Belfast, Presbyterian Church in Ireland, since 1895; *b.* Ballymoney, Co. Antrim. *Educ.*: Coleraine Academical Institution; Queen's College, Belfast; theological course at Assembly's College, Belfast; University, Edinburgh. Ordained, 1879; minister, Presbyterian Church, Omagh, Co. Tyrone, 1879-84; Lurgan, Co. Armagh, 1884-95; Moderator of the General Assembly, 1915. *Address*: College Park, Belfast. *T.A.*: Professor Hamill. Belfast. (*Died 17 Feb. 1919*.)

HAMILTON, Hon. Brig.-Gen. Alex. Be mish, retired pay; C.B. 1915; *b.* 22 Dec. 1860. Entered army, 1881; Captain K.O.S.B. 1889; Adjutant, 1890-1903; Major, 1901; Lt.-Col. 1908; Col. 1911; D.A.A.G. Egypt, 1893-98; China and Hongkong, 1891-94; D.A.Q.M.G. S. Africa, 1905-8; Embarkation Staff Officer, S. Command, 1911-13; Embarkation Commandant

since 1914; served Chin-Lushai Expedition, 1899-90 (medal with clasp); Nile Expedition, 1898 (despatches, Bt. Major); European War, 1915 (despatches, C.B.). *Club*: Junior United Service. (*Died 30 Dec. 1918*.)

HAMILTON, Allan M'Lane, M.D., LL.D., F.R.S.E.; one of the Consulting Physicians at the Manhattan State Hospital for the Insane, New York; *s.* of Philip Hamilton, *y. s.* of Alexander Hamilton the statesman, and author of the Federalist, and Rebecca, *d.* of Louis M'Lane, U.S. Senator and Secretary of the Treasury, Minister to England, 1829-30; *m.* 1902, May C. Tomlinson; no *c. Educ.*: preparatory school; Medical Department, Columbia University, New York. Took 1st Faculty and 1st Ilarren Prizes at Graduation; 1st Prize Am. Med. Ass. 1879; has since made special study of Nervous and Mental Disease and Legal Medicine; expert witness for Government in case of U.S. *v.* Guiteau, assassin of President Garfield; also connected with Czgolz, Thaw, and most important cases for past 40 years; ex-President Psychiatrical Society; Honorary Member American Neurological Association, Psychiatrical Society, N.Y. Medical and Surgical Society; Fellow Medical Society of London; has made contributions to Study of Eugenics, and in 1896 further elaborated a suggestion of vocational fitness in young people; introduced Educational System in American Asylums. *Publications*: Prize Thesis on Galvano-Puncture, 1870; A Treatise on Nervous Diseases, 1878; A System of Legal Medicine, 1900; Accidents and Injuries of the Nervous System, 1904; An Intimate Life of Alexander Hamilton, 1911; Recollections o. an Alienist, 1916; besides many contributions to special journals and encyclopædias. *Recreations*: writing, reading, fishing, photography, mechanical work. *Address*: 43 East 25 Street, New York; Great Barrington, Mass. *Club*: Beefsteak. (*Died 23 Nov. 1919*.)

HAMILTON, Charles Boughton, C.M.G. 1895.; Order S. John of Jerusalem; *b.* British Guiana, 2 May 1850; *o. s.* of Rev. Wm. Hamilton, M.A.; *m.* Elizabeth Hermina (*d.* 1897), *d.* of P. van Eeden of British Guiana; one *s.* two *d. Educ.*: Queen's Coll., British Guiana; South Devon Collegiate School, Exeter. Entered Colonial Civil Service, 1865; acted Receiver-General and Auditor-General of British Guiana, 1881-86, in which Colony thanked by Council for services; Receiver-General of Trinidad, 1886-1892; acted as Colonial Sec. twice; returned to British Guiana, 1892; Receiver-General of British Guiana, 1892; member of Executive Council of Government, 1895; member of Court of Policy of British Guiana, 1898; Govt. Director of Demerara Railway, 1910-23; Chm. of various important Commissions; Chairman Education Commission, 1902; thanked by Combined Court for special services gratuitously rendered in Public Road Administration, 1905; Secretary of State for Colonies recorded high appreciation of his services, 1908; freeman of city of Exeter, Devon. *Recreations*: fishing, shooting, boating, tropical bush life. *Address*: Orbieston, Purley, Surrey. (*Died 13 Mar. 1927*.)

HAMILTON, Sir Charles Edward, 1st Bt.; *cr.* 1892; *s.* of late J. Hamilton, and Jessie, *d.* of P. Kemble, late Capt. 4th Regt.; *b.* 28 May 1845; *m.* Mary (*d.* 1906), *d.* of late G. M'Corquodale, Gladys, Anglesey, 1867; one *d.* M.P. Southwark (Rotherhithe Div.) 1885-92. *Heir*: None. *Address*: 38 Eaton Place, S.W.1. *T.*: Victoria 5181. *Clubs*: Carlton. Constitutional. (*Died 15 Nov. 1928*.)

HAMILTON, Rt. Hon. Lord Claud (John), P.C. 1917; High Steward, Borough of Great Yarmouth, and of the Borough of Harwich; Knight of Justice of St. John of Jerusalem; *b.* Middlesex, 20 Feb. 1843; 2nd *s.* of 1st Duke of Abercorn and Lady Louisa Russell, 2nd *d.*

of Duke of Bedford; *m.* 1878, Carolina (*d.* 1911), *d.* of late Edward Chandos Pole, Radbourne Hall, Derby, and Lady Anna Chandos Pole; one *s.* one *d. Educ.:* Harrow. Entered Grenadier Guards, 1862; retired, 1867; Col. 5th Battalion Royal Inniskilling Fusiliers, 1867; Hon. Col. 1892; Aide-de-Camp to the Queen, 1887; M.P. Londonderry, 1865-68; Lord of the Treasury, 1868; M.P. King's Lynn, 1869-80; Liverpool, 1880-88; South Kensington, 1910-18. *Recreations:* cricket, football, racquets, all sports. *Address:* 28 Cambridge Square, W.2. *T.:* Paddington 4919. *Clubs:* Carlton, 1900. Bachelors'. (*Died 26 Jan. 1925.*)

HAMILTON, Rev. Charles James, M.A.; Hon. Canon of Southwell; *b.* 1840; *s.* of Rev. J. H. Hamilton, Canon of Rochester; *m.* 1870, Alice Catherine, *d.* of Elliot Macnaghten of H.M. Indian Council; three *s.* two *d. Educ.:* Harrow; Trinity College, Cambridge; B.A. (Sen. Opt.), 1863. Deacon, 1864; Priest, 1865; Curate of Southwold, 1864-66; St. Michael's, Chester Square, 1866-70; Vicar of Doveridge, Derbyshire, 1870-99; St. John's, Derby, 1899-1908; Rural Dean of Derby, 1901-8; Proctor in Convocation for Diocese of Southwell 1891-1916. *Address:* Walton-on-Trent, near Burton-on-Trent. (*Died 15 Nov. 1917.*)

HAMILTON, Edwin, M.A., M.R.I.A.; barrister; J.P.; *o. s.* of late Rev. Hugh Hamilton, Rochfort House, Balbriggan; *m.* Helen, 2nd *d.* of late Daniel Delacherois, D.L., Manor House, Donaghadee, 1891; one *s. Educ.:* Durham Grammar School (King's Scholar 1864-1868); Trin. Coll. Dublin. Prizeman in classics, honourman in science, Vice-chancellor's prizeman in English verse, 1872; M.A. 1877. Edited several Dublin weekly papers, annuals, etc.; contributed to many London weeklies, chiefly humorous verse; Member of the Royal Irish Academy, 1879; called to Irish Bar, 1887; secretary Queen's Jubilee Local Committee, same year; Chairman, Conservative Club, Dublin, 1892-94; received Com. of the Peace, 1898; Chairman, Dublin District, Institute of Journalists, 1900. *Publications:* Ariadne, a Drama (University prize poem); Dublin Doggrels; Mongrel Doggrels; Waggish Tales (prose); The Moderate Man, and other verses; Ballymuckbeg (political satire); Dublin University Tercentenary Prologue, 1892; Gaiety Theatre, Dublin, Silver Jubilee Address, 1896; New Theatre Royal, Dublin, Opening Prologue, 1897; numerous libretti, comediettas, etc., produced in Dublin theatres, and elsewhere. *Address:* The Crossways, Donaghadee, Co. Down.
(*Died June 1919.*)

HAMILTON, Sir Frederic Harding Anson, 7th Bt.; *cr.* 1647; late Maj. 60th Rifles; *b* 24 Sep. 1836; 2nd *s.* of 6th Bart. and Constantia, 3rd *d.* of Gen. Sir George Anson, G.C.B.; *S.* father 1887; *m.* 1865, Mary (*d.* 1918), *d.* of H. Willan; two *s.* four *d. Educ.:* Eton. *Heir: s.* Robert Caradoc [Lieut. Norfolk Regt.; *b.* 22 Mar. 1877; *m.* 1907, Irene, 3rd *d.* of Sir C. Mordaunt, 10th Bart.; one *s.* one *d.*]. *Recreation:* shooting, etc. *Address:* Avon Cliffe, Alveston, Stratford-on-Avon.
(*Died 19 Sept. 1919.*)

HAMILTON, Lord Frederic (Spencer), *b.* 13th Oct. 1856; 4th *s.* of 1st Duke of Abercorn, K.G. *Educ.:* Harrow. Formerly in Diplomatic Service, and successively Secretary in the British Embassies at Berlin and Petrograd and in the Legations at Lisbon and Buenos Ayres; has travelled much; M.P. (C.) S.W. Manchester, 1885-86; North Tyrone (U.), 1892-95; Editor Pall Mall Magazine to 1900.

Publication: The Holiday Adventures of Mr. P. J. Davenant, 1915; Some Further Adventures of Mr. P. J. Davenant, 1915; The Education of Mr. P. J. Davenant, 1916; The Beginnings of Mr. P. J. Davenant, 1917; Lady Eleanor,

Private Simmons, and others, 1918; The Vanished Pomps of Yesterday, 1919; Here, There, and Everywhere, 1921. *Address:* 13 Great College Street, Westminster, S.W.1. *T.:* Victoria 6180. *Clubs:* Carlton, St. James's. Beefsteak. (*Died 11 Aug. 1928.*)

HAMILTON, Adm. Sir Frederick Tower, G.C.B., *cr.* 1917; K.C.B., *cr.* 1913; C.V.O. 1908; Commander-in-Chief, Rosyth, since 1916; Grand Officer of the Legion of Honour; *b.* 8 March 1856; *m.* 1889, Maria, *d.* of late Admiral of the Fleet Hon. Sir Henry Keppel; two *s.* two *d.* Entered Navy, 1869; Commander, 1892; Captain, 1898; Rear-Adm. 1907; Adm., 1916; served Zulu War, 1879 (despatches, promoted, Zulu medal and clasp); A.D.C. to the King, 1906-7; Inspector of Target Practice, 1907-9; commanding 5th Cruiser Squadron Atlantic Fleet, 1909-11; 2nd and 3rd Fleets, 1911-13; 2nd Sea Lord of the Admiralty, 1914-16. *Address:* Admiral's Office, Rosyth, Scotland; Anmer Hall, Lynn, Norfolk. *Clubs:* United Service, Naval and Military, Marlborough. (*Died 4 Oct. 1917.*)

HAMILTON, G. E.; Hon. M.A., Cambridge; late Chairman of Finance Committee, National Union of Teachers, and Treasurer, 1884-1916. *Address:* Hamilton House, Mabledon Place, W.C.

HAMILTON, Rt. Hon. Lord George (Francis), P.C.; D.C.L.; LL.D. Glasg.; G.C.S.I., *cr.* 1903; Captain of Deal Castle, 1899-1923; Provincial Grand Master, Middlesex, 1892-1924; Chairman of Governors of Harrow School, 1913-24; *b.* Dec. 1845; 3rd *s.* of 1st Duke of Abercorn; *m.* Maud, *y. d.* of 3rd Earl of Harewood, 1871. *Educ.:* Harrow. M.P. (C.) County of Middlesex, 1868-85; Ealing Division, 1885-1906; Under-Secretary of State for India, 1874-78; Vice-President of Council, 1878-80; First Lord of the Admiralty, 1885-86, 1886-92; Chairman London School Board, 1894-95; Secretary of State for India, 1895-1903; Chairman of Royal Commission upon Poor Law and Unemployment, 1905-9; Chairman Mesopotamia Commission, 1916-17. *Publications:* Parliamentary Reminiscences and Reflections, 1868-1885, 1916, and 1886-1906, 1922. *Recreations:* shooting, golf. *Address:* 17 Montagu Street, Portman Square, W.1; *T.:* Mayfair 700. *Club:* Carlton.
(*Died 22 Sept. 1927.*)

HAMILTON, Henry; Dramatic Author; *b.* Nunhead, Surrey; *y. s.* of late James Hamilton, Captain H.E.I.C.S.; unmarried. *Educ.:* Christ's Hospital. Originally an actor. *Plays:* first play produced Prince's Theatre, Manchester; Blank-verse Drama, A Shadow Sceptre; Moths (adaptation of Ouida's novel); Our Regiment, 1884; The Lady of the Locket, Musical Play, 1884; Harvest, 1886; Lord Anerley (in collaboration), 1889; La Tosca (adaptation), 1889; The Three Musketeers, 1898; Robin Hood (collaboration), 1906. Musical Plays: The Duchess of Dantzic, 1903; (adaptations)—Veronique, 1904; The Little Michus, 1905; Autumn Manœuvres, 1912. Plays (in collaboration) at Drury Lane—The Armada, 1888; The Royal Oak, 1889; The Derby Winner, 1894; Cheer, Boys, Cheer! 1895; The White Heather, 1897; The Great Ruby, 1898; The Sins of Society, 1907; The Whip, 1909; The Hope, 1911; Sealed Orders, 1913; The Best of Such, 1916. *Address:* The Haven, Sandgate. *T.:* Sandgate 16. *Club:* Isthmian. (*Died 3 Sept. 1918.*)

HAMILTON, Col. Henry Blackburne; *e. s.* of late Rev. Henry Hamilton, M.A., Devonshire Place, London, formerly Rector of Thomastown, Co. Kildare, Ireland, previously Ensign 85th (Duke of York's Own) Light Infantry, and Frances Margaret, *d.* of late Ralph Peters, Platbridge House, Lancashire; *b.* 1841; *m.* 1874, Isabella Lottie (*d.* 1881), *d.* of J. K. Wedderburn; one *s.*; 2nd, 1888, Florence

Emily, *e. d.* of Lieut.-Gen. C. B. Ewart, C.B., R.E.; *Educ.*: Eton; Christ Church, Oxford. **M.A.** 1868. Cornet, 6th Dragoon Guards (Carabiniers), 1864; Lieutenant-Colonel, 1886; commanded 14th Hussars, 1887-91; Brevet-Colonel, 1890; retired, 1896; served Afghan Campaign, 1880 (despatches, medal); awarded Order of Mercy, 1901; Member of the Westminster City Council, 1900-3; President of St. George's, Hanover Square District, League of Mercy, 1909-19; Knight of Grace of the Order of St. John of Jerusalem in England, since 1916. *Publications*: Regimental Almanac of 14th (King's) Hussars, 1889-91; Regimental Standing Orders for the 14th (King's) Hussars, 1891; Historical Record of 14th King's) Hussars from 1715 to 1900. *Recreations*: field sports in early life, then riding, golf, croquet, and walking. *Address*: Cumloden, Bournemouth. *T.*: Bournemouth 1293. *Clubs*: Carlton, Wellington, Royal Automobile; Bournemouth; Kildare Street, Dublin. *(Died 2 April 1920.)*

HAMILTON, Very Rev. James, Dean of Clonmacnois since 1913. *Educ.*: Trinity College, Dublin. Ordained, 1878; Curate of Fivemiletown, 1878-79; Rector of Donoughmore, 1879-1882; Curate of St. Matthew, Irishtown, 1882-84; Incumbent of Dunboyne, 1884-88; Ardmurcher, 1888-94; Rector of Mayne, 1894-1906; Incumbent of Kilbride, Clara, since 1906-13. *Address*: The Deanery, Clara, King's Co., Ireland.

HAMILTON, James Fetherstonhaugh, M.V.O. 1911; Secretary to Messrs. Coutts, bankers; *b.* 11 July 1850; *s.* of late Lt.-Col. T. T. Hamilton; *m.* 1879, Ellen Bertha, *d.* of Robert Schofield, Rochdale. *Educ.*: Old Trafford School, Manchester. *Address*: 9 Chepstow Mansions, Bayswater, W.

HAMILTON, Capt. Keith Randolph, D.S.O. 1900; late D.A.A. and Q.M.G. Lowland Division, Territorial Force, Oxfordshire Light Infantry; *b.* 28 Feb. 1871; 4th *s.* of Lt.-Gen. Henry Meade Hamilton, C.B.; *m.* 1895, Ella Marcella, *d.* of late Major John Finlay (late 78th Highlanders) of Castle Toward, Argyllshire; one *s.* Entered army, 1892; Captain, 1899; served North-West Frontier India, 1897-98 (medal with two clasps); South Africa, 1899-1902 (severely wounded, D.S.O., Queen's medal 5 clasps, King's medal 2 clasps); retired 1913.

(Died 7 Dec. 1918.)

HAMILTON, Lillias, M.D.; Warden, Studley Horticultural College for Women, 1908-1924; private practice in Calcutta, 1890-94; Physician in charge of the Dufferin Hospital, Calcutta, 1893-94; Physician to the late Ameer of Afghanistan, 1894-97. *Publications*: A Vizier's Daughter, 1900; A Nurse's Bequest, 1907; The Powers that Walk in Darkness, 1924. *Address*: c/o Studley College, Warwickshire.

(Died 6 Jan. 1925.)

HAMILTON, Pryce Bowman, J.P.; *b.* 1844; *o. s.* of late John Hamilton of Hilston Park, and Anne, *e. d.* of late Pryce Jones of Cyfronydd, Co. Montgomery; *m.* 1873, Julia Annie, *o. d.* of late George H. Reynard-Cookson of Whitehill Park, Co. Durham. *Educ.*: Harrow. Late Lieut. 13th Hussars. *Address*: Seaford, Ryde; Villa Valetta, Nice. *Clubs*: Army and Navy; Royal Yacht Squadron, Cowes.

(Died 8 Dec. 1918.)

HAMILTON, Very Rev. Robert Smyly Greer; Dean of Armagh since 1924; *b.* Castle Caulfield, Co. Tyrone, 1861; *m.* Constance Helen Kinahan. *Educ.*: Trinity College, Dublin. Curate of Cavan, 1884-86; Rector of Six-mile Cross, 1886-96, Cookstown, 1896-1905, Dundalk, 1905-24. *Recreations*: tennis, golf. *Address*: The Library, Armagh. *M.*: IB 2661.

(Died 23 Oct. 1928.)

HAMILTON, Rt. Hon. and Rev. Thomas, P.C. Ireland, 1921; M.A., D.D., LL.D.; President and Vice-Chancellor of the

Queen's University of Belfast, 1908 - 23; *b.* Belfast, 28 Aug. 1842; *s.* of late Rev. David Hamilton (Moderator of General Assembly, 1854-1855); and Eliza, *d.* of Henry Weir, Banbridge, Co. Down; *m.* Frances, *d.* of Robert Allen, The Farm, Co. Londonderry, 1876; one *s.* two *d.* *Educ.*: Royal Academical Institution, Belfast; Queen's Coll., Belfast; B.A., M.A., with 1st Class Honours and two gold medals in Natural Science in Queen's Univ. of Ireland, 1863 and 1864; D.D. (hon.) Belfast and Aberdeen; LL.D. (hon.) Ireland, 1891: Ordained 1865: Examiner in Botany and Zoology to Intermediate Education Board, Ireland, 1878-80; President of Queen's College, Belfast, 1889; Senator of Royal University of Ireland, 1890. *Publications*: Faithful unto Death, a Memoir of Rev. David Hamilton, 1875; Irish Worthies, 1875; Our Rest Day (A Prize Essay), 1885; History of the Irish Presbyterian Church, 1886; Beyond the Stars, 1888; many articles in Nat. Dict. of Biography, 1886-1912. *Recreations*: autograph collecting, gardening. *Address*: Chlorine Gardens, Belfast. *T.*: Belfast 50. *(Died 18 May 1925.)*

HAMILTON, Colonel Thomas William O'Hara, B.A., M.B.; C.M.G. 1900; late R.A.M.C.; *b.* 24 May 1860; *e. s.* of late Col. T. Hamilton, Maldon, Surrey; *m.* 1891, Hannah, *d.* of late C. de Gallye Lamotte, M.D., of the Cloisters, Sunderland; one *s.* *Educ.*: King's School, Canterbury; Trinity College, Dublin. Entered army, 1883; Major, 1895; served South Africa, 1899-1902 (despatches, Queen's medal, 6 clasps, King's medal, 2 clasps, C.M.G.); Reserve of Officers. *(Died 22 April 1918.)*

HAMILTON, William Frederick, K.C.; Chancery Division; *b.* 25 Dec. 1848; *e. s.* of late Andrew Hamilton of Southampton; *m.* 1884, Ada Margaret, *e. d.* of W. Morris of Caversham House, Brixton Rise; one *s.* *Educ.*: London University (LL.D); Bencher Middle Temple. Called to Bar, 1879; Q.C., 1900; Member of War Compensation Court. *Publications*: Hamilton's Company Law; Compulsory Arbitration in Industrial Disputes. *Address*: 4 Whitehall Court, S.W.1. *T.*: 3100 Victoria. *Clubs*: Reform, Argentine. *(Died 17 Sept. 1922.)*

HAMLEY, Colonel Francis Gilbert, C.M.G. 1900; Army Pay Department; *b.* 1 Feb. 1851; *s.* of General Hamley, C.B.; *m.* 1878, Grace (*d.* 1916). *Educ.*: St. John's College, Auckland, New Zealand. Royal Cornwall Rangers (Militia), 1872-73; Control Department, 1873; Army Pay Department, 1878. Decorated for South Africa. *Address*: Cox and Co., Charing Cross, S.W. *(Died 14 Sept. 1918.)*

HAMMERSLEY, Major-General Frederick, C.B. 1908; *b.* 21 Oct. 1858; *s.* of Maj.-Gen. F. Hammersley; *m.* Edith, *d.* of George Grant; two *d.* *Educ.*: Eton; Sandhurst. Joined army, 1876; posted to 20th Regt., now Lancashire Fusiliers, 1877; raised and commanded 4th Batt. of the regiment; served on the staff at Aldershot, Dublin, and the War Office; served Egypt, 1884-5; Soudan, 1898; South Africa, 1899-1900. *Club*: Naval and Military.

(Died 28 Mar. 1924.)

HAMMERSTEIN, Oscar; *b.* Berlin, 1847. Built Haarlem Opera House, New York, 1889; Columbus Theatre, New York, 1890; Manhattan Theatre, New York, 1892; Victoria Theatre, New York, 1899; Republic Theatre, 1900; opened Manhattan Opera House, New York, 1906; and London Opera House, 1911. *Works*: Koh-i-noor; Santa Maria; War Bubbles; Sweet Marie; Marguerite; Mrs. Radley Bradley Bore; etc. *Address*: New York, Opera House, Manhattan, U.S.A. *(Died 1 Aug. 1919.)*

HAMMICK, Ven. Ernest Austen, M.A.; *b.* 3 Jan. 1850; 4th *s.* of Rev. Sir St. V. Hammick, 2nd Bt.; *m.* 1897, Mary Elizabeth Amy, widow of Wm. Popham, Bray Hill,

Natal. *Educ.*: Exeter College, Oxford. Ordained, 1874; Curate of Christ Church, Albany Street, 1874-77; Rector of Forrabury, 1877-85; St. John, Westminster, 1885-6; Priest in Charge of Kwamagwaza, Zululand, 1888-9; Archdeacon of Zululand, 1886-89; Incumbent of Blackall, Rockhampton, 1889-92; Pitsworth, Brisbane, 1892-94; Priest in Charge, Buluwayo, 1895-97; Vicar of Ulhmatulzi, 1897-1904; St. James, Umgeni, 1904-7; Archdeacon of Durban, 1899-1907; Rector of Elford, 1909-17. *Address:* Manor Road, St. Marychurch, Torquay.
(*Died 2 Sept. 1920.*)

HAMMICK, Vice-Adm. Robert Frederick, J.P.; *b.* 22 Oct. 1843; 2nd *s.* of Rev. Sir Vincent L. Hammick, 2nd Bt., and *b.* and *heir-pres.* of 3rd Bt.; *m.* 1884, Grace, *d.* of William Longman of Ashlins, Herts; two *s.* one *d.* China medal, 1856; Acting Lieut. commanding the Ant at Rangarei, 1863 (promoted); served with Naval Brigade, Pukehinahina, 1864 (medal); good service pension, 1897. *Address:* Beaumont House, Stoke, Devonport.
(*Died 3 Dec. 1922.*)

HAMMICK, Sir St. Vincent Alex., 3rd Bt., *cr.* 1834; Col. retired, 1896; *b.* Devonshire, 10 April 1839; *e. s.* of late 2nd Bart. and Mary, *d.* of Robert Alexander, E.I.C.S.; *m.* 1st Penelope Sarah Blanche (*d.* 1886), 2nd *d.* of late C. W. Beauclerk, 1869; 2nd, Elinor, 2nd *d.* of late Rev. Sir Gilbert Frankland Lewis, 3rd Bt.; two *d.* *Educ.* : Harrow; Balliol Coll., Oxford. B.A. 1861. Joined 43rd Light Infantry 1861; served in New Zealand War, 1863-66 (medal, despatches). *Heir: n.* George Frederick Hammick, R.N.V.R. [*b.* 1885; *m.* 1916, Eileen Laura, *d.* of Lt.-Col. F. Newton-King; one *d.*]. *Address:* Treneere, Torquay. *T.:* 868.
(*Died 8 Nov. 1927.*)

HAMMOND, Col. Sir Arthur George, K.C.B. *cr.* 1903; D.S.O. 1889; V.C. 1879; *b.* 28 Sept. 1843; *m.* 1886, Edith Jane, *d.* of Maj. J. H. Wright, I.S.C.; one *s.* two *d.* Entered I.S.C. 1861; Col., 1890; served Jowaki Afridee (despatches, medal with clasp), 1877-78; Afghan War (despatches, V.C., medal with two clasps), 1878-80; Hazara Expedition (D.S.O., clasp), 1888; A.D.C. to the Queen, and Colonelcy, 1890; Hazara Expedition (despatches, C.B., clasp), 1891; Isazai Expedition, 1892; Chitral Relief Force (received thanks of Govt. of India, despatches, medal with clasp), 1895; Tirah Expedition, 1897-98, commanding a brigade (two clasps, despatches). *Address:* Camberley, Surrey.
(*Died 20 April 1919.*)

HAMMOND, Basil Edward; Fellow of Trinity College, Cambridge, since 1867; *b.* Sopley, near Ringwood, Hants, 10 Aug. 1842; *s.* of late Rev. J. P. Hammond, Vicar of Sopley; *m.* 1900, Margaret Dorothea, *d.* of late Rev. Francis Slater, Vicar of St. Giles, Cambridge. *Educ.* : Rugby; Trinity College, Cambridge. B.A. 1865; Assistant-Master, Haileybury College, 1865-66; Wellington College, 1868-70; Lecturer of Trinity College, 1871-97; Tutor of Trinity, 1881-85; Lecturer on History for Cambridge University, 1884-1912. *Publications:* The Political Institutions of the Ancient Greeks, 1895; Outlines of Comparative Politics, 1903; Bodies Politic and their Governments, 1915. *Recreations:* variable. *Address:* Trinity College, and Wentworth House, Cambridge. *Club :* Savile.
(*Died 6 Dec. 1916.*)

HAMOND-GRAEME, Sir Graham Eden William, 4th Bt., *cr.* 1783; J.P., D.L.; *b.* 20 Aug. 1845; *e. s.* of 3rd Bt. and Mary, *d.* of Edward Miller; *S.* father 1874; *m.* Evelyn, *d.* of R. B. Lawes, Old Park, Dover, 1876; one *s.* late 16th Lancers; served Abyssinian War, 1867-1868 (medal). *Heir: s.* Egerton Hood-Murray, Major Hampshire Carabiniers [*b.* 23 May 1877. *Educ.* : Cambridge (B.A.). *Club:* Brooks's]. *Address:* Norton, Yarmouth, Isle of Wight;

St. James's Court, Buckingham Gate, S.W. *Club:* Cavalry.
(*Died 12 Jan. 1920.*)

HAMPSON, Sir Robert Alfred, Kt., *cr.* 1904; J.P.; Chairman of C. Tinling & Co., Ltd., Liverpool, proprietors of The Liverpool Daily Courier, The Liverpool Weekly Courier, and The Liverpool Evening Express; *b.* 23 Sept. 1852; *s.* of William Hampson of Plas Onn, Mold, Co. Flint; *m.* 1884, Kate Bolland, *d.* of Walter Ashton, Warrington, Co. Lancaster; one *s.* three *d.* *Educ.* : Liverpool College. Solicitor; Lord Mayor of Liverpool, 1903-4. *Address:* Brown Howe, Ulverston. *Clubs:* Conservative, Athenæum, Liverpool.
(*Died July 1919.*)

HAMPSON, William, M.A. (Oxford), L.M.S.S.A. (London); late Medical Officer in charge of Electrical and X-ray Departments, Queen's Hospital for Children, and St. John's Hospital, Leicester Square; Member of the Council of the Röntgen Society; 2nd *s.* of late William Hampson; *m.* Amy, *d.* of late J. Bolton, Nannerch. *Educ.:* Liverpool College; Manchester Grammar School; Trinity College, Oxford (open scholarship). Inventor of the self-intensive method of refrigeration of gases, by which air was first liquefied cheaply, and by which hydrogen and helium were subsequently liquefied; his self-intensive air liquefier is now used in most of the universities of this country and on the Continent, and in the United States, Canada, and Australia; inventor of the first apparatus for making surgical pencils of carbonic acid snow; inventor of the Hampson radiometer for measuring doses of X-rays; discoverer of the method of controlling the beats of the heart by electrically stimulated muscle contractions. *Publications:* Radium Explained; Paradoxes of Nature and Science; Modern Thraldom—a New Social Gospel; numerous contributions to Nature and other scientific journals. *Address:* 8 West Chapel Street, Mayfair, W.1. *T.:* Mayfair 65; 12 Royal Crescent, W.11. *T.:* Park 1258.
(*Died 1 Jan. 1926.*)

HANBURY, Evan, J.P., Master of the Cottesmore Foxhounds; 2nd *s.* of late Robert Culling Hanbury, M.P., of Poles, Herts, and Caroline, *e. d.* of Abel Smith, of Woodhall, Herts; *b.* 1854; *m.* 1886, Gwendoline, 2nd *d.* of George Henry Finch, M.P., of Burley-on-the-Hill, Oakham. *Educ.* : Eton; Christ Church, Oxford. High Sheriff, Rutland, 1892. *Address:* Braunston, Oakham. *Clubs:* Boodle's, Turf.
(*Died 8 Sept. 1913.*)

HANCOCK, Rev. Frederick, M.A.; S.C.L., F.S.A.; Vicar of Dunster, since 1898; Prebendary of Wells since 1899; Proctor in Convocation for diocese of Bath and Wells, 1899-1910; Treasurer of Wells Cathedral, 1914; J.P. Somersetshire; *b.* 30 Aug. 1848; *s.* of Philip Hancock of Ford, and Anne Blake, *d.* and *heiress* of Robert Hancock of Lydeard St. Lawrence; *m.* 1874, Baptista J. W., *d.* of Rev. John Woodhouse of Huish Champflower, Somerset; four *s.* two *d.* *Educ.* : Sherborne; Wadham Coll. Oxford. 2nd class in Law and History, 1872; B.A. and S.C.L. 1872; M.A. 1885; deacon, 1873; priest, 1874; Curate of Luccombe, Somerset, 1876-77; domestic chaplain to Rt. Hon. Sir T. D. Acland, Bart. 1877-78; Rector of Meshaw, Devon, 1879-1884; Rector of Selworthy, Somerset, 1884-98; Assistant Dioc. Inspector of Schools, 1884-90; Rural Dean of Dunster, 1899; J.P. Somerset; C.C. for Minehead division of Somerset, 1896-1913; Treasurer of the Cathedral Church of St. Andrew, Wells, 1913. *Publications:* A History of Selworthy; A History of Minehead; Dunster Church and Priory; Wifela's Combe; A History of the Parish of Wivelliscombe. *Address:* The Priory, Dunster; Combe End, Huish Champflower, Somerset. *Clubs:* Royal Societies; Somerset County, Taunton.
(*Died 7 Jan. 1920.*)

HANCOCK, Commander Reginald L., R.N., D.S.O. 1916; *b.* 4 June 1880; *m.* 1905, Millicent George, 2nd *d.* of D. T. Stuart, of Wellington, New Zealand; two *s.* Served European War, 1914-17; surveying operations (D.S.O.). *Address:* 36 Vineyard Hill, Wimbledon Park. *Club:* Junior Army and Navy.
(Died 4 Aug. 1919.)

HANCOCK, Rev. William Edward, Hon. Canon of Ripon; Vicar of Knaresborough, 1888-1920; *m.* Margaret Patience (*d.* 1926), *d.* of late Charles Carr, of Seghill House and Cramlington Hall, Northumberland. *Educ.:* Trinity Hall, Cambridge. Deacon, 1869; Priest, 1870. *Address:* Chunocke Hotel, Winchester. *(Died 25 Feb. 1927.)*

HANDFIELD-JONES, Montagu, M.D. (Lond.), F.R.C.P.; Obstetric Surgeon to St. Mary's Hospital and to the British Lying-in Hospital; lecturer on Midwifery and Diseases of Women to St. Mary's Hospital Medical School; examiner in Midwifery and Gynæcology in the University of Cambridge; *b.* 12 May 1855; *e. s.* of Charles Handfield-Jones, F.R.S.; *m.* Maud Kathleen Dawson. *Educ.:* Rugby; London University. *Publications:* contributions to various medical journals and to works on Obstetric Medicine and Surgery. *Address:* 26 Cavendish Square, W.1. *T.:* Mayfair 1207. *M.:* Y 382. *(Died 2 July 1920.)*

HANDLEY, Lt.-Col. Arthur, C.B. 1918; Director of Cammell, Laird & Company; *b.* 30 Sep. 1861; *m.* Clara Mabel, *e. d.* of George Wilson, J.P., late of Banner Cross, Sheffield; four *d. Educ.:* Marlborough; R.M. Academy, Woolwich. Entered Royal Artillery, 1881; Capt. 1889; Major, 1899; retired, 1905; Instructor in Gunnery, 1900-2; Assistant Director of Artillery, War Office, 1902-5, and 1917-19; Officer of the Order of the Crown of Italy, 1919. *Address:* Rusthall Elms, Tunbridge Wells. *Club:* United Service.
(Died 22 July 1927.)

HANDS, Rev. Thomas, M.A.; *b.* Shipston-on-Stour, 19 Dec. 1856; father a corn-merchant. *Educ.:* All Saints' School, Bloxham; Cowbridge Grammar School; Queen's College, Oxford (Mathematical Scholar) Degree, 1878, 1st Class Math. Mods., 1st Class Math. Greats, 2nd Class Physics; 2nd Master, Carlisle Grammar School, 1880-84; Assistant Master Clifton College, 1885-1886; Deacon, 1885; Curate of S. Agnes, Bristol; Priest, 1886; Curate, S. Margaret's Leicester, 1887-88; Hinckley, 1889-90; Vicar of S. Lawrence, Northampton, 1890-1921; Hon. Canon of Peterborough, 1919. *Recreations:* walking and gardening. *Address:* Holy Trinity Vicarage, Shoreditch, E.2 *(Died Nov. 1926.)*

HANINGTON, Rev. Canon Edward A. W., B.A.; Rector of St. Bartholomew's Church, and Canon of Christ Church Cathedral, Ottawa; *b.* New Brunswick, grandparents English; *m.* 1866; one *s.* six *d. Educ.:* University of New Brunswick. Rector of Princetown, New Brunswick; Rural Dean of Woodstock, N.B.; Chaplain to Government House, Ottawa; Secretary of the Diocese of Ottawa. *Publication:* Short Tracts. *Recreations:* cricket, boating, chess. *Address:* S. Bartholomew's Rectory, Ottawa, Canada. *T.A.:* Hanington, Ottawa. *T.:* Rideau 2115. *(Died 13 May 1917.)*

HANLEY, Allan Hastings, C.M.G. 1903; Medical Superintendent Peamdunt Sanatorium since 1913; *b.* 19 May 1863; *s.* of Lt.-Col. Dudley Hanley of Ballycomin, Co. Roscommon; late Deputy Principal Medical Officer, Southern Nigeria. *Address:* Peamdunt, Hazlehatch, Dublin. *(Died 1921.)*

HANMER, Admiral John Graham Job; *b.* 1836; 2nd *s.* of Capt. T. J. S. Hanmer, R.N., of Holbrook Hall, Suffolk; *m.* 1864, Mary Caroline, *d.* of Rev. John Cobbold Aldrich; one *s.* three *d.* Served China War, 1858; North

460

China Expedition, 1860. *Address:* The Priory, Little Waldingfield, Suffolk.*(Died 21 May 1919.)*

HANMER, Sir Wyndham Charles Henry, 6th Bt., *cr.* 1620, *re-cr.* 1774; *b.* 17 Sep. 1867; *S.* father 1893; *m.* 1890, Essex, *d.* of W. Selby Lowndes, Whaddon Hall, Bucks, 1890; one *s.* four *d. Educ.:* Eton; Christ Church, Oxford. Major in Remount Service, 1917-18. Owns about 9000 acres. *Heir: s.* Griffin Wyndham Edward, Lieut. Shropshire Yeomanry, *b.* 30 Aug. 1893. *Address:* Bettisfield Park. Flintshire. *Club:* Carlton.
(Died 3 June 1922.)

HANNA, Hon. William John, K.C.; Provincial Secretary and Registrar-General, Ontario, 1905-16; Food Controller for Canada, 1917-18; President The Imperial Oil Co., Ltd., and of Imperial Oil, Ltd.; *b.* Adelaide, Ontario, 13 Oct. 1862; *s.* of Geo. Hanna and Jane Murdock; *m.* 1st, 1891, Jean G. Neil; 2nd, Maud MacAdams, Sarnia; one *s.* two *d. Educ.:* Public Schools, Brooke, Lambton. Contested West Lambton, 1896, 1900; M.P.P. 1902, 1905. Methodist. *Address:* Toronto, Ontario. *Clubs:* Toronto, York, Toronto. *(Died 20 Mar. 1919.)*

HANNAH, Rev. Joseph Addison, M.A.; Chaplain Norwich Training College, 1926; Principal Diocesan Training College at Norwich, 1895-1924; Hon. Canon of Norwich, 1918; *b.* Warrington, 1 Dec. 1867; *e. s.* of late James Hannah of Whitehaven and Warrington. *Educ.:* The Boteler Grammar School, Warrington, 1880-86; Queens' Coll. Cambridge, 1886-90; Classical Scholar; 1st class Classical Tripos, 1889; special mention for Berney University Prize. Assistant master at Warrington Grammar School, 1890-91; chaplain and tutor St. John's College, Battersea, 1892-95; deacon (Rochester diocese) gospeller, 1892; priest, 1893. *Address:* 14 Clarendon Road, Norwich.
(Died Oct. 1928.)

HANNYNGTON, Col. (temp. Brig.-Gen.) John Arthur, C.B. 1918; C.M.G. 1911; D.S.O., 1916; 129th D.C.O. Baluchis; *b.* 26 Feb. 1868; *s.* of late John Child Hannyngton, I.C.S.; *m.* 1907, Mary Gertrude, *d.* of late Surgeon-Major J. R. Lewis, A.M.D., F.R.S., one *d. Educ.:* United Service College, Westward Ho. Joined 1st Batt. Worcestershire Regt. 1889; transferred to Indian Army, 1892; served British E. Africa, 1896, operations against Mazrui rebels (medal); Uganda, 1897-99; operations against Soudanese mutineers and rebel Waganda (medal and clasp); Somaliland, 1908-10; in command of troops (despatches, medal and clasp, C.M.G.); European War, 1914-1917 (despatches, D.S.O., Bt. Col.). *Club:* United Service. *(Died 21 Aug. 1918.)*

HANSARD, Col. Arthur Clifton, C.M.G. 1917; retired, late Royal Artillery; *b.* 11 June 1855; *s.* of Colonel L. H. Hansard, J.P.; *m.* Marion S., *d.* of H. Minchin Simons; one *s.* one *d. Educ.:* Winchester College; R.M.A. Woolwich. Commissioned in Royal Artillery, 1874; held several appointments including D.A.Q.M.G. at Headquarters; Lt.-Col. R.A. 1900; Colonel, 1906; retired, 1912; re-employed, Oct. 1914: retired on account of health, Nov. 1916 (mentioned for distinguished service in connection with the War, 1917; awarded C.M.G. *Publications:* Handbook and articles on professional subjects. *Recreation:* golf. *Address:* 17A Cadogan Gdns., S.W.3. *T.:* Kensington 2498. *Clubs:* Junior United Service, Hurlingham. *(Died 6 Jan. 1927.)*

HANSON, Sir Charles Augustin, 1st Bt., *cr.* 1918; D.L., J.P., M.P. (Coal.), Bodmin Division of Cornwall since 1916; *e. s.* of Joseph Hanson (*d.* 1870) and Mary Ann (*d.* 1905), *d.* of late William Hicks; *b.* 1846; *m.* 1868, Martha Sabina, *d.* of late James Appelbe of Trafalgar, Halton, Canada; one *d. Educ.:* Fowey. Alderman, City of London until 1921; High Sheriff, Cornwall, 1907; Sheriff of London,

HANDS, Rev. John Compton. See page xx.

1911-12; Lord Mayor of London, 1917-18; Knight of the Order of Francis Joseph; Knight Commander of the Order of the Saviour (Greece); Commander Legion of Honour (France); Grand Officer of Crown of Italy; Order of the Rising Sun, 3rd Class, Japan. *Heir:* Major Charles Edwin Bourne Hanson, W. Riding Regt. [*b.* 17 May 1874; served South African War, 1899-1902 (Queen's medal and clasp, King's medal and two clasps). *Club:* United University]. *Address:* Fowey Hall, Cornwall. *Club:* Carlton. (*Died 17 Jan. 1922.*)

HARBEN, William Nathaniel; novelist; *b.* Dalton, Ga., July 5, 1858; *e. s.* of Nathaniel Parks Harben, planter, and Myra, *d.* of Hiram Lewis Richardson; *m.* Maybelle, *d.* of Joseph B. Chandler; one *s.* one *d.* *Educ.:* high schools; privately. Travelled extensively; associate editor, The Youth's Companion, Boston, 1891-93; Member of the National Institute of Arts and Letters. *Publications:* White Marie, 1889; Almost Persuaded, 1890; A Mute Confessor, 1892; The Land of the Changing Sun, 1894; From Clue to Climax, 1896; The Caruthers' Affair, 1898; Northern Georgia Sketches, 1900; The Woman Who Trusted, 1901; Westerfelt, 1901; Abner Daniel, 1902; The Substitute, 1903; The Georgians, 1904; Pole Baker, 1905; Ann Boyd, 1906; Mam' Linda, 1907; Gilbert Neal, 1908; The Redemption of Kenneth Galt, 1909; Dixie Hart, 1910; Ann Boyd, a drama produced in Boston, 1911; Jane Dawson, 1911; Paul Rundel, 1912; The Desired Woman, 1913; The New Clarion, 1914; The Inner Law, 1915; Second Choice, 1916; The Triumph, 1917; The Hills of Refuge, 1918. *Recreations:* long walks and character study. *Address:* 854 West 181st Street, New York City; Dalton, Georgia. *T.:* St. Nicholas 9892. *Club:* Authors', New York City. (*Died 7 Aug. 1919.*)

HARBOTTLE, Frank, D.S.O. 1917; *b.* Hobart, 1872; *s.* of Joseph Harbottle; *m.* 1912, Olive, *d.* of Major P. W. Grant Pinnock, Brisbane; one *s.* one *d.* *Educ.:* Christ College, Hobart. Entered Civil Service; remained two years and left to follow business pursuits as Accountant and Company Secretary; joined Volunteer Artillery, 1889; Hon. Secretary to Tasmanian Rifle Association for some years before War; invented mechanical miniature rifle target, which was approved by British War Office about 1910; also an apparatus explaining gunnery problems and working of automatic sight, which was adopted by Australian military authorities; took keen interest in trout fishing, and personally introduced English and rainbow trout into several mountain lakes in Tasmania; served European War, 1914-17; first six months as O.C. Australian Garrison Artillery, Fort Nelson, Tasmania; eight months as Camp Commandant Tasmanian Reinforcement Camp, and joined 2nd Australian Division Field Artillery, Sep. 1915; was in Egypt Dec. 1915-Mar.. 1916; and in France (D.S.O.). Gassed at Paschendaale, Nov. 1917; invalided to Australia, Jan. 1918; joined Censor's Staff on reaching Australia; held position of Censor for Tasmania to end of War. *Recreations:* trout - fishing, golf, motoring, music. *Address:* Undruba, Queenborough, Tasmania. *Club:* Naval and Military, Hobart. (*Died Sept. 1923.*)

HARBOTTLE, Sir John George, Kt., *cr.* 1918; J.P.; *b.* 17 May 1858; *s.* of William Harbottle of Great Ayton; *m.* Mary Cowper, *d.* of Cowper Cain, Darlington; four *d.* *Educ.:* Preston Grammar School; Stokesley, Cleveland. Entered Municipality of Darlington,1896; Mayor, 1900 and 1914-17; presented with the freedom of the borough, 1917; Hon. M.A. Cambridge, 1917. *Recreations:* golf, tennis, and climbing. *Address:* Millburn, Darlington. *T.A.:* Harbottle, Darlington. *T.:* 2385. *Club:* National Liberal. (*Died 18 Aug. 1920.*)

HARCOURT, 1st Viscount, *cr.* 1916; **Lewis Harcourt,** P.C. 1905; Baron Nuneham, *cr.* 1916; a Trustee of the Wallace Collection, British Museum, London Museum and National Portrait Gallery; Member of Council and Executive of British School at Rome; Hon. Fellow R.I.B.A.; D.C.L. (Oxford); *e. surv. s.* of late Rt. Hon. Sir William Harcourt and Thérèse, *d.* of Thomas Henry Lister and Lady Theresa Lewis, *sister* of 4th Earl of Clarendon; *b.* 1863; *m.* 1899, Mary Ethel, G.B.E., *o. d.* of late Walter H. Burns of New York and North Mymms Park, Hatfield; one *s.* three *d.* *Educ.:* Eton. Secretary of State for the Colonies, 1910-15; First Commissioner of Works, 1905-10, and 1915-17; M.P. (L.) Rossendale Division, Lancashire, 1904-17. *Heir: s.* Hon. William Edward Harcourt, *b.* 1908. *Address:* 69 Brook Street, W.1; Nuneham Park, Oxford. *T.A.:* Harcourt, Wesdo, London. *T.:* Mayfair 5702. *Clubs:* Reform, National Liberal. (*Died 24 Feb. 1922.*)

HARDCASTLE, Joseph Alfred; Astronomer at the Armagh Observatory since 1917; *b.* 27 Aug. 1868; *s.* of Henry Hardcastle, *g.s.* of Sir John Herschel, Bart., and of Joseph Alfred Hardcastle, M.P.; *m.* Theresa S. C., *d.* of late Sir E. Clive Bayley, K.C.S.I., C.I.E.; one *s.* one *d.* *Educ.:* Harrow; Trinity College, Cambridge. Lecturer to University Extension Delegacy, Oxford, 1901; lecturer to University Extension Syndicate, Cambridge, 1908. *Address:* The Observatory, Armagh. *Club:* Athenæum. (*Died 10 Nov. 1917.*)

HARDIE, Charles Martin, R.S.A., 1895; J.P. County of Fife; painter of portraits, subject pictures, and landscapes; *b.* 16 March 1858, East Linton, Haddingtonshire. *Educ.:* Free Church School; East Linton. Entered School of Design, Edinburgh, 1875; Royal Scottish Academy's Life School, 1877; Stuart Prize for composition, 1878; Keith Prize for best work by R.S.A. student in Exhibition, 1880; A.R.S.A. 1886. *Principal pictures:* An Unrecorded Coronation, 1889; Burns reading his poems to the Edinburgh literati, 1887; The meeting of Burns and Scott, 1893; The Judgment of Paris, 1897; Stepping Stones and The Ford, 1913. *Recreations:* golf. *Address:* Lynedoch Studio, Edinburgh; Garthhill, North Queensferry, Fife. *Clubs:* Scottish Arts, Scottish Conservative, Edinburgh.

(*Died 1 Sept. 1916.*)

HARDIE, W. R., M.A. Edin. and Oxon.; Hon. LL.D. St. Andrews; Prof. of Humanity, Edin. Univ., since 1895; *b.* Edinburgh, 1862; *m.* Isabella Watt, 3rd *d.* of Rev. W. Stevenson. *Educ.:* Edin. Univ.; Balliol Coll. Oxford; Hertford and Ireland Scholarships, 1882; Gaisford Prizes (Prose and Verse), 1882; Latin Verse, 1883; 1st class in Literæ Humaniores, 1884; Craven Scholarship, 1884; Derby Scholarship, 1885. Fellow and tutor of Balliol College, 1884-95; Junior Proctor, 1893-94. *Publications:* Lectures on Classical Subjects, 1903; Latin Prose Composition, 1908; Silvulæ Academicæ, Verses and Verse Translations, 1912. *Address:* 4 Chalmers Crescent, Edinburgh. *Clubs:* Scottish Arts, Hon. Company of Edinburgh Golfers, Edinburgh. (*Died 3 May 1916.*)

HARDING, Rt. Rev. Alfred, D.D., LL.D., Bishop of Washington since 1909; *b.* Lisburn, Ireland, Aug. 15, 1852; *s.* of Richard Harding and Mary Ferguson; *m.* 1887, Justine Butler Prindle; two *s.* one *d.* *Educ.:* Pyper's Academy, Belfast; Public Schools, Dublin; Trinity College (America), and Berkeley Divinity School. Served as Deacon at Trinity Church, Geneva, N.Y., 1883-1887; Assistant St. Paul's Church, Baltimore, Maryland, and Rector St. Paul's Church, Washington, D.C., 1887-1908. *Address:* Bishop's House, Cathedral Close, Mount St. Alban, Washington, D.C. *T.:* Cleveland 948. *M.:* 13337 DC, 88831 Md.

Clubs: Alpha Delta Phi, New York City; Cosmos, Washington.   (*Died 30 April 1923.*)

HARDING, Rev. John Taylor, M.A.; Prebendary of St. Nicholas in Llandaff Cathedral; Rural Dean of Monmouth, 1884-1919; Proctor in Convocation for Chapter of Llandaff, 1886-1919; *b.* 1835; *e. s.* of John Harding of Henbury Hill, Gloucestershire; *m.* Patty (*d.* 1919), *d.* of John Etherington Welch Rolls of the Hendre, Monmouthshire; three *s. Educ.:* Eton; Merton College, Oxford. Deacon, 1859; Priest, 1860; Curate of Cirencester, 1859-61; Curate of Stratton, Gloucestershire, 1861-64; Vicar of Rockfield, 1873-1902. *Address:* Pentwyn, Rockfield, Monmouth. *M.:* AX 765 and AX 5796.   (*Died 30 May 1928.*)

HARDING, Col. T. Walter; High Steward of the Borough of Cambridge; D.L. counties of Camb. and Hunts; J.P. West Riding of York, County Borough of Leeds, and County of Cambridge; *b.* 1843; *s.* of T. R. Harding, D.L., J.P. of Leeds and Doddington, Camb.; *m.* Annie Heycock (*d.* 1923), *d.* of Ambrose Edmund Butler of Kirkstall, Leeds; one *s. Educ.:* France and Germany. Commanded for 20 years the 1st West York Artillery Volunteer Brigade at Leeds; President for 2 years of the Leeds Chamber of Commerce; Lord Mayor of Leeds, 1898-99; High Sheriff of the Counties of Camb. and Hunts, 1900; Hon. Freeman of the City of Leeds; contested West Leeds, 1900; Chairman of Harding, Rhodes, and Co., Ltd., Leeds; Hon. LL.D. *Address:* Madingley Hall, Cambridge. *T.A.:* Harding, Madingley. *T.:* 2 Madingley. *Clubs:* Constitutional, Leeds County, Cambridge.   (*Died 26 Mar. 1927.*)

HARDING, Warren Gamaliel; President of the United States of America since 1920; *b.* Corsica, Morrow Co., Ohio, 2 Nov. 1865; *s.* of George Tyron Harding and Phebe Elizabeth Dickerson; *m.* 1891, Florence Kling, of Marion, Ohio. *Educ.:* Ohio Central College, Iberia. Engaged in newspaper business at Marion, Ohio, since 1884; President, Harding Publishing Co., publishers of Star (daily); member Ohio Senate, 1900-4; Lieut.-Gov. of Ohio, 1904-6; Republican nominee for Governor of Ohio, 1910; member U.S. Senate from Ohio, 1915-21; Baptist. *Address:* The White House, Washington, U.S.A.; Marion, Ohio, U.S.A. *Club:* Marion, Marion.   (*Died 2 Aug. 1923.*)

HARDINGE, 3rd Viscount (of Lahore, and of King's Newton, Derbyshire, *cr.* 1846), **Henry Charles Hardinge,** C.B. 1911; late Capt. Rifle Brigade; late Col. commanding 7th Batt. Rifle Brigade; A.D.C. on Staff of Lord Roberts; A.D.C. to the King; *b.* 1 Aug. 1857; *s.* of 2nd Viscount and Lavinia, *d.* of 3rd Earl of Lucan; *S.* father, 1894; *m.* 1891, Mary, *d.* of Hon. Ralph Nevill, Birling Manor, Kent, *b.* of 1st Marquis of Abergavenny; one *s.* two *d. Educ.:* Harrow. Served in Nile Expedition, 1885. *Heir: s.* Hon. C. N. C. Hardinge. *Address:* South Park, Penshurst, Tonbridge. *Clubs:* Carlton, Pratt's.   (*Died 30 April 1924.*)

HARDINGE, Sir Edmund Stracey, 4th Bt., *cr.* 1801; J.P.; D.L.; *b.* 27 Mar. 1833; *S. b.* 1873; *m.* 1877, Evelyn, *d.* of late Maj.-Gen. Maberly, C.B.; one *s.* two *d. Educ.:* Tonbridge School; Univ. Coll. Oxford. *Heir: s.* Charles, *b.* 15 Nov. 1878. *Address:* 15 Durham Villas, W.8. *T.:* Western 4509. *Club:* Junior Carlton.   (*Died 8 April 1924.*)

HARDWICK, John Jessop, A.R.W.S. 1882; *s.* of William Hardwick, Beverley, Yorks; *b.* Bow-by-Stepney, 22 Sep. 1831; *m.* 1862, Caroline, 3rd *d.* of John Humphrey of Coptgilders Hall, Chessington, Surrey; one *s.* one *d. Educ.:* Bow, under Rev. John Dawson; studied under Royal Academicians, Redgrave, Herbert, and Danby. Apprenticed to Mr. Henry Vizetelly, draughtsman and engraver on wood, 1847; attended School of Art, 462

Somerset House (first prize for water-colour landscape painting from nature, 1851); on staff of The Illustrated London News, 1858; first exhibited Royal Academy, 1860. Friend of late John Ruskin, and assisted him with his classes at the Working Men's College, Great Ormond Street; Trustee and Churchwarden for Parish of Thames Ditton since 1881. *Recreation:* working in his garden. *Address:* The Hollies, Thames Ditton, Surrey.
   (*Died 15 Jan. 1917.*)

HARDWICK, Lt.-Col. Philip Edward, D.S.O. 1916; Commanding 10th Royal Hussars; *b.* 1875; *s.* of late Philip Hardwick, F.S.A.; *m.* 1904, Guina, *d.* of late W. Hargrave Pawson and the Hon. Mrs. Howard; one *s. Educ.:* Eton. Joined Royal Dragoons, 1897; Captain, 1905; Major, 1914; Lt.-Colonel, 10th Hussars, 1916; served with Royal Dragoons in South African War, 1899-1902 (Queen's medal 5 clasps. King's medal 2 clasps); served European War in Belgium, Flanders, and France (twice wounded, despatches, D.S.O., 1914 Star). *Address:* 7 Albert Place, Kensington, W.8. *T.:* Western 4727. *Clubs:* Army and Navy, Cavalry.
   (*Died 9 June 1919.*)

HARDWICKE, Herbert Junius, M.D., F.R.C.S., M.R.C.P.; 3rd *s.* of late Junius Hardwicke of Chilton Lodge, Rotherham, M.D., F.R.C.S., M.R.C.P., and *g.-s.* of William Hardwicke of Diamond Hall, Bridgnorth, solicitor and Proctor of Bridgnorth Royal Peculiar, and *g.-g.-s.* of William Hardwicke of Burcott Hall, Salop; *m.* Mary Elizabeth, *o. c.* of late William Allen of Southfield Grange and Wink House, Yorkshire; two *s.* two *d.* Late Fellow Lond. Med. Soc., and corresponding Fellow Med. Soc. Paris, Madrid, and Athens; formerly editor of The Specialist, and Surgeon in Tewfikiyeh Service, Upper Egypt; founder and formerly Physician to Sheffield Public Hospital for Ear, Throat, etc. *Publications:* Medical Education and Practice in all Parts of the World; European Health Resorts and Spas; Evolution and Creation; The Popular Faith Unveiled; Rambles Abroad; From Alps to Orient; Egypt for Invalids; Alpine Climates for Consumption; Medical Notes on the Spanish Peninsula and Marocco; Ascent of Mind; Evolution of the Special Senses; Mr. Gladstone and Supernaturalism, etc. *Address:* Southfield Mount, St. Leonards-on-Sea. (*Died 13 Aug. 1921.*)

HARDY, Dudley, artist; R.I., R.M.S.; *b.* Sheffield, 15 Jan. 1867; *e. s.* of T. B. Hardy, marine painter; *m.* 1st, 1899, Mrs. Burnside, *née* Mulholland (*d.* 1906); 2nd, 1907, Annie Morrison; one *s.* one *d. Educ.:* Boulogne School; Univ. Coll. School, London. Studied at Düsseldorf, Antwerp, Paris; Member Royal Institute Water-colour Painters, Society Oil Painters, Society 25 English Painters, Royal Miniature Society, and Pastel Society. *Publications:* in Illustrated London News, The Sketch, Pictorial World, Lady's Pictorial, Gentlewoman, Pick-me-up, Black and White, Graphic, and foreign papers, Punch, Sphere, etc.; book illustrations, and many posters. *Recreation:* cycling. *Clubs:* Savage, Ye Punch Bowle, London Sketch.
   (*Died 11 Aug. 1922.*)

HARDY, Ernest George, M.A., D.Litt. ; Principal of Jesus College, Oxford, since 1921; formerly Vice-Principal and Tutor; *b.* Hampstead, 15 Jan. 1852; *e. s.* of George Hardy, sometime Chief Clerk in the G.P.O.; *m.* 1st, 1877, Mary, *d.* of late John Mann; 2nd, 1920, Daisy Anne, widow of Dr. Percy Gardiner, and *d.* of late John Spear, surgeon. *Educ.:* Highgate School, 1867-70. Scholar of Exeter College, 1871-74; 1st class in Classical Moderations; 1st class in final Classical School; Fellow of Jesus College, 1875; Assistant Master, Felstead School, 1877-79; Headmaster of Grantham School, 1879-87; Fellow and Tutor of Jesus College, 1894; Public Examiner in final

Classical School, 1900-1901. *Publications:* translator (with J. S. Mann) of Schömann's Greek Antiquities; editor of Plato's Republic, book i. ; Juvenal's Satires; Pliny's Correspondence with Trajan; Plutarch's Lives of Galba and Otho; author of Christianity and the Roman Government; a History of Jesus College; Studies in Roman History, first series, 1907 ; second series, 1910 ; Roman Laws and Charters, translated with introductions, etc., 1912; Monumentum Ancyranum, edited with notes, 1923 ; Some Problems in Roman History, 1924 ; Catilinarian Conspiracy, 1924 ; articles in Classical Review, Journal of Philology, Journal of Roman Studies, etc. *Address:* The Lodgings, Jesus College, Oxford ; Jesmond, Chester Road, Bournemouth.   (*Died 26 Oct. 1925.*)

HARDY, Rev. E. J., M.A.; Chaplain to H.M. Forces ; retired ; *b.* Armagh, Ireland, 7 May 1849 ; *s.* of Rev. James Hardy, Rector of Moylary, Ireland ; *m.* Margaret, *d.* of Rev. Wm. Noble, 1876. *Educ.:* Royal School, Portora ; Trin. Coll. Dublin. Senior Moderator and Gold Medallist; Elrington, etc., Prizeman. Deacon, 1874 ; Priest, 1875 ; army chaplain, 1878-1908 ; served at Cork, Bermuda, Halifax, Dover, Gosport, Netley, Malta, Plymouth, Dublin, Hong-Kong, Egypt, Lichfield, Winchester, Aldershot. Donnellan Lecturer, Trin. Coll. Dublin, 1898-99. When at Hong-Kong visited Japan and many parts of China; gave some lectures in the large towns of England. *Publications:* How to be Happy though Married, 1884 ; Manners Makyth Man, 1885 ; Faint yet Pursuing, 1886 ; Uncle John's Talks with his Nephews, 1886 ; The Five Talents of Woman, 1888 ; The Business of Life, 1892 ; Sunny Days of Youth, 1895 ; The People's Life of their Queen, 1896 ; In the Footprints of St. Paul, 1896 ; The Love Affairs of Some Famous Men, 1897, which is dedicated to his "only wife"; Doubt and Faith, 1899. How to be Happy, etc., has been translated into many languages; Mr. Thomas Atkins, 1900 ; Concerning Marriage, 1901 ; Love, Courtship, and Marriage, 1902 ; Pen Portraits of Our Soldiers, 1902 ; Love Rules the World, and John Chinaman at Home, 1905 ; How to be Happy Though Civil, 1909 ; The Unvarying East, 1912 ; The British Soldier, His Courage and Humour, 1915. *Recreations:* riding on horse, camel, ass, bicycle, top of a motor bus ; talking to simple, hard-working people; looking at flowers and picking fruit in a garden ; taking a sun bath ; thinking of the queer things of life ; swimming. *Address:* c/o Rev. F. Stoney, Tashinny Rectory, Mullingar, Ireland. *Club:* his wife's tea-table.   (*Died 11 Oct. 1920.*)

HARDY, Maj.-Gen. Frederick, C.B. 1907 ; Colonel York and Lancaster Regiment, 1905 ; *b.* 25 Dec. 1830 ; *m.* 1863, Kate, *y. d.* of Ven. S. M. Kyle, Archdeacon of Cork. Entered army, 1849 ; Maj.-Gen. 1885 ; retired, 1889 ; served Indian Mutiny, 1857-59 (despatches twice, medal with 2 clasps). *Address:* Ashton, Wyke Hall, Winchester. *Club:* Junior United Service.
        (*Died 24 Feb. 1916.*)

HARDY, George Alexander, J.P.; Alderman of L.C.C. ; Member L.C.C., Dulwich Division ; Captain 2/12 C. of L.V.T.C. ; *b.* Islington, 29 Dec. 1851 ; *s.* of late Edward Septimus Hardy ; *m.* 1875, Florence Marianne, *d.* of late Francis Deacon Wilson ; one *s. Educ.:* privately. Merchant and manufacturer since 1874 ; J.P. for County of London ; Director London Missionary Society ; Chairman of Governors, Cheshunt College ; Chairman Managing Committee, National Liberal Club ; Member of Tribunal, Camberwell ; interested in social and philanthropic work; M.P. (L.) Stowmarket, Suffolk, 1906-10 ; contested Bath, 1910. *Recreations:* golf, chess, tennis, etc. *Address:* Highlands, Champion Hill, S.E.   *T.A.:* Osprey, London. *T.:* 430 Brixton. *Clubs:* National Liberal, Reform.   (*Died 2 Oct. 1920.*)

HARDY, Iza Duffus, *o. d.* of the late Sir Thomas and Lady Duffus Hardy. *Publications:* A New Othello ; Glencairn ; Only a Love Story ; A Broken Faith; Love, Honour, and Obey; Hearts are Diamonds ; The Love that he Passed By ; Love in Idleness ; Between Two Oceans ; Oranges and Alligators ; The Lesser Evil ; A Woman's Loyalty ; MacGilleroy's Millions ; Man, Woman, and Fate ; A Butterfly, His Silence ; The Silent Watchers, etc. *Address:* c/o London County and Westminster Bank, Temple Bar Branch, E.C.
        (*Died 30 Aug. 1922.*)

HARDY, Richard Gillies, C.S.I. 1900 : J.P. and C.C., Gloucestershire; Member Board of Revenue, U. Provinces, India, 1902-6 ; *b.* London, 12 Feb. 1852 ; *s.* of late Rev. R. Hardy of Anerley ; *m.* Charlotte Annie, *e. d.* of Admiral Sir W. G. Luard, K.C.B., of The Lodge, Witham, Essex ; three *d. Educ.:* Victoria College, Jersey. Served in Indian Civil Service since 1871 ; was Magistrate and Collector of Jhansi and Moradabad districts ; Commissioner Lucknow Division, 1896-1900 ; Member of Legislative Council, U. Provinces, 1899-1901 ; Chief Secretary, U.P. Govt., 1901 ; Member Viceroy's Legislative Council, 1901-2 ; Acting Sec. to Government of India, Revenue and Agriculture, 1902. *Decorated* for general and famine services. *Club:* East India United Service.   (*Died 1 June 1923.*)

HARDY, Rev. Theodore Bayley, V.C. 1918 ; D.S.O. 1917 ; attached Lincoln Regt. ; M.C., C.F.; Priest in Charge, Hutton Roof, since 1913 ; Chaplain to the Forces since 1916 ; *b.* 1866 ; widower; one *s.* one *d. Educ.:* City of London School ; University of London. Ordained 1898 ; Curate Bulcott, Notts, 1898-1902 ; Assistant Master, High School, Nottingham, 1891-1907 ; Curate New Basford, 1902-7 ; headmaster Bentham Grammar School, 1907-13. *Address:* Hutton Roof, Kirkby, Lonsdale.
        (*Died 18 Oct. 1918.*)

HARDY, Thomas, author; O.M. 1910 ; Hon. LL.D. Aberdeen ; Litt.D. Cambridge and D.Litt. Oxford ; LL.D. St. Andrews and Bristol ; Hon. Fellow Magdalene College, Cambridge, and Queen's College, Oxford ; J.P. Dorset ; *b.* Dorsetshire, 2 June 1840 ; *s.* of late Thomas and Jemima Hardy ; *m.* 1st, 1874, Emma Lavinia (*d.* 1912), *d.* of J. A. Gifford, and *niece* of Archdn. Gifford; 2nd, 1914, Florence Emily, J.P. for Dorchester, *d.* of Edward Dugdale, and author of numerous books for children, magazine articles, and reviews. *Educ.:* Dorchester ; King's College, London. Pupil of John Hicks, ecclesiastical architect, 1856-61 ; read Latin and Greek with a fellow-pupil, 1857-60; sketched and measured many old country churches now pulled down or altered ; removed to London and worked at Gothic architecture under Sir A. Blomfield, A.R.A., 1862-67 ; prizeman of Royal Institute of British Architects, 1863 ; the Architectural Assoc., 1863 ; wrote verses, 1865-1868 ; gave up verse for prose, 1868-70 ; but resumed it later. Holds Gold Medal of Royal Society of Literature : Member of the Council of Justice to Animals; is against blood-sport, dog-chaining, and the caging of birds. *Publications:* Prose— Desperate Remedies, 1871 ; Under the Greenwood Tree or The Mellstock Quire, 1872 ; A Pair of Blue Eyes, 1872-73 ; Far from the Madding Crowd, 1874 ; Hand of Ethelberta, 1876 ; Return of the Native (with map), 1878 ; The Trumpet-Major, 1879 ; A Laodicean, 1880-81 ; Two on a Tower, 1882 ; The Life and Death of the Mayor of Casterbridge, 1884-85 ; The Woodlanders, 1886-1887 ; Wessex Tales (collected), 1888 ; A Group of Noble Dames, 1891 ; Tess of the d'Urbervilles, 1891 ; Life's Little Ironies (collected), 1894 ; Jude the Obscure, 1895 ; The Pursuit of the Well-Beloved, serially 1892, revised and re-written as The Well-Beloved, 1897 ; A Changed

Man, etc. (collected), 1913. Verse—Wessex Poems (written 1865 onwards), 1898 ; Poems of the Past and the Present, 1901 ; The Dynasts (epic-drama), Part I., 1903 ; Part. II., 1906 ; Part III., 1908 ; Select Poems of William Barnes, with Preface, 1908 ; Time's Laughing-stocks and other Verses, 1909 ; Satires of Circumstance (serially), 1911 (with Lyrics and Reveries), 1914; Selected Poems, 1916; Moments of Vision, 1917 ; Late Lyrics, 1922 ; Queen of Cornwall (Play), 1923; Human Shows, 1925; definitive Wessex edition of works in prose and verse with new prefaces and notes, 1912 onwards ; complete Poetical Works, 2 vols., 1919 ; limited Mellstock Edition of works, 1920. *Address :* Max Gate, Dorchester, Dorset. *Club :* Athenæum.
(*Died 11 Jan. 1928.*)

HARDY, William John, Hon. M.A. Durham Univ. (Univ. Coll.), 1909 ; F.S.A., legal and genealogical record searcher and translator ; *b.* London, 29 Sept. 1857 ; 2nd *s.* of Sir William Hardy, Deputy-Keeper of the Public Records, and Miss E. C. S. Lee, West Cholderton Manor, Wilts ; *m.* 1886, Margaret (*d.* 1911), *e. d.* of Henry Page, London and Oporto ; one *s.* one *d.* *Educ. :* privately. Council Society of Antiquaries, 1887-89, 1891-93, 1895-97, 1907, 1912-13 ; Inspector Historical MSS. Commission ; editor of Calendar of State Papers, William and Mary (Master of the Rolls Series) ; Middlesex and Hertfordshire Notes and Queries, 1895-98 ; Home Counties Magazine, 1899-1904. *Publications :* Handwritings of the Kings and Queens of England, 1893; Book Plates, 1893, 2nd ed. 1897 ; Lighthouses, their History and Romance, 1895 ; Documents Illustrative of English Church History (jointly with Rev. H. Gee), 1896 ; The Stamp Collector (jointly with E. D. Bacon), 1898. *Recreations :* archæology, entomology, the collection of book-plates. *Address :* The Firs, St. Albans, Herts ; 15 Old Square, Lincoln's Inn, W.C. (*Died 17 July 1919.*)

HARE, Henry Thomas; President of Royal Institute of British Architects ; *b.* Scarborough ; *m.* 1884, 2nd *d.* of late W. H. Ferons, Durham ; one *d.* *Educ. :* Privately at Sheffield and Harrogate. Articled in 1876 ; studied subsequently at Ecole des Beaux Arts, Paris ; A.R.I.B.A., 1887 ; F.R.I.B.A., 1898 ; Vice-President, 1904-8 ; Hon. Secretary, 1909-13 ; Ashpitch Prizeman, 1886 ; Buildings executed : City Buildings, Oxford ; County Buildings, Stafford ; Westminster College, O bridge ; North Wales University, Bangor, and others. *Address :* 2 Gray's Inn Square, W.C.1 ; *T.:* Central 2507 ; Egypt, Farnham Common, Bucks.
(*Died 10 Jan. 1921.*)

HARE, Sir John, Kt., *cr.* 1907 ; *b.* London, 16 May 1844 ; *m.* 1864, Mary Adela Elizabeth, *d.* of John Hare Holmes ; one *s.* two *d.* *Educ. :* Giggleswick Grammar School, Yorkshire. First appearance on the stage, Prince of Wales' Theatre, Liverpool, 28 Sep. 1864 ; in London, 25 Sep. 1865, where he appeared in the entire series of Robertson Comedies, Sir Peter Teazel in School for Scandal, and other parts ; became manager of the Court Theatre, 13 March 1875, when he produced Olivia and other plays ; manager of St. James' Theatre in partnership with Mr. Kendal, 1879 ; opened and became manager of the Garrick Theatre, 1889-94 ; amongst other characters played by him during this period were Col. Daunt in Queen's Shilling, Lord Kilclare in Quiet Rubber, Duke of St. Olpherts in Notorious Mrs. Ebbsmith, Goldfinch in Pair of Spectacles, and Lord Quex. *Address :* 47 Westbourne Terrace, W.3. *T.:* Paddington 6060. *Clubs :* Garrick, Beefsteak.
(*Died 28 Dec. 1921.*)

HARE, Sir Lancelot, K.C.S.I., *cr.* 1907 ; C.S.I. 1906 ; C.I.E. 1900 ; Indian Civil Service, Bengal ; *b.* London, 7 Jan. 1851 ; *y. s.* of late Thomas Hare of Hook, Surrey ; *m.* 1st,

464

1881, Laura Maud (*d.* 1916), *e. d.* of late General Sir John Nation, K.C.B. ; 2nd, Marjorie Edith, *d.* of late Capt. Eustace Maudslay. *Educ. :* Hurstpierpoint, Sussex ; City of London School. Served in Bengal and Assam from 1873 ; member Board of Revenue ; member of Governor - General's Council, 1905-6 ; Officiating Lt.-Governor, Bengal, 1906 ; Lieut.-Gov. East Bengal and Assam, 1906-11. *Decorated* for service in India. *Address :* 8 Embankment Gardens, Chelsea, S.W. *Club :* Albemarle.
(*Died 7 Oct. 1922.*)

HARE, Col. Richard Charles, C.B. 1900 ; retired pay ; *b.* 8 Aug. 1844 ; *e. s.* of late Col. Hon. R. Hare and *g.g.s.* of 1st Earl of Listowel ; *m.* 1875, Mary, *o. d.* of late Lieut.-Gen. Sir Charles A. Windham, K.C.B. Appointed Ensign in 22nd Foot, 1863 ; was Adj. for 1st Batt., and commanded the 2nd Batt., 1892-96 ; commanded 63rd Regimental District, 1898-1900 ; and the 24th Regimental District, 1900-1902 ; passed the Staff College ; served as A.D.C. to Commander-in-Chief of Canada, 1867-70 ; D.A.Q.M.G. under Lord Wolseley in Cyprus, 1878-79 ; Brigade-Major, Aldershot, 1879-83 ; served in Ashanti Expedition, 1873-74 (medal and clasp), as Acting R.E. Officer ; also in Egyptian Campaign, 1882, as Brigade - Major (despatches, and Brevet-Major, Egyptian medal and Khedive's bronze star, 4th class Medjidie). *Address :* Reymerston Hall, Attleborough, Norfolk. *Club :* United Service. (*Died 31 Oct. 1917.*)

HARFORD, Charles Forbes, M.A., M.D., M.R.C.S., L.R.C.P. ; Refraction Assistant St. Bartholomew's Hospital ; Oculist to School Clinics Lond. and Herts. C.C. ; Emeritus Lecturer, late Principal of Livingstone Coll. ; Instructor in Health and Outfit to Royal Geog. Society ; Joint Secretary Fédération Internationale pour la Protection des Races Indigènes contre l'Alcoolisme ; *y. s.* of late Rev. Canon Harford-Battersby, Keswick ; *m.* Adeline, *d.* of Wm. Clapton, F.R.C.S. ; one *d.* *Educ. :* Repton ; Trinity College, Cambridge ; St. Thomas's Hospital. Medical Missionary of the C.M.S. in West Africa, 1890-92 ; with others founded Livingstone College and became its 1st Principal, 1893 ; Honorary Secretary (now Chairman of Executive) of Native Races and the Liquor Traffic United Committee, 1896-1904 ; Physician of C.M.S. 1903-11 ; Secretary Medical Committee C.M.S., 1911-19 ; Joint Secretary Society of Tropical Medicine and Hygiene, 1908-17 ; Temp. Captain, R.A.M.C. ; Secretary Church of England Temperance Society, 1919 ; Diocesan Reader in London, St. Albans, and Chelmsford Dioceses. *Publications :* Pilkington of Uganda ; Do you Pray? Daily ; Hints on Outfit for Travellers in the Tropics ; Mind as a Force. *Address :* 30 Finsbury Square, E.C.2 ; Shirley, Ox Lane, Harpenden. *T.:* Clerkenwell 1258 : Harpenden 165.
(*Died 4 July 1925.*)

HARFORD, Rev. Edward John, Canon Residentiary of Wells since 1903 ; Rural Dean of Keynsham ; *m.* 1864, Gertrude Emma, *y. d.* of Rev. Sir Thomas Pym Bridges, 7th Bt. ; one *s.* four *d.* *Educ. :* Oxford (2nd class Law and History). Ordained, 1857 ; Curate of Deal, also Curate and Lecturer of Henbury, Bristol, 1860-70 ; Vicar of Bathford, 1870-92 ; Rector of Marston-Biggott, 1892-1905 ; late Rural Dean of Frome. *Address :* The Liberty, Wells, Somerset. *T.A. :* Nunney, Frome. (*Died 27 Aug. 1917.*)

HARFORD, Rev. George, M.A. ; Vicar of Mossley Hill, Liverpool ; Hon. Canon of Liverpool ; Joint Editor of The Hexateuch according to the Revised Version, and of the Prayer Book Dictionary ; *b.* 1860 ; *s.* of T. D. Harford-Battersby, late Vicar of St. John's, Keswick, and Hon. Canon of Carlisle ; *m.* 1889, Helen Antoinette, *d.* of Col. E. C. Impey, C.I.E. ; one *s.* three *d.* *Educ. :* Harborne

HARE, Francis, M.D. See page xx.

Vicarage ; Repton School ; Balliol College, Oxford (1st Class Math. Mods., 2nd Class Math. Finals, 1st Cl. Theol.) ; Liverpool (M.A. by Diss. in Philos. 1915). Held curacy in South Lambeth and benefice of Middle w. East Claydon, Bucks. *Publications:* articles in Hastings' Dictionary of the Bible ; the Church Congress Manual ; Church Song and Prayer with Tunes. *Address:* Mossley Hill Vicarage, Liverpool. *T.:* 3 X Mossley Hill.

(*Died 21 Feb. 1921.*)

HARGREAVES, John, M.F.H. ; *e. s.* of late John Hargreaves of Broad Oak, Whalley Abbey, and Maiden Erleigh, Berkshire, and Mary Jane, *o. d.* of Alexander Cobham Cobham of Shinfield Manor, Berks ; *b.* Leighton Park, near Reading, 1 Mar. 1864 ; *m.* 1889, Evelyn Kennard, 5th *d.* of William Bunce Greenfield ; three *d.* *Educ.* : Eton. Entered 15th Hussars, 1887 ; Master of the Cattistock, 1897 - 1900 ; Master of the Blackmore Vale, 1900-5. *Address* : Templecombe House, Templecombe, Somerset. *Club* : Junior Carlton.　(*Died 21 April 1926.*)

HARKER, Ven. Archdeacon Ernest Gardner, Archdeacon of Matabeleland and Rector of Bulawayo, 1913-27. *Educ.* : Exeter College, Oxford (M.A.). Ordained 1893 ; Curate of St. Paul, Burton-on-Trent, 1893-96 ; Holy Cross, Shrewsbury, 1897 ; Rector of Castle Bromwich, 1897-1911 ; Diocesan Inspector of Schools, Birmingham, 1897-98 ; Dean and Archdeacon of Salisbury, Rhodesia, 1911 ; Vicar-general of Diocese of Southern Rhodesia, 1923-1924 and 1926 ; Chaplain of Queen Margaret's School, Scarborough, 1927. *Address* : 1 Princess Royal Park, Scarborough, Yorkshire.

(*Died 25 Dec. 1928.*)

HARKER, John Allen, O.B.E., D.Sc., F.R.S. ; Member of the firm of J. T. Crowley and Partners, Consulting Engineers ; Director of Research, Ministry of Munitions, 1916-21 ; formerly Chief Assistant at the National Physical Laboratory, Teddington ; *b.* Alston, Cumberland, 23 Jan. 1870 ; *s.* of late Rev. John Harker, Congregational minister ; *m.* Ada, *d.* of late Thomas Richardson, C.C., J.P., of Alston ; two *s.* three *d.* *Educ.* : Stockport Grammar School ; Universities of Manchester and Tübingen. Dalton Chemical Scholarship at Owens College, 1891 ; Berkeley Fellowship in Physics, 1892 ; Member of the Councils of the Physical Society of London and of the Faraday Society ; Member of the British Association Committee on Gas Engines ; Member of the Royal Institution ; was the delegate of the British Government at the International Petroleum Congress, Vienna, 1912 ; Superintendent (*pro tem.*) Eskdalemuir Observatory, 1913 ; was responsible during the war for the organisation of the work of the Nitrogen Products Committee of the Ministry of Munitions, and was Director of the Research Laboratories set up to study modern nitrogen fixation processes ; was on board the Cunard liner Andania torpedoed off the north coast of Ireland Jan. 1918 ; later visited the United States and Canada on behalf of the Ministry at the request of the American Government ; was member during the war of a large number of Government Committees on Scientific Problems, including the Oxygen Committee and the Gas Cylinders Committee of the Dept. Sci. and Ind. Research. *Publications:* a number of papers, mostly on thermal and electrical subjects, in Philosophical Transactions and Proceedings Royal Society, Philosophical Magazine, etc. *Address:* 16 Victoria Street, S.W.1 ; 6 Cambridge Terrace, Regent's Park, N.W.1 ; Clarghyll Hall, Alston, Cumberland. *Club* : National Liberal.　(*Died 10 Oct. 1923.*)

HARKER, Joseph Cunningham ; painter ; *b.* Levenshulme, Manchester, 17 Oct. 1855 ; father was well-known character actor

in Manchester ; mother before her marriage was Maria O'Connor, an actress, sister of John O'Connor, artist ; *m.* 1877, Sarah Hall, *d.* of scene painter of that name ; six *s.* three *d.* Came to London, 1870 ; apprenticed to T. W. Hall, scene painter, and assisted in many notable productions at the Haymarket Theatre under Buckstone's management ; then followed seasons in Glasgow and Dublin in 1882-83 ; in 1885-6-7-8 went for seasons to United States to paint some huge panoramic pictures, then much in vogue ; returning to England, was then engaged by Sir Henry Irving for all of his productions until his death, and has been associated with all the leading London theatrical managements. *Publication:* Studio and Stage, 1924. *Recreations:* music and sailing. *Clubs:* Savage, London Sketch.

(*Died 15 April 1927.*)

HARKNESS, James, M.A. ; *s.* of late John Harkness, Derby ; *b.* Derby, 24 Jan. 1864 ; *m.* 1908, Katherine E., *e. d.* of Rev. W. H. Cam, Paulers-Pury Rectory, Towcester ; two *s.* one *d.* *Educ.* : Derby School ; Trinity Coll., Cambridge (Major Scholar) ; first in Mathematics in the Honour Examinations for the Intermediate and B.A. at London University ; successively Associate, Associate Professor, and Professor of Mathematics at Bryn Mawr College, Pennsylvania, U.S.A. 1888-1903 ; Peter Redpath Prof. of Pure Mathematics, McGill University, Montreal, 1903-13 ; formerly Vice-President of the American Mathematical Society, and sub-editor of Transactions of the American Mathematical Society ; Fellow of Royal Society of Canada, 1909 ; LL.D. McGill University, 1921. *Publications:* (with Prof. Frank Morley) two treatises on the Theory of Functions ; assisted in the article on Elliptic Functions in the German Encyclopædia of Mathematics ; scientific papers in the Transactions of Royal Society of Canada, etc. *Recreation:* lawn tennis. *Address:* Arts' Building, McGill University, Montreal ; 23 Lorne Avenue, Montreal, Canada.

(*Died Dec. 1923.*)

HARLEY, Lt.-Col. Henry Kellett, D.S.O. 1895 ; late 7th Hussars ; *b.* 2 Dec. 1868 ; *m.* 1st, 1899, Hon. Margaret Holland, *d.* of 1st Baron Rotherham ; one *s.* one *d.* ; 2nd, Thella, *d.* of Henri Bluston, of Kovno, Russian Poland ; three *s.* Entered army, 1890 ; served Chitral Expedition, 1895 ; defence of Chitral Fort (despatches, D.S.O., medal and clasp) ; Sudan Expedition, 1897 (medal and clasp) ; Sudan Expedition, 1898 ; Battle of Atbara (despatches, severely wounded, clasp, and English - Sudan medal, 4th Class Medjidie) ; Brevet of Major, 1898 ; South African Field Force, 1901 - 1902 (medal, 5 clasps) ; served European War, in France with R.F.A. and R.G.A., 1916-17 (Croix de Guerre, Bronze Military Medal for valour, despatches) ; now on the Staff of British Mission, G.H.Q., Italy. *Address:* Raycroft, Maidenhead. *Clubs:* White's, Cavalry.

(*Died 9 Jan. 1920.*)

HARLEY, Vaughan, M.D., M.R.C.P. ; late Professor University College ; Physician ; *b.* London, 28 Dec. 1863 ; *s.* of late Dr. George Harley, F.R.S., and Emma, *d.* of James Muspratt, Seaforth Hall ; *m.* 1905, Mary, *e. d.* of Rev. Canon Blagden, of Peverel Court, Aylesbury ; two *d.* *Educ.* : Edinburgh Univ., Paris, Leipzig, Vienna, Buda Pest, Turin, etc. M.D. Edinburgh, Gold Medallist ; Bronze Medallist in Pathology ; Grocer Research Scholarship. Travelled round the world, 1887-88 ; studied at Foreign Universities, 1888-92 ; since 1892 practising in London as a physician. *Publications:* The Chemical Investigation of Diseases of the Stomach and Intestines ; numerous—in Royal Soc. Transactions, English and foreign physiological journals, and medical papers. *Recreations:* travelling, farming. *Address:* 25 Harley

465

Street, W.1; Walton Hall, Bletchley, Bucks. *T.*: Mayfair 2643. *Club*: Junior Carlton.

(*Died 21 May 1923.*)

HARMAN, Edward George, C.B. 1911; *b.* 28 Nov. 1862; 2nd *s.* of late Rev. Edward Harman. *Educ.*: Uppingham (Scholar); King's College, Cambridge. Entered the Home Civil Service, Admiralty, 1886; Home Office, 1886; Treasury, 1889; seconded for service under Lord Kitchener of Khartoum as Financial Secretary to the Soudan Government, 1898-1900; accompanied Sir David Barbour on financial mission to South Africa, 1900-1901; a Principal Clerk in H.M. Treasury, 1907-1912; retired, 1912. *Address*: 3 Middle Temple Lane, E.C.4. *Club*: New University. (*Died 20 Dec. 1921.*)

HARMER, Frederic William, J.P., M.A. (Hon.), Cantab., F.G.S., F.R.Met.S., Mém. Hon. Soc. Belge Géol. 1904, Mém. Géol. Soc., France; *b.* Norwich, 24 April 1835; *s.* of Thomas and Emily Harmer; *m.* Mary, *d.* of Adam Lyon; four *s.* one *d. Educ.*: Norwich. Mayor of Norwich, 1887-8; Alderman, 1880-1902; Geological Society, London, Council, 1896-1900; Murchison Medallist, 1902; Palæontographical Soc., Council, 1878-82; Norfolk and Norwich Nat. Soc., Pres., 1887-9; late Chairman and Man. Director, Norwich Electricity Co., Ltd.; Trustee King Ed. VI. Grammar School, Norwich; Dep. Chairman, 1909-13; Member of Mousehold Heath Conservators; Committee Norfolk and Norwich Horticultural Soc.; Norwich Castle Museum; Norwich Public Library; Income Tax Commissioners, etc.; during 1864-72 carried out with the late Searles V. Wood, Jr., the first survey of the glacial beds of the East of England, a portion of the map being published in 1872 by the Palæont. Soc.; has travelled some thousands of miles in the investigation of the Pliocene and Pleistocene deposits of the eastern and midland counties, and of those of Belgium and Holland. *Publications*: Pliocene Mollusca of Great Britain, six parts issued by the Palæontographical Soc. during 1914-21, still in progress; many original papers on Geology, Palæontology, and Palæometeorology, by the Geol. Soc. of London, Geol. Assoc. Lond., Soc. Belge de Géol., Norfolk and Norwich Nat. Soc., Yorks. Geol. Soc., etc. *Recreations*: horticulture, scientific work. *Address*: Oakland House, Cringleford, nr. Norwich. *T.A.*: Harmer, Eaton, Norwich. *T.*: Eaton 81.

(*Died 11 April 1923.*)

HARMOOD-BANNER, Sir John Sutherland, 1st Bt., *cr.* 1924; Kt., *cr.* 1913; J.P., D.L.; M.P. (C.) Everton Division, Liverpool, 1905-24; *b.* Liverpool, 8 Sep. 1847; *m.* 1st, Elizabeth, *d.* of late Thomas Knowles of Darnhall, Cheshire, M.P. for Wigan; 2nd, 1908, Ella, *d.* of John Ernest Herbert Linford. *Educ.*: Radley. Entered father's office, Harmood-Banner and Sons, Accountants, Liverpool, 1865; partner, 1870; Auditor Bank of Liverpool; High Sheriff, Cheshire, 1902; Lord Mayor of Liverpool, 1913. *Heir*: *s.* Harmood Harmood-Banner. *Address*: 63 Lowndes Square, S.W.; *T.*: Victoria 377; Ingmire Hall, Sedbergh, Yorkshire. *Clubs*: Junior Carlton, Carlton.

(*Died 24 Feb. 1927.*)

HARNESS, Major-Gen. Arthur, C.B. 1879; retired from Royal Artillery; *b.* 2 June 1838; *s.* of General Sir Henry Harness, K.C.B.; not married. *Educ.*: Carshalton; Woolwich. Entered army, 1857; served in Cape and Zulu Wars, 1877-78-79; Brevet of Lieut.-Colonel and C.B.; extra A.D.C. to H.R.H. the Commander-in-Chief, 1887-92; Maj.-Gen., 1894; Colonel Commandant R.A., 1906. *Decorated for* service in the field. *Address*: 19 Montpelier Villas, Brighton. *Club*: Army and Navy.

(*Died 15 Oct. 1927.*)

HAROLD, John, M.B., B.Ch., B.A.O., M.R.C.S., L.R.C.P. Lond.; *b.* Dublin; 2nd *s.*

466

of William Harold, Dublin; *m.*; three *s.* two *d. Educ.*: Belvedere College, Dublin; University College, London; Charing Cross Hospital, London. Physician to Hospital of St. John and St. Elizabeth; Senior Assistant Editor of Quain's Dictionary of Medicine; Advisory Editor of The International Clinics; late Medical Registrar, Charing Cross Hospital. *Publications*: many contributions to Quain's Dictionary of Medicine. *Recreation*: country life. *Address*: 65 Harley Street, W. *T.*: 1039 Pad. and 3, Milford, Surrey. *Clubs*: Garrick, Caledonian; West Surrey Golf. (*Died 27 May 1916.*)

HARPER, Lt.-Gen. Sir George Montague, K.C.B., *cr.* 1918; C.B. 1915; D.S.O. 1900; G.O.C. Southern Command since 1919; *b.* 11 Jan. 1865; *s.* of late Charles Harper; *m.* 1893, Hon. Ella Constance Jackson, 2nd *d.* of 1st Baron Allerton. Entered army, 1884; Captain, 1892; Lt.-Col. 1907; Col. 1911; served South Africa, 1899-1900 (despatches four times, Queen's medal, four clasps, D.S.O.); European War, 1914-18 (despatches, C.B., prom. Maj.-Gen., K.C.B.); Commander Legion of Honour. *Club*: Naval and Military.

(*Died 15 Dec. 1922.*)

HARPER, Ven. Henry William. *Educ.*: Eton; Merton College, Oxford (M.A.). Ordained 1857; Curate of Waimakariri District, 1857-64; Commissary of Bishop of Christchurch in England, 1864-66; Vicar of Hokitika, 1866-75; Canon of Christ Church Cathedral and Archdeacon of Timaru, 1875-1911. *Address*: 58 Kensington Palace Mansions, De Vere Gardens, W.

(*Died 20 Jan. 1922.*)

HARPIGNIES, Henri Joseph; *b.* Valenciennes, 1819. *Educ.*: Paris, under Achard; two years in Italy. First exhibited in Salon, 1853; accompanied Corot to Italy, 1860; Legion of Honour, 1875; Médaille d'Honneur of the Salon, 1897. *Address*: Rue Coetlogon 9, Paris. (*Died 29 Aug. 1916.*)

HARRIES, Arthur John, M.D., etc., Consulting Physician; *b.* 1856; father, colliery owner; *m.* 1st, 1879; 2nd, 1907; five *s.* one *d. Educ.*: University College, London; Brussels University; Fellow Royal Society Medicine. Formerly Physician and Lecturer on Clinical Dermatology to St. John's Hospital for Diseases of Skin, Leicester Square; later Physician to Electrical Department, Western Skin Hospital; in 1885 first suggested aseptic vaccination in his appendix to his translation of Warlomont's Animal Vaccination; in 1886, lecturing at St. John's Hospital, expressed reasons why the bacillus of lupus was different to that of human tuberculosis; showed intimate relation between band alopœcia and hyperthyroidism in exophthalmic goitre; was a pioneer of electro-therapeutics in England; demonstrated discomfort and fixation points for battery-produced alternating currents at Institution Electrical Engineers in 1890, and for dynamo currents at British Association the same year; also showed how local anæsthesia could be produced by cataphoresis (Lancet, 1890); Past-President Bartholomew Club, City, and Past President City of London Tradesmen's Club. *Publications*: Animal Vaccination (Warlomont), Translator and Editor, with Appendix, 1885; Lectures on Lupus, 1886; Electrolysis in Stricture, 1891; Manual of Electro Therapeutics, 1890; papers on Cataphoric Medication, 1889 (Med. Press and Circ.); Dangers and Uses of Electricity (Trans. Soc. of Arts, 1891), and Therap. Application of Continuous Current (Therap. Soc., now Royal Soc. Med. 1904). *Address*: 30 St. James's Square, St. James's, S.W.; 118 Dartmouth Road, Brondesbury, N.W. *T.*: Gerrard 938. (*Died 27 July 1922.*)

HARRIES, Robert Henry, J.P., Master of the Carmarthenshire Foxhounds 1902-14; *b.* 11 Dec. 1859; *o. s.* of late Essex Harries of

Upper Scolton, nr. Haverfordwest; *m.* 1893, Arabella, *d.* of late George Blaney Meager of Marine Villa, The Mumbles, Glamorganshire, and The Penrhyn, Goodwick, Pembrokeshire: one *s.* one *d.* *Educ.:* Cowbridge. Began his hunting career at the age of 8 with the Pembrokeshire, which he followed until he took over the Carmarthenshire; a hunter judge in all the shows in England, Ireland, and Wales; during the summer months he acts as Deputy-Master of the Pembrokeshire and Carmarthenshire Otter Hounds; joined the A.S.C. at the Remount Depot, Shirehampton, and was made lieutenant, 12 Mar. 1917. *Recreations:* keen on shooting and other sports. *Address:* The Croft, St. Clears, Carmarthenshire. *Club:* County, Carmarthen.   *(Died 25 Dec. 1918.)*

HARRINGTON, 8th Earl of (*cr.* 1742), **Charles Augustus Stanhope;** Baron Harrington, 1729; Viscount Petersham, 1742; C.E. (retired); A.D.C. to the King; Commandant of the South Derbyshire Battalion Home Guards; Lieut.-Colonel commanding Cheshire Yeomanry; M.F.H. (Harrington); *b.* 9 Jan. 1844; *S.* father 1881; *m.* Hon. Eva Elizabeth Carington, *y. d.* of 2nd Lord Carrington, 1869. *Educ.:* Queen's Coll. Belfast; Christ Church, Oxford. *Publication:* Polo-Pony Stud Book, vol. i. *Recreations:* M.F.H., South Notts, polo, yachting, gardening. Owns about 13,000 acres. *Heir:* b. Hon. Dudley Henry Eden Stanhope [*b.* 13 Jan. 1859; *m.* 1883, Kathleen, *d.* of J. C. Wood, Felcourt, Sussex; one *s.* two *d.* *Address:* Bartley Close, Totton, Hants]. *Address:* Elvaston Castle, Derby; Gawsworth, Macclesfield; Harrington House, Charing Cross, S.W. *Clubs:* Carlton, White's, Hurlingham, Marlborough; Royal Yacht Squadron, Cowes.   *(Died 5 Feb. 1917.)*

HARRINGTON, 9th Earl of (*cr.* 1742), **Dudley Henry Eden Stanhope;** Baron Harrington, 1729; Viscount Petersham, 1742; *b.* 13 Jan. 1859; 6th *s.* of 7th Earl and Elizabeth Still, *d.* of Robert Lucas de Pearshall, Wartensee Castle, Switzerland; *S.* brother, 1917; *m.* 1883, Kathleen, *d.* of J. C. Wood, Felcourt, Sussex; one *s.* one *d.* Owns about 6000 acres. *Heir:* *s.* Viscount Petersham. *Address:* Elvaston Castle, Derby; Gawsworth, Macclesfield.   *(Died 13 Nov. 1928.)*

HARRINGTON, Sir John Lane, K.C.M.G., *cr.* 1909; K.C.V.O., *cr.* 1903; C.V.O. 1901; C.B. 1902; late Major, Indian Army; Lt.-Col. (Hon.) 1917; *b.* 16 Jan. 1865; *s.* of late Nicholas Harrington, M.R.C.S.; *m.* 1907, Amy, *d.* of late U.S. Senator Macmillan. *Educ.:* Stonyhurst Coll. Entered army, 1884; Vice-Consul at Zaila, 1895-98; Consul, 1898; Minister Plenipotentiary at Court of Emperor Menelek of Ethiopia, 1903; Minister Plenipotentiary and Envoy Extraordinary, 1908-9; Agent, 1898; Agent and Consul-General, 1900; contested (C.) Crewe Division, Cheshire, 1910, and Battersea, 1910 (I.U.) North Southwark, 1918; served with B.E.F. France, 1915-16, in command of a Batt. (despatches). *Address:* Midland Bank, Ltd., 36 Old Bond Street, W.1. *Clubs:* Turf, Carlton, Marlborough, White's, Beefsteak.   *(Died 8 Sept. 1927.)*

HARRIS, Hon. Addison C.; late U.S. Minister to Austria; *b.* Wayne Co., Ind., 1840. *Educ.:* N.W. University. Member State Senate, 1870-79. Pres. Board Trustees, Perdue University. *Publication:* Indiana (9th ed. Ency. Brit.). *Address:* Indianapolis, Ind., U.S.A.   *(Died 1916.)*

HARRIS, Rt. Hon. Frederick Leverton, P.C. 1916; Officer of the Legion of Honour (France); Officer St. Maurice and St. Lazarus (Italy); Parliamentary Secretary to Ministry of Blockade, 1916-18; *b.* 17 Dec. 1864; *s.* of late F. W. Harris, J.P.; *m.* 1886, Gertrude, *d.* of John G. Richardson of Moyallon and Bessbrook,

Ireland; no *c.* *Educ.:* Winchester; Cambridge (M.A.). Member of Tariff Commission, 1904; M.P. (C.) Tynemouth, 1900-1906; M.P. (U.) Stepney, 1907-11; M.P. E. Worcestershire, 1914-1918; L.C.C. Stepney, 1907-10; Hon. Capt. R.N.V.R. *Publications:* various articles in National Review and other Journals; pamphlets on Tariff Reform. *Recreations:* shooting, fishing, painting, travelling. *Address:* 70 Grosvenor Street, W.; Small Downs House, Sandwich. *Club:* Carlton.   *(Died 14 Nov. 1926.)*

HARRIS, Frederick Rutherfoord, J.P., financier and surgeon; M.P. (U.), Dulwich, since 1903; resigned seat through going abroad, 1906; elected M.P. (C.) Monmouth District, 1900; unseated on petition; *b.* 1856; *m.* 1884, Florence, *d.* of W. Ling of Hempstead Hall, Norfolk. *Educ.:* Leatherhead Grammar School; Baden; matriculated at Edinburgh University, and graduated at Royal College of Surgeons. Went to South Africa, 1882; became Mr. Rhodes's confidential agent; appointed first Secretary to British South Africa Company; elected to Cape Parliament as one of four members for Kimberley, 1894-96; re-elected, 1898; one of Whips for Rhodes' Administration; gave evidence before House of Commons Committee (Jameson Raid) of 1897; was one of chief members of Progressive party in Cape Colony. *Recreations:* coursing, shooting, fishing. *Address:* Llangiby Castle, Usk, Monmouthshire. *Clubs:* Carlton, Union.   *(Died 1 Sept. 1920.)*

HARRIS, Frederick William, J.P. Co. Glamorgan; on the Commission of Lieutenancy for the City of London; Member of the Council of the University College of Wales; Past Master of the Drapers' Company; Chairman of Harris and Dixon, Ltd.; Director of the Commercial Union Assurance Co., Ltd.; Founder of the Deep Navigation Colliery, and of the Town of Treharris in Glamorganshire; *b.* 1833; *s.* of late Edward Harris and Isabella, *d.* of late John Tindall of Knapton Hall, Co. York; *m.* Elizabeth Rachel, *d.* of late Peter Macleod Wylie, Edinburgh; Chairman of the Coal Factors Society, 1887-1905. *Educ.:* Private School of Society of Friends. *Address:* 23 Devonshire Place, W.; Park Grove, Withyham, Sussex. *Clubs:* City of London, Oriental.
    (Died 4 Feb. 1917.)

HARRIS, George, D.D., LL.D.; President Emeritus of Amherst College; *b.* East Machias, Maine, U.S.A., 1 April 1844; *o. s.* of George and Mary A. Harris; *m.* 1873, Jane A. Viall, Providence, Rhode Island; one *s.* *Educ.:* Amherst College; Andover Theological Seminary. Pastor High Street Congregational Church, Auburn, Maine, 1869-72; pastor Central Congregational Church, Providence, Rhode Island, 1872-83; Professor of Theology in Andover Theological Seminary, 1883-99; President of Amherst College, 1899-1912. *Publications:* Moral Evolution, 1896; Inequality and Progress, 1897; A Century's Change in Religion, 1914. *Address:* 35 West 81st Street, New York City.   *(Died 1 Mar. 1922.)*

HARRIS, John Mitchell, J.P.; *b.* Sep. 1856; *e. s.* of Thomas Harris, of Calne, J.P.; *m.* 1881, Emma, *d.* of James Cox, The Elms, Stow on the Wold; two *s.* two *d.* J.P. Co. Wilts.; has given evidence before various Royal and Parliamentary Commissions. *Publications:* Writer of various pamphlets, also articles to Live Stock Jour., Farmer and Stock Breeder, and other papers. *Recreations:* fond of any kind of sport, but principally shooting. *Address:* Chilvester Hill, Calne. *T.A.:* Chilvester, Calne. *T.:* Calne 57. *M.:* HR 9702. *Club:* Junior Constitutional.
    (Died 12 Oct. 1927.)

HARRIS, Lloyd, M.P., 1908-11; *b.* Beamsville, Ont., 14 March 1867; *s.* of John and Alice Jane Harris; *m.* Evelyn F. Blackmore; one

467

d. Educ.: Brantford Public School; Woodstock College; Brantford Collegiate Institute. President Russell Motor Car Co., Ltd., Canada Glue Co., Ltd.; Vice-President Willys Overland, Ltd., Canada Cycle and Motor Co., Ltd.; Director Steel Co. of Canada, Ltd., Massey-Harris Co., Ltd., Dominion Power and Transmission Co., Trusts and Guarantee Co.; Ex-Chairman Canadian War Mission, Washington; Ex-Chairman Canadian Mission in London; a Liberal. *Address:* 110 Brant Avenue, Brantford, Ont. *Clubs:* Brantford, Toronto, National, Toronto Hunt, R.C.Y.C., York, Toronto; Rideau, Ottawa.   (*Died Sept. 1925.*)

HARRIS, Sir Matthew, Kt., *cr.* 1899; late Mayor of Sydney; *b.* Magherafelt, Co. Derry, 1840; *s.* of John Harris of same place, merchant; *m.* 1868, Frances Snowden, *d.* of William Owen Lane of Windsor, N.S.W. *Educ.:* Sydney Grammar School and University (B.A. 1863). Alderman of City of Sydney; member of Legislative Assembly for Denison Division; vice-president of Royal Agricultural Society; Justice of the Peace; director of Sydney Hospital; chairman of Wanset Commission. *Recreations:* cricket, bowls. *Address:* Warrane, Ultimo, N.S. Wales.   (*Died 8 June 1917.*)

HARRIS, Richard Hancock William Henry, C.B. 1900; retired, 1906; late commanding Regimental District of West Riding; *b.* 17 July 1851. *Educ.:* Cheltenham Coll. East Surrey Regt.; half-pay; served South Africa 1899-1900 (dangerously wounded, despatches, Queen's medal two clasps, C.B.). *Address:* 26 St. Aubyn's, Hove.   (*Died 11 Feb. 1927.*)

HARRIS, Robert, C.M.G. 1902; *b.* Wales; *s.* of W. Critchlow Harris; taken by parents as a child to Charlottetown, Prince Edward Island, 1856; *m.* 1885, Elizabeth, *d.* of late L. N. Putnam, Montreal. *Educ.:* Prince of Wales's College, Charlottetown. Painted in Charlottetown as a self-taught artist. Studied Slade School, London, and at Paris atelier Bonnat, Italy, Belgium, and Holland; after a few years in Toronto settled in Montreal; Director of Art School, Montreal, 1883-87; Pres. of the Royal Canadian Academy, 1893-1906. *Works:* has produced many pictures of Canadian life; best known as a portrait painter, very many prominent Canadians having sat to him; awards for pictures exhibited in the International Exhibitions of Paris and Chicago, and gold medals at the Pan-American at Buffalo and the St. Louis International, 1904. *Address:* 11 Durocher Street and Art Association, Montreal. *T.:* Uptown, 2278.   (*Died 27 Feb. 1919.*)

HARRIS, Admiral Sir Robert Hastings, K.C.M.G., *cr.* 1898; K.C.B., *cr.* 1900; *b.* 12 Oct. 1843; *s.* of Capt. Robert Harris, R.N.; *m.* 1875, Florence, *d.* of late Commander Henn-Gennys, R.N.; two *s.* five *d.* Royal Naval School, New Cross; Inspecting Captain of Training Ships, 1890-93; Commodore commanding Training Squadron, 1893-95; second in command Mediterranean Squadron, 1896-98; Commander-in-Chief Cape of Good Hope and West Coast of Africa Station, 1898-1902; President Royal Naval College, Greenwich, 1903-6; Admiral, 1904; J.P. Devon. *Address:* The Brake, Yelverton, R.S.O., S. Devon. *Club:* United Service.   (*Died 25 Aug. 1926.*)

HARRIS, Sir Walter Henry, Kt., *cr.* 1919; C.M.G., 1895; J.P. Surrey and Kent; Lt. for City of London, Officer of the Order of Leopold of Belgium; Director Neath and Brecon Railway Company; *b.* 6 Dec. 1851; *o. s.* of Henry Harris (*d.* 1889), builder, Clapham, Surrey; *m.* Grace, *o. d.* of late Captain Thomas Hylands of Brighton, Sussex. *Educ.:* Clapham Park School. Member of London Stock Exchange since 1884; British Royal Commission, Chicago, 1892-94; British Committee, Antwerp, 1894; British Committee, Amsterdam, 1895; British Committee, Vienna, 1895; British Committee,

Tasmania, 1895; M. Council Soc. of Arts, 1892-95. Sheriff City of London, 1889-90; Master of the Loriners' Company, 1896-97; Master of the Innholders' Company, 1902-3; Prime Warden of the Blacksmiths' Company, 1917-18, 1918-19; a Grand Officer of Freemasons, 1890; President City of London General Pension Society since 1902. *Decorated* for services to the Colonies at Chicago. *Publication:* History of the Royal Windsor Tapestry Works. *Recreation:* golf. *Address:* Rothley House, Macaulay Road, Clapham Common, S.W.4. *T.:* Battersea 572. *Clubs:* Junior Carlton, Orleans; Mid-Surrey Golf.   (*Died 3 Mar. 1922.*)

HARRIS, William; Chairman, Mappin and Webb, Carlton Hotel, Ritz Hotel, and Meux's Brewery Company; President, Ritz-Carlton Hotel, New York; *b.* 16 June 1864; *m.* 1st, 1883, Elizabeth (*d.* 1902), *d.* of William Sumner Edge, Manchester; 2nd, Madeleine, *d.* of Samuel Kordy, London; one *s.* one *d. Educ.:* Victoria University, Manchester. *Address:* Westfield, Reigate. *T.:* Reigate 132.   (*Died 26 Oct. 1923.*)

HARRIS-BURLAND, John Burland, *b.* 1870; *e. s.* of late Major-General W. Harris-Burland, 9th and 19th Foot, and *g.s.* of late J. B. Harris-Burland, J.P., of New Court, Newent, Glos.; *m.* 1906, Florence, *d.* of late Albert Marley. *Educ.:* Sherborne; Exeter College, Oxford. Theological Scholarship, Durham (won, but not accepted), 1892; Newdigate Prize, 1893; while at Oxford edited Isis for a year, and was secretary of Union Oct. term, 1894; B.A. 1895. *Publications:* Dacobra, 1903; Dr. Silex, 1905; The Black Motor Car, The Financier, The Broken Law, 1906; The Gold Worshippers, Love the Criminal, 1907; Workers in Darkness, 1908; The House of the Soul, The Disc, 1909; The Secret of Enoch Seal, The Torhaven Mystery, 1910; The Shadow of Malreward, 1911; Lord of Irongrey, 1912; The Grey Cat, 1913; Baldragon, The Curse of Cloud, 1914; The White Rook, 1917; The White Yawl; The Builder; The Avalanche; The Temple of Love; The Watchman; The Lion's Claws; Gabrielle Janthry; The Golden Sword; The Spy; The Greed of Conquest, 1919; The Poison League, 1921; The Red Moon, 1922; The Brown Book, 1923; The Hidden Hour, 1925. *Recreations:* motoring, gardening. *Address:* The Lyon's Close, Pevensey, Sussex; Stanton, nr. Broadway, Worcesters. *T.:* Pevensey 37. *M.:* PM 5339. *Club:* Savage.   (*Died 22 July 1926.*)

HARRISON, Alfred Bayford; *b.* 1845; *y. s.* of George Harrison of Grosvenor Street and Walton-on-Thames; *m.* 1871, Frances Annie, *d.* of Inspector-General John Robert Taylor, C.B.; one *s.* three *d. Educ.:* Cheltenham College. Appointed a Junior Clerk in the Parliament Office, House of Lords, 1864; Clerk attending the Table of the House, 1876; Clerk of Printed Papers, 1896; Principal Clerk of Public Bills, 1902; Chief Clerk, House of Lords, 1903-10; Barrister, Inner Temple, 1869. *Recreations:* golf, music. *Club:* Bournemouth. (*Died 6 May 1918.*)

HARRISON, Austin; late Editor of The English Review; *b.* 27 March 1873; *s.* of late Frederic Harrison; *m.* Mary Medora Greening, U.S.A.; one *s.* two *d. Educ.:* Harrow; subsequently at various foreign universities. *Publications:* The Pan-Germanic Doctrine; England and Germany; The Kaiser's War; Then and Now; Lifting Mist; Pandora's Hope; Frederic Harrison: Thoughts and Memories; Essays of To-day and Yesterday. *Recreation:* travel. *Address:* Lychgate House, Seaford. *T.:* Seaford 97.   (*Died 13 July 1928.*)

HARRISON, Constance Cary (Mrs. Burton Harrison), novelist; *b.* Virginia; *d.* of Archibald Cary, Carlsbrooke, Virginia, and Monimia, *d.* of 9th Lord Fairfax; *m.* Burton Harrison, Louisiana, a barrister of New York (*d.* 1904).

Youth spent in country house of Virginia; educated at home by governess; was in Richmond with her widowed mother during war as refugees from their home in Fairfax county; after war resided abroad with her mother for a year or two, then married, and has since lived in New York; has travelled a great deal in Europe, visiting most of its countries, as well as Africa, Syria, Turkey, and Asia Minor. *Publications:* Golden Rod, an Idyll of Mt. Desert, 1880; Woman's Handiwork, 1881; Old Fashioned Fairy Book, 1884; Folk and Fairy Tales, 1885; Bar Harbour Days, 1887; The Anglomaniacs, 1887; Flower-de-Hundred, 1891; Crow's Nest and Belhaven Tales, 1892; A Daughter of the South, 1892; Sweet Bells out of Tune, 1893; A Bachelor Maid, 1894; An Errant Wooing, 1895; Externals of Modern New York, 1896; A Merry Maid of Arcady, and other Stories, 1896; A Son of the Old Dominion, 1897; Good Americans, 1897; A Triple Entanglement, 1898; A Princess of the Hills, 1901. Her play, The Unwelcome Mrs. Hatch, was brought out by Mrs. Minnie Maddern Fiske, at the New Manhattan Theatre, New York, 1901. *Recreations:* country life and travel. *Address:* 43 East Twenty-Ninth Street, New York; Sea Urchins, Bar Harbour, Mount Desert, Maine.   *(Died Nov. 1920.)*

HARRISON, Frederic; president of English Positivist Committee, 1880-1905; *b.* London, 18 Oct. 1831; *e. s.* of late Frederick Harrison, Threadneedle Street, E.C., and Sutton Place, Guildford, and Jane, *o. d.* of Alexander Brice, Belfast; *m.* 1870, Ethel (*d.* 1916), *o. d.* of William Harrison, Craven Hill Gardens, W.; three *s.* one *d. Educ.:* King's Coll. London; Wadham Coll. Oxford (M.A., Fellow and Tutor, 1854-56); Hon. Fellow, 1899; Hon. D.C.L. Oxford; Hon. Litt.D. Cambridge; Hon. LL.D. Aberdeen; Barr. Lincoln's Inn, 1858; member of Royal Commission of Trades Unions, 1867-69; secretary Royal Commission for Digesting the Law, 1869-70; Prof. of Jurisprudence and International Law to Inns of Court, 1877-89; alderman, London County Council, 1889-93; Rede's Lecturer, Cambridge, 1900; Washington Lecturer, Chicago, 1901; Herbert Spencer Lecturer, Oxford, 1905; Vice-Pres. Royal Historical Society, and London Library; J.P. Kent and Somerset. *Publications:* Meaning of History, 1862; Order and Progress, 1875; Social Statics—Comte's Positive Polity, vol. ii. 1875; The Choice of Books, 1886; Oliver Cromwell, 1888; Annals of an Old Manor House, 1893, new ed. 1899; (editor and part author) The New Calendar of Great Men, 1892; The Meaning of History, enlarged 1894; Victorian Literature, 1895; Introductions to Comte's Positive Philosophy, to Carlyle's Past and Present, 1896; Carlyle's Essays, 1903; Bacon's Essays, 1905; Trollope's Barsetshire Tales, 1906; to Trollope's Phineas Finn and Phineas Redux, 1911, and to Miss Betham-Edwards' Lord of the Harvest; William the Silent, 1897; The Millenary of King Alfred, 1897; Tennyson, Ruskin, Mill, and others, 1899; Byzantine History in the Early Middle Ages, 1900; American Addresses, 1901; Life of Ruskin, 1902; Theophano, 1904; Chatham, 1905; Herbert Spencer Lecture, Oxford, 1905; Nicephorus: A Tragedy of New Rome, 1906; Memories and Thoughts, 1906; Carlyle and the London Library, 1907; The Creed of a Layman, 1907; The Philosophy of Common Sense, 1907; My Alpine Jubilee, 1908; National and Social Problems, 1908; Realities and Ideals, 1908; Autobiographic Memoirs, 1911; Among My Books, 1912; The Positive Evolution of Religion, 1912; The German Peril, 1915; On Society, 1918; Jurisprudence and Conflict of Nations, 1919; Obiter Scripta, 1919; Novissima Verba, 1920. *Address:* 10 Royal Crescent, Bath. *Club:* National Liberal.   *(Died 14 Jan. 1923.)*

HARRISON, Frederick, M.A.; Esquire of the Order of St. John of Jerusalem in England; *s.* of Frederick Burgoyne Harrison and Ellen Maria Norton. *Educ.:* King's College School; Trinity College, Cambridge. Private tutor and lecturer; travelled extensively for some years; went on stage, 1886; several years with Mr. Tree; joint manager of Lyceum with Mr. Forbes Robertson, 1895-96; sole lessee of the Haymarket Theatre since 1896; joint manager of Haymarket with Mr. Cyril Maude, 1896-1905. *Recreations:* gardening and motoring. *Address:* Kemnal, Haslemere, Surrey. *Clubs:* Conservative, Bath, Royal Automobile.
    (Died 13 June 1926.)

HARRISON, James J., J.P.; *s.* of late Jonathan Stables Harrison, J.P., D.L., of Brandesburton Hall, Yorks, and 70 Harley Street, London, and Eliza Whitehead, sister of George Whitehead, J.P., D.L., of Deighton Grove, York; *m.* 1910, Mrs. Sumner Clarke, of Peoria, Illinois. *Educ.:* Elstree; Harrow; Christ Church, Oxford. Took his first big game shoot 1885, and has hardly missed a year since; has a collection of trophies—birds and small animals collected in all parts of the globe; joined the Prince of Wales Yorkshire Hussars, 1884; retired, after 21 years' service, with the rank of Lt.-Colonel. *Recreations:* hunting, shooting, cricket. *Address:* Brandesburton Hall, Hull. *T.A.:* Brandesburton. *Clubs:* Carlton, Bachelors', Oxford and Cambridge, Hurlingham, Ranelagh; Yorkshire, York.
    (Died 12 Mar. 1923.)

HARRISON, Jane Ellen, Hon. LL.D. Aberdeen; Hon. D.Litt. Durham; sometime Fellow and Lecturer in Class. Archæology Newnham Coll., Camb.; *b.* Yorkshire, 9 Sep. 1850; 3rd *d.* of late Charles Harrison, Cottingham, Yorks, and Elizabeth Hawksley, *d.* of Thomas Nelson, Limber, Lincolnshire; unmarried. *Educ.:* Home; Cheltenham; Newnham College, Cambridge. Vice-President Hellenic Society, 1889-96; Corr. Member of K. Arch. Institute, Berlin. *Publications:* Myths of the Odyssey in Art and Literature, 1882; Introductory Studies in Greek Art, 1885; Mythology and Monuments of Ancient Athens, 1890, joint-author Mrs. A. W. Verrall; Greek Vase Painting (joint-author Mr. D. S. MacColl), 1894; Prolegomena to Study of Greek Religion; Religion of Ancient Greece: Themis, 1912; Ancient Art and Ritual in Home University Library, 1913; Alpha and Omega, 1915; Russia and the Russian Verb, 1915; Aspects Aorists and the Classical Tripos, 1919; Epilegomena to Study of Greek Religion, 1921; (with Hope Mirrlees) Life of the Archpriest Avvakum, trans. from the Russian, 1925; Reminiscences of a Student's Life, 1925; (with Hope Mirrlees) The Book of the Bear—translations from the Russian. *Address:* Newnham College, Cambridge. *Club:* University Women's.
    (Died 15 April 1928.)

HARRISON, John, C.B.E. 1918; D.L., LL.D. Edin. University; F.R.S.E.; Chairman Public Library, Savings Bank; *b.* 17 Aug. 1847; *s.* of late Sir George Harrison, M.P., Lord Provost of the city of Edinburgh; *m.* 1879, Helen Georgina, *d.* of George Roberts, Manufacturer, Selkirk; two *s.* three *d. Educ.:* Royal High School, Edinburgh. Head of the firm of Harrison and Son, clothiers, Edinburgh; now retired from business; has given much work in connection with the public life of Edinburgh, especially to the institutions carrying on the education of the city. *Publications:* The Scot in Ulster: Oure Tounis Colledge; The History of the Monastery of Holyrood and of the Palace of Holyrood House. *Recreations:* golf, walking. *Address:* Rockville, Napier Road, Edinburgh. *T.:* Central, Edinburgh 6958. *Clubs:* Northern, Edinburgh; Gullane Golf.   *(Died 10 July 1922.)*

HARRISON, Sir John Burchmore, Kt. *cr.* 1921; C.M.G. 1901; Government Analyst and

Professor of Chemistry, British Guiana, since 1889; Director of the Department of Science and Agriculture since 1904; Member Executive Council, 1918; *b.* Birmingham, 29 May 1856; *e. s.* of John Harrison; *m.* 1881, M. E. Hortense, *d.* of late J. P. Carter, Barbados; one *d. Educ.:* Edgbaston Proprietary School Christ's Coll. Camb. (M.A.). Island Prof. of Chem. and Agricultural Science, Barbados, West Indies, 1879-89; travelled for Geological purposes in the West Indian Islands and in the interior of British Guiana: awarded the balance of the Wollaston Donation Fund 1899 by the Geological Society of London. *Publications:* many reports and papers dealing with agricultural chemistry of tropical products, and with the geology of the West Indian Islands and British Guiana. *Decorated* for scientific services in connection with the West Indian Colonies. *Recreations:* microscopy, geology. *Address:* Georgetown, Demerara, British Guiana.   *(Died 8 Feb. 1926.)*

HARRISON, Rev. Robert, President of the Primitive Methodist Connexion, 1904; *b.* Carlisle, 6 Dec. 1841; *m.* 1st, Maria E. Wright, Hull; 2nd, S. A. Andrew, Hull. Entered ministry, 1864; served at Selby, Market Rasen, Gainsborough, Hornsea, Hull, Grimsby, Driffield, Sunderland; was Governor of Elmfield College, York, and Chairman of the Primitive Methodist Insurance Company and Chapel Aid Association. *Address:* West Gable, Hymers Avenue, Hull.   *(Died 27 Jan. 1927.)*

HARRISON, Robert Francis, K.C. 1899; *o. s.* of late Mr. Justice Harrison and Fanny Letitia Bolden Davison; *b.* 26 Dec. 1858; *m.* Agnes Blanche, *e. d.* of late John Bagwell, 1884; two *s.* two *d. Educ.:* Temple Grove, East Sheen; Wellington College (Scholar); Trinity College, Dublin (Senior Exhibitioner, Scholar, and Senior Moderator). Scholar in Constitutional and International Law, and also in the Law of Real and Personal Property, Middle Temple, and John Brooke Scholar at King's Inns, Dublin. Called to the Bar, King's Inns, Dublin, 1882; Professor of Equity at that Inns, 1892; Bencher, 1904. *Recreation:* golf. *Address:* 17 Fitzwilliam Square, Dublin. *T.:* 62072. *M.:* XP 8867. *Club:* Kildare Street, Dublin.   *(Died 24 Nov. 1927.)*

HARRISON, Robert Hichens Camden, J.P., D.L.; 4th *s.* of late Frederick Harrison; married. *Educ.:* Blackwater. High Sheriff, Oxfordshire, 1900. *Heir: s.* Cecil Eustace [Capt. Rifle Brigade; *b.* 1878; *m.* 1912, Alice, *d.* of Sir Frederick Wodehouse]. *Address:* Shiplake Court, near Henley-on-Thames, Oxfordshire. *Club:* Junior Athenaeum.   *(Died 21 Oct. 1924.)*

HARRISON, Thomas Fenwick, J.P. Herts; *b.* 9 Jan. 1852; *s.* of Thomas Harrison of Liverpool (*d.* 1888) and Mary Anne, *d.* of Cuthbert Fenwick, Newcastle; *m.* 1881, Florence Emily (*d.* 1899), *d.* of Henry Edwards of Winchester. *Educ.:* Rugby. In business at Liverpool until retirement in 1889. *Recreations:* hunting and shooting. *Address:* Kings Walden Bury, Hitchin, Herts. *Club:* Junior Carlton.   *(Died 29 Dec. 1916.)*

HARRISON, Rt. Rev. William Thomas, D.D.; Assistant Bishop of Ely 1903-1917; *b.* 22 Sep. 1837; *y. s.* of Rev. T. T. Harrison, Rector of Thorpe Morieux; *m.* 1870, Elizabeth B. Colvin, *d.* of Col. John Colvin, C.B., Leintwardine House, Ludlow; two *s.* three *d. Educ.:* Brighton College; Marlborough; Trinity College, Cambridge. Curate at Parish Church, Great Yarmouth, 1861; in charge of St. John's Church, Great Yarmouth, 1864; Rector of Thorpe Morieux, 1868; Vicar of Christ Church, Luton, 1875; Hon. Canon of Ely, 1881; Rural Dean of Luton, 1881; Vicar of St. James's, Bury St. Edmunds, 1883; Rural Dean of Thingoe, 1886; Bishop of Glasgow and Galloway, 1888-1903; Rector of Thorpe Morieux, 1903-12. *Address:* Olivers, Colchester. *(Died 11 Dec. 1920.)*

HARRISON - SMITH, Sir Francis, K.C.B., *cr.* 1919; C.B. 1911; Chairman of Grand Trunk Pacific Railway 4 per cent Debenture Committee; Paymaster Rear-Admiral (retired), 1920; *s.* of Horace Harrison-Smith, M.D., R.N., and Georgiana Amelia Way; one *s.* one *d. Educ.:* R.N. School, New Cross. Joined R.N. as Assistant Clerk, 1878; Egyptian Campaign, 1882 (medal and bronze star); Eastern Soudan Campaign, 1883-84 (El Teb and Suakim clasps, Mejidieh 5th Class, despatches); Admiral Sir Wm. Hewett's Mission to Abyssinia, 1884 (despatches); sent by Lord Salisbury on Mission to Abyssinia, 1885-86 (received thanks of H.M. Government); specially promoted for services, 1889; Naval Sec. to Commander - in - Chief, Plymouth, 1896 - 1900; China, 1901-4; Plymouth, 1908-11; Portsmouth, 1911-16; Private Sec. to H.E. the Governor of New South Wales, 1904-8. *Publications:* Through Abyssinia: an Envoy's Ride to the King of Zion; (part) The Manual of Naval Law; The King's Regulations 100 Years ago; The Curiosities of an Old Navy List; Office Work in the Navy; various magazine articles on African and Naval subjects. *Recreation:* restoration of old clocks and furniture. *Address:* Wilcot Lodge, Marlborough, Wilts.   *(Died 10 June 1927.)*

HARRISSON, Damer, F.R.C.S.E. M.Ch. *(hon. causa);* late Hon. Surgeon to the King; Hon. Consulting Surgeon, Liverpool Northern Hospital; late Clinical Lecturer on Surgery, Liverpool University; Colonel, A.M.S., T.F.; *b.* 1852; *y. s.* of John Harnett Harrisson of Sandwich; *m.* 1880, Constance, 2nd *d.* of Rev. John Vaughan Lloyd, M.A. (Oxon.), Rector of Hope. Resident Medical Officer, Liverpool Royal Infirmary, 1877-79; late Surgeon Lancashire Hussars Imp. Yeo.; late Assistant Director Medical Services, West Lancs Division (Territorial decoration). *Publications:* Papers on General Surgery; Cerebral Surgery; Surgery of Nerves; The Eugenic Aspect of the Feeble-Minded Child. *Recreations:* golf, riding, fishing, and other kinds of sport. *Address:* 53 Rodney Street, Liverpool. *T.:* 2574 Royal. *Clubs:* Athenaeum, University, Liverpool.

HART, Charles Henry, Lawyer, Art Expert and Writer; Director of Pennsylvania Academy of Fine Arts, Philadelphia; resigned 13 Jan. 1902, at the close of 20 years' service; *b.* Phila. Pa., 4 Feb. 1847; *s.* of Samuel Hart of Phila., and Julia Leavey of London, England; *m.* 1869, Armine Nixon (*d.* 1897), *g.g.d.* of Robert Morris, Signer Declaration of Independence and Financier of American Revolution; 2nd, 1905, Marianne Livingston Phillips; 3rd, 1912, Anita Arabe; one *s. Educ.:* private schools; University of Pennsylvania. Studied Law; admitted to Bar, 1868; practised until 1894, when met with severe railroad accident that left him on his back for 14 months; since recovery abandoned the Law, and devoted to Literature and Art; recognised as first Art Critic and Expert in Historical Portraiture in America; was Chief Commissioner on Retrospective Art at World's Columbian Exposition, Chicago, 1893; exposed frauds in so-called portraits of celebrities; has made the work of Gilbert Stuart, America's master painter, a special study; member of twenty learned societies. *Publications:* Life Portraits of Great Americans; Turner the Dream Painter; Bibliographia Lincolniana; Mary White—Mrs. Robert Morris; Browere's Life Masks of Great Americans; Gilbert Stuart's Portraits of Women; Catalogue Raisonnée of the Engraved Portraits of Washington; Abraham Lincoln's Place in History; Hints on Portraits and how to Catalogue them; The Last of the Silhouettists; First Century and a half of American

Art; Franklin in Allegory; The Earliest Painter in America; The Original Portraits of Washington; Benjamin West Not a Quaker; Register of Portraits painted by Thomas Sully; Memoirs of the Life and Works of Jean Antoine Houdon, sculptor, of Voltaire, and of Washington; the Wright Portrait of Franklin in Royal Society, London; Descriptive Catalogue of the Collection of Miniatures owned by Lucy Wharton Drexel, 1911; articles Philadelphia in Ency. Brit., 1885 and 1903: Who was the Mother of Franklin's Son?; editor of Letters from William Franklin to William Strahan; Frauds in Historical Portraiture, or Spurious Portraits of Historical Personages, 1913; Charles Willson Peale's Allegory of William Pitt, 1915; Peter Harrison (1716-1775), First Professional Architect in America, 1916; is contributing to Art in America a series of articles on American Portrait Painters and their Works; also about 150 magazine articles on art and history; selected and edited the illustrations for Elson's History of the United States, 1905; Lodge's Story of the American Revolution; Tarbell's The American Woman, 1910, etc. *Address:* 970 Park Avenue, New York. *T.:* Lenox 8513. *Clubs:* Royal Societies; Players', New York. (*Died Aug. 1917.*)

HART, Colonel Charles Joseph, C.B. 1909; C.B.E. 1919; V.D.; T.D.; an Officer of Order of Crown of Belgium; Temporary Lt.-Col. in the Army, 1914-20, as Recruiting Officer, Officer Commanding Troops, Competent Military Authority for Arms and Ammunition, Birmingham, and President Northern Area Quartering Committee Southern Command; *s.* of late Chas. Hart, The Hall, Harborne, Staffordshire; unmarried. *Educ.:* Haileybury College. D.L., J.P. Warwickshire; Member of the Warwickshire Territorial Army Association. *Publications:* History of the 1st V.B. The Royal Warwickshire Regt. and its Predecessors; The Antiquity of Iron; The Old Ironwork of Warwickshire; Old Church Chests. *Recreations:* archaeology, golf, Leamington Tennis Court Club. *Address:* South Bank, Warwick New Road, Leamington. (*Died Mar. 1925.*)

HART, Henry George, M.A.; *b.* 16 April 1848; *s.* of W. Hart, I.C.S.; *m.* H. L. Lawrence, *d.* of late Sir Henry Lawrence, K.C.B. *Educ.:* Rugby; St. John's Coll. Camb. (Scholar, afterwards Fellow); 7th in 1st class Class. Tripos, 1866; Assist. Master, Haileybury Coll. 1866-73; Harrow School, 1873-80; Head Master of Sedbergh School, 1880-1900. *Publication:* Sedbergh School Sermons, 1901. *Recreation:* fishing. *Address:* Sedbergh, Hillside, Wimbledon. (*Died 12 Jan. 1921.*)

HART-DAVIES, Thomas, F.R.G.S.; *s.* of late Ven. Archdeacon Hart-Davies; *m.* 1913, Cora, 3rd *d.* of George Boothby, R.N., Ashbourne, Derbys., and widow of Colonel G. B. Wanhope, Lancs. Fusiliers. *Educ.:* Marlborough; Pembroke College, Oxford (Exhibitioner). Entered I.C.S., 1869; served in numerous departments in Bombay Presidency, chiefly in Sind, where he was Educational Inspector, Assistant Commissioner, and Manager of Estates; subsequently Judge of Karachi, and Acting Judicial Commissioner; retired, 1897; contested Rotherhithe, 1900; has travelled extensively: eight times round the world, in Siberia, Persia, South America, and nearly every other country of the globe; is fond of languages; M.P. (L.) North Hackney, 1906-1910. *Publications:* has translated works from Russian, and written short stories for magazines. *Recreations:* music, conjuring, fishing, golf, and travelling. *Clubs:* Reform, East India United Service, Savile. (*Died 3 Jan. 1920.*)

HARTING, James Edmund, F.L.S., F.Z.S.; formerly Librarian and Assistant Secretary Linnean Society of London, retired, 1902; *b.* London, 1841; *s.* of James V. Hart-

ing, Lincoln's Inn Fields, Harting, Sussex, and Kingsbury, Middlesex, and Alexine, *d.* of Col. R. H. Fotheringham, R.E.; *m.* Elizabeth, *d.* of James M. Lynch, Whiteleas, Co. Kildare, and Newcastle, Co. Dublin, 1868: one *s.* one *d. Educ.:* Downside College; University of London. Admitted to practice as a solicitor, 1866; retired, 1878. Gave evidence before the Select Committee of the House of Commons on Wild Birds Protection, 1873; travelled in France, Holland, Belgium, Italy, Greece, and Thessaly; went to Paris in 1889 for The Field, to report on guns and rifles at the Paris Exhibition; and to Thessaly in 1893 for the Board of Agriculture, to report on the Vole Plague; prepared a catalogue of the Library of the Zoological Department, British Museum, published by order of the Trustees, 1884, and a catalogue of the Library of the Society of Apothecaries, 1913, for which he was awarded the gold medal of the Society; the Acclimatization Society of Paris also awarded him a medal of the 1st class for scientific publications. *Publications:* The Birds of Middlesex, 1866; The Ornithology of Shakespeare, 1871; A Handbook of British Birds, 1872; new and revised edition, with coloured plates, 1901; Our Summer Migrants, 1875; White's Natural History of Selborne, 1875-76; Rambles in Search of Shells, 1876; Ostriches and Ostrich Farming, 1877; British Animals Extinct within Historic Times, 1880; Glimpses of Bird Life, 1880; Rodd's Birds of Cornwall, 1880; Essays on Sport and Natural History, 1883; A Perfecte Booke for Kepyng Sparhawkes (1575), 1886; Bert's Treatise on Hawks (1619), 1891; Bibliography of Falconry, 1891; Walton's Angler, Tercentenary Edition, 1893; Hints on the Management of Hawks, 1897; the vol. on the Rabbit in Fur and Feather Series, 1898; The Encyclopedia of Sport (24 articles), 1897-98; Recreations of a Naturalist, 1906; editor of The Zoologist, 1877-96; and of the Natural History and Falconry Columns in the Field, 1871-1925. *Recreations:* shooting, hawking, fishing, lawn-tennis. *Address:* Portmore Lodge, Weybridge, Surrey. *Club:* Royal Societies.
(*Died 16 Jan. 1928.*)

HARTLAND, Edwin Sidney, Honorary LL.D. St. Andrews; Honorary D.Litt. University of Wales; F.S.A.; Honorary F.S.A. Ireland; Registrar County Court, Gloucester and District Registrar of the High Court, 1889-1923, and District Probate Registrar, 1918-24; *b.* Islington, 23 July 1848; *e. s.* of Rev. E. J. Hartland, Congregational minister; *m.* 1873, Mary Elizabeth, *d.* of Rev. M. R. Morgan, Vicar of Llansamlet. Solicitor at Swansea, 1871-90; Clerk to Swansea School Board, 1872-90; Chairman of Folk-tale Section of the International Folklore Congress, London, 1891; President of the Folklore Society, 1899; Mayor of Gloucester, 1902; President of the Anthropological Section of the British Association, 1906; President of Section I. (Religions of the Lower Culture), Congress for the History of Religions, Oxford, 1908; 1st Frazer Lecturer, Oxford, 1922; awarded Huxley Medal, 1923. *Publications:* English Fairy and other Folktales, 1890; The Science of Fairy Tales, 1890; The Legend of Perseus (3 vols.), 1894, 1895, 1896; Primitive Paternity, 1910; Ritual and Belief, 1914; Primitive Society, 1921; Primitive Law, 1924; edited Walter Map's De Nugis Curialium, 1923; and numerous essays and papers, chiefly on archaeological and anthropological subjects. *Address:* 13 Alexandra Road, Gloucester. (*Died 19 June 1927.*)

HARTLEY, C. Gasquoine (Mrs. Arthur D. Lewis), Author and Journalist; *b.* Antananarivo, Madagascar, 1869; 2nd *d.* of Rev. Richard Griffiths Hartley, M.A., London, and Catherine Gasquoine; *m.* 1st, Walter M.

Gallichan; 2nd, Arthur D. Lewis; one s. *Educ.*: private; almost no education until the age of 16. First occupation teaching; Headmistress of Babington House School, Eltham, Kent, 1894-1902; came to London in 1903 and began to write; first book a novel which was not successful; afterwards wrote on Spain and Spanish Art; in later years has been entirely occupied with books on education, social questions, and in particular subjects of feminist interest. *Publications*: Life the Modeller; Stories of Early British Heroes; Stories from the Greek Legends; The Weaver's Shuttle: Pictures in the Tate Gallery; The Story of Santiago de Compostela; The Cathedrals of Southern Spain; History of Spanish Painting; Moorish Cities; Spain Revisited; The Truth about Woman; The Position of Woman in Primitive Society: a study of the matriarchy; Motherhood and the Relationships between the Sexes; Women's Wild Oats; Sex Education and National Health; Divorce, To-day and To-morrow; The Mind of the Naughty Child; Mother and Son: a psychological study of character formation in children; Women, Children, Love and Marriage, etc. *Recreations*: country walks and gardening, reading. *Address*: c/o Bate & Co., 35 Bedford Row, W.C.

(*Died 7 June 1923.*)

HARTLEY, Edmund Baron, V.C.; C.M.G. 1900; Colonel (retired), Medical Staff, Cape Mounted Riflemen; Colonel Commanding Cape Medical Corps; Principal Medical Officer, Cape Colonial Forces, since 1878; *b.* Ivy Bridge, S. Devon, 6 May 1847; *e. s.* of Dr. Edmund Hartley; *m.* 1886, Ellen, *d.* of J. Rose-Innes, C.M.G., Under Secretary, Native Affairs, Cape Town. *Educ.*: private school; St. George's Hospital, London. M.R.C.S., England; L.R.C.P., Edinburgh. Clerk in H.M. Inland Revenue, 1867-69; District Surgeon, Basutoland, 1874-77; joined Colonial Forces, 1877; served in Galeka, Gaika, Morosi (V.C.), Tembu (medal and clasps), Basuto Campaigns, 1877-80; Bechuanaland, 1897 (wounded); S. Africa (medal, clasps, 1877-78-79); S. Africa, 1900-2 (despatches, C.M.G., medals, five clasps). Decorated for rescuing wounded under fire at Morosi's Mountain, 5th June 1879. *Recreation*: travelling. *Club*: Royal Societies.

(*Died 20 Mar. 1919.*)

HARTLEY, Rev. Marshall; Wesleyan Minister, retired, 1926; President of Wesleyan Conference, 1903-4; *b.* Stamford Hill, 26 Jan. 1846; *m.* Millie Ryall (*d.* 1914), *d.* of late Rev. W. W. Rouch, Wesleyan Minister. *Educ.*: Woodhouse Grove School; Richmond College. Entered Wesleyan Ministry, 1868; ordained, 1872; Secretary of the Schools Fund, 1881; Assistant Secretary of the Conference, 1886; elected into the Legal Hundred, 1890; Secretary, Conference, 1895-1902; Secretary, Wesleyan Missionary Society, 1888-1919; Connexional Funds Secretary, 1919-26; visited Mission Stations in India, China, and Ceylon, 1898; South Africa, 1902; India, Ceylon, and Burma, 1915. *Address*: 27 Cedar Road, Sutton Surrey. *T.*: Sutton 498. (*Died 21 Dec. 1928.*)

HARTLEY, Sir William Pickles, Kt., *cr.* 1908; J.P.; Pres. Primitive Methodist Church, 1909; *b.* Colne, Lancs, 1846; *s.* of John Hartley; *m.* Martha, *d.* of H. Horsfield; one *s.* seven *d.* *Educ.*: Colne Grammar School. Manufacturer of grocers' sundries, and jam, marmalade, and table jellies at Colne; removed to Bootle, Liverpool, 1874; to Aintree, 1886; benefactor to Liverpool University, to hospitals and chapels. *Publication*: The Use of Wealth, published by the National Council of the Evangelical Free Churches. *Recreations*: none except driving. *Address*: Sea View, Southport. *T.*: Southport 349. *M.*: FY 282. *Club*: Reform, Liverpool. (*Died 25 Oct. 1922.*)

HARTMANN, William, J.P.; *b.* Bremen, 21 March 1844; *s.* of Henry and Meta Hartmann. *Educ.*: Bremen. Came to England, 1864; established as merchant in London, 1866; founder of Suter Hartmann and Rahtjens Compo. Co. Ltd. (The Red Hand Compositions, Ltd., of which he is the chairman). *Recreations*: shooting, fishing, and foreign travels. *Address*: Milburn, Esher, Surrey. *T.A.*: Hartmann, Esher, Surrey. *T.*: Esher 10. *M.*: XH 6259. *Club*: Ranelagh. (*Died 11 Dec. 1926.*)

HARTOG, Marcus, M.A. (Cantab.), D.Sc. (Lond. and R.U.I.), F.L.S., Hon. F.R.H.S., late Fellow Royal University, Ireland; 2nd *s.* of Prof. Alphonse Hartog, and Marion, *d.* of Joseph Moss; *m.* 1874, Blanche, *d.* of R. Levy-Brandeis of Paris; one *s.* one *d.* *Educ.*: N. London Collegiate School; University College, London; Trin. College, Cambridge. 1st Class Nat. Sci. Tripos, 1874; Assistant to Director Royal Botanic Gardens, Ceylon, 1874-77; Demonstrator, and later Lecturer in Natural History, Owens College, Manchester, 1888; Professor of Natural History, Queen's College, Cork, 1882-1909; of Zoology in University College, Cork, 1909-21; Member Scientific Committee R.H.S. *Publications*: chiefly memoirs in zoology, botany, and general biological science; The Dual Force of the Dividing Cell, Pt. I., P.R.S., 1905; and other researches on the physics of nuclear division; A Study on the Irish Dialect of English (with Miss Mary Hayden, M.A.); Problems of Life and Reproduction, 1913; The Function of Examinations in Education, Merit Proficiency, 1919. *Recreations*: cycling, walking, music. *Address*: 33 rue d'Alsace-Lorraine, Choisy-le-Roi, France (Seine). *Club*: Maccabeans (*Died 21 Jan. 1923.*)

HARTRIDGE, Gustavus, F.R.C.S.; late Ophthalmic Surgeon to the Royal Flying Corps Hospital; Consulting Surgeon to the Royal Westminster Ophthalmic Hospital; Consulting Ophthalmic Surgeon and Lecturer on Ophthalmology to the Westminster Hospital; Consulting Ophthalmic Surgeon to St. Bartholomew's Hospital, Rochester, etc.; *s.* of James Hartridge, Yalding, Kent; *m.* Susan C., *e. d.* of Colonel Murray, 42nd Highlanders (Black Watch). *Educ.*: King's College. *Publications*: Refraction of the Eye, 16th Ed., and numerous other works on the Eye. *Recreations*: yachting and cycling. *Address*: 12 Wimpole Street, W.1. *T.*: 881 Paddington. *Clubs*: Bath, Royal Auto. (*Died 8 Sept. 1923.*)

HARTVIGSON, Frits, Knight of Dannebrog and Dannebrogsmand; pianist to H.M. Queen Alexandra; *b.* Grenaae, Denmark, 1841; unmarried. *Educ.*: Copenhagen and Berlin. Studied piano-playing, etc., with Niels W. Gade and Anton Rée in Copenhagen, and with Dr. Hans von Bülow in Berlin; appeared in public in Denmark, Berlin, Leipzig, Munich, St. Petersburg, Moscow, Helsingfors, Christiania, Edinburgh, and in the Crystal Palace Saturday concerts, the Philharmonic Society, the Richter and Henschel orchestral concerts in London; lived in London, 1864-72; in Russia, 1872-75; in London, 1875-1911; Professor and Examiner Royal College of Music; Hon. R.A.M. *Recreations*: pistol-shooting, dancing, mountaineering, collects old Japanese colour-prints and old Nankin porcelain. *Address*: 3 Martensens Allé, Copenhagen.

HARTZELL, Dr. Joseph Crane, Methodist Episcopal Bishop of Africa, 1896-1916; *b.* Moline, Illinois, 1 June 1842; *m.* 1869, Miss Jennie Culver, Chicago. *Educ.*: High School, Moline, Illinois; Illinois Wesleyan University, Bloomington, Illinois, B.A., M.A., D.D.; B.D., Garrett Biblical Institute, Chicago, Illinois; LL.D. U.S. Grant University, Tennessee; and Hedding College, Illinois. Pastor Methodist Episcopal Church, Pekin, Illinois, 1868-69; New

Orleans, La., 1870-72; Presiding Elder New Orleans District, and founder and editor South-Western Christian Advocate, 1872-81; Member Public School Board of Education, New Orleans, 1873-76; Assistant Corresponding Secretary, 1882-87; Chief Secretary, 1888-95, of Southern Education Society, Methodist Episcopal Church, Member General Conference Methodist Episcopal Church, 1876, 1880, 1884, 1888, 1892; and of Methodist Œcumenical Conference, Washington, 1878; and London, 1898. *Publications:* Methodism and the Negro; Africa Mission; Address World Exposition, Congress of Religions, Chicago; and many addresses and magazine articles on educational and racial topics in America and Africa; also several sermons. *Recreations:* only such as are incident to an intensely active and very responsible administration, while secretary over forty-five institutions of learning of higher grade, or superintending work of missions in Eastern Rhodesia and Portuguese East Africa, on East Coast and in Liberia, on the Congo and in Angola, in the West Coast and in Madeira Islands; during twenty-six years in America and twenty years in Africa travelled over 1,300,000 miles and administered over $6,000,000.00 in educational, industrial, and church work. *Address:* Cincinnati, Ohio. (*Died 6 Sept. 1928.*)

HARVEY, Alexander Gordon Cummins; M.P. (L.) Rochdale 1906-18; *b.* Manchester, 1858; cotton manufacturer and merchant, Manchester and Littleboro'; *s.* of Cummins Harvey. Co. Alderman of Lancs; J.P. Lancashire. *Address:* Town House, Littleborough. *Club:* Reform. (*Died 6 Nov. 1922.*)

HARVEY, Sir Charles, 2nd Bt., *cr.* 1868; J.P.; *b.* 25 Feb. 1849; *S.* father 1870; *m.* 1st, 1870, Jane (*d.* 1891), *d.* of B. Green, Newcastle; 2nd, 1893, Edith, *d.* of G. F. Cooke, Holmwood, Norwich; two *s.* two *d.* *Educ.:* Magdalene Coll., Cambridge; formerly Hon. Col. 4th Batt. Norfolk Regt. *Heir: s.* Charles Robert Lambart Edward [*b.* 16 April 1871; *m.* 1891, Jessie (*d.* 1913), *d.* of late Ebenezer Turnbull, of Smedley, Manchester; one *d.* *Club:* Bath]. *Publication:* History of Norfolk Militia and Militias. *Recreations:* hunting, shooting, yachting. *Address:* Rainthorpe Hall, Norwich. *T.A.:* Saxlingham, Norfolk. *Clubs:* Royal Thames Yacht, Junior United Service.
(*Died 30 Jan. 1928.*)

HARVEY, Rev. Clement Fox, M.A.; Hon. Canon of St. Carantoc in Truro Cathedral since 1878; *b.* 28 Oct. 1847; *s.* of late Prebendary Harvey, Rector of Truro; *m.* 1st, Emma Mary, *d.* of Rev. J. Hardwicke Drury; 2nd, Helen Cornelia, *d.* of J. G. Chilcott; four *s.* three *d.* *Educ.:* Winchester; Trinity College, Oxford. Student of Lincoln's Inn, 1869-70; ordained deacon, 1872; priest, 1873; Assistant Curate of Prittlewell, 1872-75; Rector of Truro, 1875-85; Vicar of Probus, Cornwall, 1885-1910; of Probus-with-Cornelly, 1897-1910; Commissioner under Pluralities Acts Amendment Act for Chapter of Truro Cathedral, 1897-1915; Surrogate for Diocese of Truro since 1878. *Publications:* several sermons. *Address:* Lanprobus, Falmouth. (*Died 25 Sept. 1917.*)

HARVEY, Sir Ernest Maes, K.B.E., *cr.* 1920; banker; partner of Allen, Harvey & Ross since 1904; *b.* Ipswich, 1 Jan. 1872; *s.* of Julius Harvey, Engineer, Ipswich; *m.* 1898, Blanche, *d.* of Edward Pogson, St. Kitts, West Indies; two *s.* *Educ.:* Ipswich; Germany. Partner, firm of Clare & Harvey (Bankers), 1894; served as Treasury Representative in Archangel, 1918; as Financial Adviser to the British Representative on the Inter-Allied Rhineland Commission, 1919; Inter-Allied Financial Adviser to the Austrian Section of the Reparations Commission in Vienna, 1920; Hon. Consul-General for Austria. *Publications:* articles on money matters. *Recreations:* golf and bridge. *Address:* 6 Cornwall Terrace, Regent's Park, N.W.1; *T.:* Mayfair 6346; Hill House, Aldeburgh, Suffolk. *T.:* Aldeburgh 65. *Clubs:* Union, City of London. (*Died 13 Sept. 1926.*)

HARVEY, Rev. Francis Clyde, Prebendary of Chichester; Vicar of Hailsham since 1872. *Educ.:* Trinity College, Cambridge. Deacon, 1868; Priest, 1869. *Address:* The Vicarage, Hailsham, Sussex.(*Died 18 Sept. 1922.*)

HARVEY, Colonel George, Editor and proprietor of N. American Review, 1899-1926; American Ambassador at the Court of St. James, 1921-24; formerly editor Harvey's Weekly; *b.* 16 Feb. 1864, of Scotch and English descent, in New England; *m.* 1887, Alma Parker. *Educ.:* Peacham, Vermont. Entered journalism at age of 20, becoming managing editor of New York World at 27; withdrew because of ill-health; bought North American Review, 1899; was elected president of publishing house of Harper and Brothers, 1900; Editor of Harper's Weekly and its successor, Harvey's Weekly. Served as A.D.C. on staff of Governor Green, and chief of staff of Governor Abbett of New Jersey; Hon. Doctor of Laws, Erskine Coll. of South Carolina, 1905; University of Nevada, 1908; Middlebury College, 1912; and Univ. of Vermont, 1914; Hon. Dr. of Letters, Dartmouth College, 1916; Hon. Member Phi Beta Kappa Alpha Chapter, 1914; was Bromley Lecturer on Journalism at Yale, 1908; Trustee Stevens Institute of Technology; Hon. Member Cottage Club of Princeton. *Publications:* Women, etc.; The Power of Tolerance. *Recreations:* golf, automobiling. *Address:* 9 East 37th Street, New York City. *Clubs:* Savage, Royal Automobile; Stoke Poges, Hanger Hill; Racquet, Metropolitan, Lotos, New York; Metropolitan, Washington; Travellers', Paris.
(*Died 20 Aug. 1928.*)

HARVEY, John Edmund Audley, J.P., D.L.; *o. s.* of late John Harvey and Anne Jane, *d.* of Henry Tennant, Cadoxton Lodge, co. Glamorgan; *b.* 1851; *m.* 1873, Rosa Frances (*d.* 1880), 6th *d.* of Admiral Hon. Keith Stewart, C.B. High Sheriff, Beds., 1886; Patron of 1 living; late Capt. 42nd Highlanders. *Heir: s.* Captain John Harvey, Irish Guards [*b.* 1875; *m.*; one *s.*]. *Address:* Ickwellbury, Biggleswade; Finningley Park, Bawtry.
(*Died 15 May 1927.*)

HARVEY, Lieut.-Col. John Robert, D.S.O. 1902; J.P. Norfolk; *b.* 31 July 1861; *e. s.* of late Col. John Edmund Harvey, 41st Regiment, of Springfield, Taplow, Bucks, and Thorpe, Norfolk, and Octavia Lettice, *d.* of Rev. R. Stephens; *m.* 1st, 1888, Nora (*d.* 1889), 2nd *d.* of H. Adams, of Canon Hill, Bray, Berks; 2nd, 1890, Florence, *d.* of F. W. Parsons of Risley Hall, Derby; one *s.* two *d.* *Educ.:* Rugby; Trinity Coll. Camb. Served in 5th Lancers; Commanded 25th Battalion Imperial Yeomanry in South Africa, 1900-1902 (despatches, Queen's medal, 3 clasps, King's medal, 2 clasps); 4th Norfolk in Gallipoli, 1915; Mayor of Norwich, 1902-3. *Publications:* Records of the Norfolk Yeomanry Cavalry, 1782 to 1908; Hunting in Norfolk; Shannon and its Lakes. *Recreations:* hunting, polo, shooting, fishing, yachting. *Address:* Holmwood, Thorpe, Norfolk. *T.:* Thorpe 44. *Club:* Army and Navy.
(*Died 2 July 1921.*)

HARVEY, William, B.A., LL.B., Advocate; Sheriff-Substitute of Lanarkshire since 1917; of Caithness, Orkney and Shetland at Kirkwall, 1904-12; of Ross and Cromarty, 1912-17; *b.* 8 Dec. 1859; *s.* of Thomas Harvey, M.A., LL.D., late Rector of the Edinburgh Academy; *m.* 1902, Evelyn Cecil la Cour; two *s.* two *d.* *Educ.:* Edinburgh Academy; King's Coll., Camb. (Exhibitioner and Scholar); Edinburgh Univ. First Class Mathematical Tripos, Parts I. and

II. ; Div. I., Pt. III., 1883 ; called to the Scottish Bar, 1886 ; Editor of the Scottish Law Reporter, 1895-1900 ; additional Examiner for degrees in Mathematics and Science in Edinburgh University, 1888-94. *Publications:* Lectures on Law of Insurance, delivered to Faculty of Actuaries, Edinburgh,1895. *Address:* Eddlehurst, Lanark. *T.:* Lanark 12. *Clubs:* University, Edinburgh ; Western, Glasgow.
(*Died 1 June 1927.*)

HARVIE-BROWN, John A., LL.D., F.R.S.E., F.Z.S.; member British Ornithologists' Union ; Hon. Life Fellow of the American Ornithologists Union ; J.P. Stirlingshire ; landed proprietor ; *b.* Scotland, 27 Aug. 1844 ; *o. s.* of John Harvie-Brown, Quarter and Shirgarton, who took the name Brown by the will of the late Alexander Brown, Quarter, and Elizabeth Spottiswoode, *d.* of late Thomas Spottiswoode, Dunipace. *Educ.:* Merchiston Castle, near Edinburgh ; Edinburgh and Cambridge Universities. Has devoted much time to the Vertebrate Fauna of Scotland, Britain, and foreign countries ; to a study of Migration of Birds (member of the British Association Committee on the subject) ; Dispersal and Distribution of Species and kindred subjects ; and for the purposes of natural history observations has travelled in Norway, Russia, and Transylvania, Faroe Isles and Rockall, and all around Scottish coasts and amongst Scottish Archipelago of islands. *Publications:* some 250 books and papers and notices of Natural History facts, etc. Owns about 2100 acres. *Recreations:* travel, shooting, fishing (salmon and trout), collecting objects of natural history in connection with work above mentioned, library do. *Address:* Dunipace House, Larbert, Stirlingshire, N.B. *Clubs:* University, Edinburgh ; County, Stirling. (*Died 26 July 1916.*)

HARWOOD, Henry William Forsyth, Editor of the Genealogist since 1894 ; *b.* Porchester Terrace, London, 9 March 1856 ; *c. s.* of late Henry Harwood Harwood, J.P. and D.L. for Middlesex, and Mary Elizabeth, *o. c.* of John Forsyth, Bengal Civil Service. Called to Bar, Middle Temple, 1880. *Address:* 15 Rugby Mansions, Addison Bridge, Kensington, W.
(*Died 3 Jan. 1923.*)

HASLAM, Sir Alfred Seale, Kt., *cr.* 1891 ; principal proprietor Haslam Engineering Co., Derby ; *b.* 27 Oct. 1844 ; 4th *s.* of William Haslam, Derby; *m.* 1875, Annie(*d.* 1924), *d.* of Thomas Tatam, The Elms, Little Eaton, Derbys. ; one *s.* two *d.* Trained as engineer at Midland Railway Works, Derby, later under Lord Armstrong's Co. ; started the Haslam Engineering Works, Derby, 1868 ; first to invent, manufacture, and to fit up Haslam's patent refrigerating plant in Colonies, and to fit up the machinery and cold chambers on board ship and on shore, which established an important business in conveying perishable food from the Colonies to Great Britain ; Mayor of Derby, 1890-91, when he received H.M. Queen Victoria when she paid a State visit to the town ; Mayor of Newcastle-under-Lyme, 1901-2-8-4 ; contested Derby as Liberal Unionist, 1892 ; M.P. (L.U.) Newcastle-under-Lyme, Staffords., 1900-6 ; contested Newcastle-under-Lyme, 1906 ; donated to the Nation statues of Queen Victoria erected in the City of London, Newcastle-under-Lyme, and Derby. *Recreations:* riding, shooting. *Address:* Breadsall Priory, near Derby. *T:* Duffield 13. *Clubs:* Reform, Devonshire, City of London.
(*Died 13 Jan. 1927.*)

HASLAM, Lewis; J.P. Co. Lancaster; M.P. (L.) Newport (Mon.) since Dec. 1918 ; *s.* of John Haslam, Gilnow House, Bolton, Lancashire, and Jane, *d.* of J. Crook, White Bank, Bolton ; *b.* Bolton, 25 April 1856 ; *m.* 1893, Helen Norma, *d.* of Henry Dixon of Watlington, Oxon. *Educ.:* University College School and University College, London ; M.P. (L.) Mon-
474

mouth Boroughs, 1906-18. *Address:* 8 Wilton Crescent, S.W. 1. *Clubs:* Reform, National Liberal, Bath, Ranelagh. (*Died 14 Sept. 1922.*)

HASLAM, Rev. Samuel Holker, Hon. Canon of Truro, 1918 ; Rector of Week St. Mary, 1900 - 1919. *Address:* 2 King's Road Villas, Paignton, Devon. (*Died 1922.*)

HASSARD, Rev. Richard Samuel, M.A. ; Canon Residentiary and Sub-Dean of Truro Cathedral ; Rector of Truro ; Proctor in Convocation for Chapter of Truro ; *b.* 1848 ; *s.* of late Rev. Henry Hassard, Rector of Stockton Forest, Yorks ; *m.* Edith (*d.* 1920), *d.* of late John Costeker, of Midhurst, Sussex. *Educ.:* Queen's College, Oxford, B.A. 1869. Ordained 1871 ; incumbent of St. Matthew's, Auckland, New Zealand, 1874-79 ; Vicar of Holy Trinity, Dalston, 1879-93 ; St. James', Norlands, Kensington, 1893-1906 ; a Vice-President of S.P.G. ; and was one of the Mission of Help to the Church in South Africa, 1904 ; Rural Dean of Powder, 1912-15. *Publications:* Confirmation and Holy Communion. *Address:* Rectory, Truro. *Club:* The Church Imperial.
(*Died 24 Oct. 1921.*)

HASTINGS, Admiral Alexander Plantagenet, C.B. 1882 ; J.P. ; *b.* India, 31 Dec. 1843 ; 2nd *s.* of late Capt. Hon. E. P. R. Hastings, and Caroline, *e. d.* of G. J. Morris, B.C.S. ; *m.* Edith Caroline, 2nd *d.* of Col. Fred. Rodolph Blake, C.B.; one *s.* one *d. Educ.:* Elm Grove, Ealing ; H.M.S. Britannia ; entered R.N. 31 Dec. 1858 ; Vice-Admiral, 1900 ; served Egyptian War, 1882 (Egyptian medal, Khedive's bronze star, C.B.) ; Soudan, 1884 ; commanded Naval Brigade landed for protection of Suakim, 1884 ; Governor of Massowah, 1884 (clasp); Captain of Royal Naval College, Greenwich, 1885-89 ; A.D.C. to the Queen, 1891-93. *Decorated* for engagement at Chalouf in the Suez Canal during Egyptian Campaign, being Capt. H.M.S. Euryalus at the time. *Address:* Bayford Hall, Bayford, nr. Hertford. *T.A.:* Bayford. *Club:* Army and Navy. (*Died 7 Dec. 1925.*)

HASTINGS, Basil Macdonald; author; *b.* London, 20 Sep. 1881 ; 2nd *s.* of S. J. E. Hastings, solicitor ; *m.* Wilhelmina Creusen White ; one *s.* one *d. Educ.:* Stonyhurst. On War Office Staff for eight years ; then assist. editor of The Bystander for three years ; during War, 2nd Lt. R.A.F., and Cpl., K.R.R.C.; founder and editor of The Fledgling ; subsequently Roosters And Fledglings (the R.A.F. Journal). *Publications:* The Tribe ; Letters of Sympathy ; Faithful Philanderers ; My Permitted Say (Essays); Memoirs of a Child ; Essays of To-day and Yesterday ; Ladies Half-Way ; The Laughers ; and the following plays : The New Sin ; Love, and What Then ? ; The Tide ; Such Nice People : Advertisement ; Bed Rock (with Eden Phillpotts) ; Played Out (one act); The Angel in the House (with Eden Phillpotts) ; The Fourth Act (one act) ; A Best Seller (one act) ; Q (one act, with Stephen Leacock); Razzle-Dazzle (Drury Lane revue); The Johnson 'Ole (with Capt. B. Bairnsfather) ; A Certain Liveliness ; Victory (from Conrad's novel) ; Pep ; Hanky-Panky John ; Any Woman Would ; If Winter Comes (with A. S. M. Hutchinson) ; The Jackdaw of Rheims (vocal ballet); Faithful Philanderers. *Address:* 30 Holland Road, Kensington, W. *T.:* Park 3393. *Club:* Savage.
(*Died 21 Feb. 1928.*)

HASTINGS, Charles Godolphin Wm., C.I.E. 1897 ; *b.* 1854 ; 2nd *s.* of late Rev. Hon. Richard Godolphin Hastings, 4th *s.* of 11th Earl of Huntingdon ; *m.* 1882, Margaret Logie, *d.* of late Gen. Sir J. D. Macpherson, K.C.B. ; one *s. Educ.:* Haileybury. Entered Punjab Police, 1873 ; Political Officer, Kurram, served Jowaki Expedition (medal with clasp); Afghan War (medal); Chitral Relief Force (medal with clasp) ; Tirah Campaign (medal, 3 clasps) ;

Inspector - General Police, N.W.F. Province, 1901; Punjab, 1904; Under-Secretary to Government, 1904-7; retired, 1909. (*Died 26 Feb. 1920.*)

HASTINGS, Graham, K.C. 1875; *b.* London, 7 Oct. 1880; 2nd *s.* of late Dr. John Hastings; *m.* Constance Arabella, *e. d.* of Rev. E. C. Holt. *Educ.:* Paris, Edinburgh, King's Coll. and Worcester Coll. Oxford. Called to Bar. 17 Nov. 1854; Bencher of Lincoln's Inn, 1877; retired 21 Dec. 1897. *Address:* 19 Hyde Park Street, W.2. *Club:* Lords.
(*Died 5 Dec. 1922.*)

HASTINGS, Rev. James, editor of The Expository Times, Dictionary of the Bible, Encyclopædia of Religion and Ethics, etc.; *b.* Huntly, Aberdeenshire; *m.* 1884, Ann Wilson Forsyth; one *s.* one *d. Educ.:* Public School, Huntly; Old Aberdeen Grammar School; Aberdeen University (M.A. and Hon. D.D.); Hon. D.D. Halifax, 1920; Divinity College of Free Church in Aberdeen. Ordained minister at Kinneff in Kincardineshire, 1884; called to Willison Church, Dundee, 1897; St. Cyrus Church, 1901; surrendered pastoral charge of St. Cyrus, 1911, and removed to Aberdeen; Mem. of the General Council of the Palestine Exploration Society; Dyke - Acland Medallist, 1913. *Publications:* The Expository Times (vols. i.-xxxii.), 1890-1921; Dictionary of the Bible (vols. i., ii., iii. and iv.), 1898-1902, with extra volume, 1904, as editor; Dictionary of Christ and the Gospels, in two vols., 1906-7; a Dictionary of the Bible in a single volume, 1908; Encyclopædia of Religion and Ethics, vols. i.-xii. 1908-1922; Dictionary of the Apostolic Church, vol. i. 1915, vol. ii. 1918; commenced in 1910 the publication of a series of volumes entitled The Great Texts of the Bible, and in 1913 a similar series entitled The Greater Men and Women of the Bible; also a series on the Great Christian Doctrines, vol. i. on Prayer, 1915; vol. ii. on Faith, 1919; vol. iii. on Peace, 1921; editor of The Scholar as Preacher series. *Recreation:* bowling. *Address:* King's Gate, Aberdeen.
(*Died 15 Oct. 1922.*)

HASTINGS, Lt.-Col. Wilfred Charles Norrington, D.S.O. 1902; late Manchester Regiment; *b.* Devonport, 24 Dec. 1873; *s.* of Rev. Francis Henry Hastings, retired Captain R.N.; unmarried. *Educ.:* Trinity College School, Stratford - on - Avon. Entered 4th Batt. South Wales Borderers, 1892; seconded for Sierra Leone Frontier Force, 1898; served in Hut Tax War, 1898-99 (wounded, medal and clasp); entered Manchester Regiment, 1899; served South African Campaign, 1900-1902 (South African and King's medals, despatches, D.S.O.); with 1st Batt. Northern Nigerian Regt. 1903; Munshi Expedition, 1906; France, 1914; Cameroon, 1915-16; Commanded Sierra Leone Batt. W. African Frontier Force, 1915; West African Regiment, 1920; retired pay, 1923. *Recreations:* shooting, fishing, boxing. *Address:* Daylesford Lodge, Stratford-on-Avon. *Club:* Sports. (*Died 19 Jan. 1925.*)

HASWELL, Prof. William A., M.A., D.Sc., F.R.S. (1897); C.M.Z.S; Challis Prof. of Biology, Sydney University, 1890-1917; Dean of the Faculty of Science, University of Sydney, 1913-17; Emeritus Professor of Biology since 1917; *b.* Edinburgh, 5 Aug., 1854; *m.* Josephine Gordon, *d.* of W. Gordon Rich, Toi Toi, New Zealand, 1894; one *d. Educ.:* Edinburgh Institution and University (Baxter scholar). Curator of Queensland Museum. 1880; zoological cruise on coasts of tropical Queensland (as guest on H.M.S. "Alert"), 1881; Demonstrator of Zoology, Comparative Anatomy, and Histology, Sydney University, 1882; Acting Curator of Australian Museum, 1882; President of Section D of Australasian Association for Advancement of Science, 1891; President of Linnean Society of N.S. Wales. 1892-93; Clarke

Memorial Medal, Royal Society, N.S.W., 1915; Editor of the Biological Reports of the Australasian Antarctic Expedition since 1916. *Publications:* A Text Book of Zoology (with T. Jeffrey Parker), 1897; A Manual of Zoology, 1899. *Recreations:* trout - fishing, golf, gardening. *Address:* 33 Wolseley Road, Edgecliff, Sydney. *Club:* Australian, Sydney. (*Died 24 Jan. 1925.*)

HATCH, Sir Ernest Frederic George, 1st Bt., *cr.* 1908; K.B.E., *cr.* 1920; founder and Chairman of Hatch, Mansfield and Company; director Fine Art and General Insurance Co.; *b.* 12 Apr. 1859; *s.* of late John William Hatch and Matilda, *o. d.* of late Hugh Snell; *m.* 1900, Lady Constance Blanche Godolphin Osborne, *y. d.* of 9th Duke of Leeds; one *d.* Contested (C.) Gorton Div. of Lancashire, 1889, 1892; M.P. (C.) Gorton Division, 1895-1906; travelled in United States, Canada, India, South Africa, Japan, and China; takes a special interest in South African affairs and in the Colonies generally throughout the Empire; has acted as special Commissioner of various industrial matters for Home Office, and been Chairman of many Departmental Committees (Home Office, Board of Trade, and Insurance Commissioners); Chairman of Government Commission for Belgian Refugees; is Treasurer and Chairman of University College Hospital; Commander of the Order of the Crown (Belgium), Knight of Grace, Order of St. John of Jerusalem. *Publications:* Far Eastern Impressions, 1904; In Support of Free Trade, 1905. *Recreations:* takes a keen interest in athletics. *Heir:* none. *Address:* 20 Portland Place, W.1.; Ridge Mount, Sunningdale. *T.:* Ascot 27. *Clubs:* Reform, Ranelagh. (*Died 17 Aug. 1927.*)

HATCH, Lieut.-Col. George Pelham, C.M.G. 1898; late Commandant of Military Force in British East Africa; *b.* 1855; *s.* of late Gen. George Cliffe-Hatch; *m.* 1895, Helen Sophia, *d.* of late Rev. C. H. Raikes. *Educ.:* Rugby. Served Afghan War, 1879-80 (medal); Egypt, Tel-el-Kebir, 1882 (medal and clasp, bronze star); in command of Troops and Police of Sultan of Zanzibar, 1891-94 (twice thanked by British Government, received the Brilliant Star of Zanzibar); present at the operations in the Witu District, 1893 (British medal and clasp, and Sultan's medal, with two clasps); raised and commanded the troops in the East Africa Protectorate, 1895-1903; served with the Somaliland Field Force, 1901-2 (medal and clasp). *Address:* 10 Clarence Road, Walmer, Kent. (*Died 23 May 1923.*)

HATFIELD, Henry, I.S.O.; Barrister-at-Law; *b.* 1854; *e. s.* of late A. Hatfield of Stockport; *m.* 1879, Mary Homena, *e. d.* of late T. Stafford of Macclesfield; one *s. Educ.:* Owens College; Royal College of Science, Dublin. Entered Patent Office, 1878; Examiner, 1884; Chief Examiner, 1888; authorised by Board of Trade to act for Comptroller-General; retired, 1919. *Recreation:* golf. *Address:* North Bank, New Barnet.
(*Died 26 Feb. 1926.*)

HATHERELL, William, R.I. 1888; R.W.A.; illustrator and painter; on the Staff of the Graphic since 1892; *b.* 18 Oct. 1855; *y. s.* of late Abraham Hatherell, Westbury-on-Trym; *m.* 1887, Emily Agnes, *d.* of John Newell Logan. *Educ.:* private schools. Entered Royal Academy Schools, 1877; made a member of the Society of Oil Painters, 1898; hon. member of the Langham Sketching Club, 1900; member of Royal West of England Academy, 1903; member of the American Society of Illustrators, 1905; first illustrating work done for Cassell's; has illustrated many works by Thomas Hardy, William Black, J. M. Barrie, etc., for Graphic, Harper's, Scribner's, etc. *Recreations:* cycling, fishing. *Address:* 15 Cavendish Road, Brondesbury, N.W. *Club:* Arts. (*Died 7 Dec. 1928.*)

HATTON, Richard George, M.A., Hon. A.R.C.A. (Lond.); Professor of Fine Art and Director King Edward VII. School of Art, Armstrong College, Newcastle - upon - Tyne; *b.* 1864; *e. s.* of George Hatton, Birmingham, and Ellen, *d.* of Richard Timmins; *m.* 1892, Gertrude Helen, 3rd *d.* of George Young, London; one *d. Educ.* : King Edward's School, Birmingham; Birmingham School of Art. President, National Society of Art Masters, 1911; Member of the Board of Education's Standing Committee of Advice for Education in Art, 1911. *Publications* : Design, 1902; Perspective for Art Students, 1902; Figure Drawing, 1905; Figure Composition, 1905; The Craftsman's Plant-Book, 1910; The Principles of Decoration, 1925. *Address* : 31 Elmfield Road, Gosforth, Newcastle.
(Died 19 Feb. 1926.)

HAUGHTON, Benjamin, landscape painter; *b.* 1865; *o. s.* of late David Haughton, J.P., of Sutton Hall, E. Yorks; *m.* 1894, Janet, 2nd *d.* of late Thomas Mason, J.P., of Alkincoats, Lancs; one *d. Educ.* : Caius College, Cambridge (B.A., 1885). *Address* : East Downe House, near Barnstaple. *(Died 31 July 1924.)*

HAUPT, Dr. Paul, W. W. Spence Professor of the Semitic Languages and Director of the Oriental Seminary in the Johns Hopkins Univ., Baltimore; Associate in Historic Archæology in the U.S. Nat. Museum, Washington; *b.* Görlitz, Germany, 1858. *Educ.* : Görlitz Gymnasium; Universities of Leipzig and Berlin under Friedrich Delitzsch in Assyriology, and Franz Delitzsch in Hebrew; for Rabbinical Hebrew as found in the Talmud he went to the local rabbis; studied Arabic with H. L. Fleischer; and A. Dillmann taught him Ethiopic. Appointed *privat-docent* at the University of Göttingen, 1880; Professor of the Semitic languages in the Johns Hopkins University, 1883, retaining his connection with the University of Göttingen until 1889 as Professor Extraordinarius of Assyriology. *Publications:* editor, with Friedrich Delitzsch, of the Johns Hopkins Contributions to Assyriology and Comparative Semitic Grammar, as well as of the Assyriological Library, and has published a number of important works, including a critical edition of the cuneiform text of the Babylonian Nimrod Epic with the Chaldean account of the Deluge, besides contributing to many philological journals; editor of The Polychrome Bible; bibliography of his publications (more than 500 numbers) is given in the Haupt Memorial Volume, 1926. *Address* : 215 Longwood Road, Roland Park, Baltimore, Md., U.S.A. *(Died 15 Dec. 1926.)*

HAUSSONVILLE, Othenin Bernard Gabrielle de Cleron Comte d'. Chev. de la Légion d'Honneur; Membre de l'Académie Française; *m.* 1865, Pauline (*d.* 1922), *d.* of 4th Marquis d'Harcourt; four *d.* Député de Seine-et-Marne, 1871-75. *Publications:* Misères et Remèdes; Socialisme et Charité; A travers les Etats Unis; Sainte-Beuve, sa vie et ses œuvres; Le Salon de Mme. Necker (with G. Hanotaux); Souvenirs sur Mme. de Maintenon; Mémoires et lettres inédites de Mlle. d'Aumale; Les Cahiers de Mlle. d'Aumale; Mme. de Maintenon et St-Cyr; La Duchesse de Bourgogne et l'Alliance Savoyarde. *Address* : 6 rue Fabert (*T.* : 703·53), Paris; Chateau de Coppet, Canton de Vaud, Suisse. *(Died 1 Sept. 1924.)*

HAVERFIELD, Francis John, Camden Prof. of Ancient History in the Univ. of Oxford since 1907; *b.* Shipston-on-Stour, 1860; *o. s.* of late Rev. W. R. Haverfield, and Emily, *sis.* of Rt. Rev. John Mackarness, late Bishop of Oxford; *m.* 1907, Winifred Breakwell. *Educ.* : scholar of Winchester (1873-79); scholar of New College, Oxford (1879-84); M.A. Oxon. Hon. LL.D. Aberdeen; Hon. D.Litt. Leeds; F.S.A.; Hon. F.S.A. Scot.; Fellow of the British

Academy. Schoolmaster, 1884-91; Senior Censor, Student, Tutor, and Librarian of Christ Church, Oxford, between 1891 and 1907; Rhind Lecturer, Edinburgh, 1905-6; Ford Lecturer, Oxford, 1906-7; Creighton Lecturer, London University, 1910; a Governor of Westminster School, 1900-8; member of the Hebdomadal Council, Oxford, 1908-14. Visitor of the Ashmolean Museum, Oxford, since 1901; Fellow of Brasenose College, Oxford; Member of General Board of Faculties, Oxford; Member of Royal Commission on Ancient Monuments, England; a Governor of Roysse's School, Abingdon; first President Society for Promotion of Roman Studies, 1910-16; President of several English local archæological societies. *Publications:* The Romanization of Roman Britain, 3rd ed. 1915; Ancient Town-planning, 1913; Military Aspects of Roman Wales; and other monographs on Roman History, and on Roman Britain; fifth edition of Conington and Nettleship's Virgil; Guide to the Portraits in Christ Church Hall; Relief Map of Syracuse (with J. B. Jordan); editor of H. Nettleship's Lectures and Essays (1895) and H. Pelham's Essays (1911); occasional contributor to Edinburgh Review, Quarterly, etc. *Address* : Winshields, Oxford. *T.* : Oxford, 110. *Clubs* : Athenæum; County, Carlisle. *(Died 1 Sept. 1919.)*

HAVERSHAM, 1st Baron, *cr.* 1906, of Bracknell; **Arthur Divett Hayter,** Bt. *cr.* 1858; P.C. 1894, M.A., J.P., D.L.; *b.* London, 19 Aug. 1835; *o. s.* of 1st Bt. and Ann, *d.* of Wm. Pulsford, Linslade Manor, Bucks; *m.* Henriette, *y. d.* of Adrian J. Hope, and *niece* of late Rt. Hon. A. J. Beresford-Hope, M.P., 1866. *Educ.* : Eton; Balliol and Brasenose Colls. Oxford. Open classical Scholarship Brasenose Coll., classical Honours, Moderations and Final Schools. M.P. (L.) Wells, 1865 - 68; Bath, 1873-85; Walsall, 1893-95; 1900-1905; served ten years in Grenadier Guards, of 2nd Batt. of which he acted as Adjutant; was in command of London Rifle Brigade for nine years; moved resolution against Earl Russell's Redistribution of Seats Bill in 1866; a Lord of the Treasury, 1880; Financial Secretary at War Office, 1882; remained in office during the two expeditions to Egypt and Suakin, until defeat of the Government, 1885; Chairman Public Accounts Committee, 1901-5; served for 15 years on the Executive Committee of the Royal Patriotic Fund; Chairman Macedonian Relief Committee; Chairman Berks Territorial Association. *Publications* : Essays on Production and its Increase; articles in Reviews. *Recreations* : cricket (played 3 years in Eton Eleven at Lord's); formerly winner of running at Eton and Oxford, and a public match at Lord's of 100 yards. *Heir* : none. *Address* : 9 Grosvenor Square, W.; *T.* : Mayfair 2195; South Hill Park, Bracknell, Berks; Tintagel, Camelford, Cornwall; Linslade Manor, Leighton Buzzard, Bucks. *M.* : 1958. *Clubs* : Brooks's, Travellers', Devonshire, National Liberal.
(Died 1 May 1917.)

HAWARD, J. Warrington, F.R.C.S., L.R.C.P.; Consulting Surgeon to St. George's Hospital, to Cripples Nursery and to Santa Claus Home; Vice - President of Society for Relief of Widows and Orphans of Medical Men; Director Guardian Assurance Company; Director and Member of Medical Board of Royal Sea - bathing Hosp., Margate; Vice-President of Invalid Children's Aid Association; *b.* 1841; *s.* of James Haward; *m.* 1876; Amy Cecilia, *d.* of James Nicholls, M.D., F.R.C.S. Formerly President of Royal Medical and Chirurgical Society, and of Surgical Section Royal Society of Medicine; Vice-President Clinical Society and Pathological Society; Hunterian Professor, Royal College of Surgeons; Assist. Surgeon to Hospital for Sick Children, Great Ormond Street; Surgical Registrar, Curator of Museum, Demonstrator of Anatomy, Lecturer on Practical Surgery and Clinical Surgery, Assistant Surgeon and Surgeon to St. George's Hospital, and Treasurer of Medical School. *Publications:* Lecture on Liberty and Authority in Relation to Medicine; and various surgical works, essays, lectures, and scientific papers. *Address:* Manor End, Berkhamsted, Herts. *Club:* Athenæum.   *(Died 20 Aug. 1921.)*

HAWES, Alexander Travers, J.P.; Solicitor; *b.* 1851; *s.* of late Wm. Hawes, of Russell Square, W.C.; *m.* 1st, 1874, Catherine (*d.* 1891), *d.* of Henry Honey; 2nd, 1897, Ada Lucy, *d.* of Col. P. S. Court; two *s.* two *d.* Partner in firm Baker, Blaker and Hawes; Treasurer and Chairman Royal Humane Society; Director Phœnix Assurance Company. *Address:* Nizels, Chislehurst, Kent. *T.A.:* Chislehurst 46. *Clubs:* Conservative, City Carlton.
(Died 20 May 1924.)

HAWKER, Squadron Commander Lanoe George, V.C. 1915; D.S.O. 1915; Royal Engineers and Royal Flying Corps; *b.* 30 Dec. 1890. Entered R.E. 1911; Squadron Commander, 1916; served European War, 1914-15 (D.S.O. for dropping bombs on the German airship shed at Gontrode from a height of only 200 feet, under circumstances of the greatest risk; V.C. for attacking three German aeroplanes, damaging one and destroying another).
(Died Nov. 1916.)

HAWKINS, Major-Gen. Alexander Caesar, C.B. 1871; *b.* Kelston Park, near Bath, 3 Nov. 1823; 8th *s.* of Sir John C. Hawkins, 3rd Bt.; *m.* Janet, *d.* of Lieut.-Gen. E. A. Williams, C.B., 1895. *Educ.:* R.M.A., Woolwich. Joined Royal Artillery, 1842; served West Indies as Fort Adjutant, 1842-47, and as Captain, 1848-50; in the trenches of the left attack in the Crimea, Mar. 1855 to Aug. 1856, and was engaged in five bombardments of Sebastopol (despatches); served in India as Lt.-Col. 1868-70. *Decorated* for service in the Crimea; C.B., 5th class Medjidie, Turkish medal, Crimean medal, Sardinian medal. *Address:* St. Winifred's Lodge, Bath.   *(Died 17 Dec. 1916.)*

HAWKSHAW, J. C., M.A., M.I.C.E., F.G.S., F.E.S., J.P. (Sussex); *b.* 17 Aug. 1841; *s.* of late Sir John Hawkshaw; *m.* Cicely (*d.* 1917), *d.* of F. Wedgwood of Barlaston, Staffordshire; one *s.* four *d.* *Educ.:* Westminster (Triplet Scholarship); Trinity College, Cambridge; Mathematical Tripos Senior Op. No. 9. President of the C.U.B.C., won Colquhoun Sculls, Capt. of 3rd Trinity Boat (Head of the River), rowed at Putney, 1863 and 1864; Hon. Col., late Lt.-Col. commanding Engineers and R.T. Staff Corps; President of the Institution of Civil Engineers, 1902; retired from professional work as Civil Engineer, 1915. *Publications:* papers on various subjects published in Proceedings of Institution of Civil Engineers (Telford Medal); Journal of Geological Society, Journal of Linnean Society, British Association Reports, and Society of Arts (medal). *Recreations:* alpine climbing (Member of Alpine Club since 1860), natural history, arboriculture, etc. *Address:* Hollycombe, Liphook, Hants. *Club:* Athenæum.
(Died 12 Feb. 1921.)

HAWLEY, Sir Henry Cusack Wingfield, 6th Bt., *cr.* 1795; *e. s.* of 5th Bt., and Frances Charlotte, *d.* of John Wingfield-Stratford of Addington Park, near Maidstone; *b.* 23 Dec. 1876; *S.* father, 1909; *m.* 1913, Marjorie Florence, *o. d.* of R. M. Curteis, Winkenhurst, Hellingley. *Educ.:* Eton; Magdalen Coll., Oxford. Owns about 8500 acres. *Heir: n.* David Henry, *b.* 13 May 1913. *Address:* The Manor House, Lytchett Maltravers, Poole, Dorset.
(Died 18 Nov. 1923.)

HAWLEY, Maj.-Gen. William Hanbury; *b.* 9 May 1829; 4th *s.* of late

Capt. R. T. Hawley of the King's Dragoon Guards, and a Waterloo Officer, and *o. d.* of late John Hanbury Beaufoy of Upton Grey, Hants; *m.* 1864, Eliza Jane, 2nd *d.* of late Henry Warner, Barrister, Trinidad; four *s.* two *d.* Ensign 14th Foot, 1846, with which regiment he served 31 years; Maj.-General, 1886; retired, 1890; served Crimea, 1855 (medal with clasp, Turkish medal); commanded troops Mauritius, 1882-87; Colonel Prince of Wales Own West Yorkshire Regiment, 1904. *Address:* Shiplake, Henley-on-Thames.
(Died 20 Mar. 1917.)

HAWTAYNE, Lionel Edward, Puisne Judge, Gold Coast since 1912; *s.* of late George Hammond Hawtayne, C.M.G.; Barrister, British Guiana, 1891; Stipendiary Magistrate. 1905. *Address:* Accra, Gold Coast.(*Died 28 Mar. 1920.)*

HAWTREY, Sir Charles, Kt., *cr.* 1922; actor-manager; 6th *s.* of late Rev. John Hawtrey, Slough; *m.* 1919, Hon. Mrs. Albert Petre. *Educ.:* Eton; Rugby; Oxford University. Made wonderful success in the Private Secretary and A Message from Mars. *Address:* 37 Hertford Street, Mayfair, W.1. *Club:* Orleans.   *(Died 30 July 1923.)*

HAY, Hon. Claude George Drummond; director of the Fine Art and General Insurance Co., Ltd.; 5th *s.* of 11th Earl of Kinnoull; unmarried. *Educ.:* Radley College; abroad. Was first Secretary of Primrose League, and Assistant Secretary, Lloyd's; contested Hoxton, 1892 and 1895; M.P. (C.) Hoxton Division of Shoreditch, 1900-10; temp. Capt., H.M. Army, 1915. *Recreations:* fond of outdoor sports, pictures, music, and has travelled a good deal. *Clubs:* St. James's, Turf.   *(Died 24 Oct. 1920.)*

HAY, Francis Stuart, Vice-Lieutenant and Convener Berwickshire; *b.* 22 July 1863; 2nd *s.* of late Major-General A. C. Hay; *m.* 1903, Laura Elizabeth, *e. d.* of late Colonel G. Fordyce-Buchan of Kelloe, Berwickshire. *Educ.:* Repton. *Recreation:* shooting. *Address:* Duns Castle, Duns, Berwickshire. *T.A.:* Hay, Duns. *T.:* Duns 11. *Clubs:* Junior United Service; New, Edinburgh. (*Died 27 Nov. 1928.)*

HAY, Colonel Sir George Jackson, Kt., *cr.* 1906; K.C.B., *cr.* 1911; C.B. 1896; C.M.G. 1902; J.P., D.L. Co. Durham; J.P., N.R. Yorkshire; late Lieut.-Col. commanding 3rd Batt. Prince of Wales's Own (W. Yorks) Regt.; Hon. Colonel Militia, and Hon. Lieut.-Col. in the Army; *b.* 18 Feb. 1840; *e. s.* of late John Hay, J.P., D.L., of Creswell, Sunderland, Co. Durham, and Hilton Manor, Yorkshire; *m.* Minnie, *o. c.* of Richard Cail, J.P., of Beaconsfield, Low Fell, Co. Durham, 1865. *Educ.:* private schools. *Publications:* The History of the Constitutional Force, 56 B.C. to 1905, etc. *Club:* Junior Army and Navy.(*Died 7 Oct. 1921.)*

HAY, Sir Hector Maclean, 7th Bt., of Alderston; *cr.* 1703; *b.* 28 Mar. 1821; *S.* father 1873; *m.* 1st, 1852, Anne (*d.* 1888), *d.* of Dr. J. White, 17th Light Dragoons; 2nd, 1889, Julia (*d.* 1906), widow of W. Johnson, Appleby, Lincolnshire; 3rd, Florence Anne, widow of Maj. A. Dingwall Fordyce of Aberdeen. Formerly Major London Rifle Brigade. *Heir: n.* William Henry, *b.* 30 May 1867. *Address:* 30 Holland Road, Hove, Sussex.   *(Died 15 Sept. 1916.)*

HAY, Colonel James Adam Gordon Richardson-Drummond-, of Seggieden and Aberargie, Perthshire; J.P. Co. Perth; a Lieut.-Colonel in the Reserve of Officers, Coldstream Guards; commanded Coldstream Guards Regiment and Regimental District, Aug. 1914 to Feb. 1917; *b.* 5 Aug. 1863; *s.* of Henry Maurice Drummond (*y. s.* of Admiral Sir Adam Drummond, K.H., of Megginch Castle, Perthshire), who assumed name of Hay on marriage with Charlotte Elizabeth, *d.* and *heiress* of Captain James Richardson-Hay (late the Carbineers), of Seggieden and Aberargie, Perthshire; *m.* 1903, Evelyn, 2nd *d.* of late Sir James T. Stewart-Richardson, 14th Bt. of Pitfour Castle, Perthshire; three *s.* one *d. Educ.*: Twyford School, near Winchester; Winchester; Sandhurst. Joined Coldstream Guards, 1884; Capt., 1895; Major, 1899; Bt. Lieut.-Colonel, 1900; Bt. Colonel, 1906; Substantive Lieut.-Colonel to command 2nd Battalion, 1907; retired, 1911; served with 1st Battalion at Suakim, Alexandria and Cyprus, 1884 (Egyptian Medal and Clasp and Khedive's Star); granted Jubilee Commemoration Medal for services in command of a Rest Camp at the Tower of London, 1897; served with the 1st Battalion at Gibraltar, 1899, and in South Africa, 1899-1902 (Queen's medal and six clasps, King's medal and two clasps; despatches and Bt. Lieut.-Colonel); Major 2nd in command 3rd Battalion at Cairo, Oct. 1906, March 1907. *Recreations*: shooting, fishing, gardening, entomology, ornithology (M.B.O.U.), philately. *Heir*: *e. s.* James, *b.* 1905. *Address*: Seggieden, by Perth. *T.A.*: Glencarse. (*Died 27 Dec.* 1928.)

HAY, James Paterson, M.V.O. 1906; *b.* 1863; *m.* 1899, Janey, *d.* of William Alexander, Alticane, Pinwherry, Ayrshire, N.B. Late manager, Irrawaddy Flotilla Co., and late Member, Burma Legislative Council. *Address*: Craigweil, Ayr, N.B. *Club*: Oriental.

(*Died 12 Dec.* 1925.)

HAY, Brig.-Gen. James Reginald Maitland Dalrymple, C.B. 1910; D.S.O. 1900; *e. s.* of late Col. George James Dalrymple Hay, B.S.C.; *b.* 31 July 1858; Scotch; *m.* 1892, Catherine Margaret, *yr. d.* of late Henry Billingshurst, M.D., Stedham Hall, Sussex. Joined 21st Royal Scots Fusiliers, 1879; Captain, 1890; Major, 1895; served Boer War, 1880-81; siege of Potchefstroom (wounded, despatches); with West India Regt. West Coast Africa, in operations Hinterland of Lagos, 1897-98 (despatches, Bt. Lt.-Col., medal, clasp); Hinterland, Sierra Leone, 1898-99 (medal, clasp); Boer War, 1899-1901, Special Service Officer; District Commissioner, Wakkerstroom, 1900-1901; Commandant, Paarl District, Cape Colony, 1901 (despatches, Queen's medal and four clasps, D.S.O.); commanded troops St. Lucia, B.W.I. 1902; Acting Administrator of the Colony, Feb.-Nov. 1902; commanded 2nd W.I.R. 1904-1907; Brevet of Col. 1904; wounded in Jamaica Earthquake, 1907; Brig.-Gen. commanding troops in Jamaica and Inspector of West India Local Forces, 1910-14; European War, commanded Infantry Brigade Colchester and East Coast, Nov. 1914-17 (despatches); retired with rank of Brig.-Gen. 1917; special appointment Commandant Corps Troops 6th Corps B.E.F. 1917-19. *Address*: c/o Cox's Branch, 6 Pall Mall, S.W.1. (*Died 6 Nov.* 1924.)

HAY, Sir James Shaw, K.C.M.G., *cr.* 1889; *b.* 25 Oct. 1839; *s.* of late Colonel Thomas Pasley Hay and cousin of Sir Hector Hay, 7th Bt., of Alderston: *m.* 1st, Jane, *e. d.* of John Morin, Allington, Dumfries; one *d.*; 2nd, Frances Marie (*d.* 1893), *d.* of Jacques Polatza of Brussels; 3rd, 1894, Isabella, *d.* of late G. F. Cockburn and *g. d.* of Lord Cockburn. Was Lieutenant 89th Foot; served Indian Mutiny; C.M.G. 1887; served Yonnie Expedition, 1887-88 (medal and clasp); Administrator of the Gambia, 1886-88; Governor of Sierra Leone and Consul-Gen. for Liberia, 1888-92; Governor of Barbados 1892-1900. *Club*: United Service. (*Died 20 June 1924.*)

HAY, Rt. Hon. Lord John, G.C.B., *cr.* 1886; Admiral of the Fleet, 1888; *b.* Geneva, 23 Aug. 1827; 4th *s.* of 8th Marquis of Tweeddale; *m.* Christina, *y. d.* of N. G. Lambert, M.P., Denham Court, Bucks, 1876. Entered Navy, 1839; served in China War, 1842; before Sebastopol; Commodore East India Station, 1861-63; M.P. for Wick, 1857-59; for Ripon, 1866-67 and 1868-71; a Lord of the Admiralty, 1866, 1868-71, 1880-83,

478

1886; commanded Channel Squadron, 1877-79; took possession of and administered Cyprus, 1878; commanded Mediterranean Station, 1883-86; Com.-in-Chief, Devonport, 1887-88; retired 1897. *Address*: Fulmer Place, Fulmer, Slough.

(*Died 4 May 1916.*)

HAY, Sir Lewis John Erroll; 9th Bt. of Park, *cr.* 1663; indigo planter; retired; *b.* Stirling, N.B., 17 Nov. 1866; *e. s.* of 8th Bt. and *d.* of John Brett Johnston, of Ballykilbeg, Co. Down; *S.* father 1889; *m.* 1895, Lizabel Annie, *o. d.* of late Lachlan Mackinson Macdonald, Skeabost, Isle of Skye; one *s.* eight *d. Educ.*: Fettes Coll. Edin. *Recreation*: golf. *Heir*: *s.* Arthur Thomas Erroll, *b.* 13 Apr. 1909. *Address*: 6 Ravelston Park, Edinburgh. *T.*: Central 4286. (*Died 14 May 1921.*)

HAY, Sir Robert Hay-Drummond-, Kt., *cr.* 1906; C.M.G. 1902; *b.* Tangier, 25 July 1846; *o. s.* of late Rt. Hon. Sir J. H. Drummond Hay, K.C.B., G.C.M.G., H.M.'s Envoy Extraordinary and Minister Plenipotentiary in Morocco; *m.* 1st, 1868, Euphemia Katharine (*d.* 1918), *e. d.* of late Thomas Willis-Fleming, formerly of South Stoneham, Hampshire; two *s.* one *d.*; 2nd, 1920, Grace Marguerite, *e. d.* of Sidney Thomas Lethbridge, Hampstead. *Educ.*: Eton; Trinity College, Camb. Attached to British Legation at Tangier, 1869-75; Consul at Mogador, 1876; transferred to Stockholm, 1879; to Tunis, 1889; Consul-General there, 1891; Consul-General in Syria, to reside at Beirut, with superintendence over Consuls at Damascus and Jerusalem, 1894; retired 1908; received the Jubilee medal, 1897. *Recreations*: field sports. *Club*: Travellers'.

(*Died 15 Oct. 1926.*)

HAY-DRUMMOND, Col. Hon. Charles Rowley, J.P.; *y. s.* of 10th Earl of Kinnoull, and Louisa Burton, 2nd *d.* of Adm. Sir Charles Rowley, 1st Bart., G.C.B.; *b.* 1836; *m.* 1858, Arabella Augusta (*d.* 1899), *d.* of late Col. William Henry Meyrick, of Goodrich Court, Herefordshire. *Educ.*: Sandhurst. Assumed additional surname of Drummond, 1900; formerly Capt. and Lt.-Col. Scots Guards; served Crimea. *Address*: Harewood Lodge, Sunninghill; 8 Eccleston Square, S.W. *T.*: Victoria 5476. (*Died 23 May 1918.*)

HAYCRAFT, Prof. John Berry, M.D., D.Sc., Gold Medallist; F.R.S.E.; Emeritus Prof. of Physiology, University College, S. Wales; formerly interim Professor of Physiology, Edinburgh University. *Publications*: Darwinism and Race Progress; The Human Body; papers before the Royal Societies of London and Edinburgh; papers in Brain, the Journal of Physiology, Text-book of Physiology (Schafer), in several German and French periodicals. *Address*: 8 Whitehall, Royston, near Cambridge. (*Died 30 Dec. 1922.*)

HAYDEN, Sir Henry Hubert, Kt., *cr.* 1920; C.S.I. 1919; C.I.E. 1911, B.A., B.A.I., F.G.S.; F.R.S. 1915; Hon. D.Sc., Calcutta; late Director, Geol. Survey of India; *b.* 1869; *s.* of late James Hayden of Lisardahla, Londonderry. *Educ.*: Hilton College, Natal; Trinity College, Dublin. Joined Geological Survey of India, 1895; attached to Tirah Expeditionary Force, 1897-98; Tibet Frontier Commission, 1903-04; services lent to Amir of Afghanistan, 1907-08. *Publications*: Papers in Records and Memoirs of the Geological Survey of India; In conjunction with Colonel S. G. Burrard, F.R.S., Sketch of the Geography and Geology of the Himalaya Mountains and Tibet. *Clubs*: Oriental; Bengal, Calcutta. (*Died Aug. 1923.*)

HAYES, Claude, R.I., R.O.I.; landscape painter; *b.* Dublin; 2nd *s.* of late Edwin Hayes, R.H.A., and Ellen Brisco. *Educ.*: Loughborough. Began life as a sailor at 19 years of age; was in the Abyssinian Expedition; left the calling of the

HAY, Sir William Henry, 8th Bt. See page xxi.

sea and went to America; returned and studied at Heatherley's School of Art; entered the Royal Academy as student at 22 years of age, and was exhibiting on the walls of R.A. at 24 years of age; elected Royal Institute of Painters in Water Colours at 32 years of age. *Recreations:* bicycling, golf, hockey. *Address:* c/o Messrs. Bourlet, 17 Nassau Street, Mortimer Street, W.1. *Club:* Arts.

HAYES, Frederick William, A.R.C.A., F.R.G.S. ; landscape painter, illustrator, author ; *b.* 13 July 1848 ; *e. s.* of W. W. Hayes, Freshfield, Lancs ; *m.* 1st, 1876, Margaret, and 2nd, 1886, Elise, *ds.* of John Robinson, of Talysarn Hall, late High Sheriff of Carnarvonshire ; two *s.* two *d.* *Educ.:* Liverpool College and privately. Brought up as architect, but abandoned this for landscape painting, especially of North Wales scenery ; one of the founders and for some years hon. secretary of Liverpool Water Colour Society ; exhibited at Royal Academy from 1871 onwards ; active worker in Fabian Society since 1891, also in the Psychical Research, Land Nationalisation, and Commons and Footpaths Preservation Societies. *Publications:* (novels, with own illustrations) A Kent Squire, 1900 ; Gwynett of Thornhaugh, 1900 ; The Shadow of a Throne, 1904 ; A Prima Donna's Romance, 1905 ; Captain Kirke Webbe, 1907 ; (sociological) The Story of the Phalanx, 1894 ; The United Kingdom, Ltd., 1910 ; miscellanea ; comedy, Medusa, at St. James's Theatre, 1882 ; various songs. *Recreations:* music, Royal Choral Society since 1882, local parliaments, cycling, walking. *Address:* 12 Westcroft Square, W.   (*Died 7 Sept. 1918.*)

HAYES, John, M.P. (S. Fein) West Cork Dec. 1918-22 ; member Dail Eireann, Cork, 1921-23 ; late Editor of Skibbereen Southern Star. *Address:* Skibbereen, Co. Cork.

HAYES, Captain William, D.S.O. 1917 ; The Queen's Regt. ; *b.* 11 April 1891 ; *e. s.* of late Major P. A. Hayes, and Edith Mary, Lady Babtie, *d.* of late W. H. Barry, of Ballyadam, Co. Cork ; unmarried. *Educ.:* Beaumont ; R.M.C., Sandhurst. Entered army, 1911 ; Captain, 1915 ; Temp. Major, 1916-18 ; served European War, 1914-18 (despatches, D.S.O.). *Address:* 7 Campden Hill Gardens, W.8. *Club:* Junior United Service.   (*Died 20 Oct. 1918.*)

HAYMAN, Ven. Reginald John Edward, Archdeacon of Geelong since 1916 ; Organising Secretary Bishop of Melbourne's Fund, 1913 ; Organising Secretary for Completion of St. Paul's Cathedral, Melbourne, 1925 (pro tem.); *b.* Axminster, 1861 ; *s.* of Philip Hayman, medical practitioner ; *m.* 1890, Mercy, *d.* of Supt. Barclay; four *s.* three *d.* *Educ.:* Oakhouse School, Axminster; Hamilton College, Victoria; Moore College, N.S.W. (First Class honours). Ordained, 1884 ; Curate of Dimboola, 1885-86 ; Casterton, 1887-88 ; Incumbent of Branxholme, 1888-89 ; Vicar of Stawell, 1889-98 ; Incumbent of Hamilton, 1898-1906 ; Archdeacon of Grampians, 1902-6 ; Vicar of Maryborough, 1906-13 ; Canon of Ballarat Cathedral, 1895-1913 ; Archdeacon of Loddon, 1906-13 ; Chairman of Committees in Ballarat Diocesan Synod, 1901-12 ; took part in securing Federal Provident Fund for Diocesan clergy. *Address:* St. Paul's Cathedral, Melbourne, Australia.   (*Died Nov. 1927.*)

HAYNE, Louis Brightwell, M.B.E., M.D.Cantab, M.A. ; Hon. Physician, Harrogate Infirmary ; *b.* 19 July 1869 ; *s.* of late Henry Hayne, The Ferns, Tunbridge Wells ; *m.* Margaret L., *d.* of late Murdoch Shaw Morison ; no *c.* *Educ.:* Tonbridge School ; Gonville and Caius College, Cambridge ; St. George's Hospital, London (House Surgeon and House Physician) ; House Physician, Victoria Hospital for Children, Tite Street, Chelsea ; Private Practice in Harrogate since 1901 ; Hon. Medical Officer

in charge of Grove House Hospital, Harrogate, 1914-19. *Recreations:* fishing, shooting, natural history. *Address:* Sheen House, Harrogate. *T.:* Harrogate 199.   (*Died 14 Feb. 1926.*)

HAYNES, Richard Septimus, K.C. 1904 ; practising in the city of Perth ; *b.* Picton, N.S.W., 14 Aug. 1857 ; *s.* of late John Haynes, Sydney, Civil Servant ; *m.* 1st, 1881, Marion Adelaide Goodwin, Sydney ; 2nd, 1907, A. D'Arcy, Perth ; three *s.* four *d.* *Educ.:* Sydney Grammar School. Admitted Solicitor, N.S.W., 1881 ; Barrister, etc., W.A., 1885 ; City Councillor, 1886-95 ; Member Legislative Council, 1896-1902 ; Mayor North Perth, 1901-4 ; Consul for Norway, 1906-14 ; Trustee Public Library and Museum since 1913 ; Member Barristers' Board since 1889. *Publications:* The Licensing Law of W.A., 3 editions ; The Trespass Law of W.A. *Recreations:* angling. *Address:* Windsor Hall, Queen's Crescent, Mt. Lawley, Perth, W. Australia. *T.A.:* Senyah. *T.:* A 1042, A 3257.(*Died 20 Feb. 1922.*)

HAYSOM, Sir George, Kt., *cr.* 917 ; Sheriff, City of London, 1917 ; Chairman, G. Haysom, Ltd., and Miller, Rayner & Haysom, Ltd. ; *b.* London, 6 May 1862 ; *m.* 1881, Lydia, *d.* of Samuel Archer; one *s.* four *d.* Member of Court of Common Council, Aldgate Ward, since 1903 ; Liveryman Basket Makers' and Spectacle Makers' Companies. *Recreations:* golf, fishing. *Address:* The Welkin, Lindfield, Sussex. *Club:* Constitutional.   (*Died 7 Sept. 1924.*)

HAYTER, Sir William Goodenough, K.B.E., *cr.* 1920 ; C.B.E. 1917 ; *b.* 28 Jan. 1869 ; *s.* of Henry Goodenough Hayter of Winterbourne, Sidmouth ; *m.* Alethea, 2nd *d.* of Rev. J. H. Slessor ; one *s.* two *d.* *Educ.:* Winchester ; New College, Oxford. Barrister, Lincoln's Inn, 1895 ; Civil Judge in the Sudan, 1904 ; Assist. Legal Adviser in Egypt, 1904 ; Khedivial Counsellor, 1913 ; Counsel to the Sultan of Egypt, 1915 ; Legal Adviser to H.B.M. Residency, Cairo, 1918 ; and to Egyptian Govt. ; Chairman, Cotton Control Commission, 1919 ; has acted as Judicial Adviser, and in 1919 as Financial Adviser ; Grand Officer of Orders of Medjidieh and Nile. *Recreation:* golf. *Address:* Zamalek, Gezira, Cairo.

   (*Died 5 Aug. 1924.*)

HAYTHORNTHWAITE, Rev. John Parker, M.A. ; Vicar of King's Langley since 1916 ; *b.* 22 May 1862 ; *s.* of late Rev. Richard Haythornthwaite, Vicar of Cleator Moor, Cumberland; *m.* 1892, Iszct Mead, L.R.C.P., L.R.C.S., Lucknow Medical Mission ; one *s.* two *d.* *Educ.:* Sedbergh School ; St. John's College, Cambridge. Curate of St. Luke's, Barrow-in-Furness, 1885-88; Organising Secretary for the Church Missionary Society in the South of Ireland, 1888-90 ; Principal of St. John's College, Agra, in North India ; Fellow of Allahabad University ; Examiner in Logic, History, etc., 1890-1911 ; Educational Deputation of the Church Missionary Society, 1911-14; Metropolitan Secretary of the Church Missionary Society, 1914-16. *Publications:* History of Parish of Kings Langley, its Ancient Church and Historic Associations, 1924 ; The Romantic Life and Notable Tomb of Edmund de Langley, 1927 ; articles in C.M. Review, East and West, etc. *Recreations:* cricket, tennis, cycling. *Address:* The Vicarage, Kings Langley, Herts. *Club:* Church Imperial.   (*Died 12 Aug. 1928.*)

HAYWARD, Wm. Thornborough, Col. (retd.) ; C.M.G. 1918 ; LL.D. (Hon.) (Aber. and Adel.), M.R.C.S., L.R.C.P. ; Consulting Physician, Adelaide Hospital ; Vice-President of British Medical Association ; *b.* 26 June 1854 ; *e. s.* of W. G. Hayward, Reading ; *m.* Florence Burden, Adelaide ; seven *s.* two *d.* *Educ.:* St. John's College, Hurstpierpoint ; Liverpool School of Medicine. Hon. Physician Adelaide Hospital, 1885-1914 ; Hon. Medical Officer Children's Hospital ; Lecturer on Clini-

479

HAYES, Hugh, M.P. See page xxi.

HAYFORD, John Fillmore. See page xxi.

cal Medicine, Materia Medica, Therapeutics, Adelaide University; Member of Council of Adelaide University; Chairman of Australian Federal Committee British Medical Association, 1913-22; O.C. 1st Australian Auxiliary Hospital, Harefield, 1915-17 (despatches); Physician to 3rd Australian Gen. Hosp., France. *Publications:* Various papers to Medical Journals. *Recreations:* bowls, bridge. *Address:* 20 Alexandra Avenue, Rose Park, South Australia. *Club:* Adelaide.

(Died 21 Dec. 1928.)

HAZELL, Walter; *o. c.* of Jonathan Hazell; *m.* Anna, *e. d.* of James Tomlin; three *s.* two *d. Educ.:* privately. Chairman, Hazell, Watson and Viney, Ltd., printers; first President of the Federation of Employing Printers of the United Kingdom; actively connected with various social reform and philanthropic movements; Treasurer British Institute of Social Service; Treasurer Land Law Reform Assoc.; President and Joint Founder of Children's Fresh Air Mission; Chairman, Women's Settlement Canning Town; Chairman Emigration Committee of Central Unemployed Body; and in furtherance of emigration has travelled through Australasia and Canada; carried on a farm for unemployables, 1892-1900; President Bloomsbury House Club, and also of Cartwright Gardens Ladies' Club; Chairman, Homes for Little Boys at Farningham and Swanley; M.P. (L.) Leicester, 1894-1900; Mayor of Holborn, 1911-12; J.P. for Bucks; a Commissioner of Income Tax. *Recreations:* farming and travel. *Address:* 52 Long Acre, W.C.; 32 Bedford Avenue, W.C.; Walton Grange, Aylesbury. *T.:* Gerrard 313 and Aylesbury 15. *Clubs:* Reform, New City.

(Died 12 Feb. 1919.)

HAZELL, Captain William, C.B. 1911; R.D., R.N.R.; *b.* 9 Dec. 1857; *e. s.* of late Joseph Hazell and late Frances Helen Hornsby; *m.* E. Hooper of Mount Pleasant, Warfield, Bracknell, Berks; no *c. Educ.:* Clewer House, Windsor. Has served in ships and vessels employed in, or otherwise associated with, the following wars: Egyptian, 1882; Burma, 1886; China-Japan, 1894-95; Boer, 1900-1902; European War, 1914-18; in the ranks successively of the late Royal Naval Artillery Volunteers, the East Indian Railway Volunteers, and the Calcutta Naval Volunteers, 1877-90; the Rangoon Pilot Service, as Mate of the pilot brig Guide, and Probationary Pilot for the Rangoon River, Burma, 1884; equal service in Merchant Service and in Royal Navy; at the Admiralty, in the Office of the Admiral Commanding Coast Guard and Reserves, 1904-5; member of the Military Council of the British League for the Support of Ulster and the Union, 1914; Sub-Lieutenant, 1890; Lieutenant, 1895; Commander (retired), 1910; and Captain (retired), 1918 (in recognition of services rendered during the war). Constitutional Imperialist and Royalist. Church of England; student and practician in divine metaphysics. *Address:* 8 Sheet Street, Windsor, Berks. *(Died 26 June 1927.)*

HAZLEHURST, Thomas Francis, J.P., D.L.; *o. s.* of late John Hazlehurst, and Sarah, *d.* of late F. Salkeld; *m.* 1867, Hon. Blanche, *y. d.* of 15th Viscount Hereford; was Capt. 3rd Warwickshire R.V.; High Sheriff, Northampton, 1900. *Address:* Cold Ashby Hall, Rugby. *Clubs:* Junior Carlton, Orleans.

(Died 26 Jan. 1918.)

HEAD, Lieut.-Col. Arthur Edward Maxwell, D.S.O. 1917; late R.F.A.; *b.* 18 June 1876; 2nd *s.* of late H. H. Head, J.P.; unmarried. *Educ.:* Charterhouse; R.M.A., Woolwich. Joined R.A. 1896; Lieut. 1899; Captain, 1902; Major, 1913; Lt.-Col., 1917; served China, 1900 (medal); European War (despatches twice, D.S.O.); retired pay, 1920. *Address:* Ferry Quarter, Strangford, Co. Down. Ireland. *Club:* Army and Navy. *(Died 15 Nov. 1921.)*

480

HEAD, Ernest, News Editor and Chief Sub-Editor, Pall Mall Gazette; *b.* 16 April 1871; formerly on staff of the Western Morning News and Managing Editor Cornish Telegraph; *s.* of Rev. A. T. Head, Ford, Devonport. *Address:* 85 Harborough Road, Streatham, S.W. *(Died 16 June 1923.)*

HEAD, George Herbert; M.A., County Court Judge, Circuit No. 16 since 1922; holds courts at Beverley, Bridlington, Goole, Great Driffield, Howden, Kingston-upon-Hull, New Malton, Scarborough, Thorne and Whitby, with jurisdiction in Admiralty at Hull and in bankruptcy at Hull and Scarborough; *e. s.* of late Rev. George Frederick Head, Vicar of Clifton Parish Church and Hon. Canon of Bristol Cathedral, and Mary Henrietta (*d.* 1912), *d.* of late Captain Charles Nelson Bolton, R.N.; *m.* 1913, Geraldine Maria, *y. d.* of late Major-General Pipon, C.B., His Majesty's Resident Governor of the Tower of London and of Louisa Ann (*d.* 1921) *d.* of the late Admiral Sir William Edmonstone, 4th Bart. C.B. of Duntreath, Stirlingshire; two *s. Educ.:* Repton School (Entrance Exhibitioner); Pembroke Coll. Cambridge (Classical Scholar); Called to the Bar Inner Temple; joined Western Circuit; J.P. for E. Riding and Ouse and Derwent Division of Yorkshire, Hull and Scarborough. *Recreations:* golf, sailing. *Address:* The Lodge, Acomb, York. *T.:* York 2837. *Clubs:* New University; Yorkshire, York.

(Died 11 Feb. 1927.)

HEAD, John Joshua, I.S.O. 1902; Collector of Customs (retired); *b.* 30 Sep. 1838; *e. s.* of late John Head of Ipswich; *m.* 1868, Charlotte, *d.* of late Henry St. John Diaper; two *d. Educ.:* Queen Elizabeth's School, Ipswich. Entered the Customs Service at Ipswich, 1856; and has since held the appointment of Collector of Customs at the ports of Cardigan, Deal, Dartmouth, Newhaven, Swansea, Harwich, Leith, Newcastle-on-Tyne, Hull, and Belfast, and for some years was the senior collector in the United Kingdom. *Address:* Highlands, Seaford, Sussex.

(Died 5 Nov. 1925.)

HEAD, Sir (Robert Pollock) Somerville, 4th Bt., *cr.* 1838; F.R.G.S.; 1st Secy., Diplomatic Service; *b.* 7 Apr. 1884; *S.* father 1907; *s.* of 3rd Bt. and Florence Julia, *d.* of R. Pollock, 8th Madras Cavalry, *g. d.* of Sir Frederick Pollock, 1st Bt.; *m.* 1915, Grace Margaret, *d.* of late David Robertson; two *s.* one *d. Educ.:* Wellington Coll. Nominated an Attaché in H.M. Diplomatic Service, 1905; passed a competitive examination, 1906; appointed to Lisbon, 1907; transferred to Madrid, 1907; 3rd Secretary, 1908; transferred to Peking, 1911; 2nd Secretary, 1914; transferred to Vienna, 1914; to Petrograd, 1914; to Peking, 1917; 1st Secretary, 1919; to Berlin, 1920. *Heir: s.* Francis David Somerville, *b.* 17 Oct. 1916. *Address:* 13 Sussex Square, W.2. *T.:* Padd. 1143; British Embassy, Berlin.

(Died 21 June 1924.)

HEADINGTON, Arthur Hutton; Capt. Berks Yeomanry; Joint-Master of the Berks and Bucks Farmers Staghounds since 1907; Member Maidenhead Board of Guardians; *b.* Scarletts, Twyford, Berks, 6 Oct. 1878; *s.* of Frederick and Fanny Headington; unmarried. *Educ.:* St. Leonard's; Uppingham. Member of National Rifle Association, Bisley. *Recreations:* hunting, shooting, fishing. *Address:* Highway, Maidenhead. *T.:* 231 Maidenhead. *M.:* LH 8565. *(Died Nov. 1917.)*

HEADLAM, Rev. Stewart Duckworth; member London School Board, 1888-1904; L.C.C. (P.) S.W. Bethnal Green since 1907. *Educ.:* Wadhurst; Eton; Trin. Coll. Camb. Ordained, 1870; Curate of St. John's, Drury Lane, 1870-73; St. Matthew's, Bethnal Green, 1873-77; St. Thomas's, Charterhouse, 1879-81; St. Michael's, Shoreditch, 1881-84. *Publications:* Laws of Eternal Life; Lessons from the Cross;

Priestcraft and Progress ; The Ballet ; Theory of Theatrical Dancing ; The Place of the Bible in Secular Education ; The Meaning of the Mass ; The Socialist's Church ; Fabianism and Land Values ; Some Old Words on the War. *Address :* Wavertree, St. Margaret's on Thames.
          (*Died 18 Nov. 1924.*)

HEADLAND, John, I.S.O. 1904 ; late a Principal Clerk in Supreme Court Pay Office ; *b.* 1840. *Address :* Russell Villa, New Barnet.
          (*Died 22 Jan. 1927.*)

HEALY, Most Rev. John, D.D., LL.D., M.R.I.A. ; Archbishop of Tuam ; *b.* Ballinafad, Co. Sligo, 14 Nov. 1841 ; *e. s.* of Mark Healy. *Educ. :* Summer Hill College, Athlone ; Maynooth College. First Honours. Classical Professor, 1867-70 ; Missionary Priest , Professor of Theology, Maynooth College ; Præfect of the Dunboyne Establishment, Maynooth College ; Senator Royal University of Ireland and of new Dublin University; ex-Member Board of Agriculture for Ireland, ; Commissioner for publication of the Brehon Laws ; Vice - President Royal Society of Antiquaries of Ireland ; member Royal Commission on University Education in Ireland, 1901. *Publications :* Ireland's Ancient Schools and Scholars ; Centenary History of Maynooth College ; Centenary Record of Maynooth College ; Life of St. Patrick ; Irish Essays, literary and historical ; Papers and Addresses. *Recreations :* fishing and yachting, where chance offers ; otherwise, recreation spent in antiquarian researches throughout Ireland. *Address :* St. Jarlath's, Tuam. Ireland. (*Died 16 Mar. 1918.*)

HEALY, Maurice, solicitor ; M.P. (I.N.) Cork (N.E.), 1910-18 ; *b.* 1859 ; *s.* of Maurice Healy, Bantry ; *y. b.* of Tim Healy, M.P. ; *m.* Annie, *d.* of late A. M. Sullivan, M.P., 1887 ; two *s.* one *d.* *Educ. :* Christian Bros., Lismore. M.P. (N.), Cork City, 1885-1900. 1909-1910. *Address :* Ashton Lawn, Cork.(*Died 9 Nov. 1923.*)

HEALY, Thomas Joseph, solicitor ; *b.* 1854 ; *s.* of Maurice Healy, Bantry, Cork ; *m.* 1879, Kathleen, *d.* of M. F. Shine, Dungarvan. Admitted a solicitor, 1888. M.P. (N.) Co. Wexford, N., 1892-1900. *Address :* Tullow. Co. Carlow. (*Died 1925.*)

HEAN, Hon. Alexander, C.M.G. 1912, M.H.A. ; a Member for Franklin, House of Assembly, Tasmania, since 1909 ; *b.* 11 June 1859 ; *s.* of late Captain A. B. Hean, Dundee, Scotland ; *m.* Amy Mary, *d.* of late J. W. Allanby, of Dunalley, Tasmania ; four *s.* four *d.* *Educ. :* Highlanders' Academy ; privately, Greenock. Arrived in Australia from Scotland, 1877 ; Council of Sorell Municipality, 1886-1906 ; Warden, 1899-1904 ; Member for Sorell, House of Assembly, 1903, and 1906 ; sometime Minister for Mines ; Attorney - General, Tasmania, 1923 ; Minister of Lands and Works, Agriculture and Railways, and Commissioner of Main Roads, 1904 ; for some time in 1911 held Office of Acting Premier ; is a Coroner and Magistrate for the Territory, and Member of the Licensing Bench of Sorell. *Recreations :* cricket ; is engaged in pastoral pursuits. *Address :* Parliament House, Hobart. *Club :* Athenæum, Hobart. (*Died 11 Jan. 1927.*)

HEARD, Rev. William Augustus, M.A. ; Hon. LL.D. Edinburgh ; F.R.S.L. ; Headmaster of Fettes College, Edinburgh, 1890-1919 ; *b.* 9 Aug. 1847 ; *s.* of James Heard, Spey Lodge, Withington, Manchester ; *m.* Elizabeth, *d.* of Henry Burt, Southport ; three *s.* three *d.* *Educ. :* Manchester Grammar School ; Trinity College, Oxford (Scholar). House-Master at Fettes College, subsequently House-master at Westminster School ; on committee of St. George's Training College, Edinburgh, St. Leonard's College, St. Andrews ; President Classical Association (Scotland). *Address :* Fettes College, Edinburgh. *T. :* 19 Central, Edinburgh. *Club :* New University. (*Died 12 Mar. 1921.*)

HEATH, Col. Edward, C.M.G. 1918 ; late Army Ordnance Department ; *b.* 5 July 1854; *m.* ; one *s.* First Commission in the Control Dept., 1873 ; Col. 1901 ; retired, 1904 ; served Bechuanaland, 1884-5 ; re-employed as Chief Ordnance Officer, Tidworth, Salisbury Plain, 1915-19. *Address :* Parkstone.
          (*Died 4 June 1927.*)

HEATH, Col. Harry Heptinstall Rose, C.B. 1905 ; *b.* 24 June 1850. Entered 10th Hussars, 1872 ; Captain Indian Staff Corps, 1884 ; Major, 1892 ; Lt.-Col., 1898 ; Col., 1900 ; served Jowaki Expedition, 1877-78 (despatches, medal with clasp) ; Afghanistan, 1878-79 (despatches, medal with clasp) ; Hazara Expedition, 1891 (clasp) ; Chitral, 1895 (despatches, Bt. Lt.-Col.) ; employed with Afghan Boundary Commission, 1884-86 ; retired, 1910. *Address :* Dunley, Bovey Tracy, S. Devon.
          (*Died 17 Dec. 1922.*)

HEATHCOTE, Justinian Heathcote Edwards-, J.P., D.L. ; *b.* 1843 ; *e. s.* of Rev. Edward James Justinian Edwards, Vicar of Trentham, Co. Stafford, and Elizabeth Anne, *d.* of late Richard Edensor Heathcote, of Apedale and Longton Halls ; *S.* uncle,1869 ; *m.* 1870, Eleanor (*d.*1927), *d.* of Spencer Stone, of Callingwood, Co. Stafford ; one *s.* one *d.* *Educ. :* Winchester. Was Capt. 68rd Foot and Staffordshire Yeomanry ; M.P. N:W. Staffordshire, 1886-92. *Heir :* *s.* Justinian John [*b.* 1874 ; *m.* 1905, Hon. Evelyn Isabella Clegg-Hill, *o. d.* of 3rd Viscount Hill. Late Lieut. Shropshire R.H.A.]. *Address :* Betton Hall, Market Drayton, Shropshire ; Longton Hall, Stoke-on-Trent. *Clubs :* Carlton, Windham.
          (*Died 21 Jan. 1928.*)

HEATHCOTE, Rev. Sir William Arthur, 7th Bt., *cr.* 1733 ; S.J. ; *b.* 22 July 1853 ; *S.* father 1903 ; *e. s.* of 6th Bt. and Letitia Maria, *d.* of David Daly. *Educ. :* Beaumont College. Is in remainder to the earldom of Macclesfield. *Heir :* *b.* Lt.-Col. Gilbert Redvers [*b.* 25 Dec. 1854 ; *m.* 1st, 1891, Pauline (*d.* 1897), *d.* of Sir Alfred Trevelyan, 7th Bt. ; 2nd, 1901, Mabel, *y. d.* of late H. D. Silvertop, of Minster Acres, Northumberland. Late 1st Battalion Cameronians ; J.P. Hants. *Address :* Bighton Wood, Alresford, Hants ; 27 Green Street, Park Lane, W.1. *T.A. :* Bighton. *T. :* Alresford 42 ; Mayfair 3951. *Club :* Army and Navy]. *Address :* Stonyhurst College, Blackburn.
          (*Died 9 Sept. 1924.*)

HEATON - ARMSTRONG, William Charles, M.P. (L.) Sudbury Division, Suffolk, since 1906 ; Fellow of the Royal Astronomical, Zoological, Botanical, Statistical, and other learned Societies ; Lord of the Manor of Roscrea ; Merchant and Banker ; *b.* 1 Sept. 1853 ; *s.* of John Heaton - Armstrong, succeeded on the death of his father to the senior representation of the families of Heaton-Armstrong, Armstrong of Mangerton, Mount Heaton and Farney Castle, Macdonnell of New Hall, and Heaton of Yorkshire ; *m.* 1885, the Baroness Bertha Maxmiliana Zois-Edelstein, *o. surv. d.* of 4th Baron Zois-Edelstein, of Austria ; two *s.* one *d.* *Educ. :* abroad and privately. Has visited nearly all our Colonies, and has travelled very extensively : though a Liberal in politics, contested Mid-Tipperary in 1892 against the separation of Ireland from England ; stood as a Loyalist in favour of granting local self-government to the greatest possible extent to Ireland ; contested the Sudbury Division of Suffolk in the Liberal interests. *Publications :* Calculation of the Sun's Meridian Altitude. *Recreations :* big game shooting, billiards, and motoring. *Address :* 5 Cornwall Gardens, S.W. ; *T.A. :* Heatonarm, London. *T. :* Western 7151. *Clubs :* Union, Royal Automobile. (*Died 20 July 1917.*)

HEAVEN, Rev. Hudson Grosett, M.A., lord of the manor and sole landowner of Lundy Island ; *b.* 1826 ; *s.* of late W. H. Heaven, of

Lundy Island; unmarried. *Educ.:* Trinity Coll. Oxford (B.A. 1851, M.A. 1852). Deacon, 1852; Priest, 1854; Vicar of Lundy Island since 1886; Curate of Knowle St. Giles, and Assistant Master, Ilminster Grammar School, 1852-54; Assistant Master Taunton College School, 1855-58; Head Master, 1858-64; Curate of Lundy Island, 1864-1886. *Address:* Blenheim, Torrington, North Devon. *Club:* Junior Conservative. *(Died 28 Feb. 1916.)*

HEAVISIDE, Arthur West, I.S.O. 1904; *b.* 1844; *m.* 1869, Isabel Sarah Bell. Retired Superintending Engineer to H.M. post office; Inventor of the Bridge system of Telephony and original investigator of Wireless Telegraphy. *Address:* 8 Elmswood Gardens, Acton Hill, W.3. *(Died 22 Sept. 1923.)*

HEAVISIDE, Oliver, F.R.S.; Hon. Mem. Lit. Phil. Soc. Manchester. *Address:* Homefield, Lower Warberry, Torquay. *(Died 4 Feb. 1925.)*

HEBB, R. G., M.A., M.D., F.R.C.P.; Consulting Physician and Physician Pathologist to Westminster Hospital; Consulting Pathologist to Queen Charlotte's Hospital; Lecturer on Pathology at Westminster Hospital Medical School; Reader in Morbid Anatomy, University of London; editor Journal Royal Microscopical Society; *m.* 1903, Henrietta Frances, *o. d.* of late Nathaniel Sharp. *Address:* 50 Ridgmount Gardens, W.C. *(Died 12 May 1918.)*

HEBBLETHWAITE, Percival, M.A.; *b.* 28 Oct. 1849; *m.* 1877; two *s.* three *d. Educ.:* Rossall School; King's College, London; Trinity College, Cambridge (Foundation Scholar, 1871; Latin Verse Prizeman, 1871, 1872; Fifth Classic, 1873). Vice-Master, Royal Institution School, Liverpool, 1875-78; Private Tutor, 1878-82; Assistant Lecturer in Classics, University College, Liverpool, 1882-98; Lecturer in Classics and Hon. Assistant Professor, 1898-1904; Secretary, 1900-4; Registrar, University of Liverpool, 1904-13. *Address:* Birch Road, Oxton, Cheshire. *T.:* Birkenhead 1964. *(Died 23 Feb. 1922.)*

HEBERDEN, Charles Buller, Hon. D.C.L., Principal of Brasenose College, Oxford, since 1889; Fellow of Winchester College, 1914; *b.* 1849; *s.* of Rev. W. Heberden. *Educ.:* Harrow; Balliol College, Oxford (Exhibitioner, 1868). First class Classical Mods. and Lit. Hum.; Fellow and Lecturer of Brasenose, 1872; Tutor, 1881; Proctor, 1881; Vice-Principal, 1888; member of Hebdomadal Council, 1896, 1902, and 1906-14; Vice-Chancellor, Oxford University, 1910-13. *Address:* Brasenose College, Oxford. *Club:* Oxford and Cambridge. *(Died 30 May 1921.)*

HEBERDEN, Surg. Capt. George Alfred, D.S.O. 1900; Medical Officer, Kimberley Light Horse; *b.* 27 April 1860; *s.* of late Rev. George Heberden; *m.* 1895, Winifred, *d.* of late Rev. Henry Cottam. *Educ.:* Malvern College; Jesus College, Cambridge; St. George's Hospital, London. B.A. Cantab. 1882; M.R.C.S. Eng.; L.R.C.P. London, 1888. District Surgeon of Predasdorp, 1888-89; Surgeon Cape Govt. Railway, 1890-92; Dist. Surgeon Kenhardt, 1893-94; Barkly West, 1895; Medical Officer to Mounted Forces during siege of Kimberley (despatches, D.S.O.); J.P., Barkly West. *Address:* Victoria West, Cape Colony. *Club:* Kimberley. *(Died 23 Jan. 1916.)*

HEBERDEN, William Buller, C.B.; 1898; J.P. for Devon; *b.* 6 July 1838; *e. s.* of late Rev. W. Heberden, Vicar of Broadhembury, Devon. *Educ.:* Harrow; Christ Church, Oxford; Hon. Fourth in Classics and Mathematics, 1860. Entered Inland Revenue Department, 1861; appointed Assistant Secretary, 1887; Sec. 1894; retired, 1898. *Address:* Elmfield House, Exeter. *Clubs:* M.C.C.; Devon and Exeter, Exeter. *(Died 30 Nov. 1922.)*

HEBERT, Louis Philippe, C.M.G. 1903; Sculptor; French-Canadian; *b.* Prov. Quebec, 27 Jan. 1850; *m.* 1879, Marie, *d.* of Thomas Roy, Montreal. *Educ.:* at common schools of his native village. In early days became clerk in a country store; went to Rome as Papal Zouave; obtained prize at Provincial Exhibition, Montreal, for wood-carving in 1873; afterwards studied in Paris; won prize given by Dominion Government for full-length statue of George Cartier 1882; Knight of Legion of Honour, 1901. *Principal Works:* Statues, among which are those to Maisonneuve, in Montreal; Monuments—Queen Victoria, Ottawa; Hon. Joseph Howe, Halifax; Sir Leonard Tilly, St. John; Mgr. de Laval, Quebec; Hon. John Young, Montreal; King Edward VII., Montreal; To South African Soldiers, Calgary. *Address:* 309 Elm Ave., Montreal. *(Died 13 June 1917.)*

HEBRARD, Emile A.; editor of Le Temps, 1915-25; *b.* Paris, 1862. *Address:* 5 rue des Italiens, Paris. *(Died April 1927.)*

HEDDERWICK, Thomas Charles Hunter, M.A., J.P.; Barr. Middle Temple, N.-E. circuit; Metropolitan Police Magistrate for North London since 1910; *b.* Scotland, 6 April 1850; 2nd *s.* of late Robert Hedderwick, Queen's printer and publisher, Glasgow; founder of old Glasgow Weekly Citizen newspaper in the Liberal interest, 1843, and of Anna M. W. Hunter, Dumfries; *m.* 1884, Jemima, *o. surv. c.* of Jas. Neilson, Biggar Park, Biggar, Lanarkshire; two *d. Educ.:* Universities of Glasgow and Leipsic. Barr. Middle Temple, 1876; in the Tichborne Appeal Case for "the Claimant"; founded the Bar Committee; contested South Lanarkshire 1892, Northern Burghs 1895, 1896, 1900, Newbury Division, Berks, 1910; M.P. (L.) Northern Burghs, 1896-1900; member of Select Committee on Election Law, 1898, of Select Committee on Pensions for the Aged Deserving Poor, 1899, and of the Board of Visitors for H.M. Convict Prison, Aylesbury, 1902; acting Deputy-Chairman, County of London Sessions, 1907-10. *Publications:* The Old German Puppet Play of Dr. Faust, a translation with notes, 1887; A Manual of Parliamentary Election Law, 1892 (new ed. 1900); The Sale of Foods and Drugs, 1894 (new ed. 1900); contributions of a literary character to various periodicals. *Recreations:* golf, book collecting. *Address:* The Manor House, Weston Turville, Wendover; Biggar Park, Biggar, N.B. *Clubs:* Reform, Eighty. *(Died 6 Feb. 1918.)*

HEDLEY, John, M.V.O. 1910; late R.A.; *b.* 21 Jan. 1834. Served Crimea, 1854-56 (Crimean and Turkish medals, clasps for Sebastopol and Inkerman); Secretary, Royal Choral Society, 1872-1910. *Address:* Laxton Vicarage, Howden, Yorkshire. *(Died 18 May 1916.)*

HEDLEY, Lt.-Col. John Ralph, D.S.O. 1916; Northumberland Fusiliers (T.F.); commanding 5th Batt. Border Regiment (T.F.); *b.* Woolley, Wantage, 21 March 1871; *y. s.* of John Hedley, Woolley, formerly of The Leaguer House, Stamfordham, Northumberland; *m.* Ada Marie, 2nd *d.* of late T. H. Bambridge, J.P., Eshott Hall, Felton, Northumberland; one *s.* one *d. Educ.:* privately; Royal Grammar School, Newcastle. In business, Newcastle, 1885-1910; Chairman of Unionist Association, 1909-10; of Northern Conservative Club, 1906-10; founded Salisbury Club for training young men to speak in public; invited twice to stand for Parliament but declined; on permanent staff Valuation Department, Inland Revenue, in charge of quarter of million acres, Hull District, 1910; Chairman Hull and East Riding Club, 1913-14; Commission in 3rd Vol. Batt. Northumberland Fusiliers, 1901; promoted to field rank, Sep. 1912; called up on mobilisation of T.F. Aug. 1914; went abroad with unit, 1915; served in France, 1915-16 (D.S.O., despatches twice). *Recrea-*

tions: cricket, tennis, shooting, and hunting. *Address:* Westgate House, Hornsea, East Yorks; Twyford, Alnmouth, Northumberland. *T.:* Hornsea, P.O. 30. *Clubs:* Northern Conservative, Newcastle; Hull and East Riding, Hull.
(*Died July 1917.*)

HEFFERNAN, Sir John Harold, K.C.B. *cr.* 1911; C.B. 1891, R.N.; *b.* 1834; *m.* 1861, Elizabeth (*d.* 1914), *d.* of late W. Hilton, Ollerton Lodge Nutsford; three *s.* two *d.* Assistant engineer, 1855; gold medal, Atlantic Telegraph 1858; served Alexandria, then promoted to Inspector of Machinery, and to Chief Inspector of Machinery in 1885; retired, 1892.
(*Died 17 Sept. 1921.*)

HEGAN, Colonel Edward, C.B. 1908; *b.* 19 Jan. 1855; *s.* of late John Hegan, 20 Queen's Gate, S.W.; *m.* 1882, Sarah, *o. d.* of late Lt.-Col. W. H. Goodair, J.P., of Ashton Park, Ashton-on-Ribble. *Educ.:* Harrow. Entered army, 1876; Captain, 5th Dragoon Guards, 1882; Major, 1887; Lt.-Col., 1899; Bt. Col., 1903; Col. 1906; Commandant School of Auxiliary Cavalry, Aldershot, 1882-84; A.D.C. to G.O.C. Western District, 1889-90; D.A.A.G., Cork, 1890-93; D.A.Q.M.G., Tirah, 1897; special service, South Africa, 1900-1900; A.A.G., South Africa, 1900; Commandant Cavalry Depôt, 1899-1904; staff officer for Imperial Yeomanry, 1906-8; Colonel in charge Cavalry Records, 1909-11; served S. Africa, 1891; Tirah, 1897-98 (despatches, medal with 2 clasps); South Africa, 1899-1900 (Queen's medal, 3 clasps); retired, 1911. *Club:* Naval and Military.
(*Died 4 Dec. 1922.*)

HEGER, Dr. Paul, M.D., Hon. LL.D. St. Andrews; Hon. Professor; Hon. President University of Brussels; *b.* Brussels, 13 Dec. 1846; *s.* of Professor Constantin Heger; *m.* Léonie Van Mons (*decd.*); one *s.* two *d.* *Educ.:* Brussels; Vienna; Leipzig. Professor of Physiology at University of Brussels, 1873-1907; practised medicine until he undertook, in 1889, the post of Principal and Director of the Institute of Physiology founded in that year by M. Ernest Solvay, Parc Léopold, Brussels. *Publications:* Archives Internationales de Physiologie (with Prof. L. Fredericq); numerous reports and essays on the work of the laboratory of the Institut Solvay. *Address:* 23 Rue des Drapiers, Brussels. *T.:* 22235.
(*Died Nov. 1925.*)

HEINEMANN, William, publisher; *b.* Surbiton, 18 May 1863. Founded the publishing house which bears his name in 1890. President of the Publishers' Association of Great Britain and Ireland, 1909-11; President of the National Booksellers' Provident Society, 1913-20. *Publications:* The First Step, a play in 3 acts, 1895; Summer Moths, a play in 4 Acts, 1898; War, a play in 3 Acts, 1901. *Recreations:* travelling and play-writing. *Address:* 32 Lower Belgrave Street, S.W.1; *T.:* Victoria 6426; 21 Bedford Street, W.C.2; *T.:* Gerrard 5675. *Clubs:* Conservative, National, Bath, etc.
(*Died 5 Oct. 1920.*)

HELLARD, Frederick, I.S.O. 1915; late a Secretary of H.M.'s Woods, Forests, etc.; *b.* 11 April 1850; *s.* of late C. B. Hellard, Portsmouth, Solicitor and formerly Mayor of that town; *m.* 1877, Harriette M., *d.* of late John Williamson; one *s.* four *d.* *Educ.:* private schools. Admitted a Solicitor, 1872; entered the Solicitor's branch of the Office of Woods, 1879; principal clerk to one of the Commissioners, 1885, and subsequently a secretary: retired 1915, but rejoined and served again till 1919. *Address:* Wayside Cottage, New Milton, Hants.
(*Died 16 May 1925.*)

HELLEU, Paul-César; Chevalier de la Légion d'honneur; peintre et graveur; *b.* Vannes, 17 déc. 1859. *Œuvres:* Envois aux Salons de la Société nationale des Beaux-Arts, Nom-

breux portraits; tableau au musée du Luxembourg. *Address:* 45 rue Emile Ménier, Paris.
(*Died Mar. 1927.*)

HELLIER, John Benjamin, M.D. London, M.R.C.S. Eng.; Emeritus Professor of Obstetrics, University of Leeds, and Consulting Obstetric Physician, Leeds General Infirmary; Leeds Maternity Hospital and Hospital for Women; *s.* of Rev. Benjamin Hellier, formerly of Headingley College; *b.* Seacombe, Cheshire; *m.* Eliza, *y. d.* of H. B. Harrison, J.P., Manchester; two *s.* two *d.* *Educ.:* Kingswood; Leeds School of Medicine; University College, London. Graduate University, London, 1876; First-Class Honours Medicine; University Scholar and Gold Medallist in Obstetric Medicine; practises as consulting specialist in Obstetrics and Gynæcology in Leeds; Honorary Fellow Glasgow Obstetrical and Gynæcological Society; late President of North of England Obstetrical and Gynæcological Society. *Publications:* many contributions to literature of Obstetrics and Gynæcology, and Pædiatrics. *Recreations:* touring, literature. *Address:* Chapel Allerton, Leeds; 27 Park Square, Leeds. *T.A:* Dr. Hellier, Leeds. *T.:* Leeds 25878.
(*Died 8 Nov. 1924.*)

HELM, Henry James, I.S.O., 1903; F.I.C., F.C.S; late Deputy Principal of the Government Laboratory, London; *b.* 1889; *s.* of Henry Helm, Cotton Manufacturer, Padiham, Lancashire; *m.* 1867, Lucilla, *d.* of John Smith, Padiham. *Educ.:* Private School, Burnley; Grammar School, Whalley. Entered Inland Revenue Service, 1859; passed by competition into Inland Revenue Laboratory, 1861, which became the Government Laboratory, 1894; and retired under the age limit, 1904; Juror at the Paris Exhibition, 1900. St. Louis, 1904, and at Brussels, 1910. *Address:* Simonstone, Bromley, Kent.
(*Died 24 Mar. 1918.*)

HELMER, Colonel (Temp. Brig.-General) Richard Alexis, C.M.G. 1918: Canadian Permanent Staff; Director-General of Musketry since 1916; Acting-Director of Military Training since 1914; *b.* 12 Oct. 1864; *s.* of Nathaniel Helmer and Melissa Johnson; *m.* 1885, Elizabeth I. Hannum. *Educ.:* Ottawa and Toronto, Ontario. Licentiate Chemist of Provinces Ontario and Quebec; joined 43rd Battalion Canadian Militia, 1883; served therein until 1906; transferred to Permanent Force of Canada as Deputy-Assistant Adjutant-General for Musketry, 1906; A.A.G. 1908; Director of Musketry, 1911; Commandant, Canadian School of Musketry, 1907; Adjutant Canadian Rifle Team, Bisley, 1899; Canadian Palma Team, Sea Girt, 1903; Ottawa, 1907; Commandant, Camp Perry, 1912; Alderman, City of Hull, Quebec, for twelve years, twice elected Mayor. *Address:* Department of Militia and Defence, Ottawa, Canada. *Club:* Laurentian, Ottawa.
(*Died 1 Feb. 1920.*)

HELMSLEY, Viscountess (Muriel); 3rd *d.* of 19th Earl of Shrewsbury; *m.* 1st, Viscount Helmsley, *e. s.* of 1st Earl of Feversham; mother of 2nd and grandmother of 3rd Earl; 2nd, Hugh Owen; Founder and President L.M.S. (Women's Branch); Chairman of Council National Society of Day Nurseries; President Islington and Brixton Unionist and Conservative Association; Hon. Secretary Women's Institute Training College Branch for Nurses; Executive Committee Lambeth Infirmary (Rescue Branch); Chairman Douglas Day Nursery; Executive St. Clement Danes Day Nursery. *Address:* 48 Pont Street, S.W.1. *T.:* Ken. 4909.
(*Died 2 Mar. 1925.*)

HEMPHILL, 2nd Baron (*cr.* 1905), Rt. Hon. Stanhope Charles John Hemphill, K.C., M.A., D.L., J.P.; *b.* Cashel, 13 March 1853; *s.* of 1st Baron Hemphill and Augusta, *d.* of late Hon. Sir Francis Stanhope, *s.* of 3rd Earl of Harrington; *m.* 1913, Hon.

May Hamilton, 2nd *d.* of 9th Baron Belhaven and Stenton; *S.* father 1906. *Educ.:* Shrewsbury School; Trinity College, Dublin (1st Classical Prize, Honours Moderatorship, and Medallist). Called to Bar, Middle Temple, 1877; Irish Bar, 1878. *Heir: b.* Capt. Hon. **F.** Hemphill. *Address:* 8 Lower Sloane Street, S.W.; *T.:* Vic. 3053; Clifton House, Shankill, Co. Dublin. *Clubs:* Reform, National Liberal; University, Royal Irish Yacht, Dublin.
(Died 26 Mar. 1919.)

HEMPHILL, Ven. Samuel, D.D., Litt.D.; Rector of Drumbeg near Belfast, 1920; Archdeacon of Down, 1923; Examining Chaplain to Archbishop of Armagh, 1920, and to Bishop of Down, 1923; *b.* Clonmel, 5 July 1859; *e. s.* of late Robert Hemphill, Springhill, Co. Tipperary; *m.* Flora Margaret, *d.* of Rev. Alexander Delap, Rector of Valencia, Co. Kerry, 1885; three *s.* four *d.* *Educ.:* Clonmel; Tipperary; Dublin University. Professor of Biblical Greek, Dublin University, 1888-98; Select Preacher in Dublin University, 1892-93, 1899; Canon of St. Patrick's Cathedral, Dublin, 1909-14; Chancellor of Christchurch Cathedral, Dublin, 1919-26; Member of the Royal Irish Academy, 1893. *Publications:* The Diatessaron of Tatian, 1888; My Neighbour, 1897; The Satires of Persius translated, 1900; A History of the Revised Version of the New Testament, 1906. *Address:* Drumbeg Rectory, Dunmurry, Co. Antrim.
(Died 12 Jan. 1927.)

HEMSLEY, William Botting, LL.D., F.R.S., F.L.S.; late Keeper of Herbarium and Library, Royal Botanic Gardens, Kew; Hon. Member Natural History Society, Mexico; Corr. Memb. Deutsch. Botan. Gesell.; Hon. Memb. R. Hort. Society; Hon. Member Royal Society, New South Wales; Hon. Member New Zealand Institute; V.M.H.; *b.* Easthoathley, Sussex, 29 Dec. 1843. *Educ.:* privately; entered Kew, 1860. *Publications:* Handbook of Hardy Trees, Shrubs, and Herbaceous Plants, 1873 and 1877; Botany of the "Challenger" Expedition; Botany of Salvin and Godman's Biologia Centrali-Americana; Flora of China; Flora of Tibet; Flora of Seychelles (Journal of Botany, 1916-17); Flora of Aldabra (Kew Bulletin, 1919); numerous articles, translations, and reviews, largely relating to geographical botany and insular floras; etc. *Address:* 9 Walmsley Road, Broadstairs, Kent. *(Died 7 Oct. 1924.)*

HEMY, Charles Napier, R.A. 1910; A.R.A. 1898; R.W.S. 1897; marine painter; *b.* Newcastle-on-Tyne, 24 May 1841; *e. s.* of late Henri F. Hemy, distinguished musician, and Margret, *d.* of Angus Macdonald; *m.* Amy Mary, *d.* of W.G.Freeman, Falmouth,1881; six *s.* four *d.* *Educ.:* Newcastle Grammar School; St. Cuthbert's College, Durham; Art studies, Newcastle Art School, under W. Bell Scott, as a boy, and Antwerp Academy, 1867, afterwards pupil of Baron Henri Leys. Made three voyages to sea as a youth; joined the Dominicans at Lyons at 19, but left at 22, and decided to become a painter; at 24 exhibited first picture at the Royal Academy; dissatisfaction with the results of these attempts resulted in going to Antwerp to study under Baron Leys; returned to England, 1870; lived in London till 1881, exhibiting at R.A., Grosvenor, New Gallery; left London and built Churchfield, at Falmouth, 1882, where most of his pictures have since been painted. *Principal pictures:* Homeward (Birmingham Corporation); Oporto; Silent Adieu; Pilchards (Chantrey Bequest); Lost, 1897; Smugglers, 1899; Home Wind (Australian Government); Birds of Prey, 1901 (Leeds Corporation); The Crew, 1902; Youth, 1903; The Lifeboat; Haul Aft; London River (Chantrey Trustees); The Crab Merchant (Union Club, Sydney), 1904; Caught Out, 1907; Plymouth, Through Sea and Air, 1910; Life, The Trawler, Home at Last, 1913; Life, 1914; The Black Flag, 1915. *Recreation:* yachting on board the "Van der Meer." *Address:* Churchfield, Falmouth. *Clubs:* hon. member Royal Yacht Squadron, and marine painter to the club; hon. member Royal Cruising Yacht. *(Died 30 Sept. 1917.)*

HENDERSON, Amos, Professor of Education and Principal of Mapperley Hall Hostel, University College, Nottingham, since 1905; *b.* 18 July 1864. *Educ.:* Borough Road College, London; University College, Nottingham. Second Master People's College, Nottingham, 1885-90; Normal Master, Department of Education, University College, Nottingham, 1890-1905. *Publication:* Some Notes on Teaching. *Recreations:* cricket, tennis, golf. *Address:* Mapperley Hall, Nottingham. *T.:* 2291.
(Died Oct. 1922.)

HENDERSON, Rev. Archibald, M.A., D.D. (Glasgow); Senior Minister of the South United Free Church, Crieff; *b.* 9 Aug. 1837; *s.* of Rev. Dr. Henderson, Glasgow; *m.* 1863, *d.* of Principal Candlish, Edinburgh; two *s.* three *d.* *Educ.:* Glasgow University; Glasgow Free Church College; New College, Edinburgh; University of Göttingen. Ordained in Crieff, 1862; Member of Crieff School Board, 1873-1906; Chairman, 1892-1906; Junior Principal Clerk of Free Church General Assembly, 1888; Senior Clerk, 1907-16; Convener of the Foreign Mission Committee, 1900-1904; nominated for Moderatorship of General Assembly, 1907, but declined office; Moderator of General Assembly, 1909; Joint-Convener of Committee on Conference with Church of Scotland, 1908-26; Hon. Chaplain to Territorial Forces, Scotland, 1910; Territorial Decoration (T.D.), 1911; Long Service Medal; D.D. St. Andrews University, 1911; Principal of Glasgow College of United Free Church of Scotland, 1918-21. *Publication:* Historical Geography of Palestine. *Address:* Crieff. *T.:* 78. *Club:* Scottish Liberal, Edinburgh.
(Died 11 April 1927.)

HENDERSON, Lt. - Gen. Sir David, K.C.B., *cr.* 1914; K.C.V.O., *cr.* 1919: D.S.O. 1902; Director-General, League of Red Cross Societies, Geneva; late Argyll and Sutherland Highlanders; Colonel Highland Light Infantry since 1918; *b.* 11 Aug. 1862; *s.* of late David Henderson, Glasgow; *m.* 1895, Henrietta Caroline, *d.* of Henry R. Dundas. Entered army, 1883; Captain, 1890; served Soudan, 1898 (despatches, brevet of Major, British medal, Khedive's medal with clasp); South Africa, 1899-1900 (wounded, despatches twice, D.S.O., brevet Lieut.-Colonel; Queen's medal, four clasps, King's medal, two clasps); European War, 1914 - 17 (prom. Maj. - Gen. and Lt. - Gen.); Director-General of Military Aeronautics 1913-1918; Knight of Grace, Order of St. John of Jerusalem, 1920; Commander Legion of Honour, 1915; Grand Officer, 1919; Grand Officer Order of the Crown of Belgium; Grand Crown of the Sacred Treasure of Japan, and of the White Eagle of Russia; Grand Officer of the Order of the Crown of Italy. *Publication:* The Art of Reconnaissance, 1907. *Address:* 22 Hans Crescent, S.W.1. *T.:* Victoria 449. *Club:* Naval and Military. *(Died 17 Aug. 1921.)*

HENDERSON, Vice-Admiral Frank Hannam, R.N., C.M.G. 1900; retired; *b.* 2 June 1850; *s.* of John Henderson, J.P., Felderland, near Sandwich, Kent; *m.* 1888, Agnes Jane, *d.* of John Burgess, Derry. *Educ.:* privately. Promoted to Lieutenant for capture of slave dhow with 180 slaves off coast of Arabia; Lieut. for transport duties Ashantee War, 1874 (medal); Senior Lieut. of "Eclipse" during Egyptian War, 1882 (medal, Khedive's star); commanded several expeditions on east coast, Africa; Humane Society's medal and Jubilee medal; in command of African West Coast Division during rebellion in Sierra Leone, 1898 (despatches, C.M.G.). *Recreations:*

golf, etc. *Address:* 15 St. Mark's Road, Anglesey, Gosport. *Clubs:* Constitutional; Royal Naval, Portsmouth. (*Died 26 June 1918.*)

HENDERSON, Lt.-Col. Hon. Harold Greenwood, C.V.O. 1910; Military Secretary to the Duke of Devonshire since 1916; *b.* 29 Oct. 1875; *e. s.* of 1st Baron Faringdon; *m.* Lady Violet Charlotte Dalzell, *y. d.* of 12th Earl of Carnwath; three *s.* one *d. Educ.:* Eton. Served 1st Life Guards, of which regiment was Adjutant; S.A. War (medal, two clasps, invalided home after a severe attack of enteric fever); retired, 1st Life Guards, 1906; contested N. Berks, 1906; M.P. (C.), Abingdon division Berkshire, 1910-16; Lt.-Col. commanding 1/1st Berks Yeomanry, Sept. 1914-Oct. 1915; D.A.A.G. War Office, 1916. *Recreations:* hunting, shooting, fishing. *Address:* 18 Arlington Street, S.W.; Buscot Park, Faringdon. *Clubs:* Carlton, Marlborough. (*Died 1 Nov. 1922.*)

HENDERSON, John M'Donald, M.P. (L.) Aberdeenshire, West, 1906-18; Chartered Accountant and Barrister-at-law; *b.* 1846; *m.* 1872, Kate Mary, 2nd *d.* of Thomas Francis Robins; one *s.* one *d. Educ.:* Gordon's College, and Marischal College, Aberdeen. *Address:* White House, Felixstowe; Cambisgate, Wimbledon, S.W. *T.:* PO Wimbledon 119. *Club:* Reform. (*Died 20 Nov. 1922.*)

HENDERSON, John Robertson, C.I.E. 1918; M.B., C.M.; F.L.S.; F.R.S.E.; *b.* Melrose, 21 May 1863; *s.* of Edward Henderson; *m.* 1st, 1888, Alice Roberta (*d.* 1915), *d.* of late David Sinclair, Madras; one *s.* one *d.*; 2nd, 1921, Eliza Beatrice, *d.* of late W. J. Adie, of Voe, Shetland. *Educ.:* Dulwich College; Dollar Academy; Edinburgh University. Professor of Zoology, Madras Christian College, 1886-1911; Superintendent Government Museum and Principal Librarian Connemara Public Library, Madras, 1911-19; Fellow Madras University; President Caledonian Society of Madras; 1917-18. *Publications:* Report on the Challenger Anomura, 1888; papers chiefly on Indian Crustacea and on South Indian numismatics. *Recreations:* fishing, field natural history. *Address:* 14 Murrayfield Avenue, Edinburgh. (*Died 26 Oct. 1925.*)

HENDERSON, Lt.-Col. Malcolm, D.S.O. 1917; the Royal Scots; 2nd *s.* of J. Henderson, Clifton, Ashbourne, Derbyshire. *Educ.:* Repton; R.M.C., Sandhurst. 1st Commission, 1908; Lieut. 1907; Adjutant the 2nd Royal Scots, Feb. 1911-14; Captain, 1914; Brevet Major, 1916; Bt. Lt.-Col. 1919: served European War, 1914-18 (Legion of Honour, Croix Chevalier, D.S.O., St. Maurice and Lazarus, Chevalier). *Clubs:* Naval and Military, Caledonian. (*Died 1 Mar. 1923.*)

HENDERSON, Maj.-Gen. Philip Durham, C.S.I. 1876; Unemployed Supernumerary List; *b.* 19 Aug. 1840; 2nd *s.* of late Maj.-Gen. R. Henderson, R.E.; *m.* 1864, Rose, 2nd *d.* of late Lt.-Gen. P. Cherry of the Madras Cavalry; two *s.* two *d. Educ.:* Private school. Joined 2nd Madras Cavalry, 1857; Attaché, 1870; Under Secretary to the Foreign Dept. of the Govt. of India, 1872; officer on special duty in Cashmere, 1874; General Superintendent of operations for the suppression of Thuggee and Dacoity, 1878; Resident in Mysore, 1892; left India, 1895. *Decorated* C.S.I. for services on Staff of H.M. the King, then Prince of Wales, during his visit to India. *Address:* 47 Warwick Road, S.W.
(*Died 19 April 1918.*)

HENDERSON, Robert, C.B. 1904; *b.* 1842; 3rd *s.* of Robert Henderson, Kinneff, Kincardineshire; *m.* 1st, Jane Skene, *d.* of Capt. Jas. Dow, Port-Glasgow (*d.*); 2nd, Mary Lewin, *o. d.* of W. S. Trevitt, of Holdingham, Lincolnshire, and *g. d.* of late W. Lewin, C.E. and J.P., Boston. *Educ.:* Parish School, Kinneff; Grammar School, Aberdeen; King's College, Old Aberdeen. Entered the Service of H.M.

Customs, 1862; Collector, 1871; held that position at Ardrossan, Cowes, Shoreham, Gloucester, Newry, Dover, Folkestone, Southampton, Belfast, Glasgow, and London; Secretary, 1900; Commissioner, 1909; retired 1910. *Address:* The Hermitage, Beckenham. (*Died 1 May 1925.*)

HENDERSON, Maj. - Gen. Sir Robert Samuel Findlay, K.C.M.G., *cr.* 1919; C.B. 1917; M.B. Edin.; *b.* Calcutta, 11 Dec. 1858; *s.* of Rev. Robert Henderson, Senior Chaplain, Bengal. *Educ.:* Bedford Grammar School; Fettes College; St. Mary's Hospital, London; Edinburgh Univ. M.B., C.M., 1882; entered Army Medical Service, 1884; served Sudan, 1885 (medal with clasp, bronze star); Burmah, 1886-91 (despatches, medal 3 clasps); Chin-Lushai Expedition, 1890 (1 clasp); N.W. Frontier, 1891-8 (medal with clasp); S. African War, 1901-2 (Queen's medal 5 clasps); European War, 1914-17 (C.B.); retired 1917; Sec. to R.V.H. Netley, 1907; to D.M.S. India, 1908-12; Honorary Physician to the King, 1911; A.D.M.S.-Quetta Division, 1914; 17th Division, 1915; Director-General, New Zealand Medical Services, 1915-19, with rank of Temp. Surg.-General; Hon. Major-General, 1917; retired, 1919. *Address:* Holt & Co., 3 Whitehall Place, S.W.1. *Club:* Junior United Service.
(*Died 5 Oct. 1924.*)

HENDERSON, T. F.; *b.* Lathones, Fifeshire, 24 May 1844, 2nd *s.* of Rev. Archibald Henderson and Catherine Finlayson. *Educ.:* University of St. Andrews (Hon. LL.D. 1914). For several years on the staff of the Encyclopædia Britannica; contributor of numerous Scottish lives to Dictionary of National Biography, and of several chapters to the Cambridge History of English Literature. *Publications:* The Casket Letters and Mary, Queen of Scots, 1889, 2nd ed. 1890; Old-World Scotland, 1893; Centenary Burns (with W. E. Henley), vols. I.-IV. 1896-97; History of Scottish Vernacular Literature, 1898; 2nd ed. 1900; 3rd ed. 1910; Anthology of Scottish Verse, 1899; annot. ed. of Scott's Border Minstrelsy, vols. I.-IV. 1902; Life of Robert Burns, 1904; James I. and VI. (Goupil Historical Series), 1904; Life of Mary Queen of Scots, 2 vols., 1905; The Auld Ayrshire of Robert Burns, 1906; selected edition of Burns's Poems (Englische Textebibliothek), Heidelberg, 1906; annotated edition of Macaulay's History of England, 1907; Scotland of To-day (with Mr. Francis Watt), 1907; 2nd ed. 1908; 3rd ed. 1913; The Ballad in Literature, 1912; The Royal Stewarts, 1914. *Address:* The Wraes, by Bridge of Weir, Renfrewshire.
(*Died 25 Dec. 1923.*)

HENDLEY, Brig.-Gen. Charles Edward, C.B. 1916; commanding Ambala Brigade; *b.* 26 Dec. 1868; *s.* of late Surgeon-General John Hendley, C.B. *Educ.:* Trinity College, Stratford-on-Avon. East Kent Militia, Welsh Regiment, and 81st Pioneers, I.A.; served Burma, 1886-87 (medal, 2 clasps); N.E. Frontier of India, 1892-93 (clasp, despatches); Tirah Expedition, 1897-98 (medal, 3 clasps); European War, Indian Expeditionary Force, Dardanelles, 1915 (despatches twice, C.B.); staff appointments, D.A.A.G., Brigade-Major, A.Q.M.G. *Club:* United Service. (*Died 10 Jan. 1920.*)

HENDLEY, Col. Thomas Holbein, C.I.E., 1891; V.D.; Indian Medical Service; retired; *b.* 1847, *e. s.* of T. Hendley; *m.* Jane Elizabeth, *d.* of Rev. John Dawson Hull, Vicar of Wickhambrook, Suffolk, 1872; one *s. Educ.:* privately, and St. Bartholomew's Hospital. M.R.C.S., L.R.C.P. London, 1869. 27 years under Foreign Dept. India, of which 24 were as Residency surgeon, Jeypore, the last 3 also as Admin. Med. officer, Rajputana; Inspec. Gen. of Civil Hosps., Bengal, 1898-1903; and officiating N.W. Provinces and Oudh, 1897; acting President Plague Commission, Calcutta, 1898; Fellow Calcutta University, 1899-1903; and

Member of Syndicate, 1899; Vice-President Asiatic Society of Bengal and Trustee Indian Museum, 1899-1903; Hon. Associate St. John of Jerusalem, 1904; Knight of Grace, 1909. Chairman Executive Committee, Jeypore Exhibition, 1883; Member of Executive Council and a Governor of Imperial Institute, 1891-92, and organised its first exhibition (Indian Art Metal Work) 1892; President, Decennial (2nd) Art Conference at Lahore, 1894; and Member Judging Com. Delhi Exhibition, 1903; Chairman, Indian Section Festival of Empire, 1911; Hon. Vice-Pres. (Trop. sect.), International Congress of Hygiene, 1894. *Publications:* author of several works on Indian Art; Rulers of India and Chiefs of Rajputana, 1897; Medico-Topographical Histories of Jeypore and Rajputana, etc. *Address:* 4 Loudoun Road, N.W.   *(Died 2 Feb. 1917.)*

HENDRIE, Colonel Sir John Strathearn, K.C.M.G., *cr.* 1915; C.V.O. 1907; *b.* Hamilton, Canada, Aug. 1857; *e. s.* of William and Margaret Hendrie; *m.* 1885, Lena Maud, *d.* of Peter R. Henderson, Kingston, Ont.; one *s.* one *d. Educ.:* Hamilton School; Upper Canada College. Mayor of Hamilton, 1901-2; Member Ontario Legislature, 1902-14; Lieut.-Governor of Ontario, 1914-19; Member Battlefields Commission; Minister without Portfolio, 1905-14; joined Canadian Militia, 1883; Col. Canadian Field Artillery Militia, R.O.; director in several manufacturing and financial companies. *Recreations:* fishing, shooting. *Address:* Strathearn, Hamilton, Ont. *Clubs:* Hamilton Tamahaac, Country, Hamilton; York, Toronto, Ontario Jockey, Albany, Toronto.   *(Died 18 July 1923.)*

HENEAGE, 1st Baron (*cr.* 1896), Edward Heneage, P.C. 1886; J.P., D.L.; High Steward of Grimsby; Trustee Lincolnshire Agricultural Society and Mablethorpe Convalescent Home; *b.* 29 Mar. 1840; *e. s.* of George Fiesche Heneage, Hainton Hall, Lincoln, and Frances, *d.* of late Michael Tasburgh, Burghwalls Hall, near Doncaster; *m.* Lady Eleanor Cecilia Hare (*b.* 1845), *d.* of 2nd Earl of Listowel, 1864; three *s.* four *d. Educ.:* Eton. 1st Life Guards, 1857-63; succeeded to family estates, 1864; M.P. Lincoln 1866-68; Grimsby, 1880-95; was Vice-Chairman of Lindsey Quarter Sessions; Chancellor of Duchy of Lancaster; Vice-President of Committee of Agriculture, 1886; retired from office and joined Liberal Unionist party; Chairman of Liberal Unionist Council from 1893-98; was Vice-Chairman of Agricultural Chamber, 1870; Chairman, 1871; President of Fisherman's Provident Association (Grimsby Branch); Member of Central Council; Chairman of South Wold Hunt Club till 1904; owns about 10,800 acres. *Recreations:* prior to 1880 owned Freeman and other racehorses and steeplechasers. *Heir: s.* Hon. Geo. E. Heneage.   *Address:* Hainton Hall, Lincoln. *Clubs:* Brooks's, Turf.   *(Died 10 Aug. 1922.)*

HENEGAN, Lt.-Col. John, D.S.O., 1893; commandant, 10th Gurkha Rifles; *b.* 1865. Entered army, 1884; Captain, 1895; Major, 1904; Lt.-Col. 1909; served Burmah, 1886-89 (medal with two clasps); Northern Chin Hills, 1892-93 (despatches, D.S.O.). *Address:* Maymyo, Burma.   *(Died 19 April 1920.)*

HENEY, Thomas William; *b.* Sydney, 5 Nov. 1862; *e. s.* of T. W. Heney, Cooma, Monaro, N.S.W.; *m.* 1898, Amy Florence, *e. d.* of Hon. Henry Gullett, M.L.C.; one *s.* two *d. Educ.:* State Schools and privately. Entered newspaper service, 1878, and thereafter connected with journalism, city and country; Editor Sydney Morning Herald, 1903-18; in England, 1910 and 1918, with Australian Press Delegation; Editor Brisbane Telegraph, 1921-23; Sydney Daily Telegraph, 1924-26; attended Empire Press Conference, Melbourne, Oct. 1925; Melbourne, 1927, working at Australian Official War History. *Publications:* Fortunate Days (poems), 1886; In Middle Harbour(poems), 1890; The Girl at Birrell's (novel), 1896; A Station Courtship (novel), 1898-99; magazine contributions, etc. *Address:* Field Place, Exeter, N.S.W. *Club:* Warrigal, Sydney.   *(Died Aug. 1928.)*

HENLEY, 4th Baron (Ireland), *cr.* 1799; Frederick Henley, Baron Northington U.K.), *cr.* 1885; *b.* 17 April 1849; *e. s.* of 3rd Baron and Julia Peel, *d.* of Dean of Worcester; *S.* father 1898; *m.* 1900, Augusta Frederica (*d.* 1905), *sister* of Sir Herbert H. Langham, 12th Bt. Attaché in the Diplomatic Service, 1868-73. Owns about 5450 acres. *Heir: b.* Hon. Anthony Ernest Henley.   *Address:* Watford Court, Rugby.   *(Died 23 Dec. 1923.)*

HENLEY, 5th Baron (Ireland), *cr.* 1799; Anthony Ernest Henley, Baron Northington (U.K.), *cr.* 1885; *b.* 3 July 1858; *s.* of 3rd Baron and Julia Peel, *d.* of Dean of Worcester; *m.* 1st, 1882, Georgiana (*d.* 1888), *d.* of late Lt.-Col. R. M. Williams; 2nd, 1889, Emmeline, *d.* of G. Maitland; one *d.*; *S. brother,* 1923. Owns about 5450 acres. *Heir: half-b.* Hon. Francis Robert Henley. *Address:* Watford, Rugby. *(Died 23 Oct. 1925.)*

HENLEY, Brig.-Gen. Hon. Anthony Morton, C.M.G. 1919; D.S.O. 1916; Director Arthur Capel and Co., Shipowners and coal exporters; 3rd *s.* of 3rd and *heir-pres.* to 5th Baron Henley: *m.* 1906, Sylvia Laura, 3rd *d.* of 4th Baron Sheffield   three *d. Educ.:* Eton; Balliol College, Oxford. Called to Bar, 1897; enlisted I.Y. 1899; served with Scots Greys, 1900-7; with 5th Lancers, 1907-14; G.S. 1914-1917; commanding 127th Infantry Brigade, 1917-19 (despatches, C.M.G., D.S.O., Brevet Maj. and Col.). *Address:* 9 Oxford Square, W.2. *Clubs:* Brooks's, Wellington.
    (Died 17 May 1925.)

HENNELL, Col. Sir Reginald, Kt., *cr.* 1902; D.S.O. 1887; C.V.O. 1910; O.B.E. 1919; Lieut. The King's Body-Guard of the Yeomen of the Guard; *b.* 11 June 1844. Joined Bombay Infantry, 1861; Lieut. 1863, Capt. 1871; Major, 1881; Col. 1887; retired, 1889; served Abyssinian Expedition, 1867-68 (medal); Afghan War, 1879-80 (services acknowledged by Government, medal); Burmah Campaign, 1886-87 (specially mentioned in despatches, D.S.O., 1886, medal and clasp); Col.-Commanding 1st Vol. Batt. Middlesex Regt. 1891, retired 1901; one of H.M.'s Honorable Corps of Gentlemen-at-Arms, 1892; Exon of H.M.'s Royal Body-Guard of the Yeomen of the Guard, 1894; Clerk of the Cheque and Adjutant of this Guard, 1895; Hon. Colonel, 3rd Cadet Battalion, Middlesex Regt., 1911. *Publications:* History of the Yeomen of the Guard. 1485-1904; Our Birthright; Looking Ahead; and other military essays. *Address:* 47 Coleherne Court, S.W.5. *Club:* United Service.
    (Died 22 May 1925.)

HENNESSY, Rt. Hon. Sir David Valentine, Kt., *cr.* 1915; J.P.; Lord Mayor of Melbourne, 1912-17, record for the city; *b.* Melbourne, Jan. 1855; *s.* of James Hennessy, of Waterford, Ireland; *m.* Mary (C.B.E., Medaille de la Reconnaissance Francaise, Medal of Queen Elizabeth), *d.* of late Michael Quinlan, Ballarat; one *s.* three *d. Educ.:* Model High Schools and Fitzroy College, Melbourne. Entered municipal life, city of Brunswick, 1892; Mayor, 1894; Member of Melbourne City Council since 1895; M.P. South Carlton for 4½ years; President of the Overseas Club, Melbourne; Member of the Royal Colonial Institute, London and Victoria League; Chairman and Director of several Companies; Member British Empire League, Melbourne; Order Commander of the Crown of Belgium, 1920; Order of St. Sava, 1916. *Address:* White

Lodge, Toorak Road, S. Yarra, Melbourne, Australia. *Club:* Athenæum, Melbourne.
(Died 16 June 1923.)

HENNESSY, Richard M., K.C.; *b.* 1854; *s.* of John C. Hennessy and Mary Kenifeck. Called to Irish Bar, 1877; Inner Bar, 1902; Bencher King's Inns, 1913. *Address:* 16 Hume Street, Dublin. *(Died 24 Oct. 1926.)*

HENNESSY, Wm. John, Painter; *b.* Thomastown, Co. Kilkenny, Ireland. Member National Academy, and Hon. Member Water Colour Society, N.Y.; Member Society of Oil Painters, and Pastel Society, London; Member Union Internationale des Beaux-Arts et des Lettres, Paris; paints figures and landscape subjects; lived alternately in France and England, but mostly in Calvados, Normandy, and in Sussex, and always in the country.

HENNIKER, Hon. Mrs. Arthur; novelist; *d.* of 1st Baron Houghton, and sister to 1st Marquis of Crewe; *m.* 1882, Maj.-Gen. Hon. A. H. Henniker-Major (*d.* 1912); President of Society of Woman Journalists, 1896. *Publications:* Sir George, 1891; Foiled, 1893; Outlines, 1894; In Scarlet and Grey, 1896; Sowing the Sand, 1898; Contrasts, 1903; 4 Act Play, The Courage of Silence, King's Theatre, London, 1905; Our Fatal Shadows, 1907; Second Fiddle, 1912. *Address:* 2 Hyde Park Square, W.2. *T.:* Paddington 237. *(Died 4 April 1923.)*

HENNIKER-HUGHAN, Admiral (retired) **Sir Arthur John**, 6th Bt.; *cr.* 1813; R.N.; C.B. 1919; M.P. (C.) Galloway since 1924; *b.* 24 Jan. 1866; *s.* of 4th Bt. and Justina Louisa, *y. d.* of Thomas Hughan, of Airds, N.B.; *S.* brother 1908 [succeeded to the property of his maternal grandmother on the death of his aunt Mrs. Houghton-Hughan, and took additional name of Hughan, 1896]; *m.* 1904, Inger Margueretta, (*d.* 1923) *o. d.* of Graham Hutchison of Balnaghie, Kirkcudbright; three *d.* Rear-Adm. 1916; Vice-Adm. 1920; retired, 1920; served in World War as Captain of H.M.S. Ajax, Grand Fleet, 1914-1916; A.D.C. to King George V., 1914-16; Admiral Superintendent Devonport Dockyard, 1916-19; promoted Admiral, retired list, 1925. *Heir: c.* Robert John Aldborough [*b.* 26 May 1888; *m.* 1914, Lucy Mabel, *d.* of late Edward Swan Hennessy of Hazelbrook, Roscommon]. *Address:* The Airds, Parton, Kirkcudbright. *Club:* Naval and Military. *(Died 4 Oct. 1925.)*

HENNIKER-MAJOR, Hon. Edward Minet, British Vice-Consul at St. Malo, 1888; retired on pension, 1919; *b.* 3 Feb. 1848; 2nd *s.* of 4th Baron Henniker; *m.* Eveline Talvera, *widow* of W. Harvey, and *e. d.* of late Capt. Henri de St. Maur, French Army. *Educ.:* Eton. *Address:* 10 Havre des Pas, Jersey.
(Died 20 Dec. 1924.)

HENRICI, Olaus M. F. E., Ph.D., LL.D., F.R.S.; Emeritus Professor of Mechanics and Mathematics, City and Guilds (Engineering) College; *b.* 1840; *m. e. d.* of late Rev. John Kennedy, D.D.; one *s.* Past Pres. of London Mathematical Society. *Publications:* Skeleton Structures, especially in their Application to the Building of Steel and Iron Bridges, 1866; Congruent Figures, 1879; Vectors and Rotors, 1903; various papers on Mathematics. *Address:* Hiltingbury Lodge, Chandlers Ford, Hants.
(Died 10 Aug. 1918.)

HENRIQUES, Henry Straus Quixano, K.C. 1921; *b.* 8 Nov. 1866; *e s.* of late E. M. Henriques, J.P., Manchester; *m.* 1894, Henrietta (*d.* 1922), 2nd *d.* of late Ferdinand Sichel; one *s.* one *d. Educ.:* Manchester Gram. School; Worcester Coll., Oxford (Sen. Class. Scholar), M.A., B.C.L., Vinerian Law Scholar, 1891; Common Law Scholarship at the Inner Temple, 1892, Examiner for the degree of B.C.L. 1897; Member of the Northern Circuit; President of the Jewish Board of Deputies; Vice-President and Ex-President of the Jewish Historical Society of England: President of the St. George's-in-the-East Jewish Settlement and of the West London Synagogue of British Jews; on the Executive Committees of the Grotius Society and International Law Association. *Publications:* The Law of Aliens and Naturalisation; The Jews and the English Law; The Return of the Jews to England; Jewish Marriages and the English Law; part of the treatise on Ecclesiastical Law in Halsbury's Laws of England. *Address:* 4 Harcourt Buildings, Temple, E.C.4; 176 Gloucester Terrace, W.2. *T.A.:* 69 Temple. *T.:* Central 9945; Paddington 2505. *Clubs:* Union, Maccabæans.
(Died 12 Nov. 1925.)

HENRY, Sir Charles Solomon, 1st Bt. *cr.* 1911; M.P. (L.) Wellington Div. of Shropshire, 1906-18; Wrekin Div., since 1918; J.P.; *b.* 28 Jan. 1860; 2nd *s.* of late J. S. Henry of Adelaide; *m.* 1892, *e. d.* of late Leonard Lewisohn of New York. *Educ.:* St. Marylebone and All Souls Grammar School in connection with King's College; University of Göttingen. Established the firm of C. S. Henry and Co., 1882, which was converted into a Limited Liability Company, 1902; contested Chelmsford Division of Essex in Liberal interest, 1900. *Heir:* none. *Recreations:* riding, golf, and motoring. *Address:* 5 Carlton Gardens, S.W.1. *T.A.:* Liegeoise. Parkwood, Henley-on-Thames. *T.:* Hurley 5. Brooklands, Wellington, Salop. *T.:* Wellington 4. *Clubs:* National Liberal, Royal Automobile, British Empire, Portland, Devonshire.
(Died 27 Dec. 1919.)

HENRY, Rt. Hon. Sir Denis Stanislaus, 1st Bt., *cr.* 1922; P.C. Ireland, 1919; Lord Chief Justice of Northern Ireland since 1921; Attorney-General for Ireland, 1919-1921; Solicitor-General, Ireland, 1918; M.P. (U.) Derry, 1916-21; K.C., Ireland, 1896; *b.* 7 Mar. 1864; 6th *s.* of late James Henry, Cahore, Draperstown; *m.* 1910, Violet, 3rd *d.* of Rt. Hon. H. Holmes: two *s.* three *d. Educ.:* Mount St. Mary's Coll., Chesterfield; Queen's College, Belfast. Called Irish Bar, 1885; Bencher of King's Inns, 1898; J.P., D.L., Co. Londonderry; Commissioner Charitable Bequests, 1912; LL.D. (hon.) Queen's, Belfast; contested (U.) North Tyrone, 1906 and 1907. *Address:* The Rath, Draperstown, Co. Derry. *Clubs:* Constitutional; University, Dublin; Ulster, Belfast; Northern Counties, Londonderry; Royal Ulster Yacht. *(Died 1 Oct. 1925.)*

HENRY, Lieut.-Gen. George, C.B. 1903; R.E.; retired list; *b.* 23 Aug. 1846; *s.* of Rev. T. Henry; *m.* 1874, Mary Helen, *d.* of late Surg.-Gen. H. H. Massy, C.B. Entered army 1868; Captain, 1880; Major, 1887; Lieut.-Col. 1892; Col. 1894; Major-Gen. 1901; Lieut.-Gen. 1907; Q.M.G. India, 1900-3; Command 7th (Meerut) Division, India, 1903-8; Col. Commandant R.E. 1916; served Afghan War, 1878-80 (medal); Burmese Expedition, 1885 (despatches, medal with clasp); Chin-Lushai Expedition, 1889-90, commanding R.E. (despatches, Brevet Lieut.-Col., clasp). *Address: c/o* Cox & Co., Charing Cross, S.W.1. *(Died 19 Nov. 1922.)*

HENRY, William Alexander, K.C.; LL.B.; member of the legal firm of Henry, Stewart, Smith & McCleave, Halifax, N.S.; *b.* Antigonish, Nova Scotia, 19 March 1863; *s.* of Hon. William Alexander Henry, Judge of Supreme Court of Canada, and Christianna McDonald; *m.* 1892, Minna H. Troop; one *s.* one *d. Educ.:* Halifax Grammar School; Lycée de Tours; Merchiston Castle School, Edinburgh; Dalhousie University, Halifax, N.S. (LL.B. 1886); Harvard University, Cambridge, Mass., U.S. Admitted to Nova Scotia Bar, 1887; K.C. 1907; President, Nova Scotia Barristers' Soc., 1917 and 1918; played in Harvard Univ. football, cricket, and lacrosse teams, 1881-82, 1883-84; member of Gentlemen of Canada

Cricket Team in Great Britain, 1887; played for Canada v. United States at cricket, 1886, 1888, 1892, 1896. *Recreations:* formerly cricket, football, baseball, hockey, running, jumping, lacrosse, lawn tennis; now golf, badminton. *Address:* 16 South Street, Halifax, Nova Scotia. *T.A.:* Henry, Halifax. *Clubs:* Halifax, Saraguay, Brightwood Golf, Halifax Golf, Gorsebrook Golf.   (*Died 11 Dec. 1927.*)

HENSHALL, John Henry, R.W.S. 1897; *b.* 11 Apr. 1856; *s.* of Benjamin Henshall, Manchester; married. *Educ.:* S. Kensington, Royal Academy Schools. Medals, S.K.; Royal Academy; Chicago International Exhibition: Paris Universal Exhibition and Brussels International Exhibition; Exhibits Royal Academy, Royal Society of Painters in Water Colours, Salon, and leading exhibitions; pictures purchased by Birmingham, Leeds, Hull, Manchester, Bristol, Preston and Blackpool Corporations for permanent collections; A.R.W.S., 1883. *Recreations:* motoring and yachting. *Address:* The Cottage, Bosham, Sussex.
(*Died 18 Nov. 1928.*)

HENSLOW, Rev. George, M.A., F.L.S., F.G.S., F.R.H.S., and V.M.H.; late Professor of Botany to Royal Hort. Society; President of Ealing Nat. Hist. Soc. 1882-1904; *b.* 1835; *s.* of late Rev. J. S. Henslow, Prof. of Botany, University of Cambridge, and Rector of Hitcham, Suffolk; *m.* 1s, Georgina, *d.* of late Rev. J. Bailey (*d.* 1875); 2nd, 1882, Katharine (*d.* 1919), *d.* of late Robert Forster, of Southwell, and widow of Rd. Yeo, Ealing: one *s. Educ.:* Sawston Parsonage, Cambs.; Grammar School, Bury St. Edmunds. Christ's College, Camb., 1854, Scholar and Medallist; 4th Sen. Op.; 2nd class, Divinity; 1st class. Natural Science Tripos. Ordained, 1858; Curate of Steyning, Sussex; Headmaster, Hampton Lucy Grammar School, Warwick, 1861-65 Curate, St. John's Wood Chapel, 1868-70; Assist. Minister of St. James, Marylebone, 1870-87; Headmaster, Grammar School, Store Street, London, 1865-1872; Examiner Natural Science Tripos, Camb., 1867; Examiner in Botany to College of Preceptors, 1874-1912; Lecturer on Botany at St. Bart.'s Med. School, 1866-90; at Birkbeck, Queen's College, etc. *Publications:* Origin of Floral Structures; Origin of Plant Structures; Floral Dissections; Botany for Beginners; How to Study Wild Flowers; The Making of Flowers; South African Flowering Plants; The Story of Wild Flowers; Poisonous Plants; Medical Works of XIV. Century; Introduction to Plant-Ecology; The Heredity of Acquired Characters in Plants; British Wild Flowers; Origin and History of our Garden Vegetables; Floral Rambles in Highways and By-ways; Theological — Evolution and Religion; Christian Beliefs reconsidered in the Light of Modern Thought; The Argument of Adaptation; Christ, no Product of Evolution; The At-one-ment, or the Gospel of Reconciliation; Spiritual Teachings of Bible Plants; Present-Day Rationalism Critically Examined; Plants of the Bible; The Spiritual Teaching of Christ's Life; The Vulgate, the source of False Doctrines; Spirit-Psychometry; Proofs of the Truths of Spiritualism; The Religion of the Spirit-World. *Recreation:* gardening. *Address:* Danehurst, Branksome Wood Road, Bournemouth.
(*Died 30 Dec. 1925.*)

HENSMAN, Howard, author and journalist; *b.* Manchester; *o. s.* of Howard Hensman; *m.* 1904; one *s.* one *d. Educ.:* privately. Contributor to most journals, magazines, and reviews on social, military, naval, Indian, and South African topics. *Publications:* A History of Rhodesia, 1900; Cecil Rhodes: A Study of a Career, 1901; When and Where of Famous Men and Women, 1908. *Recreations:* yachting,

488

boating and punting, photography, cricket, cycling, lawn-tennis, and all out-door sports.
(*Died 12 June 1916.*)

HEPBURN, Sir Thomas Henry, Kt., *cr.* 1912; J.P., Devon; *b.* 6 June 1840; *s.* of Thomas Hepburn, J.P., of Clapham Common, Surrey; *m.* 1st, 1871, Alice, *d.* of Rev. Dr. Gotch of Bristol; 2nd, 1875, Josephine, *d.* of John Robinson of Backwell House, Somerset; three *s.* three *d. Educ.:* Amersham School; University College, London; B.A., London University, 1860. Has been engaged in paper-making since 1862; at St. Mary Cray, Kent, for 11 years, and afterwards at Hele, Bradninch, Devon; is chairman of the Hele Paper Co., Ltd., established in 1892; has been concerned with Local Govt. since 1884; member Devon County Council, 1888; Alderman, 1905; Vice-Chairman, 1913; Chairman, 1916; Chairman of the Finance Committee; member of the Mid-Devon Advisory Committee for the appointment of J.P.s; a Governor of University College, Exeter, Exeter School and Hele's School,.Exeter, and Blundell's School, Tiverton. *Address:* Bradninch, nr. Cullompton, Devon. *T.A.:* Hepburn, Bradninch. *T.:* Exeter 6. *M.:* T 334. *Clubs:* Reform; Devon and Exeter, Exeter.
(*Died 2 Feb. 1917.*)

HEPWORTH, Captain Melville Willis Campbell, C.B. 1902; R.D. 1910; Royal Naval Reserve; retired; *b.* 27 Apr. 1849; *s.* of late Rev. Robert Hepworth, B.A., Cheltenham. *Educ.:* Bromsgrove School. Served in H.M.'s Indian Marine, principally in Mercantile Marine, but also in R.N.; is a Younger Brother of Trinity House; appointed Marine Superintendent of Meteorological Office, 1899; Expert Assessor to International Conference on Safety of Life at Sea, 1913. *Publications:* Notes on Maritime Meteorology; The Seaman's Handbook of Meteorology (official); The Effect of the Labrador Current upon the Surface Temperature of the North Atlantic, and of the latter upon the Temperature and Pressure over our Islands; the Gulf Stream, and many other papers and memoirs on Meteorology, Oceanography, and Navigation. *Address:* 2 Amherst Road, Ealing. *T.:* Ealing 1308.
(*Died 25 Feb. 1919.*)

HERBERT, Sir Arthur (James), G.C.V.O., *cr.* 1908; C.V.O. 1905; *b.* 22 Aug. 1855, 2nd *s.* of J. A. Herbert, of Llanarth, Monmouthshire; *m.* Helen L. Gammell, Providence, Rhode Island, U.S.A.; one *s. Educ.:* Christ Church, Oxford; M.A. Entered diplomatic service, 1879; has been Secretary at H.M.'s Embassies at Petrograd and Washington, and to Legations at Buenos Ayres, Tehran, Brussels, Berne, Stockholm; was attached to Sir Peter Lumsden's mission for demarcation of Afghan frontier, 1884-85; received allowance for knowledge of Russian and Persian; Secretary of Legation, Copenhagen, 1901; Consul-General Buda-Pesth, 1902; Chargé d'Affaires Darmstadt and Carlsruhe, 1903-5; H.M.'s Minister at Christiania, 1905-10; was appointed Minister to Mexico, 1911, but did not proceed; master of the Monmouthshire Hounds since 1907. *Address:* 1 Hill Street, Knightsbridge, S.W.7; *T.:* Western 3901; Coldbrook, Abergavenny, Monmouthshire. *Clubs:* St. James's, Oxford and Cambridge, Brooks's, Ranelagh, Travellers'.
(*Died 31 Aug. 1921.*)

HERBERT, Hon. Aubrey Nigel Henry Molyneux, F.R.G.S., J.P., D.L., M.P. (U.) Southern Division of Somerset, 1911-18; Yeovil Division since 1918; 2nd *s.* of 4th Earl of Carnarvon; *b.* 3 April 1880; *m.* 1910, Hon. Mary Vesey, only *c.* of 4th Viscount de Vesci; one *s.* three *d. Educ.:* Eton; Balliol, Oxford. After leaving University entered the Diplomatic Service and was appointed Hon. Attaché at Tokio, and afterwards Constantinople; contested S. Somerset in Conservative interest,

Jan. 1910 and Dec. 1910; has travelled extensively both in Near and Far East, including Japan, China, Turkey, Macedonia, Balkans, Yemen; Lieut. Irish Guards, Aug. 1914; wounded and prisoner, France, Sep. 1914; Capt. on General Staff Mediterranean Forces, Dec. 1914; Capt. with Forces, 1915; served in Egypt; 1st landing in Dardanelles and Suvla (White Eagle of Serbia); Temp. Lt.-Col. Adriatic Mission, Dec. 1915; served in Mesopotamia, 1916 (despatches); also Salonica; Parliamentary Sec. to the Chief Secretary for Ireland; served in Italy, 1917-18. *Publications:* Eastern Songs, 1911; Mons, Anzac, and Kut, 1919. *Address:* Pixton Park, Dulverton, Somersetshire; 28 Bruton Street, W. *T.:* Dulverton 5, Mayfair 2292. *M.:* AA 3311, Y 965. *Clubs:* Travellers', Bath, St. James's, Athenæum.   *(Died 26 Sept. 1923.)*

HERBERT, Lt. - Col. Charles, C.S.I. 1909; *b.* 16 May 1854; *e. s.* of late Maj.-Gen. Charles Herbert; *m.* 1882, Edith Helen, *d.* of Edward Sharpe Marriott; three *d.* Entered army, 45th Regt., 1874; Extra A.D.C. to Viceroy of India, 1878-82; Adjutant Deoli Irregular Force, 1880; Magistrate of Abu, 1882; Assistant Commissioner, Ajmer, 1889; officiating Political Agent in Eastern States, Rajputana, 1891-92; Political Agent, Kotah, 1894; Eastern States of Rajputana, 1900; Resident, Gwalior, 1901; in charge of ex-Ameer, 1904; Resident Jaipur, 1905-9. *Address:* Wyvern Cottage, Frant, Sussex.   *(Died 24 June 1919.)*

HERBERT, Col. Edward William, C.B. 1902; late King's Royal Rifles; retired; *e. s.* of Robert C. Herbert, 4th *s.* of 2nd Earl of Powis; *b.* 22 March 1855; *m.* 1887, Beatrice Anne, *d.* of Sir Hedworth Williamson, 8th Bt.; two *s.* two *d.* Entered army, 1874; Captain, 1888; Major, 1884; Lieut.-Col. 1898; Colonel, 1902; commanding Rifle Depot, Winchester, 1904; served Zulu War, 1879 (medal with clasp); Soudan, 1884 (brevet Major, medal with clasp, Khedive's Star); South Africa, 1901-2 (despatches, medal with 2 clasps, C.B.). *Address:* Herbert Park, Armidale, New South Wales. *Clubs:* Carlton, Naval and Military.   *(Died 28 Dec. 1924.)*

HERBERT, Sir Jesse, Kt., *cr.* 1911; F.R.G.S.; J.P.; Political Secretary to Liberal Chief Whip; Hon. Treasurer Liberal Central Association; *b.* Reading, 1851; 3rd *s.* of late Jesse Herbert, Reading, and Jane Anne, *d.* of late James Knight, Reading; *m.* 1888, Eveline, *d.* of Charles Warner, St. George's Square, London; three *s.* one *d.* *Educ.:* Reading; London University (matriculated 1872). Called to Bar, Middle Temple; First Mayor of Royal Borough of Sutton Coldfield; Professor of International Law at Canton University; Legal Adviser to South China Government. *Recreations:* chess, painting, and fishing. *Address:* 21 Abingdon Street, S.W.; Sudbury Hill, Harrow; The Shameen, West Mersea, Essex. *T.A.:* Animation, London. *T.:* Victoria 2119, P.O. Harrow 164.   *(Died 26 Dec. 1916.)*

HERBERT, William de Bracy, Barrister-at-law; Recorder of Newcastle-under-Lyme, since 1927; *b.* 14 Mar. 1872; *e. s.* of William Hawkins Herbert, J.P., Painswick, Glos.; *m.* 1899, Frances Winifred, *d.* of late Major Thomas Berington. *Educ.:* Harrow; Trinity College, Cambridge (M.A., LL.M.). Called to Bar, Inner Temple, 1893; Editor of Law Times, Law Times Reports, Cox's Criminal Cases, and Paterson's Practical Statutes; Secretary of Prime Minister's Committee as to persons not of British or allied parentage in Government offices, 1918-19; Secretary of Ministry of Health enquiry into London Lock Hospitals, 1928. *Publications:* Law of Banks and Bankers; Law of Fixtures and Repairs; Editor of Evans on Commission Agents and Saunders on Affiliation. *Address:*

4 Elm Court, Temple, E.C. *T.:* Central 1350; Windsor House, Bream's Buildings, E.C. *T.:* Holborn 3682. *Clubs:* Savile, M.C.C.   *(Died 10 Nov. 1928.)*

HERDMAN, Robert Duddingstone, A.R.S.A. 1908; *b.* 1863; 2nd *s.* of Robert Herdman, R.S.A.; *m.* 1896, Edna, *d.* of Henry Norman of Leicester; one *s.* one *d.* *Educ.:* Edinburgh Academy and University; studied Art at the R.S.A. school, studios in Paris, and the galleries of Madrid and Holland. Chairman of the Society of Scottish Artists, 1898; exhibited figure subjects and portraits chiefly in Edinburgh, London, Paris, Vienna, Munich, etc. *Recreation:* mechanics. *Address:* St. Bernard's Tower, Bruntsfield Crescent, Edinburgh.   *(Died 9 Jan. 1922.)*

HERDMAN, Sir William Abbott, Kt. *cr.* 1922; C.B.E. 1920; D.Sc., Hon. D.Sc. Harvard, Durham, Sydney, and Western Australia, Hon. LL.D. Edinburgh, F.R.S., F.L.S.; Professor of Natural History, University of Liverpool, 1881-1919; Professor of Oceanography 1919-21; *b.* Edinburgh, 8 Sep. 1858; *e. s.* of Robert Herdman, R.S.A.: *m.* 1st, Sarah Wyse Douglas; 2nd, Jane Brandreth Holt (*d.* 1922); three *d.* *Educ.:* Edin. Academy and University. Graduated 1879; assist. to Sir Wyville Thomson in "Challenger" Expedition office; Demonstrator of Zoology in Edinburgh University, 1880; President Zoological Section British Association, 1895; General Secretary British Association, 1903; President of British Association for 1920; President of Linnean Society, 1904; Foreign Secretary Royal Society, 1916; has (along with others) established a Marine Biological Station at Port Erin, Isle of Man, and a Sea-Fish Hatchery at Piel, near Barrow; is Honorary Director of Scientific Work to the Lancashire Sea-Fisheries Committee; was sent to Ceylon in 1901-2 to investigate the Pearl-Oyster Fisheries for the Government. *Publications:* Report upon the Tunicata collected during the voyage of the "Challenger," 3 vols. 1882-89; The Invertebrate Fauna of the Firth of Forth; (with others) The Fauna of Liverpool Bay, 5 vols. 1886-1900; Oysters and Disease, 1896-99; The Phylogenetic Classification of Animals; Fishes and Fisheries of the Irish Sea, 1902; Report to the Government on the Ceylon Pearl-Oyster Fisheries, Royal Society, 5 vols. 1903-6; Spolia Runiana I.-V. and about fifty other papers on Zoological subjects. *Recreations:* yachting (S. yacht Runa); much interested in early archæology. *Address:* Croxteth Lodge, Liverpool; Rowany, Port Erin, Isle of Man. *T.A.:* University, Liverpool. *T.:* Wavertree 691. *M.:* O 7646. *Clubs:* Athenæum, University, Athenæum, Liverpool; Royal Mersey Yacht.   *(Died 21 July 1924.)*

HERDT, Louis A., D.Sc., E.E., F.R.S.Can.; Professor of Electrical Engineering, McGill University, Montreal, since 1909; Hon. Secretary, A.I.E.E.; Member, I.E.E.; Officier d'Académie France; *b.* Trouville, France, 1872; widower; two *s.* *Educ.:* McGill University, Montreal; École Supérieure d'Electricité, Paris; Institut Electrotechnique, Montefiore, Liège, Belgium; On Staff of Electrical Dept. McGill University since 1899; has also carried on a consulting practice; Consulting Electrical Engineer for the City of Winnipeg on a large Hydro Electric Development; Technical Expert, Ottawa Electric Co., Ottawa, Can., City of Montreal, Montreal, Can., Dominion Government, Canada, etc.; Chairman Canadian National Committee, International Electrotechnical Commission; Chairman Montreal Electric Service Commission; Vice - Chairman Montreal Tramways Commission. *Publications:* Predetermination of Alternator Characteristics, Proceedings A.I.E.E., 1902; Use of Electricity on Canals,

HERBERT, Hilary A., LL.D. See page xxi.

Proceedings Can. Soc. C.E., 1904; Oscillographic Researches, Proceedings Can. Soc. C.E., 1904; Armature Reaction - Alternators, Electrical Review, 1906; Chart Calculation, Transmission Lines; Electrolytic Lightning Arresters; Electrolysis in Water Mains; Constant Voltage Operation of a High Voltage Transmission System; The Problem of the Electrical Railways, Electrical News. *Address:* Electrical Department, McGill University, Montreal, Canada. *Clubs:* Engineers', Montreal, Montreal. (*Died Mar. 1926.*)

HERIOT, Maj.-Gen. Mackay A. H. J.; *b.* 1889; *s.* of William Mackay Heriot, Major, Royal Marines; *m.* 1867, Rosa, *d.* of Thomas Fisher, M.D. of Canterbury, New Zealand; two *s.* one *d. Educ.:* private tutor. Served in China Expedition, 1857-59-60; was at the capture of Taku Forts and final surrender of Pekin, storming of Canton, etc.; Colonel Commandant, Plymouth Division, Royal Marine Light Infantry, 1889-1902; commanded Plymouth Volunteer Brigade, 1893-1901. *Recreations:* fishing, hunting, and shooting. *Address:* 19 Campden Hill Gardens Kensington, W. *T.:* Park 599. *Club:* Flyfishers'.(*Died 18 Nov. 1918.*)

HERKLESS, Very Rev. Sir John, Kt., *cr.* 1917; D.D.; LL.D.; Vice-Chancellor and Principal of the University of St. Andrews, and Principal of the United College of St. Salvator and St. Leonard since 1915; *b.* Glasgow, 9 Aug. 1855; *y. s.* of William Herkless, engineer, Glasgow. *Educ.:* Glasgow High School; Glasgow University; Jena University. Tutor in English Literature, Queen Margaret College, Glasgow; assistant-minister, St. Matthew's Parish Church, Glasgow, 1881-83; minister of the parish of Tannadice, 1883-94; Regius Professor of Ecclesiastical History, St. Andrews Univ., 1894-1915; Provost of St. Andrews, 1911-15; Chairman of Fife County Insurance Committee, 1913-15. *Publications:* Cardinal Beaton, Priest and Politician, 1891; Richard Cameron (Famous Scots Series), 1896; The Church of Scotland (Our Churches, and why we belong to them), 1897; Francis and Dominic, 1901; Introductions and Notes to Hebrews, etc., in Temple Bible, 1902; The Early Christian Martyrs, 1904; The College of St. Leonard, 1905; The Archbishops of St. Andrews, vol. i. 1907, vol. ii. 1909, vol. iii. 1910, vol. iv. 1913, vol. v. 1916; The Robert Lee Lecture, 1913. *Recreation:* golf. *Address:* The University House, St. Andrews. *Clubs:* Royal and Ancient, St. Andrews; University, Edinburgh.
(*Died 11 June 1920.*)

HERMAN, Mrs. (E.); Author and Journalist; *m.* Rev. M. Herman, F.R.G.S., a minister of the Presbyterian Church of England. *Educ.:* London. Regular contributor to British and American journals and periodicals; Assist. Editor of Everyman, 1913; Editor of The Presbyterian, 1913 until its suspension on account of the War: Assistant-Editor of The Challenge, 1921-2. *Publications:* Eucken and Bergson; their Significance for Christian Thought, 1912; 5th edition, 1914; The Meaning and Value of Mysticism, 1915; 3rd edition, 1922; Christianity in the New Age, 1919; Creative Prayer, 1921; 2nd edition, 1922; article Quietism in Hastings' Encyclopædia of Religion and Ethics, vol. x., 1918; under pseudonym of Hugh Sinclair— Voices of To-day: Studies of Representative Modern Preachers, 1912. *Recreations:* country rambles; walking; Celtic mythology, poetry, and folklore. *Address:* 42 Upper Clapton Road, E.5. *Club:* Writers'. (*Died 2 Dec. 1923.*)

HERON, Rev. James, D.D.; Professor of Ecclesiastical History, Church Polity, and Pastoral Theology, Assembly's College, Belfast, Presbyterian Church in Ireland; *b.* 5 Dec. 1836; closely related to late Capt. Mayne Reid, both being *g. g. s.* of Rev. Thomas Mayne, who came

490

from Scotland to Co. Down in the middle of the 18th century; *m.* 1862. *Educ.:* Royal Academical Institution, Belfast; Queen's College, Belfast; Assembly's College, Belfast; New College, Edinburgh. Graduated in the old Queen's University. Ordained in Muckamore, 1861; installed in Kilrea, Co. Derry, 1869; removed to Dundela, a Belfast suburban congregation, 1874; unanimously called by the General Assembly to succeed Dr. W. D. Killen in the Chair of Church History, 1889; Moderator of General Assembly of Irish Presbyterian Church, 1901. *Publications:* The Church of the Sub-Apostolic Age; The Celtic Church in Ireland; A Short History of Puritanism; with numerous minor works and articles. *Recreation:* reading. *Address:* Assembly's College, Belfast.(*Died 18 April 1918.*)

HERON-MAXWELL, Mrs. (Beatrice), author, journalist, and dramatist; *d.* of late E. B. Eastwick, C.B.; M.P.; F.R.S.; *m.* 1st, Lane Huddart of Brynkir, Carnarvonshire; two *d.*; 2nd, S. H. W. Heron-Maxwell, *s.* of Sir John Heron-Maxwell, 6th Bt. of Springkell. *Educ.:* home. *Publications:* Adventures of a Lady Pearl Broker; What may Happen; A Woman's Soul (with her sister, Florence Eastwick); The Queen Regent; Anne's Sister and The Fifth Wheel (with Florence Eastwick); Through a Woman's Eyes (Essays) in War Museum Library, 1917; The Cup of Trembling (with Florence Eastwick); The Tenth Step; The Silken Noose; and over 700 short stories and serials in leading Magazines; and verses illustrated by herself in Pall Mall Magazine, Pearson's, etc.; Plays—The Moon Spell; The Scarlet Terror The Housekeeper (with Mr. Metcalfe Wood) St. James's Theatre and on tour; The Long Arms; The Call of Birth; An Englishman's Lie; The Caravanners; Fear; Gerrard Double One Double O; The Bull's Eye; The Advocate; The Blue Room, Doña Quixota; Film Play, Atonement; Vice-President of the Society of Women Journalists; Member of Institute of Journalists. *Recreations:* theatres, bridge, petits jeux. *Club:* Ladies' Army and Navy. (*Died 7 Mar. 1927.*)

HERON-MAXWELL, Capt. Sir Ivor Walter, 8th Bt. of Springkell, *cr.* 1683; M.C.; *b.* 13 Nov. 1871; *e. s.* of 7th Bt. and Caroline, *d.* of R. Howard-Brooke, Castle Howard. Avoca, Co. Wicklow; *S.* father, 1910; *m.* 1910, Norah, *d.* of Hon. Francis Parker; one *s.* three *d. Educ.:* Harrow; Trinity College, Cambridge (M.A.). Served European War, 1916-18 (M.C.). *Heir: s.* Patrick Ivor, *b.* 26 July 1916.
(*Died 19 Feb. 1928.*)

HERRICK, Colonel Henry, C.M.G. 1919, D.S.O. 1917; late R.A.M.C.; *b.* 1872; served South African War, 1902 (medal); European War, 1914-17 (despatches, D.S.O.); retired pay, 1927. (*Died 10 May 1928.*)

HERRIES, Hon. Sir William Herbert, K.C.M.G., *cr.* 1920; late Minister of Native Affairs, Customs, and Marine; Minister for Railways and Native Affairs, Government of New Zealand, 1912-19; *b.* London, 19 April 1859; *s.* of H. C. Herries, Barrister-at-Law, and Leonora Emma, *d.* of H. Wickham; *m.* 1889, Catherine Louisa (*d.* 1912), *d.* of E. F. Roche, late of Johnstown, Ireland, and Shaftesbury, N.Z.; no *c. Educ.:* Eton College; Trinity College, Cambridge (B.A.). Left England for New Zealand, 1881; farming in North Island of New Zealand, near Te Aroha, Auckland province; entered N.Z. Parliament, 1896, and sat continuously for Bay of Plenty and afterwards Tauranga electorate. *Address:* Wellington, N.Z. *Clubs:* Athenæum; Northern, Auckland; Wellington, Wellington. (*Died 22 Feb. 1923.*)

HERRING, Lieut.-Col. William, J.P., Norfolk; *b.* 1889; *o. s.* of late Wm. Herring, J.P., of St. Faith's House, Norwich, and Maria Elizabeth (*d.* 1896), *d.* of late George Robinson, of Knapton House, Norfolk ; *m.* 1876, Jessie, *d.* of William Welsby, J.P. Hon. Col. 3rd Batt. King's (Liverpool) Regt. ; Lt.-Col. retired, late Major 27th Inniskillings ; patron of one living. *Address:* Narborough House, Narborough, Norfolk. (*Died 16 May 1917.*)

HERSCHEL, Col. John, R.E., F.R.S. 1871 ; F.R.A.S. 1872 ; Member of Senate, Calcutta University ; late Deputy-Supt. Great Trigonometrical Survey of India ; 3rd and *y. s.* of Sir J. F. W. Herschel, 1st Bt., and *b.* of 2nd Bt. ; *b.* Cape of Good Hope, 29 Oct. 1837 ; *m.* 1867, Mary Cornwallis (*d.* 1876), *d.* of Rev. F. Lipscomb, R. of Welbury, Yorks, and widow of D. Power, Q.C. *Educ.:* Clapham Grammar School, under late Rev. C. Pritchard ; Addiscombe, where he passed through at head of his term. Entered Bengal Engineers, 1856 ; landed India, Jan. 1859, and after 6 months at Rurki was appointed to Gr. Trigonometrical Survey, in which department he served till date of his retirement, 1886 ; was employed by Royal Society to observe total eclipse of sun, 1868 (and again 1871), spectroscopically, and was among the earliest to view the coloured flames through the prism (also without eclipse, shortly after the earlier of these) and thus help to lay foundation of our present vastly extended knowledge of sun's constitution ; he also observed many of southern nebulæ with same instruments : the results of these observations are printed in Proceedings of R. Society, vols. xvi. xvii. etc. *Address:* Observatory House, Slough, Bucks. (*Died 31 May 1921.*)

HERSCHEL, Sir William James, 2nd Bt. ; *cr.* 1838 ; Civil Service, India, 1853-78 ; one of the Secretaries to the Board of Revenue, Calcutta ; Commissioner of Dacca, 1872 ; Cooch Behar, 1874 ; *b.* 9 Jan. 1833 ; *S.* father 1871 ; *m.* Anne Emma Haldane, *d.* of A. Hardcastle, Hatcham House, Surrey, 1864 (*d.* 1873) ; two *s.* one *d. Educ.:* Clapham Grammar School ; Haileybury ; M.A. Oxford. Discovered the use of finger prints, 1859, and after proving their individuality and their persistence for fifteen years, initiated the modern system of identification for civil purposes in Bengal, 1878. *Publications:* A Gospel Monogram ; The Origin of Finger-Printing. *Recreations:* scientific. *Heir: s.* Rev. John Charles William, F.R.A.S. [Vicar of Braywood, 1914 ; *b.* 22 May 1869 ; *m.* 1908, Catharine Margaret, *y. d.* of Col. E. T. Browell, R.A. *Educ.:* Winchester ; Christ Church, Oxford (M.A.) ; Wells Theological College. Ordained, 1906 ; Curate of Bracknell, 1906-8 ; Wooburn, 1908-10 ; Crowthorne, 1910]. *Address:* Rectory House, Warfield, Berks. (*Died 24 Oct. 1917.*)

HERTSLET, Harry Lester, M.V.O., 1902 ; *b.* 1856 ; *y. s.* of late G. T. Hertslet, C.V.O. ; *m.* Marion, *d.* of late C. Matthews of Fouchers, Essex. Entered Lord Chamberlain's Department, 1874 ; Chief Clerk Lord Chamberlain's Department, 1901-8 ; retired, 1908 ; Jubilee medal, 1887, bar, 1897 ; one of the Gold Staff Officers in Westminster Abbey at Coronation of King Edward VII. (medal), and George V. (medal). *Address:* The Old Rectory, Itchenor, nr. Chichester. *T.A.:* Birdham, nr. Chichester. (*Died 6 Aug. 1925.*)

HERVEY, Arthur ; composer and writer on music ; *b.* Paris, 26 Jan. 1855 ; *o. s.* of late C. J. V. Hervey of Killiane, Wexford ; *m.* Clare, *d.* of late Sir Edmund Harrison, and widow of late J. H. Webster. *Educ.:* The Oratory School, near Birmingham. At first intended to enter the diplomatic service, but finally decided to devote himself to music ; studied under Berthold Tours. Orchestral compositions : Dramatic Overture ; Youth, a concert overture composed for Norwich Festival ; Two Tone Pictures, composed for Cardiff Festival ; The Gates of Night, a descriptive ballad for voice and orchestra, composed for Gloucester Festival ; In the East, Tone Poem composed for Cardiff Festival ; Prelude, Ione, Philharmonic Society, 1907 ; Summer, Tone Poem composed for Cardiff Festival of 1907 ; Life Moods, Variations for Orchestra, Brighton Festival of 1910 ; Ilona, opera, 1914, etc. ; has written a large number of songs, including three albums of German Lieder, and many to English, French, or Italian words ; also much music for the piano, violin, and violoncello. *Publications:* Masters of French Music ; French Music in the XIX. Century ; Alfred Bruneau ; Franz Liszt and his Music, 1911 ; Meyerbeer ; Rubinstein ; Saint-Saëns, 1921 ; contributions to supplement of Encyclopædia Britannica. Was for some time musical critic to Vanity Fair, and musical critic, Morning Post, 1892-1908. *Recreations:* music, reading, walking. *Address:* 1 Norfolk Crescent, Hyde Park, W.2 *T.:* 6389 Paddington. *Club:* St. James's. (*Died 10 Mar. 1922.*)

HERZOG, Right Rev. Edward, D.D. ; Bishop of the Old Catholic Church in Switzerland ; *b.* 1841. Ordained priest of Roman Catholic Church, 1867 ; retired, with Dr. von Döllinger and others, from communion with Rome on the definition of papal infallibility by Pius IX., 1870 ; assisted in the inauguration of the Old Catholic movement ; consecrated as first Old Catholic Bishop for Switzerland by the Old Catholic Bishop Reinkens of Bonn, who was consecrated by the Archbishop of Utrecht, 1876. *Address:* 39 Willadingweg, Bern. (*Died Mar. 1924.*)

HESKETH, Lieut.-Colonel James Arthur, C.M.G. 1917 ; D.S.O. 1915 ; Assistant Engineer, Western Lines, Canadian Pacific Railway ; *b.* 1868. *Educ.:* Royal Military College, Canada. Served European War, 1914-1919 (despatches, C.M.G., D.S.O.). *Address:* Winnipeg, Canada.

HESKETH, Sir Thomas George Fermor-, 7th Bt. ; *cr.* 1761 ; late Ensign Rifle Brigade ; Hon. Col. 5th and 6th Batts. Liverpool Regt. ; *b.* 9 May 1849 ; *S.* brother 1876 ; *m.* Florence, *d.* of W. Sharon, San Francisco, 1880 ; two *s.* Owns about 15,200 acres. *Heir: s.* Thomas Fermor-. *Address:* 9 Montagu Square, W.1 ; Park Hall, Towcester ; Eydon Hall, Byfield, Northants. *Clubs:* Carlton, Junior Carlton. (*Died 19 April 1924.*)

HESLOP, Richard Oliver, M.A., F.S.A., J.P. ; Iron and Steel Merchant ; Consul for The Netherlands ; *b.* Newcastle-upon-Tyne, 14 Mar. 1842 ; *s.* of late Joseph Heslop of Wide Open Dykes and The Mount, Co. Cumb., and Elizabeth, *d.* of Capt. Hy. Brough Oliver, 8th (King's) Regt. of Foot ; *m.* 1867, Margaret Webster, *d.* of late Cuthbert Harrison of Newcastle ; one *d.* two *s. Educ.:* Royal Grammar School, Newcastle. Hon. M.A. Dunelm., 1901 ; a Vice-President, Newcastle Society of Antiquaries ; a Vice-President of the Surtees Society, and President of the Literary and Philosophical Society, Newcastle. *Publications:* Northumberland Words, a Glossary (English Dialect Society, 1892) ; A Bibliography of the Northumberland Dialect (English Dialect Society, 1896) ; papers contributed to various societies on philological, historical, and archæological subjects. *Address:* 12 Eskdale Terrace, Newcastle upon-Tyne. (*Died 3 Mar. 1916.*)

HESPELER, Hon. Wilhelm ; late German Consul ; retired ; *b.* 29 Dec. 1850, Baden-Baden, Germany ; *m.* Katherine Keutshie ; one *s. Educ.:* Karlsruhe ; Baden. Miller and distiller for 14 years up to 1872, at Waterloo, Ontario, afterwards Immigration Commissioner for the Dominion of Canada at Winnipeg ; Speaker of the Legislature of the Province of Manitoba, 1902-6 ; member of the Royal Trust Company of Canada, and member of the Winnipeg Board ; also member of the Board of the

North of Scotland Mortgage Company, Winnipeg branch. *Address:* Winnipeg, Manitoba, Canada. *T.:* Main 8400. *M.:* 4146. *Club:* Manitoba, Winnipeg.

HETHERINGTON, Ivystan; *s.* of Henry Mellor Hetherington (formerly of the Bank of England); *m.* 1912, Edith May Madeleine, *d.* of late Alfred Howlett. *Educ.:* home; Univ. Coll. School. From Heatherley's School of Art became a student at the Royal Academy, and first exhibited there, 1877; has frequently exhibited at the Grosvenor and New Galleries. *Pictures:* When Autumn wreathes its Spell around the Year; An Old-fashioned Summer; Osiers, Langdale Farm; The Manor Garden; A Misty Moonrise; The Silent Marsh; With rushing Wind and gathering Storm, etc. *Recreations:* various. *Address:* 18 Loudoun Road, St. John's Wood, N.W. *Club:* Arts.   (*Died 23 Dec. 1917.*)

HEWAT, Col. Sir John, Kt., *cr.* 1919; M.B., C.M. (Edin.); J.P.; medical practitioner; Captain (retired) of Cape Garrison Artillery; J.P. for Cape; late M.L.A. for Woodstock, C.P., 1904-10 and 1910-20; *b.* Sarawak, Borneo, 26 Dec. 1863; *s.* of late Capt. John Hewat, Dock Superintendent, Cape Town; *m.* 1886, Lily, *d.* of late A. Teesdale, Liverpool; two *s.* two *d.* *Educ.:* Edinburgh; S.A. College, Cape Town. Chief Whip Union Party; Government Nominee School Board, Cape Division; Vice-Pres. S.A. National Union; S.A. Delegate to Coronation King George V.; Chairman S.A. Delegates to War Zone, 1915; Chairman S.A. Branch Empire Parliamentary Association; Chief M.O. General Life and Accident Insurance Co.; a Steward of the S.A. Turf Club; President of the Cape Colony Athletic and Cycling Union; Medals—Coronation, Union, Boer War, General Service 1914-19, despatches, 1914 Star; Officer of the Crown of Belgium. *Address:* Woodstock, Cape Colony. *Clubs:* Sports; City, Civil Service, Cape Town.   (*Died 21 Aug. 1928.*)

HEWBY, Louis John, C.B. 1912; *b.* 1871; *s.* of late J. P. Hewby; unmarried. *Educ.:* St. Paul's School; Magdalen College, Oxford. Served as a clerk in the Treasury, 1895-1908; Treasury Remembrancer and Deputy Paymaster for Ireland, 1908; returned to the Treasury as a Principal Clerk, 1912; Assistant Secretary, 1919; retired, 1921. *Address:* 29 Ladbroke Grove, W. *Clubs:* Oxford and Cambridge; University, Dublin.   (*Died 3 Jan. 1925.*)

HEWITT, Edgar Percy, K.C. 1912, LL.D.; *s.* of late William Henry Hewitt, Lancaster Gate, Hyde Park, and Shanklin, Isle of Wight, afterwards of Purlieu, Hythe, Southampton; *m.* 1898, Mabel, *d.* of late George Fuller Sandys; one *s.* two *d.* Called to Bar; passed first in the 1st class of Honours for LL.B. at University of London and was awarded Law Scholarship, 1888; LL.D. London, 1890; Bencher, Lincoln's Inn, 1916. *Publications:* Hewitt on the Statutes of Limitations; The Taxes on Land Values; edited 4th ed. of Kerr on Injunctions, and 9th ed. of White and Tudor's Leading Cases. *Address:* 46 Harrington Gardens, S.W.7; 14 Old Square, Lincoln's Inn, W.C.2; *T.:* Holborn 0419. *T.:* Kens. 4827. *Clubs:* Carlton, 1900, United, 1912.
     (*Died 24 Dec. 1928.*)

HEWITT, Sir Frederic (William), Kt., *cr.* 1911; M.V.O. 1902; Anæsthetist to His Majesty the King; Physician - Anæsthetist to St. George's Hospital; Consulting Anæsthetist and Emeritus Lecturer on Anæsthetics at the London Hospital; Fellow of the Royal Society of Medicine. M.A., M.D., Cantab.; M.R.C.S., Eng.; *b.* 2 July 1857; *s.* of late George Frederick Hewitt of Badbury, Wilts; *m.* 1891, Eve, *d.* of late George Clare; one *s.* two *d.* *Publications:* Anæsthetics and their Administration, 4th edition, 1912; and articles on anæsthetics in Treves's

492

System of Surgery and other works. *Address:* 24 Harcourt House, Cavendish Square, W. *Club:* Savile. *T.:* Paddington 369.
     (*Died 6 Jan. 1916.*)

HEWITT, Lt.-Col. Sir Joseph, 1st Bt., *cr.* 1921; Kt., *cr.* 1919; Hon. Lieut.-Col. in the Army; J.P., Barnsley; Solicitor and colliery owner; *b.* 14 Oct. 1865; *m.* 1891, Margaret Eliza, *d.* of George Guest of Barnsley; one *s.* four *d.* *Heir:* *s.* Joseph, *b.* 8 Sep. 1907. *Address:* Ouslethwaite Hall, Barnsley, Yorks; The Crescent, Filey, Yorks. *Clubs:* Junior Carlton, Constitutional.   (*Died 8 Feb. 1923.*)

HEWITT, Sir Thomas, Kt., *cr.* 1904; K.C., Sheriff of Devon, 1908; J.P. for Devon and London; Barrister - at - law; 3rd *s.* of Halford Wotton Hewitt, J.P. Lichfield; *m.* 1st, Elizabeth Jane, *d.* of Mrs. Keppel of Snettisham Hall, Norfolk, and her 1st husband, R. R. Wilson; 2nd, Fanny Dugard, *d.* of John R. Powles, Eastwood Park, Greta Bridge, Yorks; three *s.* one *d.* *Educ.:* Lichfield Grammar School; High School, Darmstadt; Inner Temple. Captain 40th Middlesex R.V. (Gray's Inn), 1866-70; Captain National Reserve, London Division, 1913; late Counsel and Clerk to Commissioners of Taxes for City of London; Q.C. 1899; President London Arbitration Court, 1901-6; contested N.W. Cornwall, 1906; Mayor of the Royal Borough of Kensington, 1912-13; practised chiefly in Revenue cases; for 23 years Director, and 20 years Chairman of The Ocean Accident and Guarantee Insurance Corporation; Chairman of Lynton and Barnstaple Railway Co; Director of Lynton Cliff Railway Co. *Publications:* Westminster Papers, edited, 1862-1864; Hewitt on Corporation Duty, 1892. *Address:* 9 Queen's Gate, S.W.7; The Hoe, Lynton, Devon. *T.:* Kensington 415. *Clubs:* Reform, Albemarle, Ranelagh.
     (*Died 8 Jan. 1923.*)

HEWLETT, Maurice Henry; *b.* 22 Jan. 1861; *e. s.* of Henry Gay Hewlett of Shaw Hill, Addington, Kent; *m.* 1888, Hilda Beatrice, 2nd *d.* of late Rev. George William Herbert, Vicar of St. Peter's, Vauxhall. *Educ.:* London International College, Spring Grove, Isleworth. Barr. 1891; Keeper of Land Revenue Records and Enrolments, 1896-1900; Academic Committee, R.S.L., 1910; J.P., County Alderman, Wilts. *Publications:* Earthwork out of Tuscany, 1895; The Masque of Dead Florentines, 1895; Songs and Meditations, 1897; The Forest Lovers, 1898; Pan and the Young Shepherd, 1898; Little Novels of Italy, 1899; Richard Yea-and-Nay, 1900; New Canterbury Tales, 1901; The Queen's Quair, 1904; The Road in Tuscany, 1904; Fond Adventures; The Fool Errant, 1905; The Stooping Lady, 1907; Half-way House, 1908; Open Country, 1909; Artemision: Idylls and Songs, 1909; Rest Harrow, 1910; Brazenhead the Great, 1911; The Agonists, 1911; The Song of Renny, 1911; Mrs. Lancelot, 1912; Helen Redeemed and Other Poems; Lore of Proserpine, 1913; Ben-dish: A Study in Prodigality, 1913; A Lovers' Tale, 1915; The Little Iliad, 1915; Frey and his Wife; Gai Saber: tales and songs, 1916; The Song of the Plow, 1916; Thorgils of Treadholt, 1917; Peridore and Paravail, 1917; The Village Wife's Lament, 1918; Flowers in the Grass (poems) 1920; In a Green Shade, 1920; Wiltshire Essays, 1922. *Address:* Broadchalke, Salisbury. *Club:* Athenæum.
     (*Died 15 June 1923.*)

HEXT, Rear-Admiral Sir John (retired), K.C.I.E., *cr.* 1897; *b.* 14 Oct. 1842; *s.* of Rev. J. Hext; *m.* 1st, 1874, Lilian Mary (*d.* 1893), *d.* of David Mitchell; 2nd, 1902, Jean (*d.* 1913), *d.* of Rev. W. Davidson. *Educ.:* Marlborough. Entered R.N. 1857; Ashantee, 1873; Egyptian War, 1882; Director of Royal Indian Marine, 1883 to Feb. 1898. *Address:* St. Benets, Newton Abbot, Devon.   (*Died 8 May 1924.*)

HAYDON, Hon. Louis Francis, M.L.C. since 1887; *b.* Sydney, 1848; *m.* Mary, *d.* of Edward Gell; one *s.* one *d.* M.L.A., 1881; Minister of Justice, N.S.W., 1884. *Address:* 117 Pitt Street, Sydney, N.S.W.

HEYGATE, Capt. Richard Lionel, J.P., late M.F.H. N. Herefordshire; 2nd *s.* of Major Edward Nicholas Heygate, R.E. (*d.* 1896); *b.* 1859; *m.* 1895, Eleanor Mary, *d.* of E. J. Evans; two *d.* Captain R.A., 1889-96; Major, 1915. *Address:* The Wells, Bromyard. *Club:* Naval and Military. (*Died 26 Nov. 1926.*)

HEYGATE, Colonel Robert Henry Gage, D.S.O., late Lieut.-Colonel commanding 1st Border Regiment: *b.* London, 26 July 1859; 2nd *s.* of Sir Frederick W. Heygate, 2nd Bt. of Bellarena. *Educ.:* Eton; Sandhurst. Entered army, 1878; Maj. 1896; employed on staff Egyptian Army, 1893-98; served Egyptian Campaign, 1896-98 (despatches); Dongola Campaign, 1896, including engagement at Firket (D.S.O., Khedive's medal, two clasps); in operations, 1897-98 (British medal, 4th class Osmanieh, clasp); South Africa, 1899-1900 (wounded, Colenso, despatches, Queen's medal, 2 clasps); retired 1909. *Address:* Bellarena, Co. Derry. *Club:* Naval and Military.

(*Died 28 Aug. 1923.*)

HEYWOOD, Sir Arthur Percival, 3rd Bt., *cr.* 1838; J.P. Cos. Derby and Stafford; *b.* 25 Dec. 1849; *s.* of 2nd Bt. and Margaret (*d.* 1894), *d.* of late Thomas Heywood of Hope End, Herefordshire; *S.* father 1897; *m.* 1872, Margaret Effie, *e. d.* of Rt. Rev. G. H. Sumner (Bp. of Guildford); three *s.* six *d.* *Educ.:* Trinity Coll. Camb., M.A.; High Sheriff, Derbyshire, 1899. *Publication:* Bell Towers, 1914. *Heir:* *s.* Graham Percival, J.P., D.L., *b.* 14 July 1878. *Address:* Doveleys, Rocester, Staffs.; Claremont, near Manchester; Duffield Bank, near Derby. *T.A.:* Rocester. *Club:* Athenæum. (*Died 19 April 1916.*)

HEYWOOD, Bertram Charles Percival, M.A., J.P., T.D.; *b.* 10 Nov. 1864; 2nd *surv. s.* of Sir T. Percival Heywood, 2nd Bart., of Claremont, Lancashire, and Doveleys, Rocester; *m.* 1889, Florence Maud, *d.* of late E. David Meynell, of Kirk Langley, Derby. *Educ.:* Winchester; Trinity College, Cambridge. Served in S.A. War as Capt. commanding 1st Vol. Co. Manchester Regt. (Queen's medal with three clasps); Hon. Capt. in Army, 1901; commanded 2nd V.B. (now 6th Batt.) Manchester Regt., 1902-6; Manchester Infantry Brigade, 1906-11. *Address:* Wootton Lodge, Ashbourne. *Club:* Arts. (*Died 27 Oct. 1914.*)

HEYWOOD, James Barnes, I.S.O. 1905; formerly Secretary to the Treasury, New Zealand; *m.* *Address:* Abbey Hill, Winchester, Hants. (*Died 2 Aug. 1924.*)

HEYWORTH, Brig.-Gen. Frederic James, C.B., 1915; D.S.O. 1900; *b.* 25 Mar. 1863; *m.* 1913, Mrs. Hatfeild-Harter. Entered army, 1883; Captain, 1896; Major, 1900; Lt.-Col. 1908; Col. 1911: served Soudan, 1885 (medal with clasp, Khedive's star); South Africa, 1899-1902 (despatches, D.S.O., Queen's medal, 6 clasps, King's medal, 2 clasps); European War, 1914-15 (despatches, C.B.). *Address:* Biddlesden Park, Brackley. *Clubs:* Guards', Turf. (*Died 10 May 1916.*)

HIBBERT, Col. Godfrey Leicester, C.B. 1917; C.M.G. 1919; D.S.O. 1900; late The King's Own; *s.* of Leicester Hibbert of Crofton Grange, Orpington; *b.* 31 Jan. 1864; *m.* 1902, Mabel, *y. d.* of late Lieut.-Gen. E. Faunce. *Educ.:* Cheltenham College. Entered army, 1884; Captain, 1891; Major, 1900; served South Africa, 1900-1902 (despatches, Queen's medal, 3 clasps); European War, 1915-18 (despatches C.M.G.). *Club:* Naval and Military.

(*Died 28 Mar. 1924.*)

HIBBERT, Sir Henry Flemming, 1st Bart., *cr.* 1919; Kt., *cr.* 1903; J.P.; D.L.; LL.D. (Victoria); F.R.G.S.; F.Z.S.; Chairman Lancashire County Council, 1921-27; *b.* 4 April 1850; *e. s.* of Isaac Hibbert; *m.* 1883, Marion, *d.* of E. Reuss; three *d.* Mayor of Chorley, 1889-1891; Freeman of London, 1903, and of Borough of Chorley; M.P. (U.) Chorley Division, Lancs, 1913-18; late member of Consultative Committee of Board of Education; Member of Science in Education Committee. *Heir:* none. *Address:* Dalegarth, Chorley, Lancs. *T.A.:* Hibbert Chorley. *T.:* Chorley 24. *Club:* Constitutional. (*Died 15 Nov. 1927.*)

HICHENS, Rev. Frederick Harrison, M.A.; Honorary Canon Canterbury Cathedral since 1897; *b.* East Dulwich, 22 April 1836; *s.* of Robert Hichens, stockbroker, and Jane Snaith; three *s.* two *d.* *Educ.:* Chudleigh Grammar School; King's College, London; Exeter College, Oxford (scholar). Deacon, 1861; Priest, 1862; Curate of Sunningdale, Berks, 1861-63; Speldhurst, Kent, 1863-79; resident at Clifton, Bristol, 1879-85; Rector of Hackington (or St. Stephens), Canterbury, 1885; removed from Kent to Cornwall, ten or eleven years ago; composed many hymns, chants, and kyries, some of which were used at Canterbury Diocesan Choral Festivals. *Recreation:* music. *Address:* Pennance House, Falmouth, Cornwall. (*Died 13 Oct. 1921.*)

HICHENS, Rev. Thomas Sikes, M.A.; Hon. Canon Peterboro', 1899. *Educ.:* Exeter College, Oxford. Vicar of Guilsborough, 1864-1902. *Address:* Woodlane House, Falmouth. (*Died 24 Mar. 1916.*)

HICKEY, Emily Henrietta, poet and prose-writer; lecturer on English Language and Literature; Macmine Castle, Co. Wexford; *b.* 12 April 1845, 2nd *d.* of Rev. Canon Hickey, and *g.d.* of "Martin Doyle." *Educ.:* home; private school; lectures at University College, and Cambridge Correspond. Classes. Holds Cambridge University 1st Class Honours Certificate with various marks of Distinction (Higher Local Examination). Co-founder, with Dr. Furnivall, of the Browning Society, 1881. *Publications:* A Sculptor, and other Poems, 1881; Verse Tales, Lyrics, and Translations, 1889; Michael Villiers, Idealist, and other Poems, 1891; Poems, 1896; Strafford, by Robert Browning (edited and annotated), 1884; Our Lady of May and other Poems, 1902; Havelok the Dane (from Old English), 1902; The Dream of the Holy Rood, 1903; Thoughts for Creedless Women, 1905; A Parable of a Pilgrim, etc.. Selections from Walter Hylton (edited), 1907; Lois, 1908; Our Catholic Heritage in English Literature, 1910; Litanies of the Most Holy Rosary, 1910; George Leicester, Priest, 1910; Prayers from the Divine Liturgy, 1910; Later Poems, 1913; Devotional Poems, 1922; Jesukin and other Christmastide Poems, 1924; several Short Stories; many literary papers; contributed to many English and American magazines. *Address:* c/o National Bank, Ltd., High Street, N.W.1.

(*Died 9 Sept. 1924.*)

HICKLEY, Victor North, C.I.E. 1913; V.D.; Late Commandant Behar Light Horse; *b.* 31 Dec. 1858; *s.* of late Thomas Allen Hickley, Walton-on-Thames; *m.* 1886, Alice, 3rd *d.* of late John Haig; one *d.* *Educ.:* Eton; Exeter College, Oxford. *Recreations:* polo and other sports. *Address:* c/o H. S. King and Co., 65 Cornhill, E.C.3. *Club:* Junior Army and Navy. (*Died 16 Feb. 1923.*)

HICKS, Rt. Rev. Edward Lee, Bishop of Lincoln since 1910; *b.* Oxford, 18 Dec. 1843; *m.* 1876, Agnes Mary, *d.* of Rev. Edwin Trevelyan-Smith, sometime Vicar of Cannock; two *s.* two *d.* *Educ.:* Magdalen College School, Oxford; Brasenose Coll. Oxford (Scholar); B.A.

493

1866; 1st Class in Classics in Moderations and in Greats; Chancellor's University Prize (Latin Essay), 1867; Craven Univ. Scholar. Fellow and Tutor of Corpus Christi Coll. Oxford, 1866; Rector of Fenny Compton, near Leamington, 1873; 1st Principal of Hulme Hall, Manchester, 1886; Canon Residentiary of Manchester Cathedral and Rector St. Philip's, Salford, 1892-1910; Rural Dean of Salford; Vice-President and late Hon. Sec. of United Kingdom Alliance; Select Preacher at Oxford; Examining Chaplain to Bishop of Manchester; Hon. Fellow of C.C.C. Oxford. *Publications:* Greek Inscriptions in the British Museum, 1874, 1886, 1890; Manual of Greek Historical Inscriptions, 1882; 2nd ed., 1901; Inscriptions of Cos (with W. R. Paton), 1891; Henry Bazely the Oxford Evangelist, 1886: Addresses on the Temptation, 1903; various articles in the Hellenic Journal; Building in Troublous Times (visitation charge), 1912. *Recreations:* music, temperance agitation, reading. *Address:* Old Palace, Lincoln.

(*Died 14 Aug. 1919.*)

HICKS, Rev. Herbert S., M.A. Cath. Coll., Camb.; V.D.; Rural Dean of Tynemouth; Hon. Canon of Newcastle; *b.* Sturmer Rectory, Essex; his father was Lieut. R.N. before taking orders, and was a midshipman on H.M.S. Conqueror at the battle of Trafalgar; *m.* Minnie, *d.* of late Rev. W. Syer, Rector of Kedington, Suffolk; one *s.* five *d. Educ.:* private schools. Ordained by Bishop of Manchester to Curacy of St. Peter, Halliwell, 1858; Curate of Whixoe, Suffolk, 1860; Vicar of St. Peter's, North Shields, 1860; Vicar of Tynemouth Priory, 1881-1910; Senior Chaplain to T.R.G.A. Vol., 1881-1902. *Publications:* Sermons; History of England in Rhyme; History of Tynemouth Priory. *Recreations:* interested in all outdoor sports and recreations. *Address:* The Orchard, Great Cornard, Sudbury, Suffolk. *M.:* CF 7343. *Club:* Conservative, Sudbury.

(*Died 11 Nov. 1928.*)

HICKS, William Edward, editor Western Daily Press since 1891; *b.* 1852. *Educ.:* private school; University College, Bristol. Journalist Worcester Herald, 1872; Western Daily Press, 1872-77; editor Bristol Evening News, 1877-83; leader-writer and assistant editor Western Daily Press, 1883-91; has contributed literary and political articles to various magazines; ex-president Clifton Shakespeare Society. *Recreations:* cricket, golf, cycling, and the drama. *Address:* 8 All Saints' Road, Clifton, Bristol. *T.:* 492. *Club:* Bristol Liberal.

(*Died 7 Feb. 1921.*)

HICKS BEACH, William Frederick; *y. s.* of Sir Michael Hicks Beach, 8th Bart. of Williamstrip Park, Glos., and Netheravon House, Wilts.; *heir. pres.* to baronetcy held by great-nephew, Earl St. Aldwyn; *b.* 16 July 1841; *m.* 1st, 1865, Elizabeth Tyrwhitt-Drake (*d.* 1901); four *s.* three *d.*; 2nd, 1903, Susan Christian. *Educ.:* Eton; Christchurch, Oxford. Has been Magistrate for Gloucestershire since 1879; Chairman of Cheltenham Bench for 8 years; Master of Cotswold Hounds for 8 years, and is Chairman of Hunt Committee; has been Chairman of Board of Guardians for 46 years; is Alderman of C.C. and Chairman of its Public Health Committee; Chairman of Board of Diocesan Finance; Chairman R.D.C. for 46 years, etc.; Patron of one Living; Lord of the Manors of Great Witcombe, Cranham, and Buckle Wood; M.P. (U.) Tewkesbury Division of Gloucestershire, 1916-18; presented with the Freedom of Borough of Cheltenham, 1922. *Address:* Witcombe Park, nr. Gloucester. (*Died 7 Sept. 1923.*)

HICKSON, Robert Rowan Purdon, I.S.O. 1910; M.Inst.C.E., J.P.; Consulting Engineer in connection with Harbour Work, Suva, Fiji; President of the Sydney Harbour

494

Trust since 1901; Chairman of the Managing Committee, Government Dockyard, Biloela, Sydney, N.S.W.; *b.* Dingle, Co. Kerry, 15 Sep. 1842; *s.* of Rev. George Hickson; *m.* 1866, Sophia, *d.* of Rev. Hamilton Haire; five *s.* two *d. Educ.:* private schools; St. Columba College, Dublin. Articled to James Barton, M.Inst.C.E., Engineer-in-Chief of the principal works in the north of Ireland, 1860; Harbour Engineer, Barrow-in-Furness Railway Company, 1871; Engineer-in-Chief for Harbours and Jetties, South Australia, 1876; Engineer-in-Chief and Commissioner for Roads and Bridges, 1889; Engineer-in-Chief for Public Works, 1895; Under Secretary and Commissioner for Roads; retired, 1913. *Recreations:* motoring and aquatic sports. *Address:* Belcoo, Lindfield, New South Wales. *T.A.:* Lindfield. *T.:* J1206. *M.:* 206. *Club:* Australian, Sydney. (*Died 21 June 1923.*)

HICKSON, Maj.-Gen. Sir Samuel, K.B.E., *cr.* 1919; C.B. 1915; M.B.; late R.A.M.C.; *b.* 14 Nov. 1859; 4th *s.* of late Capt. R.M. Hickson, of Dingle, Co. Kerry; *m.* 1903, Elizabeth Constance, *widow* of R. Fry, *y. d.* of late Rev. Canon Bolsher, Cork. *Educ.:* Trinity College, Dublin. Major, 1897; Lt.-Col. 1905; Bt. Col. and Hon. Surgeon to the King, 1913; served South Africa, 1896-97 (despatches, medal with clasp); S. African War, 1899-1901 (despatches, Bt. Lt.-Col., Queen's medal 2 clasps, King's medal 2 clasps); European War, 1914-18 (despatches, C.B., 1914 Star).

(*Died 22 Mar. 1928.*)

HIERN, William Philip, F.R.S. 1903; J.P., F.L.S.; Botanist and Mathematician; Devon County Alderman; *b.* Stafford, 19 Jan. 1839; *s.* of late J. G. Hiern and Ann, *d.* of James Webb; *m.* 1868, Martha Bamford. *Educ.:* St. John's College, Cambridge (Fellow 1863-68); has given attention to Systematic Botany and to Mathematics; has made contributions to the Flora of Tropical Africa, British India, S. Africa, etc. *Publications:* Monograph of Ebenaceæ, 1873; Catalogue of African Plants collected by Dr. F. Welwitsch, 1853-61: Dicotyledons, 1896-1900. *Address:* The Castle House, Barnstaple, Devon. (*Died 29 Nov. 1925.*)

HIGGENS, Charles, L.R.C.P., F.R.C.S.; Senior Consulting Ophthalmic Surgeon, Guy's Hospital; Ophthalmic Surgeon to the French Hospital; late Ophthalmic Surgeon, County of London War Hospital. *Publications:* A Manual of Ophthalmic Practice; Hints on Ophthalmic Out-patients Practice; Notes on 925 Extractions of Cataract, Lancet, 1894; on 130 Consecutive Extractions of Cataract without a Failure, Lancet, 1907; other Papers on Cataract and other Eye Affections in Medical Journals. *Address:* 52 Brook Street, W.1. *T.:* Mayfair 4820. *Club:* Bath.

(*Died 28 Dec. 1920.*)

HIGGINS, Clement; *b.* 10 Jan. 1844; *y. s.* of W. Mullinger Higgins of Wrexham; *m.* 1870, Augusta Mary, *o. c.* of Richard Wright of West Bank, near Mansfield; two *s.* one *d. Educ.:* Downing College, Camb. (M.A., Foundation Scholar, Natural Science Tripos). Called to Bar, Inner Temple, 1871; formerly went North Wales, Chester, and Glamorganshire circuit; Recorder of Birkenhead, 1882-1907. *Publications:* A Digest of Patent Cases; The Law and Practice of Patents for Inventions; The Pollution and Obstruction of Water Courses; joint-author of the Electric Lighting Act of 1882. *Address:* 3 Paper Buildings, Temple, E.C.; Winterdyne, Bournemouth West.

(*Died 4 Dec. 1916.*)

HIGGINS, Henry Vincent, C.V.O. 1905; Solicitor; *b.* 18 April 1855; *e. s.* of late Matthew James Higgins ("Jacob Omnium" of The Times), and Emily Blanche, *y. d.* of Sir Henry Tichborne, 8th Bart.; *m.* 1st, 1876, Lady

Hilda Jane Sophia Finch Hatton, *y. d.* of 11th Earl of Winchilsea and Nottingham ; two *s.* ; 2nd, Marie Louise, *d.* of George Parsons of Columbus, Ohio, U.S.A., and *widow* of late W. L. Breese of New York. *Educ.* : Oratory School, Edgbaston ; Merton College, Oxford. Lt. 1st Life Guards, 1876-83 ; Chairman of the Grand Opera Syndicate and Director of the Carlton and Ritz Hotels Companies, London, and Ritz Hotel, Paris. *Address* : 1 Upper Berkeley Street, W.1 ; *T.* : Mayfair 3338 ; 7 Bloomsbury Square, W.C. *Clubs* : Turf, Guards', Beefsteak, Garrick.
(Died 21 Nov. 1928.)

HIGGINS, Right Rev. Michael, D.D., V.G., Canon Theologian of Tuam Chapter since 1905 ; R.C. Auxiliary Bishop of Tuam since 1912 ; *b.* Ballyheane, Castlebar, Co. Mayo, Sep. 1863. *Educ.* : St. Jarlath's College, Tuam ; St. Patrick's College, Maynooth. Student to the Dunboyne Establishment, 1887 ; Priest, 1888 ; spent 13½ years doing Missionary work, 11½ years as Curate and 2 years as Parish Priest ; 11 years teaching in St. Jarlath's College, 4 as Professor and 7 as President ; Hon. D.D. of the Propaganda College, Rome, 1904 ; Parish Priest of Cummer, 1910 ; one of the members of the first Governing Body of University College, Galway. *Address* : St. Mary's, Castlebar, Co. Mayo. *(Died 20 April 1918.)*

HIGGINSON, Gen. Sir George Went-worth Alexander, G.C.B., *cr.* 1903 ; G.C.V.O. ; K.C.B., *cr.* 1889 ; J.P. ; D.L. Bucks.; retired, 1893 ; *b.* 21 June 1826 ; *o. s.* of Gen. George Higginson and Frances, *d.* of 1st Earl of Kilmorey ; *m.* Hon. Florence *(d.* 1912), *d.* of 1st Baron Castletown of Upper Ossory, 1858 ; one *s.* one *d. Educ.* : Eton. Ensign Grenadier Guards, 1845 ; in which regiment served thirty years ; was with it during whole of Crimean War, and twice promoted for service in the field ; commanded Brigade of Guards and Home District, 1879-84 ; Lieut.-Governor of the Tower of London, 1888-93 ; is a Knight of the Legion of Honour ; Knight Grand Cross of the Crown of Italy ; Crimean medal with 4 clasps. *Publication* : Seventy-One Years of a Guards-man's Life, 1916. *Address* : Gyldernscroft, Marlow-on-Thames. *Clubs* : Carlton, Guards'.
(Died 1 Feb. 1927.)

HIGGS, Colonel Frederick William, C.B.E. 1919, M.D., B.S., M.R.C.P. (Lond.), T.D. ; Medical Officer, Ministry of Health ; Assistant Director of Medical Services, 47th (2nd London) Division, Territorial Army ; *e. s.* of Augustus Wm. Higgs, L.R.C.P., of Chelsea, originally of East Hagbourne, Berks, and Jane Fell Parker ; *b.* Harlesden, Middlesex, 18 May 1881 ; *m.* 2nd *d.* of John Walter Scott, M.R.C.S., formerly R.N., of Chandlers Ford, Hants ; two *d. Educ.* : St. George's Hospital. Obtained Medical Qualification, 1904 ; Wm. Brown Exhibi-tioner ; House Surgeon and Physician, Medical Registrar and Tutor, Assistant Curator, Demon-strator of Pathology and Materia Medica, etc., St. George's Hospital, between 1904 and 1912 ; Physician to Belgrave Hospital for Children, 1907-12 ; Divisional Medical Officer, L.C.C. School Medical Service, 1912-20 ; served Queen's Westminster Volunteers, 1897-1901 ; joined Terri-torial Force, 1909 ; served as M.O. to 2nd London Division R.E. and in 2nd London C.C.S. ; com-manded Ambulance Train (Home), C.C.S. (France), A.D.M.S. 66th Division (Belgium) (despatches thrice, C.B.E.) ; A.D.M.S. 47th Div. ; Military Member of County of London Territorial Army Association, and Representa-tive of City and County of London Territorial Army Associations on the Central Joint V.A.D. Council (War Office) ; Assistant District Com-missioner, Sutton Rover Scouts. *Publications* : Contributions to Medical Journals on Children's Diseases, Tuberculosis, etc. *Recreation* : Archæ-ology. *Address* : Dell Quay, Sutton, Surrey ; Ministry of Health, S.W.1. *(Died 26 Mar. 1924.)*

HIGHMORE, Sir Nathaniel Joseph, G.B.E., *cr.* 1920 ; K.C.B., *cr.* 1913 ; Kt., *cr.* 1907 ; *b.* 13 Nov. 1844 ; *s.* of William Highmore, M.D., of Sherborne *(d.* 1883) ; *m.* 1881, Annie Louisa, Order of Mercy, 1918, *d.* of late John Lane Cutcliffe, J.P., Stoke Damerel ; one *d. Educ.* : Sherborne School. Entered Inland Revenue Department, 1864 ; Barr. Middle Temple, 1881 ; assistant solicitor In-land Revenue, 1890-1903 ; solicitor for H.M.'s Customs, 1903-13, and H.M.'s Excise, 1909-13 ; retired, 1913 ; on the panel of Chairmen of Courts of Arbitration under the Conciliation Act 1896 ; resumed duty at the Custom House, 1914, as representative of the Board of Customs and Excise on the Committee on Trade with the Enemy ; Secretary to the War Trade Department, 1915-19. *Publications* : The Ex-cise Laws ; The Stamp Laws ; The Customs Laws, and other works on revenue law. *Ad-dress* : Harbybrowe, Worcester Park, Surrey. *T.* : Malden 69. *(Died 16 April 1924.)*

HILBERS, Ven. George Christopher, M.A., V.D., F.R.N.S. ; Rector of St. Thomas, Haverfordwest, since 1874. *Educ.* : Exeter Coll. Oxford. Archdeacon of St. David's, 1888-1900. *Address* : St. Thomas Rectory, Haverfordwest. *Club* : Oxford and Cambridge. *(Died 3 Nov. 1918.)*

HILDEBRAND, Arthur Hedding, C.I.E. 1888 ; Superintendent and Political Officer, South Shan States, 1887-1902 ; *b.* 1843 ; *m.* 1879, Alice Mary, *d.* of Oliver Gourley Miller, Dundee. *Address* : Ilsington Lodge, Puddletown, Dorsets.
(Died 1 Jan. 1918.)

HILDYARD, Gen. Sir Henry John Thoroton, G.C.B., *cr.* 1911 ; K.C.B., *cr.* 1900 ; Colonel H.L.I. ; *b.* 5 July 1846 ; *s.* of late Thomas Blackborne Thoroton Hildyard, M.P., of Flintham Hall, Newark ; *m.* 1871, Annette, *d.* of late Admiral J. C. Prevost ; three *s. Educ.* : Royal Naval Academy, Gosport. Royal Navy, 1859-64 ; entered army 1867 ; Capt. H.L.I. 1876 ; Major, 1882 ; Bt. Lieut.-Col. 1882 ; Col. 1886 ; temporary Maj.-Gen. 1898 ; Maj.-Gen. 1899 ; served with Egyptian Expedition, 1882, as D.A. and Q.M.G. ; present at Kassassin and Tel-el-Kebir (despatches, medal and clasp, bronze star, 4th class Osmanieh, Brevet Lieut.-Col.) ; was D.A.A.G. and A.A.G. at Headquarters ; A.A.G. Aldershot and Commandant Staff College, 1893-98 ; commanded 3rd Brigade, Aldershot, 1898-99 ; 2nd Brigade, South Africa, 1899-1900 (despatches) ; command 5th Division, South Africa, 1900-1901 (despatches, medal and five clasps, K.C.B.) ; Director-General of Military Education, 1903-4 ; Lieut.-Gen. on Staff com-manding troops, South Africa. 1904-5 ; General Officer Commanding in Chief, S. Africa, 1905-8 ; retired, 1911. *Address* : 20 Eccleston Square, S.W. *T.* : Victoria 1232. *Club* : United Service.
(Died 25 July 1916.)

HILL, 4th Viscount (*cr.* 1842), **Rowland Richa** *d* **Clegg-Hill,** J.P. ; Bt. 1726-27 ; Baron Hill of Almarez and of Hawkstone, Salop, 1814 ; *b.* 12 Feb. 1863 ; *s.* of 3rd Viscount and Mary, *d.* of William Madax ; *S.* father 1895 ; *m.* 1890, Annie, *d.* of William Irwin, Tanrago, Co. Sligo. Capt. 3rd Batt. Royal Warwickshire Regt. 1884-88 ; Member L.C.C. 1910-18 ; Alder-man, 1921 ; doing Home Service duties, 1915-1918. *Heir* : *b.* Hon. F. W. Clegg-Hill ; *b.* 1866. *Address* : 61 Cadogan Square, S.W.1. *Club* : Wellington. *(Died 19 Dec. 1923.)*

HILL, 5th Viscount, *cr.* 1842 ; **Francis Wil-liam Clegg-Hill,** Bt. 1726-27 ; Baron Hill of Almarez and of Hawkstone, Salop, 1814 ; *s.* of 3rd Viscount Hill ; *b.* 4 Nov. 1866 ; *S.* brother 1923 ; *m.* 1905, Caroline, *d.* of Captain F. Corbett of Greenfields, Presteign. *Educ.* : Radley. *Heir* : *half-b.* Lieut.-Col. Hon. Charles Rowland Clegg-Hill, D.S.O. *Club* : Wellington.
(Died 6 July 1924.)

HILL, Alfred John, J.P., C.B.E. 1919 ; M.Inst.C.E., M.I.Mech.E., M.Inst. Transport ;

Past President of Institute of Locomotive Engineers; Whitworth Scholar; b. Peterborough, 1862; s. of late Thomas Hill; m. 1892, Margaretta, d. of late John Bressey, Bournemouth; no c. Educ.: privately. Entered the Locomotive Carriage and Waggon Works of the Great Eastern Railway at Stratford, 1877; promoted by various stages until in 1912 appointed Head of Department (title altered to Chief Mechanical Engineer in 1915); during War was Chairman of Southern Group of Railways for manufacture of munitions, and was sent by H.M. Govt. to U.S.A. on special mission connected with the supply of railway material. Publications: Papers to Inst. Civil Engineers on the Use of Cast Steel in Locomotives, and Repairs and Removals of Railway Rolling Stock. For the first awarded a Miller prize, and for the second a Watt medal and Crampton prize. Recreation: golf. Address: 12 Marina Court Avenue, Bexhill-on-Sea. T.: Bexhill 560. Club: Union. (Died 14 Mar. 1927.)

HILL, Arthur, C.I.E. 1903; Chief Engineer for Irrigation (retired), Bombay Presidency; b. 11 Jan. 1858; s. of Rev. A. Hill, Leicester. Educ.: Coopers Hill. Entered Public Works Department as assistant engineer, 1880. Address: Babbacombe Cliff, Torquay.
(Died 25 April 1927.)

HILL, Arthur, I.S.O.; b. 1854. Was attached to the Marine Department of the Board of Trade for over 47 years. Address: Collins, Westleigh Avenue, Leigh-on-Sea.
(Died 5 Sept. 1927.)

HILL, Capt. Arthur Blundell George Sandys; late Rifle Brigade; b. 13 May 1837; e. s. of Lord George Augusta Hill and Cassandra Jane, y. d. of Edward Knight of Godmersham Park, Kent; m. 1871, Helen Emily, 3rd d. of Richard Chenevix Trench, D.D., Archbishop of Dublin; three s. three d. Capt. Rifle Brigade; served Indian Mutiny (battle of Cawnpore, siege and capture of Lucknow), Doab and Oude campaigns, and with Camel Corps in Central India; Inspector of Prisons in Ireland; succeeded to Gweedon estates, Donegal, 1878. Heir-pres. to Barony of Sandys. Heir: s. Capt. Arthur Fitzgerald Sandys Hill, R.E. [b. 4 Dec. 1876. Educ.: Haileybury. Served Tibet Expedition, 1904. Club: Army and Navy]. Address: The Ashes, Hothfield, Kent.
(Died 16 June 1923.)

HILL, Arthur George, M.A., D.Litt., F.S.A.; Author and Antiquary; b. 12 Nov. 1857; e. s. of Thomas Hill of Belsize Avenue, Hampstead, and Sophia, y. d. of late Rev. Charles Thorold. Educ.: Westminster; Jesus College, Cambridge. M.A.; University of Lille, Docteur ès Lettres (D.Litt.); Director of Wm. Hill & Son and Norman & Beard, Ltd., Organ Builders; has travelled throughout Europe in the pursuit of archæology, particularly in Spain, also in Palestine. Publications: Churches of Cambridgeshire, 1878; Tourists Guide to the Co. of Camb., 1880; The Organ Cases and Organs of the Middle Ages and Renaissance, two large folio volumes, 1883 and 1891, illustrated by the Author; The Architectural History of the Christian Church, 1908; Christian Art in Spain, 1913; numerous papers in Archæologia and the Transactions of other societies, English and Foreign. Recreations: travel, drawing, music, languages, and fine art, especially architecture. Address: 41 Pall Mall, S.W.1. T.: Gerrard 7108. Clubs: United University, Oxford and Cambridge Musical. (Died 16 June 1923.)

HILL, Ven. Arundel Charles, D.D. Archdeacon of Elgin since 1894; b. 22 May 1845; s. of late Rev. B. C. Hill, M.A. (T.C.D.), Rector of York, County of Haldimand, Ontario, 1838-1870. Educ.: University College, Toronto; Huron College, London. Ordained 1869; Curate of St. Paul, London, 1869-70; St. James',

Toronto, 1870-73; Church of Ascension, Hamilton, 1873-75; Incumbent of Burford, 1875-78; Rector of Strathroy, 1878-85; Rector of Trinity Church, St. Thomas, 1885-1915; Canon of Huron, 1885-1904; Degree of D.D. conferred by Western University, London, Ont. 1913; promoted to rank of Hon. Major and Chaplain of 25th Regiment; Elgin Infantry, St. Thomas, 1908; Captain and Chaplain, 1898; now on retired list of officers retaining rank of Major. Address: Shelburne, Ontario, Canada.

HILL, Brig.-Gen. Augustus West, C.B. 1900; The Duke of Cambridge's Own (Middlesex Regiment); commanded a Division, 1908-10; b. 4 May 1853; s. of Henry Worsley Hill, Capt. R.N.; m. 1878, Alice, d. of Hon. George Vane, C.M.G., Treasurer of Ceylon; two s. Educ.: Keir House, Wimbledon; Cheltenham Coll. Joined 57th Foot, 1873; Captain, 1880; Major, 1885; Lieut.-Col. 1895; Brevet Col. 1900; served Zulu War, 1879, including relief of Echowe and capture of Cetewayo (medal with clasp); served Boer War, 1900-1901, including relief of Ladysmith, operations in Upper Natal, Orange River Colony, and Transvaal (despatches, medal with 7 clasps, C.B.); retired 1910. Club: Army and Navy. (Died 4 Feb. 1922.)

HILL, Ernest George; Principal, Muir College, University of Allahabad since 1913 and Professor of Chemistry; Meteorologist to United Provinces Government; b. 1872; s. of Rev. George Hill, D.D., Nottingham; m. 1896, Margaret Brend, d. of Rev. Eustace Rogers Conder, D.D. of Leeds; no c. Educ.: Leeds; Magdalen College, Oxford. Honour School, Natural Science, 1895; Sc.D. Dublin, 1906; appointed to Indian Educational Service as Professor of Chemistry, Muir College, Allahabad, 1895; Fellow of Allahabad University, 1896; since Dean of Faculty of Science and member of Syndicate; Director of Education Section of United Provinces Exhibition, 1910. Publications: numerous papers in scientific journals. Recreations: polo, cricket, golf. Address: Muir College, Allahabad, India. Club: East India United Service. (Died 28 June 1917.)

HILL, Sir G. Rowland; Kt., cr. 1926; Past President of the Rugby Football Union, for which he was for many years Hon. Sec.; b. Queen's House, Royal Hospital Schools, Greenwich, 21 Jan. 1855; s. of late Rev. James Hill, D.D. of the Royal Hospital Schools. Educ.: Christ's Hospital. Late Record Keeper in the Principal Probate Registry, Somerset House; Chairman of the Boro' of Greenwich Conservative Association since 1887. Clubs: Junior Carlton, Sports'. (Died 25 April 1928.)

HILL, Headon, nom de plume of F. Grainger, novelist; b. Lowestoft, Suffolk; e. s. of late Rev. J. Grainger, M.A., formerly Assist. Master at Eton College, and Vicar of Penn, Bucks.; married. Educ.: Eton. In the army a few years; has been in India, Egypt, and the United States of America; afterwards engaged in journalism in London. Publications: over sixty novels. Club: Authors'. (Died 2 Feb. 1927.)

HILL, Henry William, b. Eton, 1850; s. of late Henry Hill; m. 2nd, 1892, Fanny, d. of late Henry Lee Hogg of Cleobury Mortimer. Followed commercial pursuits for many years; a church worker, taking part in catholic movement in the Church of England; retired from business, 1890, to become lay-organising secretary, English Church Union; Secretary, 1902-1920; Vice-President, 1920; has organised several large demonstrations, including that of the Lancashire men in London against the Education Bill, 1906, the Welsh procession in London, 1912; the Hyde Park protest against the Welsh Disestablishment Bill, 1913; and Victoria Park protest, 1914; Member of Canterbury House of Laymen, 1900-20; Member National

Assembly Church of England, 1920; re-elected, 1925; Diocesan Reader (Southwark and London); Director Fidelity (Church) Trust; Treasurer of the Guild of All Souls; Secretary, Marriage Defence Council, 1920. *Publications:* has written much in the Press on social and ecclesiastical subjects. *Address:* Mole End, Hambledon, Godalming. (*Died 11 April 1926.*)

HILL, Lt.-Col. Hugh, M.V.O. 1906; D.S.O. 1915; F.R.G.S.; *b.* 16 May 1875. *Educ.:* Rugby; Sandhurst; Staff College, Quetta. Entered Royal Welsh Fusiliers, 1895; 'Capt. 1903; Major, 1913; Adjutant, 1904 - 7; served S. Africa, 1899-1900 (Queen's medal, two clasps); European War as Brigade-Major to Jullundur Brigade and D.A.A. and Q.M.G. 5th Army Corps Headquarters, 1914-15 (despatches twice, D.S.O., promoted Brevet Lt. - Col.); extra A.D.C. to the Prince and Princess of Wales during their tour in India, and when as King and Queen they were in India for the Durbar. *Address:* 45 Argyll Road, Kensington, W.; The Thatched Cottage, Beaconsfield, Bucks.
(*Died 10 Sept. 1916.*)

HILL, James Bastian, R.N., F.G.S.; Geological Adviser, Ministry of Health; *b.* 28 Dec. 1861; *s.* of late George Hill; *m.* 1886, Lucia Mary (*d.* 1912), *d.* of late D. R. Comyn; one *d.* *Educ.:* private schools; University College, London; Royal School of Mines. Served in Royal Navy, 1877-83; present at bombardment of Alexandria, 1882 (Egyptian medal one clasp, Khedive's star); on the Staff of H.M. Geological Survey of Great Britain, 1884-1911. *Publications:* numerous geological memoirs and papers. *Recreations:* shooting, fishing. *Address:* Ministry of Health, Whitehall, S.W. *Club:* Junior Army and Navy. (*Died 18 Dec. 1927.*)

HILL, James J.; LL.D. hon., Yale; *b.* near Guelph, Upper Canada, 16 Sept. 1838. *Educ.:* Rockwood Academy. In steamboat offices in St. Paul, 1856-65; agent, North-Western Packet Co. 1865; later established general fuel and transportation business on his own account; head of Hill, Griggs, and Co. 1869-75; established The Red River Transportation Co. 1870; formed North-Western Fuel Co. 1873; organised syndicate which secured control of St. Paul and Pacific Railroad from Dutch owners of the securities, 1877; reorganised system as St. Paul, Minneapolis, and Manitoba Railroad; General Manager, 1879-81; Vice-President, 1881-82; President since 1882; it became part of Great Northern system, 1890, of which he was President to April 1907; Chairman of Board of Directors, 1907-12. Has retired from active work. *Publication:* Highways of Progress. *Address:* Great Northern Railway Building, St. Paul, Minnesota, U.S. (*Died 29 May 1916.*)

HILL, James S., R.I. *Address:* 1A Steele's Studio, Haverstock Hill, N.W
(*Died 12 June 1921.*)

HILL, Colonel Joseph, C.B. 1904; 3rd Batt. Northamptonshire Regiment; *b.* 29 Dec. 1850; *s.* of Charles Hill of Wollaston and Mariette, *d.* of John Berkeley Monck, M.P., of Coley Park, Reading; *m.* 1883, Katherine, *d.* of George Miller of Brentry, Glos; one *s.* one *d.* *Educ.:* Eton. J.P., D.L., Northamptonshire; High Sheriff, 1885; served South Africa, 1902 (Queen's medal, 2 clasps); County Commandant, Northamptonshire. *Recreations:* hunting, cricket. *Address:* Wollaston Hall, Wellingborough. *Club:* Badminton. (*Died 19 May 1918.*)

HILL, Col. Peter Edward, C.B. 1907; R.A. retired; *b.* 7 June 1834; *m.* 1868, Emily Mary, *d.* of William Clarke, M.D. *Educ.:* Cheltenham; R.M.A. Woolwich. Entered army 1853; col. 1883; served Crimea, 1854-6 (medal, three clasps, 5th Medjidie, Turkish medal); Indian Mutiny, 1858-59 (medal); Afghan War, 1878-79 (despatches, medal). *Address:* Paxton House, Bath Road, Reading. (*Died 13 July 1919*)

HILL, Reginald Duke; D.L., J.P., High Sheriff of Essex, 1911; Master East Essex Foxhounds; *s.* of late James Duke Hill of Terlings Park, Harlow, Essex; *b.* 4 Jan. 1866; *m.* 1893, Flora, *o. d.* of Major Francis Tower of Thremhall Priory, Essex, and widow of Osgood Beauchamp Hanbury of Holfield Grange; two *s.* *Address:* Holfield Grange, Coggeshall, Essex. *T.:* 9 Coggeshall. *Club:* Boodle's.(*Died 16 Jan.1922.*)

HILL, Lt.-Col. Walter de Marchot, C.B.E., M.R.C.S., L.R.C.P. (Lond.); *b.* Bedford, 12 Feb. 1877; *s.* of Major.-Gen. W. Hill and Charlotte Miller, *d.* of Beauchamp Colclough Urquhart, Meldrum and Byth, Scotland; *m.* Margaret Ethel, *d.* of Robert Reed of Bristol; one *d.* *Educ.:* Blairlodge; St. Bart.'s Hospital. Master of E. E. Bliss School Electricity, Washington, U.S.A., 1905; House Surgeon, House Physician, Seaman's Hospital, Greenwich; M.O. 23 Fusiliers, 1914; M.O. 82 Brigade R.F.A., 18th Div., 1915; in command Special Military Surgical Hospital, Shepherd's Bush, 1916; Assistant Inspector of Military Orthopædics · and Liaison Officer, Ministry of Pensions, War Office, 1919; Adviser in Special Orthopædic Surgery, Ministry of Pensions, 1922; Associate of the Order of St. John of Jerusalem, 1914-15 Star. *Publications:* Treatment of Rheumatoid Arthritis; The Organisation and Administration of a Military Orthopædic Hospital in Jones's Orthopædic Surgery of Injuries, 1921. *Recreation:* golf. *Address:* 26 Thomas Street, W.1. *T.:* Mayfair 4841. *Club:* Wellington.
(*Died 20 June 1927.*)

HILL, William, B.Sc., M.D. Lond., Consulting Surgeon for Diseases of the Ear, Nose, and Throat, St. Mary's Hospital, London; Endoscopic Surgeon for Diseases of the Gullet), Metropolitan Ear and Throat Hospital; *s.* of late George Hill of Tregassick, Cornwall; *m.* Flora Hastings, *d.* of David Robert Comyn. *Educ.:* King's and University Colleges, London; St. Mary's Hospital; formerly Senior Entrance Science Scholar; Scholar in Pathology; Assistant Curator of Museum and Assistant Lecturer on Anatomy, St. Mary's Hospital; Registrar and Pathologist, Central London Throat and Ear Hospital; and Teacher of Botany, Univ. College School, etc.; Past President of the Harveian Society of London, of Section of Laryngology, Royal Society of Medicine, and of Section of Oto - rhino - laryngology, British Medical Association. *Publications:* Introductory Lecture on Occultism and Quackery in Medicine, 1902; many papers on professional subjects published in various medical journals. *Address:* Weymouth Street, Portland Place, W.1. *T.:* Langham, 2468. *Clubs:* Savage; Royal Temple Yacht.
(*Died 24 Nov. 1928.*)

HILLIER, Edward Guy, C.M.G. 1904; of the Hong Kong and Shanghai Banking Corporation; *b.* 1857; *s.* of late Charles Batten Hillier, H.B.M. Consul to Siam; *m.* 1st, 1894, Ada (*d.* 1917), *d.* of late Frederick Everett, Erith, Kent; one *s.* two *d.*; 2nd, 1919, Eleanor, *d.* of late Dr. Timothy Richard, of Shanghai, China. *Educ.:* Blundell's School, Tiverton; Trinity College, Cambridge. Entered the service of the Hong Kong and Shanghai Banking Corporation, 1883; Agent of the Bank in Peking, 1891; engaged in negotiation of various Chinese Government loans issued between 1895 and 1913; British Delegate on the Commission of Bankers for the Chinese Indemnity, 1902. Failure of sight in 1896 resulted in total blindness. *Address:* Peking, China. (*Died 12 April 1924.*)

HILLIER, Frederick James, Director, Daily News and the Star; Chairman, Technical Committee, Newspaper Proprietors' Association; *b.* Southampton, 1869; *m.* 1890, Anne Henry; three *s.* Night Editor, Morning Leader and Daily News until 1913; News Editor, Daily

News, until 1918. *Address:* 19-22 Bouverie Street, E.C.4. *T.:* Central 313.

(*Died 1920.*)

HILLIER, Joseph H., M.V.O. 1910; was Controller of Supplies, H.M. Office of Works. *Address:* Seafield Cottage, Seafield Road, Broadstairs.

HILLIER, Sir Walter Caine, K.C.M.G., *cr.* 1897; C.B. 1903; Adviser to Chinese Government, 1908-10; Adviser to Military Authorities in China, 1900 (despatches, medal); *b.* Hong Kong, 1849; *s.* of C. B. Hillier, late Consul at Bangkok; *m.* 1906, Marion Ellen, *d.* of late Sir C. U. Aitchison, K.C.S.I. *Educ.:* Bedford Gram. School; Blundell's School, Tiverton. Student Interpreter in China, 1867; Assist. Chinese Sec. Peking, 1879-85; Chinese Secretary, 1885-89; Consul-General, Corea, 1889-96; Professor of Chinese, King's College, London, 1904-8. *Publications:* The Chinese Language, and How to Learn it, 1907; English-Chinese Dictionary, 1910. *Address:* The Oaks, Bracknell, Berks.

(*Died 9 Nov. 1927.*)

HILLINGDON, 2nd Baron (*cr.* 1886), **Charles William Mills,** D.L.; Bt. 1868; partner in Glyn, Mills and Co., Bankers; *b.* 26 Jan. 1855; *e. s.* of 1st Baron and *e. d.* of 3rd Earl of Harewood; *S.* father, 1898; *m.* 1886, Hon. Alice Marion Harbord, 2nd *d.* of 5th Baron Suffield; one *s.* M.P. (C.) West Kent, 1885-92. Owns about 4500 acres. *Heir:* s. Hon. Arthur Robert Mills [*b.* 19 Oct. 1891; *m.* 1916, Hon. Edith Mary Winifred Cadogan, *d.* of late Viscount Chelsea]. *Address:* Hillingdon Court, Uxbridge; Wildernesse, Sevenoaks.

(*Died 6 April 1919.*)

HILLS-JOHNES, Lt.-Gen. Sir James; G.C.B., *cr.* 1893; K.C.B., *cr.* 1881; V.C.; LL.D. University of Wales, 1917; *b.* 20 Aug. 1833; *s.* of late James Hills, Neechindipore, Bengal, India, and Charlotte, *d.* of Signor Angelo Savi, Moisgunge; *m.* Elizabeth, *d.* and co-heir with her sister Mrs. Johnes, of late John Johnes, Dolaucothy, Carmarthenshire, 1882; assumed in 1883 by Royal licence additional name and arms of Johnes. *Educ.:* Academy, Edinburgh; Military College, Edinburgh; Addiscombe. Entered Bengal Artillery, 1853; served throughout Indian Mutiny, 1857-58; present at Hindun River. Badlee-Ka-Serai, Nujjefghur, siege and storming of Delhi, 1857; Lucknow, 1858; Bareilly, Allygunge and Mohamdee, 1858; dangerously wounded, 1857 (V.C. Brevet Majority, medal and two clasps); A.D.C. to Viceroy (Lord Canning), 1859-62; Assistant Resident, Nepal, 1862-63; commanded 8-inch mortar battery throughout Abyssinian campaign, 1867-1868; present at capture of Magdala (Bt.-Lt.-Col., medal); served throughout Lushai campaign, 1871-72 (C.B., medal and clasp); served as A. A.-G. Kandahar Field Force, 1878-79; joined Sir F. S. Roberts' column in Kurrum Valley, 1879; accompanied it to Kabul; present at battle of Charasiab and occupation of Kabul; Military Governor, city of Kabul, 1879-1880; assumed command 3rd Division Northern Afghanistan Field Force, 1880; directed operations of cavalry action at Padkoa Shana Logar Valley (received vote of thanks of Houses of Parliament, 5th May 1881, K.C.B., medal and clasp); J.P., D.L. Carmarthenshire; Hon. Colonel 4th Batt. the Welsh Regt.; Chairman Carm. County Association Territorial Forces and of Joint Counties' Association. *Address:* Dolaucothy, Llanwrda, R.S.O., South Wales. *T.A.:* Pumpsaint. *Clubs:* United Service, Junior Constitutional.

(*Died 3 Jan. 1919.*)

HIME, Lt.-Col. Rt. Hon. Sir Albert Henry, K.C.M.G., *cr.* 1900; C.M.G. 1886; P.C., 1902; Hon. LL.D. Dublin, Edin., and Camb.; *b.* Kilcool, Co. Wicklow, Ireland, 29 Aug. 1842; 7th *s.* of late Rev. Maurice C. Hime and Harriette, *d.* of late Rev. Bartholomew Lloyd, Provost of

498

Trin. Coll. Dublin; *m.* Josephine Mary, *d.* of late J. Searle of Plymouth, 1866; five *s.* two *d.* *Educ.:* Portora Royal School, Enniskillen; by private tutor; Trinity Coll. Dublin; Royal Military Academy, Woolwich. Entered Royal Engineers, 1861, became Captain 1874, and Major 1881; retired with honorary rank of Lieut.-Col. 1883; was employed in Bermuda, under the Colonial Government, 1869-71, in the construction of a causeway and swing-bridge connecting the island of St. George with the main island, for the successful completion of which works received the thanks of the Legislature and the acknowledgments of the Secretary of State for the Colonies; Colonial Engineer of Natal, 1875; member of Executive and Legislative Councils, 1876; retired when Natal assumed responsible government, 1893; M.L.A. Pietermaritzburg, 1897; served Zulu War, 1879 (medal with clasp); employed on survey of boundary between Orange Free State and Natal in 1884-85; thanked by Secretary of State for Colonies for successfully carrying out that survey; Minister of Lands and Works and Minister of Defence, Natal, 1897-99; Prime Minister and Minister of Lands and Works and Minister of Defence, 1899, resigned 1903. *Decorated* for services generally and specially for assistance rendered to Imperial Government in connection with the war in South Africa. *Recreations:* sport of all kinds, but especially fishing. *Address:* Lymbrook, Marlow, Bucks. *Clubs:* Marlow; Victoria, Pietermaritzburg.

(*Died 13 Sept. 1919.*)

HIND, C. Lewis; writer; *b.* 1862; *s.* of late Charles Hind, J.P.; *m.* 1907, Henriette Richardson Hitchcock. *Educ.:* privately; Christ's Hospital. Sub-editor of the Art Journal, 1887-92; editor Pall Mall Budget, 1893-95; editor of the Academy, 1896-1903. *Publications:* The Enchanted Stone, 1898; Things Seen (printed for private circulation), 1899; Life's Little Things, 1901; Adventures among Pictures, 1904; Life's Lesser Moods, 1904; Days With Velasquez, 1905; Rembrandt, 1905; The Education of an Artist, 1906; Days in Cornwall, 1907; The Diary of a Looker-on. 1908; Turner's Golden Visions, 1910; The Post Impressionists, 1911; The Consolations of a Critic, 1911; Brabazon: His Art and Life, 1912; The Soldier Boy, 1916; The Invisible Guide, 1917; What's Freedom? also the play of Freedom with Lyall Swete, produced at the Century Theatre, New York, 1918; Things Seen in America (printed for private circulation), 1920; Art and I, Authors and I, 1921; More Authors and I, 1922; Landscape Painting: From Giotto to Turner, vol. i., 1923; Life and I, 1923; Landscape Painting: From Constable to the Present Day, vol. ii., 1924; The Uncollected Work of Aubrey Beardsley; Life and You; One Hundred Second-Best Poems; Naphtali: Being Influences and Adventures while Earning a Living by Writing, 1925; From My Books: An Anthology: One hundred Best Poems; The Great Painters; In Art and Life; One hundred Best Books, 1927. *Address:* 24 Queen Anne's Gate, Westminster, S.W.1. *T.:* Victoria 857. *Clubs:* Arts, Authors'. (*Died 31 Aug. 1927.*)

HINDE, George Jennings, Ph.D., F.R.S., F.G.S. *Publication:* Fossil Sponge Spicules from the Upper Chalk, Munich, 1880; Catalogue of Fossil Sponges in British Museum, 1883; Report on the Materials from the Borings at the Funafuti Atoll, 1904; other papers on Fossil Sponges, Radiolaria, and Corals. *Address:* 24 Avondale Road, South Croydon. (*Died 18 Mar. 1918.*)

HINDLE, Frederick George, Solicitor; Clerk to Darwen Boro' Justices since 1882; M.P. (L.) Darwen Division of Lancashire, Jan. to Dec. 1910; *b.* Darwen, 1848; *m.* 1876, Helen, *d.* of Thomas Gillibrand, cotton manufacturer, Darwen; one *s.* *Educ.:* Grammar School, Black-

burn; Senior Prizeman at Examination as Solicitor in 1870. Practised in Manchester and at Darwen; contested (L.) Darwen Division, 1906; 1910 Dec. *Publication:* The Legal Status of Licensed Victuallers, 1883. *Recreations:* golf, motoring, etc.; served 19 years as an officer in East Lancashire Volunteers and retired with rank of Major. *Address:* Astley Bank, Darwen. *T.:* 3 Darwen.
(Died Mar. 1925.)

HINDS, John, H.M.'s Lieut. and Custos Rotulorum, Co. Carmarthen, since 1917; *b.* Cwnin Farm, near Carmarthen, 26 July 1862; *s.* of late William Hinds and *d.* of David Jones Penronw, Llanpumpsaint; *m.* 1893, Lizzie, *d.* of R. Powell, Cefntrefna, Llandovery; one *d. Educ.:* academy of late Alcwyn Evans, Carmarthen. Went to London, 1881; engaged at various drapery establishments; founded Hinds & Co. (Limited); Chairman of the Drapers' Fire Insurance Corporation; and Past President of the Drapers' Chamber of Trade; Ex-President of the Blackheath Liberal Association; President West Carmarthen Liberal Association; Chairman of the Welsh Liberal Federation; Member of Board of Management of the Warehousemen, Drapers, and Clerks' School; Treasurer of Council of Honourable Society of Cymmrodorion; Treasurer of National Eisteddfod Association; Ex-President Baptist Union of Wales; Past Master of several Freemasons' lodges; and Past Senior Deacon of the Grand Lodge of England; Ex-President of the London Welsh Literary Union, and a Member of the Charitable Aid Society; M.P. (L.) West Carmarthenshire, 1910, Carmarthen Division (Co. L.) 1918-23. *Address:* 14 Clarendon Court, W.9; *T.:* Paddington 8506; Neuadd-Deg, Carmarthen; *T.:* Carmarthen 89. *M.:* BX 5424. *Clubs:* Reform, National Liberal.
(Died 23 July 1928.)

HINE, George T., Architect in private practice; *b.* Nottingham, 1841; *e. s.* of late T. C. Hine, F.S.A.; *m.* Florence Deane, *y. d.* of late E. Cooper of Failand House. Somersetshire; one *s.* one *d. Educ.:* privately in England and abroad. Articled to his father and practised for many years with him as an architect; in 1890 came to London and practised exclusively as an asylum architect; Fellow of the R.I.B.A. and late member of Council, also of the Surveyors' Institute; Consulting Architect to H.M. Commissioners in Lunacy. *Publications:* several works on asylum construction and hygiene. *Recreations:* hunting, shooting. *Address:* 35 Parliament Street, Westminster, S.W.; 37 Hertford Street, Mayfair, W.; Old Farm, nr. Berkhamsted, Herts. *T.A.:* Asyla, London. *T.:* 4415 Gerrard. *Clubs:* Union, St. Stephen's, Constitutional, Ranelagh, etc. *(Died 25 April 1916.)*

HINGLEY, Sir George Benjamin, 2nd Bt.; *cr.* 1893; Chairman N. Hingley and Sons, Ld., and Harts Hill Iron Co., colliery proprietors and ironmasters, Netherton, Dudley, and Brierley Hill; High Sheriff for Worcestershire, 1900; *b.* 9 Sept. 1850; *s.* of Hezekiah Hingley of Grassendale Park, Liverpool; *e. b.* of 1st Bt. and Fanny Georgina, *d.* of William Thompson, Liverpool; *S.* uncle 1905. *Heir:* none. *Address:* High Park, near Droitwich. *Club:* Union. *(Died 19 Aug. 1918.)*

HINGSTON, George, I.S.O. 1903; was Collector of Customs, Glasgow. *Address:* Delgany House, Crown Hill, Devonshire.
(Died 7 Dec. 1925.)

HINKSON, Henry Albert, M.A.; author and barrister; Resident Magistrate for South Mayo since 1914; *b.* Dublin, 18 April 1865; *m.* 1893, Katharine Tynan; two *s.* one *d. Educ.:* Dublin High School; Trin. Coll. Dublin (Scholar); Germany. M.A. in Classical Honours, Royal University of Ireland, 1890; Barrister

of the Inner Temple; formerly Senior Classical Tutor at Clongowes Wood College, Kildare. *Publications:* Dublin Verses (edited), 1895; Golden Lads and Girls, 1895; O'Grady of Trinity, 1896; Up for the Green, 1898; When Love is Kind, 1898; The King's Deputy, 1899; The Point of Honour, 1901; Sir Phelim's Treasure, 1901; Fan Fitz-Gerald, 1902; Silk and Steel, 1902; Copyright Law, 1903; The Wine of Love, 1904; The Splendid Knight, 1905; Golden Morn; The Castaways of Hope Island, 1907; Father Alphonsus, 1908; The King's Liege, 1909; The House of the Oak, 1911; The Considine Luck; Glory of War, 1912; Gentleman Jack, 1913; many short stories. *Recreations:* tennis, golf, shooting. *Address:* Brookhill, Claremorris, Co. Mayo. *T.A.:* Claremorris. *Club:* Savage. *(Died 11 Jan. 1919.)*

HINTON, Lt.-Col. Godfrey Bingham, C.M.G. 1915; R.F.A.; *b.* 19 March 1871. Entered army, 1890; Captain, 1899; Major, 1905; Lt.-Col. 1914; Adjutant Volunteers, 1897-1902; served European War, 1914-15 (despatches, C.M.G.). *(Died 21 Mar. 1918.)*

HIRSCH, Emil G., L.H.D., LL.D., D.C.L., D.D., A.M.; Rabbi of Chicago Sinai Congregation since 1880; Professor of Rabbinics in the University of Chicago; Commissioner of Charities of the State of Illinois; Editor of the Reform-Advocate (a weekly); *b.* Luxemburg, May 1851; *s.* of Dr. Samuel Hirsch, Rabbi, and Louise Mickolls; *m.* 1878, Matilda, *d.* of Dr. David Einhorn and Julia Ochs; two *s.* three *d. Educ.:* Luxemburg (Gymnasium); University of Pennsylvania; Berlin; Hochschule für Wissenschaft des Judentum, Berlin. Rabbi at Baltimore, 1877; Louisville, 1878-80; Elector at Large during Presidential Election for McKinley, 1896; President of Chicago Public Library; Member of the State Board of Charities; Chaplain of Illinois Naval Reserve; Vice-President of Parliament of Religions, Chicago, 1893; of Congress of Religion, 1894; often acted as Arbitrator in disputes between Labour and Employers; Orator at many public gatherings in the U.S. *Publications:* one volume of selected addresses; The Crucifixion from the Jewish Point of View; Translator and Editor of Olath Tamid, a Jewish Prayer-book; many contributions to Jewish and other religious publications; Editor of the Biblical Department of Jewish Encyclopedia. *Recreation:* travel. *Address:* 4608 Drexel Boulevard, Chicago. *T.A.:* Rabbi. *T.:* Drexel 628. *Clubs:* Standard, Press, Quadrangle, Literary, the Book and Play, Society for Biblical Research, Chicago. *(Died 7 Jan. 1923.)*

HISLOP, Hon. Thomas William, Officer of Legion of Honour; barrister and solicitor; member of Legislative Council of N.Z.; *b.* Edinburgh, 1850; *s.* of John Hislop, LL.D., F.R.S., Edinburgh, and Johanna, *d.* of Major Horn of Stirkook, Caithness; *m.* A. Simpson of New South Wales; two *s.* three *d. Educ.:* Shaw's Grammar School, Otago; High School and University, Dunedin. Commenced practice of law at Oamaru, 1871; returned M.H.R., Waitaki District, 1875; and again, 1879; resigned, 1880; re-elected, 1885, 1887, and 1889; Colonial Secretary, 1887; afterwards Minister of Education; resigned, 1891; joined firm Brandon, Hislop & Brandon, barristers, Wellington; Mayor, Wellington, 1904-8; advocated and carried through purchase for city of Electric Works for lighting and power; initiated Zoological Gardens; carried out tramway system and drainage for suburbs, also a scheme for gradual paving of streets out of revenue instead of borrowing; while Minister of Education initiated amendment of Land Act giving option of tenure to purchaser of Govt. Lands, also bills regulating hours of shops and factories, shipping, seamen, and many other social measures and legal reforms. *Publications:* frequent contributor to daily papers; pamphlets on social and political subjects. *Recreations:* tennis, swimming, and motoring. *Address:* Sayes Court, Wellington, New Zealand. *T.:* 75. *M.:* 67. *Club:* Wellington, Wellington. (*Died 2 Oct. 1925.*)

HISSEY, James John, Author; *o. s. of* James Hissey of Longworth, Berks.; *m.* 1st, 1880, Elizabeth (Bee), *e. d.* of Sir Thomas Bouch, C.E., and Lady Bouch, Edinburgh; 2nd, 1890, Katherine Mary, *e. d.* of Richard Ridcock of Woolwich; *three s. two d. Publications:* An Old-Fashioned Journey; A Drive Through England; On the Box Seat; A Tour in a Phaeton; Over Fen and Wold; Untravelled England; An English Holiday; The Charm of the Road; A Leisurely Tour in England; and other works on British topography. *Recreations:* sketching from nature, motoring, photography, engineering. *Address:* Trevin Towers, Eastbourne, Sussex. *T.:* Eastbourne 249. *M.:* HC 27. *Clubs:* Authors', Royal Automobile, Thatched House, Royal Societies; Devonshire, Eastbourne. (*Died 5 Mar. 1921.*)

HITCHCOCK, Rev. Wm. Maunder, M.A.; Hon. Canon of Durham, 1874; retired; *b.* 18 July 1835; *s.* of George Hitchcock; *m.* 1858, Margaret Ellen (*d.* 1918); *three s. one d. Educ.:* King's College, London; Wadham College, Oxford. B.A. 1858; M.A. 1861; Deacon, 1858; Priest, 1859; Curate of St. James', Cheltenham, 1858-59; Perpetual Curate of Bussage, Gloucestershire, 1859-61; Curate of Edgbaston, 1861; Perpetual Curate of Shildon, Co. of Durham, 1862-66; Rural Dean of Chesterle-Street, 1872-80; Rector of Whitburn, Co. Durham, 1866-81; Rural Dean of Wearmouth, 1880-81; Vicar of Romford, Co. Essex, 1881-88; Vicar of East Farleigh, Co. Kent, 1888-93; Private Chaplain to Bishop of Durham, 1862-66; Examining Chaplain, 1866-79.
(*Died 18 Sept. 1921.*)

HJELT, Edvard Immanuel, Vice-Chancellor at the Univ. of Helsingfors; *b.* Wichtis, Finland, 28 June 1855; *s.* of Otto E. A. Hjelt, Professor of Medicine; *m.* 1878, Ida Ostroem; *two s. five d. Educ.:* Lyceum; and University, Helsingfors (Ph.D., 1879). Docent of Chemistry, 1880; Hon. LL.D. University of Aberdeen, 1906; Professor of Chemistry 1882-1907, and Rektor 1899-1907, at the University of Helsingfors; Vice-Pres. Senate of Finland, 1907-9; Membre de Société des Sciences de Finlande and Academie Royale des Sciences de Suède. *Publications:* numerous researches of Organic Chemistry; Principles of Organic Chemistry; continued with Brühl and Aschan the Ausführliches Lehrbuch der Chemie von Roscoe-Schorlemmer; Aus J. Berelius und G. Magnus Briefwechsel; Berelius, Liebig, Dumas, ihre Stellung zur Radikaltheorie; Geschichte d. organ. Chemie; and other biographical works. *Address:* Helsingfors. *T.:* 337.
(*Died 2 July 1921.*)

HOARE, Lieut.-Col. Arthur Fanshawe, M.A., V.D., C.B., 1911; Assistant Master, Haileybury College, 1879-1914; *s.* of Rev. Arthur Malortie Hoare and Maria Faithfull Fanshawe; *b.* 14 Aug. 1854; *m.* 1894, Gertrude J. Hoare; *four s. one d. Educ.:* Twyford School; Marlborough College; Balliol College, Oxford. Brackenbury History Scholar; Organising Secretary of Public Schools Brigade Camp, 1889-1909. *Publications:* A few essays on military subjects. *Address:* 10 Staverton Road, Oxford. (*Died 25 May 1925.*)

HOARE, Rev. John Gurney, M.A., Surrogate; Hon. Canon of Norwich; Hon. Life Governor of Church Missionary Society; *b.* Holloway, 16 March 1847; 2nd *s.* of late Rev. Edward Hoare, Hon. Canon of Canterbury and
500

Vicar of Holy Trinity, Tunbridge Wells, and Maria, *d.* of Sir Benjamin C. Brodie, 1st Bt.; *m.* 1873, Alice, *d.* of late John Woodfall, M.D.; *two s. three d. Educ.:* Tonbridge School; Trinity College, Cambridge; B.A. (Class. tripos) 1869, M.A. 1872. Winner of high jump, University sports, 1869, 1870; ordained deacon, 1873; priest, 1874; Curate of Christ Church, Sculcoates, Hull, 1873; Sunderland, 1873-75; Holy Trinity, Tunbridge Wells, 1875-1877; Vicar of St. Dunstan, Canterbury, 1877-88; of Aylsham, Norfolk, 1888-1922. *Publications:* Righteousness and Life; Lessons on Joshua and Judges; From Adam to Abraham; Christ revealed in Type, Title, and Prophecy; Life in St. John's Gospel; The Foundation Stone of Christian Faith; editor of Great Principles of Divine Truth. *Recreations:* books, gardening, golf, cycling. *Address:* Belaugh House, Wroxham, Norfolk. (*Died 20 Feb. 1923.*)

HOARE, Rt. Rev. Joseph, R.C. Bishop of Ardagh and Clonmacnoise; cons. 1895; *b.* Ballymahon, Co. Longford, 1842; *s.* of John Hoare and Maria Donohoe. *Educ.:* Mount Melleray, Longford, and Maynooth; Curate of Longford, 1867; president of St. Mel's, 1874; parish priest of Street, 1881; parish priest of Carrick-on-Shannon, 1887. *Address:* Bishop's House, St. Michael's, Longford, Ireland.
(*Died 14 April 1927.*)

HOARE, Rev. Richard Whitehead, F.K.C.; Hon. Canon of Canterbury since 1910; Fellow of King's College, London, 1912; *b.* London, 1840; *m.* 1872, Isabella Anna Maria Neale of Croydon; *two s. two d. Educ.:* home. Deacon, 1863; Priest, 1864; Assistant Curate at All Saints, Clapham Park, 1863-65; St. Barnabas, Kennington, 1865-66; St. Saviour's, Croydon, 1866-69; Minister-in-charge of the new parish of St. Michael and All Angels, Croydon, 1871; Vicar of St. Michael and All Angels, Croydon, 1883-1918. *Address:* 14 Aberdeen Road, Croydon.
(*Died 22 Feb. 1924.*)

HOARE, William Douro, C.B.E. 1920; Director Bank of England since 1898; Lieut. City of London; *b.* 1 Aug. 1862; *s.* of late Richard Hoare of Marden Hill, Hertford, and Susan, *d.* of Col. Tomkinson of Willington Hall, Tarporley, Cheshire; *m.* 1891, Ida Mary, *d.* of late Lachlan M. Rate of Milton Court, Dorking, and 9 South Audley Street, W. *Educ.:* Winchester, 1875-80; Trin. Coll., Camb., 1880-83 (M.A.). *Address:* Guessens, Welwyn; 8 and 9 Austin Friars, E.C.; 88 St. James's Street, S.W.1; North Lodge, Cromer, Norfolk. *T.A.:* Taurus, London. *T.:* London Wall 6756. *Clubs:* Brooks's, Argentine, Beefsteak.
(*Died 10 April 1928.*)

HOBART, Sir Robert Henry, 1st Bt., *cr.* 1914; K.C.V.O., *cr.* 1902; C.B. 1885; *b.* 13 Sept. 1836; *e. s.* of late Hon. and Very Rev. Henry Lewis Hobart, D.D., Dean of Windsor and Wolverhampton, Registrar of the Order of the Garter, 4th *s.* of George, 3rd Earl, and Albinia, Countess of Buckinghamshire; *m.* 1869, Hon. Julia Trollope, *d.* of 1st Baron Kesteven; *one s. one d. Educ.:* Charterhouse; Trinity Hall, Cambridge (LL.B.). Private Secretary to Marquis of Hartington (8th Duke of Devonshire) as Sec. of State for War (twice), Postmaster-Gen., Chief Sec. for Ireland, and Sec. of State for India, 1863-74, and 1880-85; to four Secretaries for Scotland, 1886-1887, 1892-95; Secretary to the Earl Marshal (Duke of Norfolk) for the purposes of the coronation of their Majesties King Edward VII. and Queen Alexandra, 1901-2 (Coronation Medal); Gold Stick Officer at the Coronation of their Majesties King George V., and Queen Mary, 1911 (Coronation Medal); Official Verderer of the New Forest, 1906; D.L. and J.P. Co. Middlesex; J.P. Co. London and Southampton; M.P. (L.) New Forest, 1906-10. *Heir: s.* Claud

HOARE, Edward Wallis, F.R.C.V.S. See page xxi.

Vere Cavendish Hobart. *Address:* Lang-down, Hythe, Southampton. *T.:* Hythe 25. Southampton. *Clubs:* Travellers', National Liberal.   *(Died 4 Aug. 1928.)*

IOBBINS, Robert, I.S.O.; 3rd *s.* of late Rev. F. C. T. Hobbins, Vicar of Bedingham, Norfolk; *m.* 1873, Jane, *o. d.* of Arthur Jones of Priors Lee, Shifnal, Shropshire; one *d. Educ.:* Norwich Grammar School. Formerly Collector of Customs at Southampton and Belfast. *Address:* 2 Lavington Road, West Ealing, W.
     (Died 21 Sept. 1922.)

HOBHOUSE, Sir Charles Parry; 3rd Bt.; *cr.* 1812; J.P.; *b.* Calcutta, 2 Jan. 1825; 3rd *s.* of H. W. Hobhouse, who was 3rd *s.* of Sir Benjamin Hobhouse, Bt.; *S. u.* 1869; *m.* 1st, Edith Lucy, *d.* of Sir T. E. M. Turton, Bt., 1855 *(d.* 1867); 2nd, Anna Maria, *d.* of Alexander Sawers, merchant, Calcutta, 1868; two *s.* eight *d. Educ.:* East Sheen, Dr. Pinckney; Rugby, Dr. Arnold; E.I.C. Hailey-bury. Bengal Civil Service, 1844-71; member Bengal Council and Imperial Legislative Council, East Indies; Judge of High Court, Calcutta. Owns 1600 acres. *Recreations:* captain cricket club, Calcutta. *Heir: s.* Rt. Hon. Charles E. H. Hobhouse. *Address:* Manor House, Monkton Farleigh, Bradford-on-Avon, Wilts. *T.A.:* Bathford.   *(Died 30 Dec. 1916.)*

HOBHOUSE, Rev. Walter, D.D.; Canon of Gloucester 1913-20; Examining Chaplain to the Bishop of Birmingham since 1905; *b.* 1862; 2nd *s.* of late Right Rev. Bishop Hobhouse and first wife, Mary, *d.* of Gen. Hon. John Brodrick; *m.* 1st, 1887, Mary Violet *(d.* 1901), *y. d.* of Edmund M'Neill, D.L., Craigdunn, Co. Antrim, Ireland; one *s.* one *d.*; 2nd, 1904, Edith *(d.* 1921), *y. d.* of Rev. William Owen, Vicar of Damerham, Wilts.; one *s.* two *d. Educ.:* Eton (Newcastle Scholar, 1880); New College, Oxford (Scholar, 1880-84. 1st class Moderations, 1881; 1st class Literæ Hum. 1884; Chancellor's Prize English Essay, 1885; Chancellor's Prize Latin Essay, 1886; Proxime accessit Ireland scholarship, 1883-84); Fellow and Lecturer of Hertford College, 1884-87; Student and Tutor of Christ Church, Oxford, 1887-1894. Headmaster of Durham School, 1894-99; editor of the Guardian, 1900-5; Bampton Lecturer at Oxford for 1909; Hon. Canon and Chancellor of Birmingham Cathedral, 1905-13; Archdeacon of Aston, 1912-13, of Gloucester, 1917-19. *Publications:* Theory and Practice of Ancient Education, 1885; The Spiritual Standard and other Sermons, 1896; Otium Didascali, 1898; The Church and the World in Idea and in History (Bampton Lectures, 1909). *Recreations:* golf, travel. *Club:* Athenæum.   *(Died 30 Oct. 1928.)*

HOBSON, Sir Albert John, Kt., *cr.* 1922; Chairman of Thomas Turner and Co., Ltd.; Director of the Birmingham Small Arms Co., Smallheath, Birmingham; Chairman of Wm. Jessop and Son, Ltd., steel manufacturers, Brightside Works, Sheffield; Vice-Chairman of the High Speed Steel Alloys Co., Widnes; and Chairman of J. J. Saville and Co., Ltd., steel manufacturers, Sheffield; ex-Master Cutler; J.P., Sheffield; ex-Pres. of Association of British Chambers of Commerce, London, 1920; Pro-Chancellor and LL.D. of the Sheffield University; Chairman of the Council for University Superannuation, London; President, Fisher Institution (Pension Charity); Alderman of the City of Sheffield; Lord Mayor, Sheffield, 1911-12; *s.* of Alderman John Hobson, scissors manufacturer, and Thyrza A. Carr, *d.* of Alderman John Carr, a member of the first Council of the borough, now city, of Sheffield; *m.* Maude L. (*dec.*), 2nd *d.* of late G. H. Faber, M.P. *Recreations:* politics, public work generally. *Address:* Esholt, Ranmoor, Sheffield. *T.A.:* Esholt, Sheffield. *T.:* Sheffield 1721. *M.:* WA 1295.

Clubs: Devonshire, Junior Constitutional; Sheffield, Sheffield.   *(Died 20 April 1923.)*

HOBSON, Ven. Edward Waller, M.A.; Archdeacon of Armagh since 1915; Examining Chaplain to Lord Primate of All Ireland; *b.* 5 Dec. 1851; *s.* of late Canon John Meade Hobson, M.A.; *m.* 1891, Frances Maria, *d.* of late Robert Westley Hall-Dare, of Theydon Bois, Essex, and Newtownbarry, Ireland; no *c. Educ.:* Atherstone School, Warwickshire; Royal School, Dungannon; Trinity Coll. Dublin University (ex-Royal Scholar, ex-University Scholar, First Honours and Silver Medallist). Curate of The Mariners' Church, Kingstown, Co. Dublin, 1876-78; Portadown, Ireland, 1878-1881; Rector of Moy, Co. Tyrone, 1881-95; Rector of Derryloran (Cookstown), Ireland, 1895-96; Portadown, Ireland, 1896-1915; Librarian Public Library, Armagh, since 1915. *Recreations:* formerly football, played for All Ireland (Rugby Union) against All England, 1875. *Address:* The Library, Armagh.
     (Died 17 April 1924.)

HODDER-WILLIAMS, Sir (John) Ernest, Kt., *cr.* 1919; C.V.O., 1921; Knight of Grace, Order of St. John of Jerusalem; Officer of the Crown of Italy, 1920; Commander, 1921; King Albert's Medal, 1920; publisher; *b.* Bromley, Kent, 16 Sep. 1876; *e. s.* of John Williams, Bromley, Kent; *g.s.* of Matthew Henry Hodder; *m.* 1st, Ethel Oddy *(d.* 1918); 2nd, Lilian, 2nd *d.* of J. R. Pakeman. *Educ.:* City of London School; University College, London; Paris; Berlin. Chairman of the firm of Hodder & Stoughton, Ltd., of London, book publishers and newspaper proprietors; Chairman Wakley & Son, Ltd., proprietors of The Lancet; Member of the City of London Corporation. *Publications:* The Life of Sir George Williams, Founder of the Y.M.C.A.; (with E. C. Vivian) The Way of the Red Cross (Preface by Queen Alexandra). *Address:* 23 Cadogan Place, S.W.1; St. Paul's House, Warwick Square, E.C.4. *T.:* Sloane 3540; City 3704. *Clubs:* Devonshire, Whitefriars. *(Died 8 April 1927.)*

HODDING, Colonel John, C.I.E. 1903; V.D.; Chief Manager of the Estates of The Hon. Sir Khajeh Salimollah, K.C.S.I. Nawab Bahadur of Dacca; formerly commanding Behar Light Horse; *b.* 1854; *m.* 1880, Mary, *d.* of Thomas Macgregor, Inverness. *Address:* Dacca, Eastern Bengal, India. *Club:* Sports.
     (Died 21 Mar. 1919.)

HODGE, Albert H., R.B.S.; sculptor; *b.* 1875; Scotch; *m.* Jessie Dunn Dunlop; one *s.* one *d. Educ.:* Glasgow. Trained at the Glasgow School of Art, in architecture (gold medal, silver medal, and 4 bronze medals); in the National Competition, also passed; 1st place in the United Kingdom in Architectural designs examination; exhibited works at the Royal Academy; executed groups of sculpture for Town Halls, Hull, Cardiff, Glamorgan, Deptford; Public Statues — Queen Victoria, Glasgow; Robert Burns, Stirling. *Recreations:* golf and angling. *Address:* 50 Bedford Gardens, Kensington, W. *Club:* Arts.   *(Died 27 Jan. 1918.)*

HODGE, Rev. Canon Edward Grose, M.A., F.E.S.; Canon of Birmingham, 1919; *m.* Florence Amy, *y. d.* of Col. J. T. Smith, R.E., F.R.S.; two *s. Educ.:* Trinity Hall, Cambridge. Ordained to the curacy of St. Matthew's, Bayswater, 1878; after seven years was asked to organise the Diocese of London for the C.E.T.S.; Vicar of Holy Trinity, Leicester, 1890; Vicar of St. James', Holloway, 1893; Rector of Holy Trinity, S. Marylebone, 1897, and became Rural Dean; Vicar Paddington, 1911-19, and Rural Dean; Rector and Rural Dean of Birmingham, 1919-25; Prebendary of St. Paul's Cathedral, 1911-19; Whitehead

501

Professor at the London College of Divinity, 1895-1919; Proctor in Convocation and Member of the National Assembly, 1921-25; a member of most of the larger Church Patronage Trusts, the great Church Societies; and many Diocesan Committees. *Publications:* pamphlets on Church Finance; series of papers on Confirmation. *Recreations:* Natural History, chiefly entomology; golf. *Address:* Halfacre, Woking.   (*Died 2 April 1928.*)

HODGES, Right Rev. Edward Noel, D.D.; Rector of St. Cuthbert's, Bedford, 1907-1916; Archdeacon of Bedford, 1910-24; Assistant Bishop of St. Albans, 1914-24; *b.* 1849; *m.* 1877, Alice, *d.* of Capt. Shirreff, Moray, N.B.; one *s.* two *d. Educ.:* Queen's College, Oxford. Ordained 1873; Tutor Mission College, Islington, 1873-77; Principal, Noble College, Masulipatam, 1877-86; Trinity College, Candy, 1886-89; Bishop of Travancore and Cochin, 1890-1904; Assistant Bishop of Durham, 1904-6; Assistant Bishop of Ely, 1907-14; retired, 1924. *Address:* Silverburn, Hoddesdon, Herts.
    (*Died 18 May 1928.*)

HODGES, Ven. George, M.A.; Hon. Canon of Ely, 1898-1912; Canon Residentiary since 1912; Commissary to the Bishop of Ely since 1903; Archdeacon of Sudbury since 1902; *b.* 1851; *s.* of Rev. George Hodges, Vicar of St. Andrew's, Hastings; *m.* Agnes Helena (*d.* 1916), *e. d.* of William Sanders, M.D.; six *s.* one *d. Educ.:* St. John's Coll. Cambridge; private tuition. B.A. 1873; M.A. 1888; ordained to curacy of Milton-next-Sittingbourne, 1878; Curate of Stoke-by-Nayland, 1877; Vicar of Stoke-by-Nayland, 1881-88; Vicar of St. James's, Bury St. Edmunds, 1888-1912; Rural Dean of Thingoes, 1888-1902; Examining Chaplain to Bishop of Ely, 1906-14; to Bishop of S. Edmundsbury, 1914; nominated to St. James's, Piccadilly, 1894, but the Marquis of Bristol lost the patronage, and he was not instituted; preached before Queen Victoria in the private chapel, Windsor, 1892; Select Preacher before the University of Cambridge, 1894; late Chaplain of 3rd Suffolk Vol. Batt.; Past Provincial Grand Chaplain of Suffolk P.M. Lodge 1008; Grand Chaplain in the Grand Lodge of England, 1908; Chaplain to the High Sheriff of Cambs, 1919. *Address:* Archdeacon's Lodgings, Ely. *Club:* Constitutional.   (*Died 30 Aug. 1922.*)

HODGES, Hon. Sir Henry Edward Agincourt; Kt., *cr.* 1918; Puisne Judge of the Supreme Court, Victoria, since 1889; Chancellor of Diocese of Melbourne since 1889; *b.* Liverpool, Oct. 1844; *m.* 1878, Margaret, *d.* of George Knox; one *s.* two *d. Educ.:* Church of England Grammar School and University of Melbourne. Went to Australia, 1854. *Address:* Homeden, Toorak, Melbourne, Victoria. *Club:* Melbourne.   (*Died 8 Aug. 1919.*)

HODGETT, Rev. Richard, Pastor, Ballymena Baptist Church since 1922; Lecturer, Irish Baptist College; *b.* Dungannon, Co. Tyrone, 30th April 1884; *s.* of Edward and Mary Hodgett; *m.* 1912, Mary Elizabeth Kerr; two *s.* three *d. Educ.:* The Irish Baptist College. Pastor, Phibsborough Baptist Church, Dublin, 1912-14; Sharkill Road Baptist Church, Belfast, 1914-22; President, Baptist Union of Ireland 1925-1926. *Publications:* The Spirit Filled Church; The Doctrines and Practices of The Irish Baptists. *Address:* The Manse, Mount Street, Ballymena, Co. Antrim. *T.A.:* Hodgett Ballymena. *M.:* IA 6530. (*Died 26 Sept. 1927.*)

HODGINS, Lieut.-Col. Frederick Owen, D.S.O. 1917; Royal Canadian Engineers: 2nd *s.* of Major-General W. E. Hodgins; *b.* Ottawa, 6 Oct. 1887; *m.* 1921, Rebecca Kathleen, *e. d.* of Henry Blakeney, Ottawa; one *d. Educ.:* Royal Military Coll. of Canada (graduated with honours, 1907). Lt. Royal Canadian Engineers, 1907; Major, 1915; Bt. and Temp. Lt.-Col., 502

1918; went to France with 1st Canadian Division, Feb. 1915; served continuously till formation of Canadian Army Corps, Sep. 1915; Staff Officer to Chief Engineer, Sep. 1915-Feb. 1917; Staff Capt., War Office (Directorate of Fortifications and Works (aviation), Aug. 1917-March 1918, specially employed, Headquarters Canadian Army Corps March 1918-Aug. 1918 on re-organisation Canadian Engineers 1918-19, Staff Officer to G.O.C. Canadian Engineers and Chief Engineer Canadian Army Corps, specially employed Militia Headquarters, Ottawa, 1919; passed Staff College, Camberley, 1920; General Staff Officer, Military District No. 3, Kingston, Ont., 1921 (despatches thrice, D.S.O.); Associate Member, The Engineering Institute of Canada. *Recreation:* golf. *Address:* 1 Villa St. Clare Apartments, Barrie Street, Kingston, Ont. *Clubs:* Junior Naval and Military; Country, Ottawa; Frontenac, Kingston; Cataraqui Golf and Country, Kingston.   (*Died 13 Nov. 1924.*)

HODGINS, Rev. Joseph Rogerson Edmond Cotter, M.A.; Rector of Whitstone, Exeter, 1917; Vicar of St. James's, Birkdale, 1905-17; Hon. Canon of Liverpool, 1896; Proctor in Convocation for Archdeaconry of Liverpool, 1906; Rural Dean of North Meols, 1913-17; *s.* of late Rev. E. P. Hodgins, D.D., Vicar of St. Stephen's, Edge Hill, and Margaret Anne, *d.* of Rev. Prebendary J. R. Cotter, M.A., *g.s.* of Sir James Cotter, 1st Bt., M.P.; *m.* 1880, Theresa Georgina Adelaide, *d.* of Robert Conway Hickson, J.P. of Fermoyle, Co. Kerry, High Sheriff, 1855; one *s.* three *d. Educ.:* Liverpool College; Emmanuel College, Camb. (Foundation scholar, Thorpe scholar, Hubbard exhibitioner and prizeman). B.A. (26th wrangler), 1873; M.A. 1876. Ordained Deacon, 1874; Priest, 1875, by Bishop of Chester; Curate of St. Jude's, West Derby, 1874-75; Curate of St. Luke's, Liverpool, 1875-81; Vicar of St. Cyprian, Edge Hill, 1881-1905; Rural Dean of Liverpool (South), 1902-5; Surrogate, 1887. *Publications:* The Sunday School in relation to the Daily Life of the Young; While there's Life there's Hope, etc. *Recreations:* cricket, boating, golf. *Address:* Whitstone Rectory, Exeter.
    (*Died May 1919.*)

HODGSON, Rev. Francis Greaves, Rector of Aldwincle, Northamptonshire, since 1891; Hon. Canon of Peterborough Cathedral since 1901; Rural Dean of Higham; *s.* of F. R. Hodgson, Oakley, near Manchester; *b.* 8 Sep. 1840; *m.* 1868, Fanny Satterfield (*d.* 1917), *d.* of James Bellhouse, Victoria Park, Manchester; two *s.* two *d. Educ.:* Rugby; Exeter College, Oxford; Cuddesdon College. Curate at Buxton, 1867-70; Rector of Pilton, 1870-91. *Address:* Aldwincle, St. Peter's Rectory, Thrapston. *T.A.:* Aldwincle. *Club:* Royal Societies. (*Died 12 June 1920.*)

HODGSON, Rev. Francis Roger, M.A.; *m.*; no *c. Educ.:* Rugby School; Corpus Christi College, Oxford. Deacon, 1877; Priest, 1878; Missionary Incumbent (U.M.C.A.) of St. John the Evangelist, Mbweni, Zanzibar, 1877-89; Curate of Higher Mediety of Malpas, 1878-79; Archdeacon of Zanzibar, 1882-89; Vicar of Frithelstock, 1890-93; U.M.C.A. Secretary for West of England and Wales, 1893-1909; for South of England and Oxford, 1909-18; Curate in charge of St. Anne's, Saunton, 1920. *Address:* St. Anne's, Saunton, N. Devon.
    (*Died 4 Nov. 1920.*)

HODGSON, Sir Frederic Mitchell, K.C.M.G., *cr.* 1899; C.M.G. 1891; *b.* 22 Nov. 1851; *s.* of late Rev. O. A. Hodgson, Rector of East Stoke, Wareham; *m.* 1883, Mary Alice, Lady of Grace of the Order St. John of Jerusalem (author of The Siege of Kumassi), *d.* of late W. A. G. Young, C.M.G., Governor of Gold Coast; one *d.* Was in Secretary's Office, Post Office Dept., 1868-82; Postmaster-General,

British Guiana, 1882-88 ; Colonial Sec., Gold Coast, 1888-98 ; administered the Govt. on several occasions ; Governor, 1898-1900 ; Govr. and Commander - in - Chief, Barbados, 1900-4 ; Govr. British Guiana, 1904-11 ; formerly Capt. in 24th Middlesex R.V. ; Capt. British Guiana R.V. 1886-88 ; Maj. commanding Gold Coast R.V., which he raised in 1892 ; Maj. comm. Barbados Volunteer Force, which he raised in 1901 ; V.D. 1897 ; Knight of Grace of the Order of the Hospital of St. John of Jerusalem. *Address:* 21 Rosary Gardens, South Kensington, S.W.7.   *T.:* Kensington 6047.   *Clubs:* Conservative, Ranelagh, West Indian.

                        (Died 6 July 1925.)

HODGSON, George Bryan, J.P. ; Joint General Manager, Press Association ; *b.* 29 July 1863 ; *s.* of John Hodgson of Toft Hill, Bishop Auckland ; *m.* 1888, Mary, *d.* of Thomas Forster of Benwell. *Educ.:* privately. Editor, Shields Daily Gazette, 1892-1917 ; Assistant Manager, Press Association, 1917-18 ; President Institute of Journalists, 1911-12. *Publications:* The Life Story of James Annand ; The Borough of South Shields ; The Banks of Tyne, etc. *Address:* Byron House, 85 Fleet Street, E.C.4. *Club:* Authors'.   *(Died 31 Mar. 1926.)*

HODGSON, Rt. Rev. Henry Bernard, D.D. ; 1st Bishop of St. Edmundsbury and Ipswich since 1914 ; *b.* Barton Hall, Penrith, 10 March 1856 ; *s.* of George Courtenay Hodgson, Vicar of Barton, and Elizabeth Buckham ; *m.* 1882, Penlope, *d.* of Admiral Richard Laird Warren ; three *s.* one *d.* *Educ.:* Shrewsbury School ; Queen's College and Christ Church, Oxford. 1st class Mods. 1876 ; 1st class Final Classical School, 1878 ; student of Christ Church, 1878-85 ; assistant master Elizabeth College, Guernsey, 1879-81 ; Deacon, 1879 ; Priest, 1880 ; Vicar of Staverton, Northants, 1881-85 ; Headmaster of Birkenhead School, 1885-86 ; Vicar of Thornbury, Gloucestershire, 1886-97 ; Rural Dean of Norham, 1897 ; Vicar of Berwick-on-Tweed, 1297-1914 ; Archdeacon of Lindisfarne, 1904 -14 ; Honorary Canon of Newcastle Cathedral and Examining Chaplain to the Bishop, 1900-14. *Address:* Bishop's House, Ipswich.   *(Died 28 Feb. 1921.)*

HODGSON, Rev. Professor James Muscutt, Principal and Baxter Professor of Theology in the Theological Hall of the Congregational Churches of Scotland, 1894-1916 ; *b.* Cockermouth ; *e. s.* of late John Hodgson of Rose Bank, Cockermouth ; *m.* Emily A., *e. d.* of late Charles Williams, J.P., of Salisbury. *Educ.:* Cockermouth Grammar School ; Glasgow University (M.A., D.D.) ; Lancashire Independent College. D.Sc. Edinburgh University. Congregational Minister, Uttoxeter, Staffs, 1865-1875 ; Professor of Apologetics and Comparative Religion at Lancashire Independent College, Manchester, 1875-94. *Publications:* Religion— the Quest of the Ideal ; Theologia Pectoris ; Outlines of Religious Faith and Doctrine, founded on Intuition and Experience ; Philosophy and Faith ; Philosophy and Revelation ; Facts and Ideas in Theology. *Address:* Bryn Glas, Conway, North Wales. *(Died 12 Mar. 1923.)*

HODGSON, Ven. Robert, Archdeacon of Stafford, 1898-1910 ; Prebendary of Lichfield since 1894 ; *b.* Hoxne, Suffolk, 11 July 1844 ; *e. s.* of Rev. John Hodgson, vicar of Hoxne ; *m.* 1st, 1870 ; 2nd, 1878. *Educ.:* Eton (gained a Foundation scholarship, 1858) ; Oriel Coll. Oxford (M.A.). Scholar and Exhibitioner, 1863 ; 1st Class in Moderations, 1864 ; 3rd Class in Lit. Hum., 1867. Curate of Stoke-upon-Trent, 1868-72 ; Vicar of Christ Church, West Bromwich, 1872-1888 ; Rural Dean of Handsworth, 1893-98 ; Vicar of Walsall and Rural Dean, 1883-92 ; Proctor for Archdeaconry of Stafford, 1895 ; Rector of Handsworth, 1892 - 1904 ; Canon-Residentiary of Lichfield, 1907. *Recreations:*

gardening, golf. *Address:* Lombard Croft, Lichfield.   *(Died 29 Jan. 1917.)*

HODGSON, Robert Kirkman, J.P. ; *o. s.* of late Kirkman Daniel Hodgson, M.P., of Ashgrove, Kent, and Frances, *d.* of late John Laforey Butler of Southgate ; *b.* 1850 ; *m.* 1875, Lady Honora Janet (Nora), 3rd *d.* of 9th Earl of Cork ; three *s.* (two killed in action) one *d.* *Educ.:* Eton ; Trinity College, Cambridge ; M.A. *Address:* Gavelacre, Longparish, Hampshire ; 77 Eaton Square, S.W.1.   *T.:* Vic. 480. *Clubs:* Athenæum, Brooks's, Travellers'.

                        (Died 26 May 1924.)

HODGSON, Ven. Thomas, Archdeacon of Huntingdon since 1915 ; Vicar of St. Neot's since 1912 ; Rural Dean, 1902. *Educ.:* Hatfield Hall ; Durham University (Foundation Scholar). Ordained, 1878 ; Curate of St. Andrew, Bishop Auckland, 1878-9 ; Assist. Master, St. George's School, Brampton, 1879-1883 ; Curate, 1883-90 ; Head-Master, Huntingdon Grammar School, 1884 - 90 ; Rector of Eynesbury, 1890-1912 ; Hon. Canon, Ely, 1911. *Address:* The Vicarage, St. Neot's Huntingdon.   *(Died 28 Sept. 1921.)*

HODGSON, Rev. William, M.A. ; Vicar of Aston, Birmingham, since 1917 ; Hon. Canon of Birmingham, 1917 ; Examining Chaplain to Bishop of Sodor and Man, 1916 ; *s.* of late Rev. William Hodgson, Vicar of Christ Church, Colne, Lancs, 1837-74, and Curate of Haworth, Yorks, under Rev. Patrick Brontë, 1835 - 37 (father of Charlotte and Emily Brontë) ; *m.* ; two *s.* three *d.* *Educ.:* University of London, Int. B.A. 1883 ; Merton College, Oxford, B.A. (1st Class Theological School), 1887 ; M.A. 1891 ; Deacon, 1887 ; Priest, 1888 ; Curate at St. Peter - le - Bailey, Oxford, 1887-90 ; Curate in charge of St. Michael's, Claughton, 1890-98 ; Vicar of St. Mary and St. Paul, Widnes, 1893-98 ; Emmanuel Church, Everton, Liverpool, 1898-1901 ; St. John, Waterloo, Liverpool, 1901-12 ; Vicar of St. Andrew, Southport, 1912-17 ; Hon. Canon of Liverpool, 1916. *Address:* Aston Vicarage, Birmingham.   *(Died 25 Dec. 1919.)*

HODGSON, William Hope; 2nd Lieut. R.F.A. ; *b.* 15 Nov. 1877 ; 2nd *s.* of Rev. Samuel Hodgson. *Educ.:* abroad. Some years at sea as an officer in Mercantile Marine ; commenced writing, 1902 ; first book published, 1907 ; commissioned July 1915 (R.F.A.) ; gazetted out of the army, 10 June 1916, owing to ill-health due to injuries received on active service ; eventually regained health and was recommissioned, 18 March 1917. *Publications:* The Boats of the Glen Carrig, 1907 ; The House on the Borderland, 1908 ; The Ghost Pirates, 1909 ; The Night Land, 1912 ; Carnacki the Ghost Finder, 1913 ; Men of the Deep Waters, 1914 ; The Luck of the Strong, 1916 ; Captain Gault, 1917. *Address:* Lisswood, Borth, S.O., Cardigan, Wales ; Chalet Mathilde, Sanary, Var, France.   *(Died 17 April 1918.)*

HODSDON, Sir James (W. B.), K.B.E., *cr.* 1920 ; C.B.E. 1919 ; J.P. ; M.D., F.R.C.S. Ed. ; President of Royal College of Surgeons, Edinburgh, 1914 -17 ; Vice-President, 1917 -19 ; Consulting Surgeon, Royal Infirmary. Edinburgh ; Representative of R.C.S. Edinburgh on General Medical Council ; Member of the Dental Board of the United Kingdom ; late Senior Surgeon, Royal Infirmary, Edinburgh ; late Senior University Lecturer on Clinical Surgery ; late Chairman of Committee of Management of Scottish Conjoint Board ; Chairman of Governing Board, School of Medicine of Royal Colleges ; late Examiner in Surgery, R.C.S. Edin. ; late Major R.A.M.C. (T.), 2nd Scottish General Hospital (C.B.E., despatches twice) ; *b.* 1858 ; *s.* of late Francis E. Hodsdon ; *m.* Joan, *d.* of late William Raffin, Edinburgh. *Educ.:* Sherborne School ; Queen's College, Belfast ; Uni-

503

versity and School of Medicine, Edinburgh; London; Vienna; Paris; late Lecturer on Surgery, Surgeons' Hall, Edinburgh; Examiner in Surgery, Universities of Edinburgh and Durham and Queen's University of Belfast. *Publications:* papers on various surgical subjects. *Recreations:* fishing, shooting, curling, golfing. *Address:* 6 Chester Street, Edinburgh. *T.:* 2330. *Clubs:* Royal Societies; University, Edinburgh. (*Died 28 May 1928.*)

HODSON, Colonel Frederic Arthur, C.B.E. 1919; Commandant Northern Rhodesia Police, 1912-19; retired with rank of Colonel, 1919; *b.* 20 Oct. 1866; *s.* of late M. Storr Hodson, Crayhe, Easingwold, Yorkshire; unmarried. Enlisted 65th Regt. 1st Batt. York and Lanc. Regt., 1889; transferred 84th Regt. 2nd Batt., Natal, 1892; served through Matabeleland Rebellion with Mounted Infantry Company Y. and L. Regt., 1896; joined British South Africa Police, S. Rhodesia, Nov. 1896; South Africa War, 1900-1 (Queen's and King's medal); Sub.-Inspector B.S.A. Police, 1902; seconded to Barotse Native Police, North-Western Rhodesia, with rank of Captain, 1903; Major, 1906; Second in Command Barotse Native Police, 1906; Lieut.-Colonel Commandant Northern Rhodesia Police, 1912; temporary rank Colonel 1916 to end of Campaign; O.C. Lines of Communication General Northey's Column; Commanded Forces North Eastern Border, German East Africa Campaign, 1914 1916 (despatches, C.B.E.). *Recreations:* tennis, golf. *Address:* The Cottage, Fulford, York. *T.:* Fulford 34. *Clubs:* Sports; Yorkshire, York. (*Died 31 Jan. 1925.*)

HODSON, Col. George Benjamin, C.B. 1911; D.S.O. 1902: A.Q.M.G. Indian Army; *b.* 3 Oct. 1863; *m.* 1910, Dorothy Clara, *d.* of Mr. Murray of 42 Clanricarde Gardens, S.W.; one *d.* Entered army, 1882; Captain, 1893; Major, 1901; Lt.-Col. 1905; Colonel, 1909; served Egypt, 1882 (medal, bronze star); Burmese Expedition, 1885-1887 (despatches, medal with clasp); Hazara, 1891 (clasp); N.W. Frontier, India, 1897-98 (despatches, medal and clasp); Southern Nigeria, 1902; Aro Expedition (despatches, medal with clasp, D.S.O.). *Address:* Lahore, Punjab, India. *Club:* United Service.
(*Died 25 Jan. 1916.*)

HODSON, Sir Robert Adair, 4th Bt.; *cr.* 1789; Lieut.-Col. commanding 4th Batt. Royal Irish Fusiliers; retired, 1907; Hon. Col. 1907; *s.* of 3rd Bt. and Meriel Anne, *d.* of Rev. Richard Neville; *b.* 29 Sep. 1853; *S.* father 1888; *m.* 1911, Emily Frances Louisa, *e. d.* of late Colonel G. Beresford, R.A., of Woodhouse, Co. Waterford. *Educ.:* Haileybury College. Owns about 1000 acres. *Heir: u.* E. A. Hodson. *Address:* Holybrooke, Bray, Co. Wicklow.
(*Died 3 Jan. 1921.*)

HOERNLE, Augustus Frederic Rudolf, M.A. (Oxford), Ph.D. (Tübingen), C.I.E. 1897; *b.* Agra (East India), 19 Oct. 1841; 2nd *s.* of late Rev. T. C. Hoernle, C.M.S.; *m.* 1877, Sophie, *d.* of R. Romig of Bonn (Germany); one *s. Educ.:* public school in Esslingen and Stuttgart; Universities of Basel, Tübingen, and London. Church Missionary in Mirat, 1865; Professor in Jay Narain's Coll. Benares, 1870; returned to England, 1874; Principal Cathedral Mission College, Calcutta, 1877; joined Indian Educational Service, 1881; Principal of the Calcutta Madrasah, 1881; retired 1899; specially interested in archaeology, epigraphy, palæography, etc. *Decorated* for linguistic, numismatic, and archæological research. *Publications:* Comparative Grammar of the North Indian Languages; Comparative Dictionary of the Bihari Language; Edition of the Bower Manuscript, of Chanda's Prakrit Grammar, of the Seventh Anga of the Jains; Report on the British Collection of Central Asian Antiquities;

Studies in the Medicine of Ancient India: Part I. Osteology; History of India; numerous contributions to the Journal of Royal Asiatic Society, the Asiatic Society of Bengal, the Indian Antiquary, etc. *Address:* 8 Northmoor Road, Oxford. (*Died 12 Nov. 1918.*)

HOEY, William, M.A., D.Lit., Q.U.I., and M.A. Oxon., M.R.A.S.; *b.* Dungannon, 2 July 1849; *s.* of late Rev. W. Hoey; *m.* 1882, Eleanor, *d.* of late Nathaniel Ferguson, of Mount Pottinger House, Belfast; three *s. Educ.:* Grammar School, Drogheda; Connexional School, Dublin; Queen's College, Belfast. Entered Indian Civil Service, 1870; proceeded to India, 1872; appointed to Oudh, and subsequently N.W.P.; Commissioner of Gorakhpur, 1897; Fellow of Allahabad University; Member of Provincial Numismatic Committee; retired, 1900; Lecturer on Indian History and Hindustani, Dublin University, 1903; Lecturer on Hindustani, Oxford University, 1906. *Publications:* Trades and Manufactures of Northern India; Translation of Oldenberg's Buddha: His Life, his Doctrine, his Order, from the German, and of The Life of Asafuddaulah, and Memoirs of Delhi and Fyzabad from the Persian; Urdu Praxis; Going East; contributions to the journals of the Royal Asiatic Society and Asiatic Society of Bengal. *Recreations:* interested in Indian history, archæology and numismatics, and in Persian. *Address:* 8 Bradmore Road, Oxford. (*Died April 1919.*)

HOFFERT, Hermann H., D.Sc. (London); Fellow of the Physical Society of London; H.M. Inspector (Divisional) of Schools. Board of Education, Technological Branch; *b.* Liverpool, 25 Dec. 1860; *o. surv. s.* of late Henry A. Hoffert, of German descent, naturalised Englishman; *m.* 1891, Annie, *e. d.* of late E. Ward, of Reading, Berks; two *s.* two *d. Educ.:* Crediton Grammar School; Weymouth Collegiate School. Royal College of Science and Royal School of Mines (1876-81); Associate Royal School of Mines in Geological, Metallurgical, and Mining Divisions, with De la Beche medal in mining; Neill Arnott medal for Experimental Physics, London University; D.Sc. in Experimental Physics, 1885; Assistant and afterwards Demonstrator of Physics, Royal College of Science; Inspector of Schools under the Science and Art Department, 1893; now in charge of the North-Western Division of England for Inspection of Science and Technical Schools under the Board of Education. *Publications:* papers to Physical Society of London on Colour-combining Apparatus and Intermittent Lightning Flashes. *Recreations:* cycling, tennis, photography.

HOGAN, Henry Charles, Member of National Assembly of the Church of England; *b.* 29 Sep. 1860; 2nd *s.* of late Cole Hogan; *m.* 1883, Emma Maud Mary, *o. d.* of late George Alexander Stead; three *s.* one *d. Educ.:* privately. Entered ecclesiastical journalism 1881; Sub-Editor of the Record, 1881-1905; Editor of the Layman, 1905-8; Editor of the Record since 1908, also Editor of the Churchman since 1914, and of other Church and Homiletical publications; late Hon. Secretary of Church of England Young Men's Society; Life Governor Cheltenham Training College; Vice-President Church Pastoral Aid Society; Chairman Barbican Mission to the Jews. *Recreation:* change of work. *Address:* 10 Longley Road, Tooting Graveney, S.W.17. *T.:* Streatham 2980.
(*Died 31 Dec. 1924.*)

HOGAN, James Francis; author, journalist; *b.* Tipperary, 29 Dec. 1855; while an infant, parents emigrated to Australia and settled near Melbourne. Unmarried. *Educ.:* St. Patrick's College, Melbourne. Entered Education Department, Victoria, 1873; joined literary staff of Melbourne Argus, 1881; settled in London, 1887; M.P. Mid Division of Tipperary

504

HOFMEYR, George Morgan. See page xxi.

1898-1900. *Publications:* An Australian Christmas Collection, 1886; History of the Irish in Australia, 1887; The Australian in London, 1888, The Lost Explorer, 1890; The Convict King, 1891; Robert Lowe, Viscount Sherbrooke, 1893; The Sister Dominions, 1895; The Gladstone Colony, 1898. *Recreations:* walking, touring, music, and the drama. *(Died 9 Nov. 1924.)*

HOGAN, Rt. Rev. Mgr. John F., D.D.; President, St. Patrick's College, Maynooth, since 1912; *b.* Coolreagh, Co. Clare, 1858. *Educ.:* Ennis Diocesan College; St. Sulpice, Paris; Freiburg in Breisgau. Ordained, 1882; spent some years for special studies in France and Germany; Professor of Modern Languages at Maynooth, 1886; has edited Irish Ecclesiastical Record for close on twenty years; gave evidence on Irish University Education before the Robertson Commission; took part in organising reception of King George and Queen Mary, 1911; Senator of the National University of Ireland, 1913; Pro-Vice-Chancellor, 1914. Domestic Prelate of His Holiness the Pope, 1914. *Publications:* The Life and Works of Dante; Irish Catholics and Trinity College; Maynooth College and the Laity; many historical and theological essays in various reviews. *Address:* St. Patrick's College, Maynooth. *T.A.:* Maynooth, Ireland.
(Died 24 Nov. 1918.)

HOGARTH, David George, C.M.G. 1918; M.A.; D.Litt.; Hon.Litt.D. Cantab.; Keeper of the Ashmolean Museum since 1909; President of the Royal Geographical Society since 1925; Statutory Commissioner under the Oxford and Cambridge Universities Act, 1923; Fellow Magdalen College, Oxford; Fellow of the British Academy; Radcliffe Trustee; Schweich Lecturer, 1924; F.S.A., F.R.G.S. (Founder's Gold Medal, 1917); Vice-Pres. Hellenic Soc.; Comdr. R.N.V.R. 1915-19, and Director of Arab Bureau, Cairo, 1916; Order of Nile 3rd class, 1917; Order of Nahda (Hejaz) 2nd class, 1919; *b.* Barton-on-Humber, 23 May 1862; *e. s.* of Rev. G. Hogarth, Vicar; *m.* 1894, Laura V., *y. d.* of Charles Uppleby, Barrow Hall; one *s. Educ.:* Winchester; Magdalen College, Oxford. Craven Fellow, 1886; Tutor of Magdalen, 1886-98; Director, British School at Athens, 1897-1900; explored Asia Minor, Syria, etc., and conducted excavations in Cyprus, Egypt, Crete, Syria and Melos. *Publications:* Devia Cypria, 1890; Modern and Ancient Roads in Eastern Asia Minor, 1892; A Wandering Scholar in the Levant, 1896; Philip and Alexander of Macedon, 1897; Authority and Archæology, 1899; The Nearer East, 1902; The Penetration of Arabia, 1904; The Archaic Artemisia of Ephesus, 1908; Ionia and the East, 1909; Accidents of an Antiquary's Life, 1910; The Ancient East, 1914; Carchemish I., 1914; The Balkans, 1915; Hittite Seals, 1920; Arabia, 1922; The Wandering Scholar, 1925; Kings of the Hittites (Schweich Lectures), 1926; C. M. Doughty, A Memoir, 1928. *Address:* 20 S. Giles or Ashmolean Museum, Oxford. *T.:* Oxford 3219. *Clubs:* Athenæum, Savile.
(Died 6 Nov. 1927.)

HOGBEN, George, C.M.G. 1915; M.A., F.G.S.; *b.* 14 July 1853; *e. s.* of Rev. G. Hogben, Congregational Minister, and Mary B. McLachlan; *m.* 1885, Emily Frances, *y. d.* of late Edward Dobson, M.I.C.E.; two *s. Educ.:* Congregational School, Lewisham; University School, Nottingham; Birkbeck Institution; St. Catharine's College, Cambridge (Mathematical Sizarship); Gold Medallist, Royal Geographical Society, 1871; Haberdashers' Co.'s and Goldsmiths' Co.'s Exhibitions; 1st Class Mathematical Honours (Wrangler), 1877. In Accountant and Controller-General's Dept., Inland Revenue, 1872-3; Mathematical Master, Aldenham School, 1877-81; subsequently at High School, Christchurch, N. Zealand; Head-Master, Timaru High School, 1889-99; Inspector-General of Schools, N.Z., 1899-1914, and late Director of

Education (title changed); has been President of many learned societies; now Member of the General Council of Education for N.Z.; Fellow of Senate, University, N.Z., 1908-15. *Publications:* Methode Naturelle: Mathematical Geography; Earthquakes and other Earth Movements; many pamphlets. *Recreations:* bowling, seismology, proportional representation. *Address:* Wellington, New Zealand. *Club:* Civil Service, Wellington. *(Died 25 April 1920.)*

HOGG, Rev. Andrew Albert Victor; Rector of Gowran since 1906; Prebendary Killamary since 1907; Chancellor of Ossory, 1925; *b.* 9 Jan. 1864; *s.* of Rev. Dr. Hogg, Rector of Cavan, and Ann Caroline Brushe; unmarried. *Educ.:* Trinity College, Dublin. Ordained, 1891; Vicar of St. John, Kilkenny, 1901-6; Minor Canon of St. Canice's Cathedral, 1905-6; Rural Dean of Odagh, 1906; Member of Diocesan Council, 1907; Secretary of Diocesan Synod, 1920; Member of the Senate T.C.D., 1892; F.R.S.A.I., 1897. *Recreations:* tennis and gardening. *Address:* St. Mary's Rectory, Gowran, Co. Kilkenny. *(Died 11 Nov. 1927.)*

HOGG, Sir Frederick Russell, K.C.I.E., *cr.* 1888; C.S.I., 1887; Indian Civil Service, retired 1889; *b.* Paris, 1836; 5th *s.* of Rt. Hon. Sir James Weir Hogg, 1st Bt., and Mary, *d.* of Samuel Swinton, Swinton; *m.* 1st, 1857, Emily, 3rd *d.* of Gen. Eckford; 2nd, 1885, Harriett Venn, *d.* of late William Stephens Dicken; three *s.* one *d. Educ.:* Eton; Haileybury Coll. Arrived at Calcutta in 1857; Postmaster-Gen., Punjab, 1863; Bombay, 1867; Bengal, 1868; Deputy-Director-General Post Office of India, 1869; Director-General Post Office of India, 1880; late partner in firm of Messrs. Hogg, Curtis, Campbell, and Company. *Recreations:* Took second prize for diving at Eton; won mile swimming race at Haileybury; Captain of term four-oar boat at college; used to play cricket, football, rackets, lawn-tennis; generally fond of all games and fond of shooting. *Address:* 6 Bickenhall Mansions, W. *Club:* Oriental.
(Died 4 Sept. 1923.)

HOGG, Maj.-Gen. George Crawford, C.B. 1896; *b.* 18 Sep. 1842; *m.* 1878, Henrietta Isabella, *d.* of C. N. Minchin; three *s. Educ.:* Cheltenham College. Entered Bombay Cavalry, 1858; Maj.-Gen. 1897; served Afghan War, 1878-1880 (despatches several times, medal); Q.M.G. Bombay Army, 1891-95; commanding Deesa District, 1895-1900; Colonel 34th Prince Albert Victor's Own Poona Horse, 1904; transferred to unemployed supernumerary list, 1904. *Address:* Ablington, Cheltenham. *Club:* New, Cheltenham. *(Died 12 Oct. 1921.)*

HOGG, Sir Stuart Saunders, Kt., *cr.* 1875; *b.* Calcutta, 1833; 4th *s.* of Rt. Hon. Sir James W. Hogg, 1st Bt., M.P.; *m.* Selina Catherine, *e. d.* of Sir T. E. Perry, 1860; two *s.* one *d. Educ.:* Eton. Entered Indian Civil Service, 1853; served in Punjaub, where he was Assistant-Commissioner during time of Mutiny; served as civil officer attached to flying column under Gen. John Nicholson (despatches); transferred later to Oude, and subsequently down to Bengal, where he was Magistrate and Collector of Burdwan, and afterwards Chief Commissioner of Police and Chairman of the Municipality, Calcutta. *Address:* Villa Céline, Beaulieu-sur-Mer, France. *Club:* East India United Service.
(Died 23 Mar.1921.)

HOGGE, James Myles, M.A.; M.P. (L.) East Edinburgh, 1912-24; associated with B. Seebohm Rowntree in social investigation, etc.; *b.* Edinburgh, 19 April 1873; *m.* 1905, Florence R. Metcalfe, Malton, Yorkshire; one *s.* two *d. Educ.:* Edinburgh Normal School and Edinburgh University; Moray House Training College; New College, Edinburgh. Began as pupil teacher in Edinburgh; 1st class King's Scholar, Moray House Training College, Edinburgh; Licentiate of United Free Church of

Scotland; engaged in Settlement work in Edinburgh slums; joined B. Seebohm Rowntree, Joseph Rowntree, and Arthur Sherwell, in social investigation; joint editor, Scottish Students' Song Book, British Students' Song Book; President, Edinburgh University Liberal Association; Senior President, Edinburgh Students' Representative Council; editor, Student, Edinburgh University; founded Young Scots' Society; President National Federation of Discharged Sailors and Soldiers, 1919-20. *Publications:* War Pensions and Allowances; Betting and Gambling; The Facts of Gambling; Licensing in Scandinavia; Aims and Achievements of Liberalism; Scotland Insured; Scots Home Rule; Pensions and Separation Allowances; A Book of Consolation; Joint Chief Whip Independent Liberal Party, 1918-22. *Recreation:* work. *Club:* Press. (*Died 27 Oct. 1923.*)

HOGUE, Hon. James Alexander; *b.* Clarence Town, New South Wales, 2 Sep. 1846; 3rd *s.* of late Fitzarthur Hogue and Elizabeth Mackay; *m.* Jessie, 4th *d.* of late John Robards, Clarence Town; five *s.* four *d. Educ.:* National Schools, and Newcastle Grammar School. After leaving school learnt printing; acquired knowledge of shorthand; became newspaper reporter; joined Sydney Evening News staff, 1875; Sub-Editor five years, Editor ten years; Minister of Public Instruction and Labour, 1898-99; Colonial Secretary, 1904-7; M.L.A., Glebe, 1894-1910; Minister of Public Instruction and Minister for Labour and Industry, 1907-10; Trustee, National Park, N.S.W.; Councillor, Royal Australian Historical Society. *Publications:* newspaper and magazine articles, etc. *Recreations:* music, bowls. *Address:* Mosman, Sydney, N.S.W. *Clubs:* Athenæum, Tattersall's, Sydney.
(*Died 2 Aug. 1920.*)

HOHLER, Henry Booth, J.P., D.L.; 2nd *s.* of Rev. Frederick Williams Hohler, Rector of Winstone and Colesborne, Gloucestershire, and Jane Harriet, *e. d.* of late Thomas Theobald, of Greys Thurrock, Essex; *b.* 1835; *m.* 1st, 1856, Henrietta Wilhelmina (*d.* 1902), *o. d.* of late Robert Lawes of Kingston Hill, Surrey; 2nd, 1914, Ida Marion, *y.d.* of late Rev. William and Mrs. Stracey-Clitherow, formerly of Boston House, Middlesex. *Heir:* Frederick Scott [a magistrate for Berkshire, *b.* 1859; *m.* 1884, Frances Amelia, 3rd *d.* of Sir Jacob Henry Preston, 2nd Bart.; one *s.* one *d.*]. High Sheriff, Kent, 1901. *Address:* Fawkham Manor, Kent. *Club:* Junior Carlton.(*Died 14 Feb. 1916.*)

HOLCROFT, Sir Charles, 1st Bt., *cr.* 1905; *b.* 16 July 1831; 4th *s.* of late Thomas Holcroft of Brierley Hill, Staffs; unmarried; took a prominent part in establishing Birmingham University. *Heir:* none. *Address:* The Shrubbery, Summerhill, Kingswinford, Staffs.
(*Died 11 Mar. 1917.*)

HOLDEN, Captain Edward Charles Shuttleworth, D.S.O. 1900; J.P.; Lt.-Col., Derbyshire Yeomanry Cavalry; *b.* 7 Jan. 1865; *o. c.* of Charles Shuttleworth Holden; *m.* 1906, Aimée Marguerite (*d.* 1913), *y. d.* of late Vicomte de Labrosse and *widow* of William R. Cookson of Binfield Park, Berks; one *s.* Served South Africa, 1899-1900 (despatches, D.S.O.); resigned, 1910. *Address:* The Cottage, Doveridge, Derby. *Clubs:* Boodle's, Carlton. (*Died 17 May 1916.*)

HOLDEN, Sir Edward Hopkinson, 1st Bt., *cr.* 1909; M.P. (L.) Heywood Division, Lancs, 1906-10; Chairman of the London City and Midland Bank, Ltd.; *s.* of late Henry Holden of Tottington, Lancashire; *b.* 11 May 1848, Tottington, near Manchester; *m.* 1877, Annie, *y. d.* of William Cassie, late of Aberdeen, two *s. Educ.:* Summerseat; Owens College, Manchester. *Recreation:* golf. *Heir: e. s.* Harry Cassie Holden [*b.* 20 Oct. 1877; *m.* 1905, Edith Ross, *d.* of John Pryor. *Educ.:* Trinity Hall,
506

Cambridge. Barrister-at-law of the Inner Temple, 1901; B.A., LL.B.]. *Address:* 5 Threadneedle Street, E.C.; *T.:* Paddington 2023; 19 New Cavendish Street, W.; The Grange, Thorpe, Chertsey, Surrey. *Clubs:* Reform, National Liberal. (*Died 23 July 1919.*)

HOLDEN, Sir Edward Thomas, Kt., *cr.* 1907; J.P.; *b.* 1831; *m.* 1st, 1854, Caroline (*d.* 1901), *e. d.* of Robert Glass, Edinburgh, 2nd, 1902, Helen Sarah, 2nd *d.* of F. H. Yates of Great Barr; one *s.* M.P. (L.) Walsall, 1891-1892; three times Mayor of Walsall, and member of the Town Council for over sixty years. *Address:* Glenelg, Walsall. (*Died 13 Nov. 1926.*)

HOLDEN, Sir John Henry, 1st Bt., *cr.* 1919; Managing Director Tunncliffe & Hampson, Ltd.; Mayor of Leigh, and Military Representative Leigh Area during the war. *Heir: s.* George, *b.* 16 April 1890. *Address:* The Firs, Leigh, Lancs; 7 Argyle Road, Southport. *T.:* Leigh 1; Southport 1181. (*Died 4 May 1926.*)

HOLDEN, Rev. Robert; *b.* 16 Sep. 1853; 4th *s.* of Rev. A. A. Holden of Nuthall Temple, Nottingham; *m.* 1880, Alice, *d.* of John Trotter of Dyrham Park, Barnet; two *s.* two *d. Educ.:* Brentwood. Rector of Nuthall, 1879-1914. *Recreation:* gardening. *Address:* Nuthall Temple, nr. Nottingham. *T.:* Bulwell 77. *M.:* NN 4343.
(*Died 10 May 1926.*)

HOLDER, Rear-Adm. Henry Lowe; *b.* 1832; *m.* 1868, Isabella, *d.* of late Gen. J. S. Fraser, of Ardachie, Inverness. Entered Navy, 1852; Commander, 1864; Capt. 1871; retired, 1873; Rear-Adm. 1888; served Russian War, 1854-55 (Crimean and Turkish medals, Sebastopol clasp, 5th Class Medjidie); Straits of Simonoseki, 1864 (promoted, specially mentioned). *Address:* 5 Sussex Place, Southsea. (*Died 5 Jan. 1924.*)

HOLDER, Sir John Charles, 1st Bt.; *cr.* 1898; Knight of Grace of the Order of the Hospital of St. John of Jerusalem in England; J.P., Birmingham; J.P., D.L., Worcestershire (High Sheriff, 1908); *b.* Birmingham, 10 Dec. 1838; *o. s.* of late Henry Holder, of Birmingham and Malvern; *m.* 1872, Geraldine Augusta, *d.* of John Williams Knipe, of Worcester; four *s.* six *d. Educ.:* Camp Hill; privately. Chairman of Building Committee of New General Hospital, which has cost upwards of £200,000, and was opened free of debt by Princess Christian, 1897; Treasurer of Birmingham Bishopric Endowment Fund; takes an active part on Council of Birmingham University; presented to Birmingham Corporation Art Gallery La Petite Classe, by J. Geoffroy; The Marseillaise, by Gustave Doré; Dominicans in Feather (a group of penguins), by H. Stacy Marks; The Sea Shall Give up Her Dead, by Sir Frederick Leighton; The Wizard, by Burne Jones; Rosa Trixplex, by Rossetti. Possesses pictures by Alma-Tadema, Langley (Disaster), Sidney Cooper, Vicat Cole, Frank Hollt, Kate Greenaway, William Geets, Leader, Keeley Halswelle, Rossetti, Henry Moore, Miss Kemp Welch, David Cox, Ansdell, etc. *Heir: s.* Henry Charles [*b.* Edgbaston, 1 May 1874; *m.* Evelyn, *d.* of Sir Robert Ropner, 1st Bt.; two *s.* three *d. Educ.:* Repton; Brasenose Coll. Oxford (B.A.)]. *Address:* Pitmaston, Moseley, Worcestershire. *T.:* 3080. *Clubs:* Union; Conservative, Birmingham.
(*Died 26 April 1923.*)

HOLDER, Rt. Rev. Mgr. Joseph, Provost; Prot. Ap. *ad instar* V.G.M.R., Diocese of Dunkeld (R.C.). *Address:* St. Joseph's Rectory, Dundee.

HOLDERNESS, Sir Thomas William, 1st Bt., *cr.* 1920; G.C.B., *cr.* 1917; K.C.B., *cr.* 1914; K.C.S.I., *cr.* 1907; I.C.S., B.A.; *b.* 11 June 1849; *m.* 1885, Lucy Shepherd, *d.* of G. R. Elsmie, I.C.S., C.S.I.; one *s.* one *d. Educ.:* Cheltenham; University College, Oxford. Indian Civil

HOLBOROW, Col. William Hillier, C.M.G. See page xxi.

Service, 1872 ; Member of Famine Commission, 1897 ; Sec. to Government of India, Revenue and Agricultural Department, 1898-1901 ; received Kaiser-i-Hind medal, 1st class, 1899 ; Secretary Revenue Statistics and Commerce Department, India Office, 1901-12 ; Permanent Under-Secretary of State, India Office, 1912-19. *Publications :* Narrative of the Indian Famine, 1896-97 ; fourth edition revised of Strachey's India, 1911 ; Peoples and Problems of India, 1912 ; Article India Supplementary Volumes, Encyclopaedia Brittanica. *Heir :* o. s. Ernest William Elsmie, *b.* 1890. *Address :* Flagcourt, Tadworth, Surrey. *T. :* Burgh Heath 29 *Club :* Athenæum.   (*Died 16 Sept. 1924.*)

HOLDICH, Lt.-Col. Godfrey William Vanrennen, D.S.O. 1916 ; R.A. ; *e. s.* of Sir T. H. Holdich ;   *b.* 1882 ; *m.* 1909, Winifred, *d.* of Arthur Fraser. *Educ. :* Wellington. Served European War, 1914-18 (despatches, D.S.O., Order of the Nile and of Crown of Italy, Batt. Lieut.-Col.).   (*Died 13 April 1921.*)

HOLDSWORTH, Lieut.-Col. John Joseph, C.I.E. 1899 ; *b.* 1844 ; *s.* of late John Hall Holdsworth, M.D. ; *m.* 1st, 1871, Lucy (*d.* 1880), *d.* of late John Hall Bridgman, J.P., of Lehra, Gorakhpur, India ; 2nd, 1888, Maria Teresa (*d.* 1898), *d.* of late William James Howard of Sea Point Manor, Blackrock, Dublin ; one *d.* Commandant Gorakhpur Light Horse ; late Lt.-Col. commanding United Provinces Light Horse ; a landed proprietor in India ; Hon. A.D.C. to the Viceroy of India (Baron Curzon of Kedleston), 1899. *Address :* Lehra, Gorakhpur U.P., India. *Club :* East India United Service.
          (*Died 29 June 1920.*)

HOLE, William, R.S.A., 1889 ; R.P.E. ; Painter and Etcher ; *b.* Salisbury, 7 Nov. 1846 ; *o. c.* of Richard Brassey Hole, M.D., and Anne Burn Fergusson ; *m.* 1876, Elizabeth, *o. d.* of Jas. Lindsay, W.S. ; three *s.* two *d. Educ. :* Edin. Acad. Served apprenticeship as a civil engineer in Edinburgh ; travelled in Italy before settling down ; sketches commended by artists in Rome ; adopted Art as a profession, 1870 ; studied in Royal Scottish Academy School ; practised etching, both original and interpretative, in addition to painting, and more recently has turned his attention to mural decoration ; A.R.S.A. 1878. *Principal paintings :* End of the '45, 1879 ; Prince Charlie's Parliament, 1882 ; The Night's Catch, 1883 ; The Fill of the Boats, 1885 ; " If Thou hadst known," 1887 ; The Canterbury Pilgrims, 1889 ; The Ascension ; The Life of Jesus of Nazareth, a series of 80 water-colour pictures completed 1906. *Original etchings :* " Quasi Cursores," 1884 ; The Canterbury Pilgrims, 1888 ; Illustrations of Burns's Poems, 1896 ; " Pro Nobis," 1897. *Interpretative etchings :* The Mill (after J. Crome), 1888 ; The Sawyers (after Millet), 1890 ; Jumping Horse (after Constable), 1890 ; He is Coming (after M. Maris), 1889 ; Admiral Pulido Pareja (after Velasquez), 1893. *Mural paintings :* The Chancel of St. James's Church, Edinburgh, 1896 ; Series of Historical Paintings in the National Portrait Gallery of Scotland, 1900 ; do. in the Municipal Buildings, Edinburgh, 1903. *Address :* 13 Inverleith Terrace, Edinburgh.   (*Died 22 Oct. 1917.*)

HOLFORD, Lt.-Col. Sir George (Lindsay), K.C.V.O. *cr.* 1910 ; C.I.E. 1890 ; C.B.E. 1919 ; C.V.O. 1901 ; Equerry-in-Waiting to H.M., 1901-14 ; *b.* 2 June 1860 ; *s.* of late Robert Stayner Holford and Mary Ann, *d.* of General James Lindsay, M.P. ; *m.* 1912, Susannah West, *d.* of late Arthur Wilson of Tranby Croft, and *widow* of J. Graham Menzies. *Educ. :* Eton. Joined 1st Life Guards, 1880 ; Equerry to Duke of Clarence, 1888-92 ; Lt.-Col. 1st Life Guards since 1908 ; Equerry-in-Waiting to Prince of Wales, 1892-99 ; Equerry-in-Waiting to King Edward to 1910 ; since then Equerry-in-Waiting to Queen Alexandra ; Extra Equerry to King George, 1910 ; commanded Reserve Regt. 1st Life Guards during the war. Owns about 16,400 acres, and the Dorchester House Picture Gallery. *Address :* Weston Birt House, Tetbury ; Dorchester House, Park Lane, W.1. *T. :* Gerrard 4479. *Clubs :* Carlton, Marlborough, White's.
          (*Died 11 Sept. 1926.*)

HOLFORD, James Price William Gwynne, D.L. County of Brecon ; Chairman Conservative Association for Breconshire ; *b.* 25 Nov. 1888 ; *m.* 1891, Mary Eleanor, 3rd *d.* of P. R. Gordon Canning, Hartpury, Gloucester ; one *d. Educ. :* Eton ; Christ Church, Oxford. M.P. Breconshire 1870-90. *Address :* Buckland Bwlch S.O., Breconshire ; Treholford and Cilgwyn, Carmarthenshire. *Clubs :* Carlton, Junior United Service, Wellington. (*Died 6 Feb. 1916.*)

HOLIDAY, Henry ; *b.* London, 17 June 1899 ; *s.* of G. H. Holiday, teacher of classics and mathematics, and Climène Gerber of Mulhouse. Alsace ; *m.* 1864, Catherine (*d.* 1924), *d.* of Rev. T. Raven ; one *d. Educ. :* home. Went to Leigh's, 1854 ; student at R.A., 1854 ; early impressed with imagination and beauty of Pre-Raphaelite pictures ; kindly received by Millais, Rossetti, and Holman Hunt ; formed lifelong friendship with Holman Hunt and Burne-Jones ; while at R.A. formed sketching club with Albert Moore, Marcus Stone, and Simeon Solomon ; first picture at R.A., Durlestone Bay, painted 1857, hung on line in 1858 and sold first day ; the Burgess of Calais painted 1858, R.A. 1859, recently presented to Guildhall Gallery ; Dante's First Meeting with Beatrice when a Child, painted 1859, rejected 1860, hung on line 1861 ; subsequent time largely occupied with decorative work, mural painting, stained glass, mosaic, etc., but found time for painting and sculpture ; exhibited at R.A. and Grosvenor, Diana, Adam, The Duet, Sleep (a life-size statue), Aspasia, Dante and Beatrice (bought by Corporation of Liverpool), etc. etc. ; invented a new form of enamel on metal in relief, to extend the use of the material to large scale work, 1899. *Publications :* a series of articles on wood engraving in the Magazine of Art ; Stained Glass as an Art ; Reminiscences of my Life ; edited Aglaia, the journal of the Healthy and Artistic Dress Union. *Recreations :* chiefly mountain-climbing (English) and music ; follows progress of science with interest, and accompanied Sir Norman Lockyer's eclipse expedition to India in 1871. *Address :* Wansfell, 18 Chesterford Gardens, Hampstead, N.W.3. *T.A. :* Henry Holiday, Hampstead. *T. :* Hampstead 1030.   (*Died 15 April 1927.*)

HOLLAND, Sir Arthur, Kt., *cr.* 1913 ; J.P., D.L., M.A. ; senior partner of Arthur Holland and Company, shipowners and insurance brokers, 2 East India Avenue, E.C. ; *b.* Liverpool, 13 July 1842 ; 2nd *s.* of Charles Holland, merchant ; *m.* 1868, Barbara, *o. d.* of Frederick Schwann of Gloucester Square, Hyde Park ; five *s.* one *d. Educ. :* privately ; Trinity College, Cambridge. Honours in Mathematical Tripos, 1864 ; entered office of Lamport and Holt, 1864 ; partner, 1870 ; on death of Mr. Lamport fresh arrangements were made ; has taken active part in politics and local affairs at Wimbledon, where he has resided since 1874 ; first chairman of the Urban District Council of Wimbledon ; 2nd Mayor of Wimbledon, 1906-7 ; contested Wimbledon Division of Surrey, 1910. *Publications :* pamphlets on social and political questions. *Recreation :* golf. *Address :* Holmhurst, Wimbledon, S.W.20. *T.A. :* Spartan, London. *T. :* Wimbledon 367. *M. :* P 2617 and P 7524. (*Died 8 Jan. 1928.*)

HOLLAND, Lt.-Gen. Sir Arthur Edward Aveling, K.C.B., *cr.* 1918 ; K.C.M.G., *cr.* 1919 ; C.B. 1915 ; D.S.O. 1900 ; M.V.O. 1903 ; Commandeur Légion d'Honneur ;

Commandeur l'ordre de Leopold ; Belgium Croix de Guerre ; R.F.A. ; M.P. (C.) Borough of Northampton since 1924 ; late Commandant, Royal Military Academy, Woolwich ; *b.* 13 April 1862 ; *y. s.* of Major-General A. Butcher ; *m.* Mary Kate Duval, *o. d. of* Lewis Duval Hall, J.P., D.L. ; one *d.* Entered Army, 1880 ; Captain, 1888 ; Major, 1898 ; Lt.-Col. 1905 ; Colonel, 1910 ; served Burmah, 1885-89 (medal with two clasps) ; South Africa, 1900-1 (despatches twice, medal with four clasps, D.S.O.) ; European War, France and Flanders, 1914-18 ; Commanded Artillery, 8th Division, 1914-15 ; Artillery, 3rd Army, 1916 ; 1st Division, 1915-1916 ; 1st Army Corps, 1917-18 (despatches eight times, C.B., prom. Maj.-Gen., K.C.B., prom. Lieut.-Gen., K.C.M.G.). *Address:* 45 Carlisle Mansions, Westminster, S.W. ; Hanslope Lodge, Stony Stratford. *T.:* Franklin 6240 ; Wolverton 22. *Clubs:* Naval and Military, Ranelagh.
(Died 7 Dec. 1927.)

HOLLAND, Bernard Henry, C.B. 1904 ; *e. s.* of late Rev. F. J. Holland, Canon of Canterbury, and Mary Sibylla, *d.* of Rev. Alfred Lyall of Harbledown ; *b.* 23 Dec. 1856 ; *m.* 1895, Florence Helen, *d.* of Rev. W. A. Duckworth ; one *s.* two *d. Educ.:* Eton ; Trinity Coll., Cambridge (M.A.). Called to Bar, Inner Temple, 1882 ; The Charity Commission Office, 1884-90 ; Priv. Sec. Duke of Devonshire, 1892-94 ; Sec. to various Royal Commissions, 1891-1908 ; Private Secretary to Secretary of State for Colonies, 1903-8 ; Alderman of London County Council, 1910-20 ; Sub-Commissioner for National Service for East Kent area, 1917 ; Member of Kent Education Committee, 1921 ; Chairman of the Kent and Canterbury Hospital Board, 1922. *Publications:* Selection from Crabbe's Poems, 1899 ; Onyx, 1899 ; Imperium et Libertas, a study in Politics, 1901 ; Life of the Duke of Devonshire, 1911 ; Verse, 1912 ; The Fall of Protection, 1913 ; The Lancashire Hollands, 1917 ; Memoir of Kenelm Digby, 1919 ; Belief and Freedom, 1923. *Address:* Harbledown Lodge, Canterbury. *Club:* Athenæum.
(Died 25 May 1926.)

HOLLAND, Com. Gerald Edward, C.M.G. 1911 ; C.I.E. 1900 ; D.S.O. 1890 ; Temp. Col. R.E. ; Dock and Marine Superintendent, L. and N. W. Railway, Holyhead ; *b.* Dublin, 21 Oct. 1860 ; 2nd *s.* of late Denis Holland of Dublin ; *m.* 1896, Mary (*d.* 1913), *e. d.* of late Edmund Dwyer Gray, M.P., of Vartry Lodge, Ballybrack, Ireland ; one *s.* two *d. Educ.:* Ratcliffe College, Leicestershire. Joined Royal Indian Marine, 1880 ; Lieut. 1882 ; Commander, 1893 ; served with Burma Expeditionary Forces, 1887-89 (medal, 2 clasps), Chin-Lushai Expedition, 1889-90 (clasp, despatches, D.S.O.) ; commanded Royal Indian Marine troopship "Warren Hastings" when that vessel was unfortunately lost on Reunion Island at 2 A.M. on 14 Jan. 1897 ; tried by Court-Martial ; result, a simple reprimand ; commendatory order containing warm praise published simultaneously with Court-Martial finding by Viceroy and Governor-General in Council ; served on Naval Transport Staff, Durban, 1899-1900 ; as Divisional Officer, ditto, 1900-1 (despatches thrice, medal, clasp, C.I.E.) ; Principal Port-Officer, Rangoon, Burma, 1901-4 ; retired from Royal Indian Marine, 1905 ; served European War, 1914-16 (despatches twice, C.M.G.) ; Officier Ordre de Leopold de Belgium. *Recreations:* cricket, golf, yachting, motoring. *Address:* Bryn-y-Mor, Holyhead. *M.:* P 1374. *Club:* Oriental.
(Died 26 June 1917.)

HOLLAND, Lt.-Col. Guy Lushington, M.V.O. 1911 ; in command of Pioneer Depot ; *b.* 21 Feb. 1861 ; *s.* of Maj.-Gen. H. W. Holland. Entered Army, 1883 ; Captain, I.S.C., 1894 ; Major, Indian Army, 1901 ; Lieut.-Col., 1908 ;

served Sikkim Expedition, 1888 (despatches, medal with clasp) ; Chitral, 1895 (medal with clasp) ; China, 1900 (medal) ; Waziristan, 1901-2 (clasp). *Address:* 21 Havelock Road, Croydon.

HOLLAND, Capt. Herbert Christian, M.V.O. 1905 ; Chief Constable of Derbyshire since 1897 ; *b.* 1858 ; *s.* of Edward Holland, J.P., D.L., M.P. (Evesham), of Dumbleton Hall, Evesham ; *m.* ; four *s. Educ.:* Eton : Radley ; Sandhurst. 8th and 15th Hussars ; served Afghan War, 1879-80 ; Boer War, 1881 ; Egyptian War, 1882 (wounded) ; Capt. Derbyshire Yeomanry ; J.P. Derbyshire. *Address:* The Wheathills, Kirk Langley, Derby. *T.A.:* Holland, Kirk Langley. *T.:* 2 Kirk Langley. *Clubs:* Boodle's, Pratt's.
(Died 5 May 1916.)

HOLLAND, Rev. Henry Scott, M.A., D.D. Aberdeen ; D.Litt. Oxford, 1907 ; editor of The Commonwealth ; Regius Professor Divinity, Oxford, and Canon of Christ Church, since 1910 ; *s.* of George Henry and Hon. Charlotte D. Holland, Gayton Lodge, Wimbledon. *Educ.:* Eton ; Balliol Coll. Oxford. First class Lit. Hum. 1870 ; senior student, Christ Church, 1870 ; tutor, 1872 ; ordained, 1872-74 ; Select Preacher to University of Oxford, 1881-82, 1894-96 ; Censor of Christ Church, 1882-84 ; Canon, Truro, 1882-84 ; Exam. Chaplain to Bishop of Truro, 1882-1904 ; Canon of St. Paul's, 1884-1910 ; Precentor, St. Paul's Cathedral, 1886-1910. *Publications:* Logic and Life ; Creed and Character ; Christ and Ecclesiastes ; On Behalf of Belief ; Pleas and Claims ; God's City ; Personal Studies, 1905 ; Vital Values, 1906 ; article on Justin Martyr in Smith's Eccles. Dict. ; Apostolic Fathers ; Life of Jenny Lind ; Old and New ; Fundamentals, pamphlet, 1909 ; Fibres of Faith, 1910 ; A Bundle of Memories, 1915 ; So as by Fire, 1916 ; Essay in Lux Mundi, and in volumes on Church Reform, and on Good Citizenship. *Recreations:* cycling, formerly rowing, racquets, football, swimming. *Address:* Oxford.
(Died 17 Mar. 1918.)

HOLLAND, Maj.-Gen. Henry William, C.B. 1869 ; retired ; *b.* Bombay, 1825 , *e. s.* of late Major Henry Colson Holland of Bombay Army ; *m.* 1st, 1850, Ellen (*d.* 1863), *d.* of James Farquharson, Bombay C.S. ; 2nd, 1870, May (*d.* 1881), *d.* of late R. H. Ellis, Dublin, and widow of Colonel Giles Keane ; 3rd, Laura Marie (*d.* 1920). *Educ.:* Cheltenham ; Woolwich. Joined 18th Bombay Native Infantry, 1841 ; Captain, 1856 ; Major, 1861 ; Lieutenant-Colonel, 1867 ; Colonel, 1868 ; Major-General, 1877 (retired) ; appointed a S.A. Commissary-General, 1847 ; served in Abyssinian War as Controller of Supply and Transport, 1867-68 (despatches, brevet of Col., medal, and C.B.) ; was Commissary-General of Bombay Army, 1870-77. *Address:* 21 Havelock Road, Croydon. *(Died 20 Sept. 1920.)*

HOLLAND, Major Hugh, D.S.O. 1919 ; late G.S.O.2, War Office ; *b.* 20 Jan. 1884 ; 2nd *s.* of Dr. J. F. Holland, St. Moritz, Switzerland ; *m.* 1911, Dorothy, *d.* of the late J. A. F. Bennett of North Breache Manor, Ewhurst, Surrey ; one *s. Educ.:* Tonbridge School ; Royal Military Academy, Woolwich. Joined Royal Artillery, 1903 ; retired, 1910 ; served European War, 1914-18 (despatches, D.S.O.). *Publications:* contributions to various periodicals. *Recreations:* golf, tennis, and winter sports. *Address:* 4 Paulton's Square, Chelsea, S.W. *Club:* Sports.
(Died 15 Jan. 1922.)

HOLLAND, Admiral Swinton Colthurst, F.R.G.S. ; J.P. ; *b.* 8 Feb. 1844 ; *m.* 1881, Eva A. Williams ; one *s.* two *d.* Entered R.N. 1857 ; Rear-Admiral, 1899 ; Vice-Admiral, 1903 ; Admiral, 1907 ; A.D.C. to Queen, 1895 ; Commodore in Charge, Hong-Kong, 1896 ; Superintendent of Chatham Dockyard, 1899-1902 ; retired 1908. *Address:* Langley House, Chichester. *(Died 8 June 1922.)*

HOLLAND, Sir (Thomas) Erskine, Kt., *cr.* 1917; K.C. 1901; D.C.L., LL.D.: *b.* 17 July 1835; *e. s.* of Rev. T. A. Holland, Rector of Poynings, Sussex; *m.* 1st, Louise (*d.* 1891), *d.* of M. Jean Delessert; 2nd, Ellen, *widow* of the Rev. Stephen Edwardes; four *s.* one *d. Educ.:* Brighton Coll.; Balliol and Magdalen Colls., Oxford. Demy of Magdalen; 1st Class, final classical school; Fellow of Exeter Coll., 1859-71; Chancellor's Prizeman, 1860; Barr. Lincoln's Inn, 1863; Bencher, 1907; Vinerian Reader in English Law, 1874; Professor of Inter. Law and Diplomacy, 1874-1910; Fellow of All Souls Coll., Oxford, from 1875; Assessor (sole judge) of the Chancellor's Court, 1876-1910; D.C.L. Oxford; Hon. LL.D. Bologna, Glasgow, Dublin, Brussels; Hon. Professor in University of Perugia; Hon. Member of the University of Petrograd, of the Juridical Society of Berlin, and of the American Society of International Law; Hon. Citizen of Sanginesio; Fellow of British Academy; Correspondent of the Academies of the Moral and Political Sciences of the Institut de France, of the Istituto di Bologna, and of Padua and Brussels; Member of the Institut de Droit International (President, 1913); Corresponding Member of the Institut Américain de Droit International; Commander of the Order of the Crown of Italy; Grand Commander of the Rising Sun of Japan; member of the Royal Commission on the Supply of Food, etc., in Time of War, 1903-5; British Plenipotentiary at the Geneva Conference, 1906; Bencher, Lincoln's Inn, 1907. *Publications:* An Essay on Composition Deeds, 1864, 1865; Essays on the Form of the Law, 1870; The Institutes of Justinian, as a recension of the Institutes of Gaius, 1873, 1881; Albericus Gentilis, a lecture, 1874; tradotto da Aurelio Saffi, 1884; Alberici Gentilis De Iure Belli, 1877; The Elements of Jurisprudence, 1880 (which gained the Swiney Prize, 1894), 13th English edition, 1924; The European Concert in the Eastern Question, 1885; The Admiralty Manual of Naval Prize Law, 1888; Studies in International Law, 1898; The War Office Manual of the Laws and Customs of War on Land, 1904; Neutral Duties in a Maritime War, 1905; The Laws of War on Land, 1908; A Valedictory Retrospect, 1910; Proposed Changes in the Law of Prize, 1911; R. Zouch Ius Feciale, 1911; Io. de Lignano De Bello, 1917; Letters to the Times on War and Neutrality, Ed. iii., containing the letters of forty years (1881-1920), 1921 *Address:* Poynings House, Oxford; 3 Brick Court, Temple, E.C. *Club:* Athenæum.
(Died 24 May 1926.)

HOLLEY, Major-Gen. Edmund Hunt, Col. Commandant R.A.; J.P., Devon, and Lord of Manor of Okehampton; *b.* 24 May 1842; 4th *s.* of J. H. Holley, late of Oaklands, Okehampton; *m.* 1879, 2nd *d.* of Rev. H. E. Hayter-Hames; one *s.* two *d. Educ.:* Carshalton; Woolwich. Obtained commission in Royal Artillery, 1860; commanded a battery in Soudan Campaign, 1884 (despatches, received brevet promotion); was Colonel on Staff commanding R.A., Cork District, 1894-98; succeeded to the family estates on the death of his eldest brother, 1898. *Recreations:* hunting and shooting. *Address:* Oaklands, Okehampton, Devon. *Club:* United Service. *(Died 9 April 1919.)*

HOLLINGDRAKE, Sir Henry, Kt., *cr.* 1921; J.P., Cheshire; engineer; *b.* 15 April 1872; *s.* of late Robert Hollingdrake and Emma Hollingdrake of Edgeley House, Stockport; *m.* 1898, Esther Emily, *d.* of late Thomas Lewis and late Elizabeth Elstub Lewis of Dynas Powis, Glam.; one *s.* one *d. Educ.:* Manchester Grammar School. Formed and was Chairman of the Stockport and district Prisoners of War Committee; formed the Stockport and District Comforts Fund, Member of the Cheshire Prisoners of War Aid Society; Member of the Lancashire and Cheshire Civilian Prisoners Relief Fund; rendered considerable service in connection with organizing transport for the conveyance of wounded in Cheshire; Member of the Soldiers and Sailors Families Association. *Address:* The Cleeve, Porlock, Somerset. *T.A.:* Hollingdrake, Porlock. *(Died 2 May 1923.)*

HOLLINGS, Herbert John Butler, J.P., D.L.; *b.* 1855; *e. s.* of John Hollings, J.P., of Wheatley Hall, Yorks, and The Watchetts, and Mary Jane Hope, *e. d.* of late Rev. Canon Mitton; *m.* 1886, Nina Augusta Stracey, *d.* of Gen. John Hall Smyth, C.B.; one *s.* one *d. Educ.:* Winchester, Oxford (B.A. 1878). Called to Bar, Inner Temple, 1880; patron of 1 living. *Address:* The Watchetts, Frimley, Surrey. *Clubs:* Constitutional, Junior Constitutional.
(Died 6 Mar. 1922.)

HOLLINGTON, Alfred Jordan, J.P.; Lieut. of City of London; F.R.H.S.; textile merchant; senior partner in the firm of Hollington Bros.; *s.* of Thomas and Ann Hollington; *b.* 12 May 1845; *m.* 1st, 1875, Alice, *d.* of William Dear, Hyde Park Corner; two *s.* four *d.*; 2nd, 1890, Alice, *d.* of Henry Clarke, J.P., Hampstead. *Educ.:* City of London School. Member of Corporation of London; Chairman of many Committees; Member of 1st L.C.C.; Chairman of Improvements Committee; Chairman of Wholesale Clothiers' Federation; Member of the London Textile Association and London Chamber of Commerce; P.M. of Lodge of Felicity, No. 58; one of the founders and P.M. of Bishopsgate Lodge; P.M. of Tinplate Workers Co.; P.M. of Gold and Silver Wire Drawers' Co.; Member of Loriners' Co. *Recreations:* breeder of horses and shorthorn cattle; grower of orchids. *Address:* Forty Hill, Enfield, Middlesex. *T.A.:* Enfield. *T.:* Enfield 142.
(Died 3 Dec. 1926.)

HOLLINS, Sir Frank, 1st Bt., *cr.* 1907; J.P.; Chairman of Horrockes, Crewdson and Co., Ltd., Cotton - spinners; *b.* 16 April 1843; *s.* of late Edward Hollins of Pleasley, Mansfield; *m.* 1875, Dora Emily, O.B.E., 3rd *d.* of Caleb Cox; four *s.* two *d. Heir: s.* Arthur Meyrick [*b.* 16 July 1876; *m.* 1908, Mary Prudence, *d.* of late John Thwaites]. *Address:* Greyfriars, nr. Preston. *(Died 27 Jan. 1924.)*

HOLLIS, William Ainslie, M.A., M.D., F.R.C.P.; an Ex-President, British Medical Association; Consulting Physician, Royal Sussex County Hospital; ex-President, Brighton and Sussex Medico - Chirurg. Society; ex-President, Brighton and Hove Natural History and Philosophical Society; *b.* Lewisham, Kent, 1839; *m. d.* of Charles Lever; one *s.* two *d. Educ.:* Brighton College; Trinity College, Cambridge; St. Bartholomew's Hospital, London. House Physician to St. Bartholomew's Hospital when the appointment was first made. *Publications:* numerous medical and scientific papers in current periodicals. *Recreations:* cycling and cactus culture. *Address:* Salisbury Lodge, Salisbury Road, Hove, Brighton. *T.:* 646 P.O. Brighton. *Clubs:* New University; Hove.
(Died 26 Mar. 1922.)

HOLLOWAY, Maj.-Gen. Benjamin, C.I.E. 1915; Indian Army; *s.* of Lt.-Col. E. V. P. Holloway of Charlbury, Oxon; *b.* 27 Aug. 1861; *m.* 1901, Muriel Aimée Becher; four *s.* Entered Indian Army, 1883; Captain, 1892; Major, 1901; Lt. - Col. 1907; Col. 1912; D.A.Q.M.G., India, 1900; Assist. Secretary Military Dept., Govt. of India, 1901-6; Commandant 29th Lancers, 1909; Deputy Secretary Army Dept., Govt. of India, 1912, Secretary, 1914; G.O.C. Southern Brigade, 1916; served Burma, 1885-86 (despatches, medal with clasp). *Address:* Wellington, Nilgiris, India.
(Died 12 May 1922.)

509

HOLLOWAY, Sir Henry, Kt., cr. 1917; J.P.; Governing Director of Holloway Brothers (London), Ltd., Contractors; b. 5 Aug. 1857; 4th s. of late Thomas Holloway, Lavington; m. 1881, Annie Jane, e. d. of late John Gollop, Clapham, S.W.; seven c. Educ.: privately. Founded the business of Holloway Brothers (London), Ltd., in conjunction with his late brother, Thomas Holloway, J.P., 1882; Past President of the Institute of Builders; Past President of the London Master Builders' Association. Address: Bridge Wharf, Grosvenor Road, S.W.1. T.A.: Antefixa, Churton, London. T.: Victoria 8560. Club: Reform.
(Died 5 Aug. 1923.)

HOLME, Charles, Chevalier, Rising Sun of Japan; Vice-President, Japan Society; founder and for 25 years editor of the Studio; b. Derby, 7 Oct. 1848; s. of Geo. Holme, silk manufacturer, Derby. Educ.: Derby (private school). East India merchant, 1868-86; travelled in Russia, Asia Minor, China, Japan, etc. Publications: Reviews, Magazine articles and lectures upon the fine and decorative arts. Recreation: farming. Address: Upton-Grey House, nr. Basingstoke, Hants. T.A.: Upton-Grey.
(Died 14 Mar. 1923.)

HOLME, Charles Henry, of Rawburn, Berwickshire; b. 1853; e. s. of Bryan Holme Holme, of Paull Holme, Yorks., and Catharine Margaret, d. of Gen. Hon. Sir Patrick Stuart, G.C.M.G., of Eaglescarnie; m. 1886, Eva Magdalen, d. of Rev. Canon and Hon. Mrs. Machell; three s. two d. Educ.: Bath College; R.I.E. College, Coopers Hill. Served the Govt. of India in P.W. Dept. 1876-99; M.Inst.C.E. Address: Rathburne, Duns, Berwickshire. Club: New, Edinburgh.
(Died 12 Feb. 1928.)

HOLME, George A.; s. of S. Holme, Holmestead, Liverpool; b. 28 March 1848; m. 1886, Ada Laura, e. d. of Thomas Allen Hickley of Elm Grove, Walton on Thames. Educ.: Repton School, and University College, Oxford; 3rd Class Classical Mods. 1869; 3rd Class Law and History, 1871; B.A., 1871. Solicitor, 1876; Examiner in Common Law for Final Law Exam. (Honours); Chancery Taxing Master, 1901; Master of Supreme Court of Judicature, 1903. Address: 238 Royal Courts of Justice, Strand, W.C.; Angle, Harrow on the Hill. T.: 186 P.O., Harrow. Clubs: United University; Northwood Golf; Vincent's, Oxford.
(Died 9 Nov. 1917.)

HOLMES, Arthur Bromley, M. Eng. (Liverpool), M.Inst.C.E.; b. 8 June 1849; s. of late Arthur East Holmes of Derby; m. Elizabeth, d. of late Richard Stone. Educ.: Repton School. Served apprenticeship with Andrew Handyside and Co., Ltd., engineers, Derby, and was afterwards employed by them in the management of their business of constructors of bridges, roofs, and other steel and iron structures, and ultimately held the position of works manager; commenced business as consulting engineer in Liverpool in partnership with J. C. Vaudrey, 1882; one of the founders of the Liverpool Electric Supply Co., 1883; Engineer and Manager of that Company till its purchase by the Corporation of Liverpool, 1896; City Electrical Engineer, 1896-1903; one of the Founders and Engineers of the Birmingham Electric Supply Company; Consulting Engineer to the Liverpool Corporation, 1903-1913. Publications: books and papers on electrical subjects. Address: 2 Princes Gate East, Liverpool. T.: Royal Liverpool 481. Club: Athenæum, Liverpool. (Died 27 Dec. 1927.)

HOLMES, Ven. Bernard Edgar, Chaplain S.A.M.R. (Lt.-Col., retired); b. 1860; 7th s. of John Holmes, Somerfield, Maidstone; m. Grace Pauline, e. d. of late Sir Jacob Barry. Educ.: St. John's College, Cambridge

510

(M.A.). Ordained, 1883; Curate of West Felton, Salop, 1883-87; Priest-Vicar of Truro Cathedral, 1888-90; Chaplain of Colonial Forces, 1892; Chaplain to the Forces, S. Africa, 1897-1902; Canon of Grahamstown. 1907-21; Rector of King William's Town, 1891-1921; Rural Dean, 1892-1921; Archdeacon of King William's Town, 1910-21; British Chaplain at Rome, 1920-24. Recreations: golf, gardening. Publication: The Source of Civic Power. Address: c/o Standard Bank of S. Africa, 10 Clement's Lane, E.C.4.
(Died 7 July 1928.)

HOLMES, Sir George (Charles Vincent), K.C.B., cr. 1911; K.C.V.O., cr. 1906; C.B. 1904; C.V.O. 1903; Chairman of Board of Public Works, Ireland, 1901-13; Hon. Member Institute of Naval Architects; b. 9 October 1848; 3rd s. of Robert Holmes, of Moycashel, Co. Westmeath; m. 1880, Louisa, d. of late Charles Greenstreet Addison, Barr.-at-law, London; one s. Educ.: Downing College, Cambridge. Obtained an Entrance Scholarship, 1870, and Whitworth Engineering Scholarship, 1871; educated as an engineer at the Crewe Locomotive Works of the L. & N.-W. Railway; Resident Engineer to the building of great iron Rotunda of the Vienna International Exhibition of 1873; Member of the International Jury of this Exhibition, section of Prime Movers; Secretary of the Institution of Naval Architects, 1878-1901. Publications: Text-Book of the Steam Engine; Marine Engines and Boilers, and Ancient and Modern Ships (both Handbooks of the Victoria and Albert Museum, South Kensington); also wrote Official Reports on Prime Movers for the Royal British Commission of the Vienna International Exhibition of 1873. Recreations: fishing and shooting. Club: St. James's. (Died 13 Feb. 1926.)

HOLMES, Brig.-Gen. Hardress Gilbert, C.M.G. 1916; C.B.E. 1919; J.P.; 2nd s. of Bassett Holmes of St. David's, D.L. and J.P.; b. 7 July 1862; m. 1908, Alys Maude Josephine, d. of late John Lloyd, Gloster, King's Co.; one d. Entered army, 1885; Major, 1905; retired, 1908; served N.-W. Frontier, India, 1897-98 (medal 2 clasps); S. Africa, 1899-1902; Commanded Mounted Infantry Regt. and a Column (despatches twice, Bt. Major, Queen's medal 5 clasps, King's medal 2 clasps); rejoined army at beginning of the European War; commanded 9th Batt. the Yorkshire Regiment, B.E.F., 1914-16; Brig.-Gen. 1916; retired pay, 1920; served 1914-19 (despatches 4 times, C.M.G., and C.B.E., Bt. Lt.-Col.); High Sheriff Co. Tipperary, 1910. Recreations: hunting, shooting, fishing. Address: St. David's, Nenagh, Co. Tipperary. Clubs: Naval and Military; Kildare Street, Dublin. (Died 4 Sept. 1922.)

HOLMES, Rev. Henry Comber, Hon. Canon of York; Rector of Birkby since 1876, and Vicar of Hutton, Bonville, since 1885; s. of late Rev. William Rusbridge Holmes; married; one d. Educ.: Winchester; Exeter College, Oxford; B.A., 1868; M.A., 1872. Ordained, 1870; Curate of East Retford, Notts, 1870; Blyth, 1874; Rural Dean of Northallerton, 1897; Chaplain to 1st V.B. Yorks Regt., now 4th Batt. Yorks Regt., 1882-1915; member of North Riding Territorial Association. Address: Birkby Rectory, Northallerton. T.: Great Smeaton. (Died 16 June 1920.)

HOLMES, Rt. Hon. Hugh, P.C.; Lord Justice of Appeal, 1897; b. 17 Feb. 1840; s. of late William Holmes, Dungannon; m. 1869, Olivia (d. 1901), d. of J. W. Moule. Educ.: Trin. Coll. Dublin. Irish Barr. 1865; Solicitor and Attorney-General for Ireland, 1878-80; M.P. (C.) Dublin Univ. 1885-87; Judge of High Court of Justice, Ireland, 1887-97. Address: 3 Fitz-William Place, Dublin. Club: Carlton.
(Died 19 April 1916.)

HOLMES, Thomas; late Police Court Missionary, North London Police Court; b.

Walsall, 1846 ; *s.* of William Holmes, iron-moulder ; *m.* 1872, Margaret, *d.* of Ralph Brammar, carpenter, Rugeley ; five *s. Educ.:* National School, Rugeley. For many years an ironworker; owing to an accident and subsequent illness had to give up his trade ; taught night school, etc., for some years ; in 1885 appointed Police Court Missionary at Lambeth Police Court ; in 1889 transferred to North London Court ; lecturer on criminology and social subjects ; Associate Society for Study of Inebriates ; has established Home of Rest for women engaged in the Home Industries ; The Home Workers' Aid Association, of which he is Hon. Organiser, 1903 ; and intends to devote the remainder of his life to the housing of London's poorest toilers, and hopes to improve the conditions under which home workers live and labour. *Publications:* Pictures and Problems from London Police Courts ; Known to the Police ; London's Underworld ; articles in contemporary reviews; Editor of The London Homeworker. *Address:* 12 Bedford Road, Tottenham.(*Died 26 Mar. 1918.*)

HOLMES, Rev. Thomas Scott, D.D., M.A. ; F.R. Hist. Soc.; Chancellor and Canon Residentiary of Wells Cathedral ; Examining Chaplain to the Bishop of Bath and Wells ; *b.* 20 Aug. 1852 ; *s.* of Rev. I. Holmes, B.A., of Anfield, Liverpool ; *m.* 1880, Katharine, *d.* of E. A. Freeman, D.C.L., of Somerleaze, Wells ; one *d. Educ.:* Royal Inst. School, Liverpool. Foundation Scholar and Prizeman, Sidney-Sussex College, Cambridge ; B.A., Sen. Opt., 1875 ; M.A. 1878 ; B.D. 1909, ; D.D. 1910 ; Tutor, St. Aidan's College Birkenhead, 1875 ; Vice-Principal, Wells Theological Coll. 1877-80 ; Vicar of Wookey, Somerset, 1879-1900 ; Prebendary of Wells, 1895 ; Rural Dean of Axbridge, 1897-1900 ; Birkbeck Lecturer in Eccles. Hist., Trinity Coll. Cambridge, 1906-8 ; Proctor in Convocation for the Chapter of Wells, 1909. *Publications:* History of the Parish of Wookey ; Glastonbury Custumaria ; Bruton and Montacute Cartularies ; Bp. R. de Salopia's Register, 2 vols. (Somerset Record Society); Bishop Giffard and Bishop Bowett's Register, 1 vol.; Historical and Legendary Glastonbury ; History of Wells and Glastonbury, 1908 ; The First Six Centuries of the Church in Gaul, 1910 ; an account of the Ecclesiastical Records and Plate of the Diocese of Bath and Wells, 1914 ; Register of Bishop Nicholas Bubwith, 1914 ; Register of Bishop John Stafford, 1916. *Address:* East Liberty, Wells, Somerset.
(*Died 10 Feb. 1918.*)

HOLMES, Col. William, C.M.G. 1916; D.S.O. 1901 ; Commanded 5th Infantry Brigade, Australian Expeditionary Force, Dardanelles, 1915 ; *b.* 12 Sep. 1862 ; *s.* of late Captain William Holmes, General Staff, N.S.W. Military Forces ; *m.* 1887, Susan Ellen (*d.* 1912), *d.* of Lieut. Henry Green, Reserve of Officers, N.S.W., late R.H.A.; one *s.* one *d.* 2nd Lieut. (1st N.S.W. Inf. Regt.), 1886 ; 1st Lieut., 1890 ; Captain, 1894 ; Major, 1900 ; Bt. Lt.-Col., 1902 ; Lt.-Col.. 1905 ; Col., 1912; commands 6th Australian Inf. Brig.; served with 1st N.S.W. Contingent, S. African Campaign, 1899-1900 · Relief of Colesburg, advance on Bloemfontein with Clement's Column, with Ian Hamilton's Column from Bloemfontein to Thabanchu, Hout Nek, Winburg, Ventersburg, Kroonstad, Lindley, Heilbron, Doorn Kop, Roodepoort, Johannesburg, Pretoria, Diamond Hill ; wounded, 1900, and invalided (despatches, S. African War medal, with four clasps); European War, 1914-16 (despatches, C.M.G.); commanded Australian Naval and Military Force which occupied German New Guinea, 1914 ; British Administrator, 1914-15 ; A.D.C. to the Governor-General of Australia, 1904-11. *Address:* Bondi, New South Wales, Australia.
(*Died 5 July 1917.*)

HOLMES-A-COURT, Hon. Edward Alexander ; late Chief-Constable of Oxford-

shire ; 5th *s.* of 2nd Lord Heytesbury ; *b.* 23 Oct. 1845 ; *m.* 1880, Adelaide Sophie, *y. d.* of Hugh Hamersley of Pyrton Manor, Oxfordshire ; one *s.* two *d.* Lt.-Col. the King's L.I., retired. *Address:* The Rosary, Freshwater Bay, Isle of Wight.
(*Died 23 June 1923.*)

HOLROYD, Sir Charles, Kt., *cr.* 1903 ; Hon. Litt.D. Leeds ; F.R.S. of Painter Etchers, and member of the Art Workers' Guild ; Director of National Gallery, 1906-16 ; F.S.A. ; formerly Keeper, National Gallery of British Art (Tate Gallery) ; *b.* Leeds, 9 April 1861 ; *s.* of William Holroyd, merchant of that town, and Lucy Woodthrope of Aveley, Essex ; *m.* 1891, Fannie Fetherstonhaugh, *d.* of Hon. J. A. Macpherson of Melbourne ; one *s. Educ.:* Leeds Grammar School ; Yorkshire College of Science ; The Slade School of Fine Art, University College, London. Medal for Painting from Life, 1st prizes for Landscape Painting, Etching and Composition ; Travelling Studentship for two years, spent in Italy. Assistant to Professor Legros at the Slade School for four years ; frequently exhibited pictures at the Royal Academy, the R. Institute of Painters in Water Colours, etc., and etchings in the Royal Society of Painter Etchers. *Publications:* Etchings, including the Monte Olivetto Series, and the Icarus Series, etc. ; Michael Angelo and his Works ; Life of A. Legros for the Supplement to Encyclopædia Britannica. *Recreation:* gardening. *Address:* Sturdie House, Beechwood Avenue, Weybridge. *T.:* Weybridge, 305. *Clubs:* Athenæum, Arts, Burlington Fine Arts. (*Died 17 Nov. 1917.*)

HOLROYD, Hon. Sir Edward Dundas, Kt., *cr.* 1903 ; *s.* of Edward Holroyd, Senior Commissioner London Bankruptcy Court, 1831-1869, *g. s.* of Sir George Sowley Holroyd, Justice of the Court of King's Bench, described by Lord Brougham as "high amongst the greatest of any age " ; *b.* 25 Jan. 1828 ; *m.* Anna Maria Hoyles, *d.* of Henry Compton, 1862 ; two *s.* three *d. Educ.:* Winchester (Queen's gold medal for Latin and English Essays, 1845, 1846) ; Trinity College, Cambridge (1st Class Class. Tripos, M.A. 1854). English Bar, 1855 ; Melbourne Bar, 1859 ; Tasmanian Bar, 1867 ; offered a Judgeship, 1872 and 1873, but declined ; Q.C. 1879 ; Justice of the Supreme Court of Victoria, 1881-1906 ; retired 1906. President of Athenæum and Savage Clubs, Melbourne. *Address:* Fernacres, St. Kilda, Melbourne, Victoria. *Club:* Junior Conservative. (*Died 5 Jan. 1916.*)

HOLT, Sir Edward, 1st Bt., *cr.* 1916 ; C.B.E. 1920 ; has been twice Lord Mayor of Manchester ; *e. s.* of Joseph Holt ; *b.* 9 Sep. 1849 ; *m.* 1879, Elizabeth, *d.* of Joseph Brooks, Cheatham, Manchester ; one *s.* three *d.* Heir : *s.* Edward, *b.* 16 April 1888. *Address:* Woodthorpe, Prestwich, Lancs. ; Blackwell, Windermere.
(*Died 11 April 1928.*)

HOLT, Henry ; author, publisher ; editor Unpartizan (lately Unpopular) Review, 1914-21 ; *s.* of Dan and Ann E. Holt ; *b.* Baltimore, Md., 3 Jan. 1840 ; *m.* 1st, 1863, Mary Florence (*d.* 1879), *d.* of J. Selby West of New York ; 2nd, 1886, Florence, *d.* of Charles Corey Taber of New York ; three *s.* three *d. Educ.:* Yale (A.B. 1862) ; Columbia (LL.B. 1864) ; Hon. LL.D., University of Vermont, 1901 ; Hon. Phi Beta Kappa Johns Hopkins Univ., 1914. Began publishing business with G. P. Putnam, 1863 ; now President Henry Holt & Co. ; Trustee Simplified Spelling Board ; Trustee American Geographical Soc., 1892-1909 ; Fellow American Association for Advancement of Science ; first Chairman New York University Settlement Society ; first Chairman University Club Library ; Member Harvard Visiting Committee on Philosophy and Psychology ; has lectured at Yale, Columbia, University of Vermont, and Union Theological Seminary. *Publications:* Calmire: Man and Nature, 1892; Talks on Civics, 1901; Sturmsee: Man and Man, 1905; On the Civic Relations, 1907; On the Cosmic Relations, 1914; second edition, enlarged, under title The Cosmic Relations and Immortality, 1919; Sixty Years a Publisher, 1924; The Hopeful Borderland, 1925; and sundry review articles. *Recreations:* music, landscape gardening. *Address:* 19 West 44th Street, New York; 57 East 72nd Street, N.Y.; Fairholt, Burlington, Vermont. *Clubs:* Authors' (Presiding Officer, 1908-11), Century, City, University, Yale, New York; Ethan Alen, Country, Burlington.

(*Died 13 Feb. 1926.*)

HOLT, L. Emmett, M.D., LL.D., Emeritus Professor of Diseases of Children, Columbia University, and Physician-in-Chief to the Babies' Hospital, New York; Secretary Board of Scientific Directors, Rockefeller Institute of Medical Research. *Address:* 155 West 58th Street, New York. (*Died 14 Jan. 1924.*)

HOLT, Sir Vesey (George Mackenzie), K.B.E., *cr.* 1920; a managing partner in Glyn Mills, Currie, Holt & Co., Bankers and Army Agents; J.P. Kent; *b.* 1854; *e. s.* of late Vesey Weston Holt; *m.* 1880, Mabel Mary, *e. d.* of late Walter Drummond; four *s.* one *d.* *Educ.:* private schools. *Address:* 67 Cadogan Place, S.W.1; Mount Mascal, Bexley, Kent. *Clubs:* Arthur's, Travellers', Union.

(*Died 6 Dec. 1923.*)

HOLT, William R., Journalist and Special Correspondent; *b.* Rochdale, 1870; *m.* Mary (Minnie) Holt, Rochdale; two *s.* one *d.* *Educ.:* St. Peter's, Rochdale. Trained as newspaper man on the Rochdale Observer, where his first important work was in connection with the death and burial of John Bright; was under Sullivan on the Birmingham Daily Mail; came to London, 1897; was in Belgrade immediately after assassination of King Alexander and Queen Draga, and attended the Skuptshina at which King Peter was elected to the throne; under fire during labour riots in Belgium, also in Sidney Street! Went to Constantinople for the jubilee of Sultan Abdul Hamid; accomplished a rapid transit journey by going from London to Washington and back, and interviewing President Taft, within twelve days. *Club:* Press.

HOLTZE, Maurice, I.S.O., Ph.D.; Director Botanic Gardens, Adelaide, S. Australia, 1892-1918; *b.* Hanover, 9 July 1840; *s.* of C. Holtze, Chief Inspector of Orphan Houses; *m.* Evelampia, *d.* of Surgeon-Captain Simon Mesenzoff, Russian Army; two *s.* one *d.* *Educ.:* Hildesheim; Marburg. Studied Horticulture and Botany at Royal Gardens, Hanover, and Imperial Gardens, Petrograd; went to Australia, 1872; Curator Botanic Gardens, Port Darwin, Northern Territory, 1876. *Address:* American River, Kangaroo Island, S. Australia.

(*Died 12 Oct. 1923.*)

HOLWELL, Capt. Raymond Vernon Doherty-, D.S.O. 1915; R.E.; *b.* 18 July 1882. Entered army, 1901; Captain, 1911; served European War, 1914-15 (despatches, D.S.O.). (*Died 9 Jan. 1917.*)

HOME, 12th Earl of (*cr.* 1604), **Charles Alexander Douglas-Home,** K.T.1899, D.L. J.P.; Baron Home, 1473; Baron Dunglass, 1604; Baron Douglas (U.K.), 1875; Lord-Lieut. of Lanarkshire, 1890-1918; Maj.-Gen. Royal Company of Archers; *b.* The Hirsel, Coldstream, 11 Apr. 1834; *s.* of 11th Earl and Lucy, *e. d.* of 2nd and last Baron Montagu of Boughton; *S.* father 1881; *m.* 1870, Maria, *o. d.* of Capt. Charles Conrad Grey, R.N.; one *s.* four *d.* *Educ.:* Eton; Trin. Coll. Camb. Cornet of Berwickshire, 1879-90. *Heir: s.* Lord Dunglass. *Address:* The Hirsel, Coldstream, Berwickshire; Douglas

512

Castle and Bothwell Castle, Lanarkshire. *Clubs:* Carlton, Travellers'.(*Died 30 April 1918.*)

HOME, Colonel Frederick Jervis, C.S.I. 1892; Royal Engineers (Retired List, 1895); *b.* Calcutta, 22 Oct. 1839; *o. surv. s.* of late Maj.-Gen. Richard Home, Bengal Army; *m.* Constance Stanley (*d.* 1894), *e. d.* of J. S. M'Gowan; two *s.* one *d.* *Educ.:* Kensington Proprietary Grammar School; H.E.I.C. Military Seminary, Addiscombe. Corps of Bengal Engineers, 1858; proceeded to India, 1860; Irrigation Branch of the Public Works Department, 1861-94; Inspector-General of Irrigation and Deputy-Secretary to the Government of India, Public Works Dept., 1890-94. *Decorated* for services in the Irrigation Department, India. *Address:* Aveland, Crieff, Perthshire. *T. A.:* Crieff.

(*Died 5 Nov. 1919.*)

HOME, Major-Gen. Hon. William Sholto; *b.* 25 Feb. 1842; 3rd *s.* of 11th Earl of Home. Entered Grenadier Guards, 1860; Lieut. and Capt. 1863; Capt. and Lieut.-Col. 1871; Major-Gen. 1895; served Egypt, 1882 (medal with clasp, 4th class Osmanieh, Khedive's star); Suakin, 1885; Soudan, 1895 (clasp). *Address:* Cliveden Chambers, 105 Mount Street, W. (*Died 22 Dec. 1916.*)

HOMOLLE, Jean Théophile, Administrateur Général de la Bibliothèque Nationale depuis 1913; *b.* Paris, 19 déc. 1848; *s.* of Eugène Homolle, Dteur en Médecine, et Florence Morlière; *m.* Léonie Marthe Congnet; two *s.* two *d.* *Educ.:* Paris. Elève de l'Ecole Normale Supérieure, 1869-1873; membre des Ecoles fr. d'Athènes et de Rome, 1874-78; Maître de Conférences à l'Université de Nancy, 1878-84; Professeur Suppléant au Collège de France, 1884-90; Directeur de l'Ecole française d'Athènes, 1891-1904, 1912-13; Directeur des Musées Nationaux, 1904-11; Membre de l'Académie des Inscriptions, 1892; Membre de l'Académie des Beaux-Arts, 1910. *Publications:* Les Archives de l'Intendance Sacrée à Délos; De antiquissimis Dianae simulacris Deliacis; Collaboration au Bulletin de Correspondance Hellénique depuis 1877; Direction de la publication des Fouilles de Delphes, et de Délos; Monuments figurés de Delphes. *Récréations:* promenade à pied et jardinage. *Address:* 8 rue des Petits Champs, Paris. *T.:* Gutenberg 62-66. (*Died June 1925.*)

HONE, Nathaniel, R.H.A. *Address:* St. Dolough's Park, Rahene, Co. Dublin.

(*Died 14 Oct. 1917.*)

HOOD, Captain Basil, dramatic author; *b.* 5 April 1864; *y. s.* of late Sir Charles Hood. *Educ.:* Wellington College; Royal Military College, Sandhurst. Gazetted Lieutenant in Princess of Wales's Own (Yorkshire) Regt. 1883; served 12 years; promoted Captain, 1893; afterwards half-pay; 3 years in 3rd Batt. same regiment; retired, 1898. Author of The Gypsies; Gentleman Joe; The French Maid; Dandy Dan; Duchess of Dijon; Orlando Dando; Her Royal Highness; The Rose of Persia; Ib and Little Christina, first serious play; The Emerald Isle; Sweet and Twenty; Merrie England, 1902; My Pretty Maid; A Princess of Kensington; dramatic versions of Hans Andersen's Tales; English versions of Merry Widow, Dollar Princess, The Count of Luxembourg, A Waltz Dream, and Gipsy Love; The Pearl Girl, 1913. *Recreations:* reading and travelling. *Address:* 88 St. James's Street, S.W. *Clubs:* Naval and Military, Garrick, Beefsteak. (*Died 7 Sept. 1917.*)

HOOD, Basil F., D.S.O. 1916; Paymaster (acting), Royal Navy; Secretary to Vice-Admiral Sir John de Robeck, K.C.B.; *b.* 20 Sep. 1886; 2nd *s.* of late Rev. John F. Hood and M. C. du plat Richardson Griffiths; unmarried. *Educ.:* St. John's School, Leatherhead. Entered Royal Navy, 1904; Assistant Paymaster, 1907; Secretary to Admiral of Patrols, 1912-14; to 9th Cruiser Squadron, 1914-15; to Vice-Admiral

commanding Eastern Mediterranean Squadron, 1915-16; served during Gallipoli operations (despatches twice, D.S.O.). *Clubs*: Junior United Service, Junior Army and Navy.
(Died 6 Aug. 1917.)

HOOD, David Wilson, C.B.E., M.Inst.C.E.; Engineer-in-Chief, Trinity House; *b.* 18 March 1874; 2nd *s.* of late J. Hood, J.P., Lilliesleaf, Roxburghshire; unmarried. *Educ.:* Daniel Stewart's College and University, Edinburgh. *Address:* 5 Beech Mansions, W. Hampstead, N.W. *T.A.:* Dioptric, Fen, London. *T.:* Hampstead 7564. *Club:* Caledonian.
(Died 29 Oct. 1924.)

HOOD, Donald Wm. Charles, C.V.O. 1901; M.D. (Cantab.), F.R.C.P. (Lond.); late Examining Physician Foreign Office; late Manager Royal Institution of Great Britain; Governor and Member Committee of Management of Bethlem and Bridewell Royal Hospitals; Consulting Physician and Member Board of Management of Earlswood Royal Institution; late Examiner in Medicine, Cambridge Univ.; Vice-President West London Hospital; Senior Physician West London Hospital; practises as consulting physician; *b.* Market Lavington, Wilts, 23 June 1847; *e. s.* of late Sir Charles Hood, Lord Chancellor's visitor in lunacy; *m.* Alice, *d.* of John Wickham Flower of Park Hill, Croydon; one *s.* three *d. Educ.:* Harrow; Caius College, Cambridge. *Decorated,* 1901, for services rendered in connection with the Duke of Abercorn's and Georgina Countess of Dudley's fund for the relief of wounded and sick officers during the Boer War. *Recreations:* fishing, shooting. *Address:* 64 Boundary Road, St. John's Wood, N.W.8. *T.:* Maida Vale 2372. *Club:* Athenæum. *(Died 15 Mar. 1924.)*

HOOD, Rear-Admiral Hon. Horace Lambert Alexander, R.N.; C.B. 1911; D.S.O. 1904; M.V.O. 1906; Naval Secretary to First Lord of the Admiralty since 1914; 2nd *s.* of 4th Viscount Hood; *b.* 2 Oct. 1870; *m.* 1910, *d.* of late A. E. Touzalin, and *widow* of George Nickerson; two *s.* Joined "Britannia," 1883; "Temeraire," 1885; "Calliope," 1889 (Hurricane at Samoa); obtained five first-class certificates, Beaufort Testimonial, Goodenough Medal, and Ryder Prize; Lieut., 1890; served Soudan Expedition, 1897-98 (Medjidieh, 4th class, despatches, medal, promoted to Commander); Captain, 1903; Rear-Admiral, 1913; served in "Hyacinth" in Somaliland Expedition, 1903 (despatches, medal, D.S.O.); A.D.C. to the King, 1912; in command of Royal Naval College, Osborne, 1910-14; served European War, 1914-15 (despatches). *Address:* East Sheen Lodge, Sheen, Surrey, S.W. *T.:* Richmond 72. *Clubs:* Naval and Military, Roehampton.
(Died 31 May 1916.)

HOOD, Hon. Sir Joseph Henry, Kt., *cr.* 1920; M.A., LL.B.; Judge of Supreme Court, Victoria, since 1890; *b.* 1 June 1846. *Educ.:* Melbourne University. Called to Bar, 1868; member of Council, Univ. of Melbourne, since 1891. *Address:* Supreme Court, Melbourne, Victoria. *(Died 29 Jan. 1922.)*

HOOKINS, Rev. William, President of the Methodist New Connexion, 1903-4; *b.* Bridgwater, 10 Oct. 1845; *m.* Ellen Jane Fisher, Oldbury; four *s.* three *d. Educ.:* St. Mark's College Schools; Ranmoor College, Sheffield. Entered Ministry, 1870; Superintendent of Irish Missions, 1890-93. *Address:* 2 Crown Hill Park, Torquay. *(Died 14 Feb. 1917.)*

HOOLE, Lieut.-Col. and Hon. Col. James, C.M.G. 1900; 3rd Batt. Yorkshire Regt.; *b.* 1850; *s.* of late Francis Hoole of Moor Lodge, Sheffield, and of Edgefield, Bradfield, Yorks; *m.* 1882, Mary Violet, *o. d.* of Rev. R. Hickman, of Birdingbury, Warwicks; three *s.* two *d.* Served South Africa, 1900-1 (despatches, Queen's medal, three clasps); J.P. Oxfordshire;

1896; Lord of Manor of Headington. *Address:* Manor House, Headington, Oxford.
(Died 8 Aug. 1917.)

HOOPER, Rev. William, D.D.; Missionary, C.M.S.; Translator, Mussoorie, India, since 1892; *b.* 27 Sep. 1887; *s.* of retired Lieut. R.N., and *d.* of Thomas Bramston, M.P.; *m.* 1st, 1862; 2nd, 1891; four *s.* one *d. Educ.:* Cheltenham Preparatory School; Bath Grammar School; Wadham College, Oxford; Hebrew Exhibition; Sanskrit Scholarship; 1st class in Lit. Hum.; B.A., 1859; M.A., 1861. Went to India, C.M.S., 1861; Benares, 1861-1866; Calcutta, 1867-68; Vicar of Cressing, Essex, 1870-72; Benares, 1873; Lahore, 1874-1879; Benares, 1881; Allahabad, 1882-87; Canon of Lucknow, 1906-19; Vicar of Mount Albert, New Zealand, 1889-90. *Publications:* translation of Old Testament in Hindi; Commentary on Epistle to Hebrews in English and Hindi; Hindi translation of Commentary on Epistle to Philippians; four lectures on Palestine; sermons on the Lord's Prayer; tract on the Lord's Day; Outline of Hinduism, in Hindi; Doctrine of Salvation as set forth in Christianity, Hinduism and Islam; Helps to Hindustani Idiom; The Hindustani Language; Hindi translation of St. Clement's (of Rome) Epistle; Hebrew-Urdu Dictionary; Greek-Hindi Dictionary; Greek Grammar in Hindi; Urdu translation of Book of Common Prayer; Urdu Manual on the Holy Communion; Notes on the Bible; many sermons, lectures, etc. *Address:* Mussoorie, India.
(Died 3 Oct. 1922.)

HOOPER, Colonel Sir William Roe, K.C.S.I., *cr.* 1903; C.S.I. 1887; *b.* 12 Jan. 1837; *s.* of J. W. Hooper of Bathwick; *m.* 1859, Lucy Fanny (*d.* 1919), *d.* of Henry Benson Cox; one *d.* President India Office Medical Board, 1895-1904; served in India, 1859-95; Hon. Surgeon to the King; F.R.C.S.; Knight of Grace of St. John of Jerusalem. *Address:* Abertarff, Blackford Road, Edinburgh. *(Died 29 Sept. 1921.)*

HOPE, Adrian Elias, V.D.; *b.* 8 April 1845; *e. s.* of late Capt. Adrian John Hope and Countess Rapp; *m.* 1st, 1867, Lady Ida Duff, 2nd *d.* of 5th Earl of Fife; three *d.*; 2nd, Mildred Henrietta (*d.* 1914), *e. d.* of Sir Francis Scott, 3rd Bart.; two *d.* Late Hon. Col. 1st London Rifle Volunteers. *Address:* 9 Clifton Place, Hyde Park, W.2. *T.:* Paddington 7147. *Clubs:* Carlton, Bachelors', Marlborough, St. James's, Royal Thames Yacht: Royal Yacht Squadron, Cowes. *(Died 18 Nov. 1919.)*

HOPE, Sir Alexander, 15th Bt.; *cr.* 1628; J.P. for Midlothian; *b.* 22 Oct. 1824; *S.* brother 1898. *Educ.:* Haileybury. Bengal C.S., 1845-75. *Heir:* *n.* Major J. A. Hope. *Address:* Pinkie House, Musselburgh, N.B. *Club:* New, Edinburgh. *(Died 7 Mar. 1918.)*

HOPE, Sir Edward Stanley, K.C.B. *cr.* 1908; C.B. 1895; *b.* 1 Feb. 1846; *e. surv. s.* of late George W. Hope of Luffness, East Lothian, formerly M.P. for Windsor, and the Hon. Caroline Georgiana, *d.* of last Lord Montagu of Boughton; *m.* 1881, Constance Christina, *d.* of Sir John and Lady Constance Leslie of Glasslough, Ireland; one *s.* one *d. Educ.:* Eton; Christ Church, Oxford. Barr. Inner Temple; Charity Commissioner for England and Wales, 1879-99; Registrar of Privy Council, 1899-1909; Lunacy Commissioner (unpaid), 1908-14. *Address:* Coulsdon Grange, Surrey. *T.:* Purley 547. *Clubs:* Travellers'. Turf.
(Died 15 Feb. 1921.)

HOPE, George Everard, J.P., D.L.; Captain Grenadier Guards; *o. c.* of late Henry Walter Hope, and Lady Mary Catherine Constance, *sis.* of 5th Earl of Rosebery; *b.* 4 Nov. 1886; *m.* 1911, Margaret, *d.* of late John Cockton, J.P., of Kirkborough, Cumberland; one *s.* one *d. S.* 1913. *Address:* 65 Lowndes Square, S.W.; Luffness Castle, Aberlady, N.B.;

Rankeillour House, Springfield, Fife. *Clubs:* Wellington, Travellers'. (*Died 10 Oct. 1917.*)

HOPE, Graham; *d.* of Col. W. Hope, V.C., and *sis.* of late Adrian Hope. Acted as Organising Secretary of the Women's Unionist and Tariff Reform Association for nearly four years. *Publications:* A Cardinal and his Conscience; My Lord Winchenden; The Triumph of Count Ostermann, 1908; The Gage of Red and White, 1904; The Lady of Lyte, 1905; Amalia, 1907; The Honour of X, 1908. (*Died 20 April 1920.*)

HOPE, Jas. Edward, *b.* 6 Nov. 1852; *s.* of James Hope of Belmont, Midlothian, and the Hon. Gertrude Elphinstone; *m.* 1880, Sophia, *d.* of Admiral Sir William Edmondstone 4th Bt., of Duntreath Castle; two *s.* one *d.* *Educ.:* Harrow; Oxford. Registrar of Estate Duties for Scotland till 1903; Member of Royal Company of Archers, King's Body Guard for Scotland; J.P., Midlothian. *Address:* Belmont, Murrayfield, Midlothian. *T.* 4065 Edinburgh. *M.:* S 1331. *Clubs:* Carlton; New, Edinburgh. (*Died 8 Dec. 1917.*)

HOPE, Lt.-Col. Sir John (Augustus), 16th Bt., *cr.* 1628; M.P. (U.), Midlothian, 1912-18; (Co. U.) North Midlothian and Peebles, Dec. 1918-1922; *b.* 7 July 1869; *s.* of late Rev. Canon Hope, rector of Barwick in Elmet, Yorks; *S.* uncle 1918; *m.* 1910, Hon. Mary Bruce, O.B.E., *e. d.* of 6th Lord Balfour of Burleigh; three *s.* one *d.* Contested Midlothian, 1910; entered army, 1889; Major, 1905; served South Africa, 1901-2 (Queen's medal, 4 clasps); European War, with the 9th Batt. King's Royal Rifles (wounded); O.B.E. 1918; Lieut.-Col., Reserve of Officers. *Heir: s.* Archibald Philip, *b.* 1912. *Address:* Pinkie House, Musselburgh, N.B. *Clubs:* Naval and Military, Carlton; New, Edinburgh. (*Died 17 April 1924.*)

HOPE, John Owen Webley, C.M.G. 1918; Senior Commissioner, Kenya Colony; *s.* of late Rear-Adm. Charles Webley Hope; *b.* 1875. *Club:* Caledonian. (*Died 15 Sept. 1927.*)

HOPE, Robert Charles, F.S.A.; *b.* Derby, 1855; *m.* Mary, *d.* of late Joseph Edgerley Purser, Dublin; two *s.* one *d.* *Educ.:* Derby School; Peterhouse, Cambridge. Late of Lincoln's Inn; Hon. Consul in Italy for the Univs. of Scotland; resided in Scarborough, 1875-1900; since then in Geneva and Florence; hon. secretary of the Yorkshire Lawn Tennis Association and County Club for first two years; founder and hon. sec. of the Town of England Lawn Tennis Club and Filey L.T.C.; invented the net adjuster and folding umpire's chair used at all first-class tournaments; manager and stage director of the Scarborough Dramatic Club for twelve years; conductor of the Scarborough Orchestral Society, 1899-1901, and of the Choral and Orchestral Society, 1890; manager and stage director of English Dramatic Club in Geneva, 1901-3, and of the English Dramatic Club, Florence, since 1907; travelled in America, Canada, China, Japan, Ceylon, S. Africa, and Europe generally. *Publications:* Holy Wells of England; Mediæval Music; The Temples and Shrines of Nikko, Japan; The Leper in England; A Dialectal Glossary of Place-Nomenclature; The Church Plate in Rutland; English Goldsmiths, etc.; composer of Church Service in D; editor of The Popish Kingdome or Reigne of Antichrist, by Barnabe Googe. *Recreations:* music, drama. *Address:* Wood Hall, Dulwich, S.E.21. *T.:* Sydenham 0483. (*Died 18 Dec. 1926.*)

HOPE, Colonel Thomas, J.P., D.L.; late Captain Bombay Staff Corps; *b.* 3 Feb. 1848; 2nd *s.* of late Hon. Charles Hope, and Lady Isabella Helen Douglas, *d.* of 5th Earl of Selkirk; *m.* 1909, Mary Louisa, *d.* of General Horace Albert Browne, Indian Army, and widow of Col. W. G. Cumming, R.E. M.P., Linlithgow, 1898-95. *Address:* Summerhill, Dumfries. *Club:* New, Edinburgh. (*Died 28 Mar. 1925.*)

HOPE, Sir William H. St. John, Kt., *cr.* 1914; Litt.D., Hon. D.C.L. (Durham); Knight of Grace of the Order of the Hospital of St. John of Jerusalem; Assistant Secretary of the Society of Antiquaries to 1910. *Publications:* The Stall Plates of the Knights of the Garter, 1901; The Abbey of St. Mary-in-Furness, 1902; Heraldry for Craftsmen and Designers, 1913; A Grammar of English Heraldry, 1913; Windsor Castle, its Architectural History, 1913; joint author of The Chronicles of the Collegiate Church of All Saints, Derby; and of the Corporation Plate and Insignia of Office of the Cities and Towns of England and Wales; author of numerous papers in various transactions on archæological subjects. *Address:* Galewood, Great Shelford, Cambridge. (*Died 18 Aug. 1919.*)

HOPE, Lieut.-Col. William Henry Webley, C.M.G. 1918; R.A.; a Director of Inspection, Royal Small Arms Factory, Enfield; *s.* of late Rear-Adm. Charles Webley Hope; *b.* 1871; *m.* 1900, Florence, *d.* of late Charles Walter Hill of Clapham, Sussex; one *s.* *Educ.:* Royal Military Academy, Woolwich. *Address:* R. Small Arms Factory, Enfield. (*Died 13 May 1919.*)

HOPKINS, Arthur Antwis, J.P.; Metropolitan Police Magistrate, Bow Street, since 1913; *b.* 2 June 1855; *e. s.* of late John Satchell Hopkins, Edgbaston, Birmingham; *m.* Ada, *y. d.* of late Rev. James Butler, D.C.L., All Souls Coll. Oxford, 1880. *Educ.:* Rugby School; Trin. Coll. Camb. (M.A.). Barr. 1879; Metropolitan Police Magistrate, Lambeth, 1890-1913. *Address:* 63 North Gate, N.W. *Clubs:* United University, Portland. (*Died 6 July 1916.*)

HOPKINS, Paymaster-in-Chief David Bertie Lyndsay, M.V.O. 1904; Assist. Clerk, 1878; Paymaster, 1894; Fleet-Paymaster, 1902; Paymaster-in-Chief (retired) 1911; clerk to secretary in Minotaur during Egyptian War, 1882 (Egyptian medal, bronze star); Secretary to Commanders-in-Chief China, Australia, Mediterranean and Portsmouth Stations. *Address:* The Corner, Horley, Surrey. (*Died 21 Mar. 1925.*)

HOPKINS, Everard, artist; contributor to Punch, Illustrated London News, Black and White, etc.; *b.* Hampstead, 5 Feb. 1860; *y. s.* of Manley Hopkins, Hawaiian Consul. *Educ.:* Charterhouse; Slade School of Art, Gower Street. Slade Scholar, 1878; Assistant Editor of the late Pilot newspaper. *Publication:* Novel, Lydia. *Recreations:* cycling, tennis, golf. *Address:* 85A Linden Gardens, W.2. *T.:* Park 1104. *Club:* Savile. (*Died 17 Oct. 1928.*)

HOPKINS, Right Rev. Frederick C., S.J., titular Bishop of Athribis; Vicar Apostolic of British Honduras since 1899; *b.* 1844; *s.* of William Hopkins, Birmingham. *Educ.:* Ratcliffe College; Oscott. Attended Birmingham Hospital Medical School; M.R.C.S., London; entered the Society of Jesus, 1868; edited the Angelus (a Belize Catholic Church magazine), 1888-99. *Address:* Bishop's House, Belize, British Honduras. (*Died 11 April 1928.*)

HOPKINS, John Castell, F.S.S., F.R.G.S., P.R.S.L.; Author The Canadian Annual Review of Public Affairs, 1901-20; Managing Director The Canadian Review Co., Ltd.; *b.* Sunset Park, Dyersville, Iowa, U.S., 1 April 1864; *s.* of late John Castell Hopkins of The Cliffs, Duncan, B.C., and *g.s.* of late John Castell Hopkins, J.P., Rowchester House, Berwickshire; *m.* 1907, Anne Beatrice Bonner, Toronto; two *d.* *Educ.:* Bowmanville; Toronto. Associate Editor Toronto Daily Empire, 1890-93; seven years in Imperial Bank of Canada; Founder of the 1st Branch Imperial Federation League in Ontario; Hon. Secretary of the League in Canada for some years ; a Founder and ex-President of the Empire Club of Toronto ; Pres. in 1891-92 of the Ontario and Toronto Conservative Associations. *Publications*: 30 volumes in Canadian and British History or Biography ; many pamphlets on public topics ; Editor of Canada: An Encyclopaedia of the Country, in 6 Vols. ; special contributor to N.Y. Tribune, London Times, Sheffield Telegraph, Glasgow Herald ; many magazine articles. Canadian contributor to Appleton's Encyclopædia, the Americana, and others. *Recreations*: golfing, reading novels. *Address*: 121 Farnham Avenue, Toronto, Canada. *Clubs*: Albany, Royal Canadian Yacht, Rosedale Golf, Toronto.

(*Died Nov. 1923.*)

HOPKINS, Sir John Ommanney, G.C.B., *cr.* 1899 ; K.C.B., *cr.* 1892 ; J.P. ; Admiral 1896 ; *b.* 1834 ; *s.* of Rev. W. T. Hopkins, rector of Nuffield, Oxon ; *m.* 1st, *d.* of Metcalfe Larken, 1875 ; 2nd, Minna, *d.* of Admiral Sir Sydney Colpoys Dacres, G.C.B., 1882 ; one *s.* one *d.* *Educ.*: Marlborough Coll. In Black Sea, 1854-55 ; at Sebastopol ; private secretary to First Lord of the Admiralty, Earl of Northbrook, 1881-83 ; A.D.C. to the Queen, 1881-85 ; Director of Naval Ordnance, 1883-86 ; Admiral Superintendent of Portsmouth Dockyard, 1886-88 ; Naval Lord of the Admiralty and Controller of the Navy, 1888-92 ; Commander-in-Chief North American and West India Station, 1892-95 ; Commander-in-Chief on the Mediterranean Station. 1896-99 ; medal and clasp for Sebastopol. *Recreations*: riding, shooting, fishing, cycling. *Address*: Greatbridge House, Romsey, Hants. *T.A.*: Romsey. *Clubs*: United Service ; Royal Naval, Portsmouth ; Union, Malta. (*Died 30 July 1916.*)

HOPKINS, Livingston, cartoonist and part proprietor Sydney Bulletin ; *b.* Bellefontaine, Ohio, U.S.A., 1846 ; *s.* of Daniel and Sarah Hopkins ; *m.* 1875, Miss Commager of Ohio ; five *c.* Left school at the age of fourteen ; after various experiments in commerce, journalism, etc., the opportunity came for cultivating long-existing taste for humorous illustration ; went to New York in 1870, and between that and 1883 contributed to most of the current American illustrated publications of that period ; engaged by the Sydney Bulletin for three years (1883), which term renewed from time to time has led to present share in the business ; now retired. *Recreations*: music, fiddle-making, mechanics, and outdoor amusements. *Address*: Raglan Street, Mosman, near Sydney, N.S.W. *T.*: Mosman 1117. *Clubs*: Imperial Service, Sydney ; Recreation, Mosman.

(*Died 21 Aug. 1927.*)

HOPKINS, Tighe, writer ; *b.* 5 Dec. 1856 ; *o. s.* of late Rev. W. R. Hopkins, Vicar of Moulton, Cheshire ; *m.* 1881, Ellen (*d.* 1914), *o. d.* of late Rev. H. J. Crump, and *step-d.* of late Mortimer Collins, novelist ; one *d.* *Educ.*: St. John's, Leatherhead ; Oundle Grammar School. *Publications*: Twixt Love and Duty, 1886 ; For Freedom, 1888 ; Nugents of Carriconna, 1890 ; Incomplete Adventurer, 1892 ; Lady Bonnie's Experiment, 1895 ; Kilmainham Memories, 1896 ; Pepita of the Pagoda (Arrowsmith's Annual), 1897 ; Dungeons of Old Paris, 1898 ; An Idler in Old France, 1899 ; The Silent Gate : A Voyage into Prison, 1900 ; Man in the Iron Mask, 1901 ; The Women Napoleon Loved, 1910 ; Some forty chapters in London Stories, 1911 ; Wards of the State, an Unofficial View of Prison and the Prisoner, 1913 ; Romance of Fraud ; Prisoners of War, 1914 ; Romance of Escapes, 1916 ; Your Unsuspected Self, 1917 ; Literary Staff of the Daily Chronicle, Nation ; Carleton's Traits and Stories in Red Letter Library ; De Quincey in Newnes's Classics ; has written largely on Penal Reform. *Recreations*: cycling, walking. *Address*: Frayne, Herne Bay. (*Died 14 Feb. 1919.*)

HOPKINS, William Joseph, M.V.O. ; *b.* 22 Aug. 1863 ; *s.* of Joseph Hopkins, Salisbury, Wilts. ; *m.* Harriett Jane, *d.* of John Barber, Southampton ; three *s.* two *d.* *Educ.*: Salisbury Grammar School. Joined Metropolitan Police, 1885 ; served in all ranks ; Superintendent of K Limehouse Division, D Marylebone Division, and A Whitehall Division ; retired ; Officier de l'Ordre Leopold II. of Belgium ; 1st and 2nd Jubilee, Edward VII. and George V. Coronation medals ; Chairman of County Society — Wiltshiremen in London. *Recreations*: swimming and amateur theatricals. *Address*: 399 Fulham Palace Road, Fulham, S.W.6. *Club*: Stadium. (*Died June 1927.*)

HOPKINSON, Bertram, C.M.G. 1917 ; F.R.S. 1910 ; M.A., M.I.C.E. ; Professor of Mechanism and Applied Mechanics, Cambridge University since 1903 ; Professorial Fellowship at King's College, 1914 ; *b.* 11 Jan. 1874 ; *e. s.* of late Dr. J. Hopkinson, F.R.S. ; *m.* 1903, Mariana, *e. d.* of Alex. Siemens ; seven *d.* *Educ.*: St. Paul's School ; Trinity College, Cambridge. Called to Bar, 1897 ; on death of Dr. J. Hopkinson, 1898, started business as a consulting engineer in partnership with Chas. Hopkinson and Ernest Talbot ; jointly with partners was responsible for the design of the electric tramways at Leeds and Newcastle-on-Tyne and numerous other works. *Publications*: edited Original Papers by Dr. J. Hopkinson, with a memoir ; author of several scientific and technical papers, read before the Royal Society, Institution of Civil Engineers, and other bodies. *Recreations*: sailing, walking, rowing, ski-ing. *Address*: 10 Adams Road, Cambridge. *T.*: 103 and 268 Cambridge. (*Died 26 Aug. 1918.*)

HOPKINSON, Edward, D.Sc. (London) ; M.A. (Cambridge) ; M.Inst.C.E., M.I.Mech.E. (Past President) ; M.I.E.E. ; M.P. (C.U.) Clayton Division of Manchester since Dec. 1918 ; *b.* Manchester, 28 May 1859 ; 4th *s.* of late John Hopkinson, sometime Mayor of Manchester, and Alice, *d.* of late John Dewhurst, Skipton ; *m.* Minnie, *e. d.* of late John Campbell of Rathfern, Co. Antrim ; one *s.* one *d.* *Educ.*: Owens College, Manchester ; and Emmanuel College, Cambridge (Scholar and Fellow). Mechanical and electrical engineer ; designed the electrical equipment of the Bessbrook and Newry Tramroad, also the original City and South London Railway, opened 1890, for papers on which he received the Telford and George Stephenson medals and premiums of the Inst.C.E. ; Chairman David Lewis Colony for Epileptics ; Member of Executive Committee Manchester Steam Users' Association ; a Director of Mather & Platt. Ltd., and of the Chloride Electrical Storage Coy., Ltd. ; Indian Industrial Commission, 1916-18. *Publications*: technical papers in the Transactions of the Royal Society and Proceedings of the Inst.C.E. and Inst.Mech.E. *Recreations*: travelling and climbing. *Address*: Ferns, Alderley Edge, Cheshire. *T.*: Alderley Edge 20. *Clubs*: Athenæum, Reform, Alpine.

(*Died 15 Jan. 1922.*)

HOPKINSON, John, F.L.S., F.G.S., F.Z.S., F.R.M.S., F.R.Met. Soc., Assoc.Inst.Ç.E. ; Secretary Ray Society since 1902 ; Director St. Albans Gas Co. ; Income Tax Commissioner (St. Albans) ; *b.* Leeds, 1844 ; *m.* Kate, *d.* of Thomas Willshin of Kingsbury, St. Albans ; two *d.* *Educ.*: Leeds ; London ; Berkhamsted. In business (J. & J. Hopkinson, pianoforte manufacturers), 1860 - 1913 ; editor Herts Natural History Society since 1875, Hon. Secretary 1875-91, President 1891 - 93 ; Treasurer Ray Society, 1899-1902 ; founded the Hertfordshire Natural History Society, 1875, and the Conference of Delegates to British Association in 1880 (first Chairman), and chiefly instrumental in founding the Herts County Museum at St. Albans, built in 1898, establishing a Meteorological Observatory at the Museum in

1900 by presenting the instruments; Conservative; Church of England. *Publications:* Bibliography of the Tunicata, 1912; British Freshwater Rhizopoda (with J. Cash and G. H. Wailes), 3 vols. published; numerous papers in Geological Magazine, Annals Natural History, British Association Reports, Trans. Herts Natural History Society, etc.; several articles in works on Yorks, Herts, and Beds. *Recreations:* mountain walking and photography (especially geological). *Address:* Weetwood, Watford. *(Died 5 July 1919.)*

HOPLEY, Hon. William Musgrove, Senior Judge, Southern Rhodesia, since 1914; *b.* 1858; *e. s.* of Frederick Hurlingh Hopley, M.L.A., and Wilhelmina Johanna von Abo; *m.* 1832, Annie Catherine, *e. d.* of Hon. John Van der Byl, M.L.C.; one *s.* one *d. Educ.:* St. Andrew's Coll. Grahamstown; Diocesan College, Rondebosch, Cape Colony; Pembroke College, Cambridge. M.A., LL.M., 1st class Law Tripos, 1877. Called to Bar, Inner Temple, and joined Cape Bar, 1878; practised at Cape Town and Grahamstown till 1883; at Kimberley from 1883; Crown Prosecutor for Griqualand West, 1885-1892; Q.C. 1890; Puisne Judge of the Supreme Court, Cape Colony March 1892, and assigned to the High Court of Griqualand; on staff of Field Marshal Lord Roberts as legal adviser at Bloemfontein, March, April, May, 1900; assigned to Supreme Court, Cape Town, temporarily 1904 and permanently 1907; late Puisne Judge, Cape Colony; retired on pension from the Bench of the Supreme Court of S. Africa, C.P.D., 30 Sep. 1914. *Address:* Judges Chambers, Salisbury, Rhodesia. *Clubs:* Civil Service, Cape Town; Salisbury, Salisbury. *(Died Mar. 1919*

HOPTON, Rev. Prebendary Michael; *b.* 1838; 2nd *s.* of Rev. W. Parsons Hopton, Bishop Frome-Bromyard; *m.* 1872, Mary Lucy (*d.* 1910), 4th *d.* of Sir W. Rouse Boughton, 10th Bart., Downton Hall, Salop; one *d. Educ.:* Harrow; Trinity Coll. Camb. (M.A.) Vicar of Staunton Long, 1866-76; Canon Frome, 1876-1903; Prebendary of Hereford Cathedral, 1901; J.P. Herefordshire; late Hon. Sec. to Hereford Three Choir Festival, the Clergy Widows and Orphan Charity; Hon. Treasurer Clergy Pension Fund for Hereford Diocese; Hon. Treasurer Diocesan Board of Finance. *Address:* Holmer Hall, Hereford. *T.A.:* Hereford. *(Died 20 April 1928.)*

HOPWOOD, Aubrey, author; *b.* Edinburgh, 4 April 1863; 2nd *s.* of late John Turner Hopwood of Ketton Hall, Stamford. *Educ.:* Cheam School; Charterhouse. Lieut. Northamptonshire Regiment, 1882; travelled round the world, 1889; Secretary of Arthur's Club, 1893-1907. *Publications:* Down by the Suwanee River, 1897; The Sleepy King, 1898; The Bunkum Book, 1900; Rhymes without Reason, 1903; The Old English Sheep Dog, 1905; author of lyrics for A Runaway Girl, The Lucky Star, Alice in Wonderland, Bluebell, The Cherry Girl, The Merry-go-Round, The Lady Wrangler, You and I, and many songs for music. *Recreations:* shooting, fishing. *Address:* The Beeches, Malmesbury. *T.:* Malmesbury 33. *Clubs:* Authors', Garrick, Orleans. *(Died 25 Oct. 1917.)*

HOPWOOD, Avery, playwright; *b.* Cleveland, O.; *s.* of James Hopwood and Jule Pendergast. *Educ.:* University of Michigan, A.B., 1905; went to New York as Special Correspondent for Cleveland Leader, 1905. *Publications:* (plays) This Woman and This Man; Seven Days (with Mary Roberts Rinehart); Judy Forgot; Nobody's Widow (produced in England as Roxana); Fair and Warmer; Sadie Love; Our Little Wife; Double Exposure; The Gold Diggers; The Bat, and Spanish Love (both with Mary Roberts Rinehart); The Girl in the Limousine; Ladies'

Night; The Demi-Virgin; Why Men Leave Home; Little Miss Bluebeard; The Alarm Clock; The Best People (with David Gray); Naughty Cinderella; The Garden of Eden, etc. *Address:* c/o Farmers' Loan and Trust Co., 475 5th Avenue, New York, N.Y. *Clubs:* Lambs, University of Michigan, Coffee-House. New York. *(Died 1 July 1928.)*

HOPWOOD, Charles Augustus, C.B. 1897; *b.* 27 Dec. 1847; *s.* of late Rev. Canon Hopwood, and *d.* of 13th Earl of Derby; *m.* 1888, Georgie Florence Louisa, *d.* of late George Lear Curtis. Entered Foreign Office, 1872; Assistant Clerk, 1894; Senior Clerk, 1899; retired, 1906. *Address:* 18 Beaufort Gardens, S.W.3. *T.:* Western 1719. *(Died 21 Mar. 1922.)*

HORE, Col. Charles Owen, C.M.G. 1900; late Lieut.-Col. 2nd Batt. Royal Garrison Regt.; retired, 1907; *b.* 2 Sept. 1860; *m.* 1889, Dulcibella Eden, *d.* of General George T. Radcliffe. *Educ.:* Cheltenham College. Late South Staffs Regiment; served Egypt, 1882, 1884-85, 1898; South Africa, 1899-1900 (despatches thrice, Queen's medal, 8 clasps). *Address:* 23 South Eaton Place, S.W. *Club:* Army and Navy. *(Died 14 Feb. 1916.)*

HORE, Maj.-Gen. Walter Stuart; retired, 1899; Bombay Infantry; *b.* 1843; *s.* of late Capt. William Hore, Bengal Army; *m.* 1876, *d.* of General W. S. Hatch, R.A.; one *s.* one *d. Educ.:* Cheltenham College. Served Abyssinian Campaign, 1867-68 (medal); Hon. Colonel 120th Rajputana Infantry; J.P. Herefordshire. *Address:* Lemore, Eardisley, Herefordshire. *(Died 1 April 1918.)*

HORLICK, Sir James, 1st Bt., *cr.* 1914; D.L., J.P.; High Sheriff, Gloucestershire, 1902; Lord of the Manor of Cowley; *b.* 1844; *m.* Margaret Burford; two *s. Educ.:* Privately. For many years actively engaged in promoting the interests of Horlick's Malted Milk Co., of which concern he is the founder and Chairman; latterly he has taken great interest in the agricultural matters of Gloucestershire, and in country pursuits. *Recreations:* shooting; motoring. *Heir: s.* Ernest Burford [*b.* 29 Feb. 1880. *Educ.:* Wellington College; Christ Church, Oxford; *m.* 1902, Jane, *d.* of late Col. Cunliffe Martin; one *s.* two *d.*]. *Address:* 2 Carlton House Terrace, S.W.1; Kidbrooke Park, Forest Row, Sussex. *T.A.:* Horlick, Charles, London. *T.:* Regent 2458. *Clubs:* Bath, Constitutional, Carlton. *(Died 7 May 1921.)*

HORN, David Bayne, C.I.E. 1905; F.C.H.; M.I.C.E.; Irrigation, Marine, and Railway Branches, Public Works Department Government of Bengal (retired); *b.* 1851; *s.* of late David Horn of Middle Douglie, Perthshire, and latterly of Dollar. *Educ.:* R.I.E. College. Appointed Assistant Engineer, 1874; Executive Engineer, 1882; Under-Secretary, Public Works Department, 1885-1886; Superintending Engineer, 1896; Member Legislative Council, Bengal, 1902; Chief Engineer and Secretary to Government, 1902-6; retired, 1906. *Club:* Oriental. *(Died 3 Jan. 1927.)*

HORN, William Austin; *b.* 24 Feb. 1841; *s.* of late E. K. Horn; *m.* Penelope, *d.* of late W. C. Belt, Barrister-at-Law, Middle Temple; five *s.* two *d. Educ.:* St. Peter's College; Worcester College, Oxford. For fifty years engaged in development of outlying portions of the British Empire in Australia, Ceylon, Malay States, India, Papua; had several minor exploring expeditions in Australia between 1868 and 1879; explored scientifically Central Australia in 1894; holds Australian record for long ride on horseback, 164 miles in 22¼ hours; represented district of Flinders in S. Australia, for which State he has been a J.P. for 52 years; Governor of Middlesex Hospital; Chairman of Knula Selangor Rubber Co., British New Guinea Devt. Co., and Robinson River Rubber and Coconut

Co., Director of Bank of Adelaide, London. *Publications:* Results of Horn Scientific Exploration; Notes by a Nomad; Bush Echoes. *Recreations:* shooting. golf. *Address:* 5 Onslow Gardens. S.W. *T.:* Kensington 6695; Old Stoke Lodge, Stoke Charity, Hants. *Clubs·* Carlton, Junior Carlton.   *(Died 23 Dec. 1922.)*

HORNABROOK, Ven. Charles Soward, Archdeacon of Adelaide since 1918; Priest in Charge of St. Mary Magdalene, Adelaide, since 1908; Canon of Adelaide, 1911; *m.* Ordained, 1889; Curate of Tarree, 1889-92; St. John's, Adelaide, 1892-94; Rector of Kapunda, 1894-1901; Port Adelaide, 1901-5; general licence, Diocese of Adelaide, 1908; Archdeacon of Mt. Gambier, 1908-11. *Address:* Adelaide, South Australia.   *(Died 25 Sept. 1922.)*

HORNBY, Albert Neilson; *b.* Blackburn, 10 Feb. 1847; *s.* of late W. H. Hornby. *Educ.:* Harrow. Played cricket with marked success for 31 years—first for Harrow against Eton, 1864, and then for Lancashire, which he captained for many years. *Recreations:* cricket. football, fox-hunting, and shooting. *Address:* Parkfield, Nantwich. *Clubs:* M.C.C.; Lancashire County Cricket.   *(Died 17 Dec. 1925.)*

HORNBY, Sir (William) Henry, 1st Bt., *cr.* 1899; M.P. (C.) Blackburn, 1886-1910; J.P., D.L.; head of W. H. Hornby & Co., cotton spinners and manufacturers; *b* 9 Aug. 1841; *s.* of late W. H. Hornby, M.P. for Blackburn; *m.* Letitia, *d.* of Capt. W. R. Clayton Browne, 1887; one *s.* three *d.* Served as a Naval Cadet in 1855 in the Baltic during the Crimean War. *Heir:* s. Henry Russell [*b.* 12 Sep. 1888; *m.* 1913, Dorothy Elma, o. *d.* of Maj.-Gen. Sir W. Fry; one *s.*; was on active service in France]. *Address:* 34 Ennismore Gardens, S.W.7. *T.:* Kensington 5269. *Club:* Carlton.   *(Died 22 Oct. 1928.)*

HORNE, Sir Andrew (John), Kt., *cr.* 1913; *b.* Ballinasloe, Co. Galway, 18 Aug. 1856; *m.* 1884, Margaret (*d.* 1920), *d.* of late Francis Norman, solicitor, Rutland Square, Dublin; two *s.* two *d.* *Educ.:* Clongowes Wood College; Vienna. On obtaining medical degrees was elected assistant to the Master, Rotunda Hospital; Fellow Royal Coll. Physicians, Ireland, 1885; Vice-Pres., 1894-1896; Pres., 1908-10; elected Master of National Maternity Hospital on its foundation, 1894; was Vice-President of obstetrical section of British Medical Association held at Swansea; President obstetrical section Royal Academy of Medicine, Ireland; Ex-President Royal College Physicians; Extern Examiner in Obstetrics, University of Dublin. *Publications:* various papers on medical subjects. *Recreations:* golf, tennis, hunting. *Address:* 94 Merrion Square, Dublin. *T.:* Dublin 1476. *Clubs:* Royal Societies; Stephen's Green, Dublin   *(Died 5 Sept. 1924.)*

HORNE, Frederic, O.B.E. 1918; J.P.; Small Holdings Commissioner, Ministry of Agriculture and Fisheries; retired, 1924; *b.* Cuckfield, Sussex, 14 Aug. 1868; *s.* of late Charles Horne, M.A., and Harriet Silvester, *d.* of Leonard Simpson; *m.* Jean Picken, 2nd *d.* of late Andrew Thomson, The Manor, Shifnal; one *s.* one *d.* *Educ.:* Newport, Shropshire; Adams Grammar School. After leaving school, studied farming in Bucks. and Shropshire, and owing to ill-health went to Central Queensland, 1881; returned after seven years, and farmed for fifteen years at Hinnington, Shifnal; was for some years Vice-Chairman of the Shropshire Chamber of Agriculture; contested Ludlow Division of Shropshire, 1904 and 1906, and Barkston Ash Division of Yorks. twice in 1910; formerly on Committee of National Liberal Club. *Publications:* several pamphlets dealing with Rural Depopulation, Land Reform, and Food Supply in time of War. *Address:* Dickley-Wood, Harrietsham, near Maidstone, Kent. *Club:* National Liberal.   *(Died 2 Feb. 1927.)*

HORNE, Herbert P., architect, writer, and connoisseur; has built Church of the Redeemer, Bayswater Road, the new buildings in Brewhouse Court, Eton College, the Baptistery, St. Luke's, Camberwell, and various private houses. Has contributed to the Saturday Review, Fortnightly Review, Monthly Magazine, Burlington Magazine, Revue Archéologique, Rassegna d'Arte, etc.; editor of the Hobby Horse, 1887-91. *Publications:* Diversi Colores, 1891; The Binding of Books, 1894; Life of Leonardo da Vinci, done into English, with a Commentary, 1903; Condivi's Life of Michelangelo, done into English, 1904; Sandro Botticelli, 1908. *Address:* Palazzo proprio, 6 Via dei Benci, Florence, Italy. *Club:* Burlington Fine Arts.   *(Died 23 April 1916.)*

HORNE, John, F.R.S., LL.D., F.R.S.E., F.G.S.; *b.* Campsie, Stirlingshire, 1 Jan. 1848; *s.* of late James Horne, Newmill, Campsie; *m.* Anna Leyland (*d.* 1926), *d.* of late Henry Taylor and Anna M. Harrington, Pernambuco, Brazil, and *step-d.* of Robert Arbuckle, M.D., Brazil, and of Auchenhay, Kirkcudbrightshire; two *s.* one *d.* *Educ.:* High School and Univ., Glasgow. Entered Geol. Survey of Scot. 1867; Wollaston Fund, Geological Society, 1888; Murchison Centenary Fund (with Dr. Peach), 1892; Neill Medallist, Royal Society, Edinburgh, 1893; Murchison Medallist, Geological Society (with Dr. Peach), 1899; Assistant Director, Geological Survey, Scot. 1901; President (geological section), British Association, Glasgow, 1901; Hon. LL.D. Aberdeen, 1902; retired from Geological Survey, 1911; Hon. LL.D. St. Andrews, 1911; President, Royal Society, Edinburgh, 1915-19; Hon. LL.D. Edinburgh, 1920; Wollaston Medal, Geological Society (with Dr. Peach), 1921; Hon. Member of the Physical and Natural History Society, Geneva, 1920; Corresponding Member of the Geological Society of Belgium, 1922; Foreign Hon. Member of American Academy of Arts and Sciences, 1925. *Publications:* The Silurian Rocks of Scotland (with B. N. Peach, F.R.S., and J. J. H. Teall, F.R.S.), parts of several Geological Survey Memoirs, and various papers in journals and transactions of scientific societies. *Recreations:* travelling in new geological fields, reading. *Address:* 20 Merchiston Gardens, Edinburgh.
    (Died 30 May 1928.)

HORNE, Lancelot Worthy, C.B.E. 1918; M.V.O. 1920; Superintendent of the Line, London & North Western Railway, 1914; retired 1923 when grouping of railways took place; *b.* 1875; *e. s.* of late Octavius Horne and Harriet, *d.* of late John Rowland Gibson, F.R.C.S.; unmarried. *Educ.:* Shrewsbury. Entered service of L. & N.W. Rly. in General Manager's office, 1893; transferred to office of Superintendent of Line, 1895; has been Superintendent in charge of the Chester and Holyhead, the Birmingham and the London Districts; also Goods Manager of Liverpool District; Assistant to Superintendent of the Line, 1911; Major Engineer and Railway Staff Corps. *Recreations:* shooting and fishing. *Address:* The Manor House, Cheddington, Bucks. *Club:* Conservative.(*Died 7 Mar. 1924.*)

HORNER, Andrew L., K.C. 1904; M.P. (U.) South Tyrone since Jan. 1910; Crown Prosecutor, Co. Cavan; *b.* Limavady, 1863; *m.* Annie M., *y. d.* of late John Robb, J.P., Belfast; two *s.* one *d.* *Educ.:* Foyle College, Londonderry; Queen's University, Belfast. Member of North-West Irish Circuit; Bencher King's Inns, Dublin; contested South Tyrone, 1906. *Address:* 34 Fitzwilliam Place, Dublin. *Clubs:* Constitutional, Carlton.   *(Died 26 Jan. 1916.)*

HORNER, Egbert Foster, Mus.D., F.R.C.O., Director of Examinations, Trinity College of Music, London; *b.* London, 1864; *m.* Emily Anna Charlesina, *d.* of late Charles Fox, Tunbridge Wells; one *s.* one *d.* *Educ.:*

pupil of Sir Frederick Bridge. Mus.B. Durham University, 1895 ; Mus.D. 1900; Organist of St. John's Church, Westminster, 1890-1919 ; Vice-President Union of Graduates in Music ; Member of the Court of Assistants, Royal Society of Musicians ; Member of the Board of Studies in Music, Member of the Faculty of Music, and Recognised Teacher in Music, University of London ; Examiner for Degrees in Music, University of Durham, 1924-27; Professor Harmony and Counterpoint, Trinity College of Music ; Examiner for Degrees in Music, University of Birmingham, 1927-28 ; Dean of the Faculty of Music, University of London, 1928 ; Examiner for Degrees in Music, University of London, 1928. *Publications:* Organ Music, Church Music, etc. *Address:* 6 Alexandra House, St. Mary's Terrace, W.2.

(Died 8 Oct. 1928.)

HORNER, Sir John (Francis Fortescue), K.C.V.O., *cr.* 1907 ; J.P., D.L. ; Barrister ; High Sheriff of Somerset, 1885 ; Commissioner of Woods and Forests, 1895-1907; *b.* 28 Dec. 1842 ; *m.* 1883, Frances, O.B.E., 4th *d.* of William Graham, M.P. ; two *d. Educ.:* Eton ; Balliol College, Oxford, M.A. *Address:* 16 Lower Berkeley Street, W.1. *T.:* Langham 1660 ; Manor House, Mells, Frome. *Clubs:* United University, Athenæum, Brooks's.

(Died 31 Mar. 1927.)

HORNING, Lewis Emerson; Professor of Teutonic Philology, University of Toronto (Victoria College), since 1905 ; *b.* 2 April 1858 ; *s.* of James Horning and Eliza Macklem, of United Empire Loyalist descent ; *m.* 1885, Beatrice Lillian, *d.* of Charles Nixon ; one *s.* two *d. Educ.:* Brantford Collegiate Institute, Victoria College ; Postgraduate at Breslau, Goettingen, and Leipzic. Matriculated, 1880 ; four scholarships, B.A., 1884 ; taught Peterboro Collegiate Institute, 1884-86 ; Adjunct Professor Classic and Modern Languages, Victoria College, 1886-89 ; abroad, 1889-91 ; Ph.D. Goettingen, 1891 ; Professor of German Language and Literature and of Old English, 1891-1905 ; public lecturer on literature, politics, and history. *Publications:* various High School and College Textbooks ; translation of Witkowski, History of German Drama in 19th Century ; numerous magazine articles on Canadian literature, present day politics, etc. ; bibliography of Canadian (English) fiction with L. J. Burpee. *Recreation:* gardening. *Address:* Victoria College, Toronto, Canada.

(Died 6 Jan. 1925.)

HORNUNG, Ernest William, novelist and journalist; *b.* Middlesborough, 7 June 1866 ; *y. s.* of late John Peter Hornung, Middlesborough ; *m.* Constance, *d.* of late Charles Altamont Doyle, and *g. d.* of John Doyle, " H. B." 1893. *Educ.:* Uppingham School. In Australia, 1884-86 ; literary work ever since. *Publications:* A Bride from the Bush, 1890 ; Under Two Skies, 1892 ; Tiny Luttrell, 1893 ; The Boss of Taroomba, The Unbidden Guest, 1894 ; The Rogue's March. Irralie's Bushranger, 1896 ; My Lord Duke, 1897 ; Young Blood, Some Persons Unknown, 1898 ; The Amateur Cracksman, Dead Men Tell No Tales, 1899 ; The Belle of Toorak, Peccavi, 1900 ; The Black Mask, 1901 ; The Shadow of the Rope, 1902 ; No Hero, Denis Dent, 1903 ; Stingaree, A Thief in the Night, 1905 ; Mr. Justice Raffles, 1909 ; The Camera Fiend, 1911 ; Fathers of Men, 1912 ; Witching Hill, 1913 ; The Thousandth Woman, The Crime Doctor, 1914 ; Notes of a Campfollower, 1919 ; The Young Guard (verse); *Address:* Midway Cottage, Partridge Green, Sussex. *Clubs:* Savile, Royal Automobile, M.C.C. *(Died 22 Mar. 1921.)*

HORSFALL, Jeremiah Garnett, C.I.E. 1890 ; Indian Civil Service (retired); *b.* Fairfield Hall, Bolton Abbey, Yorkshire, 1840 ; *y. s.*

518

of late Jeremiah Horsfall, J.P.; *m.* 1875, Mary Isabella, 2nd *d.* of late F. J. Howson of Huntingdon. *Educ.:* Giggleswick ; Christ's College, Cambridge (Scholar ; B.L.). Entered Madras Civil Service, 1862 ; retired, 1890. *Decorated* for famine work in Ganjam District, 1888. *Address:* Hollenden, Exmouth. Devon.

(Died 28 Mar. 1920.)

HORSFALL, Sir John Cousin, 1st Bt.; *cr.* 1909 ; County Alderman, West Riding of Yorkshire County Council; *b.* 8 Dec. 1846 ; *s.* of John Foster Horsfall, Oxenhope, near Keighley ; *m.* 1st, Elizabeth Ann, *d.* of James Hartley, Ilkley ; 2nd, Sarah Emily, *d.* of John Crossley Fawcett Greenfield, Brearley, nr. Halifax ; one *s.* four *d. Educ.:* privately, Rev. J. B. Grant, The Vicarage, Oxenhope ; Commercial College, Rippenden, nr. Halifax. Worsted spinner, Glusburn, nr. Keighley ; built Institute in Glusburn village, used for various purposes : Baptist religious worship and Sunday school, technical and art classes and lectures, recreation and library, swimming and slipper baths. *Heir: s.* John Donald, Captain T.F. Reserve [*b.* 1 June 1891 ; *m.* 1914, Henrietta. *d.* of W. Musgrave, Shorbridge House, Eastbourne. *Address:* Beanlands, Crosshills, near Keighley]. *Address:* Hayfield, Crosshills, near Keighley. *T.A.:* Horsfall, Crosshills. *T.:* Crosshills 20 and 30. *M.:* C 7006, C 8095. *Clubs:* National Liberal ; Union. Bradford.

(Died 18 Oct. 1920.)

HORSLEY, Gerald Callcott, F.R.I.B.A.; Past - President Architectural Association ; *b.* 31 Oct. 1862 ; *y. s.* of late John Callcott Horsley, R.A.; *m.* 1895, Susan, *d.* of late Peter Black, Glasgow. *Educ.:* Kensington School. Articled pupil to R. Norman Shaw, R.A., 1879 ; became student of the Royal Academy, Owen Jones travelling student of Royal Institute of British Architects (1887, 1888); designed many buildings, including St. Paul's Girls' School, Brook Green, W. ; St. Chad's Church, Longsdon ; Framewood, Stoke Poges ; Coverwood, Surrey ; additions, Balcombe Place ; offices for Universities Mission to Central Africa, Westminster, Harrow, and Pinner Stations for London and North-Western Railway. *Publications:* various papers and addresses on the Art of Architecture ; a contributor to Architecture ; A Profession of an Art, 1895. *Recreations:* sketching, golf. *Address:* 2 Gray's Inn Square, W.C. ; 28 Bedford Gardens, Kensington, W. *T.:* Central 2507. *Club:* Athenæum. *(Died 2 July 1917.)*

HORSLEY, Rev. J. W., M.A. Oxon ; Vicar of Detling, Kent, 1911 - 21 ; Hon. Canon of Southwark ; late Hon. Sec. Southwark Diocesan Temperance Society ; Borough Councillor and Chairman of Health Society of Southwark ; Mayor of Southwark, 1910 ; Chairman of Clergy Friendly Society since 1882 ; *b.* 14 June 1845, at Dunkirk, near Faversham, whereof his father, Rev. J. W. Horsley, M.A. Oxon, the first incumbent ; *m.* Mary Sophia, *e. d.* of Capt. Codd, Governor H.M. Prison, Clerkenwell ; two *s.* four *d. Educ.:* King's School, Canterbury ; Pembroke College, Oxford. Curate, Witney, Oxon (with Bishop Jacob), 1870 ; Curate, St. Michael's, Shoreditch ; Chaplain, H.M. Prison, Clerkenwell, 1876-86 ; Cler. Sec. Waifs and Strays Society ; Vicar, Holy Trinity, Woolwich ; Rector of St. Peter's, Walworth, 1894 - 1911 ; member of Royal Commission on Venereal Disease, 1914. *Publications:* Practical Hints on Parochial Missions (in conjunction with his brother-in-law, Bishop Dawes); Jottings from Jail ; Prisons and Prisoners ; I remember, 1911 ; How Criminals are Made and Prevented, 1912 ; Commentary on the Litany, 1915 ; and many papers and pamphlets. *Recreations:* natural history in most branches, especially botany and conchology; social reform, especially as regards temperance and sanitation ; Freemason.

Grand Chaplain, 1906. *Address :* c/o Detling Vicarage, Kent. *Club :* Swiss Alpine.

(*Died 25 Nov. 1921.*)

HORSLEY, Reginald Ernest, M.D., F.R.C.S. Edin.; J.P.; author; *b.* Sydney, N.S.W., 1863 ; *s.* of late Capt. Charles Henry Horsley, 51st Madras N.I., H.E.I.C. ; Provost Royal Burgh of Crail, and Ex-officio Admiral of the Forth ; *m.* Mary, *d.* of late William Inglis, of Kirkmay. *Educ.:* Sydney Grammar School ; Trinity College, Melbourne University ; Universities of Edinburgh and Berlin. Was on editorial staff of Challenger Expedition Commission ; was Assistant, Ear and Throat Wards, Edinburgh Royal Infirmary ; Surgeon, Edinburgh (New Town) Ear and Throat Hospital ; Aurist to the Edinburgh Institution for the Education of the Deaf and Dumb ; Lecturer on Biology at Stonyhurst College affiliated Medical School ; retired in 1903 from the profession of medicine ; since then engaged in literary work ; has travelled extensively in Australia, New Zealand, South Sea Islands and U.S.A. *Publications :* The Yellow God ; The Blue Balloon ; Stonewall's Scout ; Hunted through Fiji ; In the Grip of the Hawk ; The Romance of New Zealand (Romance of Empire) ; The Red Hussar, Hunting U - Boats, etc. *Recreations :* travelling, natural history. *Address :* Kirkmay House, Crail, Fife.

(*Died 22 July 1926.*)

HORSLEY, Sir Victor Alexander Haden, Kt., *cr.* 1902 ; F.R.S., B.S., F.R.C.S., M.D. (Halle) ; Surgeon to National Hospital for Paralysis and Epilepsy, 1886 ; Emeritus Professor of Clinical Surgery and Consulting Surgeon at University College Hospital since 1906 ; *b.* Kensington, 1857 ; *s.* of late J. C. Horsley, R.A. ; *m.* 1887, Eldred, 3rd *d.* of Sir Frederick Bramwell, 1st Bt. ; two *s.* one *d.* *Educ. :* Cranbrook School ; Univ. Coll. Hospital. Professor-Superintendent of Brown Institution, 1884-90 ; Secretary to Royal Commission on Hydrophobia, 1885 ; Fullerian Professor at Royal Institution, 1891-93 ; Professor of Pathology, University College, 1893-96 ; 1st Medallist of the Lannelongue International Prize in Surgery, 1911 ; Royal Medallist of the Royal Society ; LL.D. and D.C.L. Montreal and M'Gill Univ. ; Foreign Associate of the Academy of Medicine, Paris, of the Academy of Wissenschaft, Berlin ; Member of the Science Society of Sweden in succession to Lord Lister ; Member of Learned Societies in Rome, Petrograd, Buda Pesth, Vienna, Philadelphia, etc. ; in 1884 he proved by experiment that the disease myxœdema was caused by the absence of the thyroid gland, and was subsequently awarded the Cameron gold medal and the Fothergill gold medal ; was 1st Chairman of the Representative Meeting of the British Medical Association ; a keen supporter of all Progressive measures and of National Sick Insurance ; contested (L.) University of London ; he was prospective candidate of Market Harborough on temperance and woman suffrage lines, though on these grounds he was afterwards refused the support of the officials ; was Vice-Chairman of the L.C.C. Sub-Committee of Enquiry into the Medical Inspection and Treatment of School Children, and is Vice-President of the English League for the Taxation of Land Values. *Publications :* many papers, principally on the nervous system, in the Phil. Trans., Roy. Soc., Brit. Med. Journal, etc. *Address :* 25 Cavendish Square, W. *T. :* Mayfair 2413. *Clubs :* Athenæum, National Liberal.

(*Died 16 July 1916.*)

HORT, Edward Collett, F.R.C.P. (Edinburgh) ; Consulting Physician ; *b.* 1868 ; *s.* of late Professor Hort, some time Hulsean Professor in the University of Cambridge ; *m.* 1896, Ethel Augusta, *d.* of late Rev. A. P. Gordon ; two *d.* *Educ.:* Emmanuel College, Cambridge ; Guy's Hospital. Member Advisory

Council for Medical Research, National Health Insurance Commission ; Member Pathological Society, Great Britain and Ireland ; Member Association Physicians ; Fellow Royal Society of Medicine ; Fellow of Royal Academy of Medicine, Ireland ; author of a new method of diagnosing Cancer by examining the blood, and of a new method of treating Gastric and Duodenal Ulcer with serum and dry protein. *Publications :* Rational Immunization in the Treatment of Pulmonary Tuberculosis, 1909 ; Autotoxæmia and Infection, Proc. Roy. Soc., 1910 ; Gastric Ulcer, B.M.J., 1908, 1909, 1910 ; Diagnosis of Cancer by Examination of the Blood, ibid., 1909 ; Bacterial Vaccines and Rational Immunization, Pract., 1909 ; Normal Serum Therapy, Lancet, 1908 ; Use and Abuse of Tuberculin, Quart. Journ. of Medicine, 1911 ; Immune and Normal Serum Therapy, B.M.J., 1911 ; Obscure Cases of Fever without Physical Signs, ibid. ; The Dangers of Saline Injections, British Medical Journal, 1911 ; A Critical Study of Experimental Fever, Proc. Royal Society, 1912 ; Micro-organisms and their Relation to Fever, Journal of Hygiene, 1912 ; Salvarsan Fever and other Forms of Injection Fever, Proc. Royal Society Medicine, 1912 ; Fever, its Causes and Treatment, Lecture to Medical Graduates College, Medical Press, 1912 ; Vaccines and Fever, B.M.J., 1913 ; The Etiology of Typhus Fever, B.M.J., 1914 ; The Causal Organism of Typhus Fever, Journ. of Hygiene, 1914, B.M.J., 1915 ; Hæmic Infections of the Urine, B.M.J., 1914 ; The Sterility of Normal Urine, Journ. of Hygiene, 1914 ; The Etiology of Epidemic Cerebrospinal Fever, B.M.J., 1915 ; engaged in research work in private laboratory at Lister Institute. *Recreations :* music and fishing. *Address :* 8 Harley Street, W.1 ; Thornlea, Harrow. *T. :* Gerrard 2319, Harrow 29.

(*Died 15 Oct. 1922.*)

HORTON, Major James ; *b.* 21 Jan. 1845 ; served in 4th Dragoon Guards, 1860-87 ; Inspector of Saddlery, Royal Dockyard, Woolwich, 1887-1911 ; invented service saddle employed South African War ; also the service 1910 riding saddle with automatic self-adjusting side bars, which has been patented. *Recreation :* painting. *Address :* Mentmore Lodge, Copers Cope Road, Beckenham, Kent.

(*Died 14 Nov. 1925.*)

HORTON, Lt.-Col. James H., D.S.O., 1904 ; Major I.M.S. ; M.R.C.S. and L.R.C.P. London ; *b.* 27 Dec. 1871. *Educ.:* Guy's Hospital ; Arthur Durham prize, 1891 ; Member and Cert. Medical Psychol. Association ; House Physician Guy's Hospital, 1895. Entered I.M.S. 1902 ; served East Africa, 1903 (despatches, D.S.O.) ; Captain, 1905 ; Major, 1913 ; Indian Frontier War, 1908 ; Balkan War, 1912 ; Indian Expeditionary Force, Mesopotamia, 1914-15. *Address:* Personal Assistant to the Surgeon-General with the Govt. of Bombay, Poona, India. *Club :* Junior Naval and Military. (*Died July 1917.*)

HORTON-SMITH, Richard Horton, M.A., K.C. ; Bencher, late Senior Trustee, and Treasurer of Lincoln's Inn ; Lincoln's Inn representative Governor of Tancred's Charities ; Chairman of H.M.'s Commissioners for Land Tax for the Holborn District ; a Vice-President of the S.P.C.K. ; *b.* 4 Dec. 1831 ; *e. s.* of late Richard Smith, of the City of London, and of The Lodge, Littlehampton, Sussex, and Elizabeth, *d.* of late Wm. Lumley ; *e. b.* of Sir Lumley Smith, K.C. ; *m.* 1864, Marilla, *e. d.* of late John Baily, Q.C. ; two *s.* two *d.* *Educ. :* University College School ; Univ. Coll. Lond. St. John's Coll. Camb. 4th Classic and Senior Opt. 1856 ; Members' Latin Essay Prize, 1857 ; Fellow St. John's Coll. 1859 ; Founder Raymond Horton-Smith Prize, 1900 (Camb. Univ.). Classical Lecturer, King's Coll. Lond. 1857. Called to Bar, 1859 ; Joint-Editor, De G. J. & S. (Chanc. Reports), 1862-65 ; Joint-Author (with De Gex),

519

Arrangements between Debtors and Creditors, 1867-8-9 ; Q.C. 1877. Member of Original Liberal Unionist Committee for Maintenance of the Union, 1886 ; late Vice-Chairman of Committee University College Hospital, and presently on those of Brompton Hospital for Consumption, and Public Dispensary, Drury Lane (Chairman) ; late on Council, and also Committee of Hosp., King's Coll. London. *Publications:* Theory of Conditional Sentences in Greek and Latin, 1894 ; Various Papers relative to the Drama, etc. *Recreations:* Literature, Music (Director and V.-P., R.A.M. ; Hon. Counsel Philharmonic Society, and V.-P. late Bar Musical Society), Freemasonry (P.J.G.W.-P.G.S.N.). *Address:* 53 Queen's Gardens, Hyde-Park, W. *T.:* Paddington 2786. *Clubs:* Athenæum ; Pitt, Cambridge.
(*Died 2 Nov. 1919.*)

HOSE, Rt. Rev. George Frederick, D.D. ; *b.* 3 Sep. 1838 ; *m.* 1867, Emily Harriet, *d.* of J. Kerbey, M.R.C.S., H.E.I.C. *Educ.:* St. John's Coll. Camb. (M.A.). Ordained 1861 ; Curate of Roxton and Gt. Barford, Beds, 1861-65 ; Curate of H. Trinity, Marlebone, 1865-68 ; Chaplain of Malacca, 1868-72 ; Chaplain of Singapore, 1872-81 ; Archdeacon of Singapore, 1874-81. Bishop of Singapore, 1881-1908. *Address:* The Manor House, Normandy, Guildford. *T.A.:* Hose, Normandy, Surrey.
(*Died 26 Mar. 1922.*)

HOSIE, Sir Alexander, Kt. ; *cr.*1907 ; M.A. ; LL.D. ; F.R.G.S. ; *b.* 16 Jan. 1853 ; *s.* of late A. Hosie ; *m.* 1st, 1887, Florence Lindsay (*d.* 1905) ; one *s.* ; 2nd, 1913, Dorothea (author of Two Gentlemen of China, 1924), *o. d.* of Rev. W. E. Soothill, Professor of Chinese, Oxford University. *Educ.:* Grammar School, Old Aberdeen ; King's College and University, Aberdeen. Student Interpreter in China, 1876 ; employed on special service at Chungking, 1882 ; 2nd Assist. 1886 ; 1st Assistant, 1891 ; Consul at Wuchow, 1897 ; Kiu-kiang, 1900 (did not proceed) ; Consul - General for Province of Szechuen, 1902 ; Tientsin, 1908-12 ; Commercial Attaché to the British Legation in China, 1905 - 9 ; British Delegate to the Shanghai International Opium Commission, 1909 ; appointed personally to investigate the production of Opium in China, 1910 ; Coronation Medal, 1911 ; retired, 1912 ; Special Attaché to the British Legation, 24 Nov. 1919 to 11 Feb. 1920. *Publications:* Three Years in Western China ; Manchuria, its People, Resources, and Recent History ; On the Trail of the Opium Poppy, 1914 ; Szechwan, its Products, Industries and Resources, 1922 ; Editor of Philips' Commercial Map of China, 1922. *Address:* Coleford, Sandown, I.W. (*Died 10 Mar. 1925.*)

HOSKIN, John, LL.D., K.C., D.C.L. ; one of the Board of Governors of University of Toronto ; *b.* Holsworthy, Devon, May 1836 ; *s.* of Richard Hoskin ; *m.* 1866, Mary Agnes, *d.* of late Walter Mackenzie, Barrister-at-Law, of Castle Frank, Toronto. *Educ.:* London. Went to Canada, 1854 ; called to Bar, 1863 ; Q.C. 1873 ; Bencher of Law Society of Upper Canada, 1876 ; now Treasurer ; for many years Senator of Toronto University (Hon. LL.D. 1889) ; D.C.L. (hon.) Trinity University ; Chairman of Board of Trustees of University of Toronto until its reorganization in 1906 ; Chairman of the New Board of Governors, 1906 ; Guardian *ad litem,* and Official Guardian of Infants, 1874-1904 ; Advisory Counsel to his Successor in Office since 1904 ; on the directorate of the Bank of Commerce, of the British American Assurance Company, of The Canada Life Assurance Co., and the Western Assurance Co. ; President of the Canadian Landed and National Investment Company ; a Director, late President Toronto General Trusts Company ; a Director of the Toronto Gas Company, Vice - President the Western Assurance Company, and British American Assurance Company. *Address:* Toronto. *Club:* York, Toronto. (*Died 6 Oct. 1921.*)

520

HOSKING, Hon. Sir John Henry, Kt., *cr.* 1925 ; late Chairman of War Pensions Appeal Board ; *b.* Penzance, 1854 ; *m.* 1890 ; two *s.* one *d.* Went to Auckland, N.Z., 1856 ; Barrister and Solicitor,1875 ; K.C. 1907 ; Judge, Supreme Court, Wellington, 1914-25. *Address:* 24 Sefton Street, Wellington, New Zealand.
(*Died 30 May 1928.*)

HOSKINS, William, I.S.O. 1907. Was Controller of Accounts and Stores for Prison Commissioners. *Address:* Glenroy, Southbourne Road, Bournemouth. (*Died 8 Nov. 1928.*)

HOSKINS, Rt. Rev. Sir Edwyn, Bishop of Southwell (1904) ; 12th Bt., *cr.* 1676 ; 4th *s.* of Canon Sir John Leigh Hoskyns, 9th Bart. ; *b.* 22 May 1851 ; *S.* brother, 1923 ; *m.* 1883, Mary Constance Maude, *d.* of Robert Benson ; one *s.* two *d. Educ.:* Jesus College, Cambridge (Fellow). Ordained, 1874 ; Curate, Welwyn, Herts; Quebec Chapel, 1879-81; St. Clements, North Kensington, 1881-86 ; Rector, St. Dunstan, Stepney, 1886-95 ; Vicar of Bolton, 1895-1901 ; Hon. Canon of Manchester since 1899 ; Rector of Burnley, 1901-4 ; Bishop of Burnley, 1901-5. *Address:* Bishop's Manor, Southwell. (*Died 2 Dec. 1925.*)

HOSKYNS, Sir Leigh, 11th Bt., *cr.* 1676 ; *b.* 14 Feb. 1850 ; *s.* of late Canon Sir John Leigh Hoskyns, 9th Bt., and Emma, *d.* of late Admiral Sir John S. Peyton, K.C.H. ; *S.* brother 1914 ; *m.* 1882, Frances Hester Frederica, *d.* of John Samuel Bowles, Milton Hill, Berks ; three *d. Educ.:* Haileybury ; Trinity College, Oxford. Barrister-at-Law ; formerly Crown Prosecutor, Kimberley ; J.P. and High Sheriff for Oxfordshire, 1907. *Heir:* *b.* Bishop of Southwell. *Address:* 78 Cadogan Square, S.W.1. *Clubs:* Arthur's, New University. (*Died 12 Sept. 1923.*)

HOSKYNS, Rear-Admiral Peyton, C.M.G. 1900 ; M.V.O. 1896 ; R.N. ; commanded special service ships, Portsmouth ; *b.* Aston Tyrrold, Berks, 15 Sept. 1852 ; 5th *s.* of Sir John Leigh Hoskyns, 9th Bt., and Emma, *d.* of Sir John Strutt Peyton, K.C.H. ; *m.* 1882, Grace Macduff, *d.* of D. M. Latham, J.P., D.L., Gourock House, Renfrewshire ; two *s.* two *d. Educ.:* Haileybury; H.M.S. "Britannia." Joined Navy, 1866, as Naval Cadet ; retired 1907 ; served in the Sierra Leone rebellion, 1898 (despatches). *Decorated:* C.M.G. for services in the Sierra Leone rebellion ; M.V.O. for services to Prince Henry of Battenberg, who was taking passage in H.M.S. "Blonde" after Ashanti Expedition of 1895, and died *en route* to Sierra Leone. *Recreations;* shooting, fishing, golf. *Address:* The Brookside, Bedhampton, Havant. *Club:* United Service. (*Died 20 Dec. 1919.*)

HOSMER, James Kendall, author ; *b.* 29 Jan. 1834 ; graduated at Harvard, 1855 ; A.B., A.M. 1867 ; Minister in Deerfield, Mass. 1860-1866 ; Prof. Rhetoric and Eng. Lit. at Antioch College, Ohio, 1866-72 ; Prof. Eng. and History, University of the State of Missouri, 1872-74 ; Ph.D. Univ. of Mo. 1874 ; Prof. Eng. and Germ. Lit. Washington Univ., St. Louis, Mo. 1874-92 ; LL.D. 1897 ; President American Library Association, 1902-3 ; Librarian Minneapolis Public Library, 1892-1904, Emeritus since 1926 ; Member Minnesota Historical Society, Corresponding Member of Massachusetts Historical Society, Colonial Society of Mass., New England Historical and Genealogical Society, Fellow of the American Academy of Arts and Sciences, 1915 ; LL.D. Harvard University, 1925. *Publications:* Color Guard, 1864 ; Thinking Bayonet, 1865 ; Short History of German Literature, 1878 ; Life of Samuel Adams, 1884 ; Story of the Jews, 1885 ; Life of Young Sir Henry Vane, 1888 ; Short History of Anglo-Saxon Freedom, 1890 ; How Thankful was Bewitched, 1894 ; Life of Thomas Hutchinson, Royal Governor of Mass. Bay, 1896 ; History of the Mississippi Valley, 1901 ; History of the Louisiana Purchase, 1902 ; Appeal to Arms ; Outcome of the Civil War, 1907 ; edited

Journal of John Winthrop, 1908; The Last Leaf, 1912. *Address:* Public Library, Minneapolis, Minnesota, U.S.A. *(Died 11 May 1927.)*

HOSTE, Sir William Graham; 4th Bart., *cr.* 1814; 2nd Lieut., 2nd Rifle Brigade; *b.* 12 Aug. 1895; *s.* of 3rd Bart. and Alice, *d.* of James Healy, of Sydney; *S.* father 1902. *Educ.:* Royal Naval College, Osborne; Dartmouth; Harrow; Royal Military College, Sandhurst. Served European War,1914-15(wounded). *Heir:* none. *Address:* 48 Berkeley Square, W.
(Died 9 May 1915.)

HOTHAM, 6th Baron, *cr.* 1797, **Frederick William Hotham;** Bt. 1621; *b.* 19 March, 1863; *s.* of late Rev. W. F. Hotham and Emma, *d.* of John Carbonell; *m.* 1902, Benita, *d.* of late T. Sanders; two *d.*; *S.* cousin 1907. Owns about 15,000 acres. Possesses the portrait of the famous Mrs. Siddons, the actress, in The Fatal Marriage. *Heir: c.* Henry Frederick Hotham; *b.* 13 Aug. 1899. *Address:* Dalton Hall, Beverley; 32 Prince's Gate, S.W.7; *T.:* Kens. 2290; Bucklands, Churt, Farnham. *T.:* Hindhead 74. *Clubs:* Junior Constitutional; Yorkshire, York. *(Died 7 Oct. 1923.)*

HOTHAM, Sir Charles Frederick, G.C.B., *cr.* 1902; K.C.B., *cr.* 1895; G.C.V.O., *cr.* 1901; Admiral of the Fleet, 1903-1913; *b.* 1843; *m.* 1872, Margaret (*d.* 1918), *d.* of David Milne-Home of Wedderburn, Berwickshire. Served New Zealand, 1860-64 (despatches, medal, severely wounded); Bombardment of Alexandria, 1882 (medal, clasp, bronze star, 3rd class Osmanieh); late Naval A.D.C. to the Queen; Lord of Admiralty, 1889; Commander-in-Chief, Pacific Station, 1890-92; at Nore, 1897-99; at Portsmouth, 1899-1903. *Address:* 67 Eccleston Square, S.W.1. *T.:* Victoria 3469. *Clubs:* Army and Navy; New Edinburgh; Yorkshire, York. *(Died 22 Mar. 1925.)*

HOTHFIELD, 1st Baron, *cr.* 1881, **Henry James Tufton,** D.L., J.P.; Bt. 1851; Lord-Lieut. of Westmorland since 1881 and Vice-Admiral of the coast of Cumberland and Westmorland; *b.* Paris, 4 June 1844; *e. s.* of Sir Richard Tufton, Bt., and Adelaide A. Lacour; *m.* 1872, Alice (*d.* 1914), 2nd *d.* of late Rev. William James Stracey-Clitherow; three *s.* one *d.* *Educ.:* Eton; Christ Church, Oxford. Lord-in-Waiting, 1886; Mayor of Appleby, 1895-96. *Heir: s.* Hon. S. R. Tufton. *Address:* 2 Chesterfield Gardens, W.1; *T.:* Mayfair 7056; Appleby Castle, Westmorland; Skipton Castle, Yorkshire. *Clubs:* Carlton, Garrick.
(Died 29 Oct. 1926.)

HOUGH, Edwin Leadam, C.B.E. 1920; late Senior Official Receiver in Bankruptcy, High Court of Justice; *b.* Carlisle, 22 Oct. 1852; *e. s.* of Edwin Hough; *m.* Emma, *d.* of Joseph Chambers, Oxford, Lieut.-Col. H.M. Bengal Army, 1878. *Educ.:* Rossall; Queen's Coll., Oxon. Solicitor in Carlisle, 1878-90; Official Receiver Carlisle District, 1884; Official Receiver in High Court, 1890; retired, July 1919. *Recreations:* fishing, golf. *Address:* Kildonan, Enfield. *T.:* Enfield 320. *(Died 14 May 1928.)*

HOUGH, John Stanley, K.C.; Member of firm of Hough, Campbell & Ferguson, Barristers, Solicitors, etc., Winnipeg; *b.* County of Prince Edward, Province of Ontario, 29 Sep. 1856; *m.* 1896, Julia Frances Chaffey; one *s.* one *d.* *Educ.:* University of Toronto; Osgoode Hall. Called to Bar and admitted as Solicitor, 1882; has practised ever since in City of Winnipeg; Member Canadian Board of Royal Exchange Corporation, and Member of Advisory Board of Royal Trust Company; President of Winnipeg General Hospital. *Recreations:* golf, yachting. *Address:* 280 Roslyn Road, Fort Rouge, Winnipeg, Canada. *T.:* Fort Rouge 6448. *M.:* 3434 for Manitoba. *Clubs:* Bath; Mount Royal, Manitoba; St. Charles Country, Winnipeg.
(Died June 1928.)

HOUGH, Sydney Samuel, F.R.A.S., F.R.S., 1902; H.M. Astronomer, Royal Observatory, Cape of Good Hope, since 1907; *b.* 11 June 1870; *m.* 1906, Gertrude Annie, *y. d.* of late J. H. Lee of Halstead, Essex; formerly Fellow of St. John's College, Isaac Newton student in the University of Cambridge; Fellow Royal Society of South Africa. *Publications:* various mathematical memoirs relating to astronomical subjects in Phil. Trans. of the Royal Society and elsewhere. *Address:* Royal Observatory, Cape of Good Hope. *T.A.:* Astronomer, Cape Town. *Club:* Civil Service, Cape Town.
(Died 8 July 1923.)

HOUGHTON, Rev. Edward James, M.A.; Hon. Canon of Worcester Cathedral; Rural Dean and Vicar of Blockley since 1879; Diocesan Secretary, Society for Promoting Christian Knowledge; Hon. Secretary, Worcester Diocesan Joint Committee on Education, 1882-1908; Joint Hon. Secretary, Worcester Diocesan Council for Promoting Higher Religious Education in Secondary Schools; one of the examiners appointed by the Board of the National Society; Acting Chaplain of the 2nd Vol. Battalion of the Gloucestershire Regiment; retired after 20 years' service; Hon. Secretary, Worcester Archidiaconal Board of Education, 1882-1920; *b.* Lytham, Lancashire, 28 May 1838; *s.* of Edward Houghton and Sarah Jane Villiers; *m.* Hannah Maria Walford (*d.* 1916), The Grange, Alvechurch; three *s.* three *d.* *Educ.:* Rossall; Christ Church, Oxon. 2nd Master of Twyford School, under present Dean of Durham, and Curate of Twyford, 1860-63; Senior Curate of Alvechurch, 1863-66; Lecturer and Curate in charge of St. Philip's, Birmingham, 1866; Vicar of Boston Spa, Yorks, 1866-71; Diocesan Inspector of Schools, Worcester, 1871-1879. *Publications:* Confirmation Address; Latin Sermon, Oxford. *Recreations:* captain of Rossall Cricket Eleven 2 years, Christ Church Eleven. *Address:* Blockley Vicarage, R.S.O., Worcestershire. *T.A.:* Blockley. *Clubs:* Constitutional, M.C.C.; Worcester County. *(Died 21 Oct. 1919.)*

HOULDSWORTH, Sir William Henry, D.L.; 1st Bt., *cr.* 1887; landed proprietor; *b.* Manchester, 20 Aug. 1834; *s.* of late Henry Houldsworth, Coltness, Lanarkshire; *m.* Elisabeth, *d.* of Walter Crum, Thornliebank, Renfrewshire; two *s.* three *d.* *Educ.:* St. Andrews University. Member Royal Commission on Depression of Trade; Gold and Silver Commission; Delegate of Great Britain to Monetary Conference, Brussels, 1890; Labour Conference, Berlin, 1892; member Royal Commission on Liquor Licensing Laws, 1896; M.P. (C.) N.W. Manchester, 1883-1906. *Recreations:* golf, shooting, music. *Heir: s.* Henry, *b.* 17 Sept. 1867. *Address:* Coodham, Kilmarnock, N.B. *Clubs:* Conservative, Carlton. *(Died 18 April 1917.)*

HOULT, Joseph, J.P.; steamship owner of Liverpool; late City Councillor and Chairman of the Watch Committee; Magistrate for Liverpool; *b.* 1847; *s.* of late John Hoult of Liverpool; *m.* 1872, Julia (*d.* 1901), *d.* of late James Murray of Edinburgh; one *s.* three *d.* M.P. (C.) Wirral Division of Cheshire, 1900-1906. *Recreations:* fishing, shooting. *Address:* The Rocklands, Thornton Hough, Cheshire; Bowscar, Penrith. *Clubs:* Carlton, 1900; Liverpool Conservative. *(Died 19 Oct. 1917.)*

HOUNDLE. Henry Charles Herman Hawker, C.B.E. 1918; I.S.O. 1903; *b.* 1851. Chief Clerk Local Government Board, Whitehall. *Address:* 3 Paper Buildings, Temple, E.C.1.
(Died 30 Sept. 1919.)

HOUSTON, Sir Robert Paterson, 1st Bt., *cr.* 1922; M.P. (C.) Liverpool. W. Toxteth, 1892-1924; shipowner; head of Houston line of steamers; *b.* Liverpool, 31 May 1853; *m.* 1924, Dame Fanny Lucy, D.B.E. *cr.* 1917, *d.* of late Thomas Radmall and widow of 9th Baron Byron. *Educ.:* Liverpool College and privately. *Heir:* none. *Address:* Beaufield, St. Saviour's, Jersey, C.I. *Clubs:* Carlton, Royal Thames Yacht. (*Died 14 April 1926.*)

HOUSTON - BOSWALL - PRESTON, Thomas Alford, *b.* 1850; *s.* of 2nd Bt. and *heir pres.* to nephew, Sir T. R. Houston-Boswall, 5th Bt.; *m.* 1883, Alice Mary, *d.* of late William Cunard; two *s.* one *d.* [Assumed additional name of Preston by Royal Licence, 1886.] *Address:* Tweed Hill, Berwick-on-Tweed. *Clubs:* Travellers', Orleans New.
(*Died 3 Jan. 1918.*)

HOVELL, Lieut.- Colonel Hugh De Berdt, D.S.O. 1900; *b.* 15 April 1863; 3rd *s.* of late D. De Berdt Hovell of Boreham Holt, Elstree, Herts. *Educ.:* Wellington College; Sandhurst. Entered 2nd Batt. Worcestershire Regiment, 1884; served South Africa, 1900-02 (despatches, Queen's medal 3 clasps, King's medal 2 clasps, D.S.O.); Royal Humane Society's medal, 1891; commanded and trained 2nd Batt. Worcestershire Regt. before the war, on Sir John Moore's and Sir Charles Napier's methods of command, for Gheluvelt, 1914; enlisted in his old 2nd Batt., 1915; served as private with his old comrades (1915 Star, War and Victory medals); originated in 1886 the use of telephones on rifle-ranges, and in 1888 the use of field telephones. *Publications:* Soldiers' Shooting; Soldiers' Training. *Club:* Junior United Service. (*Died 27 Nov. 1923.*)

HOVELL, T. Mark, F.R.C.S.; Medical attendant to the late Emperor Frederick III. of Germany (Companion of Crown Order); Consulting Aural Surgeon, London Hospital; Consulting Surgeon, Hospital for Diseases of Throat, Golden Square; Aural Surgeon, British Home for Incurables; *e. surv. s.* of late Dennis De Berdt Hovell and Mary, *d.* of A. De Horne; *m.* 1905, Hon. Margaret Cecilia Bateman-Hanbury, *d.* of 2nd Baron Bateman; one *s. Publication:* A Treatise on Diseases of the Ear, 2nd edit.; papers on throat, nose, and ear. *Address:* 105 Harley Street, W.1. *T.:* Paddington 1171; Lemsford House, Lemsford, near Hatfield. *T.:* Hatfield 81. (*Died 30 June 1925.*)

HOW, Ven. Henry Walsham; *b.* Whittington, Shropshire, 17 May 1856; *s.* of late Bishop Walsham How, of Wakefield; *m.* 1886, Katharine, *d.* of Prebendary Hutchinson, of Blurton, Staffs; three *s.* one *d. Educ.:* Marlborough; Wadham College, Oxford; Leeds Clergy School. Curate, Stoke-on-Trent, 1879-1885; St. Anne's, Haughton, Lancs, 1885-86; Rector, 1886-89; Vicar of Mirfield, Yorks, 1889-1902; Chaplain to Bishop of Wakefield, 1891-97; Vicar of Meltham, 1902-17; Hon. Canon of Wakefield, 1899-17; Rural Dean of Huddersfield, 1905-17; Proctor in Convocation, 1905 - 17; Archdeacon of Halifax and Canon of Wakefield, 1917-23. *Publications:* edited The Closed Door, Addresses by Bishop Walsham How; editor of Wakefield Diocesan Calendar, 1891-1906. *Address:* Elmhurst, Pickersleigh Road. Malvern Link. *Club:* Royal Societies (*Died 29 Nov.1923.*)

HOWARD of Glossop, 2nd Baron (cr. 1869), **Francis Edward Fitzalan - Howard,** D.L., J.P.; *b.* 9 May 1859; *s.* of 1st Baron and Augusta, *e. d.* and heir of Hon. George Henry Talbot; *S.* father, 1883; *m.* 1st, 1883, Clara, *d.* of J. Greenwood of Swarcliffe, Ripley, Yorks (*d.* 1887), one *s.* one *d.*; 2nd, 1891, Hyacinthe, *d.* of late William Scott-Kerr, of Chatto and Sunlaws, Roxburghshire; one *d. Educ.:* Oratory School, Edgbaston. *Heir: s.* Hon. Bernard Edward Fitzalan-Howard. *Address:* Glossop Hall, Derbyshire; Dorlin House, Acharach, Argyllshire, N.B. *Clubs:* Bachelors', White's. (*Died 22 Sept. 1924.*)

HOWARD, Sir Ebenezer, Kt., *cr.* 1927; O.B.E. 1924; J.P.; Director of First Garden

City Limited and Welwyn Garden City Limited; shorthand writer; President International Federation for Housing and Town Planning; *b.* City of London, 29 Jan. 1850; *s.* of Ebenezer Howard of London and Ann Tow of Colsterworth; *m.* 1st, 1879, E. A. Bills of Coventry; 2nd, 1908, E. A. Hayward of Letchworth; one *s.* three *d. Educ.:* private schools, Sudbury, Cheshunt and Ipswich. Stockbrokers' and merchants' offices; short time private secretary, Dr. Joseph Parker; solicitor's office; in 1872 went to Nebraska, U.S.A., afterwards to Chicago; practised as stenographer in courts there; joined staff of Gurney & Sons, official shorthand writers to Houses of Parliament, 1877; afterwards became partner of William Treadwell; spent spare time preparing scheme social reform, especially seeking solution of twin problems of overcrowded city and depopulated country; in 1899 formed Garden City Association (which in turn formed "First Garden City Limited") to carry out a large and comprehensive scheme of town planning; career closely associated with town-planning movement. *Publications:* To-morrow, a Peaceful Path to Real Reform, 1898; in subsequent editions called Garden Cities of To-morrow. *Recreation:* new fields of activity. *Address:* 3 Gray's Inn Place, W.C.1; 5 Guessens Road, Welwyn Garden City. *Club:* National Liberal.
(*Died 1 May 1928.*)

HOWARD, Sir (Edward) Stafford, K.C.B., *cr.* 1909; C.B., 1900; J.P., D.L.; *b.* Greystoke Castle, Cumberland, 28 Nov. 1851; 2nd *s.* of Henry Howard, Greystoke; *m.* 1st, 1876, Lady Rachel Campbell (*d.* 1906), *d.* of 2nd Earl Cawdor; one *s.* two *d.*; 2nd, 1911, Catharine Meriel, *d.* of late Sir Arthur Cowell-Stepney and Hon. Lady Cowell-Stepney of The Delf, Llanelly; one *s.* one *d. Educ.:* Harrow; Trinity College, Cambridge (B.A. Classical Tripos). Barrister, Inner Temple; M.P. East Cumberland, 1876-85; Thornbury Division of Gloucestershire, 1885-86; Under-Secretary for India in Mr. Gladstone's Government, 1886; Commissioner of H.M.'s Woods Forests, and Land Revenues, 1893 - 1912; an Ecclesiastical Commissioner since 1914. *Address:* Cilymaenllwyd, Llanelly, S. Wales. *Clubs:* Travellers', Bath, Cavendish.
(*Died 8 April 1916.*)

HOWARD, Capt. (Temp.-Major) Guy Robert, D.S.O. 1914; Royal Flying Corps; late Essex Regiment, 2nd Batt. (Special Reserve); *b.* 5 Feb. 1886; *s.* of Col. W. Howard. Served European War, 1914-15 (wounded, despatches, D.S.O.); while in command of a Patrol of the 2nd Battalion, made a valuable reconnaissance through a thick wood. *M.:* LM 9741. *Clubs:* Junior United Service, Royal Flying Corps. (*Died 24 Oct. 1918.*)

HOWARD, Sir Henry, G.C.M.G., *cr.* 1916; K.C.B., *cr.* 1907; K.C.M.G., *cr.* 1899; C.B. 1874; *b.* 11 Aug. 1843; *s.* of late Sir Henry F. Howard, G.C.B.; *m.* 1867, Cecilia (*d.* 1907), *d.* of late Geo. W. Riggs of Washington, D.C.; one *s.* three *d.* Attaché in Diplomatic Service, 1865; 3rd Secretary, 1869; 2nd Secretary, 1873; 1st Secretary, 1885; Secretary of Embassy, 1890; Minister Plenipotentiary, 1894; Envoy Extraordinary and Minister Plenipotentiary, 1896; has served in the United States of America, the Netherlands, Guatemala, Greece, Denmark, China, Russia, and France; Jubilee Medal, 1897; Coronation Medal, 1902; British Minister at the Hague and Luxemburg, 1896-1908; Minister Plenipotentiary in British Mission to the Pope, 1914-16. *Club:* Travellers'. (*Died 4 May 1921.*)

HOWARD, Colonel Henry Richard Lloyd, C.B. 1900; late Col. Cheshire Royal Engineers Railway Battalion; Hon. Col. Denbighshire Hussars, Imperial Yeomanry; late a Gentleman-at-Arms; late Major, 16th Lancers; *b.* 9 July 1853; *s.* of Rev. R. H. Howard, and

Julia Elizabeth, d. of late William Ripley; m. 1881, Violet Mary (d. 1913), d. of the late Captain H. B. Hankey, R.N., of West Leigh, Havant; one s. one d. Educ.: Eton; Christ Church, Oxford. Contested Flintshire (C.) 1895, 1900, and 1910; Flint Boroughs, 1910; C.C. for St. Asaph Div. of Flintshire; served Zulu War, 1879 (medal with clasp); commanded 9th batt. Imperial Yeomanry, South Africa, 1900-1 (despatches, medal with 4 clasps, C.B.). Recreations: hunting, shooting, fishing. Address: Wygfair, St. Asaph. T.A.: Howard, Meriadog. T.: 14 Trefnant. M.: DM 19. Club: Naval and Military.   (Died 22 Dec. 1922.)

HOWARD, Hon. Hugh Melville, D.L.; b. 28 March 1883; s. of 6th Earl of Wicklow and 2nd wife, Fanny Catherine, e. d. of Richard Robert Wingfield; m. 1908, May, o. c. of Benjamin Aymar Sands of New York and Southampton, Long Island; one s. one d. Educ.: Eton; Trinity College, Oxford, M.A. Contested (U.) E. Wicklow, Dec. 1910. Address: Bellevue, Delgany, Co. Wicklow. Clubs: Bachelors'; Kildare Street, Dublin.
    (Died 17 Feb. 1919.)

HOWARD, Joseph, J.P.; one of H.M.'s Lieutenants for the City of London; b. 1834; s. of late J. E. Howard, F.R.S., Tottenham; m. Ellen, d. of H. Waterhouse, 1859; five s. two d. Educ.: University College, London. Barr. Lincoln's Inn, 1856. M.P. (C.) Tottenham, Middlesex, 1885-1906. Address: 18 Kensington Court, W.8. T.: Western 4863; Winchester House, E.C. Club: Carlton.
    (Died 2 Mar. 1923.)

HOWARD, Robert Jared Bliss, M.D., F.R.C.S.; m. See Baroness Strathcona. Educ.. M'Gill University; London Hospital. Fellow Royal Society of Medicine. Address: 46 Green Street, Park Lane, W.1. T.: Mayfair 4800.
    (Died 9 Jan. 1921.)

HOWARD, Robert Mowbray, J.P., D.L., B.A.; 3rd s. of Henry Howard, of Greystoke Castle, Cumberland, and of Thornbury Castle, Gloucestershire (d. 1875), and Charlotte Caroline Georgiana (d. 1896), e. d. of late Henry Lawes Long, of Hampton Lodge; b. 1854; m. 1st, 1881, Louisa Georgina (d. 1910), e. d. of late Rev. Walter Sneyd, of Keele Hall, Staffordshire; 2nd, 1912, Audrey Cecilia Campbell (d. 1926), 3rd d. of late Charles Hallyburton Campbell, B.C.S.; 3rd, 1927, Louisa Felicia, o. d. of late William Earle Welby, of Bainton House, Stamford. Heir: s. Henry Ralph Mowbray, of Hampton Lodge [Major Rifle Brigade; b. 1883; m. 1911, Millicent, d. of late W. D. James]. Educ.: Trinity College, Cambridge. Address: Ignora, Compton, Guildford. Club: Arthur's.
    (Died 2 Oct. 1928.)

HOWARD, T. Henry; Commissioner; Chief of the Staff of the Salvation Army, 1912-19; b. Walsall, 12 July 1849; m. M. Wassell, of Sedgeley; three s. Educ.: privately; Tipton, Staffs; Ilkeston. Entered the Salvation Army as an officer, 1881; Commissioner for Australasia, 1884; appointed to the direction of the Field Work in the United Kingdom, 1892; became Principal of the International Training College in Clapton, and subsequently Foreign Secretary; placed on Retired List, 1919. Publications: Standards of Life and Service; numerous spiritual articles in the Salvation Army press. Address: 101 Queen Victoria Street, E.C.; T.: Dalston 2375.
    (Died 1 July 1923.)

HOWARD, Walter; Actor, Manager, Dramatic Author; b. Leamington, 1866. Educ.: Stratford-on-Avon. First appearance as an actor at Stratford-on-Avon, 1889; London, 1896; New York, 1914. Plays: The Wearin' o' the Green, 1896; A Life's Revenge, 1898; For the King, 1899; Two Little Drummer Boys, 1899; Man and Wife, 1900;

Why Men Love Women, 1901; Two Little Sailor Boys, 1901; Under the Russian Flag, 1902; The Midnight Wedding, 1905; Her Love Against the World, 1906; The Prince and the Beggar Maid, 1908; Second to None, 1908; The Boy King, subsequently re-named The Ragged Prince, 1910; The Life Guardsman, 1911; The Soldier Princess, 1912; The Story of the Rosary, 1913; The Silver Crucifix, 1915; Seven Days' Leave, 1917; Boy of my Heart, 1920. Address: 23 Haymarket, S.W.1. T.: Regent 1147. Clubs: Green Room, Devonshire, Eccentric.   (Died 6 Oct. 1922.)

HOWARD-BROOKE, Colonel Richard Edward Frederic; of Castle Howard, Ovoca, Co. Wicklow, and Roskelton, Queen's County; J.P. Hampshire; b. 1 Nov. 1847; 3rd s. of late Richard Howard-Brooke; m. 1878, Alice Eliza, d. of late Samuel Ridley of The Castle, St. Helens, Isle of Wight. Address: Faircroft, Ryde, Isle of Wight. T.A.: Ryde Wight. T.: Ryde,75. Clubs: United Service; Royal Victoria Yacht, Ryde.   (Died 13 Jan. 1918.)

HOWARD-VYSE, Howard Henry, J.P., D.L.; b. 7 March 1858; e. s. of Col. R. Howard-Vyse and Julia Agnes, d. of 1st Lord Hylton; m. 1882, Mabel Diana, o. d. of late Rev. G. Granville Sykes Howard-Vyse; one s. Educ.: Eton. Royal Horse Guards, 1879-88. Address: Stoke Place, Slough, Bucks. T.A.: Vyse, Wexham. Clubs: Naval and Military. Turf.
    (Died 29 May 1927.)

HOWARTH, William James, C.B.E. 1919; M.D., B.Ch., D.P.H. Victoria University of Manchester; Medical Officer of Health, City of London. Educ.: Manchester Grammar School and Owens College. Formerly House Surgeon at Manchester Royal Infirmary and Loughborough General Hospital; has held the position of Medical Officer of Health of Bury, Lancs, Derby (10 years), and the County of Kent (5 years); in Kent was also School Medical Officer, and Executive Officer for tuberculosis work, and control of midwives; appointed to the City Corporation, 1912; Milroy Lecturer, Royal College of Physicians 1917; Fellow, Past-President and Vice-President of the Incorporated Society of Medical Officers of Health, and Past-President of the Metropolitan, Midland, and Home Counties Branches; Fellow of the Royal Sanitary Institute and of the Royal Institute of Public Health; Chairman Meat Preservation Committee of the Food Investigation Board; member of the Meat Inspection Committee, and of the Insanitary Areas Sub-Committee of the Ministry of Health; representative of the Ministry of Health on the Sanitary Inspectors' Examination Board; University nominee, Board of Management, Low Temperature Research Station, Cambridge; formerly Chief Rationing Officer under London and Home Counties Rationing Scheme. Publications: The Organisation and Administration of the Medical Inspection of Scholars, in Kelynack's Medical Inspection of Schools and Scholars: The Treatment of Enlargements of the Thyroid Gland, and some Observations on the Functions of that Organ; various contributions to Public Health literature. Address: Guildhall, E.C.2; 80 Westbourne Gardens, Folkestone, Kent.
    (Died 15 June 1928.)

HOWE, Hon. James Henderson, M.L.C. Northern District since 1897; a Member of the Council of School of Mines; b. Scotland, 4 March 1839; m. 1864, Harriette, d. of Richard Keynes. Went to Australia, 1856; M.H.A., Stanley, 1881 and 1884; Gladstone, 1887, 1890, and 1893; Commissioner of Crown Lands, 1885-7, 1890, 1892-3; Commissioner of Public Works, 1889-90; a Member of Convention, 1897; succeeded in carrying an Amendment to the Constitution Bill for Invalid and Old Age Pensions. Address: Mambray, St.

Peter's, Adelaide. Club: Australasian National
(Died 5 Feb. 1920.)

HOWELL, Colonel (temp. Brig.-Gen.)
Arthur Anthony, C.M.G. 1915 ; T.D. 1916 ;
M.R.C.S. Eng. 1886 ; L.R.C.P. Edin. 1891 ;
3rd London Regt. (R. Fusiliers) (T.F.) ; b. 1362 ;
3rd s. of late Very Rev. David Howell, Dean of
St. David's ; m. 1805, Charlotte Isabel, d. of late
John Firth, of Abbeydale, Sheffield. Educ. :
Shrewsbury School ; London Hospital. Joined
the 3rd Vol. Batt. Royal Fusiliers as a Lieut.
1896 ; served South African War with the C.I.V.
as a Captain, receiving Queen's medal and four
clasps ; Lt.-Col. Commanding 3rd Batt. The
London Regt. Royal Fusiliers (T.F.) 1910-16 ;
served European War, 1914 - 16 (C.M.G.), despatches twice, Order of St. Anne) ; appointed
to command 1st London Reserve Brigade, 1916,
with temp. rank of Brig. - Gen. ; promoted
Colonel in T.F. 1917. Address: St. David's,
Worplesdon Hill, Brookwood, Surrey. T. :
Woking 503.   (Died 15 Jan. 1918.)

HOWELL, Rev. G. ; Hon. Canon of Liverpool ; Rural Dean of Walton since 1910. Ordained
1874 ; Assistant Curate, Christ Church, Everton,
1874-79 ; Vicar, 1879 - 1916. Recreation : walking. Address: Christ Church Vicarage, Everton.
(Died 16 Aug. 1918.)

HOWELL, Hon. Hector Mansfield ;
Chief Justice of Manitoba since 1909 ; b.
Ontario, 17 Sep. 1842 ; m. 1875, Harriette
Lally ; one s. three d. Educ. : Albert College.
Called to Bar of Ontario, 1871 ; Manitoba Bar,
1879 ; Q.C., 1884 ; Chief Justice of the Court
of Appeal for Manitoba, 1906. Address: 66
Carlton Street, Winnipeg. Clubs: Manitoba,
St. Charles' Country, Hunt, Winnipeg.
(Died April 1918.)

HOWELL, Lt.-Col. Herbert Gwynne,
D.S.O. 1915 ; O.B.E. ; late R.F.A. ; b. 15 Nov.
1879 ; s. of late Major M. G. Howell, Llanelwedd
Hall, Radnorshire ; m. Annable, d. of Capt.
Martin, late The Buffs, of Dunmore, Galway,
Ireland ; one s. one d. Entered army, 1900 ;
Captain, 1911 ; employed with West African
Frontier Force, 1904-9 ; served Bechuanaland,
1897 (medal with clasp) ; South Africa, 1900-2
(despatches twice, Queen's medal 4 clasps,
King's medal 2 clasps) ; N. Nigeria, Dakkakerri
Campaign, 1908 ; European War, Cameroons,
1914-16 (D.S.O. despatches 3 times) ; Egypt,
1916-18 ; Palestine Campaign, Battle of Gaza
and Capture of Jerusalem (despatches, O.B.E.) ;
retired pay, 1923. Recreations: polo, big game
hunting. Address: Llanelwedd Hall, Builth,
Wales ; 26 South Park, Sevenoaks, Kent.
Clubs: Army and Navy, Sports.
(Died 16 Nov. 1925.)

HOWELL, John Aldersey, D.S.O. 1917 ;
M.C. ; b. 13 Aug. 1888 ; s. of Rev. J. A. Howell,
M.A., Vicar of Penmaenmawr, and Alice Mary,
d. of Canon C. F. Royds, Chester Cathedral ;
m. 1922, Angel Helen Sibell. o. d. of Brig.-Gen.
Hugh Archdale, C.B., C.M.G. ; one d. Educ. :
Rossall. Stage, started with F. R. Benson ;
acted in . London prior to war ; served in
Cheshire Regt. during the war, 2nd in Command
of 10th Batt. ; invalided with the hon. rank of
Major, 1918 (D.S.O., M.C., despatches). Re-
creation : golf. Address: 23 Chepstow Crescent,
W.11. Club: Savage.   (Died 4 Aug. 1928.)

HOWELL, Mortimer Sloper, C.I.E.,1886;
b. Bath, 3 Feb. 1841 ; o. s. of late John Warren
Howell, M.R.C.S. ; m. 1895, Laura Sabina (d.
1909) ; d. of late Rev. Edward Wilton, West
Lavington, Wilts ; one d. Educ.: Christ's
Hospital ; Corpus Christi Coll.Oxford. Emeritus
Fellow of the Universities of Calcutta and
Allahabad ; Hon. LL.D. Edin. Entered Indian
Civil Service, 1862 ; retired, 1896 ; was then
Judicial Commissioner of Oudh. Decorated
for official services and attainments in Oriental
Literature. Publications: Grammar of the

Classical Arabic Language, after the method of
the native Grammarians. Recreations: Arabic
literature, cycling, boating, golf. Address:
Woodbury, Clevedon, Somerset. T.: Clevedon,
53 Y. Club: East India United Service.
(Died 9 Sept. 1925.)

HOWELL, Brig. - Gen. Philip, C.M.G.
1915 ; 4th (Queen's Own) Hussars ; b. 7 Dec.
1877 ; s. of late Lieut.-Col. Horace Howell ; m.
1911, Rosalind, d. of late H. E. Buxton, Fritton,
Norfolk ; one d. Entered Indian army, Queen's
Own Corps of Guides, 1897 ; Captain, 1906 ;
Major, 4th Hussars, 1913 ; Lt.-Col. 1914 ; Staff-
Capt., Intelligence, India, 1904-6 ; passed Staff
College, 1907 ; Brig.-Maj. to I. G. Cavalry,
India, 1908 ; General Staff Officer, 3rd grade,
War Office, 1909-11 ; General Staff Officer, 2nd
grade, Staff College, 1912-13 ; Brig. - Gen.,
General Staff, 1915 ; served N.W. Frontier, India,
1908 (medal with clasp) ; European War, 1914-
15 (despatches four times, C.M.G.).
(Died 10 Oct. 1916.)

HOWELL-PRICE, Lieut.-Col. Owen
Glendower, D.S.O. 1917 ; M.C., Aust. Forces ;
b. Australia. Educ. : Sydney. Served European War, 1915-17 (despatches, M.C., D.S.O.).
Address: Candahar Barracks. Tidworth.

HOWELLS, William Dean, Hon. D.Litt.
Oxon. ; man of letters ; b. 1837, Martin's Ferry,
Belmont County,Ohio ; s. of William Cooper and
Mary Dean Howells ; m. 1862, Elinor G. Mead ;
one s. two d. Educ.: self-taught. M.A. Harvard
and Yale ; Litt. D. Yale ; D. Litt. Oxon.: Litt. D.
Columbia ; LL.D. Adelbert ; Litt. D. Princeton.
Printer, 1848-58 ; journalist, 1858-61 ; United
States Consul at Venice, 1861-65 ; editor of the
Atlantic Monthly, 1866-81 ; author of travels,
novels, essays, plays, criticisms, poems, from 1859
till the present time. Publications: some seventy
books of the kinds indicated ; among others :
A Foregone Conclusion ; A Chance Acquaintance ; Their Wedding Journey ; A Counterfeit
Presentment ; The Lady of the Aroostook ; Out
of the Question ; The Undiscovered Country ;
April Hopes ; The World of Chance ; The Land-
lord of Lion's Head ; The Son of Royal Lang-
brith ; Venetian Life ; Italian Journeys ; Tuscan
Cities ; Modern Italian Poets ; The Rise of Silas
Lapham ; Indian Summer ; The Shadow of a
Dream; An Imperative Duty; The Albany Depôt,
1897, and 24 other farces ; An Open-Eyed Con-
spiracy, 1898 ; The Story of a Play, 1898 ; The
Ragged Lady, 1899 ; Their Silver Wedding
Journey, 1899 ; Literary Friends and Acquaint-
ance, 1900 ; A , Pair of Patient Lovers,
Heroines of Fiction, 1901 ; The Kentons, Litera-
ture and Life, 1902 ; Questionable Shapes, 1903;
Letters Home, 1903 ; Miss Bellard's Inspiration.
1905 ; London Films, 1905 ; Certain Delightful
English Towns, 1906 ; Through the Eye of the
Needle, 1907 ; Fennel and Rue, 1908 ; Roman
Holidays, 1908 ; Seven English Cities, 1909 ;
The Mother and the Father, 1909 ; Imaginary
Interviews, 1910 ; My Mark Twain, 1910 ; New
Leaf Mills, Familiar Spanish Travels, 1913 ; The
Seen and Unseen in Stratford-on-Avon, 1914 ;
Years of my Youth, 1916 ; The Daughter of the
Storage, 1916 ; The Leatherwood God, 1916.
Recreations: theatre, reading, walking, garden-
ing. Address: c/o Harper Bros., New York.
Clubs: Century, New York : Tavern, Boston.
(Died 11 May 1920.)

HOWEY, Maj. - Gen. William, Bengal
Infantry ; b. 7 Aug. 1838 ; m. 1860, Annie Isabella, d. of Major Henry Christian Talbot of
Stone, Kent. Entered army, 1858 ; Maj.-Gen.
1894 ; unemployed supernumerary list, 1894 ;
served Indian Mutiny, 1858-59 (medal). Address: Naval and Military Hotel, Harrington
Road, South Kensington, S.W.7.
(Died 18 July 1924.)

HOWIE, Rev. Robert, D.D. ; Moderator of the General Assembly of the U.F. Church of Scotland in 1902 ; *b.* parish of Kilwinning, 4 Feb. 1836 ; *s.* of John Howie, personally related to Howie of Lochgoin (author of Scots Worthies), and Mary Stevenson ; *m.* 1st, 1861, Catherine Coulson Davy (*d.* 1910), related to Sir Humphry Davy and Dr. Walter Coulson of London ; 2nd, 1911, Martha Elder Dunsmore, Principal of Emgwali Training School, S. Africa. *Educ. :* Irvine Academy ; Glasgow Univ.; Glasgow F.C. Coll. ; Edinburgh F.C. Coll. Minister of Wynd Free Church, Glasgow, 1860-64 ; Trinity Free Church Congregation, 1864 - 72 ; St. Mary's Free Church, Govan, 1872-1906, of which he is still minister emeritus ; as the Senior Minister now living, who was connected with what was known as the Wynd Mission, and as Convener of the Church Extension Committee of the Free Church Presbytery of Glasgow, he has been more or less identified with movements resulting in the erection of upwards of forty new churches, and involving an outlay of upwards of £300,000 ; Convener of Home Mission and Church Extension Committee of Free Church and then of United Free Church during the ten years ending May 1906 ; Convener of Committee on Statistics of the said Churches during thirteen years. *Publications :* volume— The Churches and Churchless in Scotland ; Plea for Equity in the Scottish Churches' Case ; and sundry publications of a more ephemeral and controversial character, in defence of the orthodox views in regard to Holy Scripture. *Recreations :* has travelled a good deal in different countries on the Continent, in Egypt, Palestine, India, and America. *Address :* 15 Clarendon Place, Stirling, Scotland.
(Died 4 Mar. 1918.)

HOWISON, George Holmes, M.A., LL.D., Professor of Philosophy, *emeritus,* at the University of California ; *b.* Montgomery County, Maryland, 1834 ; *e. s.* of Robert and Eliza (Holmes) Howison ; *m.* 1863, Lois Thompson Caswell, of Norton, Massachusetts. *Educ. :* Marietta College, Ohio (B.A. 1852 ; M.A. 1855) ; Lane Theological Seminary, Cincinnati (1852-55) ; studied, later, at University of Berlin. Engaged in various educational offices in academies and public schools, as instructor, town superintendent, and headmaster, in Ohio and Massachusetts, 1855-64 ; Assist. Prof. of Mathematics, Washington Univ., St. Louis, 1864-67 ; Tileston Prof. of Political Economy, 1867-69 ; Senior Master in the English High School, Boston, 1869-71 ; Prof. of Logic and the Philosophy of Science, Massachusetts Institute of Technology, 1871-79 ; Lecturer on Ethics, Harvard Univ., 1879-80 ; student in Europe, chiefly at the University of Berlin, 1880-82 ; Lecturer on Logic and Metaphysics, University of Michigan, 1883-84 ; Mills Professor of Philosophy, University of California, 1884-1909. Editor of the Philosophical Publications of the University of California, and of the Publications of the Philosophical Union ; Member American Editorial Board Hibbert Journal, London. Fellow American Association Advancement of Science ; Member American Historical Association, American Political Science Association, New York Academy of Political Science, National Geographic Society, St. Louis Philosophical Society ; Hon. Member Philosophical Union, University of California, and of American Philosophical Association, 1915 ; LL.D., Marietta, 1883 ; Michigan, 1909 ; California, 1914. *Publications :* Treatise on Analytic Geometry, 1869 ; The Limits of Evolution, and other Essays in Philosophy, 1901; 3rd ed., 'enlarged, with Reply to Prof. James Ward, 1916 ; Philosophy, its Fundamental Conceptions and its Methods (in Congress of Arts and Science, Vol. i., St. Louis Universal Exposition), 1906 ; The Conception of God (jointly with Professors Royce, Le Conte, and Mezes), 1897. *Address :* 2681 Piedmont Ave., Berkeley, California.
(Died 31 Dec. 1916.)

HOWLAND, William Bailey ; President The Independent, New York, since 1913 ; publisher The Outlook, New York, 1890-1913 ; *b.* Ashland N.Y., 1849 ; *m.* 1873, Ella M. Jacobs ; two *s.* Founded Outing Magazine, 1882 ; Treasurer Congregational Home Missionary Society, 1893-1907 ; Trustee Chautauqua Institution ; President Commissioners State Reservation at Niagara Falls ; Treasurer Society for Italian Immigrants ; Treasurer American Civic Association ; President National Institute of Efficiency. *Address :* 119 W. 40th Street, New York City. *Clubs:* Royal Societies ; Manor House, Bredon ; National Arts, Republican, City, Italian, Lake Placid, New York.
(Died 27 Feb. 1917.)

HOWLETT, Richard, F.S.A. ; *b.* 17 Aug. 1841 ; *s.* of S. B. Howlett of War Office ; *m.* Alice (*d.* 1901), *d.* of James Holderness Featherstone ; two *s. Educ. :* King's College School ; Corpus Christi College, Cambridge. Barr. Middle Temple, 1871 ; served in the Civil Service Commission (1862-1906), retiring as Assistant Secretary of that Department. *Publications :* edited for the Master of the Rolls Series the Chronicles of William of Newburgh and Robertus de Monte, the Gesta Stephani, and several other 12th cent. chronicles. *Address :* c/o R. R. Howlett; 1 Sunnyside, Wimbledon.
(Died 4 Feb. 1917.)

HOWORTH, Sir Henry Hoyle, K.C.I.E., *cr.* 1892 ; D.C.L., F.R.S. 1893 ; F.S.A. ; Trustee and Hon. Librarian of the Chetham College ; Trustee of British Museum since 1899 ; Member of the Royal Commission on Ancient Monuments ; *b.* Lisbon, 1 July 1842 ; *o. s.* of late Henry Howorth, Lisbon, merchant, and Elizabeth Beswiche, Rochdale ; *m.* 1869, Katherine (*d.* 1921), *e. d.* of late J. P. Brierley, Lauriston, Rochdale ; three *s. Educ. :* Rossall. Barr. Inner Temple, 1867 ; took an active part for many years in Lancashire politics and public life ; has written a large number of political letters in the Times ; president Royal Archæological Institute and the Viking Society ; Vice-President Asiatic and Numismatic Societies ; M.P. (C.) South Salford, Lancashire, 1886-1900. *Publications:* A History of the Mongols ; Chinghis Khan and His Ancestors ; The Mammoth and the Flood ; The Glacial Nightmare and the Flood ; Ice and Water ; St. Gregory the Great ; St. Augustine of Canterbury ; The Golden Days of the Early English Church, 1916 ; more than a hundred scientific memoirs on geological, archæological, historical, and ethnological subjects, and a number of communications to the Reviews. *Address :* 45 Lexham Gardens, W.8. *T. :* Western 1748. *Clubs:* Carlton, Athenæum, Burlington Fine Arts.
(Died 15 July 1923.)

HOWSE, Francis ; one of H.M.'s Lieutenants for City of London ; J.P. County of London ; *b.* 20 June 1851 ; 4th *s.* of Thomas Howse, late of Silvermere, Woodberry Down, N. ; *m.* 1876, Bessie, 2nd *d.* of Charles Gatliff, late of Lakefield, Woodberry Down, N. ; three *s.* two *d. Educ. :* Clapham Grammar School. Admitted a solicitor, 1878 ; member of London School Board, 1891-94, also 1897 ; member of Hackney Borough Council, 1900-3 ; Under - Sheriff for City of London, 1904-5 ; Mayor of Hackney, 1905-6 ; Alderman, Walbrook Ward, City of London, 1906-9 ; Trustee of the Hackney Benevolent Society, the Stoke Newington Dispensary, the British Asylum for Deaf and Dumb Females, Clapton ; Church - warden of St. Thomas, Clapton Common, for 27 years. *Recreation :* angling. *Address :* 112A Holland Road, Kensington, W.14. *Club:* City Carlton.
(Died 13 Sept. 1925.)

HOWSON, G. W. S., Head Master Gresham's School, Holt, Norfolk, since 1900 ; *s.* of W.

Howson, Head Master of Penrith School ; *g.s.* of Rev. J. Howson, 2nd Master Giggleswick School. Unmarried. *Educ.:* Giggleswick School. Scholar Merton College, Oxford, 1879 ; 1st Class Final Honours School of Natural Science, 1883 ; M.A. 1886 ; Assistant Master Newton College, 1883-86 ; Assistant Master, Uppingham School, 1886 - 1900. *Recreations :* riding, fives, trout-fishing. *Address :* Gresham's School, Holt, Norfolk. *T.A. :* Holt, Norfolk. *Club :* Cavendish. 　　　　　　　　　*(Died 7 Jan. 1919.)*

HOYLE, Hon. Henry Clement, M.L.A. ; *b.* 28 Nov. 1852 ; *m.* 1877 ; three *s.* four *d. Educ. :* Convent School, Balmain, N.S.W. ; private study. Apprenticed to engine smithing and went through engineering trades ; took prominent part in establishing trades unionism in N.S.W. ; being strong protectionist, was foremost in advocacy of manufacture of requirements of N.S.W. within the State, and took prominent part in every movement since 1870 to advance democracy of Australia ; at age of 22 was a member of Trades and Labour Council of N.S.W., and was President of eight-hours conference of Iron Trades ; instrumental in inaugurating Association of Employees of Government Railways and Tramways of the State, and was first President of the Association ; entered Parliament, 1891, in protectionist interest ; defeated at 1894 general elections, and engaged in commercial pursuits for some years, re-entering Parliament in 1910 ; became Parliamentary Secretary of the State Labour Party in 1913 ; Assistant Colonial Treasurer and Minister for Railways of New South Wales, 1914. *Recreations :* cricket and reading. *Address :* Leoncliffe, New South Head Road, Vaucluse, Sydney, N.S.W. *(Died 20 July 1926.)*

HOYLE, J. Rossiter, M.I.C.E. ; J.P. City of Sheffield ; Master Cutler, Sheffield, 1912-13 ; Director, Thomas Firth & Sons, Ltd., steel and gunmakers ; *b.* Manchester, 1856 ; *s.* of Wm. Jennings Hoyle of Manchester and Newcastle-on-Tyne ; *m.* 1883, Augusta, *e. d.* of Alexander Muir of Manchester and Liverpool. Member of Council of Mechanical Engineers' Institute ; Director of the Projectile and Engineering Co., Ltd. ; two years President of Sheffield Society of Engineers and Metallurgists. *Address :* Norfolk Works, Sheffield ; 8 The Sanctuary, Westminster. S.W.1. 　　　　*(Died 14 Mar. 1926.)*

HOYLE, William Evans, M.A., D.Sc., F.Z.S., M.R.C.S. ; *b.* Manchester ; *s.* of Wm. Jennings Hoyle, Manchester and Newcastle-on-Tyne ; *m.* 1st, 1883, Edith Isabel Sharp *(d.* 1916), Manchester ; one *d.* ; 2nd, 1918, Florence Ethel Mabel, *d.* of late T. Hurry Riches, J.P., and widow of J. H. Hallett, J.P., of Radyr Chain ; one *d. Educ. :* Owens Coll., Manchester ; Christ Church, Oxford ; St. Bartholomew's Hospital. Demonstrator of Anatomy, Owens College ; Naturalist on Challenger Expedition Editorial Staff ; Director Manchester Museum, 1889-1909 ; late Vice-Pres. and Hon. Librarian, Manchester Literary and Phil. Society ; ex-President Section D, British Association ; Corresponding Member, Academy of Sciences, Philadelphia ; ex-Pres., Museums Association ; ex-Pres., Conchological Society, Great Britain and Ireland ; Director of the Welsh National Museum, 1909-24. *Publications :* papers on museums and zoology, chiefly Cephalopoda. *Address :* Glenroy, Blundell Avenue, Porthcawl. *T. :* Porthcawl 186. 　　　　　　　　　*(Died 7 Feb. 1926.)*

HOYLES, Newman Wright, K.C., Hon. LL.D. ; Principal, Law School, Osgoode Hall, Toronto, 1894-1923 ; *b.* St. John's, Newfoundland, 14 Mar. 1844 ; *e. s.* of late Sir Hugh William Hoyles, Chief-Justice of Newfoundland ; *m.* 1873, Georgina M., *d.* of late Lewis Moffatt of Toronto ; one *s.* two *d. Educ. :* Upper Canada Coll., Toronto ; King's Coll., Windsor, Nova Scotia ; Trinity Coll., Camb. (B.A. 1867). Called

526

to Ontario Bar, 1872 ; Q.C. 1889 ; a member of the Church of England ; President Corporation and Chairman of the Council of Wycliffe College, Toronto ; President (Hon.) of the Upper Canada and Canadian Bible Societies ; Vice - President British and Foreign Bible Society ; a member of the Senate of the University of Toronto ; Vice-President of the Church Missionary Society of England ; President of Havergal College, Toronto. *Publications :* has written numerous articles in legal magazines. *Recreation :* rowing. *Address :* 567 Huron Street, Toronto. *T. :* Hillcrest 0488. *Club :* University of Toronto (Hon. President). 　　　　　　　*(Died 6 Nov. 1928.)*

HUBBARD, William Egerton, J.P. ; Russia merchant ; *e. s.* of late William Egerton Hubbard of Leonardslee, Sussex ; *m.* 1st, Jane Clifford, *d.* of late Rev. Carey Borrer, Rector of Hurstpierpoint ; 2nd, Mary Emily, *d.* of late Thomas Jesson of Clarendon Terrace, Brighton ; one *s.* one *d. Educ. :* Eton ; Trin. Coll., Camb. (B.A.) Entered firm of John Hubbard & Co. of 17 St. Helen's Place, E.C., 1865 ; Director London, County, and Westminster Bank ; commanded company of 2nd Sussex R.V. 1872-87 ; retired Hon. Major ; took part in various philanthropic works ; was Chairman Reformatory and Refuge Union ; is Treasurer National Refuges for Homeless and Destitute Children. *Address :* 5 South Park, Sevenoaks. *(Died 10 Jan. 1918.)*

HUDSON, Rev. Joseph, M.A., Hon. Canon Carlisle ; *b.* 12 July 1834 ; *e. s.* of Rev. Joseph Hudson, M.A., Vicar of Chillingham, Northumberland ; *m.* 1st, 1857, Mary Anne, *d.* of John Unsworth of The Thorne, Penrith ; 2nd, 1880, Emily Valence, widow of Rev. H. W. Cookson, D.D., Master of Peterhouse, Cambridge ; four *s.* four *d. Educ. :* Durham School ; Peterhouse, Camb. *Address :* Crosby House, Carlisle. *T.A. :* Crosby House, Crosby-on-Eden. *M. :* AO 1853. 　　*(Died 14 Nov. 1919.)*

HUDSON, Major Robert Arthur, D.S.O. 1916 ; 1/8th P.W.O. (West Yorks) Regt. (Leeds Rifles), T.F. ; *b.* Gildersome, nr. Leeds, 16 June 1880 ; 3rd *s.* of late Robert and Hannah Hudson of St. Ives, Wood Lane, Headingley, Leeds ; *m.* Mary Vere, *e. d.* of Mark Senior, Ossett ; one *s.* one *d. Educ. :* Giggleswick Grammar School. Took a commission in the 3rd Vol. Batt. P.W.O. West Yorks, 1898 ; entered business of Robert Hudson, 1897 ; now a Permanent Director of Robert Hudson, Ltd., Portable Railway Manufacturers, Gildersome, nr. Leeds ; Hon. Colonel of the 1st (Leeds) Batt. Ripon Regiment of the Church Lads' Brigade ; served European War, 1914-15 (D.S.O.). *Recreations :* golf, motoring, Territorial and Church Lads' Brigade work. *Address :* 64 Headingley Lane, Leeds. *T. :* Headingley 193. *M. :* U 86. 　　　*(Died Oct. 1917.)*

HUDSON, Sir Robert (Arundell), Kt., *cr.* 1906 ; G.B.E., *cr.* 1918 ; J.P. London, and Suffolk ; *b.* 30 Aug. 1864 ; *e. s.* of late Robert Hudson, of Lapworth, Warwickshire, and Jessie *(d.* 1921), *d.* of late J. Kynoch, of Peterhead ; *m.* 1st, 1889, Ada *(d.* 1895), *d.* of late Henry Hammerton, of Coventry ; one *d.* ; 2nd, 1923, Viscountess Northcliffe, G.B.E., R.R.C., *widow* of Viscount Northcliffe.

Is Chairman of the Joint Finance Committee of the British Red Cross Society and the Order of St. John ; Knight of Grace, Order of St. John ; Chevalier of the Legion of Honour ; a Trustee of Westminster Abbey Fund ; Joint Treasurer of Westminster Hospital ; Treasurer of the Sulgrave Manor Board ; Trustee of Cassel Hospital, Swaylands ; Member of the Imperial War Graves Commission, and of the Voluntary Hospitals Commission ; Director of Sun Insurance Office and Sun Life Assurance Society ; Patron of the living of Theydon Mount with Stapleford Tawney. *Publication :* edited the late Robert Hudson's Memorials of

HOZUMI, Baron Nobushige, L.L.D. See page xxi.

HUBBARD, Robert Richard, Bey. See page xxi.

a Warwickshire Parish. *Address:* Hill Hall, Theydon Mount, Epping, Essex. *T.:* Epping 21. *Clubs:* Marlborough, Reform, Burlington Fine Arts. *(Died 25 Nov. 1927.)*

HUDSON, William Henry; Staff Lecturer in Literature to the Extension Board of London University; *b.* London, 2 May 1862; *s.* of Thomas Hudson, F.S.S.; *m.* 1890, Florence Amy Leslie of London. *Educ.:* privately. Engaged in journalism in London; for several years private secretary to Herbert Spencer: Assistant Librarian, Cornell University, New York, 1890-92; Professor of English Literature, Stanford University, California, 1892-1901. Professorial Lecturer in the University of Chicago, 1902-3. *Publications:* The Church and the Stage, 1886; Introduction to the Philosophy of Herbert Spencer, 1894 (new ed. 1904); Studies in Interpretation, 1896; Idle Hours in a Library, 1897; The Study of English Literature, 1898; The Sphinx and other Poems, 1900; The Meaning and Value of Poetry, 1901; Life of Sir Walter Scott, 1901; The Famous Missions of California, 1901; The Strange Adventures of John Smith, 1902; Rousseau and Naturalism in Life and Thought, 1903; Introduction to Sartor Resartus in Everyman's Library, 1908; Herbert Spencer (in Philosophies, Ancient and Modern), 1909; An Introduction to the Study of Literature, 1910 (new ed. 1913); Keats and his Poetry, 1911; Gray and his Poetry, 1911; Lowell and his Poetry, 1911; Milton and his Poetry, 1912; Introduction to Dryden's Essays in Everyman's Library, 1912; The Story of the Renaissance, 1912; An Outline History of English Literature, 1913; Schiller and his Poetry, 1913; Wordsworth and his Poetry, 1913; The Man Napoleon, 1915; A Quiet Corner in a Library, 1915; France: the Nation and its Development, 1917; Whittier and his Poetry, 1918; Johnson and Goldsmith and their Poetry, 1918; A Short History of English Literature in the 19th Century, 1918; editor of The Vicar of Wakefield, 1898; Sir Roger de Coverley Papers, 1899; Bacon's Essays, 1901; Dryden's Essay of Dramatic Poesie, 1904; Spenser's Faery Queene, Book i., 1904; Shakespeare's Henry V.; Macaulay's Essay on Clive, 1910; Macaulay's Essay on Warren Hastings, 1911; Representative Passages from English Literature, 1914; The Elizabethan Shakespeare; the Poetry and Life Series.
(Died 12 Aug. 1918.)

HUDSON, W. H. *Publications:* The Purple Land, 1885; Argentine Ornithology, 1888-89; The Naturalist in La Plata, 1892; Birds in a Village, 1893; Idle Days in Patagonia, 1893; British Birds, 1895; Birds in London, 1899; Nature in Downland, 1900; Birds and Man, 1901; El Ombú, 1902; Hampshire Days, 1903; Green Mansions, 1904; A Crystal Age, 1906; A Little Boy Lost, 1907; The Lands End, 1908; Afoot in England, 1909; A Shepherd's Life, 1910; Adventures among Birds, 1913; Far Away and Long Ago; History of My Early Life, 1918; Birds of La Plata, 1919; Birds in Town and Village, 1919; The Book of a Naturalist, 1919; Dead Man's Plack. 1921. *(Died 18 Aug. 1922.)*

HUGEL, Anatole, Baron von, K.C.S.G.; M.A., Hon. Sc. D., F.R. Anthrop. Inst., F.R.G.S.; *b.* Florence. 1854; *y. s.* of Charles, Baron von Hügel, Austrian Minister at Florence and at Brussels, and Elizabeth, *d.* of late General Francis Farquharson (East Indian Co., etc.) and *niecs* of late General Sir James Outram, Bart.; *m.* 1880, Eliza Margaret, *e. d.* of late William Froude, F.R.S. *Educ.:* Jesuit Colleges of Kalksburg (Vienna) and Stonyhurst. Curator of the University Museum of Archæology and of Ethnology, Cambridge, 1883-1921; travelled and collected in Australasia, and spent three years (1875-77) with the natives of Fiji; Founder and first President of the Cambridge University Catholic Association, 1895-1922; President of St. Edmund's House, Cambridge, 1917-

1920. *Publications:* contributions to Encyclopædia Britannica and to archæological, ethnological, and ornithological societies and journals. *Recreation:* gardening. *Address:* Croft Cottage, Cambridge. *T.:* Cambridge 632. *Club:* Athenæum. *(Died 15 Aug. 1928.)*

H U G E L, Friedrich, Baron von, Hon. LL.D., St. Andrews; Hon. D.D., Oxford; Baron of Holy Roman Empire; *b.* Florence, May 1852; *s.* of B. Karl von Hügel, Austria, and *g.n.* of Gen. Sir James Outram; *m.* Lady Mary Catherine Herbert, *e. d.* of late Sidney, Lord Herbert of Lea, and *sister* of the 13th and 14th Earls of Pembroke; two *d.* *Educ.:* His father's Embassies in Florence and Brussels, under advice of Alfred von Reumont, the historian. Rendered deaf, and some fifteen years incapable of sustained mental work, by typhus fever, 1871; settled in England spring 1871; worked at Greek and Hebrew; devoted life to historical critici$_m$ as applied to biblical documents, to psychology and philosophy as applied to religious experience, and to the consolidation of such studies amongst his fellow Roman Catholics; much intercourse with W. G. Ward, 1873-82. A naturalized British subject. *Publications:* Paper on Pentateuch criticism at Friburg Catholic Scientific Conference, 1897; numerous articles on Biblical Criticism and Philosophy of Religion in English, American, French, and Italian Reviews; The Papal Commission and the Pentateuch, with Prof. Charles Briggs, 1906; The Mystical Element of Religion, 2 vols., 1908, 1909, new ed. 1923; Eternal Life, 1912, 1913; The German Soul, 1916; Essays and Addresses, 1921; Some Notes on the Petrine Claims, 1930. *Address:* 13 Vicarage Gate, Kensington, W.8. *(Died 27 Jan. 1925.)*

HUGGINS, Lt.-Col. Ponsonby Glenn, C.B., 1909; D.S.O. 1887; late 81st Pioneers (Indian Army); *b.* 21 Jan. 1857; 4th *s.* of late H. J. Huggins, Chief-Justice, Sierra Leone, and Letitia, *d.* of late William Laborde: *m.* 1st, 1883, Elizabeth Sophia (*d.* 1893), *o. d.* of Commander W. Grierson, R.N.; one *s.* one *d.*; 2nd, 1912, Margaret Rose, *d.* of late J. E. M. Wylie and *widow* of G. F. W. Grierson. *Educ.:* private schools, Würtemberg and Switzerland; Royal Naval School, New Cross; R.M.C., Sandhurst. Entered army, 1876; Lieut.-Col. 1902; served Afghan War, 1878-79 (medal); Burmah, 1885-89 (despatches, D.S.O., medal with two clasps); Chin Hills, 1892-93 (clasp); Tirah, 1897-98 (despatches, medal with two clasps). *Address:* c/o Parry, Murray & Co., 54 Old Broad Street, E.C.2. *(Died 4 Jan. 1925.)*

HUGHES, Captain Arthur Beckett, C.B.E. 1919; R.N. (retired); *b.* 1873; *s.* of late Rev. John Edward Hughes of Cheswardine, Salop, and Mary Anne Chadwick of Daresbury Hall, Cheshire; unmarried. *Educ.:* Park House, Reading; Naval Academy, Stubbington. Entered R.N. 1887; Lieutenant, 1896; Commander, 1907; Captain, 1915; served S. African War, 1899-1902, as lieutenant of Philomel (medal); European War, 1914-19 (despatches, C.B.E.); second in command of Ocean, when that ship, together with Irresistible, was sunk during the attack on the Chanak Forts 18 March 1915; retired, 1922. *Club:* United Service. *(Died 8 April 1925.)*

HUGHES, Elizabeth Phillipps, LL.D., M.B.E.; on the governing body of the University of Wales, of the University College, Cardiff, etc.; Member of the Glamorgan Education Committee, etc.; *b.* Carmarthen, 22 June 1851; *d.* of Dr. John Hughes, Carmarthen. *Educ.:* Hope House, Taunton; Ladies' College, Cheltenham; University of Cambridge. On the staff of the Ladies' College, Cheltenham, for five years; student of Newnham College, 1881-85; Moral Sciences Tripos Class I., History Tripos Class II.; Principal of the Cambridge Training College for Secondary Teachers, 1885-99; went round the

527

HUDON, Lt.-Col. Joseph Alfred George, C.M.G. See page xxii.

world, lectured a good deal in America, Japan, etc., 1899-1902; Professor of English for six months in three colleges in Japan; settled in Wales and undertook a good deal of unpaid public work, educational, insurance, tuberculosis, etc.; Bardic name Merch Myrddin; has sat on three Government Departmental Committees, and has been witness before several Royal Commissions; has done work in connection with the Red Cross; started the first Red Cross Women's Camp, helped to start the first Red Cross Hospital in S. Wales in the late war. *Publications:* chiefly educational pamphlets and sections in educational books. *Recreations:* travelling, alpine climbing, etc. *Address:* Penrheol, Barry, S. Wales. (*Died 19 Dec. 1925.*)

HUGHES, Col. Emilius, C.B. 1887; C.M.G. 1879; Retired List, Army Service Corps; *b.* London, 6 June 1844; *y. s.* of Philip Hughes of War Office; *m.* 1st, 1864, Mary Sandys Emily (*d.* 1869), *d.* of late Lieut.-Col. M. Louis, R.H.A.; 2nd, 1872, Ada Elizabeth (*d.* 1904), *d.* of Henry Grainger of High Ireby, Cumberland; one *s.* four *d.* *Educ.:* King's Coll., London. Joined Commissariat Department, 1862; served in South African War, 1878-79; operations against Sekukuni; Zulu Campaign, in Commissariat charge with Sir Evelyn Wood's Flying Column; action at Kambula and Battle of Ulundi (despatches, medal with clasp; C.M.G.); promoted Commissary; Transvaal Campaign 1881, Newcastle Field Force (despatches); Egyptian Expedition 1882, senior Commissariat officer 2nd Division, including Battle of Tel-el-Kebir (medal with clasp, bronze star; 3rd class Medjidieh; promoted Lieut.-Colonel): Soudan Expedition, 1884-85; with Force up the Nile, as Senior Commissariat Officer (despatches, clasp, promoted Colonel); Headquarters, 1885-1887; A.A.G. Dublin District, 1887-91, A.A.G., Malta, 1891-95; retired 1895; Chairman, Church of England Soldiers' and Sailors' Institutes Association, Church House, Westminster, 1922. *Address:* Allens, Plaxtol, Sevenoaks. *T.A.:* Colonel Hughes, Plaxtol. *T.:* Plaxtol 18. (*Died 30 July 1926.*)

HUGHES, Col. George Arthur, D.S.O. 1898; late Colonel Royal Army Medical Corps; retired, 1905; *b.* 18 May 1851; 5th *s.* of late James Hughes, Curragh Priven, Rathcormac, Co. Cork. *Educ.:* Trin. Coll. Dublin. Bachelor of Arts; Bachelor of Medicine; Master of Surgery. Entered army, 1877; served Afghan War, 1878; Bechuanaland Expedition, South Africa, 1884; Ashanti Expedition, 1896; Soudan Expedition. 1898 (despatches, D.S.O.) *Club:* Army and Navy. (*Died 13 April 1926.*)

HUGHES, John Williams Gwynne-, Lord-Lieutenant of Carmarthenshire since 1913; J.P., D.L.; *b.* 22 Nov. 1858; *e. s.* of late John Williams Morgan Gwynne-Hughes, and 2nd wife, Mary, *d.* of late W. Lewis; *m.* 1880, Emily Beatrice, *y. d.* of late George Henfrey; one *d.* *Educ.:* Cheltenham: Jesus College, Cambridge. High Sheriff, Carmarthenshire, 1888; C.C. Carmarthenshire (Chairman 1903). *Recreations:* shooting, fishing. *Address:* Tregeyb, near Llandilo, Carmarthenshire. (*Died 2 Jan. 1917.*)

HUGHES, Herbert, C.B. 1911; C.M.G. 1901; *b.* 25 Apr. 1853; *s.* of James Hughes; *m.* 1884, Loetitia, *d.* of H. Birkinyoung; three *d.* Colonel Commanding 3rd West Riding Brigade, Territorial Force, 1908-12; Member, Territorial Forces Advisory Committee at War Office, 1908-12; Lord Mayor of Sheffield, 1905-6. *Decorated* for Territorial service and services at International Industrial Conferences, 1886-1900; Commander of Royal Order of the Sword of Sweden. *Address:* Ashdell Grove, Sheffield. *T.:* 440 Sheffield. *Club:* Junior Carlton. (*Died 16 Jun. 1917.*)

HUGHES, Rev. Llewelyn Robert, M.A.; Rector of Llandudno since 1902; Canon of Bangor Cathedral since 1919; *s.* of late Robert Hughes of Aberllefenny, Merionethshire; *m.* 1890, May E., *d.* of late Charles Sweetapple; two *s.* *Educ.:* Queen's College, Oxford. Curate of Festiniog, 1883-1885; of, Carnarvon, 1885-88; Vicar of Portmadoc, 1888-1902; member of the Governing Body of the Church in Wales; Treasurer of the Bangor Diocesan Board of Finance; Chaplain to the Forces, 1914-19 (despatches); formerly Chaplain to Volunteer and Territorial Forces. *Publications:* Essays on Church and Educative Subjects; sermons; articles in Church periodicals. *Recreations:* travelling and architecture. *Address:* The Rectory, Llandudno. *Club:* Royal Societies. (*Died 15 Jan. 1925.*)

HUGHES, M. K., A.R.E.; Member Water Colour Society of Ireland; *e.* of late Sir Frederic Hughes, K.L.S., D.L., of Rosslare Fort. Co. Wexford, and Lady Hughes. *Educ.:* privately. Studied at the Westminster School of Art under Mr. Mouat Loudan; Engraving and Etching School, Royal College of Art, under Sir Frank Short, R.A., P.R.E., and Miss Pott, R.E.; exhibited in the Royal Academy; Salon, Paris; Royal Hibernian Academy, etc.; exhibitions of Etchings in New Dudley Galleries, 1909; Dublin, 1910. *Publications:* Illustrations in Art Journal, Studio, etc.; various plates of old London and old Dublin, Norway, Palestine, etc. *Address:* Little Nutcombe, Hindhead, Surrey. (*Died 21 Aug. 1918.*)

HUGHES, Hon. Lt.- Gen. Hon. Sir Sam, K.C.B., *cr.* 1915; M.P., Minister of Militia and Defence, 1911-16; *b.* Darlington, Co. Durham, Ont., 8 Jan. 1853; *s.* of John Hughes, a native of Tyrone, Ireland, and Caroline Laughlin, of Scotch-Irish-Huguenot descent; *m.* 1st, 1872, Caroline J. (*decd.*) *d.* of late Major Preston, Vancouver, B.C.; 2nd, 1875, Mary, *d.* of H. W. Burk, ex-M.P. West Durham; one *s.* two *d.* *Educ.:* public schools; Toronto Model and Normal Schools; Toronto Univ. Lecturer in English Language, Literature and History in Toronto Collegiate Institute until 1885, when he purchased the Lindsay Warder, which he edited until 1897; identified with amateur athletics; has been in the Active Militia since his thirteenth year; declined position of Deputy Minister of Militia in 1891, and of Adjt.-General, Canada, 1895; Lt.-Col. commanding 45th Batt., 1897; took part in the Queen's Jubilee celebration, 20 June 1897 (medal); president of the Dominion of Canada Rifle Association; president, Small Arms Committee, Canada; chairman, Board of Visitors, Royal Military College, Kingston; Railway Intelligence Officer, Headquarters Staff; served in the Fenian Raids, 1870 (medal); since 1872 has advocated and made personal offers of Colonial Military Assistance to the Empire in Imperial Wars; personally offered to raise corps for the Egyptian and Soudanese campaigns, the Afghan Frontier War, and the Transvaal War; visited Australia and New Zealand in 1897-98 in the interest of Colonial Assistance in Imperial Wars; served South African War, 1899-1900 (despatches several times); European War, in France, 1914-15; raised Canadian contingents for European War, 1914-16; contested House of Commons for N. Victoria, 1891; elected 1892, 1896, and 1900; Victoria and Haliburton 1904, 1908, and 1911; member of the Orange Order, Foresters, and Masonic Order; Methodist; Conservative. *Address:* Lindsay, Ont. *Clubs:* Rideau, Country, Hunt, Ottawa. (*Died 24 Aug. 1921.*)

HUGHES, Spencer Leigh, M.P.(L.) Stockport since 1910; parliamentary journalist; *s.* of late Rev. James Hughes; *m.* Ellen Wayland (*d.* 1916), *d.* of late James Groves, Newport, Isle of Wight; one *d.* *Educ.:* Woodhouse Grove School, near Leeds. Connected with Ransomes, Sims, and Jefferies, Ltd., the Ipswich engineers, for ten years, with the Morning Leader from its start, and with the Star since 1891. *Pub-*

lications: The English Character, 1912; The Art of Public Speaking, 1913; Things that don't Count, 1916; Press, Platform, and Parliament, 1918; Parliamentary Tales in the Windsor and Cassell's Magazines. *Recreation:* attempting to catch fish. *Address:* 40 Lexham Gardens, Kensington, W.8. *T.:* Victoria 6168. *Clubs:* National Liberal, Eighty, Wigwam.

(*Died 22 Feb. 1920.*)

HUGHES, Sir Thomas, Kt., *cr.* 1898; J.P., Liverpool; head of firm Thomas Hughes and Son, timber importers; Hon. Freeman of the City of Liverpool; *b.* Liverpool, 3 Aug. 1838; *e. s.* of Thomas Hughes, timber merchant; *m.* 1866, Miss Stott; two *s.* five *d.* *Educ.:* Liverpool Institute. Elected member City Council, 1878; re-elected three times without opposition; elected Alderman, 1891; Mayor of Liverpool, 1889; Lord Mayor, 1897; Chairman of Parliamentary Committee for the Creation of Greater Liverpool. *Recreation:* fishing. *Address:* Springwood, Linnet Lane, Liverpool. *T.A.:* Planks. *T.:* Royal, 1575. *Club:* Conservative, Liverpool. (*Died 31 Oct. 1923.*)

HUGHES, Thomas M'Kenny, M.A., F.R.S., F.E.S., F.S.A.; Woodwardian Professor of Geology, Cambridge University; Chevalier St. Maur and St. Laz; *m.* Mary Caroline (*d.* 1916), *d.* of Rev. G. F. Weston. *Publication:* Cambridge, in Cambridge County Geographies. *Address:* Ravensworth, Cambridge. *Club:* Athenæum. (*Died 9 June 1917.*)

HUGHES, Sir Walter Charleton, Kt., *cr.* 1906; C.I.E., 1900; M.Inst.C.E.; *b.* 22 Sep. 1850; *m.* 1889, Evelyn Isabel Rose, *e. d.* of late Col. H. S. Hutchinson, I.S.C.; two *s.* one *d.* *Educ.:* private schools; King's College, London. Fellow of King's College, London, and Fellow (appointed) of the University of Bombay. Joined Indian Public Works Department, 1868; Secretary to the Government of Bombay, P.W.D., 1887-92; Chairman Board of Trustees for the Port of Bombay, 1892-98 and 1900-10; additional member Bombay Legislative Council, 1897-1910; Chairman Bombay Improvement Trust, 1898-1900. *Address:* Dartmouth House, 2 Queen Anne's Gate, S.W. *Clubs:* National, Byculla, Royal Bombay Yacht, Bombay. (*Died 30 Mar. 1922.*)

HUGHES, Walter Tatham, I.S.O. 1905; Assistant Secretary to the Commissioners, Royal Hospital, Chelsea; *s.* of Rev. Henry Hughes, M.A., Vicar of All Saints, Gordon Square, London, and Anne Amelia, *d.* of Thomas James Tatham, J.P., D.L.; *m.* Charlotte, *d.* of Francis Wheatley Preston, of Tenbury, Worcestershire; two *d.* *Educ.:* Blackheath; Marlborough; France. Appointed to the Royal Hospital, Chelsea, 1867. *Address:* 12 Somerset Place, Lansdown, Bath.

(*Died 24 July 1917.*)

HUGHES-HALLETT, Col. James Wyndham, C.B., 1900; D.S.O. 1896; C.V.O. 1905; commanding Gordon Volunteer Infantry Brigade, 1906; commanding 72nd and 79th Regimental Districts, 1902; retired, 1906; *b.* Petham, Kent, 15 Sep. 1852; 3rd *surv. s.* of late Rev. J. Hughes-Hallett of Higham, Canterbury and Dunmow, Essex, and Mary Frances, *d.* of late Gen. Sir Thomas Gage Montresor, K.C.K.H.; *m.* 1893, Alice, *d.* of late Capt. Henry Wm. Landers. *Educ.:* Haileybury; Sandhurst. Entered army 1872; served during Afghan War, 1878-79, present at capture of Peiwar Kotal (despatches, medal with clasp); Captain 72nd Highlanders, 1880; with Egyptian Expedition 1882, including Tel-el-Kebir (despatches, medal with clasp, and bronze star); Major, Seaforth Highlanders, 1890; with Chitral relief force, 1895, in command of his regiment (despatches, medal with clasp, and D.S.O.); South Africa, 1899-1902, in command of regt. and temporarily in command of Highland Brigade (wounded, despatches thrice, C.B. and Brev. Col.). *Recreations:* shooting and cricket.

Address: 22 Campbell Avenue, Murrayfield, Edinburgh. *T.:* Central 2220. *Clubs:* Naval and Military, Sports. (*Died 2 June 1927.*)

HUISH, Marcus Bourne, LL.B. Camb.; Barr. Inner Temple; editor Art Journal, 1881-98; Chairman Japan Society; Cavaliere Order Crown of Italy; Chevalier Order Sacred Treasure, Japan; *e. s.* of Marcus Huish and Margaret Bourne; *m.* Catherine, *e. d.* of T. E. Winslow, Q.C.; one *s.* *Publications:* Greek Terra Cotta Statuettes; Year's Art; Japan and its Art; The Seine and the Loire; Meryon; Samplers and Tapestry Embroideries; Happy England; His Majesty's Water-colours; American Pilgrims Way. *Recreation:* golf. *Address:* 21 Essex Villas, Kensington, W.8. *T.:* Park 3263. *Club:* New University.

(*Died 4 May 1921.*)

HULBERT, Rev. Charles Augustus, M.A.; Rector of Castor, Peterborough, since 1911; Hon. Canon of Peterborough, 1899; Surrogate, 1901; *b.* 23 May 1838; *e. s.* of Rev. Canon C. A. Hulbert, Vicar of Almondbury, Yorkshire; *m.* 1st, Louisa, *d.* of Rev. B. Powell, J.P., Vicar of St. George's, Wigan; 2nd, Julia Margaret, *d.* of Rev. F. P. Seymour, M.A., Rector of Havant; three *s.* *Educ.:* Caius College, Cambridge. Curate of Holy Trinity, Tunbridge Wells, 1861-65; Bowdon, Cheshire, 1865-67; Incumbent of Slaithwaite, Yorks, 1867-79; Vicar of St. Stephen's, Leeds, 1879-81; Rector of Nether Broughton, Leicestershire, 1881-1901; Rural Dean of Framland III. 1885-1901; Vicar of Towcester, Northamptonshire, 1901-11. *Address:* The Rectory, Castor, Peterborough. (*Died 24 Mar. 1919.*)

HULETT, Hon. Sir (James) Liege, Kt., *cr.* 1902; J.P., ex-M.L.A.; Member of Senate of Union Parliament, 1910-20; *b.* 17 May 1838; *o. s.* of late J. L. Hulett of Gillingham, Kent, and Natal; *m.* 1869, Mary Ann, *o. d.* of late B. Balcomb; six *s.* one *d.* Entered Natal Legislative Council as Member for Victoria County, 1883; nominated to Executive Council, 1889; upon advent of responsible government in 1893 elected for old constituency to Legislative Assembly; retained seat until union, 1910, having served as Minister of Native Affairs and Speaker; Chairman and Managing Director of Sir J. L. Hulett and Son, Ltd., tea and sugar growers, manufacturers, and refiners. *Address:* The Manor House, Mentone Road, Durban, Natal. (*Died 5 June 1928.*)

HULL, Arthur Eaglefield, Mus. Doc. Oxon; F.R.C.O.; Editor Monthly Musical Record; Editor-in-Chief International Dictionary of Modern Music and Musicians; Principal of College of Music, Huddersfield; organ recitalist; *b.* Market Harborough, 1876; 2nd *s.* of S. Hull, Byfield, Market Harborough; *m.* 1906, Bertha Constance Barrett, F.R.C.O., 2nd *d.* of Alfred Slapps Barrett of Bishop Stortford; one *s.* one *d.* *Educ.:* privately. Principal Huddersfield College of Music, 1908; founder Huddersfield Chamber Music Society, now Huddersfield Music Club, 1900; editor Monthly Musical Record since 1913; founder British Music Society, 1918, and Hon. Director, 1918-1921; founder and first editor of The Music Bulletin, 1918; founder London Contemporary Music Centre (now also the British Section of International Society for Contemporary Music), 1920; founder Composers' Advisory Board, 1920. *Publications:* Modern Harmony, 1915 (Spanish ed. 1921, German ed. 1926); Organplaying: its technique and expression (6th ed. 1922); monograph on Scriabin (3rd ed. 1923); Handbook to Bach's Complete Organ Works, 1928; Music; Classical, Romantic and Modern, 1926; etc.; composer of songs, pf. pieces, organ music. *Address:* 19 Berners Street, W.1; Melbourne House, Huddersfield. *T.:* Regent

2481; Huddersfield 1094. *Club:* Oxford and Cambridge Musical. (*Died 4 Nov. 1928.*)

HULL, Major-General Sir Charles Patrick Amyatt, K.C.B., *cr.* 1918; C.B. 1916; Commanding Wessex Division T.F. since 1919; *b.* 3 July 1865; *s.* of late H. C. Hull, Barrister-at-law; *m.* 1901, Muriel, *d.* of late R. R. Dobell, Quebec, Canada; one *s.* two *d. Educ.:* Charterhouse; Trinity College, Cambridge (B.A.). Joined Royal Scots Fusiliers, 1887; Brevet-Col. 1915; Col. 1916; in India till 1896; A.D.C. to the Viceroy, 1895-96; served South African War as Adjutant of 2nd Batt. R.S.F. (severely wounded, Brevet-Major); on Staff, 1903-7 and 1909-12; Lt.-Col. to command the 4th Batt. Middlesex Regt. 1912; served European War, 1914-18 (C.B., prom. Maj.-Gen., K.C.B.); holds Russian Order of St. Vladimir, 4th class, with swords. *Recreations:* hunting, polo, shooting, and fishing. *Club:* Naval and Military. (*Died 24 July 1920.*)

HULL, Professor Edward, LL.D., F.R.S.; consulting geologist; *b.* Antrim, Ireland, 21 May 1829; *e. s.* of late Rev. John Dawson Hull, Vicar of Wickhambrook, Suffolk; *m.* 1857, *d.* (*d.* 1901) of late Dr. C. T. Cooke, Cheltenham; two *s.* four *d. Educ.:* Trin. Coll. Dublin (M.A.). Appointed to Geological Survey of United Kingdom, 1850; Scot. District Surveyor, 1867; Ireland Director, 1869; Prof. of Geology in the Royal College of Science; retired 1890; President Royal Geological Society, Ireland, 1873; conducted a scientific expedition through Arabia Petraea and Palestine, sent out by Committee of Palestine Exploration Fund, 1883-84; a member of Royal Commission on Coal Reserves, 1891; Secretary to the Victoria Institute in 1900. *Publications:* A Treatise on Building and Ornamental Stones of Great Britain and Foreign Countries, 1872; The Coal Fields of Great Britain, 5th ed. 1905; Contributions to the Physical History of the British Isles, 1882; Mount Seir, Sinai, and Western Palestine, 1885; Memoir on the Physical Geology of Arabia Petraea and Palestine, 1886; Physiology (Physical Geography), 1888; Physical Geology and Geography of Ireland, 2nd ed. 1891; Volcanoes, Past and Present (Contemporary Science Series), 1892; Our Coal Resources at the Close of the Nineteenth Century, 1897; Reminiscences of a Strenuous Life, 1910; Monograph on the Sub-oceanic Physiography of the North Atlantic Ocean, 1912. *Recreation:* music — the organ. *Address:* 14 Stanley Gardens, W. *Club:* Constitutional. (*Died 19 Oct. 1917.*)

HULTON, Sir Edward, 1st Bt., *cr.* 1921; formerly Newspaper Proprietor; *s.* of Edward Hulton, of Ashton-on-Mersey; *b.* 1869; *m.* Millicent, *d.* of John Warriss; one *s.* one *d. Address:* 51 Great Cumberland Place, W.1. *T.:* Paddington 5168; Downside, Leatherhead, Surrey. (*Died 23 May 1925.*)

HULTON, Rev. Henry Edward, Hon. Canon of Chelmsford Cathedral since 1914; St. Alban's, 1900-14; *b.* 21 June 1839; *e. surv. s.* of late William Adam Hulton (Judge of H.M. County Courts), Hurst Grange, Preston, Lancashire, and Dorothy Ann, *d.* of late Edward Gorst. *Educ.:* Cheltenham College; Trinity College, Oxford (B.A. 1862, M.A. 1864). Ordained Deacon, 1863; Priest, 1865; Curate of Sonning, 1863-69; Vicar of All Saints', Dunsden, 1870-76; Vicar of Great Waltham, 1876-1906; Rural Dean of Chelmsford, 1886-1913. *Address:* Boreham Manor, Chelmsford. *Club:* New University (*Died 24 Dec. 1922.*)

HULTON-HARROP, William Edward Montagu, J.P., D.L.; *b.* 30 Aug. 1848; 2nd *s.* of late Rev. Arthur Hyde Hulton and Elizabeth Margaret, 2nd *d.* and co-heir of Jonah Harrop, D.L., of Bardsley, and *g.-s.* of late William Hulton, D.L., of Hulton Park, whose name he

assumed; *m.* 1878, Margaret Henrietta Elizabeth, *e. d.* of late Calverly Bewicke, of Close House, Northumberland; four *s.* two *d. Educ.:* Magdalene College, Cambridge. High Sheriff, Shropshire, 1885. *Address:* Lythwood Hall, Shrewsbury. *Club:* New University. (*Died 7 April 1916.*)

HUMBLE-CROFTS, Rev. William John, M.A. Oxon; Rector of Waldron, Sussex; Prebendary of Chichester; Rural Dean of Dallington; Surrogate; *b.* 9 Dec. 1846; *s.* of Rev. M. M. Humble, Rector of Sutton Scarsdale, Derbyshire; *m.* Bridget, *d.* of Rev. Taylor White, Rector of Norton Cuckney, Notts; two *s.* two *d. Educ.:* Exeter College, Oxford. Second Class Moderations, Oxford, 1868. *Publications:* various poems and letters. *Recreations:* cricket, rowing, tennis, fencing; Captain of the Magnus School, Newark-on-Trent, and stroke of the Magnus boat; played cricket for Derbyshire, County, and for the Gentlemen of Yorkshire, Derbyshire, and Notts, and Free Foresters, and Exeter College. *Address:* Waldron Rectory, Sussex. *M.:* O 4423. (*Died 1 July 1924.*)

HUME, George Haliburton, M.D.; F.R.C.S. Ed.; D.C.L.; Consulting Surgeon to Royal Victoria Infirmary, Hospital for Sick Children, Maternity Hospital, City Asylum, Newcastle-on-Tyne and Barrasford Sanatorium; *b.* Berwickshire, 17 Sep. 1845; *m.* 1878, Frances Diana, *e. d.* of Minchin Jackson, Canada; two *s.* four *d. Educ.:* Kelso Grammar School; Edinburgh University. Practised as a surgeon in Newcastle 1868-1914; for some years was Lecturer on Physiology in the University of Durham College of Medicine; retired from the post of Senior Surgeon to the Royal Infirmary, 1905; took a prominent part in promoting the building of the Royal Victoria Infirmary, opened 1906. *Publications:* papers on surgical subjects in medical journals; The Evolution of Surgical Principles, address at British Medical Association, Newcastle, 1893; History of the Newcastle Infirmary. *Address:* Gosforth, Newcastle-on-Tyne. (*Died 8 May 1923.*)

HUMMEL, Rt. Rev. Francis Ignatius, Vicar Apostolic of the Gold Coast and titular Bishop of Trapezopolis since 1906; *b.* Alsace, 1870. *Educ.:* Ecole des Missions, Clermont; African Missions Seminary, Lyons. Missionary on the Niger, 1896-1906. *Address:* Cape Coast Castle, British West Africa. (*Died 15 Mar. 1924.*)

HUMPHREYS, Rev. Alfred Edward, M.A.; Vicar of St. Michael, Stonebridge Park, Willesden, since 1907; Hon. Canon of Norwich Cathedral since 1901; *b.* Oswestry, Salop, 1843; *m.* 1883, H. A., *d.* of T. J. Boileau, Judge, H.E.I.C.S., Madras. *Educ.:* King Edward School, Birmingham; Trinity College, Camb.; Browne Medal for Greek Ode and Davies' Classical Univ. Scholarship; Scholar, Fellow, Assistant Tutor, Lecturer in Divinity, at Trinity Coll. 1862-77; Examiner, Proctor, and Preacher in the Univ. 1866-87; Vicar of St. Matthew's, Cambridge, 1877-87, and Chaplain of Cambridge Union, 1884-87; Vicar of Hempton, Norfolk, 1887-95; Rector of Fakenham, Norfolk, 1887-1907. *Publications:* Commentary on 1 and 2 Tim. and Titus (Cambridge Bible), 1895; Christ's Daily Orders, 1898; Commentary on Philippians, 1900; Commentary on Caesar, Bell. Gall. Bk. vi., 1900; Christ our Overlord, 1900; The Plain Truth about the Education Act, 1902; Fair Play, an Appeal for Justice in Tithe Rating, 1904. *Recreations:* rowing, cycling. *Address:* St. Michael's Vicarage, Stonebridge Park, N.W. (*Died 17 Aug. 1922.*)

HUMPHREYS, Major Dashwood William Harrington, D.S.O. 1904; *b.* 6 Feb. 1872. Entered army, 1894; Captain, 1903; served Thibet, 1903-4 (slightly wounded,

530

HUME, Alexander Williamson. See page xxii.

despatches, D.S.O.); A.D.C. to Political Resident, Aden. *Address*: Aden Brigade, Aden.
(*Died 17 Feb. 1917.*)

HUMPHREYS, Eng. Rear-Adm. Sir Henry, R.N., K.C.M.G., *cr.* 1919; C.B. 1916; *s.* of late Major D. Humphreys, R.A.; *m.* A. Josephine, *d.* of late Edward Eckersley, R.N. Gained Royal Humane Society's Bronze Medal, 1897; served European War, Dardanelles, 1914-16 (despatches, C.B., Officer Legion of Honour); retired list, 1921. *Address*: 4 Penlee Gardens, Stoke, Devonport.(*Died 27 May 1924.*)

HUMPHREYS, Noel Algernon, I.S.O. 1902; *b.* London, 12 Sep. 1837; *e. s.* of Henry Noel Humphreys, author and artist; *m.* Gertrude, 2nd *d.* of Thomas Spencer Cobbold, M.D., F.R.S.; two *s.* one *d. Educ.*: private. Junior Clerk in Registrar-General's Office (England), 1856; engaged on preparation of census statistics, based upon the five census enumerations, 1861-1901; Secretary in the Census Office, 1890-93; Assistant Registrar-General, 1898-1900; late Hon. Secretary of the Royal Statistical Society; Member of the Departmental Committee on the Financial Aspect of Old Age Pensions, 1898; Chief Clerk in Registrar-General's Office (England), 1898-1905. *Publications*: edited, for Royal Statistical Institute, the Vital Statistics of Dr. William Farr, D.C.L., F.R.S.; contributed many papers on various branches of vital statistics to the Journal of the Royal Statistical Society and to the periodical press. *Address*: Glenside, East Liss, Hants.(*Died 6 Mar. 1923.*)

HUMPHREYS, Very Rev. Robert, M.A.; Dean of Killaloe since 1886; Incumbent of Ballinaclough 1891-1911. *Educ.*: Trinity College, Dublin. Ordained 1853; Curate of Bromcliffe, 1855-57; Borrisokane, 1857; Broadford, 1857; Kilfenora, 1857-64; Lisdoonvarna, 1864; Prebendary of Killaloe, 1864-81; Incumbent of Quin, 1881-91; Dean of Kilfenora, 1884-86; Member of General Synod of Church of Ireland; Member of Representative Body of Church of Ireland. *Address*: Beechlands, Shankill, Co. Dublin. (*Died Mar. 1917.*)

HUMPHRY, Alfred Paget, M.V.O. 1909; D.L., J.P., County Alderman, Cambridgeshire; Member of Council, National Rifle Association; Member of Cambridge Territorial Force Association; *b.* Cambridge, 20 June 1850; *o. s.* of Sir George Murray Humphry, M.D., F.R.S., and Mary, *d.* of D. R. M'Nab, Epping Place, Epping, Essex; *m.* 1st, Elizabeth, *d.* of T. Boycott, M.D., 1876; 2nd, Clara Edyth, *d.* of C. Murchison, M.D., F.R.S., 1887; three *s.* two *d. Educ.*: Rugby; Trin. Coll. Camb.; Lincoln's Inn. Barr. 1875. Winner of Queen's Prize, Wimbledon, 1871; member of various national rifle teams, 1872-83; Exec. Officer, National Rifle Association, 1881-91; Lieut.-Col. commanding Cambridge University R.V. 1886-89; Member of War Office Small Arms Committee, 1900-5; Senior Esquire Bedell, Cambridge University, 1877-1913; Bursar, Selwyn College, 1884-1900; Steward, Trinity College, 1887-97. *Publication*: History of the National Rifle Association. *Address*: Horham Hall, Thaxted, Essex; Trinity College, Cambridge. *Clubs*: Athenæum; Cambridge County.
(*Died 6 Oct. 1916.*)

HUMPHRY, Mrs. C. E., journalist; *d.* of late Rev. James Graham, Londonderry Cathedral; *m.* 1881; one *d. Educ.*: Dublin. *Publications*: Manners for Men; Etiquette for Every Day; Three Cookery Books. *Recreations*: reading, gardening, the play. *Address*: Carrig-Cleena, Maidenhead. (*Died 2 April 1925.*)

HUMPHRY, Laurence, M.A., M.D. (Camb.), F.R.C.P. (Lond.); Physician to Addenbrooke's Hospital, Cambridge; Lt.-Col. R.A.M.C. (T.), 1st Eastern General Hospital; formerly Assessor to the Regius Professor of Physic; Lecturer in Medicine in the University; Examiner in Medicine, Conjoint Board, London;

President Cambridge and Huntingdon Branch Brit. Med. Assoc., 1905; *b.* 1856; *s.* of J. T. Humphry, barrister-at-law, London, and J. O. M'Nab of Epping; *m.* 1889, Isabel L., *d.* of Prof. Sir George Stokes, 1st Bart., M.P. *Educ.*: Haileybury College; Trinity College, Cambridge; St. Bartholomew's Hospital. B.A. Nat. Sc. Trip., 1st Part, 1876; 1st Class Final M.B., 1880; Resident Medical Officer City of London Chest Hospital, 1881-83; teacher of Pathology Cambridge University, 1884; Examiner in Medicine, Cambridge University, on several occasions; President Cambridge Medical Society, 1899-1900; Examiner in Medicine, Royal Army Med. Corps. *Publications*: Manual of Nursing; Art., Congenital Malformation of Heart, Allbutt's System of Medicine; Contrib., Severe Symptoms following Puncture of Hydatid Cysts of Liver, Lancet, 1887; The Parathyroid Glands in Graves' Disease, ibid. 1905; Rupture of Coronary Artery, ibid. 1898; Aneurysm of the Aorta communicating with the Sup. Vena Cava, Brit. Med. Journ. 1910; Case of Acromegaly; Pressor substances in Urine (with Dr. Dixon), ibid. 1910; Multiple Embolic Aneurysms of the Pulmonary Artery, Journal of Pathology and Bacteriology, vol. xvii. 1912; The Urinary Diastase Test and Loewi's Reaction in Pancreatic Lesons, Brit. Med. Journ. 1914. *Address*: Lensfield, Cambridge. *T.*: 414.
(*Died 5 Feb. 1920.*)

HUNEKER, James Gibbons, critic; *b.* Philadelphia, 1860; Irish-Hungarian descent; *g.s.* of Jas. Gibbons, Irish poet, former vice-pres. Fenian Brotherhood. *Educ.*: Paris. Studied music with distinguished masters; adopted journalism as a profession; former musical, art, and dramatic editor of the New York Sun; music editor, New York Times; corresponding member Hispanic Society, New York; member Academy Natural Sciences, Philadelphia; member Institute Arts and Letters. *Publications*: Mezzotints in Modern Music, 1899; Chopin: the Man and his Music, 1900; Melomaniacs, 1902; Overtones, 1904; Iconoclasts, 1905; Visionaries, 1905; Egoists, 1909; Promenades of an Impressionist, 1910; Franz Liszt, 1911; The Pathos of Distance, 1913; New Cosmopolis, 1915; Ivory, Apes, and Peacocks, 1915; Unicorns, 1917; Bedouins, 1920; Steeplejack, 1920. *Address*: The World Office, New York. *Club*: Authors'.
(*Died 9 Feb. 1921.*)

HUNT, Edmund Langley, C.M.G. 1902; L.R.C.P. and S.I.; *b.* 1868. *Educ.*: Kingsley College; Royal College of Surgeons, Ireland. Civil Surgeon S.A. Field Force, 1899-1902; Medical Officer on personal staff Com.-in-Chief, Feb. 1902 to termination of war (despatches, 2 medals, 6 clasps); Medical Officer, Anglo-German Boundary Commission to Lake Chad, N. Nigeria, 1903-4 (despatches, received thanks of Mr. Secretary Lyttleton and Government of Northern Nigeria, the thanks of the Emperor of Germany, and the Insignia of 3rd class, Crown of Prussia); M.O., W.A.M.S., 1905; received thanks of S. of S. for services in connection with outbreak of plague at Accra, Gold Coast, 1908; transferred to Ceylon as Inspecting Medical Officer (I.M.O.), 1912; promoted Assistant P.C.M.O. and I.G.H., 1915; transferred on promotion to Jamaica as S.M.O. 1920. *Address*: Kingston, Jamaica, West Indies.
(*Died 30 Sept. 1925.*)

HUNT, Capt. George Percy Edward, R.N.; D.S.O. 1900; *m.* Cecilia Teresa, *d.* of late Rt. Hon. Sir Cecil Clementi Smith. Served South Africa, 1899-1900 (D.S.O.); retired, 1913. *Address*: The Great House, Almeley, Herefordshire. (*Died 22 Aug. 1917.*)

HUNT, Major Gerald Ponsonby Sneyd, C.M.G. 1916; R. Berks Regt.; *b.* 24 July 1877; *m.* 1911, Helen Pennal, *sis.* of Sir A. E. Dunbar, Bt. Served S. African War,

1899-1902 (Queen's medal 3 clasps, King's medal 2 clasps); European War. 1914-16 (despatches, C.M.G.). *(Died 23 Mar. 1918.)*

HUNT, Rev. Henry de Vere, M.A.; Canon of Clonfert and Kilmacduagh, 1913; Rector of Ahascragh since 1888; *b.* 12 Mar. 1856; *s.* of late Major Henry Leslie Hunt, Adjutant, 7th West York Rifle Volunteers, formerly of 67th Regt.; *m.* 1882, Mary Caroline, *d.* of late Rev. Peter William Browne, Rector of Blackrod, Lancashire; one *s.* three *d.* *Educ.:* Bedford Grammar School; Clare College, Cambridge. Ordained, 1882; Curate of Wavertree, 1882-4; Littleton, Middlesex, 1884-6; Incumbent of Ennisnag, Kilkenny, 1886-8. *Address:* Ahascragh Rectory, Ballinasloe. *(Died 27 Jan. 1919.)*

HUNT, Rev. H. G. Bonavia, Mus.D., F.R.S.E.; *b.* 1847. *Educ.:* privately; also King's College, London; afterwards student in the Musical Faculty, Christ Church, Oxford; Mus.B. Christ Church, Oxon. 1876; Mus.D. Trinity College, Dublin, 1887; member of the Senate, 1890; sub-editor and editor of the *Quiver*. 1865-1905; editor of Cassell's Magazine, 1874-96; editor and founder of Little Folks from commencement to 1876; founder and first Warden of Trinity College, London, 1872-92; founder and first Warden of the Kilburn Grammar School, 1897-1904; Teacher of Musical History, University of London, 1900-7. Ordained by Bishop of Winchester to curacy of Esher, 1878; afterwards curate of St. Philip's, Regent Street, and St. James's, Piccadilly; Vicar of St. Paul's, Kilburn; now Vicar of Burgess Hill, Sussex. *Publications:* A Concise History of Music, 19th ed. 1915; sermons, anthems, and services. *Recreations:* cycling, musical composition. *Address:* Burgess Hill Vicarage, Sussex. *T.:* Burgess Hill 67. *Club:* Royal Societies. *(Died 27 Sept. 1917.)*

HUNT, Rev. Thomas Hankey; *b.* Hatton, nr. Runcorn, Cheshire, 1842; *m.* 2nd *d.* of late Rev. Dr. William Antliff, President of the Conference, 1863-65; three *s.* one *d.* Member of the Council of Forty of the United Kingdom Alliance, and of the National Temperance Federation; edited the Primitive Methodist World from 1883 until its amalgamation with the Leader, 1909; Sec. Sunday School Union, 1892-97; Pres. of the Primitive Methodist Connexion, 1903-4; Sec. of P. M. Temperance Society, 1897-1914; Pres. of P. M. Temperance Society. 1906-15; Secretary of the Liverpool District Education Committee; Director of the Primitive Methodist Leader. *Publications:* The Liquor Problem, and How to Solve It; The Christian Citizen and Temperance Reform; Martin Luther: A Study for Protestants; Sunday School Reform, a Problem for the Times (Morse Lecture, 1908), etc. *Address:* 152 South Bank Road, Southport.

HUNT, Major William Morgan, D.S.O., M.C.; Royal Artillery; *b.* 1881; *s.* of Langford Hunt, C.E., of Owen Doon, and Augusta Morgan. Entered Army, 1900; served Mesopotamia, 1914-16, No. 23 M.B. (twice wounded, despatches thrice); North-West Frontier, India, Mohmand Expedition, No. 8 M.B., 1917-18 (despatches); Afghanistan, 1919 (despatches). *Recreations:* rowing, football, boxing, big game shooting. *Address:* Owendoon House, Bawnboy, Co. Cavan. *(Died 19 July 1925.)*

HUNT-GRUBBE, Admiral Sir Walter James, G.C.B., *cr.* 1899; K.C.B., *cr.* 1882; J.P. Hants; *b.* 1833; *s.* of Rev. James A. Hunt-Grubbe; *m.* Mary (*d.* 1908), *d.* of William Codrington, Wroughton, Wiltshire, 1867; one *s.* two *d.* Entered Navy, 1845; served on W. Coast of Africa, 1845-48, 1854-57, 1865-66, in suppressing slave trade; Commander, 1861, for operations on River Gambia; Capt. 1866; in charge of Ascension Island, 1866; in command of Naval Brigade in Ashantee War (severely wounded), 1874; C.B. 1874; A.D.C. 1879-84; in command of N.

Division of Mediterranean fleet at Alexandria, 1882; Commander-in-Chief of Cape and W. Coast of Africa Station, 1885-88; Admiral Superintendent of Devonport Dockyard, 1888-91; President Royal Naval College, Greenwich, 1894-97. *Club:* United Service. *(Died 11 April 1922.)*

HUNTER, Sir Charles Roderick, 3rd Bt., *cr.* 1812; M.P. (C.) Bath, 1910-18; Inspector of Musketry, Imperial Yeomanry, 1900; late Capt. Rifle Brigade, retired 1890; *s.* of 2nd Bt. and Constance, *d.* of W. I. Bosanquet; *b.* 6 July 1858; S. father 1890; *m.* Agnes, *d.* of A. S. Kennard, Crawley Court, Hants, 1887. *Educ.:* Eton. *Heir:* none. *Address:* 36 Draycott Place, S.W.3. *T.:* West 6970. *Clubs:* Carlton, Travellers'. *(Died 24 June 1924.)*

HUNTER, Captain Douglas William, D.S.O. 1916; M.B., R.A.M.C., A.I.F.; M.B., Ch.B. Glas., D.P.H. Camb. *Educ.:* Glasgow University. Served European War, 1914-17 (D.S.O.). *Address:* 10 Hallfield Road, Bradford. *(Died 25 Mar. 1918.)*

HUNTER, Major-Gen. George Douglas, C.B. 1917; C.M.G. 1916; D.S.O. 1896; M.R.C.S., L.S.A.; Army Medical Service (retired); Director of Medical Services, British East African Expeditionary Forces, Dec. 1915-Mar. 1918; *b.* 28 Aug. 1860; 2nd *s.* of late Brig. Surgeon George Yeates Hunter, Indian Army; *m.* 1895, Elfrida Hannah, *d.* of late T. W. U. Robinson of Houghton-le-Spring, Durham; one *s.* one *d.* Entered R.A.M.C., 1884; Surg.-Major, 1896; served Nile Expedition, 1884-85 (medal with clasp, Khedive's star); Soudan Frontier Field Force, 1885-86; Soudan, 1888-89 (clasp); Dongola Expeditionary Force, 1896 (despatches, D.S.O., British medal, Khedive's medal with two clasps); operations of 1898, including the battle of Khartoum (despatches, clasp to Khedive's medal, 4th class Osmanieh); Lt.-Col. 1904; Principal Medical Officer, Egyptian Army, 1905-8 (2nd class Medjidieh); European War, 1914-18 (despatches, C.M.G., C.B.). *Address:* Cadbury, Yatton, Somerset. *(Died 15 April 1922.)*

HUNTER, G. Sherwood, R.B.A. 1889; *b.* Aberdeen, N.B.; 2nd *s.* of James Hunter, granite merchant of that city; *m.* Constance Mary, *d.* of Ed. Montague Suart, H.E.I. *Educ.:* Edinburgh, Paris, Rome. Painted in Scotland, Holland, Spain, Italy, France, Egypt and Palestine; medals Crystal Palace, 1896, 1898; Hon. mention, Paris International, 1900. *Address:* The Malt House, Newlyn, Penzance. *(Died 18 June 1920.)*

HUNTER, Hamilton, C.M.G. 1900; *b.* 1845; *s.* of Walter John Hunter, H.E.I.C.S., formerly of Baughurst House, Hants; *m.* 1882, Isabella Jane, *d.* of late Sir John Gorrie; two *d.* Magistrate for Taviuni, Fiji, 1874; Stipendiary Magistrate, Cakandrovi, 1875; Chief Police Magistrate, Fiji, 1877; Deputy Commissioner for W. Pacific, 1881; Acting Registrar-Gen. 1892; Official Receiver in Bankruptcy, 1894; Registrar Supreme Court, and Curator Intestate Estates, 1895; Judicial Commissioner to visit Islands, 1896; Acting Consul, Samoa, 1899; Consul at Tonga, 1901. *Address:* 18 South Parade, Southsea. *Club:* Royal Corinthian Yacht, Southsea. *(Died 19 Jan. 1923.)*

HUNTER, John, J.P.; *b.* 19 Feb. 1833; *m.* 1862; one *d.* Merchant Taylors School in the City, 1840-50; articled to his uncle and godfather, 1850; in his office, 1850-60; further 10 years, 1870-80; became his partner, 1880; continued there until 1900. *Publications:* addresses as an ex-President of the Council of the Law Society. *Address:* 4 Morton Crescent, Exmouth. *T.A.:* Hereford Chasseur.

HUNTER, Rev. John, D.D. (Glas.), 1893; late Minister of Trinity Church, Glasgow; *b.* Aberdeen, 14 July 1849; *m.* 1883, Marion, *e.d.* of D. Martin, York; one *s.* *Educ.:* Aberdeen; Nottingham; Springhill College, Birmingham, now Mansfield College, Oxford. Ordained Minister

532

of the Congregational Church at York in succession to the Rev. James Parsons, 1871; Minister of Wycliffe Church, Hull, 1882; Trinity Church, Glasgow, 1887-1902; was elected the first Nonconformist President of the Theological Society of the University of Glasgow, 1895; King's Weigh House Church, Grosvenor Square, London, 1901; returned to the pastorate of Trinity Church, Glasgow, 1904-13. *Publications:* Devotional Services for Public Worship; Hymns of Faith and Life; A Plea for a Worshipful Church; Angels of God, and other sermons; The Coming Church; De Profundis Clamavi, a volume of Discourses preached on special occasions, 1908; God and Life, a volume of sermons delivered in the United States and elsewhere, 1910; and many contributions to religious and other journals. *Recreation:* walking. *Address:* 8 Prince Arthur Road, Hampstead, N.W.   *(Died 15 Sept. 1917.)*

HUNTER, Maj.-Gen. John Gunning, C.B. 1913; Indian Army (retired); *b.* 1 Nov. 1859; *s.* of late Colonel Alexander Hunter, Indian Army; *m.* 1st, 1885, Louisa, *d.* of late Donald McCallum, Perth; 2nd, 1921, Helen Barbara, *widow* of John Slater, Chorley Wood, Herts. *Educ.:* Cheltenham; Sandhurst. First Commission, 70th Foot, 1878; served throughout Afghan War, 1878-79, with 70th Foot, including its march to Kandahar and to the vicinity of the Helmund River; transferred to Indian Army; served as Commandant, 10th Jâts, and vacated on completion of 7 years' tenure of command and after 25 years' service in the corps; served through the Burma War, 1887-90 (official thanks, Chief Commissioner, and despatches); served throughout the Chin-Lushai Expedition (Burma Column), and commanded march and attack on Hanta (despatches); served as Brigade Commander at Home and in France in European War, 1914-17 (despatches); promoted to permanent rank of Maj.-Gen.; Special Appointment under the War Office, Sep. 1917 to the signing of peace; retired 1919; Colonel, 10th Jâts, 1922; awarded a Good Service Pension, 1922. *Address:* La Collinette, Morgat, Brittany. *Club:* East India United Service.
    (Died 11 June 1926.)

HUNTER, Lieut.-Col. John Muir, C.S.I. 1899; O.B.E. 1920; Indian Staff Corps, late Royal Artillery; *b.* Mauritius, 31 May 1844; *s.* of Captain Hugh Hunter, R.N., and Elizabeth Mather; *m.* Emily Jean, *d.* of J. Patison Thom, Assistant Secretary India Office, London, 1870. *Educ.:* Royal Naval School, Newcross; King's Coll.School, London; abroad and private tuition; Royal M. Academy, Woolwich; Political Agent in Kathiâwar, Bombay Presidency, India, to 1901; Hon. Sec., War Pensions Committee and Hon. Sec., Sailors' Vegetable Fund. *Address:* c/o Bank of England, Burlington Gardens, W.   *(Died 13 Dec. 1920.)*

HUNTER, Sir Thomas, Kt., *cr.* 1911, LL.D.; D.L.; W.S.; Town Clerk, Edinburgh, 1895-1918; *b.* 16 June 1850; *s.* of late Robert Hunter, Hawick. *Educ.:* Hawick Academy; Edinburgh University. *Address:* 6 Albany Street, Edinburgh; House, Inverarbour, Inverleith Place, Edinburgh. *Clubs:* Royal Societies; University, Edinburgh.   *(Died 25 Aug. 1919.)*

HUNTER, Sir (William) Bernard, Kt., *cr.* 1916; Managing Governor, Imperial Bank of India; *b.* 1868; late Secretary and Treasurer, Bank of Madras. *Address:* 2 Princes Street, E.C.   *(Died 12 May 1924.)*

HUNTER, William Henry, M.Inst.C.E., M.Am.Soc.C.E., etc.; Civil and Consulting Engineer; Consulting Engineer to the Manchester Ship Canal Co. since 1910; to the Marine Board of Launceston, Tasmania; to the Greenock Harbour Trust,.etc.; *b.* 1849; *s.* of late Henry Hunter, Sunderland; *m.* 1st, 1880, Eliz. Jane (*d.* 1893), *o. d.* of late Councillor Grainger of

Sunderland; 2nd, 1895, Florence, 2nd *d.* of late William Clayton, New Ferry, Birkenhead; one *s.* two *d. Educ.:* private schools; College of Physical Science, Newcastle-upon-Tyne. After pupilage on Harbour and Dock Works, Sunderland, became, in 1872, Resident Engineer on Hylton and Monkwearmouth Railway (Durham), then Assistant Engineer on the reconstruction of Weaver Navigation (Cheshire); engaged on pioneer and parliamentary work for the Manchester Ship Canal, river Dee, etc., 1882-87; Chief Assistant Engineer on the design and construction of the Ship Canal, 1887; Chief Engineer, 1895; Member of the Board of Consulting Engineers for the Panama Canal, 1905; A Past President of the Manchester Association of Engineers, etc. *Publications:* Rivers and Estuaries; many papers published in Technical Transactions, in the Proceedings of the Navigation Congresses, etc. *Recreations:* resting and reading. *Address:* 42 Spring Gardens, Manchester; Bank House, Woodley, Cheshire. *T.:* City 1956, Manchester. *Clubs:* Whitehall; Brasenose, Engineers', Manchester.
    (Died 27 Feb. 1917.)

HUNTINGTON, Sir Charles (Philip), 3rd Bart.. *cr.* 1906; late Lieut. 3rd Batt. Royal Irish Regiment (Reserve); *b.* 17 Jan. 1888; 5th *s.* of 1st Bart. and Jane Hudson, *d.* of Walter Sparkes of Merton, Surrey; *S.* brother, 1907; *m.* 1st, 1909, Delia Dorothy (who obtained a divorce, 1922), *d.* of late Daniel John O'Sullivan of the Grange, Killarney, Co. Kerry; 2nd, 1925, Madeleine, *y. d.* of late Capt. William Birch, R.N., of Kilcool, Co. Wicklow. *Educ.:* Eton; King's College, Cambridge. Entered at the Inner Temple, 1908; called to Bar, 1911; served European War, 1914-18 (wounded). *Heir:* none. *Recreations:* golf, motoring. *Address:* The Chauntry, Burnham Abbey, Bucks. *T.:* Burnham 102. *Club:* Garrick.
    (Died 28 Jan. 1923.)

HUNTINGTON, Henry Edwards; *b.* Oneonta, N.Y., 27 Feb. 1850; *s.* of Solon Huntington and Harriet Saunders; *m.* 1st, 1873, Mary E. Prentice; 2nd, 1913, Arabella D. Huntington. *Educ.:* private and public schools. In hardware business in Oneonta and New York; lumberman, St. Albans, Va., 1874-80; superintendent of construction, Chesapeake, Ohio and South Western Railway, 1880-1884; V.P. and General Manager Ohio, and Big Sandy R.R. and Ohio Valley Rly., 1886; Assistant to President Southern Pacific Co., 1892; First V.P. Southern Pacific Co., 1900; Chairman and Director of many companies. *Address:* San Gabriel, California, U.S.A.
    (Died 23 May 1927.)

HURLE, Colonel Edward Forbes Cooke-; D.S.O. 1918; J.P. Hants, 1922; late Major Somerset Light Infantry, and Colonel Territorial Force; *b.* 1866; 3rd *surv. s.* of late J. Cooke-Hurle, Brislington Hill, near Bristol; *m.* 1st, 1893, Grace (*d.* 1908), *d.* of late T. Davey, Bannerleigh, Leigh Woods, Bristol; one *d.*; 2nd, 1913, Muriel Penelope, *d.* of Major Maitland of Bartley Manor, Southampton; one *s.* Served European War, 1914-18 (D.S.O.). *Address:* Northerwood Farm, Lyndhurst, Hants.
    (Died 21 Dec. 1923.)

HUSBAND, Thomas Fair, I.S.O. 1911; Civil Servant since 1881; *b.* Wigtown, Scotland, 5 Sep. 1862; 7th *s.* of James William Husband and Margaret Fair Anderson; *m.* 1895, Mary Sophia, *y. d.* of Samuel Gilliland and Frances Knox, Brook Hall, Co. Derry; one *d. Educ.:* Wigtown Normal School; Edinburgh University (M.A. 1881). *Publication:* (with M. F. A. Husband) Punctuation, its Principles and Practice, 1905. *Recreation:* open air. *Address:* 60B Belsize Park Gardens, N.W.3.; *T.:* Hampstead 3132. *Clubs:* National Liberal; Edinburgh University.   *(Died 24 Jan. 1921.)*

HUSON, Thomas, J.P., R.I., R.E., R.C.A.; analytical chemist, painter, etcher, and engraver; *b.* Liverpool, 18 Jan. 1844; *e. s.* of late George Canning Huson, analytical chemist; *m.* 1873, *d.* of W. Fabian; four *d. Educ.:* privately in Liverpool. An analytical chemist in Liverpool, 1864; carrying on at same time profession of painter, etcher, and engraver (now retired from profession of chemistry, and devotes his time to art pursuits). *Publications:* Six landscape mezzotints, 1880; Round about Snowdon (in conjunction with Jas. J. Hissey), 1894; Round about Helvellyn, 1895; Photoaquatint and Photogravure, 1897, and many etchings and engravings. *Recreations:* music, violin and viola, photography, mechanical pursuits, turning, and carpentry. *Address:* Pen-y-Garth, Bala, North Wales. *T.A.:* Huson, Bala. *Club:* Royal Societies.   *(Died 2 Feb. 1920.)*

HUSSEY, Col. Arthur Herbert, C.B. 1915; C.M.G. 1918; late R.A.; *b.* 2 June 1863; 3rd *s.* of late Edward Hussey, of Scotney Castle, Sussex. Entered army, 1882; Captain, 1891; Major, 1900; Lt.-Col. 1908; Colonel, 1912; Commanding R.A. Northumbrian Division, Northern Command, 1913; served S. African War, 1902 (Queen's medal 4 clasps); European War, 1914-1918 (despatches twice, C.B., C.M.G.); holds Order of Danilo (Montenegro), 2nd Class, 1917. *Club:* Naval and Military.   *(Died 27 May 1923.)*

HUSSEY-WALSH, Lt.-Col. William late Reserve of Officers; *b.* 1863; *s.* of Walter Hussey-Walsh, of Cranagh and Mul Hussey; *m.* 1892, Mary, *d.* of Mrs. Fazakerley Evered, of Wadhurst Castle, Sussex; one *d. Educ.:* France; Austria; Oratory School, Edgbaston; Sandhurst. Entered Cheshire Regt., 1884; served Burma War, Chin-Lushai Expedition, on preliminary Chinese Boundary Commission, and during Wunth-ho Rebellion; paid Attaché Intelligence Branch, Burma, 1890 (Simla despatches); retired as Captain, 1899; joined 4th Batt. Essex Regt. shortly after outbreak of S. African War, and employed with S.A. Constabulary, 1901-6; Recruiting Staff Officer, S.A.C., Cape Town, 1903-6; Major (R. of O.), 1908; Secretary to the British Branch of the Spanish Red Cross Soc. during war in Morocco, 1909 (Order of St. John Lateran); raised and trained 26 (3 Tyneside Irish) Northumberland Fusiliers and 2nd G.B. Royal Welsh Fusiliers for service abroad, 1914-15; Commandant of Cairo Citadel, 1916; Western Frontier Force, Egypt, 1917-18 (despatches); Base Commandant, Beirut, Syria (graded A.A.G.), 1918-9, and at Port Said, 1919-20; Hon. Secretary for the Levant of the Officers' Association (Lord Haig's Appeal), with headquarters at Cairo, 1920; collected in the spring of 1921 £10,900 in Egypt, the Sudan and Palestine; Order of the Nile, 1919; Officer of Crown of Italy and of French Legion of Honour, 1920; Medaille d'Honneur, France (1st Class), 1921; on Council of Naval and Military Emigration League; Fellow, R. Colonial Institute, and United Service Institute. *Recreations:* all aquatic sports, and riding, shooting and lawn tennis. *Address:* 24 Ennismore Gardens, S.W.7. *T.:* Western 4025. *Club:* Naval and Military.   *(Died 2 Jan. 1925.)*

HUTCHINS, Sir David Ernest, Kt., *cr.* 1920; J.P. (Cape), F.R.G.S.; Chief Conservator of Forests, British East Africa (retired); *b.* 22 Sep. 1850; *m.* Violet B., *d.* of Frederic J. Walker, The Priory, Bathwick, Bath; no *c. Educ.:* Blundell's, Tiverton; School of Forests, Nancy. Served ten years in the Indian Forest Service; twenty-three in that of S. Africa, and four in that of British East Africa; has a unique acquaintance with the extra-tropical forest of Africa, which extends in patches from the extreme south of the African coast to the Equator, altitude compensating latitude;

534

has specially studied extratropical trees; sent on a special mission to explore the forest girdling Mount Kenia, 1908; passed two months in the Alpine region, under the Equator, of snowy Kenia; visited Cyprus and reported to the colonial office on its forestry, 1909; made a forest tour through each of the Australian States, and prepared a study on Australian Forestry for the West Australian Government, 1914-15; made an official tour through the New Zealand Forests, and reported to the New Zealand Government, 1916; Brachlyaena Hutchinsii, one of six most valuable trees in the extra-tropical forest of Africa, has been so named at Kew. *Publications:* various works on African Forestry; Report on Forests of British East Africa, illustrated, 1909; Forests of Mount Kenia, 1907; S. African Forestry, visit of British Association to S. Africa, 1905; Extra-tropical Forestry, illustrated, 1906; Report on Transvaal Forestry illustrated, 1908; on Rhodesia, 1904; The Cluster-pine at Genadendaal; Tree-planting in Cape Colony, etc.; Cyprus Forestry, 1909; A Forest Tour in Australia; Report on Forestry to W. Australian Government, 1914-15; British Forestry; Journal of a Forest Tour (in Germany). *Recreations:* mountaineering, cycling, running, gardening. *Address:* Medo House, Cobham, Kent. *Club:* Authors'. *(Died 1920.)*

HUTCHINS, Sir Philip Percival, K.C.S.I., *cr.* 1891; *b.* London, 28 Jan. 1838; 5th *s.* of William Hutchins, and Isabella, *d.* of Honoratus Leigh Thomas, sometime President of the College of Surgeons; *m.* 1860, Fanny Annie, *d.* of B. T. Norfor. *Educ.:* Merchant Taylors' School; E.I.C. College, Haileybury. Joined Madras Civil Service, 1857; district judge of Madura, 1872-82; called to the Bar, Inner Temple, 1875; judge of the Madras High Court, 1888; member of Council, Madras, 1886; member of the Governor-General's Council, 1888-93; joined India Office, 1893, as Judicial and Public Secretary; Member of Council of India, 1898-1908; C.S.I. in 1888. *Publication:* An Indian Career, 1858-1908. *Recreations:* cricket, cycling, bowls. *Address:* Danesfort, Camberley. *T.A. and T.:* Camberley 67. *Club:* East India United Service. *(Died 21 May 1923.)*

HUTCHINSON, Colonel Charles Alexander Robert, D.S.O. 1916; F.R.G.S.; Indian Army, retired; *b.* Bulandshahr, India, 31 May 1872; *y. s.* of late Surg.-Gen. J. A. C. Hutchinson, I.M.S.; *m.* 1916, Barbara Anne Betsy, 2nd *d.* of late James Fowler Allan, Aberdeen; one *d. Educ.:* Bedford School; Sandhurst. 2nd Lieut. 18th Royal Irish Regiment, 1891; Indian Army (3rd Sikhs, Frontier force), 1896; 41st Dogras, 1900; entered the Indian Staff College, 1906; Brigade Major, Assam Brigade, 1908-12; served N.W. Frontier of India, 1897; Tochi (medal and clasp), Samana (clasp), Tirah (clasp); actions of Dargai, Sampagha Pass, Arhanga Pass, operations against Khani Khel Chamkannis and in Bazar Valley, 1897; Abor Expedition, 1911-12, General Staff Officer (despatches, Brevet Lieut.-Colonel, medal and clasp); European War, 1914 (very severely wounded, despatches, D.S.O.); retired, 1920. *Recreations:* rowing, tennis, golf, photography, and water-colour painting.   *(Died 25 July 1923.)*

HUTCHINSON, Lieut.-Gen. Henry Doveton, C.S.I. 1908; Indian army; retired; Col. 3rd (Queen Alexandra's Own) Gurkha Rifles, 1904; *b.* 13 Sep. 1847; *e. s.* of late Dr. T. Cayley Hutchinson, D.I.G. of Hospitals; *m.* 1874, Annie Alice Campbell (*d.* 1924), *sister* of Sir J. F.Stuart-Menteth, Bt.:   two *s.* Served Sikkim Campaign, 1887-88; Relief of Chitral, 1895 (medal and clasp); Tirah Campaign, 1897-98 (2 clasps); raised for service the 2nd battalion 3rd Gurkha Rifles, 1891; commanded troops in Chitral after British occupation, 1896; Director of Military Education in India, 1896-1901; Special duty (China Expedition) in the India Office, 1901-2; Assist. Military Secretary (for Indian Affairs), 1902-4; Director of Staff Duties, War Office, 1904-8. *Publications:* Military Sketching Made Easy (5th ed.); Field Fortification (5th ed.); The Story of Waterloo; The Story of 1812; The Story of Corunna; The Campaign in Tirah, 1897-98, etc. *Clubs:* United Service, Pilgrims

(Died 21 Nov. 1924.)

HUTCHINSON, Rev. Henry Neville, M.A. Camb., F.G.S., F.R.G.S., F.Z.S.; *b.* Chester, 1856; *e. s.* of Rev. T. Neville Hutchinson, late Science Master at Rugby, and Sarah K. Turner, Winson, Birmingham; *m.* 1902, Bertha, *d.* of late Daniel Sydney Hasluck, Olton Court, Warwicks. *Educ.:* Rugby; St. John's College, Cambridge. Student-Master at Clifton College, 1879-80; Curate to St. Saviour's, Redland Park, 1884; private tutor to sons of Earl of Morley, 1886-87; travelled for health; began literary work in London, 1891. *Publications:* Autobiography of the Earth, 1890; The Story of the Hills, 1891; Extinct Monsters, 1892; Creatures of Other Days, 1894; Prehistoric Man and Beast, 1896; Marriage Customs in Many Lands, 1897; Primæval Scenes, 1899; Living Races of Mankind (editor and part author of), 1900; The Living Rulers of Mankind, 1901. *Recreation:* country rambles. *Address:* 17 St. John's Wood Park, N.W.8. *T.:* Primrose Hill 3297. *M.:* XR 1172. *Club:* Royal Societies.

(Died 30 Oct. 1927.)

HUTCHINSON, Lieut. - Col. Hugh Moore, C.M.G. 1918; D.S.O. 1900; York and Lancaster Regiment; late Connaught Rangers; *b.* 18 June 1874; *s.* of late Rev. S. Hutchinson, M.A.; *m.* 1914, Eileen Millicent, *y. d.* of Minton Goode; one *s. Educ.:* Cheltenham College; Sandhurst. Entered army, 1894; served Sierra Leone, 1898-99 (medal with clasp); South Africa, 1899-1901; relief of Ladysmith (dangerously wounded, 5 wounds, 23 Feb. 1900); operations in Transvaal, Free State, and Cape Colony (severely wounded, 3 wounds, 14 July 1901, despatches, D.S.O., medal and 6 clasps); attached Egyptian army, 1902-12; commanded 12th Sudanese, 1906-12; Egypt, 1902; commanded 1st Egyptian Battalion on cholera duty (4th class Medjidieh); Sudan, operations against Nyam - Nyams (medal and clasp), 1904-5; Sudan, operations against Talodi Arabs, 1906 (clasp); Sudan, 1911; operations in Southern Kordofan (medal with clasp, 3rd class Osmanieh); European War, 1914-18 (American Distinguished Service Medal, 1914 Star, severely wounded, C.M.G.). *(Died 26 Dec. 1924.)*

HUTCHINSON, Colonel James Bird, C.S.I. 1904; Indian Army; unemployed supernumerary list, 1902-5; Member of Council of Lieut.-Governor Punjab; *b.* 22 Mar. 1844; *m.* 1869, Annie Charlotte, *d.* of Major-General Hugh Rose; four *s.* two *d. Educ.:* Blackheath Proprietary School; Cheltenham College. Joined South Lancashire Regt., 1863; served with 5th Ghoorka Rifles, 1865-68; Commissioner and Superintendent, Lahore, 1894-99; Governor, Aitchison Coll., Lahore, 1900-5; J.P. Surrey. *Address:* Waverley Drive, Camberley.

(Died 6 Sept. 1921.)

HUTCHINSON, John; *b.* Ballingham, Hereford; *s.* of Geo. Hutchinson (brother-in-law of the poet Wordsworth); *m.* 1871, Helen Taylor, *d.* of Edward Meredith, M.D., of Bath. *Educ.:* at Chelsea, under the Rev. Derwent Coleridge; Paris. Many years engaged in educational work at Harrow, Hereford, Doncaster, and other schools; Fellow of the Educational Institute of Scotland and College of Preceptors; Keeper of the Library of the Hon. Society of the Middle Temple, 1880-1909; retired, 1909. *Publications:*

Ariconia, or Recollections of Wyeside, a poem, 1858; Herefordshire Biographies, 1890; Men of Kent, 1892; Llandrindod Legends and Lyrics (under pseudonym Ladylift), 1895; The Legend of Hereford Cathedral, a poem, 1897; Notable Middle Templars, 1902; Middle Temple Records; An Inquiry into the Origin and Early History of the Inn, 1904; The Sonnets of Shakespeare, 1912; Literary Legends, 1913; contributor to Dictionary of National Biography and periodical literature. *Recreations:* fishing, ruralising, and (olim) cricket, etc. *Address:* Dullatur House, Hereford. *Clubs:* United; Hereford Constitutional.

(Died 4 April 1916.)

HUTCHINSON, Hon. Sir Joseph Turner, Kt.; *cr.* 1895; Chief Justice of Supreme Court of Ceylon, 1906-11; *b.* 1850; *m.* 1897, Constance Mary, *d.* of J. Lucas of Stapleton House, Upper Tooting. *Educ.:* St. Bees School; Christ's Coll., Cambridge (Scholar; M.A., 1876). Barr. Middle Temple, 1879; Chief Justice Gold Coast Colony, 1889; Chief Justice of Grenada, 1895-97; Chief Justice of Cyprus, 1897-1906. *Address:* Braystones, Beckermet, Cumberland. *Club:* Reform. *(Died 20 Jan. 1924.)*

HUTCHINSON, Teasdale H., agriculturist; *b.* 31 May 1837; *m.* 1880, a niece of J. B. Booth of Killerby; two *s.* (one killed in the War), two *d. Educ.:* Durham Grammar School. Commenced farming, 1865; won Royal Agricultural Society's prize for best managed farm in Yorkshire twice; has won many prizes for shorthorns and hunters. *Recreations:* hunting and riding. *Address:* Manor House, Catterick, Yorks. *T.A.:* Catterick. *(Died 27 May 1928.)*

HUTCHINSON, Maj. - Gen. William Francis Moore, R.A.; *b.* 3 Feb. 1841. Entered army, 1857; Maj.-Gen. 1898; retired, 1901; D.A.G., R.A., Headquarters, 1897-99; Commandant, Staff College, 1899-1901. *Address:* Bendemeere, Old Wish Road, Eastbourne.

(Died 22 April 1917.)

HUTCHISON, Sir George Aitken Clark, Kt.; *cr.* 1924; M.P. (U.) North Midlothian, 1922-23 and since 1924; *b.* Renfrew, 6 July 1873; *s.* late Rev. John Hutchison, D.D., Bonnington United Free Church, Leith, and late Jane, *d.* of late John Clark, Paisley; *m.* Margaret, *d.* of late John Blair, W.S., Edinburgh; three *s. Educ.:* Edinburgh Academy; Edinburgh University. Advocate, 1896; K.C. 1922; contested Argyllshire Unionist interest in 1906, 1910 (Jany.) and 1910 (Dec.); North Midlothian, 1923; J.P. Argyllshire; Honorary Sheriff-Substitute of Argyll at Oban; Director of Royal Victoria Tuberculosis Hospital Trust, Edinburgh; served Recruiting Staff and Ministry of National Service; Director of Hospital for Diseases of Women, Edinburgh; has been Vice-Commodore of Royal Clyde Yacht Club and Rear - Commodore Royal Northern and Royal Eastern and Royal Forth Yacht Clubs. *Recreations:* tennis, yachting, horticulture. *Address:* Island of Eriska, Ledaig, Argyllshire; 24 Hans Place, S.W.1; *T.:* Sloane 4320. *M.:* SB 91, SB 560. *Clubs:* Carlton, Junior Carlton, 1900; New, University, Conservative, Edinburgh; Conservative, Glasgow; numerous Yacht. *(Died 22 Dec. 1928.)*

HUTCHISON, Very Rev. Michael Balfour, Dean of Glasgow since 1908; Rector of St. Ninian, Glasgow, 1870-1920; Examining Chaplain to Bishops of Glasgow since 1881; *b.* Isle of Cumbrae, Buteshire, 18 July 1844; *s.* of John Hutchison (*b.* 1765), Burgess of Glasgow and merchant there; *m.* 1869, Margaret, o. *d.* of Rev. James Stewart, Rector of Holy Trinity, Paisley; two *s.* two *d. Educ.:* High School and University of Glasgow; Worcester and Lincoln Colleges, Oxford (B.A. 1867, M.A. 1870, D.D. 1905). Ordained, 1867; Curate

of St. Stephen, Norwich, 1869-70; Holy
Trinity, Paisley, 1870; Diocesan Inspector of
Schools, 1879-90. *Publication:* vol. of Trans-
lations of Hymns into Latin Verse, etc.
Address: The Deanery, Glencairn Drive, Pollok-
shields, Glasgow. *Clubs:* Glasgow Literary,
Provand's Lordship.

HUTCHISON, Sir Thomas, 1st Bt., *cr.*
1923; J.P., D.L., L.L.D.; Consul for Belgium
in Leith; a Brigadier of K.B.G.S., R.C.A.; *b.* 16
Dec. 1866; *e. s.* of late Robert Hutchison,
Carlowrie Castle, Kirkliston; *m* 1894, Jane
Moir Ogilvy, *d.* of late Alex. Ogilvy Spence,
banker; one *s.* *Educ.:* Collegiate School,
Edinburgh; Edinburgh University. Director
of Commercial Bank of Scotland, Ltd.;
Director of J. G. Thomson & Co., Ltd., Wine
Merchants; Chairman Longmorn Glenlivet
Distillery Co., Ltd.; Lord Provost of Edin-
burgh, 1921-23. *Recreations:* shooting. golf,
archery. *Heir:* *s.* Eric Alexander Ogilvy, *b.*
28 Feb. 1897. *Address:* 12 Douglas Crescent,
Edinburgh; Hardiston, Kinross-shire. *Clubs:*
Junior Constitutional; Caledonian United
Service, Edinburgh.   *(Died 12 April 1925.)*

HUTCHISON, William, M.A., LL.B.,
Solicitor in Glasgow; M.P. (U.) Glasgow
(Kelvingrove) since 1922; *b.* Greenock; *s.* of
William Hutchison, Printer Lithographer; *m.*
Agnes Hood, *d.* of William Grant, Dunoon; one
d. *Educ.:* Greenock Academy (dux); Glasgow
University. Most distinguished student of
his year in Law, Civil Law Prizeman and
others; contested Bridgeton Division of Glas-
gow, 1910; stood down for Coalition Liberal,
1918. *Address:* 10 University Gardens, Glas-
gow. *T.A.:* Appellants, Glasgow. *T.:* Western
Glasgow 1854. *Clubs:* Constitutional, St.
Stephen's; Conservative, Art, Glasgow.
                                    (Died 1 May 1924.)

HUTSON, Ven. Eyre; Rector, All Saint's,
St. Thomas, D.W.I. since 1872; H.B.M. Consular
Chaplain; Archdeacon of Virgin Islands; *b.*
Barbados, 6 Sep. 1830; *s.* of Rev. John Hutson.
also a native; *m.* 1858, Sarah Agnes Curll, a
native; four *s.* two *d.* *Educ.:* Codrington
College, Barbados (Scholar). Ordained 1853;
Acting Chaplain, Soc. Chapel; Curate, St.
Fernando, Trinidad; St. Thomas', and Holy
Innocents, Barbados; M.A. Emeritus; Knight
of Dannebrog; as Senior Archdeacon three
times administered the diocese during the
vacancy. *Recreation:* parish work. *Address:*
St. Thomas, Danish W. Indies.

HUTTON, Arthur Hill, Metropolitan Police
Magistrate 1906-15; *o. surv. s.* of late John
Hill Hutton of Houghton Hall, Houghton-le-
Spring, Co. Durham; *b.* 17 Mar. 1859; *m.* 1892,
Sarah Elizabeth, *niece* and adopted *d.* of late
John Edward Taylor of 20 Kensington Palace
Gardens, W. *Address:* Houghton Cottage,
Walton Heath, Surrey. *T.:* Burgh Heath 258.
Clubs: Union, Garrick.   *(Died 12 Jan. 1922.)*

**HUTTON, Lieut.-Gen. Sir Edward
(Thos. Henry)**, K.C.B., *cr.* 1912; K.C.M.G.,
cr. 1900; D.L.; retired; Colonel Commandant
The King's Royal Rifle Corps; Hon. Colonel 6th
Light Horse (N.S.W. Northern Rivers Lancers),
and 15th Light Horse (N.S.W. Mounted Rifles),
and 6th Reserve Batt. K.R.R.C. 2nd Class
Japanese Order of the Rising Sun; *b.* Torquay, 6 Dec. 1848; *s.* of Edward Thomas
Hutton, Beverley, Yorks; *m.* Eleanor, *o. d.* of
Lord Charles Paulet, and *g.d.* of 13th Marquess
of Winchester, 1889. *Educ.:* Eton. Joined 60th
Rifles 1867; Colonel, 1892; Major-General (temporary), N. S. Wales, 1893-96; Canada, 1898-1900;
South Africa, 1900; Lieut.-Gen. 1907; served
Zulu War, 1879; battle of Gingihlovo (desp.,
medal); Boer War, with Mounted Infantry,
1881; Egyptian War, 1882; Mil. Secy., and in command of Mounted Infantry, including the reconnaissance in force, 5 Aug., and other operations

at Alexandria; battle of Tel-el-Kebir (horse
killed, despatches, Brevet Major, medal and
star); Nile Expedition, 1884-85, in command of
Mounted Infantry; also on the staff; raised
and commanded Mounted Infantry at Aldershot, 1888-92; A.D.C. to the Sovereign, 1892-
1901; commanded the Military Forces, N.S.
Wales, 1893-96; president Military Conferences
in Australia, 1896; Assistant Adjutant-General,
Ireland, 1896-98; Gen. in Command of the Dominion Militia, 1898-1900; commanded the
Mounted Troops, other than Cavalry, on the
flank of Lord Roberts's advance, and subsequently an independent column in the operations in the Eastern Transvaal (despatches,
medal and 5 clasps); commanded and organised
the Military Forces of Australia, 1901-4; Gen.
of Administration Eastern Command and commanding 3rd Division, 1905-6; organized and
commanded 21st Division, 3rd Army, 1914-15.
Publications: Brief History of the K.R.R.C.;
pamphlets upon military and other questions.
Recreations: cricket, shooting, hunting. *Address:* Fox Hills, Chertsey. *T.A.:* Longcross.
T.: Long Cross 11. *Club:* United Service.
                                    (Died 4 Aug. 1923.)

HUTTON, Rev. Henry Wollaston,
M.A.; Prebendary Lincoln Cathedral since
1877; *b.* Gate Burton, Lincolnshire, 6 Nov.
1835; *s.* of Rev. H. F. Hutton, of Spridlington,
Lincolnshire; *m.* 1860, Frances Annie, *d.* of
John Bromhead, of Reepham and Lincoln;
one *s.* one *d.* *Educ.:* Southwell; Rugby; privately; Oxford. Curate of Southwell, 1859-61;
Rector of St. Mary Magdalene, Lincoln, 1862-
1877; Priest-Vicar, Lincoln, 1861-1913; Alderman of Lindsey (Lincolnshire) County Council
since 1889; J.P. Lincolnshire. *Address:* Vicars'
Court, Lincoln. *T.:* 243 Lincoln.
                                    (Died 9 Oct. 1916.)

HUTTON, John, J.P., D.L.; C. Alder-
man; *b.* Solberge, 10 Jan. 1847; *e. s.* of John
Hutton, and Caroline, *d.* of Thomas Robson,
Holtby Hall, Yorkshire; *m.* 1870, Hon. Caro-
line Shore, *d.* of 2nd Lord Teignmouth; one *s.*
Educ.: Eton; Christ Church, Oxford. M.P. (C.)
Northallerton, 1868-74; M.P. Richmond Div.
N.R. Yorkshire, 1895-1906; Chairman of North
Riding Quarter Sessions, 1892-99; and of the
County Council 1895-1915; formerly a repre-
sentative of York Diocese in House of Laymen;
formerly a Captain in North York Rifles (Militia).
Publications: Northallerton Farm Account
Book; The Columnar Farm Account Book,
pamphlets, etc. *Address:* Sowber Gate,
Northallerton. *T.A.:* Northallerton. *T.:*
Northallerton 25. *Clubs:* Constitutional;
Yorkshire, York.   *(Died 19 Dec. 1921.)*

**HUXTABLE, Lieut.-Col. Robert
Beveridge**, C.M.G. 1918; D.S.O. 1917; Aus-
tralian Army Medical Corps; *b.* 1867; *m.* 1898,
Teresa, *d.* of M. F. Shine, Dungarvan, Ireland.
Educ.: Otago; Edinburgh University, M.B.,
C.M. Served European War, 1915-18 (de-
spatches, C.M.G., D.S.O.). *(Died 11 May 1920.)*

**HUYSHE-ELIOT, Hon. Reginald
Huyshe**, M.L.C., Ceylon; *b.* 18 March 1868;
e. s. of late R. Ffolliott Eliot, J.P., D.L., and
Mary Milborough, *o. d.* of late General George
Huyshe, C.B.; *m.* 1893, Annie Buckland, *d.*
of G. B. Fletcher, Tapio, N.S. Wales; two *s.*
Assumed additional name of Huyshe by Deed
Poll, 1912. *Educ.:* privately; H.M.S. Wor-
cester; Commission, R.N.R.; engaged in tea
and rubber planting in Ceylon for past thirty
years; Assistant Commissioner for Govern-
ment of Ceylon at St. Louis Exhibition, 1904;
Member of Legislative Council since 1914, repre-
senting planting interests. *Address:* Norwood
House, Norwood, Ceylon. *Clubs:* Badminton,
Oriental, Royal Automobile. *(Died 7 Jan. 1920.)*

HYDE, Lt.-Colonel Dermot Owen,
M.B., R.A.M.C.; C.B.E., D.S.O.; O.C. British
Station Hospital, Maymyo, Burma; *b.* 1 Dec.

1877; *s.* of Lt.-Colonel Robert Hyde, A.M.S., and Jean. *d.* of Gen. Sir Patrick Craigie. K.C.B.; *m.*1908, Hilda Edith Richmond, *d.* of Lt.-Col. F. de R. Mauduit; two *s.* *Educ.*: Trinity College, Dublin, B.A., M.B., D.P.H. Received a commission in R.A.M.C., 1900; visited Australia, New Zealand and Tasmania with Imperial Representative Corps; served S. African War with Kavanagh's Column and Calwell's Column; appointed in 1911 to West Riding Division T.F., and worked on the Mobilisation Schemes of the medical units, including the Territorial General Hospitals of Leeds and Sheffield; proceeded with the Division to France and completed in 1916 five years as D.A.D.M.S. of an Infantry Division; commanded a Field Ambulance with the 5th Division during the Somme battle; O.C. No. 1 Casualty Clearing Station, 1917; A.D.M.S. 21st Division, 1918-19; appointed for three years Senior Medical Officer Bermuda, and served as a Member of the Board of Health of the Colony; returned to England, 1922, and proceeded to the Dardanelles, being appointed A.D.M.S. to 28th Division. *Recreations:* tennis, golf. *Address:* No. 2 British Infantry Lines, Maymyo, Burma; Glyn, Mills & Co., 8 Whitehall Place, S.W.1.
(*Died 19 April 1928.*)

HYDE, James Wilson, I.S.O. 1904; *b.* Paisley, 6 Feb. 1841; *s.* of John Hyde and Mary Wilson; *m.* Joanna Stuart Gibb, Glasgow; one *d.* *Educ.*: Parish School, Govan; Free Church Normal Seminary, High School, Mechanics' Institution, and School of Design, Glasgow. Appointed Clerk, P.O. Glasgow, 1860; Money Order Office, London, 1864; Secretary's Office, London, 1870; Controller, Sorting Office, G.P.O., Edin., 1878-1906; now retired. *Publications:* The Royal Mail, its curiosities and romance; A Hundred Years by Post; The Post in Grant and Farm. *Recreations:* literature, music, and painting. *Address:* c/o Chief Clerk, Sorting Office, General Post Office, Edinburgh.
(*Died 1 May 1918.*)

HYDE, William De Witt, LL.D., D.D.; President of Bowdoin Coll. since 1885; *b.* Winchendon, Mass., 23 Sept. 1858; *s.* of Joel and Eliza Hyde; *m.* Prudence M. Phillips, 1883; one *s.* *Educ.*: Phillips' Exeter Acad.; Harvard Coll. and Andover Seminary. *Publications:* Social Theology; Practical Ethics; Practical Idealism; God's Education of Man; Jesus' Way; The College Man and the College Woman; Self-Measurement; The Teacher's Philosophy; The Five Great Philosophies of Life; The Quest of the Best; The Gospel of Good Will. *Address:* Brunswick, Me., U.S.A. (*Died 29 June 1917.*)

HYMAN, Hon. Charles Smith, late Minister of Public Works for Canada; resigned, 1906; *b.* London, Ontario, 1854; *s.* of Ellis W. Hyman and Annie Niles, *d.* of late Wm. Niles, M.L.A., Canada; *m.* 1st, 1876, Elizabeth (*d.* 1917), *d.* of late John Birrell of London, Ont.; 2nd, 1918, Alexandra, *d.* of late Alexander Brenner, London, Ont. *Educ.*: Hellmuth College, London, Ont. Was Alderman and Chairman of Finance Committee of London, 1882-83; President Board of Trade, 1881-82, and Mayor in 1884; Secretary Dominion Liberal Convention, 1893; first returned to Parliament, 1891; elected London, 1900 and 1904; was Chairman of Select Standing Committee of House of Commons on Railways, Canals, and Telegraph Lines; Chairman of the Redistribution Committee of 1903; sworn of the Privy Council and made a Member of the Cabinet without portfolio, 1904; Acting Minister of Public Works, 1904-5. *Address:* Idlewild, London, Ont. *Clubs:* London, London; Toronto, Toronto; Rideau, Ottawa; St. James's, Montreal; Union, St. John. (*Died 9 Oct. 1926.*)

HYNDMAN, Henry Mayers; *b.* London, 7 Mar.1842; *e. s.* of late John Beckles Hyndman,

M.A. Trin. Coll. Cambridge, barrister-at-law (donor £150,000 to build and endow churches East End, London, see Hyndman Trustees, Clergy List), and Caroline Seyliard Mayers; *m.* 1st, 1876, Matilda Ware (*d.* 1913); 2nd, 1914, Rosalind Caroline, *o. d.* of Major Travers, Tortington House, Arundel. *Educ.*: privately; Trin. Coll. Camb. (B.A.). Sussex County Eleven, 1863-68; correspondent Pall Mall Gazette, War, 1866; friends, Mazzini, Garibaldi and Saffi, 1867; article Cavour, Fortnightly Review, 1868; Australia, New Zealand, Polynesia, America, 1869-71, wrote the leaders Melbourne Argus for free education during winning fight, 1869; journalist 1871-1874; visited America, 1874-80 at intervals; 1881, founded Social Democratic Federation; 1881-84, member Irish Land League, and Central Executive Land League of Great Britain; founded *Justice,* Unemployed agitation; debated St. James's Hall Socialism against Bradlaugh, 1884; tried Old Bailey West End Riots, acquittal; 1887-95, active agitator for social remedies; stood general election Social-Democratic candidate for Burnley, 1895; delegate and chairman at International Socialist Congress, London, 1896; Eight Hours, 1890; vigorous agitator against South African War, 1899-1900; took very active part establishing new "International" at International Socialist Congress, Paris, 1900; constant writing and speaking for justice to India, 1900 onwards; active agitator against Transvaal War, 1901-2; member of International Socialist Bureau, 1900-1910; Agitation, London and Provinces, 1903-4; Warnings against German Menace, 1905-14; contested Burnley, 1906 and 1910 (twice); Member National Workers' Committee (War Emergency), 1914-19; helped to Constitute National Socialist Party against Anti-National Socialist Groups, 1916; Member of Food Consumers' Council, 1918-20. *Publications:* Indian Policy and English Justice, 1874; Bankruptcy of India, 1878, book, 1886; England for All, 1881; Nationalisation of Land in 1772 and 1882; Historical Basis of Socialism, 1883; Emigration Fraud Exposed, 1884; Socialism and Slavery, reply to Herbert Spencer; A Commune for London, 1888; Mr. Gladstone and the Eight Hours Law; Commercial Crises of the 19th Century, 1892; Economics of Socialism, 1896; The Record of an Adventurous Life, 1911; Further Reminiscences, 1912; The Future of Democracy, 1915; The Awakening of Asia, 1919; Clemenceau: The Man and His Time, 1919; The Evolution of Revolution, 1920; Debate, Duke of Northumberland, Industrial Unrest, Committee Room, House of Commons, 1921; Marx Made Easy, 1921. *Recreations:* cricket, racquets. *Address:* 13 Well Walk, N.W.3. *T.:* Hampstead 3554. (*Died 22 Nov. 1921.*)

HYNDMAN-JONES, Sir William Henry, Kt., *cr.* 1906; Chief-Justice Straits Settlements, 1906-14; *b.* 9 Aug. 1847; *m.* 1882. *Educ.*: Marlborough; Trinity College, Cambridge; LL.B. 1870. Called to Bar, Lincoln's Inn, 1878; acting Senior Police Magistrate, and Commissioner to inquire into administration and working of Police Force, Barbadoes, 1880; acting Judge of Court of Appeal, 1880; Magistrate, 1st District, St. Lucia, 1881; Member of Executive and Legislative Council, 1881; Delegate to West Indian Telegraph Conference, 1882; acting Chief Justice of St. Lucia and Tobago, 1883; acting Attorney-General, 1883; acting Chief Justice of St. Lucia and Tobago; Member of Windward Court of Appeal, 1886; Magistrate and Member of Executive and Legislative Council, Grenada, 1887; Resident Magistrate for Westmoreland, Jamaica, 1888; St. Thomas-Ye-East, 1890; St. Catherine, 1891; City and Parish of Kingston, 1892; acting Puisne Judge, 1893; acting Attorney General and Member of Privy Council,

1895 ; Supernumerary Resident Magistrate for Jamaica, 1896 ; Puisne Judge, Straits Settlements, 1896 ; acting Judicial Commissioner for Federated Malay States in addition to other duties, 1903 ; Judicial Commissioner, F.M.S. 1904 ; Chief Judicial Commissioner, 1906 ; Chairman of Committee to draft Civil and Criminal Procedure Codes, S.S. ; President of Statute Law Revision Commission, S.S. ; President of Commission to inquire into the state of Johore Bahru Prison. *Club:* Albemarle.

(*Died 20 Aug. 1926.*)

HYSLOP, Rev. Archibald Richard Frith, M.A. ; Vicar and Rural Dean of Kingston-on-Thames, Surrogate ; Hon. Canon of Southwark Cathedral ; Examining Chaplain to the Bishop of St. Andrews ; *b.* 20 July 1866 ; *s.* of late Archibald Hyslop, J.P., of Lotus, Dumfries ; *m.* 1st, 1893, Alice Sophia (*d.* 1901), *d.* of late Dr. Maynard of Rangoon ; 2nd, 1902, Elizabeth Lucy, 2nd *d.* of Rev. W. Done Bushell, of Harrow ; one *s.* one *d. Educ.:* St. Paul's School (Captain, 1884-85) ; King's College, Cambridge (Scholar). Carus Prize, 1887 ; honourably mentioned, Porson Prize, 1888, and Chancellor's medals, 1889 ; Assistant Master in Harrow School, 1892-1902 ; ordained deacon, 1900 ; priest, 1901 ; Warden of Glenalmond, 1902-13 ; Canon of St. Ninian's, Perth, 1909-13 ; Rector of Stoke, Coventry, 1913-18. *Publications:* editor of Euripides' Andromach (Macmillan's Classical Series). *Recreations:* golf, figure-skating. *Address:* Vicarage, Kingston-on-Thames. *T.:* Kingston 0648.

(*Died 19 Oct. 1926.*)

HYSLOP, Col. James, D.S.O. 1900 ; Deputy Director Medical Services, Union of South Africa ; President Natal Medical Council, etc.; *b.* 3 Mar. 1856 ; *s.* of Thos. Hyslop, Wood Park, Kirkcudbrightshire ; *m.* 1st, 1882, Clementina Flemming Cullen Elphinstone Brown ; 2nd, Barbara, *widow* of Sir J. Steel, 1st and last Bt. *Educ.:* Hutton Hall ; Edinburgh University ; Berlin, Vienna, Munich. M.B., C.M., Edinburgh University. Formerly P.M.O., Natal Militia ; Physician Superintendent, Natal Mental Hospital ; Assistant Medical Officer, Border Counties Asylum, Melrose ; Assistant Physician, Royal Edinburgh Asylum, Morningside ; Delegate from Natal Government to Conference of South African States and Colonies on Plague, held at Pretoria, 1899 ; Chairman Plague Conference held at Durban, 1899. *Decorated* for services in South African War, 1899-1901 ; Natal Native Rebellion, 1906 (despatches). *Publication:* Investigation Anatomy of Central Nervous System. *Address:* The Huts, Pietermaritzburg, Natal. *Club:* Victoria, Pietermaritzburg.

(*Died 5 Oct. 1917.*)

HYSLOP, Sir Thomas, Kt., *cr.* 1911 ; J.P. ; *b.* Bank House, New Cumnock, Scotland, 9 Oct. 1859 ; *s.* of John Hyslop, of Bank and Agnes Kirkland ; *m.* Margaret Torrance ; one *s.* three *d. Educ.:* Ayr Academy. In business in Glasgow, 1876-82, when proceeded to Natal, where engaged in farming ; President Natal Farmers' Conference, 1899-1903 ; Member Invasion Losses Inquiry Commission, 1899-1903 ; Member for Umgeni Division, 1902-10 ; joined Hime Ministry as Treasurer, 1903 ; one of Natal delegates to Bloemfontein Customs Conference, 1903 ; delegate to Johannesburg Intercolonial Railway Conference, 1905, and Maritzburg Customs Conference, 1906 ; Treasurer in Smythe Ministry, 1905 and 1906 ; one of the Natal delegates to the National Convention in 1908 and 1909, which drafted the South African Constitution ; with other delegates proceeded to London in 1909 to afford information in connection with the Draft South Africa Act to H.M.'s Ministers ; Member of the Financial Relations Commission pro-

vided for in the South Africa Act, 1911 ; Member of the Board of Railways and Harbours of the Union of South Africa since 1914. *Address:* Commercial Road, Maritzburg, Natal. *Clubs:* Victoria, Maritzburg ; Pretoria, Pretoria.

(*Died Dec. 1919.*)

I

IBANEZ, Vicente Blasco, Spanish novelist ; Commandeur de la Legion d'Honneur ; *b.* 1867 ; *m.* 1st (wife died 1925) ; 2nd, 1925, Dona Elena Ortuzar Bulnes. *Publications:* The Shadow of the Cathedral ; The Four Horsemen of the Apocalypse ; Sonnica ; The Dead Command ; Blood and Sand ; The Fruit of the Vine ; Mare Nostrum ; Woman Triumphant ; Enemies of Woman ; The Mayflower ; The Torrent ; The Temptress ; In the Land of Art ; La Bodega ; Alfonso XIII. Unmasked, 1925 ; Queen Calafia ; The Old Woman of the Movies ; The Mad Virgins ; A Novelist's Tour of the World, 1927 ; The Pope of the Sea ; The Mob. *Address:* Villa Fontana Rosa, Menton, A.M., France. *T.A.:* Fonrosa, Menton.

(*Died 28 Jan. 1928.*)

IDDESLEIGH, 2nd Earl of (U.K.) (*cr.* 1885) ; **Walter Stafford Northcote** ; Bt. 1641 ; Viscount St. Cyres, 1885 ; *b.* 7 August 1845 ; *e. s.* of 1st Earl and Cecilia, *d.* of Thomas Farrer ; *S.* father, 1887 ; *m.* Elizabeth Lucy, *e. d.* of Sir Harry S. Meysey-Thompson, 1st Bt., 1868 ; one *d. Educ.:* Eton ; Balliol College, Oxford. Private secretary to his father, 1867-68 and 1874-77 ; member of Inland Revenue Board, 1877-92. *Publications:* Belinda Fitzwarren, 1901 ; Luck e' Lassendale, 1902 ; Charms, 1904 ; Dowland Castle, 1907 ; Ione Chaloner. Owns about 2500 acres in Devonshire. *Heir:* *n.* Henry Stafford Northcote [*b.* 1901. *Educ.:* Rugby ; Magdalen College, Oxford]. *Address:* Pynes, near Exeter. (*Died 26 May 1927.*)

IDINGTON, Hon. John ; Judge, Supreme Court, Canada, 1905, retired 1927 ; *b.* 14 Oct. 1840 ; *m.* Maggie, *d.* of George Colcleugh ; four *s.* four *d. Educ.:* Galt Grammar School ; Toronto Univ., LL.B. ; gold medallist, 1864. Barrister, 1864 ; K.C. 1876 ; Judge, High Court of Justice, Ontario, 1904. *Address:* 325 Stewart Street, Ottawa. *Club:* Rideau, Ottawa.

(*Died 7 Feb. 1928.*)

IDRIS, Thomas Howell Williams, J.P. Merioneth and London ; High Sheriff for Merioneth, 1912-13 ; M.P. (L.) Flint Boroughs, 1906-10 ; chemist and mineral water manufacturer ; *b.* Pembrokeshire, 5 Aug. 1842 ; 2nd *s.* of Benjamin Williams ; *m.* 1873, Emeline, *d.* of John Trevena, Pembroke Dock ; five *s.* one *d.*; [assumed additional surname of Idris by deed poll, 1893]. *Educ.:* National School ; privately. Member of London County Council from formation to 1906 ; Mayor of St. Pancras Borough, 1903-4 ; Director First Garden City, Ltd.; President Pharmaceutical Conference, 1903 and 1904 ; President of Public Pharmacists Association ; Fellow of Chemical Society ; Member of Society of Chemical Industry ; Freeman of City of London. *Publications:* Notes on Essential Oils (1st and 2nd editions); various papers on chemical subjects. *Recreations:* gardening and forestry. *Address:* 120 Pratt Street, Camden Town, N.W. ; Dolycae, Cader Idris, Corris R.S.O., Merionethshire. *T.A.:* Idris, London. *T.:* North 521 and 522. *M.:* XN 853. *Club:* National Liberal.

(*Died 10 Feb. 1925.*)

IPTIKHAR-UD-DIN, C.I E. 1916 ; Fakir Sayad ; Settlement Collector, Punjab, since 1910 ; joined the Service, 1886 ; Revenue Member of Council of Tonk State, 1906 ; Special duty with Amir of Afghanistan, 1906 ; British

Agent at Cabul, 1907. *Address* : Lahore, India.
(*Died 12 Jan. 1914.*)

ILBERT, Sir Courtenay Peregrine,
G.C.B., *cr.* 1911 ; K.C.B., *cr.* 1908 ; K.C.S.I.,
cr. 1895 ; C.I.E. 1882 ; C.S.I. 1885 ; Clerk
of the House of Commons, 1902 - 21 ; *b.*
12 June 1841 ; *m.* Jessie, *d.* of Rev. C.
Bradley and *niece* of Dean Bradley, 1874 ;
five *d. Educ.* : Marlborough College, Balliol
College, Oxford (Scholar, Fellow, Bursar) ;
Hertford, Ireland, Craven, Eldon Scholar.
Barr. Lincoln's Inn, 1869 ; Legal Member of
Council of Governor - General of India, 1882 -
1886 ; President of Governor-General's Council,
1886 ; Vice-Chancellor of Calcutta Univ. 1885-
1886 ; Assistant Parliamentary Counsel to the
Treasury, 1886-99 ; Parliamentary Counsel to the
Treasury, 1899-1901 ; Chairman of Statute Law
Committee ; Member of Council of Marlborough
College; of Board of Governors of London School
of Economics ; Vice-Pres. of London Library ;
J.P., Bucks. *Publications :* The Government of
India, 1898 ; Legislative Methods and Forms,
1901 ; Parliament, 1911 ; The Mechanics of
Law-making, 1914. *Address :* 24 Pelham
Crescent, South Kensington, S.W. 7 ; Trout-
wells, Penn, Bucks. *T.* : Kensington 2751.
Club : Athenæum. (*Died 14 May 1924.*)

ILIFFE, Frederick, M.A., Mus. Doc.
(Oxon) ; *e. s.* of John Iliffe ; *m.* Katherine (*d.*
1915), *d.* of Frederick Willson Marvel, Kibworth.
Educ. : Kibworth Grammar School ; privately.
Organist of St. Barnabas' Church, Oxford,
1879-83 ; St. John's College, 1883 ; Organist
to the University of Oxford, 1900-25 ; conductor of Queen's College Musical Society,
1883-1904, a number of male-voice cantatas being
composed by eminent musicians expressly for
its concerts ; Examiner for Musical Degrees
University of Oxford, 1908. *Publications :* Oratorio—Visions of St. John the Divine ; eight-part
Motett—Sweet Echo (Milton), composed for the
Cheltenham Festival Society, 1898 ; cantatas—
Morning, 1896 ; Evening, 1899 ; Power of Song,
1901 ; Via Crucis (a Lenten Cantata), 1905 ; various
anthems, services, and part songs ; Analysis of
of J. S. Bach's Das Wohltemperirte Clavier
(forty-eight preludes and fugues). *Recreations :*
canoeing, fishing, and gardening. *Address :*
18 Warnborough Road, Oxford.

(*Died 2 Feb. 1928.*)

ILSLEY, Most Rev. Edward, D.D. ;
b. Stafford, 11 May 1838. *Educ.* : Sedgley
Park ; Oscott College. Ordained, 1861 ; for
12 years Assistant Priest, Longton ; Rector
of Olton Seminary, 1873-88 ; Canon of Birmingham R.C. Cathedral, 1876 ; Bishop of Fesse,
1879-88 ; Bishop of Birmingham, 1888-1911 ;
Archbishop of Birmingham, 1911-21 ; retired,
1921. Governor of Birmingham University ;
Pres. of Birmingham Catholic Diocesan Schools
Association ; retired from all duty. *Address* :
Oscott College, Birmingham. *T.* : 890 East.
(*Died 1 Dec. 1926.*)

INAYAT-KHAN, Pir-o-Murshid, poet,
musician and philosopher ; Representative
General of the Sufi Movement ; *b.* Baroda, 1882 ;
g.s. of Moula Bux, the founder of Indian
Music Notation ; *m.* 1913, Ameena Begum ; two
s. two *d. Educ.* : Gayan Shala (Academy of
Music at Baroda). Began public career as
musician at the age of 18 and received
Gold Medals from the citizens of Madras,
Bangalore, Mysore, Rangoon, Travancore, Coimbatore, Bombay, and Calcutta ; endeavoured to
introduce a uniform system of music for all
India, and in recognition of his work in this
direction the Sangit Samilani of Bengal named
him The Morning Star of the Renaissance of
Indian Music ; received the title of Tansen
from Nizam of Hyderabad ; initiated a Sufi,
1906, by Sayed Abu Hashim Madani and thereafter made a pilgrimage to all the holy men
of India ; began to travel, 1910 ; lectured in
America, Russia, France, Switzerland, Holland,
Belgium, Germany, England, Italy, Scandinavia, and made the headquarters of his Movement in Geneva. *Publications :* A Sufi Message
of Spiritual Liberty ; Diwan of Inayat-Khan ;
Songs of India : Hindustani Lyrics : In an
Eastern Rosegarden ; Gayan ; The Inner Life ;
The Way of Illumination ; The Mysticism of
Sound ; The Soul, Whence and Whither ; The
Unity of Religious Ideals ; Sufi Mystic Philo-
sophy ; Vadan. *Recreations :* music and travel-
ling. *Address :* 51 Rue de la Tuilerie, Suresnes,
Seine, France. (*Died 5 Feb. 1927.*)

INCHES, Sir Robert Kirk, Kt., *cr.* 1915 ;
Lord Provost of the City of Edinburgh ; *b.* 16
Feb. 1840 ; *s.* of Robert Inches and Sarah
Johns ; *m.* 1868 ; two *s.* two *d. Educ.* : Royal
High School, Edinburgh. King's Clockmaker
for Scotland ; Senior Partner of Hamilton &
Inches, Goldsmiths, Edinburgh ; Lord Provost,
Past Bailie and Judge of Police ; Treasurer
Edinburgh Merchant Company ; Chairman
Royal Tradesmen ; Member of the Court of the
Clockmakers' Co., London ; Deputy Lieutenant
of County of City of Edinburgh ; Extra-
ordinary Director of the National Bank, and
Scottish Widows' Fund ; Senior Elder of St.
Giles' Cathedral, Edinburgh. *Address :* Strath-
earn House, Edinburgh. *Clubs :* Junior Con-
stitutional ; Scottish Conservative, Edinburgh.
(*Died 19 July 1918.*)

INFIELD, Henry John, J.P. ; Newspaper
Proprietor. Has for more than 30 years
taken an active interest in Newspapers
and other Publications, and been closely
associated with many and varied commercial
undertakings. Started the first halfpenny
Morning Daily Newspaper in the United Kingdom at Brighton, 1868 ; converted the halfpenny daily into an enlarged penny paper, the
Sussex Daily News, in 1873, at the same time
issuing an evening edition at a halfpenny ;
established the Southern Weekly News, 1876 ;
published the Evening Argus, a halfpenny
paper, 1880 ; and the Morning Argus, a halfpenny morning paper, in 1896 ; converted his
business into the Southern Publishing Co.
Ltd., of which he is chairman and permanent
director ; chairman Ingram and Royle, Ltd.,
London, importers and exporters of natural
mineral waters ; Brighton Theatre Royal, Ltd. ;
and The Brighton Grand Hotel Co., Ltd. ; director of the Brighton West Pier Co. ; Brighton,
Hove, and Preston United Omnibus Co. Ltd. ;
Hanningtons, Ltd., Brighton ; and is a member of the Southern Counties Board of the
Liverpool and London and Globe Insurance
Company, Ltd. *Recreation :* motoring. *Ad-
dress :* 130 North Street, Brighton. *Clubs :*
Reform, Royal Automobile ; New, Brighton.
(*Died 24 July 1921.*)

INGHAM, Rt. Rev. Ernest Graham,
M.A., D.D. ; Vicar of St. Jude's, Southsea,
since 1912 ; *b.* 1851 ; *s.* of late Hon. S. S.
Ingham, Speaker of House of Assembly,
Bermuda. *Educ.* : Bishop's College School,
Lennoxville, Canada ; St. Mary Hall (now
Oriel College), Oxford. Organizing Secre-
tary C.M.S. for West Yorks, 1878-80 ; Vicar
of St. Matthew's, Leeds, 1880-83 ; Bishop of
Sierra Leone, 1883-97 ; Rector of Stoke-next-
Guildford, 1897-1904 ; Rural Dean, 1904 ; Home
Secretary Church Missionary Society, 1904-12 ;
Proctor in Convocation for Diocese of Win-
chester. *Publications :* Sierra Leone after a
Hundred Years, 1894 ; From Japan to Jerusalem,
1911 ; Sketches in Western Canada, 1913. *Ad-
dress :* St. Jude's Vicarage, Southsea.
(*Died 9 April 1926.*)

**INGHAM, His Honour Judge Robert
Wood**, D.L., J.P. ; Judge of County Court,
Circuit 22, since 1892 ; *b.* 1846 ; 2nd *s.* of Sir
James Taylor Ingham ; *m.* 1876, Mary, *d.* of

Rev. J. D. Penrose; four *s.* one *d.* Barr. Inner Temple, 1873. *Address:* Sugwas Court, Hereford. *(Died 10 Jan. 1928.)*

INGILBY, Sir William, 3rd Bt., *cr.* 1866; of Ripley Castle, Yorkshire, and Harrington Hall, Spilsby, Lincoln; *b.* 13 Dec. 1829; *y. s.* of 1st Bart. and Elizabeth, 2nd *d.* of Day Hort Macdowall; *S.* brother, 1911; *m.* 1874, Eleanor Isabella, *d.* of late Henry Macdowall of Garthland, Co. Renfrew; two *s.* (twins). *Educ.:* Addiscombe. Formerly Lieut. in Bengal Horse Artillery; J.P. West Riding, Yorkshire. *Heir:* *s.* William Henry Ingilby [Bt. Lt.-Col. Scots Guards; *b.* 28 Dec. 1874; *m.* 1906, Hon. Alberta Diana, 3rd *d.* of 1st Baron Swansea; one *s.*]. *Address:* Ripley Castle, Harrogate. *T.:* Ripley 3. *Club:* Boodle's. *(Died 17 Dec. 1918.)*

INGLEBY, Holcombe, J.P., M.A., *b.* 18 March, 1854; 2nd *s.* of late Clement Mansfield Ingleby, LL.D.; *m.* 1886, Harriet Jane, *d.* of late C. F. Neville-Rolfe; one *s.* one *d.* *Educ.:* Corpus Christi College, Oxford. Mayor of King's Lynn, 1909-10 and 1919-22; High Sheriff of Norfolk, 1923; edited the Red Register of Lynn; M.P. (C.) King's Lynn, 1910-18. *Address:* Sedgeford Hall, Norfolk. *T.:* Snettisham 3. *T.A.:* Sedgeford. *Clubs:* Athenæum; Norfolk. Norwich. *(Died 6 Aug. 1926.)*

INGLEFIELD, Admiral Sir Frederick Samuel, K.C.B., *cr.* 1911; F.R.G.S.; a Younger Brother of the Trinity House; D.L. J.P. Derbyshire; *s.* of late Col. S. H. S. Inglefield, R.A.; *b.* 1854; *m.* 1903, Cecil, *d.* of J. G. Crompton, D.L., J.P., of Flower Lilies, Derbyshire; two *s.* Entered navy, 1868; Rear-Admiral, 1906; retired voluntarily, June 1916; served Egypt, 1882 (medal, bronze star); Suakim, 1884-1885 (clasp); Assistant Director of Naval Intelligence, 1902-4; Naval A.D.C. to King Edward, 1905-6; a Lord of Admiralty, 1904-7; commanded 4th Cruiser Squadron, 1907-9; Admiral commanding Coast Guard and Reserves, 1909-12; Grand Officer of the Crown of Italy, 1910 (Messina, 1908). *Address:* Flower Lilies, Windley, Derbyshire; 15 Beaufort Gardens, E.W.3. *Clubs:* United Service; Derby County. *(Died 8 Aug. 1921.)*

INGLES, Rev. David, M.A., Vicar of Witham, 1886-1915; Hon. Canon of St. Albans, 1893; *b.* 28 May 1836; *m.* Clementina Louisa (*d.* 1918); six *d.* *Educ.:* Trinity College, Cambridge. Curate of Chorleywood, 1861-62; Stoke-on-Trent, 1862-64; Cookham Dean, 1864-67; Frogmore End, 1867-70; Vicar of Apsley End, Herts 1872-74; Halstead, 1874-86. *Recreations:* in Cambridge University Boat, 1860, which won; in First Trinity Boat, Henley, 1860, which won Grand Challenge and Stewards Cups; won University Sculls, 1858, University Pairs, 1859; Captain of the Sheringham Golf Club, 1903-4. *Address:* The Priory, Brentwood, Essex. *(Died 14 Jan. 1921.)*

INGLIS, Captain Arthur McCulloch, D.S.O. 1916; Gloucestershire Regt. (attached Tank Corps, as temp. Major); *b.* 14 July 1884. *Educ.:* Cheltenham College. Lt. 3rd Batt. Wiltshire Regt. 1901; in St. Helena till the end of S. African War; joined 2nd Batt. Gloucestershire Regt. 1906; A.D.C. to Sir Henry L. Galway, Governor of Gambia, 1911; joined the Gambia Co. West African Frontier Force, 1913; served on the G.O.C.'s Staff (Gen. Dobell) in Cameroons till May 1916; joined the Tank Corps, July 1916, since in France (D.S.O.). *Recreations:* games and shooting. *Address:* Inglisby, Prestbury, Gloucestershire. *Clubs:* Army and Navy, Sports. *(Died 12 May 1919.)*

INGLIS, Col. Henry Alves, C.M.G. 1918; retired pay,- late R.A.; *b.* 5 Oct. 1859; *s.* of Thomas Inglis, M.D., H.E.I.C.S.; *m.* 1899, Ethel, *d.* of George Robinson of Green Lane, Dalston, Cumberland. J.P. Cumberland. Entered army, 1879; retired, 1910; served

Afghan War 1879-80, including relief of Kandahar (medal and clasp, bronze star); Zhob Valley Expedition, 1884; commanded R.A., Weymouth, 1914-18. *Address:* Green Lane, Dalston, Cumberland. *(Died 17 Feb. 1924.)*

INGLIS, Lt.-Col. Sir Robert William; Kt., *cr.* 1910; V.D.; President of the Stock Exchange Rifle Club; *b.* 22 July 1843; 5th *s.* of late Rev. Robert Inglis, M.A., Edzell, Forfarshire; *m.* 1st, 1869, Ellen Rose (*d.* 1916); no *c.*; 2nd 1919, Rebecca, *y.d.* of late Frederick William Fairclough, Southwark. *Educ.:* Free Church Normal School, Edinburgh. Member of the Stock Exchange, 1872; dinner chairman of Benevolent Fund, 1895; member of the General Purposes Committee, 1895; Chairman, 1907-17; Member of Benevolent Fund Committee, 1896; Chairman since 1907; Queen's Edinburgh Rifle Volunteers, 1859-1866; Ensign London Irish Rifles, 1872; promoted to Lieutenant, Captain, and Major, and retired with rank of Lieut.-Col. and right to wear the uniform, 1891; erected, endowed, and presented the Inglis Memorial Hall, Edzell, with 8500 volume Library and Parish Council Rooms, 1898; built and endowed the Rifle and Revolver Club, Borers' Passage, Devonshire Square, E., for use of the Stock Exchange Rifle Club, and the city banks rifle clubs, insurance offices, etc., 1903-4. *Recreations:* shooting, fishing. *Address:* Craigendowie, Reigate.
(Died 10 April 1923.)

INGPEN, Arthur Robert, LL.B., K.C.; 4th *s.* of Robert Frederick Ingpen; married. *Educ.:* London University. Called to Bar, Middle Temple, 1879, and Lincoln's Inn (*ad eundem*); Q.C. 1900; Bencher of Middle Temple, 1907. *Publications:* Joint Editor with late Lord Justice Vaughan Williams of the 10th ed. of Williams on the Law of Executors and Administrators (2 vols.); author of A Concise Treatise on the Law relating to Executors and Administrators; joint-author of titles Copyholds and Copyright and Literary Property in The Laws of England, edited by Lord Halsbury; joint-editor of the 7th ed. of Seton on Judgments and Orders (3 vols.); editor of Master Worsley's Book on the History of the Middle Temple; author of Middle Temple Bench Book, and of An Ancient Family: a Genealogical Study. *Address:* 12 New Square, Lincoln's Inn, W.C. *T.:* Central 9858. *Club:* Junior Carlton. *(Died 5 Sept. 1917.)*

INGRAM, John H.; *b.* London, 16 Nov. 1849. Has travelled over various parts of Europe, and is conversant with the languages and literatures of several countries. *Publications:* Flora Symbolica, 1868; edited Poe's Works with Memoir, 1874; Life of E. A. Poe, 1880; Philosophy of Handwriting, 1879; The Bird of Truth, from Spanish of Fernan Caballero, 1881; Claimants to Royalty, 1882; Eminent Women Series, edited, 1883, etc.; Haunted Homes, 1883, 2nd series, 1884; Oliver Madox-Brown, a Biography, 1884; Poe's Tales and Poems, with Biographical Essay, 1884; Poe's Poems and Essays, with new Memoir (Tauchnitz edition), 1884; Poe's Tales (Tauchnitz edition) 1884; The Raven, edited with Commentary, 1885; Poe's complete Poetical Works, annotated, with Memoir, 1888; E. B. Browning's Poetical Works, with Memoir, 1886; Life of E. B. Browning, 1888; annotated edition of Lockhart's Life of Burns, 1890; Darley's May Queen, with Biographical Sketch, 1892; Christopher Marlowe and his Associates, 1904; Poe's Poems, with sketch of the author, 1909 (The Muses Library); Chatterton, a Biography, 1910; Marlowe and his Poetry, 1914; Chatterton and his Poetry, 1915; Editor of Eminent Women Series; contributor to leading reviews of Europe and America. *Address:* 1 Hollingbury Terrace, Preston, Brighton. *(Died Feb. 1916.)*

INGRAM, Thomas Allan, M.A., LL.D.; Editor Hazell's Annual since 1913; *b.* Castlederg, 26 July 1870; *e. s.* of Wm. Ingram, Letterkenny, Co. Donegal; *m.* Alice E., *y. d.* of R. J. Martin; one *s.* three *d. Educ.*: Elphin Grammar School; Trinity College, Dublin. Departmental Editor, Law and Economics, Encyclopædia Britannica, 1903-12; formerly in business; Alderman of the Woolwich Borough Council; Governor of the Woolwich Polytechnic; etc. *Publications:* Adam Smith on Free Trade and Protection; Woolwich Records (joint author); many articles in Encyclopædia Britannica, monthlies (Fortnightly, etc.), and daily press. *Recreations:* freemasonry, gardening, photography. *Address:* 17 Warwick Square, E.C.4.; 27 Wrottesley Road, Woolwich.
(Died 28 July 1922.)

INGRAM, Capt. Thomas Lewis, M.A. Cantab., M.R.C.S., L.R.C.P., D.S.O. 1916; R.A.M.C. attached 1st King's Shropshire Light Infantry; *b.* Brighton, 1875; *e. s.* of T. Lewis Ingram, of The Priory, Wimbledon Common, S.W.; *m.* 1909, Lilian, *e. d.* of late Lt.-Col. Donnithorne, Scots Greys; one *s.* one *d. Educ.:* Monkton Combe, Bath; Trinity College, Cambridge; London Hospital. Served S. African War as trooper in 34th Coy. Imperial Yeomanry (Middlesex) (Queen's medal with three clasps); M.R.C.S., L.R.C.P. 1903; House Surgeon at Poplar Hospital, 1903 - 4; Senior House Surgeon Westminster Hospital, 1905; Medical Practice at Welford, near Rugby, 1906-14; Commission R.A.M.C. Sep. 1914; served European War, 1914-16 (wounded, despatches, Military Cross, D.S.O.). *Recreations:* hunting, fishing, shooting. *Address:* Welford, near Rugby. *T.A.:* Welford. *T.:* Welford 4 *M.:* LC 7260.
(Died Sept. 1916.)

INGRAM, Sir William James, 1st Bt., *cr.* 1893; late Managing Director Illustrated London News and Sketch, Limited; *b.* 27 Oct. 1847; *s.* of late Herbert Ingram, M.P. Boston, originator of Illustrated London News, and Anne, *d.* of William Little, Eye (who afterwards married Sir E. Watkin, 1st Bt.); *m.* Mary, *d.* of Hon. Edward Stirling, Adelaide, 1874; three *s. Educ.:* Winchester; Trin. Coll. Camb. Barr-Inner Temple, 1872. M.P. (L.) Boston, 1874-1880, 1885-86, and 1892-95. *Heir: s.* Herbert [*b.* 26 Sep. 1875; *m.* 1908, Hilda Vivian, *d.* of late Col. Carson Lake, New York; one *s.* one *d. Address:* Tayside, Westgate - on - Sea. *Clubs:* Devonshire, Bath]. *Address:* The Bungalow, Westgate-on-Sea; 65 Cromwell Road, S.W.; 198 Strand, W.C. *Club:* New University.
(Died 18 Dec. 1924.)

INMAN, Arthur Conyers, M.A., M.B., B.Ch. (Oxon); Superintendent of the Laboratories of the Brompton Hospital for Diseases of the Chest, London, since 1907; *b.* 1879; *e. s.* of Rev. H. T. Inman, M.A. (Cantab.), 69 Warwick Road, Kensington, S.W.; *m.* 1st, 1909, Dorothy Marguerite (*d.* 1917), *o. c.* of F. J. Wethered, M.D.; 2nd, 1919, Colette, *y. d.* of M. Frey, Paris. *Educ.:* Haileybury; St. Edward's School, Oxford; Wadham College, Oxford; St. Thomas's Hospital, London; Marburg; Dresden; Paris. B.A. (Oxon), Honour Schools of Nat. Science, 1900; M.A., M.B., B.Ch. (Oxon), 1904; held resident appointments at St. Thomas's Hospital and Brompton Hospital; Hilfärztlicher Externat, Pathological Dpt. Dresden; worked at the Pasteur Institute, Paris, in the laboratories of late Prof. Metchnikoff; went on special duty to Nepal in 1909 and 1920; Hon. Capt. R.A.M.C., Specialist Bacteriologist in B.E.F. during European War. *Publications:* numerous contributions on scientific subjects in English, American, German, and French scientific journals. *Recreations:* travelling, golf. *Address:* 27 Cornwall Gardens, S.W.1. *T.:* Western 2023; Ken. 2075. *Clubs:* Oxford and Cambridge, M.C.C.
(Died 9 June 1926.)

INMAN, Canon Edward, M.A.; Canon and Prebendary of Salisbury Cathedral; *s.* of T. Gibson Inman, Barrister, J.P.: *m.* 1867, Eleanora M., *d.* of Rev. S. Slade-Gully, Rector of Berrynarbor, Devon; M.A., J.P. of Trevennen House, Cornwall; two *s.* two *d. Educ.:* Oriel College, Oxford. Rector of W. Knoyle, Wilts, 1872 - 82; Vicar of Gillingham, Dorset, with Motcombe, Enmore Green, E. Stour, W. Stour, and Milton, 1882-91; Vicar of Potterne, Wilts, and Rural Dean of Potterne, 1891-1900. *Address:* Sandecotes Lodge, Parkstone. Dorset. *T.A.:* Parkstone. *(Died 14 May 1924.)*

INNES, Sir James, 13th Bt., *cr.* 1628; *b.* 20 Jan. 1846; *s.* of 11th Bt. and Elizabeth, *d.* of Alexander Thurburn of Keith; *S.* brother 1912. *Heir: n.* James Bourchier; *b.* 1883. *Address:* Edengight House, Keith, Banffs. *Club:* Junior Constitutional. *(Died 7 Jan. 1919.)*

INNESS, George, painter; *b.* Paris, France, 5 Jan. 1854; *s.* of George Inness; *m.* Julia G. Roswell - Smith. *Educ.:* under his father in Rome; Paris. Exhibited annually at Paris Salon; hon. mention, Paris Salon, 1896, and gold medal, 1900; Officier Academie des Beaux Arts, Paris, 1902; A.N.A. 1895; N.A. 1899. *Publications:* Art, Life, and Letters of George Inness, 1917. *Address:* Tarpon Springs, Florida; Cragsmoor, Ulster Co., N.Y., U.S.A.
(Died 27 July 1926.)

INVERCLYDE, 3rd Baron, *cr.* 1897; **Sir James Cleland Burns,** 4th Bt., *cr.* 1889; J.P. Lanarkshire, Renfrewshire, and County of City of Glasgow; Lord-Lieut. Dunbartonshire; D.L. Renfrewshire; *b.* 14 Feb. 1864; 2nd *s.* of 1st Baron and Emily, *d.* of G. C. Arbuthnot of Mavisbank; *S. b.* 1905; *m.* 1891, Charlotte Mary Emily, *y. d.* of late Robert Nugent-Dunbar of Machermore Castle, Co. Kirkcudbright; one *s.* two *d. Educ.:* Repton. Hon. Colonel Clyde Royal Garrison Artillery; Hon. Colonel, 1st Cadet (Dunbartonshire) Battalion, A. & S. Highlanders; Commander, R.N.V.R.; Principal Director Shipping Firm of G. & J. Burns, Ltd.; Chairman Burns S.S. Company, Limited; a Director Cunard Steamship Company, Ltd.; Deputy-Chairman, The Clydesdale Bank, Limited; and Director of Clyde Steamship Owners' Association; President Chamber of Shipping of United Kingdom, 1899; Chairman of Glasgow Shipowners' Association since 1900; Hon. Member Advisory Committee on New Lighthouse Works, etc.; Member of Lloyd's Register General Committee, London, and Local Committee, Glasgow; Associate Member of Council. Institution of Naval Architects; Associate Member Institution of Engineers and Shipbuilders in Scotland; Warden of the Worshipful Company of Shipwrights; Chairman Glasgow City Mission; Commodore Royal Clyde Yacht and Royal Largs Yacht Clubs; Vice-Commodore Royal Northern Yacht Club; President Dumbartonshire Volunteer Force. *Heir: s.* Hon. John Alan Burns. *Recreations:* shooting, yachting, curling, lawn-tennis (President Scottish Hockey Association). *Address:* Castle Wemyss, Wemyss Bay, Renfrewshire; Hartfield, Cove, Dunbartonshire; 10 Berkeley Square, W.1. *T.A.:* Inverclyde, c/o Burns, Glasgow. *T.:* Kilcreggan 7; Wemyss Bay 4; Mayfair 3048. *Clubs:* Travellers', Carlton, Royal Thames Yacht; Royal Yacht Squadron, Cowes; Ulster. Belfast; Western. Glasgow; New. Edinburgh. *(Died 16 Aug. 1919.)*

IPSWICH, Viscount, William Henry Alfred Fitzroy; Lieut. 5th (Reserve) Batt. Coldstream Guards; *b.* 24 July 1884; *e. s.* of Earl of Euston; *m.* 1913, Auriol, *o. d.* of Major Brougham, Potters Pury House, Northants; one *s.* one *d. Educ.:* Harrow; Trinity College, Cambridge. *Heir: s.* John Charles William Fitzroy; *b.* Aug. 1914. *Address:* Whittlebury, Towcester; 11 Alfred Place West. S.W *Club:* Guards'. *(Died 23 April 1918.)*

541

IREDELL, Lt.-Gen. Francis Shrubb; b. 1837; s. of late Lieut.-Col. F. M. Iredell; m. 1867, Katharine Helen, d. of John Green, Dublin, and g.d. of Hon. Edward Massy of Chester, and of Ballynort, Co. Limerick; one s. two d. Educ.: Cheltenham College. Served Indian Mutiny, 1857-58; Kathiawar, 1860-61; Afghan War, 1880-81; Lt.-Gen. Indian Army, U.S. List, 1898; Colonel, 114th Mahrattas, 1903. Address: Vernon Lodge, Preston Park, Brighton. Club: Junior Conservative. (Died 10 Nov. 1924.)

IRELAND, Most Rev. John, R.C. Archbishop of St. Paul since 1888; b. Ireland, 11 Sep. 1838. Educ.: Cathedral School, St. Paul; Petit Seminaire, Meximeux; Grand Seminaire, Hyeres, France. Ordained Priest, 1861; co-adjutor Bishop, St. Paul, 1875. Publication: The Church and Modern Society, 1896. Address: 977 Portland Avenue, St. Paul, Minn. U.S.A. (Died 25 Sept. 1918.)

IRELAND, Col. Sir Robert Megaw, K B.E., cr. 1919; C B. 1911; C.M.G. 1900; Army Pay Department; retired, 1911; b. 5 June 1849; s. of R. S. Ireland, M.D.; m. 1872, Evaline Alice, d. of Col. EardleyHoward, B.S C.; two s. four d. Served South Africa, 1899-1902 (despatches, Queen's medal, 6 clasps, King's medal, 2 clasps, C.M.G.) Address: Montrose, Yarborough Road, Southsea. (Died 3 Sept. 1919.)

IRVINE, Lieut.-Col. Acheson Gosford, I.S.O. 1908; y. s. of late Lieut.-Col. J. G. Irvine, many years Principal A.D.C. to Governors - General of Canada; b. 1837. Educ.: Quebec. Is Lt.-Col. (retired) Canadian Militia; served Fenian Raids, Canada, 1866 and 1870; with Red River Expedition, 1870, as Major 2nd Battalion or Quebec Rifles (medal with three clasps); North - West Rebellion, 1885 (medal); commanded Dominion Troops in Manitoba, 1871-74; and was a member of Lieut.-Governor's Administrative Council of N.W. Territories of Canada, 1882-87; a Vice-President of the American Prison Association; Assistant Commissioner North-West Mounted Police, Canada, 1875; Commissioner, 1880, and Warden of Manitoba Penitentiary, 1892; first President Manitoba Rifle Association (which he organised), 1871; President of Red River Expedition Association, 1895; Warder, Kingston Penitentiary, 1913. Club: Frontenac, Kingston, Canada.

IRVINE, Alexander Forbes, D.L., J.P.; b. 17 Aug. 1881; e. s. of late Francis Hugh Forbes Irvine and Mary Agnes, o. d. of John Ramsay of Barra, N.B.; m. 1905, Dorothy Isabel, 2nd d. of late Col. Henry Crawford of Rothie Norman, Aberdeenshire; five s. Educ.: Winchester; New College, Oxford (Hons. Modern History). Address: Drum Castle, Drumoak S.O., Aberdeenshire. (Died 29 April 1922.)

IRVINE, Admiral Sir St. George Caufield D'Arcy-, K.C.B., cr. 1902; C.B. 1882; b. 23 May 1838; m. 1868, Katherine, o. d. of late Vice-Admiral Sir Horatio Austin. Entered R.N. 1845; Admiral, 1897; served Nicaragua; China; Crimea, 1854-55 (Crimean and Turkish medals, Sebastopol clasp, Baltic medal); Turco-Russian War, 1878; bombardment Alexandria, 1882 (C.B., Egyptian medal, Khedive's bronze star). Address: 2 Hans Crescent Mansions, S.W. Club: United Service. (Died 2 July 1916.)

IRVING, Charles John; C.M.G., 1881; retired Government officer; b. 7 Feb. 1831; m. 1866, Mary Jane, d. of Charles Tompkins; three s. one d. Colonial Land and Emigration Office, 1852-53; clerk, Audit Office, 1853-64; special clerk, Audit Office, Mauritius, 1864-67; auditor-general, Straits Settlements, 1867-79; resident councillor, Malacca, 1879-82; Penang, 1882-87. Address: Sarlsdown, Exmouth. (Died 23 Feb. 1917.)

IRVING, Dan, M.P. (Soc.) Burnley since Dec. 1918; b. 1854; m. 1882, d. of Henry Brock, Bristol. Was in Mercantile Marine and a railway servant; Secretary and agent to the Socialist Party for over twenty years; contested Accrington, Rochdale, and North-West Manchester. Address: 80 Glen View Road, Burnley, Lancs. (Died 25 Jan. 1924.)

IRVING, Henry Brodribb, actor-manager; b. London, 5 Aug. 1870; e. s. of late Sir Henry Irving, Kt., and Florence, d. of Surg.-Gen. O'Callaghan; m. 26 July 1896, Dorothea, d. of John Forster Baird, barrister - at - law. Miss Baird appeared as Trilby at the Haymarket Theatre, 1895, and left the stage in 1912; one s. one d. Educ.: Marlborough College; New College, Oxford; M.A. Appeared first on stage at Garrick Theatre in School, 1891; called to Bar, Inner Temple, 1894; lessee Shaftesbury Theatre, 1903; Queen's Theatre, 1909-11; Australian tour, 1911-12; South African tour, 1912-13; Lessee of Savoy Theatre since 1913. Publications: The Life of Judge Jeffreys, 1898; French Criminals of the 19th Century, 1901; Occasional Papers, 1906; The Trial of Franz Müller, 1911; Trial of Mrs. Maybrick, 1913; A Book of Remarkable Criminals, 1918. Address: 10 Sudbury Hill, Harrow. T.: Harrow 164; The Mill, Whitstable. Clubs: Athenæum, Garrick, Beefsteak. (Died 17 Oct. 1919.)

IRVING, Sir Henry Turner, G.C.M.G., cr. 1888; b. 1833; m. 1884, Emma P. (d. 1903), d. of Sir D. Barclay, 10th Bt., and widow of Sir H. F. F. Johnson, 3rd Bt. Entered Colonial Office, 1854; Colonial Secretary of Jamaica, 1866-69; of Ceylon, 1869; Governor of Leeward Islands, 1873-74; of Trinidad, 1874-1880; of British Guiana, 1882-88. Address: The Gap, Westhill, Ottery St. Mary, Devon. (Died 22 Nov. 1923.)

IRVING, Hon. Paulus Æmilius, D.C.L.; Puisne Judge, Victoria, British Columbia; b. 3 Apr. 1857; 3rd s. of Sir Æmilius Irving, Toronto; m. 1883, Diana, d. of Hon. W. Hamley; two s. two d. Educ.: Trinity College School, Port Hope; Trinity College, Toronto. B.A., 1877; M.A., B.C.L., 1880. Called to Bar of Ontario, 1880; British Columbia, 1882; Deputy Attorney-General, B.C., 1883-90; Puisne Judge of Supreme Court of British Columbia, 1897; as special commissioner he settled mining disputes in Atlin, B.C., 1899; his services on this occasion were acknowledged in the speech from the throne (vide B.C. Sessional papers, 1890); promoted to Court of Appeal, 1909. Address: Halwyn, 29 Richardson Street, Victoria, B.C. Clubs: Union, Victoria, B.C; Vancouver, Vancouver, B.C. (Died 4 Feb. 1916.)

IRVING, Rev. Robert, M.A.; Vicar of Christ Church, Sefton Park, Liverpool, since 1877; Hon. Canon of Liverpool since 1896; b. Bracken Hill, near Longtown, 1840; y. s. of Wm. Irving; m. 1872, Anne Maria, d. of Peter Tasker, merchant, Liverpool; two s. one d. Educ.: Sedbergh; Christ's Coll. Camb. Graduated, 1863; first class ordinary B.A.; Deacon, 1864; Priest, 1866; Curate of St. Matthias, Salford, 1864-66; St. Saviour, Liverpool, 1866-71; Curate and Ev. Lect. Walton-on-the-Hill, 1871-73; in charge of St. Mary, Wavertree, Liverpool, 1873-77; Hon. Sec. Local Charities since 1878; Member of Toxteth School Board before its dissolution; Examiner for Liverpool School Board, 1876 and 1877; Rural Dean, Toxteth, 1908; President Liverpool Clerical Society. Publications: sermons on Future Punishment, Working Men's Clubs, Sundry papers. Recreations: cricket, boating, football, cycling. Address: 25 Ivanhoe Road, Sefton Park, Liverpool.

IRVING, Rev. Thomas Henry, Vicar of Hawkshead and Rural Dean of Ambleside since

1909; Hon. Canon of Carlisle, 1913; *b.* 21 Dec. 1856; *s.* of Rev. James Irving and Isabella Lawson; *m.* Margaret Anne, 2nd *d.* of late James Varley, The Croft, St. Helens; two *s.* one *d. Educ.:* St. Bees; St John's College, Cambridge. Curate of Farlam, 1879; Kendal, 1885; Vicar of Lindale in Cartmel and Rural Dean of Cartmel, 1889. *Address:* Hawkshead Vicarage, Ambleside.   (*Died 11 Nov. 1926.*)

IRWIN, Sir Alfred (Macdonald Bulteel), Kt., *cr.* 1910; C.S.I. 1904; *b.* 26 Dec. 1853; *s.* of Ven. Henry Irwin, B.D., Archdeacon of Elphin; *m.* 1884, Alice Kathleen (*d.* 1809), *d.* of Christopher French, J.P., D.L., of Clooniquin, Co. Roscommon; one *s.* two *d. Educ.:* Kingstown School, Co. Dublin. Indian Civil Service, Panjab, 1876; Burma, 1877; Deputy Commissioner, 1886; Commissioner, 1898; Acting Judge, Lower Burma Chief Court, 1902; Member of Legislative Council, Burma, 1903; Acting Judicial Commissioner, Upper Burma, 1908; Judge, Lower Burma Chief Court, 1905-9; Acting Chief Judge, 1908; retired, 1909. *Publications:* The Burmese Calendar, 1901; The Burmese and Arakanese Calendars, 1909. *Address:* 49 Ailesbury Road, Dublin. *T.:* Ballsbridge 110. *Club:* University, Dublin.   (*Died 1 Feb. 1921.*)

IRWIN, Colonel De la Cherois Thomas, C.M.G. 1901; Hon. A.D.C. to Earl of Minto and Earl Grey, Governors-General; late Hon. Secretary Canadian Patriotic Fund Association; retired, Royal Canadian Artillery; *b.* Armagh, Ireland, 31 March 1843; *m.* 1367, Isabella (*d.* 1926), *d.* of Robert Hamilton of Hamwood, Quebec; three *s.* one *d. Educ.:* privately; Royal Military Academy, Woolwich. Entered Royal Artillery, 1861; retired as Lt.-Col. 1882; entered Canadian Military Service, 1872; retired, 1909; R.M. Staff College, 1871-72; Inspector of Artillery for Dominion of Canada, 1882-98; commandant Royal School of Artillery, 1873-82; commanding Royal Canadian Artillery, 1883-97; President Dominion Artillery Association, 1900-1901; President St. John Ambulance Association, 1923-24; Hon. Col. Commandant Canadian Artillery, 1925. *Recreations:* Ottawa Golf Club, Rideau Curling Club, Denholm Angling Club. *Address:* 170 Cooper Street, Ottawa; Carnagh, Co. Armagh, Ireland. *Club:* Rideau, Ottawa.   (*Died 19 Mar. 1928.*)

IRWIN, Henry, C.I.E. 1888; M.I.C.E.; *b.* 1841; *m.* 1871, Henrietta Helen, *d.* of Rev. Robert Irwin. Joined Public Works Department, 1868; consulting architect to Government, 1889; retired, 1896. *Address:* Loch End, Ootacamund, India.   (*Died 5 Aug. 1922.*)

IRWIN, Lt.-Gen. John Staples, C.B. 1906; Mid Ulster Artillery, Dungannon; *b.* 1846. *Address:* Dungannon, Co. Tyrone.
    (*Died 4 Oct. 1917.*)

IRWIN, Thomas Lennox, secretary of Strand and St. George's Registration Associations since 1885; member of Grand Council of the Primrose League; chairman of Finance Committee, 1904-5, and of General Purposes Committee, 1915; *b.* Brompton, 9 Sept. 1846; *e. s.* of late Thos. Irwin of the Exchequer and Audit Department, and Agnes, *d.* of late William Jerdan of the Literary Gazette; *m.* Elizabeth, *d.* of late Wm. Freeman, Lincoln's Inn, 1882. *Educ.:* Cholmeley School, Highgate. Barr. Lincoln's Inn, 1875; Secretary of Westminster Conservative Association, 1874-85. *Publication:* Pocket Guide to the Corrupt Practices Act, 1883. *Recreations:* cricket, football, lawn tennis, golf. *Address:* 6 Longfield Road, Ealing, W.; Parliament Mansions, Victoria Street, S.W.1. *Club:* Junior Carlton.   (*Died 27 Aug. 1918.*)

ISAACS, Godfrey Charles; Managing Director Marconi's Wireless Telegraph Co., Ltd.; 4th *s.* of Joseph M. Isaacs; married; two *s.*

Educ.: London; Hanover and Brussels Universities. At an early age entered his father's firm of fruit and ship brokers; this business afforded occasion for considerable travel in almost all European countries, the opportunity of acquiring foreign languages and becoming acquainted with the characteristics of peoples of the Continent; in several years of a busy and active life acquired considerable business and financial experience; upon retiring from his father's firm, he continued to take considerable interest in business at home and abroad, until in 1910, at the invitation of Mr. Marconi, consented to take the managing direction of Marconi's Wireless Telegraph Co., Ltd. *Recreation:* golf. *Address:* Lyne Grove, Virginia Water, Surrey. *T.:* Chertsey 86. *M.:* LC 1174; LE 8474.   (*Died 17 April 1925.*)

ISHERWOOD, John Henry Bradshaw- J.P.; *b.* 27 Aug. 1841; *e. s.* of late Thos. Bradshaw-Isherwood and Mary Ellen, 2nd *d.* of Rev. Henry Bellairs; *m.* Elizabeth, (*d.* 1921), *d.* of Thomas Luce, Malmesbury; three *s.* one *d. Educ.:* Rugby; Cambridge. Late Lieutenant 84th Regiment. *Address:* Marple Hall, Marple, Cheshire. *T.A.:* Marple.
    (*Died 9 May 1924.*)

ISHIBASHI, Kazunori, R.O.I.; Member of the Royal Society of Portrait Painters; Member of the Imperial Art Society of Japan; *b.* Matsuye, Japan. *Educ.:* Buddhist Temple, Kyoto. Became pupil of the late Taki Katei, Imperial Court Artist, 1892; entered Army School, 1899; went through Boxer Campaign, 1890 (Sun Rising Order, Class 6); Studied Royal Academy School five years; Exhibited R.A. first time, 1908; Paris Salon first time, 1911; Associate Société Nationale des Beaux-Arts, 1922; member Société Nationale des Beaux-Arts, 1923. *Address:* 11 Doria Road, Parson's Green, S.W. *Club:* Chelsea Arts.
    (*Died 2 May 1928.*)

ISMAY, Rev. William, M.A.; Vicar of Eckington, 1877-1919; Hon. Canon of Worcester since 1913, and Rural Dean of Pershore since 1908; *b.* 10 May 1846; *m.*; one *s.* two *d. Educ.:* Emmanuel College, Cambridge; Ordained, 1871; Curate of St. Stephens, Canonbury, 1871-73; St. Marks, Hamilton Terrace, 1873-77. *Address:* St. Barnabas, Newland, Malvern.   (*Died 11 May 1922.*)

ISRAEL, John William, I.S.O., Auditor General for the Commonwealth of Australia since 1901; *b.* Launceston, Tasmania, 4 July 1850; *s.* of John Cashmore Israel and Adelaide Maria Israel; *m.* 1883, Jane M'Donald of Ulverstone, Tasmania; one *s. Educ.:* Abraham Barrett's Academy, and Church of England Grammar School, Launceston. Audit clerk in the office of the Launceston and Western Railway Company, Launceston, 1870; after the Railway was transferred to the Government of Tasmania promoted to the position of Stationmaster, Launceston, and subsequently to office of Accountant of Tasmanian Government Railways; transferred to position of chief clerk of the Government Audit Office, Hobart, Tasmania, 1882; later deputy Auditor; Auditor-General for Tasmania, 1895; was Hon. Treasurer of late Royal Geographical Society of Australia, Victorian Branch; many years President of the Board of Benevolence, Grand Lodge of Freemasons, Tasmania; also was First Principal of Royal Arch Chapter; Past Senior Grand Warden of Grand Lodge of Victoria; first honorary member of the Australasian Corporation of Public Accountants. *Recreations:* gardening, reading. *Address:* Eshcol, Sackville Street, East Kew, Victoria. *T.A.:* Commonwealth Audit Office. *T.:* Central 9978.   (*Died 30 May 1926.*)

IVEAGH, 1st Earl of (cr. 1919); Edward Cecil Guinness, K.P. 1897; G.C.V.O., *cr.* 1910; F.R.S., LL.D.; Viscount Elveden, *cr.* 1919;

Viscount Iveagh (*cr.* 1905), Baron (*cr.* 1891); Bt. 1885; *b.* 10 Nov. 1847; 3rd *s.* of Sir Benjamin Lee Guinness and Elizabeth, *d.* of Edward Guinness; *b.* of 1st Baron Ardilaun; *m.* 1873, Adelaide (*d.* 1916), *d.* of late Richard Samuel Guinness, M.P., Deepwell, Co. Dublin; three *s.* *Educ.:* Trinity Coll., Dublin (Hon. LL.D. 1891). Chancellor Dublin University, 1908. *Heir: s.* Viscount Elveden. *Address:* 5 Grosvenor Place, S.W.1; *T.:* Vic. 4567; Kenwood, Hampstead Lane, N.W.3.; *T.:* Mountview 2664; 80 St. Stephen's Green, Dublin; Elveden Hall, Suffolk; Farmleigh, Castleknock, Co. Dublin. *Clubs:* Athenæum, Carlton, Turf; Kildare Street, Dublin. *(Died 7 Oct. 1927.)*

IVERACH, Rev. James, M.A., D.D.; Principal since 1905; Professor of New Testament Language and Literature, United Free Church College, Aberdeen, since 1907; *b.* Caithness, 1839; 3rd *s.* of James Iverach, Halkirk, Caithness; *m.* Margaret, *d.* of Donald Macdonald, Thurso; one *s.* four *d.* *Educ.:* the Univ. and New Coll. Edinburgh. Ordained at West Calder, 1869; translated to Ferryhill, Aberdeen, 1874; Prof. Apologetics, etc., U.F. Church College, Aberdeen, 1887-1907; Moderator United Free Church, 1912-13. *Publications:* Life of Moses; Life and Times of St. Paul; Is God Knowable?; Evolution and Christianity; The Truth of Christianity; Theism, in the light of present Science and Philosophy; Descartes, Spinoza, and the New Philosophy, etc.; was for years a contributor to the Spectator. *Recreation:* golf. *Address:* 12 Ferryhill Place, Aberdeen. *Club:* Scottish Liberal, Edin. *(Died 6 Aug. 1922.)*

IYENGAR, S. Kasturi Ranga, B.A., B.L.; proprietor and editor, The Hindu, since 1905; *b.* 1859; *s.* of Sesha Iyengar, Revenue Official, Tanjore Dt.; *m.* Kanakammal, *d.* of Gopala Iyengar, landlord, Tanjore; two *s.* two *d.* *Educ.:* The Presidency College, Madras. Sub-Registrar; resigned and studied for the Bar under the late Sir V. Bashyam Iyengar; practised at Coimbatore and at Madras, 1885-1905; connected with Indian national political organisations; Member of the All-India Congress Committee and President of the Madras Provincial Congress Committee; a member of the Indian Press Deputation in 1918, and visited the Western Front and Great Britain; Fellow of the Institute of Journalists. *Recreations:* chess and indoor games. *Address:* 100 Mount Road Madras. *T.A.:* Hindu, Madras. *T.:* 305. *M.:* 2650. *Club:* Cosmopolitan, Madras.*(Died 12 Dec. 1923.)*

IZAT, Alexander, C.I.E. 1898; M.I.C.E.; Director of Bengal and North-Western Railway Company; *b.* 1844; *m.* 1873, Margaret Dewar, *d.* of James Rennie; four *s.* two *d.* Entered Indian Public Works Department, 1863, as Assistant-Engineer, Hyderabad; transferred to Railway Branch, 1870, and served in various parts of India, being instrumental in initiating and carrying out many metre-gauge extensions; services lent to Bengal and North-Western Railway as Agent and Chief Engineer, 1888, and continued in that capacity, carrying through many important extensions, until retirement from India, 1904; joined Board of Directors, 1902. *Address:* Balliliesk, Dollar, N.B.*Died 2 Jan. 1920.)*

J

JACK, A. G. Mackenzie, C.B.E.; J.P.; M.Inst.C.E.; retired; *b.* 1851; *s.* of Alex. Jack, Avoch, Scotland; *m.* Marian, *d.* of J. Herdman Bey, Constantinople; one *s.* four *d.* *Educ.:* Presbyterian Schools, Woolwich. Served apprenticeship in Engineering Dept., Woolwich

544

Arsenal; engineer in U.S. Navy; Supt. Imperial Arsenal, Tientsin; General Manager, Managing Director, and Deputy Chairman from 1888 to retirement in 1921, of Hadfields, Ltd., Sheffield. *Recreations:* outdoor exercises, study of the Chinese language, violin. *Address:* Rock Hills, Brincliffe, Sheffield; 51 West Kensington Mansions, W.14. *T.:* Sheffield 754. *Clubs:* Constitutional; Sheffield, Sheffield.
(Died 2 Aug. 1927.)

JACK, Robert Logan, LL.D., F.G.S., F.R.G.S., Mem. Inst. Mining and Metallurgy; Consulting Geologist and Mining Engineer; *b.* Irvine, Ayrshire, 1845; *s.* of Robert Jack; *m.* 1877, Janet, *d.* of Dr. James Simpson, Fintry, Stirlingshire; one *s.* *Educ.:* Irvine Academy; Edinburgh University. Assistant Geologist, Geol. Survey of Scotland, 1866-77; Govt. Geologist of Queensland, 1877-99; Explorations in N. Queensland before settlement took place and had some narrow escapes, having been speared by the natives; took prominent part in mining development of Colony and in inception of artesian water supply; President Geological Section Australasian Assoc. for Advancement of Science at first meeting in Sydney; President Royal Society, Queensland, 1896; represented Queensland at Greater Britain Exhibition, London, 1899; resigned 1899 and led an expedition in Korea and China in the interests of an English Company; the Boxer movement led to the withdrawal of the party from China into Burma across the Yangtse, Salwen, Mekong, and Irrawadi and the mountainous regions inhabited by Lolo and Tibetan tribes; Member of Council Geol. Soc. London, 1902-3; returned to London, 1901; practised his profession there till 1903, and subsequently in Western Australia and New South Wales; has held several Royal Commissions in Western Australia. *Publications:* numerous official publications; Mineral Wealth of Queensland; Explorations in the Cape York Peninsula; Artesian Water in the Western Interior; Handbook of Queensland Geology; (with Robert Etheridge) Geology and Palæontology of Queensland and New Guinea; The Back-Blocks of China, 1904; Report of the Royal Commission on the Collie Coalfield, Western Australia, 1905; Report on the Probability of Obtaining Artesian Water in the Kimberley District, Western Australia, 1906; Report of Royal Commission on Miners' Lung Diseases, Western Australia, 1911; Northwest Australia, 1922. *Address:* Norwich Chambers, Hunter Street, Sydney.

JACK, William, M.A., LL.D., D.Sc., F.R.S.E.; *b.* Stewarton, Ayrshire, 29 May 1834; *s.* of Robert Jack, Irvine; *m.* Agnes Jane Nichol (*d.* 1901), *d.* of J. P. Nichol, LL.D., Professor of Astronomy, University of Glasgow; two *s.* *Educ.:* Glasgow and Cambridge. Assistant Commissioner Primary Education (Ireland) Commission, 1878; served on Queen's Colleges (Ireland) Commission, 1882; formerly Fellow of Peterhouse, Camb.: H.M. Insp. of Schools in S.W. district of Scotland, 1860-66; Professor of Natural Philosophy, Owens Coll. Manchester, 1866-70; editor Glasgow Herald, 1870-76; publisher (Macmillan and Co.), 1876-1879; Professor of Mathematics, Glasgow University, 1879-1909. *Address:* 5 St. John's Terrace, Hillhead, Glasgow. (*Died 20 Mar. 1924.*)

JACK, William Robert, M.D.Glasg., B.Sc., F.R.F.P.S.G.; Visiting Physician, Glasgow Royal Infirmary; Lecturer in Clinical Medicine, Glasgow University; *b.* 1866; *e. s.* of late Professor William Jack; *m.* 1904, Helen, *d.* of Alexander Montgomery, Hamilton. *Educ.:* Fettes College, Edinburgh; Glasgow University; continental medical schools. *Publications:* Wheeler's Handbook of Medicine, 2nd to 7th editions; various contributions to Glasgow Medical Journal. *Address:* 16 Woodside Place, Glasgow. *T.:* Charing 1216.*(Died 11 July 1927.)*

JACKSON, Benjamin Daydon, Ph.D.; Secretary of the Linnean Society, 1880-1902; General Secretary, 1902-26; Curator of the Linnean Collections since 1926; Secretary to Departmental Committee of H.M. Treasury on Botanical Work, 1900-1; Hon. Ph.D. Upsala; Knight of the Swedish Order of the Polar Star, 1907; b. London, 3 April 1846; m. 1884, Jane, y. d. of late Charles Hunt, Manchester. Educ.: private schools. Publications: Life of John Gerard, 1877; Life of Dr. William Turner, 1878; Guide to the Literature of Botany, 1881; Vegetable Technology, 1882; Pryor's Flora of Herts (edited), 1887; Index Kewensis (engaged nearly 14 years on its preparation), 1893-95; Supplement to the same (with Th. Durand) 1901-6; Glossary of Botanic Terms, 1900, 3rd ed. 1916; Life of George Bentham (English Men of Science), 1906; New Genera and Species of Cyperaceae, by late C. B. Clarke (edited), 1906; Illustrations of Cyperaceae, by the same (edited), 1909; Darwiniana, 1910; Index to the Linnean Herbarium, 1912; Catalogue of Linnean Specimens of Zoology, 1913; Notes on a Catalogue of the Linnean Herbarium, 1922; Linnæus: the Story of his Life, 1923; many shorter articles, chiefly on Botany, Botanic History and Bibliography. Recreation: change of work. Address: Burlington House, Piccadilly, W.1; 21 Cautley Avenue, Clapham Common, S.W.4. *(Died 12 Oct. 1927.)*

JACKSON, Hon. Cecil Gower, J.P.; Judge, Native High Court, Natal, since 1910; b. 1872; s. of Rev. N. Jackson; m. 1904, Catherine Annie, d. of R. Burkitt of Alford, Lincolnshire; no c. Educ.: privately; silver medal Natal Lit. Ex. 1891. Held first appointment in Natal Civil Service, 1888; clerk of court in various Magisterial Offices and deputy clerk of Peace, and acted frequently as Magistrate 1894-1901; Assistant Magistrate Ladysmith, Mazinto and Newcastle, 1902-3; Civil Magistrate, Durban, 1904; Magistrate Weenen, 1905; Magistrate for special purposes Mahlabatun, 1908 and Nongoma, 1909; Commissioner to revise sentences on native rebels, 1909; served S.A. War, 1899-2, and Native Rebellion, 1906. Address: Maritzburg, Natal. Club: Victoria, Maritzburg.
(Died 15 April 1920.)

JACKSON, Sir Charles James, F.S.A.; b. Monmouth, 24 May 1849; s. of late James Edwin Jackson of Monmouth. Called to Bar, Middle Temple, 1888; J.P. Glamorgan; worked as a member of the Silver Committee of the Red Cross Society during the war; admitted to the Freedom and Livery of the Worshipful Company of Goldsmiths of London prior to being admitted to the Freedom of the City of London, 1922. Publications: English Goldsmiths and their Marks; Illustrated History of English Plate. Address: 6 Ennismore Gardens, S.W. Clubs: Junior Carlton, Ranelagh.
(Died 23 April 1923.)

JACKSON, Sir Cyril, K.B.E., cr. 1917; M.A.; s. of late Laurence M. Jackson of South Park, Bodiam; b. 6 Feb. 1863. Educ.: Charterhouse; New College, Oxford. Barrister, Inner Temple; Toynbee Hall, 1885-96; Central Secy. Children's Country Holidays Fund, 1888-96; Member of London School Board, 1891-96; Inspector-General of Schools, and Permanent Head of Education Department, West Australia, 1896-1903; Chief Inspector, Board of Education, 1903-6; reported to the Manx Government on the Education of the Island, 1906; Expert Investigator on Unemployment in England and Ireland and on Boy Labour to the Royal Commission on the Poor Law, 1906; Member London County Council, Limehouse Division, 1907-13; Chairman Education Committee, 1908-10, and 1922; Chairman L.C.C. Unemployment Committee, 1921-23; Acting Agent-General for Western Australia, 1910-11; Vice-Chairman,

L.C.C., 1911; Alderman, L.C.C., 1913-16, and 1919; Chairman, L.C.C. 1915; Member of Senate London University, 1908-21; Governor Imperial College of Science, 1908-16 and since 1919; Member of Special Committee Home Office on Van Boys, 1912; on Distribution of Public Work, 1913; Chairman of London Intelligence Committee on Unemployment and Distress, Local Government Board, 1914; Chairman of Advisory Committee on National Register, 1915; Vice-Chairman War Pensions, etc., Statutory Committee, 1916, 1917; Member of Central Tribunal, 1915-16 and 1917-19; one of the Chairmen of the Committee on Production and Court of Arbitration, 1918-19; Member of Port of London Authority, 1915-16 and 1919; Representative of Board of Education at Conferences in U.S.A. (St. Louis, 1904, Washington, 1919); Member of Royal Commission on Indian Services, 1923; Chairman, Groceries Trade Board, Labour Ministry, 1924; Member of Admiralty Committee on Officers' Pensions, 1924; is a Director (West End Board) of the Eagle Star and British Dominions Insurance Company. Publications: Unemployment and Trade Unions; Outlines of Education in England; The Religious Question in Public Education (with Michael Sadler and Athelstan Riley); articles in Edinburgh and other reviews. Address: Ballards Shaw, Limpsfield; 12 St. James's Place, S.W.1. T.: Gerrard 4009. Club: Savile.
(Died 3 Sept. 1924.)

JACKSON, Frank Stather; Judge of the Mayor's and City of London Court since 1921; b. Torquay, Nov. 1853; e. of J. H. Jackson, Salisbury; m. Edith, y. d. of late James Easton, 44 Princes Gardens, S.W. Educ.: Sherborne. Admitted Solicitor, 1875; called to Bar, 1884; Registrar of the Mayor's Court, 1890; Assistant Judge of Mayor's Court, 1900. Publication: The Mayor's Court Practice (with Lewis Glyn, K.C.). Recreation: golf. Address: 18 Brunswick Gardens, W.8; Lord Mayor's Court, E.C. Clubs: St. Stephen's. St. George's; Richmond Golf.
(Died 17 Oct. 1922.)

JACKSON, Frederick Hamilton, R.B.A. 1889; b. 1848; y. s. of N. Jackson, of Hamilton, Adams and Co., wholesale booksellers. Educ.: private schools. Entered his father's house of business, but gave it up to follow art; student and first-class medallist, Royal Academy Schools; exhibitor R.A. New Gallery, and other leading Galleries since 1870; Master of Antique School, Slade School, University College, under Sir E. J. Poynter, P.R.A. and M.A. Legros; founder of the Chiswick School of Art in 1880, in conjunction with E. S. Burchett, Perspective Lect. at the Schools, South Kensington; member of Art Workers' Guild, 1887; Society of Decorative Designers (committee) from its formation; Vice-Pres. 1903; Cantor Lecturer, 1907; late examiner to the Board of Education in principles of design; has of late years given special attention to decoration and design, writing and lecturing also upon technical and archæological subjects; practises, in addition to easel picture-painting, in oil and water colour, ecclesiastical decoration, including mosaic in the east end of St. Bartholomew's, Brighton, the apse of St. Basil's, Deritend, Birmingham, and design for many purposes. Publications: Hand-books for the Designer and Craftsman; Intarsia and Marquetry, and Mural Decoration; True Stories of the Condottieri; A Little Guide to Sicily; The Shores of the Adriatic, the Italian side and the Austrian side; Rambles in the Pyrenees and the adjacent districts. Recreations: principally travel, and in turning from one form of art production to another or to literary work, and gardening. Address: The Fair Haven, 15 Melrose Road, Southfields, S.W. *(Died 13 Oct. 1923.)*

JACKSON, Rt. Hon. Frederick Huth, P.C. 1911; partner in Frederick Huth and

Co.; Director Bank of England; President of the Institute of Bankers, 1909-11; one of H.M.'s Lieutenants for the City of London; b. London, 26 Apr. 1863; e. s. of Thomas Hughes Jackson, The Manor House, Birkenhead; g. s. of late Sir Wm. Jackson, Bt.; m. Clara, e. d. of Rt. Hon. Sir Mountstuart E. Grant Duff, 1895; one s. (Frederick, m. 1920, Helen, d. of Sir Paul Vinogradoff; three d. Educ.: Harrow; Balliol Coll. Oxford. B.A. Oxford 1887 (Honours School History); M.A. 1890. Address: 64 Rutland Gate, S.W.7; T.: Western 3191; Possingworth, Cross-in-Hand, Sussex; La Maison du Diable, Aix les Bains, France. Clubs: Athenæum, Oxford and Cambridge, Reform, New University.
(Died 3 Dec. 1921.)

JACKSON, Henry, O.M., 1908; Litt.D.; Hon. LL.D. St. Andrews, Aberdeen, and Glasgow; Hon. D.Lit. Oxford; Hon. Litt.D. Manchester and Sheffield; F.B.A.; Regius Professor of Greek, Cambridge, since 1906; Fellow of Trinity College, Cambridge, since 1864, Vice-Master, 1914-19; Foreign hon. member of American Academy of Arts and Sciences; b. Sheffield, 1839; e. s. of late Henry Jackson, surgeon, and late Frances Swettenham; m. Margaret Edith, d. of late Canon F. V. Thornton, 1875; two s. three d. Educ.: Sheffield Collegiate School; Cheltenham Coll.; Trin. Coll. Camb. B.A. 1862; Assistant Tutor, 1866; Prælector in Ancient Philosophy, 1875-1906; Litt.D. 1884; Member of the Council of the Senate, 1882-86, 1888-92, 1892-96, 1900-2, 1902-6; Fellow of Winchester College, 1905-17. Publications: Translations (with R. C. Jebb and W. E. Currey), 1878; Aristotle's Nicomachean Ethics, Bk. v., 1879; On some Passages in the Seventh Book of the Eudemian Ethics, 1900; Texts to illustrate the History of Greek Philosophy from Thales to Aristotle, 1901; Plato's Later Theory of Ideas, in Journal of Philology, Nos. 20, 22, 25, 26, 28, 30, 49; articles on Greek Philosophers in Encyclopædia Britannica; papers in the Journal of Philology, and in Transactions and Proceedings of the Cambridge Philological Society, etc.; About Edwin Drood, 1911. Address: Trinity College, Cambridge; Sunny Hill, St. Stephen's Road, Bournemouth. Club: Athenæum. (Died 25 Sept. 1921.)

JACKSON, Rev. Henry Latimer, D.D.; Rector of Little Canfield since 1911; b. 1851; o. s. of late John Henry Jackson of Richmond, Surrey; m. 1st, Annie (d. 1906), d. of late Robert Fell of Corbridge-on-Tyne; two s. two d.; 2nd, Caroline Harriot Leili (d. 1921), d. of late Walter Watson of Guildford; 3rd, 1923, Eleanor Hyde, 2nd d. of late Mathias Sidney Smith Dipnall, of Christ's Hospital, and widow of W. H. Woodroffe, of British Guiana. Educ.: Highgate Grammar School; Germany; Christ's College, Cambridge. Ordained to Curacy of St. Neots, Hunts; then in charge of Houghton, Hunts.; Rector of St. James's, Sydney, and Fellow and Lecturer of St. Paul's College, University of Sydney, of which M.A. ad eund, 1885; appointed to Crown Living of St. Mary's, Huntingdon, 1895; Hulsean Lecturer at Cambridge, 1912; Select Preacher, 1906 and 1920; Lecturer in Modern and Medieval Dutch Literature, 1918; Lady Margaret Preacher, 1919; F.R.Hist.S. Publications: On the Path of Progress, 1901; Born of the Virgin Mary, 1903; The Fourth Gospel and some recent German Criticism, 1906; The Synoptic Problem (in Cambridge Biblical Essays), 1909; The Eschatology of Jesus, 1913; The Problem of the Fourth Gospel, 1918; Mediævalist and Modernist, 1919; A Manual of the Dutch Language (with B. W. Downs), 1921; articles in Hastings' Dictionary of Christ and the Gospels. Recreations: motoring, cycling, foreign travel. Address: Little Canfield Rectory, Dunmow, Essex. T.: Dunmow 49Y1.(Died 21 Mar. 1926.)

JACKSON, Capt. Henry Mather-; b. 27 Feb. 1894; e. s. of Sir Henry Mather-Jackson, Bt.; m. 1920, Florence, d. of late Granville W. Garth, New York; one d. Educ.: Eton; R.M.C. Served European War, 1914-1919; Capt. 9th Lancers. Address: Hellidon House, Daventry, Northants. T.: Daventry 18. Club: Buck's. (Died 2 April 1928.)

JACKSON, Sir John, Kt., cr. 1895; C.V.O 1911; M.P. (U.) for Devonport, 1910-Dec. 1918; LL.D., F.R.S. Edinburgh, F.R.G.S., J.P.; one of the largest contractors for Public Works; b. York, 4 Feb. 1851; y. s. of late Edward Jackson, York; m. 1876, Ellen Julia, y. d. of late George Myers, London; five d. Educ.: York; Univ. of Edinburgh. Trained civil engineer; was contractor for last section of Manchester Ship Canal; Foundations Tower Bridge, Dover Harbour, and other works of magnitude; recently completed the Admiralty Docks at Keyham, Devonport; the Admiralty Harbour, Simon's Bay, South Africa, and Singapore Harbour, the great railway across the Andes from Arica on the Pacific Coast to La Paz, the capital of Bolivia; and the Great Barrage across the Euphrates at Hindia, near Babylon; at present carrying out Mesopotamia Irrigation Works, Harbour Works in Canada and other places, and other large works; was a member of the Royal Commission appointed to enquire into the War in South Africa; holds highest Chilian Order of Merit and Spanish Order Grand Cross of Naval Merit. Recreations: yachting, cycling, motoring, Commodore R.S.W. Yacht Club. Address: 51 Victoria Street, Westminster, S.W.1; 48 Belgrave Square, S.W.1; T.: Victoria 153; Henley Park, Henley-on-Thames. T.: Henley 48. Clubs: Carlton, Junior Carlton, Royal Automobile; United Service, Edinburgh; Royal Yacht Squadron, Cowes; Royal Western Yacht, Plymouth.
(Died 14 Dec. 1919.)

JACKSON, John Brinckerhoff; b. Newark, New Jersey, 19 Aug. 1862; s. of late Frederick Wolcott and Nannie Nye Jackson; m. 1886, Florence A., d. of Matthew Baird of Philadelphia, Penn. Educ.: private schools at Newark; United States Naval Academy, Annapolis, Maryland. Graduated, 1883; served for two years in American European Naval Squadron, principally in the Mediterranean; Ensign, 1885; resigned from Navy, 1886; studied law, and was admitted to the Bar in New York, 1889; Hon. A.M., Princeton University; Second Secretary of Legation, Berlin, 1890; Secretary of Embassy, 1894; served frequently as Chargé d'Affaires; Minister to Greece, Roumania and Servia, Bulgaria and Montenegro, 1902-7; Persia, 1907-9; Cuba, 1909-11; Roumania, Servia and Bulgaria, 1911-13; Volunteer Assistant at the American Embassy in Berlin, 1914, and Special Agent of the Department of State at same, Jan. 1915; visited England in 1915 to inspect places where German prisoners of war were interned, and after return to Germany was engaged in work connected with British prisoners until Feb. 1917; Delegate to the International Maritime Law Conference at Hamburg, 1902; repres. the United States at Coronation of King Peter of Servia, 1904; Delegate to First International Archæological Congress at Athens, 1905; American Representative at Olympic Games at Athens, 1906; Special Ambassador at the coming of age of the Crown Prince of Bulgaria, 1912; Member of N.Y. Bar Association. Recreations: golf, swimming. Address: U.S. Government Despatch Agency, 53 Victoria Street, Westminster, S.W.1. Clubs: Union League, University, Army and Navy, New York; Rittenhouse, Philadelphia; Metropolitan, Washington; Casino, Berlin; Imperial Yacht, Kiel; Jockey, Bucharest. (Died 20 Dec. 1920.)

JACKSON, Sir Keith George, 4th Bt.; cr. 1815; late Lieut. 83rd Foot; b. 2 Aug. 1842;

S. brother (who was murdered at Delhi) 1857 ; *m.* 1875, Alice, *d.* of late C. F. Montrésor, B.C.S. ; two *s.* *Educ.*: Ordnance School, Carshalton ; Magdalene College, Cambridge. *Heir*: *s.* Robert Montrésor [*b.* 11 March 1876 ; *m.* 1913, Katherine, *y. d.* of late John Abry of The Glen and Barden Park, Tonbridge ; one *s.*]. *Address*: La Paz, Entre Rios, Argentine.

(Died 3 Sept. 1916.)

JACKSON, Maunsell Bowers, K.C., Barrister ; clerk of the crown for Ontario since 1864 ; *b.* Co. Wexford, Ireland ; *s.* of Benjamin Jackson ; *m.* 1868, Claire Edith Cull ; two *s.* three *d.* *Educ.*: Toronto Academy. Called to bar, Ontario, 1855. *Address*: Drumsnab, Castle Frank Road, Rosedale, Toronto, Canada. *T.*: North 2349. *(Died 29 Mar. 1922.)*

JACKSON, Col. Sir Robert Whyte Melville, K.C.M.G., *cr.* 1918 ; K.B.E., *cr.* 1919 ; C.B. 1908 ; C.M.G. 1900 ; *b.* 3 June 1860 ; *o. s.* of late Robert Jackson, Registrar-General of Shipping ; *m.* 1887, Frances, *d.* of Capt. Hugh MacTernan, J.P., D.L., of Heapstown House, Sligo ; one *s.* two *d.* *Educ.*: Marlborough. Entered 2nd Batt. Royal Inniskilling Fusiliers, 1881 ; Army Ordnance, 1886 ; Capt. R. Inniskilling Fusiliers, 1870 ; Major, 1897 ; Lt.-Col., 1901 ; Col., 1907 ; Brig.-Gen., 1915 ; served S. Africa, 1900-1901 (despatches twice, brevet of Col., Queen's medal 3 clasps, King's medal 2 clasps, C.M.G.) ; Chief Ordnance Officer Cape Colony, 1903-5 ; Director Royal Army Clothing Factory, Pimlico, 1907-Feb. 1915 ; was made Director of Ordnance for Mediterranean Exped. Force (despatches thrice, K.C.M.G., K.B.E.) ; Order of the White Eagle, Serbia, 1916. *Recreations*: yachting, shooting. *Address*: 50 Hurlingham Court, S.W.6. *T.*: Putney 295.

(Died 25 Feb. 1928.)

JACKSON, Sir Robert William, Kt., *cr.* 1882 ; C.B. 1874 ; Deputy Surgeon-Gen. retired 1882 ; *b.* 1826 ; *m.* 1st, 1860, Anne (*d,* 1888), *d.* of John Jones Simpson ; 2nd, 1891, Gertrude, *d.* of Robert P. Daye ; three *s.* one *d.* Entered Army Med. Department, 1854 ; served Crimea, 1854-56 ; Indian Mutiny, 1857-58 ; Ashanti War, 1874 ; Zulu War, 1880 ; Egyptian Campaign, 1882. *Address*: Eglinton, New Grove Avenue, Sandymount, Dublin. *(Died 12 May 1921.)*

JACKSON, Colonel Sydney Charles Fishburn, C.M.G. 1919 ; D.S.O. 1889 ; *b.* Dedham Grove, near Colchester, 21 April 1868 ; *s.* of late Commander W. T. F. Jackson, R.N. ; *m.* Lucy Beatrice, 2nd *d.* of late Sir W. H. Drake, K.C.B. 1898 ; two *s.* *Educ.*: Wellington ; Royal Military College, Sandhurst. Gazetted R.I. Rifles, Sep. 1882 ; transferred to Hampshire Regiment, Oct. 1882 ; Capt. 1890 ; Major, 1901 ; Lieut.-Col. 1904 ; Brevet Col. 1910 ; Subst. Colonel, Dec. 1914 ; retired, 1920 ; served Burma Campaign, 1885-89 (medal and two clasps, despatches twice, D.S.O.) : Zhob Valley Expedition, 1890 ; A.D.C. to G.O.C. Upper Burma Field Force, 1886-89 ; A.D.C. to G.O.C. Quetta District, 1889-93 ; A.D.C. to H.E. the Com.-in-Chief in India, 1893-94 ; Station Staff Officer 1st class, Punjab, Apr. 1897 ; D.A.A.G. Bombay Command Headquarters, 1897-1902 ; D.A.A. and Q.M.G. 6th Division, 1906-10 ; served with Somaliland Field Force, 1903-1904, in command of detachment Hampshire Regt. (despatches, medal with 2 clasps, brevet of Lieut.-Colonel) ; A.Q.M.G. Eastern Command, 1917-18 ; A.A. and Q.M.G. Gibraltar, 1918-20 ; European War 1914-18, in command of 1st Hampshire Regt. (despatches, severely wounded, 1914 Star, British War Medal, Victory Medal, C.M.G.). *Recreations*: hunting, golf, rowing. *Club*: Army and Navy.

(Died 27 June 1928.)

JACKSON, Sir Thomas Graham, 1st Bt., *cr.* 1913 ; R.A. 1896 ; Hon. D.C.L. Oxford, 1911 ; Associé de l'Academie Royale de Belgique, 1910 ; Hon. LL.D. Camb. 1910 ; M.A. ; architect ; *b.* Hampstead, 21 Dec. 1835 ; *s.* of Hugh Jackson, solicitor, and Eliza, *d.* of Thomas Graham Arnold, M.D. ; *m.* 1880, Alice Mary (*d.* 1900), *y. d.* of William Lambarde, J.P., D.L., of Beechmont, Kent ; two *s.* *Educ.*: Brighton College ; Wadham College, Oxford (Scholar, 1854) ; Fellow Wadham College, 1864 ; vacated Fellowship by marriage, 1880 ; Hon. Fellow, 1882 ; A.R.A. 1892. Pupil of Sir George Gilbert Scott, R.A., 1858 - 61. *Works*: at Oxford : new Examination Schools of University ; Restoration of Bodleian Library, St. Mary's and All Saints Churches ; new buildings for Brasenose, Lincoln, Corpus, Trinity, Balliol, and Hertford Colleges, new Radcliffe Library, Electric Laboratory, Somerville Hall, City High School and High School for Girls, etc. ; new Sedgwick Memorial Museum, Archæological Museum, Physiological and Psychological Laboratories, and new Law Library and Law School at Cambridge ; restorations at Eltham Palace, Rushton Hall, Longleat, Great Malvern Priory, Portsmouth Church, Grimsby Church, Bath Abbey, Trinity Church, Coventry, Christchurch Priory, Hospital of St. Cross, and Winchester Cathedral ; new churches at Annesley, Hornblotton, Wimbledon, Stratton, Aldershot, Northington, Curdridge, and Narberth ; new buildings for the following public schools : Eton, Westminster, Rugby, Harrow, Radley, Uppingham, Brighton, Giggleswick, Aldenham, Cranbrook, Sandwich ; new buildings for Inner Temple, Drapers' Hall ; several private houses. *Publications*: Modern Gothic Architecture, 1873 ; Dalmatia, the Quarnero, and Istria, 1887 ; Wadham College, Oxford : its History and Buildings (with illustrations), 1893 ; The Church of St. Mary the Virgin, Oxford : its History and Architecture ; Reason in Architecture, 1906 ; Byzantine and Romanesque Architecture, 1913 ; Gothic Architecture in France, England, and Italy, 1915 ; A Holiday in Umbria, 1917 ; The Renaissance of Roman Architecture, 1921-22 ; Memories of Travel, 1923. *Heir*: *s.* Hugh Nicholas [Major R.F.A. ; *b.* 21 Jan. 1881 ; late Lieut. R. W. Fusiliers]. *Recreations*: boating, gardening, music, travel. *Address*: 49 Evelyn Gardens, S. Kensington, S.W. *Clubs*: Athenæum, Royal Societies. *(Died 7 Nov. 1924.)*

JACKSON, William Henry, C.M.G. 1914 ; retired civilian ; 3rd *s.* of late, Lt.-Col. Thomas Jackson, Harbledown Lodge, Harbledown, Kent ; *m.* ; two *s.* five *d.* *Educ.*: King's School, Canterbury ; R.I.E.C., Coopers Hill. Entered Ceylon Civil Service, 1879 ; Police Magistrate, Colombo, 1892 ; Assistant Government Agent, 1895 ; Chairman of the Colombo Harbour Board, Principal Collector of Customs, and Member Legislative Council, 1901 ; Controller of Revenue and Member Executive Council, 1911 ; retired, 1913. *Recreations*: cricket and golf. *(Died 14 Dec. 1920.)*

JACOB, Rt. Rev. Edgar, D.D. Oxon. ; Hon. D.D. Durham ; Bishop of St. Albans (1908-19) ; *b.* Crawley Rectory, near Winchester, 16 Nov. 1844 ; *s.* of late Ven. Philip Jacob, Archdeacon and Canon of Winchester, and of Anna, *e. d.* of late Hon. and Rev. Gerard T. Noel, Canon of Winchester. *Educ.*: Winchester ; New College, Oxford (Scholar). Curate of Taynton, Oxon., 1868 ; Witney, 1869-71 ; charge of St. James's, Bermondsey, 1871-72 ; domestic chaplain to Bishop (Milman) of Calcutta, 1872 - 76 ; charge of Wilberforce Memorial Mission, S. London, 1877 ; Vicar of Portsea, 1878-96 ; Hon. Canon of Winchester, 1884-96 ; hon. chaplain to the Queen, 1887-90 ; chaplain-in-ordinary, 1890-96 ; examining chaplain to Bishop (Browne) of Winchester, 1876-91 ; chaplain to Bishop (Thorold) of Winchester, 1891-95 ; to Bishop (Davidson) of Winchester, 1895-96 ; Rural Dean of Landport,

1892-96 ; proctor in Convocation for Hants and Isle of Wight, 1895-96 ; Select Preacher, Oxford, 1895-96 ; Bishop of Newcastle, 1896-1903. *Publications :* The Divine Society (Cambridge Lectures on Pastoral Theology), 1890. *Address :* Verulam House, St. Albans. *Club :* Athenæum.
(Died 25 Mar. 1920.)

JACOB, Sir (Samuel) Swinton, I.A., K.C.I.E. ; *cr.* 1902 ; C.V.O., 1911 ; A.I.C.E., Hon. Assoc. R.I.B.A. ; late Chief Engineer Jaipur State, Rajputana, India ; *b.* 14 Jan. 1841 ; *s.* of Col. W. Jacob, Bombay Artillery ; *m.* Mary, *d.* of Robert Brown, Edinburgh, 1874. *Educ. :* Cheam School ; Addiscombe H.E.I.C. College. Gained commission in Bombay Artillery. Lieut. 1858 ; joined Indian Staff Corps, 1862 ; Capt. 1870 ; Major, 1878 ; Lieut.-Col. 1884 ; Colonel, 1888 ; served in P.W.D. 1862-96 ; 1st grade Exec. 1881 ; 1st class Sup. Engineers, 1896 ; officiated as Sup. Engineer and Secretary to the A.G.G. for Rajputana, and C.I. on several occasions ; services lent by the Govt. of India in the Foreign Dept. to the Maharajah of Jaipur in Rajputana, 1867 ; served at Aden, 1861-66 (thanked by Secretary of State) ; received thanks Govt. of India for exertions during famine in Rajputana, 1868-69 ; commended by Govt. of India for services in the P.W.D. of the Jaipur State, 1872 ; again thanked 1873 and 1890 ; served as Assist. Field Engineer with the Aden Force, 1865-66 ; blown up in the destruction of an Arab fort, 6 Jan. 1866. Attended coronation of King Edward VII. as Political Officer with H.H. the Maharajah of Jaipur, bringing him and his suite from India and back to Jaipur, 1902 ; appointed by Govt. of India on special duty as Consulting Engineer for Irrigation in Rajputana, 1902-5. In architectural work in India, among other works, has designed the following : the Sandeman Memorial Hall at Quetta ; Secretariat Offices for the Govt. of India at Simla ; the Victoria Memorial Hall at Peshawar ; the Bank of Madras at Madras ; the Albert Hall at Jaipur ; the Jubilee Clock Tower at Jacobabad ; St. Stephen's College at Delhi ; the Public Offices at Jodhpur and at Dholpur ; the Hospital at Bharatpur ; College for the Begum of Bhopal ; a Palace for the Maharajah of Kotah ; a Palace and other buildings for the Maharajah of Bikaner ; the Church at Jaipur ; the R.C. Church at Ajmere ; the new Daly College at Indore and subsidiary buildings ; the Marble Canopies over the Statues of the late Queen Victoria at Lahore, Lucknow, and Ajudhya ; Drinking Fountains at Calcutta and Bombay ; Marble Altars, Fonts, Pulpits, *etc.*, in different parts of India. Decorated for services as Engineer to the Jaipur State ; for publication of the Jaipur Portfolios, title conferred by the French Govt. Officer de l'Academie des Beaux Arts ; owns Kaiser-i-Hind gold medal ; C.I.E. 1890 ; and Coronation medals for England and India. *Publications :* Jaipur Portfolios of Architectural Details ; a work on Jaipur Enamels, letterpress by Surgeon-Col. T. H. Hendley, C.I.E. *Address :* c/o H. S. King and Co., 9 Pall Mall, S.W.
(Died 4 Nov. 1917.)

JACOB, Lieut.-Colonel Walter Henry Bell, D.S.O. 1919 ; late Royal Garrison Artillery ; *b.* 13 June 1871 ; *s.* of Thomas Walter Jacob, Irish, late of War Office, and Louisa, *d.* of late William Bell, English ; *m.* 1st, Mildred Jessie (*d.* 1920), 2nd *d.* of late Capt. Horatio Paul ; 2nd, 1922, Adah Louisa, *d.* of late T. Harbridge Jones. *Educ. :* St. Paul's School ; Royal Military Academy, Woolwich. 2nd Lieut. Royal Garrison Artillery, 1889 ; served South African War (Queen's medal and 2 clasps) ; European War (D.S.O., Serbian White Eagle with swords 4th class, Italian Croce di Guerra) ; retired pay, 1921. *Recreations :* polo, boating. *Address :* 20 Dietro La Chiesa, Sliema, Malta.
(Died 24 Mar. 1925.)

JACOB, Maj.-Gen. William, Indian Army ; *b.* 14 Dec. 1837 ; 2nd *s.* of late Lt.-Col. W. Jacob, Bombay Artillery ; *m.* 1861, Eliza, *d.* of Rev. G. A. Jacob, Teignmouth ; two *s.* two *d.* Entered army, 1855 ; Maj.-Gen 1894 ; unemployed list, 1897 ; served Indian Mutiny, 1858 (medal with clasp) ; Afghan War, 1880-81 (despatches, medal). *Address :* Brookands, Tavistock, Devon.
(Died 9 Mar. 1917.)

JACOBS, Joseph, author and journalist ; *b.* Sydney, N.S.W., 29 Aug. 1854 ; *m.* Georgina, 2nd *d.* of late T. Horne ; two *s.* one *d.* *Educ. :* Sydney Grammar School, St. John's Coll. Camb. (Senior Moralist, 1876). Visited Spain for historical purposes, 1868 ; United States on a lecturing tour, 1896 ; is corresponding member of Royal Academy of History, Madrid, and of the Brooklyn Institute ; sometime editor of Folk Lore, Literary Year-Book, Jewish Year-Book ; late Secretary of the Russo-Jewish Committee ; President of the Jewish Historical Society ; Literary Editor of the Jewish Encyclopedia ; Editor, American Hebrew ; Director, Bureau of Jewish Statistics, 1914. *Publications :* English Fairy Tales, 1890 ; Studies in Jewish Statistics, 1896 ; Celtic Fairy Tales, 1891 ; Indian Fairy Tales, 1892 ; Tennyson and In Memoriam, 1892 ; Jews of Angevin England, 1893 ; More English Fairy Tales, 1893 ; More Celtic Fairy Tales, 1894 ; Studies in Biblical Archæology, 1894 ; Æsop's Fables, 1894 ; Literary Studies, 1895 ; Reynard the Fox, 1895 ; As Others Saw Him (a Jewish Life of Christ), 1895 ; Sources of the History of the Jews in Spain, 1895 ; Jewish Ideals, 1896 ; Wonder Voyages, 1896 ; Story of Geographical Discovery, 1898 ; Europa's Fairy Book, 1915 ; Mr. Jacobs has also translated Balthasar Gracian's Art of Worldly Wisdom from the Spanish, 1892, and Tales from Boccaccio, 1899 ; he has likewise published editions of North's Fables of Bidpai, 1887 ; Caxton's Æsop, 1889 ; Painter's Palace of Pleasure, 1891 ; Howell's Familiar Letters, 1892 ; Day's Daphnis and Chloe, 1890 ; and has written Introduction to the Arabian Nights, Morris's Old French Romances, Goldsmith's Comedies, and Thackeray's Esmond, all in 1896 ; Austen's Emma and Chamisso's Peter Schlemihl, 1898. *Recreations :* chess, novels, cycling, book collecting (8000 vols.). *Address :* 11 Greystone Terrace, Yonkers, N.Y. *Clubs :* Maccabeans, New Vagabonds' ; Authors'. New York.
(Died 3 Feb. 1916.)

JAFAR, Raja Sir Saiyid Abu, K.C.I.E., *cr.* 1922 ; C.I.E. 1918. *Address :* Pirpur, Fyzabad District, U.P., India. (Died 14 Feb. 1927.)

JAFFRAY, Sir John Henry, 3rd Bt. ; *cr.* 1892 ; *b.* 9 Dec. 1893 ; *s.* of 2nd Bt. and Alice Mary, *d.* of Francis Galloway ; *S.* father, 1914. *Educ. :* Eton ; Trinity Hall, Cambridge. 2nd Lieut. Worcestershire Yeomanry, since 1914. *Heir :* *b.* William Edmund Jaffray, 2nd Lieut. King's Dragoon Guards, *b.* 29 July 1895. *Address :* Skilts, Studley, Warwickshire.
(Died 23 April 1916.)

JAFFREY, Francis, F.R.C.S. Eng. ; L.R.C.P. Lond. ; Consulting Surgeon to St. George's Hospital ; Consulting Surgeon to the Belgrave Hospital for Children ; Hon. Secretary Fowey Cottage Hospital ; *b.* Adelaide, South Australia, 1861. *Educ. :* privately ; St. George's Hospital. Formerly Demonstrator and Lecturer on Anatomy and Surgery in St. George's Hospital Medical School ; and visiting Surgeon to the Atkinson Morley Convalescent Hospital, Wimbledon. *Publications :* articles in medical papers, and an article on the general treatment of Dislocations in the System of Treatment edited by Latham and English. *Recreations :* sea-fishing, yachting, and shooting. *Address :* Cliff Lawn, Fowey. *Club :* Royal Fowey Yacht.
(Died 20 May 1919.)

JAIPUR, Maharaja of, Lt.-Gen. H. H. Saramad-i-Rajhai-Hindustan

Raj Rajendra Shree Maharajadhiraj, Sir Sawai Madho Singh Bahadur, K.G.C.S.I., cr. 1888 ; G.C.I.E., cr. 1901; G.C.V.O., cr. 1903 ; G.B.E., cr. 1918 ; Donat of the Order of the Hospital of St. John of Jerusalem, 1912 ; LL.D. Edin. 1908 ; Hon. Lieut.-General ; Hon. Col. of 13th Rajputs (Shekhawati) Regt. 1904 ; Member of the First Class of the Order of the Crown of Prussia, 1910 ; b. 1861 ; S. 1880. Salute, twenty-one guns. The Maharaja is head of Kuchhwaha clan of Rajputs, tracing descent from Rama, the celebrated king of Ayodhya (modern Oudh). The modern capital, Jaipur, was built in A.D. 1728 by Maharaja Jai Singh, the ancient capital being Amber, founded in A.D. 1150. The administration is carried on by a council consisting of ten members, the Maharaja exercising the supreme civil and criminal authority within his territories. The State of Jaipur comprises an area of 15,579 square miles, and has a population of 2,658,666. The State maintains a Transport Corps, organised in 1890, the strength of which is 1 superintendent, 8 officers, and 695 non-commissioned officers and men. The present Maharaja, apart from being a wise and capable administrator, takes a deep interest in all matters affecting the welfare of the British Empire. Among his many princely liberalities may be mentioned his subscription of Rs.1,600,000 towards founding a permanent Famine Fund for India, Rs.100,000 towards the Transvaal War Fund, Rs.400,000 added to the Famine Fund in memory of the Queen-Empress Victoria, Rs.250,000 towards the All India Victoria Memorial, Rs.300,000 for the promotion of the Imperial Institute, London, and Rs.75,000 towards King Edward's Hospital Fund; in commemoration of the visit of the Prince of Wales to Jaipur in 1905 he gave an additional Rs.300,000 to the Famine Fund; on the occasion of the Delhi Durbar of January 1903, his senior Maharanee, Her late Highness Maharanee Jadanjee, subscribed Rs.100,000 to the Famine Fund, and added to the same fund another Rs.100,000 in honour of the visit of the Princess of Wales in 1905 ; to the Women's Medical College, Hospital and Nursery School, Delhi, he gave Rs.300,000 ; to Prince of Wales's Relief Fund Rs.100,000 ; to Imperial Indian Relief Fund Rs.100,000 ; his total contributions in connection with the Great War amount to Rs.23,83622. Is a very catholic Hindu in his religion, and when invited in 1902 to be present at the coronation of King Edward VII. he travelled to England in a strict orthodox style with 125 of his officers and attendants, a whole ship being chartered for the voyage, and all eatables and drinking-water being brought from India. *Heir*: Maharaj-Kumar Man Singh (adopted 24 March 1921). *Address*: Jaipur, Rajputana, India.   (*Died 7 Sept. 1922.*)

JAMAL, Sir Abdul Karim Abdul Shakur, Kt., cr. 1920; C.I.E. 1915; merchant; b. 1862 ; m.; four s. five d. *Educ.*: Jamnager (Kathiawar); Rangoon. Proprietor of the firm Jamal Bros. & Co., Ltd. ; founder and half owner of Indo-Burma Petroleum Co., Ltd.; Member Burma Legislative Council. *Address*: Jamal Manzie, Rangoon, Burma.
             (*Died 2 Sept. 1924.*)

JAMES, Charles Canniff, C.M.G. 1911 ; M.A., LL.D. ; b. Napanee, Ontario, 14 June 1863 ; s. of late Charles James, J.P., and Ellen Canniff (U.E.L.); m. 1887, Frances L., d. of James Crossen of Cobourg, Ontario ; one s. *Educ.*: Napanee High School ; University of Victoria College (University of Toronto). Graduated, 1883 ; Master in Cobourg Collegiate Institute, 1883-86 ; Professor of Chemistry at Ontario Agricultural College, Guelph, Ontario, 1886-91 ; Deputy Minister of Agriculture for the Province of Ontario, Canada, 1891-1912 ; Special Commis-

sioner on Agricultural Instruction, Canadian Department of Agriculture, 1912 - 13 ; Ex-President of Ontario Historical Society ; Fellow of Royal Society of Canada. *Publications*: Text-book on Agriculture ; various pamphlets on Agricultural work ; Bibliography of Canadian Poetry (English) ; Contributions to the History of Ontario. *Recreation*: golf. *Address*: 144 St. George Street, Toronto. *Clubs*: National, University, Lambton Golf and Country, Toronto.
             (*Died 23 June 1916.*)

JAMES, Edmund Janes, A.M., Ph.D., LL.D., President State University of Illinois, 1904-20 ; President Emeritus since 1920 ; b. Jacksonville, Illinois, 21 May 1855 ; s. of Rev. Colin D. James and Amanda K. Casad ; m. 1879, Anna Margaret, d. of Rev. Wm. Roderick Lange of Halle a/S., Prussia ; two s. one d. *Educ.*: North-Western Univ. ; Harvard Univ.; Universities of Halle, Leipsic, and Berlin. LL.D. Queen's Univ., Harvard Univ., North-western Univ., and Univ. of Michigan ; Principal of Public High School, Evanston, Illinois, 1877-79 ; of the Model High School, Normal, Illinois, 1879-82 ; Professor of Public Finance and Administration in the University of Pennsylvania at Philadelphia, 1883-96 ; Professor of Public Administration and Director of Extension Division, University of Chicago, 1897-1901 ; President Northwestern University, 1902 - 4 ; founder and for eleven years Pres. American Academy of Political and Social Science ; founder and for six years Pres. of the American Society for the Extension of University Teaching at Philadelphia ; past Vice-Pres. of American Association for the Advancement of Science ; Vice-Pres. of American Social Science Association ; Pres. Board of Trustees of the Illinois State Historical Library ; Chairman Illinois State Highway Commission ; Delegate of United States Government to Pan-American Congress at Rio Janiero, 1906 ; Hon. Sec. of State Geological Commission ; of State Tax Commission ; Pres. of American Economic Association, 1910 - 11, *Publications*: Translation of the Panegyricus of Isocrates ; History of American Tariff Legislation ; The City Government of Philadelphia ; The Modern Municipality and the Gas Supply ; City Administration in Germany ; The City Charters of Chicago ; Government Regulation of Railways ; Our Legal Tender Decisions ; The Education of Business Men in Europe ; the Origin of the Land Grant Act of 1862 ; and more than one hundred papers, essays, and monographs on educational, political, and social questions. *Recreations*: wheeling, mountain climbing, horseback riding, golf, occasional trips to Europe. *Address*: Urbana, Illinois. *Clubs*: Harvard, New York ; University, Washington ; University, Union League, Chicago, Cliff-Dwellers, Chicago ; Evanston ; University, Champaign ; University, Urbana.
             (*Died 17 June 1925.*)

JAMES, Sir Edward Burnet, Kt., cr. 1908 ; J.P.; b. 7 May 1857 ; s. of late Stephen James of Bristol and Chew Magna, Somerset, and Mary, d. of late George Bush, Bristol ; m. 1888, Mabel Amelia, d. of Sir G. W. Edwards, J.P. ; one s. [Captain Gilbert Sydney James, R.F.A. ; m. 1918, Evelyn, d. of Brig.-Gen. Vizard, 10 The Avenue, Colchester]; one d. Councillor (Bristol), 1891-1913 ; Alderman, 1906-13 ; High Sheriff, 1900-1 ; Lord Mayor, 1904-5 and 1907-8 ; Master of Society of Merchant Venturers, 1895 ; Chairman, Bristol South Conservative Association, 1905-7 ; President, Colston Dolphin Society, 1906-7. *Address*: Springfort, Stoke Bishop, Bristol. *T.*: Stoke Bishop, 65 *Club*: Constitutional, Bristol.   (*Died 27 Dec. 1927.*)

JAMES, Francis Edward, R.W.S. ; Water-Colour Painter ; Member New English Art Club ; s. of Rev. Henry James, Rector of Willingdon, Sussex ; m. Anna Georgiana, widow

549

of late Phillip Scholfield of Maltby Hall, and d. of Captain Gooch, R.N. *Educ.:* private school. *Address:* 42 South Street, Torrington, North Devon. (*Died 25 Aug. 1920.*)

JAMES, Henry, author; *b.* 15 Apr. 1843; *s.* of late Rev. H. James. *Educ.:* France; Switzerland; Harvard Law School. Became a naturalized Englishman, 1915. *Publications:* Watch and Ward, 1871; A Passionate Pilgrim, 1875; Roderick Hudson, 1875; Transatlantic Sketches, 1875; The American, 1877; French Poets and Novelists, 1878; The Europeans, 1878; Daisy Miller, 1878; An International Episode, 1879; Life of Hawthorne, 1879; A Bundle of Letters, 1879; Confidence, 1879; Diary of a Man of Fifty, 1880; Washington Square, 1880; The Portrait of a Lady, 1881; Siege of London, 1883; Portraits of Places, 1884; Tales of Three Cities, 1884; A Little Tour in France, 1884; The Bostonians, 1886; Princess Casamassima, 1886; Partial Portraits, 1888; The Aspern Papers, 1888; The Reverberator, 1888; A London Life, 1889; The Tragic Muse, 1890; Terminations, 1896; The Spoils of Poynton, 1897; What Maisie Knew, 1897; In the Cage, 1898; The Two Magics, 1898; The Awkward Age, 1899; The Soft Side, 1900; A Little Tour in France, 1900; The Sacred Fount, 1901; The Wings of the Dove, 1902; The Ambassador, 1903; The Golden Bowl, 1905; English Hours, 1905; The American Scene, 1907; The High Bid, 1909; Finer Grain, 1910; The Outcry, 1911; A Small Boy and Others, 1913; Notes on Novelists, 1914. *Club:* Athenæum.
(*Died 28 Feb. 1916.*)

JAMES, Sir Henry Evan Murchison, K.C.I.E., *cr.* 1901; C.S.I. 1898; *b.* 20 Jan. 1846; 3rd *s.* of late William Edward James, Barrock Park, Cumberland; unmarried. *Educ.:* Durham School. Assist. Collector, 1865; Under-Secretary to Govt. of Bombay, 1873; Postmaster-General, Bombay, 1875; Postmaster-General, Bengal, 1880; Director-General of the Post Office, 1886; Collector and Commissioner of Ahmedabad, 1889-91; Commissioner in Sind, 1891-1900; member of the Gov.-General's Legislative Council, 1895-97; officiating member of Council, Bombay, 1898-99; Retired 1900; Member of Port-of-Spain Commission, 1903; Member of Council, Central Asian Society, Indian Section, Royal Society of Arts, and F.R.G.S. *Publication:* Long White Mountain, or Travels in Manchuria, 1888. *Address:* Glenshee, Cambridge Park, Twickenham. *T.:* Richmond 123. *Clubs:* Carlton, East India United Service.
(*Died 20 Aug. 1923.*)

JAMES, John Arthur, M.V.O. 1909, J.P.; *b.* 1853; *m.* 1885, Mary Venetia, *d.* of late Rt. Hon. G. A. F. C. Bentinck. *Address:* 3 Grafton Street, W.; Coton House, Rugby. *Clubs:* Carlton, Travellers', Turf, Marlborough, Bachelors'. (*Died 30 April 1917.*)

JAMES, Lt.-Col. Walter Haweis; late Royal Engineers; *b.* 9 July 1847; *y. s.* of late H. C. James and Elizabeth Jane Page; *m.* 1871, Fanny Eugenia Mabel Caunter, *o. d.* of Rev. G. Akehurst; three *s.* one *d.* *Educ.:* privately; R.M. Academy, Woolwich. Entered Royal Engineers, 1867; Captain, 1879; passed Staff College with Honours, 1877; served in the Intelligence Dept. War Office, and as Dep.-Assist. Quartermaster-General, Zulu War; retired, 1880; re-employed, 1901; appointed to War Office as assistant to Permanent Under-Secretary, and promoted Major; Lieut.-Col. 1903; contested West St. Pancras, 1885 (C.); Member of London County Council, 1889-92; Chairman of Sanitary Committee and Whip of the Moderate Party; many years a member of the Grand Council of the Primrose League; Vice-Chairman, 1899; recalled to the Army, 14 Sep. 1914; served in the Censor's Department till 31 May 1918 as 2nd Grade S.O.; retired then, having reached age limit. *Publications:*

Modern Strategy; The Waterloo Campaign; numerous articles in the magazines and newspapers. *Recreations:* shooting, tennis. *Address:* 6 St. Mary's Mansions, W.2. *Club:* Authors'.
(*Died 13 Jan. 1927.*)

JAMES, Colonel William Reginald Wallwyn, C.M.G. 1916; retired 1917; *b.* 23 Oct. 1860; *s.* of Edward Wallwyn James; *m.* 1889, Aline, *d.* of Rev. Canon Hayman; one *s.* *Educ.:* Royal Military Academy, Woolwich; Lieut. R.A., 1880; substantive Colonel, 1912; served S. Africa, 1901 (clasp); European War, 1914-1916 (despatches, C.M.G.). *Club:* United Service. (*Died 6 Nov. 1925.*)

JAMESON, John, J.P., D.L.; Chairman and Managing Director, John Jameson & Son, Ltd.; *e. s.* of late John Jameson of St. Marnock's, and Anne, *d.* of William Haig, Provost of St. Andrews, N.B.; *m.* 1870, Elizabeth, *e. d.* of late Thomas Collins Banfield. *Educ.:* Trin. Coll. Dublin (M.A.); High Sheriff, Co. Dublin, 1880. Owns 4600 acres. *Address:* St. Marnock's, Malahide, Co. Dublin.(*Died 25 Feb. 1920.*)

JAMESON, Lt.-Col. John Eustace-; Commdg. 24th (Reserve) Batt. the London Regt. since 1914; *b.* Ireland, 22 Mar. 1858; 3rd *s.* of James Jameson, Anfield, Co. Dublin, and Alice, *d.* of Alicia Eustace, and *g. d.* of Viscount Baltinglass; *m.* Mary, *d.* of J. B. Cabbell, Cromer Hall, Cromer. *Educ.:* Wimbledon, Sandhurst. Late 18th Royal Irish, 20th Hussars, and Q.O. Worcestershire Hussars; Lt.-Col. commanding the 24th (Reserve) County of London Battalion, The London Regiment (The Queen's), which he raised, 1 Sep. 1914; raised and commanded the 3/24th Battalion, London Regiment (The Queen's) from 22 May 1915; attached to the Staff in Dublin as A.A.G. (Advisory), 1 Aug. 1916; attached to the Staff (Irish) Division in Flanders from 5 Dec. (despatches); late H.M. Inspector of Factories; manager of William Jameson and Co., distillers, Dublin; M.P. (N.) W. Clare, 1895-1906. *Recreations:* Hurlingham, All Ireland, and Wanderers' Polo Clubs. *Address:* 37 Cranley Gardens, S.W. *Clubs:* Naval and Military, Hurlingham, Reform.
(*Died 22 Dec. 1919.*)

JAMESON, Rt. Hon. Sir Leander Starr, 1st Bt.; *cr.* 1911; C.B. 1894; P.C. 1907; President British South Africa Company; M.P. Harbour Division, Capetown, 1910-12; *b.* Edinburgh, 9 Feb. 1853; *s.* of late R. W. Jameson, W.S. *Educ.:* London Univ.; M.D. 1877; M.B. and B.S. 1875; M.R.C.S. Eng. 1875. Administrator of Rhodesia, British South Africa Company, 1891-95; led raid on Transvaal, 29 Dec. 1895; battle of Krugersdorp, 1 Jan.; surrendered to Boers, 2 Jan. 1896; tried in London, and sentenced to 10 months' imprisonment, May 1896; released in December owing to ill-health; served S. Africa, 1899-1900; elected member of Cape Legislative Assembly for Kimberley, 1900; appointed Director of De Beers Consolidated Company, 1900, and of the British South Africa Company, 1902; Premier, Cape Colony, 1904-8. *Heir:* none. *Address:* 2 Great Cumberland Place, W. *T.:* Paddington 1453. *Clubs:* Beefsteak, Orleans.
(*Died 26 Nov. 1917.*)

JAMIESON, George, C.M.G. 1897; Director of the British and Chinese Corporation, Chinese Central Railways and Yangtse Valley Company; *b.* 1843; *m.* 1873, Margaret, *d.* of late Patrick Inkson of Berrleys, Banffs.; one *s.* three *d.* Entered Consular Service, 1864; Barr. Middle Temple, 1880; Consul and Judge of Supreme Court, Shanghai, 1991; Consul-Gen., 1897-99. *Publications:* various papers on the Revenue and Statistics of China; prize essay on Bimetallism. *Address:* 43 Onslow Square, S.W.7. *T.:* Kensington 2226. *Clubs:* Reform, Thatched House.
(*Died 30 Dec. 1920.*)

JAMIESON, William Allan, LL.D., M.D., C.M., F.R.C.P.E.; Knight of Grace of St. John

of Jerusalem ; Royal Household Jubilee Medal, 1897 ; Surgeon the King's Bodyguard for Scotland, the Royal Company of Archers ; Consulting Physician for Diseases of the Skin, Edinburgh Royal Infirmary ; Consulting and Visiting Physician to the Edinburgh City Hospital for Infectious Diseases, 1886-91 ; *b.* Dreghorn Manse, Ayrshire, 1 April 1839. *Educ.*: Irvine Academy ; University of Glasgow (Arts) ; University of Edinburgh and Vienna (Medicine) ; Coronation Medal, 1911 ; President, Royal College of Physicians, 1909-10. *Publications:* A Manual of Diseases of the Skin, 4th edition, 1894 ; The Care of the Skin in Health, 1912 ; many contributions on Dermatology and allied subjects. *Recreations:* archery, cycling, travel. *Address:* 35 Charlotte Square, Edinburgh. *T.:* 3154. *Club:* University, Edinburgh.
(Died 21 April 1916.)

JANE, Fred. T.; naval author and journalist, etc. ; *b.* 6 Aug. 1870 ; *e. s.* of Rev. John Jane, Vicar of Upottery, Devon ; *m.* 1st, 1892, Alice, *d.* of late Hamilton Beattie ; one *d.* ; 2nd, 1909, Edith Frances Muriel, *o. d.* of late Captain Henry Chase Carré, R.N.; one *d. Educ.:* Exeter School. Inventor of the Naval War Game ; naval correspondent for the Engineer, Scientific American, and Standard ; contested Portsmouth as Navy Interests Candidate, 1906. *Publications:* Blake of the "Rattlesnake," 1895 ; The Incubated Girl, 1896 ; To Venus in Five Seconds, 1897 ; The Lordship, the Passen, and We, 1897 ; The Violet Flame, The Port Guard Ship, 1899 ; Fighting Ships (naval annual) ; The Torpedo in Peace and War, 1898 ; The Jane Naval War Game (naval kriegspiel), 1898 ; The Imperial Russian Navy, 1900 ; Ever Mohun, 1901 ; Hints on Playing the Jane Naval War Game, 1902 ; The Jane Coast Operations War Game for the Instruction of Garrison Artillery in Coast Defence, 1903 ; The Imperial Japanese Navy, 1904 ; Heresies of Sea Power, 1906 ; The Ought-to-go, 1907 ; A Royal Bluejacket, 1908 ; All the World's Aircraft (Annual), 1910 ; How to play the Naval War Game, 1912 ; The British Battle Fleet, 1912 ; Your Navy as a Fighting Machine, 1914 ; various small war handbooks, 1914 ; The World's Warships, 1915. *Recreations:* motoring, scouts. *Address:* Hill House, Bedhampton, Havant, Hants. *T.A.:* Jane, Bedhampton. *T.:* 115 Havant. *M.:* BK 97, BK 264, BK 1616.
(Died 8 Mar. 1916.)

JANES, Emily. *Educ.:* private school. Diocesan Secretary G.F.S. St. Albans diocese, 1877-78 ; voluntary parish work at Apsley, 1865-80 ; a Matron, Magdalen Hospital, Streatham, 1880-81 ; Private Secretary to Miss Ellice Hopkins, 1882-86, these years being spent in petitioning for the Amendment of the Laws for the Protection of Girls ; Hon. Org. Sec. Ladies' Associations for the Care of Girls, 1886-95 ; Secretary of the National Union of Women Workers (now the National Council of Women), which had grown out of conferences and associations she had helped to organise from 1895 until 1917, when she resigned ; Founder, Distaff Guild, Hampstead Garden Suburb, 1923. *Publications:* A Threefold Cord (a Magazine for Charitable Workers), 1891-93 ; editor, the Englishwoman's Year-Book, 1899-1908 ; The Associated Work of Women in Philanthropy — a paper in the Baroness Burdett Coutts' book, Woman's Mission ; occasional magazine articles. *Recreations:* reading, music, conversation. *Address:* Dunclutha, Hastings, Sussex.
(Died 26 Oct. 1928.)

JANJIRA, H.H. Nawab Sir Sidi Ahmad Khan Sidi Ibrahim Khan, G.C.I.E., *cr.* 1906 ; *b.* 1862 ; *S.* 1879 ; descendant of the Sarul Khan family ; *m.* 1st, Ahmedbibi (*d.* 1885) ; 2nd, 1886, Nazli Begum, of the Fyzee family of Bombay; 3rd, 1913, Kalsumbibi,

a grand-daughter of the Nawab's great uncle ; one *s. Heir: s.* Sidi Mahamad Khan, *b.* 7 Mar. 1914. The State has an area of 324 square miles and a population of 88,717 ; entitled to a salute of 13 guns. *Address:* Janjira, Kolaba, Bombay.
(Died 2 May 1922.)

JANVRIN, Rev. William Langston Benest, M.A., Rector of Cradley, Malvern, since 1917 ; Prebendary in Hereford Cathedral ; *b.* London, 15 Aug. 1853 ; *s.* of William and Jane Matilda Janvrin, both of Jersey ; *m.* 1879, Maud Madeleine Beavis ; three *s.* one *d. Educ.:* Clare College, Cambridge. Ordained 1878 ; Priest, 1879 ; Curate of S. Saviour's, S. Pancras, London ; Sherington, Bucks ; Perpetual Curate in Beverley Minster, Yorkshire ; Vicar of Southwold, Suffolk ; and Vicar of S. Peter's, Hereford. *Address:* Cradley Rectory, Malvern. *T.A.:* Cradley. *T.:* Ridgway Cross 5. *M.:* CJ 9457.
(Died 26 Dec. 1927.)

JAPP, Francis Robert, M.A., LL.D., F.R.S. ; Emeritus Professor of Chemistry, Aberdeen University ; *b.* Dundee, 8 Feb. 1848 ; *y. s.* of James Japp, minister of Catholic Apostolic Church ; *m.* 1879, Elizabeth, *o. d.* of F. Tegetmeyer ; two *d. Educ.:* Universities of St. Andrews, Edinburgh, Heidelberg, and Bonn. Research Assistant and, later on, Lecturer on Chemistry in Normal School of Science, S. Kensington (Royal Coll. of Science), 1878-90 ; Foreign Secretary of Chemical Society, 1885-91, and Vice-President, 1895-99 and 1915-18 ; Longstaff Medallist of Chemical Society, 1891 ; President Chemical Section, British Association, 1898 ; Vice-President of the Institute of Chemistry of Great Britain and Ireland, 1901-4. *Publications:* Inorganic Chemistry, jointly with Professor Sir Edward Frankland, F.R.S., 1884 ; and numerous researches published in Journal Chemical Society from 1879 on. *Address:* 25 Ellerker Gardens, Richmond, Surrey.
(Died 1 Aug. 1925.)

JARDINE, David Jardine, of Applegarth; J.P., Dumfriesshire ; F.R.G.S. ; *s.* of James Jardine of Dryfeholm, Tinwald, and Torthorwald, Dumfriesshire, and Larriston, Roxburghshire ; *m.* Angela, *d.* of Sir Charles Bright, Bart., M.P., late of Badsworth Hall, Yorkshire, and Carbrook Hall, Yorkshire ; one *d. Educ.:* Trinity Coll. Cambridge. M.A. After leaving the university travelled in India, Java, China, Japan, Australia, New Zealand, Tasmania, America, Canada, Egypt, and South Africa. Spent four years in India shooting big game. Member Royal Company of Archers (King's Bodyguard for Scotland). *Recreations:* fond of racing, trains with Peacock at Middleham, Yorkshire. Won the Royal Hunt Cup at Ascot with "Refractor," 1899 ; and Northumberland Plate with "Sir Harry," 1909. *Address:* Jardine Hall and Dryfeholm, Lockerbie, Dumfriesshire ; Larriston Hall, Roxburghshire ; 9 Upper Grosvenor Street, W.1. *T.:* Mayfair 3934. *Clubs:* Carlton. Boodle's.
(Died 23 Aug. 1922.)

JARDINE, Sir John, 1st Bt., *cr.* 1916 ; K.C.I.E., *cr.* 1897; Hon. I.L.D. Aber.; M.P. (L.) Roxburghshire since 1906; Judge of High Court, Bombay, 1885 ; Acting Chief Justice, 1895 ; retired 1897 ; *b.* England, 27 Sep. 1844; 3rd *s.* of William Jardine, J.P., Dunstable; *m.* 1880, Minnie D., *d.* of J. Hogg, M.R.C.S.; six *s. Educ.:* Christ College, Cambridge. Chancellor's Gold Medal English Verse, Cambridge, 1864 ; Fellow University of Bombay, 1872 ; sometime Dean of Arts and Dean of Law ; Vice-Chancellor, 1895 ; President Royal Asiatic Soc. Bombay. Entered Bombay C.S. 1864 ; Political Officer in Native States of Kattywar, 1871 ; Secretary for trial of the Gaekwar of Baroda, 1875 ; Secretary to Treaty with Portugal and Law Officer to Government of India, 1877 ; Judicial Commissioner of Burma, 1878 ; President Burma School Board, 1881 ; Chief Secretary to Bombay Government, holding the Political, Secret, Educational,

Persian, and Judicial portfolios, 1885 ; contested Roxburghshire (L.), 1900. *Publications*: Notes on Buddhist Law, with translations of the Burmese Law of Manu ; Preface to Dr. E. Forchhammer's King Wagaru's Code ; editor of Customary Law of the Chin Tribe, and of Father Sangermano's Burmese Empire 100 Years Ago. *Recreation*: travel. *Heir*: *e. s.* Capt. John Eric Birdwood Jardine, 5th Queen's West Surrey Regt. *Address*: Applegarth, Godalming. *Clubs*: Reform ; Scottish Liberal, Edinburgh ; Byculla, Bombay. (*Died 26 April 1919*.)

JARDINE, Major Sir John Eric Birdwood, 2nd Bt., *cr.* 1916 ; 5th Batt., The Queen's Regiment ; *b.* London, 30 Sep. 1890 ; *e. s.* of 1st Bt., K.C.I.E., LL.D., and Minnie Dunbar, *d.* of Jabez Hogg, F.R.C.S. ; *S.* father 1919 ; unmarried. *Educ.*: Charterhouse ; C.C.C. Oxford, B.A. 1914. Commissioned in 5th Batt. The Queen's R. W. Surrey Regt. 1911 ; served in India, 1914-15, and in Mesopotamia, 1915-19 (despatches) ; Captain, 1916 ; Major, 1921. *Heir*: *b.* Capt. C. A. Jardine. *Recreations*: soldiering, books, tennis, and bridge. *Address*: Black Gates, W. Byfleet, Surrey. *Club*: New University.
(*Died 24 Mar. 1924*.)

JARDINE, Sir Robert William Buchanan, 2nd Bt., *cr.* 1885 ; *b.* 21 Jan. 1868 ; *s.* of 1st Bt. and Margaret, *d.* of J. Buchanan Hamilton, Leny, Perthshire ; *m.* Ethel Mary, O.B.E., *d.* of late Benjamin Piercy, of Marchwiel Hall, Wrexham, and Macomer, Sardinia, 1894 ; one *s.* one *d. Educ.*: Eton ; Magdalene College, Cambridge. *Heir*: *s.* William, (*b.* 7 Mar. 1900 ; *m.* 1921, Jean, *yr. d.* of Lord Ernest Hamilton ; M.F.H. Dumfriesshire.) *Address*: Castlemilk, Lockerbie, N.B. ; 24 St. James's Place, S.W.1 ; *T.*: Regent 980 ; The Kremlin, Newmarket. *Clubs*: Arthur's, Carlton, Turf.
(*Died 30 Jan. 1927*.)

JARMAN, John Robert, I.S.O. 1909 ; a Sub-Inspector Board of Education, 1875-1909, in Sunderland and Durham districts ; *b.* 1844. *Address*: 13 Tunstall Vale, Sunderland.
(*Died 19 April 1922*.)

JARRETT, Col. Henry Sullivan, C.I.E. 1895 ; Colonel on the Supernumerary List ; *b.* 17 June 1839 ; 2nd *s.* of late Thomas Jarrett, Speldhurst, Kent, and Eliza, *d.* of late Capt. Chambers, 89th Foot ; *m.* Agnes Delacour, *d.* of late Francis Beaufort, Bengal Civil Service, 1874 ; three *s. Educ.*: Prior Park, Bath. First commission, 1856 ; served in India during the Mutiny (medal) ; also in the Mahsud-Waziri Expedition, 1860 (medal and clasp) ; and the second Yusufzai Expedition as A.D.C. to Sir Neville Chamberlain and Sir John Garvock (clasp) ; Secretary and Member, Board of Examiners, Fort-William, Calcutta ; and Asst.-Secretary, Legislative Dept., Govt. of India, 1870-94. *Decorated* for general services. *Publications*: History of the Caliphs ; Institutes of the Emperor Akbar ; Heine's Book of Songs into English verse ; Stratheir. *Recreations*: fishing, shooting. *Address*: South Lodge, Imberhorne, East Grinstead. *Club*: United Service.
(*Died 15 April 1919*.)

JARVIS, Lt.-Col. Arthur Leonard Fitzgerald, I.S.O. 1905 ; *b.* 1852 ; *s.* of late George Murray and Elizabeth Arnold Jarvis ; *m.* Frances Geraldine, *d.* of late Capt. C. L. J. Fitzgerald, 1st W.I. Regt. ; one *s.* Entered Canadian Government Service, 1868 ; Private Secretary to Postmaster-General, 1882 ; to Minister of Agriculture, 1885-92 ; Secretary, Department of Agriculture, 1896 ; commanded the Governor-General's Foot Guards, 1899-1904 ; Assistant Deputy Minister of Agriculture, 1908 ; retired 1925. General Service Medal with one clasp, Long Service Medal, and Long Service Decoration. *Club*: Rideau. (*Died Mar. 1927*.)

JASTROW, Morris, Jr., Ph.D., LL.D. ; Professor of Semitic Languages in the University of Pennsylvania since 1885 ; *b.* 13 Aug. 1861 ; *s.* of Marcus Jastrow (*d.* 1903) and Bertha Wolffsohn (*d.* 1908) ; *m.* 1893, Helen Bachman ; no *c. Educ.*: Public and Private Schools, Philadelphia, 1866-81 ; University of Pennsylvania, 1881-85 (A.B.) ; Breslau and Leipzig Universities, 1881-84 Paris (Collège de France, École des Hautes Études, École des Langues Orientales Vivants), 1884-85 ; Strasburg University, 1885. President of the American Oriental Society, 1914-1915 ; President of the Society of Biblical Literature, 1916 ; Member of American Philos. Society ; U.S. Delegate to various Congresses ; Haskell Lecturer at Oberlin College, Oberlin, O., 1913 ; Lewison Lecturer (Free Synagogue of New York), 1915, etc. *Publications*: Religion of the Babylonians and Assyrians, 1898 ; two grammatical treatises of Abu Zakariyya Hayyug, 1897 ; A Fragment of the Babylonian Dibbarra Epic, 1891 ; The Study of Religion, 1902 ; Die Religion Babyloniens und Assyriens, 1902-12 ; Atlas of Illustrations for the Religion of Babylonia and Assyria, 1912. Editor : (with memoir) Selected Essays of James Darmesteter (transl. by Helen Bachman Jastrow), 1895 ; series Handbooks on the History of Religion ; Semitic Dept., International Encyclopedia ; Editor of Rand, M'Nally and Co.'s Linguistic Map of Europe and the Near East, 1919 ; Aspects of Religious Belief and Practice in Babylonia and Assyria, 1911 ; Hebrew and Babylonian Traditions, 1914 ; Babylonia-Assyrian Birth-Omens and their Cultural Significance, 1914 ; The Civilization of Babylonia and Assyria, 1915 ; The War and the Baghdad Railway, 1917 ; The War and the Coming Peace, 1918 ; Zionism and the Future of Palestine, 1919 ; A Gentle Cynic, 1919 ; The Eastern Question and its Solution, 1920 ; The Book of Job, 1920 ; in conjunction with A. T. Clay, An Old Babylonian Version of the Gilgamesh Epic, 1920 ; numerous articles and monographs in American and European periodicals and serials. *Recreations*: walking, chess, reading novels. *Address*: 248 S. 23rd Street, Philadelphia, Pa., U.S.A. *T.*: Locust 2481. *Club*: Franklin Inn, Philadelphia. (*Died June 1921*.)

JAYNE, Rt. Rev. Francis John D.D. ; *b.* 1845 ; *s.* of John Jayne, J.P., and Elizabeth Haines; *m.* Emily, *d.* of Watts J. Garland, Lisbon, 1872 ; three *s.* three *d. Educ.*: Rugby ; Wadham Coll. Oxon. Hody Greek Exhibition, 1st class Mods. Greats, Law and History ; Fellow of Jesus College, 1868 ; Senior Hall and Houghton Greek Testament Prizeman, 1870 ; Curate, St. Clement's, Oxford, 1870-71 ; Tutor, Keble College, 1871-79 ; Preacher at Whitehall, 1875-77 ; Principal, St. David's Coll. Lampeter, 1879-86 ; Select Preacher, Oxford, 1884 ; Vicar, Leeds, 1886 ; Bishop of Chester, 1889-1919. *Address*: The Quarry, Oswestry, Salop. *Club*: Athenæum.
(*Died 23 Aug. 1921*.)

JEANS, Sir Alexander Grigor, Kt., *cr.* 1918 ; Managing Director and Editor of the Liverpool Post and Mercury and of the Liverpool Echo since 1904 ; *b.* Elgin, 27 June 1849 ; *s.* of Robert Jeans, J.P., Elgin ; *m.* 1877, Ellen (*d.* 1889), *d.* of Thomas Gallon, Birkenhead ; four *s.* one *d. Educ.*: Elgin Academy. Been connected with the Liverpool Post since 1872 ; Manager, 1879 ; has been Chairman of the Liverpool Reform Club, the Press Association, and the Cheshire Automobile Club ; twice Captain of Wallasey Golf Club. *Recreations*: golf and motoring. *Address*: Inchbroom, Bidston Road, Birkenhead. *T.*: Birkenhead 664. *Clubs*: National Liberal ; Liverpool Reform, Liverpool Exchange. (*Died 6 Mar. 1924*.)

JEANS, Hon. Maj.-Gen. Charles Gilchrist, C.B. 1917 ; retired ; late A. O. Dept. ; *b.* 4 Aug. 1854. Entered Army, 1873 ; Col. 1908 ; retired, 1913. (*Died 5 Jan. 1920*.)

JEANS, Sir Richard Walter, Kt., cr. 1922; late Director and General Manager, Bank of Australasia, and Chairman Australasian Bank Managers' Committee; b. 2 July 1846; m. 1902, Lucia Ellinor, d. of Robert Fremuth, Dantzig. Address: Ridgeway, Langley Avenue. Surbiton, Surrey. T.: Kingston, 525. M.. LO 5410. Clubs: Constitutional, Australasian.
(Died 13 April 1924.)

JEANS, William, journalist, retired; b. Edinburgh. Educ.: Elgin Academy; Edinburgh University. Has been a journalist all his life; entered the Press gallery, 1863, and was there continuously till 1911, with the exception of the years 1866-67-68, which he spent in the press in Melbourne, Victoria; was for over 40 years the London editor and Parliamentary correspondent of the Dundee Advertiser, and has during the same period also represented at Westminster the Leeds Mercury, the Yorkshire Observer, and the Liverpool Daily Post. Recently published a volume of Parliamentary Reminiscences covering the period from 1868 to 1886. Recreation: golf. Address: Deanfield, Belmont Road, Reigate. Club: National Liberal. (Died 5 Feb. 1916.)

JEFFERS, Le Roy, F.R.G.S.; Librarian, Author, Lecturer; b. Ipswich, Mass., Aug. 1878; s. of Charles P. Jeffers and Elizabeth B. Stalker; m. 1918, R. E. Miller. Manager for the Booklovers Libraries, 1901-4; Manager, Book Order Office, New York Public Library, for its system of 52 branch Libraries, since 1905; also in main reading-room for evening service, 1906-14; visited European Libraries, 1908; Member American Library Association, New York Library Club; published through A.L.A. comparative lists of books issued in various editions, showing the most economical method of purchasing desirable editions for library use; contributor on mountaineering, travel, psychology, and library economy to periodicals; author of The Call of the Mountains, 1922; Lecturer on the Natural Wonders of the United States and Canada, and on Mountaineering in North America; Librarian American Alpine Club; Organiser and Secretary, Bureau of Associated Mountaineering Clubs of North America; Member National Institute of Social Sciences; California Academy of Sciences. Address: 476 Fifth Avenue and 106 Central Park West, New York. Clubs: Alpine, Authors; Explorers, American and Canadian, French Alpine; Adirondack Mountain, Appalachian Mountain, Fresh Air, Green Mountain, Harvard Travellers, Sierra. (Died 25 July 1926.)

JEFFERSON, Frederick Thomas, Head of Kenrick & Jefferson, West Bromwich; Chairman and Managing Director of the Britannic Assurance Corporation; m. 1917, Millie Robinson, Brighton. Address: Lapworth Hall, Warwickshire. (Died 15 Nov. 1920.)

JEFFERY, Walter, Managing editor Evening News, Sunday News, and Woman's Budget, Sydney, N.S.W.; M. Institute of Journalists, Lond.; b. Portsmouth, 1861. Educ.: Portsmouth. Went to sea, 1876; and was in different parts of the world until 1884; then began journalism, and arrived in Sydney in 1886; is a Trustee of the Public Library of N.S.W., Sydney. Publications: A Century of Our Sea Story, 1900; The King's Yard, etc. Recreation: student of early Australian history and English naval history. Address: S. Bennett Ltd., 49 Market Street, Sydney, Australia.
(Died 14 Feb. 1922.)

JEFFREY, Rev. Norman Stuart, Hon. Canon of Manchester. Address: Rylea, Thornton-le-Fylde, Preston. (Died Sept. 1919.)

JEFFREYS, Admiral Edmund Frederick, R.N.; C.V.O. 1903; b. 1 Oct. 1846; s. of late General E. R. Jeffreys, C.B. Entered Navy, 1860; Capt. 1885; Beaufort Testimonial, 1874; served Egyptian war, 1882; Assist.

Director of Torpedoes, 1889-93; Director of Naval Ordnance Admiralty, 1897-1901; late Senior Officer Coast of Ireland, 1901-4. Club: United Service. (Died 19 Mar. 1925.)

JEFFREYS, Brig.-General Patrick Douglas, C.B. 1896; O.B.E. 1919; late 1st Batt. The Connaught Rangers; retired; b. 29 July 1848; 2nd s. of late Gen. E. R. Jeffreys, C.B.; m.1897, Maude Maynard, o. d. of late Sir Richard Oldfield, Kt. Educ.: Marlborough College. Entered army, 1866; served Zululand, 1879 (medal with clasp); Burmah, 1886-87 (despatches, medal with clasp); Zhob Field Force, 1890 (despatches); commanded, with temporary rank of Brigadier General, 2nd Brigade of Malakand Field Force during operations on N.W. Frontier, 1897-98, including operations in Bajour, in the Mamund country, and in Buner (despatches twice, medal with clasp); Commanded East Group, Kent Vol. Regt. 1915-1919; J.P. and C.C. Kent. Address: Doddington Place, Sittingbourne, Kent. T.: Doddington-Kent. Club: United Service. (Died 12 April 1922)

JELF, Sir Arthur Richard, Kt., cr. 1901; b. Pankow, near Berlin, 1837; s. of late Rev. Richard William Jelf, D.D., Principal of King's College, London, and Emmy, Countess Schlippenbach of Prussia, Maid of Honour to the Queen of Hanover; m. 1867, Jane, y. d. of late Rev. William Clark King, Vicar of Norham; three s. three d. Educ.: Eton; Christ Church, Oxford (2nd class Mods, 2nd class Greats, hon. 4th Mathematics). Barr. Inner Temple, 1863; Q.C. 1880. Recorder of Shrewsbury, 1879-1901; Judge of King's Bench Division of High Court of Justice, 1901, 1910. Address: Oak House, Carlton Road, Putney Hill, S.W. T.: Putney 1184. Club: Athenæum.
(Died 24 July 1917.)

JELLICORSE, Rev. William, M.A.; Prebendary of Wellington in Hereford Cathedral since 1891. Address: Maryvale, Ludlow. (Died 8 July 1920.)

JENKINS, Rev. David, Hon. Canon of Truro. Address: Tideford Vicarage, St. Germans, Cornwall. (Died 18 Dec. 1926.)

JENKINS, Lieut.-Col. Francis, C.M.G. 1918; Officier de la Légion d'Honneur; Secretary Southern Provinces and Colony of Nigeria since 1921; s. of H. L. Jenkins of Clanacombe, Kingsbridge, Devon; b. 31 May 1877; m. 1914, Margaret Campbell, d. of late Capt. W. T. Fraser, 42nd Highlanders, and Mrs. Fraser of Moorside, Cookham; two d. Educ.: Harrow; R.M.C., Sandhurst. First commission Coldstream Guards, 1896; Capt. 1904; Major, 1911; temp. Lt.-Col. 1916; seconded for service with the West African Frontier Force, 1903-6, 1908-10, and 1911-19; Staff Officer for West African Frontier Force at the Colonial Office, 1911-16; served South Africa with Coldstream Guards, 1900-2 (Queen's medal 5 clasps, King's medal 2 clasps); West Africa, with Northern Nigeria Regt., 1903 (African Gen. Service medal and clasp); European War, with Nigeria Regt., Nigerian Frontier (mention, C.M.G.); retired from Army, 1919; Colonial Secretary, Barbados, 1919-21. Address: Lagos, Nigeria. Clubs: Guards, Travellers, Sports.
(Died 8 Nov. 1927.)

JENKINS, Herbert; Author and Managing Director of the publishing house of Herbert Jenkins, Ltd.; s. of George J. Jenkins, Norwich; unmarried. Educ.: Greyfriars College. In spare moments snatched from the commerce of books, contributed articles, stories, etc., to reviews and periodicals; founded the publishing house of Herbert Jenkins, Ltd. Publications: The Life of George Borrow, 1911; Bindle, 1916; The Night Club, 1917; Adventures of Bindle, 1918; John Dene of Toronto, 1919; Malcolm Sage, Detective, 1920; Mrs. Bindle, 1921. Recreation: walking. Address: 3 York

555

JEFFERY, Edward Turner. See page xxii.

Street, St. James's, S.W. *T.A.:* Booklover. *T.:* Gerrard 7846 *(Died 8 June 1923.)*

JENKINS, Huntly E., Barrister. *Address:* 1 Brick Court, Temple, E.C. 4. *T.:* Central 1596 ; 21 Craven Hill, W.2 ; Paddington 4852. *(Died 1 Nov. 1923.)*

JENKINS, Hon. John Greeley ; 4th *s.* of Evan Jenkins and Mary Davis of South Wales ; *b.* Pennsylvania, U.S., 8 Sep. 1851 ; *m.* 1883, Jeannie Mary, *o. d.* of W. H. Charlton of Adelaide : one *s.* one *d. Educ.:* public schools in America ; Wyoming Seminary, Pa. Worked on father's farm until 1872 ; travelled in Canada and United States for publishing company, 1872-78 ; arrived Adelaide, Australia, 1878 ; entered Town Council, Unley, 1885 ; mayor, 1886 ; Member of Parliament for District of Sturt, 1887-1902 ; Torrens, 1902-5 ; served on several Royal Commissions; Minister of Education, 1891-92; introduced the Free Educational Bill, which was passed 1891 ; Minister for Works, 1892 and 1894-99 ; Chief Secretary, 1899-1901 ; Premier and Chief Secretary, 1901-5; Agent-General for S. Australia, 1905-8 ; attended several important conferences between premiers of States and Commonwealth ; during his premiership introduced and passed an amendment to the Constitution, reducing the number of members of Parliament and materially lessening the expense of Government ; always strong advocate land settlement and progressive legislation ; was for several years Deputy Grand Master of S.A. Grand Lodge ; represented Commonwealth Government, International Telegraph Conference, Lisbon, 1908; Member of Council and Hon. Treasurer of the London Chamber of Commerce ; Vice-President of the British Empire Products organisation ; Vice-Chairman British Imperial Council of Commerce ; attended International Congress of Commerce in Boston, 1912, and Paris, 1914 ; and International Trade Conference in Atlantic City, 1919, Paris, 1920 ; on the Directorate of the International Chamber of Commerce, Vice-President and on the Council of the Royal Colonial Institute ; Member of the Council, the Empire Cotton Growing Corporation ; Member of Council, British Empire Exhibition, 1924. *Publications:* Australian Products ; Social Conditions of Australia; Edited Australasian Section Encyclopedia Americana. *Recreations:* walking, gardening. *Address:* 12a Windsor Court, Bayswater, W. ; 27 Clement's Lane, E.C.4. *T.A.:* Starproof, London. *T.:* Central 4727. *Club:* City Carlton. *(Died 22 Feb. 1923.)*

JENKINS, Rt. Hon. Sir Lawrence Hugh, Kt., *cr.* 1899; K.C.I.E., *cr.* 1903; P.C. 1916 ; *b.* 22 Dec. 1858 ; 2nd *s.* of R. D. Jenkins, Cilbronnau, Cardigan, J.P. ; *m.* 1892, Catherine Minna, 2nd *d.* of late Andrew B. Kennedy ; one *s. Educ.:* Cheltenham College ; Oxford University. Called to Bar, 1883 (Lincoln's Inn) ; Bencher of Lincoln's Inn, 1909 ; Judge of Calcutta High Court, 1896-99 ; Chief Justice of the High Court of Judicature, Bombay, 1899-1908 ; Member of Council of India, 1908-9 ; Member of the Judicial Committee of the Privy Council since 1916 ; Chief Justice, High Court, Bengal, 1909-15 ; Chairman of Quarter Sessions, Cardiganshire ; Past District Grand Master of Freemasons for Bombay and Bengal. *Address:* Cilbronnau, near Cardigan. *(Died 1 Oct. 1928.)*

JENKINS, Brig.-Gen. (Hon.) Noble Fleming, C.M.G. 1916 ; C.B.E. 1919 ; *b.* 29 Oct. 1860 ; *s.* of late D. J. Jenkins, M.P. Penryn and Falmouth ; *m.* 1st, Mabel (*d.* 1918), *d.* of late Major General J. F. Richardson, C.B. ; three *d.* ; 2nd, Edith Muriel, *d.* of Major L. B. Edgar one *s.* two *d. Educ.:* Rugby ; Sandhurst. Captain Border Regt., 1888 ; served South African War, 1899-1901 ; rejoined 3rd Border Regt. on outbreak of war ; served European War, 1914-18 (despatches, C.M.G., C.B.E.); is Deputy-Secretary of the S.P.G. *Address:* 32 Greycoat Gardens, S.W.1. *T.:* Victoria 3207. *(Died 19 Aug. 1927.)*

JENKINS, William Henry Phillips, J.P., D.L. ; *b.* 1842 ; *o. surv. s.* of late John Jenkins of Caerleon, Co. Monmouth, and Elizabeth, *d.* and co-heiress of late Henry Phillips of Llantarnam House, Co. Monmouth ; *m.* 1st, 1872, Lady Caroline Anne (*d.* 1912), *y. d.* of 6th Earl of Jersey ; 2nd, 1914, Kathleen, 2nd *d.* of late John H. Abernethy. *Educ.:* Rugby ; Merton College, Oxford. *Address:* Frenchay Park, Bristol. *Clubs:* Boodle's, New University. *(Died 26 Dec. 1916.)*

JENKINS, Rev. William Owen, D.D. (Oxon.); *b.* 1863 ; *s.* of late W. Jenkins, of Abercastell, and Mary, *e. d.* of late Daniel Owen of Ty Gwyn, Pembs. ; Principal, The Diocesan College, Rondebosch, S.A.; Canon and Chancellor of St. George's Cathedral, Cape Town ; Examining Chaplain to the Archbishop of Cape Town ; *m.* 1891, Margaret Collinson (*d.* 1915), *e. d.* of late W. G. Steel of Carlisle ; two *s.* four *d. Educ.:* Haverfordwest School ; Classical Exhibitioner of Jesus Coll. Oxford. B.A. (Classical Honours), 1885. Chaplain of St. Andrew's Coll. Grahamstown, 1888-91 ; Rector of East London East (S. Africa), 1891-94 ; Rector and Rural Dean of Graaff Reinet, 1894-99; Member of Provincial Synods, 1898, 1904, 1909, 1915, and of Provincial Standing Committee, 1910-15 ; Examiner in Divinity and Philosophy and Member of Council Cape Univ. *Publications:* The Incarnation in St. Paul's Theology ; The Christian Hope of Immortality ; Lilies, Corner Stones, and Pearls ; The Philosopher as Statesman, a Study in Plato's Republic. *Address:* Rondebosch, S.A. *(Died 19 July 1919.)*

JENKINSON, Sir Edward George, K.C.B.; *cr.* 1888 ; *b.* 1835 ; *m.* 1865, Annabella (*d.* 1915), *d.* of Capt. T. Monk Mason, R.N. *Educ.:* Harrow ; Haileybury Coll. Indian Civil Service, 1856-80 ; served Indian Mutiny ; late Private Secretary to Lord Spencer, Lord-Lieut. of Ireland, 1882-84. *(Died 1 Mar. 1919.)*

JENKINSON, Francis John Henry, Hon. D.Litt., Oxford ; Librarian, University Library, Cambridge, since 1889 ; *b.* 20 August 1853 ; *s.* of John Henry Jenkinson ; *m.* 1902, Margaret Clifford, *o. d.* of late Ludovick C. Stewart. *Educ.:* Marlborough ; Trinity Coll., Cambridge (Fellow and late assistant tutor). *Address:* Southmead, Chaucer Road, Cambridge. *(Died 21 Sept. 1923.)*

JENNER, George Francis Birt, C.M.G. 1902 ; Jubilee medal, 1897 ; *b.* Paris, 26 May 1840 ; *e. s.* of Albert Lascelles Jenner, Wenvoe Castle, Glamorgan, and Henrietta Morris, *e. d.* of Sir John Morris, Bt., Sketty Park, Glamorgan ; *m.* Stephanie Emilianoff, *d.* of Alexis Emilianoff, Ragatova, etc., in the Government of Orel, Russia. *Educ.:* abroad. Entered Diplomatic Service, 1857 ; Attaché, Washington, 1859 ; accompanied Lord Lyons in attendance on the Prince of Wales when in Canada and U.S., 1860 ; Turin, 1860 ; Athens, 1862 ; Dresden, 1866 ; Berne, 1866 ; Constantinople, 1867 ; Teheran, 1868 ; Acting Consul-General at Tabreez, 1868 ; Berne, 1872 ; Stockholm, 1876 (Acting Charge d'Affaires, 1879) ; Secretary of Legation and Oriental Secretary, Tehran 1882 ; Secretary of Legation, Mexico, 1884 (Charge d'Affaires, 1885); Buenos Ayres, 1887 (Charge d'Affaires, 1888-89); Chargé d'Affaires, Lima, 1891-92 ; Minister Resident and Consul-General, Bogota, 1892-97; transferred to Central America, 1897 ; retired on a pension, 1902. *Address:* Les Alouettes, Cannes. *Club:* St. James's.

JENNINGS, Arthur Seymour, F.J.I., F.I.B.D.; Founder and Editor of The Decorator, and Paint and Wallpaper ;

Chairman and Managing Director Trade Papers Publishing Co., Ltd.; Past President and Fellow Incorporated Institute of British Decorators; Author and Journalist since 1882; Expert and Lecturer in Decoration, Paints, Colours, and Varnishes; *b.* Camberwell, S.E., 3 Jan. 1860; *s.* of William Jennings, leather technologist; *m.* 1885, Jennie Marguerite, *d.* of Thomas Higenbotham, Yonkers, N.Y., U.S.A.; one *d.* Educated as architect; late Lecturer Science and Art Department Board of Education; late Associate Editor Scientific American and Oils, Colours, and Drysalteries; Fellow Institute of Journalists; member of Technical and Scientific Circle; Consulting Examiner City and Guilds of London Institute; Weekly Newspaper Proprietors' Association; member Society of Authors; member Paint and Varnish Committee British Engineering Standards Association; honorary Life member International Association of Master Painters and Decorators, of the United States and Canada; member of Council, Oil and Colour Chemists' Association; member Research Association of British Paint, Colour and Varnish Association. *Publications:* The Modern Painter and Decorator; The Decoration and Renovation of the Home; The House Beautiful; Painting by Immersion and by Compressed Air; Wall Papers and Wall Coverings; Paint and Colour Mixing; The Builders' Pocket Book; Motor and Coach Painting; The Painters' Pocket Book; Commercial Paints and Painting, Paints and Varnishes, etc. *Recreations:* freemasonry and music. *Address:* 4 Brunswick Square, Hove, Brighton. *T.A.:* Polystyle (Holb.), London. *T.:* Holborn 4776; Hove 6641. *Club:* Authors'.

JENNINGS, Brig.-Gen. Herbert Alexander Kaye, C.I.E. 1916; R.A.; Retired List; *b.* 1862; *s.* of Maj.-Gen. C. J. Jennings; *m.* 1893; one *d. Educ.:* Wellington College; R.M.A. Woolwich. Entered R.A. 1882. *Address:* Simla, India. *Club:* Naval and Military.
(Died 15 Jan. 1921.)

JENNINGS, James George, M.A., C.I.E. 1919; Director of Public Instruction, Bihar and Orissa; *b.* 14 June, 1866; *s.* of James Jennings; *m.* 1894, Maud Walrond, *d.* of Gateward Coleridge Davis, Bar.-at-Law; three *d. Educ.:* Ashby-de-la-Zouch Grammar School; privately; Lincoln College, Oxford. Indian Educational Service, 1892; Professor of English Literature, Government College, Benares, 1892; Government College, Allahabad, 1895; Inspector of Schools, United Provinces, 1906; Principal, Government College, Allahabad, 1907; Director of Public Instruction, Bihar and Orissa, 1913-17 and 1920-21; Vice-Chancellor, Patna University, 1917-20; Member of the Legislative Council, Bihar and Orissa, 1913-16 and 1917-20; Additional member (temporary) of the Viceroy's Legislative Council, 1917; Fellow of Allahabad University, 1895-1913; Hon. Fellow since 1913; ex officio Fellow of Calcutta University, 1913-17. *Publications:* Addresses to Students, 1918; Essay on Metaphor; Select Passages on Duty to the State; Selections from Marcus Aurelius Antoninus; Sakuntala, adapted from Kalidasa; From an Indian College. *Address:* 16 Charlbury Road, Oxford. *Club:* East India United Service.
(Died Jan. 1921.)

JENNINGS, Rev. Canon John Andrew; Canon of Christ Church Cathedral, 1913; Wallace Lecturer in Divinity since 1902, Trinity College, Dublin; Rector of Harold's Cross, Dublin, since 1901; Rural Dean, 1905; *b.* 1855; *o. s.* of John Jennings, Blackrock, Co. Dublin; *m.* 1881, Jane Charlotte, *y. d.* of Rev. Samuel McCutcheon, Longford; two *s.* one *d. Educ.:* Trinity College, Dublin. Downes' Divinity Prize, 1st; B.A. 1880; M.A. 1883; ordained, 1880; priested, 1881; Curate of St. Peter's, Drogheda,

1880; Rector of Portnashangan (Meath), 1881; Rector of Donaghpatrick (Meath), 1882; Rector of St. Mary's, Dublin, 1896; Hon. Chaplain Lord Lieut. 1901, and to all subsequent Lord Lieuts.; member of Senate, T.C.D.; member of General Synod of Church of Ireland; member of Dublin Diocesan Council; governor of King's Hospital (Blue Coat School); trustee of Mageough Home; Professor of Pastoral Theology, Trinity College, Dublin, 1912-17; Select Preacher, Dublin University, 1914, 1915, 1916, 1917, and 1921. *Publications:* Modern Elocutionist, 1879, many editions; Wayside Restings (poems), 1880; six volumes of Readings, 1880-96, many editions; editor of Church of Ireland Parish Magazine, circulation 13,000 monthly, 1888-98; Unto the Perfect Day, 1883; Liturgical Reading, 1883; Reverence, 1891; The True Order, 1907; various articles, sermons, and verses. *Recreations:* sketching, photography. *Address:* Harold's Cross Rectory, Dublin.
(Died Dec. 1923.)

JENNINGS, Colonel Robert Henry, C.S.I. 1904; R.E.; *b.* 18 Oct. 1852; *e. s.* of late R. Jennings, Woodlawn, Cork; *g.s.* of late Lt. T. Jennings, R.N. Lakeville, Cork; *m.* 1892, Bessie, *d.* of late Archibald Gray and Mrs. Gray of 97 Holland Park, W. and St. Mary's Tower, Birnam, Perthshire; one *s.* one *d. Educ.:* Royal Military Academy, Woolwich. Travelled much in Europe and the East; entered R.E. 1872; Colonel, 1903; served Afghan War, 1879-80; Chief Political Officer, Sir C. MacGregor's Force Mari Expedition (despatches, medal); Chief Political Officer, Toba Column, 1882; made exploration, Persia, Baluchistan, Helmund, 1884-85 (thanked by Commander-in-Chief; high approval Government of India); Army Staff till 1890; Consul to H.B. Majesty, Basra, Turkish Arabia, 1892; Resident, Jeypore, 1898; Indore, 1899-1902; W. Rajputana States, 1903-5; on special duty representing H.E. the Viceroy as host of King of Afghanistan's eldest son during latter's tour in India, 1904-5; decorated for special services, 1904; Member Royal Society of Arts; Fellow, Royal Botanic Society. *Publications:* numerous articles in Gazetteer of Baluchistan, 1891, of Persia, 1892; description of country and routes, between Baghdad, Nejf, and Karbela, in Mesopotamia, 1892; and Baluchistan and Persia, 1886, with scientific appendices and illustrated Diary. *Recreations:* shooting, fishing, literary works, politics. *Address:* 20 Roland Gardens, S.W. *Clubs:* Junior United Service, Authors'.
(Died 21 Nov. 1918.)

JENNINGS, General Sir Robert Melvill, K.C.B.; *cr.* 1909; C.B. 1896; *b.* 20 Nov. 1841; *s.* of Rev. M. J. Jennings, M.A.; *m.* 1873, Dame Agnes Mary (*d.* 1920), *d.* of Rev. J. S. Gilderdale; one *s.* one *d.* Entered Bengal Cavalry, 1859; Maj.-Gen. 1895; Lt.-Gen. 1900; General, 1904; served North-West Frontier, India, 1863-64 (medal with clasp); Egyptian war, 1882 (despatches, brevet of Col., 4th class Osmanieh, Khedive's star); Hon. Colonel 6th P.W. Cavalry. *Address:* c/o H. S, King & Co., 9 Pall Mall, S.W.1. *(Died 16 Aug. 1922.)*

JENNINGS, William Thomas, J.P., Member House of Representatives since 1902; *b.* Auckland, New Zealand, 1 Jan. 1854; father from Lancaster, and mother from. Fermanagh (I.), maiden name M'Ivor; *m.* 1886, Dora Mary Brannigan, of Australia. *Educ.:* St. Paul's and St. Peter's Schools, Auckland. Was apprenticed to his uncle, the then proprietor of the New Zealander, daily paper, and learned the printing business; was manager Dunedin Age, evening paper, and filled responsible positions in other offices throughout the colony; late Member Legislative Council, New Zealand; was enthusiastic volunteer for number of years, attaining position Acting-Lieut. Hobson Rifles, and at present is Hon. Lieut. Auckland Engineer Corps; took part in three annual contests N.Z. Rifle Association's shooting tournaments ; active member friendly societies for over 20 years, attaining positions President Hibernian Society, and Grand District President United Ancient Order of Druids ; President Typographical Union, and President Tailoresses' Union, Auckland. *Publications:* written for various newspapers and periodicals. *Address:* Parliamentary Buildings, Wellington, N.Z.   *(Died 6 Feb. 1923.)*

JERDAN, Rev. Charles, M.A., D.D. (Edin.), LL.B. (Lond.), senior minister of Sir Michael Street United Free Church, Greenock, since 1884 ; *b.* 25 March 1843 ; *s.* of David Jerdan and Elisabeth Smiles ; *m.* 1st, 1870, Jane Forbes (*d.* 1902), *d.* of George Paterson, Glasgow ; one *s.* ; 2nd, 1905, Agnes, *d.* of John Haddow Carmichael, Greenock. *Educ.:* Edinburgh University ; Divinity Hall of United Presbyterian Church. Ordained at Dennyloanhead, Stirlingshire, 1867, and minister there till 1878 ; minister of Tay Square Church, Dundee, 1879-84 ; junior Principal Clerk of United Free Church General Assembly, 1907 ; Senior Clerk, 1916-20 ; served on many important committees of United Presbyterian and United Free Church Supreme Courts. *Publications:* Messages to the Children, 1897 ; For the Lord's Table, 1899 ; For the Lambs of the Flock, 1901 ; Gospel Milk and Honey, 1905 ; Pastures of Tender Grass, 1909 ; Manna for Young Pilgrims, 1912 ; Seed-Corn and Bread, 1915 ; The Wells of Salvation, 1917 ; Scottish Clerical Stories and Reminiscences, 1920 ; The One Saving Name, 1922 ; contributions to the Pulpit Commentary, Hosea, Hebrews, James. *Address:* 68 Union Street, Greenock.   *(Died 1926.)*

JERMYN, Sir Alfred, Kt., *cr.* 1919 ; *b.* 4 June, 1845 ; *s.* of William and Harriott Jermyn ; *m.* Ellen, 3rd *d.* of late James Horatio Bobby of Diss, Norfolk ; eight *c. Educ.:* King Edward VI. Grammar School, Wymondham. Until 1915 senior partner in the firms of Jermyn & Perry and Jermyn & Sons of King's Lynn, Hunstanton and Oakham, drapers ; Founder and Chairman of Berry & Stanyon, Ltd., Sheerness ; Jermyn, Smart & Smith, Ltd., New Brompton ; Chairman and Director Hobbie's Manufacturing Co., Ltd., Dereham and London ; Chairman and Director Foster & Bird, Ltd., King's Lynn ; also of the East Coast Steamship Co., Ltd., of King's Lynn, Hull and Newcastle ; Director of Savage's Engineering Co., Ltd., and of the King's Lynn Docks & Railway Co., Ltd. ; formerly member of the Norfolk County Council for 15 years ; Commissioner of Taxes (Land and Income) ; Chairman and Governor of High School for Girls ; Governor of King Edward VII. Grammar School ; J.P. and Alderman of the Borough ; Mayor of King's Lynn, 1898 ; Member of the Wheelwrights' Company, City of London ; Member of Philanthropic Lodge of Freemasons, and of the Foresters, Rechabites, Shepherds, and Good Templar Societies ; is widely known in Wesleyan Methodist and Free Church circles ; President of the West Norfolk Federation of Free Church Councils. *Recreations:* public service and golf. *Address:* Burleigh House, King's Lynn. *T.:* 34. *Club:* West Norfolk, King's Lynn and County, King's Lynn.

(Died 27 June 1921.)

JERNINGHAM, Charles Edward Wynne ; a J.P. for the County of London ; appointed a Member of the Cable Censors' Committee at the Press Bureau, 1914 ; *b.* 26 March 1854 ; *y. s.* of Charles William Edward Jerningham, late of Painswick, Gloucestershire, and Emma, *d.* of Evan Wynne Roberta, of Grove House, Surrey ; *heir-pres.* to the baronetcy of Jerningham. *Educ.:* Beaumont and Stonyhurst ; for some time Senior Philosopher at the latter. Was the last

to receive a nomination for the Grenadier Guards before the adoption of the competitive examination system ; for twenty-two years wrote the Letter from the Linkman in Truth over the signature of Marmaduke, and for fourteen years contributed a weekly article to the Graphic over the same signature ; with Sir Reginald Beauchamp—the originator—helped to found the Self-Help Emigration Society, and is on the Executive Council of the Commons and Footpaths Protection Society, and the Coal-Smoke Prevention Association ; is a corresponding Member of the Archæological Society of France ; founded The Art Collectors' Protection Association ; and with W. Lacon Threlford, The Institute of Linguists, 1910 ; in 1906 presented to the nation the collection of prints of the Royal London Parks now permanently exhibited at the London Museum ; joint author, with Mr. Ralph Nevill, of Piccadilly to Pall Mall, 1908 ; published The Maxims of Marmaduke, 1910 ; The Bargain Book, 1911 ; editor of Vanity Fair, 1912 ; is a collector of old English glass, and has composed waltzes and songs ; Catholic ; Radical. *Clubs:* St. James's, Bachelors', New, Ranelagh, etc.   *(Died 7 Feb. 1921.)*

JEROME, Jerome Klapka, writer ; *b.* Walsall, 2 May 1859 ; *o. sur. s.* of Rev. Jerome Clapp Jerome ; *m.* Georgina Henrietta Stanley, *d.* of Lieut. Nesza of the Spanish Army, 1888 ; one *d. Educ.:* Marylebone Grammar School. Clerk ; schoolmaster ; actor ; journalist ; editor of Idler (with Robert Barr), 1892-97 ; of To-Day, 1893-97. *Publications:* On the Stage and Off, 1888 ; Idle Thoughts of an Idle Fellow, 1689 ; Three Men in a Boat, 1889 ; Diary of a Pilgrimage, 1891 ; Novel Notes, 1893 ; John Ingerfield, 1894 ; Barbara, 1886 ; Fennel, 1888 ; Sunset, 1888 ; New Lamps for Old, 1890 ; Ruth, 1890 ; Wood Barrow Farm, 1891 ; Prude's Progress, 1895 ; Rise of Dick Halward, 1896 ; Sketches in Lavender, 1897 ; Letters to Clorinda, 1898 ; The Second Thoughts of an Idle Fellow, 1898 ; Three Men on the Bummel, 1900 ; Miss Hobbs, 1900 ; Paul Kelver, 1902 ; Tea Table Talk, 1903. Tommy & Co., 1904 ; Idle Ideas in 1905 ; Susan in Search of a Husband, 1906 ; Passing of the Third Floor Back, 1907 ; The Angel and the Author, 1908 ; Fanny and the Servant Problem, 1908 ; They and I, 1909 ; The Master of Mrs. Chilvers, 1911 ; Esther Castways, 1913 ; The Great Gamble, 1914 ; Malvina of Brittany, 1917 ; Cook, 1917 ; All Roads lead to Calvary, 1919 ; Anthony John, 1923 ; My Life and Times, an Autobiography. *Address:* 41 Belsize Park, Hampstead, N.W.   *(Died 14 June 1927.)*

JEROME, Thomas Stroud, I.S.O. 1903 ; Chief Inspector of Works, War Office. *Address:* War Office, S.W.   *(Died 1 April 1917.)*

JERRED, Sir Walter (Tapper), K.C.B., *cr.* 1918 ; C.B. 1912 ; Assistant Secretary, Local Government Board ; *b.* 1864 ; *m.* 1901, Gertrude, *d.* of John Kirkbank-Lamin. *Address:* Local Government Board, S.W.   *(Died Oct. 1918.)*

JERROLD, Laurence ; *b.* London, 1873 ; *e. s.* of Evelyn (*e. s.* of Blanchard, *e. s.* of Douglas Jerrold) and Florence Yapp ; *m.* 1906, Germaine, *d.* of late Paul Leprince-Ringuet, Paris ; two *s.* one *d. Educ.:* Paris Univ.(Bachelor of Letters and Philosophy). Founded at 20 with other Jeunes, a Jeune Revue : The Magazine International, in which he published translations into French of the most Whitmanish of the Leaves of Grass, and which started a new French literary movement in praise of Nature and Life, and thereupon died ; has written in French on English literature (Revue Blanche ; Humanité Nouvelle, etc.); and in English on French literature and life (political questions, drama, art, music, in English and American reviews and in special journalistic correspondence); The Real France, 1911 ; The French and the English, 1913 ; France To-day, 1916 ; chief Paris correspondent of the Daily Telegraph. *Address:* 45 Rue Ampère, Paris; Les Peupliers, Petites Dalles, Seine Inf., France.   (*Died Oct. 1918.*)

JERSEY, 8th Earl of (*cr.* 1697), **George Henry Robert Child Villiers,** Viscount Grandison, 1620; Viscount Villiers and Baron Hoo, 1691; D.L., J.P. Oxon, and J.P. Middlesex; C.A. Oxfords and Middlesex; High Steward of City of Oxford; *b.* 2 June 1873; *o. s.* of 7th Earl of Jersey and Margaret, Countess of Jersey;   *S.* father, 1915; *m.* 1908, Lady Cynthia Almina Constance Mary Needham, *o. d.* of 3rd Earl of Kilmorey; two *s.* two *d.   Educ.:* Eton; New College, Oxford. Owns about 19,400 acres.   *Heir: s.* Viscount Grandison.   *Address:* Osterley Park, Isleworth; Middleton Park, Bicester; Baglan House, Briton Ferry, S. Wales. *Clubs:* Carlton, Turf, Bachelors', Jockey.   (*Died 31 Dec. 1923.*)

JERVOISE, Sir Eustace James Clarke, 6th Bart., *cr.* 1813; late Capt. South Lancashire Regt.; *b.* 14 Mar. 1870; *s.* of Alan Arthur Clarke Jervoise, *nephew* of 1st Bt., and Helen Jane, *d.* of Major J. Cruickshank; *S.* uncle, 1911. *Heir: half-b.* Dudley Alan Lestock [*b.* 27 Nov. 1876; *m.* 1908, Grace Estre, *y. d.* of Walter Ellison of Eastbrook, Wellingborough. *Address:* Evesham Cottage, Hailsham]. *Address:* Idsworth, Horndean, Hants.(*Died 11 May 1916.*)

JERWOOD, Rev. Thomas Frederick, Hon. Canon of Peterborough since 1915; Rural Dean of Rothwell II., 1900-21; Rector of Little Bowden, 1874-1924. *Address:* 8 Webster Gardens, Ealing, W.5.   (*Died 29 Dec. 1926.*)

JESSEL, Albert Henry, K.C. 1906; *b.* 81 Oct. 1864; *y. s.* of late Henry Jessel and Julia, *d.* of late Louis Cohen; *m.* Ella, 3rd *d.* of late George C. Raphael; three *s.* three *d.   Educ.:* Clifton; Balliol College, Oxford (M.A.). Called to Bar, 1889; practises in Chancery Division; Vice-President of United Synagogue; late President South London Jewish Schools, and Hon. Sec. Jewish Voluntary Schools Association; contested (C.) Accrington Division, Lancs. January 1910; Central Hackney, December 1910. *Publications:* joint editor of volume on Companies in Encyclopædia of Forms and Precedents; article on Executors and Administrators in the Encyclopædia of the Laws of England. *Recreations:* riding, shooting, golf. *Address:* 6 Gloucester Square, W. *T.:* 3322 Paddington. *Clubs:* Carlton, Junior Carlton, United, Cecil, 1900.   (*Died 2 Jan. 1917.*)

JESSEL, Sir Charles James, 1st Bt., *cr.* 1883; M.A., J.P., D.L.; Chairman of the Imperial Continental Gas Association; *b.* London, 11 May 1860; *e. s.* of late Rt. Hon. Sir George Jessel, Master of the Rolls; *m.* Edith, 2nd *d.* of late Rt. Hon. Sir Julian Goldsmid, 3rd Bt., M.P. 1890; two *s.* two *d.   Educ.:* Rugby; Balliol Coll. Oxford (M.A.). Barr. Lincoln's Inn, 1885; does not practise. *Recreation:* shooting. *Heir: s.* George [M.C., Capt. T. F. Reserve; *b.* 28 May 1891; *m.* 1923, Muriel, *d.* of late Col. J. W. Chaplin, V.C., and *widow* of Major F. Swetenham]. *Address:* 81 Hill Street, W.1; *T.:* Grosvenor 1696; Ladham House, Goudhurst, Kent. *Clubs:* Garrick, Brooks's, Beefsteak.(*Died 15 July 1928.*)

JESSON, Charles, late Organiser of the Musicians' Union; M.P. (Co.-Lab.) for Walthamstow, W., Dec. 1918-22; *b.* Leicester, 1862; *father,* boot and shoe manufacturer; *m.* 1889, Emily Roberts; one *d.   Educ.:* Public Schools in Leicester. Served as Musician in the Army. *Recreation:* politics. *Address:* 88 Meteor Road, Westcliffe-on-sea, Essex. *T.:* Southend 1100.

JESSOP, Lt.-Comdr. John de Burgh, D.S.O. 1917; R.N., retired; *o. s.* of late William de Burgh Jessop of Overton Hall, Derbys, and Judith, 2nd *d.* of Sir John Gay Newton Alleyne, 3rd Bart.; *b.* 28 Aug. 1885; *m.* 1917, Ethel Joane, *d.* of Capt. C. H. Hill, late Gloucester Regt.; one *d.* Served European War, 1914-18.   (*Died 23 Mar. 1924.*)

JESSOP, Walter Hamilton Hylton, J.P.; Senior Ophthalmic Surgeon to and Lecturer on Ophthalmic Medicine and Surgery, St. Bartholomew's Hospital; Ophthalmic Surgeon, Foundling Hospital; Examiner in Ophthalmology, Queen's University, Belfast; President, Ophthalmological Society, U.K.; *b.* 1858.   *Educ.:* Bedford; Caius College, Camb. M.A., M.B., F.R.C.S.; late Hunterian Professor of Comparative Anatomy and Physiology, Royal College of Surgeons.   *Publications:* Manual of Ophthalmic Surgery and Medicine. *Address:* 78 Harley Street, W.; *T.:* Pad. 1077; The Mill House, Sutton Courtenay, Berks. *T.:* Abingdon 87. *M.:* 6453LC; 7557LB. *Clubs:* Reform, Burlington Fine Arts; Berkshire.
(*Died 16 Feb. 1917.*)

JETTE, Sir Louis Amable, K.C.M.G., *cr.* 1901; LL.D.; Chief Justice of the Court of King's Bench, Quebec, 1909; retired 1911; *b.* L'Assomption, P.Q., 15 Jan. 1836; *s.* of late Amable Jetté, merchant, and Caroline Gauffreau, *g. d.* of a St. Domingo planter; *m.* 1862, Berthe, *d.* of Toussaint Lafiamme. Called to the Bar, 1857; engaged in journalism; elected to House of Commons for Montreal (East), 1872. re-elected in 1874; appointed Judge Super. Court, 1878; re-appointed, 1908; Chief Justice. Province of Quebec, 1909-11; Professor of Civil Law, Laval University, LL.D. 1878, subsequently Dean of the Faculty at Montreal; Commander of the Legion of Honour of France, 1898; Member of the Alaskan Boundary Tribunal, 1903; Lieutenant-Governor of the Province of Quebec, 1898-1908. *Address:* 71 d'Auteuil Street, Quebec. *Clubs:* St. James's, Montreal; Garrison, Quebec. (*Died May 1920.*)

JEUNE, John Frederic Symons-, Examiner of Standing Orders for the Houses of Lords and Commons; Knight of Grace Order of St. John; J.P. Co. Oxon.; Barrister Inner Temple; *b.* 10 Dec. 1849; 2nd *s.* of late Francis Jeune, Bishop of Peterborough, and *b.* of late Lord St. Helier, P.C., G.C.B.; *m.* Frances Susannah, *d.* of Richard Hanmer Bunbury, Capt. R.N.; one *s.* one *d. Educ.:* Rugby. Late Lt. W. Somerset Yeomanry. Assumed additional name and arms of Symons under the will of his great-uncle, Rev. B. P. Symons, D.D., Warden of Wadham College, Oxford. *Address:* Runnymede House, Old Windsor. *Clubs:* Travellers', Windham, Wellington, Beefsteak.   (*Died 8 Feb. 1925.*)

JEVONS, Shirley Byron; editor of The Sportsman, 1903-11; *b.* Doncaster; *s.* of late John William Jevons, founder and proprietor of the Nottingham Daily Express; *m.* 1887, Mary Wigley of Nottingham. *Educ.:* Makepeace Hall College, Yorkshire. *Publications:* Private Lawrie and his Love; Baffled; The Livingstone Mystery; and other tales. Served in the Army; sub-editor Birmingham Daily Gazette, 1885-90; dramatic critic and assistant editor of the Sportsman, 1890-1903; retired, 1923. *Recreation:* study. *Address:* Flat 7, Orchard House, S.E.5.   (*Died 6 Oct. 1928.*)

JODHPUR, H.H. Raj Rajeshwar Maharaja Dhiraj Maharaja Sri Sumer Singhji Sahib Bahadur of, K.B.E., *cr.* 1918; Rajhai-Hind; *b.* 14 Jan. 1898; *s.* of late Maharaja Sir Sirdar Singhji Sahib Bahadur; ascended the gaddi 5th Apr. 1911; *m.* sister of H. H. the Jamsahib of Nawanagar; one *d. Educ.:* Wellington College. Placed the whole of the resources of the State at the disposal of the British Government during European War; served at the head of the Jodhpur Lancers at the front; made an Hon. Lieut. in the British Army; is head of the great Rathore clan of Rajputs, which is a branch of the great Solar race of antiquity; the State of Marwar over which he rules is the largest State in Rajputana. *Recreations:* polo and hunting. *Address:* Jodhpur, Marwar State, India. (*Died 3 Oct. 1918.*)

JESSE, Richard Henry. See page xxii.

JOHNS, Rev. Claude Hermann Walter, Litt.D., D.D.; *b.* Banwell, Somersetshire, 4 Feb. 1857; *e. s.* of late Rev. W. P. Johns, and Eleanor, *d.* of Charles Gilbert, of Mutford Hall; *m.* Agnes Sophia, *d.* of late Rev. J. Griffith, LL.D. *Educ.:* Faversham Grammar School; Queens' College, Cambridge (School and College Exhibitioner, Foundation Scholar); 27th Wrangler 1880; M.A. 1885; Litt.D. 1909; Hon. D.D. 1915. Second Master Horton College, Tasmania, 1880-84; Paston Grammar School, 1885-87; Tutor at St. Peter's College, Peterborough, 1887-92; Ordained 1887; Curate of St. Botolph's, Helpston; St. John's, Peterborough; St. Mark's, Peterborough; Assistant Chaplain of Queens' College, Cambridge, to 1901; Edwardes Fellow of Queens' College, 1908-09; Lecturer in Assyriology at Queens' College, 1895-1909; at King's College, London, 1904-10; Rector of St. Botolph's Parish, Cambridge, 1892-1909; Hon. Fellow, Queens' College, 1915; Master of St. Catharine's College, Cambridge, 1909-19, and *ex officio* Canon Residentiary of Norwich. *Publications:* Assyrian Deeds and Documents of the 7th century B.C.; An Assyrian Doomsday Book; The Oldest Code of Laws; Babylonian and Assyrian Laws, Contracts and Letters; The Year Names of the First Dynasty of Babylon; The Bohlen Lectures on the Religious Significance of Semitic Proper Names; History of Assyria; History of Babylonia; The Schweich Lectures on the relations between the Laws of Babylonia and the Laws of the Hebrew Peoples; numerous articles and notes on Assyriology and Biblical Archæology in Scientific Journals and Dictionaries. *Recreations:* cricket, football, tennis, collector of insects, ferns, and birds' eggs in Tasmania. *Address:* Rathmines, Barnes Close, Winchester. (*Died 20 Aug. 1920.*)

JOHNS, Col. Sir William Arthur, Kt. *cr.* 1914; C.B. 1917; C.I.E. 1910; A.M.I.C.E.; temp. Col. in army; Superintending Engineer since 1906. *Educ.:* St. Columba's, Ireland; Uppingham; R.I.E. College. Entered India P.W. Department, 1880; employed with Seistan Boundary Commission, 1902-3; Frontier Surveys, 1912-13; served German East Africa, 1915-17 (despatches, C.B.). *Address:* Sunnylands, Carrickfergus, Ireland. *Club:* East India United Service. (*Died 2 June 1918.*)

JOHNSON, Rev. Arthur Henry, M.A.; Fellow and Chaplain of All Souls College, Oxford; Modern History Lecturer at University College, Oxford, since 1885; *b.* 8 Feb. 1845; 2nd *s.* of Captain George J. Johnson, of Castlesteads, Cumberland, and Frederica, *yr. d.* of Sir Frederick Hankey, K.C.M.G.; *m.* 1873, Bertha Jane, *y. d.* of Robert Bentley Todd, M.D. (Oxon), F.R.S.; two *s. Educ.:* Eton; Exeter College, Oxford. Fellow of All Souls College, Oxford, 1869-74 and since 1906; Priest, 1872; Chairman of the Modern History Board, 1893-1912; Hon. Secretary to Curators of the University Parks, 1911-24; Ford Lecturer for 1909; Modern History Lecturer to Pembroke College, 1874-84, St. John's College, 1875-84, Wadham College, 1875-84, Trinity College, 1876-1903, Hertford College, 1876-1903, Worcester College, 1883-85, Corpus Christi College, 1884-85, Balliol College, 1884-90, Merton College, 1884-1923. *Publications:* Europe in the XVI. Century; The Enlightened Despot; The Disappearance of the Small Landowner; The History of the Drapers' Company; Letters of Charles Greville and Henry Reeve. *Recreations:* Oxford Running Blue; fishing, shooting, hunting. *Address:* All Souls College and 5 South Parks Road, Oxford. *M.:* BY 9892.
(*Died 31 Jan. 1927.*)

JOHNSON, Bertha Jane, M.A.(Oxon.) by decree, 1920; Poor Law Guardian since 1894; *b.* London, 1846; *y. d.* of late Robert Bent-

558

ley Todd, M.D. (Oxon), F.R.S., sometime Professor of Anatomy and Physiology, King's College, London; *m.* 1873, Rev. Arthur H. Johnson, M.A., Fellow and Chaplain and tutor, All Souls College, Oxford; two *s. Educ.:* Home; Slade School of Art. Artist, portraits exhibited at Royal Academy, etc.; Member of Council of Lady Margaret Hall, Oxford, 1879-1926; for many years Vice-Chairman of Oxford Charity Organisation Society; Member of the original Committee of the Association for the Education of Women in Oxford; Hon. Secretary with supervision of Home Students, 1883-94; Principal of Home Students, 1894-1910; Principal of the Society of Oxford Home Students, appointed by the University, 1910-21; on the original Committee of Lady Margaret Hall, Hon. Secretary, 1880-1914; member of Education Committee, Oxfordshire County Council, 1903-1922, and co-opted Member of its Examining Board till 1924. *Address:* 5 South Parks Road, Oxford. *Club:* University Women's.
(*Died 24 April 1927.*)

JOHNSON, Ven. Charles, J.P., Archdeacon of Zululand and Missionary at St. Augustine's; *b.* Barnesley, Yorkshire 8 Sep. 1850; *s.* of Wm. Johnson; *m. d.* of Canon Jenkinson; five *s.* five *d. Educ.:* Maritzburg College; private tuition. Began mission work as missionary at Springvale, Natal; after work in other places, was sent to the people of Hlubi, the well-known Basuto chief, then in Natal, who asked that he might go with him to that part of Zululand which had been given to him as a reward for his services in the Zulu war; first began the Memorial Mission on the battlefield of Isandhlwana; after a year, went to a place about 10 miles away, nearer the chief's own house; this place was then called St. Augustine's, Rorke's Drift; the people were all heathen and very ignorant; now has 67 native teachers under him, and has established 38 out-stations round his central place, besides a large number of places where services are held, called preaching centres; he has about 8000 baptized Christians, and 1700 under regular instruction. *Publications:* various Zulu books and translations. *Address:* St. Augustine's, Zululand. *T.A.:* Vaut's Drift, Natal.
(*Died 1 Nov. 1927.*)

JOHNSON, Claude Goodman; Managing Director of Rolls-Royce, Ltd., London, Derby, Bombay; Managing Director of Automobiles Rolls-Royce (France), Ltd., Paris; Managing Director of Rolls-Royce of America, Incorporated; *s.* of late William Goodman Johnson, Science and Art Department, South Kensington. *Educ.:* St. Paul's School; Art School, South Kensington. Principal clerk, Imperial Institute, from its inception for 10 years; first Secretary Royal Automobile Club, 5½ years; as such, organised the first purely automobile Exhibition held in this country, 1899; the 1000 miles reliability trial of automobiles, 1900, and the campaign throughout the country with a view to educating County Councils as to the utility and safety of motor vehicles; Joint Manager with late Hon. Charles S. Rolls, of C. S. Rolls & Co.; this Co. acquired the whole of the output of motor cars designed by Mr. F. H. Royce of Royce, Ltd. (the Rolls-Royce cars); these subsequently became Rolls-Royce, Ltd. *Address:* Adelphi Terrace House, W.C.2; *T.:* Gerrard 7161; Villa Vita, Kingsdown, Deal; *T.:* Kingsdown, Deal 12. *Clubs:* Royal Thames Yacht, Ranelagh, Royal Automobile.
(*Died 11 April 1926.*)

JOHNSON, Cyrus, R.I.; *b.* 1 Jan. 1848. *Educ.:* Perse Grammar School, Cambridge. First exhibited in R.A. 1871, genre and then landscape; and as a portrait painter in 1877; among his sitters have been Mrs. Luttrell (1877), Mrs. Perceval, W. H. C. Plowden, F.R.S.,

JOGLEKAR, Rao Bahadur Ramchandra Narayan. See page xxii.

Sir John Duckworth, the Rev. Edward Thring, R. Neville Grenville, Rt. Hon. Edward Gibson, Lord Ebury, Canon Kynaston, Dr. Merry, Lord Halsbury, Sir George Macfarren, and Sir Bryan Donkin. *Address:* 8 Margravine Gardens, Baron's Court, W.6. *Club:* Arts.

(*Died 27 Feb. 1925.*)

JOHNSON, Rev. Frank; Editor of Sunday School Chronicle and Times since 1899; British Congregationalist and Examiner, 1909-12; Publications Secretary National Sunday School Union since 1911; Founder and Editor of the Graded Quarterlies (Primary, Junior, Intermediate, and Senior); Hon. Sec. British International Lessons Council since 1913; *m.* 1894, Alice, *d.* of William Cottom, of Birmingham; one *s.* two *d. Educ.:* Wolverhampton; London University; New College (Pye Smith Scholar of latter and Associate of the Theological Senatus). Schoolmaster for two years; Assistant Master, Model School, Borough Road Training College; minister of Congregational Church, Stone, Staffs, 1893-1899, during which period held the post of Secretary to Staffs. Cong. Union; minister, Hemel Hempstead Congregational Church, 1916-18. *Publications:* Under Cross and Crescent (1904); Faith and Vision, 1906; Bible Teaching by Modern Methods, 1907; Life of Sir Francis F. Belsey, 1914; The Disciples' Prayer, 1915; The Way of Success, 1925; contributes largely to his own and various other periodicals. *Recreations:* rose culture, cycling, and music. *Address:* 57 and 59 Ludgate Hill, E.C.4. (*Died 13 Sept. 1927.*)

JOHNSON, Major Frederick Henry, V.C. 1915; B.Sc. (1st Hons. Lond.); Temp. Major while in command of a Field Co., 231st Field Co. R.E.; *b.* Streatham, 15 Aug. 1890; *s.* of Samuel Rogers Johnson; unmarried. *Educ.:* Whitgift Middle School; St. Dunstan's College, Catford; Battersea Polytechnic; University of London. Worked as engineering apprentice and improver, 1907-11; Whitworth Exhibitioner, 1910; Day Student at Battersea Polytechnic, 1911-14; Chairman, Students' Council, editor of Polytechnic Magazine, 1914; graduated in Engineering, University of London, as internal student, 1914; Member of London University Officer's Training Corps, 1914; temp. 2nd Lt. R.E. 1914; served European War, 1914-16 (wounded on Hill 70, despatches, V.C.). *Recreations:* cycle, rowing. *Address:* 24 Cranworth Gardens, Brixton, S.W. (*Died Dec. 1917.*)

JOHNSON, George William, C.M.G. 1905; M.A.; Principal Clerk in Colonial Office, 1900-17; *e. s.* of late W. H. F. Johnson, M.A., J.P., of Llandaff House, Cambridge; *b.* 1857; *m.* 1883, Lucy, 6th *d.* of late James Nutter of Cambridge; two *s.* two *d. Educ.:* his father's school; Perse Grammar School; Trin. Coll., Camb. (Foundation Scholar 1877), 8th Wrangler and 3rd class Classical Tripos, 1880. Appointed 2nd class Clerk Colonial Office, 1881. *Publications:* Dickens' Dictionary of Cambridge; editor of the Christian Socialist, 1891; occasional reviews in the Spectator, etc.; (in conjunction with his wife) Memoir of Josephine E. Butler, 1909; The State and Sexual Morality, 1920. *Recreations:* reading and chess. *Address:* 22 Westbourne Park Villas, W.2. *T.:* Park 1948. *Club:* National Liberal. (*Died 13 Feb. 1926.*)

JOHNSON, Sir Henry James, Kt., *cr.* 1911; Solicitor; *b.* 14 June 1851; *s.* of Manuel John Johnson, Radcliffe Observer, Oxford, and Caroline, *d.* of Prof. J. A. Ogle, Oxford; *m.* 1884, Pauline, *d.* of Julius Hinterhuber, Salzburg; one *s. Educ.:* Winchester; Oxford, M.A. President, Law Society, 1910-11; firm, Waltons and Co., 101 Leadenhall Street, E.C. *Address:* 55 Sloane Gardens, S.W. *T.:* Victoria 3481. *Clubs:* United University, Savile.

(*Died 1 Mar. 1917.*)

JOHNSON, Rt. Rev. James, D.D. (Durham), M.A.; Assistant Bishop of Western Equatorial Africa since 1900. *Educ.:* Freetown Grammar School; Fourah Bay College, Sierra Leone. Catechist, C.M.S., 1858; Tutor C.M.S. Grammar School, 1860; Catechist, Christ Church, 1861; ordained, 1863; Missionary Curate of Christ Church till 1873; Native Missionary in charge of St. Paul's Church, Lagos, Yoruba Country, 1874; Superintendent of interior Yoruba Mission, 1877; Pastor of St. Paul's Church, Lagos, 1881; Secretary Native Church Committee and Church Missions; Diocesan Inspector; Bishop's Examining Chaplain; Member of Bible Translation Committee; Member of Legislative Council and Board of Education, 1886. *Publication:* Yoruba Heathenism. *Address:* Lagos, West Africa.(*Died 18 May 1917.*)

JOHNSON, Brig.-Gen. Ronald Marr, C.M.G.1 919; D.S.O. 1917; late R.F.A.; *b.* 4 Nov. 1873; *s.* of late Thomas Marr Johnson and Mrs. A. Gunning Keen; *m.* 1904, Gladys, *d.* of Maj.-General Sir John Leach, K.C.V.O.; one *s. Educ.:* Fonthill; Radley; R.M.A., Woolwich; Staff College, Quetta. Served China, 1900; European War, 1914-18; retired pay, 1923. *M.:* PD 5677. *Clubs:* Army and Navy; Royal St. George's Golf. (*Died 15 Nov. 1925.*)

JOHNSON, Lieut.-Col. Thomas Gordon Blois-, C.M.G. 1916; C.I.E. 1918; Commandant 22nd Punjabis; *b.* 27 Jan. 1867; 4th *s.* of late Major W. T. Johnson. *Educ.:* United Service College, Westward Ho; Sandhurst. Entered army, 1888; Indian Staff Corps, 1890; served N.W. Frontier of India, 1897-98; Relief of Malakand; operations in Bajaur Mohmand (medal, 2 clasps); Tirah, 1897-98 (clasp); N.W. Frontier of India, 1902; operations against Darwesh Khel - Waziris; commanded a detachment despatched to quell the rising in Bastar Native State; Mesopotamian Campaign, 1915 (severely wounded at Kut-El-Amara, C.M.G.). *Recreations:* riding, sailing, golf, Champion of Northern India (Coulmarg Kashmir), 1904; shooting. *Club:* Junior United Service. (*Died 6 Nov. 1918.*)

JOHNSON, Lt.-Col. T. Pelham, D.S.O. 1916; A.S.C.; Officer Commanding 15th Div. Train, B.E.F., France; *b.* Stratford Rectory, Saxmundham, 16 June 1871; *s.* of Rev. F. A. Johnson, B.A., and Ellen, *d.* of Richard Garrett of Carlton Hall, Saxmundham; *m.* Lilian Dora, *e. d.* of late Colonel Henry Vere Hunt, Indian Staff Corps; one *d. Educ.:* Woodbridge Grammar School; Queen's College, Cambridge; Royal Military College, Sandhurst. First Commission to Bedfordshire Regt. 1892; India, 1893-95; served Chitral campaign, 1895 (medal and clasp); transferred to A.S.C. 1896; served in East Africa and Uganda, 1898-1903 (East and Central African medal, 1900; African General Service medal, 1899-1900, despatches); served in South Africa, 1904-9; went to France with 4th Division, Aug. 1914; took 15th Div. Train to France, July 1915 (despatches 4 times, D.S.O.); Croix de Chevalier du Mérite Agricole, April 1917. (*Died June 1918.*)

JOHNSON, William, M.B.E. 1918; M.P. (Lib.-Lab.) Nuneaton Division of Warwickshire since 1906; Police Committee and Standing Joint - Committee since 1890; Member, Foleshill Board Guardians and Rural District Council since 1902; *b.* Chilvers Cotton, 1849; father, collier; grandfather, collier; *m. d.* of a Butty collier; four *s.* one *d. Educ.:* Collycroft School. Factory worker twenty years, with brief intervals colliery worker with father; General Sec. and Agent, Warwickshire Miners' Association since 1885; Treasurer of Midland Miners' Federation; County Councillor for Bedworth since 1889; Alderman, 1915; Education Committee, Warwickshire County Council, 1903; Chairman of Bedworth Parish Council since 1894; Governor of Nicholas Chamberlain's Charity, J.P. Warwickshire. *Publications:* Essay: Mazzini's Duties of Man; Machinery

JOHNSON, Rt. Rev. Joseph Horsfall, D.D. See page xxii.

v. Human Labour, based on Pattison's Mental
Science. *Recreations:* cricket and music.
Address: Bedworth, Warwickshire. *T.:* Bed-
worth 8Y. *Club:* National Liberal.
(*Died 20 July 1919.*)

**JOHNSON, Rt. Hon. Sir William
Moore**, 1st Bt., *cr.* 1909; P.C. 1881; *b.* 1828;
s. of late Rev. William Johnson, Chancellor
Diocese of Cloyne, Cork; *m.* Susan, *d.* of
R. Bayly, J.P., Green Park, Kilmalloch,
Limerick, 1884. *Educ.:* Trin. Coll. Dublin
(M.A.). Irish Barr. 1853; Law Adviser to the
Crown in Ireland 1868-74; Q.C. 1872; Solicitor-
General for Ireland, 1880-81; Attorney-General,
1881-83; M.P. Mallow, 1880-83; Judge High
Court of Justice, King's Bench Division, Ire-
land, 1883-1909; Judge High Court of Admiralty
(Ireland), 1893-1909. *Heir:* none. *Address:* 26
Lower Leeson Street, Dublin. *Clubs:* Reform;
Dublin University; St. George Yacht, Kings-
town. (*Died 9 Dec. 1918.*)

JOHNSON, Rev. William Cowper,
M.A.; Hon. Canon Norwich, 1901. *Educ.:*
Trinity College, Cambridge. Curate of St.
Mary's, Nottingham, 1870-72; St. Giles on the
Fields, 1872-75; Flitton, Beds, 1875; Vicar
Pulloxhill, Beds, 1875-80; Rural Dean of Hing-
ham, 1896; Rector of Yaxham, 1880-1915.
Address: 6 Christ Church Road, Newmarket
Road, Norwich. (*Died 6 April 1916.*)

JOHNSON, Ven. William Percival,
Archdeacon of Nyasa since 1896; Central
Africa Itinerant Missionary. *Educ.:* Bedford
School; University College, Oxford (M.A.;
D.D. 1911). Ordained, 1876. *Address:* Uni-
versities' Mission, Likoma, Nyasaland.
(*Died 11 Oct. 1928.*)

JOHNSTON, Andrew, J.P., D.L.; *b.* 23
May 1835; *s.* of Andrew Johnston, M.P. for St.
Andrews Boroughs, and Priscilla, *e. d.* of Sir T.
Fowell Buxton, Bart., M.P.; *m.* 1858, Charlotte,
e. d. of Rev. George Trevelyan. *Educ.:* Rugby;
Univ. Coll. Oxford. M.P. South Essex, 1868-
1874; High Sheriff, 1880-81; Chairman of Quarter
Sessions, 1880-1910; Chairman Essex County
Council, 1889-1915; Director Commercial Union
Assurance Co., Ltd.; New River Co., Ltd.
Address: Forest Lodge, Woodford Green, Essex.
(*Died 28 Feb. 1922.*)

JOHNSTON, Col. Charles Arthur, C.B.
1917; D.S.O. 1917; M.B.; D.P.H. (London);
Indian Medical Service (retired); *b.* 28 Feb.
1867; *m.* Isabel Mary, *d.* of late Dr. J. H.
Honeyman; one *s.* Capt. 1890; Major, 1902;
Lt.-Col. 1910; Col. 1920; served Manipur, 1891
(medal with clasp); Burma, 1891-92 (despatches,
clasp); Tirah, 1897-98 (medal with clasp);
China, 1900 (medal); European War, 1914-18
(D.S.O., C.B., despatches twice); retired, 1920.
Address: 6 Grosvenor Street, W.1. *Club:*
Junior United Service. (*Died 23 April 1926.*)

**JOHNSTON, Lieut.-Col. Charles
Evelyn,** D.S.O. 1918, M.C. 1918; *b.* 29 May
1878; *e. s.* of Reginald Eden Johnston, of Terlings, Harlow, Essex; *m.* 1905, Pleasance, *y. d.*
of Col. W. J. Alt, C.B.; three *s.* one *d.* *Educ.:*
Eton; New College, Oxford (M.A.). Member
of E. Johnston & Co., Ltd., 20 King William
Street, E.C.; Director London Joint City and
Midland Bank, London and Brazilian Bank, San
Paulo Railway, Indemnity Mutual Marine Assurance, Brazilian Warrant Co.; Lieut.-Col. London Regt. (T.A.R.); served European War,
1914-18 (despatches, D.S.O., M.C.). *Recreations:* Oxford VIII. 1899 and 1900. *Address:*
Little Offley, Hitchin; 160 St. James' Court,
S.W. *Clubs:* Oxford and Cambridge, Leander,
City of London. (*Died 27 Aug. 1922.*)

**JOHNSTON, Ven. Charles Francis
Harding,** M.A.; *b.* Barnstaple, 8 Oct. 1842;
s. of Rev. G. Johnston, and Elizabeth, *d.* of
James Gordon Morgan, M.D.; *m.* Kate, *d.* of
Richard Mallam, M.R.C.S., Kidlington; two *s.*
Educ.: Barnstaple Grammar School; Christ's

College, Cambridge (Wrangler, 2nd Classical
Tripos). In Inland Revenue Dept., Somerset
House, 1859-62; Civil Service Commission,
1862-68; Master, Trinity College, Glenalmond,
1867-68; ordained, 1867; Chaplain of H.M.
I.E., 1869-90; Domestic Chaplain to Bishop of
Bombay, 1869-75; Archdeacon of Bombay, 1888-
1890; Curate of All Saints, Oxford, 1890-91;
Vicar of Headington Quarry, Oxford, 1891-1916;
Editor St. Basil on the Holy Spirit, revised
text, 1892. *Address:* Thelwall Vicarage, War-
rington. (*Died 22 Aug. 1925.*)

JOHNSTON, Brig.-Gen. Francis Earl,
C.B. 1915; the Prince of Wales's (North Staffs
Regt.); *m.* Morna (*d.* 1915). Served expedition
to Dongola, 1896 (Egyptian medal with clasp,
medal); S. African War, 1900-2 (despatches
twice, Queen's medal, 3 clasps, King's medal,
2 clasps); Dardanelles, 1914-15 (C.B.).
(*Died 8 Aug. 1917.*)

JOHNSTON, George Jameson, M.A.,
M.B., F.R.C.S.I.; Visiting Surgeon and Clinical
Lecturer Royal City of Dublin Hospital; Pro-
fessor of and Examiner in Surgery, Royal Coll. of
Surgeons in Ireland; Consulting Surgeon Royal
Hospital for Incurables, Dublin, and Masonic
Orphan Boys' School; *b.* 18 April 1866; *s.* of
Ronald Johnston, Mullaghmore, Co. Tyrone;
unmarried. *Educ.:* Royal School, Dungannon;
School of Physic, Trinity College, Dublin. Ex-
Demonstrator of Anatomy and Operative Sur-
gery, School of Physic, T.C.D.; ex-Assistant
Surgeon Richmond Hospital; ex-Examiner in
Anatomy Conjoint Board, R.C.P. and S.I.;
Examiner in Surgery Conjoint Fellowship and
Dental Boards, R.C.P.I. and R.C.S.I.; ex-
Examiner in Clinical Surgery, Univ. Dub.; and
in Surgery, National University of Ireland;
ex-Member of Council Roy. Coll. of Surgeons in
Ireland; ex-Tem. Lt.-Col. R.A.M.C. in charge
of Surgical Division of a base hospital, B.E.F.;
ex-Visiting Surgeon Dublin Castle Red Cross
Hospital; mentioned for war work. *Publica-
tions:* papers on various surgical subjects.
Recreations: golf, philately. *Address:* 13 Lower
Fitzwilliam Street, Dublin. *T.:* 1362. *Club:*
Hibernian United Services, Dublin.
(*Died 8 Oct. 1926.*)

JOHNSTON, Sir Harry (Hamilton);
G.C.M.G., *cr.* 1901; K.C.B., *cr.* 1896; D.Sc.
Camb.; J.P.; War Medal, 1914-18; Gold
Medallist Zoological, Royal Geographical, and
Royal Scottish Geographical Societies; Hon.
Member Italian Geographical Society, and Royal
Irish Zoological Societies; Trustee of the Hun-
terian Collection, Royal Coll. of Surgeons; Hon.
Member R.W.S.; Hon. Life Member of the
New York Zoological Society; *b.* Kennington,
London, 12 June 1858; *s.* of John Brookes
Johnston and Esther Laetitia Hamilton; *m.* Hon.
Winifred Irby, O.B.E., *d.* of 5th Lord Boston,
and *step-d.* of Sir H. Percy Anderson, K.C.B.,
1896. *Educ.:* Stockwell Grammar School;
King's Coll., London; student Royal Academy
of Arts, 1876-80. Medallist S. Kensington
School of Art, 1876; silver medallist Zoological
Society, 1896. Studied painting at R.A. and
also in France; travelled in North Africa,
1879-80; explored Portuguese West Africa and
River Congo, 1882-83; commanded Scientific
Expedition of Royal Society to Mt. Kilimanjaro,
1884; H.M. Vice-Consul in Cameroons, 1885;
Acting Consul in Niger Coast Protectorate,
1887; Consul for province of Mozambique, 1888;
expedition to Lakes Nyasa and Tanganyika
(founding of the British Central Africa Protectorate), 1889; C.B. 1890; Commissioner and Consul-General B.C.A., 1891; Consul-Gen. Regency
of Tunis, 1897-99; Special Commissioner, Commander-in-Chief and Consul-General for
Uganda Protectorate, etc., 1899-1901. *Publications:* essays on the Tunisian Question,
1880-81; River Congo, 1884; Kilimanjaro,
1885; History of a Slave, 1889; Life of

Livingstone, 1891 ; various blue-books and reports on West Africa, Central Africa, North Africa, and East Africa, 1888-1901 ; British Central Africa, 1897 ; A History of the Colonisation of Africa by Alien Races, 1899-1913 ; The Uganda Protectorate, 1902 ; British Mammals, 1903 ; The Nile Quest (History of the Exploration of the Nile), 1903 ; Liberia, 1906 ; George Grenfell and the Congo, 1908 ; A History of the British Empire in Africa, 1910 ; The Negro in the New World, 1910 ; The Opening-up of Africa. 1911 ; Views and Reviews, 1912 ; Common Sense in Foreign Policy, 1913 ; Phonetic Spelling, 1913 ; Pioneers in West Africa, Canada, India, Australasia, Tropical America, and South Africa (6 vols.), 1911-13 ; A Gallery of Heroes and Heroines, 1915 ; The Truth about the War, 1916 ; The Black Man's Part in the War, 1917 ; The Gay Dombeys (a novel), 1919 ; Comparative Study of the Bantu and Semi-Bantu Languages, vol. i., 1919 ; vol. ii., 1922 ; Mrs. Warren s Daughter, 1920 ; The Backward Peoples, 1920 ; The Man who did the Right Thing, 1921 ; The Veneerings, 1922 ; Little Life-Stories, 1923 ; The Story of my Life, 1923 ; Relations, 1925. *Recreations* : painting, biological studies, music. *Address* : St. John's Priory, Poling, Arundel.
(*Died 31 July 1927.*)

JOHNSTON, Rev. Hugh William ; Rector of North Cray since 1864 ; Hon. Canon of Canterbury, 1904. *Educ.* : Trinity Coll. Camb. Ordained 1861 ; curate of Chaddesley-Corbett, Worcestershire, 1861-63 ; Salehurst, Sussex, 1863-64 ; Rural Dean East Dartford, 1894-1913.
(*Died 1 Sept. 1918.*)

JOHNSTON, Rt. Hon. Sir James, P.C. Ireland, 1919 ; Kt., *cr.* 1918 ; Member of Senate of Northern Ireland ; *b.* 29 Nov. 1849 ; *m.* 1876, Jeannie, *d.* of George Cleland, of Ballywoolen, Co. Down. High Sheriff of Belfast, 1912 ; Lord Mayor, 1917 and 1918. *Address* : Belvoir Park, Newtownbreda, Co. Down. *Clubs* : Constitutional ; Ulster Reform, Belfast.
(*Died 13 April 1924.*)

JOHNSTON, Sir John Barr, Kt., *cr.* 1899 ; merchant ; *b.* 9 Aug. 1843 ; *e. s.* of John Johnston, Beragh, Co. Tyrone, Ireland ; *m.* Isabel, *d.* of Alexander Weir, Ballindrait, Co. Donegal, 1877 ; one *s.* three *d.* Alderman and Justice of the Peace for the City of Londonderry ; Mayor of Londonderry, 1897-98 ; Justice of the Peace and Grand Juror for County Tyrone ; High Sheriff of the County of the City of Londonderry, 1900 *Address* : Londonderry. (*Died 12 Feb. 1919.*)

JOHNSTON, Rev. John Octavius, M.A. ; Cathedral Chancellor, Lincoln ; *b.* Barnstaple, 1 Nov. 1852 ; *y. s.* of Rev. George Johnston and Elizabeth, *d.* of James Gordon Morgan, M.D., Barnstaple ; *m.* Harriette Louisa, *d.* of Dalton Mallam, Oxford ; two *s.* one *d.* *Educ.* : Barnstaple Grammar School ; Keble Coll., Oxford, 1874-79. B.A. 1878 ; 2nd class Classics, 1st class Theology ; Senior Hall Houghton Greek Testament Prize, 1880 ; M.A. 1881. Curate of Kidlington, Oxon., 1879-81 ; Principal of St. Stephen's House, Oxford, 1881-84 ; Theological Tutor of Merton College, 1883-95 ; Chaplain, 1885-95 ; Vicar of All Saints', Oxford, 1885-95 ; Examiner in Honour School of Theology, 1896-92 ; Examining Chaplain to the Bishop of Oxford, 1889-1913 ; Vicar of Cuddesdon and Principal of Cuddesdon Theological College, 1895-1913 ; Honorary Canon of Christ Church, 1902-13 ; Proctor in Convocation for the Diocese of Oxford, 1902-17 ; Proctor for Lincoln Chapter, 1918. *Publications* : joint-editor of Three Anti-Pelagian Treatises of St. Augustine ; Dr. Liddon's Life of Dr. Pusey ; Dr. Pusey's Spiritual Letters ; Life and Letters of H. P. Liddon, D.D. ; Men of God. *Address* : Subdeanery, Lincoln. (*Died 6 Nov. 1925.*)

JOHNSTON, Reginald Eden, J.P. ; Director Bank of England ; *b.* 1847 ; *s.* of Edward Johnston, 23 Queen's Gate Terrace, S.W. ; *m.* Alice (*d.* 1907), *d.* of Rev. C. Eyres, Great Melton, Norfolk, 1875 ; two *s.* three *d.* *Address* : Terlings, Harlow. *Club* : Union.
(*Died 20 Nov. 1922.*)

JOHNSTON, Robert Mackenzie, I.S.O. 1903 ; F.S.S. ; Registrar-General and Government Statistician ; Fellow and Member of Council of the Royal Society of Tasmania ; Member of Council and of Senate of the University of Tasmania ; Fellow and Past President of Section .F (Economics and Statistics) of the Australasian Association for the Advancement of Science ; Fellow of the Royal Geographical Society of Australia ; Hon. Foreign Corresponding Member of the Geological Society of Edinburgh. *Publications* : Systematic Account of the Geology of Tasmania ; numerous publications relating to the Natural History of Tasmania. *Address* : Hobart, Tasmania.
(*Died 20 April 1918.*)

JOHNSTON, Robert Matteson, M.A.Cantab., and of the Inner Temple, barrister-at-law ; Professor of Modern History, Harvard University, since 1919 ; editor of The Military Historian and Economist ; Secretary of the Military Efficiency Association ; Major 'U.S. army, attached to General Staff, A.E.F., 1918-19 ; *b.* Paris, 11 April 1867 ; *s.* of W. E. Johnston, M.D. *Educ.* : schools, England, France, U.S.A. ; Pembroke College, Cambridge. Engaged in business until 1900 ; first lectured at Harvard University, 1904 ; Professor of History, Bryn Mawr College, 1907 ; Assistant Professor History, Harvard, 1908-19. *Publications* : The Roman Theocracy and the Republic, 1901 ; Napoleon, a short biography, 1904 ; The Napoleonic Empire in Southern Italy, 1904 ; Memoirs of Malakoff, 1906 ; The French Revolution, a short history, 1906 ; Leading American Soldiers, 1907 ; The Corsican, 1910 ; The Holy Christian Church, 1911 ; Mémoire de Marie Caroline, reine de Naples, 1912 ; Bull Run, 1913 ; Arms and the Race, 1915. *Recreations* : fencing, motoring. *Address* : Littlewood, Norfolk, Mass., U.S.A. *Clubs* : Savile : Harvard, Boston. (*Died 1 Jan. 1920.*)

JOHNSTON, Samuel, inventor ; *b.* Shelby, Orleans Co., N.Y., 9 Feb. 1835 ; *m.* 1856, Arsula S. Vaughan, Cattaraugus Co., N.Y. *Educ.* : common schools. Inventor of corn planters, rotary and disk harrows, self-rakes for harvesters, mowing machines, corn harvesters, self-raking reapers, platform reapers and binders, cold-rolling rolling-mills, roller reamers, roller forging mills ; also a metal-working process by which finished articles are produced in duplicate from ores or metals ; a method of veneering hard metals with soft. or *vice versâ*. Discoverer of a method of coking fuels of all kinds in particles so fine that they float in air, and the fuel is transported in pipes or burned within the apparatus to the desired temperature up to one equalling the electric furnace, or making it into water gas ; a continuous roasting and smelting furnace which separates and recovers the various impurities of ores and recovers the metals ; a method of treating the chimney gases and converting them to heat ; an apparatus for filling all forms of moulds for sand-moulding and making cores, giving uniform texture to the moulds or core—saving 90 per cent of labour. *Address* : 420 Ashland Avenue, Buffalo, N.Y.

JOHNSTON, Sir William, 9th Bt. ; *cr.* 1625 ; J.P. ; *b.* 31 July 1849 ; *S.* father 1865 ; unmarried. *Educ.* : Merchiston Castle School, Edinburgh. Was in Oriental Bank, China ; now Director of the Ceylon Tea Plantations Co., Ltd., London. *Recreations* : fencing, shooting, gardening. *Heir* : kinsman, George Johnston,

JOHNSTON, Rt. Rev. James Steptoe, D.D. See page xxii. **561** *b.* 21 Apr. 1845. *Address:* The Ranche, Buckhurst Hill, Essex. *Clubs:* Caledonian; Royal Northern. Aberdeen. (*Died 22 Nov.* 1917.)

JOHNSTONE, Vice-Admiral Charles; retired list; *b.* 1843; *s.* of James Johnstone; *m.* 1878, Janet, *d.* of George Schonswar, J.P., D.L., Co. Gloucester; one *s.* five *d.* *Educ.:* Naval Academy, Gosport; H.M.S. Illustrious. Specially promoted to Captain for services in Madagascar when in command of H.M.S. Dryad; gained Gold Medal of Royal United Service Institution, 1884. *Publications:* articles on Naval Prize Law. *Address:* Mouswald Place, Ruthwell R.S.O., Dumfriesshire
(*Died 2 Dec.* 1927.)

JOHNSTONE, Sir Donald (Campbell), Kt., *cr.* 1915; Chief Judge, Chief Court, Punjab, since 1915; *b.* 23 Feb. 1857; *s.* of Maj.-Gen. H. C. Johnstone, C.B.; two *s.* one *d.* *Educ.:* Edinburgh Academy. Passed into Indian Civil Service, 1877; proceeded to India, 1879; Secretary Revenue Board, Punjab, 1887-91; Sessions Judge, Punjab, 1894-1905; Puisne Judge, Chief Court, Punjab, till April 1915. *Address:* Chief Court, Lahore, Punjab.
(*Died 26 Nov.* 1920.)

JOHNSTONE, James William Douglas, C.I.E. 1911; late Inspector-General of Education, Gwalior State, Central India; *b.* Murree, Punjab, 30 Aug. 1855; *e. s.* of late Major-General Henry Campbell Johnstone, C.B., of the Indian Staff Corps. *Educ.:* Edinburgh Academy and University. Appointed to Punjab Educational Dept., 1877; transferred to Foreign Dept. of Govt. of India, an appointment as Head-master, Mayo College, Ajmere; appointed principal Daly College, Indore, 1885; was official representative of Central India for collecting art products for Colonial and Indian Exhibition of 1886; services lent by Government of India to Gwalior State for employment as tutor to H.H. Maharaja Scindia, 1890; on H.H.'s attaining his majority, was appointed Inspector Gen. of Education in the State, 1894; was also Census Comm., Gwalior State, 1900-2 and 1910-11, in addition to ordinary duties; was employed on famine duty in 1897 and 1900; accompanied His Highness to England in 1902, to be present at the Coronation of King Edward, and received Coronation medal; was political officer with the Maharaja of Gwalior at King George V.'s Coronation (medal); R.G.S., and a Fellow of the Allahabad University; was a member of the Majlis-i-Khas or State Council, Gwalior State; retired 1911. *Publications:* Census Report of Gwalior State, 1901; Gwalior, 1905. *Recreations:* golf, tennis, shooting. *Address:* Queen Anne's Mansions, S.W. *T.:* Victoria 5510. *Clubs:* East India United Service; Royal and Ancient, St. Andrews, N.B. (*Died 18 Oct.* 1925.)

JOHNSTONE, John Andrew, R.F.A.; *b.* 1893; *e. s.* of late Major James Henry L'Estrange Johnstone, M.V.O., J.P., R.E., and Amy Octavia, *y. d.* of late Andrew Wauchope. *Address:* The Hangingshaw, nr. Selkirk.
(*Died May* 1918.)

JOHNSTONE, Colonel Montague George, D.S.O. 1900; Hon. Col. and late Col. Commanding 3rd King's Own Yorkshire Light Infantry; *b.* 21 March 1848; 2nd *s.* of late Gen. Montague Cholmeley Johnstone and Louisa, *d.* of late Lt.-Gen. Sir Henry Somerset, K.C.B., K.H., and *g.d.* of Lord Charles Somerset; *m.* 1880, Agnes (*d.* 1923), *widow* of Capt. Johnston Stansfeld and *yr. d.* of late Joseph Harrison, J.P., D.L., of Galligreaves and of Samlesbury Hall, Lancashire, Lord of the Manor of Hadley, Essex; two *s.* one *d.* *Educ.:* Cheltenham College. Formerly Maj. 2nd Dragoons (Royal Scots Greys); an extra A.D.C. to Lord Lieut. of Ireland, 1880 (Duke of Marlborough); served on Headquarters Staff in

Bechuanaland Expedition, 1884-85; in former year assisted in raising the 2nd Mounted Rifles (Carrington's Horse), and in South Africa, 1900-1 (despatches, medal with 3 clasps, D.S.O. and Lt.-Colonelcy); employed by Master of the Horse and by Colonial Office, also was Commandant of Lambeth Palace Camp during Coronation of King Edward VII.; commanded his present regiment during its embodiment in the Mediterranean, 1902; was a Lt.-Col. Reserve of Officers; commanded 1st Westminster Battalion, National Reserve; has held several military appointments and belonged for many years to the King's Bodyguard for Scotland; employed by the War Office, on the Staff, 1914-18; Coronation medal, 1911. *Address:* 66 Beaufort Mansions, Chelsea, S.W. *T.:* Kensington 2968. *Club:* Naval and Military.
(*Died 12 June* 1928.)

JONES, Lt.-Col. Alfred Stowell, V.C., C.E.; M. Inst. C.E.; J.P., Berks; Consulting Engineer for Sewage Disposal; *b.* Liverpool, 24 Jan. 1832; *s.* of late Archdeacon J. Jones; *m.* 1863, Emily (*d.* 1918), *y. d.* of late John Back, Aldershot Place, Surrey; one *s.* one *d.* *Educ.:* Liverpool Coll.; Staff Coll., Sandhurst. Entered 9th Lancers, 1852; served throughout siege of Delhi as D.A.Q.M.G. to the cavalry (despatches thrice, promoted Captain and Brevet-Major); wounded at Agra by bullet through bridle-arm and 22 sabre cuts. 10th October 1857; graduated at Staff Coll., 1861; Staff, Cape of Good Hope, 1861-67; retired, 1872; Manager of all Sewage Works of the 1st Army Corps, Aldershot, 1895-1912; retired 1912. *Decorated:* taking a nine-pounder gun from the enemy, 8 June 1857. *Publications:* Will a Sewage Farm Pay? (three editions), 1874-87; Natural and Artificial Sewage Treatment, 1902; many papers in professional journals. *Address:* Ridge Cottage, Finchampstead, Berks. *Club:* Junior United Service.
(*Died May* 1920.)

JONES, Rev. Basil M., M.A.; Vicar of Llanfair, nr. Ruthin, with Jesus Chapel, since 1870; Chaplain of H.M. Prison, Ruthin, since 1904; *e. s.* of Rev. James Jones, M.A., Rector of Llanfwrog, Denbighshire; *m.* Emily (*d.* 1910), *y. d.* of Francis Willis, M.D., of Shillingthorpe, Lines; two *s.* two *d.* *Educ.:* Ruthin and Newport Salop Grammar Schools; Jesus Coll., Oxford (Scholar). B.A. 1863; M.A. 1866; Deacon, 1866; Priest, 1867; Curate of Llanwenarth, 1866; Llanfwrog, 1868; Prebendary of St. Asaph, 1899; Chaplain to the High Sheriff of Denbighshire, 1878; Governor of County School for Girls at Ruthin, 1900; Vice-Chairman, 1907; Chairman of Parish Council of Llanfair, 1907; Rural Dean of Dyffryn Clwyd, 1916. *Publications:* occasional sermons and addresses. *Address:* Llanfair Vicarage, Ruthin.
(*Died 9 Mar.* 1925.)

JONES, Major Bryan John, D.S.O. 1916; Leinster Regiment; *b.* 13 May 1874; *e. surv. s.* of Colonel T. J. Jones, late Royal Artillery, of Lisnawilly, Dundalk, and Margaret Gertrude, *d.* of late Sir Theophilus Shepstone, K.C.M.G.; *m.* 1911, Grace, *o. d.* of late S. H. Stephens, County Inspector, Royal Irish Constabulary. *Educ.:* privately. First Commission in Leinster Regiment, 1894; served South African War, 1900-2 (despatches, Queen's and King's medals); European War, 1914-18 (despatches, D.S.O., thrice wounded). *Publications:* contributor of articles on Irish archæology and folklore to various periodicals. *Recreations:* riding, gardening, military history. Irish subjects. *Address:* Lisnawilly, Dundalk.
(*Died 20 Sept.* 1918.)

JONES, Chester, J.P.; Metropolitan Police Magistrate, Bow Street, since 1920; *b.* 1854; 4th *s.* of John Henry Jones of Elmwood, Streatham, S.W.; *m.* 1888, Ellen, *d.* of late John Shyane. *Educ.:* University College, London; Trinity

Hall, Cambridge, B.A. 1876. Called to Bar, Middle Temple, 1879; Police Magistrate, Thames, 1907-11; Old Street, 1911-14; Lambeth, 1914-1920; presided over many Home Office Enquiries on Industrial Matters; Member of Vice-Regal Commission on loss of Dublin Crown Jewels. *Recreation*: yachting. *Address*: 3 Marine Parade, Brighton. *Clubs*: New University, United University.   (*Died 9 July 1922.*)

JONES, Rt. Hon. Sir David Brynmor, Kt., *cr.* 1906; P.C. 1912; LL.B., Hon. LL.D. (Wales), K.C.; a Master in Lunacy since 1914; *e. s.* of late Rev. Thomas Jones, Swansea, Chairman Congregational Union of England and Wales; *b.* 1852; *m.* 1892, Florence (*d.* 1920), widow of A. de M. Mocatta, and *d.* of Major Lionel Cohen; J.P. Glamorganshire. *Educ.*: University School and College, London. Barr. Middle Temple, 1876; Bencher, 1899; Reader, 1911; Judge of County Courts, 1885; resigned, 1892; Recorder of Merthyr Tydfil, 1910; M.P. Stroud Division of Gloucestershire, 1892; Member Welsh Land Commission, 1893; Chairman County Court Departmental Committees, 1893 and 1899; Chairman Metropolitan Police Commission, 1906; Member Welsh Church Commission, 1907; Member Venereal Diseases Commission, 1913; M.P. (L.) Swansea District, 1895-1914; Recorder of Cardiff, 1914-15; Member Court of Referees, 1896-1914, and a Chairman of Standing Committees, House of Commons, 1906-14; Hon. Counsel to and member of Court of University of Wales; a Vice-President and Chairman of Council of the Cymmrodorian Society. *Publications*: Essay on Home Rule and Imperial Sovereignty, 1886; edited The Divine Order and other Sermons, by the Rev. Thomas Jones, with an introduction by Robert Browning, 1884; Address on Welsh History in the Light of Recent Research, 1891; The Welsh People, 1900 (with Principal Rhys), etc. *Recreations*: travel, sculling, tennis. *Address*: 27 Bryanston Square, W.; *T.*: Paddington 2091. *Clubs*: Reform, Devonshire, Ranelagh.   (*Died 6 Aug. 1921.*)

JONES, Rev. Donald, B.D. (Durham); Principal of Bede College, Durham, 1903-25; Lecturer in the University of Durham; *b.* 1857; *s.* of Thomas Evan Jones of The Precincts, Canterbury; *m.* 1923, Mary Edith Macray, Whitefield, Cumberland, *d.* of Rev. Dr. Macray, Rector of Ducklington, Oxfordshire. *Educ.*: The King's School, Canterbury; Lichfield Theological College. Assistant Master at the King's School, Canterbury, and Victoria College, Jersey, 1877-1886; Deacon, 1887; Priest, 1888; Curate of Aughton, Lancashire, 1887-89; Priest-Vicar in Lichfield Cathedral, and Vice-Principal and Lecturer at the Theological College, Lichfield, 1889-1903. *Publications*: An Analytical Sketch of Jewish History and a First Index to Early Church History. *Recreations*: golf, cycling, fishing.   (*Died Aug. 1925.*)

JONES, Major Evan Rowland, Author and Writer, editor and proprietor of The Shipping World, and the publications of the Shipping World Company; *b.* Penylan Farm, by Tregaron, Cardiganshire; *s.* of William Jones and Mary, *d.* of Evan Rowlands, of Wenallt, Cardiganshire; *m.* 1867, Kate Alice, *d.* of William Evans, of Llanwnda, Carnarvonshire; no *c.* *Educ.*: public and private schools, military classes, and by private tutors. Went to America at age of 15; organised the Welsh citizens of Milwaukee into the Lincoln Anti-Slavery Society, 1860; enlisted (under age) for the American War in 5th Wisconsin Infantry, 1861; served on Non-Commissioned Staff; as Second Lieut., Captain, and Brevet Major; filled the office of Judge Advocate of a Brigade Court Martial, 1864-65; held a position in Department of State, Madison, until appointed by President Grant in 1869 American Consul

for the N.E. Coast, resident in Newcastle-on-Tyne; Consul for South Wales, resident at Cardiff, 1884-92; reported upon the whole Consular System by instructions from the Department of State: member of Council and Court of Governors of University College of South Wales and Monmouthshire; President of Cymmrodorion Society; M.P. Carmarthen Boroughs, 1892-5. *Publications*: author of Lincoln, Stanton, and Grant; Historical Sketches; Four Years in the Army of the Potomac; Heroes of Industry; Life of (his friend) Joseph Cowen; papers on economic subjects; Una Montgomery; first and present editor of the Shipping World, and the Shipping World Year Book. *Recreations*: formerly tennis, riding, and swimming; now walks and books. *Address*: The Pryors, Hampstead, N.W.3. *T.A.*: Shipping World, London. *T.*: Hampstead 5092, Gerrard 2381. *Clubs*: Savage and National Liberal.

(*Died 16 Jan. 1920.*)

JONES, Miss E. E. Constance; D. Litt. (Hon.) Wales; Mistress of Girton College, Cambridge, 1903-16; Vice-Mistress, 1896-1903, and Resident Lecturer in Moral Sciences, 1884-1903; *d.* of J. Jones, M.D., J.P., of Langstone Court, Herefordshire, and Llancayo House, Monmouthshire, and Emily Edith, *d.* of Thomas Oakley, J.P., of Lydart House, Monmouth; kin to Dr. David Lewis, 1st Principal of Jesus College, Oxford. *Educ.*: at home; Miss Robinson's, Alstone Court, Cheltenham; Girton Coll. Camb. First Class in Moral Sciences Tripos, 1880; Examiner in Logic in the Cambridge Higher Local, 1902-3-4; Governor of the Univ. College of Wales, Aberystwyth; Member of the Aristotelian Society, and the Soc. for Psychical Research, etc. *Publications*: translator (with Miss E. Hamilton) of Lotze's Mikrokosmus; author of Elements of Logic as a Science of Propositions, of General Logic, of a Primer of Logic (2nd ed. 1913); of a Primer of Ethics, of A New Law of Thought and its Logical Bearings, of vol. on Girton College, in Beautiful Britain series, of The Three Great Questions: an outline of Private and Public Duty, 1915; article, Henry Sidgwick in Hastings' Encyclopædia of Religion and Ethics, 1920, and of various articles and reviews; was entrusted with carrying through the press the 6th and 7th editions of late Prof. Sidgwick's Methods of Ethics and with editing his Lectures on the Ethics of Green, Spencer, and Martineau, and National and International Right and Wrong (a Reprint of two Essays from Practical Ethics). *Recreations*: architecture and languages. *Address*: Meldon House, Weston-super-Mare; Ar-y-Bryn, Llanddewi Skyrrid, Abergavenny. *Club*: Writers'.

(*Died 17 April 1922.*)

JONES, Francis, M.Sc., F.R.S.E., F.C.S.; *b.* Edinburgh, 1845; *s.* of Francis and Esther Jones; *m.* 1872, Jessie Ferguson, *d.* of Thomas Chapman, Edinburgh; one *s.* five *d.* *Educ.*: Edinburgh Institution; Edinburgh University; Heidelberg University. Research Assistant to Prof. Roscoe, 1866; Demonstrator in Chemistry, Owens College, Manchester, 1870-71; Senior Chemistry Master, The Grammar School, Manchester, 1872-1919; Fellow of Royal Society of Edinburgh and Chemical Society of London; Vice-President of the Manchester Literary and Philosophical Society of Manchester, and President, 1909-11. *Publications*: Junior Course of Practical Chemistry; Questions on Chemistry; German Science Reader; The Air of Rooms: An Examination of the effect produced on the air of rooms by the use of gas, coal, electric light, etc., for heating and lighting purposes; Address on the History of the Introduction of Science in Schools and Colleges; various papers read before the Chemical Society of London and Manchester Literary and Philosophical

Society on Boron Hydride, Stibine, **Volatility** of Sulphur, Action of Alkalies on Glass, etc. *Recreations:* golf, photography. *Address:* 17 Whalley Road, Whalley Range, Manchester.
(*Died 22 Oct. 1925.*)

JONES, Lt.-Col. Frank Aubrey, D.S.O. 1900; late Welsh Regt.; *b.* 4 Aug. 1873. Entered army, 1895; served Sierra Leone, 1898-99 (wounded, medal with clasp); South Africa, 1899-1902 (severely wounded; despatches; Queen's medal, 3 clasps; King's medal, 2 clasps; D.S.O.). (*Died 11 July 1916.*)

JONES, Hon. George, Member Legislative Council of New Zealand since 1895; editor and proprietor of The Oamaru Mail; *b.* Hutt Valley, New Zealand, 24 Oct. 1844; *s.* of George Jones of Shropshire and London, and Ann Eliza Adams of London; *m.* Dorothy Tweedy of Sunderland; four *s.* four *d.* *Educ.:* common schools, Rev. Mr. Scales' Academy, and Rev. G. O. Vance's Grammar School, Geelong. Served part apprenticeship as printer at Heath and Cordell's of that time; then employed for a year at Government Printing Office at Brisbane. At age of 17 worked as journeyman compositor on the Rockhampton Bulletin; arrived in Christchurch, N.Z., 1863, and was successively employed in the Standard, the Lyttelton Times, and the Press; entered into business as printer and publisher in Christchurch in 1866, eventually taking in as partner the late George Tombs, afterwards of Whitcombe and Tombs; subsequently went to Auckland and started the Waikato Times and Auckland Echo; on the demise of the Echo, in conjunction with Messrs. Reed and Brett, established the News in Dunedin, in the Provincialist interest; purchased the Oamaru Mail, 1877; was brought into political prominence through a State prosecution which was consequent on his libelling Attorney-General Sir F. Whitaker, when he appeared at the Bar of the House, and subsequently in the Supreme Court, by whom he was acquitted; sat in House of Reps., 1880-81; resigned owing to ill-health; is an advocate of liquor prohibition; as a boy was a member of the first musical society in Australia shortly after its establishment, and has taken a prominent part in music throughout that country and New Zealand. *Recreations:* music, gardening. *Address:* Mail, Oamaru. *T.:* 148, 159, 27.
(*Died Dec. 1921.*)

JONES, Harry, Parliamentary Correspondent, Daily News; Barrister-at-Law (Middle Temple); *b.* Llanelly, South Wales, 27 Mar. 1866; *m.* Emily Margaret, *d.* of Thomas Mainwaring, 1895; one *s.* Assistant-editor South Wales Daily News; acting editor Weekly Sun, editor Evening Sun; managing editor Western Daily Mercury; deputy editor Daily Chronicle. *Publications:* Liberalism and the House of Lords; War Letters of a Public Schoolboy, 1918. *Recreations:* golf, walking. *Address:* 29 Half Moon Lane, Herne Hill, S.E. *T.:* Brixton 726. *Clubs:* National Liberal; Dulwich and Sydenham Golf. (*Died 11 Jan. 1925.*)

JONES, Sir Henry, Kt., *cr.* 1912; M.A., LL.D.; F.B.A. 1904; D.Litt. Wales, 1905; Professor of Moral Philosophy, University of Glasgow, since 1894; *b.* Llangernyw, North Wales, 1852; *m.* 1882, Annie Walker, Kilbirnie, Ayrshire; three *s.* one *d.* *Educ.:* University of Glasgow (M.A. 1879); hon. LL.D. St. Andrews, 1895. Professor of Philosophy and Political Economy at University College of North Wales, Bangor; Professor of Logic and Metaphysics at University of St. Andrews; Hibbert Lecturer on Metaphysics at Manchester College, Oxford; D.Litt. University of Wales; Fellow of the British Academy. *Publications:* Browning as a Religious and Philosophical Teacher; The Philosophy of Lotze; Idealism as a Practical Creed; The Working Faith of the Social Reformer; Social Powers. *Address:* The University, Glasgow; Noddfa, Tighnabruaich, Argyllshire. (*Died 4 Feb. 1922.*)
564

JONES, Sir Henry, Kt., *cr.* 1919; *b.* Hobart, 1862; *m.* 1883, Alice, *d.* of W. Glover, Manchester. Founder and Managing Director of H. Jones & Co., Ltd.; Chairman of Directors of Henry Jones Co-operative, Ltd., Melbourne; Director of Tongkah Harbour Tin Dredging Co.; part owner Bendena Station, Queensland. *Address:* Old Wharf, Hobart, Tasmania.
(*Died 29 Oct. 1926.*)

JONES, Canon Henry David, M.A.; V.D.; Canon Residentiary of Chichester since 1900; *b.* 1842; *e. s.* of Robert Jones, D.I.. of Middlesex, and of Glanbrane Park, Llandovery; *m.* 1st, Emily, *e. d.* of W. Leetham, J.P., Hull; 2nd, Elizabeth Lucy (*d.* 1918), 3rd *d.* of Rev. James Kirkpatrick, of Holydale, Keston, Kent; five *s.* two *d.* *Educ.:* Shrewsbury School; St. John's College, Cambridge (Exhibitioner, 1861; B.A., 1864; M.A., 1868). Curate of St. James', Kingston-upon-Hull, 1865-67; St. Gabriel's, Pimlico, 1867-69; Aberaman, Glamorganshire, 1869; Rector of St. Mary's, Aberdeen, 1869; Chaplain at Genoa, 1874; Curate of St. Michael's, Bournemouth, 1875; Prebendary of Colworth in Chichester Cathedral, 1891-1903; of Gates, 1903; Treasurer, 1911; Precentor, 1918; Rural Dean of Hastings, 1889-1905; Rector of Upper St. Leonards, 1879-1915. *Address:* The Chantry, Chichester.
(*Died 26 April 1925.*)

JONES, Henry Festing, Author; *b.* 1851; 2nd *s.* of Thomas Jones, Q.C., of the Northern Circuit, Barrister-at-law, and Ellen, *o. c.* of Rev. William Carmalt of Putney School. *Educ.:* private tuition; Rottingdean; Radley; Trinity Hall, Cambridge. Articled to a solicitor, 1873; met Samuel Butler, Author of Erewhon, 1876; admitted a solicitor, 1876; retired from the law, 1887, and joined Butler, assisting him in his work and travelling with him in Italy. *Publications:* About 20 songs and 6 four-part songs, words by various poets, 1886-1907; King Bulbous: a Comic Opera for schools and classes, words by P. R. Crib, 1897; Diversions in Sicily, 1909; Castellinaria and other Sicilian Diversions, 1911; The Note Books of Samuel Butler, 1912; Samuel Butler, Author of Erewhon, a Memoir, 1919 (James Tait Black Prize); Mount Eryx and other Diversions of Travel, 1921; several pamphlets about Butler; In collaboration with Butler—Gavottes, Minuets, Fugues, etc., for the piano, 1885; Narcissus, a Cantata, 1888; Ulysses, an Oratorio, 1904; (with A. T. Bartholomew) Joint-editor of the Shrewsbury Edition of the complete Works of Samuel Butler. *Recreation:* sketching. *Address:* 120 Maida Vale, W.9. *T.:* Maida Vale 2652. *Club:* New University.
(*Died 23 Oct. 1928.*)

JONES, Capt. Henry Michael, V.C. Entered army, 1849; served in Crimea; severely wounded at Alma; Capt. 1855; dangerously wounded at Redan; left army, 1857; entered Diplomatic Service, 1858; Consul-Gen. at Tabreez, 1868; at Christiania, 1875; Philippopolis, 1880; Minister Resident at Bangkok, 1889; Minister Resident at Lima, 1894, and at Quito, 1895-98; retired; Knight of the Legion of Honor. *Clubs:* United Service, Junior United Service. (*Died 18 Dec. 1916.*)

JONES, Rt. Rev. Herbert Edward, Suffragan Bishop of Lewes since 1914; Archdeacon of Chichester since 1914; *b.* 6 April 1861; *s.* of Sir Willoughby Jones, 3rd Bt., of Cranmer Hall, Norfolk; *m.* Madeleine, *d.* of Edward Long Fox, M.D., Clifton; one *s.* one *d.* *Educ.:* Eton; Trinity College, Cambridge. Curate of St. Andrews, Westminster, 1884-86; Rector of Knebworth, 1888-1897; Rector of Petworth, 1897-1905; Examining Chaplain to the Bishop of Chichester, 1903-7; Vicar of Hitchin, 1907-13; Hon. Canon of St. Albans; Examining Chaplain to the Bishop of St. Albans. *Address:* 2 Eaton Gardens, Hove, Sussex. (*Died 19 Feb. 1930.*)

JONES, Howard Parker, M.A., Ph.D.; M'Leod Professor of Modern Languages, Dalhousie University, Halifax, N.S., since 1906; *b.* 27 Sep. 1863, 3rd *s.* of St. Clair Jones of Weymouth, Nova Scotia; *m.* 1893, Isabel, *y. d.* of Thomas Ridd, Barnstaple, England; one *s.* two *d. Educ.:* The Collegiate School and King's College, Windsor, Nova Scotia (B.A. 1884, M.A. 1891). Ph.D. Heidelberg University, 1886; Professor of Modern Languages, King's College, Windsor, N.S., 1888-92; Instructor in German at Cornell University, Ithaca, N.Y., 1893-98; Professor of Modern Languages at Hobart College, Geneva, N.Y., 1898-1906; honorary member of the Phi Beta Kappa Society. *Publications:* A German Reader; articles in various periodicals. *Recreations:* croquet, rowing. *Address:* King Street, Dartmouth, Nova Scotia. (*Died 29 April 1924.*)

JONES, Sir James Edward, Kt., *cr.* 1914; J.P.; merchant; *b.* 14 July 1843; *s.* of Ellis and Ann Jones, Castlemere, Rochdale; *m.* 1869, Hannah Hoyle, Crossfield, Rochdale; two *d. Educ.:* Rochdale; Collegiate School, Sheffield. *Recreations:* golf, riding, driving. *Address:* Sparthfield, Rochdale. *T.:* Rochdale 114. *Club:* Reform, Manchester. (*Died 8 Jan. 1922.*)

JONES, Sir John Bowen Bowen-, 1st Bt., *cr.* 1911; D.L., J.P.; *b.* 25 Dec. 1840; *s.* of John Jones of the City of London, merchant, and Ann Bowen; *m.* 1863, Elizabeth Margaret (*d.* 1904), *e. d.* of Evan Bowen, Ensdon House, Montford, Shropshire; no *c. Heir:* none. *Address:* Council House Court, Shrewsbury.
(*Died 6 June 1925.*)

JONES, Josiah Towyn, M.P. (Co.L.) East Carmarthen 1912-18; Llanelly (Carmarthen), 1918-22; Governor of Cardiff and Aberystwyth Universities; Member Carmarthen County Council; Chairman of the Welsh Congregational Union, 1919-20; late Welsh Whip and Lord of the Treasury; *b.* 28 Dec. 1858; *m.* 1885, Mary Howells, Plas Cadwgan, Swansea Valley; two *d.* Worked on farm as a boy; went to sea, served as cabin-boy; entered Presbyterian College, Carmarthen, 1876; ordained Congregationalist Minister, Dowlais, 1880; Minister Cwmaman, 1884-1904; retired, 1906; Organiser for Welsh Congregational Union and member of Welsh Central Board; late member Carmarthen C.C. and Education Committee. *Address:* 22 Marine Terrace, New Quay, Card. *Club:* National Liberal.
(*Died 16 Nov. 1925.*)

JONES, Kennedy, M.P. Hornsey Division of Middlesex since 1916; *b.* Glasgow, 4 May 1865; *m.* 1892, Hetty, *d.* of J. Staniland, Birmingham; one *s.* three *d. Educ.:* High School, Glasgow. Joint Founder Daily Mail, Daily Mirror, Editor Evening News, 1894-1900; stood as Independent Candidate for Wimbledon, April 1916; Director-General (unpaid) Food Economy Dept., Ministry of Food, 1917; Chairman Select Committee on Transport (Metropolitan Area), 1919; Chairman, Advisory Committee Ministry of Transport (London Traffic), 1920. *Address:* 8 King's Bench Walk, E.C.4. *T.:* City 7007. *Clubs:* Constitutional, Royal Automobile, Royal Thames Yacht, Royal Aero. (*Died 20 Oct. 1921.*)

JONES, Capt. Kingsmill Williams, D.S.O. 1915; Medical Officer to The Buffs (1st Batt.); *b.* 11 March 1875; *s.* of late Percival Jones, Dublin. *Educ.:* Wesley College, Dublin; Trinity College, Dublin (Mathematical Scholar). B.A. Dub. 1898; M.A., M.D., D.P.H. 1903; M.B., B.Ch., B.A.O. 1901; L.M. (Rot. Hosp. Dub.), 1901; elected Member of Manchester City Council, 1913; went to France with his unit, 16th Field Ambulance, 6th Div. B.E.F. Sep. 1914 (twice wounded, D.S.O. despatches). *Publications:* Delirium in Febrile Conditions, 1908. *Recreation:* rowing. *Address:*

2 Syndall Street, Stockport Road, Manchester. *T.:* City 4568. *Club:* Arts, Manchester.
(*Died Aug. 1918.*)

JONES, Rev. Lewis; Congregational Minister; Minister of Tynycoed and Bethlehem, Abercrave, Swansea Valley; *b.* 6 April 1842 at a farmhouse called Rhydybod, Llanuwchllyn, Merionethshire; *s.* of David and Jane Jones, farmers; *m.*; one *s.* one *d. Educ.:* Bala College; Glasgow University. Ordained as Congregational Minister at Tynycoed and Bethlehem Chapels, Abercrave, 1867; resigned, 1919; took prominent part in Denominational Associations; special Preacher and President of Congregational Union of Wales; served on School Board; Chairman of Ystradgunlais Tribunal; a strict total abstainer and non-smoker; President of the Bible Society branch of the district; an extensive sphere of labour of mixed farmers and labourers; five Sunday Schools under his care; rebuilt the chapels and built three new schools, and cleared all the debt. *Publications:* Paul in Europe; Israel of the Old Testament; Is there a Word from the Lord? (special sermon); Church Independency in the Light of History; articles in periodicals. *Address:* Cœdmor, Llantwit Major, Glam.
(*Died Aug. 1928.*)

JONES, Rt. Rev. Llewellyn, D.D.; Bishop of Newfoundland and Bermuda since 1878; *b.* Liverpool, 11 Oct. 1840; *m.* Elizabeth Alice (*d.*1903), *d.* of Hon. Sir Adams G. Archibald, K.C.M.G., Lt.-Gov. of Nova Scotia, 1881; two *s.* one *d. Educ.:* Cheltenham; Harrow; Trin. Coll. Cambridge (M.A.). Ordained, 1864; Rector of Little Hereford, 1874-78. *Address:* St. John's, Newfoundland; Hamilton, Bermuda.
(*Died 9 Jan. 1918.*)

JONES, Rev. Lloyd Timothy, Hon. Canon of Peterborough. *Address:* All Saints Vicarage, Northampton. (*Died 3 Jan. 1920.*)

JONES, Brig.-Gen. Lumley Owen Williames, D.S.O. 1915; 2nd Batt. Essex Regt.; *b.* 1 Dec. 1876. *Educ.:* Winchester. Entered army, 1897; Captain, 1905; Adjutant, 1912; Bt.-Lt.-Col. 1916; employed with W.A. Frontier Force, 1904-8; served South Africa, 1901-2 (Queen's medal, 4 clasps); West Africa, 1905-6 (medal with clasp); European War, 1914-18 (despatches thrice, D.S.O., Bt. Col.); Legion of Honour. *Address:* Cefn Bryntalch, Abermule; Montgomeryshire.(*Died 14 Sept.1918.*)

JONES, Hon. Sir Lyman Melvin, Kt., *cr.* 1911; Chevalier of the Legion of Honor, 1914; *b.* Ontario, 21 Sept. 1843; of Welsh-Scotch descent; *s.* of Norman Jones and Therese Jane Patterson; *m.* 1873, Louise, *d.* of Thomas Irwin; one *d.* Alderman of City of Winnipeg and Chairman of Finance Committee, 1886; Mayor of Winnipeg and Vice-President of Board of Trade, 1887; re-elected Mayor, 1888; Provincial Treasurer, Manitoba, 1888; represented Constituency of Shoal Lake; re-elected 1888 to represent North Winnipeg; resigned office, 1889, though retaining seat in Legislature until end of term, and returned to Eastern Canada to devote his time to private business; upon amalgamation of the Massey and Harris Companies in 1891 became Managing Director of consolidated Companies; President since 1902; Member of Senate of Dominion of Canada since 1901 (L.); President, Bain Wagon Co., Ltd., Woodstock, and Johnston Harvester Co., Batavia, N.Y., U.S.A.; Vice-President, Ontario Jockey Club; Director Canadian Bank of Commerce; Director, Blackstone Mutual Fire Insurance Co. and Merchants' Mutual Fire Insurance Co., Providence, R.I., U.S.A.; Verity Plow Co., Ltd. *Recreations:* golf, motoring. *Address:* Llawhaden, St. George St., Toronto, Canada. *T.A.:* Melvin, Toronto. *Clubs:* National, York, Toronto Hunt, Royal Canadian Yacht, Toronto; Rideau, Ottawa; Manitoba, Winnipeg.
(*Died 15 April 1917.*)

JONES, Lt. - Col. Michael Durwas Goring-, C.M.G. 1916; D.S.O. 1918; 2nd Durham L.I.; *b.* 13 Jan. 1866; Lieut. 1886; Capt. 1896; Major, 1908; Lt.-Col. 1915; Adjutant Indian Vols. 1901-6; served European War, 1914-18 (despatches, C.M.G., D.S.O.).
(Died 19 May 1919.)

JONES, Major Percy Arnold Lloyd-, D.S.O. 1915; R.A.M.C.; *b.* 17 Oct. 1876. Served one year in ranks; Lieut. R.A.M.C., 1904; Capt. 1908; served South Africa, 1900 (Queen's medal, 3 clasps); European War, 1914-16 (despatches twice, D.S.O.). *(Died 29 Dec. 1916.)*

JONES, Sir Philip Sydney, Kt.; *cr.* 1905; M.D., F.R.C.S.; *b.* 15 April 1886; 2nd *s.* of David Jones, Sydney; *m.* 1863, Hannah Howard, *d.* of Rev. G. Charter; three *s.* four *d.* *Educ.:* private schools; University College, London. M.D., University of London, 1860; F.R.C.S. (Eng.), 1861; Fellow of Senate, University of Sydney; Vice-Chancellor, 1904-5; Hon. Consulting Physician, Royal Prince Alfred and Sydney Hospitals; President, Inter-Colonial Medical Congress, 1892. *Recreations:* travel, croquet. *Address:* Llandilo, Strathfield, New South Wales. *Club:* Union, Sydney.
(Died 18 Sept. 1918.)

JONES, Rev. Richard Thomas, Vicar of Glanogwen, Bethesda, since 1898; Canon of Bangor Cathedral since 1910. *Educ.:* Lampeter. Ordained, 1885; Curate Pwllheli, 1895-8; Vicar of Nevin, 1888-98. *Address:* Glanogwen Vicarage, Bethesda, N. Wales. *(Died 1 April 1917.)*

JONES, Maj.-Gen. Robert Owen, C.B. 1885; R.E.; *b.* 14 Nov. 1837; *s.* of late William Jones, Bryn Tegid, and Ann, *d.* of Owen Owen, Dolgadfa; *m.* 1878, Harriette (*d.* 1922), *d.* of Rt. Hon. Sir James Parker Deane, P.C., Q.C., D.C.L.; four *d.* *Educ.:* Cowbridge; Woolwich. Commissioned in Royal Engineers, 1856; served Ashanti War, 1873-74; engineer in charge of communications from the Prah to the coast; Boundary Commissioner, 1884-85; retired, 1887; J.P. County Merioneth. *Address:* Bryn Tegid, Bala, N. Wales. *Club:* Junior United Service. *(Died 19 Feb. 1926.)*

JONES, Rev. Thomas, Canon of St. David's Cathedral, 1908; *b.* 14 June 1839; *m.* 1865; two *s.* one *d.* *Educ.:* St. David's College, Lampeter. Ordained 1862; Curate of Llanelly, Brecon, 1862; Llanfigon, 1864; Llandyssuil, Cardigan, 1865; Vicar of Llanwnen, W. Silian, 1868; Llywel, Brecon, 1878; Rector of Penboyr, Carmarthen, 1889; retired, 1914. *Address:* Millbank, Lampeter, Cardiganshire. *T.A.:* Lampeter. *(Died 1927.)*

JONES, Thomas Ridge, M.D., Aberdeen; Consulting Physician Victoria Hospital for Children; *b.* 1840; *s.* of Thomas and Ellen Jones, Rhyl, North Wales; *m.* 1876, Ruth, *d.* of Joseph Ridge, M.D., F.R.C.P.; four *s.* one *d.* *Educ.:* Liverpool Institute and private; Middlesex; St. George's Hospitals; Aberdeen University. Was awarded 1st prize in each subject, except botany, and the Governor's Prize for Clinical Medicine and Surgery, given to the most distinguished student at the Middlesex Hospital; for twenty-six years Physician, and for last fifteen years Consulting Physician to the Victoria Hospital for Children; Fellow of the Royal Society of Medicine. *Publications:* On the Recent Outbreak of Smallpox at St. George's Hospital, St. George's Hospital Report, vol. v.; Lymphatic Leukæmia, Pathological Society, 1878; Observations on Cerebral Hæmorrhage from Forty Fatal Cases (serial), B.M.J., 1863-64; Colalepsy, ibid. 1863; On Anæsthetics (serial), ibid. 1872. *Recreations:* riding, mountaineering. *Address:* 4 Chesham Place, S.W.; Iford Manor House, near Lewes, Sussex. *T.:* 746 Victoria. *Clubs:* Reform, Wellington. *(Died 4 April 1924.)*

JONES, Walter, M.I.M.E., J.P.; Founder of Jones & Attwood, Ltd., heating and hydraulic engineers; *b.* 1846; *m.* 1876, *e. d.* of Thomas Noke. *Publications:* Heating by Hot Water; National and Municipal Finance; Capital and Labour, etc. *Address:* The Uplands, Stourbridge. *T.:* Stourbridge 381. *(Died 25 Aug. 1924.)*

JONES, Lieut. - Col. Walter Dally, C.M.G. 1917; *b.* 21 May 1855; *y. s.* of late John Jones of The Clock House, Wandsworth, S.W.; *m.* 1886, Marion Isabella, 2nd *d.* of late Colonel Frank Crossman, 12th Bengal Cavalry; three *d.* *Educ.:* Harrow; Trinity College, Cambridge. 2nd Lieut. 99th Duke of Edinburgh's Lanarkshire Regt. 1878; Captain Wiltshire Regt. 1885; passed Staff College, 1889; D.A.A.G. Gibraltar, 1891-98; retired 1901; Secretary Wiltshire T.F. Association, 1908-12; Assistant Secretary Committee of Imperial Defence, Nov. 1914; Senior Assistant Secretary War Cabinet, Dec. 1916; served S. African War, 1879, Zulu Campaign, Defence of Eshowe (medal with clasp); S. African War, 1899-1900, Press Censor on Sir R. Buller's Staff, Relief of Ladysmith (despatches twice, Queen's medal with 6 clasps, brevet of Lieut.-Col.); Chevalier of the Legion of Honour, 1916. *Address:* 53 Belgrave Road, S.W. *Clubs:* Army and Navy, Garrick, Beefsteak.
(Died 20 Feb. 1926.)

JONES, Lieut.-Col. Walter Thomas Cresswell, C.B. 1921; D.S.O. 1900; Royal Marine Light Infantry; *b.* 31 Jan. 1874; *s.* of late Rev. George Jones; *m.* 1909, Hildred, *e. d.* of A. St. Clair Buxton; one *s.* three *d.* *Educ.:* Bradfield College, Berks; Rev. J. Scott Ramsay, Army Tutor. Served with Naval Brigade, S. Africa (despatches thrice, D.S.O.); Dardanelles, 1915 (despatches). *Address:* Forton Barracks, Gosport, Hants. *(Died 16 Aug. 1923.)*

JONES, Sir William Hollingworth Quayle, Kt., *cr.* 1892; *b.* 6 Feb. 1854; *e.s.* of late Rev. C. W. Jones, Vicar of Pakenham, and Rural Dean of Thedwastre, Suffolk; *m.* 1st, 1884, Alice (*d.* 1890), *d.* of Charles Kent of Woodcot, Oxford; 2nd, Claire (whom he *div.* 1905), *d.* of E. Berdoe-Wilkinson, 1893; 3rd, 1906, May Bradley (whom he *div.* 1910), 5th *d.* of late William Dyer. *Educ.:* Caius Coll., Camb. (B.A. 1876; M.A. 1879). Barr. Middle Temple, 1877; Acting Judge Gold Coast, 1882; Queen's Advocate, Gold Coast, 1883; Chief Justice of the West African Settlements, 1887; title subsequently changed to Chief Justice of Sierra Leone, retired invalided, 1895; was Deputy Governor on various occasions, and acting Governor, Sierra Leone, 1892; belongs to S.E. Circuit; appointed in 1897, 1898, 1899, 1900, 1901, 1902, 1903, 1904, and 1905 to act as a Chairman at Courts of London Sessions during absence of 1st, the Chairman, and 2nd, the Deputy Chairman, also Feb. 1906, as Deputy for the Chairman under the Quarter Sessions (London) Act, 1896; formerly Captain in the West Suffolk Militia, retired 1889; was reappointed Captain, 3rd Batt. Suffolk Regiment, 1896; Hon. Major 1899; retired, 1900, with rank of Major; J.P. Suffolk. *Address:* Barton Mere, Bury St. Edmunds. *Club:* New University.
(Died 6 Jan. 1925.)

JONES, W. Lewis, M.A.; Professor of English Language and Literature, University College of North Wales, since 1897; *b.* 1866; *s.* of William Jones, of Llangefni, Anglesey; *m.* 1901, Edith, *d.* of Elias Owen, Menai Bridge; one *d.* *Educ.:* Friars School, Bangor; Queen's Coll. Camb. (Scholar). Graduated Classical Tripos, 1888; Members' (University) Prizeman for English Essay, 1887; Assistant Lecturer in English, Univ. Coll. of N. Wales, 1891; Examiner in English in the University of Glasgow, 1903-6; Examiner in English in the University of Birmingham, 1909-11; Vice-Principal of University College of N. Wales, 1903-5; Member of Court and of Senate of University of Wales. *Publications:* editor of Caniadau Cymru (an anthology of Welsh poetry), 1897; second ed. 1907; articles in Quarterly Review, Modern

Language Review, Transactions of Cymmrodorion Society and other periodicals; The Univ. of Wales (with W. Cadwaladr Davies) in College Histories, 1905; King Arthur in History and Legend, 1911; Land of my Fathers (a patriotic anthology), 1915; contributor to Cambridge History of English Literature. *Recreations:* golfing, cycling. *Address:* Ceinwen, Bangor, N. Wales. *(Died 2 Feb. 1922.)*

JONES-PARRY, Rear-Admiral John Parry; retired; J.P., Cheshire; inventor of non-recoil gun carriage, and mantle to protect crew; *b.* 7 Oct. 1829; *s.* of late Rev. J. Jones-Parry; *m.* 1st, 1861, Çatherine (*d.* 1895), *d.* of J. de Winton; two *s.* one *d.*; 2nd, 1898, Marion, *d.* of H. Roome. *Educ.:* sea. Served at Odessa and Sebastopol; a gunnery officer on board H.M.S. "Terrible" stationed in the Black Sea from beginning to end of the war; retired 1873. *Address:* Edern, Parkwood Road. Boscombe.*(Died 18 April 1920.)*

JONES-VAUGHAN, Maj.-Gen. Hugh Thomas, C.B. 1894; J.P. Carnarvons.; *b.* 1841, Glanywern, Merionethshire; *e. s.* of late Canon Jones, and Catherine, *d.* of Liston Vaughan; *m.* Eva, *e. d.* of E. Owen, Hengwrtucha, Dolgelly, 1883; one *s. Educ.:* R.M.C. Sandhurst. Passed Staff College, 1871; Maj.-Gen. 1899; Served in the Indian Mutiny, 1857-58; present at the actions of Chanda, Umineerapore, and Sultanpora; final siege and capture of Lucknow (medal and clasp); Afghan War, 1878-79-80, as Brigade-Major with 1st division Peshawur Field Force; capture of Ali Musjid; and in expeditions to the Bazar and Lugman valleys; Brigade-Major in the Zaimusht Expedition, and at assault and capture of Zawa (three times mentioned in despatches, Brevet of Lieut.-Colonel, medal and clasp); A.A.G. Western District, 1887-92; appointed Colonel on the Staff with temporary rank of Major-General, 1894; General Officer commanding troops, Straits Settlements, 1894-99; Distinguished Service Record, 1899; Colonel, Loyal North Lancashire Regiment, 1909. *Recreations:* shooting, hunting, rowing. *Address:* Tyddynllydyn, Rhydyclafdy, Carnarvon. *Club:* United Service. *(Died 11 April 1916.)*

JONNART, Celestin Auguste, French Ambassador Extraordinary to the Vatican; member of French Academy, 1923; *b.* Flechin, Pas-de-Calais, 1857. Has rendered eminent service to France in Politics, in the Colonies in the diplomatic service. *Address:* French Legation to the Holy See, Rome.
(Died 30 Sept. 1927.)

JOPP, Col. John, C.B. 1894; Indian Army; *b.* 13 Mar. 1840; *m.* 1886, Annie Florence Mead, *d.* of late Surgeon-Major John Memsie, I.M.S. Entered army, 1856; Colonel, 1886; served Aden, 1858; Abyssinian War, 1868 (medal); Afghan War, 1879-80 (medal, despatches); Political Resident, Aden, and commanding 2nd Class District, 1890-95; A.D.C. 1895-97.
(Died 16 June 1923.)

JORDAN, Rt. Hon. Sir John (Newell), P.C. 1915; K.C.M.G., *cr.* 1920; K.C.B., *cr.* 1909; K.C.M.G., *cr.* 1904; C.M.G. 1897; G.C.I.E., *cr.* 1911; Member of the League of Nations Advisory Committee, Geneva; *b.* 5 Sep. 1852, Balloo, Co. Down, Ireland; *m.* Annie Howe, *d.* of Dr. Cromie, Clough, Co. Down, 1885; three *s. Educ.:* Royal Belfast Academical Institution; Queen's College, Belfast. 1st class Honours. Appointed Student Interpreter in China, 1876; Assistant Chinese Secretary to H.B.M. Legation, Pekin, 1889; Chinese Secretary, 1891; Consul-General, Corea, 1896-98; Chargé d'Affaires, 1898-1901; Minister Resident at Seoul, 1901; H.B.M. Minister Resident at Court of Corea, 1901-6; H.B.M. Envoy Extraordinary and Minister Plenipotentiary, Peking, 1906-20; received the Jubilee Medal, 1897, and the Coronation Medal,

1902. *Publications:* Translations of the Pekin Gazette. *Recreation:* riding. *Address:* 12 Portinscale Road, S.W.15. *(Died 14 Sept. 1925.)*

JORDAN, Rev. Louis Henry, B.D.; Special Lecturer on the History and Comparison of Religions; *b.* Halifax, Canada, 27 July 1855; *s.* of late William Jordan, merchant, Halifax; *m.* 1890, Catherine Pollok, 2nd *d.* of Hon. James McDonald, Chief-Justice of Nova Scotia. *Educ.:* Dalhousie University, Halifax (Lord Dufferin Gold Medallist, being premier member of the Graduating Class of 1875); Edinburgh (Medallist in Philosophy, 1882); Princeton; Oxford; Marburg; Leipsic; Berlin. Minister of St. Andrew's Church, Halifax, 1882-85; Erskine Church, Montreal, 1885-90; St. James Square Church, Toronto, 1894-1900; Lecturer on Church Polity, Montreal Theological College, 1887-89; Special Lecturer on Comparative Religion, University of Chicago, 1902; all the years since 1890 (excepting pastorate in Toronto) have been devoted to travel, reading and lecturing, in different parts of the world. *Publications:* Comparative Religion: Its Genesis and Growth, 1905; Comparative Religion: A Survey of its Recent Literature, 1906, 1910, 1914; Comparative Religion: Its Method and Scope, 1908; The Study of Religion in the Italian Universities (with Professor Labanca), 1909; Modernism in Italy: its Origin, its Incentive, its Leaders and its Aims, 1909; Comparative Religion: its Adjuncts and Allies, 1915; contributions to the Review of Theology and Philosophy, Expository Times, Hibbert Journal, Princeton Theological Review, American Journal of Theology, Biblical World, etc. *Recreation:* foreign travel. *Club:* Authors'. *(Died 4 Oct. 1923.)*

JORDAN, William George; author and educator; *b.* New York City, 6 March 1864; *s.* of Henry and Mary Moat Murdock; *m.* 1922, Nellie B. Mitchell. *Educ.:* The College of the City of New York. Editor of Book Chat, 1884; Editor of Current Literature; retired from this position to lecture on his new system of education; Managing Editor of The Ladies' Home Journal, 1897; Editor-in-Chief of the Saturday Evening Post, 1898; Editor of the Search-Light, 1905. In 1907 wrote a pamphlet on the House of Governors, which led, in 1908, to a meeting of the Governors of all the States in Washington, and the organization of the State Executives for annual meetings as a House. *Publications:* The Kingship of Self-Control; The Majesty of Calmness; The Power of Truth; Mental Training: A Remedy for Education; The Crown of Individuality; Little Problems of Married Life; The Wood Carver; The Power of Purpose; What every American should know about the League of Nations; Feodor Vladimir Larrovitch, a memoir; The Trusteeship of Life; The Vision of High Ideals; educational works. *Recreation:* book collection. *Address:* 317 East Seventeenth Street, New York. *Clubs:* Authors', Dutch Treat, The Musketeers, New York.
(Died 20 April 1928.)

JOSA, Ven. Fortunato Pietro Luigi, Rector of S. Endellion since 1917; *b.* 5 June 1851; *m.* Beatrice Mary, *d.* of A. Cleaver of Nottingham; one *s.* three *d. Educ.:* Collegio Romano, Rome; St. Augustine's College, Canterbury; St. Boniface, Warminster. Ordained; 1874; Sub-Warden of the Bishop's College for Training Schoolmasters, 1874; Assistant Curate of St. Philip's; East Indian Missionary, Non Pareil, 1876; Rector of Holy Trinity, 1884; Canon of the Cathedral, 1892-1914; Rural Dean of Demerara, 1893-95; Government Examiner in Oriental Languages, 1878; Vicar-General Diocese of Guiana, 1912-14; Archdeacon of Demerara, 1910-14; Vicar of Christ Church, Demerara, 1890-1914. *Publications:* The Apostle of the Indians; The Life of S. Francis of Assisi; Manual of the Hindi Language; English Church

567

JORDAN, Edwin Oakes, Ph.D. See page xxii.

History of the West Indian Province ; The Tale of a Roaming Catholic ; and many pamphlets in English and Hindi, etc. *Recreations :* golf, philately. *Address :* The Rectory, S. Endellion, Port Isaac, N. Cornwall. *Club :* Corona.
(Died 19 Dec. 1922.)

JOSEPH, Delissa, F.R.I.B.A., since 1889 ; in practice as an architect since 1882 ; *b.* Jan. 1859 ; *e. s.* of late Isaac Solomon Joseph; *m.* 1887, Leah (Lily), *d.* of late Joseph Solomon. *Educ.:* Durham House School and Jews' College. Has been member of Council of Royal Institute of British Architects, 1922-23, of City of London Conservative Association, of United Synagogue, of Jews' College, and of Anglo - Jewish Association ; has exhibited Architectural Works at Royal Academy, and held a one-man show at Suffolk Street Galleries, 1924. *Principal Works :* Whole of Fitzgeorge Avenue, Chelsea Embankment Gardens, and Rangoon Street ; Adelaide Court, Rutland Court, Chelsea Court, Castlenau Gardens, Exeter Mansions, Stanhope Court, Brookfield House, Oxford Circus House, Bartlett House, Peninsular House, West India House St. George's House, Bush Lane House, Chester-field House ; Hotel Rembrandt, Coburg Court Hotel, Jermyn Court Hotel, Park View Hotel, Park Gate Hotel ; seven Synagogues ; thirteen superstructures of Tube Stations, and buildings in St. Paul's Churchyard, Old Jewry, Walbrook, Langham Place, Great St. Helen's, Kingsway, Fleet Street, Cheapside, St. Swithin's Lane, Tottenham Court Road, Oxford Street, Hanover Street, Albemarle Street, etc. *Publications :* Higher Buildings for London, and Building Heights and Ancient Lights, R.I.B.A. Journal; Numerous Letters to the Times on Higher Buildings for London. *Recreations:* motoring, golfing, reading, smoking. *Addresses :* 2 Basing-hall Avenue, E.C.2 ; 4 Cornwall Mansions, 33 Kensington Court, W.8. *T.:* London Wall 1138. *T.A.:* Rebuilding London. *Club:* Maccabaeans. *(Died 10 Jan. 1927.)*

JOSHI, Rev. Canon D. L., Canon of St. Thomas' Cathedral, Bombay ; Hon. Chaplain to Bishop of Bombay ; Marathi Priest-in-charge, Emmanuel Church, Bombay ; *b.* 8 May 1864 *s.* of late Rev. Lucas M. Joshi and Karunabai ; *m.* Anubai, *d.* of late D. Nana ; one *s. Educ. :* Robert Money School, Bombay ; College of Science, Poona ; Divinity School, Poona. Left Civil Engineering for Theology, 1882 ; after being a schoolmaster, ordained, 1893 ; for sixteen years in charge of the C.M.S. Marathi Church in Bombay. *Publications:* Editor of Dharma-dipika, an Anglo-Marathi Magazine ; translator of Walker's Commentary on Philippians ; Oxenden's Family Prayers ; and several other books and booklets ; engaged on the revision of the Marathi Bible. *Address:* Molesworth, Girgaum, Bombay. *T.A.:* Testimony, Bombay.
(Died Oct. 1925.)

JOULAIN, Rt. Rev. Henry, D.D., O.M.I., Bishop of Jaffna since 1893 ; *b.* St. Romans, 24 Sept. 1852 ; *s.* of James Joulain and Mary Morillon. *Educ.:* Petit Séminaire de Mont Morillon ; Grand Seminary of Poictiers ; Priest, 1875 ; Assistant parish-priest at St. Andre de Niort, 1876-80 ; entered Congregation of Oblates of Mary Immaculate, 1880 ; sent to Ceylon same year ; Missionary till 1893. *Address:* Jaffna, Ceylon. *T.A.:* Bishop, Jaffna. *Club:* Jaffna Catholic (Hon. Pres.). *(Died 7 Feb. 1919.)*

JOURDAIN, Lt.-Col. Charles Edward Arthur, D.S.O. 1900 ; Commanding 2nd. Batt. Loyal North Lancashire Regt.; *b.* 7 May 1869 ; *s.* of late Rev. F. Jourdain ; *m.* 1912, Alexia Grace, *y. d.* of Captain Frederick Papillon, R.N. Entered army, 1888 ; Captain, 1895 ; Major, 1906 ; Lt.-Col., 1913 ; served South Africa, 1899-1902 (despatches, D.S.O.) ; European War, 1914-17. *Club :* Junior United Service. *(Died 29 July 1918.)*

JOURDAIN, Eleanor Frances, Principal, St. Hugh's College, Oxford, since 1915 ; *d.* of late Rev. Francis Jourdain, Vicar of Ashburne, Derbyshire. *Educ.:* home ; Lady Margaret Hall, Oxford (Scholar) ; second class in the Final Honour School of Modern History, 1886 ; Assistant Mistress in High Schools (Totten-ham and Clifton) ; Headmistress of the School for Girls, Corran, Watford, 1892 ; Vice-Principal, St. Hugh's College, Oxford, 1902 ; obtained the Degree of Doctor of the University of Paris for a thesis on the Divina Commedia, 1904 ; M.A. Oxon. 1920 ; Taylorian Lecturer in French, Oxford 1920 ; Fellow of the Huguenot Society ; Member of the Aristotelian Society ; on the Council of the Dante Society. *Publications :* Le Symbolisme dans la Divine Comédie de Dante ; The Theory of the Infinite in Modern Thought ; An Introduction to the Study of the French Classical Drama ; Methods of Moral Instruction and Training of Girls in France (a contribution to a volume edited by Prof. Sadler) ; Dramatic Theory and Practice in France, 1690-1808, etc. *Address:* St. Hugh's College, Oxford. *T.:* Oxford 782. *Club:* Women's University. *(Died 6 April 1924.)*

JOWETT, Rev. John Henry, C.H. 1922 ; M.A., D.D. Edinburgh, 1910 ; New York, 1911 ; Minister of Westminster Chapel 1918-23 ; *b.* 1864 ; *s.* of Josiah and Hannah Jowett ; *m. d.* of Francis Winpenny, Barnard Castle. *Educ.:* Hipperholme Grammar School ; Edin-burgh University ; Oxford University. Minister of St. James's Congregational Church, New-castle - on - Tyne, 1889 - 95 ; Carr's Lane, Birmingham, 1895-1911 ; Pres. Free Church Council, 1910 ; Minister of Fifth Avenue Presby-terian Church, N.Y., 1911 - 18. *Publications:* Apostolic Optimism ; From Strength to Strength ; Meditations for Quiet Moments ; Brooks by the Traveller's Way ; Thirsting for the Springs ; The Passion for Souls ; Silver Lining ; The Trans-figured Church ; The Preacher: his Life and Work ; Things that Matter Most ; Daily Medita-tions ; The Eagle Life ; The Friend on the Road. *Recreation:* walking. *Address:* 10 Chichester Road, Croydon. *(Died 19 Dec. 1923.)*

JOWITT, Frederick McCulloch, C.B.E. 1918 ; J.P. ; *b.* 1868 ; *m.* 1900, Helen Dorothy, *d.* of W. T. Benson, Montreal. *Address:* Hollins Hall, Ripley, Leeds. *Club:* Reform.
(Died Sept. 1919.)

JOY, George William, artist ; *s.* of W. Bruce Joy, M.D.; *b.* 7 July, Dublin, 1844 ; *m.* 1877, Florence, *d.* of Thomas Masterman ; four *d. Educ.:* Harrow. Studied Kensington ; Royal Academy ; Paris (under Charles Jalabert and Bonnat) ; served 21 years in Artists' Corps, repre-senting them at Wimbledon, Bisley, etc. ; also shot 6 times in International Match for Ireland. *Pictures:* Domenica ; Chess-players ; Laodamia ; Young Nelson's First Farewell ; Wellington at Angers ; Prince Charlie and Flora Macdonald ; The King's Drum shall never be beaten for Rebels, in Russel-Cotes Municipal Art Gallery, Bourne-mouth ; Princess Alice of Albany, for Queen Victoria ; Reverie, for New Zealand Govern-ment ; Truth, to German Government ; Joan of Arc, sold to French Government ; Lear and Cordelia, and The Death of General Gordon, in Leeds Municipal Art Gallery ; The Danaids ; The Drummer of the Penin-sular ; Christ and a Little Child, at Church House, Westminster ; A Merchantman Seeking Goodly Pearls ; A Dinner of Herbs, in Oldham Municipal Art Gallery ; Britannia ; The King's Daughter ; Dreams on the Veldt ; Griselda ; The Sword ; A Dream of Fair Women ; A Herald, temp. Edward III., Eve ; Tancred and Clorinda, 1919 ; Card Houses ; and many portraits, including Sir Theodore Martin, Countess Cranbrook, Countess Ferrers, Lady Craig as a child, R. Bowerman ; also impression-

ist flower pictures and studies, etc. ; obtained Gold Medals at Paris, Munich, and Berlin ; also the Chicago Medal. *Publication :* autobiographical sketch in The Work of George W. Joy, 1904. *Recreations :* music, rifle shooting, cricket. *Address :* Woodside, Purbrook, Hants. *T. :* Waterlooville 79. *Club :* Arts.
                           (Died 28 Oct. 1925.)

JOYCE, Thomas Heath ; *b.* London, 9 July 1850; *s.* of Thomas Joyce, Freshford, Somerset ; editor and proprietor of the Atlas ; *m.* 1st, 1874, Ellen Margaretta (*d.* 1916), *d.* of George Murphy ; 2nd, Emma, *d.* late W. Frances Knight, Overton, Hants ; two *s.* *Educ. :* mainly abroad. Joined staff of the Graphic at its start in Dec. 1869 ; editor of Daily Graphic, 1890-91 ; joint-editor with Hammond Hall, 1891-1906 ; editor of the Graphic, 1891-1906 ; F.R.G.S. *Publications :* miscellaneous journalistic and magazine contributions ; translated Victor Hugo's History of a Crime. *Recreations :* travel, walking, photography ; journeyed round the world, 1907. *Clubs :* Whitefriars ; Royal Albert Yacht, Southsea.   *(Died 13 May 1925.)*

JOYNER, Robert Batson, C.I.E. 1898 ; M.Inst.C.E., F.R.G.S. ; *b.* 1 March 1844 ; 3rd *s.* of late H. St. John Joyner, and Frances, *e. d.* of Alfred Batson, Ramsbury, Wilts ; *m.* Margaret Vye, *e. d.* of late N. Milne, 1879 ; one *s.* two *d.* *Educ. :* Privately. Appointed by Sec. of State to Bombay Public Works Department, 1868 ; constructed Mutha Canal Irrigation Work and Poona Water Supply ; twice thanked by Government for work done in Great Famine, 1876-77; designed and constructed Gokak Canal Works and other large schemes ; employed in designing and constructing works for utilising Falls of Gokak, 1886-87, services being specially lent by Government of India ; sent to Sindh to specially report on irrigation matters, 1889 ; appointed Superintending Engineer of that Province, 1891 ; and 1st Class Superintending Engineer, 1894 ; had charge of Famine Relief Works, 1896-98 ; specially thanked by Government. *Decorated* for work in India. *Publications :* Report on Utilisation of River Indus and Irrigation Management of Province of Sindh ; paper on Proper Management of Indian Famines ; Bombay Hydro-Electric Works design. *Recreations :* rowing, polo, and pig-sticking formerly; now photography, sketching, cycling, etc. *Address :* Woody Bay, N. Devon.   *(Died 30 July 1919.)*

JUDD, George William, I.S.O., 1913 ; Superintendent Preventive Service, Karachi, since 1881 ; *b.* 11 Nov. 1854 ; *s.* of Captain George William Judd, Ordnance Department ; *m.* 1878, M. F. S. Malvery, *d.* of late editor and proprietor of Our Paper, published at Karachi ; four *s.* three *d.* *Educ. :* K.E. and I.E. School, Karachi. Entered Commissioner's Office, 1872 ; holds silver medal, Delhi Durbar. *Recreations :* cricket, shooting, fishing. *Address :* Andrew Road, Keomari, Karachi. *T. :* 107.

JUDD, John Wesley, C.B. 1895 ; LL.D., F.R.S., F.G.S. ; *b.* Portsmouth, 18 Feb. 1840 ; *m.* 1878, Jeannie Frances, *d.* of John Jeyes ; one *s.* one *d.* *Educ. :* Camberwell ; Royal School of Mines. Geological Survey of England and Wales, 1867-70 ; Inspector of Schools, 1871 ; President Geological Society, 1887-88 ; Prof. of Geology, 1876-1905 ; Dean of Royal College of Science, London, 1895-1905 ; Emeritus Professor of Geology in the Imperial College of Science and Technology, 1913. *Publications :* Geology of Rutland, 1875 ; Volcanoes : What they are and what they Teach, 1878 ; The Student's Lyell, 1896 and 1911 ; The Coming of Evolution, 1910 ; and many scientific memoirs in the Transactions of the Royal and other Societies. *Recreations :* geological exploration, gardening. *Address :* 30 Cumberland Road, Kew ; Beachside, Walmer, Kent.   *(Died 3 Mar. 1916.)*

JUDGE, Mark Hayler, A.R.I.B.A., senior partner Mark H. Judge & Son; retired,

1921 ; chief surveyor to Sanitary Assurance Association since 1880 ; hon. secretary Sunday Society for Opening Museums, etc., on Sundays, since 1875 ; *b.* Battle, Sussex, 26 Feb. 1847 ; *e. s.* of late George Hayler, Battle, and Mary, *e. d.* of late John Brignall, Wittersham, Kent ; adopted surname of Judge, 1861 ; *m.* 1875, Emily, *e. d.* of late John Harwood Simpson, M.Inst.M.E., Stokesley, Yorks ; one *s.* two *d.* *Educ. :* St. Mary's National School, Hastings ; Parker's Endowed School, Hastings. Founded Sunday Society, 1875 ; Director of Artizans', Labourers', and General Dwellings Co., Ltd., since 1877 ; member of Vestry of Paddington, 1886-92 ; chairman Metropolitan Board of Works Enquiry Committee, 1886-89 ; curator Parkes Museum of Hygiene, Univ. Coll. 1878-82; secretary International Medical and Sanitary Exhibition, Kensington, 1881 ; trustee Paddington Free Public Library ; Founder University Extension Guild, 1903 ; Hon. Sec. Further Strand Improvement Committee since 1903 ; founded the British Constitution Association, 1905 ; Chairman Sandgate and Shorncliffe Sir John Moore Centenary Memorial Committee ; Chairman Committee on War Damage, instituted 1915. *Publications :* Sanitary Arrangements of Dwelling-Houses, 1884 ; Sanitary Architecture, 1901 ; Communal and Individual Responsibility as regards Health Conditions, 1909 ; and other works on Hygiene, including articles in Reviews on cognate subjects and Individualism ; Political Socialism—A Remonstrance (Editor) ; The War and the Neutral Powers—International Law, 1914.   *(Died 25 Jan. 1927.)*

JUDSON, Harry Pratt, LL.D. ; President of the University of Chicago, 1906-23 ; President Emeritus since 1923 ; *b.* Jamestown, N.Y., 20 Dec. 1849 ; *s.* of Rev. Lyman P. Judson and Abigail C. Pratt ; *m.* 1879, Rebecca A. Gilbert, Troy, N.Y. ; one *d.* *Educ. :* Williams College. A.B. 1870 ; A.M. 1883 ; LL.D. 1893 ; LL.D. Queen's University, Canada, 1903 ; State University of Iowa, 1907 ; Washington University, 1907; Western Reserve, 1909 ; Harvard, 1909 ; University of Michigan, 1911 ; North-Western University, 1913 ; Dalhousie University, Halifax, N.S., 1919 ; teacher and principal High School, Troy, N.Y., 1870-85 ; professor history, University of Minnesota, 1885-92 ; professor political science and head dean of the colleges, University of Chicago, 1892-94 ; prof. and head dept. political science, and dean of faculties arts, literature and science, 1894-1907 ; acting president, 1906-7 ; President, 1907-23 ; co-editor American Historical Review, 1895-1902 ; member General Education Board, 1906 ; member of the Rockefeller Foundation, 1913-23 ; Chairman, Commission on Medical Education in China, Rockefeller Foundation, 1914 ; Chairman, University of Chicago War Service, 1917-18 ; Director American Persian Relief Commission, 1918-19; Knight Royal Prussian Order of the Crown, 1904 ; Officer Legion of Honour, 1918 ; First Class Order of the Lion and Sun (with brilliants), Persia, 1919 ; Commander of the Order of St. Sava, 1921; gold medal, National Institute of Social Sciences, 1920. *Publications :* History of the Troy Citizens' Corps, 1884; Caesar's Army, 1885; Caesar's Commentaries (co-editor), 1885 ; Europe in the Nineteenth Century, 1894, 1898, revised, 1901 ; The Growth of the American Nation, 1895, 1900; The Higher Education as a Training for Business, 1896 ; The Mississippi Valley (in Shaler's United States of America), 1894 ; The Young American, 1895 ; The Government of Illinois, 1900; The Essentials of a Written Constitution (Decennial Publications, The University of Chicago, vol. iv.); Our Federal Republic, 1925. *Recreations :* golf and fly-fishing. *Address :* The University of Chicago, Chicago. *Clubs :* Quadrangle, University, Union League, Cliff Dwellers, Chicago ; Uni-

versity, Washington ; Century, New York.
(*Died 4 Mar. 1927.*)

JULER, Henry Edward, F.R.C.S. ;
b. Suffolk ; *s.* of H. C. Juler, M.D. ; *m.*; two
s. three *d. Educ.* : London ; Paris · Berlin. St.
Mary's Hospital Medical School. House
Surgeon, Female Lock Hospital ; Medical Super-
intendent of St. Mary's Hospital ; Demonstrator
of Anatomy, St. Mary's Hospital Medical School;
Pathologist, Royal Westminster Ophthalmic
Hospital ; Consulting Ophthalmic Surgeon, St.
Mary's Hospital ; Consulting Ophthalmic Sur-
geon to the Royal Westminster Ophthalmic
Hospital, and to the London Lock Hospitals.
Publications: A Handbook of Ophthalmic Science
and Practice ; and other works on the Eye.
Recreations: fond of horse exercise, golf, and
motor cars. *Address :* 24 Cavendish Square, W.1.
T. : Mayfair 1633. (*Died 23 April 1921.*)

**JULIAN, Maj.-Gen. Sir Oliver Richard
Archer,** K.B.E., *cr.*, 1921 ; C.B. 1916; C.M.G.
1900; C.B.E. 1919; late Army Medical Service; *b.*
26 July 1863; *s.* of Captain Thomas Archer Julian,
late 52nd Regt., of Broomhill, Ivybridge ; *m.*
1888, Lily, *d.* of late Sampson Taylor Rowe.
Entered army, 1887, Major, 1899 ; served South
Africa, 1899-1902 (despatches twice ; Queen's
medal 4 clasps—Talana, Defence of Ladysmith,
Laing's Nek, Belfast ; King's medal 2 clasps ;
C.M.G.) ; Zakka Khel Expedition, 1908 ;
Mohmand Expedition, 1908 (despatches, Bt.
Lt. - Col.) ; European War, France and Belgium,
1915-17 (despatches, C.B.) ; D.D.M.S. Western
Command, 1917-1919 (C.B.E.) ; D.M.S., Meso-
potamia, 1919-21 (despatches, K.B.E.) ; Phy-
sician and Surgeon, Royal Hospital, Chelsea,
1913-15 ; retired pay, 1921. *Address :* Ivydene,
South Molton. Devon. (*Died 13 June 1925.*)

K

KADOORIE, Sir Ellis, Kt., *cr.* 1917, of
Hong-Kong ; Merchant ; *b.* Baghdad, 7 Dec.
1865 ; *s.* of Silas Kadoorie and Remah Eleazar ;
unmarried. *Educ. :* privately. *Recreation :*
racing. *Address :* 10 Ice House Street, Hong-
Kong. *Clubs:* Hong-Kong ; Shanghai.
(*Died Feb. 1922.*)

KAGWA, Sir Apolo, K.C.M.G., *cr.*,
1925 ; Principal Minister, 1914 - 26, formerly
Regent, of Buganda. Visited England, 1902.
Address: Mengo, Uganda. (*Died 21 Feb. 1927.*)

KAINE, Hon. John Charles, M.L.C.,
Stadocona division ; in Cabinet, without port-
folio, since 1906 ; *b.* 18 Oct. 1854 ; *m.* 1st, 1879,
Theresa Maria Tucker ; 2nd, 1904, Helen Smith.
Address: 5 Ste. Ursule Street, Quebec
(*Died 23 April 1921.*)

**KAMBAL, Miralai (Colonel) Beshir
Bey,** D.S.O. 1917; Inspector Kordofan Arab
Tribes since 1900 ; *b.* Halfayet El - Melouk,
Khartoum North District, Khartoum Province,
1855; descendant of Malik Shawish Kambal,
last King of Dongola till 1817 ; *m.* 1870 ; six *s.*
fourteen *d. Educ. :* in his own house at Halfayet El - Melouk. Under the former Sudan
Government—Service rendered in Khartoum,
Sennar, Red Sea Coasts, Expedition of Darfur
with Gordon Pasha in 1876, Kassala and Aby-
sinian frontiers with the following ranks in
the Irregular troops : Bulukbashi, Head of 25
Irregular Cavalry; Bimbashi, Head of 100
Irregular Cavalry ; Sangak, Head of 200, 300,
and 400 Irregular Cavalry. Under Dervishes
Rule, 1885-98—under captivity in Omdurman,
1885-90 ; Bahr-el-Jebel, 1891-93 ; Omdurman,
1894-95 ; passed in prison in Omdurman 1896-
1898 ; mentioned in Ten Years' Captivity in
the Sudan, by Father Ohrwalder, and Fire
and Sword, Slatin Pasha, as well as in Arabic
publications of Ibrahim Fawzi Pasha and Naoum

Bey Shoukair. Under present Government,
1899-1918 ; O.C. Irregular Battalion and then
as Sub-Governor Kordofan, 1899 ; 4th Medjidie,
4th Osmanieh, English and Egyptian Sudan
medals with clasps of Djebel-Dayer Talodi,
Djebel Nimi, Victoria medal, 1912. *Recreations:*
the only recreation he enjoys is cultivation
during three months' leave every year. *Address:*
El-Obeid, Kordofan, Sudan. (*Died 6 Sept. 1919.*)

KANE, Admiral Sir Henry Coey,
K.C.B., *cr.* 1911 ; C.B. 1891 ; retired 1899 ;
b. 1843 ; *s.* of Sir Robert Kane, F.R.S.,
Fortlands, Killiney. Sub-Lieutenant R.N.
1863 ; Naval Attaché to Maritime Courts,
1883-87 ; Director of Naval Ordnance, 1894-97.
Address : 201 Ashley Gardens, S.W. *T. :* Victoria 7711. *Club:* United Service.
(*Died 30 Jan. 1917.*)

**KANE, Captain Robert Romney
Godred,** D.S.O., 1915 ; Royal Munster Fusiliers ; *b.* 11 Oct. 1888 ; *s.* of late Judge R. R.
Kane, 4 Fitzwilliam Place, Dublin, and Glendree,
County Clare; unmarried. *Educ. :* Oratory
School, Edgbaston ; Sandhurst. Entered army
1908 ; joined the 1st Batt. R. Munster Fusiliers
in India (Rawal Pindi) ; was in India and Burma
till Aug. 1914 ; served European War, on Staff in
Gallipoli from the first landing till 18 July 1915
(twice wounded) ; on Staff in France, 1915-16
(D.S.O., Chevalier, Legion of Honour, despatches). *Recreations:* hunting, polo, big and
small game shooting. *Address:* 201 Ashley
Gardens, S.W. *Club:* Junior Army and Navy.
(*Died 1 Oct. 1918.*)

KANE, William Francis de Vismes,
D.L., J.P., M.R.I.A. ; member Diocesan
Council, Dio. Clogher, Ch. of I. ; *b.* Exmouth,
19 Apr. 1840 ; *o. s.* of Joseph Kane, of Dublin,
and Withycombe Grange, Devon, and Eliza, *d.*
of Col. the Count de Vismes, Coldstream
Guards ; *m.* 1st, 1863, Emily, *d.* of Rev. C. J.
Hamilton ; one *d.* ; 2nd, 1902, Hon. Louisa
Catherine, *d.* 1st Lord Bateman, relict of late
Col. Green Wilkinson, Scots Guards. *Educ. :*
Brighton College ; Dublin Univ. (M.A.). High
Sheriff, Co. Monaghan, 1865 and 1909; sometime
a Director and Chairman of the Grand Canal
Coy., Ireland, in which he initiated large re-
forms. *Publications :* Handbook of European
Butterflies ; a Catalogue of the Lepidoptera of
Ireland ; articles on Entomology, and Micro-
scopic Crustacea, etc. ; in various scientific
magazines. *Recreations:* archæology, horticul-
ture, nat. history, and microscopy. *Address :*
Drumreaske, Monaghan. *T.A. :* Ballinode.
(*Died 18 April 1918.*)

KANTARAJ URS, Sir M., K.C.I.E., *cr.*
1921 ; C.S.I. 1914 ; Dewan (Chief Minister) of
Mysore 1918-22 ; retired 1922 ; *b.* 20 Sep. 1870 ;
s. of Narasaraj Urs and Kempananja Ammanni,
of the Kalale family, Mysore; *m.* Mahara-
jakumari Jayalakshmi Ammanni, *e. sis.* of
Maharaja of Mysore; one *d. Educ.:* Maharaja's
Coll., Mysore ; The Christian Coll., Madras. As-
sistant Commissioner, 1894 ; Asst. Private Secre-
tary to H.H. the Maharani Regent, 1895-99 ;
Special Asst. Commissioner, Bangalore, 1899 ;
Deputy Commissioner, Mysore District, also
President, Mysore City Municipal Council,
1902 ; Chairman, Mysore City Improvement
Trust Board, 1908 ; Excise Commissioner in
Mysore, 1912 ; Chairman, Industries and Com-
merce Committee, 1912-16 ; Member of the
Executive Council, Mysore, 1913-18 ; visited
Japan, Mar.-Aug. 1916 ; Chairman, Agricultural
Committee, 1916-18 ; created Rajaseva Dhurina
(Gandabherunda Order), Oct. 1916. *Recrea-*
tions: riding and tennis. *Address:* Jayalakshmi
Vilas, Mysore, India. *Clubs:* United Service
(Hon.) ; Bangalore, Ursu, Mysore.
(*Died 3 Oct. 1923.*)

KAPP, Dr. Gisbert, *b.* Mauer, near Vienna ;
father of German family, mother of Scotch ; *m.*

1884, Therese Mary Krall; two s. *Educ.*: Polytechnic School, Zürich. In practical engineering work, partly in England, partly abroad, since 1876; Manager to the works of Messrs. Crompton and Co., Chelmsford, 1882-84; set up as Consulting Engineer in Westminster, 1884; went to Berlin and became General Secretary to the German Association of Electrical Engineers and Lecturer of Electrical Engineering at Charlottenburg, 1894; Telford Medallist, 1886-1888; Hon. D.Eng. Karlsruhe and Dresden; Past President Institution of Electrical Engineers; President of the Engineering Section British Association, 1913; Professor of Electrical Engineering, the University, Birmingham, 1905-1918. *Publications*: for 11 years editor of Elektrotechnische Zeitschrift; Electric Transmission of Power; Transformers; Dynamo Machines; Construction of Electric Machinery; Alternating Currents; Principles of Electrical Engineering and their Application; various papers at the Institutions of Civil and Electric Engineers. *Recreations*: golfing, yachting. *Address*: Selly Park, Birmingham.
(Died 10 Aug. 1922.)

KARAULI, H.H. Maharaja Dhiraj Sir Bhanwar Pal, Deo Bahadur, Yadukul Chandra Bhal, G.C.I.E., *cr.* 1897; K.C.I.E. 1894; *b.* 24 July 1864; married, six wives; no *c*. *Educ.*: Mayo College, Ajmere. *S.* 1886. Recognized as head of Jadon Rajputs (Lunar dynasty), and as the lineal descendant of Sri Krishna, the god. Is a patron of learning, especially Sanskrit. The State has an area of 1242 square miles and a population of over 150,000. Entitled to a salute of 17 guns. Received Coronation medal, 1912. *Recreation*: shooting. *Address*: Karauli, Rajputana.
(Died 3 Aug. 1927.)

KARKARIA, R. P.; *b.* Bombay, 16 May 1869. *Educ.*: St. Xavier's School and College. B.A. 1888; Senior Fellow and Professor St. Xavier's College, Bombay, 1891; Principal and Professor of English Language and Literature, Collegiate Institutions, 1898; Examiner in History and Philosophy, Bombay University; F.R.Hist.S., M.R.A.S.; *m.* cousin; no *c*. *Publications*: discovered the Anstey MS. of, and edited, 1892, with notes, Carlyle's hitherto Unpublished Lectures on European Literature and Culture, originally delivered in 1838; Parnell's Poems, and Golden Treasury, Book IV.; India—Forty Years of Progress and Reform, 1896, India since the Mutiny, Historical Sketch of the Parsis, Shivaji, Akbar, and other Essays; Bibliography of Bombay; European Travellers in Gujarat; translated Parsi Sacred Book, the Pahalavi Dinkard; Cicero's De Natura Deorum and a Teleological Treatise of the Avesta; Zoroaster and Comte—some Zoroastrian traits in Positivism; Purim and Farwardigan—in the Hoshang Memorial Volume, 1909; The French Revolutionary and the Parsi Calendars: a study in chronology—in the Cama Memorial Volume; Firdausi: his Editors and Translators; Proselytism among the Parsis and among the Jews: a Historical Parallel; Death of Shivaji, 1905; edited Lord Curzon's Farewell Speeches in India, with Essays on his Viceroyalty, 1906; Lord Curzon's Indian Viceroyalty, 1908; The Scientific Study of Mahratha History, 1907; Mahmud Begurra, Sultan of Gujarat; edited Dean Church's Dante, with Introduction, 1906; Essays in English History, 1908; Charm of Bombay, an Anthology with notes, 1914; was the first to give in India a series of lectures on the present Great War—its historical causes, course, etc.—which he began in Bombay in September 1914; contributed to a Parsi paper during 1915-16, a Calendar of Eminent Parsis for every day in the year; organised with Bombay Jashan Committee the Historical Celebration at Sanjan, 1916, of the 1200th anniversary of Parsis' first

arrival in India at that place. *Recreations*: book-hunting and coin-collecting; visiting historical places in Western India. *Address*: Gowalia Tank, Grant Road, Bombay, 7.
(Died 13 May 1919.)

KASHMIR and JAMMU, Lt.-Gen. H.H. Sir Pratab Singh Indar Mahindar Bahadur Sipar-i-Saltanat, Maharaja of; G.B.E., *cr.* 1918; G.C.I.E., *cr.* 1911; G.C.S.I.; LL.D. Punjab University; Hon. Col. 47th Dogras; *b.* 1850; is the third of his line, and *g.s.* of the founder of the dynasty, Maharaja Ghulab Singh; *S.* 1885. Area of 84,432 square miles; population of 3,320,518; is entitled to a salute of twenty-one guns within the limits of his State, and twenty-one guns in the rest of India; British Government conferred additional powers on the Maharaja in 1905; H.H. signalised this by inaugurating public works of importance, a motor road *viâ* Banihal Pass to Srinagar, etc.; The Govt. again conferred full powers on the Maharaja in 1921. *Recreations*: religious and historical discussion. *Address*: Srinagar, Kashmir; Jammu, Punjab. *(Died 23 Sept. 1925.)*

KATO, Viscount Takaaki, Viscount, *cr.* 1916; G.C.M.G.; Baron, *cr.* 1911; Prime Minister of Japan since 1924; *b.* 3 Jan. 1860; *m.* 1886, Haruji, *sister* of Baron Hisaya Iwasaki; one *s.* one *d.* *Educ.*: Univ. of Tokio Private Sec. to the Minister for Foreign Affairs, 1888-90; Director of Banking Bureau and Director of Taxation Bureau, Finance Department, 1891-94; Envoy Extraordinary and Minister Plenipotentiary at the Court of St. James's, 1894-99; Minister for Foreign Affairs, 1900-1901 and 1906; Ambassador of Japan at the Court of St. James's, 1908-1913; Minister for Foreign Affairs, Jan. 1913; resigned, Feb. 1913; Leader of the Kensei Kwai since 1913; Minister for Foreign Affairs, 1914-15; Member of the House of Peers, 1915. *Address*: Shimo-Nibancho, Tokio, Japan.
(Died 28 Jan. 1926.)

KATO, Admiral Baron Tomosaburo, Juhnii; Insignia of the First Class of the Order of the Paulownia and Rising Sun, Insignia of the First Class of the Order of the Sacred Treasure, and Insignia of the Second Class of the Order of the Golden Kite; Japanese Prime Minister and Minister of Marine since June 1922; *b.* Hiroshima, Japan, 1859. Entered navy at age of 12; midshipman, 1888; Captain, 1899; Professor at the Naval College; Construction Supervisor in the Navy Department; Chief of Staff of Standing Squadron, 1902; of the Kamiura Fleet; of the combined Fleet under Admiral Togo in the Russo-Japanese war of 1904-5; Vice-Minister of Marines, 1906; Commander-in-Chief, Kure Naval Station, 1909-1914; also served in the Navy Department; Commander-in-Chief of the First Fleet when war broke out in 1914; promoted to Admiral, 1915; Minister of Marine in 1918 in the Terauchi Cabinet; created Baron in recognition of war services; one of the three chief Japanese Delegates, Washington Conference, 1921-22. *Address*: Ichichome, Nagatacho, Kohjimachi-Ku, Tokio, Japan. *(Died 24 Aug. 1923.)*

KAUFMANN, Rev. Moritz, M.A.: Rector of Ingworth since 1892, and Vicar of Calthorpe, Norfolk, since 1898; *b.* 7 Oct. 1839; *s.* of Leopold and Babetta Kaufmann, of Gross-sachsen Weinheim, in the Grand Duchy of Baden; *m.* Mary Josephine, *d.* of William Pilkington and Eliza Campbell Watson, of Cloughton, Birkenhead; three *s.* one *d.* *Educ.*: Grammar School of Weinheim; Trinity College, Dublin. Respondent, Prizeman in Hebrew, Syriac, Chaldee, and modern languages; English Composition Prize awarded by late Prof. Dowden. After serving several cures at home and abroad he was tutor at St. Aidan's Theological College, Birkenhead, 1877-83; subsequently curate in charge of Erpingham, 1884-92; Donnellan Lecturer for the

University of Dublin, 1899-1900. *Publications:* Utopias or Social Schemes of Improvement from Sir Thomas More to Kárl Marx ; Christian Socialism ; Charles Kingsley, Christian Socialist and Social Reformer ; Socialism and Communism in their Practical Application ; Socialism and Modern Thought, Social Development under Christian Influence ; The Housing of the Working Classes and of the Poor, in Social Problems Series, etc. ; contributor to Cambridge Modern History ; Pascal's Thoughts, translated and selected (Devotional Works). *Recreations:* country walks, perusal of fiction. *Address:* Ingworth, Norwich. *T.A.:* Aylsham. *Club:* New Athenæum. (*Died 8 Mar. 1920.*)

KAULBACH, Ven. James Albert, M.A., D.D. ; Rector of Truro, Nova Scotia, since 1903 ; Archdeacon of Nova Scotia and Canon of St. Luke's Cathedral since 1889 ; Examining Chaplain since 1896 ; *b.* Lunenburg, N.S., 30 Aug. 1889 ; 3rd *s.* of J. H. Kaulbach, High Sheriff of Lunenburg, N.S. ; *m.* 1876, Mary Sophia, *d.* of James F. Bradshaw, Quebec ; one *s.* *Educ.:* Collegiate School and King's College, Windsor, N.S. Ordained Deacon, 1864 ; Priest, 1865 ; Curate at River John, 1864-70 ; Vicar of Truro, Nova Scotia, 1870-1903. *Address:* Truro, Nova Scotia. *Club:* Clericus, Halifax, N.S.
(*Died 25 Feb. 1913.*)

KAVANAGH, Rt. Hon. Walter Mac-Murrough, P.C. Ire. 1916 ; J.P., D.L. ; *b.* Jan. 1856 ; *e. s.* of Right Hon. Arthur McM. Kavanagh ; *m.* 1887, Helen Louisa, *d.* of Colonel J. S. Howard ; two *s.* *Educ.:* Eton ; Christ Church, Oxford. High Sheriff, Co. Carlow, 1884 ; M.P. (N.) Carlow, 1908-10. *Address:* Borris House, Borris, Co. Carlow. *Clubs:* Reform ; Sackville Street, Dublin.
(*Died 18 July 1922.*)

KAY, Lt.-Col. Sir William Algernon Ireland, 6th Bt., *cr.* 1803 ; C.M.G. 1918 ; D.S.O. 1914 ; K.R.R.C. ; *b.* 21 March 1876 ; *s.* of 5th Bt. and Emily, *d.* of late Thomas James Ireland, Ousden Hall, Suffolk ; *S.* father, 1914. Entered army, 1896; Captain, 1901; Major, 1914; Adjutant Volunteers, 1906-8, and Territorials, 1908-9 ; served Sierra Leone, 1898-9 (medal with clasp) ; South Africa, 1899-1902 (despatches, Queen's medal, 4 clasps ; King's medal, 2 clasps) European War, 1914-18 (D.S.O., Bt. Lt.-Col., C.M.G.). *Heir:* none. *Club:* Naval and Military. (*Died 4 Oct. 1918.*)

KAYE, Lt.-Col. James Levett; temp. employed at War Office since 1916 ; *b.* 27 Dec. 1861 ; *s.* of James Kaye, Barrister of Lincoln's Inn ; *m.* Edith Mary, *o. d.* of late Stephen Harvey-James, Indian Civil Service ; no *c.* *Educ.:* Winchester ; Sandhurst. Entered army, 1882 ; served with the Royal Berkshire Regt. in Egypt and Gibraltar till 1885, including Suakin campaign, 1885 ; joined Indian Army and served with 25th Punjab Infantry, 5th Bengal Cavalry and Central India Horse ; joined the Political Department of the Government of India, 1889 ; Settlement Commissioner in Kashmir, 1895-1904 ; Political Agent, Alwar, 1905 ; Resident at Indore, 1907 ; Resident in Mewar, Rajputana, India, 1911-16. *Recreations:* shooting, motoring, and golf. *Address:* Whitehall Court, S.W. *Club:* East India United Service.
(*Died 17 Nov. 1917.*)

KAYE, Sir Joseph H., 1st Bt., *cr.* 1923 ; *b.* 6 Sep. 1856 ; *s.* of late Henry Kaye of Lindley, Huddersfield ; *m.* 1885, Emily, *d.* of Alfred Crowther, J.P., of Greenroyd, Huddersfield ; one *s.* *Educ.:* locally. Woollen and worsted cloth manufacturer ; Chairman of Kaye & Stewart, Ltd., Huddersfield ; Chairman of Gledhill Bros. & Co., Ltd., Huddersfield ; Director of Lloyd's Bank ; Director of London Midland and Scottish Railway ; Past President of Huddersfield Chamber of Commerce ; Past Chairman, Huddersfield Fine Cloth Manufacturers' Association ; Trustee of the Hudders-

field Royal Infirmary ; J.P. County Borough of Huddersfield, etc. ; President of the Huddersfield Conservative Association ; Member of the Royal Commission in 1916-17 on the Textile Trades after the war ; Prominent Member of Committee of the Huddersfield War Hospital, 1915-19. *Recreations:* foreign travel, formerly mountaineering, etc., golf. *Heir:* *s.* Captain and Flight-Commander Henry Gordon Kaye. *Address:* Norwood, Huddersfield. *T.:* Huddersfield 2099. *Clubs:* Carlton, Junior Carlton, Constitutional. (*Died 24 Dec. 1923.*)

KAY-SHUTTLEWORTH, Edward James, B.A. ; *y. s.* of 1st Baron Shuttleworth; *b.* 16 March 1890 ; *m.* 1914, Sibell, 2nd *d.* of C. R. W. Adeane. *Educ.:* Eton ; Balliol College, Oxford. Bar, Inner Temple, 1913 ; holds temporary commission, 7th Service Batt. Rifle Brigade since 1914 ; served European War, 1915.
(*Died 10 July 1917.*)

KAY-SHUTTLEWORTH, Hon. Lawrence Ughtred ; J.P. (Lancashire) 1912 ; Private Sec. (unpaid) to the Rt. Hon. Walter Runciman, 1913-14 ; Temp. 2nd Lieut. R. Field Artillery ; *b.* 21 Sep. 1887 ; *e. s.* of 1st Baron Shuttleworth ; *m.* 1913, Selina Adine, *d.* of Col. Hon. F. Bridgeman ; one *s.* one *d.* *Educ.:* Eton ; Balliol College, Oxford ; B.A. 2nd Class (History Honour School), 1910. Called to Bar, Inner Temple, 1913 ; contested Altrincham Div. of Cheshire, 1913. *Address:* 7 Queensberry Place, S.W. *T.:* Kensington 5402 ; Gawthorpe Hall, Burnley ; Barbon Manor, Kirkby Lonsdale. *Clubs:* Brooks's, Reform, Cobden, Eighty. (*Died 30 Mar. 1917.*)

KEABLE, Robert, novelist ; *b.* 6 March 1887; *s. of Rev.* Robert Henry Keable and Margaret Clarke Hopkins, late of Pavenham Vicarage, Bedfordshire. *Educ.:* Whitgift Grammar School ; Magdalene College, Cambridge (Open Latimer-Neville History Exhibition and School Scholarships) ; B.A., 1st Class History Tripos, 1908 ; Westcott House Clergy Training School. Ordained, 1911 ; Curate of Bradford Parish Church, Yorks, 1911 - 12 ; The Universities Mission to Central Africa, 1912-14 ; Rector Leribe, Basutoland, 1914-20 ; Chaplain to the S. African Forces on service in France, 1917-18 ; resigned orders, 1920 ; first novel published, 1921 ; Assistant Master, Dulwich College, 1921 ; Dunstable Grammar School, 1922 ; M.A. 1914. *Publications:* Darkness and Light, 1913 ; Songs of the Narrow Way, 1914 ; The Loneliness of Christ, 1914 ; A City of the Dawn, 1915 ; The Adventures of Paul Kangai, 1915 : The Perpetual Passion, 1916 ; The Drift of Pinions, 1917 ; This Same Jesus, 1918 : Standing By, 1919 ; Pilgrim Papers, 1920 ; Simon Called Peter, 1921 ; The Mother of All Living, 1921 ; Peradventure, 1922 ; Recompense, 1924 ; Numerous Treasure, 1925 ; Tahiti : Isle of Dreams, 1925 ; Lighten our Darkness (in U.S.A., Ann Decides), 1927 ; Monty Mad, 1928 ; contributor to various magazines. *Recreations:* travel, swimming, rowing, shooting. *Address:* c/o A. P. Watt & Son, 10 Norfolk Street, Strand, W.C.2.
(*Died Dec. 1927.*)

KEANE, Lt.-Colonel Richard Henry, C.B.E. 1919, O.B.E. 1918 ; *b.* 1881 ; 3rd *s.* of late Sir Richard Francis Keane, 4th Bart., of Cappoquin, Co. Waterford ; *m.* 1906, Alice, *y. d.* of late Sir Lumley Smith, Judge of the City of London Court ; one *s.* two *d.* *Educ.:* Clifton ; Royal Agricultural College, Cirencester. Joined Royal Naval Division, 1915 ; transferred to the Army, 1916 ; commanded 15th Batt. (Transport Workers) South Lancs, 1917-19 (O.B.E., C.B.E.). *Address:* Fortwilliam, Glencairn, Co. Waterford, Ireland. (*Died 22 Nov. 1925.*)

KEARNS, Major Reginald Arthur Ernest Holmes, C.M.G., 1916 ; A.S.C., T.F. Served European War, 1914-16 (despatches, C.M.G.) (*Died 24 Nov. 1918.*)

KEARNS, Col. Thomas Joseph, C.B. 1918; C.M.G. 1917; Serjeant-at-Arms City of London since 1907; and commanding Army Service Corps, 1st London Division Territorial Force; *b.* 6 Jan. 1861; *o. s.* of late Philip Kearns, Belfast; *m.* Haidee Ida, *o. d.* of late Henry Holmes, Toronto; no *c. Educ.*: Dagmar House School, Hatfield, Herts. Served in ranks until commissioned Riding Master Army Service Corps, 1896; retired on appointment as City Marshal, London, 1904; served South African War, 1879; Zulu Campaign (medal with clasp);´Ashantee Expedition, 1895-96 (star, honourably mentioned); South African War, 1899-1902; on staff (despatches twice, Queen's medal with six clasps, King's medal with two clasps); European War, 1914-19 (despatches five times); Diamond Jubilee Medal; Coronation Medals, King Edward VII. and King George V.; 1914-15 star; Officer of the Order of Leopold II., Belgium. *Address:* Mansion House, E.C. *Club:* Royal Automobile. (*Died 30 June 1920.*)

KEARTON, Richard, F.Z.S., field naturalist, author and lecturer; *b.* Thwaite in Swaledale, Yorks, 2 Jan. 1862; 2nd *s.* of late John Kearton, yeoman farmer, and Mary, *e. d.* of Richard Hunter of Winton, Westmorland; *m.* Ellen Rose Cowdrey, 1889; three *s.* two *d. Educ.*: Muker National School. Farmer in Swaledale, Yorks, until 1882; sub-manager of Publicity Department, Cassell & Co., publishers; retired, 1898. *Publications:* Birds Nests, Eggs and Egg Collecting; British Birds' Nests: How, Where, and When to Find and Identify Them, illustrated entirely by photos taken direct from Nature; With Nature and a Camera, being the Adventures and Observations of a Field Naturalist and an Animal Photographer; Wild Life at Home: How to Study and Photograph It; Our Rarer British Breeding Birds; Our Bird Friends; Strange Adventures in Dickybird Land (a Book of Natural History Fiction for Children); A Photographically Illustrated Edition of White's Selborne, 1902; Wild Nature's Ways; The Adventures of Cock Robin and his Mate; Pictures from Nature; Nature's Carol Singers; The Fairyland of Living Things; Kearton's Nature Pictures; The Adventures of Jack Rabbit; Baby Birds at Home; Wonders of Wild Nature; At Home with Wild Nature; Wild Bird Adventures; The Pocket Book of Birds (with Howard Bentham); A Naturalist's Pilgrimage; contributor to various papers and magazines. *Address:* Ashdene, Caterham Valley, Surrey. (*Died 8 Feb. 1928.*)

KEARY, Charles F., novelist and writer on history and philosophy. *Educ.*: Marlborough; Trin. Coll., Camb. *Publications:* A Wanderer, 1888; A Mariage de Convenance, 1889; The Two Lancrofts, 1893; Herbert Vanlennert, 1895; The Journalist, 1898; Twixt Dog and Wolf, 1901; High Policy, 1902; Bloomsbury, 1905; The Mount, 1909; The Brothers: a masque (verse), 1902; Rigel: a mystery (verse), 1904; Religious Hours (verse), 1916; The Dawn of History (ed.), 1879; Outlines of Primitive Belief, 1882; The Mythology of the Eddas, 1882; The Vikings in Western Christendom, 1890; Norway and the Norwegians, 1892; The Pursuit of Reason, 1911; and other writings on antiquarian subjects; formerly on the staff of the British Museum; has contributed to the Edinburgh, Nineteenth Century, Fortnightly, and other reviews and magazines. *Club:* Savile.
(*Died 25 Oct. 1917.*)

KEATING, Most Rev. Frederick William, D.D.; R.C. Archbishop of Liverpool since 1921; *b.* Birmingham, 1859. *Educ.*: St. Chad's Grammar School, Birmingham; Sedgley Park; Benedictine Coll., Douai; Olton Seminary. Ordained, 1882; Administrator of St. Chad's Cathedral, Birmingham, 1898-1908; Bishop of Northampton, 1907-

1921. *Address:* Archbishop's House, Belvidere Road, Liverpool. *T.:* Royal 465.
(*Died 7 Feb. 1928.*)

KEATINGE, Henry Pottinger, C.M.G. 1913; M.B., F.R.C.S.; Corresponding Member Royal Zoological Society; Hon. Fellow Royal Academy of Medicine in Ireland; Member of the Egyptian Institute; *b.* 31 July 1860; *s.* of Gen. R. H. Keatinge, V.C., C.S.I. *Educ.*: Uppingham; Guy's Hospital; Durham University College of Medicine. Served with Egyptian Army, 1884-90; Nile and frontier campaigns during that period (medal, three clasps; bronze star and 4th class Osmanieh); appointed to the Cairo School of Medicine, 1890; later as Director of it and of the Kasr el Ainy Hospital (2nd class Medjidieh) (despatches, Egypt, 1915); retired from Egyptian Government Service, 1919 (2nd class Order of the Nile). *Address:* 21 Regent Road, Jersey. *Clubs:* Garrick, Fly-fishers'. (*Died 21 June 1923.*)

KEBTY-FLETCHER, J.; *b.* Liverpool, 1868. *Educ.*: Liverpool College; abroad. Linguist; past President of the Liverpool Produce Exchange; contested Rossendale Division, 1906 and 1910; M.P. (C.) Altrincham Division, Cheshire, 1911-13. *Address:* Hooton, Cheshire. (*Died 12 July 1918.*)

KEELING, Rev. William Hulton, M.A. Oxon.; LL.D. Leeds; Head Master of Bradford Grammar School since 1871; *b.* Blackley Rectory, Manchester, 1840; *e. s.* of Rev. William Robert Keeling; *m.* 1870, Henrietta Frances (*d.* 1905), *d.* of Rev. Sydney Gedge; five *s.* four *d. Educ.*: Manchester Grammar School; Wadham College, Oxford. 1st cl. Classical Mods. 1859; 2nd cl. Lit. Hum., 1862; VIth Form Master Bromsgrove School, 1863-65; VIth Form Master Rossall School, 1865-67; Head Master Northampton Grammar School, 1867-71; Member of the Committee of the Head Masters' Conference, 1894-97 and 1899-1902. *Address:* Bradford Grammar School (*Died 30 Mar. 1916.*)

KEEN, Austin, Hon. M.A. (Cantab.), F.C.S.; Education Secretary to the Cambridgeshire County Council since 1894; Permanent Member of Executive (ex-Hon. Secretary and ex-Chairman) of the Association of Directors and Secretaries of Education in Counties and County Boroughs; Member of the Education Committee of the County Councils Association; Member of the Court of Governors and of the Council of the University College of Wales, Aberystwyth; Co-opted Member of Cambridge University Board of Agricultural Studies; Member of the Joint Scholarships Board; Chairman of the East Anglian Musical Competition; Commissioner for National Savings in Cambridgeshire; Member of the Horticultural Advisory Committee of the Board of Agriculture, etc.; Hon. Local Secy. for Cambridgeshire for the Royal Automobile Club. *Educ.*: University College of Wales, Aberystwyth. Science Master at Ardwyn School, 1881-82; Organising Secretary of the Huddersfield Technical School, 1882-94. *Publications:* Ten Years' Work in Cambridgeshire under the Technical Instruction Act; various papers on education administration and the training of teachers; The Catalogue of the Cambridgeshire County Library. *Recreations:* fruit-growing, shooting, croquet. *Address:* Cefn Llys, Cambridge. *T.A.:* Keen, Cefnllys, Cambridge. *T.:* 176. *M.:* CB 1728. *Clubs:* Royal Automobile; Cambridge Union Society. (*Died 20 Jan. 1922.*)

KEENE, Col. Alfred, D.S.O. 1887; *b.* 17 April 1855; *s.* of late H. G. Keene, C.I.E.; *m.* 1894, Janet Frances, widow of Colonel Ayrton Pullan. Entered army, 1874; Col. 1904; retired 1905; served Afghan War, 1878-80 (despatches, medal); Burmah, 1885-86 (despatches, D.S.O., medal with clasp). *Address:* Down Close, The Ridgeway, Guildford. (*Died 21 April 1918.*)

WHO WAS WHO, 1916-1928

KEENE, Charles James, C.I.E., V.D.; Public Works, India (Railways), retired 1905; Secretary, Madras and Southern Mahratta Railway, and Major Railway Rifles, retired 1912; b. 25 May 1850; m. 1881, Mary Victoria Josephine, y. d. of late Wellington Shegog of Dublin; four s. one d. Address: Ealing.
(Died 9 April 1917.)

KEENE, Most Rev. James Bennett, Bishop of Meath (Church of Ireland) since 1897; b. Dublin, 25 Oct. 1849; y. s. of Arthur Bennett Keene, M.A.; m. 1913, Henrietta Sophia, o. surv. d. of Rev. W. Streatfeild. Educ.: Rathmines School, and Trinity College, Dublin. First Honourman and Prizeman in Classics, 1867; first of the First Honourmen in Science, 1867, 1868, 1869; first Primate's Hebrew Prizeman, 1867, 1868, 1869; Mathematical Scholar and Lloyd Exhibitioner, 1870; Senior Moderator and Gold Medallist in Mathematics, Logic, and Ethics, 1871; Wall Biblical Scholar in Hebrew, Syriac, and Chaldee, 1872; M'Cullagh Prize and Bishop Law's Mathematical Premium, 1872; Elrington Theological Prize, 1874; Extra Prize at Theological Exhibition and Divinity Testimonium (First Class), 1875; Rector of Navan, 1879; Prebendary of Tipper and Canon of St. Patrick's; Examining Chaplain to the Bishop of Meath, 1885; Headmaster of Navan College; Diocesan Nominator and Secretary of Board of Education; Member of Senate. T.C.D. Address: Bishopscourt, Ardbraccan, Navan; 26 Clyde Road, Dublin. Clubs: New Oxford and Cambridge; University, Dublin.
(Died 5 Aug. 1919.)

KEENE, William, C.B.E. 1918; M.V.O. 1909; b. Ewe Cote, Whitby, Yorks, 13 May 1851; 2nd s. of late Rev. William Keene and Mary Loy, d. of George Merryweather; m. 1885, Louisa Catharine, d. of late Rev. Frederick Pitman of Iddesleigh, Devon, and Mrs. H. M. Northcote. Educ.: Shrewsbury; Uppingham. Passed an examination, 1887; Consul at Madeira, 1888; Consul for Island of Madeira and its Dependencies, to reside at Funchal, 1894; Consul for Departments of the Nord (with exception of the town of Dunkirk), Pas de Calais, and Somme. to reside at Calais, 1894; Consul for Piedmont, and for the Provinces of Porto Maurizio, Genoa, Massa, Piacenza, Parma and Reggio to reside at Genoa, 1897; Consul General with the same district, 1900; Member of the British Commission for the Milan Exhibition, 1906; Member of the Superior Jury at Turin International Exhibition, 1911, and at the Genoa International Exhibition, 1914; retired on a pension, 2 Jan. 1918; received the Coronation medal, 1911. Recreations: all sports. Address: Villa Erin, San Remo, Italy. T.: 224. Clubs: St. James's, Constitutional, New Oxford and Cambridge.(Died 1 April 1920.)

KEETON, Haydn; Mus.D., Oxon; Organist and Master of the Choristers, Peterborough Cathedral, since 1870; b. Mosborough, Derbyshire, 26 Oct. 1847; s. of Edwin and Ruth Keeton; m. 1st, 1872, Eliza, 2nd d. of Thomas Southam, Surgeon, Peterborough; one s. one d.; 2nd, 1908, Anne, e. d. of Thomas Southam. Educ.: St. George's Chapel, Windsor. Chorister boy at St. George's Chapel, Windsor, 1858; articled pupil to Sir G. Elvey, Organist of St. George's Chapel, 1862-68; Organist of Datchet Church about 1865; Assistant Music Master at Eton College, 1868; Mus.B. (Oxon), 1869; Mus.D., 1877; Organist of Aldin House, Slough, the Rev. J. Hawtrey's Preparatory School, 1869; conducted the Peterborough Orchestral Society for 25 years, and the Peterborough Choral Union for about 20 years; Examiner for Oxford University, 1895, and for Durham University, 1899, 1900, 1916; Examiner for the Royal College of Organists. Publications: chants, services, anthems, organ voluntaries, part-songs, and madrigal. Recreation: bridge. Address: Thorpe Road, Peterborough. T.A.: Peterborough.
(Died 27 May 1921.)

KEILY, Right Rev. John, D.D.; R.C. Bishop of Plymouth since 1911; b. 23 June 1854; s. of Bartholomew and Margaret Keily, Limerick. Educ.: Plymouth; Roulers; Bruges. Ordained, 1877; after various appointments, including the Cathedral, Rector of Holy Cross, Plymouth, for 25 years, Diocesan Inspector, and Member of Central Education Council, etc., Canon of the Diocese; Bishop Assistant at the Pontifical Throne, etc., 1927. Address: Bishop's House, Cecil Street, Plymouth. T.: 1479 Plymouth.(Died 23 Sept. 1928.)

KEITH, Col. James, D.S.O., 1891; Late R.A.; b. 5 Nov. 1842; s. of William Keith, M.D. Entered army, 1861; Captain, 1875; Major, 1881; Lieut.-Col. 1890; Colonel, 1894; served Afghanistan, 1878-79 (medal); Sikkim, 1878 (despatches, medal with clasp); Hazara, 1891 (despatches, D.S.O.); Izazai, 1892. Address: Queen Anne's Mansions, S.W.(Died 5 Feb. 1919.)

KEITH, Skene; b. Edinburgh, 1858; s. of Thomas Keith. Educ.: Edinburgh University and in New York. Was a special Assistant Surgeon in the Edinburgh Royal Infirmary until removed to London, 1888; Consulting Surgeon to the Hounslow Hospital. Publications: Text-Book of Abdominal Surgery; Gynæcological Operations; Cancer, the Relief of Pain and Possible Cure. Recreation: gardening. Address: 7 Manchester Square, W. (Died 19 Aug. 1919.)

KEKEWICH, Sir George William, K.C.B., cr. 1895; D.C.L.; M.P. (L.) Exeter, 1906-10; b. 1 Apr. 1841; 4th s. of late Samuel Trehawke Kekewich, M.P. S. Devon, and Louisa, d. of Lewis William Buck, M.P. N. Devon; married. Educ.: Eton; Balliol Coll. Oxford. 1st class Classics Moderations; 2nd class Classics Final Schools, Oxford; Examiner in Education Department, 1867; Senior Examiner, 1871; Secretary Education Department, 1890-1900; Secretary also of Science and Art Department, 1899-1900; Secretary of Board of Education, 1900-1903; Hon. D.C.L., Durham. 1897; J.P. Middlesex. Recreations: salmon-fishing, gardening. Address: 6 Sackville Gardens, Hove. Clubs: Reform, National Liberal; Union, Brighton. (Died 5 July 1921.)

KELK, Sir John William, 2nd Bt.; cr. 1874; J.P.; b. 13 Jan. 1851; S. father 1886. Educ.: Jesus Coll. Camb. Sheriff Co. Wilts, 1892; late Major Wilts Yeomanry Cavalry. Heir: none. Address: 40 Grosvenor Square, W.1. T.: Mayfair 3349. Club: Junior Carlton.
(Died 23 Mar. 1923.)

KELLAS, A. M., B.Sc.; Ph.D.; Lecturer on chemistry, Middlesex Hospital Medical School. Educ.: Aberdeen Grammar School; University and Heriot-Watt College, Edinburgh; University College, London; Heidelberg University. Recreations: mountaineering and travel; interested in geographical exploration. Address: 4 St. Mark's Crescent, Regent's Park, N.W. Club: Alpine. (Died 5 June 1921.)

KELLEHER, Stephen B.; Fellow of Trinity College, Dublin, since 1904; Erasmus Smith's Professor of Mathematics in the University of Dublin; b. Cork, June 1875; s. of late William Kelleher, Cork; m. 1910, Isabel Marion Johnston, Londonderry; two d. Educ.: Christian Brothers' Schools, Cork. Entered Royal University of Ireland, 1892; M.A. 1896; studied at Queen's College, Cork, 1892-96; entered Trinity College, Dublin, 1898; B.A. 1902. Address: 46 Leeson Park, and 24 Trinity College, Dublin. Club: University, Dublin.
(Died 18 Aug. 1917.)

KELLETT, Sir Henry de Castres, 3rd Baronet (U.K. of Lota, cr. 1801); S. 2nd Bart. 1886 (by special remainder) but did not assume the title until Feb. 1906; b. 15 Sep. 1851; e. s. of late Henry de C. Kellett, who was 3rd s. of

Henry de C. Kellett, 3rd *s.* of Richard Kellett, father of the 1st Baronet; *m.* 1880, Joan R. M., 2nd *d.* of William Harrison of Richmond, Victoria; three *s.* four *d.* Member of Kew Borough Council, Victoria, Metropolitan Fire Brigades Board, Victoria, and Tramways Trust, Victoria. *Heir: s.* Henry de C. Kellett [*b.* 2 Oct. 1882; *m.* 1905, Rubie Septima, 7th *d.* of Easton Johnston]. *Address:* High Street, Kew, Victoria, Australia. (*Died 20 June 1924.*)

KELLEY, Major Sir Frederic Arthur, Kt., *cr.* 1923; O.B.E. 1919; M.P. (U.) Rotherham, Dec. 1918-23; *b.* 6 May 1863; *m.* 1888, *d.* of Charles Henry Pickles. *Educ.:* Tettenhall College, Wolverhampton; Giggleswick Grammar School. A National Service representative in South Yorkshire; for several years a member of the Sheffield City Council; contested Hallamshire and Spen Valley; J.P. West Riding Yorks, Sheffield, Harrogate. *Address:* Grey Cauds, Harrogate.

(*Died 29 May 1926.*)

KELLEY, Howard G.; President of the Grand Trunk Railway Company of Canada and the Grand Trunk Pacific Railway Co. 1917-22; *b.* Philadelphia, Pa., 12 Jan. 1858; *s.* of Edwin A. Kelley and Mary B. Peterson; *m.* 1899, Cora J. Lingo, Denison, Texas; *Educ.:* Polytech. College, Pa. Entered Railway Service, 1881; Superintendent, Montana, 1884-87; Resident Engineer and Superintendent, bridges and buildings, St. Louis S.W. Railway System, 1887-90; Chief Engineer, 1890-98; Minneapolis and St. Louis Railway, 1898; Iowa Central Railway, 1900; Consulting Engineer St. Louis S.W. Railway, 1898-99; President American Railway Engineering and Maintenance of Way Association, 1905-6; Chief Engineer Grand Trunk Railway System, 1907. *Address:* 731 Sherbrooke St., W., Montreal. *Club:* Engineers', Montreal. (*Died 15 May 1928.*)

KELLOCK, Thomas Herbert, M.A., M.D., M.Ch. (Camb.), F.R.C.S. (Eng.), L.R.C.P. (Lond.); Surgeon to and Lecturer on Surgery, Middlesex Hospital; Consulting Surgeon, Hospital for Sick Children, Great Ormond Street; Consulting Surgeon to the Yarrow Home, Broadstairs; and the Lord Mayor Treloar's Cripple's Hospital and College, Alton; Captain R.A.M.C. (T.); Examiner in Surgery, University of Cambridge; *b.* Totnes, Devon, 1863; *s.* of T. C. Kellock, Solicitor; *m.* 1915, Margaret, *y. d.* of Alexander Brooke; one *s. Educ.:* Totnes Grammar School; Emmanuel College, Cambridge (Exhibitioner); St. Thomas's Hosp. Medical School. Honours in Mathematical Tripos, 1883; Cheselden Medallist, 1891. Medical Superintendent (3 years) at the Hospital for Sick Children, Great Ormond Street; Surgical Registrar and Tutor in Surgery, Middlesex Hospital. *Publications:* A Surgical Report of the Middlesex Hospital, 1897; also various contributions to Medical Journals and Transactions of Medical Societies. *Address:* 2 Upper Wimpole Street, Cavendish Square, W.1. *T.:* Langham 1465. *Club:* New University. (*Died 19 Dec. 1922.*)

KELLY, Right Rev. Denis, R.C. Bishop of Ross since 1897; *b.* Kilnaneave, Nenagh, Co. Tipperary, 29 Feb. 1852; *e. s.* of William Kelly and Bridget, *d.* of late James Butler. *Educ.:* The College, Ennis; Collège des Irlandais, Paris. 1st prizeman in Classics, Mathematics, Mental Philosophy, Theology, Scripture and Canon Law; Doctor in Divinity. Received priest's orders, 17 March 1877; appointed curate of Roscrea; after four months appointed professor, later on Vice-President, and finally President, of the Ennis College; Member of the Agricultural Board for Ireland 1900-21; Royal Commissioner on Poor Laws and the Relief of Distress, 1906-9; Member of

Cabinet Committee on Irish Finance, 1911; of National Education Committee of Inquiry (Ireland), 1913, etc. *Publications:* Letters and pamphlets, mostly on educational topics. *Address:* Bishop's House, Skibbereen, Co. Cork.

(*Died 18 April 1924.*)

KELLY, Frederick Septimus, *b.* Sydney, N.S.W., 29 May 1881; *s.* of late T. H. Kelly. *Educ.:* Eton; Balliol College, Oxford (Nettleship musical scholar; B.A. 1903; M.A. 1912). Stroked Eton eight, 1899; rowed in Oxford eight, 1903; competed at Henley Regatta, 1902-6, winning, among other races, the Diamond Sculls in 1902, 1903, 1905; won Wingfield Sculls, 1903, and rowed in winning Leander eight at the Olympic Sports of 1908; studied music, 1903-8, at Dr. Hoch's Konservatorium, Frankfort o/M, under Professors Knorr (composition), and Engesser (pianoforte), and had some further lessons in composition from Mr. D. F. Tovey; made formal début as pianist and composer in Sydney, 1911, and in following spring, 1912, gave a series of concerts in London; Sub-Lieutenant in the Royal Naval Division, 1914; sailed for the Mediterranean with the Hood Battalion, 1915; landed on Gallipoli Peninsula in April; wounded, June; returned to active service, July; Lieutenant, June 1915. *Publication:* article on sculling in The Complete Oarsman. *Musical Publications:* ops. 1-7, consisting mostly of songs, and works for the pianoforte. *Recreations:* rowing, the usual games, motoring, travel. *Address:* Bisham Grange, Marlow. *T.:* Marlow 38. *Club:* Union. (*Died 13 Nov. 1916.*)

KELLY, Capt. Hubert Dunsterville Harvey-, D.S.O. 1915; late Squadron Comdr. R.F.C.; late Royal Irish Regt.; *b.* 9 Feb. 1891. Entered Army, 1910; Captain, 1915; served European War, 1914-18 (despatches, D.S.O.).

KELLY, Col. James Graves, C.B. 1895; late A.D.C. to Queen; Unem. Super. List; late Col. on Staff, Sialkot; *b.* 28 Nov. 1848; *m.* 1st, 1873, Lavinia (*d.* 1900), *d.* of late R. MacMullen; four *d.*; 2nd, 1901, Eleanor, *d.* of late P. Riley. Entered army, 1863; Col. 1895; served Hazara Expedition, 1891 (medal with clasp); Miranzai Expedition, 1891 (clasp); Chitral, 1895; Relief of Chitral; Commanded the Force from Gilgit (thanks of Govt. of India, despatches, C.B., brevet of Col., A.D.C. to Queen, medal with clasp). *Club:* United Service.

(*Died 20 June 1923.*)

KELLY, John, I.S.O.; late Secretary and Assistant Registrar-General, Ireland, retired. *Address:* 2 Royal Terrace, West Kingstown.

KELLY, Sir Malachy, Kt., *cr.* 1912; Chief Crown Solicitor for Ireland, since 1905; *s.* of late Ignatius Kelly, Crown Solicitor, Co. Mayo, and Mary, *d.* of late Peter Thoby; *b.* 25 May 1850; *m.* 1894, Annie, *d.* of Rt. Hon. Sir Patrick Coll, K.C.B. (*d.* 1899); one *s.* two *d. Educ.:* privately. Admitted a Solicitor, 1871; Sessional Crown Solicitor, Co. Mayo, 1881-85; Crown Solicitor, 1885-1905. *Address:* Thorndale, Temple Road, Milltown, Co. Dublin; Maryland, Castlebar. *Club:* Stephen's Gn., Dublin. (*Died 25 Mar. 1916.*)

KELLY, Mark Jamestown, Consul-General of Honduras in London; resigned Consulate-General of Salvador, 1911, after fifteen years' service; F.R.G.S.; F.S.A.; Chevalier Order of the Legion of Honour; Officer of Public Instruction of France; *b.* 1848. As Financial Agent of Salvador in Europe carried out the financial arrangements which discharged the foreign debt of that Republic, and enabled the building of a railway system there, and negotiated a new loan for the country in London, 1908; appointed by Salvador Government to attend the International American Conference at Buenos Ayres as Delegate of the Republic, 1910, Chairman of the Salvador Railway Company of London; President of the Salvador Chamber of Commerce in London; identified with railway construction, formerly, in Ecuador. *Recreations:* collecting old china and travelling. *Address:* Beech House, Redhill, Surrey. *T.:* Redhill 402. *Club:* City Carlton.

(*Died 13 Dec. 1916.*)

KELLY, Surgeon Peter Burrowes, R.N., D.S.O. 1915; Lieut.-Surg. R.N. College, Osborne, I.W.; *b.* 23 Sep. 1888; *s.* of Gilbert Graves Kelly; *m.*; one *d. Educ.:* Dublin; London. Served Dardanelles, 1914-15 (wounded, despatches, D.S.O.), at landing of Expeditionary Force. *Recreations:* rugby, football, cricket, shooting. *Address:* The Abbey, Athy, Co. Kildare. (*Died 6 April 1920.*)

KELLY, Rev. Thomas, Pastor St. F. de Sales' Church, Smith's Falls, since 1898; *b.* Waterford. *Educ.:* Catholic University High School, Waterford; St. Vincent's College, Castleknock; St. John's College, Waterford. Ordained, 1877; went to Canada as Private Secretary to late Archbishop Cleary, 1881; Rector, Cathedral St. Mary Immaculate, Kingston. *Address:* Smith's Falls, Ontario.

(*Died 4 June 1926.*)

KELLY, Right Rev. William Bernard, First Bishop of Geraldton since 1898; *b.* 1855. *Address:* Bishop's House, Geraldton, Western Australia. (*Died 26 Dec. 1921.*)

KELTIE, Sir John Scott, Kt. *cr.* 1918; F.R.G.S., F.S.S., F.S.A. (Scot.), LL.D. St. Andrews; Commander of the Swedish Order of North Star, 1898, of the Norwegian Order of St. Olaf, 1907; Finnish Order of the White Rose, 1921; Hon. Member Geographical Societies of Edinburgh, Paris, Berlin, Petrograd, Rome, Brussels, Amsterdam, Geneva, Marseilles, Lisbon, Philadelphia, etc.; *b.* Dundee, 29 March 1840; *m.* 1865, Margaret Scott (*d.* 1922); one *d. Educ.:* Perth; Univ. of St. Andrews and Edinburgh. Editorial staff of W. and R. Chambers, 1861; of Macmillan and Co. 1871-84; for several years sub-editor of *Nature;* inspector of geographical education, R.G.S., 1884; Librarian R.G.S., 1885-92; Secy. Royal Geographical Society, 1892-1915; Joint Editor of Geographical Journal, 1915-17; retired, 1917; President Geographical Section, British Association, 1897; awarded Cullum Gold Medal (American Geographical Society), Gold Medals of Paris and Royal Scottish Geographical Societies, 1915, and Victoria Medal R.G.S. 1917. *Publications:* History of Scottish Highlands and Clans, 1874; Report on Geographical Education, 1886; Applied Geography, new ed. 1908; The Partition of Africa, 1894; The History of Geography (with O. J. R. Howarth), 1914; editor of Statesman's Year Book since 1880; editor of The Story of Exploration; has written largely on geographical and scientific subjects to the leading daily, weekly, and monthly periodicals. *Recreation:* golf. *Address:* 88 Brondesbury Road, N.W.6. *T.:* Willesden 1040. *Club:* Royal Societies.

(*Died 12 Jan. 1927.*)

KEMBALL, Col. Arnold Henry Grant, C.B. 1912; Lieut.-Col. 54th Canadian Infantry Batt. since 1915; Fruit-rancher; *b.* 4 Jan. 1861; *s.* of late Major-Gen. John Shaw Kemball; *m.* 1895, Alvilda Sundt; two *d. Educ.:* Wellington College. Entered army, 1880; Captain I.S.C. 1891; Major, Indian army, 1897; Lt.-Col. 1905; Col. 1907; D.A.A.G. Malakand Field Force, 1897; D.A.G.M.G. Tirah Force, 1897-98; served Hazara expedition, 1898 (medal with clasp); Hazara, 1891; Isazai, 1892; N.W. Frontier, 1897-98 (despatches, medal with clasp); Tirah, 1897-98 (despatches, clasp, brevet-major). *Address:* Kaslo, British Columbia. (*Died 1 Mar. 1917.*)

KEMNAL, Sir James, Kt., *cr.* 1920; F.R.S.E.; Managing Director of Babcock & Wilcox, Ltd., London and Renfrew, Scotland;

Chairman of Worthington, Simpson, Ltd., London and Newark; Vice-President of Sociedad Espanola de Construcciones, Babcock & Wilcox, Bilbao; Director of French Babcock & Wilcox Co., Paris; Director of Power Securities Corporation, London; President of the British and Latin-America Chamber of Commerce; *b.* London, 1864; *m.* 1905, Linda Larita, *d.* of Clement De Leuze, Nyallo, Victoria, formerly of Nice; one *s.* Member Institution Mechanical Engineers, Member Institution Naval Architects, Electrical Engineers, and other learned Societies; Liveryman, Shipwrights Co. *Recreations:* yachting, fishing. *Address:* Kemnal Manor, Chislehurst. *T.A.:* Manor, Chislehurst. *T.:* Sidcup 248. *Clubs:* St. Stephen's, City Carlton, Conservative; Glasgow. (*Died 8 Feb. 1927.*)

KEMP, Stephen, F.R.A.M., Member of the Philharmonic Society; Professor of Pianoforte at the Royal Academy of Music, Royal College of Music, and Guildhall School of Music; *b.* Gt. Yarmouth, 8 Nov. 1849; *s.* of Robert and Jane Kemp; *m.* 1st, 1880, Clara Beasley (*dec.*); three *s.* three *d.;* 2nd, 1906, Gertrude Thorne. *Educ.:* Gt. Yarmouth Grammar School; Royal Academy of Music (Free Scholarship); toured through England and Wales as Solo Pianist with Lazarus' Anemoic Union, 1871; in Norway with Svendsen the flautist, 1878; began giving Annual Chamber Concerts at Prince's Hall, Piccadilly, 1885; Editor of Modern Music. *Address:* 80 Oxford Gardens, Notting Hill, W. (*Died 30 Oct. 1918.*)

KEMP, Admiral Thomas Webster, C.B. 1917; C.M.G. 1918; C.I.E. 1905. Entered Navy, 1880; Lieutenant, 1890; Commander, 1900; Senior Naval Officer, Persian Gulf, 1905; Rear-Admiral retired, 1917; Vice-Admiral retired, 1922; Admiral retired, 1926; served China, 1900. *Club:* United Service.

(*Died 13 Jan. 1928.*)

KEMPE, Sir Alfred Bray, Kt., *cr.* 1912; D.C.L. (Hon. Durham), F.R.S.; Chancellor, Diocese of London, since 1912; also Chancellor of the Dioceses of Southwell, St. Albans, Peterborough, Chichester, and Chelmsford; Bencher of Inner Temple, 1909; *b.* Kensington, 6 July 1849; 3rd *s.* of late Rev. John Edward Kempe, Rector of St. James's, Piccadilly; *m.* 1st, Mary (*d.* 1893), 2nd *d.* of late Sir W. Bowman, Bt.; 2nd, 1897, Ida, *d.* of His Honour Judge Meadows White, Q.C.; two *s.* one *d. Educ.:* St. Paul's School; Trin. Coll. Camb. (M.A.); 22nd Wrangler. Barr. Inner Temple and Western Circuit, 1873; Treas. and Vice-Pres. of the Roy. Soc. 1899-1919; Secretary Royal Commission on Ecclesiastical Courts, 1881-83; Chancellor of the Diocese of Newcastle, and Official to the Archdeacons of Essex, Southwark, and Kingston to 1912. *Publications:* How to Draw a Straight Line, 1877; A Memoir on the Theory of Mathematical Form (Philosophical Transactions), 1886. *Recreations:* mathematics, music. *Address:* 2 Paper Buildings, Temple, E.C.4; *T.:* Central 179; 22 Pembridge Square, W. *T.:* Park 1566. *Club:* Athenæum.

(*Died 21 April 1922.*)

KEMPE, Rev. Edward Wood, M.A.; Hon. Priest to the King, 1901; Vicar of Jesus Church, Forty Hill, Enfield, since 1874; *b.* Hadley, Middlesex, 9 July 1844; *s.* of late Rev. Prebendary Kempe, Rector of St. James's, Piccadilly; *m.* Margaret Millar (*d.* 1909), *d.* of W. H. Challis, of Enfield, 1878; two *s.* three *d. Educ.:* St. Paul's School, Trinity Coll. Camb. Junior Optime, 1867. Curate of St. Andrew's, Enfield, 1868-74; Priest in Ordinary to Queen Victoria, 1878-1901. Member of Edmonton Board of Guardians, 1882-1905; Member of Enfield Education Committee, 1908-7; Member of London Diocesan Conference since 1899. *Publication:* Enfield and its Environs, 1896.

Recreations : music and drawing.   *Address :* Forty Hill Vicarage, Enfield.(*Died 12 May 1918.*)

KEMPE, Sir John Arrow, K.C.B., *cr.* 1909; C.B. 1900 ; B.A. ; *b.* 5 Jan. 1846 ; *s.* of late Rev. J. E. Kempe, Rector of St. James's, Piccadilly ; *m.* 1872, Mary Jane (*d.* 1926), *d.* of Rev. J. Edwards, Vicar of Barrow-on-Trent; three *s.* three *d. Educ. :* St. Paul's School ; Trinity College, Cambridge. Silver Medal ; winning trial eight for University boat, 1866. Clerkship in Treasury, 1867 ; Assistant Private Secretary to Mr. Disraeli, 1868 ; Private Secretary to Chancellor of Exchequer (Sir S. Northcote), 1874-80 ; to Sir R. Lingen, 1880-81 ; to Lord Frederick Cavendish, 1881 ; member of Commission on Agricultural and Dairy Schools, 1887-88 ; Principal Clerk in Treasury 1888-94 ; Deputy Chairman Board of Customs, 1894-1904 ; Assistant Comptroller and Auditor, 1904 ; Comptroller and Auditor-General, 1904-11 ; member of Royal Commission on Electrical Communication with Lighthouses and Light Vessels, 1892-97 ; Chairman of Local Taxation Committee, 1911-1914 ; Member of Royal Commission on the Civil Service, 1915. *Address:* Coram Court, Lyme Regis. *T. :* Lyme Regis 12.(*Died 4 April 1928.*)

KEMPSTER, Col. Francis Jas., D.S.O. 1887 ; late A.A.G. Madras ; *b.* 12 Mar. 1855. Entered army, 1876 ; Col. 1896 ; served Afghan War, 1880 (medal); Bechuanaland, 1884-85 ; Soudan Frontier Field Force, 1887 (despatches, D.S.O., 3rd class Medjidie, medal, Khedive's star); Suakim, 1888 (despatches, clasp); Soudan Frontier, 1889 (despatches, brevet of Lieut.-Col., clasp); Ashanti, 1896 (despatches, A.D.C. to Queen, star); N.W. Frontier, 1897 (despatches, medal with two clasps); retired, 1902.

(*Died 29 Dec. 1925.*)

KENDAL, William Hunter (Mr. Grimston), actor and manager; *b.* London, 16 Dec. 1843 ; *m.* Madge Robertson, 7 Aug. 1869 *Educ. :* private school ; tutor. Commenced his career on the stage in London at the Soho Theatre (now called the Royalty), 1861, Glasgow in 1862, where he remained till 1866, supporting such stars as Mr. and Mrs. Charles Kean, Helen Faucit, G. O. Brooks, etc. ; made his second appearance in London at the Haymarket Theatre, 31 Oct. 1866, in A Dangerous Friend ; with Mr. and Mrs. Charles Matthews ; remained there five or six years, playing such parts as Charles Surface, Captain Absolute, Romeo, Orlando, Pygmalion, etc. ; thence to Court Theatre for couple of seasons ; from there to Old Prince of Wales Theatre for Diplomacy, Lond. Assur. and Peril ; back to Court Theatre for a season ; then became Lessee and Manager, in partnership with John Hare, of St. James's Theatre from 1879-88 ; producing there The Queen's Shilling, The Squire, Impulse, The Ironmaster, A Scrap of Paper, Lady of Lyons, As You Like It, William and Susan, Ladies' Battle, etc. ; toured with Mrs. Kendal in the United States of America and Canada from 1889-95 with phenomenal success. *Recreations:* fishing, shooting, riding, motoring, collecting pictures. *Address:* 12 Portland Place, W. ; The Lodge, Filey, Yorkshire. *M. :* LD 3670, LD 7858. *Clubs:* Junior Carlton, Garrick, Beefsteak, Royal Automobile.

(*Died 6 Nov. 1917.*)

KENDALL, H. Bickerstaffe; editor of The Holborn Review, 1902-16 ; *b.* Wakefield, 1844 ; *s.* of Rev. Charles Kendall, President of Conference, 1881. *Educ. :* Durham University. Connexional Editor, 1892-1901 ; President of Conference, 1901. *Publications:* Handbook of Primitive Methodist Church Principles and Polity ; Christ's Kingdom and Church in the Nineteenth Century ; The Origin and History of the Primitive Methodist Church ; section Primitive Methodism in A New History of Methodism, 1909. *Address :* 29 Castlemain

20

Road, Stourfield Park, Bournemouth.

(*Died 10 Mar. 1919.*)

KENEALY, Noel Byron; editor of periodicals dealing with Automobilism ; 5th *s.* of late E. V. Kenealy, LL.D., Q.C.; *m.* 1905, Isabel, *e. d.* of late Col. St. Leger Shervinton. commdg. Malagasy army. Founded the Hertfordshire Automobile Club and the British Motor Boat Club ; Adviser on art matters ; has had an Art education at Slade, Herkomer, and Paris Schools ; and has exhibited at Royal Academy. *Recreations :* motoring, golf. *Club:* Royal Automobile.   (*Died 18 Dec. 1918.*)

KENNAN, George, Litt.D. ; Writer and Lecturer ; *b.* Norwalk, Ohio, U.S.A., 16 Feb. 1845 ; *s.* of John Kennan and Mary Ann Morse ; *m.* 1879, Emeline, *d.* of J. R. Weld. *Educ. :* in common and high schools of Norwalk and Columbus, Ohio. Telegraph Operator, Norwalk, Ohio, 1857 ; Assistant Manager W.U. Telegraph Office, Cincinnati, O., 1863-64 ; went to N.E. Siberia as explorer and telegraphic engineer, 1865 ; Superintendent of Construction, Middle Division Russo-American Telegraph Co. in Siberia, 1866-68 ; made an exploration of Eastern Caucasus, 1870-71 ; Night Manager of Associated Press at Washington, D.C., 1877-85 ; made investigation of Russian exile system in Siberia, 1885-86 ; lectured throughout United States, 1889-98, and in Great Britain in 1894 ; reported the Spanish-American war in 1898 as special correspondent in Cuba of The Outlook (N.Y.); expelled from Russia by order of the Minister of the Interior, 1901 ; went to Martinique, 1902, to report for The Outlook (N.Y.) the eruption of Mont Pelee and the destruction of St. Pierre ; Special Correspondent in the Far East, 1904-6 ; staff writer, M'Clure's Magazine, 1906-8 ; and the Outlook since 1909 ; received war medal, Japan, 1907 ; Order of the Sacred Treasure, Japan, 1908 ; Member of National Institute of Arts and Letters. *Publications:* Tent Life in Siberia, 1870 ; new edition, 1910 ; Siberia and the Exile System, 2 vols., 1890 ; Campaigning in Cuba, 1899 ; Folk Tales of Napoleon, 1902 ; The Tragedy of Pelee, 1902 ; A Russian Comedy of Errors, 1915 ; The Chicago and Alton Case, 1916 ; Misrepresentation in Railroad Affairs, 1916 ; E. H. Harriman's Far Eastern Plans, 1917 ; The Salton Sea, 1917 ; E. H. Harriman : A Biography, 2 vols. 1922 ; various articles. *Recreations:* yachting, cycling, and flower-gardening. *Address:* Medina, N.Y., U.S.A. *Club:* Authors', New York.   (*Died 10 May 1924.*)

KENNARD, Major Arthur Molloy, D.S.O. 1900 ; *b.* 7 July 1867 ; *s.* of Arthur C. Kennard ; *m.* 1912, Evelyn Mary, *widow* of Charles H. Helbert and *o. d.* of Lord David and Lady Mary Kennedy ; one *s.* Entered R.A. 1886 ; Captain, 1897 ; Major, 1900 ; served South Africa, 1899-1902 (despatches ; Queen's medal, 3 clasps ; King's medal, 2 clasps ; D.S.O.) ; J.P., D.L. Stirlingshire ; promoted temp. Lt.-Col. of 95th Brigade Royal Field Artillery, 21st Div. Kitchener's 3rd Army, 1915 ; wounded, Battle of Loos, Sep. 1915 ; now commanding 179th Brigade R.F.A. in France. *Address :* Kershiill, Falkirk, Scotland. *Club :* Naval and Military.   (*Died 2 Jan. 1917.*)

KENNARD, Right Rev. Monsignore Charles H. (Canon), Canon of the Diocese of Clifton, Domestic Prelate of His Holiness Pius X. ; *b.* 1840 ; *y. s.* of John Pierse Kennard of Hordle Cliff, Hants, and Sophia, *d.* of Sir John Chapman. *Educ. :* Harrow ; University College, Oxford. Played against Cambridge at racquets three years in succession ; holder of the gold racquet at Oxford, 1861 ; Member of the Harlequin and Perambulator Cricket Clubs ; received into the Catholic Church by Dr. Newman, 1868 ; President of the Burnham and Berrow Golf Club. *Address :*

Westleigh, Burnham, Somerset. *Clubs:* Oxford and Cambridge; R.N. Devon Golf.
(*Died 6 Aug. 1920.*)

KENNARD, Martyn Thomas; *b.* 14 Sep. 1859; *s.* of late H. Martyn Kennard, J.P., D.L.; *m.* 1903, Cora, widow of 3rd Earl of Strafford. *Educ.:* Eton; Christ Church, Oxford. Has spent most of his life big game shooting, chiefly in India. *Clubs:* Marlborough, Turf.
(*Died 12 May 1920.*)

KENNARD. Capt. Willoughby Arthur, D.S.O. 1915; 13th Hussars; *b.* 20 May 1881. Entered army, 1900; Captain, 1906; served S. African War, 1899-1902 (Queen's medal 4 clasps); European War, 1914-16 (despatches, D.S.O., severely wounded). *Clubs:* Cavalry. Bath. Orleans. (*Died Oct. 1918.*)

KENNAWAY, Rt. Hon. Sir John Henry, 3rd Bt., *cr.* 1791; C.B. 1902: P.C. 1897; Col. 3rd Vol.Batt. Devon Regt.; president Church Missionary Society and London Society for promoting Christianity among Jews; *b.* 6 June 1837; *e. s.* of 2nd Bt. and Emily, *d.* of Thomas Kingscote, Kingscote; *m.* 1866, Fanny, *d.* of Archibald F. Arbuthnot; one *s.* two *d.*; *S.* father 1873. *Educ.:* Harrow; Balliol Coll. Oxford. First Class in Law and Modern History School. M.P. (C.) East Devon, 1870-1910; Father of House of Commons, 1908-10. *Publications:* On Sherman's Track, Owns about 4100 acres. *Heir: s.* John, *b.* 7 Apr. 1879. *Address:* Escot, Ottery St. Mary, Devon. *Clubs:* Athenæum, National. (*Died 6 Sept. 1919.*)

KENNAWAY, Sir Walter, Kt., *cr.* 1909; C.M.G. 1891; *b.* 1835; Secretary to the Department of the High Commissioner for New Zealand in London, 1874-1909; *m.* 1864, Alicia, *d.* of J. E. Jones; four *s.* three *d.* *Address:* Malda, Thicket Road, Anerley, S.E(*Died 24 Aug. 1920.*)

KENNEDY, Sir Alexander (Blackie William), Kt., *cr.* 1905; created a Pasha by H.M. King Hussein, 1924; LL.D. (Glas. and Birm.); D. Eng. (Liverpool); F.R.S., Past President Inst. C.E., Past President Inst.M.E., and elected Hon. Member of both Institutions; President Camera Club; Hon. F.R.S. Edin.; Hon. F.R.S., New South Wales; emeritus Professor of Engineering in University College, London; senior partner in Firm Kennedy and Donkin, civil engineers; *b.* Stepney, 17 Mar. 1847; *e. s.* of late Rev. John Kennedy, D.D., and Helen Stodart, *sister* of late Professor Blackie; *m.* 1874, Elizabeth Verralls (*d.* 1911), *e. d.* of late William Smith, LL.D., Edinburgh; two *s.* one *d.* *Educ.:* City of London School; Royal College of Mines. Pupil to marine engineers, then in various engineering works; Professor of Engineering in Univ. College, London, 1874-89, where established first engineering laboratory; has designed electric works for lighting and power in Edinburgh, Manchester, Calcutta, Loch Leven, Japan, etc.; Director of St. James' and Pall Mall Electric Supply Company; Associate Member of Ordnance Committee, 1909; Member of Lord Parker's Committee on Wireless Telegraphy, 1913; Vice-Chairman of the (late) Anti-Aircraft Equipment Committee; Chairman of the Electric Railway Advisory Committee under the Ministry of Transport. *Publications:* Translation of Reuleaux's Kinematik, 1876; The Mechanics of Machinery, 1886; Moore's Alps in 1864, 1902; Yprès to Verdun, 1921; Petra, its History and Monuments, 1925. *Recreations:* music, mountaineering, photography, golf. *Address:* 7A The Albany, W.1; *T.:* Regent 5663; Broadway Court, S.W.1; *T.:* Victoria 3601. *M.:* XP 302. *Clubs:* Athenæum, Garrick, Alpine. (*Died 1 Nov. 1928.*)

KENNEDY, Major-Gen. Alfred Alexander, C.B. 1921; C.M.G. 1915; Colonel 3rd (King's Own) Hussars; commanding the West Riding Area and the 49th (West Riding) Division, with headquarters at York,

since 1923; *b.* 10 Dec. 1870; *s.* of late Myles Kennedy, Stone Cross, Ulverston; *m.* 1898, Dora Campbell, *d.* of W. T. Rowley, Birkdale, Lancashire; one *s.* *Educ.:* Harrow; R.M.C., Sandhurst. Entered army, 1891; Capt. 1896; Major, 1902; Lt.-Col. 1913; Brevet Col. 1915; Maj.-Gen. 1919; served South African War, 1902 (Queen's medal 3 clasps); European War, 1914-19 (despatches seven times, Bt. Col., Major-Gen., C.B., C.M.G., Officier Légion d'honneur). *Clubs:* Cavalry, Ranelagh.
(*Died 31 Mar. 1926.*)

KENNEDY, Brig.-Gen. Charles Henry, C.B. 1914; Royal Marines; Commandant. Chatham Division, Royal Marine Light Infantry; *b.* Wellington, Madras Presidency, India; *s.* of late Major-General H. F. Kennedy, 60th King's Royal Rifle Corps; *m.* Georgina Frances, *d.* of William Loudon Gordon, Inspector-General of Hospitals and Fleets, R.N.; two *s.* *Educ.:* Bath College. Joined Royal Marine Lt. Infantry, 1880; served in the R. Marine Battalion throughout the war, 1882, in Egypt; present at occupation of Port Said, the actions at Tel-el-Mahuta, Mahsaneh, Kassassin 28 Aug., Kassassin 9 Sep., Tel-el-Kebir (medal, Tel-el-Kebir clasp, and Khedive's star); commanded the Royal Marines at the storming of Illig, 1904, and capture of the Sultan and the Dervish garrison on the Somali coast, 1904 (mentioned in official report; General East African medal; Somaliland, clasp). *Recreations:* fishing, shooting, riding, etc. *Address:* Chatham. (*Died 14 Nov. 1916.*)

KENNEDY, Frederick Charles, C.I.E. 1886; *b.* 1849; *m.* 1881, Mary, *d.* of John Cuddie, of Falkirk. Late manager of Irawaddy Flotilla Co., Ltd. *Club:* Oriental. (*Died 17 April 1916.*)

KENNEDY, Rev. James Houghton, D.D. ; Rector of Stillorgan since 1879; Canon of St. Patrick's Cathedral, Dublin, since 1913; *Educ.:* Trinity College, Dublin (M.A.). Curate of Trory, 1866-67; Headford, 1869-70; Dalkey, 1870-73; Monkstown, 1873-78; Select Preacher, University of Dublin, 1906, 1909, and 1913; Canon of Christ Church Cathedral, Dublin, 1900-13. *Publications:* Natural Theology and Modern Thought, 1891; Editor Second and Third Epistles to the Corinthians, 1900. *Address:* The Rectory, Stillorgan, Dublin.

KENNEDY, Brig.-Gen. John, C.M.G. 1918; D.S.O. 1916; Argyll and Sutherland Highlanders; *b.* 1878; *m.* 1919, Mrs. C R. Pawson. Entered Army, 1898; Major, 1915; served European War, 1914-18 (despatches, D.S.O. and bar, C.M.G., Bt. Col.). *Club:* Army and Navy. (*Died Oct. 1921.*)

KENNEDY, Sir John Charles, 3rd Bt., *cr.* 1836; D.L., J.P.; *b.* London, 23 Mar. 1856; *e. s.* of 2nd Bt., and Augusta, *y. d.* of Viscount Glentworth; *m.* Sydney, *d.* of Sir James Macaulay Higginson, 1879; two *s.* two *d.*; *S.* father 1880. *Educ.:* Eton; Trin. Coll. Camb. (B.A.) Lived at home since father's death, farming 400 acres. *Recreations:* hunting, shooting, cricket. *Heir: s.* John Ralph Bayly, *b.* 9 Apr. 1896. *Address:* Johnstown Kennedy, Hazlehatch, Co. Dublin. *Club:* Kildare Street, Dublin. (*Died 22 Mar. 1923.*)

KENNEDY, Col. John Murray, M.V.O. 1905 ; V.D., J.P., D.L.; late Hon. Colonel 5th K.O.S.B. Vols. (retired); *b.* 5 April 1841; *m.* 1880, Frances Eleanor Catherine, *d.* of Lt.-Col. John James Brandling, C.B., R.A.; one *d.* *Educ.:* Cambridge University (B.A.). *Address:* Knocknalling, Dalry, Kirkcudbrightshire.
(*Died 24 Mar. 1928.*)

KENNEDY, Captain Macdougall Ralston, C.M.G. 1912: D.S.O. 1899; Director of Public Works, Soudan ; R.E., retired, 1909 ; *b.* 20 Dec. 1873; *s.* of Rev. A. Kennedy; *m.* 1904, *d.* of Maj.-Gen. W. H. Ralston. *Educ.:* Edinburgh Academy; R.M.A. Woolwich. Entered army, 1893; served Crete, 1898

KENNEDY, George, LL.D., K.C. See page xxiii.

(despatches); Egypt, 1899 (D.S.O., 4th class Medjidie). *Recreations:* yachting, golfing, shooting. (*Died 2 Nov. 1924.*)

KENNEDY, Myles, J.P., D.L. Co. Lancaster; High Sheriff, 1922; *b.* 3 June 1862; *e. s.* of late Myles Kennedy, J.P., of Stone Cross, Ulverston, and Margaret, *d.* of late A. B. Rowley; *m. c.* Ethel Campbell, 3rd *d.* of late Joseph Rowley, J.P., Co. Flintshire; two *s.* two *d.* *Educ.:* Harrow; Royal School of Mines. Chairman, North Lonsdale Iron and Steel Co. Ltd. *Recreations:* shooting, fishing, golf. *Address:* Stone Cross, Ulverston, Lancashire. *M.:* B 4425 and TB 250. *Clubs:* Windham, Royal Automobile.

(*Died 9 Aug. 1928.*)

KENNEDY, Capt. Myles Arthur Claude, D.S.O., 1912; 8th Gurkha Rifles; *b.* 12 Aug. 1885; *o. s.* of Col. Claude Kennedy; *m.* 1913, Nora Constance Marion, *d.* of late W. L. Mumford, M.D.; one *d.* Entered army, 1905; Indian army, 1906; served Abor Expedition, 1912 (despatches, medal with clasp, D.S.O.). (*Died 2 Nov. 1918.*)

KENNEDY, Hon. Lord Kennedy, Neil J. D., M.A. (Aber.), LL.D. (Edin.); K.C. Scot., 1906; Chairman Scottish Land Court since 1912; *b.* April 1855, Rosehall, Sutherlandshire; *s.* of Rev. John D. Kennedy, Free Church, and Catharine Mackay, Inverness; *m.* 1902, Hilda, *y. d.* of Walter Stevenson, Westhorpe, Hendon. *Educ.:* High School, Inverness; Aberdeen and Edinburgh Universities; New College, Edinburgh; first bursar in Divinity, and Grierson Scholar in Law; called to Bar, 1877; was recommended by the Faculty of Advocates for the Chair of Civil Law in Edinburgh University, 1889 and 1893; lecturer on Private International Law in Edinburgh University, 1898; Professor of Civil and Scots Law, University of Aberdeen, 1901-7; contested the county of Inverness in the Liberal interest, 1895; appointed a member of the Royal Commission on Registration of Titles, 1907; Sheriff of Renfrew and Bute, 1907-12; Chairman of Crofters' Commission and Member of the Congested Districts Board, 1908-12. *Publications:* wrote many articles on literary and legal subjects in the Juridical Review and other legal publications. *Address:* 22 Ainslie Place, Edinburgh. *Clubs:* Scottish Liberal, Edinburgh; University, Aberdeen.

(*Died 13 Feb. 1918.*)

KENNEDY, Robert, M.A., M.D. D.Sc., D.L., J.P.; St. Mungo Professor of Surgery in the University of Glasgow and ex-officio Surgeon in the Royal Infirmary since 1911; *b.* Glasgow, 20 Dec. 1865; *m.* 1895, Janet Lyon (*d.* 1922), *d.* of John Miller, M.D.; one *d.* *Educ.:* Univ. of Glasgow, Edin. and Berlin. Graduated in Univ. of Glasgow with highest honours in Arts and Medicine; John Clark Scholar, 1886-87; George A. Clark Scholar, 1888-92; Surgeon to out-door department, Glasgow Victoria Infirmary, 1892-96, and of Western Infirmary, 1896-1900; Assistant Surgeon, Western Infirmary, 1900-10, and Lock Hospital, 1893-94; Examiner in Surgery, St. Andrews University, 1901-4; Lecturer in Applied Anatomy, University of Glasgow, 1906-1911; Surgeon and Lecturer in Clinical Surgery, Western Infirmary, 1910-11; Senior and Consulting Surgeon in Charge Orthopædic Department, Scottish National Red Cross Hospital, Bellahouston, 1917-19; Director and Consulting Surgeon, Shakespeare Hospital (Ministry of Pensions), Glasgow, 1918-19; Surgeon-in-Chief, Bellahouston Hospital (Ministry of Pensions), Glasgow, 1919-22. *Publications:* On the Regeneration of Nerves, 1897; On the Restoration of Co-ordinated Movements after Nerve-Crossing with Interchange of Function of the Cerebral Cortical Centres, 1901; Experiments on the Restora-

tion of Paralysed; Muscles by means of Nerve Anastomosis, Parts I., II., and III., 1911, 1914, 1915; Phil. Trans., Suture and Anastomoses des Nerfs in Chipault's L'Etat Actuel de la Chirurgie Nerveuse, 3 vols., Paris, 1903; Suture of the Brachial Plexus in Birth Paralysis of the Upper Extremity, Brit. Med. Journal, 1903 and 1904; Operative Procedure in Nerve Injuries, British Journal of Surgery, 1918; numerous papers in various departments of surgery in the medical journals and transactions of societies. *Address:* 14 Woodside Terrace, Glasgow. *T.:* Ch. X. 501.

(*Died 3 June 1924.*)

KENNEDY, Robert Gregg, C.I.E. 1907; *b.* 1851; *m.* 1889, Mabel Sarah, *d.* of G. B. M. Wyse. *Educ.:* R.I.E. College. Entered service, 1873; Executive Engineer, 1881; Superintending Engineer, 1898; Chief Engineer and Commissioner to Sec. Central Provinces, 1903; joint Sec. to Punjab Irrigation, 1904; Sec. (Irrigation) to Chief Commissioner N.W. Frontier Provinces, 1905; retired 1906. *Publication:* Report on Irrigation in the U.P. *Address:* c/o British Linen Bank, West End Branch, Edinburgh. (*Died 2 Mar. 1920.*)

KENNEDY, Lt.-Col. William Magill, C.I.E. 1916; Indian Army, retired; in Civil Employ as Deputy Commissioner, Assam; *b.* 1868; *s.* of late Charles George Blagrave Kennedy, J.P., of Mullantean, Stewartstown, Co. Tyrone; *m.* 1922, Violet Hope, *e. d.* of Robert Ponsonby Staples, Lissan, Cookstown, Co. Tyrone. *Educ.:* Royal School, Dungannon; Trinity College, Dublin. Joined the 4th Batt. Royal Inniskilling Fusiliers (Tyrone Militia), 1887; 2nd Batt. 1890; transferred to the Indian Staff Corps and posted to the 9th Madras Infantry, 1892; took part in Chin Hills Expedition, 1892-93; Assistant Commissioner, Assam, 1894; Deputy Commissioner, 1905; Commissioner of Excise and Salt, and Inspector-General of Registration, Eastern Bengal and Assam, 1905-11; Member and Secretary of Assam Labour Enquiry Committee, 1906; Second Secretary to the Chief Commissioner of Assam, 1912-13; officiating Chief Secretary, 1913; Member of Legislative Council, Eastern Bengal and Assam, 1910-11; Assam Legislative Council, 1912-15; Tea Commissioner for India, 1917-19; Chairman, Assam Labour Board, 1915-20. *Recreations:* fishing, shooting, and golf. *Address:* Mullantean, Stewartstown, Co. Tyrone; c/o King, Hamilton & Co., Calcutta. *Clubs:* East India United Service; Bengal, Royal Calcutta Turf, Calcutta.

(*Died 22 Sept. 1923.*)

KENNEDY, Admiral Sir William Robert, G.C.B., *cr.* 1911; K.C.B., *cr.* 1897; *b.* 4 Mar. 1838; *s.* of John Kennedy, Chargé d'Affaires, Naples; *m.* 1868, Edith L., *d.* of Capt. E. Stopford, R.N.; one *d.* *Educ.:* Cheam; Dr. Maldon's, Brighton. Navy Cadet, 1851; Sub-Lt. 1857; Lt. 1857; Com. 1867; Capt. 1874; Rear-Admiral, 1889; Vice-Admiral, 1896; Admiral, 1901; served Crimea (two medals); China, 1856-59 (medal and clasps); Commander-in-Chief, East Indies, 1892-95; at the Nore, 1901-1902; has Royal Humane Society's medal. *Publications:* Sporting Adventures in the Pacific; Sport Travel in Newfoundland; Sporting in South America; Hurrah for the Life of a Sailor. *Recreations:* shooting, fishing. *Address:* Falconer's Hill, Daventry. *Club:* United Service. (*Died 9 Oct. 1916.*)

KENNEDY, Lt.-Col. Willoughby Pitcairn, C.S.I. 1906; *b.* 10 Dec. 1850; *e. s.* of Gen. Sir Michael Kavanagh Kennedy, K.C.S.I., *m.* 1887; one *d.* Entered army, 1870; served Afghan War, 1880 (medal); Special Political Agent, Cambay, 1890-94; Administrator, Raj-Piplah estates, 1890-94; Navanagar estate, 1895; Political Agent Kathiawar, 1901; Agent to

Governor there, 1902; retired, 1906. *Address:* Lynedoch, W. Byfleet, Surrey.
(Died 7 Aug. 1928.)

KENNEY, Colonel Arthur Herbert, C.M.G. 1893; D.S.O. 1900; Royal Engineers; late commanding R. Engineers, Devon Sub-District; retired; *b.* Plymouth, 4 Jan. 1855; 2nd *s.* of late Captain E. H. Kenney, R.N, and Charlotte Mary, *d.* of late Captain Bignell, R.N. *Educ.:* private tuition; Roy. Mil. Acad., Woolwich. Lieut. R.E., 1873; Captain, 1885; Major, 1892; Lt.-Col. 1900; served in India, 1876-83; Egypt and Soudan, 1884-85; West Africa, 1890-92; Assistant Field Engineer, Kuram Valley, and Kabul Field Force, during Afghan War, 1879-80 (medal); Nile Expedition, 1884-85 (medal, two clasps, and Khedive's star), and was in charge of Boat Repairing Party River Column (despatches); South African War, 1809-1900, as O.C. Advance Depot R.E., C.R.E. 10th Division, and C.R.E. Gen. Ian Hamilton's Force (despatches, medal, 3 clasps, and D.S.O.); re-employed from the retired list 1 Sep. 1914, as C.R.E. of a Division till 31 July 1915, and as Commandant of a Training Centre till 30 May 1916 (despatches, 1915 Star, British War medal, Victory medal and oak leaf); was British Commissioner of the Anglo-French Commissions for delimiting the frontiers of the Colonies of the Gambia, and of Sierra Leone, 1890-92 (C.M.G.). *Address:* 44 Preston Park Avenue, Brighton.
(Died 4 Sept. 1923.)

KENNEY - HERBERT, Edward Maxwell, J.P. Bucks; late H.M. Divisional Inspector of Schools, Board of Education; *b.* 10 Dec. 1845; *s.* of Rev. A. R. Kenney-Herbert, Rector of Bourton-on-Dunsmore, Co. Warwick; *m.* 1876, Lady Jane White, *d.* of 3rd Earl of Bantry; one *s.* one *d.* *Educ.:* Rugby School; Merton College, Oxford. *Address:* 6 Woodfield Road, Ealing, W. *T.:* Ealing 1215.
(Died 26 Jan. 1916.)

KENNINGTON, T. B., painter of portraits, genre pictures; *b.* Great Grimsby, Lincolnshire. *Educ.:* private school; Liverpool School of Art. Gold medal, South Kensington; scholarship medal while at Liverpool; two years at South Kensington, afterwards Paris under Bouguereau and Tony Fleury; formerly member N.E.A.C., also R.B.A.; Vice-President, Institute of Oil Painters; member of Royal British Colonial Society of Artists; Bronze medal, Paris, 1889; Bronze medal, Paris, 1900. *Recreation:* chess. *Address:* 8 Netherton Grove, Chelsea, S.W. *Club:* Arts.
(Died 14 Dec. 1916.)

KENNION, Rt. Rev. George Wyndham; D.D. *hon.* Glas.; *b.* 1845; *s.* of George Kennion, M.D., Harrogate, and Catherine Elfrida, *d.* of late T. J. Fordyce, of Ayton Castle, Berwickshire; *m.* Henrietta, *d.* of Sir Charles Dalrymple Fergusson, 5th Bt., 1882. *Educ.:* Eton; Oriel Coll. Oxford (M.A.). Ordained 1869; Domestic Chaplain to Bishop of Tuam, 1869-70; Curate of Doncaster, 1870-71; Vicar of St. Paul, Hull, 1873-76; Vicar of All Saints, Bradford, 1876-82; Bishop of Adelaide, 1882-94; Lecturer in Pastoral Theology, University of Cambridge, 1900; Ramsden Preacher Univ. Camb. 1901. *Recreations:* in former years boating and all school-boys' games, hunting, shooting; in Australia, riding, swimming, boating; at present, cycling, reading. *Address:* The Palace, Wells, Somerset. *Club:* Athenæum.
(Died 19 May 1922.)

KENNY, The Rt. Hon. William, Hon. Mr. Justice Kenny, Judge of the King's Bench Division of the High Court of Justice, Ireland, since 1897; P.C. 1902; *b.* Dublin, 14 Jan. 1846; *o. s.* of late Edward Kenny, solicitor, Ennis, Co. Clare; *m.* Mary, *e. d.* of David Coffey Master in Chancery, 1873. *Educ.:* privately; Trinity Coll. Dublin (M.A.) Irish Bar, 1868; Q.C. 1885; Bencher,

580

King's Inns. 1890; member of Senate of University of Dublin; a leader at Chancery Bar; mainly instrumental in establishing the Liberal Union of Ireland after the defeat of Home Rule Bill of 1886, and in organising the memorable visit of Lord Hartington and Mr. Goschen to Dublin in 1887; M.P. (U.) Dublin (Stephen's Green), 1892 - 97; Solicitor - General for Ireland, 1895-97; elected M.P. 1892 by majority of 15; there being three candidates Nationalist vote was divided, but in 1895, when Nationalist vote was solid against him, he was elected by 456; a Nationalist again contested seat on his appointment as Solicitor-General when he retained it, hitherto deemed an impregnable Nationalist stronghold with a practically undiminished majority; Judge for Probate and Matrimonial Business, 1919; Chairman Irish Railway and Canal Commission. *Address:* Marifield, Cabintely, Co. Dublin. *Club:* Kildare Street, Dublin.
(Died 4 Feb. 1921.)

KENRICK, John Arthur, J.P.; *b.* 1829; *e. s.* of late Archibald Kenrick of Berrow Court and Anne, *d.* of late William Paget of Loughborough, Co. Leicester; *m.* 1866, Clara, *d.* of Rev. John Taylor. *Address:* Berrow Court, Edgbaston. *(Died 23 April 1926.)*

KENRICK, Rt. Hon. William, P.C. 1899; J.P.; *b.* 1831; *s.* of late Archibald Kenrick, W. Bromwich; *m.* Mary, *d.* of late J. Chamberlain, *sister* of Rt. Hon. J. Chamberlain, 1862 [Mr. Chamberlain's first wife was a sister of Mr. Kenrick]; two *s.* two *d.* *Educ.:* private school, Hove; Univ. Coll. Lond. Gold medal for chemistry, 1850. Was a hardware manufacturer; Alderman and Town Councillor (Mayor 1877), Birmingham; M.P. (U.L.) Birmingham, N. Div. 1885-99. *Recreation:* landscape painting. *Address:* The Grove, Harborne, Birmingham. *Club:* Burlington Fine Arts. *(Died 31 July 1919.)*

KENSINGTON, Sir Alfred, Kt., *cr.* 1914; *b.* 26 April 1855; *s.* of Arthur Kensington (*d.* 1886); *m.* 1881, Alice H. M., *d.* of late Maj.-General H. C. Johnstone, C.B.; two *s.* one *d.* *Educ.:* Marlborough; Univ. Coll. Oxford. Entered Indian Civil Service, 1877; held various appointments in the Indian Civil Service in the Punjab, and under Government of India; Judge, Chief Court, Punjab, 1904; Chief Judge, 1914; retired, 1915. *Address:* 3 Buckingham Gate, S.W.1; *T.:* Victoria 5861. *Club:* Albemarle.
(Died 2 Nov. 1918.)

KENSINGTON, William Charles, I.S.O. 1909; J.P.; Permanent Under-Secretary for Lands and Immigration, New Zealand, 1901-1912; *b.* Werndu, Criccieth, N. Wales, 3 Aug. 1845; *e. s.* of late Charles J. W. Kensington, Prince Hill, Worton, Wilts; *m.* 1st, Emily Selena (*d.* 1869), *d.* of G. Owen Ormsby; 2nd, 1873, Amy (*d.* 1906), *d.* of Lt.-Col. Hon. W. H. Kenny, 73rd Rgt.; three *s.* two *d.* *Educ.:* Grosvenor School, Bath; King's School, Bruton, Somerset. Went N.Z. 1862; Ensign 1st. Batt. New Zealand Militia, 1865, later Captain; served Maori War, 1863-65 (war medal); Captain Auckland Rifle Brigade, 1871. *Address:* Cheverell, Marton, Rangiteikei, N.Z. *Club:* Marton.
(Died 20 Aug. 1922.)

KENT, Lieut.-General Henry, Colonel, Middlesex Regiment since 1900; *b.* 3 Aug. 1825; *m.* Caroline (*d.* 1891), *d.* of William Ward, Wolverhampton. Entered army, 1845; Maj.-Gen. 1883; retired, 1886; served Crimea, 1854-55 (medal with three clasps, 5th class Medjidie, Turkish medal); commanded 77th Regiment, 1868-80; 7th and 57th Regimental Districts, 1880-83. *Address:* Glenthorne, The Downs, Wimbledon, S.W.19. *Clubs:* United Service, Junior United Service, Army and Navy.
(Died 24 Feb. 1921.)

KENT, Professor Thomas Parkes, M.A.; Professor of Mathematics in the Uni-

versity of Cape Town; *b.* Nevis, West Indies; *e. s.* of Rev. Alfred Kent; *m.* 1906, Constance, *y. d.* of Henry Beard of Cape Town and Kenilworth; three *s.* one *d.* *Educ.:* Kingswood School, Bath; Christ Church, Oxford (Scholar); Exhibitioner, London Univ.; First Class Honours in Final, School of Mathematics; Honours in Final, Natural Science School; Assistant Master at Fettes College, Edinburgh, and Cranleigh School, Surrey; Professor in Mathematics at the Diocesan College, Rondebosch, 1902; at the South African College, Cape Town, 1908. *Publications:* Articles and verse in educational and other journals; The Flick of Fortune (novel). *Address:* Nevis, Claremont, near Cape Town. *Clubs:* Civil Service; Owl, Cape Town.
(Died 4 Aug. 1925.)

KENYON, 4th Baron; *cr.* 1788; **Lloyd Tyrell-Kenyon**, D.L., J.P., K.C.V.O., T.D.; Bt. 1784; Baron of Gredington, 1788; A.D.C. to King George V.; Lord-in-Waiting, 1916; Ld.-Lt. Denbighshire; *b.* London, 5 July 1864; *o. s.* of late Hon. Lloyd, and *d.* of 1st Baron Harlech, Brogyntyn, Shropshire; *S.* grandfather, 1869; *m.* 1916, Gwladys Julia, *d.* of late Col. H. R. Lloyd Howard, C.B.; one *s.* one *d.* *Educ.:* Eton; Christ Church, Oxford. Late Col. commanding Shropshire Imperial Yeomanry; Pres., North Wales Univ. Coll.; Pro-Chancellor, University of Wales; Lord-in-Waiting, 1900-5; Col. commanding 2/1 Welsh Horse, Dec. 1914-Dec. 1916; Chairman Advisory Committee on Milk, 1924; President National Museum of Wales; Chairman Agricultural Wages Board, 1924, etc. Owns about 10,000 acres. *Recreations:* hunting, shooting. *Heir: is* Hon. Lloyd Tyrell-Kenyon, *b.* 13 Sep. 1917. *Address:* 2n The Albany, Piccadilly, W.1; *T.:* Gerrard 2893; Gredington, Whitchurch, Shropshire; Peel Hall, Bolton, Lancs; Boreham House, Chelmsford. *Clubs:* Carlton, Turf. *(Died 30 Nov. 1927.)*

KENYON, Edith C., novelist; *b.* Hooton Pagnell, Doncaster, Yorks; 3rd *d.* of late John Kenyon, M.R.C.S., and Ellen (Wilton), of Hooton Pagnell and Brynllwydwyn, N. Wales. *Educ.:* chiefly at home. Lived at Hooton Pagnell and in Wales; later, for several years, in Bradford with brother, Dr. J. E. Kenyon; went to Hastings, 1895, and after three years to London; began writing early; several of her first novels were published in New York. *Publications:* Altogether 40 books; latest, A Queen of Nine Days, 1903; A Girl in a Thousand, 1904; Sir Claude Mannerley, 1905; Love's Golden Thread, 1905; Gladys's Repentance, 1906; The Adventures of Timothy, 1907; Two Girls in a Siege; Chats with Women, 1908; A Girl from Canada, 1911; The Wooing of Mifanwy, 1912; The Winning of Gwenora, 1913; Pickles: a Red Cross Heroine, 1916; The Blue Eyes of Nansi; In Another Woman's Shoes, 1919. *Recreations:* fiction, chess. *Address:* 14 Manor Road, Twickenham, S.W. *(Died 21 June 1925.)*

KENYON, James, J.P., woollen manufacturer; chairman of Liverpool Storage Co.; *b.* Bury, 1846; *s.* of James Kenyon of Crimble, nr. Bury; *m.* 1875, Elise, *y. d.* of F. Genth of Burnage; four *s.* one *d.* *Educ.:* Bury Grammar School; Liverpool Collegiate. M.P. (C.) Bury, Lancashire, 1895-1902. *Recreations:* shooting, cricket, racing. *Address:* Walshaw Hall, Bury, Lancashire. *Clubs:* Carlton, Conservative.
(Died 25 Feb. 1924.)

KENYON-SLANEY, Major Philip Percy, M.C.; M.P. (C.) Tavistock since 1924; *er. s.* of late Percy Robert Kenyon-Slaney and Geraldine Ellen Georgina, *d.* of Rev. George Whitmore; *b.* 1896. *Educ.:* Bradfield College, Berks. Served European War, 1914-21 (M.C., despatches); contested Tavistock Division, 1923. *Recreations:* shooting, fishing, hunting. *Address:* Beechwood House, Plympton, Devon; *T.:* Plympton, 13Y2; 7 Chester Terrace, S.W.1. *T.:* Sloane 3119 and 6240. *Club:* Junior Army and Navy. *(Died 9 Sept. 1928.)*

KEPPEL, Sir George Roos-, G.C.I.E., *cr.* 1917; K.C.S.I., *cr.* 1913; K.C.I.E., *cr.* 1908; C.I.E. 1900; Member of the Council of the Secretary of State for India, 1920; Chief Commissioner and Agent to Governor-General North-West Frontier Province, India, 1908-19; Hon. Col. Khyber Rifles, 1909; *b.* 7 Sep. 1866; joined Royal Scots Fusiliers, 1886; Captain, 1895; Brevet Major, 1899; Bt. Lt.-Col. 1907; transferred to Indian Staff Corps, 1897; served Burmese Expedition, 1885-89 (medal with two clasps); Tirah Expedition, 1897-98 (medal with three clasps); commanded operations against the Para Chamkannis, 1899 (C.I.E. and Brevet of Major); Bazar Valley Field Force, 1908, as Chief Political Officer, and in command of a column (despatches, medal with clasp, K.C.I.E.); holds Swedish Military Order of the Sword; employed in France, 1914, as extra King's Messenger; operations on N.W. Frontier of India, 1915-17; Afghan operations, 1919 (despatches three times, G.C.I.E.); Military Governor Martial Law Area, N.W.F.P., 1919 (despatches); Temp. Major-General, 1919; retired Dec. 1919; President, Indian Branch League of Mercy, 1915-19; Knight of Grace, Order of St. John of Jerusalem, 1916. *Address:* Whitehall Court, S.W.1. *T.:* Victoria 3160, Ex. 35. *Clubs:* Marlborough, Wellington, United Service, Arts, Royal Automobile.
(Died 11 Dec. 1921.)

KEPPEL, Rear-Admiral Leicester Chantrey; retired; 2nd *s.* of late Rev. Canon the Hon. Thomas Robert Keppel; *m.* Emily (*d.* 1913), *d.* of Geo. Robinson of Bagatelle Moka, Mauritius; one *s.* three *d.* Served as midshipman in H.M.S. Bellerophon, 1854; was actively engaged in embarking the army at Varna and landing at Old Fort; served at Eupatoria in defence of that town; at bombardment of Sevastopol, 1854, and bombarded Fort Constantine at 600 yards; served in H.M.S. Magicienne, at bombardment in destruction of Friedericksham, 1855; in charge of boat under fire against Viborg, and lifted two infernal machines when under fire and cleared passage; in charge of mortar vessel at bombardment of Sevesborg, 1855; was engaged with Russian artillery at Ravenoari in Finland, 1855; engaged in suppression of Slave Trade on East Coast of Africa and captured several slave dhows under fire, 1861; served in expedition up Zambesi with Dr. Livingstone; in command of gun-boats Janus and Insolent at Chefoo, 1867-69; kept Neinfe Rebels in check; obtained redress for outrages on British subjects at Jamone, Formosa, 1868 (received thanks of Commander-in-Chief and Her Majesty's Minister); punished piratical natives for attack on Sharp Peak River Min, Chefoo, and attacked Pington and subdued natives at Foochowfoo (received official thanks, 1869); West Coast of Africa—served in Niger Expedition when several piratical villages were destroyed, and severe punishment inflicted on river pirates, 1877 (despatches); as Commander in H.M.S. Avon up Congo, commanded expedition for punishment of pirates, who had attacked and pillaged American vessel Joseph Nickeroon (received approval of Lord Derby, also approval from their Lordships for skill and gallantry with which the operations were conducted, as well as approval of the Secretary of State for Foreign Affairs); commanded H.M. ships Constance and Cleopatra in China and Japan; Flag-Capt. to Commander-in-Chief at Nore, etc. *Address:* Guelderland, West Worthing. *Club:* Junior Naval and Military. *(Died 24 Sept. 1917.)*

KER, Hon. John Errington, M.R.C.S. (Eng.), L.R.C.P. (London); Superintending Medical Officer, Jamaica Government Medical Service, since 1904; Member Legislative Council of Jamaica; *b.* Port Rush, Co. Antrim, 22 June 1860; *s.* of late C. B. Ker, M.I.C.E., late resident engineer on the G.I.P. Railway, India; *m.*

KEOGH, Martin Jerome, LL.D. See page xxiii.

Naomi, *d.* of Henry Morley, Nottingham; no *c.* *Educ.*: Clifton College; privately; France and Germany. St. Thomas's Hospital, London; Rotunda, Dublin; House-Surgeon Birmingham General Hospital, 1887 - 8; Hertford British Hospital, Paris, 1888-9; Birmingham Homœopathic Hospital, 1889; Assistant - Surgeon, Colonial Hospital, Gibraltar, District Medical Officer, Police Surgeon, etc., 1889; later on appointed Port Surgeon, Gibraltar; Civil Surgeon during the war, 1899-1900; attached to No. 3 General Hospital, Rondebosch, Cape Colony, and Springfontein, O.R.C., and later to No. 2 General Hospital, Pretoria, also to Railway Department (medal and 3 clasps). *Recreations*: riding and gardening and travelling. *Address*: Halfway Tree, St. Andrews, Jamaica. *Club*: Jamaica.   (*Died 25 Oct. 1918.*)

KER, William Paton, F.B.A., M.A., Fellow of All Souls College; Professor of Poetry, Oxford, since 1920; *b.* 1855; *s.* of William Ker, merchant, Glasgow. *Educ.*: Glasgow Academy; Glasgow University; Balliol College (Snell Exhibitioner) Taylorian Scholar, 1878; Professor of English Literature and History in the University College of South Wales, Cardiff, 1883-89; Professor of English Literature, University College, London, 1889-1922. *Publications*: Epic and Romance, 1897; The Dark Ages, 1904; Essays on Medieval Literature, 1905; Sturla the Historian, 1906; the Art of Poetry, 1920. *Address*: 95 Gower Street, W.C. *Clubs*: Alpine, Athenæum, United University; Western, Glasgow.   (*Died 17 July 1923.*)

KERR, Hon. James Kirkpatrick, K.C.; P.C. Can.; Life Senator since 1903; *b.* Puslinch, near Guelph, Ontario, Canada, 1 Aug. 1841; *s.* of Robert Warren Kerr and Jane Hamilton, *d.* of late James Kirkpatrick; *m.* 1st, 1864, Anne Margaret, *d.* of Hon. William Hume Blake, Chancellor of Upper Canada; 2nd, 1883, Adelaide Cecil, *d.* of Rev. G. Stanley - Pinhorne, Cumberland, and *niece* of late Rt. Hon. Alexander Staveley Hill of Oxley Manor, Staffordshire; one *s.* four *d.* *Educ.*: Dr. Tassie's School, Galt, Ontario. Called to Bar, 1862; Q.C. for Ontario, 1874, and Canada, 1881; Bencher of Law Society, 1879; contested (L.) Centre Toronto, 1891; Grand Master of Masonic Grand Lodge of Canada, 1874-77; Member of Supreme Council, 33rd Degree Ancient and Accepted Scottish Rite, for England, Canada, and United States; Provincial Great Prior Masonic Knight Templar and Knight of Grand Cross of the Temple, 1883 (England and Wales); Vice-Pres. of Canadian General Electric Co., and director of several large industrial and other companies; President of Liberal Association for Ontario, 1892-1904; The Speaker of the Senate, Canada, 1909-11. *Address*: Rathnelly, Toronto, Canada. *T.A.*: The Senate of Canada, Ottawa, and Kerdason, Toronto. *Clubs*: Toronto, York, Hunt, Ontario, Ontario Jockey, Toronto; Rideau, Ottawa.
     (*Died 4 Dec. 1916.*)

KERR, John, M.A. LL.D.; *b.* 15 July 1830; *s.* of John Kerr, Dalry, Ayrshire; *m.* Elizabeth Jackson, *d.* of Dr. Thomas Jackson Graham, R.N., 1866; five *s.* four *d.* *Educ.*: Dalry Parish School; Glasgow and Edinburgh Universities; Trinity College, Cambridge. Honours in Classics, 1858; Silver Goblet Declamation Prize, 1858; Historical Essay Prize, Life and Character of Wm. III., 1859; Assistant Master in King Edward VI.'s School, Bury St. Edmund's, 1859; H.M. Inspector of Schools in Scotland N. district, 1860-78; Chief Inspector in S.W. district, 1878-88; Senior Chief Inspector of Schools and Training Colleges, 1888-96; Classical Examiner for degrees in Edinburgh University, 1867-70, in Glasgow University, 1872-75; in the course of forty-seven years examined the majority of the Secondary Schools in Scotland, and gave evidence before almost all important

Education Commissions. *Publications*: Cambridge Burney Prize Essay, 1860; Memories Grave and Gay, 1902; Other Memories Old and New, 1904; Leaves from an Inspector's Logbook, 1913; Scottish Education, Primary, Secondary, and University from the 12th Century to 1913; a considerable number of magazine articles. *Recreations*: travelling, curling, fishing, golf. *Address*: 15 Royal Terrace, Edinburgh.   (*Died 1 Dec. 1916.*)

KERR, John, *b.* 1852; *m.* 1877, Helen Margaret, *d.* of Thomas Melville of Kershill, Stirlingshire; two *s.* four *d.* M.P. (U.), Preston, 1903-1906. *Address*: Bramshill, Frinton-on-Sea, Essex.

KERR, Rev. John, M.A. (Edin.); minister Church of Scotland, parish of Skelmorlie, 1876-78; Dirleton since 1878; Member of Editorial Committee, Church Service Society; Clerk to Synod of Lothian and Tweeddale, 1907-15; *b.* Dumfries, 1852; *m.*; two *s.* four *d.* *Educ.*: Glencairn School; Edinburgh University. *Publications*: The History of Curling, the Jubilee volume of the Royal Caledonian Curling Club; the Golf-Book of East Lothian; Golf Song-Book; Curling in Canada and the United States; article Curling in Badminton volume on Ice Sports, and in World of Sport; Archery, Golf, and Curling in Scottish History and Life; Parish Councils in Country Parishes; Fellowship with the Father; Rich and Poor; The Renascence of Worship (Lee Lecture for 1905); North Berwick in Health Resorts Series. *Recreations*: curling, golf, travel; Captain Scottish Curling Team which visited Canada and United States, 1902 - 3; Chaplain Royal Caledonian Curling Club, 1897-1913; M.W. Past Grand Chaplain Grand Lodge of Scotland; Retired Chaplain (Lt.-Col.) 8th Royal Scots (T.F.). *Address*: Dirleton, R.S.O., East Lothian.
     (*Died 8 Dec. 1920.*)

KERR, Lord Ralph Drury, K.C.B. *cr.* 1911; C.B.; *b.* 11 Aug. 1837; *m.* 1878, Lady Anne Fitzalan Howard, *d.* of 14th Duke of Norfolk; one *s.* three *d.* Entered 10th Hussars, 1857; Maj.-Gen. 1890; retired, 1898; served Afghan campaign, 1879; Inspecting Officer for auxiliary cavalry, 1883-88; commanded Curragh District, 1891-96. *Address*: Woodburn, Dalkeith, N.B.
     (*Died 18 Sept. 1916.*)

KERR, Admiral of the Fleet Lord Walter Talbot, G.C.B., *cr.* 1902; K.C.B., *cr.* 1896; *b.* Scotland, 28 Sep. 1839; 4th *s.* of 7th Marquis of Lothian, and Cecil, *d.* of 2nd Earl Talbot; *m.* 1873, Lady Amabel Cowper (*d.* 1906), *d.* of 6th Earl Cowper; four *s.* two *d.* *Educ.*: Radley College. Entered Navy, 1853; served in Baltic, 1854-55; with Naval Brigade at relief and battle of Lucknow; has Royal Humane Society medal for saving life; Capt. 1872; Rear-Admiral 1889; Vice-Admiral 1895; Admiral 1900; Private Secretary to First Lord of Admiralty, 1885-90; second in command Mediterranean, 1890-92; Junior Lord of Admiralty, 1892; 2nd Lord, 1894-95; commanded Channel Squadron, 1895-97; Senior Naval Lord of Admiralty, 1899-1904; Admiral of the Fleet, 1904. *Recreations*: cycling, photography, botany. *Address*: 58 Cromwell Road, S.W.7; *T.*: Western 6248; Melbourne Hall, Derby. *Club*: Junior Carlton.   (*Died 12 May 1927.*)

KERR, Captain William, D.S.O. 1916; 2nd Batt. The Border Regt.; *b.* 2 March 1877; *m.* 1st, Ester Isobel; one *c.*; 2nd, Emily, daughters of R. Dalton, Cummersdale, Carlisle. *Educ.*: St. Patrick's, Carlisle. Entered Army, 1895; served South African Campaign (Queen's medal, 7 clasps); European War, 1914-17; present at battles of Ypres, Neuve Chapelle, Festubert, Loos (wounded at Festubert, despatches thrice, Military Cross, D.S.O.). *Address*: c/o R. Fulton, Cummersdale, Carlisle.   (*Died May 1918.*)

KERR, Capt. William Alexander, V.C. Late Southern Mahratta Horse; served

Indian Mutiny, 1857 (despatches, medal with clasp, V.C.). *Publications:* Riding ; Riding for Ladies ; Peat and its Products ; Imperial Horse Supply ; etc. *Address:* 73 Bouverie Road, W., Folkestone. (*Died 21 May 1919.*)

KERRISON, Roger, J.P.; *e. s.* of late Roger Allday Kerrison, Norwich, and Adelaide Thorp, *d.* of John Stokes ; *b.* 1842 ; *m.* 1st, 1867, Florence Lucy (*d.* 1903), 3rd *d.* of Rev. Sir Charles Clarke, 2nd Bart. ; two *d.* ; 2nd, 1905, Ellen, *d.* of James Smith, Alderton. *Educ.:* Harrow ; Trinity College, Cambridge, M.A. ; High Sheriff, Suffolk, 1900 ; late Lieut. Norfolk Artillery Militia. *Address:* Colne House, Earls Colne, Essex. *Clubs:* Wellington, New University, Hurlingham, Royal Yacht Squadron, Cowes. (*Died 6 Mar. 1924.*)

KERSHAW, John Felix; late Judge of Court of Appeal, Cairo (Egyptian Government) ; *b.* 20 Nov. 1873 ; *s.* of late Sir Louis Kershaw, K.C., late Chief Justice of Bombay ; *m.* Anne Winston, *d.* of Overton Price and Anne Rodgers, Kentucky, U.S.A. ; two *s.* one *d. Educ.:* Shrewsbury School ; Balliol College, Oxford. Honours in History and Law, Oxford, 1895 and 1896 ; called to Bar, 1897 ; practised N.E. Circuit ; Judge, Khartoum, 1902 ; Judge, First Instance, Cairo, 1905 ; appointed to Native Appeal Court, 1913 ; President of Court of Enquiry, Australian Red Cross, 1915 ; President, Military Court (trading with the Enemy), throughout War ; Legal Adviser (temp. Lt.-Col.) to 20th Corps during troubles in Egypt, 1919, and later same to G.H.Q. British Army in Egypt ; Legal Adviser to Court of Enquiry, Alexandria Riots, 1921 ; President of Cairo Assize Court, and resigned, June 1926, in consequence of adverse verdict in case of instigators of Sirdar's murder ; 2nd Class, Order of the Nile ; 3rd Class, Medjidieh. *Publications:* Hints on Criminal Investigation, 1907 ; Reply to Charge of Atrocities Alleged against British Soldiers, 1919 (Blue Book) ; Causes of Alexandria Riots, 1921 (Blue Book). *Recreations:* rowing, shooting, tennis, racing, swimming, golf. *Address:* Zeenalek, Gezira, Cairo, Egypt. *M.:* YL 5348 (G.B.). *Clubs:* White's ; Gezira Sporting, Cairo. (*Died 16 June 1927.*)

KESTELL-CORNISH, Rt. Rev. George Kestell, Anglican Bishop of Madagascar since 1919 ; Archdeacon of Madagascar, 1901-19 ; S.P.G. Missionary since 1882 ; *b.* 4 Sep. 1856 ; *e. s.* of late Rt. Rev. R. K. Kestell-Cornish, Bishop of Madagasgar ; *m.* 1885, Sarah Louisa Champernowne. *Educ.:* Keble College, Oxford (M.A. 1885). Ordained 1880 ; Curate of St. James', Great Grimsby, 1880-82 ; Principal, High School, Tanarive, Madagascar, 1884-90 ; Mahanoro, 1891-94 and 1899-1901 ; Principal, St. Augustine's Theological College, Ambinanindrano, 1902-19. *Address:* La Mission Anglicane, Ambatobe, Tananarive, Madagascar. (*Died 23 June 1925.*)

KESTEVEN, Sir Charles Henry, Kt., *cr.* 1920 ; Solicitor to Govt. of Bengal since 1919 ; *m.* 1921, Annie Lander (Nancy), *d.* of late James Wilson. Solicitor to the Government of India, 1904-19. *Address:* Calcutta. *Clubs:* White's, Oriental. (*Died 13 Jan. 1925.*)

KESWICK, Major Henry, M.P. (U.) Epsom Division of Surrey, 1912-18 ; J.P. ; *b.* 1870 ; *e. s.* of late William Keswick, M.P. ; *m. d.* of late William Johnston, I.C.S. ; three *s. Educ.:* Eton ; Trinity Coll. Camb. (M.A.). Entered Jardine, Matheson & Co. of Hong-Kong, China, and Japan ; Captain in 3rd Batt. King's Own Scottish Borderers ; served South African War ; Chairman Municipal Council and of Chamber of Commerce, Shanghai; member Legislative and Executive Councils, Hong-Kong, and Vice-Chairman of the Hong-Kong Chamber of Commerce ; Chairman of Directors of the Hong-Kong and Shanghai Banking Corporation, Hong-Kong

and Whampoa Dock Company, and many other public companies ; first Chairman of the Far Eastern Section of the London Chamber of Commerce ; Member of the London Committee of the Hong-Kong and Shanghai Banking Corporation ; Member of the Royal Company of Archers ; at outbreak of war rejoined his old battalion, and was given command of the 3rd V.B. K.O.S.B., which he relinquished on its disbandment ; Member of County Council of Dumfriesshire ; President of the Dumfriesshire Unionist Association. *Address:* Cowhill Tower, Dumfries. *Clubs:* Carlton ; Scottish Conservative, Edinburgh. (*Died 29 Nov. 1928.*)

KETCHEN, Maj.-Gen. Isaac, R.A. ; 2nd *s.* of Isaac Ketchen, J.P., of Kingillie, Nairn ; *b.* 13 Feb. 1839 ; *m.* 1872, Celia Catherine Caroline (*d.* 1896), *d.* of Col. W. L. Twentyman ; one *d.* Entered army, 1857 ; Maj.-Gen. 1890 ; retired, 1893 ; served Jowaki Expedition, 1876. *Address:* Hotel Rembrandt, Thurloe Place, S.W.7. *Club:* United Service. (*Died 12 Jan. 1920.*)

KETTLE, Thomas Michael ; Irish Bar ; Journalist ; Professor of Economics of Ireland, University College, Dublin ; *b.* 1880 ; *s.* of A. J. Kettle, farmer and a pioneer of the Land Movement, and Margaret, *d.* of Laurence M'Court of St. Margaret's, Co. Dublin ; *m.* 1909, Mary, *d.* of David Sheehy, M.P. *Educ.:* Christian Brothers' School, N. Richmond St. ; Clongowes ; Univ. College, Dublin. M.P. (N.) East Tyrone, 1906-10 ; contributor to various journals and reviews. *Address:* Clonmore, Glasnevin, Dublin. (*Died Sept. 1916.*)

KEY, Ellen ; lives in her own house, built on a little piece of ground, owned by the state, in the country ; *b.* Sundsholm, Province of Smaland, Sweden, 11 Dec. 1849 ; *d.* of Emil Key, and Countess Sophia Posse ; unmarried. *Educ.:* in parents' home. After father's loss of his fortune, commenced, 1880, to teach in Stockholm in the school of a friend; also to lecture at the working-men's institute, 1884 ; had begun in 1870 to write articles ; left the school 1899, and the lectures 1903, and went abroad ; made several lecturing tours and has passed most of the time between 1899-1910 abroad. *Publications:* in English, The Century of the Child ; Love and Marriage ; The Morality of Women ; Love and Ethics ; The Woman Movement ; Rahel Varnhagen ; The Renaissance of Motherhood ; War, Peace, and the Future ; The All Conqueror, 1924 ; biography (in English), Ellen Key, her Life and her Work, a study by Louise Nyström-Hamilton ; in her own and other languages has written about thirty greater or smaller works. *Recreations:* nature, books, music, art. *Address:* Strand, Alvastra, Sweden. (*Died April 1926.*)

KEY, Rev. Sir John Kingsmill Causton, 3rd Bt., *cr.* 1831 ; M.A. ; *b.* at Wandsworth, 22 Aug. 1853 ; *e. s.* of 2nd Bart. and Mary Sophia, *d.* of G. H. Hahn of the Orchard, Wandsworth ; *S.* father 1899 ; *m.* 1891, Emily, 3rd *d.* of William Woodward of Hardwicke Bank, Tewkesbury. *Educ.:* Clifton ; Lincoln Coll., Oxford. B.A. 1877 ; M.A. 1878 ; curate of St. George's, Kidderminster, 1878-81 ; missionary of the Universities Mission to Central Africa, Zanzibar, 1882-1904 ; Rhodesia, 1912-14 ; canon of Zanzibar, 1899 ; Vicar of Moulsford, 1915-21 *Heir:* *b.* K. J. Key. *Address:* Pemba, Southbourne-on-Sea, Hants. (*Died 27 April 1926*)

KEYES, Commander Adrian St. Vincent, R.N., C.B.E., 1919 ; D.S.O. 1915 ; *s.* of late Gen. Sir Charles Keyes, G.C.B., ; *b.* 1882 ; *m.* 1916, Eleanor, *d.* of Lt.-Col. Walter Campbell, The Ivy House, Hampton Court ; one *s.* Served Dardanelles, 1914-18 (despatches, D.S.O.) ; present at landing of Expeditionary Force in Gallipoli ; retired. (*Died 6 Oct. 1926.*)

KEYMER, Rev. Nathaniel, M.A. ; a Canon Missioner in the Diocese of Southwell since 1888 ; a Proctor in Convocation for Diocese of Southwell 1906 - 16 ; *b.* 13 April 1844 ; *e. s.* of Rev. Nathaniel Keymer, Head Master of Christ's Hospital, Hertford ; *m.* 1869, Susan Anne, *d.* of Francis Eugenia Scoble Willesford ; two *s. Educ.:* Christ's Hospital ; Kensington Grammar School ; Pembroke College, Cambridge ; Cuddesdon College. B. A. 1866 ; M.A. 1870 ; Deacon, 1867 ; Priest, 1868 ; Curate of Bingham, Notts, 1867-77 ; First Vicar of Middlestown, Wakefield, 1877 ; Rural Dean of Tuxford, 1884-1902 ; Rector of Headon, 1879-1911. *Publications:* Durham Mission Tune-Book, 1886 ; A Help to Intercession, 1874 ; Instructions on Confirmation, 1890 ; The Holy Eucharist in Type and Shadow, 1897 ; Instructions on the Holy Eucharist, 1918 ; Life in Christ, or What it is to be a Christian, 1918 ; The Anointing of the Sick for Healing, 1920. *Address:* Derby House, Nottingham. *T.:* 1549.

(Died 10 Dec. 1922.)

KEYSER, Arthur Louis ; *s.* of late Alfred Keyser of Cross Oak, Berkhamsted, Herts. *Educ.:* Clifton College ; Steffisburg, Thun, Switzerland. Travelled in Australia, 1882 ; also visited New Zealand and New Guinea on board H.M.S. Nelson when Admiral Sir James Erskine hoisted the British flag in New Guinea ; Secretary to Governor of Fiji, 1884 ; entered service of Malay States, 1888 ; held various posts in Selangor, including that of Ulu Selangor ; subsequently Collector and Magistrate, Jelebu, 1890-97 ; and officer in charge of the Negri Sembilan ; Commissioner on board H.M.S. Æolus to the Keeling Cocos Islands and Christmas Islands, receiving thanks of Secretary of State for his report, 1897 ; in same year received similar thanks for saving life in Jelebu floods ; seconded for service under Foreign Office ; Acting Consul in Borneo-Brunei and Sarawak, 1898 ; Consul, 1899 ; transferred to Foreign Office ; Consul at Berbera, Somali Coast, 1900 ; at Zaila, 1901 ; has Somaliland medal, with clasp ; H.B.M. Consul for provinces of Cadiz, Cordova, Huelva, and Seville, 1903-18 ; Consul-General, 1916-18 ; Consul - General, Ecuador, First Sec. H.M. Legation, Quito, and Chargé d'Affaires during absence of H.M. Minister, 1918 ; retired, 1920. *Publications:* Description of Visit to New Guinea ; also Java ; several novels ; People and Places, a Life on Five Continents, 1922 ; Trifles and Travels, 1928. *Recreations:* won lawn-tennis championship of Australia, 1882 ; of New South Wales, 1884. *Address:* Tangier, Morocco. *Clubs:* White's, Junior Carlton, Ranelagh, Royal Automobile.

(Died 7 Mar. 1924.)

KEYSER, Colonel Frederick Charles, C.B. 1882 : *e. s.* of late Alfred Keyser of Cross Oak, Great Berkhampstead ; *b.* London, 8 April 1841 ; *m.* 1st, 1872, Louisa Frances Marshall (*d.* 1909), *d.* of late Lt.-Gen. George C. Vialls, C.B. ; 2nd, 1909, Mabel Laura, *d.* of late Lt.-Gen. Sir B. L. Gordon, K.C.B. *Educ.:* Totteridge and Neuwied, Germany ; Royal Academy, Gosport. Gazetted Ensign to Royal Fusiliers, 1858 ; commanded 2nd Batt. 1885 ; Inspector of Signalling, Aldershot, 1889 (retired under age clause, 1898) ; Colonel, 1885 ; Afghan War, 1879-80 ; covering of retreat from Maiwand ; defence of Kandahar, and Battle of 1 Sept. (despatches, medal with clasp) ; in command Signallers, Egyptian Expedition, 1862 ; commanded Corps of Signallers. Battles: Kassassin, severely wounded, Tel-el-Kebir (despatches, medal and clasp, Bronze Star, 3rd class Medjidie and C.B.) Commanded 3rd Battalion (now disbanded) Royal Northern Reserve Regt. 1900-1901 ; appointed to Command Home Counties Volunteer Brigade, with rank of Brig.-Gen., 1902. *Recreations:* racing, shooting, yachting. *Address:* 87 Prince of Wales Mansions, Battersea Park, S.W. *Clubs:* United Service, Sports.

(Died 4 April 1920.)

584

KHAIRPUR STATE, H.H. Mir Imam Baksh Khan, Ruler of, G.C.I.E., *cr.* 1911. Population about 130,000. *Address:* Khairpur State, Bombay Presidency. *(Died Feb. 1921.)*

KIBBLEWHITE, Ebenezer Job ; editor of the Weekly Times, 1884-1910, Building News and Engineering Journal, and English Mechanic and World of Science, 1878 - 1922 ; Director, Strand Newspaper Co., Ltd., 1894 - 1922 ; *b.* London, 7 Dec. 1846 ; *e. s.* of Ebenezer Heather Kibblewhite ; *m.* 1st, 1868 ; 2nd, 1873 ; five *s. Educ.:* Royal Asylum of St. Anne's Society ; Sion College. Commenced life as a pupil teacher, then in a solicitor's office, and afterwards became associated with John Passmore Edwards in journalistic work. *Publications:* The Gospel of Humanity ; The Record of Our Race. *Recreations:* gardening, walking. *Address:* 10 Lancaster Place, Strand, W.C. *T.:* Gerrard 1991. *(Died 2 Dec. 1924.)*

KIDD, Benjamin ; author ; *b.* 9 Sept. 1858; *m.* 1887, Maud Emma Isabel, *d.* of late John Perry, of Weston-super-Mare ; three *s.* Occupied with the development of system of social philosophy outlined in his books. Formerly Member of the Inland Revenue Office. Travelled for economic studies, Eastern, Southern, and Western United States, and Canada, 1898 ; South Africa, 1902 ; Special Correspondent of the Times. *Publications:* Social Evolution, 1894 (trans. German, 1895 ; Swedish, 1895 ; French, 1896 ; Russian, 1897 ; Italian, 1898 ; Chinese, 1899 ; Czech, 1900 ; Danish, 1900 ; Arabic, 1913) ; The Control of the Tropics 1898, published in U.S.A., Mr. Joseph Chamberlain spoke of its effect on British colonial policy ; Principles of Western Civilisation, 1902 (trans. Spanish 1903) ; also author of prefatory article on Application of Doctrine of Evolution to Sociological Theory, 10th ed. Ency. Brit. 1902, and of the article Sociology in 11th ed. 1911 ; The Significance of the Future in the Theory of Organic Evolution (two lectures Royal Institution, London, 1906) ; Individualism and After (Herbert Spencer Lecture, University of Oxford, 1908) ; The Two Principal Laws of Sociology, Bologna, 1909 ; articles Civilisation, Darwinism, Ency. Relig. and Ethics, 1910-11. *Clubs:* Athenæum, Savile.

(Died 2 Oct. 1916.)

KIDD, Henry, J.P., D.L. ; *b.* 1862 ; 2nd *s.* of Robert Charles Kidd (*d.* 1866), and Mary Jane, *y. d.* of Rev. George Mason, of Cuckney, Notts ; *m.* 1897, Lady Mary Kerr, *d.* of 9th Marquis of Lothian ; one *d.* one *s.* ; late Capt. Lothian and Berwick Imp. Yeo. 1896-1901 ; Lieut. Imp. Yeo. S. Africa, 1900. *Clubs:* St. James's, Orleans.

(Died 23 June 1923.)

KIDD, James ; M.P. (U.) Linlithgowshire, 1918-22 and since 1924 ; solicitor ; *b.* 11 Mar. 1872 ; *m.* 1899, Jessie, *d.* of Thomas Turnbull. *Educ.:* Carriden Public School ; Edinburgh University. Parliamentary Secretary to the Scottish Board of Health, 1922. *Address:* Muiredge, Carriden, Bo'ness, Scotland. *Clubs:* Constitutional ; Scottish Conservative, Edinburgh. *(Died 2 Mar. 1928.)*

KIDSTON, Robert, LL.D., D.Sc., F.R.S., F.R.S.E., F.G.S., F.R.P.S.E. ; Foreign Member Kaiser. Mineral. Gesell., Petrograd ; Hon. Mem. Soc. Russe de Minéralogie, Petrograd ; Foreign Mem. Soc. Géol. de Belgique ; J.P. Stirlingshire ; *b.* at Bishopton House, Bishopton, Renfrewshire ; *y. s.* of late Robert Alexander Kidston ; *m.* Agnes Marion Christian, *y. d.* of late Major Patrick Oliphant of Over Kinnedar, Fife ; two *d. Educ.:* Stirling High School ; Univ. of Edinburgh. *Publications:* Catalogue of Palæozoic Plants in the Geological Collection of the British Museum ; Végétaux houil. dans le Hainaut-Belge dans les Collections du Musée royal d'Histoire nat. à Bruxelles, 1911 ; and over 100 papers and memoirs on the Carboniferous Flora, published in Transactions of Royal Societies, Edinburgh and London, Geological Society London, Linnean Society, Royal Physical Society, Edinburgh, Geological Soc. of Glasgow, Nat. Hist. Soc. Glasgow, Geol. and Polytechnical Soc. Leeds, Geol. Soc. of Manchester, Yorkshire Nat. Union, Bot. Soc. of Edinburgh, etc. (Murchison Fund, Geol. Soc. London, 1887; Neill medal, Roy. Soc. Edin., 1890; Murchison medal, Geological Society, London, 1916). *Recreations:* gardening, curling, and fishing. *Address:* 12 Clarendon Place, Stirling. *T.:* Stirling 156.

(*Died 13 July 1924.*)

KIDSTON, Hon. William, b. Falkirk, 1849; widower. Emigrated to Australia, 1882; established a bookseller's and stationer's business at Rockhampton; M.L.A. Rockhampton, 1896; Treasurer and Postmaster-General of Queensland, 1899; Treasurer, 1903; Premier, 1908-7, and since 1908. *Address:* Brisbane, Queensland. (*Died 27 Oct. 1919.*)

KIDSTON-KERR, Col. Alex. Ferrier, C.B. 1896; retired; b. 24 Sep. 1840; 6th s. of late Archd. Glen Kidston of Newton House, Newton, Lanarkshire; m. 1873, Jean Howe, d. of late James Howe M'Clure, Solicitor, Glasgow. *Educ.:* Merchiston Castle School, Edinburgh; privately in France. Entered 42nd Royal Highlanders, 1858; Capt., 1873; Maj., 1881; Brevet Lieut.-Col. 1884; Colonel, 1888; served Ashanti War, 1874; Battle of Amoaful; capture and destruction of Becquah; Battle of Ordansu and capture of Coomassie (despatches, medal with clasp); Egyptian Expedition, 1882-84; Battle of Tel-el-Kebir (medal with clasp, bronze star, 4th class Osmanieh); Soudan, 1884; Battle of El Teb (despatches, 2 clasps); Brevet of Lieut.-Col. Soudan Expedition, 1884-85; Nile, action of Kerbekan (2 clasps); has Jubilee Medal; assumed the additional surname of Kerr on succeeding to entailed estate of Gairney, Kinross-shire; J.P., D.L. for Kinross-shire. *Recreations:* hunting, golf, shooting. *Address:* Gairney, Kinross; The Grange, Grange, Edinburgh. *T.A.:* The Grange, Edinburgh. *T.:* Central 6829. *M.:* 3579. *Clubs:* Army and Navy; New, Edinburgh.

(*Died 2 Mar. 1926.*)

KIKUCHI, Baron Dairoku, cr. 1902; Privy Councillor, 1912; President of Imperial Academy, 1st class Order of Sacred Treasure, 2nd class Rising Sun, Rigakuhakushi (D.Sc. Japan); Hon. LL.D. Glasgow, Manchester, and Rutger's; M.A. Camb.; B.A. London; Hon. Professor of Imperial Universities of Tokyo and Kyoto; corresponding member of British Association for the Advancement of Science; b. Yedo (now Tokyo), 17 Mar. 1855; 2nd s. of Dr. Shūhei Mitsukuri (born Kikuchi, adopted into Mitsukuri family); m. Tatsu, d. of H. Fukuda; three s. five d. *Educ.:* Kaiseijo (Yedo); University College School, London; St. John's College, Cambridge. Professor of Mathematics (Tokyo Imp. Univ.), 1877-98; Vice-Minister of Education, 1897-98; President Imperial University, Tokyo, 1898-1901; Minister of Education, 1901-3; President of Peers' School, 1904-5; President, Kyoto Imperial University, 1908-12; Life member of the House of Peers, 1890; resigned, 1912; Member of the Imperial Academy since 1889; President of the Earthquake Investigation Committee. *Publications:* several books on Mathematics, etc.; Education in Japan, in English. *Heir:* Taiji Kikuchi. *Address:* 124 Takehayacho, Koishikawa, Tokyo, Japan.

(*Died 19 Aug. 1917.*)

KILBRIDE, Dennis, M.P. (N.) Kildare, S., 1906-18; tenant farmer; b. 1848; s. of Thomas Kilbride, Lugnacurran, Queen's Co. *Educ.:* Clongowes. M.P. South Kerry, 1887-95; M.P. (N.) Co. Galway, N. 1895-1900; returned for both North Galway and South Kerry, elected

to sit for North Galway. *Address:* Duke Street, Athy, Co. Kildare. (*Died Oct. 1924.*)

KILBURNE, George Goodwin, R.I., painter (figure pictures); b. Norfolk, 24 July 1839; e. s. of late Goodwin Kilburne, Hawkhurst, Kent; m. 1st, 1862, d. of late Robert Dalziel, painter, niece to the Bros. Dalziel, to whom he was apprenticed; three s. two d.; 2nd, 1899, Edith Golightly; two d. *Educ.:* Hawkhurst. On leaving school, five years apprenticed to Dalziel Bros., wood-engravers, London; worked at wood-engraving for one year more, then gave it up for painting; followed the profession of an artist ever since. Takes particular interest in hunting, and in ancient arms and armour, possesses good collection of arms and armour, principally swords. *Recreations:* hunting, cycling, golf. *Address:* Normanton, 16 Albion Road, Swiss Cottage. *Club:* Artists' Society. (*Died 21 June 1924.*)

KILLANIN, 2nd Baron, cr. 1900; **Martin Henry Fitzpatrick Morris;** Bt., cr. 1885; P.C. Ire. 1920; H.M. Lieutenant and Custos Rotulorum, Co. Galway; J.P. Co. Cavan; Hon. LL.D. Royal University of Ireland; Knight of Grace of the Grand Priory of St. John of Jerusalem; a Commissioner of National Education in Ireland; Governor, University College, Galway; a Director of the Bank of Ireland and Barrister, Lincoln's Inn; b. 22 July 1867; e. s. of Rt. Hon. Michael Baron Morris and 1st Baron Killanin, P.C., and Anna, d. of Hon. H. G. Hughes, a Baron of Court of Exchequer, Ireland; S. father, 1901. *Educ.:* Trinity College, Dublin (B.A.), essay gold medallist of Univ. Philosophical Society. Circuit Registrar and Private Sec. to his father, when Lord Chief Justice of Ireland, 1887-89; High Sheriff Galway, 1897; Senator, Royal Univ. of Ireland, 1904-9; Member of Irish Agricultural Wages Board. 1917-19; C.C. for Spiddal Division of Co. Galway; 1899-1920; contested Borough of Galway, 1895; M.P. (C.) 1900-1; served on Select Committee, House of Lords, on Chantrey Trust, 1904; Chairman of Viceregal Commission on Primary Education (Ireland), 1918-19. *Heir:* n. Michael Morris, b. 30 July 1914. *Publications:* an essay on Spiritual Realism, 1892; Transatlantic Traits, 1897; and contributions to the Nineteenth Century and other magazines. *Address:* Galvia, Lee on the Solent, Hampshire; Spiddal House, Co. Galway. *Clubs:* Athenæum; County, Galway. (*Died 11 Aug. 1927.*)

KILNER, Group-Captain Cecil Francis, D.S.O. 1915; R.A.F.; b. 8 Oct. 1883; s. of late W. A. Kilner, Kemsing, Kent. Entered R.M.L.I. 1902; Captain, 1913; served European War, 1914-18 (despatches, D.S.O. and bar); promoted Wing-Comdr. 1918; Group-Captain, 1924.

(*Died 20 Oct. 1925.*)

KILNER, Right Rev. Francis Charles, D.D.; Suffragan Bishop of Richmond since 1913; Hon. Canon of Ripon and Rector of Stanhope, Co. Durham. *Educ.:* Rugby School, Keble College, Oxford; Cuddesdon College. Ordained 1874, Curate of Christ Church, Bootle. 1874-79; Missioner, Diocese of Winchester, 1879-81; Vicar of Bingley, Yorks, 1892-1906; Rural Dean of South Craven, 1892-1906; Warden, Diocesan Home for Women Workers, 1900-6; Archdeacon of Craven, 1896-1913; Vicar of Gargrave, 1906-13. *Address:* The Rectory, Stanhope, Co. Durham.

(*Died 19 Mar. 1921.*)

KILVERT, Sir Harry Vernon, Kt., cr. 1921; J.P.; b. 28 June 1862; s. of late Nicholas Kilvert, The Lodge, Ashton-upon-Mersey, Cheshire; m. 1889 Annie Gertrude, d. of Henry S. Pemberton. *Address:* The Lodge, Ashton Lane, Ashton, Cheshire. (*Died 12 Mar. 1924.*)

KIM, Tan Jiak, C.M.G., 1911; unofficial member Legislative Council, Straits Settlements. *Address:* Singapore. (*Died 23 Oct. 1917.*)

KIMBER, Sir Henry, 1st Bt., *cr.* 1904; M.P. (C.) Wandsworth (1st member) 1885-1913; Vice-Chairman of Capital and Counties Bank; Chairman of South Indian Ry. Co.; founder or reconstructor of several colonial and other undertakings; *b.* 13 July 1834; *s.* of Joseph Kimber of Canonbury; *m.* Mary Adelaide (*d.* 1901), *d.* of late Gen. Chas. Dixon, R.E., 1861; four *s.* two *d. Educ.:* private schools; tutors; University College, London. First Prizeman of Incorporated Law Society, 1858, and Second in Law at Univ. Coll., London. Solicitor, 1858; founded firm of Kimber and Ellis, now Kimbers, Williams and Co.; retired in favour of his sons, 1890; favourite work to rescue and reform commercial enterprise; is one of the founders of New Rugby, Tenn., U.S.A.; six times contested Wandsworth, eight times elected, twice unopposed. *Recreations:* parliamentary and business; travelling, globe-trotting. *Heir: s.* Henry D. *Address:* Lansdowne Lodge, East Putney, S.W.15; Albany Chambers, Petty France, Westminster, S.W.1; 79 Lombard Street, E.C. *T.:* Putney 154, Victoria 484. *Clubs:* Carlton, City Carlton (of which he is a founder), St. Stephen's, Ranelagh, Royal Automobile. (*Died 18 Dec. 1923.*)

KINCH, Prof. Edward, F.I.C.; Professor of Chemistry, Royal Agricultural Coll., Cirencester, 1881-1915; *b.* 19 Aug. 1848; 3rd *s.* of Charles Kinch; *m.* 1889, Edith (*died*), 3rd *d.* of Rev. George Huntington. *Educ.:* Grammar School, Henley-on-Thames; Royal College of Chemistry, Oxford Street, W. Chief Assistant to Professor of Chemistry, R.A. College, 1869-73; on Teaching Staff, Royal College of Chemistry and Royal School of Mines, South Kensington, 1873-75; Superintendent of Minerals, India Museum, London, 1875-76; Prof. of Chemistry, Imperial College of Agriculture, Tokio, Japan, 1876-81. *Publications:* Papers in Transactions of the Asiatic Society of Japan, Journal of the Chemical Society, Mineralogical Magazine, Journal of the Royal Agricultural Society, Transactions of the Surveyors' Institution, Agricultural Students' Gazette, etc. *Recreations:* rowing, gardening. *Address:* Konbaba, Haslemere, Surrey. *Clubs:* Savile, Farmers'. (*Died 6 Aug. 1920.*)

KING, Alfred John, B.Sc.; *b.* 14 Feb. 1859; 2nd *s.* of late Alderman J. King, formerly Mayor of Manchester; *m.* 1888, Julia Constance, *d.* of late Thomas Oliver of Bollington; two *s.* one *d. Educ.:* Oliver's Mount School, Scarborough; Owens College. Bleacher and finisher; Chairman, Bollington District Council, 1896-1906; member, Society of Friends; M.P. (L.) Knutsford Div. of Cheshire, 1906-10. *Address:* Elleray, Windermere. *T.:* Windermere 174. *Clubs:* Devonshire; Reform, Clarendon, Manchester. (*Died 16 Mar. 1920.*)

KING, Arthur Thomas, I.S.O. 1903; Chief Clerk, National Debt Office; retired, 1910; *b.* 1845. *Address:* The Summit, Stevenage, Herts. (*Died 26 Mar. 1922.*)

KING, Sir Charles Albert, Kt., *cr.* 1912; C.B. 1907; Comptroller and Accountant-General of Post Office, 1901-19; *b.* 1853; *s.* of late Rev. W. King of Fordham, Essex. *Address:* 46 The Avenue, Beckenham. *T.:* Bromley 444. (*Died 1 Feb. 1922.*)

KING, Charles Macintosh, Convener of County of Stirling; Chairman of Stirlingshire Territorial Force Association; Joint Convener of the Smaller Livings Committee of the Church of Scotland; D.L., J.P.; *b.* 1836; *s.* of John King of Campsie; *m.* 1867, Jane Margaret, *d.* of Dr. Andrew Buchanan, Professor of the Institutes of Medicine in Glasgow University; two *s.* three *d. Educ.:* Glasgow High School and University. Hon. Colonel 4th Vol. Batt. Argyll and Sutherland Highlanders; Chairman of Campsie Parish School Board for forty-three years, etc. *Recreations:* walking, shooting. *Address:* Antermony House, Milton of Campsie. *Clubs:* County, Stirling; Western, Glasgow; Conservative, Edinburgh. (*Died 11 Feb. 1920.*)

KING, Sir Charles Simeon, 3rd Bt., *cr.* 1821; *b.* 8 Dec. 1840; *S.* father 1874; *m.* Sophia Louisa, *d.* and heir of late R. S. Bolton-Davis, Swerford Park, Oxon. 1891. A writer on religious and political subjects. Edited (1892) Henry's (Rev. William, F.R.S.) Upper Lough Erne in 1789; and A Great Archbishop of Dublin, William King, D.D. (1650-1729), 1906. *Heir:* none. *Address:* The Highlands House, St. Leonards-on-Sea. (*Died 3 April 1921.*)

KING, George, Director and one of the founders of The Sphere and The Tatler; Chairman of Technical Journals, Ltd., proprietors of The Architect's Journal and The Architectural Review; *m.* Sister Janet (*d.* 1911), Royal Red Cross, *d.* of Benjamin Wells, A.R.A.M.; two *d.* Winner of the £500 Prize Competition given by Tit-Bits for best scheme of National Old Age Pensions. *Recreations:* golf and fishing. *Address:* Vardin, Purley. *Clubs:* Devonshire, Constitutional. (*Died 12 July 1922.*)

KING, Sir George Anthony, Kt., *cr.* 1924; Chief Master Supreme Court Taxing Office since 1921; *b.* 23 Oct. 1858; *o. s.* of George Farquharson King, Solicitor; *m.* 1888, Mabel, *y. d.* of Rev. Henry Ralph Blackett; one *s. Educ.:* Winchester; Corpus Christi College, Oxford. B.A. 1881; 2nd class Jurisprudence; M.A. 1884; Solicitor, 1885; Master of the Supreme Court, 1902-21; London Diocesan Reader, 1896; Member of the House of Laymen, 1906, and of the National Assembly; Treasurer Pan-Anglican Congress, 1908; Vice-President B. and F.B.S. and C.M.S.; Treasurer, C.E.M.S. and R.T.S., and of National Mission of Repentance and Hope, 1916. *Publications:* In Our Tongues, 1900; Costs on the High Court Scale, 1910; joint-editor of the Annual Practice. *Address:* Penn Road House, Croydon. *T.:* Croydon 574. *Club:* National. (*Died 17 Jan. 1928.*)

KING, George Kemp, M.V.O. 1911; Acting Principal, Territorial and Volunteer Forces Directorate, War Office, since 1917; Assistant Principal, Territorial Directorate, 1913-17; *b.* 25 March 1880; *s. s.* of George King, Eltham, Kent; *m.* 1917, Mary Lilian Wenonah, *e. d.* of Robert N. Helme, Netherleigh, Lancaster; one *s. Educ.:* Christ's Hospital; St. John's College, Cambridge (Foundation Scholar). Bracketed 13th Wrangler, 1902; 1st Class, Natural Sciences Tripos, Part I., 1903; B.A., 1902; Clerk of the Higher Division, War Office, 1903; Editor, War Office List, 1905-6; Resident Clerk, 1906-13; Private Secretary to Sir Edward Ward, Permanent Under-Secretary of State for War, 1908-1912; acted as Private Secretary to Mr. (now Viscount) Haldane, when Secretary of State for War, April to Aug. 1908; Private Secretary to Col. Seely, Secretary of State for War, 1912-1913. *Address:* 1 K. Montagu Mansions, Portman Square, W.1. (*Died 5 Aug. 1920.*)

KING, Sir Gilbert, 4th Bt., *cr.* 1815; country gentleman; *b.* 30 May 1846; *e. s.* of 3rd Bt.; *m.* 1st, Charlotte, *d.* of Robert Heard, Pallastown, Co. Cork, 1888 (*d.* 1892); one *d.*; 2nd, Louisa, *d.* of late Lieut.-Colonel Henry Baker Sweet, 1897; *S.* father 1895. *Educ.:* Blackheath Proprietary School; Trinity Coll. Dublin (M.A.). High Sheriff, Co. Roscommon, 1892; Co. Leitrim, 1894 and 1904; Co. Sligo, 1909. *Heir: c.* George Adolphus, *b.* 8 Sep. 1864. *Address:* Charlestown, Drumsna, Ireland. (*Died 9 July 1920.*)

KING, Mrs. Harriet Eleanor Baillie Hamilton; *d.* of Admiral W. A. and Lady Harriet Baillie Hamilton; *m.* Henry Samuel King, J.P., of Manor House, Chigwell, Essex (*d.*

1878); seven c. ; Roman Catholic. *Publications:* Aspromonte, and other Poems ; The Disciples ; A Book of Dreams ; Ballads of the North, and other Poems ; The Prophecy of Westminster ; The Foreshadowing of a Saint ; The Hours of the Passion ; Letters and Recollections of Mazzini. *Address:* 1 Woburn Square, W.C.

(Died 10 May 1920.)

KING, Sir Henry Clark, Kt., *cr.* 1906 ; Solicitor and Notary Public and Commissioner, High Court, Madras ; *b.* 20 June 1857 ; *s.* of Rev. C. W. King, H.M.'s Inspector of Schools, and Mary Anne King, *d.* of Rev. Canon Douglas of Durham ; *m.* Ethel, *e. d.* of G. Alderson Smith of Wheatcroft, Scarborough ; one *s.* two *d. Educ.:* Durham ; Marlborough. Articled to A. S. Field of Leamington in 1875, and went to India in 1880 as assistant to Tasker and Wilson ; afterwards senior partner in the firm of King and Josselyn, Madras ; was one of the three secretaries appointed by the Presidency of Madras in connection with the reception of T.R.H. the Prince and Princess of Wales at Madras, 1906.. *Recreations:* Marlborough College XI. 1874-75 ; Marlborough College XX. 1874 : for many years played for the Madras Presidency XI. *Address:* 26 First Avenue, Hove. *T.:* 8888. *Clubs:* Durham County ; Madras. *(Died 23 July 1920.)*

KING, Rev. Henry Hugh ; Rector of Falmouth since 1912 ; *b.* 1869 ; *y. s.* of Ridley King, Architect, Ipswich and Leeds, and Eliza, *d.* of James Fenton, C.E., Low Moor, Bradford ; *m.* Enid Mary, *d.* of Edward Anketell - Jones, of Ettrick, Victoria ; two *d. Educ.:* Royal Masonic School ; Felsted ; private tutors ; Trinity College, Dublin. Crammed for Indian Civil Service ; invalided by football accident ; read for Holy Orders at Truro, Scholae Cancellarii ; ordained 1895 ; remained in diocese ever since ; held curacies at Hessenford and Penzance ; Chaplain for 3 years to Lord St. Levan ; Vicar of Marazion for 7 years ; Rural Dean of Penwith, 3 years ; Chaplain at Santa Cruz, Teneriffe ; Vicar of Bodmin, Cornwall, to 1912 ; Hon. Canon of Truro Cathedral ; P.G.C. Cornwall, 1912. *Recreations:* reading, illuminating, and gardening. *Address:* The Rectory, Falmouth. *(Died 17 Aug. 1918.)*

KING, John Charles, I.S.O. 1911 ; late Assistant Colonial Secretary of Gibraltar ; *b.* 20 May 1847 ; *s.* of David King, Perth, N.B. ; *m.* Louise, *d.* of late J. Gregory (mossi, Gibraltar ; one *s.* one *d. Educ.:* under private tuition abroad. Appointed to Gibraltar Civil Service, 1866 ; Official Trustee, 1913. *Address:* Prince Edward's Road, Gibraltar. *(Died 24 Mar. 1918.)*

KING, Leonard William, M.A., Litt.D., F.S.A. ; Assistant Keeper of Egyptian and Assyrian Antiquities, British Museum, since 1913 ; Professor of Assyrian and Babylonian Archaeology in the University of London, King's College, since 1915 ; *b.* London, 8 Dec. 1869 ; 5th *s.* of Robert King (*d.* 1886) and Mary, *o. d.* of late John Henry Scarborough ; *m.* 1906, Anna, 3rd *d.* of late Henry Anthony Burke of Tully, Co. Galway ; one *s.* one *d. Educ.:* Rugby ; King's College, Cambridge. Excavated at Kouyunjik (Nineveh) for the British Museum, 1903-4 ; collected rock-inscriptions in Assyria, Persia, and Kurdistan, 1901,1903-4 ; F.R.G.S.1905; Lecturer in Assyrian, King's College, London, 1910-15. *Publications:* Babylonian Magic and Sorcery, 1896 ; Cuneiform Texts in the British Museum, 1896-1914 ; Assyrian Chrestomathy, 1898 ; Letters of Hammurabi, 1898-1900 ; Babylonian Religion and Mythology, 1899, and Assyrian Language, 1901 (Books on Egypt and Chaldaea, vols. iv. and v.) ; Annals of the Kings of Assyria, 1902, and Guide to the Babylonian and Assyrian Antiquities in the British Museum, 1900, 2nd ed. 1908 (with Dr. Wallis Budge) ; Seven Tablets of Creation, 1902 ; Sculptures and Inscription

of Darius at Behistûn (with R. C. Thompson, M.A.), 1907 ; Egypt and Western Asia, Amer. ed. 1906, Eng. ed. 1907 (with H. R. Hall, M.A.) ; Studies in Eastern History 1904-7 ; History of Sumer and Akkad, 1910 ; Boundary-Stones in the British Museum, 1912 ; Catalogue of the Kouyunjik Collection in the Brit. Mus. (Supplement), 1914 ; Gates of Shalmaneser ; History of Babylon ; has also contributed to Dic. of Nat. Biog. ; Encycl. Bibl. ; Encycl. Brit. etc. *Address:* 29 St. Edmund's Terrace, Regent's Park, N.W. ; British Museum, W.C.

(Died 20 Aug. 1919.)

KING, Sir Lucas White, Kt., *cr.* 1919 ; C.S.I. 1898 ; LL.D., F.S.A. ; *b.* 28 Sep. 1856 ; *e. s.* of late Dep. Surg.-Gen. Henry King, Principal, Medical School, Madras ; *m.* 1891, Geraldine, *e. d.* of late Alfred Harmsworth, barrister-at-law, Middle Temple, and Mrs. Harmsworth, of Poynter's Hall, Herts ; one *s.* three *d. Educ.:* Ennis College and Dublin University. Exhibitioner and Honourman, Trinity Coll., Dublin, where he took the degrees of B.A. and LL.B. (1878), and LL.D. (1896). Entered Indian Civil Service 1878, and has since held, among others, the following appointments : Assist. Resident, Mysore, 1887 ; First Assistant to the A.G.G., Central India, 1888 ; Deputy Comr. Derah Ismail Khan, 1890-95 ; Political officer, Zhob Valley Field Force, 1890 ; Political officer, Waziristan Field Force, 1894 (despatches, medal and clasp) ; Boundary officer Indo-Afghan Demarcation Commission, 1895 ; Deputy Comr. Peshawar, 1895 ; Deputy Comr. Kohat, 1897-1900 ; Political officer Kohat-Kurram Field Force, and subsequently of the Tirah Expeditionary Force, 1897-98 (despatches, medal with three clasps, C.S.I.) ; Deputy Commissioner Kangra ; Commissioner Lahore ; Salt Revenue, Northern India ; Multan ; Rawal Pindi ; Coronation (Durbar) medal, 1902 ; resigned I.C.S., 1905 ; Professor of Oriental Languages, Dublin University, 1905-22 : J.P. Co. Dublin, 1906-22. *Publications:* Memoirs of Babur ; Sa'di's Odes ; Life of Tamerlane ; Brochures on Oriental Numismatics, and Monograph on the Orakzai Country and Clans. *Recreations:* shooting, archæology, Persian literature, and first editions ; member of the following societies : Antiquaries of London, Antiquaries of Ireland, Royal Asiatic, First Edition. *Address:* Craig Veigh, Aboyne, Aberdeenshire ; 20 Abercorn Place, N.W.S. *Club:* Junior Carlton. *(Died 23 Aug. 1925.)*

KING, Thomas Mulhall, I.S.O. 1908 ; *b.* 4 Aug. 1842 ; 2nd *s.* of late Alexander King, Melbourne ; *m.* 1st, 1866, Jane Maria, *e. d.* of late Captain Robert Harkness MacDonnell, 56th Regt. and Royal Dublin Fusiliers, afterwards Chief Clerk in Insolvency, Melbourne ; three *s.* six *d.* ; 2nd, Anniella Victoria, *d.* of late George Zichy-Woinarski. *Educ.:* Melbourne. Entered Customs Service as Clerk, 1863 ; Collector of Customs (head of Dept.), 1882 ; in conjunction with this appointed Chief Inspector of Distilleries and Excise, 1888 ; Member Immigration Board, 1884 ; Under-Secretary Treasury, 1893 ; Auditor-General, 1901 ; Deputy Railway Commissioner, Queensland, 1907-11 ; Commissioner, 1911. *Recreations:* none in particular. *Address:* Kilmorna, Coorparoo ; Brisbane, Queensland.

KING, William Benjamin Basil; writer ; *b.* Charlottetown, Prince Edward Island, Canada, 26 Feb. 1859 ; *s.* of William King, originally of Bucks, England ; *m.* Esther Manton Foote, Boston, U.S.A. *Educ.:* St. Peter's School, Charlottetown ; King's College, Windsor, Nova Scotia. *Publications:* Let Not Man Put Asunder ; In the Garden of Charity ; The Steps of Honour ; The Giant's Strength ; The Inner Shrine ; The Wild Olive ; The Street Called Straight ; The Way Home ; The Letter of the Contract ; The Side of the Angels ; The Lifted Veil ; The High Heart ; The City of

587

Comrades; The Thread of Flame; The Empty Sack; The Dust Flower; The Conquest of Fear; The Happy Isles; Faith and Success; The High Forfeit; The Spreading Dawn, 1927. *Address*: 1 Berkeley Street, Cambridge, Mass., U.S.A. *T.A.:* Basilking, Boston.
(*Died 22 June 1928.*)

KING, William Frederick, C.M.G., 1908; LL.D. 1904; Chief Astronomer of the Department of the Interior of Canada since 1890; Member of Board of Examiners for Dominion Land Surveyors, since 1885; *b.* Stowmarket, Suffolk, 19 Feb. 1854; *s.* of William King and Ellen Archer; *m.* 1881, Augusta Florence, *d.* of John Allen Snow, of Ottawa; two *s.* one *d. Educ.:* Grammar School, Port Hope, Ontario; Univ. of Toronto. B.A. 1875, Gold Medallist in Mathematics; Dominion Land and Topographical Surveyor, 1876; Inspector of Surveys, Department of the Interior, 1881; Chief Inspector, 1886; H.M. Commiss. for the International Boundary between Canada and the United States under Treaties of 1892, 1903, 1906, and 1908; also under Agreements, entered into in 1899, 1901, and 1906; Member of International Waterways Commission, 1904-7; Director of Dominion Astronomical Observatory from its opening in 1905; Fellow (and Hon. President since 1906) of the Royal Astronomical Society of Canada; Fellow of the Royal Society of Canada, and President, 1911-12; Fellow of the American Association for the Advancement of Science; Superintendent of the Geodetic Survey of Canada, 1909. *Publications:* Various scientific papers. *Address:* Observatory House, Ottawa. *Club:* Rideau, Ottawa. (*Died 23 April 1916.*)

KING, Yeend, R.I.; Vice-President R.I.; *b.* London, 21 Aug. 1855; *o. s.* of Henry King; *m.* 1881, Edith Lilian, 4th *d.* of T. L. Atkinson, mezzotint engraver; one *d. Educ.:* Temple Choir School; Philological School. Apprenticed to Messrs. O'Connors, glass painters, Berners Street, London; left after three years; first studied painting under William Bromley, R.B.A., afterwards in Paris under Bonnat and Cormon; on returning made specialty of landscape with figure; an exhibitor in R.A. since 1876. *Pictures:* From Green to Gold, bought for permanent collection, Liverpool; The Lass that Loves a Sailor; Sweet September; The Miller's Daughter; Hay in September, R.A., 1896; The Garden by the River, purchased by Council of R.A. as trustees for the Permanent Collection, New South Wales, 1897; Milking Time, also purchased by the Council of R.A. under terms of Chantrey Bequest, 1898. *Medals:* Paris, Berlin, Chicago. *Recreation:* gardening. *Address:* 219 Maida Vale, W. *Clubs:* Arts, Savage, Wigwam, St. John's Wood Arts. (*Died 10 June 1924.*)

KING-HARMAN, Col. Wentworth Henry, J.P., D.L.; *b.* 27 Mar. 1840; 2nd *s.* of late Hon. L. H. King-Harman and *d.* of late J. R. Johnstone of Alva, N.B.; *m.* 1863, Annie Kate, *d.* of D. J. Smith, of Kingston, Canada; one *s.* three *d. Educ.:* Cheltenham; Royal Military Academy, Woolwich. Late R.A. Entered Army, 1856; Captain, 1867; Major, 1875; Lieut.-Col. 1882; Colonel, 1886; late Chief Government Inspector of Small Arms. *Address:* Newcastle, Ballymahon.
(*Died 1 April 1919.*)

KING-WOOD, William, C.I.E. 1909; C.B.E. 1919; Director Persian Section, Indo-European Telegraph Department; *b.* 1 May 1867; *m.* 1904, Daisy Grace, *o. d.* of Sir Hugh Adcock; three *s.* one *d. Educ.:* Dollar Academy, N.B. Served in South Africa, 1899-1901 (medal, 3 clasps, despatches). *Recreations:* tennis, shooting, fishing, *Address:* Tehran, Persia. *Club:* Junior Naval and Military. (*Died 27 Jan. 1921.*)

KINGSFORD, Charles Lethbridge, M.A., F.B.A.; *b.* Ludlow, 25 Dec. 1862; 3rd *s.* of late Rev. Sampson Kingsford, formerly Fellow of St. John's College, Cambridge, and Vicar of St. Hilary, Cornwall; and Helen, *d.* of William Lethbridge of Kilworthy, Tavistock; *m.* Alys, *d.* of late C. T. Hudson, LL.D., F.R.S. *Educ.:* Rossall; St. John's College, Oxford (Scholar). 2nd Moderations, 1st, Lit. Hum.; 2nd, Modern History; Arnold Essay, 1888; on editorial staff of Dictionary of National Biography, 1889; Examiner Education Department, 1890; Assistant Secretary, 1905-12; Private Secretary to Sir A. Boscawen, Ministry of Pensions, 1917-18; Vice-President of Society of Antiquaries, 1920-23; Ford Lecturer in English History at Oxford, 1923-24; Fellow of the British Academy, 1924; Vice-President of the Royal Historical Society and the London Topographical Society. *Publications:* Song of Lewes, 1890; The Crusades (with late T. A. Archer), 1894; Henry V. (Heroes of the Nations), 1902; Chronicles of London, 1905; Stow's Survey of London with Introduction and Notes, 1908; Sir Otho de Grandison (Transactions of Royal Historical Society, 1909); J. Pecham, De Paupertate (with A. G. Little and F. Tocco), 1910; The First English Life of Henry V., 1911; English Historical Literature in the Fifteenth Century, 1913; The Grey Friars of London, 1915; The Story of the Middlesex Regiment, 1916; Stonor Letters (Camden 3rd Series), 1919; The Story of the Royal Warwickshire Regiment, 1921; Prejudice and Promise in Fifteenth-Century England (Ford Lectures), 1925; Calendar of MSS. of Lord De L'Isle and Dudley, vol. i. (Royal Commission on Historical MSS.), 1925; The Early History of Piccadilly, Leicester Square, and Soho, 1925; numerous articles in Dictionary of National Biography; contributions to English Historical Review, Encyclopædia Britannica, 11th ed., Camden Miscellany, vols. xii. and xiii.; Archæologia, London Topographical Record, Cambridge Mediæval History. *Address:* 15 Argyll Road, Kensington, W.8. *T.:* Park 4117. *Club:* United University. (*Died 27 Mar. 1926.*)

KINGTON-BLAIR-OLIPHANT, Lieut.-Colonel Philip Lawrence, D.S.O. 1916; Capt. Reserve of Officers; Temp. Lt.-Col. commanding 11th R. Irish Rifles since Aug. 1916; *b.* 1867; *o. s.* of Philip Oliphant Kington-Blair-Oliphant of Ardblair, Perthshire; *m.* 1901, Laura Geraldine Bodenham, 2nd *d.* of Frederick Bodenham, Hereford; three *s.* one *d. Educ.:* Harrow. Gazetted 2nd Lieut. Rifle Brigade, 1888; Capt. 1895; retired (Reserve of Officers), 1903; in 1914 joined the Ulster Volunteer Force, and was serving with that force at the outbreak of the War; on the formation of the Ulster Division he was appointed second in Command of the 11th Batt. Royal Irish Rifles (D.S.O. for action in Battle of the Somme, despatches twice). *Publications:* several novels, under the name of Philip Lawrence Oliphant, among them The Little Red Fish, Maya, and The Tramp. *Address:* Ardblair Castle, Blairgowrie, Perthshire. *Club:* Authors'.
(*Died 8 April 1918.*)

KINKEAD, Richard John, A.B.; M.D. Dublin; L.R.C.S.I.; J.P. Co. Galway; Professor Obstetrics and Lecturer in Medical Jurisprudence and Hygiene, Univ. Coll. Galway; Physician and Gynæcologist, late The Galway Hospital; Surgeon H.M. Prison, Galway; *b.* Ballina, Co. Mayo; *s.* of Rev. Francis Kinkead and Elizabeth, *d.* of Robert Croften, J.P., Croften Park, Ballina; *m.* 1st, Alice, *d.* of Thos. S. Langley; 2nd, Emily, *widow* of Col. Poulett Somerset, C.B., M.P., and *d.* of John Hubert Moore; four *d. Educ.:* Rossall Coll.; Arlington House, Portarlington; Royal Coll. of Surgeons, Ireland, and Univ. of Dublin. Silver medals, Medicine and

Surgery; practised in Tuam, 1865-77; Hon. Secretary Tuam Diocesan Synod; Professor, 1876; Ex-Member Governing Body, Univ. Coll., Galway; Examiner National University, Ireland, and of late Queen's University in Ireland; Past President Irish Medical Association; Fellow Royal Acad. of Medicine, Ireland; Provincial Grand Master South Connaught; Member Representative Church Body. *Publications:* Financial Scheme and Supplemental Scheme, Diocese of Tuam; numerous contributions to medical and other journals; Our Homes; The Irish Medical Practitioner's Guide; Insanity, Inebriety, and Crime; Our Senses and How they Serve us; The Use and Abuse of Alcohol. *Recreations:* none. *Address:* University College, and Forster House, Galway. *T.A..* Kinkead, Galway. *T.:* 3 Galway. *Club:* Galway County. *(Died 18 Mar. 1928.)*

KINLOCH, Major-General Alexander Angus Airlie, C.B. 1893; D.L., J.P.; retired pay; *b.* Sidmouth, 27 December 1838; *e. s.* of late Colonel John Grant Kinloch of Logie and Kilrie, and *Agnes, d.* of F. Garden Campbell of Troup and Glenlyon; *m.* 1867, Constance Emma Mary (*d.* 1916), *d.* of late Fred. Beckford Long; five *s.* one *d.* *Educ.:* Royal Military Academy, Woolwich. Entered Rifle Brigade, 1855; exchanged to King's Royal Rifle Corps, 1871; D.A.A.G. for musketry, India, 1870-1877; D.A.Q.M.G. throughout Afghan war, and afterwards in India; mentioned in despatches; Brevets of Major and Lieutenant-Colonel; medal and 2 clasps; commanded 2nd and 4th Batt. K.R.R., and afterwards three 2nd class districts in India, and 1st Brigade Chitral Relief Force (medal and clasp); retired under age clause, 1895, with honorary rank of Major-General in recognition of services in the Army. *Decorated* for service in the field. *Publications:* Large Game Shooting in Thibet, the Himalayas, Northern and Central India. Owns about 2000 acres. *Recreations:* shooting, fishing, and hawking. *Address:* Logie, Kirriemuir, N.B.
(Died 17 Jan. 1919.)

KINNAIRD, 11th Baron (cr. 1682), Arthur FitzGerald Kinnaird, K.T. 1914; F.R.G.S., D.L., J.P.; Lord High Commissioner to the Church of Scotland 1907, 1908, and 1909; Baron Kinnaird of Rossie (U.K.), 1860; Hon. Col. of late Tay Division R.E. (Vol.) Submarine Miners from 1893; President Football Association; Director of Barclay's Bank, Limited, bankers; President, Y.M.C.A.; *b.* 16 February 1847; *s.* of 10th Baron and Mary, *d.* of W. H. Hoare, The Grove, Mitcham, Surrey; *S.* father 1887; *m.* Mary Alma, *d.* of Sir Andrew Agnew, 8th Bt., 1875; two *s.* one *d.* *Educ.:* Eton; Trin. Coll. Camb. (M.A.). Owns about 11,900 acres. *Heir: s.* Master of Kinnaird. *Address:* 10 St. James's Square, S.W.1; *T.:* Regent 685; Rossie Priory, Inchture, Perthshire. *Clubs:* Athenæum; New, Edinburgh.
(Died 30 Jan. 1923.)

KINNEAR, 1st Baron (cr. 1897), Alexander Smith Kinnear; P.C. 1911; Judge of the Court of Session, Scotland, 1882-1913; *b.* Edinburgh, 3 Nov. 1833; *s.* of John Kinnear and Mary, *d.* of Alexander Smith, banker, Edinburgh. *Educ.:* Glasgow and Edinburgh Universities. Bar. Scotland, 1856; Q.C. 1881; Dean of Faculty of Advocates, 1881. *Heir:* none. *Address:* 2 Moray Place, Edinburgh. *Clubs:* Athenæum, Brooks's. (*Died 20 Dec. 1917.*)

KINNEAR, John Boyd, of Kinloch (late of Kinnear); landowner; *b.* 1828; *e. s.* of C. Kinnear of Kinloch, and Christian Boyd Greenshields; *m.* 1st, 1852, Sarah Harriet, *o. d.* of G. Frith (*d.* 1866); 2nd, 1868, Teresa, 4th *d.* of Clemente Bassano of Venice. *Educ.:* Home; Universities of St. Andrews and Edinburgh. Called to Scottish Bar, 1850; Political Secretary to Lord Advocate, 1852-56; called to English

Bar, 1856; leader-writer on Daily News, Morning Star, London Review, and Pall Mall Gazette, 1860-70; served as volunteer in Italian war of 1866; owing to bad health lived in island of Guernsey, 1870-84; M.P. (R.U.) E. Div. of Fife, 1885-86; 1882-1905 farmed about 600 acres of his own land, applying the latest knowledge of chemistry and physiology with successful results, and giving to his workpeople an interest in the form of profit-sharing. He has no special recreations apart from the subjects above indicated. *Publications:* besides several law books, Principles of Reform, Political and Legal, 1864; Principles of Property in Land, 1880; Principles of Civil Government, 1887; Foundations of Religion, 1905; Teaching of the Lord, 1906; articles—Land in Encyclopædia Britannica, 9th ed., and Chambers's Cyclopædia; articles on Farming Tenure and Game Laws in Dictionary of Political Economy; and several pamphlets on Corn-Laws, the Eastern and Irish questions, Laws affecting women, etc. Owns about 900 acres. *Address:* Kinloch, Collessie, Fife. *(Died 10 Nov. 1920.)*

KINNOULL, 12th Earl of (cr. 1633), Archibald Fitzroy George Hay, D.L., J.P.; Viscount Dupplin and Lord Hay, 1627, 1633, 1697; Baron Hay (Great Brit.) 1711; Lieut. 1st Batt. Black Watch, retired; *b.* London, 20 June 1855; *s.* of 11th Earl and Emily, *d.* of 7th Duke of Beaufort; *S.* father 1897; *m.* 1st, 1879, Josephine Maria (*d.* 1900), *d.* of John Hawke, solicitor, London; 2nd, 1903, Florence Mary, *y. d.* of late Edward Darell; two *d.* Formerly Colonel of Egyptian Gendarmerie; served with staff of Baker Pasha in Egypt. *Heir: g.s.* Lord Hay of Kinfauns. *Recreations:* shooting, fishing, all games, music, etc. *Address:* 74 Eaton Place, S.W.; Balhousie Castle, Perth. *T.:* 4575 Kensington. *M.:* LN 6033. *Clubs:* Carlton, Orleans. *(Died 7 Feb. 1916.)*

KINO, Major Algernon Roderick, D.S.O. 1915; late East Yorkshire Regt.; *b.* 17 June 1880; *m.* 1907, Alice Elsie, *d.* of H. G. Beard. Entered army, 1900; Captain, 1910; Major, 1915; served European War, 1914-18 (despatches, D.S.O.). *(Died 10 Feb. 1924.)*

KIPPEN, William James, J.P., D.L.; K.C. 1919; Chairman, Standing Joint Committee, Dumbartonshire; Ex-Convener, Western Divisional Council, Scottish Unionist Association; *o. s.* of James Hill Kippen of Busby and Westerton. *Educ.:* Clifton College; Trinity College, Oxford (B.A.); Edinburgh University (LL.B.). Advocate, 1890. *Recreations:* country pursuits. *Address:* Westerton, Balloch, Dumbartonshire. *(Died 1 Dec. 1928.)*

KIRALFY, Imre; author; Kt. Commander Royal Order of Leopold; Kt. Commander of the Portuguese Order of Villa Viçosa; and of the Imperial Japanese Order of the Sacred Treasure; Officier de L'Instruction Publique of France; *m.* Marie, *d.* of John Graham, Carlisle; five *s.* one *d.* Created and was Commissioner-General of the following International Exhibitions held in London: Franco-British Exhibition, 1908, the Imperial International Exhibition, 1909, the Japan-British Exhibition, 1910; the Coronation Exhibition, 1911, the Latin-British Exhibition, 1912; Anglo-American Exposition, 1914; Director-General of the Empire of India Exhibition, 1895; India and Ceylon Exhibition, 1896; Victorian Era Exhibition, 1897; Universal Exhibition, 1898; Greater Britain Exhibition, 1899; Woman's International Exhibition, 1900; Military Exhibition, 1901; Paris in London Exhibition, 1902; Fire Exhibition, 1903; also British Commissioner-General of the Liège Universal Exposition, 1905; author of Nero, 1888-91; Venice in London, 1891-93; Columbus, 1892-93; America, 1893; India, 1895-96; Our Naval Victories, 1898; China, or the Relief of the Legations, 1901; Created and designed The Great White City and the Stadium for the

Olympic Games, London, 1908. *Publications:* Babylon; Rome; Nero; The Bride of the Sea; Columbus; America; India; China, etc. *Recreations:* photography. *Address:* Tower House, Cromwell Road, S.W. *T.:* Western 1440. *T.A.:* Kiralfy, London. *Clubs:* British Empire, Constitutional.   *(Died 27 April 1919.)*

KIRBY, Colonel Norborne, C.I.E. 1917; retired; *b.* 19 Sep. 1863; 5th *s.* of late Rev. H. T. Murdoch Kirby, Mayfield, Sussex; *m.* 1898, *c.* Evelyn Rivers, *d.* of Rev. R. R. Kirby, Ventnor; three *s.* one *d.* *Educ.:* Cheltenham College; R.I.E. College, Cooper's Hill. Lieut. R.E. 1886; Capt. 1895; Maj. 1903; Lt.-Col. 1911; Col. 1915; served N.E. Frontier, India, 1892-93 (medal with clasp). *Address:* The Towers, Ventnor, I. of W. *(Died 6 April 1922.)*

KIRK, Sir Amos Child, Kt., *cr.* 1922; J.P.; Alderman of City of Cardiff since 1920; Lord Mayor of Cardiff, 1918-19; *b.* Leeds, 14 Jan. 1856; *s.* of George and Sarah Ann Child Kirk; *m.* 1881, Mary Elizabeth, *d.* of Charles and Ann Garland, Leeds; one *s.* two *d.* *Educ.:* St. Marks N. School, Woodhouse, Leeds. Agent, Liverpool Victoria Insurance Offices, 1876; Director, 1908; Divisional Manager for South Wales, for above office; Councillor, City of Cardiff, 1907. *Recreation:* literature. *Address:* Clifton House, Newport Road, Cardiff. *T.:* Cardiff 1577. *Clubs:* Conservative, Central, Cardiff.   *(Died Oct. 1928.)*

KIRK, Sir John, G.C.M.G., *cr.* 1886; K.C.M.G., *cr.* 1881; K.C.B., *cr.* 1890; F.R.S. M.D., LL.D., D.Sc., D.C.L.; Member of Government Committee for Construction of Uganda Railway since 1895; Foreign Secretary Royal Geographical Society; *b.* Scotland, 19 Dec. 1832; 2nd *s.* of Rev. John Kirk, Arbirlot, Forfarshire; *m.* 1867, Helen (*d.* 1914). *d.* of Charles Cooke; one *s.* three *d.* *Educ.:* Edin. Univ. Served in Turkey during Russian War; Chief Officer on Dr. Livingstone's Govt. Expedition to Africa, 1858-64; Political Agency, Zanzibar, 1866; H.M. Agent and Consul-General; retired from Consular Service, 1887; British Plenipotentiary at Brussels to African Conference, 1889-90; H.M. special Commissioner to Niger Coast, 1895. *Address:* Wavertree, Sevenoaks Kent. *Club:* Athenæum. *(Died 15 Jan. 1922.)*

KIRK, Sir John, Kt., *cr.* 1907; J.P., County of London, 1909; *b.* Kegworth, Leicestershire, 10 June 1847; *m.* 1872; four *s.* three *d.* *Educ.:* Castle Donnington Grammar School. Spent part of boyhood in France; at sixteen became clerk to Pure Literature Society; then Assistant Secretary to Ragged School Union, 1873-79; Secretary Open Air Mission; Secretary, Director, and now Treasurer of Shaftesbury Society and Ragged School Union since 1879; organises Pearson's Fresh Air Fund, and other Press Funds; Fellow Royal Chartered Institute of Secretaries. *Publications:* contributions to journalism. *Recreations:* reading, foreign travel; has visited most European countries, Canada, Australasia, America, and South Africa; interest in child-cripples and children generally. *Address:* 32 John Street, Theobald's Road, W.C.1.; Westcott, Surrey. *T.:* Museum 1951, and Westcott 16. *Club:* National Liberal. *(Died 3 April 1922.)*

KIRKE, Henry, M.A., B.C.L. (Oxon); J.P.; retired civilian; *b.* 4 June 1842; *m.* 1864, Agnes, *d.* of Admiral Sir S. Lushington, G.C.B.; two *s.* six *d.* At different times Sheriff of Demerara; Police Magistrate of Georgetown; Judge of Supreme Court in British Guiana; Attorney-General of Jamaica; Special Commissioner for British Guiana at Calcutta International Exhibition, 1883-4, etc. *Publications:* Twenty-five years in British Guiana; From the Gun-room to the Throne; The First English Conquest of Canada. *Address:* The Haywards, Middle Wallop, Hants. *(Died 9 July 1925.)*

KIRKMAN, Hon. Thomas, was Member of the late Legislative Council, Natal; *b.* Dec. 1843; 2nd *s.* of late Rev. T. P. Kirkman, M.A., F.R.S., Rector of Croft, near Warrington; unmarried. *Educ.:* Rossall School. In various subordinate positions in Manchester for eight years; went to Natal in 1868 with brother John; settled on Government grant of land in Alexandra County; was fourteen years in Volunteer force, and had eight months' active service during Zulu War, 1879; elected a Member of Legislative Assembly for Alexandra County at inauguration of responsible Government, 1893; appointed to Upper House, 1897, re-appointed, 1907; F.R.M.S. 1898. *Recreation:* microscopical studies. *Address:* Croftlands, Esperanza, Natal, S. Africa. *Clubs:* Quekett Microscopical; Victoria, Pietermaritzburg. *(Died 29 Oct. 1919.)*

KIRKPATRICK, Hon. Andrew Alexander, Minister of Mines, Minister of Marine and Minister of Immigration, South Australia, 1924-27; *b.* London, 4 Jan. 1848; *m.* 1878, Catherine Maria Cooper; three *s.* four *d.* Arrived in South Australia, 1861; has been Chairman of the United Labour Party, the Trades and Labour Council, and the Eight Hours' Celebration Union; M.C.L. Southern District, 1891-97; Central District since 1900; Chief Secretary and Minister of Industry, 1905-9; Agent-General for South Australia, 1904-14; his mother accompanied Florence Nightingale to the Crimea. *Address:* Adelaide, S. Australia. *(Died Aug. 1928.)*

KIRKPATRICK, Francis, I.S.O. 1903; J.P.; *b.* 21 Dec. 1840; *s.* of late Alexander Kirkpatrick of Crumlin Road, near Belfast, Ireland; *m.* 1867, Agnes Mackie, *d.* of late Henry Longfield Black of Newry, Ireland; two *s.* four *d.* *Educ.:* Edenderry National School, Crumlin Road, near Belfast. Arrived in New South Wales, 1858; obtained an appointment as Cadet in the Audit Department of the Civil Service; transferred to the Treasury from that Department, 1864; appointed successively Book-keeper, Accountant (1872), Consulting Accountant and Chief Inspector of Accounts (1888); and Under-Secretary for Finance and Trade, The Treasury, New South Wales (1891); retired from the Civil Service of New South Wales after 46 years' service, 1904. *Address:* 4 Parkview Road, Manly, near Sydney, New South Wales. *(Died 10 June 1921.)*

KIRKPATRICK, Lt.-Col. Henry Pownall, D.S.O. 1902; late 2nd in command of 16th Queen's Lancers; *b.* 1862; *e. s.* of late Edward Kirkpatrick, Tyldesley, Lancs., and Agnes, *y. d.* of late James Pownall, Pennington Hall, Leigh, Lancashire; *m.* 1898, Ruby, *o. c.* of Major W. B. Morris, 7th Hussars. *Educ.:* Uppingham; Brasenose College, Oxford. *Clubs:* Naval and Military, Cavalry, Boodle's. *(Died 30 Aug. 1919.)*

KIRKPATRICK, John, M.A. (Cantab.), Dr. Jur. (Heidelb.); LL.B. (Edin.); Hon. LL.D. (Glasgow and Edin.); Advocate; Officier de l'Instruction Publique; *s.* of late John Kirkpatrick, Advocate, formerly Chief Justice of Ionian Islands; *b.* 1835; *m.* 1st, Louisa, *sis.* of late Prof. J. Henslow of Cambridge; 2nd, 1907, Alma, *d.* of late Gen. Davidson Smith. Secretary of Senatus and Dean of Law Faculty, 1886-97; Professor of History in Edinburgh University, 1881-1909. *Publications:* Digest of Scottish Law of Evidence; many historical and legal papers; account of Octocentenary Festival of Bologna; translator of Baedeker's guide-books, 1861-81; editor of Lord Mackenzie's Roman Law, Fischer's Scots in Sweden; author of Handbook of Idiomatic English, 1912, and War Studies, 1915; one of founders, now Hon. Member, of Franco-Scottish Society; Hon. Secretary of Edinburgh Vacation Courses. *Recreations:* modern languages, travel. *(Died 12 Jan. 1926.)*

KIRKWOOD, Major John Hendley Morrison, J.P.; D.S.O. 1917; *o. s.* of late J. M. Kirkwood of Yeo, Devon, and Glencarha, Co. Mayo; *b.* 11 May 1877; *m.* 1902, Gertrude, *d.* of Sir Robert Lyle, Bart.; two *s.* one *d. Educ.:* Harrow. Was in 7th Dragoon Guards; served S. Africa, 1899-1901 (wounded, medal, 5 clasps, despatches); Captain in the Royal North Devon Hussars; served with 4th Dragoon Guards, 1914-15 (wounded); with 1st Life Guards and Household Batt. (D.S.O.), and commanded 1st Batt. Royal Irish Rifles: M.P. (C.) S.-E. Essex, 1910-12. *Address:* Yeo, Fairy Cross, S.O., N. Devon. *Clubs:* Turf, Carlton.   (*Died 7 Feb. 1924.*)

KIRKWOOD, William Montague Hammett, Legal Adviser, His Imperial Japanese Majesty's Government, Tokyo, 1885-1902; Knight Grand Cross of the Rising Sun; Knight Grand Cross of the Sacred Treasure; Japanese Constitution Medal; *b.* 1850; 4th *s.* of late John Townsend Kirkwood of Yeo Vale, N. Devon, and Gore Court, Kent; *m.* 1st, Harriet Alice, *d.* of Hugh Darby Owen of Bettys Hall, Montgomeryshire; 2nd, Ethel, *d.* of Edward Morris. *Educ.:* Marlborough College. Old Marlburian Scholar; Member of Inner Temple; Her Majesty's Crown Advocate in Japan, and Legal Adviser, British Legation and Consulates, 1882-85; assisted in drafting the Japanese Constitution and Codes of Law; has travelled extensively through the Far East; spent several months amongst the head-hunting tribes of Formosa in 1897, and was engaged to organise the administration of that island when ceded to Japan; was Adviser to the first U.S. Phillipine Commission, and received the thanks of Congress for his services; was a censor in the War Office during the War, and Commandant of Boy Scout Camps working for the Flax Branch of the Board of Agriculture; Commissioner of Boy Scouts for Kensington. *Address:* 12 Egerton Gardens, S.W. *T.:* Western 3823.   (*Died 28 Mar. 1926.*)

KISHANGARH, Lt.-Col. H.H. Umdai Rajhae Buland Makan Maharajadhiraj Maharaj Sir Madan Singh Bahadur, K.C.S.I., *cr.* 1911; K.C.I.E., *cr.* 1909; *b.* 1 Nov. 1884; S. his father, the late Maharaja Sir Sardul Singh Bahadur, G.C.I.E.; *cr.* 1892; *m.* 2nd *d.* of present chief of Udaipur, and *y. sis.* of H.H. the Maharani of Bhavnagar; two *d. Educ.:* privately; served as Member of the Imperial Cadet Corps and European War, 1914-15 (despatches). The State has an area of 858 square miles and a population of over 90,000. *Recreations:* polo, tennis, coursing, pigsticking, shikar. *Address:* Kishengarh, Rajputana, India.   (*Died Oct. 1926.*)

KITCAT, Mrs. S. A. P.; pen name, Mrs. Murray Hickson; Mabel, *d.* of His Hon. Judge Greenhow late of Leeds (for 29 years Recorder of Berwick-on-Tweed); *great-n.* of Harriet and James Martineau; *m.* Sidney A. P. Kitcat. *Educ.:* Birklands, Highgate. Began to write for pleasure and in leisure hours; continues to write for the same reason and in the same way; has written a good deal about cricket, both tales and articles; has written articles, verses, short stories, for Longmans' Magazine, The Gentlewoman, Vanity Fair, The Bystander, and many other publications; (with Keighley Snowden) a play, The Whip Hand. *Publications:* A Latter-Day Romance; Concerning Teddy; Chronicles of Teddy's Village; Shadows of Life. *Recreations:* amateur theatricals, gardening, reading, motoring. *Address:* Warling Dean, Esher, Surrey.

      (*Died 12 Nov. 1922.*)

KITCHENER of Khartoum, 1st Earl, *cr.* 1914, of Khartoum and of Broome; **Horatio Herbert Kitchener,** Baron, *cr.* 1898; Viscount, *cr.* 1902, of Khartoum; of the Vaal, Transvaal, and Aspall, Suffolk; Viscount

Broome, *cr.* 1914, of Broome, Kent; Baron Denton, *cr.* 1914, of Denton, Kent; K.G. 1915; G.C.I.E., *cr.* 1908; G.C.S.I., *cr.* 1909; G.C.B., *cr.* 1898; G.C.M.G., *cr.* 1902; K.P., *cr.* 1911; O.M.; P.C. 1914; Secretary of State for War since 1914; Col. Commandant Corps R.E. 1906; Col. Irish Guards, 1914; Field-Marshal, 1909; *b.* Crotter House, Ballylongford, Co. Kerry, 24 June 1850; *s.* of late Lt.-Col. H. H. Kitchener, of Cossington, Leicesters., and Frances, *d.* of Rev. J. Chevallier of Aspall Hall, Suffolk. *Educ.:* R.M. Academy, Woolwich. Entered Royal Engineers 1871; Major-General, 1896; Palestine Survey, 1874-78; Cyprus Survey, 1878-82; commanded Egyptian Cavalry, 1882-84; Nile Expedition, 1884-85 (despatches, brevet Lieut.-Col., medal with clasp, 2nd cl. Medjidie, Khedive's star); Governor of Suakim, 1886-88 (despatches, clasp); Soudan Frontier, 1889, including engagement at Toski (despatches, C.B., and clasp); Adjutant-Gen. Egyptian army, 1888-92; Sirdar, 1890; commanded Dongola Expeditionary Force, 1896 (promoted Major-Gen., K.C.B., 1st cl. Osmanieh, British medal, Khedive's medal with two clasps); commanded Khartum Expedition, 1898 (thanks of Parliament, raised to Peerage, grant of £30,000, G.C.B., two clasps to Khedive's medal); Chief of Staff of Forces in South Africa, 1899-1900; Commander-in-Chief, 1900-1902 (despatches, promoted Lieut.-General and General, received Viscounty, grant of £50,000, thanks of Parliament); Commander-in-Chief, India, 1902-9; Member of Committee of Imperial Defence, 1910; H.M.'s Agent and Consul-General in Egypt, 1911-14; Lord Rector of Edinburgh University, 1914; holds Grand Cordon Order of Leopold. *Publications:* contributions to Blackwood's Magazine. *Heir: b.* Lieut.-Colonel H. E. C. Kitchener. *Address:* York House, St. James's Palace, S.W.; Broome Perk, Canterbury. *Clubs:* Athenæum, United Service, Junior United Service.   (*Died 5 June 1916.*)

KITCHIN, Ven. Arthur, M.A.; Vicar of Hardingstone, Northants, since 1913; *b.* 14 Mar. 1855; 3rd *s.* of late Joseph Kitchin of Dunsdale, Westerham, Kent; *m.* Edith Ann, *y. d.* of late Thomas Everard of New Hall Park, Thurlaston, Leicestershire; one *s.* three *d. Educ.:* Westminster; Christ Church, Oxford. Deacon, 1878; Priest, 1879; Curate of Bexley Heath, Kent, 1878-82; Gulval, Cornwall, 1882-83; Chaplain (Bengal Ecclesiastical Establishment), St. James', Calcutta, 1883; St. Paul's Cathedral, Calcutta, 1884-89; Mussoorie, 1889-92; St. Thomas', Calcutta, 1894-1905; officiating Archdeacon of Calcutta, 1887, 1900, and 1902; Furlough, 1892-94, 1899, and 1905; Exam. Chaplain to the Bishop of Calcutta, 1902-5; Archdeacon of Calcutta, 1903-7; Rector of Rushden, 1905-13; Rural Dean of Higham Ferrers I., 1906-13. *Address:* Hardingstone Vicarage, Northants
      (*Died 17 Feb. 1928.*)

KITSON, Col. Charles Edward, D.S.O. 1916; Colonel in charge of Record Office, Lichfield, since 1925; *b.* 3 Nov. 1874; *s.* of late Col. J. E. Kitson, C.B.; *m.* 1905; one *d. Educ.:* Wellington College. Joined Kent Artillery Militia, 1891; 2nd Royal West Kent Regt., 1893; served South African War (Queen's medal 3 clasps, King's medal 2 clasps); European War (Bt. Lt.-Col., D.S.O.); commanded 2nd Bn. The Queen's Own Royal West Kent Regiment, 1920-24. *Club:* Army and Navy.   (*Died 11 Oct. 1928.*)

KLEIN, Edward Emanuel, M.D., F.R.S., late Lecturer on advanced Bacteriology, Medical School, St. Bartholomew's Hospital; has been connected with Medical Department of Local Government Board since 1871, in carrying out pathological and bacteriological inquiries; *b.* 1844; *m.* 1877, Sophia Amelia (*d.* 1919). *Publications:* several text-books on Histology and Bacteriology; numerous reports on Pathological and Bacteriological subjects in the Reports of

591

KITTSON, Rev. Henry, D.C.L. See page xxiii.

the Medical Officer of the Local Government Board, 1871-1907; The Bacteriology and Etiology of Oriental Plague, 1906. *Recreation: gardening. Address:* 13 Wilbury Villas, Hove, Sussex.
(Died 9 Feb. 1925.)

KLOTZ, Otto, LL.D., D.Sc., F.R.A.S., F.R.S.C., Hon. Fellow, New Zealand Institute; Director Dominion Observatory; *b.* Preston, Ont., 31 March 1852; *m.* 1873, Marie Widenmann; three *s. Educ.:* Univ. of Toronto; Univ. of Michigan. Early days Surveyor and Explorer in Canadian North-West; exploratory survey to Hudson's Bay, 2000-mile canoe trip,1884; Astronomer since 1885; connected with Alaska Boundary Survey, 1893-94; completed first astronomic girdle of the world, wiring the British empire together astronomically, 1903-4; Chairman Carnegie Library, 1910-12; President of the Canadian Club, 1912-13; of the University Club, 1914-15; Delegate for Canada at International Seismological Meeting at The Hague, 1907; at Zermatt, 1909; at Manchester, 1911; and at Petrograd, 1914; Chairman National Committee of Canada, International Astronomical Union, 1920; President American Seismological Society, 1920-21; Delegate for Canada at Rome, International Astronomers' Union, May 1922. *Publications:* numerous papers on Astronomy, Gravity, Terrestrial Magnetism, and Seismology. *Recreation:* golf. *Address:* 437 Albert Street, Ottawa, Canada. *Clubs:* Authors'; Rideau, Rivermead, University, Ottawa. *(Died Dec. 1923.)*

KNAGGS, Sir Samuel William, K.C.M.G., *cr.* 1920; C.M.G., 1908; *b.* 25 Dec. 1856; *s.* of Robert Knaggs, M.R.C.S.E.; *m.* 1893, Violet Grey, *d.* of J. A. Harragin, S.I.P.; one *s.* four *d. Educ.:* Royal College, Trinidad. Entered Trinidad Service, 1876; Chief Commissioner, Port of Spain, 1899; Receiver-General, Trinidad, 1901; Colonial Secretary, Barbados, 1903; Colonial Secretary, Trinidad and Tobago, 1907; administered the Government of Barbados in 1903, 1904, 1905, 1906, and 1907; and of Trinidad and Tobago in 1907, 1908, 1909, 1910, 1912, 1913, 1915, and 1916; retired, 1918.
(Died 31 Dec. 1924.)

KNAPP, Charles Welbourne, President the St. Louis (Mo.) Republic; member of Board of Directors Associated Press; *b.* St. Louis, Missouri, 23 January 1848; *e. s.* of John Knapp. *Educ.:* St. Louis (Mo.) University, A.B., 1865; A.M., 1867; LL.D., 1904; Columbia College (N.Y.), and Univ. of Kentucky Law School, LL.B., 1867. *Recreation:* golf. *Address:* The Republic, St. Louis, Mo. *Clubs:* Noon-day, Commercial, Round Table, Aztec, Gridiron. *(Died 6 Jan. 1916.)*

KNATCHBULL, Major Reginald Norton, D.S.O. 1900; 2nd Batt. The Leicestershire Regt.; *b.* 7 Feb. 1872; *s.* of Col. Norton Knatchbull, late Derbyshire Regt.; *m.* 1906, Winifred, *d.* of W. F. Peel; one *d.* Entered army, 1891; Capt. 1900; Major, 1906; served S. Africa, 1899-1900 (despatches, Queen's medal, 5 clasps, D.S.O.); European War, 1914-15 (wounded). *(Died Aug. 1917.)*

KNATCHBULL, Sir Wyndham, 12th Bt.; *cr.* 1641; 2nd *s.* of 10th Bt. and Mary, *e. d.* of Jesse Watts-Russell of Ham Hall, Stafford; *b.* 9 Aug. 1844; S. *B.* 1871; *m.* 1902, Margaret Elizabeth, *widow* of John Dillon Browne. M.P. East Kent, 1875-76. *Heir: e.* Lord Brabourne. *Address:* Mersham Hatch, Ashford, Kent. *Clubs:* Carlton, Junior Carlton.
(Died 30 July 1917.)

KNATCHBULL - HUGESSEN, Herbert Thomas, M.A.; *b.* Mershani Hatch, near Ashford, Kent, 1 Dec. 1835; *y. b.* of 1st Baron Brabourne and 4th *s.* of late Rt. Hon. Sir Edward Knatchbull, 9th Bart., M.P., and 2nd wife, Fanny Catherine, *e. d.* of Edward Knight of Godmersham Park, Kent, and Chaw-

592

ton House, Hants. *Educ.:* Eton; Trinity College, Oxford. M.A. 1859; Barr. 1860; M.P. North-East Kent, 1885 - 95. *Recreation:* cricket. *Club:* Carlton. *(Died 15 May 1922.)*

KNECHT, Edmund, Ph.D.(Zurich), M.Sc. Tech. (Manchester), F.I.C.; Associate Professor of Technological Chemistry, Manchester University, Manchester; Editor, Journal of Dyers and Colourists; *b.* Liverpool, 1861; 3rd *s.* of late Gustav Knecht, B.Sc. *Educ.:* private tuition; Zurich University; Swiss Federal Polytechnic. Demonstrator in Chemistry at the Polytechnic, 1883-84; Head of Chemistry and Dyeing Department, Bradford Technical College, 1884-90; Lecturer in Chemistry, Manchester Technical College, 1890-1902; Prof. of Tinctorial Chemistry, Municipal School of Technology, 1902-9. *Publications:* (with Eva Hibbert) New Reduction Methods in Volumetric Analysis, 1925; numerous contributions to current scientific and technical literature, and Encyclopædia Britannica; several books on bleaching, dyeing, textile printing, and analytical chemistry. *Recreations:* golf, cycling. *Address:* Marple Cottage, Marple. *(Died 8 Dec. 1925.)*

KNEELAND, Abner W., B.A., M.A., B.C.L., Ph.D.; retired Professor of English Language and Literature in Macdonald College, P.Q.; *b.* 22 May 1853; *s.* of Gardner Kneeland, contractor, and Susan Goddard; *m.*; four *s.* two *d. Educ.:* Victoria and McGill Universities. Began teaching, 1877; Principal of a public school in Montreal, 1879; Prof. of English in M'Gill Normal School, 1892; Member of the Council of Public Instruction for the Province of Quebec, 1890; Chairman of the Text-book Committee for P.Q., 1890 - 1914; Liberal; Methodist; a Member of the Senate of Wesleyan Theological College and of the Board of Governors L'Institute Methodiste Française, Montreal. *Publications:* writes for The Montreal Daily Star, Weekly Witness, The New Outlook, etc.; articles on Travel, Civics, Forestry, Fertilization, Education, Religion, Physiography; and has contributed many poems to various magazines and newspapers. *Recreations:* fishing, horticulture. *Address:* Macdonald College, P.Q., Canada. *T.:* Ste. Anne de Bellevue 267. *T.A.:* Ste. Anne de Bellevue, P.Q. *(Died 20 Nov. 1928.)*

KNEEN, Thomas, Clerk of the Rolls, Isle of Man. *Address:* Douglas, Isle of Man.
(Died 23 Nov. 1916.)

KNEEN, William; artist, painter; R.B.A., 1897-1904; member New English Art Club, 1899-1904; and Society of Painters in Tempera; Art Master at Westminster School; *b.* Isle of Man, 1 Dec. 1862; 4th *s.* of late John Kneen, Isle of Man, and Elizabeth Cleator; *m.* 1901, Winifred Ida Mary, *e. d.* of late J. P. Leech, Kensington; one *d. Educ.:* Isle of Man; the Grammar School, Manchester; under Professor Fred. Brown. Has exhibited usually at the New English Art Club; the International Society of Sculptors, Painters and Gravers; The Goupil Gallery Salon. *Recreation:* reading. *Address:* Westridge, Marchmont Road, Richmond, Surrey. *T.:* Richmond 2695. *Club:* Chelsea Arts. *(Died Oct. 1921.)*

KNIGHT, Edward Frederick, Morning Post special war correspondent in S. Africa; barrister, journalist and author; *b.* 28 Apr. 1852; *e. s.* of Edward Knight, Papcastle, Cumberland. *Educ.:* Westminster; Caius Coll., Camb. (B.A.). On staff of Morning Post. Travelled in South America, Turkey, South Africa, Central Asia, etc.; Barr. 1879. Times correspondent in Hunza-Nagar Campaign, 1891 (throughout which served as officer, medal and despatches); Matabeleland, 1893-95; Madagascar, 1895; Sudan Campaign, 1896; Greece, 1897; Sudan, 1897-98;

Cuba, 1898 ; Spain, 1899 ; Morning Post correspondent, South Africa, 1899-1900 (severely wounded Belmont, right arm amputated) ; with Ophir Tour round the World. 1901-2 ; South Africa, 1902-3 ; with Kuroki's Army in Russo-Japanese War, 1904 ; Turkey, 1908. *Publications :* Albania and Montenegro ; The Cruise of the Falcon ; The Threatening Eye ; Sailing (All England Series of Sports) ; The Falcon on the Baltic ; The Cruise of the Alerte ; Save Me from My Friends ; Where Three Empires Meet ; Madagascar in War Time ; Rhodesia of To-day ; Letters from the Sudan ; A Desperate Voyage ; Small Boat Sailing ; With the Royal Tour ; South Africa after the War ; Over Sea Britain ; The Awakening of Turkey ; Reminiscences, 1923, etc. *Recreation :* yachting ; undertook voyages in command of small sailing yachts, Falcon, Alerte, etc., to South America, West Indies, the Baltic, etc.   *(Died 3 July 1925.)*

KNIGHT, Sir Henry Edmund, Kt., *cr.* 1833 ; J.P. ; Alderman City of London ; *b.* 25 Mar. 1833 ; *s.* of John William Knight, St. Marylebone and St. Albans ; twice married ; five *s.* five *d. Educ. :* City of London School. Member of Corporation of London, Cripplegate Ward, 1867 ; alderman, 1874 ; Sheriff of London and Middlesex, 1875 ; Lord Mayor, 1882 ; Member of Court of Lieutenancy for City of London ; a Governor of the Royal Hospitals. *Address :* 41 Hill Street, W. ; Stainhill Park, Hampton-on-Thames.   *Club :* City Liberal.
            (Died 21 Nov. 1917.)

KNIGHT, Rev. Henry Joseph Corbett, D.D. ; Bishop of Gibraltar since 1911 ; late Fellow and Lecturer of Corpus Christi College, Cambridge, and Principal of the Clergy Training School ; *s.* of late Rev. J. L. Knight ; *m.* 1st, Clara Gwyn Kerslake (*d.* 1911) ; 2nd, 1915, Bridget, 3rd *d.* of late Horace Swete, M.D. *Educ. :* Islington Proprietary School ; St. Catharine's College, Cambridge (Scholar). B.A. ; 1st Class Classical Tripos, 1882 ; 1st Class Theol. Tripos, 1884 ; Scholefield and Evans (University) Prizes, 1884 ; M.A. 1885. Deacon, 1885 ; Priest, 1886 ; Classical and Theological Lecturer of Selwyn College, Cambridge, 1884-95 ; Tutor, 1885-1895 ; Rector of Marnhull, 1895-1901 ; Examining Chaplain to Bishop of Salisbury, 1896 ; Fellow of C.C.C. 1901 ; Principal of C.T.S. 1901 ; Commissary for the Bishops of Wellington and Rangoon ; Hulsean Lecturer, 1905-6 ; Preacher before the University, 1887, 1895, 1905, 1913, 1919 ; Examiner in Theological Tripos, 1888, 1896 ; Member of the Board of Examiners, S.P.G., 1906 ; Sub-Prelate of the Order of St. John of Jerusalem, 1913. *Recreations :* chiefly cycling. *Address :* 23 Old Park Road, Hitchin.
            (Died 27 Nov. 1920.)

KNIGHT, Capt. John Peake, D.S.O. 1914 ; Lieut. R.F.A. ; *b.* 3 Aug. 1890. Entered army, 1910 ; served European War, 1914-15 (despatches ; D.S.O.).   *(Died 31 Aug. 1916.)*

KNIGHT, Chief Engr. T. H., O.I.E. 1917 ; M.I.N.A. ; R.I.M. ; Inspector of machinery, Bombay Dockyard. *Address :* Royal Indian Marine Dockyard, Bombay. *(Died 18 Oct. 1918.)*

KNIGHT, William Angus, LL.D. (Glas.) ; Commander of the Order of the Saviour of Greece, 1910 ; Professor of Moral Philosophy University of St. Andrews, 1876-1902 ; Examiner to University of St Andrews, 1871-73 ; Examiner to University of London, 1883-93, 1894-99 ; Examiner to Civil Service Commission since 1878 ; Examiner in Victoria University, 1892-95 ; Examiner to University of New Zealand, 1878, etc. ; *b.* Scotland, 22 Feb. 1836 ; 2nd *s.* of late Rev. Geo. Fulton Knight, Mordington, Berwickshire ; *m.* Mary (*d.* 1915), *d.* of David Landale, St. Mary's, Kirkcaldy ; one *s.* one *d. Educ. :* Circus Place School, High School, and University, Edinburgh. *Publications :* Poems from the Dawn of English Literature to the Year 1699,

1863 ; Colloquia Peripatetica, or Deep Sea Soundings, 1870 ; Studies in Philosophy and Literature, 1879 ; Spinoza Essays, edited, 1882 ; (Edited) Philosophical Classics for English Readers, 15 vols., 1880-90 ; Hume, in same series, 1886 ; Memorials of Coleorton, 1387 ; Wordsworth's Poetical Works and Life, 11 vols., 1881-1889 ; Transactions of the Wordsworth Society, 8 vols., 1880-88 ; Principal Shairp and His Friends, 1888 ; Essays in Philosophy, Old and New, 1890 ; Selections from Wordsworth, 1889 ; The White Doe of Rylstone, edited 1891 ; Wordsworth's Prose, 1893 ; Stories and Rhymes of Golf, 1893 ; (Edited) University Extension Manuals, 25 vols., 1891-99 ; The Philosophy of the Beautiful ; Its History, 1891 ; Its Theory, 1893 ; Aspects of Theism, 1894 ; The Christian Ethic, 1894 ; The English Lake District, as Interpreted in the Poems of Wordsworth, 1878-91 ; Through the Wordsworth Country, 1892 ; Wordsworthiana, 1889 ; edited Rectorial Addresses delivered at the University of St. Andrews, 1894 ; The Literature of the Georgian Era, by Prof. Minto, edited with Biographical Introduction, 1894 ; Memoir of John Nichol, Professor of English Literature in Glasgow University, 1895 ; The Works of William Wordsworth and Dorothy Wordsworth, 12 vols. 1896-97 ; Nugæ Viatoris, 1897-1903 ; Lord Monboddo and some of his Contemporaries, 1900 ; Dove Cottage from 1800-1900 ; Varia, being Studies on Problems of Philosophy and Ethics, 1901 ; Inter Amicos, 1901 ; Pro Patria et Regina, 1901 ; Early Chapters in the History of the University of St. Andrews and Dundee, 1902 ; Some Nineteenth Century Scotsmen, 1902 ; Andreapolis, 1902 ; Official Catalogue of the Contents of Dove Cottage, 1902 ; Catalogue of Portraits of Philosophers, Poets, etc., presented to the University of St. Andrews, 1902 ; Retrospects, 1903 ; Reciprocity in Trade, the Empire's Safeguard, 1903 ; The Poems of Coleridge, edited ; Biographical Sketch of Sir Thomas Thornton, 1905 ; Prayers, Ancient and Modern, 1905 ; Letters of the Wordsworth Family, 1907 ; The Poems of Sir Walter Scott, edited ; Memorials of Thomas Davidson, 1907 ; The Poets on Christmas, 1907 ; Things New and Old, Sunday Addresses, 1909 ; A Psalter for Daily Use, 1909 ; Coleridge and Wordsworth in the West Country, their Friendship and Surroundings ; The Golden Wisdom of the Apocrypha, 1910 ; A Book of Sacred Verse, 1910 ; The Glamour of Oxford, 1911 ; An Easter Anthology, 1912 ; The Browning Centenary, 1912 ; Prayers, Ancient and Modern, 1912 ; Pro Patria et Rege, Poems on War, British and American, two series, 1515. *Recreations :* mountaineering, golf, rod, gun. *Address :* Greta Lodge, Keswick. *Clubs :* Athenæum ; Royal and Ancient Golf, St. Andrews.
            (Died 4 Mar. 1916.)

KNIGHT-ADKIN, Harry Kenrick, Hon. Secretary Diocesan Board of Missions, 1921-25 ; Public Preacher and Hon. Canon of Bristol, 1922 ; *e. s.* of Rev. Henry Adkin ; *b.* 1851 ; *m.* Georgina Elizabeth, *o. c.* of Jas. Peter Knight, Cheltenham ; three *s.* one *d. Educ. :* Northleach Grammar School ; University of London, B.A., 1877. Private Tutor Cheltenham, 1870-77 ; Assistant Master New College, Eastbourne, 1877-78 ; Curate of St. John's, Cheltenham, 1879-84 ; Vicar of Cold Salperton, 1884-97 ; Rector of Crudwell (Wilts), 1898-1909 ; Vicar of Hankerton (Wilts), 1902-10 ; Rector of Horfield Bristol and O.C.F. Horfield Barracks, 1910-21 ; took name of Knight-Adkin by deed poll, 1910 ; Freemason, P.M., 82, 2388, P.P.G.C. (Gloucestershire), P.P.J.G.W. (Wilts). *Publications :* Sermon, Religion and Science ; Pamphlet, Mathematical Formulæ. *Recreation :* gardening. *Address :* 69 Alma Road, Clifton, Bristol.   *(Died 3 Jan. 1927.)*

KNOLLYS, 1st Viscount, cr. 1911; **Francis Knollys,** 1st Baron of Caversham, cr. 1902; G.C.B., cr. 1908; G.C.V.O., cr. 1901; K.C.M.G., cr. 1886; K.C.B., cr. 1897; C.B. 1876; P.C. 1910; I.S.O. 1903; Private Secretary to King Edward when Prince of Wales, 1870-1901; and from 1901-1910; to King George, 1910-1913; Lord-in-Waiting to Queen Alexandra since 1910; 2nd s. of late Gen. Rt. Hon. Sir W. T. Knollys, K.C.B., and Elizabeth, d. of late Sir J. St. Aubyn, Bt.; b. 16 July 1837; m. 1887, Hon. Ardyn Mary Tyrwhitt (d. 1922), d. of Sir H. Tyrwhitt, 3rd Bt., and Baroness Berners; one s. one d. Groom-in-Waiting to King Edward when Prince of Wales, 1886-1901; Gentleman Usher to Queen Victoria, 1868-1901. Heir: s. Hon. E. G. W. Tyrwhitt Knollys.   Address: St. James's Palace, S.W.; Blount's Court, Henley-on-Thames.
(Died 15 Aug. 1924.)

KNOLLYS, Rev. Erskine William, M.A.; Hon. Canon of Canterbury, 1905; b. 31 July 1842; e. s. of Canon W. F. E. Knollys; m. Caroline, d. of Prebendary J. E. Kempe; three s. two d. Educ.: Radley; Brasenose College, Oxford. Deacon, 1866; Priest, 1867; Diocesan Inspector of Schools; Vicar of Addington, Surrey; Rector of Great Chart; Vicar of South Norwood; of Folkestone, 1898; Rural Dean of the Deanery of Elham, 1909. Address: Charlton, Goodrich, Ross-on-Wye.   T.A.: Goodrich, Ross.   M.: CG 4891.
(Died 23 Nov. 1923.)

KNOLLYS, Major Louis Frederic, C.M.G. 1877; b. 26 Feb. 1847; 3rd s. of late Canon W. F. E. Knollys; unmarried. Educ.: Radley; Marlborough. Joined 32nd Light Infantry, 1866; Major in the Cameronians (Scottish Rifles), 1881; A.D.C. to the Governor of Mauritius, 1872; A.D.C. Fiji, 1875; Commandant Armed Native Constabulary, Fiji, 1877; A.D.C. to the Governor of New Zealand, 1880; A.D.C. to the Governor of Ceylon, 1883; Inspector-General of Police and Prisons, Jamaica, 1886; Inspector-General of Police, Ceylon, 1891; Inspector-General of Police and Prisons, Ceylon, 1898; Provisional Member of the Legislative Council, Ceylon, 1899; retired, 1902. Decorated: commanded an expedition to suppress a rising in the mountains in Fiji, and restored order, 1876. Address: The Graig, Ross, Herefordshire.
(Died 15 Dec. 1922.)

KNOTT, Cargill Gilston, F.R.S.; D.Sc.; LL.D. (St. Andrews); General Secretary, Royal Society of Edinburgh; Reader in Applied Mathematics Edinburgh University since 1892; b. Penicuik, Scotland, 30 June 1856; s. of Pelham Knott; m. Mary, e. d. of Rev. J. M. Dixon, Paisley, 1885; one s. three d. Educ.: Arbroath High School; Edinburgh University. Assistant to Chair of Natural Philosophy, Edinburgh University, 1879-83; Prof. of Physics, Imperial University, Japan, 1883-91; conducted Magnetic Survey of Japan, 1887; decorated Fourth Order of the Rising Sun, 1891; awarded Keith Prize (Roy. Soc. Edin.) for original work on magnetic strains, 1897; Thomson Lecturer, U.F. Church College, Aberdeen, 1905-6 (Earthquakes), and 1913-14 (Radio-activity); Hon. Secretary of Napier Tercentenary Celebration, Edinburgh, 1914, and Editor of the Memorial Volume. Publications: Electricity and Magnetism; Physics; Physics of Earthquake Phenomena; Memoir of Professor P. G. Tait; Four-Figure Mathematical Tables; article Pneumatics, Encyclopædia Britannica; Light in Supplement; Photometry in 11th ed.; revised Kelland and Tait's Quaternions (3rd ed. 1904); Earthquake Waves in Dictionary of Applied Physics, 1922; papers on Electricity, Magnetism, Seismology, Elasticity, etc. Recreations: golf, chess. Address: 42 Upper Gray Street, Edinburgh.   T.: 7640.
(Died 26 Oct. 1922.)

594

KNOTT, John, A.M., M.D., Ch.B., and D.P.H. (Univ. Dubl.); F.R.C.S.I., M.R.C.P.I., M.R.I.A.; practising physician, scientist, author, critic; b. Kingsland, Co. Roscommon, 5 June 1853; o. s. of William Knott. Educ.: Kingsland National School; Schools of Surgery, R.C.S.I.; first prize at every competitive examination, and First Senior Exhibition with gold medal; both Mapother medals, and gold medal of the Pathological Society; licentiate of the R.C.P.I., and licentiate and Fellowship, R.C.S.I.; University of Dublin (two Moderatorships and medals). House-Surgeon and House-Physician at the Houses of Industry Hospitals for a year respectively; visited the Universities of Heidelberg, Leyden, Paris, Vienna, Buda-Pesth, Cracow, Bologna, and Moscow; for several years Senior Demonstrator of Anatomy, and afterwards College Anatomist, Schools of Surgery, R.C.S.I.; formerly Examiner in Physics, Conj. Exam. R.C.P. & S.I.; also Examiner in Biology, afterwards in Pathology and in Physiology, Apothecaries' Hall, Ireland. Publications: Pathology of the Œsophagus (gold medal of the Pathological Society), 1878; Mapother's Physiology, third edition (wholly re-written), 1882; Use of Organic Acids in Gout and Rheumatism, 1887; The Fever of Over-exertion, 1887; Hey's Internal Derangement of the Knee-joint, 1905; Dupuytren's Contraction of the Palmar Fascia, 1905; Spontaneous Combustion, 1908; Aconite, Queen-Mother of Poisons, 1908; Heat Waves and Ocean Currents; the Gulf Stream Myth, 1909; Dies Caniculares, 1907; Normal Ovariotomy, Female Circumcision, Clitoridectomy and Infibulation, 1908; The Origin of Syphilis and the Invention of its Name, 1909; Phthiriasis, 1910; Sir Walter Raleigh's Royal Cordial, 1910; The King's Evil and its Cures, 1911; Introduction to Eugenics, 1911; Iron, Metallic and Magnetic, Medicinal and Philosophical, 1909; The Last Illness of Lord Byron, 1910; The Last Illness of Napoleon Bonaparte, 1912; Influenzal and other Therapeutics, 1918; etc. Recreations: travel; study of art, ethnology, of comparative religion; (listening to) music. Address: 2 Sally-mount Terrace, Ranelagh, Dublin.   T.A.: John Knott, Ireland. Clubs: Authors', Royal Societies.
(Died Jan. 1921.)

KNOWLES, Maj.-Gen. Sir Charles Benjamin, K.C.B., cr. 1908; C.B. 1881; b. 14 Aug. 1835; s. of late John Knowles of The Lawn, Rugby; m. 1892, Constance Mary, O.B.E., d. of late James Elmslie, and widow of Rev. G. Elliott (Lady of Grace, Order of St. John of Jerusalem). Entered army,1855; Maj.-Gen. 1890; served Crimea, 1855 (wounded, medal with clasp, Turkish medal); Afghan War, 1878-80 (despatches twice, C.B., medal with two clasps). Address: Eastfields, Camberley, Surrey. Club: Army and Navy.
(Died 29 July 1924.)

KNOWLES, Sir Charles George Frederick, 4th Bt., cr. 1765; Vice-Admiral (retired), 1894; b. 14 Mar. 1832; S. father 1892; m. 1861, Elizabeth, d. of late John Chapman; 2nd, Mary, d. of C. Thomson, Halifax, Nova Scotia, 1882 (d. 1890); three s. four d. Entered R.N. 1845; served in Burmese War, 1853; commanded Niger Expedition, 1864. Heir: s. Francis [b. 13 Jan. 1886; m. 1914, Kathleen, d. of late W. Lemon. Educ.: Oriel College, Oxford]. Address: 3 Moreton Road, Oxford. Club: United Service.   (Died 3 Mar. 1918.)

KNOWLES, Rev. Francis, Honorary Canon of Christchurch Cathedral, New Zealand since 1894; Secretary and Treasurer to the Church Property Trustees of the Diocese of Christchurch; b. 5 Aug. 1830; s. of William Barnard Knowles and Elizabeth Andsley; m. 1st, 1855, Charlotte (d. 1890), d. of Nathaniel and Mary Wiles, Cheltenham; two s.; 2nd, 1891, Annie, widow of Rev. Charles Alabaster, M.A.

Educ.: Stebonheath House Academy, Stepney, London. Associate College of Preceptors, London, 1848; Assistant Master, The Proprietary School, Cheltenham, 1847-50; Scripture Reader, Halesworth, Suffolk, 1850; Deacon, 1857; Priest, 1859; Vicar of Lyttelton, 1859-72; Merivale, 1872-76; Balclutha, 1876-78; Gladstone, 1878-79; Diocesan Registrar, Christchurch, since 1879. *Recreations:* walking and general reading. *Address:* Christ's College, Christchurch, N.Z. *T.:* Christchurch, 1267.
(*Died 11 Sept. 1916.*)

KNOWLES, Frederick Arthur, C.M.G. 1914; F.R.C.I.; *b.* 17 Apr. 1872; *e. s.* of late Col. F. Knowles, 2nd Lancers, Indian Army; *m.* 1914, Elsie Anna, *o. d.* of late Richard Seeman; one *s.* one *d. Educ.:* Wellington. Assistant Collector, Uganda Protectorate, 1898; served in Uganda, 1898 (medal); 1st Class Magistrate, 1902; Sub-Commissioner, 1906; Sessions Judge, N. and W. Provinces, 1908; Provincial Commissioner and Sessions Judge, Buganda Kingdom, 1908; N. and W. Provinces, 1911; Acting Chief Secretary during 1911; Provincial Commissioner, Buganda Kingdom, 1913-16; retired Sep. 1916. *Address:* St. Chad's, Woodfield Road, W.5. *T.:* Ealing, 476.
(*Died 22 Sept. 1922.*)

KNOWLES, Lieut.-Col. John George, C.I.E. 1913; V.D. Commandant Surma Valley Light Horse; Hon. A.D.C. to Viceroy and Governor-General, Cachar; tea planter. *Address:* Surma Valley, Cachar, Assam.
(*Died 28 Feb. 1919.*)

KNOWLES, Sir Lees, 1st Bt., *cr.* 1903; C.V.O.; O.B.E.; T.D.; D.L.; M.A.; LL.M.; *b.* 16 Feb. 1857; *e. s.* of late John Knowles; *m.* 1915, Lady Nina Ogilvie-Grant, O.B.E. (Dame of Justice of St. John of Jerusalem), *y. d.* of 10th Earl of Seafield. *Educ.:* Rugby; Trinity Coll., Cambridge (M.A., LL.M., 1882). Has endowed three annual three-yearly Exhibitions for Rugby boys, and one yearly for a graduate in his fourth year, at Trinity Coll., Cambridge; formerly Hon. Sec. to Guinness Trust for Housing the Poor; Private Secretary (unpaid) to Mr. Ritchie; President of the Local Government Board, 1887-92; President of the Board of Trade, 1895-1900; 2nd Church Estates' Commissioner (unpaid), 1896-1906; Trustee of the London Parochial Charities; Hon. Secretary to the Lancashire Conservative M.P.'s Association; President Cambridge University Athletic Club, 1878; an Amateur-Champion Athlete; Barrister Lincoln's Inn, 1882; contested Leigh Division, 1885; M.P. (C.) Salford, W., 1886-1906; Lt.-Col.Terr. Force, retired 1918; late Commandant, 7th and 8th Batts. Lancs Fus. (Terr.); Vice-Chairman of Lancs Territorial Army Association, and Chairman of that of East Lancs.; Knight of Grace of St. John of Jerusalem; Member of Merchant Taylors' Company and the Plumbers Company; formerly on Council of Rossall School; a Governor of Chetham's Hospital, Manchester; Past-President of the Hackney Horse Society; Lord of the Manor of Turton. *Publications:* A Day with Corps-Students in Germany; The War in the Peninsula: The Battle of Minden, etc.; edited Letters of Capt. Engelbert Lutyens, St. Helena, 1820-23, 1915; The British in Capri, 1906-8, 1918; A Gift of Napoleon, 1921; Fun, Fact and Extract; and The Taking of Capri, 1923. *Heir:* none. *Address:* Westwood, Pendlebury, and Turton Tower, Lancs; 4 New Square, Lincoln's Inn, W.C.; 4 Park Street, W.1. *T.:* Grosvenor 1293. *Clubs:* Carlton, Junior Carlton; Union, Constitutional, Manchester. (*Died 7 Oct. 1928.*)

KNOWLES, Lilian Charlotte Anne, Litt.D.; Professor of Economic History, University of London; *d.* of late Philip Tomn and Mrs. Tomn, of Killagorden, Truro; *m.* 1904. C.M. Knowles, barrister-at-law; one *s. Educ.:* Truro High School; the Continent; Girton College, Cambridge. History Tripos, First Class, 1893; Law Tripos (Part I.), First Class, 1894; Litt.D. Trinity College, Dublin, 1906. Trained under Archdeacon Cunningham; lecturer in Modern Economic History at the London School of Economics and Political Science, 1904; Reader in Economic History in the University of London, 1907; Member of the Departmental Committee on the rise in the cost of living to the working classes, 1918; Member of the Royal Commission on the Income Tax, 1919-1920; Member of the Council of the Royal Economic Society; Member of the Council of the Royal Historical Society; Dean of the Faculty of Economics in the University of London, 1920-24. *Publications:* The Industrial and Commercial Revolutionism Great Britain in the Nineteenth Century; The Economic Development of the Overseas Empire, 1763-1914; various papers on economic history subjects; edited English edition of The Referendum in Switzerland, by Simon Deploige; editor of series of Girton College Studies. *Address:* 47 St. Mary's Mansions, Paddington, W.; Killagorden, Truro, Cornwall. *Club:* University of London.
(*Died 25 April 1926.*)

KNOWLES, Robert Millington, J.P., D.L.; *b.* 1843; *e. s.* of late James Knowles, J.P., of Eagley Bank, and Mary Elizabeth, *d.* of late Robert Millington, of Ordsall; *m.* 1st 1867, Ellen Marsden (*d.* 1872), *e. d.* of late John Haslam, J.P., of Bolton; 2nd 1875, Hon. Alice Catherine Brooks (*d.* 1892), *e. d.* of 1st Lord Crawshaw, two *d. Educ.:* University College, London. High Sheriff, Notts, 1885; Hon. Major late 8. Notts Yeomanry. *Address:* Colston Bassett Hall, Bingham, Nottinghamshire. *Clubs:* Wellington, Brooks's. (*Died 28 Nov. 1924.*)

KNOWLING, Hon. George; *b.* Exeter, 15 September 1841; *s.* of George and Elizabeth Knowling; *m.* Elizabeth Upham of Silverton, Devon; three *s.* four *d. Educ.:* Marlborough House School, Exeter. Went Newfoundland, 1858; *s. u.* in business, 1886; member of Legislative Council, 1898. *Address:* Thornlea, Riverhead, St. John's, Newfoundland. *T.A.:* Knowling, St. John's. *T.:* 405, 405A, 527. *Club:* City, St. John's.
(*Died Nov. 1923.*)

KNOWLING, Rev. Richard John, D.D.; Canon of Durham and Professor of Divinity in the University of Durham since 1905; Professor of New Testament Exegesis in King's College, London, 1894-1905; *b.* Devonport, 16 Sept. 1851; *e. s.* of Prebendary Knowling, Vicar of Wellington, Somerset; *m.* 1893, Ellen (*d.* 1914), *e. d.* of Major-General Raban. *Educ.:* Blundell's School, Tiverton; Balliol College, Oxford. Fellow of King's College, London, 1899; Emeritus Professor, 1905; Examiner for Hall-Houghton Prizes at Oxford, 1897, and for Denyer and Johnson Scholarships, 1905; Select Preacher at Cambridge, 1895; Boyle Lecturer, 1903-5; Examining Chaplain to Archbishop of Canterbury, 1903, and to Bishop of Exeter, 1903-16; Examiner for B.D. in University of London, 1905-6. *Publications:* Witness of the Epistles; Acts of the Apostles, in Expositor's Greek Testament; Our Lord's Virgin Birth; Epistle of St. James (Westminster Commentaries); contributions to Smith and Wace's Dict. of Christian Biog., the Critical Review, Ency. Brit. 10th edit., Biblical World; Critical Questions, 1903; The Testimony of St. Paul to Christ (Boyle Lectures), 1905; Manchester Cathedral Lectures, 1907; Messianic Interpretation, 1910; articles in Hastings' Dictionary of Christ and the Gospels, 1906. *Address:* Durham.
(*Died 4 July 1919.*)

KNOX, Major Arthur Rice, D.S.O. 1900; retired; *b.* 8 March 1863; *s.* of late Major-Gen. T. Knox, R.A. *Educ.:* Cheltenham College.

Entered R.A., 1883; Captain, 1892; Major, 1900; served South Africa, 1899-1900 (despatches, Queen's medal, 5 clasps, D.S.O.); European War, 1914-15 (wounded).
(*Died 22 April 1917.*)

KNOX (Edmund Francis) Vesey; K.C. 1906; *b.* 23 Jan. 1865: *s.* of late Vesey Knox, of Shimnah, Newcastle, Co. Down; *m.* 1st, 1891, Anne (*d.* 1907), *d.* of W. Lloyd; two *s.* one *d.*; 2nd, 1917, Agnes, *d.* of Julian Beerbohn and widow of R. Nevill. *Educ.*: Keble Coll., Oxford. Fellow of All Souls College, 1886-93; Barrister, Gray's Inn, 1889; Bencher, 1906; Treasurer, 1913; practises at the Parliamentary Bar; M.P. W. Cavan, 1890-95; M.P. (N.) Londonderry, 1895-99. *Address*: 25 Carlyle Square, Chelsea, S.W.3; Shimnah, Newcastle, Co. Down; Goldsmith Building, Temple, E.C.4. *T.*: Central 639. ' *Club*: Reform.
(*Died 15 May 1921.*)

KNOX, Sir George Edward, Kt., *cr.* 1906; I.S.O. 1915; LL.D. Allahabad; Knight of Grace, St. John, Jerusalem, 1915; Judge High Court, N.-W. Provinces, India, since 1890; *m.* 1868, Katherine Anne Louise, *d.* of late Major W. Loch, 1st Bombay Lancers. *Educ.*: Merchant Taylors' School; University College, London. Entered I.C.S. 1864; Legal Remembrancer, 1887. *Publications*: Digest of the Criminal Law of the Bengal Presidency; Digest of Civil Procedure; The Legal Remembrancer, 1879-82; Treatise upon the Indian Stamp Law. *Address*: Braemar, Naini Tal, India. (*Died 20 July 1922.*)

KNOX, Sir James, Kt., *cr.* 1905; J.P. Co. Ayr; Director, Linen Thread Co., Ld.; *b.* 4 Jan. 1850: *s.* of James Knox of Riverside, Kilbirnie, and Janet Muir, Beith; *m.* 1875, Anne Eliza (*d.* 1919), *o. d.* of James McCosh of Merksworth, Dalry; two *d.* *Address*: Place, Kilbirnie, Ayrshire. *Clubs*: New, Western, Glasgow.
(*Died 30 Sept. 1926.*)

KNOX, Richard, Lieutenant-Colonel, retired 1888; *b.* 23 Dec. 1848; *e. s.* of late Lieut.-Gen. Richard Knox, 18th Hussars, and Mary, *d.* of General Bryce M'Master, H.E.I.C.S.; *m.* Mary Eliza, *o. c.* of late Clement Milward, Q.C., 1882; one *s.* Joined 18th Hussars 1867; exchanged as Captain to 13th Hussars, 1878. *Address*: Holt Hatch, Alton, Hants. (*Died 4 Feb. 1918.*)

KNOX, Robert, M.B., C.M., M.D. Edin.; M.R.C.S. England; M.R.C.P. Lond.; L.R.C.P., F.R.P.S. Lond.; M.I.E.E.; D.M.R.E. Camb.; late Honorary Radiologist, King's College Hospital; Director, Electrical and Radiotherapeutic Department, Cancer Hospital (Free), Fulham Road, S.W.; Consulting Radiologist, Great Northern Central Hospital; Consulting Radiologist, Chelsea Hospital for Women; Honorary Consulting Radiologist, Queen Alexandra Hospital, Millbank; Honorary Radiologist, Royal Sea-bathing Hospital; *b.* Leith. *Educ.*: Edin. University; Guy's Hospital. Fellow of the Royal Society of Medicine; Past. President Electro-therapeutic Section; Fellow of the Medical Society of London; Member, British Medical Association; Vice-President, British Institute of Radiology; Past Pres. Röntgen Society; Hon. Fellow American College of Radiology; Hon. Mem. American Röntgen Ray Society, Radium Society, New York Röntgen Society, Scandinavian Röntgen Society. *Publications*: Radiography, X-Ray Therapeutics and Radium Therapy, 2nd edition, 1917; 3rd edition, 1919; 4th edition, 1924; Joint editor British Journal of Radiology; author article on Radium Therapy in Eden and Lockyer's Gynæcology; various articles on X-Rays and Radium in medical journals; Radiography of the Gall Bladder, Acta Radiologica, 1924. *Address*: 38 Harley Street, W.1; 15 South Grove, Highgate, N.6. *T.*: Langham 1563, and Mountview 0068. (*Died 21 Sept. 1928.*)

KNOX, Major-General Sir William George, K.C.B. 1900; C.B. 1889; Col. Comdt. R.A.; *b.* 20 Oct. 1847; 2nd *s.* of late General T. E. Knox, C.B.; *m.* 1889, Alice, *d.* of Sir Robert Dundas, 1st Bt. *Educ.*: R.M. Academy, Woolwich. Royal Artillery, 1867; Abyssinian Campaign, 1867-68 (medal); Ashanti Campaign, 1874, including Battles of Amoaful, Ordashu, capture of Coomassie (medal and clasp); Afghan Campaign, 1878-79, including capture of Ali Musjid (despatches, medal and clasp); Zulu and Transvaal Campaign, 1879, capture of Sekikuni's stronghold (despatches, Brevet of Major, medal and clasp); Turkish War medal from Sultan of Turkey for services with Red Crescent Society in winter Balkan Campaign, Russo-Turkish War, 1877, and present at several actions; defence of Ladysmith and operations in O.R.C. (despatches 5 times, Queen's medal, 4 clasps, King's medal, 2 clasps, K.C.B.); commanding R H.A Curragh to 1899; late commanding 23rd Brigade, South Africa; late G.O.C. 8th Division, Irish Command. *Recreations*: hunting, shooting, fishing. *Address*: 24 Portman Square, W.; *T.*: Mayfair 1532; Sherborne St. John, Hants. *Club*: Naval and Military. (*Died 14 Dec. 1916.*)

KNOX LITTLE, Rev. William John, M.A.; Canon of Worcester since 1881; Sub-Dean, 1902; Proctor for Chapter in Convocation of Canterbury, 1888-1911; Vicar of Hoar Cross 1885-1907; Acting Chaplain to Brigade of Guards and subsequently to Household Cavalry during part of S. African War (despatches, Queen's medal and clasps); *b.* 1889; *s.* of John Little, Stewartstown, Co. Tyrone; *m.* Annie, *d.* of Henry Gregson, Moorlands, Lancs.; six *s.* four *d.* *Educ.*: Trin. Coll. Camb. Assist. master Sherborne School; curate Christ Church, Lancaster; curate of Turweston, Bucks; curate of St.Thomas's, Regent St.; Rector of St. Alban's, Cheetwood, Manchester, 1875-85. *Publications*: Meditations on the Three Hours' Agony of Our Blessed Redeemer, 1877; Characteristics and Motives of the Christian Life, 1880; Mystery of the Passion, 1881; Witness o. the Passion of Our Most Holy Redeemer, 1884; The Broken Vow, a Story of Here and Hereafter, 1887; The Child of Stafferton, 1888; The Journey of Life; The Light of Life, 1888; Sunlight and Shadow in the Christian Life, 1889; The Waif from the Waves; A Story of Three Lives, 1890; The Christian Home—its Foundation and Duties, 1891; The Perfect Life, 1899; Sketches and Studies in South Africa, 1899; Manual of Devotion for Lent, 1900; Holy Matrimony, 1900; A Treasury of Meditation; Confirmation and Holy Communion, 1901; The Conflict of Ideals in the Church of England, 1905. *Address*: The College, Worcester. (*Died 3 Feb. 1918.*)

KOEBEL, W. H., author and traveller; *b.* 1872; *e. s.* of late Oscar Koebel of Murley Grange, Bishopsteignton, Devon; *m.* Eleanor, *y. d.* of late Anthony Garstin of New Zealand; one *d.* *Educ.*: privately; and in France, Switzerland, Germany. *Publications*: The Great South Land; Argentina, Past and Present; Modern Chile; The Romance of the River Plate; British Exploits in South America; Portugal, its Land and People; In the Maoriland Bush; South America; Uruguay; The South Americans, from the social and industrial point of view; Paraguay; Madeira, Old and New; In Jesuit Land; Modern Argentina; Central America; Hodson's Voyage; The Singular Republic; The Anchorage; The Butterflies' Day; The Return of Joe; The Seat of Moods, etc.; Editor-in-Chief of the Encyclopædia of South America, 1913; contributor to many newspapers and magazines; has undertaken special commissions for South America for The Times, Sphere, Standard, etc., 1918; proceeded on a special mission to South America for the British Government, receiving the thanks of the War Council, 1921 ; founded and edited the Anglo South American Handbook. *Recreations:* sports and games, bibliography. *Address:* 23 Gilston Road, The Boltons, S.W. *Clubs:* St. James's, Argentine, Authors'; Barnstaple and North Devon.

(*Died 20 June 1923.*)

KOHLER, Kaufmann, Ph.D. ; President of the Hebrew Union College, Cincinnati, Ohio, 1903 ; President Emeritus, 1921 ; *b.* Fürth, Germany, 10 May 1843 ; *s.* of Moritz Kohler and Babette Loewemayer ; *m.* 1870, Johanna, *d.* of Rev. Dr. David Einhorn ; two *s.* two *d.* *Educ.:* Universities of Munich, Berlin. Leipzig, and Erlangen. Rabbi of the Beth El congregation in Detroit, 1869 ; Minister of Sinai Temple, Chicago, Ill., 1871-79 ; of Temple Beth El, New York, 1879-1903 ; hon. minister for life since 1903, being relieved of active ministerial work in order to accept the Presidency of the Hebrew Union Coll. in Cincinnati ; introduced Sunday services, in addition to the regular Saturday service, during ministry in Chicago, being their first introduction into Jewish pulpits in America ; convened the Pittsburg Conference, 1885 ; President for many years of the New York Board of Jewish Ministers ; Hon. Pres. of Central Conference of American Rabbis, 1903 ; editor in charge of the departments of Theology and Philosophy of the Jewish Encyclopædia. *Publications:* Der Segen Jacobs, 1869 ; On Capital Punishment according to Jewish Law, 1869 ; On the Song of Songs, 1878 ; Ethical Basis of Judaism, 1887 ; Jewish Ethics ; Moses and Jesus ; Church and Synagogue in their Mutual Relations; Backwards or Forwards; Lectures on Reform Judaism, 1885 ; The Testament of Job ; On the Psalms ; A Guide to Instruction in Judaism ; Principles of Jewish Theology upon a Historical Basis, 1910 (German), Hebrew Union College and other Addresses, 1916 ; Jewish Theology, Historically and Systematically Considered, 1918 ; Heaven and Hell in Comparative Religion, with special reference to Dante's Divine Comedy, 1923 ; edited Collected Writings of Rev. Dr. David Einhorn, 1880 ; editor of weeklies Sabbath Visitor, 1881-1882, and Jewish Reformer, 1886. *Recreations:* theatre, symphony concerts, and walks. *Address:* 2 W. 88th Street, New York City. (*Died 28 Jan. 1926.*)

KOLHAPUR, His Highness Sir Shahu Chhatrapati, Maharaja of, G.C.I.E., cr. 1911; G.C.S.I., cr. 1895; G.C.V.O.; LL.D.; Camb.; M.R.A.S.; Hon. Colonel in British Army, 1915 ; Hon. Colonel 108rd Mahratta Light Infantry ; direct descendant of Shivaji, the founder of the Maratha Empire ; *b.* 26 June 1874 ; adopted, on 17 March 1884, from the Kagal Bargirdar's family, being the natural born son of Jayasingrao Ghatge Sarjarao Vazarat Ma-ab, Jabagirdar of Kagal ; *m.* Lakshmibai Saheb, *g. d.* of a sister of H.H. the late Ganapatrao Gaikwad, Maharaja of Baroda ; one *s.* one *d.* *Educ.:* privately under a European tutor and guardian, Mr. S. M. Fraser ; Rajkumar Coll., Rajkote. Has been administering the affairs of the Kolhapur State from 2nd April 1894. *Decorated* for loyalty, good government, and in recognition of the dignity of the house. Has a salute of 21 guns. *Recreations:* polo, shikar, and other manly sports. *Address:* Kolhapur, Bombay Presidency, India. (*Died 6 May 1922.*)

KOUROPATKIN, Alexei Nicholaevitch, General of Infantry since 1901 ; A.D.C. to the Emperor, 1902-17 ; *b.* 17 Mar. 1848 ; nobleman of Government Pskov ; married ; one *s.* *Educ.:* after having finished the courses of the I. Corps of Cadets and of the I. Military School, Emperor Paul I., ended with the diploma of the first Category at the Academy of the General Staff of army, Emperor Nicholas I. Member of honour at the Academies;

of the General Staff of army, Emperor Nicholas I. ; of Engineering, Emperor Nicholas I. ; of Military Jurisprudence, Emperor Alexander II.; of artillery, Grand Duke Michael, and at the Imperial Academy of Military Medicine. Officer since 1866 ; attached to the General Staff of army since the year 1874 ; Col. 1878 ; Maj.-Gen. 1882 ; Lt.-Gen. 1890 ; sent to foreign countries for scientific purposes, 1874-75; officer of the General Staff of army, district Turkestan, 1876-77 ; Bulgaria, 1877-78 ; chief of the Asiatic bureau of the Main Staff of army, 1878-79 ; assistant-professor of Military Statistics at the Academy of the General Staff of army, Emperor Nicholas I.; commander of the rifle-brigade, Turkestan, 1879-83 ; General for treating the questions of Strategy at the Main Staff of army, 1883-90'; Governor of the Trans - Kaspian district and commander of the troops of this district, 1890-98; head of the Ministry of War, 1898 ; served in Turkestan against Bucharia, 1867 - 68 ; in Algeria in the expedition of French troops, 1874; in Turkestan against Kokand, 1876 ; in Bulgaria against the Turks, 1877 - 78 ; in Middle Asia against Akhal-Teke, 1880 - 81, where he commanded the main detachment and stormed Geok-Tepe (twice wounded) ; received the Order of St. Stanislaus of the 3rd class with swords and knot ; the Order of St. Anne of the 3rd class with swords and knot, and the rank of Lieut. 1869 ; the rank of Second Captain, 1870 ; the rank of Captain and the Order of St. Georges of the 4th class, 1876 ; the Order of St. Woldemar of the 4th class with swords and knot and the rank of Lieut. Colonel, the Order of St. Stanislaus of the 2nd class with swords and "the Golden Arm," 1877 ; the rank of Col. and the Order of St. Anne of the 2nd class with swords, 1878 ; the Order of St. Woldemar of the 3rd class with swords, 1879 ; the order of St. Georges of the 3rd class, 1881 ; the rank of Major-Gen. 1882 ; the Orders of St Stanislaus and St. Anne of the 1st class ; of St. Woldemar of the 2nd class ; and the Orders of the White Eagle and St. Alexander Nevsky (French) Légion d'honneur, grande croix, grand croix d'officer, croix de commandeur et croix de chevalier ; (Mecklenburg-Schwerin) the Crown of the Wends ; (Servian) cross of officer of the Order Takova and the golden medal for courage ; (Roumania) the great cross of the Order of Star and the Iron Cross ; (Montenegro) the golden medal "for courage," and the Order of Daniel of the 1st class ; (Persian) the image of the Shah with diamonds, and the golden ribbon with knot, and the Order of Lion and Sun of the 2nd class ; (Bucharia) the Orders of Tskender-Salis, of the Crown and of the Star of the 1st class with diamonds ; (Tunis) the great cross of officer of the Order Nishan Tphtikhar ; (Japan) the Order of the Rising Sun of the 1st class. Commanded Russian Forces in first part of Russo - Japanese War, 1904. *Publications:* Algeria, 1877 ; Kashgaria (gold medal of Imperial Russian Geographical Society), 1879 ; The Operations of the Troops of General Skobeleff during the War of Russia with the Turks 1877-1878, 1885 ; The Blockade of Plevna, 1885 ; The Crossing of the Balkan by the Detachment of General Skobeleff and the Battle near the Village Sheinovo the 28th of December 1877, 1889 ; The Conquest of Turkomania and the Expedition against Akhal-Teke in the years 1881-1882, with the Description of the Battles in the Middle Asia from the year 1839 till the year 1876, 1899 ; Russia for Russians : the Past and Future Problems of the Russian Army, 1910. *Address:* St Sbg Tavritcheskaia 3, Petrograd ; (in summer) Tcheschourino, Gouv. de Pskow, Russia.

(*Died 10 Feb. 1921.*)

KRETSER, Edward, de, J.P., I.S.O. ; *b.* 31 July 1854 ; *s.* of Peter Cornelius de Kretser ; *m.* 1877, Alice Grace Anjou. *Educ.:* Colombo

597

KOHLSAAT, Herman H. See page xxiii.

KRAUS, Adolf. See page xxiii.

Academy, now Royal College. Clerk, Colonial Secretary's Office, 1872; Chief Clerk, 1892; Director of the Widows' and Orphans' Pension Fund since 1897; a Manager of the Public Service Mutual Guarantee Association since 1901; Secretary Ceylon Savings Bank since 1908; ex-officio Secretary of the Public Service Mutual Provident Association, 1892-1900, and President since 1901; Auditor of the Departmental Funds of the Police Dept.; Assistant Auditor-General, Ceylon Civil Service, 1901-7; Assistant Controller of Revenue, 1907-21; retired on pension, 1921. *Address:* Gracelyn, Bambalapitiya, Colombo. *M.:* 6,345.   (*Died 6 Oct. 1925.*)

KRISHNAN, Hon. Mr. Justice Cheruvari, M.A. (Cantab.); Barrister-at-law; Dewan Bahadur: Judge, High Court of Judicature, Madras, since 1920; *b.* Cannanore, North Malabar, India, in the Cheruvari Tarwad, Nov. 1868; *m.* 1895, Kinathi Madhavi of Tellicherry; two *s.* five *d. Educ.:* High School, Cannanore; Presidency College, Madras; Christ's College, Cambridge. Took degree at Cambridge in Natural Science; called to Bar, Middle Temple, 1891; enrolled as Advocate, High Court of Madras, 1892; entered Government Service as Assistant Chemical Examiner and acting Professor of Chemistry, Presidency College, Madras; resigned and returned to practice, 1893; elected Fellow of the Madras University; Judge of the Court of Small Causes, Madras, 1906; acted as Chief Presidency Magistrate, 1911; Chief Judge of the Court of Small Causes, Madras, 1912; received the title of Dewan Bahadur; acted as Judge of the High Court, 1916, and subsequently several times. *Recreations:* cricket, tennis, billiards. *Address:* Shenstone Park, Chetput, Madras. *T.:* 208. *M.:* 6531 and 8004. *Club:* Cosmopolitan, Madras.   (*Died 9 Nov. 1927.*)

KROPOTKIN, Prince Peter Alexeievitch, Geographer; *b.* 9 Dec. 1842; *s.* of Prince Alexei Petrovitch and Ekaterina Nikolaevna Kropotkin (*b.* Sulima). *Educ.:* Corps of Pages, Petrograd, 1857-62; Petrograd Univ. 1869-73. Gold Medal of Russian Geographical Society for journey across North Manchuria in 1864; Aide-de-Camp to military Governor of Transbaikalia; Attaché for Cossack's Affairs to Governor-General of Eastern Siberia; crossed North Manchuria from Transbaikalia to the Amur, 1864; up the Sungari to Kirin, 1864; Secretary to Physical Geography Section of Geographical Society; explored the glacial deposits in Finland and Sweden, 1871; joined International Working Men's Association, 1872; arrested and confined in fortress St. Peter and St. Paul, 1874; escaped from military hospital, 1876; came to England; founded at Geneva the anarchist paper Le Révolté; expelled from Switzerland, 1881; condemned at Lyons to five years' imprisonment, 1883; liberated, 1886. *Publications:* Report of the Olekma and Vitim Expedition, with Catalogue of Heights in East Siberia, 1874; Researches on the Glacial Period, vol. i. 1876; General Sketch of the Orography of East Siberia, 1876; all in Russian in Memoirs of Russian Geographical Society (French translation, with additions, of the latter, Brussels, 1904); In Russian and French Prisons, 1886; Russia, in Enc. Britannica, 9th and 10th ed.; Russia, Asia, and France, in Chambers' Enc., last edition; Recent Science in Nineteenth Century, 1892-1901; Paroles d'un Révolté, 1884; La Conquête du Pain, 1888; L'Anarchie, sa Philosophie, son Idéal, Paris, 1896 (Engl. transl. 1897); La Science moderne et l'Anarchie, 1912; The State, its Part in History, 1898; Fields, Factories, and Workshops, 1899; 2nd edition, 1901; 8th edition, 1912; Memoirs of a Revolutionist, 1900 (French, German, Dutch, Swedish, Danish, Spanish, Italian, Russian transl.) 3rd ed 1908; Mutual Aid, a Factor of Evolution, 1902; cheap ed. 1915;

598

Modern Science and Anarchism, 1903; revised ed. 1912; The Orography of Asia, with maps, 1904; The Desiccation of Asia (Geographical Journal), 1904 and 1914; Ideals and Realities in Russian Literature, 1905; cheap ed. 1916; The Conquest of Bread, 1906; new edition, 1913; The Great Revolution, 1789-1793, 1908; Terror in Russia, 1909. *Recreations:* bookbinding, carpentry.   (*Died 8 Feb. 1921.*)

KUENEN, Johannes Petrus, Ph.D., LL.D.; Professor of Physics, University, Leiden, Holland; *b.* Leiden, Holland, 11 Oct. 1866; *e. s.* of Professor Abraham Kuenen, Theological Professor, University, Leiden; *m.* Dora Wicksteed, 3rd *d.* of Rev. P. H. Wicksteed, Childrey, Berks; three *s.* two *d. Educ.:* Grammar School and University of Leiden, Ph.D.; gold medal for prize essay. Demonstrator and Lecturer, University, Leiden; Professor, University College, Dundee, 1895-1907. *Publications:* Books on Heat; Theory of Mixtures; Equation of State; various scientific papers. *Recreations:* cycling, gardening, boating. *Address:* Leiden, Holland.   (*Died 25 Sept. 1922.*)

KUROKI, General Count; Hon. G.C.M.G. 1906; *b.* Satsuma, 1844; a Kagoshima Samurai; commanded Left Column in war with China, General, 1903; served Russo-Japanese War; victorious at Yalu, Kiu-lien-ling, etc. *Address:* Tokyo, Japan.   (*Died 4 Feb. 1923.*)

KUSEL, Baron de, (Selig) Bey; *b.* Liverpool, 12 June 1848; *m.* 1876, Elvira, *e. d.* of Cleto Chini of Leghorn and Cairo; one *d. Educ.:* Cheltenham. Bey, 1882; present at Bombardment of Alexandria (war medal, Khedive's Star); was Controller-general of Egyptian Customs and of the Gunpowder Department; Inspector-General of the Coastguards; Egyptian Delegate on International Sanitary Board of Egypt; Kt. Commander of Villa Vicosa; and of Order of Christ; Commander of the Medjidie, Osmanieh, and Nichan-ifshar; Chevalier of Crown of Italy; Capt. East Surrey Regt. (retired). *Publication:* An Englishman's Recollections of Egypt, 1915. *Address:* Tanglelands, Dormanspark, Surrey. *Club:* Junior Army and Navy.   (*Died 1917.*)

KUYPER, A., D.D., LL.D.; *b.* Maassluis, 29 Oct. 1837; *m.* 1863, I. H. Schaay (*d.* 1899); four *s.* three *d. Educ.:* University of Leiden. Candidatus philologiæ, Doctor Theologiæ. Golden medal from the University of Groningen for paper on Calvini et Lasci de ecclesia sententiarum comparatio; Pastor of the Reformed Church at Beest, 1863; Utrecht, 1868; Amsterdam, 1870; member of the States-General for Gonda, 1874-77; for Sliedrecht, 1894-1901; Prime-minister after the elections of July 1901; Minister of State, 1907; Member of States General, 1908; Member of Senate, 1913; founded Free University, Amsterdam, 1880; professor, Free University; lecturer, Encyclopædia, Dogmatics, Hebrew, Exegesis N.T.; Dutch Literature, Æsthetics; founded the daily The Standard and became its chief editor 1872, the Heraut (weekly), 1878; founded Reformed Free Churches, 1886; lectured in America in twenty places; Stone lecturer, 1898; Commander of Order of Dutch Lion, 1912; Grand Cross of Order of Leopold of Belgium, of Medjidie of Turkey; of Christ, Portugal; Hon. Doctor of Laws, Princeton, New Jersey; Hon. Doctor of Technical Science, Delft; Hon. Doctor of Philology, Hope College, Holland, Mich.; Hon. Doctor of Jurisprudence, University of Leuven, 1910; Minister of State, 1910; Hon. President of Netherland Press Association, 1897; President of the Netherland Council for Internationalism, 1911; Hon. Member of the Flemingue Royal Academy of Literature, Ghent, 1906. *Publications:* Joannes a Lasco opera, 2 vols.; edited Encyclopædia S. Theologie, 3 vols.; E voto Dordraceno, 4 vols.; The Work of the Holy Spirit, 3 vols.; Calvinism; From the

KUTLEHR, Raja Ram Pal of, C.S.I. See page xxiii.

Scriptures ; Political Platform of the Anti-Revolutionary Party; The Incarnation; Socialism and Christianity ; The Evolution ; The South African Crisis ; Common Grace, 3 vols. ; Varia Americana, 1899 ; Around the Old World, etc., 2 vols. ; and many other publications ; Anti-revolutionary Politics, 2 vols. Two hundred and fourteen volumes altogether. *Address :* The Hague, 5 Kanaalstraat. *T. :* 710.   (*Died 8 Nov. 1920.*)

KYLLACHY, Lord ; William Mackintosh, M.A., LL.D., J.P., D.L. ; *b.* 9 April 1842 ; *e. s.* of late William Mackintosh, Inshes House, Inverness-shire ; *m.* Jane (*d.* 1909), *d.* of David Stevenson, C.E., 1869 ; two *s.* one *d. Educ. :* Edinburgh Academy and University ; Hon. LL.D.,1889. Advocate, 1865 ; Procurator, Church of Scotland, 1880 ; Sheriff of Ross, Cromarty, and Sutherland, 1881 ; Q.C. and Dean of Faculty of Advocates, 1886 ; raised to Bench as Lord Kyllachy, 1889 ; Judge of the Court of Session and Justiciary, retired, 1907. *Address :* Kyllachy, Tomatin, Inverness-shire ; 6 Randolph Crescent, Edinburgh. *Clubs :* Brooks's ; New, Edinburgh. (*Died 9 Dec. 1918.*)

KYNNAIRD, Viscount, Sigismondo Maria Giuseppe ; Duca di Mondragone ; *b.* 20 June 1886 ; *e. s.* of 10th Earl of Newburgh ; *m.* 1910, Teresa, *d.* of Principe Ugo Boncompagni Ludovisi, *e. s.* of Principe di Piombino. *Address :* 1o Via Virginio Orsini, Rome.
    (*Died 4 Nov. 1918.*)

L

LABORDE, Edward Daniel, C.B.E. 1922 ; I.S.O. 1908 ; *b.* 1863 ; *s.* of late Edward Laborde, C.M.G., Administrator of several West Indian Colonies. Chief Clerk to Governor Windward Islands, 1885 ; Private Secretary to Governor Sir Walter Sendall, 1888 ; Chief of Police St. Vincent, 1889 ; Supervisor of Customs, 1897 ; Acting Colonial Secretary, Member Executive and Legislative Council, 1901 ; Chief of Police and Inspector of Prisons, St. Lucia, 1902; Acting Administrator of St. Vincent, 1904 ; Acting Administrator and Colonial Secretary, St. Lucia, 1905 ; Treasurer, Island of Grenada, 1915 ; Acting Administrator, St. Lucia, 1907 ; has acted as Administrator, Colonial Secretary, Grenada, on various occasions ; Administrator, Government of St. Lucia, June 1921-Aug. 1922, when he retired ; London Representative of St. Lucia and Hon. Treasurer for West Indian and Atlantic Colonies at British Empire Exhibition ; Member of West Indian Conference, 1926. *Club:* West Indian.   (*Died 29 June 1928.*)

LA BILLOIS, Hon. Charles H. ; *b.* Dalhousie, Restigouche, County New Brunswick, 18 Dec. 1856 ; *s.* of Joseph H. La Billois, for many years a merchant and postmaster in Dalhousie ; his grandfather came from Brittany and was a surgeon under Napoleon Bonaparte, reaching America in 1816 ; his grandparents, on his mother's side, came from Ireland after the Rebellion ; *m.* Charlotte, *y. d.* of John M'Naughton, lumber merchant, of Quebec ; two *s.* two *d. Educ. :* Grammar School, Dalhousie ; Model School, Carleton, province of Quebec. Returned to the House of Assembly, New Brunswick, to represent Restigouche, his native county, at the General Election, 1882, and has been re-elected at every election since ; appointed a Member of the Executive Council, 1891, under leadership of Hon. A. G. Blair. Commissioner of Agriculture, 1897 ; Acting Commissioner, Board of Works, 1900 ; Chief Commissioner, Board of Works, 1900. *Address :* Dalhousie, New Brunswick. (*Died 22 Nov. 1928.*)

LABORI, Fernand, Avocat à la Cour d'Appel de Paris, ancien bâtonnier ; ancien député de l'Arrondissement de Fontainebleau ; Fondateur de la Revue du Palais et de la Grande Revue ; Ancien rédacteur en chef de la Gazette du Palais ; Membre du Conseil de l'Ordre, 1905 ; bâtonnier de l'Ordre des Avocats à la Cour de Paris, 1911-13 ; *b.* Reims, France, 18 April 1860 ; *s.* of Adolphe Labori, Inspecteur Principal hon. aux Chemins de Fer de l'Est ; *m.* 1893, Marguerite Okey ; three *d. Educ. :* Reims ; two years in Germany and England ; Paris. Called to Bar, 1884 ; has taken part in many famous cases, including the Zola Case, the Dreyfus Appeal, and the Humbert Case. *Publications :* The Répertoire encyclopédique du droit français, 12 vols. *Address :* 12 rue Pigalle, Paris.   (*Died 14 Mar. 1917.*)

LACE, John Henry, C.I.E. 1913 ; Chief Conservator, Burma, 1908, retired 1913. Joined India Forest Department, 1881 ; Conservator, 1902 : retired 1913.   (*Died 9 June 1918.*)

LACON, Capt. Henry Edmund ; J.P. County of Suffolk ; *o. s.* of late Henry James Lacon, Captain R.N. of the Goldrood, Ipswich, *y. s.* of Sir Edmund Lacon, 2nd Bart., of Ormesby Hall, Norfolk ; *m.* 1890, Hon. Margaret Erskine, *o. d.* of 5th Lord Erskine of Spratton Hall, Northampton. *Educ. :* Harrow. Late Captain in the 71st Highland Light Infantry. *Address :* The Lodge, Bramford, Ipswich.
    (*Died 18 Mar. 1924.*)

LACOSTE, Hon. Sir Alexandre, Kt. ; *cr.* 1892 ; P.C., LL.D., D.C.L. ; Chief Justice, Quebec, 1891-1907; *b.* Boucherville, Canada, 12 Jan. 1842 ; *s.* of Hon. Louis Lacoste, senator (member of an old Languedoc family which settled in Canada) and Mary Antoinette Thaïs Proulx ; *m.* 1866, Marie Louise, *d.* of Leon Globensky of Montreal ; three *s.* seven *d. Educ. :* St. Hyacinthe Coll. ; Laval Univ., Quebec. Barr. 1863 ; Q.C. 1880 ; Bâtonnier of the Bar, Montreal, 1879-81 ; Professor of Law, Laval University ; Member of Legislative Council, 1882-84 : Member of Senate, 1884-91 ; Speaker, 1891 ; Privy Councillor of Canada, 1892 ; Administrator for the Province of Quebec, 1898 ; resigned. 1907. *Address :* 71 St. Hubert Street, Montreal. *Club:* Mount Royal, Montreal.   (*Died 16 Aug. 1923.*)

LADD, Professor George Trumbull, LL.D. ; Clark Professor of Metaphysics and Moral Philosophy in Yale University (Emeritus) ; *b.* 19 Jan. 1842 ; *m.* 1st 1869, Cornelia Ann Tallman ; 2nd 1895, Frances Virginia Stevens ; two *s.* one *d. Educ. :* Western Reserve College ; Andover Theological Seminary. Preached, Edinburgh, Ohio, 1869-71 ; Pastor, Spring St. Congl. Church, Milwaukee, Wis., 1871-9 ; Prof. of Philosophy, Bowdoin Coll., 1879-81 ; Yale, 1881-1905 (Emeritus, 1905) ; Lecturer, Andover Theol. Sem., 1879-81 ; at Doshisha and Summer School, Japan, 1892 ; and in 1899 and 1906-7, before the Imperial Universities and Commercial Colleges of Japan ; and in 1899-1900 at Bombay, under the auspices of the Bombay University, and in Calcutta, Madras, and elsewhere in India ; several times lecturer at Harvard, and conducted Graduate Seminary in Ethics in 1895-6 ; Delegate to World's Congress of Psychologists at Paris, 1900 ; Guest and Unofficial Adviser of Prince Ito, in Korea, 1907 ; Decorated Order of the Rising Sun, 3rd class, 1899 ; 2nd class, 1907 ; Gold Medallist of the Imperial Educational Soc. of Japan, 1907 ; several times admitted to audience with the Emperor of Japan ; Founder of American Psychological Association, and President in 1893 ; Member American Phil. Soc. ; American Oriental Soc. ; Society of American Naturalists ; Vice-Pres. Amer. Soc. of Associated Sciences, 1911-12. *Publications :* Principles of Church Polity, 1882 ; Doctrine of Sacred Scripture, 2 vols., 1884 ; Lotze's Outlines, trans. 6 vols., 1887 ; Elements of Physiological Psychology, 1887 (revised ed. with Prof. R. S. Woodworth, 1911) ; What is the Bible? 1888 ; Introd. to Philosophy, 1889 ; Outlines of Physiological Psychology, 1890 ;

Philosophy of Mind, 1891; Primer of Psychology, 1894; Psychology, Descriptive and Explanatory, 1894; Philosophy of Knowledge, 1897; Outlines of Descriptive Psychology, 1898; Essays on the Higher Education, 1899; A Theory of Reality, 1899; Lectures to Teachers (in Japanese only), 1899; Philosophy of Conduct, 1902; Philosophy of Religion, 2 vols., 1905; In Korea with Marquis Ito, 1908; Knowledge, Life, and Reality, 1909; Rare Days in Japan, 1910; What Can I Know? 1914; What Ought I to Do? 1915; What Should I Believe? 1915; What May I Hope? 1915; The Secret of Personality, 1917; Intimate Glimpses of Life in India, 1919. *Recreations:* music and gardening. *Address:* New Haven, Connecticut. *T.:* Center 3333. *(Died Aug. 1921.)*

LAFFAN, Rev. Robert Stuart de Courcy, M.A.: Rector of St. Stephen, Walbrook with St. Benet Sherehog since 1899: *b.* 18 Jan. 1853; *e. s.* of late Lieut.-Gen. Sir Robert Michael Laffan, K.C.M.G.; *m.* Bertha Jane (*d.* 1912), *d.* of Frederick Grundy, and *widow* of Surg.-Gen. Leith-Adams. *Educ.:* Winchester; Merton Coll., Oxford (Exhibitioner), 1st class Mods. 1876; B.A. (1st Lit. Hum.), 1878; M.A. 1884; Deacon, 1882; Priest, 1883; Officer of Order of Redeemer (Greece), 1907; Officier de l'Instruction Publique (France), 1907; Commander II. Class of the Swedish Royal Order of Wasa, 1912; Senior Classical Master and Chaplain, Derby School, 1880-84; Headmaster King Edward the VI.'s School, Stratford-on-Avon, 1884-95; Select Preacher to University of Oxford, and Select Preacher to University of Cambridge for 1898 and 1899; Principal of Cheltenham College, 1895-99; Chaplain to 12th London Batt. (Rangers), 1904-12; rejoined Aug. 1915; in charge of St. George's Garrison Church, Aldershot, 1916-19; Member of International Olympic Committee since 1899, and of Technical Education Board L.C.C., 1900 - 1904; Member of Council, Shakespeare Memorial Association, Stratford - on - Avon; Member of British Olympic Council since 1905. *Publication:* Aspects of Fiction, 1885. *Address:* 1 Brunswick House, Palace Gardens Terrace, Kensington, W.8. *T.:* Park 2524. *(Died 16 Jan. 1927.)*

LAFLEUR, Paul Theodore, M.A., Professor of Comparative Literature, McGill University, since 1907; Molson Professor of English, 1920. *Educ.:* High School, Montreal; McGill University. *Address:* 215 Peel Street, Montreal. *Club:* University, Montreal. *(Died 9 Feb. 1924.)*

LA FOLLETTE, Robert Marion, Senator; *b.* Primrose, Wisconsin, 14 June 1855; *s.* of Josiah La Follette and Mary Ferguson; *m.* 1881, Belle Case of Baraboo, Wis. *Educ.:* University of Wisconsin; LL.D. Admitted to Bar, 1880; District Attorney Dane Co., 1880-84; Member of Congress, 1885-91; took prominent part in framing McKinley Bill; Governor of Wisconsin, 1901-3, 1903-5, 1905-7; elected U.S. Senator, 1905 for term 1905-10, and resigned Governorship; re-elected United States Senator three terms, 1910-29. *Publication:* Autobiography—A Personal Narrative of Political Experiences, 1913. *Address:* Maple Bluff Farm, Madison, Wis.; 2112 Wyoming Avenue, Washington, D.C., U.S.A. *(Died 18 June 1925.)*

LAING, Malcolm Alfred, Lord-Lieut. of Orkney and Shetland since 1892; late Captain 14th Hussars; *b.* 20 May 1846; *s.* of Samuel Laing, late Chairman Brighton Railway Co. *Educ.:* Harrow; Sandhurst. Passed 1st out of Sandhurst, 1864; gazetted 14th Hussars, 1865; Captain, 1870; retired, 1873. *Recreations:* shooting, fishing, racing, golf. *Address:* 18 Queen Street, Mayfair, W. *T.:* 2092 Gerrard; Crook, Orkney. *Clubs:* Turf, Arthur's, Jockey. *(Died 10 Dec. 1917.)*

LAIRD, Thomas Patrick, C.A.; Professor of Accounting and Business Method, University

of Edinburgh; senior partner of Moncreiff and Horsburgh, C.A., Edinburgh; *b.* 1860; *m.* 1st, Mary Jane, *d.* of Rev. James Macgregor; 2nd, Caroline Grizel, *d.* of James Edward Barclay; one *s.* one *d. Educ.:* Sharp's Institution and Academy, Perth. Admitted Member Society of Accountants, Edinburgh; Secretary of that Society, 1916-20; Member of the University Court, University of Edinburgh; Chairman of British Assets Trust, Ltd. *Address:* 35 Inverleith Row, Edinburgh; 46 Castle Street, Edinburgh. *T.A.:* Monarch, Edinburgh. *T.:* Central 999. *Club:* Northern, Edinburgh.*(Died 11 June 1927.)*

LAKE, Sir St. Vincent Atwell, 7th Bt.; *cr.* 1711; *b.* 8 Jan. 1862; *S. u.* 1897; *m.* 1885, Elizabeth Daisy (*d.* 1900), *d.* of Charles Day. *Heir: c.* Arthur Johnstone [*b.* 1849; *m.* 1884, Emily Burton (*deceased*); three *d.*].
(Died 12 Nov. 1916.)

LAKE, Sir Arthur Johnstone, 8th Bt., *cr.* 1711; *b.* 15 Oct. 1849; *S.* cousin, 1916; *m.* 1884, Emily Burton (*deceased*); three *d. Heir: c.* Atwell Henry, Lieut. R.N., *b.* 13 Feb. 1891.
(Died 10 Nov. 1924.)

LAKING, Sir Guy Francis, 2nd Bt., *cr.* 1902; C.B., 1914; M.V.O., F.S.A.; Knight of Grace of the Order of ·St. John of Jerusalem; Knight Commander of the Charles III. of Spain; Knight of the Crown of Italy; Officer of the Leopold of Belgium; Officer of St. John the Lateran; Keeper of the King's Armoury; Keeper of the Armoury of the Wallace Collection; Keeper and Sec. and Accounting Officer of the London Museum, Lancaster House, St. James, since 1911; *b.* 21 October 1875; *s.* of 1st Bt. and Emma (*d.* 1905), *d.* of Joseph Mansell; *S.* father, 1914; *m.* 1898, Beatrice, *d.* of Charles Mylne Barker; one *s.* one *d. Educ.:* Westminster School. Went to the Architectural Museum, Westminster, to learn drawing; was going to be artist, but joined the firm of Christie, as took such deep interest in pictures and works of art. *Publications:* The Armoury at Windsor Castle, 1904; The Armoury of the Knights of St. John, 1905; The Furniture of Windsor Castle, 1905; The Sevres Porcelain of Buckingham Palace, 1907; articles upon art subjects in Magazine of Art, The Art Journal, etc.; the *catalogue raisonné* of the European and Eastern Armour at Hertford House, etc. *Recreations:* riding, drawing, reading; all matters connected with the stage. *Heir: s.* Guy Francis William, *b.* 1903. *Address:* Meyrick Lodge, Avenue Road, Regent's Park, N.W.; York Gate House, Broadstairs. *Clubs:* Marlborough, Conservative, Garrick. *(Died 22 Nov. 1919.)*

LALAING, Count de, Hon. G.C.V.O. 1915; *b.* London, 1856; *s.* of late Count and of Julia Maria Vibart; *S.* father 1881; *m.* Christine, *d.* of Baron du Tour de Bellinchaye, grand master of the ceremonies at the Dutch Court; *heir: s.* Jacques, *b.* 1889; one *d. Educ.:* Brussels (LL.D.). Entered Belgian Foreign Office, 1879; 2nd Secretary, Vienna, 1881; Chargé d'Affaires, Bucharest, 1883; Attaché au Cabinet du Roi, 1884; 1st Secretary, Berlin, 1886; the Hague, 1887; Councillor in London, 1889; Minister, Rio de Janeiro, 1893; Bucharest, 1896; Envoy Extraordinary and Minister Plenipotentiary, 1898; Berne, 1899; London, 1903-15; Commander, Order of Leopold; Grand Cross, Order of the Crown of Belgium; Grand Cross of the Star of Roumania, and of the Crown of Italy, etc. *Recreations:* golf, shooting. *Address:* 15 West Halkin Street, Belgrave Square, S.W.1; *T.:* Victoria 3919; 43 Rue Ducale, Brussels; Santbergen, Flandre orientale, Belgium. *Clubs:* Travellers', Royal Automobile, Bachelors'; Cercle du Parc, Brussels. *(Died 13 Nov. 1919.)*

LALL, I. C., M.A., O.B.E. 1918; I.S.O.; *b.* 27 April 1865; *s.* of Chandu Lall, Educational Department, Lahore; *m.* 1888, Georgiana, 3rd *d.* of A. Athim, E.A. Commissioner in the Punjab;

two s. three d. *Educ.*: Baring High School, Batala; Government Coll., Lahore. B.A. Calcutta University, 1884; M.A. Punjab University, 1885; entered the Punjab Provincial Civil Service, 1885; Settlement Officer, 1902-12; Deputy Commissioner, Gujerat, 1912; retired from service, 1918. *Recreations:* tennis, riding. *Address:* Lahore, Punjab. (*Died 27 Mar. 1922.*)

LAMB, Sir Archibald, 3rd Bt.; *cr.* 1795; D.L.; late Maj. 2nd Life Guards; Maj. Imperial Yeomanry; served South Africa; *b.* 5 Nov. 1845; *S.* grandfather 1860; *m.* Louisa, *y. d.* cf Sir H. E. Durrant, 3rd Bt. (widow of J. R. Fenwick), 1875. *Educ.:* Eton; Trinity Coll. Camb. Owns about 2700 acres. *Heir: b.* Lt.-Col. C. A. Lamb. *Address:* Beauport, Battle, Sussex. *Club:* Carlton. (*Died 6 Nov. 1921.*)

LAMB, Rev. Benjamin, Hon. Canon of Ripon. *Address:* Belford. Devonshire Place, Bath. (*Died 19 Jan. 1925.*)

LAMB, Edmund, M.A. (Oxon.), F.C.S., F.R.G.S.; County Councillor, West Sussex; *b.* 8 July 1863; 2nd *surv. s.* of late Richard Westbrook Lamb, J.P. and D.L. of West Denton, Northumberland, and Georgiana, *d.* of Stephen Eaton of Ketton Hall, Co. Rutland, and *g. s.* of Joseph Lamb, J.P. and D.L. of Temon, Co. Cumberland; *m.* 1898, Mabel, *o. d.* of Stephen Winkworth, Holly Lodge, Campden Hill, W., and *g. d.* of Thomas Thomasson, the friend and supporter of Cobden and Bright; one *d. Educ.:* Oratory School, Edgbaston, Birmingham; Merton Coll., Oxford (honours degree); University Coll., London. A colliery proprietor in Northumberland, and a landowner in Northumberland and Sussex; M.P. (L.) Leominster Div. of North Herefordshire, 1906-10; Member of Institute of Mining Engineers. *Recreations:* horse breeding, and farming. *Address:* Borden Wood, Liphook, Hants; Holly Lodge, Campden Hill, W.8. *T.:* Park 4791. *Clubs:* Oxford and Cambridge, Union, Bath. (*Died 3 Jan. 1925.*)

LAMB, Sir Richard A. See page xxiii.

LAMBART, Lieut.-Col. Sir Gustavus Francis, 1st Bart., *cr.* 1911; C.V.O. 1903; late Major and Lt.-Col. 5th Leinster Regiment; *b.* 25 Mar. 1848; *e. s.* of Gustavus W. Lambart of Beau Parc, Co. Meath; *m.* 1911, Kathleen Moore Brabazon; one *s.* Formerly Chamberlain to Duke of Marlborough; Comptroller to H.E. The Earl of Dudley, 1902-3; Chamberlain, 1904; Secretary to Order of St. Patrick. *Heir: s.* Oliver Francis, *b.* 6 Apr. 1913. *Address:* Beau Parc, Co. Meath. *Clubs:* Carlton; Kildare Street, Dublin. (*Died 16 June 1926.*)

LAMBART, Richard, D.S.O. 1914; *b.* 26 June 1875; *s.* of late Maj. Fred Lambart, Scots Fusiliers; *m.* 1913, Faith Bevan. *Educ.:* Radley. Entered army, 1914; served European War, 1914-15 (despatches, D.S.O.). *Address:* 30 Milner Street, Cadogan Square, S.W. *Club:* Royal Automobile. (*Died 6 Jan. 1924.*)

LAMBERT, Agnes; *b.* Milford Hall, Salisbury; *y. d.* of late Rt. Hon. Sir John Lambert, K.C.B., Permanent Secretary of the Local Government Board, and Ellen, *d.* of Henry Shorto, of Salisbury. *Publications:* A School Bank Manual; edited The Free Trade Speeches of Charles Pelham Villiers; numerous articles in the Nineteenth Century, Dublin Review, and other periodicals. *Recreations:* music, gardening. *Address:* Milford House, Elms Road, Clapham Common, S.W. (*Died Nov. 1917.*)

LAMBERT, Alfred Uvedale Miller; M.A., J.P., F.R. Hist. Soc., F.S.A., M.F.H. Burstow Foxhounds, 1900-1905; *y. s.* of late Henry Thomas Lambert, J.P., of Sandhills, Bletchingley, Surrey, and Georgina Emily, *d.* of late Rev. Sir Thomas Combe Miller, 6th Bt., of Froyle Park, Hants (*d.* 1902); *m.* 1st, 1894, Violet (*d.* 1894), *d.* of late Walter James Marshall, J.P., D.L., of Patterdale Hall, Westmorland; 2nd, 1904, Cecily, *o. d.* of late Gerard Hoare, J.P., M.F.H. Burstow Foxhounds, of Stansted House.

Godstone; one *s. Educ.:* Eton; Trinity Coll., Camb. 2nd Lieut. Middlesex Yeomanry Cavalry, 1891-95. *Publication:* Blechingley, a Parish History, 1921. *Address:* South Park Farm, Bletchingley, Surrey. *Club:* Windham.
(*Died 6 June 1928.*)

LAMBERT, Admiral Sir Cecil Foley, K.C.B., *cr.* 1920; *b.* 28 May 1864; 3rd *s.* of late Sir H. E. F. Lambert, 6th Bt., and *heir-pres.* to Sir J. F. Grey; *m.* 1896, Rosina, *d.* of Francis Drake. Served Egypt, 1882 (medal and star); 4th Sea Lord Admiralty, 1913-19; Director of Personnel, Air Ministry, 1919-21; additional member of the Air Council, 1920-21; Vice-Admiral, 1921; retired list, 1921; Adm. retired list, 1926. *Address:* 8 Palace Street, S.W.1. *Club:* Orleans. (*Died 29 Feb. 1928.*)

LAMBERT, Francis L., I.S.O.; *b.* Roscommon, Ireland, 1838; *m.* 1865, Josephine Amelia, 3rd *d.* of late B. H. Hickey, Anerley; two *s.* one *d. Educ.:* privately. Entered Excise Department, 1858; passed into Government Laboratory, 1862, obtaining a prize for proficiency in Practical and Theoretical Chemistry; returned to Excise Branch, and having passed through all the grades, reached the highest post, that of Chief Inspector of Inland Revenue, from which he retired in 1902. *Recreations:* historical and scientific studies and gardening. *Address:* 17 Heathhurst Road, Sanderstead.
(*Died 31 July 1925.*)

LAMBERT, Rev. Frederick Fox, M.A.; Hon. Canon St. Albans, 1898. *Educ.:* Corpus Christi College, Oxford; Curate of Kidderminster, 1866-68; Vicar of Loversall, 1868-72; Chaplain to the Marquis of Salisbury, 1872-77; Claremarket Mission, 1877; Bedington, 1878-79; Rector of Clothall, 1879-91; Vicar of Cheshunt, 1891-1911. *Address:* Aston Dene, Stevenage.
(*Died 25 April 1920.*)

LAMBERT, Sir George Thomas, Kt.; *cr.* 1903; C.B. 1897; Director of Greenwich Hospital; *b.* 9 Nov. 1837; *y. s.* of late Henry Lambert, M.P., and Catherine, *d.* of Wm. Talbot of Castle Talbot; descended from the second Earl of Shrewsbury. *Educ.:* Downside Coll., Bath; London Univ.; matriculated in first class, 1856. Acted as private secretary to members of the Government in several administrations, including the 16th Earl of Derby, Sir George Trevelyan, Earl of Camperdown, Sir Massey Lopes, and Lord Brassey. *Address:* 7 Park Place, St. James's, S.W. *Clubs:* White's Arthur's.
(*Died 20 Nov. 1918.*)

LAMBERT, Sir John, K.C.I.E.; *cr.* 1898; Member of Legislative Council, 1892; retired, 1897; *b.* 1838; *m.* 1869, Annie, *d.* of Lieut.-Gen. F. D. Atkinson. Entered Bengal Police, 1863, as Assistant and District Superintendent; Visitor Jail and Lunatic Asylums, 1872; Deputy Commissioner of Police, Calcutta, 1874; Foreign Dept., 1882-84; Acting Commissioner, Calcutta, 1885-86; Commissioner, 1889. *Address:* 81 Harcourt Terrace, S.W. *T.:* Kensington 4178. *Club:* Oriental. (*Died 31 Aug. 1916.*)

LAMBERT, Col. (temp. Brig.-General) Thomas Stanton, C.B. 1918; C.M.G. 1918; Com. 13th Infantry Brigade; *b.* 27 Jan. 1871; *s.* of late Rev. R. U. Lambert, M.A., Vicar of Christ Church, Bradford-on-Avon, Wiltshire and Agnes, *d.* of Archdeacon Stanton, Burbage, Wilts; *m.* Geraldine Rachel Foster; two *s.* one *d. Educ.:* Charterhouse; R.M.C., Sandhurst. East Lancashire Regt. 1891; India, 1897-1904; Staff College, Camberley, 1905-7; Staff Captain, Harrismith O.R.C., S. Africa, 1907-9; War Office, 1910-14; served with B.E.F. Aug. 1914-Nov. 1914 with 4th Div.; present at Le Cateau, Nery, Marne, Aisne, Ploegsteert (severely wounded); commanded 1st Batt. East Lancashire Regt. at Marne and Aisne; D.A.A.G. 37th Div., March-May 1915; commanded 2nd Batt. East Lancashire Regt. June-Oct. 1915; Bridoux Salient (Loos operations), 26-28 Sep.

1915; Acting A.A.G., G.H.Q. Oct-Dec. 1915; commanded 69th Infantry Brigade, 1916-18, including capture of Contalmaison, and actions of Le Sars, and Hill 60, Menin Road, Cameron Covert (Polygon Wood); Italy, 1917-18; commanded 32nd Division, 1918-19; Operations of 4th Army, Aug. to Nov. 1918, including actions at Damery, Huleville, passage of Somme at Brie and St. Christ, Holnon Wood, Hindenburg Line, Sequehart, passage of Oise and Sambre Canal at Ors, relief of Avesnes; commanded 1st King's Brigade, Lancashire Division, Army of the Rhine; Commanded Dublin Brigade, Oct. to Dec. 1919. *Recreations:* tennis, riding, winter sports. *Club:* United Service.
(Died 20 June 1921.)

LAMBERT, Lieut.-Col. Walter Miller, J.P. Dorset; D.S.O. 1887; *b.* 8 May 1843; *y. s.* of Richard Lambert of Lyston Hall, Essex, and Charlotte, *d.* of John Campbell; *m.* 1878, Frances, *o. c.* of F. B. Courtenay; one *s.* two *d. Educ.:* Cheltenham College. Entered Royal Marine Artillery, 1860; Lieut.-Col. 1886; served Burmah, 1885-86 (despatches, D.S.O., medal with clasp). *Recreation:* fishing. *Address:* 25 Princess Road, Bournemouth.
(Died 25 Jan. 1924.)

LAMBERT, Rev. William Henry, M.A.; *b.* 1833; 5th *s.* of Sir Henry John Lambert of Aston House, Oxon.; *m.* 1866, Georgiana Joyce (*d.* 1920), 3rd *d.* of Robert Biddulph of Ledbury; one *s. Educ.:* Eton; Merton College, Oxford. Ordained, 1857; Curate of St. Mary's, Bridgnorth, 1857-8; Rector of Stoke Edith with Westhide, 1858-1905; Rural Dean of Weston, 1886-96 and 1904-11; Prebendary of Hereford Cathedral, 1887-1918; Pres. of the Woolhope Naturalists Field Club, 1893. *Address:* Fenton House, Hereford.
(Died 23 Feb. 1924.)

LAMBOURNE, 1st Baron, *cr.* 1917; **Amelius Richard Mark Lockwood;** P.C. 1905; G.C.V.O., *cr.* 1927; C.V.O. 1905; J.P., D.L.; Lord-Lieutenant of Essex; Vice-President R.S.P.C.A.; President Royal Horticultural Society; President of the Bribery and Secret Commissions Prevention League Incorporated; *b.* 17 Aug. 1847; *e. s.* of late General Mark Wood; *m.* 1876, Isabella (*d.* 1923), 2nd *d.* of Sir John R. Milbanke, 8th Bart., Minister at Munich and The Hague. *Educ.:* Eton. Entered Coldstream Guards, 1866; retired, 1883; Provincial Grand Master of Essex Freemasons, 1902; M.P. (C.) Epping Division of Essex, 1892-1917. *Heir:* none. *Address:* 5 Audley Square, W.1; *T.:* Grosvenor 1972; Bishop's Hall, Romford, Essex. *T.:* Chigwell 16. *T.A.:* Audlesque, London; Bishop's Hall, Chigwell Row. *M.:* LC 5677; F 1625; A 8290. *Club:* Carlton.
(Died 20 Dec. 1928.)

LAMBTON, Lieut.-Col. Francis W., retired; J.P. Pembrokeshire; *b.* Naples, 1834; 3rd *s.* of William Henry, *y. b.* of 1st Earl Durham and Henrietta Lambton, co-heiress of Cuthbert Ellison, jr., of Durham; *m.* Lady Victoria Alexandrina Elizabeth Campbell (*d.* 1909), *e. d.* of 2nd Earl Cawdor. *Educ.:* Eton. Served in the Crimea in the Scots Guards, 1854 to end of war. *Recreations:* all sorts of sports. *Address:* Brownslade, near Pembroke. *Club:* Travellers'. *(Died 6 Oct. 1921.)*

LAMBTON, Lieut. - Colonel George Charles, D.S.O. 1900; O.B.E.; late Worcestershire Regiment; 4th *s.* of late Lieut.-Colonel F. W. Lambton and Lady Victoria Alexandrina Elizabeth Campbell (*d.* 1909), *e. d.* of 2nd Earl Cawder; *b.* 10 Nov. 1872. *Educ.:* Wellington. Entered K.R.R.C. 1892; Worcesters. Regt. 1895; Captain, 1900; served S. Africa, 1899-1902, with 5th Mounted Infantry (despatches, Queen's medal four clasps, King's medal, two clasps, D.S.O.); European War, 1914-15 (despatches twice, Bt. Lt.-Col.); retired pay, 1922. *Address:* Brownslade, near Pembroke. *(Died 30 Aug. 1927.)*

602

LAMPLUGH, George William, F.R.S. 1905; *b.* Driffield, East Yorkshire, 8 April 1859; *m.* 1887; two *s.* one *d. Educ.:* private schools. Mercantile occupation until 1892; joined the Staff of the Geological Survey as Assistant-Geologist; District Geologist, 1901; President Geological Society, 1918-20; Assistant Director, H.M. Geological Survey of Great Britain, 1914-20 (retired); *Publications:* numerous geological, geographical, etc., papers and memoirs. *Address:* 13 Beaconsfield Road, St. Albans.
(Died 9 Oct. 1926.)

LAMY, Etienne Marie Victor, homme de lettres; Membre, et depuis 1913 Secrétaire Perpetuel, de l'Académie Française; Officier de la Légion d'Honneur; *b.* Cize Jura, 2 June 1845. *Educ.:* Collège Stanislas. Docteur en droit, 1870; Député de Jura, 1871-81. *Publications:* Le Tiers Parti, 1868; Rapport sur le Budget de la Marine, 1878; Discours, 1879; La République en 1883; L'Armée et la Démocratie, 1889; La France du Levant, 1898; La Femme de demain, 1899; Aimée de Coigny, 1900; Etudes sur le Second Empire, 1900; Témoins de jours passés, 1909 (2e Série, 1913); Au Service des idées et des lettres, 1909; Quelques Œuvres et quelques Ouvriers (2 séries), 1910 et 1913. *Address:* 3 Place d'Jéna, Paris; Château de Vannoz par Champagnole, Jura; L'Estagnol, Antibes.
(Died 9 Jan. 1919.)

LANCASTER, William Joseph Cosens, A.M.I.C.E.; civil engineer, British Admiralty Service; *b.* Weymouth, 23 May 1851; *o. s.* of Capt. Wm. Lancaster; *m.* 1878; one *s. Educ.:* Royal Naval Coll. Greenwich (medallist); went to sea at age of 15; obliged to abandon the profession in consequence of extreme shortsight; adopted profession of civil engineer, making specialty of sea and harbour work; travelled in Baltic and Mediterranean, East and West Indies, East, West, and South Coasts of Africa, etc.; began to write sea stories, under pseudonym of "Harry Collingwood," 1878. *Publications:* The Secret of the Sands, 1879; Under the Meteor Flag, 1884; Voyage of the Aurora, 1885; Pirate Island, 1885; The Congo Rovers, 1886; Log of the Flying Fish, 1887; The Rover's Secret, 1888; Missing Merchantman, 1889; Doctor of the Juliet, 1892; Cruise of the Esmeralda, 1894; The Pirate Slaver, 1895; Jack Beresford's Yarn, 1896; Log of a Privateersman, 1896; The Homeward Voyage, 1897; An Ocean Chase, 1898; The Castaways, 1899; A Pirate of the Caribbees, 1900; Dick Leslie's Luck; Across the Spanish Main, 1906; With Airship and Submarine; Geoffrey Harrington's Adventures, 1907; A Middy in Command; Under the Chilian Flag; Blue and Grey, 1908; The Cruise of the Thetis, 1909; Harry Escombe; A Middy of the Slave Squadron; Overdue, 1910. *Recreations:* yachting (especially yacht racing), yacht designing, swimming, shooting, riding, painting in water colours, photography, cycling, music. *Club:* Whitefriars'. *(Died June 1922.)*

LANDON, Perceval, Barrister - at - law; special correspondent, dramatist and author; *b.* 29 Mar. 1869; *s.* of late Rev. Edward Henry Landon and Caroline, *d.* of late Rev. and Hon. Arthur P. Perceval; unmarried. *Educ.:* Hertford College, Oxford; B.A. 1893. Called to Bar, Inner Temple, 1895; special correspondent for The Times, S.A. War, 1899-1900; private secretary to Governor of New South Wales, 1900; special correspondent Daily Mail, Delhi Durbar, China, Japan, Siberia, 1903; special correspondent The Times, expedition to Lhasa, 1903-4; special correspondent the Daily Telegraph, Prince of Wales' visit to India, 1905-6; Persia, India, and Nepal, 1908; Russian Turkestan, 1909; Egypt and Sudan, 1910; N.E. frontier of India, Delhi Durbar, 1911; Mesopotamia and Syria, 1912; Scandinavia, British and French lines, 1914-15; Italian Lines, 1917; Peace Conference, Paris,

1919; Constantinople, 1920; India, Mesopotamia, Syria, Palestine, 1921; Prince of Wales' Tour, India and Japan, 1921-22; China, North America, 1922; Peace Conference, Lausanne, 1923; China, Nepal, Egypt, 1924; China, 1925; on staff Daily Telegraph; Silver Medal of the Royal Society of Arts, 1915. *Publications:* Heliotropes, 1903; Lhasa, 1905; Under the Sun, 1906; 1857: The Story of the Indian Mutiny, 1907; Raw Edges, 1908; The House Opposite; For the Soul of the King (transl. from the French), 1909. *Address:* 1 The Studios, Gunter Grove, Chelsea, S.W. *T.:* Kensington 8846. *Club:* Beefsteak.

(Died 23 Jan. 1927.)

LANDOR, A. Henry Savage, M.R.I., F.R.G.S.; Hon. Cor. Member École d'Anthropologie of Paris; Hon. Member and Gold Medallist Geographical Society, Marseilles; Hon. Member Italian Anthropological Society, Founder Member of International Anthropological Institute, Paris: painter, sculptor, explorer; *b.* Florence; 2nd *s.* of late Charles Savage Landor; *g.s.* of Walter Savage Landor. *Educ.:* Liceo Dante, Istituto Tecnico, Florence; Atelier Thaddeus, and Atelier Julian, Paris. Travelled in the East several years; also United States of America, etc. First white man to reach both sources of the great Brahmaputra River and establish their exact position (Tibet, 1897); first white man to settle the geographical problem that no range higher than the Himalayas existed north of the Brahmaputra River in Tibet; first white man to explore Central Mindanao Island, where he discovered the "white tribe" (Mansakas); held until Duke of Abruzzi's expedition world's record in mountaineering, having reached an altitude of 23,490 ft. on Mount Lumpa (Nepal), 1899; accompanied Allied troops on the march to Pekin, 1900; was the first Anglo-Saxon to enter the Forbidden City, side by side with the doyen General Linievitch on the day of Allies' entry; went from Russia to Calcutta overland, across Persia, Afghanistan, and Beluchistan, 1901-2; spent one year cruising in the Philippine and Sulu Archipelagos, visiting some 400 islands, 1903; was in the American War against the Malanaos (Mindanao Island), 1903; also in the war between Sultans Abdul Aziz and Mulai Hafid in Morocco; witnessed Belgian campaign, battles of Malines, Termonde, siege and bombardment of Antwerp, Ostende, Nieuport, Roulers, Ypres; visited French and British Fronts, 1914; bombardment Arras; visited Austro-Italian Front, 1916; made extensive journey in Albania, Macedonia, and Greece, 1918, visiting Italian, French, Serbian, and English front lines, thus completing inspection of entire Western Front in Europe, from Antwerp to Salonica; crossed Africa in its widest part, 1906; crossed South America from Rio de Janeiro to Lima, traversing unexplored Central Brazil and over the Andes, 1910-12. Inventor of two types of improved armoured cars, of a new type of rigid airship, of a device for destroying barbed-wire entanglements, and of an armoured motor-cycle with mitrailleuse. *Publications:* Alone with the Hairy Ainu, or 3800 Miles on a Pack-saddle; Corea, or the Land of the Morning Calm; A Journey to the Sacred Mountain of Siao-ou-tai-shan; In the Forbidden Land, 1898; China and the Allies, 1901; Across Coveted Lands, 1902; The Gems of the East, 1904; Tibet and Nepal, 1905; Across Widest Africa, 1908; The Americans in Panama, 1910; An Explorer's Adventures in Tibet, 1910; Across Unknown South America, 1913; Mysterious South America, 1914. *Address:* c/o Grindlay, 54 Parliament Street, S.W.1; Calappiano, Empoli per Vinci, Italy; 10 Via Farini. Florence, Italy. *Club:* Royal Aero.

(Died 26 Dec. 1924.)

LANDOUZY, Louis Joseph, Professeur de clinique médicale et Doyen de la Faculté de Médecine de Paris; Médecin de Hopitaux (Hôpital Laënnec); Membre de la Société de Biologie, de l'Académie de Médecine et de l'Institut; *b.* Reims (Marne); de père et de grandpère, médecins; *m.* Louise, fille de feu le chirurgien A. Richet, de l'Institut; no *c.* *Educ.:* Education classique, au lycée de Reims (Marne); Education médicale; École de médecine de Reims, puis Faculté de Médecine et Hôpitaux de Paris. *Publications:* La Pleurésie, dite *a frigore*, fonction de Tuberculose; La Typhobacillose; Asthme et tuberculose; Tuberculose chez les enfants du premier âge; Tuberculoses professionnelles; Hérédité de la tuberculose: A. Hérédité de graine; B. Hérédité terrain: dystrophisme tuberculeux: études cliniques et expérimentales; Tuberculose: maladie sociale; Cent ans de Phtisiologie, 1808-1908; Empoisonnements non professionnels par l'Aniline; Localisations angiocardiaques typhoidiques; Atrophies myopathiques: myopathie type Landouzy Déjerine; Paralyses dans les Maladies aigues; Enquête sur l'alimentation d'une centaine d'ouvriers et d'employés parisiens, 1905, avec D. H. Labbé; Education alimentaire rationnelle, 1911; Tableaux muraux d'Éducation alimentaire, rationnelle, hygiénique et économique, 1906; Les Sérothérapies, 1898; Glossaire médical, 1902, avec Dr. Jayle; Pneumococcie, Pneumonie, and Pleurésie, in Traité de Médecine de Brouardel et Gilbert; Crénothérapie, cures hydro-minérales, avec A. Gautier, Moureu et de Launay, 1910; Eléments d'Anatomie et de Physiologie médicales, avec Dr. L. Bernard, 1913; avec Dr. Jean Heitz, Le Substratum scientifique de la Balnéothérapie, etc.: Congrès de Physiothérapie, Berlin, 1913, Congrès international de Médicine, Londres, 1913; Fièvres typhoïde et paratyphoïdes, Presse Médicale, 1914; La Guerre et la Réforme du Soldat tuberculeux, in Revue d'Hygiène, 1915; La Syphilis avant la guerre, in Bulletin de l'Académie de Médicine, 1915 et 1916; Médicine Allemande et Médicine Française, in Les Allemands et la Science, 1916, etc. Rédacteur en chef de la Revue de Médecine; Directeur scientifique de la Presse Médicale. *Récréations:* Voyages, Tableaux, Livres. *Address:* 15 rue de l'Université, Paris.

(Died 10 May 1917.)

LANDRY, Col. Hon. Auguste Charles Philippe Robert, Senator since 1892; Speaker of the Senate since 1911; *b.* 15 Jan. 1846; *m.* 1st, 1868, Wilhelmina (*d.* 1903), *d.* of late Étienne Couture, St. Gervais, P.Q.,; 2nd, 1908, Marie Clara Amelie, *d.* of late Hon. Elisée Dionne, M.L.C. *Educ.:* Quebec Seminary; Laval University. M.P. (C.) Montmagny, 1878-87. *Address:* Notre Dame de Quebec. *Club:* Garrison, Quebec. *(Died 20 Dec. 1919.)*

LANDRY, Major-General Joseph Philippe, C.M.G. 1917; *b.* 1870; *s.* of late Hon. Philippe Landry, President of the Senate of Canada; *m.* 1896, Blanche, *d.* of late Hon. Sir Alexandre Lacoste, P.C., LL.D. *Educ.:* Quebec and Ottawa Universities; Lille University; McGill University. Barrister, Canada, 1896; served European War, 1914-18 (despatches twice, C.M.G.). *Club:* Garrison. Quebec. *(Died July 1926.)*

LANDRY, Hon. Sir Pierre Armand, Kt. *cr.* 1916; Chief Justice of the King's Bench Division of the Superior Court of New Brunswick; *b.* 1 May 1846; *m.* 1870; six *s.* one *d.* *Educ.:* St. Joseph's University (M.A.), Laval. Bar, New Brunswick, 1870; Q.C., 1881; M.L.A., 1870-74, 1878-83; Chief Commissioner of Public Works, 1878-82; Provincial Secretary, 1882-83; Member Canadian House of Commons for seven years; Judge Supreme Court of New Brunswick, 1893. *Address:* Dorchester, New Brunswick.   (*Died 28 July 1916.*)

LANE, Col. Clayton Turner, C.I.E. 1895; J.P., D.L., Supernumerary List, Indian Army; *b.* 20 Feb. 1842; 3rd *s.* of late James Lane of Knockeevan, Camberley; *m.* 1867, Nicola Arbuthnot, *d.* of late William Allardyce of Aberdeen; four *s.* two *d. Educ.:* private school. Ensign, Bengal Army, 1858; Assist. and District Superint. of Police, Punjaub, 1863; Berar, 1865; Inspector-General of Police, Hyderabad Assigned District, 1877; Deputy-Comm. 1895; U. S. List, 1896. *Address:* Downfold, Guildford. *T.:* 280 Guildford.   (*Died 11 June 1920.*)

LANE, Sir Harry Philip Parnell, Kt., *cr.* 1925; C.B.E. 1918; M.V.O. 1913; Chief Constable of Lancashire since 1912; *b.* 1870; *m.* 1903, Flora Emma, *d.* of late Capt. E. R. Peel, Rockferry, Cheshire. *Address:* Ellel Hall, Lancaster. *Clubs:* Flyfishers'; County, Lancaster.
     (*Died 24 April 1927.*)

LANE, James Ernest, F.R.C.S.; Senior Surgeon, London Lock Hospital; Consulting Surgeon, St. Mary's Hospital; Major R.A.M.C.(T.); formerly Member of the Council and of the Court of Examiners of the Royal College of Surgeons of England; Member of Royal Commission on Venereal Diseases. *Publications:* editor of Heath's Practical Anatomy, 9th edit.; many articles on the treatment of Venereal Diseases. *Address:* 47 Queen Anne Street, W.1. *T.:* Langham 1035.
     (*Died 4 Nov. 1926.*)

LANE, John, publisher; *b.* West Putford, N. Devon, 14 Mar. 1854; *e. s.* of Lewis and Mary Grace Lane; *m.* 1898, to Annie E. King. *Educ.:* Chulmleigh. Joint-founder with Mr. Elkin Mathews of the Bodley Head Publishing business, 1887; dissolved partnership, 1894; has since conducted the Bodley Head publishing business in Vigo Street, London; Founder of the Yellow Book, 1894, and art editor of it from vol. iv. *Publications:* edited and wrote Introduction Life of Sir Thomas Bodley, 1894; Sir Caspar Purdon Clark, 1905; edited Memoirs of the Count de Cartrie, 1906. *Recreation:* collecting objets d'art. *Address:* 8 Lancaster Gate Terrace, W.2. *T. A.:* Bodleian, London. *T.:* Padd. 7177. *Clubs:* Reform, Cocoa-Tree, Whitefriars, Pilgrims, Odd Volumes; Union, Brighton; National Arts, New York. (*Died 2 Feb. 1925.*)

LANE, Mrs. John (Annie E. Lane), *b.* Geneva, Switzerland; *o. c.* of late Julius Eichberg, Boston. U.S.A., Superintendent of Music in the Public Schools of Boston, and Director and founder of the Boston Conservatory of Music; *m.* 1st, Tyler Batcheller King, LL.D., Boston; 2nd,1898, John Lane (*d.*1925), London, publisher. *Educ.:* Boston. Author of the words of the American national hymn To Thee O Country, set to music by Julius Eichberg. *Publications:* Kitwyk; The Champagne Standard; According to Maria; Talk of the Town; Maria Again; War Phases according to Maria; translations—Balthasar and Honey Bee, from the French of Anatole France; Peterkins, from the German of Ossip Schubin; articles in The Fortnightly Review, The Nineteenth Century, Blackwood's, The Atlantic Monthly, The Century, Lippincott's Magazine, etc. *Recreation:* music. *Address:* 8 Lancaster Gate Terrace, W.2. *T.:* Paddington 7177. (*Died 23 Jan. 1927.*)

LANE, John Henry Hervey Vincent, J.P., D.L.; *b.* 1867; *e. s.* of late John Henry Bagot Lane, J.P., D.L., of King's Bromley Manor and Lily Hill, and Susan Anne, *d.* of late Henry William Vincent of Lily Hill; *m.* 1902, Hon. Grace Louisa Edwardes, 3rd *d.* of 4th Baron Kensington; two *s.* five *d. Educ.:* Eton. Was Captain 4th Batt. South Staffordshire Regt.; patron of King's Bromley. Owns 2500 acres. *Address:* King's Bromley

604

Manor, Lichfield. *Clubs:* Carlton, Travellers', Wellington.   (*Died 22 Feb. 1917.*)

LANE, John Macdonald, late Commissioned Officer, Indian Navy; retired; *b.* 1840; *s.* of James Lane, late of Knockevan, Camberley; *m.* 1872, *d.* of late Rev. W. Powell; three *s.* (one killed in War), two *d. Educ.:* Private School; Naval College, Southsea. Joined Indian Navy, 1856; passed final exams. qualifying for command of Man-of-War, 1861; took part in Persian War, 1856 (medal and clasp); Indian Mutiny, 1857; abolition of slavery on Arabian Coast, 1858; service abolished, 1862; joined Indian Telegraph Dept., 1862; with Bhootan Expedition, 1864; constructed line to Darjeeling and through Assam to Gowhatty, 1864; latter country completely undeveloped; surveyed for line to Bankok *via* Tenasserim River, and shot the rapids, 1883; laid sea cable, Kenery Island, Bombay Harbour, to main land, 1885; retired 1890 with rank of Chief Superintendent. *Publications:* Creator and Created; Varied Life by Sea and Land; A Revolution in Diet; Nation's Loss of Beauty. *Recreations:* fishing, gardening, etc. *Address:* Dudley House, Montpelier Road, Twickenham.
     (*Died 19 Jan. 1927.*)

LANG, Col. Arthur Moffatt, C.B., 1908; R.E. (retired); *b.* 15 Nov. 1832; *e. s.* of Arthur Lang, I.C.S., of Westhill, Harrow, and Sarah, *o. d.* of General R. Tickell, C.B.; *m.* 1st, Sarah (*d.* 1889), *d.* of General F. B. Boileau, R.A.; 2nd, Edith Mina (*d.* 1903), *y. d.* of Rev. Owen C. Seymour Lang, M.A., of Bentley, Hants; 3rd, Ida F. C., *d.* of James C. Richardson, J.P., Glanrafon, Glamorganshire. *Educ.:* Rugby; Cheltenham; Military College, Addiscombe. Entered Army, 1852; Lieut.-Col. 1877; Col. 1881; retired, 1888; served Indian Mutiny, 1857-58; siege, assault of Delhi, Agra, relief of Lucknow, Cawnpore, siege and capture of Lucknow (despatches four times, medal 3 clasps); held appointments in P.W.D. and M.W.D., India, including Principal of Roorkee Engineering College, Deputy Inspector-Gen. for Fortifications, Chief Engineer in Baluchistan, in Burmah, in North-West Provinces. *Address:* Box Grove Lodge, Guildford, Surrey.
     (*Died 6 Aug. 1916.*)

LANG, Lt.-Colonel Godfrey George, D.S.O. 1916; late 2nd Batt. West Yorkshire Regt.; *b.* 24 April 1867; *e. s.* of late George Lukis Lang, I.C.S., and Louisa Astell; *m.* 1899, Isabel Frances Emily, *y. d.* of late R. P. Ebden, C.B.; one *d. Educ.:* Clifton College; Bedford Grammar School; Sandhurst. Entered Army, 1887; Captain, 1894; Major, 1907; Lt.-Colonel, 1916; served N.W. Frontier India, 1907 (medal with clasp); European War (despatches twice, D.S.O.); retired pay, 1921. *Recreations:* polo, cricket, hunting, golf, shooting, fishing. *Address:* c/o Cox & Co., Charing Cross, S.W.1.
     (*Died 29 July 1923.*)

LANG, Sir Peter Redford Scott, Kt., *cr.* 1921; Regius Professor of Mathematics, University of St. Andrews, 1879; retired, 1921; Col. 1st Fifeshire Vol. Artillery and T.F.; retired, 1914; *b.* Edinburgh, 8 Oct. 1850. *Address:* Mansefield, St. Andrews. *Clubs:* Royal and Ancient, St. Andrews; Scottish Conservative, Edinburgh. (*Died 5 July 1926.*)

LANG, William Lindsay Holmes, Joint Editor The Financial News since 1921; *b.* Glasgow, 27 April 1888; *o. s.* of William Lang, L.D.S., of Glasgow, and Margaret Lindsay, Possil Park; *m.* Felicia, 4th *d.* of late William Lindsay, J.P., last Provost of Broughty Ferry; one *d. Educ.:* various schools, including Dundee High School and Harris Academy. Apprenticed to Scots Law on staff of The Times, 1906-8; legal practice, politics and journalism, 1908-12; Editor Manchester Weekly Times, 1912-15; Naval Service with Grand Fleet,

1915-19 ; Founder and Editor of The Dolphin (organ of the Imperial Merchant Service Guild), and leader writer and literary critic to the Liverpool Courier, 1919-21. *Publications:* A Sea Lawyer's Log, 1919 ; several monographs on political and economic questions ; articles to philosophical periodicals throughout the world. *Recreations:* football (formerly), cricket, trainping, reading, and the theatre. *Address:* 55 Holland Park Avenue, W.11. *Club:* Royal Societies. (*Died 19 May 1928.*)

LANG, Col. William Robert, D.Sc. ; F.R.S.C. ; J.P. ; Director of Military Studies, University of Toronto, since 1919 ; Professor of Chemistry there, 1900-19 ; *y. s.* of late John Lang, Downanhill, Glasgow ; *m.* 1909, Edith, *y. d.* of A. J. Hollington, J.P., of Forty Hill, Enfield, one of H.M.'s Lieutenants for City of London ; one *s.* three *d.* *Educ.:* Universities of Glasgow and Paris ; on staff of former, 1890-1900 ; F.C.S., F.I.C. ; T.D. ; late Major of R.E. (T.) ; Col. Canadian Militia (C.O.T.C.) ; 5 years' war service, General Staff, C.E.F. (G.S.O. 1st Grade), (mentioned for valuable services, thanked by Army Council). *Publications:* some fifty original papers in English, French, and American scientific journals ; also Part II. of The Guide, by General Sir W. D. Otter, K.C.B. *Address:* The University of Toronto, Canada. *Clubs:* Caledonian ; York, Toronto ; Scottish Conservative, Edinburgh. (*Died 20 Nov. 1925.*)

LANGBRIDGE, Rev. Frederick, Rector of St. John's and Canon of St. Munchin's, St. Mary's Cathedral, Limerick ; Chaplain District Asylum ; *b.* Birmingham, 17 Mar. 1849 ; *m.* Jane, *d.* of John Wilson, Kendal, 1878 ; three *d.* *Educ.:* King Edward VI.'s School, Birmingham ; St. Alban Hall ; Merton College, Oxon. (M.A.) D.Litt., T.C.D., 1907. *Publications:* poems—Gaslight and Stars, 1892 ; Sent Back by the Angels, 1885 ; Poor Folk's Lives, 1887 ; A Cracked Fiddle, 1892 ; A Cluster of Quiet Thoughts, 1896 ; The Scales of Heaven, 1896; Clear Waters, 1897; Little Tapers, 1899 ; The Distant Lights, 1902 ; Ballads and Legends (Collected Issue of narrative poems); The Peaks of Proud Desire ; The Power of Red Michael, 1909 ; Restful Thoughts for Dusty Ways, 1912. *Novels:* The Dreams of Danis, 1897 ; Love has no Pity, 1901 ; also many books for children and for boys ; editor, What to Read, 1889; Poets at Play, 1888; Ballads of the Brave, 1890. *Plays* (with Freeman Wills): The Only Way ; Rouget de L'Isle ; After All ; (sole author) The Chevalier de St. George ; The Devil's Trap : (with A. H. Ferro) The Children of Kings. *Recreations:* billiards, croquet, chiefly reading. *Address:* St. John's Rectory, Limerick. (*Died 10 Jan. 1922.*)

LANGDALE, Henry Joseph, J.P., D.L. ; *e. s.* of Charles Joseph Langdale (*d.* 1895) and Henrietta (*d.* 1898), *e. d.* and co-heir of late Henry Grattan, M.P., of Celbridge Abbey, Co. Kildare ; *b.* 2 June 1853. *Educ.:* Beaumont. Late Capt. 4th Batt. R. Irish Fusiliers (Militia). *Address:* Houghton Hall, Sancton, E. Riding, Yorks.

LANGDON, Rev. Alfred, Prebendary of Lincoln. *Address:* The Vicarage, New Sleaford. (*Died 16 Nov. 1925.*)

LANGDON, Col. Harry, C.B. 1911 ; V.D. ; T.D. ; retired ; *b.* 29 March 1855 ; 3rd *s.* of John Langdon, Huyton Park, Liverpool ; *m.* Elizabeth Day, *y. d.* of John Hind Talbot, Liverpool ; three *s.* four *d.* *Educ.:* Liverpool Institute ; High School. Governing Director J. Langdon and Sons, Ltd., Government contractors, Liverpool. Commanded the Royal Naval Artillery Volunteers, 1878-92 ; transferred to Mersey Div. Submarine Miners as Capt. 1893 ; Major, 1894 ; Lieut.-Colonel, 1905-1908 ; transferred to Lanc. Fortress R.E. (T.) as Lt.-Col. and Honorary Colonel, 1908. *Re-*

creations: shooting, riding, yachting. *Address:* Oxton Hall, Oxton, Cheshire. *T.A.:* Military, Liverpool. *T.:* Birkenhead 619. *Clubs:* Royal Mersey Yacht, Lyceum, Liverpool. (*Died 7 July 1925.*)

LANGELIER, Hon. Chas., K.C. 1897 ; Judge of Court of Sessions of the Peace, Quebec, since 1910 ; *b.* 23 Aug. 1852 ; *m.* 1882, Marie Lucile La Rue ; one *d.* *Educ.:* Laval Univ., Quebec (Doctor in Law, Dufferin medal) ; one of the Governors of Laval University ; President of the Licence Commission for the city of Quebec. Admitted to Bar, 1875 ; sat one Parliament as Member of the House of Commons of Canada, and eleven years as Member of the Quebec Legislature ; Minister of the Crown as Secretary of the Province, 1890 ; Sheriff of Quebec, 1900. *Publications:* Souvenirs Politiques, two vols. ; Histoire de la Confédération, 1916. *Address:* 111 Grande Allée, Quebec. *T.:* 966. *Club:* Garrison, Quebec. (*Died 7 Feb. 1920.*)

LANGFORD, 4th Baron (cr. 1800), **Hercules Edward Rowley,** K.C.V.O.; Representative Peer for Ireland since 1884 ; Lieut.-Colonel Grenadier Guards (retired) ; *b.* 1 June 1848 ; *e. s.* of 3rd Baron and *e. d.* of Edward Michael Conolly, M.P. ; *S.* father 1854 ; *m.* 1st, 1889, Georgina (*d.* 1901), 6th *d.* of Sir Richard Sutton, 4th Bart. ; one *s.* ; 2nd, 1915, Margaret Antonia, *e. d.* of Rev. W. M. Carruthers, of Little Munden, Herts. *Educ.:* Eton. Ensign Grenadier Guards, 1867 ; State Steward to Viceroy of Ireland, 1886-92. *Heir:* *s.* Hon. John Hercules William Rowley. *Address:* Summerhill House, Enfield, County Meath. *Clubs:* Carlton ; Kildare Street, Dublin. (*Died 29 Oct. 1919.*)

LANGFORD, 5th Baron, cr. 1800, **John Hercules William Rowley ;** *b.* 16 Dec. 1894 ; *e. s.* of 4th Baron and Georgina (*d.* 1901), 6th *d.* of Sir Richard Sutton, 4th Bart. ; *S.* father 1919. *Heir:* *u.* Hon. William Charles Rowley, *b.* 1849. *Address:* Summerhill House, Enfield, County Meath. (*Died 29 Sept. 1922.*)

LANGFORD, Surgeon Martyn Henry, R.N., D.S.O. 1915. Served Dardanelles, 1914-15 (despatches, D.S.O.) ; was serving in the Inflexible when she was mined, and attended the wounded under great difficulties. (*Died 15 Dec. 1918.*)

LANGLER, Sir Alfred, Kt., cr. 1927 ; sole executor of the Hackett Estate, and governing director of the West Australian Newspaper Co., Ltd. since 1917 ; *b.* Ipplepen, Devonshire, 1865. Some time on the literary staffs of different Devonshire journals, and a contributor to various London papers ; on the editorial staff of the Register, Adelaide, 1890-95 ; joined the West Australian literary department, 1895 ; after some years, in addition to his literary work, became actively concerned in the business management of the paper ; editor-in-chief of the West Australian and Western Mail, 1916-1928 : Australian delegate to Second Imperial Press Conference, Ottawa, 1920 ; Chairman Western Australian Committee Third Imperial Press Conference, 1925 ; Justice of the Peace for Western Australia. *Address:* West Australian Office, Perth, W.A. *Club:* Weld, Perth. (*Died 26 Mar. 1928.*)

LANGLEY, John Newport, F.R.S. ; Sc.D. Cambridge, Hon. LL.D. St. Andrews ; Hon. Sc.D. Dublin ; Hon. M.D. Groningen, Hon. Dr. Strasbourg ; Fellow of Trinity College, Cambridge ; Professor of Physiology, Cambridge ; Editor Journal of Physiology ; 2nd *s.* of John Langley and Mary, *e. d.* of Richard Groom ; *b.* 1852 ; *m.* 1902, Vera Kathleen, *d.* of Frederick G. Forsyth-Grant of Ecclesgreig, Kincardineshire ; one *d.* *Educ.:* Exeter Grammar School and private ; St. John's College, Cambridge (Scholar). 1st class

Natural Sciences Tripos. Lecturer Trinity College, Cambridge, and University Lecturer, 1884-1903 ; Royal Medallist of Royal Society, 1892 ; Baly Medal, Roy. Coll. Physic., 1903 ; Andreas Retzius Medal, Swedish Soc. Physic., 1912 ; Memb.Council Royal Society,1897-98; Vice-Pres. 1904-5 ; Memb. Council Cambridge Univ., 1898-1900 ; President Section I. Brit. Assoc., 1899 ; President Neurol. Soc. of Great Britain, 1893 ; Corr. Memb. Société de Biologie, Paris ; Phys. Med. Soc. Florence ; Imp. Mil. Acad. of Med., Petrograd ; Hon. Memb. Soc. de Neurol. Kasan ; K.K. Gesell. d. Aertze, Vienna ; Swedish Society of Physicians ; (Gesell.) Deutsch. Nervenärtze ; Soc. de Biol., Buenos Aires ; and of Amer. Physiol. Soc. ; For. Memb. Acad. Roy. de Méd. de Belgique ; Kong. Danske Vidensk. Selskab. Copenhagen ; R. Accad, d. Lincei, Rome ; k. Svenska Vetensk.-Akad., Stockholm ; k. Vetensk. Soc. Upsala ; Bavarian Acad. Sci. Munich ; Member Soc. Belge de Biol., Soc. Roy. de Sci. Med. et Nat. de Bruxelles, and Portuguese Soc. Nat. Sci. *Publications:* Autonomic Nervous System, Pt. I.; numerous scientific papers. *Recreations:* gardening, golf. skating. *Address:* Hedgerley Lodge, Cambridge. *T.:* Cambridge 445. *M.:* ER 1665 and 3011. *Club:* Athenæum. (*Died 5 Nov. 1925.*)

LANGLEY, Sir Walter Louis Frederick Goltz, K.C.M.G., *cr.* 1912 ; C.B., 1899 ; Assistant Under-Secretary of State in the Foreign Office since 1907 ; *b.* 22 Feb. 1855 ; *m.* 1894, Gertrude Mary, *d.* of William Ramsay (*d.* 1895); one *s.* Was private secretary to successive Parliamentary Under Secretaries of State for Foreign Affairs, 1887-98. *Address:* 10 Warwick Square, S.W. *Club:* Travellers'.
(*Died 30 Sept. 1918.*)

LANGMAN, Sir John Lawrence, 1st Bt., *cr.* 1906 ; *b.* 24 June 1846 ; *s.* of late Joseph Langman, Plymouth and London, and Eleanor James, *d.* of John Lawrence, Aberdeen; *m.* 1868, Mary (*d.* 1904), *d.* of late James Marks ; one *s.* Equipped and maintained the Langman Field Hospital in South African War, 1900 (despatches, Queen's medal with three clasps); Knight of Grace of the Order of St. John of Jerusalem. *Heir: s.* Archibald Lawrence. *Address:* 97 Eaton Square, S.W.1. *T.:* Sloane 3233. *Club:* Devonshire. (*Died 3 Oct. 1928.*)

LANSDELL, Rev. Henry, D.D.; F.R.G.S., M.R.A.S.; *b.* Tenterden, 10 Jan. 1841 ; *e. s.* of Henry and Julia Lansdell; *m.* Mary, *d.* of Charles Colyer, of Farningham and Greenhithe, Kent. *Educ.:* at home; St. John's Coll. Highbury. Ordained 1867 ; curate, Greenwich, 1868 ; and in charge of St. Peter's, Eltham, 1885-86 ; Reader, St. Germans, Blackheath, 1881-82 ; Lecturer, St. James's, Plumstead, 1891; Chaplain of Morden College, Blackheath, 1892 - 1912 ; travelled in every country of Europe and Asia, 5 countries of Africa, and across America, 1870-1904 ; visited 170 foreign mission stations in Europe, Asia, and Africa, 1888-90 ; prospected for missionary purposes, took photographs, and collected specimens of fauna in Russian and Chinese Turkestan. *Publications:* originator and editor Clergyman s Magazine, 1875-86; Through Siberia, 1882 ; Russian Central Asia, 1885, abridged into Through Central Asia, 1887 ; Chinese Central Asia, 1893 ; The Sacred Tenth, 1906 ; The Tithe in Scripture, 1908 ; Princess Ælfrida's Charity, Parts i.-vii. Part owner of about 700 acres. *Recreation :* literary composition. *Address:* Dimsdale, 4 Pond Road, Blackheath Park, S.E.3. *T.A.:* Lansdell, Blackheath. *T.:* 1594 Lee Green.
(*Died 5 Oct. 1919.*)

LANSDOWNE, 5th Marquess of (Gt. Brit.), *cr.* 1784 ; **Henry Charles Keith Petty-Fitzmaurice**, K.G. P.C., G.C.S.I., G.C.I.E., G.C.M.G., D.C.L. (Hon. Oxford), LL.D. 26th Baron of Kerry and Lixnaw

1181 ; Baron of Keith and Nairne, 1681 ; Earl of Kerry, Viscount Clanmaurice, 1723 ; Viscount Fitz-Maurice and Baron Dunkeron, 1751 ; Earl of Shelburne, 1753 ; Baron Wycombe, 1760 ; Earl of Wycombe and Viscount Calne, 1784 ; Trustee of National Gallery since 1894 ; late Lord-Lieut. of Wilts ; *b.* 14 Jan. 1845 ; *e. s.* of 4th Marquis and *e. d.* of Comte de Flahault and Baroness Keith and Nairne ; *S.* father, 1866, mother 1895 ; *m.* 1869, Lady Maud Evelyn Hamilton (C.I., Comp. of Honour, G.B.E.), *d.* of 1st Duke of Abercorn ; one *s.* two *d.* Lord of Treasury, 1869-72 ; Under Secretary for War, 1872-74 ; Under-Secretary for India, 1880 ; Gov.-Gen. of Canada, 1883-88 ; Gov.-Gen. of India, 1888-93 ; Secretary for War, 1895 - 1900 ; Foreign Secretary, 1900-1905 ; Minister without Portfolio, 1915-16. *Heir: s.* Earl of Kerry. *Address:* 65 Brook Street, W. ; *T.:* Mayfair 6999 ; Bowood Park, Calne, Wiltshire ; Derreen, Kenmare, Co. Kerry. *Clubs:* Brooks's, Travellers'. (*Died 3 June 1927.*)

LANSING, Robert; Diplomatist and Adviser in International Law ; *b.* Watertown, N.Y., 17 Oct. 1864; *s.* of John Lansing and Maria L. Dodge; *m.* 1890, Eleanor, *d.* of John W. Foster (a former Secretary of State). *Educ.:* Amherst ; LL.D. Amherst, 1915 ; Princeton, 1917; Columbia, 1918 ; University of State of N.Y., 1919. Admitted to Bar, 1889 ; Counsel for U.S. Behring Sea Arbitration, 1892 - 3 ; Counsel for U.S. Behring Sea Claims Commission, 1896-7 ; Solicitor for U.S. Alaskan Boundary Tribunal, 1903 ; Counsel North Atlantic Coast Fisheries Arbitration, 1909-10; Agent of U.S., American and British Claims Arbitration, 1912-14; Counsellor for Department of State, 1914-15; Secretary of State, U.S.A., 1915-20 ; Commissioner to Peace Conference at Paris, 1918-19 ; Counsel for Chile in Tacna - Arica Arbitration, 1923-24. *Publications:* Government, its Origin, Growth, and Form in the United States (joint), 1902 ; The Peace Negotiations, 1921 ; Notes on Sovereignty, 1921 ; The Big Four of the Peace Conference, 1921. *Address:* 1823 18th Street, Washington, D.C. *Clubs:* Metropolitan, Chevy Chase, Congressional Country, Washington.(*Died 30 Oct. 1928.*)

LANTERI, Edward, R.B.S. ; Professor of Sculpture, Royal College of Art, since 1880 ; *b.* Burgundy ; naturalised Englishman, 1900. *Educ.:* Ecole des Beaux Arts, Paris, under Cavelier, Aimé, Millet, and Guillaume. Was assistant to Sir Edgar Boehm for twenty years ; Exhibitor at the Royal Academy since 1876. *Principal works:* Bust Portraits : King Edward VII. ; late Duchess of Leinster ; late M. Waddington, French Ambassador ; Paul Cambon, French Ambassador ; Admiral Lord C. Beresford ; Sir W. Richmond, R.A.; Sir Archibald Geikie, O.M. (Geological Museum); Alfred Stevens (Tate Gallery); Paysan (Musée du Luxembourg, Paris, Tate Gallery, and Preston Museum). *Statues:* Omphale, marble acquired by King Edward VII. ; Peace (Victoria and Albert Museum) ; Sir Samuel Sadler, Middlesborough ; etc. *Statuettes:* Fencing Master ; Sir A. Harris ; Sir Edgar Boehm, R.A.; etc. *Groups:* The Duet, marble acquired by A. Carnegie ; The Fisherman and the Mermaid ; etc. *Publications:* Modelling : a Guide for Teachers and Students (3 volumes). *Address:* Royal College of Art, S. Kensington, S.W.
(*Died 1917.*)

LAPWORTH, Charles, F.R.S., LL.D., M.Sc., F.G.S. ; *b.* Farringdon, 1842 ; *o. s.* of James Lapworth; *m.* Janet, *d.* of Walter Sanderson, Galashiels ; two *s.* one *d.* *Educ.:* Certificated Teacher, Culham, 1862-3 ; Galashiels, N.B., 1864-75 ; Madras College, St. Andrews, 1875-81. Hon. LL.D. Univ. Aberdeen, 1883 ; Univ. Glasgow, 1912 ; Bigsby Medallist (1887) and Wollaston Medallist (1889) of the Geological

LANGLEY, Walter. See page xxiii.

iety; Royal Medallist Royal Society (1891); wilde Medallist Manchester Phil. Soc. 1905; President, Section C, Brit. Assoc., 1892; Pres., Geol. Soc., 1902-4; Member of Council Royal Society, 1895-96; Member Royal Coal Commission, 1902-4; Prof. of Geology and Physiography, Birmingham University, 1881-1913; M.Sc.; Emeritus Professor, 1914; Consulting Geologist on matters of mining and civil engineering — Water Bills of Birmingham, Gloucester, Harrogate, Leicester, etc. *Publications:* scientific papers and memoirs in Geology and Palæontology, dealing mainly with researches among Graptolites and the Lower Palæozoic Rocks; editor Page's Textbooks, Geology and Physical Geography; editor Monograph, British Graptolites, Palæontographical Soc. 1900-8; Intermediate Textbook of Geology, 1899. *Recreations:* field geology, music. *Address:* 38 Calthorpe Road, Edgbaston, Birmingham. *T.A.:* Geology, Birmingham.

(*Died 13 Mar. 1920.*)

LARCOM, Arthur, C.B. 1904; Senior Clerk in H.M. Foreign Office; Barrister-at-Law; 4th *s.* of Major-Gen. Rt. Hon. Sir Thomas Aiskew Larcom, 1st Bt.; *b.* 9 Nov. 1847; *m.* 1884, Sophie (*d.* 1913), *d.* of Alex. Perceval of Temple House, Co. Sligo. *Educ.:* Oriel College, Oxford; M.A. 1872. Appointed to a Clerkship in the Foreign Office, 1871; Acting 3rd Secretary to the Legation at Tehran, 1875-77; Acting Oriental Secretary, Tehran, 1879-81; Acting 2nd Secretary, Tokio, 1884-87; Senior Clerk and Head of U.S. Dept. in F. O., 1899; H.M. Agent before the International Court of Arbitration at the Hague in the matter of the Venezuelan Claims, 1903. *Address:* Villa Miramare, San Remo, Italy. *Clubs:* Travellers', Oxford and Cambridge. (*Died 19 Mar. 1924.*)

LARCOMBE, Thomas, I.S.O. 1903; appointed to the War Office, 1857; retired, 1903; *s.* of late William Larcombe; *b.* 1842; *m.* 1st, 1876, Elizabeth Ellen (*d.* 1903), *e. d.* of Richard James, 207 Adelaide Road, South Hampstead; 2nd, 1905, Agnes, *y. d.* of William Adam Oldaker, 54 Ladbroke Road, Holland Park, Kensington. Twice elected head of the poll as Member of Local Board and District Council, Hampton, Middlesex; served as Vice-Chairman of the Council, and Chairman of Finance and Education Committees; elected Trustee of Hampton Charities, and Representative Governor of Hampton Grammar School; for many years President of Hampton (Middlesex) Liberal Association; Member of Northbrook Society. *Recreation:* travel. *Address:* 15 Oakwood Court, Kensington, W. *Club:* National Liberal. (*Died 14 Dec. 1916.*)

LARDNER, James Carrige Rushe, K.C. 1921; M.P. (N.), North Monaghan, 1907-18; *b.* 1879; *s.* of Hugh Lardner, Swan Park, Monaghan; *m.* 1920, Rita, *d.* of Sir Joseph Downes, South Hill; two *s. Educ.:* St. MacCartan's College, Monaghan; Clongoweswood College, Co. Kildare. Barrister, King's Inns, Dublin, and Gray's Inn, London; Bencher, King's Inns, 1924; Director Dublin South Eastern Railway Co.; Member of Committee to consider on Medical Benefits under National Insurance Act (Ireland). *Address:* 22 Ailesbury Road, Dublin. *T.:* Ballsbridge 261. *Clubs:* Devonshire; Royal Dublin, Stephen's Green, Dublin.

(*Died 3 May 1925.*)

LARGE, Captain Edwin Ryder, D.S.O. 1917, O.B.E. 1919; R.D. 1923; R.N.R.; F.R.G.S.; *b.* 31 Dec. 1878; 3rd *s.* of late A. R. Large, Woolston, Hants; *m.* Elsa Marguerite, *y. d.* of late Hon. Thomas King, Minister of Education, South Australia; two *s. Educ.:* Woolston College, Hants. Entered Mercantile Marine, 1893; Younger Brother of Trinity House, 1913; served in Calcutta Naval Volunteers, 1895-96; various periods of service in H.M. Fleet; served European War, 1914-19; attached to Gallipoli Expedition (1915-16) from First Landing until Final Evacuation (despatches); successful gunnery actions against enemy submarines (D.S.O., monetary awards); presentation from Admiral Sir Lewis Bayly, Commander-in-Chief, Coast of Ireland; Appreciation of High Commissioner for Australia for services under Australian Government; Appreciation of Lords Commissioners of Admiralty on three occasions; General Service and Mercantile Marine War Medals; Lloyd's Silver Medal for Meritorious Services; Lloyd's Silver Medal for saving life at sea; Royal Humane Society's Bronze Medal for jumping overboard at sea and rescuing a seaman; whilst commanding H.M.T. Karroo, acted as Commodore of Convoys; represented the Mercantile Marine at the Admiralty, on Mercantile Marine Awards Committee, Feb. 1918-Feb. 1919; O.B.E. for services in connection with inquiries into submarine attacks on British merchant vessels; Fellow of Royal Colonial Institute; Captain R.N.R. 1926. *Address:* 42 Corringham Road, Golders Green, N.W.11. *T.:* Speedwell 2500. *T.A.:* Rydelar, London. *Clubs:* Cocoa Tree; Royal Bombay Yacht: Sind. (*Died 10 Nov. 1928.*)

LARKWORTHY, Falconer, late Chairman of Ionian Bank, Ltd., Commander of the Order of the Saviour (Greece); Director Commercial Union Assurance Co., Ltd., and Palatine Insurance Co.; Fellow Institute of Bankers; *b.* Weymouth, 22 March 1833; *s.* of Dr. Ambrose Larkworthy, Bombay, and Amelia, *d.* of John Cooke, shipowner, Calcutta; *m.* 1st, Mary, *d.* of Captain Balston, Cape Town; 2nd, Elizabeth, *d.* of J. W. Clover, The Wood, Aylsham, Norfolk; three *s.* three *d. Educ.:* High School, Liverpool. colonial and international banker; political economist; strong advocate of a new national and international currency and exchange system. Church of England. *Publications:* Ninety-one years, Being the Reminiscences of Falconer Larkworthy, ed. by Harold Begbie, 1924; numerous papers on Currency and Exchange. *Address:* 35 Belsize Avenue, N.W.3. *T.:* Hampstead 492. (*Died 14 May 1928.*)

LARNACH, James Walker, J.P.; *b.* 10 June 1849; *e. surv. s.* of late Donald Larnach of Brambletye, Sussex; *m.* 1889, Lady Isabel Lettice Theodosia (*d.* 1904), *d.* of 9th Earl of Cork; one *d. Educ.:* Eton; Trinity College, Cambridge (M.A.) Hon. Major late Suffolk Hussars Yeomanry Cavalry; High Sheriff Oxfordshire, 1904. Won the Derby with Jeddah, 1898. *Address:* Brambletye, Sussex; Lanwades Hall, Suffolk. *Clubs:* Jockey, Turf, Marlborough, Junior Carlton. Windham.

(*Died 24 Jan. 1919.*)

LA ROCQUE, Rt. Rev. Paul, D.D., D.C.L., R.C. Bishop of Sherbrooke since 1893; *b.* Marieville, P.Q., 28 Oct. 1846. *Educ.:* Colleges Ste. Therese and St. Hyacinthe. Ordained, 1869; Rector Cathedral St. Hyacinthe, 1884-93. *Address:* Bishop's House, Sherbrooke, P. Quebec. (*Died Aug. 1926.*)

LASCELLES, Rt. Hon. Sir Frank (Cavendish), P.C., 1894; G.C.B., cr. 1897; G.C.M.G., cr. 1892; G.C.V.O., cr. 1904; *b.* 23 Mar. 1841; 5th *s.* of late Rt. Hon. W. S. S. Lascelles, M.P., and Caroline, *e. d.* of 6th Earl of Carlisle; *m.* 1867, Mary Emma (*d.* 1897), *e. d.* of late Sir J. F. Olliffe, M.D., Physician to British Embassy, Paris; one *d.* Entered Diplomatic Service, 1861; 2nd Secretary Diplomatic Service, 1871; Agent and Consul-General, Bulgaria, 1879; Minister, Roumania, 1886; Persia, 1891; Ambassador to Russia, 1894; to Germany, 1895-1908. *Address:* 14 Chester Square, S.W.1. *T.:* Ken. 1287. *Clubs:* Travellers', St. James's, M.C.C.

(*Died 2 Jan. 1920.*)

LARIVIERE, Hon. Alphonse Alfred Clément. See page xxiv.

LASCELLES, Hon. Frederick Canning; 2nd *s.* of 4th Earl of Harewood and 1st wife, Elizabeth Joanna, *e. d.* of 1st Marquess of Clanricarde; *b.* 8 May 1848; *m.* 1878, Frederica Maria (*d.* 1891), *d.* of late Hon. Sir Adolphus Liddell, K.C.B.; one *s.* four *d.* Commander R.N.; retired. *Address:* Sutton Waldron House, Blandford.

(*Died 31 Dec. 1928.*)

LASCELLES, Hon. Gerald William, C.B. 1914; B.A., F.Z.S.; Deputy Surveyor, New Forest, 1880-1914; President of Land Agents' Society, 1911; *b.* 26 Oct. 1849; *s.* of 4th Earl of Harewood; *m.* 1875, Constance Augusta Mary Fitzclarence, *o. c.* of late J. Burton Phillipson of Bramshaw House Lyndhurst, Hants, and of Sunninghill, Berks; one *s.* one *d. Educ.:* Eton; Magdalene College, Cambridge. *Publications:* Badminton vol. on Falconry; do. Shooting vol. (part of); Thirty-five Years in the New Forest, 1915; portions of Fur and Feather Series; various articles, mainly on sport. *Recreations:* manager of Old Hawking Club since 1872. *Address:* Tillington House, Petworth. *Clubs:* Carlton, St. James's, Beefsteak, Authors'. (*Died 11 Feb. 1928.*)

LASH, Zebulun Aiton, K.C.; LL.D.; Barrister-at-Law; *b.* St. Johns, Newfoundland, 29 Sep. 1846; *s.* of William Lash, Banker; *m.* 1871, Elizabeth Ann, *d.* of late Judge Miller of Galt, Ontario; three *s.* one *d. Educ.:* Dundas Ontario Grammar School; University of Toronto. Called to Bar of Ontario, 1868; lecturer to Law Society, 1872-76; practised law in Toronto, Ontario, till 1876; Deputy of the Minister of Justice of Canada, 1876-82; returned to Toronto; Bencher of Law Society, 1883; re-elected till after 20 years of service, became Bencher for life by statute; Q.C. 1879; Hon. LL.D., University of Toronto, 1910; Vice-Chairman, Board of Governors of University of Toronto; President, Great North Western Telegraph Co.; Vice-President, Canadian Bank of Commerce; Director and Senior Counsel, Canadian Northern Railway Co.; Vice-President, National Trust Co.; Director, Bell Telephone Co., and other companies. *Publications:* Defence and Foreign Affairs: a Suggestion for the Empire; Pamphlets and Articles on Legal Subjects. *Recreations:* fishing and shooting, canoeing. *Address:* 59 Admiral Road, Toronto, Canada. *T.A.:* Lash, Toronto. *T.:* Hillcrest 3846. *M.:* 1560 and 1561, Ontario, 1917. *Clubs:* York, Toronto, University, Toronto; Rideau, Ottawa; Mount Royal, Montreal.

(*Died 24 Jan. 1920.*)

LASSETTER, Brig.-Gen. Harry Beauchamp, C.B. 1902; C.M.G. 1917; late Comm. 2nd Australian Light Horse Brigade; *b.* 19 March 1860; *s.* of late F. Lassetter, of Sydney; *m.* 1891, Elizabeth Anne, *d.* of late J. M. Antill; one *s. Educ.:* Eton; Cheltenham; R.M.C., Sandhurst. Joined H.M. 38th Regt. as 2nd Lieut. 1880. Lieut. 80th Regt. 1881; Captain, 1887; proceeded to N.S. Wales, 1888 (with local rank of Major); raised and trained Mounted Rifles in the Colony; Lieut.-Colonel, 1894; went to England with detachment Queen Victoria's 60th Jubilee, 1897; commanded the Colonial escort in the Queen's procession; served Nile Expedition (medal with clasp, bronze star); South Africa in command of New South Wales Mounted Rifles, 1902 (despatches, medal and clasp, C.B.); European War 1915-17 (C.M.G.). *Address:* Sydney, New South Wales. *T.A.:* Lassetter, Sydney. *Club:* Naval and Military. (*Died 17 Feb. 1926.*)

LATHAM, Charles, Professor of Mining, University of Glasgow, since 1907; *b.* Birkdale, Lancashire, 1868; 2nd *s.* of late James Beven Latham; *m.* Nellie, 2nd *d.* of William White, Nottingham; one *d. Educ.:* Wigan High School; Rivington Grammar School; School of Mines, Wigan. Articled to Moss Hall Coal Co.,

Wigan; Assistant General Manager, Moss Hall Coal Co., 1891-93; Director of Mining, University College, Nottingham, 1893-1902; Dixon Lecturer in Mining, University of Glasgow, 1902-7; Examiner in Mining, University of Manchester, 1908; Member of the Institute of Mining Engineers. *Publications:* Colliery Winding Machinery; Coal Cutting by Machinery; Detection and Estimation of Inflammable Gases in Mine Air by means of Flame Caps. *Recreations:* golf, cycling, fishing. *Address:* 16 Queensborough Gardens, Glasgow, W. *Club:* College, Glasgow. (*Died 27 Sept. 1917.*)

LATHAM, Peter Wallwork, M.A., M.D., F.R.C.P. Lond.; Consulting Physician Addenbrooke's Hospital, Cambridge (Physician, 1863-1890); *b.* Wigan, Lancashire, 21 Oct. 1832; *e. s.* of John Latham, physician; *m.* 1st, 1862, Jamima Burns (*d.* 1877), *y. d.* of John M'Diarmid, Dumfries; one *d.*; 2nd, 1884, Marianne Frances, *d.* of J. F. Bernard, M.D., Clifton, and Marianne, *s.* of the brothers Sir Henry and John, 1st Lord Lawrence. *Educ.:* Neuwied, Germany; Glasgow University; Caius College, Cambridge (Scholar 1855); St. Bartholomew's Hospital, London. 19th Wrangler, 1858; 1st in Natural Sciences Tripos, 1859, with distinction in Chemistry, Physiology, Comp. Anatomy, Botany, and Mineralogy; Fellow of Downing College, 1860; Councillor of the Royal Coll. of Physicians, 1886-87; Censor, 1887-89; Senior Censor, 1894-95; Harveian Orator, 1888; Downing Professor of Medicine, Cambridge, 1874-1894; formerly Assistant Physician to the Westminster Hospital. *Publications:* among others, On the Early Symptoms of Phthisis, 1864; On Nervous or Sick Headache, 1873; On the Formation of Uric Acid in Animals, 1884; On Some Points in the Pathology of Rheumatism, Gout, and Diabetes (Croonian Lectures), 1886; The Harveian Oration, 1888; On Blood Changes in Disease; articles in Quain's Dictionary of Medicine. *Address:* 15 Royal York Crescent, Clifton, Bristol. *Clubs:* Royal Societies; Cambridge County.

(*Died 29 Oct. 1923.*)

LATHBURY, Daniel Conner, Journalist; *b.* 11 Apr. 1831; *m.* Bertha, *y. d.* of late Professor Bonamy Price. *Educ.:* King's College, London; Brasenose College, Oxford (M.A.). President of the Union; Barrister, Lincoln's Inn, but has never practised; joint-editor of The Economist, 1878-81; editor of The Guardian, 1883-99; editor of The Pilot from its foundation to its death, 1900-4. Editor of Correspondence on Church and Religion of W. E. Gladstone, 1910. *Address:* Hascombe, Godalming. *Club:* Athenæum. (*Died 14 June 1922.*)

LATIMER, Rev. William Thomas, M.A., D.D.; Senior Minister of Eglish Presbyterian Church, Dungannon, since 1872; *o. s.* of Rev. John Latimer, Ballynahatty, Omagh, Co. Tyrone; *m.* Frances, *d.* of Andrew Macbeth, mill-owner, Ballindrait, Strabane; one *s.* one *d. Educ.:* Queen's College, Belfast (Queen's University). B.A.; M.A. Belfast; D.D., Belfast and Derry United Theolog. Faculty. *Publications:* The Doctrines of the Plymouth Brethren (seventh edition), 1908; The Life and Times of Rev. H. Cooke, D.D., LL.D., Belfast, 1888 (new edition, 1899); A History of the Irish Presbyterians, 1893 (second edition, 1902); Popular History of the Irish Presbyterian Church, 1897 (Guild edition, 1897); Ulster Biographies, 1897; Presbyterianism in Omagh, Belfast, 1913; Tom Eccles, the Robber, 1913; many historical articles and reviews in the Journal of the Royal Society of Antiquaries, the Northern Whig, the Witness, Belfast, the Irish Presbyterian, and in other periodicals. *Recreations:* walking, reading, etc. *Address:* Eglish Manse, Dungannon, Co. Tyrone. (*Died 19 July 1919.*)

LATHROP, Rose Hawthorne. See page xxiv.

LA TOUCHE, Sir James John Digges, K.C.S.I., cr. 1901; Member of Council of India, 1907-14; b. 16 Dec. 1844; s. of W. D. La Touche, Dublin; m. 1878, Julia, d. of T. W. Rothwell. Educ.: Trin. Coll. Dublin. Entered I.C.S. 1867; Lieut.-Gov. of the United Provinces of Agra and Oudh, 1901-6; retired, 1906.
(Died 5 Oct. 1921.)

LA TOUCHE, Robert Percy O'Connor, J.P., of Harristown, Co. Kildare; b. 12 July 1846; o. s. of John La Touche and Maria, o. d. of Robert Lambart Price of Treng-wainton, Cornwall; m. 1870, Lady Annette Louisa Scott, 2nd d. of 3rd Earl of Clonmell. Address: Harristown, Brannockstown, Co. Kildare. Clubs: Marlborough; Kildare Street, Dublin.
(Died 13 Mar. 1921.)

LATULIFE, Rt. Rev. E. A.; Bishop of Haileybury since 1915; b. St. Anicet, county of Huntingdon, P.Q., 3 Aug. 1859; s. of Antoine Latulipe and Lucie Bonneville. Educ.: Montreal College and Grand Seminary, Montreal. Ordained 1885; Professor in Montreal College, 1885; Curate in the Parish of St. Henri, 1886-88; Chaplain, Motherhouse of the Sisters of St. Ann, 1888-91; Chaplain Provincial Monastery of the Good Shepherd, Montreal, 1891-94; Rector of the Cathedral, Pembroke, Ontario, 1894-1906; Parish Priest at Haileybury, Ontario, 1906-8; Vicar Apostolic of Temiscamingue, 1908-15. Publications: Visite pastorale chez les Sauvages du Lac Barriere et du Grand Lac Victoria; Pastoral Letters. Address: Haileybury, Ontario.
(Died 14 Dec. 1922.)

LAUDER, Chas. Jas., R.S.W.; Member of Royal Institute Fine Arts, Glasgow; s. of James Thompson Lauder, artist, portrait painter, and Rachael, d. of Peter Currie, Greenock; m. 1st, Mary M'Callum, Glasgow; 2nd, Gertrude Annie Ashton, artist, London. Educ.: village school, Maryhill, Glasgow. Bred to designing; studied art under Heath Wilson, School of Design, Glasgow; Medallist Crystal Palace, 1884; painted much in Venice and in various cities of Italy, France, and Holland; lived 15 years at Richmond on Thames; painted on the Thames from Hampton Court to the Pool; pictures shown in several one-man shows in London and Glasgow. Publications: Picturesque London; Hampton Court; Royal Richmond. Recreations: reading (mainly history) and gardening. Address: Asolo, Thorntonhall, Lanarkshire. T.: Clarkston 205. Club: Art, Glasgow.
(Died April 1920.)

LAUDER, Sir Thomas North Dick-; 9th Bt.; cr. 1688; late Lieut. 60th Rifles; b. 28 April 1846; e. s. of 8th Bt. and Lady Anne Dalrymple, 2nd d. of 9th Earl of Stair; Knight of Justice, Order of St. John of Jerusalem; S. father 1867. Heir: b. George William Dalrymple [b. 4 Sep. 1852; m. 1882, Jane Emily Clifford, d. of W. P. Woodward; one s. Address: Gorton House, Hawthornden, Edinburgh. Club: New, Edinburgh]. Address: Fountain Hall, Pencaitland, Haddington; Grange House, Edinburgh. Clubs: Army and Navy, Junior Carlton; New, Edinburgh. (Died 19 June 1919.)

LAUDERDALE, 13th Earl of, cr. 1624, **Frederick Henry Maitland,** D.L., J.P.; Baron Maitland, 1590; Viscount Lauderdale, 1616; Viscount Maitland, Baron Thirlestane and Boltoun, 1624; Baronet of Nova Scotia, 1672; Representative Peer for Scot. since 1889; retired Lt.-Col. Bengal Staff Corps, 1886; Lord-Lt. of Berwickshire, 1890-1901; b. 16 Dec. 1840; s. of Gen. Frederick Colthurst Maitland, g. s. of 4th s. of 6th Earl and Anne, d. of Stephen Williams; S. cousin, 1884; m. 1st, Charlotte, d. of Lieut.-Col. Sleigh, 77th Regt., 1864; 2nd, Ada, d. of Rev. H. T. Simpson, Rector of Adel, Yorkshire, 1883; two s. two d. Served in 8th and in 4th

Hussars, 1861-74; served under Foreign Dept. Government of India, 1869-86; Hereditary Royal Standard Bearer for Scotland, 1670 to 1910. Heir: s. Viscount Maitland. Address: Lauriston, Hollington Park, St. Leonard's-on-Sea; T.: Hastings 82; Thirlestane Castle, Lauder, Berwickshire. Clubs: Carlton, United Service.
(Died 1 Sept. 1924.)

LAURIE, Rev. Sir (John Robert Laurie) Emilius, 3rd Bt.: cr. 1834 (assumed name of Laurie on succeeding to Maxwelton, 1886, under the will of his great-u. Sir Robert Laurie); b. 16 May 1823; s. of Sir John Bayley, 2nd Bt.; S. father 1871; m. 1855, Marianne Sophia (d. 1909), d. of late Edward R. Rice, M.P., of Dane Court, Kent; three s. one d. Educ.: Eton; Trinity Coll. Camb. Vicar of Woburn; St. John's, Paddington; Rector of St. George's, Bloomsbury. Heir: s. Claude. Address: Maxwelton House, Thornhill, N.B.; 14 Hyde Park Street, W. Club: National.
(Died 5 Dec. 1917.)

LAURIE, Ranald Macdonald, D.S.O. 1917; T.D., D.L.; Member of Stock Exchange: Lt.-Colonel late commanding 2nd East Anglian Brigade R.F.A. (T.); b. 1869; s. of R. P. Laurie, C.B., M.P. for Canterbury and Bath, and Amy, d. of Sir Ranald Martin, C.B.; m. 1894, Florence Albreda, d. of Hon. Greville Vernon; one s. Educ.: Eton; Christ Church, Oxford. Served European War in France, Egypt, and Palestine, 1914-19 (D.S.O., Order of the Nile 3rd Class, despatches). Address: Ford Place, Grays, Essex. Clubs: Carlton, United University.
(Died 21 Oct. 1927.)

LAURIER, Rt. Hon. Sir Wilfrid, P.C. 1897; G.C.M.G.; cr. 1897; D.C.L.; LL.D.; K.C.; b. St. Lin, Quebec, 20 Nov. 1841; o. c. of late Carolus Laurier, P.L.S., and Marcelle Martineau; m. 1868, Zoë, d. of G. N. R. Lafontaine of Montreal. Educ.: L'Assomption Coll. M'Gill University; Roman Catholic. B.C.L. of M'Gill, 1864; Barr. 1864; Q.C. 1880; entered Parliament, 1871; re-elected 1874; member of Federal Assembly, 1874; Minister of Inland Revenue in the Mackenzie Ministry, 1877; defeated at General Election of 1878, but was immediately afterwards elected for Quebec East; was re-elected at the General Elections in 1878, 1882, 1887, 1891, and 1911; Leader of Liberal Party, 1891; Premier of Canada, 1896-1911 (the first French Canadian to hold that post). Address: 335 Laurier Avenue, Ottawa. Clubs: Rideau, St. James's, National, Union, Ottawa.
(Died 17 Feb. 1919.)

LAVERACK, Frederick Joseph; b. Leeds; s. of George and Elizabeth Laverack; m. Rose, e. d. of Robert Roberts, Leeds; one s. two d. Educ.: Ranmoor College, Sheffield; privately. Studied law, but afterwards became a Congregational minister with pastorates in Yorkshire and Fulham; joined the late Sir Arthur Pearson in 1916 and organised The Blinded Soldiers' Children Fund, raising £100,000; reorganised chaplains Dept. National Institute for the Blind; Joint Sec. Greater London Fund for the Blind; late Director of Association for the General Welfare of the Blind; has been very successful in raising large funds for charitable purposes; is a well-known organiser and business expert; contested Brixton Nov. 1922; M.P. (L.) Brixton Division of Lambeth, Dec. 1923-Oct. 1924; in much request as a speaker and lecturer. Publications: Life's Asides; These Sayings of Mine; many articles. Recreations: reading, chess, motoring. Address: Invergordon, 48 Harold Road, Upper Norwood, S.E.19. T.: Sydenham 4773. Club: National Liberal.
(Died 11 April 1928.)

LAVERGNE, Hon. Mr. Justice Joseph, a Judge of the Court of the King's Bench for the Province of Quebec since 1906;

21

609

b. 29 Oct. 1847; *s.* of late Louis David Lavergne, J.P., and Marie Geneviève Delagrave; *m.* 1876, Marie Louise Emilie, *d.* of late J. G. Barthe, M.P., barrister and writer; one *s.* one *d.* *Educ.:* St. Ann's College, P.Q. Admitted at Bar, 1871; practised law for twenty-six years in partnership with Sir Wilfrid Laurier in Arthabaska; was Mayor of town of Arthabaska, and Warden of County of Arthabaska for some years; during same period edited a weekly newspaper, and was a member of Canadian House of Commons, 1887-97, representing the constituency of Drummond and Arthabaska; Judge of Superior Court for district of Ottawa, 1897; Montreal, 1901; King's Bench, 1906. *Publications:* Le Journal d'Arthabaska; L'Union des Cantons de l'Est. *Recreations:* books, billiards, cards. *Address:* Court House, Montreal; 340 Kensington Avenue, Westmount, P.Q., Canada. *T.:* Westmount 422. *Club:* Rideau, Ottawa. *(Died Jan. 1922.)*

LAVISSE, Ernest, Académie française; Professeur à l'Université de Paris; Directeur de l'Ecole normale supérieure; Directeur de la Revue de Paris; Corresponding Fellow of the British Academy; né au Nouvion-en-Thiérache (Aisne), 17 déc. 1842. *Educ.:* Paris, au lycée Charlemagne; à l'Ecole normale supérieure. Professeur aux lycées de Nancy, Versailles et Henri IV (Paris), 1865-75; maître de conférences à l'Ecole normale supérieure, 1875-80; Professeur à la Faculté des Lettres de l'Université de Paris. *Publications:* Publications pédagogiques: Questions d'éducation nationale; Etudes et étudiants; Publications historiques: Etudes sur l'histoire de Prusse; la Jeunesse du Grand Frédéric; le Grand Frédéric avant l'avènement; l'Allemagne impériale; Trois Empereurs d'Allemagne; vue générale de l'histoire de l'Europe; a dirigé en collaboration avec M. A. Rambaud la publication d'une grande "Histoire générale"; a dirigé la publication d'une "Histoire de France jusqu'à la Révolution française," et y a écrit deux volumes sur Louis XIV. *Address:* rue de Médicis 51, Paris. *(Died 18 Aug. 1922.)*

LAW, Lt.-Col. Alfred, Chief Constable of Hertfordshire since 1911; *b.* 1871; *y. s.* of Major-General Samuel Crozier Law and Annie Emily Cotgrave, *d.* of Colonel Charles Hogg; *m.* 1896, Katherine, *y. d.* of Edward Rotheram, of Crossdrum, Oldcastle, Co. Meath; one *s.* one *d.* *Educ.:* Wellington; Sandhurst. Joined 2nd Batt. North Staffordshire Regiment, 1890; Adjutant, North Down Rifles, 1899-1904; called to Bar, Middle Temple, 1909; rejoined army, April 1915; appointed A.A. and Q.M.G., South Midland Division. *Address:* The Dell, Hertingfordbury, Herts. *T.A.:* Hertingfordbury. *T :* Hertford 149. *(Died 8 Nov. 1928.)*

LAW, Right Hon. Andrew Bonar, P.C. 1911; LL.D. Glas.; M.P. (U.) Central Division, Glasgow, since Dec. 1918; Lord Rector Glasgow University since 1919; J.P. Dumbartonshire; *b.* New Brunswick, 16 Sep. 1858; *s.* of Rev. James Law, M.A., of New Brunswick, and Eliza, *d.* of William Kidston of Glasgow; *m.* 1891, Annie Pitcairn (*d.* 1909), *d.* of Harrington Robley of Glasgow; two *s.* two *d.* *Educ.:* New Brunswick; Gilbertfield School, Hamilton; High School, Glasgow. Parliamentary Secretary of the Board of Trade, 1902-6; M.P. (U.) Blackfriars Div. of Glasgow, 1900-1906; M.P. (U.) Dulwich Div. of Camberwell, 1906-1910; contested Manchester, N.W., 1910; M.P. (U.) Bootle Division, Lancs, 1911-18; Leader of Opposition in House of Commons, 1911-15; Secretary of State for the Colonies, 1915-16; Chancellor of the Exchequer, 1916-18; Lord Privy Seal, 1919-21 (resigned); Plenipotentiary, Peace Conference; Leader of the House of Commons, 1916-21 (resigned); Member of the War Cabinet, 1916-19; Leader of Unionist Party, 1911-21 (resigned); Prime Minister and

First Lord of the Treasury, 1922-23; formerly Chairman of Glasgow Iron Trade Association; was a member of William Kidston and Sons, iron merchants, Glasgow, and William Jacks & Co., iron merchants, Glasgow. *Recreations:* golf, chess, tennis. *Address:* 24 Onslow Gardens, S.W.1. *(Died 30 Oct. 1923.)*

LAW, Sir Archibald Fitzgerald, Kt., *cr.* 1908; Chief Judicial Commissioner, Federated Malay States since 1906; *b.* 1853; *m.* 1883, Louisa Alice, *d.* of E. P. Squarey, Downton, Wilts. *Educ.:* Oriel College, Oxford. Called to Bar, Inner Temple, 1879; Assistant Commissioner, Cyprus, 1880; President of District Court, Famagusta, 1883; Director of Survey and Principal Forest Officer, 1886; M. L. Council, 1887; Queen's Advocate, 1892; Puisne Judge, Straits Settlements, 1893. *Address:* Stourbridge, Wimborne, Dorset. *Club:* Oxford and Cambridge. *(Died 26 July 1921.)*

LAW, Mary, violinist; *b.* London 1889; *d.* of Edward Gibbon Law. *Educ.:* Guildhall School of Music; London; Chicago. Made *début*, 1900. *Recreation:* riding. *T.:* London Wall 5753. *(Died 1919.)*

LAW, Rev. Robert, D.D.; Professor of New Testament Literature and Exegesis, Knox College, Toronto; *b.* 1860; *s.* of James Law, farmer, East Mains, Broxburn, West Lothian; *m.* Ralphina Melville, *d.* of Rev. Robert Brown, Markinch, Fife; five *s.* one *d.* *Educ.:* Daniel Stewart's College, Edinburgh; Edinburgh and Tübingen Universities; United Presbyterian Theological Hall. Minister of United Presbyterian (and United Free) Church in Mearns, 1885-91; Kilmarnock, 1891-97; Bridge of Allan, 1897-1901; Lauriston Place Edinburgh, 1902-9; Kerr Lecturer, 1905; D.D. Edinburgh University, 1911. *Publications:* The Tests of Life: a Study of the First Epistle of St. John, being the Kerr Lectures for 1909 (third edition, 1914); The Emotions of Jesus, 1914; The Grand Adventure, 1916; various encyclopaedia and magazine articles. *Address:* 70 St. Albans Street, Toronto. *T.:* North 5732. *(Died 7 April 1919.)*

LAWES, Edward Thornton Hill, M.A., B.C.L.; Barrister-at-Law; Recorder of Salisbury 1908-18; *b.* 1869; *e. s.* of late Henry Fricker Lawes, barrister-at-law; *m.* 1907, Eleanor Stokes, 2nd *d.* of late Samuel Saudars of Chalfont Grove, Bucks, and 7 De Vere Gardens, W. *Educ.:* Clifton; Corpus Christi, Oxford. Called to Bar, Lincoln's Inn, 1894; Western Circuit, Revising Barrister, 1904. *Publications:* edited the second edition of Wills on Evidence jointly with the late author; The Law of Compensation for Industrial Diseases, 1909. *Address:* Ennox Lodge, Hinton Charterhouse, Bath.
(Died 13 Oct. 1921.)

LAWLESS, Col. Hon. Edward; *b.* and *heir-pres.* of 4th Baron Cloncurry; *b.* 1841; *m.* 1880, Mary Elizabeth, *d.* of late Rev. R. Burton. Formerly Capt. Rifle Brigade; Hon. Col. Royal Dublin Fusiliers. *Address:* Bryanstown, Maynooth, Co. Kildare. *(Died 24 April 1921.)*

LAWRENCE of Kingsgate, 1st Baron, *cr.* 1923; **Charles Napier Lawrence,** Chairman of North British and Mercantile Insurance Company and Antofagasta and Bolivia Railway; *b.* 27 May 1855; *s.* of 1st Lord Lawrence of the Punjab; *m.* 1881, Catherine Sumner of New York. *Educ.:* Marlborough College. Formerly a merchant; Chairman, London and North-Western Railway, 1921-24; Chairman, London Midland and Scottish Railway, 1923-24; served on Royal Commissions, St. Louis Exhibition, and Shipping Bounties and Rebates; Chairman of Royal Commission on Insurance Acts of 1911, 1912, which sat 1924-26. *Recreations:* shooting, golf. *Address:* 23 Eaton Square, S.W.1. *T.:* Victoria 441. *Clubs:* Brooks's, Garrick, St. James's, Athenæum. *(Died 17 Dec. 1927.)*

LAWRENCE, Hon. (Alfred) Clive, C.B.E. 1918; H.M. Procurator General and Solicitor to the Treasury since 1923; *b.* 1876; *e. s.* of 1st Baron Trevethin; *m.* 1924, Mildred; *yr. d.* of late Rev. Edward Parker Dew, Breamore, Hants; one *d. Educ.:* Hailey-bury; Trinity Hall, Camb. Bar., Middle Temple, 1902; 8. Wales Circuit; Revising Barrister, 1914; Junior Counsel to Ministry of Labour, March 1919; Solicitor to Ministry of Labour, August 1919; Director of Intelli-gence Branch, Procurator-General's Dept., 1914-19; Officer of the Order of St. Maurice and St. Lazarus, Italy, 1919. *Recreations:* shooting, fishing, golf. *Address:* 15 Grove End Road, N.W.8. *Clubs:* Travellers', Garrick.
(Died 13 Mar. 1926.)

LAWRENCE, Sir Joseph, 1st Bt., *cr.* 1918; Kt., *cr.* 1902; J.P. Co. Surrey; Chairman of Lino-type and Machinery, Ltd.; and of International Linotype, Ltd.; Director of Mergenthaler Lino-type Co., New York; Commissioner of Lieuten-ancy for City of London; Alderman of Surrey County Council; *b.* 23 Sept. 1848; *s.* of late Philip Lawrence, Zante, Ionian Isles; *m.* 1873, Mar-garet Alice, *d.* of late Joseph Jackson, South-port; one *d. Educ.:* privately; Owens Coll. Manchester. Captain of 40th Lancashire Vols. 1873-78; was one of the principal and earliest pioneers of the Manchester Ship Canal; took an active part in the passage of the Patents Acts 1902-1907; contested Cardiff, 1900; Sheriff of City of London, 1900-1901; M.P. (C.) Mon-mouth Boroughs, 1901-1906. Conservative and Imperialist. *Heir:* none. *Address:* Oaklands, Kenley, Surrey. *Clubs* Carlton, City Carlton, Constitutional.
(Died 24 Oct. 1919.)

LAWRENCE, Roger Bernard, K.C. 1913; barrister, Lincoln's Inn; Bencher, 1919; Vice-Chancellor of the Co. Palatine of Lan-caster, 1919; B.A. London University; *s.* of late Philip Henry Lawrence, barrister; *m.* Clara Mabel, *d.* of the Rev. Philip Henry Wick-steed ; two *s.* two *d. Address:* The Beeches, Poplar Road, Oxton, Birkenhead; 9 Cook Street, Liverpool. *Clubs:* Reform, Athenæum, Liverpool; Union, Manchester.
(Died 8 Dec. 1925.)

LAWRENCE, Rev. Thomas Joseph, M.A., LL.D., J.P.; Hon. Canon of Salis-bury, 1919; Rector of Upton Lovel, Wilts, since 1902; *b.* Chesterton, near Cambridge, 23 April 1849; *m.* Elizabeth Anna, *d.* of Edward Ede, J.P., of Plymouth; one *s.* one *d. Educ.:* Perse Grammar School, Cambridge; Downing Coll. Camb. (Scholar and prizeman). Whewell Univ. Scholar; Senior Moral Sciences Tripos; Senior Law and History Tripos. Fellow and tutor of Downing Coll. 1873-76; ordained 1874; Vicar of Tadlow, Cambs, 1877-88; Deputy-Professor of International Law at Camb. 1883-1885; Professor of International Law in the Univ. of Chicago, U.S.A., 1892-93; Rector of Nailstone, Leicestershire, 1894; Rector of Girton, Cambs, 1895-1902; Hon. Fellow of Downing College, 1908; Assistant-Chaplain, Chapel Royal, Savoy 1894-1909; Lecturer on International Law at Royal Naval College, Greenwich, and at Royal Naval War College, Portsmouth, 1884-1909; Preacher before the University of Cam-bridge on several occasions; Member of the Institut de Droit International; Reader in International Law in the University of Bristol. *Publications:* Disputed Questions in Modern International Law, 1884; Handbook of Public International Law, 1885, 10th ed., revised and brought up to date, 1918; Principles of Inter-national Law, 1895, 6th ed., brought up to date, 1915; contributions to History of the Nine-teenth Century, 1902, and to King's College Lectures on Colonial Problems, 1913; War and Neutrality in the Far East, 1904; International Problems and Hague Conferences, 1908; Docu-ments Illustrative of International Law, 1914. *Recreation:* gardening. *Address:* Upton Lovel Rectory, Wilts.
(Died 16 Aug. 1919.)

LAWRENCE, Maj.-Gen. William Alexander, Indian Army; *b.* 5 July 1843; *m.* 1884, *d.* of G. F. White; one *s.* Entered army, 1861; Maj.-Gen. 1897; retired list, 1902; served Afghan War, 1878-80 (despatches, medal with clasp, brevet Lt.-Col.). *Address:* 23 Pembroke Gardens, Kensington, W.8. *T.:* Western 3034.
(Died 8 July 1924.)

LAWRIE, Allan James, K.C. 1924; Deputy Chairman County of London Quarter Sessions since 1911; *e. s.* of late J. D. Lawrie of Monk-rigg, East Lothian; *b.* 1873; *m.* Ethel, *y. d.* of late Judge Adams; three *s. Educ.:* Fettes College, Edinburgh; Trinity College, Oxford. Called to Bar, Lincoln's Inn, 1899; contested (L.) Holderness Division, Yorkshire, 1900; Treasury Counsel, Middlesex Sessions, 1908. *Recreations:* shooting, fishing, golf. *Address:* 36 Scarsdale Villas, W.8; *T.:* Western 1681; Sessions House, Newington, S.E. *Clubs:* Brooks's, National Liberal Eighty, Public Schools.
(Died 1 Feb. 1926.)

LAWS, Rev. George Edward, Vicar of Congresbury, Somerset; Hon. Canon of Bristol. Deacon, 1879; Priest, 1880; Curate, St. John, Upper Holloway, 1879; St. Matthew, Luton, 1882-3; Emmanuel, Clifton, 1884-7; Vicar of St. Clement's, Bristol, 1887-1905; St. Peter, Bristol, 1905. *Address:* The Vicarage, Congres-bury, Somerset.
(Died Dec. 1923.)

LAWSON, Abercrombie Anstruther, D.Sc.; F.R.S.E.; F.L.S.: Professor of Botany, University of Sydney since 1912; 4th *s.* of late William Lawson, Fife, Scotland. *Educ.:* Uni-versity of Glasgow; Bonn. Travelled in Europe, 1906-7; student at Bonn, 1906; Lecturer in Botany, Glasgow University, 1907-12. *Publi-cations:* Memoirs; On the Morphology of the Gymnosperms and Cytology. *Recreations:* golf, mountain climbing, travelling. *Address:* The University, Sydney, N.S.W. *Club:* Australian, Sydney.
(Died 26 Mar. 1927.)

LAWSON, Alexander, Professor of English Literature at St. Andrews, 1897-1920; *o. s.* of late Alexander Lawson and Catharine Mac-Quarrie; *b.* Lowvalleyfield, Culross, 18 Sep. 1852. *Educ.:* Geddes School, Culross; Uni-versities of St. Andrews and Heidelberg. M.A. with 1st class Honours in Philosophy, 1874; Tyndall-Bruce Scholar, 1874; Ramsay Scholar, 1875; B.D. 1877; Assistant to Professor Thomas Spencer Baynes, LL.D., during session 1876-1877; Assistant Clergyman successively in St. Michael's, Dumfries, and Maxwell Parish, Glasgow; ordained Collegiate Minister of Elgin, 1882; Examiner in English and Philosophy in University of St. Andrews, 1886-89; Chairman of Elgin Parochial Board, 1889-93; presented to Parish of Deer, Aberdeenshire, by Presbytery of Deer and inducted 1898; Dean of the Faculty of Arts, St. Andrews, 1902-7; Hon. D.D. of Edinburgh Univ. 1905. *Publications:* literary articles in various journals, 1888-97; Letters on Golf, 1889; A Book of the Parish of Deer, 1896. Poems of Alexander Hume, edited for Scottish Text Society, 1902; Kingis Quair, 1910; edited a St. Andrew's Treasury of Scottish Verse, 1920. *Recreations:* golf, bridge, piquet. *Address:* 4 Gillespie Terrace, St. Andrews, N.B. *Club:* Scottish Conservative, Edinburgh.
(Died 22 Jan. 1921.)

LAWSON, Rev. Frederick Pike, Hon. Canon of Peterborough. *Address:* Sudborough Rectory, Thrapston.
(Died 3 Nov. 1920.)

LAWSON, Major Frederick Washing-ton, D.S.O. 1918; Engineer for Metropolitan Water Supply and Sewerage, Perth, Western Australia; *b.* Launceston, Tasmania, 12 June 1869; *m.* 1892, Christina Vernon; three *s.* one *d. Educ.:* Public Schools, Victoria. Served articles

Mechanical Engineering with J. Buncle & Sons, Melbourne; entered Public Service of N.S.W., 1892; attached to Water Supply, Drainage, and Irrigation Branch of Public Works Dept.; transferred to Public Works Dept., Western Australia; engaged on Water Supply and Drainage Works; served with Australian Engineers in France (promoted Major, despatches, D.S.O.); Member Inst.C.E.; M.Inst.M.E.; M. Royal San. Inst.; Vice-President Inst. Engineers Aust.; Member Faculty Eng. W.A. University. *Publications:* technical papers, Instituté of Engineers, Australia, *Recreations:* interested in all sports. *Address:* King's Park, Perth, Western Australia. *T.:* 4556. *Clubs:* Naval and Military, Masonic, Perth.

(*Died 17 Nov. 1924.*)

LAWSON, Henry Hertzberg, *b.* near Grenfell, New South Wales, 17 June 1867; *s.* of Peter Hertzberg Larsen, a Norwegian, and Louisa Albury, of New South Wales. Went to London, 1900; returned to Sydney, 1903; contributed verse and prose to the Bulletin. *Publications:* Short Stories in Prose and Verse, 1895; In the Days when the World was Wide, and Other Verse, 1896; While the Billy Boils, 1898; Verses, Popular and Humorous, 1900; The Country I Come From,1901; Joe Wilson and His Mates, 1901; Children of the Bush, 1902; On the Track and Over the Sliprails; When I Was King and Other Verses, 1905; The Rising of the Court; The Skyline Riders, and other works.

(*Died 3 Sept. 1922.*)

LAWSON, H. S., M.A. Cantab; Headmaster of Buxton College; temp. Sec. Lieut. R.F.A. (T.); *b.* Weston-in-Gordano, Somerset, 19 Oct. 1876; *s.* of late Rev. Robert Lawson of Camerton, Somerset, and *d.* of late John Mason Neale; *m.* 1908, J. K., *d.* of late O. J. Trinder of Tadorne, Surrey; two *s.* one *d.* *Educ.:* Haileybury; Peterhouse, Cambridge. Ministry of Education, Cairo; Wellington College, Berks; Wolverhampton Grammar School; Tutor to sons of Earl of Morton. *Recreations:* cricket, football, golf. *Address:* Buxton College, Derbyshire. *T.:* Buxton 122. *M.:* LD 6271. *Club:* New Oxford and Cambridge.

(*Died 5 Feb. 1918.*)

LAWSON, Sir John Grant, 1st Bt.; *cr.* 1905; J.P. and D.L.; *b.* Yorkshire, 28 July 1856; 2nd *s.* of late Andrew Lawson, Aldborough, Yorkshire, and Isabella, *d.* of John Grant, Nuttall Hall, Lancashire; *m.* 1902, Sylvia, *y.* *d.* of Charles Hunter, Selaby Hall, near Darlington; two *s.* one *d.* *Educ.:* Harrow; Christ Church, Oxford (M.A.). Parliamentary Charity Commissioner, 1895-1900; Secretary of Local Government Board, 1900-5; Chairman of Ways and Means and Deputy Speaker, 1905; M.P. (C.) Thirsk and Malton Division, York, 1892-1906. *Recreation:* hunting. *Heir:* *s.* Peter Grant, *b.* 28 July 1903. *Address:* Middlethorpe Lodge, York; Nuttall Hall, Lancashire. *Clubs:* Carlton; Yorkshire, York. (*Died 27 May 1919.*)

LAWSON, Thomas William, Banker and Broker, Yachtsman, Author, Farmer; *b.* Charlestown, Mass., 26 Feb. 1857; *s.* of Thomas Lawson and Anna Maria Loring; *m.* 1878, Jeannie Augusta Goodwillie. *Educ.:* Public Schools, Cambridge, Mass. In business as Banker and Broker since 1870. *Publications:* The Krank, 1887; History of the Republican Party, 1888; Secrets of Success, 1888; Collection of Poems and Short Stories from Magazines, 1888; Lawson History of the America Cup, 1902; Frenzied Finance,1905; Friday the Thirteenth, 1907. (*Died 7 Feb. 1925.*)

LAWSON, Victor F., newspaper editor and publisher; *b.* Chicago, 9 Sep. 1850. *Educ.:* Phillip's Academy, Andover, Mass. Took charge of his father's interest in a printing establishment, 1872; bought Chicago Daily News, 1876; started morning edition, 1881; sole proprietor,

1888; changed name of morning issue to the Chicago Record (now Chicago Herald and Examiner); ex-President of the Associated Press; established Daily News Fresh-Air Fund, which maintains the Lincoln Park Sanatorium for sick poor children; inaugurated popular movement for establishment of Postal Savings Banks in America; Hon. Degree Doctor of Laws, Columbia University, New York, 1924, and University of Michigan, 1923. *Address:* 15 North Wells Street, Chicago. *Clubs:* Royal Automobile; Commercial, Chicago, University, Union League, Mid-day, Chicago Athletic, Press, Onwentsia, South Shore Country, Saddle and Cycle, Wayfarers, Chicago; Century, New York. (*Died 19 Aug. 1925.*)

LAYARD, George Somes, Author and Reviewer; *b.* 4 Feb. 1857; *s.* of Rev. C. C. Layard; *m.* Eleanor Byng, *d.* of Thomas Gribble; one *s.* one *d.* *Educ.:* Harrow; Trin. Coll., Camb. B.A. Cambridge; Barrister-at-law; Western Circuit; member of the Inner Temple; one of the Malvern Hills Conservators, 1900-2; contributor to Dictionary of National Biography and Times Supplement of Encyclopædia Britannica; inventor of a system for the federation of private libraries, and originator (in the Nineteenth Century) of a scheme which had its development in the London distributing kitchens. *Publications:* Charles Keene; Mrs. Lynn Linton; Portraits of Cruikshank, by himself; Tennyson and his Pre-Raphaelite Illustrators; His Golf Madness, and other Queer Stories; Society Straws; The Gentle Art of Booklending (privately printed); Dolly's Governess; Kate Greenaway (with M. H. Spielmann); Sir Thomas Lawrence's Letterbag; Suppressed Plates, 1907, A Great Punch Editor (Shirley Brooks), 1907. Wax: a novel, 1909. Peter Layard: a memoir (privately printed), 1919; Pierre Lombart's Headless Horseman, 1922. *Recreations:* book-hunting, print-collecting, and croquet. *Address:* 5 Pelham Place, S.W.7. *T.:* Kensington 6894. (*Died 30 May 1925.*)

LAZIER, Stephen Franklin, M.A., L.L.B., K.C.; head of firm of Lazier and Lazier, Barristers, Hamilton, Ont.; *b.* Picton, Prince Edward Co., Ont., Canada, 1 July 1841; *s.* of Benjamin Franklin Lazier and Leonora Clark; *m.* Alice Maude Mary Lister of Hamilton, Ontario, Canada; two *s.* two *d.* *Educ.:* Dundas Grammar School; University of Victoria College, Ontario. Ex-President Ontario Bar Association; President Hamilton Law Association; for over 25 years School Trustee of Hamilton Board of Education; for 23 years Recording Steward of Hamilton Centenary Methodist Church; four times Delegate to Methodist General Conference; Trustee for 35 years of Centenary Methodist Church; Ex-President Hamilton Branch of Bible Society; Ex-Chairman Board of Education, Hamilton; Ex-President Hamilton Young Men's Christian Association. *Recreations:* travelling and motoring. *Address:* 131 Charles Street, Hamilton, Ontario, Canada. *T.:* 520 Hamilton, Ontario. *M.:* 33534. *Club:* Hamilton, Hamilton.

(*Died Sept. 1916.*)

LEA, Hugh Cecil; newspaper proprietor; *s.* of C. A. Lea and Elizabeth Maria, *d.* of late Thos. Matthews. *Educ.:* Boulogne; Reims; Munich. M.P. (L.) for E. St. Pancras, 1906-1910; L.C.C. 1910-13. *Address:* 14 Grafton Street, Bond Street, W.1. *Club:* Reform.

(*Died 29 Jan. 1926.*)

LEA, Colonel Samuel Job, C.B. 1899; retired pay; *b.* Hoylake, Cheshire, 13 July 1851; *s.* of Rev. J. Lea Vicar of Shocklach, Cheshire, and Jane Bell, Perth; *m.* 1872, Annie (*d.* 1912), *d.* of T. Parker of Aldford, Cheshire. *Educ.:* private schools. Entered army, 1872; Lt.-Col., 1890; served in Egypt, 1882; Nile Expedition, 1884-85; Soudan, 1885-86; (Egypt), medal with clasp, 4th class Medjidie and Khedive's star;

(Nile), two clasps ; D.A.A.G. Ireland, 1897-1900 ; special service South Africa, 1900 - 1901 (despatches, Queen's medal, 2 clasps). *Decorated* for service abroad. *Recreations :* hunting, shooting, fishing. *Address :* 20 Beach Road, Fairbourne, N. Wales.   (*Died 29 June 1919.*)

LEACH, Charles, D.D., M.P. (L.) Colne Valley, West Riding of Yorkshire. 1910-16 ; *b.* in a Yorkshire village, near Halifax, 1847 ; *m.* Mary Jane, *y. d.* of Charles Fox. *Educ. :* Private tutors ; Ranmoor Theological College, Sheffield. Trained and educated for the Nonconformist ministry ; carried on his ministry at Sheffield, Birmingham, Manchester, and London ; founded the Queen's Park College and Institute in West London, now carried on by the London County Council ; has written a large number of books and stories ; has travelled on the Continent, in Syria, Turkey, Canada, and America, and made nine visits to Palestine and Egypt ; has been recognised as one of the founders of the Sunday afternoon movement ; retired from the Pastorate and became a Parliamentary candidate ; one of the founders and now Vice-Chairman of the Abstainers and General Insurance Co., Ltd. *Publications :* Is my Bible True ; Sunday afternoons with Working Men ; How I reached the Masses ; Bethesda Chapel ; The Romance of the Holy Land, &c. *Recreations :* cycling and story writing. *Address :* Springfield, Canonbury Park South, N.   (*Died 24 Nov. 1919.*)

LEACH, Major-General Sir Edmund, K.C.B., *cr.* 1907 ; C.B. 1885 ; Colonel Queen's Own, 1904-21 ; *b.* 28 Nov. 1836 ; 6th *s.* of late Henry Leach of Corston, Pembroke ; *m.* 1869, Frances Elizabeth, 2nd *d.* of late W. H. Ince ; two *s. Educ. :* Sandhurst. Entered Queen's Own Regiment, 1854 ; Captain, 1864 ; Major, 1866 ; Lt.-Col. 1876 ; Lt.-Col. commanding 1st Batt. Queen's Own (Royal West Kent) Regt. 1883 ; Col. 1884 ; Maj.-Gen. 1894 ; retired 1898 ; served Crimea, 1855-56 ; New Zealand War, 1863-66 (despatches thrice, medal, Bt. Major) ; Egyptian War, 1882 (medal, 4th class Osmanie, Khedive's star) ; Nile Expedition, 1885 (despatches, C.B.) ; was A.A.G. Eastern District, 1886-91 ; commanded troops Barbados, 1894-95. *Address :* 27 Thurloe Square, S.W.   (*Died 7 Aug. 1923.*)

LEACH, Frederick, *s.* of late Henry Leach, J.P., D.L., of Corston, Pembrokeshire ; *b.* 1843 ; unmarried. I.S.O. 1902 ; late Senior Clerk, War Office. *Address :* The Holt, Lindfield, Hayward's Heath ; 7 Stanford Road, Kensington Court, W.   (*Died 27 Feb. 1916.*)

LEACH, Rev. Henry, M.A. ; Hon. Canon, Gloucester, 1897 ; *m.* Lucy (*d.* 1913), *o. d.* of late William Peel, Ackworth Park, Yorks. *Educ. :* Emmanuel College, Cambridge ; Master Ipswich Grammar School, 1853-58 ; Curate of St. Thomas's, Portman Square, 1858-63 ; Vicar of All Saints, Horton, Bradford, 1864-76 ; Framfield, Sussex, 1876-83 ; St. Peter's, Islington, 1883-86 ; Rector of Ash Church, Gloucester, 1886-98 ; Vicar of Staunton-on-Arrow, Herefords, 1900-8. *Address :* Southover, East Grinstead, Sussex.
     (*Died 4 June 1921.*)

LEACH, Sir John, K.C.V.O., *cr.* 1904 ; *b.* May 1848 ; *s.* of late Thos. Leach Seaford Lodge, Ryde, Isle of Wight ; *m.* 1st, 1878, Agnes Jane (*d.* 1921), *d.* late Henry Beck of Herne Bay, Kent ; 2nd, 1923, Marian, *d.* of late Francis Norvall. *Educ. :* Royal Military Academy. Commissioned Royal Artil. 1869 ; served in Afghan Campaign, 1879, and Bazzar Valley Expedition (medal) ; Major, R.H.A., 1890 ; Lieut.-Colonel, R.H.A., 1895 ; Colonel on the Staff R.A. (Brigadier-General) Bengal, 1900 - 1904 ; Major-General, 1904 ; appointed to command Coast Defences, Plymouth, 1905. *Club :* Naval and Military.
     (*Died 22 Jan. 1927.*)

LEACH, Rear-Adm. Robert Owen ; *b.* 1832 ; *m.* 1869, Mary, *d.* of late Captain William Donaldson Davies. Entered Navy, 1846 ; Lieut. 1854 ; Commander, 1863 ; Captain, 1869 ; retired, 1873 ; Rear-Adm., 1886 ; served Baltic (medal) ; New Zealand (medal). *Address :* Conway House, Charlton Kings, Cheltenham.
     (*Died 21 Dec. 1920.*)

LEACHMAN, Colonel Gerard Evelyn, C.I.E. 1916 ; D.S.O. 1918 ; Royal Sussex Regt. ; Political Officer, Ramadi, Mesopotamia ; *b.* 27 July 1880 ; *s.* of Dr. Leachman, Fairley, Petersfield. *Educ. :* Charterhouse. Entered army, 1900 ; Capt. 1910 ; Major, 1915 ; served S. Africa, 1899-1902 (despatches, Queen's medal 4 clasps, King's medal 2 clasps) ; European War (Mesopotamia) 1914-17 (Bt. Lt.-Col., C.I.E., D.S.O.). Holds Gill Medal, R.G.S., 1911, for travels in N.E. Arabia ; Macgregor Medal for Exploration, 1910. *Club :* United Service.
     (*Died 12 Aug. 1920.*)

LEAF, Walter, Litt.D., D.Litt. ; Chairman Westminster Bank ; Fellow of London University ; Member of the L.C.C. (E. Marylebone), 1901-4 ; *b.* Norwood, 1852 ; *e. s.* of Charles John Leaf, F.L.S., F.S.A., and Isabella Ellen, *d.* of late John Tyas of The Times ; *m.* 1894, Charlotte Mary, *d.* of late J. A. Symonds ; one *s.* one *d. Educ. :* Harrow ; Trinity College, Cambridge (Minor Scholar, 1869 ; Scholar, 1871 ; Fellow, 1875 ; Hon. Fellow, 1920) ; Craven Univ. Scholar, 1873 ; B.A., Senior Classic (bracketed), 1874 ; M.A., 1877 ; Litt.D., 1888 ; D.Litt. (Oxford), 1904. Entered firm of Leaf, Sons & Co., 1877 ; Chairman Leaf & Co. Ltd., 1888 - 92 ; President of Hellenic Society, 1914-19 ; one of founders and first Members and Vice-President of London Chamber of Commerce ; Deputy Chairman, 1885-86 ; Chairman, 1887 ; Vice-President Alpine Club, 1902-3-5 ; Deputy Chairman Committee of London Clearing Banks, 1917 ; Chairman, 1918-19 ; President of the Inst. of Bankers, 1919-21 ; Pres. of the Classical Association, 1921 ; Member of Council and Chairman of British National Committee International Chamber of Commerce ; President of the Chamber, 1925-6. *Publications :* The Story of Achilles (with, J. H. Pratt), 1880 ; The Iliad of Homer trans. into English Prose (with Messrs. Lang and E. Myers), 1882 ; The Iliad, edited with English Notes and Introduction, 1886-88 (2nd ed. 1900-2) ; Companion to the Iliad, 1892 ; A Modern Priestess of Isis (trans. from Russian), 1894 ; Versions from Hafiz, an Essay in Persian Metre, 1898 ; Troy, a study in Homeric Geography, 1912 ; Homer and Histoy, 1915 ; Little Poems from the Greek, 1922 ; Strabo on the Troad, 1923 ; numerous papers in Journal of Philology, Hellenic Studies, Geographical Journal, etc. *Recreations :* mountaineering, cycling, photography, travelling, skating, motoring. *Address :* 6 Sussex Place, Regent's Park, N.W.1. *T. :* Paddington 3270. *Clubs :* Athenæum, Alpine, Skating.   (*Died 8 Mar. 1927.*)

LEAH, Samuel Dawson, I.S.O. 1904 ; Chief-Inspector of Excise, Inland Revenue Department, 1902 ; retired 1906 ; *b.* 1844, *y. s.* of late Edward Leah, Wellington, Salop ; *m.* 1884 ; one *s.* one *d. Educ. :* Admaston, Salop ; High Ercal Grammar School, Salop. Entered Inland Revenue Department, 1869 ; Assistant Chief Inspector of Excise from 1898. *Recreation :* literature. *Address :* 18 Applegarth Road, Brook Green, W.   (*Died 2 May 1916.*)

LEAHY, Arthur Herbert ; Emeritus Prof. of Mathematics, Univ. of Sheffield ; *b.* Corfu, 25 May 1857 ; *e. s.* of late Col. Arthur Leahy, R.E., Flesk, Killarney, and Harriet, *d.* of B. M. Tabuteau, Dublin ; *m.* 1913, Margaret, *o. d.* of W. J. Chichele Nourse ; one *s.* one *d. Educ. :* Temple Grove ; Upping-

WHO WAS WHO, 1916-1928

ham ; Trinity College, Dublin ; Pembroke College, Cambridge. B.A. as 9th Wrangler, and 3rd class Class. Tripos, 1881 ; M.A. 1884 ; Instructor, R.M.A., Woolwich, 1882-83 ; Mathematical Master, Bradfield College, 1883 - 85 ; Fellow of Pembroke College, 1887 ; Bursar, 1888-92 ; Mathematical Lecturer, 1887-92 ; Professor of Mathematics in the University of Sheffield, and in Firth College, Sheffield, 1892-1922 ; Dean of Faculty of Science, 1905-11, Dean of the Faculty of Arts, 1919-22 ; Public Orator, 1912-22 ; President of Sheffield Literary and Philosophical Society, 1909 ; Vice-President Section A, British Association, 1910. *Publications :* papers on oscillatory actions in ether, on functions connected with spherical harmonics, and other mathematical subjects ; The Courtship of Ferb, 1902 ; Heroic Romances of Ireland, 1905. *Recreation :* Ancient Irish Literature. *Address :* Flesk, 3 Goda Road, Littlehampton, Sussex.   *(Died 16 May 1928.)*

LEAN, Maj.-Gen. Kenneth Edward, C.B. 1911 ; *b.* 28 May 1859 ; *s.* of late James Lean, B.C.S. ; *m.* 1887, Nina, *d.* of Captain G. Quin, late 79th Highlanders. *Educ. :* Clifton College. Entered Army, 1879 ; Captain, 1887 ; Major, 1897 ; Lt.-Col. 1904 ; Col. 1908 ; Brig.-Gen. 1912 ; served S. Africa, 1879-81 (medal with clasp) ; Burma, 1885-6 (medal with clasp) ; commanded 5th Mounted Infantry and Independent Mobile Column, South Africa, 1899-1902 ; present at actions of Belmont, Graspan, Modder River, Majesfontein, Johannesburg, Diamond Hill, Wittebergen, and Bothaville (despatches, Brevet Lt.-Col., Queen's medal 5 clasps ; King's medal 2 clasps) ; European War, 1914-18. *Address :* Fairfield, Walmer, Kent. *Club :* United Service.   *(Died 13 Nov. 1921.)*

LEANE, Colonel Edwin Thomas, C.B.E. ; V.D. ; *b.* Prospect, South Australia, 25 Aug. 1867 ; *s.* of T. J. Leane ; *m.* Katie Mary, *d.* of James Machin, Adelaide, S.A. ; three *s.* three *d.* *Educ. :* Public School, North Adelaide. Joined S. Australian Militia Garrison Artillery, 1888 ; Commissioned 3rd Regiment (Infantry), 1890 ; served S. African War, 1899-1902 (King's medal 2 clasps, Queen's medal 3 clasps, despatches) ; at outbreak of European War joined 12th Batt. A.I.F. with rank of Captain ; Major, 1915 ; D.A.D.O.S. 2nd Australian Division, 1915-16 ; Lieut.-Colonel, 1916 ; A.D.O.S., A.I.F. Headquarters, London, 1916-1917 ; A.D.O.S. Australian Army Corps, 1917-1918 ; A.D.O.S., A.I.F., France and C.O. Australian Army Ordnance Corps and temp. Colonel, 1918 ; Colonel, 1918 ; proceeded to London as Director of Ordnance Services Repatriation and Demobilisation Dept. A.I.F., 1918 ; returned to Australia Nov. 1919 (C.B.E., Belgian Croix de Guerre, V.D., despatches 6 times) ; Administrator and Chief Magistrate, Norfolk Island, 1924-26 ; Deputy Administrator, Northern Territory, Feb.-May 1925. *Recreations :* rifle shooting, horticulture. *Clubs :* Imperial Service, Sydney ; Naval and Military, Royal Automobile, Stock Exchange, Melbourne.   *(Died Aug. 1928.)*

LE BAS, Sir Hedley Francis, Kt., *cr.* 1916 ; Governing Director, Caxton Publishing Co., Ltd. ; *b.* Jersey, 19 May 1868 ; *s.* of late Capt. T. A. Le Bas ; *m.* 1900, Mary, *d.* of Joseph Barnes, Dorchester ; one *s.* one *d.* *Educ. :* Jersey. At 18 years of age enlisted in the 15th Hussars, in which regiment he served seven years in the ranks ; founded the Caxton Publishing Co., 1899. Knight of Grace, St. John of Jerusalem, 1916 ; Joint Hon. Secretary Prince of Wales' Fund ; Member of National War Savings Committee ; Hon. Treasurer English Golf Union ; Hon. Organiser Lord Kitchener National Memorial Fund ; edited Lord Kitchener Memorial Book. *Recreations :* golf and swimming (holds Royal Humane Society Award

for saving life). *Address :* Chussex, Walton Heath, Tadworth. *Clubs :* Reform, Aldwych ; Walton Heath Golf.   *(Died 25 Mar. 1926.)*

LE BLANC, His Honour Sir Pierre Evariste, K.C.M.G., *cr.* 1916 ; K.C., 1893 ; Lieut.-Governor of Quebec since 1915 ; *b.* 10 Aug. 1854 ; *y. s.* of late Joseph Le Blanc of St. Martin and late Adèle Bélanger of Ste Thérèse ; *m.* 1886, Hermine, *d.* of late Théodose Beaudry and late Catherine Vallée of Montreal ; one *s.* two *d.* *Educ. :* Jacques-Cartier Normal School ; McGill University, Montreal. A member of the Quebec Legislature, 1882-1908 ; Speaker of the Legislative Assembly, 1892-97 ; Leader of the Opposition, 1904-8 ; called to Bar at Montreal, 1879 ; LL.D., Laval University, 1915. *Address :* Montreal ; Spencer Wood, Quebec. *Clubs :* St. James, Mount - Royal, Montreal Hunt, Jockey, Montreal ; Garrison, Quebec.
      (Died 20 Oct. 1918.)

LEBOUR, George Alexander Louis, M.A., D.Sc., F.G.S. ; Prof. of Geology since 1879 and Vice-Principal since 1902, Armstrong Coll. (formerly Durham Coll. of Science), Newcastle-upon-Tyne ; *b.* 1847 ; *s.* of Alexander Lebour, artist ; *m.* Emily, *d.* of Dr. W. Hodding of London. *Educ. :* Royal School of Mines. On H.M. Geological Survey, 1867-73 ; Lecturer in Geological Surveying in Durham College of Science, 1873-79 ; Murchison Medallist of the Geological Society, 1904 ; Member of several Research Committees of the British Association ; Sub-editor for Foreign Geology of the Geological Record, 1874-80. *Publications :* Geology of Northumberland and Durham, 3 editions, 1878-89 ; Geological Map of Northumberland, 1877 ; more than 100 papers on Carboniferous Geology, Heat-conductivity of Rocks, Underground Temperature, and many reviews on scientific subjects ; Geology of Durham in Victoria County History, etc. etc. ; papers on relations between Public Health and Geology ; Reports on Foreign and British Coal-fields. *Address :* Armstrong College, Newcastle-upon Tyne ; Radcliffe House, Corbridge-on-Tyne.
      (Died 7 Feb. 1918.)

LE BRAZ, Anatole ; Prof. of French Literature, University of Rennes ; Officier Legion of Honour ; Docteur ès Lettres ; *b.* Duault, Côtes-du-Nord, 2 Apr. 1859. *Educ. :* Lycée St. Louis ; Faculté des Lettres de Paris ; Professor of Philosophy, College of Etampes, 1884-86 ; Professor Lycée of Quimper, 1886-1900 ; Lecturer at Harvard, 1906 ; United States and Canada, 1907, 1912, and 1915. *Publications :* Soniou Breiz-Izel ; La Chanson de la Bretagne, 1892 ; Pâques d'Islande ; Le Sang de la Sirène ; Le Gardien du Feu ; La Terre du Passé ; Au Pays des Pardons ; La Legende de la mort chez les Bretons-armoricains ; Vieilles Histoires du pays Breton ; Le Théatre celtique ; Les contes du soleil et de la brume ; Au Pays d'exil de Chateaubriand ; Ames d'Occident. *Address :* 12 Rue José-Maria de Heredia, Paris, VIIc.   *(Died Feb. 1926.)*

LE BRETON, Clement Martin, K.C. 1904 ; O.B.E. 1918 ; Recorder of Sudbury, 1918 ; Barrister-at-law, South Eastern Circuit ; *b.* 1852 ; 2nd *surv. s.* of late Very Rev. William Corbet le Breton, M.A., Dean of Jersey. *Educ. :* Victoria Coll., Jersey ; Royal Military Coll. Sandhurst. Honours, Ensign, Northumberland Fusiliers, 1870 ; Lieut. 1871 ; retired, 1874 ; Barrister, Inner Temple, 1879 ; Military Services (Civil Liabilities) Commissioner, 1916 ; Arbitrator in Industrial Disputes for Ministry of Labour, 1917 ; Chairman Shirt-making and Tailoring Trade Boards, 1918 ; *Address :* 1 Harcourt Buildings, Temple, E.C. ; 19 Half Moon Street, W.1. *Clubs :* Orleans, Reform.
      (Died 1 July 1927.)

LECK, David Calder ; K.C. 1912 ; Barrister, Middle Temple ; *b.* 1857 ; 2nd *s.* of late Rev. Alexander Leck, Kilmacolm, Renfrewshire ; *m.* ;

two s. *Educ.*: Glasgow University, LL.B. *Address:* 5 Paper Buildings, Temple, E.C.4; Ravenshoe, Burgh Heath. *T.*: Burgh Heath 230.
(*Died 18 Mar. 1927.*)

LECKY, Colonel Frederic Beauchamp, D.S.O. 1900; retired; late Royal Horse Artillery; *b.* 11 October 1858; *s.* of John Frederick Lecky, D.L., of Ballykealey, Tullow, Co. Carlow, Ireland; unmarried. *Educ.:* Uppingham School; R.M.A., Woolwich. Entered Royal Artillery, 1878; Captain, 1886; Major, 1896; served in Egyptian Expedition, 1882; present at Battle of Tel-el-Kebir (medal and clasp and bronze star); South Africa, 1900-1 (despatches, Queen's medal 6 clasps, King's medal 2 clasps, D.S.O.). *Club*: Naval and Military.
(*Died 15 Nov. 1928.*)

LECLEZIO, Sir Eugene Pierre Jules, Kt. *cr.* 1887; Chief Justice of Mauritius, 1883-1898; *b.* 1832; *m.* 1859, Camille, *e. d.* of Capt. J. C. Accary, French Army. *Educ.:* Royal College, Mauritius. Barr. Middle Temple, 1858; Judge of Mauritius, 1882. *Address:* Port Louis, Mauritius.

LECOCQ, Charles, *b.* Paris, June 3, 1832. *Educ.:* Conservatoire national de musique. Officier de la Legion d'honneur; membre de la société des Auteurs et Compositeurs dramatiques; membre de la société des Artistes musiciens. Works: Fleur de The, 1868; les Cent vierges, 1871; La Fille de Mme. Angot, 1872; Giroflé, Girofla, 1874; le Petit Duc, 1878; le Jour et la Nuit, 1881; le Cœur et la Main, 1882; Plutus, 1886; Ali-Baba, 1887; le Cygne, 1899; Yetta, 1903. *Address:* 28 rue de Surène. Paris. (*Died Oct. 1918.*)

LEDGER, Edward, proprietor and editor of The Era; retired, 1905. *Educ.:* Collegiate and Commercial School, Denmark Hill. Surrey. *Recreation:* collects armour, antique marquetry, old silver and oak furniture, old delft, oriental china, and bric-à-brac. *Address:* The Three Gables, Fitz-John's Avenue, N.W.3; *T.:* Hampstead 441; Villa Plage, Royal Parade, Eastbourne. (*Died 24 Sept. 1921.*)

LEDLIE, James Crawford, O.B.E. 1918; M.A., B.C.L.; Barrister-at-law; Deputy-Clerk of the Privy Council, 1909-21; *b.* 29 April 1860; *o. surv. s.* of late Alexander Holmes Ledlie, of Calcutta. *Educ.:* Heidelberg University; Lincoln College, Oxford. 1st Class Lit. Hum., 1884; Taylorian Scholar (German), 1883; entered the Judicial Department of the Privy Council Office, 1893; Chief Clerk of the Judicial Department 1902-9. *Publication:* Translator of Sohm's Institutes of Roman Law. *Address:* Verney House, Kilternan, Co. Dublin.
(*Died 18 Nov. 1928.*)

LEE, Hon. Charles Alfred; *b.* 13 Nov. 1842; *m.* 1865, *widower* 1915; three *s.* two *d.* M.L.A. Tenterfield, 1884-1920; was Father of N.S.W. Parliament, retired 1920; Minister for Justice, 1898-99; Minister for Public Works, 1904-10. *Address:* Tenterfield, New South Wales.
(*Died 15 Aug. 1926.*)

LEE, Gordon Ambrose de Lisle, C.B. 1920; C.V.O. 1926; Clarenceux King of Arms since 1926; *b.* Aberdeen, 11 July 1864; 2nd *s.* of Rev. Dr. F. G. Lee, of All Saints', Lambeth; *m.* 1888, Rose (*d.* 1922), *e. d.* of Robert Wallace, Secretary to the Earl Marshal. *Educ.:* St. Mary's College, Harlow; Westminster School. An artist and designer in black and white, 1885-1889; Blue-mantle Pursuivant of Arms, 1889-1905; York Herald of Arms, 1905-22; Norroy King of Arms, 1923-26; Secy. to the Deputy Earl Marshal (Lord Fitz Alan of Derwent); Secy. to the Earl Marshal of England (Duke of Norfolk), 1911-17; Deputy Registrar of the Heralds' College in 1899; Member of Council, Japan Society, 1909-15. *Publications:* B. Margaret of Salisbury, a Sketch of the Life and Times of the Last of the Plantagenets

(1887); Lives of V. Philip Howard, Earl of Arundel, Queen Mary Tudor, and St. Philip Neri; Some Notes on Japanese Heraldry, 1909; (with Mr. K. Tomita) Japanese Treasure Tales, 1906; editor The Episcopal Arms of England and Wales, 1906; arranged and superintended the heraldry, ceremonial and ecclesiology in Mr. Tree's revivals of Richard II. and Much Ado about Nothing, and of Raymond Rôze's opera, Joan of Arc; part author and producer of the Chelsea Pageant, 1908. *Recreations:* the play, the study of Japanese art, antiquities, etc. *Address:* Zenda, Cumberland Road, Kew Gardens, Surrey; Heralds' College, E.C.4. (*Died 12 Sept. 1927.*)

LEE, Sir Henry Austin, K.C.M.G., *cr.* 1902; C.B. 1892; Counsellor of Embassy in Diplomatic Service; late Commercial Attaché for France, Belgium, and Switzerland; *b.* 6 April 1847; *s.* of George A. Lee of Frogmore Guernsey, and Ceylon Civil Service; *m.* Madeleine de Wolff, *d.* of B. Franklin Smith of New York, 1892. *Educ.:* Elizabeth College, Guernsey; Pembroke College, Oxford (M.A., Hon. Fellow). Entered Foreign Office, 1870; transferred to Diplomatic Service, 1892; attached to the Marquis of Salisbury's Special Embassy to Constantinople, 1876-77; Assistant Private Secretary to the Earl of Beaconsfield, at the Congress of Berlin, 1878; at various times Private Secretary to Sir Charles Dilke, Lord Fitzmaurice, Viscount Bryce, Sir James Fergusson, M.P., Earl of Lytton, Marquis of Dufferin and Ava. *Recreation:* shooting. *Address:* 14 bis Avenue du Trocadero, Paris: Isle of Jethou, near Guernsey. *Clubs:* Arthur's, Brooks's, St. James's. (*Died 7 Nov. 1918.*)

LEE, Maj.-Gen. Henry Herbert, C.B.E. 1918; J.P., D.L.; *b.* 1838; *m.* 1873, Constance (*d.* 1890), *e. d.* of G. Lyall of Headley Park, Surrey. *Educ.:* Marlborough. Served Abyssinia, 1868 (despatches, medal); Egypt, 1885; represents Diocese of Llandaff in House of Laymen. *Address:* The Mount, Dinas Powis, Cardiff. *Club:* United Service.
(*Died 19 Mar. 1920.*)

LEE, Rev. James Wideman, D.D.; *b.* Rockbridge, Georgia, U.S.A., 28 Nov. 1849; *e. s.* of Zachry J. Lee and Emily H. Wideman; *m.* 1875, Emma Eufaula, *d.* of Rev. L. L. Ledbetter of Cedartown, Ga.; three *s.* three *d.* *Educ.:* Bawsville Academy; Grantville High School; Emory Coll., Oxford, Ga. Ordained to ministry, Methodist Episcopal Church, South, 1876; pastor of churches in Georgia at Rockmart, Long Cane, Carrolton, Dalton, Rome, and Atlanta; pastor St. John's Church, St. Louis, Mo., 1893, 1901-5 and 1911-15; head of an expedition to Palestine, 1894; Presiding Elder St. Louis District, 1897-1901 and 1915, 1916; Chaplain, Barnes' Hospital, and Assistant to the Trustees, 1917; Pastor Trinity Church, Atlanta, Ga., second time, 1905-1909; Pastor Park St. Church, second time, 1910. *Publications:* The Making of a Man, 1892, translated Japanese 1893, Chinese 1904, Korean 1908; Christ the Reason of the Universe, in an Address before the World's Parliament of Religions, held in Chicago, 1893; The Earthly Footsteps of the Man of Galilee, 1895; Henry W. Grady, Editor, Orator, and Man, 1897; edited and illustrated The Self-Interpreting Bible, 1897; Illustrated History of Methodism, 1900; History of Jerusalem, 1904; The Real Uncle Remus, 1908; Abraham Lincoln, 1909; Religion of Science, 1912 (translated into Japanese, 1916); Magnetizing the Commonplace, A Lesson in Human Geography, 1914; Robert Burns, or The Geography of Genius, 1915; Climate and Unity, 1916; The Bible and Life, 1916; The Inner and the Outer Half of Man, 1917. *Recreation:* travelling. *Address:* 5043 Washington Avenue, St. Louis, Mo., U.S.A. *T.:* Forest 4262.
(*Died 4 Oct. 1919.*)

LEE, John, C.B.E. 1923; Director of Automatic Telephone Manufacturing Co. and of other companies; Controller of the Central Telegraph Office, 1919-27; *b.* 1867; *m.* 1902, Mary Emily, *d.* of H. R. Nickson, Birkenhead; one *s.* one *d.* M.A.; M.Com.Sc., Belfast; Lecturer at various Industrial Conferences at Oxford and Cambridge; delegate to International Telegraph Conference, Paris, 1925. *Publications:* Modern Telegraph Practice; Economics of Telegraphs and Telephones; Plain Economics; Management, a Study of Industrial Organisation; The Social Implications of Christianity; The Principles of Industrial Welfare; Christian Social Duty; An Introduction to Industrial Administration; Letters to an Absentee Director; Editor of the Dictionary of Industrial Administration. *Address:* Mulgrave Lodge, Sutton, Surrey. *T.:* Sutton 337. *Club:* National Liberal.
(*Died 24 Dec. 1928.*)

LEE, Rev. Richard, M.A. Cambridge; *ad eundem,* M.A. Dublin; *s.* of late Rev. Richard Lee, Ex. Sch. T.C.D. *Educ.:* Christ's Hospital; Jesus Coll. Camb. Foundation Scholar; Rustat Scholar; 1st (bracketed) 2nd class Classical Tripos, 1869. Assistant Master at Christ's Hospital, 1871-76; Curate of Holy Trinity, Finchley, 1873-75; Lecturer of St. Benet, Paul's Wharf, 1875-76; Head Master of Christ's Hospital, London, 1876-1902; Fellow (Hon.) of College of Preceptors, 1921.
(*Died 27 Feb. 1922.*)

LEE, Richard Henry; *o. s.* of late John Henry Lee of 15 Collingham Gardens, S.W.; *g.-g.s.* of James Lee of Pinchinthorp, Yorkshire; *m.* Rosina, *y. d.* of late Charles Wigg of Hoole Bank, Chester. *Address:* Yarner, Bovey Tracey, S. Devon.   (*Died 8 Sept. 1923.*)

LEE, Sir Sidney, Kt., *cr.* 1911; engaged at King George's request, on full biography of King Edward VII. from original papers, of which vol. i. (from Birth to Accession) appeared in March 1925, and vol. ii. (the Reign) is near completion; editor of Dictionary of National Biography, 1891-1917; Professor of English Language and Literature in the University of London (East London College), 1913-24; Dean of Faculty of Arts, University of London, 1918-22; President of English Association, 1917; Hon. D.Litt. Oxford, 1907; Hon. LL.D. Glasgow, 1907; Hon. Litt.D. Victoria University, Manchester, 1900; Fellow of the British Academy; Foreign Member, American Academy of Arts and Sciences; Corresponding Member, Massachusetts Historical Society; Member of Royal Commission on Public Records since 1910; Chairman of the Executive, Shakespeare's Birthplace Trust, Stratford-on-Avon, since 1903; Registrar of Royal Literary Fund, 1907; Emeritus Professor of English in University of London, 1924; Trustee of National Portrait Gallery, 1924; *b.* London, 5 Dec. 1859. *Educ.:* City of London School; Balliol College, Oxford. Clark Lecturer in English Literature, Trinity College, Cambridge, 1901-2; Lecturer at Lowell Institute, Boston, U.S.A., 1903; Lecturer for the Common University Fund at Oxford, 1909. *Publications:* Stratford-on-Avon from the Earliest Times to the Death of Shakespeare, 1885, new ed. 1906; Lord Herbert of Cherbury's Autobiography, with a continuation of his Life, 1886, new ed. 1906; A Life of William Shakespeare, 1898 (illustrated ed. 1899, popular ed. 1900, 1907, 1915, revised 1925); A Life of Queen Victoria, 1902 (new ed. 1904); Shakespeare First Folio Facsimile, with Introduction, and Census of Extant Copies, 1902; Elizabethan Sonnets, 1904; Great Englishmen of the 16th Century, 1904, 1925; Shakespeare's Poems and Pericles, 1905; Shakespeare and the Modern Stage, 1906; America and Elizabethan England in Scribner's

616

Magazine, 1907; The French Renaissance in England, 1910; Principles of Biography, 1911; Shakespeare and the Italian Renaissance, 1915; Comment on Prefatory Pages of First Folio, 1923; editor, A Year's Work in English Studies (English Association), 1921, 1922, 1923, 1924. *Address:* 108A Lexham Gardens, Kensington, W.8. *T.:* Western 7183. *Club:* Athenæum.
(*Died 3 Mar. 1926.*)

LEE-DILLON, Hon. Harry (Lee Stanton), F.S.A.; *b.* 25 July 1874; *o. c.* of 17th Viscount Dillon; *m.* 1st, 1904, Brenda Mary (marriage dissolved, 1911), *e. d.* of Thomas Smith, L.S.A., M.R.C.S.; one *d.*; 2nd, 1913, Kathleen Clare, 2nd *d.* of late James Atchison, Civil Engineer, of Cardigan, Lavender Bay, Sydney, N.S.W. *Educ.:* Charterhouse; Sandhurst. Late Lieut. Rifle Brigade. *Address:* 146 Rue de la Paix, Boulogne, France. *Clubs:* White's, Army and Navy.   (*Died 7 Feb. 1923.*)

LEE WARNER, Philip Henry; *b.* 1877; *e. s.* of late Sir William Lee Warner, G.C.S.I., Hon. LL.D. Cantab.; *m.* 1907, Mary King, 2nd *d.* of General Thomas Sherwin, Boston, Mass.; one *s.* two *d. Educ:* Rugby; University College, Oxford; Honours Mod. History. Partner Chatto & Windus, Publishers, 1905; incorporated the Medici Society, Ltd., 1908; Managing Director and Publisher to above, 1908-21, when resigned; Chairman, Charles Whittingham and Griggs (Printers), Ltd. (from incorporation), 1919-21; Managing Director, 1922; incorporated (and became Managing Director) Martin Hopkinson & Co. Ltd., Publishers, 1923. *Address:* 14 Henrietta Street, Covent Garden, W.C.2; *T.:* Gerrard 8321; The Manor House, Bletchingley, Surrey; *T.:* Bletchingley 11; *T.A.:* Bletchingley. *Clubs:* Athenæum, Arts.   (*Died 28 Jan. 1925.*)

LEEBODY, Prof. John R., M.A., D.Sc.; F.I.C.; President Magee Presbyterian College; *b.* 1840; 2nd *s.* of Rev. H. Leebody, Ballindery, Co. Antrim; *m.* 1866, Mary Isabella Welsh (*d.* 1911), *d.* of John Welsh, Kirkcubbin, Co. Down; two *s.* two *d. Educ.:* Royal Acad. Instit. Belfast; Queen's College, Belfast; Queen's University (First Science Scholar in College and First Honourman and Gold Medallist in mathematics and physics in the University). Professor of Mathematics and Physics in Magee College, 1865. *Publications:* Religious Teaching and Modern Thought, 1889, and various magazine and review articles. *Recreations:* fishing, shooting, golf. *Address:* Magee Presbyterian College, Derry.   (*Died 21 Aug. 1927.*)

LEECH, Henry Brougham, LL.D.; *b.* 15 Nov. 1843; 2nd *s.* of Rev. John Leech, D.D., late of Mitchelstown, Co. Cork; *m.* 1875, Annie Louise, *d.* of Wm. Garbois of Dublin; five *s.* one *d. Educ.:* Trinity College, Dublin and Cambridge; Fellow of Gonville and Caius College, 1873. Called to the Irish Bar, 1871; Professor of Jurisprudence and International Law, University of Dublin, 1878-1888; Lecturer in Hindoo and Mohammedan Law, 1881; Deputy Regius Professor of Feudal and English Law, 1883-1884; Regius Professor of Laws, 1888-1908; Registrar of Deeds in Ireland, 1891-1908; Registrar of Titles in Ireland, 1893-1908; Associé de L'Institut de Droit International, 1893; Member of the American Acad. of Political and Social Science, 1902. *Publications:* Essay on Ancient International Law, 1878; Registration of Titles *v.* Registration of Assurances, 1891; The South African Republics, their History and International Position, 1901; The Irish University Question: its History and its Solution, 1905; A Handbook for Unionist Speakers, 1910; The Continuity of the Irish Revolutionary Movement, 1847-1912; Prolusiones Emeriti, 1919, being Translations into Latin and Greek Verse; and other pamphlets and essays. *Address:* 19 Porchester Square,

W.2. *Clubs*: Authors', Junior Constitutional.
(*Died 2 Mar. 1921.*)

LEECH, Sir Stephen, K.C.M.G., *cr.* 1919; *b.* 8 July 1864; 2nd *s.* of late John Leech of Gorse Hall, Dukinfield, Cheshire. *Educ.*: Eton; Magdalen Coll., Oxford. Entered H.M.'s Diplomatic Service as Attaché, 1888; 3rd Secretary, 1890; 2nd Secretary, 1894; 1st Secretary, 1904; Councillor of Embassy, 1907; Minister Resident, 1909; Envoy Extraordinary and Minister Plenipotentiary, 1913; employed at Berlin, Brussels, Constantinople, Lisbon, Rome, Copenhagen, Christiania, Peking, Cuba, Hayti and Santo Domingo; retired, 1920. *Address*: Parkhill, Lyndhurst, Hampshire. *Club*: Travellers'.
(*Died 12 May 1925.*)

LEEDS, 10th Duke of (*cr.* 1694), **George Godolphin Osborne**; Baronet, 1620; Viscount Latimer, Baron Osborne, 1673; Earl of Danby, 1674; Viscount Osborne of Dunblane, 1675; Marquis of Carmarthen, 1689; Baron Godolphin, 1832; Prince of the Holy Roman Empire; M.F.H. Bedale; *b.* 18 Sep. 1862; 2nd *s.* of 9th Duke and Fanny, 2nd *d.* of 4th Baron Rivers (*ext.*); *S.* father, 1895; *m.* 1884, Lady Katherine Frances Lambton; one *s.* four *d. Educ.*: Eton; Trinity College, Cambridge. M.P. (C.) Lambeth Brixton Division, 1887-95; Treasurer of the Household, 1895-1901; L.C.C. (City of London) since 1898. Owns about 24,300 acres. *Recreation*: owner of yacht "Corisande." *Heir*: *s.* Marquis of Carmarthen. *Address*: 11 Grosvenor Crescent, S.W.1; Hornby Castle, Bedale, Yorkshire. *Clubs*: Carlton; Royal Yacht Squadron, Cowes (Commodore). (*Died 10 May 1927.*)

LEEDS, Sir Edward Templer, 5th Bt.; *cr.* 1812; *b.* 11 Oct. 1859; 2nd *s.* of 3rd Bt. and 2nd wife, Fanny, *o. d.* of Maj.-Gen. Templer, E.I.C.S.; *m.* 1906, Charlotte Augusta, *d.* of Rev. Edward Crow, M.A.; *S. half-b.* 1894. *Heir*: *c.* Reginald Arthur St. John Leeds; *b.* 13 May 1899. *Address*: 1 Queen's Parade, Cheltenham.
(*Died 31 May 1924.*)

LEEDS, Lieut.-Col. Thomas Louis, C.M.G. 1918; D.S.O. 1917; late Commandant 59th Scinde Rifles (Frontier Force); *b.* 25 July 1869; 3rd *s.* of late Edward Montagu Leeds and Jessie, *d.* of Thomas Spears, Kirkcaldy; *m.* 1904, Clara Guion, *d.* of Col. Kilburn, U.S.A. Army; one *d. Educ.*: Sherborne. Joined 3rd Batt. Derbyshire Regt. 1889; 1st Batt. Sherwood Foresters (Derbyshire Regt.), 1891; transferred to Indian Army, 1894; joined 6th Punjab Infantry, P.F.F. (now 59th Rifles, F.F.), 1896; served in China, Zakka Khel, and Mohmand Expeditions (medal and clasp for China), 1900; Zakka and Mohmand Expedition, 1908; France, Sep. 1914-Dec. 1915 (despatches, Bt. Lt.-Col.); Mesopotamia, 1916 (despatches 4 times, D.S.O., C.M.G., 3rd class Order of St. Stanislas); retired, 1921. *Recreations*: fishing, golf. *Address*: Amor Hall, Washbrook, near Ipswich. *Club*: United Service.
(*Died 8 July 1926.*)

LEEDS, William Henry Arthur St. John, late Commissioner I.C.S., Burma; *b.* 3 Mar. 1864; *c.* and *heir-pres.* to Sir E. T. Leeds, 5th Bt.; *m.* 1908, Edith Mabel, *d.* of late Maj.-Gen. Muspratt-Williams; two *s.* one *d. Address*: 10 Cranley Gardens, S.W. *T.*: Kensington 5476. *Club*: East India United Service.
(*Died 22 Aug. 1917.*)

LEEFE, Gen. John Beckwith, R.M.A.; *b.* 6 June 1849; *m.* 1880, Julia Mary, *d.* of Capt. J. G. Gurney. Entered R.M.A. 1867; Captain, 1877; Major, 1886; Lt.-Col. 1896; Col. 1902; Maj.-Gen. 1905; Lt.-Gen. 1908; Gen. 1912; Professor of Fortification, R.N. College, 1883, 90; served S. Africa, 1900 (Queen's medal with clasp); retired 1914. *Address*: Foxwood, Farnham, Surrey. (*Died 30 Mar. 1922.*)

LEEKE, Rev. Edward Tucker, Canon since 1877, and Sub-Dean of Lincoln Cathedral

---

since 1898; *b.* 1841; *s.* of Rev. William Leeke, Vicar of Holbrooke, near Derby; *m.* 1880, Dora, *d.* of Rt. Rev. Christopher Wordsworth, Bishop of Lincoln; five *s.* two *d. Educ.*: Trinity College, Cambridge (Fellow). Ordained, 1867; Assistant Tutor, Trinity College, 1864-68; Curate of St. Andrew the Less, Cambridge, 1868-69; Vicar, 1869-77; Chancellor of Lincoln Cathedral and Examining Chaplain to Bishop of Lincoln, 1877-98; Chaplain, Lincoln Hospital, 1887-1902, 1906-7; Vicar of St. Nicholas, W. St. John, Lincoln, 1902-19. *Address*: The Chancery, Lincoln. (*Died 23 May 1925.*)

LEEKE, Rt. Rev. John Cox, D.D., M.A.; Sub-Dean of Southwark since 1905; *b.* Holbrooke, Derbyshire, 1843; *s.* of Rev. W. Leeke; *m.* Alice, *d.* of John Meynell of Meynell Langley, Derbyshire; two *s.* one *d. Educ.*: private tuition; Trinity College, Cambridge. Curate of Wanstead, 1867-1870; Holbrooke, 1870-74; Rector of Kidbrook, Blackheath, 1875-1901: St. Mark's, Plumstead, 1901-5; Rural Dean of Woolwich, 1892-1905; Hon. Canon of Rochester, 1900-1905; Bishop of Woolwich (Suffragan) 1905-18. *Recreations*: various. *Address*: Stone Cross House, Byfield, Northants.
(*Died 28 Nov. 1919.*)

LEES, Sir Harcourt James, 4th Bt.; *cr.* 1804; *b.* 24 April 1840; *s.* of 3rd Bt. and Maria Charlotte, *d.* of Edward Sullivan; *S.* father 1892; *m.* 1st, 1860, Charlotte (who divorced him 1872), *d.* of W. M'Taggart; two *s.* two *d.*; 2nd, 1872, Harriet Helen Constance (who divorced him 1887), *d.* of Henry Morgan Howard; 3rd, 1899, Louise Hayes. Late Lieut. 60th Rifles. *Heir*: *s.* Arthur Henry James [*b.* 18 Jan. 1863; unmarried]. *Address*: Upperton and Co., 14 Lincoln's Inn Fields, W.C.
(*Died 22 Mar. 1917.*)

LEES, Sir John M'Kie, K.B.E., *cr.* 1919; K.C.1901; *b.* 18 Nov. 1843; *o. surv. s.* of Walter Lees, Glasgow; *m.* 1st, 1873, Eliza (*d.* 1875), *e. d.* of Sir John Gillespie; 2nd, 1881, Alice Susan, 3rd *d.* of James Clark, of Crossbasket, Lanarkshire; three *s. Educ.*: Ayr and Edinburgh Academies, and Edinburgh University; M.A., Edinburgh, 1864; LL.B., 1867. Examiner to Glasgow University for Degrees in Law, 1874-80; and to Edinburgh University, 1877-80. Bar, 1867; Sheriff-Substitute of Lanarkshire at Airdrie, 1872-75, and at Glasgow, 1875-91; Sheriff of Stirling, Dumbarton, and Clackmannan, 1891-1917; and of Forfarshire, 1917-22; Commissioner of Northern Lighthouses, 1917; Convener of the Sheriffs of Scotland, 1907-19. *Publications*: Sheriff Court Styles; Small Debt Handbook; Pleading in Sheriff Court; Analysis of Small Debt Amendment Act; Forms of Interlocutors, etc. *Recreations*: golf, cycling, fishing. *Address*: 4 Darnaway Street, Edinburgh. *T.*: Central, Edinburgh 1873. *Club*: University, Edinburgh. (*Died 5 Nov. 1926.*)

LEES, Thomas Orde Hastings, M.A.; J.P., Barr.-at-Law; *b.* 1846; *s.* of Rev. John and Lady Louisa Lees (*d.* of 11th Earl of Huntingdon); *m.* Grace, *d.* of Joshua Wigley Bateman of Guilsborough, Northamptonshire (secretary to the Duchy of Cornwall). *Educ.*: Royal Naval School; Newcross; Royal Academy, Gosport; M.A., Trinity College, Dublin. Obtained (1868) a cadetship in the Royal Irish Constabulary; served as D.I. in counties Longford, Mayo, Louth, and Tipperary; appointed Chief Constable of Northamptonshire, 1875; called to the Bar (Mid. Temple), 1881; for some years went Midland Circuit, contested (C) Northampton 1886, opposing Messrs. Labouchere and Bradlaugh; the first Chief Constable of Isle of Wight, 1890; retired 1899; received special thanks and jubilee medal for services rendered Court at Osborne, 1896-7. *Publications*: The Constable's Pocket Book, and other technical works; Editor of Snowden's Police

Officers' Guide. *Recreations :* field sports, travel, ornithology (F.Z.S.). *Address :* Guilsborough, Northamptonshire ; 3 Temple Gardens, E.C. *Club :* Junior Carlton. (*Died 30 Sept. 1924.*)

LE FANU, William Richard ; Secretary and Treasurer to the Governors of Queen Anne's Bounty ; *b.* 1861 ; unmarried. *Educ. :* Hailey-bury ; St. John's College, Cambridge. *Address :* The Albany, Piccadilly, W. *Club :* Arts.
(*Died 22 Mar. 1925.*)

LEFROY, A. H. F., K.C., M.A. ; Professor of Roman and English Law and General Jurisprudence, and Special Lecturer on English Constitutional law, Colonial law, and Federal law, University of Toronto ; *b.* Toronto, 21 June 1852 ; *s.* of late General Sir J. H. Lefroy, K.C.M.G., etc., and Emily Merry, *d.* of late Sir John Beverley Robinson, 1st Bt., Chief Justice of Upper Canada ; *m.* 1884, Mary Theodora, *d.* of Henry Seton Strathy of Toronto, Banker ; two *s.* (3rd *s.* Frazer Keith Lefroy, 2nd Lieut. R.F.A., killed on Western Front, 7 April, 1917). *Educ. :* Rugby ; New Coll. Oxford. 2nd Class Honours in Literæ Humaniores, 1873 ; called to English Bar, 1877 ; called to Bar of Upper Canada, 1878 ; has since then practised as barrister and solicitor in Toronto. *Publications :* Legislative Power in Canada, 1897-1898 ; Canada's Federal System, 1913 ; article on The Dominion of Canada, in *Corpus Juris,* 1917 ; Canadian Constitutional Cases ; contributor to Nelson's Encyclopædia of Canada ; and joint translator with J. H. Cameron of A Short History of Roman Law, by P. F. Girard, 1906 ; editor of the Canadian Law Times, and writer of numerous articles in the Law Quarterly Review. *Recreations :* golf and bicycling. *Address :* 163½ Church Street (Athena Building), Toronto. *Clubs :* New University ; Toronto, Toronto.
(*Died 8 Mar. 1919.*)

LEFROY, Rev. Frederick Anthony, M.A. ; Hon. Canon of Gloucester Cathedral ; *b.* 19 Dec. 1846 ; *s.* of Very Rev. Jeffrey Lefroy, Rector of Ahaderg, Dean of Dromore, Ireland, and Helena, *d.* of Rev. F. S. and Lady Helena Trench ; *m.* 1881, Henrietta (*d.* 1920), *d.* of George Gurney, Shincliffe, Eastbourne ; three *s.* two *d. Educ. :* Harrow ; Trinity College, Cambridge. Curate of St. George's, Brandon Hill, Bristol, 1870-76 ; Vicar, 1876-92 ; Examining Chaplain to Bishop of Gloucester and Bristol, 1891 ; Vicar of South Petherton, Somerset, 1892-1902 ; Vicar of Haresfield, Glos., 1902-17 ; Examining Chaplain to the Bishop of Gloucester. *Address :* Glassfall Lodge, Cheltenham. *Club :* Constitutional. (*Died 25 Dec. 1920.*)

LEFROY, Right Rev. George Alfred, D.D. ; Bishop of Calcutta since 1913 ; *b.* Co. Down, Aug. 1854 ; *s.* of Very Rev. Jeffrey Lefroy, Dean of Dromore, *g. s.* of Chief Justice Lefroy (of the Queen's Bench, Ireland). *Educ. :* Marlborough and Trin. Coll. Camb. ; 1st class in Theological Tripos. Ordained 1879 ; joined the Cambridge Mission in Delhi same year ; became head of United S.P.G. and Camb. Mission in Delhi, 1891 ; Bishop of Lahore, 1899-1912. *Address :* The Palace, Calcutta.
(*Died 1 Jan. 1919.*)

LEFROY, Harold Maxwell-, M.A., F.E.S., F.Z.S. ; Professor of Entomology, Imperial College of Science and Technology, S. Kensington, since 1912 ; *b.* 20 Jan. 1877 ; 4th *s.* of C. J. Maxwell-Lefroy and Elizabeth Catherine M'Clintock, Itchel Manor, Crondall, Hants ; *m.* 1904, Kathleen Hamilton, *d.* of William O'Meara of British Guiana ; one *s. Educ. :* Marlborough College ; King's College, Cambridge. First-class Natural Science Tripos, 1898 ; Entomologist to Imperial Department of Agriculture for the West Indies, 1899-1903 ; Imperial Entomologist for India, 1903-12 ; Hon. Curator, Insect House, Zoological Gardens, since 1913 ; Imperial Silk Specialist, India, 1915-16 ; Temp. Lieut.-Col. Mesopotamia E. Force, 1916 ;

attached Royal Commission on Wheat Supplies, 1917-18. *Publications :* Indian Insect Pests, 1906 ; Indian Insect Life, 1910 ; Manual of Entomology, 1923 ; many contributions to West Indian Bulletin, Agricultural Jour. of India ; Memoirs of the Agricultural Department of India, etc. *Address :* Imperial College of Science, S. Kensington, S.W. *T.A. :* Lefroy, Scientist, Southkens, London. *T. :* Kensington 6444.
(*Died 14 Oct. 1925.*)

LEGARD, Albert George ; sometime Divisional Inspector of Schools for Wales ; now retired ; *b.* 31 May 1845 ; *y. s.* of George Legard, Westhorpe House, Scarborough ; *m.* 1875, Mildreda (*d.* 1920) *d.* of Matthew R. Biggs of Islip Grange, Northants. *Educ. :* Durham School ; Balliol College, Oxford. 1st Class Classical Moderations, 1866 ; 1st Class Lit. Hum. 1868 ; one of H.M. Inspectors of Schools 1871 ; Sheffield District, 1871-72 ; Leeds District, 1872-96 ; sometime Member of Welsh University Court, and Member of South Wales University College Council, and Governor of various schools. *Recreations :* riding, walking. *Address :* 5 Kensington, Bath. (*Died 18 Feb. 1922.*)

LEGARD, Sir Algernon Willoughby, 12th Bart., *cr.* 1660 ; *b.* 14 Oct. 1842 ; *s.* of Henry Willoughby Legard, 2nd *s.* of 7th Bart., and Charlotte Henrietta, *d.* of Henry Willoughby ; *m.* 1872, Alicia Egerton, *y. d.* of Rev. G. Brooks, late Rector of Hampden, Bucks. *S.* cousin, 1901. *Educ. :* Marlborough ; Trin. Coll., Camb. *Heir : n.* D. A. H. Legard. *Address :* 18 Victoria Road, Kensington, W.8. *Club :* Boodle's.
(*Died 9 Sept. 1923.*)

LEGARD, Rev. Cecil Henry, M.A., LL.B. ; Rector of Cottesbrooke, 1887 - 1914 ; heir to the Legard Baronetcy ; *b.* 28 Nov. 1843 ; *m.* 1873, Emily (*d.* 1915), *d.* of James Hall ; one *s.* one *d. Educ. :* Magdalene College, Cambridge. Vicar of Boynton, Yorks, 1870-79 ; Aylesby, Great Grimsby, 1879-80 ; Rector of Healing, Lincolnshire, 1880-87 ; Curate of Riby, Lincolnshire, 1884-87. *Heir : s.* Digby [*b.* 7 Dec. 1876 ; *m.* 1904, Georgina, *d.* of W. J. S. Barber-Starkey ; three *s. Address :* Headon Lodge, Brompton, Yorks]. *Address :* Langham Lodge, Cottesbrooke, Northampton. *Clubs :* Arthur's ; Yorkshire, York. (*Died Feb. 1918.*)

LE GEYT, Maj.-Gen. Philip Harrison, Indian Army ; *b.* 22 Dec. 1834. Entered army, 1851 ; Maj.-Gen. 1892 ; retired list, 1892 ; served Persian Expedition, 1856-57 (medal with clasp) ; Indian Mutiny, 1858-59 ; served in Political Dept. as Assistant Political Agent, Kathiawar and Cutch, 1863 ; Mahi Kantha, 1872-80 ; Political Superintendent, Palanpur, 1880 ; returned to Europe, 1889. *Address :* Littledale, 45 Blackwater Road Eastbourne. (*Died 23 May 1922.*)

LEGG, Captain Sir George Edward Wickham, K.B.E., *cr.* 1920 ; M.V.O. 1902 ; Secretary, Soldiers', Sailors', and Airmen's Families Assoc. since 1896 ; *b.* 13 July 1870 ; 3rd *s.* of late Rev. W. Legg, Rector of Hawkinge, Kent ; *m.* 1895, Kathleen (Lady of Grace, Order of St. John of Jerusalem), *d.* of late Col. Sir James Gildea, G.B.E., K.C.V.O., C.B. ; one *s. Educ. :* Radley ; Trinity College, Cambridge ; R.M.C., Sandhurst. Joined South Staffordshire (80th) Regt. 1891 ; and subsequently the 3rd Batt. Royal West Kent Regt. (Militia) ; Capt. in the Reserve of Officers, 1905-1920 ; Knight of Grace, Order of St. John of Jerusalem, 1899 ; Chevalier, Légion d'Honneur, 1919 ; Member of the Council of St. Peter's College, Radley, since 1914. *Publications :* editor of the Radley College Register (2nd edition), 1847-1904 ; (3rd edition), 1847-1912. *Address :* 14 Pembroke Gardens, Kensington, W.8. *T. :* Western 0509. (*Died 1 Sept. 1927.*)

LEGG, John Wickham, Hon. D.Litt. Oxon. ; F.S.A. ; Chairman of the Council of the Henry Bradshaw Society for Editing Rare Liturgical Texts, 1895-1915 ; *b.* 1843 ; widower since

1908. Tutor to late Duke of Albany, 1866-7; Demonstrator of Morbid Anatomy, 1874 ; Lecturer on Pathological Anatomy and Assistant Physician at St. Bartholomew's Hospital, London, 1878-87 ; Bradshaw Lecturer at the Royal College of Physicians of London, 1883 ; Member of the Canterbury House of Laymen, 1909-13. *Publications:* Edited numerous volumes for Henry Bradshaw Society ; Breviarium Romanum Quignonianum for Cambridge University Press, 1888 ; Sarum Missal from three early MSS. for Clarendon Press, Oxford, 1916; English Church Life from 1660 to 1833, 1914 ; Collected Essays, Liturgical and Historical, 1917 ; Church Ornaments and their Civil Antecedents, 1917 ; contributions to Archaeologia, Proceedings of Royal Society, Archaeological Journal, Journal of Theological Studies, Transactions of Bibliographical Society. *Address:* 82 Woodstock Road, Oxford.   *(Died 28 Oct. 1921.)*

LEGGE, Colonel Hon. Sir Harry Charles, G.C.V.O., *cr.* 1920 ; K.C.V.O., *cr.* 1910 ; Equerry-in-Waiting to the Queen, 1893, and to the King, 1901-15; Paymaster of the King's Household, 1915-20 ; Extra Equerry to the King, 1915 ; Secretary and Registrar of the Order of Merit since 1907 ; *b.* Patshull, Staffordshire, 4 Nov. 1852 ; 2nd *s.* of 5th Earl of Dartmouth ; *m.* Amy Gwendoline, *d.* of Gustavus and Lady Fanny Lambart, Beau Parc, Ireland, 1884 ; one *d.* *Educ.* : Eton. Coldstream Guards, 1872-99 ; Adj. 1st Battalion, 1878-85 ; Soudan Campaign, Brevet Major, 1885 ; Groom-in-Waiting to Queen Victoria, 1889. *Recreations:* none. *Address* : Fulmer Gardens, Slough. *T.A.* : Stoke Poges T. : Fulmer 8. *Club* : Carlton.
    (Died 20 Jan. 1924.)

LEGGETT, Major Eric Henry Goodwin, D.S.O. 1915 ; R.A. ; *b.* 31 Dec. 1880. Entered army, 1899 ; Captain, 1907 ; Major, 1914 ; employed with Malay States Guides, 1905-8 ; Staff Captain R.A. 4th Division Eastern Command, 1911-13 ; Brigade-Major, 1913-14 ; served European War, 1914-15 (despatches, D.S.O.).   *(Died 30 July 1916.)*

LE GRAVE, Rev. William, D.S.O. 1902 ; Chaplain to the Forces, R.C. ; retired 1908 ; *b.* 5 Sep. 1843. *Educ.* : St. Edmund's Coll. Ware. Ordained, 1867 ; taught mathematics at above college, 1866-78 ; became Chaplain to the Forces, 1878 ; served in Malta, Bermuda, Ashanti Expedition, 1895-96 ; Senior R.C. Chaplain in South Africa, 1899-1900 (despatches twice, D.S.O.). *Address:* 30 Park Road, Abingdon, Berks.   *(Died 20 April 1923.)*

LEHFELDT, Robert Alfred, B.A. Camb. D.Sc. Lond., F.R.S.S.A.; Professor of Economics, University of the Witwatersrand, Johannesburg, since 1917 ; *b.* Birmingham, 7 May 1868 ; *s.* of late Dr. F. C. Lehfeldt. *Educ.* : St. John's College, Cambridge. Demonstrator of Physics, Firth College (now University of) Sheffield, 1890-96 ; Professor of Physics, East London College, London, 1896-1906; Professor of Physics, S.A. School of Mines and Technology, 1906-17 ; Correspondent for S. Africa of the Royal Economic Society. *Publications:* Text-Book of Physical Chemistry, 1902 ; Electro-chemistry, 1906, in Sir W. Ramsay's series on Physical Chemistry ; Economics in the Light of War, 1916 ; Gold, Prices, and the Witwatersrand, 1919 ; Restoration of the World's Currencies, 1923 ; Money (World's manual series), 1926 ; numerous papers. *Address:* P.O. Box 1176, Johannesburg, South Africa. *T.A.* : University, Johannesburg. *Club* : Royal Societies.
    (Died Sept. 1927.)

LEHMANN, Liza (Mrs. Herbert Bedford), retired on marriage, 1894 ; appointed Vocal Professor at the Guildhall School of Music, 1914 ; *b.* London ; *d.* of Rudolf Lehmann, artist, and *g. d.* of Robert Chambers. Studied singing under her mother and Signor Randegger ; composition under Raunkilde, Rome ; Freudenberg, Wiesbaden ; and Hamish MacCunn, London ; made professional début as soprano at a Monday Popular Concert in 1885, and from then until marriage sang at principal concerts in the kingdom. *Publications:* song-cycle for four solo voices, with pianoforte accompaniment, entitled In a Persian Garden, the words being from the Rubaiyát of Omar Khayyám ; a setting for baritone solo, chorus and orchestra of Scott's Young Lochinvar ; two musical dualogues (words by Austin Dobson), The Secrets of the Heart, and Goodnight, Babette ; Endymion (Longfellow) Scena for soprano and orchestra ; In Memoriam (words selected from Tennyson), a song-cycle for a solo voice with pianoforte accompaniment ; The Daisy-Chain (Twelve Songs of Childhood) ; More Daisies ; Once Upon a Time (a Fairy Cantata); and Sergeant Brue (a musical farce, book by Owen Hall), Romantic Suite, for Violin and Piano ; The Vicar of Wakefield (light romantic opera) ; The Golden Threshold, an Indian songgarland (cantata) ; Nonsense Songs from Alice in Wonderland (song-cycle); Practical Hints for Students of Singing ; also many separate songs. *Recreation:* gardening. *Address:* 40 Warwick Avenue, Paddington, W. *T.* : Paddington 6873.   *(Died 19 Sept. 1918.)*

LE HUNTE, Sir George Ruthven, G.C.M.G., *cr.* 1912 ; K.C.M.G., *cr.* 1903 ; C.M.G. 1898 ; *b.* 20 Aug. 1852 ; *s.* of George Le Hunte of Wexford ; *m.* 1884, Caroline Rachel, *d.* of John Clowes of Burton Court, Herefords. ; one *s.* one *d.* *Educ.* : Eton ; Trinity College, Cambridge. B.A. 1873 ; M.A. 1880 ; Barrister, Inner Temple, 1881 ; Private Secretary to Sir A. Gordon, K.C.M.G. (Lord Stanmore) ; first Governor of Fiji, 1875 ; served in various offices in Fiji, 1875-87 ; Judicial Commissioner for High Commission Western Pacific, 1883 ; President of Dominica, 1887-94; Colonial Secretary, Barbados, 1894-97 ; Colonial Secretary, Mauritius, 1897 ; Lieut.-Governor British New Guinea, 1898-1903 ; Governor South Australia, 1903-1908 ; Governor and Commander-in-Chief of Trinidad and Tobago, 1908-15 ; retired, Jan. 1916. Decorated for Colonial service. *Recreations:* general. *Address:* Sandridge, Crowborough, Sussex.
    (Died 29 Jan. 1925.)

LEIGH, Egerton, J.P., D.L. ; *s.* of late Egerton Leigh, D.L., and Lydia Rachel, *d.* and co-heir of late John Smith Wright of Bulcote Lodge, Notts ; *b.* 13 July 1843 ; *m.* 1st, 1874, Lady Elizabeth Mary (*d.* 1880), *e. d.* of 3rd Earl of Bantry (*ext.*) ; one *d.* ; 2nd, 1889, Violet Cecil Mary, 2nd *d.* of Col. Alfred Tippinge, of Longparish House, Whitchurch, Hants ; one *s.* one *d.* High Sheriff, Co. Chester, 1882 ; was Captain 1st Royal Dragoons. *Address* : 20 Cadogan Place, S.W.1. *T.* : Victoria 7591. *Clubs:* Arthur's, Cavalry. *(Died 18 Oct. 1923.)*

LEIGH, Lt.-Col. Henry Percy Poingdestre, C.I.E. 1892 ; Indian Army ; U.S.I. 1907 ; retired ; late Commissioner, Punjab ; *b.* Jamaica, 28 Dec. 1851; *e. s.* of late Col. Henry Leigh, 98th Regt. and A.P.D., and Ursula, *d.* of late J. Davison ; *m.* 1879, Annie, *d.* of late W. R. Maxwell, 95th Regt. ; one *s.* three *d.* *Educ.:* private school ; R.M.A., Woolwich. Joined Royal Artillery, 1871 ; Indian Staff Corps, 1877 ; served in 2nd and 16th Bengal Cavalry ; entered Punjab Commission, 1879 ; special duty in Kurrum Valley 1886 ; 1st and 2nd Miranzai expeditions as political officer, 1891 (despatches, medal and clasp, C.I.E.) *Club:* Bath and County, Bath.
    (Died 25 Feb. 1928.)

LEIGH, Hon. and Very Rev. James Wentworth, D.D., F.S.A.; Dean of Hereford 1894-1919 ; Provincial Grand Master of Freemasons for Herefordshire ; *b.* Paris, 21 Jan. 1838 ; 3rd *s.* of 1st Lord Leigh ; *m.* Frances (*d.* 1910), *d.* of Pierce Butler, Georgia, U.S.A., and Frances A.

Kemble ; one *d. Educ.*: Harrow ; Trin. College, Cambridge. *Publication :* Other Days, 1921. *Recreations:* formerly cricket and riding, etc. *Address :* Brent House, 63 Pont Street, S.W. *Clubs :* Royal Societies, Wellington.

(Died 5 Jan. 1923.)

LEIGH, Roger, J.P. ; *b.* 27 Apr. 1840 ; adopted *s.* of Sir Robert Holt Leigh, 1st Bart. (*ext.*), of Hindley Hall ; *m.* 1st, 1861, Elizabeth Jane (*d.* 1884), *d.* of late Captain Thomas Eden Blackwell, Argyllshire Highlanders ; three *d.* ; 2nd, 1885, Agatha Elizabeth, *o. d.* of late Alfred Shaw. *Educ.:* Christ Church, Oxford / Trinity Coll., Camb. M.P. Rochester, 1880-85. *Address :* Hindley Hall, Wigan ; 3 Queen's Parade, Bath.

(Died 29 Feb. 1924.)

LEIGH, Hon. Rupert ; *b.* and *heir-pres.* to 3rd Baron Leigh ; *b.* 10 Dec. 1856 ; *m.* 1906, Beatrice Mary, 2nd *d.* of late D. R. Smith ; one *s. Educ.:* Wellington Coll. Late Major, 4th Dragoon Guards ; served Afghanistan, with 15th Hussars, 1878-79 (medal) ; Egypt, 1882 (medal with clasp, bronze star) ; Bechuanaland, 1884-85 ; N.W. Frontier India, 1897 (medal with 2 clasps) ; A.D.C. to two Governors of New South Wales, 1890-94 ; Military Secretary to Governor of Bombay, 1900 ; employed under the War Office since 1915. *Address :* 7 Beaufort Gardens, S.W. *Club :* Naval and Military.

(Died 14 Aug. 1919.)

LEIGHTON, Major Sir Bryan Baldwin Mawddwy, 9th Bt. ; *cr.* 1692 ; J.P. for Shropshire ; Colonel Westmoreland and Cumberland (late Shrops) Imperial Yeomanry since 1914 ; passed through Upavon Flying School and gazetted Flying Officer Royal Flying Corps, 1914 ; *b.* 26 Nov. 1868 ; *e. s.* of 8th Bt. and Hon. Eleanor Leicester Warren, *d.* of 2nd Lord de Tabley ; *S.* 1897 ; *m.* Margaret Frances, *d.* of late John Fletcher, Saltoun Hall, Haddingtonshire, 1890. Joined Americans in Spanish-American war ; served South Africa, 1896-97, also 1900-1 ; served Bechuanaland, 1896-97 (medal and clasp) ; present in Manchuria, Russo-Japanese War ; with the Turkish Army in Thrace, Balkan Campaign ; served European War. Owns about 4100 acres. *Heir : o. surv. s.* Richard Tiel Leighton, Yeomanry and R.F.C. (missing, Aug. 1917). *Address :* 8 Wellington Court, Knightsbridge, S.W. ; Loton Park, Shrewsbury. *T. :* Kensington 3478. *Clubs :* Bachelors', Carlton. *(Died 19 Jan. 1919.)*

LEIGHTON, Edmund Blair, R.I., artist ; *b.* Lond. 21 Sep. 1853; *s.* of Charles Blair Leighton, artist ; *m.* Katherine, *e. d.* of late W. Nash, 1885 ; one *s.* one *d. Educ.:* Univ. Coll. School. Student Royal Academy, and exhibitor there every year from 1887. *Works :* Boyhood of Alfred the Great, 1913. *Photogravures and Engravings :* Lay thy Sweet Hand in mine, etc. ; The Question ; Just by Chance ; Two Strings ; Goodbye ; Next-door Neighbours ; In 1816 ; Sorrow and Song ; Launched in Life ; Waiting for the Coach ; The New Governess ; In Time of Peril ; Elaine ; God Speed ; The Accolade ; Home ; Adieu ; Alain Chartier and Queen Margaret of Scotland, R.A., 1903 ; Ribbons and Laces, etc. ; Vox Populi, 1904 ; A Foundling, 1905 ; Vows, 1906 ; Tristram and Isolde, 1907 ; The Dedication, 1908 ; The Shadow, 1909 ; Pelléas and Mélisande, 1910 ; To the Unknown Land, 1911 ; A Hostage, 1912 ; Boyhood of Alfred the Great, 1913 ; St. Elizabeth of Hungary, 1915 ; Affections, 1916 ; Maternity, 1917 ; Crusaders, Royal Academy 1918 ; Evicted, Suppression of Religious Houses in 1540, Royal Academy 1919 ; Mated, Royal Academy 1920. Has a collection of old musical instruments, of arms, and old furniture, etc. *Address :* 14 Priory Road, Bedford Park, W. *Club :* Arts. *(Died 1 Sept. 1922.)*

LEINSTER, 6th Duke of (*cr.* 1766), **Maurice FitzGerald,** Baron of Offaly, 1205 ; Earl of Kildare, 1316 ; Viscount Leinster (Gt. Brit.),

620

1747 ; Marquess of Kildare, 1761 ; Earl of Offaly, 1761 ; Baron Kildare, 1870 ; Premier Duke, Marquess, and Earl, of Ireland ; *b.* Kilkea Castle, Co. Kildare, 1 Mar. 1887 ; *s.* of Gerald, 5th Duke, and Hermione, *d.* of 1st Earl of Feversham ; *S.* father 1893. *Educ.:* Eton. *Heir :* *b.* Lord Edward FitzGerald. *Address :* Carton, Maynooth, Co. Kildare.

(Died 4 Feb. 1922.)

LEIPER, William, J.P., R.S.A. (1896), F.R.I.B.A. (1881) ; architect, retired ; *b.* Glasgow, 21 May 1839 ; *s.* of Wm. Leiper and Jane Mellis. *Educ.:* High School, Glasgow, and private school. A.R.S.A., 1891. Pupil of Boucher and Cousland, architects ; afterwards with Wm. White, F.S.A., and J. L. Pearson, R.A.; designed Dowanhill, Camphill, and Hyndland churches ; also St. James' Church, Kilmacolm ; Sun Fire Offices, Glasgow ; Messrs. Templetons' factory ; Kinloch-Moidart ; Kelly, Cairndhu, Cornhill, Ballimore, Glendaruel, Auchenbothie, and other mansions ; Dumbarton and Partick Burgh buildings ; also designed the decorations for Imperial Yacht "Livadia," and the decoration of the Banqueting Hall, Municipal Buildings, Glasgow ; silver medal, Paris Exhibition, 1900. *Recreations :* painting, sketching. *Address :* Terpersey, Helensburgh. *(Died 28 May 1916.)*

LEISHMAN, John G. A. ; late American Ambassador to Germany ; *b.* Pittsburgh, Penn., 28 March 1857, of Scotch-Irish descent ; *m.* 1880, Julia Crawford ; one *s.* two *d. Educ.:* Public Schools. Former President of the Carnegie Steel Co., from which office he resigned to accept the nomination tendered by President M'Kinley as American Minister to Switzerland, 1897 ; Ambassador to Turkey, 1901-9 ; Rome, 1909-11. *Clubs :* Union League, New York Yacht, New York ; Metropolitan, Washington ; Duquesne, Pittsburgh, Pittsburgh ; Travellers', Paris ; Cercle d'Orient, Club de Constantinople, Constantinople ; Caccia, Rome ; Union, Berlin.

LEISHMAN, Major-General John Thomas, R.A. ; retired ; *b.* 1835 ; 2nd *s.* of James Leishman, Bromrigg, Dollar, and Dymchurch ; *m.* 1860, Annie (*d.* 1910), *d.* of late Capt. Weir, 6th Dragoons ; one *s.* two *d. Educ.:* Edinburgh University ; Addiscombe College. Commissioned (Bombay Artillery), 1855 ; served with Sir Hugh Rose's force in the Hyderabad District, 1859 ; transferred to Royal Artillery, 1861 ; Captain, 1864 ; Major, 1872 ; Colonel, 1884 ; retired as Major-General, 1885. *Recreations :* interested in church, school, and hospital work. *Address :* Chatsworth, Craneswater Park, Southsea. *Club :* Royal Albert Yacht, Southsea. *(Died 5 Aug. 1920.)*

LEISHMAN, Lt.-Gen. Sir William Boog, Kt., *cr.* 1909 ; K.C.B., *cr.* 1924 ; K.C.M.G., *cr.* 1918 ; C.B. 1915 ; F.R.S. 1910 ; M.B., C.M. ; F.R.C.P. London ; F.R.F.P.S. Glasgow ; M.R.C.P. Edin. ; Hon. LL.D. Glasgow University and McGill University, Montreal ; Director-General Army Medical Service since 1923 ; Hon. Physician to the King, 1912 ; *b.* 6 Nov. 1865 ; *s.* of late Professor W. Leishman ; *m.* 1902, Maud Elizabeth, *e. d.* of late Lieutenant-Colonel E. Gunter ; one *s.* three *d. Educ.:* Westminster ; Glasgow University. Surgeon, A.M.S., 1887 ; Major, R.A.M.C., 1899 ; Bt. Lt.-Col., 1905 ; Lt.-Col., 1911 ; Brevet Col., 1912 ; Colonel, 1915 ; Major-General, 1918 ; Lt.-Gen. 1923 ; served Waziristan Expedition, 1894-95 (medal with clasp) ; European War, 1914-18 (despatches thrice, K.C.M.G., C.B., Commander Legion of Honour, Distinguished Service Medal, U.S.A.) ; Knight of Grace of the Order of St. John of Jerusalem ; Assist. Prof. Pathology, Army Med. School, Netley, 1900-8 ; Professor of Pathology, Royal Army Medical College, 1903-13 ; late Examiner in Pathology, University of Oxford ; and in Tropical Medicine University

of Cambridge ; Harben Lecturer, 1910 ; Linacre Lecturer, Cambridge, 1925 ; President, Society of Tropical Medicine and Hygiene, 1911-12 ; Member of the Yellow Fever Commission, W. Africa, 1913-15 ; the Medical and Sanitary Advisory Committee for Tropical Africa, Colonial Office, 1913 ; the Medical Research Council, 1913-23 ; Chairman, Foot and Mouth Disease Research Committee, Ministry of Agriculture, 1924 ; Member of the Scientific Advisory Committee of British Empire Cancer Campaign, 1924. *Publications:* contributions to medical and scientific literature. *Address:* War Office, S.W. ; Wyberton, Park Hill Road, Croydon. *Clubs:* Athenæum, Junior United Service.
(Died 2 June 1926.)

LEITCH, Hon. James, Judge, Supreme Court of Ontario, Appelate Division, since 1913 ; *b.* South Branch, Stormont Co., Ont., 2 June 1850. Scotch descent; *s.* of William and Nicholas Bryden Leitch ; *m.* 1876, Elizabeth, *d.* of E. Strickland, merchant, Buckingham, Que.; one *s.* four *d. Educ.:* private tutor ; Williamstown and Cornwall Grammar Schools. Called to Ontario Bar 1876 ; K.C. 1889 ; practised profession in Cornwall, Ont. ; Reeve of Cornwall, 1884 ; Mayor, 1885, 1886 ; President of Bar Association, united counties of Stormont, Dundas, and Glengarry, 1904-1905 ; Member of High School Board, 1887-1906 ; Chairman, 1903-1906 ; Life Governor and a Director, Cornwall General Hospital ; Candidate for election to Ontario Legislature for Stormont, 1886 and 1890 ; Candidate for election to House of Commons of Canada for Stormont, 1896 ; Chairman, Ontario Railway and Municipal Board, 1906-1912 ; Judge of the Supreme Court of Ontario, 1912 ; a Conservative ; a Presbyterian. *Address:* Toronto. *Clubs:* Cornwall, Lambton Golf and County.

LEITCH, Rev. Matthew, D.D., D.Lit. ; President and Professor of Biblical Criticism, Assembly's College, Belfast, Presbyterian Church in Ireland. *Address:* College Park, Belfast. *(Died 30 April 1922.)*

LEITH of Fyvie, 1st Baron, *cr.* 1905, **Alexander John Forbes-Leith,** J.P., D.L., Aberdeenshire ; *b.* 6 August 1847 ; *e. s.* of Admiral John Leith and Margaret Forbes of Blackford ; *m.* 1871, Mary L., *d.* of D. A. January of St. Louis, U.S.A. ; one *d.* Entered R.N. 1860 ; Lieut. 1869 ; retired, 1871 ; served New Zealand War, 1864-65 ; received Humane Society's Silver Medal for Saving Life, 1866. *Recreations:* yachting, shooting, motoring. *Heir:* none. *Address:* Fyvie Castle, Aberdeen ; *T.A.:* Alleith, Fyvie ; *T.:* Fyvie 8 ; Hartwell House, near Aylesbury ; *T.:* Stone 2 ; 23 St. James' Place, S.W.1 ; *T.:* Gerrard 6134. *Clubs:* Carlton, Coaching, Naval and Military, Marlborough ; Royal Yacht Squadron, Cowes ; New, Edinburgh.
(Died 14 Nov. 1925.)

LEITH, Major Thomas, J.P., D.L. ; *b.* 1830 ; *m.* 1874, Lady Mary Isabella Dalzell, *sister* of 12th Earl of Carnwath. *Educ.:* Royal Military Academy, Edinburgh. Formerly in Bombay Staff Corps, and A.D.C. to Sir Bartle Frere, Governor of Bombay ; served with the Bombay Fusiliers at the storming of Mooltan, 1848 ; with Sind Horse in Persian Expedition, 1857, and Indian Mutiny. *Address:* Petmathen, Oyne, Aberdeenshire. *Clubs:* Wellington ; Royal Northern, Aberdeen. (*Died 30 Jan. 1920.*)

LEITH-BUCHANAN, Sir Alexander Wellesley George Thomas, 5th Bt., *cr.* 1775 ; *b.* 5 Dec. 1866 ; *S.* father 1903 ; *s.* of 4th Bt. and Eliza, *d.* of T. Tod, Drygrange, Roxburghshire, N.B. ; *m.* 1888, Maude Mary, *d.* of late Alexander Grant ; two *s.* J.P., D.L. Dumbartonshire ; Vice-Chairman Territorial Army Association, County of Dumbarton ; Lt.-Col. commanding 9th Batt. Argyll and Sutherland Highlanders, 1911-17.

Heir: s. George Hector Macdonald, *b.* 30 Jan. 1889. *Address:* Ross Priory, Dumbarton, Scotland. *(Died 29 April 1925.)*

LEMAN, Count Georges, G.C.O.L., G.C.L.H. ; G.C.M.G. ; Lieutenant-General in the Belgian Army ; *b.* Liège, 8 Jan. 1851 ; one *s.* one *d. Educ.:* Athenæum, Brussels ; Military School, Brussels. Officer in the Engineer Service ; Commander-in-Chief of the Military School ; Military Governor of the fortress of Liège, which he defended in 1914. *Publications:* works on mathematics, mechanics, fortification, etc. *Address:* 60 quai St. Léonard, Liège, Belgium. *(Died 17 Oct. 1920.)*

LE MARCHANT, Sir Denis, 3rd Bt., *cr.* 1841 ; *b.* 8 June 1870 ; *s.* of 2nd Bart. and Hon. Sophia Strutt, *e. d.* of 1st Lord Belper ; *S.* father 1915 ; *m.* 1915, Katherine, *d.* of William Mackay, of Bonar Bridge, N.B. *Educ.:* Trinity Hall, Cambridge. *Heir: b.* Brig.-Gen. E. T. Le Marchant. *Clubs:* Travellers', Wellington.
(Died 29 April 1922.)

LE MESSURIER, Col. Augustus, C.I.E. 1886 ; *b.* 23 June 1887 ; *m.* 1871, Kathleen, *d.* of Maj.-Gen. Moxon, B.S.C. Entered army, 1856 ; Col. 1885 ; served Okamundel Field Force, 1859 Abyssinian Campaign, 1866 (despatches, medal); Afghan War, 1879-80 (Brevet of Lieut.-Col., medal); Hazara Expedition, 1891 (medal with clasp). *Address:* 57 Mount Avenue, Ealing. *T.:* Ealing 1164. *Clubs:* United Service, Sports.
(Died 19 Feb. 1916.)

LE MESURIER, Captain Charles Edward, R.N., C.B. 1916 ; Commodore, 2nd class. Served European War, 1914-17, including Jutland Bank (despatches, C.B.).
(Died 10 Nov. 1917.)

LE MESURIER, Colonel Frederick Augustus, R.E., C.B. 1893 ; LL.B. ; *b.* Newbury, 17 Mar. 1839; *y. s.* of F.H. Le Mesurier, Com. R.N., and Jane, *d.* of T. C. Maunsell of Thorpe Malsor; *m.* 1866, Louisa, *d.* of John Dens Browne, M.P. for Co. Mayo; one *s.* two *d. Educ.:* Royal Naval School, New Cross ; R.M.A., Woolwich. Barr. Middle Temple ; LL.B. Univ. of Lond. Entered Royal Engineers, 1857 ; Superintendent Public Works, Trinidad, 1861-68 ; Inspector of Army Signalling, 1875-80 ; Commandant of Pretoria, 1880-81 ; organised and trained a battalion of rifles to take part in defence of town against Boers (despatches, Bt.-Lt.-Col.); C.R.E. base at Suakin, 1885 (despatches, medal with clasp and bronze star); Chief Engineer Ireland, 1889-94. *Decorated* for services in S. Africa and Suakin. *Address:* 31 St. Margaret's Road, Oxford.
(Died 9 June 1926.)

LEMMON, Colonel Sir Thomas Warne, K.C.B., *cr.* 1922 ; C.B., *cr.* 1897 ; Colonel 3rd Batt. (Mil.) East Surrey Regt.; *b.* 1838 ; *s.* of Mr. Lemmon of Gatcombe House, Hants ; *m.* 1st, 1864, Emma Louisa (*d.* 1885), *d.* of late Thomas Warne; 2nd, 1886, Ellerie, *d.* of late James Bayliss ; one *s.* Appointed Ensign North Middlesex Regt., 1860 ; Brig.-Gen. 1900 ; transferred to 1st R. Surrey Militia, 1866 ; commanded 3rd East Surrey Regt. as Lt.-Col. 1887-98, when appointed Hon. Colonel of Battalion, received Jubilee commemoration medal. *Recreations:* shooting, riding. *Address:* Burleigh, Brimscombe, Gloucestershire. *Club:* Junior United Service.
(Died 8 Jan. 1928.)

LE MOINE, J. de St. Denis, I.S.O. ; Sergeant-at-Arms of the Senate of Canada; *b.* 13 July 1850 ; *s.* of Robert Auguste Le Moine of Chateau Richer, Quebec, and Emma Juchereau du Chesnay ; *m.* Margaret Louisa Mackey ; two *d. Educ.:* Quebec Seminary ; St. Mary's College, Montreal. Served on gunboat La Canadienne, also in Ottawa troop of Cavalry ; was Captain and Quartermaster in 5th Princess Louise Dragoon Guards. *Address:* 505 Wilbrod Street, Ottawa. *M.:* 151,229. *T.:* 1239. *Clubs:*

LEMASS, Peter Edmund.   See page xxiv.

Golf, Country, Hunt, Connaught Park, Jockey, Ottawa. *(Died 1922.)*

LEMON, Sir James, Kt., *cr.* 1909; J.P., M.I.C.E., F.R.I.B.A., F.S.I.; Past-President of the Institution of Municipal and County Engineers, and Hon. Treasurer; F.G.S., F. San. Inst.; retired Civil Engineer; *b.* in Lambeth, 15 Jan. 1833; *s.* of James Lemon and Sophia Glannon; *m.* 1859; no *c.* *Educ.:* Private School, Westminster. Seven years assistant to the late Sir Joseph Bazalguette, Metropolitan Board of Works; Borough Engineer, Southampton, 1866-78; Consulting Engineer, 1878-81; went into private practice, Southampton and Westminster, 1878; served the offices of Councillor, Alderman, and Mayor, Southampton; Mayor, two years; Member of County Council of Hants, six years. *Publications:* Professional Reports; Reminiscences of Public Life in Southampton, two vols. *Recreation:* bowls. *Address:* 11 The Avenue, Southampton. *Clubs:* National Liberal; South Hants, Gladstone, Southampton.
(Died 10 May 1923.)

LENG, Christopher David, J.P.; Director Sir W. C. Leng & Co.; *b.* 1861; *e. s.* of late Sir Wm. C. Leng of Oaklands, Sheffield; *m.*; one *s.* one *d.* *Educ.:* Collegiate School; Lausanne. *Recreations:* hunting, motoring, golf. *Address:* Sandygate, Sheffield. *T.:* 656. *M.:* W 6, W 7, W 1894. *Club:* Junior Constitutional.
(Died 1 Jan. 1921.)

LENNARD, Lt.-Col. Sir Henry Arthur Hallam Farnaby, 2nd Bt., *cr.* 1880; J.P., D.L.; *b.* 7 Nov. 1859; *s.* of 1st Bt. and Julia, *d.* of late H. Hallam, F.R.S.; *S.* father, 1899; *m.* 1894, Beatrice, *d.* of A. Cator of Woodbastwick Hall, Norfolk; one *s.* three *d.* *Educ.:* Eton; Christ Church, Oxon. Owns about 1200 acres. *Heir:* s. Stephen Arthur Hallam Farnaby, *b.* 31 July 1899. *Address:* Wickham Court, West Wickham, Kent. *Clubs:* Arthur's, Travellers'. *(Died 26 Feb. 1928.)*

LENNARD, Sir Thomas Barrett-, 2nd Bt., *cr.* 1801; *b.* 29 Dec. 1826; *S.* grandfather 1857; *m.* 1853, Emma *(d.* 1916), *d.* of late Rev. Sir J. P. Wood, 2nd Bt.; two *s.* four *d.* *Educ.:* St. Peter's Coll. Camb. (M.A.) Owns about 6000 acres. *Heir:* s. Thomas, J.P., D.L. [*b.* 25 Oct. 1853; *m.* 1884, Mary, *d.* of late Canon Price. *Educ.:* Harrow. Barrister, Middle Temple. *Address:* Horsford Manor, Norwich. *Clubs:* Brooks's, Travellers']. *Address:* Belhus, Aveley, Essex; 7 Lewes Crescent, Brighton. *Clubs:* United University, Farmers'. *(Died 17 Jan. 1919.)*

LENNARD, Sir Thomas Barrett-, 3rd Bt., *cr.* 1801; J.P., D.L.; *b.* 25 Oct. 1853; *s.* of 2nd Bt. and Emma *(d.* 1916), *d.* of late Rev. Sir J. P. Wood, 2nd Bt.; *S.* father 1919; *m.* 1884, Mary, *d.* of late Canon Price. *Educ.:* Harrow. Barrister, Middle Temple; a Chairman of Quarter Sessions, Norfolk. Owns about 4000 acres. *Heir:* b. Richard Fiennes, *b.* 17 May 1861. *Address:* Horsford Manor, Norwich. *Club:* Brooks's.*(Died 19 Sept. 1923.)*

LEON, Sir Herbert Samuel, 1st Bart., *cr.* 1911; J.P.; *b.* 11 Feb. 1850; 2nd *s.* of late George Leon; *m.* 1st, 1873, Esther *(d.* 1875), 2nd *d.* of late Edward Henry Beddington; 2nd, 1880, Fanny, 3rd *d.* of David Hyam, M.P. (N.) Div. of Bucks, 1891-95; two *s.* two *d.* *Educ.:* privately. Alderman of Bucks County Council; Chairman of Finance Committee. *Heir:* s. George Edward Leon [*b.* 7 May 1875; *m.* 1899, Mildred Ethel, *d.* of late L. J. Jennings, M.P.; one *s.* one *d.* *Address:* 48 Brompton Square, S.W.]. *Address:* Bletchley Park, Bletchley, Bucks; 7 Cleveland Row, St. James's, S.W.1. *T.:* Bletchley 31, Regent 749. *Clubs:* Devonshire, Reform, Portland. *(Died 23 July 1926.)*

LEONCAVALLO, Ruggiero, composer; *b.* Naples, 8 Mar. 1858. *Educ.:* Naples Conservatoire. *Works:* I Pagliacci, 1892; Medici,

622

1898; Chatterton, 1896; La Bohème, 1897; Zazà, 1900; Roland von Berlin, 1904; Maià, 1910; Malbruk, 1911. *(Died 9 Aug. 1919.)*

LE-POER-TRENCH, Col. Hon. William, C.V.O. 1912; late R.E.; *b.* 17 June 1837; *s.* of 3rd Earl of Clancarty and Lady Sarah Juliana Butler, *d.* of 3rd Earl of Carrick; *m.* Harriet *(d.* 1909), *o. c.* of Sir W. Martins, 1864; one *s.* Entered R.E. 1854; Capt., 1861; Major, 1872; Col., 1879; served in China 1857-58 (despatches, medal with clasp); in charge of operations to connect the triangulation of England with Germany through France and Belgium in 1860-61; M.P. (C.) Co. Galway 1872-74; contested Whitechapel in 1886 and 1893; Chairman of Poor Law and Lunacy Inquiry Commission, Ireland, 1877-79; J.P. for London, Westminster, Middlesex, and Bucks. *Address:* St. Huberts, Gerrard's Cross, Bucks. *Clubs:* Carlton, Constitutional, United Service. *(Died 16 Sept. 1920.)*

LE QUEUX, William Tufnell, novelist; traveller; Commander of Orders of St. Sava of Serbia, Danilo of Montenegro, Crown of Italy, San Marino Order; Ex-Consul of Republic of San Marino; *b.* London, 2 July 1864; *e. s.* of William Le Queux, Châteauroux, Indre. *Educ.:* privately in London; Pegli, near Genoa. Studied art in Paris; forsook the Quartier Latin; made a tour through France and Germany on foot; became journalist and special correspondent; foreign editor of Globe, 1891; resigned to devote time to novel writing, 1893; travelled in Algeria, Morocco, Kabylia, the Areg region of the Sahara, etc.; journeyed through Macedonia, Turkey, Montenegro, Serbia, Albania, 1907; Arctic, 1908; Sudan, 1909; correspondent of Daily Mail during Balkan war; collector of mediæval manuscripts, codices, and monastic seals, of which he possesses a large and valuable collection; has intimate knowledge of secret service of Continental Powers; consulted by the Government on such matters. Forecasted the war in his book The Invasion, 1908. *Publications:* Guilty Bonds, 1890; Secrets of Monte Carlo, 1899; An Observer in the Near East, 1907; German Spies in England, 1915; Rasputin, the Rascal Monk; The Secret Life of the Ex-Tsaritza, The Intriguers, 1920; Landru, 1921; Things I Know, 1923; Where the Desert Ends, 1923; The Crystal Claw, 1924; The Broadcast Mystery, 1924; Hidden Hands, 1925; The Blue Bungalow, 1925; The Fatal Face, 1926; The Chameleon, 1927; Blackmailed, 1927; and many other books; lectures on Spies and Spying. *Recreations:* revolver practice; ski-ing in Switzerland; the study of Egyptology and criminology; experiments in wireless telephony; Member of the Institute of Radio Engineers; President of Wireless Experimental Association; was first wireless experimenter to broadcast. *Address:* c/o Camelot Press, 34 Strand, W.C. *Clubs:* Devonshire; Swiss Alpine. *(Died 13 Oct. 1927.)*

LE SAGE, Sir John Merry, Kt. *cr.* 1918; Lieutenant of the City of London; late managing editor, Daily Telegraph; retired June 1923; *b.* Clifton, 28 April 1837; *s.* of John Le Sage, Clifton; *m.* Elizabeth Lord Martin. *Educ.:* Clifton; Bath; London. After a brief provincial career was engaged on the staff of the Daily Telegraph, and served for many years under the direction of the late J. M. Levy and Lord Burnham; acted as special correspondent in France, Germany, Italy, Russia, Egypt, America, Canada; with the German army in the campaign of 1870-71; and with Lord Wolseley's Force in Egypt in 1882; was in Paris during the whole period of the Commune; managing editor for many years. *Recreation:* cricket. *Address:* 25 Ranelagh Avenue, Hurlingham, S.W.6. *T.:* Putney 1089.
(Died 1 Jan. 1926.)

LESCHER, Joseph Francis, Baron of the old Kingdom of France by grant, Louis XIII., of Kertsfeld, Alsace; Hereditary Count of the Holy Roman Empire by Brief of Pope Pius X.; J.P. counties of Essex, Middlesex, and London; D.L. Essex; b. 6 Aug. 1842; m. Mira Charlotte, d. of Capt. Hankey, 9th Lancers, and Charlotte, d. of the Marquis d'Etampes; two d. Educ.: Stonyhurst College. High Sheriff of Essex, 1885-86. Recreations: travel, hunting, and shooting. Address: Boyles Court, near Brentwood, Essex. Clubs: Reform, St. George's.
(Died 8 Jan. 1923.)

LESLIE, Lt.-Col. Archibald Stewart, C.M.G. 1918; T.D.; Yeomanry; J.P., D.L.; b. 1873; m. 1910, Margaret Isobel, d. of Col. E. W. Horne; four s. Educ.: Oxford University. Late Secretary, Grouse Disease Inquiry; served European War, 1914-18 (despatches, C.M.G.). Address: Kininvie, Banffshire; 1 Eton Terrace, Edinburgh. T.: 6793. Club: New, Edinburgh. (Died 1 May 1928.)

LESLIE, Sir Bradford, K.C.I.E., cr. 1887; Civil Engineer; Chairman of the Southern Punjab Railway Co. Ltd.; original designer and builder of large bridges in Bengal, including the highway bridge over the river Hooghly at Calcutta; b. 1831; s. of late Charles R. Leslie, R.A.; m. 1855, Mary Jane Eliza (d. 1886), d. of late W. Honey, M.Inst. C.E.; one s. one d. Fellow of University of Calcutta; Officier de l'instruction publique, France. Address: 171 Maida Vale, W.9. T.: Maida Vale 2661.
(Died 21 Mar. 1926.)

LESLIE, George Dunlop, R.A. 1876; b. London, 2 July 1835; y. s. of C. R. Leslie, R.A.; married; four s. two d. Educ.: Mercers' School. Student at Royal Academy, 1856; A.R.A. 1868; figure and landscape painter. Publications: Our River, 1881; Letters to Marco, 1894; Riverside Letters, 1896; The Inner Life of the Royal Academy, 1914. Pictures: Midsummer Morn, 1904; The Deserted Mill, 1905. Recreations: gardening, boating. Address: Compton House, Lindfield, Sussex. Club: Athenæum.
(Died 21 Feb. 1921.)

LESLIE, Sir John, 1st Bt., cr. 1876; D.L.; late Lieut. 1st Life Guards; b. 16 Dec. 1822; e. s. of late Charles P. Leslie, Glasslough, Co. Monaghan, M.P., and his 2nd wife, Christiana, d. of George Fosberry, Clorane, Co. Limerick; m. Lady Constance Damer, sister of 5th Earl of Portarlington, 1856; one s. four d. Educ.: Harrow; Christ Church, Oxford (B.A.). M.P. Co. Monaghan, 1871-80. Owns about 44,500 acres. Heir: s. Col. John Leslie [b. 1857; m. 1884. Leonie Blanche, d. of Leonard Jerome of New York; three s. Address: 46 Great Cumberland Place, W. Club: Turf]. Address: Glaslough, Co. Monaghan; 22 Manchester Square, W. Clubs: Carlton, Athenæum, Travellers'.
(Died 23 Jan. 1916.)

LESLIE, Robert Murray, M.A., B.Sc., M.D. (Edinburgh), M.R.C.P. (London); Officier d'Académie Francaise; Senior Physician, Prince of Wales General Hospital; Physician, Royal Hospital for Diseases of the Chest, London; Civil Physician, Bermondsey Military Hospital; Physician, Canning Town Hospital for Women and Children; Lecturer on Medicine, N.E. London Post-Graduate College; Deputy Chairman and Examiner, Incorporated Institute of Hygiene; Chairman of Council, Women's Imperial Health Association of Great Britain; b. 23 June 1866; s. of Alexander Leslie, J.P. Rossshire, and Isabella Murray, Old Meldrum, Aberdeenshire; m. 1920, Gwladys Olive, y. d. of Capt. Knox Keith, R.N. Educ.: George Watson's College, Edinburgh; Universities of Edinburgh and London. Sir Edward Baxter Scholar, Natural Science, 1889; Ettles Scholar, 1892; University Medallist in Medicine and Obstetric Medicine and Stark Scholar in Clinical Medicine, 1892; Fellow of Royal Society of Medicine; Member of Eugenics and other Scientific Societies; Late Assistant to Professor of Pathology and Professor of Clinical Medicine, University of Edinburgh; Senior Resident Physician, Edinburgh Royal Infirmary; and House Physician, Brompton Hospital for Consumption; Assistant to Examiners in Medicine, London University; Senior Medical Registrar and Lecturer on Practical Medicine, King's College Hospital; President; N.E. London Clinical Society. Publications: The Health of a Woman, 1917; Hæmorrhage from the Lungs, in Encyclopædia Medica, 1917; Disordered Action of the Heart, in Clinical Journal, 1919; Vaccine Treatment of Influenza and Pneumonia, in Medical Press, 1919. Recreations: travel, mountaineering, golf. Address: 143 Harley Street, W.1. T.: Mayfair 897. Clubs: Royal Automobile, Albemarle, Roehampton.
(Died 29 Mar. 1921.)

LESLIE-ELLIS, Lieut.-Col. Henry, F.S.A., F.R.G.S., J.P. and D.L. Co. Wicklow; High Sheriff, 1902; e. s. of late Robert Francis Ellis of Magherymore Co. Wicklow; m. 1894, Margaret, d. of Rev. S. Rolleston, Rector of St. Minver, Cornwall; three s. one d. Educ: Harrow; Sandhurst. Late Major Inniskilling Dragoons, and Lieut.-Col. Royal Bucks Hussars, joined Inniskilling Dragoons, 1872; served Boer War. 1881-82; was Staff Officer to Colonel Curtis's column to Potchefstroom, 1882; later, Adjutant and second in command, Royal Bucks Hussars. Recreations: hunting; travel; collector of Greek, Roman, and English gold coins. Address: Magherymore, Wicklow; Clubs: Army and Navy, Wellington; Kildare Street, Dublin.
(Died 1919.)

LE SOUËF, W. H. Dudley; Director Zoological Gardens since 1901, and Manager Royal Park, Melbourne; b. Victoria, Australia; English parentage; s. of A. A. C. Le Souëf; m. 1888, Edith E. Wadeson, England; three s. three d. Educ.: Melbourne; Crediton Grammar School, Devon. Has travelled extensively in various parts of the world in the interests of his Society; took part in the Zoological Congress at Boston, U.S.A., and in the Ornithological Congress in Cambridge, England; C.M.Z.S.; M.B.O.U.; C.M.S.N.G. Frankfort; Corres. Fell. Amer. O.U.; M.B.O.C.; Past-President and Hon. Member Royal Australian Ornithological Union; C.M. Washington Park Zool. Society; Life Vice-President and Member Melbourne Camera Club. Publications: Wild Life in Australia; Animals of Australia (jointly); Birds of Australia (jointly); Description of Birds' Eggs from North Australia (Ibis, 1896-98); Visit to Albatross Island (Ibis, 1895); Mound-building Birds of Australia (Ibis, 1899); Visit to Queensland (Vict. Nat. 1891); many papers on Ornithology and on Geographical subjects; has taken many photos, mostly of Natural History subjects, which have been used in many publications; Ascent of Mount Peter Botte. Address: Zoological Gardens, Parkville, Melbourne. (Died 6 Sept. 1924.)

LESSARD, Major-General Francois Louis, C.B. 1900; b. 9 Dec. 1860; m. 1882, Florence, d. of Thomas Conrad Lee, Quebec; three d. Educ.: College St. Thomas, P.Q.; Commercial Academy, Quebec. 2nd Lieut. Quebec Garrison Artillery, 1880; transferred to 65th Batt. Infantry, Montreal, 1884; Rebellion, Canadian North-West, 1885 (medal); appointed to Cavalry School Corps, 1884; Captain Royal Canadian Dragoons, 1888; Major, 1894; Lieut.-Col. 1898; Brevet Colonel, 1901; Adjutant-Gen. Canadian Militia, 1907-12; G.O.C. 2nd Division, 1912-15; Substantive Colonel, 1907; Brigadier-General, 1911; Major-General, 1912; Inspector-General Eastern Canada, 1915; G.O.C. M.D. No. 6 and O.C. Halifax Fortress Command, 1917-18; A.D.C. to Governor-General of Canada, 1901-11. Served S. African War. 1899-

1901 (despatches, medal 5 clasps). *Address:* Meadowvale, Ontario. *Clubs:* Junior Army and Navy; Hunt, Toronto. *(Died Aug. 1927.)*

LESTER, Rev. Henry Arthur; Director, Bishop of London's Sunday School Council; *s.* of Edward Lester of Bedford; *m.* Alice, *d.* of John Perrin of Thurnham, Kent; three *s.* one *d. Educ.:* Bedford Modern School; Oxford University. B.A. 1896, Honours Mod. History; M.A. 1899; ordained, 1896; Assistant Chaplain and Tutor, St. John's Training College, Battersea, 1896-98; Vice-Principal Warrington Training College, 1898-1911; University Extension Lecturer of Manchester and Liverpool Universities. *Publication:* Sunday School Teaching. *Recreation:* golf. *Address:* 108 Muswell Hill Road, N.10. *(Died 24 July 1922.)*

LE STRANGE, Hamon, F.S.A.; *b.* 25 Nov. 1840; *e. s.* of Henry L, Styleman le Strange, of Hunstanton Hall, Norfolk, and Jamesina, *d.* of John Stewart, M.P., of Belladrum, Inverness-shire; *m.* Emmeline, *d.* of William Austin, of Boston, Massachusetts; three *s.* three *d. Educ.:* Eton; Christ Church, Oxford. 1st class in Law and Modern History; 3rd Secretary in H.M. Diplomatic Service at Mexico, Paris, and Washington, 1865-71; Chairman of Quarter Sessions for Norfolk; County Alderman; Provincial Grand Master of Freemasons; Chairman of Eastern Sea Fisheries Joint Committee. *Heir: s.* Roland, J.P., D.L. [*b.* 5 March 1869; *m.* 1891, Hon. Agneta Frances Delaval, *o. d.* of 18th Baron Hastings; two *s.*]. *Publications:* Norfolk Official Lists; History of Freemasonry in Norfolk; Le Strange Records, 1100-1310. *Address:* Hunstanton Hall, Norfolk. *Club:* Athenæum. *(Died 25 Mar. 1918.)*

LE STRANGE, Roland, J.P., D.L.; *b.* 5 March 1869; *e. s.* of late Hamon Le Strange and Emmeline, *d.* of William Austin, of Boston, Massachusetts; *m.* 1891, Hon. Agneta Frances Delaval, *o. d.* of 18th Baron Hastings; two *s.* Late Lieut. P.W.O. Norfolk Artillery. *Address:* Hunstanton Hall, Norfolk.
(Died 20 Feb. 1919.)

LESUEUR, Daniel, Officier de la Légion d'honneur; femme de lettres, ex-vice-présidente de la Société des Gens de Lettres; Présidente du Denier des Veuves des Gens de Lettres; *b.* a Paris; *m.* Henry Lapauze, Conservateur du Palais des Beaux-Arts de la Ville de Paris, Officier de la Légion d'honneur. *Educ.:* en France et en Angleterre. *Publications:* Poésies; Trad. de Lord Byron; Romans: Marcelle; Un Mystérieux Amour; Amour d'aujourd'hui; Névrosée; Une Vie tragique; Passion slave; Justice de femme; Haine d'amour; A force d'aimer; Invincible Charme; Lèvres closes; Comédienne; Au delà de l'amour; L'Honneur d'une femme; Fiancée d'outre-mer; Le Cœur chemine; La Force du passé; L'Or sanglant; Fleur de joie; Lys royal; Le Meurtre d'une âme; Le Marquis de Valcor; Madame de Ferneuse; Le Fils de l'Amant; Madame l'Ambassadrice; Nietzschéenne; Le Droit à la Force; Flaviana Princesse; Chacune son Rêve; Une Ame de Vingt ans; Au Tournant des Jours; Sociologie: L'Évolution féminine. *Recreations.:* sports, équitation. *Address:* Petit Palais, Champs Elysées, Paris; *T.:* Elysées, 17.88; La Valeorie, Parmain (Seine-et-Oise); *T.:* 15.
(Died 3 Jan. 1921.)

LETCHWORTH, Rev. Arnold, M.A., Hon. Canon of Southwark Cathedral; *b.* 6th July 1840; *s.* of Henry Finch and Maria Elizabeth Letchworth; *m.* 1886, Mary Frances Oldman. *Educ.:* Kensington Proprietary Grammar School; Exeter College, Oxford; Deacon, 1864; Priest, 1865; Curate, Christ Church, Folkestone, 1864-6; Saltburn-by-Sea, 1867-9; Vicar, St. John's, Kingston-on-Thames, 1870-1915. *Address:* 12 St. Augustin's Road, Bournemouth. *(Died 18 Jan. 1923.)*

624

LETCHWORTH, Sir Edward, Kt.; *cr.* 1902; F.S.A.; late Grand Secretary of Freemasons; *b.* 18 Mar. 1833; *e. s.* of late Henry Finch Letchworth, Oak Hill, Surbiton; *m.* 1902, Mary Constance, widow of Thomas Blaikie of Aberdeen. Formerly a solicitor, and for many years one of the Chief Stewards of Her Majesty's Manors; was a promoter of the Volunteer movement in 1859, and from 1860 to 1867 served as Captain in both the 33rd and 49th Middlesex Volunteer Corps; is a Governor of the Foundling and St. Bartholomew's Hospitals. *Address:* 14 Cornwall Gardens, S.W.; *T.:* 2093 Kensington; Freemasons' Hall, W.C.; Lynn Court, 30 Broadwater Down, Tunbridge Wells, Kent. *Clubs:* Junior Carlton, Garrick. *(Died 8 Oct. 1917.)*

LETCHWORTH, Rev. Henry Howard, M.A.; Hon. Canon of Canterbury, 1911; *b.* 24 Aug. 1836; 2nd *s.* of late Henry Finch Letchworth of Oak Hill, Surbiton; *m.* 1885, Mary Georgina, *d.* of late Lieut. J. Strettell, R.N., and widow of Frederick Fortreath Smart; three *s. Educ.:* Kensington Grammar School; Oriel College, Oxford. Deacon, 1859; Priest, 1860; held various curacies; Vicar, Holy Trinity, Southampton, 1885; Rector, Exton, Hants, 1886; Vicar, S. Peter's, Maidstone, 1889; Vicar, Detling, 1898-1911; Rural Dean of Sutton, 1904-11. *Address:* 62 Old Dover Road, Canterbury. *(Died 18 Oct. 1921.)*

LETHBRIDGE, Alan Bourchier; author and writer on Russian affairs; *b.* Sandhill Park, Taunton, Jan. 1878; *s.* of Sir Wroth Lethbridge, 4th Bart.; *m.* 1912, Marjorie Colt, o. *d.* of General Byrne, United States Army (ret.). *Educ.:* Eastman's Naval Academy; Sherborne; Heidelberg. Intended for the Navy, failed medically; a year tea-planting in Ceylon and then travelled extensively—S. America, the Near East, Russia and Europe generally; political officer in Northern Nigeria, 1903-7; visited Siberia and later Canada and the United States; after marriage lived chiefly in Russia; during European War was attached to the Foreign Office, having previously served as interpreter; subsequently transferred to the Ministry of Information; Fellow of United States Geographical Soc.; Special Correspondent, Daily Telegraph, in West Africa, 1919; Fellow Royal Historical Society. *Publications:* The New Russia; The Soul of the Russian; Germany as it is To-day; West Africa—the Elusive, etc. *Recreations:* travel, books, and carnations. *Address:* 2316 Nineteenth Street, Washington, D.C. *Clubs:* Wellington; Royal Dorset Yacht. *(Died 25 Feb. 1923.)*

LETHBRIDGE, Lieut.-Colonel Sir Alfred Swaine, K.C.S.I., *cr.* 1896; J.P. Hants; *b.* Tirhoot, Bengal, 30 Sept. 1844; *s.* of W. F. Lethbridge, Woolborough, Devonshire, and Susan, *d.* of Robert Swaine, Musbury, Devonshire; *m.* 1899, Edith Seymour, widow of George Bellett, and *d.* of H. F. Waring of Lyme Regis, Dorset. *Educ.:* King's Coll. London; Aberdeen (M.D.). Entered Bengal Medical Service, 1867; Lieut.-Col. 1887; served in Burmah and Bengal; Additional Member of Council of Viceroy of India, 1895-97; retired April 1898. *Address:* Windhover, Bursledon, Hants. *(Died 11 Mar. 1917.)*

LETHBRIDGE, Sir Roper, Kt., *cr.* 1885; K.C.I.E., *cr.* 1890; D.L., J.P., Devon, and J.P. Kent; Lord of the Manor of Exbourne; patron of one living; President of Anti-Tea-Duty League; President of the Devonshire Association for 1901; member of the Exeter Diocesan Board of Education, and of the Standing Committee of the Exeter Diocesan Conference; Chairman of Council of the Devon and Cornwall Record Society; Vice-President of the Okehampton Agricultural Society; Commissioner for Income Tax appeals, Okehampton; Vice-President of Tariff Reform League, and Chairman of Devonshire Branch of League; *b.* Devonshire, 23 Dec. 1840; *e. s.* of late E. Lethbridge; *m.* 1st, Eliza, *d.* of W. Finlay, and *g.-g.-d.* of Henry, 11th Baron Teynham, 1865 (*d.* 1895); one *s.* one *d.*; 2nd Emma, *d.* of John Neave and widow of late Frederick Burbidge, Micklefield, Herts, 1897. *Educ.*: Plymouth and Mannamead Coll.; Exeter Coll. Oxford (Scholar), M.A.; graduated in double Classical and Mathematical Honours, Barr. Inner Temple, 1880; Bengal Education Service, 1868-76; Secretary Simla Education Commission, 1877; created C.I.E. 1878; Indian Political Agent, 1878; candidate for Whitby, 1884; a founder and one of the original Committee of the Imperial Federation League, 1884; M.P. North Kensington, 1885, 1886; retired 1892. *Publications*: The Golden Book of India; History of India; History and Geography of Bengal; Selections from Modern English Literature; High Education in India; India and Imperial Preference; Life of Ramtanu Lahiri, the Bengali Reformer; The Indian Offer of Imperial Preference; many other educational and political books and pamphlets; editor Calcutta (Quarterly) Review, 1871-78. *Address*: Exbourne Manor, Exbourne, Devon. *T.A.*: Lethbridge, Exbourne. *Club*: Carlton. (*Died 15 Feb. 1919*.)

LETT, Rev. Henry William, M.A., M.R.I.A.; Rector of Aghaderg, Co. Down, since 1886; Chancellor of Dromore Cathedral; Rural Dean and Member of the Diocesan Council and General Synod of the Church of Ireland; *b.* 1838; *s.* of Rev. Canon Charles Lett of Tincurry, County Wexford, Rector of Finvoy, and Elizabeth Mary, *d.* of Lieut.-Col. Marcus Corry, D.L., of Ballyhomra; *m.* 1865, Louisa Kathleen, *d.* of John Tandy, of Dublin; one *s.* three *d. Educ.*: Trinity College, Dublin. Curate of Derryaghy, Co. Antrim, 1861; Incumbent of Meigh and Curate of Camlough, Co. Armagh, 1863; Rector of Montiaghs, Co. Armagh, 1875. *Publication*: Descriptive Notes of all the Hepatics found in the British Islands, 1902; Census Report on the Mosses of Ireland, 1915. *Address*: Aghaderg Glebe, Loughbrickland, Banbridge, Co. Down.
(*Died 26 Dec. 1920*.)

LETTS, Edmund Albert, D.Sc. (Hon.), F.R.S.E., F.C.S., F.I.C. and C. Emeritus Professor of Chemistry in the Queen's University, Belfast; Fellow of the Royal Sanitary Institute; *b.* Sydenham, Kent, 27 August 1852; 3rd *s.* of Thomas Letts of Clare Lodge, Sydenham, and South View, Isle of Wight, and of Emma Horwood, 3rd *d.* of Frederick Barry of Boxhill, Surrey. *Educ.*: Bishop Stortford School; King's College, London; Universities of Vienna and Berlin. Chief Assistant Chemical Laboratory, University of Edinburgh, 1872; First Professor of Chemistry in University College, Bristol, 1876; Keith Prizeman, R.S. Edinburgh, 1890. *Publications*: (with Dr. Adeney) Appendix VI. to 5th Report of the Royal Commission on Sewage Disposal, and (with Eric H. Richards) Appendix III. to 7th Report of ditto; on The Pollution of Estuaries and Tidal Waters; Some Fundamental Problems in Chemistry—Old and New; various papers on scientific subjects. *Address*: Queen's University, Belfast; 6 Dunelin, Malone Road, Belfast. (*Died 19 Feb. 1918*.)

LEUCHARS, Col. Hon. Sir George, K.C.M.G., *cr.* 1915; C.M.G. 1903; D.S.O. 1907; *b.* 16 April 1868; *m.* 1891, Marion, *d.* of late W. Mackenzie, M.A. Served S. Africa, Umvoti Mounted Rifles, 1899-1902 (despatches, Queen's medal 4 clasps, C.M.G.); Native Rebellion, Natal, 1906; Bt. Col. O.C. Troops, Natal (medal and clasp, D.S.O.); represented Umvoti Co. Natal Parliament, 1898-1906; Minister of Native Affairs and Public Works, 1903-5; returned to Union Parliament, Umvoti Division, 1910; J.P.; Minister of Commerce and Industries,

Union of S. Africa, 1911; Minister Public Works and Acting Minister Posts and Telegraphs, 1912; resigned, 1912; O.C. Troops, Natal, 1914-15. *Address*: Bracken, Greytown, Natal.
(*Died Feb. 1924*.)

LEUDESDORF, Charles, M.A., Fellow of Pembroke College, Oxford, since 1873; Registrar of the University of Oxford since 1906; *b.* Manchester, 30 Jan. 1853; *s.* of Henry Leudesdorf, Manchester; unmarried. *Educ.*: private school; The Owens College, Manchester; Worcester College, Oxford; Exhibitioner 1869, Scholar, 1870-73; Mathematical Lecturer, Pembroke College, 1873-1906; Proctor, 1887; Secretary to Boards of Faculties, 1889-1906. *Publications*: A translation of Cremona's Elements of Projective Geometry, 1885; various papers on mathematical subjects in the Proceedings of the London Mathematical Society. *Address*: 8 Bardwell Road, Oxford. *T.*: Oxford 309.
(*Died 10 Aug. 1924*.)

LEVANDER, F. W., F.R.A.S. 1871; Editor of the British Astronomical Association since 1900; Librarian, 1895-1906; on Council, 1895-1911; President, 1906-8. *Address*: 30 North Villas, Camden Square, N.W.(*Died 20 Dec. 1916*.)

LEVER, Col. Sir Arthur Levy, 1st Bart., *cr.* 1911; J.P. Essex; *b.* 17 Nov. 1860; *s.* of late Joseph Levy of Leicester; *m.* 1896, Beatrice (*d.* 1917), 3rd *d.* of late Philip Falk, when added the name of Lever for family reasons; one *s. Educ.*: University Coll. School; privately and abroad. Member of the Royal Commission on Coast Erosion and Afforestation, 1906-11; M.P. (L.) Harwich Division N.E. Essex, 1906-10; (N.L.) Central Hackney 1922-1923; contested South Wolverhampton, 1910; Member of the London War Pensions Committee; Deputy Director of Recruiting for South-Eastern Region, 1917; served in European War first as Major 2/1st Batt. The London Regiment, Royal Fusiliers, and subsequently on Headquarters' Staff, Southern Command, with rank of Colonel (temp.) and retired as Colonel. *Recreations*: hunting, and outdoor sports. *Heir*: *s.* Tresham Joseph Philip, *b.* 8 Sep. 1900. *Address*: 20 Hans Crescent, S.W.1; *T.*: Victoria 202; The Grange, Knockholt, Kent; *T.*: Knockholt 14. *Clubs*: Reform, Bath, Ranelagh. (*Died 23 Aug. 1924*.)

LEVERHULME, 1st Viscount, *cr.* 1922, of the Western Isles; Baron, *cr.* 1917; **William Hesketh Lever,** Bt., *cr.* 1911; Hon. R.I.; Grand Officer of the Belgian Order of Leopold II.; Hon. LL.D. Edin.; F.R.G.S.; Hon. F.R.I.B.A.; Chairman of Lever Brothers, Ltd., and founder of Port Sunlight: *b.* Bolton, Lancashire, 1851; *m.* 1874, Elizabeth Ellen (*d.* 1913), *d.* of Crompton Hulme of Bolton; one *s. Educ.*: Bolton Church Institute. Entered father's business in Bolton, 1867; removed to Wigan, 1877, and afterwards to Warrington and Wirral; Congregationalist; contested (R.) Wirral, 1900; Birkenhead 1892, 1894, and 1895; M.P. (L.) Wirral Div., Cheshire, 1906-10; High Sheriff, Lancs, 1917; Junior Warden for Grand Lodge of England, 1918; Mayor of Bolton, 1918-19. *Heir*: *s.* Hon. W. H. Lever. *Address*: Borve Lodge, Leverburgh, Harris, Scotland; The Hill, North End, N.W.3; The Bungalow, Rivington, near Bolton. *T.*: Hampstead 1324. *Clubs*: Reform, National Liberal, Royal Automobile, Caledonian.
(*Died 7 May 1925*.)

LEVESON GOWER, Maj. Lord Alastair St. Clair Sutherland-, M.C.; Royal Horse Guards; *b.* 24 Jan. 1890; *o. b.* and *heir-pres.* of 5th Duke of Sutherland; *m.* 1918, Elizabeth Helene, *d.* of Warren Gardener, Demarest, New York. Late Lieut. Lovat's Scouts Yeomanry; served European War, 1914-18 (wounded, despatches, M.C.).
(*Died 28 April 1921*.)

LEVESON GOWER, Arthur Francis Gresham, F.S.A.; *b.* 25 April 1851; *y. s.* of late Wm. Leveson Gower of Titsey Place, Surrey, and Emily, 3rd *d.* of Maj.-Gen. Sir Francis Hastings Doyle, Bt.; *m.* 1881, Caroline Frederica (*d.* 1895), *y. d.* of late George Savile Foljambe of Aldwark, Yorks, and Osberton, Notts; two *d. Educ.:* Eton; Christ Church, Oxford; B.A. 1874, M.A. 1877. Entered Diplomatic Service, 1876; 3rd Sec. 1879; 2nd Sec. 1881; Sec. of Legation, 1895; employed at Constantinople, Rio de Janeiro, Vienna, Berlin, Berne, Belgrade, Athens; Secretary of Legation at the Hague, 1898-1905; retired, 1905; F.S.A., Knight of Justice Order of St. John of Jerusalem in England; one of three representatives of Order on occasion of German Emperor's visit to Palestine, 1898; admitted to Freedom of City of London, 1913; a Special Constable Headquarters Central Department Section XI., stationed at Buckingham Palace during the war. *Address:* Hadleigh House and Clifford Lodge, Windsor. *Clubs:* Athenæum. Travellers'.
(*Died 26 Dec. 1923.*)

LEVETT, Ernest Laurence, M.A., K.C. 1891; *m.* Mary Jeudwine (*d.* 1912). Called to the Bar, Lincoln's Inn, 1873; Bencher; retired from practice; late Fellow of St. John's College, Cambridge. *Address:* 78 Cambridge Terrace, Hyde Park, W.; North Bank, Alnmouth, Northumberland. (*Died 3 Oct. 1916.*)

LEVEY, Charles Joseph, R.M.; I.S.O. 1904; *b.* Grahamstown, Cape Colony, 1846; *m.* 1876, Sarah Randall. *Educ.:* Lovedale Seminary, Cape Colony. Commanded a column of Tembus in Transkein War (medal); Hon. Lieut.-Colonel D. D. V. Guard, Dordrecht, Cape Colony; Commandant, Dordrecht, in Boer War, 1900; captured rebel chief Sandillis in Kafir rebellion, Cape Colony; fortified and successfully defended Residency, Southeyville, Cape Colony, 1879; commanded native volunteers against chiefs Stock and Mfanta, Cape Colony, 1880; Political Officer with Colonel Wavell's column in Tembu War, 1880; Clerk to British Resident, Fingoland, Cape Colony, 1880; Political Agent with emigrant Tembus, 1875; Magistrate, Southeyville, 1877; Magistrate, Xalanga, 1883; Civil Commissioner and Resident Magistrate, Wodehouse, Cape Colony, 1900; succeeded Lord Cecil, Imperial Commissioner, Western Transvaal, 1901; Resident Magistrate, Marico, Transvaal Colony, 1902. *Address:* Malmani Kloof Road, Seapoint, Cape-town, S.A. (*Died 9 Oct. 1920.*)

LEVEY, George Collins, C.M.G. 1878; *b.* Devonshire, 1835; *s.* of late George Levey, Camberwell Grove; *m.* 1st, 1868, Euphemia Dalton (*d.* 1874); *e. d.* of Charles Whybrow Ligar, Surveyor-General of Victoria; 2nd, 1877, Mary Elizabeth (*d.* 1908), *d.* of George Parker, Washington, and widow of late Hon. J. E. Bouligny, Member of Congress for City of New Orleans. *Educ.:* Univ. Coll. London. First person in Victoria to employ machinery in quartz-crushing; travelled all over Europe, 1859-1861; M.L.A. Normanby, 1861-68; editor and proprietor of Melbourne Herald, 1863-68, which paper he issued at 1d., and thus founded cheap journalism in Australia; editor and contributor to Melbourne Age, 1869-81; Secretary to Commissioners for Victoria at the Exhibitions in London, Paris, Vienna, Philadelphia, Melbourne, 1873, 1876, 1878, 1880-81; Executive Commissioner, Amsterdam, 1883; Secretary Royal Commission, Hobart Exhibition, 1894-95; Secretary Adelaide Exhibition, 1887; Colonial Committee of Royal Commission to Paris Exhibition, 1900. *Publications:* Handbooks to Australasia and River Plate; Australian Ency. *Address:* Royal Colonial Institute. (*Died 13 April 1919.*)

LEVY, Joshua Moses, retired General Foreign Merchant; *b.* Gibraltar, 19 Dec. 1854; *e.*

s. of Moses de Joshua Levy and Esther Pariente; unmarried. *Educ.:* Northwick College. Elder and Past Warden, Spanish and Portuguese Jews' Synagogue; Member London Committee of Deputies of the British Jews; Member Council Jews' College; Committee of Delegates of Sir Moses Montefiore's Endowment at Ramsgate; Member London Chamber of Commerce; Member of Council British Merchants' Morocco Association; Member Council of League of British Jews. *Recreations:* travelling, horse riding. *Address:* 98 Sutherland Avenue, W.9. *Clubs:* Maccabeans; Ramsgate, Ramsgate.
(*Died 2 Mar. 1922.*)

LEVY, Major Walter Henry, D.S.O.; *b.* 1 Nov. 1876; *e. s.* of late Henry Levy, 11 Hyde Park Place, W., and Annette, *d.* of E. H. Beddington; *m.* 1903, Nellie, *e. d.* of Lord Bearsted; one *s.* three *d. Educ.:* Rugby. Director of M. Samuel & Co., Ltd., Gresham Life Assurance Society Ltd., Gresham Fire and Accident Society Ltd.; Has travelled extensively; served European War in France and Belgium, 1914-18 (despatches twice, D.S.O.). *Recreations:* shooting, rowing. *Address:* 54 Lowndes Square, S.W.1. *T.:* Kensington 8337. *Clubs:* Carlton, Wellington, Ranelagh.
(*Died 9 June 1923.*)

LEWIN, Lt.-Col. Thomas Herbert, J.P.; *b.* 1 April 1839; *s.* of G. H. Lewin, barrister; *m.* 1876, Margaret, 3rd *d.* of late John R. McClean, M.P. for East Staffordshire, and widow of Ralph, *e. s.* of late Sir George Elliot, Bart., M.P. for Durham; one *s.* two *d. Educ.:* private schools; Addiscombe College. Major Indian Army, 1877; retired, 1878, Lt.-Col.; served Indian Mutiny, 1854-57; defence of Cawnpore, siege of Lucknow (medal with clasp); Lushai Expedition, 1871-72 (medal with clasp). *Publications:* A Fly on the Wheel, or How I helped to govern India; Life and Death; Wild Tribes of the South-East Frontier. *Recreations:* lawn tennis, billiards, music. *Address:* Parkhurst, Abinger Common, Dorking. *Club:* United Service. (*Died 12 Feb. 1916.*)

LEWIS, Mrs. Agnes Smith; *e. twin d.* of John Smith, Irvine, Ayrshire; *m.* late Rev. Samuel Savage Lewis, Fellow of Corpus Christi College, Cambridge. *Educ.:* Irvine Academy till the age of 12, private schools (Birkenhead and London) till the age of 18, afterwards entirely by the private tuition of distinguished university graduates. Hon. Phil. Doc., Halle; LL.D. St. Andrews; D.D. Heidelberg; Litt.D. Dublin. Discoverer (Feb. 1892) of the Syro-Antiochene, or Sinaitic Palimpsest, the most ancient known MS. of the Four Gospels in Syriac, and of other valuable Oriental MSS.; Gold Medallist of Royal Asiatic Society, 1915. *Publications:* Before marriage—Eastern Pilgrims; Effie Maxwell; Glenmavis; Brides of Ardmore; Monuments of Athens (translation); Glimpses of Greek Life and Scenery; Through Cyprus. After marriage—Life of Rev. S. S. Lewis; Introduction to the Four Gospels from the Sinaitic Palimpsest; Some Pages of the Sinaitic Palimpsest retranscribed; A Translation of the Syriac Gospels; In the Shadow of Sinai; co-editor of The Story of Ahikar; The Palestinian Syriac Lectionary of the Gospels; and of Palimpsest Fragments of Palestinian Syriac; Studia Sinaitica I., Catalogue of the Sinai Syriac MSS.; VI. A Palestinian Syriac Lectionary from the Pentateuch Prophets, etc.; IX. X. Select Narratives of Holy Women from the Sinai Palimpsest, with a Translation; The Transitus Mariæ, in Syriac; Horæ Semiticæ, III., IV.; Acta Mythologica Apostolorum, in Arabic, with translation; Codex Climaci Rescriptus; The Old Syriac Gospels, or Evangelion da Mepharreshe; co-editor of, Leaves from Three Ancient Qurâns, 1914; Margaret Atheling and other Poems, 1917. *Recreation:* travel. *Ad-*

dress: Castle-brae, Chesterton Lane, Cambridge. *M.:* CE 2078.   (*Died Mar. 1926.*)

LEWIS, Angelo, M.A. (Prof. Hoffmann); author, editor, journalist; *b.* London, 23 July 1839; *m.* Mary Ann Avery, 1864; one *d. Educ.:* North London Collegiate School; Wadham College, Oxford; Barr. Lincoln's Inn, 1861; practised until 1876; on staff of Saturday Review, under J. Douglas Cook; contributor to Chambers' Journal, the Cornhill, Temple Bar, London Society, St. Paul's, and many other serials; winner of prize of £100 offered by Youth's Companion, Boston, for best short story for boys; took up conjuring as a hobby, and in 1876, under *nom de plume* of Professor Hoffmann, produced Modern Magic, the first English book of any importance on the subject. The popularity of this book led to the production of others, as below. *Publications:* Modern Magic; More Magic, 1890; Later Magic, 1903; Drawing-room Amusements; Conjurer Dick; Tricks with Cards; Home Gymnastics; Puzzles, Old and New; The Book of Card and Table Games; Baccarat, Fair and Foul; Every Boy's Book of Sport and Pastime; The Modern Hoyle; Hoyle Modernised; The Secrets of Conjuring and Magic (Robert-Houdin); The Secrets of Stage Conjuring (Robert-Houdin); The Sharper Detected and Exposed (Robert-Houdin); Drawing-room Conjuring; Magic at Home; The Game of Skat; The Book of Patience Games; Dominoes; The Chess Games of Greco; Latest Magic, 1918; Handbooks on Piquet, Ecarté, Bridge, Auction Bridge, Rubicon Bézique, Hearts, Heartsette, Ombre, Five Hundred, and Quinto; also Progressive Whist and Euchre; King Koko, 1904; Magical Tit-bits, 1910. Inventor of card games, Quinto, Schnapps, Bimbo, Frisco, Queen Mab, San Tan, Zigzag, Knock Out and Boss. *Recreations:* chess, billiards. *Address:* Manningford, Upper Bolebrooke Road, Bexhill-on-Sea. *Club:* Whitefriars.
      (*Died 23 Dec. 1919.*)

LEWIS, Arthur Cyril Wentworth, Editor The Straits Times, Singapore, F.M.S. since 1927; *b.* Nottingham, 4 Oct. 1885; *e. s.* of Arthur Lewis, Felbrigge, Roughton, Norwich, and Margaret (*decd.*), *d.* of Rev. W. H. Cornforth; *m.* 1923, Josette Eugenie Nöel of Le Faouët, Morbihan, Brittany. *Educ.:* Felsted; Exeter College, Oxford, B.A. (History Honours), 1908. Entered journalism on Nottingham Daily Express, 1909; Literary Editor Sheffield Telegraph, 1910-13; on staff of The Times, 1914-23; special correspondent, Denmark and Morocco, and Chief Correspondent of The Times in Paris, 1921-22; Editor, The Englishman, Calcutta, 1923-27; served in World War, 1914-19, France, Egypt, Palestine, and Salonika; Lieut.-Colonel, A.D.A.P. & S.S. *Recreations:* travelling, lawn tennis, and golf. *Address:* The Straits Times, Singapore, F.M.S. *Clubs:* New University, Authors', Press; Bengal, Calcutta.
      (*Died 15 Mar. 1928.*)

LEWIS, Arthur Hornby, D.L., J.P.; *b.* 1843; *e. s.* of James Owen Lewis of St. Anne's Mount, Aigburth, Lancs.; *m.* 1879, Helen, *e. d.* of James Reid Stewart, D.L., J.P., of Calder Park, Lanarkshire, N.B. High Sheriff of Cheshire, 1905-6. *Recreations:* shooting and hunting. *Address:* Danesfield, Great Marlow, Bucks.; 29 Park Lane, W.1; Chaseley, Eastbourne, Sussex. *Club:* Conservative.
      (*Died 22 Sept. 1926.*)

LEWIS, Brig.-Gen. Bridges George, C.B. 1918; D.S.O. 1900; late Commanding 1st Batt. East Lancs. Regt.; *b.* 3 March 1857; *s.* of Rev. G. B. Lewis; *m.* 1st, 1879, Mary (*d.* 1917), *d.* of Rev. Canon Burn-Murdoch; one *s.* one *d.*; 2nd, Laura Montgomery, *d.* of Rev. W. Glenn; one *s.* two *d. Educ.:* Uppingham; Sandhurst. Entered army, 1878; Captain, 1885; Adjutant 2nd Batt. 1887-91; Major, 1895; served South Africa, 1900-1 (despatches,

Queen's medal four clasps, D.S.O.); European War, 1914-18 (C.B., despatches); Temp. Brig.-Gen. Comd. 56th Infantry Brigade, 2nd New Army, Sep. 14; J.P. Co. Carlow. *Address:* Sandbrook, Tullow, Co. Carlow.
      (*Died 24 April 1925.*)

LEWIS, Col. David Francis, C.B. 1898; A.D.C. to King; *b.* Buttington, near Welshpool, 21 Oct. 1855; *e. -. of* late Rev. D. P. Lewis and Louisa, *y. d.* of late Capt. F. Hallowes, R.N., of Glapwell Hall, Derbyshire; *m.* 1910, Edith Marion, *o. surv. d.* of late Henry Smith, J.P., D.L., of Summerhill Court, Staffs. *Educ.:* private school; Sandhurst, 1875. Joined 2nd Bn. The Buffs, 1876-90; promoted Major in Cheshire Regt.; served Zulu War, 1879 (wounded, despatches); Egyptian Army, 1886-1900 (medal with clasp, Khedive's star, 3rd Class Medjidie); Sudan, 1896-99 (Egyptian medal 8 clasps, Queen's medal, Brevets Lt.-Col. and Col., C.B., A.D.C. to the Queen, despatches 6 times, thanks of both Houses of Parliament); was in command at action of Rosaires; was Times Correspondent with the French Army, Morocco, 1907, and with the Spanish Army round Melilla, 1909; Spanish Order of Military Merit; raised 16th Batt. R. Warwick. Regt., Oct. 1914; County Comdt. Warwick. Vol. Corps (despatches); J.P. Warwickshire and Gloucestershire. *Recreation:* hunting. *Address:* Hungerdown, Seagry, Chippenham, Wilts. *T.:* Seagry 3. *Club:* Naval and Military.
      (*Died 2 Feb. 1927.*)

LEWIS, Lieut. Donald Swain, D.S.O. 1915; R.E. and Royal Flying Corps; *b.* 5 Apr. 1886. Entered army, 1904; served European War, 1914-5 (D.S.O.).   (*Died 10 April 1916.*)

LEWIS, Edgar Samuel, Editor and Director Daily Mail, Hull, and Hull Times, Co. Hull, since 1890; *b.* Worcester, 22 Dec. 1853; 2nd *s.* of Edmund Lewis, Deputy-Clerk of Peace; *m.* Emma Bourner Sprigg, 1878; one *s.* one *d. Educ.:* Worcester Upper and Middle School. Journalist; Editor Westmorland Gazette, 1888-89; Preston Herald, 1889-90. *Publication:* Bonny Westmorland Lass. *Address:* 22 Whitefriargate, Hull. *T.:* 4304 Hull.
      (*Died 16 April 1922.*)

LEWIS, Sir George James Graham, 2nd Bt., *cr.* 1902; Head of firm Lewis and Lewis, solicitors; *b.* 12 Sep. 1868; *s.* of 1st Bt. and Elizabeth, *d.* of F. Eberstadt; *S.* father, 1911; *m.* 1896, Marie, *d.* of Emil Hirsch; one *s.* two *d. Educ.:* Harrow; Balliol College, Oxford. Admitted a solicitor, 1894. *Heir: s.* George James Ernest, *b.* 25 Feb. 1910. *Address:* 21 Montagu Square, W.1; *T.:* Mayfair 166; The Grange, Rottingdean, Sussex: (Office), Ely Place, Holborn, E.C.1; *T.:* Holborn 536. *M.:* A 193. *Clubs:* Bath, Royal Automobile.
      (*Died 8 Aug. 1927.*)

LEWIS, Harold; Literary Editor of the Globe until its cessation Feb. 1921; *b.* Bath, 22 June 1856; *e. s.* of William Lewis, J.P.; *m.* Isabella (*d.* 1913), *d.* of Wakefield Simpson of Whitby; two *s.* two *d. Educ.:* Grosvenor School, Bath, B.A. Lond., 1879. On staff of Bath Herald till June 1883; specially interested in the condition of the poor and in children's education; Member of the Institute of Journalists; editor of the Bristol Mercury, 1883-1901; staff of Nottingham Guardian, 1901-14. *Publications:* The Church Rambler; the Original Bath Guide; and various pamphlets and articles on archæological questions. *Recreations:* Captain, 1886-96, 2nd Gloucester V.R.E.; a lover of the drama. *Address:* 31 Epperstone Road, West Bridford, Nottingham.   (*Died 30 Sept. 1924.*)

LEWIS, Sir Henry, Kt., *cr.* 1911; J.P.; *b.* 21 Nov. 1847; *s.* of Thomas Lewis, M.P. for Anglesey; *m.* Annie, *d.* of Rev. Roger Edwards, D.D.; two *s.* two *d. Educ.:* Friars School, Bangor; The College, Bala. Alderman of

City of Bangor; Co-opted Member of North Wales Counties Training College; Member of Council of University College of N. Wales. *Publications*: History of Friars School, and other local histories. *Recreations*: motoring and walking. *Address*: Pendyffryn, Bangor. *T.* : 94. *M.* : CC 3941. *(Died 16 Nov. 1923.)*

LEWIS, Col. Henry, O.B.E. 1919; J.P., D.L., Joint M.F.H., Tredegar and Pentyrch; *b.* 1847; *e. s.* of Henry Lewis (*d.* 1881), and 1st wife, Anne, *d.* of late Walter Morgan; *m.* 1879, Mabel, *d.* of Capt. P. F. Durham. Hon. Col. late 1st Royal Devon Imperial Yeomanry. *Address*: Green Meadow, Tongwynlais, Cardiff. *Club* : Cavalry. *(Died 9 July 1925.)*

LEWIS, Isaac; partner in Lewis and Marks; Director, Johannesburg Consolidated Investment Coy.; Swaziland Corporation; South African Breweries, Ltd.; Victoria Falls and Transvaal Power Co., Ltd.; *b.* Neustadt, Province of Kovno, Russia, 1849; *m.* Sarah Ann (*d.* 1919); went to South Africa, 1870. *Address*: Vereeniging, South Africa.
(Died 29 Mar. 1927.)

LEWIS, James Henry, D.C.L., Mus.D., F.E.I.S.; Freeman of the City of London and Liveryman of the Worshipful Company of Basketmakers; Principal, Victoria College of Music, London; Warden and Licensed Lay Chaplain to the Incorporated Guild of Church Musicians, London; *b.* 23 Feb. 1856; *m.* Annie, *d.* of late William Roff, Malvern, 1881; one *s.* four *d.* *Educ.*: Malvern. Trained for the musical profession; composer of numerous pianoforte solos, songs, organ music, anthems, services, etc. *Publications*: many text-books, etc., including Harmony, Counterpoint, Double Counterpoint and Canon, Fugue, Elements of Music, History of Church Music, Dictionary of Musical Terms, Pronouncing Vocabulary of Musical Terms, The Material of Melody, and Early Steps in Musical Art. *Recreation*: photography. *Address*: Thornton Lodge, Twickenham, S.W.; Victoria College of Music, 158 Holland Park Avenue, W.11.
(Died 20 Nov. 1924.)

LEWIS, Hon. John, C.M.G. 1923; M.L.C. since 1898; Director of Bagot, Shakes & Lewis, Ltd., Stock and Station Agents, Adelaide, S.A.; pastoralist; *b.* Brighton, S.A., 12 Feb. 1842; *s.* of late James Lewis; *m.* 1876, Martha Ann Brook; four *s.* two *d.* *Educ.*: Private school, Brighton. Pioneer and Explorer; crossed the Continent from Adelaide to Darwin in 1872; explored in the Northern Territory in 1872 and 1873; J.P. for 50 years; on Licensing Bench for 42 years; for seven years President of the Royal Geographical Society (S.A. Branch); for three years President of the Horticultural and Floricultural Society; on various Councils and Boards, including Pastoralists' Association, Aborigines' Friends' Association, South Australian Soldiers' Fund, Adelaide Children's Hospital, Botanic Garden, etc. *Publication*: Fought and Won : Autobiography, 1922. *Recreations*: takes a keen interest in all sport, including horse racing; owned Wee Gun, winner of the Adelaide Cup in 1919. *Address*: Benacre, Glen Osmond, South Australia. (*Died 25 Aug. 1923.*)

LEWIS, John Christopher, I.S.O., 1910; J.P.; Commissioner of Affidavits; retired Civil Service Officer; *b.* Barbados, 1842; *m.* 1871; three *s.* two *d.* *Educ.*: Barbados. Entered Civil Service, Trinidad, 1861; 5th Clerk G.P.O., 1868; Acting 2nd Clerk, 1868; Postmaster San Fernando, 1869; Acting Postmaster-General, 1886, 1891, and 1899; Member of Municipal Council, 1903; Mayor of San Fernando, 1904; re-elected, 1905; Manager of the Government Boys' and Girls' Central School since 1890. Has travelled in the West Indies and British Guiana, and has visited America, Canada, The Azores, France, Great Britain, Sweden, Finland and Russia. *Publications*: Christ the Saviour of the World; Kathleen. *Address*: Lewisville, San Fernando, Trinidad, B.W.I. *(Died 11 June 1918.)*

LEWIS, John Hardwicke, water-colour painter; *b.* Hyderabad, Deccan, 1840; *e. s.* of Frederic Christian Lewis, jun., known as the "Indian Lewis," for his many canvasses of Durbars, etc., at all the native Courts in India; *m.* 1st, Ellen, *d.* of Rev. Dr. Wm. Andrews; 2nd, Elizabeth Eugenie, *d.* of Wm. Steele, artist; two *s.* two *d.* *Educ.*: privately after 2½ years at Kensington Grammar School. Studied oil painting in Paris under Thomas Couture; painted portraits and genre in London, and exhibited many years at the R.A. prior to 1885; since 1889 has lived at Veytaux in Switzerland, and devoted all his time to Swiss landscape painting in water-colours; the interval between 1885 and 1889 was spent in California. *Publications*: illustrated Our Life in the Swiss Highlands, by Addington Symonds; The Upper Engadine, by Rev. Spencer C. Musson; three books on the Lake of Geneva, by Gribble, la Côte d'Emeraude. Brittany, by Spencer C. Musson. *Recreations*: writing and reading. *Address*: Veytaux, Switzerland.
(Died 3 Oct. 1927.)

LEWIS, John Penry, C.M.G. 1911; Ceylon Civil, Service, retired; *b.* 17 Sep. 1854; 2nd *s.* of late Rev. John Lewis; *m.* 1894, Violet Marion, *d.* of late Joseph Anderson of Ankerwyke, Wraysbury; one *s.* two *d.* *Educ.*: Mill Hill School; Queen's University, Ireland, B.A. 1876; M.A. 1882; a Member of the Middle Temple; Ceylon Civil Service, 1877-1910; retired as Government Agent, Central Province, and Member Executive and Legislative Councils, 1910; was Superintendent of Pearl Fisheries, Ceylon, 1904, 1905, and 1906; first Special Officer under Waste Lands Ordinance, 1907-10; belongs to Church of England. *Publications*: compiled A Manual of the Vanni Districts, 1895; Tombstones and Monuments in Ceylon, 1913; Ceylon in Early British Times, 1913; papers to Folklore, Architectural Review, and Journal of Ceylon Branch of Royal Asiatic Society. *Recreations*: sketching, archaeology, etc. *Address*: Canford Cliffs, Dorset. *T.A.*: Canford Cliffs. *Club* : Authors'.
(Died 29 Sept. 1923.)

LEWIS, Very Rev. Julius, Dean of Ballarat since 1915. *Educ.*: Moore College, N.S.W. Ordained, 1875; curate of Hamilton, 1876-79; Portland, 1879-81; Christ Church Cathedral, Ballarat, 1881-84; Canon, 1887-88; Vicar of Maryborough, 1884-88; Incumbent of St. Jude's, Melbourne, 1888-97; Archdeacon of Tamworth, 1897; Vicar of Tamworth, 1897-1902; of Armidale, 1902; Canon Residentiary St. Peter's Cathedral, Armidale; Archdeacon of Armidale, 1902-14. *Address*: The Deanery, Christ Church Cathedral, Ballarat, Victoria.
(Died 1920.)

LEWIS, Thomas, F.R.A.S.; Assistant, Royal Observatory, Greenwich; Secretary, Royal Astronomical Society; awarded Lalande Prize by French Academy, 1907. *Publications*: Memoir on Double Stars : Joint - Editor The Observatory. *Address*: Royal Observatory, Greenwich. *Club* : Royal Astronomical.
(Died 5 June 1928.)

LEWIS, Thomas Arthur, Barrister; M.P. (Co. L.) Pontypridd Division of Glamorgan, Dec. 1918 - 22; Junior Lord of the Treasury, unpaid, 1922; *b.* 21 Sep. 1881; *s.* of Rev. J. M. Lewis, Cemaes, Pembrokeshire, and Phœbe, *d.* of Thomas Griffiths, Pantygroes, Pembrokeshire; *m.* 1919, Marjorie, *d.* of late William Culross, Adelaide, S. Australia; one *d.* *Educ.*: University College, Cardiff; joined Inns of Court O.T.C., 1915; commissioned April 1916; served Salonica, 1916-18; Parliamentary Private Secretary to Capt. Hon. F. Guest,

M.P., Chief Government Whip, Feb. 1919;
called to Bar, Middle Temple, 1919. *Address:*
Cemaes, Pontypridd. *Club:* National Liberal.
(Died 18 July 1923.)

LEWIS, Sir Thomas William, Kt., *cr.*
1918; J.P., D.L.; Stipendiary Magistrate,
Cardiff, 1887-1923; *y. s.* of late Thomas William
Lewis of Abercanaid House, Merthyr, J.P.; *b.*
1852; *m.* 1st, Elizabeth Agnes, *d.* of late Robert
Tidman, Ipswich; 2nd, Henrietta Catherine, *d.*
of late Rev. H. Willmott, Rector of Kirkley-
Bar, Middle Temple, 1879. *Address:* Gilestone
Manor, near Cardiff. *Club:* Oxford and Cam-
bridge. *(Died 28 April 1926.)*

LEWIS, Rev. Canon William; Canon
Residentiary of Llandaff Cathedral, 1908-14;
Rector of Ystradyfodwg since 1869; Curate of
Nantyglo, 1862-64; Pentredach, 1864-68; per-
petual Curate of St. John Baptist, Llandrisant;
Precentor of Llandaff, 1891; Rural Dean of
Rhondda, 1895; Examining Chaplain, Bishop of
Llandaff, 1905-14. *Address:* Ystradyfodwg,
Pentre, R.S.O. *(Died 27 Jan. 1922.)*

LEWIS, William George, I.S.O. 1908; a
Commissioner of Customs and Excise, 1910;
retired, 1912; *b.* 1844. *Address:* Evesham
Lodge, Reigate. *T.:* Reigate 367.
(Died 27 July 1926.)

LEWIS, William James, F.R.S. 1909;
Professor of Mineralogy, Cambridge, since 1881;
Fellow of Oriel Coll., Oxford; *b.* 16 Jan. 1847;
s. of Rev. J. Lewis, late of Bonvilston; un-
married. *Educ.:* Jesus Coll., Oxford (M.A.). 1st
Math. Mods.; 1st Math. Final Schools; 1st
Natural Science Schools; Senior Math. Scholar.
Author of a treatise on Crystallography, 1899;
North Wraxhall, 1913. *Address:* Trinity Col-
lege, Cambridge. *(Died 16 April 1926.)*

LEWTAS, Lieut.-Col. John, C.B.E,
1918; late Commissioner of Medical Services,
Ministry of National Service; *b.* Liverpool; *s.*
of Dr. T. Lewtas; *m.* Annie Chambers, *d.* of
Henry Threlfall Wilson, The Cranes, Surbiton;
one *s. Educ.:* Liverpool College; Edinburgh
University; St. Thomas' Hospital Medical
School. Entered the Indian Medical Service,
1875; served with the Guides in the Afghan
campaigns of 1878-79 and 1880 (despatches
twice, medal 2 clasps); Lecturer on Ophthalmology, and Ophthalmic Surgeon Medical
College Hospital, Calcutta; Surgeon to the
Mayo Hospital; late Fellow of the Calcutta
University. *Publications:* various contributions to medical journals. *Recreation:* fishing.
Address: 15 Cheyne Place, S.W.3. *T.:* Kensington 5098. *(Died 23 Sept. 1920.)*

LEWTHWAITE, Sir William, 1st
Baronet, *cr.* 1927; D.L., J.P. Cumberland,
since 1875; C.A., Cumberland: *b.* 29 Oct.
1853; *s.* of Wm. Lewthwaite of Broadgate,
J.P., D.L., and Mary, *d.* of Wm. Challinor of
Leek, Co. Stafford; *m.* 1881, Helena Jane, *d.* of
Charles Challinor of Basford Hall, Co. Stafford;
one *s.* one *d. Educ.:* Rugby; Trinity College,
Cambridge. *Heir: s.* William Lewthwaite, Old
Broadgate. *Address:* Broadgate, Broughton-
in-Furness. *T.:.:* The Green.
(Died 18 Dec. 1927.)

LEWTON-BRAIN, Lawrence, B.A.,
F.L.S.; Director of Agriculture, Federated
Malay States since 1910; of Federated Malay
States and Straits Settlements since 1919; *b.* 1879,
s. of J. Lewton-Brain of The Rookery, Yaxham,
Norfolk; *m.* 1904, Annie, *d.* of late W. O'Meara
of Ossory and Colonial Civil Service, British
Guiana; three *s. Educ.:* Firth College, Sheffield;
St. John's College, Cambridge. (Foundation
scholar and Hutchinson student); Demonstrator
in Botany, Cambridge University, 1900;
Mycologist and Agricultural Lecturer to the
Imperial Department of Agriculture for the
W.I., 1902; studied the diseases of sugar-cane,
cacao, cotton, and other tropical plants, also

the breeding and hybridization of the sugar-
cane; proceeded to Hawaii and became
Assistant Director of the Division of Pathology
and Physiology of the Hawaiian Sugar Planters'
Association, Experiment Station, 1905; Director
of the Division, 1907; worked on sugar-cane
and its diseases, the bacteria of sugar, etc.
Publications: The Anatomy of the Leaves of
British Grasses (Trans. Linn. Soc.), 1902;
numerous bulletins and papers on the botany
and pathology of tropical cultivated plants,
1902-10. *Recreations:* tennis, photography. *Address:* Kuala Lumpur, Federated Malay States.
T.A.: Agriculture, K. Lumpur. *M.:* SL 17.
(Died 24 June 1922.)

LEY, Sir Francis; 1st Bt., *cr.* 1905; J.P.;
Knight of Grace of the Hospital of the Order
of St. John of Jerusalem in England; *b.* 3 Jan.
1846; *o. s.* of late George Phillips Ley of Burton-
on-Trent, and Sarah, *d.* of John Pott, Yoxall,
Staffs; *m.* 1st, 1870, Georgina Townsend (*d.* 1886),
d. of late Capt. George Willis of Aislaby Hall,
Yorks; one *s.* two *d.;* 2nd, 1888, Alison Catherine,
d. of late John Jobson, J.P., of Spondon,
Derbys.; one *s. Educ.:* privately. Lord of the
Manors of Epperstone and Kirkoswald, Lazonby,
Staffield, and Glassonby in Cumberland; High
Sheriff, Notts, 1905; founded in 1874, and is
Governing Director of Ley's works in Derby;
ex-President Nottingham General Hospital,
Derbyshire Children's Hospital, Notts County
Cricket Club, and Notts Agricultural Society.
Owns about 6500 acres of agricultural property;
Heir: s. Henry Gordon [*b.* 12 March 1874; *m.*
1899, Rhoda, *d.* of Herbert Prodgers, J.P., of
Kington, St.-Michael's House, Wilts; two *s.* one
d. Major Notts Imp. Yeo. *Address:* Willington
House, Derbyshire]. *Recreations:* salmon fish-
ing, shooting. *Address:* Epperstone Manor,
Notts; Lealholm Lodge, Grosmont, Yorks.
Clubs: Royal Automobile, Notts County.
(Died 27 Jan. 1916.)

LEY, William Henry; *b.* London 26 Dec.
1847. *Educ.:* Winchester College. Became a
clerk in journal office, House of Commons,
1868; became Clerk of the Journals, 1895;
retired 1908. *Address:* 36 St. George's Road,
S.W.1. *Club:* Wellington. *(Died 21 July 1919.)*

LEYCESTER, William Hamilton; one
of the Magistrates of the Police Courts of the
Metropolis since 1912; at Bow Street since
1922; *b.* 1864; *s.* of William Leycester, for
many years chief of The Times Parliamentary
Staff; *m.* Frances Eliza, *d.* of J. C. Warne,
Captain 24th Regiment (S.W. Borderers).
Educ.: King's College School; Peterhouse,
Cambridge. (Scholar). 18th Wrangler, 1888;
called to Bar, 1888; practised chiefly at the
London Sessions and Central Criminal Court,
where he was one of the Treasury Counsel.
Club: Garrick. *(Died 23 Oct. 1925.)*

LEYLAND, Christopher John, J.P.
Northumberland; *b.* 19 Sep. 1849; *e. s.* of late
John Naylor of Leighton Hall, Montgomery-
shire; *m.* 1st, 1874, Everilda Elizabeth (*d.* 1890),
e. d. of late Ralph Creyke, Rawcliffe, Yorkshire;
one *d.;* 2nd, 1892, Helen Dora, *e. d.* of Digby
Cayley, Norton Grove, Yorkshire; three *s.*
three *d.* Entered Navy, 1862; retired Sub-
Lieutenant in 1872; Director, The Parsons
Marine Steam Turbine Co. Ltd.; Parsons
Foreign Patents Co. Ltd.; Cleveland Ship-
building Co. Ltd. *Heir: e. s.* Christopher
Digby Leyland, late Capt. 1st Life Guards,
Household Cavalry [*b.* 24 Dec. 1892; *m.* 1916,
Sylvia Evelyn, *e. d.* of Sir John Cotterell;
one *s.*]. *Address:* The Mead, Beal, Northum-
berland. *Club:* Carlton. *(Died 21 Oct. 1926.)*

LEYLAND, John, writer on naval, inter-
national, and historical subjects; *s.* of Francis
A. Leyland, author of The Brontë Family; *m.*
Fanny Julia, (*d.* 1921), *d.* of T. Duncan; two *s.*
Has written for the Times, Daily Chronicle,

Observer, Nineteenth Century, Quarterly and Edinburgh Reviews, Country Life, New York Herald, and other English and American papers and magazines; editor of the Army and Navy Gazette, 1904-9; of The Navy 1910-12; author of articles and statistics in the Naval Annual since 1896; edited the volume, 1901, 1915, and 1916; part editor, 1906 and 1914; attached to Admiralty War Staff, 1917-18; wrote, in collaboration with Com. C. N. Robinson, R.N., In the Queen's Navee and For the Honour of the Flag; Hon. Member R.U.S.I. *Publications:* The Blockade of Brest, 1803-1805 (Navy Records Society), The Royal Navy, its Influence in English History and the Growth of Empire; The Achievement of the British Navy in the World War, etc. *Address:* Crimsworth Dene, Forest Hill. *T.:* Sydenham 923.

(*Died 5 Jan. 1924.*)

LEYTON, Albert Sidney Frankau, M.A., M.D., Sc.D., F.R.C.P., D.P.H.; Director of Clinical Laboratory, Addenbrookes Hospital, Cambridge; ex-Prof. of Pathology, University of Leeds; *b.* London, 5 Jan. 1869; *m.* 1909, Helen Gertrude, widow of Robert S. Stewart, M.D.; two s. *Educ.:* City of London School; Gonville and Caius Coll. Camb. Lecturer on Experimental Medicine, Univ. of Liverpool; Director of the Liverpool Cancer Research; Assist. Physician, Hospital for Consumption; Goulstonian Lecturer, Royal Coll. of Physicians; Member of the Physiological and Pathological Societies. *Publications:* author of scientific and medical papers, chiefly on the nervous system, cancer, and enteric fever, and Essentials of Morbid Histology. *Address:* The Chestnuts, Great Shelford, near Cambridge. *T.:* Shelford 46; *T.A.:* Leyton, Great Shelford. *M.:* F.C. 1066.

(*Died 21 Sept. 1921.*)

LIAS, Rev. Chancellor John James, Chancellor of Llandaff Cathedral; *b.* 30 Nov. 1834; *s.* of Charles Lias, silver plate manufacturer, London; *m.* 1st, 1865, Miss E. Attenborough; 2nd, 1890, Miss Mortlock; five *s.* one *d.* *Educ.:* King's College, London; Emmanuel College, Camb. (Foundation Scholar; M.A. Was compelled, from ill-health, to give up reading for Mathematical Honours at Cambridge; ordained, 1858, to curacy of Shaftesbury, Dorset; by another breakdown in health forced to give up regular clerical work for five years; Curate of Folkestone, 1865-66; Vicar of Eastbury, 1866-68; Minor Canon of Llandaff Cathedral, 1868-71; Professor of Modern Literature at St. David's College, Lampeter, 1871-80; Vicar of St. Edward's, Cambridge, 1880-92; Preacher at the Chapel Royal, Whitehall, 1884-86; Examining Chaplain to the Bishop of Llandaff, 1887-1900; Rector of East Bergholt, 1892-1903; also formerly Hulsean Lecturer and Lady Margaret Preacher, Cambridge; member of Council of the Imperial Federation League from foundation until it was dissolved. *Publications:* Rector and His Friends (Dialogues), 1868; Doctrinal System of St. John, 1875; Commentaries on Joshua (Pulpit Commentary), Judges, 1st and 2nd Corinthians (Cambridge Bible for Schools), 1st Epistle to St. John, Hulsean Lectures on the Atonement, Are Miracles Credible? Miracles, Science and Prayer, Principles of Biblical Criticism, Nicene Creed; articles in Encyclopædia Britannica, Murray's Bible Dictionary, and Murray's Shorter Dictionary of Ecclesiastical Biography; papers read before the Victoria Institute, etc. *Recreations:* music and light reading. *Address:* The Lodge, Abington, Cambridge.

(*Died 16 Mar. 1923.*)

LIBERTY, Sir Arthur Lasenby, Kt., *cr.* 1913; D.L., J.P., C.C. Bucks; Founder and Chairman of Liberty and Co. Ltd., and promoter of other industries connected with the decorative arts; *b.* Chesham, Bucks 13 Aug. 1843; *e. s.* of

the late Arthur Liberty, of Chesham; *m.* 1875, Emma Louise, *d.* of late Henry Blackmore, of Exmouth. *Educ.:* University School, Nottingham. Member of Council of London Chamber of Commerce; Member of Advisory Committee Royal School of Art Needlework; Vice-President of the Silk Association of Great Britain and Ireland; a Director of the British Produce Supply Association; Past Master of the Glass-Sellers' Company; President of the English Monumental Inscriptions Society; Chairman of Council of the Bucks Architectural and Archæological Soc., and of the Bucks Association for loan of Pictures to Country Schools; County Council Representative on the Bucks Territorial Association; Member of the Royal Institute; Fellow of the Asiatic Society of Japan; Member of the Organising Council of the Japan Society; Fellow of the Royal Historical Society; Fellow of the Royal Statistical Society; Past President of the Sette of Odd Volumes; Juror at Paris International Exhibition, 1900; member of London Committee of the Milan Exhibition, 1906; Lord of the Manor of The-Lee, Bucks; High Sheriff for the county of Bucks in 1899; Chairman of The-Lee Parish Council; has travelled in the Far East; awarded medals for papers read before the Society of Arts in 1890 and 1900. *Publications:* Springtime in the Basque Mountains; De Libertat; Pictorial Records of Japan; A Day in Tangier; The Treasure Hunt. *Recreations:* travelling, sketching, and shooting. *Address:* Lee Manor, The-Lee, Bucks; 28 Warwick Street, Regent Street, W. *T.A.:* The-Lee. *T.:* The-Lee 2. *M.:* BH 1258, BH 1356. *Club:* Devonshire. (*Died 11 May 1917.*)

LICHFIELD, 3rd Earl of (cr. 1831), Thomas Francis Anson, D.L., J.P.; Viscount Anson and Baron Soberton, 1806; Director National Provincial Bank of England, Ltd.; Bank of Australasia, etc.; *b.* 31 Jan. 1856; *s.* of 2nd Earl and Lady Harriet Georgiana Louisa Hamilton, *d.* of 1st Duke of Abercorn; *S.* father 1892; *m.* 1878, Lady Mildred Coke, *d.* of 2nd Earl of Leicester, three *s.* three *d.* *Educ.:* Harrow; Trinity College, Cambridge; B.A. Owns about 20,000 acres in Staffordshire. *Heir:* s. Viscount Anson. *Address:* 38 Great Cumberland Place, W.; *T.:* Mayfair 3716; Shugborough Park, Stafford. *Club:* Brooks's.

(*Died 29 July 1918.*)

LIDDELL, Adolphus George Charles, C.B., 1908; *s.* of Hon. Sir A. F. O. Liddell, K.C.B. and F. E. L. Lane-Fox; *b.* 29 June 1846; unmarried. *Educ.:* Eton; Balliol Coll., Oxford. 2nd Class Lit. Hum., 1869; called to Bar, 1871; North Eastern Circuit; Secretary to Royal Commission on Municipal Corporations, Reformatory and Industrial Schools, and Trawling; Revising Barrister for S. Division of West Riding of Yorks, 1884-86; Counsel to the Mint on the Durham and Northumberland Sessions; Chief Clerk, Crown Office in Chancery, 1886; Assistant Secretary, Lord Chancellor's Department 1888-1919; Private Secretary to Lord Chancellor 1909-15. *Publication:* Notes from the Life of an Ordinary Mortal, 1911. *Address:* 6 Seville Street, Lowndes Square, S.W. *Clubs:* Travellers', Wellington.

(*Died 12 Aug. 1920.*)

LIDDELL, Charles; *b.* 1856; *y. s.* of John Liddell of Benwell Hall, Northumberland; *m.* 1894, Madeline, *d.* of late J. A. Dease, Turbotston, W. Meath; one *d.* *Educ.:* Ushaw College, Co. Durham; High Sheriff for Cumberland, 1917. *Address:* Warwick Hall, Carlisle. *T.A.:* Warwick Bridge.

(*Died 9 July 1922.*)

LIDDELL, Sir Robert Morris, Kt., *cr.* 1916; D.L., Ex-High Sheriff, Co. Down; Managing Director, William Liddell & Co., Ltd., of Donacloney, Belfast, London, New York, etc.; *b.* 20 July 1870; *s.* of William Liddell; *m.* 1896, Charlotte Walton, *d.* of late John Arnott Taylor

LIDDELL, Colin. See page xxiv.

of Belfast ; three *s.* three *d.* *Educ. :* Christ College, Finchley. Hon. Treasurer the U.V.F. Hospital Fund, and the U.V.F. Patriotic Fund. *Address:* Banoge House, Donacloney, Co. Down. *T.A.:* Banoge, Donacloney, Co. Down. *Clubs:* Constitutional ; Union, Belfast.
(*Died 16 April 1928.*)

LIDDELL, T. Hodgson, R.B.A.; landscape painter ; *b.* Edinburgh, 1860 ; *y. s.* of W. H. Liddell; *m.* 1885, May, *e. d.* of late Henry Pitman; three *s.* *Educ.:* Royal High School, Edinburgh. Travelled in China, and held exhibition of water-colours painted there, at the Fine Art Society, 1909 ; author and illustrator of China, its Marvel and Mystery. Principal pictures exhibited in R.A. and other galleries : Sabbath of Still Rest ; An Old Waterway ; A Fen Flood ; Springtime ; A Bend of the Avon ; Borderland (and at St. Louis) ; The Estuary at Aberdovey, 1904 (purchased for the M'Kelvie Gallery, Auckland, N.Z.) ; Cleeve Mill, and Mill Pool, 1905. *Recreations :* travelling, riding, shooting.
(*Died June 1925.*)

LIDDLE, R. W., Organist and Rector Choir Southwell Cathedral since 1888 ; *b.* Durham, 1864 ; married ; no *c.* *Educ. :* Durham. Organist St. Baldred's, North Berwick, 1886-88 ; Conductor Mansfield Harmonic Society, 1898 ; Orchestral Society, 1906 ; Organist and Choirmaster St. Peter's Church, Mansfield, 1904 ; Conductor Newark and District Orchestral Society, 1908 ; Manager and 1st violin of the Liddle String Quartette. *Publications :* Evening Services ; Anthems : O Send Out Thy Light, Save Lord and Hear Us, As for Me, etc. ; Hymn tunes and Chants. *Recreations :* the practice and performance of Chamber Music. *Address :* Vicar's Court, Southwell, Notts.
(*Died 30 Dec. 1917.*)

LIFFORD, 6th Viscount (*cr.* 1781), **Archibald Robert Hewitt** ; Baron Lifford, 1768 ; *b.* 14 Jan. 1844 ; *s.* of 4th Viscount and Lady Mary Acheson, *d.* of 2nd Earl of Gosford ; *S.* brother, 1913 ; *m.* 1878, Helen Blanche, *d.* of late C. S. Geach ; one *s.* two *d.* Entered Navy, 1858 ; retired Capt. 1890. *Heir :* s. Lt.-Col. Hon. E. J. Hewitt, D.S.O. *Address :* Hill House, Lyndhurst, Hants. (*Died 21 May 1925.*)

LIGHTFOOT, Rev. John, D.Sc., M.A., Mus. Bac. ; Vicar of Cross Stone since 1882 ; Hon. Canon of Wakefield, 1910 ; *b.* Tunstall, 18 Dec. 1853 ; *s.* of Peter and Catherine Lightfoot ; *m.* ; five *d.* *Educ. :* University of Edinburgh ; Theological College, Lichfield. Ordained, 1875 ; Curate, Heath Town, Bradford, Halifax. *Publications :* Studies in Philosophy ; Text Book, XXXIX Articles ; Pastor Meus Dominus ; Logic and Education ; Theory of Music; Elementary and Intermediate Algebra ; Advanced Arithmetic ; The Complete Arithmetic ; Alexander the Great ; Short Methods in Arithmetic ; Graphic Algebra, etc. *Recreation :* golf. *Address :* Cross Stone, Todmorden.
(*Died 9 Aug. 1917.*)

LIGHTFOOT, Rev. John Alfred, Vicar of Haile, Cumberland, since 1926 ; *b.* 18 May 1861 ; *s.* of George Lightfoot of Birkby, Maryport, Cumberland ; *m.* Marianne F., *d.* of David Marshall Lang, Lay Sec. of Church Missionary Society. *Educ. :* Merchant Taylors' School, London ; Hertford Coll., Oxford (B.A. 1883, M.A. 1887). Deacon, 1885 ; Priest, 1886 ; Tutor and Assist. Chaplain of St. John's Hall, Highbury, 1886-93 ; Afternoon Lecturer at Christ Church, Highbury, 1886-91 ; Curate of St. Augustine's, Highbury, 1892-93 ; Vicar of St. Stephen's, Canonbury, 1898-99 ; Principal of the Church Missionary College, Islington, 1899-1917 ; Vicar of Christ Church, Chislehurst, 1917-25 ; Examining Chaplain to Bishop of Durham, 1901-12. *Recreations* lawn tennis, cycling. *Address :* Haile Vicarage, Beckermet, Cumberland.
(*Died 2 Jan. 1928.*)

LILLEY, Capt. James Lindsay, D.S.O. 1900 ; Victorian Mounted Rifles ; *b.* 1871 ; *m.* 1913, Olive Agatha Hope, *y. d.* of late Rev. C. E. Cummings and Mrs. Geoffrey ffolkes of Sinytham, Little Torrington, Devon. Served South Africa, 1900-1 (despatches, Queen's medal 3 clasps, D.S.O.). (*Died 1 Dec. 1923.*)

LILLY, William Samuel, M.A., J.P. ; barrister ; Secretary to Catholic Union of Great Britain since 1874 ; *b.* 10 July 1840 ; *e. s.* of late William Lilly, Windout House, near Exeter ; *m.* 1907, Anna Marie, *d.* of M. Félix Emery of Geneva. *Educ. :* Peterhouse, Cambridge. Hon. Fellow of Peterhouse. Under-Secretary to Govt. of Madras, 1869. *Publications :* Ancient Religion and Modern Thought, 1884 ; Chapters in European History; 1886 ; A Century of Revolution, 1889 ; On Right and Wrong, 1890 ; On Shibboleths, 1892 ; The Great Enigma, 1898 ; A Manual of the Law specially affecting Catholics (with Sir J. P. Wallis), 1893 ; The Claims of Christianity, 1894 ; Four English Humorists of the Nineteenth Century 1895 ; Essays and Speeches, 1897 ; First Principles in Politics, 1899 ; A Year of Life, 1900 ; Renaissance Types, 1901; India and its Problems, 1902 ; Christianity and Modern Civilisation, 1903 ; Studies in Religion and Literature, 1904 ; Idola Fori, 1910 ; Many Mansions, 1907 ; The New France, 1913. *Recreations :* riding, rackets, cycling. *Address :* 36 Fitzgeorge Avenue, West Kensington, W. *T. :* Hammersmith 1486. *Club :* Athenæum (elected under Rule 2, 1887).(*Died 29 Aug. 1919.*)

LIMA, Sir Bertram Lewis, K.B.E. *cr.* 1918 ; Captain in the Canadian Army ; Chairman of the Daily Mirror, Sunday Pictorial, Glasgow Daily Record, and Leeds Mercury newspaper companies. *Address :* 1 Duchess Street, Portland Place, W. *T. :* Mayfair 1741.
(*Died 24 Feb. 1919.*)

LINCOLNSHIRE, 1st Marquess of (*cr.* 1912), **Charles Robert Wynn-Carrington**, K.G., P.C., G.C.M.G. ; Earl Carrington, 1895 ; Baron Carrington, 1796 ; Viscount Wendover, 1895 ; Joint-Hereditary Lord Great Chamberlain of England ; *b.* 16 May 1843 ; *m.* 1878, Hon. Cecilia Margaret Harbord, *e. d.* of 5th Lord Suffield ; five *d.* Liberal. Protestant, L.C.C. *Educ. :* Eton ; Trin. Coll., Camb. (B.A.). M.P. High Wycombe, 1865-68 ; Captain Royal Bodyguard, 1881-85 ; Governor, New South Wales, 1885-90 ; Lord Chamberlain of the Household, 1892-95 ; Pres. Board of Agriculture, 1905-1911 ; Lord Privy Seal, 1911 ; Lord-Lieut. of Bucks, 1915-23. Owns 23,000 acres. *Heir :* (to Barony) *b.* Hon. Rupert Carington. *Address :* Daws Hill Lodge, High Wycombe, Bucks. *T. :* High Wycombe 67 ; 53 Princes Gate, S.W.7 ; *T. :* Kensington 74. *Clubs :* Brooks's, National Liberal. (*Died 13 June 1928.*)

LINDLEY, Baron (Life Peer), *cr.* 1900 ; **Rt. Hon. Nathaniel Lindley** ; P.C. ; F.R.S. ; Hon. LL.D. Edin. and Camb. ; D.C.L. Oxford; *b.* Acton Green, Middlesex, 1828; *o. s.* of John Lindley, Ph.D., F.R.S., Professor of Botany, Univ. Coll. London ; *m.* Sarah (*d.* 1912), *e. d.* of Edward John Teale, Leeds, 1858 ; four *s.* two *d.* *Educ. :* Univ. Coll. London. Barr. Middle Temple, 1850 ; Q.C. 1872 ; Judge of Court of Common Pleas, 1875 ; Lord Justice of Appeal, 1881-97 ; Master of the Rolls, Oct. 1897-1900 ; Lord of Appeal in Ordinary, 1900-5. *Publications :* Introduction to the Study of Jurisprudence ; Treatises on the Law of Partnership and Companies. *Address :* The Lodge, East Carleton, Norwich.
(*Died 9 Dec. 1921.*)

LINDLEY, Rear-Ad. George Robert (retired), C.B. 1913 ; *b.* 5 July 1850 ; *s.* of late Robert Charles Lindley of Mansfield, and Elizabeth, *d.* of Chas. Delmar of Elmstone, Kent ; *m.* 1896, Kate Louisa, *d.* of late Mr. Windebanks of Southsea ; one *s.* two *d.* *Educ. :* Dover ; on board H.M.S. "Britannia."

Entered Navy 1863; served on board H.M.S. "Achilles" during the Egyptian War, medal and Khedive's star; commanded a Naval brigade landed in Witu territory, East Coast of Africa, in 1893 (C.B., South African medal and clasp). *Address:* Watersend, Temple Ewell, Dover. (*Died 1 Aug. 1918.*)

LINDLEY, Maj.-Gen. Hon. John Edward; late Colonel, Royal Dragoons; J.P. Norfolk and Suffolk; *b.* 15 Sep. 1860; *e. s.* of late Baron Lindley; *m.* 1887, Isabel, *d.* of late Francis Morgan Nichols, Lawford Hall, Essex; one *d.* D.A.A.G. Aldershot, 1893-96; Jersey, 1899; Commandant, School of Instruction, Imperial Yeomanry, 1901-3; A.A.G., N.E. District and Northern Command, 1903-5; Commandant Cavalry School, 1905-7; Brigadier-General Commanding 3rd Cavalry Brigade, 1907-10; Commanded Welsh Division, 1913-15; served S. Africa, 1899-1900 (Queen's medal 2 clasps); Gallipoli, 1915. *Address:* The Maultway House, Camberley, Surrey. *Club:* Naval and Military. (*Died 7 April 1925.*)

LINDLEY, Sir William Heerlein, Kt., *cr.* 1911; M.I.C.E., F.G.S., Dr.ing. h.c.; Consulting Engineer; *b.* 30 Jan. 1853; *s.* of William Lindley, Civil Engineer; *m.* Fanny H. Getz of Frankfurt-on-Main; one *s.* two *d.* *Educ.:* Mr. Thompson's School, Kidbrook House, Blackheath; Mr. George Valentine's School, Blackheath; private tuition: matriculated London University, 1869; his father's resident engineer on Budapest Waterworks, 1870-73; Engineer-in-Chief of the City of Frankfurt-on-Main, 1873-95, for sewage and water-works, harbour works and regulation of River Main, electrical supply works, streets, and roads, town planning and other engineering works and for the technical administration; at same time and till present, consulting engineer for designing and execution of various municipal works in other towns. *Works:* waterworks—Warsaw (with his father), Bucharest, Crajova, Ploesti Pitesti, Baku; designed new water supply of Petrograd from Lake Ladoga, 1912; sewage works—Elberfeld, Warsaw, Homburg, Mannheim, Hanau, Wurzburg, Prague, Crajova, Samara; Electrical Supply Works, Elberfeld; was a member of the Commission for the regulation of the Danube at Vienna and for the water supply of Amsterdam; President of the Engineering Standards Commission of the German Gas and Waterworks Engineers; President of Commission on Vagabond Currents from Electric Tramways and Rules for Abating same; Member of International Committee on Pipe-Screw Thread; and Assistant Commissioner of Royal Commission on Canals and Waterways. *Recreations:* mountaineering, riding. *Address:* c/o Institution of Civil Engineers, Great George Street, S.W. (*Died 30 Dec. 1917.*)

LINDSAY, 11th Earl of (*cr.* 1633), **David Clark Bethune,** J.P.; Lord Lindsay of The Byres, 1445; Baron Parbroth, 1633; Viscount Garnock; Baron Kilbirny, Kingsburne, and Drumry, 1703; *b.* 18 April 1832; *s.* of David Aytone Lindsay and Jane Emilia, *d.* of John Aytone of Kippo, Fifeshire; *S.* cousin 1894; *m.* 1866, Emily Marian, *d.* of Robert Crosse, Doctors' Commons, and widow of Capt. E. C. Barnes, 91st Regt.; two *s.* one *d.* *Educ.:* St. Andrews, Edinburgh Universities. Owns about 2300 acres. *Heir: s.* Viscount Garnock. *Address:* Wormistone House, Crail; Kilconquhar Castle, Kilconquhar, Fifeshire. (*Died 20 Mar. 1917.*)

LINDSAY, David; *b.* Goolwa, South Australia, of Scotch parents, 20 June 1856; married; four *s.* one *d.* *Educ.:* private schools. Entered Survey Department, South Australia, 1872; Junior Surveyor Northern Territory, 1878; Surveying and Control of Public Works till 1882; explored Arnhem Land, N.T., 1883;

exploring in north-west of South Australia, 1884; exploring and surveying from the Southern boundary to the Gulf of Carpentaria, 1885-86; rode across Australia from North to South with only a small black boy as companion, 1888; surveying, exploring, and prospecting in the MacDonnell Ranges, Central Australia, 1889-90; leader of the Elder Scientific Exploring Expedition; crossed the great Victoria District, 550 miles in 35 days, the 42 camels having only 7½ gallons of water each for the whole journey, during the journey discovered and reported the existence of a great auriferous area—on this report prospectors went out and found the great goldfield of West Australia; overlanded a mob of camels from Pt. Augusta to Coolgardie, 1891-93; stayed in the goldfields till 1895, assisting in the exploration and exploitation of that great mineral belt; visited London in connection with mining, 1895-96; since which time has been intimately associated with the development of the mining industry in various states of Australia; was a member of the Commonwealth Royal Commission to advise as to railways and new ports to develop the Northern Territory, 1913; exploring in Northern Territory, 1916-20. *Publications:* Journals of Exploration; Territoria. *Address:* 56 Market Street, Sydney, N.S.W. (*Died 18 Dec. 1922.*)

LINDSAY, Col. Henry Arthur Peyton, C.B. 1924; C.S.I. 1921; C.M.G. 1915; C.B.E. 1919; Indian army, retired; *b.* 29 Jan. 1868; *m.* Charlotte Eliza, *d.* of late Maj. F. Stewart. Entered West India Regt., 1887; Capt. Indian Army, 1898; Major, 1905; Lieut.-Col. 1913; Colonel, 1916; served N.W. Frontier, India, 1897-98 (medal with clasp); European War, 1914-18 (despatches, C.M.G., Bt. Col.); retired, 1924. (*Died 30 Dec. 1926.*)

LINDSAY, Rev. Dr. James; philosopher, theologian, and man of letters; *e. s.* of late John Cowan Lindsay; *m.* 1908, Margaret, *e. d.* of late James Cook, Glasgow, and *widow* of R. Barclay Shaw, of Annick Lodge and Knockgerran, Ayrshire. *Educ.:* under his father; Glasgow University. M.A. 1878; B.Sc. 1879; B.D. 1882; D.D. 1899; F.R.S.L. 1910; F.R.S.E. 1889; F.G.S. 1888; M.R.A.S. 1897; declined Principalship of Calcutta College, 1882; University Extension Lecturer, 1886-87; Corresponding Member of Royal Academy of Sciences, Letters, and Arts, Padua, 1894; Member Aristotelian Society, 1897; Examiner to the Associated Theological Colleges, British and Colonial—Philosophy, 1897-99, and Honours Theology, 1899; Hugh Waddell Lecturer, Queen's University, Canada, 1899-1900; Member of International Congress of Psychology, Paris, 1900; Associate Editor of Bibliotheca Sacra since 1903; Associate Philosophical Society of Louvain, 1903; Member of the Kant Society, Halle, 1904; Member of International Congress of Philosophy, Heidelberg, 1908; Request by German Commission to write on present English Philosophy declined, 1910; Member of Goethe-Gesellschaft, and of English Goethe Society, 1913. *Publications:* Progressiveness of Modern Christian Thought, 1892; Essays, Literary and Philosophical, 1896; Significance of the Old Testament for Modern Theology, 1896; Recent Advances in Theistic Philosophy of Religion, 1897; Momenta of Life, 1901; Studies in European Philosophy, 1909; The Fundamental Problems of Metaphysics, 1910; The Psychology of Belief, 1910; New Essays, Literary and A Critical Essay on European Literature, 1913; A Philosophical System of Theistic Idealism, 1917; Seven Theistic Philosophers, 1920; Great Philosophical Problems, 1922 *Address:* Annick Lodge, Irvine; Broadstone, Stranraer. (*Died 25 Mar. 1923.*)

LINDSAY, Sir John, K.B.E., *cr.* 1924; Kt.,
cr. 1915; Town Clerk of Glasgow, 1912-27; *b.*
Glasgow, 16 Dec. 1860; *s.* of late Alex. Lindsay,
Marine Engineer; *m.* 1893, Charlotte Elizabeth,
(*d.* 1922), 3rd *d.* of late David Douglas, retired
Valuator, Arbroath; one *s.* one *d.* *Educ.:*
Gorbals and Hutchesontown Sessional Schools;
Glasgow University. Entered the service of
the Sheriff Clerk of Lanarkshire, 1875; Assist-
ant Clerk of Police, Glasgow, 1891; Clerk of
Police and Town Clerk Depute (Police Depart-
ment); D.L. for the County of the City of
Glasgow; J.P. for the Counties of the Cities of
Glasgow, Dundee and Aberdeen, and Counties
of Lanark, Dumbarton and Argyll; Honorary
Sheriff - Substitute of Lanarkshire. *Publica-
tions:* Treatises on the Statutory Police Law
of Glasgow; Municipal Glasgow: its evolution
and enterprises; etc. *Recreation:* bowling.
Address: St Mungo, Pollokshields, Glasgow.
T.: Central 6400.   (*Died 23 Sept. 1927.*)

LINDSAY, William Alexander, C.V.O.
1924; K.C., M.A., J.P., D.L.; Peerage-Counsel;
Clarenceux King of Arms since 1922; *b.* 8 June
1846; *e. s.* of late Hon. Colin Lindsay and Lady
Frances Howard, *d.* of 4th Earl of Wicklow;
m. 1870, Lady Harriet Gordon, *d.* of 5th Earl
of Aberdeen; three *s.* two *d.* *Educ.:* Eton;
Cambridge. Member of Lloyd's, 1868; M.A.
1871; Barr. Middle Temple, 1873; Q.C. 1897;
Bencher, 1906; Norroy King of Arms, 1919-22
(previously Windsor Herald and Portcullis
Pursuivant); Royal Commissioner to inquire
into Corrupt Practices, 1880; contested Burnley,
1874, 1876, 1894, 1896; Huddersfield, 1880;
Forfarshire, 1885; F.S.A. *Publications:* articles
on Earldom of Mar, the O'Briens, and various
genealogical subjects; the Stewart and Guelph
Pedigrees; The Royal Household, 1837-97;
Charters of Inchaffr y; contributor to Encyclopædia Britannica and Lord Halsbury's Laws
of England. *Address:* 17 Cromwell Road, S.W.7;
T.: Western 3595; Goldsmith Building, Temple,
E.C.4; College of Arms, E.C.4; *T.:* Central
485. *Clubs:* Athenæum, Carlton.
    (*Died 13 Sept. 1926.*)

LINDSAY-HOGG, Sir Lindsay, 1st Bt.,
cr. 1905; J.P.; late Member of E. Sussex C.C.;
b. 1853; *s.* of late W. Hogg of Oakleigh, Pem-
bury, near Tunbridge Wells, and Lancaster Gate,
London, Consul for the Hanseatic States; *m.*
1880, Alice, *d.* of J. C. Cowley of Heathfield,
Addington, Surrey, and Luke, *e. d.* of late Sir
William Baynes, Bart.; one *s.* three *d.* *Educ.:*
Harrow. M.P. (C.) Southern and Eastbourne
Div. of Sussex, 1900-6. Owns property in
Sussex. *Recreations:* coaching and any kind of
sports; has done much towards the Rifle Clubs
and the formation and improvement of the
agricultural and other societies throughout
England, and is president of a large number.
Heir: g.s. Anthony Henry [*b.* 1 May 1907, *e. s.*
of late William Lindsay Lindsay-Hogg and
Nora Cicely, *d.* of late Capt. J. J. Barrow of
Holmewood, nr. Tunbridge Wells, Dornoch,
N.B., and 35 Hyde Park Gardens, W. *Ad-
dress:* Hayward's Grange, Rotherfield, Sussex].
Address: Rotherfield Hall, Jarvis Brook, Sussex. *T. :* Rotherfield 7. *Club:* Carlton.
    (*Died 25 Nov. 1923.*)

LINDSELL, Henry Martin, C.B. 1904;
b. 7 May 1846; *e. s.* of Lieutenant-Colonel
Lindsell, J.P., D.L., of Fairfield, Biggleswade,
Beds, and Emma, *d.* of Rev. Martin Hogge,
Vicar of Southacre, Norfolk; unmarried.
Educ.: Harrow (Head of the School); Trinity
College, Oxford (scholar). 1st class Mods.;
2nd class Litteræ Humaniores; M.A. Oxon.
Called to the Bar, Inner Temple, 1874; ap-
pointed Examiner to the Education Depart-
ment, 1876; Advising Counsel, 1891; Principal
Assistant Secretary (Legal), 1903 (retired); J.P.
and C.C. Beds; Chairman of Quarter Sessions.

Address: 67 Albert Hall Mansions, S.W.;
Shortmead, Biggleswade, Beds. *Club:* United
University.   (*Died 30 Jan. 1925.*)

LINES, Rt. Rev. Edwin S., D.D. Yale,
1897, Berkeley Divinity School, 1904, Princeton, 1911; Rutgers, 1917; Bishop of the Diocese
of Newark, U.S.A., since 1903; *b.* Naugatuck,
Connecticut, 23 Nov. 1845; *m.* 1880, Mary L.
Morehouse; two *s.* *Educ.:* The Cheshire School;
Yale University; Berkeley Divinity School.
Rector Christ Church, West Haven, Conn.,
1874-79; St. Paul's Church, New Haven, Conn.,
1879-1903; Member, Board of Missions, 1901-
1925; sometime Member of National Churches
Council, Educational and Social Service Boards,
etc. *Publications:* a number of historical papers
and addresses, lectures, and contributions to
periodicals. *Address:* 21 Washington Street,
Newark, N.J., U.S.A. *Clubs:* Graduates, New
Haven; Nassau, Princeton. (*Died 25 Oct. 1927.*)

LINKLATER, John Edmund, Barrister-
at-Law; Registrar in Bankruptcy, High Court
of Justice since 1887; *b.* 14 Nov. 1848; *s.* of
late John Linklater, Solicitor of Walbrook,
E.C.; *m.* 1876, Emma, *d.* of late Walter Lindesay
Willson; two *d.* *Educ.:* Eton; Christ Church,
Oxford (B.A., S.C.L., 1871; M.A., 1874).
Called to Bar, Inner Temple, 1872. *Address:*
3 Collingham Road, S.W. *T.:* Western 1225.
Club: New University.   (*Died 11 Jan. 1917.*)

LINTON, Sir James Dromgole, Kt.;
cr. 1885; P.R.I.; Hon. Member Royal Scottish
Water Colour Society; Member of the Royal
Institute of Oil Painters; Hon. Associate of
the Royal Institute of British Architects;
corresponding member of the Society of
Water Colour Painters, Vienna; Hon. Presi-
dent of the Royal Society of Miniature
Painters; Knight of the Order of St. John
of Jerusalem; Officier of the Order of Leopold,
Belgium; Jubilee Medal, 1897; *b.* London, 26
Dec. 1840; *o. s.* of late James Linton, London,
and Jane Scott, Carlisle; *m.* 1867, Harriet
Maria, *d.* of late Henry Allen; three *s.* three *d.*
Educ.: Cleveland House, Barnes. President
of the Royal Institute of Painters in Water
Colours, 1884-99, and since 1909. *Address:* 4
The Mall, Parkhill Road, Haverstock Hill,
N.W. *Club:* Savage.   (*Died 3 Oct. 1916.*)

LIPSETT, Major-Gen. Louis James,
C.B. 1918; C.M.G. 1915; Royal Irish Regt., attached to Canadian Forces; *b.* 15 June 1874; *o.
surv. s.* of late Richard Lipsett and Mrs. Lipsett,
The Cottage, Merthyr-Tydfil. Entered army,
1894; Capt. 1901; Maj. 1913; D.A.A. and Q.M.G.
1905-7; A.D.C. to Maj.-Gen. 2nd Div. Aldershot,
1907-8; General Staff Officer, 2nd Grade, Canadian Forces, 1911; served N.-W. Frontier,
India, 1907-8 medal 2 clasps); European War,
1914-18 (despatches, Bt. Lt.-Col. and Col.
C.B., C.M.G.). *Club:* Army and Navy.
    (*Died 14 Oct. 1918.*)

LISH, Joseph J., Past President, S.A.
(London), and a Gold Medallist of the Society of
Architects; *m.* Nancy Bentley Hozier Roberton,
d. of late Edward M'Leod of Natal, S.A., and
g.d. of late John Roberton of Lauchope, Lanarkshire; two *s.* two *d.* *Publications:* editor, and,
with W. H. Hudleston and Prof. A. Meek,
joint author, of The Dove Marine Laboratory,
containing a history of the Dove family and
their descendants; also, Cullercoats and Marine
Biology; and articles upon Reinforced Concrete and Portland Cement, showing the position this country can claim to have occupied
in the origination and development of these
materials. *Address:* Croftlands, Thornthwaite,
near Keswick.   (*Died 17 Jan. 1923.*)

LISLE, 6th Baron, *cr.* 1758, **George
William James Lysaght,** Irish Peer; *b.*
29 Jan. 1840; 2nd *s.* of 5th Baron, and Henrietta,
d. of John Church; *S.* father, 1898; *m.* Amy
Emily, *d.* of late Ayliffe Langford, Ventnor, Isle
633

of Wight, 1868 ; one s. one d. Educ.: private tutors ; Plymouth Grammar School. Formerly Lt. in Devon Militia Artillery, and in Jackson's Forest Rangers Waikato Militia ; served Maori War, 1864-65. Owns about 7000 acres in Counties Cork and Limerick. Heir: s. Hon. Horace George Lysaght. Address: West End, Mallow, Co. Cork. (Died 16 Mar. 1919.)

LISTER, Joseph Jackson, F.R.S. ; late Fellow of St. John's College, Cambridge ; s. of late Arthur Lister, F.R.S. ; m. 1911, Dorothea Charlotte Edith, d. of late George Selwyn Marryat. Publications: articles on Foraminifera, Mycetozoa, etc., in Lankester's Treatise on Zoology ; part author of chapters on Arthropoda in Sedgwick's Students' Textbook of Zoology, and of various zoological memoirs. Address: Merton House, Grantchester, nr. Cambridge ; St. John's College, Cambridge. Club: Savile.
(Died 5 Feb. 1927.)

LISTER, Thomas David, C.B.E. 1920 ; late Physician to Mt. Vernon Hospital for Consumption, and to Royal Waterloo Hospital for Children ; Member of Senate of London University, elected in 1919 by Medical Graduates in Convocation ; Head Office Medical Adviser of the Royal Exchange Assurance Corporation, Friends' Provident Institution, and North British and Mercantile Insurance Company (West End) ; Consulting Physician to the National Union of Teachers ; Consulting Physician to the Post Office Sanatorium Society ; Consulting Physician to the Association of Local Government Officers ; Consulting Physician for Chest Cases to the Prince of Wales' Hospital for Officers, St. Marylebone, 1917-1919 ; b. London, 30 Jan. 1869 ; s. of late Francis Wilson Lister, and Elizabeth Wishart, o. d. of David Roy, of Glasgow ; m. Louise Edna Bertha, e. d. of Eugen Ritter, London. Educ.: Aske's School (Haberdashers' Company) ; Guy's Hospital. M.D. Lond. 1894, F.R.C.S. Eng. 1894, M.R.C.P. 1900 ; House Surgeon at Guy's, 1893-94 ; Pathologist to East London Hospital for Children, 1897-1900 ; Member and Hon. Advisory Physician of Council of National Association for Establishment and Maintenance of Sanatoria for Workers suffering from Tuberculosis, and as Chairman of Sites and Buildings Sub-committee drafted the scheme of the Benenden Sanatorium ; Pres. and Treas. of Assurance Medical Society ; Fellow of the Royal Society of Medicine ; an invited member of Panel Committee of the County of London and of the Hospital Saturday Fund Board of Delegates. Publications: Industrial Tuberculosis, 1910 ; section (jointly) on Heart and Lungs in Knocker's Medico-Legal Aspects of Accidents ; contributions to transactions and medical journals on Life Assurance, Children's Diseases, Consumption, and allied subjects. Address: Nenthorn, Henley-on-Thames. Club: Royal Societies. (Died 30 July 1924.)

LISTER, Rev. Thomas Llewellyn, M.A., V.D. ; Hon. Canon of Llandaff, 1909-22 ; Rural Dean of Newport, 1905. Educ.: Jesus College, Oxford (M.A.). Ordained 1862 ; Curate of St. Woolos, Newport, 1862-75 ; Vicar of St. Mark's, Newport, 1895-1916. Address: 31 Fields Road, Newport, Mon. (Died 25 July 1926.)

LISTER-KAYE, Sir John Pepys, 3rd Bt. ; cr. 1812 ; D.L. ; Groom-in-Waiting to King Edward VII., 1908-10 ; late Lieutenant Royal Horse Guards ; b. 18 Feb. 1853 ; s. of L. Lister-Kaye and Lady Caroline Pepys, 3rd d. of 1st Earl of Cottenham ; S. grandfather 1871 ; m. Natica, d. of Antonio Yznaga del Valle, New York, U.S.A. Educ.: Eton ; Trin. Coll., Camb. Heir: b. Cecil Edmund. Address: Overton Lodge, Wakefield. Clubs: Marlborough, Carlton, Turf, Guards'. (Died 27 May 1924.)

LISTOWEL, 3rd Earl of (cr. 1822), William Hare, K.P., P.C., J.P. ; Baron Ennismore,

1800 ; Viscount Ennismore, 1816 ; Baron Hare (U.K.), 1869 ; Capt. Scots Guards (retired 1856) ; b. Convamore, 29 May 1833 : e. s. of 2nd Earl and 2nd d. of late Vice-Admiral William Windham ; S. father 1856 ; m. Lady Ernestine Mary Brudenell-Bruce, y. d. of 3rd Marquess of Ailesbury (one s. two d. Lieut. Scots Guards, 1852 ; severely wounded at the Alma ; Lord-in-Waiting, 1880. Heir: s. Viscount Ennismore. Address: Kingston House, Prince's Gate, S.W. ; Convamore, Ballyhooly, Co. Cork. Club: Brooks's ; Royal Yacht Squadron, Cowes.
(Died 5 June 1924.)

LITTLE, Mrs. Archibald.; b. Madeira ; y. d. of late Calverley Bewicke of Hallaton Hall, Leicestershire, and Mary Amelia Hollingsworth ; m. 1886, late Archibald Little, Pioneer of Upper Yangtse and author of The Far East and Through the Yangtse Gorges. Worked on many philanthropic committees in England ; then founder, organizing Secretary, and finally President of the Tien Tsu Hui, or Anti-foot-binding Society of China ; Vice-President of the Women's Conference at Shanghai, 1900 ; delivered lectures before the Geographical Societies of Glasgow, Edinburgh, Aberdeen, Dundee, Manchester, Liverpool, Newcastle, South Shields, also at Glasgow Exhibition ; read a paper of Mr. Little's before the British Association at Glasgow. Publications: Intimate China ; The Land of the Blue Gown ; Round About my Peking Garden ; Li Hung Chang, his Life and Times ; A Marriage in China ; Out in China, a Novelette ; A Millionaire's Courtship ; Fairy Foxes, a Chinese Legend ; Mother Darling, written to establish the rights of mothers to their own children ; A Noble Army and a Holy War ; many novels, among these Margery Travers ; Onwards ! but Whither ; The Last of the Jerninghames ; and many magazine and newspaper articles ; edited Mr. Archibald Little's Across Yunnan ; also Gleanings from Fifty Years in China. Recreations: travel and sightseeing. Club: Ladies' Empire. (Died 31 July 1926.)

LITTLE, James, M.D. Univ. Edin. ; M.R.I.A. ; Hon. LL.D. Edinburgh, Hon. Physician to His Majesty in Ireland, 1908 ; Regius Professor of Physic, Dublin University, since 1898 ; Fellow Royal Coll. of Physicians, Ireland ; b. Newry ; s. of Archibald Little and Mary, d. of Richard Coulter ; m. Anah (d. 1914), d. of Robert Murdoch, Dublin ; two s. one d. Educ.: Armagh Royal School ; Medical School, T.C.D., and University, Edinburgh ; M.D., Hon. Causâ, Univ. Dub. In 1866 became Physician, Adelaide Hospital ; has been Professor of Practice of Medicine, Royal College of Surgeons, Ireland ; president of the Royal College of Physicians, Ireland, and of the Royal Academy of Medicine, Ireland, and is consulting physician to four Dublin hospitals, and Crown Representative for Ireland on General Medical Council. Publications: First Steps in Clinical Study ; Chronic Diseases of the Heart. Recreations: field sports. Address: 14 St. Stephen's Green, Dublin. Clubs: Athenæum, Junior Carlton ; Kildare Street, University, Dublin. (Died 23 Dec. 1916.)

LITTLEJOHN, Harvey, M.A., M.B., B.Sc. (Pub. Health), F.R.C.S., F.R.S.E. ; Professor of Forensic Medicine since 1906 ; and late Dean of the Faculty of Medicine, Edinburgh University ; s. of the late Sir H. D. Littlejohn. Educ.: Edinburgh University ; Vienna ; Berlin ; Paris. Formerly M.O.H., Sheffield ; President, Section of Forensic Medicine, International Medical Congress, 1913 ; Major R.A.M.C. (T.) Commanding Medical Unit O.T.C. ; President Medico-Legal Society of London. Publications: Illustrations of Forensic Medicine, and numerous papers on Forensic Medicine and Public Health. Address:

11 Rutland Street, Edinburgh. *T.:* 2106. *Clubs:* Savile; University, Edinburgh.
(*Died 15 Aug. 1927.*)

LITTLEJOHN, Robert; Director of the African Banking Corporation since 1900; Member of Tariff Commission. General Manager African Banking Corporation, 1891-1900. *Address:* 8 Cavendish Square, W.1. *Clubs:* Constitutional, Caledonian, Gresham.
(*Died 24 May 1920.*)

LITTLER, Captain Charles Augustus, D.S.O. 1916; 12th Batt. Australian Imperial Forces; *b.* Launceston, Tasmania, 26 Mar.; *s.* of Augustus Littler and Hannah Murray; *m.* 1892, Helen Cotgrave Thomas; three *s.* *Educ.:* Edinburgh College. Trained as a Banker; several years Commercial Agent for Tasmania in Far East; travelled largely in Java, Malay States, Philippines, China, Borneo, Manchuria, Japan, and Siberia; served with Russians and Americans in the field; explored the interior of Mindanao, Southern Philippines, and spent much time amongst the wild people; has been a member of many economic, traffic, harbour, and tariff commissions; served European War, 1915-16 (D.S.O.). *Address:* Silwood, Devonport West, Tasmania. (*Died 3 Sept. 1916.*)

LITTLEWOOD, Bt.-Colonel Harry, C.M.G. 1917; Hon. M.Sc. (Leeds); F.R.C.S. (Eng.) 1886; L.R.C.P. (Lond.) 1884; J.P.; Examiner in Surgery University of Cambridge; Consulting Surgeon General Infirmary, Leeds; *b.* Norfolk, 18 April 1861; 2nd *s.* of late Charles F. Littlewood, Hempstead Hall, Norfolk, and Mary, *d.* of Augustine Worts, Lessingham, Norfolk; unmarried. *Educ.:* Norwich; University College, London; University College Hospital. Atkinson - Morley Surgical Scholar, 1884; late Senior Surgeon and Chairman of the Faculty, Leeds Infirmary, and President of the Leeds and West Riding Medico-Chirurgical Society; Consulting Surgeon to the Victoria Hospital, Keighley, and Malton Cottage Hospital; late Professor of Surgery and Lecturer on Practical and Operative Surgery in the University of Leeds, and Resident Surgical Officer to the Leeds Infirmary; late House Surgeon, House Physician, and Resident Obstetric Officer, University College Hospital and Senior Demonstrator of Anatomy, University College, London; and Clinical Assistant, Royal London Ophthalmic Hospital; Examiner in Surgery in the National University of Ireland; gazetted to the Territorial Force, R.A.M.C., as Surgeon Lt.-Col. 2nd Northern Division General Hospital, Leeds, 1908; Administrator 2nd Northern General Hospital, Leeds, 1915-19; Lord of the Manor of Hempstead, Norfolk; Knight of Grace of the Order of the Hospital of St. John of Jerusalem. *Publications:* Several contributions on surgical subjects to medical societies and medical journals. *Recreations:* farming and motoring. *Address:* Erpingham Lodge, Ingworth, Norfolk. *T.A.:* Aylsham, Norfolk. *M.:* U 790. (*Died 19 Dec. 1921.*)

LIVEING, Edward, M.D. (Cantab.); Fellow (1874) and Registrar of the Royal College of Physicians, 1889 - 1909; Emeritus Registrar, 1909; Fellow and late Member of Council, King's College, London; formerly Assistant Physician to King's College Hospital; Consulting Physician, St. Marylebone General Dispensary; *b.* Nayland, Suffolk, 8 Feb. 1832; 2nd *s.* of Edward Liveing and Catherine, *o. d.* of Geo. Downing, Barrister, Lincoln's Inn; *m.* 1st, 1854, Frances (*d.* 1885), *o. d.* of Lieut. Henry Torlesse, R.N., Police Magistrate at Hobart; three *s.* two *d.*; 2nd, 1898, Harriet Susan, *e. d.* of Rev. J. Wilson Brown, Rector of Stowlangtoft, Suffolk, and Hon. Canon of Ely. *Educ.:* King's College, London; Gonville and Caius College, Cambridge; B.A. Math. Honours, 1858; M.B. 1859; M.D. 1870. Examiner in Medicine,

University of Cambridge, 1870-71. *Publication:* On Megrim, a contribution to the pathology of Nerve Storms. *Address:* 52 Queen Anne Street, Cavendish Square, W. (*Died 2 April 1919.*)

LIVEING, George Downing, M.A., Sc.D., F.R.S., J.P.; President of St. John's Coll. since 1911; *b.* Nayland, Suffolk, 21 Dec. 1827; *e. s.* of Edward Liveing and Catherine, *o. d.* of George Downing, Lincoln's Inn; *m.* Catherine, 2nd *d.* of Rowland Ingram, rector of Little Ellingham, Norfolk (*d.* 1888). *Educ.:* St. John's College, Cambridge (M.A., Hon. Sc.D. 1908); Fellow, 1853-60, and since 1880; 11th Wrangler, 1850; 1st in Natural Sciences Tripos, 1851; Lecturer on Natural Science, St. John's Coll., Camb. 1853; Professor of Chemistry, Staff and Royal Military Colleges, 1860; Professor of Chemistry, Cambridge, 1861 - 1908; started the first laboratory for students in Cambridge, 1852; active in organizing. *Publications:* many papers on Spectroscopy, Crystallisation, etc.; On the Transmutation of Matter, Camb. Essays, 1st ser. 1855; Chemical Equilibrium the Result of Dissipation of Energy, 1885; jointly with Mr. Warren, Report on University Colleges, 1897; jointly with Sir J. Dewar, Collected Papers on Spectroscopy, 1915. *Recreations:* field geology, gardening. *Address:* St. John's College, Cambridge.
(*Died 26 Dec. 1924.*)

LIVEING, Robert, A.M. and M.D. Cantab.; Consulting Physician to the Skin Department, Middlesex Hospital; *b.* Nayland, Suffolk, 30 Mar. 1834; *s.* of Edward Liveing, M.R.C.S.; *m.* Adelaide (*d.* 1906), *d.* of Admiral Edward Hawker; one *s.* one *d.* *Educ.:* Christ's Coll. Cambridge (Scholar). Math. Hons. 1856; Fellow of King's Coll. London; formerly Lecturer on Anatomy and Physician to Middlesex Hospital; Gulstonian Lecturer, 1873; Vice-President Alpine Club, 1869 and 1870. *Publications:* Handbook on Diseases of the Skin; Notes on the Treatment of Skin Diseases; Lectures on Leprosy. *Recreations:* travelling and gardening. *Address:* 11 Manchester Square, W. *Club:* Alpine.
(*Died 22 Feb. 1919.*)

LIVERSIDGE, Archibald, M.A. Cambridge, LL.D. Glasgow; F.R.S. 1882; Hon. F.R.S. Edin.; 1900; Associate Royal School of Mines; Emeritus Professor of Chemistry in the University of Sydney (Professor, 1873-1908), and First Dean of the Faculty of Science, 1879-1904; F.I.C., F.C.S., F.G.S., F.R.G.S.; Vice-President Chemical Society, 1910-13; Vice-President Society of Chemical Industry, 1909-12; *b.* Turnham Green, 17 Nov. 1847; *s.* of late John Liversidge, Bexley, Kent; unmarried. *Educ.:* private school and tutors; Royal School of Mines and Royal College of Chemistry, Royal Exhibitioner, 1867; Christ's College, Cambridge (Scholar in Natural Science); Instructor in Chemistry, Royal School of Naval Architecture, 1867; Univ. Demonstrator in Chemistry, Camb., 1870; Hon. Sec. of the Royal Soc. N.S.W., 1875-1889; President, 1886, 1890, and 1901; Member Phil. Society, Cambridge, Physical Society, London; Mineralogical Societies, Great Britain and France; Hon. Member Royal Society N.S.W., 1908; Royal Society Victoria, 1892; New Zealand Inst., 1890; Royal Historical Society, London, 1877; K. Leop.-Car. Akad. Halle, 1894; Corr. Mem. New York Acad. Sci. 1899; Royal Society, Tasmania, 1875; Queensland, 1886; Soc. d'Acclim. Mauritius, 1876; Edinburgh Geological Society, 1893; Trustee of the Australian Museum, 1874-1908; Member of the First Board of Technical Education, Sydney; Originated the Faculty of Science, 1879, and the School of Mines, Sydney University, 1890; the Australasian Association for the Advancement of Science, 1885; the Sydney Section of the Society of Chemical Industry, 1902; and was first Chairman, 1903-5;

a member of the original Board of three of the Technological Museum, Sydney, 1879; Hon. Sec. Australasian Association for the Advancement of Science, 1888-1909; Hon. Member, 1902; President, 1888-90; Vice-President since 1890; a Vice-President British Association, 1896. *Publications:* The Minerals of New South Wales; Report upon Technical Education and Museums; and over 100 papers, researches, etc., upon Chemistry and Mineralogy, published by the Roy. Soc. London, Chemical Soc., Roy. Soc. N.S.W. *Address:* Fieldhead, Coombe Warren, Kingston Hill, Surrey.   *T.:* Kingston 1775.   *Clubs:* Athenæum, Carlton.   (*Died 26 Sept. 1927.*)

LIVESEY, James, Senior member, Livesey, Son & Henderson. Civil and Mechanical Engineers; *s.* of Joseph Livesey, Preston; *b.* 1831. *Educ.:* Preston. Commenced his career on the Caledonian Railway; served pupilage at locomotive works of Beyer and Peacock, Manchester; Locomotive Superintendent, and Assistant Engineer on construction work, Isabel Segunda Railway in Spain, Santander to Alar del Rey, 1859; one of the earliest advocates of the use of steel, and devoted considerable time to its manufacture and general application; reported for the Buenos Ayres and Great Southern Railway on the advantages of steel rails over iron, and his recommendations were adopted 1869; laid out and arranged a new and extensive steel works for the Freedom Iron and Steel Company of Pennsylvania; the first pair of reversing engines ever made were sent to these works; designed and erected a large and novel grain elevator at Carcarana, on the River Plate, in Argentina; commissioned by the Canadian Government to visit the United States of America to make an exhaustive examination of the principal railways in that country, and to report thereon; Consulting Engineer to the Buenos Ayres Great Southern Railway and afterwards to many railways in all parts of the world; inventor of the iron and steel permanent way, largely adopted in South America, India, Egypt, etc., and of the patent switch lock, which prevents a signalman splitting a train when passing over the facing points, and which the Government ordered to be adopted on all the railways in the United Kingdom; inventor of the newspaper folding machine (fifty-six years ago) now incorporated in the printing machine by which all newspapers are folded. *Address:* 4 Whitehall Court, S.W.1.   *Clubs:* Royal Thames Yacht, Hurlingham.   (*Died 3 Feb. 1925.*)

LIVINGSTONE, Matthew, I.S.O. 1902; *s.* of John Livingstone, Hilltown, Dundee; *b.* 1837; *m.* Elizabeth Jane Stirling, *o. d.* of John Adam Ewart, late Chief Assistant Keeper of the Register of Sasines; two *d.* *Educ.:* Dundee; Edinburgh University. Appointed Chief Clerk of the General Register of Sasines for Scotland, 1871; Chief Assistant Keeper, 1891; Deputy Keeper of the Records of Scotland, 1892-1903. *Publications:* Guide to the Public Records of Scotland, 1905; Editor of The Register of the Privy Seal of Scotland, 1908. *Address:* Sidlaw, 32 Hermitage Gardens, Edinburgh. (*Died 26 April 1917.*)

LLANGATTOCK (of the Hendre), 2nd Baron (*cr.* 1892) **John Maclean Rolls,** J.P., D.L.; *e. s.* of 1st Baron Llangattock, and Georgiana, *d.* of Sir Charles Fitzroy Maclean, 7th Bart. of Morvaren; *b.* 25 Apr. 1870. *Educ.:* Eton; Christ Church, Oxford; B.A. 1893; M.A., B.C.L., 1896. Bar. Inner Temple, 1896; Captain and Hon. Major (retired) 1st Monmouthshire Volunteer Artillery; Major 2/4th Welsh R.F.A.(T.), 1915; High Sheriff, Monmouth, 1900; Mayor of Monmouth, 1906-7; owns property in Monmouthshire; has land in Southwark, Newington, Camberwell, Bermondsey. *Heir:* none. *Address:* The Hendre, Mon-

mouth.   *T.:* Monmouth 26.   *M.:* AX 57, 60, 202.   *Clubs:* Carlton, Junior Constitutional, Royal Automobile.   (*Died 1 Nov. 1916.*)

LLEWELYN, Sir John Talbot Dillwyn-, 1st Bt., *cr.* 1890; J.P., D.L.; *b.* 26 May 1836; *e. s.* of John Dillwyn-Llewelyn, F.R.S., Penllergare, Swansea, and Emma, *d.* of T. M. Talbot, Margam; *m.* 1861, Julia (*d.* 1917), *d.* of Sir M. Hicks-Beach, 8th Bt.; one *s.* two *d.* *Educ.:* Eton; Christ Church, Oxford (M.A.). M.P. (C.) Swansea, 1895-1900: late Director G.W. Railway; was Chairman Quarter Sessions of Glamorganshire, and an Alderman of the County Council. Owns about 14,900 acres. *Heir:* s. C. L. Dillwyn-Venables-Llewelyn. *Recreations:* was some years captain of the South Wales cricket eleven; and President of the Welsh Rugby Football Union. *Address:* Penllergare, Swansea. *Clubs:* Athenæum, Carlton.
    (*Died 6 July 1927.*)

LLEWELYN, Sir Leonard (Wilkinson), K.B.E., *cr.* 1917: late Controller of Non-Ferrous Metals, Ministry of Munitions; *b.* 11 June 1874; *s.* of late Llewelyn Llewelyn, J.P., High Sheriff, Monmouthshire, 1913, and *d.* of Geo. Wilkinson; *m.* 1st, 1899, Edith (*d.* 1913), *d.* of late Edward Jones, J.P., D.L., of Snatchwood Park, Pontypool, Monmouthshire; one *s.* three *d.*; 2nd, 1922, Mrs Elsie Louise Jones, Glen Usk, Caerleon, Newport, Mon. *Educ.:* Monmouth Grammar School; Cheltenham; Heidelberg; Officer of the Legion d'Honneur; Officer of the Order of Leopold; Officer of the Order St. Stanislav; Silver Medal of the Royal Humane Society; High Sheriff Monmouthshire, 1920; J.P. Cos. Glamorgan and Monmouth; Director of Duffryn Aberdare Colliery Co. Ltd., Cambrian Collieries, Glamorgan Collieries, Fernhill Collieries, John Lysaght, Ltd., Sankey and Sons, Ltd., Harwood Bros. Ltd., Phœnix Patent Fuel, Ltd., Arrow Fuel, Ltd., Consolidated Cambrian Collieries, D. Davis and Sons, Welsh Navigation Colliery Co., Managing Director of North's Navigation Collieries (1889) Ltd., Celtic Collieries Ltd., Crown Preserved Coal Co. Ltd., Frenchwood Mill Co. Ltd., and other large steel and colliery undertakings; contested North Monmouthshire General Election, 1918. *Recreations:* polo, horse-breeding, golf. *Address:* Malpas Court, Newport, Mon.; Glen Usk, Caerleon, Mon. *T.:* Newport 2887. *Clubs:* Junior Carlton, Bath, Sports.   (*Died 13 June 1924.*)

LLEWELYN, Sir Robert Baxter, K.C.M.G., *cr.* 1898; *s.* of John Llewelyn; *b.* 1845; *m.* 1873, Theodora Louisa, *d.* of Charles Harvey of Campbeltown; two *d.* Extra Clerk Colonial Office, London, 1868; Registrar Colonial Secretary's Office, Jamaica, 1869; Private Secretary to Sir J. P. Grant, 1873; Clerk of Privy Council, Jamaica, 1877; Commissioner for Turks Islands, 1878; Administrator of Tobago, 1885; of St. Vincent, 1888; of St. Lucia, 1889; of the Colony of the Gambia, 1891-1900; Governor of Windward Islands, 1900-6. *Club:* Junior Carlton.   (*Died 19 Feb. 1919.*)

LLOYD, Charles Harford, M.A., Mus.D. Oxon., Hon. R.A.M., and F.R.C.O.; Organist, Choirmaster, and Composer at H.M. Chapel Royal, St. James's Palace, 1917; *b.* at Thornbury, Gloucestershire, 1849; *y. s.* of late Edmund Lloyd, Solicitor. *Educ.:* Thornbury Grammar School, Rossall School; Magdalen Hall (Hertford College), Oxford; Open Classical Scholarship; 2nd Class Mod.; 2nd Class Final Theol. Sch. First President of Oxford University Musical Club; Organist of Gloucester Cathedral, 1876; Organist of Christ Church Cathedral, Oxford, 1882; Precentor and Musical Instructor, Eton College, 1892-1914; Conducted, while at Gloucester, the Three-Choir Festivals of 1877 and 1880; at Oxford, the Choral and Orchestral Societies; at Eton, the

Windsor and Eton Choral and Orchestral Societies; has at various times been Examiner in Music in the Univs. of Oxford, Cambridge, London, and Durham; Member of Council Royal College of Music and Past President of Royal College of Organists; Grand Organist of English Freemasons, 1917. *Musical publications:* Hero and Leander, Song of Balder, Andromeda, Longbeards' Saga, Song of Judgment, Alcestis, etc. Anthems, Services, Organ Pieces, Trio for Pianoforte, Clarionet, and Bassoon, Characteristic Pieces for Violin and Pianoforte, etc. *Recreations:* figure skating, cycling, boating, golf. *Address:* Hillcrest, Slough. *T.:* Slough 182. *Club:* United University. *(Died 16 Oct. 1919.)*

LLOYD, Edward, singer; *b.* 7 March 1845; *s.* of Richard Lloyd (*d.* 1850), vicar choralist in Westminster Abbey, and Miss Hopkins; *m.* 1921, Mrs Clement Walter Hann. *Educ.:* Grey's School, Southwark; Choir, Westminster Abbey, 1852-60; tenor, St. Andrew's, Well St., and Chapel Royal; first appeared Gloucester Musical Festival, 1871; has sung at all principal festivals. *Recreations:* golfing, walking, tennis. *(Died 31 Mar. 1927.)*

LLOYD, Lieut.-Col. Fitzwarren, C.I.E., 1914; V.D.; late Commandant, Assam Valley Light Horse; *b.* 16 August 1859; *s.* of late Col. Lloyd, Aston Hall, Oswestry; *m.* 1891; no *c.* *Educ.:* Eton. *Address:* Grindlay & Co., 54 Parliament Street, S.W.1. *(Died 15 Feb. 1923.)*

LLOYD, Lt.-Gen. Sir Francis; G.C.V.O., *cr.* 1918; K.C.B., 1911; C.V.O. 1909; C.B. 1900; D.S.O. 1898; a Commissioner Duke of York's Royal Military School since 1920; Col. Royal Welch Fusiliers, 1915; Hon. Col. 13 County of London, Kensington Batt., 1920; retired pay, 1920; *b.* 12 Aug. 1853; *s.* of Col. R. T. Lloyd and The Lady Frances, *d.* of Thomas Robert, 10th Earl of Kinnoull; *m.* Mary, *d.* of George Gunnis Leckie, Stirling, 1881. *Educ.:* Harrow. Joined 33rd Duke of Wellington Regt., 1874; transferred Grenadier Guards, 1874; Capt. 1885; Major, 1892; Lieut.-Col. 1898; Col. 1902; Brig.-Gen. 1904; Maj.-Gen. 1909; Lieut.-Gen. 1917; Suakin Expedition as Signalling Officer Guards Brigade, 1885; battle of Hasheen (medal with c asp, Khedive's star, despatches); Nile Expedition, 1898; battle of Khartoum (despatches, D.S.O., British medal, Khedive's medal); South Africa, 1900-2 (severely wounded, despatches, C.B., South African medals, Queen's and King's); commanded 2nd Batt. Grenadier Guards, and subsequently 1st Batt. Grenadier Guards; Commanded 1st Guards Brigade, 1904-1908; Welsh Division T.F., 1909-13; London District, 1913-19; Danish Order of Dannebrog, II. Class; Grand Cross St. Sava (Serbia); Grand Officer Crown of Belgium; White Eagle, Russia; is a Knight of Grace of St. John of Jerusalem, 1916; one of H.M. Lieutenants for the City of London; J.P., D.L. Salop; J.P. Essex; Food Commissioner for London and Home Counties, 1919-20. *Address:* Aston Hall, Oswestry, Shropshire; *T.A.:* Queenshead; Rolls Park, Chigwell, Essex; *T.:* Chigwell 7. *Club:* Carlton. *(Died 26 Feb. 1926.)*

LLOYD, His Hon. Sir Horatio, Kt., *cr.* 1890; Recorder of Chester since 1866; Chairman of Quarter Sessions, Cheshire, since 1883; *b.* 29 Sep. 1829; *s.* of late Edward Watson Lloyd, Prothonotary and Clerk of the Crown; *m.* 1856, Harriette (*d.* 1902), *d.* of late Honoratus Leigh Rigby, Hawarden, Flintshire; three *s.* *Educ.:* Rossall, and privately. Bar, 1852; Counsel to H.M.'s Mint and Post Office, and revising barrister; Judge of County Courts, Chester, 1874-1906; Royal Commissioner to inquire into Welsh Sunday Closing Acts, 1889. *Publications:* The Law of Quarter Sessions, 1875; Chitty's Statutes, 1865-80; Papers on archæological subjects. *Recreations:* aquatics, watercolour painting. *Address:* 8 Stanley Place, Chester. *Club:* Royal Societies. *(Died 24 Dec. 1920.)*

LLOYD, Howard, J.P., Worcestershire; was Director of Lloyd's Bank, Ltd.; *b.* 16 Aug. 1837, 3rd *s.* of Isaac Lloyd; *m.* Marabella, 3rd *d.* of John Eliot Howard, F.R.S.; seven *s.* *Educ.:* private schools. For 31 years General Manager of Lloyd's Bank, Limited. *Address:* Grafton Manor, Bromsgrove. *T.:* Bromsgrove. *T.:* 52 Bromsgrove. *Clubs:* New Oxford and Cambridge; Union, Conservative, Birmingham. *(Died 17 Sept. 1920.)*

LLOYD, Rev. Iorwerth Grey, M.A., F.S.A.; Prebendary or Canon of Llandewi Aberarth in St. David's Cathedral; a Surrogate for Diocese of St. David's; *e. s.* of late Rev. Henry Robert Lloyd, M.A., Rector of Cliffe-at-Hoo, Kent, and Harriett, 4th *d.* of Hon. and Rt. Rev. Edward Grey, D.D., sometime Bishop of Hereford and Prebendary of Westminster Abbey; *b.* 22 Oct. 1844; *m.* 1871, Nina, 3rd *d.* of late Charles Eastland de Michele, sometime H.B.M. Consul at Petrograd; three *s.* three *d.* *Educ.:* Durham School; Exeter College, Oxford (3rd class in Law and Modern History, 1867). Curate of Ashford, Kent, 1868-69; Cliffe-at-Hoo, 1869-71; Coulsdon, 1871-79; Chaplain to 3rd Marquis of Ailesbury, 1878-86; Vicar of Hersham, Surrey, 1879-83; Wiston, Pembrokeshire, 1883-87; Clarbeston, 1885-87; Rector of Bosherston, Pembrokeshire, 1887-1903; Rural Dean of Castlemartin, 1898-1903; formerly a Member of Croydon (Surrey) Board of Guardians, and afterwards Chairman of Walten-on-Thames School Board; Vicar of Slebech with Minwear and Newton North, Pembrokeshire, 1908-19; Rural Dean of Dungleddy to 1919; Hon. Sec. to Building Committee of St. David's Diocesan Board, 1911-18. *Publications:* Parish Church of Cliffe in the Archæologia Cantiana, vol. xi.; Preparation for Confirmation, a paper read before the Clergy of the Rural Deanery of Castlemartin in the St. David's Diocesan Gazette, No. 20. *Recreations:* fly-fishing. *Address:* 5 Staverton Road, Oxford. *(Died 24 Dec. 1920.)*

LLOYD, Colonel Sir Morgan George, K.C.B. *cr.* 1911; C.B. 1897; commanding 3rd Battalion the Royal Irish Regiment, 1885-1903; now Hon. Colonel; *b.* 1843; *s.* of Owen Lloyd of Lisadurn, Co. Roscommon, J.P. and D.L., and Harriet, *d.* of Arthur French of French Park, Co. Roscommon, and *sister* of Lord de Freyne and Right Hon. Fitzstephen French, M.P.; *m.* 1870, Emily Olivia (*d.* 1912), 2nd *d.* of Thomas Bell, Brookhill, Co. Wexford, Ireland; óne *s.* two *d.* *Educ.:* private school; Royal Military Coll. Sandhurst. Late King's Dragoon Guards. Decorated for length of service in the Militia. *Recreations:* shooting, golf, etc. *Address:* Raheen, Tenby, S. Wales. *(Died 25 June 1917.)*

LLOYD, Colonel Robert Oliver, C.B. 1919; J.P. and D.L., Pembrokeshire; Chairman Pembrokeshire Territorial Force Association, 1909-20; *b.* 20 March 1849; 4th *s.* of Rev. Canon Charles Lloyd, late Rector of Chalfont, St Giles, Bucks; *m.* 1877, Mary Isabella (*d.* 1912), *d.* of Major-General D. G. Pollard of Castle Pollard, Westmeath; one *s.* one *d.* *Educ.:* Marlborough College; Royal Military Academy, Woolwich. Joined Royal Engineers, 1870; served in India, 1872-1901; on active service in Burmah, 1885-88 (severely wounded, despatches, medal with 2 clasps); promoted Colonel in the Army, 1899; Chief Engineer Bombay Army, Poona, 1899-1901; retired, 1902. *Recreations:* racing, polo, cricket, shooting. *Address:* 16 Forest Road, Branksome Park, Bournemouth, W. *Club:* Pembroke County, Haverfordwest. *(Died 20 July 1921.)*

LLOYD, Colonel Thomas, C.B. *cr.* 1897; J.P. Cardiganshire and Pembrokeshire; *b.* 12 June 1853; *e. s.* of late Edmund Lloyd, and *g. s.* of late Thomas Lloyd of Coedmore, Lord-Lieut. of Cardiganshire. *Educ.:* Clifton Coll.; Shrews-

bury School. Commanded Cardigan Royal Gar. Artillery Militia, 1887-1904. *Recreations:* riding, rowing, fishing. *Club:* United Service.
(Died 12 June 1916.)

LLOYD, Maj.-Gen. Thomas Francis, J.P., D.L., Co. Limerick; retired; *b.* 21 April 1839; *s.* of Thomas Lloyd of Beechmount, J.P. for counties of Clare, Limerick, and Tipperary, D.L. for Co. Limerick; *g.s.* of Thomas Lloyd of Beechmount, D.L., M.P. for Co. Limerick; *m.* 1870, Mary Henrietta, *d.* of Christian Allhusen of Stoke Court, D.L. Bucks. *Educ.:* Cheltenham Coll. Ensign, 98th Regt. (Prince of Wales's), 1855; served in N.W. Frontier campaign, 1860; action of Poluteen, forcing the Burrarah Pass, and taking of the stronghold Makin (medal and clasp); commanded the 98th P. of W. Regt. for 5½ years; commanded the 2nd Regimental District 5 years, and was Assist. Adjt. and Q.M.G. Cork District for 4 years, when he was promoted Maj.-Gen.; High Sheriff, 1894; Colonel-in-Chief, North Staffordshire Regiment, 1911. Owns 1500 acres. *Address:* Beechmount, Rathkeale, Co. Limerick. *Club:* United Service.
(Died 8 Nov. 1921.)

LLOYD, William Harris, M.D.; Hon. Surgeon to the King since 1901; *b.* 1836; *s.* of William Lloyd of Waterford, and of Kyle, Templemore, Co. Tipperary; *m.* 1870, Phœbe, *d.* of late Lt.-Gen. Vincent; two *d.* Served China, 1857-58; Inspector-General of Hospitals and Fleets, 1890; retired, 1896. *Address:* 4 Alfred Place West, S. Kensington, S.W. *Club:* United Service. *(Died 2 April 1923.)*

LLOYD-BAKER, Granville Edwin Lloyd, J.P., D.L., Gloucester; County Councillor, 1889-1910; *b.* 1841; *e. s.* of T. B. Lloyd Baker of Hardwicke Court, and Mary, *o. c.* of Nicholas Lewis Fenwick of Besford Court, Worcestershire; *m.* 1868, Catherine (*d.* 1890), 4th *d.* of Hon. Arthur Lascelles of Norley, Cheshire; one *s.* five *d. Educ.:* Eton; Christ Church, Oxford. High Sheriff, Gloucestershire, 1898; served in various committees in the County Council and as Magistrate; Chairman of the Reformatory Committee, and of the Visiting Justices of the Prison. *Publications:* Dairying in Denmark; The Metayer System in Italy; French Agricultural Schools; Old Age Pensions, an Ounce of Fact; Large and Small Holdings in Denmark. *Recreation:* travelling. *Address:* Hardwicke Court, near Gloucester. *T.A.:* Lloyd-Baker, Hardwicke. *T.:* Hardwicke District 2. *Club:* Carlton. *(Died 3 Oct. 1924.)*

LLOYD OWEN, David Charles, M.D. (Birm.) 1902; M.B., B.Ch. 1901; F.R.C.S.I. 1880; M.R.C.S. (Eng.) 1865; J.P. Warwickshire Knight of Grace, Order of St. John of Jerusalem; *s.* of Rev. D. Owen, originally of Darowen, Mont. *Educ.:* Birmingham; Paris. Past Acting Honorary and now Consulting Honorary Surgeon to the Birmingham and Midland Eye Hospital, Children's Hospital, and General Hospital; Vice-Chairman of the British Ophthalmic Hospital at Jerusalem; Past Vice-President of the Ophthalmological Society of Great Britain; one of the founders and First President of the Midland Ophthalmological Society; Past President of the Ophthalmological Section of the British Medical Association; Past President of the Midland Medical Society. *Publications:* numerous books and papers on subjects connected with his speciality, including Ophthalmic Therapeutics, Pain in Eye Diseases, Hereditary Nystagmus, etc.; translations of Giraud Teulon ou Vision, etc. *Recreations:* archæology and genealogy. *Address:* Bron-y-Graig, Harlech, N. Wales.
(Died 25 Dec. 1925.)

LOANE, Miss M.; *d.* of late Captain J. Loane, R.N. *Publications:* The Queen's Poor; The Next Street but One; From Their Point

of View; An Englishman's Castle; Neighbours and Friends; The Common Growth; Shipmates. *Address:* 22 Elmdale Road, Clifton.
(Died 23 Feb. 1922.)

LOBB, John, F.R.G.S., F.R.Hist.Soc.; Senior Bridgemaster of the City of London; Chairman of the Law and City Courts Committee of the Corporation of the City of London for 1905; on the Editorial Staff of the Sun Evening Newspaper, 1891-1903; *b.* Tower Hamlets, 7 August 1840; *e. s.* of late John and Louisa Lobb; *m.* 1st, 1868, Ann, *o. d.* of Rev. Samuel Bruton of Kingswood, Gloucester; two *s.* three *d.*; 2nd, 1884, 2nd *d.* of Henry Moon of Clayhidon, near Wellington, Devon; three *s.* one *d. Educ.:* privately. Called to the Primitive Methodist ministry, 1862; resigned for commercial sphere; editor and proprietor of the Kingsland Monthly Messenger, 1871-73; became manager of the Christian Age, 1872-90; chief proprietor, 1880-90; Chairman of the Epping Forest Committee, 1899; member of the Court of Common Council for the Ward of Farringdon Without, 1887-1905; for 15 years member of the London School Board; 9 years Chairman of the Stores Committee; Chairman of the Finance Committee; Guardian of the City of London Union for 18 years; Chairman of the Lunatic Visiting Committee for 5 years; member of the Metropolitan Asylum Board for 3 years; Chairman of the Freemen's Orphan School for 2 years; 12 years Governor of Lady Holles's Trust, and St. Bride's Foundation; is a Governor of the Haberdashers' Schools and Sir John Cass's Institute; Member of the Institute of Journalists since 1886; during 1905-13 travelled 80,000 miles, lectured to 220,000 persons on Spiritualism; visited Mexico and the U.S.A., 1909. *Publications:* Story of the Life of Rev. Josiah Henson; The Life and Times of Frederick Douglass, 1886; Life of the Rev. T. de Witt Talmage, D.D., 1879; Talks with the Dead, 1906; The Busy Life after Death, 1908; The Banished Christ and the Bible; A Sketch of the Life of Sarah Flower Adams, 1910; Startling Revelations from the Heaven Worlds. 1920. *Address:* 14 Emmanuel Road, Balham, S.W.12. *(Died July 1921.)*

LOCH, Sir Charles Stewart, Kt., *cr.* 1915; B.A.; Tooke Professor of Economic Science and Statistics, King's College, London, 1904-8; Secretary to the Council of the London Charity Organisation Society, 1875-1914; resigned 1914; *b.* Bengal, 4 Sept. 1849; 5th *s.* of late George Loch, Indian Civil Service, judge, High Court, Calcutta (*d.* 1883), and Louisa Gordon, his first wife; *m.* Sophia E., *e. d.* of late Edward Peters, I.C.S., 1876; one *s.* one *d. Educ.:* Trin. Coll., Glenalmond; Balliol Coll., Oxford. Clerk, Royal College of Surgeons, 1873-75; member Royal Commission on Aged Poor, 1893-95; Dunkin Trust Lecturer, Manchester Coll., Oxford, 1896 and 1902; Guy medal, Royal Statistical Society, 1909; a Member of the Institut International de Statistique; Member of the Royal Commission on the Care and Control of the Feeble-minded; Member of the Royal Commission on the Poor Laws; Hon. D.C.L., Oxford; Hon. LL.D., St. Andrews. *Publications:* Charity and Charities in Encyclopædia Britannica, 1902; Charity Organisation; Old Age Pensions and Pauperism; Charity and Social Life, 1910. *Poems:* Things Within, 1922; articles on charitable, social, and economic subjects, published in Aspects of the Social Problem, 1895, Methods of Social Advance, 1904, the Statistical and Economic Journals, and elsewhere. *Address:* Little Bookham, Surrey.
(Died 23 Jan. 1923.)

LOCHHEAD, John, R.B.A.; *b.* Glasgow; father a publisher in that city; *m.* 1893, *y. d.* of late Sir Daniel Macnee, P.R.S.A.; one *s. Educ.:* Glasgow. Started studies in Edinburgh at Life

School there; afterwards travelled in France, Holland, Belgium, Switzerland, etc., for further study; exhibitor at New Salon, Munich, Budapest, Berlin, and America; represented in the National Gallery, Berlin, and Fine Art Society, Prague; also exhibitor at all the important picture exhibitions in Britain. *Chief Pictures:* Decking the May Queen; Summertime in the Fen Country; The Evening Hour; All Things Bright and Beautiful; Country Content; By the Ferry, Summertime; A Garden of Sunbeams; *Publications:* A Riverside Idyll; illustrated Quiet Folk, by R. Menzies Fergusson, D.D. *Recreations:* travelling, golf, and walking; also viewing and collecting various phases of art, and art objects. *Addresses:* Abinger, West Kilbride, Ayrshire; Studio, 113 St. Vincent Street, Glasgow. *Club:* Glasgow Art.

(*Died June 1921.*)

LOCHHEAD, William, B.A., M.Sc., F.A.A.S.; Prof. of Biology, Macdonald College-McGill University, since 1906; President Quebec Society Protection of Plants since 1908; President Quebec Pomological Society, 1916-17; President Ont. Entomological Society, 1902-4; Editor, Journal of Agriculture for Quebec, 1908-1920; Fellow American Association Advancement of Science; *b.* 3 April 1864; *s.* of W. Lochhead and Helen Campbell; *m.* 1889, Lilias Grant; one *s. Educ.:* McGill and Cornell Universities. Scholarships every year of University course, 1881-85; Fellowship in Cornell University, 1886-87. Attended Cornell (post graduate), 1886-87, 1894-95, and several summer sessions; Teacher of Science in Perth, Galt, and London Collegiate Institutes, 1887-94, 1895-98; Professor of Biology, Ontario Agricultural College, 1898-1906. *Publications:* Bulletins-The San Jose and Allied Scales; The Hessian Fly; The Pea Weevil; Nature Studies; Spray-Calendar; Heredity and Genetics; Class Book of Economic Entomology. *Recreations:* tennis and bowling. *Address:* Macdonald College, Quebec, Canada. *T.:* 38. *Clubs:* University, Montreal; Gamma Alpha Society, Cornell.

(*Died 26 Mar. 1927.*)

LOCK, His Honour Judge B. Fossett, County Court Judge, Circuit 16 (East Riding of Yorkshire and parts of North and West Ridings), since 1913; *b.* 19 Dec. 1847; 3rd *s.* of Henry Lock of Dorchester, Solicitor; *m.* 1879, Jane Elizabeth (*d.* 1920), 2nd *d.* of Rev. J. P. Hammond, Vicar of Sopley, Hants; one *s.* one *d. Educ.:* Dorchester Grammar School; Eton (King's Scholar); King's Coll., Camb. (Scholar). B.A. 1871 (aegrotat, Classical Tripos); M.A. 1877. Called to Bar (Lincoln's Inn), 1877, joined the Chancery Bar, Western Circuit and Dorset Sessions; Hon. Secretary of Positivist Society, 1880-86; held Commission in the Royal Naval Artillery Volunteers, 1890-92; Hon. Examiner to the Council of Legal Education, 1896-1906; Chairman of Committee of the Social and Political Education League, 1887-1913; is Chairman of the central Legal Aid Society; Member of Admiralty Volunteer Committee; a Vice-President of the Dorset Men in London; a member of the Council of the Selden Society; and of the Yorkshire Archæological Society. *Publications:* Joint Editor of the Annual Practice, 1910-11; Memoir of Professor Maitland, in the Dictionary of National Biography; sundry articles and pamphlets on the Defence of Poor Prisoners and Legal Aid for the Poor, etc. *Recreations:* sailing, rowing, walking, sketching. *Address:* The Toft, Bridlington, Yorkshire; *T.A.:* Bridlington. *T.:* 99 Bridlington; 11 New Square, Lincoln's Inn, W.C. *Clubs:* Royal Societies; Royal Cruising; Royal Yorkshire Yacht.

(*Died 11 Aug. 1922.*)

LOCK. Rev. John Bascombe, M.A., Fellow and Bursar of Gonville and Caius College, Camb.; *b.* Dorchester, 18 March 1849; *s.* of late

Joseph Lock, Dorchester; *m.* 1873, Emily, 3rd *d.* of late Edwin Baily, Cirencester; three *s.* one *d. Educ.:* Grammar School, Bristol; Caius Col., Camb. (scholar 1868). 3rd wrangler Mathematical Tripos, 1872; moderator and examiner in Mathematical Tripos, 1876-77. Curate of Horningsea, 1872; assistant master at Eton, 1872-84; Lecturer on Mathematics and assistant tutor at Caius College, 1884-89; member of Financial Board, of the Press, University Buildings, Syndicates, and of the Building Committee in the University of Cambridge; late Chairman of Addenbrooke Hospital. *Publications:* many Mathematical Books for schools and colleges; chiefly Arithmetic, Trigonometry, and Mechanics. *Recreations:* motoring, formerly rowing, bicycling, lawntennis, fives, skating. *Address:* Herschel House, Cambridge. *T.:* Cambridge 150. *M.:* CE 2629.

(*Died 8 Sept. 1921.*)

LOCKHART, Sir Simon Macdonald, 5th Bt.; *cr.* 1806; M.V.O.; retired; *b.* 18 Mar. 1849; *S. b.* 1870; *m.* Hilda Maud, 2nd *d.* of Col. Macdonald Moreton, late Coldstream Guards, 1898. *Educ.:* Eton. Served Egyptian Campaign, 1882; Colonel 1st Life Guards, 1892-98; Brig.-Gen. on Staff commanding cavalry at Curragh, 1900-1901. *Heir:* none. *Address:* The Lee, Lanark, N.B. *Clubs:* Carlton, United Service; Royal Yacht Squadron, Cowes. (*Died 25 Mar. 1919.*)

LOCKYER, Sir (Joseph) Norman, K.C.B., *cr.* 1897; F.R.S.; Hon. LL.D. Glasgow, Aberdeen, and Edinburgh; Hon. Sc.D. Cambridge and Sheffield; Hon. D.Sc. Oxford; Director of Hill Observatory, Salcombe Regis, Sidmouth; late Director of Solar Physics Observatory, South Kensington, 1885-1913; *b.* Rugby, 17 May 1836; *s.* of Joseph Hooley Lockyer and Anne, *d.* of Edward Norman, Cosford; *m.* 1st, 1858, Winifred (*d.* 1879), *y. d.* of William James, Trebinshon, near Abergavenny; 2nd, 1903, Thomazine Mary, *y. d.* of late Samuel W. Browne of Bridgwater and Clifton, and widow of Bernard E. Brodhurst, F.R.C.S.; four *s.* two *d. Educ.:* private schools; Continent. Appointed to War Office, 1857; editor of Army Regulations, 1865; Secretary, Duke of Devonshire's Royal Com. on Science, 1870; transferred to Science and Art Department, 1875; elected F.R.S. 1869; Pres. of British Assoc. for Advancement of Science, 1903-4; Rede Lecturer at Cambridge, 1871; correspondent of Institute of France, 1875 (Janssen Medal); chief of English Govt. Eclipse Expeditions, 1870, 1871, 1882, 1886, 1896, 1898, 1900, 1905; observed the eclipse of 1878 in the United States. *Publications:* Elementary Lessons in Astronomy, 1870; contributions to Solar Physics, 1873; Spectroscope and its Applications, 1873; Primer of Astronomy, 1874; Studies in Spectrum Analyses, 1878; Star-gazing Past and Present, 1878; Chemistry of the Sun, 1887; Movements of the Earth, 1887; Meteoritic Hypothesis, 1890; Dawn of Astronomy, 1894; Rules of Golf, 1896; The Sun's Place in Nature, 1897; Recent and Coming Eclipses, 1897; Inorganic Evolution, 1900; Stonehenge, and other British Stone Monuments Astronomically Considered; Education and National Progress, 1906-1907; Surveying for Archæologists, 1909; Tennyson as a Student and Poet of Nature, 1910, etc. *Recreations:* tennis, golf (St. George's Club). *Address:* 16 Penywern Road, S.W.5; Salcombe Regis, Sidmouth. *T.A.:* Phusis, London; Lockyer, Sidmouth. *T.:* Western 5383. *Club:* Athenæum.

(*Died 16 Aug. 1920.*)

LODER, Sir Edmund Giles, 2nd Bt.; *cr.* 1887; J.P.; *b.* 7 Aug. 1849; *e. s.* of 1st Bt. and Maria Georgiana, 4th *d.* of Hans Busk; *S.* father 1888; *m.* Marion, *d.* of W. E. Hubbard, Leonardslee, Horsham, 1876; one *d. Educ.:* Eton; Trin. Coll. Camb. (M.A.). High Sheriff, Northampton, 1888. *Heir: g.s.* Giles Rolls [*b.*

673

10 Nov. 1914]. *Address*: Leonardslee, Horsham, Sussex. *Club*: Athenæum.(*Died 14 April 1920.*)

LODGE, Henry Cabot; *b.* Boston, U.S.A., 12 May 1850; *m.* Anna Cabot Davis, 1872; two *s.* one *d.* *Educ.*: Harvard (Ph.D.); Harvard Law School (LL.B.). Suffolk Bar, 1876; Member of Congress (Republican), 1887-93; Senator since 1893; served two terms Member of House of Representatives, Mass.; elected to 50th, 51st, 52nd, and 53rd Congresses; LL.D. Harvard; Williams, 1893; Yale, 1902; Clarke, 1902; Amherst College, 1914; Union College, 1915; Princeton, 1916; Dartmouth, 1917; Brown, 1918; President Massachusetts Historical Society; Fellow Royal Historical Society, 1917. *Publications*: Essays on Anglo-Saxon Land Law; Life and Letters of George Cabot, 1877; A Short History of the English Colonies in America, 1881; Daniel Webster, 1883, Alexander Hamilton, 1882, George Washington, 1889 (in American Statesmen series); Studies in History, 1886; Speeches, 1892; Hero Tales from American History (with Theodore Roosevelt), 1895; History of Boston, 1891; Historical and Political Essays, 1892; Certain Accepted Heroes, 1897; The Story of the American Revolution, 1898; Ballads and Lyrics; Story of the Spanish War, 1899; A Fighting Frigate and other Essays and Addresses, 1902; One Hundred Years of Peace, 1913; The Democracy of the Constitution; War Addresses, 1917, etc. *Address*: Nahant, Mass., U.S.A.
(*Died 9 Nov. 1924.*)

LOEB, Prof. Jacques, Member Rockefeller Institute for Medical Research, New York, since 1910; *b* 7 April 1859; *m.* 1890, Anne L. Leonard; two *s.* one *d.* *Educ.*: Ascanisches Gymnasium, Berlin; Universities of Berlin, Munich, Strassburg (M.D. 1884); Hon. D.Sc. Cantab. 1909; Hon. M.D. Geneva, 1909; Hon. Ph.D. Leipzig, 1909; Hon. D.Sc. Yale, 1923; Doctor (Hon.) Strasbourg, 1923; Assistant in Physiology, Univ. of Wurzburg, 1886-88; Strassburg, 1888-90; Stazione zoologica, Naples, 1890-91; Associate in Biology, Bryn Mawr Coll., Bryn Mawr, Pa., 1891-92; Assistant Professor of Physiology, Univ. of Chicago, 1892-95; Associate Professor, 1895-1900; Professor, 1900-3; Professor of Physiology, Univ. of California, 1903-10; Member, Nat. Acad. of Sciences; American Philosophical Society; American Physiological Society; American Society Biol. Chemists; Corr. mem., Académie des Sciences de l'Institut de France; Academy of Sciences, Cracow; Med. Gesellsch., Budapest; Bataafsch Genootschap der Proefondervindelijke Wijsbegeerte te Rotterdam; Foreign Fellow Linnean Society, London; For. Mem. Acad. Royale des Sciences de Belgique, Brussels; Hon. mem. Royal Institution of Gt. Britain; Société de Biologie, Paris; Acad. Royale de Med. de Belgique, Brussels; Soc. Impériale des Amis des Sciences Naturelles, Moscow; Cambridge Philosophical Society, England; Med. Geselsich. Wien; Assoc. mem. Société Royale des Sciences Medicales et Naturelles, Brussels; Société Belge de Biologie; Fellow Am. Acad. Arts and Sciences. *Publications*: Animal Heliotropism and its Identity with the Heliotropism of Plants, 1890; Physiological Morphology, Part I. Heteromorphosis, 1891; Physiological Morphology, Part II. Organisation and Growth, 1892; Comparative Physiology of the Brain and Comparative Psychology, 1900; Studies in General Physiology, 1905; The Dynamics of Living Matter, 1906; Investigations on Artificial Parthenogenesis, 1906; The Mechanistic Conception of Life, 1912; Artificial Parthenogenesis and Fertilisation, 1913; The Organism as a Whole, 1916; Forced Movements, Tropisms, and Animal Conduct, 1918; Proteins and the Theory of Colloidal Behavior, 1922. *Address*: Rockefeller Institute, 66th Street and Avenue A, New York. (*Died 12 Feb. 1924.*)

LOEWENSTEIN-WERTHEIM, H.S.H. Princess, Lady Anne Savile; *d.* of 4th Earl of Mexborough; *b.* 1866; *m.* 1897, H.S.H. Prince Ludwig Karl zu Loewenstein-Wertheim-Frendenberg (*d.* 1899). *Address*: 8 Upper Belgrave Street, S.W.
(*Died 31 Aug. 1927.*)

LOFTIE, Rev. Arthur Gershom, Rector of Wetheral and Warwick, Cumberland, 1904-1916; Hon. Canon of Carlisle Cathedral, 1908; Chaplain to the High Sheriff of Cumberland, 1912; *b.* Nice, 22 Oct. 1843; *s.* of John Henry Loftie, J.P., Co. Down and Co. Armagh, Ireland, of Tanderagee, Co. Armagh; *m.* 1874, Jamesina Roberta, *y. d.* of James Robert Grant of the Hill, Cumberland; no *c.* *Educ.*: Portarlington School; Trinity College, Dublin. Ordained to Curacy of Arthuret, Cumberland, 1867; Vicar of Beckermet, St. Bridget's, W. Cumberland, 1871; Collated to Rectory of Great Salkeld, Cumberland, near Penrith, 1894; a Member of the Cumberland and Westmoreland Archæological and Antiquarian Society; Hon. Chaplain to the Bishop of Carlisle, 1920. *Publications*: Calder Abbey, its Ruins and History, 2nd edition, 1892; Great Salkeld, its Rectors and History, 1900; editor of The Rural Deanery of Gosforth; Diocese of Carlisle, its Churches and Endowments, 1889; compiled a Catechism for Children, 1872; fourth edition translated into Hindustani, 1881. *Recreations*: archæology, architecture, and gardening. *Address*: Undermount, Rydal, near Ambleside, Westmorland.
(*Died Oct. 1922.*)

LOGAN, Brig. - Gen. David Finlay Hosken, C.B. 1917; C.M.G. 1916; R.A.; *b.* 28 Dec. 1862; *s.* of late David Logan, Chief Engineer, South Indian Railway, and late Jean Hosken; *m.* Ethel Mayzod Evans; one *d.* *Educ.*: private school, Reading; R.M. Acad., Woolwich. 1st Commission, 1888; Adjutant, 1st Glamorgan V.A.; Adjutant, Cape Garrison Artillery; served South Africa (King's and Queen's medals); European War, 1914-17 (despatches, C.B., C.M.G.); Humane Society's bronze medal; Brig.-Gen. 1916. *Recreations*: golf, fishing. *Address*: c/o Cox & Co., 16 Charing Cross, S.W.1. *Club*: United Service.
(*Died 17 June 1923.*)

LOGAN, John William, A.M.I.C.E.; J.P.; M.P. (L.) Harborough Div. Leicestershire, 1891-1904, and 1910-16; *b.* Newport, Mon. 1845; *s.* of John Logan, The Maindee, Newport Mon. *Educ.*: Gloucester Collegiate School. *Recreations*: hunting, shooting, fishing. *Address*: East Langton Grange, Market Harborough. *Clubs*: Reform, Cobden. (*Died 25 May 1925.*)

LOGUE, His Eminence Cardinal Michael, R.C. Archbishop of Armagh since 1888; Roman Catholic Primate of all Ireland since 1887; *b.* Co. Donegal, 1840; formerly Bishop of Raphoe (cons. 1879) and coadjutor to the late Primate, 1887; created Cardinal, 1893. *Address*: Ara Cœli, Armagh.
(*Died 19 Nov. 1924.*)

LOHR, Hervey, A.R.A.M., composer, pianist, and conductor; *b.* Leicester, 13 June 1856; *s.* of George Augustus Löhr. *Educ.*: privately; Royal Academy of Music, under Sir Arthur Sullivan, W. H. Holmes, and Dr. Prout (Lucas Medal (twice), Potter Exhibition, Santley Prize for accompaniment); is an Associate of Philharmonic Society, Member Royal Society of Musicians. Compositions: five symphonies; a grand opera (Kenilworth); oratorio (The Queen of Sheba); trio for piano and strings; quartet and quintet for piano and strings; two string quartets; pianoforte music, songs, part-songs, Church music, etc. (*Died 16 Jan. 1927.*)

LOMAS, Surg.-Capt. Ernest Courtney, C.B. 1916; D.S.O. 1901; M.B.; F.R.C.S. (Ed.); R.N.; *b.* 24 Dec. 1864; *m.* 1901, Eleanor Mary Ruthven, *d.* of Robert Howden, East Lothian.

Educ.: Owens Colle ›, Manchester. M.B., Ch.B., Vict.; M.R.C.S., Eng., 1888; Surgeon, R.N. 1891; landed with Naval Brigade; attached Ladysmith Relief Column, South African War, 1899-1900 (despatches, medal with 2 clasps, D.S.O.); specially promoted Staff-Surgeon, 1900; Fleet-Surgeon, 1904; Surgeon-Capt., 1918; F.R.C.S. (Edin.), 1907; S.M.O. of Hospital Ships Maine and Rohilla, when these vessels were totally wrecked, 1914; S.M.O. Hospital Ship Garth Castle, 1915 (C.B. 1916, for services during the War); retired, 1919. *Address:* Boggs, Pencaitland, East Lothian.   (*Died 24 Feb. 1921.*)

LOMAS, John; prominent Anglican Churchman in the jurisdiction of North and Central Europe, and estate owner in Switzerland; *b.* Manchester, 2 Nov. 1846; *s.* of George Lomas; *m.* 1875, Maria Thurston, *d.* of Christopher Gabriel, Norfolk House, Streatham Hill; three *s.* two *d.* *Educ.:* Manchester Grammar School; Victoria University, Manchester. Editor of the Anglican Church Magazine, 1886 - 1912; General Secretary of North and Central Europe Church Conferences since 1912; President and Director of various educational, charitable, social, and commercial undertakings. *Publications:* Sketches in Spain from Nature, Art, and Life; In Spain; Don Luis; numerous magazine articles; also Church music, Communion offices, anthems, etc. *Recreations:* church and organ music. *Address:* St. Jean, Territet, Switzerland. *T.A.:* Lomas. Territet. *T.:* Montreux 225. *Clubs:* Constitutional, Church Imperial; Montreux International.
    (*Died 1 Mar. 1927.*)

LOMAX, John A., Member of Society of Oil Painters; *b.* 1857; *s.* of John Lomax. Manchester; *m.* Lily *d.* of James Lings, of Manchester. *Educ.:* Stuttgart; Munich. *Works:* How the Old Squire caught the Big Sack; To bring the Roses back; Overtaken; The Elopement: Reconciliation; Run to Earth, etc. etc. *Recreations:* tennis, billiards, cycling, golf. *Address:* 17 Marlborough Road, St. John's Wood, N.W. *Clubs:* Arts, St. John's Wood Arts.
    (*Died 13 Dec. 1923.*)

LONDESBOROUGH, 2nd Earl of (*cr.* 1887), **William Francis Henry Denison,** Baron Londesborough, 1850; Viscount Raincliffe, 1887; K.C.V.O., *cr.* 1908; *b.* 30 Dec. 1864; *e. s.* of 1st Earl and Lady Edith Frances Wilhelmina Somerset, *y. d.* of 7th Duke of Beaufort, K.G.; *S.* father, 1900; *m.* Lady Grace Augusta Fane, *e. d.* of 12th Earl of Westmorland, 1887; two *s.* one *d.* Deputy-Lieut. East Riding of Yorkshire; late Lieut. Yorks. Hussars; late Hon. Col. 2nd Vol. Batt. East Yorks Regt.; Hon. Col. 5th (Cyclist) Batt. East Yorks Regt. Owns about 52,700 acres. *Heir: s.* Viscount Raincliffe. *Address:* Blankney Hall, Lincoln; Londesborough Park, Market Weighton; Londesborough Lodge, Scarborough; The Island, Walton on the Hill, near Epsom; 7 Chesterfield Gardens, W. *T.:* Mayfair 5606. *Clubs:* Marlborough, Orleans.
    (*Died 30 Oct. 1917.*)

LONDESBOROUGH, 3rd Earl of, *cr.* 1887 **George Francis William Henry Denison,** Baron Londesborough, 1850; Viscount Raincliffe, 1887; *b.* 17 July 1892; *e. s.* of 2nd Earl and Lady Grace Augusta Fane, *e. d.* of 12th Earl of Westmorland; *S.* father 1917. Owns about 52,700 acres. *Heir: b.* Hon. Hugo W. C. Denison. *Address:* Blankney Hall, Lincoln; Londesborough Park, Market Weighton.
    (*Died 12 Sept. 1920.*)

LONDON, Jack; writer; *b.* San Francisco, 12 Jan. 1876; *s.* of John London; *m.* 1st, 1900, Bessie Maddern; two *d.*; 2nd, 1905, in Chicago, Charmian Kittredge. *Educ.:* Univ. of California. Sailor, gold - miner, tramp, writer, socialist, lecturer, journalist, etc. In his search for adventures among the scum marine population of San Francisco Bay he soon lost his ideal

romance and replaced it with the real romance of things; he became, in turn, a salmon fisher, an oyster pirate, a schooner sailor, a fish patrolman, a longshoreman, and general bay-faring adventurer; when he was seventeen he shipped before the mast as able seaman; went to Japan and seal-hunting on the Russian side of Behring Sea, among other things, and served at divers times in various forecastles; he became possessed of an interest in sociology and economics; swayed partly by this, and partly by the fascination of the enterprise, he tramped over the United States and Canada, many thousands of miles, and having more than one jail experience because he possessed no fixed place of abode, and no visible means of support; later on he repeated his vagabond career in the East End of London; he went over Chilcoot Pass with the first of the Klondike rush of 1897; went as war correspondent to Japan, Korea, and Manchuria, 1904; war correspondent, Mexico, 1914; started on a seven years' cruise around the world in a fifty-foot ketch-rig yacht, 1906. *Publications:* The Son of the Wolf, 1900; The God of His Fathers; A Daughter of the Snows; The Children of the Frost; The People of the Abyss; The Cruise of the Dazzle; The Call of the Wild; The Kempton-Wace Letters; The Faith of Men; The Sea Wolf, 1904; The War of the Classes; The Game, 1905; Tales of the Fish Patrol, 1905; Moon-Face; Scorn of Women, 1906; White-Fang, 1906; Love of Life, 1907; Iron Heel; The Road, 1908; Before Adam, 1908; Martin Eden, 1909; Lots Face, Revolution, Theft, Burning Daylight, 1910; Adventure, 1911; The Cruise of the Snark, 1911; South Sea Tales, 1911; When God Laughs, 1912; A Son of the Sun, 1912; The House of Pride, 1912; Smoke Bellew Tales, 1912; The Night Born, 1913; The Abysmal Brute, 1913; John Barleycorn, 1913; The Valley of the Moon, 1913; John Barleycorn; The Strength of the Strong; The Mutiny of the Elsinore, 1914; The Jacket, 1915; The Little Lady of the Big House, 1916; The Acorn Planter (play); The Turtles of Tasman; Jerry and Michael; The Human Drift; Hearts of Three. *Recreations:* kite-flying, yacht-sailing, fencing, boxing, horseback riding, swimming, agriculture. *Address:* Glen Ellen, Sonoma County, California. *Club:* Bohemian. San Francisco. (*Died 22 Nov. 1916.*)

LONG, 1st Viscount, *cr.* 1921, of Wraxall; **Walter Hume Long,** P.C., J.P.; F.R.S.; Hon. LL.D. Birmingham; Lord - Lieut. for Wilts; Colonel commanding Royal Wilts Imperial Yeomanry (Prince of Wales's Own), 1898-1906; *b.* Bath, 13 July 1854; *e. s.* of late Richard Penruddocke Long, Rood Ashton, Wilts, and Dolforgan, Montgomeryshire [M.P. Chippenham, 1859-65; N. Wilts, 1865-68], and Charlotte, *d.* of Rt. Hon. W. W. Fitz-William-Hume Dick [M.P. Wicklow, 1850-80]; *m.* 1878, Lady Dorothy Blanche (Doreen), 4th *d.* of 9th Earl of Cork and Orrery; one *s.* one *d.* *Educ.:* Harrow; Christ Church, Oxford (Hon. Student). M.P. (C.) North Wilts, 1880-85; Devizes Division, 1885 - 92; Parliamentary Secretary to Local Government Board, 1886-92; M.P. (C.) West Derby, Liverpool, 1892-1900; President Board of Agriculture, 1895-1900; President of Local Government Board, 1900 - 5; M.P. (C.) South Bristol, 1900 - 6; M.P. (C.) South Dublin, 1906-10; M.P. (C.U.) Strand Division, 1910; St. George's, Westminster, 1919-21; Chief Secretary for Ireland, 1905-6; President Local Government Board, 1915-16; Secretary of State for the Colonies, 1916-18; First Lord of the Admiralty, 1919 - 21; Chairman of Harrow Governors, 1924; Hon. Student Christ Church, Oxon. *Publication:* Memories, 1923. *Recreations:* cricket, hunting. *Heir: g.s.* Walter Francis David Long, *b.* 1911. *Address:* Rood Ashton, Trowbridge, Wilts. *Clubs:* Carlton, Cavalry.   (*Died 26 Sept. 1924.*)

LONG, George Bathurst, M.V.O. 1910; H.M. Privy Purse, 1901-11; Comptroller's Office, 1874-1901; *b.* 28 July 1855; *s.* of late Walter Bathurst Long, Special Commissioner, Somerset House; *m.* 1883, 2nd *d.* of John Kenshole of Heavitree, Exeter; one *d. Educ.:* St. Paul's School. *Address:* Clarehurst, Baldslow Road, Hastings. *Clubs:* Junior Conservative; Hastings, St. Leonards and County Conservative, Hastings.   (*Died 2 Jan.* 1917.)

LONG, Sir James, Kt., *cr.* 1910; J.P.; late Chairman of Cork Harbour Commission; Member of the Governing Body, University College, Cork; *b.* Nov. 1862; *m.* 1884, Mary (*d.* 1923), *d.* of William Elliott of Plymouth; two *s.* two *d. Address:* Spy Hill Villa, Queenstown, Co. Cork.   (*Died 17 Sept.* 1928.)

LONG, John Luther; *b.* 1861. *Plays and Publications:* The Darling of the Gods; Madame Butterfly, 1898; Miss Cherry Blossom of Tokyo; The Fox Woman, 1900; The Prince of Illusion, 1901; Naughty Nan; Heimweh, and other Stories, 1906; Adrea, play; Lady Betty Martingale, play; Crowns, play, 1923; War, novel; Seffy, novel. *Address:* 250 Ashbourne Road, Elkins Park Branch, Philadelphia, Penna., U.S.A.   (*Died 31 Oct.* 1927.)

LONG, Lt.-Col. Walter, C.M.G., 1916; D.S.O. 1902; Royal Scots Greys; temp. Lt.-Col. 6th Batt. Wiltshire Regt. since 1915; *b.* 26 July 1879; *e. s.* of Rt. Hon. W. H. Long, M.P.; *m.* 1910, Sibell, *d.* of Hon. Francis Johnstone. *Educ.:* Harrow. Entered army, 1899; Captain, 1902; Major, 1915; A.D.C. to Maj.-Gen. Scobell, 1st Cavalry Brigade, Aldershot; Adjutant of the Scots Greys, 1906-9; served South African campaign, 1899-1902 (despatches, Queen's medal, 2 clasps, King's medal, 2 clasps, D.S.O.); European War, 1914-15 (despatches twice, C.M.G.); Holds Order of St. Stanislas (3rd Cl.). *Recreations:* hunting, polo, shooting, and cricket. *Clubs:* Cavalry, Bath.   (*Died 27 Jan.* 1917.)

LONG, Lieut.-Col. and Hon. Col. William, C.M.G. 1900; 4th Batt. Somerset Light Infantry; retired; Provincial Grand Master of Somerset, and of Mark M. Masons, Somerset; *b.* 22 Jan. 1843; *e. s.* of William Long, F.S.A., J.P., of Wrington, Somerset, and Elizabeth Hare, o. c. of late James Hare Jolliffe, of Bathford, Somerset; *m.* 1867, Anna Mary, *d.* of late Henry Hunter, Capt. 5th Dragoon Guards; one *s.* seven *d. Educ.:* Eton. Served South Africa, 1900-2 (despatches, Queen's medal with clasp, King's medal 2 clasps, C.M.G.); D.L. and J.P., Somerset; High Sheriff, 1899. *Address:* Newton House, Clevedon. *Club:* Junior United Service.   (*Died 9 May* 1926.)

LONGE, Colonel Francis Bacon, late R.E.; C.B. 1910; J.P.; of Spixworth Park, Norwich; *b.* 31 Oct. 1856; *m.* 1905, May, *d.* of late Deputy Surg.-Gen. John Meane. *Educ.:* Cheltenham Coll.; Royal Military Academy, Woolwich. Lieut. Royal Engineers, 1876; transferred to Indian Establishment, and posted to the Bengal Sappers and Miners, 1878; appointed to Survey of India, 1880; Substantive Colonel in army, 1905; served with Kurram, Kabul, and Kandahar Field Forces, 1879-81; Kabul-Kandahar march, 1880 (despatches twice received thanks of Governor-General, medal 3 clasps, and bronze star); with Suakim Expeditionary Force, 1885 (medal and clasp, Egyptian Star); Wuntho Expedition (Upper Burma), 1891 (medal and clasp); served as Survey Officer with the Chin-Manipur and Burma-China Boundary Commissions, 1894 and 1897-98, respectively, and as a Member of the Indian Survey Committee of 1904-5; Surveyor-General of India, 1904-1911; Hon. A.D.C. to the Viceroy and additional Member of the Legislative Council of the Governor-General, 1909-10. *Address:* c/o Cox & Co., Charing Cross, S.W.1. *Club:* Junior United Service.   (*Died 2 June* 1922.)

LONGFELLOW, Ernest Wadsworth, artist; *b.* Cambridge, Mass., 1845; *s.* of the poet; pupil of Couture, Paris. *Works:* Morning on the Ægean; Evening on the Nile; Italian Phifferari; A Wind came up out of the Sea; Stirling Castle; Misty Morning; various portraits. *Address:* Century Association, 7 W. 43rd Street, New York.   (*Died 24 Nov.* 1921.)

LONGFORD, Joseph Henry; Emeritus Professor of Japanese, King's College, London University, 1916; Vice-Pres., Japan Society, London, 1922; *b.* 25 June 1849; *s.* of late Charles Longford of Blackrock, co. Dublin, and of Mary, *d.* of late Capt. Ralph Manning, 24th Regt.; *m.* Alice, *d.* of late Walter Johnston, Trench Hall, Northumberland; one *s.* two *d. Educ.:* Royal Academical Institution and Queen's College, Belfast; B.A. Queen's University in Ireland; D. Litt. Queen's University of Ulster, 1919. Entered H. M. Consular Service in Japan as Student Interpreter, 1869; served for 33 years, travelling during this period throughout the whole of the Japanese Empire, from the Kurile Islands in the extreme north to Formosa in the extreme south; successively H.M. Consul and Judge of H.M. Consular Courts at Tokio, Hiogo, Hakodate, Tainan, Tamsui, and Nagasaki; retired on a pension in 1902; called to Bar, Middle Temple, 1889; Professor of Japanese, King's College, London, 1903-16; nominated on H.M.'s behalf, as one of the suite of Prince Komatsu, the official representative of the Emperor of Japan at King Edward's Coronation (Coronation medal); received from Emperor of Japan, silver wedding medal, Order of the Rising Sun, and, on occasion of visit to London of Crown Prince, Order of the Sacred Treasure; Chairman of Japan Society, London, 1921-22. *Publications:* Penal Code of Japan, 1877; Japan (Living Races of Mankind), 1905; The Regeneration of Japan (Cambridge Modern History), 1910; The Story of Old Japan, 1910; The Story of Korea, 1911; Japan of the Japanese, 1911; The Evolution of New Japan, 1913; Japan (Spirit of the Allied Nations), 1915; Japan (Harmsworth Encyclopedia), 1920; Japan (Nations of To-day) 1923; contributions to the Transactions of the Asiatic Society of Japan, and of the Japan Society, London, and, principally on Japanese subjects, to the Quarterly, Fortnightly and National Reviews, The Nineteenth Century and other Reviews, and to the Press; numerous Reports, principally on industrial subjects in Japan, issued by the Foreign Office. *Recreations:* boating; walking; cricket (spectator); bridge. *Address:* 10 Esmond Road, Bedford Park, W. T.: Chiswick 2387. *Clubs:* Reform; Royal Irish Yacht. (*Died 12 May* 1925.)

LONGHURST, Sir Henry Bell, Kt., *cr.* 1902; C.V.O. 1910; L.D.S.R.C.S. Eng.; Hon. Surgeon-Dentist to H.M. the King; *b.* London, 20 Jan. 1835; *s.* of late James Longhurst; *m.* 1865, Mary (*d.* 1923), *d.* of late Samuel Wilmot, Nottingham; six *s.* two *d. Educ.:* private school; Univ. College, London. *Recreations:* shooting, fishing, gardening. *Address:* Grove House, Park Road, Hampton Hill, Middlesex.   (*Died 5 Aug.* 1926.)

LONGLEY, Hon. James Wilberforce, statesman, jurist, and littérateur; a Judge of the Supreme Court of Nova Scotia since 1905; *b.* Paradise, Nova Scotia, Canada, 4 Jan. 1849; *m.* 1st, 1877, Annie, *y. d.* of N. Brown; two *s.* one *d.*; 2nd, 1901, Lois E., *y. d.* of late George Fletcher; three *s.* A lecturer and public speaker, and a regular contributor to the magazines; is a Liberal in politics, and an advanced thinker on social and religious questions; graduated from Acadia University, 1871; admitted to the Bar of Nova Scotia, 1875; first elected to Parliament, 1882; entered Government, 1884; Attorney-

General, 1886-1905, having sat in Parliament without interruption since 1882; Q.C. 1892; D.C.L. 1897; L.L.D., 1905; elected Fellow of the Royal Society of Canada, 1898. *Publications*: Love; Socialism, its Truths and Errors; The Greatest Drama; A Material Age; Canada and Imperial Federation; Religion in 19th Century; Life of Joseph Howe, etc. *Address*: 18 Green Street, Halifax, N.S. *T.A.*: Halifax, N.S. *T.*: 1599.
(Died 16 Mar. 1922.)

LONGSTAFF, George Blundell, M.A., M.D., Oxon.; F.R.C.P., F.S.A., F.L.S., F.C.S., F.G.S.; J.P., London and Devon; *b.* 12 Feb. 1849; *s.* of George Dixon Longstaff, M.D., of Wandsworth, and Maria, *d.* of Henry Blundell of Hull; *m.* 1st, 1875, Sara Leam (*d.* 1903), *d.* of Ed. Dixon of Southampton; two *s.* two *d.*; 2nd, 1906, Mary Jane. *Educ.*: Rugby; New Coll. Oxon. (Scholar, First Class in Natural Science); St. Thomas's Hospital (Mead medal). Has devoted much time to municipal and philanthropic work; has served on many committees of the Charity Organisation Society; been a Guardian of the Poor; L.C.C. for Wandsworth, 1889-1903; as Chairman of its Building Act Committee took a principal part in drafting and getting through Parliament the London Building Act, 1894; has been Vice-President of the Royal Statistical and Entomological Societies. *Publications*: Studies in Statistics, 1891; The Langstaffs of Teesdale and Weardale, 1907; Marriage and the Church, 1910; Butterfly Hunting in Many Lands, 1912. *Recreations*: travelling, botany, entomology, skating. *Address*: Highlands, Putney Heath, S.W. *T.A.*: Roehampton. *Clubs*: Savile, Conservative, Skating. *(Died 7 May 1921.)*

LONGSTAFF, Llewellyn Wood; Lieut.-Col., formerly commanding 1st V.B. East Yorkshire Regt.; retired 1880; Surrey National Reserve; Divisional V.P. Red Cross; F.R.G.S. (formerly on Council), F.Z.S., F.R.Met.Soc., etc.; *b.* 23 Dec. 1841; *e. s.* of late G. D. Longstaff, M.D., and Maria, *d.* of H. Blundell, J.P.; *m.* 1873, Mary L., *d.* of late Thomas W. Sawyer of Southampton; four *s.* three *d. Educ.*: Wandsworth Proprietary School; by Tutor on the Continent; Royal School of Mines. Twice President of the Hull Incorporated Chamber of Commerce and Shipping; by his support made practicable the British National Antarctic Expedition, 1899-1904. *Recreations*: voyaging and travelling. *Address*: Ridgelands, Wimbledon, S.W. *T.A.*: Swordsmen Wim, London. *T.*: Wimbledon 749 and 1837. *Clubs*: Royal Societies, Royal Yorkshire Yacht. *(Died 20 Nov. 1918.)*

LONGUEVILLE, Thomas, *b.* 29 April 1844; *e.* and *o. surv. s.* of Thomas Longueville of Prestatyn, Trelogan, and Penyllan; *m.* 1868, Mary Francis, *o. surv. c.* of Alexander Robertson of Balgownie; three *s.* one *d. Educ.*: Christ Church, Oxford. Cornet in the North Shropshire Yeomanry, 1865-8; for some years a partner in Croxon's Bank, Oswestry; J.P. Co. Salop; for 20 years a constant contributor to The Saturday Review; also frequent contributor to other journals and magazines. *Publications*: The Life of a Prig; A Life of Sir Kenelm Digby; Rochester and other Literary Rakes; Policy and Paint; A Life of James II.; Turenne; Vices in Virtues, etc. *Recreations*: incapacitated from taking any; formerly painting, hunting, and attending races. *Heir*: *e. s.* Lt.-Col. Regina d Longueville [*b.* 26 Mar. 1869; *m.* 1912, Dorothy Mary Catherine, 2nd *d.* of W. J. Fitzherbert-Brockholes; one *s.* Commanded 7th Batt. R. Welsh Fusiliers, late Major Coldstream Guards]. *Address*: Llanforda, Oswestry.
(Died 18 Aug. 1922.)

LONSDALE, Rev. Henry, M.A., Hon. Canon of Carlisle, 1901. *Educ..*: Magdalene College Cambridge (Scholar). M.A. Deacon,

1875; Priest, 1876; Vicar of Thornthwaite, 1881-89; Upperby, 1889-1904; Corbridge-on-Tyne, 1904-17. *Address*: Arlaw Banl s, Winston, Darlington. *(Died 17 June 1926.)*

LONSDALE, James Rolston, M.P. (U.) Mid-Armagh since Jan. 1918; *b.* 31 May 1865; *s.* of James Lonsdale, D.L., of the Pavilion, Armagh; *b.* of 1st Baron Armaghdale; *m.* 1902, Maud, *d.* of John Musker, Shadwell Court, Norfolk. *Educ.*: Royal School, Armagh; Trinity College, Dublin. High Sheriff of Co. Armagh, 1907; a Unionist. *Address*: 12 Sussex Square, W.2. *Clubs*: Carlton, Bachelors'.
(Died 23 May 1921.)

LORAINE, Sir Lambton, 11th Bt.; *cr.* 1664; J.P.; Rear-Admiral (retired); *b.* Northumberland, 17 Nov. 1838; *e. s.* of 10th Bt.; *m.* Frederica M. H., *d.* of Charles Acton Broke, co-heiress of the Brokes of Nacton, 1878; one *s.* two *d.*; *S.* father 1852. *Educ.*: Burlington House School, Fulham (extinct); a short time at Cambridge. *Recreations*: usual recreations of country and town. *Heir*: *s.* Percy Lyham, *b.* 5 Nov. 1880. *Address*: 7 Montagu Square, W.; Bramford Hall, near Ipswich. *T.A.*: Loraine, Bramford. *Clubs*: United Service, Naval and Military. *(Died 13 May 1917.)*

LORAINE, Rev. Nevison; Prebendar of St. Paul's Cathedral, and Canon non-resid nt-ary; Vicar of Grove Park-West, W., since 1870; *b.* Northumberland; *s.* of Nevison and Jane Loraine; *m.* Agnes May, (*d.* 1915) *d.* of John and Hannah Howard; three *s.* one *d. Educ.*: Northumberland Grammar School; Croft House; Private Tutors; College of Divinity. Ordained 1860; Curate of St. Giles in the Fields, 1860-61; Incumbent of Holy Trinity, Liverpool, 1861-70; Fairchild Lecturer, 1899; Golden Lecturer, 1908-9; Biblical Examiner, London Reading Union, 1884. *Publications*: Discourses on the Lord's Prayer; The Voice of the Prayer Book; Home Reunion, pub. Letter to Archbishop of Canterbury; The Eastern Question, an Ecclesiastical Political Brochure; The Sceptic's Creed; The Church and Liberties of England; The Battle of Belief; Half-Hours with Busy Men; Golden Lectures; sundry reviews, articles, lectures, etc. *Recreations*: travel, lit erature, athletics, motoring. *Address*: Grove Park Vicarage, Chiswick. *T.A.* Prebendary Loraine, Chiswick. *M.* LC 3957. *(Died 10 Sept. 1917.)*

LORD, Herbert Owen; Master Cotswold Hounds since 1904; *b.* 2 Nov. 1854; 2nd *s.* of Captain Arthur Owen ord, 72nd Highlanders (Seaforth), and Lucy Sophia, *d.* of late Henry Taylor, T.C.S.; *m.* Mary Ollivant, *e. d.* of late William Dugdale, J.P., D.L., of Simonstone Hall, Lancashire, and Lilley Brook, Charlton Kings; two *d. Educ.*: Eton. *Recreations*: hunting; shooting; golf; cricket, etc. *Clubs*: Boodle's, Orleans, Pratt's, Bath, Sandown, Roehampton. *(Died 2 April 1923.)*

LORD, John King; Professor (Emeritus) of Latin Language and Literature; Trustee Dartmouth College, United States, America. *b.* Oct. 21, 1848; *s.* of John King Lord and Laura Esther Smith; *m.* Emma Fuller Pomeroy; three *s.* one *d. Educ.*: Dartmouth College, 1868. *Publications*: New Hampshire in 9th ed. Ency. Brit.; also in Johnson's Cyclopædia; Cicero: Laelius; Livy: Books i., xxi., xxii.; Atlas of the Geography and History of the Ancient World; editor, Chase's History of Dartmouth College, and the Town of Hanover, vol. i.; wrote History of Dartmouth College, vol. ii. *Address*: Hanover, New Hampshire, U.S.A. *T.*: W 44.
(Died 26 June 1926.)

LORD, Sir Riley, Kt., *cr.* 1900; *s.* of late George Lord, Accrington; *b.* Accrington, 24 Feb. 1838; *m.* 1857, Mary, *d.* of John and Susannah Haggas, Keighley (*d.* 1894). Represented the Prudential Life Assurance Co. for over

44 years ; entered Newcastle-upon-Tyne Council, 1885 ; was Sheriff of Newcastle, 1892-1893 ; Mayor, 1895-96 and 1899-1900 ; during first mayoralty inaugurated Victoria Diamond Jubilee Fund to build new Infirmary ; raised £100,000, another £100,000 was bequeathed by John Hall for same purpose, and £100,000 more contributed by Lord Armstrong ; foundation stone of Royal Victoria Infirmary laid 20 June 1900 by Prince of Wales on behalf of the Queen, and opened by His Majesty 11 July 1906 ; J.P. Newcastle-upon-Tyne and Northumberland. *Address :* Highfield Hall, Gosforth, Newcastle-upon-Tyne.
(Died 17 Aug. 1920.)

LOREBURN, 1st Earl, cr. 1911 ; **Robert Threshie Reid,** 1st Baron, cr. 1906 ; Kt., cr. 1894 ; G.C.M.G., cr. 1899 ; J.P. ; D.C.L., Oxon. ; *b.* 3 April 1846 ; 2nd *s.* of Sir James John Reid, Mouswald Place, Dumfries, and Mary, *d.* of Robert Threshie, Barnbarroch, Kirkcudbrightshire ; *m.* 1st, 1871, Emily Douglas (*d.* 1904), *d.* of Capt. Fleming : 2nd, 1907, Violet Elizabeth, *e. d.* of W. F. Hicks-Beach of Witcombe Park, Gloucs. *Educ. :* Cheltenham College ; Balliol College, Oxford. First Class in Moderations and in Lit. Hum. ; Demy of Magdalen Coll. ; Scholar of Balliol Coll. ; Ireland Univ. Scholar, 1868. Barr. 1871 ; Q.C. 1882 ; M.P. Hereford, 1880 ; Solicitor-Gen. 1894 ; Attorney-General, Oct. 1894 ; M.P. (L.) Dumfries, 1886-1905 ; University Counsel, Oxford, 1899-1906 ; Lord Chancellor, 1905-12. *Decorated* for his services in connection with the Venezuelan Boundary Arbitration Commission. *Publication :* Capture at Sea, 1913 ; How the War Came, 1919. *Recreations :* Oxford University XI., 1866-68 ; represented Oxford v. Cambridge at racquets, 1865-67. *Heir :* none. *Address :* 8 Eaton Square, S.W. ; Kingsdown, Dover. *Clubs :* Brooks's, National Liberal.
(Died 30 Nov. 1923.)

LORIMER, John Campbell, K.C., M.A., LL.B., Advocate ; Sheriff-Principal of Aberdeen, Kincardine, Banffs., since 1911 ; *s.* of Rev. Dr. John Gordon Lorimer, Glasgow, and Jane, *d.* of Rev. Dr. John Campbell, Tolbooth Church, Edinburgh ; *m.* 1875, Jemima Margaret, *d.* of Rev. Prof. Bannerman, D.D., of Abernyte, Perthshire. *Educ. :* Glasgow Academy ; Glasgow and Edinburgh Universities. Scottish Bar, 1866 ; Counsel for Inland Revenue, Scotland, 1882-86 ; Advocate Depute, 1886 and 1892-95 ; Parliamentary Counsel to Secretary for Scotland, 1900-8 ; K.C. 1903 ; Member of Court University of Edinburgh, 1901-9 ; Sheriff-Principal of Ayr, 1908-11 ; and Director, Century Insurance Company. *Publications :* Lectures on Company Law ; New Death Duties (commentary on) ; Appendix on the Law of Scotland to Lord Lindley's Law of Partnership. *Recreations :* formerly mountaineering. *Address :* 9 Gloucester Place, Edin. *Club :* Royal Northern, Aberdeen.
(Died 20 Jan. 1922.)

LORIMER, Sir William, Kt., cr. 1917 ; *b.* 4 Nov. 1844 ; *s.* of William Lorimer and Margaret Kirkhope Whigham ; *m.* 1st, 1869, Jane (*d.* 1902), *d.* of Alex. Smith ; 2nd, 1913, Mary Elizabeth, *d.* of John Sieber, of Irwell Springs, Lancashire ; four *s.* four *d. Educ. :* Sanquhar, Dumfriesshire. Has for practically the whole of his business life been connected with the locomotive industry ; was for many years managing partner of the firm of Dubs & Co., of Glasgow, now absorbed in the North British Locomotive Co., of which he has been Chairman since its formation in 1903 ; until last year, Chairman for over twenty years of the Steel Co. of Scotland, and is a Director of the Glasgow and South Western Railway ; has been a member of the Dominions Royal Commission since it was appointed in 1912, and in that capacity has visited all the self-governing Dominions ; is LL.D. of the University of Glasgow and a member of the

University Court. *Address :* Kirklinton, Langside, Glasgow. *Clubs :* Reform ; Western, Glasgow.
(Died 9 April 1922.)

LORT PHILLIPS, Lt.-Col. John Frederick, J.P., D.L. ; *e. s.* of Richard Ilbert Lort Phillips (*d.* 1860) and Frederica Maria Louisa, *e. d.* of late Baron de Rutzen of Slebech Hall, Pembrokeshire ; *b.* 1854 ; *S.* uncle, 1866 ; *m.* 1895, Hon. Maude, late Maid of Honour to Queen Victoria, 2nd *d.* of late Haughton Charles Okeover of Okeover, Staffordshire, and *widow* of Sir Andrew Barclay Walker, 1st Bart. of Osmaston Manor, Derbyshire. High Sheriff, Pembrokeshire, 1880. *Address :* Lawrenny, Kilgetty, Pembrokeshire.
(Died 15 May 1926.)

LOTE, Thomas Alfred, J.P. ; M.F.H. Teme Valley ; *b.* 1863 ; *s.* of Henry Lote, Croydon ; *m.* 1890, Hannah, *d.* of George Townsend, Shrewsbury. *Address :* Brook House, Knighton.

LOTI, Pierre (Louis Marie Julien Viaud) ; Capt. French Navy ; French novelist ; member of the French Academy since 1891 ; *b.* Rochefort, 14 Jan. 1850 ; *s.* of M. Viaud. Entered Navy, 1867 ; 2nd Lieutenant, 1873 ; Lieutenant, "Oceania," 1881 ; served Pacific, Tonkin campaign, China ; Comm. Legion of Honour 1910, Grand Cross, 1921. *Publications :* Aziyadé, 1876-1877 ; Le mariage de Loti (1st called Rarahu), 1880 (trans. 1890) ; Le roman d'un Spahi, 1881 (trans. 1890) ; Fleurs d'ennui, 1882 ; Mon frère Yves, 1883 (trans. 1887) ; Les trois dames de la Kasbah, 1884 ; Pêcheur d Islande, 1886 (trans. 1888) ; Madame Chrysanthème, 1887 (trans. 1888) ; Propos d'exil, 1887 ; Japonneries d'automne, 1889 ; Au Maroc, 1890 ; Roman d'un enfant, 1890 (trans. 1891) ; Le livre de la pitié et de la mort, 1891 (trans. 1892) ; Fantôme d'orient, 1892 (trans. 1892) ; Le desert : Ramuntcho ; La Galilée ; Jérusalem ; and others ; Figures et choses qui passaient, 1898 ; L'Inde sans les Anglais, 1903 ; La Troisième jeunesse de Mme. Prune, 1905 ; Disenchanted, 1906 ; Pélérin d'Angkor, 1912. *Address :* L'Académie Française, Paris.
(Died 10 June 1923.)

LOTON, Sir William Thorley, Kt., cr. 1923 ; Director W. Australian Bank since 1882 ; *b.* England, 1839. Went to Western Australia, 1863 ; founded firm of Padbury, Loton & Co. ; was Member Legislative Council. *Address :* Weld Chambers, St. George's Terrace, Perth, W. Australia.
(Died 22 Oct. 1924.)

LOUCH, Ven. Thomas ; *b.* Hadleigh, Suff., 1848 ; *s.* of Thomas Frederick Louch, of H.M. Inland Revenue, and Mary Ann, *d.* of Charles Steane ; *m.* 1889, Mary Grace, *d.* of George Baston, J.P., Geraldton, Western Australia ; one *s.* one *d. Educ. :* Sandbach Grammar School ; Owens College ; S. Aidan's Theological College. Resided in Cork (Ireland), 1852 ; Sandbach (Cheshire), 1854 ; Manchester, 1862 ; St. Aidan's College, Birkenhead, 1877 ; Curate of Holy Trinity, Warrington, 1879-81 ; St. Stephen's, Poplar, London, 1881-86 ; Rector of Geraldton, Western Australia, 1886-1900 ; Rector of Albany, 1900-22 ; Archdeacon of the Bunbury Diocese 1905-22 ; Examining Chaplain to the Bishop of Bunbury ; Administrator of the Bunbury Diocese, 1917 and 1920 ; Hon. Chaplain to the Defence Forces, 1890-1910, retiring with the rank of Lieutenant-Colonel. *Address :* Albany, Western Australia. *Clubs :* Albany, Western Australia.
(Died 19 Oct. 1927.)

LOUCKS, Rev. Edwin, late Rector of Pictou, Diocese of Ontario, Canada ; Canon of St. George's Cathedral, Kingston, Ontario ; *b.* 1 March 1829 ; *m.* 1864 ; three *s.* three *d. Educ. :* Bishop's College, Lennoxville, Quebec. Curate in sole charge at Lennoxville ; Senior Curate, Christ Church, Ottawa, Ontario ; now retired. *Address :* 37 Division Street, Kingston, Ontario.
(Died 20 July 1919.)

LOUDAN, Mouat, R.S.P. ; Member National Portrait Society and Art Workers' Guild, etc. ; *b.* of Scottish parentage in London, 1868 ; *m.* 1898 ; two *s. Educ.:* Dulwich College. Entered Royal Academy Schools, where worked for nearly four years, obtaining medals for drawing, painting, modelling, also the gold medal and travelling studentship ; after this studied in Paris ; here of late years devoted himself almost entirely to portraiture. *Recreations:* mechanics, cabinet work, etc. ; golf. *Address:* 48 Circus Road, N.W.

(Died 26 Dec. 1925.)

LOUDON, James, President of the University of Toronto, 1892-1906, and Professor of Physics, 1887-1906 ; *b.* Toronto, 1841, of Irish parentage ; *m.* 1872, Julia, *d.* of John Lorn M'Dougall of Renfrew ; three *s.* one *d. Educ..* The Toronto Grammar School, Upper Canada College and Univ. of Toronto. B.A., M.A., LL.D., Univ. of Toronto ; LL.D. Queen's, Princeton, Johns Hopkins, McMaster, and Glasgow Universities ; D.C.L., Trinity University (Toronto) ; F.R. Soc. of Canada ; Pres. R.S.C. (1901-2). Math. Tutor in Univ. Coll. Toronto, 1863 ; Classical and Math. Tutor, 1864 ; Math. Tutor and Dean of Residence, 1865 ; Prof. of Mathematics and Natural Philosophy, 1875. *Publications:* various Mathematical and Physical papers in Journal of Canadian Institute, the Philosophical Magazine, the American Jour. of Math. and the Trans. of Roy. Soc. of Canada. *Address:* 88 St. George St., Toronto, Canada. *T.:* Coll. 1259, Toronto.

(Died 28 Dec. 1916.)

LOUDOUN, 11th Earl of (*cr.* 1633), **Charles Edward Hastings Abney-Hastings,** D.L., J.P. ; Baron Botreaux, 1368 ; Baron Hungerford, 1426 ; Baron de Moleyns, 1445 ; Baron Hastings (England) 1461 ; Baron Loudoun, 1601 ; Baron Donington (U.K.), 1880 ; *b.* 5 Jan. 1855 ; *s.* of Countess of Loudoun and Charles F. Abney-Hastings ; S. mother 1874 ; *m.* 1880, Hon. Alice Mary Elizabeth Fitzalan - Howard (*d.* 1915), 3rd *d.* of 1st Lord Howard of Glossop. Owns about 33,000 acres. *Heir:* Edith Maud Rawdon-Hastings, *b.* 13 May 1883, *d.* of late Hon. Paulyn Rawdon-Hastings, *b.* of 11th Earl. *Address:* Willesley Hall, Ashby-de-la-Zouche ; Loudoun Castle, Galston. *T.A.:* Galston. *Clubs:* Carlton, Marlborough ; Royal Yacht Squadron, Cowes. *(Died 17 May 1920.)*

LOUGH, Rt. Hon. Thomas, Parliamentary Secretary to the Board of Education, 1905-8 ; M.P. (L.) Islington, W., 1892-1918 ; H.M. Lieutenant of Co. Cavan since 1907 ; tea merchant in London since 1880 ; *b.* Ireland, 1850 ; *s.* of Matthew Lough, Killynebber House, Cavan, and Martha, *d.* of Wm. Steel ; *m.* Edith, *d.* of late Rev. John Mills, 1880. *Educ.:* Royal School, Cavan ; Wesleyan Connexional School, Dublin. Contested Truro, 1886 ; founder Home Rule Union, 1887 ; London Reform Union, 1892. *Publications:* England's Wealth, Ireland's Poverty, 1896 ; The Brussels Sugar Convention, 1903 ; Ten Years' Tory Rule in Ireland, 1905 ; Parliament during the War, 1917. *Recreation:* golf. *Address:* 97 Ashley Gardens, S.W.1 ; Drom Mullac, Killeshandra, Co. Cavan. *T.:* Victoria 7646. *Clubs:* Reform, National Liberal, Eighty ; Stephen's Green, Dublin ; Royal Irish Yacht, Kingstown. *(Died 11 Jan. 1922.)*

LOUGHEED, Hon. Sir James Alexander, K.C.M.G., *cr.* 1916 ; P.C. Canada ; K.C. ; Leader of Opposition in Senate of Canada ; *b.* 1 Sep. 1854 ; *m.* 1884, *e. d.* of late William L. Hardisty of Hon. Hudson's Bay Co. ; four *s.* one *d. Educ.:* Toronto, Canada. Practised law, Toronto, 1881 ; moved to North - West Territories, 1883 ; Q.C. 1889 ; called to Senate of Canada, 1889 ; Minister of the Interior, 1920-1921 ; Leader of Government in Senate, 1911-21. *Address:* Calgary, Alberta, Canada. *T.A.:* Lougheed, Calgary. *Clubs:* Rideau, Ottawa ; National Toronto ; Ranchmen's, Calgary.

(Died Nov. 1925.)

LOUISSON, Hon. Charles, J.P. ; Member Legislative Council, New Zealand ; *b.* London, 1842 ; *s.* of George Louisson, merchant ; *m.* 1877, Hannah, *d.* of Maurice Harris, J.P., of Christchurch, N.Z. ; two *s.* two *d. Educ.:* Gravesend, England. Emigrated to Victoria, 1855 ; settled in N.Z. 1865 ; served as a city councillor for ten years ; twice presented with silver service, etc., by citizens ; Mayor of Christchurch, N.Z., 1888, 1889, 1898, 1899 ; Commissioner for N.Z., 1888, at the International Exhibition in Melbourne ; District Grand Master for Canterbury, N.Z., for Scotch Masonic Constitution from 1889-99. *Recreations:* Member, Canterbury Jockey Club ; President, N.Z. Metropolitan Trotting Club. *Address:* 214 Gloster St., Christchurch. *T.:* 726. *Club:* Canterbury, Christchurch.

(Died 19 April 1924.)

LOUSADA, Duc de, Commander Francis Clifford de Lousada, R.N. ; *b.* 17 Oct. 1842 ; 3rd *s.* of late Marquis de Lousada and Marianne, *d.* of Sir Charles Wolseley, 7th Bt. ; *m.* 1879, Emily Florence, widow of Sir Eardley G. C. Eardley, 4th Bt. ; S. *bro.* 1905. *Address:* 4 Lancaster Street, Hyde Park, W. *T.:* 2857 Pad. *Club:* Naval and Military

(Died 5 Feb. 1916.)

LOUYS, Pierre ; *b.* 10 Dec. 1870 ; *g. n.* of Duke of Abrantès ; *g.-g.-s.* of Sabatier, president of the Institut de France and surgeon in ordinary to Napoleon the First ; *b.* of French Ambassador to Russia ; *m. y. d.* of late José-Maria de Heredia, poet, member of the Académie Francaise. *Educ.:* Lycée Janson de Sailly, Paris. Six visits to North Africa ; when aged 19, founded the review La Conque, to which Swinburne, Leconte de Lisle, Heredia, Verlaine, Mallarmé, Maeterlinck, and Moréas were contributors ; his book Aphrodite had the greatest circulation ever reached by any living writer in France—350,000 copies were printed, not including translations ; ten dramas and operas were written under this title and subject, and several of them played in Russia, Austria, Argentina, France, etc., including one at the Opera Comique, Paris, with music by Camille Erlanger. *Publications:* Astarté, 1892 ; Les Chansons de Bilitis, 1895 ; Aphrodite, 1896 ; La Femme et le Pantin, 1898 ; Les Aventures du Roi Pausole, 1901 ; Sanguines, 1903 ; Archipel, 1906 ; Psyché, 1909 ; several translations from the Greek (Meleagros, Lucian). *Recreations:* bibliophilism (ancient books), musical composition, painting, etching, etc. ; Persian cats ; Greek, Egyptian, and Japanese collections. *Address:* 29 Rue de Boulainvilliers, Paris. *T.:* 683-64. *(Died 4 June 1925.)*

LOVELAND, Richard Loveland, K.C. ; D.L. (Middlesex) ; J.P. London and Middlesex ; Knight of Grace St. John of Jerusalem ; *b.* London, 18 July 1841 ; *o. surv. s.* of late John Perry Loveland, J.P., Middlesex, and Harriet Hannah, *o. d.* of late Richard Errington, Beaufront, Hexham, Northumberland ; *m.* Maria Elizabeth Oddie (*d.* 1913), 5th *d.* of Rev. F. P. H. Nind, Vicar of Woodcote - cum - Southstoke, Oxon. ; two *s.* three *d. Educ.:* Kensington Grammar School ; Pembroke College, Oxford. Barrister, 1865 ; Deputy-Chairman of Middlesex Sessions, 1889-1896 ; Deputy - Chairman of the County of London Sessions, 1896-1911. *Publications:* editor of Sir John Kelying's Crown Cases ; Shower's Cases in Parliament ; Hall on the Seashore Rights ; Griffith and Loveland on the Judicature Acts, etc. *Address:* Bury House, Alverstoke, near Gosport, Hants.

(Died 21 Sept. 1923.)

LOVELL, Sir Francis Henry, Kt., *cr.* 1900 ; C.M.G. 1893 ; LL.D., F.R.C.S. ; Dean of the London School of Tropical Medicine ; Chief Medical Officer of Mauritius and member of the Legislative Council, 1878-93 ; Surgeon-General and member of the Executive and Legislative Councils of the Colonies of Trinidad and Tobago, 1898 - 1901 ; retired from the Colonial service, 1901. *Address:* London School of

Tropical Medicine, Royal Albert Dock, E.
(*Died 28 Jan. 1916.*)

LOVERSEED, John Frederick; M.P. (L.), Sudbury Division of West Suffolk. 1923-24; *b.* 1881; *s.* of late Henry Loverseed, builder and contractor, Nottingham; *m.* 1910, Katherine Annie, *d.* of Wm. Thurman, Grantham; one *s. Educ.:* Southwell Grammar School; Gosberton Hall. Farming, 1899-1905; Agent to Sir R. Winfrey, M.P., 1908-13; to Major S. G. Howard, 1922; Capt. and Adjt. 5th Batt. Suffolk V.T.C., 1914; Military Rep. Tribunals West Suffolk, 1916; County Councillor, West Suffolk. 1919; Town Councillor, Sudbury, 1919; Mayor of Sudbury, 1921-23; Chairman of Governors, Sudbury Grammar School; Governor of East Anglian School, Bury St. Edmunds; of King Edward's Grammar School, Bury St. Edmunds; of Girls' Secondary School, Sudbury; Governor Court of Guardians, Sudbury; West Suffolk Education Committee and Standing Joint Committee; Member of Wesleyan Methodist Conference, 1924; J.P. Suffolk, 1924. *Recreations:* cricket, tennis, bowls. *Address:* Newland, Queen's Road, Sudbury, Suffolk. *T.A.:* Loverseed, Sudbury, Suffolk. *T.:* Sudbury 9. *Club:* National Liberal. (*Died 1928.*)

LOVETT, Col. (Brig.-Gen.) Alfred Crowdy, C.B. 1915; *b* 22 Nov. 1862; *m.* 1903, Fannie, *e. d.* of Col. E. W. Rumsey, of Trellick, Monmouth. Entered army and gazetted to Gloucestershire Regt. 1883; Capt. 1891; Major, 1903; Lt.-Col. 1911; Col. 1915; Instructor R.M.C. 1901-6; served European War, 1914-17 (despatches, C.B.). *Club:* Army and Navy.
(*Died 27 May 1919.*)

LOVETT, Maj.-Gen. Beresford, C.B. 1889; C.S.I. 1873; F.R.G.S., F.R.S.A.; *b.* 16 Feb. 1839; *s.* of late Rev. Robert Lovett of Marbœuf Chapel, Paris, and Rector of Pickwell, Leicestershire; *m.* 1876, Agnes (*d.* 1914), *d.* of W. Turnbull Blewitt; one *d.* After passing through Addiscombe Military College entered R.E. 1358; Maj.-Gen. 1892; employed in Persia, 1866-70, in the Telegraph Dept., and 1870-72 on the Special Mission to Seistan, for which service was given the C.S.I.; served Jowaki-Afreedee Expedition, 1878 (medal with clasp); Afghan War, 1878-79 (brevet of Lieut.-Col., medal with clasp); H.M. Consul in Persia, 1880-83; Hazara Expedition, 1888 (C.B., clasp); retired, 1894. *Address:* Hillside, 58 Harvey Road, Guildford. *Clubs:* East India United Service; County, Guildford. (*Died 12 Sept. 1926.*)

LOVETT-CAMERON, Rev. Charles Leslie, M.A.; *b.* 26 Jan. 1843; *s.* of late Rev. J. H. Lovett-Cameron, Vicar of Shoreham, Kent; *m.* 1876, Caroline, *d.* of Edward A. Holden, D.L., of Aston Hall, Derbyshire. *Educ.:* Eton; Merton College, Oxford (Scholar); 1st Class Mod. 1865; B.A. (2nd Class Lit. Hum.) 1867; M.A. 1869; Deacon, 1876; Priest, 1877. Assistant Master at Eton College, 1868-80; Vicar of Stratfield Mortimer, 1880-1913; Rural Dean of Reading, 1903-11; Hon. Canon of Christ Church, Oxford, 1907; Treasurer of the Berks Clergy Charity, 1897-1916; takes an interest in archæology and horticulture. *Address:* Abbeycroft, Mortimer, Berks. (*Died 24 Jan. 1927.*)

LOVIBOND, Joseph Williams, F.R.M.S.; J.P. City of Salisbury and Co. Wilts; Chairman of John Lovibond & Scns, Ltd., and of The Tintometer, Ltd.; Lord of the Manor of Lake, Wilts; 3rd *s.* of John Locke Lovibond of Long Sutton, Somerset, Greenwich, and Starts Hill, Kent; *b.* 1833; *m.* Charlotte, *d.* of Edward Steer, Crockham Hill, Kent; three *d. Educ.:* privately. Entered Mercantile Marine, 1846; Californian gold miner, 1849; Lovibond's Brewery, Greenwich, 1854; Mayor of Salisbury, 1878-90; Silver Medallist, St Louis Exposition, 1906, for a new theory of Light and Colour, also two bronze medals for its practical application, all awarded by the International Juries; Inventor

and Patentee of apparatus for measuring and recording colour sensations, also a gold and two silver medals at the Brussels Exhibition, 1910; holder of three medals awarded by the Royal Sanitary Association for apparatus dealing with Sanitary Hygiene and with Colour Education. *Publications:* Light and Colour Measurement; Colour Phenomena; a pamphlet on Free Trade; The Teachers' Handbook of Colour. *Recreations:* trout-rearing. *Address:* The Pleasaunce, Lake, near Salisbury. (*Died 1918.*)

LOW, Charles Rathbone, F.R.G.S.; Commander Indian Navy; *b.* Dublin, 30 Oct. 1837; *s.* of Maj. J. H. Low, 39th Bengal Native Infantry; *m.* Catherine, *d.* of General Boileau, R.E., F.R.S. Went to sea, 1853; served in Indian and China Seas, Persian Gulf, Red Sea, and East Coast of Africa, in suppression of piracy and the slave trade. First Librarian and Assist. Sec. Royal United Service Institution, 1865-68; represented the Indian Navy at the Thanksgiving Service in St. Paul's for the Recovery of the Prince of Wales, 1872; in the Abbey at the Jubilee Service of Queen Victoria, 1887; in the Funeral Procession of Her late Majesty; at the Coronation of King Edward VII.; in the Funeral Procession of His late Majesty; and at the Coronation of King George V.; in 1856 saved a seaman from drowning in the Hooghly, and was congratulated by the Governor-General, Lord Canning. *Publications:* Tales of Old Ocean, 1866; Land of the Sun, 1870; History of the British Navy, 1872; Life of Field-Marshal Sir G. Pollock, 1873; Life and Voyages of Captain James Cook, 1876; History of the Indian Navy, 1877; Life of Lord Wolseley, 1878; The First Afghan War, 1879; Soldiers of the Victorian Age, 1880; History of Maritime Discovery, 1881; Life of Lord Roberts, 1883; History of the British Army, 1889; Great African Travellers, 1890; Her Majesty's Navy, 1892; Britannia's Bulwarks, 1895; The Olympiad, 1903; also many minor works, and hundreds of magazine articles and contributions to The Times. *Address:* Lowville, Bournemouth; 27 Russell Road, Kensington, W. *T.:* Park 2864. *Club:* Junior Naval and Military. (*Died 7 Feb. 1918.*)

LOW, F. Harrison, M.B., M.R.C.S., L.S.A.; practising as X-ray specialist, and electrical worker; *b.* 1854; *e. s.* of Edwin Low, Solicitor; *m.* 1879, Fanny, *d.* of John Standring, Lee, S.W. *Educ.:* Private school; King's College, Aberdeen. Qualified M.B. C.M., Aberdeen, at 21; went into private practice, and so remained for twenty years; founded the Röntgen Society for study of X-rays, 1897; Hon. Sec. of same ever since; first medical officer in charge of X-ray Dept., King's College Hospital, Children's Hospital, Paddington Green, and Polyclinic Post-Graduate College. *Recreations:* photography, gardening.

LOW, Hon. Sir Frederick, Kt., *cr.* 1909 (**The Hon. Mr. Justice Low**); Judge of High Court of Justice, King's Bench Division, since 1915; *b.* 21 Nov. 1856; *s.* of late Stephen Philpot Low, D.L., J.P., Kent; *m.* 1882, Katherine, 4th *d.* of late Charles Thompson; one *s.* two *d. Educ.:* Westminster; privately. Admitted a Solicitor, 1878; called to Bar, Middle Temple, 1890; K.C., 1902; Bencher, 1911; S.E. Circuit; contested Salisbury (L.), 1900; Battersea, Clapham Division, 1906; Captain in the 4th V.B. Royal West Surrey Regiment and 22nd Middlesex R.V., 1880-90; Commissioner of Assize, Western and Midland Circuits, 1913-15; M.P. (L.) Norwich, 1910-15; Recorder of Ipswich, 1906-15. *Address:* 51 Sloane Gardens, S.W.; 373 Royal Courts of Justice, Strand, W.C. *T.:* Vict. 484. *Clubs:* Athenæum, Reform. (*Died 4 Sept. 1917.*)

LOW, George Macritchie, F.F.A., F.R.S.E.; Manager and Actuary of the Scottish Equitable Life Assurance Society 1900 - 20:

a Director National Bank of Scotland, 1904-1918; Member of the Royal Company of Archers (King's Bodyguard for Scotland); *b.* Edinburgh, 1849; *m.* 1891, Charlotte Ellen (*d.* 1916), *d.* of late David McLaren, merchant. *Educ.:* Edinburgh. Secretary, 1875, and Manager, 1883, of the Edinburgh Life Assurance Company; President of the Faculty of Actuaries in Scotland, 1900-3 and 1915-19. *Publications:* article, Life Insurance, in the 9th Edition of the Encyclopædia Britannica; various papers and addresses on actuarial and other cognate subjects. *Recreations:* golf, fishing. *Address:* 11 Moray Place, Edinburgh. *T.:* 2796. *M.:* SG 4099. *Clubs:* University, Edinburgh; Honourable Company of Edinburgh Golfers, Muirfield.
(*Died 29 Nov. 1922.*)

LOW, Sir James, 1st Bt., *cr.* 1908; D.L., J.P.; Kt., *cr.* 1895; managing director of Lindsay and Low, Limited, Dundee; *b.* 10 Feb. 1849; *s.* of William Low; *m.* 1890, Katherine, *d.* of Wm. Munro; one *s.* two *d.* Lord Provost of Dundee, 1893-96. *Heir: s.* Walter John, *b.* 27 May 1899. *Address:* Kilmaron Castle, near Cupar, Fifeshire.
(*Died 30 June 1923.*)

LOW, Lt.-Col. Robert Balmain, D.S.O. 1896; late Hodson's Horse, Indian Army; *b.* 7 Oct. 1864; *e. s.* of Gen. Sir R. C. Low, G.C.B.; *m.* 1st, 1899, Mabel Violet, *d.* of Maj.-Gen. O'Grady Haly, C.B.; 2nd, 1918, Leslie Dumville (*d.* 1919), *d.* of Francis C. D. Smythe of Cambridge Gardens, W., and widow of Alex. G. Macmillan. Entered Army, 1885; Captain 1896; Major, 1903; served Lushai Expedition, 1889 (clasp); Hazara Expedition, 1891 (medal with clasp); Chitral Relief Force, 1895 (despatches, D.S.O., medal with clasp); Tirah Expedition, 1897-98 (two clasps); China, 1900-1; Provost-Marshal and Headquarters Camp Commandant (despatches, brevet majority, medal with clasp). *Address:* Ambala, India.
(*Died 20 April 1927.*)

LOW, Robert Bruce, C.B. 1919; M.D., D.P.H.; Assistant Medical Officer, Local Government Board (retired); Inspector of Examinations under the Gen. Medical Council; *s.* of John Low; *b.* Edinburgh, 1846; *m.* 1874, Henrietta Jane, *d.* of Samuel Spencer of Howsham, Lincolnshire; two *s.* four *d.* *Educ.:* Royal High School and University of Edinburgh; Post Graduate Studies at St. Thomas's Hospital, London, and at Universities of Würzburg and Berlin. After graduation in 1867 was House Surgeon at Royal Infirmary, Edinburgh; and after a year's post-graduate study, practised as a rural general practitioner for nineteen years, fifteen of which were in North Yorkshire; was Deputy Coroner for North Riding; M.O.H. for Helmsley Rural District; Medical Inspector to the Local Government Board, 1887; Assistant Medical Officer, 1900; late Examiner in Sanitary Science, State Medicine and Public Health at the Universities of Cambridge, Edinburgh, Glasgow, and Leeds; served on the War Office Anti-Typhoid Inoculation Committee, 1904-12; Member of Council of the Epidemiological Section of the Royal Society of Medicine; Fellow of the Society of Tropical Medicine. *Publications:* Reports on the Progress and Diffusion of Plague, Cholera, and Yellow Fever throughout the World, 1896-1918; Reports on the Epidemiology of Exanthematic Typhus Fever 1914, Cerebrospinal Fever 1915, Acute Anterior Poliomyelitis 1916, Smallpox 1918, &c.; German Methods of Isolating Smallpox Cases, 1903; the State Animal Vaccine Establishments of Germany, 1905; the Tenure of Office and Appointment of Medical Officers of Health, 1886. *Address:* 98 York Mansions, Battersea Park, S.W.11. (*Died 12 May 1922.*)

LOW, Hon. Seth, LL.D.; *b.* 18 Jan. 1850; married. *Educ.:* Brooklyn Polytechnic Institute; Columbia University. Mayor of Brooklyn, 1881-85; contested Greater New York, 1897; President of Columbia University, New York, 1889-1901; Mayor of New York City, 1902-3; President, National Civic Federation, New York; President, Chamber of Commerce of State of New York, 1914-16. *Address:* Bedford Hills, N.Y. (*Died 18 Sept. 1916.*)

LOW, William Malcolm, J.P., D.L.; *b.* 1835; *e. s.* of General Sir J. Low, G.C.S.I., K.C.B., Clatto, Co. Fife, and Augusta, *d.* of John Talbot Shakespear; *m.* 1872, Lady Ida Feilding (*d.* 1915) *d.* of 7th Earl of Denbigh. *Educ.:* Haileybury College. Indian Civil Service, 1856-76; received special letter conveying thanks of Her Majesty for services in the field during Indian Mutiny; retired from ill-health, as Commissioner of the Nerbudda Districts; M.P. Grantham, 1886-92. *Recreations:* gardening, fishing, boating. *Address:* 22 Roland Gardens, S.W. *Clubs:* Carlton; New, Edinburgh. (*Died 14 June 1923.*)

LOWE, Lieut.-Col. Arthur Cecil, C.M.G. 1918; D.S.O. 1900; H.A.C.; *b.* 1868; *s.* of Henry W. Lowe of Holywood House, Walton-on-Thames; *m.* 1910, Amy Louisa, 2nd *d.* of late S. W. Partridge, Lynn Court, Tunbridge Wells. Served South Africa, 1900 (despatches, Queen's medal, 3 clasps, D.S.O.). *Address:* 7 East India Avenue, E.C. (*Died 24 Nov. 1917.*)

LOWE, Arthur Labron, M.A., LL.B.; C.B.E. 1919; *b.* Edgbaston, 1861; *y. s.* of late Henry Lowe, of Southfield, Norfolk Road; *m.* 1st, 1890, Mary Letitia (*d.* 1918), *d.* of late A. Bruce Mitchell, Edgbaston; three *d.*; 2nd, 1923, Emma Mary, *y. d.* of late Rev. G. A. Smallwood, Ashby-de-la-Zouch, Leicestershire. *Educ.:* Clifton College; Clare College, Cambridge. Admitted Solicitor, 1887; member of firm of Johnson, Barclay, Johnson & Lowe, 1900-5; Registrar, Birmingham County Court and District Registrar of the High Court of Justice there since 1905; Joint Editor of Costs and Fees Section of Annual County Court Practice; member of the Standing Committee for framing County Court Rules; elected a Fellow of the College of Teachers of the Blind, 1914; member of the Advisory Committee on the Welfare of the Blind Ministry of Health since 1919; Pres. Association of County Court Registrars, 1910-20, President Birmingham Law Society, 1916-18; Chairman of Birmingham Branch British Red Cross Society since its formation to 1922; Chairman of Committee Birmingham Royal Institution for the Blind, 1902-13; Chairman of the Midland Counties Association for the Blind, 1916-24. *Recreations:* farming and gardening. *Address:* Monkspath Hall, Shirley, Warwickshire; 52 Westfield Road, Edgbaston. *T.:* Edgbaston 432. *Club:* Union, Birmingham.
(*Died 7 Feb. 1928.*)

LOWE, Rev. Joseph, Hon. Canon of Newcastle. *Address:* Haltwhistle.
(*Died 22 Aug. 1920.*)

LOWELL, Amy, Litt.D.; author; *b.* 9 Feb. 1874, Brookline, Mass.; *d.* of Augustus Lowell and Katharine Bigelow Lawrence. *Educ.:* Private Schools. Phi Beta Kappa Poet, Tufts College, 1918; Columbia University, 1920; Hon. Litt.D. Baylor University, 1920; Hon. Member Phi Beta Kappa Society, Columbia, 1920; Member Poetry Society America; N.E. Poetry Club; Member American Geographical Society; N.E. Woman's Press Association; Boston Proof-Readers' Association. *Publications:* A Dome of Many-Coloured Glass, 1912; Sword Blades and Poppy Seed, 1914; Six French Poets, 1915; Men, Women, and Ghosts, 1916; Tendencies in Modern American Poetry, 1917; Can Grande's Castle, 1918; Pictures of the Floating World, 1919; Legends, 1921; (with Florence Ayscough) Fir-Flower Tablets: Poems translated from the Chinese, 1921; A Critical Fable, 1922; John Keats,

1924. *Address:* Sevenels, Brookline, Mass., U.S.A. *Clubs:* Lyceum; Colony, MacDowell, P.E.N., The Poets, New York; Chilton, Boston.
(*Died 12 May 1925.*)

LOWELL, Percival, A.B. cum laude, Harvard, 1876; Non-Resident Professor of Astronomy, Mass. Institute of Technology, since 1902; LL.D. Amherst College, 1907, Clark University, 1909; Director of the Lowell Observatory, Flagstaff, A.T.; *b.* Boston, U.S.A., 13 March 1855; *s.* of Augustus Lowell and Katharine Bigelow, *d.* of Abbott Lawrence, Minister Plenipotentiary to Great Britain, 1851; *m.* 1908, Constance Keith, of Boston. *Educ.:* Harvard College (2nd year Honours in Mathematics; Bowdoin prize medallist). Counsellor and Foreign Secretary to Korean Special Mission to U.S., and guest of Korean Government in Söul, 1883; lived in Japan at intervals, 1883-93; Phi Beta Kappa Poet at Harvard, 1889; established Lowell Observatory, 1894; undertook Eclipse Expedition to Tripoli, 1900; sent Expedition to the Andes to photograph the planet Mars, 1907; has made discoveries on the planets, especially Mars, and formulated theory of its habitability; Fellow American Academy Arts and Sciences; Member Royal Asiatic Society of Great Britain and Ireland; American Philosoph. Society; Société de Astronomique de France; Astronomische Gesellschaft; De La Société Belge D'Astronomische; Hon. Mem. Sociedad Astronómica De Mexico; Hon. Fellow Royal Astronomical Society of Canada; Janssen Medallist of the Société Astronomique de France, 1904, for researches on Mars. *Publications:* Chosön, 1885; The Soul of the Far East, 1886; Noto, 1891; Occult Japan, 1894; Mars, 1895; Annals of the Lowell Observatory, vol. i. 1898; vol. ii. 1900; vol. iii. 1905; The Solar System, 1903; Mars and its Canals, 1906; Mars as the Abode of Life, 1909; The Evolution of Worlds, 1910. *Address:* 53 State Street, Boston, U.S.A. *Clubs:* Royal Societies; Somerset, Union; Saint Botolph, Boston; Century, Aero, Authors', New York; Imperial, Tokio, Tokio.
(*Died 13 Nov. 1916.*)

LOWNDES, Maj.-Gen. Thomas; joined Madras Army, 1854; Political Agent, Bhamo, 1872-3; Inspector-General of Police, Rangoon, 1875-86. *Address:* 71 Oxford Terrace, W.2. *Club:* Constitutional. (*Died 15 Feb. 1927.*)

LOWNDES, William Selby-, J.P.; *b.* 13 Nov. 1836; *e. s.* of late William Selby-Lowndes and 1st wife, Lucy, *d.* of late Isaac Rawlins Hartman; *m.* 1867, Jessie Mary, *d.* of Lieut.-General Lechmere Worrall, and widow of Eyre Coote of West Park, Hants; one *s. Heir: s.* Col. William, O.B.E., T.D., J.P., D.L. [*b.* 27 June 1871; *m.* 1894, Florence, *o. d.* of Frederick Norton of Auckland, New Zealand, and widow of Sir Edwin Abercromby Dashwood, 8th Bart. *Educ.:* Eton. Served South African War with Bucks Yeomanry Cavalry, European War with Beds. Yeomanry 1st Cav. Div. (Legion of Honour, Croix de Guerre, despatches twice, O.B.E., T.D.); Director of West End Branch Royal Insurance Co., Director of Investment Registry Office, Chairman of the County Gentleman's Association]. Master of the Whaddon Chase Hunt; patron of three livings. *Address:* Whaddon Hall, Stony Stratford.
(*Died 3 Nov. 1920.*)

LOWRY, Charles, M.A., J.P.; Headmaster Tonbridge School 1907-22; *b.* 19 Oct. 1857; *s.* of Rev. C. H. Lowry of Stanwix House, Carlisle; *m.* 1883, Frances Maria, *d.* of Rev. C. C. Lowndes of Windermere; one *s.* two *d. Educ.:* Eton; Corpus Christi College, Oxford. Assist. Master at Wellington College, 1883; Eton College, 1883-1900; Headmaster Sedbergh School, 1900-1907. *Recreations:* rowing, golf. *Clubs:* Cavendish, Leander. (*Died 13 Dec. 1922.*)

LOWRY, Admiral Sir Robert Swinburne, K.C.B., *cr.* 1913; *b.* Zante, 4 Mar.

1854; *e. s.* of late Lt.-Gen. R. W. Lowry, C.B.; *m.* Helena, *d.* of T. Greer, Sea Park, Belfast, and Grove House, Regent Park, 1893; one *s.* one *d. Educ.:* H.M.S. "Britannia." Dartmouth. Entered Navy Dec. 1867; Lieut. 1875; served in "Serapis" during Prince of Wales's trip to India in that year; Gunnery Lieut. 1880; Commander, 1890; Commanded H.M.S. "Ganges"; received Royal Humane Society's bronze medal for saving life, 1873; thanks of French Government with a piece of Sèvres china for exertions in rescuing the corvette "Seigneley" when ashore at Jaffa, 1892; Captain, 1896; Assist. Director of Naval Intelligence, 1897-1900; Flag-Captain to Rear-Admiral Lord C. Beresford in H.M.S. "Ramillies"; Captain of H.M.S. "Hood," 1902; Capt. R.N.E. College, Devonport; Capt. H.M.S. "Russell" and A.D.C. to the King; Rear-Admiral in the Channel Fleet. 1907; Pres. Royal Naval War College, 1907-8; commanded 2nd Cruiser Squadron, 1908-10; Vice-Admiral 1911; Admiral 1913; Admiral Commanding in Scotland 1913-16; Commander-in-Chief, Rosyth, 1916; retired, 1917; Chairman Committee on Naval Education, 1916-17; Chairman Admiralty Committee on Mercantile Marine, 1917-18. *Recreations:* shooting, fishing, cycling, golf. *Address:* Wickham Lodge, Wickham, Hants. *Club:* United Service.
(*Died 29 May 1920.*)

LOWRY-CORRY, Admiral Hon. Armar; *b.* 25 May 1836; *s.* of 3rd Earl of Belmore; *m.* 1868, Geraldine (*d.* 1905), *d.* of late James King-King, M.P., of Staunton Park, Herefordshire; five *s.* three *d.* Entered Navy, 1849; Admiral, 1894. *Address:* 15 Warwick Square, S.W. *Club:* United Service.
(*Died 1 Aug. 1919.*)

LOWRY-CORRY, Col. Hon. Henry William, late commdg. Coldstream Guards; *b.* 30 June 1845; *s.* of 3rd Earl of Belmore; *m.* 1876, Hon. Blanche Edith Wood (*d.* 1921), *d.* of 1st Viscount Halifax; one *s.* two *d.* M.P. Co. Tyrone, 1873-80; served Egypt, 1885 (medal with clasp, Khedive's star); J.P. and late Chairman of Quarter Sessions for W. Suffolk; Chairman Suffolk Terr. Army Assoc. *Address:* Edwardstone Hall, Boxford, Suffolk. *Club:* Travellers'.
(*Died 6 May 1927.*)

LOWTHER, Rt. Hon. Sir Gerard Augustus, 1st Bt., *cr.* 1914; G.C.M.G., *cr.* 1911; K.C.M.G., *cr.* 1907; C.B., *cr.* 1904; P.C. 1908; *b.* 16 Feb. 1858; 2nd *s.* of late Hon. William Lowther, *b.* of 3rd Earl of Lonsdale, and Hon. Charlotte Alice, *d.* of only Baron Wensleydale; *m.* 1905, Alice, *d.* of Atherton Blight of Philadelphia, U.S.A.; two *d. Educ.:* Harrow. Entered Diplomatic Service, 1879; has served in Madrid, Paris, Constantinople, Vienna, Sofia, Bucharest, Tokio, Budapest; Secretary of Embassy, Washington; Envoy Extraordinary and Minister Plenipotentiary for Chile, 1901-4; Minister at Tangier, 1904-8; H.B.M. Ambassador at Constantinople, 1908-13. *Heir:* none. *Address:* 23 Belgrave Square, S.W. *T.:* Vic. 6495. *Clubs:* Travellers', St. James's, Prince's.
(*Died 5 April 1916.*)

LOYD, Archie Kirkman, D.L., K.C.; *b.* 1847; M.P. (U.), North or Abingdon Division of Berks, 1895-1905, and 1916-18; *s.* of late Thomas Kirkman Loyd and Annie, *d.* of late James Haig; *m.* Henrietta, *d.* of late E. L. Clutterbuck, Hardenhuish, Wilts, 1885; three *s.* Barr. 1868; Midland Circuit; Bencher Middle Temple, 1894; retired from bar, 1895; Alderman Berks County Council; V.P. of Council of British Red Cross Society. *Address:* Downs House, East Hendred, Berks; 60A Cadogan Square, S.W.1. *T.:* Ken. 4052. *Clubs:* Carlton Windham, 1900; Berks County.
(*Died 1 Dec. 1922.*)

LUARD, Lt.-Col. Charles Eckford, C.I.E. 1923; Indian Army, retired; *b.* 11 Oct. 1869; *s.* of late Col. C. H. Luard, R.E.; *m.* 1903,

Alice Margaret, *d.* of James Todd, Aberdeen: two *s.* one *d.* *Educ.:* Marlborough; Christ Church, Oxford, M.A. Indian Army (8th Gurkhas); Political Dept. Govt. of India; Political Agent, Bhopal; sometime Private Secretary to Maharajah of Indore; retired, 1925. *Publications:* History of States in Central India; joint author of Official History of the King-Emperor's Visit to India; Bibliography of Central India History, etc.; Census of Central India, 1901, 1911, and 1921; University Member Oxford City Council. *Address:* Woodsend, Boars Hill, Oxford. *T.:* Oxford 24. *M.:* FC 7952.   *(Died 17 May 1927.)*

LUARD, Major Edward Bourryau, D.S.O. 1915; 1st Batt. the King's (Shropshire Light Infantry); *b.* 20 Sep. 1870; *s.* of late Lt.-Gen. R. G. A. Luard, C.B.; *m.* 1905, Louise Henrietta Smith. Entered army, 1891; Captain, 1900; Major, 1910; served S. African War, 1899-1902 (Queen's medal, 3 clasps); European War, 1914-15 (D.S.O.). *Club:* Sports.   *(Died 24 April 1916.)*

LUBBOCK, Frederic; Chairman, London Board, Bank of New Zealand; Chairman London Merchant Bank, Ltd.; Director London Assurance Corporation; Director British Bank of South America, Ltd.; *b.* 1 May 1844; 6th *s.* of Sir John W. Lubbock, 3rd Bt.; *m.* 1869, Catherine, *o. d.* of John Gurney of Earlham Hall, Norfolk; six *s.* one *d.* *Educ.:* Eton. *Address:* 26 Cadogan Gardens, S.W.3; Emmets, Ide Hill, Sevenoaks. *T.:* Ken 2604. *Club:* Arthur's.   *(Died 22 June 1927.)*

LUBBOCK, Hon. Harold (Fox-Pitt); 3rd *s.* of 1st Baron Avebury, and 2nd wife Alice Augusta Laurentia Laura, *d.* of General Fox-Pitt-Rivers; *b.* 10 June 1888; *m.* 1914, Dorothy, *e.-d.* of H. W. Forster; one *s.* *Educ.:* Eton; Trinity College, Cambridge; M.A. Capt. West Kent Yeomanry. *Address:* 48 Grosvenor Street, W.   *(Died 4 April 1918.)*

LUBBOCK, Montagu, M.D. (Lond. and Paris), F.R.C.P.; formerly Assistant Physician to the West London Hospital, Physician to Outpatients, Charing Cross Hospital, and Assistant Physician to the Children's Hospital, Great Ormond Street; *b.* 24 May 1842; 5th *s.* of late Sir J. W. Lubbock, 3rd Bart., of High Elms, Kent, and Harriet Hotham, *d.* of Col. Hotham: *m.* 1st, 1872, Lora (*d.* 1882), *y. d.* of Capt. Geo. Hotham, R.E.; one *s.*; 2nd, 1888, Nora (*d.* 1918), *e. d.* of Nottidge Charles Macnamara, F.R.C.S., of the Lodge, Chorley Wood, Herts. *Educ.:* Eton College; football and cricket elevens; boating eight; won the running, hurdle race, and fives contests; President of the Debating Society. Upon leaving Eton, was Captain of the 11th Kent Volunteers in 1859. Was in the City for a short time; became M.D. Paris; returning then to England, he became M.D. London, and has been since that time practising as a physician in London. *Publications:* has contributed articles to medical works and papers to medical journals. *Recreations:* walking and golf. *Address:* 127 Mount Street, Berkeley Square, W. *Club:* Athenæum.   *(Died 8 April 1925.)*

LUBBOCK, Hon. Norman; *b.* 16 Dec. 1861; 2nd *s.* of 1st and *b.* and *heir-pres.* of 2nd Baron Avebury; *m.* 1919, *c.* Edith Harriet, *e. d.* of late Sir Nevile Lubbock, K.C.M.G. *Address:* Fishleigh House, Hatherleigh, N. Devon.   *(Died 11 Nov. 1926.)*

LUCAS (*cr.* 1663) **and DINGWALL** (*cr.* 1609), Baron of, **Auberon Thomas Herbert;** P.C. 1912; Royal Flying Corps; *b.* 25 May 1876; *o. surv. s.* of Hon. Auberon Herbert and Lady Florence Amabel, *d.* of 6th Earl Cowper. *Educ.:* Bedford Grammar School; Balliol Coll. Lieutenant Hants Yeomanry; Under-Secretary of State, War Office, 1908-11; Under-Secretary of State for Colonies, 1911;

Parliamentary Secretary, Board of Agriculture, 1911-14; President of the Board of Agriculture, 1914-15. Is *co-heir* to Barony of Butler. *Recreation:* ornithology. *Heir-pres.: sis.* Hon. Nan Ino Herbert. *Address:* 32 Old Queen Street, S.W.; *T.:* Victoria 938; Picket Post, Ringwood. *Clubs:* Brooks's, Travellers'. *(Died 3 Nov. 1916.)*

LUCAS, Rev. Arthur, M.A.; Hon. Canon of Rochester; *b.* 1851; *s.* of W. S. Lucas, of St. Bartholomew's Hospital; *m.* 1884 (*d.* 1920), Lilian, 4th *d.* of Ven. Arthur Davenport, Archdeacon of Hobart, Tasmania. *Educ.:* Uppingham; Clare College, Cambridge (Scholar and Exhibitioner). Assistant Master and Chaplain, Tonbridge School, 1878-1910; Acting Headmaster, 1907. *Recreations:* travel, golf. *Address:* 3 Bina Gardens, S.W.5. *T.:* Kensington 1590.   *(Died 18 Feb. 1921.)*

LUCAS, Sir Arthur, Kt., *cr.* 1919; *b.* 1845; *s.* of Louis Lucas; *m.* 1893, Juliana Violet, *d.* of Alfred G. Henriques, J.P., Brighton. *Educ.:* University College School and College, London. Civil Engineer; A.M.I.C.E. and M.I.M.E.; pupil of Sir John Hawkshaw; Director of Imperial Continental Gas Association; and Deputy Chairman of Continental Union Gas Co.; Vice-President of the Hospital for Sick Children, Great Ormond Street; Chairman of the Hospital Convalescent Home, Swanley. *Address:* 27 Bruton Street, W. 1. *T.:* Gerrard 5108. *Clubs:* Athenæum, Burlington Fine Arts.   *(Died 9 Jan. 1922.)*

LUCAS, Charles James; *b.* 25 Feb. 1853; *s.* of late Charles Thomas Lucas and Charlotte Emma, *d.* of C. Tiffin; *m.* 1881, Mildred Frances, *y. d.* of Eric Carrington Smith of Ashfold, Sussex; two *s.* *Educ.:* Harrow. Lt.-Col. (retired) Engineer and Railway S.C. V.D.; one of H.M. Lieutenants for City of London; High Sheriff for Sussex, 1904-5; D.L., J.P. Sussex. *Address:* Warnham Court, Horsham. *T.A.:* Lucas-Warnham. *T.:* Broadbridge Heath 9. *Clubs:* Carlton, Royal Automobile.   *(Died 17 April 1928.)*

LUCAS, Col. Francis Alfred, V.D.; *b.* 7 June 1850; *m.* 1887, Alice, *y. d.* of late Viscount de Stern. Contested Louth Div. of Lincs, 1895; M.P. (C.) Lowestoft Div. of Suffolk, 1900-6; contested Kennington, Jan. and Dec. 1910; Supply and Transport Officer, S. London Vol. Brigade, 1890-1900; commanding Harwich Vol. Brigade, 1900-6; 41 years' service in Reserve Forces; J.P. Suffolk; Deputy Chairman, Alliance Assurance Co., Ltd. *Address:* Stornoway House, Cleveland Row, S.W. *T.A.:* Sobriety, London. *T.:* Regent 3985. *Clubs:* Athenæum, Carlton, St. James's, Garrick.   *(Died 11 Dec. 1918.)*

LUCAS, Francis Herman, C.B. 1911; C.V.O. 1917; Financial Secretary India Office; *b.* 1878; *m.* 1903, Helen Mary, *e. d.* of late Morris Smith, Dalbeattie, Kirkcudbrightshire; one *s.* three *d.* *Educ.:* Winchester College (Scholar); Trinity College, Cambridge (Scholar). Entered India Office, 1901; Assistant Private Secretary to Lord George Hamilton, 1902-3; to Rt. Hon. St. John Brodrick, M.P., 1903-5; and to Rt. Hon. John Morley, M.P., 1905-7; Principal Private Secretary to Viscount Morley, 1909-10, to the Marquess of Crewe, 1910-15, and to Rt. Hon. Austen Chamberlain, M.P., 1915-1917. *Address:* 50 Oakley Street, Chelsea, S.W.3.   *(Died 13 April 1920.)*

LUCAS, Brigadier-General Frederic George, C.B. 1918; C.S.I. 1919; C.I.E. 1921; D.S.O. 1898; *b.* Falmouth, 20 Oct. 1866; *e. s.* of late Frederic Lucas, Paymaster, R.N.; *m.* 1920, Ethel Fanny Whitelock, *widow* of Lt.-Col. A. J. Menzies, D.S.O.; one *d.* *Educ.:* Royal Naval School, New Cross; Royal Acad. Gosport (Burney's); Royal Military College, Sandhurst. Joined East Lancashire Regt. 1886; Indian Staff Corps, 1888; Captain, 1897; Bt. Major 1898; Major, 1904; Lt.-Col. 1911; Col. 1917: served

Hazara Expedition, 1891 (medal and clasp); Isazai Expedition, 1892; commanded the Gurkha Scouts, Tirah Expedition, 1897-98 (despatches twice, brev. of Maj. and D.S.O., medal with two clasps); Waziristan, 1901-2 (despatches, clasp); Bazar Valley, 1908(despatches, medal and clasp); European War, including Mesopotamia, 1914-1918 (Bt. Col., C.B., C.S.I., Legion d'Honneur, Croix d'Officier); Afghanistan, 1919 (despatches, clasp); Waziristan, 1919-20 (despatches, C.I.E., 2 clasps); retired, 1921. *Clubs:* United Service, Alpine. *(Died 5 Oct. 1922.)*

LUCAS, John Seymour; R.A. 1898; F.S.A.; historical and portrait painter; *b.* London, 21 Dec. 1849; *s.* of Henry Lucas; *n.* of John Lucas, portrait painter; *m.* 1877, Marie Elizabeth (*d.* 1921), *d.* of Louis Dieudonne de Cornelissen and Marianne Bath. *Educ.:* Royal Academy School of Art. Practised as painter of genre and historical pictures, and portraits; A.R.A. 1886; visitor at Royal Academy Schools of Art, from 1886; Examiner Department of Science and Art, South Kensington; painted (1898) fresco for Royal Exchange, representing William the Conqueror granting the first charter to the City of London, presented by the Corporation of London; commissioned by King Edward VII. to paint the reception of the Moorish Embassy, 1901, and in 1914 commissioned to paint for the House of Commons, a large fresco of The Flight of the Five Members, 1642. *Engraved works:* Armada in Sight; The Surrender of Don Pedro de Valdez to Drake on board the "Revenge"; Eloped; The Toper; The Smoker; The Loving Cup, etc. *Address:* New Place, Woodchurch Road, N.W.; Blythborough, Suffolk. *(Died 8 May 1923.)*

LUCAS, Keith, Sc.D.; F.R.S. 1913; Fellow and Lecturer in Natural Sciences, Trinity Coll. Cambridge; *b.* Greenwich, 1879; *s.* of Francis Robert and Katharine Lucas; *m.* 1909, Alys, *d.* of Rev. C. E. Hubbard; three *s. Educ.:* Rugby; Trinity College, Cambridge. Fellow of Trinity College, 1904; Sc.D., Cambridge, 1911; Croonian Lecturer, Royal Society, 1912. *Publications:* papers on Physiology of Nerve and Muscle in Journal of Physiology. *Address:* Fen Ditton, Cambs; Trinity College, Cambridge. *T.:* Cambridge 739 and 580. *(Died 5 Oct. 1916.)*

LUCAS, Marie Elizabeth Seymour; *b.* Paris, 23 Apr. 1855; *d.* of Louis Dieudonne de Cornelissen and Marianne Bath; lineally descended from Antonius Cornelissen of Antwerp, patron of the Fine Arts, and friend of Van Dyck, who painted his portrait. A daughter of Rubens married into the Cornelissen family; *m.* 1877, John Seymour Lucas. *Educ.:* at home; London; Germany; Royal Academy. *Paintings:* Types of English Beauty; We are but Little Children weak; Weighed and found Wanting, etc. *Address:* New Place, Woodchurch Road, West Hampstead.
(Died 25 Nov. 1921.)

LUCAS-TOOTH, Sir (Archibald) Leonard (Lucas), 2nd Bt., *cr.* 1906; Major Hon. Artillery Company; *b.* 3 June 1884; *s.* of 1st Bt. and Helen, *d.* of Frederick Tooth, of Goderich, Sydney; *S.* father 1915; *m.* 1916, Rosa Mary, *y. d.* of Charles A. Bovill, 60 Pont Street, S.W.; one *d: Heir:* none. *Address:* Holme Lacy, Herefordshire; Kameruka, Co. Auckland, N.S. Wales. *(Died 12 July 1918.)*

LUCCHESI, Andrea Carlo, R.B.S., sculptor; *b.* London (City), 19 Oct. 1860. *Educ.:* Euston Coll.; West London; School of Art; Royal Academy Schools. Began life as a sculptor's moulder and drifted into carving and afterwards modelling; exhibited at Royal Academy and other exhibitions since 1881. *Address:* 1 and 2 Camden Studios, Camden Street, N.W. *Clubs:* Savage, St. John's Wood Arts.
(Died 9 April 1925.)

LUCE, Rev. Edward; Rector of St. Saviour, Jersey; Canon of Winchester; *b.* 1851; *s.* of late Francis Edward Luce of St. Lawrence, Jersey, and Louisa, *d.* of late John Orange of St. Brelade; *m.* 1882, Catherine Wynne, *d.* of late John Este Vibert of the Grange, St. Mary, Jersey; one *s.* four *d. Educ.:* Victoria College, Jersey; Pembroke College, Oxford. Deacon, 1874; has held in succession the Rectories of St. John, St. Mary, and St. Saviour in the Island of Jersey; Vice-Dean of Jersey since 1898; a member of the States of Jersey, and has been on several occasions deputed by that body to represent them before His Majesty's Privy Council. *Recreations:* agricultural pursuits; was for many years President of the Royal Agricultural and Horticultural Society of Jersey. *Address:* St. Saviour's, Jersey.
(Died 1 July 1917.)

LUCK, General Sir George, G.C.B., *cr.* 1909; K.C.B., *cr.* 1897; *b.* 24 Oct. 1840; family to which he belongs resides at Malling, Kent; *m.* 1867, Ellen Georgina, *d.* of Maj.-Gen. Frank Adams, C.B. *Educ.:* private schools. Joined army, 1858; Capt. Inniskilling Dragoons, 1867; Lt.-Col. 15th Hussars, 1879; Brig.-Gen. commanding Sind District, 1884; Inspector-General of Cavalry in India, 1887-93; commanding Quetta District, 1893; Inspector-General of Cavalry in Great Britain and Ireland, 1895-98; commanded 15th Hussars in Afghan and Boer wars; in command of Bengal Army, 1898-1903; Colonel of the 15th the King's Hussars, 1904; General, 1905; H.M.'s Lieutenant the Tower of London, 1905-7. *Address:* Landford Lodge, Salisbury. *Club:* Army and Navy.
(Died 10 Dec. 1916.)

LUCK, Richard; Recorder of Richmond, Yorks. since 1920; *b.* 14 Sep. 1847; *s.* of late Ald. Richard Luck, J.P., Mayor of Darlington, 1872. *Educ.:* Queen Elizabeth Grammar School, Darlington; St. John's College, Cambridge (11th Senior Optime; M.A., LL.M.). Called to Bar, Inner Temple, 1871; North Eastern Circuit; President Darlington Conservative and Unionist Club. *Address:* Central Chambers and Osborne Villa, Darlington. *T.A.:* Richard Luck, Darlington. *T.:* Chambers 2416; Residence 2417. *(Died Nov. 1920.)*

LUCKES, Eva C. E.; C.B.E. 1917; matron, London Hospital, Whitechapel, E.1.; Lady of Grace of the Order of St. John of Jerusalem; member of the British Red Cross Society; Royal Red Cross (1st class). *Publications:* General Nursing, ninth and revised edition, 1914; Hospital Sisters and their Duties, fourth and revised edition, 1912. *Address:* London Hospital, Whitechapel, E.1. *T.:* Avenue 5020.
(Died 16 Feb. 1919.)

LUCKMAN, Ven. William Arthur Grant, V.D.; *e. s.* of Rev. W. Grant Luckman; *b.* 25 June 1857; *m.* Sophia Carolina, *d.* of Rev. Prebendary Ommanney of Chew Magna, Somerset. *Educ.:* Keble College, Oxford (M.A.). Ordained, 1881; Master of Boys' High School, Allahabad, 1882-86; Chaplain of St. Paul's Cathedral, 1881-91 and 1893-94; Naini-tal, 1891-1893; St. John, Calcutta, 1893-95; Canon of Calcutta, 1900-7; Archdeacon, 1907-11. *Address:* The Rectory, Colinton, Midlothian. *Clubs:* East India United Service, Oriental.
(Died 8 Jan. 1921.)

LUCY, Sir Henry, J.P.; Kt., *cr.* 1909; "Toby, M.P." of Punch; *b.* Crosby, 5 Dec. 1845; *m.* Nancy, *d.* of John White, headmaster, Crescent School. *Educ.:* Crescent School, Liverpool; Paris. Apprenticed to Liverpool merchant; joined staff Shrewsbury Chronicle as chief reporter, 1864; went to Paris to study language and literature, 1869; returned to London, joined staff of new morning edition Pall Mall Gazette, 1870; joined Daily News as special correspondent, chief of Gallery staff, and writer of Parliamentary summar7, 1873; editor of the Daily News, 1886; resigned, preferring earlier vocation in Press Gallery, 1887; began to contribute Cross Bench articles to the Observer, 1880; joined the staff of Punch, creating the character of "Toby, M.P.," from whose Diary the Essence of Parliament, commenced by Shirley Brooks, was extracted, 1881; retired, 1916. *Publications:* Handbook of Parliamentary Procedure; Men and Manner in Parliament, 1875; Gideon Fleyce, a novel, 1882; East by West, 1884; A Diary of Two Parliaments: The Disraeli Parliament, 1880, and the Gladstone Parliament, 1885; A Diary of the Salisbury Parliament, 1892; A Diary of the Home Rule Parliament, 1895; Faces and Places, 1895; Mr. Gladstone, a Study from Life, 1896; The Miller's Niece, 1896. A Diary of the Unionist Parliament, 1901; Peeps at Parliament, 1903; Later Peeps at Parliament, 1905; The Balfourian Parliament, 1906; Memories of Eight Parliaments, 1908; Sixty Years in the Wilderness, 1909 (second series, 1912); Nearing Jordan (third series), 1916; The Diary of a Journalist, 1920; second vol. 1922, third vol. 1923; Lords and Commoners, 1921. *Recreation:* travel; made journey round the world, crossing U.S., visiting Japan, returning through India, 1883-84; visited the Cape, 1894; West Indies, 1902; United States, 1908. *Address:* Whitethorn, Hythe, Kent. *Club:* National Liberal.

(Died 20 Feb. 1924.)

LUDLOW of Heywood, 2nd Baron (*cr.* 1897), **Rt. Hon. Henry Ludlow Lopes,** J.P. Wilts and Northampton; D.L. Wilts; *b.* Wiltshire, 30 Sep. 1865; *s.* of 1st Baron Ludlow and Cordelia Lucy, *e. d.* of Erving Clark, Efford Manor, Devon; *m.* 1st, 1908, Blanche (*d.* 1911), *widow* of 7th Lord Howard de Walden; 2nd, 1919, Lady Wernher (see Lady Ludlow). *Educ.:* Eton; Balliol College, Oxford; B.A., 1885 (2nd class Honours); M.A., 1890; Barr; Capt. Royal Wiltshire Imp. Yeomanry; L.C.C.; Pres. of Cancer Hospital; late Treasurer of St. Bartholomew's Hospital; European War, 1917-1918, Staff; M.F.H. Hertfordshire Hounds *Recreations:* shooting, hunting, stalking, and coaching. *Heir:* none. *Address:* Bath House, Piccadilly, W.; Luton Hoo, Luton, Beds. *Clubs:* Carlton, Marlborough, Bachelors'.

(Died 8 Nov. 1922.)

LUKIN, Maj.-Gen. Sir Henry Timson, K.C.B., *cr.* 1918; C.B. 1916; D.S.O. 1900; C.M.G. 1902; Permanent Force, Union of South Africa (retired); *b.* 24 May 1860; *s.* of R. H. Lukin, Barrister-at-Law; *m.* 1891, Lily, *d.* of M. H. Quinn, Fort Hare, S.A. *Educ.:* Merchant Taylors' School. Served South African War, 1879; Zulu Campaign; attached to Cavalry Brigade in advance on Ulundi; present at battle (severely wounded, medal with clasp); operations in Basutoland, 1881 (medal and clasp); Field Adjutant Bechuanaland Field Force, Langeberg Campaign, 1896-97 (despatches several times); South African War; Lieut.-Colonel 1900; commanded artillery, Wepener siege, 1900; commanded 1st Colonial Division, Cape Colony, 1901 (despatches thrice, Queen's medal four clasps, King's medal two clasps, D.S.O.); Colonel Commanding Cape Mounted Riflemen, 1903-12; Commandant-General Cape Colonial Forces, 1904-12; Inspector-General Permanent Force Union of South Africa, 1912; served South-West Africa, 1914-15; European War, 1915-18; commanded South African Infantry Brigade, Egypt and France, 9th Division, B.E.F., and 64th Division (Order of the Nile, 3rd Class, K.C.B., Commandeur Legion d'Honneur); Hon. Major-General in the Army, 1919. *Recreations:* golf, polo, tennis, etc. *Address:* Ascot, Kenilworth, Cape, South Africa. *Clubs:* Windham; Civil Service, Cape Town. *(Died 16 Dec. 1925.)*

LUKIS, Surg.-Gen. Hon. Sir Charles Pardey, K.C.S.I., *cr.* 1911; C.S.I. 1910; M.D., Lond.; F.R.C.S., Eng.; Director-General I.M.S. since 1910, and Member of the Viceroy's Legislative Council, India; Chairman Executive Committee, Indian Council, St. John Ambulance Association; and Commissioner for the St. John Ambulance Overseas Brigade within the Empire of India, 1915; Hon. Surg. to H.E. the Viceroy of India, 1905; Good Service Pension, 1910; Knight of Grace of the Order of St. John of Jerusalem, 1911; Hon. Surgeon to H.M., 1913; V.D. 1915; *b.* 9 Sept. 1857; *s.* of late W. H. Lukis; *m.* 1885, Lilian, *e. d.* of late Col. John Stewart, R.A., C.I.E., of Ardvorlich; two *s.* three *d. Educ.:* St. Bartholomew's Hospital. Late Principal and Professor of Medicine, Medical College, Calcutta; and first Physician, College Hospital; served Waziri Expedition, 1881; Zhob Valley Expedition, 1884. *Publications:* A Manual of Tropical Hygiene; Editor of The Indian Journal of Medical Research, Ghosh's Materia Medica, and Waring's Bazaar Medicines of India. *Address:* Home Department, Government of India, Simla. *Clubs:* East India United Service; Bengal, Calcutta; United Service, Simla. *(Died 24 Oct. 1918.)*

LUMHOLTZ, Carl; exploring countries and author; *b.* near Lillehammer, in the central part of Norway, 1851. *Educ.:* Lillehammer Latin og Realskole; University of Christiania. Sent by the Museums of Christiania University to Australia as zoological collector, 1880-84; camped for nearly a year with the blacks of the coast range near Cardwell, Queensland; discovered the tree kangaroo of Australia and other mammals; turned to anthropology and travelled seven years among the Indians of Mexico, mostly in the little known Sierra Madre of Northern Mexico; his faculty to gain the confidence of the natives was largely due to his ability of learning and rendering their songs; between the years 1914 and 1917 he spent two years travelling in Dutch Borneo, making a journey through the central part of the island; is planning an expedition to New Guinea (Dutch part), 1920. *Publications:* Among Cannibals, 1889; Unknown Mexico, 1902; New Trails in Mexico, 1912; Through Central Borneo, two years travel in the Land of the Headhunters, 1920; Symbolism of the Huichol Indians; Decorative Art of the Huichol Indians, published as Memoirs of the American Museums of Natural History. *Recreations:* ski-ing, skating, dancing. *Address:* Christiania, Norway; c/o Norwegian Consulate General, New York.

(Died 5 May 1922.)

LUMLEY, Colonel Francis Douglas, C.B.E. 1919; C.B. 1902; late Middlesex Regt.; *b.* 13 Nov. 1857; *m.* Leonora Constance (*decd.*), *d.* of Arthur Kenyon. Entered army, 1875; Captain, 1884; Major, 1893; Lieut.-Col. 1901; Brevet Colonel, 1904; Substantive Col. 1907; Commanding No. 10 District, 1908-11; served South Africa, 1899-1902 (despatches, C.B., medal with five clasps); European War, 1914-1919 (despatches). *Club:* Naval and Military.

(Died 4 Dec. 1925.)

LUMLEY, Brigadier-General Hon. Osbert (Victor George Atheling), C.M.G. 1917; *b.* and *heir* of Earl of Scarbrough, and *b.* of late Lady Bolton, Lady Bradford, Lady Zetland, and Lady Grosvenor; *b.* 18 July 1862; *m.* 1892, Constance Eleanor, O.B.E., *e. d.* of late Captain Eustace John Wilson-Patten, 1st Life Guards, and Emily Constantia, *d.* of Rev. Lord John Thynne (she *m.* 2nd, 3rd Marquess of Headfort); one *s.* one *d.* Formerly A.D.C. and Military Private Secretary to Lord-Lieutenant of Ireland (Marquess of Zetland), A.D.C. to Major-General Sir R. Thynne, K.C.B., commanding N.E. District, and Colonel-in-Charge, Cavalry Records (Hussars), 1910-14. *Heir:* *s.* Lawrence Roger, *b.* 27 July 1896, late Lieut. Hussars.

Address: 50 Cadogan Square, S.W.1; *T.:* Victoria 2095. *(Died 14 Dec. 1923.)*

LUMLEY, Theodore, J.P.; Member Special Local Tribunal for London; Consul-General for Monaco in London; Knight of the Order of St. Charles. *Educ.:* Paris. Solicitor; prizeman, Law Society, 1868; Commissioner for the Strichen and Auchmedden Estates, Aberdeenshire; Solicitor to the Government of Portugal and to the Imperial Persian Legation in London; Hon. Solicitor, Royal General Theatrical Fund, and St. Peter's Hospital; conducted the Langworthy case and many other *causes célèbres*; member of the Court of Assistants of the Company of Turners; member of the firm of Lumley and Lumley, 37 Conduit Street, W.1, 15 Old Jewry Chambers Bank, E.C.; 32 Boule. vard Haussmann, Paris. *Address:* 25 Upper Grosvenor Street, W.1. *T.A.:* Lumbulus, London. *T.:* Gerrard 3582. *Clubs:* Devonshire, Royal Automobile, Royal Aero. Royal Motor Yacht.
(Died 2 July 1922.)

LUMSDEN, Gen. Sir Peter Stark, G.C.B., *cr.* 1885; K.C.B., *cr.* 1879; C.S.I. 1870; D.L. and J.P. for the Counties of Aberdeen and Banff; *b.* 9 Nov. 1829; *s.* of late Colonel T. Lumsden, C.B.; Belhelvie Lodge, Aberdeenshire; *m.* Mary, *d.* of J. Marriott, 1862. *Educ.:* Military Coll. Addiscombe. Entered Indian Army, 1847; served in the Quartermaster-Gen.'s Department in frontier campaign in the N.W. of India, 1851-54; on special military mission to Afghanistan, 1857-58; in Central India campaign, 1857-58; in China at capture of Taku Forts and occupation of Pekin, 1860; with Bhootan Field Force, 1865; as Deputy Quartermaster-Gen., 1864-68; as Quartermaster-Gen. of the Army, 1868-73; Acting Resident, Hyderabad, 1873; Adj.-Gen. of the Army, 1874-79; Chief of the Staff in India, 1879; A.D.C. to the Queen, 1870-81; British Commissioner for demarcation of N.W. boundary of Afghanistan, 1884-85; member of the Council of India, 1883-93. *Publication:* Lumsden of the Guides, 1899. *Address:* Buchromb, Dufftown, N.B. *Club:* United Service. *(Died 9 Nov. 1918.)*

LUND, Niels M., Associate of Royal Society of Painter-Etchers; *b.* 30 Nov. 1863. *Educ.:* Royal Academy of Arts, London; Paris. Honourable mention and Gold Medallist, Paris Salon, 1894-95. First exhibited at R.A., 1887; Salon, 1894; Pictures in the Luxembourg, Paris; and other public Galleries. *Address:* 169 Adelaide Road, N.W. *(Died 28 Feb. 1916.)*

LUSCOMBE, Ven. Popham Street; authorised to officiate in Diocese of Sydney. *Educ.:* Moore Theological College, N.S.W.; Queens College, Camb. (M.A.). Incumbent of Wollombi, 1879-93; Gresford, 1893; Canon of Christ Church Cathedral, Newcastle; Rector of Waratah, 1901-11; Dungog, 1911-22; Archdeacon of Northumberland, 1908-11; Rector of Paterson, 1922-24; Archdeacon of Gloucester, N.S.W., 1911-24. *Address:* Kanawha, West Ryde, New South Wales. *(Died 6 Feb. 1927.)*

LUSHINGTON, Alfred Wyndham, C.I.E. 1915; *s.* of James Law Lushington, I.C.S.; *m.* Elizabeth Alice, *d.* of Capt. S Cordue, Bagshot, Surrey; one *s.* two *d. Educ.:* Malvern College. Joined India Forest Dept., 1882. Imperial Forest Service, Conservator of Forests, Madras, 1905 (retired). *Address:* Dyces House, Waltair, India.
(Died 26 Mar. 1920.)

LUTTMAN-JOHNSON, Lieut.-Col. Frederic, D.S.O. 1900; late Lieut.-Col. commanding and Hon. Col. 3rd Leinster Regt.; *b.* 22 Jan. 1845; *s.* of Rev. H. W. R. Luttman-Johnson, of Binderton, Chichester. Entered army, York and Lancaster Regiment, 1865; retired 1900; served South Africa, 1900-2 (despatches, Queen's medal, 3 clasps, King's medal, 2 clasps, D.S.O.); J.P. West Sussex. *Address:*

Redhill House, Petworth, Sussex. *Club:* Army and Navy. *(Died 11 Aug 1917.)*

LUTTRELL, Hugh Courtenay Fownes; *b.* Woodlands, W. Somerset, 10 Feb. 1857; *s.* of late George Fownes Luttrell and Elizabeth, *d.* of Sir Alexander Hood, 2nd Bt., M.P.; *m.* 1904, Dorothy Hope Wedderburn, *e. d.* of Sir William Wedderburn, 4th Bt.; two *s.* four *d. Educ.:* Cheltenham Coll. Capt. in Rifle Brigade; A.D.C. to Lord Cowper and Lord Spencer, Viceroys of Ireland; A.D.C. to General Sir John Adye, Governor of Gibraltar; was Captain and Hon. Major 3rd Battalion Duke of Cornwall's Militia from 1887-96. M.P. (L.) Tavistock Division of Devonshire (W. Devon), 1892-1900 and 1906-10. *Recreations:* gardening and painting. *Address:* Ward House, Bere Alston, Devon. *(Died 14 Jan. 1918.)*

LUTWYCHE, Hudson Latham, J.P., D.L.; *b.* Homefield Houses, Lancashire, 10 July 1856; *o. surv. s.* of late Hudson Lutwyche, Kynaston, Ross, Herefordshire; *m.* 1888, Alice Metta, *o. d.* of Otis Hopkins, Milwaukee, U.S.A.; one *s. Educ.:* Rugby; Cheltenham College. Captain 3rd Batt. Royal Lancaster Regiment; travelled a good deal; takes great interest in county business, especially in all matters of sport; High Sheriff, Herefordshire, 1889. *Recreations:* hunting, shooting, fishing, and all field sports. *Address:* Kynaston, Ross, Herefordshire. *T.A.:* Hoarwithy. *Clubs:* Boodle's, St. James's. *(Died 19 July 1925.)*

LÜTZOW, Count, Ph.D. of the Bohemian University of Prague; Hon. F.R.S.L.; F.R.G.S.; D. Litt. Oxon; Chamberlain of H.M. the Emperor of Austria since 1881; *m.* Anna, *y. d.* of late Baron vbn Bornemann, minister of Mecklenburg in Paris. *Educ.:* Vienna and Innsbruck Universities. Member of Austrian Parliament, 1885-89; Member of Royal Society of Sciences, Bohemia, and of the Bohemian Academy of Francis Joseph; Ilchester Lecturer, Oxford, 1904; lectured at American Universities, 1912. *Publications:* Bohemia, an Hist...ul Sketch; History of Bohemian Literature, 1899; Prague (Mediæval Towns Series); The Labyrinth of the World (edit. and trans. from the Bohemian of Comenius), 1901; The Historians of Bohemia, 1904; The Life and Times of Master John Hus, 1909; The Hussite Wars, 1914; many literary and political articles. *Recreations:* racing, hunting, fencing. *Address:* Château de Zampach, Hnátnice, Bohemia. *T.A.:* Lützow Hnátnice, Bohemia. *Clubs:* Jockey, Vienna; Bohemian Art (Ümelecky, Klüb) Chicago.
(Died 13 Jan. 1916.)

LUXFORD, Maj. Rev. John Aldred, C.M.G. 1916; C.F., 3rd class, N.Z. Chaplain Dept. Served S.A. War, 1902 (Queen's medal with clasp); European War, 1914-16 (despatches, C.M.G.). *Address:* Christ Church, New Zealand.
(Died 1921.)

LUXMOORE, Henry Elford, M.A.; retired ex-Senior Assistant Master, Eton College; 2nd *s.* of Rev. Henry Luxmoore, Vicar of Barnstaple, Devon. *Educ.:* Stoke Poges; Eton College (K.S. 1852-59); Pembroke College, Oxford (Rouse Scholar); 1st Class Mods., 1862; 1st Class Lit. Hum., 1864. Assistant Master at Eton, 1864-1904; Bucks County Council and Education Committee; ex-Chairman Eton Society for Improvement of Cottage Accommodation; Oxford Diocesan Board; ex-Master of Guild of St. George, 1922-26; Advisory Committee, St. Albans Diocese. *Publications:* mainly pamphlets, English Manners, Tudor and Stuart; Noblesse Oblige; Eton Chimneys; Layman's Argument; Confirmation; Ut casti sint; Addresses to Guild of St. George; Reproductions of water-colour drawings, "Eton from a Backwater"; contributions to Nat. Biog. Hortic. Journal, Quarterly Review. *Recreations:* ethics and economics, rural reconstruction,

art, gardening. *Address:* Baldwin's End, Eton, Bucks. *T.A.:* Eton. *Club:* Savile.
(*Died 11 Nov. 1926.*)

LUZZATTI, Luigi, Member Chamber of Deputies, 1870-1921; Senator, 1921; Professor of Public Law, University of Rome; *b.* Venice, 1 March 1841. *Educ.:* Gymnase and Lycee, Venice; University of Padua. Professor of Political Economy, Technical Institute, Milan, 1863; Professor of Constitutional Law, University of Padua, 1866; General Secretary to Minister of Agriculture, 1869 - 73; Chancellor of the Exchequer, 1891, 1896, 1903, 1906, 1920; Minister of Agriculture, Industry, and Commerce, 1909; President of the Council of Ministry and Home Minister, 1910; Member of the Institute of France and Grand Cross of the Legion of Honour, 1898; Minister of State, 1906; Knight of Savoia's Order; Grand Cross of Sts. Mauritius and Lazarus; Grand Cross de l'ordre de Leopold, Belgique, etc. *Publications:* La Diffusion du Credit et les Banques populaires, 1863; L'Eglise et l'Etat en Belgique avec applications à l'Italie, 1866; La Liberté de conscience et de science, 1910 (traduite en français, en allemand, en japonais, etc.); Pro italico nomine; Reports on Popular Banks instituted by him in Italy; A Book on Small Property, 1913; Scienza e patria, 1916; Sul filosofo dalmata Giorgio Politeo, 1919; Grandi Italiani, Grandi Sacrifizi per la Patria, 1924; articles on social, financial, and religious questions; Dio nella Liberta, 1926, etc. *Address:* Via Vittorio Veneto 84, Rome. *T.:* 10-51.
(*Died 29 Mar. 1927.*)

LYALL, Sir Charles James, K.C.S.I., *cr.* 1897; C.I.E. 1880; M.A. Oxon.; Hon. LL.D. Edin.; Hon. Ph.D., Strassburg; Hon. D.Litt. Oxford; Fellow, British Academy; Fellow of King's College, London; *b.* 9 Mar, 1845; *s.* of late Charles Lyall, 55 Sussex Gardens, W.; *m.* 1870, Florence Lyall, *d.* of Henry Fraser; two *s.* five *d.* *Educ.:* King's College School; King's College; Balliol College, Oxford. Entered B.C.S. 1867; Assist. Magistrate Meerut, Bulandshahr, and Allahabad Districts, 1867-71; Under - Secretary to Govt. N.W. Provinces, 1871-72; Assist. Under-Secretary, Foreign Department, 1872; Under-Secretary to Govt. of India in Revenue, Agriculture, and Commerce Department, 1873-80; Secretary to Chief Commr. of Assam, 1880-83; Judge and Commr. Assam Valley Districts, 1883-84; Secretary to Govt. of India in Revenue and Agricultural Department, 1886; again Secretary to Chief Commr. Assam, 1887; Judge and Commissioner of Assam Valley Districts, 1888-89; Secretary to Govt. of India in Home Department, 1889-94; Chief Commissioner, Assam, 1894; Chief Commissioner Central Provinces, India, 1895-98; Secretary Judicial and Public Department, India Office, 1898-1910. *Publications:* Translations of Ancient Arabic Poetry, 1885; edition of Ten Ancient Arabic Poems, 1894; articles in Ency. Brit., 9th and 11th editions; edition of two ancient Arabic *Diwáns,* with translation, 1913. *Address:* 82 Cornwall Gardens, S.W.7. *T.:* Western 7083. *Club:* Athenæum.
(*Died 1 Sept. 1920.*)

LYALL, David Robert, C.S.I., 1891; *b.* Ochterlony House, Forfarshire, N.B., 24 Nov. 1841; *e. s.* of late David Lyall; *m.* 1866, Laura Agnes, *d.* of late Maj.-Gen. W. J. B. Knyvett; two *s.* three *d.* *Educ.:* Edinburgh Academy; Capt. of the XI. and Football XX. Entered Bengal Civil Service, 1861; Inspector-General of Police L.P. 1883-87; Commr. of Chittagong, 1887-91; Commr. of Patna, 1891-92; member of Board of Revenue and of Legislative Council, Bengal, 1892-96; retired 1896; Civil Political officer with Chin Lushai Expedition, 1888 (medal and clasp, C.S.I.); President of Committee to inquire into Military and Public Works Expenditure, Simla, 1894; Superintendent of

the Cooch Behar State, 1896-99. *Recreations:* cricket, racquets, pig-sticking, shooting. *Address:* Netherclay House, Bishop's Hull, Taunton. *T.A.:* Bishop's Hull. *Clubs:* East India United Service; Somerset County. (*Died 3 Jan. 1917.*)

LYALL, Sir James Broadwood, K.C.S.I., *cr.* 1892; G.C.I.E., *cr.* 1888; retired officer Indian Civil Service; director Hand in Hand Insurance Company; *b.* England, 4 Mar. 1838; *s.* of Rev. Alfred Lyall, Rector of Harbledown, Kent, and Mary, *d.* of James Broadwood, Lyne, Sussex; *m.* Katherine, *d.* of Rev. J. Cautley, 1874. *Educ.:* Eton; Haileybury Coll. Appointed Bengal C. S., 1857; landed in India, 1858; joined Punjab Commission, 1859; Resident in Mysore and Chief Commissioner of Coorg, 1888-1887; Lieut.-Governor of the Punjab, 1887-92; visited China, Japan, Canada, and U.S., 1892; member Royal Commission on Opium, 1893; revisited India in that capacity; President Indian Famine Commission, 1898. *Publications:* only official. *Recreations:* golf, cycling, shooting. *Address:* Statenborough House, Eastry, Dover. *Club:* Athenæum. (*Died 4 Dec. 1916.*)

LYE, Lt.-Col. Robert Cobbe, D.S.O. 1904; 34th Sikh Pioneers; *b.* 27 Nov. 1865. Entered army, 1885; Capt. 1896; Major, 1903; served Burmah, 1885-87 (slightly wounded, despatches, medal with clasp); Miranzai Expedition, 1891; Chitral, 1895 (medal with clasp); N.W. Frontier, India, 1897-98 (clasp); Thibet, 1903-4 (severely wounded, despatches, D.S.O.). *Address:* Sialkot, India. (*Died 28 June 1917.*)

LYELL, 1st Baron of Kinnordy, *cr.* 1914; **Leonard Lyell,** Bt., *cr.* 1894; D.L.; *b.* 21 Oct. 1850; *e. s.* of late Col. H. Lyell and Katherine, *d.* of Leonard Horner, F.R.S., and *nephew* of Sir Charles, the geologist; *m.* Mary, *d.* of Rev. J. M. Stirling, 1874; one *d.* M.P. Orkney, 1885-1900. *Heir: g.s.* Charles Antony Lyell, *b.* 1 June 1913. *Address:* Kinnordy, Kirriemur, Forfarshire. *Club:* Athenæum. (*Died 18 Sept. 1926.*)

LYELL, Hon. Charles Henry, M.P. (L.) South Edinburgh since 1910; *b.* 18 May 1875; *o. s.* of 1st Lord Lyell of Kinnordy; *m.* 1911, Rosalind Margaret, *e. d.* of Vernon J. Watney; one *s.* one *d.* *Educ.:* Eton; New College, Oxford. Parliamentary Private Secretary to Rt. Hon. Sir Edward Grey, Bart., M.P., Secretary of State for Foreign Affairs, 1906 and to Rt. Hon. H. H. Asquith, Prime Minister, 1910; J.P. Forfarshire; Lieut. Forfar and Kincardine Artillery Militia, 1900 - 8; Vice-Chairman County Territorial Association, Forfarshire, 1908; M.P. (L.) East Dorset, 1904-10; gazetted Capt. in Fife R.G.A., Sep. 1914; Major in Highland Battery, Fife R.G.A., May 1915. *Recreations:* shooting, motoring. *Address:* 1 Cadogan Gardens, S.W.; Kinnordy, Kirriemuir, N.B. *Clubs:* Brooks's, Reform.
(*Died 18 Oct. 1918.*)

LYELL, William Darling, M A.; Advocate; Sheriff - Substitute of Lanarks. since 1912; *b.* Edinburgh, 12 Jan. 1860; *s.* of David Lyell, Solicitor before the Supreme Courts of Scotland; *m.* 1st, 1891, Helen (*d.* 1903), *d.* of James Earl Moreton, F.R.C.S.; 2nd, 1907, Viola, *d.* of John Williams, Carmarthen. *Educ.:* Edinburgh University. Admitted to the Bar of Scotland, 1882; appointed an Extra Advocate Depute, 1889; Sheriff-Substitute of Dumfries and Galloway, 1890-1900; Renfrew and Bute, 1900-12. *Publication:* The House in Queen Anne Square, 1920; The Justice-Clerk, 1923. *Address:* 29 Park Circus, Glasgow. *T.:* Charing Cross, Glasgow, 1278. *Clubs:* Caledonian; Scottish Conservative, Edinburgh; Western, Glasgow. (*Died 5 Mar. 1925.*)

LYLE, Sir Harold, K.B.E., *cr.* 1925; C.M.G. 1916; *b.* Newcastle-on-Tyne, 17 Jan. 1873; *m.* Rose Hilda Sawer; one *s.* one *d.* Student Interpreter Siam. 1893; Vice-Consul

at Bangkok, 1902 ; Consul at Chiengmai, 1907 ; called to Bar, Middle Temple, 1910 ; British Consul-General, Bangkok, with local rank of First Secretary of Legation, 1918 ; retired, 1924. *Address :* Longfield, Kingswear, S. Devon.
(*Died 16 July 1927.*)

LYLE, Henry Samuel, M.R.C.S., Eng.; Senior Surgeon Liverpool Hospital for Cancer and Skin Diseases since 1899 ; *b.* Bideford, 24 Oct. 1857 ; *s.* of late D. Lyle of Bideford ; *m.* Millicent, *widow* of G. O'Brien of Liverpool ; no *c. Educ.:* Bideford Grammar School. Entered Liverpool Royal Infirmary School of Medicine, 1874 ; subsequently went to King's College, London, qualified as M.R.C.S., Eng., 1880 ; Assistant Surgeon to Liverpool Hospital for Cancer and Skin Diseases, 1892 - 99. *Publications :* Treatment of Ringworm ; Treatment of Vesicular Eczema ; Case of Cancer cured by *x*-Rays ; Relations between Cancer and Chronic Inflammation ; Improved Mouth Gag. *Address :* 209 Upper Parliament Street, Liverpool. *T. :* Royal, 5008. *Club :* Liverpool Chess.
(*Died 29 Mar. 1916.*)

LYLE, Sir Robert Park, 1st Bt., *cr.* 1915 ; Chairman and Managing Director Abram Lyle & Sons, Limited, Sugar Refiners, London, when this firm and Henry Tate & Sons, Limited amalgamated in 1921, became Chairman of Tate & Lyle, Limited ; Chairman British Sugar Refiners' Association ; A Member of the Royal Commission on the Sugar Supply ; *b.* 1859 ; 6th *s.* of late Abram Lyle, J.P., of Oakley, Greenock, and Mary *d.* of late William Park, Greenock ; *m.* 1882, Agnes, 4th *d.* of the late William Jamieson, Shipowner, Greenock ; one *d. Educ.:* Madras College ; St. Andrews. On leaving school joined the family business in Greenock ; became a partner in 1882, and was more particularly identified with the Shipowning branch of the firm ; transferred to London, 1897, to take up position as a Managing Director of the sugar refining business ; became Chairman, 1908 ; served over twenty years in 1st Vol. Batt. Argyll and Sutherland Highlanders ; retired with rank of Major, 1897 ; is a Fellow Zoological Society, and an Associate Institute Naval Architects. *Heir :* none. *Address :* 81 Cadogan Square, S.W.1. *T. :* Kensington 1289. *Clubs :* Caledonian, Royal Thames Yacht, Ranelagh. (*Died 11 July 1923.*)

LYNCH, George, F.R.G.S., author and war correspondent ; *b.* Cork, Ireland, 27 March 1868. *Educ. :* under John Henry, Cardinal Newman. Travelled and explored in deserts of Western Australia, in the Pacific Islands, etc. ; acted as war correspondent for the London Daily Chronicle during the Spanish-American war ; represented the Illustrated London News during the Boer war ; wounded at the battle of Reitfontein, in the early part of the siege of Ladysmith ; captured by the Boers while making an attempt to go from Ladysmith to General Buller's force ; kept prisoner for a month in Pretoria ; liberated ; invalided home after-enteric fever ; acted as war correspondent for the Daily Express and the Sphere in the China campaign and relief of the Legations ; acted as special correspondent for London Daily Mail, United States ; for the New York Journal, Macedonia, 1903 ; and London Daily Chronicle, Japan and Manchuria with Japanese army, 1904 ; in Petrograd during the disturbances of spring, 1905 ; correspondent for the Illustrated London News and Westminster Gazette during World War ; invented gloves for handling barbed wire and several patents adopted by the War Office and Admiralty ; has travelled six times around the world. *Publications :* The War of the Civilisations ; Realities ; Impressions of a War Correspondent ; The Path of Empire ; Old and New Japan. *Recreations :* war-corresponding, yachting, fox-hunting, tak-

ing out patents. *Address :* 248 Gloucester Terrace, Hyde Park, W.2. *T. :* Park 3918. *Clubs :* Savage, City of London.
(*Died 29 Dec. 1928.*)

LYNCH, John Gilbert Bohun; author and caricaturist ; *b.* London, 21 May 1884 ; *o. s.* of late Trueman Lynch and Renira, *d.* of late Capt. G. B. Martin, C.B., R.N. ; *m.* twice ; one *s.* one *d. Educ. :* Haileybury ; University College, Oxford. *Publications:* Glamour, 1912 ; Cake, 1913 ; Unofficial, 1915 ; The Complete Gentleman, 1916 ; The Tender Conscience, 1919 ; Forgotten Realms, 1920 ; A Perfect Day, 1923 ; Menace from the Moon, 1924 ; Respectability, 1927 ; The Complete Amateur Boxer, 1913 ; Knuckles and Gloves, 1922 ; Max Beerbohm in Perspective, 1921 ; The Prize Ring, 1926 ; A History of Caricature, 1926 ; The Italian Riviera, 1927 ; Collecting, 1928 ; Decorations and Absurdities (with Reginald Berkeley) ; edited Isles of Illusion ; A Muster of Ghosts, 1924 ; has contributed to Home Chat, Quarterly Review, Answers, London Mercury, Chums, Fortnightly Review, and other periodicals. *Address :* Northlew Manor, Beaworthy, N. Devon. *Club :* Savage.
(*Died 2 Oct. 1928.*)

LYNCH, Sir John Patrick, Kt., *cr.* 1911 ; President Incorporated Law Society of Ireland, 1905-6 ; Vice Chairman, Dublin Castle Red Cross Hospital ; Governor of the House of Industry Government Hospitals ; J.P. Co. Dublin ; *b.* 1858 ; *e. surv. s.* of late Standislaus John Lynch, J.P., member of the Irish Land Commission ; *m.* 1896, Frieda, *d.* of late William Ottmann, of Irving Place, New York ; three *d. Educ. :* Clongowes Wood College. *Address :* Belfield, Booterstown, Co. Dublin. *T.A. :* Okandl, Dublin. *T. :* Ball's Bridge, No. 2. *M. :* IK 212 and 1244. *Clubs :* Stephen's Green, Dublin ; Royal Irish Yacht.
(*Died 4 Mar. 1921.*)

LYNCH, Richard Irwin, Curator, Botanic Garden, Cambridge, 1879 - 1919 ; *b.* St. Germans, 1850. Entered Kew, 1867 ; held responsible positions, 1870-79 ; Associate Linnean Society, 1881 ; awarded Veitch Memorial medal in silver, 1901, in gold, 1924 ; Hon. M.A. Cantab, 1906 ; Victoria Medallist in Honour, 1906 ; Associate Royal Botanic Society ; Corresponding Member Royal Horticultural Society ; raised many Hybrids, especially the Gerberas cultivated on Riviera ; raised (at Kew) the universal window plant Campanula isophylla alba. *Publications :* Book of the Iris ; Papers in Journal Royal Horticultural Society ; Journal Linnean Society ; the Gardeners' Chronicle, etc. *Recreation :* photography. *Address :* Granta, Upper Walnut Road, Chelston, Torquay.
(*Died 7 Dec. 1924.*)

LYNDEN-BELL, Col. Edward Horace Lynden, C.B. 1915 ; M.B., A.M.S. ; Knight of St. John of Jerusalem ; *b.* 18 Dec. 1858 ; *e. s.* of Major-General T. Lynden-Bell of Brook Hill, Co. Wexford ; *m.* 1891, Mary Haigh, *e. d.* of Major Guyon, Royal Fusiliers. Major, 1895 ; Lt.-Col. 1903 ; Colonel, 1912 ; Deputy Director of Medical Services, London District, 1912 ; served Burma, 1885-9 (medal, 2 clasps) ; European War as D.D.M.S. 1914-17 (C.B.). *Club :* Junior United Service. (*Died 1 Sept. 1922.*)

LYNE, Rev. Leonard Augustus, Hon. Canon of Gloucester ; Hon. Diocesan Missioner. *Address :* St. Mark's Vicarage, Gloucester.
(*Died 18 Dec. 1919.*)

LYNN - JENKINS, Frank ; sculptor ; H.M. Examiner for the Board of Education, S. Kensington ; *b.* Torquay, 1870 ; *m.* 1901, Phœbe, *d.* of Charles and Henriette Le Fèvre ; no *c. Educ. :* Weston College. Studied at Lambeth School of Modelling ; Royal Academy student ; won several prizes and medals, and British Institution Exhibition ; exhibited at Royal Academy, Paris Salon, and numerous International Exhibitions, since 1895 ; silver medallist

Paris Exhibition, 1900 ; executed many important decorative schemes (Lloyd's Registry, United Kingdom Prov. Assoc., etc.), also portrait statues and busts ; formerly, for several years, collaborated with Prof. Gerald Moira in many large decorative schemes in coloured relief ; member of Art Workers' Guild, and Royal Society of British Sculptors (one of the founders of the latter). *Publications :* occasional contributor to contemporary Art magazines. *Recreations :* golf, music. *Club :* Chelsea Arts.   *(Died Sept. 1927.)*

LYON, Sir Alexander, Kt., *cr.* 1906 ; D.L., Lord Provost of Aberdeen, 1905-8 ; *b.* 1850 ; *m.* 1875, Elsie, *d.* of late William Inglis ; one *s.* four *d. Educ. :* Aberdeen. *Address :* 10 Queen's Road, Aberdeen.   *(Died 26 April 1927.)*

L Y O N, Admiral Herbert ; *b.* 28 Dec. 1856 ; 4th *s.* of A. W. Lyon, J.P., Abbotsclownholme, Rocester, Stafford ; *m.* Frances Violet Inglis, *d.* of late Major-Gen. T. Inglis, C.B. R.E. ; one *d. Educ. :* Mr. Malden's School, Windlesham House, Brighton ; the Rev. H. Burney's, Royal Academy, Gosport. Entered navy as Cadet, 1870 ; Midshipman, 1872 ; Sub - Lieut., 1876 ; Lieut., 1880 ; Commander, 1894 ; Captain, 1900 ; Rear-Admiral, 1910 ; served as midshipman in Charybdis in the Lingi and Lukut river expeditions, Straits of Malacca, Perak (medal and clasp) ; as Sub-Lieut. (medal and clasp) in Zulu War, relief of Ekowe, Battle of Ginginhlovo ; as Captain of Retribution at the blockade of Venezuela ; last appointment Commodore at Hong-Kong ; Foreign Orders ; Crosses of Naval and Military 3rd class Order of Merit (Spain), gold and silver medal 2nd and 3rd class of the Nichau-Imtiaz (Turkey). Collar Order of the Commander of the Order of Redeemer (Greece). *Recreations :* polo, shooting, fishing, hunting. *Address :* Stoke Cottage, Devonport. *T. :* 26X Devonport. *M. :* OO 527. *Clubs :* Royal Naval, M.C.C.   *(Died 6 Mar. 1919.)*

LYONS, Sir Joseph, Kt., *cr.* 1911 ; D.L. County of London ; chairman J. Lyons and Co., Ltd. ; *b.* London ; *s.* of late Nathaniel Lyons, of Newmarket and London ; *m.* Psyche, *d.* of late Isaac Cohen. *Educ. :* borough Jewish schools and private academy. For some years followed the profession of an artist, exhibiting at various exhibitions ; after which became a caterer and now the head of J. Lyons and Co. Ltd. ; Director of Trafford Park Estates, Manchester ; Chairman Hancocks, Ltd., N.Z. ; Vice-Chairman Trafford Park, Ltd. ; Chairman Strand Palace Hotel, Ltd. *Publications :* (part author) Master Crime and Treasures of the Temple. *Recreations :* painting, writing, motoring. *Address :* 26 West Kensington Gardens, W. *T. :* Hammersmith 168. *M. :* LD 8200. *Clubs :* Royal Automobile, Eccentric.   *(Died 21 June 1917.)*

LYONS, Rt. Hon. William Henry Holmes, P.C. 1922 ; *b.* 1843 ; *m.* 1888, Lily, *e. d.* of late George Evans, Gortmerron House, Co. Tyrone ; two *d. Educ. :* Harrow. Grand Master of Grand Orange Lodge of Ireland, and Grand Master of Imperial Grand Black Chapter of the British Commonwealth ; Chairman of South Antrim Constitutional Association ; Sheriff of Antrim, 1904. *Address :* Newlands, 30 Deramore Park, Belfast. *T :* Malone 456. *Club :* Ulster, Belfast.   *(Died 26 Mar. 1924.)*

LYSAGHT, Hon. Horace George, J.P. for Co. Cork ; *b.* 16 Feb. 1873 ; *e. s.* of 6th Baron Lisle, of Mount North ; *m.* 1899, Alice Elizabeth, *d.* of Sir John Wrixon Becher, 3rd Bt. ; three *s.* two *d. Address :* Newmarket Cottage, Co. Cork.   *(Died 30 Sept. 1918.)*

LYSTER, Cecil Rupert Chaworth, M.R.C.S. ; Medical Officer in charge of Electrical Department of Middlesex Hospital since 1902 ; M.O. in charge of Electrical Massage and X-Ray Department, 2 A.M. Hospital, Mill-bank ; Surgeon to the Bolingbroke Hospital, S.W., since 1902 ; Fellow Royal Society of Medicine ; Vice-Pres. of Radiological Section of Royal Society of Medicine ; *b.* 14 Dec. 1859 ; *e. s.* of Alfred Chaworth Lyster and Elizabeth, *d.* of Capt. Charles Leighton Kennett ; *m.* 1903, Edith, (*d.* 1919) *d.* of late George J. Thompson ; no *c. Educ. :* privately. Charing Cross Hospital Resident Medical Officer ; Resident Obstetrical Officer Charing Cross Hospital, 1881-82 ; Travelled in America and the Continent ; Medical Superintendent and Hon. Secretary to Bolingbroke Hospital, S.W., 1885-1903 ; has made a special study of Electro-Therapeutics. *Publication :* The Treatment of Disease by Different Forms of Rays. *Recreation :* yachting. *Address :* 50 Gordon Mansions, W.C.1 ; 70 Wimpole Street, W.1. *T. :* Museum 2502 ; Mayfair 1769.   *(Died 26 Jan. 1920.)*

LYSTER, Lt.-Gen. Harry Hammon, C.B., 1881 ; V.C., 1858 ; *b.* 24 Dec. 1830 ; *s.* of Anthony Lyster of Stillorgan Park, Dublin. Served throughout Central India campaign, 1857-1858 ; Afghan campaigns, 1878-79 ; commanded 3rd Ghoorka Regt., 1879-87 ; I.S.C. on U.S. List, 1892 ; served as special constable in 1847, in London during the time of the Chartist Riots. *Address :* 1 St. Mark's Square, Gloucester Gate, N.W.1. *T. :* Hampstead 4997.   *(Died 1 Feb. 1922.)*

LYSTER, Thomas William, M.A. ; Librarian, National Library of Ireland, 1895-1920 ; *b.* Co. Kilkenny, 17 Dec. 1855 ; *s.* of Thomas Lyster, Rathdowney and Jane Smith, Roscrea. *Educ. :* Wesleyan School, Dublin ; Dublin University. First Senior Moderatorship at degree. Assistant Librarian, National Library of Ireland, 1878-95 ; Examiner in English under Intermediate Education Board, 1880, and several subsequent years ; Vice-President of Library Association, 1899. *Publications :* translator, with notes, revision, and enlargement, of Düntzer's Life of Goethe, 1883 ; editor of English Poems for Young Students, 1893, 5th edition 1904 ; critical papers in The Academy, etc. ; papers on library technique and theory. *Address :* 10 Harcourt Terrace, Dublin.   *(Died 12 Dec. 1922.)*

LYTTELTON-ANNESLEY, Lt.-Gen. Sir Arthur Lyttelton, K.C.B., *cr.* 1.23 ; Kt. and K.C.V.O., *cr.* 1903 ; Hon. Colonel 11th Prince Albert's Own Hussars ; *b.* 2 Sep. 1837 ; *e. s.* of Arthur Lyttelton-Annesley of Arley Castle, Staffordshire, and Camolin Park, County Wexford, J.P. and D.L. ; unmarried. *Educ. :* Harrow. Joined 11th Hussars, 1854 ; was present at siege and capture of Sevastopol (medal and clasp, Turkish medal) ; King Edward's and King George's Coronation medals, Knight Commander of the Order of Christ of Portugal, and Kaiser-i-Hind medal ; served ten years in India with the 11th, and commanded the regiment for some years, and brought it home ; was Aide-de-Camp to Field-Marshal H.R.H. the Duke of Cambridge ; was Assistant Adjutant-General of the Forces ; Adjutant-General of the Bombay Army ; commanded the troops in Scotland for five years ; was awarded the good service pension for distinguished and meritorious service ; is representative in the female line of the Annesleys, Earls of Anglesey, Earls of Mount Norris, and Viscounts Valentia, and of George, 1st Lord Lyttelton ; was on the Staff of Prince of Wales, 1875-76, and returned to England with H.R.H. through Egypt, Spain, and Paris. *Recreations :* travelling, boating, yachting, reading, gardening. *Address :* Templemere, Weybridge. *Club :* Carlton.   *(Died 16 Feb. 1926.)*

LYTTON, Lady Constance (Georgina) ; *b.* Vienna, 1869 ; *d.* of 1st Earl of Lytton. *Educ. :* Home. Childhood and youth spent chiefly abroad ; in 1908, aged 39, realised that women, together with men, participate in life's responsibilities, and should have an equal share in self-government; that the Government had always prevented this; became a Suffragette; four times imprisoned, two hunger-strikes; at the first of these was released because of heart condition, at the second (Walton Jail, Liverpool), disguised as a working woman, heart condition not noticed, and she was forcibly fed; May 1912 had a stroke; invalided since then. *Publications:* No Votes for Women, pamphlet, 1909; Prisons and Prisoners, 1914. *Recreations:* my friends, music, flowers. *Address:* Homewood, Knebworth, Herts. *T.A.:* Knebworth. *T.:* 5 Knebworth.

(*Died 22 May 1923.*)

LYVEDEN, 3rd Baron (*cr.* 1859), **Courtenay Percy Robert Vernon;** Lieut. R.N.V.R. (Transport Service); Pres. of British Committee, Study of Foreign Municipal Institutions; has been a member of dramatic profession since 1882; *b.* Grafton Underwood, Kettering, 29 Dec. 1857; *s.* of Rev. Hon. Courtenay John Vernon and Alice Gertrude, *d.* of late Rev. M. FitzGerald S. Townshend; *S.* uncle, 1900; *m.* 1890, Fanny Zelie (*d.* 1924), *d.* of Major Hill of Wollaston Hall, Wellingboro; one *s.* one *d.* *Educ.:* Eton. For some years Capt. 1st Royal Lanark Militia. *Recreations:* boating, hunting, shooting. Owns about 4200 acres. *Heir:* *s.* Hon. Robert Fitzpatrick Courtenay Vernon. *Club:* Royal Thames Yacht. (*Died 25 Dec. 1926.*)

M

MAASDORP, Hon. Christian George, Puisne Judge of Supreme Court, Cape Colony, 1885-1910; appointed Judge President of Cape Provincial Division of Supreme Court by first Union Ministry, 1910; *b.* Malmesburg, 1848; 3rd *s.* of G. H. Maasdorp, M.D.; *m.* 1876, Ella Elizabeth, *d.* of late Hon. C. W. Hutton; three *s.* two *d.* *Educ.:* Graaff Reinet College; Cape University (M.A.). Called to Bar, Inner Temple, 1871. *Address:* Hillside, Church Street, Rondebosch, Cape Town. (*Died May 1926.*)

MABERLY, Colonel Charles Evan, D.S.O. 1900; Royal Horse Artillery; retired; *s.* of late Maj.-Gen. Evan Maberly, C.B., of Avonmonth House, Christchurch; *b.* 5 Apr. 1854. *Educ.:* R.M.A., Woolwich. Served Nile Campaign, 1884-85 (Egyptian medal, clasp, bronze star); South Africa, 1899-1900 (severely wounded, despatches, Queen's medal with clasp, D.S.O.). *Address:* 98 Piccadilly, W.1. *T.:* Mayfair 4779. *Clubs:* St. James's, Naval and Military, Pratt's, Arthur's, Boodle's; Kildare Street, Dublin.

(*Died 7 Sept. 1920.*)

MABIE, Hamilton Wright, editor and writer; associate editor of The Outlook since 1879; *b.* Cold Spring-on-Hudson, New York; *m.* 1876. *Educ.:* Williams Coll.; Columbia University; LL.D. Union College; B.A., M.A., L.H.D., Williams College; LL.B. Columbia University; LL.D. Western Reserve University. Practised law six or seven years; abandoned it for editorial and literary work. *Publications:* Norse Stories; My Study Fire (first series); Under the Trees and Elsewhere; Short Studies in Literature; Essays in Literary Interpretation; My Study Fire (second series); Essays on Nature and Culture; Essays on Books and Culture; Essays on Work and Culture; The Life of the Spirit; William Shakespeare, Poet, Dramatist, and Man; A Child of Nature; Parables of Life; In Arcady; Backgrounds of Literature; Works and Days; The Great Word; Christmas To-day; Introductions to Notable Poems; American Ideals, Character and Life; Japan, To-day and To-morrow, 1914. *Recreations:* cycling, golf. *Address:* 381 Fourth Avenue,

New York City. *Clubs:* Century, Authors', Aldine, Graduates, Alpha Delta Phi, Canoe Brook.

(*Died Jan. 1917.*)

MACALISTER, Alexander, LL.D., M.D., D.Sc., M.A., F.R.S., F.S.A.; Professor of Anatomy, Cambridge University, since 1883; Fellow of St. John's College; *b.* Dublin, 9 April 1844; 2nd *s.* of Robert Macalister and Margaret Anne, *y. d.* of Col. James Boyle, Dungiven; *m.* 1866, Elizabeth (*d.* 1901), *d.* of James Stewart, Perth. *Educ.:* Trin. Coll. Dublin. Demonstrator of Anatomy, College of Surgeons, 1860; Professor of Zoology, University of Dublin, 1869; Professor of Anatomy and Chirurgery, Dublin, 1877. *Publications:* Introduction to Animal Morphology, 1876; Morphology of Vertebrate Animals, 1878; Text-Book of Human Anatomy, 1889; Evolution in Church History, 1879; Memoir of James Macartney, 1900; besides numerous papers and smaller text-books for students in Zoology and Physiology. *Recreation:* travel. *Address:* Torrisdale, Cambridge. (*Died 2 Sept. 1919.*)

MacALISTER, Sir John Young Walker, Kt., *cr.* 1919; O.B.E.; F.S.A., F.R.G.S.; Sec., and Editor Proceedings of Royal Society of Medicine; F.I.J.; *b.* 1856; *s.* of Donald MacAlister, Tarbert, Cantyre; *m.* 1874, Elizabeth, 2nd *d.* of George Batley, Blackhall, Edinburgh; two *s.* *Educ.:* High School, Liverpool; Edinburgh University. Studied medicine for three years; compelled by ill-health to give it up; sub-librarian, Liverpool Library; librarian of Leeds Library; engaged in journalism in connection with Leeds Mercury and Yorkshire Post; 1st librarian, Gladstone Library, 1887; founded The Library, 1889; Hon. Secretary Library Association, 1887-98; President, 1914-19; promoted Consolidating and Amending Library Act, 1892; Chairman of Editing Committee of 7th International Congress of Hygiene; Hon. Sec. Gen. and Organiser of the 2nd Internat. Library Conference, 1897; Commissioner for Paris Exposition, 1900; member of Committee of Internat. Congress on Tuberculosis, 1901; in 1905 formulated scheme for amalgamating the Medical Societies of London, which led to the amalgamation of all the leading societies, with a new Charter under the name of The Royal Society of Medicine; Member of Committee of Japan Exhibition, London, 1910, of College of Ambulance, Village Centre (Enham, Hants), Federation of Medical Societies and Society for prevention of Venereal Diseases, People's League of Health; Founder and first Chairman of the University of London Press, 1910; Hon. Sec. Surgical Advisory Committee, War Office; Organiser and Hon. Sec. Emergency Surgical Aid Corps for Admiralty, War Office, and Metropolitan Police. *Recreation:* sleeping. *Address:* 33 Finchley Road, N.W.8. *T.:* Hampstead 2448. *Clubs:* Athenæum, Garrick, Savage (Hon. Life Member), Bath. (*Died 1 Dec. 1925.*)

MACALPINE, Sir George Watson, Kt., *cr.* 1910; LL.D. M'Master (Toronto); J.P.; Chairman of the Altham Colliery Company, Ltd.; Great Harwood Colliery Company, Ltd.; Accrington Brick and Tile Company, Ltd.; Whinney Hill Plastic Brick Company, Ltd.; Vice-President of the British and Foreign Bible Society; Ex-President of the Baptist Union; *b.* Paisley, 10 Mar. 1850; *m.* 1877, Marianne, *y. d.* of James Barlow, J.P., Accrington; four *s.* one *d.* *Educ.:* John Neilson and Grammar Schools, Paisley. *Publication:* The Days of the Son of Man. *Recreation:* golf. *Address:* Broad Oak, Accrington. *T.:* Accrington 2743 *M* N 4476, etc. *Club:* National Liberal. (*Died 18 April 1920.*)

MACANDREW, Maj.-Gen. Henry John Milnes, C.B. 1918; D.S.O. 1900; Indian Army, 5th Cavalry; *b.* 7 Aug. 1866; *s.* of late Sir Henry Macandrew, Aisthorpe, Inver-

ness; m. 1892, Esther, y. d. of Henry Ritchie Cooper, J.P. ' of Ballindalloch, Stirlingshire; one s. one d. Educ.: The Inverness College. Joined 2nd Batt. Cameron Highlanders, 1884; transferred to Lincoln Regt. 1886; joined 5th Bengal Cavalry,1889; served as Brigade Transport Officer 2nd Brigade Tirah Expeditionary Force 1897; as Brigade Transport Officer Khyber Force, 1898 (Indian Frontier medal with 2 clasps, despatches); served in Kitchener's Horse, South Africa, Feb.-June 1900; Intelligence Officer, Delagoa line, July-Sep. 1900; D.A.A.G.I. General Clement's Column, Sept. 1900 to Feb. 1901; Feb.-May 1901 D.A.A.G.I. to Gen. Hon. Neville Lyttelton, and Gen. Bruce Hamilton from May 1901 to June 1902; as D.A.A.G. Intelligence Army Headquarters Staff, S. Africa (S. African medal and 4 clasps, King's medal and 2 clasps, D.S.O., despatches twice); European War, 1914-18 (despatches, C.B.); Brigade Major to the Inspector-General of Cavalry in India, 1903-5. Recreation: gentleman rider across country and on flat. Address: Aisthorpe, Inverness, Scotland. Club: Cavalry.
(Died 16 July 1919.)

M'ARDLE, John Stephen, J.P.; M.Ch. R.U.I. (Hon. Caus.), F.R.C.S.I., etc.; Member of Senate National University of Ireland; Member of Governing Body, Dublin University College; Professor of Surgery, University College, Dublin, since 1910; Lecturer on Surgery and Senior Surgeon, St. Vincent's Hospital, Dublin, since 1886; Consulting Surgeon, Children's Hospital, Temple Street; Consulting Surgeon, Maternity Hospital, Holles Street; b. Dundalk, 1859; m.; two s. two d. Educ.: St. Mary's College, Dundalk. House Surgeon, St. Vincent's Hospital, 1879-81; Demonstrator of Anatomy, Cecelia Student Medical School, 1880; Staff Surgeon, St. Vincent's, 1881; Professor of Surgery, Catholic University, 1900. Publications: The Surgery of the Abdomen, 1888; Hydrocele and its Treatment, 1888; Diseases of Joints, 1889; Clinical and Operative Surgery, 1900; Renal Surgery, 1895; Operative Surgery, 1905. Recreations: shooting, farming. Address: 72 Merrion Square, Dublin; Ballytregue, Wicklow. T.: 293 Dublin. M.: IK 463-464. (Died 14 April 1923.)

MACARDLE, Sir Thomas Callan, K.B.E., cr. 1920; J.P.; D.L.; Chairman, Macardle, Moore & Co. Ltd., The Dundalk Brewery; Dundalk and Newry Steampacket Co., Ltd.; Dundalk Race Co., Ltd.; Kinahan Bros., importers and bonders, Ltd.; and Alpha Trust, Ltd.; President Dundalk Chamber of Commerce; b. 14 Jan. 1856; s. of E. H. Macardle, J.P., Cambricville, Dundalk, and Margaret Callan, Tullagee, Co. Louth; m. 1888, Minnie, d. of Lt.-Colonel James Clarke Ross, late Scots Greys; two s. two d. Educ.: St. Mary's College, Dundalk. High Sheriff, County Louth, 1917. Address: St. Margaret's, Dundalk, Co. Louth, Ireland. T.A.: Macardle, Dundalk. T.: Dundalk 50. M.: IY 54. Clubs: Stephen's Green, Dublin; Dundalk.
(Died 18 Dec. 1925.)

MACARTHUR, Rt. Rev. James, Assist. Bishop-in-charge of the Isle of Wight since 1921; Archdeacon of Isle of Wight since 1906; b. 7 June 1848; m. 1879, Emily Harriette (d. 1905), d. of Richard Gardnor, solicitor and high bailiff, Carmarthen; one d. Educ.: Glasgow Univ. (M.A. 1868). Hon. D.D. Oxon.. 1898. Late Fellow University, Bombay; called Scottish Bar, 1871; Inner Temple, 1874; Cuddesdon Theological College, 1877-78; ordained, 1878; curate, St. Mary, Redcliffe, 1878-80; Rector, Lamplugh, Cumberland, 1880-87: Vicar, St. Mary's, Tothill Fields, 1887-92; Vicar, All Saints, South Acton, 1892-98; Rural Dean of Ealing, 1894-98; Bishop of Bombay, 1898-1903; Bishop Suffragan of Southampton, 1903-20. Address: Luccombe Hill, Shanklin, Isle of Wight. T.A.: Shanklin. T.; Shanklin 42. Club: Athenæum. (Died 2 Feb. 1922.)

MACARTHUR, Mary R., Secretary, Women's Trade Union League and National Federation of Women Workers; Hon. Secretary Central Committee on Women's Employment; Member, National Insurance Advisory Committee; b. 13 Aug. 1880; m. 1911, William C. Anderson, M.P. (d. 1919); one d. Educ.: Glasgow and Germany. Recreation: playgoing. Address: 42 Woodstock Road, Golder's Green, N.W.4. T.: Finchley 2234. (Died 1 Jan. 1921.)

M'ARTHUR, William Alexander, D.L.; b. Sydney, 1857; s. of Alexander M'Arthur, M.P.; m. 1890, Florence Creemer, d. of J. C. Clarke, M.P. M.P.E. Riding of York (Buckrose Div.) 1886-87; unseated on scrutiny; a Junior Lord of Treasury, 1892-95; M.P. (G.L.) Cornwall. Mid. St. Austell, 1887-1908; one of the Liberal Whips. Clubs: Garrick, Devonshire.

MACARTNEY, John William Merton, C.B. 1911; C.V.O. 1921; late Colonel commanding Royal Guernsey L.I.; b. 15 Nov. 1850; e. s. of William Merton Macartney, barrister, who was e. surv. s. of Rev. Arthur Chichester Macartney, formerly Vicar of Belfast and Templepatrick; at one time Captain in Royal Artillery; is the representative of the Macartneys of Blacket who migrated from Kirkcudbright to Co. Antrim, 1629; m.; three s. two d. Educ.: H.M.S. Britannia. Joined 54th Foot as Ensign, 1869; Captain in Dorsetshire Regiment, 1881; Major, 1889; Lieut.-Col. 1900; served in India, Egypt, Burmah, and at home; D.A.A.G. Rawal Pindi, 1884-86; Guernsey and Alderney Dist. 1900-3; Secretary to the Government in the Island of Guernsey, 1913; resigned command, 2nd R.G.L.I., 1913. Publications: History of Development of Tactics; Studies of Waterloo. Recreations: much interested in rifle-shooting; member N.R.A. Address: Elmgrove, Guernsey. T.A.: Guernsey. T.: 2333.
(Died 24 May 1925.)

MACARTNEY, Rt. Hon. Sir William (Grey) Ellison-, K.C.M.G., cr. 1918; P.C. 1900; b. Dublin, 7 June 1852; e. s. of late John William Ellison-Macartney and Elizabeth Phœbe, e. d. of Rev. John Grey Porter; m. 1897, Ettie, e. d. of late John Edward Scott, Outlands, Devonport; one s. one d. Educ.: Eton; Exeter College, Oxford (B.A. 1st class Honours). J.P. England and Wales; Parliamentary Secy. to the Admiralty, 1895-1900; M.P. (U.) S. Antrim, 1885-1903; High Sheriff, Co. Antrim, 1908; Deputy-Master, Royal Mint, 1903-13; Governor of Tasmania, 1913-17; Western Australia, 1917-20; Chairman, Governors of the People's Palace, Mile End Road, and of Council of the East London College, University of London. Address: 48 Elm Park Road, Chelsea, S.W.3. T.: Kensington 5957. Club: St. Stephen's.
(Died 4 Dec. 1924.)

MACBEAN, Major-Gen. Forbes, C.B. 1900; C.V.O. 1905; A.D.C. to the King, 1907-11; b. 3 Jan. 1857; s. of late Col. Forbes Macbean, 92nd Highlanders; m. 1889, Mary Katherine Fishburn, d. of late Capt. W. T. Forbes Jackson, R.N. Educ.: Uppingham. Entered 92nd Highlanders, 1876; Capt. 1884; Major, 1893; Brevet Lieut.-Col. 1898; served Afghan War, 1879-80; present at engagements in and around Kabul; present on march from Kabul to Kandahar (medal with three clasps and bronze star); served with 92nd Highlanders, Transvaal Campaign, 1881; with 1st Batt. in Tirah Campaign, 1897-98 (severely wounded, despatches, medal with two clasps, Brevet Lt.-Col.); S. African War, 1899-1902 (despatches, C.B., medal with five clasps, King's medal with two clasps, Bt.-Col.); commanded 1st Batt. Gordon Highlanders, 1900-4; Highland Territorial Division, 1908-11; Bareilly Brigade, 1911-15. Club: Army and Navy. (Died 20 Feb. 1919.)

McBEE, Silas; Hon. D.C.L. University of the South; editor of the Churchman, 1896-1912; founder and editor of The Constructive Quarterly since 1912; b. Lincolnton, N.C., 14 Nov. 1858. *Educ.:* Univ. of the South. *Publication:* An Eirenic Itinerary. *Address:* 244 Madison Avenue, New York. *(Died 3 Sept. 1924.)*

MACBETH, Rev. John, LL.D., Rector of Killegney and Rossdroit since 1873; Precentor of Ferns Cathedral; b. 21 May 1841; s. of Robert Macbeth, of Kilcreevy, Co. Armagh; m. 1869, Isabella Jemima (d. 1914), y. d. of Richard Star, of Ballytore, Co. Kildare; one s. four d. *Educ.:* Trinity College, Dublin. Held Curacies of Maryborough and of Ferns; was in 1873 presented to his present living; has added a chancel to Killegney Church, restored St. Peter's Church, Rossdroit, built a schoolhouse, and enlarged the Glebe House; an examiner under the Intermediate Board of Education, and also under the Board of Religious Education of the General Synod. *Publications:* The Story of Ireland and her Church; Notes on the Book of Common Prayer; Notes on the Thirty-nine Articles; numerous pamphlets. *Recreations:* a frequent speaker on temperance and foreign missions; has done much to advance the cause of religious instruction in the secondary schools, and is founder of the Ferns Exhibition with that object. *Address:* Killegney Parsonage, Enniscorthy. *T.A.:* Clonroche, Co. Wexford. *(Died 23 Sept. 1924.)*

M'BRIDE, Hon. Sir Peter, Kt., cr. 1915; Agent-General for Victoria in London 1918-22; formerly Minister of Mines, Minister of Forests, Minister of Railways, and Acting Chief Secretary, State of Victoria, Australia; b. Dunolly, Victoria, 9 Feb. 1867; m.; one s. one d. *Educ.:* Wesley College, Melbourne. Member of Parliament of Victoria since 1897; Cabinet rank since 1909; Order of St. Sava; Belgian Order of the Crown; Grande Officier of the Order of Leopold II. (Belgian). *Recreations:* racing, tennis. *Address:* c/o Melbourne Place, Strand, W.C. *T.A.:* Yarra, Estrand, London. *T.:* City 8656. *Clubs:* Royal Automobile, Junior Naval and Military, Constitutional, British Empire, Sports, City Carlton, Australian, Royal Thames Yacht; Phyllis Court, Henley; Athenæum, Royal Yacht, Melbourne.
(Died Mar. 1923.)

M'BRIDE, Sir Richard, K.C.M.G., cr. 1912; LL.D. California, 1913; K.C. 1905; barrister-at-law; Agent General for British Columbia in London since 1916; b. New Westminster, B.C., 15 Dec. 1870; 2nd s. of Arthur H. M'Bride; m. 1896, Margaret, y. d. of Neil M'Gillivray; five c. *Educ.:* Public and High Schools, New Westminster; Dalhousie University, Halifax, Nova Scotia (LL.B. 1890). Barrister British Columbia, 1892; contested Westminster District for Canadian House of Commons, 1896; returned as member for Dewdney in local elections, 1898, 1900 and 1903; Victoria City, 1907; Victoria City and Yale, 1909; Victoria, 1912; Minister of Mines; Prime Minister, British Columbia, 1908-16; Conservative. *Address:* British Columbia House, 1 and 3 Regent Street, S.W.
(Died 6 Aug. 1917.)

McBRYDE, Hon. Duncan Elphinstone; member of the Legislative Council, Victoria, since 1893; b. Argyleshire, Scotland, 1853; m. Ellen, d. of late Archibald Menzies, Melbourne; two d. *Educ.:* private school. Left Scotland for Australia; arrived in Melbourne Jan. 1872; directed his attention to pastoral pursuits, finally bought Mount Poole Station, New South Wales; about 1885, silver lead mining in the Broken Hill district (about 200 miles from Mount Poole), was largely engaging public attention; bought an interest in the Broken Hill Proprietary Company, of which he has been a Director for 30 years; Director of the Commercial Bank of Australia; one of the original shareholders of the Silverton Tramway Company; was Minister for Public Works; J.P. for Victoria and New South Wales; Presbyterian. *Recreations:* gardening, fishing, and motoring. *Address:* Kamesburgh, Wallace Avenue, Toorak, Victoria. *T.:* Brighton 1007. *M.:* 284 and 1060. *Club:* Australian, Melbourne.
(Died Nov. 1920.)

M'CABE, Sir Daniel, Kt. cr. 1916; J.P.; D.L.; Lord Mayor, Manchester, 1914-15; Knight of St. Sylvester; Director of Manchester Ship Canal; Alderman of the City of Manchester; b. 1852. *Address:* 104 Rochdale Road, Blackley, Manchester. *(Died 29 Sept. 1919.)*

MACCALL, Hon. Maj.-Gen. Henry Blackwood, C.B. 1896; comdg. 2nd Class District, India, 1901-1902; retired; b. 15 Aug. 1845; s. of late Col. George Maccall; m. 1885, Grace Mabel, d. of P. J. Farquharson, Langton House, Blandford. Entered army, 1864; Col. 1895; served Izazai Expedition 1892; Chitral Relief Force, 1895 (despatches, C.B., medal with clasp). *Club:* Army and Navy.
(Died 22 July 1921.)

M'CALL, Hon. Sir John, Kt., cr. 1911; M.D., LL.D.; Agent-Gen. for Tasmania in London since 1909; Member of House of Assembly and Member of the Executive Council; Warden of Leven Municipality and Chairman of Leven Harbour Trust; b. Devonport, Tasmania, 20 Aug. 1860; s. of late Hon. John Hair M'Call; m. twice; three s. one d. *Educ.:* Glasgow University. Has given a large amount of time to service of the public, both in Local Government and Parliament; was Chief Secretary in Propsting Government, and Pres. of Central Board of Health; President of the Australian Natives Association in London; Medical Officer in charge of Australian Officers' Hospital in London. *Recreations:* practically none. *Address:* 56 Victoria Street, S.W.; 30 Nevern Mansions, S.W. *T.:* Western 3562. *Clubs:* British Empire, Australasian. *(Died 27 June 1919.)*

McCALLUM, Col. Sir Henry Edward, R.E.; G.C.M.G., cr. 1904; K.C.M.G., cr. 1898; Governor of Ceylon, 1907-13; b. Yeovil, 28 Oct. 1852; e. s. of Major H. A. M'Callum, R.M.L.I., and Eleanor, d. of Major Brutton, R.M.L.I.; m. 1897, Maud, 3rd d. of Lieut.-Col. Creighton, R.M.L.I.; one s. three d. *Educ.:* privately; Royal Military Academy, Woolwich. Passed from Woolwich first out of fifty-two cadets, 1871; Pollock medallist, 1871; Fowke medallist, 1874. Chatham, 1871-74; Superintendent Telegraphy Southern District, 1874; Inspector-General Fortifications office, 1874-75; Private Secretary to Sir William Jervois, Governor Straits Settlements, 1875-77; several times mentioned in despatches, Perak medal and clasp; Superintendent Admiralty Works, Hong-Kong, 1877-78; Singapore, 1878-79; Royal Arsenal, Woolwich, 1879-80; Deputy Colonial Engineer, Penang, 1880-84; Colonial Engineer and Surveyor-General, Straits Settlements, member Executive and Legislative Councils, 1884-97; Commandant Singapore Volunteer Artillery, 1888-97; Special Commissioner in Pahang, Malay Peninsula, to suppress outbreak (received thanks of H.M. Government), 1891; Governor and Commander-in-Chief, Lagos, 1897-99; special mission to Hinterland in connection with French aggression in Lagos (received thanks of H.M. Government), 1898 (West African medal and clasp); Governor of Newfoundland, 1898-1901 A.D.C. to H.M., 1900-1; Governor of Natal, 1901-7 (South African medal with four clasps; Natal Rebellion Medal). *Decorated:* C.M.G., 1887, construction of fortifications, Singapore; K.C.M.G. 1898, special services, Lagos Hinterland; G.C.M.G., special services in South Africa. *Recreations:* cricket, shooting, fishing, golf. *Address:* Lauriston, Crawley Ridge,

Camberley. *Club:* Junior United Service.
(Died 24 Nov. 1919.)

M'CALLUM, Sir John Mills, Kt., *cr.* 1912; M.P. (L.) Paisley since 1906; J.P. Co. Renfrew; *s.* of late John M'Callum, senior, of J. and J. M'Callum, dyers, Paisley; *b.* 1847; *m.* 1875, Agnes, *d.* of Stephen Oates, J.P., ship-broker, Grimsby. *Educ.:* John Neilson Institution, Paisley. Chairman of firm of Isdale and M'Callum, Ltd., soap-makers, Paisley; since early manhood has taken active interest in the social and religious progress of the town and has been closely associated with the Paisley Liberal Club; he was for a number of years a member of the Town Council, and served a period on the magisterial bench. *Address:* Southdene, Castlehead, Paisley. *T. :* 409. *Clubs:* National Liberal; Scottish Liberal, Edinburgh; Glasgow Liberal.
(Died 10 Jan. 1920.)

McCALMONT, Maj.-Gen. Sir Hugh, K.C.B., *cr.* 1900; C.V.O. 1903; *b.* 9 Feb. 1845; *e. s.* of late James McCalmont, Abbeylands, Co. Antrim, and Emily, *d.* of late James Martin, Ross, Co. Galway; *m.* 1885, Hon. Rose Elizabeth Bingham, 3rd *d.* of 4th Baron Clanmorris; one *s. Educ.:* Eton. M.P. (C.) North Antrim, 1895-99. Entered army, 1865; Capt. 1869; Major, 1878; Lieut.-Col. 1885; Maj.-Gen. 1896; served Red River Expedition, 1870 (despatches, medal); Gold Coast, 1873 (medal); Armenia, 1877 (brevet of Major, medal); A.D.C. to Sir Garnet Wolseley, South Africa, 1879 (despatches, Brevet Lieut.-Col., medal with clasp); expedition against Murris, 1880 (despatches); Egypt, 1882, including Kassassin twice, Tel-el-Kebir, and capture of Cairo (despatches, medal with clasp, 3rd class Medjidie, Khedive's Star); Nile Expedition, 1884-85 (despatches, brevet of Col., C.B. and clasp); commanded Cork District, 1898-1903; retired, 1906; Colonel, 7th Hussars, 1907. *Recreations:* hunting, shooting, cycling, etc. *Address:* 5 Carlos Place, W.1; Mount Juliet, Thomastown, Co. Kilkenny. *Clubs:* Carlton, Army and Navy, Bachelors'; Kildare Street, Dublin; Royal St. George Yacht, Kingstown. *(Died 2 May 1924.)*

McCANN, P., M.P. (S.F.) East Tipperary since 1918. *(Died 6 Mar. 1920.)*

McCARTHY, Sir Frank, Kt., *cr.* 1923; C.B.E.; journalist. *Address:* Rangoon, Burma. *(Died 13 Feb. 1924.)*

M'CARTHY, James Desmond, C.M.G. 1891; Surgeon R.N., 1872-74; assistant surgeon, Lagos, W. Africa, 1877; Colonial surgeon, 1880; Chief Medical Officer, Gold Coast, 1884; retired, 1893; served Ashanti Expedition, 1873 (despatches, medal and clasp). *Decorated* for services on Gold Coast. *Publications:* report on Ventilation and Analysis of Air in H.M.S. "Devastation"; various sanitary reports and papers, including analysis of water-supply of Gold Coast and Lagos; paper on Disposal of Sewage in Tropical Climates, read before the Congress of the Royal Institute of Health, Dublin, Aug. 1898. *Recreations:* yachting, shooting. *Address:* Pitmore Cottage, Sway, Hants. *(Died 29 July 1923.)*

M'CARTHY, Jeremiah, M.A., M.B., F.R.C.S.; Consulting Surgeon London Hospital. *Educ.:* Trinity College, Dublin; London Hospital. Was Lecturer on Surgery London Hosp. Medical College. *Address:* 1 Cambridge Place, Victoria Road, W.
(Died 26 April 1924.)

McCARTHY, Michael John Fitzgerald, Barrister-at-law; author; *b.* Midleton, Co. Cork; *s.* of Denis McCarthy and Catherine Fitzgerald of Clonmult; *m.* 1887, Margaret, *d.* of John Ronayne of Douickmore. *Educ.:* Vincentian Seminary, Cork; Midleton College, Co. Cork; Trinity College, Dublin. B.A. 1885; called to the Bar, 1889; took no part in public life until the appearance of Five Years in Ireland, 1901; since then has written and spoken against the power exercised by the Roman Catholic Church in politics and in education. Stood for Stephen's Green Parliamentary Division of Dublin, 1904, but retired to avoid a split in the Unionist vote; started and conducts Christian Defence Effort in opposition to Papal aggression. *Publications:* Five Years in Ireland, 1895-1900, 1901; tenth edition, 1903; Priests and People in Ireland, 1902; fifth edition, 1905, popular edition, 1908; Rome in Ireland, 1904; Gallowglass, or Life in the Land of the Priests, 1904; Catholic Ireland and Protestant Scotland, 1905; The Coming Power, a Contemporary History of the Far East, 1905; Church and State in England and Wales, 1906; Irish Land and Irish Liberty, 1910; The Nonconformist Treason, 1912; The Irish Revolution, vol. i., 1912; The Dictators, 1913; many Letters to Parliament, and other publications in opposition to Home Rule, 1913-20; The British Monarchy and the See of Rome, 1924; The Irish Papal State, 1925; Church and Empire Breaking, 1927; Anglo-Catholic Bolshevism, 1927; The Bishops and the House of Commons, 1928. *Recreations:* reading, observing, walking. *Address:* 13 Alwyne Mansions, Wimbledon, S.W. *(Died 26 Oct. 1928.)*

M'CARTHY, Robert Henry, C.M.G. 1906; J.P.; *s.* of Jeremiah M'Carthy of Cork; *m.* Mary Emily, *d.* of Richard Beamish, of Ballinora, Co. Cork; one *d. Educ.:* privately. Imperial Customs, 1875-95; formerly Collector of Customs and Member of the Executive and Legislative Councils of Trinidad; retired, 1908; Special Services; Missions in connection with commercial treaties to Washington, 1899 and 1900; Ottawa and Caracas, 1900; to Barbadoes West Indian Conferences on Quarantine, 1904 and 1907; and in 1908 Conference at Barbadoes on West Indian trade with Canada; Reported upon and reorganised Malta Customs, 1908-10; technical adviser Royal Commission on Trade between Canada and the West Indies, 1909 and 1910. *Recreations:* billiards, chess, and golf. *Address:* Lampton, Hounslow. *(Died 12 Mar. 1927.)*

McCARTHY, Tim; Editor Irish News, Belfast, since 1906; *e. s.* of late Denis McCarthy of Cloghroe, Cork; *m.* Katie, *d.* of late Denis M'Lynn, Sligo. *Educ.:* National Schools; privately. Reporter and Editor Cork Herald and Cork Weekly Herald; Sub-Editor, News Editor and Leader-writer Evening Sun; Sub-Editor and Leader Writer Dublin Evening Telegraph; Acting-Editor Irish People (organ of the United Irish League); sentenced to imprisonment, 1902-3; editor series of Provincial papers in Ulster, 1904-6. *Publications:* Many articles in magazines; a short History of the Irish Brigade in France. *Recreations:* walking, travelling in Ireland. *Address:* 131 Antrim Road, Belfast. *(Died 30 Dec. 1928.)*

MACCARTHY, Rt. Rev. Welbore, D.D.; *m.* 1872, Emily Fearon, *d.* of William Delves; two *d. Educ.:* St. Aidans, Birkenhead; Trin. Coll., Dublin. Curate of Preston-Patrick, 1867-68; Ulverston, 1868-71; Christ Church, Battersea, 1871-72; Balham, 1872-73; Chaplain at Jhansi, 1874-75; Rangoon, 1875-77; St. Paul's Cathedral, Calcutta, 1877-82; Bishop's Commissary, 1879-1882, and 1891-98; Mussoorie, 1882-84; Meerut, 1884-85; Shahjehanpore, 1885-87; Lucknow, 1888-89; Chaplain, St. Paul's Cathedral, Calcutta, 1889-98; Archdeacon of Calcutta, 1892-98; Rector of Ashwell, 1898-1901; Vicar of Gainsborough, 1901-5; Prebendary of Lincoln Cathedral, 1901; Rural Dean of Corringham, 1901; Vicar of Grantham, 1905; Rural Dean of North Grantham and Prebendary of Empingham in Lincoln Cathedral, 1905; Rector of North and South Stoke and

Rural Dean of Beltisloe, 1910-18; Bishop of Grantham (Suffragan to Lincoln), 1905-18. *Address:* 20 Somerset Road, West Ealing. *Club:* Oriental. (*Died 21 Mar. 1925.*)

MACCARTIE, Lieut.-Col. Frederick Fitzgerald, C.I.E. 1898; I.M.S., M.B., J.P.; retired; *b.* 6 Aug. 1851; *s.* of late Justin Maccartie of Carrignavar, Cork; *m.* 1881, Julie Charlotte, *d.* of Capt. J. A. Vanrenen; two *d.* Surgeon, 1878; Lieut.-Col. 1898; served Afghan War, 1878-80 (medal). *Address:* Carrignavar, Co. Cork. *Clubs:* Bombay Yacht; Cork County.
(*Died Nov. 1916.*)

M'CAUGHEY, Hon. Sir Samuel, Kt., *cr.* 1905; member of Legislative Council, New South Wales since 1899; *b.* Ballymena, Ireland; unmarried. Went to Australia 1876; presented twenty battle-planes to the State. *Address:* North Yanco, Yanco, N.S.W. *Club:* Union, Sydney. (*Died 28 July 1919.*)

McCAULEY, Ven. George James, Archdeacon of Sierra Leone and Canon of St. George's Cathedral since 1901. Ordained 1863; Assistant Native Missionary at Wilberforce, 1863-67; Pastor of Wellington, 1867-80; Pastor of Kissy, 1880-94; Assistant Colonial Chaplain for six months at the Gambia, 1882; Pastor of St. John's, Brookfield, 1900-1908; Pastor of Cl rist Church, 1908-11; Hon. M.A., University of Durham, 1912. *Address:* Freetown, Sierra Leone.

M'CAUSLAND, Lieut.-Gen. Edwin Loftus, *y. s.* of late Rev. W. H. M'Causland; *m.* Georgina, *o. c.* of Very Rev. James Mitchell, D.D.; two *s.* one *d.* *Educ.:* privately. Joined Royal Marine Light Infantry, 1876; took part in Egyptian War, 1882; severely wounded at Tel-el-Kebir (medal and clasp, Khedive's bronze star); Commandant Chatham Division, 1909-10; Major-General, 1910; retired pay, 1922. *Recreations:* golf and sketching. *Address:* Solent Lodge, Lee-on-Solent, Hants. *Club:* Cocoa Tree.
(*Died 12 Oct. 1923.*)

McCAUSLAND, Maj.-Gen. William Henry, R.A.; *b.* 11 May 1836; *m.* Mary (*d.* 1915). Entered army, 1854; Maj.-Gen. 1889; retired, 1890; served China War, 1860 (medal with clasp). (*Died 17 Nov. 1916.*)

MACCAW, William John MacGeagh, F.R.G.S.; M.P. (U.) West Down, 1908-18; *s.* of Rev. William MacCaw, D.D., and Sarah, *d.* of John MacGeagh, J.P.; *m.* Eleanor Elizabeth (*d.* 1918), *d.* of Walter Hardy, solicitor; two *s.* two *d.* *Educ.:* privately. Lived for twenty years in India; has travelled extensively in the East and in Europe; contested (U.) East Tyrone, Jan. and July 1906. *Recreations:* golfing and shooting. *Address:* 103 Eaton Square, S.W.1; Rooksnest Park, Godstone, Surrey. *Clubs:* Carlton, Oriental, City of London. (*Died 3 Mar. 1928.*)

McCAWLEY, Hon. Thomas William, Chief Justice of the Supreme Court of Queensland since 1922, and President of the Court of Industrial Arbitration since 1917; *b.* Toowoomba, Queensland, 24 July 1881; *s.* of late James McCawley; *m.* 1911, Margaret Mary, *d.* of late Thomas O'Hogan; three *s.* one *d.* *Educ.:* St. Patrick's Boys' School, Toowoomba. Entered Public Service of Queensland, 1898; First Clerk, Dept. of Justice, 1905; called to Bar, 1907; Crown Solicitor, 1910-17; Under-Secretary for Justice, 1915-17; Judge of the Supreme Court of Queensland, 1917; Member of Senate of University of Queensland. *Address:* Windermere Road, Ascot, Brisbane.
(*Died 16 April 1925.*)

M'CLELAN, Hon. Abner Reid, *b.* 1831; *y. s.* of late Peter M'Clelan, a Justice of the Court of Common Pleas; *g. s.* of Peter M'Clelan, who, with Miss Wilson, whom he subsequently married, came to Nova Scotia from Londonderry, Ireland; re-

660

moter ancestry from Galloway, Scotland; *m.* Anna B., *d.* of late W. J. Reid, Collector of Customs at port of Harvey. *Educ.:* Mount Allison, Sackville (D.C.L.). LL.D. Univ. of New Brunswick. Elected to Provincial Parliament of New Brunswick, 1854, and each subsequent election till 1867, when he resigned seat and office of Chief of Public Works in the Government to enter the Dominion Senate; appointed Lieut.-Gov. 1896; always a Liberal in politics, favouring free trade and a closer union with Great Britain and the Empire. *Address:* Riverside, Albert County, N.B. (place of his birth). *Club:* Union, St. John. (*Died 30 Jan. 1917.*)

M'CLELLAN, Rev. John B., M.A.; Hon. Member Surveyors' Institution; and late Principal Royal Agricultural College, Cirencester. Formerly Fellow of Trinity College, Cambridge, and Rural Dean of North Camps, Diocese of Ely. *Publications:* New Translation of New Testament, vol. i., from a Revised Greek Text, with Harmony of the Four Gospels, Notes, and Dissertations; Treatise on the Election and Consecration of Bishops. *Address:* Ruthven, The Avenue, Kew Gardens, S.W.
(*Died 24 April 1916.*)

M'CLELLAND, Prof. John Alexander, F.R.S. 1909; M.A., D.Sc. (R.U.I.), M.A. (Camb.), ScD. (Dubl.) Professor of Experimental Physics, University College, Dublin; Commissioner of National Education, Ireland; *b.* 1870; *s.* of Wm. M'Clelland of Dunallis, Coleraine; *m.* 1901, Ina, *d.* of J. Esdale; two *s.* three *d.* *Educ.:* Academical Institution, Coleraine; Queen's College, Galway, Royal University; (First Science Scholar, Galway; Special Prizeman, M.A. degree (R.U.I.), 1893; 1851 Exhibition Scholarship, 1894; Junior Fellowship (R.U.I.), 1895, Fellowship, 1901); Trinity College, Cambridge (Research degree, Cambridge, 1897). Prof. of Physics, University College, Dublin, 1900; Member of Senate of National University of Ireland and of Governing Body of University College, 1908; Secretary of Royal Irish Academy; member of Advisory Council for Scientific and Industrial Research. *Publications:* Papers on Physical Subjects in various journals. *Recreation:* golf. *Address:* Rostrevor, Orwell Road, Rathgar, Dublin.
(*Died 13 April 1920.*)

McCLELLAND, Sir Peter Hannay, K.B.E., *cr.* 1918; *b.* 1856; *s.* of Thomas McClelland and Margaret Davidson. *Educ.:* Wigtown Normal School; George Watson's Col., Edinburgh. A partner of Duncan, Fox & Co., Liverpool, London, and South America; a Liveryman of the Girdlers' Guild; a Life Governor of the Royal Scottish Corporation; Director of the South American Export Syndicate, Ltd. *Recreations:* motoring, horsemanship. *Address:* Eaton House, 66a Eaton Square, S.W.1; *T.:* Victoria 6648; Springfield, Northaw, Herts. *Clubs:* Royal Automobile, Argentine. (*Died 14 Jan. 1924.*)

McCLINTOCK, Very Rev. Francis George le Poer, Rector of Drumcar since 1886; Dean of Armagh since 1908; Chaplain to Lord-Lieutenant since 1908. *Educ.:* Trinity College, Cambridge (M.A.). Curate of Kilsaran, 1878-79; Rector, 1879-86. *Address:* Drumcar, Dunleer S.O., Co. Louth. (*Died 3 Feb. 1924.*)

M'CLURE, Rev. Edmund, M.A., M.R.I.A.; Secretary of the Society for Promoting Christian Knowledge, 1875-1915; Hon. Canon, Bristol; *b.* Ireland of Scotch parentage; *m.* twice; two *s.* one *d.* *Educ.:* Trinity College, Dublin; Germany. Curate in Belfast for ten years; has travelled in Australia, South Seas, South America, and United States, etc.; acquainted with French, German, Dutch, Danish, Spanish, Italian, Celtic, Latin, Greek, Hebrew, Aramaic, Syriac, and other languages. *Publications:* a chapter of English Church History, 1888;

a Star Atlas (2nd ed. 1901), translated and adapted from German of Professor Klein ; Historical Church Atlas, 1897 ; (Joint) History of S.P.C.K., 1898 ; British Place-Names in their Historical Setting, 1909 ; Modern Substitutes for Traditional Christianity, 1913 ; 2nd ed. with additional section on Modernism, 1914 ; Spiritualism, Historical and Critical Sketch, 1916 ; Translator of Hommel's Hebrew Tradition, 1897 ; Prof. Kittel's Babylonian Excavations and Early Bible History, new ed. 1903 ; of Prof. Pellat's (from French), The New State of Matter, 1905 ; of Dr. Troelstra's De Naam Gods in den Pentateuch, 1912 ; and Pfarrer Dahse's Is a Revolution in Pentateuch Criticism at hand ? 1912. *Recreations*: study is his chief recreation ; chiefly interested in recent scientific research and in linguistic questions concerning the Bible. *Address*: 80 Eccleston Square, S.W.1 ; *T.*: Victoria 3418 ; St. Leonard's, Malvern Link. *M.*: LA 8401. *Club*: Reform.
(Died 18 Nov. 1922.)

McCLURE, Sir John David, Kt., *cr.* 1913; headmaster of Mill Hill School since 1891 ; *b.* 9 Feb. 1860 ; *s.* of late John McClure, J.P., Wigan ; *m.* 1889, *d.* of late J. Johnstone, Holcombe, Lancs ; one *s.* two *d. Educ.*: privately ; Owens Coll. Manchester; Trin. Coll. Cambridge; LL.D., M.A. (Cantab.) ; D.Mus.Lond. ; Assistant Master, Hinckley Grammar School, 1878-82; entered Trinity College, Cambridge, of which College afterwards Exhibitioner and Prizeman ; graduate in Mathematics and Law ; from 1885-1891 Lecturer under the Camb. Univ. Extension Syndicate ; Prof. of Astronomy, Queen's Coll. London, 1888-94; Barr. Inner Temple, 1890 ; elected by the Graduates in Arts to the Senate of the newly constituted University of London, 1900. but resigned owing to ill-health, 1901; Jc Hon. Secretary I.A.H.M. 1904-13 ; Chairman of the Congregational Union of England and Wales, 1919-20. *Recreations*: travel, curling. *Hobby*: music. *Address*: Mill Hill School, N.W. *T.A.*: Millhillian, London. *T.*: 208 P.O. Finchley. *Club*: Savile. *(Died 18 Feb. 1922.)*

M'CLYMONT, Right Rev. James A., C.B.E.; V.D. ; D.D. (Edin.) ; editor of Church of Scotland Guild Text-Books and Guild Library; Convener of Committee on Chaplains to H.M. Forces ; Principal Clerk of the General Assembly ; Moderator of General Assembly of Church of Scotland, 1921 - 22 ; Principal Chaplain of Church of Scotland in this country with rank of Brigadier General (1917 - 19); Trustee of Iona Cathedral ; *b.* Girvan, Ayrshire, 26 May 1848 ; 4th *s.* of late Samuel M'Clymont, J.P., Milburne, Girvan ; *m.* Agnes, 5th *d.* of late Thomas Smith, J.P., Ashwood, near Dundee, 1886. *Educ.*: Girvan Grammar School ; Ayr Academy ; Edinburgh University ; Tübingen. *Publications*: Beck's Pastoral Theology of The New Testament, joint-translation ; The New Testament and its Writers, an Introduction to the Books of the New Testament; volume on St. John's Gospel in The Century Bible ; text of Greece (Beautiful Books series); New Testament Criticism, its History and Results (Baird Lecture, 1910-11). *Recreations*: travelling, curling, golfing. *Address*: 22 Murrayfield Drive, Edinburgh. *Clubs*: Authors; Conservative, Edinburgh. *(Died 19 Sept. 1927.)*

M'CONAGHEY, Lt.-Col. Allen, C.I.E. 1911 ; *b.* 31 Mar. 1864. Entered army, 1884 ; Captain I.S.C. 1895 ; Major, Indian Army, 1902 ; Lt.-Col. 1910 ; Political Assistant Quetta-Pishin, 1896 ; Political Agent, Sinjawi, 1902 ; Chagai, 1904 ; Kalat, 1904 ; Deputy Commissioner, Sibi, 1905 ; Political Agent, Zhob, 1906 ; Political Agent and Deputy Commissioner in Quetta-Pishin, 1907-19 ; retired, 1919. *Club*: United Service. *(Died 31 May 1925.)*

McCONNEL, John Wanklyn, M.A. (Cantab.), J.P., Ayrshire and Manchester ; Chairman Fine Cotton Spinners and Doublers Association,

Limited ; Director, The Williams Deacon's Bank, Ltd. ; *b.* 14 Feb. 1855 ; *s.* of William McConnel of Manchester and Knockdolian, Ayrshire, and Margaret Bradshaw Wanklyn; *m.* 1885, Edith, *yr. d.* of Rev. R. H. Cobbold, Rector of Ross, Herefordshire ; no *c. Educ.*: Repton ; Caius College, Cambridge. Called to Bar, Lincoln's Inn, 1880 ; Managing Director and Chairman of McConnel Co. Ltd., Fine Spinners, until its incorporation in the Fine Spinners Association ; interested in cotton growing since 1907 ; served on the Empire Cotton Growing Committee. *Publications*: A Century of Fine Cotton Spinning ; various pamphlets on Cotton Growing. *Recreations*: fishing, shooting, golf, etc. *Address*: Knockdolian, Colmonell, Ayrshire ; 6 St. James Square, Manchester. *Clubs*: British Empire; Union, Manchester ; Prestwick and Formby Golf. *(Died 25 May 1922.)*

M'CONNELL, Sir Robert John ; 1st Bt., *cr.* 1900 ; D.L. ; *b.* 6 Feb. 1853 ; *s.* of Joseph M'Connell of Clogher ; *m.* 1st, 1874, Mary (d. 1896), *d.* of Charles Smylie; three *s.* two *d.* ; 2nd, 1897, Elsie, *d.* of George Hewson (whom he *div.*, 1904). Was created a Baronet on the occasion of Queen Victoria's visit to Belfast ; Lord Mayor of Belfast. *Heir*: *s.* Joseph [b. 17 Sep. 1877 ; *m.* 1900, Lisa, *d.* of late Jackson M'Gown ; two *s.* one *d. Address*: Glen Dhu, Belfast]. *Address*: Glen Dhu, Belfast. *Club*: Constitutional. *(Died 22 April 1927.)*

McCORKILL, Hon. John Charles, D.C.L., University of Bishops College ; LL.D., Laval University ; a Puisne Judge, Superior Court, since 1906 ; *b.* 31 Aug. 1854 ; *s.* of Robert and Margaret McCorkill ; *m.* 1884, Apphia Mary, *y. d.* of late Hon. Elijah Leonard. *Educ.*: St. John's High School ; McGill Normal School and McGill College, Montreal. Advocate, 1878 ; K.C. 1899 ; M.P.P. (L.), Missisquoi, 1897 ; Legislative Councillor, District of Bedford, 1898-1903 ; M.P.P. Co. Brome, Quebec, 1903-1906 ; Treasurer of the Province and Member of the Executive Council, 1908 - 6 ; Major (retired) Fifth Royal Scots, Montreal. *Recreation*: golf. *Address*: Braeside, 189 Grande Allee, Quebec. *Clubs*: Garrison, Quebec; St. James's, Montreal. *(Died 10 Mar. 1920.)*

McCORMICK, Rev. James, Rector of Moyrus - Roundstone, since 1878 ; Canon of Tuam since 1892 ; *m.* ; six *s.* one *d. Educ.*: Trinity College, Dublin (M.A., D.D.). Ordained, 1876 ; Curate of Tuam, 1876-78 ; Superintendent, Irish Church Mission ; Member of the General Synod, Church of Ireland, since 1890 ; Diocesan Nominator since 1903 ; Member of Diocesan Council since 1889. *Address*: Roundstone, S.O., Co. Galway. *(Died 6 May 1921.)*

McCORMICK, Very Rev. Joseph Gough, D.D. ; Dean of Manchester since 1920 ; *b.* London, 1874 ; *s.* of late Rev Joseph McCormick, D.D., Rector of St. James, Piccadilly, and Frances Harriett, *d.* of Col. and Hon. Mrs. Haines ; *m.* Alison Mary, *d.* of Rev. E. Conybeare; two *s.* two *d. Educ.*: Foster School ; St. John's College, Cambridge (Winchester Prizeman). Ordained 1897 ; Curate at Great Yarmouth ; Vicar of St. Paul's, Princes Park, Liverpool, 1901 ; Vicar of St. Michael's, Chester Square, 1909-20 ; Hon. Chaplain to the King, 1915 ; Chaplain to the King, 1918 ; Proctor in Convocation for the Diocese of London, 1919 ; Chaplain to I.Z. 1923 ; Vice-President Lancs. Co. Cricket Club, 1924. *Publications*: Plain Words on Vexed Questions ; Christ and Common Topics. *Recreations*: cricket, Norfolk County XI., from 1899. *Address*: The Deanery, Manchester. *Club*: New Oxford and Cambridge. *(Died 30 Aug. 1924.)*

M'CORMICK, Robert; Ambassador of the United States to France, 1905-7 ; *b.* Rockbridge, Co. Virginia; *s.* of William Sanderson

McCOMB, Col. Robert Brophy, C.B. See page xxiv.

M'Cormick and Mary Ann Grigsby; *m.* 1876, Katharine Medill, *d.* of Joseph Medill, Chicago. *Educ.*: University of Virginia. Secretary United States Legation, London, 1889-92; Official Representative in London of Chicago Columbian Exposition, 1892-93; United States Minister to Austria-Hungary, 1901-1902, when raised to rank of Ambassador; at Petrograd, 1902-5. *Recreations:* shooting, riding, golf, etc. *Address:* American Embassy, Paris. *Clubs:* St. James's; Chicago, Washington Park, Chicago Golf, Chicago; Union, University, Players, New York; Metropolitan and County, Washington; Jockey, Petrograd.   (*Died 18 April 1919.*)

MACCRACKEN, Henry Mitchell, D.D., LL.D.; Chancellor Emeritus, 1910; Chancellor of New York University, 1885-1910; *b.* Oxford, Ohio, 28 Sept. 1840; *e. s.* of late Rev. John Steele Maccracken; *m.* Catherine, *o. d.* of Rev. Thomas Swan Hubbard, Vermont; three *s.* one *d. Educ.*: Miami University, Oxford, Ohio; Princeton Theological Seminary; Germany. In charge of Presbyterian parishes in Columbus, Ohio, and Toledo, Ohio, 1863-81; Chancellor of University of Pittsburgh, Pa., 1881-84. *Publications:* Lives of Church Leaders; Book of the Hall of Fame, which foundation he organised, 1900. *Address:* University Heights, New York City. *T.*: Tremont 4332.
(*Died 24 Dec. 1919.*)

M'CRAE, Sir George, Kt., *cr.* 1908; D.S.O. 1917; J.P. for County of the City of Edinburgh; M.P. (L.) Stirling and Falkirk District of Burghs, 1923-24; *b.* 29 Aug. 1860; *m.* 1880, Eliza Cameron Russell (*d.* 1918); four *s.* (one killed in the War) five *d. Educ.*: Edinburgh Lancastrian School; Heriot-Watt College, Edinburgh. Entered Town Council of Edinburgh, 1889; elected Treasurer of the city, 1891; Chairman of Finance Committee, 1891-1899; was successful in promoting various financial and other reforms in the City Council; M.P. East Edinburgh, 1899-1909; Vice-President and Chairman of the Local Government Board for Scotland, 1909; Chairman Scottish Board of Health, 1919-22; Hon. Colonel Territorial Force (V.D.) and Hon. Lt.-Col. in the Army. Raised a Battalion of 1550 in twelve days in 1914, and two reserve companies of 250 men each later; this Battalion became the 16th (S.) Battalion The Royal Scots, which he commanded in European War (despatches twice, D.S.O.). *Publications:* Lectures on Municipal Finance, etc. *Recreations:* riding, golf. *Address:* Torluish, North Berwick. *Club:* Reform.
(*Died 27 Dec. 1928.*)

McCRAITH, Sir James William, Kt., *cr.* 1918; J.P.; *b.* 19 Mar. 1853; *s.* of William McCraith, Kirkcudbrightshire, and Sarah, *d.* of James Yorke, Northamptonshire; *m.* 1876, Maria Elizabeth, *d.* of Thomas and Elizabeth Dickinson of Holly Mount, Notts; three *s.* one *d. Educ.*: King's School, Grantham. Chairman City of Nottingham Unionist Association; Trustee Nottingham Savings Bank; ex-President Nottingham Law Society; ex-President Notaries of England and Wales. *Recreations:* shooting, golf, tennis. *Address:* The Park, Nottingham. *T.*: 852. *Club:* Carlton.
(*Died 9 July 1928.*)

M'CRAITH, Sir John Tom, Kt., *cr.* 1904; J.P.; *b.* 8 Nov. 1847; *s.* of late W. M'Craith, Director of Nottingham and Notts Banking Co.; Trustee, Nottingham Savings Bank; Chairman of Nottingham and County Constitutional Club; Alderman of the City of Nottingham; Vice-Chairman of the Nottinghamshire Territorial Assoc. *Address:* Park Terrace, Nottingham.
(*Died 5 Dec. 1919.*)

McCRAKEN, Sir Robert, Kt., *cr.* 1922; Chairman of Steel Brothers & Co. Ltd.; *b.* 4 Nov. 1846; *s.* of James McCraken of Ardwell,

662

Ayrshire; *m.* 1890, Pauline, *d.* of late Edouard Chrestien; three *d. Educ.*: Ayr Academy. *Address:* 23 Kensington Palace Gardens, W.S. *T.*: Park 3962. *Clubs:* Oriental, Ranelagh.
(*Died 3 Nov. 1924.*)

McCUBBIN, Frederick; Australian Artist; landscape and portrait painter; Drawing Master at the National Gallery, Melbourne, since 1884; *b.* West Melbourne, 25 Feb. 1855; *s.* of A. McCubbin, Garvin, Ayrshire; *m.* 1889, Annie Moriarty. *Educ.*: St. Paul's, Swanston Street, and Wilmot's School, West Melbourne. First Examiner in Drawing Matriculation, Melbourne University, from 1900; Exhibited at Paris Salon, 1897, and at the Grafton Galleries, London. *Pictures:* Down on his Luck (Perth Gallery); A Bush Burial (Geelong Gallery); The Pioneers and Winter Evening (Melbourne Gallery); On the Wallaby Track (Sydney Gallery); Ti-tree Glade, and portrait of the artist (Adelaide Gallery). *Address:* Carlsberg, Kensington Road, South Yarra, Melbourne, Australia.
(*Died 22 Dec. 1917.*)

MACCULLAGH, Sir James Acheson; *cr.* 1896; J.P.; Medical Inspector Local Gov. Board; *b.* Dublin, 4 Oct. 1854; *e. s.* of late John MacCullagh, R.M.; *m.* 1880, Ida M'Clelland. *Educ.*: Ennis Coll.; Dublin University (B.A., M.D.) (Stip. Cond.). House Surgeon Londonderry City and County Infirmary. Has been Mayor of Londonderry thrice. *Recreations:* president N.W. Football Association, president Londonderry Cycling Club, capt. Londonderry Cricket Association. *Address:* Lisgorm, Galway. *Club:* County, Galway. (*Died July 1918.*)

McCULLOCH, Allan Riverstone; Zoologist of the Australian Museum, Sydney, since 1906; Specialist in ichthyology; *b.* 20 June 1885; *s.* of Herbert Riverstone McCulloch and Ella Maud Backhouse; unmarried. *Educ.*: Sydney. Entered service of the Australian Museum as a Voluntary Cadet, 1898; joined the salaried staff, 1902; fishes trawled by the Federal Investigation Vessel Endeavour and the collection of the Australian Museum provided most of the material for his studies; engaged on a Catalogue of Australian Fishes; elected to the Councils of the Linnean and Zoological Societies of N.S. Wales and the Great Barrier Reef Committee; the gathering of natural history and ethnological collections has carried him far into Western Papua, the New Hebrides, and along the Australian coastline from south of Tasmania to the Torres Straits. *Publications:* Fifty odd papers dealing with fishes, and others with mammals, reptiles, and crustaceans of Australia, in the publications of various scientific societies and institutions of Australia; more generally known as a writer of popular articles in semi-scientific journals. *Recreations:* keen on drawing and painting; and a little music when time permits; has also managed a fair amount of travelling around on anything from warships to pearling-luggers along the Australian coasts and South Seas. *Address:* Australian Museum, College Street, Sydney.
(*Died 1 Sept. 1925.*)

M'CULLOCH, Rev. James Duff, D.D.; Minister of Hope Street Free Church, Glasgow, since 1889; Senior Minister since 1921; Principal of Free Church College, Edinburgh, since 1905; *b.* 1836; 5th *s.* of late Andrew M'Culloch and Catherine Ross; *m.* 1870, Anne Isabella, 3rd *d.* of late Rev. George Davidson of Latheron; five *s.* three *d. Educ.*: Fearn F.C. School; Tain Royal Academy; Edinburgh Univ.; New Coll. Edinburgh. Minister of the Free Church at Latheron, 1867-89; Moderator of the General Assembly of the Free Church of Scotland, 1901. *Address:* Free Church College, Edinburgh; Torbeg, 52 Eastwood Mains Road, Giffnock, Glasgow. *T.*: Giffnock 127.
(*Died 11 Dec. 1926.*)

McCUBBIN, Lt.-Col. Thomas, C.M.G. See page xxiv.

MACCUNN, Hamish, composer of music and conductor; *b.* Greenock, Scotland, 22 Mar. 1868; twin 2nd *s.* of James MacCunn, formerly shipowner, Greenock; *m. o. d.* of late John Pettie, R.A., 1889; one *s. Educ.*: various schools in Greenock; private tutors; Royal College of Music, London; Scholar, 1883-87; studied there; composition under Dr. C. H. H. Parry; also pianoforte and viola. Conductor with the Carl Rosa Opera Company, The Moody-Manners Opera Company, and of light operas, etc., at the Savoy, Adelphi, Lyric, Apollo, Prince of Wales', Queen's and Daly's theatres, and with Mr. Thomas Beecham at Covent Garden and His Majesty's Theatres, 1910. *Publications:* overtures, etc.—The Land of the Mountain and the Flood, Chior Mhor, The Ship o' the Fiend, The Dowie Dens o' Yarrow, and Highland Memories; dramatic cantatas, etc.—Lord Ullin's Daughter, Bonny Kilmeny, The Cameronian's Dream, Queen Hynde, The Lay of the Last Minstrel, The Death of Parcy Reed, The Wreck of the Hesperus, Kinmont Willie, Livingstone the Pilgrim; (with Rev. Silvester Horne—Livingstone Centenary Meeting, Albert Hall, 1913); Conductor of Stock Exchange Orchestra, 1913-14; Lamkin, The Jolly Goshawk; music in English productions of Earl and the Girl, Talk of the Town, A Waltz Dream, and Autumn Manœuvres; operas—Jeanie Deans (with Joseph Bennett); Diarmid (with the Duke of Argyll); The Pageant of Darkness and Light (with John Oxenham and Hugh Moss); Orient Exhibition, 1908; songs, about 100; part songs, about 20; and various other miscellaneous works. *Recreations:* fishing, golf, billiards. *Address:* 6 Abbey Court, N.W. *T.:* 2066 P.O. Hampstead. (*Died 2 Aug. 1916.*)

M'CUTCHEON, George Barr; author; *b.* Indiana, U.S.A., 26 July 1866; *s.* of John Barr and Clara Glick M'Cutcheon; *m.* 1904, Marie Van Antwerp Fay. *Educ.:* Purdue University. City editor, Lafayette Evening Courier, 1893-1901. *Publications:* Graustark; Castle Craneycrow; The Sherrods; Brewster's Millions; The Day of the Dog; Beverly of Graustark; The Purple Parasol; Nedra; Cowardice Court; Jane Cable; The Flyers; The Daughter of Anderson Crow; The Husbands of Edith; The Man from Brodney's; The Alternative; Truxton King; The Butterfly Man; The Rose in the Ring; What's-his-Name; Mary Midthorne; Her Weight in Gold; The Hollow of her Hand; A Fool and his Money; Black is White; The Prince of Graustark; Mr. Bingle; The Light that Lies; From the Housetops; Green Fancy; Shot with Crimson; The City of Masks; Sherry; Anderson Crow, Detective; West Wind Drift; Quill's Window; The Court of New York, 1920; Yollop; Viola Gwyn; Oliver October; East of the Setting Sun; Romeo in Moon Village; Kindling and Ashes; The Inn of the Hawk and Raven; Blades; various magazine stories and serials. *Address:* c/o Dodd, Mead & Co., 443 Fourth Avenue, New York City. (*Died 23 Oct. 1928.*)

MACDERMOT, Captain Ffrench (The MacDermot-Roe); descended from the Princes of Leinster; holds the above ancient chieftain title, and is also the Lord of Moylurg, as recorded in the history of the county of Roscommon; is head of the Protestant branch of the MacDermot sept or clan. It was the Princess Eva, daughter of Dermot, Prince of Leinster, who married Richard St. Clair, Earl of Pembroke, of Chepstow Castle, near Bristol, an alliance which led to the conquest of Ireland in the reign of King Henry II., given in English history. The MacDermot family suffered heavily in days gone by through confiscation and suppression of their titles, particularly during the reign of Queen Elizabeth and later on in Cromwell's time, when their estates and castles were taken from them and bestowed upon Colonel King, an officer of the Parliamentary forces. The head of the family is the MacDermot, Prince of Coolavin Roe (or rua), signifying red, a nom de guerre of Feudal times. *Address:* Villa Elise, Pont de la Russe, Monte Carlo. *Club:* Royal Societies. (*Died 8 Nov. 1917.*)

MACDERMOT, Rev. Henry Myles Fleetwood, *b.* 24 March 1887; *s.* of Theodosia and Henry MacDermot, M.D.; *m.* Mary Emily Langdon; eight *s.* three *d. Educ.*: home. Ordained, 1860; Curate, 1860-80; Rector of St. Joseph, Grove, 1880-82; St. Michael and All Angels, Kingston, 1882-85; St. Mark, Craigton, 1885-1911; Chaplain to Archbishop of West Indies; Chaplain to the Forces at Newcastle Jamaica; Canon and Tutor of Ch. Theological College, Jamaica; Retired, 1914. *Recreations:* reading, chess. *Address:* 788 Shuter Street, Montreal. (*Died 23 Sept. 1918.*)

M'DERMOTT, Peter Joseph, C.M.G. 1918; I.S.O. 1905; Under Secretary, Chief Secretary's Dept., Queensland; *m.* 1895, Mary Fleming. Entered Public Service, 1872. *Address:* Chief Secretary's Dept., Brisbane. (*Died 9 Nov. 1922.*)

MACDONALD of Earnscliffe (Ontario), 1st Baroness, *cr.* 1891; **Susan Agnes Macdonald** [was created a peeress in own right on death of her husband in consideration of his public services]; *b.* 1836; *d.* of Hon. T. J. Bernard, P.C. Jamaica; *m.* 1867, Right Hon. Sir John Alexander Macdonald, P.C., G.C.B., LL.D., D.C.L., Prime Minister of Canada, 1867-73, and 1878-91; one *d. Heir:* none. *Address:* Earnscliffe, Ottawa. (*Died 5 Sept. 1920.*)

MACDONALD, Alexander, M.A.; Ruskin Master of Drawing in the University of Oxford. *Address:* Ruskin Drawing School, Beaumont Street, Oxford. *T.:* Oxford 44.
(*Died 16 Oct. 1921.*)

M'DONALD, Sir Andrew, Kt., *cr.* 1897; *b.* 1836; *s.* of Thomas M'Donald, Kirkhill, Midlothian; *m.* Isabella, *d.* of late William Fisher, Lanark, 1857; one *s.* Master of Edinburgh Merchant Co., 1888-89; Lord Provost of Edinburgh, 1894-97. *Address:* 40 Lauder Road, Edinburgh; Toftcombs, Biggar, N.B.
(*Died 15 July 1919.*)

MACDONALD, Sir Archibald John, 4th Bt.; *cr.* 1813; *b.* 2 Feb. 1871; *s.* of 3rd Bt. and Catharine Mary, *d.* of late John Coulthurst, and widow of Hon. Edward T. Stonor; *S.* father, 1901; *m.* 1900, Constance Mary, *d.* of Rev. H. M. Burgess. *Heir:* none. *Recreations:* golf, motoring, shooting, fishing, tennis. *M.:* AA 1797, 1069. (*Died 11 Oct. 1919.*)

MACDONALD, Augustine Colin, Lieut.-Governor of Prince Edward Island; *s.* of Hugh Macdonald, who came to Prince Edward Island in 1805 from Moidart, Invernesshire, and Catherine, *d.* of A. Macdonald of Rhue Arisaig, Invernesshire; *b.* Panmure, Prince Edward Island, 30 June 1837; *m.* Mary Elizabeth, sixth *d.* of late Hon. John Small Macdonald, Charlottetown; three *s.* four *d. Educ.:* Grammar School, Georgetown; Central Academy, Charlottetown, P.E.I. First returned to Local Assembly, 1870; sat for three sessions; Elected to represent King's Co. on the Province entering Confederation; and has sat for twenty sessions in Parliament at Ottawa. *Address:* Charlottetown, Prince Edward Island. (*Died July 1919.*)

M'DONALD, Hon. Charles, M.P., Speaker House of Representatives, Commonwealth Parliament, Australia, 1910-13 and 1914-17; *b.* Melbourne, Victoria; *s.* of late Charles Thomas Young M'Donald of Charters Towers, Queensland; *m.* 1892, *e. d.* of Alfred Tregear, Charters Towers, Queensland; one *d. Educ.:* State School, Victoria and N.S.W. Watchmaker by trade; been connected with the labour movement in Queensland since its inception; President Australian Labour Federation, 1890-92; M.L.A. of Queensland for district of Flinders, 1893-1901; returned to first House of Representatives, 1901 (Commonwealth Parliament); Chairman of Committees of House of Representatives, 1907-10; a Fellow of the Art Society of Queensland. *Recreations:* golf, is a keen lover of all kinds of sport. *Address:* Hughenden, Studley Avenue, Kew, Melbourne. *T.:* Hawthorn 497. (*Died Nov. 1925.*)

MACDONALD, Maj.-Gen. Sir Donald Alexander, Kt. *cr.* 1918; C.M.G. 1908; I.S.O. 1903; Quartermaster-General Canadian Militia, 1904-17; *b.* 31 Oct. 1845; *s.* of late Alexander Eugene Macdonald, Deputy-Clerk of the Crown and Registrar of the Surrogate Court of Cornwall, Canada; *m.* 1876, Mary, 2nd *d.* of Hon. Mr. Justice Hugh Richardson, formerly of the Superior and Supreme Court of the North-West Territories of Canada; one *d. Educ.:* County High School. Joined Militia, Rifle Company of Cornwall as Ensign, 1863; Lieut. 59th Regt. 1865; Capt. 1866; Adjt. 59th Regt. 1869; Major, 1871; Lieut.-Col. 1877; Col. 1900; Brig.-Gen. 1907; Maj.-Gen. 1912; served during Fenian Raids, 1866; Red River Expedition, 1870 (medal, two clasps); North-West Rebellion, 1885 (medal); holds Long Service Decoration; sometime Chief Superintendent Military Stores; Director-General of Ordnance, Canada, 1908-4; third military member Militia Council. *Address:* Chateau Laurier, Ottawa, Canada. *T.:* Q 3625, Q 1919. *Clubs:* Ottawa, Canada, Rideau, Golf, Country, Ottawa; Royal Canadian Yacht, Toronto. (*Died 3 May 1920.*)

MACDONALD Rev. Frederic Wm., President of the Wesleyan Methodist Conference, 1899; *b.* 25 Feb. 1842; *s.* of Rev. G. B. Macdonald; *m.* Mary (*d.* 1909), *y. d.* of late Benjamin Cork of Burslem. *Educ.:* St. Peter's Collegiate School and Owens College, Manchester. Entered Wesleyan ministry, 1862; joint editor of London Quarterly Review, 1871-75; represented British Methodist Conference at General Conference of Methodist Episcopal Church of America, 1880; appointed Professor of Theology, Handsworth College, 1881; appointed Secretary of Wesleyan Missionary Society, 1891; visited Australia and New Zealand, 1903. *Publications:* Life of Fletcher of Madeley; Life of William Morley Punshon; Latin Hymns in the Wesleyan Hymn Book; In a Nook with a Book; As a Tale that is Told, 1919. *Recreations:* those of a book-lover. *Address:* 18 Wellington Road, Bournemouth. (*Died 16 Oct. 1928.*)

MACDONALD, Rev. Frederick William, J.P.; Hon. Canon of Salisbury; late Rural Dean of Wylye; late Alderman of County Council of Wiltshire; *b.* 1848; *s.* of W. Macdonald, M.A., Archdeacon of Wiltshire and Residentiary Canon of Salisbury; *m.* 1874, Frances Lucy Matthews Pimperne, Dorsetshire; no *c. Educ.:* Marlborough College; Somerset College, Bath; Oxford. Travelled Australian Colonies, South America, Europe; Curate of Coggs, Oxon, 1874-76; Brizenorton, Oxon, 1876-77; Vicar of Stapleford, Wilts, 1877-95; Rector of Wishford, Wilts, 1895-1924. In Freemasonry—Past Grand Chaplain of England; late Provincial Grand Mark Master for Wiltshire. *Publications:* Brochures on Local Government; educational matters. *Recreations:* fishing, golf, freemasonry. *Address:* Pinehurst, Clevedon, Somerset.
(*Died 24 Nov. 1928.*)

M'DONALD, Hugh Campbell, C.M.G. 1914; Resident and District Magistrate; *b.* 12 Oct. 1869, *s.* of Donald Wm. M'Donald, J.P., and Sarah Bisset, *niece* of late General Bisset; *m.* 1st, 1901, Jean, *d.* of James Bladon, Edenbridge; two *s.*; 2nd, 1919, Elsie May, *y. d.* of T. J. Wall, Southampton, and widow of Capt. F. Hardie, R.A.M.C.; one *d. Educ.:* South Africa. Joined Sir Harry Johnston's Administration, Nyasaland, 1894; Judicial Officer, Lower Shire

664

District, 1897; Resident 1st Grade. 1907. *Address:* Zomba, Nyasaland. (*Died 16 Mar. 1921.*)

MACDONALD, James Alexander; Managing Editor, The Globe, Toronto, 1902-16; *b.* Middlesex Co., Ontario, Canada, 22 Jan. 1862; *s.* of late John A. Macdonald, a native of Pictou Co., Nova Scotia; *m.* 1890, Grace Lunsden Christian; two *s.* one *d. Educ.:* Hamilton and Toronto, Ontario; Edinburgh. Graduated at Knox Coll. Toronto, 1887; ordained to ministry of the Presbyterian Church, and inducted pastor of Knox Church, St. Thomas, Ontario, 1891; resigned pastoral charge, 1896; entered journalism in Toronto as first editor of The Westminster; Member of Board of Governors of the University of Toronto since 1906; LL.D. Hon. Glas. and Oberlin; Member first Imperial Press Conference, London, 1909; President of Westminster Co., Toronto; Vice-Pres. Toronto Conservatory of Music. *Publications:* From Far Formosa, volume on life-work of late Dr. G. L. MacKay; The Significance of Lincoln; What a Newspaper Man saw in Britain; Democracy and the Nations. *Address:* The Globe, Toronto. *Club:* Ontario, Toronto. (*Died 14 May 1923.*)

MACDONALD, Maj.-General Sir James Ronald Leslie, K.C.I.E.: *cr.* 1904; C.B. 1900; LL.D.; D.L. (Aberdeenshire) 1914; Colonel Comdt. Royal Engineers since 1924; *b.* 8 Feb. 1862; *s.* of Surgeon-Major James Macdonald, M.D., F.R.C.S.E. (retired); *m.* 1894, Alice Margaret, *y. d.* of General George Pringle, I.S.C. *Educ.:* Grammar School, Aberdeen; Aberdeen University. Entered R.E. 1882; Capt. 1890; Brevet Major, 1895; Brevet Lt.-Col. 1899; Major, 1899; B-evet Col. 1900; Col. 1905; Brig.-Gen. commanding Presidency Brigade, India, 1905; served with Hazara Expedition, 1888 (despatches, medal and clasp); Chief Engineer Preliminary Survey for Uganda Railway, 1891-1892; Uganda, 1892; Nouma Expedition, 1893; acting Commissioner Uganda Protectorate, 1893; commanded operations against rebels, Uganda, 1893 (acknowledgment of Govt., medal); Chief Staff Officer Unyoro Expedition, 1893-94 (medal, brevet of Major, Brilliant Star of Zanzibar, 2nd class); chief command of operations in Uganda, 1897-98; commanded at action of Lubwa's Hill, siege of Lubwa's Fort, engagements of Kizalera, Kijembo, etc. (medal with 2 clasps, brevet of Lt.-Col., thanks of Govt.); commanded Juba Expedition, 1898-99; Director of Railways, China Expeditionary Force, 1901 (despatches, brevet of Col., medal); commanded operations in Thibet, 1903-4, including engagements at Guru, Niani, Tsechen, capture of Gyantse and advance to Lhasa (medal and clasp, K.C.I.E.); commanding Presidency Brigade, 1905-7; commanding Lucknow Infantry Brigade, 1907-9; commanding troops in Mauritius, 1909-12. *Decorated* for services in Uganda and Thibet. *Publications:* Soldiering and Surveying in British East Africa. *Address:* c/o Grindlay & Co., 54 Parliament Street, S.W.1. (*Died 27 June 1927.*)

MACDONALD, James Smith; editor Farmer and Stockbreeder since 1895, and Agricultural Correspondent of the Morning Post; Director in firm of Macdonald & Martin, Ltd.; formerly acting editor of Farming World; *b.* 1873; *s.* of late William Macdonald, editor North British Agriculturist; *m.* 1900, Jeannie, *d.* of George Kerr, Edinburgh; two *s. Educ.:* George Watson's College, Edinburgh; attended science course affecting agriculture and live stock. Holder of first-class certificates; written extensively on agricultural and live stock subjects in home and foreign publications from experience in Great Britain and abroad; Chairman Institute of Journalists (London District), 1918. *Recreation:* golf. *Address:* The Rookery, 7 Dorset Road, Merton

Park, S.W.19. *T.:* P.O. Wimbledon 767. *Clubs:* Farmers', Aldwych. *(Died 9 Dec. 1923.)*

MACDONALD, John, I.S.O.; Collector of Inland Revenue at Edinburgh, 1902-7; *b.* 1843; *e. s.* of Robert B. W. MacDonald, Glen Urquhart, Inverness; *m.* 1887, Annie, *e. d.* of Roderick Finlayson, Tain, Ross-shire; two *s.* two *d. Educ.:* local schools. Entered Inland Revenue Department, 1867; held several offices in the country and Somerset House. *Publications:* one of the editors of Ham's Inland Revenue Year-Bo)k since first publication to 1907; Smuggling in the Highlands. *Recreation:* angling. *Address:* 66 Polwarth Terrace, Edinburgh. *(Died 19 Feb. 1928.)*

MACDONALD, Col. John Andrew, of Glenaladale; C.B. 1897; Hon. Col. and late Lt.-Col. com. 3rd (Militia) Batt. Queen's Own Cameron Highlanders; *b.* Borrodale, Inverness-shire, 29 July 1837; *e. s.* of late Angus Macdonald of Glenaladale and Mary, *d.* of Hugh Watson, Torsonce, Midlothian; *m.* 1st, 1862, Helen *(d.s.p.* 1864), *d.* of Edward Chaloner, Liverpool; 2nd, 1901, Margaret Mary Teresa, widow of George Edmund Wicksted, and *y. d.* of late Sir Edward Blount, 8th Bt. *Educ.:* Ushaw Coll. near Durham. *Decorated:* Diamond Jubilee. *Address:* Glenfinnan, Inverness-shire, N.B.; Betley Hall, Crewe. *Clubs:* Caledonian; New, Edinburgh. *(Died 25 Feb. 1916.)*

MACDONALD, Rt. Hon. Sir John Hay Athole, P.C., K.C.; G.C.B., *cr.* 1916; K.C.B., *cr.* 1900; LL.D., F.R.S., F.R.S.E., M.I.E.E., J.P., D.L., V.D. 1892; Lord Justice-Clerk of Scotland, Lord President Second Division Court of Session, 1888-1915; a Brigadier-General, 1891 (and the Adj.-Gen. 1896-1902), Ensign-Gen. 1904, of the Royal Company of Archers (King's Royal Bodyguard); Hon. Col. Army Motor Reserve; Member of H.M. Road Board; *b.* Edinburgh, 27 December 1836; *s.* of late Matthew Norman Macdonald Hume, W.S., Ninewells, and Grace, *d.* of Sir John Hay, Bt., Smithfield and Haystoune; *m.* Adelaide Jeanette, *d.* of Maj. Doran, Ely House, Wexford, 1864 *(d.* 1870); two *s. Educ.:* Edin. Acad. and University (LL.D. 1884); Basle University; LL.D. St. Andrews, 1911; Advocate, 1859; Q.C. 1880; Sheriff of Ross, Cromarty, and Sutherland, 1874-76; Sheriff of Perthshire, 1880-1885; Commissioner of Northern Lighthouses, 1876-80 and 1885-88; Member of H.M. Prison Board, 1880-85; Member of H.M. Board of Supervision, 1880-85; Solicitor-General for Scotland, 1876-80; Dean of the Faculty of Advocates, 1882-85; Lord Advocate of Scotland, 1885-89; C.B. 1882; P.C. 1885; Member Committee of Privy Council on Education, 1885-89; Chairman Royal Commission on Boundaries of Glasgow, 1888; M.P. Universities of Edinburgh and St. Andrews, 1885-89; Colonel Commandant of Queen's R.V. Brigade, 1882-92; Brig.-Gen. Commanding the Forth Brigade, 1888-1901; Hon. Col. Queen's Brigade, 1900; Hon. Col. of Motor Volunteer Corps, 1903; Vice-President Royal United Service Institution; Vice-President National Rifle Association; President Royal Scottish Society of Arts, 1890-92; Royal Commemoration medals (two), 1897: one as Adj.-Gen. of the Royal Bodyguard, the other as Brig.-Gen. of Troops on duty at Royal Procession; Royal Coronation Medal; obtained many medals and diplomas for life-saving inventions, military works, and electrical inventions, including decorations from H.M. the King of the Belgians and the United States Government. It was through his exertions with the Postmaster-General and the Government that post-cards were introduced into Great Britain; inventor of a Holophote Course Indicator for preventing collisions at sea; a Military Field Telegraph; a Barothermotelemeter, and other electrical appliances. *Publications:* Common Sense on Parade, or Drill without Stays; Macdonald on Tactics; A New Form of Infantry Attack; A Treatise on the Criminal Law of Scotland; Prisoners on Oath; Our Trip to Blunderland; Electricity in the Household; Power Traction in War; Infantry in a New Century; The Future of Motor Traction; Infantry Training, Dress, and Equipment; the Making of the Infantry Soldier; Criminal Law and Procedure; The Volunteers in 1905; The Past and Future of Power Traction on Roads; Roads; Fifty Years of It, or the Experiences and Struggles of a Volunteer of 1859; Life Jottings of an Old Edinburgh Citizen, 1915; and numerous books, pamphlets, and lectures on Tactics, Law, and Electricity. *Recreations:* captain of the Royal and Ancient Golf Club, 1887-88; president Scottish Amateur Athletic Association; Steward, Royal Automobile club; golf, cricket, lawn-tennis, curling, electrical inventions and research, driving; President Scottish Automobile Club; strong supporter of autocar movement; is the arbiter in disputes in international football matches. *Address:* 15 Abercromby Place, Edinburgh. *Clubs:* Constitutional, Royal Societies, Royal Automobile; New, Edinburgh; Golf, Wimbledon; New, Luffness. *T.:* 196 Edinburgh. *M.:* S 1. *(Died 9 May 1919.)*

MACDONALD, John Ronald Moreton of Largie, J.P., D.L. for Argyll; landed proprietor; *b.* 1873; *s.* of late Charles Moreton Macdonald, of Largie, and Elizabeth Hume Campbell, of Glendaruell; *m.* 1906, Daisy, *d.* of late General Eyre Crabbe, C.B.; two *s.* two *d. Educ.:* Eton; Magdalen College, Oxford (M.A.). Has been chiefly resident on his own property since he inherited it in 1894, and occupied in its management, in local affairs, in county business, and in literary work. *Publications:* A History of France, 1916; Contributions to Cambridge Modern History, and other Historical Essays. *Address:* Largie Castle, Tayinloan. *Clubs:* Travellers', Cavendish; New, Edinburgh. *(Died 10 Sept. 1921.)*

MACDONALD, Ranald Mackintosh, C.B.E. 1919; N.Z. Red Cross Service, England; *b.* 1860; *e. s.* of late W. K. Macdonald, Orari, N.Z.; *m.* 1885, Gertrude, *d.* of George Gould, N.Z.; three *s.* two *d.* Mechanical Engineer, N.Z. Railways; Managing Director Christchurch Tramways; Christchurch City Council; Canterbury Agricultural and Pastoral Association, C. J. C.; Director several companies. *Recreation:* motoring. *Address:* Hambledon, Christchurch, N.Z. *Clubs:* Royal Automobile, Junior Athenæum; Christchurch, Christchurch, N.Z. *(Died 21 Oct. 1928.)*

MACDONALD, Lieut.-Col. Reginald Percy, D.S.O. 1889; reserve of officers; late Hampshire Regt.; *b.* 10 June 1856; *e. s.* of Maj. Gen. J. C. Macdonald; *m.* 1890, *d.* of Thomas Chard, Ramsgate, and *widow* of Alex. Murray of Old Polmaise, Stirling. *Educ.:* Clifton Coll. Served in Royal Pembroke Artillery Militia, 1875 and 1876; joined 67th Hampshire Regt., 1878; promoted Captain, 1884, Major, 1892; Lieut.-Col., 1903; gazetted 2nd in command, 1897; voluntarily retired, 1897; served in Afghan War, 1879-80, with the 67th Regt. (medal); served in Burma Expedition, 1885-87, with the 2nd Batt. Hampshire Regt., including the surrender of Mandalay (medal with clasp); also with the 1st Batt. Hampshire Regt., 1887-89, including the expedition to Mogaung (despatches, D.S.O., and clasp); South Africa, 1899-1900. *Recreations:* all sports.

M'DONALD, Rev. Walter, D.D.; Prefect of the Dunboyne Establishment, St. Patrick's College, Maynooth; *b.* 1854, of tenant farmer stock, at Emil, Piltown, Co. Kilkenny. *Educ.:* St. Kieran's College, Kilkenny; St. Patrick's

College, Maynooth. Priest. 1876 ; Professor of St. Kieran's College, Kilkenny, where for five years he taught philosophy, theology, and English literature ; Professor of Theology at St. Patrick's College, Maynooth, 1881. Founded The Irish Theological Quarterly, 1906, of which he was chief editor for three years, when he retired. *Publications :* Motion : its Origin and Conservation (this book was condemned by the S. Congregation of the Index at Rome, and withdrawn from circulation by order of that body) ; The Principles of Moral Science ; Some Ethical Questions of Peace and War with Special Reference to Ireland, 1919. *Recreation :* walking. *Address :* St. Patrick's College, Maynooth, Ireland. (*Died 2 May 1920.*)

MACDONALD, Sir William Christopher, Kt., *cr.* 1898 ; Governor of M'Gill University, Montreal, to which he has given large endowments ; Director of the Bank of Montreal ; Governor of Montreal General Hospital ; merchant ; *b.* Glenaladale, Prince Edward Island, 1831 ; *y. s.* of late Hon. Donald Macdonald, President Legislative Council of Prince Edward Island. *Educ. :* Central Academy, Charlotte Town, Prince Edward Island. *Address :* 449 Sherbrooke Street, West, Montreal, Canada. *Club :* Mount Royal, Montreal.
(*Died 11 June 1917.*)

MACDONALD, William Rae, Actuary ; Carrick Pursuivant, 1898 - 1909 ; Albany Herald since 1909 ; *b.* Edinburgh, 25 Dec. 1843 ; *o. s.* of William Rae Macdonald of Mont Albion, Surinam, South America, and his wife, Isabella Johnston ; *m.* Annie S. Johnston, 1880. *Educ. :* Edinburgh Institution. Fellow Faculty of Actuaries in Scotland. *Publications :* On the Calculus of Finite Differences, 1876 ; On the Theory of Logarithms, 1885 ; a translation from the Latin of The Construction of the Wonderful Canon of Logarithms, by John Napier of Merchiston, with a bibliographical account of the various editions of his works, 1889 ; article on John Napier in the Dictionary of National Biography, 1894 ; The Heraldry of Elgin, in the Proceedings of the Society of Antiquaries of Scotland, 1899-1900 ; Heraldry in Churchyards between Tain and Inverness, in the Proceedings of the Society of Antiquaries of Scotland, 1901-2 ; Scottish Armorial Seals, 1904. *Recreations :* heraldic and archæological investigation. *Address :* Neidpath, 4 Wester Coates Avenue, Edinburgh.
(*Died 1923.*)

MACDONELL, Angus Claude, D.C.L., K.C. ; Senator ; Barrister-at-law, of Osgoode Hall, Toronto ; *b.* Toronto, 23 June 1861 ; *s.* of Angus Duncan Macdonell, a United Empire Loyalist, and Pauline Rosalie De-La-Haye (French descent) ; unmarried. *Educ. :* Toronto Model School and Trinity University. Member House of Commons, 1904-17 ; Conservative ; a Catholic. *Recreations :* aquatics, and general field athletics. *Address :* Toronto. *Clubs :* Toronto, Albany, Toronto Hunt, Royal Canadian Yacht, Argonaut Rowing, Ontario Jockey, Empire, Toronto ; Rideau, Ottawa.
(*Died April 1924.*)

MacDONELL, Edgar Errol Napier, C.M.G. 1918 ; *b.* 10 Oct. 1874 ; *s.* of late Rt. Hon. Sir Hugh MacDonell, G.C.M.G., P.C. ; *m.* 1906, Violet, *o. d.* of Frank Forrester ; one *d. Educ. :* Eton. Served at the Consulate of Lisbon, 1896 ; Vice-Consul and Agent for British Central Africa to reside at Chinde, 1898 ; Acting Consul, Beira, 1900 ; Consul at Moçambique, 1900 ; Acting Consul-General, Lourenço Marques, 1901-2 ; Consul for Liberia, 1903 ; Consul for Continental Greece, 1906 ; Consul for Roumania, 1910 ; Consul - General, Portuguese East Africa, 1912 ; received Queen's S. African War Medal ; appointed Chief Liaison Officer to Portuguese G.E.A. Expeditionary Force, with rank of Staff Major, 1917 (Commendador

of the Portuguese Order of Aviz, despatches) ; subsequently promoted Staff Colonel ; H.B.M. Consul-General for States of Rio de Janeiro, 1921 ; retired on pension, 1924. *Recreations :* shooting, fishing, and sports generally. *Club :* Eccentric. (*Died 4 Dec. 1928.*)

MACDONELL, Sir John, Kt., *cr.* 1903 ; K.C.B., *cr.* 1914 ; C.B. 1898 ; LL.D., M.A. ; King's Remembrancer, 1912-20, and Master of Supreme Court, 1889-1920 ; *b.* 1846 ; *s.* of James Macdonell of Rhynie, Aberdeenshire ; *m.* 1873, Agnes, 3rd *d.* of Daniel Harrison of Shirly House, Beckenham, Kent ; two *d. Educ. :* Aberdeen and Edinburgh Universities. Barrister Middle Temple, 1873 ; appointed Revising Barrister for Middlesex, 1884 ; one of the Counsel to the Board of Trade and London Chamber of Commerce ; Membre de l'Institut International de Statistique ; late Vice-President of the Royal Statistical Society ; President of Grotius Society ; editor of State Trials, 1887 ; editor of Civil Judicial Statistics since 1894, of the Criminal Judicial Statistics, 1900, and of the Journal of Comparative Legislation ; elected Associate of the Institut de Droit International, 1900 ; Member, 1912 ; Member of Board of Studies of Economics, London University, and the first Dean of the Law Faculty of that University ; Fellow of the British Academy, 1913 ; Quain Professor of Comparative Law, University College, London, 1901-20 ; President of Society of Public Teachers of Law, 1912-13 ; Member of Royal Commission on Shipping Combinations and of Sub-Commission to South Africa, and of Lord Gorell's Committee on High Court and County Courts ; and Chairman of Committee of Enquiry into Breaches of the Laws of War ; Vice-President of Medico-Legal Society. *Publications :* Survey of Political Economy ; The Land Question ; The Law of Master and Servant ; edited Smi*th's* Mercantile Law ; articles in reviews, magazines, and periodical press. *Recreations :* golf, bicycle. *Address :* 31 Kensington Park Gardens, W. ; 173 Royal Law Courts, W.C. *Clubs :* Athenæum, Reform. (*Died 17 Mar. 1921.*)

MACDONNELL, 1st Baron, *cr.* 1908 ; **of Swinford ; Antony Patrick Macdonnell,** G.C.S.I., *cr.* 1897 ; K.C.S.I., *cr.* 1893 ; P.C. (Gt. Br.) 1902 ; P.C. (Ir.) 1903 ; K.C.V.O., *cr.* 1903 ; D.Litt., D.C.L. (Oxon) ; *b.* 1844 ; *m.* 1878, Henrietta, *d.* of Ewen Macdonell (Keppoch) ; one *d. Educ. :* Queen's Col., Galway. Entered Indian Civil Service, 1865 ; Acting Chief Commissioner in Burmah, 1889 ; Chief Commissioner of Central Provinces, 1891 ; Acting Lieut.-Governor, Bengal, 1893 ; Member of Council of Viceroy of India, 1893-95 ; Lieut.-Governor of N.W. Provinces and Chief Commissioner of Oudh, 1895-1901 ; Member of the Council of India, 1902 ; Under-Secretary of State in Ireland, 1902-8 ; Member of the Irish Convention, 1917-18. *Heir :* none. *Address :* 3 Buckingham Gate, S W.1. *T. :* Victoria 5861. *Clubs :* Reform ; St. Stephen's Green, Dublin.
(*Died 9 June 1925.*)

MACDONNELL, Henry, C.B. 1897 ; Inspector-General of Hospitals and Fleets ; *b.* 1839 ; *s.* of late Wm. Macdonnell of Dublin ; *m.* 1886, Francis Alice, *e. d.* of late Sir William R. Holmes, Consular Service, of Kilrea, Ireland. *Educ. :* Dublin ; L.R.C.S.I. 1860 ; L.R.C.P.I. 1861. Entered R.N. as Surgeon, 1861 ; became Staff-Surgeon, 1874 ; Fleet-Surgeon, 1882 ; Deputy Inspector-General, Hospitals and Fleets, 1890 ; Inspector-General, 1897 ; served at bombardment of Alexandria, 1882, and during subsequent Egyptian War (medal with clasp, bronze star) ; served as Deputy Inspector-General at Haslar, Malta, and Chatham Hospitals ; Inspector-General, Haslar, 1898-99 ; retired 1899. *Decorated* on the occasion of Her Majesty's Diamond Jubilee ; awarded the Jubilee Medal of 1897. *Add ess:* Keith House, Villiers Road, Southsea. *(Died 31 Aug. 1922.)*

McDONNELL, Col. John, C.B. 1900; R.A.; retired 1903; *b.* 28 May 1851; *s.* of Luke J. McDonnell D.L., Merrion Square, Dublin; *m.* 1890, Pau ne, *d.* of late Colonel Hannay, and *widow* of late Captain Milford, R. W. Fusiliers; one *s. Educ.:* Stoneyhurst College; R.M. Academy. Joined R. A., 1872; Captain, 1881; Major, 1889; Lieutenant-Colonel, 1897; Colonel, 1901. Served Afghan War, 1879-1880 (medal); Boer War, 1900 (commanded the Artillery, 6th Division); severely wounded at Klip Kraal (medal with two clasps, C.B., despatches); Commandant, R. Hibernian Military School, 1914-19. *Address:* 18 Clyde Road, Dublin. *Clubs:* Kildare Street, Dublin; Royal St. George Yacht, Kingstown.

(Died 25 Aug. 1928.)

M'DONNELL, Richard Grant Peter Purcell, C.I.E. 1905; late Burma Police Dept.; Inspector of Police, 1886; District Superintendent, 1896; Commissioner Rangoon Town Police, 1899-1908; retired, 1908. *Club:* East India United Service. *(Died 24 April 1927.)*

MACDONNELL, Rt. Rev. William Andrew; Bishop of Alexandria since 1906; *b.* 1853. *Educ.:* Ottawa University; Grand Seminary, Montreal. Ordained, 1881. *Address:* The Palace, Alexandria, Ont.*(Died 10 Nov.1920.)*

M'DOUALL, William; Member Royal Asiatic Society; *b.* Owsden Rectory, Suffolk, 13 April 1855; *e. s.* of late Rev. W. S. M'Douall, Rector of Owsden; unmarried. *Educ.:* Uppingham School, 1868-1873. Joined Indo-European Government Telegraph Department in Persian Gulf in June 1875, and proceeded to Bushire; stationed at various places in Persian Gulf until 1890, when services transferred to consular service, and appointed to open new Vice-Consulate at Mohammerah, on the Karun River, 1904; Consul 1904; Consul, Kermanshah, 1909; Hamadan, 1916; retired 1918; Mesopotamia Civil Administration, 1918-21; Assistant Political Officer, Badrah; Anglo-Persian Oil Co., 1923. *Address:* Khaniqin, Iraq.

(Died 2 Nov. 1924.)

M'DOUGALD, John, C.M.G., 1912; J.P.; Commissioner, Customs Dept., Ottawa, Canada, since 1896; *b.* Blue Mountain, Pictou N.S., 13 March 1848; *m.* Margaret Jane Macleod of Westville, N.S.; two *s. Educ.:* Grammar School, New Glasgow, N.S.; M.P. Pict u, 1881-96. *Address:* 149 Daly Avenue, Ottawa.

(Died 14 June 1919.)

MACDOUGALL, Brig.-General Alexander, C.M.G. 1918; Canadian Forestry Corps; *s.* of late J. T. MacDougall, C.M.G.; *b.* 1878. Served European War, 1915-18 (C.B., Legion of Honour). *(Died Jan. 1927.)*

MACDOUGALL, Major-Gen. James Charles, C.M.G. 1916; *b.* Toronto, 16 July 1863; *s.* of Alex. Duncan MacDougall, Barrister, of Osgoode Hall, Toronto, and *g.s.* of Captain Duncan MacDougall, 79th Cameron Highlanders; *m.* 1889, Josephine, *d.* of George Macaulay Hawke, Toronto; one *s. Educ.:* Collegiate Institute and Royal Military College, Kingston, Ontario. Joined Canadian Permanent Force, (Royal Canadian Regt.), 1885; Lt.-Col. same Regt. 1910; served South Africa (Queen's medal with clasp); held various staff appointments in Canada and was acting Adjutant-General at the beginning of European War; joined first Canadian Contingent as Military Secretary to G.O.C.; commanded Canadian Training Division, Shorncliffe, Kent, 1915 and 1916; brought to the notice of the Secretary of State for War, for valuable services rendered in connection with the War; employed on special duty, 1917-18; retired, 1919. *Clubs:* Caledonian; Royal Bermuda Yacht. *(Died 30 Jan. 1927.)*

MACDOUGALL, Sir James Patten, K.C.B., *cr.* 1914; C.B. 1906; M.A. Oxon.; Keeper of the Records of Scotland, Deputy Clerk Register, and Registrar-General since 1909; Barrister Inner Temple since 1873; Advocate of the Scottish Bar, 1874; Legal Secretary to Lord Advocate, 1886, and 1892-1894; Legal Member of Local Government Board, 1894-1904; Vice-President and Chairman of Local Government Board for Scotland, 1904-1909; D.L., J.P., Vice-Convener (1901-4, 1910), Argyllshire; *b.* 29 May 1849; *e. s.* of John Patten, Writer to the Signet, and of Jane Maxwell Campbell, *e. d.* of D. MacDougall of Gallanach, Argyllshire; assumed surname of Mac-Dougall on succeeding to his mother in 1891; *m.* 1884, Alice Mary, *e. d.* of late Major Horne of Stirkoke, Caithness-shire; no *c. Educ.:* Edinburgh Academy; Christ Church, Oxford. Chairman of Departmental Committee on Poor Law Medical Relief in Scotland, 1902; Member of Royal Commission on Poor Laws and Relief of Distress, 1905; a Boundary Commissioner for Scotland, 1917. *Address:* Gallanach, Oban, N.B.; 39 Heriot Row, Edinburgh. *Clubs:* Brooks's; New, Edinburgh; Royal Highland Yacht, Oban; Honourable Company of Edinburgh Golfers, Muirfield. *(Died 10 Mar. 1919.)*

M'DOUGALL, Sir John, Kt., *cr.* 1902; late Chairman London County Council; *b.* 1844; *s.* of Alexander M'Dougall, Manchester, and Jane Shenwell of Youlgrave; *m.* 1st, 1867, Lucy Armstrong; two *s.* thre *d.*; 2nd, 1882, Ellen Mary, *d.* of George Lidgett, J.P., Blackheath; one *s.* two *d. Address:* Clifton House, Greenwich Park, S.E. *T.:* 205 Deptford. *Club:* National Liberal. *(Died 8 May 1917.)*

MACDOUGALL, Lt.-Col. Stewart, of Lunga, Argyll; J.P. and D.L. Co. Argyll, and County Councillor; Landed Proprietor; *b.* 1854; 2nd but o. *surv. s.* of John MacDougall of Lunga and Richmond Margaret, *d.* of Don. Stewart; *m.* Wilhelmina, 2nd *d.* and co-heiress of Wm. Liddell of Sutton and Keldy Castle, Yorkshire; three *d. Educ.:* at home. Entered 93rd Highlanders, 1876; served Egyptian Campaign, 1882 (seriously wounded Tel-el-Kebir, despatches, medal and clasp and Khedive's Star); Adjutant 4th Batt. Argyll and Sutherland Highlanders, 1884-89; retired as Major, 1892; Lt.-Col. in command 10th Batt. Gordon Highlanders, 1914; Gentleman-at-Arms in Household of H.M. since 1900; received Coronation medals. *Recreations:* shooting, golf, hunting, and all outdoor sports, yachting. *Address:* Lunga, Ardfern, Argyll. *T.A.:* Lunga, Ardfern; Engine Court, St. James's Palace, S.W. *Clubs:* Carlton, Naval and Military; New, Edinburgh. *(Died 21 July 1916.)*

McEVOY, Ambrose; A.R.A. 1924; *b.* 1878; *s.* of Captain A. McEvoy; *m.* 1902, Mary Spencer, *d.* of Col. Spencer Edwards of Freshford, Bath; one *s.* one *d.* Studied at the Slade School; Member of the New English Art Club, International Society of Painters, National Portrait Society, etc.; Associate of Royal Society of Painters in Water Colours, 1926; Royal Society of Portrait Painters; works have been acquired by the Luxemburg Gallery, the National Gallery of British Art (Tate Gallery), Manchester Art Gallery, Ottawa Gallery, National Gallery of Canada, the Municipal Gallery of Johannesburg, and other Galleries. *Address:* 107 Grosvenor Road, S.W.1; *T.:* Victoria 5901; Duffield Cottage, Duffield, Derbyshire. *T.:* Duffield 116.

(Died 4 Jan. 1927.)

MACEWAN, David, M.D., C.M. Edin., LL.D. St. Andrews University; Emeritus Professor of Surgery, University College, Dundee (Univ. of St. Andrews); Consulting Surgeon, Dundee Royal Infirmary; *b.* Kinross-shire, 1846; *m.* 1st, Bertha Elizabeth, *e. d.* of

667

MACDONNELL, Col. William, C.B. See page xxiv.

M'EACHRAN, Duncan, F.R.C.V.S., LL.D. See page xxiv.

Rev. Robert Templeton, Grahamstown, South Africa ; 2nd, Margaret, *d.* of late R. S. Stronach, Hillhead, Glasgow. *Educ.:* Perth Academy ; University of Edinburgh. *Publications:* papers to medical journals. *Address:* 2 Airlie Place, Dundee. (*Died 31 Mar. 1927.*)

MACEWAN, Peter, F.C.S., editor of The Chemist and Druggist ; corresponding member Société de Pharmacie, Paris ; *b.* Lochee, Forfarshire, 29 May 1856 ; *m.* Euphemia, *d.* of R. Thomson, Edinburgh ; three *s.* two *d.* *Publications:* The Art of Dispensing ; Pharmaceutical Formulas, etc. *Recreation:* golf. *Address:* 64 Southwood Lane, Highgate, N. *T.:* Hornsey 1760 ; 42 Cannon Street, E.C. *Clubs:* National Liberal ; Highgate Golf.
(*Died 16 May 1917.*)

MACEWEN, Dr. Alexander R.; Moderator General Assembly U.F. Church, 1915; Professor of Church History, New College, Edinburgh, since 1901 ; *b.* Edinburgh, 1851 ; *s.* of Rev. Alex. MacEwen, D.D., Glasgow, and Eliza Robertson, Dunfermline ; *m.* 1885, Margaret, *d.* of R. H. Begg, Moffat ; two *s.* one *d.* *Educ.:* Glasgow Academy (Medallist) ; Glasgow Univ. ; Balliol College, Oxford ; Göttingen University ; U.P. Theological College. Foundation Bursar, Jeffrey Greek Medallist, Muirhead (Latin) and Moral Philosophy First Prizeman at Glasgow ; Snell Exhibitioner and Arnold Historical Essayist at Oxford ; M.A. (Honours) of Oxford ; B.D. and Hon. D.D. of Glasgow. Deputy Professor of Greek, Assistant Professor of Latin, Classical Examiner for Degrees at Glasgow University ; U.P. minister at Moffat, at Anderston, and at Claremont Church, Glasgow ; Chairman of Moffat School Board ; member of Glasgow School Board ; Governor of Hutcheson's Schools ; Secretary of Christian Unity Association ; director of other trusts and societies ; educational, charitable, and religious. *Publications:* Memoir of Alexander MacEwen, D.D., 1876; Roman Satiric Poetry, 1877 ; St. Jerome, 1878 ; Life of Principal Cairns, 1894 ; The Eastern Church in Greece, 1890 ; The Erskines, 1900 ; Antoinette Bourignon, Quietist, 1910 ; A History of the Church in Scotland, vol. i., 1913 ; various articles and reviews. *Recreations:* riding and travel. *Address:* New College, Edinburgh.
(*Died 26 Nov. 1916.*)

McEWEN, Robert Finnie, D.L., J.P. Co. Berwick ; J.P. Co. Ayr ; F.S.A. (Scot.): Member of the King's Bodyguard in Scotland ; *b.* 1861 ; *o. s.* of late Rev. John McEwan, M.A., of Kirkmichael, and Isabella, *d.* of Wm. Finnie of Kilmarnock ; *m.* 1893, Mary Frances, *e. d.* of late Henry Dundas ; one *s.* one *d.* *Educ.:* Edinburgh University, M.A. ; Cambridge, B.A. Called to Scottish Bar, 1888 ; member of Council, Royal College of Music, London, since 1906. *Publications:* Church music, songs and part songs. *Recreations:* shooting, fishing, music. *Address:* Marchmont House, Greenlaw, Berwickshire ; Bardrochat, Colmonell, Ayrshire. *Clubs:* Carlton ; New, Edinburgh.
(*Died 31 Mar. 1926.*)

MACEWEN, Sir William, Kt., *cr.* 1902; C.B. 1917 ; M.D., Hon. LL.D., Glasgow and Liverpool Universities ; D.C.L. Durham, 1921 ; Hon. F.R.C.S., England and Ireland ; Hon. D.Sc., Oxon and Trinity College, Dublin ; F.R.S. ; Hon. Surgeon to H.M. in Scotland ; Surg.-Gen. R.N. for Scotland ; President British Medical Association, 1922 ; Hon. Member Imperial Medical Academy, St. Petersburg ; of Royal Medical Academy of Rome ; of American Surgical Society, and of German Surgical Congress ; President International Surgical Society, 1920-23 ; corresponding member Surgical Society of Paris ; Professor of Surgery, Glasgow University since 1892 ; *b.* 22 June 1848 ; *m.* Mary Watson, *d.* of late Hugh Allan of Crosshill, Glasgow ; three *s.* three *d.*

668

Publications: Osteotomy, 1880 ; On Pyogenic Infective Disease of the Brain and Spinal Cord ; Meningitis, Abscess of the Brain, Infective Sinus Thrombosis, 1893 ; On Hernia and its Radical Cure ; On a Method of Cure of Aneurism; On Transplantation of Bone by Bone Grafting ; On the Growth of Bone ; The Growth and Shedding of the Antler of the Deer, 1921. *Address:* 8 Woodside Crescent, Glasgow ; Garrochty, Kingarth, Bute. *T.:* National 194, Charing Cross, Glasgow. (*Died 22 Mar. 1924.*)

MACFADYEN William Allison, M.A. Oxon ; LL.D Cape ; Professor of Philosophy at the Transvaal University College since 1912 ; *b.* 24 Feb. 1865 ; *s.* of Rev. J. A. Macfadyen, M.A., D.D., of Manchester, England ; *m.* 1893, Marian, *d.* of Rev. Dr. Roberts, Professor of Latin, St. Andrews University, N.B. ; one *s.* one *d.* *Educ.:* Manchester Grammar School ; Brasenose College, Oxford. Vice-Principal of Graaff Reinet College, Cape Colony, 1889-91 ; at the Bar, Capetown, 1891-1892 ; joined Pretoria Bar, S.A.R. 1892 ; Docent in English Literature and Philosophy, 1893-99 ; Official Translator of Laws of Transvaal and Free State, 1900-1 ; Assistant Director of Education, Transvaal, 1901-2 ; at the Transvaal Bar and Lecturer in Law, 1902-6 ; Professor of Law, Rhodes University College, Grahamstown, 1906-1911 ; Chairman of Senate, 1907-10 ; Acting Professor of English and Philosophy, Grey University College, Bloemfontein, 1911-12. *Publications:* Official Translation of Laws ; Political Laws of Transvaal ; two vols. Law Reports ; essays and lectures. *Address:* P.O. Box 14, Pretoria, S.A. *Club:* Pretoria, Pretoria.
(*Died Oct. 1924.*)

MACFALL, Haldane; Major (retired) ; *b.* 24 July 1860 ; *e. s.* of late Lieut.-Col. D. Chambers Macfall ; *m.* Mabel, *d.* of Admiral Sir James Hanway Plumridge, K.C.B., M.P., of Hopton Hall, Suffolk. *Educ.:* Norwich Grammar School ; Sandhurst. Gazetted to West India Regiment, 1885 ; served in Jamaica and West Africa ; retired as lieutenant, 1892 ; in the European War—Captain, The Essex Regiment, Jan. 1915 ; Major (2nd in command), The Sherwood Foresters. *Publications:* The Wooings of Jezebel Pettyfer, 1897 (called The House of Mirth and The House of the Sorcerer in America) ; The Masterfolk, 1903 ; Whistler, 1905 ; Irving, Ibsen, part author of Rouge, 1906 ; Old English Furniture (Connoisseur), Boucher, Fragonard, Vigée Le Brun, 1908 ; Beautiful Children, 1909 ; The French Pastellists of the Eighteenth Century, 1900 ; History of Painting (8 volumes), 1910 ; The Splendid Wayfaring, 1913 ; The Nut in War, 1914 ; Battle, 1914 ; Germany at Bay, 1917 ; Beware the German's Peace, 1918 ; The Book of Lovat, 1923 ; The Three Students, 1926, and The Perfect Lady, and Life of Beardsley—decorated ; Songs of the Immortals and Persuasions to Joy, 1927 ; pen-name of Hal Dane. Awarded Civil List pension for distinction in literature, 1914. Exhibited Royal Academy, International and elsewhere. *Recreations:* the playhouse ; books ; designing covers and decorations for books ; the study of life and people. *Address:* The White House, Challoner Crescent, West Kensington, W.14. *T.:* Western 2294. *Club:* Whitefriars. (*Died 25 July 1928.*)

MACFARLAND, Robert Arthur Henry, M.A., Headmaster of Campbell Coll., Belmont, near Belfast, since 1907 ; *s.* of John MacFarland of Omagh, Co. Tyrone, and *g.s.* of Rev. William Henry, D.D., of Newtownards, Co. Down, and Letterkenny, Co. Donegal ; unmarried. *Educ.:* Royal Academical Institution, Belfast ; Queen's College, Belfast ; Gonville and Caius College, Cambridge (Foundation Scholar). B.A. with First Class Honours in Mathematical Science in Queen's University, Ireland, 1880 ;

Ninth Wrangler in Mathematical Tripos, 1888; Chief Master of the Army Class at Repton School, 1889-1907; commanded the Contingent of the Officers' Training Corps at Repton School, 1900-3, and Campbell College Contingent, 1915-20. *Recreations:* golf, cycling. *Address:* Campbell College, Belfast. *T.:* Knock 102. *Club:* Ulster Reform, Belfast.
(Died 11 April 1922.)

MACFARLANE-GRIEVE, William Alexander, M.A. and S.C.L. Oxford; M.A. Cambridge; J.P. Roxburgh, Cambridge, and Berwick: F.S.A. Scot.; *b.* 1844; *o. surv. s.* of William Macfarlane, M.D., F.R.C.S., R.N., and Margaret Verner (Jane), *o. d.* of George Grieve, of Eastfield, Berwickshire. *Educ.:* Royal High School, Edinburgh; Universities of Edinburgh and Bonn; Balliol College and St. John's College, Oxford (Scholar); 2nd class in Classical Moderations, 1865, name appearing in the class list as Comyn-Macfarlane; B.A. and S.C.L. 1866. A Master at St. Peter's College, Radley, 1867-68; in residence at Oxford engaged in literary work, 1869-72; on succeeding to the Edenhall entail ceased to use the surname of Comyn and assumed the surname and arms of Grieve, both by Royal Licence; of Lincoln's Inn; owner of about 9000 acres of land in the counties of Roxburgh, Cambridge, and Berwick; member of Licensing Committee, Co. Cambridge; a Commissioner of Supply for the Counties of Roxburgh and Berwick; Lord of the Manors of Eleswell and Impington Ferme-part; patron of one living; has been for many years actively engaged in agriculture and forestry. *Recreations:* book-collecting, farming and stock-breeding, sylviculture (medal of R.A.S.E. 1911), heraldry, music. *Address:* Impington Park, Cambridgeshire; Penchrise Peel, via Hawick; Edenhall House, near Kelso. *Clubs:* Conservative, New University, Constitutional; Cambridge County; Oxford County; Border, Hawick; Scottish Conservative, Edinburgh.
(Died 8 Mar. 1917.)

MACPETRIDGE, Ven. Charles, Rector of Kilgariffe since 1874; Archdeacon of Ross since 1904. *Educ.:* Trinity College, Dublin. Ordained, 1869; Curate of Christ Church, Cork, 1869-73; Kinsale, 1873-74. *Address:* Clonakilty, Co. Cork.

MACGIBBON, Rev. James, D.D., M.C.; Minister of Glasgow Cathedral since 1916; *b.* Edinburgh, 1865; *s.* of George Ramsay MacGibbon; *m.* 1906, Margaret, *d.* of late Robert Robin, Castlehill, Hamilton; three *s. Educ.:* George Watson's College, and University Edinburgh. M.A. 1884; B.D. 1887; Assistant to Very Rev. Sir James Cameron Lees, St. Giles's Cathedral, Edinburgh, 1887-90; Minister of Blackford, Perthshire, 1890; Collegiate Minister of Hamilton, 1901; served as Chaplain to the B.E.F. in France, 1915-16 (despatches, Military Cross); D.D. Glasgow University, 1920. *Recreations:* walking, cycling. *Address:* 6 Bute Gardens, Glasgow, W. *T.:* Western 4357. *Clubs:* Conservative, Edinburgh; New, Glasgow. *(Died 18 Nov. 1922.)*

MACGILL, Major Campbell Gerald Hertslet, M.V.O. 1911; T.D.; *b.* 1876; *o. s.* of late Campbell MacGill, of Stratford-sub-Castle, Salisbury; *m.* 1910, Evelyn Ross, *y. d.* of late Allan Burnett, of Blackheath; one *s.* three *d.* Entered the Board of Green Cloth, 1898; Assistant Sec., 1908; Establishment Officer of the King's Household, 1922; Coronation medals, 1902 and 1911; one of the Gold Staff Officers at the Coronation of King George V.; late Major of the London Rifle Brigade; Adjutant 2nd Battalion London Rifle Brigade, Sep. 1914-June 1915; Staff Capt., July 1915-May 1916; Brig.-Maj., Group B, 1st Lond. Div., 1916. *Address:* 8 Prince of Wales Mansions, Battersea Park, S.W.11. *T.:* Latchmere 4515.
(Died 22 Nov. 1922.)

MACGILL, Admiral Thomas, C.B. 1897; R.N.; *b.* Clapham, 16 Aug. 1850; 2nd *s.* of late Rev. Thomas MacGill; *m.* Maria, *d.* of J. West, 1884. *Educ.:* Western College, Brighton. Naval Cadet, 1863; Lieutenant, 1874; Commander, 1885; Captain, 1892; served as Lieut. of Humber during Egyptian War, 1882 (medal and star); also at Suakim, 1884 (clasp, Suakim); Harbourmaster at Suakim, 1885 (clasp, despatches, and promoted Commander); Captain of Phœbe, employed against chief M'baruk, capture of stronghold Mwele, E. Africa (medal, despatches); served in Benin Expedition, 1897 (despatches, clasp, C.B.); Captain in charge, Bermuda Dockyard. *Club:* Royal Naval, Portsmouth. *(Died 16 April 1926.)*

MACGILLIVRAY, Hon. Angus, J.C.C.; *b.* Bailey's Brook, Picton Co., N.S., January 22, 1842; *e. s.* of John and Catharine MacGillivray, and *g. s.* of Angus MacGillivray of Inverness-shire, Scotland; *m.* 1st, Maggie, *d.* of Alexander McIntosh (*d.* 1879); 2nd, Mary, E., *e. d.* of John Doherty of New York; three *s.* four *d. Educ.:* common schools; St. F. X. College, Antigonish. M.A. Studied law under late Hugh M'Donald (afterwards Judge Sup. Court); admitted barrister and attorney, 1874; elected to House of Assembly, N.S., 1878 and 1882; Speaker of Nova Scotia Legislature, 1883-86, and in 1886 became member of the Fielding Ministry; resigned, March 1887, and ran against Sir John Thompson, Minister of Justice for House of Commons, Canada; defeated by 40 votes; elected House of Assembly, 1887, and became member of Govt.; resigned, 1891, and again unsuccessfully opposed Sir John Thompson; appointed member, Legis. Coun. of Nova Scotia, 1892; resigned, 1895, and elected for House of Assembly, 1895; member of the Murray Ministry, 1896; re-elected 1897 and 1901; Lecturer on Constitutional History in St. F. X. University; Judge of the County Court for one of the Judicial Districts of the Province, 1902. *Address:* Antigonish, Nova Scotia.
(Died 4 May 1918.)

MACGILLIVRAY, William, J.P.; Writer to the Signet since 1870; and senior partner of the firm of Lindsay, Howe & Co., W.S., Edinburgh, since 1907; *b.* 1823; *e. s.* of Alexander MacGillivray of Stonehaven; *m.* 1868, Margaret Dods, Musselburgh; three *s. Educ.:* Stonehaven; Edinburgh University. Clerk to John Monro, Advocate, Edinburgh; Court Manager, Dundas & Wilson, C.S., Edinburgh; partner of Messrs. Lindsay, Howe & Co., W.S., Edinburgh, 1870; Director of John Watson's Educational Institution, Edinburgh; also of the Orphan Hospital, Dean; Director of the British Linen Bank, Edinburgh; and of the Edinburgh Life Assurance Company. *Publications:* Rob Lindsay and his School, 1905; Auld Drainie and Brownie, 1906; The Story of Little Janet, 1907; The Elder and His Wife, 1910; Cotbank and its Folks, 1911; all collected into one volume under title Memories, 1912; Tante Claire, her Life and her Wisdom, 1908; Life of Professor MacGillivray, Aberdeen, 1910; Men I Remember, 1913. *Recreations:* literature and natural history. *Address:* 4 Rothesay Place, Edinburgh. *T.:* 378 Central. *Club:* University, Edinburgh.
(Died 23 Nov. 1917.)

McGILLYCUDDY, Denis Donough Charles (The McGillycuddy of the Reeks), J.P.; *b.* 14 May 1852; *e. surv. s.* of late Richard McGillycuddy of The Reeks, and Anna, *d.* of Capt. John Johnstone, 23rd Welsh Fusiliers, of Mainstone Court, Co. Hereford; *m.* 1881, Gertrude Laura, *y. d.* of Edmond Howd Miller of Ringwood, Passaic Co., New Jersey, U.S.; one *s.* Was in R.N. *Heir:* Major Ross Kinloch McGillycuddy. *Address:* The Reeks, Killarney; Bauncluone, Beaufort, Co. Kerry. *(Died 16 Mar. 1921.)*

M'GILP, Major Clyde, D.S.O. 1917; O.C. 1st Battery, N.Z.F. Artillery; *b.* N.Z., 12 Oct.

1885 ; *s.* of A. M'Gilp, Birkenhead, Auckland, N.Z. ; unmarried. *Educ.:* Auckland. At the age of 17 served in South Africa as a trooper ; on return to N.Z. entered Artillery (Volunteer) as a gunner, passed through all ranks ; commanded the Battery as Major, 1909 ; commanded Battery in Egypt, Gallipoli, and France (despatches twice, D.S.O.) ; total service, 17 years. *Address :* c/o The Director of Base Records, N.Z. Military Forces, Wellington, New Zealand.

M'GINNESS, Brig.-General John R., U.S.A., retired ; planter ; *b.* near Dublin, 17 Sep. 1840 ; *e. surv. s.* of Francis M'Ginness and Annie Hartford ; unmarried. *Educ. :* United States Military Academy, West Point, N.Y. First Lieutenant Ordnance, 1863 ; Captain, 1869 ; Major, 1881 ; Lieut.-Col. 1898 ; Col. 1902 ; Brig.-General, retired 1904 ; served at various arsenals in United States ; Asst. Ordnance Officer and Chief Ordnance Officer, Department of the South, 1864 ; breveted Capt. and Major for gallant and meritorious conduct at siege of Charleston and vicinity, 1864 ; Asst. Ordnance Officer, War Department, 1864-69 ; served on plains with General Sherman, 1866 ; Chief of Ordnance of Philippine Islands, 1898-1901. *Publications :* Official reports as Commandant of Rock Island and various other arsenals in the United States. *Recreations :* riding, walking, tennis, golf, snowshoeing, hunting big game, etc. *Address :* c/o War Department, Washington, U.S.A. *Clubs :* Union League, Hamilton ; Army and Navy, Washington ; Army and Navy, Catholic, Manhattan, New York ; Westover, Norfolk, Va. ; Union, Cleveland.   (*Died 17 Dec. 1918.*)

M'GOUN, Archibald, M.A., B.C.L., K.C. ; Professor of Civil L w, M'Gill University, Montreal, since 1888 ; *b.* Montreal, 1853 ; *s.* of Archibald M'Goun, a native of Douglas, Lanarkshire, Scotland, and Jane Mackay, *d.* of Samuel Mackay of Ayr, Scotland ; *m.* 1887, Abigail, *d.* of Thomas Mackay of Toronto ; one *s.* one *d. Educ. :* M'Gill Univ., Mo itreal ; L'Ecole de Droit, Paris, France. Twice President University Literary Society 1884-85 ; one of the founders of the Imperial Federation League in Canada, 1885 ; delegate to Imperial Federation Council in London, 1886 ; Vice-President of League (now the British Empire League) in Canada ; Fellow Royal Colonial Institute ; Chairman of meeting, Montreal, to promote Free Trade within the Empire, 1907 ; President Graduates' Society, M'Gill University, 1887 ; course of lectures on Constitutional Law, 1897 ; now lectures on Corporations and on Agency and Partnership ; Q.C. 1899 ; Attorney as practising advocate for various commercial corporations ; Pres. Montreal Economic and Statistical Society, 1907. *Publications :* Federation of the Empire, Address as President of University Literary Society, 1884 ; Economic Study, Commercial Union with the United States, with a word on Imperial Reciprocity, 1886 ; A Federal Parliament of the British People, 1890 ; article on Imperial Reciprocity in Canadian Encyclopædia ; articles in The Commonwealth, Ottawa, 1900-1 ; A Revenue Tariff within the Empire, 1905. *Recreations :* experiments in Phonetics ; articles in an International Phonetic Alphabet Neotype, based on Ellis's Palæotype ; member Victoria Rifles Reserves. *Address :* British Empire Building, Montreal ; Dunaven, Bellevue Avenue, Westmount.   (*Died 5 June 1921.*)

McGOWEN, Hon. James Sinclair Taylor ; Prime Minister and Colonial Treasurer, New South Wales, 1910-13 ; *b.* at sea, 16 Aug. 1855, of English parentage ; *m.* ; six *s.* two *d. Educ. :* at private and denominational schools ; began work at an early age ; was boilermaker's apprentice, Sydney, 1870 ; afterwards at Atlas Works, and Railway Department till 670

1910 ; Member for Redfern, 1891-1920 ; Secretary and President Boiler-makers' Society ; President Eight-Hour Demonstration Committee. *Recreations :* formerly cricket, now fishing and bowls. *Address :* 177 Pitt Street, Redfern, N.S.W.   (*Died April 1922.*)

M'GRATH, Sir Joseph, Kt., *cr.* 1911 ; LL.D. ; *b.* 25 Aug. 1858 ; *m.* 1898, Eleanor Mary, *d.* of Patrick McAlister, Dublin ; one *s.* two *d. Educ. :* St. Stanislaus' College, Tullabeg, Tullamore. Called to Irish Bar, 1892 ; Registrar and Member of the Senate of the National University of Ir land, 1908 ; one of the Secretaries of the Royal University of Ireland ; Life Governor of the Royal Veterinary College of Ireland ; a Vice-Chairman of the National Society for the Prevention of Cruelty to Children ; Hon. Secretary of the Clongowes Union since foundation in 1897 ; a Vice-President of the Royal Dublin Society. *Address :* 11 Clyde Road, Dublin.   *Died 15 Mar. 1923.*)

MACGREGOR, Sir Evan, G.C.B., *cr.* 1906 ; K.C.B., *cr.* 1893 ; I.S.O. 1902 ; J.P. ; *b.* 31 March 1842 ; 3rd *s.* of late Sir J. A. B. MacGregor, 3rd Bt., and Mary, *d.* of late Admiral Sir T. M. Hardy, 1st Bt., G.C.B. *m.* 1884, Annie Louise (*d.* 1922), *d.* of late Col. W. A. Middleton, C.B. ; one *d. Educ. :* Charterhouse. Permanent Secretary to Admiralty, 1884-1907. *Address :* Aynsome, Cartmel, Lancs. *Club :* Caledonian.   (*Died 21 Mar. 1926.*)

MACGREGOR, Gregor, B.A. ; member of London Stock Exchange ; *b.* 31 Aug. 1869 ; *s.* of late Donald MacGregor, J.P., and Euphemia Watt, Ardgartan, Arrochar, N.B. ; *m.* 1902, Ruby, *e. d.* of late T. W. N. Oliver, 26 Brunswick Terrace, Brighton ; two *s. Educ. :* Cargilfield, Edin. ; Uppingham ; Jesus College, Cambridge. Cambridge XI. 1888-91 ; went to Australia with Lord Sheffield's XI. 1891 - 92 ; Middlesex XI. 1892-1907 ; played for England *v.* Australia, all matches, 1890 and 1893. *Rec eations :* cricket, golf ; football formerly (Cambridge XV. and Scottish International). *Address :* 39 Craven Hill Gardens, W. *T.:* Paddington 2754. *Clubs :* Sports, M.C.C. ; Honourable Company of Edinburgh Golfers, Muirfield.   (*Died 20 Aug. 1919.*)

MACGREGOR, Col. Henry Grey, C.B. 1889 ; *b.* Belfast, 15 Jan. 1838 ; *y. s.* of late Gen. Sir D. Macgregor (*d.* 1881), and Elizabeth, *d.* of late Sir William Dick, Bt. ; *m.* 1863, Rosetta (*d.* 1891), *d.* of late Rt. Hon. Sir Joseph Napier, Bt. *Educ. :* Trin. Coll., Cambridge. Joined 17th Regt. 1858 ; passed throug Staff College, 1865 ; special service, Zulu War, 1878-79. A.Q.M.G. and D.A.Q.M.G. Transvaal War, 1880 - 81 ; D.A.Q.M.G. Egyptian expedition, 1882 ; A.A.G. Suakim expedition, 1885 ; Instructor R.M. Coll., 1867-69 ; A.D.C. Gen. Officer commanding S.E. Dist., 1869-71 ; Garrison Instructor, 1872-77 ; D.A.A.G. Northern Dist., 1883-85 ; A.D.C. to the Queen, 1886-95 ; A.A.G. of Army, 1890-95 ; retired from Army, 1895 ; despatches, Zulu War, twice, 1879 (promoted Major) ; despatches, Egyptian expedition, 1882 (promoted Lieut.-Col.) ; despatches, Suakim expedition, 1885. *Decorated* for Zulu War, 1879 (medal and clasp) ; Egyptian expedition, 1882 (medal, bronze star, and 4th class Osmanieh) ; Suakim expedition, 1885 (clasp). *Address :* 4 Brechin Place, South Kensington, S.W. *Club :* National.   (*Died 13 Oct. 1925.*)

M'GREGOR, Rt. Rev. Mgr. James, Rector of Blairs College since 1899 ; *b.* Keith, 1860. *Educ. :* Blairs College ; Scots College, Rome ; Priest, 1883 ; Curate at Aberdeen Cathedral, 1888-91 ; Priest in Charge of Dufftown Mission, 1891-95 ; Administrator, Aberdeen Cathedral, 1895-99 ; Domestic Prelate to the Pope, 1908 ; Canon of Aberdeen Chapter, 1912. *Address :* Blairs College, Aberdeen.

     (*Died 10 Feb. 1928.*)

McGREGOR, His Honour, James Drummond, Lieutenant-Governor of Nova Scotia since 1910 ; *s.* of Roderick McGregor and Janet Chisholm ; *b.* New Glasgow, N.S., 1 Sep. 1838 ; *m.* 1st, 1867, Elizabeth McColl, of Guysboro (*d.* 1891); 2nd, 1894, Roberta Ridley of Peterborough. Merchant and shipowner ; senior partner in firms of R. McGregor & Sons and J. D. & P. A. McGregor ; twice elected to Local Legis. and once defeated ; contested House of Commons, 1900 ; twice Mayor of New Glasgow ; summoned to the Senate, 1903 ; a Presbyterian. *Address:* Government House. Halifax, N.S.
(*Died 4 Mar. 1919.*)

MACGREGOR, Robert, R.S.A. 1889 ; married. *Address:* 62 Hanover Street, and Kenmure Cottage, Portobello, Edinburgh. *Club:* Scottish Arts, Edinburgh.

MACGREGOR, Hon. Robert Malcolm; Member Provincial Parliament of Nova Scotia for Pictou County since 1904 ; also Member Executive Council of the Province since 1911; *b.* 9 Jan. 1876 ; *s.* of late Lieut.-Governor James D. MacGregor and first wife, Elizabeth M'Coll ; *m.* 1905, Laura MacNeil ; one *s.* two *d. Educ.:* Dalhousie College, B.A. Director Nova Scotia Steel and Coal Co., Ltd. ; Director Bank of Nova Scotia ; Director Eastern Trust Company. *Recreations:* curling and tennis. *Address:* New Glasgow, Nova Scotia. *Club:* Halifax, Halifax.
(*Died 10 Sept. 1924.*)

MACGREGOR, Robert Roy, I.S.O. 1902 ; Secretary of the Congested Districts Board for Scotland, 1897-1912 ; *e. s.* of late Rev. Alexander MacGregor, M.A., West Parish, Inverness ; *b.* 3 Nov. 1847 ; *m.* 1875, Henrietta (*d.* 1906), *d.* of late Rev. Thomas Davidson of Abbey St. Bathans, Berwickshire ; one *s.* one *d. Educ.:* Aberdeen and Edinburgh Universities. Entered H.M. Exchequer, Edinburgh, by competition, 1867 ; secretary to Committee on System of Land Registration in Scotland, and three other committees on various subjects, 1888-96; author of several works. *Recreation:* golf. *Club:* Conservative, Edinburgh.

MACGREGOR, Rt. Hon. Sir William, P.C. 1914 ; G.C.M.G., *cr.* 1907 ; K.C.M.G., *cr.* 1889 ; C.B. 1897 ; M.D. Aber. ; Hon. D.Sc. Camb. ; Hon. LL.D. Edin. ; LL.D. Aber. ; LL.D. Queensland ; F.F.P.S. Glas. ; First Chancellor, University of Queensland ; *b.* Scotland, 1847 ; *e. s.* of late John MacGregor ; *m.* 1883, Mary, *d.* of R. Cocks ; one *s.* three *d. Educ.:* Aberdeen ; Glasgow. Formerly Resident Surgeon and Resident Physician Glasgow Royal Infirmary, and Royal Lunatic Asylum, Aberdeen ; Assist. Government Medical Officer, Seychelles, 1873 ; Surgeon Civil Hospital, Port Louis, Mauritius, 1874 ; Chief Medical Officer, Fiji, 1875; was Receiver-General and Administrator of the Government, and Acted as High Commissioner and Consul-General for the Western Pacific ; Administrator of British New Guinea, 1888 ; Lieut.-Governor, 1895 ; Governor of Lagos, 1899-1904 ; Governor of Newfoundland, 1904-9 ; Governor of Queensland, 1909-14 ; Fellow of Royal Geographical Societies of England and Scotland and Berlin, and of Roy. Anthropological Society of Italy ; has Albert medal, 2nd class, and Clarke gold medal, for saving life at sea ; Watson gold medal, 1872 ; also Founder's medal Royal Geographical Society of England ; and Mary Kingsley Medal, 1910. Declared Queen Victoria's sovereignty over British New Guinea, 4 Sep. 1888. Represented the West African Colonies and Protectorates at the Coronation, 1902 ; Knight of Grace of St. John of Jerusalem; retired 1914. *Address:* Chapel on Leader, Earlston, Scotland.
(*Died 3 July 1919.*)

MACGREGOR, W. Y., R.S.A. 1921 ; *b.* Finnart, Dumbartonshire, 1855 ; *s.* of John Macgregor, shipbuilder, Glasgow. *Educ.:* Glasgow Academy. Studied Art in Glasgow, and afterwards for some years was a pupil of M. Legros at the Slade School, University College, London. *Address:* Albyn Lodge, Bridge of Allan, N.B. *Clubs:* Scottish Arts, Edinburgh; Glasgow Art, Glasgow.
(*Died Sept. 1923.*)

M'GRIGOR, Brig.-Gen. Charles Roderic Robert, C.B. 1904 ; C.M.G. 1916 ; late commanding 3rd Batt. King's Royal Rifles ; *b.* 5 Sept. 1860 ; *s.* of Sir Chas. M'Grigor, 2nd Bt.; *m.* 1892, Ada Rosamond, *d.* of late Robert Bower of Welham, Yorkshire ; one *s.* one *d. Educ.:* Eton. Officer ; served Griqualand East (medal, clasp) ; Boer War, 1881 : Egyptian War, 1882 (medal, clasp, and Khedival Star) ; Suakin Expedition, 1884 (two clasps) ; Suakin Expedition, 1885 (clasp, Medjidieh, and Brevet) ; South African War, 1899-1902 (despatches twice, Queen's medal six clasps, King's medal two clasps, and Brevet) ; Brig.-General in charge of Administration, Western Command, 1909 ; various positions on Staff ; served European War, 1914-16 (C.M.G.). *Recreation:* shooting. *Club:* Naval and Military.
(*Died 9 July 1927.*)

M'GRIGOR, Captain Sir James Rhoderick Duff, 3rd Bt. ; *cr.* 1831 ; *b.* London, 27 April 1857 ; *S.* father 1890 ; *m.* Helen, *d.* of J. G. Meiggs, an American, 1890 ; one *s.* one *d. Educ.:* Eton ; Christ Church, Oxford. Entered army (85th Light Infantry), 1877 ; transferred to Rifle Brigade, 1878 ; retired as Capt. 1890. *Recreations:* shooting, fishing. *Heir: s.* Charles Colquhoun, Rifle Brigade [*b.* 26 April 1893 ; *m.* 1919, Amabel, *o. d.* of E. L. Somers Cocks, 47 Wilton Crescent, and Bake, St. Germans]. *Address:* 58 Sloane Street, S.W.1. *Clubs:* Junior United Service, Travellers'.
(*Died 4 Feb. 1924.*)

McGUINNESS, Joseph, M.P. (Sinn Fein, Longford Co. since Dec. 1918 ; draper. M.P. South Longford, 1917.
(*Died 31 May 1922.*)

McGUIRE, Hon. Thomas Horace, LL.D. Hon. ; Chief Justice of Supreme Court, North-West Territories ; retired, 1903; *b.* Kingston, 21 April 1849 ; *m.* 1877, Mary Victory, *e. d.* of late John Cunningham, Kingston. *Educ.:* Collegiate Institute and Queen's University, Kingston. First Chief Justice of this Court. Formerly the Court (by statute) consisted of " Five Puisne Judges," but by Act of 1900 the Court consists of " a Chief Justice and four Puisne Judges " ; Chairman of the Educational Council of Province of Saskatchewan, and Member of Senate of Provincial University ; President of Board of Trade. *Address:* Prince Albert, Sask., Canada.
(*Died 13 July 1923.*)

McHARDY, Lt.-Col. Sir Alexander Burness, K.C.B., *cr.* 1911 ; C.B. 1900 ; late R.E.; F.S.A.; *s.* of late David McHardy, Cranford, Aberdeen ; *b.* 11 June 1842 ; *m.* 1865, Elise (*d.* 1906), *o. d.* of late Sir J. and Lady Anderson ; one *s.* two *d. Educ.:* Aberdeen University. Served in the Royal Engineers, 1862-77, and for part of that time acted as Surveyor-General, Hong Kong ; in 1877 transferred from Home District to Prison Department, England ; served on Committee on Metropolitan Police Stations, 1881 ; Secretary Dept. Committee on Employment of Convicts, 1882 ; appointed Surveyor of Prisons, 1882 ; Sec;. Royal Commission on Irish Prisons, 1884 ; in 1886 appointed Prison Commissioner, Scotland ; served on Dept. Committee on Prisoners Awaiting Trial, 1889, and on Dept. Committee on Habitual Offenders, 1894, chairman Prison Commission. Scotland, 1896-1909, and chairman of Dept. Committee on Inebriates Acts, 1898. *Address:* 3 Ravelston Park, Edinburgh ; Crauford, Aberdeen.
(*Died 10 Aug. 1917.*)

MACHELL, Percy Wilfrid, C.M.G. 1906 ; *b.* 1862 ; *s.* of late Rev. Canon Machell and Hon. Emma, sister of 8th Lord Middleton ;

671

m. 1905, Countess Victoria Alice Leopoldine Ada Gleichen, *d.* of late H.S.H. Prince Victor of Hohenlohe Langenburg (Lady Valda Machell); one *s. Educ.*: Clifton; Sandhurst. Joined 56th Regiment as Lieutenant, 1882; Captain 1888; temporary Major, 1893; retired (Reserve of Officers), 1896; served with the Nile Expeditionary Force, 1884-85 (medal with two clasps, bronze star); joined Egyptian Army, 1886; in command at capture of Fort Khormoussa, 1888 (4th class Osmanieh); operations round Suakin and action of Gamaizah, 1888 (horse shot, clasp); Soudan, 1889-91; Toski Expedition; Brigade-Major No. 2 column; capture of Tokar (clasp, and clasp on bronze star, 4th class Medjidie); commanded 12th Soudanese Battalion, 1891-95; Inspector-General, Egyptian Coastguard, 1896; Adviser to the Ministry of the Interior, Egypt, 1898-1908; Grand Cordon of Medjidie, 1902; Alderman, L.C.C., 1912-13; J.P. Westmorland, 1913; Lieut-Col. commanding the Lonsdale Batt. Border Regiment, 1914. *Address:* Crakenthorpe Hall, Appleby, Westmorland. *Club:* Naval and Military. *(Died July 1916.)*

MACHUGH, Rt. Rev. Charles, D.D.; R.C. Bishop of Derry since 1907; *b.* 1855. *Educ.:* Maynooth. Professor St. Colomb's Diocesan Seminary, 1890-1905; Parish Priest at Strabane, 1905-7; Vicar-General, Derry. *Address:* Bishop's House, Derry.
(Died 12 Feb. 1926.)

MACHUGH, Lt.-Col. Robert Joseph, War Correspondent on staff of the Daily Telegraph. Represented that paper in the Cuban Campaign during the Spanish-American War, 1898; in the Boer War, South Africa, 1899-1901; in the Russo-Japanese War, 1904; during the latter war he was attached to the staff of General Baron Kuroki and accompanied the First Japanese Army from Korea to the Shaho; was present at the battles of the Yalu, Mo-tien-ling Pass, To-wan, An-ping, and Liaoyang (medal with clasp); accompanied the Serbian Army in the Balkan War of 1912 (Commander Order of St. Sava), Mexico early in 1913, and witnessed the revolution; has travelled extensively in United States, Canada, West Indies, Africa (South and East), Europe, Mexico, China, and Japan; joined the late 1st City of London Royal Garrison Artillery, 1895; transferred to the Territorial Army, 1908; commands the 6th London Brigade, Royal Field Artillery, with which he served as Lieut.-Col. in France; is a member of the Q Club. *Publications:* The Siege of Ladysmith; Modern Mexico; introductions to various works, and numerous contributions on military and historical subjects in the magazines.
(Died 6 July 1925.)

McILLREE, John Henry, I.S.O.; late Assistant Commissioner Royal N.W. Mounted Police; *b.* Jamaica, 28 Feb. 1849; *s.* of late Surgeon-General McIllree of the British Army; *m.* 1884, Lily, *d.* of J. Winter Humphrys of Ballyhaise House, Co. Cavan, Ireland; one *d.* one *s. Educ.:* Halifax School; Windsor University, N.S.; Sandhurst. Member of the Royal North-West Mounted Police since it was formed, 1873; retired, 1911; has 1885 Rebellion Medal. *Recreations:* shooting, fishing, golf. *Clubs:* Union of B.C., Victoria Golf.
(Died 17 May 1926.)

MACINNES, Lt.-Col. Duncan Sayre, C.M.G. 1917; D.S.O. 1900; R.E.; General Staff Officer, Staff College; *b.* 19 July 1870; *s.* of late Hon. Donald Macinnes, of Hamilton, Canada; *m.* 1902, Millicent, *d.* of F. Wolferstan-Thomas; one *s.* one *d.* Entered army 1891; Captain, 1902; Major, 1911; Bt. Lt. Col., 1915; served Ashanti, 1895-96 (star); South Africa, 1899-1900 (despatches twice, Queen's medal, 3 clasps, King's medal, 2 clasps, D.S.O.); European War, 1915-17 (C.M.G.). *Address:* The Ridge, Camberley, Surrey. *Club:* Army and Navy.
(Died 23 May 1918.)

McINNIS, Lt.-Col. Edward Bowater, C.M.G. 1890; *b.* 22 May 1846; *m.* 1889, Maud Susanna, *d.* of Capt. Wearing, R.M., and *g.d.* of (T.) Gen. Wearing, R.M., A.D.C. (of Trafalgar). Major, Lt.-Col. 1887; served Afghan War, 1878-80 (despatches); march to Candahar and battle of Candahar (despatches, medal with two clasps, bronze decorations); Adjutant 9th Lancers; Inspector-General of Police, Gold Coast, and British Guiana, 1891; commanded Militia, British Guiana, 1892-1902; on special duty to Urnan Venezulean frontier, 1896; commanded the Cavalry of the Colonial Forces at Queen Victoria's Diamond Jubilee, 1897; proceeded on Special Mission to Malta, 1909-10, to inquire into the organization of police of that island; acted as Political Officer and A.D.C. to the Sultans of Perak and Kedah during the Coronation of King George. *Clubs:* Army and Navy; Radnor, Folkestone. *(Died 4 April 1927.)*

M'INROY, Col. Charles, C.B. 1894, of The Burn and Arnhall, N.B.; D.L. (Kincardinesh.); J.P. Kincardine and Forfar shires unemployed Supernumerary List, Indian Army, *b.* 3 March 1833; *s.* of late J. P. M'Inroy, Lude, Blair Atholl, and *n.* of late Lieut.-Colonel W. M'Inroy of The Burn and Arnhall, Vice-Lt. of Kincardineshire; *m.* 1862, Emelia Katherine, *e. d.* of late Alex. Hamilton, LL.B., W.S.; two *s.* two *d. Educ.:* private and Wimbledon School. Entered army 1855; Lieut. 1858; Capt. 1867; Major, 1875; Lieut.-Col. 1881; Col. 1885; served Indian Mutiny, 1857-59; present at surrender of Kirwee, at Sahao (despatches), Girwasa (despatches); commanded in cavalry actions of Maharajpore, Jakoli, (thanked in despatches), and Mow Mahoni (medal and clasp for Central India); Abyssinian Campaign, 1868 (despatches and medal); Egyptian War, 1882, present at Kassassin and Tel-el-Kebir (medal with clasp, Khedive's star); Burmah Expedition, 1885-86; principal Commissariat Officer in Upper Burmah, 1888-89 (medal with two clasps). *Recreations:* fishing, shooting, curling (vice-pres. Royal Caledonian Curling Club, 1896-97), golf. *Address:* The Burn, Edzell, Brechin. *T.A.:* Burn Edzell. *Club:* New Edinburgh. *(Died 4 Feb. 1919.)*

MACINTYRE, John, M.B., C.M., F.R.S.E., F.R.M.S.; LL.D. Glasgow University; Knight of Grace of the Order of St. John of Jerusalem: F.R.F.P.S.G.; D.L., J.P.; M.I.E.E.; Hon. Lieut.-Commander R.N.V.R.; late University Lecturer on Diseases of the Nose and Throat, Glasgow University; Consulting Surgeon for Diseases of the Nose and Throat, and Consulting Medical Electrician, Glasgow Royal Infirmary; Vice-President of Medical Faculty and Emeritus Professor of Laryngology, Anderson College of Medicine, Glasgow; Senior Editor British Journal of Laryngology: President of West of Scotland Branch British Medical Association: Membre de la Société d'Otologie, de Laryngologie, et de Rhinologie, Paris; Corresponding Member of the American Laryngological Association; Fellow of the London Laryngological Society, British Laryngological, Rhinological, and Otological Association; Röntgen Society, London; and Hon. Member of the British Electro-Therapeutic Society, London; *b.* 2 Nov. 1859; *m.* 1892, Agnes Jean, *d.* of late Henry Reid Hardie. *Educ.:* Glasgow University; Vienna. Held various appointments, such as assistant and afterwards Dispensary Surgeon to the Glasgow Royal Infirmary; Demonstrator of Anatomy in the School of Medicine attached to that hospital; President of the British Laryngological, Rhinological, and Otological Association, London, 1893 and 1900. *Publications:* numerous papers on surgery, X-rays, electrical and physical science in relation to medicine, and demonstrations upon these subjects before the Royal Societies of London and Edinburgh, International Medical Congresses, and British Medical Association, published in the different Transactions and Proceedings of the societies or in the Lancet, British Medical Journal, Nature, and other scientific journals published at home or abroad. *Recreations:* yachting and naval volunteering. *Address:* 179 Bath Street, Glasgow. *T.:* Nat. 162 Douglas, Glasgow. *Clubs:* Services; College, Art, Glasgow. (*Died 29 Oct. 1928.*)

M'IVER, Sir Lewis, 1st Bart., *cr.* 1896; M.P. (U.L.) Edinburgh, W., 1895-1909; Hon. Colonel of Forth Royal Garrison Artillery; *b.* 6 Mar. 1846; *s.* of J. M'Iver, Madras; *m.* Charlotte, *d.* of N. Montefiore, 1884; two *d.* *Educ.:* Bonn University. Barr. 1878; Indian Civil Service, 1868-84; M.P. Torquay Division, Devon, 1885-86; contested South Edinburgh, 1892. *Heir:* none. *Address:* 25 Upper Brook Street, W.1. *T.:* Mayfair 1209. *Clubs:* Ranelagh, Brooks's, Baldwin, St. James's, Royal Automobile. (*Died 9 Aug. 1920.*)

MACK, Sir Hugh, Kt., *cr.* 1908; J.P.; Chairman of Directors of Hugh Mack & Co.; Ltd., Belfast, Wholesale Woollen and Manchester Warehousemen; *b* 1832; 3rd *s.* of David Mack of Lisburn; *m.* 1st, Emma, *d.* of late Wm. Gilbert of Belfast; 2nd, Margaret, *d.* of late James Moore of Drumbadmore, Co. Fermanagh; three *s.* four *d.* *Educ.:* Lisburn. Founded business of which he is now Chairman, 1859; Vice-President Ulster Liberal Association. *Address:* Dalboyne, Lisburn.
(*Died Sept. 1920.*)

MACK, Hon. Jason Miller, President of Legislative Council of Nova Scotia since 1920; *b.* 17 March 1843; *m.* 1878, Minnie, *o. d.* of Daniel Kellaher, Liverpool, N.S. *Educ.:* Normal School and King's College, University, Windsor. Barrister, 1869; K.C. 1907; M.L.C. since 1907; Minister without portfolio, which position he resigned later; D.C.L. King's College, 1921. *Address:* Liverpool, Nova Scotia.
(*Died Jan. 1927.*)

MACKARNESS, Ven. Charles Coleridge, D.D.; Examining Chaplain to the Archbishop of York; Canon of York since 1896; Fellow of Denstone College since 1901; *b.* 22 July 1850; *e. s.* of late Bishop Mackarness of Oxford: *m.* Grace Emily, *e. d.* of Rev. Canon Milford, formerly Rector of East Knoyle, Wilts, 1882; four *s.* two *d.* *Educ.:* Winchester; Exeter College, Oxford. B.A., 2nd class Final Classical School, 1873; M.A. 1876; B.D. and D.D. 1914; Assistant Curate of St. Mary's, Reading, 1874-79; Chaplain, Censor, and Theological Lecturer in King's College, London, 1879-81; Vicar of Aylesbury, 1882-89; Rural Dean of Aylesbury, 1887-89; Vicar of St. Martin's, Scarborough, 1889-1916; Archdeacon of the East Riding, 1898-1916; *Publications:* The Message of the Prayer-Book, 1887; The Poetry of Keble as a Guide to the Clergy, 1891; Memorials of the Episcopate of Bishop Mackarness, 2nd ed., 1892; Faith and Duty in time of War (sermons), 1916. *Recreations:* formerly in Winchester Cricket XI., 1868; Capt. of Ex. Coll. Oxford XI., 1873; member of Oxford Univ. Association Football XI., 1873; cycling. *Address:* 1 Polstead Road, Oxford.
(*Died 1 Mar. 1918.*)

MACKARNESS, His Hon. Frederic Coleridge, M.A.; County Court Judge, Circuit 50 (Sussex) since 1911; *b.* 1854; *s.* of Rt. Rev. J. F. Mackarness, Bishop of Oxford; *m.* 1882, Amy (*d.* 1916), *d.* of Rev. Richard Chermside. *Educ.:* Marlborough; Keble College, Oxford. Called to Bar, Middle Temple, 1879; Advocate of Cape Supreme Court, 1882; Revising Barrister for London, 1889; Recorder of Newbury, 1894; Professor of Roman-Dutch Law Univ. Coll. London, 1905-6;

23

M.P. (L.) Newbury Div. Berks, 1906-10. *Address:* 21 Montpelier Square, S.W.7; *T.:* Kens. 2412; Kingsmead, Bramber. *Club:* Reform.
(*Died 23 Dec. 1920.*)

MACKAY, Alexander Grant, M.A., K.C., Minister of Municipal Affairs and Minister of Health since 1918; M.P.P. Athabasca District, Alberta; Member of the Legislature of the Province of Alberta since 1913; Leader of the Liberal Opposition in the Legislature of the Province of Ontario, 1907-1911; *b.* 7 Mar. 1860; Scotch parentage; unmarried. *Educ.:* Toronto University. Four years High School Principal; Member Legislature of Province of Ontario, 1902-13; Minister of Crown Lands, Ontario, 1904-1905. *Address:* Edmonton, Canada. (*Died April 1920.*)

MACKAY, Ebenezer, B.A., Ph.D.; M'Leod Professor of Chemistry in Dalhousie University since 1896; *b.* Plainfield, Pictou County, Nova Scotia, 1864; *s.* of Angus Mackay, a native of Rogart, Sutherlandshire. *Educ.:* Pictou Academy; Dalhousie University; Johns Hopkins University. Principal of Schools, New Glasgow, N.S., 1886-92; Fellow, Johns Hopkins University, 1895. *Address:* Dalhousie University, Halifax, N.S. *Club:* Halifax.
(*Died 6 Jan. 1920.*)

MACKAY, John, I.S.O. 1911; Port-master and Chairman of Marine Board of Queensland since 1902; *b.* Bonar Bridge, Sutherlandshire, 26 March 1889; *e. s.* of George Mackay, Tongue, Sutherlandshire, and Annie Munro; *m.* 1883, Marion, *e. d.* of John MacLennan of Invervanie, Armidale District, New South Wales; three *s.* one *d.* *Educ.:* Free Church Academy, Inverness. Came to Australia with parents and settled in New England district, 1854; led expedition into Queensland and discovered the Mackay District and Pioneer River in Central Queensland, 1859; formed Greenmount Station in the Mackay District, 1860; sold Greenmount and left Queensland, adopting a sea life, 1864; shipmaster in the Pacific and South Seas, also planting in Fiji, 1869-82; entered the Queensland Marine Department as Harbour-Master at Cooktown, North Queensland, 1883; Harbour-Master at Brisbane, 1888; Liberal; Presbyterian. *Publications:* Echoes of the Great Barrier Reef; The Stone Ruins of the Caroline Islands; several stories of Australian and South Sea Island life. *Recreations:* reading, walking, writing, historical research work. *Address:* Brisbane. *T.A.:* Kangaroo Point, Brisbane. *T.:* Brisbane, Central 2953. *Club:* Johnsonian, Brisbane.

MACKAY, Ven. John Alexander, D.D.; Archdeacon of Saskatchewan and Superintendent of Indian Missions; *b.* Hudson's Bay Territories, 1838; *s.* of William Mackay, an officer of the Hon. Hudson's Bay Company, and Mary Bunn; *m.* 1864, Margaret Drever of Winnipeg; one *s.* four *d.* *Educ.:* by Rev. E. A. Watkins and Rev. J. Horden, afterwards Bishop Horden, missionaries of the C.M.S.; St. John's College, Winnipeg, under Bishop Anderson. Ordained deacon, 1862; priest, 1863; for fifty-nine years missionary among the Cree Indians in the Canadian North-West. *Publications:* translation of Oxenden's Pathway of Safety; A Manual of Family Prayer; Psalms and Hymns, all in Cree; revision of the Bible in Cree for the British and Foreign Bible Society; Revision Hordon's Cree Grammar and Hunter's Translation of Book of Common Prayer in Cree. *Address:* Prince Albert, Saskatchewan, N.W.T., Canada.
(*Died Nov. 1923.*)

MACKAY, Hon. Robert; Senator since 1901; *b.* Scotland, 1840; *m.* 1871, *d.* of late George Baptist, Three Rivers, P.Q.; four *s.* two *d.* Went to Canada, 1855; director of many companies. *Address:* Kildonan Hall, 681 Sherbrooke Street W., Montreal. *Clubs:* St. James's, Mount

Royal, Canada, Montreal; Rideau, Ottawa.
(*Died 16 Dec. 1916.*)

M'KAY, Hon. Thomas; Senator since 1881; *b.* 8 Jan. 1839; *m.* 1868, Jessie, *d.* of late John Blair, Truro, N.S. M.P. (C.) Cumberland, 1874-1881. *Address:* Elmhurst, Truro, Nova Scotia.

M'KAY, William D., R.S.A., 1888; LL.D. Edin.; *b.* Gifford, East Lothian, 1844; *e. s.* of Peter M'Kay, parish schoolmaster there. *Educ.:* parish school, Gifford. Entered at Trustees' Academy, Edinburgh, 1860; afterwards studied at the Royal Scottish Academy's School; A.R.S.A., 1877; R.S.A. 1883; Librarian, 1896; Secretary, 1907; practises the landscape and landscape with figures department of Art. *Publications:* George Manson and his works, in collaboration with P. W. Adam, R.S.A., and late John M. Gray, 1880; The Scottish School of Painting, 1906; Raeburn's Technique, special article for The Studio, Feb. 1908; in collaboration with Frank Rinder, The Royal Scottish Academy, 1826-1916, 1917. *Address:* 1 Warrender Park Crescent, Edinburgh. *Club:* Scottish Arts, Edinburgh.
(*Died 10 Dec. 1924.*)

M'KEAN, Capt. George Burdon, V.C. 1918, M.C., M.M.; late Corps of Military Accountants; *b.* Bishop Auckland, Co. Durham, 4 July 1890; *s.* of James M'Kean, merchant, and Jane Ann Henderson. *Educ.:* Robertson College and University of Alberta, Edmonton. Went to Canada alone, 1905; lived and worked on a cattle ranch, and later on a farm owned by brother, until 1911, when he entered Robertson College; registered with the University of Alberta as a student in Arts and Medicine, 1912; enlisted in Canadian Expeditionary Force, 1915; Sergeant, 1916; France, 1916; Commission, 1917; Captain, 1919 (twice wounded, V.C., M.C., M.M.); retired pay, 1926. *Publication:* Scouting Thrills, 1919. *Recreations:* tennis and football. *Address:* c/o Lloyds Bank, Ltd., Cox and King's Branch, 6 Pall Mall, S.W.1. (*Died Nov. 1926.*)

McKEE, Rev. Robert Alexander, M.A., Vicar of Farnsfield, 1882-1928; Canon of Rampton in Southwell Cathedral, 1915; Rural Dean of Southwell, 1910; *b.* Ward House, Co. Leitrim, 1847; *e. s.* of Rev. James McKee, D.D., late Vicar of Wymynswold, Co. Kent; *m.* 1872, Mary, 2nd *d.* of John Jeffery, Northampton; four *s.* two *d. Educ.:* St. John's College, Cambridge; Deacon, 1871; Priest, 1872; Curate of Atherton, 1871-73; Curate in charge of St. Anne, Hindsford, 1873-77; Vicar of Lumb-in-Rossendale, 1877-82; Secretary to the Board of Education for the County of Notts, 1897; Secretary to the Notts Church Schools' Association, 1903; Secretary to the Southwell Diocesan Education Committee, 1904; Organising Secretary of S.P.G. for the Archdeaconry of Nottingham, 1903. *Address:* Bickerton Vicarage, Malpas, Cheshire. (*Died 19 Feb. 1926.*)

MACKEEN, Hon. David; Senator since 1896; *b.* 20 Sep. 1889; *m.* 1st, 1867, Isabel (dead), of late Henry Poole, Derby, England; 2nd, 1877, Francis M. (dead), *d.* of late William Lawson, Halifax, N.S.; 3rd, 1888, Jane K., *e. d.* of late John Crerar, Halifax, N.S. *Address:* Maplewood, Halifax, N.S. *Clubs:* Halifax, Halifax; Rideau, Ottawa. (*Died 13 Nov. 1916.*)

MACKELLAR, Hon. Sir Charles Kinnaird, Kt., *cr.* 1912; K.C.M.G., *cr.* 1916; M.B., C.M.; Member of the Legislative Council of New South Wales since 1886; President of the State Children Board New South Wales for 14 years; *b.* Sydney, N.S.W., 5 Dec. 1844; *s.* of Frederick Mackellar, M.D., of Sydney, N.S.W.; *m.* 1877, Marion, *d.* of Thomas Buckland of Sydney; two *s.* one *d. Educ.:* Sydney Grammar School; University of Glasgow. Representative of the Jennings Dibbs Government, and Minister for Mines, 1886; Member of the

Senate of the Commonwealth, 1900; sometime President of the Board of Health and Medical Adviser to the Government of N.S.W. *Address:* Rosemount, Ocean Street, Woollahra, Sydney. *Club:* Australian, Sydney. (*Died July 1926.*)

M'KENDRICK, John Gray, LL.D. (Hon. Aberdeen and Glasgow), M.D., F.R.S., F.R.S. Edin., F.R.C.P.E., M.R.I.; Professor of Physiology, Glasgow University, 1876-1906; now Emeritus Prof.; formerly Examiner in Physiology, University of London, Victoria University, University of Birmingham, Universities of Oxford, Cambridge, Durham, and Aberdeen (1916); *b.* Aberdeen, 1841; *o. s.* of James M'Kendrick, merchant, Aberdeen; *m.* 1867, Mary (*d.* 1898), *d.* of W. Souttar, Aberdeen; two *s.* two *d. Educ.:* Aberdeen and Edinburgh Universities (M.D., Ch.M. Aberdeen). Formerly Assistant to Professor of, and Lecturer on, Physiology, Edinburgh; Fullerian Professor of Physiology at Royal Institute of Great Britain; has twice delivered the Thomson Lectures at the Free Church College of Aberdeen; formerly one of the lecturers in connection with the Gilchrist Trust; has served on the Councils of the Royal Society and of Royal Society of Edinburgh; President of Physiological Section of British Association; spends most of the year at Maxieburn, Stonehaven. *Publications:* Animal Physiology, 1876; Lectures on the History of Physiology, 1879; A Text-Book of Physiology, 1888; Life in Motion, or Muscle Nerve, 1892; Physiology, 1896; Life of Helmholtz, 1899; Boyle (Oxford) Lecture on Hearing, 1899; Science and Faith, 1899; Christianity and the Sick, 1901; and various papers on physiological acoustics and experimental phonetics. *Address:* Maxieburn, Stonehaven. *T.:* Stonehaven 8. (*Died 2 Jan. 1926.*)

MACKENZIE, Col. Sir Alfred Robert Davidson, K.C.B., *cr.* 1907; C.B. 1886; late Bengal Cavalry; *b.* 30 Sept. 1835. Entered army, 1854; Colonel 1882; served Indian Mutiny, 1857-1858 (medal with 2 clasps); Afghan War, 1879-80 (despatches, medal with clasp, bronze decoration). *Club:* East India United Service.
(*Died 8 May 1921.*)

M'KENZIE, Lieut.-Col. Archibald Ernest Graham, D.S.O. 1916; Commanding 26th (New Brunswick) Batt. Canadians since 1916; *b.* Campbellton, New Brunswick, Canada, 21 Jan. 1878; *s.* of Archibald M'Kenzie; *m.* 1904, Charlotte B., *d.* of James M. Troy, Newcastle, N.B. *Educ.:* University of New Brunswick (B.A. 1902, M.A. 1904); King's College, B.C.L. 1907. After graduation Principal of Harkin's Academy, Newcastle, New Brunswick; admitted to Bar of New Brunswick in 1907, and commenced practice in Campbellton; contested (L.) the County of Restigouche, 1912; has always taken deep interest in militia, being Adjutant of Batt. at outbreak of war. *Recreations:* fishing, curling. *Address:* Campbellton, N.B., Canada. *Clubs:* Union, St. John; Campbellton. (*Died 8 Sept. 1918.*)

MACKENZIE, David James; advocate; *b.* 8 March 1855; *s.* of Thomas Mackenzie, Ladyhill, Elgin; *m.* 1886, Margaret Jane, *d.* of George Wilson, M.D., Huntly, Aberdeenshire. *Educ.:* schools in Elgin and Aberdeen; Universities of Aberdeen and Edinburgh. Admitted a Member of the Faculty of Advocates, 1879; appointed Sheriff-Substitute of Caithness, Orkney, and Zetland at Lerwick, 1885; transferred to Wick, 1891; to Kilmarnock, 1902, and to Lanarkshire at Glasgow, 1914; retired, 1920; F.S.A. Scot., 1887. *Publications:* Byways among Books, 1900; Poems, 1920, etc.; a contributor to various magazines, including Blackwood's, All the Year Round, Good Words, and Chambers's. *Recreations:* reading, book-hunting, scribbling with pen and pencil. *Ad-*

dress: Deansford, Bishopmill, Elgin.

(*Died 27 May 1925.*)

M'KENZIE, Donald Duncan, K.C.: Judge of Supreme Court of Nova Scotia since 1923; M.P.P.C.; *b.* Lake Ainslie, Nova Scotia, 8 Jan. 1859; *s.* of Duncan M'Kenzie and Jessie M'Millan; *m.* 1891, Florence.N. M'Donald of Sydney Mines, N.S.; one *s. Educ.:* Sydney Academy. Admitted to the Nova Scotia Bar, 1889; elected to the Local Legislature of Nova Scotia, 1900; resigned, 1904; elected to House of Commons; re-elected 1908, 1911, 1917, and 1921; Leader of Liberal Opposition, House of Commons, Ottawa, 1919-21; Solicitor - General, Canada, 1921-23; Presbyterian. *Recreations :* quoits, horses and fishing. *Address:* Halifax, Nova Scotia. (*Died June 1927.*)

MACKENZIE, Ven. Gaden Crawford, Archdeacon of Perth, Huron, since 1905. *Educ.:* Trinity College, Toronto (Hon. D.C.L.). Ordained, 1869; Incumbent of Dysart, 1869-70; Curate, 1870-72; Chaplain, 1872-73; Rector of Kincardine, 1873-79; Gracechurch, Brantford, 1879-1905. *Address:* Brantford, Ontario.

(*Died 20 Mar. 1920.*)

MACKENZIE. Sir James, Kt., *cr.* 1915; M.D. Ed.; F.R.S. 1915, F.R.C.P., LL.D., Aberdeen and Edinburgh; Consulting Physician to the King in Scotland; Consulting Physician to the London Hospital; *b.* 12 Apr. 1858; *s.* of Robert Mackenzie, Scone; *m.* 1887, Frances, *d.* of George Jackson, Boston; one *d. Educ.:* Perth Academy; Edinburgh University. After graduation (1878) appointed House Physician and Assistant to Professors of Clinical Medicine, Royal Infirmary, Edinburgh; in medical practice in Burnley, 1879-1907; in consulting practice in London, 1907 - 18; Oliver-Sharpey Lecturer, Royal College of Physicians, 1911; Schorstein Lecturer, London Hospital, 1911; Gibson Memorial Lecturer, Edinburgh College of Physicians, 1914. *Publications:* The Study of the Pulse, etc., 1902 (German Translation); Diseases of the Heart, 1908, 3rd ed. 1913 (German, French, and Italian Translations); Symptoms and their Interpretation, 3rd ed. 1918 (German. Italian. Danish and Spanish Translations); Principles of Diagnosis and Treatment in Heart Affections, 1916 (Italian Translations; The Future of Medicine, 1919; numerous papers to scientific journals. *Address:* 58 Albert Hall Mansions, Kensington Gore, S.W.7. (*Died 26 Jan. 1925.*)

MACKENZIE, J. Hamilton, A.R.S.A. 1923; R.S.W. 1910; A.R.E. 1910; President Glasgow Art Club, 1923-25; *b.* Glasgow, 1875; *m.* Margaret Thomson Wilson, Artist (*decd.*). *Educ.:* Glasgow School of Art (Haldane Travelling Scholarship); R. Instituto de Belli Arti, Florence; exhibits at Glasgow Institute, R.S.A., etc.; Fleeting Shadows was purchased by Glasgow Corporation Art Gallery, 1913; Army Service, R.A.S.C., Motor Transport, 1915-19 — Rank, Private; East Africa, 1916. *Publications:* amongst his etchings are: Cathedral of St. Francis, Assisi; L'Ancien Greffe and Cathedral Tower, Bruges. *Address:* 204 West Regent Street, Glasgow; Studio, 104 West George Street, Glasgow. *Clubs:* Glasgow Art : Scottish Arts, Edinburgh.

(*Died 29 Mar. 1926.*)

MACKENZIE, J.J., B.A., M.B.; F.R.S. Canada; Professor of Pathology and Bacteriology, University of Toronto, since 1900; *b.* 1865; a Canadian by birth, of Scottish parentage; *m.* 1892, Agnes Kathleen, *d.* of W. Vesey - Rogers, Dublin. *Educ.:* Univ. of Toronto; Univs. of Leipzig and Berlin. Sometime Fellow in Biology, Univ. of Toronto; subsequently Bacteriologist to the Ontario Provincial Board of Health; has written on bacteriological and pathological subjects;

member of the American Public Health Association, the Society of American Bacteriologists, and American Association of Pathologists and Bacteriologists; Past President, Royal Canadian Institute; served European War attached to No. 4 Canadian General Hospital (University of Toronto) in Greece. *Address:* 56 Wychwood Park, Hillcrest, Toronto. *T.:* Hillcrest 7007. *Clubs:* Royal Societies; Toronto Golf, York, Toronto. (*Died 1 Aug. 1922.*)

MACKENZIE, Kenneth James Joseph, M.A., A.S.I., etc.: Reader in Agriculture in the University of Cambridge and Consultant to the Institute of Animal Nutrition; *b.* 1867; *s.* of late Major A. C. C. Mackenzie, R.E., and Melesina, *d.* of late J. H. Woodward; unmarried. *Educ.:* Fort Augustus College; the S.E.A. College, Wye; B.D.F.A. Institution, Reading; abroad. Late Professor of Agriculture, S.E.A.S.C.; Member of the Agricultural Board of Studies and Examiner, London University; late Editor of the Journal and now Governor of the Royal Agricultural Society of England; has been chairman of the Cambridge-shire and Isle of Ely Chamber of Agriculture and many other agricultural societies, and has judged all sorts of classes at agricultural shows; represented the British Government on the International Exhibition at Brussels, 1910; and went in 1918 to France on behalf of the War Office and Y.M.C.A. to lecture to the B.E.F. concerning the home food supply, etc. *Publications:* Cattle, 1919, a reconstructive work on animal husbandry; many articles in the various agricultural periodicals, and wrote in all classes of publications upon the feeding of England during the war. *Address:* Christ's College, Cambridge. *T.:* Cambridge 913. *Clubs:* Savile, Farmers. (*Died 5 June 1924.*)

McKENZIE, Marian, F.R.A.M.; leading contralto vocalist and teacher; *b.* Plymouth; *e. d.* of Capt. Joseph McKenzie; wife of Richard Smith Williams (*d.* 1926). *Educ.:* privately at Plymouth: musical education under Dr. Samuel Weekes, Plymouth; Roy. Acad. of Music, under Cavaliere Alberto Randegger, etc. Parepa Rosa Scholar; Westmoreland Scholar, R.A.M.; bronze, silver, and gold medallist, R.A.M.; principal contralto of the Handel and Bach Festivals, and of the Leeds, Birmingham, Norwich, Chester, etc., Festivals, and of the Welsh Eisteddfodd, also of H.M. State concerts, and the Viceregal Court; Associate Philharmonic Society; member Royal Society of Musicians. *Recreation:* bridge. *Address:* 83 Carlisle Mansions, Victoria Street, S.W.1. *T.:* Victoria 5353. (*Died 16 June 1927.*)

MACKENZIE, Colonel Robert Holden, Esquire of the Order of St. John of Jerusalem; Gentleman of the King's Body-Guard for Scotland; F.S.A. 1887; F.S.A. Scot. 1904: late Major Worcestershire Regiment and Colonel commanding 4th (Special Reserve) Batt. the Cameronians (Scottish Rifles); raised the 1st (Highlanders) Cadet Batt. the Royal Scots in Edinburgh in 1911; was in H.M.S. Lively when that vessel was wrecked and lost, while attached to Royal Commission on the Highland Crofters, 1883; A.D.C. to Sir Walter Sendall, G.C.M.G., Governor of the Windward Islands, 1885-86; to Sir Henry Bulwer, G.C.M.G., Governor of Natal and afterwards Cyprus, 1886-89; to Lieut.-General Sir F. M. Colvile, K.C.B., 1891-93; and to Major - General Sir A. E. Turner, K.C.B., Inspector-Gen. of Auxiliary Forces, 1900-1901; served operations in Soudan, 1889; South African War, 1900-2; has been a member of Council of the Royal United Service Institution, and was for some years on the Staff of the Royal Military Tournament. *Publications:* The Trafalgar Roll; Papers and contributions to Dictionary of National Biography, Scottish Historical Review, the Cornhill, Chambers's Journal, Macmillan's, the United Service. the

McKENZIE, Hon. Robert Donald. See page xxiv.

Cavalry, and other magazines. *Recreations:* Military and Scottish History and Antiquities. *Clubs:* United Service; New, Edinburgh.

MACKENZIE, Maj.-Gen. Roderick, Knight of the Legion of Honour; 5th class Medjidie; J.P. and D.L. for Aberdeenshire; *b.* 1830; *s.* of late Major Forbes Mackenzie; *m.* 1878, Caroline, *d.* of J. A. Beaumont; one *d. Educ.:* Military Academy, Woolwich. Served in the Royal Artillery throughout the Crimean War. *Address:* Foveran House, Aberdeenshire; 14 Charles Street, Berkeley Square, W. *T.:* Mayfair 5772. *Clubs:* Carlton, United Service, Turf; New, Edinburgh. *(Died 19 May 1916.)*

MACKENZIE, Sir William, Kt., *cr.* 1911; President of the Canadian Northern Railway; member of Mackenzie, Mann & Co.; *b.* Kirkfield, Ont., 30 Oct. 1849, of Scottish parentage; Presbyterian; *m.* 1872, Margaret, (*d.* 1917) *d.* of John Derry. Knight of Grace, St. John of Jerusalem; two *s.* six *d. Address:* Benvenuto, 350 Avenue Road, Toronto. *Clubs:* Toronto; Toronto; St. James's, Montreal; Manitoba, Winnipeg; Rideau, Ottawa. *(Died 5 Dec. 1923.)*

MACKENZIE, William Dalziel; *b.* Renfrewshire, 1840; *e. s.* of Edward Mackenzie, of Fawley Court; J.P., D.L. Oxon and Mary Dalziel; *m.* 1st, 1868, Mary Anna (*d.* 1900), *e. d.* of Henry Baskerville, of Crowsley Park, Oxon; 2nd, 1902, Mary Catherine (*d.* 1924), 2nd *d.* of Adam S. Gladstone, and *widow* of Sir Francis G. Stapleton, 8th Bt.; one *s.* four *d. Educ.:* Harrow; Magdalen Coll., Oxford, M.A. Barrister-at-law, Inner Temple, 1863; Conservative candidate, Reading, 1874; later at Truro and Woodstock; J.P. Oxon (High Sheriff, 1878) Bucks. Cos. Dumfries, Kirkcudbright, Inverness; D.L.; Lt.-Col. late Queen's Own Oxfordshire Hussars, Imperial Yeomanry; Director of L. and N.W. Ry. Co. 1873-82. *Publications:* On Agricultural Depression and Fiscal Question, etc. *Heir: e. s.* Roderick, J.P. [late Major 3rd Batt. Cameron Highlanders; *m.* 1888, Maud Evelyn (*d.* 1924), *e. d.* of late Gen. Sir George Wentworth Higginson, G.C.B., G.C.V.O.; one *s.* one *d. Address:* Sunnyclose, Henley] *Recreations:* farms largely, estate improvements, planting, etc. *Address:* House of Farr, Inverness; Fawley Court, Henley-on-Thames. *T.:* Henley 201. *Clubs:* Carlton, Cavalry, Constitutional, Caledonian.
(Died 4 Dec. 1928.)

MACKENZIE, W. G., A.R.H.A. *Educ.:* Old School of Art, Belfast (National Scholarship); London, under E. J. Poynter, R.A.; Julian's, Paris. Specimens of his painting from the figure have been purchased by the authorities of South Kensington and elsewhere, and are used as examples in the Government Schools of Art; Adjudicator at the School of Art, Belfast. *Works:* Portrait of late C. C. Connor (last Mayor of Belfast), City Hall, Belfast; Presentation Portrait of Sir Crawford McCullagh, ex-Lord Mayor of Belfast, Royal Hibernian Academy, Dublin. *Address:* Studio, Clarence Place, Belfast.

MACKENZIE, Lieut.-Col. William Scobie, D.S.O. 1917; O.B.E. 1920; R.A.O.C.; *m.* 1906, Geraldine, *d.* of late Col. Francis Moore; three *s.* two *d.* Served European War, 1914-18 (despatches, D.S.O.). *Address:* Forthside House, Stirling. *(Died 1 Sept. 1926.)*

McKEOWN, Robert John, M.P., Director, Milford Weaving and Finishing Co. Ltd., Belfast and other companies; *b.* Coagh, Co. Tyrone, 12 May 1869; *m.* 1899, Elizabeth J., *d.* of John McVea, Whitehead; two *s.* one *d. Educ.:* Moneymore Intermediate School; Private tuition. Chairman of the Irish Power-loom Manufacturers Association, 1914-20; member of the Flax Control Board, London, during the War; Unionist Member for North Belfast in Northern Parliament, and Parliamentary

676

Secretary for the Ministry of Education and also for the Ministry of Commerce; President of the Ulster Reform Club, 1920, and Chairman of the Ulster Liberal Unionist Association, 1921. *Recreations:* golf and boating. *Address:* Cliff Lodge, Whitehead, Co. Antrim. *T.:* Whitehead 12. *M.:* OI 7643. *Clubs:* Constitutional; Ulster Reform, Belfast; Co. Antrim Yacht. *(Died 9 April 1925.)*

McKEOWN, Walter, C.B.E. 1919; B.A., M.D., M.R.C.S. Eng.; Col. C.A.M.C.; President of the Academy of Medicine, Toronto; *b.* Toronto, 10 Feb. 1866; *m.* 1892, Minnie, *e. d.* of late John Woods, Toronto; one *s.* two *d. Educ.:* Upper Canada College and University, Toronto; Middlesex Hospital. Continuously in practice in Toronto since 1891; Associate Professor of Clinical Surgery, University of Toronto; Surgeon-in-Chief, St. Michael's Hospital, Toronto; served in N.W. Rebellion, 1885; European War, C.E.F., 1915; Member of the Royal Commission on Pensions appointed by Dominion Government, 1922. *Recreation:* music. *Address:* 140 Wellesley Crescent, Toronto. *(Died 6 Sept. 1925.)*

McKERRELL, Brig.-Commander Augustus de Ségur, C.B. 1908; *b.* 28 Aug. 1863; *s.* of late Robert McKerrell. *Educ.:* Cheam; Eton; R.M.C. Sandhurst. Joined the Cameron Highlanders, 1884; Captain 1892; Major 1899; Bt.-Lt.-Col. 1899; Bt.-Col. 1904; employed with Egyptian army, 1893-1903; served Soudan, 1884-85 (medal with clasp, bronze star); Soudan, 1885-86; Dongola, 1896 (Egyptian medal); Nile Expedition, 1897 (clasp), 1898 (despatches, brevet Lt.-Col., clasp and medal), 1899 (clasp, 3rd class Medjidie and 3rd Osmanieh); Governor, Dongola, 1900-2; Berber, 1902-3; commanded 2nd Batt. Cameron Highlanders, 1910-12. *Address:* Headquarters, Black Watch Infantry Brigade, Dundee. *Club:* Naval and Military. *(Died 24 April 1916.)*

MACKESY, Col. Charles Ernest Randolph, C.M.G. 1917; C.B.E. 1919; D.S.O. 1917; J.P.; retired; landowner; *b.* Dublin, 1861; *s.* of Captain E. R. Mackesy, late 97th Regt.; *m.* Jessie (*d.* 1920), *d.* of Thomas Adam, Kilmarnock; three *s. Educ.:* France; Switzerland; Germany. Took first prize on several occasions for all-round athletics; spent several years in Western U.S.A.; since 1891 in N.Z.; 20 years Vol. and Terr. Officer; left with main body, 1914, in command of Auckland Mt. R.; served 5½ years abroad; several times in command of Mounted Brigade; Military Governor and Administrator East of Jordan (despatches five times, C.M.G., C.B.E., D.S.O.); served on County Council and Harbour Boards. *Publications:* pamphlets on Chronology, etc. *Address:* The Hill, Whangarei, Auckland, New Zealand. *(Died 20 Nov. 1925.)*

MACKEY, Brig.-Gen. Hugh James Alexander, C.M.G. 1917; M.V.O. 1901; D.S.O. 1915; late R.F.A.; *b.* 19 Mar. 1876; *s.* of late Capt. Hugh A. Mackey, R.A.; *m.* 1904, Violet Alice, *e. d.* of Henry Edgar Rodwell; three *d.* Entered R.A. 1896; Captain, 1902; Major, 1912; Adjutant R.M.A. 1909-13; Lt.-Col. 1917; Col. 1921; served European War, 1914-19, including Mesopotamia (despatches six times, D.S.O., C.M.G., Order of St. Stanislas, 1914 Star, G. S. and Victory medals); retired pay, 1921. *Address:* c/o Lloyds Bank, Cox's Branch, 6 Pall Mall, S.W.1. *Club:* Army and Navy.
(Died 1 May 1927.)

MACKEY, Hon. Sir John Emanuel, Kt., *cr.* 1921; M.A., LL.B.; M.L.A. Gippsland West, 1902; Speaker of the Legislative Assembly, Victoria, since 1917; *b.* 7 Aug. 1865; *m.* Zella, *y. d.* of late Hon. William Bates, Minister of Trade and Customs; two *s.* two *d.* Was Minister of Lands; Chief Secretary; Minister for Labour; Solicitor-General; Barrister-at-law; Lecturer on Equity, University of Melbourne;

Member of the Council of the University of Melbourne, Trustee and Treasurer of the Melbourne Public Library and National Gallery; Member of the Board of Visitors of the Melbourne Observatory; Chairman of Trustees of the Melbourne Cricket Ground. *Address:* Selborne Chambers, Melbourne, Victoria, Australia. *(Died April 1924.)*

MACKIE, Charles H., R.S.A. 1917; A.R.S.A. 1902; R.S.W. 1902; *b.* 1862; *s.* of Captain William Mackie, 2nd Regt. (Queen's Royals); *m.* 1891, 2nd *d.* of Provost Walls, Dunfermline; one *s. Educ.:* Edinburgh University; Royal Scottish Academy Schools. Painter of landscapes, portraits, and mural decorations; Chairman of Society of Scottish Artists, 1900-1901; exhibited at Munich, Venice, Berlin, Buda-Pesth, Dresden, and Amsterdam International Exhibitions; received Gold Medal at Amsterdam, 1912, also R.A., R.S.A., Pittsburg, P.A., etc. *Publications:* several wood-block colour prints. *Recreations:* golf and bicycling. *Address:* Coltbridge Studio, Murrayfield, N.B. *Club:* Scottish Arts.
(Died 12 July 1920.)

MACKIE, Rev. George M., M.A., D.D., Missionary to the Jews and Minister of Anglo-American Congregation, Beyrout, since 1880; *b.* Banchory-Ternan, near Aberdeen, 1854; *s.* of Rev. James Mackie. *Educ.:* Graduated in Arts at Aberdeen Univ. with honours in Ment. Phil.; entered Edinburgh Divinity Hall as First Bursar, 1876, and shortly after completing his theological studies offered himself as a missionary on behalf of Israel. In his Arabic and Hebrew studies, while chiefly seeking to qualify himself for the work of an evangelist, he has by long residence in the East and contact with Jews, Moslems, and Oriental Christians, become deeply conscious of the family background of the Bible and of the helpfulness of Oriental life and folklore in explaining its meaning. He has contributed various articles on such matters to Hastings' Bible Dictionary and the Expository Times, and is the author of the text-book, Bible Manners and Customs, belonging to the Guild Library Series of the Church of Scotland. In 1901 the degree of D.D. was conferred upon him by Aberdeen University. *Recreations:* golf, sketching. *Address:* Beyrout, Syria.
(Died 1922.)

MACKIE, John Beveridge, F.J.I.; editor and proprietor Dunfermline Journal, Dunfermline Express, West Fife Echo; Rosyth and Forth Mail; *b.* Dunfermline, 2 June 1848; 3rd *s.* of John Mackie and Janet Syme; *m.* Lilias, *d.* of late James Robb, editor of Scottish Farmer, Feb. 1885; two *s.* three *d. Educ.:* Free Abbey Acad. Dunfermline. Reporter Dunfermline, Cupar-Fife, Edin. and Glasgow; sub-editor Glasgow Herald, 1870-77; with his brothers William and Robert conducted Daily Review, Edin. 1877-86; leader-writer Newcastle Daily Leader, 1886-89; editor of North-Eastern Daily Gazette, 1890-1903. *Publications:* Life and Work of Duncan M'Laren, 1888; Modern Journalism, 1894; Memories; Pitcairnie: a Tale of the Press-Gang; Friends of the People; Pittencrieff Glen, its History, Antiquities, and Legends; Essays on Influence; Margaret, Queen and Saint; Dunfermline Men of Mark; Dunfermline Born Princes and Princesses; Idylls of Dunfermline; The Model Member: Sir Henry Campbell-Bannerman's Forty Years' Connection with the Stirling Burghs, 1914; Andrew Carnegie: his Dunfermline Ties and Benefactions; etc. *Address:* Park Place, Dunfermline. *T.A.:* Journal, Dunfermline. *T.:* 11. *(Died 22 May 1919.)*

MACKIE, Sir Peter Jeffrey, 1st Bt., *cr.* 1920; F.S.A., J.P.; *b.* 26 Nov. 1855; *e. s.* of Alexander Mackie; *m.* 1889, Jessie, *d.* of Thomas Abercrombie; two *d.* Chairman White Horse Distillers, Ltd.; travelled extensively and written on Tariff Reform, Empire Federa-

tion, and other political subjects; Unionist; Episcopal; owns 12,000 acres. *Publications:* Empire; The Keeper's Book (16 editions). *Recreations:* all sports. *Heir:* none. *Address:* Corraith, Symington, Ayr. *T.:* Troon 19. *T.A.:* Symington, Kilmarnock; Glenreasdell, Whitehouse, Argyll. *Clubs:* Caledonian; County, Ayr. *(Died 22 Sept. 1924.)*

MACKIE, Sir Richard, Kt., *cr.* 1909; J.P.; Ship Owner and Coal Exporter; *b.* Dunfermline, April 1851; *m.* Isabella, *d.* of late Laurence Thomson, St. Andrews; two *s.* two *d. Educ.:* Dunfermline. Came to Leith, 1865; entered an office of Shipbrokers and Coal Exporters; has been in the same office since above date and acquired the business, 1873; has carried on the firm of Mackie, Koth and Co. since 1873 as Shipbrokers and Coal Exporters; established the firm of Richard Mackie & Co., Steamship Owners, 1882; both firms are still in existence and he is senior partner of both; Provost of Leith, 1899-1908; Italian and Swedish Vice-Consul; Knight of the Polar Star Sweden; Cavaliere of the Crown of Italy. *Recreations:* golf, bowling, yachting. *Address:* Trinity Grove, Leith. *T.A.:* Mackie, Leith. *T.:* Granton 223. *M.:* WS 1, WS 2. *Clubs:* Junior Constitutional, Conservative, Edinburgh; Royal Forth Yacht, Merchants', Leith. *(Died 30 June 1923.)*

MACKINLAY, Lt.-Col. George; *b.* 1847; 2nd *s.* of late John Mackinlay, M.R.C.S.; *m.* 1871, Lucy Teshmaker, *d.* of late David Graham Johnstone, J.P.; one *d. Educ.:* Kensington Grammar School; R.M. Academy, Woolwich. Joined R.A. 1866; served in the Punjab and in Malta six years; Instructor, R.M. Academy, Woolwich, seven years; passed Artillery College; Observer, transit of Venus Expedition to Jamaica, 1882; retired, 1889; took part in Missionary work in Galicia, Spain, 1892-94; rejoined the army at Woolwich during Boer War, 1900-2; retired half-pay Lt.-Col.; Assistant Inspector of Steel under the Admiralty in Yorkshire, 1915-16, during World War; Vice-President of the Victoria Institute. *Publications:* The Text Books of Gunnery, 1888 and 1887; The Magi, how they recognised Christ's Star (in which it was first demonstrated that 8 B.C. was the date of the Nativity), 1907; Recent Discoveries in St. Luke's Writings (in which the existence of three parallel narratives in St. Luke's Gospel was first pointed out), 1921. *Address:* Coverley, 4 Thornlaw Road, West Norwood, S.E.27. *(Died 1 Oct. 1928.)*

MACKINNON, Hon. Donald Alexander, K.C., LL.B.; M.P. for Queen's County, Prince Edward Island, since 1921; *b.* 21 Feb. 1863, of Scottish parentage; *m.* 1892, Louisa Owen (*d.* 1912) of Georgetown; one *s.* one *d. Educ.:* Prince of Wales College; Dalhousie University, Halifax; LL.B. Admitted to the Bar of P.E.I. 1887; Q.C. 1900; President Law Society of P.E.I. 1901; a Member of House of Assembly of P.E.I. 1893; re-elected 1897 for Murray Harbour Electrical District; Attorney-General in Provincial Cabinet; M.P. East Queen's, P.E.I., to House of Commons, Canada, 1900-4; Lieut.-Governor of P.E.I., Canada, 1904-10; Hon. Colonel, 82nd Regiment, 1909; President Law Society of P.E.I., 1916; Vice-President, British and Foreign Sailors Society for P.E.I.; Chief of Caledonian Club; Commissioner for Boy Scouts, P.E.I. appointed Honourable for life, 1927. *Publications:* The Constitution (P.E.I.); History of Queen's County; P.E.I. in 1950; joint editor of Past and Present Prince Edward Island. *Address:* Charlottetown, Prince Edward Island. *T.A.:* Fingon. *T.:* 64. *(Died April 1928.)*

MACKINNON, Sir Lauchlan Charles, Kt., *cr.* 1916; *b.* Corry, Broadford, Isle of Skye, 12 Apr. 1848; *s.* of late Alex. K. Mackinnon and Barbara, *d.* of Capt. Reid: *m.* 1876, Emily Grace

677

Mackinnon (*d.* 1923); one *s.* two *d.* *Educ.*: Bath; Finchley College, London. Went to Australia, 1870; General Manager of the Argus and Australasian, 1880-1920; proprietor of the Mackinnon share on the death of the original proprietor, Lauchlan Mackinnon, 1888. *Address:* Downes, Crediton, Devon. *Clubs:* Reform, Oriental; Melbourne, Australian, Melbourne. (*Died 3 Dec.* 1925.)

MACKINTOSH, Rt. Rev. Monsignor Alexander, Catholic Priest, Fort William; *b.* Inverness-shire, 1854 (Gaelic-speaking Highlander). *Educ.:* Blair's College, Aberdeen; Douai; Paris; St. Peter's Seminary, Glasgow. Ordained, 1877; Canon Theologian of Argyll and the Isles since 1907; Vicar General, 1917-18; Vicar Capitular (*sede vacante*), 1918-19; Protonotary Apostolic and Domestic Prelate, 1920. *Address:* The Presbytery, Fort William, Scotland.

MACKINTOSH, Charles Rennie, F.R.I.B.A., I.A.; corresponding member of the Künstler Osterreiche, Vienna; architect; artist; *b.* Glasgow, 1869; *y. s.* of William Mackintosh; *m.* 1900, Margaret. *Educ.:* Glasgow School of Art; Paris. Greek Thomson Scholar, 1889; travelled in France and Italy. *Works:* public, ecclesiastic, and domestic, executed in Scotland, England, Belgium, Germany, Austria, Italy, and Russia. *Publication:* Meister der Inner Kunst. *Recreations:* travel, research. *Address:* 2 Haus Studios, 43A Glebe Place, Chelsea, S.W.3. (*Died 10 Dec.* 1928.)

MACKINTOSH, Most Rev. Donald A.; Archbishop of Chersona, and Coadjutor-Archbishop of Glasgow, with the right of succession, since 1912; Provost of the Chapter; *b.* 1845. *Educ.:* France; Blairs College, Aberdeen. Ordained Priest, 1871; Vicar-General of the Archdiocese of Glasgow, 1909-12. *Address:* 5 Westbourne Gardens, Kelvinside, Glasgow. (*Died 13 Oct.* 1919.)

MACKINTOSH, Rev. William Lachlan, M.A. Oxon; Rector of St. Michael and All Angels, Inverness, since 1910, and Canon of the Cathedral since 1911; *e. s.* of late Eneas Mackintosh, J.P. and D.L. of Balnespick, Inverness-shire (*d.* 1893), and Isabella Lachlan, *d.* of Isaac Barker of Itonfield, Cumberland; *b.* Ballifeary (then Eilenach), Inverness, 31 Aug. 1859. *Educ.:* Marlborough College; Pembroke College, Oxon; Ely Theological College. Deacon, 1886; Priest, 1887; Assistant Curate, Wantage, Berks, 1887-91; Canon Residentiary of Inverness Cathedral with the charge of the Mission-Chapel of the Holy Spirit, 1891; succeeded to the property of Balnespick and Clune, Inverness-shire, on the death of his father, 1893; resigned his Canonry in order to work entirely at the Mission, 1902; endowed the Mission Chapel, so that it became an incumbency (St. Michael and All Angels), 1910. *Publications:* The Will of God in Daily Life, 1895; The Life of Archbishop Laud, 1907. *Recreation:* ecclesiology. *Address:* St. Michael's Lodge, Abban Street, Inverness; Balnespick, Tomatin, Inverness-shire. *Club:* Highland, Inverness. (*Died 20 April 1926.*)

M'KISACK, Henry Lawrence, M.D., F.R.C.P. (London); Consulting Physician; *b.* Carrickfergus, 27 Oct. 1859; *s.* of late James M'Kisack, Belfast, and Eleanor Sophia, *d.* of late Hill Willson of Purdysburn and Carrickfergus; *m.* Emily (*d.* 1927), *d.* of late Henry Matier, Dunlambert, Belfast; one *s.* one *d.* *Educ.:* Hillbrook, Holywood; Alfred House, Broadstairs; Queen's College, Belfast; post-graduate study in Dublin, London, and Birmingham. Graduated M.B. in R.U.I. with honours in 1887; Consulting Physician, Royal Victoria Hospital, Belfast; Ulster Volunteer Force Hospital, Lisburn and Hillsborough District Hospital, and to the Ministry of Pensions (Ulster Region); Pres. of Ulster Branch British Medical Associa-

678

tion, 1914-15; President of Ulster Medical Society, 1911-12; University Clinical Lecturer, Queen's University, Belfast; Fellow of Royal Society of Medicine, Member of Association of Physicians of Great Britain and Ireland, and of other Medical Associations; Director of Henry Matier and Co., Ltd., Belfast. *Publications:* Dictionary of Medical Diagnosis, 2nd edition; Aids to Case-Taking, 2nd edition; various papers on medical subjects. *Address:* 88 University Road, Belfast. *T.:* Belfast 829. *Clubs:* Royal Societies; Ulster, Belfast. (*Died 26 Mar.* 1928.)

MACKLIN, His Honour Albert Romer; Judge of County Court Circuit No. 37 (West London, Barnet, St. Albans, and Chesham), since 1919; *b.* 14 Nov. 1863; *s.* of late Albert Macklin and Mary, *d.* of Frank Romer; *m.* 1889, Martha Kate, *d.* of Benjamin John Warren, Deal; one *s.* one *d.* *Educ.:* City of London School; Caius College, Cambridge. 1st Class Classical Tripos, Part I., 1884; 1st Class Law Tripos, 1886; Chancellor's Medal for English Verse, 1886; Tancred Law Studentship; B.A., LL.B., 1886; called to Bar, 1889; joined South-Eastern Circuit; Revising Barrister, 1907-14; Legal Adviser to War Trade Department, Oct. to Dec. 1915; C.C. Judge Circuit 11, 1916-19. *Publication:* (with Lord Justice Vaughan Williams) the Article on Libel and Slander in Lord Halsbury's Laws of England. *Address:* 138 Gloucester Terrace, Hyde Park, W.2. (*Died 18 Aug.* 1921.)

MACLACHLAN, Lt.-Col. Alexander Fraser Campbell, D.S.O. 1902; 3rd Batt. K.R.R.C.; *b.* 23 July 1875. *Educ.:* Eton; Magdalen College, Oxford. B.A. 1897. Entered army, 1899; served South Africa, 1899-1902 (wounded, despatches, medal, four clasps, and King's medal); European War, 1914-17 (despatches, Bt. Lt.-Col.). *Address:* Newton Valence, Alton, Hants. (*Died 22 Mar.* 1918.)

MACLACHLAN, Brig.-Gen. Ronald Campbell, D.S.O. 1916; commanding 8th Batt. Rifle Brigade since 1914; *b.* 24 July 1872; *s.* of Mrs. Maclachlan, Newton Valence, Alton, Hants; *m.* Elinor Mary, *d.* of J. C. Cox, Sydney, and widow of Hon. Sidney Trench. *Educ.:* Cheam; Eton; R.M.C., Sandhurst. Hon. M.A. Oxford University; entered army, 1893; Capt. 1900; Major, 1910; Lt.-Col. 1915; served S. Africa, 1899-1900 (despatches, Queen's medal, 4 clasps); Tibet Expedition, 1903-4 (medal); European War, 1914-16 (D.S.O.). *Address:* Newton Valence, Alton, Hants. *Club:* Army and Navy. (*Died 11 Aug.* 1917.)

MACLACHLAN, Col. Thomas Robertson, C.M.G. 1915; 92nd Punjabis; *b.* 8 Apr. 1870. Served Thibet, 1903-4 (despatches, medal with clasp); N.W. Frontier, India, 1908 (medal with clasp); European War, Mesopotamia, 1914, 17 (C.M.G., Bt. Col.). (*Died 30 Oct.* 1921.)

McLAGAN, Archibald Gibson, C.I.E., of Pumpherston, Mid Calder, Scotland; senior partner in Turnbull, Gibson & Co.; *b.* 2 June 1853; *y. s.* of late Charles Gibson, Pitlochry, Perthshire; *m.*; one *s.* two *d.* *Educ.:* Church of Scotland School, Pitlochry; Perth Grammar School. Three years in a Liverpool merchant and shipping office; several years in India with a mercantile firm; returned from India for private family reasons and joined Turnbull, Gibson & Co. *Recreation:* fishing mostly. *Address:* 21 Bury Street, St. Mary Axe, E.C. 3. *T.A.:* Affreter, Ald, London. *T.:* Avenue 5701. *M.:* YN 8218. *Club:* Oriental. (*Died 15 May* 1928.)

M'LAREN, Hon. Francis (Walter Stafford); Flight Lieut. R.F.C.; M.P. (L.) Spalding Division, Lincs, since 1910; *s.* of 1st Baron Aberconway of Bodnant; *m.* 1911, Barbara, *d.* of Sir Herbert Jekyll; two *s.* *Educ.:* Eton; Balliol College, Oxford. Parlia-

M'KINNON, Rev. W. See page xxv.

mentary Secretary to Rt. Hon. Lewis Harcourt; Lieut. R.N.V.R. since 1914; on active service Dardanelles campaign with R.N. Armoured Car Squadron. *Address:* 8 Little College Street, S.W. *T.:* Victoria 8400. *Clubs:* Bachelors', Queen's.   (*Died 30 Aug. 1917.*)

MACLAREN, James Anderson, K.C. 1922; Member of Scottish Bar; *b.* Glasgow, 13 Sep. 1866; father, one of the magistrates of Glasgow; *m.* 1st, 1905, Margaret, *d.* of Robert Young, Crieff, Perthshire; three *s.* two *d.*; 2nd, 1926, Janet (*d.* 1926), *d.* of James Davie, Dunfermline. *Educ.:* Glasgow and Edinburgh Universities. Called to Scottish Bar, 1888; served South African War (Queen's medal with 5 clasps); settled for a time at Crieff, Perthshire, when became a magistrate of that borough and member of the Crieff School Board; returned to the Bar, 1909. *Publications:* Court of Session Practice—the standard work; Bill Chamber Practice; Expenses in the Supreme and Sheriff Courts. *Recreation:* walking.   (*Died 23 May 1926.*)

McLAREN, Sir John, K.B.E. *cr.* 1919, M.Inst.C.E., M.Inst.M.E., J.P., Chairman of J. & H. M'Laren, Ltd., Engineers, Leeds; *s.* of Henry M'Laren of Hylton Castle, Sunderland, and Jean, *d.* of John Buchanan, Gilchorn, Arbroath; *b.* 1 April 1850; *m.* 1881, Jane, *d.* of James M'Cracken, Glenapp; one *s.* three *d. Educ.:* Privately. Served on Royal Commission on International Exhibitions, Brussels, 1910; Turin and Rome, 1911; President Chamber of Commerce, Leeds, 1918-19; Chairman of the Management Board, and Board of Control of the National Ordnance Factories, Leeds, 1915-19. *Publications:* Contributor of papers to the Institution of Civil Engineers, Mining Engineers, Farmers' Club, etc. *Recreations:* shooting, fishing, etc. *Address:* Highfield House, Headingley, Leeds. *T.A.:* McLaren, Leeds. *T.:* Headingley, 292. *Clubs:* British Empire, Farmers', Leeds. (*Died 12 Oct. 1920.*)

MACLAREN, Hon. John James, D.C.L., LL.D.; Justice of Appeal, 1902-23; *b.* Lachute, Quebec; *s.* of late John Maclaren, a native of Callander, Scotland; *m.* 1st, 1870, Margaret G. Mathewson (*d.* 1875); 2nd, 1878, Mary E. Mathewson (*d.* 1906); one *s.* two *d. Educ.:* Victoria University; B.A. and Prince of Wales' Gold Medallist, 1862; LL.B. 1868; LL.D. 1886; McGill University, B.C.L. 1868; D.C.L. 1887. Was British Secretary of British and American Joint Commission on Oregon Claims, 1867-69; Advocate, Quebec, 1868; Q.C. 1878; Member of Bar Council and Law Examiner; removed from Montreal to Toronto, 1884; Barrister, Ontario, 1884; Hon. Lecturer on Comparative Jurisprudence, University of Toronto, 1886-90; Vice-Chancellor, Victoria University, and a Regent since 1870; Senator of University of Toronto since 1891; President of the World's Sunday School Convention at Tokyo, Japan, 1920. *Publications:* Bills, Notes, and Cheques, 1st edition 1892, 5th edition 1916; Banks and Banking, 1st edition 1896, 4th edition 1914; Roman Law in English Jurisprudence, 1887. *Address:* Osgoode Hall, Toronto, Canada.   (*Died July 1926.*)

MACLAREN, Major Kenneth, D.S.O. 1900; 13th Hussars; retired; *b.* 18 Oct. 1860; *m.* 1st, Leila Evelyn (*d.* 1904); one *d.*; 2nd, 1910, Ethel Mary Wilson. *Educ.:* Harrow School. Entered army, 1880; Captain, 1887 served North-West Frontier, India, 1897-1898 (despatches, medal with clasp); S. Africa, 1899-1900 (severely wounded, despatches, Queen's medal 3 clasps, D.S.O.). *Address:* Dunmar, Tighnabruaich, Argyllshire. *Club:* Naval and Military.   (*Died 20 Sept. 1924.*)

McLAREN, Rev. William David, M.A.; *b.* 31 Jan. 1856; *s.* of David McLaren and Helen Muir. *Educ.:* Edinburgh University. Con-

gregational Minister, Northampton, 1883-94; disabled by partial blindness; Biblical Lecturer, Free Churches' Council of England, 1898-1906; on Staff Congregational College, Melbourne, 1906-17. *Publications:* Our Growing Creed, 1912; articles, etc. *Address:* c/o National Provincial Union Bank, Putney, S.W.   (*Died 11 Nov. 1921.*)

McLAUGHLIN, Sir Henry, K.B.E., *cr.* 1919; Chairman McLaughlin & Harvey, Ltd., Belfast, Dublin, and London; *b.* 21 March 1876; *s.* of W. H. McLaughlin, D.L., of Macedon, Co. Antrim; *m.* 1899, Ethel, *d.* of W. S. Mollan, Belfast; two *d. Educ.:* Belfast Royal Academy; Mount Radford, Exeter. Past President Building Employers'Association, Dublin; Hon. Director Irish Recruiting, 1915-16; Director Red Cross Our Day Fund (Ireland), 1917; Member Lord French's Recruiting Council, 1918. *Recreations:* breeder of Scottish deerhounds, golf, swimming, tennis. *Address:* Riversdale, Monkstown, Co. Dublin. *Clubs:* National; St. Stephen's Green, Dublin.   (*Died 21 Nov. 1927.*)

M'LAURIN, Duncan, R.S.W.; Hon. Member of the Glasgow Art Club; *b.* Glasgow, 1848; *s.* of Duncan M'Laurin, Bank Agent; unmarried. *Educ.:* High School of Glasgow; Glasgow School of Design; Heatherly's Academy, London. Painting, Cattle by Stream, bought by the Corporation of Glasgow; painting, Home from the Plough, bought by the Scottish Modern Arts Association. *Address:* Bloomfield, Helensburgh.   (*Died 25 Jan. 1921.*)

MACLAURIN, Richard Cockburn, M.A., Sc.D., LL.D.; President, Massachusetts Institute of Technology, since 1909; *b.* Lindean, Scotland, 1870; *s.* of Rev. R.C. Maclaurin, M.A.; *m.* 1904, Margaret Alice Young; two *s. Educ.:* Auckland Grammar School; St. John's College, Cambridge. New Zealand University Scholar; Foundation Scholar, St. John's Coll. Cambridge; Class i. div. i. part ii. Mathematical Tripos; studied Strassburg University, 1895; Smith's Prizeman (Mathematics), Cambridge University, 1897; M'Mahon Studentship (Law), St. John's College, 1897; Member Lincoln's Inn; Yorke Prizeman (Law), Cambridge University, 1898; Fellow of St. John's College, 1897-1903; Prof. Mathematics, Victoria College, New Zealand Univ., 1898-1905; Dean Faculty of Law, N.Z., 1905-7; Prof. Mathematical Physics, Columbia Univ., New York, 1907-9; LL.D. (Cambridge), 1905; Sc.D. (Cambridge), 1908; Sc.D. (Dartmouth), 1909; LL.D. (Wesleyan), 1909; LL.D. (Harvard), 1910; LL.D. (Denison), 1914. *Publications:* Title to Realty; The Theory of Light; Light; numerous papers published by Royal Society, Philosophical Magazine, Revue Scientifique, Cambridge Philosophical Society, etc. *Recreation:* travelling. *Address:* Cambridge, Mass. *Clubs:* St. Botolph, University, Tavern, Union, Engineer's, Commercial, Boston; Technology New York; Cosmos, Washington.   (*Died 15 Jan. 1920.*)

MACLAVERTY, Edward Hyde East, I.S.O. 1907; late Senior Collector of Revenue, Jamaica; *b.* 19 Mar. 1847; *s.* of Rev. Colin Maclaverty, M.A.; *m.* 1875, Elizabeth, *d.* of late Edward Claver Smith of Spanish Town, Jamaica. *Address:* Dulce Domum, Kingston, Jamaica.   (*Died 5 Oct. 1922.*)

MACLEAN, Rev. Alexander Miller, C.M.G. 1916; D.D. (Edin.); Minister of the First Charge of the Abbey of Paisley since 1910; Chaplain in Ordinary to His Majesty for Scotland since 1914; *b.* Argyllshire, 1865; *e. s.* of late Rev. Lachlan Maclean, Minister of North Knapdale; *m.* 1890, Mary, *o. c.* of Robert Brown, Edinburgh; one *d. Educ.:* Royal High School and University, Edinburgh. Graduated in Arts, 1884, in Divinity in 1887; ordained Minister of Turriff, Aberdeenshire, 1889; translated to Cramond, Midlothian, 1896; Peebles,

1906; represented the Church of Scotland in India and inaugurated the Scots Church of St. Andrew, Simla, 1904; promoted in 1911 a scheme of restoration and improvement of surroundings of the Abbey for which nearly £70,000 has been subscribed, and the work is now in progress; Vice-Convener of the Highland Committee of the Church of Scotland, 1914; Chaplain (successively) to the 5th Gordons, Edinburgh City Artillery, and Renfrewshire R.E.; served at the Front with the British Expeditionary Force, 1914-16, also 1918-19 (despatches, C.M.G.). *Publications:* With the Gordons at Ypres; Queen Victoria and her Time; Paisley Abbey Restoration; articles in various magazines and newspapers. *Recreations:* fishing, golfing, curling. *Address:* The Abbey Manse, Paisley. *T.A.:* Paisley. *T.:* Paisley 2527.

(*Died 6 Mar. 1925.*)

MACLEAN, Allan, C.M.G. 1916; Consul-General, Valparaiso, since 1918; *b.* 18 Mar. 1858. Consul at Dar-al-Baida, 1893; Bilbao, 1906; Dantzig, 1910. *Address:* Valparaiso, Chile.

(*Died Oct. 1918.*)

MACLEAN, Charles Donald, M.A., Mus. Doc.; *b.* Cambridge, 27 March 1843; *e. s.* of late Rev. A. J. Macleane. *Educ.:* Shrewsbury; Exeter Coll., Oxford (scholar); studied music under Ferd. Hiller of Cologne. Indian Civil Service (Madras), 1865-93, and was there Inspector of Schools, Cantonment Magistrate, Supervisor Government Press, Small Cause Court Judge, Sub-Secretary Board of Revenue, Under-Secretary to Government, Government Translator in Tamil and Canarese, Judge and Collector in Chingleput, Madras, Nellore, Neilgherry, Salem districts; various special duties, etc.; Organist Exeter College, Oxford, 1868-65; Organist and Music-director, Eton Coll. 1871-75; Organist, Crystal Palace, 1880; Lecturer; many orchestral works performed at Crystal Palace and elsewhere; Vice-President Orchestral Association and Musical Association of Great Britain, and Royal College of Organists; member Philharmonic Society, and Society of British Composers; General Secretary and English Editor of the International Musical Society. *Publications:* Madras Manual of Administration, 3 vols., Polyglot report of London Congress, History of Modern English Music in Paris Encyclopédie, and many contributions to Press. *Recreation:* Captain, National Reserve. *Address:* 61 Drayton Gardens, South Kensington, S.W. *T.:* 2087 Western. *Clubs:* Athenæum, United University, Services, Playgoers.

(*Died 23 June 1916.*)

MACLEAN, Maj.-Gen. Charles Smith, C.B. 1881, C.I.E. 1888; Indian Staff Corps; *b.* 15 Dec. 1836; *m.* 1869, Margaret, *d.* of Peter Bairnsfather. Entered army, 1853; Maj.-Gen. 1898; served Indian Mutiny, 1857 (severely wounded, medal with clasp); China, 1860 (medal with two clasps); Afghan War, 1878-80 (despatches several times, Brevet Lieut.-Col., C.B., medal with clasp): Mahsood-Wuzeeree Expedition, 1881; Consul-General for Khorassan and Sistan, 1889-91. (*Died 15 July 1921.*)

M'LEAN, Hon. Sir George, Kt. *cr.* 1909; C.M.G. 1909; J.P.; Memb. of Legislative Council, N.Z., since 1882; *b.* Elgin, N.B., 10 Sep. 1834; *y. s.* of James M'Lean (and Jane Proctor) of Scotston Hill, Co. Elgin; *m.* 1867, Isabel, *d.* of Hon. Matthew Holmes, M.L.C., Wellington; one *s.* five *d.* *Educ.:* Elgin Grammar School; St. Andrews. Came out to Melbourne about 1852; joined Oriental Bank, 1859; appointed Manager of Bank of New Zealand, Dunedin, 1862; became member of mercantile firm, Cargills and M'Lean, 1868, returned member of Provincial Council for Waikonaiti; Provincial Treasurer, 1869; returned member of House of Representatives for Waikonaiti; Postmaster-General, 1876; and a member of two

later ministries. *Address:* Hazelwood, Dunedin, N.Z. *T.A.:* Dunedin. *T.:* 238. *Club:* Fernhill, Dunedin. (*Died 17 Feb. 1917.*)

MACLEAN, Lt.-Col. Henry Donald Neil, D.S.O. 1900; late K.O.S.B.; *b.* 24 June 1872. Entered army, 1893; Capt. 1900; served North-West Frontier, India, 1897-98 (medal with two clasps); South Africa, 1899-1902 (despatches, Queen's medal 3 clasps, King's medal 2 clasps, D.S.O.); European War, 1914-17 (despatches, Bt. Lt.-Col.); retired pay, 1922. (*Died 25 Aug. 1926.*)

McLEAN, Col. James Reynolds, C.B.E. 1918; Deputy Director General of Recruiting; *b.* 1872; *m.* 1900, Emma Margaret, *d.* of Lawrence Steele, Southampton. *Educ.:* Edinburgh and Cambridge Universities. *Address:* Greenaleigh, Fydian Road, Cardiff.

(*Died 3 July 1921.*)

MACLEAN, John Cassilis Birkmyre, C.B. 1917; Surgeon Rear-Admiral, retired; *b.* 26 Aug. 1849; *s.* of Rev. A. Maclean, D.D.; *m.* 1892, Maude, *e. d.* of late E. Hewlett, The Priory, Totnes; one *s.* *Educ.:* Aberdeen University Entered R.N. 1872; retired, 1907; present at bombardment of Alexandria and in Egyptian Campaign, 1882 (specially promoted). *Address:* 12 Penlee Gardens, Devonport. *T.:* Devonport 360. *M.:* CO 7136. *Club:* Royal Western Yacht. (*Died 25 Dec. 1925.*)

McLEAN, John Roll, proprietor of the Cincinnati Enquirer; *b.* Cincinnati, 17 Sep. 1848. *Educ.:* public schools, Cincinnati; Harvard. Bought interest of his father, Washington McLean, in Cincinnati Enquirer, afterwards purchasing the other interests; prominent in State and National Democratic politics; Democratic candidate for governor, Ohio, 1899; is Ohio Member Democratic National Committee. *Address:* Washington. (*Died 9 June 1916.*)

MACLEAN, Kaid, General Sir Harry Aubrey de, K.C.M.G.; *cr.* 1901; C.M.G. 1898; *b.* 15 June 1848; *s.* of Andrew Maclean of the Macleans of Drimnin); *m.* 1st, Catherine Coe (whom he divorced 1905); three *d.*; 2nd, 1913, Ella, *d.* of late General Sir Harry Prendergast, V.C. Formerly in 69th Foot; became Instructor to the Moorish Army under the late Sultan, and accompanied him in his expeditions; Colonel of Sultan of Morocco's Bodyguard; captured by Raisuli, July 1907, while on a mission from the Sultan, and held a prisoner for seven months. *Decorated* for services rendered to British Government. *Address:* Tangier, Morocco. *Clubs:* Junior Carlton, Caledonian, St. Stephen's, Royal Automobile.

(*Died 4 Feb. 1920.*)

MACLEANE, Rev. Douglas, M.A.; Public Preacher, Salisbury Diocese; Canon of Salisbury since 1910; Proctor in Convocation since 1906; *b.* at Bath, 1856; *s.* of Rev. Arthur Macleane (Editor of Bibliotheca Classica; First Principal of Brighton College); *b.* of Bishop of Moray and Ross, and of late Charles Maclean, Mus. Doc., I.C.S.); *m.* 1887, Augusta S. Wightwick; two *d.* *Educ.:* Christ's Hospital (2nd Grecian), Scholar and Fellow, Pembroke College, Oxford; Curate of Great Witley, Worcester, 1879-82; Domestic Chaplain to Earl of Craven, 1882-85; Fellow of Pembroke, Oxford, 1882-91; Rector of Codford St. Peter, Wilts, 1885-1914; Vicar of Branksome Park, Dorset, 1915-22; Diocesan Warden of Sacred Study since 1907; Examining Chaplain to Bishop of Moray since 1904; Fellow of SS. Mary and Andrew, Taunton, since 1911; President, East Dorset Branch of E.C.U., 1914-25; of Sarum District Union, 1923. *Publications:* A History of Pembroke College, Oxford, 1897; Oxford College Histories (Pembroke), 1900; The Great Solemnity of the Coronation, 1902; Reason, Thought, and Language, 1906; Our Island Church, 1909;

Lancelot Andrewes, 1910.; Statutes of Salisbury Cathedral (co-editor), 1913; Equality and Fraternity, 1924; many contributions to reviews and magazines; on staff of Saturday Review and Church Times. *Recreations:* rowed in College boat. *Address:* The Close, Salisbury, *T.A.:* Salisbury. *Club:* Authors'.
(*Died 31 Aug. 1925.*)

MACLEAR, Lt.-Col. Harry, D.S.O., 1915; 2nd Batt. East Lancs. Regt.; *b.* 16 Feb. 1872. Entered army, 1891; Captain, 1900; Major, 1910; special service Somaliland Field Force, 1903-4; employed with West African Frontier Force, 1905-1907; Provost Marshal Mohmand Field Force, 1908; served Chitral, 1895 (medal with clasp); N.W. Frontier, India, 1897-98 (clasp); East Africa, 1903-4 (medal with clasp); European War, 1914-15 (D.S.O.).   (*Died 15 Mar. 1916.*)

McLEARN, Sir William, Kt., *cr.* 1900; Head of William McLearn and Co., Railway Contractors; *b.* 1837; Mayor of Londonderry 1899 and 1900; Chair. Technical School Com.; also representing the Londonderry Borough Council on the Agriculture and Technical Instruction Board for Ireland. *Address:* Carrickmore, Londonderry. (*Died 14 April 1918.*)

M'LEISH, Col. Duncan, C.M.G. 1900; C.B.E.; V.D.; commands 3rd Brigade Australian Light Horse (V.M.R.); *b.* 20 July 1851; 2nd *s.* of Duncan and Catherine M'Leish, formerly of Scotland; unmarried. *Educ.:* private tuition. Entered Victorian Mounted Rifles, 1886; served with that corps up till leaving for service in South Africa, 1899; Major, 1900; returned to Australia, 1900, and rejoined his old regiment; commanded 2nd Batt. Australian Horse, 1902 to end of war; returned to Australia shortly afterwards; Lt.-Col. 1908; retired list, 1911; served European War, 1914-16. *Address:* Glenmore, Yea, Victoria, Australia. *Clubs:* Naval and Military; Melbourne Stock Exchange. (*Died 17 April 1920.*)

M'LELLAN, C. M. S., playwright; *b.* Bath, Maine, U.S.A., 1865. *Educ.:* Boston. Editor and dramatic critic in New York until 1897, since lived in England; plays produced in London: Leah Kleschna, Glittering Gloria, On the Love Path The Jury of Fate; and The Strong People, 1910; wrote under the name of Hugh Morton the libretti of The Belle of New York, An American Beauty, The Girl from Up There, and Nelly Neil, produced in London; and In Gay New York, The Whirl of The Town, Yankee Doodle Dandy, Puritania, The Honeymooners, and The Telephone Girl.
(*Died 22 Sept. 1916.*)

M'LENNAN, Lt.-Col. Bartlett, D.S.O. 1917; O.C. 42nd Canadian Battalion The Royal Highlanders of Canada; *b.* Montreal, 10 Nov. 1868; *y. s.* of late Hugh M'Lennan; unmarried. *Educ.:* Lyall School, Sorel; Royal Military College, Kingston. In business in Montreal; Director Montreal Telegraph Co., Canada Sugar Refining Co., Canadian Explosives Co., Mundeth & Co. Ltd.; went to France, Oct. 1915, with 42nd Canadian Batt. (despatches twice, D.S.O.); Lt.-Col. 1917. *Recreations:* hunting and polo. *Address:* 50 Ontario Avenue, Montreal, Canada. *Clubs:* Bath; Mount Royal, Montreal.   (*Died 3 Aug. 1918.*)

MACLENNAN, Hon. Farquhar Stuart; Puisne Judge Superior Court and Deputy Local Judge in Admiralty. *Address:* Montreal, Canada.   (*Died 18 June 1925.*)

M'LENNAN, John Ferguson, K.C. 1905; Advocate; Sheriff of Caithness, Orkney, and Zetland since 1905; *b.* Inverness, 3 Oct. 1855; *o. s.* of late Malcolm M'Lennan, Procurator-Fiscal of Caithness, and author of Peasant Life in the North; unmarried; *Educ.:* Inverness Academy; Grammar School, Old Aberdeen; Universities: Aberdeen (M.A.), 1875; Edinburgh (LL.B.), 1879; Forensic Prizeman, 1878; Edinburgh University Endowment Association Law Fellowship, 1879. Scotch Bar, 1881. *Ad-*

dress: 20 Heriot Row, Edinburgh. *Clubs:* Royal Societies; Northern, Scottish Arts, Edinburgh.   (*Died 1 June 1917.*)

MACLEOD, Admiral Angus, C.V.O. 1904; *b.* 11 June 1847; *m.* 1st, Rose, *d.* of R. Hickson, and *widow* of J. R. Pollock; 2nd, Jane Margaret (*d.* 1906), *d.* of Captain J. B. Forster, 62nd Wiltshire Regiment; one *s.* [Major Murray Macleod, O.B.E., R.A.; *m.* 1919, Phillis, *y. d.* of William Boosey, Streatley]. Entered navy, 1860; Lieut. 1868; Commander, 1881; Captain, 1888; Rear-Admiral, 1901; Vice-Admiral, 1905; Admiral, 1910; served Gold Coast, 1874 (slightly wounded, despatches, Ashantee medal, Coomassie clasp); Senior Naval Officer, Gulf of Siam, 1893; A.D.C. to Queen Victoria and to King Edward VII., 1899-1901; Director of Naval Ordnance, Admiralty; Senior Officer, Coast of Ireland, 1904-6; retired, 1910. *Address:* 87 Victoria Street, S.W.; Holmisdal, Glendale, Isle of Skye. *Clubs:* United Service, National.
(*Died 29 April 1920.*)

M'LEOD, Clement Henry, F.R.S. Canada and Member American Astronomical Society; Professor of Geodesy, M'Gill Univ., Montreal, since 1888; Vice-Dean of the Faculty of Applied Science, 1908. *Educ.:* M'Gill University. Consulting Engineer; Superintendent of the Observatory, M'Gill College; Fellow of M'Gill University; Member of the Canadian Society of Civil Engineers. Determined difference of longitude, in co-operation with Greenwich Observatory, Montreal and Greenwich, in 1892, and other longitudes in Canada; various astronomical expeditions. *Publications:* publications in the Transactions of the Royal Society of Canada, astronomical, meteorological, and physical subjects; Transactions, Canadian Soc. of Civil Engineers; meteorological reports. *Address:* M'Gill College, Montreal, Canada.
(*Died 26 Dec. 1917.*)

MACLEOD, Very Rev. Donald, D.D., V.D.; Chaplain in Ordinary to the King in Scotland; acting editor of Good Words, 1872-1905; Emeritus Minister of Parish of The Park, Glasgow; *b.* Campsie, Stirlingshire; *s.* of Norman Macleod, D.D., Dean of the Chapel Royal; Celtic Scholar and Author; *b.* of Norman Macleod, D.D., Dean of Chapel Royal and Dean of the Thistle, first editor of Good Words, and author; *m.* Isabella, *d.* of James Anderson of Highholm, Renfrewshire; three *s.* one *d.* *Educ.:* different schools; Univ. of Glas. (B.A.). Travelled two years; first parish Lauder; subsequently Linlithgow; Moderator of the Assembly of the Church of Scotland, 1895-96; Convener of the Home Mission Committee of the Church of Scotland from 1888-1900. *Publications:* Memoir of Norman Macleod, D.D.; Sunday Home Service; Christ and Society; The Doctrine and Validity of the Ministry and Sacraments of the National Church of Scotland, Baird Lecture, 1903; many contributions to Good Words; lectures on the Reformation, the Parochial System, and Dr. Chalmers, in the St. Giles' Series. *Address:* 8 Tipperlinn Road, Edinburgh. *Clubs:* Western, Glasgow; University, Edinburgh.
(*Died 11 Feb. 1916.*)

M'LEOD, Gen. Sir Donald James Sim, K.C.B., *cr.* 1913; K.C.I.E., *cr.* 1906; C.B., 1898; D.S.O. 1887; Colonel 28th Light Cavalry; retired, 1906; *b.* India, 22 Feb. 1845; 2nd *s.* of Lt.-Gen. W. C. M'Leod; *m.* Camilla, *e. d.* of Major J. Nicholas, 1877; one *s.* one *d.* *Educ.:* Kensington Proprietary School. Joined Madras Cavalry, 1861; served on Army Staff, India, 1877-88; D.Q.M.G. Madras Army, on service in Burma, 1886-87 (medal, D.S.O.); commanding 3rd Madras Lancers, 1890-93; A.A.G. District, 1893-95; Brig.-Gen. commanding a 2nd Class District, 1895-1900; Maj.-Gen. commanding 1st Class District, 1901-1908; Lt.-Gen. commanding Burma Division, 1903-6. *Address:* 99 Barkston

M'LEOD, Hon. Donald. See page xxv.

Gardens, S.W.5. *T.:* Western 2789. *Club:* United Service. *(Died 16 Jan. 1922.)*

McLEOD, Hon. Sir Ezekiel, Kt. *cr.* 1917; Chief Justice Supreme Court, New Brunswick, since 1914; *b.* 29 Oct. 1840. *Educ.:* High School, Cardwell, King's Co., N.B.; Harvard. Called to Bar, 1868; Q.C., 1882; Member Provincial Legislature, 1882-86; Attorney-Gen., 1882-83; Member House of Commons, 1891-96; a Senator of the University of New Brunswick; late Judge, Supreme Court, and Judge, Vice-Admiralty, New Brunswick. *Address:* St. John, New Brunswick. *(Died 11 June 1920.)*

M'LEOD, Hon. Harry Fulton, B.A., K.C. 1910; M.P.; represented York County in New Brunswick Parliament, 1908; Solicitor-General for Province, 1908; Provincial Secretary and Receiver-General, New Brunswick, 1911; resigned from N.B. Government. Dec. 1913; M.P. 1913, and as supporter of Union Government and Conscription, 17 Dec. 1917; *b.* Fredericton, N.B., 14 Sep. 1871; United Empire Loyalist descent; *s.* of Rev. J. M'Leod, D.D.; *m.* 1909, Ina F., *d.* of Lt.-Col. G. W. Mersereau; one *s.* two *d.* *Educ.:* Fredericton Collegiate School; University N.B. (first Honour Man and Gold Medallist). Admitted to Bar of N.B. 1895; contested N.B. Parliament, 1903; Mayor of Fredericton, 1907-8. Grand Master L.C.L. of New Brunswick, 1906-7; Lieut.-Col. of 71st York Regiment since 1909; O/C 12th Batt. 1st Division Canadian Expeditionary Force, Aug. 1914-July 1916; Colonel, with command Divisional troops, Shorncliffe, England, July 1916. *Address:* Fredericton, N.B., Canada. *Clubs:* Fredericton City, Fredericton Bicycling and Boating; Union, St. John, N.B.; Laurentian, Ottawa.

(Died 7 Jan. 1920.)

M'LEOD, Herbert, Hon. LL.D. St. Andrews; F.R.S., F.C.S.; Hon. Director Royal Society Catalogue of Scientific Papers; *b.* Stoke Newington, 19 Feb. 1841; *o. s.* of Bentley M'Leod. *Educ.:* Stockwell Grammar School; private school at Deal. Assistant Chemist in the School of Mines, 1860-71, under Professors A. W. Hofmann and E. Frankland; Professor of Chemistry, Royal Indian Engineering College, Cooper's Hill, 1871-1901; President of Section B. British Association, 1892; formerly Examiner in Chemistry in the Universities of Oxford, London, Birmingham, and Cambridge, and to the Pharmaceutical Society; has contributed papers to the Royal, Chemical, and Physical Societies. *Address:* 109 Church Road, Richmond, Surrey. *(Died 1 Oct. 1923.)*

MACLEOD, James John, C.I.E. 1896; Indigo planter, Tirhoot, India; *b.* Snizort, Isle of Skye, 9 Nov. 1841; 4th *surv. s.* of Rev. Roderick Macleod of Snizort. *Educ.:* Edinburgh Institution and University of Edinburgh. Lieut.-Col. Behar Light Horse. *Decorated* as a leading planter and a prominent member of the Behar Light Horse; officiated commandant on several occasions. *Recreations:* steeplechase-riding, polo, pig-sticking. *Address:* Lalseriah, Segowlie, Chumparun, India. *Club:* Bengal, Calcutta. *(Died 24 Feb. 1919.)*

MACLEOD, John, I.S.O. 1902; late H.M. Inspector of Schools; retired; *b.* Bonar Bridge, 1839; *s.* of Roderick Macleod; *g.-g.-g.s.* of Roderick Macleod of Assynt, and *c.* Elizabeth, *d.* of Macleod of Assynt; *m.* 1st, Jane Emily, *d.* of Lieutenant-Colonel Myers, 71st H.L.I.; one *s.* one *d.*; 2nd, 1903, Katharine Louisa, *e. d.* of late Wadham Locke Sutton of Rossway, Herts; one *d.* *Educ.:* Glasgow University. Was successively Professor of Mathematics in King's College, N.S.; Assistant to the Professor of Mathematics in the University of Glasgow; Mathematical Instructor in the Royal Military Academy, Woolwich; elected Fellow of the Mathematical Society of London, 1872. *Publications:* Reminiscences; numerous original theorems in pure geometry. *Recreation:* golf;

was twice elected Captain of the Moray Golf Club. *Address:* Fairfield, Nairn.

(Died 5 July 1927.)

MACLEOD, Colonel Kenneth, M.D., F.R.C.S.E.; Hon. Physician to the King; Indian Medical Service (retired); *b.* North Uist, Inverness-shire, 23 July 1840; *s.* of Rev. Norman Macleod, relative of Rev. Norman Macleod, D.D., Glasgow; twice married; four *s.* six *d.* *Educ.:* Aberdeen and Edinburgh Univs. A.M., LL.D., Aberdeen University; Fellow of University of Calcutta; Hon. Fellow, Royal College of Surgeons of England. Graduated in Edinburgh with distinction, 1861; Assistant Medical Officer, Durham County Asylum, 1861-65; entered Indian Medical Service, 1865; retired, 1892; held successively appointments of Civil Surgeon of Jessore, medical charge of 6th Bengal Light Infantry; Member and Secretary, Cattle Plague Commission; Secretary, Medical Department, Professor of Anatomy and of Surgery, Calcutta Medical College; appointed Member of Medical Board, India Office, 1893; appointed Professor of Military Medicine, Army Medical School, Netley, 1897. *Publications:* Medico-legal Experience in Bengal, 1876; Operative Surgery in the Calcutta Medical College Hospital, 1885; Epidemic Dropsy, 1893; Nerve Splitting and Stretching, 1894; numerous communications to medical periodicals and societies, and official reports; editor, Indian Medical Gazette, 1870-1892. *Recreation:* golf. *Address:* Duncaple, Westend, Hampshire. *T.A.:* Westend, Southampton. *(Died 17 Dec. 1922.)*

M'LEOD, Norman F., *b.* Madras, India, June 1858; *s.* of General W. C. M'Leod, Madras Army; unmarried. *Educ.:* Clifton College; R.I.E. College, Cooper's Hill. Public Works Department, United Provinces, India, 1878; Superintending Engineer, 1903; Chief Engineer and Secretary to Government Irrigation, 1905-11; Member of Legislative Council, United Provinces, 1909-11; retired, 1911. *Address:* c/o H. S. King & Co., Pall Mall, S.W.1. *Club:* East India United Service.

(Died 20 April 1921.)

McLEOD, Brig.-Gen. William Kelty, C.S.I. 1919; late R.A.; *s.* of late Lt.-Gen. W. K. McLeod; *b.* 1862; *m.* 1920, Mary Forrester, *d.* of late James Lumsden, Huntingtowerfield, Perth; one *d.* *Educ.:* Trinity College, Glenalmond; Royal Military Academy, Woolwich. Served N.W. Frontier of India, 1897-98 (medal with clasp); European War, 1914-19 (despatches, C.S.I.). *Address:* Greenbank, Perth. *T.:* Perth 114. *(Died 22 Nov. 1928.)*

McMAHON, Col. Bernard William Lynedoch, C.M.G.; C.V.O. 1925; Equerry to Princess Louise, Duchess of Argyll; *b.* 10 Oct. 1865; *s.* of Major William McMahon, late 14th Light Dragoons; unmarried. *Educ.:* Wellington College. Durham Light Infantry, 1885-1915; served S. African war, 1899-1902 (Queen's medal with four clasps, King's medal with two clasps, Brevet of Major); Commandant School of Musketry; served European War (1914 Star, British War Medal, Victory Medal, C.M.G.). *Address:* The Mount, Penshurst, Kent. *T.A.:* Penshurst. *Club:* Junior United Service.

(Died 23 Dec. 1928.)

M'MAHON, Sir Lionel, of the City of Dublin, 4th Bt.; *cr.* 1815; *b.* 30 June 1856; *s.* of 2nd Bt. and Maria Catherine, *sis.* of Sir Thomas Bateson, Bt. (*cr.* 1st Baron Deramore); *m.* 1888, Annie Cecilia Austin-Cooke (*d.* 1923). *Educ.:* Rugby. Late Lieut. 58th Regt.; Barrister-at-law, Inner Temple, 1888; D.L. Co. Tyrone; High Sheriff, Co. Tyrone, 1914. *Heir:* none. *Address:* Mountfield Lodge, Omagh, Co. Tyrone.

(Died 20 Feb. 1926.)

MACMANUS, Joseph Edward; First Acting Editor of the Daily Mail, 1896-98; Editor of The Morning, 1898; Assist. Director for Great

Britain of Le Figaro, Paris, 1905. Author of many short plays, verses, and songs. Qualified as a Solicitor, but has never practised. *Recreations:* sailing, motoring. *Address:* 85 Eldon Chambers, Fleet Street, E.C. *T.:* Bearable, London. *Clubs:* Press, Amateur Camping, London.

(*Died 17 June 1921.*)

MACMASTER, Sir Donald, 1st Bt., *cr.* 1921; K.C., D.C.L.; Barrister Quebec, 1871; Ontario, 1882; Q.C. 1882; Lincoln's Inn, 1906; M.P. (U.), Chertsey Division, Surrey, since 1910; (Co.U.) since 1918; *b.* Williamstown, 3rd Sep. 1846; *o. s.* of Donald Macmaster and Mary Cameron; *m.* 1st, 1880, Janet (*d.* 1883), *d.* of Ranald Sandfield Macdonald, Lancaster, Ont.; 2nd, 1890, Ella Virginia, *d.* of Isaac Deford, Baltimore, Md.; two *d.* *Educ.:* Grammar School, Williamstown, Ont.; M'Gill University, Montreal. B.C.L.; Elizabeth Torrance gold medal, prize essayist and valedictorian, 1871; D.C.L. 1894; served as Crown prosecutor in several Canadian *causes célèbres*, and as Arbitrator between Newfoundland Government and Reid-Newfoundland Railway, 1904-5; Counsel for United States Government in Gaynor and Green Extradition Inquiry and Appeals thereon to Judicial Committee of Privy Council, before which he now practises his profession; appointed on Royal Commission to inquire into matters concerning good government of Quebec, 1892; Pres. of Montreal Bar, 1904; twice elected Pres. of McGill Soc. and President of St. Andrews Society, Montreal; member for Glengarry in Ontario Legislature, 1879-82; M.P. Conservative, Canadian House of Commons, 1882-86; Unionist candidate for Leigh Division of Lancashire, 1906; Member of the Speaker's Conference for reform of representation and franchise. *Publication:* Monograph, The Seal Arbitration at Paris, 1894. *Recreations:* golf and travel. *Address:* 57 Sloane Gardens, S.W.1. *Clubs:* Carlton, Constitutional; St. James's, Montreal.

(*Died 3 Mar. 1922.*)

M'MICHAEL, Solon William, I.S.O. 1908; Chief and General Inspector of Customs for Dominion of Canada since 1894, and Member of the Board of Customs for Canada since 1895; *b.* Waterford, Ontario, 18 Nov. 1848; *e. s.* of late Aaron M'Michael, J.P.; *m.* Josephine, *d.* of Charles Shoemaker, Muncy, Penn., U.S.A.; one *s.* one *d.* *Educ.:* Simcoe Grammar School. Appointed to Customs, 1878; Financial Inspector of Customs for Dominion, 1885. *Address:* 101 St. George Street, Toronto, Canada. *T.A.:* M'Michael, Toronto. *T.:* College 6006. *M.:* 20200. *Club:* National, York Downs Golf and County, Toronto. (*Died 24 Sept. 1923.*)

McMILLAN, Alec, M.A.; 2nd *s.* of late John McMillan, J.P., Castramont, Stewartry of Kirkcudbright; *m.* 1888, Nellie, *d.* of James Fortescue Harrison, J.P. (M.P. 1874-80), author of The Evolution of Daphne and other novels, author and composer of Night Winds and other songs. *Educ.:* Aldenham School; Brasenose College, Oxford. Exhibitioner, Merton College, Scholar, Brasenose College, 1864; 1st class Classical Moderations, 1866. In I.C.S., 1868-94; Under-Secretary to Government, N.W.P. and Oudh, 1874-77; District Judge, Meerut, 1884; Agra, 1886; Cawnpore, 1890; Lucknow, 1892; Barr., Inner Temple, 1883; Professor of Indian Jurisprudence and Indian History, King's College, London, 1899-1902; H.M. Consul for the Alpes Maritimes and Monaco, 1902-10; originated Memorial Scheme that eventuated in erection of Queen Victoria Memorial Hospital at Nice. *Publications:* Divers Ditties, 1895; Portentous Prophets and Prophetesses, 1898; Mainly About Robert Bruce, 1901; Essence of Ecclesiastes, in Metre of Omar Khayyám (under nom de plume Alastair Buchanan), 1904. *Club:* Hurlingham.

(*Died 11 June 1919.*)

McMILLAN, Rev. Charles D. H., Vicar of Malmesbury with St. Mary, Westport, since 1907; Hon. Canon of Bristol Cathedral, 1911; Rural Dean of Malmesbury, 1912; *s.* of late Charles S. McMillan, of Bristol; *m.* 1890, Alice Mary, *e. d.* of late Samuel Mackenzie, of Bayswater. *Educ.:* King's School, Bruton; Wadham College, Oxford. B.A. 1888 (2nd Class Modern History); M.A. 1892; Curate of Stanley, Yorks, 1889-91; Wakefield Cathedral, 1891-92; Vicar of St. John's Church, Wakefield, 1892-1907; Hon. Canon of Wakefield Cathedral, 1906-7; Chairman of Wakefield School Board, 1901-3. *Publication:* The Sleeping Cardinal and other Sermons. *Address:* Malmesbury.

(*Died 6 May 1919.*)

MACMILLAN, Rev. Donald, M.A., D.D.; Clerk to Synod of Glasgow and Ayr since 1913; Hastie Lecturer in the University of Glasgow, 1906-9; *b.* Skipness, Argyllshire, May 1855; *m.* 1889, Edith, 2nd *d.* of John H. Worthington, Manchester; two *s.* *Educ.:* Glasgow University; Jena. Ordained to parish of Wanlockhead, 1883; translated to parish of Auchtertool, 1886; translated to Kelvinhaugh Parish, Glasgow, 1891; retired, 1923; editor of Church of Scotland Sabbath School Magazine, 1899-1900; editor of Saint Andrew, 1899-1905; Pres. of the Knox Club, 1911; Convener of Church of Scotland's Pension Fund for Ministers, 1917; Senior Grand Chaplain Grand Lodge of Scotland, 1918; Vice-Convener of Aged and Infirm Ministers Fund and Pension Fund, 1921. *Publications:* edited late Professor Hastie's Outlines of Pastoral Theology, 1904; John Knox, A Biography, 1905; George Buchanan, A Biography, 1906; Life of the Rev. Dr. George Matheson, 1907; The Aberdeen Doctors, 1610-88, 1909; A Short History of the Scottish People, 1911; Life of Professor Flint, 1914; Patriotism and Religion, 1917; Socialist and Proletarian Sunday Schools: A Menace to the Church, 1923; The Life of Professor Hastie, 1926; articles on theological subjects to various journals, magazines, and reviews. *Recreation:* golf. *Address:* Knapdale, Forest Row, Sussex. *Club:* Conservative, Glasgow.

(*Died 27 Mar. 1927.*)

MACMILLAN, Michael, D.Litt.; Fellow Bombay Univ.; Wilson Philological Lecturer, 1882, 1891, 1895, 1901, 1905; English Lecturer, Birmingham University, 1905-20; *b.* Newton-Stewart, N.B., 23 Jan. 1853; *m.* 1879, Tilly, *d.* of Rev. Stephen Balmer, Portpatrick. *Educ.:* Rugby; Marlborough; B.N.C., Oxford (scholar). 1st class Classical Moderations; 2nd class Final Classical Schools; B.A. 1876. Joined Bombay Educational Department, 1878, as Professor of Logic and Moral Philosophy at Elphinstone College; Principal of Elphinstone Coll., Bombay, 1900-7, and Professor of English Literature, 1891-1907; Delegate of Bombay Asiatic Society to Hanoi Congress, 1902. *Publications:* Simple Essays; Essays for the Young; Questions and Answers on Elementary Logic; Annotated editions of Marmion, Rokeby, Paradise Lost I.-IV., Vicar of Wakefield, Southey's Nelson, Ivanhoe, Pope's Homer's Iliad, Pride and Prejudice, Othello, Julius Cæsar, Twelfth Night, Kenilworth, Vanity Fair; School History of India; Promotion of General Happiness; Globe Trotter in India Two Hundred Years Ago, and other Indian Studies; Tales of Indian Chivalry (translated into Marathi, Gujarati, Kanarese, and Telugu); Princess of Balkh; In Wild Mahratta Battle; The Last of the Peshwas; Bruce of Bannockburn (Modernized Version of Barbour); with D. B. Hakim, Handbook of English Grammar and Composition; with A. Barrett, English Idioms, Indian English Corrected, and Notes on the Siege of Corinth. *Recreations:* played Rugby XV. Oxford *v.* Cambridge, 1876; walking and cycling. *Address:* University, Birmingham. (*Died 28 Aug. 1925.*)

MACMILLAN, Rev. Robert Alexander Cameron, M.A., D.Phil.; Minister of St. John's Presbyterian Church, Kensington, since 1913; *b.* 11 May 1883; *s.* of Rev. John Macmillan, Minister of Lochbroom, Ross-shire; unmarried. *Educ.:* High School and University of Glasgow. Ordained 1909; transferred to Johannesburg, 1911; Doctor of Philosophy, 1912. *Publication:* The Crowning Phase of the Critical Philosophy — A Study in Kant's Critique of Judgment 1912. *Address:* 98 Holland Road, W.   (*Died 11 April 1917.*)

M'MILLAN, Hon. Sir William, K.C.M.G.; *cr.* 1901; *b.* Londonderry, Ireland, 14 Nov. 1850; *s.* of Rev. Gibson M'Millan, Wesleyan minister; *m.* 1st, 1877, Ada Charlotte, *d.* of Frederick Graham; 2nd, 1892, Helen, *d.* of Rev. William Gibson; one *s.* four *d. Educ.:* Wesley College, Dublin; private school, London. Arrived Australia, 1869; member of firm of W. & A. M'Arthur, London and Sydney; President of Sydney Chamber of Commerce, 1886; entered New South Wales Parliament, 1887; Colonial Treasurer, 1889; Member of Federal Conference, 1890; Delegate to Federal Convention, 1891 and 1897; Member of House of Representatives Federal Parliament, 1901 - 3. *Address:* Althorne, Woollahra, Sydney, New South Wales. *Clubs:* Devonshire; Australian, Sydney; Melbourne, Melbourne.
    (*Died 21 Dec. 1926.*)

McMILLAN, William Bentley, C.B.E. 1918; J.P.; Provost of Greenock since 1909; Hon. Sheriff Substitute for Renfrew and Bute; *b.* 5 Nov. 1871; *s.* of late Matthew and Mary McMillan; *m.* Margaret Campbell, *d.* of late Duncan and Jessie Campbell; one *s.* two *d. Educ.:* Motherwell. Entered Corporation, 1894; Member Northern Lighthouses Trust, etc. *Recreations:* public work, yachting, and golf. *Address:* The Craigs, Greenock. *T.A.:* Provost McMillan, Greenock. *T.:* Greenock 477. *M.;* VS No. 1. *Clubs:* Greenock, Royal Gourock Yacht; Royal Clyde Yacht; Scottish Automobile; Scottish Constitutional.
    (*Died 1 June 1922.*)

McMILLAN, Sir William Northrup, Kt., *cr.* 1918; Hon. Member of Legislative Council, B.E.A.; F.R.G.S., C.M.Z.S.; Member of the Order of the Cross of Solomon, and Star of Ethiopia; Captain 25th (Service) Battalion Royal Fusiliers (Frontiersmen); *b.* St. Louis, Missouri, U.S.A., 19 Oct. 1872; *s.* of William and Eliza McMillan, of Hamilton, Ontario, Canada; *m.* 1894, Lucie Fairbanks Webber, of Northampton, Mass., U.S.A.; no *c. Educ.:* Pottstown, Pennsylvania, U.S.A. Ranching, New Mexico, 1890-93; business, St. Louis, U.S.A., 1893-98; business, London, 1898-1901; exploration and big-game hunting in Africa, 1901-5; ranching in British East Africa since 1905. *Publications:* maps and pamphlets Royal Geographical Society. *Recreations:* big game hunting, fishing, shooting, yachting. *Address:* Nairobi, Colony of Kenya; 19 Hill Street, Berkeley Square, W.1. *T.:* Mayfair 6647. *T.A.:* McMillan, Nairobi. *Clubs:* St. James's, Ranelagh, Royal Automobile; Union League, Manhattan, New York; Tuna, California.   (*Died 22 Mar. 1925.*)

MACNAB, Brig.-Gen. Colin Lawrance, C.M.G. 1918; *b.* Halifax, Nova Scotia, 2 Dec. 1870; *m.* Beatrice Marian, *d.* of Rev. W. B. Bliss, Wicken, Essex; two *s. Educ.:* St. Edward's; Oxford; Westminster. Joined 1st Border Regt. 1891; Asst. Adjutant, 1894-97; Adjutant, 1897-1900; Captain, Northumberland Fusiliers, 1900; Major, The Royal Sussex Regt. 1903; commanded Royal Sussex Regt. 1911-15; Brig.-Gen. Mesopotamia, 1915; France, 1916-1917; served South African War (despatches); European War (despatches twice, C.M.G.). *Recreations:* fishing, shooting. *Address:* Littlebury, Saffron-Walden, Essex. *T.A.:* Littlebury, Essex. *Club:* United Service(*Died 13 Oct. 1918.*)

M'NAB, Hon. Robert, M.A.; LL.B.; Litt.D.; Minister of Justice and Marine, New Zealand; *b.* 1864. *Educ.:* Invercargill Grammar School; Otago University. Called to Bar, 1889; M.H.R., Mataura, 1893-96 and 1898-1908; M.P. Hawkes Bay, 1914; Minister for Lands, 1906. *Publications:* Murihiku, 1909; The Old Whaling Days, 1913; From Tosman to Marsden, 1914; editor Historical Records of New Zealand. *Address:* Wellington, New Zealand.
    (*Died 17 Feb. 1917.*)

MacNACHTAN, Colonel Neil F., C.V.O. 1912; Clerk and Treasurer, United Counties Northumberland and Durham; *b.* 5 Feb. 1850; *s.* of Edmund A. MacNachtan; *m.* 1st, Jeannie Hervey Lawder; 2nd, Edith Isabell Radclyffe; one *s.* two *d. Educ.:* Cobourg Grammar School; Victoria College. Enlisted in Cobourg Garrison Artillery, 1868; commanded same, 1891-1900; commanded 14th Battery Canadian Field Artillery, 1901-6; commanded 10th Brigade Canadian Field Artillery, 1907-12; retired as Colonel; commanded Canadian Artillery team which competed with British Territorial Artillery in England, 1911 (C.V.O.). *Recreations:* of late years, shooting and fishing. *Address:* Cobourg, Ontario, Canada. *T.:* Residence 229; Office 36.
    (*Died 10 Dec. 1928.*)

MACNAGHTEN, Rev. Henry Alexander, M.A.; late Rector of Tankersley; Hon. Canon of Sheffield; *e. s.* of late Elliot Macnaghten and 1st wife, Isabella, *o. d.* of late John Law; *b.* 1850; *m.* 1st, 1873, Louisa (*d.* 1921), *d.* of Ross D. Mangles; two *s.* one *d.*; 2nd, 1925, Evelyn Vere, *o. d.* of late William Lewis Boyle and Mrs. Boyle, Evelyns, Hingham. *Educ.:* Eton; King's College, Cambridge. Curate of St. Mary, Beverley, 1876-77; Vicar of Wentworth, Yorkshire, 1877-82; Prescott. Lancs, 1882-86. *Address:* 2 Manson Place, S.W.7.   (*Died 17 July 1928.*)

MACNAGHTEN, Sir Melville Leslie, Kt., *cr.* 1907; C.B. 1912; *b.* 16 June 1853; *y. s.* of late Elliot Macnaghten of Ovingdean, Sussex, sometime Chairman of the East India Company; *m.* 1878, Dora, *e. d* of Rev. Dr. Sanderson, Canon of Chichester; two *s.* two *d. Educ.:* Eton. Manager of family estates, Bengal, 1873-88; Chief Constable of Criminal Investigation Department, Scotland Yard, 1889-1903; appointed to represent police on Hon. H. H. Asquith's Committee to enquire into the identification of Criminals, 1893-94; late Assistant Commissioner of Metropolitan Police; Chief of the Criminal Investigation Department, 1903-13; Knight Commander of the White Military Order of Spain, and Second Class Commander of the Order of Dannebrog. *Publication:* Days of My Years, 1914. *Address:* Queen Anne's Mansions, St. James's Park, S.W. *T.:* Victoria 7598. *Club:* Garrick.   (*Died 12 May 1921.*)

M'NAIR, Lieut.-Gen. Edward John, Bengal Infantry; *b.* 9 July 1838; *m.* Catherine Louisa Spry Dyas (*d.* 1910). Entered army, 1856; Lt.-Gen. 1891; retired list, 1892; served Indian Mutiny, 1857 (medal with clasp for Delhi); Hazara Campaign, 1868 (medal with clasp); Afghan War, 1879-80 (despatches, medal). *Address:* 9 St. James's Square, Bath.
    (*Died 15 April 1921.*)

McNAIR, Captain Eric Archibald, V.C. 1916; 9th (Service) Batt. R. Sussex Regt. *Educ.:* Charterhouse; Magdalen College, Oxford. Served European War, 1914-17 (V.C.). *Address:* c/o Chartered Bank of India, Australia, and China, 38 Bishopsgate, E.C. *Club:* Bath.
    (*Died Aug. 1918.*)

MACNAMARA, N. C., F.R.C.S. England, and of Ireland, Fellow of Calcutta University; late Professor, Ophthalmic Medicine, Calcutta; Vice-President of the Royal College of Surgeons; Surgeon and Founder of Mayo Hospital, Cal-

cutta ; Consulting Surgeon to Westminster Hospital, and of the Royal Westminster Ophthalmic Hospital ; Vice-President of the British Medical Association ; Member of the War Office Committee on Army Medical Service, and Government Committee on Leprosy ; Chairman of the Committee of British Medical Association on Medical Education, and of Teaching University for London ; Surg.-Maj. Bengal M.S. and of Staff in Sonthal Rebellion ; also of Tirhout Volunteers in Indian Mutiny ; *m. d.* of Hon. Henry Vincent Bayley, B.C.S. *Publications:* Origin and Character of the British People ; Story of an Irish Sept ; Human Speech, 1908 ; The Evolution of Purposive Living Matter, vols. 95 and 97 of International Scientific Series, 1910 ; Hunterian Oration, 1901 ; Diseases of the Eyes, 5th ed. ; Hist. of Asiatic Cholera, 3rd ed. ; Diseases of Bones and Joints, 3rd ed. ; Instinct and Intelligence, 1915, etc. *Address:* The Lodge, Chorleywood, Herts. *Club:* Athenæum.
(*Died 21 Nov. 1918.*)

MACNAMARA, Walter Henry; a Master of Supreme Court ; Secretary and Registrar of Railway and Canal Commission ; Registrar to Court under Benefices Act (1898) ; *b.* 1851 ; *e. s.* of late Henry Macnamara, Barrister and Railway Commissioner ; *m.* 1882, Florence (*d.* 1917), *d.* of F. de Mauduit. *Educ.:* Repton : Christ Church, Oxford. Barr. 1874. One of delegates appointed by Foreign Office to represent Great Britain at International Railway Congress in Paris, 1900 ; Washington, 1905 ; Berne, 1910 ; Vice-President of the Norwegian Club. *Address:* Apsley Cottage, Banstead, Surrey ; The Hut, Birchington, Thanet ; Royal Courts of Justice, W.C.2. *Club:* Reform. (*Died 17 Sept. 1920.*)

M'NAUGHT, W. G., Mus. Doc., F.R.A.M., Assistant Inspector of Music Ed. Dept. 1883-1901 ; Examiner Society of Arts ; editor of Messrs. Novello & Co.'s School Music and other Series ; *b.* Mile End, 30 Mar. 1849 ; 2nd *s.* of Donald M'Naught, Greenock ; *m.* Clara Weybret Waller, 1878 ; two *s.* one *d.* *Educ.:* private school, Stepney ; Royal Acad. of Music, 1872-76. Music Director Bow Bromley Institute, 1876-1900 ; Adjudicator at competitions, etc. *Publications:* editor The Musical Times and School Music Review. *Recreation:* general reading. *Address:* Annandale, Woodside Park, Finchley, N.12 *T.:* 950 P.O. Finchley (*Died 13 Oct. 1918.*)

McNAUGHT, William Kirkpatrick, Hon. Col. ; C.M.G. 1914 ; President American Watch Case Co., Ltd., 509 King Street West, Toronto ; Member Hydro-Electric Commission of the Province of Ontario ; Member of the Land Transport Commission of Canada appointed by Department of Militia and Defence ; Member of the Royal Commission on Unemployment for the Province of Ontario ; Chairman Industrial Commission of Province of Ontario ; Hon. Col. 109th Regiment Infantry Canadian Militia ; Ex-President and Chairman of Art Committee of Canadian National Exhibition ; *b.* Fergus, Ontario, 6 Sep. 1845, *s.* of John McNaught and Sarah Kirkpatrick of Penpont, Scotland ; *m.* 1872, Caroline Eliza, *d.* of Ladds William Lugsdin, Toronto ; three *s.* one *d.* *Educ.:* Public and Grammar Schools, Brantford ; Bryant and Stratton Commercial College, Toronto. Began as invoice clerk ; elected for North Toronto to Ontario Legislature, 1906 ; re-elected, 1908 and 1911 ; founded The Trader and Canadian Jeweler and edited it for 26 years ; Liberal-Conservative ; Baptist. *Publications:* Lacrosse and How to Play it ; Canadian Pioneers ; Ontario's True National Policy in regard to Black and White Coal ; The Milk Question ; Why a Protective Tariff Policy is necessary for Canada ; Imperial Federation ; Canada First in the Empire. *Recreations:* lacrosse, rowing, sailing, rifle shooting. *Address:* 614 Huron Street, Toronto,

Canada. *Clubs:* National, Royal Canadian Yacht, Toronto. (*Died Feb. 1919.*)

MACNAUGHTAN, S., author ; 4th *d.* of late Peter Macnaughtan, J.P. *Educ.:* at home. Worked at music and painting ; travelled in South America, South Africa, Canada and United States, Turkey, Macedonia, Palestine, Egypt, Greece, India, Kashmir, Nepal, Burma, etc. ; helped with Red Cross Society's work (comforts for sick and wounded) in S. Africa ; has written some books, articles, etc. ; holds Belgian Order of Leopold. *Publications:* Selah Harrison ; The Fortune of Christina M'Nab ; The Gift ; A Lame Dog's Diary ; The Expensive Miss du Cane ; Three Miss Graemes ; Us Four ; The Andersons ; Peter and Jane ; Four Chimneys ; Some Elderly People ; A Woman's Diary of the War. *Address:* 1 Norfolk Street, Park Lane, W. *T.:* Mayfair 4049. (*Died 24 July 1916.*)

MACNAUGHTON - JONES, Henry, M.D., M.Ch., Q.U.I.-M.A.O. (Honoris Causa), R.U.I., F.R.C.S.I. and Ed. ; Consulting Surgeon ; *b.* Cork ; *s.* of William Thomas Jones, M.D., and Helen Macnaughton Jones ; *m.* Henrietta, 3rd *d.* of Wm. Verling Gregg, of Cork ; three *c.* *Educ.:* Queen's College, Cork. Demonstrator of Anatomy, Queen's College, Cork, at age of 19 ; ten years Demonstrator and Lecturer on Descriptive Anatomy in this college ; Professor of Midwifery, 1876 ; Examiner in Midwifery (obstetrics and gynæcology) in the Royal University of Ireland, 1881 ; did duty in eight of the Poor Law dispensary districts of Cork city, resigned in 1872 ; eleven years physician to the Cork Fever Hospital ; surgeon to the County Hospital ; in 1868 founded the Cork Eye, Ear, and Throat Hospital ; in 1872 founded the Cork Maternity ; in 1874 was principal mover in the foundation of the Women and Children's Hospital, now the Victoria Hospital ; founded the Premier Branch of the British Medical Association in Ireland ; came to London, 1883 ; thrice President of the Irish Medical Schools and Graduates Association ; twice President of the British Gynæcological Society ; hon. member Obstetrical Societies, Belgium, Leipzig, Munich, Rome ; Vice-President and President Obstetrical and Gynæcological section of the Royal Society of Medicine for 1909-10 and 1910-11 ; President of the Irish Association (in London), 1909-10 ; Hon. President International Congresses of Obstetrics and Gynæcology, Amsterdam, Rome, Paris, Petrograd, and Berlin ; Raconteur for Great Britain and Ireland, International Congress of Obstetrics and Gynæcology, Berlin, 1912. *Publications:* Diseases of Women (2 vols.), 9th edition, 1904 ; Diseases of the Ear and Nasopharynx, 6th edition, 1902 ; Noises in the Head and Ear ; Surgical Essays : Affections of the Hip, Knee, and Ankle, 1885 ; Practical Points in Gynæcology, 1890 ; Hints to Midwives. *Recreations:* rowing, writing verse (A Piece of Delf and Other Fragments, 1st and 2nd series ; The Dawn of Life and other Poems ; The Thames, etc.). *Address:* 13 Harley Street, W. ; *T.:* Mayfair 2243 ; The Rest, 6 Ravenscroft Park, Barnet ; *T.:* Barnet 451. *T.A.:* Macnaughton - Jones, London. (*Died 16 April 1918.*)

MACNEECE, Major-Gen. James Gaussen, C.B. 1911 ; Director Medical Services, Indian Army ; *b.* 27 Feb. 1856 ; *s.* of Rev. James MacNeece, M.A., late of Clonfeacle Rectory, Moy, and Mulnagore Lodge, Dungannon, Co. Tyrone ; *m.* Josephine Alice, 2nd *d.* of Nicholas Coulthurst, Malabar, Southsea ; no *c.* ; Major R.A.M.C. 1890 ; Lt. -Col. 1898 ; Col. 1907 ; Surg.-Gen. 1910 ; P.M.O. Malta, 1905 ; India, 1910 ; D.D.M.S. Southern Command, 1912 ; Director Med. Services, Indian Army, 1915-16 ; served Bozdar Field Force, 1881 ; Zhob Valley Expedition, 1884 ; Afghan War, 1878-80 (medal with clasp) ; S. Africa, 1900-1 (despatches, Queen's medal, three clasps) : Maj.-

Gen. on Retired List, 1918; Commander St. Maurice and St. Lazarus (Italy). *Address:* 9 Spenser Road, Southsea, Hants. *Club:* Junior United Service. (*Died 13 Dec. 1919.*)

M'NEIL, Daniel, K.C. 1907; Barrister-at-law; *b.* Hillsborough, Inverness County, 31 Jan. 1853; 2nd *s.* of Malcolm M'Neil and Ellen Meagher; *m.* 1881; two *s.* three *d.* *Educ.:* Hillsborough High School; College of St. Francis Xavier, Antigonish. Admitted to Bar of Nova Scotia, 1879; elected to represent his native county in 1886 in the Local Legislature of this province, and also in 1890; a member of the Government of Nova Scotia, 1886-93; contested his native county in 1901 and 1906. *Address:* Inverness, County of Inverness, Nova Scotia. *T.:* 8 Inverness. *Club:* Inverness.

MACNEILL, John Gordon Swift, M.P. (N.) S. Donegal, 1887-1918; Professor of Constitutional Law and of the Law of Public and Private Wrongs since 1909, Clerk of Convocation since 1910, and Dean of Faculty of Law, National Univ. of Ireland, since 1912; K.C.; *b.* Dublin, 11 March 1849; *o. s.* of Rev. John Gordon Swift MacNeill, M.A., and Susan Colpoys, *d.* of Rev. Henry Tweedy, M.A., formerly Lieut. 7th Dragoon Guards; unmarried. *Educ.:* Trinity College, Dublin (Three First Honours Classics); Christ Church, Oxford (Classical Exhibition); 2nd class Classical Mods., 1870; 2nd class Final School Law and Modern History, 1872; M.A. 1875. Irish barr.; First Place and First Exhibition at Final Examination for call to Irish Bar, 1875; Auditor of Irish Law Students' Debating Society, 1875; called to Irish Bar, 1876; Professor of Constitutional and Criminal Law, King's Inns, Dublin, 1882-1888; was severely criticized and caricatured for protesting in the House of Commons against the cession of Heligoland to Germany, 1890; proposed motion disallowing votes of directors of Mombasa Railway which resulted in defeat of Unionist Government, 1892; Q.C. 1893; was commended by Sir H. Campbell-Bannerman, as Premier, in the House of Commons for his success in procuring, after years of agitation, the abolition of flogging in the Royal Navy, 1906; by repeated motions in the House of Commons established the principle that the position of Minister of the Crown is incompatible with the holding of directorships in Public Companies; proposed motion with reference to the conduct of the trial of the Great Yarmouth Election Petition, 1906; one of the seven members of the House of Commons who constitute the Committee of Privileges, 1908; by persistent questions to Ministers in the House of Commons from November 1914, pressed the Government to introduce the legislation embodied in The Titles Deprivation Act 1917. *Publications:* The Irish Parliament, what it was and what it did, 1885; English Interference with Irish Industries, 1886; How the Union was carried, 1887; Titled Corruption, 1894; The Constitutional and Parliamentary History of Ireland, 1917; Studies in the Constitution of the Irish Free State, 1925; What I have Seen and Heard, 1925. *Recreations:* pedestrianism, pet dogs, travel, original research, visits to places of archæological, historic, or architectural interest; collections of old plate, china, and historic relics. *Address:* 17 Pembroke Road, Dublin; Barra, Baily, Co. Dublin. *Club:* National Liberal.

(*Died 24 Aug. 1926.*)

M'NEILL, Capt. Malcolm, C.M.G. 1916; D.S.O. 1902; late Argyll and Sutherland Highlanders: temp. Lt.-Col. commanding a Service Batt.: *b.* 30 Jan. 1866; *s.* of late Lt.-Col. A. C. M'Neill, C.S.I. (Madras Army). Entered army, 1885; Captain, 1894; served Waziristan, 1894-95, assistant superintendent of signalling (medal and clasp): Tochi Valley, 1897 (medal and clasp),

686

Somaliland, 1901 (D.S.O., despatches, medal and clasp); retired, 1906; served European War, 1914-16 (despatches, C.M.G.). *Publications:* In Pursuit of the Mad Mullah; Service and Sport in the Somali Protectorate, 1902. *Recreations:* big game hunting, fishing, and shooting. *Address:* Dun-Grianach, Oban. *Clubs:* Junior United Service; New, Edinburgh. (*Died 3 June 1917.*)

McNEILL, Sir Malcolm, Kt., *cr.* 1904; C.B. 1901; late Chairman of the Local Government Board for Scotland; retired; *b.* 15 Nov. 1839; *y. s.* of Captain McNeill; Colonsay, Gigha, and Ardlussa; *m.* 1st, 1864, Clara Elizabeth, *y. d.* of Robert Buchanan of Ardoch; 2nd, 1871, Susan Carruthers (*d.* 1914), *e. d.* of Archibald McNeill, P.C.S.; two *s.* two *d.* *Educ.:* Eton; Sandhurst. Retired from army, 1861, and entered the Civil Service, 1867, under the Board of Supervision for the Relief of the Poor and of Public Health in Scotland; became Secretary of the Board of Supervision, 1892; of the Local Government Board, 1894; and Vice-president and Chairman, 1897. *Recreations:* golf and wood-carving. *Address:* 53 Manor Place, Edinburgh. *T.:* Edinburgh 1025. *Club:* New, Edinburgh.

(*Died 4 May 1919.*)

McNUTT, Hon. Peter, Minister without Portfolio, Prince Edward Island; *b.* Darnley, 5 April 1834; *s.* of late Hon. Peter S. McNutt of Darnley, Prince Edward Island, whose father, James McNutt, a native of Londonderry, Ireland, came to Prince Edward Island as private secretary to Governor Patterson in 1770; *m.* 1861, Anna Stewart McNutt of Malpeque, Prince Edward Island. *Educ.:* Darnley; Prince of Wales College, Charlottetown. Was Commissioner of Small Debts until the County Courts were established; a Coroner for Prince County since 1868; High Sheriff of County, 1875-77; first returned at a bye-election in 1882 to Legislative Council; re-elected at General Elections, 1882 and 1897, for 4th District of Prince County, and again at General Election, 1900, to the Legislative Assembly; member of the Executive Council of Prince Edward Island, without portfolio, continuously since Oct. 1897; merchant and farmer, Presbyterian, Liberal. *Address:* Malpeque, Prince Edward Island. (*Died Nov. 1919.*)

MACNUTT, Hon. Thomas, Member of the Dominion House of Commons for Saltcoats, Sask., 1908-25; *b.* Campbelton, N.B., 3 Aug. 1850; *s.* of Charles S. MacNutt, of Scotch descent, and Emily Allison Sims, English; *m.* 1885, Margaret M'Fadyen; two *s.* one *d.* *Educ.:* Collegiate and Commercial College, Ottawa. Went west on staff of special survey, 1874; spent three years at that work, then took up land and has been farming ever since, doing considerable work in meantime in connection with colonisation and immigration; was contractor and later Inspector of Public Works for Territorial Government; President Saltcoats District Telephone Company and Agricultural Society; Director of several local institutions; Justice of the Peace and Coroner for many years; served in Militia during Fenian raid, 1866, and Rebellion, 1885 (Service Medal and Ontario Land Grant); defeated for old Territorial Assembly, 1892; elected, 1902; for New Sask. Legislature in 1905; Speaker of Saskatchewan Legislative Assembly, 1905-8; re-elected 1908, but resigned; Presbyterian; Independent. *Address:* Saltcoats, Sask. (*Died Feb. 1927.*)

MACONOCHIE, A. White, Managing Director of Maconochie Bros., Ltd., London, Lowestoft, Fraserburgh, and Stornoway; *b.* 1855; married; one *s.* three *d.* *Educ.:* Shrewsbury. Member of Tariff Commission, 1904; M.P. (L.U.) for East Aberdeenshire, 1900-1906; contested (C.) East Aberdeenshire, 1906; Partick Division, Lanarks., 1910-11; Wednesbury Division of Staffordshire, 1918. *Address:* 8 Porchester Gate, Hyde Park, W.2. *T.:* Park

4619. *T.A.:* c/o Maconochie, Milleast, London ; Cudham Hall, Cudham, Kent. *M.:* LF 7687.
(Died 3 Feb. 1926.)

MACONOCHIE, Sir Evan, K.C.I.E., *cr.* 1921 ; C.S.I. 1918 ; I.C.S., retired ; *b.* 8 July 1868 ; *s.* of Alexander Maconochie, late of the Home Office, Whitehall ; *m.* 1899, Margaret Lucy, *d.* of late Sir Denzil Ibbetson, K.C.S.I. ; three *s.* one *d. Educ.:* Sherborne School ; New College, Oxford. Joined Bombay Civil Service, 1889 ; served as Assistant Collector and Settlement Officer ; Under-Secretary to Govt. of India Dept. of Rev. and Agriculture, 1897-1900 ; Private Secretary to Maharaja of Mysore, 1902-9; Collector and Commissioner of Division ; Agent to the Governor in Kathiawar, 1915-22 ; J.P. Devon. *Publication:* Life in the Indian Civil Service, 1926. *Recreations:* shooting, fishing, golf. *Address:* Upway, Seaton, Devon. *Club:* East India United Service. *(Died 4 Dec. 1927.)*

MACOUN, James Melville, F.L.S.; C.M.G. 1912 ; Head of Biological Division, Geological Survey of Canada since 1917 ; *b.* Belleville, Ontario, 7 Nov. 1862 ; *e. s.* of Prof. John Macoun, Dominion Naturalist, and Ellen Terrill Macoun ; *m.*; one *d. Educ.:* Albert University, Belleville. Assistant Botanist and Naturalist to Geological Survey of Canada, 1883-1917 ; has travelled over whole Dominion in that capacity ; Joint-Secretary of British Fur-Seal Commission, 1891 ; British Agent in Behring Sea, 1892 ; at Paris Arbitration, 1893, as fur-seal expert ; one of the British Fur-Seal Commissioners, 1896-98 ; represented Canada at Paris Exposition, 1900, as Forestry Commissioner ; assisted Ambassador Bryce and Sir Joseph Pope at settlement of fur-seal question at Washington, 1911 ; elected Cor. Member of Zoological Society of London, 1893, and Fellow of the Linnæan Society of London, 1914. *Publications:* numerous reports of the Geological Survey and other departments ; Flora of the Pribyloff Islands ; Catalogue of Canadian Birds. *Recreation:* walking. *Address:* Department of Mines, Ottawa. *T.A.:* Ottawa. *T.:* Q 8527. *Club:* University.
(Died 8 Jan. 1920.)

MACOUN, John, M.A.,F.R.S.Can.; Naturalist to Dominion of Canada ; *b.* Maralin, County Down, 17 April 1831 ; *m.* 1862, Ellen Tyrrell ; two *s.* three *d. Educ.:* self-educated. Emigrated to Canada, 1850 ; farmed in the bush till 1857 ; taught in public schools until 1874 ; while still teaching in public schools became Professor of Botany in Albert College, Belleville, Ont., 1868 ; Professor of Natural History, 1875-79 ; explorer for the Dominion Government, 1879 ; placed on Civil List with title of Dominion Botanist, 1881 ; Dominion Naturalist and Assistant Director of the Geological Survey of Canada, 1886. *Publications:* The Great North-West ; Catalogue of Canadian Plants ; Catalogue of Canadian Birds ; many reports and short papers. *Recreation:* field work in the summer. *Address:* Sidney, Vancouver Island, Canada. *T.:* 129.
(Died 18 July 1921.)

MᶜPEAKE, James Young, Vice-Chairman National Magazine Co. Ltd. Editor of Nash's Magazine since 1915 ; *b.* Belfast, 18 Dec. 1868 ; *e. s.* of Robert MᶜPeake, Belfast; *m.* Gertrude, 3rd *d.* of Denis Sheils, Skerries, Co. Dublin ; two *s. Educ.:* St. Malachy's College, Belfast. In 1890 joined staff Dublin Daily Express, of which successively Sub-Editor and Editor ; Editor Dublin Evening Mail, 1900-1912; Managing Director London Budget, 1912-1914. *Recreation:* golf. *Address:* 40 Montagu Mansions, W.1. *T.:* Mayfair 4743. *M.:* XE 9707. *Clubs:* Savage ; Highgate Golf.
(Died 19 Sept. 1924.)

MACPHAIL, Rev. William Merry, M.A.; General Secretary of the Presbyterian Church of England since 1907 ; Moderator of the Synod of the Presbyterian Church of England, 1916-17 ; *b.* Newcastle, 31 Oct. 1857 ; 3rd *s.* of Late Dugald Macphail, author of well-known Gaelic songs; *m.* 1882, Sarah Stone, 3rd *d.* of late William Goldie, of Ashmore, Dorsetshire ; one *s.* two *d. Educ.:* Sherborne ; George Watson's College,Edinburgh ; Edinburgh University ; Glasgow Free Church College. Took the M.A. degree with Honours in Mental Philosophy at Edinburgh University ; Holder of the Hamilton Fellowship and the Ferguson Scholarship in Mental Philosophy ; Ministerial Assistant at the West Free Church, Rothesay, 1881-82; and at Mayfield Free Church, Edinburgh, 1882 ; Minister of Maybole Free Church, Ayrshire, 1882-85 ; Streatham Presbyterian Church, London, S.W., 1885-1907 ; Clerk of the Synod of the Presbyterian Church of England, 1895-1908. *Publication:* The Presbyterian Church, its Doctrine, Worship and Polity. *Recreation:* golf. *Address:* 58 Blenheim Gardens, Cricklewood, N.W. ; Offices of the Presbyterian Church of England, 7 East India Avenue, E.C. *T.A.:* Byterian Led. London. *T.:* Central 1011⁶. *(Died 23 Sept. 1916.)*

MACPHERSON, Lieut.-Colonel Archibald Duncan, C.I.E. 1926 ; *b.* 14 Jan. 1872 ; *s.* of late Sir William and Lady Macpherson ; *m.* 1911, Viva Tertia Pevensey Duke ; three *s. Educ.:* Charterhouse ; Sandhurst. Joined 77th Middlesex Regt., 1891 ; 2nd (Sam Brown's) Cavalry P.F.F., 1893 ; Political Department of the Government of India, 1898 ; retired, 1927. *Address:* c/o Grindlay & Co., Ltd., 54 Parliament Street, S.W.1. *Club:* Junior Naval and Military.
(Died 27 Aug. 1928.)

MACPHERSON, Sir Arthur George, K.C.I.E.; *cr.* 1889 ; *b.* 26 Sept. 1828 ; *y. s.* of Hugh Macpherson, M.D.; *m.* 1860, Frances Caroline (*d.* 1918), *d.* of late William Martin ; four *s.* one *d. Educ.:* Aberdeen ; Edinburgh. Barr. Inner Temple, 1852 ; Legislative Secretary, Government of Bengal, 1862-64 ; Government of India, 1864 ; Judge of High Court at Calcutta, 1864-1877 ; legal adviser to Secretary of State for India, 1879-82 ; Judicial Secretary, India Office, 1882-93. *Address:* Tenerife, Trefusis Terrace, Exmouth.
(Died 22 Jan. 1921.)

MACPHERSON, Charles, Mus. Doc. Dunelm (*honoris causâ*), F.R.A.M., F.R.C.O.; Hon. Member American Guild of Organists ; Organist of St. Paul's Cathedral since 1916 ; President Royal College of Organists, 1920-22 ; Sub-organist, 1895-1916 ; Professor of Harmony, Royal Academy of Music ; an Examiner for the Associated Board of the R.A.M. and R.C.M.; *b.* Edinburgh, 10 May 1870 ; *e. s.* of late Charles Macpherson, Burgh Architect to City of Edinburgh, and Mrs. Macpherson (afterwards *m.* late Rev. W. Fancourt, M.A., St. Mungo's, West Linton, Peeblesshire) ; *m.* 1910, Sophia Menella, *y. d.* of Rev. W. C. E. Newbolt; one-*s. Educ.:* St. Paul's Choir School; Royal Academy of Music ; Charles Lucas Medallist (for Composition), 1893. Organist of St. David's, Weem, Aberfeldy, N.B., 1887-89 ; of private chapel at Luton Hoo, Beds. (the late Madame de Falbe), 1889-95 ; conductor of the London Church Choir Association since 1914 ; Hon. Conductor of Choir at opening ceremony and Thanksgiving Service, 24 May, at the British Empire Exhibition, Wembley, 1925. *Publications:* various musical compositions for church use, also orchestral and other secular works ; A Short History of Harmony ; lectures, etc. *Recreations:* sketching, golf. *Address:* 8 Amen Court, St. Paul's, E.C.4. *(Died 28 May 1927.)*

McPHERSON, Col. David William, C.M.G. 1917 ; Canadian Army Medical Corps ; Officer commanding Ontario Military Hospital, 1916 ; *b.* Toronto, of Scotch parents, 13 June 1869 ; *m.* 1905, Margaret, *d.* of late William and Margaret Sloane, Quebec. *Educ. :* Wellesley Public School and Toronto Collegiate ; Toronto University, M.B. ; M.D., C.M. Trinity University, Fellow of the American College of Surgery, 1913. Practised Surgery in Toronto and was Surgeon to Grace Hospital, Toronto ; when Canadian Army Medical Corps was established, 1899, joined as Lieut. and worked his way up to Lieut.-Col. in command of No. 11 Canadian Field Ambulance ; D.A.D.M.S. Canadian Military District No. 2, 1913 ; offered services for France, 6 Aug. 1914 ; organised No. 2 Canadian Field Ambulance, came overseas as Commanding Officer, Sep. 1914, went to France with the 1st Canadian Division, Feb. 1915 ; through 2nd Battle of Ypres ; Officer commanded Canadian Convalescent Hospital, Epsom, 1915 (temp. Col. 5 Dec. 1916, despatches thrice, C.M.G.). *Address :* 556 Bathurst Street, Toronto, Canada. *(Died 1923.)*

MACPHERSON, Rev. Ewen George Fitzroy, B.A., C.M.G. 1915 ; C.B.E. 1919 ; Rector of Chawton since 1926 ; late Chaplain to the Forces, 1st Class ; *b.* 31 Oct. 1863. *Educ. :* Durham University. Ordained, 1888 ; Curate of Medomsley, 1888-92 ; Chaplain to Forces Portsmouth, 1892-94 ; Curragh Camp, 1894-99 ; Natal, 1899-1900 ; Johannesburg, 1900-1904 ; Winchester, 1904-9 ; Gibraltar, 1909-13 ; served South Africa, 1899-1902 (despatches, Queen's medal 6 clasps, King's medal 2 clasps) ; European War, 1914-19 (despatches, C.M.G.) ; Assist. Chaplain-General, Southern Command, 1916 ; Western Command, 1920-22 ; Vicar of Reculver with Hoath, 1922. *Address :* Chawton Rectory, Hants. *(Died 28 Nov. 1926.)*

MACPHERSON, George, J.P. and D.L. County of Stafford ; J.P. County of Worcester ; 3rd *s.* of G. Macpherson, J.P. of Gibston, Aberdeenshire ; *m.* 1st, 1880, Emma Stone (*d.* 1889), 3rd *d.* of late H. Addenbrooke of Sutton Coldfield ; 2nd, 1894, Hilda Mary, *o. d.* of late E. Bindon Marten, C.E. ; one *d. Educ. :* Chanonry House, Aberdeen. Commenced business at Tudhoe Iron Works, Co. Durham ; became partner in firm of Philip Williams & Sons, Coal and Ironmasters, Tipton ; is a Director of the London and North-Western Railway and Barclay Bank, Ltd. ; is Chairman Birmingham Canal Comm. and S.S. Mond Gas Co. ; is Chairman of the S. Staff. Ironmasters' Association and the Midland Wages Board. *Recreations :* fishing and shooting. *Address :* The Lloyd House, nr. Wolverhampton ; Edinglassie Lodge, Glass, Huntly, N.B. *T. :* Wolverhampton 866. *M. :* E 454. E 1103. *Club :* Caledonian. *(Died 24 April 1924.)*

MACPHERSON, Hector, F.R.S.E. ; Author and Journalist. *Publications :* Mr. Gladstone, His Political Career, 1892 ; Thomas Carlyle, 1896, and Adam Smith, 1899, in Famous Scots Series ; Herbert Spencer, 1900 ; new and condensed edition of Adam Smith's Wealth of Nations, 1903 ; Books to Read, and How to Read Them, 1904 ; The Scottish Church Crisis, 1904 ; Scotland's Battles for Spiritual Independence, 1905 ; A Century of Intellectual Development, 1907 (translated into Japanese) ; A Century of Political Development, 1908 (translated into Japanese) ; Intellectual Development of Scotland, 1911 ; Scotland's Debt to Protestantism, 1912 ; The Jesuits in History, 1914 (translated into Hungarian). *Address :* 5 Merchiston BankAvenue, Edinburgh. *(Died Oct. 1924.)*

MACPHERSON, Major-Gen. Sir William (Grant), K.C.M.G., *cr.* 1918 ; C.B. 1915 ; C.M.G. 1902 ; Col. Commandant R.A.M.C. since 1925 ; late Army Medical Service ; *b.* Kilmuir, Ross-shire, 27 Jan. 1858 ; 3rd *s.* of late Rev. W. Macpherson of Kilmuir Easter, Ross-shire ; *m.* 1st, 1884, E. A. (*d.* 1907), 2nd *d.* of late J. Clunas of New Orleans, U.S.A., and Nairn, N.B. ; 2nd, 1910, G. E., *y. d.* of

688

late General Sir John Doran, K.C.B. *Educ. :* Fettes College, Edinburgh ; Edinburgh, Tübingen, and Leipzig Universities. Editor-in-Chief Official Medical History of the War, and author of several articles and works on military medical subjects. Served at the War Office as a Deputy Assistant and Deputy Director-General of the Army Medical Service, and as a member of the Advisory Board for Medical services and of the Army Sanitary Committee ; was in medical charge of Sir C. Euan Smith's Mission to Fez, 1892, and of Sir A. Nicolson's Mission to Morocco City, 1896 ; represented H.M. Govt. and War Office at several International Conferences ; Hon. Secretary of Central British Red Cross Committee from formation till·1902 ; on special duty S. Africa, 1902-3, and Panama and Cuba, 1908 ; Senior Medical Officer, N. China Command, and attached to Japanese Army in the Field, Russo-Japanese War, 1904-5 ; one of the British Plenipotentiaries at the Conference for the Revision of the Geneva Convention, 1906 ; attached to Directorate of Military Operations, War Office, 1906-10 ; P.M.O. Malta, 1910 ; Assist.-Director Medical Services, 4th Quetta Division, and Lecturer Medical Services, Staff College, Quetta, 1911-14 ; served European War, 1914-18, as Director of Medical Services 1st Army and as Deputy Director-General, G.H.Q. ; also as Director of Medical Services British Force in Macedonia, 1915-16 (despatches nine times, K.C.M.G., C.B.): M.A. (Honours, Classics and Greek Travelling Scholar), M.B. of Edinburgh University ; LL.D. (Edin. Univ.); D.P.H. of Cambridge University ; formerly Hon. Physician to H.M. ; F.R.G.S. ; F.R.S.Med.; Knight of Grace, Order of St. John of Jerusalem ; 3rd Class Sacred Treasure of Japan ; Commander, Legion of Honour and Crown of Italy ; Japanese Red Cross Society's decoration for meritorious services, and Japanese war medal ; U.S.A. Distinguished Service Medal. *Address :* 14 Evelyn Gardens, S.W.7. *Clubs :* Savile, Junior United Service. *(Died 15 Oct. 1927.)*

MACQUOID, Katharine Sarah, novelist ; writer of travel books ; *b.* Kentish Town, 26 Jan. 1824 ; 3rd *d.* of late Thomas Thomas and Phœbe Gadsden ; *m.* 1851, Thomas Robert Macquoid, R.I. (*d.* 1912) ; two *s. Educ. :* home. *Publications :* first short story appeared in Welcome Guest, 1859 ; Piccalilli, 1862 ; A Bad Beginning, 1862 ; Chesterford,[1863 ; Hester Kirton, 1864 ; By the Sea, 1865 ; Elinor Dryden, 1867 ; Charlotte Burney, 1867 ; Wild as a Hawk (Marjorie), 1868 ; Forgotten by the World, 1869 ; Rookstone, 1871 ; Patty, 1871 ; Miriam's Marriage, 1872 ; Pictures across the Channel, 1872 ; Too Soon, 1873 ; Through Normandy, 1874 ; My Story, 1874 ; The Evil Eye, 1875 ; Diane, 1875 ; Lost Rose, 1876 ; Through Brittany, 1877 ; Doris Barugh, 1877 ; Pictures and Legends from Normandy and Brittany, 1878 ; The Berkshire Lady, 1879 ; In the Sweet Spring Time, 1880 ; Beside the River, 1881 ; Little Fifine, 1881 ; In the Ardennes, 1881 ; A Faithful Lover, 1882 ; Her Sailor Love, 1883 ; About Yorkshire, 1883 ; Under the Snow, 1884 ; Louisa, 1885 ; A Strange Company, 1885 ; At the Red Glove, 1885 ; A Little Vagabond, 1886 ; Joan Wentworth, 1886 ; Sir James Appleby, 1886 ; Mère Suzanne, 1886 ; At the Peacock, 1887 ; Puff, 1888 ; Elizabeth Morley, 1889 ; Roger Ferron, 1889 ; Pepin, 1889 ; Cosette, 1890 ; The Haunted Fountain, 1890 ; At an Old Chateau, 1891 ; Drifting Apart, 1891 ; The Prince's Whim, 1891 ; Maisie Derrick, 1892 ; Miss Eyon of Eyoncourt, 1892 ; Berris, 1893 ; In an Orchard, 1894 ; Appledore Farm, 1894 ; His Last Card, 1895 ; In the Volcanic Eifel, 1896, and In Paris, 1900 (jointly with Gilbert S. Macquoid) ; The Story of Lois, 1898 ; A Ward of the King, 1898 ; His Heart's Desire, 1903 ; Pictures in Umbria, 1905 ; A Village Chronicle, 1905 ; Captain Dallington, 1907 ; Molly Montague's Love Story, 1911 ;

many stories in magazines and newspapers. *Recreation:* visits from my friends. *Address:* The Edge, 8 Lucien Road, Tooting Common, S.W.   *(Died 24 June 1917.)*

MACQUOID, Percy, R.I.; J.P.; artist, designer and decorator; *s.* of late T. R. Macquoid; *m.* 1891, Theresa I., *d.* of Thos. Dent. *Educ.:* Marlborough; Royal Academy Schools. *Publications:* A History of English Furniture; Costume, Furniture, and Domestic Habits in Shakespeare's England, 1916; Theatrical Designs for Scenery and Costume in Paolo and Francesca, Nero, The School for Scandal, Antony and Cleopatra, Romeo and Juliet, Joseph and his Brethren, False Gods, Henry VIII., If I were King, The Aristocrat, Mary Rose, The Dover Road, and other plays, etc. *Address:* The Yellow House, 8 Palace Court, Bayswater, W.2; Hoove Lea, Hove. *T.:* Park 2400. *Clubs:* Garrick, Arts; Union, Brighton.
         (Died 20 Mar. 1925.)

MACRAE, Col. Alexander William, C.I.E. 1911; Hon. Col. Malabar Volunteer Rifles; J.P. Hampshire; *b.* 15 June 1858; *s.* of Dr. Charles Mackenzie Macrae. *Address:* Kerala, Yateley, Hants.   *(Died 1 Feb. 1920.)*

MACRAE, Charles Colin, J.P.; *b.* 6 Aug. 1843; *s.* of A. C. Macrae, M.D., Inspector-General of Hospitals; *m.* Cecilia, *d.* of Samuel Laing, once Finance Minister of India and for many years M.P. for Orkney and Shetland. *Educ.:* Eton; University College, Oxford. Called to Bar, 1868; practised for 8 years in Calcutta, where he was Secretary to the Legislative Council, Govt. of Bengal; then practized in this country at the Common Law and Parliamentary Bar, and before the Privy Council, and was standing Counsel to the India Office; retired 1889; is Chairman of the London, Brighton, and South Coast Rly. Co., London Caledonian Trust, British and China Corporation, and Director of the Gresham Life and Fire Insurance Societies, and various other companies. *Publications:* The Law of Divorce in India; The Indian Contract Act, with notes. *Recreations:* shooting, fishing, golf, sketching. *Address:* Ravenshall, Bournemouth West. *T.A.:* Pavy, London. *T.:* Bournemouth 1500. *Clubs:* Windham, City of London; Bournemouth.   *(Died 28 Nov. 1922.)*

MACRAE, Sir Colin George, Kt., *cr.* 1900; *b.* 30 Nov. 1844; *m.* 1877, Flora Maitland *(d.* 1921), 3rd *d.* of John Colquhoun, 1 Royal Terrace, Edinburgh; one *s.* one *d. Educ.:* Edinburgh Academy and University; M.A. Writer to His Majesty's Signet, 1871; J.P. for Counties of Edinburgh, Forfar, and Dumbarton; Chairman of School Board of Edinburgh, 1890-1900. *Decorated* for services to education. *Recreations:* shooting, fishing, cycling, etc. *Address:* Glenflora, Colinton. *T.A.:* Macrae, Edinburgh. *T.:* 2495 Edinburgh Central. *Club:* New, Edinburgh.
         (Died 9 Dec. 1925.)

MACRAE, Robert Scarth Farquhar, C.I.E. 1917; C.B.E. 1919; Indian Police, retired; Chief Police Officer, Port of London Authority's Police, since 1925; *b.* 18 May 1877; *s.* of late John Macrae, Procurator-Fiscal of Orkney, and Mrs. Garson of Grindelay, Orphir, Orkney; *m.* 1911, Beatrice Reid, *d.* of late Andrew McGeoch, Glasgow; one *s.* one *d. Educ.:* Trinity College, Glenalmond; St. Andrews University. Somaliland Expeditionary Force, 1903-4; Political officer, Somaliland, 1904-5; Comr. of Police, Baroda, 1912-16; Controller of Native Craft, Mesopotamia Expeditionary Force, 1916-19; Dep. Inspector General of Police, Bihar and Orissa, 1919-25; retired, 1925. *Address:* 88 Finchley Road, N.W.3.
         (Died 20 Feb. 1926.)

MACRAY, Rev. William Dunn, M.A., Hon. Litt.D., F.S.A.; Rector of Ducklington,

1870-1912; antiquary, author, and editor. Assist. in Bodleian Library, 1840-1905; *b.* 1826. *Educ.:* Magdalen Coll. School and Magdalen Coll. Oxford (Fellow); *m.* 1856, Adelaide Otilia Alberta *(d.* 1905), 2nd *d.* of Otto Schmidt of Berlin; three *s.* two *d. Publications:* editor of numerous works for the Record Office, Rolls Series, Clarendon Press, Roxburghe Club; Catalogues of the Rawlinson and Digby MSS. in Bodleian Library, 1862-98; Index to the Catalogue of Ashmolean MSS., 1867; Annals of the Bodleian Library, 1868, 1890; Calendar of the Clarendon State Papers in the Bodleian, 1867-76 (vols. ii. iii.); edited Clarendon's History of the Rebellion (6 vols.) for the Oxford University Press, 1888; Register of Fellows of Magdalen College, 8 vols., 1894-1915; Breviarium Bothanum, 1901, etc. *Address:* Bloxham, Oxfordshire; Magdalen College, Oxford.   *(Died 5 Dec. 1916.)*

MACRITCHIE, David, F.S.A., Scot. and Ireland; Fellow of Royal Anthropological Institute of Great Britain and Ireland; Author; *b.* Edinburgh, 16 April 1851; *y. s.* of William Dawson MacRitchie, M.D., surgeon in the Hon. East India Company's Service. and Elizabeth Elder, *d.* of John MacRitchie of Craigton, Perthshire, Writer, Edinburgh; unmarried. *Educ.:* Edinburgh Southern Academy, Edinburgh Institution, and Edinburgh University. Became a member of the Society of Chartered Accountants, Edinburgh, but soon thereafter turned his attention to ethnology and antiquarian research, largely from the point of view of traditional lore; has written on the subject of dwarf races, in tradition and in fact; on the archaic underground dwellings of the British Isles; and on the history and character of the gypsies; in 1888 he founded the cosmopolitan Gypsy Lore Society, the quarterly Journal of which he edited in collaboration with his friend Francis Hindes Groome until 1892, when the society became dormant; on its revival, in 1907, he was made first President; one of the founders, 1906, of the St. Andrew Society, Edinburgh, the aim of which is to define Scotland's position in history. *Publications:* Ancient and Modern Britons, 1884; The Gypsies of India, 1886; The Testimony of Tradition, 1890; The Ainos, a work chiefly drawn from Japanese sources, 1892; Fians, Fairies, and Picts, 1893; Scottish Gypsies under the Stewarts, 1894; The Savages of Gaelic Tradition, 1920; in 1897 he edited and published the Diary of a Tour through Great Britain in 1795, by his grandfather, the Rev. William MacRitchie, Perthshire. He has contributed a number of articles to magazines and scientific journals, and to the Harmsworth Encyclopædia, the Encyclopædia of Religion and Ethics, and the Encyclopædia of Occultism. *Recreation:* travel. *Address:* 4 Archibald Place, Edinburgh. *Club:* Scottish Arts, Edinburgh.   *(Died 14 Jan. 1925.)*

M'ROBERT, Sir Alexander, 1st Bt., *cr.* 1922; Kt., *cr.* 1910; K.B.E., *cr.* 1919; LL.D. Aberdeen; F.R.G.S.; Chairman of British India Corporation, Limited, Cawnpore; *b.* 21 May 1854; *e. s.* of John M'Robert, Douneside, Tarland, N.B.; *m.* 1st, 1883; 2nd, 1911, Rachel, *d.* of Dr. William Hunter Workman, of Worcester, Massachusetts, U.S.A.; three *s. Educ.:* Public Schools, Newhills, N.B.; Royal College of Science. Before going to Cawnpore in 1884, held the appointment of Neil Arnott Lecturer in Experimental Physics, Mechanics' Institution, Aberdeen; and was Lecturer in Chemistry in Robert Gordon's College, Aberdeen; invested with the Order of Honour of Afghanistan, 1918. President of the Upper India Chamber of Commerce for nine years, and represented that body in the Legislative Council of the United Provinces of Agra and Oudh for five successive terms of two years each;

McSWEENY, George, K.C. See page xxv.

represented Chamber at the Congresses of Chambers of Commerce of the Empire at Montreal 1903, London 1906 and 1912, Sydney 1909, and Toronto 1920; Fellow of the University of Allahabad in the Faculty of Science since 1904; Member of Committee of Management, Government Engineering College, Roorkee, since 1900; Governor of Agricultural College, Cawnpore; Lieut.-Colonel Commanding Cawnpore Volunteer Rifles (V.D.) 1899-1912; pioneered the movement for providing sanitary dwellings for factory workers in India; has travelled extensively all over the world. *Heir:* s. Alasdair Workman, *b.* 11 July 1912. *Address:* The Shieling, Cawnpore. *T.A.:* M'Robert, Cawnpore. *Clubs:* Bath, Oriental, National Liberal; Cawnpore; Royal Northern, Aberdeen.   (*Died 22 June 1923.*)

MacSWINEY, Terence Joseph, M.P. (S.F.) Mid Cork since Dec. 1918. Lord Mayor of Cork, 1920.   (*Died 25 Oct. 1920.*)

M'TAGGART, John M'Taggart Ellis, Litt.D.; Hon. LL.D. St. Andrews; Fellow of the British Academy; Fellow since 1891 and Lecturer, 1897-1923, of Trinity College, Cambridge; *b.* 1866; *s.* of late Francis Ellis M'Taggart, Judge of County Courts, and late Caroline Ellis; *m.* 1899, Margaret, *d.* of late Joseph Bird, Auckland, New Zealand. *Educ.:* Clifton College; Trinity College, Cambridge. *Publications:* Studies in the Hegelian Dialectic, 1896; Studies in Hegelian Cosmology, 1901; Some Dogmas of Religion, 1906; A Commentary on Hegel's Logic, 1910; The Nature of Existence, vol. i., 1921. *Recreation:* novel-reading. *Address:* Trinity College, Cambridge. *Club:* Savile.   (*Died 18 Jan. 1925.*)

McTAGGART, Captain W. B., D.L., J.P.; *m.* 1st, Letitia, *d.* of A. Thompson of Blackrock, Dublin; 2nd, Louisa, *d.* of Admiral Joseph Grant Bickford, R.N.; one *s. Educ.:* Harrow. Joined 14th Hussars, 1868; retired 1879; Chairman, Mysore Gold Mining Co., Ltd., etc.; Master of the Surrey Staghounds fourteen years, resigned 1915. *Publications:* Absolute Relativism, and many philosophical treatises and essays. *Recreations:* hunting, shooting, fishing. *Clubs:* Naval and Military, Carlton.   (*Died 9 Nov. 1919.*)

M'VAIL, Sir David Caldwell, Kt., *cr.* 1910; M.B.; F.R.F.P.S. Glasgow; Hon. F.R.C.P.I.; Ex-Professor of Clinical Medicine, St. Mungo's College; Hon. Consulting Physician to Glasgow Royal Infirmary; Crown Member for Scotland General Medical Council, 1892-1912; *b.* Kilmarnock, 6 Oct. 1845; *s.* of late James M'Vail; *m.* 1877, Lily Neilson, *d.* of late Thomas N. Brown; one *s.* one *d. Educ.:* Anderson's College; Glasgow University. Was the Annual Lecturer to the Faculty of Physicians and Surgeons of Glasgow, 1882—on the Mechanism of Respiration. Has written various papers on Pulmonary, Cardiac, and Physiological subjects; Member of the Court of Glasgow University since 1891. *Address:* 3 St. James's Terrace, Glasgow. *T.:* 443 Hillhead, Glasgow. *Clubs:* Liberal, Glasgow University.   (*Died 4 Nov. 1917.*)

McVAIL, John Christie, M.D., LL.D., F.R.F.P.S.; D.P.H. Cambridge; (retired); late Member Scottish Board of Health; late Deputy Chairman National Health Insurance Commission, Scotland; Crown Member for Scotland, Gen. Med. Council, 1912-22; late County Medical Officer, Stirlingshire and Dunbartonshire; late Member, Highlands and Islands Medical Service Board; late Examiner in Medical Jurisprudence and Public Health, Universities of Edinburgh, Glasgow, and St. Andrews; now Univ. of Aberdeen and Scottish Conjoint Board; ex-President Society Medical Officers of Health of Great Britain and Incorporated Sanitary Association of Scotland, and

of Glasgow and West of Scotland Branch, British Medical Association; Lane Lecturer, Cooper Medical College, San Francisco, 1906; now President Epidemiological Section, Royal Society of Medicine; Medical Investigator Royal Commission on Poor Laws, 1907 (Appendix Report, vol. xiv.); Milroy Lecturer, Royal College of Physicians, London, 1919; Jenner Medallist Royal Society of Medicine, 1922; Stewart prize, British Medical Assoc. 1922; Member of Court of Governors, London School of Hygiene and Tropical Medicine, 1924; *b.* Kilmarnock, 22 Oct. 1849; *s.* of late James McVail; *m.* Jessie Shoolbred, *d.* of late John Rowat, Kilmarnock; two *s.* two *d. Educ.:* Anderson's College; Glasgow University. Practised medicine in Kilmarnock, 1878-91; was physician to Infirmary, Medical Officer of Health, and Crown Examiner in Medico-legal cases for North Ayrshire; late Member Council British Medical Association. *Publications:* Evidence before Royal Commission on Vaccination, vol. vi. of Report; The Prevention of Infectious Diseases, 1907; numerous writings on public health subjects, especially on Smallpox and Vaccination; Ethics of Preventive Medicine, published in Public Health, 1901; County Health Reports; Half a Century of Smallpox and Vaccination, 1919; The British Medical Association: Its Constitution and Government, a Historical Survey, 1924. *Address:* 44 Rotherwick Road, Golders Green, N.W.11. *T.:* Speedwell 1567.   (*Died 29 July 1926.*)

M'VITTIE, Surg.-Gen. Charles Edwin; Surg.-Gen. 1895; served Afghan War, 1880 (medal); Burmese Expedition, 1886-87 (despatches, medal with 2 clasps); Hon. Physician to H.M. since 1910.   (*Died 27 Feb. 1916.*)

MACWATT, Hay, M.A., LL.B., Sheriff-Substitute of Ross and Cromarty and Sutherland (retired 1912); *b.* 1855; 2nd *s.* of David MacWatt, late Procurator-Fiscal of Clackmannanshire; *m.* 1897, May, *d.* of late R. C. MacWatt, M.D., Medical Officer of Health for Berwickshire. *Educ.:* Edinburgh Collegiate School; Edinburgh University. Called to Scots Bar, 1881; Sheriff-Substitute of Argyll 1897-1904. *Address:* Elsick House, Strathpeffer, Ross-shire. *T:* Strathpeffer 42. *Club:* University, Edinburgh.   (*Died 13 Oct. 1920.*)

M'WHAE, Hon. Sir John, Kt., *cr.* 1924; Agent-General for Victoria in London, 1922-1924; late Member for Melbourne City, Legislative Council, Victoria, 1909-22; Minister of Public Works, Bowser Administration; Member of Executive Council in the State of Victoria; Hon. Minister Lawson Administration; for 30 years Member Stock Exchange of Melbourne; six years chairman of latter; *b.* Ballarat, 1858; of Scotch parentage; *m.* E. H. Douch, Williamstown, Australia; three *s.* two *d. Educ.:* Dumfries Academy; Ballarat Grammar School. Started life in Union Bank of Australia; afterward Member of the Ballarat and Melbourne Stock Exchanges; connected with pastoral properties in Victoria, Queensland. *Address:* 314 Collins Street, Melbourne. *T.A.:* M'Whae, Melbourne. *Clubs:* Australian, Stock Exchange, Melbourne(*Died 17 Sept. 1927.*)

McWHINNIE, Hugh, F.J.I.; *b.* farm of Merkland, Kirkoswald, Ayrshire; *m.* Elizabeth, *d.* of George Hoyle, Ashton-under-Lyne; two *s. Educ.:* Parochial School, Dailly; Kirkoswald. Joined the Oldham Standard as a reporter; subsequently became connected with the Liverpool Albion, and later joined the Liverpool Courier; Editor of the Demerara Daily Colonist for 3 years; connected with the Editorial Department of the Liverpool Daily Post for 17 years; Editor of Bristol Daily Mercury and Bristol Evening Echo, 1901-4; was on literary staff of the Tribune; for

MACVICAR, Hon. John. See page xxv.

McWEENEY, Edmond J., M.D. See page xxv.

the past 17 years Managing Director of the North Devon Press, Ltd., North Devon Herald. *Recreations:* cycling, horticulture, and mechanics. *Address:* Rozelle, Victoria Road, Barnstaple. *T.:* 6 Barnstaple. *Club:* Press. *(Died 1923.)*

M'WILLIAM, Andrew, C.B.E. 1919; D.Met., A.R.S.M.; Consulting Metallurgist, formerly Metallurgical Inspector to Indian Government; Assistant Professor of Metallurgy in the University of Sheffield; *s.* of John A. M'William and Agnes M'Pherson; *m.* 1900, Georgina Beebee, *d.* of George Croome, of Gloucestershire; one *s.* *Educ.:* Allan Glen's School, Glasgow; Royal School of Mines, London; Associate of the Royal School of Mines, 1887; 1st Class in Metallurgy; Demonstrator in Metallurgy in Sheffield Technical School, 1887-91; Chemist and Steel Manager in works, 1891-94; Lecturer in Metallurgy to Staffs C.C. 1894-96; manager of danger area to British Explosives Syndicate, 1896; Lecturer in Metallurgy, University College, Sheffield; visited Sweden for general tour of steel works, 1899; again in 1907 to study electric melting; went to Spitsbergen for a Sheffield syndicate to investigate coal and mineral prospects, 1908; late Consulting Metallurgist to the Tata Iron and Steel Co., Jamshedpur, India; Member Iron and Steel Institute and Institute of Metals; Hon. Member and President Sheffield Society of Engineers and Metallurgists; Hon. Life Fellow of Permanent Way Institution; Capt. and O.C. "E" Co. Chota Nagpur Light Horse. *Publications:* General Foundry Practice (with Dr. Longmuir); many papers on original investigations to Iron and Steel Institute, Institute of Metals, Society of Engineers and Metallurgists, Odontological Section of the Royal Society of Medicine; popular series Notes on Metals in local newspaper; reviews and articles in Nature and elsewhere. *Address:* 221 Upperthorpe, Sheffield.
(Died 5 April 1922.)

MADDEN, Archibald Maclean, C.M.G. 1908; *b.* 31 May 1864; *e. s.* of late Surgeon-General Chas. D, Madden, C.B., Hon. Surgeon to the King; *m.* C. C., *e. d.* of late Canon A. P. Moor, of Truro; three *s. Educ.:* Cheltenham; Trinity College, Cambridge (B.A.). Clerk, Librarian's Depart., Foreign Office, 1890-93; Acting Vice-Consul, Dar-al-Baida, 1894; employed on Special Service in Morocco, 1894 and 1895; Act. Consul, 1894; Clerk to Legation, Tangier, 1894; accompanied Sir E. M. Satow's special mission to Fez, 1894-95; Sir A. Nicolson's (now Lord Carnock) special mission to Morocco, 1896; Acting Consul, Tangier, 1896 and 1898; Vice-Consul, 1897; Vice-Consul, Mogador, 1900-1907; Consul, Dar-al-Baida (Casablanca), 1907-1914; present at bombardment and siege of Casablanca and Franco-Spanish military occupation, Aug. 1907; H.B.M. Consul at Bilbao, 1914; in Foreign Office, 1923-25, when he retired. *Address:* 53 Sisters Avenue, S.W.11.
(Died 15 Oct. 1928.)

MADDEN, Right Hon. Dodgson Hamilton; P.C. (Ir.), M.A., LL.D. and Litt.D. (hon.) Trin. Coll. Dublin; Judge of High Court of Justice, Ireland (King's Bench Div.), 1892; retired, 1919; Vice-Chancellor of Dublin Univ. 1895-1919; *b.* 28 Mar. 1840; *o. s.* of Rev. Hugh Hamilton Madden, M.A., Chancellor of Cashel; *m.* 1st, 1868, Minnie (*d.* 1895), *d.* of Lewis Moore, D.L., Cremorgan, Queen's Co.; 2nd, 1896, Jessie Isabelle, *d.* of Richard Warburton, D.L., Garryhinch, King's Co. *Educ.:* Trinity College, Dublin (Classical Scholar and Medallist; Gold Medallist in Ethics and Logics). Barr. Ireland, 1864; Q.C. 1880; third Serjeant-at-Law, 1887; Solicitor-General for Ireland, 1888; Attorney-General, 1889-92; M.P. (C.) for Dublin University, 1887-92. *Publications:* Treatise on Registration of Deeds, etc., 1868; 2nd ed. 1901; Practice of Land Judges

Court, 1870, 3rd ed. 1888; The Diary of Master William Silence; a Study of Shakespeare and of Elizabethan Sport, 1897; new edition, 1907; Some Passages in the Early History of Classical Learning in Ireland, 1907; Shakespeare and his Fellows, an attempt to decipher the Man and his Nature, 1916; A Chapter of Mediæval History: The Fathers of Literature, of Sport, and Horses, 1923. *Recreations:* riding, fishing, literature. *Address:* The Orchard, East Sheen, Surrey. *Clubs:* University, Kildare Street, Dublin. *(Died 6 Mar. 1928.)*

MADDEN, Hon. Sir Frank, Kt., *cr.* 1911; Speaker of Legislative Assembly Victoria, since 1904; *b.* Cork, 1847; *m.* Annie Eliza, *d.* of late Hon. Goodall Francis. *Educ.:* London; Beauchamp; Melbourne. Went to Australia, 1857; M.L.A. Eastern Suburbs, 1884-1904; Boroondara since 1904. *Address:* Mooroolbeck, Studleigh Park, Kew, Melbourne.
(Died Feb. 1921.)

MADDEN, Hon. Sir John, G.C.M.G., *cr.* 1906; K.C.M.G., *cr.* 1899; Kt., *cr.* 1893; Chief Justice of Supreme Court, Victoria, since 1893; Lieut.-Governor, 1899; Chancellor of Melbourne University, 1897; administered Government of Victoria, Jan. 1900 to Oct. 1901; *b.* 16 May 1844; *m.* 1872, Gertrude Frances, *d.* of F. J. S. Stephen; one *s.* five *d. Educ.:* Melbourne University (B.A. 1863; LL.D. 1866; Hon. D.C.L. Oxford, 1906); Hon. LL.D. Aberdeen. Australian Barr. 1866. *Address:* Cloyne, St. Kilda, Melbourne; Yamala, Frankston, Victoria. *Club:* Melbourne, Melbourne.
(Died 9 Mar. 1918.)

MADDEN, Hon. Walter, J.P.; Member Victorian Executive Council; Chairman and Managing Director National Trustees Executors and Agency Company, Melbourne; Vice-Chairman, National Mutual Life Association of Australasia Limited; *b.* Cork, Ireland, 1848; *s.* of John and Margaret Madden; unmarried. *Educ.:* Clapham; France; Melbourne. Began as a midshipman on board H.M.S. Victoria, and for a time was engaged in marine survey of Victorian coast; then became land surveyor in Victorian public service; entered Parliament, 1880; Minister of Lands, 1881-82; was member for the Wimmera District and Chairman of the Country party in the Legislative Assembly; took a prominent part in dealing with land, water-supply, railway, and rabbit questions; was Vice-President of Royal Commission on vegetable products, which was appointed on his motion in 1886; was member of Royal Commission with reference to the Transfer of Land Statute and the Management of the Titles Office, and of the Royal Commission on Irrigation and Water-Supply. *Recreations:* no special recreations. *Address:* Queen Street, Melbourne. *T.A.:* National, Melbourne. *T.:* 1784. *Clubs:* Melbourne Australian, Reform. *(Died 3 Aug. 1925.)*

MADDISON, Rev. William, M.A.; Vicar of Gosforth, Newcastle-on-Tyne, since 1893; Hon. Canon of Newcastle, 1908; *b.* 1853; *s.* of Thomas Maddison; *m.* 1879, Elizabeth, *o. d.* of George Blagdon of Red-hill, Durham; two *s.* two *d. Educ.:* Durham School, K.S. and Head of School; University College, Durham (Classical Scholar, 1872-75). B.A. 1st Class Classics, 1875; Fellow of the University, 1875; Deacon, 1876; Priest, 1877; Curate of East Rainton, 1876; Bedlington, 1879; Vicar of Blyth, 1882-87; St. Augustine's, Tynemouth, 1887-93; Chaplain to City of Newcastle Asylum, 1893-1906. *Address:* Gosforth Vicarage, Newcastle-on-Tyne.
(Died 8 July 1920.)

MADDOCK, Sir Simon, Kt., *cr.* 1922; J.P., D.L.; Chairman Urban Council of Rathmines; Member County of Dublin County Council; Member of Council, Royal Dublin Society; Council Dublin Chamber of Commerce; Director Johnston, Mooney & O'Brien,

Limited; James H. Webb & Co. Limited; Housing of the Very Poor Association, Ltd.; Governor Meath Hospital, National Children's Hospital, and Westmoreland Government Hospital; *b.* 4 May 1869; *s.* of late Benjamin Maddock, 52 Dartmouth Square, Dublin; *m.* 1901, Randalina Augusta Caroline, *d.* of Colonel J. D. Johnstone, D.L., and Hon. Mrs. Augusta Johnstone of Snow Hill, Lisbellaw, Co. Fermanagh; one *d. Educ:* High School, Dublin. *Address:* Mount Jerome House, Dublin. *T.:* Rathmines 269. *Clubs:* Constitutional; Hibernian United Service, Dublin.*(Died 15 Dec. 1927.)*

MADELEY, Earl of; Richard George Archibald John Lucien Hungerford Crew-Milnes; *e. s.* and *heir* of 1st Marquess of Crewe; *b.* 7 Feb. 1911. *(Died 31 Mar. 1922.)*

MADEN, Sir John Henry; Kt., *cr.* 1915; J.P. for Lancashire; C.C.; M.P. (L.) Rossendale, N.E. Lancs, 1892-1900, and (Coal.) 1917-18; *b.* 11 Sep. 1862-18; *s.* of late Henry Maden; *m.* 1891, Alice, *d.* of late Joshua Meller, Lytham, Lancashire; one *s. Educ.:* Gram. School, Manchester. First Freeman of Bacup; Mayor of Bacup, 1896-97, 1900-10, 1917. *Recreations:* golf, billiards, etc. *Address:* Rockcliffe House, Bacup, Lancashire. *T.A.:* Magpie, Manchester. *T.:* Bacup 121. *Clubs:* Reform. Devonshire, National Liberal.
(Died 18 Feb. 1920.)

MADGE, Sir William Thomas; 1st Bt., *cr.* 1919; *b.* Plymouth, 1845; *m.* 1st, 1865. Mary Helen Webber (*d.* 1891); two *s.* (decd.) two *d.* ; 2nd, 1892, Judith Ketchell. Six years on the Western Morning News at Plymouth; joined The Globe in London in 1866; soon became publisher, and subsequently manager; resigned in 1908 after 42 years' active service; became Proprietor, 1912-14; started The People Newspaper (Limited), the first Conservative Sunday penny paper, 1881; jointly with the late Sir G. C. H. Armstrong acquired the whole paper, which soon became a phenomenal success under his management; in 1914 became sole proprietor, retiring in 1922; ran the Sun, 1904-6; was responsible for the now historic journalist coup, in the publication in The Globe of 30th May 1878 of the Salisbury-Schouvaloff Treaty; appeared at the Bar of the House of Commons in Aug. 1901, with the then editor, in connection with a leading article reflecting on the Irish Party. *Heir: g.s.* Frank William, *b.* 2 Mar. 1897. *Recreations:* motoring, an ardent politician. *Address:* Broughton Lodge, Putney, S.W.15; Devonia, St. Margaret's Bay, Kent. *T.:* Putney 2012, and St. Margaret's Bay 27. *M.:* YL7167, NP8514. *Clubs:* Constitutional, United.
(Died 29 Jan. 1927.)

MAPLIN, Major George Hamilton, I.S.O. 1913; V.D.; Chief Inspector Customs Preventive Service, Calcutta. *Address:* Customs Service, Calcutta.

MAGNAY, Sir William, 2nd Bt., *cr.* 1844; *b.* 30 Nov. 1855; *S.* father 1871; *m.* Margaret, *d.* of Matthew Soulsby, 1879; two *s.* one *d. Publications:* The Fall of a Star, 1897; The Pride of Life; The Heiress of the Season, 1899; The Man-Trap, 1900; The Red Chancellor, 1901; The Man of the Hour, 1902; Count Zarka, 1903; The Master Spirit, 1906; The Mystery of the Unicorn, 1907; The Duke's Dilemma, 1907; The Amazing Duke, 1907; The Red Stain, 1908; The Powers of Mischief, 1909; The Long Hand, 1911; Paul Burdon, 1912; The Players, 1913; The Fruit of Indiscretion, 1913; The Price of Delusion, 1914; The Black Lake, 1915. *Heir: s.* Christopher Boyd William [*b.* 27 Mar. 1884. *Educ.:* Harrow; Pembroke College, Cambridge]. *Address:* 8 Gloucester Place, Portman Square, W. *T.:* Mayfair, 3653. *Club:* Union.
(Died 8 Jan. 1917.)

MAGNUS, Katie (Lady Magnus); *b.* 2 May 1844; *d.* of late E. Emanuel, J.P., South-

sea; *m.* 1870, Sir Philip Magnus, Bt., M.P.; two *s.* one *d. Educ.:* home. *Publications:* First Makers of England; Minor Moralities and Heresies; Outlines of Jewish History; Jewish Portraits; Picture Stories from the Bible; Book of Verse; Boys of the Bible; Little Miriam's Bible and Holiday Stories; numerous contributions in prose and verse to Westminster Gazette; articles in National Review, Spectator, and other magazines, etc. *Address:* 16 Gloucester Terrace, W.2; Tangley-Hill, Chilworth, Surrey. *T. A.:* Chilworth, Surrey.
(Died 2 Mar. 1924.)

MAGRATH, Maj.-Gen. Beauchamp Henry Whittingham; Indian Army; *b.* 4 Feb. 1832; *m.* 1871, Manie, *d.* of H. Greene, Bray, Co. Wicklow. Entered army, 1849; Maj.-Gen. 1890; unemployed list, 1890. *Address:* Mountjoie, London Road, Camberley, Surrey. *Club:* Junior Constitutional.*(Died 13 Nov. 1920.)*

MAGUINNESS, Rev. John Thomas, Hon. Canon of Ripon. *Address:* Lagg Cottage, Maxwell Road, Bournemouth.*(Died 20 Oct. 1920)*

MAGUIRE, James Rochfort, C.B.E. 1918; M.A.; *b.* 1855; *m.* Julia Beatrice, *e. d.* of 1st Viscount Peel, 1895. *Educ.:* Cheltenham; Merton Coll., Oxford. Formerly Fellow of All Souls Coll., Oxford. Barr. Inner Temple, 1883; M.P. (N.) N. Donegal, 1890-92; W. Clare, 1892-1895; Chairman of the British South Africa Company since 1923; Chairman of the Rhodesian Railways, Ltd. *Address:* 3 Cleveland Square, S.W.1. *T.:* Regent 382.
(Died 18 April 1925.)

MAGUIRE, Most Rev. John A., D.D.; R.C. Archbishop of Glasgow since 1902; *b.* Glasgow, 8 Sept. 1851. *Educ.:* St. Mungo's Academy, and St. Aloysius College, Glasgow; Stonyhurst College; Glasgow University; Propaganda, Rome. Assistant Cathedral, Glasgow, 1875; Diocesan Secretary, 1879; Incumbent of Partick, 1883; Canon, 1884; Vicar-General, 1885; Provost of Chapter, 1893; Auxiliary Bishop (titular of Trocmadae), 1894. *Address:* 160 Renfrew Street, Glasgow.
(Died 14 Oct. 1920.)

MAHAFFY, His Honour Arthur William, O.B.E. 1919; Administrator of Dominica since 1915; *b.* 22 Oct. 1869; *s.* of late Sir John Pentland Mahaffy, Provost of Trinity College, Dublin, and Frances, *d.* of William MacDougall of Drumleck, Howth, Ireland; *m.* 1903, Enid, *d.* of Captain Boyd of the Devonshire Regiment and Australia; two *s.* one *d. Educ.:* Marlborough; Magdalen College, Oxford; Trinity College, Dublin. Second Lieut. R. Munster Fusiliers, 1892-5; Govt. Agent Gilbert Islands, 1896; Assistant to Resident, British Solomon Islands, 1897; Deputy Commissioner W. Pacific and Magistrate W. Solomon, 1898; Colonial Secretary Fiji, 1904; Assistant High Commissioner W. Pacific, 1908: Member of Anglo-French Conference on New Hebrides, 1914. *Publications:* occasional contributions to Blackwood. *Recreations:* rowing, fishing, shooting, and cricket; all outdoor sports; winning Varsity Four, Oxford (record time, 6 mins. 30 secs.), 1889; winning Trial viii., 1890; rowed at Henley several years; captain of Dublin U. Boat Club three years in succession. *Address:* Government House, Dominica, B.W.I. *T.A.:* Accentors, Dominica. *Clubs:* New University, Leander; Dominica. *(Died 28 Oct. 1919.)*

MAHAFFY, Rev. Gilbert; Canon of Christ Church Cathedral, Dublin, 1905-16; Incumbent of Booterstown, Co. Dublin, 1913-1916. *Educ.:* Royal Belfast Academical Institution; Trinity College, Dublin (M.A.). Ordained 1873; Curate of Strabane, 1873-75; St. George's, Dublin, 1875-79; Monkstown, 1879-86; Incumbent of St. Paul, Dublin, 1886-94; St. Mary, 1894-96; St. Peter's, 1896-1913.; Prebendary of

St. Michael's, 1914-16. *Address:* 27 Wellington Place, Clyde Road, Dublin. (*Died 20 Dec. 1916.*)

MAHAFFY, Sir John Pentland, G.B.E., *cr.* 1918; C.V.O. 1904; J.P. for Co. Dublin; Scholar, Graduate, now Provost, Trinity Coll. Dublin; Hon Phil.D. of Louvain, 1908; late Fellow and Professor of Ancient History; late precentor of the College chapel; M.A.; D.D.; Mus.D. of Dublin; Hon. D.C.L. of Oxford; Hon. LL.D. St. Andrews, and of Athens, 1912; Hon. Fellow of Queen's Coll.' Oxford; Knight Commander of the Order of the Redeemer in Greece; Corresponding Member of Imperial Academy of Vienna; of Royal Academy, Berlin; of the Lincei, Rome; Hon. Member of Academy of Sciences, Utrecht; of the Parnassus at Athens; of the Archæol. Society of Alexandria; of the Royal Society of Bavaria; Commissioner of Intermediate Education, Ireland; President Royal Irish Academy, 1911-16; Member of the Irish Convention, 1917-18; Vice-Provost of Trinity College, 1913; *b.* Switzerland, 26 Feb. 1839; *y. c.* of Rev. Nath. B. Mahaffy and of William MacDougall, Howth, 1865; two *s.* two *d.* *Educ.:* home, but in Switzerland and Germany, where his parents resided, till age of 11. Owns property in Co. Monaghan, where he sits on the Grand Jury; High Sheriff, 1901-1902 and 1918-19. *Publications:* A translation of Kuno Fischer's Commentary on Kant, 1866; Twelve Lectures on Primitive Civilisation, 1868; Prolegomena to Ancient History, 1871; Kant's Critical Philosophy for English Readers, 1871; Greek Social Life from Homer to Menander, 1874, 7th ed. 1900; Greek Antiquities, 1876, now a school-book in France, Russia, and Hungary; Rambles and Studies in Greece, 1876, 5th ed. 1905; Greek Education, 1879; A History of Classical Greek Literature, 1880; Report on the Irish Grammar Schools, 1880-81; The Decay of Modern Preaching, 1882; The Story of Alexander's Empire, 1890; Greek Life and Thought from Alexander to the Roman Conquest, 1887; The Art of Conversation, 1889; The Greek World under Roman Sway; Greek Pictures, 1890; Problems in Greek History, 1892; Sketch of the Life and Teaching of Descartes; edited Duruy's Roman History, 1883-86; Alexander's Empire, 1887; The Petrie Papyri deciphered and explained; 3 vols. (viii., ix., xi.) of the Cunningham Memoirs, published by the Royal Irish Academy, 1891-1905; Empire of the Ptolemies, 1896; Petrie's History of Egypt, vol. iv.; An Epoch in Irish History, 1904; The Silver Age of the Greek World, 1906; What have the Greeks done for Modern Civilisation? Lowell Lectures, 1909. *Recreations:* played cricket for many years in Gentlemen of Ireland, after playing for his College; shot in Irish Eight at Wimbledon; game-shooting, salmon fishing, music. *Address:* Provost's House, Dublin; Earlscliff, Baily, Ireland. *Clubs:* Athenæum; Fellows Trin. Coll. Dublin.
(*Died 30 April 1919.*)

MAHDI HUSAIN, Khan, Wahud-ud-Daula, Azod-ul-Mulk, Nawab Mirza, Khan Bahadur, C.I.E. 1911; *b.* 1834. *Educ.:* India; Arabia. Travelled extensively in Arabia, Persia, Afghanistan, Baluchistan, and Europe; visited Mecca, Medina, Kaymiani; Kaiser-i-Hind gold medal, 1907. *Publication:* Takhullus. *Recreations:* riding and shooting. *Address:* Tirminigaz, Lucknow, U.P.

MAHER, Maj.-Gen. Sir James, K.C.M.G., *cr.* 1918; C.B. 1916; late A.M.S.; *b.* 27 Dec. 1858; *m.* 1902, Gertrude, *d.* of J. F. Browne, B.C.S. Entered R.A.M.C. 1885; Maj.-Gen. 1918; served Soudan, 1885 (medal with clasp, bronze star); Ashanti, 1895-1896 (honour) ably mentioned, prom. Surgeon-Major, star); European War, 1914-18 (K.C.M.G., C.B.);

Director Medical Services Headquarters, Egypt, 1916-17; retired pay, 1917. *Address:* The Moorings, Boundary Road, Worthing.
(*Died 7 Jan. 1923.*)

MAHON, Sir William Henry, 5th Bt., *cr.* 1819; D.S.O. 1900; J.P., D.L.; late Col. commanding 4th West Yorkshire Regt.; *b.* 31 Dec. 1856; *S.* father, 1893; *m.* 1905, Hon. Edith Dillon, 2nd *d.* of 4th Lord Clonbrock; two *s.* one *d.* Served South African War, 1900-2 (despatches). *Heir: s.* George Edward John, *b.* 22 June 1911. *Address:* Castlegar, Ahascragh, Co. Galway. *Clubs:* Carlton; Kildare Street, Dublin.
(*Died 13 Aug. 1926.*)

MAHONY, Rt. Rev. Mgr. John Mathew, J.C.D., V.G., Dean of Hamilton Diocese, Ontario, 1906, and Vicar-General since 1909; Rector of Cathedral since 1899; *b.* Hamilton, Ont., 1862. *Educ.:* Hamilton; St. Jerome's College, Berlin; Grand Seminary, Montreal; Laval University. Ordained, 1894; Privy Chamb. to the Pope, 1908; Domestic Prelate, 1912. *Address:* 56 Mulberry Street, Hamilton, Ontario. (*Died 8 May 1918.*)

MAHONY, Major Michael Joseph, D.S.O. 1916; M.D., R.U.I.; Hon. Physician, St. Vincent's Hospice for the Dying; *s.* of Richard Mahony, Tramore. *Educ.:* Castleknock College, Dublin. Major R.A.M.C.; served South African War, 1900-1 (Queen's medal four clasps); European War, 1914-18 (despatches, D.S.O., immediate award, Somme 1916, T.D.); Médaille de Reconnaissance Française (en argent). *Address:* 33 Derby Lane, Stoneycroft, Liverpool. (*Died Dec. 1927.*)

MAIDEN, Joseph Henry, F.R.S. 1916; I.S.O., J.P., F.L.S., Director of the Botanic Gardens, Sydney; retired, 1924; Government Botanist, N.S.W.; *b.* St. John's Wood, London, 25 April 1859; *e. s.* of Henry Maiden; *m.* 1883, Jeanie, *y. d.* of John Hammond of Manchester; four *d.* *Educ.:* City of London Middle Class School, and as assistant to late Prof. Frederick Barff, M.A. First Curator Technological Museum, N.S.W., 1881; late Superintendent of Technical Education; Consulting Botanist, Forest Department, and Department of Agriculture; hon. or corresponding member of a large number of scientific societies; Linnean Medal, 1915. *Publications:* Useful Native Plants of Australia; Illustrated Flowering Plants and Ferns of New South Wales; Manual of the Grasses of New South Wales; Wattles and Wattle-barks; Forest Flora of New South Wales; Critical Revision of the genus Eucalyptus; Sir Joseph Banks, the Father of Australia, etc. *Address:* Botanic Gardens, Sydney. (*Died 16 Nov. 1925.*)

MAIN, Lt.-Commdr. Frank Morgan, R.D., R.N.R., D.S.O. 1915; served on patrol duty, European War, 1914-17 (despatches, D.S.O.).
(*Died 21 Oct. 1924.*)

MAINWARING, Colonel Charles Salusbury; Colonel late 1st V.B. Royal Welsh Fusiliers; J.P., D.L., Co. Denbigh; J.P. Merioneth and Carnarvon; *b.* 7 July 1845; *e. s.* of T. Mainwaring, M.P. for Denbigh; *m.* 1901, Gertrude, *d.* of Thomas Loverock; one *s.* one *d.* *Educ.:* Eton; Christ Church, Oxford; M.A. 1870. Served in Denbighshire Yeomanry, Royal Denbigh Militia and Denbighshire Volunteers; commanded the Battalion, 1890-99; was the first Commanding officer to receive the Q. distinction for passing in all military subjects: contested (C.) West Denbighshire, 1885. *Recreations:* agriculture, garden; County Council; Welsh University Court; Education. *Address:* Galltfaenan, Trefnant, R.S.O.; Cerrigydruidion, N. Wales. *Clubs:* Carlton. Junior Carlton, Boodle's, Hurlingham. (*Died 14 June 1920.*)

MAINWARING, Hon. Maj.-Gen. Rowland Broughton, C.M.G. 1899; retired; *b.* 11 Sep. 1850; *s.* of late Rev. C. H. Mainwaring of Whitmore, Stafford; *m.* 1880, Evelyn Louisa

Jane, d. of late Capt. Mervyn Archdale. *Educ.*. Marlborough. Entered army, 1871 : Col. 1899 ; served Gold Coast, 1873 (Ashanti medal); Burmese expedition, 1885-86 ; commanded expedition from Bhamo, Mogoung, 1886 (medal with clasp) ; served Hazara expedition, 1891 (clasp) ; commanded 2nd Batt. Royal Welsh Fusiliers, Crete, 1898 (Bt. of Col., C.M.G.); A.A.G. Portsmouth, 1899 ; A.A.G. S. Africa, 1899-1900 (despatches, Queen's medal 2 clasps); commanded 23rd Regimental Dist. 1900-1906 ; 68th Welsh Div., 1915-17. *Address :* The Lodge, Bembridge, Isle of Wight. *T.A. :* Bembridge. *T. :* Bembridge 47. *Club :* Army and Navy.
(*Died 22 Nov. 1926.*)

MAIR, Alexander, M.A. ; Professor of Philosophy, University of Liverpool, since 1910 ; *b.* Glasgow, 1870 ; *m.* 1903, Isabel Hewitt, Bangor ; one *s.* four *d. Educ. :* Edinburgh University. Graduated M.A. (1st Class Honours in Philosophy), 1898 ; Assistant Lecturer in Philosophy and English Literature, University College of North Wales, 1899 ; Assistant Lecturer in Philosophy, Liverpool, 1900 ; Independent Lecturer in Philosophy, Liverpool, 1904; Dean of the Faculty of Arts, Liverpool, 1908-11 ; Examiner in Philosophy, Aberdeen, 1904-8 ; Edinburgh, 1909-12 ; President of University Club, Liverpool, 1921 ; President of Liverpool Psychological Society, 1924 ; President of Association of University Teachers, 1925. *Publications :* Belief, Hallucination, Ency. of Religion and Ethics ; Philosophy and Reality, 1911 ; various articles and reviews. *Recreations :* walking, and golf. *Address :* 26 Parkfield Road, Liverpool. *Club :* University, Liverpool. (*Died 8 Oct. 1927.*)

MAIR, Prof. Alexander W. ; Litt.D. Aber. 1911 ; Professor of Greek, Edinburgh University, since 1903 ; *m.* 1906 ; five *s.* six *d. Educ. :* Aberdeen Univ., 1889-93 (1st Class Honours Classical Literature, Liddell Prize for Verse Composition, 1890, 1891, 1892, 1893 ; Simpson Prize for Greek, 1893) ; Fullerton Scholar, 1893 ; Ferguson Scholar, 1894 ; Caius College, Camb. University, 1893-98 (1st Division 1st Class Classical Tripos, Part I., 1896; 1st Class with Special Distinction Class. Tripos, Part II., 1898) ; Craven Scholar, 1897 ; Sir W. Browne Medal, 1897 ; Senior Chancellor's Medallist, 1898 ; Schuldham Plate, 1898 ; Fellow Gonville and Caius, 1899-1905; Lecturer Aberdeen University, 1898-99 ; Lecturer Edinburgh Univ. 1899-1903 ; Classical Examiner to London University, 1919-23. *Publications :* Hesiod, Introduction, Translation and Appendices, 1908 ; Callimachus, 1921 ; Lycophron, 1921 ; in Hastings' Encyclopædia of Ethics, etc., articles on Hesiod, Pindar, Life and Death, Sin, Suicide, Worship ; much verse contributed to various magazines. *Recreation :* golf. *Address :* 9 Corrennie Drive, Edinburgh. *T. :* 52632. (*Died 13 Nov. 1928.*)

MAIR, Charles, LL.D. (Hon.) Queen's University, Kingston, Ont., 1904 ; author ; for many years in Canadian Government Civil Service; superannuated, 1921; Canadian Government Immigration Agent in charge of the Fort Steele District of East Kootenay, B.C. ; *b.* Canada, 21 Sep. 1838 ; *s.* of late James Mair, Scotland ; *m.* 1869, Eliza L. Mackenney, *niece* of late Sir John Schultz ; one *s.* three *d. Educ. :* Grammar School, Perth, Canada; Queen's University, Kingston. Paymaster for Dominion Government to men engaged in opening immigration road from Fort Garry to Lake of the Woods, 1868 ; prisoner in the hands of the insurrectionists, 1869-70 ; sentenced to death, but escaped, and joined expedition from Portage la Prairie to Fort Garry ; one of the founders of the "Canada First" party ; was acting Quartermaster of the Governor-General's Body Guard, the Toronto Cavalry Regiment, commanded by Lieut.-Col George T. Denison in Riel's North-West Rebellion of 1885 ; ex-Fellow Royal

Society of Canada. *Publications :* Dreamland and other poems, 1868 ; Tecumseh, 1886 ; Through the Mackenzie Basin, a Narrative of the Athabasca and Peace River Expedition of 1899 ; The American Bison, an article contributed to the Royal Society of Canada. *Address :* 1601, 15th Ave. W., Calgary, Alberta, Canada.
(*Died July 1927.*)

MAIR, George Herbert, C.M.G. 1920 ; Assistant Director on League of Nations Secretariat since 1919 ; *b.* 8 May 1887 ; *e. s.* of late Fleet Surgeon G. Mair, R.N. ; *m.* 1911, Maire O'Neill ; one *s.* one *d. Educ. :* Aberdeen University (M.A., Seafield Gold Medal); Christ Church, Oxford (Scholar, B.A. 1st Cl. Mod. Hist.). Joined editorial staff Manchester Guardian, 1909, and acted as leader writer, special correspondent, literary editor and political correspondent in London, 1911-14; Assistant Editor Daily Chronicle, 1914, but resigned to devote full time to Government work first under Home Office and later with Foreign Office (News Dept.) Department of Information and Ministry of Information; Assistant Secretary Ministry of Information, 1918 ; Director of Press Section British Peace Delegation, Paris, 1919 ; Chevalier of the Legion of Honour, 1919. *Publications :* Edition of Wilson's Arte of Rhetorique, 1908; English Literature : Modern, 1911 ; enlarged edition of above, 1914 ; articles in many papers and reviews. *Recreation :* walking. *Address :* 34 Walpole Street, S.W.3. *T. :* Vict. 4999. *Clubs :* Garrick, Savile, St. James's. (*Died 2 Jan. 1926.*)

MAIR, John Bagrie, O.B.E. 1920 ; M.V.O. 1909; J.P. Morayshire: Chief Constable of Morayshire; *b.* Drumblade, Aberdeenshire, 8 May 1857; *s.* of late John Mair, farmer, Pitscurry, Huntly; *m.* 1883, Jessie, *e. d.* of Wm. Blackley, High Blantyre, Lanarkshire; three *s.* three *d. Educ. :* Longhill School ; privately. At the age of 21 years appointed a constable in the Lanarkshire Constabulary ; a Sergeant in the Burgh of Johnstone, 1883 ; a Detective Inspector in the Burgh of Paisley, 1885 ; a Superintendent in the Burgh of Elgin, 1890 ; Chief Constable of County and Burgh of Elgin, 1892 ; has been in charge of the Police arrangements when Royalty visited this county on 14 different occasions ; has received valuable presents from King George when Prince of Wales ; awarded the King's Police Medal, 1922. *Recreations :* golf, fishing, and curling. *Address :* Maida View, Elgin. *T. :* 18. *M. :* SO 505. *Clubs :* Moray Golf, Elgin, Elgin.
(*Died 26 Jan. 1927.*)

MAIR, Very Rev. William, M.A., D.D., retired Parish Minister ; *b.* Savoch, 1830 ; *s.* of Rev. James Mair, M.A., schoolmaster ; *m.* 1866, Isabella, *d.* of David Edward of Balruddery. *Educ. :* Savoch Parish School ; Aberdeen Grammar School ; Marischal College and University, Aberdeen. Minister at Lochgelly, 1861-64 ; Parish Minister of Ardoch, 1864-69 ; of Earlston, 1869-1903 ; Moderator of the Church of Scotland, 1897 ; retired to Edinburgh, 1903. *Publications :* A Digest of Laws and Decisions, Ecclesiastical and Civil, relating to the Constitution, Practice, and Affairs of the Church of Scotland, 4th edit. 1911 ; Speaking, 4th edit. 1908 ; The Truth about the Church of Scotland, 1891 ; Jurisdiction in Matters Ecclesiastical, 1896; Loyalty : The Christ our King, address to the General Assembly, 1897 ; pamphlets on Union of Scottish Churches—Churches and the Law, 1904 ; The Scottish Churches, two papers, 1907 ; The Scottish Churches : National Religion, 1907 ; The Scottish Churches : The Hope of Union, 1909 ; The Scottish Churches : External Relations, 1912 ; The Scottish Churches, Jan. 1914 ; The Scottish Churches, Jan. 1915 ; My Young Communicant, 1906 ; several other pamphlets ; My Life, 1911 ; Action Sermons, 1917 ; The Scottish Churches, 1918. *Address :* 145 Mayfield Road, Edinburgh. *T. :* 5076.
(*Died 27 Jan. 1920.*)

MAIRIS, Gen. Geoffrey, late R. Marines ; *b.* 23 May 1834 ; *y. s.* of late Major V. H. Mairis, formerly 78th Highlanders and 6th Dragoon Guards, of Marston and Collingbourne, Wilts., and Elizabeth, *y. d.* and *co-heiress* of late Thomas Edwards, The Manor House, West Lavington, Wilts., and *g. s.* of late Rev. Wm. Mairis, D.D., of Exeter College, Oxford, Rector of Wallingford, Berks., Vicar West Lavington, Wilts., Prebendary of Wells Cathedral, and Chaplain to late Duke of Kent; *m.* 1867, Barbara, 3rd *d.* of late Richard Brouncker of Boveride, Dorset. Entered army, 1852 ; General, 1896 ; retired, 1899 ; served Crimea, 1854 - 55, including battle of Balaclava and siege of Sevastopol (medal with 2 clasps; 5th Cl. Medjidie, Turkish medal); China, 1857 - 61, including storm and capture of Taku Forts and occupation of Pekin (wounded, despatches, medal with 2 clasps) ; Zulu War, 1879 ; Commanded Battalion, Ireland, 1881-82 ; Depôt, 1883-85 ; 1st Division (Chatham), 1885-86. *Recreations:* shooting, hunting. *Address:* 51 St. Aubyn's, Hove, Sussex. *Club:* United Service.   (*Died 22 April 1917.*)

MAITLAND, Rev. Adam Gray, LL.D. ; Hon. Canon of Worcester ; Deacon, 1878 ; Priest, 1879 ; Vicar of Dudley, 1892-1918.   (*Died 16 Aug. 1928.*)

MAITLAND, Dalrymple, J.P. ; C.P. ; Speaker of House of Keys since 1909 ; Chairman of the Isle of Man Steam Packet Co. Ltd. ; the Isle of Man Railway Co. ; and the Isle of Man Banking Co. Ltd. ; Director of the Liverpool Daily Post and Mercury ; *b.* Liverpool, 1848 ; *s.* of John Maitland, Editor and one of the Proprietors of the Liverpool Mercury, and Agnes, *d.* of James Dalrymple, Isle of Man ; *m.* 1879, Fanny, *d.* of Charles Caley, Merchant, Douglas, Isle of Man. *Educ.:* Private schools, Liverpool and Douglas. On leaving school went into business with William Dalrymple at the Union Mills, Isle of Man, as Woollen Manufacturer and Corn Miller ; retired from business, 1887 ; one of the members for Middle Sheading, House of Keys, since 1890. *Address:* Brook Mooar, Union Mills, Isle of Man. *Clubs:* National Liberal ; Junior Reform, Liverpool ; Ellan Vannen, Douglas.   (*Died 25 Mar. 1919.*)

MAITLAND, Air-Comm. Edward Maitland, C.M.G. 1919 ; D.S.O. 1917 ; A.F.C. 1919 ; R.A.F. ; B.A. ; F.R.G.S. ; senior Airship Officer ; took part in R 34's Atlantic crossing, 1919 ; *b.* '21 Feb. 1880 ; *e. s.* of late Arthur Maitland, M.A., J.P. *Educ.:* Haileybury ; Trinity Coll., Camb. 2nd Lt. The Essex Regt. 1900 ; Adjutant 3rd Batt. 1906-1909 ; appointed to Balloon School, South Farnborough, 1909; Air Battalion, 1910; Commanding Officer, No. 1 Squadron, R.F.C. (Airships), on formation of Royal Flying Corps, 1913 ; early in 1914, when the Admiralty took over the Army Airships, was gazetted to the Royal Naval Air Service, as Wing Commander ; Wing-Captain, 1915 ; Brig.-Gen. on formation of Royal Air Force, April 1918 ; served in South African War, 1901 - 2, Transvaal and Orange River Colony (medal and 4 clasps) ; served with Expeditionary Force, Belgium, early in 1914 with observation balloons co-operating with British fleet ; American Distinguished Service Medal, 1917 ; American Navy Distinguished Service Cross, 1921. *Publication:* Log of the R 34. *Recreations:* ballooning, ski-running, tennis. *Address:* 16 Chelsea Court, S.W. *T.:* Western 1387. *Clubs:* White's, Orleans, Bath, Garrick.   (*Died 24 Aug. 1921.*)

MAITLAND, Sir Herbert Lethington, Kt., *cr.* 1915 ; M.B. ; *s.* of late Duncan Mearns Maitland and Emily, *d.* of Duncan Dalgetty ; *b.* 12 Nov. 1868 ; *m.* 1898, Mabel Agnes, *u.* of Samuel Cook ; two *s. Educ.:* Newington College and Sydney University, M.B., M.Ch. ;

Surgeon, Sydney Hospital ; Lecturer in Clinical Surgery, Sydney University. *Address:* 147 Macquarie Street, Sydney. Australia.   (*Died 23 May 1923.*)

MAITLAND, William James, C.I.E. 1887 ; late Deputy Gov. Director of Indian Guaranteed Railways ; *b.* 22 July 1847 ; *s.* of late Augustus Maitland, and *g. s.* of late Sir Alexander Maitland, Bart., of Clifton Hall, Midlothian ; *m.* 1878, Agnes (*d.* 1908), *e. d.* of late Ralph Neville - Grenville of Butleigh Court, Glastonbury ; one *d. Educ.:* Edin. Academy. *Address:* 18 Lennox Gardens, S.W. *T.:* 5000 Kensington ; Witley Manor, Witley, Surrey. *Clubs:* Carlton, Travellers'. (*Died 8 May 1919.*)

MAITLAND, William Whitaker, C.V.O. 1921 ; O.B.E. 1918 ; Secretary to the Government, Jersey, C.I., since 1904 ; *b.* 15 June 1864 ; *e. s.* of Rev. J. Whitaker Maitland of Loughton Hall, Essex, and Venetia, *d.* of Sir R. Digby Neave of Dagnam, Essex ; *m.* 1902, Lindisfarne, *d.* of Archdeacon of Northumberland, and Lady Louisa Hamilton ; one *s.* one *d. Educ.:* Harrow ; Trinity Hall, Cambridge. Was in Ceylon, 1889-1902 ; Lord of the Manor of Loughton and patron of one living. *Recreations:* shooting and fishing. *Address:* Government Office, Jersey ; Loughton Hall, Essex. *T.:* Loughton 112. *Clubs:* Junior Carlton, Badminton.   (*Died 5 Nov. 1926.*)

MAITLAND - KIRWAN, Lionel ; of Gelston and Collin ; *b.* Dalgan Park, Co. Mayo, Ireland, 16 Apr. 1849 ; *s.* of Charles Lionel Maitland-Kirwan, D.L., of Co. Mayo, Ireland, and Matilda Elizabeth Maitland - Kirwan of Gelston Castle, Castle Douglas, N.B. ; *m.* Agnes, *y. d.* of Willwood Herries Maxwell of Munches, Dalbeattie, N.B. ; one *s.* two *d. Educ.:* Tutor and Crammer, Southsea. *Recreations:* shooting and fishing. *Address:* Collin, Castle Douglas, Kirkcudbrightshire. *T.:* Auchencairn 7. *T.A.:* Auchencairn. *Clubs:* Junior Carlton ; New, Edinburgh.   (*Died 5 June 1927.*)

MAJOR, Albany Featherstonehaugh, O.B.E. 1918 ; F.S.A. ; Principal, War Office (retired) ; Hon. Secy. Committee on Ancient Earthworks (Congress of Archæological Societies) ; *b.* 3 Dec. 1858, *e. s.* of late Charles Messenger Major and Emily, *e. d.* of late William Storey Featherstone ; *m.* 1901, Margit, *e. d.* of Albert Grön, Sandefjord, Norway. *Educ.:* Dulwich College. Appointed to Admiralty, 1878 ; transferred to War Office (after open competition), 1884 ; Hon. Secretary, Viking Club, 1894-1904 ; Hon. Editor, 1904-9 ; Hon. Vice-President, 1917 ; President, Croydon Natural History and Scientific Society, 1919-20. *Publications:* A Throw of the Dice ; An Ancient Tale Retold, 1884 ; Sagas and Songs of the Norsemen, 1894 ; Stories from the Northern Sagas (joint author), 1899 ; Early Wars of Wessex : being Studies from England's School of Arms in the West, 1913. *Recreation:* field archæology. *Address:* 30 The Waldrons, Croydon. *Club:* Authors'. (*Died 7 Dec. 1925.*)

MAJOR, Dr. Charles Immanuel Forsyth, F.R.S. 1908 ; F.Z.S., etc. ; scientist and explorer ; *b.* 1848 ; *s.* of Charles Forsyth Major, scholastic divine—a younger son of Capt. John Major and Ann, *d.* of Capt. John Forsyth, Royal Navy. Member and corresponding member of various British and foreign scientific societies ; and author of numerous scientific publications in England and abroad. *Address:* British Museum, South Kensington, S.W. ; Bastia, Corsica.   (*Died 25 Mar. 1923.*)

MAJOR, Francis William, C.M.G. 1917 ; I.S.O. 1910 ; *b.* 1863 ; *s.* of Charles Henry and Frederica Frances Sage Major; *m.* 1895, Eleanor Laura Louisa, *d.* of William Rowland Pyne ; no *c. Educ.:* The Philberds, near Maidenhead, Berks. Treasury, Trinidad, 1885 ; secretary to Road and Crown Lands Commission, Agricultural Contracts Commission, and Civil Service Commission, Trinidad, 1887-90 ; private secretary to Sir W. Robinson, 1888; assistant Comptroller of Customs, 1891; assistant Treasurer, 1891; Comptroller of Customs, 1895; Receiver-General Bermuda, and member Executive and Legislative Council, 1899; prepared scheme (which was approved by Secretary of State) for improvement of financial administration of Bermuda; Commissioner of Customs, 1908-22, M.L.C. and Currency Officer, Kenya; Government Representative, Homeward Loading Sub-Committee, 1917; Chairman, Port Advisory Board, Mombasa, 1920; served European War, 1914-18 (despatches); received thanks of Admiralty for services rendered; Croix de Chevalier, Belgium. *Recreations:* ordinary. *Address:* Mombasa, British East Africa. *(Died 7 Aug. 1923.)*

MAKGILL, Sir George, 11th Baronet of Kemback, *cr.* 1627; *b.* 12 Dec. 1868; *e. s.* of 10th Bart. and Margaret Isabella, *d.* of Robert Haldane, of Cloanden, Perthshire; *S.* father, 1906; *m.* 1891, Frances Elizabeth, *e. d.* of Alexander Innes Grant, of Merchiston, Otago, N.Z., and Frances Anne, *e. d.* of Colonel Henry Rutherfurd, Bengal Artillery; two *s.* two *d. Educ.:* privately. Has written novels, magazine articles, and stories, chiefly of Colonial life. *Publications:* Outside and Overseas; Cross Trails; Blacklaw, Felons, etc. *Heir:* s. John Donald Alexander Arthur Makgill, late Lieut. Coldstream Guards, *b.* 31 Dec. 1899. *Address:* Kemback, nr. Cupar, Fife; Yaxley Hall, Eye, Suffolk. *T.:* Eye 7. *Clubs:* Authors', Caledonian; New, Edinburgh. *(Died 17 Oct. 1926.)*

MALCOLM, Sir James William, 9th Bt., *cr.* 1665; *b.* 29 March 1862; *S.* cousin, 1901; *m.* 1885, Evelyn Alberta, 3rd *d.* of late Albert George Sandeman, and *g.d.* of late Viscount de Moncorvo; two *s.* two *d. Educ.:* Magdalene College, Cambridge; Administrative Assistant Ministry of Munitions, 1916. Late Captain Pembroke Artillery Militia; J.P. Counties Norfolk and Suffolk. *Heir:* s. Michael Albert James [*b.* 9 May 1898; *m.* 1918, Hon. Geraldine M. Digby, *d.* of 10th Baron Digby; one *s.* one *d. Educ.:* Eton. Lieut. Scots Guards, Special Reserve; served European War, 1914-18; wounded in France, 1918]. *Address:* Itchin, Stoke House, Alresford, Hants. *T.A.:* Alresford, Hants. *T.:* Alresford 79. *Clubs:* Boodle's, Royal Automobile. *(Died 30 April 1927)*

MALCOLMSON, Major-General John Henry Porter, C.B. 1897; retired; *b.* 20 Oct. 1832. *Educ.:* Private school; Addiscombe. Joined Bombay Artillery, 1849; served in the Indian Mutiny and Afghan campaign, 1878-80. *Decorated* for the rearguard action at Kushki na Khud in 1879. *Recreations:* has participated in cricket, boating, hunting, cycling, and shooting big and small game. *Club:* Junior United Service. *(Died 30 June 1920.)*

MALDEN, Charles Edward, M.A.; Recorder of Thetford since 1885; *b.* Chertsey, 1845; *e. s.* of late Henry Malden and Georgina, *d.* of Col. Drinkwater-Bethune; *m.* Sarah Fanny, 2nd *d.* of late Sir Richard Mayne, K.C.B., 1877; two *s.* two *d. Educ.:* Univ. Coll. School; Ipswich School; Trin. Coll. Camb. (Scholar and Prizeman); 1st class Classical Tripos, 1867. Barr. Inner Temple, 1870; practises on South-Eastern Circuit; Revising Barrister, 1884; Commissioner Civil Liabilities, 1916-20. *Address:* 15 Collingham Place, S.W.5. *T.:* Western 4323. *(Died 29 Nov. 1926.)*

MALET, Sir Charles St. Lo, 6th Bt., *cr.* 1791; *b.* 1 Nov. 1906; *s.* of 5th Bt. and Louise Michelle, *d.* of Philibert Dubois. *S.* father, 1909. *Heir:* u. Harry Charles, J.P. *b.* 1873; *m.* 1906, Mildred Laura, *d.* of Capt. H. S. Swiney, Gensing House, St. Leonards; one *s.* two *d.* Formerly in Cape Mounted Rifles and Capt. 8th Hussars; served South Africa, 1899-1902 (Queen's medal, four clasps, King's

medal, two clasps). *Address:* Wilbury, Salisbury]. *Address:* St. Lo, Westcliff Road, Broadstairs; 34 Corso d'Italia, Rome. *(Died 21 Nov. 1918.)*

MALET, Guilbert Edward Wyndham; Kt. of Grace, Order of S. John of Jerusalem; R.A., retired 1879; *b.* 12 July 1839; *e. s.* of W. W. Malet, Priest, and Eliza, 2nd *d.* of E. J. Esdaile, J.P., of Cothelstone House, Somerset; *m.* 1st, Florence, *d.* of C. W. Wilshere, J.P., of The Frythe, Welwyn; 2nd, Gertrude, *s. d.* of Sir P. Cunliffe Owen, K.C.B.; four *s.* two *d. Educ.:* Winchester. Lieut., Bengal Artillery, 1858; Royal Artillery, 1861; Royal Horse Artillery, 1865; Capt. and Adjt., 22nd Brigade R.A., 1872; R.H.A., 1874; Major, 1879; Capt., 1st Herts R.V., 1880-86; founder of the Army Guild, Holy Standard, 1873, and S. Helena, 1875; Secretary, W.I. Section, R. Colonial and Indian Exhibition, 1886; founder of Military and Naval Exhibitions, Chelsea, and Director of R.M.E., 1890 (surplus £10,100, for Soldiers' Church Institutes); Secretary, European Commission, Chicago Exposition, 1893, of Soldiers and Sailors Help Society, 1899, of Capetown Cathedral Memorial Fund, 1902, of S. Stephen's College Delhi Building Fund, 1913, Cambridge-Delhi Mission. *Publications:* History of J Battery Royal Horse Artillery; Soldiers' and Sailors' Friends Handbook. *Address:* 52 Penywern Road, S.W.5; Austin House, Frome. *(Died 15 Oct. 1918.)*

MALING, Captain Irwin Charles, C.M.G. 1892; *b.* 2 Feb. 1841; 2nd *s.* of late Commander Robert Saunders Maling, R.N., sometime H.M. Salt Commissioner, India; *m.* Emily Ann, *o. d.* of late Rev. Benjamin Whitelock, M.A., of Groombridge, Kent, 1868. *Educ.:* Wimbledon School and Royal Military Acad.; Neustadt, Austria. Formerly in 89th, 35th, and 23rd Regts.; retired 1879; served during Indian Mutiny, 1858-59 (medal); was private sec. and A.D.C. to Sir A. E. Kennedy, C.B., Gov.-in-Chief of W. African Settlements (successfully carried out several special missions to native chiefs), 1868-70; private sec. to Marquess of Normanby, G.C.M.G. (successively Gov. of Queensland and New Zealand), 1871-79; Colonial Sec. and Registrar-Gen. Grenada, 1879-89, and Administrator of St. Vincent, 1889-93; administered Govt. of Grenada, 1880, 1882, 1884, 1885, and 1886-87; acted as Colonial Sec. of Leeward Islands and Pres. of Antigua, 1888, and as Administrator of Leeward Islands, 1889; retired from official life, 1893. *Recreations:* shooting and fishing. *Address:* 5 St. John's Park, Blackheath, S.E. *Club:* Junior United Service. *(Died 13 June 1918.)*

MALINS, Sir Edward, Kt., *cr.* 1919; M.D. Edin., F.R.C.P. Lond., M.Sc. Birm.; J.P. Co. Warwick; J.P. City of Birmingham; Consulting Obstetric Physician to the General Hospital, Birmingham; Professor of Midwifery, University of Birmingham; *b.* Liverpool, 22 Dec. 1841; *s.* of Samuel Malins, M.D.; *m.* 1869, Mary (*d.* 1920), *d.* of Henry Owen, C.E.; five *s.* one *d. Educ.:* King Edward's School, Birmingham; Univ. of Edin. Appointed Medical Officer to Hospital for Women, Birmingham, 1876, and to the Lying-in Charity; Obstetric Physician to the General Hospital, 1877; Pres. Midland Medical Society, 1882; Pres. Birm. Branch Brit. Med. Assoc. 1901; Pres. Univ. Graduates' Club, 1876; President Birmingham Debating Society, 1880; President Obstetrical Society of London, 1903-4; Governor of King Edward's School; Bailiff, 1900; Examiner in Midwifery, Roy. Coll. Physicians, London; University of Manchester, etc. *Publications:* various papers in connection with Diseases of Women and Midwifery. *Recreations:* contributions to literature; arts; Church work, etc. *Address:* 50 Newhall Street, Birmingham.

T.A.: Malins, Birmingham. *T.*: 2114.
(*Died 23 July 1922.*)

MALLOCK, Major Charles Herbert,
D.S.O. 1917; Special Reserve, R.F.A.; *e. s.* of
late Richard Malloch and 1st wife, Mary Jones,
d. of T. A. H. Dickson, Liverpool; *b.* 15 May
1878; *m.* 1906, Margaret Iris, 4th *d.* of John
Bazley-White; three *s.* J.P., C.C., Patron
of one living and Lord of the Manor of Cockington; served S. Africa, 1901 (Queen's medal,
4 clasps); European War, 1914-17 (D.S.O.).
Address: Cockington Court, Torquay.
(*Died 5 Nov. 1917.*)

MALLOCK, William Hurrell, *s.* of William Mallock, and *e. d.* of Ven. R. H. Froude,
Archdeacon of Totnes (*sister* to J. A. Froude the
historian). *Educ.*: private tuition; Rev. W. B.
Philpot, Littlehampton; Balliol Coll. Oxford.
Third Class in Moderations; Second Class
Final Classical Schools; Newdegate prize
poem, 1872. Never adopted any profession,
though at one time intended for diplomacy; has spent a considerable portion of
his life since leaving Oxford in London
and Devonshire; also in South of France and
Italy; has travelled and resided in Cyprus and
East of Europe. *Publications*: The New Republic; religion and philosophy—Is Life Worth
Living? The New Land and Virginia; Studies of
Contemporary Superstitions; economic and
social science—Social Equality; Property and
Progress; Labour and the Popular Welfare,
1893; Classes and Masses, 1896; Aristocracy and
Evolution, 1898; Doctrine and Doctrinal Disrup-
tion, 1900; Religion as a Credible Doctrine,
1902; The Reconstruction of Belief, 1905; The
Nation as a Business Firm, 1910; Social
Reform, 1914; The Limits of Pure Democracy,
1918; novels—A Romance of the Nineteenth
Century; The Old Order Changes; A Human
Document; The Heart of Life: The Indi-
vidualist; The Veil of the Temple, 1904; two
small volumes of verses; Lucretius on Life and
Death, a Poem; An Immortal Soul, 1908;
Capital, War, and Wages, 1918; his main object
in his political and economic writings has been
to expose the fallacies of Radicalism and Socialism; his philosophic writings have aimed at
showing that science taken by itself can supply
man with no basis for religion. *Club*: Bachelors'.
(*Died 2 April 1923.*)

MALTBY, Lt.-Comdr. Gerald Rivers,
R.N.; M.V.O. 1902; *s.* of late Rev. Henry
Joseph Maltby, Canon of Durham; *b.* 1851; *m.*
1876, Hersey Eliza Cecilia (*d.* 1918), *d.* of late
Admiral Sir George Elliot, K.C.B. Entered
Navy; 1866; retired, 1876; served Ashanti, 1874
(despatches, promoted, medal and clasp); Assis-
tant Hon. Secretary General Committee R.N.
Exhibition, 1891; Hon. Secretary Royal Naval
Fund, 1892; Secretary Royal United Service
Institution, 1893-98; Assistant Secretary Im-
perial Institute, 1898-1902. *Address*: 54 St.
George's Square, S.W.1. *T.*: Victoria 2089.
Clubs: United Service, Naval and Military.
(*Died 3 April 1922.*)

MALTHUS, Colonel Sydenham, C.B.
1879; J.P. for Surrey; *b.* 29 May 1831; *m.* 1867,
Henrietta, *e. d.* of late Rev. T. Maberly. Entered
army, 1852; Colonel (retired), 1880; commanded
94th Regiment in Zulu war, 1879, present at
Ulundi (medal). *Address*: Dalton Hill, Albury,
Guildford. *Club*: Constitutional.
(*Died 26 May 1916.*)

MAN, Edward Garnet, Barrister; J.P.,
s. of Henry Man, Commander R.N., of Hal-
stead Hall, Kent; *b.* 8 Feb. 1837; *m.* 1867,
Catherine, *d.* of J. Matthews of 21 Manchester
Square and Halliford, Middlesex; four *s.* five *d.*
Barr. 1866; formerly Assist. Commissioner and
J.P. Bengal; served with 3rd Sikh Irregular
Cavalry during mutiny; Government Advocate,
Burmah; Special Correspondent, Times, in Perak

War; J.P. Surrey and Kent; Chairman of Kent
County Bench (Elham); Diocesan Lay Reader,
Canterbury. *Publications*: Our Trade and Com-
merce; Santalia and the Sonthals; Papal Aims
and Papal Claims. *Recreations*: riding and
driving, cycling. *Address*: Halstead, Riviera,
Sandgate, Kent. *T.*: 39 Sandgate. *Clubs*: St.
Stephen's, United; Radnor, Cinque Ports.
(*Died 15 Nov. 1920.*)

MANBY, Sir Alan (Reeve), Kt., *cr.* 1903;
K.C.V.O., *cr.* 1918; M.V.O. 1901; Physician
Extraordinary to the King; late Surgeon Apothe-
cary to the King and the Household at Sand-
ringham; also to H. M. Queen Alexandra; late
Physician Extraordinary and Surgeon Apothe-
cary to King Edward VII.; *b.* 4 June 1848;
s. of late Frederic Manby, East Rudham,
Norfolk; *m.* 1876, Charlotte Annie, *d.* of late
Edmund Farrer, Petygards Hall, Swaffham,
Norfolk: one *s.* one *.d. Educ.*: Epsom; Guy's
Hospital. M.D. Durh., M.R.C.S., L.S.A.;
F.R.C.S. Eng.; Fellow Royal Society of
Medicine; Member (Pres. 1892-93) Norfolk and
Norwich Medical Chir. Society; President East
Anglian Br. B.M.A. 1896; Vice-President Obs.
Section B.M.A. Oxford, 1904; Vice-President
Therapeutical Section, B.M.A., Toronto, 1906;
Surgeon Apothecary to the Prince and Princess
of Wales at Sandringham, and to Duke of York,
1885; in attendance on Prince and Princess of
Wales during Colonial tour, 1901; Kt. Com-
mander 2nd Class Danish Royal Order of Danne-
brog, 1903; inventor of various instruments;
author of various papers, British and American
Medical Journals, etc. *Address*: East Rudham,
Norfolk. *T.A.*: East Rudham. *T.*: 2 East
Rudham. *M.*: AH 1051. (*Died 29 Sept. 1925.*)

MANCE, Sir Henry Christopher; Kt. *cr.*
1885; C.I.E. 1888; past Pres. Inst. E.E.; Mem.
Inst.C.E.; inventor of the heliograph; LL.D.;
Dir. West African Telegraph Co.; *b.* 1840; *s.* of
late Henry Mance, Brockley; *m.* Annie, *d.* of
John Sayer, of Yatton, 1874; three *s.* two *d.*
Educ.: privately. Entered service of Indian
Government, Persian Gulf Telegraph Depart-
ment, 1863; became engineer and electrician of
the line; was Capt. in Sind Volunteers; retired
from the service, 1885; is member of Physical
Society. *Publications*: various papers on
electrical subjects; Mance's Method, etc.
Address: 25 Linton Road, Oxford. *Club*:
Thatched House. (*Died 21 April 1926.*)

MANCINELLI, Signor L.; Conductor
and Composer; pupil of Malbellini of Florence.
Works: operas, Ero e Leandro, Isora di
Provenza, Paolo and Francesca; two Masses;
Ouverture Romantica, 1910; several oratorios,
including Isaia, and orchestral suites; a great
number of songs; La Priere des Oiseaux, from
Rostand's Chantecler, for small orchestra (for
private performances), contralto voice and girls'
chorus; three acts opera, 1916, fantasia lirica
on Shakespeare's Midsummer Night's Dream,
and six songs, including one on Shelley's Indian
Serenade; two symphonic and choral orchestral
poems, Frate Sole and Giuliano l'Apostata,
both illustrated with a vision on the stage.
Twenty years conductor at Covent Garden,
London; Grand Collar of San Ehiago of
Portugal; Commander of the Crown of Italy.
Address: Rome, via Scipioni 287.
(*Died 2 Feb. 1921.*)

MANDER, Captain John Harold;
O.B.E. 1920; Chief Constable of Norfolk, 1915;
b. The Mount, near Wolverhampton, 1869; *s.*
of late Charles B. Mander; *m.* 1894, Elinor,
d. of late J. P. A. Lloyd-Philipps of Dale
Castle, Milford Haven, and Mabys, Cardigan-
shire; two *d. Educ.*: Rugby; Trinity Hall,
Cambridge. Lieut. 3rd N. Stafford Regt.,
1888-90; gazetted Duke of Cornwall's Light
Infantry, 1890; Captain, 1899; served S. African
War, 1899-1900 (despatches); Adjutant 4th V.B.
Durham L.I., 1901-5; Brigade Major, Durham

L.I. Brigade, 1904-5 ; Chief Constable, Isle of Ely, 1906-15. *Recreations :* shooting, cricket, golf, etc. *Address :* Thorpehurst, Thorpe St. Andrew, Norwich. *T. :* Norwich, Thorpe 5. *Club :* Naval and Military.   (*Died 9 Dec. 1927.*)

MANDERSON, Maj.-Gen. George Rennie, C.B. 1881 ; Royal Bengal Artillery ; *b.* 17 Feb. 1834 ; *m.* 1st, 1873 (*d.* 1875) *d.* of late Sir W. H. Walker ; 2nd, 1880, Harmine, *d.* of late C. Herring-Cooper. Entered army, 1851 ; Major-General 1885 ; served Burmah, 1852-53 (despatches, medal with clasp) ; Indian Mutiny, 1857 (despatches, medal with three clasps) ; Jowaki campaign, 1877-78 (despatches, clasp) ; Afghan war, 1878-79 (despatches, C.B., medal and clasp). *Address :* Fullands, Taunton, Somerset.(*Died 8 Jan. 1918.*)

MANFIELD, Harry, M.P. (L.) Mid-Northants, 1906-18 ; J.P., C.A. ; *e. s.* of late Sir Philip Manfield ; *m.* 1909, Louisa, *d.* of late Sir John Barran, 1st Bt., of Chapel Allerton Hall, Leeds. *Address :* Moulton Grange, Northants. *Clubs :* Reform, National Liberal, Eighty, Bath.   (*Died 9 Feb. 1923.*)

MANGAN, Right Rev. John, D.D. ; R.C. Bishop of Kerry since 1904 ; *b.* Listowel, Co. Kerry, 1852 ; *s.* of John Mangan, Bedford, Listowel. *Educ. :* Maynooth College. Served for a few years in the Liverpool Mission ; Professor at St. Michael's College, Listowel ; Parish Priest of Glengariffe, Sneem, and Kenmare ; was Archdeacon of Aghadoe and Vicar-General of Kerry. *Address :* The Palace, Killarney, Co. Kerry.   (*Died 1 July 1917.*)

MANIFOLD, Hon. Sir Walter Synnot, Kt., *cr.* 1920 ; J.P. Queensland ; Pres. of Legislative Council of Victoria, Australia, 1919-23 ; *b.* 30 March 1849 ; *s.* of late Thomas Manifold of Waiora, Danderong Road, Melbourne, pastoralist, and Jane Elizabeth M., *d.* of late Walter Synnot, H.M. 66th Regiment, 2nd *s.* of Sir Walter Synnot, of Ballymoyer, County Armagh ; *m.* 1885, Fanny M., *d.* of late Alexander John Smith, Commander, R.N. ; no *c. Educ. :* Church of England Grammar School, and University, Melbourne. Solicitor, 1875 ; pastoralist in North West Queensland, pastoralist at Wollaston, Warrnambool, Victoria, 1886-1914 ; Member of Legislative Council of Victoria for Western province, 1901-24. *Address :* Kyalite, Toorak Road, Toorak, Victoria. *T. :* U 2465. *Clubs :* Melbourne ; Warrnambool ; Hamilton.   (*Died 15 Nov. 1923.*)

MANN, Rt. Rev. Monsignor Horace K., D.D. ; Rector of the Collegio Beda, Rome, since 1917 ; *b.* London, 27 Sep. 1859 ; *s.* of Robert K. Mann, Hull, and Jane Mountain, Yorkshire. *Educ. :* St. Cuthbert's College, Ushaw. Taught for some years at Ushaw ; ordained priest for the diocese of Hexham and Newcastle, 1886 ; Corresponding Member Royal Historical Academy of Spain ; Member of the Accademia d'Arcadia, and of the R. Società Rom. di Storia Patria ; assistant master at St. Cuthbert's Grammar School ; Headmaster, 1890-1917. *Publications :* The Lives of the Popes, from the life of St. Gregory I. (590-604) to Gregory IX. (1227-1241), thirteen vols. ; Life of Hadrian IV., the English Pope. *Address :* Collegio Beda, Via S. Niccolo da Tolentino, 67, Roma. *Club :* Authors'.
  (*Died 1 Aug. 1928.*)

MANNERS, 3rd Baron (*cr.* 1807), **John Thomas Manners**, J.P. ; late Captain 3rd Hampshire Regt. ; *b.* 15 May 1852 ; *s.* of 2nd Baron and *d.* of Vice-Admiral William Bateman Dashwood ; *S.* father, 1864 ; *m.* 1st, Constance (*d.* 1920), *d.* of Col. Henry E. H. Fane, M.P., of Clovelly Court, Devonshire, 1885 ; one *s.* two *d.* ; 2nd, 1922, Mrs Claud Guinness, Christchurch. *Educ. :* Trin. Coll., Camb. (M.A.). Entered Grenadier Guards 1875 ; retired, 1888. *Heir : s.* Hon. Francis Henry Manners [late Capt. Grena-

698

dier Guards ; *b.* 21 July 1897]. *Address :* Avon Tyrrell, Christchurch ; 38 Great Cumberland Place, W.1. *T. :* Paddington 2279. *Club :* Carlton.   (*Died 19 Aug. 1927.*)

MANNERS, J. Hartley, dramatic author ; *b.* London, 10 Aug. 1870 ; *m.* Laurette Taylor. *Educ. :* private schools. An actor, 1898-1905 ; first appearance Bijou Theatre, Melbourne ; last, California Theatre, San Francisco ; in America, 1902-14. *Publications :* Plays—The Cross-Ways ; As Once in May ; The Girl in Waiting ; The Panorama of Youth ; A Queen's Messenger ; A Woman Intervenes ; The Wooing of Eve ; Peg o' my Heart ; Zira ; A Marriage of Reason ; Happiness ; The Day of Dupes ; Just as Well ; The Harp of Life ; Out There ; One Night in Rome ; The National Anthem ; All Clear ; God of my Faith ; God's Outcast. *Clubs :* Devonshire ; Lotos, New York.
  (*Died 19 Dec. 1923.*)

MANNERS, Major Lord Robert William Orlando, C.M.G. 1917 ; D.S.O. 1900 ; King's Royal Rifle Corps ; Reserve of Officers ; Brigade Major ; *b.* 4 Feb. 1870 ; 4th *s.* of 7th Duke of Rutland ; *m.* 1902, Mildred Mary, *d.* of Rev. Charles Buckworth, widow of Major H. E. Buchanan Riddell ; one *d.* Served Isazai, 1892 ; South Africa, 1899-1902 (despatches, Queen's medal with 6 clasps, King's medal with 2 clasps, D.S.O.) ; European War, 1914-17 (wounded, C.M.G.). *Address :* Knipton, Grantham. *Club :* Wellington.
  (*Died 8 Sept. 1917.*)

MANNERS-SUTTON, Francis Henry Astley ; Private Secretary to the Duke of Devonshire since 1908 ; *b.* 10 Feb. 1869 ; *e. s.* of late Hon. Graham Manners-Sutton, 2nd *s.* of 3rd Viscount Canterbury ; *c.* and *heir-pres.* to 5th Viscount. Colonial Civil Service, 1891-93 ; was Private Secretary to late Lord James of Hereford ; attached War Staff, Admiralty. *Address :* 4 Down Street, Piccadilly, W. *Clubs :* Carlton, St. James's.   (*Died 7 Mar. 1916.*)

MANSEL, Colonel Alfred, D.S.O. 1891 ; late commanding Northern Section R.A., Plymouth ; retired ; *b.* 5 Feb. 1852 ; *s.* of late Captain W. H. Mansel. Entered army, 1872 ; Lieut.-Col. 1898 ; served Naga Expeditionary Force, 1879-80 (despatches, medal with clasp) ; Mahsood-Wuzeeree expedition, 1881 ; Burmah, 1886-87 (despatches, two clasps). *Address :* Plymouth.   (*Died 7 July 1918.*)

MANSFIELD, Cyril James, M.V.O. 1909 ; Deputy Surgeon-General R.N. Hospital, Haslar ; *y. s.* of late Rev. Edward Mansfield, B.A., Vicar of Highnam, near Gloucester. *Educ. :* Cheltenham College ; Aberdeen University. M.B. C.M. Entered Royal Navy, 1885 ; M.D. Aberdeen, 1896 ; Medical Officer in charge R.N. College, Osborne, 1905-9, during the time Prince of Wales was a cadet. *Recreations :* golf, shooting, fishing. *Address :* Haslar. *Clubs :* Junior United Service ; Royal Naval, Portsmouth.   (*Died 7 May 1916.*)

MANSFIELD, Walter, Financial Editor of the Daily Chronicle, 1907-15 ; Echo and Evening Chronicle, 1915 ; controlled City pages of Westminster Gazette, 1908-12 ; *b.* 1870 ; *y. s.* of Charles E. Mansfield, a former City Editor of the Morning Post ; *m.* 1893, Helen, *y. d.* of Robert Hall, Chester ; one *d.* Assistant Financial Editor of the Morning Post for several years. *Publications :* many works of fiction, partly in collaboration under the nom de plume of Huan Mee ; at one time contributor to Punch and other journals ; part author of musical plays produced in London and Australia. *Recreations :* cycling, billiards. *Address :* 9 West Lodge Avenue, West Acton, W. *Club :* Eccentric.   (*Died 30 April 1916.*)

MANSON, Edward, B.A. ; Registrar of the High Court in Bankruptcy for companies and winding up ; Barrister, Middle Temple ; *b.* 1

Aug. 1849; father, London physician; *m.* 1st, 1880, *widow* of Rev. W. P. Manson (*d.* 1891); four *s.* two *d.*; 2nd, 1914, Eileen, *d.* of George Beck. *Educ.:* St. Paul's School; Brasenose College, Oxford; Scholar and Hulmeian Exhibitioner; graduated with honours (Lit. Hum.). Called to Bar, 1878. *Publications:* joint editor with Sir John Macdonell, C.B., of the Journal of Comparative Legislation; Law of Trading Companies; Law of Debentures; Practical Guide to Company Law; Builders of our Law, 2nd ed.; contributor to Encyclopædia Britannica, and Encyclopædia of the Laws of England. *Recreation:* cycling. *Address:* High Court of Justice, Bankruptcy Buildings, W.C.
(Died 20 Nov. 1919.)

MANSON, James Alexander, editor of Cassell's Encyclopædia (vols. vii. to x.) and of The Makers of British Art Series; *b.* Alloa, 18 Aug. 1851; *e. s.* of James Bolivar Manson, editor of Edinburgh Daily Review (*d.* 1868), and Jane (*d.* 1913), *d.* of Robert Graham; *m.* Margaret Emily, *y. d.* of Charles Deering; four *s.* (one killed in action at Richebourg, 1915), two *d. Educ.:* High School and Univ. of Edinburgh. Member of editorial staff of Cassell, Petter, and Galpin, 1870-94; chief editor, Cassell and Company, 1894-1900; editorial staff The Times Supplement to the Encyclopædia Britannica, 1900-5; Harmsworth Educational Staff, 1908-10; dramatic critic, Weekly Dispatch, 1890-92; literary editor of the Daily Chronicle, 1891. *Publications:* In Memoriam edition of Burns's Poetical Works, in 2 vols. 1896, in 1 vol. 1901; 'Valour for Victoria, 1901; Sir Edwin Landseer, R.A., 1902; Indoor Games, 1906; Daily Sea Trips, 1906; The Bowler's Handbook, 1906; The Slums of Auld Reekie, 1907; Curiosity Land for Young People, 1908; Indoor Amusements, 1911; The Complete Bowler, 1912; contributor of articles on Bowls to the Field over the pen-name of Jack High, and of articles on Royal Bowls to the Sunday Times. *Recreations:* bowls, whist, chess, dominoes; captain of Herne Hill Bowling Club, 1885-1910; Hon. Member of English Bowling Association; Member of the Old Edinburgh Club. *Address:* 4 Cornwall Avenue, Church End, Finchley. *Clubs:* Savage, Edinburgh University (London).
(Died 8 Feb. 1921.)

MANSON, John, I.S.O. 1903; late Controller of Money Order Department, G.P.O.; *b.* 9. Oct. 1842; *m.* 1875, Marion, *d.* of John de Putron, Guernsey. *Address:* 3 George Place, Guernsey. *(Died 6 June 1923.)*

MANSON, Sir Patrick, G.C.M.G., *cr.* 1912; K.C.M.G. *cr.* 1903; F.R.S., M.D., LL.D. (Aberdeen and Hongkong); F.R.C.P. (London); Hon. D.Sc. Oxon; late Physician and Medical Adviser to Colonial Office; distinguished as a Parasitologist; first to enunciate hypothesis (since proved correct by Maj. Ross) that the mosquito was the host of the malarial parasite at one stage of its existence, and thus an active agent in diffusing the disease; C.M.G. 1900; *b.* 3 Oct. 1844; *s.* of John Manson of Fingask, Aberdeen; *m.* 1875, Henrietta Isabella, *d.* of Capt. J. P. Thurburn; one *s.* three *d. Publications:* Goulstonian Lectures, 1896; Tropical Diseases, 1907; various scientific papers. *Address:* The Sheiling, Clonbur, Co. Galway. *(Died 9 April 1922.)*

MANTON, Sir Henry, Kt., *cr.* 1912; *b.* Dec. 1835; *s.* of Alderman Henry Manton; *m.* Mary, *d.* of William Woodroffe of Normanton-on-Soar, Leicestershire, yeoman farmer; two *s.* three *d. Educ.:* King Edward's School, Birmingham. In trade as silversmith; City Councillor since 1881; J.P. City of Birmingham since 1892; Deputy Chairman of Justices, 1911-1913; Guardian of the Poor since 1876; Acting President Poor Law Unions Association, 1910-18. *Publications:* sundry pamphlets on poor

law and social subjects. *Recreation:* social work. *Address:* Rowington, Norfolk Road, Edgbaston, Birmingham. *T.A.:* Mantonia. *T.:* Edgbaston 1116. *Club:* Liberal, Birmingham.
(Died 12 Oct. 1924.)

MANVELL, Rev. Arnold Edward William, M.A.; Vicar of Peterborough since 1920; Hon. Canon of Peterborough Cathedral, 1925; *b.* Dover, 1868; *s.* of W. Manvell; *m.* 1903, Gertrude Theresa, *d.* of C. Baines, Leicester; one *s. Educ.:* Dover College; Oxford University; Wycliffe Hall, Oxford. Ordained, 1892; Curate of Sherborne Abbey, Dorset, 1892; Priest in Charge, St. James', Leicester, 1897; Vicar of St. Barnabas, Leicester, 1904; Chaplain, Leicester Mental Hospital, 1906; Chaplain to Peterborough Workhouse, 1920. *Address:* The Vicarage, Peterborough.
(Died 3 May 1927.)

MANVERS, 4th Earl (*cr.* 1806), **Charles William Sydney Pierrepont,** D.L., Viscount Newark and Baron Pierrepont, 1796; Capt. Notts Yeomanry Cavalry; Lieut.-Col. and Hon. Col. 4th Batt. Sherwood Foresters; *b.* 2 Aug. 1854; *s.* of 3rd Earl, and Georgina, *d.* of Augustin, Duc de Coigny; *S.* father, 1900; *m.* 1880, Helen, *d.* of Sir Michael Shaw-Stewart, 7th Bt.; one *s.* three *d. Educ.:* Eton. M.P. (C.) Nottinghamshire, 1885-95 and 1898-1900; formerly Lieut. Grenadier Guards. *Recreation:* Master of the Rufford Hunt since 1900. Owns about 38,000 acres. *Heir: s.* Viscount Newark. *Address:* 6 Tilney Street, W.1; *T.:* Mayfair 5954; Thoresby Park, Ollerton, Nottinghamshire; Holme Pierrepont, Nottingham.
(Died 17 July 1926.)

MAPLESON, Henry; V.D., J.P., D.L., Col. Royal Field Artillery (retired); President Société Internationale de Musique; *b.* London, 17 Feb. 1851; *s.* of Colonel J. H. Mapleson, D.L., J.P. *Educ.:* St. Mary's College; Bonn University. Originally destined for the army, on leaving Univ. of Bonn, underwent a course of training at Woolwich, where he successfully passed his examination for the Royal Artillery; abandoning the idea of the army as a calling, Colonel Mapleson was gazetted to the Reserve of Officers in order to enable him to follow his father's profession as Director of Italian Opera in London, New York, etc.; made tour of the world and visited the principal cities of both hemispheres; was shipwrecked in the Gulf of Mexico and was one of the five survivors who reached New Orleans; organised by Command of King Edward VII. the fête given by His Majesty at the British Embassy, Paris, in honour of the President of the French Republic (M. Loubet) on 3 May 1903; holds the Royal Victoria Decoration for officers of 20 years' service; is Chevalier Legion of Honour, France, and has the Grand Army of Republic Medal, U.S.A.; Coronation Medal, King and Queen of Spain; Orders of Leopold, Belgium; Isabella la Catholique, Spain; Sauveur, Greece; de Wasa, Sweden and Norway; Medjidie, Turkey, and Sainte Anne, Russia; received a public subscription of £8000 with a testimonial and service of plate as a recognition of his public services, 1908. Performed active duties as a Recruiting Officer during the European War, and received letter of appreciation from Army Council. *Publications:* contributions to several English and American magazines; is a musical, dramatic, and art critic. *Recreations:* riding, driving, hunting, shooting, yachting. *Club:* Junior Army and Navy. *(Died 26 Sept. 1927.)*

MAPPIN, Sir Frank, 2nd Bt., *cr.* 1886; *b.* 6 Sep. 1846; *s.* of 1st Bt. and Mary, *d.* of J. Wilson, Sheffield; *S.* father, 1910. Retired Captain and Hon. Major, 1st West York Yeomanry Cavalry; J.P. *Heir: b.* Wilson [*b.* 14 Jan. 1848; *m.* 1876, Emily Kingsford, *d.* of

George Wilson, Tapton Hall, Eccleshall; two *s.* one *d.*). *Address:* Birchlands, Sheffield. *Clubs:* Reform, National Liberal. (*Died 30 May 1920.*)

MAPPIN, Sir Wilson, 3rd Bt., *cr.* 1886; *b.* 14 Jan. 1848; *s.* of 1st Bt. and Mary, *d.* of J. Wilson, Sheffield; *S.* brother, 1920; *m.* 1876, Emily Kingsford, *d.* of George Wilson, Tapton Hall, Eccleshall; one *d. Heir: g.s.* Charles Thomas Hewitt, *b.* 7 March 1909. *Address:* Thornbury, Fulwood Road, Sheffield.
(*Died 8 June 1925.*)

MARAIS, Rev. Johannes Izak, B.A., D.D.; Professor of Natural Theology and Speculative Philosophy, Theological College, Stellenbosch, since 1877; *b.* Cape Town, 1848, of Huguenot parentage; *m.* 1876, *d.* of Oloff Fehrsen, M.D.; two *s.* three *d.* *Educ.:* private schools; South African College, Cape Town (Gold Medallist, 1866); Theological College of the Dutch Reformed Church, Stellenbosch; Universities of Edinburgh and Utrecht. B.A. of the University of the Cape of Good Hope; Hon. D.D. of St. Andrews; minister of the Dutch Reformed Church, Hanover, Cape Colony, 1873-77; Member of Council of the University of the Cape of Good Hope since 1884; President of Council, Victoria College, Stellenbosch, and Lecturer in Hebrew since 1888; Examiner in Old Testament, University of Cape of Good Hope; Contributor to International Bible Dictionary; Author of Government Report on Bishop Grundtvig and the People's High School in Denmark. *Address:* Victoria College, Stellenbosch, South Africa. (*Died 1919.*)

MARCH, George Edward, C.M.G. 1881; *b.* 1884; *m.* 1st, 1858, Florence, *d.* of late Wentworth Beaumont; 2nd, 1873, Virginia (*d.* 1877), *d.* of late Gen. Gabriel, C.B.; 3rd, 1883, Margaret Mary, *d.* of late A. T. Roberts of Coeddu, Flint. Clerk in Librarian Dept. Foreign Office, 1855; transferred to Treaty Dept. 1860; supt. Treaty Dept. 1873; Acting Sec. of Legation and Diplomatic Sec. to Gen. Sir Alfred Horsford, British delegate at Conference on Rules of Military Warfare at Brussels, 1874; secretary to Royal Commission on Extradition, 1877; retired on pension, 1881. *Address:* 61 Cadogan Square, S.W. (*Died 29 May 1922.*)

MARCHAMLEY, 1st Baron, *cr.* 1908, of Hawkstone; **Rt. Hon. George Whiteley,** P.C. 1907; J.P.; *b.* 1855; *s.* of G. Whiteley, Halifax; *m.* Alice (*d.* 1913), *d.* of W. Tattersall, Quarry Bank, Blackburn; two *s.* two *d.* M.P. (C.) Stockport, 1893-1900; Patronage Secretary of Treasury, 1905-8; M.P. (L.) West Riding, Pudsey Div. of Yorks. 1900-8. *Heir: s.* Hon. W. T. Whiteley. *Address:* 29 Prince's Gardens, S.W.7; *T.:* Kensington 5299. *Club:* Reform.
(*Died 21 Oct. 1925.*)

MARCHANT, Maj.-Gen. Alfred Edmund, C.B. 1900; A.D.C.; retired list; *b.* 26 Feb. 1863; *s.* of late W. L. Marchant, of Adelaide, South Australia; *m.* 1st, Mary Collett, *d.* of late S. C. Homersham; 2nd, 1897, Edith Mary, *d.* of late A. P. Turner, Jersey; two *d.* Joined Royal Marines, 1881; A.D.C. to the King, 1910; served Soudan, 1884-85 (wounded, M'Neill's Zeriba, medal with two clasps, Khedive's star); H.M.S. Calliope during severe hurricane at Samoa; South Africa, 1899-1900 (C.B., despatches thrice, Queen's medal 7 clasps); Antwerp, 1914; Coronation medal. *Clubs:* Junior United Service, Sports. *Address:* Milton House, Fareham. (*Died 21 Jan. 1924.*)

MARCHMONT, Arthur Williams, novelist; *s.* of late Rev. Henry Marchmont; *b.* Southgate, Middlesex, 1852; *m.* 1892. *Educ.:* privately; Pembroke College, Oxford, B.A. Entered Lincoln's Inn, 1888. After leaving Oxford engaged in journalism, at first in London, and subsequently in provinces, editing in succession the North Eastern Daily Gazette

and Lancashire Daily Post; contributing meanwhile constantly to reviews and magazines; abandoned journalism for fiction, 1894. *Publications:* Isa, 1887; By Right of Sword, 1897 (dramatized and produced in America, 1902); A Dash for a Throne, 1898; The Greatest Gift, 1899; In the Name of a Woman, 1900; For Love or Crown, 1901; Sarita the Carlist, 1902; When I was Czar, 1903; By Snare of Love; The Queen's Advocate, 1904; A Courier of Fortune (produced as play), 1905; By Wit of Woman, 1906; In the Cause of Freedom; The Man who was Dead, 1907; A Millionaire Girl; My Lost Self, 1908; An Imperial Marriage, 1909; At the Call of Honour; The Case of Lady Broadstone, 1910; Elfa; In the Name of the People, 1911; The Ruby Heart of Kishgar; The Mystery of Engrave Square, 1912; Under the Black Eagle; When Love Called, 1913; The Heir to the Throne, 1914; The Lady Passenger; A Tight Corner, 1915; Because of Misella, Her Sentinel, 1916; The Unguarded Hour, 1918; The Man Without a Memory, 1919; His Majesty, 1920; When the Empire Crashed, 1921; By Hand Unseen, 1922. *Recreations:* golf and travel. *Address:* 33 Bloomfield Road, Bath. *T.:* Bath 283. *Club:* Authors'. (*Died 1 July 1923.*)

MARDEN, Orison Swett, Author; founder and editor of Success Magazine; *b.* Thornton, N.H., about 1850; *s.* of Louis and Martha (Cilley) Marden; *m.* 1905, Clare Evans; one *s.* two *d.* *Educ.:* Coll. of Liberal Arts, Boston Univ. (B.S. A.B., A.M., B.O., LL.B.), and Harvard Univ. (M.D.). President, The Aldine Club; National Institute of Social Sciences. *Publications:* Pushing to the Front, or Success under Difficulties, 1894; Rising in the World, or Architects of Fate, 1895; How to Succeed, 1896; Success, 1897; The Secret of Achievement, 1898; Character the Grandest Thing in the World, 1899; Cheerfulness as a Life Power, 1899; The Hour of Opportunity, 1900; Good Manners and Success, 1900; Winning Out, 1900; Elements of Business Success, 1900; Talks with Great Workers, 1901; How They Succeeded, 1901; An Iron Will, 1901; Economy, 1901; Stepping Stones, 1902; The Young Man Entering Business, 1903; Stories from Life, 1905; The Making of a Man, 1905; Choosing a Career, 1905; Every Man a King, 1906; Success Nuggets, 1906; The Power of Personality, 1906; The Optimistic Life, 1907; He Can Who Thinks He Can, 1908; Peace, Power, and Plenty, 1909; Do It To A Finish, 1910; Not the Salary, but the Opportunity, 1910; Be Good to Yourself, 1910; Getting On, 1910; The Miracle of Right Thought, 1910; Self Investment, 1911; The Joys of Living; The Exceptional Employee; The Progressive Business Man; Training for Efficiency, 1913; I Had a Friend; Hints for Young Writers; Keeping Fit, 1914; Woman and Home; The Crime of (Sex) Silence, 1915; The Victorious Attitude; Making Life a Masterpiece; Selling Things; Everybody Ahead, 1916; How to Get What You Want, 1918; Published Success Magazine; Thrift, 1918; Ambition and Success, 1919; You Can, But Will You, 1920; Success Fundamentals; Masterful Personality, 1921; Round Pegs in Square Holes; Self-Discovery; Prosperity, How to Attract It, 1922; Making Yourself, 1923; Inspiration Magazine, 1923. *Address:* 251 4th Ave., New York City; Glen Cove, Long Island, New York. *T.:* Gramercy 6221. (*Died 10 Mar. 1924.*)

MARESCAUX, Vice-Admiral Gerald Charles Adolphe, C.B. 1919; C.M.G. 1915; *b.* 1860; *s.* of late Laurence M. Marescaux, Agra Bank, Karachi; *m.* 1894, Kathleen Louisa Rose, 2nd *d.* of late Maj.-Gen. J. B. Dennis, R.A., Ennel Lodge, Mullingar; two *s.* *Educ.:* Royal Naval Academy, Gosport. Entered navy, 1873; Lieutenant, 1883; Commander, 1896; Captain, 1903; Rear-Adm. 1913; District Captain North of Ireland Coast Guards, 1910-12 ; Captain-in-Charge, Portland, 1913 ; received thanks of English and Dutch Governments, also from Colonial Governor (Gambia) for various services; served European War, 1914 - 19 (despatches thrice, C.M.G., C.B.); Commander of the Legion of Honour ; D.A.Q.M.G., Base Commandant ; temp. Lieut.-Colonel, 1914-17 ; temp. Colonel, 1917 ; retired 1915. *Address :* Inchiholohan, Kilkenny. *Club :* Junior Constitutional.

(Died 3 Sept. 1920.)

MARGOLIOUTH, Rev. G., M.A. ; Biblical and Oriental scholar and writer ; *b.* (of Jewish parents) Wilkowiczky, Russian Poland, 4 Dec. 1853 ; *m.* 1886, Marian, *d.* of John Fearon, of Cockermouth. *Educ. :* Düsseldorf ; University of Bonn ; Cuddesdon College, Oxon ; Queen's College, Cambridge. Ordained, 1881 ; naturalised British subject, 1887 ; Semitic Languages Tripos in Honours (Ægrotat), 1890 ; Tyrwhitt Hebrew Scholar (1st class), 1891 ; Appointment at the British Museum (in charge of Hebrew, Syriac, and Ethiopic MSS.), 1891 (retired 1914) ; founded the Text and Translation Society for the publication of Oriental works, 1900 ; and served as Hon. Secretary, 1900-1903 ; Member of the Aristotelian Society, 1905-8 ; Examiner in Hebrew and Aramaic in the University of London, 1909-13 and since 1917 ; Member of the Board of Studies in Theology, 1914. *Publications :* Descriptive List of the Hebrew and Samaritan MSS. in the British Museum, 1893 ; The Superlinear Punctuation, 1893 ; The Liturgy of the Nile, Palestinian-Syriac and English, 1896 ; The Palestinian-Syriac Version of the Holy Scriptures, four recently discovered portions, 1896 ; Ibn-al-Hiti's Arabic Chronicle of Karaite Doctors, 1897 ; Descriptive List of Syriac and Karshuni MSS. in the British Museum, 1899 ; Catalogue of the Hebrew and Samaritan MSS. in the British Museum, vol. i. 1899 ; vol. ii. 1905 ; vol. iii., section 1, Kabbalah, 1909 ; sections 2-7, 1912 ; sections 8-9, 1915 ; Original Hebrew of Ecclesiasticus, xxxi., etc., 1899 ; Hebrew Babylonian Affinities, 1899 ; The Problem of Immortality, 1904 ; articles in the Contemporary Review, the Jewish Quarterly Review, etc. *Recreations :* country life and general literature. *Address :* 4 Albany Villas, Hove, Sussex. *(Died 14 May 1924.)*

MARILLIER, Frank William, O.B.E. 1919 ; C.B.E. 1920 ; *b.* 22 Nov. 1855 ; *s.* of Rev. J. F. Marillier, M.A., late Vicar of Much Dewchurch, Hereford ; *m.* 1891, Katherine Maud Brooke ; two *d. Educ. :* Bristol Grammar School. Engineering pupil to the late Major J. Pearson, late Bristol and Exeter Railway, Bristol, 1872 ; draughtsman, Great Western Railway, 1876 ; Works Manager G.W.R. Depôt, Saltney, Chester, 1898 ; Carriage and Wagon Superintendent, G.W.R.,Swindon,1914 ; during the war Chairman of the Ambulance Trains Committee ; retired from G.W.R., 1921 ; Town Council ; Churchwarden Swindon Parish Church; Director Swindon Permanent Building Society. *Publications :* Sundry Railway Papers ; Steam Heating on Trains, etc. *Recreations :* cycling, motoring, golf, tennis, croquet, billiards. *Address :* Deva, Westlecott Road, Swindon, Wilts. *T.A. :* Marillier, Deva, Swindon. *M. :* HR 2445. *Club :* North Wilts Golf. *(Died 14 June 1928.)*

MARIS, Matthew, painter ; *b.* The Hague, 1839. *Educ. :* Hague Art School ; Antwerp. Travelled in Germany and Switzerland, 1860 ; enrolled in Municipal Guard of Paris, 1870. *Works :* Souvenir d'Amsterdam ; The Little Daughter of the Artist, Swan : A Fairy Tale.

(Died 22 Aug. 1917.)

MARJORIBANKS, Hon. Coutts; 2nd *s.* of 1st Baron Tweedmouth and *heir-pres.* to 3rd Baron ; *b.* 1860 ; *m.* 1895, Agnes Margaret, *d.* of late Col. Kinloch, R.A., and *widow* of Commander Jasper E. T. Nicolls, R.N. Formerly Lieut. Cameron Highlanders. *Address :* Invercraig, Kalemalka Lake, Vernon, British Columbia. *(Died 1 Nov. 1924.)*

MARKER, Richard; J.P. Devon and Dorset; D.L. Devon ; *b.* 10 Aug. 1835 ; *s.* of T. J. Marker, Rector of Gittisham, Devon ; *m.* 1865, Hon. Victoria Alexandrina, *d.* of 9th Baron Digby ; one *s.* one *d. Educ. :* Harrow. *Address :* Combe, Honiton. *Clubs :* Travellers', Wellington.

(Died 8 Mar. 1916.)

MARKHAM, Admiral Sir Albert Hastings, K.C.B., *cr.* 1903 ; R.N. ; retired 1906 ; *b.* Bagnères, 11 Nov. 1841 ; 4th *s.* of Capt. John Markham, R.N., and Marianne, *d.* of John Brock Wood ; *m.* Theodora, *d.* of F. T. Gervers, Amat, Ross-shire, 1894 ; one *d. Educ. :* home ; Eastman's R.N. Academy, Southsea. Entered R.N. 1856 ; served 8 years on China station ; took active part in operations leading to fall of Pekin, and suppression of Taiping rebellion ; Lieut., 1862 ; served on Mediterranean and Australian stations ; received an expression of their Lordships' approval for his activity in suppressing so-called labour traffic in South Sea Islands ; Commander, 1872 ; commander of Alert in Arctic Expedition, 1875-76, when he succeeded in planting Union Jack in highest northern position reached up to then, viz. 83° 20′ 26″ ; for this promoted to capt. and received gold watch from Royal Geographical Society ; Flag Captain in Pacific, 1879-82 ; Capt. of Naval Torpedo School at Portsmouth, 1883-86 ; Commodore Training Squadron, 1886 - 89 ; A.D.C. to the Queen ; Rear - Admiral and 2nd in command of Mediterranean Squadron, 1892-94 ; Commander - in - Chief at the Nore, 1901-4 ; during periods of professional unemployment made various voyages of exploration to Davis Strait, Lancaster Sound, Novaya Zemlya, and Hudson's Bay ; received thanks of Canadian Government for his valuable services in the exploration of Hudson's Strait and Bay ; on Council of British Empire League, Navy Records, and Hakluyt Societies. *Publications :* The Cruise of the Rosario, 1873 ; A Whaling Cruise to Baffin's Bay, 1874 ; The Great Frozen Sea, 1877 ; Northward Ho ! 1878 ; The Life of John Davis the Navigator, 1882 ; A Polar Reconnaissance, 1880 ; Life of Sir John Franklin, 1890 ; Life of Sir Clements R. Markham, 1917 ; is a frequent contributor to Good Words, North American Review, Youth's Companion, Badminton Magazine, and other Serials. *Recreations :* fond of all kinds of sport ; has made large collections in natural history. *Address :* 19 Queen's Gate Place, S.W. *T. :* Western 336. *Club :* United Service. *(Died 28 Oct. 1918.)*

MARKHAM, Sir Arthur Basil, 1st Bt., *cr.* 1911 ; M.P. (L.) for Mansfield Division of Nottinghamshire since 1900 ; J.P. ; *b.* 25 Aug. 1866 ; *s.* of late Charles Markham of Tapton House, Derbyshire, and *d.* of Sir Joseph Paxton ; *m.* 1898, Lucy, *d.* of Capt. A. B. Cunningham, late R.A. ; three *s.* one *d. Educ. :* Rugby. Formerly Captain, 3rd Sherwood Foresters ; J.P. Leicestershire and Derbyshire. *Heir : s.* Charles, *b.* 28 Aug. 1899. *Address :* 43 Portland Place, W. ; *T. :* Mayfair 610 ; Newstead Abbey, Mansfield ; Beachborough Park, Shorncliffe. *Club :* Reform.

(Died 7 Aug. 1916.)

MARKHAM, Br.-Gen. Charles John, C.B.E. 1919 ; retired Army Officer ; *b.* 21 June 1862 ; *s.* of Rev. C. W. Markham ; *m.* Isabella Cameron, *d.* of Col. Gardner, R.M.A. ; one *s. Educ. :* Westminster ; R.M.C., Sandhurst. Gazetted to King's Royal Rifle Corps, 1882 ; served in India, Burma, England, Gibraltar, Malta. S. Africa and Egypt ; commanded 1st Batt. K.R.R.C., 1904-8 ; 42nd Infantry Brigade, 14th Light Division, Sep. 1914-July 1915 at home and in France ; 205th Infantry Brigade, 68th Division, at home, Sep. 1915-March 1917 ;

served Manipur Expedition, 1891; N.E. Frontier, 1891-92; European War, 1914-19 (C.B.E.). *Address*: 52 Campden House Court, W.8. *T.*: Park 4397. *Club*: Naval and Military. (*Died 7 July 1927.*)

MARKHAM, Sir Clements Robert, K.C.B.; *cr.* 1896; F.R.S.; D.Sc. Cam. and Leeds; late President Royal Geographical Society, International Geographical Congress, 1894-99, Hakluyt Society, and Geographical, Elizabethan and Royal Society Clubs; one of the Governors of Westminster School, and Trustee of Dr. Busby's charities; *b.* Stillingfleet, Co. York, 20 July 1830; *s.* of Rev. David F. Markham, Vicar of Stillingfleet and Canon of Windsor, and of Catherine, *d.* of Sir William Mordaunt Milner, Bt., Nunappleton, Co. York; *m.* 1857, Minna, *d.* of Rev. J. H. Chichester, Rector of Arlington, Co. Devon. *Educ.*: Cheam; Westminster School. Entered the Navy in 1844; served in the Arctic Expedition of 1850-51; left the Navy 1852; travelled in Peru, 1852-54; introduced the cultivation of the quinine-yielding chinchona trees from Peru into British India, 1859-62; geographer to the Abyssinian Expedition; Secretary to the Royal Geographical Society, 1863-88; Secretary to the Hakluyt Society, 1858-87; Assistant Secretary in the India Office, 1867-77. *Publications*: Life of the Great Lord Fairfax; The Fighting Veres; History of Peru; Threshold of the Unknown Region; Memoir of the Indian Surveys; History of Persia; History of the Abyssinian Expedition; Missions to Tibet; Lives of Columbus, John Davis, and Major Rennell; Travels in Peru and India; Ollanta, an Inca drama, translated from the Quichua; The Paladins of Edwin the Great, 1896; Richard III.: His Life and Character, 1907; Quichua Dictionary, 1908; Life of Sir Leopold M'Clintock, 1909; The Story of Majorca and Minorca, 1900; The Incas of Peru, 1910, and other works; edited twenty-two volumes for the Hakluyt Society, two for the Navy Records Society, one for the Roxburghe Club. *Recreations*: travelling, topographical research. *Address*: 21 Eccleston Square, S.W. *Clubs*: Athenæum, Royal Societies.
(*Died 30 Jan. 1916.*)

MARKHAM, Lieut.-Gen. Sir Edwin, K.C.B., *cr.* 1897; Col.-Commandant R.H.A.; *b.* 28 March 1833; *s.* of W. Markham, Becca Hall, Yorks; *m.* Evelyn, *d.* of Admiral Hon.. Sir Montagu Stopford, 1877; two *s.* one *d.* Served in Crimea, 1854-55; and India, 1857-58; Deputy-Adj.-General R.A. Headquarters, 1887-1892; Lt.-Governor, Jersey, 1892-95; Inspector-General of Ordnance at Headquarters, 1895-98; Governor of Military College, Sandhurst, 1898-1902. *Address*: 51 Brunswick Place, Brighton.
(*Died 31 Mar. 1918.*)

MARKIEVICZ, Mme. Constance Georgine, Member Dail Eireann for Dublin City, South, since 1923; has been Secretary for Labour; M.P. (S.F.), St. Patrick's, Dublin, Dec. 1918-22; sister of J. A. R. Gore Booth; *m.* 1900, Casimir Dunin de Markievicz; one *d.* Took part in Dublin Rebellion, 1916; sentenced to death; subsequently commuted to penal servitude for life; released, 1917.
(*Died 15 July 1927.*)

MARKS, B. S., R.C.A.; *b.* Cardiff, 8 May 1827; *s.* of Mark Lyon Marks and Anne Michael; *m.* 1858, Zipporah (*d.* 1905), *d.* of Michael Marks; two *s.* four *d.* *Educ.*: private school in Cardiff. Studied art from earliest days as a portrait painter and organised classes for artisans in the subject of drawing; president for some years of the Cardiff Hebrew Congregation; part founder of the Cardiff and Ealing Free Public Libraries; one of the earliest volunteers; a vice-president of the Industrial Committee of the Jewish Board of Guardians; Past Master of the Buckingham and Chandos

Lodge of Freemasons; president of Art Section (1883) of the Cwmmrodorion Society in connection with the National Eisteddfod of Wales. *Portraits*: H.M. King Edward VII. (as Prince of Wales); Maharajah of Kuch Behar; 7th Earl of Shaftesbury, K.G.; 1st Earl of Lathom, G.C.B.; 1st Lord Rothschild, G.C.V.O.; Lord James Crichton-Stuart; Baroness Charlotte de Rothschild; Dr. Lloyd, Bishop of Bangor; Very Rev. F. W. Farrar, Dean of Canterbury; Chief Rabbi Dr. N. M. Adler; Very Rev. Dr. Hermann Adler, C.V.O., Chief Rabbi; Sir Morgan Morgan and Lady Morgan; Sir John and Lady Monckton; Sir Edward Hill, M.P.; Sir Philip Magnus, M.P.; Sir T. Marchant Williams; Sir E. M. Nelson, K.C.M.G.; Sir Horace Brooks Marshall, etc. etc.; also painter of genre works. *Publications*: Presidential Address (in official publication) before the Art Section of the Cymmrodorion Society in connection with the National Eisteddfod of Wales, 1883; Fleeting Shadows, Fair Maidens three (words set to music by F. Helena Marks). *Address*: 10 Matheson Road, West Kensington, W.
(*Died 6 Dec. 1916.*)

MARKS, Harry Hananel, editor and chief proprietor of The Financial News; *b.* London, 9 April 1855; 5th *s.* of late Rev. Professor D. W. Marks, and Cecilia, *d.* of late Moseley Wolff, Liverpool; *m.* Annie Estelle Marks (*d.* 1916); one *s.* one *d.* *Educ.*: Univ. College, London; Athenée Royale, Brussels. Journalist in United States, 1871-88; L.C.C. for East Marylebone, 1889; contested North-East Bethnal Green, 1892; L.C.C. for St. George's in the East, March 1895; J.P. for Kent; M.P. (C.) St. George, Tower Hamlets, 1895-1900; M.P. Isle of Thanet Div. of Kent, 1904-10; Major (officer commanding) 1st Cadet Batt. The Buffs (East Kent Regiment). *Publications*: Leaves from a Reporter's Note-Book, 1881; The Metropolitan Board of Works, 1888; The Case for Tariff Reform, 1905. *Address*: 6 Cavendish Square, W.; *T.*: Gerrard 3503; Callis Court, St. Peter's, Thanet. *M.*: D 600. *Clubs*: Carlton; Cinque Ports, Royal Temple Yacht.
(*Died 22 Dec. 1916.*)

MARKWICK, Colonel Ernest Elliott, C.B. 1905; C.B.E. 1919; retired, Army Ordnance Department; *b.* 19 July 1853; *e. s.* of the late William Markwick of East Acton, W.; *m.* Amy, *o. c.* of late F. M. Murton; two *s.* one *d.* *Educ.*: private school; King's College School. Entered the late Control Department of the Army, 1872; served Zulu War, 1879; Boer War, 1880-81; siege of Pretoria (despatches); Bechuanaland Expedition, 1884-85 (hon. mentioned and specially promoted); Chief Ordnance Officer Cork District, 1887-93; Gibraltar, 1893-1898; Western District, 1898-1903; 2nd Army Corps, 1903-4; Assistant Director of Ordnance Stores, Southern Command, 1905; A.D.O.S., Irish Command, 1914-19; is a Fellow of the Royal Astronomical Society and a Past President of the British Astronomical Association. *Address*: c/o Glyn, Mills, Currie, Holt & Co., 3 Whitehall Place, S.W.1. (*Died 4 July 1925.*)

MARLING. Sir William Henry, 2nd Bt., *cr.* 1882; D.L., J.P.; *b.* Stroud, 1 July 1835. *S.* father, 1883; *m.* 1860, Mary Emily (*d.* 1918), *d.* of John Abraham Longridge, Lancashire; four *s.* *Educ.*: Trin. Coll. Camb. *Heir*: *s.* Col. P. S. Marling. *Address*: Stanley Park, Stroud, Gloucestershire. *T.*: 35 Stroud. (*Died 19 Oct. 1919.*)

MARRABLE, Brig.-Gen. Arthur George, C.B. 1916; K.O.York.L.I.; *b.* 26 April 1863; *s.* of late George Marrable, H.M.'s Paymaster. *Educ.*: Rugby; Oxford. P.s.c.; served Burma, 1886-89 (medal 2 clasps); N.W. Frontier of India, 1897-98 (severely wounded, medal 2 clasps); S. African War, 1899-1902 (despatches twice, Queen's medal 4

clasps, King's medal 2 clasps, Bt. Major); Bt. Lt.-Col.; European War, 1914-16 (despatches thrice, Bt. Col., C.B., 1914 Star, General Service Medal, Victory medal, Officer Legion of Honour, Commander Order of the Crown (Belgium), Croix de Guerre, Belgium). *Clubs:* United Service, Junior Constitutional.
(Died 31 Dec. 1925.)

MARRABLE, Mrs.; President Society of Women Artists; father (Cockburn) Lieut. 17th Lancers; *g.c.* of Mrs. Dunlop of Dunlop, Burns's first patroness; *m.* Frederick Marrable, architect, *s.* of Sir Thomas Marrable; her uncle, Ralph Cockburn, was one of the original members R.W.S.; one *s. Educ.:* Queen's College, under Henry Warren, Alfred Newton, R.W.S. and Prof. C. Welsch; Rome. Member Royal Belgian Society; Member Verein der Schripstellerin und Kunstlerinnen in Wien. Has travelled much in Italy, Austria, and Switzerland; was for many years the only English artist in the Engadine; has painted pictures for King Edward, King George, Her Majesty the Queen, late Duchess of Teck, etc.; has exhibited in the R.A., R.B.A., New Gallery, Women Artists, and in Rome, Belgium, America, and Australia. *Recreations:* reading, travelling in beautiful scenery, and music. *Address:* 12 Zetland House, Cheniston Gardens, Kensington, W.
(Died 21 May 1916.)

MARRIOTT, Ernest, Artist and Author; *b.* Manchester, 9 July 1882; *s.* of Rhodes Marriott. Studied under Walter Crane at Manchester Municipal School of Art; for ten years acted as Librarian to the Portico Library; has travelled considerably in Europe, and made many paintings of Continental scenes; for two and a half years acted as Chief Assistant to Gordon Craig in Florence at the School for the Art of the Theatre; has produced a number of caricatures, book-plate designs, book illustrations, and theatre-scene designs; is a collector of oriental paintings, Japanese prints, and carvings; has organised and arranged picture exhibitions at Zürich, Cologne, Warsaw, and at several towns in England; has delivered lectures on art, and contributed poetry, verses, articles, and criticisms to many journals; during the war has been acting as Hon. Quartermaster of an Auxiliary Military Hospital. *Publications:* Jack B. Yeats, his Pictorial and Dramatic Art; Giovanni Segantini; A Catalogue of Works on Architecture; Continental Vignettes; Illustrations to Stories from Don Quixote; Bruges and the Ardennes; On the Zuider Zee, etc.; writes verses for children under the *nom de plume* of Timothy Quince. *Address:* 9 Albert Square, Manchester.
(Died 8 Mar. 1918.)

MARRIOTT, Very Rev. John Thomas; Incumbent of All Saints, Bathurst, N.S.W., and Dean of Bathurst, 1882-1912. *Educ.:* University of Giessen (Ph.D.); Trinity College, Toronto (Jure Dignitatis D.D.); Melbourne University (M.A. 1887); Fellow Australian College of Theology, 1900. Headmaster Andover Grammar School, 1867-72; Curate of Edmondthorpe, Leicestershire, 1872-76 and 1878-79; Headmaster Wymondham Grammar School, 1872-79; Incumbent of St. Saviour, Redfern, 1880-81; St. Luke, Burwood, 1881-82. *Address:* Oakwood, Burgess Hill, Sussex.
(Died 15 April 1924.)

MARRIOTT, Major Richard George Armine, D.S.O. 1900; J.P. Essex; *b.* 26 Jan. 1867; *s.* of late Humphrey R. G. Marriott of Abbot's Hall, Shalford, Essex; *m.* 1912, Eileen Anita, *o. d.* of Brig.-Gen. R. A. Hickson; one *s.* three *d. Educ.:* Harrow. Entered army (The Buffs), 1887; Captain, 1896; Major, 1905; served South Africa, 1899-1902 (severely wounded, despatches, Queen's medal 3 clasps, King's medal 2 clasps, D.S.O.); retired pay, 1907. *Address:* Arthington, Torquay, Devon.
(Died 15 Dec. 1924.)

MARRIOTT, William, F.R.Met.Soc.; Corresponding Member Hertfordshire Natural History Society; Assistant Secretary of Royal Meteorological Society, 1872-1915; *b.* 9 Aug. 1848; *s.* of William Marriott; *m.* Jane S. Old. *Educ.:* Colfe's Grammar School, Lewisham; University College, London. Engaged at Royal Observatory, Greenwich, 1869-72; Inspector of the Stations of Royal Meteorological Society, 1878-1911; appointed Lecturer on Meteorology, 1905. *Publications:* Hints to Meteorological Observers, seven editions; Some Facts about the Weather, two editions; numerous papers on meteorological subjects; editor of the Meteorological Record, 1881-1911; (with J. S. Fowler) Our Weather. *Address:* 70 Victoria Street, Westminster, S.W. *T.:* 2721 Victoria.
(Died 28 Dec. 1916.)

MARSDEN, Capt. George, D.S.O. 1900; 3rd (S.R.) Battalion The Cheshire Regiment; late S. African Light Horse; *b.* 9 Feb. 1874; *s.* of late Capt. Richard Marsden, R.N.R., J.P.; *m.* 1904, Mary Julia, *o. d.* of late George Booker of Kenogue, Co. Louth, Ireland; two *d. Educ.:* St. Paul's School. Joined 3rd West Yorkshire Regiment; passed school of instruction, Chelsea; resigned commission; joined Perth (Western Australia) Artillery; employed on special mission to inquire into the condition of the aborigines of W. Australia, 1896-97; appointed A.D.C. to Governor of W. Australia (Sir Gerard Smith, K.C.M.G.); resigned, 1899; joined South African Light Horse, 1899 (despatches thrice). *Decorated* for services in South African Boer War. *Club:* Sports.
(Died 24 Sept. 1916.)

MARSDEN, R. Sydney, D.Sc., M.D., Ch.M., D.P.H. (Edin. etc.); L.A.H. (Dub) Hon. Causa, 1911; Medical Officer of Health for Birkenhead; *b.* Sheffield, 1856; *s.* of late Robert Marsden; *m.* Beatrice Eva, *e. d.* of Rev. C. Cotterell Ward, M.A. (Cantab.), Rector of Salford, Oxon; one *d. Educ.:* Universities of Edinburgh, Göttingen, Berlin, and Paris. F.R.S. Edin., F.R.P.S., M.R.I.A., F. Inst. Chem., etc. President, Royal Medical Society, 1881; thrice President Med. Soc., and President Lit. and Sci. Soc., Birkenhead; Lect. on Chem. Univ. Coll. Bristol, 1879; has received grants for original research from Govt. Research Fund, the Royal and Chem. Societies of London, and has frequently been called to give evidence before Royal Commissions and Select Parliamentary Committees; was the first person to produce the "Diamond" artificially. *Publications:* A Short Account of Edinburgh University Tercentenary Festival, 1884; History of Birkenhead Literary and Scientific Society, 1907; Genealogical Memoirs of the Family of Marsden (with B. A. and J. A. Marsden), 1914; The Artificial Preparation of the Diamond, 1881; numerous papers on Chemistry and Physics to the Transactions and Proceedings of Royal and other learned Societies, British and Foreign, and also many papers to the Medical Journals, and contributions to the literature of sanitary science; he is an acknowledged authority on all matters dealing with public health. *Recreations:* gardening, and collecting pictures, china, books, bijoutry, etc. *Address:* 6 Cearns Road, and Town Hall, Birkenhead. *T.:* 668 Birkenhead.
(Died Mar. 1919.)

MARSDEN, Sir Thomas Rogerson, Kt., *cr.* 1918; C.B.E. 1918; J.P.; Managing Director of Platt Brothers & Co., Ltd., Oldham. *Address:* Brookhurst, Alexandra Road, Oldham.
(Died 24 Jan. 1927.)

MARSDEN, Lieut.-Colonel William, late Royal Irish Fusiliers, and South Lancashire Regiments; M.A. Cambridge; *b.* 1841; *e. s.* of Canon Marsden of Grey Friars, Colchester; *m.* 1873, Katharine, *d.* of B. Rigby Murray of Parton, N.B.; two *s.* one *d.* Captain Instructor, School of Musketry, 1873-5; D.A.A.G. Southern and Western Districts, 1875-80; D.A.A.G. School of

Musketry, 1880-83 ; Head of Range Department, National Rifle Association, 1876-81 ; appointed Secretary, 1890 ; Member of Council, 1881-1909 ; Vice-President, 1909. *Address :* Cedar Court, Farnham, Surrey.   (*Died 3 June 1925.*)

MARSH, Maj.-Gen. Frank Hale Berwick, Bengal Infantry ; 2nd *s.* of late Col. Hippisley Marsh and Louisa, *e. d.* of Gen. Sir R. H. Cunliffe, 4th Bart. ; *b.* 26 July 1841 ; *m.* Sophia Frederica Augusta (*d.* 1918), *d.* of Col. R. Taylor ; one *s.* five *d.* Entered army, 1859 ; Maj.-Gen. 1897 ; returned England, 1897 ; served N.W. Frontier of India Campaign, 1863 (despatches, medal with clasp) ; Abyssinian Expedition, 1867-68 (medal). *Address :* Acton Lodge, 12 Radnor Park West, Folkestone.
(*Died 25 Jan. 1923.*)

MARSHALL, Alfred, M.A. and Hon. D.Sc. Oxon. and Camb. ; Hon. LL.D. Edin. and Bristol ; Hon. Dr. Jur. Cracow and Christiania ; Hon. Fellow of Balliol College and of St. John's College, Cambridge ; Fellow of the British Academy ; Foreign Member or Fellow of the Institute or Academies of France and Sweden, and of Rome, Milan and Turin ; Awarded the Prix Emile de Laveleye of the Belgian Academy, 1921 ; Vice-President of the Royal Economic Soc., etc. ; *b.* London, 26 July 1842 ; *m.* Mary, *d.* of Rev. Thomas Paley. *Educ. :* Merchant Taylors' School ; St. John's Coll. Camb. Title to probationary classical Fellowship at St. John's Coll., Oxford, 1861 ; Second Wrangler, 1865 ; Fellow of St. John's College, Cambridge, 1865-77 and 1885-1908 ; Principal of Univ. Coll., Bristol, 1877-82 ; Lecturer at and Fellow of Balliol Coll., Oxford, 1883-84 ; Professor of Political Economy, Camb. Univ., 1885-1908 ; Emeritus Professor, 1918 ; Member of Royal Commission on Labour, 1891. *Publications :* Economics of Industry (in conjunction with his wife), 1879 ; Principles of Economics, vol. i., 1890, translated into several languages ; Elements of Economics, vol. i., 1891 ; Memorandum on the Fiscal Policy of International Trade, published as a White Paper, 1903 ; Industry and Trade, 1919 ; Money, Credit and Commerce, 1923, etc. *Address :* Balliol Croft, 6 Madingley Road, Cambridge. *T. :* Cambridge 286.   (*Died 13 July 1924.*)

MARSHALL, Col. Sir Arthur Wellington, Kt. *cr.* 1898 ; D.L. ; J.P. for Huntingdonshire ; Hon. Col., late Lieut.-Col. commanding 5th Batt. (Militia) King's Royal Rifle Corps ; *b.* 18 July 1841 ; *s.* of James Marshall of Goldbeaters, Middlesex ; *m.* 1867, Constance (*d.* 1915), *d.* of late W. H. Desborough of Hartford, Hunts ; three *s.* one *d.* Sheriff of the counties of Cambridge and Huntingdon, 1890. *Address :* The Towers, Buckden, Huntingdon.
(*Died 1 Dec. 1918.*)

MARSHALL, Charles Devereux, F.R.C.S. ; Surgeon to the Royal London (Moorfields) Ophthalmic Hospital ; Ophthalmic Surgeon to the Victoria Hospital for Children, Chelsea ; Surgeon (late Lieutenant) Royal Naval Volunteer Reserve ; *b.* 8 Dec. 1867 ; *s.* of William Marshall, solicitor, Southsea ; unmarried. *Educ. :* University College, London. Has held various appointments at University College Hospital and at the Royal London Ophthalmic Hospital. *Publications :* Diseases of the Eyes ; many papers relating to scientific subjects, chiefly ophthalmological, published in various journals and books. *Recreation :* yachting. *Address :* 112 Harley Street, W. *T. :* 181 Mayfair ; 28 Merton Road, Southsea. *Clubs :* Royal Cruising, Primrose, Royal Albert Yacht.   (*Died 24 Sept. 1918.*)

MARSHALL, George Balfour, M.D., C.M. (Edin.), F.R.F.P.S. (Glas.) ; Con. Gynæcological Surgeon, Glasgow Royal Infirmary ; Professor of Obstetrics and Gynæcology, St. Mungo's Medical College, Glasgow ; Past Pres.

704

Glasgow Obstetrical and Gynæcological Society ; Examiner in Obstetrics and Gynæcology for the Fellowship of the Royal Faculty of Physicians and Surgeons, and for the Triple Qualification of the Edinburgh and Glasgow Colleges ; *b.* Edinburgh, 1863 ; *e. s.* of T. R. Marshall ; *m.* 1901, Anna Morrison, 3rd *d.* of John Stewart, Greenhill House, Paisley ; two *s.* one *d. Educ. :* George Watson's College and University (graduated with honours), Edinburgh ; Jena ; Berlin ; Doctor of Medicine, Edinburgh, with honours, 1894. Settled in Glasgow, 1894 ; on Gynæcological Staff of the Glasgow Royal Infirmary, 1896 ; Visitor to the Examinations of the Pharmaceutical Society of Great Britain. *Publications :* Manual of Midwifery ; numerous papers on gynæcological and obstetrical subjects. *Recreations :* fishing, photography. *M. :* GB 8383. *Address :* 19 Sandyford Place, Glasgow. *T. :* 4837 Douglas.   (*Died 31 Jan. 1928.*)

MARSHALL, Sir Herbert, Kt., *cr.* 1905 ; J.P. County and Borough of Leicester ; *b.* 13 June 1851 ; *s.* of late James Marshall of Leicester ; *m.* Clara Ann, *d.* of late Vittore Albini of Garzeno, Como, Italy ; two *s.* two *d. Educ. :* privately. Hon. Representative of the Royal Academy and the Royal College of Music ; Mayor of Leicester, 1896-97 ; Member of the Council of the National Union ; President Leicester Borough Conservative Association ; Vice-President, Leicestershire Automobile Club ; Musical Director, Leicester Philharmonic Society ; twice contested Harborough Division, Leicestershire. *Recreations :* travelling, motoring, politics, Freemasonry. *Address :* Ratcliffe Lodge, Knighton, Leicester. *T.A. :* Duetto. Leicester and London. *T. :* 2021 Leicester ; Mayfair 1330, London. *M. :* BC 6. *Clubs :* Carlton, Junior Conservative.
(*Died 1 Sept. 1918.*)

MARSHALL, Sir James Brown, K.C.B., *cr.* 1911 ; C.B. 1902 ; Director of Dockyards and Dockyard Work, 1906-17 ; *b.* 23 Feb. 1853 ; *s.* of Samuel Marshall, Berwick ; *m.* Alice E., *d.* of late Joseph Pharaoh, Bedhampton. *Educ. :* Royal School of Naval Architecture and Royal Naval College, Greenwich. Entered Royal Dockyard, Portsmouth, 1867 ; since engaged in progressive positions at the Royal Dockyards and Admiralty. *Address :* Mornington Hall, West Cowes, Isle of Wight.   (*Died 22 July 1922.*)

MARSHALL, Rev. James M'Call, M.A. ; Rector of Croft, Darlington, since 1894 ; a governor of St. Peter's School, York ; Vice-President of Surtees Society ; *b.* 1838 ; *s.* of late James Marshall, of Harper's Hill ; *m.* Annette, *d.* of late Joseph Blakemore of Edgbaston ; four *s.* two *d. Educ. :* Manchester School and Trinity Coll., Oxford (1st class Mod., 1st class Lit. Hum., B.A. 1862). Ordained, 1874 ; Fellow of Brasenose Coll., Oxford, 1863-66 ; Lecturer, 1863-65 ; also of Wadham Coll., 1864-65 ; Assistant Master, Clifton Coll., 1865-69 ; 2nd Master, Dulwich College, 1869-84 ; Member of Council, Girls' Public Day School Co., 1876-84 ; Headmaster, Durham School, 1884-94 : strong supporter of women's education. *Publications :* edited Greek Irregular Verbs ; The Odes and Epodes of Horace, 1874. *Recreations :* gardening, travelling. *Address :* Croft Rectory, nr. Darlington.
(*Died 10 Jan. 1926.*)

MARSHALL, Rev. John Turner, M.A. ; D.D. ; Pres. Baptist College, Manchester, 1898-1920 ; now Lecturer in Biblical Languages ; *b.* Farsley, near Leeds, 13 May 1850 ; *s.* of Jonathan Marshall ; *m.* 1877, Hettie, *d.* of W. G. Cooper, Burnley ; one *d. Educ. :* Tottington Boarding School ; Rawdon, Owens, and Manchester Baptist Colleges. Appointed Classical Tutor of the Baptist College, Manchester, 1877. Lecturer on the History of Christian Doctrine in the University of Manchester, 1904 ; President of the Baptist Union of Great Britain and Ireland, 1909 ; Dean of Faculty of Theology in Manchester University, 1915. *Publications :* Job and his Comforters ; wrote a series of articles in the Expositor 1891, to show that the divergences of the Synoptic Gospels are, in many cases, due to variant translation of a common Aramaic original ; has contributed numerous articles to the Critical Review, the Expository Times, and Hastings' Dictionary of the Bible. He has written Commentaries on Job and Ecclesiastes. *Recreation :* an occasional round of golf. *Address :* 23 Ladybarn Road, Fallowfield, Manchester.   (*Died 23 June 1923.*)

MARSHALL, Brig. - Gen. John Willoughby Astell, C.B. 1905 ; late Brig.-Gen. commanding Troops, Jamaica ; *b.* 13 March 1854. Entered army, 1876 ; Captain, 1887 ; Major, 1893 ; Lt.-Col., 1898 ; served W. Africa (despatches, medal with clasp), 1892 ; Gambia (despatches, Brevet Major), 1892 ; Ashanti (star), 1895-96 ; Sierra Leone (despatches, Brevet Col.), 1896-99 ; retired, 1911. *Address :* 206 Gloucester Terrace, Hyde Park, W.   (*Died 14 Nov. 1921.*)

MARSHALL, John Wilson, M.A. ; Professor of Greek and Vice-Principal University College of Wales, Aberystwyth ; *s.* of Alexander Marshall, M.D., Kilmarnock. *Educ. :* Glasgow University ; Balliol College, Oxford. Captain, Officers' Training Corps (retired). *Address :* University College of Wales, Aberystwyth.   (*Died 30 Mar. 1923.*)

MARSHALL, Lieut.-Col. Noel George Lambert, Knight of Grace of the Order of St. John of Jerusalem in England ; Commander of the Order of the Legion of Honour of France ; Commander of the Order of the Crown of Italy ; Grand Officer of the Order of St. Sava, Serbia ; Chairman of the Canadian Red Cross during European War ; President, 1922 ; *b.* London, England, 30 Dec. 1852 ; *s.* of Kenric R. and Charlotte A. Marshall ; *m.* 1879, Harriette Isobel, *d.* of John Hogg, M.P. ; two *s. Educ. :* Toronto Grammar Schools. Chairman the Standard Fuel Co. of Toronto ; President Dominion Automobile Co., and Faramel, Ltd. ; Chartered Trust and Executor Co. ; Director Standard Bank Western Canadian Flour Mills, and Canadian Northern Prairie Lands Co. ; Conservative, Anglican ; has devoted a large portion of his life to public service, and is a member of the Boards of many charitable institutions ; a member of the Ontario Parole Commission for the past sixteen years (now Chairman). *Address :* 623 Sherborne Street, Toronto, Canada. *Clubs :* York, Toronto Hunt, National, Toronto.   (*Died 9 Dec. 1926.*)

MARSHALL, Colonel Sir Thomas Horatio, Kt., *cr.* 1906 ; C.B. 1892 ; *b.* Hartford Beach, Cheshire, 5 Jan. 1833 ; *o. s.* of Thomas Marshall, barrister - at - law, and of Agnes Phœbe, *d.* of Digby Legard of Wotton Abbey, Co. Yorks ; *m.* 1st, 1857, Laura Anne (*d.* 1858), *d.* of Rev. Martin Stapylton ; one *s.* ; 2nd, 1862, Lucy Martina (*d.* 1916), *d.* of Rev. Edward Nugent Bree ; four *s.* two *d. Educ. :* Eton ; Exeter Coll. Oxford (M.A.). 3rd (Militia) Batt. Cheshire Regt., 1862-88 ; retired as Major and Hon. Lt.-Col. ; 3rd Volunteer Battalion Cheshire Regt., 1860-98 (Lieut. - Col. commanding, 1865-98) ; Hon. Col. 1898 ; Earl of Chester's Yeomanry Cavalry, 1852-62 ; J.P. for Counties of Cheshire, Anglesey, and Carnarvon ; patron of one living. *Decorated* for service in Auxiliary Forces. *Recreations :* hunting, shooting, rowing, golf. *Address :* Bryn - y - Coed, Bangor, N. Wales. *T.A. :* Bangor. *Club :* Junior Carlton.
          (*Died 29 Mar. 1917.*)

MARSHALL, Thomas Riley, LL.D. ; Vice-President of the United States, 1913-21 ; *b.* North Manchester, Ind., 14 Mar. 1854 ; *m.* 1895, Lois I. Kimsey, Angola, Ind. *Educ. :* Wabash College. Admitted to Bar, 1875 ; Governor of Indiana, 1909-13. *Address :* Columbia City, Indiana, U.S.A.   (*Died 1 June 1925.*)

MARSHALL, Major W. R., D.S.O. 1915 ; 15th Batt. Canadian Forces. Served European War, 1914-15 (D.S.O.).   (*Died May 1916.*)

MARSHALL, Lt.-Col. William Thomas, V.C. ; Secy. Fife County Territorial Assoc. ; *b.* 5 Dec. 1854. *Educ. :* privately. Joined 19th Hussars, 1873 ; commissioned, 1885 ; served Egyptian War, 1882-84, present at battle of Tel-el-Kebir (medal with clasp and Khedive's star) ; Soudan Expedition, 1884, present in engagements at El Teb and Tamai (despatches, V.C., two clasps) ; served South Africa, 1899-1900, operations in Natal including actions at Lombard's Kop, Defence of Ladysmith, Laing's Nek (Queen's medal with four clasps) ; late Camp Quartermaster, Aldershot, 19th (Queen Alexandra's Own Royal) Hussars, retired 1907 ; mentioned in despatches, 6 Aug. 1917, for valuable services rendered in connection with the War. *Address :* St. Helen's, Kirkcaldy, Fife, N.B. *T.* 246. *T.A. :* Kingdom, Kirkcaldy.
          (*Died 11 Sept. 1920.*)

MARSHALL-HALL, Sir Edward, Kt., *cr.* 1917 ; K.C. 1898 ; Recorder of Guildford since 1916 ; *b.* Brighton, 16 Sep. 1858 ; *y. s.* of late Dr. Alfred Hall, F.R.C.P., and Julia Elizabeth, *d.* of James Sebright ; *m.* Henriette Kroeger ; one *d. Educ. :* Rugby (Mathematical prizeman) ; St. John's College, Cambridge. B.A. 1882 ; Barr. Inner Temple, 1883 ; Bencher, 1910 ; practised in London and on the South - Eastern Circuit and Sussex Sessions ; M.P. (C.) Southport Div. of Lancs, 1900-6 ; East Toxteth Div., Liverpool, 1910-16. *Recreations :* shooting, golf. *Address :* 3 Temple Gardens, E.C.4 ; *T. :* Central 700 ; 57a Wimpole Street, W.1 ; Overbrook, Brook, Godalming. *Clubs :* Carlton, Garrick, Beefsteak, M.C.C.   (*Died 24 Feb. 1927.*)

MARSHAM, George, D.L., J.P., C.B.E. ; *b.* 10 April 1849 ; *s.* of Rev. George Marsham, Allington Rectory, Maidstone. *Educ. :* Eton ; Merton College, Oxford. Kent County Council ; Chairman, 1900-10 ; Chairman, Royal Insurance Co., Maidstone Branch ; Maidstone Gas Co. ; Director, Royal Insurance Co., Maidstone Waterworks Co. ; President, Mote Cricket Club ; Committee West Kent General Hospital (Chairman for over 30 years) ; Churchwarden for over 30 years ; Member Kent County Cricket Club Committee. *Recreation :* cricket. *Address :* Hayle Cottage, Maidstone. *T. :* Maidstone 90. *Club :* Junior Carlton, M.C.C.   (*Died 2 Dec. 1927.*)

MARSHAM, Rev. Hon. John ; *b.* 25 July 1842 ; 2nd *s.* of Charles, 3rd Earl of Romney ; *m.* 1866, Penelope Jane, *y. d.* of Rev. W. Wheler Hume, St. Leonards-on-sea ; five *s.* six *d. Educ. :* Eton ; Oxford ; Cambridge ; Cuddesdon. Ordained, 1866 ; Rector of Barton Segrave, 1868-1908 ; Rector and Arch Priest of Haccombe, Devon, 1908 ; retired, 1911. *Recreations :* cricket and shooting. *Address :* St. Clair, Seaford, Sussex.   (*Died 16 Sept. 1926.*)

MARSTON, Robert Bright, F.Z.S. ; Fellow Institute of Journalists ; Member Japan Society ; *b.* London, 30 May 1853 ; *s.* of late Edward Marston ; *m.* 1881 ; four *s.* (two killed in France) three *d. Educ. :* Croydon, Bonn, Islington Proprietary School. Has been in the publishing business for over 50 years ; for nearly 50 years has been editor of the Fishing Gazette ; founder of the Fly-Fishers' Club, 1884, President, 1897 and 1910 ; late Hon. Sec. Publishers' Association ; editor Publishers' Circular ; Chairman Thames Angling Preservation Society ; Member Government Fresh - Water Fish Committee, 1917 ; Member of the Joint Committee of the Ministry of Agriculture and the Ministry of Transport, 1919-22 ; Member Executive Council Fisheries Organisation Society. *Publications :* War, Famine, and our Food Supply, 1897 ; Walton, and some Earlier Writers on Angling ; editor of the 100th edition of

24

The Compleat Angler; of Angling, and How to Angle; translator of Liesegang's Carbon Process of Photography; Tissandier's History and Handbook of Photography; Rohlff's Travels in Morocco; Mechanical Traction in War; Articles on Food Supply in War Time in the Nineteenth Century, etc. *Recreations:* salmon, trout, and general angling; archery; shooting; cycling; formerly captain of football and cricket clubs; amateur photography. *Address:* Surrey Lodge, 160 Denmark Hill, S.E.5. *Club:* The Fly-Fishers'. *(Died 2 Sept. 1927.)*

MARTELLI, His Honour Ernest Wynne, K.C.: County Court Judge for Hampshire since 1916. Called to Bar, Lincoln's Inn, 1888; Bencher, 1913. *Address:* 14 Ladbroke Road, W. *(Died 2 May 1917.)*

MARTI, Prof. Karl, Dr. theol., ordentlicher Professor für das Alte Testament an der Universität, Bern, since 1895; zugleich auch Professor für semitische Philologie since 1901; *b.* Bubendorf (Baselland), 25 April 1855; *m.* Fräulein Lina Rieder von Basel, 1879; one *s.* eight *d. Educ.:* Pädagogium von Basel, 1870-73; Universität zu Basel (Kautzsch, Socin), Göttingen (Ritschl), und Leipzig (Fleischer, Delitzsch), 1873-78. Licentiat der Theologie (Basel), 1879; zum Doctor theologiae honoris causa ernannt von der theolog. Fakultät zu Basel, 1895. 1877 das Examen für den Pfarrdienst in der reformierten Kirche der Konkordatskantone der Schweiz bestanden; 1878-85 Pfarrer in Buus (Baselland); 1885-95 Pfarrer in Muttenz (Baselland); gleichzeitig von 1881 an, zuerst als Privatdozent, dann von 1894 an als ausserordentlicher Professor, an der Universität Basel thätig. *Publications:* der Prophet Jeremia von Anatot, 1889; der richtige Standpunkt zur Beurteilung der abweichenden theologischen Anschauungen, 1890; der Prophet Sacharja, der Zeitgenosse Serubbabels, 1892; der Einfluss der Ergebnisse der neuestenalttest. Forschungen auf Religionsgeschichte und Glaubenslehre, 1894, ins Schwedische übersetzt von K. O. Tellander, 1894; August Kayser's Theologie des Alten Testaments, 2. Aufl. 1894; 3. Auflage unter dem Titel: Geschichte der israelitischen Religion, 1897, 5. Aufl. 1907; kurzgefasste Grammatik der biblisch-aramäischen Sprache, 1896, 2 Aufl. 1911; das Buch Jesaja (Tübingen, 1900), das Buch Daniel erklärt (Tübingen, 1901) und Dodekapropheton I. (Tübingen, 1903), II. (Tübingen, 1904) im kurzen Hand-Commentare zum Alten Testament, der seit 1897 von mir herausgegeben und 1904 vollständig geworden ist; various articles (Chronology of Old Testament and others) in Ency. Bib.; Die Religion des Alten Testaments unter den Religionen der vorderen Orients, 1906; ins Englische übersetzt unter dem Titel: The Religion of the Old Testament: Its Place among the Religions of the Nearer East, London, 1907; ins Japanische übersetzt, Tokyo 1914; Stade's Nachfolger in der Herausgabe der Zeitschr. für die alttestamentl. Wissenschaft, 1907-23; Stand und Aufgabe der alttestamentlichen Wissenschaft in der Gegenwart, Rektoratsrede, Bern, 1912; Herausgeber der Studien zur semit. Philol. u. Religionsgesch. zu Wellhausens 70. Geburtstag, Giessen, 1914; der Beiträge zur alttest. Wissenschaft zu Karl Buddes 70. Geburtstag, Giessen, 1920. *Address:* Bern, Marienstrasse 25. *T.A.:* Prof. Marti, Bern. *T.:* 3774. *(Died 23 April 1925.)*

MARTIN, Lieut.-Gen. Sir Alfred Robert, K.C.B., *cr.* 1910; C.B. 1902; Col. of the 5th Royal Gurkha Rifles; *b.* 30 March 1853; *e. s.* of late Colonel D. W. Martin; *m.* 1882, Bessie Charlotte St. George, 2nd *d.* of late Surg.-Gen. Sir A. C. C. De Renzy, K.C.R.; two *s.* three *d. Educ.:* Harrow. Entered army (34th Cumberland Regiment), 1874; 5th Gurkha Rifles, 1877; Captain, 1886; Major, 1894;

Lt.-Col. 1900; Col. 1899; Maj.-Gen. 1904; Lt.-Gen. 1909; served against Jowaki-Afreedees, 1877-78 (medal with clasp); Afghan War, 1878-80 (despatches three times, medal with four clasps, bronze star; served expedition against Atekzai tribe, 1880; Marri tribe, 1880; Hazara, 1888 (clasp); Miranzai, in command of 1st Batt. 5th Gurkha Rifles (despatches, brevet of Major, clasp); served Isazai expedition; Waziristan, 1894-95 (despatches, brevet Lieut.-Col., clasp), Tochi expedition, 1897; Tirah, 1897-98 (despatches, medal with two clasps); has held several Staff appointments, including A.M.S. for Indian affairs, Horse Guards; Brigade Commander, India, 1904-6; Adjutant-General in India, 1906-8; Divisional Commander, India, 1908-12; retired, 1912; awarded Distinguished Service Award. *Address:* Saint Peters, Farringdon, nr. Alton, Hants. *(Died 27 Oct. 1926.)*

MARTIN, Arthur Anderson, M.D., Ch.B., F.R.C.S. Ed.; Senior Surgeon, Palmerston North Hospital, New Zealand; late Field Ambulance, 5th Division, 2nd Army; late Surgical Specialist, No. 6 General Hospital, Rouen, France, British Expeditionary Force; late Civil Surgeon, South African Field Force, 1901 (medal, 4 clasps); retired Captain, New Zealand Medical Corps. *Publication:* A Surgeon in Khaki, 1915. *Address:* The Hospital, Palmerston North, New Zealand. *(Died Oct. 1916.)*

MARTIN, Cornwallis Philip Wykeham-, J.P., C.C.; *o. s.* of Philip Wykeham-Martin (*d.* 1878) and Elizabeth (*d.* 1893), *d.* of late John Ward; *b.* 19 Mar. 1855; *m.* 1876, Anna Bertha (*d.* 1923), *e. d.* of Major William Pitt Draffen. *Educ.:* Eton; Merton College, Oxford. Late Captain 1st Kent R.V. *Address:* Leeds Castle, Maidstone; Chacombe Priory, Banbury; Packwood Hall, Knowles, Warwicks. *Club:* United University. *(Died 23 Feb. 1924.)*

MARTIN, Colonel Cunliffe, C.B. 1881; retired; *b.* 3 Feb. 1834; 5th *s.* of late Sir Ranald Martin, C.B.; *m.* 1870, Frances Mary, *d.* of late T. R. Colledge, M.D., F.R.S.Ed.; three *s.* four *d. Educ.:* Cheltenham College. Joined 1st Bengal Light Cavalry, 1852; served with the Governor-General's bodyguard in the suppression of the Santhal rebellion, 1855; with 14th Light Dragoons, 1857 (severely wounded, despatches, medal and clasp); as A.D.C. to late F.M. Sir Donald Stewart in Expedition to Abyssinia, and with 12th Bengal Cavalry at taking of Magdala, 1868 (medal, despatches); commanded Central India Horse, Afghan War, in operations in Besud and Khama Valleys, 1880, in march from Kabul to Kandahar and battle of Kandahar under Earl Roberts (despatches thrice, medal and clasp, star, and C.B.). *Address:* Delmar, Cheltenham. *T.A.:* Cheltenham. *T.:* 1041. *Club:* New, Cheltenham. *(Died 10 July 1917.)*

MARTIN, Capt. Edward Harington, C.M.G. 1917; R.N. Capt.-Supt., Halifax Dockyard, Nova Scotia. *Address:* Halifax Dockyard, Nova Scotia. *(Died 26 May 1921.)*

MARTIN, Colonel Ernest Edmund, C.M.G. 1916; C.B.E. 1919; F.R.C.V.S., D.V.H.; Deputy Director of Veterinary Services; *b.* 20 June 1869; 2nd *s.* of late T. J. Martin of Osborne House, Taunton; *m.* 1913, Alexine Aimée Samuelson. *Educ.:* Queen's College, Taunton. Served S. Africa, 1902 (Queen's medal 2 clasps); European War, 1914-18 (despatches, C.M.G.). *Club:* Junior Naval and Military. *(Died 23 Aug. 1926.)*

MARTIN, Col. George Blake Napier, C.B. 1881; R.A. (retired); *b.* 28 Feb. 1847; *m.* 1889, Evelyn Henrietta, *o. d.* of late Col. Henry Clement Swinnerton-Dyer, R.A. Entered army, 1866; Capt. 1878; Major, 1884; Lt.-Col. 1893; Col. 1897; served Egypt, 1882, including Tel-el-Kebir (despatches, brevet of Major, medal with clasp, 4th class Medjidie, Khedive's Star); Nile, 1884-85 (two clasps); Burmah, 1886 (medal with clasp). *(Died 20 Jan. 1917.)*

MARTIN, Sir George Clement, Kt.; cr. 1897; M.V.O.; Mus. Doc.; Hon. Mus. Doc. Oxford; Hon. R.A.M.; F.R.C.O.; Organist St. Paul's Cathedral since 1888; b. 11 Sep. 1844; m. 1879, Margaret, d. of T. M. Cockburn. Educ.: privately. Organist, Lambourn; Dalkeith. Compositions mainly for the Church. Recreations: shooting, bicycling, photography, golf. Address: 4 Amen Court, St. Paul's, E.C. T.: City 160. T.A.: Martin, St. Paul's. Club: Constitutional.
(Died 23 Feb. 1916.)

MARTIN, Rev. Canon Henry, M.A.; b. 1844; s. of Rev. R. M. Martin, Vicar of Thorpe, Surrey, and Charlotte, d. of J. R. Buttemer; m. 1st, 1874, Constance Clare Lawton (d. 1905), d. of Major-Gen. Trafford, Plas Panthoel, Carmarthenshire; two s. one d.; 2nd, 1906, Frances Eliza Mary, d. of Maj.-Gen. Griffith, Maesgwyn, Winchester; one s. one d. Educ.: Merchant Taylors' School; Oxford. Graduated with Honours in Theology, 1872; Classical Master Elizabeth College, Guernsey, 1872 - 73; Curate All SS., Guernsey, 1873; Vice - Principal Cheltenham Training College, 1873-78; Curate of Ch. Ch. Cheltenham, 1876-78; Principal, Training College, Winchester, 1878-1912; Hon. Canon of Winchester, 1898; Hon. Lt.-Col. (retired) 1st Vol. Batt. Hampshire Regt.; V.D. Recreations: bicycling, golf, mountaineering. Address: Clifton Mount, Winchester. T.A.: Canon Martin, Winchester. T.: 121. Clubs: Alpine, Swiss Alpine, New Oxford and Cambridge, Hampshire County.
(Died 27 July 1919.)

MARTIN, Rev. Henry, M.A.; Hon. Canon of Durham, 1899; Vicar of Kelloe since 1916; b. Dore, 1844; s. of Rev. Richard Martin of Killaloe; m. 1874, Mary, d. of W. J. Lunn, M.D., Hull; six s. five d. Educ.: Sheffield Collegiate School; Clare College, Cambridge (scholar, prizeman), senior optime, 1867. Curate, Chapel en le Frith; Earls Heaton; St. Paul's, Hull; Vicar St. John's, Sunderland, 1875-85; Vicar Stockton-on-Tees, 1885-1916; Rural Dean of Stockton, 1903; Proctor, York Convocation, 1903-18; served on Boothill, Sunderland, and Stockton School Boards; Chairman, Durham Dio. C.E.T.S.; Commissary to Bishop of Barbados, 1906. Recreations: bicycling, gardening. Address: Kelloe Vicarage, Coxhoe, Co. Durham. M.: J1551.
(Died 13 June 1923.)

MARTIN, Howard, P.P.S.I.; Official Arbitrator under the Acquisition of Land Compensation Act, 1919, since 1920; s. of late Rev. Samuel Martin of Westminster; m. e. c. of late C. E. Smith, of Silvermere, Cobham, Surrey, and Colwood Park, Bolney, Sussex; three s. three d. Educ.: University College School, London; private tuition. Articled as a pupil to Robert Jacomb Hood, C.E., and afterwards employed for some years as assistant engineer on the construction of new railways in Surrey and Sussex and the Newhaven Harbour works; joined as partner a firm of surveyors in Croydon, 1870; joined the late Herbert Thurgood, surveyor, in partnership at 27 Chancery Lane, 1882; practised there as surveyor, land agent, etc., till 1920; Member of Council of Surveyors Institution since 1892; President, 1908-9. Publications: A number of contributions to the Transactions of the Surveyors Institution on professional subjects. Recreations: golf and hunting, reading and music. Address: South Lawn, Reigate; 12 Great George Street, Westminster, S.W.1. T.: Redhill 278; Victoria 5322. Club: St. Stephen's.
(Died 19 Jan. 1924.)

MARTIN, Hon. Joseph; b. Milton, Ontario, Canada, 24 Sep. 1852; s. of Edward and Mary Ann Martin; m. 1881, Mrs. Elizabeth Jane Eaton (d. 1913), Ottawa, Canada; no c. Educ.: Canadian and Michigan Public Schools;

Toronto University. Barrister in Canada since 1882; Canadian K.C.; Member of Legislature, Manitoba, 1882 - 92; Attorney-General and Minister of Education, Manitoba, 1888-91; Member of Dominion of Canada House of Commons for Winnipeg, 1893-96; Member of Legislature, British Columbia, 1898 - 1903; Attorney-General and Minister of Education, British Columbia, 1898-99, Premier of British Columbia, 1900; contested (L.) South-West Warwickshire, 1909; M.P. (L.) East St. Pancras, 1910 - 18; took active part in Manitoba against Canadian Pacific Railway monopoly, Abolition of French as official language and of separate schools, and in favour of introduction of Torrens System of Land Registry; strong Free Trader and advocate of unrestricted reciprocity between United States and Canada. Publications: owned and edited daily newspapers in Vancouver, Canada, for some time. Clubs: Royal Automobile; Vancouver, Vancouver.
(Died 2 Mar. 1923.)

MARTIN, Sir Richard, Kt., cr. 1921; J.P., ex-Mayor of Swansea. Address: c/o Town Hall, Swansea.
(Died 16 Sept. 1922.)

MARTIN, Rev. Richard; Prebendary of Exeter Cathedral since 1894; b. Staverton Vicarage, Devon, 1 March 1836; 3rd s. of Rev. William Martin and Jane Champernowne of Dartington Hall; m. Eliza Rose (d. 1919). Educ.: Marlborough; Corpus Christi College, Oxford. Curate of Swymbridge, 1859-1861; Rector of Challacombe, 1861-80; Vicar of Swymbridge, 1880-87; Ilfracombe, 1887 - 1905; Rural Dean of Shirwell, 1871-87; Barnstaple, 1894-1905; Proctor in Convocation, 1895; Sub-Dean of Exeter Cathedral, 1911. Recreations: rowed in the Oxford boat against Cambridge, 1857. Address: Carlton Close, Exmouth.
(Died 20 Feb. 1927.)

MARTIN, Sir Richard Biddulph, 1st Bt.; cr. 1905; banker; Chairman Martin's Bank, Ltd.; b. London, 12 May 1838; m. Mary Frances, o. d. of late Admiral Richard Crozier, K.T.S., Westhill, Isle of Wight, 1864. Educ.: Hardenhuish; Harrow; Exeter College, Oxford (M.A.). Chairman Assets Realisation Co., Debenture Corporation, and Anglo-American Debenture Corporation; formerly Chairman British North Borneo Company; Director Sun Fire and Life Offices, etc.; Fellow and formerly President of Institute of Bankers, of which he was one of the founders; President (1906) and Treasurer of the Royal Statistical Society; Fellow of the Anthropological Institute; F.R.G.S.; Hon. Secretary to the Metropolitan Hospital Sunday Fund; Treas. of St. Mark's Hospital for Fistula, and of the Royal National Orthopædic Hospital, of the Childhood Society, and of Association for Promoting Welfare of Feeble-Minded; Prime Warden of the Fishmongers' Company, 1906; M.P. Tewkesbury, 1880 - 85; Mid or Droitwich Division of Worcestershire, 1892-1905; J.P. for Co. of Kent, Co. of Worcester, and Co. of Gloucester; a Lieut. of City of London. Heir: none. Recreations: photography, and formerly archery, sketching. Address: Overbury Court, Tewkesbury; 10 Hill Street, Mayfair, W. T.: 2946 Gerrard. Clubs: Athenæum, Windham, Ranelagh; Travellers', Paris. M.: AB 1434; AB 670.
(Died 23 Aug. 1916.)

MARTIN, Col. Rowland Hill, C.B. 1898; retired; C.M.G. 1901; b. 30 Oct. 1848; s. of late Col. A. P. Martin of Fleetlands, Fareham; m. 1902, Emily, widow of John Nugent, C.S.I. Educ.: Cheltenham College. Entered Army, 1869; Colonel, 1896; served Bechuanaland Expedition, 1884-85; Nile, 1898 (despatches, Queen's medal, Egyptian medal with clasp, C.B.); commanded 21st Lancers in charge at Omdurman; South Africa, 1902 (despatches, Queen's medal with clasp, C.M.G.); late commanding 21st Lancers, 1892-98; J.P. Hants. Club: Cavalry.
(Died 31 Jan. 1919.)

MARTIN, Sidney, M.D., F.R.S.; Physician to University College Hospital; Professor of Clinical Medicine, University College Hospital; *b.* Jamaica, 8 April 1860; 2nd *s.* of late John Ewers Martin, Jamaica; *m.*; one *d. Educ.:* University College, London. Pathologist and Assistant Physician, Victoria Park Chest Hospital; Pathologist and Medical Tutor, Middlesex Hospital; Assistant Physician, Hospital for Consumption, Brompton. *Publications:* Diseases of the Stomach, 1895; Appendix to Report of Royal Commission on Tuberculosis, 1896; A Manual of Pathology, 1903; Papers on Medical and Scientific Subjects in Proc. Roy. Soc.; etc. *Address:* 51 Wimpole Street, W.1. *T.:* Paddington 1705. *(Died 22 Sept. 1927.)*

MARTIN, Stapleton, M.A.; *b.* 1846; 2nd *s.* of Marcus Martin, Barrister, and Harriett Mary, *o. c.* of John Stapleton of Calcutta; *m.* 1895, Helen Gertrude, 2nd *d.* of Walker Busfeild, J.P., of Charlton, Somerset; two *s.* three *d. Educ.:* privately; Christ's College, Cambridge. Called to Bar, Middle Temple, 1871. *Publications:* Izaak Walton and his Friends, 1903; and various articles and pamphlets. *Recreations:* hunting and billiards. *Address:* The Firs, Norton, Worcester. *Clubs:* Oxford and Cambridge, M.C.C. *(Died 26 Sept. 1922.)*

MARTIN, Sir T. Carlaw, Kt., *cr.* 1909; LL.D. (St. Andrews); J.P.; F.R.S.E.; Director Royal Scottish Museum, 1911-16; edited Scottish Morning Journals, 1890-1910; Chairman Scottish Agricultural Commission to Canada, 1908; to Australia, 1910-11. *Address:* 18 Blackford Road, Edinburgh. *Clubs:* National Liberal; Scottish Liberal, Edinburgh.*(Died 26 Oct. 1920.)*

MARTIN, Colonel Thomas Morgan, C.M.G. 1916; late Acting Commissioner New South Wales District, St. John Ambulance Brigade, Overseas; Col. A.A.M.C. Reserve; late Officer Commanding No. 2 Australian General Hospital; *b.* 30 Nov. 1854; *s.* of John W. Martin, LL.D., Blackrock, Dublin, and Grace Morgan; *m.* Mary, *d.* of Dr. J. Marshall, Dromore, Co. Tyrone; three *s.* three *d. Educ.:* Rev. R. North's School, Dublin; Trinity College, Dublin. Practised for five years in Piltown, Ireland, and for forty-two years in Sydney, N.S.W.; served South African War, 1899-1900. with the 1st N.S.W. Field Hospital, and as Secretary to Surg.-Gen. Williams, P.M.O., Gen. Ian Hamilton's, and later Gen. Hunter's Forces; served European War, first in Egypt, afterwards in France, 1915-16 (C.M.G.). O.C. No. 2 Australian Auxiliary Hospital (Southall), 1917. *Recreation:* golf. *Address:* 21 Oxford Street, Sydney, N.S.W. *Club:* Imperial Service, Sydney. *(Died 23 May 1928.)*

MARTIN, Victoria Claflin Woodhull, financier and reformer; editor Humanitarian Magazine; writer; *b.* Homer, Ohio, U.S., 23 Sep. 1838; 7th *c.* of Reuben Claflin and Roxanna Hummel; *m.* 1st, Canning Woodhull (*d.* 1873); 2nd, John Biddulph Martin (*d.* 1897); one *s.* one *d.* Banker; editor and proprietor The Humanitarian Magazine; memorialised Congress in 1870 for Women's Suffrage; lectured throughout U.S. on Finance, Women's Suffrage, Religious and Scientific Improvement of Human Race; nominated for Presidency of U.S. in 1872 by the Equal Rights Party; organised conventions for the discussion of social reform; carried on a continuous propagandist work in the interests of the working classes both in America and Europe for over 30 years. *Publications:* The Origin, Tendencies, and Principles of Government; Social Freedom; Garden of Eden Stirpiculture; Rapid Multiplication of the Unfit; The Human Body the Temple of God; Argument for Woman's Electoral Rights, etc. *Recreations:* scientific agriculture, psychical research, motoring, collecting works of art. *Address:* Bredon's Norton, near Tewkesbury, Worcestershire. *T.A.:* Bredon. *T.:* 2 Bredon. *M.:* AB 110. *Club:* Ladies' Automobile. *(Died 9 June 1927.)*

MARTIN, Sir William, Kt., *cr.* 1919; J.P.; F.S.A. (Scot.); *b.* 24 Feb. 1856; *m.* 1880, Helen Amelia Dyer; three *s.* two *d. Educ.:* Glasgow University. Hon. Representative Royal Humane Society; Member, Scottish National War Savings Committee; President of Toynbee House, Glasgow; Hon. Vice - President, National Citizens Council; Vice-Chairman Westerton Garden Suburb. *Recreations:* literature, walking. *Address:* 24 Atholl Gardens, Kelvinside, Glasgow; *T.:* Douglas 3440; Oakvale, Hunter's Quay, Argyll. *Club:* Liberal, Glasgow. *(Died 13 Sept. 1924.)*

MARTIN, W. A. P., D.D., LL.D.; ex-President of Imperial University, Peking; *b.* Livonia, Indiana, 10 April 1827. *Educ.:* Indiana State Univ.; Presby. Theol. Seminary. Arrived China, 1850; stationed as Missionary at Ningpo; went as Interpreter with U.S. Minister, Reid, to Tientsin, where new treaties were made after storming of forts by British and French 1858; went with U.S. Minister, Ward, to Peking; witnessed defeat of Allies at Taku, 1859; accompanied Mr. Ward to Japan, then under Shogun; made President and Professor of International Law in Imperial College, Peking, 1867; held position 25 years, and resigned on account of health; appointed by Imperial Decree President of New University, 1898; in Siege in Peking, shut up eight weeks in H.B.M.'s Legation, 1900; President Viceroy's University, Wuchang, 1905-5. *Publications:* In Chinese—Evidences of Christianity; Natural Philosophy; Mathematical Physics; Mental Philosophy, with preface by Li Hung Chang; Translations of four Text-books of International Law, Wheaton, Woolsey, Bluntschli, and Hall. In English—A Cycle of Cathay; The Lore of Cathay; The Siege in Peking; Chinese Legends and other poems; The Awakening of China, 1907. *Recreation:* verse-making. *Address:* A. P. Mission, Peking, China. *(Died 17 Dec. 1916.)*

MARTIN-LEAKE, Vice-Admiral Francis, C.B. 1922; D.S.O. 1917; R.N. (retired); *s.* of late Stephen Martin Leake of Thorpe Hall, Essex, and Marshalls, Ware, Herts; *b.* 1869; unmarried. Served European War, 1914-19; commanded cruiser Pathfinder, 1914, and Achilles in Grand Fleet, 1915-17; Chief of Staff to Admiral Commanding at Queenstown, 1918-19; Rear-Admiral retired, 1921; Vice-Adm. retired, 1926. *Addrses:* Marshalls, Ware, Herts. *M.:* NK 3229. *Club:* United Service. *(Died 21 Jan. 1928.)*

MARTINEAU, George, C.B. 1902; *b.* 24 Sep. 1835; *s.* of George Martineau of Tulse Hill; *m.* 1861, Ida, *d.* of late Major Roderick Mackenzie of Kincraig; three *s.* one *d. Educ.:* University College, London. Adviser to British Delegates at International Conferences on Sugar Bounties, Brussels, 1875, 1898, 1902, and Paris 1876, 1877; Assistant British Delegate to International Sugar Commission, 1903-5. *Publications:* Free Trade in Sugar, 1889; The Statistical Aspect of the Sugar Question, 1899; The Brussels Sugar Convention, 1904; Sugar: Cane and Beet, 1917; A Short History of Sugar, 1856-1916, a Warning; Sugar from several Points of View, 1918; magazine articles. *Address:* Gomshall Lodge, Gomshall, Surrey. *(Died 5 Feb. 1919.)*

MARTYN, Edward; dramatist; *b.* Masonbrook, Co. Galway, 31 Jan. 1859; *e. s.* of late John Martyn, J.P. of Tulira, Co. Galway, and late Anne, *d.* of late James Smyth, J.P., of Masonbrook; is a Catholic and Nationalist. *Educ.:* Belvedere, Dublin; Beaumont, Windsor; Christ Church, Oxford; chiefly self-educated. One of the original founders of the Irish Dramatic Movement in 1899; Founder of the Palestrina Choir of men and boys at Dublin for the reform of liturgical music, in same year, which in 1903 became the Schola Cantorum of that Archdiocese; organised a

reform of church architecture, stained glass, etc., 1903 ; was President of Sinn Fein from 1904 until he resigned in 1908 ; founded at Dublin, 1914, The Irish Theatre, for the production of native non-peasant plays, plays in the Irish language, and translations of Continental master dramas ; promoter of Gaelic League and other educational improvements for Ireland ; is a Governor of the Galway College of the National University. *Publications :* Morgante the Lesser ; Preface to Robert Elliot's Art and Ireland ; Ireland's Battle for her Language ; the following plays—The Heather Field, 3 acts ; Maeve, 2 acts ; The Tale of a Town, 5 acts ; The Placehunters, 1 act ; Romulus and Remus, 1 act ; Grangecolman, 3 acts ; The Dream Physician, 5 acts ; The Privilege of Place, 3 acts ; Regina Eyre, 4 acts ; poems ; many articles on Art, Politics, etc. *Recreations :* Mr. George Augustus Moore. *Address :* Tulira, Ardrahan, Co. Galway ; 15 Leinster Street South, Dublin. *M. :* IM 262. *Club :* Kildare Street, Dublin.
(*Died 5 Dec. 1923.*)

MARZBAN, Jehangier B., C.I.E. 1920 ; J.P. ; proprietor of the Jamé Jamshed, the leading Anglo-Vernacular daily of Bombay (30 years) ; *b.* Bombay, 1848 ; grandfather was the first founder of Vernacular Journalism (128 years ago) in the Presidency ; *m.* ; three *s.* two *d. Educ. :* Elphinstone College, Bombay. Assistant Manager of the Times of India (7 years) ; Manager of the Bombay Gazette (9 years) ; proprietor Advocate of India (5 years) ; late Chairman Consumption Home at Deolali. *Publications :* thirty books on travels, wit and humour, and fiction. *Address :* Jame Jamshed Printing Works, Bombay, India.(*Died Dec. 1928.*)

MASEFIELD, Col. Robert Taylor, C.B. 1897 ; J.P., D.L., Salop ; *b.* Ellerton Hall, Newport, Shropshire, 1839 ; *e. s.* of late Robt. Masefield, Ellerton Hall ; *m.* 1864, Emily, *d.* of T. Rylands of Banshee House, Newport, Salop. *Educ. :* privately. Joined 31st Regt., 1860 ; served Chinese War, 1860-62 (medal and clasp) ; occupation of Pekin (medal and clasp) ; Lt.-Col. commanding 2nd Volunteer Batt. King's Shropshire Light Infantry, 1876-1904 ; Hon. Col. 1904. *Recreations :* all country sports. *Address :* Springhayes, Woodbury, S. Devon.
(*Died 1 Nov. 1922.*)

MASHAM, 2nd Baron (*cr.* 1891), **Samuel Cunliffe-Lister,** J.P. (title taken from the town of Masham, chiefly his property) ; *b.* 1857 ; *s.* of 1st Baron and Anne, *d.* of John Dearden, Hollins Hall, Halifax. Protestant. Conservative. *Educ. :* Harrow ; Oxford University. Possesses' some first-class pictures—Gainsborough, Sir Joshua, Romney, etc. Owns about 24,000 acres ; Manningham Mills (chief shareholder). *Heir :* b. Hon. John Lister. *Address :* Swinton, Masham, Yorks.
(*Died 24 Jan. 1917.*)

MASHAM, 3rd Baron, *cr.* 1891 ; **John Cunliffe-Lister ;** *s.* of 1st Baron and Anne, *d.* of John Dearden, Hollins Hall, Halifax. Protestant, Conservative ; *b.* 9 Aug. 1867 ; *m.* 1906, Elizabeth Alice, *d.* of W. R. Brockton ; S. brother 1917. Possesses some first-class pictures—Gainsborough, Sir Joshua, Romney, etc. Owns about 24,000 acres ; Manningham Mills (chief shareholder). *Heir :* none. *Address :* Swinton, Masham, Yorks.
(*Died 4 Jan. 1924.*)

MASHAM, William George, I.S.O. ; late first-class clerk, Board of Education ; *b.* 1843. *Address :* 70 Norwood Hill, S.E.
(*Died 14 Feb. 1916.*)

MASHITER, Col. Sir George Coope (formerly Helme), K.C.B., *cr.* 1909 ; C.B. 1898 ; C.M.G. 1900 ; *b.* Warley Lodge, Essex, 25 Nov. 1843 ; 2nd *s.* of Thomas Mashiter (*ne* Helme) of Manor House, Little Bookham,

Surrey, and Hornchurch Lodge, Essex ; *m.* 1874, Florence Sophia, 2nd *d.* of Rev. J. Pearson of East Horneon, Essex. *Educ. :* Winchester ; Sandhurst. Joined 10th Foot, 1862 ; Captain, 1876 ; Major, 1881 ; exchanged to Wiltshire Regiment, 1883 ; Lieut.-Col., half-pay, 1888 ; retired, 1889 ; Jubilee Decoration, 1897 ; served South Africa, in command of 6th Batt. Middlesex Regt. 1900-2 (despatches, Queen's medal with clasp, King's medal 2 clasps, C.M.G.) ; Lt.-Col., retired pay, since 1889 ; Lt.-Colonel (and Hon. Colonel) commanding 6th Battalion Duke of Cambridge's Own Middlesex Regt. 1889-1904 ; Colonel commanding West Yorkshire Vol. Inf. Brigade, 1906-7 ; Colonel commanding 1st West Riding Brigade, Territorial Force, 1907-9 ; Hon. Col. 6th Batt. West Yorkshire Regt. since 1907 ; Hon. Col. 6th Batt. Middlesex Regt. since 1921 ; J.P., D.L. Wilts. *Recreations :* hunting, shooting. *Address :* Rowden Lodge, Chippenham, Wilts. *T. :* Chippenham 78. *Club :* Naval and Military.
(*Died 11 Aug. 1927.*)

MASKELYNE, John Nevil ; Lessee of St. George's Hall, London ; *b.* Cheltenham, 22 Dec. 1839 ; *s.* of John Nevil and Harriett Maskelyne of Cheltenham ; *m.* 1861, Elizabeth, (*d.* 1911) ; two *s.* one *d. Educ. :* Cheltenham. Appeared as conjurer at age 16 ; exposed Davenport Brothers' Cabinet and Dark Seance, 1865 ; first appeared London, 1873 ; at Egyptian Hall, Piccadilly, to 1904. *Publications :* Modern Spiritualism ; Sharps and Flats ; The Supernatural ? ; etc., etc. *Recreations :* music and hill-climbing. *Address :* St. George's Hall, Langham Place, W. *T.A. :* Maskelyne, London. *T. :* 1545 Mayfair. *Clubs :* Junior Constitutional, Aero.(*Died 18 May 1917.*)

MASON, Alfred John, I.S.O. 1902 : Superintendent of Deposit, Reference, and Binding Department, Local Government Board, 1866-1913 ; *b.* 1853. (*Died 5 Sept. 1913.*)

MASON, Rev. Arthur James, D.D. ; *b.* 4 May 1851 ; 3rd *s.* of G. W. Mason, Morton Hall, Notts ; *m.* 1899, Margaret, *d.* of late Rev. G. J. Blore, D.D. ; two *s.* one *d. Educ. :* Repton School ; Trinity College, Cambridge. Fellow of Trinity College, 1873-84 ; Assistant Tutor, 1874-77 ; Canon of Truro, 1877-84 ; Vicar of All Hallows, Barking, 1884-95 ; Fellow of Jesus College, 1896-1903 ; Lady Margaret Professor of Divinity, Cambridge University, 1895-1903 ; Hon. Fellow of Jesus College, 1909 ; Vice-Chancellor, Cambridge, 1908 ; Master of Pembroke College, Cambridge, 1903-12 ; Hon. Fellow since 1912 ; Canon of Canterbury since 1895 ; Hon. Chaplain to H.M. *Publications :* The Persecution of Diocletian, 1875 ; Commentary on Thessalonians and 1st Epistle of St. Peter, 1879 ; The Faith of the Gospel, 1887 ; The Relation of Confirmation to Baptism, 1893 ; The Conditions of our Lord's Life upon Earth, 1896 ; Thomas Cranmer, 1898 ; Historic Martyrs of the Primitive Church, 1905 ; Memoir of Bishop Wilkinson, 1909 ; Memoir of Bishop Collins, 1912 ; The Church of England and Episcopacy, 1914 ; What Became of the Bones of St. Thomas, 1920 ; edited the Five Theological Orations of Gregory of Nazianzus ; History of the Papacy in the 19th Century, by Bishop Nielsen. *Address :* The Precincts, Canterbury.
(*Died 24 April 1928.*)

MASON, Hon. Sir Arthur Wier, Kt., *cr.* 1922 ; Puisne Judge, Supreme Court, Transvaal, 1902 ; Judge President since 1923 ; *s.* of Rev. Frederick and Maria Mason of Durban ; *b.* 1860 ; *m.* 1890, Ellen Lavinia (*d.* 1912), *d.* of John Harwin of Maritzburg ; one *s.* one *d. Educ. :* New Kingswood School, Bath ; New College, Eastbourne. B.A. (Lond.). Admitted to Bar in Natal as Solicitor, 1881, and as Advocate from 1884 ; a Puisne Judge of the

Supreme Court, Natal, 1896 ; Commissioner of the Special Court (for treason cases), 1900 ; and President, 1901 ; Delimitation Commissioner, 1919 ; Chairman, 1923. *Address :* Supreme Court, Pretoria. *T. :* 288. (*Died 8 June 1924.*)

MASON, Charlotte Maria Shaw, Principal of the House of Education, Ambleside ; Director of the Parents' Union School ; Editor of the Parents' Review ; *b.* Bangor, 1 Jan. 1842 ; *d.* of Joshua Mason, merchant, Liverpool ; spinster ; churchwoman. *Educ. :* home. After a short training and some experience in schools of various grades, and in a Training College (Chichester), perceived certain principles leading to a reformed theory and practice of education ; to further such reform, wrote several volumes ; lectured ; founded the Parents' National Education Union, 1887 ; the House of Education, 1891 ; the Parents' Union School, 1891 ; the Parents' Review, 1890, etc. ; has lived to see a pretty wide adoption of her principles and methods in Elementary Schools, Secondary Schools, and home schoolrooms. *Publications :* Home Education ; Parents and Children ; School Education ; Some Studies in the Formation of Character ; Ourselves ; The Forty Shires ; The Ambleside Geography Books (vols. i., ii., iii., iv., v.), (revised and brought up to date, 1922). The Saviour of the World (a Life of Christ in verse) ; vol. i., The Holy Infancy ; vol. ii., His Dominion ; vol. iii., The Kingdom of Heaven ; vol. iv., The Bread of Life ; vol. v., The Great Controversy ; vol. vi., The Training of the Disciples ; The Basis of National Strength (series of Letters to The Times) and A Liberal Education for All (three pamphlets, dealing with Elementary, Continuation, and Secondary Schools) ; articles in magazines. *Recreations :* reading and driving. *Address :* Scale How, Ambleside.
(*Died 16 Jan. 1923.*)

MASON, Rev. Edmund Robert, M.A. (Oxon.) ; Hon. Canon of Ely Cathedral ; 2nd *s.* of Henry Mason and Isabella Russell of Deptford ; *m.* 1883, Lilly Marian Williams, *e. d.* of Ebenezer R. Williams of Handsworth two *s.* one *d.* privately ; Queen's College, Oxford (B.A., 3rd Class Theological School). Ordained, 1871 ; Curate of St. George's, Edgbaston, Birmingham, 1871-76 ; Association Secretary of the Church Missionary Society, 1876-81 ; Vicar of Christ Church, Birmingham, 1881-88 ; Prebendary of Lichfield Cathedral, 1881-88 ; Commissary to Bishop of Sierra Leone, 1883-97 ; Vicar of Oxton, Notts., 1888-97 ; Vicar of Luton, Beds., 1897-1910 ; Rural Dean, 1905-1910 ; Chaplain to the High Sheriff of Bedfordshire, 1907 ; Select Preacher, Cambridge, 1911-1912. *Publications :* sermons and papers, chiefly on missionary subjects, contributed to the press. *Address :* Foxley, Barton Road, Cambridge. (*Died 6 July 1922.*)

MASON, Rev. George Edward ; *b.* 20 Oct. 1847 ; *s.* of George William Mason of Morton Hall, Retford ; unmarried. *Educ. :* Repton : Trinity College, Cambridge. Curate at St. John's, Red Lion Square, London ; then presented by late Duke of Portland to living of Whitwell, Derbyshire ; resigned the living after having held it for 34 years, 1908 ; resigned at same time Hon. Canonry of Southwell Cathedral ; Principal of St. Bede's College, Umtata, Cape Colony, 1908 ; resigned, 1920 ; Long Service Medal (King Edward) as Hon. Chaplain to the 4th Battalion Notts and Derbyshire Regiment. *Publications :* Round the Round World on a Church Mission ; Claudia, the Christian Martyr.
(*Died 30 Mar. 1928.*)

MASON, Lt.-Colonel James Cooper, D.S.O. 1900 ; banker ; Commanding 10th Regiment Royal Grenadiers Militia of Canada ; *b.*

710

Toronto, 1875 ; *e. s.* of late Brigadier-General Hon. James Mason, Senator ; *m.* 1904, Jean Florence, *d.* of late Alexander MacArthur. *Educ. :* Toronto Collegiate Institute. Served as Lieut. and Capt. Royal Canadian Regt., South Africa, 1899-1900 (severely wounded) (despatches, brevet of Major, D.S.O., medal and three clasps). *Address :* 268 St. George Street, Toronto, Canada. *Clubs:* Royal Canadian Yacht ; Scarborough Golf. (*Died 6 Aug. 1923.*)

MASON, Robert, J.P. ; M.P. (Coal.), Wansbeck Division of Northumberland, 1918-22 ; Alderman, J.P., Northumberland ; *b.* Belford, Northumberland, 17 Dec. 1857 ; *m.* Rosa Elizabeth Thompson ; two *s.* three *d.* *Address :* Marden House, Whitley Bay, Northumberland. *T. :* Whitley Bay 83. *M. :* TY 7 and TY 8. *Clubs:* National Liberal ; Liberal, Union, Pen and Palette, Newcastle-upon-Tyne.
(*Died 1 Aug. 1927.*)

MASON, Sir Thomas, Kt., *cr.* 1909 ; J.P., D.L. County of City of Glasgow ; A.I.C.E. London. Deacon Convener of the City of Glasgow, 1889-1890 ; Dean of Guild of the City of Glasgow, 1906-8 ; President of the Incorporated Old Men and Women's Home ; Chairman of the Clyde Navigation Trust ; Chairman of the General Board of Control for Scotland ; Caledonian Canal Commissioner. *Address :* Craigie Hall, Bellahouston, Glasgow.
(*Died 26 April 1924.*)

MASPERO, Sir Gaston Camille Charles, Hon. K.C.M.G., *cr.* 1909 ; Egyptologist ; *b.* Paris, 1846 ; *m.* 1st, 1871, Harriet Yapp ; 2nd, 1880, Louise d'Estournelles Constant de Rebecque ; two *s.* one *d.* *Educ. :* Lycée Louisle-Grand ; Ecole normale, Paris. Professeur d'Egyptologie Ecole des Htes. Etudes, 1869 ; Docteur ès Lettres, 1873 ; Professor of Egyptian Philology and Archæology, Coll. of France, 1874 ; Director of the Boulaq Museum, succeeding Mariette Bey, 1881-86 ; Académie des Inscriptions, 1883 ; Hon. Fellow Queen's College, et Hon. D.C.L. Oxford, 1887 ; Director of Excavations, Egypt, 1899-1914 ; Secrétaire perpétuel Académie des Inscriptions, 1914. *Publications :* in English—Egyptian Archæology, 1889 ; Life in Ancient Egypt and Assyria, 1891 ; Dawn of Civilisation, 1894 ; The Struggle of the Nations, 1896 ; The Passing of the Empires, 1900 ; New Light on Ancient Egypt, 1908 ; Egypt, Ancient Sites and Modern Scenes, 1910 ; Art in Egypt, 1912. *Address :* Palais Mazarin, 25 Quai Conti, Paris ; le Pavillon, à Milon-la-Chapelle, Seine-et-Oise. (*Died 30 June 1916.*)

MASSEY, Rev. Edwyn Reynolds, M.A. Rural Dean of Claydon, 1893 ; Hon. Canon of Christ Church, 1915 ; Surrogate for Bucks Archdeaconry ; 3rd *s.* of Rev. Thos. Massey, rector of Hatcliffe, Lincs. ; *b.* 28 April 1847 ; *m.* 1879, Jessie Margaret Hawkins ; four *s.* three *d.* *Educ. :* Newark-on-Trent ; Exeter College, Oxford (Exhibitioner). 1st Class Mods. ; B.A., 1870 ; M.A., 1872 ; Deacon, 1871 ; Priest, 1872, Curate of Summertown, 1871-74 ; Vice-principal of Lichfield Theological College, 1874-80 ; Tyrrell Diocesan Chaplain, 1876-79 ; Vicar of Merton, Oxon., 1880-93 ; Diocesan inspector of schools, 1888-93 ; Rector of Marsh Gibbon, Bucks, 1893. *Publications:* contributor to Revised Marginal References to R.V. of the Bible, 1898 ; various articles in magazines, etc. ; Editorial Secretary of Oxfordshire Archæological Society, 1905-11. *Recreations :* Bowls ; cycling ; archæology.
(*Died 19 Sept. 1923.*)

MASSEY, Rev. John Cooke, M.A. Rector of Risley, Derby, 1892-1927 ; 2nd *s.* of Rev. Thomas Massey, Rector of Hatscliffe ; *b.* 1 Feb 1842 ; *m.* 1869, Elizabeth, 2nd *d.* of Andrew Irwin ; one *s.* five *d.* *Educ. :* Pocklington Grammar School ; Exeter College, Oxford. Lieutenant in King's Own Staffordshire Regiment, 1862-66 ; ordained, 1866 ; Curate of

Rugeley, Staffordshire, 1866-69; South Normanton, Derbyshire, 1869-71; Rector, 1871-92; Rural Dean of Alfreton, 1883-92; Ilkeston, 1899-1909; Hon. Canon of Southwell Cathedral, 1885; Hon. Diocesan Inspector of Schools in Religious Knowledge; late Chairman of Southwell Diocesan Sunday School Committee. *Publications:* Several Sermons, etc.; Articles for Press; Editor of Southwell Diocesan Magazine, 1894-1901. *Recreation:* cycling. *Address:* Chislehurst, 37 Marlborough Road, Bournemouth West. Hants.(*Died 21 Aug. 1928.*)

MASSEY, Rt. Hon. William Ferguson, P.C. 1914; Hon. LL.D. Edinburgh, 1917; Prime Minister of New Zealand since 1912; *b.* Limavady, Co. Derry, 26 Mar. 1856; *s.* of John Massey and Marian Ferguson; *m.* 1882, Christina, C.B.E., *e. d.* of Walter Paul, Auckland, N.Z.; three *s.* two *d.* *Educ.:* Public School and Secondary Schools at Londonderry. Went out to New Zealand 1870 to join his parents, who had emigrated with the Nonconformist settlers, 1862; followed farming pursuits, and eventually settled at Mangere, near Auckland; was early associated with Local Government, and at different times held positions of Member of Road Board, Chairman of School Committee, President of Auckland Agricultural and Pastoral Association, President of Farmers' Club, etc.; entered New Zealand Parliament as Member for Waitemata, 1894; Member for Franklin since 1896; Chief Opposition Whip, 1895; Leader of the Opposition, 1903; Prime Minister, 1912; has held office as Minister of Finance, Railways, Lands, Labour, Agriculture, Industries, and Commerce; a Representative of New Zealand, Imperial War Cabinet and Conference, 1917-18; Plenipotentiary Peace Conference, Paris, 1919; Imperial Conference, 1921; Imperial and Economic Conferences, 1923; Grand Officer Legion of Honour, France; Grand Officer of the Order of the Crown of Belgium. *Publications:* pamphlets and miscellaneous articles. *Recreations:* general interest in all sport. *Address:* Wellington, New Zealand. *T.A.:* Wellington. *Clubs:* Northern, Auckland; Auckland; Wellington, Wellington.

(*Died 10 May 1925.*)

MASSIE, John, M.A., Hon. D.D. (Yale); M.P. (L.) Cricklade Division, Wilts, 1906-1910; J.P. Co. Oxford; Yates Professor of New Testament Exegesis, Mansfield College, Oxford, 1886-1903; *b.* 3 Dec. 1842; *e. s.* of Rev. R. Massie, Newton-le-Willows; *m.* 1876, Edith Mary, 2nd *d.* of late Alexander Ogilvie, 4 Great George Street, S.W., and Sizewell House, Suffolk. *Educ.:* Atherstone Grammar School; St. John's Coll., Camb. (Scholar); incorporated Corpus Christi Coll., Oxford, 1886. Classical Prof. Spring Hill Theological College, Birmingham, 1869-86; Prof. also New Testament Exegesis, 1871-86; Councillor and Alderman of Leamington, 1878-87; Vice-Chairman of Council of Leamington High School for girls since 1890; Assistant Commissioner to Royal Commission on Secondary Education, 1894; Member of Executive of National Liberal Federation, 1894-1906, and since 1910; Treasurer, 1903-6; President of Liberation Society; President of Oxford and District Free Church Council 1896-1921; Member of Council and Education Board of Mansfield College; President National Education Association, and of Body of Protestant Dissenting Deputies; Chairman of Council (1918-21) and Chairman of Education Committee, Congregational Union; Chairman of Oxfordshire Committee under War Pensions Act, 1916-21; and of Higher Education Sub-Committee of Oxfordshire County Council. *Publications:* contributions to Hastings's Dictionary of the Bible, Cheyne's Encyclopædia Biblica, and other theological publications; commentary on I. and II. Corinthians in Century Bible, 1902; articles on educational and other sub-

jects in various reviews and magazines; pamphlets on Drift towards Dogmatic Teaching in Schools, 1898; Clericalism and Primary Education, 1895; The Proposed University for Roman Catholics in Ireland, 1899; etc. *Recreations:* outdoor games, fly-fishing, music. *Address:* Charlton Lea, Old Headington, Oxford. *T.A.:* Headington. *T.:* 10 Oxford. *Clubs:* Reform, National Liberal. (*Died 11 Nov. 1925.*)

MASSIE, Brig.-Gen. Roger Henry, C.B. 1919; C.M.G. 1919; *b.* 2 July 1869; *e.* and *o. surv. s.* of Edward Massie, of Coddington, Cheshire; *m.* 1902, Cecil Dorothea, *e. d.* of late Maurice J. Hall, of The Willows, Middleburg, Cape Colony; one *s.*; two *d.* *Educ.:* Stubbington House, Fareham; Royal Military Academy, Woolwich; commissioned in R.A. 1888; served Soudan, 1896; Indian Frontier and Tirah, 1897-98; S. Africa, 1899-1902; Staff-Capt. D.A.A.G. (Intelligence), and D.A.Q.M.G., S. Africa, 1901-5; France and Belgium, 1916-18; C.R.A. Portsmouth, 1919-20; Brig.-Gen. commanding Heavy Artillery, Canadian Corps, B.E.F., 1917-18; commanded Royal Garrison Artillery, Western Command, 1920-22; retired pay, 1922. *Address:* Wick Vale, Finchampstead, Berks. *T.:* Eversley 59. *Club:* Army and Navy. (*Died 23 Feb. 1927.*)

MASSINGBERD, Stephen Langton, J.P.; D.L.; Lord of Manor of Gunby and Patron of Welton-cum-Gunby, Lincs.; *o. s.* of late Edmund Langton and Emily (*d.* 1897), *e. d.* and *heiress* of late Charles Langton Massingberd; *b.* 12 May 1869; *m.* 1895, Margaret (*d.* 1906), 2nd *d.* of Vernon Lushington, K.C., 36 Kensington Square, W.; no *c.* *Educ.:* Charterhouse; Trinity College, Cambridge, History Tripos, 1891. Assistant Secretary to the Royal Statistical Society of London, and Editor of the Society's Journal, 1895-98; Member of the Lindsey County Council since 1904; Alderman, 1922; Vice-Chairman Spilsby Board of Guardians since 1908; Chairman since 1914; late Major 3rd Batt. the Lincolnshire Regt.; served in South Africa, 1902, and in France, 1916-18 (despatches). *Address:* Gunby Hall, Burgh, Lincolnshire. *M.:* BE 908. (*Died 21 May 1925.*)

MASSINGHAM, Henry William; *b.* Old Catton, Norwich, 1860; *s.* of Joseph Massingham, Norwich; *m.* 1st, Emma (*d.* 1905), *d.* of late Henry Snowdon of Norwich; 2nd, 1907, Ellen, *d.* of the same. *Educ.:* Norwich Grammar School, under Dr. Jessopp. On staff of Norfolk News and Daily Press, Norwich; subsequently editor of National Press Agency; assistant editor and editor of the Star; literary editor, special Parliamentary representative, assistant editor, and editor of the Daily Chronicle; special Parliamentary representative of the Daily News; editor of the Nation, 1907-23; is a Commander of the Order of the Redeemer. *Publications:* The London Daily Press; Labour and Protection; many articles in the magazines. *Recreation:* travel. *Address:* 21 Bedford Square, W.C.1. (*Died 28 Aug. 1924.*)

MASSON, Frederic; ci-devant Bibliothécaire au Ministère des Affaires Ftrangères, destitué en 1880; Secretaire perpetuel de l'Academie Française; Fondateur de l'Assistance Mutuelle des Veuves, de la Guerre; président de la Maison Chinoise; Administrateur de l'Hôpital de l'Institut (Fondation Dosne, Hôtel Thiers); *b.* Paris, 1847; *m.* M. Cottin. *Publications:* Napoléon et les Femmes; Napoléon chez lui, 1894; Cavaliers de Napoléon; Josephine Imperatrice, 1898; Napoléon et sa Famille, 1897-1912; Napoléon et son Fils, 1908, etc. *Address:* 15 rue de la Baume, Paris; Clos des Fées. Asnières sur-Oise, Seine-et-Oise. (*Died 19 Feb. 1925.*)

MASSON, John, M.A., LL.D. Senior Classical Lecturer in Edinburgh Provincial College; *s.* of Rev. John Masson, of Dundee. *Educ.:* Dundee High School; Universities of St.

Andrews, Leipzig, Berlin, and Paris. Rector of Waid Academy, Anstruther; Examiner in Classics in St. Andrews University; Classical Lecturer in University College, Dundee. *Publications:* collaborated in Professor Lewis Campbell's large edition of Sophocles, to which he contributed a chapter on The MSS. of Sophocles; articles on Lucretius and Sophocles in British Quarterly Review, Journal of Philology, Classical Review, and Quarterly Review (Jan. 1897, on "Epicurus and his Sayings"); articles on Classical Literature in Chambers's Encyclopædia, Book on the Atomic Theory of Lucretius, 1884; Lucretius, Epicurean and Poet, 1907-9; Selections from the Georgics, 1921. *Recreations:* walking, fly-fishing. *Address:* 123 Mayfield Road, Edinburgh.   (*Died 17 Dec. 1927.*)

MASSY, 7th Baron, *cr.* 1776; Hugh Somerset John Massy; *s.* of 6th Baron and Lady Lucy Maria Butler (*d.* 1896), *d.* of 3rd Earl of Carrick; *b.* 15 Feb. 1864; *S.* father, 1915: *m.* 1886, Ellen Ida Constance, *d.* of Charles W. Wise, Rochestown, Tipperary; two *s.* three *d.* Heir: *s.* Hon. Hugh Hamon Charles George Massy [*b.* 13 July 1894; *m.* 1919, Margaret, *d.* of late Richard Leonard of Meadsbrook, Ashbourne, Co. Limerick, and *widow* of Dr. Moran, Tara, Co. Meath]. *Address:* Killakee, Rathfarnham, Co. Dublin. *T.A.:* Rathfarnham.

     (*Died 20 Oct. 1926.*)

MASSY, Colonel Harry Stanley, C.B. 1908; late Commandant 19th Bengal Lancers and A.A.G.; *b.* 12 July 1855; 3rd *s.* of late Major H. W. Massy of Grantstown Hall, Tipperary; *m.* 1894, Geraldine Aileen, *d.* of George Massy of Glenville, Limerick; one *s.* one *d.* Entered army, 1874; Capt. 1885; Major, 1894; Lieut.-Col. 1900; served against Jowaki Afreedees, 1877-78 (medal with clasp); Afghan War, 1878-80 (wounded, medal with clasp, despatches); Burmah, 1886-1888 (despatches, clasp); 2nd Miranzai Expedition, 1891 (clasp); N.W.F. India, 1897-98 (despatches, medal with two clasps). *Recreation:* aviation. *Address:* Grantstown Hall, Tipperary. *T.:* Richmond 1554.

     (*Died 10 Oct. 1920.*)

MASSY-BERESFORD, John George; J.P. Peeblesshire and Fermanagh; D.L.; *b.* 7 Feb. 1856; *s.* of Very Rev. J. M. Massy-Beresford, Dean of Kilmore, and Emily Sarah Massy-Beresford of Macbichill; *m.* 1892, Hon. Alice Mulholland, *y. d.* of 1st Baron Dunleath; two *s.* one *d.* *Educ.:* Malvern; Jesus Coll. Camb. B.A. 1879; High Sheriff, Co. Fermanagh, 1900; served in Lanarkshire Yeomanry Cavalry, 1876-84; British Red Cross in France, 1915-16. *Recreations:* hunting, yachting, shooting, fishing. *Address:* St. Hubert's, Belturbet, Ireland. *T.A.:* Belturbet. *M.:* IL 6. *Clubs:* Royal Automobile; Royal St. George Yacht, Kingstown.

     (*Died 27 July 1923.*)

MASTERMAN, Rt. Hon. Charles Frederick Gurney, P.C. 1912; M.A.; M.P. (L.) Rusholme Division of Manchester 1923-1924; 4th *s.* of late Thomas William Masterman of Rotherfield Hall, Sussex; *b.* 1873; *m.* 1908, Lucy, *e. d.* of Rt. Hon. Gen. Sir Neville Lyttelton; one *s.* two *d.* *Educ.:* Weymouth; Christ's College, Cambridge. First class in Natural Sciences Tripos, 1895; 1st class in Moral Sciences, 1896; President of the Union, 1896; Fellow of Christ's College, 1900; has written for Nation, Athenæum, etc.; was Literary Editor Daily News; Secy., Children's County Holiday Fund, London, 1900-3; Guardian of the Poor, Camberwell, 1901-4; Lecturer, Cambridge and London University Extension Societies; contested Dulwich as Liberal Candidate, 1903; Parliamentary Secretary Local Government Board, 1908-1909; M.P. (L.) West Ham (North), 1906; unseated on petition, 1911; Under-Secretary of State, Home Department, 1909-12; Financial Secretary to Treasury, 1912-14;

late Chairman of National Insurance Commission; M.P. (L.) South-West Bethnal Green, 1911-14; Chancellor Duchy of Lancaster, 1914-15; Director of Wellington House (Propaganda Dept.) 1914-18. *Publications:* Tennyson as a Religious Teacher, 1899; The Heart of the Empire, 1901; From the Abyss, 1902; In Peril of Change, 1905; F. D. Maurice, 1907; The Condition of England, 1909; The New Liberalism, 1920; How England is Governed, 1921; England after War, 1922. *Address:* 46 Gillingham Street, S.W.1. *T.:* 1036 Victoria. *Clubs:* Reform, National Liberal.

     (*Died 17 Nov. 1927.*)

MASTERS, Rev. James Hoare; Canon Residentiary of Chichester Cathedral; Prebendary of Wisborough in Chichester Cathedral; Custos and Chaplain of St. Mary's Hospital, Chichester; *s.* of Captain Masters, R.N., of Ryde, Isle of Wight; *m.* 1859, Margaret, *d.* of John Atkinson of Leeds, Solicitor; one *s.* *Educ.:* Clapham Grammar School; Emmanuel College, Cambridge. Curate of Limpsfield, Surrey, and All Saints, Southampton; Vicar of Lower Beeding, Horsham, for 21½ years, 1861-83; Rector of Slinfold, Horsham, 19 years, 1883-1902; Rural Dean for 30 years; Surrogate in the Diocese of Chichester. *Address:* The Close, Chichester. *Club:* Constitutional.

     (*Died 6 Jan. 1918*)

MASTERS, Rev. William Caldwall, M.A.; Rector of Stanton Fitzwarren, Wilts, 1885-1919; Hon. Canon of Bristol, 1912; *b.* 1843; *s.* of Rev. J. Smalman Masters, M.A., Jesus College, Oxford, Incumbent of Christ Church, Shooter's Hill, Kent; *m.* 1870, Ellen (*d.* 1918), *sister* of J. Ashfordby - Trenchard of Stanton Fitzwarren, and of Nyn Park, Herts; two *s.* one *d.* *Educ.:* St. Mary Magdalen College, Oxford. Curate of St. Mary's, Hitchin, Herts, 1866-69; Vicar of Long Marston and Assistant Priest of Tring, Herts, 1870. *Publications:* Some Notes on the Ancient Church of St. Leonard, Stanton Fitzwarren, and otherwise, dedicated to the Lord Bishop of Bristol, Dr. G. Forrest Browne; Christian Architecture; Two Addresses, etc., dedicated to the same; The Soldier and the Cross, an address at the dedication of the Churchyard Soldiers' Cross, Stanton Fitzwarren, Jan. 1916; In Memoriam, E. M. 1919. *Recreations:* literature, mediæval architecture, wood - carving and designing. *Address:* 29 York Gardens, Clifton, Bristol.

     (*Died 19 Aug. 1924.*)

MATHER, Rt. Rev. Herbert, D.D.; Chancellor of Hereford Cathedral, 1906; *b.* 1840; *m.* 1872. *Educ.:* Trinity Coll. Camb. Ordained Deacon, 1866; Priest, 1867; Vice-Principal Carmarthen Training College, 1865-7; Principal, 1867-8; Curate of Newland, 1868-70; Chaplain to Bishop of Newfoundland and Incumbent of St. John's Cathedral, 1870-2; Chaplain to Bishop of Nova Scotia, 1872-3; Rector of All Saints, Huntingdon, 1874-7; Vicar of Loddington, 1877-93; Rural Dean of Gartree, 1886-92; Provost of St. Andrew's Cathedral, Inverness, 1891-97; Bishop of Antigua, 1897-1904; Assistant Bishop to Bishop of Hereford, 1905-12; Rector, Hampton Bishop, Hereford, 1908-12; in charge of diocese of Accra, 1912-13. *Address:* Trevathan, Beckenham, Kent.

     (*Died 30 July 1922.*)

MATHER, James Marshall, Nonconformist Minister; *b.* Darlington, 9 May 1851; *s.* of John Mather and Sarah, 2nd *d.* of James Marshall, Darlington; *m.* Helena, 2nd *d.* of S. R. de Ville, Staffordshire; one *s.* one *d.* *Educ.:* Lincoln. Pupilled to a firm of architects, Lincoln, in which city his father was the minister of a large Nonconformist church; when out of his articles, studied for and entered same ministry, and lived since in Lancashire. *Publications:* Life and Teachings of John Ruskin (gone through nine editions); Popular Studies in

Nineteenth Century Poets ; Lancashire Idylls ; The Sign of the Wooden Shoon ; By Roaring Loom ; Rambles round Rossendale (2 Series). *Recreations :* walking, the novels of Balzac. *Address :* 7 Granville Avenue, Broughton Park, Manchester.   (*Died May 1916.*)

MATHER, Rt. Hon. Sir William, P.C., Kt., *cr.* 1902 ; J.P. ; Hon. LL.D. Princeton and Victoria Universities ; *b.* 1888 ; *s.* of late William Mather, of Manchester, and Amelia, *d.* of late James Tidswell, of Manchester ; *m.* 1863, Emma, *d.* of Thomas Watson, of Highbury ; one *s.* four *d. Educ. :* private schools, and in Germany. Late Chairman of Mather and Platt, Ltd., Manchester ; M.I.C.E. and M.I.Mech.E. ; a Governor and member of Council of Owens College, and of Victoria University ; a Trustee of the Gordon College, Khartoum ; has interested himself largely in the question of cotton growing in the Sudan ; Ex-Pres. of the British Science Guild ; President of Textile Institute ; member of the Royal Commission Exhibitions Branch Board of Trade ; investigated Technical Education in America and Russia for Royal Commission on Technical Instruction, 1883 ; established the system of 8 hours' day at Mather & Platt's, Ltd., Salford Works, in 1893, which has since been continued at their Park Works ; has been engaged in promoting technical education for many years ; Chairman of Froebel Educational Institute of London ; Chairman of British Education Section of Franco-British Exhibition, 1908 ; was member of the Committee appointed by the Minister of War in 1901 to report on the reorganisation of the War Office ; a Liberal ; M.P. S. Div. of Salford, 1885-86 ; Gorton Div. of Lancashire, S.E., 1889-95 ; Rossendale Div. of Lancashire, N.E., 1900-4. *Address :* Manchester ; Bramble Hill, New Forest, Hampshire. *Clubs :* Reform, Brooks's Devonshire.   (*Died 18 Sept. 1920.*)

MATHERS, Edward P. ; newspaper proprietor, editor, author ; *b.* Edinburgh, 19 Aug. 1850 ; *s.* of late David Mathers, publisher, newspaper proprietor ; *m.* Mary A., *d.* of late R. H. Powys. *cousin* of Lord Lilford ; one *s.* four *d. Educ. :* High School, Edinburgh ; Edinburgh Institution. English journalist till 1878 ; emigrated then to South Africa, and held positions on press, founding and editing the Natal Advertiser ; in early 'eighties travelled throughout Transvaal goldfields ; wrote about them, being the only journalist who foretold their greatness ; returned to England, 1888 ; founded his weekly paper South Africa, and inaugurated annual South African dinners in London, being Chairman of Committee ; Life Member of Royal Geographical Society and Royal Colonial Institute. *Publications :* Trip to Moodie's ; Goldfields Revisited ; Golden South Africa ; South Africa and How to Reach it ; Zambesia, England's El Dorado in Africa. *Recreation :* travel. *Address :* 10 Stanley Crescent, W.11. *T.A. :* Eddies, London. *T. :* Park 119. *Club :* Ranelagh.   (*Died 13 Oct. 1924.*)

MATHERS, Helen (Mrs. Henry Reeves), novelist ; *b.* Misterton, Crewkerne, Somerset, 26 Aug. 1853 ; 3rd *d.* of late Thomas Mathews, Misterton, and Maria Buckingham ; *m.* Henry Albert Reeves (*d.* 1914), orthopedic surgeon. *Educ. :* Chantry School, Frome. *Publications :* Comin' thro' the Rye ; Cherry Ripe ; My Lady Greensleeves ; Sam's Sweetheart ; Story of a Sin ; Eyre's Acquittal ; A Man of To-Day ; The Lovely Malincourt ; The Sin of Hagar ; Venus Victrix ; Murder or Manslaughter ; Found Out ; Blind Justice ; Bam Wildfire ; The Juggler and the Soul ; Becky ; Cinders ; Honey ; Griff of Griffiths Court ; Side-Shows ; The Ferryman ; Tally Ho ! ; Pigskin and Petticoat ; Gay Lawless ; Love, the Thief. *Recreation :* needlework. *Club :* Ladies' Park.   (*Died 11 Mar. 1920.*)

MATHERS, Hon. Thomas Graham ; Chief Justice of the King's Bench, Manitoba,

since 1910 ; *b.* 1859 ; *s.* of late Christopher Mathers and Rachel Graham, both of North of Ireland ancestry ; *m.* 1892, Jessie, *d.* of late Richard Waugh, journalist ; one *s.* one *d. Educ. :* Lucknow and Kincardine, Ont. Came to Manitoba, 1888 ; called to Bar of Manitoba, 1889 ; Head of Law Department, Manitoba Government Railways, 1888-90 ; Puisne Judge of the King's Bench, 1905 ; Agent Minister of Justice for Manitoba and Counsel for the several departments of the Dominion Government, 1896-1905 ; Alderman of Winnipeg, 1898-99 ; Chairman Board of License Commissioners, 1899-1900 ; contested Mayoralty, 1900. *Recreations :* golf, shooting. *Address :* 16 Edmonton Street, Winnipeg, Man. *T. :* 936 Main. *M. :* 440. *Clubs :* Manitoba, Winnipeg ; Brandon, Brandon ; St. Charles Country, St. Charles.
    (*Died 16 Aug. 1927.*)

MATHESON, Annie ; *b.* Blackheath, 1853 ; *d.* of late Rev. James Matheson, of Nottingham. *Publications :* (poems) As Months go by, Religion of Humanity, Love's Music, Love Triumphant, Selected Poems, Snowflakes and Snowdrops, Roses and Loaves, Maytime Songs ; Hal's Book ; (prose) editor and joint author of By Divers Paths ; author of Leaves of Prose ; Story of a Brave Child (Joan of Arc), Florence Nightingale ; A Plain Friend ; Our Hero of the Golden Heart. Anthologist and editor of : Sayings from the Saints ; A Little Book of Courage ; Songs of Love and Praise ; A Daybook for Girls ; originator and editor of Rose and Dragon books, including Young Citizen series. *Club :* Lyceum.   (*Died 16 Mar. 1924.*)

MATHESON, Charles Louis, M.A. ; K.C. (Irish), 1891 ; Recorder of Belfast and C.C. Judge, Antrim, since 1919 ; *b.* Dublin, 3 Feb. 1851 ; 2nd *s.* of Robert N. Matheson, Clerk of the Privy Council, Ireland, and Victorine, *d.* of Mons. Jean Phillipe Jossevel, Juge du Pays, of Moudon, Switzerland ; *m.* Elinor, *o. d.* of Charles Tuthill, Barrister-at-Law, of Newstead, Roebuck, Co. Dublin ; two *s.* three *d. Educ. :* Rathmines School ; Trinity Coll. Dublin. First Honours ; auditor of the College Historical Society, 1874 ; Irish Barr. 1874 ; H.M. First Serjeant at Law in Ireland 1913-19. *Address :* 62 Merrion Square, Dublin. *T. :* Dublin 1550. *Club :* University, Dublin.   (*Died 20 May 1921.*)

MATHESON, Sir Kenneth (James), 2nd Bt. *cr.* 1882 ; D.L., J.P. ; *b.* London, 12 May 1854 ; *e. s.* of 1st Bt. and 2nd wife, Lavinia Mary, *sis.* of 8th Lord Beaumont ; *m.* 1913, Ada Juliana, *d.* of late George E. B. Lousada, and *widow* of Daniel C. Stiebel ; *S.* father 1886. *Educ. :* Harrow ; Christ Church, Oxford. *Heir :* *half-b.* Alexander Percival [*b.* 6 Feb. 1861 ; *m.* 1884, Eleanor, *d.* of late Rev. K. E. A. Money ; four *d. Address :* Anderun, Littlehampton. *Clubs :* National Liberal, Hurlingham]. *Address :* Follaton, Totnes, Devon ; 48 Grosvenor Square, W.1 ; *T. :* Mayfair 6030 ; 19 Sussex Square, Brighton. *Club :* Carlton.
    (*Died 25 Jan. 1920.*)

MATHESON, Rt. Hon. Sir Robert Edwin, P.C. Ireland, 1910 ; Kt., *cr.* 1907 ; LL.D. ; Barrister-at-law ; *e. s.* of late R. N. Matheson, Clerk of the Privy Council for Ireland ; *b.* 6 May 1845 ; *m.* 1866, Cherrie M. Hardy (*d.* 1918) ; one *s.* four *d. Educ. :* Rathmines ; Trinity College, Dublin. Studied law at King's Inns, Dublin, and Middle Temple, London ; called to Irish Bar, 1875 ; Secretary General Register Office, Dublin, 1877 ; Assistant Registrar-General, 1879-1900 ; Registrar-General for Ireland, 1900-1909 ; Commissioner of Irish Census, 1881, 1891, 1901 ; Hon. LL.D. Royal University, 1901 ; Examiner in Vital Statistics, etc., Dublin University, 1901-9 ; President Statistical Society of Ireland, 1905-6. *Publications :* Digest of the Irish Marriage Law ; Varieties and Synonyms of Surnames and Christian Names in Ireland ; Report on Sur-

713

names in Ireland ; Insects, Fungi, and Weeds injurious to Farm Crops ; Housing of People of Ireland, 1841-1901 ; Results of Census of 1901, etc. *Address:* 44 Belgrave Square, Monkstown, Co. Dublin. *(Died 10 Jan. 1926.)*

MATHEW, Charles James, K.C. 1913 ; C.B.E. 1917 ; L.C.C. (P.) St. George's in the East, 1910-19 ; Alderman since 1919 ; *b.* 24 Oct. 1872 ; *y. s.* of late Lord Justice Mathew ; *m.* Anna, *d.* of late James Archbold Cassidy of Monasterevan, Co. Kildare ; two *s.* one *d. Educ.:* The Oratory School, Birmingham ; Trinity Hall, Cambridge (B.A.). Called to Bar, 1897 ; Bencher, Lincoln's Inn, 1918. *Address:* 75 Albert Hall Mansions, S.W.7 ; 10 Old Square, Lincoln's Inn, W.C.2. *T.:* Kensington 5272, Holborn 1586. *Club:* Athenæum. *(Died 8 Jan. 1923.)*

MATHEW, Frank, novelist and barrister-at-law ; *b.* Bombay, 1865 ; *s.* of late Frank Mathew, C.E. ; *n.* of late Sir James Charles Mathew ; *m.* 1899, Agnes *d.* of James Tisdall Woodroffe, Advocate-General of Bengal ; two *s. Educ.:* Beaumont College ; King's College School ; London Univ. Inglis Scholarship, King's College, London, 1886 ; Stephen Endowment, 1887. *Publications:* Father Mathew : his Life and Times, 1890 ; At the Rising of the Moon ; Irish Stories and Studies, 1893 ; The Wood of the Brambles, 1896 ; A Child in the Temple, 1897 ; The Spanish Wine, 1898 ; Defender of the Faith, 1899 ; One Queen Triumphant, 1899 ; Love of Comrades, 1900 ; The Royal Sisters, 1901 ; Ireland, 1905 ; An Image of Shakespeare, 1922. *Address:* 1 Hermes Road, Oxford.
(Died 25 Oct. 1924.)

MATHEWS, Sir Charles, 1st Bt., *cr.* 1917 ; Kt., *cr.* 1907 ; K.C.B., *cr.* 1911 ; Director of Public Prosecutions since 1908 ; Barrister-at-Law, Western Circuit ; *b.* 16 Oct. 1850 ; *s.* of William and Elizabeth West, and stepson of late Charles James Mathews, the Comedian, whose surname he assumed by deed poll ; *m.* Lucy, *d.* of Lindsay Sloper, 1888 ; no *c. Educ.:* Eton. Called to Bar, Middle Temple, 1872 ; Bencher, 1901 ; joined W. Circuit ; Junior Counsel to the Treasury at the Central Criminal Court, 1886 ; Senior Counsel, 1888 ; contested Winchester (L.G.), 1892 ; Recorder of Salisbury, 1893-1908 ; Hon. Member of the Jockey Club. *Address:* 88 Sloane Street, S.W.1. *Clubs:* Turf, Garrick, Beefsteak. *(Died 6 Jan. 1920.)*

MATHEWS, George Ballard, M.A., F.R.S., LL.D. (Glasg.) ; *b.* London, 23 Feb. 1861. *Educ.:* Ludlow Grammar School ; University College, London ; University of Cambridge. Assistant-Lecturer in Pure Mathematics at the University College of N. Wales, Bangor, Professor of Mathematics there, 1884-96 ; late Fellow of St. John's College, Cambridge ; Examiner in Mathematics for the Universities of Ireland (National) and Manchester. *Publications:* Theory of Numbers, part I. ; A Treatise on Bessel Functions (conjointly with Prof. A. Gray, F.R.S., LL.D.) ; Tract on Algebraic Equations ; articles on Universal Algebra and on Number in the Encyclopædia Britannica ; Projective Geometry ; and various papers on mathematical subjects. *Address:* 7 Menai View Terrace, Bangor. *(Died 19 Mar. 1922.)*

MATHEWS, Rev. William Arnold, M.A., Hon. Canon of Carlisle ; *b.* Hatfield, Yorkshire, 1839 ; *s.* of William Mathews, M.D., J.P. ; *m.* 1866, Caroline Sara Georgina, *d.* of William H. Stuart of Lennoxville, Canada ; five *s.* four *d. Educ.:* Uppingham ; Corpus Christi College, Oxford. Ordained, by Bishop Jackson of Lincoln, Curate of St. Peter's, Old Radford, Nottingham, 1862 ; Vicar of Laughton, Lincolnshire, and a Diocesan Inspector of Schools, 1865 ; Vicar of Dacre, Cumberland, 1871 ; Rector of Skelton, Cumberland, and Rural Dean of Greystoke, 1877 ; Vicar of St. Mary's, Carlisle, 1879 ; Appleby, 1883 ; Rural Dean of Appleby, 1886 ; Proctor in Convocation

for the Archdeaconry of Carlisle ; Rector of Bassingham, 1896-1913 ; Vicar of St. Wendron, Helston, 1918-23. *Publications:* The National Church of a Christian Nation ; Constitutional Church Reform, 1886 ; The Witness of the World to Christ, 1889. *Recreations:* fishing, carpentry. *Address:* 27 Rockliffe Road, Bath.
(Died 23 Nov. 1925.)

MATTHEW, Frederic David ; Hon. D.Litt. Oxford ; *b.* 14 Oct. 1838 ; *m.* 1874, Gertrude, *e. d.* of late Rev. J. W. v. R. Hoets ; four *s.* three *d. Educ.:* King's College School. Co-founder with the late Dr. F. J. Furnivall of the Wyclif Society, 1882 ; Member of Executive Committee of Wyclif Society. *Publications:* Edited English Works of Wyclif for E.E.T.S. 1880 ; Life of John Wyclif, 1884. *Address:* 70 Belsize Park Gardens, N.W.
(Died 23 Jan. 1918.)

MATTHEW, Reginald Walter, C.M.G. 1921 ; Director in the Department of Overseas Trade ; *b.* 14 Sep. 1879 ; *e. s.* of late Walter E. Matthew, Archdeacon of Colombo ; *m.* 1908, Dorothy, *y. d.* of late George Chambers, of Clarendon Road, Holland Park. *Educ.:* St. Paul's School ; Jesus College, Oxford. Entered War Office, 1903 ; transferred to Board of Trade, 1904 ; Secretary to Committee on Supply and Training of British Boy Sailors, 1906 ; Secretary, Merchant Shipping Advisory Committee, 1910-1914 ; Secretary to British Delegation at International Conference on Unification of Maritime Law, Brussels, 1909, 1910, and 1912 ; Private Secretary to Mr. H. J. Tennant, Parliamentary Secretary, Board of Trade, 1909-10 ; and to following Presidents—Mr. Sydney Buxton, 1911-1913 ; Mr. John Burns, 1914 ; Mr. Walter Runciman, 1914-16 ; Sir Albert Stanley, 1917 ; joined Department of Overseas Trade, Dec. 1917 ; Chevalier, Legion of Honour, 1918. *Recreation:* lawn tennis. *Address:* 21 Riverview Gardens, Castelnau, Barnes, S.W.13.
(Died 8 Nov. 1923.)

MATTHEWS, Col. Godfrey Estcourt, C.B. 1911 ; C.M.G. 1915 ; *b.* 17 June 1866. Entered Royal Marines, 1884 ; Captain, 1894 ; Major, 1902 ; Lieut.-Colonel, 1910 ; Col. 1915 ; employed with Egyptian army since 1907 ; served in Nile Expedition, 1897 (medal with clasp), 1898 (despatches twice, brevet of Major, two clasps, medal), 1899 (clasp) ; served with Plymouth Batt., R.N. Division, in Gallipoli, 1915. *Club:* Naval and Military. *(Died 13 April 1917.)*

MATTHEWS, Joseph Bridges, K.C. 1913 ; Recorder of Dudley since 1923 ; of Tewkesbury, 1912-23 ; *s.* of John Matthews, late of Worcester ; *m.* Florence Louisa, *e. d.* of Henry William Batson, late of Worcester ; two *d. Educ.:* Worcester Cathedral School. Solicitor at Worcester, 1884-95 ; Sheriff of Worcester, 1895-96 ; called to Bar, Middle Temple, 1896 ; Bencher, 1924 ; Oxford Circuit. Bronze Medal Royal Humane Society. *Publications:* Law Relating to Married Women ; Covenants in Restraint of Trade ; Moneylending ; joint editor of Pritchard's Quarter Sessions, 2nd ed. ; editor of Hayes and Jarman on Wills, 12th and 13th ed. *Address:* Bickley Court, Kent ; 2 Paper Buildings, Temple, E.C.4. *T.:* Temple 57 ; Holborn 1885. *(Died 5 Aug. 1928.)*

MATTHEWS, Col. Valentine, C.B.E., V.D., M.R.C.S., L.S.A. ; late R.A.M.C. (Vol.) ; late Temp. Lt.-Col. in Army ; organised arrangements for meeting, housing, feeding, and transport of travelling soldiers on leave ; late Senior Surgeon Westminster General Dispensary ; Inspector of Rest Houses, London District ; *b.* 14 Feb. 1855 ; *s.* of William Matthews ; *m.* Maude, *d.* of J. H. Garlant ; one *s. Educ.:* St. Paul's School ; King's College, London. First Jefe (Hon.) No. 3 Ambulance, Cruz Roja, Madrid ; Hon. Life Member St. John Ambulance Association ; late County Director V.A.D., T.F. Association, County of

MATSUMURA, Jinzo, D.Sc. See page xxv.

London; Medical Registrar, House Physician, and Assistant Demonstrator of Anatomy, King's College Hospital. *Publications:* (with Capt. J. Harper) Handbook for Vol. Medical Officers; various communications to Medical Journals. *Recreations:* fishing, sculling, etc. *Address:* 29 Onslow Square, S.W.7. *T.:* Kensington 225. *Club:* Reform. *(Died 6 Oct. 1921.)*

MATTHEWS, Sir William, K.C.M.G., *cr.* 1906; Consulting Engineer for Harbour and Dock Works; *b.* 8 March 1844; *s.* of late John Matthews of Penzance. *Educ.:* privately in Cornwall. A civil engineer and a member of the firm of Coode, Matthews, Fitzmaurice & Wilson, consulting engineers for harbours to the Crown Agents for the Colonies; chief engineers of the National Harbour at Dover; consulting engineers for harbours and docks at Colombo, Singapore, and other ports; advisers on these and kindred subjects to the Admiralty, Board of Trade, and Colonial governments; consulting engineers to the Mersey Conservancy, the Humber Conservancy, the Tyne Commissioners; Member of a Committee appointed by the Admiralty in 1901 to inquire into the naval works at Gibraltar; appointed by the Admiralty in 1900 to report upon the Naval Harbour at Malta; Member of Royal Commission on Coast Erosion, 1906; Past-President Inst. C.E., 1908; Member of International Technical Commission on Suez Canal, 1908; Member of Royal Commission on Oil Fuel, 1912; C.M.G. 1901; Officer of Order of Leopold, 1894. *Address:* 14 Strathray Gardens, Hampstead, N.W.; 9 Victoria Street, Westminster, S.W.1. *T.A.:* Penlee, London. *T.:* 47 Westminster; 1939 P.O. Hampstead. *Clubs:* Junior Carlton, St. Stephen's. *(Died 8 Jan. 1922.)*

MATTHEY, Col. Edward, C.B. 1902; Lieut.-Col. and Hon. Col. late London Rifle Brigade; *b.* 1836; *m.* 1861. *Address:* 31a Weymouth Street, W. *T.A.:* Eked, London.
(Died 21 Oct. 1918.)

MATZ, Bertram Waldrom; Publisher; Editor of The Dickensian; *b.* London, 5 March 1865; *m.* one *s.* two *d.* A Founder and President of the Dickens Fellowship, and its first Hon. Secretary, 1902-3; Editor of the National Edition of Dickens's Works; Dickens's Miscellaneous Papers, Plays, and Poems; the memorial edition of Forster's Life of Dickens; first Editor of The Odd Volume; contributor to the Fortnightly Review, Bookman, Strand, and various magazines and newspapers on Dickens, Meredith, and other subjects. *Publications:* Charles Dickens: the Story of his Life and Writings; Thomas Carlyle: a brief Account of his Life and Work; The Dickens Birthday Book; The Humour of Pickwick; The Sayings of Sam Weller; The George Inn, Southwark; The Dickens Calendar; The Inns and Taverns of Pickwick; Dickensian Inns and Taverns; Character Sketches from Dickens; Dickens in Cartoon and Caricature, etc. *Address:* 29 Woodfield Avenue, Streatham, S.W.16.
(Died 17 July 1925.)

MAUDE, Ven. Charles Bulmer; Archdeacon of Salop, 1896-1917; *s.* of late Edmund Maude of Middleton, Yorks; *b.* 1848; *m.* 1878, Geraldine, *d.* of late Alex. Donovan of Framfield Place, Sussex, J.P., D.L. *Educ.:* Exeter Coll., Oxford (M.A.). Vicar of S. Cyprian, Kimberley, 1875-81; Wilnecote, 1881-86; Leek, 1886-96; S. Chad's, Shrewsbury, 1896-1906. *Address:* The Castle, Ludlow. *T.A.:* Ludlow.
(Died 11 May 1927.)

MAUDE, Edith Caroline, C.B.E. 1920; *d.* of late Major H. W. Briscoe, R.A., of Tinvane, Co. Tipperary; *b.* 1865; *m.* 1894, Gerald Edward Maude, *s.* of late Captain Hon. Francis Maude, R.N., Barrister-at-law, and late Major 4th Battalion East Surrey Regiment. Secretary of the Shipwrecked Mariners' Society since 1896; Hon. Secretary Soldiers' and Sailors' Families' Association (Kennington and S. Lambeth Branch), 1911-18; President since 1918 and Hon. Secretary (County of London Branch); Member of Council, Women's Holiday Fund, Association for the Welfare of the Blind; Chairman of Evelyn Convalescent Cottage, Upper Wargrave, and of Committee of Royal Home for Soldiers' Daughters, Hampstead, etc. *Address:* 14 Cranley Place, S.W.7. *T.:* Kensington 1610. *(Died 6 Oct. 1922.)*

MAUDE, Lt. - Gen. Sir Frederick Stanley, K.C.B. *cr.* 1916; C.B. 1915; C.M.G. 1901; D.S.O. 1900; late Coldstream Guards, G.C.B., V.C.; *m.* 1893, Cecil Cornelia Marianne St. Leger, *d.* of late Col. Rt. Hon. Thomas Edward Taylor, M.P., of Ardgillan Castle, Co. Dublin; one *s.* two *d.* *Educ.:* Eton; Sandhurst. Entered army, 1884; Capt. 1896; Major, 1899; Lt.-Colonel, 1907; Colonel, 1911; Maj.-Gen. and Divisional Commander, 1915; passed Staff College, 1896; served Soudan, including engagement at Hasheen, and destruction of Tamai, 1885 (medal with clasp, Khedive's star); South African War, 1899-1901, including advance on Kimberley; operations in the Orange Free State, actions at Poplar Grove, Driefontein, Karee Siding, Vet River, and Zand River; and operations in the Transvaal, actions near Johannesburg, Pretoria, Diamond Hill, and Belfast; operations in Cape Colony (despatches, Queen's medal with six clasps, D.S.O.); European War, 1914-15 (wounded, despatches seven times, C.B.); Adjutant 1st Batt. Coldstream Guards, 1888-92; Brigade Major Brigade of Guards. 1897-99; Brigade Major Guards Brigade, 1900-1; Military Secretary to Governor-General of Canada, 1901-4; Private Secretary to Secretary of State for War, 1905; D.A.A., Q.M.G. Plymouth, 1906-1908; General Staff, 2nd London Division, Territorial Force, 1908-9; Assistant Director Territorial Force, War Office, 1909-12; Chief of General Staff, 5th Division, 1912-14; General Staff, War Office, 1914; Staff, 3rd Army Corps, 1914; Brig.-Gen. 1914, and commanding 14th Infantry Brigade; Maj.-Gen. 1915, and commanding 33rd Division, afterwards 13th Division; Temp. Lt.-Gen. in command of Tigris Army Corps, July 1916; Commander-in-Chief in Mesopotamia, August 1916; Lt.-Gen., Feb. 1917; Officer of the Crown of Italy, March 1917. *Address:* Mardale, Watford, Herts; 6 Lower Sloane Street, S.W. *Club:* Guards'.
(Died 18 Nov. 1917.)

MAUDE, Major Ralph Walter, D.S.O. 1919; Secretary Guards' Club; *b.* 1873; *y. s.* of late Hon. Mrs. Maude, *d.* of 2nd Baron Sudeley, and Captain Charles Henry Maude; *m.* 1905, Alice Thomson (whom he divorced 1914); one *s.* *Educ.:* Charterhouse. Journalist from the age of twenty-one till outbreak of war; for a long period closely associated with the late C. N. Williamson; contributor to most of the leading publications; joined Army 1914, and was first attached to 2/8th Gurkhas, with whom he served as interpreter throughout first year of war; afterwards sent to G.H.Q. for instruction as A.P.M. under the present Commissioner of Police; subsequently A.P.M., Bethune, Dieppe, Rouen, Amiens, and Cologne (D.S.O. French Croix de Guerre, despatches thrice). *Publication:* The Haymarket Theatre (with eldest brother, Cyril Maude). *Recreations:* The society of congenial companions, fishing. *Address:* Guards' Club, Brook Street, W.1. *T.:* Mayfair 870. *Club:* Junior Naval and Military.
(Died 17 Jan. 1922.)

MAUDSLAY, Walter Henry; *b.* 23 Sep. 1844; *g. s.* of Henry Maudslay, engineer; *m.* 1st, 1869, Emily (*d.* 1885), *e. d.* of Charles Lucas of Warnham Court, Sussex; one *s.*; 2nd, 1889, Violet, *e. d.* of Bevil Granville of Wellesbourne, Warwickshire, and Northchurch, Herts. *Educ.:* Brighton College;

Trinity Hall, Cambridge. For 33 years a member of the firm of Maudslay, Sons & Field, Marine Engineers, Lambeth ; for 35 years (since its establishment) a Director of the Employers' Liability Assurance Corporation, Ltd. ; for several years Chairman, in the South of England, of the Iron Trades Employers Association, and later Vice-President of the Federated Employers of Great Britain ; Managing Director since its establishment of The Birmingham Aluminium Casting 1903 Co., Ltd., and also Chairman since 1913 ; for 40 years Member of the Committee and subsequently Treasurer of the General Lying-In Hospital, Lambeth. *Recreations :* shooting and fishing. *Address :* 69 Cadogan Gardens, S.W.3 ; *T. :* Kensington 1013 ; Nausidwell, nr. Falmouth, Cornwall. *Club :* Wellington. **(Died 25 Aug. 1927.)**

MAUDSLEY, Henry, M.D., LL.D., F.R.C.P. ; physician; *b.* Rome, near Settle, Yorkshire, 1835 ; 3rd *s.* of late Thomas Maudsley ; *m.* Ann Caroline, *y. d.* of late John Conolly, M.D., D.C.L., Lawn House, Hanwell. *Educ. :* Giggleswick School ; privately ; Univ. Coll. London. M.D. Lond. 1857 ; medical superintendent of Manchester Royal Lunatic Hospital, 1859-62 ; editor of Journal of Mental Science, 1862-78 ; physician, West London Hospital, 1864-74 ; Professor of Medical Jurisprudence in Univ. Coll. London, 1869-79; Goulstonian Lecturer, Roy. Coll. Phys. 1870. *Publications :* Responsibility in Mental Disease, 1874 ; Physiology of Mind, 1876 ; Pathology of Mind, 1879, 2nd ed. 1895 ; Body and Will, 1883 ; Natural Causes and Supernatural Seemings, 1886, 3rd ed. 1897 ; Life in Mind and Conduct, 1902; Heredity, Variation and Genius, 1908 ; Organic to Human, Psychological and Sociological, 1917. *Address:* Heathbourne House, Bushey Heath, Herts. *Clubs :* Reform. Savile.
(Died 23 Jan. 1918.)

MAUNDER, Edward Walter, F.R.A.S. ; Secretary, Victoria Institute, 1913-18 ; Superintendent, Solar Department, Royal Observatory, Greenwich, 1873-1913, and 1916-19 ; *b.* 12 April 1851 ; *y. s.* of Rev. George Maunder, Wesleyan minister ; *m.* 1st, 1875, Edith Hannah Bustin ; 2nd, 1895, Annie Scott Dill Russell three *s.* two *d.* *Educ. :* University College School, and King's College, London. Entered Royal Observatory, Greenwich, as assistant, 1873 ; elected Fellow, Royal Astronomical Society, 1875 ; on the Council, 1885-89, and 1891-92 ; Secretary, 1892-97 ; Vice-President, 1897 ; founded British Astronomical Association, 1890 ; President, 1894-96 ; Eclipse Expeditions —West Indies, 1886; Lapland, 1896; India, 1898; Algiers, 1900 ; Mauritius, 1901 ; Labrador, 1905. *Publications:* Royal Observatory, Greenwich, its History and Work ; Astronomy without a Telescope, 1902 ; The Astronomy of the Bible, 1908 ; Science of the Stars, 1912 ; Are the Planets inhabited ? 1913 ; Sir W. Huggins, and Spectroscopic Astronomy, 1913; and jointly with Mrs. Maunder, The Heavens and their Story, 1908 ; edited, The Observatory, 1881-87 ; The Journal and Memoirs of the British Astronomical Association, 1890-94, and 1896-1900 ; Astronomical Department of Knowledge, 1895 to 1904 ; Indian Eclipse of 1898 ; Total Solar Eclipse of 1900. *Address:* 8 Maze Hill, Greenwich Park, S.E. *Club:* Royal Societies. **(Died 21 Mar. 1928.)**

MAUNG KIN, The Hon. Sir, K.C.I.E., *cr.* 1924 ; Home Member of the Executive Council of the Governor of Burma since 1923 ; *b.* Aug. 1872 ; *o. s.* of U. Po Kyaw, A.T.M., *g.s.* of U. Aung, K.S.M., A.T.H. ; *m.* Ma Than May, *d.* of U. Po, rice-miller ; one *s.* one *d.* *Educ. :* Government College, Rangoon. Called to Bar, 1896 ; Law Lecturer at Government College, 1902 ; Assistant Public Prosecutor, Rangoon, 1905 ; Assistant-Govt. Advocate, Burma, 1912; Chief Judge, Small Cause Court, Rangoon, 1913-14 ; Judge of the

716

Chief Court, 1915 ; officiated as Chief Judge of the Chief Court, 1920 ; Judge of the High Court of Judicature at Rangoon, 1922. *Recreations :* tennis, riding. *Address :* Windermere Park, Rangoon, Burma ; Sherwood, Maymyo, Burma. *Clubs :* Orient, Paperchase, Rangoon ; Country, Maymyo. **(Died 22 Oct. 1924.)**

MAUNG PE, I.S.O. 1913 ; K.S.M. 1901 ; was Additional Judge, Court of Small Causes, Rangoon, Burma ; *b.* 30 July 1858 ; *s.* of U Zan, of Bassein, Burma; *m.* ; two *s.* one *d.* *Educ. :* Rangoon. Held ministerial appointments under Government since 1877 ; was on special duty in the Office of the Deputy Superintendent of Census of Burma, and was gazetted as an Extra Assistant Commissioner, 1881 ; Township Officer, Pegu ; Akunwoon of the Bassein District ; served as Township Officer in the Districts Henzada and Thongwa, 1883-87 ; Assistant Town Magistrate of Rangoon, 1887 ; Township Officer in Magwe and Tharrawaddy Districts, 1890 ; in charge of Myanaung Sub-Division in the Henzada District, 1895 ; Magistrate of Eastern Sub-Division, Rangoon, 1896. *Address :* 47 Crisp Street, Rangoon.
(Died 15 May 1924.)

MAUNSELL, General Sir Frederick Richard, K.C.B., *cr.* 1897 ; unemployed ; *b.* Co. Wicklow, Ireland, 4 Sept. 1828; *m.* 1863, Mary, *d.* of Don. M. Velez (*d.* 1883) ; three *s.* three *d.* *Educ. :* King Edward's School, Birmingham ; Grosvenor College, Bath ; Addiscombe College. Served at siege of Mooltan, battle of Goojerat (medal and two clasps), 1848-49 ; battle of Budli serai, sieges of Delhi and Lucknow, Oudh Campaign (medal and two clasps), 1857-58 ; Afghan Campaign (medal and one clasp), 1878 ; C.B. 1873 ; K.C.B. 1897. Lieutenant, B.E. 1846 ; Captain, R.E. 1858 ; Major, 1858 ; Lieut.-Colonel, 1869 ; Colonel, 1874 ; Major-General, 1878 ; Lieut.-General, 1884 ; Col. Commdt., 1886 ; General, 1887 ; Hon. Colonel 1st K.G.O. Sappers and Miners, 1904. *Address :* 32 Ashley Gardens S.W.; Laleham, Middlesex. *Club :* United Service.
(Died 29 Oct. 1916.)

MAUREL, Victor, singer ; *b.* Marseilles, 1848 ; *m.* *Educ. :* Paris Conservatoire under Faure. Created Iago in Verdi's "Otello."
(Died 23 Oct. 1923.)

MAURICE, Lt.-Col. David Blake, D.S.O. 1900 ; late Royal Berkshire Regiment ; *e. s.* of late Oliver Calley Maurice, J.P., London Street, Reading, and Manton Grange, Marlborough, Wilts ; *b.* 24 Dec. 1866 ; *m.* 1903, Cecilia Evelyn, *e. d.* of James Simonds, J.P., Redlands, Reading. *Educ. :* Uppingham, in XI. and XV. Entered 3rd Royal Berks, 1885 ; 1st Royal Berks, 1889 ; Adjutant, 1st Royal Berks, 1894-98 ; served in Mounted Infantry and Staff, S. Africa, 1899-1901 (despatches, Queen's medal five clasps, D.S.O.) ; Adjutant Q.V.B. West Yorkshire Regt., 1903-6 ; commanded Depôt Royal Berks Regt. 1908-12. **(Died 4 Dec. 1925.)**

MAVOR, James, Ph.D. ; F.R.S. of Canada ; Professor of Political Economy in the University of Toronto, 1892-1923 ; Emeritus, 1923 ; *b.* Stranraer, 8 Dec. 1854 ; *s.* of late Rev. James Mavor, M.A., and Mary Ann Taylor Bridie; *m.* 1883, Christina, *d.* of P. B. Watt, London ; two *s.* one *d.* *Educ. :* High School and University of Glasgow. Assistant editor of Industries, editor Scottish Art Review ; University Extension Lecturer in Political Economy ; Professor of Political Economy, St. Mungo's College, Glasgow, 1888 ; has travelled extensively in America, in the Far East, and in Russia. *Publications:* Wages Theories and Statistics, 1888 ; Economic Theory, and History Tables and Diagrams, 1890 ; Scottish Railway Strike, 1891 ; Currency Reform, 1891 ; Economic Study, and Public and Private Charity, 1892 ; Report on Labour Colonies in Germany, etc., to H.M. Board of Trade, Parliamentary Paper, 1893 ; English Railway Rate Question, 1894 ;

edited Handbook of Canada, 1897; Notes on Art, 1898: Report on Immigration into Canada from Europe (to Canadian Government), 1900; Report on Workmen's Compensation Acts (to Provincial Government of Ontario), 1900; Papers on Municipal Affairs, 1904; Report to H.M. Board of Trade on the North-West of Canada, Parliamentary Paper, 1905; Taxation of Corporations in Canada, 1909; Railway Transportation in America, 1909; Taxation in Upper Canada, 1913; Economic Survey of Canada, 1914; Applied Economics, 1914; An Economic History of Russia, 1914 (new edition 1925); My Windows on the Street of the World, 1923; The Russian Revolution, 1926. *Recreation:* chess. *Address:* 145 Isabella Street, Toronto. *Clubs:* Savile; Toronto, York, Arts and Letters, Toronto; City, New York.

(Died Nov. 1925.)

MAW, William Henry, LL.D., Pres. Inst.C.E., Past-Pres. Inst.Mech.E., Past-Pres. R.A.S., F.R.G.S., F.R.M.S.; joint-ed. of Engineering since 1866; *b.* Scarborough, 6 Dec. 1838; *s.* of W. M. Maw, Scarborough; *m.* 1867, Emily, *d.* of Thomas Chappell; three *s.* five *d.* Professional training in works of Great Eastern Railway, 1855-65; Member of Royal Commission for St. Louis Exhibition, 1904; Member of the Advisory Panel, Munitions Inventions Department, Ministry of Munitions of War. *Publications:* joint-author of The Waterworks of London, and Road and Railway Bridges; author of Recent Practice in Marine Engineering; Double-Star Observations (Memoirs R.A.S.), etc. *Recreations:* astronomy and microscopy. *Address:* 18 Addison Road, Kensington, W.14; Outwood, Surrey; 35 and 36 Bedford Street, W.C.2. *T.A.:* Engineering, Westrand, London. *T.:* Gerrard 3663 and 8598 and Park 2208. *Clubs:* Royal Thames Yacht, Garrick.

(Died 19 Mar. 1924.)

MAXIM, Sir Hiram Stevens, Kt., *cr.* 1901; C.E., M.E.: late of the firm Vickers Sons and Maxim; Civil, Mechanical, and Electrical Engineer; Chevalier of the Legion of Honour; inventor of the automatic system of firearms; *b.* Maine, U.S.A., 5 Feb. 1840; *m.* Sarah, *d.* of late Charles Haynes. *Educ.:* Maine. Has conducted extensive experiments with a view of ascertaining how much power was required to perform artificial flight, and has prepared various scientific papers for publication. *Recreations:* reading scientific books and studying the abstract sciences. *Publication:* My Life, 1915. *Address:* Sandhurst Lodge, High Road, Streatham, S.W. *(Died 24 Nov. 1916.)*

MAXWELL, Col. Francis Aylmer, V.C. 1900; C.S.I. 1911; D.S.O. 1898; 18th Bengal Lancers; Military Secretary to Lord Hardinge, 1910-16; *b.* 7 Sep. 1871; *s.* of T. Maxwell; *m.* 1906, Charlotte Alice Hamilton, 3rd *d.* of late P. H. Osborne of Currandooley, N.S.W.; two *d.* Joined Royal Sussex Regt., 1891; Captain, 1901; Major, 1909; Bt. Lt.-Col., 1915; served Waziristan, 1895 (medal with clasp); Chitral, 1895 (despatches, medal with clasp); North-West Frontier, India, 1897-98 (despatches, D.S.O., three clasps); South Africa, 1900-2 (medal with 6 clasps, King's medal with 2 clasps, V.C.; Brevet majority); European War, 1914-17 (Bar to D.S.O.; Bt. Col.). *Decorated* for gallantry in saving Q Battery at Koorn Spruit. *Address:* The Grange, Guildford. *Club:* Cavalry.

(Died 23 Sept. 1917.)

MAXWELL, Hamilton, R.S.W.; *b.* Glasgow, 27 Dec. 1830; parents Scotch. *Educ.:* High School, Glasgow. Trained to business at an early age; sailed to Melbourne, Australia, 1852; had some experience of the Bush and Gold Digging and returned home, 1856; lived two years in Derbyshire in charge of farm, colliery and brickwork; went to Bombay, 1859; Sheriff of Bombay and Chairman of the Bank of Bombay, 1878; returned to Scotland, 1881;

has been since then a professional artist, a Vice-President Royal Institute of the Fine Arts, Glasgow; President of the Glasgow Art Club, 1909; member of the Royal Scottish Water Colour Society; 33rd degree of Scottish Freemasonry. Had a studio in Paris 1893-1908: made many water colour drawings of ancient towns and villages in France, Italy, and Germany. *Publication:* Artist's Wanderings, in Glasgow Herald, signed H.M. *Recreations:* shooting, fishing, golf, cricket, painting. *Address:* 8 St. James' Terrace, Hillhead, Glasgow. *Club:* Glasgow Art. *(Died 5 Feb. 1923.)*

MAXWELL, Colonel Hon. Henry Edward, D.S.O. 1900; The Black Watch; *b.* 27 Nov. 1857; *s.* of late Hon. Richard Maxwell; *bro.* of 10th Baron Farnham; *m.* 1887, Edith, *d.* of Col. R. A. G. Cosby of Stradbally Hall Queen's Co.; one *s.* one *d.* Entered army, 1876; Captain, 1885; Major, 1895; Lt.-Col., 1903; Brevet-Col., 1906; served South Africa, 1899-1902 (wounded, despatches, Queen's medal, 4 clasps, King's medal, 2 clasps, D.S.O.); J.P.; D.L.; High Sheriff, Co. Cavan, 1910. *Address:* Arley, Mount Nugent, County Cavan. *Clubs:* Naval and Military; Kildare Street, Dublin; Royal St. George Yacht. *(Died 2 Mar. 1919.)*

MAXWELL, Lieut.-Col. Henry St. Patrick, C.S.I. 1892; late Deputy Commissioner 1st grade Assam; *b.* 17 Mar. 1850; *s.* of Gen. William Maxwell, R.A.; *m.*; one *d.* Entered army, 1869; Lt.-Col. 1895; served Daffla Expedition, 1874-75 (despatches); against Naga Hill tribes, 1879-80 (despatches, medal with clasp); Akha Expedition, 1883-84 (despatches): Manipur, 1891 (despatches, clasp). *Address:* 20 Oakley Avenue, Ealing, W. *Club:* United Service. *(Died 15 Aug. 1923.)*

MAXWELL, Richard Ponsonby, C.B. 1903; late Senior Clerk Foreign Office; *b.* 21 Oct. 1853; *s.* of late Rev. Charleton Maxwell. *Educ.:* Winchester; St. John's Coll., Camb. Entered F.O. 1877; acting 3rd Secretary in Diplomatic Service, 1880; assisted British Agent on Behring Sea Arbitration, Paris, 1893; Private Secretary to Sir T. H. Sanderson, 1894-96; Assistant Clerk, 1896; Secretary to British Plenipotentiaries at Peace Conference, The Hague, 1899; acting Secretary of Legation, 1899; acting Senior Clerk, 1900; retired, 1913. *Address:* 3 Whitehall Court, S.W.1. *Clubs:* Travellers'; Kildare, Dublin. *(Died 23 May 1923.)*

MAXWELL, Lt.-General Sir Ronald Charles, K.C.B., *cr.* 1915; K.C.M.G., *cr.* 1918; C.B. 1900; Colonel Commandant R.E. since 1920; *b.* 26 Dec. 1852; *s.* of late Lieut.-Col. C. F. Maxwell; *m.* 1903, Emily Mary, *e. d.* of T. F. Burnaby Atkins of Halstead Place, Kent. Entered army 1872; Captain, 1884; Major, 1891; Lt.-Col. 1899; Colonel, 1902; Major-General, 1909; Lieut.-General, 1916; retired list, 1919; served Afghanistan, 1879-80 (medal with clasp, bronze star); S. Africa, 1900-2 (despatches, Queen's medal 3 clasps, King's medal 2 clasps, C.B.); European War, 1914-18; Inspector-General of Communications in France, 1914; Quartermaster-General to the Armies in France, 1915-17 (despatches, K.C.B., K.C.M.G.); A.A.G. War Office, 1902-6; Brig.-Gen. i/c Administration Western Command, 1906-9; Maj.-Gen. i/c Administration Southern Command, 1909-11; commanding East Coast Defences, 1911-14; Grand Officer Legion of Honour, 1915; Grand Officer of the Crown, Belgium, 1915; Commandeur de l'Ordre de Mérite Agricole, 1917. *Address:* Poplars, Burghfield Common, nr. Reading. *Club:* Naval and Military.

(Died 20 July 1924.)

MAXWELL, Captain Sir William, K.B.E., *cr.* 1919; Chevalier of the Legion of Honour; traveller, publicist, War Correspondent, formerly of The Standard and The Daily Mail; accompanied Lord Kitchener

717

MAXWELL, Lawrence, LL.D. See page xxv.

in the march on Khartoum; present at the battle of Omdurman (medal with clasp); accompanied the German Emperor through the Holy Land and Syria; was at first Peace Conference at The Hague; was besieged in Ladysmith; on relief of garrison went to Kimberley; was with Lord Roberts' army in every engagement from the capture of Bloemfontein to Lydenburg and Komati Poort; saw Kruger at Delagoa Bay; accompanied the Duke and Duchess of York in their tour through Australia, Canada, and the Colonies; travelled in Morocco, interviewed Sultan Abdul Aziz at Fez; accompanied Mr. Chamberlain in his South African tour, 1902-3; also King Edward in his yacht to Lisbon, Gibraltar, Malta, Naples, Rome; with General Kuroki's army from the battle of the Yalu to the battle of the Sha-ho; with General Nogi at the last assaults on and surrender of Port Arthur (Order of Rising Sun); joined the Daily Mail, 1905; accompanied the Prince of Wales in Indian tour; present at coronation of the Shah of Persia; travelled through Persia and along line of projected German railway from Persian Gulf to Constantinople; present at Delhi Durbar; journeyed up the Yang-tsi and from Hankow to Pekin during the revolution; in Pekin during the mutiny; made report on Borkum and German island defences; with the Bulgarians in the Balkan War; represented Daily Telegraph in beginning of European War, 1914-15; with the Belgians till the Germans entered Brussels; was taken prisoner by a British cavalry patrol outside Mons; present at battles of Marne and Aisne; received commission as Captain attached to Imperial General Staff; attached to Headquarters Staff in the Dardanelles Expedition; afterwards head of section in Secret Service; Director of public companies. *Publications:* With the Ophir round the Empire, 1902; Sixteen Famous Battles; With the Japanese from the Yalu to Port Arthur; Canada of To-day. *Address:* Wraysbury, Bucks. *Clubs:* St. James's, Royal Automobile.

(*Died 23 Dec. 1928.*)

MAXWELL, Sir William Francis, 4th Bt.; *cr.* 1804; D.L., J.P.; *b.* 19 June 1844; 2nd *s.* of 3rd Bt. and 1st wife, Mary, *d.* of John Sprot; *S.* father 1886; *m.* 1884, Jessidora, *o. d.* of late John Anthony Macrae, LL.D., of Macrae; one *d.* Owns about 6400 acres. *Heir:* none. *Address:* Cardoness, Gatehouse, Kirkcudbrightshire. *Clubs:* Carlton; New. Edinburgh.

(*Died 26 Jan. 1924.*)

MAXWELL, Admiral William Henry; retired list; J.P. Sussex; *b.* 13 June 1840; *s.* of Lt.-Col. Charles Francis Maxwell, 82nd Regt.; *m.* 1871, Catherine Penelope, *d.* of Colonel F. T. Maitland; one *s. Educ.:* various. Entered the Navy, 1854; served in H.M.S. Euryalus as midshipman, the Baltic during war with Russia, 1854-56, and Boscawen, Cape Station, 1857-60; Lieutenant in Lyra, East Coast of Africa, 1860-1862, suppressing slave trade; Sutlej, in Pacific, 1863-66; Commander H.M.S. Octavia, 1868-69, Abyssinian Expedition, East Indies; Dryad, 1869, captured a slaver on Madagascar coast, freed 200 slaves; Excellent, School of Gunnery, 1869-72; Captain H.M.S. Emerald, Australian Station, 1878-82; Neptune, Channel Fleet, 1888-1885; Commodore Hong Kong, 1887-88; A.D.C. the Queen, 1887-88; Rear-Admiral, 1889; Vice-Admiral, 1895; retired, 1895; retired Admiral, 1900; Conservator Thames, 1896-1906. *Address:* Holywych House, Cowden, Kent. *Club:* United Service.

(*Died 1 July 1920.*)

MAXWELL, William Henry, M.A., Ph.D., LL.D.; City Superintendent of Schools; Emeritus Superintendent City of New York since 1898; *b.* Stewartstown, Ireland, 5 March 1852; *m.* 1877, Marie A. Folk; one *s.* one *d. Educ.:* Royal Academical Institution, Belfast; Queen's Colls., Galway and Belfast. Teacher, Victoria Coll., Belfast, 1872-74; journalist, N.Y.,

718

1877, 1880; teacher, Public Schools, Brooklyn, N.Y., 1880-82; Ass. Superintendent of Schools, Brooklyn, 1882-87; Superintendent of Schools, Brooklyn, N.Y., 1887-98. *Publications:* A series of text-books on English Grammar and Composition. *Recreations:* Pedestrianism, bicycling, golf. *Address:* 500 Park Avenue, New York. *T.:* 5580 Plaza, New York. *Clubs:* Century Association, City, New York.

(*Died 3 May 1921.*)

MAXWELL-STUART, Herbert Constable, J.P., D.L.; *b.* 1842; *e. s.* of late Hon. Henry Constable-Maxwell, of Traquair, and Juliana, *d.* of Peter Middleton, of Stockeld Park, Co. York. *Address:* Scarthingwell Hall, Tadcaster; Traquair House, Innerleithen, N.B.; Terregles, Dumfries, N.B. (*Died 13 April 1921.*)

MAY, Sir Arthur William, K.C.B., *cr.* 1914; C.B. 1911; K.H.P. 1913; Surgeon-Vice-Admiral R.N. retired; *b.* 13 June 1854; *s.* of late Rev. H. T. May, Fellow of New College, Oxford; *m.* 1892, Adelaide Gibson, *d.* of William Baldock, Cooling Castle, Kent. *Educ.:* Sherborne School; King's College Hospital. Entered Royal Naval Medical Service, 1878; served Egyptian War, 1882; Suakim Expedition, 1884; Nile Expedition for relief of General Gordon, 1884-85, Camel Corps; Deputy Director-General Medical Dept., R.N., 1905-9; Director-General, 1913-17; D.L., J.P. Cornwall; Knight of Grace St. John of Jerusalem; 1st Class Order of Sacred Treasure, Japan; Commander of the Order of Leopold, Belgium. *Address:* Tremeer, St. Tudy, Cornwall. *M.:* AF 509. *Club:* Army and Navy.

(*Died 20 April 1925.*)

MAY, Sir Francis Henry, G.C.M.G., *cr.* 1919; B.A., LL.D., D.C.L.; *b.* Dublin, 14 March 1860; 4th *s.* of late Rt. Hon. G. A. C. May, Lord Chief-Justice of Ireland, and Olivia, 4th *d.* of Sir Mathew Barrington, 2nd Bart. of Glenstal, Co. Limerick; *m.* 1891, Helena, *d.* of late Gen. Sir Geo. Digby Barker, G.C.B.; four *d. Educ.:* Harrow; Trinity College, Dublin. 1st Honourman and Prizeman Classics and Modern Languages; B.A. 1881. Appointed, after competitive exam., to Hong-Kong Cadetship, 1881; Assist. Protector of Chinese, 1886; private sec. to Governor Sir Wm. Des Vœux, to Acting Governor Sir F. Fleming, and to Acting Governor Lieut.-Gen. Digby Barker, 1889-91; Assist. Col. Sec. 1891; Acting Col. Treas. 1892; member Legis. Council and C.M.G. 1895; Captain Superintendent of Police, 1893-1902, and Superintendent Victoria Gaol and Fire Brigade, Hong-Kong, 1896-1902; Colonial Secretary, Hong-Kong, 1902-10; administered the Government of Hong-Kong during 1903, 1904, 1906-7, and 1910; Governor of Fiji and High Commissioner Western Pacific, 1910-12. Governor of Hong-Kong, 1912-19; Knight of Grace of St. John of Jerusalem; J.P., Suffolk. *Publications:* Guide to Cantonese Colloquial; Yachting in Hong-Kong. *Recreations:* hunting, polo, shooting, rifle-shooting, fishing, yachting. *Address:* Clare Priory, Suffolk. *Club:* Windham.

(*Died 6 Feb. 1922.*)

MAYCOCK, Sir Willoughby Robert Dottin; K.C.M.G., *cr.* 1913; C.M.G. 1905; *b.* 7 July 1849; *o. s.* of late Colonel Dottin Maycock, formerly of 6th Inniskilling Dragoons; *m.* Emma Leah (*d.* 1919), *o. d.* of John Prigge. Served temporarily in Exchequer and Audit Department, 1870-72; obtained a clerkship in the Foreign Office, 1872; attached to Royal Commission for negotiation of a treaty of commerce with France, 1881, and to Rt. Hon. Joseph Chamberlain's special mission to Washington, 1887; received a Royal Commission as Acting Second Secretary in H.M. Diplomatic Service, 1887; Assistant in Treaty Department of Foreign Office, 1897; Superintendent, 1903-13; joint editor of British and Foreign State Papers; received Jubilee medal, 1897; Coronation medals, 1902 and 1911; retired on pension, 1913; entered

2nd Middlesex Rifle Militia, 1870; promoted to rank of Captain, 1873; resigned, 1880. *Publication:* With Mr. Chamberlain in the United States and Canada, 1887-88. Is a Director of the Pilbara Copper Fields, Ltd. *Recreations:* field sports, cycling, music and drama. *Address:* 80 St. George's Square, S.W. *Clubs:* St. James's; Roehampton; Epsom; Sandown Park.
(*Died 23 Nov. 1922.*)

MAYDON, The Hon. John George, late Member of Union Parliament, Legislative Assembly; *b.* Morhanger, Bedfordshire, Oct. 1857; *s.* of John Maydon, of Morhanger and Salden, Bucks; *m.*; two *s.* two *d.* *Educ.:* City of London School, under Dr. E. A. Abbott. Entered shipping office of Natal Direct Line in Mark Lane; went to Natal to volunteer for the Zulu War, throughout which he served with the Durban Mounted Rifles; spent a year in the O.F.S., then returned to England for a year, at the end of which came out again to Natal to manage the affairs of the Natal Direct Line of Steamers in S.A.; entered the first Natal Parliament under Responsible Government. 1893; was in England on holiday at the outbreak of the Boer War in 1899, and immediately sailed to offer his services in S.A., which were not accepted, and he proceeded to the front as newspaper correspondent, being present at all the battles of the western campaign from Magersfontein to the capture of Bloemfontein; called back to Natal in May 1901, he re-entered Parliament and led an attack on the Natal Government which led to Colonel Hime's resignation, and Sir George Sutton forming a ministry in which he became Colonial Secretary, shortly after taking also the portfolio of Railways and Harbours; sent by his Government to London in 1905 to represent it at the Shipping Conference on Rebates; elected Greyville, Durban, for Union Parliament. *Publications:* Natal, its History, Government, and Products, 1896; French's Cavalry Campaign. *Recreations:* hunting and shooting. *Address:* Netherley, Maritzburg. *Clubs:* City Carlton, Junior Constitutional; Durban, Maritzburg.
(*Died Aug. 1. 19.*)

MAYGAR, Lt.-Col. Leslie Cecil, V.C. 1901; D.S.O. 1917; 8th Australian Light Horse Regiment; *b.* 26 May 1871. *Educ.:* privately. Served South Africa, 1901-2 (Queen's medal, 3 clasps, V.C.). European War, 1915-17 (D.S.O.). *Address:* Strathearn, Longwood, Victoria, Australia. (*Died Nov. 1917.*)

MAYNARD, Lieut.-Colonel Frederic P., M.B., F.R.C.S., I.M.S. 1887; retired; Ophthalmic Surgeon, Crewe Memorial Cottage Hospital; School Oculist, Cheshire County Council; late Fellow Calcutta University; Professor of Ophthalmic Surgery, Medical College, and Ophthalmic Surgeon, College Hospital, Calcutta; Surgeon-Superintendent, Mayo Native Hospital, Calcutta; Medical Officer and Naturalist, Baluch-Afghan Boundary Commission. *Educ.:* St. Bartholomew's Hospital; Paris, etc. Editorial Staff, British and American Journals of Ophthalmology; Fellow of Royal Society of Medicine, London; Member of Ophthalmolog. Society of London and North of England Ophthalmic Society. *Publications:* Manual of Ophthalmic Operations (2nd ed.); Manual of Ophthalmic Practice. *Address:* Prudential Chambers, Market Street, Crewe. *T.:* Crewe 223; Threotynerode, Audlem, Cheshire. *Club:* Bengal United Service, Calcutta.
(*Died 30 Sept. 1921.*)

MAYNARD, John Percy Gordon, D.L.; *s.* of William Joseph Maynard; *m.* 1874, Haida, *d.* of Weldon Molony, and *g.* *d.* of Sir Anthony Weldon, Bart.; two *s.* one *d.* Master of Ward Union Hounds, which pack he has hunted with continuously for last 35 years. *Recreations:* hunting, racing. *Address:* Ratoath

Manor, co. Meath. *Club:* Sackville Street, Dublin. (*Died 13 Mar. 1918.*)

MAYNE, Ven. Joseph; Incumbent of Larah, 1894-1923; Archdeacon of Kilmore, 1910-23; *b.* 18 Oct. 1848. *Educ.:* Trinity College, Dublin, M.A. Ordained, 1874; Incumbent of Garrison, 1874-78; Killasnett, 1878-90; Killenkere, 1890-94. *Address:* 6 Crofton Mansions, Dunleary, Co. Dublin.(*Died 7 Mar. 1927.*)

MAYO, 7th Earl of (*cr.* 1785), **Dermot Robert Wyndham Bourke,** K.P., P.C., D.L., J.P.; Baron Naas, 1766: Viscount Mayo, 1781; Representative Peer for Ireland, 1890; Senator Irish Free State, 1921; Cornet, 10th Hussars, 1870; Lieut. Co. Kildare; Lieut. Grenadier Guards, retired 1876; *b.* 2 July 1851; *s.* of 6th Earl and Blanche, *d.* of 1st Lord Leconfield; *S.* father, 1872; *m.* 1885, Geraldine, *d.* of late Hon. Gerald Ponsonby. Conservative; Church of Ireland. *Educ.:* Eton. *Publications:* Sport in Abyssinia; De Rebus Africanis: The War Cruise of the Aries; History of the Kildare Hunt. *Recreations:* fox-hunting; promoting the agricultural and industrial welfare of Ireland; collector of English china and miniatures. *Heir:* *c.* Major Walter Longley Bourke. *Address:* Palmerstown, Straffan, Co. Kildare. *Clubs:* White's, Stratford; Kildare Street, Dublin. (*Died 31 Dec. 1927.*)

MAYO, Arthur, V.C. 1857; *b.* Oxford, 18 May 1840; 5th *s.* of Herbert Mayo, F.G.S., Cheshunt, Herts, and Sarah Harman, Theobalds, Cheshunt: *m.* 1865, Ellen, *d.* of Joseph Baker; five *c.* *Educ.:* Berkhamsted School, Herts. Went voyage in Wellesley East Indiaman, 1855-56; entered Indian Navy, 1857; served in steam frigate Punjaub, and with I. N. Brigade ashore, June 1857-Jan. 1860, when invalided home; entered Magdalen Hall, Oxford, 1862; B.A. 1865; ordained, 1866; Assistant Curate, St. Peter's, Plymouth; was received into the Roman Catholic Church, 1867.
(*Died 18 May 1920.*)

MAYOR, Rev. Joseph Bickersteth, M.A.; Emeritus Professor of King's Coll. Lond.; Hon. Fellow of St. John's Coll. Camb.; Hon. Litt.D. of Dublin University; *b.* 1828; *s.* of Rev. Robert Mayor and Charlotte Bickersteth (sister of Henry Bickersteth, Lord Langdale, and of Edward Bickersteth of Watton); *m.* Miss A. J. Grote (niece of Geo. Grote, the historian, and of John Grote, Professor of Moral Philosophy at Cambridge), 18 3; two *s.* two *d.* *Educ.:* Rugby, 1841-47; St. John's College, Cambridge, 1847-63; B.A. 1851; 2nd in 1st class of Classical Tripos; Fellow and Lecturer, 1852; Tutor, 1860; Deacon, 1859; Priest, 1860; Headmaster of Kensington Proprietary School, 1863-1868; Professor of Classics at King's College, 1870-79. *Publications:* Greek for Beginners, 1899; Cicero de Natura Deorum, 3 vols. 1880-85; Guide to the Choice of Classical Books, 3rd ed. 1885; Supplement to ditto, 1896; Sketch of Ancient Philosophy, 1881; Chapters on English Metre, 2nd ed. 1901; Epistle of St. James with Introduction, Notes, and Commentary, 3rd ed. 1910; with further studies, 1913; Clement of Alexandria, Seventh Book of the Stromateis, edited from Dr. Hort's Notes, with English translation, Commentary, and Dissertations, 1902; Handbook of Modern English Metre, 1903, 2nd ed. 1912; The World's Desire, and other Sermons, 1906; Epistle of St. Jude and Second Epistle of St. Peter, with Introduction, Notes, and Commentary, 1907; Tolstoi as Shakespearian Critic in R.S.L. Transactions for 1908; part author of the book entitled Virgil's Messianic Eclogue, 1907; Select Readings from Psalms, with Essay on the Growth of Revelation, 1908; editor of Prof. Grote's posthumous works, viz. Examination of the Utilitarian Philosophy, 1870; Treatise on Moral Ideals, 1876; Exploratio Philosophica, Part II., 1900; editor of Classical Review from March 1887 to Dec. 1893. *Address:*

Queensgate House, Kingston Hill, Surrey.
(*Died 29 Nov. 1916.*)

MccGWIRE, Maj.-Gen. Edward Thomas St. Lawrance; *b.* 13 Mar. 1830. Entered army, 1849; Maj.-Gen. 1886; retired, 1890. *Address:* 32 Royal Crescent, W
(*Died 16 Mar. 1917.*)

MEAD, Percy James, C.S.I. 1921; C.I.E. 1914; Chief Secy. to Government, Bombay; *b.* 15 Nov. 1871; *s.* of late Lt.-Col. C. J. Mead, late Bengal Royal Artillery; *m.* 1st, 1904, Frances Alexandra, *d.* of George Cowie; 2nd, 1913, May Gertrude, *d.* of late Canon Maddock; two *s.* two *d.* *Educ.:* Haileybury; King's College, Cambridge. Entered Indian Civil Service, 1894; Under-Secretary to Govt. of Bombay, Revenue and Finance, 1901; Talukdari Settlement Officer, 1905; Superintendent, Census Operations, 1910; Junior Collector, 1911; Senior Collector, 1916; Director of Industries, 1917; Chief Secretary to Government, 1919. *Recreations:* cricket, tennis, golf, etc. *Address:* c/o Grindlay & Co., 54 Parliament Street, S.W.1. *Club:* East India United Service.
(*Died 7 April 1923.*)

MEADE, Rev. Hon. Sidney, Canon of Salisbury since 1891; *b.* 29 Oct. 1839; 3rd *s.* of 3rd Earl of Clanwilliam; *m.* 1868, Lucy Emma, 2nd *d.* of late John Henry Jacob, of The Close, Salisbury; one *s.* one *d.* *Educ.:* Oxford. Ordained, 1866; Curate of S. Mary's, Reading, 1866-69; Rector of Wylye, Wilts, 1869-82; Assistant Curate of Ch. Ch. Bradford-on-Avon, 1882-1901. *Address:* Frankleigh House, Bradford-on-Avon, Wilts. (*Died 11 Feb. 1917.*)

MEAGHER, Michael, M.P. (N.) North Kilkenny, 1906-18; farmer; *b.* 27 Feb. 1846; *s.* of Patrick Meagher, J.P., Tullaroan, and Mary Josephine O'Dwyer, Graystown Castle, Co. Tipperary; *m.* 1881, Johanna, o. *d.* of William Corcoran, Ballingarry, Co. Tipperary. *Educ.:* St. Patrick's College, Mountrath. Queen's Co. Took part in the Fenian rising, 1867. *Address:* Chestnut Villa, Tullaroan, Co. Kilkenny.
(*Died Dec. 1927.*)

MEARA, Rev. Henry George Jephson, Hon. Canon of Oxford. *Address:* Steventon Vicarage, Berks. (*Died 4 June 1921.*)

MEARNS, Andrew Daniel, J.P.; Director, The Cunard Steamship Co., Ltd. and America-Levant Line, Ltd.; Chairman, Liverpool Steamship Owners Association, 1922; President, Liverpool Shipping Staffs Association, 1922; *b.* 6 Mar. 1857; *s.* of late Captain Daniel Mearns of Montrose; *m.* Laura Cannington, *d.* of late Edwin Phillips, Liverpool; one *s.* two *d.* *Educ.:* Russell's Academy, Belfast. *Recreation:* golf. *Address:* Uplands, Burbo Bank Road, N. Blundellsands. *T.A.:* Cunard, Liverpool. *T.:* Crosby 39. *M.:* TC 4097. (*Died 6 Dec. 1925.*)

MEASE, Very Rev. Charles William O'Hara, M.A.; Incumbent of Castleknock since 1903; Dean of the Chapel Royal, Dublin, since 1913; Chaplain to the Household of the Lord Lieutenant; *b.* Dublin, June 1856; *y.* *s.* of late Andrew Mease, F.R.C.S.I.; *m.* 1896, Martha Gertrude, *d.* of late Alfred Billing, J.P., Helsby, Cheshire; one *d.* *Educ.:* Armagh and Cavan Royal Schools; Trinity College, Dublin (Royal Scholar); 1st Honourman in Classics; M.A., Divinity Testimonium. Ordained, 1881; Curate of Monaghan, 1881-3; Incumbent Killoughter, 1883-4; Curate St. Stephen's, Dublin, 1884-8; Rector, Killiskey, 1888-93; Dean's Vicar St. Patrick's Cathedral, Dublin, 1893-1902. *Recreations:* tennis, golf. *Address:* Mt. Hybla, Castleknock, Dublin. *T.:* 24 Castleknock. *Club:* University, Dublin.
(*Died 21 May 1922.*)

MECREDY, Richard James, B.A.; Director R. J. Mecredy and Co., Ltd.; Mecredy, Percy and Co., Ltd.; Editor Motor News; Joint

Editor, with Sir J. C. Percy, of Irish Cyclist; *b.* Ballinasloe, 18 May 1861; *s.* of Rev. James Mecredy, D.D.; *m.* 1887; three *s.* three *d.* *Educ.:* Portora School, Enniskillen; Trinity College, Dublin. Apprenticed to T. T. Mecredy; solicitor, 1882; abandoned the law for journalism, 1886; became proprietor of Irish Cyclist, 1886, jointly with brother Alec, and has edited it ever since; started Motor News, 1900; one of the first to recognise the merits of the pneumatic tyre, Director of the first Dunlop Company; went off the Board when the Company was refloated. *Publications:* Encyclopædia of Motoring; Health's Highway; Road Books of Ireland; etc. *Recreations:* touring, cycling, motoring, camping; principal hobby, scenery. *Address:* Vallombrosa, Bray, Co. Wicklow. *T.:* 26 Bray; Motor News, Dublin. *T.:* Dublin 2453. *Club:* Irish Automobile, Dublin. (*Died April 1924.*)

MEDLICOTT, William Norton; Southwark Local War Pensions Committee, 1919-22; *b.* Birmingham; *s.* of Thomas and Eliza Medlicott; *m.* 1894, Margaret, *d.* of John Macmillan of Stoke-on-Trent; two *s.* one *d.* Assistant editor Birmingham Daily Gazette, 1889; editor Manchester Evening Mail, 1890-92; managing editor Staffordshire Evening and Weekly Post, 1893-94; Church Family Newspaper, 1895-1911, editor 1905-11; Secretary Ada Leigh Homes, Paris, 1913-17. *Address:* 19 Gloucester Place, Greenwich, S.E.10.
(*Died 17 May 1923.*)

MEDLYCOTT, Rev. Sir Hubert James, 6th Bt.; *cr.* 1808; *b.* 9 Dec. 1841; *s.* of 2nd Bt. and Sarah, *d.* of Rev. Edward Bradford; *S.* brother, 1908; *m.* 1870, Julia Ann, *d.* of Rev. C. T. Glyn; one *s.* two *d.* *Educ.:* Harrow; Trinity College, Cambridge. Ordained, 1866; Curate, Brington, Northants, 1866-70; Vicar of Milborne-Port, 1870-88; Hill, Gloucs., 1883-86. *Heir:* *s.* Hubert Mervyn [*b.* 29 Sep. 1874; *m.* 1906, Nellie Adah, *d.* of Hector E. Monro, Edmonsham, Dorset, two *s.* *Educ.:* Harrow; Trinity College, Cambridge (B.A.). Major Dorset Yeomanry. *Address:* Milborne Port, Sherborne]. *Address:* 31 Chester Street, S.W.1; *T.:* Victoria 7347; Ven House, Sherborne, Dorset. *Club:* Wellington.
(*Died 25 May 1920.*)

MEE, Arthur ("Idris"), Journalist; *b.* Aberdeen, 1860; *o.* *s.* of late George S. Mee (sometime editor Bradford Observer); *m.* 1888, Claudia, *d.* of late David Thomas, Llanelly. Connected with the Welsh press since 1876; on the editorial staff of the Western Mail since 1892; also edited the Western Mail Almanac, Literary Supplement, Illustrated Guide to Cardiff, Cambrian Notes; Who's Who in Wales, 1920. *Publications:* Llanelly Parish Church, its History and Records, 1888; Observational Astronomy, 1893 (2nd ed. 1897); and a number of astronomical and astrological brochures. *Address:* Tremynfa, Llanishen, Cardiff.
(*Died 15 Jan. 1926.*)

MEESON, Engineer Commander Edward Hickman Tucker, D.S.O. 1915; R.N.; *b.* 20 Dec. 1877; *s.* of Frederick Richard Meeson, Eastbourne; *m.* 1908, Glady May, *d.* of George Robert Gordon Joy, Solicitor; one *d.* *Educ.:* Westminster; R.N.E. College. Assistant Engineer, 1899; Engineer Lieut. 1904; Engineer Lieut.-Commander, 1912; served in H.M.S. Laurel in action off Heligoland Bight (D.S.O. and specially promoted to Engineer Commander 1 June 1915). *Address:* 32 Arundel Road, Eastbourne. (*Died 31 May 1916.*)

MEHARRY, Rev. J. B., B.A., D.D.; ex-Moderator, Presbyterian Church of England. *Educ.:* Queen's Colleges, Belfast and Galway; Assembly's College, Belfast. *Publications:* From Natural to Spiritual; The Principles of Presbyterianism; The Advantages of Presbyterianism as a Form of Church Government; The Christian Priest. (*Died 20 Jan. 1916.*)

MEARS, Thomas Lambert, LL.D. See page xxvi.

MEHTA, Khan Bahadur, Sir Bezonji Dalabhoy, Kt., cr. 1912. *Address:* Nagpur, India. *(Died 5 May 1927.)*

MEIKLE, Andrew; Editor Wolverhampton Express and Star; b. Dunfermline, Fifeshire, 24 May 1847; 3rd s. of James Meikle, handloom weaver; m. 1878, o. d. of Robert Parker. Leicester; no c. *Educ.:* Roland Street School, Dunfermline. Served seven years' apprenticeship as compositor in Dunfermline Press, subsequently became reporter on that paper; afterwards reporter on the Teviotdale Record, Jedburgh; Bolton Guardian; chief reporter Bolton Chronicle; editor Somerset County Herald; editor and manager Warrington Examiner; and for 38 years associated with the Wolverhampton Express and Star and allied papers owned by the Midland News Association, Ltd. *Recreations:* cards and walking. *Address:* 33 Merridale Road, Wolverhampton. *T.:* Wolverhampton 953. *Club:* Wolverhampton Liberal. *(Died 14 Aug. 1922.)*

MEISSAS, Gaston. Member of the Société de Géographie. *Publications:* Marseilles; part author Paris in 9th edition Ency. Brit. *Address:* Avenue Bosquet 3, (VIIᵉ) Paris.

MELDON, Sir Albert, Kt., cr. 1910; b. 25 May 1845; s. of late James Dillon Meldon, J.P., 24 Merrion Square, Dublin, and Coolarne, Athenry, Co. Galway; m. 1st, 1873, Mary (d. 1914), d. of late Bernard Doherty of Buncrana, Co. Donegal; 2nd, 1917, Lily, d. of Andrew Levins Moore, J.P., of Ashton, Co. Dublin; three s. *Educ.:* Stonyhurst Coll., Lancashire. Called to Bar, 1868; Resident Magistrate, 1883-1910, and voluntarily during the war 1915-17 (received thanks of Government six times); D.L., J.P. Co. Wicklow and County Director R.C.J. and St. J.A.B. *Address:* Vevay, Bray, Co. Wicklow. *T.:* Bray 36. *M.:* TI 133. *Clubs:* Stephen's Green, Royal Irish Automobile, Dublin.

(Died 27 Nov. 1924.)

MELHADO, Carlos, C.M.G. 1911; Member Executive Council, British Honduras; Represented Colony of British Honduras at the Coronation, 22 June 1911; b. 30 April 1852; m. 1874, Florence Irene Stevenson; three s. two d. *Address:* Belize, British Honduras. *(Died 15 Oct. 1922.)*

MELINE, Felix Jules; Deputy for the Vosges; Avocat à la Cour; Leader of Moderate and Protectionist Republicans; b. Remiremont, Vosges, 20 May 1838. *Educ.:* Faculté de Paris. Elected to National Assembly (Vosges), 1872; re-elected for Remiremont, 1876; Minister of Agriculture, 1883-85; President of the Council, 1888; Premier, 1896-98; Candidate for Presidency, 1899. *Address:* Rue de Commaille 4 (VIIᵉ) Paris. *(Died Dec. 1925.)*

MELITUS, Paul Gregory, C.S.I. 1912; C.I.E. 1894; I.C.S.; b. 1858; s. of G. P. Melitus; m. 1906, Janet Douglas, d. of J. D. Cowan. *Educ.:* Marlborough; Wren and Gurney; Balliol College, Oxford. Entered I.C.S. 1878; Assistant Magistrate, etc., Bengal, 1880; Assist. and Deputy Com. and Assistant Secretary to Chief Commissioner, Assam, and Acting Postmaster-General, Bengal, 1886-91; Under-Sec. Home Dept. Govt. India, 1891; Deputy Sec., 1893; Sec. to Chief Comm. Assam, 1894; Judge and Commissioner, Assam Valley Districts, 1898; Member, Board of Revenue, Eastern Bengal and Assam, 1905; retired, 1913. *Address:* 17 Gwydyr Mansions, Hove, Sussex. *Club:* East India United Service. *(Died 23 Feb. 1924.)*

MELLIS, Rev. James, M.A. Edinburgh; b. Manse of Tealing, Forfarshire, 1843; e. s. of Rev. David Barclay Mellis, and Mary, d. of Rev. John Campbell, D.D., Tolbooth Parish, Edinburgh; m. 1872, Jane Anne, d. of Rev. John Roxburgh, D.D., Glasgow; one s. two d. *Educ.:* privately, High School, University, and New College, Edin-

burgh; Erlangen. Licensed preacher, 1867; ordained Free Church, Carnbee, Fife, 1869; Clerk of Free Synod of Fife; translated to Southport, 1879; Clerk of the Presbytery of Liverpool, 1894-1919; served on numerous Church Committees; Joint-Convener of Committee on Intercourse with other Churches, 1896-1910; Convener of Welsh-English Committee, 1906-24; Moderator of Synod of Presbyterian Church of England, 1910; on Board of Southport Infirmary, 1882-1919, Vice-Chairman, 1895-1919; President of Southport Free Church Council, 1898-99 and 1917-18, and Past Vice-President of the District Council; present at Coronation of King George V. in Westminster Abbey, 1911; Minister Emeritus since 1919. *Publications:* Occasional Sermons and Appreciations; From My Study: Reflections and Recollections, 1913; Talks and Tales, 1919; Quiet Reflections, 1924. *Address:* The Elms, Normans Place, Altrincham, Cheshire.

(Died 13 Sept. 1925.)

MELLIS, Col. William Andrew, C.B. 1919; Aberdeen T.F. Association, County of Aberdeen. *Address:* T.F. Association, Aberdeen. *(Died 4 June 1925.)*

MELLISH, Lt.-Col. Henry, C.B. 1917; J.P., D.L. Notts; Alderman and Vice-Chairman, Notts County Council; Chairman, Notts Education Committee and Notts Territorial Association; Chairman, Quarter Sessions (Retford Division); b. 31 Oct. 1856; s. of late Lt.-Col. William Leigh Mellish and Margaret, d. of Sir Samuel Cunard, Bart.; unmarried. *Educ.:* Eton; Ball College, Oxford. 1st class moderations (mathematics), 1877; 1st class science, 1879; held a commission in Notts Volunteers and Territorial Force, 1876-1912; commanded 4th (Notts) V.B. Sherwood Foresters, 1901-5; President, Royal Meteorological Society, 1909-1910. *Recreations:* rifle shooting; represented England in match for Elcho Shield at Wimbledon and Bisley on over twenty occasions. *Address:* Hodsock Priory, Worksop. *T.:* North Carlton 3. *Club:* New University.

(Died 2 Feb. 1927.)

MELLISS, Col. Sir Howard, K.C.S.I., cr. 1897; late Inspector-General of the Imperial Service Troops of India; b. 2 April 1847; s. of George Melliss, Talbot Square, London, and St. Helens; m. Edith Mary d. of General Conran, R.H.A., 1877. *Educ.:* privately; R.M.C. Sandhurst. Served in the 33rd (Duke of Wellington's) Regt., and Royal Scots Fusiliers; was present at the storming and capture of Magdala, 1868; was on special service, Baroda; in Intelligence Branch, Q.M.G.'s Dep. Simla; A.Q.M.G. of the Indian Division in Egypt, 1882; on Staff of Bombay army as Brigade-Major and A.Q.M.G.; was Military Attaché to Admiral Sir F. Richards in Burmah, 1885; was organiser and afterwards Inspector-General of Imperial Service troops in India; has Abyssinian, Burma, Indian Frontier, Jubilee, and Egyptian medals; Knight Commander of Star of India; in receipt of distinguished service pension; Order of Medjidie, Egyptian Bronze Star. *Address:* 6 Buckingham Palace Gardens, S.W.1. *Club:* Naval and Military. *(Died 21 June 1921.)*

MELLOR, Francis Hamilton, C.B.E. 1918; K.C., C.C. Judge, Manchester, since 1911; J.P., Cheshire and Lancashire; late Chairman of the Conciliation Boards under the Coal Mining Minimum Wage Act for Lancashire, Cheshire, and North Staffordshire; of the Conciliation Boards connected with the Lancashire and Yorkshire Railway Companies, and also the Cheshire Lines and Wirral Railway Co.; b. 13 May 1854; 10th s. of late Rt. Hon. Sir John Mellor; m. 1886, Mabel, e. d. of Herbert Knowles of Barnagore, Calcutta; one d. *Educ.:* Cheltenham College; Trinity College, Cambridge (M.A.). Called to Bar, Inner Temple, 1890; was a member of General Council of Bar, 1898-

721

1911; Recorder of Preston, 1898-1921; Chairman of Salford Hundred Appeal Tribunal; part author of Short and Mellor's Crown Office Practice. *Address:* Heathfield, Knutsford, Cheshire. *Clubs:* New University, M.C.C.; Union, Manchester. *(Died 26 April 1925.)*

MELLOR, Sir James (Robert), Kt., *cr.* 1911; LL.M. Cantab.; late Senior Master of the Supreme Court, King's Remembrancer, and King's Coroner; Master of the Crown Office; Registrar of the Court of Criminal Appeal, 1908; *b.* 4 May 1889; 3rd *s.* of late Rt. Hon. Sir John Mellor; *m.* 1868, Anne Jane (*d.* 1921), *e. d.* of Thomas Shaw; three *s.* four *d.* *Heir: s.* Brig.-Gen. Sir G. Mellor. *Address:* Eastgate, Tenterden, Kent. *(Died 19 Feb. 1926.)*

MELLOR, John Edward, C.B. 1919; late Chairman Denbighshire, T.F. Association; *b.* Ashton-under-Lyne, Lancashire; *s.* of late Thomas Walton Mellor, M.P. for Ashton under Lyne, 1868; *m.* 1st, Miss Andrew, of Ashton-under-Lyne (*d.* 1889); 2nd, 1895, Miss Rhodes of Hadfield, Derbyshire; one *s.* one *d.* *Educ.:* Rossall. J.P. for Lancaster, Chester, and Denbighshire; D.L. and Vice-Lieutenant for Denbighshire; late Hon. Col. 9th T.B. Manchester Regiment. *Recreations:* shooting, fishing. *Address:* Tan-y-Bryn, Abergele, North Wales. *T.A.:* Mellor, Abergele. *T.:* Abergele 4. *M.:* CA 993. *Club:* Carlton.
(Died 20 Aug. 1925.)

MELLOR, John James, J.P., D.L.; Hon. Col., retired, 1st Vol. Batt. Lancashire Fusiliers; chairman of J. & J. Mellor, Ltd., Bury, and of the Brook Mills Co. Ltd., Heywood, cotton spinning and manufacturing concerns; *b.* Oldham, 12 August 1830; *y. s.* of late Jon. Mellor, of Hope House; *m.* Jennette, *o. c.* of late Robert Clegg, Clayton-le-Moors. *Educ.:* private schools and private tutors. Since 1851 largely interested in cotton-spinning and manufacturing and in railway working and administration; an officer of volunteers 27 years, and for many years commanding officer of the regiment; devoted to scientific and engineering work; M.P. (C.) for the Radcliffe-cum-Farnworth Division of Lancashire, 1895-1900. *Address:* The Woodlands, Whitefield, near Manchester.
(Died 12 Jan. 1916.)

MELLOR, Captain William, D.S.O. 1915; R.N. (retired); *b.* 20 Aug. 1874; *m.* 1920, Emily Constance, *d.* of late John Whitmore, J.P., of Kilsallaghan, Dublin; one *s.* Served Dardanelles, 1914-15, in charge of trawler mine-sweepers (D.S.O., despatches). *Address:* Oaklands, Blundellsands, Liverpool. *Club:* United Service. *(Died 10 May 1928.)*

MELLOWES, William Joseph, M.P. (S.F.), North Meath and East Galway, Dec. 1918-22. *(Died Dec. 1925.)*

MELLY, George Henry, O.B.E.; Director Lamport & Holt, Ltd., Liverpool, London, Manchester, New York, Rio de Janeiro, and Buenos Aires; Director Liverpool and London and Globe Insurance Co., Ltd., Thames and Mersey Marine Insurance Co., Ltd., Liverpool and London War Risks Insurance Association, Ltd.. Excess Values (Liverpool and London), War Risks Insurance Association, Ltd., Royal Mail Steam Packet Co. (Liverpool Local Board), Archibald McMillan & Son, Ltd.; Dumbarton, Liverpool, Brazil, and River Plate Steam Navigation Co. Ltd.; *b.* March 1860; *s.* of George Melly, 90 Chatham Street, Liverpool; *m.* Elizabeth, *d.* of Edward Edmonds, London; no *c.* *Educ.:* Rugby. *Address:* 101 Royal Liver Buildings, Liverpool; The Lane Cottage, Freshfield. *T.:* Bank 8880, Formby 254. *M.:* CM 6943. *Clubs:* City of London, Windham, Palatine, Racquet, Liverpool.*(Died 20 Oct. 1922.)*

MELROSE, James, C.B., 1904; J.P. for Portsmouth; Chief Inspector of Machinery Royal Navy (retired); *b.* 1841; *s.* of James Melrose, engineer, of Hawick; *m.* 1880, Jane Foot, *d.* of

Capt. J. Milton. *Educ.:* Devonport; Stoke Grammar School. Entered Navy as Assistant Engineer, 1861; served with distinction through all ranks in engineering branch up to time of retirement, 1901; after that specially employed at the Admiralty conducting experimental investigations on oil fuel, north country coal, etc. *Address:* Winton House, South Hayling. *Club:* Hayling Island Golf. *(Died 18 July 1922.)*

MELROSE, John, C.B.E., J.P.; *b.* 1853; *s.* of John Melrose, engineer; *m.* 1876, Grace French Taylor. *Educ.:* Hawick High School. Engineer in Hawick; Provost of Hawick, 1902-19. *Address:* Hopehill, Hawick. *T.:* Hawick 64. *Clubs:* Scottish Conservative, Edinburgh; Border, Hawick.
(Died 7 April 1927.)

MELVILL, Major-General Charles William, C.B. 1919; C.M.G. 1918; D.S.O. 1917; G.O.C. New Zealand Military Forces since 1924; *b.* 5 Sep. 1878; *y. s.* of late Lieutenant Teignmouth Melvill, V.C., 24th Regiment, and Mrs. Melvill of Lanarth, Bournemouth; *m.* 1911, Rita, 3rd *d.* of William Burnett, Te Tarata, Dunedin, N.Z., and *niece* of General Sir Charles Burnett, K.C.B.; no *c.* *Educ.:* Wellington College. 2nd Lieut. S. Lancs Regt. 1897; left as Capt. and Adj. 1906; on Staff of N.Z. Forces, 1911; Staff College, Camberley, 1913; p.s.c.; went France with S. Lancs Regt., Sep. 1914 (wounded); Chief Instructor School of Instruction, Western Command, Jan.-May 1915; Brigade Major, Tay Defences, May-Sep. 1915; G.S.O. to N.Z. Forces, Gallipoli, 1915; remained till evacuation; Brig. Major, N.Z. Rifle Brigade, Egypt; commanded 4th Batt. N.Z. Rifle Brigade, 1916-17 (including Somme); Commander 1st N.Z. Inf. Brig., till Feb. 1919 (despatches four times, Officer of Order of the Crown of Belgium, 1917; Croix de Guerre, 1918); G.O.C. Wellington Military District, 1919-21; Central Command, N.Z., 1921-24. *Recreations:* fishing, shooting, polo. *Address:* G.H.Q., Wellington, N.Z.; Lanarth, Bournemouth. *Club:* Junior Naval and Military. *(Died Sept. 1925.)*

MELVILLE, 6th Viscount (cr.1802), Charles Saunders Dundas; Baron Dunira, 1802; I.S.O., 1902; *b.* 27 June 1843; *s.* of Rev. Hon. Charles Dundas, 4th *s.* of 2nd Viscount, Rector of Epworth, Lincolnshire, and Louisa, *d.* of Sir William Boothby, 9th Bt.; S. brother, 1904; *m.* 1st, 1872, Grace Selina Marion (*d.* 1890), *o. c.* of William Scully; four *s.*; 2nd, 1891, Mary (*d.* 1919), *d.* of late George Hamilton, M.D., Falkirk; two *d.*; 3rd, 1920, Margaret, *e. d.* of late William James Todd, Edinburgh, and *g.d.* of late Samuel Bishop Todd, Belfast. Consul, Santos, 1869; Canary Islands, 1877; Stettin, 1882; Consul-General, Hamburg, 1885; Kingdom of Norway, 1897-1907. *Heir: s.* Hon. Henry C. C. Dundas. *Address:* Melville Castle, Lasswade, Edinburgh.*(Died 21 Sept. 1926.)*

MELVILLE, Sir George, K.C.M.G., *cr.* 1900; C.M.G. 1891; *b.* Aberdeen, 1 July 1842; *s.* of late G. Melville of Culross, N.B.; *m.* Marie Elise Louise, *d.* of late Capt. FitzLanders of Charlton Hall, Northumberland, 1869; two *d.* one *s.* *Educ.:* Edinburgh Acad., and by private tutors. Entered Imp. Civil Service, after competitive examination, June 1862; Lieut. Kent Artillery Militia, 1873; transferred to the Colonial Civil Service, Nov 1874, when appointed to act as Treasurer of Sierra Leone; acted also as Colonial Secretary of that colony, 1875; Assistant Government Secretary of British Guiana, 1879; acted on several occasions as Government Secretary; in 1889 appointed Colonial Secretary of British Honduras; administered the Government, 1890-91; administered the Government of the Falkland Islands, 1893; Colonial Secretary of the Bahamas, 1894; administered the Government, 1894-95; Colonial Secretary, Leeward Islands, and Island Sec., Antigua, 1895-

1902 ; administered the Government of the Leeward Islands, 1895-7, 1899-1902 ; administrator of St. Lucia, 1902 ; administered the Government of the Windward Islands, 1903 ; retired on pension, 1905. *Decorated* for services while officer administering the Government of British Honduras. *Address :* c/o Cox & Co., Charing Cross, S.W.1. *Club :* Constitutional.

(Died 24 Feb. 1924.)

MELVILLE, Lt.-Col. Harry George, I.M.S. ; Professor of Materia Medica, Lahore Medical College ; *b.* Edinburgh, Mar. 24., 1869 ; *s.* of late Francis S. Melville, D.C.S., Edinburgh ; *m.* 1903, Isobel, *y. d.* of late Alexander Lawson, J.P. of Burnturk, Fife, N.B. one *d. Educ. :* Collegiate School and University Edinburgh. M.B., CM., Ed. 1890 ; joined Indian Medical Service, 1892 ; Medical Officer, 5th Punjab Cavalry, 1896 ; appointed to Lahore Medical College, 1901 ; F.R.C.S.E., 1900 ; M.D., 1906 ; Fellow, Punjab University ; served Waziristan, 1894-95 (medal and clasp) ; Punjab Frontier, 1897 (medal and two clasps) ; Tirah, 1897-98. *Publications :* contributions to Medical Journals. *Recreations :* polo, riding, golf, shooting. *Address :* c/o H. S. King & Co., 9 Pall Mall, S.W. *Club :* East India United Service ; United Service, Simla ; Punjab, Lahore.

(Died 7 Dec. 1918.)

MELVILLE, Robert Dundonald ; K.C. 1914 ; Professor of Civil Law, Royal School of Law, Cairo, 1906-24 ; *b.* 16 July 1872 ; 4th *s.* of late Francis Suther Melville, D.C.S., Edinburgh. *Educ. :* Collegiate School ; University of Edinburgh, M.A. 1893 ; LL.B. 1896 ; Forensic Prizeman, 1894. Called to Scottish Bar, 1897 ; Order of the Nile, 1921. *Publications :* A Manual of the Principles of Roman Law, 1st ed. 1915, 2nd ed. 1918, 3rd ed. 1921 ; (Joint) A Treatise upon the Law of Arbitration in Scotland ; and "Burgh Government" ; many articles on legal, historical, and general subjects to various periodicals. *Recreations :* golf, tennis. *Address :* c/o Mitchell & Baxter, W.S., Edinburgh. *Clubs :* Royal Automobile ; Scottish Conservative, Edinburgh ; Turf, Cairo ; Union, Alexandria. *(Died 7 Sept. 1927.)*

MELVILLE, William, M.V.O. 1903 ; J.P. ; Chevalier of the Order of Dannebrog, Denmark ; Order of Christ, Portugal ; Crown of Italy ; Officier de la Legion d'Honneur ; Commander of the Order of Isabel la Catolica, Spain ; *b.* 1852 ; *s.* of late James Melville of County Kerry. Entered the Metropolitan Police, 1872 ; has been several years on the Continent and taken an active part in the suppression of Anarchism ; has accompanied the late Queen and King Edward VII. and other members of the Royal Family in various Continental tours ; has also been in attendance on several foreign sovereigns while visiting this country ; late Chief of the Special Police Service, New Scotland Yard ; Chevalier of the Order of Francis Joseph of Austria ; Knight of Order of St. Silvester of Holy Roman Empire, 1908. *Address :* Kenmare, Orlando Road, Clapham, S.W. *Club :* National Liberal. *(Died 1 Feb. 1918.)*

MENDEL, William, D.L. ; *b.* 19 June 1854. *Educ. :* Privately. Director Harrod's Stores, Ltd. ; D. H. Evans and Co., Ltd. ; Paquin, Ltd. *Address :* 31 Hans Mansions, S.W. *T. :* Kensington 3210. *Clubs :* Reform, Royal Automobile. *(Died 6 Jan. 1917.)*

MENTETH, Sir James Stuart-, 3rd Bart., *cr.* 1838 ; *b.* 29 July 1841 ; *e. s.* of T. L. Stuart-Mentèth and Isabella Maria, 2nd *d.* of James Tobin, Dublin. *S. u.* 1870 ; *m.* 1872, Helen Gertrude, *d.* of Darwin E. Fay of Fulton, N.Y. ; two *d. Heir :* 1st *c.,* Lt.-Col. James Frederick [*b.* 26 Feb. 1846 ; *m.* 1st, 1868, Frances Octavia Moore (*d.* 1887), *d.* of Gen. Sir James Wallace Sleigh, K.C.B. ; three *s.* one *d.* ; 2nd, 1888, Elizabeth Alyson, *d.* of Capt. E. A. Blackett, R.N., of Wylaw ; one *s.* three *d.* Late

2nd Dragoon Guards. *Address :* Rownhams Mount, near Southampton]. *Address :* Canandaigua, New York. *(Died 28 Oct. 1918.)*

MENTETH, Lt.-Col. Sir James Frederick Stuart-, 4th Bart., *cr.* 1838 ; *b.* 26 Feb. 1846 ; *m.* 1st, 1868, Frances Octavia Moore (*d.* 1887), *d.* of Gen. Sir James Wallace Sleigh, K.C.B. ; three *s.* one *d.* ; 2nd, 1888, Elizabeth Alyson, *d.* of Capt. E. A. Blackett, R.N., of Wylam ; one *s.* three *d.* ; *N. c.* 1918. Late 2nd Dragoon Guards. *Heir :* *s.* William Frederick [*b.* 1874 ; *m.* ; one *s.*]. *Address :* Rownhams Mount, near Southampton. *Club :* Army and Navy.

(Died 7 Sept. 1926.)

MENZIES, Rev. Allan, B.D., D.D. ; Professor of Divinity and Biblical Criticism, St. Mary's College, St. Andrews, since 1889 ; *b.* Edinburgh, 23 Jan. 1845 ; 3rd *s.* of Prof. Allan Menzies, Edinburgh University, and Helen, *d.* of Alexander Cowan, of Valleyfield ; *m.* Mary Elizabeth, *d.* of Rev. John Adamson Honey, D.D., Inchture, Perthshire ; two *d. Educ. :* Edinburgh Acad. ; German Schools ; Edinburgh and St. Andrews Univs. (M.A.). Minister of Abernyte, Perthshire, 1873. *Publications :* translated Baur's First Three Centuries of Christianity ; The Apostle Paul ; Pfleiderer's Philosophy of Religion ; author of National Religion (1888) ; History of Religion (1895) ; The Earliest Gospel (1901) ; Second Corinthians, 1912 ; editor of supplementary issue of the Ante - Nicene Fathers ; editor of Review of Theology and Philosophy. *Recreations :* swimming, boating, golf, cycling. *Address :* St. Andrews, Fifeshire ; St. Mary's, Innellan, Argyllshire. *Club :* Royal and Ancient, St. Andrews. *(Died 8 May 1916.)*

MENZIES, Captain Arthur John Alexander, D.S.O. 1915 ; M.B. ; R.A.M.C. ; *s.* of late Alexander Menzies, Lankat Estate, Sumatra ; *m.* 1916, Ethel Fanny Whitelock, *y. d.* of late Rev. D. L. Boyes, Melrose. Served European War, 1914-17 (D.S.O.). *Address :* c/o Holt & Co., 3 Whitehall Place, S.W.

(Died 9 Aug. 1918.)

MENZIES, James Acworth, M.A. (Dunelm.), M.D.(Edin.) ; Professor of Physiology, University of Durham, since 1915 ; *s.* of late Rev. R. Menzies, Riding Mill, Northumberland ; *m.* Florence E., *d.* of late Rev. A. McLaren, D.D., Manchester ; one *d. Educ. :* Edinburgh University. M.B., C.M., 1890 ; Demonstrator of Physiology, Owens College, Manchester, 1890-96, and 1898-99 ; M.D., Gold Medallist, Edinburgh University, 1894 ; House Surgeon, Royal Eye Hospital, Manchester, 1896-97 ; Honorary Ophthalmic Surgeon, Rochdale Infirmary, 1905-11 ; Lecturer on Physiology, University of Durham College of Medicine, 1911-15. *Publications :* (with Professor Bainbridge) Essentials of Physiology ; papers in Journal of Physiology, British Medical Journal, Ophthalmoscope, etc. *Recreation :* golf. *Address :* University of Durham College of Medicine, Newcastle-upon-Tyne.

(Died 9 July 1921.)

MERCADIER, Elie ; Director of the Agence Havas in London ; Officer of the Legion of Honour ; *b.* Monestier, Tarn, 1844. *Educ. :* Toulouse. *Address :* Agence Havas. 113 Cheapside, E.C. *(Died 30 Sept. 1916.)*

MERCER, Major - Gen. Sir David, K.C.B., *cr.* 1918 ; C.B. 1915 ; Adjutant-General Royal Marine Forces since 1916 ; *b.* London, 1 July 1864 ; *s.* of late D. D. Mercer ; *m.* 1893, Katherine Frances, *d.* of late W. F. Lawrence, Boston, U.S.A. ; two *s.* one *d. Educ. :* Dulwich College. Entered R.M.L.I. 1883 ; Adjutant Portsmouth Division, 1891-95 ; Staff-Officer, Depot R.M., Deal, 1899-1903 ; D.A.A.G., R.M. 1903-8 ; A.A.G., R.M. 1911-14 ; Brig.-General commanding 1st R.N. Brigade, R.N. Division, 1914-16 : served throughout the operations in Gallipoli (despatches twice, C.B), elsewhere 1915-18 (K.C.B., Commander Legion of Honour). *Recreations :* golf, fishing, shooting.

Address: 7 Bickenhall Mansions, W.1.   *T.:* Mayfair 1685. *Clubs:* United Service; Huntercombe Golf.   *(Died 1 July 1920.)*

MERCER, Colonel Edward Gilbert, C.M.G. 1916; late commanding 1st Lond. Regt. (Royal Fusiliers); *s.* of late E. J. B. Mercer, Bath; unmarried. *Educ.:* King's School, Gloucester; Magdalen College, Oxford (M.A.). Assistant Master at Harrow School and Commandant Harrow School O.T.C.; served S. African War with 2nd Batt. Royal Fusiliers (Queen's medal 4 clasps); European War, 1914-18 (despatches, C.M.G.). *Address:* West Hill House, Harrow-on-the-Hill. *Clubs:* New University, Oxford and Cambridge Musical.   *(Died 19 Dec. 1926.)*

MERCER, Rt. Rev. John Edward, D.D. hon. causa, Oxon.; Canon Residentiary Chester Cathedral since 1916; Archdeacon of Macclesfield, 1919; *b.* Bradford; *s.* of Rev. Edward Mercer; *m.* 1st, 1882, Josephine Archdall; 2nd, 1916, H. Ethel Bennion. *Educ.:* Rossall School; Lincoln College, Oxford. Ordained, 1880; Curate of Tanfield, 1880-82; Penshaw, 1882-83; Rossall School Missioner, Newton Heath, 1883-89; Rector of St. Michael, Manchester, 1889-97; St. James, Gorton, 1897-1902; Bishop of Tasmania, 1902-14; first Moorhouse Lecturer, Melbourne. *Publications:* What is the World External to Mind?; The Soul of Progress; Social Equality; The Spiritual Evolution of the Race; The Science of Life and the Larger Hope; Nature Mysticism; The Problem of Creation, etc. *Address:* Lumley House, Chester.   *(Died 27 April 1922.)*

MERCIE, Jean Marius Antonin, Sculptor and Painter; Grand Prix de Rome; Member of the Institute; Grand Officer, Legion of Honour; Professor École des Beaux-Arts; President Société Artistes Francais; *b.* Toulouse, 29 Oct. 1845. *Works:* Sculpture—David avant combat, David après le combat, Gloria Victis, Quand même, Tombeaux du roi Louis Philippe (Dreux, France), Baudry, Thiers, Michelet (Père Lachaise, Paris); Monument, Général Lee (Washington); Tombeau Pellegrini (Buenos Ayres); Monument, Francis Scott Key (Baltimore), etc.; Picture Portraits—Vénus, Galathie et Pygmalion, etc. *Address:* 15 avenue Observatoire, Paris. *(Died 14 Dec. 1916.)*

MERCIER, Charles Arthur, M.D., F.R.C.P., F.R.C.S.; Physician for Mental Diseases to Charing Cross Hospital; Examiner in Mental Diseases at the London University; *b.* 1852; *s.* of late Rev. L. P. Mercier; *m.* 2nd, 1913, Mary, *y. d.* of late Donald MacDougall. *Educ.:* Merchant Taylors' School; London Hospital. Cabin boy, warehouseman, clerk, medical student; medical officer of various asylums. *Publications:* Sanity and Insanity; Nervous System and the Mind; Lunacy Law for Medical Men; Psychology, Normal and Morbid; Text-book of Insanity, Criminal Responsibility, etc. *Recreations:* mechanics, chess, photography, motoring. *Address:* 34 Wimpole Street, W. *T.:* Paddington 986. *M.:* A 4422. *Clubs:* Savile, Casual.   *(Died 2 Sept. 1919.)*

MERCIER, Cardinal (Desiré), a Belgian; Archbishop of Malines and Cardinal since 1907; *b.* Braine l'Alleud, 1851. Professor of Philosophy at Louvain University, 1882-1906; Founder of the Institute of Philosophy and the Revue Neo-scholastique. *Publications:* Criteriologie Metaphysique Generale; Les Origines de la Psychologie Contemporaine; A Manual of Modern Scholastic Philosophy, 1917; a mes Séminaristes; Retraite Pastorale; La Vie Intérièure. *Address:* Malines, Belgium.   *(Died 23 Jan. 1926.)*

MEREDITH, Rt. Hon. Richard Edmund, P.C.; *b.* 18 Nov. 1855; *s.* of late William Rice Meredith, solicitor; *m.* 1880, Annie, *d.* of late John Pollock, solicitor; three *s.* two *d.* Barr, Hilary 1879; appointed Q.C.

1892; elected a Bencher of King's Inns, 1894; Judge of the Supreme Court of Judicature in Ireland, and Judicial Commissioner of the Irish Land Commission, 1898-1906; Master of the Rolls in Ireland, 1906-12. *Address:* 32 Molesworth Street, Dublin. *Clubs:* University, Dublin; Royal St. George Yacht, Kingstown.   *(Died 23 Jan. 1916.)*

MEREDITH, William Appleton, F.R.C.S.Eng., M.B. C.M. Edin. Consulting Surgeon Samaritan Free Hospital, London; J.P. Norfolk; *b.* 3 March 1848; *e. s.* of Samuel Ogden Meredith of Philadelphia; *m.* Caroline, *d.* of late Henry Atkinson Green of Boston, U.S.A.; naturalised a British subject in 1886. *Educ.:* abroad; University College, London; University of Edinburgh. *Publications:* various papers on Abdominal Surgery. *Address:* Little Massingham Manor, King's Lynn, Norfolk.   *(Died 6 Oct. 1916.)*

MEREDITH, Hon. Sir William Ralph, LL.D.; Kt., *cr.* 1896; Chief Justice of Ontario since 1912; *b.* 31 Mar. 1840; *s.* of John Cooke Meredith, London, Ontario; *m.* 1862, Mary, *d.* of Marcus Holmes, Ontario; three *d.* *Educ.:* London, Ontario; University of Toronto (LL.B., LL.D.). Member of Legislative Assembly for London, Ontario, 1872-94; Chief Justice of the Common Pleas, 1894-1912; Chancellor of the University of Toronto. *Address:* Toronto, Ontario. *Club:* Toronto.   *(Died 22 Aug. 1923.)*

MEREDYTH, Sir Henry (Bayly), 5th Bt., *cr.* 1795; J.P.; *b.* 14 Jan. 1863; *e. s.* of Henry William Meredyth and Harriet Anne, *e. d.* of Rev. William Le Poer Trench; *S.* grandfather 1889; *m.* 1st, 1866, Kathleen (whom he divorced, 1894), *o. c.* of late Robert O'Hara, Raheen, Co. Galway; 2nd, 1897, Mildred Beatrice (*d.* 1912), *d.* of Edmund B. Liebert; one *d.* Late Lieut. 4th Brig. N. Irish Division R.A., and West Somerset Yeomanry. Owns over 20,000 acres. *Heir:* none. *Address:* Hollymount, Co. Down. *Clubs:* Carlton, Bachelors', Cavalry; Kildare Street, Dublin.   *(Died 30 Sept. 1923.)*

MEREWETHER, Rev. Wyndham Arthur Scinde, M.A.; Canon of Salisbury Cathedral since 1919; Rural Dean of Wilton; *b.* 12 Sep. 1852; *s.* of H. A. Merewether, Q.C.; *m.* 1888, Harriot Edith Fox (*d.* 1928), *d.* of Wilson Fox, F.R.S., M.D., Physician-in-Ordinary to Queen Victoria. *Educ.:* Winchester; Oriel College, Oxford. Curate of Bradford-on-Avon, 1876-80; St. George, Hanover Square, 1880-86; Vicar of North Bradley, Wilts, 1886-1908; Bradford-on-Avon, 1908-14; St. Thomas, Salisbury, 1914-22. *Recreations:* cricket, Winchester XI. 1870-71; Oxford *v.* Cambridge Association football, 1874. *Address:* 38 The Close, Salisbury.   *(Died 3 Dec. 1928.)*

MERK, William Rudolph Henry, C.S.I. 1887; LL.D.; Indian Civil Service; *b.* Simla, India, 12 Dec. 1852; *e. s.* of Rev. J. N. Merk; *m.* 1894, Rosamond, *d.* of A. Savory of Kirkham Abbey, and Sun Rising, Banbury. *Educ.:* private schools in Switzerland and Germany; King's Coll., Aberdeen. Passed 3rd for I.C.S.; joined in India, 1875; on political duty in Afghan War, 1879-81; Under-Sec. Punjab Govt., 1882-84; with Afghan Boundary Commission, 1884-87; Deputy-Commissioner, Peshawar, 1887-1892; in charge of Kurram, 1892-94; Commissioner, Peshawar, 1896-98; with Black Mountain Expedition, 1888; Chief Political Officer, Mohmand Field Force, 1897; Chief Secy. Punjab Government, 1898-99; Commissioner, Derajat, 1900-1901; in charge of Mahsud Waziri blockade, 1900-1902; Commissioner, Multan, 1903; Chief Commissioner Andaman and Nicobar Islands, 1904-6; Commissioner, Delhi, 1906-7; Multan, 1908; member, Legislative Council, Govt. of India, 1909; Financial Commissioner Punjab; Chief Commissioner of N.W.F. Province; retired from service, 1910. *Decorated* for services

724

with Afghan Boundary Commission. *Recreations:* riding, shooting, fishing, etc. *Address:* c/o Lloyds Bank, Ltd., 9 Pall Mall, S.W.1. *Club:* East India United Service.
(Died 15 Jan. 1925.)

MERRIMAN, Rt. Hon. John Xavier, P.C. 1909; M.L.A., Union of South Africa, since 1910; J.P.; surveyor,farmer; mem. Cape Parliament for Namaqualand, Wodehouse, now of Victoria West; *b.* Street, Somersetshire, 1841; *s.* of Bishop N. J. Merriman, Grahamstown; *m.* Agnes Vintcent (*d.* 1923), *d.* of Hon. J. Vintcent, M.L.C. *Educ.:* Rondebosch Diocesan College; Radley, near Oxford. Went to South Africa 1849 and 1861; entered politics, 1869; joined Molteno Ministry, 1875-78; Scanlen Govt., 1881-84; Commissioner Crown Lands. 1875-78, 1881-84; Treasurer-General, 1890-93; member of Cape Jameson Raid Committee; drew up Report; Treasurer-General, 1898-1900; Prime Minister and Treasurer, 1908-10; Member of National Convention for Union. *Address:* Schoongezigt, Stellenbosch, Cape Colony. *Clubs:* Reform; Civil Service, Cape Town. *(Died 2 Aug. 1926.)*

MERRIMAN, Col. William, C.I.E. 1890; R.E.; retired; *b.* Kensington, 2 Apr. 1838; 5th *s.* of late Dr. Merriman of Kensington and Marlborough; *m.* Emily J. A. E., *c. d.* of late Col. Fitzroy Somerset, R.E., 1872; one *s.* three *d.* *Educ.:* Kensington School and Addiscombe College. Fellow of Bombay University. Commission in R.E. (Bombay), 1856; served in India, South Africa (Boer Campaign); Headquarters Staff, Bombay, etc. *Decorated* for services in connection with the Coast Defences of Bombay, Karachi, Aden, etc. *Recreations:* cricket, football, hunting, shooting, rowing, golf, etc. *Address:* Creffield,Colchester. *T.A.:* Colchester. *Clubs:* East India United Service, Sports; Byculla, Bombay. *(Died 11 Mar. 1917.)*

MERRY, Rev. William Walter, D.D. Oxon.; Hon. D.Litt., Victoria University; LL.D., Aberdeen; Rector of Lincoln Coll. since 1884; *b.* Worcestershire, 6 Sept. 1835; *o. s.* of late Walter Merry and Elizabeth Mary Byrch; *m.* Alice Elizabeth (*d.* 1914), *o. d.* of late Joseph Collings, Jurat of Royal Court of Guernsey, 1862; two *s.* two *d.* *Educ.:* Cheltenham; Balliol College, Oxford (M.A.) Scholar; 1st class mods. 1855, 2nd class Lit. Hum. 1857; Chancellor's Prize, Latin Essay, 1858; Select Preacher, 1878-79, 1889-90; Whitehall Preacher 1883-84; Member of the Hebdomadal Council, 1896-1908; Vice-Chancellor, 1904-5; public orator University of Oxford, 1880-1910; life member of the Council of Cheltenham College. *Publications:* Greek Dialects, 1875; Aristophanes' Clouds, 1879, 3rd ed.; Acharnians, 1880, 4th ed.; Frogs, 1883, 3rd ed.; Knights, 1887, 2nd ed.; Birds, 1889, 3rd ed.; Wasps, 1893; Peace, 1900; Selected Fragments of Roman Poetry, 1891, 2nd ed.; Homer's Odyssey, i.-xii. 66th thousand, xiii.-xxiv. 16th thousand. *Address:* Lincoln College. Oxford.
(Died 5 Mar. 1918.)

MERZ, John Theodore, Ph.D., Hon. D.C.L. Durham; Hon. LL.D. Aberdeen; Vice-Chairman Newcastle-upon-Tyne Electric Supply Co. Ltd.; director of several companies; former Member of Senate University of Durham; *b.* Manchester, 1840; *s.* of Philip Merz; *m.* 1873, Alice Mary Richardson; two *s.* one *d.* *Educ.:* Darmstad ; Giessen, Göttingen, Heidelberg, and Bonn Universities. *Publications:* Leibnitz (Philosophical Classics), 1884; History of European Thought in the Nineteenth Century, vol. i. 1896, 3rd edition, 1907; vol. ii. 1903, 2nd edition, 1912; vol. iii. 1912; vol. iv. 1914; Religion and Science, 1915; A Fragment on the Human Mind, 1919. *Recreations:* Bibliophily, gardening. *Address:* The Quarries, Newcastle-upon-Tyne. *Clubs:* Reform; Union, Newcastle.*(Died 21 Mar. 1922.)*

MESSEL, Rudolph, F.R.S., 1912; Ph.D.; manager, Royal Institute; President, Society Chemical Industry, and Past Foreign Secretary of same; P.V.P. Chemical Society; Member Board of Studies in Chemistry, University of London; Member of Governing Body, Imperial College of Science and Technology, London; Managing Director of Spencer, Chapman & Messel, Ltd.; *b.* Darmstadt, Germany, 14 Jan. 1848; *s.* of L. Messel,/Banker; unmarried. *Educ.:* Darmstadt; Universities of Zürich, Heidelberg, Tübingen, D.Sc. nat. Tübingen. Came to England, 1870; assistant, J. C. Calvert; later appointed assistant to Sir Henry Roscoe, both at Manchester; entered into Chemical Industry and introduced numerous new processes; was the first, prior to Winkler, to devise conjointly with Squire, a successful process for the manufacture of sulphuric anhydride by the catalytic process. *Publications:* Various, mainly in relation to industrial chemistry. *Recreations:* art and literature. *Address:* 147 Victoria Street, S.W.1; Silvertown, Essex. *T.:* Victoria 2400. *Clubs:* Devonshire, Savage.
(Died 18 April 1920.)

MESSENT, Philip Glynn, C.I.E. 1914; M.Inst.C.E.; Consulting Engineer (with A. J. Barry, K. A. Wolfe Barry, and J. Lumsden Rae) to the Trustees of the Port of Bombay, and Consulting Engineer (with A. J. Barry and K. A. Wolfe Barry) to the Trustees of the Port of Aden, 2 Queen Anne's Gate, Westminster, S.W.; *b.* 1862; *e. s.* of late Philip J. Messent, M.Inst.C.E., and Elizabeth, *d.* of late Joseph Glynn, F.R.S., M.Inst.C.E. *Educ.:* Charterhouse. Articled pupil and Assistant to Philip J. Messent, M.Inst.C.E., Chief Engineer to the Tyne Improvement Commissioners, 1880-84; Assistant Engineer to the Bombay Port Trust, 1884-99; Chief Engineer to the Bombay Port Trust, 1899-1922; has carried out many important works, including the Alexandra Dock (50 acres) and the Hughes Dry Dock, 1000 ft. long and 100 ft. wide at entrance; extensive reclamations and Bombay Port Trust Railway. *Address:* 6 Grosvenor Hill, Wimbledon, S.W.19. *T.:* Wimbledon 1112. *Clubs:* Northern Counties; Byculla, Royal Bombay Yacht, Bombay; Club of Western India, Poona.
(Died 4 Aug. 1925.)

MESSER, Adam Brunton, M.D., Edin.; Hon. Physician to King; Inspector-General of Hospitals and Fleets Royal Navy (retired); Member of Royal Anthropological Institute; *y. s.* of late Adam Messer of Blainslie; *m.* Elizabeth Mary, *y. d.* of late Capt. Belches, R.N. *Educ.:* Edinburgh Academy; Universities of Edinburgh and Paris. Joined Royal Navy, 1859; specially promoted for distinguished service in New Zealand War, 1863-64; Coronations of Edward VII. and George V., New Zealand War, and Sir Gilbert Blane's gold medals. *Address:* Kinclune, Carlisle Road, Eastbourne. *Club:* Caledonian United Service, Edinburgh.
(Died 11 Oct. 1919.)

METAXA, Andrea, The Count; *b.* 23 Mar. 1844; *m.* 1871, Louisa Elizabeth, *d.* of late Thomas White of Congelow, Yalding, Kent (*d.* 1896); one *d.* *Educ.:* Cheltenham. Special war correspondent, 1870. *Publications:* Round the Wight in an Open Canoe; Journal of a Tour in the Mediterranean; Walking Tour through Isle of Wight, 1870. *Recreations:* rowing, public and political speaking on Eastern Question, Women's Suffrage Bill, Deceased Wife's Sister's Bill, and Married Woman's Property Act. *Heir:* *g. s.* Andrea-Richard-Dudley, *b.* 20 Jan. 1902. *Address:* 4 Park Place, St. James's, S.W.
(Died 15 Mar. 1921.)

METAXAS, Sir D. G., G.C.V.O., cr. 1906; Greek Minister to Rome, 1908; *b.* Syra, Greece; 2nd *s.* of George L. Metaxas, lawyer; *m.* 1st, Helène C. Cantacuzène (*d.* 1909); one *d.* ; 2nd, 1915, Amelie Mavrogordato. *Educ.:* Athens. Diplomatic service at the Foreign Office, Constantinople, Rome, Berlin, Belgrade, London ; Secretary, Conference, Berlin, 1880 ; and during negotiations, Prevesa, for delimiting new Greco-Turkish frontiers ; Envoy Extraordinary and Minister Plenipotentiary of King of the Hellenes to Great Britain, 1895-1908.

(Died 1 Feb. 1928.)

METCALFE, Sir Charles Herbert Theophilus, 6th Bt., *cr.* 1802 ; C.E. ; *b.* 8 Sep. 1853 ; *o. c.* of 5th Bt. and 1st wife, Charlotte, *d.* of Lieut.-Gen. Sir John Low, K.C.B. ; *S.* father, 1883. *Educ.:* Harrow ; University Coll., Oxford (M.A.). *Heir:* cousin Theophilus, *b.* 19 June 1866. *Address:* Winkworth Hill, Hascombe, Godalming. *Club:* Carlton.

(Died 29 Dec. 1928.)

METCALFE, Hon. Thomas Llewellyn ; Justice of Court of King's Bench, Manitoba, since 1909 ; *b.* St. Thomas, Ontario, 21 Feb. 1870 ; unmarried. *Educ.:* Portage la Prairie. Came West, 1876 ; early life farming and ranching ; admitted Manitoba Bar, 1894 ; afterwards to Bar of Saskatchewan and Alberta ; practised at Winnipeg ; was Counsel for prisoner in Molson's Bank Robbery Case ; Member Royal Commission last Revision Dominion Statutes ; also Fisheries Commission, 1909. *Recreations:* active generally ; special—polo, riding. *Address:* Court House, Winnipeg. *T.:* Fort Rouge 328. *M.:* 655. *Clubs:* Manitoba ; St. Charles Country ; Polo ; Hunt. *(Died 2 April 1922.)*

METCALFE, Rev. W. M., D.D. (St. Andrews, 1892), F.S.A. Scot. ; minister of South Parish, Paisley ; Assessor to Lord Rector of University of St. Andrews, 1892-1899 ; Clerk to the Presbytery of Paisley ; *b.* York, 14 Sept. 1840 ; *s.* of John and Hannah Metcalfe ; *m.* Cecilia, *d.* of James and Cecilia Simpson, Dundee ; two *s.* three *d. Educ..* New Coll. London. Minister of Tighnabruaich. Editor Scottish Review, 1882-1900. *Publications:* The Natural Truth of Christianity, 1880 ; The Reasonableness of Christianity, 1882 ; Pinkerton's Vitæ Antiquæ Sanctorum Scotiæ, 1889 ; Ancient Lives of Scottish Saints, 1895 ; Legends of the Saints in the Scottish Dialect of the Fourteenth Century, 1896 ; The John Neilston Institution : Its First Fifty Years, 1902 ; Charters and Documents relating to the Burgh of Paisley, 1902 ; the Legends of SS. Ninian and Machor in the Scottish Dialect of the Fourteenth Century, 1904 ; History of the County of Renfrew, 1905 ; A History of Paisley, 1909 ; Supplementary Dictionary of the Scottish Language, 1910 ; The Lordship of Paisley, 1912 ; Specimens of Scottish Literature (1325-1835), 1913 ; Robert Henryson's Poems, 1916 ; many articles on literary and other topics. *Recreations:* reading, golfing. *Address:* South Manse, Paisley. *(Died 8 Aug. 1916.)*

METCHNIKOFF, Elie ; Professor at the Pasteur Institute, Paris ; Membre de l'Académie de Médecine ; Foreign Member of the Royal Society of London and of the Académie des Sciences ; awarded Nobel Prize for Medicine, 1908. *Publications:* The Nature of Man, 1903 ; Immunity in Infective Diseases, 1906 ; The Prolongation of Human Life : Optimistic Essays, 1907. *Address:* rue Dutot 18 (XVe), Paris.

(Died 15 July 1916.)

METHUEN, Sir Algernon Methuen Marshall, 1st Bart., *cr.* 1916 ; M.A. ; head of Methuen & Co., Ltd., publishers ; *b.* Southwark, 23 Feb. 1856 ; 3rd *s.* of J. B. Stedman, F.R.C.S., Godalming ; *m.* 1884, Emily C., *d.* of Edwin Bedford, Ladbroke Terrace, W. *Educ.:* Berkhampstead School ; Wadham College, Oxford. Head of High Croft Preparatory School, Milford, 1880-95 ; founded Methuen and Co., June 1889 ; assumed surname of Methuen, Aug. 1899 ; J.P. Surrey, 1909 ; contested (L.) Guildford Division, Surrey, 1910. *Publications:*

726

Peace or War in South Africa ; England's Ruin ; An Anthology of Modern Verse : Shakespeare to Hardy ; also some school books. *Heir:* none. *Address:* New Place, Haslemere, Surrey. *Clubs:* Reform, National Liberal .

(Died 20 Sept. 1924.)

METTAM, Professor A. E., Principal of Royal Veterinary Coll. of Ireland since 1900 ; President of the Royal College of Veterinary Surgeons, 1911-12-13 ; Professor of Bacteriology and Pathology since 1900 ; Professor of Anatomy and Histology, Royal Dick Veterinary College, Edinburgh, 1890-1900 ; George Heriot Research Fellow Edinburgh University, 1896 ; Past President of the Scottish Microscopical Society ; Examiner in National University of Ireland and in the Universities of London and Manchester ; member Royal Irish Academy. *Address:* Royal Veterinary College, Dublin. *(Died Nov. 1917.)*

MEULEMAN, Most Rev. Brice, S.J. ; Catholic Archbishop of Calcutta since 1902 ; *b.* Ghent, 1 March 1862. *Educ.:* St. Barbe's Coll. Ghent. Joined the Society of Jesus, 1879 ; after three years' philosophical and scientific studies at Louvain joined the Jesuit Mission in Bengal, 1886 ; taught philosophy for six years in St. Xavier's College, Calcutta, and theology for three years in St. Mary's Seminary Kurseong ; nominated Superior of the Jesuit Mission in Bengal, 1900. *Address:* Calcutta.

(Died 15 July 1924.)

MEXBOROUGH, 5th Earl of (*cr.* 1766), **John Horace Savile**, D.L., J.P. ; Baron Pollington, 1753 ; Viscount Pollington, 1766 ; *b.* 17 June 1843 ; *s.* of 5th Earl and Rachel, *d.* of 3rd Earl of Orford ; *S.* father, 1899 ; *m.* 1st, 1867, Venetia (*d.* 1900), *d.* of Sir R. S. Errington, 11th Bt. ; 2nd, 1906, Donna Sylvia Cecilia Maria (*d.* 1915), *d.* of the Noble Carlo de Ser Antoni of Lucca and Naples, and widow of Captain C. Clerk. *Educ.:* Eton ; Trin. Coll. Camb. (M.A. 1868). Buddhist. Owns about 7600 acres. Contested the first election by ballot ever held in the United Kingdom, Pontefract, York. *Heir-pres.: half-b.* Hon. John Henry Savile. *Recreations:* gardening, reading. *Address:* Albert Court, Kensington Gore, S.W. ; Cannizaro, Wimbledon Common, S.W. ; Methley Park, Leeds. *T.:* Wimbledon 103. *M.:* A 1956. *Clubs:* Carlton, Hurlingham, Lords, Travellers'.

(Died 4 June 1916.)

MEYER, Arthur ; Director of the Gaulois ; Publicist ; *b.* Paris, 16 June 1845 ; *m.* Marguerite de Turenne, *g.d.* of Duke de Fitz-James. *Publications:* Ce que mes yeux ont vu, 1911 ; Ce que je peux dire, 1912 ; Ce qu'il faut taire, pièce, 1914 ; numerous articles. Collections : books, drawing, autographs. *Address:* Rue Drouot 4, Paris. *T.A.:* Arthur Meyer, Paris. *T.:* 212 ; 21. *Club:* Cercle interallie, Paris.

(Died 2 Feb. 1924.)

MEYER, Sir Carl, 1st Bt., *cr.* 1910 ; J.P., Essex ; Lieutenant of the City of London ; Director of the National Bank of Egypt; Chairman of the London Committee of De Beers ; *b.* Hamburg, 23 Dec. 1851 ; *m.* 1883, Adele, *d.* of Julius Levis, of Belsize Grove, Hampstead ; one *s.* one *d. Educ.:* Abroad. *Recreations:* music, shooting. *Heir: s.* Frank Cecil [*b.* 7 May 1886 ; *m.* 1920, Marjorie, 2nd *d.* of Frederick Seeley, Hale, Cheshire]. *Address:* 12 Park Crescent, Portland Place, W.1. *T.:* Langham 2116 ; Shortgrove, Newport, Essex. *Club:* Junior Carlton. *(Died 18 Dec. 1922.)*

MEYER, George von Lengerke ; *b.* Boston, U.S.A., 24 June 1858 ; *s.* of George Augustus Meyer and Grace Helen, *d.* of William Parker, Boston, and *g.d.* of Bishop Parker, Massachusetts ; *m.* 1885, Alice, *d.* of Charles H. Appleton and Isabella, *d.* of Jonathan Mason, Boston ; one *s.* two *d.* Graduated, Harvard, 1879 ; Member of the City Government of Boston, 1889-92 ; Member of the Massachusetts

Legislature, 1892-97 ; Speaker of the House of Representatives, 1894-97 ; Chairman of the Massachusetts Board, Paris Exposition Commissioners, 1898 ; Member, Republican National Committee from Massachusetts, 1898 - 1904 ; United States Ambassador to Italy, 1900-5 to Russia, 1905-7 ; Postmaster-General, 1907-9 ; Secretary of the Navy, 1909 - 13 ; Chevalier Grand Cross, Grand Cordon of SS. Maurizio e Lazzaro, Italy ; of Alexander Nevsky, Russia ; of Rising Sun, Japan ; LL.D. Harvard, 1911. *Recreations :* fishing, shooting, and hunting. *Address :* Hamilton, Mass. *Clubs :* Somerset, Boston ; Knickerbocker, New York, Metropolitan, Washington. *(Died 10 Mar. 1918.)*

MEYER, Paul ; member of the Institute of France ; Associate of the British Academy ; Commandeur de la Légion d'Honneur ; directeur de l'Ecole Nationale des Chartes, Paris ; professeur honoraire au Collège de France ; Editor of Romania (1872) ; author of many publications concerning the Romance languages and literatures ; *b.* Paris, 17 Jan. 1840. *Educ. :* Lycée Louis le Grand ; Ecole des Chartes. *Address :* 16 Labourdonnais, Paris. *(Died 1917.)*

MEYER, Sir William Stevenson, G.C.I.E., *cr.* 1918 ; K.C.S.I., *cr.* 1915 ; K.C.I.E., *cr.* 1909 ; C.I.E. 1901 ; Indian Civil Service ; High Commissioner for India since 1920 ; President, Central Recruiting Board, India, 1917 - 18 ; Ordinary Member of Council of Governor-General of India, 1913-18 ; *b.* 13 Feb. 1860 ; *m.* 1895, Mabel Henrietta (*d.* 1914), *d.* of late Major W. W. Jackson, I.A. *Educ. :* Blackheath ; University College School ; University College. Entered I.C.S. 1881 ; retired 1918 ; Assistant Secretary to Madras Government, 1886-89 ; Secretary Board of Revenue, 1890-94 ; Deputy Secretary Government of India, Financial Department, 1896-1901 ; Editor, Imperial Gazetteer of India, 1902-4 ; Financial Secretary, Government of India, 1905-9 ; Chief Secretary, Government of Madras, 1909 ; Member of Royal Commission on Decentralization in India, 1907-9 ; a British Delegate to The Hague International Conference, 1911-12 ; Member of Lord Nicholson's Committee on the Indian Army, 1912-13. *Address :* St. James's Court, Buckingham Gate, S.W.1. *Clubs :* Reform, Overseas. *(Died 19 Oct. 1922.)*

MEYERHEIM, Robert Gustav, R.I. 1898 ; belongs to family of Berlin artists of same name ; is a native of Dantzic. *Educ. :* Academy at Carlsruhe under Professor Gude ; Düsseldorf under Professor Oswald Achenbach ; settled in England 1875, taking up water-colour in addition to oil - painting. *Address :* Lindeneck, Wimblehurst Road, Horsham. *(Died 16 May 1920.)*

MEYNELL, Alice, poet and essayist, *y. d.* of late T. J. Thompson ; *m.* to Wilfrid Meynell. *Educ. :* by her father, who, having completed his own education at Trin. Coll. Camb., married early and devoted himself to his two daughters, of whom the elder is Lady Butler, the battle-painter. Spent much of her early life in Italy. *Publications :* Preludes, a volume of poems written in girlhood ; Poems, the same republished with some changes and additions, 1893 ; The Rhythm of Life, 1893 ; The Colour of Life, 1896 ; The Children, 1896 ; The Flower of the Mind : a general Anthology of English Poetry, 1897 ; The Spirit of Place, 1898 ; John Ruskin, 1900 ; Later Poems, 1901 ; Children of the Italian Masters ; Prefaces to the Red Letter Library ; selections from the Poets ; a selection from the verses of John B. Tabb, 1906 ; Ceres' Runaway, 1910 ; Mary, Mother of Jesus, 1912 ; Collected Poems, 1913 ; Selected Essays, 1914 ; A Father of Women, and other Poems, 1917 ; Hearts of Controversy, 1917 ; The Second Person Singular, and other Essays, 1921 ; also contributor to a number of periodicals. *Recreation :*

music. *Address :* 2A Granville Place, W. ; Greatham, Pulborough, Sussex. *(Died 27 Nov. 1922.)*

MEYNELL, Edgar, Recorder of Doncaster since 1921 ; *b.* 6 Sep. 1859 ; *o. surv. s.* of late Judge Meynell ; unmarried. *Educ. :* The Oratory, Edgbaston. Called to Bar, Middle Temple, 1884 ; joined the North Eastern Circuit ; was a revising Barrister in Hull and the East Riding of Yorkshire, 1892-1912. *Address :* Old Elvet, Durham. *T. :* Durham 133. *Clubs :* Union ; Northern Counties, Newcastle-upon-Tyne ; Durham County, Durham. *(Died 4 July 1923.)*

MEYNELL, Everard ; author, journalist ; *b.* 1882 ; 2nd *s.* of Wilfrid Meynell ; *m.* 1907, Grazia Carbone, singer, Buffalo, U.S.A. ; two *s.* two *d.* *Publications :* Life of Francis Thompson ; Corot and his Friends, etc. ; contributor to Illustrated London News, Dublin Review, etc. *Address :* Greatham, near Pulborough, Sussex. *(Died 7 Jan. 1926.)*

MEYRICK, Sir George Augustus Eliott Tapps-Gervis-, 4th Bt., *cr.* 1791 ; *b.* 9 March 1855 ; *S.* father, 1896 ; *m.* 1884, Jacintha, *d.* of C. Phipps ; two *s.* two *d.* *Heir :* *s.* George Llewellyn. *Address :* Hinton Admiral, Christchurch, Hants ; Bodorgan, Anglesey. *(Died 12 May 1928.)*

MEYRICK, James Joseph, C.B. 1882 ; F.R.C.V.S. ; *b.* London, 6 Sept. 1834 ; *o. s.* of late Theobald Meyrick of Ballinasloe, Ireland ; *m.* Elizabeth Henrietta, *d.* of late James Westbeare, 1881. *Educ. :* City of London School ; Royal Veterinary College, London. Gazetted Veterinary Surgeon to Royal Artillery, 1860 ; became Vet.-Surgeon, 1st class, 1870, and Inspecting Vet.-Surgeon, 1881 ; served Canada, 1862-67 (including Fenian raids, 1866, medal) ; India, 1868 - 80 ; Egypt, 1882 - 83 ; superintended Government horse-breeding operations in Punjab, 1878-80 (thanks of Government of India and Punjab Government) ; Egyptian Campaign, 1882 (despatches, medal, Egyptian medal, 3rd class Osmanieh). *Decorated* for services in Egyptian Campaign. *Publications :* Stable Management, and Prevention of Disease among Horses in India ; Veterinary Manual for Use of Salootris and Native Horse-owners in India (translated into Hindustani ; published and distributed by Indian Government). *Recreations :* shooting and painting. *Address :* 45 The Chase, Clapham Common, S.W.4. *(Died 14 Feb. 1925.)*

MEYSEY - THOMPSON, Col. Richard Frederick, late Rifle Brigade ; 2nd *s.* of Sir H. S. Meysey-Thompson, 1st Bart ; *b.* 17 April 1847 ; *m.* 1879, Charlotte, *y. d.* of Sir James Walker, 1st Bart. ; one *s.* one *d.* *Educ. :* Eton. Has medal for Ashanti campaign, and clasp for Coomassie, and also Royal Humane Society's Medal, and Commanded 4th West Yorkshire Regiment ; Local Director of Barclays Bank, York ; Member of York Race Committee, formerly member of Irish National Hunt Steeplechase Committee. *Publications :* A Fishing Catechism ; A Shooting Catechism ; A Hunting Catechism ; The Course, The Camp, The Chase ; The Horse. *Address :* Westwood Mount, Scarborough. *T. :* Scarborough 367. *Clubs :* Army and Navy ; Yorkshire County, York. *(Died 1 Sept. 1926.)*

MIALL, Louis Compton, D.Sc., F.R.S. ; *b.* Bradford, 1842 ; *m.* Emily (*d.* 1918), *d.* of Joseph Pearce ; three *c.* Professor of Biology, University, Leeds, 1876-1907 ; Fullerian Professor of Physiology in the Royal Inst. 1904-5 ; President Zoological Section, British Association, 1897 ; Education Section, 1908. *Publications :* Special Memoirs on Natural History, Object Lessons from Nature, 1891 ; Natural History of Aquatic Insects, 1895 ; Round the Year, 1896 ; Thirty Years of Teaching, 1897 ; Injurious and Useful Insects, 1902 ; House, Garden,

MEYER, Kuno, Ph.D. See page xxvi.

and Field, 1904; The Early Naturalists, 1912, etc. *Address:* Thornycroft, Ben Rhudding, Leeds.   (*Died 21 Feb. 1921.*)

MICHAEL, Albert Davidson, F.L.S., F.Z.S., F.R.M.S., F.R.H.S., F.R.G.S., etc.; *b.* 5 May, 1836; *s.* of J. Michael, Solicitor London; *m.* 1865, Anne Smith. *Educ.:* King's College, London. Practised as a solicitor in London; also known in connection with the Conservative organisation in Surrey; late President of the Royal Microscopical Society, and the Quekett Microscopical Club; late Vice-Pres. of the Linnean Society, and member of the Scientific Committees of the Zoological and Royal Horticultural Societies; Vice-President of Ray Society, etc. *Publications:* numerous books and papers on the Acarina and on microscopical subjects published by the Ray, Linnean, Zoological, and Royal Microscopical Societies, Das Tierreich and in other English, French, Belgian, and German scientific publications. *Recreations:* the microscope, travel gardening. *Address:* The Warren, Studland, Dorset.
    (*Died 29 May 1927.*)

MICHELHAM of Hellingly, 1st Baron (*cr.* 1905), **Herbert Stern;** K.C.V.O., *cr.* 1912; Bt., *cr.* 1905; a Baron of Portugal; *b.* 28 Sep. 1851; *s.* of late Baron Hermann de Stern and Julia, *d.* of late A. A. Goldsmid; *m.* 1898, Aimée Geraldine (despatches twice, Order of Mercy, Mons Star; Medaille d'Or, Legion d'Honneur), *d.* of Octavius Bradshaw; two *s.* Senior partner in firm of Herbert Stern and Co., 33 Cornhill, E.C., and Paris; D.L. of City of London; Alderman, L.C.C., 1906-12. *Heir: s.* Hon. Herman Alfred Stern. *Address:* 26 Princes Gate, S.W.; *T.:* Kensington 502; Strawberry Hill, Twickenham; Imber Court, Thames Ditton; 23 Rue Nitot, Paris. *Club:* Carlton.   (*Died 7 Jan. 1919.*)

MICHELHAM, Aimée Geraldine, Baroness; Lady President of the League of Mercy; *d.* of Octavius Bradshaw; *m.* 1st, 1899, 1st Baron Michelham (*d.* 1919); 2nd, 1926, Frederick, *s.* of late Frederick Almy, of Cedarhurst, Long Island, N.Y. Order of Mercy, Legion of Honour, Medaille des Epidemies, 1914 Star, despatches twice. *Address:* 20 Arlington Street, S.W.1; *T.:* Regent 603; The Mansion, Strawberry Hill; *T.:* Richmond 164; 23 Rue Nitot, Paris.   (*Died 1 Jan. 1927.*)

MICHELL, Rev. Francis Rodon; Vicar of Ash, next Sandwich, Canterbury; *b.* Ilfracombe, 6 Aug. 1839; *e. s.* of John Michell, solicitor, and Mary Elizabeth Bryan; *m.* 1866, Adelaide Lachlan, *d.* of Lieutenant Maclean, 67th Regt. Beng. N.I.; four *s.* four *d.* *Educ.:* Penzance Grammar School; St. Augustine's College, Canterbury. Ordained, 1862; sent to Pekin by the S.P.G. as their first ordained missionary, when mission closed in 1864 he went to Shanghai, China, and thence in 1866 to Calcutta; Chaplain on the Bengal Ecclesiastical Establishment, 1867; Archdeacon of Calcutta and Examining Chaplain to the Bishop of Calcutta, 1887; Fellow of the University of Calcutta, 1889; retired from the Service, 1892. *Recreations:* carpentering and bookbinding. *Address:* Ash Vicarage, Canterbury. *Club:* Primrose.   (*Died Aug. 1920.*)

MICHELL, John; I.S.O., 1903; H.M. Con.-Gen., St. Petersburg, 1894-1903; *b.* Cronstadt, 20 Aug. 1836; *s.* of John Michell of Bodmin and Amelia, *d.* of T. Bishop of St. Petersburg; *m.* Louisa, *d.* of R. C. Dangar of St. Neots; three *s.* *Educ.:* abroad. Home, Civil, and Consular Services; clerk in the Admiralty, 1860; Vice-Consul, St. Petersburg, 1866; assisted late Capt. Glascott, R.N., in verifying the Turco-Persian boundary Maps, 1867-69; Consul-General for Northern, North - Eastern, and Central Russia, 1886; Consul-General, 1894; received Jubilee decoration. *Address:* Hotakka, Ayrupää Rly. Station, Wiborg, Finland.   (*Died 11 Sept. 1921.*)

MICHELL, Hon. Sir Lewis Loyd, C.V.O., *cr.* 1910; Kt., *cr.* 1902; J.P.; Director British South Africa Co., Rhodesia Railways, and Mashonaland Railway; Fellow of the Bankers' Institute, South Africa; Fellow Royal Colonial Institute; *b.* Plymouth, 11 Aug. 1842; *s.* of John Michell, solicitor, of Ilfracombe; *m.* 1871, Maria Agnes, *d.* of Edward Philpott, Civil Commissioner, Uiterhage, Cape Colony. *Educ.:* Christ's Hospital. For 30 years with the Standard Bank of S. Africa, latterly as General Manager; was President of the Martial Law Board and Treasurer of Lord Milner's Relief Fund during the Boer War; late Minister without portfolio, Cape Colony; Chairman of De Beers Consolidated Mines; Member of the Legislative Assembly for Cape Town. *Publication:* Life of Cecil Rhodes, 1910. *Address:* Rondebosch, Cape Province.   (*Died 29 Oct. 1928.*)

MICHELSON, Christian; former Prime Minister, Norway; *b.* 1857; admitted to Bar, 1879. Became partner in a Bergen Shipping firm; Chairman of Board of Aldermen, Bergen; returned to Storthing for Bergen, 1891; went back to business and municipal life, 1894; and again returned to Storthing for Bergen, 1903; member of Cabinet under M. Hagerup's Premiership; succeeded M. Hagerup as Prime Minister, 1905; Chief of Provisional Norwegian Government after separation of Union with Sweden, 7 June - 25 Nov. 1905; again Prime Minister to 1907. *Address:* Fjösanger, Norway.
    (*Died 28 June 1925.*)

MICHIE, J. Coutts, A.R.S.A.; artist; *b.* 29 July, 1861; 3rd *s.* of late Henry Michie; *m.* 1909, Mrs. MacCulloch. *Educ.:* Edinburgh, Rome, Paris. Received medal in Paris Salon, 1898; acted on the Executive Committee for Franco-British Exhibition, 1907, and for Rome, 1911; travelled in France, Italy, Spain, Morocco, living in Tangier for several years. *Recreations:* cycling, billiards. *Address:* 184 Queen's Gate, S.W.; *T.:* Kensington 241; Oak Hall, Haslemere. *Clubs:* Arts; University, Aberdeen.
    (*Died 18 Dec. 1919.*)

MICHIE, Robert James, M.A.; leader-writer Bristol Times and Mirror; *b.* Banffshire, 3 Aug. 1856; *m.* 1900, Annie Crawford Smith. *Educ.:* schools in Scotland and Newcastle-on-Tyne; University of Aberdeen (Honours in Philosophy and Classics). Entered journalism, 1881; on sub-editorial staffs successively of Reading Mercury till 1890 and Birmingham Daily Gazette till 1897; editor of Western Morning News, Western Weekly News, and Naval and Military Record, 1897-1902. *Recreation:* gardening. *Address:* Times and Mirror Office, Bristol.
    (*Died 31 Dec. 1928.*)

MICHOLLS, E. Montefiore, M.A.; Barrister-at-law; *b.* 27 July 1852; *s.* of late Horatio L. Micholls; *m.* Ada, *d.* of late Maurice Beddington, J.P.; two *s.* two *d.* *Educ.:* Rugby; New College, Oxford. Called to Bar, 1877; Chairman of the Executive Committee of the National Society for Epileptics; Manager of Elementary Schools in the East End of London, and of two Industrial Schools; and on the Committees of other Charitable and Educational Societies. *Recreations:* fishing, shooting, golf. *Address:* 11 Queen's Gate, S.W.7; *T.:* Kensington 747.   (*Died 11 Sept. 1926.*)

MICKS, William Lawson; *b.* 25 Jan. 1851; *s.* of late Sir Robert Micks, sometime Secretary to Board of Inland Revenue, and Ellen, *d.* of James Lawson of Waterford; *m.* Isabel, *d.* of late Rev. Canon Meyrick, Rector of Blesinton, Co. Wicklow; three *s.* one *d.* *Educ.:* Kilkenny College; Trinity College, Dublin. Entered Irish Church Temporalities Commission as Clerk, 1872; Registrar, 1878; Assistant-Secretary Irish Land Commission on its formation, 1881; transferred to temporary post of Comptroller under the Arrears of Rent (Ireland) Act 1882, 1882 ; reverted to former post, 1883 ; a General Inspector under Local Government Board for Ireland, 1885 ; acted as a Commissioner on the County Donegal Light Railway Commission, 1890 ; first Secretary of Congested Districts Board for Ireland, 1891 ; was a Commissioner on the Local Government Board for Ireland, 1898-1910 ; was seconded to act as Chairman of the Viceregal Poor Law Reform Commission for Ireland, 1908, which reported in 1906 ; nominated to be a member of the Viceregal Committee of Inquiry into the Agriculture and Technical Instruction (Ireland) Act 1899, and the administration of that Act, 1906 ; dissented from his colleagues and submitted a Minority Report in 1907 ; hon. member of Congested Districts Board for Ireland, 1909, Permanent Member, 1910 ; retired from the public service on pension, 1924. *Publication :* History of the Congested Districts Board, 1925. *Address :* 3 Palmerston Villas, Palmerston Park, Dublin.   *(Died 4 April 1928.)*

MIDDLEMORE, Sir John Throgmorton, 1st Bt., *cr.* 1919 ; M.P. (L.U.) Birmingham, North, 1899-1918 ; *b.* 9 June 1844 ; *m.* Mary, *d.* of late Rev. Thomas Price, Selly Oak, Birmingham. *Educ.:* for a Surgeon. Founder of the Children's Emigration Homes, Birmingham, and of the Middlemore Home, Halifax, Nova Scotia ; member of Birmingham City Council, 1883-92 ; J.P. Birmingham and Worcestershire. *Heir : s.* William Hawkslow, *b.* 10 April 1908. *Address :* Lark Hill, Worcester.   *(Died 17 Oct. 1925.)*

MIDDLETON, 9th Baron (*cr.* 1711), **Digby Wentworth Bayard Willoughby,** Bt. ; *cr.* 1677 ; D.L., J.P. ; Alderman E. R. Yorks C. C. ; Conservative ; President Buckrose Conservative Association ; Chairman, 1911, Advisory Council on Light Horse Breeding to Board of Agriculture ; late M.F.H. Lord Middleton's Hunt, E. R. Yorks ; *b.* 24 Aug. 1844 ; *s.* of 8th Baron and Julia, *o. d.* of Alexander Bosville, Thorpe and Gunthwaite, Yorkshire ; *S.* father 1877 ; *m.* 1869, Eliza, *o. d.* of Sir Alexander Penrose Gordon-Cumming, 3rd Bt. *Educ.:* Eton. Scots Guards, 1864 ; Lieut. and Capt. 1867 ; retired, 1869 ; late Hon. Col. E. R. Yorkshire Volunteer Artillery. Owns about 99,600 acres. Possesses minerals in Notts. *Recreations:* farming, forestry, and sport. *Heir : b.* Hon. Godfrey E. P. Willoughby. *Address :* Wollaton Hall (built by John of Padua), Nottingham ; Birdsall House, and Settrington House, York ; Middleton Hall, Tamworth ; Applecross, R.S.O., Ross-shire *Clubs :* Carlton, Junior Carlton.
    (Died 28 May 1922.)

MIDDLETON, 10th Baron (*cr.* 1711), **(Godfrey) Ernest (Percival) Willoughby,** Bt., *cr.* 1677 ; *b.* 18 June 1847 ; *s.* of 8th Baron and Julia, *o. d.* of Alexander Bosville, Thorpe and Gunthwaite, Yorkshire ; *S.* brother, 1922 ; *m.* 1881, Ida Eleanora Constance (*d.* 1924), *d.* of G. W. H. Ross ; two *s.* four *d. Educ.:* Eton. Formerly Captain 9th Lancers ; owns about 99,600 acres ; possesses minerals in Notts. *Heir : e. s.* Major Hon. Michael Guy Percival Willoughby. *Address :* Wollaton Hall (built by John of Padua), Nottingham ; Birdsall House, and Settrington House, York ; Middleton Hall, Tamworth ; Applecross, R.S.O., Ross-shire. The Green, Brompton, R.S.O., Yorkshire. *Clubs :* Army and Navy ; Yorkshire, York.
    (Died 11 Nov. 1924.)

MIDDLETON, Reginald Empson, M.Inst.C.E., M.Inst.Mech.E., F.S.I., F.R. Sanit.Inst., F.R.M.S. ; late Joint Engineer to the Staines Reservoirs Joint Committee, Engineer of Higham Ferrers and Rushden Water Board, Huntingdon, Welwyn, etc. ; *b.* 30 May 1844 ; *s.* of Rev. Joseph Empson Middleton, Vice-Principal of St. Bees College and Vicar of Belton, Leicestershire ; *m.* E. A., *d.* of Henry

White of Silverdale, Sydenham, S.E. ; four *s.* two *d. Educ.:* St. Bees Grammar School, Cumberland ; Charterhouse. Articled to Robert Stephenson & Co., Newcastle-on-Tyne ; engaged in the locomotive department of Whitehaven, Cleator, and Egremont Railway, and of the Great Eastern Railway, afterwards on the Moldo-Wallachian bridges ; Resident Engineer Solway Junction Railway and Cadiz Waterworks, etc. ; District Engineer Honduras Interoceanic Railway ; engaged on Southport and Ventnor Piers, Whitby and Redcar Railway ; engineer in charge of survey department, Forth Bridge Works ; Consulting Engineer for Waterworks at Dauntsey, Honiton, Stoney Stanton, Wymington, Glamorgan County Council, etc., and for several sanitation works ; assistant commissioner to Royal Commission on London Water Supply, 1891-93 ; Joint Engineer for New River Water Company's Bill, 1896 ; Highland Water Power Bill, 1899 ; Charing Cross, Hammersmith, and District Railway Bills, 1901, 1902, etc. ; Chief Engineering Witness for London Water Companies before the Royal Commission on London Water Supply, 1898-1899 ; has appeared for and advised the Metropolitan Water Companies and a large number of water companies, corporations, and councils ; was engaged for some of the London Waterworks Companies in connection with the arbitration for purchase. *Publications :* pamphlets on triangulation at the Forth Bridge ; London (Welsh) Water Supply ; Village Water Supplies ; The Pollution of Water and its Correction ; Pollution of Rivers ; the Relative Value of Percolation Gauges ; The Desirability of making Watershed Areas and Sanitary Districts Coterminous ; a Treatise on Surveying (part author), 4th Edition 1920. *Recreations :* rowing ; Tyne Amateur Rowing Club, Kingston Rowing Club ; Tyne Grand Challenge Cup, Clydesdale Cup ; Steward's Plate, Durham ; Plate, York ; Garland Challenge Cup and Championship, Tyne. *Address :* 90 Kensington Park Road, W.11.
    (Died 1 July 1925.)

MIFFLIN, Lloyd ; Litt.D. ; *b.* Columbia-on-the-Susquehanna, Pennsylvania, 15 Sept. 1846 ; *s.* of J. Houston Mifflin, portrait painter and author of vol. of lyrics. *Educ.:* Washington Classical Institute ; private tutors ; studied in Europe, 1871-73. In early life devoted himself to landscape painting ; a pupil of Moran, N.A., and of Herzog, Germany ; health failing, gave up art, retired to country and devoted himself to literature, especially to the sonnet, of which he has written more than five hundred. *Publications :* The Hills, 1896 ; At the Gates of Song, 1897 ; The Slopes of Helicon, and Other Poems, 1898 ; Echoes of Greek Idyls, 1899 ; The Fields of Dawn and Later Sonnets, 1900 ; Castalian Days, 1903 ; The Fleeing Nymph and Other Verse, 1905 ; Collected Sonnets of Lloyd Mifflin, 350, 1905 ; My Lady of Dream, 1906 ; Toward the Uplands, 1908 ; Flower and Thorn, 1909 ; As Twilight Falls, 1916. *Recreations :* painting, riding, driving and the pursuit of literature. *Address :* Norwood, near Columbia, Pennsylvania, U.S.A.   *(Died 16 July 1921.)*

MILBANK, Sir Powlett Charles John, 2nd Bt. ; *cr.* 1882 ; J.P., D.L. ; Lord-Lt. Radnorshire, 1895 ; M.F.H. Radnors and West Herefords since 1902 ; *b.* Edinburgh, 1 May 1852 ; *o. surv. s.* of Sir F. Milbank, Bt. (*d.* 1898), and Lady Milbank, *d.* of Sir Alexander Don, 6th Bt. ; *m.* 1875, Edith Mary, *d.* of Sir Richard Green-Price, 1st Bt. ; one *s.* three *d. Heir : s.* F. R. P. Milbank. *Educ.:* Eton. M.P. (C.) Radnorshire, 1895-1900. *Address :* Barningham Park, Barnard Castle, Yorks ; Norton Manor, Norton, R.S.O., Radnorshire. *T.A.:* Norton, Prestign ; Barningham, Barnard Castle. *Clubs :* Carlton, Bachelors'.   *(Died 30 Jan. 1918.)*

MILBURN, Sir Charles Stamp, 2nd Bart.; *cr.* 1905; *b.* 5 Dec. 1878; *s.* of 1st Bt. and Clara Georgiana, *d.* of late Wm. C. Stamp, Tulse Hill, Surrey; *S.* father 1907. *Educ.*: Christ's College, Cambridge (M.A. 1904). *Heir*: *b.* Leonard John, *b.* 14 Feb. 1884. *Address*: Guyzance, Acklington, and Wardrew House, Gilsland, Northumberland; Milburn House, Newcastle-on-Tyne.   *(Died 16 July 1917.)*

MILBURN, James Booth, Editor of the Tablet since April 1920; *b.* York, 1860; *e. s.* of late W. C. Milburn, York; *m.* 1895, Caroline, *yr. d.* of late W. Moody of the Bank of England, Manchester; one *s.* one *d. Educ.*: St. Cuthbert's College, Ushaw; Master at Ushaw and afterwards at St. Bede's College, Manchester; Assistant Editor of the Tablet, 1895-1920. *Publications*: The Oxford Movement, 1895; A Martyr of Old York, 1902; Joan of Arc, 1905; The Restoration of the Hierarchy, The Rise of the Christian School, 1907; numerous articles in the Dublin Review the Ushaw Magazine and the Tablet. *Address*: The Retreat, Field Lane, London Road, Brentford. *(Died 21 April 1923.)*

MILDMAY, Major Sir Henry Paulet St. John, 6th Bt.; *cr.* 1772; J.P. co. Hants; *b.* 28 Apr. 1853; *e. s.* of 5th Bt. and Hon. Helena Shaw-Lefevre, 2nd *d.* of Viscount Eversley, G.C.B. Late Grenadier Guards; served Egyptian War, 1882 (medal with clasp, Khedive's star); Suakin Expedition, 1885 (despatches, brevet Major, clasp). Owns about 10,900 acres. *Heir*: *b.* Gerald Anthony Shaw-Lefevre St. John-Mildmay [*b.* 30 Oct. 1860; *m.* 1892, Isabel Emily, 2nd *d.* of Rev. C. A. St. John-Mildmay of Hazelgrove; one *s.* one *d. Address*: Dockham House, Coates, Cirencester. *Clubs*: Travellers', Isthmian]. *Address*: Dogmersfield Park, Winchfield, Hants. *(Died 24 April 1916.)*

MILDMAY, Lt.-Col. Herbert Alexander St. John-, M.V.O. 1911; Gentleman-at-Arms; *b.* 1836; *m.* 1884, Susan, *d.* of late Hon. J. Lothrop Motley, U.S. Minister in London. Late Rifle Brigade; served Crimea, 1855 (medal with clasp, Turkish medal); N.W. Frontier India, 1864 (medal). *Address*: 31 Gloucester Street, S.W.1. *T.*: Victoria 5447.   *(Died 21 Oct. 1922.)*

MILES, Colonel Charles Napier, C.B. 1900; M.V.O. 1901; *b.* 9 Apr. 1854; *s. s.* of Col. C. W. Miles of Burtonhill, Malmesbury; *m.* Emily, *d.* of late J. W. G. Spicer, 1880. *Educ.*: Eton. Played against Harrow, 1871-72. Entered 1st Life Guards as Lieut. 1875; Capt. 1882; Major, 1895; served Egyptian Campaign, 1882 (medal and clasp, Khedive's bronze star); commanded Household Cavalry Regt., from July till their return to England, in the South African War, 1900 (despatches; Queen's medal, 3 clasps; C.B.); Lieut.-Col. 1st Life Guards, 1895-1902; retired 1906; High Steward for Malmesbury since 1892; Lord of the Manor of Burtonhill; Patron of one living. *Address*: Ingelburne Manor, Malmesbury; Cardigan. *T.*: 44 Malmesbury. *Clubs*: Arthur's, Pratt's, Carlton, Orleans.   *(Died 25 May 1918.)*

MILES, Lt.-Gen. Sir Herbert (Scott Gould), G.C.B., *cr.* 1914; G.C.M.G., *cr.* 1916; K.C.B., *cr.* 1908; C.B. 1900; G.B.E. 1918; C.V.O. 1903; M.V.O. 1897; *b.* 31 July 1850; *m.* 1877, Alice, C.B.E., *y. d.* of late Joseph Parker of Brettenham Park, Suffolk; two *d. Educ.*: Wellington College; Royal Military College, Sandhurst. Entered army, 1869; Colonel, 1893; A.A.G., Aldershot, 1893-98; Commandant of the Staff College, 1898-99; served South Africa (D.A.G.), 1899-1900 (despatches twice, Queen's medal 6 clasps, C.B.); Commandant, Staff College, Camberley, 1900-3; General Commanding Troops Cape Colony, 1903; Director of Recruiting and Organisation, Headquarters, 1904; Q.M.G. to the Forces, 1908-12; Governor and Commander-in-Chief, Gibraltar, 1913-18; Colonel, Royal Munster

Fusiliers; Governor, Wellington College; Commissioner, Chelsea Hosp.; Grand Officer Legion of Honour; Grand Officer Crown of Italy; Grand Cross of Isabel la Catolica of Spain. *Address*: Satis House, Yoxford, Suffolk. *Clubs*: Army and Navy, Marlborough, Travellers'.   *(Died 6 May 1926.)*

MILES, Lieut.-Gen. Nelson Appleton; late Commanding U.S. Army; *b.* Westminster, Mass., 8 Aug. 1839. Entered army as volunteer, 1861, attaining rank of maj.-gen. of Vols., grade by grade, and at age of 25 commanded an army corps; entered regular army at close of Civil War; rose by regular grades to be lieut.-gen., succeeding to command of U.S. army, 5 October 1895; conducted successfully several campaigns against hostile Indians on Western frontiers, notably against Sitting-Bull, Chief Joseph, and Geronimo; was in command of U.S. troops at Chicago during the riots in 1894; represented U.S. army at seat of Turko-Grecian war, and also at Queen Victoria's Diamond Jubilee, 1897; commanded army during war of 1898 with Spain, and during war in the Philippines; Harvard University conferred degree of LL.D. *Publications*: Personal Recollections, or From New England to the Golden Gate; Military Europe; Serving the Republic; also many magazine articles and military reports. *Address*: Washington, D.C. *(Died 15 May 1925.)*

MILEY, Col. James, C.S.I. 1897; *b.* 22 Oct. 1846; 2nd *s.* of late James Miley; *m.* 1868, Kate, *d.* of William Watson. *Educ.*: private schools, Ireland and France; R.M.C., Sandhurst. Appointed 12th Foot, 1865; Indian Army, 1870; Regiment duty till 1875; Departmental Staff till 1893; Military Accountant-General and ex-officio Dn. Secretary for Finance, Military Department, Government of India, 1893-1902. *Address*: 7 Sloane Street, S.W. *T.*: Victoria 2625. *Clubs*: Naval and Military, Portland. *(Died Feb. 1919.)*

MILFORD HAVEN, 1st Marquess of, *cr.* 1917; **Admiral of the Fleet Louis Alexander Mountbatten**; Earl of Medina, *cr.* 1917; Viscount Alderney, *cr.* 1917; P.C., 1914; G.C.B. (Military); G.C.B. (Civil); G.C.V.O., K.C.B. (Military), K.C.M.G.; Personal A.D.C. to the King; D.L. Isle of Wight; LL.D.; *b.* Gratz (Austria), 24 May 1854; *e. s.* of Prince Alexander of Hesse, and *g.s.* of Louis II., Grand Duke of Hesse; *m.* 1884, his cousin, Princess Victoria, *d.* of Louis IV. Grand Duke of Hesse, K.G., and of Princess Alice, Queen Victoria's daughter, 1884; two *s.* two *d.* Protestant. Was naturalised British subject as Prince Louis of Battenberg, and entered Royal Navy as Naval Cadet, 1868; Sub-Lieut. 1874; Lieut. 1876; Commdr. 1885; Capt. 1891; Commodore, 1902; served in Egyptian War, 1882 (medal and Khedive's star); Director of Naval Intelligence, 1902-5; Rear-Admiral, 1904; Commanding Second Cruiser Squadron, 1905-7; second in Command Mediterranean, 1907-8; Commander-in-Chief Atlantic Fleet, 1908-10; Commanding 3rd and 4th Divisions Home Fleet, 1911; Second Sea-Lord of Admiralty, 1911-12; First Sea-Lord of Admiralty, 1912-14, when he resigned; in 1917 he relinquished at the King's request his German titles, assumed by Royal Licence the surname of Mountbatten, and was created a Peer as above; Rede Lecturer, Cambridge University, 1918; Adm., retired 1919; Adm. of the Fleet, retired 1921; Elder Brother of Trinity House; Fellow Royal Numismatic Society and Royal Geographical Society. *Publication*: Men-of-War Names; British Naval Medals. *Heir*: *s.* Earl of Medina. *Address*: Kent House, East Cowes, I.W. *Clubs*: United Service, Naval and Military, Bachelors', Bath, Athenæum.   *(Died 11 Sept. 1921.)*

MILLAIS, Sir John Everett; 3rd Bt.; *cr.* 1885; *o. s.* of 2nd Bt. and Mary St. Lawrence, *o. d.* of W. E. Hope Vere of Craigie Hall,

Midlothian and Blackwood, Lanarkshire; -b. 28 Nov. 1888; *S.* father 1897. *Educ.*: H.M.S. Britannia. Served in H.M.S. Amethyst, 1914; is a Lieut.-Commander, R.N. (retired); J.P. Kent, 1919. *Heir*: *u.* Geoffrey William [b. 18 Sep. 1863; *m.* 1901, Madeleine Campbell, *d.* of Col. C. H. Grace; one *s.* one *d.*]. *Address*: Leacon Hall, Warehorne, Ashford, Kent. *Clubs*: Junior Naval and Military, Royal Automobile.   (*Died 30 Sept. 1920.*)

MILLAR, A. H., LL.D. (St. Andrews), 1909; F.S.A. Scot., 1882; F.R.S.A., F.L.A.1914; J.P.; Chief Librarian and Curator, Dundee Free Library and Museum, since 1908; *b.* Glasgow, 25 Nov. 1847; *y. s.* of Andrew Millar, manufacturer. and Mary Browning; *m.* 1st, 1872, Margaret (*d.* 1912), *d.* of James Small, manufacturer, Kinross; one *s.*; 2nd, 1919, Margaret, *d.* of David Smart, chemist, Port Glasgow. *Educ.*: St. Peter's School, Glasgow, and privately; studied music at Andersonian University, Glasgow. Highest certificates in Theory and History of Music from John Hullah, and in Original Composition from Sir George A. Macfarren; was Assistant to Colin Brown, Professor of Music, Andersonian Univ., 1869. Began to write art-criticism for Art Journ. 1879; joined staff of Dundee Advertiser, Jan. 1881, as leader-writer, art-critic, and reviewer, also writing historical serials for People's Journal and People's Friend; Literary Editor, 1889-1908, music critic and art critic, 1886-1908, Dundee Advertiser; Editor of Valentine's Shire Series of Illustrated County Histories; President Scottish Library Association, 1912-13, 1913-14, and 1914-15; was on staff of Dictionary of National Biography and has written over 100 articles for it. *Publications*: The History of Rob Roy, 1883; The Castles and Mansions of Ayrshire, 1885; The Black Kalendar of Scotland (first series), 1885; Miniature Series of Historical Works, 1886-92; Quaint Bits of Glasgow, 1887; The Roll of Eminent Burgesses of Dundee, 1513-1887, 1887; The Castles and Mansions of Renfrewshire and Buteshire, 1889; The Glamis Book of Record, 1890; The Historical Castles and Mansions of Scotland, 1890; Fife, Pictorial and Historical: its People, Castles, Mansions, and Burghs; 1895; Contemporary Writers, 1895-97; Bygone Glasgow, 1896; Book of Glasgow Cathedral (with Archbishop Eyre, George Eyre Todd, and others), 1898; Compt-Buik of David Wedderburn of Dundee, 1586-1632; Glasgow in the "Forties," by William Simpson, R.I., edited with biography, 1899; Scottish Burgh Life, 1903; Mary, Queen of Scots, her Life-Story, 1905; Story of Robert the Bruce, 1908; Scottish Forfeited Estates Papers, 1909; The First History of Dundee, 1918; Haunted Dundee, 1923; Glimpses of Old and New Dundee, 1925; James Bowman Lindsay, Pioneer of Wireless Telegraphy, 1926; Gregarach: The Strange Adventure of Rob Roy's Sons, 1926. *Address*: Albert Institute, Dundee.   (*Died 27 Feb. 1927.*)

MILLAR, James Gardner, K.C., 1909; Sheriff of Lanarkshire since 1908; *b.* Glasgow, 1 May 1855; *s.* of John Millar, Merchant, Glasgow, one of the Magistrates of the City; unmarried. *Educ.*: Glasgow High School; Glasgow University (M.A.); Edinburgh University (LL.B.); LL.D. (Glas.). Called to Bar, 1881; Sheriff Court Depute, 1894; Extra Depute on Western Circuit, 1895; acted as interim Sheriff-Substitute in Ayr, Kilmarnock, and during winter of 1904-5 in Glasgow; Legal Secretary to Lord Advocate, 1905; Sheriff-Substitute of the Lothians and Peebles at Edinburgh, 1906-8. *Recreations*: golf and fishing. *Address*: 5 Park Circus, Glasgow. *Clubs*: National Liberal; University, Scottish Liberal, Edinburgh; Western, New, Glasgow.
    (*Died 28 June 1917.*)

MILLER, Vice-Admiral Charles Blois, C.B. 1916; *b.* 22 March 1867; *s.* of Sir

Alexander Edward Miller, C.S.I., K.C., LL.D., of Ballycastle, Co. Antrim, and Elizabeth Furley Miller; *m.* 1919, Ethel Margaret, *widow* of John Stevenson. *Educ.*: Lockers Park, Hemel Hempstead. Entered H.M.S. Britannia, 1880; served in H.M.S. Northumberland during Egyptian Campaign of 1882 (medal, bronze star); Commander, 1903; Captain, 1908; served European War, including Battle of Jutland Bank (C.B.), 1916; retired list, 1924. *Recreations*: general. *Address*: Crowmarsh Battle, Wallingford. *Clubs*: Naval and Military, Naval, Portsmouth.   (*Died 14 July 1926.*)

MILLER, Sir Denison Samuel King, K.C.M.G., *cr.* 1920; J.P.; Governor, Commonwealth Bank of Australia since 1912; *b.* Fairy Meadow, near Wollongong, New South Wales, 8 Mar. 1860; *s.* of the late Samuel King Miller, Headmaster Demliquin Public School, New South Wales; *m.* Laura Constance, *e. d.* of late Doctor John Theophilus Heeley; four *s.* two *d.* *Educ.*: Demliquin Public School; joined Bank of New South Wales, 1876; rose to position of Accountant in the Head Office; General Managers' Inspector, 1907; Metropolitan Inspector, 1909; one of the founders and of the Institute of Bankers of New South Wales, and till quite recently its Honorary Treasurer; is Chairman of the Executive of the Hospital Saturday Fund, and Life Governor of the Sydney Hospital, and Royal Alexandra Hospital for Children, Sydney; takes an active part in all patriotic and charitable organisations. *Recreation*: golf. *Address*: Cliffbrook, Coogee, New South Wales. *T.*: Commonwealth Bank, Sydney. *T.*: Randwick 205. *M.*: 2086. *Club*: Australian, Royal Sydney Yacht, Australian Golf, Sydney.   (*Died 6 June 1923.*)

MILLER, Fred, M.A.; Managing Editor Daily Telegraph since 1923; *e. surv. s.* of late Dr. James W. Miller, Dundee; *b.* Dundee, June 1863; *m.* 1887, Jane Cairns, *e. d.* of James Johnston, drysalter, Dundee; one *s.* three *d.* *Educ.*: Dundee Institution; Royal High School, Edinburgh; Edinburgh University. Joined staff of Daily Telegraph in 1883; Chief Sub-Editor, 1895-1900; Assistant Editor, 1910-23. *Address*: 102 Dartmouth Road, N.W.2. *T.*: Willesden 1557.   (*Died 5 Nov. 1924.*)

MILLER, George, I.S.O., 1903; J.P.; *b.* Sydney, 19 Dec. 1842; *s.* of George Miller, formerly a Deputy Assistant Commissary-General, who settled in the Colony in 1836, and was afterwards Managing Trustee of the Savings Bank of N.S.W.; unmarried. *Educ.*: St. Philip's Grammar School, Sydney; Upton Park Academy, Slough, Bucks; Brighton College. Clerk, N.S.W. Civil Service, 1860; was for 2 years Private Secretary to the Hon. Charles Cowper, when Premier and Chief Secretary; and for 1 year Private Secretary to the Hon. William Forster, when Chief Secretary; resigned, 1865, to engage in squatting pursuits in Queensland; appointed to Education Department, N.S.W., 1867, of which he was Chief Clerk for 15 years and Acting Under Secretary for two periods of 18 months and 10 months respectively; was appointed Comptroller General of Prisons, 1890; Under Secretary of Justice, 1896; Under Secretary combined departments of Attorney-General and of Justice, 1901-5; retired from service, 1905. *Decorated* for faithful service. *Recreations*: cycling, sculling. *Clubs*: Australian, Union, Sydney.

MILLER, Henry, C.I.E. 1917; *b.* 1859; *s.* of late William Charles Miller, Liverpool; *m.* 1892, Frances Margaret Adams; late Member of Council, Assam. *Address*: Halton, Adelaide Road, Walton-on-Thames. (*Died 11 April 1927.*)

MILLER, Hon. Sir Henry John, Kt., *cr.* 1901; Speaker of the Legislative Council, New Zealand, 1892-1903; Member since 1903; *b.* 9 Sep. 1830; 2nd *s.* of Rev. Sir Thomas

Combe Miller, 6th Bt., and *heir-pres.* to 8th Bt. ; *m.* 1864, Jessie, *d.* of John Orbell, of Hawkesbury, Waikonati, N.Z. ; five *s.* one *d.* *Address:* Legislative Council, Wellington, N.Z. ; Fernbrook, Oamaru, Otago, N.Z.
(Died 9 Feb. 1918.)

MILLER, Sir John Alexander, 3rd Bt., *cr.* 1874 ; D.S.O. 1900 ; D.L. ; *b.* 27 Sep. 1867 ; *s.* of 1st Bt. and Mary Anne, *d.* of late J. F. Leith ; *S.* brother 1906 ; *m.* 1st, 1889, Inez (who divorced him 1901), *e. d.* of late Capt. W. M. Innes ; 2nd, 1901, Ada Mary (whom he divorced 1906), *o. c.* of Francis H. Paget ; 3rd, 1907, Eveline Francis, *e. d.* of J. P. Cookson, C.B. *Heir:* none. *Address:* Manderston, Duns, Berwickshire. *(Died 16 Feb. 1918.)*

MILLER, Sir Leslie Creery, Kt., *cr.* 1914 ; C.B.E. 1919 ; Chief Judge in Mysore, 1914-22 ; *b.* 28 June 1862 ; *s.* of late Sir Alexander Edward Miller, K.C., C.S.I. ; *m.* 1886, Margaret Julia, O.B.E., *d.* of Robert Lowry ; no *c. Educ.:* Charterhouse and Trinity College, Dublin. Entered Indian Civil Service, 1881 ; served Madras as Assistant Collector and Magistrate ; Manager Pittapur estate, 1891-92 ; Principal Assistant and District Magistrate, 1895 ; Collector and Magistrate, 1899 ; District and Sessions Judge, 1900 ; Judge High Court of Madras, 1906-14. *Address:* Glen Morgan Estate, Pykara P.O., Nilgiri Hills. *Club:* East India United Service. *(Died 17 Feb. 1925.)*

MILLER, Philip Homan, A.R.H.A. 1890 ; paints portraits and figure subjects and contributes to leading illustrated papers ; *b.* Londonderry ; *s.* of Rev. J. H. Miller, headmaster, Foyle College, and Margaret Irwin ; *m.* Sophia, *d.* of Rev. J. P. Holmes, Corbeg, King's Co. *Educ.:* under brother, Prof. Dr. T. Miller ; Queen's College, Belfast ; Royal College of Surgeons, Dublin. Studied architecture and painting, and entered R.A. schools, gaining 1st prize figure-drawing from life ; began exhibiting R.A. 1879 ; some 40 drawings of noted members in White's Club are his work ; he suggested the club for Irish artists in London, and is hon. sec. *Recreation:* gardening. *Address:* 1 Campden Hill Road, W. ; Moyleen, Great Marlow.
(Died 23 Dec. 1928.)

MILLER, Willet G., M.A., LL.D., F.R.S.C., F.G.S. ; Provincial Geologist of Ontario since 1902 ; *b.* of Canadian parents in the Province of Ontario; not married. *Educ.:* Port Rowan High School ; University of Toronto. Fellow, 1890-1893, and Examiner in Mineralogy and Geology, 1893-95 ; assistant in field geology, Geological Survey of Canada, in the region north of Lake Huron, 1891-93 ; Lecturer, and later Professor, in Geology in Queen's University, Kingston, Canada, 1893-1902 ; in charge of field work in geology in Eastern Ontario for the Bureau of Mines, 1897-1901 ; has been a post-graduate student at the American Universities, Chicago and Harvard, and at the at Heidelberg, Germany ; LL.D., hon., Queen's University, Kingston, 1907 ; and University of Toronto, 1913 ; President Canadian Mining Institute, 1908-1910 ; Life member Geological Society of America, Geological Society of London, British Association for Advancement of Science, Canadian Mining Institute, American Institute of Mining Engineers, and Hon. Member and Gold Medallist, 1914, of the Institution of Mining and Metallurgy ; Member Washington Academy of Sciences ; Society of Economic Geologists ; American Association for Advancement of Science ; Member Royal Ontario Nickel Commission, 1915-17 ; Canada's Representative on Imperial Mineral Resources Bureau, 1918-19, 1922. *Publications:* writings chiefly on the Pre-Cambrian and Economic Geology of Ontario ; Papers and Reports on Corundum-bearing Rocks, Iron Ores. Gold Deposits, Cobalt-Silver Ores, etc., in Annual Reports of Ontario Bureau of Mines, American

Geologist, Journal of Geology, Canadian Mining Institute, etc., etc. *Recreations:* canoeing and exploring. *Address:* Department of Mines, Toronto. *Clubs:* National, Victoria. Rosedale Golf. Toronto. *(Died Feb. 1925.)*

MILLER, Rev. William, C.I.E. 1884 ; M.A., LL.D., D.D. ; Kaiser-i-Hind Gold Medal, 1907 ; Principal of Madras Christian College, Madras, 1863-1908 ; Hon. Principal since 1908 ; *b.* Thurso, 13 Jan. 1838 ; unmarried. *Educ.:* Bellevue Academy, Marischal College, Aberdeen ; New College, Edinburgh. Member of the Legislative Council of Madras, 1893-97, and 1899-1902 ; Moderator of the Assembly of Free Church of Scotland, 1896-97 ; Vice-Chancellor of the University of Madras, 1901-4. *Publications:* Our Scandinavian Forefathers, 1862 ; The Plan of History, 1863 ; The Greatest of the Judges, 1878 ; The Least of All Lands, 1888 ; Criticisms on several of Shakespeare's Plays ; and many addresses and lectures. *Address:* Burgo Park, Bridge of Allan. Scotland.
(Died 15 July 1923.)

MILLER, Major William Arch., D.S.O. 1916 ; M.C., M.B. ; R.A.M.C. ; S.R. ; *s.* of late Rev. Rob. Miller, M.A., F.E.I.S. *Educ.:* George Watson's College, and University, Edinburgh. Served European War, 1914-17 (D.S.O., M.C. and bar, despatches). *Address:* Anneville, 9 Canaan Lane, Edinburgh. *Club:* United Sport.
(Died 1925.)

MILLEVOYE, Lucien, Député de Paris 16e arrondissement (quartier de l'Etoile) depuis 1898 (nationale Libérale); s'est signalé à la Chambre par de nombreux et importants discours sur la politique extérieure, sur les veaux arts et sur les questions sociales ; *b.* Grenoble, 1 Aug. 1850 ; petit-fils du poète Charles Millevoye, l'auteur célèbre de l'Anniversaire, et de la Chute des feuilles ; fils d'Alfred Millevoye, ancien premier président de la cour d'appel de Lyon ; *m.* A été magistrat à Lyon ; il donna sa démission, refusant d'exécuter les décrets de 1880 contre la liberté religieux ; ami du général Boulanger, il fit une ardente campagne politique de 1888 à 1890 ; député d'Amiens de 1889 à 1893 ; prépara par une longue série de conférences l'alliance franco-russe ; redacteur à La Patrie depuis 1896. *Recreations:* Escrime à la épée et au pistolet, a eu de nombreux duels. Les plus connus sont eux contre Goldmann, correspondant de la Gazette de Francfort ; Berteaux, ancien ministre de la guerre ; Comte de Noailles, son dernier concurrent ; grand amateur de musique ; s'occupe beaucoup de questions artistiques, a présenté un rapport très remarqué sur l'opéra. *Address:* 16 rue Spontini, Paris. *(Died 25 Mar. 1918.)*

MILLS, Hon. Algernon Henry; managing partner Glyn, Mills, Currie & Co. ; 2nd *s.* of 1st Lord Hillingdon ; *b.* 13 Feb. 1856 ; *m.* 1880, Lady Mary Frances Seymour (d. 1895), *o. d.* of 4th Earl of Portarlington ; one *s.* Director Sun Insurance Office, Central London Railway Coy. and Great Western Railway. *Address:* Wood Norton, Evesham. *(Died 21 Oct. 1922.)*

MILLS, Charles A., A.R.H.A. *Address:* 55 Millmount Avenue, Drumcondra, Ireland.

MILLS, Hon. Charles Houghton; M.L.C. ; retired ; *b.* Nelson, New Zealand, 1844 ; *s.* of late Richard Mills of Portsmouth ; *m.* Margaret, *d.* of John Morison of Nelson ; two *s.* four *d. Educ.:* public schools, Nelson and Wellington, in which was pupil-teacher for four years. Subsequently engaged in mercantile pursuits ; holds master mariner's certificate ; member of House of Representatives for Waimea, Picton, district of Marlborough, 1890 ; Waimea, Sounds, 1893 ; Wairau since 1896 ; Chairman of Public Petitions Committee ; Government Whip, 1893-1900 ; member of the Seddon Ministry, 1900-6 ; Member of Hall-

Jones Government until the Ward Ministry was formed, when he retired ; called to Legislative Council, 1909. *Address:* Leitrim Street, Blenheim, New Zealand. *T.:* 2443.

(Died 3 April 1923.)

MILLS, Prof. Edmund James, D.Sc. Lond. ; Hon. LL.D. Glasgow ; F.R.S. 1874 ; F.I.C.; Emeritus Professor of Technical Chemistry at Glasgow Royal Technical Coll.; *b.* London, 8 Dec. 1840; *s.* of Charles F. and Mary Anne Mills; *m.* Amelia, *d.* of late William Burnett, London. *Educ.:* Cheltenham Grammar School ; Royal School of Mines. Assistant to the late Dr. John Stenhouse, F.R.S., 1861 ; Chemical Tutor at Glasgow University, 1862-65 ; appointed Professor of Technical Chemistry, Glasgow, 1875. *Publications:* many original memoirs and essays on Chemistry ; amongst them — Destructive Distillation, 1877 (4th ed.); Fuel and its Applications 1889 : also My Only Child (poems), 1895 ; The Secret of Petrarch, 1904. *Address:* 64 Twyford Avenue, West Acton, W.3 *Club:* Athenæum.

(Died 21 April 1921.)

MILLS, Capt. Hon. Geoffrey (Edward), R.N.V.R. ; Naval Provost Marshal, London ; *b.* 15 March 1875 ; *y. s.* of 1st Baron Hillingdon ; *m.* 1st, 1901, Grace Victoria (whom he divorced 1914), *d.* of late Hon. Hungerford T. Boddam, Judge of the High Court, Madras ; two *s.* ; 2nd, 1917, Hilda Susan Ellen, *y. d.* of Sir Daniel Cooper, 2nd Bt., and widow of late Viscount Northland. Late Lieut. West Kent Imperial Yeomanry. *Address:* 28 Welbeck Street, W.1. *Club:* White's. *(Died 14 Aug. 1917.)*

MILLS, Brig.-Gen. George Arthur, C.B. 1900 ; *b.* 28 March 1855 ; *s.* of Captain George Longley Mills, Bombay Army ; *m.* 1885, Helen Henrietta, *d.* of John Garland Baker, of Mahagastotte, Ceylon ; one *d. Educ.:* Clifton College. Gazetted to Royal Madras Fusiliers (102nd), 1873 ; A.D.C. to General Officer Commanding Ceylon, 1879-1882 ; Captain, 1880 ; Egyptian Army and served in Egypt, 1885-87 ; Major 1st Royal Dublin Fusiliers, 1888 ; Lieut.-Col., 1898 ; Lieut.-Col. commanding 1st Bn. Royal Dublin Fusiliers till 1902 ; served with 1st Bn. during South African War, 1899-1902 ; severely wounded (left hand and arm disabled) at the battle of Alleman's Nek, 1900 (despatches four times); Commanded No. XI. District, 1906-10 ; retired 1910 ; Commanding 7th Reserve Brigade, 1914 ; Combatant Member Travelling Medical Board to 20 Jan. 1917 ; landed in France, 17 Oct. 1917 ; Area Commandant Vraignes ; Mar. 1918, O.C. Corps Troops, Cavalry Corps ; Apr. 1918, Special Service 4th Army, B.E.F., France ; Headquarters 4th Army Staff, B. Branch, 1912-1919 (despatches, War and Victory medals); served in Gibraltar, Ceylon, Egypt (medal and Khedive's Star), India, Baluchistan, and South Africa, 1899-1902 (despatches 4 times, Queen's medal 5 clasps, King's medal 2 clasps, C.B.). *Recreations:* racing (India), pig-sticking (won Guzerat pig-sticking cup in 1897), shooting (big and small game), fishing, hunting, polo, etc. *Address:* Bridge House, Padworth, Reading. *Club:* Junior Naval and Military.

(Died 19 Sept. 1927.)

MILLS, Harry Woosnam; Director, Times of Ceylon Co., Ltd. ; London Representative, Times of Ceylon ; *b.* 1873 ; *m.* 1901, Kathleen (*d.* 1923), *y. d.* of George Nagington, Comberley Hall, Staffs; three *s.* one *d.* In Colombo since 1901, previously 2 yrs. in Paris ; 3 yrs. in India on Civil and Military Gazette. *Publications:* The Pathan Revolt in North-West India ; The Tirah Campaign ; Ceylon : A Traveller's Paradise. *Address:* Firgrove House, West End, Southampton. *Clubs:* Sports ; Colombo.*(Died Mar. 1925.)*

MILLS, Colonel Herbert James, C.B. 1887 ; retired ; *b.* 13 Aug. 1836 ; *s.* of late John Mills and Louisa Hubbard ; *m.* 1st, Elizabeth

Ann (*d.* 1874), *d.* of Robert Jolly of Woolwich ; 2nd, Alice E. G., *widow* of H. J. Money. *Educ.:* private tuition. Served in Canada, 1869-74 ; with Egyptian Expedition, 1882-84 (despatches, medal, bronze star, 3rd class Medjidie) ; Soudan, as Senior Ordnance Officer, 1884 (despatches twice) ; assistant to Director of Artillery at War Office, 1886-91 ; Senior Ordnance Officer for Southern District, 1891-94. *Decorated:* for Egyptian Campaign. *Recreations:* music, athletics. *Address:* 17 Clifton Gardens, Maida Vale, W.9. *(Died 2 May 1927.)*

MILLS, James, M.A., LL.D. ; *b.* Co. of Simcoe, Province of Ontario, of Irish parentage, 24 Nov. 1840 ; *m.* 1869, Jessie Ross of Cobourg, Ontario ; one *s.* five *d. Educ.:* public schools of Ontario ; Bradford Grammar School, Simcoe County ; Victoria University, Cobourg. B.A. (Prince of Wales's Gold Medal for highest School Proficiency), 1868 ; M.A. 1871 ; LL.D. (Hon.) 1892; after graduation taught an Academy in the Province of Quebec for one year ; taught the Latin and Greek Classics in the Cobourg Collegiate Institute for three years ; went to Brantford, Ontario, as headmaster of High School, 1873 ; President Ontario Agricultural College, Guelph, 1879-1904 ; organised the Farmers' Institutes of Ontario, and took charge of them for ten years ; organised and controlled the provincial Travelling Dairies; was Director of the three Dairy Schools of the Province ; and as Chairman of Board of Directors of the Fruit Experiment Stations of Ontario assisted in testing the suitability or non-suitability of different varieties of fruit to the varying conditions of soil and climate throughout the Province ; Member of the Board of Regents of Victoria University for 20 years, and of the Senate of the University of Toronto for 16 years ; Member of the Board of Railway Commissioners for Canada, 1904-1914 ; Librarian and Supervising Officer for the Commission, 1914. *Publication:* First Principles of Agriculture. *Address:* Railway Commission Offices, Ottawa, Canada. *Clubs:* Country, Ottawa. *(Died Dec. 1924.)*

MILLS, Joseph Trueman, J.P., D.L. for Leicestershire ; High Sheriff in 1880 ; J.P. for Beds, Bucks, Herts, and Norfolk ; Director of Weymouth and Portland Railway, Union Assurance Society, and New River Co. ; *b.* 15 Jan. 1836 ; 2nd *s.* of J. Remington Mills, J.P., of Tolmers, Herts, and L. Matilda, *d.* of Jos. Trueman of Walthamstow; *m.* 1858, Eliza Anna, 4th *d.* of James Layton, J.P., Baldock, Herts ; one *s.* three *d. Educ.:* privately. *Recreations:* hunting and shooting. *Address:* Stockgrove, Leighton-Buzzard. *Club:* City. *(Died 17 Jan. 1924.)*

MILLS, Lawrence Heyworth, D.D. N.Y. ; Hon. M.A. Oxon. ; Professor Zend Philology, Oxford, since 1898 ; *b.* N.Y., 1837 ; *s.* of late P. L. Mills and Elizabeth Caroline Kane; *m.* Maria Bowen, *d.* of Robert Paige Swann of Leesburg, Virginia ; three *s.* one *d. Educ.:* New York University ; Theological Seminary, Fairfax, co. Virginia. Came to Oxford, 1887, on the invitation of Professor M. Müller, and has been since resident there. *Publications:* Sacred Books of the East, vol. xxxi., 18b:, translated into Gujrati by Palanji Madan, Bombay ; Gâthas, with Zend, Pahlavi, Sanskrit, and Persian texts, comm. etc., Leipzig, 1892-1894 ; article Nineteenth Century Rev., Zor. and Bible, transl. into Gujrati and Italian ; 2nd ed. Gâthas, verb. and metrical, 1900 ; 3rd vol. Gâthas, Dict., 1st issue, 1902 ; art. Zeitschrift Germ. Or. Soc., vol. xlii., also 1895-1910 ; Asiatic Quart. Rev., etc. ; Zarathushtra, Philo, the Achæmenids, and Israel, vol. i. 1904, vol. ii. 1906 ; Daniel and Revelations compared with Avesta, Univ. Lectures, 1907 ; Yasna I. with Avesta, Sanskrit, Pahlavi, and Persian texts, first three translated with full original Sanskrit equivalents of the Avesta, 1910; printing of Dictionary, third vol. Gāthas, recommenced 1910; suspended for the editing and translating of the Pahl. commentaries in Z.D.M.G., and J.R.A.S.; Our Own Religion in Ancient Persia, 1913, Univ. Lect.; Dictionary of Gāthas, completing them, pp. 1196, subventioned by Secretary of State for India in Council 1914; Lore of Av. in Catechetical Dialogues, published by Trustees of the Sir J. J. Transl. Fund of Bombay, 1916; The Creed of Zarathushtra, a treatise written for the Zoroastrian Association of Bombay, 1916; The Fundamental and Dominant Presence of Zoroastrian Thought in the Jewish Exilic, Christian and Muhammad Religions, and in the Greek and Gnostic Philosophies with their Modern Successors, 1917; The Vital Necessity of the Persian Theology to all Biblical Study; The Great Utility of Avesta Study to that of the Veda. *Recreations:* advanced research; formerly fencing, and small boat yachting on open sea. *Address:* 218 Iffley Road, Oxford. *T.A.:* Prof. Mills, Oxford.

MILLS, Rev. William, M.A.; Rector of Bennington since 1881; Hon. Canon of St. Albans, 1912. *Educ.:* Trinity College, Dublin. Deacon, 1875; Priest, 1876; Curate of Coleshill, 1875-76; Upton, 1876-79; L. Marlow, 1879-81. *Address:* Bennington Rectory, Stevenage.
(Died 6 April 1922.)

MILLS, Rt. Rev. William Lennox, D.D., LL.D., D.C.L; Bishop of Ontario since 1901; b. Woodstock, Ontario; s. of William Mills; m. Katharine Sophia, d. of late Stanley Clark Bagge of Montreal; one s. *Educ.:* Woodstock Grammar School; Huron Coll. Lond.; Graduate of the Western University, London, 1872; B.D. and D.D. of the Univ. of Trinity College, Toronto, in course 1884-94, D.C.L. (Honoris Causa); LL.D. Queen's University, Kingston (Honoris Causa); D.D. Bishop's Coll., Lennoxville (ad eundem). Ordained Deacon, 1872; Priest, 1873; Incumbent of Trinity Church, Norwich, Ontario, 1872; Rector of St. Thomas' Church, Seaforth, Ontario, 1874; Rector of the Crown Rectory of St. John's, Province of Quebec, 1875; Rector of Trinity Church, Montreal, 1882; Examining Chaplain to the Bishop of Montreal, and Lecturer in Ecclesiastical History in the Montreal Diocesan Theological College, 1883; Canon of Christ Church Cathedral, Montreal, 1884; Archdeacon of St. Andrew's, Diocese of Montreal, 1896; Bishop Coadjutor of Ontario, with title of Bishop of Kingston, 1900. *Address:* Bishop's Court, Kingston, Ontario, Canada. *(Died 4 May 1917.)*

MILLSPAUGH, Rt. Rev. Frank Rosebrook, D.D.; Bishop of Kansas since 1895; b. Nichols, N.Y., 12 April 1848; s. of Cornelius Madden Millspaugh and Elvira Rosebrook; m. e. d. of Rt. Rev. R. H. Clarkson, Bishop of Nebraska; one s. two d. *Educ.:* Faribault, Minn.; Shattuck Hall; Seabury Divinity School. Lay Reader at seventeen; Deacon, 1873; Priest, 1874; Missionary with seven stations, Minnesota, 1873-6; Dean of Trinity Cathedral, Omaha, 1876-86; President Standing Committee; Delegate General Convention; Rector St. Paul's, Minneapolis, Minn., 1886-94; Dean Grace Cathedral, Topeka, Kansas, 1894-1895. *Recreation:* fishing. *Address:* Bishop's House, Topeka, Kansas. *Club:* Country, Topeka. *(Died Nov. 1916.)*

MILMAN, Sir Francis John, 4th Bt., cr. 1800; Lieut. R.A., retired 1870; b. 10 Aug. 1842; S. father 1885; m. Katharine, d. of Stephen C. Moore, D.L., J.P., Barne, Clonmel, 1870; six s. one d. *Educ.:* Woolwich. Entered R.A. 1864; Hon. Maj. and Adj. 2nd Brig. Welsh Division R.A., 1879-87. *Heir:* s. Francis [b. 27 Oct. 1872; m. 1898, Georgina Maude Emma, o. c. of late Thomas Ripon Wallis].
(Died 2 June 1922.)

MILNE, Alan Hay, B.A. Cantab.; C.M.G. 1911; late (retired 1917) Secretary of the Liverpool Chamber of Commerce, the Liverpool School of Tropical Medicine, the Liverpool Merchants' Mobile Hospital (Incorporated), the Union of Tobacco Manufacturers of Great Britain and Ireland; Mersey Committee for Export of Coal to France and Italy; P.M.G.'s Telephone Advisory Committee for Liverpool; b. 1869; y. s. of late Very Rev. A. J. Milne, LL.D., of Fyvie, Moderator of the General Assembly of the Church of Scotland; unmarried. *Educ.:* Fettes College, Edinburgh; Pembroke College (Scholar), Cambridge. *Publications:* Ulysses or de Rougemont of Troy; The Life of Sir Alfred Lewis Jones. *Address:* c/o Bank of Liverpool. *(Died 21 Jan. 1919.)*

MILNE-HOME, David William, J.P. D.L., Berwickshire; Hon. Col. South-East of Scotland R.F.A., Member of Berwickshire County Council, and of Berwickshire County Association (Territorial); Major Special Reserve of Officers; employed with the R.G.A. since Oct. 1914; b. 30 April 1873; s. of late Colonel David Milne-Home, Royal Horse Guards, and Jane, 3rd d. of Sir Thos. Buchan-Hepburn, 3rd Bart.; m. 1904, Margaret Florence, o. c. of late Captain Arthur Pole, 13th Hussars, and Mrs. Pole, 7 Tedworth Square, S.W.; three d. *Educ.:* privately. Served in the South-East of Scotland Artillery from 1894 till the regiment was disbanded, 1909; as A.D.C. and Private Secretary to Sir Hubert E. H. Jerningham, K.C.M.G., Governor of Trinidad and Tobago, 1897-1900; succeeded to entailed estates of Wedderburn, Paxton, and Billie on death of his father, 1901. *Recreations:* shooting, fishing, gardening, forestry. *Address:* Paxton House, Berwick-on-Tweed; Caldra, Duns; Grange, Reston; Wedderburn Castle, Duns. *T.A.:* Home, Paxton. *M.:* SH 144. *Clubs:* Carlton, Bath; New, Edinburgh.
(Died 27 July 1918.)

MILNER, 1st Viscount, cr. 1902; **Sir Alfred Milner;** Baron, cr. 1901; K.G., 1921; G.C.B. 1901; K.C.B. 1895; G.C.M.G. 1897; Hon. D.C.L. Oxon and LL.D. Cambridge; s. of Charles Milner, M.D., and Mary, d. of Major-Gen. Ready, Governor of Isle of Man; b. 23 Mar. 1854; m. 1921, Violet Georgina, d. of late Admiral Frederick Augustus Maxse, and widow of Lord Edward Cecil, of Great Wigsell, Bodiam, Sussex. *Educ.:* Germany; King's College, London; Balliol College, Oxford; (M.A.); 1st class Classical; Fellow of New College, Oxford. Barr. Inner Temple, 1881; mainly engaged in journalism (Pall Mall Gazette, etc.), 1882-85; contested Harrow Division, 1885; Private Secretary to Mr. Goschen (Chancellor of the Exchequer), 1887-89; Under-Secretary for Finance in Egypt, 1889-92; Chairman Board of Inland Revenue, 1892-97; Governor of the Cape of Good Hope, 1897-1901; Governor of Transvaal and Orange River Colony 1901-5, and High Commissioner for South Africa, 1897-1905; Member of War Cabinet (Minister without portfolio), 1916-18; Secretary of State for War, 1918-19; Secretary of State for the Colonies, 1919-21. *Publications:* England in Egypt, 1892; The Nation and the Empire, 1913; Questions of the Hour, 1923. *Heir:* none. *Address:* 14 Manchester Square, W.1; *T.:* Langham 1488; Sturry Court, near Canterbury. *Clubs:* Athenæum, Brooks's, New University.
(Died 13 May 1925.)

MILNER, Brig.-Gen. George Francis, C.M.G. 1918; D.S.O. 1902; 5th Lancers; Brigade Commander Lowland Mounted Brigade, 1913-1914; Inspector of Cavalry since 1914, and commanding 1st Reserve Cavalry Brigade; b. 10 July 1862; s. of Henry B. W. Milner, 2nd s. of Sir W. Milner, 4th Bt., and Charlotte, d. of Rt. Rev. Marcus Beresford, Archbishop of Armagh; m. 1910, Phyllis Mary, d. of E. Lycett

Green of Ken Hill, King's Lynn; two *s.*
Educ.: Eton. Joined 17th Lancers, 1883; promoted into 1st Life Guards, 1898; commanded 5th Lancers, 1909; served South African War, 1900-1902, as Brigade-Major to Gen. Broadwood; also in command of 12th Imperial Yeomanry with rank of Lieut.-Colonel (despatches, Queen's medal five clasps, King's medal two clasps, D.S.O.); European War, 1914-18 (C.M.G., despatches twice); has the Crown of Prussia, 2nd class. *Clubs:* Turf, Bachelors'.
(Died 20 June 1921.)

MILNER, James Donald, F.S.A.; Director, Keeper, and Secretary National Portrait Gallery since 1916; b. 20 Nov. 1874; *e. s.* of late James Milner; *m.* 1902, Lily Bruton; one *s.* two *d.* Entered National Portrait Gallery, 1893; Clerk, 1895; Acting Assistant Keeper, 1896. *Publications:* Catalogue of Portraits of Botanists in the Museums of the Royal Botanic Gardens, 1906; contributions to the Second Supplement of the Dictionary of National Biography. *Address:* National Portrait Gallery, St. Martin's Place, W.C.2.
(Died 15 Aug. 1927.)

MILNER-BARRY, E. L., M.A.; Professor of German and Teutonic Philology in the University College of North Wales; Lieut. R.N.V.R., employed as Naval Intelligence Officer and Interpreter; *s.* of late Rev. E. Milner-Barry, Vicar of Scothorne, Lincoln; *m. o. d.* of Dr. W. H. Besant, F.R.S. *Educ.*: Universities of Kiel and Berlin; Caius College, Cambridge (Scholar); First-Class Medieval and Modern Languages Tripos, 1889. Assistant and Housemaster at Mill Hill School, 1891-1907; for many years an active member of the Modern Language Association, Vice-Chairman of Committee, 1907-10; examiner in German to the Univ. of London, 1897-1903; in the Univ. of Cambridge, 1898-99, 1911-12; in the University Oxford, 1914-15; in the University of Leeds, 1914-16; occasional examiner for the Civil Service Commission, etc., etc. *Publications:* Editions of Scheffel's Trompeter von Säkkingen; Hackländer's Geheimer Agent; contributor to the Morning Post, the Guardian, etc. *Recreations:* golf, travel. *Address:* Plas Lodwic, Bangor, North Wales.
(Died 7 May 1917.)

MILNER-WHITE, Sir Henry, Kt., *cr.* 1918; M.A.; LL.D.; J.P.; b. 19 Dec. 1854; *y. s.* of late Robert White, Egypt House, Cowes; *m.* 1st, 1883, Kathleen Lucy (d. 1890) *y. d.* of Charles Meeres, M.R.C.S., Sandown, I.W.; 2nd, 1894, Annie Booth (Nita), widow of W. Hubert Hall, and *o. c.* of late Robert Teasdale, J.P., Darlington; two *s. Educ.*: Pembroke College, Cambridge. Barr. Inner Temple, 1886; Chairman Eastleigh Petty Sessional Division; President of Board of Trade Inquiry, 1921, on foundering of B.I. SS. Huntspill; Treasurer of University College, Southampton, and Representative of University of Cambridge, on the Council; Member of County of Hampshire and the Isle of Wight Territorial Force Association since its formation, 1908; Chairman and Managing Director of Edwin Jones & Co., Ltd., Southampton; Member of Board of Finance and other Diocesan Committees; Member of the House of Laity, National Assembly; was General Lay Secretary Church Congress at Southampton, 1913; President for three years Southampton Chamber of Commerce; Delegate to Chicago Exhibition, 1893; Life Governor, Vice-President, Trustee, and Member of Committee of Management, Royal South Hants and Southampton Hospital; Chairman Executive Committee Red Cross Hospitals, Highfield, Southampton, throughout the War, 1914-19; Chairman Southampton Record Society. *Recreation:* travel. *Address:* The Deepdene, Southampton. *Club:* Carlton.
(Died 16 April 1922.)

MILNES, Alfred, M.A., D.Lit. (London); b. Bolton, 16 Apr. 1849; 2nd *s.* of late Benjamin Milnes; *m.* Helena Emily, *d.* of late C. J. A. Goldberg, West Malling, Kent, 1876; four *d. Educ.*: private school; Lincoln College, Oxford; University of Lond. Formerly Rector's Scholar of Lincoln Coll. Oxford. Head Master Imperial Naval School, Tokio, Japan, 1876-78; Assistant Clerk to Senate of University of London, 1878-97; Clerk, 1897-1901; External Registrar, 1901-15; University Extension Staff Lecturer on Economics and Political Science; Hon. Member of the Cobden Club. *Publications:* Elementary Notions of Logic; Problems and Exercises in Political Economy; From Gild to Factory; Economic Foundations of Reconstruction; Economics for To-day; Economics of Fairy Lore; editor of Johnson's Select Works, editor of Butler's Hudibras. *Address:* 44 Goldhurst Terrace, South Hampstead, N.W.6. *T.:* Hampstead 4660. *Clubs:* National Liberal, Lond. Univ.*(Died 1 Nov. 1921.)*

MILROY, Hugh, of Chapel; I.S.O. 1902; S.S.C.; b. Galloway, 1840. *Educ.*: Galloway; Edin. Univ. Joined the Civil Service, 1862; admitted a Solicitor before the Supreme Courts, 1866; appointed a Commissioner of Supply for Kirkcudbrightshire, 1895; J.P. 1899; late Chief Clerk, Crown Office, Edinburgh. *Recreations:* shooting, fishing, and golf. *Address:* West Grove, West Ferry Road, and Crown Office, Edinburgh.
(Died Oct. 1919.)

MILVAIN, Sir Thomas, Kt. *cr.* 1913; C.B. 1912; LL.M.; Judge Advocate General since 1905; K.C.; b. 4 May 1844; 5th *s.* of late Henry Milvain, of North Elswick Hall, and Jane Aitken, *e. d.* of Edward Davidson; *m.* Mary, 3rd *d.* of John Henderson, Durham; one *s.* one *d. Educ.*: Durham School: Trinity Hall, Cambridge. M.P. (C.) Durham City, 1885-86, 1886-92, when defeated; contested Cockermouth Division of Cumberland, 1895; Maidstone, 1901; Chancellor of the County Palatine of Durham and Sadberg, 1892; Recorder of Bradford 1892-1905; M.P. (C.), Hampstead, 1902-5. *Recreations:* shooting, fishing, golf. *Address:* Eglingham Hall, Alnwick; 3 Plowden Buildings, Temple, E.C. *Clubs:* Carlton, New, University.
(Died 23 Sept. 1916.)

MINCHIN, Maj.-Gen. Frederick Falkiner, C.B. 1917; retired; b. 17 Mar. 1860; *m.* 1st, 1887, Marjorie (d. 1904), *d.* of late Gen. H. D. Abbott, C.B.; two *s.* one *d.*; 2nd, 1905, Caroline, *d.* of John Lloyd of Astwick Manor, Herts; two *s.* one *d.* Entered R.A. 1879; Capt. 1887; Major, 1897; Lt.-Col. 1904; Col. 1911; Inspector Ordnance Dept. 1896-1903; Chief Inspector, 1903-7; Member Ordnance Board, 1908-11; Director of Ordnance Inspection, India, 1911-15; served Burma, 1889 (medal with clasp); Military Adviser, Ministry of Munitions, 1915. *Recreations:* fishing and shooting. *Address:* Annagh Coolbawn, Borrisokane, Co. Tipperary. *T.A.:* Annagh, Coolbawn, Ireland.
(Died 11 July 1922.)

MINCHIN, Col. William Cyril, C.B. 1917; b. 1856; *s.* of Major James White Minchin; *m.* 1st, E., *d.* of James Broughton Ballard, of Glenbrook, Co. Cork; 2nd, Beryl, *w.* of Henry Harker; no *c.* Joined 77th Regiment, 1875; A.P.D. 1884; served in the Nile Expedition, 1898. *Address:* Trinity Gardens, Folkestone. *Club:* Junior United Service.
(Died 9 Mar. 1924.)

MINNS, Capt. Allan Noel, D.S.O. 1916; M.C.; R.A.M.C.; L.M.S.S.A. London; b. Thetford, Norfolk, 23 March 1891; *s.* of Dr. Allan G. Minns; unmarried. *Educ.*: Guy's Hospital. Served European War, Mesopotamia, 1915-17 (despatches, D.S.O., M.C.); at present serving in Mesopotamia attached 1st Rifle Brigade, 18th Division, Baizi. *Address:* Alexandra House, Thetford.
(Died 6 April 1921.)

MIRBEAU, Octave ; *b.* Treviers, Calvados, 16 Feb. 1850; *Educ.:* Jesuites' du College du Vannes. *Publications:* Les Lettres de ma Chaumiere; Contes de ma Chaumiere; Le Calvaire; L'Abbé Jules; Sebastian Roch; Le Jardin des Supplices; Le Journal d'une Femme de Chambre; Les Vingt-et-un Jours d'un Neurasthénique; Farces et Moralités; La 628 E. 8; Dingo. Plays: Les mauvais Bergers; Les Affaires sont les Affaires; Le Foyer; L'Epidemie; La Porte feuille; Vieux menage; Scrupules. *Address:* Château de Cheverchemont, Eriel s/Seine, Seine-et-Oise. *T.:* 22.

(Died 16 Feb. 1917.)

MIREHOUSE, William Edward, Barrister-at-Law; Recorder of the Borough of Wenlock since 1889; Revising Barrister since 1888; *b.* 29 Oct. 1844; *y. s.* of Rev. William Squire Mirehouse, Hambrook Grove, county of Gloucester, and Rector of Colsterworth, county of Lincoln; *m.* 1904, Ethel, *o. d.* of the late Horace Shearly of Billinghurst, Sussex; two *d.* *Educ.:* Harrow; Clare College, Cambridge. B.A. 1867; M.A. 1870; Barr. Lincoln's Inn, 1870; member of Oxford Circuit. *Recreations:* played in Harrow cricket eleven, 1863; played in Harrow football eleven, 1862; present recreations, hunting and shooting. *Address:* Hambrook Grove, near Bristol; 4 Pump Court, Temple, E.C. *Club:* New University.

(Died 17 June 1925.)

MITCHELL, Right Rev. Anthony, D.D.; Bishop of Aberdeen and Orkney since 1912; *b.* Aberdeen, 24 Oct. 1868; *s.* of John Mitchell; *m.* 1893, Elizabeth, *d.* of Leslie Valentine, Inverurie; one *s.* one *d.* *Educ.:* Grammar School, Aberdeen; King's College; Aberdeen University; Jenkins prize for Classical Philology, 1889; Black prize, and Seafield Gold Medal for Latin, 1890; Blackwell Essay, 1893; M.A. (1st Class Honours in Classics) 1890; B.D. (Honours) 1903; Caius College, Cambridge; Edinburgh University; Episcopal Theol. College, 1890; Jamieson Bursary, Urquhart Greek Prize, and Luscombe scholarship. Ordained, 1892; Curate of St. Mary's Cathedral, Edinburgh, with charge of Church of Good Shepherd, Murrayfield, 1892; Hebrew Lecturer, Edinburgh Theological College; Curate, St. John's, Dumfries, 1893; Rector, St. Andrew's, Glasgow, 1895; Diocesan Missioner of Glasgow and Galloway, 1902; Rector of St. Mark's, Portobello, 1904; Principal, and Pantonian Professor of Theology, Theological College of the Episcopal Church in Scotland, 1905; Canon of St. Mary's Cathedral, Edinburgh, 1905, and Chancellor, 1912; Examining Chaplain to Bishop of Edinburgh. *Publications:* Verse—Tatters from a Student's Gown, 1890; History of the Episcopal Church in Scotland, 1907; Story of the Church in Scotland, 1908; Biographical Studies in Scottish Church History, 1914. *Address:* Bishops Court, Aberdeen. *T.:* 1545.

(Died 17 Jan. 1917.)

MITCHELL, Major Charles Johnstone, D.S.O. 1917; Oxfords. and Bucks L.I. R. of O.; *b.* 20 Sep. 1879; 2nd *s.* of Col. H. L. Mitchell, R.A., 28 Cornwall Gardens, S.W., and Mary Arabella Susan, *e. d.* of C. D. Reynolds of Ramslade, Bracknell; *m.* 1906, Maud Elsie, *y. d.* of Charles Arthur Galton, I.C.S.; one *s.* Served European War, 1914-17 (D.S.O.) *Address:* 28 Cornwall Gardens, S.W. *Club:* Army and Navy. *(Died 16 Oct. 1918.)*

MITCHELL, Edmund, novelist; *b.* Glasgow, 1861; *m.* 1886; four *s.* one *d.* *Educ.:* Elgin Academy; Aberdeen University (M.A. and gold medallist for English Literature). Followed the profession of journalism in India, Australia, and America, and has travelled widely as a special correspondent. Senior Lieut. Bombay Vol. Artillery, 1888-89. *Publications:* The Temple of Death, 1894; Towards the Eternal Snows, 1896; Chickabiddy

Stories, 1899; Plotters of Paris, 1900; The Lone Star Rush, 1901; Only a Nigger, 1901; The Belforts of Culben, 1902; The Despoilers, 1904; In Desert Keeping, 1905; Tales of Destiny, 1913. *Dramatic Work:* The Telephone, 1901. *Recreations:* chess and reading. *Address:* 1815 North Normandie Avenue, Los Angeles, California. *(Died 31 Mar. 1917.)*

MITCHELL, J. Campbell, R.S.A. 1919; *b.* Campbeltown, Argyllshire, 1865. *Educ.:* Grammar School, Campbeltown. Paints landscape and seascape; represented in the New Pinakothek, Munich, by A Scottish Moorland; in Corporation Art Gallery, Aberdeen, by Aberlady; and in Walker Art Gallery, Liverpool, by Springtime, Midlothian; in Public Gallery, Auckland, New Zealand, by On the Kintyre Coast; and in the Smith Institute, Stirling, by The Haunt of the Curlew. *Address:* Duncree, Corstorphine, Midlothian. *T.:* Corstorphine 65. *M.:* SG 3022. *Club:* Scottish Arts, Edinburgh. *(Died 16 Feb. 1922.)*

MITCHELL, John, J.P. for County of the City of Dundee; F.J.I.; editor Dundee Courier since 1887; *b.* Perth, 16 April 1860; three *s.* one *d.* *Educ.:* St. Leonard's School, Perth; Glasgow University. Telegraphist in Dundee Post Office; joined Scotsman reporting staff, 1882; President of Institute of Journalists, 1910-11; Temporary Major Dundee Volunteer Regiment. *Recreations:* riding, cycling, bowling, curling. *Address:* 4 Prospect Place, Dundee. *T.:* Dundee 1858. *M.:* TI 3962. *Clubs:* Eastern, New, Dundee; King James VI., Perth. *(Died 7 Nov. 1923.)*

MITCHELL, John Ames, editor of Life; *b.* New York, 17 Jan. 1845; *m.* 1885. *Educ.:* Harvard Scientific School, 1864; studied architecture in Paris, 1867-70. Practised as architect in Boston until 1876, but gradually drifted into artistic and decorative work, illustrating books, etc., and went to Paris again for study and remained four years; during that time produced several etchings, receiving an honourable mention at the Paris Exposition; studied drawing and painting in Julian's atelier, and with Albert Maignan; went to New York, 1880; started Life, 1883, and has edited that journal since its first issue. Finds recreation in literature and motoring; and in summer on his estate at Ridgefield, Conn. *Publications:* Croquis de l'Exposition, 1879, a series of etchings; The Summer School of Philosophy at Mount Desert, 1881; The Romance of the Moon, 1886; The Last American, 1889; Life's Fairy Tales, 1893; Amos Judd, 1895; That First Affair, 1896; Gloria Victis, 1897; The Pines of Lory, 1901; The Villa Claudia, 1904; The Silent War, 1906; Dr. Thorne's Idea, 1910; Pandora's Box, 1911; Drowsy, 1917. *Address:* 17 West Thirty-First Street, New York. *T.:* 3680 Madison Square.

(Died 29 June 1918.)

MITCHELL, Sir Thomas, Kt., *cr.* 1906; C.V.O. 1906; *b.* Belfast, 1844; *m. d.* of late Thomas Goble, Worthing. *Educ.:* H.M. Dockyard, Chatham. Draughtsman, Chatham Dockyard, 1871; at Admiralty three years; foreman of Portsmouth Dockyard during building of Trafalgar; Admiralty overseer, Palmer's Shipyard, Jarrow, 1889-91, where he superintended the building of the Resolution and Revenge; Constructor, Hong-Kong Dockyard, 1891-95; Senior Constructor, Devonport Dockyard, 1895-99; Chief Constructor, Bermuda, 1899-1902; Sheerness, 1902-3; next at Chatham; manager of Constructive Department, Portsmouth, during building of Dreadnought (thanks of Admiralty) and Bellerophon (*cr.* Kt.); retired 1907. *Address:* 37 Salisbury Road, Craneswater Park, Southsea. *(Died 1 April 1919.)*

MITCHELL, Col. Thomas, C.B. 1902; Magistrate County Surrey; Hon. Colonel 5th Vol. Batt. East Lancs Regiment; *b.* 1839; *s.* of John Mitchell, Fearnes Hall, Lancashire;

m. 1881, Margaret, *d.* of John Lord, J.P., of Bacup, Lancashire, and Mooswald Place, Dumfries; one *s.* one *d. Educ.:* Preston Grammar School; afterwards private tutor. Joined the 4th Lancashire Rifles, 1859. *Recreations:* athletics, hunting, shooting, travelling. *Address:* Wimbledon Lodge, Eaton Gardens, Hove, Sussex. *Clubs:* Junior Carlton, Constitutional.   (*Died 2 June 1921.*)

MITCHELL-THOMSON, Sir Mitchell, 1st Bt., *cr.* 1900; J.P. Peeblesshire; D.L., J.P., Edinburgh; Knight of Grace of the Order of St. John of Jerusalem; F.R.S.E., F.S.S.A.; Lord Provost of Edinburgh, 1897-1900; *b.* 1846; *y. s.* of late Andrew Thomson of Seafield, Alloa, and Janet, *e. d.* of William Mitchell, Alloa; *m.* 1st, 1876, Eliza (*d.* 1877), *e. d.* of late William Lowson of Balthayock, Perthshire; 2nd, 1880, Eliza Cook, *y. d.* of late Robert Cook, shipowner, Leith; one *s.* two *d. Educ.:* Alloa and Edinburgh. Member Royal Company of Archers; Director of the Bank of Scotland, the Scottish Widows' Fund, and Caledonian Railway. *Heir: s.* William. *Address:* Inglismaldie, Laurencekirk, Kincardineshire. *T.:* Central 306, Edinburgh. *Clubs:* Carlton, Junior Carlton, Constitutional.
     (*Died 15 Nov. 1918.*)

MITCHINSON, Rt. Rev. John, D.C.L., D.D., Master of Pembroke College, Oxford, and Canon of Gloucester since 1899; Assistant Bishop of Peterborough, 1881-1914; of Gloucester, 1904-5; Hon. Fellow of St. Chad's, Denstone, and of St. Andrew, Taunton; *b.* Durham, 23 Sept. 1833; *o. s.* of John Mitchinson; unmarried. *Educ.:* Durham School; Pem. Coll. Oxford (Scholar). 1st class (Classics) Moderations, 1853; 1st class Lit. Hum. and 1st class Nat. Sc. Oxford, 1854-55. Fellow of Pem. Coll. Oxford; President of the Union; Assistant Master in Merchant Taylors' School, 1858-59; Headmaster of the King's School, Canterbury, 1859-73; Hon. Canon of Canterbury, 1871-99; Select Preacher, Oxford, 1872-1873, 1893-94, 1908-4; Ramsden Preacher, Cambridge, 1883, and Oxford, 1900, 1913; Bishop of Barbados and the Windward Islands, 1878-1881; coadjutor to Bishop of Antigua, 1879-82; Rector of Sibstone, 1881-99; Archdeacon of Leicester, 1886-99; Hon. Fellow of Pembroke College, Oxford, 1882-99. *Address:* Pembroke Coll. Oxford; Cathedral Gardens, Gloucester.
     (*Died 25 Sept. 1918.*)

MITFORD, Major-General Reginald C. W. Reveley; retired list; *b.* Waterloo Manor, Hants, 23 Feb. 1839; *y. s.* of John Mitford, barrister-at-law, and *g. s.* of the historian of Greece; *m.* 1865, Margaret A., *d.* of late H. Moore. *Educ.:* Rugby School. Appointed Ensign in the Indian Army, 1855; served Indian Mutiny (severely wounded, despatches and G.G.O., recommended by Lord Clyde for V.C., 23 Oct. 1858); two N.W. Frontier Expeditions; Afghan War; retired, 1886; has travelled in China, Japan, N. America, civilised Europe, Germany and Austria. *Publications:* To Cabul with the Cavalry Brigade; Orient and Occident; edited Forbes Mitchell's Reminiscences of the Great Mutiny. *Recreations:* sketching, travelling, shooting. *M.:* 6943 I.K. *Clubs:* Wellington, Hurlingham.
     (*Died 21 Aug. 1925.*)

MITFORD, Capt. Robert Osbaldeston-, J.P.; F.R.G.S., F.Z.S.; late 73rd Regt. (2nd Batt. Black Watch); *b.* 25 Nov. 1846; *e. s.* of late Edward Ledwich Osbaldeston Mitford and Janet, *d.* of late Venerable Benjamin Bailey, Archdeacon of Ceylon; *m.* 1875, Annie, 2nd *d.* of late Major-Gen. Charles Stuart Lane; three *s.* five *d. Educ.:* Eton; Sandhurst. *S.* father, 1912. Assumed name of Osbaldeston, 1912. Lord of the Manors of Mitford, Molesdene, Pigdon, etc.; patron of the living. *Heir: s.* Bertram Lane [*b.* 1876; *m.* B. K., *e. d.* of

25

Rev. R. C. MacLeod of MacLeod]. *Address:* Mitford Castle, Northumberland. *T.A.:* Osbaldeston, Mitford. *T.:* Morpeth 52. *M.:* LK 6943 and NL 2165. *Clubs:* Naval and Military, Royal Automobile.
     (*Died 27 Dec. 1924.*)

MITRA, S. M., M.R.A.S.; Hindu author; settled in England since 1905; *b.* 30 Nov. 1856; unmarried. Connected with the Indian press for thirty years—English, Urdu, and Bengali writer; ten years Proprietor and Editor of the Deccan Post; lectured under London University, British Navy League, Central Asian Society, East India Association, etc.; selected by Calcutta Sahitya Parishad in 1901 to revise transliteration of Arabic and Persian words and phrases in vogue in Bengali language; opposed in 1907 anti-British Bengal boycott movement in The Times; often writes in reviews; represented India at the International Free Trade Congress in London, 1908; represented Hindu Medicine at the International Congress of Medicine, London, 1913. *Publications:* (English) Life of Sir John Hall; Position of Women in Indian Life (with H.H. the Maharani of Baroda); Indian Problems, British Rule in India; Anglo-Indian Studies; Peace in India—how to attain it; Moslem-Hindu entente-cordiale; Imperial Preference and India; Hindupore (an Anglo-Indian romance); Voice for Women—without votes; Yoga Mental Culture; revised Anglo-Indian terms in Standard Dictionary; (Urdu) Zibeh ul baqar, (Bengali) Nayati Prabandha, etc. *Recreations:* Hindu psychotherapy and reciting Persian poetry. *Address:* Royal Asiatic Society, 74 Grosvenor Street, W.1.
     (*Died 15 Nov. 1925.*)

MITTAG-LEFFLER, Gösta, Dr.Phil.; Professor of Mathematics, University Stockholm, 1881-1911; Editor of the international mathematical journal Acta Mathematica; possessor of probably the greatest existing library for mathematics; *b.* Stockholm, 16 March 1846; *s.* of Member of Parliament, Rector J. O. Leffler and Gustava Mittag; *m.* 1882, Signe (*d.* 1921), *d.* of General J. af Lindfors, Finland; brother of late authoress Anne-Charlotte Leffler, in her first marriage, Edgren, in her second marriage, Duchessa di Cajanello; brother of the philologist Frits Läffler. Prof. and Mrs. M.-L. have bequeathed by will all their property, including the library and their estate at Djursholm, to an International Mathematical Institution, which has already entered into activity, bearing the name Makarna Mittag-Lefflers matematiska stiftelse; author of a great number of dissertations in higher analysis; Foreign Member Royal Society; Hon. Member Philosophical Society, Cambridge, London Mathematical Society, Royal Institution, Manchester Literary and Philosophical Society, Royal Irish Academy; member of nearly all the learned societies of Europe, including Institute of France, Società Italiana (detta dei XL), Ac. dei Lincei, Ac. St. Petersburg, Göttingen, Belgium, Stockholm, Christiania, Copenhagen, Helsingfors, etc.; Hon. Doctorates from Bologna, Oxford, Cambridge, Christiania, Aberdeen, St. Andrews. *Publications:* Sur la représentation analytique des fonctions monogènes uniformes d'une variable indépendante, 1884; Sur la représentation analytique d'une branche uniforme d'une fonction monogène, 1900-20; Niels Henrik Abel (Revue du mois, 1907). *Recreation:* travelling. *Address:* Djursholm, Sweden. *T.:* Stockholm 755.11; Djursholm 809. (*Died July 1927.*)

MITTON, Rev. Henry Arthur, M.A.; Master of Sherburn House, Durham, 1874-1913; resigned, 1913; *b.* 24 Jan. 1837; *e. s.* of Rev. Canon Mitton, Vicar of St. Paul's, Manningham; *m.* 1861, Annie Eliza (*d.* 1903), *e. d.* of Rev. Theodore Dury, Rector of Westmill, Herts; four *s.* four *d. Educ.:* Bradford school; Christ's College, Cambridge (head of Modern History,

Univ. exam., under Sir James Stephen, 1858);
B.A. 1859. Ordained by Bishop of Ripon, 1860;
Curate sole charge of Heaton, Bradford, 1860-64;
Incumbent of St. Barnabas', Heaton, 1864-68;
selected by the Bishop of Durham from outside
his own diocese to be Vicar of Bishop-Auckland,
1868; broke down from fever and overwork,
1874; appointed by Bishop Baring to Sherburn
House, one of the very few ancient leper foundations (now Brethren and Sisters) remaining in
England. *Publications:* Lectures, in answer to
Dr. Parker, on the Book of Common Prayer;
short account of Christ's Hospital, Sherburn,
etc. *Recreations:* angling, pedestrianism. *Address:* The Rectory, Bowness - on - Solway,
Carlisle. *(Died 1 July 1918.)*

MIVART, Dr. Frederick St. George,
M.D. Louvain, F.R.C.S. Edinburgh; late
Medical Inspector H.M. Local Government
Board; *b.* London; *s.* of Dr. St. George Mivart,
F.R.S.; *m.* 1877, Marie Sophie, *d.* of D.
Maurigy of Brancolar, Nice, France; one *s.*
one *d.* *Educ.:* Beaumont; Catholic College
of Higher Studies, Kensington; St. Mary's
Hospital, London; Louvain University; Royal
Infirmary, Edinburgh; Paris and Vienna. F.Z.S.
Fellow of the Royal Societyof Medicine; Fellow
of the Royal Sanitary Institute; has conducted
scientific and other enquiries on behalf of the
Local Government Board. *Address:* 15 Stafford
Terrace, Kensington, W.8. *T.:* Park 1877.
Club: Reform. *(Died 5 Nov. 1925.)*

MOBERLY, Winifred Horsbrugh,
M.A.; Principal of St. Hilda's College, Oxford;
b. April 1875; *d.* of Col. Charles Morris Moberly,
Indian Staff Corps; unmarried. *Educ.:* Win-
chester and Sydenham High Schools; Lady
Margaret Hall, Oxford (scholar); Bursar at
Lady Margaret Hall, Oxford, 1910-12; Organiser
of Training Schemes for Unemployed Women for
the Central Committee on Women's Employ-
ment, 1914-15; Administrator of the "Millicent
Fawcett Hospitals" in Russia and Galicia,
1915-17; Area Secretary, Y.W.C.A. for the
W.A.A.C. in Calais, 1917-18; Lecturer in
U.S.A. for War Workers' Campaign, Oct. and
Nov. 1918. *Address:* St. Hilda's College,
Oxford. *Club:* University Women's.
(Died 6 April 1928.)

MOCKLER, Col. Percy Rice, C.M.G.
1918; retired pay; J.P. Oxon; *b.* Sep. 1860;
y. s. of late Edward Mockler, of Rockville, Co.
Cork, and Julia, *d.* of J. B. G. Ferryman, of
Leckhampton, Glos.; *m.* 1896, Augusta, *e. d.* of
late Thomas Fielden Campbell, 26 Devonshire
Place, W. *Educ.:* Cheltenham College; R.M.C.,
Sandhurst. Joined 6th Foot (Royal Warwickshire Regt.), 1879; retired, 1906; served Burmah Expedition as a Brigade Transport Officer,
1885-87 (despatches, medal and clasp); re-
employed European War, 1914-18 as a Colonel-
in-charge of Records (despatches, C.M.G.). *Recreations:* football, polo, and racquets, now
gardening. *Address:* Peppard House, Rotherfield Peppard, Oxon. *Club:* Army and Navy.
(Died 6 Mar. 1927.)

MOFFAT, Rev. John Smith, C.M.G., 1890;
retired on pension; *b.* Kuruman, Bechuanaland,
10 Mar. 1835; *s.* of late Rev. Robert Moffat, D.D.,
and Mary, *d.* of late James Smith; *m.* 1858,
Emily, *d.* of late J. S. Unwin, Brighton. *Educ.:*
private school, Newcastle-on-Tyne; Cheshunt
Coll.; New Coll., London. Missionary in
Matabelelard, 1859 - 65; Bechuanaland till
1879; Commissioner on western border of the
Transvaal during British occupation, 1880-81;
Resident Magistrate, Maseru, Basutoland, 1882-
1884; Resident Magistrate, Taungs, Bechwana-
land, 1885-87; Assistant Commissioner in
Bechuanaland Protectorate and Matabeleland,
1887-95; Resident Magistrate, Taungs, 1895-96.
Decorated for special diplomatic services in
Matabeleland. *Publication:* The Lives of Robert
and Mary Moffat. *Recreation:* honorary
738

missionary work. *Address:* Cape Town.
(Died 28 Dec. 1918.)

MOFFATT, Alexander; Sheriff-Substitute
of Stirlingshire at Falkirk since 1904; of
Linlithgowshire since 1917; *b.* 31 Aug. 1863;
s. of Alexander Moffatt, shipowner, Glasgow, and Lilly, *d.* of John Millar of Greenock;
m. 1888, Blanche Helen Isabel (*d.* 1913), *d.* of
Alexander M'Ritchie, supt. engineer P. and O.
Steamship Co., London; one *s.* one *d.* *Educ.:*
Park School, Glasgow; Universities of Glasgow
and Edinburgh; M.A., LL.B., of former.
Advocate at Scottish Bar, 1888; Sheriff-Sub-
stitute of Shetland, 1900-4; contested Paisley
(C.), 1895; volunteer officer, 1880-88, and 1900-5;
Major-Commandant 7th V.B. Gordon High-
landers, 1904. *Publications:* articles on Copy-
right, Salvage, Ports and Harbours, Pilots, and
others in Green's Encyclopædia of Scots Law;
occasional contributions to legal journals.
Recreations: yachting, shooting, walking.
Address: Arnotdale, Falkirk. *T.:* Falkirk 150.
Clubs: Junior Army and Navy; University,
Scottish Conservative, Edinburgh; Stirling
County, Stirling. *(Died 29 Mar. 1921.)*

MOGGRIDGE, Ernest Grant, C.B.
1919; late Assistant Secretary Ministry of
Transport; *b.* 18 June 1863; *s.* of late
Edward Moggridge; unmarried. *Educ.:* privately. Entered Home Civil Service (Class I.),
1886; Secretary's Office, General Post Office;
transferred to Board of Trade, 1892; Secretary
to Royal Commission on Electrical Communication with Lighthouses and Light-vessels, and to
Committee on International Code of Signals;
Private Secretary to Permanent Secretary to
Board of Trade; Assist. Secretary for Marine Department of Board of Trade, 1913-16. *Clubs:*
Union, Windham. *(Died 1 Feb. 1925.)*

MOIR, Byres M.D. Edin.; Consulting
Physician to the London Homœopathic Hospi-
tal and Bromley Cottage Hospital; *b.* 1853; *s.* of
Patrick Moir Byres, of Tonley, Aberdeenshire;
m. Evelyn, *d.* of Col. Collings Bonamy, Guern-
sey; two *s.* one *d.* *Educ.:* Manchester Gram-
mar School; Owens College; Edinburgh Uni-
versity. After qualification studied in Paris;
Surgeon to Orient Line; House Surgeon and
Physician to London Homœopathic Hospital.
Publications: contributions to medical journals.
Address: Weymouth Court, 1 Weymouth Street,
W.1. *T.:* Langham 2334. *(Died 4 July 1925.)*

MOLE, Harold Frederic, F.R.C.S. (Eng.),
L.R.C.P. (Lond.); Surgeon, Bristol Royal
Infirmary; *b.* 1866; *s.* of late Frederic M. Mole
of Edgbaston; *m.* 1913, Harriet, *d.* of late Reuben
Holmes of Heanor, Derbyshire. *Educ.:* Bristol;
St. Bartholomew's Hospital. Late Junior House
Surgeon and Anæsthetist, Junior House Phy-
sician, House Physician and House Surgeon
and Senior Resident Officer, Bristol Royal In-
firmary; Assistant Surgeon and Surgeon-in-
charge of the Aural Department, Bristol
Royal Infirmary. *Publications:* Two cases of
Intubation in Adults; Two cases Ruptured
Tubal Pregnancy; Two cases of Ruptured
Intestine; the Aural Complication of Influenza;
Bristol Medico-Chirurgical Journal. *Address:*
24 College Road, Clifton, Bristol. *T.:* 1349.
Club: Clifton. *(Died 21 Dec. 1917.)*

MOLESWORTH, Sir Guilford Lindsey,
K.C.I.E.; *cr.* 1888; late Consulting Engineer
to the Government of India for State Railways;
retired, 1889; *b.* 3 May 1928; *y. s.* of Rev.
J. E. N. Molesworth, D.D., Vicar of Rochdale;
m. Maria Elizabeth (*d.* 1919), *d.* of J. T.
Bridges, of St. Nicholas Court, Thanet, and
g.d. of Sir Robert Affleck, 5th Bt., 1854;
one *s.* two *d.* *Educ.:* King's School, Canterbury; College of Civil Engineers, Putney.
Served apprenticeship under Sir William Fairbairn, and pupilage under Mr. Dockray, Engineer-in-Chief, London and North-Western
Railway; Chief Assistant Engineer on London,

Brighton, and S. C. Railway; in Arsenal at Woolwich during Crimean War; Mechanical Engineer Ceylon Railway, 1859: subsequently Agent and Chief Engineer; Chief Resident Engineer Ceylon Govt. Railway in 1862; Director-General of Railways to Ceylon Govt. and Director of Public Works in 1867; Consulting Engineer to the Govt. of India, 1871; President of the Institution of Civil Engineers, 1904. Afghan War medal; Burma War medal and clasp; thanks of Government for services performed during the Afghan War in the enemy's country. Property in Swords, near Dublin, 850 acres. *Publications:* Conversion of Wood by Machinery; Pocket-book of Engineering Formulæ; Metrical Tables; Decimal Coinage; Light Railways; Gauge of Railways in India; Land as Property; Imperialism and Free Trade; Text-book of Bi-metallism; The Divorce of Silver and Gold; Political Economy in its Relation to Strikes; Reason and Instinct in Ants; Iron Manufacture in India; Silver and Gold (prize essay); Masonry Dams; Graphic Statics; Our Empire under Protection and Free Trade; Economic and Fiscal Facts and Fallacies; Life of John Edward Nassau Molesworth, D.D.; A Spy of the Huns, etc. *Address:* Manor House, Bexley, Kent. *Clubs:* St. Stephen's, Royal Societies. (*Died 21 Jan. 1925.*)

MOLESWORTH, Mary Louisa, Mrs.; *b.* Holland; *e. d.* of Charles Augustus Stewart, *o. s.* of Maj.-Gen. Stewart, Strath, N.B., and Agnes Janet, *d.* of John Wilson, Transy, Fife; *m.* 1861, Maj. R. Molesworth (*d.* 1900), late Royal Dragoons, *n.* of 7th Viscount Molesworth; one *s.* three *d. Educ.:* home, and partly in Switzerland. Spent several years in France and Germany. *Publications:* early novels—She was Young and He was Old, etc., under name of Ennis Graham; books for the young—Carrots; Cuckoo Clock; Herr Baby; A Charge Fulfilled; Little old Portrait; and many others. Later novels—Hathercourt Rectory; The Red Grange; Neighbours, etc.; Lives of the Saints for Children; Stories for Children in Illustration of the Lord's Prayer, 1897; Meg Langholme, 1897; Miss Mouse and her Boys, 1897; The Laurel Walk, 1898; The Magic Nuts, 1898; The Boys and I; The Old Pincushion; The Grim House, 1899; This and That; The House that Grew; The Wood Pigeons and Mary; Peterkin; The Story of a Year, 1910. *Recreation:* wrote stories as amusement when very young. *Address:* 155 Sloane Street, S.W. (*Died July 1921.*)

MOLINEUX, Rev. Arthur Ellison, Hon. Canon of Canterbury. *Address:* The Vicarage, Minster, Ramsgate. (*Died 22 Dec. 1919.*)

MOLINEUX, Rev. Charles Hurlock, Hon. Canon of Southwell. *Address:* Staveley Rectory, Chesterfield. (*Died 26 Aug. 1927.*)

MOLLISON, James W., C.S.I. 1911. Superintendent of Farms, Bombay, 1890; Deputy Director of Agriculture, 1897; Inspector-General of Agriculture in India, 1901; retired, 1912. (*Died 4 Oct. 1927.*)

MOLLOY, Bernard Charles; *b.* 1842; *s.* of late Kedo Molloy and Maria Teresa Molloy, late of Hawke House, Sunbury. Barr. Middle Temple, 1872; formerly Capt. in French Army; special gold medal Franco-German War; Private Chamberlain Court of the Vatican; M.P. (N.) Birr, King's Co. 1880-1900. *Address:* 5 Paper Buildings, Temple, E.C. *T.:* Holborn 1268. *Club:* Reform. (*Died 26 June 1916.*)

MOLONY, Rev. Henry William Eliott, M.A.; Hon. Canon of St. Albans, 1914. *Educ.:* All Souls College, Oxford; Leeds Clergy School. Ordained, 1882; Curate of St. John's, Hammersmith, 1882-85; St. Saviour, Hoxton, 1885-91; Rural Dean of Barking, 1907-12; Vicar of Great Ilford, 1892-1912; Rector of Stevenage, 1912-18. *Address:* Windsor Road, Parkstone, Dorset. (*Died 23 Aug. 1919.*)

MOLSON, Major John Elsdale, M.D., J.P. West Sussex; M.P. (U.) Gainsborough, 1918-23; *b.* 6 Aug. 1868; *s.* son of late Samuel Elsdale Molson, Montreal, Canada; *m.* Mary, *d.* of A. E. Leeson, M.A., M.D.; three *s*, one *d. Educ.:* Cheltenham College; Emmanuel College, Cambridge. Contested N.E. Bethnal Green, Jan. and Dec. 1910; served in R.A.M.C. (T.) in England and Egypt, Aug. 1914-Dec. 1918. *Recreations:* shooting, motoring and golf. *Address:* Goring Hall, Worthing; 21 St. James' Court, Buckingham Gate, S.W. *T.A.:* Molson, Goring-by-Sea. *T.:* Goring-by-Sea 8; Victoria 2360. *M.:* BP 8141. *Clubs:* Carlton, Oxford and Cambridge. (*Died 28 Nov. 1925.*)

MOLYNEUX, Rev. Sir John Charles; 9th Bt., *cr.* 1730; LL.B.; Vicar of Portesham, Dorchester, Dorset, since 1886; *b.* Ireland, 27 June 1843; *S.* father 1879; *m.* 1st, 1873, Fanny, (*d.* 1893). *d.* of Edward Jackson, Walsoken House, Wisbeach; one *s.* three *d.*; 2nd, 1895, Ada Isabel Hepzibah (*d.* 1925), *d.* of Rev. A. F. Wynter, Rector of Barnardiston, Suffolk. *Educ.:* Bradfield College; Christ College, Cambridge. Ordained 1867. *Heir:* *s.* William Arthur [*b.* 26 July 1877; *m.* 1924, Constance Cochrina Hood, of Invergeldie, Comrie, Perthshire, *d.* of Mrs. Stanley Clay, Rose Hill, Sevenoaks]. *Address:* Portesham Vicarage, Dorchester. (*Died 26 Aug. 1923.*)

MOMBER, Captain Edward Marie Felix, R.E., D.S.O. 1916; Temporary Major, O.C. 176 Tunnelling Company, R.E.; *s.* of Frederick Ernest Momber and Eugénie Ardoin. *Educ.:* Stubbington House; Cheltenham College (head of both Schools); R.M.A. Woolwich. Commissioned R.E., 1907; S.M.E. Chatham, 1909; 11th Field Company R.E., Aldershot, 1912; Capt. Oct. 1914; 25th Fortress Company R.E., Hong Kong; and Adjutant R.E. till beginning of war; Adjt. to Siege Companies R.E., Chatham, Nov.-Dec. 1914; served European War, 1914-16, in France; formed 176 Tunnelling Company R.E., April 1915 (Military Cross, despatches, D.S.O.); Temp. Major, Dec. 1915. *Recreations:* Rugby—For R.M.A., Woolwich, S.M.E. Chatham, Captain Aldershot Command, played for United Services, Portsmouth, also Army, Hampshire County, cap; Rowing—R.E.Y.C., on Medway and at Henley, Captain Hong Kong R.C.; Fencing—represented R.M.A., Woolwich, and won sabres competition, cadet at Olympia in 1907; Gymnastics—colours for R.M.A., Woolwich against Sandhurst, 1907, holder of about 40 cups for swimming, field-sports, and rowing; hunting, and rider in point-to-point. (*Died 20 June 1917.*)

MONACO, Prince of, Albert Honoré Charles; *b.* Paris, 13 Nov. 1848; *S.* father, Prince Charles III. 1889; *m.* 1st, 1869, Lady Mary Douglas-Hamilton (now Countess Tassilo Festetics); 2nd, 1889, Alice *née* Heine, Duchess de Richelieu, *b.* New Orleans, 10 Feb. 1858. Catholic. *Heir:* by 1st marriage, Prince Louis Honore Charles Antoine, *b.* Baden-Baden, 12 July 1870. *Recreation:* oceanographic studies. *Address:* The Palace, Monaco; Château Marchais, par Liesse, Aisne, France; 10 Avenue du Président Wilson, Paris. (*Died 26 June 1922.*)

MONCK, 5th Viscount (*cr.* 1800), Henry Power Charles Stanley Monck; Baron Monck, 1797; of Ballytrammon, Co. Wexford; Baron Monck (U.K.), 1866; J.P., D.L., *b.* Dublin, 8 Jan. 1849; *e. s.* of 4th Viscount and Elizabeth Louise Mary Monck, 4th *d.* of 1st and last Earl of Rathdowne; *S.* father, 1894; *m.* Lady Edith Caroline Sophia Scott, *d.* of 3rd Earl of Clonmell, 1874; one *s.* one *d.*; Church of England; Conservative. *Educ.:* Eton; Christ Church, Oxford (B.A., S.C.L.). Lt. Coldstream Guards, 1871; Captain, retired, 1885; served in Egyptian campaign, 1882; and expedition to Suakin, Feb. to May 1885 (medal with 2 clasps, bronze star). Owns about 14,200 acres in Cos. Wicklow, Kilkenny, Wexford, Westmeath, and city of Dublin. *Recreations:* shooting, cricket, racquets. *Heir: g.s.* H. W. S. Monck. *Address:* Charleville, Enniskerry, Co. Wicklow. *Clubs:* Carlton; Kildare Street, Dublin. (*Died 18 Aug. 1927.*)

MONCKTON, Arthur, M.P., J.P.; *o.* 20 July 1845; 2nd *s.* of late General Henry Monckton and Anne, *o.d.* of John Groome Smythe of Hilton; *m.* 1896, Lady Gertrude Bouverie, *d.* of 4th Earl of Radnor; two *s.* two. *d. Educ.:* Eton; Christ Church, Oxford. After leaving Oxford went to the Royal Agricultural College, Cirencester, and for a few years acted as Land Agent to his brother, Francis Monckton, Stretton Hall, late M.P. for West Staffordshire; resigned after an attack of rheumatic fever. *Recreations:* gardening, magic lantern exhibitions. *Address:* Normanston Hall, Lowestoft. *T.A.:* Lowestoft.
(*Died 2 May 1917.*)

MONCKTON, Edward Philip, barrister; I.T.; Recorder of Northampton since 1890; C.C. King's Cliffe Division, Northamptonshire; *b.* Bareilly, India, 18 July 1840; *e. s.* of E. H. C. Monckton, H.E.I.C.S., and later of Fineshade Abbey, Northamptonshire; *m.* Christabel (*d.* 1899), *d.* of Rev. C. D. Francis, Vicar of Tysoe, Warwickshire, 1866; *seven s.* three *d. Educ.:* private schools; Trin. Coll. Cambridge. M.A., F.S.A.; Barrister - at - Law, Midland Circuit; Lieut.-Col. 3rd Northamptonshire Regt. (retired 1895); member of House of Laymen; High Sheriff of Rutland, 1882-84; M.P. (C.) N. Northampton, 1895-1900; J.P. Northamptonshire. Rutland, Liberty of Peterborough. Chairman of Qr.-S. Liberty of Peterborough. Owns about 3200 acres. *Recreations:* rowing, cricket, hunting, shooting, geology, science. *Address:* Fineshade Abbey, Stamford; Laundimer House, Oundle, Northamptonshire. *Clubs:* Carlton Junior Carlton, Cavendish.
(*Died 1916.*)

MONCKTON, Francis, J.P., D.L. Staffordshire; late Hon. Major Staffordshire Yeomanry Cavalry; *b.* 7 Mar. 1844; *e. s.* of General Henry Monckton; *g.s.* of 1st Viscount Galway; *m.* 1889, Evelyn Mary, *d.* of Algernon Charles Heber-Percy of Hodnet Hall, Co. Salop; one *s.* two *d. Educ.:* Eton; Christ Church, Oxford. M.P. (C.) West Staffordshire, 1871-85; High Sheriff, 1895. *Club:* Carlton.
(*Died 30 Sept. 1926.*)

MONCKTON, Lionel; composer, and musical critic, Daily Telegraph; *b.* 1862; *s.* of late Sir John Monckton; *m.* Gertie Millar. *Educ.:* Charterhouse; Oxford. *Publications:* Songs in Gaiety plays. *Address:* 69 Russell Square, W.C.1. *T.:* Central 9235. *Clubs:* Conservative. Eccentric, Green Room.
(*Died 15 Feb. 1924.*)

MONCREIFF, Hon. James William, W.S., D.L. Kinross-shire; *b.* 16 Sep. 1845; 3rd *s.* of 1st Baron Moncreiff; *m.* 1872, Mary Lillias (*d.* 1910), *e. d.* of late George Mitchell Innes, of Bangour, Linlithgowshire; four *s. Address:* 6 Ainslie Place, Edinburgh. *Clubs:* Brooks's; New, Edinburgh. (*Died 30 Jan. 1920.*)

MONCRIEFF, Alexander Bain, C.M.G. 1909; M.I.C.E.; Member American Society Civil Engineers; C.E.; *b.* Dublin, 22 May 1845; *m.* 1877, Mary Bonson Sunter. *Educ.:* Belfast Academy. Went to South Australia, 1875; Chairman of South Australian Supply and Tender Board, 1895-99; Engineer-in-Chief, South Australia; Engineer for Harbours and Jetties, 1888-1909; President Institute of Surveyors, 1901, and of Public Service Association of South Australia, 1904; Railways Commissioner, 1909-1916; Chairman of the Municipal Tramways Trust, Adelaide; retired, 1922. *Address:* 12 Alexandra Avenue, Rose Park, Adelaide, South Australia. (*Died 11 April 1925.*)

MONCRIEFF, Lieut. - Gen. George Hay, Colonel, The Royal Scots; retired, 1900;

b. 22 Aug. 1836; *s.* of late General George Moncrieff; *m.* 1871, Flora, *sis.* of Sir Archibald Lamb, 3rd Bart. *Educ.:* Leamington College; Sandhurst. Scots Guards, 1854-86; served Crimea, 1855-56 (despatches, medal, medal, Sebastopol) and Turkish medal), V.D.; Assistant Military Sec. headquarters, 1887-90; commanded Curragh Brigade, 1890-91; commanded Dublin District, 1891-95. *Recreation:* golf. *Address:* 38 Thurloe Square, S.W.; Greenside, Sunningdale. *Clubs:* Guards', United Service.
(*Died 15 Oct. 1918.*)

MONCRIEFF, Robert Hope, author and editor; *b.* Edinburgh, 1846. *Educ.:* Edinburgh, and privately in England. Took some steps towards the Scottish Bar, but "penned a stanza," etc., at an early stage, and served a time as a school teacher. *Publications:* The World of To-day, Bonnie Scotland, and some 200 volumes of fiction, history, school-books, guidebooks, etc., under various aliases, chiefly as "Ascott R. Hope." *Club:* Athenæum.
(*Died 10 Aug. 1927.*)

MONET, Claude; *b.* Paris, 14 Nov. 1840. A soldier in Africa for two years; studied under Gleyre; visited England, 1870. *Principal works:* Views of Argenteuil, 1872; Cathedrals, 1874; Views of Vetheuil, 1875; of Pourville and cliffs of Etretat, 1881; of Bordighera, 1886; of the Creuse, 1889; Le Meules, 1891; Cathedrals, 1894; Le Bassin des Nymphéas, 1900. *Address:* Giverny, Vernon, Eure, France.
(*Died 5 Dec. 1926.*)

MONET, Hon. Dominique; Puisne Judge since 1908; President of the Court of King's Bench, Crown Side, since 1920; *b.* 2 Jan. 1865; *m.* 1887, Marie Louise La Haye. *Educ.:* L'Assomption College; Laval University. Advocate, 1889; K.C. 1905; M.P. (L.) Napierville, 1891-96; Laprairie and Napierville, 1896-1904; Napierville, 1904-5; Minister of Public Works, 1095. *Address:* Montreal, Province of Quebec.
(*Died Feb. 1923.*)

MONETA, Ernesto Teodoro; President of the Società Internazionale per la Pace; Unione Lombarda; *b.* Milan, 1833. Received the Nobel Prize, 1907; took part in the Milan uprising, 1848; General Staff Officer in Garibaldi's Army, 1860; Officer in the Italian Army, 1861-67; Director the Secolo, 1867-96; founded the Unione Lombarda, 1888; came under the influence of Hodgson Pratt in 1886, and from that time worked energetically in forming Peace Societies throughout Northern Italy; has attended most of the International Peace Congresses, and was President of the fifteenth, held at Milan, 1906; Member of Carnegie Consultative Council, and Member Emeritus of Institut Int. de la Paix; edits the fortnightly review, La Vita Internazionale, the Almanacco Pro Pace and the Storia delle guerre, delle insurrezioni, e della pace nel secolo XIX. *Address:* 21 Portici Settentrionali, Milan.
(*Died 10 Feb. 1918.*)

MONEY, Col. Charles Gilbert Colvin, C.B. 1898; Colonel, retired; *b.* 7 Sep. 1852; *s.* of Gilbert P. Money, Bengal Civil Service; *m.* Sophie Louisa, *d.* of Alex. Johnston, Bengal Civil Service, 1881. *Educ.:* Harrow. Served in 5th Fusiliers, afterwards called the Northumberland Fusiliers, from 1872; commanded 1st Batt. Northumberland Fusiliers in Soudan campaign, 1898 (despatches, C.B., medals and clasp for Khartoum); occupation of Crete, 1898-99; South Africa, 1899-1901 (despatches, Queen's medal 5 clasps, Brevet Col.); commanded 24th Regimental District, 1902-5; and Colonel in charge of Records, South Midland grouped Regimental District, 1905-7. *Address:* 7 Lypiatt Ter., Cheltenham.
(*Died 29 Feb. 1928.*)

MONEY, Walter, F.S.A.; *b.* The Dene, Donnington, Berks, 21 Aug. 1886; *m.* Charlotte Ann (*d.* 1922), *d.* of Mrs. Gillmore, Herborough

House, Newbury ; one *s.* one *d.* *Educ.:* private school. Local secretary for Berks Soc. Antiq. London, and of British Arch. Association ; Correspondent of the National Trust. Presented site and raised the funds for the erection of the Memorial to Lord Falkland on the battlefield of Newbury ; originator of the Didcot, Newbury, and Southampton, and the Lambourn Valley Railways, the Newbury District Hospital and other local institutions. *Publications:* The History of Newbury ; The History of Hungerford ; The History of Speen—the Roman *Spinæ* ; Church Goods in Berks ; The Two Battles of Newbury, 1643-44 (1st and 2nd ed.) ; The Story of the Siege of Donnington Castle ; The Siege of Basing ; A Royal Purveyance in the Elizabethan Age ; A Popular History of Newbury and the Neighbourhood, 1905 ; many memoirs on historical and archæological subjects. *Address:* Shawdene House, Donnington, Newbury.

(*Died 18 Oct. 1926.*)

MONEY - KYRLE, Ven. Rowland Tracy Ashe, Archdeacon of Hereford since 1923 ; Canon of Hereford since 1925. *Educ.:* New College, Oxford ; Wells Theological College. Curate of Portsea, 1890-95 ; Ross, 1895-98 ; Rector of Ribbesford, 1898-1902 ; Vicar of Kentish Town, 1902-10 ; Rector of Ross, 1910-26. *Address:* Cathedral Close, Hereford.

(*Died 26 Dec. 1928.*)

MONIER-WILLIAMS, Major Craufurd Victor, D.S.O. 1919 ; M.C. ; Assistant-Manager, Owen & Dyson, Ltd., Rother Iron Works, Rotherham ; *b.* Chessington, Surrey, 18 Feb. 1888 ; *s.* of M. F. Monier-Williams, Stoke d'Abernon, Cobham. *Educ.:* Rugby School. Served European War with the Territorial Force, 49th Division, being seconded from his regiment, 5th York and Lancaster to the Signal Service, R.E., France, 1915-18 ; attained rank of Lieut.-Col., Assistant-Director of Signals (D.S.O., M.C., despatches four times). *Address:* Rother Iron Works, Rotherham.

(*Died 14 May 1922.*)

MONIER-WILLIAMS, Monier Faithfull ; Solicitor ; Chairman of the English and Scottish Law Life Association ; Chairman of the British Law Insurance Company ; on the Board of Eagle Star and British Dominions Insurance Company ; and on the Board of the Solicitors' Law Stationers Society, Ltd. ; *b.* 15 April 1849 ; *e.s.* of late Sir Monier Monier-Williams, K.C.I.E., Boden Professor of Sanscrit in the University of Oxford ; *m.* Emma Georgina, *d.* of late Gordon Wyatt Clark, D.L., J.P., of Mickleham Hall, Dorking ; two *s.* one *d.* *Educ.:* Rugby. *Address:* 25 Old Court Mansions, Kensington, W.8 ; Nutlea, Nelson Road, Bognor. *Clubs:* Conservative, City of London, Alpine.

(*Died 13 Nov. 1923.*)

MONOD, Théodore ; retired pastor of the Reformed Church of France ; *s.* of late Frédéric Monod, the founder of l'Union des Eglises Evangéliques de France ; *b.* 1836 ; *m.* ; four *s.* two *d.* *Educ.:* University of Paris. Bachelier ès Sciences ; Licencié ès Lettres ; studied law, 1855-58 ; at New York became a Christian, 1858 ; studied theology in the Presbyterian Seminary, Allegheny City, 1858-60 ; Founder and Pastor of the Second Presbyterian Church of Ste. Anne, Kankakee Co., Illinois, 1860-63 ; Pastor of the Chapelle du Nord, Paris, 1864-75 ; Home Missionary among the French Protestant Churches, 1875-77 ; Pastor of the Reformed Church of Paris, 1877-1906. *Publications:* Regardant à Jésus, 1862 ; De quoi il s'agit, 1875 Le Don de Dieu ; Le Libérateur, Journal mensuel, 1875-79 ; Crucifiés avec Christ ; Jésus Laïque ; Poésies : Loin du Nid, 1882 ; Au Vent la Voile, 1898. *In English:* The Gift of God. Life more abundant (republished together in one volume, The Gift and the Life, 1912) ; Denying self, etc. Several hymns, in French

and in English. Addresses at Mildmay, Keswick, and other meetings. *Address:* 5, rue Renault, à Saint-Maudé (Seine). (*Died 1921.*)

MONRO, Alexander, C.I.E. 1904 ; M.A. ; *b.* 1847 ; *s.* of late Henry Monro ; *m.* 1879, Evelyn Agnes Dingwall. *Educ.:* Sherborne ; Oriel Coll. Oxford (Scholar). Called to Bar, 1872 ; went to India as Inspector of Schools, 1879 ; Fellow of Madras University, 1885 ; Director of Public Instruction, Central Provinces, 1888-1904 ; acting Director of Public Instruction, Madras, 1893-4 ; retired from the Indian Educational Service, 1904 ; Member of Legislative Council, Madras, 1893-94 ; Mayor of Godalming, 1909-10, and 1910-11. *Recreations:* cycling, golf. *Address:* Crawford, Frith Hill, Godalming. (*Died 20 Sept. 1916.*)

MONRO, James, C.B. 1888 ; *b.* 1838 ; *s.* of George Monro, solicitor, Supreme Courts, Edinburgh ; *m.* 1863, Ruth, *d.* of W. Littlejohn, banker, Aberdeen. *Educ.:* High School, Edinburgh ; Universities of Edinburgh and of Berlin. Served Bengal Civil Service, 1857 ; held the offices of Magistrate, Civil and Sessions Judge, Inspector - General of Police, Commissioner Presidency Division, etc. ; Assistant Commissioner Metropolitan Police, 1884 ; Chief Commissioner, 1888 ; resigned, 1890 ; returned to Bengal, and founded the Ranaghat Medical Mission. *Address:* 15 Bolton Road, Chiswick, W.4.

(*Died 28 Jan. 1920.*)

MONTAGU, Rt. Hon. Edwin (Samuel) ; P.C. 1914 ; M.P. (Co.L.) Chesterton (now Camb.) Div., Cambridgeshire, 1906-22 ; a Trustee of the British Museum, 1920 ; *b.* 1879 ; 2nd *s.* of 1st Lord Swaythling ; *m.* 1915, Hon. Venetia Stanley, *d.* of 4th Baron Sheffield: one *d.* *Educ.:* Clifton ; City of London School ; Trinity College, Camb. Parliamentary Secretary to Chancellor of Exchequer, 1906-8 ; to Prime Minister, 1908 - 10 ; Parliamentary Under-Secretary of State, India, 1910-14 ; Chancellor Duchy of Lancaster, 1915 ; Financial Secretary to Treasury, 1914-16 ; Minister of Munitions and Member of War Committee, 1916 ; Secretary of State for India, 1917-22. *Address:* 4 Gordon Place, Bloomsbury, W.C.6. *T.:* Museum 7387. (*Died 15 Nov. 1924.*)

MONTAGU, General Sir Horace Wm., K.C.B. 1905 ; C.B. 1869 ; Senior Col. Commandant Royal Engineers ; *b.* Swaffham, Norfolk, 16 May 1828 ; 3rd *s.* of late Rev. Geo. Montagu, Rector of South Pickenham ; *m.* 1859, Catherine, *d.* of late Gen. Poole Valancey England, R.A. ; three *s.* four *d.* *Educ.:* Shrewsbury. Joined R.E. Corps, 1842 ; landed Crimea and present at battles of Alma and Inkerman and siege of Sevastopol ; taken prisoner 22 March during a sortie, but was exchanged, and returned, 3 Aug., to the siege, six weeks before Sevastopol fell (Crimean medal with three clasps ; Kt. of the Legion of Honour ; Sardinian Order of Merit ; Turkish war medal and 5th class of Medjidie ; Brevets of Major and Lieut.-Col.) ; returned to England 1856, and was subsequently commanding Royal Engineers at Sheerness, Colchester, and at Halifax, Nova Scotia. *Address:* 15 Oxford Road, Colchester.

(*Died 14 Nov. 1916.*)

MONTAGUE, Charles Edward ; author ; *b.* 1 Jan. 1867 ; 3rd *s.* of late Francis Montague, of St. Margaret's, Twickenham ; *m.* 1898, Madeline, *o.* *d.* of C. P. Scott of Manchester ; five *s.* two *d.* *Educ.:* City of London School ; Balliol Coll., Oxford. Is a Director of the Manchester Guardian Limited and a Governor and hon. graduate of the University of Manchester ; served in army in France, Belgium, and Germany, 1915-1919 (despatches thrice) ; Royal Humane Society Bronze Medal for saving life from drowning. *Publications:* A Hind Let Loose, 1910 ; Dramatic Values, 1911 ; The Morning's War, 1913 ; Disenchantment,

1922 ; Fiery Particles, 1923 ; The Right Place, 1924 ; Rough Justice, 1926 ; Right off the Map, 1927 ; A Writer's Notes on His Trade, 1930. *Rec.:* mountaineering. *Address:* Kitt's Quarries, Burford. *Club:* Alpine. (*Died 28 May 1928.*)

MONTEAGLE of Brandon, 2nd Baron (*cr.* 1839), **Thomas Spring Rice**, K.P., D.L. ; *b.* 31 May 1849 ; *s.* of Hon. Stephen Edmond Spring Rice and *d.* of late Mr. Serjeant Frere ; *S.* grandfather, 1866 ; *m.* Elizabeth (*d.* 1908), *d.* of Bishop of Meath (Butcher), 1875 ; one *s. Educ.:* Harrow ; Cambridge. B.A. ; Senior Optime in Mathematics, 1872. *Heir: s.* Hon Thomas A. Spring Rice. *Clubs:* Athenæum ; Kildare Street, Dublin.
(*Died 24 Dec. 1926.*)

MONTEITH, Col. John, C.B. 1906 ; *b.* 24 June 1852 ; 2nd *s.* of Robert Thomson Monteith and Charlotte Eliza Steele ; *m.* Evelyn, *o. d.* of late Hon. H. L. Pepys. *Educ.:* Elizabeth College, Guernsey ; Sandhurst. Entered army, 1872 ; Capt. I.S.C., 1884; Major, 1892 ; Lieut.-Col. Indian Army, 1898 ; Bt. Col. 1902 ; D.A.A.G. 1902-4 ; served Afghan War, 1879-80 (despatches thrice, medal with clasp) ; Soudan Expedition, 1885 (medal with clasp, bronze star) ; Zhob Valley, 1890 ; retired, 1910 ; served as a Commandant on Lines of Communication in France during European War, 1914-17. *Address:* Villa Forster, Dinard, France. (*Died 2 June 1928.*)

MONTGOMERY, Sir Basil Templer Graham-, 5th Bt. ; *cr.* 1801 ; of Stanhope ; D.L. and J.P., Kinross ; *b.* 1 Mar. 1852 ; *s.* of 3rd Bt. and Alice, *d.* of late J. Hope Johnstone; *S. b.* 4th Bt., 1903 ; *m.* 1st, 1880, Mary, *y. d.* of Sir Thomas Moncreiffe, 7th Bt. (marriage dissolved 1905) ; one *s.* one *d.*; 2nd, 1905, Theresa Blanche, *e. d.* of late Colonel Verschoyle, Grenadier Guards. *Educ.:* Trinity College, Glenalmond ; Rugby. Joined the 60th Rifles, 1872 ; served on the staff of General Barton, C.B., in Afghanistan, 1878-79 (medal) ; retired from the army, 1880 ; a Gentleman of the King's Bodyguard for Scotland ; Lt.-Colonel and County Commandant Kinross-shire Volunteers. Owns 6000 acres. *Heir: b.* Rev. Charles Percy Graham-Montgomery, *b.* 1855. *Address:* Kinross House, Kinross, N.B. ; 25 Bruton Street, W.1. *T.:* Mayfair 81. *Club:* Turf. (*Died 4 Oct. 1928.*)

MONTGOMERY, Florence, novelist ; *b.* 1843 ; *d.* of Admiral Sir Alex. Montgomery, 3rd Bt. Began by telling stories to her younger sisters ; was induced to publish by the novelist Whyte Melville. *Publications:* A very Simple Story, 1866 ; Peggy, and other Tales, 1868 ; Misunderstood, 1869 ; Thrown Together, 1872 ; The Children with the Indiarubber Ball, 1872 ; Thwarted, 1873 ; Wild Mike and his Victim, 1874 ; Seaforth, 1878 ; The Blue Veil, 1883 ; Transformed, 1886 ; The Fisherman's Daughter, 1888 ; Colonel Norton, 1895 ; Tony, 1897 ; Prejudged, 1900 ; An Unshared Secret, and other stories, 1903 ; Behind the Scenes in a Schoolroom, 1914. *Address:* 56 Cadogan Place, S.W. (*Died 8 Oct. 1923.*)

MONTGOMERY, Rt. Hon. Hugh de Fellenberg, P.C. Ire. 1924 ; D.L. ; Senator Northern Ireland ; *o. s.* of H. R. S. Montgomery of Blessingbourne and Maria, *y. d.* of Emanuel de Fellenberg, of Hofwyl, Berne, Switzerland ; *m.*; five *s. Educ.:* privately; Christ Church, Oxford. *Address:* Blessingbourne, Fivemiletown. *M.:* JI 1919. *Clubs:* Ulster, Belfast ; University, Dublin.
(*Died 8 Oct. 1924.*)

MONTGOMERY, Walter Basil Graham, O.B.E. ; *o. s.* of Sir Basil Templer Graham-Montgomery ; *b.* 1881 ; *m.* 1912, Fanny (whom he divorced, 1914), *o. c.* of late Theodore M. Zariñl. *Educ.:* Eton ; Trinity Hall, Cambridge. D.L., J.P., County Councillor, Kinross-shire ; Provost of Kinross.

Address: 25 Bruton Street, W.1 ; Kinross House, Kinross. (*Died 23 Mar. 1928.*)

MONTGOMERY, Maj.-Gen. William Edward; *b.* 18 July 1847 ; *m.* 1891, Alberta, *d.* of late Gen. Rt. Hon. Sir Henry Ponsonby, G.C.B. Entered army, 1866 ; Maj.-Gen. 1895 ; Lieut.-Col. 1st Batt. Scots Guards, 1885-94 ; retired, 1900 ; served South African War, 1879 (despatches, medal with clasp). *Address:* Grey Abbey, Newtownards, Co. Down.
(*Died 11 June 1927.*)

MONTGOMERY-MOORE, General Sir Alexander George, K.C.B. ; *cr.* 1900 ; J.P. Belfast and D.L. Tyrone ; High Sheriff, Co. Tyrone, 1904 ; Col. 4th Hussars ; *b.* 6 Apr. 1833 ; *s.* of Alexander James Montgomery-Moore of Garvey, Co. Tyrone ; *m.* 1887, Hon. Jane Colborne, *d.* of 1st Baron Seaton. *Educ.:* Eton. A.D.C. to Commander of Forces, Ireland, 1856-1860 ; Commanded 4th Hussars, 1868-80 ; A.A.G., Dublin District, 1880-85 ; commanded Belfast District, 1886 ; S.E. District, 1887 ; troops in Canada, 1893 ; Aldershot, 1899. Owns 3500 acres. *Address:* Gipsy Lodge, Norwood, S.E. *Clubs:* Carlton, United Service.
(*Died 17 Jan. 1919.*)

MONTROSE, 5th Duke of (*cr.* 1707), **Douglas Beresford Malise Ronald Graham**, K.T., Chancellor of Order since 1917 ; A.D.C. to H.M. the King ; *cr.* Baron Graham before 1451 ; Earl of Montrose, 1505 ; Marquis of Montrose, 1645 ; Duke of Montrose, Marquis of Graham and Buchanan, Earl of Kincardine, Viscount Dundaff, Baron Aberuthven, Mugdock, and Fintrie, 1707 ; Earl and Baron Graham (Peerage of England), 1722 ; Lord-Lieut. of Stirlingshire since 1885 ; Hereditary Sheriff of Dumbartonshire ; Lord High Commissioner, Church of Scotland, 1916-17 ; Lord Clerk Registrar of Scotland since 1890 ; *b.* 1852 ; 3rd *s.* of 4th Duke and Caroline Agnes, *y. d.* of 2nd Lord Decies ; *S.* father, 1874 ; *m.* Violet Hermione, G.B.E., 2nd *d.* of Sir Frederick Graham, 3rd Bt. of Netherby, Cumberland, July 1876 ; three *s.* In politics a Tory. *Educ.:* Eton. Joined Coldstream Guards, 1872 ; transferred to 5th Lancers, 1874 ; retired 1878 ; late Colonel commanding 3rd Batt. Argyll and Sutherland Highlanders ; served South African War (medal and two clasps). Owns 115,000 acres. *Recreations:* all outdoor sports. *Heir: s.* Marquis of Graham. *Address:* Buchanan Castle, Glasgow. *T.A.:* Dundaff, Drymen. *Clubs:* Carlton, United Service ; Royal Yacht Squadron, Cowes. (*Died 10 Dec. 1925.*)

MONTY, Hon. Rodolphe, P.C. Canada, K.C. 1909; senior partner, Monty, Duranleau, Ross Angers & Monty, Advocates, Montreal, Quebec ; *b.* Montreal, 30 Nov. 1874 ; *s.* of Jacques Monty, St. Cesaire, Quebec, and Adele Beauchemin, of Beloeil, Quebec ; *m.* 1899, Eugenie, *d.* of Dr. Arthur Dorval ; six *s.* three *d. Educ.:* Ste. Marie de Monnoir Coll. ; Laval (B.A.) ; McGill (LL.D.). Called to Quebec Bar, 1897 ; in partnership with A. Duranleau, 1898-1921, firm was later changed to present title ; Sec. of State, Canada, 1921 ; President Law Students Society, Laval, 1895-96 ; Member Council of Bar for nine years ; Treasurer Council of Bar for two years ; Examiner for the Bar for five years ; now Bâtonnier of the Bar of Montreal and General Bâtonnier of the Province of Quebec, Canada ; President of La Société de Rapatriment and de Colonisation de la Province de Quebec ; Conservative ; Catholic. *Recreation:* golf. *Address:* 4238 Delorimer Avenue, Montreal, Quebec. *Clubs:* St. Denis, Delorimier, Canadian, Laval Sur Le Lac Golf, Montreal. (*Died 1 Dec. 1928.*)

MOODY, Lieut.-Col. Arthur Hatfield, C.B.E. 1919 ; T.D. ; J.P.; F.J.I. ; *b.* 1875 ; *o. s.* of George Moody of Stourbridge, journalist and newspaper proprietor ; *m.* Mary H. A., *e. d.* of C. Holroyd-Doveton ; one *s.* two *d. Educ.:*

King Edward's School, Stourbridge; Wolverley. Proprietor and Editor of the Worcestershire and Staffordshire County Express, Stourbridge; Fellow and Past Vice-President of Institute of Journalists; President Staffordshire and Warwickshire Newspaper Society, 1921; President Midland Newspaper Federation, 1923; Mayor of Stourbridge, 1921-24; Deputy Mayor, 1919-21 and 1924-25; County Councillor for Worcestershire; Member Worcestershire Territorial Association; Hon. Member Institute of Municipal Accountants, 1923; took a prominent part in obtaining Charter of Incorporation for Stourbridge in 1914; an original Alderman of the Borough; Supply Officer, 1st Mounted Brigade, and (under Forage Committee of War Office) District Purchasing Officer for Berks and Oxon; Deputy Administrator for Eastern Area; Administrator of Eastern Area; Administrator of Northern Area; and Administrator of West Midland Areas (mentions twice, Brevet Major, C.B.E., T.D.). *Publications:* Through Vigo's Golden Gates; articles upon Local Government, Trade, and Travel. *Address:* Norton Close, Stourbridge, Worcestershire. *T.:* 100 Stourbridge. *M.:* NP 6461.   **(Died 7 Feb. 1926.)**

MOODY, Maj.-Gen. Sir John Macdonald, Kt., *cr.* 1906; *b* 1839; *s.* of late John Moody, R.N.; *m.* 1873, Isabella, 3rd *d.* of Rev. J. Mainwaring of Boden Hall, Cheshire. Entered Royal Marines, 1855; Col.-Commandant R.M.L.I., 1899-1902; has taken much interest in recruiting for both the sea and land forces, and in the employment of ex-sailors and soldiers; Vice-Chairman of the National Employment Society for Reserve and Discharged Soldiers, etc.; member of Defence Committee of the London Chamber of Commerce and of Council of Marine Society (Training Ship "Warspite"); takes much interest in the Boys' Brigade, of which he is a Vice-President; also member of London Council, and Hon. President City and East London Battalion; A Director of the Sailors' Home, Well Street. *Address:* 29 Upper Berkeley Street, W.1. *T.:* 4880 Mayfair. *Club:* Junior United Service.
          (Died 13 Sept. 1921.)

MOODY, William H., Associate Justice of Supreme Court of United States, 1906-10; Secretary of the Navy, 1902; Attorney-General 1904-6; *b.* Newbury, Mass., 23 Dec. 1853; *s.* of Henry L. Moody and Melissa A. Emerson, descended from William Moody of Ipswich, Eng., who settled at Newbury, Mass., 1634. *Educ.:* Schools of Salem and Danvers; Phillip's Academy, Andover, Mass., graduating 1872; graduated at Harvard, 1876. Studied law under late Richard Dana; admitted to Bar in 1878; District Attorney for Eastern Massachusetts, 1890-95; elected to 54th Congress from Sixth Massachusetts District, 1895; re-elected to 55th, 56th, and 57th Congresses; prosecuted the "beef trust" and "peonage" cases in the Supreme Court. *Recreations:* fond of horseback riding, base-ball, and other out-door sports. *Address:* Washington, D.C.; Haverhill, Mass. *T.A.:* Boston, Mass. *T.:* Main 197. *Clubs:* Metropolitan, Washington; Chevy-Chase, Maryland; University, Boston; Pentucket, Haverhill.   **(Died 2 July 1917.)**

MOOKERJEE, Sir Asutosh; Saraswati, Sastravachaspati, Kt., *cr.* 1911; C.S.I. 1909; M.A., D.L., D.Sc., Ph.D.; one of His Majesty's Judges in the High Court of Judicature, Fort William, in Bengal, since 1904; Vice-Chancellor of the University of Calcutta, 1906-14, and 1921-23; *b.* 29 June 1864; *s.* of Dr. Ganga Prasad Mookerjee of Calcutta; *m.* 1886, Jogmaya, *d.* of Ram Narain Bhattacharjee of Krishnaghur; four *s.* three *d.* *Educ.:* South Suburban School; Presidency College; City College. M.A. 1885; Premchand Roychand Student, 1886; D.L. 1894; D.Sc. (Hon.) 1908; Fellow

and Syndic of Calcutta University since 1889; Tagore Professor of Law, 1897; enrolled a Vakil of Calcutta High Court, 1888; Professor of Mathematics at Ind. Asso. for Cultivation of Science, 1887-92; Representative of University on Council of Lieut.-Governor of Bengal, 1899-1903, and of Calcutta Corporation on same Council and Additional Member of Council of Governor-General of India, 1903-4; Bengal Member of Indian University Commission, 1902; Member on Calcutta University Commission, 1917-19; Fellow Royal Ast. Soc., Royal Society, Edinburgh; Royal Irish Academy and of other learned Societies British and Foreign; President, Asiatic Society Bengal, 1907-9 and 1921-23; Chairman, Trustees Indian Museum since 1909; Founder-President, Calcutta Mathematical Soc. since 1908; President, Council of the Imperial Library, Calcutta; President of the First Indian Science Congress, 1909; Twin President, Bengali Literary Conference, 1916 and 1918. *Publications:* Geometry of Conics, 1892; Law of Perpetuities, 1899; Vyavahara Matrika of Jimutavahana, 1912; Addresses Academic and Literary, 1915; numerous papers on Mathematics in Journals and Transactions of Learned Societies. *Recreation:* Walking. *Address:* 77 Russa Road North, Bhowanipur, Calcutta. *T.:* Cal. 646.
          (Died 25 May 1924.)

MOON, Henry E., I.S.O. 1902; late Staff Clerk, Privy Council Office. *Address:* St. Mary's Grove, Chiswick, W.4.
          (Died 28 June 1920.)

MOON, Right Hon. Sir Frederick (Robert), K.C.M.G., *cr.* 1911; P.C.; D.C.L., LL.D., M.L.A.; Premier of Natal, 1906-1910; *b.* May 1853; *m.* Charlotte Mary St. Clair, *d.* of W. J. Dunbar-Moodie; three *s.* three *d.* *Educ.:* Hermannsburg School, Natal. Commenced life as a diamond digger at Kimberley, 1872; subsequently owned claims in Kimberley mine; twice elected by fellow-diggers as member of Kimberley Mining Board; returned to Natal, 1880, settling down as a farmer, which occupation he still follows; member Legislative Assembly 1886-1910; was one of the party who carried Responsible Government for the Colony; Minister for Native Affairs, 1893-97, and 1899-1906; declined office under Sir Henry Binns, 1897; one of Natal delegates to Customs Union Conference at Cape Town, 1898, also Bloemfontein and Maritzburg, 1906; Natal delegate to inaugural festivities of Australian Commonwealth; Acting Prime Minister for Colony of Natal during Sir H. Hime's visit to England for Coronation ceremony; Chairman of Natal Industries Commission, 1905-6, of Customs Convention, 1908; called to form a Ministry in 1906; attended Colonial Conference of Premiers in London, 1907; Minister of Commerce and Industries, United South Africa, 1910; Senate as one of the members especially deputed to look after native interests, 1910-20; received Freedom of Cities of London, Manchester, and Bristol. *Address:* Greystone, Estcourt, Natal. *Club:* Victoria, Pietermaritzburg.   **(Died 18 Mar. 1927.)**

MOOR, George Raymond Dallas, V.C. 1915; Lieut. Hampshire Regt.; A.D.C. on General's Staff; 2nd *s.* of W. H. Moor, late Auditor-General, Transvaal, and nephew of late Sir Ralph Moor, K.C.M.G. *Educ.:* Cheltenham College. Entered army, 1914; served European War (Dardanelles), 1914-18 (V.C. for personal bravery near Krithia). *Address:* c/o Cox & Co., 16 Charing Cross, S.W.1.
          (Died 3 Nov. 1918.)

MOORE, Rev. Alfred Edgar, M.A.; Canon of Lincoln: Warden of Browne's Hospital, Stamford, since 1918; late Vicar of Horncastle and Rural Dean; married. *Address:* Browne's Hospital, Stamford.   **(Died 29 June 1924.)**

743

MOORE, Rev. Canon Arthur John, M.A.; Vicar of Holywood, Co. Down, since 1897; Chancellor of Down Cathedral; b. 1853; s. of late Rev. Theodore Octavius Moore, M.A.; m. 1878, Ruth Isabella O'Neill; no c. *Educ.*: Foyle College, Londonderry; Trinity College, Dublin. Curate of Shankill, Lurgan, 1876; Incumbent of St. Jude's Church, Ballingafeigh, Belfast, 1879-86; Christ Church, Lisburn, 1886-94; Rector of Coleraine, 1894-97. *Address*: The Vicarage, Holywood, Co. Down.
(*Died 8 Sept. 1919.*)

MOORE, Col. Athelstan, D.S.O. 1902; Royal Dublin Fusiliers; employed with N.Z. Military Forces; b. 9 July 1879; m. Nora Kathleen; one s. Entered army, 1899; served South Africa, 1899-1902 (despatches, Queen's and King's medals with 4 clasps); N. Nigeria, 1908 (medal with clasp). *Address*: 81 Church Road, Richmond, Surrey. (*Died 14 Oct. 1918.*)

MOORE, Dr. Benjamin, F.R.S. 1912; Professor of Bio-Chemistry, Oxford University, since 1920; Medical Research Staff, National Health Insurance. *Educ.*: Queen's College, Belfast; Leipzig University. Five years on staff of University College; then went to Yale University; late Lecturer in Physiology, Charing Cross Medical School; Professor of Bio-Chemistry, Liverpool University, 1902-14. *Publications*: The Dawn of the Health Age; The Origin and Nature of Life; Biochemistry, a Study of the Origin, Reactions, and Equilibria of Living Matter, 1921. *Address*: Oxford.
(*Died 5 Mar. 1922.*)

MOORE, Maj.-Gen. Charles Alfred, Bombay Cavalry; b. 12 Nov. 1839; m. 1873, Mary Henrietta, d. of late J. F. Moir. Entered army, 1856; Maj.-Gen. 1895; retired, 1900; served Indian Mutiny, 1858-60 (medal and clasp); Abyssinian War, 1867-68 (despatches twice, medal). *Address*: Glenarbuck, The Park, Cheltenham. (*Died 30 June 1925.*)

MOORE, Admiral Charles Henry Hodgson; b. 22 March 1858. s. of late Major-General C. W. Moore; m. Fanny Ponsonby, d. of late A. Dalrymple; one s. one d. Entered Navy, 1871; Commander, 1895; Captain, 1900; Rear-Adm. 1910; retired, 1913; Vice-Admiral, 1915; Admiral (retired). 1919. *Address*: Austhorpe, Grassington Road, Eastbourne.
(*Died 17 Mar. 1920.*)

MOORE, Maj.-Gen. Claude Douglas Hamilton, C.B. 1925; C.M.G. 1918; D.S.O. 1915; Royal Warwickshire Regt.; G.O.C. 42nd (East Lancs) Division T.A. since 1927; late Commanding Infantry Brigade, Ahmednagar, India; b. 9 Feb. 1875. M.A. Cambridge University. Entered Army, 1898; Capt. 1901; Major, 1914; D.A.A. and Q.M.G., North China, 1912; served S. African War, 1899-1901 (Queen's medal 4 clasps); European War, 1914-18 (despatches eight times, D.S.O., C.M.G., Bt. Lt.-Col. and Col., Fifth Class Order of the Rising Sun for services at Tsingtao, Third Class Order of the Nile, Legion of Honour, France); Maj.-Gen. 1925. *Club*: Junior Army and Navy.(*Died 14 Sept.1928.*)

MOORE, Rev. Courtenay, M.A., V.P.R.S.A.I.; b. 25 Mar. 1840; s. of Alexander Moore of Rossnashane, Co. Antrim; m. 1869, Jessie Mona Duff, d. of Capt. B. Duff, Gordon Highlanders, s. of Garden Duff of Hatton Castle, Aberdeenshire, and Louisa, e. d. of 5th Baron Duffus; two s. two d. *Educ.*: Trinity College, Dublin (Catechetical Premiums); Honourman in Ethics; A Respondent at Degree Examination; A Divinity Testimonium of the First Class. Deacon, 1865; Priest, 1866; Curate of Brigown, 1865; Rector of Farahy, 1871; of Castletownltoche, 1875; of Brigown, Mitchelstown, 1882-1920; Canon of Cloyne, 1885; Rural Dean, 1893; Precentor of Cloyne Cathedral, 1909; *Publications*: two Irish novels: Con Hegarty; Jer. Sharkey; several theological pamphlets;

St. Patrick's Liturgy, 3rd ed.; Prayers for the Faithful Departed, 3rd ed.; A Chapter of Irish Church History; many articles in Cork Archæological and Historical Journal. *Recreations*: cycling. archæologizing.

MOORE, Sir Edward Cecil, 1st Bt., cr. 1923; b. 1851; m. 1893, Florence, d. of James Harverson, Alderman, Bishopsgate Ward, since 1912; Sheriff, 1914-15; Lord Mayor of London, 1922-23. *Heir*: g. s. Edward Stanton, b. 28 Dec. 1910. *Address*: 1 Lancaster Gate Terrace, W.2. *Club*: City Carlton.
(*Died 7 Dec. 1923.*)

MOORE, Rev. Edward, D.D.; Hon. D.Litt. Dublin; Canon of Canterbury since 1903; Hon. Fellow of Pembroke College and of Queen's College, Oxford; Corresponding Member of the Accademia Della Crusca and Fellow of the British Academy, 1906; b. Cardiff; s. of J. Moore, M.D. *Educ.*: Bromsgrove Grammar School; Pembroke College, Oxford (Exhibitioner). Double 1st class Moderations, 1855; double 1st class in Classics and Mathematics, 1857. Fellow and Tutor, Queen's College, 1862-64; Principal of St. Edmund Hall, Oxford, 1864-1913. *Publications*: Aristotle's Ethics, bks. i.-iv.; 5th ed. 1896; Aristotle's Poetics, with notes, 1875; Time References in the Divina Commedia, 1887; Textual Criticism of the Divina Commedia. 1889; Dante and his Early Biographers, 1890; Tutte le Opere di Dante Alighieri (The Oxford Dante), 1894; Studies in Dante, 1896; 2nd Series, 1899; 3rd Series, 1903; Gli Accenni al Tempo nella Divina Commedia, Florence, 1900. *Address*: The Precincts, Canterbury. (*Died 2 Sept. 1916.*)

MOORE, Colonel Edward James, C.B. 1911; V.D.; Territorial Force Reserve; late 20th Batt. London Regiment; b. 25 May 1862; m. 1891, Helena, d. of Isaac Crookenden of Blackheath. *Address*: Park End, Blackheath Park, S.E.3. *T.*: Lee Green 233.
(*Died 7 Mar. 1925.*)

MOORE, Ven. Edward Marsham, Rector of Uppingham, 1907-20. *Educ.*: Christ Church, Oxford; Cuddesdon Theological College. Curate of Ashborne, 1867-72; Vicar, 1872-76; Rector of Benefield, 1876-1907; Archdeacon of Oakham, 1906-18; Hon. Canon Peterborough, 1899-1906. *Address*: Vale House, Loose, Maidstone. *Club*: Oxford and Cambridge.
(*Died 5 Sept. 1921.*)

MOORE, Francis William, dramatic author; b. Finsbury, 27 June 1849; 2nd s. of late Henry Moore, Croydon, and Frances Isabella Riddle; unmarried. *Educ.*: privately. *Publications*: Humorous Pieces in Prose and Verse, 1893; Original Plays and Duologues, chiefly Humorous, 1893; The Kingdom of Arcadee, 1895; When George the Fourth was King, 1896. *Recreation*: rose-growing. *Address*: Maythorne, 1 Park Hill Rise, Croydon. *T.*: 25.
(*Died 14 Dec. 1927.*)

MOORE, George Arbuthnot; b. Birkenhead, 16 March 1857; s. of Charles Moore of Easterlands, Somerset; m. 1881, Lucy Olivia, 3rd d. of William Whitmore St. George, of Clifton Park, Birkenhead; one s. one d. *Educ.*: Birkenhead School; Stuttgart; Wurtemburg. Appointed a member of the Advisory Committee to the Department of Overseas Trade by Sir A. Steel Maitland at its inception; a member of the Interim Provisional Council to the Board of Trade by Sir A. Stanley; Chairman of the Council of the Liverpool Chamber of Commerce, 1918-19; Chairman of the Taxation and Finance Committee of the Council of the Association of British Chambers of Commerce, 1921-3, and a Liverpool representative on the Council of that Association. *Recreations*: shooting, farming, mechanics, lawn tennis and squash racquets. *Address*: Rowler, Brackley, Northants. *M.*: CM 848 and M 6244. *Clubs*:

St. Stephen's, Royal Automobile.
(Died 3 Dec. 1923.)

MOORE, Rev. Henry Dodwell, M.A.; Canon or Prebendary of Lincoln since 1908; Vicar of Honington, Lincolnshire, 1867-1916; Rural Dean, 1879-1915; *b.* 1838; 2nd *s.* of late Philip Charles Moore, a Proctor in Doctors Commons; *m.* 1867, Augusta Rosina (*d.* 1901), *d.* of Sir A. J. Rugge - Price, 5th Bt., of Richmond, Surrey; three *s.* five *d. Educ.*: Pembroke College, Oxford. B.A. (2nd Class Mathematics), 1862; M.A. 1865; Deacon, 1863; Priest, 1864; Curate of Barkingside, Essex, 1863 - 65; St. Michael's, Bromley, E., 1865-67; Curate in charge of Wisborough Green, Sussex, 1867; an Inspector of Schools in Diocese of Lincoln, 1870-88; Secretary of the Grantham Clerical Society, 1896-1915. *Address:* The Hollies, Brant Broughton, Newark. *T.A.:* Brant Broughton.
(Died 2 Aug. 1919.)

MOORE, Sir John Samuel, K.C.B., *cr.* 1911; C.B. 1902; Paymaster-in-Chief, Royal Navy; retired 1891; *b.* 1831; *e. s.* of John Percy Moore, M.D., and Elizabeth, *d.* of Samuel Porter, Saltash; late Lieut. 10th (Lincoln) Regt.; *m.* 1861, Mary Anne, *d.* of Thomas Spearman, Heywood, Paymaster-in-Chief, R.N.; one *s. Educ.*: private schools. Entered Royal Navy, 1846; Served on the Cape station during Kaffir War, 1849-52 (medal); present at the capture of the forts at Bomarsund in the Baltic, 1854 (medal); present at the operations against Sebastopol, Kertch, and Yenikale, and capture of Kinburn (Crimean and Turkish medals, Sebastopol clasp); secretary to Commodore in India during the Mutiny, 1857-58; and secretary to Commodore, East Indian station, 1859-60; secretary to Commander-in-Chief, Mediterranean station, during Egyptian War, 1882 (specially mentioned in despatches, Egyptian medal, Alexandria clasp, Khedive's bronze star, Medjidie 3rd class); Fleet Paymaster H.M. yacht Victoria and Albert, 1883 - 91. *Recreations:* gardening, fishing. *Address:* Alverstoke. Hants.
(Died 21 Nov. 1916.)

MOORE, Louis Herbert, B.A.; General Manager of the American Press Telegram Company, and London correspondent of the Washington Star; *b.* Brooklyn, New York, 1 Nov. 1860; *m.* Alice, *d.* of late Theodore Mace of Montclair, New Jersey; one *d. Educ.*: Public Schools, Boston, Mass.; St. Stephen's College, Annandale, New York. Travelled extensively in Europe; was European Manager of the United and Associated Press of America, 1889-97; represented his Association at most of the notable events in Europe during that time, including the funeral of Alexander III. at St. Petersburg, the coronation of Nicholas II. at Moscow, and the Armenian troubles at Constantinople. In 1900 organised the foreign service of the Daily Express and was Foreign Editor of that paper for two years. *Recreations:* travel, golfing, and amateur photography. *Address:* 66 Burton Court, Sloane Square, S.W. *T.A.:* Luisaint, London. *T.:* 840 Victoria. *Club:* Savage.
(Died 19 Jan. 1918.)

MOORE, Sir Norman, 1st Bt., *cr.* 1919; M.D. (Cantab.); F.R.C.P. (Lond.); Consulting Physician to St. Bartholomew's Hospital, London; President of Royal College of Physicians of London, 1918-22; and Representative of the College in General Medical Council; Hon. Fellow of St. Catharine's College, Cambridge; Hon. LL.D. Camb.; *b.* Higher Broughton, Lancashire, 8 Jan. 1847; *o. s.* of Robert Ross Rowan Moore and Rebecca, *d.* of B. C. Fisher; *m.* 1st, 1880, Amy (*d.* 1901) *d.* of William Leigh Smith of Crowham, Sussex; 2nd, 1903, Milicent, *d.* of Maj.-Gen. John Ludlow; one *s.* one *d. Educ.*: Owens College, Manchester; St. Catharine's Coll. Camb. B.A. 1869; M.A. 1872; M.D. 1876; House Physician, St. Bartholomew's Hospital,

1872-74; Casualty Physician, 1875-77; Assistant Physician, 1883-1902; Physician, 1902-11; Lecturer on Comparative Anatomy, 1874 - 85; Lecturer on Pathology, 1887 - 93; Lecturer on Principles and Practice of Medicine, 1893-1911; Fellow of Royal College of Physicians, 1877; Harveian Orator, 1901; Senior Censor, 1908; Harveian librarian, 1910-18; Pres. 1918-20; Rede Lecturer, Cambridge, 1914. *Publications:* several medical treatises; the Harveian Oration for 1901; 459 lives (chiefly of medical writers) in Dictionary of National Biography; FitzPatrick Lectures on the History of Medicine; The History of St. Bartholomew's Hospital; Life of Charles Waterton, 1871; translation of the Concise Irish Grammar of E. Windisch; essay on History of Medicine in Ireland; Loss of the Crown of Loegaire Lurc (Irish text and translation). *Heir: s.* Alan Hilary [*b.* 23 Jan. 1882; *m.* 1922, Hilda Mary, *d.* of Rt. Rev. Winfrid O. Burrows, Bishop of Chichester]. *Address:* 67 Gloucester Place, Portman Square, W.1.; Hancox, Battle, Sussex. *T.:* Mayfair 537; Battle 1Y5. *Club:* Athenæum.
(Died 30 Nov. 1922.)

MOORE, Rev. Obadiah, St. George's Cathedral; Acting Pastor of Bp. Crowther Memorial Church (St. Clement's), Cline Town, Freetown, though retired; *b.* York, Sierra Leone, 28 Dec. 1848; of Mendi and Dahomian descent; *m.* 1st, 1878, *d.* of Rev. W. Quaker, one of three Foundation Pastors of the Sierra Leone Native Pastorate Church; 2nd, 1894, *d.* of Hon. T. J. Sawyerr, merchant, etc., M.L.C., Sierra Leone; three *s.* two *d. Educ.*: Wesleyan Village School; Church Elementary School, Kent, S. Leone; C.M. Grammar School, Freetown; C.M.S. College, Fourah Bay, 1867-70; Monkton Combe Collegiate School, Somerset, England, 1875-76. Junior Tutor, C.M.S. Grammar School, 1870; Senior Tutor, 1871-75; in England, 1875-76; returned to Grammar School, 1876; ordained 1877; first Pastor, Sierra Leone Native Church at Bonthe, Sherbro District, 1880-82; Native Principal, C.M.S. Grammar School, Freetown, 1882-1906; Canon, St. George's Cathedral, Freetown, 1898; retired from active service, 1906; has visited England four times. *Recreation:* boating. *Address:* Freetown, Sierra Leone, West Africa. *(Died 27 Feb. 1923.)*

MOORE, Lt.-Col. Richard St. Leger, C.B. 1902; D.L., J.P.; Master Kildare foxhounds, 1883-97; heretofore pres. Irish Amateur Athletic Assoc.; *b.* Kilbride Manor, Co. Wicklow, 12 July 1848; *e. s.* of Richard Moore, and *g. s.* of Rt. Hon. Lord Chief Justice Moore; *m.* 1878, Alice, *d.* of J. P. Tynte, Tynte Park, Co. Wicklow; one *s.* three *d. Educ.*: Harrow. Served in 9th Lancers, 12th Lancers, and 5th Lancers, 1866-1881. Since 1881 has lived at home as a country gentleman; High Sheriff, 1899; commanded 17th Batt. Imp. Yeo., South Africa, 1900 (despatches, C.B.). *Recreations:* hunting, shooting, fishing, cricket, tennis, polo, boxing, fencing, and running. Owns 2500 acres. *Address:* Killashee, Naas, Co. Kildare, Ireland. *M.:* IO 424. *Clubs:* Army and Navy, Cavalry, Hurlingham; Kildare Street, Dublin. *(Died 18 Oct. 1921.)*

MOORE, Thomas, M.V.O. 1911; *b.* 1858. In charge of Police, Great Central Railway; Supt. Executive and Statistical Branches Metropolitan Police Office. *Address:* 8 Berridge Road, East Nottingham. *(Died 20 May 1920.)*

MOORE, Sir Thomas O'Connor, 11th Bt., *cr.* 1681; *b.* 5 Nov. 1845; *s.* of the 10th Bart. and Mary Anne, *e. d.* of Andrew Ryan O'Connor, barrister, Mt. Pleasant, Co. Dublin; *S.* father, 1882; *m.* 1908, Katherine Mathilda Howard, *d.* of late Capt. J. G. Elphinstone, H.E.I.C.S. *Heir:* none. *Address:* 36 Wellington Road, St. Luke's. Cork. *(Died Jan. 1926.)*

MOORE, Hon. William; *b.* Isle of Man, 1817; President Legislative Council, 1889-

1894; Minister of Lands and Works, 1873-76 and 1877-78; Chief Secretary, 1894-99. *Address:* The Rocks, New Norfolk, Tasmania.

MOORE, William H.; *b.* Utica, N.Y.; 25 Oct. 1848; *s.* of Nathaniel F. Moore and Rachel A. Beckwith; *m.* 1879, Ada Small. Entered Amherst College, 1867; admitted to Bar, Wis., 1872; settled in Chicago, and made a specialty of Corporation Law; with his brother, James H., reorganised the Carnegie Steel Co., later forming the four great corporations known as the "Moore group," with a combined capital of $187,000,000, all now absorbed in the U.S. Steel Corporation; also promoted other large industrial corporations, including the Diamond Match Co., National Biscuit Co., American Tin Plate Co., American Steel Hoop Co., etc.; Director U.S. Steel Corporation. *Address:* E. 54th Street, New York. *(Died 11 Jan. 1923.)*

MOORE, Vice-Admiral W. Usborne, *b.* 1849; *s.* of late John Alldin Moore, barrister; *m.* 1877, Gertrude Usborne; one *s.* three *d.* *Publications:* The Cosmos and the Creeds; Glimpses of the Next State; The Voices. *Address:* 8 Western Parade. Southsea. *Club:* United Service. *(Died 15 Mar. 1918.)*

MOORMAN, Frederic William, B.A., Ph.D.; Professor of English Language, University of Leeds, since 1912; *b.* 8 Sep. 1872; *s.* of late Rev. A. C. Moorman; *m.* 1898, Frances B. Humpidge; two *s.* one *d.* *Educ.:* Caterham School; University College, London; University College of Wales; Strasburg University. Assistant Lecturer in English Language and Literature, University College of Wales, Aberystwyth, 1895; Lecturer and Professor at Yorkshire College and University of Leeds since 1898. *Publications:* William Browne and the Pastoral Poetry of the Elizabethan Age, 1897; The Interpretation of Nature in English Poetry from Beowulf to Shakespeare, 1905; An Introduction to Shakespeare, 1906; Robert Herrick: a Biographical and Critical Study, 1910; The Place-Names of the West Riding of Yorkshire, 1911; The May King, 1914; Yorkshire Dialect Poems (Anthology), 1916. *Recreations:* birdwatching, gardening, cycling. *Address:* 2 Hollin Lane, Headingley, Leeds. *(Died 8 Sept. 1919.)*

MOORSOM, Lt.-Col. Henry Martin, M.V.O. 1903; *b.* 1839; *m.* 1877. Edith Arabella Louisa Florence, *d.* of late William Thomas Bristow Lyons, Brook Hill, Co. Antrim. Entered Rifle Brigade, 1855; retired, 1877; served Indian Mutiny, 1857-58 (medal with clasp); Canada, 1866 (medal with clasp); Chief Constable, Lancs, 1880-1909; King's Police medal, 1909. *Address:* Court Manor, Westmeon, Petersfield. *Club:* Army and Navy.
(Died 29 Dec. 1921.)

MOORSOM, James Marshall, K.C. 1885; J.P.; 4th *s.* of Vice-Admiral and Mary Maude Moorsom, *g. s.* of Admiral Sir Robert Moorsom, K.C.B., who commanded the *Revenge* at the battle of Trafalgar; *m.* Emma Catherine Browne of Tallantire; two *s.* Called to Bar, Inner Temple, 1863; Bencher, 1892; Treasurer, 1914; M.P. for Yarmouth, 1892-95. *Address:* Fieldside, Keswick, Cumberland; Inner Temple, E.C. *Clubs:* Oxford and Cambridge, M.C.C.
(Died 26 Mar. 1918.)

MORANT, Adm. Sir George Digby, K.C.B., *cr.* 1901; retired; *b.* Ireland, 8 Aug. 1837; *e. s.* of late George Morant, Grenadier Guards, and Shirley House, Carrickmacross, Ireland, and Lydia, 3rd *d.* of late John Hemphill, Rathkenny, Co. Tipperary; *m.* 1866, Sophia Georgina (*d.* 1911), *y. d.* of late Col. Eyres, Grenadier Guards; two *s.* four *d.* *Educ.:* Dr. Burney's Royal Naval Academy. Entered R.N. 1850; Captain, 1873; Admiral, 1901; commanded
746

H.M.'s ships Grasshopper, Enterprise, Cockatrice, Valorous, Achilles, Victor Emmanuel (as Commodore); superintended Pembroke Dockyard, and as superintending fittings of contract-built ships under Naval Defence Act, and as Admiral Superintendent of Chatham Dockyard, 1892-95; superintendent of Irish Lights, 1875-78; war medals for Burmah, Baltic, Crimea (two clasps), China. *Recreations:* reading, drawing, shooting, and fishing. *Address:* 31 Redcliffe Square, S.W.10. *T.:* Western 1628. *Club:* United Service. *(Died 13 Feb. 1921.)*

MORANT, Sir Robert Laurie, K.C.B., *cr.* 1907; C.B. 1902; 1st Secy. of the Ministry of Health since 1919; *b.* 7 April 1863; *s.* of late Robert Morant, Hampstead; *m.* 1896, Helen, *d.* of late Edwin Cracknell of Wetheringsett Grange, Suffolk. *Educ.:* Winchester; New College, Oxford. Educational work of various kinds; tutor to Royal Family of Siam, and organiser of public education in that country; subsequently social and educational work in East London; Assistant Director of Special Inquiries and Reports in Education Department, Whitehall, 1895; Private Secretary to Sir John Gorst, and subsequently Assistant Private Sec. to Duke of Devonshire; Permanent Secretary, Board of Education, 1903-11; Chairman of Insurance Commission, 1912-19. *Address:* 17 Thurloe Square, S.W.7. *T.:* Kensington 5616.
(Died 13 Mar. 1920.)

MOREL, Edmund D.; M.P. (Lab.) Dundee since 1922; Secretary and part founder of the Union of Democratic Control, and Editor of Foreign Affairs; *b.* 10 July 1873; *s.* of Edmond Morel-de-Ville and Emmeline de Horne; *m.* 1896, Mary Richardson; four *s.* one *d.* *Educ.:* Eastbourne. Author and journalist; founded Congo Reform Association, 1904; took a leading part in movement against Congo misrule, and published many pamphlets on the subject; visited the States and inaugurated similar movement there, 1904; published with Pierre Mille, the French African explorer, Le Congo léopoldien; member of West African Lands Committee (Colonial Office), 1912-14; Liberal candidate, Birkenhead, Oct. 1912 - Oct. 1914; resigned upon outbreak of war; Hon. Secretary Congo Reform Association, 1904-12; Editor African Mail for ten years; a Vice-President of the Anti-Slavery Society; Labour candidate for Dundee, 1921-22. *Publications:* Affairs of West Africa; The British Case in French Congo; King Leopold's Rule in Africa; Red Rubber; Great Britain and the Congo; Nigeria; Morocco in Diplomacy; Ten Years of Secret Diplomacy; Truth and the War; Africa and the Peace of Europe; The Black Man's Burden; Thoughts on the War; The Peace, and Prison; Pre-War Diplomacy; Diplomacy Revealed. Holds silver medal Society of Arts for paper on British in Nigeria. *Address:* Kings Langley, Herts. *(Died 12 Nov. 1924.)*

MORESBY, Admiral John; explorer and author; retired, 1888; Admiral, 1893; *b.* 1830; *s.* of late Sir Fairfax Moresby; *m.* Jane (*d.* 1876), *d.* of P. Scott; one *s.* four *d.* Discovered (1873) finest harbour in New Guinea, on which Port Moresby now stands; also 25 large inhabited islands, and more than 100 smaller ones, and explored over 600 miles of previously unknown coast line; served in the Baltic, 1854-55 (medal); China, 1861; Japan, 1864; Senior Officer, Bermuda, 1879-81. *Publications:* Discoveries and Surveys in New Guinea; A Cruise in Polynesia and Visits to the Pearl-Shelling Stations in Torres Straits, 1876; Two Admirals, 1909. *Address:* Blackbeck, Fareham. *(Died 12 July 1922.)*

MORETON, Lord; Henry Haughton Reynolds-, D.L., J.P.; *b.* 4 Mar. 1857; *e. s.* of 3rd Earl of Ducie; *m.* Ada, *d.* of late Dudley R. Smith, Belgrave Square, W., 1888. M.P. (L.) W. Gloucestershire, 1880-85. *Address:* 37 Park

Lane, W.1; *T.*: Mayfair 4462; Sarsden House, Kingham, Oxford. *Clubs:* Brooks's, Travellers'.
(*Died 23 Feb. 1920.*)

MORETON, Hon. Sir Richard (Chas.), K.C.V.O., *cr.* 1913; C.V.O. 1913; M.V.O. 1907; D.L.; H.M.'s Marshal of the Ceremonies, 1887-1913; *b.* London, 21 Jan. 1846; 7th *s.* of 2nd Earl of Ducie and Elizabeth, *e. d.* of Lord Sherborne; *m.* 1868, Janie, *e. d.* of late Thomas Ralli, Lady of the Bedchamber to H.R.H. the Duchess of Albany; one *d.* Cadet R.N. *Address:* Crookham House, Crookham, Hants. *T.*: Fleet 60. *T.A.*: Church-Crookham. *Club:* Bachelors'. (*Died 2 Mar. 1923.*)

MORGAN, Alfred Kedington; F.S.A.; A.R.C.A.; Art Master at Rugby School and Hon. Curator of the Art Museum; *b.* S. Kensington, 23 April 1868; *e. s.* of Alfred Morgan, artist; *m.* Gertrude Ellen Hayes, A.R.E.; no *c. Educ.*: The Royal College of Art. Student in training, R.C.A.; Art Master at Cheltenham Grammar School; Peripatetic Art Master to the School Board for London, and afterwards L.C.C.; Assistant Examiner in Geometrical Drawing to the Board of Education; Art Master at Aske's School, Hatcham; sometime Associate Royal Society of Painter Etchers and Engravers (resigned); Member of National Art Collections Fund; Exhibitor at R.A. and other public exhibitions. *Recreation:* music. *Address:* The Art Museum, Rugby. *M.*: NX 427.
(*Died 14 April 1923.*)

MORGAN, Lt.-Col. Anthony Hick-man, D.S.O. 1894; D.L., J.P. Co. Cork; *e. s.* of late Capt. Anthony Morgan of Bunalun, Skibbereen, Co. Cork (late Capt. 95th Regiment), and Eliza Tymons of Riverstown, Co. Clare; *b.* 1858; *m.* 1896, Mary, *d.* of late C. E. Bagnell of Clonkennan, Limerick. Entered Army Medical Department, 1881; retired, 1896; served Egyptian War, 1882 (medal, Khedive's star); Gambia, 1891-92 (medal with clasp); West Coast Africa, 1893-94 (despatches); Gambia, 1894 (despatches, D.S.O., clasp); served on board hospital ship Princess of Wales, South Africa, 1889-90, as Officer commanding troops and P.M.O. (despatches, medal and clasp); High Sheriff, County of Cork, J.P., 1904; Kt. of Grace of St. John of Jerusalem; F.R.G.S.; F.Z.S.; contested (C.) Isle of Wight, 1906; Member of the Iron and Steel Institute. *Address:* 14 Grosvenor Place, S.W.1; Hollybrook House, Skibbereen, Co. Cork. *T.*: Kensington 2123. *Clubs:* Army and Navy, Carlton, Hurlingham; Royal St. George's Yacht; Royal Northern Yacht; Royal Yacht Squadron, Cowes; Royal Cork Yacht; Royal Highland Yacht, Oban.
(*Died 29 Sept. 1924.*)

MORGAN, Hon. Sir Arthur, Kt., *cr.* 1907; Pres. Legislative Council, Queensland, since 1906; Lieutenant-Governor of Queensland, 1908; *b.* Rosenthal, Warwick, Queensland, 19 Sept. 1856; 4th *s.* of James Morgan, formerly Member for Warwick; *m.* 1880, Alice Augusta, *e. d.* of H. E. Clinton; five *s.* three *d. Educ.*: Public School Warwick. Elected to Municipal Council, 1885; Mayor, 1886, 1887, 1888, 1889, and 1898; M.L.A. Warwick, 1887, 1888, 1893, 1898, 1899, 1902; Chairman of Committees of the Legislative Assembly, 1891; Chairman Royal Commission on Local Government, 1896; Speaker of the Legislative Assembly, 1898-1903; Premier, Chief Secretary, and Minister for Railways, 1903-6. *Publication:* Discovery and Development of the Downs, 1902. *Recreations:* shooting, fishing. *Address:* Clinton, Paddington, Brisbane. *T.*: Brisbane 311. *Clubs:* Johnsonian, Brisbane; Warwick, Warwick; Pioneers, Sydney.
(*Died Dec. 1916.*)

MORGAN, Major Cecil Buckley, D.S.O. 1900; late West India Regt.; *b.* 18 Nov. 1860; *m.* 1894, Maud Mary, *d.* of Richard Keeling of Penkridge, Staffs. Entered army, 1884; Major, 1898; served Niger Territories, 1892-93

and 1895 (twice wounded); Sierra Leone; 1898-1899 (severely wounded, despatches, D.S.O., medal with clasp). *Address:* Uitenhage, Roodewal, Orange River Colony.
(*Died 29 Mar. 1918.*)

MORGAN, D. J.; partner in Morgan, Gellibrand and Co., Russian merchants; J.P.; *b.* 1844; *m.* 1867, *d.* of A. Bigland of Liverpool *Educ.*: Forest School, Walthamstow; Switzerland. M.P. (C.) South-west or Walthamstow Div. of Essex, 1900-6. *Address:* Bentley Mill, Brentwood, Essex. *Clubs:* Carlton, City.
(*Died 28 Feb. 1918.*)

MORGAN, Brig.-Gen. Sir Hill Godfrey, K.B.E., *cr.* 1919; C.B. 1902; C.M.G. 1918; D.S.O. 1896; *b.* 20 June 1862; *s.* of late Capt. Hill Faulconer Morgan, 28th Foot; *m.* 1886, Fanny, *d.* of late J. Bousfield of Grassmere, Craneswater Park, Southsea. Joined 1st Gloucestershire Regt. (28th) from Militia (1883) as a Lt. and transferred to Army Service Corps, 1888 as Captain; Major, 1898; served Dongola Expeditionary Force, 1896-8 (despatches, D.S.O., 4th class Medjidie, British medal, Khedive's medal with two clasps); Nile expedition, including Khartoum (despatches, 4th class Osmanieh, clasp); Director of Supplies, Natal, 1899-1900, and Director of Supplies, South Africa, 1900-1902 (despatches five times, Brevet Lieut.-Col., Queen's medal six clasps, King's medal two clasps, C.B.); Lt.-Col. 1904; Bt.-Col. 1917; retired, 1906; Asst. Director of Supplies, Central Force, Home Army, 5 Aug. 1914; Military Member Organising Committee Farmers' County Committees, 9 Dec. 1914; Administrative Member Forage Committee, 27 May 1915; Temp. Brig.-Gen., 18 Aug. 1917; mentioned for valuable services in connection with War, 6 July 1918. *Clubs:* Junior United Service, Ranelagh. (*Died 4 Jan. 1923.*)

MORGAN, Rev. John, Archdeacon of Bangor, 1902-20; Rector of Trefdraeth 1902-1920. *Educ.*: Sidney-Sussex College Cambridge (Sen. Opt.). Curate, Bangor, 1868-70; Vicar, 1880-85; Curate, Llanberis, 1870-72; Vicar of Corris, Merrions, 1872-76; Rector of Dowlais, 1876-80; Rector of Llandudno, 1885-1902. *Address:* c/o The Vicarage, Carnarvon.
(*Died 1 Jan. 1924.*)

MORGAN, John Hammond, C.V.O. 1901; M.A. Oxon; F.R.C.S.; Medaille de Reconnaissance de la Republique Française; Consulting Surgeon to Charing Cross Hospital; late Treasurer of School; Consulting Surgeon to Hospital for Sick Children; Hon. Surg. 14th Middlesex R.V.; late President of Med. Soc. of London; *b.* 19 Aug. 1847; *s.* of John Morgan, F.R.C.S.; *m.* 1874, Isabel, 2nd *d.* of W. C. Lucy of Brookthorpe, Gloucestershire. *Educ.*: Harrow; Trinity College, Oxford. Examiner in Surgery, University of Oxford. Member of Council R.C.S. Was President of Oxford University Athletic Club; winner of Inter-University 3 mile race in 1868-69-70; attached as Surgeon to several London Hospitals; Knight of Grace of the Order of St. John of Jerusalem; Medical Chief of Croix Rouge Hospital for Wounded Soldiers at Nevers, 1917. *Decorated* for services in connection with Duke of Abercorn's Fund for sick and wounded officers. *Publications:* Catalogue of Museum of Charing Cross Hospital; Lettsomian Lectures, 1897; many papers on surgical subjects. *Recreations:* fishing, shooting, travel. *Address:* 3 Connaught Square, W.2; Hilliers, Bucklebury, Reading. *T.*: Paddington 6250. *Clubs:* Athenæum, New University, Beefsteak.
(*Died 11 Oct. 1924.*)

MORGAN, Lt.-Col. Stuart Williams, D.L., J.P., M.F.H., Brecon; *b.* 1867; *m.* 1893, Blanche (*d.* 1898), *o. d.* of P. K. Budworth of Greensted Hall, Essex. *Address:* Bolgoed, Brecon. (*Died 16 Nov. 1922.*)

MORGAN, Walter J., R.B.A. *Address:* 17 Radnor Road, Handsworth, Birmingham.
(Died 31 Oct. 1924.)

MORGAN, Sir Walter Vaughan, 1st Bt., *cr.* 1906; Alderman of City of London; one of H.M. Lieutenants for the City; Treasurer of Christ's Hospital; holds Orders of Saviour of Greece; St. Maurice and St. Lazare, Italy; and Rising Sun, Japan; Commander of the Legion of Honour; Kt. Commander of the Order of St. Olav; *b.* 3 May 1831; 6th *s.* of Thomas Morgan of Glasbury and Marianne, *d.* of William Vaughan of Brecon; unmarried. *Educ.:* Christ's Hospital. Entered service of National Provincial Bank of England, 1846; retired as Chief Cashier at Manchester, 1856, to join his brothers in London in founding the firm of Morgan Brothers, merchants and newspaper proprietors, and the Morgan Crucible Company; the firm consisted of six brothers, who continued in partnership for thirty years, and still so continue, except that death has reduced the number to two; one of the proprietors of The Chemist and Druggist and The Ironmonger Journals; Sheriff of City of London, 1900-1901; Lord Mayor of the City of London, 1905-6. *Heir:* none. *Recreation:* Freemason of many years' standing; Grand Treasurer of the Grand Lodge of England, 1897-98; and Past Grand Warden, 1906. *Address:* 2 Whitehall Court, S.W. *Clubs:* Reform, Gresham.
(Died 12 Nov. 1916.)

MORGAN, Rev. William, M.A., D.D.; *b.* 1862; *s.* of an Aberdeenshire farmer; *m.* 1903, *e. d.* of late Peter Esslemont, M.P. for East Aberdeenshire, and afterwards Chairman of the Scottish Fishery Board. *Educ.:* Aberdeen University; United Presbyterian College, Edinburgh; Halle. For 18 years minister of the United Free Church, Tarbolton, Ayrshire; acted as Examiner in Philosophy, Aberdeen University (hon. D.D. 1910); Professor of Systematic Theology and Apologetics, Queen's Theological College, Kingston, Canada, 1912; delivered in Glasgow the Kerr Lectures, 1914, and the Dudleian Lecture, Harvard University, 1921. *Publications:* The Religion and Theology of Paul; has also contributed largely to current periodical literature.
(Died 16 Jan. 1923.)

MORGAN, William Pritchard; *b.* 1844; *s.* of late W. Morgan, Pillgwenlly, Newport, Mon. Solicitor; practised in Queensland; returned to England 1888; now interested in gold mining property in Wales and China; M.P. (G.L.) Merthyr Tydvil, 1888-1900. *Address:* Byways, Englefield Green, Surrey; Plas Tyddyngladis, near Dolgelley, N. Wales.
(Died 5 July 1924.)

MORISON, Alexander Blackhall, M.D., F.R.C.P.; Consulting Physician, Royal Northern Hospital, London, and to Mount Vernon Hospital; *b.* 1850; *s.* of Alexander C. Morison, Surgeon, Bengal N.I., H.E.I.C.S.; *m.* Elizabeth Stewart, *e. d.* of Duncan Maclachlan, Edinburgh. *Educ.:* Universities of Edinburgh, Berlin, and Würzburg. Graduated, University of Edinburgh, 1872; after study on Continent, settled in practice in London; specialized in Medicine; appointed Physician to Great Northern Central Hospital, Paddington Green Children's Hospital, and St. Marylebone General Dispensary; F.R.C.P. Edin., 1889; Morison Lecturer, Royal College of Physicians, Edin., 1897-98; F.R.C.P. Lond., 1903; Fellow Royal Society of Medicine and of Medical Society of London; Corresponding Member Edinburgh Medico-Chir. Society; President National Medical Union, etc. *Publications:* Disorders of the Heart; The Nervous System and Visceral Disease; On the Nature, Causes, and Treatment of Cardiac Pain; The Blackhalls of that Ilk and Barra; Hereditary

Coroners and Foresters of the Garioch (New Spalding Club). *Recreations:* antiquarian research, fishing, sketching, golf. *Address:* 14 Upper Berkeley St., W.1. *T.:* Paddington 2168. *T.A.:* Benachie, London. *Club:* Caledonian.
(Died 23 Dec. 1927.)

MORISON, Hon. Donald, K.C.; *b.* 22 Apr. 1857; *m.* 1883, Catherine E., *e. d.* of Robert Trapnell, Co. Donegal; one *s.* one *d.* Admitted to Bar, 1881; M.H.A. for Bonavista District, 1888-97 and 1906-13; Attorney-General, 1894; Judge of Supreme Court, 1898-1902, when returned to active practice of the legal profession; Attorney-General, 1909-13; one of the Counsel for Great Britain at North Atlantic Fisheries Arbitration at the Hague, 1910. *Address:* St. John's Newfoundland. *T.A.:* Morison. Newfoundland. *(Died 24 April 1924.)*

MORLAND, Gen. Sir Thomas Lethbridge Napier, K.C.B., *cr.* 1915; C.B. 1903; K.C.M.G., *cr.* 1917; D.S.O. 1902; General Officer Commanding-in-Chief, Aldershot Command, 1922-23; A.D.C. General to the King since 1922; *b.* 9 Aug. 1865; *m.* 1890, Mabel Eleanor Rowena, *e. d.* of Admiral Henry C. St. John of Stokefield, Thornbury. Entered army, 1884; Captain, 1893; Major, 1899; served Nigeria, 1897-98 (despatches, Brevet Major, medal with clasp); Nigeria, 1901, 1902, 1903 (C.B.); European War, 1914-18 (despatches twice, K.C.B., prom. Lt.-Gen.); King's Royal Rifle Corps; Inspector-General, West African Frontier Force, 1905-10; Brigadier-General commanding 2nd Infantry Brigade, Aldershot, 1910-13; commanded 2nd London Division Territorial Force, 1914; General, 1923. *Club:* Naval and Military. *(Died 21 May 1925.)*

MORLEY of Blackburn, 1st Viscount, *cr.* 1908; **John Morley,** P.C., O.M., M.A., F.R.S., LL.D., D.C.L.; Hon. Fellow, All Souls, Oxon.; Chancellor of Victoria University, 1908-23; *b.* Blackburn, 24 Dec. 1838; *s.* of late Jonathan Morley, surgeon. *Educ.:* Cheltenham College; Lincoln College, Oxford. Hon. LL.D., Glasgow, 1879; Cambridge, 1892; St. Andrews, 1902; Edinburgh, 1904; Hon. D.C.L., Oxford, 1896. Barr. Lincoln's Inn, 1873; M.P. (L.) Newcastle-on-Tyne, 1883-95; twice Chief Secretary for Ireland with seat in Cabinet, 1886, and 1892-95; Bencher of Lincoln's Inn, 1891; Trustee of British Museum, 1894; M.P. (L.) Montrose Burghs, 1896-1908; Member of Historical Manuscripts Commission; Secretary of State for India, 1905-10; Lord President of the Council, 1910-14. *Publications:* Edmund Burke, 1867; Critical Miscellanies, 1871, second series, 1877; Voltaire, 1871; Rousseau, 1873: The Struggle for National Education, 1873; On Compromise, 1874; Diderot and the Encyclopædists, 1878; Burke, 1879; The Life of Richard Cobden, 1881; Studies in Literature, 1891; Oliver Cromwell, 1900; Life of Gladstone, 1903; Recollections, 1917. *Heir:* none. *Address:* Flowermead, Wimbledon Park, S.W. *Club:* Athenæum. *(Died 23 Sept. 1923.)*

MORLEY, Right Hon. Arnold, P.C.; *b.* 18 Feb. 1849; *s.* of Samuel Morley, M.P. for Bristol, and Rebecca, *d.* of Samuel Hope, Liverpool; *m.* 1911, Elsie (*d.* 1912), widow of Daniel Runyon, of New York. *Educ.:* Trin. Coll. Camb. (M.A.); took an ægrotat degree in Mathematical honours, having been 9th in the 3 days. Barrister Inner Temple, 1873; M.P. Nottingham, 1880-85; Nottingham E., 1885-95; Patronage Secretary and Chief Liberal Whip, 1886-92; Postmaster-General, 1892-95; acted as counsel for Home Office in Colliery Accident Inquiries, 1880-85; Chairman of Dominions Commission, 1912; passed as extra master, the examination of the Board of Trade, with one hundred marks. *Recreations:* shooting, fishing, stalking, cycling, yachting; owns steam yacht "Yarta"; rowed in 1st Trinity 1st boat, head of the river, 1870. *Address:* 7 Stratton Street, Piccadilly, W. *T.:*

Gerrard 3806. *Clubs:* Brooks's, Turf, National Liberal; Royal Yacht Squadron, Cowes.
(*Died 16 Jan. 1916.*)

MORLEY, Charles, Editor of the Pall Mall Magazine, 1905-11. *Publications:* Studies in Board Schools; London at Prayer, 1909. *Address:* c/o Pall Mall Magazine, Newton Street, Holborn, W.C. (*Died 20 April 1916.*)

MORLEY, Charles; *b.* 1847; *s.* of late Samuel Morley, M.P., and *b.* of late Rt. Hon. Arnold Morley. *Educ.:* Trin. Coll. Camb. (B.A. 1870; M.A. 1874). Hon. Secretary to Royal College of Music; was a partner in firm of Messrs. I. and R. Morley, Wood Street, E.C.; M.P. (G.L.) Brecknockshire, 1895-1906. *Recreations:* music and driving. *Address:* Shockerwick, Bath; 46 Bryanston Square, W. *Clubs:* Athenæum, Reform, Brooks's, National Liberal, Travellers'.
(*Died 27 Oct. 1917.*)

MORLEY, Edward Williams; *b.* Newark, N.J., 29 Jan. 1838; *s.* of Rev. Sardis Brewster Morley and Anna Clarissa Treat; *m.* 1868, Isabella Ashley Birdsall of Winsted, Connecticut. *Educ.:* Williams College. Professor of Chemistry, Western Reserve University at Cleveland, Ohio, 1868-1906; Professor emeritus since 1906; Sc.D., Yale, 1909; LL.D. Western Reserve University, 1891; Williams College, 1901; Lafayette College, 1907; University of Pittsburgh, 1915; Member National Academy of Sciences, 1897; Foreign Member Chemical Society, London; Hon. Member Royal Institution; Hon. Member American Chemical Society; Past President A.A.A.S., and of American Chemical Society; Hon. President, Eighth International Congress Applied Chemistry, 1912; Davy Medallist, 1907; Elliot Cresson Medallist, 1912; Willard Gibbs Medallist, 1917. *Publications:* On the Densities of Oxygen and of Hydrogen, and on the Ratio of their Atomic Weights; and about forty other papers. *Recreations:* automobile, camera. *Address:* West Hartford, Connecticut. *M.:* 4179 C. (*Died 24 Feb. 1923.*)

MORLEY, Rt. Rev. Samuel, M.A., D.D.; *b.* 1841. *Educ.:* London Univ.; Pembroke Coll. Camb. (M.A.). D.D., Archbishop of Cant. *jure dignitatis.* Late Chaplain of St. John's Church, San Remo; Chaplain of Assouan, Egypt, and Archdeacon of Church of England in Egypt; ordained, 1868; Curate of Ilkeston, Derbyshire, 1868-70; Curate of Sandgate, 1871-75; Chaplain of Secunderabad, India, 1875-78; Domestic Chaplain to the Bishop of Madras, 1878-96; Consecrated Bishop in Tinnevelly and Madura in St. George's Cathedral, Madras, 28 Oct. 1896, by the Bishops of Calcutta, Madras, and Travancore; retired, 1903. *Address:* Sillwood, Upper Bridge Road, Redhill, Surrey.
(*Died 6 Nov. 1923.*)

MORRIS, Edmund M., A.R.C.A. 1897; artist; *b.* Perth, Ontario, 1871; *y. s.* of late Hon. Alexander Morris, P.C., D.C.L. *Educ.:* Toronto; Art Students' League, New York; L'Academie Julian, under Laurens and Constant; returned to Canada, 1896; has painted in Holland and Scotland and latterly in the Province of Quebec; accompanied the Indian Treaty Commissioners into the James Bay district and made a series of portraits of the Ojibway Indians, 1906; commissioned by the Ontario Government to paint chiefs of the North-West Indian tribes, 1907 (now in the Royal Ontario Museum); by the Alberta and Saskatchewan Governments to paint Indian portraits for the Parliament buildings in Edmonton and Regina, 1909; a founder of New Canadian Art Club, 1908; Cap Tourmente purchased by the Dominion Government; a painter of landscape and figures in landscape; bronze medal, Pan-American exhibition, 1901; Hon. Secretary, Canadian Art Club. *Club:* Arts and Letters, Toronto.

MORRIS, Commissary-General Sir Edward, K.C.B., *cr.* 1882; C.B. 1879; J.P. City and County of Dublin; *b.* 1833; *s.* of late Robert Morris, Rosbercom House, Co. Kilkenny; *m.* 1858, Elizabeth Dorcas (*d.* 1875), *d.* of William B. Mant; one *d.* Entered Commissariat Dept., 1854; Commissary-General, 1881-86; retired 1886; served Crimea, 1854-56 (medal with clasp and Turkish medal); Zulu War, 1879 (medal with clasp, despatches twice); Egypt, 1882 (despatches twice, medal with clasp, Egyptian Star and 2nd class of the Medjidie). *Club:* Junior United Service.
(*Died 15 Feb. 1923.*)

MORRIS, Rev. Ernest Edwin, M.A., T.D., R.D., J.P., Vicar of Ashbourne and Hon. Canon of Southwell; H.C.F. (1st Class); Income Tax Commissioner and Assessor under Clergy Discipline Act, etc.; *b.* 30 Aug. 1856; *s.* of late Henry Morris of Shrewsbury; *m.* Josephine, *d.* of late Richard Knott Bolton, M.A., of Carrickmines, Co. Dublin, and Fenny Bentley, Derbyshire; three *s.* two *d. Educ.:* Shrewsbury: Jesus College, Cambridge; Ely Theological College. Formerly Vicar of Blackwell; Chaplain to High Sheriff; Chaplain to 6th Batt. Derbyshire Territorial Infantry; Chairman of Governing Body of Queen Elizabeth's Grammar School; Member of County Licensing Committee; Derbyshire Territorial Association, etc. *Address:* The Vicarage, Ashbourne. *T.A.:* Vicar. Ashbourne. (*Died 7 July 1924.*)

MORRIS, Greville; artist; *m.* Harriet Maud Catherine, *d.* of Rev. Maurice Edward Jenkins, Christ College, Cambridge, formerly Vicar of Egton, Yorkshire. *Educ.:* Cheltenham College; received art training at Paris. *Address:* Kenython, Parkstone, Dorset.
(*Died 13 Jan. 1922.*)

MORRIS, Sir Henry, 1st Bt., *cr.* 1909; M.A., M.B. Lond., F.R.C.S.; President Royal Society of Medicine, 1910-12; President Royal College of Surgeons, 1906-9; Consulting Surgeon and Emeritus Lecturer on Surgery, Middlesex Hospital; Past-Representative of Royal College of Surgeons on and Treasurer of the General Medical Council, 1905-17; Founder and Vice-President of Imperial Cancer Research Fund; Trustee of the Hunterian Museum, London; For. Corr. Member Societe de Chirurgie; Hon. Mem. Med. Soc.; State of New York; Hon. Fellow Royal College of Surgeons in Ireland; *b.* 7 Jan. 1844; *s.* of late William Morris, surgeon, of Petworth, Sussex. *Educ.:* Epsom College. University College, and Guy's Hospital. Delivered Cavendish Lecture, 1893; Hunterian Lectures, 1898; Bradshaw Lecturer, Royal College of Surgeons, 1903; Annual Oration, Medical Society of London, 1905, On the Personal Relations between the London Hospitals and their Medical Schools; Hunterian Oration on John Hunter as a philosopher, Feb. 1909, delivered before their R.H. the Prince and Princess of Wales; formerly Surgeon to, and Lecturer on Anatomy and Surgery, Middlesex Hospital Medical College; Examiner in Surgery, University of London, and in Anatomy, University of Durham; Chairman of the Court of Examiners R.C.S. for six years; Bradshaw Lecture on Cancer and its Origin; Sir Mitchell Banks Memorial Lecture, University of Liverpool, 1908. *Publications:* The Anatomy of the Joints of Man; Surgical Diseases of the Kidney and Ureter; Injuries and Disease of the Genital and Urinary Organs; Injuries of the Lower Extremity; and Injuries and Diseases of the Abdomen; Editor of Morris's System of Anatomy, 4th edition; The Treatment of Inoperable Cancer; "Suggestion" in relation to the Treatment of Disease, 1910; Looking Back, or from Superstition to Research—Christian Science Refuted, 1909; Contributor to Playfair's Gynæcology and Allbutt's Medicine, and various articles in The Outlook during the period of the war. *Heir*: none. *Address*: 42 Connaught Square, W.2. *T.*: Paddington 725.

(Died 14 June 1926.)

MORRIS, Sir Malcolm, K.C.V.O., *cr.* 1908; F.R.C.S. Edin., F.Z.S.; Chairman of British Federation of Medical and Allied Services, President of Institute of Hygiene; Vice-President of National Council for Combating Venereal Diseases; Fellow of Royal Sanitary Institute; Member of Committee of Radium Institute; *y. s.* of John Carnac Morris, F.R.S., M.C.S. *Educ.*: St. Mary's Hospital; Berlin; Vienna. Has been Surgeon to the Skin Department, St. Mary's Hospital and Seamen's Hospital; Lecturer on Skin Diseases, London School of Clinical Medicine; President of the Harveian Society; representative of National Association for the Prevention of Tuberculosis at the Berlin Congress 1899; Secretary-General, British Congress of Tuberculosis, 1901; President Dermatological Section Royal Society of Medicine; President Dermatological Section International Medical Congress, London, 1913; Member Royal Commission on Venereal Diseases, 1913-15. *Publications*: Skin Diseases, 1894; sixth edition, 1917; Light and X-Rays in Skin Diseases, 1907; The Nation's Health, 1917; Story of English Public Health, 1919. *Address*: 11 Marlborough Place, N.W.8. *T.*: Hampstead 1070. *Clubs*: Reform, M.C.C. *(Died 19 Feb. 1924.)*

MORRIS, Rev. Richard; Hon. Canon of Rochester, 1908. *Educ.*: Trinity College, Dublin. Ordained, 1868; Curate of Doon, 1869; Castle Terra, 1869-72; Vicar of St. Mark's, New Brompton, 1872. *Address*: Vittoria Walk, Cheltenham. *(Died 25 Jan. 1923.)*

MORRIS, Sir Robert Armine, 4th Bt., *cr.* 1806; D.L., J.P.; *b.* 27 July 1848; *S.* father 1898; *m.* Lucy (*d.* 1902), *d.* of Thomas Cory, Sketty House, Swansea, 1885; one *s. four d.* Owns about 3000 acres. Major 3rd Batt. Welsh Regt. 1882-84. *Heir: s.* Tankerville Robert Armine, late Lieut. 1st Batt. Gloucesters. Regt., *b.* June 1892. *Address*: Sketty Park, Swansea. *Club*: Carlton. *(Died 20 Feb. 1927.)*

MORRIS, Rev. Rupert Hugh, D.D. (Oxon.), F.S.A.; Vicar of St. Gabriel's, Pimlico; Prebendary of Mathry ("Golden Prebend") in St. David's Cathedral; *b.* Holywell, Flintshire, 1844; *s.* of William Morris, J.P., formerly editor of Y Cymro, a Welsh Church newspaper; *m.* Fanny Ada, *d.* of Lt.-Gen. C. E. Gold (late Colonel of 65th). *Educ.*: Ruthin Grammar School; Jesus College, Oxford (Scholar and Powis Scholar); 2nd class Classics, Moderations; 2nd class Classics, Final Exam. Lit. Hum. Assistant Classical Master, Rossall School, 1865-69; Curate of Poulton le Ffylde, 1867-69; Principal of Training College for S. Wales and Monmouthshire, 1869-76; Lecturer of St. Peter's, Carmarthen; Secretary of St. David's Diocesan Board of Education, 1870-76; appointed by Bishop Thirlwall to Stall in St. David's Cathedral for educational work; Curate of St. Mary's, Park Street, Grosvenor Square, London, W., 1876-78; Vicar, 1878-82; Headmaster of Godolphin School, 1876-84; Chaplain and Librarian to Duke of Westminster, 1884-95; Vice-President of Cambrian Archæological Association. *Publications*: Chester in the Times of Plantagenets and Tudors, 1893; History of the Diocese of Chester, 1895 Rules for Paraphrasing, etc. *Address*: St. Gabriel's Vicarage, 4 Warwick Square, S.W. *(Died 8 Jan. 1918.)*

MORRIS, Samuel, J.P.; merchant and shipowner; *b.* 1846; *s.* of late G. Morris, Fiddown; *m.* Catharine, *d.* of James Feehan, Tybroughny, 1874; six *s.* three *d.* M.P. (N.) Co. Kilkenny, S., 1894-1900. *Address*: Newrath House, Waterford. *T.*: 57 and 193 Waterford; 10 Carrick-on-Suir. *(Died Aug. 1920.)*

MORRIS, Rev. Silas, M.A., Principal, Baptist Coll., Bangor, since 1896; *b.* 1862; *m.* 1892, Miss M. H. Williams, Pontardulais; one *s. Educ.*: Elem. Schools, Dafen (near Llanelly, Carm) and Pontardulais; Aberavon Academy, Pontypool College, and N. Wales University College, upon entering which last he took the highest entrance Scholarship, 1884; graduated London University M.A. (in Classics), 1888. Classical Tutor at North Wales Baptist College, Llangollen, 1886; removed to Bangor, 1892; Editor of Seren Gomer, 1893-1904. *Address*: Baptist College, Bangor.

(Died 25 July 1923.)

MORRIS, Lieut.-Col. Thomas Henry, J.P., D.L.; C.B.E. 1918; *b.* 3 Feb. 1848; *e. s.* of Wm. Morris, J.P., D.L., The Lodge, near Halifax, Yorks; *m.* 1909, Florence Ethel, *y. d.* of Richard Crompton, Bury; no *c. Educ.*: Rugby. *Address*: Bolton Lodge, Bolton Percy, Yorks. *T.A.*: Bolton Percy. *T.*: 16 Tadcaster. *M.*: WY 1. *Club*: Union. *(Died 26 Nov. 1927.)*

MORRIS-AIREY, Harold, C.B.E. 1919; Technical Adviser, H.M. Signal School, Royal Naval Barracks, Portsmouth; *b.* 1880; *o. s.* of William M Airey, Crumpsall, Manchester; *m.* Eva, *d.* of late William Prescott, Manchester; three *s. Educ.*: Owen's College, Manchester; University of Bonn. Was Lecturer in Physics at the Universities of Bonn, Manchester, and Durham; carried out experimental work in Wireless Telegraphy at Armstrong College, Newcastle; at the outbreak of war offered services to Admiralty, and in 1915 was appointed to the Wireless Telegraphy Department in H.M.S. Vernon as Lieut. R.N.V.R.; took part in early development of wireless apparatus in naval aircraft; promoted to Lt.-Commander; was appointed in charge of development of Naval Wireless Transmission with rank of Lieut.-Col., R.M., 1918; appointed wireless expert to Admiralty, 1920. *Publications*: papers on Electricity and Optics in various scientific journals. *Recreation*: motoring. *Address*: 16 Villiers Road, Southsea. *T.*: Portsmouth 5802. *M.*: BK 6705. *(Died 19 June 1927.)*

MORRISBY, Major Hon. Arthur, J.P.; Acting Clerk Legislative Council 1916-18; granted the title of Honourable for life by the King, 1916; Coroner for Tasmania since 1911; *b.* Sandford, Tasmania, 29 December 1847; *s.* of late John Morrisby of Clarence, Tasmania; *m.* 1875, Isabel Snowden (*d.* 1880), of Hobart; one *s. Educ.*: Mornington School, near Bellerive, Clarence. Member Clarence Municipality, 1890-1892; Member and Chairman First Town Board, Zeehan, West Coast, Tasmania; Chairman, 1892-94 and 1896-1900, Member to 1902; Chairman Board of Advice, Cemetery Trust, 1892-1902; Member of Licensing Bench, Marine Board of Strahan, Macquarie Harbour, 1898-1902; minister without portfolio, 1903-4; formed, and was appointed Captain of the Zeehan Rifle Company, 1st Batt. Tas. Infantry, 1896; served in S. African War in command of E. Squadron 3rd Batt. Australian Commonwealth Horse, and retired with rank of Major (medal with clasp); elected by Parliament as a Member of the Council of the University of Tasmania; elected Lay Representative, Anglican Synod of Tasmania, 1907; Chairman of Committee of Synod, 1911-16; Chairman of Committee, 1919; Member of the Diocesan Council, 1914; Member of the Legislative Council of Tasmania for Gordon, 1899-1916; Chairman of Committees, 1907-16; appointed by Government as a Royal Commissioner to open Parliament, 1914. *Recreations*: rifle shooting and sporting shooting, rowing. *Address*: Bellerive, near Hobart, Tasmania. *Club*: Military, Hobart.

MORRISON, Brig.-Gen. Colquhoun Grant, C.M.G. 1915; late 1st Dragoons; *b.* 28 Jan. 1860; *m.* 1914, Vera, *d.* of Col. H. A.

Sawyer. Entered army, 1879 ; Captain, 1889 ; Major, 1897 ; Lt.-Col., 1908 ; Col., 1911 ; Instructor R.M.C., 1891-97 ; D.A.A.G. Jersey, 1899-1901 ; Commandant and Area Administrator, South Africa, 1901-2 ; D.A.A.G. Orange River Colony and Cape Colony, 1906-9 ; specially employed, War Office, 1911 ; A.A. and Q.M.G. Gibraltar, 1912-14 ; served South Africa, 1901-2 (Queen's medal, 3 clasps) ; European War, 1914-15 (C.M.G.). *Club:* Army and Navy.

(Died 23 May 1916.)

MORRISON, Major-Gen. Sir Edward Whipple Bancroft, K.C.M.G., *cr.* 1919 ; C.B. 1918 ; C.M.G. 1917 ; D.S.O. 1900 ; *b.* 6 July 1867 ; *m.* 1911, Mrs. Emma Fripp of Ottawa. Served South Africa, 1899-1900 (despatches, Bt. Capt., Queen's medal 3 clasps, D.S.O.), commanded 8th Artillery Brigade C.F.A., 1900-13 ; Director of Artillery Headquarter Staff, 1913-14 ; O.C. 1st Artillery Brigade, C.E.F. 1914-15 ; served Second Ypres, Festubert, Givenchy ; G.O.C. II. Canadian Divisional Artillery, 1915-16, St. Eloi, Third Ypres, and Somme ; G.O.C. Canadian Corps Artillery, 1916-19 ; Vimy, Hill 70, Lens, Paschendaele, 1917, Amiens, Arras, Quéant-Drocourt Line, Canal du Nord, Bourlon Wood ; capture of Cambrai, Valenciennes, Mons, 1918 ; Army of Occupation in Germany, 1919 (K.C.M.G., C.M.G., despatches, C.B., Major-General, 1918) ; Inspector-General of Artillery, 1919 ; Master-General of the Ordnance, 1920 ; President of Canadian Artillery Association, 1921. *Publication:* With the Guns. *Address:* 21 M'Leod Street, Ottawa, Canada. *Club:* Rideau, Ottawa.

(Died May 1925.)

MORRISON, Col. F. L., C.B. 1916 ; V.D. ; 5th Batt. Highland L.I. (T.F.) ; *b.* 24 Oct. 1863. Writer (M.A., LL.B., of Glasgow University). *Address:* Ashcraig, Great Western Road, Glasgow. *(Died 22 Dec. 1917.)*

MORRISON, George Ernest; Political Adviser to President, Chinese Republic, since 1912 ; Times Correspondent, Indo China, Siam, Peking, 1895-1912 ; *b.* Geelong, Victoria, Australia, 4 Feb. 1862 ; *s.* of late Dr. G. Morrison ; *m.* 1912, Jennie Wark, *d.* of Robert Robin ; three *s. Educ.:* Melbourne and Edinburgh Universities (M.D., C.M.). Crossed Australia on foot from the Gulf of Carpentaria to Melbourne, Christmas, 1882-83 ; speared in New Guinea, Oct. 1883 ; graduated, 1887 ; crossed from Shanghai to Rangoon by land, 1894 ; as special for the Times travelled from Bangkok in Siam to Yunnan city in China and round Tonquin, 1896 ; and in 1897 crossed Manchuria from Stretensk in Siberia to Vladivostok ; was in Peking during siege of Legations, June-Aug. 1900 ; was present at the triumphal entry into Port Arthur, January 1905 ; in 1907 crossed China from Peking to the French border of Tonquin ; represented Times Portsmouth Peace Conference, 1905 ; rode from Honan city in Central China across Asia to Andijan in Russian Turkestan, 3750 miles in 175 days, 1910 ; has travelled in every province of China except Tibet. Holds 1st Class Order Excellent Crop (China). *Publication:* An Australian in China : being the Narrative of a Quiet Journey Across China to Burma, 1895. *Address:* Peking. *Club:* Oriental. *(Died May 1920.)*

MORRISON, Very Rev. George Herbert, D.D. ; Minister of Wellington Church, Glasgow, since 1902, and Moderator of the United Free Church General Assembly, 1926 ; *b.* 2 Oct. 1866 ; *s.* of Doctor Thomas Morrison, Rector, Free Church Training College, Glasgow ; *m.* 1st, 1894, Agnes Gray Orr, Glasgow (*d.* 1902) ; 2nd, 1904, Christine Marie Auchinvole, Glasgow ; one *s.* two *d.* (younger son killed, 1918). *Educ.:* Glasgow Academy and Glasgow University. Sub-Editor of the New English Dictionary, Oxford, 1888-89; Assistant to Dr. Alexander Whyte, Edinburgh, 1893-

1894 ; Minister of First Free Church, Thurso, 1894-98 ; St. John's Free Church, Dundee, 1898-1902. *Publications:* Many volumes of sermons and addresses ; edited the Memoirs of Thomas Boston, and Hugh Macdonald's Rambles round Glasgow ; is a constant contributor to the Religious Press. *Recreations:* walking and field-botany. *Address:* 29 Lilybank Gardens, Glasgow, W.2. *T.:* Glasgow 1516 W.

(Died 14 Oct. 1928.)

MORRISON, Col. John, M.V.O. 1910 ; O.B.E. 1918 ; V D. ; late commanding 5th (the Sutherland and Caithness Highland) Battailon Seaforth Highlanders ; Vice-Lieutenant of Sutherland, J.P. *Address:* Rhives. Golspie, Sutherland. *(Died 1 Mar. 1919.)*

MORRISON, R. E., R.C.A. ; portrait painter ; *b.* Peel, Isle of Man, 31 Dec. 1851 ; *s.* of John Morrison, builder ; *m.* 1879 ; one *s. Educ.:* Peel ; Liverpool School of Art ; London ; Académie Julien, under Bougeureau and Tony Robert Fleury, Paris. Followed the profession of portrait painter in his adopted city, Liverpool, where he has resided for more than forty years ; has painted many noted people in Liverpool and throughout the northern counties. *Recreation:* landscape sketching. *Clubs:* Arts ; University. Artists', Liverpool.

MORRISON, Walter, J.P. ; *b.* 21 May, 1836 ; *s.* of James Morrison, of Morrison, Dillon, and Co., and Mary, *d.* of John Todd, of same firm. *Educ.:* Eton ; Balliol Coll. Oxford. 1st class Lit. Hum. 1857. M.P. Plymouth, 1861, 1874 ; contested City of London, 1880 ; M.P. Skipton Division (L.U.), 1886-92 and 1895-1900. *Publications:* some occasional papers. Owns about 13,900 acres. *Address:* Malham Tarn, Langcliffe, Settle ; 77 Cromwell Road. S.W. *Club:* United University. *(Died 18 Dec. 1921.)*

MORROW, Albert; *b.* Comber, Co. Down, 1863 ; *m.* 1901, Catherine Macnamara ; one *s.* one *d. Educ.:* Belfast ; Royal College of Art, London. Started on the English Illustrated Magazine, 1884 ; has been illustrating books and magazines ever since ; has had hundreds of posters reproduced, both theatrical and commercial, Answers posters, Lloyd's News posters, and for Cassell & Co. ; exhibited for seven consecutive years in the Royal Academy. *Recreations:* principally walking and sketching landscape. *(Died Oct. 1927.)*

MORSON, Walter Augustus Ormsby, K.C. Canada ; Barrister ; *b.* Hamilton, P.E.I., 24 Dec. 1851 ; *m.* 1891, May Elizabeth Des Brisay. Member of Legislative Assembly, P.E.I., since 1902 ; Conservative. *Address:* Charlottetown, P.E. Island. *(Died Sept. 1921.)*

MORTIMER, Rev. Christian, Canon of Lichfield 1890-1914. *Educ.:* Clare Coll. Camb. (M.A. Junior Optime). Ordained 1859 ; curate of Eaton-Bishop, Herefords., 1859-64 ; Middle, Salop, 1864-68 ; vicar of Grinshill, 1868-71 ; Ash, Salop, 1871-80 ; Diocesan Inspector, 1871-88 ; Rector of Pitchford, Salop, 1880-90 ; Preb. of Dassett-Parva, 1885-90 ; Examining Chaplain to Bishop of Lichfield, 1890-91. *Address:* Poundfields, Old Woking, Surrey.

(Died 23 Aug. 1916.)

MORTIMER, George Frederick Lloyd, Recorder of Rotherham since 1905 ; *b.* 1866 ; *m.* 1893, Mary Isabella Edith, *d.* of Sir T. Wrightson, 1st Bart. *Educ.:* Birkenhead School ; Balliol College, Oxford (1st class Lit. Hum., 1889). President Oxford Union Society ; K.C. 1919 ; Bencher of Inner Temple, 1924. *Address:* 4 Harcourt Buildings, Temple, E.C.4 ; 3 Cheyne Place, S.W.3. *T.A.:* 69 The Temple. *T.:* Central 8435. *Club:* New University.

(Died 5 Sept. 1928.)

MORTIMER, Lieut.-Col. James, C.M.G. 1916 ; 5th Batt. Yorks Regt. (T.F.). Served S. African War, 1900-1 (Queen's medal, 4 clasps) ; European War, 1914-16 (despatches,

751

C.M.G.). *Address:* Grove Cottage, Driffield, E. Yorks. *(Died 15 Sept. 1916.)*

MORTIMER, Colonel Sir William Hugh, K.C.B., *cr.* 1911; C.B. 1900; *b.* 13 Dec. 1846; *s.* of A. J. Mortimer, British Paymaster-General, English German Legion; *m.* 1877, Evelyn Maude Mary, *e. d.* of George Harries of Trevaccon and Rickerton, Pembrokeshire; three *d.* Entered army as Ensign 41st Welsh Regiment; Army Pay Department, 1878; served Egyptian-Campaign, 1882 (medal with clasp); Tel-el-Kebir (bronze star); South Africa, 1899-1902, first as Chief Paymaster Natal Forces, and afterwards as Chief Paymaster of Forces South Africa (despatches twice, C.B., Queen's medal, 4 clasps; King's medal, 2 clasps); Chief Paymaster, Army Pay Department, retired 1906. *Address:* Quarrymill, Dyke Road, Brighton.
(Died 24 Oct. 1921.)

MORTIMORE, Lt.-Col. Claude Alick, D.S.O. 1916; late R.F.A.; *b.* 28 Dec. 1875; *s.* of late Alexander Mortimore; unmarried. *Educ.:* Uppingham. Served S. Africa, 1900-2 (Queen's medal 4 clasps, King's medal 2 clasps); European War, 1914-18 (D.S.O., Chevalier Légion d'Honneur, Bt. Lt.-Col.); retired pay, 1922. *Address:* 17 Sussex Mansions, S.W.7. *T.:* Kensington 1411. *Club:* United Service.
(Died 7 April 1927.)

MORTIMORE, Frederick William, M.V.O. 1916; Paymaster-Captain, Royal Navy (retired); *b.* 27 Oct. 1858; 2nd *s.* of late Richard Mortimore of Cullompton, Devon; unmarried. *Educ.:* Sherborne School. Entered Navy, 1875; retired, 1914. *Address:* Riseholme, Elm Road, Horsell, Woking. *Club:* Junior United Service.
(Died 12 May 1928.)

MORTON, Sir Alpheus Cleophas, Kt., *cr.* 1918; M.P. (L.) Sutherlandshire, 1906-18; Architect and Surveyor; 2nd *s.* of late Francis Morton of Old Sodbury, Gloucestershire. *Educ.:* privately in Canada. Member of Corporation of London since 1882; contested Hythe Burghs, 1885; Christchurch, Hants, 1886; M.P. (L.) Peterborough, 1889-95; Deputy-Alderman of the Ward of Farringdon With-Out; Chairman of the Metropolitan Paving Committee; member of City and Guilds Institute; Guardian of City of London; Governor of St. Bartholomew's Hospital; Member of the City Lieutenancy. *Address:* 124 Chancery Lane, W.C.; 47 Gauden Road, Clapham, S.W.4. *Clubs:* National Liberal; Scottish Liberal, Edinburgh.
(Died 26 April 1923.)

MORTON, General Boyce William Dunlop, Indian Army; *b.* 24 Aug. 1829; *m.* 1855. Entered army, 1848; Lt.-Gen. 1892; unemployed list, 1887; served Cossyah and Jyntiah Hills Campaign, 1861-63 (despatches); in civil employ, 1854-84; Deputy Commissioner of seven districts in succession, including Darjeeling, 1867-73. *Publications:* Some Indian Experiences; What Follows; What I Believe. *Address:* 2 Priory Parade, London Road, Cheltenham. *(Died 15 Aug. 1919.)*

MORTON, Edward, dramatist, critic, and journalist; *m.* Rosamond, *d.* of Capt. Thomas Devereux Bingham, Wartnaby Hall, Leicestershire. *Publications:* Travellers' Tales, 1892; Man and Beast (with I. Zangwill), 1898; Miss Impudence, comedy in one act, produced at Terry's Theatre, 1892; San Toy, or The Emperor's Own, comic opera (music by Sidney Jones), produced at Daly's Theatre, 1899. *Club:* Authors'. *(Died 6 July 1922.)*

MORTON, James Elliot Vowler, C.B. 1918; R.N.; Paymaster Rear-Adm.; *b.* Chittlehamholt Parsonage, N. Devon, 27 Oct. 1861; *e. s.* of late Rev. James Henry Morton, M.A., Trinity College, Dublin; unmarried. *Educ.:* St. John's Foundation School, Leatherhead. Entered R. Navy, 1878; served in N. America and West Indies, Australia, China, W. Coast of

752

Africa, Pacific and Mediterranean Stations; Fleet Paymaster, 1902; on board H.M.S. Charybdis at the Blockade of Venezuela Coast and action at Puerto Cabello; in 1911 when in H.M.S. Carnarvon, took part in the Investiture of the Prince of Wales at Carnarvon Castle (Coronation medal); served in H.M.S. Tiger, 1914-18; present at the battles of Dogger Bank, 1915, and Jutland, 1916; Paymaster-in-Chief 1916; Paymaster Rear-Adm., 1920; Russian Military Order (2nd class) of St. Stanislaus; Officer of the Legion of Honour. *Recreations:* shooting and fishing. *Address:* Crescent Mansions, Plymouth. *(Died 21 Sept. 1924.)*

MORTON, James H., A.R.C.A.; artist; *b.* Darwen, 1881; *s.* of James and Elizabeth Morton. *Educ.:* elementary schools and Higher Grade School; Darwen (Huntingdon Scholarship and Local Exhibition); Royal College of Art (R.C.A. Scholarship). Taught Art in Darlington for twelve months; since been designing and painting; Exhibitor at the Royal Academy, International, Liverpool Exhibitions. *Recreations:* walking, botany. *Address:* 30 Sudell Road, Darwen.
(Died 5 Nov. 1918.)

MORTON, Levi Parsons, LL.D.; *b.* Shoreham, Vermont, U.S.A., 16 May 1824; *s.* of Rev. Dan. Oliver and Lucretia Parsons Morton; *m.* 1st, Lucy Kimball (*d.* 1871); 2nd, 1873, *d.* of W. L. Street; five *c.* *Educ.:* Shoreham Academy. Founded the Banking Houses of L. P. Morton and Co., Morton, Bliss, and Co., New York, and Morton, Rose, and Co., Morton, Chaplin, and Co., London, and the Morton Trust Co., New York; [descendant of George Morton of Bawtry, Yorks, financial agent in London of the Mayflower Pilgrims who arrived at Plymouth, Mass. on ship "Ann," 1623]; Member of Congress from New York, 1878-81; United States Minister to France, 1881-85; Vice-President of the United States, and President of the Senate, 1889-93; Governor of the State of New York, 1895 and 1896; Dartmouth College 1891, and Middleburg College 1893, bestowed on him LL.D. Owns 1000 acres. *Address:* Ellerslie, Rhinecliff-on-Hudson; 681 Fifth Avenue, New York. *Clubs:* Century, Union, Metropolitan, Union League of New York Lawyers Republican, Downtown.
(Died 16 May 1920.)

MORTON, Thomas Corsan; artist; Curator, Kirkcaldy Museum and Art Gallery, Fifeshire; late Keeper, National Galleries of Scotland; *b.* Glasgow, 1859; *s.* of James Morton, M.D., LL.D., and Elizabeth Corsan; *m.* 1890, Amelie Lydiard Robertson; one *s.* one *d.* *Educ.:* High School, Glasgow. Studied Art at the Slade School, London, under Professor Alphonse Legros, and thereafter at Paris under Messieurs Boulanger and Lefevbre; afterwards settled in Glasgow, and later in Edinburgh, but now resident in Kirkcaldy. *Recreations:* walking, reading. *Address:* 44 Townsend Place, Kirkcaldy, Fifeshire. *Club:* Glasgow Art.
(Died 24 Dec. 1928.)

MORVI, H.H. Thakur Saheb Sir Waghji Ravaji, G.C.I.E.; *cr.* 1897; *b.* 7 April 1858; *S.* 1870. *Educ.:* Rajkumar College. The state has an area of 822 square miles and a population of about 90,000. *Address:* Morvi, Kathiawar, Bombay. *(Died July 1922.)*

MOSCHELES, Felix; *b.* London, 8 Feb. 1833; *o. s.* of late Ignaz Moscheles, composer, godson of Felix Mendelssohn. *Educ.:* London and Leipsic; studied painting in Paris and Antwerp. Exhibited first pictures in Antwerp and at the Paris Salon; later in the Academy, Grosvenor and New Galleries; very active in the cause of International Arbitration and Peace; has written pamphlets and many articles on the subject; is member of committees of different Peace Societies; President and Chairman of the International Arbitration and Peace Association; and President of the London Esperanto Club;

Member of the International Peace Bureau, Bern. *Publications:* Felix Mendelssohn's Letters to Ignaz and Charlotte Moscheles; In Bohemia with Du Maurier; Fragments of an Autobiography, 1902. *Recreations:* propaganding and lecturing. *Address:* 80 Elm Park Road, S.W. *T.:* Western 1051. *Club:* National Liberal.
(Died 22 Dec. 1917.)

MOSELY, Alfred, C.M.G. 1900; LL.D. Knight of Grace of the Order of St. John of Jerusalem; *b.* 13 Oct. 1855; *s.* of late A. Mosely, formerly of Clifton, Bristol; *m.* Florence Louisa Roberts; two *s.* four *d. Educ.:* privately; Bristol Grammar School. Served with the Princess Christian Hospital, South Africa; Member of Tariff Commission, 1904; organised Industrial and Educational Commissions to America, 1902 and 1908 respectively, and Commission of several hundred School Teachers to United States and Canada, 1906-7; and arranged reception of 1000 Canadian and U.S. school teachers on a return visit to this country, 1908-9. *Publications:* Reports and pamphlets on Industrial and Educational matters and Economics. *Address:* West Lodge, Hadley Wood, Barnet. *T.A.:* West Lodge, Cockfosters. *Club:* Constitutional.
(Died 22 July 1917.)

MOSER, Oswald, R.I., R.O.I.; *b.* 1874; *m.* 1911, Margot Murray. *Educ.:* Skelsmergh House School, Highgate. Studied Art at St. John's Wood Art Schools; exhibited Dixisti (The Last Supper) at the Royal Academy and the Salon (mention honorable) and subsequently purchased by late Lord Winterstoke for Bristol; gold medal and the diplôme d'honneur at the Paris autumn Salon; The Adoration of the Magi, exhibited at the Royal Academy, Paris Salon, and invited to the Royal Scottish Academy 1914, and purchased by the Earl of Moray. *Recreations:* shooting, fishing, golf, tennis. *Address:* 33 Canfield Gardens, Hampstead, N.W. *T.:* Hampstead 5379. *Club:* St. John's Wood Arts. *(Died 30 Sept. 1916.)*

MOSHIER, Professor H. H., Major, 11th Canadian Field Ambulance; Professor of Physiology, Univ. of Alberta, since 1914; *b.* 11 Jan. 1889; *m.* 1914, Ida Winifred Griffith; no *c. Educ.:* Toronto University, Canada. House Physician, Toronto General Hospital, 1909-11; practised medicine at Calgary, 1911-14. *Publications:* Papers on the Wasserman Reaction, Canadian Medical Association, 1911, and Vaccine Therapy, Alberta Medical Association, 1912 *Recreations:* golf, mountain climbing. *Address:* University of Alberta, Canada. *(Died 29 Aug. 1918.)*

MOSLEY, Sir Alexander, Kt., *cr.* 1926; C.M.G. 1901; J.P.; *b.* 1847; *m.* 1881, Mercedes, *y. d.* of late Francis Francia, J.P., Gibraltar; one *s.* four *d.* Formerly President Gibraltar Chamber of Commerce and Unofficial Member Executive Council, Gibraltar. *Address:* Gibraltar. *(Died 17 April 1927.)*

MOSLEY, Sir Oswald; 5th Bt., *cr.* 1781; Captain, Derbyshire Yeomanry (T.F.); *b.* 29 Dec. 1873; *s.* of 4th Bt. and Elizabeth, *d.* of Sir Wm. White; S. father, 1915; *m.* 1895, Katharine Maud, *d.* of late J. H. Edwards Heathcote; three *s.* Owns about 3800 acres. *Heir: s.* Oswald Ernald. *Clubs:* Carlton, Turf, Pratt's; Kildare Street, Dublin. *(Died 21 Sept. 1928.)*

MOSS, Rev. Henry Whitehead, M.A.; Prebendary of Hereford since 1887; *b.* Lincoln, 23 June 1841; *e. s.* of late Henry Moss, Lincoln; *m.* Mary, *o. d.* of Rev. W. A. Beaufort, Egglestone Vicarage, Darlington, 1887; two *s.* four *d. Educ.:* Shrewsbury School; St. John's Coll. Camb. Porson Prizeman, 1861, 1862, 1863; Craven Univ. Scholar, 1862; Browne's Medallist, 1863; B.A. (Senior Classic), 1864; M.A. 1867. Lecturer and Fellow of St. John's College, Cambridge, 1864. Repeatedly elected a member of the Committee of the Headmasters' Conference, of which he was Chairman, 1899-1902; a selected speaker at the Church Congress, 1875

and 1896; Select Preacher before the Univ. of Cambridge, 1905; Headmaster of Shrewsbury School, 1866-1908. *Publications:* a contributor to Sabrinae Corolla and Florilegium Latinum. *Address:* Highfield Park, near Oxford. *Club:* Oxford and Cambridge. *(Died 14 Jan. 1917.)*

MOSS, His Honour Judge Samuel, M.A., B.C.L., J.P. (Denbighshire); County Court Judge, North Wales, Chester District (Circuit No. 29), since 1906; Barrister-at-Law; *b.* 13 Dec. 1858; 2nd *s.* of late Enoch Moss, Broad Oak, Rossett, North Wales; *m.* Eleanor, *d.* of E. B. Samuel, The Darland, Wrexham, 1895; four *s.* two *d. Educ.:* privately; Worcester Coll. Oxford. Barr. Lincoln's Inn, 1880; formerly practised on North Wales and Chester Circuit; Assistant Boundary Commissioner for whole of Wales, 1887; M.P. E. Denbighshire, 1897-1906; formerly Alderman and first Vice-Chairman of Denbighshire C.C., and 2nd Chairman; formerly member of Chester City Council. *Publication:* English Land Laws, 1886. *Recreations:* cycling, riding, and shooting. *Address:* 50 Hough Green, Chester; Accre Hall, Llandegla, nr. Wrexham, N. Wales. *M.:* FM 910.
(Died 14 May 1918.)

MOSTYN, Sir Pyers Charles, 10th Bt.; *cr.* 1670; *b.* 13 Aug. 1895; *s.* of 9th Bart., and Anna, *d.* of Thomas A. Perry, Bitham House, Warwicks.; *S.* father 1912. *Heir: c.* Pyers George Joseph, Lieut. Royal Welsh Fusiliers; *b.* 28 Sep. 1893. *Address:* Talacre, Prestatyn, Flints.; The Mount, Constitution Hill, Parkstone, Dorset. *Club:* Wellington.
(Died 16 Jan. 1917.)

MOTT, Sir Frederick Walker, K.B.E., *cr.* 1919; F.R.S., M.D., B.S. London; F.R.C.P., LL.D. Edin.; Fellow of University College, London; Consulting Physician to Charing Cross Hospital; late Pathologist to London County Asylums; Lecturer on Morbid Psychology, Birmingham University; Brevet Lt.-Colonel, late R.A.M.C.; Order of Officer of Star of Roumania, Corresponding Member of the Neurological and Psychiatrical Societies of France, of Belgium, and of the Netherlands; Fullerian Prof. of Physiology, Royal Inst., and of the American Psychiatrical Society; Croonian Lecturer, Roy. Coll. of Phys., 1900; Lettsom Lecturer Med. Soc., 1916 (The Effects of High Explosives upon the Central Nervous System); Fothergill Gold Medallist and Prize, 1910; Moxon Gold Medallist, 1918; *b.* Brighton, 23 Oct. 1853; *s.* of Henry Mott; *m.* 1885, Georgiana, *d.* of late G. T. Soley; four *d. Educ.:* Univ. Coll. and Hospital, London. University Scholar and Gold Medallist. *Publications:* Nature and Nurture in Mental Development; Brain and the Voice; War Neuroses and Shell Shock; Editor, Archives of Neurology and Psychiatry; numerous contributions to medical journals and recent text-books of medicine and in Encyclopædia Britannica; several original papers relating to Neurology in the Proceedings and Philosophical Transactions of the Royal Society, and in Brain. *Recreation:* golf. *Address:* 25 Nottingham Place, W.1. *T.:* Mayfair 1426. *Clubs:* Athenæum (hon.), Savage. *(Died 8 June 1926.)*

MOTTRAM, Rev. William; Emeritus Secretary of the Congregational Union Temperance Committee; *b.* 29 Mar. 1836; *s.* of Thomas and Frances Louisa Mottram; *m.* 1st, Lucy Hannah (*decd.*), *d.* of Thomas Mellor of Rangefiat House, Warslow; 2nd, Elizabeth, *d.* of J. H. Fruen, Salisbury; three *s.* two *d. Educ.:* Waterhouses Trustees School; private tutors. Held pastorates in the west of England 1859-87; editor Tewkesbury Weekly Record, 1879-83; pastor at Borough Road Church and Superintendent of Lambeth Baths Mission, 1887-96; missioner, lecturer, and preacher in every county of England and Wales; lecture on Adam Bede has raised £1400 for charitable

MOSSOP, Joseph Upjohn, D.S.O. See page xxvi.

753

objects. *Publications :* The True Story of George Eliot in Relation to the Characters in Adam Bede ; Manuals for Temperance Sunday ; various sermons and periodical contributions. *Recreations :* travel, reading, hymnology, old English games. *Address :* 32 Selby Road, Anerley, S.E.2.   *(Died Aug. 1921.)*

MOUBRAY, John James, J.P.; H.M. Lt. for County of Kinross ; *o. s.* of Robert Moubray (*d.* 1880), and Catherine Beveridge (*d.* 1904), *d.* of John Wilson, of Hillpark ; *b.* 1857 ; *m.* 1893, May Marianne, *e. d.* of William Calvert Booth, of Oran, Catterick, Yorkshire ; three *s.* four *d. Educ. :* St. John's Coll., Oxford (M.A., Hon. Fellow). *Address :* Naemoor, Rumbling Bridge, Kinross-shire ; Killerby, Catterick, Yorkshire. *Clubs :* Carlton, Boodle's.
(Died 21 Oct. 1923.)

MOULD, Percy, Chief Manager, The Mercantile Bank of India, Ltd., since 1913 : 2nd *s.* of late Col. J. S. Mould, R.M.L.I. ; *m.* Edith Katherine, *d.* of late Walter Langton of Barrow House, Keswick ; one *s.* two *d. Educ. :* Portsmouth. Joined Mercantile Bank of India, Ltd. 1886. *Recreations :* golf, shooting. *Address :* Broadwater House, Tunbridge Wells. *T. :* Tunbridge Wells 372. *M. :* XF 4700. *Club :* Oriental.   *(Died 14 Nov. 1923.)*

MOULE, Ven. Arthur Evans, D.D. ; Rector of Burwarton c. Cleobury North, 1908-1914 ; late Archdeacon in the Missionary Diocese of Mid China ; *b.* 10 April 1836 ; 6th *s.* of late Rev. Henry Moule, M.A., Vicar of Fordington, Dorset ; *m.* 1861, Eliza Agnes, *y. d.* of late Rev. J. H. Bernau, Vicar of Belvedere, Kent, for twenty years missionary in British Guiana ; six *s.* three *d. Educ. :* home ; Malta College ; C.M.S. College, Islington. Left England for China, 1861 ; witnessed in Dec. 1861 the storming of Ningpo by the Taipings, their expulsion by Capt. Roderick Dew in May 1862, and the second siege of Ningpo by 100,000 Taipings in Sep. 1862 ; worked in and around Ningpo, 1861-69 ; in charge of the Mission, 1864-69, when his brother, afterwards Bishop in Mid-China, moved inland to Hangchow (first inland mission residence) ; in Ningpo again, 1871-76 ; Hangchow, in sole charge, 1876-79 ; witnessed founding of the Chiiki Mission 80 miles south ; after furlough, to Shanghai as Secretary of the Mission and Archdeacon ; B.D. Lamb. given by Archbishop Tait ; worked in Shanghai, 1882-94 ; in charge temporarily of the Cathedral of the Holy Trinity ; invalided home, 1894, and retired by C.M.S., 1898 ; Rector of Compton Valence, Dorset 1898-1902 ; rejoined C.M.S., 1902 ; work in Chehkiang and Kiangsu ; at home 1910, but in reserve ; D.D. Lamb. 1912 ; Vice-President of C.M.S. *Publications :* English—Four Hundred Millions ; Chinese Stories ; Story of Chehkiang Mission (4 editions) ; The Glorious Land ; China as a Mission Field ; The China Mission ; Reasons of the Hope that is in us ; New China and Old (3rd edition) ; Tufts and Tails ; Young China ; Songs of Heaven and Home (3rd edition) ; Half a Century in China ; three essays on the Opium Question ; The Splendour of a Great Hope ; The Chinese People ; City, Hill, and Plain. Chinese—Commentary on and Translation of the Thirty-nine Articles ; Adams' Private Thoughts ; Filial Piety (illustrated) ; Sermons on the Gospels (2 vols.) ; A Letter to the Scholars of China ; Goulburn on Personal Religion ; Chinese Hymnal Companion ; Sheet Tracts. *Address :* Junior School, Weymouth College, Weymouth.
(Died 26 Aug. 1918.)

MOULE, Charles Walter, M.A. ; Senior Fellow and President, and formerly Lecturer, Tutor (1879-92), and Librarian (1895-1913) of Corpus Christi College, Cambridge ; *b.* 9 Feb. 1834 ; *s.* of Rev. H. Moule, Vicar of Fordington, Dorset ; *m.* 1885, Mary Dora, *d.* of Lieut.-Col. R. Cautley, 10th Bengal Cavalry ; one *s.* one *d.*

B.A 1857, when he was bracketed Senior Classic with the late Sir J R. Seeley and two others ; fifteen times Public Examiner for the Classical Tripos, besides examining for University Scholarships and Prizes. *Recreations :* long walks, walking-tours, and sketching. *Address :* 13 Cranmer Road, Cambridge. *(Died 1 May 1921.)*

MOULE, Rt. Rev. Handley Carr Glyn, D.D. ; Bishop of Durham since 1901 ; *b.* Dorchester, Dec. 1841 ; *y. s.* of Rev. H. Moule, M.A., Vicar of Fordington ; *m.* 1881, Mary (*d.* 1915), *d.* of Rev. C. Boileau Elliott, F.R.S. ; one *d. Educ. :* home ; Trin. Coll. Camb. Carus Greek Testament Prize, 1862 ; Browne's Classical Medallist, Camb. 1863 ; Second Classic in the Tripos of 1864 ; B.D. 1894 ; D.D. 1895. Fellow of Trin. Coll. Camb. 1865-81 ; Assistant Master at Marlborough, 1865-67 ; Dean of Trin. Coll. 1878-76 ; Select Preacher at Cambridge, 1880, and frequently later ; at Oxford, 1895 ; 1st Principal of Ridley Hall, Cambridge, 1881-99 ; Hon. Chaplain to Queen Victoria, 1898-1901 ; Norrisian Professor of Divinity, Cambridge, and Professorial Fellow of St. Catharine's Coll. 1899-1901 ; Chaplain in Ordinary to the King, 1901 ; Hon. Fellow of St. Catharine's College, 1902. *Publications :* Six Sacred Poems, awarded Seaton's Prize at Cambridge, between 1869-76 ; Commentaries on the Epistles to the Romans, Ephesians, Philippians, and Colossians, in the Cambridge Bible, and on Romans in the Expositor's Bible (between 1880 and 1894) ; Outlines of Christian Doctrine, 1889 ; Charles Simeon, in "English Leaders of Religion," 1892 ; Ridley on the Lord's Supper, a critical edition, 1895 ; Veni Creator ; Thoughts on Christian Sanctity, 1885 ; In the House of the Pilgrimage (poems), 1896 ; Ephesian Studies, 1900 ; The Secret of the Presence, Sermons, 1900 ; Thoughts for the Sundays of the Year, 1901 ; The School of Suffering (Memoir of a Daughter), 1905 ; Christus Consolator, 1915 ; Christ and Sorrow, 1916 ; The Call of Lent, 1917 ; Auckland Castle, 1918 ; and many other religious works since 1885. *Recreation :* the telescope. *Address :* Auckland Castle, Bishop Auckland.
(Died 8 May 1920.)

MOULE, Horace D'Oyly, C.S.I. 1897 ; late of Indian Civil Service ; *b.* 4 Nov. 1843 ; *s.* of Rev. Horatio Moule, Rector of Wolverton, Somerset ; *m.* 1871, Banna (*d.* 1913), *d.* of late Gen. Richard Horsford, Bengal Art. ; two *s.* two *d. Educ. :* Cheltenham. Joined I.C.S., 1863 ; served in N.W.P. and Oudh as magistrate and collector ; Commissioner of Lucknow and Rohilkhund, and Member of Board of Revenue. *Decorated* for public services ; J.P. Surrey *Address :* 7 Hereford Square, S.W.7. *T. :* Kensington 7482. *Clubs :* Reform, Wellington.
(Died 19 Dec. 1925.)

MOULTON, 1st Baron, *cr.* 1912 (Life Peerage), **John Fletcher Moulton,** P.C. ; Kt ; *cr.* 1906 ; K.C.B., *cr.* 1915 ; G.B.E., *cr.* 1917 ; M.A., F.R.S. ; Hon. LL.D. Camb. ; Judge of Court of Appeal, 1906-12 ; Lord of Appeal in Ordinary and Member of Judicial Committee of Privy Council since 1912 ; Hon. LL.D. Edin., 1911 ; *b.* Madeley, 18 Nov. 1844 ; *s.* of Rev James Egan Moulton ; *m.* 1st, 1875, Clara (*d.* 1888), widow of R. W. Thompson, Edinburgh ; one *s.* ; 2nd, 1901, Mary May (*d.* 1909), *d.* of Major Henry Davis, of the Villa Floridiana, Naples ; one *d. Educ. :* New Kingswood School, near Bath ; St. John's College, Cambridge. Whilst undergraduate at Cambridge entered for various Math. Exams. and carried all before him ; in the same year took gold medal, London ; was Senior Wrangler and First Smith's Prizeman, Camb. 1868 ; Fellow of Christ's Coll. Camb. ; resigned Fellowship, and came to London, 1873 ; Barr. Middle Temple, 1874 ; Q.C. 1885 ; Treasurer, Middle Temple, 1910 ; M.P. (L.) Clapham Division, 1885-86 ; South Hackney, 1894-95 ; Launceston Div. of Cornwall, 1898-1906 ; Fellow and Member of Senate of University of London; Commandeur de la Légion d'Honneur and Grand Officier de l'Ordre de l'Etoile Noire ; Commandeur de l'Ordre de Léopold de Belgique ; Grand Cordon Order of the White Eagle of Russia ; member of the Royal Commission on Civil Service Superannuation, Gas, etc. ; member of the Superior Jury at the last Paris Exhibition, and first Chairman of the Medical Research Committee under the National Insurance Act; President of the Institution of Gas Engineers, 1917-18 ; Chairman Advisory Committee to Home Office for Administration of the Cruelty to Animals Act, 1876 ; of Committee on Chemical Products, 1914 ; of Committee on High Explosives, 1914, and Director General of Explosive Supplies in Ministry of Munitions, since 1914. *Address:* 57 Onslow Square, S.W.7; Forest Green, Bank, Lyndhurst. *T.A.:* Snatcher, London. *T.:* Ken. 720. *Clubs:* Athenæum, Garrick, Savage, Royal Automobile.

(*Died 9 Mar. 1921.*)

MOULTON, Rev. Professor James Hope, M.A., D.Lit., D.D., D.C.L., D.Theol. ; Greenwood Prof. of Hellenistic Greek and Indo-European Philology, Manchester Univ. ; Tutor Wesleyan College, Didsbury, since 1902 ; *b.* 11 Oct. 1863 ; *s.* of Rev. W. F. Moulton, M.A., D.D., member of the New Testament Revision Company ; nephew of Lord Moulton, F.R.S., and Professor R. G. Moulton ; *m.* 1890, Eliza, *d.* of Rev. G. R. Osborn (*d.* 1915) ; two *s.* one *d.* *Educ.:* The Leys School, Cambridge King's College, Cambridge. First Class in Classical Tripos, 1884 and 1886, with distinction in Philology ; Fellow of King's College, Cambridge, 1888 ; lecturer and frequently examiner in Classical Tripos, Part II. ; Chancellor's Medal for English Poem, 1885 ; Classical Lecturer at Girton and Newnham Colleges, 1887-1901 ; Gold Medal in Classics, London, and D.Lit. ; Hon. D.D. Edinburgh, 1909—the same degree his father received 1874 ; Hon. D.C.L. Durham, 1910 ; Hon. D.Theol. Berlin (on occasion of its centenary), and Groningen (at its tercentenary, 1914). Entered Wesleyan Ministry, 1886 ; became Classical Master at The Leys. *Publications:* Grammar of N.T. Greek, vol. i., Prolegomena, 3rd edition, 1908 (translated into German, 1911, with considerable additions) ; art. Zoroastrianism in Hastings' Dictionary of the Bible ; Early Religious Poetry of Persia (Cambridge Manuals) ; Early Zoroastrianism (Hibbert Lectures, 1912) ; Religions and Religion (Fernley Lecture, 1913) ; Vocabulary of the Greek Testament, Parts I. and II. 1914-15, with Prof. Milligan of Glasgow ; numerous papers in Expositor, Expository Times, Classical Review, etc. *Recreations:* tennis and golf. *Address:* Didsbury College, Manchester. *T.:* Didsbury 85.

(*Died 9 April 1917.*)

MOULTON, Richard Green, Professor (Emeritus) of Literary Theory and Interpretation, University of Chicago, U.S.A., 1892-1919 ; *b.* 1849 ; *y. s.* of late Rev. James Egan Moulton ; *m.* Alice Maud, *y. d.* of late Skelton Cole of Sheffield. *Educ.:* New Kingswood School, Bath; Clevedon College, Northampton ; Christ's College, Cambridge. B.A. and Exhibitioner, London University ; M.A. and scholar of Christ's College, Cambridge, 1877 ; Ph.D. University of Pennsylvania, 1891. Lecturer in Literature to Cambridge University (Extension), 1874-90 ; Lecturer to the American Society for Extension of Univ. Teaching, 1890-1891 ; Lecturer to the London Society for Extension of Univ. Teaching, 1891-92. *Publications:* Shakespeare as a Dramatic Artist; The Ancient Classical Drama ; The Literary Study of the Bible, 2nd ed., enlarged and partly rewritten, 1899 ; The Modern Reader's Bible, new ed., 1907; A Short Introduction to the Literature of the

Bible, 1901 ; The Moral System of Shakespeare, 1903, republished (1907) under title, Shakespeare as a Dramatic Thinker ; World Literature, and its Place in General Culture, 1911 ; The Modern Study of Literature, 1915 ; The Bible at a Single View, 1918 ; The Modern Reader's Bible for Schools (New Testament Volume, 1920; Old Testament Volume, 1922). *Recreations:* walking, and especially music. *Address:* Hallamleigh, Frant Road, Tunbridge Wells. *T.:* Tunbridge Wells 958. (*Died 15 Aug. 1924.*)

MOUNET, Jean Sully; *b.* Bergerac, Dordogne, 27 Feb. 1841. *Educ.:* Conservatoire. First prize tragic acting, 1868 ; *début* at Odéon, Paris, 1868 ; served War of 1870 ; Knight of Legion of Honour, 1889. *Publication:* (drama) La Buveuse de Larmes. *Address:* Rue Guy Lussac, 1 (V^e) Paris. (*Died 1 May 1916.*)

MOUNTBATTEN, Maj. Lord, Leopold Arthur Louis, G.C.V.O. 1915; K.C.V.O. 1911; *yr. s.* of Princess Beatrice and late Prince Henry of Battenberg ; *b.* 21 May 1889. *Educ.:* Magdalene College, Cambridge. Served European War, 1914-18 (despatches).

(*Died 23 April 1922.*)

MOUNT EDGCUMBE, 4th Earl of, *cr.* 1789; **William Henry Edgcumbe,** Viscount Mount Edgcumbe and Valletort, 1781 ; Baron Edgcumbe of Mount Edgcumbe, Co. Cornwall (U.K.), 1742 ; P.C., G.C.V.O., D.C.L., D.L. ; Keeper of Privy Seal to H.R.H. Prince of Wales since 1907; Lord-Lt. of Cornwall since 1877; Vice-Admiral of Cornwall ; Hon. Col. 2nd Prince of Wales' Vol. Batt. Devonshire Regt. ; Member of the Council of the Duchy of Cornwall since 1889 ; Provincial Grand Master of the Freemasons of Cornwall since 1869 ; *b.* London, 5 Nov. 1832 ; *S.* father, 1861 ; *m.* 1st, 1858, Lady Katherine Elizabeth Hamilton (*d.* 1874), 4th *d.* of 1st Duke of Abercorn ; one *s.* three *d.* ; 2nd, 1906, Caroline (*d.* 1909), *d.* of Hon. George Edgcumbe, and widow of 3rd Earl of Ravensworth. Church of England ; Conservative. *Educ.:* Harrow ; Christ Church, Oxford ; Hon. D.C.L. Oxford. M.P. for Plymouth, 1859-61 ; Equerry, 1858 ; and afterwards Lord-in-Waiting to H.R.H. Prince of Wales ; Lord Chamberlain in H.M. Household, 1879-80 ; Lord Steward in H.M. Household, 1885-1886, 1886-92 ; Brig.-Gen. Plymouth Vol. Brigade, 1878-82 ; A.D.C. to the Queen, 1887-97. *Heir:* *s.* Viscount Valletort. *Recreations:* sketching and landscape gardening. *Address:* Mount Edgcumbe, Plymouth ; 3 Lowndes Square, S.W. *T.:* Vic. 1256. *Clubs:* Carlton, Travellers', Marlborough ; Royal Yacht Squadron, Cowes.

(*Died 26 Sept. 1917.*)

MOUNTGARRET, 15th Viscount of Nidd (Ireland), *cr.* 1550; **Edmund Somerset Butler;** Baron, *cr.* 1911; *b.* 1 Feb. 1875; *e. s.* of 14th Viscount Mountgarret and Mary Eleanor, *d.* of St. John Charlton of Apley Castle, Shropshire ; *S.* father 1912 ; *m.* 1897, Cecily, *d.* of late Arthur Grey, Sutton Hall, Easingwold. Owns about 14,700 acres. *Heir:* *h.-b.* Hon. Piers Henry Augustus Butler, *b.* 28 Aug. 1903. *Address:* Nidd Hall, Yorks; Ballyconra, Kilkenny.

(*Died 22 June 1918.*)

MOUNT STEPHEN, 1st Baron, *cr.* 1891, **George Stephen ;** Bt. 1886; G.C.V.O. *cr.* 1905; D.L.; *b.* 5 June 1829; *s.* of William Stephen, Dufftown, Banffshire ; *m.* 1st, 1853, Annie Charlotte, *d.* of Benjamin Kane (*d.* 1896); 2nd, 1897, Gian, D.B.E.; *d.* of late Captain Robert George Tufnell, R.N. Went to Canada, 1850 ; became Director, Vice-President, and President of Bank of Montreal ; President St. Paul and Manitoba Railway ; became head of the Canadian Pacific Railway till 1888 ; Conservative Presbyterian. *Heir:* none. *Address:* 17 Carlton House, Terrace, S.W. ; Brocket Hall, Hatfield, Hertfordshire ; Grand Metis, Quebec, Canada. *Clubs:* Carlton, Arthur's.

(*Died 29 Nov. 1921.*)

MOWAT, Robert Anderson; *o. s.* of late Joseph Mowat, Edinburgh; *b.* 1843; *m.* 1871, Jessie (*d.* 1922), *d.* of late Thos. Clarkson. Edinburgh. *Educ.:* Church of Scotland Normal School, Edinburgh; School of Arts, Edin.; University College, London. Passed a competitive examination and was appointed a Student Interpreter on the China Consular Establishment, 1864; Acting Interpreter at H.B.M.'s Consulate in Hankow during part of 1866; Acting Law Secretary of H.B.M.'s Supreme Court for China and Japan at Shanghai, 1867-68, when appointed to substantive post; called to Bar, Inner Temple, 1871; Acting Assistant Judge of the Supreme Court, 1876-78; Acting Judge, 1878; Assistant Judge and Registrar, 1878; Acting Chief Justice, 1879, 1881, and 1888-89; Judge of H.B.M.'s Court for Japan, April 1891, but remained, at the request of the Secretary of State, at Shanghai as Acting Chief Justice and Acting Consul-General till Oct. 1891, when he took up his post in Japan; retired on a pension, 1897. *Address:* 10 Grand Avenue Mansions, Hove. *T.:* Hove 8853.
(Died 7 June 1925.)

MOWATT, Rt. Hon. Sir Francis, G.C.B., *cr.* 1901; K.C.B., *cr.* 1893; P.C. 1906; I.S.O. 1902; a member of the Royal Commission of 1851; *b.* 1837; *m.* 1864, Lucy (*d.* 1896), *d.* of A. Frerichs, and widow of Count Stenbock, of Kolk, Esthonia. *Educ.:* Winchester; St. John's College, Oxford. Permanent Secretary to the Treasury, 1894-1903. *Address:* 41 Sloane Gardens, S.W.1. *T.:* Victoria 5831. *Clubs:* Reform, Athenæum. *(Died 20 Nov. 1919.)*

MOWBRAY, Rev. Sir Edmund George Lionel, 4th Bt., *cr.* 1880; M.A.; *b.* Mortimer, Berks, 26 June 1859; *s.* of late Rt. Hon. Sir J. R. Mowbray, 1st Bt., and Elizabeth Gray, *d.* of G. I. Mowbray, Mortimer, Bucks; *S.* brother, 1916; *m.* 1891, Caroline Elwes, *d.* of late Gen. G. T. Field, R.A.; one *s. Educ.:* Eton; New College, Oxford; B.A. 1882; M.A. 1885; Deacon, 1883; Priest, 1884; Assistant Curate, St. John the Evangelist, Westminster, 1883-86; travelled in America and South Africa, 1886-87; Curate, St. Bartholomew's, Dover, 1887-90; Rector of Durley, Hants, 1890-92; Vicar of St. Bartholomew's, Dover, 1892-1906; Licensed Preacher in Diocese of Ripon, 1906-8; Vicar of Freeland, Oxon. 1908-1909; Vicar of St. Michael's and All Angels, Brighton, 1909-17. *Heir: s.* George Robert, *b.* 15 July 1899. *Address:* Warennes Wood, Mortimer. Berks. *(Died 2 Feb. 1919.)*

MOWBRAY, Major John Leslie, D.S.O. 1915; R.A.; *b.* 19 July 1875. Entered army, 1900; Captain, 1911; Staff Captain, Headquarters India, 1909-13; Brigade-Major, 1914; served European War, 1914-15 (D.S.O.)
(Died 24 July 1916.)

MOWBRAY, Sir Reginald Ambrose, 3rd Bt., *cr.* 1880; *s.* of 1st Bart. and Elizabeth Gray, *d.* of G. J. Mowbray of Mortimer, Berks; *S.* brother 1916; *b.* 5 April 1852. *Educ.:* Christ Church, Oxford (M.A.). *Heir: b.* Edmund, *b.* 26 June 1859. *Address:* 90 Piccadilly, W.; Warennes Wood, Mortimer, Berks.
(Died 30 Dec. 1916.)

MOWBRAY, Sir Robert Gray Cornish, 2nd Bt., *cr.* 1880; J.P., D.L.; Chairman of Quarter Sessions and Chairman of the County Council for Berks; *b.* London, 21 May 1850; *e. s.* of 1st Bart. and Elizabeth Gray, *d.* of G. J. Mowbray of Mortimer, Berks; *S.* father 1899. *Educ.:* Eton; Balliol Coll. Oxford. 1st class Final Classical Schools, 1872; Fellow of All Souls, 1873; President Oxford Union Society, 1873; M.A. (Oxf.), 1875. Barr. Inner Temple, 1876; went the Oxford Circuit; Secretary to Royal Commission on Stock Exchange, 1877-78; M.P. (C.) Prestwich Division of S.E. Lancashire, 1886-95; and Brixton Division of Lambeth, 1900-1906; Parliamentary private secretary to Chancellor of Exchequer (Goschen),

1887-92; member of Royal Com. on Opium, 1893-1895, of Royal Com. on Indian Expenditure, 1896; member of Court of the Goldsmiths Company; Prime Warden, 1898-99 and 1914-15; director of University Life Assurance Society. *Recreation:* travelling. *Heir - pres.: b.* Reginald Ambrose [*b.* 5 April 1852. *Educ.:* Christ Church, Oxford (M.A.)]. *Address:* 90 Piccadilly, W.; Warennes Wood, Mortimer, Berks. *Clubs:* Athenæum, Carlton, Oxford and Cambridge.
(Died 23 July 1916.)

MOXON, Col. Charles Carter, C.M.G. 1916; D.S.O. 1918; Hon. Col. 5th Batt. Yorks. L.I. (T.F.); *b.* 1866; *m.* Lucia Percival. Served S. African War, 1900-1 (Queen's medal, 3 clasps); European War, 1914-18 (despatches, C.M.G., D.S.O.). *Address:* Monk Fyston Lodge, South Milford S.O. *T.:* South Milford 4.
(Died 20 Mar. 1924.)

MOXON, Ven. Robert Julius; Archdeacon of Grafton, since 1897. Ordained, 1888; Vicar of Lower Clarence, 1888-92; Tenterfield, 1892-95; Inverell, 1895-96. *Address:* The Vicarage, Grafton, N.S.W.

MOYERS, Sir George, Kt.; *cr.* 1887; A.B., LL.B., LL.D., T.C.D., D.L. (Dublin); J.P. Co. Dublin; *b.* 11 May 1836; *s.* of William Moyers, Fortfield House; *m.* 1st, 1857, Ada Constance, *d.* of Peter Lambert, of Castle Ellen, Co. Galway (*d.* 1885); two *s.* five *d.*; 2nd, 1904, Lily Pakenham, *widow* of Thomas Aiskew Mooney, LL.D. *Educ.:* Bellevue House, Bristol; Trin. Coll. Dublin (B.A.), 1856. Architect, civil engineer, and surveyor, first in London and subsequently in Dublin; Lord Mayor, 1881; entertained Lord-Lieut. and Countess Cowper at Mansion House, Dublin, this being the last occasion upon which the representatives of the Sovereign have been received there; opened the South City Markets to the public; Commissioner of Pembroke Township, 1869-1901; Chairman of Board, 1887-92; is a life Governor of the King's Hospital, Mercers' Hospital, the Meath Hospital and Co. Dublin Infirmary, the Old Men's Asylum, Dublin. *Recreations:* cricket, rifle shooting, yachting. *Address:* 27 Belgrave Square, Monkstown, Co. Dublin. *Clubs:* Junior Carlton, Constitutional; Leinster, Dublin.
(Died 4 Nov. 1916.)

MOYES, Wm. Henry; assistant editor of The Lady for four years; sub-editor on the Morning Post for three years, after having had charge of special editions; and Editor of The Local Government Journal and Officials Gazette for four years; has contributed articles for many years on home, foreign, colonial, Parliamentary, and other problems to the daily and weekly Press, monthly magazines, etc. *Publications:* The God Stone; When Least Expected; The Mormon's Daughter; The Mystic's Legacy; Quest of the Twin Soul; and other novels and serial stories; The Beauties and Antiquities of Wiltshire; Cycling Tours on the Continent; Haunted Surrey; Superstitions of the Year; How to Succeed in Parliament; Oratory and Debating Skill at St. Stephen's; Local Government in Parliament; The Mystery of Christ's Divine Humanity, etc. *Recreations:* cycling and cricket. *Address:* 3 Kenilworth Gardens, Southbourne Grove, Westcliff-on-Sea.
(Died 22 Jan. 1926.)

MOYSE, Charles E., Molson Professor of English Literature, McGill University, Montreal, 1878-1920; Dean of the Faculty of Arts and Vice-Principal of McGill University, 1903-20; Hon. President St. James' Literary Society, Montreal; President Devonian Society of Montreal; *b.* Torquay, 9 March 1852; *s.* of Charles W. Moyse and Mary Anne, *d.* of John Jenkins of Exeter; *m.* Janet McDougall, *d.* of John Stirling of Montreal, two *s. Educ.:* Independent College, Taunton; University College, London; B.A. (Lond.), 1874; Exhibitioner in English, 1st B.A. (1872); prizeman in Animal Physiology,

2nd B.A. (1874); LL.D. (Hon.) McGill, 1903 , made an Honorary Freeman of the Borough of Torquay, July 1921. *Publications:* The Dramatic Art of Shakespeare, 1879 ; Poetry as a Fine Art, 1883 ; Shakespeare's Skull (under the pseudonym of Belgrave Titmarsh), 1889 ; Editor, McGill University Magazine, 1901-5 ; Ella Lee (verse), 1910 ; The Lure of Earth (verse), 1911 ; verse and literary articles in serial literature. *Address:* 324 Sherbrooke Street, West, Montreal. *T.:* Uptown 3125. *Clubs:* University of London ; University, Montreal.

(Died July 1924.)

MOYSEY, Maj.-Gen. Charles (John), C.M.G. 1884 ; R.E. (retired); *b.* 12 June 1840 ; *s.* of Rev. F. L. Moysey and Arabella, *g.-n.* of 3rd Viscount Bangor; *m.* 1873, Frances Henrietta, 2nd *d.* of Sir Peter Benson Maxwell, Kt. ; one *s.* two *d. Educ.:* Cheltenham Coll. Entered army, 1857 ; Maj.-Gen., 1897 ; served Zulu War, 1879, including Ulundi (despatches, Brevet Lieut.-Col., medal with clasp) ; Assistant Inspector-General of Fortifications at headquarters, 1884-1889 ; commanding R.E. Thames District, 1889-1894. *Address:* Bathealton Court, Wiveliscombe, Somerset. *(Died 14 Sept. 1922.)*

MOYSEY, Henry Luttrell, I.S.O. 1903 ; Fellow Royal Colonial Institute ; *b.* 10 Dec. 1849; *s.* of late Rev. F. Luttrell Moysey of Bathealton Court, Wiveliscombe, Somerset ; *m.* 1875, Dora Kathleen, *d.* of William Hervey O'Grady, J.P. of Batticaloa, Ceylon ; two *s.* one *d. Educ.:* Cheltenham College. Entered Ceylon Civil Service, 1870 ; retired as Postmaster-General and Director of Telegraphs, 1906. *Address:* Cresswell House, Bexhill-on-Sea. *T.A.:* Loutre, Bexhill-on-Sea. *T.:* 470 Bexhill.

(Died 15 Aug. 1918.)

MUDDIMAN, Sir Alexander Phillips, K.C.S.I., *cr.* 1926 ; Kt., *cr.* 1922 ; C.S.I. 1920 ; C.I.E. 1913 ; Governor of United Provinces of Agra and Oudh since 1927 ; Home Member of Executive Council of Governor-General and Leader of the Assembly, 1924-27 ; *b.* 14 Feb. 1875. *Educ.:* Wimborne School. Entered Indian Civil Service, 1897 ; served in Behar in various capacities ; Under-Secretary to the Government of Bengal, 1903 ; Registrar of the High Court at Fort William, 1905 ; Additional Member Legislative Council, 1915 ; Secretary to the Government of India Legislative Department, 1915-21 ; Officiating Law Member, 1919 ; President of the Council of State, India, 1920-24. *Address:* Governor's Camp, United Provinces, India. *Clubs:* Oriental, Travellers'.

(Died 17 June 1928.)

MUDFORD, W. H.; *b.* 1839 ; *s.* of proprietor of Kentish Observer and Canterbury Journal. Late editor and manager of The Standard ; resigned editorship in 1900. *Recreations:* cycling, shooting, travel. *Address:* Westcombe Lodge, Wimbledon Common, S.W. *Clubs:* Carlton, Junior Carlton.

(Died 18 Oct. 1916.)

MUDHOLKAR, Hon. Rao Bahadur Rangnath Narsinh, C.I.E. 1914 ; B.A., LL.B. ; Pres. Indian National Congress, 1912 ; Advocate Central Provinces and Berar ; Pres. Amraoti City Municipality ; *b.* Bombay Presidency, 16 May 1857. *Educ.:* Dhulia High School ; Elphinstone College, Bombay (Fellow). Vakeel Bombay High Court ; Secretary Indian Industrial Conference (President, 1908) ; Delegate of Indian National Congress to England, 1890 ; Chairman of several factories and commercial concerns ; Member Imperial Legislative Council, 1910-12 ; Member Central Provinces Legislative Council since 1914. *Address:* Amraoti, India. *(Died Jan. 1921.)*

MUDIE-SMITH, Richard ; journalist, editorial staff of Daily Chronicle ; *b.* 1877 ; *s.* of Samuel Smith, of Seamer, Yorks, and Susan Elizabeth, *d.* of James Mudie, of Arbroath, N.B. ; *m.* 1904, Mabel Wesley, *y. d.* of Edwin Hunt, *g.-g.-g.-d.* of Charles Wesley ; one *s. Educ.:* Kent College, Canterbury. Fellow of the Royal Statistical Society ; assistant editor of Examiner, 1901 ; organised and superintended a census of Public Worship in London and Greater London on behalf of the Daily News, 1902-3 ; organised an exhibition of Sweated Home Industries of the United Kingdom for the same paper, 1906, which resulted in the passing of the Trade Boards Act; on staff of Daily News, 1902-6, and 1910-12 ; assistant editor of Nation, 1907 ; editor of the London Missionary Society's publications, 1907-9. *Publications:* The Religious Life of London ; Thoughts for the Day ; Sweated Industries ; The Heart of Things ; Passages from the Writings of F. W. Robertson ; (with H. R. A.) The Lost Homes of England. *Address:* 62 Rotherwick Road, Hampstead Garden Suburb, N.W. *T.:* 1539 Finchley. *Club:* National Liberal. *(Died 23 Feb. 1916.)*

MUHRMAN, Henry ; *b.* Cincinnati, Ohio, 21 Jan. 1854 ; of German parentage ; *m.* 1880 (*d.* 1900). *Educ.:* The Cincinnati Public Schools. At the age of 15 became a lithographer ; left Cincinnati 1876 to study Art at Munich ; returned to America, 1878 ; was elected a member of the New York Water-Colour Society and Society of American Artists; settled in London, 1883 ; painted mostly at Hampstead Heath and Kew Bridge; elected member of the International Society of Sculptors, Painters, and Gravers, and the Pastel Society, London, also of the Secession Societies in Munich and in Berlin ; represented in the Galleries of Dublin and Munich (Pinakothek), and largely in important private collections ; received medals of the Munich Academy of Fine Arts, 1877 ; Chicago Universal Exposition, 1893 ; gold medals at the Munich (1897) and Dresden (1901) International Exhibitions ; also gold medal at the St. Louis Universal Exposition, 1904. *Address:* The Goupil Gallery, 5 Regent Street, S.W. *(Died 30 Aug. 1916.)*

MUIR, Col. Charles Wemyss, C.B. 1902 ; C.I.E. 1887 ; *b.* 12th Apr. 1850 ; *s.* of Sir William Muir, K.C.S.I. ; *m.* 1883, Alice, *d.* of Horace Abel Cockerell, C.S.I. ; one *s.* one *d.* Entered army, 1869 ; Lieut.-Col. 1895 ; Col. 1899 ; served Afghan War, 1880 (medal); Soudan, 1885 (despatches, medal with two clasps, Khedive's star); Burmah, 1885-87 (medal with clasp); Tirah, 1897-98 (despatches, medal, three clasps); European War. *Address:* Cox Green, near Maidenhead. *Club:* United Service.

(Died 27 Dec. 1920.)

MUIR, Right Rev. Pearson M'Adam, D.D.; Minister of Glasgow Cathedral, 1896-1915 (retired); Chaplain in Ordinary to the King in Scotland since 1910 ; Acting Chaplain 8th Scottish Rifles ; *b.* Kirkmabreck Manse, Kirkcudbrightshire, 26 Jan. 1846 ; *y. s.* of Rev. John Muir, Minister of Kirkmabreck, and Gloriana M'Adam, *d.* of John Pearson, Springhill, Muirkirk ; *m.* 1871, Sophia Anne (*d.* 1907), *y. d.* of Very Rev. Jas. Chrystal, D.D., LL.D., Minister of Auchinleck, and Moderator in 1879 of the Gen. Assembly of the Church of Scotland ; two *s.* three *d. Educ.:* Kirkmabreck ; Glasgow High School and University. Ordained and became Minister of Catrine, Ayrshire, in 1870 ; Minister of Polmont, Stirlingshire, in 1872 ; Minister of Morningside, Edinburgh, in 1880 ; Secretary of Church Service Society, 1888-1907 ; Convener of Colonial Committee, 1892-97 ; Lecturer on Pastoral Theology in Universities of Edinburgh and St. Andrews, 1895-96, 1903-4, 1905-6 ; and in Universities of Aberdeen and Glasgow, 1896-97, 1902-3, 1904-5 ; Moderator of the General Assembly of Church of Scotland, 1910-11. *Publications:* Samuel Rutherford (in the St. Giles' Lectures on Scottish Divines, 1881-82); The Church of Scotland : A Sketch of its History, 1890 ; Monuments and Inscriptions in Glasgow Cathedral (in Book of Glasgow Cathedral, edited by G. E. Todd), 1898 ; Religious Writers of England, 1901 ; Modern Substitutes for Christianity (Baird Lecture), 1909 ; Seventh Jubilee of the General Assembly, 1910. *Address:* West Manse, Cambuslang, Lanarkshire. *(Died 13 July 1924)*

MUIR, Sir Richard David, Kt., *cr.* 1918 ; a Bencher of the Middle Temple since 1909 ; Recorder of Colchester since 1911 ; *s.* of late Richard Muir and Anne Burleigh, of Greenock ; *b.* 1857 ; *m.* 1889, Mary Beatrice, *d.* of late William Leycester, barrister-at-law, and chief of the Times Parliamentary corps ; one *s.* one *d.* *Educ.:* King's College, London. Was engaged on Times staff, Press Gallery, House of Commons ; called to Bar, 1884 ; Counsel to the Treasury at the North London Sessions ; Junior Counsel to the Treasury at the Old Bailey ; a Senior Counsel to the Treasury, 1901 ; Senior Treasury Counsel at Central Criminal Court, 1908. *Address:* 30 Campden House Court, W.8. *T.:* Park 504 ; 3 Temple Gardens, E.C.4. *Club:* Garrick. *(Died 14 Jan. 1924.)*

MUIR, Ward; Author and Journalist ; *b.* 1878 ; *s.* of Rev. J. J. Muir ; *m.* Dorothea Lang ; one *d.* *Educ.:* Merchant Taylors', Crosby ; Brighton College. *Publications:* Novels, Essays, and Magazine contributions. *Recreations:* land-scape photography, trout-fishing. *Address:* 44 Mecklenburgh Square, W.C.1., *T.:* Museum 6972. *Clubs:* Savage, Camera, Whitefriars. *(Died 9 June 1927.)*

MUIR-MACKENZIE, Sir John William Pitt, K.C.S.I., *cr.* 1909 ; I.C.S., M.R.A.C., and M.R.A.S. England (by examination) ; *b.* 19 Mar. 1854 ; 6th *s.* of Sir John W. P. Muir-Mackenzie, 2nd Bart. of Delvine, Dunkeld, Perthshire, N.B. ; *m.* Marie Therese, *e. d.* of Villiers Stuart of Drunana, Cappoquin, Co. Waterford, Ireland. *Educ.:* Eton, 1866-69 ; private tuition ; Rev. Alfred Green, St. David's, Pembrokeshire. Passed exam. into Indian Civil Service, 1874 ; served in India, 1876 ; deputed to study agriculture at the Royal Agricultural College, Cirencester, 1883 ; to Reunion and Mauritius in connection with coolie labour questions, 1893 ; was Under Secretary and officiated as Secretary to the Govt. of India in the Revenue and Agricultural Depts. ; subsequently Director of Agriculture ; Chief Sec. to the Govt. of Bombay and Commissioner in Sind ; Member of Indian Irrigation Commission ; Member of the Executive Council of the Government of Bombay, 1905-10 ; temporary Governor, 1907 ; retired from I.C.S., 1910. *Recreations:* golf, music. *Address:* 22 Draycott Place, S.W. *T.:* Kensington 1153. *Clubs:* East India United Service ; Byculla, West of India, Bombay. *(Died 25 Oct. 1916.)*

MUIR-MACKENZIE, Montague ; Official Referee since 1905 ; *b.* 29 Sept. 1847 ; 5th *s.* of Sir John Muir-Mackenzie, 2nd Bart. of Delvine, Perthshire, and Sophia, *d.* of J. R. Johnstone, Alva, N.B. ; *m.* 1888, Hon. Sarah Napier Bruce, *d.* of 1st Baron Aberdare ; one *d.* *Educ.:* Charterhouse ; Brasenose College, Oxford (Scholar) ; 1st class in Moderations and Final Schools ; Fellow of Hertford Coll. Oxford, 1874-88 ; Barrister, 1873 ; secretary to Lord Chief-Justice Coleridge, 1873-77 ; Recorder of Deal, 1892 ; Recorder of Sandwich and Bencher of the Middle Temple, 1894 ; standing counsel to the Board of Trade, and other public bodies ; Hon. Sec. of the Royal College of Music. *Publications:* Mackenzie on Bills of Lading ; Chalmers and Mackenzie on the Judicature Acts ; Mackenzie and Lushington on the Laws of Registration ; Mackenzie and Clarke on the Bankruptcy Acts : Notes on the Temple Organ. *Address:* 21 Hyde Park Gate, S.W. ; Royal Courts of Justice, W.C. *Clubs:*

758

United University, National, Ranelagh. *(Died 18 April 1919.)*

MUIR-MACKENZIE, Lt.-Col. Sir Robert Smythe, 4th Bt., *cr.* 1805 ; late R.A. ; *b.* 27 Nov. 1841 ; 2nd *s.* of Sir J. W. P. Muir-Mackenzie, 2nd Bart., and Sophia Matilda, 5th *d.* of J. R. Johnstone of Alva, Clackmannan ; *S. b.* 1909 ; *m.* 1872, Anne Elizabeth Augusta, *d.* of Captain Charles Kinnaird Johnstone Gordon of Craig, Aberdeenshire ; one *s.* two *d.* *Heir:* *s.* Robert Cecil ; [*b.* 17 Oct. 1891 ; *m.* 1914, Kate Brenda Blodwen, *d.* of late Henry Jones, Cardiff.] *Address:* Marldon House, Paignton. *(Died 2 Feb. 1918.)*

MUIR-MACKENZIE, Sir Robert Cecil, 5th Bt., *cr.* 1805 ; Lieut. 5th Batt. Durham L.I. ; *b.* 17 Oct. 1891 ; *o. s.* of 4th Bt. ; *S.* father 1918 ; *m.* 1914, Kate Brenda Blodwen, *d.* of late Henry Jones, Cardiff ; one *s.* *Heir:* *s.* Robert Henry, *b.* 6 Jan. 1917. *(Died 12 April 1918.)*

MUIRHEAD, Alexander, D.Sc. (Lond. Univ.), F.R.S. *Address:* The Lodge, Shortlands, Kent ; *T.A.:* Muirheads, London. *T.:* Bromley 750. *(Died 13 Dec. 1920.)*

MUIRHEAD, John ; R.B.A., R.S.W. ; *b.* Edinburgh, 1868 ; 2nd *s.* of John Muirhead, architect and builder ; *m.* Margaret Neale, *e. d.* of James Cooper, dentist, Edinburgh. *Educ.:* Royal High School, Edinburgh. Commenced studies at Board of Manufactures' School, Edinburgh, 1880 ; exhibited first pictures in R.S.A. 1881, and since then has painted a great deal in France, Belgium, and Holland ; has exhibited R.A., R.I., N.E.A.C., Liverpool, Manchester, International Rome, Pittsburg U.S.A., Munich, Dresden, and many other art centres ; illustrated Hilaire Belloc's River of London. *Publication:* Photogravure of picture Declining Day and Ebbing Tide. *Recreations:* fishing, cycling. *Address:* 148 Gipsy Hill, S.E.19 ; Monument Cottage, Houghton, Hunts. *Club:* The Three Arts. *(Died 21 Nov. 1927.)*

MULCAHY, Hon. Edward, twice Minister of Lands, Works, and Mines, Tasmania ; Commonwealth Senate, 1908-1910 and 1919-20 ; *b.* Limerick, 28 Mar. 1850 ; went Tasmania, 1854. *Educ.:* Primary Schools, Hobart. *Address:* Tara, Melville Street, Hobart, Tasmania. *(Died 23 Oct. 1927.)*

MULES, Rt. Rev. Charles Oliver, D.D. ; *b.* 1837 ; *s.* of Rev. J. H. Mules, Vicar of Ilminster ; *m.* 1870, Laura (*d.* 1925), *d.* of Capt. F. H. Blundell, Nelson ; three *s.* one *d.* *Educ.:* Cheltenham ; Trin. Coll. Camb. Senior Optime (M.A.). Ordained, 1864 ; Archdeacon of Waimea ; Bishop of Nelson, New Zealand, 1892-1912. *Address:* 25 Trafalgar Square, Nelson, New Zealand. *(Died 9 Oct. 1927.)*

MULLEN, Benjamin Henry, M.A. Director of Museums and Libraries, Salford, since 1892 ; *b.* Dublin, 19 Jan. 1862 ; *s.* of late Benjamin Mullen, Warrenpoint, Clontarf ; *m.* Essie, *d.* of late Henry Gibson, J.P., Ardnardeen, Clontarf. *Educ.:* Bective College, Dublin ; Foyle Coll., Londonderry ; Trin. Coll., Dublin ; Mus. Ex. ; B.A. 1884 ; M.A. 1887 ; Freeman of City of Dublin ; Assistant in Art and Ethnographical Department, National Museum of Ireland, Dublin, 1884-92 ; Lecturer on Manchester University Extension Staff, Lecturer under the Ogden Trust. *Publications:* numerous articles on art, archæology, and ethnography. *Address:* Royal Museum and Libraries, Peel Park, Salford. *(Died 23 Oct. 1925.)*

MULLER, W. Max, Ph.D. (Leipsic), Professor of Exegesis at the R.E. Seminary, Philadelphia, since 1890 ; Assist. Prof. of Egyptology, University of Pennsylvania ; *b.* Gleissenberg, Bavaria, 15 May 1862 ; *s.* of F. Müller, teacher ; *b.* of Dr. Ernst Müller, politician and member German Reichstag ; *m.* 1889 ; two *s.* one *d.* *Educ.:* Gymnasium of Nürnberg ; studied at

MULJI, Vasanji Trikamji, Rao Sahib Sir, Kt. See page xxvi.

Universities of Erlangen, Leipsic, Berlin, Munich, theology, classical and Oriental philology ; one of the last students of G. Ebers, the Egyptologist. Went to America, 1888 ; lived at New York ; visited the Orient, 1900, etc. Chief studies : points of contact between Egyptology and the Bible ; African languages. *Publications :* Asien und Europa nach den ägyptischen Denkmälern, 1893 ; Die Liebespoesie der alten Agypter, 1899 ; Egyptological Researches, 1906 foll. for the Carnegie Institution, Washington, etc.; Egyptian Mythology, 1918. *Recreations :* bicycling and other exercise. *Address :* 4325 Sansom Street, Philadelphia, Pa.

(*Died 12 July 1919.*)

MULLINGER, James Bass, M.A., Hon. Litt.D. Camb. , late University Lecturer in History ; Emeritus Librarian and Lecturer in History, St. John's College, Cambridge ; late President Cambridge Antiquarian Society ; *b.* Bishop Stortford, Herts ; 2nd *s.* of John Morse Mullinger and Mary, 2nd *d.* of Rev. James Bass. *Educ.:* University College ; St. John's College, Cambridge (M.A.). Graduated in double honours (third class in Classical Tripos, and second class in Moral Sciences), 1866 ; Le Bas Prizeman, 1866 ; Hulsean, 1867 ; Kaye, 1875 ; Lecturer at Bedford Coll. London, 1881-83 ; Lecturer to Teachers' Training Syndicate at Cambridge on History of Education, 1885-95 ; Birkbeck Lecturer on Ecclesiastical History to Trin. Coll. Camb., 1890-94. *Publications :* Cambridge Characteristics in the Seventeenth Century, 1867 ; The Ancient African Church, 1869 ; The New Reformation, 1875, a narrative of the Old Catholic Movement (by "Theodorus") ; The Schools of Charles the Great, 1876 ; The University of Cambridge from the Earliest Times to the Decline of the Platonist Movement, 3 vols., 1873-1911 ; Vol. IV., 1916 ; An Introduction to English History (in conjunction with late S. R. Gardiner), 1881, 1883, 1894, 1903 ; The Age of Milton (with Canon Masterman), 7th edition, 1913 ; History of St. John's College, Cambridge, 1901 ; also numerous historical articles in Encyclopædia Britannica, Dictionary of Christian Antiquities, Dictionary of National Biography, Encyclopædia of Religion and Ethics, Cambridge Modern History, and History of English Literature. *Recreations :* architecture, visiting places of historic interest, chess. *Address :* St. John's College and 68 Lensfield Road. Cambridge.

(*Died 22 Nov. 1917.*)

MULLINS, Major Charles Herbert, V.C. 1900 ; C.M.G. 1900 ; Imperial Light Horse ; Barrister ; *m.* 1902, Norah Gertrude, *d.* of S. Haslam, Brooklands, Uppingham ; two *s.* one *d.* Served South Africa, 1900 (despatches, V.C., C.M.G.). *Decorated* for gallantry at Elandslaagte. *Address :* Enduline, Parktown, Johannesburg. (*Died 23 May 1916.*)

MULLINS, Lieut.-Col. George Lane, A.A.M.C. ; Officer Commanding No. 4 Australian General Hospital ; Hon. Organising Secretary, Red Cross Society, N.S.W. Division ; Red Cross Director, N.S.W ; Hon. Consulting Physician, St. Vincent's Hospital, Sydney, etc. ; *s.* of late James Mullins, J.P., of Sydney, and Elizabeth Lane ; *b.* Sydney, 24 Aug. 1862 ; *m.* 1891, Mary Ellen, *d.* of late Patrick Burke, J.P., of Orange, N.S.W. ; four *s.* *Educ. :* St. Mary's College, Lyndhurst, Sydney ; Sydney Grammar School ; Dublin University, M.A., M.D. Filled positions at St. Vincent's Hospital, Sydney, of Assistant Physician, Hon. Physician, Consulting Physician and Medical Officer in charge of Electro-Therapeutic Department ; now Director (Hon.) Department of Special Therapeutics at Sydney Hospital ; Deputy Chairman, Lecturer, Examiner, St. John Ambulance Association, N.S.W, ; was Commissioner, St. John Ambulance Brigade in the Commonwealth (10 years) ; Knight of Grace, Order of St. John of Jerusa-

lem in England ; awarded Conspicuous Service Medal by Order of St. John ; held following positions in Commonwealth Military Forces—Adjutant, Staff Officer Medical Services, Acting P.M.O., Chief Instructor Officers' School of Instruction, Examiner in Military Sanitation, etc. ; Life Member Red Cross Society of Japan ; Consulting Medical Officer, Consulate-General of France (N.S.W.) ; Vice-President Intercolonial Medical Congress, 1896, 1899 ; travelled extensively in Europe. *Publications :* History of Smallpox and Vaccination in N.S. Wales, 1898 ; A Course of First Aid (3rd edition), 1914 ; Camps and Camp Hygiene, 1908 ; Medical Electricity, 1915. *Recreations :* Red Cross work, motoring. *Address :* 205 Macquarie Street, Sydney ; St. Meldan's, Rose Bay, Sydney. *Club :* University, Sydney.

(*Died 20 Mar. 1918.*)

MUMMERY, John Howard, C.B.E., D.Sc. (Penn.), F.R.C.S., L.D.S. (Eng.) ; retired ; *b.* 18 Jan. 1847 ; *s.* of John R. Mummery, late of 10 Cavendish Place, W. ; *m.* 1st, Mary Lily, *d.* of William Lockhart, Shanghai and Blackheath ; 2nd, Lilian B., *e. d.* of Thos. Parker, Nottingham ; three *s.* two *d.* *Educ. :* University College and Hospital, London. Examiner Dental Board of the United Kingdom ; late Lecturer on Bacteriology at Royal Dental Hospital ; member of the committee on the causes of dental disease of the Medical Research Council ; Honorary Fellow Royal Society of Medicine. *Publications :* The Microscopic Anatomy of the Teeth ; several papers in the Philosophical Trans. of the Royal Society, especially on the distribution of nerves to the dentine. *Recreation :* golf. *Address :* 79 Albert Bridge Road, S.W.11. *T. :* Latchmere 4065.

(*Died 30 Aug. 1926.*)

MUNCASTER, 5th Baron (*cr.* 1783), **Josslyn Francis Pennington ;** Bt. 1676 ; Baron U.K. 1898 ; Lord-Lt. Co. Cumberland since 1876 ; Hon. Col. Cumberland Volunteers, V.D. ; *b.* Hamilton Place, London, 25 Dec. 1834 ; *S. b.* 1862 ; *m.* Constance, *d.* of E. L'Estrange, Tynte, Co. Sligo, 1863. Protestant, Conservative. *Educ. :* Hatfield private school ; Eton. Army, Capt 90th Light Infantry ; served in Crimea, 1854-56 ; in trenches and two attacks on Redan and storming party (medal and clasp, Turkish medal) ; afterwards Capt. Rifle Brigade ; M.P. W. Cumberland, 1872-80 ; Egremont Division of Cumberland, 1885-92 ; late Col East York Militia ; late Lieut. in Yorkshire Hussars. Owns about 15,000 acres, and minerals in Lancashire. *Recreation :* country life. *Heir :* none. *Address :* Muncaster Castle, Cumberland. *Clubs :* Army and Navy, Carlton.

(*Died 30 Mar. 1917.*)

MUNDAY, Luther ; *b.* 1857 ; *m. d.* of General English, C.B. *Educ. :* by his father, a schoolmaster. Planter and estate owner, Ceylon, 1878-84 ; Member of Executive Committee, People's Palace, 1887 ; Secretary Lyric Club, 1887-93 ; founder Green Park Club, and others ; has produced 43 plays, and organised 400 charitable and other entertainments ; was director of two London theatres, and has acted as manager-in-chief to Sir Charles Wyndham and Sir Herbert Beerbohm Tree ; was delegate on Board of Governors Waterloo Hospital ; Hon. Treasurer Animals' Hospital ; Lecturer and was Member of First Committee Shakespeare Memorial National Theatre ; cartoon artist and sculptor. *Recreation :* doing nothing. *Publication :* A Chronicle of Friendships. *Address :* 37 Half Moon Street, W. ; Littlewick Green, Berks. *T. :* Littlewick Green 13. *Club :* Isthmian. (*Died 29 May. 1922.*)

MUNDY, Alfred Edward Miller, J.P. ; *b.* 28 Nov. 1849 ; *o. s.* of late Alfred Miller Mundy and Jane, 2nd *d.* of late Rear-Admiral Sir John Hindmarsh, K.H. ; *m.* 1st, 1873, Ellen Mary, *y. d.* of late Charles Rowland Palmer-Morewood.

MUMTAZUD DOWLAH MUHAMMAD FAIYAZ ALI KHAN, Nawab of Pahasu, K.C.V.O. See page xxvi.

of Alfreton Hall, Co. Derby (whom he divorced 1881, she *m*. 2nd 1882, 20th Earl of Shrewsbury); one *d.*; 2nd, 1888, Catharine Louisa, 3rd *d.* of Sir John Hartopp, 4th Bart.; one *s.* three *d*. *Educ.*: Christ Church, Oxford. High Sheriff, Derby, 1891. *Address:* Shipley Hall, Derby. *Club:* Royal Yacht Squadron, Cowes.

(*Died 15 April 1920.*)

MUNDY, Admiral Godfrey Harry Brydges, C.B. 1917; D.S.O. 1919; M.V.O. 1903; *b.* 11 Aug. 1860; *m.* 1890, Rose, 9th *d.* of late Sir Robert Miller Mundy; one *s.* one *d*. Entered Navy 1873; Commander, 1896; Captain, 1902; Rear-Adm. 1912; Vice-Adm. 1917; Adm. 1920; served Egyptian War, 1882 (medal, Khedive's bronze star); Admiral Superintendent Pembroke Dockyard, 1908-11, Devonport Dockyard, 1913-16; retired, 1917; Vice-Admiral North Atlantic Convoy, 1917-18. *Club:* Naval and Military. (*Died 7 Oct. 1928.*)

MUNRO, Sir Henry, Kt., *cr.* 1906; J.P. Inverness-shire; *b.* 1842. Was a member Royal Commission Highlands and Islands, 1892, commonly known as the Deer Forests Commission; three times elected Pres. of Inverness Chamber of Commerce; is a Bank Director and a Director of other public companies; is a member of the Extra Parliamentary Panel for Scotland under the Private Legislation Procedure (Scotland) Act of 1899; was a member of the Scottish Land Enquiry Committee which reported on the Land Question in Scotland, 1914. *Address:* Ness Mount, Inverness. (*Died 23 Dec. 1921.*)

MUNRO, Sir Hugh Thomas, 4th Bt.; *cr.* 1825; J.P., D.L.; *b.* 16 Oct. 1856; *e. s.* of 3rd Bt. and Henrietta, *d.* of John Drummond; *S.* father 1913; *m.* 1892, Selina Dorothea (*d.* 1902), *d.* of Maj.-Gen. T. E. Byrne, R.A.; one *s.* two *d.* Private Secretary to late Sir George Pomeroy Colley, Governor of Natal, 1880; served as volunteer in Basuto campaign, 1880-81 (medal and clasp); contested (C.) Kirkcaldy District of Burghs, 1885; was long on Central Council of Conservative party in Scotland, and chairman of Tay Divisional Committee of National Union of Conservative Associations for Scotland, and chairman of Forfarshire Unionist Organisation; member of County Council for Forfarshire since its formation; member of School Board, etc.; F.R.G.S. *Publications:* many articles on mountaineering, notably a catalogue universally accepted as the standard now of all the Scottish mountains. *Recreations:* shooting, mountain climbing, travel. *Heir: s.* Thomas Torquil Alfonso Munro, *b.* 7 Feb. 1901. *Address:* Lindertis, Kirriemuir, N.B. *T.A.:* Munro, Craigton. *M.:* LN 842 and SR 919. *Clubs:* Wellington, Royal Automobile, Alpine; New, Scottish Mountaineering, Edinburgh. (*Died 19 Mar. 1919.*)

MUNRO, Colonel Lewis, C.B.E. 1919; retired pay; *b.* 25 July 1859; *s.* of late Captain Lewis Munro, H.E.I.C.S.; *m.* Maud, *d.* of late C. Breed Eynaud, Malta; no *c. Educ.:* Clifton College; R.M.C., Sandhurst; Staff College. Joined 37th Regt. 1880; Adjutant 1st Hampshire Regt. 1882; commanded 2nd Hampshire Regt. 1906-9; Brigade Major, Gibraltar, 1892; Brigade Major, Aldershot, 1898; served Boer War, 1899-1901, as Brigade Major Infantry Brigade, and afterwards D.A.A.G. Headquarters; Aden Hinterland Expedition, 1902; retired as substantive Colonel, 1910; employed throughout European War as Assistant to M.G.A. and A.Q.M.G., Eastern Command, and subsequently under the Air Ministry (despatches three times, C.B.E.). *Recreations:* shooting, fishing, golf. *M.:* HC 4861. *Clubs:* Army and Navy, M.C.C. (*Died 11 Nov. 1927.*)

MUNRO, Robert, M.A., M.D., LL.D., F.R.S.E.; *b.* Ross-shire, 21 July 1835; *m.* 1875, Anna (*d.* 1907); *d.* of late William Taylor, Kilmarnock. *Educ.:* Tain Royal Academy; University of Edinburgh. Doctor at Kilmarnock till 1886, when he retired to

devote more attention to archæological and anthropological pursuits; Secretary Society of Antiquaries of Scotland, 1888-99; President of Anthropological Section of British Association, 1898; Rhind Lecturer on Archæology, 1888; Dalrymple Lecturer on Archæology, 1910 (University of Glasgow); Munro Lecturer on Anthropology and Prehistoric Archæology, 1911 (University of Edinburgh); Hon. Member of the Royal Irish Academy, of the Royal Society of Antiquaries of Ireland, Société Royale des Antiquaires du Nord, Society d'Arch. de Bruxelles, Friesch Genootschap, etc.; Associé étranger de la Soc. d'Anthropologie de Paris; Cor. M. of the Anthrop. Societies of Berlin, Vienna, and the Numismatic Society of Philadelphia. *Publications:* Ancient Scottish Lake - Dwellings, 1882; The Lake-Dwellings of Europe, 1890 (French ed. 1908); Rambles and Studies in Bosnia - Herzegovina and Dalmatia, 1895 (2nd ed. 1900); Prehistoric Problems, 1897; Prehistoric Scotland and its place in European Civilisation, 1899; Man as Artist and Sportsman in the Palæolithic Period, 1904; Archæology and False Antiquities, 1905; Munro Lectures (Palæolithic Man, and Terremare), 1912; Prehistoric Britain, 1914; Darwinism and Human Civilization, with special reference to the origin of German Military Kultur, 1917; From Darwinism to Kaiserism, 1919; numerous contributions to medical and scientific journals. *Recreation:* travel. *Address:* Elmbank, Largs, Ayrshire. *Club:* Authors'.

(*Died 18 July 1920.*)

MUNRO, Sir Thomas, Kt., *cr.* 1914; G.B.E., *cr.* 1920; K.B.E., *cr.* 1917; J.P., D.L.; Co. Clerk of Lanarks.; Clerk to Co. of Lanark Education Authority; Clerk to the Lanark District Board of Control; was chief adviser Labour Regulation Department of Ministry of Munitions, and Member of the Munition Council; adviser to Demobilisation Branch of Ministry of Labour; a member of H.M. Commission on Dilution of Labour for Clyde and Tyne Districts; Assessor to Central Board of Control (Liquor Traffic); Chairman under appointment by the Govt. of the Provisional Joint Industrial Committee, and acted as Chairman of several other Government Commissions and Committees during the War; *b.* Moorfarm Ho., Tain, 1866; *s.* of late Thomas Munro, Solicitor, Dingwall and Tain, and Helen (*d.* 1889), *d.* of late Hector Mackenzie, J.P., Ullapool; *m.* 1897, Jean Russell, *d.* of late James Smart, Balgreen, Hamilton; two *d. Educ.:* privately; Milne's Institution, Fochabers; Edinburgh University. *Address:* 2 Rothesay Place, Edinburgh. *T.A.:* 281, 282, and 283, Hamilton. *M.:* V 777. *Clubs:* Caledonian, National; University, Edinburgh.

(*Died 11 April 1923.*)

MUNSEY, Frank Andrew; owner and publisher of the Sun and the Evening Telegram, New York; *b.* Mercer, Maine, U.S.A., 21 Aug. 1854; unmarried. *Educ.:* common schools of Maine. Began in country store in Maine; became manager of Western Union Telegraph Office, Augusta, Maine; came to New York in 1882; started The Golden Argosy, a juvenile weekly (now the adult Argosy-All-story Weekly); and launched Munsey's Weekly, 1889; converted into Munsey's Magazine, 1891; has made addresses on publishing and advertising. Lectured on Journalism at Yale University, 1902. *Publications:* A Tragedy of Errors; Derringforth; Under Fire; Afloat in a Great City; The Boy Broker. *Recreations:* yachting, golf, horseback riding, automobiling. *Address:* 280 Broadway, New York City. *T.A.:* Munsey, New York. *Clubs:* Union League, New York Yacht, Riding, Lotos, Pilgrims, Turf and Field, Merchants', New York; Chevy Chase, Metropolitan, Washington. (*Died 22 Dec. 1925.*)

MUNSTER, 4th Earl of (cr. 1831), **Aubrey FitzClarence**, Viscount FitzClarence, Baron Tewkesbury, 1831; b. 7 June 1862; s. of 2nd Earl; S. brother, 1902. Was Gentleman Usher to Queen Victoria and King Edward VII. Heir: n. Geoffry William Hugh FitzClarence, b. 1906. Address: 2 Warwick Square, S.W.1. T.: Victoria 2884. Clubs: Bachelors', St. James's, Carlton.
(Died 1 Jan. 1928.)

MÜNSTERBERG, Dr. Hugo; Professor of Psychology since 1892, and Director of Psychological Laboratory, Harvard; b. Dantzig, 1 June 1863; m. Selma Oppler, Strasburg. Educ.: Dantzig Gymnasium; Leipsic; Heidelberg; Assistant Professor University of Freiburg, 1887-91. Publications: Psychology and Life, 1899; American Traits, 1902; the Americans, 1904; Principles of Art Education, 1905; Eternal Life, 1905; Science and Idealism, 1906; On the Witness Stand, 1907; Psycho-Therapy, 1908; The Eternal Values, 1909; Psychology and the Teacher, 1909; Psychology and Industrial Efficiency, 1913. Address: 7 Ware Street, Cambridge, Massachusetts, U.S.A.
(Died 15 Dec. 1916.)

MUNTZ, Frederick Ernest, J.P., D.L.; landed proprietor; b. 14 June 1845; e. s. of late G. F. Muntz, J.P., D.L.; m. 1869, Georgiana Jane, e. d. of late A. Borrowman of Edinburgh; one s. Educ.: Corpus Christi College, Cambridge; B.A., 1871; called to Bar, Lincoln's Inn, 1873. High Sheriff, Warwickshire, 1902; Capt. Hon. Major late 3rd Batt. Devonshire Regt.; Lord of the Manor of Tanworth in Arden; contested Rugby Division of Warwickshire, 1899; Patron of Tanworth in Arden. Heir: s. Gerald Douglas Ernest [b. 15 Nov. 1876; m. 1909, Elsie (whom he divorced 1917), d. of Harrison Benn of Bradford and Dawlish; one d.; late Lieut. R.N.V.R.]. Address: Umberslade, Hockley Heath, Warwickshire. T.A.: Hockley Heath. T.: Tanworth in Arden 9. Clubs: Carlton, Oxford and Cambridge, Hurlingham. M.: AC 44, AC 740, AC 2834.
(Died 25 Nov. 1920.)

MUNTZ, Sir Gerard Albert, 2nd Bt., cr. 1902; President of the Institute of Metals, 1910, 1911; Vice-President Inst. Mech. E.; b. 27 Nov. 1864; m. 1st, 1893, Katherine Blanche, d. of James Prinsep (whom he divorced, 1907); two d.; 2nd, 1909, Henrietta Winifred, 3rd d. of late Lt.-Col. F. L. Graves, R.A.; one s. two d.; S. father, 1908. Chairman Non-Ferrous Metal Committee (Board of Trade), 1916-17; Chairman Metallurgical Committee (Ferrous and Non-Ferrous) Department of Scientific and Industrial Research, 1916-1919; Member of Copper, Zinc, Lead, Sectional Committees of Imperial Mineral Resources Bureau, 1920; Member of Council of British Non-Ferrous Metals Research Association since 1920; Consultant Director of Muntz's Metal Co. Ltd. and Elliot's Metal Co. Ltd.; Chairman of the Brass and Copper Tube Association, 1911-21. Heir: s. Gerard Philip Graves, b. 12 June 1917. Address: Tiddington-House, near Stratford-on-Avon. Club: St. Stephen's.
(Died 22 Oct. 1927.)

MURDOCH, Prof. James, M.A.; Prof. of Oriental Studies, Univ. of Sydney since 1919; b. Kincardineshire, Scotland, 1856. Educ.: Universities of Aberdeen, Oxford, and Göttingen. Assist. Prof. of Greek, Aberdeen Univ., 1880-1881; Headmaster Maryborough Grammar School (Q.), 1881-85; 2nd Master Brisbane Grammar School (Q.), 1885-88; since 1888 mostly resident in Japan for purposes of study and research. Publications: History of Japan, vol. i. 1911; vol. ii. 1902; vol. iii. (1650-1868) in the Press; vol. iv. (1868-1912) on the stocks. Address: University of Sydney, Australia.
(Died 30 Oct. 1921.)

MURE, William John, C.B. 1897; M.A., J.P. Co. Edinburgh; advocate, Edinburgh; b. 1845; s. of late David Mure, Judge of the Court of Session, Scotland; m. 1878, Emily May, M.B.E.

1920, d. of J. B. Innes, W.S., Edinburgh; one d. Educ.: Loretto; Harrow; Trinity College, Cambridge. Scotch Bar, 1871; legal secretary to the Lord Advocate, 1885-86, 1886-92, and 1895-1896. Address: 39 Lennox Gardens, S.W.1. T.: Kensington 6107. Clubs: Carlton, Wellington; New, Edinburgh.
(Died 9 Nov. 1924.)

MURIE, Dr. James, M.D. Glasgow, LL.D. St. Andrews. Was naturalist to Consul Petherick's expedition to Gondokoro; pro-sector to Zoological Society; assistant librarian and secretary to Linnean Society. Address: Canvey Cottage, Leigh-on-Sea, Essex.(Died 21 Dec. 1925.)

MURLAND, William; J.P. Northamptonshire, High Sheriff, 1913; s. of J. W. Murland, Nutley, Booterstown, Co. Dublin; m. 1887, Mary Geraldine Fitzgerald; two s. Educ.: Trinity College, Dublin. Called to Irish Bar, 1878. Address: Badby House, Daventry, Northants; 28a Cadogan Place, S.W.1. T.: Victoria 3722. M.: 3722. Club: Junior Carlton.
(Died 2 Mar. 1926.)

MURPHY, George Fitzgerald, B.A.; J.P. Co. Meath; b. 1850; e. s. of late James George Murphy of The Grange, and Mary, d. of late Col. Fitzgerald of Geraldine Co., Kildare, m. 1884, Lady Mary Louisa Plunkett, e. d. of 10th Earl of Fingall. High Sheriff, County Meath, 1908. Address: The Grange, Dunsany. Clubs: Orleans; Sackville Street, Dublin.
(Died 13 Nov. 1920.)

MURPHY, Rev. Hugh Davis, D.D.; Rector of St. George's, Belfast, since 1880; Chaplain to the Lord-Lieutenant of Ireland; b. Co. Antrim, 8 June 1849; m. Francesca Barbara, d. of late Rev. Richard Burgess, B.D., Rector of Upper Chelsea and Prebendary of St. Paul's; four s. one d. Educ.: Trin. Coll., Dublin. B.A. 1873; M.A. 1884; B.D. 1890; D.D. 1891; Prizeman, English Literature; Downes Prizeman, Written Sermon; Ordained, 1874; Curate of Ballinderry, 1874-75; Assistant Chaplain, Bethesda Church, Dublin, 1875-77; Curate of St. George's, Belfast, 1878; Member of the General Synod of the Church of Ireland; Rural Dean of North Belfast; Chaplain in Belfast to the Actors' Church Union; Canon of St. Patrick's Cathedral; is a Prince Mason, and has been three times Provincial Grand Chaplain of the Masonic Province of Antrim. Publications: A Forgotten Gospel; The State of the Soul between Death and the Resurrection; poems in various periodicals. Recreations: gardening and shooting, Continental travel, modern literature. Address: 39 Wellington Park, Belfast.(Died 8 Mar. 1927.)

MURPHY, Sir James Joseph, 1st Bt., cr. 1903; Kt., cr. 1902; D.L. (City of Dublin); steamship owner; Partner, Palgrave, Murphy and Co.; 2nd s. of late Michael Murphy, J.P.; b. 24 Jan. 1843; m. 1869, Bridget Jane, d. of late Francis Norman; five d. President of Chamber of Commerce, Dublin, 1902-3-4. Heir: none. Address: Yapton, Monkstown, Co. Dublin. T.: Kingstown 8. T.A.: Yapton, Kingstown. Clubs: Constitutional; Royal Irish Yacht, Kingstown; St. Stephen's Green, Dublin.
(Died 16 Feb. 1923.)

MURPHY, James Keogh, M.A., M.D., M.C. (Cantab.), F.R.C.S. (Eng.); Consulting Surgeon; Surgeon to the Miller General Hospital for South East London; Surgeon to Paddington Green Children's Hospital; General Medical Editor to the Oxford University Press and Hodder & Stoughton; b. 12 Sep. 1869; e. s. of late Rt. Hon. Mr. Justice Murphy, P.C., LL.D., and Mary, d. of late Rt. Hon. Mr. Justice Keogh; m. 1895, Mabel Roney, d. of late Joshua K. Schofield of Cambria Kersal, Manchester; one s. Educ.: Charterhouse (Senior Scholar); Caius College, Cambridge (Scholar); St. Bartholomew's Hospital. 1st Class Natural Science Tripos; Demonstrator of Anatomy to the University of Cambridge for three years; completed medical education at St. Bartholomew's and obtained the Laurence

761

MURFREE, Mary Noailles. See page xxvi.

Scholarship and large Gold Medal ; the post of External Assistant at the Rotunda Hospital, Dublin, by competitive examination ; returned to St. Bartholomew's and acted as House Physician ; a family practitioner for five years in Princes' Square ; returned to Bartholomew's, having obtained the Fellowship of the Royal College of Surgeons whilst in practice, to devote himself especially to surgery ; there acted as Demonstrator of Anatomy for three years, and devoted himself to the work of his hospital appointments. *Publications :* The Records and Lessons of a Series of 3000 Midwifery Cases (Practitioner) ; The Radical Treatment of Tubercular Disease of the Ankle and Tarsus, read at Brit. Med. Assoc., published Brit. Med. Jour. and Lancet ; editor with Mr. D'Arcy Power of A System of Syphilis, in six volumes ; editor of the Practitioner's Encyclopaedia of Medicine, Surgery, and Midwifery, 2nd ed. 1913 ; editor and translator Kirmisson's Handbook of the Surgery of Children, etc. *Recreations :* motoring, Surgeon Royal Naval Volunteer Reserve. *Address :* 17 Devonshire Place, W. ; 16 Pembridge Crescent, W. *T.A. :* Oxymoron, London. *T. :* 1998 Park ; 878 Mayfair ; 8961 City. *M. :* LK 9914. *Club :* Constitutional.
(*Died 13 Sept. 1916.*)

MURPHY, Very Rev. John. *Address :* West Calder, N.B.

MURPHY, Rt. Rev. John Baptist Tuohill, S.Sp., S.T.D., L.L.D. ; R.C. Bishop of Port Louis (Mauritius), since 1916 ; b. Mein House, Knocknagoshil, 24 June 1854 ; s. of Bartholemew Murphy, gentleman-farmer, and Johanna Tuohill. *Educ. :* Blackrock College, Dublin ; Holy Ghost College, Paris. Won an Exhibition and Medal for Greek Verse at the Catholic University, Dublin ; Assistant Master at St. Mary's College, Trinidad, for five years ; ordained Priest, 1878 ; Dean of Studies, Rockwell College, 1879-86 ; President Pittsburg College, 1886-99 ; Blackrock College, 1899-1904 ; Trinity Park, Bath, 1904-6 ; Provincial, U.S.A., 1906-10 ; Ireland and England, 1910-16. *Publications :* several vols. of sermons ; articles in various Reviews ; brochures in special subjects. *Address :* The Palace, Port Louis, Mauritius.
(*Died 17 April 1926.*)

MURPHY, John Harvey, K.C. 1920 ; b. 1862 ; o. s. of late John Patrick Murphy, K.C., of the Middle Temple, and g. s. of late Patrick Mathias Murphy, Q.C., of Dublin ; m. 1891, Lucy, e. d. of late Edward C. Clarke ; one s. one d. *Educ. :* Downside School, Bath ; Trinity Hall, Cambridge. Called to Bar, Middle Temple, 1887 ; practised on S.E. Circuit, Herts and Essex Sessions, and Probate and Divorce Court. *Publications :* Chief Reporter to The Times in Probate and Divorce Court, June 1895-Sep. 1909. *Recreations :* books, the drama, fishing, miniature rifle - shooting. *Address :* Lowood, College Road, Upper Norwood, S.E.19 ; 3 Temple Gardens, Temple, E.C.4. *T. :* Syd. 1319 and Central 700. *Clubs :* Reform, Royal Automobile. (*Died 20 Dec. 1924.*)

MURPHY, Martin, I.S.O. 1903 ; C.E., D.Sc. ; Govt. Inspecting Engineer on the Western Division of the National Trans - Continental Railway, Canada, since 1906 ; b. Ballendaggen, Enniscorthy, 11 Nov. 1832 ; m. Maria Agnes Buckley, Bantter, Ireland ; eight s. three d. Resident Engineer, Dublin, Wicklow, and Wexford Railway, 1862-67 ; went to Canada, 1868 ; Provincial Government Engineer of Nova Scotia, 1875-1903 ; President Canadian Society of Civil Engineers, 1902-3. *Address :* Edmonton, Alberta, Canada. (*Died Jan. 1926.*)

MURPHY, Martin Joseph, J.P., M.P. (N.), East Waterford, since 1913. *Address :* Atlantic, Tramore, Co. Waterford. *Club :* National Liberal. (*Died 4 Sept. 1919.*)

MURPHY, Sir Michael, 1st Bt., cr. 1912 ; s. of Michael Murphy of 21 Merrion Square,

Dublin, J.P. ; b. 9 March 1845 ; m. 1877, Mary (d. 1882), d. of James and Mary Freeman of Rathmines, Co. Dublin ; one s. one d. Head of the firm of Michael Murphy, Ltd., steamship owners, of Dublin, Liverpool, Swansea, and Cardiff ; member of the Board of Superintendence of the Belfast Banking Company, Ltd., also ex-chairman of the Dublin Port and Docks Board ; has been largely instrumental in reviving the shipbuilding industry in Dublin. *Heir :* s. George Francis [b. 31 March 1881 ; m. 1913, Frances, d. of late Richard Davosen. *Address :* Hawthorn, Shrewsbury Road, Dublin]. *Address :* Wyckham, Taney, Dundrum, Co. Dublin. *Clubs :* Reform ; St. Stephen's Green, Dublin. (*Died 10 April 1925.*)

MURPHY, Patrick Charles, M.D. ; Senator of Canada since 1912 ; Physician and Surgeon ; b. Kinkora, P.E. Island, 14 Sep. 1868 ; m. 1st, 1893 (d. 1901) ; 2nd, 1904 (d. 1912) ; four s. three d. ; 3rd, 1915. *Educ. :* native district, Summerside High School, and New York University ; graduated in medicine, New York University, at head of class, 1893. Began practice of medicine in P.E. Island ; President Maritime Medical Association at Halifax, N.S., 1904 ; organised the Tignish Trading Co., 1904. *Publications :* contributor to contemporary medical literature and current political literature. *Address :* Tignish, Prince Edward Island.
(*Died Mar. 1925.*)

MURPHY, Sir Shirley Forster, Kt., cr. 1904 ; K.B.E., cr. 1919 ; F.R.C.S. ; Lieut.-Col. R.A.M.C.(T.F.) ; Vice-President Royal Sanitary Institute, Society of Medical Officers of Health, Epidemiological Section Royal Society of Medicine, and Royal Statistical Society ; late Examiner in Public Health, Royal Colleges of Physicians and Surgeons ; Bisset Hawkins Medallist, Royal College of Physicians, and Jenner Medallist, Royal Society of Medicine ; late Medical Officer of Health, Administrative County of London ; Member of Royal Commission on Tuberculosis ; s. of late George Murphy ; m. Ellen Theodora, d. of Henry S. King ; two d. *Educ. :* University College School ; Guy's Hospital. *Address :* 9 Bentinck Terrace, Regent's Park, N.W.8. *T. :* Hampstead 958. *Clubs :* Athenæum, Savile.
(*Died 27 April 1923.*)

MURPHY, William Martin, J.P. ; b. 29 Dec. 1844 ; e. s. of late Denis William Murphy of Bantry, Co. Cork, and Mary Anne, d. of late James Martin of Castletown Bere, Co. Cork ; m. 1870, Mary Julia (d. 1900), d. of late James Fitzgerald Lombard, J.P., of South Hill, Co. Dublin ; three s. three d. M.P. Dublin (St. Patrick's Division), 1885-92 ; carried out several railway and electric tramway and lighting undertakings in the United Kingdom, and constructed railways in the Gold Coast Colony, West Africa ; President Dublin Chamber of Commerce, 1912-13 ; Chairman Finance and General Purposes Committee, Dublin Castle Red Cross Hospital, since February 1915 ; Chairman Dublin United Tramways Company, and a director of the Great Southern and Western Railway of Ireland ; founded in 1905 the Irish Independent, the only halfpenny daily morning paper in Ireland ; principal promoter and Chairman of Committee of Irish International Exhibition held in Dublin, 1907 ; prominent in opposition to Syndicalist Strikes in Dublin, 1913. *Address :* Dartry, Rathmines, Co. Dublin. *T.A. :* Railways, Dublin ; Arenaconas, London. *T. :* Rathmines 83, Dublin. *Clubs :* Reform, Royal Irish Yacht, Kingstown. (*Died 26 June 1919.*)

MURPHY, Col. William Reed, D.S.O. ; F.Z.S. ; Lt.-Col. Indian Medical Service ; retired ; b. 23 Oct. 1849 ; unmarried. *Educ. :* Clongoweswood College, County Kildare ; Trinity College, Dublin ; Royal College of Surgeons, Ireland (took all prizes during student course there and at Meath Hospital); took 1st prize at Netley on entering Indian Medical Service, 30 March 1872; served with Indian Contingent, Malta and Cyprus, 1878; Afghanistan, 1878-80 (despatches, medal and clasp); received special thanks from the Brig.-Gen. commanding the Cavalry Brigade at the cavalry action of Pat Kao Shana, for conduct in action at great personal risk (London Gazette, 22 Oct. 1880); Hazara, 1888 (despatches, Indian medal, and clasp); Lushai, 1888-89 (clasp); P.M.O. Lushai Column, Chin Lushai Field Force, 1889-90 (despatches, mentioned by Government of India, clasp, D.S.O.); Chitral Relief Force, 1895 (medal and clasp); P.M.O. Kurram-Kohat Force, 1897 (despatches, 2 clasps); P.M.O. Kurram M. Column, Tirah Field Force, 1897-98 (despatches, clasp); Granted Indian Army Good Service Pension, 1918; Member of the Royal Institution of Great Britain. *T.A.:* Ejus, London. *T.:* Regent 683. *Clubs:* East India United Service, Junior Naval and Military.

(Died 7 Aug. 1927.)

MURRAY of Elibank, 1st Baron, *cr.* 1912; **Rt. Hon. Alexander William Charles Oliphant Murray;** P.C. 1911; Director, S. Pearson and Son; *b.* 12 April 1870; *e. s.* of 1st Viscount and 10th Baron Elibank; *m.* 1894, Hilda Louisa Janey Wolfe, *sis.* of late Lt.-Gen. Sir J. W. Murray; no *c. Educ.:* Cheltenham. Late Lt. Lothians and Berwickshire Yeomanry Cavalry; contested West Division Edinburgh (G.), 1895; also Peebles and Selkirk, and city of York bye-election, 1900; M.P. (L.) Midlothian, 1900-1905; Parliamentary Secretary to Treasury, 1910-12; M.P.(L.) Peebles and Selkirk, 1906-10, and Midlothian, 1910-12; Comptroller H.M.'s Household and Scottish Liberal Whip, 1906-10; Under Secretary of State for India, 1909; Chief Liberal Whip, 1909-12. *Heir: b.* Hon. Gideon Murray. *Address:* Elibank, Walkerburn, Scotland. *Clubs:* Brooks's, Reform, Bachelors', Marlborough. *(Died 13 Sept. 1920.)*

MURRAY, Albert E., R.H.A., F.R.I.B.A., F.R.I.A.I.; architect; ex-President of the Royal Institute of the Architects of Ireland; Professor of Architecture R.H.A.; Freeman of the City of Dublin; *b.* 14 May 1849; 2nd *s.* of late William George Murray, R.H.A., Avonmore, Co. Dublin, and M. A., *d.* of James Craig of Armagh; *m.* 1902, Amy H., *o. d.* of Andrew Johnston, Dublin; one *s.* one *d. Educ.:* privately. Hon. Sec. to Royal Institute of Architects of Ireland, 1883-1901; Examiner in the Diploma of Public Health, Royal College of Physicians, 1887-96; Hon. Sec. Military Lodge (Masonic) of Ireland since 1883; extensive practice, and consultant to many hospitals, which latter work has been a special study; Professor of Architecture in the Royal Hibernian Academy; Examiner in Architecture in the National University, Ireland; Governor of Mercers Hospital, Dublin; on visiting Committee of Dublin Hospital Sunday Fund. *Recreations:* yachting, fishing, golf, sketching. *Address:* 37 Dawson Street, Dublin. *T.:* 676; 2 Clyde Road, Dublin. *T.:* Ballsbridge 507. *Clubs:* Junior Constitutional; Royal Irish Yacht, Northern Counties, Londonderry. *(Died 20 Mar. 1924.)*

MURRAY, Major Alexander Penrose; *b.* 13 July 1863; *e. s.* of George Joseph Murray of Ayton, Fife, and Augusta Anne, *d.* of Rev. George Deane, Rector of Bighton, Hants; *m.* 1st, 1891, Nina (*d.* 1894), *d.* of Col. Alexander Solovtsoff; one *s.*; 2nd, 1895, Ethel Chorley, *d.* of Maj.-Gen. Arthur Hill; one *s. Educ.:* Eton. 2nd Lieut. Royal Aberdeenshire Highlanders, 1881; Lieut. Gordon Highlanders, 1883; Capt. 1893; served Eastern Soudan, 1884, present at battle of El Teb (medal, clasp, and Khedive's star); retired from army, 1895; has received the Royal Humane Society's silver

medal for saving life from drowning; Vice-Consul at Odessa, 1891; Acting Consul at Batoum, 1891-92; transferred to Sebastopol, 1892; Consul-General for the Governments of Poland, Kovno, Grodno, Minsk, and Vilna, to reside at Warsaw, 1897; received the Jubilee Medal, 1897; served with 1st Batt. Gordon Highlanders South African War, 1899-1901 (severely wounded); operations in the Orange Free State, including actions at Houtnek (Thoba Mountain) and Zand River; operations in the Transvaal, including actions near Johannesburg and Pretoria; operations in the Transvaal, west of Pretoria (despatches, Queen's medal with three clasps); Consul-General, Hayti, 1908-11; Consul St. Pierre Miquelon, 1912-13; retired, 1913; served European War 1914-17 with Gordon High landers (hon. rank of Major). *Address:* 16 Polwarth Grove, Edinburgh. *(Died Mar. 1926.)*

MURRAY, Maj.-Gen. Anthony Hepburn, R.A.; *b.* 31 Oct. 1840; *m.* 1871, Mary Madeline, *d.* of Gen. G. Radcliffe. Entered army, 1857; Maj.-Gen. 1896; retired, 1897. *Address:* St. Enodoc, Wellington College, Berks. *Club:* Naval and Military.

(Died 27 May 1917.)

MURRAY, Colonel Arthur Mordaunt, C.B. 1909; M.V.O. 1908; F.R.G.S.; *b.* Southfleet, Kent, 20 Jan. 1852; *m.* 1st 1895, Isabel, *d.* of Richard Pemberton of Hawthorn Towers, Co. Durham, one *d.*; 2nd 1898, Mabel *d.* of John Nicholson of Seaforth, Lancashire; two *s.* one *d. Educ.:* Uppingham School; Royal Military Academy, Woolwich. Received a commission in Royal Artillery, 1873; served as Assistant-Superintendent of Transport in the 1st Division Peshawur Valley Field Force, 1878-79 (despatches); appointed to Royal Horse Artillery, 1880; Captain, 1882; Brigade-Major R.A. Egypt, 1885-87; Major, 1889; Assistant Military Secretary to G.O.C. South Africa, 1895; Lt.-Col., 1898; Assistant-Commandant Royal Military Academy, Woolwich, 1900; Bt. Col., 1902; sent on a mission to Japan, 1906; Commandant Duke of York's Royal Military School, Chelsea, 1907-9; Member Royal United Service Institution, Whitehall. *Publications:* Imperial Outposts, 1907; Fortnightly History of the War, 1914-15; awarded the gold medal of the Royal Artillery Institution for an essay on Fire Discipline, 1892; silver medal of the same Institution The Tactics of Massed Batteries in the Field. *Recreation:* travelling. *Address:* 4 Albert Place, Kensington, W.8. *T.:* Western 2636. *Club:* Reform.

(Died 23 May 1920.)

MURRAY, Charles Oliver, R.E., artist and etcher; *b.* Denholm, Roxburghshire; 3rd *s.* of late Thomas Murray; *m.* 1869, Elizabeth, *e. d.* of late Archibald Campbell, Glasgow. *Educ.:* Minto School; Edinburgh School of Design; School of the Royal Scottish Academy. Gained Keith prize there and National Medallions Queen prize, silver and gold medals for anatomical studies and drawing from the antique in the national competitions; awarded at International Exhibitions: London, 1884; silver medal, Munich, 1893; gold medal, Paris, 1900; silver medal for etching; elected to Royal Society of Painter Etchers on its foundation, exhibiting there and at Royal Academy, yearly since 1876; engaged in drawing illustrations for books and magazines for several years, afterwards as an etcher, original and interpretive; etched pictures by many distinguished artists, and many original plates, landscape, architectural and figure subjects. *Publications:* in addition to above plates, etchings illustrating Keats's Eve of St. Agnes, Border Ballads, etc. *Recreations:* reading, travelling. *Address:* 10 Avondale Road, South Croydon. *Club:* Art Workers' Guild.

(Died 11 Dec. 1924.)

MURRAY, David, M.A., LL.D., F.S.A., F.S.A. Scot.; a Solicitor in Glasgow; *b.* Glasgow, 15 April 1842; *s.* of David Murray, Solicitor in Glasgow (*d.* 1848) and Ann Hunter Guthrie (*d.* 1901); *m.* 1872, Frances Porter (*d.* 1919), *e. d.* of late Arthur Francis Stoddard of Broadfield, Renfrewshire; three *d. Educ.:* Merchiston Castle, Edinburgh; University of Glasgow. Dean of the Faculty of Procurators in Glasgow, 1895-98; President of the Archæological Society of Glasgow, 1895 - 98; Vice - President of the Society of Antiquaries of Scotland, 1900-1903; President of the Royal Philosophical Society of Glasgow, 1904-7; Rhind Lecturer in Archæology for 1908; President Glasgow Bibliographical Society, 1912-13, 1915-20; a Member of the University Court of the University of Glasgow. *Publications:* The York Buildings Company, a Chapter in Scotch History, 1883; The Law relating to the Property of Married Persons, 1891; An Archæological Survey of the United Kingdom; The Preservation and Protection of our Ancient Monuments, 1896; Museums, Their History and their Use, 1904; and numerous others; Early Burgh Organisation in Scotland, vol. i., Glasgow, 1924; Memories of the Old College of Glasgow; Some Chapters in the History of the University, 1927. *Recreations:* travelling, yachting, and book-collecting. *Address:* 18 Fitzroy Place, Glasgow; Moorepark, Cardross, Dumbartonshire. *Clubs:* Reform, Royal Societies; Western, Glasgow; University, Edinburgh; Royal Northern Yacht.(*Died 2 Oct. 1928.*)

MURRAY, Dr. Donald, M.B., C.M.Glas.; M.P. (L.) Western Isles, Inverness, since Dec. 1918; Medical Officer of Health for Burgh of Stornoway and School Medical Officer for Lewis and the western portion of Ross-shire; *b.* Stornoway, 21 Oct. 1862; *m.* 1898, Janet Catherine Grace, *d.* of Alexander Macpherson, Stornoway. *Educ.:* Glasgow University. President of the Medico-Chirurgical Society and of the University Liberal Club. *Address:* 4 St. Alban's Road, N.W.5. *Club:* National Liberal.
(*Died 6 July 1923.*)

MURRAY, Colonel Frank, D.S.O. 1904; 8th Ghoorka Rifles; *b.* 10 June 1864. Entered Army, 1885; Capt. 1896; Major, 1903; served Burmah, 1885 - 89 (medal with two clasps); Waziristan, 1894-95 (clasp); Thibet, 1903-1904 (despatches, D.S.O.). *Address:* Shillong, Assam.
(*Died 18 April 1917.*)

MURRAY, Ven. Frederic Richardson; L.Th., M.A., D.D.; Rector of St. Mary's, Belize, since 1888; Archdeacon of Belize since 1904; *b.* 1 Sep. 1845; *m.* Mary Jane, *d.* of late Rev. John Dolphin, B.A. Oxon, Vicar of Lower Guiting, Glos.; three *s.* five *d. Educ.:* Spencer's, Newcastle-on-Tyne; Stepney Grammar School, London; Clare College, Cambridge; Scorton, Yorks; Hatfield Hall, Durham. Ordained, 1868; Priest, 1869; Curate of Grimley, 1868-70; Shepton - Beauchamp, 1870-71; Ruyton - XI. - Towns, 1871 - 72; St. Andrew's, Deal, 1872-73; S.P.G. Missionary, Newfoundland, 1873-81; Chaplain to Bishop Feild, 1873; Rector of Twillingate, 1873; Rural Dean Notre Dame Bay, 1873; Incumbent St. John's Cathedral, 1877; Rector of St. Mary's Heart's Content, 1879; offered St. George's, Halifax, 1881; Rector and Minor Canon St. Luke's Pro-Cathedral, Halifax, N.S., 1881; Assistant Rector Parish Church, Kingston, 1888; Commissary Bishop of Jamaica, 1889; Bishop Holme, 1891; Bishop Ormsby, 1893; Bishop Bury, 1905; Bishop Farrar, 1912-15; Bishop Dunn, 1919-24; Headmaster Belize High School, 1890; Acting Rector of St. John's, 1891; Archdeacon of Honduras, 1894; Canon, 1905-7; Administrator of the Diocese, 1911-17, 1920-23. *Address:* St. Mary's Rectory, Belize, British Honduras. (*Died 23 June 1925.*)

MURRAY, Sir George Sheppard, Kt., *cr.* 1906; *b.* 26 June 1851; *s.* of late Alexander Murray, Ceylon Civil Service; *m.* 1888, Lucy, *d.* of late N. B. Dennys; one *s.* one *d.* Unofficial Member of the Legislative Council of Straits Settlements, 1888 - 1906. *Address:* Cleveland House, St. James's Square, S.W.1; *T.:* Gerrard 5884; Barretstown Castle, Ballymore Eustace, Co. Kildare. *Clubs:* Wellington, Junior Carlton, Sports, Royal Automobile.
(*Died 27 Oct. 1928.*)

MURRAY, Lieut.-Gen. Sir James Wolfe, K.C.B., *cr.* 1900; D.L. Peebles, 1907; *b.* 13 Mar. 1853; *e. s.* of late James Wolfe Murray of Cringletie; *m.* 1st, 1875, Arabella (*d.* 1909), *d.* of W. Bray; two *s.* three *d.*; 2nd, 1913, Fanny, *d.* of late James S. Robson and *widow* of Sir Donald H. Macfarlane. *Educ.:* Glenalmond; Harrow; R.M.A., Woolwich. Entered R.A., 1872; Colonel, 1899; served Ashanti, 1895, in command of Lines of Communication (Bt. Lt.-Col., star); Commanding Lines of Communication, Natal, 1899-1900 (despatches twice); Quartermaster-General in India, 1903-4; Master-General of the Ordnance, 1904-7; in Command of 9th (Secunderabad) Division, India, 1907-11; General Officer Commanding-in-Chief Scotland, 1913; S. Africa, 1914; 1st Military Member of the Army Council, 1914-15; G.O.C.-in-Chief Eastern Command, 1916 - 17; holds Russian Order of St. Anne, 1st Class, with swords; and Order of White Eagle. *Address:* Cringletie, Peebles. *T.:* Peebles 69. *Clubs:* Army and Navy; New, Edinburgh. (*Died 17 Oct. 1919.*)

MURRAY, Sir John, K.C.V.O., *cr.* 1926; C.V.O. 1913; J.P., D.L., F.S.A., etc.; head of publishing house of John Murray, founded 1768; Vice-Chairman Hospital for Sick Children; High Sheriff, County of London, 1908; President of Publishers' Association, 1898-99; Chairman League of Remembrance; Commandeur de l'Ordre Royal du Sauveur (Greece); D.Ph. University of Athens; Ordre de la Couronne (Belgian); *b.* London, 1851; *m. d.* of William Leslie of Warthill, Aberdeenshire, late M.P.; one *s.* one *d. Educ.:* Eton; Magdalen College, Oxford; M.A. *Publications:* Memoirs of John Murray III.; editor of Gibbon's Autobiography; Byron's Correspondence, 1922, and other works. *Recreations:* shooting, golf, cricket, riding, etc.; Captain of Royal Wimbledon Golf Club, 1884; Treasurer Roxburghe Club. *Address:* 50 Albemarle Street, W.1. *T.A.:* Guidebook, London. *T.:* Mayfair 788. *Clubs:* Athenæum, M.C.C., etc.
(*Died 30 Nov. 1928.*)

MURRAY, Keith William, Portcullis Pursuivant of Arms since 1913; Carnarvon Pursuivant Extraordinary, 1911; Knight of Grace of the Order of St. John of Jerusalem, 1912; F.S.A., 1891; *b.* 1860; *s.* of late William Powell Murray of Lincoln's Inn, barrister-at-law, a Registrar of the High Court in Bankruptcy, and Georgina Charlotte Daysh, *o. d.* of Hon. Arthur R. Turnour, Commander R.N.; *m.* Grace, *y. d.* of late Sir George S. Abercromby of Birkenbog and Forglen, Baronet; one *d. Educ.:* Marlborough. Studied civil and mechanical engineering, 1880-86; subsequently taking up the subjects of heraldry and genealogy; edited the Genealogist, 1889-94; has since contributed to that magazine and publications of a similar nature and to the Scots Peerage; some years in the London Scottish Rifle Volunteers; Gold Staff Officer at the Coronation of H.M. King Edward VII. *Recreations:* golf, fishing, shooting, etc. *Address:* College of Arms, Queen Victoria Street, E.C.; 37 Cheniston Gardens, Kensington, W. *T.:* Central 1686. *Club:* Junior Carlton.
(*Died 11 Jan. 1922.*)

MURRAY, Sir Patrick Keith, 8th Bt.; *cr.* 1673; Capt. Grenadier Guards (retired); *b.* 27

Jan. 1885 ; *S.* father 1861 ; *m.* 1st. Frances. *d.* of Anthony Murray, Dollerie, Perthshire, 1870 (*d.* 1874); 2nd, Ione, *d.* of late Hon. Lord Kinloch, a Judge of Court of Session, 1876 (*d.* 1881) ; four *s.* one *d. Educ.:* Trin. Coll. Camb. Entered army, 1854. *Heir: s.* Capt. W. K. Murray. *Address :* Ochtertyre, Crieff, Perthshire.
(*Died* 10 *Jan.* 1921.)

MURRAY, Richard, O.B.E. ; M.V.O. ; Principal Technical Assist. Naval Store Dept. Admiralty; b. 19 June 1865; *s.* of Richard Murray of Portsmouth ; *m.* 1886, Isabella, 5th *d.* of late Thomas Sagar, Fleet Engineer, R.N. ; one *s. Address :* Naval Store Dept., Admiralty, S.W.
(*Died* 12 *Sept.* 1925.)

MURRAY, Sir Robert, Kt., *cr.* 1914 Partner in Love and Stewart Timber Merchants, Glasgow ; *b.* 1846 ; *m.* Jane Stewart (*d.* 1922). *Address:* 2 Hanover Terrace, Regent's Park, N.W.1. *T. :* Paddington 1056.
(*Died* 14 *June* 1924.)

MURRAY, Colonel Robert Davidson, M.B., I.M.S. ; retired ; *b.* 30 Aug. 1851 ; *s.* of William Murray, J.P., Kilcoy, Ross-shire ; *m.* Mary McInnes, *e. d.* of Deputy-Surg.-Gen. George Mackay, M.D., I.M.S., Madras ; three *s.* three *d. Educ.:* Inverness Royal Academy ; Aberdeen University. Graduated in Medicine with first-class honours at Edinburgh University, 1874 ; Senior Resident Physician Edinburgh Royal Infirmary, 1874-75 ; entered Indian Medical Service, 1875 ; held many important appointments under the Bengal Government, 1876-1904 ; First Resident Surgeon, Presidency General Hospital, and Superintendent of Asylums, 1882-86 ; served with the Burmese Expeditionary Force, 1886-87 ; commanded Field Hospital in Mandalay (medal and despatches) ; Civil Surgeon of Howrah, 1890-96 : Professor of Surgery, Calcutta Medical College, and First Surgeon to the Medical College Hospital, 1898 ; P.M.O., Lahore District, 1904; Inspector General of Civil Hospitals, United Provinces of Agra and Oudh, 1905-10 ; Member of the Legislative Council of the Lieut.-Governor, United Provinces, and the first Medical Officer to obtain a seat on Indian Legislature. *Publications :* numerous contributions to the Medical Press. *Address :* 5 Nevern Square, S.W.5. *T. :* Western 2382. *Club :* East India United Service.
(*Died* 12 *Jan.* 1920.)

MURRAY Maj.-Gen. Robert Hunter, C.B. 1896 ; C.M.G. 1898 ; *b.* 12 Aug. 1847 ; *y. s.* of late John Murray, J.P., and *g.s.* of late John Murray of Wooplaw, Roxburghshire, N.B. ; *m.* Florence, *d.* of late Captain H. W. Barlow, R.E., 1887 ; one *s.* one *d. Educ.:* Edinburgh Academy. Ensign 72nd Highlanders, 1867; served throughout Afghan War, 1878-80, as Adjutant ; severely wounded at Battle of Kandahar (medal with four clasps for Peiwar Kotal, Charasia, Kabul and Kandahar ; and bronze star for Kabul-Kandahar March ; Bt. of Major) ; Egyptian Campaign, 1882, as Brig. Maj. of the Indian Contingent (medal with clasp, for Tel-el-Kebir, and Egyptian bronze star ; Bt. of Lieut.-Col.) ; Sudan Campaign, 1885, as assist. to chief of the staff; actions of Hasheen, Tamai (clasp for Snakim); D.A.A.G., Guernsey, 1889-92 ; Sudan Campaign, 1898, in command of the 1st Batt. Seaforth Highlanders (severely wounded, Egyptian Sudan medal with two clasps, medal) ; Colonel, 1892 (five times despatches) ; A.D.C. to late Queen; commanding 72nd and 79th regimental districts, 1899-1900 ; 1st Batt. Seaforth Highlanders to 1899 ; Maj.-Gen. comm. Infantry Brigade, Aldershot, 1900-2 ; comm. troops at Alexandria, 1902-4 ; Col. Seaforth Highlanders, 1914-24. *Address :* The Red House, Yateley, Hants. *Club:* Army and Navy.
(*Died* 17 *Jan.* 1925.)

MURRAY, Major William, O.B.E., M.P. (Co.U.), Dumfries, since Dec. 1918; *e. s.* of late Capt. John Murray, R.N., of Murraythwaite,

and Grace Harriet, *d.* of Col. William Graham ; *b.* 1865 ; *m.* 1892, Evelyn, *d.* of John Bruce ; three *d. Educ.:* Magdalen College, Oxford. Contested Dumfriesshire several times; Member of Faculty of Advocates; late Capt. 5th Batt. K.O.S.B. *Address:* Murraythwaite, Ecclefechan, Scotland ; 98 Park Street, Mayfair, W.1. *Clubs:* Carlton, Arthur's; New, Edinburgh.
(*Died* 5 *Mar.* 1923.)

MURRAY, Colonel Sir Wyndham, K.C.B., *cr.* 1917 ; Kt., *cr.* 1905 ; C.B. 1902; late Member of Honorable Corps of Gentlemen-at-Arms ; Gentleman Usher of the Scarlet Rod in the Order of the Bath, 1913-1928 ; Grand Cross, St. John of Jerusalem ; *b.* 22 Feb. 1844 ; *s.* of late Rev. T. B. Murray, Prebendary of St. Paul's, and Helen, *d.* of Sir W. Douglas, K.H. ; *m.* 1890, Emma Cecilia (*d.* 1922), *d.* of E. Walker. *Educ.:* Marlborough College. Gloucestershire Regiment, 1863 ; Staff College, 1872 ; D.A.Q.M.G. Cork, 1875 ; Intelligence Branch, Q.M.G. Dept. Dublin, 1877 ; Brig.-Major 1st Brigade, 1878 ; Military Attaché, Turkey, 1878 (despatches); A.D.C. and D.A.Q.M.G. Zululand, 1879 (despatches, Brevet-Major, medal with clasp) ; Staff Officer, Kabul, 1880 (medal) ; Staff Officer, Pishin Outposts, Afghanistan, 1881(despatches); D.A.Q.M.G. Egypt, 1882 (despatches, medal with clasp for Tel-el-Kebir, Brevet Lt.-Col., 4th class Osmanieh, Khedive's Star) ; D.A.Q.M.G. Bechuanaland 1884-85 (despatches) ; Military King's Messenger, France, 1915-16 (War Medal, 1914-15 Star, Victory Medal); M.P. (C.) Bath, 1892-1906; late Chairman Japan Society; 3rd Class Order of Rising Sun, Japan. *Recreations :* shooting, yachting. *Address:* 10 Rutland Gate, S.W.7 ; *T.:* Kensington 4473 ; 147 King's Road, Brighton. *M.:* A 393. *Clubs:* Carlton ; Royal Yacht Squadron, Cowes.
(*Died* 1 *Nov.* 1928.)

MURRAY BAILLIE, Lieut.-Col. Frederick David; *b.* 1862 ; *er. s.* of late Col. James William Murray Baillie, of Cally and Broughton, J.P., R.H.G., and Elizabeth Florence, *d.* of late Frederick R. Magenis ; *m.* 1900, Alexandra Helen Agnes, *o. d.* of late James Cavan-Irving, of Burnfoot, 5th Dragoon Guards ; one *d. Educ.:* Eton. Formerly Major 4th Hussars ; Major and Hon. Lieut.-Col., retired, late 2nd Co. of London Yeomanry ; a Railway Transport Officer, 1914-17. *Address:* Ilston Grange, Leicester ; Cally, Gatehouse, Kirkcudbright. *Clubs:* Boodle's, Cavalry.

MURTON, Sir Walter, Kt., *cr.* 1899, C.B. 1894; *b.* East Stour, Ashford, Kent, 6 Apr. 1836 ; 2nd *s.* of late Walter Murton, and Elizabeth, *d.* of late Richard Coleman ; *m.* Mary (*d.* 1895), *y. d.* of late John Callaway of Canterbury, 1860 ; two *s. Educ.:* Tonbridge School. Admitted a solicitor, 1858 ; appointed solicitor to the Board of Trade in 1875 from the first formation of the Legal Department ; retired, 1900. *Decorated* 1894 in recognition of services at the Board of Trade ; a British Representative at Conference on German Claims arising from S. African War, 1900 ; travelled in the Dominions and other countries, 1900 to 1908. *Publications :* Wreck Inquiries ; Law and Practice. *Address:* Gipp's Close, Langton, Kent. *T.A.:* Langton Green. *Clubs:* Devonshire ; Tunbridge Wells and Counties.
(*Died* 20 *June* 1927.)

MUSCIO, Bernard, Challis Professor of Philosophy, University of Sydney, since 1922 ; *b.* N.S. Wales, 1887 ; *s.* of Bernard Muscio, Orchard Hills, N.S.W. ; *m.* 1915, Florence Mildred, *e. d.* of Charles Fry, Sydney ; no *c. Educ.:* privately; Sydney University ; Gonville and Caius College, Cambridge. B.A. Sydney, 1910 ; B.A. Cambridge, 1913 ; University Demonstrator in Experimental Psychology, Cambridge, 1914 ; Investigator to the Industrial

Fatigue Research Board, 1919-22. *Publications:* Lectures on Industrial Psychology, 1st ed. Sydney, 1917 ; 2nd ed. London, 1921 ; various reports of investigations in industrial fatigue, published by the Industrial Fatigue Research Board ; articles on Philosophy and Psychology in Mind, Monist, British Journal of Psychology, etc. *Address:* The University, Sydney, N.S. Wales. **(Died 28 May 1926.)**

MUSGRAVE, Charles Edwin, F.I.C.S. ; Secretary London Chamber of Commerce ; Chevalier, Order of St. Anne of Russia ; Officer of the Crown of Roumania ; b. 17 April 1861 ; e. s. of late E. G. Musgrave, Stotfold, Beds. *Educ.:* privately. Sub-Editor of The Citizen, 1881 ; entered service of London Chamber of Commerce, 1882 ; Assistant Secretary, 1884 ; Secretary, 1909 ; Secretary, Congress of Chambers of Commerce of the Empire, 1920, and of British Imperial Council of Commerce since formation, 1911, London Labour Conciliation and Arbitration Board, and Timber Trade Federation of United Kingdom ; President Chartered Institute of Secretaries, 1921-22 ; Member, Court of Turners' Company ; has given evidence before Royal Commissions, etc. *Publications:* (joint) Handbook, The Factory and Workshops Act, 1901 ; The London Chamber of Commerce, from 1881 to 1914. *Recreations:* rowing, touring, reading. *Address:* 97 Cannon Street, E.C. ; Temple Chambers, E.C.4. *T.A.:* Convention, Cannon, London. *T.:* City 1949. *Clubs:* Authors', Gresham. **(Died 3 Aug. 1923.)**

MUSGRAVE. Major Herbert, D.S.O. 1915 ; R.E. ; b. 11 May 1876 ; y. s. of late Sir Anthony Musgrave, G.C.M.G. ; m. 1915, Georgeanna, o. d. of Mark Hopkins ; one d. *Educ.:* Harrow. Entered army, 1896 ; Captain, 1905 ; with S. African Constabulary, 1901-4 ; D.A.A. and Q.M.G., Malta, 1908-12 ; served S. African War, 1899-1902 (despatches twice, Queen's medal 5 clasps, King's medal 2 clasps) ; European War, 1914-16 (wounded, D.S.O.). *Address:* Hurstanclays, East Grinstead. *Club:* United Service. **(Died 3 June 1918.)**

MUSGRAVE, Sir Richard George, 12th Bt. ; cr. 1611 ; D.L., J.P. ; b. 11 Oct. 1872 ; e. s. of 11th Bt. and Adora Frances Olga, d. of Peter Wells of Forest Farm, Windsor (she m. 2nd, the 3rd Lord Brougham) ; S. father, 1881 ; m. 1895, Hon. Eleanor Harbord, 7th d. of 5th Baron Suffield ; one s. Owns about 6900 acres. *Heir:* s. Nigel Courtenay, b. 11 Feb. 1896. *Address:* 17 Charles Street, W.1 ; T.: Gerrard 2136 ; Eden Hall, Langwathby, Cumberland. **(Died 21 May 1926.)**

MUSPRATT, Edmund K., J.P., F.C.S., F.I.C., LL.D. ; Chairman, British Insulated and Helsby Cables, Ltd. ; Vice-Chairman, United Alkali Co., Ltd. ; member of Council, University of Liverpool ; b. Linacre, near Liverpool, 6 Nov. 1833 ; s. of late James Muspratt, Seaforth Hall ; m. 1861, Frances Jane, d. of Thomas Baines, Liverpool ; three s. four d. *Educ.:* Pestallozian Institution, Worksop ; Universities of Giessen and Munich. Formerly member of the firms James Muspratt & Sons and Muspratt Bros. & Huntley, now incorporated in the United Alkali Co., Ltd. ; President, Liverpool Chamber of Commerce, 1875 ; Member, City Council Liverpool, 1877-86; Member, Lancashire County Council, 1889-1902; Pro-Chancellor, University of Liverpool, 1903-9; President, Society of Chemical Industry, 1885 ; President, Financial Reform Association. *Publications:* My Life and Work; Addresses to various Societies. *Recreations:* travelling and reading. *Address:* Seaforth Hall, nr. Liverpool. **(Died 1 Sept. 1923.)**

MUSPRATT-WILLIAMS, Lt.-Col. Charles Augustus, C.I.E. 1916 ; s. of General Jackson Muspratt-Williams ; b. 13 Sep. 1861 ; m. Ethel Annie, d. of late Rear-Admiral

766

A. J. Kennedy, R.N. ; one s. one d. *Educ.:* Cheltenham College. Entered Army, 1881; Captain, 1889 ; Major, 1899 ; Lt.-Col. 1909 ; Assistant Superintendent, Gunpowder Factory, Kirkee, Small Arms Factory, Kirkee, Gun Carriage Factory, Bombay, 1887-90 ; Assistant Superintendent, Gunpowder Factory, Ishapur, 1890-91 ; Superintendent, 1892-98 ; Chief Inspector of Explosives with the Government of India, 1898-1920 ; retired, 1920. *Address:* c/o Lloyds Bank, Ltd., 9 Pall Mall, S.W.1. *Club:* Public Schools. **(Died 6 May 1925.)**

MUSTERS, John Patricius Chaworth, D.L., J.P. ; b. Oxton, 1860 ; e. s. of late John Chaworth Musters and Caroline Anne, e. d. of late Henry Porter Sherbrooke of Oxton, Notts; m. Mary Anne, d. of George Sharpe; four s. five d. *Educ.:* Eton ; Christ Church, Oxford. High Sheriff, Notts, 1902 ; Farmer ; Colliery director ; magistrate ; Patron of 2 livings; owner of Annesley, Wiverton, and Edwalton, all in Nottinghamshire. *Recreations:* farming, sport, ornithology. *Heir:* s. J. N. Chaworth-Musters. *Address:* Annesley Park, Nottingham. *T.A.:* Annesley, Woodhouse. *Clubs:* Carlton ; Notts County, Nottingham. **(Died 12 Dec. 1921.)**

MYER, Horatio ; b. Hereford, 1850 ; m. 1877, Esther, d. of Henry Joseph. Engaged in wool trade, 1869-75, and in shipping iron trade, 1876-84 ; iron founder, 1876-1903 ; Member L.C.C. 1889 ; M.P. (L.) North Lambeth, 1906-10. *Publication:* pamphlet, Taxation of Landlords. *Address:* 64 Maida Vale, W. ; *T.:* Padd. 1667 ; Forthill, Henley. *Club:* National Liberal. **(Died 1 Jan. 1916.)**

MYERS, Hon. Sir Arthur, Kt., cr. 1924 ; J.P. (New Zealand) ; Director, National Bank of New Zealand, Ltd., London ; Director, New Zealand Insurance Co. ; b. 19 May 1867 ; 2nd s. of late Louis Myers, Auckland, N.Z. ; m. 1903, Vera Anita, O.B.E., d. of late B. W. Levy ; one s. two d. *Educ.:* Wellington College, New Zealand. Chairman Director The Campbell and Ehrenfried Co., Auckland, N.Z. ; Member Royal Commission on Local Government (England) ; Lieut.-Col. New Zealand Military Forces (retired) ; Mayor of Auckland, 1905-8 ; Member New Zealand Parliament for Auckland City East, 1910-21 ; Member Mackenzie Ministry, 1912, holding portfolios Finance, Defence, and Railways ; Member National Ministry New Zealand, 1915-1919, holding portfolios Customs, Pensions, and Munitions ; presented Myers Park and Kindergarten, Town Hall Clock and other benefactions to Auckland City. *Recreations:* golf, tennis, fishing. *Address:* 71 Upper Berkeley Street, W.1. *T.:* Paddington 1185. *Club:* Constitutional. **(Died 9 Oct. 1926.)**

MYLNE, Rt. Rev. Louis George, D.D. ; Hon. Canon, Worcester, 1917 ; s. of Major C.D. Mylne, Bombay Army ; b. Paris, 1843; m. Amy, d. of G. W. Moultrie, 1879; five s. *Educ.:* Merchiston Castle School, Edinburgh ; St. Andrews University; Corpus Christi College, Oxford. Curate of N. Moreton, Berks, 1867-70 ; Senior Tutor of Keble College, Oxford, 1870-76 ; Bishop of Bombay, 1876-97 ; Rector of Alvechurch, Worcestershire, 1905-17; Vicar of St. Mary, Marlborough, 1897-1905 ; Prebendary of Woodford and Wilsford in Salisbury Cathedral, 1899-1905 ; *Publications:* English Church Life in India, 1881 ; Corporate Life of the Church in India, 1884 ; Counsels and Principles of the Lambeth Conference of 1888 ; Sermons preached in Bombay, 1889 ; Churchmen and the Higher Criticism, 1893 ; Hopes for Reunion, 1896 ; The Hidden Riches of Secret Places (in Mankind and the Church), 1907 ; Missions to Hindus, 1906 ; The Holy Trinity, 1916. *Address:* Redcliffe, Battenhall, Worcester. **(Died 19 Feb. 1921.)**

N

NADIA, Maharaja of; Hon. Maharaja Kshaunish Chandra Ray Bahadur; Member Bengal Executive Council since 1924; *b.* at the Palace, Krishnagar, 29 Oct. 1890; *s.* of late Maharaja Kshitish Chandra Ray Bahadur; *m.* Maharani Jyotirmoyee Daby, *d.* of late Raja Ashutoshe Nath Ray of Cossimbazar; two *d. Educ.*: Privately. Comes of the oldest aristocratic family in Bengal; created Maharaja at Coronation Durbar, Delhi, 1911; made Maharaja Bahadur, 1917; first non-official elected Chairman of Nadia District Board, 1920-24; Member of the Bengal Legislative Council, 1921-23. *Recreations:* photography and shooting. *Address:* The Palace, Krishnagar, Nadia, Bengal; 2 Bright Street, Ballygunje, Calcutta. *T.:* Regent 198. *M.:* 1114, 3303, 5308, and .11867. *Clubs:* Calcutta.; Darjeeling Gymkhana.
(*Died May* 1928.)

NAESMYTH, Sir James Tolmé, 7th Bt.; *cr.* 1706; *b.* 6 Aug. 1864; *s.* of 6th Bt. and Mary Ann, *d.* of John Nicholls, late Clerk to the Lord Chancellor's Court, Westminster; *S.* father 1907. *Heir:* u. Douglas Arthur Bradley [*b.* 1905]. *Address.:* Posso, Peeblesshire, N.B.
(*Died 24 July* 1922.)

NAESMYTH, Sir Douglas Arthur Bradley, 8th Bt., *cr.* 1706; *b.* 1 Jan. 1905; *s.* of late Donald Luttrell Kilve Naesmyth, M.R.C.S., 3rd *s.* of 6th Bt., and Flora, *d.* of late H. W. Burrage; *S.* uncle 1922. *Heir:* none.
(*Died Jan.* 1928.)

NAIRNE, Sir Perceval Alleyn, Kt., *cr.* 1915; F.R.G.S.; Order of Mercy; Solicitor, admitted 1864, firm Baker & Nairne; Chairman Seaman's Hospital Society and London School of Tropical Medicine; Solicitor to Worshipful company of Drapers, London, to National Union of Teachers, and to League of Mercy; and King George's Fund for Sailors; *b.* 12 Feb. 1841; 5th *s.* of Captain Alexander Nairne, H.E.I.C.S., previously R.N. (Copenhagen, 1801); unmarried. *Educ.*: Clapham Grammar School. Secretary Rochester and Southwark Diocesan Conferences in succession, 1886-1911. *Address:* 176 The Grove, Camberwell, S.E.; 3 Crosby Square, Bishopsgate, E.C. *T.:* 5841 Avenue.
(*Died 10 Dec.* 1921.)

NAISH, Redmond, I.S.O. 1908; Accountant in National Education Office, Ireland; *b.* 1848; *s.* of late C. Naish, J.P.; *m.* 1882, Mary, *d.* of late Alderman Macdermot, Dublin. *Educ.*: Tullabeg. Entered Department, 1868. *Address:* 66 Northumberland Road, Dublin.

NAISMITH, Lt.-Col. William John, D.S.O. 1900; Territorial Decoration, 1902; M.D. Edinburgh, F.R.C.S. Edinburgh; *b.* 8 Sep. 1847; *m.* 1890, Edith Mary, *y. d.* of late W. R. Sanders, M.D., F.R.C.P.E., Prof. of Pathology in the University of Edinburgh; one *s.* two *d.* Surg.-Lt.-Col. Ayrshire Imperial Yeomanry; Surg. H.M. Prison of Ayr, Ayr Industrial Schools, and Ayrshire County Constabulary; Medical Officer, 6th Batt. Imperial Yeomanry; served South Africa, 1900-2 (despatches, Queen's medal 3 clasps, King's medal 2 clasps, D.S.O.); retired. *Address:* 19 Queen's Gardens, St. Andrews, Fife. (*Died 3 Jan.* 1926.)

NAND LAL, Diwan Bahadur Pandit, I.S.O. 1911; a Kashmiri Pandit of Lahore, Punjab; *s.* of Pandit Janardhan Koul: *b.* Amritsar, Nov. 1857. *Educ.*: Collegiate School, Amritsar. Served about 5 years in Financial Commissioner's Office, Punjab, and in Deputy Commissioner's Office, Lahore; transferred to Baluchistan; served for some years as Confidential Clerk and then as Head Clerk to new Quetta and Pishin District; Subordinate Judge of Quetta, 1885; Extra Assistant Commissioner; for about 4 years was Personal

Indian Assist. to Agent to the Governor-General in Baluchistan; was Secretary to the Sandeman High School at Quetta; made a Rai Saheb by Lord Curzon on the Queen's Birthday, 1899; transferred to Central India as Extra Assistant to the Agent to the Governor-General, 1902; made Rai Bahadur by Lord Minto, 1910; made Diwan Bahadur by Lord Reading, 1925; Second Assistant to Agent Governor-General, 1915; Assistant Political Agent, Bundelkhand, 1919; is President of Victoria Library and Lady O'Dwyer Girls' School, Indore; retired after 50 years' service, 1924. *Address:* Indore, India.
(*Died 28 May* 1926.)

NANJUNDAYYA, H. Velpanuru, C.I.E. 1914; *b.* 13 Oct. 1860; *e. s.* of Subbayya Garu; is descended from a high-class Brahman family of Mysore; *m.*; six *s.* five *d. Educ.*: Wesleyan Mission School, Mysore; Christian College, Madras; Madras University (Fellow, 1895). Graduated, 1880; obtained Law Degree, 1883; Advocate of the Chief Court of Mysore, but did not practise long; accepted a place as Munsiff and entered the service of the Mysore Government, 1885; Under Secretary to Government, 1895; Judge, Chief Court of Mysore, 1904; present at both the Delhi Durbars; subsequently Mem. of Council and Chief Judge Chief Court; retired from State Council, 1916; Vice-Chancellor, Mysore University. *Publications:* A Treatise on Law and a Manual of Political Economy in Kanada, the Language of the Mysore State, and of the Ethnographic Survey of the Mysore Castes. *Address:* Mallesvaaram, Bangalore, India.
(*Died 7 May* 1920.)

NANSON, Hon. John Leighton, of Gray's Inn; barrister-at-law, M.L.A. West Australia; *b.* Carlisle, England, 22 Sep. 1863; *s.* of late John Nanson, solicitor, Carlisle; *m.* Janet Drummond, *d.* of late A. Durlacher, Resident Magistrate, Geraldton, West Australia; one *d. Educ.*: Carlisle Grammar School; King William's College, Isle of Man. For many years assistant editor of the West Australian, Perth, W.A.; subsequently called to the Bar; Minister for Lands, W.A., 1901; Member Coolgardie Water Scheme Commission, 1902; Leader of Opposition, 1902-3; Minister for Works, 1904; Attorney-General, Minister for Education and Member of the Executive Council West Australia, 1909-11. *Recreations:* usual. *Address:* 1 Ord Street, Perth, West Australia. *Club:* Weld, Perth.
(*Died 29 Feb.* 1916.)

NANTON, Sir Augustus Meredith, Kt., *cr.* 1917; *b.* Toronto, 7 May 1860; *s.* of Augustus Nanton, Barrister, Osgood Hall, Toronto, and Mary Louisa, *d.* of Sheriff W. B. Jarvis of Toronto; *m.* 1st, 1886, Georgina Hope Hespeler (*d.* 1887); 2nd, Ethel Constance, *d.* of late Thomas Clark, Winnipeg; three *s.* three *d. Educ.*: Toronto Model School. Vice-President, Great West. Life Insurance Co. Dominion Bank; President, Winnipeg Electric Railway Co.; Director and Chairman, Canadian Committee, Hudson's Bay Co.; Director and Member Executive Canadian Pacific Railway; Director, Royal Trusts Co., Manitoba Bridge and Iron Works, Cockshutt Plow Co., Ogilvie Flour Mills Co., Canada Starch Co., Guarantee Co. of North America; Senior Winnipeg Partner in Osler, Hammond and Nanton, Investment Brokers. *Address:* Kilmorie, 229 Roslyn Road, Winnipeg. *Clubs:* Marlborough; Manitoba, St. Charles' Country, Hunt, Winnipeg; Toronto, Toronto; Mount Royal, Montreal; Rideau Ottawa. (*Died 24 April* 1925.)

NAOROJI, Dadabhai, LL.D. (hon.) Bombay; first Indian Member of Parliament; *b.* Bombay, 4 Sept. 1825; *s.* of a Parsi priest; *m.* Gulbai, *d.* of a Parsi priest; two *d. Educ.*: Elphinstone School and College. First Indian Professor in India Mathematics and Natural Philosophy, 1854; visited England, as partner

NANAK CHAND, Masheerud-dowal Rai Bahadur, C.S.I. See page xxvi.

in first Indian firm in England, 1855 ; Professor Gujarati, and Life Governor, University College, London ; obtained admission of Indians to the Civil Service, 1870 ; Prime Minister Baroda, 1874 ; Member of Corporation and Municipal Council, Bombay, 1875 - 1876 and 1881 - 1885 ; Member Legislative Council, Bombay, 1885-1887 ; promoted Bombay Ripon Technical School, 1885 ; M.P. (L.) Central Finsbury, 1892-95 ; great reception in India, 1893 : President Indian National Congress, 1886, 1893, and 1906 ; President London Indian Society for many years ; moved for inquiry into Indian affairs in House, 1894 ; defeated Government re Simultaneous Examinations, 1893 ; only Indian member of a Royal Commission ; Member of Inter-Parliamentary Conference at the Hague, 1894 ; Member of Royal Commission on Indian Expenditure, etc., 1895 ; gave evidence to this Welby Commission, 1897 ; Member of British Committee of Indian National Congress from beginning (1889). *Publications:* papers on Poverty of India ; England's Duties to India ; Mysore ; Expenses of the Abyssinian War ; Indian Civil Service Clause in the Governor-General of India's Bill ; Admission of Educated Natives into the Indian Civil Service ; Wants and Means of India ; Commerce of India ; Financial Administration of India ; Correspondence with Secretary of State on Condition of India, 1880 ; Note on General Education ; Minute on Technical Education ; Reply to Sir Grant Duff in Contemporary Review, 1887 ; and many papers on Indian social, political, and economic subjects ; collection published, 1887 ; Poverty and Un-British Rule in India, 1901 ; The Rights of Labour, 1906 ; Correspondence with Lord George Hamilton, 1900-1901 ; has addressed many public meetings on India. *Address:* The Sands, Vesava ; Andheri, B.B., and C.I. Railway, Bombay.   *(Died 2 July 1917.)*

NAPIER of Magdala and Caryngton, 2nd Baron (U.K.); *cr.* 1868 ; **Robert William Napier ;** *b.* 11 Feb. 1845 ; *s.* of 1st Baron and Anne, *d.* of G. Pearse, Medical Inspector-General at Madras ; *S.* father 1890 ; *m.* 1885, Eva Maria Louisa Langham, *d.* of 4th Lord Macdonald of the Isles, and *widow* of Capt. Langham, Grenadier Guards [Lady Napier is author of A Stormy Morning, How She Played the Game, Half a Lie, etc.] ; one *d.* Protestant. *Educ.:* privately. Entered Army, 1860, at age of 15 ; served in Bengal Army, 1861-82 ; Umbeyla campaign, 1864 ; Abyssinian campaign, 1868 ; retired as Lieut.-Col. in 1883. *Heir :* Hon. Edward Napier. *Address:* Lynedale, Isle of Skye.   *(Died 11 Dec. 1921.)*

NAPIER, Colonel Alexander, M.D., R.A.M.C.T.; (Ret.); late Officer Commanding 4th Scottish General Hospital, Glasgow ; Physician, Victoria Infirmary, Glasgow ; Hon. Librarian and Fellow of Royal Faculty of Physicians and Surgeons, Glasgow ; *b.* Glasgow, 21 June 1851 ; *s.* of Alexander Napier and Jane Struthers ; *m.* 1879, Elizabeth Harper ; four *s.* three *d.* *Educ.:* High School, Glasgow ; Universities of Glasgow and Berlin. Two years in practice in S. Africa ; in practice in Glasgow since 1876. *Publications:* translations : Physiology and Pathology of the Sympathetic System of Nerves (Prof. A. Eulenburg and Dr. P. Guttmann), 1879 ; A Handbook of Physical Diagnosis, comprising the Throat, Thorax, and Abdomen (Dr. P. Guttmann), 1879 ; Manual of Stretcher Drill. *Recreations:* loafing, rarely ; golfing, occasionally ; botanising, collecting old books, especially old English Bibles. *Address:* 10 Athole Gardens, Glasgow, W.2. *T.:* Western, 5411 Glasgow. *Club:* Conservative, Glasgow.   *(Died 5 Oct. 1928.)*

NAPIER, Arthur Sampson, M.A., D.Litt., B.Sc., Ph.D., Hon. Litt.D. (Manchester) ; Hon. D.Litt. (Groningen) ; Fellow of

the British Academy ; Merton Professor of English Language and Literature, Oxford, since 1885 ; also Rawlinsonian Prof. of Anglo-Saxon since 1903 ; Fellow of Merton Coll.; *b.* Cheshire, 30 Aug. 1853 ; *e. s.* of late George Webster Napier, Alderley Edge, Cheshire ; *m.* Mary Ferrier, 2nd *d.* of James Hervey, Alderley Edge ; four *s.* one *d.* *Educ.:* Rugby School ; Owens Coll. Manchester ; Exeter Coll. Oxford (M.A., D.Litt.) ; University of Berlin. Reader of English, University of Berlin, 1878 - 82 ; Professor of English Language and Literature, University of Göttingen, 1882-85 ; Corresponding Member, Royal Academy of Sciences, Göttingen ; Hon. Member, American Academy, Boston. *Publications:* Ueber die Werke des altenglischen Erzbischofs Wulfstan, 1882 ; Wulfstan-Sammlung der ihm zugeschriebenen Homilien, Berlin, 1883 ; History of the Holy Rood-tree (Early English Text Society), 1894 ; Crawford Collection of Early English Charters (in conjunction with Mr. W. H. Stevenson, Oxford), 1895 ; Old English Glosses, 1900 ; The Franks Casket, 1901 ; contributions to the Zeitschrift für deutsches Alterthum, Anglia, Englische Studien, Archiv für das Studium der neueren Sprachen, American Modern Language Notes, Academy, etc. *Address:* Merton College, Oxford ; Headington Hill, Oxford.   *(Died 10 May 1916.)*

NAPIER, Major Egbert ; late 3rd Gordon Highlanders ; Chief Constable of Norfolk ; *b.* Penbedw Hall, Flintshire, 12 Aug. 1867 ; *s.* of Col. Edward Napier, late 6th Dragoon Guards, and Marthe Louise, *d.* of late W. B. Buddicom, Penbedw Hall, Flintshire ; *m.* Evangeline, *d.* of J. G. Dreyer, Copenhagen, and Valschrivier, Orange River Colony ; two *d.* *Educ.:* Wellington College. Formerly on Staff of Commissioner of Metropolitan Police ; served South African War, 1900-1 ; Brigade Major Kroonstad District and Adjutant of Driscoll's Scouts.
          (Died 19 Nov. 1916.)

NAPIER, Hon. Mark Francis, B.A. ; Barrister ; *b.* 21 Jan. 1852 ; *s.* of 10th Baron Napier and Ettrick ; *m.* 1878, Emily, *y. d.* of 7th and last Viscount Ranelagh ; two *s.* *Educ.:* Cambridge. M.P. (L.) Roxburgh, 1892-95. *Address:* Puttenden Manor. Lingfield, Surrey.
          (Died 19 Aug. 1919.)

NAPIER, Vice-Admiral Sir Trevylyan Dacres Willes, K.C.B., *cr.* 1919 ; C.B. 1916 ; M.V.O. ; R.N. ; *b.* 19 April 1867 ; 4th *s.* of Admiral Gerard John Napier ; *m.* 1899, Mary Elizabeth, *d.* of Admiral Sir Michael Culme-Seymour, Bart.; one *s.* two *d.* *Educ.:* privately. Entered Royal Navy as Naval Cadet, 1880 ; Midshipman, 1882 : served in Egyptian War ; Lieutenant, 1887 ; Commander, 1899 ; served in H.M. Yacht ; Captain, 1903 ; commanded H.M.S. Crescent, 1904-7, as Flag-Capt. to Admiral Sir John Durnford on Cape Station ; commanded Royal Naval College, Dartmouth, 1907-10 ; H.M.S. Bellerophon, 1910-12, and 2nd Light Cruiser Squadron, 1913 ; served European War, 1914-16 (C.B.), Battle of Jutland Bank (despatches) ; Naval A.D.C. to the King, 1913 ; in command of Light Cruiser Squadrons, 1914-1917 ; Vice-Admiral, Light Cruiser Force, 1917-1919. *Club:* United Service.
          (Died 30 July 1920.)

NAPIER, Maj.-Gen. William John, C.B. 1917 ; C.M.G. 1916 ; late R.A. ; *b.* 10 Nov. 1863 ; 3rd *s.* of late Hon. William Napier, 2nd *s.* of 9th Baron Napier ; *m.* 1889, Maud Denison Gooch, *o. d.* of late Col. G. N. W. Holbrook, R.M.L.I. ; one *s.* Served S. African War, 1899-1900 (Queen's medal 3 clasps) ; European War, 1914-18 (despatches, C.M.G., C.B., Director of Artillery, War Office, prom. Maj.-Gen.) ; retired pay, 1922. *Address:* 14 Carlyle Mansions, Cheyne Walk, Chelsea, S.W.3. *T.:* Kensington 5858. *Clubs:* United Service, Royal Automobile, Ranelagh.   *(Died 18 Nov. 1925.)*

NAPIER, Colonel Wm., C.M.G. See page xxvii.

NAPOLEON, H.I.H. Prince (Victor Jerome Frederic); head of Napoleon family; *b.* Palais Royal, Paris, 18 July 1862; *e. s.* of Prince Napoleon and Princess Marie Clotilde de Savoie; *m.* 1910, H.R.H. Princess Clementine of Belgium; one *s.* one *d.* Expelled from France, 1886. *Address:* 241 Avenue Louise, Brussels; Chateau de Ronchinne, par Courrière, Province Namur; Domaine de Farnborough Hill, Farnborough, Hants. *(Died 3 May 1926.)*

NARSINGARH, H.H. Shri Huzur Raja Sir Arjun Singhji Sahib Bahadur of, K.C.I.E.; *b.* 10 Jan. 1887; *s.* of Maharaj Moti Singhji Sahib of Dkuankher; belongs to the Paramar or Ponwar branch of Agnikul Rajputs; S. 1897. *Educ.:* Daly College; Mayo College; Imperial Cadet Corps. Invested with full ruling powers, 1909; *m.* 1907, *d.* of H.H. Rajah Sahib Bahadur of Sailana; one *s.* three *d.* The State is 734 square miles in extent, and has a population of 101,426, the Chief receiving a salute of 11 guns. *Heir:* s. Shri Maharaj Kumar Shri Vikram Singh Bahadur, *b.* 21 Sept. 1909. *Address:* Narsingarh, Central India.
(Died 22 April 1924.)

NASH, Rev. Adam James Glendinning, M.A.; Rector of St. Mildred, with St. Margaret, City of London, since 1912; Hon. Canon of Ripon Cathedral, since 1900; Fellow of Sion College, 1912; Surrogate for the Master of the Faculties and the Vicar-General of Canterbury, 1912; Editor of the London Diocese Book since 1912; *s.* of Joseph and Matilda Glendinning Nash. *Educ.:* Queens' College, Cambridge (B.A., 1871; M.A., 1874). Deacon, 1871; Priest, 1872; Curate of St. John's, Fitzroy Square, London, 1871-78. Assistant Thursday Morning Lecturer at St. Peter-upon-Cornhill, London, 1877-81; Vicar- Designate of St. Thomas, Finsbury Park, 1878-81; General Secretary of Bradford Church Congress, 1898; V.P. Cambridge Church Congress, 1910; Past Provincial Grand Chaplain of West Yorkshire Freemasons; Chaplain to the Mayor of Bradford; Vicar of St. John's with St. Hilda, Bradford, 1881-1912; Official Principal to Archdeaconry of Craven, 1894-1912; Proctor in the Convocation of York, 1895-1919; Assessor under Clergy Discipline Act; Hon. Secretary to Ripon Diocesan Conference, 1898-1912; Member of Bradford Governing Body of Ripon Diocesan Education Society. *Publications:* Confirmation Day Suggestions and Meditations, 1890, 1891, and 1892; Preparation for Confirmation, 1903; Summary of Foreign Marriage Law, 1904; 2nd edition, 1910; Parish Church Anthem Book, 1905. *Address:* 4 Harley House, Regent's Park, N.W.1. *T.:* Paddington 3100.
(Died 13 Oct. 1920.)

NASH, Rev. Alexander, M.A. (Oxon.); Hon. Canon of Gloucester Cathedral since 1901; Hon. Sec. of Diocesan Board of Finance (Maintenance Committee), and Diocesan Queen Victoria Clergy Fund; *b.* Poonah, India, 1845; *s.* of Lt. A. Nash, R.E. and H.E.I.C., and Lucy Anne, *g-d.* of Sir Charles Blois, 7th Bart., Cockfield Hall, Suffolk; *m.* 1868, Elizabeth, *e. d.* of W. W. Cowslade of Erieigh, Reading; four *s.* four *d.* *Educ.:* abroad; private schools; B.N.C., Oxford. Entered Holy Orders, 1868, and for seven years was Curate of Standish with Hardwicke; Rector of Quedgeley, Gloucester, 1876-89; Vicar of Standish with Hardwicke, 1889-1923. *Recreations:* rowed in B.N.C. boat Head of River, 1867 and 1868; gardening. *Address:* Whiteknights, Tuffley, Gloucester.
(Died 29 Aug. 1924.)

NASH, John Brady, M.D. Edin. and Sydney; M.R.C.S.; Director Royal Prince Alfred Hospital, Sydney, 1917; Member of Legislative Council, New South Wales, since 1900; Director Sydney Hospital since 1905; Member of the Board of Health for New South Wales 1918; Hon. Consulting Surgeon Coast Hospital, Sydney; Hon. Surgeon State Hospital, Rookwood, Sydney; Lieutenant-Colonel, unattached list, Australian military forces; *b.* at sea, near Canary Islands, 19 May 1857; *s.* of Dr. Andrew Nash, J.P., L.R.C.P., etc., and Margaret Brady, both of Co. Cork; *m.* 1888, Agnes M'Cormick of Newcastle, N. S. Wales; four *d.* *Educ.:* St. Patrick's Coll., Melbourne, Victoria; Sydney (Matriculated, 1877) and Edinburgh Universities. Took honours in most subjects; graduated, 1882; M.D., 1892; studied in London, Dublin, and Paris before returning to New South Wales in 1883; at Newcastle, New South Wales, 1883-1900; practising as a surgeon in Sydney since 1900; Member Royal Commission on decline of the birthrate in New South Wales, 1903; Hon. Surgeon to St. Margaret's Hospital for Women, Sydney; for five years commanded the Irish Rifle Regiment in the Australian military forces; Lt.-Col. Australian Army Medical Corps, Australian Imperial Expeditionary Force, 1914-16; on service in Egypt, 1915; Anzac during October 1915. An original Anzac. *Publications:* numerous contributions on medical and surgical subjects to medical journals in Australia and to the Australian Medical Congresses; lectures on literary, especially Shakespearian, subjects before the Shakespearian Society, and other bodies. *Recreations:* literature at present. *Address:* 219 Macquarie Street, Sydney, New South Wales. *T.:* 3681 city. *Clubs:* Australian, University, Sydney.

NASH, Joseph, R.I. *Address:* The White House, Somerleyton, Suffolk. *(Died 24 May 1922.)*

NASH, Colonel Llewellyn Thomas Manly, C.M.G. 1915; late A.M.S.; *b.* 7 Apr. 1861; *m.* 1901, Editha Gertrude, *y. d.* of Rev. Charles Sloggett. Major, 1897; Lieut.-Col. 1905; served Miranzai Expedition, 1891 (despatches, medal with clasp); Hazara Expedition, 1891 (clasp); European War, 1914-18 (C.M.G., despatches twice). *Address:* 16 Queen's Road, Richmond, Surrey. *T.:* Richmond 3048. *Club:* Junior United Service. *(Died 9 Sept. 1928.)*

NASIR-EL-MULK, Abdul Kassim Khan, G.C.M.G., *cr.* 1897; K.C.M.G., *cr.* 1889; late Regent of Persia, 1911; *b.* 1858. *Educ.:* Teheran; Balliol College, Oxford. Sent on special mission to Europe, 1897; was Governor of Khurdistan. *(Died Dec. 1927.)*

NATHAN, Sir Nathaniel, Kt., *cr.* 1903; K.C.; *b.* 1843; *e. s.* of late Jonah Nathan, Pembridge Square, W.; *m.* 1870, Helen (*d.* 1906), *o. d.* of Thomas Turner, J.P. Doncaster. *Educ.:* University College School and University College, London; B.A. London, 1863. Called to Bar, 1866; joined Midland Circuit; practised at Birmingham, 1873-88; a resident magistrate in Jamaica, 1888; magistrate for Kingston, 1891; served as Acting Judge of Supreme Court, Jamaica, till 1893, when appointed Senior Puisne Judge of Trinidad; Attorney-General of Trinidad, 1898; and acted as Chief Justice, 1901-3. *Publications:* Economic Heresies, 1909. *Address:* 77 St. James' Court, S.W. *Club:* Reform.
(Died 18 Feb. 1916.)

NATHAN, Sir Robert, K.C.S.I., *cr.* 1919; C.S.I. 1911; C.I.E. 1903; B.A.; Barrister-at-Law; *s.* of late Jonah Nathan. *Educ.:* St. Peter's Coll. Cambridge. Entered Indian Civil Service, 1888 (retired, 1915), serving as assistant magistrate and collector, settlement officer, joint magistrate, etc.; Under-Secretary to Government of India, Financial and Commercial Department, 1895; Home Department, 1897; Magistrate and Collector, 1900; Secretary to Indian Universities Commission, 1902; Deputy Secretary, Home Department, 1903; on special duty in the Home and Finance Departments, 1904; Private Secretary to Viceroy, 1905. Commissioner, Dacca Division, Eastern Bengal, 1907; Officiating Chief Secretary to the

Governor of Eastern Bengal and Assam, 1910 ; President Dacca, 1912, and Patna, 1913, Universities Committees. *Publications :* Official History of Plague in India ; Progress of Education in India, 1897-98, 1901-2 ; Articles for the Imperial Gazetteer of India. *Address :* C 8 The Albany, W.1. *T. :* Gerrard 7088. *Club :* East India United Service. (*Died 26 June 1921.*)

NATHUBHAI, Tribhovandas Mangaldas, J.P. ; Hon. Magistrate, and Fellow of the University, Bombay ; Sheth or head of the Kapol Banya community ; resigned the presidentship after tenure thereof for twenty-five years, 1912 ; political representative of Bombay Hindus for the Coronation of King George V. ; *b.* 28 Oct. 1856 ; *s.* of Sir Mangaldas Nathubhai, Kt., C.S.I. (the first Hindu in India to get the honour of Knighthood) ; *m.* 1st, 1875 ; 2nd, 1883 ; two *s.* three *d.* *Educ. :* St. Xavier's College, Bombay. Was for twenty years an elected Member of the Bombay Municipal Corporation ; has been an Honorary Magistrate ever since the establishment of Courts of Bench Magistrates in Bombay ; has been nominated by Government a Member of the Bombay Provincial Advisory Committee for students proceeding to Europe ; is President, Trustee, or Member of the Committees of several Hindu public charity funds in Bombay ; President of the Hindu Mahajan Committee ; Patron of the Teachers' Association, Bombay, Sanitary Association, Bombay, and Hindu Gymkhana, Bombay ; Patron of the Hindu Ambulance Corps ; rendered eminent services during the first outbreak of plague in Bombay, which were recognised both by Government and the public ; much interested in the question of Moral Education. *Publications :* Moral Education and the Four Cardinal Truths ; Foundations of Morality and Suggestions for a Moral Code ; Hindu Castes and Customs ; Search after Truth (Series 1 and 2) ; A Discourse on the Depressed Classes ; Universal Brotherhood ; Relative Position of Man and Woman ; Moral Courts. *Address :* Sir Mangaldas House, Lamington Road, Bombay. *T. :* Bombay 1457. *Clubs :* (Hon.) Ranelagh ; Orient, Bombay ; Western India Turf. (*Died 6 April 1920.*)

NAVILLE, Henri Edouard, D.C.L., LL.D., Dr. Phil., Dr. Litt., Dr. Theol. ; Hon. F.S.A., Fellow of King's College, London ; Foreign Associate of the Institute of France ; Member of the histor.-philos. class of the Videnskabs-Selskabet of Christiania ; Foreign Member of the Academy of Buda-Pesth, and of the Academy of Vienna ; Correspondent of the Academy of History of Madrid ; Hon. Member International Committee of the Red Cross ; Hon. Knight of Grace of the Order of St. John of Jerusalem ; Commander of the Crown of Italy ; Officer of the Légion d'Honneur ; Knight of the Red Eagle, 3rd class, Prussia ; and of the Polar Star, Sweden ; Hon. Professor at the University of Geneva ; *b.* Geneva 1844 ; *s.* of Adrien Naville and Sophia Rigaud ; *m.* 1873, Marguerite, *d.* of Count Alexandre de Pourtales ; two *s.* two *d.* *Educ. :* Geneva ; King's College, London ; Universities of Bonn, Paris, and Berlin. Has been excavating in Egypt since 1883 ; member of several learned and religious societies ; ex-President of the Evangelical Alliance. *Publications :* Textes relatifs au mythe d'Horus, 1870 ; La Litanie du soleil, 1875 ; Inscription historique de Pinodjem III, 1883 ; Das ägyptische Todtenbuch der XVIIIten bis XXten Dynastie 1886 ; La Religion des anciens Egyptiens, 1906 ; L'Évolution de la langue égyptienne et les langues sémitiques, 1920 ; l'Ecriture égyptienne, 1926 ; for the Egypt Exploration Fund :—the Store City of Pithom, 1883 ; Goshen, 1886 ; the City of Onias, 1888 ; Bubastis, 1889 ; the festival-hall of Osorkon II., 1890 ; Ahnas el Medineh, 1891 ; the Temple

of Deir el bahari, 6 vols. ; the Temple Deir el bahari of the XI Dyn., 3 vols. ; The Cemeteries of Abydos, Pt. I., 1914 ;—the Papyrus of Iouiya, 1908 ; Papyrus funéraires de la XXIe Dynastie, 2 vols. ; Archæology of the Old Testament, 1913 ; Schweich Lectures : The Text of the Old Testament, 1916 ; The Law of Moses, 1920 ; La Haute Critique dans le Pentateuque, 1921. *Address :* Malagny, near Geneva.
(*Died 17 Oct. 1926.*)

NAYLOR, James Richard, C.S.I. 1890 ; J.P., Ind. Civ. Service (retired) ; *b.* 3 Sept. 1842 ; *m.* 1868, Eleanor (*d.* 1909), *step-d.* of C. Hexton, of the Bombay Rev. Survey. Entered Bombay Civil Service, 1862 ; appointed Legal Remembrancer to Govt. of Bombay, 1874 ; Member of Legislative Council, Bombay, 1884 ; acted as Member of Governor's Council, Bombay, 1887-88. *Decorated* for service to the Government of Bombay as Legal Remembrancer and Member of the Legislative Council. *Address :* Hallatrow Court, Bristol. (*Died 13 May 1922.*)

NAYLOR, Ven. William Herbert ; Archdeacon of Clarendon since 1894 ; *b.* 5 May 1846 ; *m.* ; six *s.* *Educ. :* M'Gill University, Montreal (M.A.). Ordained, 1873 ; Curate of St. Armand West, 1873-74 ; Rector, 1874-76 ; Incumbent, St. Paul's, Shawville, 1874-1907 ; Rector, St. James Church, Farnham, 1907-17 ; Rural Dean of Clarendon, 1883-94. *Address :* Philipsburg, Quebec, Canada.
(*Died 6 June 1918.*)

NEALE, Sir Henry James Vansittart-, K.C.B., *cr.* 1902 ; C.B. 1897 ; Pres. of East Berks Agricul. Assoc., 1905 ; J.P. for Berks and Westminster ; *b.* 30 Nov. 1842 ; *s.* of late Edward Vansittart-Neale of Bisham Abbey, and Frances Sarah, *d.* of J. N. Farrer of Ingleborough, York ; *m.* 1887, Florence, *d.* of Arthur Eddis, Q.C., County Court Judge, Clerkenwell ; two *d.* Assistant Sec. to Admiralty, 1896-1903. Patron of one living. *Address :* Bisham Abbey, Marlow. *Club :* St. Stephen's. (*Died 15 July 1923.*)

NEEDHAM, Sir Frederick, Kt., *cr.* 1915 ; M.D., M.R.C.P., etc. ; H.M. Commissioner of the Board of Control since 1892 ; 2nd *s.* of James P. Needham ; *m.* 1st, Charlotte (*d.* 1907), *d.* of Rev. J. Shooter, Vicar of Bishop Wilton, Yorks ; 2nd, Helen M. S., *d.* of W. L. Newman, York. *Educ. :* St. Peter's School, York ; St. Bartholomew's Hospital, London. Medical Superintendent of York Lunatic Hospital, 1858-74 ; Medical Superintendent of Barnwood Hospital for Insane, Gloucester, 1874-92 ; has been president of the Medico-Psychological Association of Great Britain and Ireland ; president of the York Medical Society ; the Gloucestershire Medical and Surgical Association ; the Psychological section of the British Medical Association ; is an honorary member of the Medico-Legal Society of New York ; Member of Royal Commission on Care and Control of Feeble-minded, 1905, etc. *Address :* Imperial Hotel, Bournemouth. (*Died 6 Sept. 1924.*)

NEEDHAM, Sir George William, Kt., *cr.* 1920 ; *b.* 9 Nov. 1843 ; *m.* 1887, Sarah, *d.* of John Ashworth ; one *s.* *Educ. :* Oldham High School ; Vice-Chairman of Platt Bros. & Co. ; Vice-President of Oldham Chamber of Commerce and of Oldham Royal Infirmary ; Governor of Oldham Grammar School and connected with various other institutions ; President of the Oldham Branch of the St. John's Ambulance Assoc., being a Knight of Grace. *Address :* Holly Bank, Oldham. *T. :* 526. *M. :* J 64. *Clubs :* Manchester Reform ; Reform, Albion, Oldham. (*Died 29 Feb. 1928.*)

NEEDHAM, Jack Francis, C.I.E., 1899, F.R.G.S. ; *b.* 14 Dec. 1842 ; *e. s.* of Hon. F. H. Needham, 3rd *s.* of 2nd Earl of Kilmorey. Entered Service, 1867 ; Assistant Supt. of Police, 1876 ; Assistant Political Officer, Sadiya, 1882. Obtained Gill Memorial, R. G. Society, 1887, for his services in exploring the Valley of the Lohit

Brahmaputra between Assam and the Zanjul Valley in Tibet; Depy.-Inspt. Gen. Bengal Police Dept. 1885-1905. *Publication:* Grammar of Miri, Singpho, and Kampti Languages. *Address:* Shillong, Assam.
(*Died 11 Nov. 1924.*)

NEEDHAM, Joseph, M.B., C.M., Univ. Aberd. (Highest Hons. and Special Hons. for G.aduation Thesis); M.R.C.P., M.R.C.S., etc.; Anæsthetist to 3rd London General Hospital, to King George Hospital, and to the Weir Hospital a Medical Officer, Board of Education, London County Council, and of Metropolitan Police; medal, Coronation King George V.; formerly Assistant Professor of Anatomy, University of Aberdeen; Demonstrator of Histology, London Hospital Medical College and London School of Medicine for Women; *b.* London 1853; *m.* 1st, 1880, Jane Robinette, (*d.* 1884), *e. d.* of Rev. J. A. Coghlan, M.A., Vicar of Tetsworth, Oxon; 2nd, 1892, Alicia Adelaide; one *s. Educ.:* Privately; London Hospital Medical College; University of Aberdeen; London Hospital Medical Scholar, 1875; and gained other Honours in Surgery, Chemistry, Anatomy, Physiology, Materia Medica, Botany, Gynæcology, etc. *Publications:* Contributions to the Medical and Scientific Press. *Recreations:* music, study of archæology, and cycling. *Address:* 150 Harley Street, W.1; Clapham Park, S.W. *T.:* Brixton 291. *M.:* LM 9377.
(*Died 2 Aug. 1920.*)

NEIL, Rev. John, D.D.; Minister of Westminster Presbyterian Church, Toronto, since 1884; Moderator of Assembly of Presbyterian Church in Canada; *b.* Mono Centre, County of Dufferin, Ontario, 5 April 1853; parents from Scotland; *m.* Louise B., *d.* of Rev. Dr. Bayne, Minister of Pictou, Nova Scotia. *Educ.:* Public School, Mono; Jarvis Street Collegiate, Toronto; Toronto University, B.A.; Knox College, Toronto; Edinburgh University; D.D. Queen's University, Kingston, Ontario. Minister Campbellville, 1882-84; spent three months in England and France conveying greetings to chaplains and men, 1917-18. *Address:* 88 Charles Street, E., Toronto. *T.:* North 1757.
(*Died Mar. 1922.*)

NEILSON, George; *b.* Ruthwell, Dumfriesfriesshire, 1858; *s.* of Capt. Edward Neilson; *m.* 1892, Jane, *d.* of Thomas Richardson; one *d. Educ.:* Cummertrees, Dumfriesshire; King William's Coll., Isle of Man. Passed law-agent, 1881; F.S.A. Scot.; President Glasgow Juridical Society, 1889; Procurator Fiscal of Police of Glasgow, 1891-1910; Stipendiary Magistrate of Glasgow, 1910-23; Hon. LL.D. Glasgow University, 1903; President Glasgow Archæological Society, 1907-10; Rhind Lecturer in Archæology, 1912; President Royal Philosophical Society of Glasgow, 1913-15; and of Sir Walter Scott Club, 1914-18. *Publications:* Trial by Combat, 1890; Per li neam Valli, 1891; Annals of Solway 1899; John Barbour, Poet and Translator, 1900; Huchown of the Awle Ryale, the Alliterative Poet, 1902; Acts of the Lords of Council, 1496-1501 (joint editor), 1918. *Address:* Wellfield, Partickhill, Glasgow.
(*Died 15 Nov. 1923.*)

NEILSON, Col. Walter Gordon, C.M.G. 1916; D.S.O. 1900; late Argyll and Sutherland Highlanders; *b.* 1 Oct. 1876; *s.* of late Col. James Neilson, C.B.; *m.* 1908. Ida Lacon Graham of Duntrune, Forfarshire, *o. c.* of late F. G. Lacon; one *d. Educ.:* Merchiston Castle School. Entered army, 1897; Bt. Lt.-Col. June 1918; Lt.-Col. 1922; Col., 1924; Passed Staff College; served South Africa, 1899-1902; advance on Kimberley, including actions at Modder River and Magersfontein; operations in the Orange Free State, and actions at Paardeberg; operations in the Transvaal, including the action at Zilikat's Nek, etc. (twice wounded, despatches twice, Queen's medal 3 clasps, King's medal 2 clasps, D.S.O.); European War, 1914-18 (despatches

six times, C.M.G.). *Address:* 15 Regents Park Terrace, N.W.1. *T.:* Hampstead 7238. *Club:* Army and Navy.
(*Died 29 April 1927.*)

NEITENSTEIN, Frederick William, I.S.O. 1906; late Commander training ships Vernon and Sobraon; Comptroller-General of Prisons, 1896-1909; member Central Board for Old Age Pensions; member Public Service Supplies Board; Retired from Public Service, April 1910; Voted special gratuity by Parliament for distinguished services; received thanks of Government; Deputy Public Service Commissioner; *b.* London, 1850; *s.* of Frederick John Neitenstein of London; *m.* 1879, Marion, *d.* of H. Walker, M.D.; one *d. Educ.:* Sherman College, Kent; Paris and London, privately. Served in the English Mercantile Marine in Devitt and Moore's ships until entering the N.S.W. Govt. Service as Lieut. of the training ship Vernon, 1873; Commander, 1878; Commander of training ship Sobraon, 1892; Magistrate for the State, 1890; has at various times acted on various Boards, Royal Commissions, etc.; reorganised the entire prison system, and has been engaged on reformatory work for the past 33 years; member Howard Association, London; Past Deputy Grand Master of Freemasons. *Publications:* various papers on reformatory and prison matters; Prevention and Treatment of Crime. *Recreations:* reform and philanthropic work. *Address:* Bank of New Zealand, Sydney, New South Wales. *Club:* Royal Colonial Institute.
(*Died 23 April 1921.*)

NELIGAN, Rt. Rev. Moore Richard; Rector of Ford since 1911; *y. s.* of late Rev. Canon Neligan, D.D., late Incumbent, Christ Church, Leeson Park, Dublin; *m.* 1894, Mary, *e. d.* of late Edmund Macrory, K.C., of 19 Pembridge Square, W.; two *s.* two *d. Educ.:* Reading School; Trinity College, Dublin; B.A., 1884; M.A., 1887; D.D. (jure dig.), 1902. Curate of St. Paul's, Sculcoates, Hull; East Dereham, Norfolk; Christ Church, Lancaster Gate, W.; Vicar of St. Stephen's, Paddington, W.; Bishop of Auckland, 1903-10. *Publications:* The Religion of Life; The Churchman as Priest; sermons, pamphlets. *Recreations:* cycling, riding, fishing. *Address:* Ford Rectory, Northumberland.
(*Died 24 Nov. 1922.*)

NELKE, Paul; Senior Partner of Nelke, Phillips & Co.; *b.* Berlin, 5 Sep. 1860; *s.* of Julius Nelke, Banker; *m.* Maria, *d.* of C. Conrad; two *d. Educ.:* abroad. *Recreation:* racing. *Address:* 10 Cadogan Square, S.W.1; *T.:* Ken. 771; Wood Lee, Virginia Water.
(*Died 22 Dec. 1925.*)

NELSON, Rev. Canon Charles Moseley, M.A.; Registrar, University College, Auckland, N.Z.; *b.* Southwark, London, 7 Oct. 1848; *e.s.* of Charles Coventry and Anne Nelson, of Southwark; *m.* Georgiana Sophia, *y. d.* of James Coates, Private Secretary to Capt. Wm. Hobson, R.N., First Governor of New Zealand; two *s.* two *d. Educ.:* City of London School; Queens' College, Cambridge (minor scholar and foundation scholar). B.A. (2nd Class Class Classics), 1867; M.A., 1871; Deacon, 1867; Priest, 1868; Curate of Phillack and Gwithian, Cornwall, and Diocesan Inspector of Schools, 1867-68; Vicar of St. Paul's (Mother Church), Auckland, N.Z., 1870-1908; Bishop's Examining Chaplain, 1870-1902; Canon, 1893; Clerical Representative and Clerical Secretary, General, Synod, 1874, 1880, 1886, 1892; Acting Professor (Classics and English) at University College, Auckland, 1891; Governor, Auckland Grammar School, 1881-99; Governor, St. John's College, Auckland, 1892-1910; Trustee, St. John's College, Auckland, since 1897; Hon. Life Governor, Orphan Home Trust Board, Auckland, 1908, elected upon retiring from position of Chairman of the Board, which he had held many years; is a Freemason of high standing in the craft. *Address:* University College, Auckland, N.Z.   *(Died 17 Feb. 1919.)*

NELSON, Rt. Rev. Cleland Kinloch, D.D. ; Bishop of Atlanta 1907-17 ; *b.* Cobham, Virginia, 23 May 1852 ; *s.* of Mr. Keating S. Nelson ; *m.* M. Bruce Matthews of Maryland. *Educ.:* St. John's College, Annapolis, Maryland. Rector St. John the Baptist, Germantown, Philadelphia, 1876 ; Rector Church of the Nativity, South Bethlehem, Penna., 1882-92 ; Bishop of Georgia, U.S.A., 1892-1907. *Publications:* sermons and addresses. *Recreations:* gardening and architecture. *Address:* 731 Piedmont Ave., Atlanta, Georgia ; *T.:* Ivy 119, and Main 842.   *(Died 15 Feb. 1917.)*

NELSON, Lieut. David, V.C. 1915 ; L Battery, R.H.A. ; *b.* 27 Dec. 1886 ; *m.* 1915. Served ten years in ranks ; 2nd Lieut. R.A., 1914 ; Lieut. 1915 ; served European War, 1914-15 (despatches twice, V.C.).   *(Died 8 April 1918.)*

NELSON, Sir Edward Montague, K.C.M.G., *cr.* 1897 ; J.P., D.L. ; *b.* 5 Mar. 1841 ; *s.* of late George Nelson, Warwick ; *m.* 1866, Mary Caroline, *d.* of F. Wallis, F.R.C.S. ; *four s. one d. Educ.:* privately. Sheriff of Middlesex, 1892. *Address:* The Lawn, Warwick ; 3 Whitehall Court, S.W. *Clubs:* Junior Carlton, etc.   *(Died 4 Feb. 1919.)*

NELSON, Sir William, 1st Bt. *cr.* 1912 ; J.P.; *b.* 1851; 2nd *s.* of James Nelson of Cooldrinagh, Co. Kildare (*d.* 1899), and Elizabeth (*d.* 1896), *d.* of late Richard MacCormack of Glainden, Co. Westmeath ; *m.* 1879, Margaret, *d.* of late Michael Hope, of Gartlandstown, Co. Westmeath ; three *s.* five *d. Educ.:* St. Edward's College, Liverpool. *Recreations:* racing, hunting, fishing, golf. *Heir:* *e. s.* James Hope Nelson [*b.* 26 Feb. 1883 ; *m.* 1913, Elizabeth Vallee, St. Louis, U.S.A. *Educ.:* Stonyhurst College]. *Address:* 16 Hill Street, Berkeley Square, W.1. *T.A.:* Navarque. *T.:* Mayfair 3919. *Club:* Bath.   *(Died 7 July 1922.)*

NESBIT, E. (Mrs. Hubert Bland), poet and novelist, and author of children's books ; *b.* London ; *y. d.* of John Collis Nesbit ; *m.* Hubert Bland (*d.* 1914) ; two *s.* two *d. Educ.:* France, Germany, London. *Publications:* Lays and Legends, 1886 ; Leaves of Life, 1888 ; Lays and Legends, 2nd series, 1892 ; A Pomander of Verse, 1895 ; In Homespun, 1896 ; Grim Tales, 1893 ; Something Wrong, 1893 ; The Marden Mystery, 1896 ; Songs of Love and Empire, 1897 ; The Secret of Kyriels, 1898, etc. ; The Story of the Treasure-Seekers, 1899 ; Pussy and Doggy Tales, 1899 ; The Book of Dragons, 1900 ; The Would-be Goods ; Nine Unlikely Tales ; Thirteen Ways Home, 1901 ; Five Children and It, 1902 ; The Red House, 1903 ; The Literary Sense, 1903 ; The Phœnix and the Carpet, 1904 ; The New Treasure Seekers, 1904 ; The Rainbow and the Rose, 1905 ; Oswald Bastable, 1905 ; The Enchanted Castle, 1906 ; Man and Maid, 1906 ; The Incomplete Amorist, 1906 ; The Railway Children, 1906 ; The House of Arden, 1908 ; Salome and the Head, 1909 ; These Little Ones, 1909 ; Daphne in Fitzroy Street, 1909 ; Harding's Luck, 1909 ; Fear, 1910 ; The Magic City, 1910 ; Ballads and Lyrics, 1910 ; Dormant ; The Wonderful Garden, 1911 ; The Magic World, 1912 ; Wings and the Child, 1913 ; Wet Magic, 1913 ; Garden Poems, 1914 ; The Incredible Honeymoon, 1921 ; The Lark, 1922 ; Poems, 1922 ; in collaboration with Hubert Bland—The Prophet's Mantle, 1885 ; in collaboration with Oswald ·Barron—The Butler in Bohemia, 1894. *Address:* The Longboat, Jesson St. Mary's, New Romney, Kent.   *(Died 4 May 1924.)*

NESBIT, Paris, K.C. : Barrister practising in the Supreme Court of South Australia ; *b.* 8 Aug. 1852 ; *s.* of Edward Planta Nesbit ; *m.* 1st, Ellen Logue ; three *s.* ; 2nd, Cecilia Elizabeth Hughes. *Educ.:* Angaston and

772

Tanunda, South Australia. Called to Bar, 1874 ; K.C. 1893 ; for 10 years, 1883-1893, drafted nearly all the principal South Australian Statutes. *Publications:* Translations from German Poets ; The Beaten Side ; numerous letters in local newspapers. *Recreations:* reading, motoring, bridge. *Address:* Barossa, St. Peter's, Adelaide. *T.A.:* Nesbit, Adelaide. *T.:* Central 212.   *(Died 31 Mar. 1927.)*

NESBITT, Rev. Allan James; Rector of Hollymount since 1873 ; Canon of Tuam since 1887. *Educ.:* Trinity College, Dublin (B.A.). Ordained, 1864 ; Curate of Westport, Castlebar, and Athenry. *Address:* Hollymount, S.O., Co. Mayo.   *(Died 19 May 1918.)*

NETHERSOLE, Sir Michael, Kt., *cr.* 1917 ; C.S.I. 1914 ; *b.* 24 Apr. 1859 ; *s.* of John Nethersole ; *m.* Margaret, 3rd *d.* of late Rt. Hon. Sir E. N. C. Braddon, K.C.M.G. *Educ.:* Sutton Valence ; R.I.E. College. Entered India Public Works Dept., 1880 ; Executive Engineer, 1892 ; lent to Kashmir State, 1893-1900 ; Chief Engineer and Secretary to Government United Provinces, 1900-11 ; Inspector General of Irrigation, 1912-17 ; retired 1917 ; Chief Hy. Engineer, Andra Valley Power Co., Tata Sons, Bombay. *Recreations:* riding, golf, all field sports, bridge. *Address:* c/o Tata Sons, Ltd., Navsari Buildings, Bombay. *Clubs:* East India United Service ; Royal Bombay Yacht.   *(Died 16 June 1920.)*

NEUMANN, Sir Sigmund, 1st Bt., *cr.* 1912 ; sole partner in S. Neumann & Co. ; on Board of African Banking Corporation, and London Joint Stock Bank, Ltd. ; partner of Neumann, Lubeck, & Co., Bankers ; *b.* Bavaria, 1857 ; *m.* 1890, Anna Allegra, *d.* of late Jacques Hakim, Alexandria ; two *s.* three *d. Heir: s.* Cecil Gustavus Jacques, *b.* London, 9 June 1891. *Address:* 146 Piccadilly, W. ; *T.:* Gerrard 2782 ; Cecil Lodge, Newmarket ; Glenmuick, N.B. ; Bamham Hall, Norfolk.   *(Died 13 Sept. 1916.)*

NEVARES, Celso, Ex-Consul-General of Ecuador in London ; *b.* Ecuador, 13 June 1850 ; *m.* an Englishwoman. Jubilee Medal, 1897 ; Coronation Medal. *Address:* Broad Lea, Beckenham, Kent. *T.:* Bromley 1067.

NEVE, Arthur, F.R.C.S.E. ; 1st Class Medal Kaiser-i-Hind, 1900 ; Back Award, Royal Geographical Society, 1911 ; Surgeon, Mission Hospital, Kashmir ; *b* Brighton, 1858 ; *m.* 1912, Betsy Sophia Havard. *Educ.:* Brighton Grammar School ; R.C.S. and University, Edinburgh. President Indian Medical Missionary Association, 1908 - 10 ; Hon. Vice-President for life ; Vice-President International Medical Congress, Bombay, 1909. Major R.A.M.C. (temp.), War Hospital, Dartford (despatches). *Publications:* Guide-book to Kashmir and N. Himalayas (10th edition) ; Picturesque Kashmir ; Thirty Years in Kashmir. 1913. *Recreation:* Himalayan exploration.   *(Died 14 Oct. 1919.)*

NEVILL, Lord George (Montacute), J.P., D.L. ; 3rd *s.* of 1st Marquess of Abergavenny ; *b.* 23 Sep. 1856 ; *m.* 1882, Florence Mary, *o. d.* of late Temple Soanes of Brenchley House, Kent ; one *s.* one *d. Heir: s.* Guy Temple Montacute, Captain Sussex Yeomanry [*b.* 15 July 1883 ; *m.* 1909, Isabel Nellie, *o. c.* of late J. W. Larnach : one *s.* one *d. Address:* Hamsell Manor, Eridge, Sussex]. *Address:* 22 Palmeira Square, Hove, Sussex. *Clubs:* Carlton, Ranelagh ; Union, Brighton.   *(Died 10 Aug. 1920.)*

NEVILL, Most Rev. Samuel Tarratt, D.D. ; Bishop of Dunedin since 1871 ; Primate of New Zealand since 1902 ; *b.* 13 May 1887 ; *s.* of Jonathan Nevill and Mary, *d.* of George Berrey ; *m.* 1st, 1868, Mary S. C. Penny of Mont le Grand, Exeter ; 2nd, Rosalind Margaret, *d.* of Rev. Geoff Fynes-Clinton of

Anderson Bay, New Zealand. *Educ.:* St. Aidan's; Magdalene College, Cambridge (Hon. Fellow); Rector of Shelton, Staffordshire, 1864–1871. *Publications:* Spiritual Philosophy; Pamphlets, etc. *Address:* Bishopsgrove, Dunedin.

NEVILLE, Admiral Sir George, R.N.; K.C.B., *cr.* 1909; C.V.O. 1905; J.P.; C.C.; *b.* 18 March 1850; 2nd *s.* of late R. Neville-Grenville of Butleigh Court, Glastonbury; *m.* 1886, Fairlis Florence, 2nd *d.* of late D. Lloyd Jones of Llandovery, Carmarthenshire, and Victoria, Australia; three *s.* Joined H.M.S. Britannia, 1863; Sub-Lieut., 1869; Lieut., 1872; Commander, 1885; Captain, 1892; was twice round the world with H.R.H. the Duke of Edinburgh in H.M.S. Galatea, and once as 1st Lieut. of H.M.S. Comus; served also under H.R.H. the Duke of Edinburgh in H.M.S. Sultan, Black Prince, Minotaur, Alexandra, and Vivid; commanded H.M.S. Dolphin, Dido, Australia, and Mars, and local naval forces at Melbourne; 1st Cruiser Squadron, 1905-7; 3rd and 4th Divisions Home Fleet, 1909-11; retired, 1913. *Address:* Murtrey, Frome. *Clubs:* Naval and Military, Royal Automobile. *(Died 5 Feb. 1923.)*

NEVILLE, Rev. Hon. Grey; Rector of Bluntisham, Hunts, since 1917; *b.* 4 Dec. 1857; *m.* 1889, Mary, *d.* of late Rev. Francis Slater; two *s.* five *d.* *Educ.:* Eton; Magdalene College, Cambridge. Ordained, 1882; Curate of Hunstanton, 1882-83;-. St. Giles's, Cambridge, 1884-85; Vicar of Waltham St. Lawrence, Berks, 1885-1912; Rector of Christchurch, Cambs. 1912-17. *Address:* Bluntisham Rectory, St. Ives. Hunts. *(Died 28 Dec. 1920.)*

NEVILLE, Nigel Charles Alfred; stipendiary magistrate of South Staffordshire since 1885; *b.* 10 April 1849; *o. s.* of late Thomas Neville of Shenstone House, Lichfield; *m.* Julia Anne, *d.* of late David Ballinger of Wolverhampton, 1892. *Educ.:* Uppingham; St. John's College, Cambridge (B.A.). Barrister, Inner Temple, 1873. *Address:* Shenstone House, Lichfield. *T.A.:* Shenstone. *(Died 12 April 1923.)*

NEVILLE, Sir Ralph, Kt., *cr.* 1906; **The Hon. Mr. Justice Neville;** Judge of High Court of Justice since 1906; *s.* of Henry Neville, surgeon, Esher; *m.* 1872, Edith Cranstoun, *e. d.* of late Henry T. J. Macnamara, one of Her Majesty's Railway Commissioners *Educ.:* Tonbridge School; Hon. Fellow Emmanuel College, Cambridge (M.A.). Barr. 1872; K.C. 1888; Bencher of Lincoln's Inn; M.P. Liverpool Exchange, 1887 - 95; sometime President of Garden City Association. *Address:* Royal Courts of Justice, W.C.; Banstead Place, Banstead, Surrey. *T.:* Burgh Heath 192. *Clubs:* Athenæum, Reform. *(Died 13 Oct. 1918.)*

NEVILLE, Colonel William Candler, D.S.O. 1900; Colonel Cheshire Regt.; retired 1909; *b.* 22 Jan. 1859; *s.* of Major Robert Neville, late 51st Regiment, of Ahanure, Co. Kilkenny, and Rockfield, Co. Dublin; *m.* 1892, Amy, *y. d.* of Colin C. Ross of Gruinards, Ross-shire; one *s.* one *d.* *Educ.:* Cheltenham College. Entered army, 1878; Captain. 1885; Major, 1896; commanding 22nd Regtl. District, 1914; served Burmese Expedition, 1887-88 (medal with clasp); S. Africa, 1900-1902 (despatches, medal with 4 clasps, D.S.O.). *Club:* Junior United Service. *(Died 28 June 1926.)*

NEWALL, Colonel Stuart, C.B., 1900; N.Z. Mounted Infantry; *b.* 9 May 1843; *s.* of late Thos. Newall of Dumfries; *m.* 1872, Georgina, *d.* of G. Roberts; one *s.* four *d.* Served New Zealand, 1863-66 (medal); South Africa, 1899-1900 (despatches, Queen's medal, 2 clasps, C.B.). *Address:* Wellington, New Zealand.
(Died 1920.)

NEWBOROUGH, 4th Baron (*cr.* 1776), **William Charles Wynn;** Bt. 1742; *b.* 4 Nov. 1873; *g.-s.* of 3rd Baron, *s.* of Hon. Thomas John Wynn and Anna, *d.* of Edwin

Corbett, H.M. minister at Athens; *S.* grandfather 1888; *m.* 1900, Grace, *d.* of Col. H. M. Carr of Kentucky. *Educ.:* Heidelberg; Trinity Hall, Cambridge. *Heir: b.* Hon. Thomas J. Wynn. *Address:* Bryn Llewellyn, Festiniog, Wales; 39 Park Lane, W. *T.:* Mayfair 5949.
(Died 13 July 1916.)

NEWCASTLE, 7th Duke of (*cr.* 1756), **Henry Pelham Archibald Douglas Pelham-Clinton,** D.L., J.P.; Earl of Lincoln, 1572; Lord High Steward of Retford; Master Forester of Dartmoor; Keeper of St. Briavel's Castle; Member of London School Board, 1894-97; *b.* 28 Sep. 1864; *s.* of 6th Duke and Adela, *d.* of late Henry Thomas Hope of Deepdene, Surrey; *S.* father, 1879; *m.* 1889, Kathleen Florence May, O.B.E., *d.* of late Major Henry Augustus, 9th Lancers, and Hon. Mrs. Candy, *d.* of 3rd Baron Rossmore. *Educ.:* Eton. Owns about 35,600 acres. *Heir: b.* Lord H. F. Pelham-Clinton Hope. *Address:* Clumber Park, Worksop; Forest Farm, Windsor Forest; 11 Berkeley House, Hay Hill, W.1. *T.:* Mayfair 4308. *Clubs:* Carlton, St. James's, Garrick.
(Died 30 May 1928.)

NEWDEGATE, Lady (A. E.) Newdigate-, 2nd *d.* of late Very Rev. Thos. Garnier, Dean of Lincoln, and of Lady Caroline Elizabeth, *d.* of 4th Earl of Albemarle; *m.* 1858, Sir E. Newdigate-Newdegate of Arbury (*d.* 1902). *Publications:* Gossip from a Muniment Room; The Cheverels of Cheverel Manor; Cavalier and Puritan. *Address:* Medecroft, Winchester.
(Died 25 Dec. 1924.)

NEWLAND, Captain H. Osman, F.R.Hist.S., *s.* of late Major O. Newland; *m.* Lois, *d.* of late F. N. Druitt; one *d.* *Educ.:* Counter Hill, City of London, and Goldsmith's Institute. Introduced Study of Citizenship into London School Board and the L.C.C. Schools; Compiled first course of Sociology in United Kingdom; special L.C.C. lecturer in Sociology, Commercial History and English Literature; assisted found Sociological Society; founder and Hon. Sec. British West African Association; Explored Sierra Leone, 1912; assisted open new route Monte Blanc for P.L.M. 1913; Recruiting, Sub-area Commander and Military Intell. 1917; Officer for Education R.A.F. 1918 - 19. *Publications:* Short History of Citizenship; Local Govt. Handbook to Education; The Model Citizen; Sierra Leone: Its People, Products, Secret Societies; The Ivory Coast; Coconuts, Kernels, Cocoa and other Vegetable Oils; Origin and Systems of Empire; Romance of Commerce; Soldiers of Empire (Song), etc. *Recreations:* mountain-climbing, cycling, sculling, swimming, music. *Address:* The Trossachs, Herne Bay; 79 Mt. Nod Road, S.W.16. *T.:* Streatham 89. *Clubs:* Authors', New Oxford and Cambridge.
(Died 27 June 1920.)

NEWMAN, David, M.D., F.R.F.P.S.G.; Consulting Surgeon to the Glasgow Royal Infirmary, and for many years Pathologist and Lecturer on Pathology to the same hospital; Medical Assessor, W. C. Act; Senior Fellow of the Association of Surgeons of Great Britain and Ireland; Fellow of the Royal Society of Medicine of London; Vice-President International Medical Congress, London Meeting; President Glasgow Medico-Chirurgical Society; President of the Clinical and Pathological Society of Glasgow; Member Assoc. International d'Urologie; *b.* 1853; *e. s.* of Edward Newman, M.D., Fleet Surgeon, R.N.; of Craig Ailey, Cove, Dumbartonshire, and Annabella, *d.* of late David Smith of Whitevale House, Glasgow, and Farthingneuk, Dumfriesshire; *m.* 1885, Jean, *d.* of William Polson, J.P. Edgehill, Paisley; one *s.* one *d.* *Educ.:* Universities of Glasgow and Leipzig. *Publications:* Surgical Diseases of the Kidneys;

Diagnosis of Surgical Diseases of the Kidneys; Malignant Disease of the Throat and Nose, etc.; numerous papers to medical and surgical journals, and contributions to Societies, especially relating to Diseases of the Kidneys and Bladder. *Address:* Craig Ailey, Cove, Dumbartonshire. *Club:* Western, Glasgow. (*Died 22 April 1924.*)

NEWMAN, Edward Braxton, I.S.O. 1902; *b.* 15 Dec. 1842. Entered the Foreign Office, 1859; First Class Clerk, 1873; Assistant to Chief Clerk, 1890; retired, 1907. *Address:* 71 Chelsham Road, Clapham, S.W.
(*Died 20 Mar. 1916.*)

NEWMAN, Ven. Ernest Frederick; M.A.; Vicar of Marystowe since 1909, and Rector of Coryton since 1912; Archdeacon of Plymouth; *b.* Coryton, Devon, 2 March 1859; *s.* of Rev. W. S. Newman, Rector of Coryton; *m.* Jessie, *d.* of late Lieut. E. Hathway, 10th Hussars; three *s.* *Educ.:* Marlborough; Keble College, Oxford; Wells Theological College. Assistant Curate, St. Mary's, Reading, 1884-86; Chaplain (A.C.S.) Bengal, 1887-88; Chaplain to the Forces: Tower of London, 1889-94; Caterham, 1894-1900; South Africa, 1900-1904 (despatches), Portsmouth, 1904-8; Rural Dean of Tavistock, 1917-20. *Address:* Marystowe Vicarage, Lew Down, Devon. *T.A.:* Chillaton. *M.:* TA 7234.
(*Died 28 April 1928.*)

NEWMAN, Philip Harry, R.B.A., F.S.A.; Remembrancer and Hon. Librarian, R.S.L.; Early Member of Society of Designers, and sometime Vice-President; retired; Hon. Member Artists' Society and Langham Sketch Club; Member of Committee and sometime Hon. Treasurer of Artists' Benevolent Fund; *b.* London, 1840; *e. s.* of Philip Robert Newman, merchant, and Margaret Eliza Barnfather; *m.* 1860, Charlotte Isabella Gibbs (*d.* 1920), Art student; one *s.* one *d.* *Educ.:* London and Paris; student London University and St. Martin's and Spitalfields Schools of Art; also in Paris. Designer of decorative works in painting, stained glass, and wall tiling pictures; frequent exhibitor at Royal Academy and R.B.A., etc. Principal works in oil: Sardanapalus, Orpheus and Eurydice, My Father's House of Many Mansions, The Temptation, Solomon dedicating the Temple, Murder of Becket, The Quarries of Cheops; black and white illustrations numerous; Judy, and A Shakespeare Reverie Tercentenary Tribute and Souvenir. Decorative paintings and stained glass at Church of St. Mary the Virgin, Aldermaston; Apse of Chapel, Royal Masonic Institute for Boys, Bushey, Herts; Spirit Fresco, Our Lord healing the Sick, St. Peter's Church, Belsize Park, etc.; Designer of War Memorials, Birkbeck College, F.M. School Chapel, Bushey, Herts, St. Mary's Church, Aldermaston, Stamford Brook. Writer and lecturer on art subjects and inventor of method of preserving ancient wall paintings, applied successfully at Canterbury, Aldermaston, and elsewhere. *Publications:* contributions to Social History of England and numerous papers in Transactions Royal Society of Literature and Archæologia; poems various. *Recreations:* music, billiards, sketching. *Address:* 5 Ravenscourt Square, W.6. (*Died 21 Dec. 1927.*)

NEWMARCH, Francis Welles, C.S.I. 1914; Financial Secretary, India Office, since 1911; *b.* 29 Dec. 1853; *e. s.* of late Rev. Charles Francis Newmarch, Rector of Leverton, Lincs. *Educ.:* Balliol College, Oxford; Corpus Christi College (Scholar); 1st class in Class Mods.; 1st class, Lit. Hum. Entered India Office, 1877; Military Dept. till 1902; then Assistant Secretary Financial Dept.; Secretary Public Works Dept. *Recreations:* mountaineering, walking. *Address:* India Office, S.W. *Clubs:* Alpine, Constitutional, Wigwam. (*Died 2 Jan. 1918.*)

NEWMARCH, Sir Oliver Richardson, K.C.S.I.; *cr.* 1894; Major-General, retired, 1887;

b. 31 Oct. 1834; *s.* of late Dr. Newmarch and Violet, *d.* of Col. Sherwood, R.A.; *m.* 1st, 1858, Mary Isabella (*d.* 1867), *d.* of Major Parke, 61st Regiment; four *d.*; 2nd 1874, Agnes Mary, *d.* of late James Norman; one *s.* *Educ.:* Charterhouse; Merton College, Oxford. Entered Bengal Army, 1855; served in Indian Mutiny (medal); Military Secretary Government of India, 1884; Military Secretary India Office, 1889-99. *Club:* United Service.
(*Died 16 Feb. 1920.*)

NEWNHAM - DAVIS, Lieut. - Col. Nathaniel, author; Lieutenant-Colonel, retired; Captain Sup. Cos. T.F.; *b.* London, 6 Nov. 1854; *e. s.* of Henry Newnham-Davis and Mary Newnham; unmarried. *Educ.:* Harrow. Joined the Buffs, 1873; served through Griqualand West and Zulu campaigns with Imperial Mounted Infantry, 1877-79 (despatches twice, medal and clasp); served in Straits Settlements, China, India; attached three years to Intelligence Department, Simla; retired 1894; joined staff of the Sporting Times same year; resigned 1912; editor Man of the World, 1894-1900; editor Town Topics, 1914; on outbreak of war applied for re-employment in army; was appointed an officer of the military guard over prisoners of war at Alexandra Palace in 1915. *Publications:* Three Men and a God, 1896; An Ideal (Palace Theatre), 1896; Jadoo, 1898; Military Dialogues, 1898; Dinners and Diners, 1899; Baby Wilkinson's V.C. 1899; The Transvaal under the Queen, 1899; Military Dialogues on Active Service, 1900; A Charitable Bequest (Criterion Theatre), 1900; The Gourmet's Guide to Europe, 1903; part author Lady Madcap (Prince of Wales's Theatre), 1904; A Day in Paris (Empire Theatre), 1908; New York (Empire Theatre), 1911; The Gourmet's Guide to London, 1914. *Recreation:* amateur theatricals. *Address:* 32 Clarence Gate Gardens, N.W. *T.:* 8722 Paddington. *Clubs:* Naval and Military, Beefsteak, Garrick, Royal Eastern. (*Died 28 May 1917.*)

NEWTON, Sir Alfred James, 1st Bart., *cr.* 1900; J.P.; Alderman of the ward of Bassishaw since 1890; Governor of the Hon. The Irish Society, 1906; orders of "Leopold," "Lion and Sun" (Persia), highest grade; Grand Cordon of Servia, Order of Medjidie (1st class), and Polar Star of Sweden; Hon. Freeman Royal Borough of Scarborough, and of Londonderry; Chairman Harrod's Stores, Ltd., and D. H. Evans & Co., Ltd.; *b.* Hull, 19 Oct. 1849; *s.* of late G. Beeforth Newton of Kottingham, East Yorks; *m.* E. Jane (Lily), *e. d.* of late Joseph Watson of Mill-house, Mitcham Common, 1874; one *s.* one *d.* Lord Mayor of London 1900, when he founded City of London Imperial Volunteers, for which service the Baronetcy was conferred; Conservative Unionist and Churchman; formerly yeast merchant (H. Love & Co.) and shipowner; contested West Southwark, 1900. Heir: *s.* H. K. Newton. *Address:* Kottingham House, Burton-on-Trent; 17 Cumberland Terrace, Regent's Park, N.W.1. *T.A.:* Newtonio, London. *T.:* 508 North. *Club:* Bath.
(*Died 20 June 1921.*)

NEWTON, Ernest, C.B.E. 1920; R.A., 1919; F.R.I.B.A.; *b.* 12 Sep. 1856; *m.* 1881, Antoinette Johanna Hoyack, Rotterdam; three *s.* *Educ.:* Blackheath; Uppingham. Articled to R. Norman Shaw, R.A., 1873; after six years spent in his office, began practice on his own account; made almost entirely domestic architecture; principal works—Bullers Wood, Chislehurst; Redcourt, Haslemere; Steep Hill, Jersey; Glebelands, Wokingham; Ardenrun Place, Blindley Heath; House of Retreat and Chapel for the Sisters of Bethany, St. Swithun's Church, Hither Green. Royal Gold Medallist, 1918; President Royal Institute of British Architects, 1914-17; Officier de l'Ordre de la Couronne, Belgium; Hon. Membre de la Société Centrale de l'Architecture de Belgique; Officier d'Academie de France; Membre Correspondant de la Société des Architectes diplomés par le Gouvernement, France. *Publications:* A Book of Houses; A Book of Country Houses. *Recreation:* novel reading. *Address:* 4 Raymond Buildings, Gray's Inn, W.C.1.; 17 Blomfield Road, W.9. *T.:* Chancery 7684; Paddington 4514. *Clubs:* Athenæum, Arts.   (*Died 25 Jan. 1922.*)

NEWTON, Hibbert Henry, J.P.; Clerk of the Parliaments and Clerk of the Legislative Council of Victoria since 1924; *b.* Ballenglen, near Oakleigh, Victoria, 1861; *s.* of late Hon. Hibbert Newton, barrister-at-law, Postmaster-General in the Nicholson Ministry; *m.* Clara Violet, *o. d.* of late W. Ravenscroft Stephen; three *s.* one *d.* *Educ.:* All Saints' Grammar School, St. Kilda; matriculated at Melbourne University. Entered the Public Service of Victoria as an officer of the Law Department in 1880; joined the staff of the Legislative Assembly in 1884; Clerk Assistant in 1902; Clerk of the Legislative Assembly, 1910; Clerk of the Parliaments, 1912; Chief Clerk Commonwealth Celebrations Staff, 1901; Clerk of the Interstate Conferences of Premiers and Ministers, held at Melbourne in 1909, 1912, and 1914. *Address:* State Parliament House, Melbourne.   (*Died 2 Jan. 1927.*)

NEWTON, Rev. Horace, M.A., Canon of York, 1885; *b.* 7 Sep. 1841; *m.*; five *d.* *Educ.:* St. John's College, Cambridge (Scholar). Ordained, 1865; Curate of St. Mary, Nottingham, 1865-8; Vicar of Holy Trinity, Heworth, 1869-77; Driffields-Ambo, Yorkshire, 1877-92; Redditch, 1892-1905. *Address:* Holmwood, Redditch. *T.:* Redditch 17. *M.:* AB 1935. *Club:* Constitutional.   (*Died 12 Nov. 1920.*)

NEWTON, John; Secretary, Native Races and the Liquor Traffic United Committee, and Member of Committee; *b.* 9 Feb. 1864; *m.* 1st, 1887, Elizabeth Lees (*d.* 1908); 2nd, 1912, Helena Bessie Ethel, 2nd *d.* of E. R. Norris of Harlesden, N.W.; two *s.* one *d.* Assist.-master, ElementarySchool; ParliamentaryAgent,United Kingdom Alliance; resigned 1909; Member of Executive Committee, Anglo-Indian Temperance Association; Vice-Chairman Executive Children's Protection League, Joint Hon. Secretary of the National Temperance Federation; Fellow of the Royal Colonial Institute. *Publications:* Life of Captain John Brown, of Harper's Ferry; W. S. Caine, M.P., a Biography; Our National Drink Bill, its direct and indirect effects upon National Health, Morals, Industry, and Trade; contributed to various literary periodicals. *Recreation:* golf. *Address:* 178 Palace Chambers, S.W.   (*Died 31 Aug. 1916.*)

NEWTON, Sir William, Kt., *cr.* 1905; K.C.; Member of Council, Mauritius; *s.* of William Newton of Bourbon, Mauritius; called to Bar, Middle Temple, 1863. *Address:* Port Louis, Mauritius.

NEWTON, William George, I.S.O. 1914; late Deputy Controller H.M. Stationery Office, retired 1917; *b.* 1859; *s.* of late John Newton of Woolwich; *m.* 1891, Blanche, *e. d.* of late George Thomas Jelley, of the War Department. Entered the Stationery Office, 1875; Private Secretary to Controller, 1879; Assistant Controller, 1904. *Address:* 17 Chariton Road, Blackheath, S.E.   (*Died 7 April 1920.*)

NEWTON-BRADY, Sir Andrew (assumed additional name of Newton 1870), Kt., *cr.* 1911; Resident Magistrate, Belfast, since 1908; *b.* 1849; *s.* of Sir Thos. Francis Brady, Kt., J.P.; *m.* 1st, Annie, *d.* of late Robt. Mecredy, of Lissoughter Lodge, Recess, Co. Galway; 2nd, Julie, *d.* of late Arthur Henry D'Esterre, M.D.; three *s.* three *d.* *Educ.:* France. Secretary to Royal Commission on Oyster Fisheries, 1869 and subsequently in the Irish Civil Service; appointed Resident Magistrate, Co. Galway,

1882; Co. Clare, 1894; has received the thanks of Government on many occasions: Barrister-at-Law. *Recreations:* golf, fishing, shooting. *Address:* Mullafairy, Greystones, Co. Wicklow. *M.:* R.I. 3453. *Club:* United Service, Dublin.   (*Died 20 Mar. 1918.*)

NIBLETT, Robert Henry, I.S.O. 1911, M.A.,J.P.; Deputy Collector, United Provinces, India; *b.* 1859; *s.* of Philip Niblett, J.P.; *m.* 1885, Kathleen Allen, *d.* of late Charles Howard; five *s.*, four *d.* M.A. (Honours) 1881; Headmaster, Boys' High School, Naini Tal, 1881; Assistant Editor, U.P. Gazetteer, 1882; joined U.P. Civil Service, 1884. *Address:* Myrtle Villa, Allahabad, U.P., India.   (*Died 5 May 1918.*)

NICHOL, R., M.P. (Lab.)East Renfrewshire since 1922; teacher in Allan Glen's School, Glasgow; *b.* 1890; *m.* 1920, *d.* of late Bailie Alston, Glasgow. *Address:* 4 Polayn Garth, Welwyn Garden City, Herts.
    (*Died 16 April 1925.*)

NICHOL, Col. Hon. Walter Cameron, LL.D.; Lieut.-Governor of British Columbia, 1921-26; *b.* Goderich, Ont., 15 Oct. 1866; *s.* of Robert K. Addison Nichol and Cynthia Jane Ballard; *m.* 1897, Quita Josephine March, *d.* of Charles Greenwood Moore, M.D., London, Ont.; one *s.* one *d.* Until recently a publisher and newspaper owner, but now retired; formerly Editor, Hamilton Herald, 1888-1896; came to British Columbia, 1897; interested in mining and various industries in British Columbia; is Hon. Colonel 16th the Canadian Scottish Regiment, Victoria, B.C.; an Officer of the Legion of Honour. *Recreations:* driving, motoring, yachting, etc. Religion: Anglican. *Clubs:* Vancouver Terminal City, Western, Royal Vancouver Yacht, Vancouver Rowing, Vancouver; Union, Oak Bay Golf, Colwood Golf, Royal Victoria Yacht, Victoria; Rainier Seattle Golf and County, Seattle.
    (*Died 19 Dec. 1928.*)

NICHOLAS, Captain John, R.A., M.V.O. 1902; Superintendent Royal Mews, Buckingham Palace 1892-1913; *b.* 30 Sep. 1851; 2nd *s.* of John Nicholas of Ely, Cambridgeshire; *m.* 1878, Mary Ann (*d.* 1906), *d.* of James Egan of Dublin, Riding Master and Hon. Lieut. R.A., 1888; Hon. Captain, 1898. Entered army, 1869; retired, 1898. *Address:* Bushy Lodge, Hampton Court, Middlesex.
    (*Died 20 April 1920.*)

NICHOLAS, Sir Walter Powell, Kt., *cr.* 1919; Solicitor, a member of the firm of Morgan, Bruce & Nicholas, Pontypridd; *b.* 12 June 1868; 5th *s.* of John Nicholas of Brynamman, Carmarthenshire; *m.* 1897, Florence (J.P. County Glamorgan), *e. d.* of Edward Edwards of Risca, Monmouthshire; one *d.* *Educ.:* privately; Alderman Davis Schools, Neath. Admitted Solicitor, 1894 (1st Class Honours; Law Society's Prizeman); Solicitor to the South Wales Miners' Federation; Clerk to the Rhondda Urban District Council 1901, the Ystradyfodwg and Pontypridd Main Sewage Board, 1901, and the Pontypridd and Rhondda Joint Water Board, 1911; Chairman of the Insurance Committee for the County of Glamorgan since 1915; and of the Executive Committee of the Urban District Councils Association of England and Wales; Member of the Royal Commissions on Local Government and Mining Subsidence; Member of the Representative Body, Governing Body, and Electoral College of the Church in Wales, and Chairman of the Legal Committee of the Representative Body. *Recreation:* motoring. *Address:* The Garth, Trealaw, Glam. *T.A.:* Trealaw. *T.:* Tonypandy 53. *M.:* L 1273. *Club:* Royal Automobile.   (*Died 10 April 1926.*)

NICHOLL, Maj.-Gen. Sir Christopher Rice Havard, K.C.B., *cr.* 1921; *b.* 15 Dec. 1836; 5th *s.* of late Rt. Hon. John Nicholl of

Merthyr Mawr, Glamorgan ; *m.* 1868, Florence, *d.* of Rev. Charles Knight of Tythegston Court, Glamorgan ; two *s.* six *d.* *Educ.:* Eton. Rifle Brigade, 1855 ; Maj.-Gen. 1890 ; retired, 1892 ; served Crimea, 1855-56 (medal with clasp, Turkish medal) ; Indian Mutiny, 1857-59 (medal with clasp) ; Ashanti War, 1874 (medal with clasp, brevet Lt.-Col.) ; commanded 3rd Battalion Rifle Brigade ; Colonel Commandant 1st Rifle Brigade. *Recreations:* illuminating, travel, walking. *Address:* 11 Tedworth Square, S.W.3. *T.:* Ken. 1065. (*Died 31 Mar. 1928.*)

NICHOLLS, Harry, comedian ; *b.* London, 1852 ; *m.* sister of late Henry Pettitt, dramatic author ; one *s.* two *d.* *Educ.:* City of London School. Went on stage at 18 ; first appearance in London Surrey Theatre ; four years at Grecian Theatre ; fourteen years principal comedian Drury Lane Theatre ; ditto five years at Adelphi Theatre. *Publications:* author of many Pantomimes (at Drury Lane and elsewhere) ; part author of Jane ; A Runaway Girl ; The Toreador, etc. ; written many comic songs, farces, etc. Hon. Treasurer of the Actors' Benevolent Fund ; a Trustee of the Actors' Orphanage Fund ; Past Master of the Worshipful Company of Joiners and Member of the Court of Assistants. *Address:* 31 Birch Grove, W.3. *Club:* Green Room (*Died 29 Nov 1926.*)

NICHOLLS, Hon. Sir Henry Alfred Alford, Kt., *cr.* 1926 ; C.M.G. 1896 ; M.D. ; late Principal Medical Officer of Dominica, West Indies ; *b.* London, 27 Sept. 1851 ; *s.* of Thomas William Nicholls of London ; *m.* 1877, Marion, 3rd *d.* of J. Corney Crompton, J.P. of Dominica ; four *s.* six *d.* *Educ.:* University, Aberdeen ; St. Bartholomew's, London ; M.B. (Honours) and C.M. Aberdeen, 1873 ; M.D. Aberdeen, 1875 ; M.R.C.S. Eng. 1873 ; F.L.S., C.M.Z.S. ; corresponding and honorary member of several learned societies at home and abroad. Medical Superintendent, Dominica Yaws Hospitals, 1877 ; Medical Officer Public Institutions, 1880 ; Health Officer, 1897 ; Senior Medical Officer, 1904 ; Crown nominee in Legislative Assembly, 1875-77 ; Chairman of Poor Law Board, 1885-1891 ; Local Commissioner Colonial and Indian Exhibition, 1886 ; in 1891, appointed Special Commissioner to inquire into prevalence of Yaws in West Indies (thanked by Secretary of State for Report, which was published as a Blue-book) ; chairman, Roseau Town Board, 1896-98 ; J.P. ; official member of the Legislative Council, 1898 ; President Dominica Agricultural Society, 1906 ; represented Leeward Islands at W.I. Agricultural Conferences in Barbados, 1899, 1901, and 1902 ; Trinidad, 1905 ; represented the Colony at W.Indian Quarantine Conference at Barbados, 1904, and at Imperial Health Conference, London, 1914 ; Commissioner for Dominica at Tropical Products Exhibition, London, 1914 ; Official Member Executive Council, 1915 ; Chairman, Road Commission, 1918 ; Member of Executive Council of Leeward Islands, 1922 ; acted several times as Administrator of Dominica. *Publications:* Text-Book of Tropical Agriculture, Dominica, illustrated and described ; numerous papers and pamphlets on medical, botanical, and agricultural subjects. *Recreations:* experimenting in tropical agriculture. *Address:* Kingsland House, Roseau, Dominica ; St. Aroment, Dominica, West Indies. *T.A.:* Nicholls, Dominica. *Clubs:* Authors', West Indian ; Dominica. (*Died Feb. 1926.*)

NICHOLS, Catherine Maude, R.E., S.M., N.B.A., Membre de l'Union International des Beaux Arts, Paris ; Painter, Etcher, and Author ; *b.* Norwich ; *e. d.* of late W. P. Nichols, F.R.C.S., Senior Consulting Surgeon of the Norfolk and Norwich Hospital, and Bethel Hospital, Norwich, and Mayor of Norwich, 1866. *Educ.:* Norwich. Many sketching tours, chiefly England and France ; travelled in France, Germany, and Switzerland ; exhibited frequently at the Salon, Academy, Royal Painter-Etchers, Venice, Melbourne, etc. ; First Lady Fellow of the Royal Painter - Etchers ; Principal paintings — Earlham, Norwich ; Strangers Hall, Norwich ; Very Rev. Canon Fitzgerald ; Brancaster Staithe ; and many others ; etched upwards of 200 plates. *Publications:* Lines of Thought and Thoughts in Lines, 1892 ; Old Norwich ; Two Norfolk Idylls ; Cromer Sketches ; Doubts Dispelled ; Zoroaster ; Why I became a Catholic ; Black and White, Norwich: Haunts of George Borrow in and around Norwich: a series of four etchings, 1913 ; contributed articles to various periodicals ; Six Dry Points after old Crome. *Recreations:* reading and the theatre. *Address:* The Studio, 73 Surrey Street, Norwich. *Club:* Forum. (*Died 30 Jan. 1923.*)

NICHOLS, Rt. Rev. William Ford, D.D. ; Bishop of California since 1893 ; *b.* 9 June 1849 ; *s.* of Charles H. and Margaret E. Nichols ; *m.* 1876, Clara Quintard ; two *s.* two *d.* *Educ.:* Trinity College, Hartford, Connecticut ; Berkeley Divinity School, Middletown, Connecticut. Deacon, 1873 ; Priest, 1874 ; Assistant Bishop of California, 1890 ; Private Secretary, Bishop Williams of Conn., 1871-76 ; Assistant, Holy Trinity, Middletown, Conn., 1873-75 ; Rector, St. James', West Hartford, Conn., and Grace, Newington, Conn., 1875-77 ; Christ Church, Hartford, Conn., 1877-87 ; St. James', Philadelphia, 1887-90 ; Member of Delegation from Connecticut to Seabury Centenary at Aberdeen, 1884 ; Professor Church History, Berkeley Divinity School, 1885-87 ; Assistant Secretary, House of Bishops, 1886 ; Deputy to General Convention, 1889 ; declined election as Assistant Bishop of Ohio, 1888 ; acted for Presiding Bishop in transfer of The Church in Hawaii to the American Church, 1902 ; and in temporary charge again of District, 1920-21 ; First President Province of the Pacific (American Church), 1915 ; Hon. President Seamen's Church Institute of America ; one of the Episcopal Canons of St. George's Collegiate Church, Jerusalem ; Hon. Life Member of Pacific Union Club, San Francisco. *Publications:* On the Trial of Your Faith ; Character ; Apt and Meet ; A Father's Story of the Fire and Earthquake of 1906 ; Some World-Circuit Saunterings ; various articles in reviews, etc. *Address:* 1215 Sacramento Street, San Francisco. (*Died 5 June 1924.*)

NICHOLSON, 1st Baron of Roundhay, *cr.* 1912 ; **Field-Marshal Lord William Gustavus Nicholson,** G.C.B., *cr.* 1908 ; K.C.B., *cr.* 1898 ; Col. Comdt. R.E. ; *b.* 2 Mar. 1845 ; *m.* 1871, Victoria, *d.* of D. Dillon. Entered R.E. 1865 ; Col. 1891 ; served Afghan War, 1878-1880 (despatches) ; Candahar Field Force, 1879 (despatches) ; march to Candahar (despatches, brevet of Major, medal, three clasps, bronze star) ; Egyptian War, 1882, including Tel-el-Kebir (4th class Osmanieh, Khedive's star) ; Burmese Expedition, 1886-87, as A.A.G. Army Headquarters (despatches, brevet of Lieut.-Col., medal with clasp) ; Tirah Expeditionary Force, 1897-98, as Chief of Staff (despatches, K.C.B., medal with two clasps) ; C.B. 1891 ; Adjutant-General in India, 1898-99 ; served South Africa as Military Secretary to Commander-in-Chief, and Director of Transport at Headquarters, 1899-1900 (despatches twice, promoted Maj.-Gen., medal with five clasps) ; Director-General of Mobilisation and Military Intelligence, War Office, 1901-4 ; Chief British Military Attaché, Japanese Army, 1904-5 ; Q.M.G. of the Forces, and 3rd Military Member of the Army Council, 1905-7 ; Chief of General Staff and 1st Military Member of the Army Council, 1908-12 ; Chairman of Commission on Indian Army Expenditure, Simla, 1912 - 13. *Heir:* none. *Address:* 51 Pont Street, S.W. *Clubs:* Athenæum, United Service, Army and Navy. (*Died 13 Sept. 1918.*)

NICHOLSON, Sir Charles Norris, 1st Bt., *cr.* 1912; LL.B., M.A.; M.P. (L.) Doncaster since 1906; 2nd Church Estates Commissioner since 1910; Vice-Chairman of London War Pensions Committee under the Statutory Committee, 1916; *b.* 30 July 1857; *e. s.* of William Norris Nicholson, late one of the Masters in Lunacy, and Emily, *d.* of James Stock Daniel; *m.* Amy Letitia, *d.* of George Crosfield of Warrington; two *d. Educ.:* Charterhouse; Trinity College, Cambridge. Called to Bar, Lincoln's Inn; many years a Member of Board of Guardians, Shoreditch. *Heir: g. s.* John Norris Nicholson, *b.* 1911. *Address:* 35 Harrington Gardens, S.W. *T. :* Kensington 439. *Clubs:* Oxford and Cambridge, Ranelagh, Queen's, etc.

(*Died 29 Nov. 1918.*)

NICHOLSON, Brig.-Gen. John Sanctuary, C.B. 1902; C.M.G. 1901; D.S.O. 1897; C.B.E. 1918; M.P. (Constit. Ind., Cons. Anti-Waste), Abbey Div. Westminster since 1921, (U.) since 1922; Capt. 7th Hussars; *b.* London, 19 May 1863; 2nd *s.* of W. Nicholson, Basing Park, Alton, Hants. *Educ.:* Harrow. Joined 7th Hussars, 1884; Comdt. of B.S.A. Police, 1896, raised corps; served Matabeleland, 1896 (despatches, D.S.O.); South Africa, 1900 (despatches. Bt. Lt.-Col.); Com.-Gen. B.S.A. Police, Rhodesia, South Africa, 1899-1900; Insp.-Gen. S.A. Constabulary, 1903-5; European War, 1914-15 (despatches); retired 1920. *Recreations:* hunting, shooting. *Address:* 2 South Audley Street, W. *Clubs:* Naval and Military, Cavalry.

(*Died 21 Feb. 1924.*)

NICHOLSON, Joseph Shield, M.A. (London); Sc. D. (Cambridge); Hon. LL.D. (St. Andrews); Fellow of the British Academy; Professor of Political Economy, University of Edinburgh, 1880-1925; *b.* Wrawby, Lincolnshire, 9 Nov. 1850; *s.* of Rev. T. Nicholson, Independent minister; *m. e. d.* of W. B. Hodgson, LL.D., late Prof. of Pol. Economy, Edinburgh University, 1885. *Educ.:* University, Edinburgh; Trin. Coll., Camb. (Scholar); Heidelberg. Cobden Prize, Cambridge (twice); Gerstenberg Prize, London (M.A.); private tutor, Cambridge, 1876-80. *Publications:* Effects of Machinery on Wages, 1878; Tenant's Gain not Landlord's Loss, 1883; editor of Smith's Wealth of Nations, 1884; The Silver Question, 1886; Money and Monetary Problems. 1888; Principles of Political Economy, vol. i. 1893; vol. ii. 1897; vol. iii. 1901; Historical Progress and Ideal Socialism, 1894; Strikes and Social Problems, 1896; Banker's Money, 1902; Elements of Political Economy, 1903; The Tariff Question, 1903; The History of the English Corn Laws, 1904; Rates and Taxes as affecting Agriculture, 1905; Rents, Wages, and Profits in Agriculture and Rural Depopulation, 1906; A Project of Empire, 1909; The Neutrality of the United States, 1915; War Finance, 1918; Inflation, 1919; Revival of Marxism, 1920; romances — Thoth, 1888; A Dreamer of Dreams, 1889; Toxar, 1890; Tales from Ariosto, 1913; Life and Genius of Ariosto, 1914. *Recreations:* fishing, golf, chess problems. *Address:* 3 Belford Park, Edinburgh.

(*Died 12 May 1927.*)

NICHOLSON, Major Randolph, D.S.O. 1919; M.C.; late Royal Horse Artillery; now partner in W. C. Hunter & Co., 6th Avenue, Nairobi, Kenya Colony; *b.* 8 April 1894; 4th *s.* of F. Frederic Nicholson and Mrs. Emily F. Nicholson, of Willoughton Manor, Lincoln; *m.* 1921, Margery, 2nd *d.* of William and Haydee Nathalie Ward-Higgs, of 29 Mincing Lane, E.C., and 197 Cromwell Road, S.W.; one *s. Educ.:* Felsted. With Borneo Co. Ltd., 1911-14; Regular Commission in R.A., 1914; served European War, France and Belgium, 1915-1919 (despatches, D.S.O., M.C. and bar); Egyptian Expeditionary Force, Syria, Palestine, and Egypt, 1919-20; on Staff 6 months during 1917; resigned, May 1920. *Recreations:* polo, tennis, golf, big-game shooting. *Address:* P.O. Box 96, Nairobi, Kenya Colony. *T.A. :* care Venator Nairobi. *T. :* 89. *M.:* B 6041. *Clubs:* Public Schools : Nairobi ; Muthaiga Country.

(*Died 4 Aug. 1928.*)

NICHOLSON, Major-Gen. Stuart (James), C.B. 1897; retired; *b.* 20 Nov. 1836; *s.* of late Wm. Henry Nicholson of St. Margaret's, Rochester; *m.* 1870, Elizabeth, *d.* of David Laing Burn of St. Andrews, N.B.; one *s.* two *d. Educ.:* Charterhouse; Royal Military Academy, Woolwich. Entered Royal Artillery, 1855; Captain, 1863; Major, 1872; Lt.-Col. 1881; Col. 1885; Maj.-Gen. 1895; A.D.C. to Insp.-Gen. R.A. 1864-69; Instr. School of Gunnery, 1872-77; commanded Chesnut Troop R.H.A., 1877-81; Assist. Director of Artillery, War Office, 1881-84; Member Ordnance Committee, 1884-85; Comdt. and Supt. School of Gunnery Shoeburyness, 1887-92; Maj.-Gen. Commd. R.A. Brigade, Malta, 1892-95; in command of R. A. Southern District, 1895-97; Colonel Commandant Royal Artillery, 1906; commanded R.A. and N.S.W. Artillery with Soudan Expedition, 1885 (despatches, medal with clasp, bronze star; promoted Colonel); J.P. for Essex. *Publication:* A B C of Fair Trade. *Recreations:* fishing and golf. *Address:* 8 Hope Street, St. Andrews. *Clubs:* United Service; Royal and Ancient Golf, St. Andrews.

(*Died 10 April 1917.*)

NICOL, John, C.M.G. 1901; *b.* Ramstone, Monymusk, Scotland, 1838; *m.* 1862, Janet M'Donald, of Catrine, Ayrshire, Scotland; one *s.* five *d.* Left Scotland for Durban, Natal, 1860; has carried on business as builder and timber merchant for 34 years; for several years a volunteer in the Durban Field Artillery; joined the Durban Town Council in 1885; has been twice Deputy Mayor and four times elected Mayor of the borough; Justice of the Peace for eight years. *Address:* Banchory, Corrie Road, Durban. (*Died 25 May 1920.*)

NICOL, Rev. Thomas, D.D., Moderator, General Assembly of the Church of Scotland, 1914; Professor of Divinity and Biblical Criticism, University of Aberdeen, since 1899; *b.* 21 Oct. 1846; *m.* Annie, *o. surv. d.* of late Rev. John Underwood, minister of Kirkcudbright, 1878; three *s.* two *d. Educ.:* Aberdeen, Edinburgh, and Tübingen Univs.; M.A. of Aberdeen, 1868, with First Class Honours in Classics and Mental Philosophy, and with Simpson Greek Prize; Hutton Prize and Fullerton Scholarship; B.D. of Edinburgh, 1871; D.D. of Edinburgh, 1893. Ordained minister of Kells, Kirkcudbrightshire, 1873; translated to Tolbooth Parish, Edinburgh, 1879; Croall Lecturer, 1897-98; Convener from 1896 to 1911 of Church of Scotland Jewish Mission Committee; Editor of Church of Scotland Mission Record, 1886-1900; Baird Lecturer, 1906-7. *Publications:* Translation jointly with Rev. Dr. J. A. M'Clymont of Beck's Pastorallehren des Neuen Testaments; Church of Scotland Sabbath School Teachers' Book, Grade I. (edited); Recent Explorations in Bible Lands; Recent Archæology and the Bible (Croall Lectures, 1897-98); The Present Position and Prospects of Biblical Science (Introductory Lecture); The Four Gospels in the Earliest Church History (Baird Lectures, 1906-7). *Recreation:* golf. *Address:* 53 College Bounds, Old Aberdeen.

(*Died 7 Aug. 1916.*)

NICOLET, Gabriel; Chevalier de la Légion d'Honneur; Member of Society of Oil-Painters and of Royal Society of Portrait Painters; Member of the Royal West of England Academy; Société internationale des Aquarellistes; Bronze Medal, Universal Exhibition, Paris, 1889; Gold Medal, Paris Salon, 1895, H.C.; Silver Medal, Universal Exhibition, Paris, 1900; *b.* Pons, Charente Inférieure, France,

5 March 1856; Father, clergyman; *m.* 1905, Amy Magnus. *Educ.:* University of Liége; Royal Academy of Arts, Liége; Dusseldorf; Paris. Has lived in England since 1885 and also in Paris. *Recreations:* riding, rowing, fencing. *Address:* 18 rue de l'Université, Paris. *Club:* Arts. (*Died April 1921.*)

NICOLL, James H., M.B., University of Glasgow; Hon. Lieut.-Col. R.A.; M.C.; J.P., Glasgow; Examiner in Surgery, University of Glasgow; Member of University Court, University of Glasgow, as representative of President Poincare, Lord Rector of Glasgow University; Surgeon to the Western Infirmary, Glasgow; Consulting Surgeon to the Royal Hospital for Sick Children, Glasgow, Glasgow Ear and Throat Hospital, and to the Glasgow Lunacy Board's Asylum; Acting and Consulting Surgeon in various war hospitals in Britain and Overseas; *b.* Glasgow, 1865; *s.* of Rev. James Nicoll, Glasgow; unmarried. *Educ.:* Glasgow Academy and Univ.; London Hospital. After graduation in Glasgow, studied surgery for four years at the London Hospital and at various other hospitals in London and on the Continent; was Professor of Surgery, Anderson's College; Hon. Secretary Glasgow Branch of British Medical Association; President Surgical Section of Glasgow Medico-Chirurgical Society. *Publications:* numerous publications on surgical subjects. *Recreations:* golf, fishing, walking. *Address:* 4 Woodside Place, Glasgow. *T.:* Charing Cross 271, Glasgow; Central 271. *Clubs:* Royal Automobile; Western, New, Glasgow.
(*Died 15 Aug. 1921.*)

NICOLL, Sir William Robertson, Kt., *cr.* 1909; C.H. 1921; M.A., LL.D. (Aberdeen and St. Andrews); D.D. Halifax (N.S.); editor British Weekly since 1886, Bookman since 1891, Expositor since 1885, etc.; *b.* Lumsden, Aberdeenshire, 10 Oct. 1851; *e. s.* of Rev. Harry Nicoll; *m.* 1st, 1878, Isa Dunlop; 2nd, 1897, Catherine, *d.* of Joseph Pollard, High Down, Herts; one *s.* two *d.* *Educ.:* Grammar School, Aberdeen; University, Aberdeen; M.A. 1870; LL.D. Aberdeen 1890; St. Andrews, 1922; D.D. Halifax N.S. 1920. Free Church Minister of Dufftown, 1874-77; of Kelso, 1877-85. *Publications:* Literary Anecdotes of the Nineteenth Century, 1895; Life of James Macdonell, 1890; Prof. Elmslie; The Lamb of God; The Incarnate Saviour; The Key of the Grave; Songs of Rest (Series i. and ii.); The Return to the Cross 1897; Sunday Afternoon Verses, 1897; Letters on Life, 1901; The Church's One Foundation, 1901; The Garden of Nuts, 1905; The Day Book of Claudius Clear, 1905; The Lamp of Sacrifice, 1906; My Father, 1908; Life of Ian Maclaren, 1908; The Round of the Clock, 1910; Emily Brontë, 1910; The Expositor's Dictionary of Texts, 1910; Sunday Evening, 1910; The Problem of Edwin Drood, 1912; A Bookman's Letters, 1913; Reunion in Eternity, 1918; Letters of Principal Denney, 1920; Princes of the Church, 1921; Ed. The Expositor's Greek Testament; and numerous theological works. *Address:* Bay Tree Lodge, Hampstead, N.W.3; The Old Manse, Lumsden, Aberdeenshire. *Clubs:* Reform, Bath, Whitefriars. (*Died 4 May 1923.*)

NICOLLS, Maj.-Gen. Oliver Henry Atkins, Col. Commandant, R.A. since 1904; *b.* 24 July 1834; *m.* 1st, 1875, Harriet (*d.* 1881), *d.* of Rev. C. Y. Crawley; 2nd, 1885, Mary (*d.* 1891), *d.* of E. Wolstenholme Lee. Entered army, 1853; Maj.-Gen. 1890; retired, 1896; served Crimea, 1854-56 (medal with clasp, Turkish medal); Perak Expedition, 1875-76 (despatches, medal with clasp, brevet Lt.-Col.); Commanding R.A., North British District, 1887-90; R.A. Brigade, Malta, 1891-92; troops in Woolwich district, 1892-94. *Address:* 4 East Pallant, Chichester. (*Died 15 Oct. 1920.*)

NICOLSON, Sir Arthur Thomas Bennet Robert, 9th Bart. of that Ilk and

778

Lasswade; *cr.* 1629; D.L., Orkney and Shetland; J.P.; Commissioner of Supply for Shetland; *b.* Morphett Vale, Adelaide, 1842; *S.* father 1879; *m.* Annie, *d.* of late John Rutherford, Bruntsfield Place, Edinburgh, formerly of Australia, 1881; four *s.* one *d.* *Educ.:* Melbourne College. *Heir: s.* Arthur John Frederick William [*b.* 8 June 1882; Advocate, M.A., LL.B.]. *Address:* Brough Lodge, Fetlar, and Grimista, Lerwick, Shetland. *T.A.:* Fetlar, Shetland.
(*Died 27 May 1917.*)

NIECKS, Frederick, Mus. Doc.; Hon. LL.D. Edin.; Reid Professor of Music, and Dean of the Faculty of Music, Edinburgh University, 1891-1914; *b.* Düsseldorf (Germany), 3 Feb. 1845; *m.* 1907, Christina, 3rd *d.* of late Professor Sir John Struthers, M.D. *Educ.:* private school and teachers at Düsseldorf; Leipsic University; musically by Dr. Langhans, Grunewald, and Auer (violin); Tausch (pianoforte and composition), Düsseldorf and Cologne. Violinist and teacher of music at Düsseldorf till 1868; then settled in Scotland, where he was engaged in teaching music, and since 1875 as a writer on music, contributing largely to musical journals. *Publications:* A Concise Dictionary of Musical Terms, to which is prefixed an Introduction to the Elements of Music, 1884; Chopin as a Man and Musician, 1888; A History of Programme Music, a Contribution to the History of Musical Expression, 1907. *Recreations:* fine arts and literature. *Address:* 40 George Square, Edinburgh. (*Died 24 June 1924.*)

NIGHTINGALE, Thomas Slingsby, C.M.G.; Secretary, Office of High Commissioner Union of S. Africa, London, since 1911; *b.* Bedford, Cape Colony, 1866; *e. s.* of late Percy Nightingale, Inspecting Commissioner Cape of Good Hope; *g.-s.* of Sir Charles Nightingale, 11th Bart., Kneesworth, Cambridgeshire; *m.* 1900, Doris Elizabeth, *d.* of late Charles Stoughton Collison, of East Bilney, Norfolk; two *s.* one *d.* *Educ.:* Royal Naval School, New Cross; St. George's School, Brampton. Entered Civil Service Cape of Good Hope, 1883; served successively in War Dept.; Civil Commissioner and Resident Magistrate's Office, King William's Town; Customs Dept. Cape Town, Kimberley, Port Elizabeth, East London; Resident Magistrate and Sub-Collector Customs, Port Nolloth, Namaqualand, 1891-96; Chief Clerk Office Agent-General, Cape of Good Hope, London, 1898; Secretary, 1905; frequently acted as Agent-General for varying periods up to May 1910 when upon establishment of Union became 1st Assistant-Secretary in Office of High Commissioner Union of S. Africa; Acting High Commissioner, Nov. 1913 till Aug. 1914; Commissioner of Supreme Court of S.A. and Member of Advisory Committee of Imperial Education Conference; represented Union of S.A. as joint Delegate with Sir Richard Solomon at the International Radio-Tel. Conference, London, 1912. *Recreations:* golf, cycling. *Address:* Kneesworth, Limpsfield, Surrey. *T.A.:* Limpsfield. *Club:* Royal Societies'.
(*Died 20 June 1918.*)

NIHAL SINGH, Rev. Canon Solomon, B.A.; Evangelistic Missionary; *b.* 15 Feb. 1852; *s.* of Thakur Himmat Singh, Mainpuri Chauhan, Rajput: a Jagirdar by birth; *m.* 1870, *d.* of Subahdar Sundar Singh, a Tilok Chandi Bais of Baiswara; three *s.* three *d.* *Educ.:* Govt. High School, Lakhimpur; Canning College, Lucknow. Second master in the C.M.S. High School, Lucknow; eventually Headmaster; Headmaster of the C.M.S. High School, Jabbulpore, 1886; ordained 1891; sent to England as delegate of the U.P. and Oudh branch of the C.M.S. to the Centenary Celebrations of the Church Missionary Society in London, 1899; Hon. Canon in All Saints Cathedral, Allahabad, 1906. *Publications:* An English Grammar for the use of the Middle

Classes in Oudh; translation into English of the Urdu Entrance Course, Majmua-Sakhun, 1873-1875; Khulasat-ul-Isaiah (in two parts); Risala-e-Saf Goi, or Plain Speaking; Verses on Temperance in Urdu; Munajat Asi, or the Prayers of a Sinner; Verses on the Coronation of King Edward VII. and George V. in Urdu, and a number of handbills in Hindi for free distribution. *Recreation:* Theological study. *Address:* 2 Pioneer Road, Allahabad. (*Died 8 May 1916.*)

NILKANTH, Rao Bahadur Sir Ramanbhai Mahipatram, Kt., *cr.* 1927; B.A., LL.D.; High Court Pleader; *s.* of Rao Saheb Mahipatram Rupram Nilkanth, C.I.E.; *m.* 1889, Vidyagauro, *d.* of Gopilal, B.A., M.B.E., Kaiser-i-Hind Gold Medallist; two *s.* five *d.* *Educ.:* Elphinstone College, Bombay; Gujarat College, Ahmedabad. President of Ahmedabad Municipality; member of the Legislative Council, Bombay; Secretary of General Societies. *Publications:* Brochure on marriage ritual; satire called Bhadram Bhadra; essays in literature and criticism; essay on humour, with humorous sketches. *Address:* Bhadra Ahmedabad, Bombay Presidency, India. *M.:* 2690. *Club:* Gujarat, Ahmedabad.
(*Died Mar. 1928.*)

NILSSON, Madame Christine (Comtesse de Miranda); Prima donna; *b.* Sweden, 20 Aug. 1843; *m.* 1st, M. Auguste Rouzaud, 1872 (*d.* 1882); 2nd, 1887, Comte de Miranda (*d.* 1902). *Educ.:* Halmstad; Stockholm, under Berwald. Went to Paris, 1860; studied under Français Wartel; made her *début* in Paris, 1864; first appearance in London, 1867; has sung in the following operas: The Magic Flute; Martha; Don Juan; Faust; Robert the Devil. *Address:* 3 rue Clément Marot, Paris. (*Died 22 Nov. 1921.*)

NINNIS, Insp.-Gen. Belgrave, R.N.; retired; 4th *s.* of Paul Ninnis of St. Austell, Cornwall; *m.* Ada Jane, *d.* of James Sutton of Streatham, Surrey; two *s.* one *d.* *Educ.:* privately. Joined Royal Navy, 1861; Naturalist to Northern Territory of South Australia Surveying Expedition, 1864-66; served in the Arctic Expedition, 1875-76, under Captain (Sir George) Nares; awarded Sir Gilbert Blane Gold Medal, C.V.O., M.D., M.R.C.S., LL.M., F.S.A.; Knight of Justice, Order of St. John of Jerusalem. *Publications:* Remarks on the Ethnology, Natural History, and Meteorology of the Northern Territory of South Australia; On an Epidemic amongst the Esquimaux Dogs, Arctic Expedition, 1875-76. *Address:* The Elms, Leigham Avenue, Streatham, S.W.16. *T.:* Streatham 1814. *Club:* Army and Navy.
(*Died 18 June 1922.*)

NIPHER, Francis Eugene; Professor of Physics in Washington University, St. Louis, 1874; Professor Emeritus, 1915; *b.* Port Byron, N.Y., 10 Dec. 1847; *s.* of Peter Nipher and Roxalana P. Tilden; *m.* 1873, Matilda Aikins; one *s.* four *d.* *Educ.:* State University of Iowa. Secretary, Academy of Science of St. Louis, 1875-85; President, 1885-90; President, St. Louis Engineers' Club, 1890; Fellow American Association for Advancement of Science; Member American Physical Society; American Philosophical Society of Philadelphia; Société Français de Physique; Royal Society of Arts; in 1902 he showed that over-exposed photographic plates which are to reverse should be developed in the light instead of the dark room; discovered the causes of magnetic disturbances in the earth's field, and has produced such disturbances in the field of a bar magnet surrounded by electrified air; has shown that water in a vapour condition can be decomposed by an electric current; has obtained experimental proof that electrification of masses of matter diminishes gravitational attraction; converted gravitational attraction between masses of matter into a repulsion, when the masses were wholly shielded from each other by metal; has shown that the electrical potential of the earth is constantly subject to enormous local variations. *Publications:* Theory of Magnetic Measurements, 1886; Electricity and Magnetism (Math.), 1895; Introduction to Graphical Algebra, 1898; Experimental Studies in Electricity and Magnetism, 1914; many papers in Transactions Academy of Science of St. Louis. Among these are A Method of Measuring Pressure due to Wind at any Point on any Structure; The Law of Contraction of Gaseous Nebulæ. *Address:* Kirkwood, St. Louis Co., Mo., U.S. *T.:* Kirkwood 934 W.
(*Died 6 Oct. 1926.*)

NISBET, Hume, author and artist; *b.* Stirling, Scotland, 8 Aug. 1849. *Educ.:* in Letters under Mr. James Culross, LL.D.; in Art under Sam Bough, R.S.A. Left Scotland at sixteen; spent seven years travelling through Australia; on return was appointed Art Master in the Watt College and Old School of Arts, Edinburgh; held this position for eight years; resigned in 1885; travelled for Messrs. Cassell through Australia and New Guinea, 1886; since then occupied as novelist, etc.; revisited Australia and other parts in 1895; visited China and Japan, etc., 1905-6. *Publications:* 46 Romances, including Bail Up, etc.; 4 vols. of poetry—Egypt, Memories of the Months, The Matador; Hathor, Colonial Tales, being vols. i. and ii. of Poetic and Dramatic Works, in 8 vols.; Travels; A Colonial Tramp; 5 Books on Art—Where Art Begins, etc; Life and Nature Studies, 1915. *Recreations:* travelling and studying Nature and Humanity. *Address:* Dhoon Villa, Willingdon Road, Eastbourne. *Club:* Yorick.

NISBET, Rev. Matthew Alexander; Rector of Ickham since 1897; *b.* Delhi, 1838; *s.* of Matthew Nisbet, 48th Bengal Native Infantry; *m.* 1875, Louisa J. Scobell, *d.* of Rev. S. G. Scobell; three *d.* *Educ.:* Cheltenham College; Jesus College, Cambridge (Scholar). Captain of College Boat; Captain of College Eleven (cricket); M.A.; M.A. (comit. caus.), Oxford; Curate of Longborough, 1861; Chipping-Campden, 1867; Vicar of St. Luke's, Gloucester, 1872; Chaplain to Volunteers; Chairman of Gloucester School Board, 1876-81; Rural Dean of Gloucester; Rector of Ringwould, 1881; Guardian and District Councillor; Hon. Sec. of the Canterbury Diocesan Education Society, 1885-1912; Hon. Sec. of the Canterbury Diocesan Sunday School Teachers' Association, 1887-1907; Hon. Canon of Canterbury, 1891; Chairman of the Finance Committee of the Diocesan Association; Member of Kent County Education Committee, 1904-18; Rural Dean of East Bridge. *Recreations:* walking and golf. *Address:* Ickham Rectory, Canterbury. *T.A.:* Wickhambreux. *M.:* N 8918. *Clubs:* Constitutional; St. George's, Sandwich; Cinque Ports, Deal; East Kent, Canterbury. (*Died 5 Sept. 1919.*)

NISBET, Pollok Sinclair, A.R.S.A., R.S.W. 1879; *b.* Edinburgh, 18 Oct. 1848; *s.* of late John Nisbet, decorator, Edinburgh; *m.* Hellen, *y. d.* of John Grieve of Loyal and Inglestone, Perthshire; one *s.* one *d.* *Educ.:* Edinburgh Institution. Travelled and painted extensively in Spain and Italy, and in Morocco, Tunis, and Algeria; studied in Rome and Venice. *Address:* Edinburgh. *Club:* Scottish Arts, Edinburgh.

NISBET, Colonel Robert Parry, C.I.E. 1885, F.R.G.S., Indian Army (retired). *Educ.:* King's College, London. Was called to the Bar at the Middle Temple, 1872; Elected a Fellow of the University of London. He passed through all the grades of the Civil Commission, Panjab, and held many important posts; as Deputy Commissioner of Lahore for five years; was also for the same term Deputy

Commissioner and Superintendent of the Hill States at Simla; and on promotion was successively Commissioner of the Delhi, Derajat, Peshawar, and Rawal Pindi Divisions, Panjab; from Commissioner of Rawal Pindi he was in 1888 appointed to be H.M.'s Resident in Kashmir, which post he held till he retired from the Service in 1892. *Address:* 229 Cromwell Mansions, Cromwell Road, S.W. *T.:* 3351 Kensington.   *(Died 5 June 1916.)*

NISBETT, Lt.-Col. George Dalrymple More, J.P.; *e. s.* of late John More Nisbett, of Cairnhill, and of The Drum, and Lady Agnes (*d.* 1900), 2nd *d.* of 9th Earl of Stair; *b.* 1850. Brevet Lt.-Col. (retired) late Bedfordshire Regt. *Address:* The Drum, Gilmerton, Midlothian. *Clubs:* United Service, Junior United Service; New, Edinburgh.   *(Died 23 Sept. 1922.)*

NISSIM, Charles; J.P.; late Member of Governor of Bombay's Legislative Council; Hon. Presidency Magistrate for Bombay, 1904; President Bank of Bombay.; Vice-President Jewish Association; Partner of the firm of David Sassoon and Co., merchants and bankers; *b.* Bombay, 28 Nov. 1845; *m.* Rachel (*decd.*), 3rd *d.* of late E. J. Abraham; one *s. Educ.:* Elphinston High School; David Sassoon Hebrew School. Speaks English, French, German, Hebrew, Arabic, Hindustani, Guzrathi, Marathi, and Chinese. Left for China, 1862, returning, 1880; visited Europe several times, and Palestine; settled down in Bombay; J.P., Fellow of University of Bombay, 1899; Director of several Joint Stock Companies; invited guest of H.E. the Governor to the Delhi Durbar. *Recreations:* reading, riding, swimming, chess. *Address:* 203 Knightsbridge, S.W. *T.:* 3290 Kensington. *Clubs:* British Empire; Royal Bombay Yacht, Bombay.   *(Died 3 Nov. 1918.)*

NIVEN, Charles, M.A., D.Sc., F.R.S.; Professor of Natural Philosophy, Aberdeen University, 1880-1922; *m.* Mary, *d.* of late Sir David Stewart; one *s.* two *d. Educ.:* Aberdeen and Cambridge. Formerly Fellow of Trinity College, Cambridge, and Professor of Mathematics in Queen's College, Cork. *Publications:* papers in Proceedings and Transactions of the Royal Society and other periodicals. *Recreation:* fishing. *Address:* 6 Chanonry, Old Aberdeen. *Club:* Royal Northern, Aberdeen.
      (Died 11 May 1925.)

NIVEN, James, M.B., B.C. Cantab.; A.M. Aberdeen; M.A. Cantab.; LL.D. Aberdeen; *b.* 12 March 1851; widower; three *d. Educ.:* Aberdeen and Cambridge Universities; Formerly Fellow of Queens' College, Cambridge; lately Medical Officer of Health for Manchester; formerly Medical Officer of Health, Oldham. *Publications:* Annual Reports; numerous papers. *Address:* 50 Granville Road, Fallowfield, Manchester.   *(Died Oct. 1925.)*

NIVEN, William, F.S.A., A.R.E., J.P. (Berks); *s.* of late D. Graham Niven, R.C.S., of Pershore. *Educ.:* private schools. Was articled to late Sir G. Gilbert Scott, R.A., 1865; subsequently practised architecture for some years; has etched plates of chiefly architectural subjects; for some years hon. editor of Recordsissued annually by the Architectural and Archæological Society for the County of Buckingham. *Publications:* Old Worcestershire Houses, 1873; Warwickshire, 1878; Staffordshire, 1882; City Churches, Destroyed or Threatened, 1887; Monograph of Aston Hall, 1884. *Recreations:* study of architecture and works of art; collector of old Wedgwood. *Address:* Marlow Place, Marlow.
      (Died 7 Nov. 1921.)

NIVEN, Sir William Davidson, K.C.B., *cr.* 1903; C.B. 1897; M.A., F.R.S.; late Director of Studies in Royal Naval College, Greenwich; *b.* 1842; *s.* of Charles Niven, Peterhead. *Educ.:* Trinity College, Cambridge (Wrangler, Fellow). *Address:* Eastburn, Sidcup. *(Died 29 May 1917.)*

780

NIXON, Alfred, F.C.A., F.S.A.A., F.C.I.S.; late Principal, Municipal High School of Commerce, Manchester—Day and Evening Departments and School of Languages; *b.* 17 March 1858; *m.*; one *s.* one *d. Educ.:* University of Manchester. In practice for many years as a chartered accountant; headmaster to organize the Municipal Evening School of Commerce, 1889; during the war conducted special business training courses for 1000 women; responsible under the Board of Education and the Ministry of Labour for the full-time training of 1500 officers and disabled men; First President Incorporated Society of Commercial Teachers; Member of Council, Chartered Institute of Secretaries; late Member of Teachers' Registration Council representing commercial teachers; late Chairman of the Finance Committee of the Sale Administrative Education Committee; late Chairman of the Exchange Ward Liberal Committee; Past President of the Manchester Society of Incorporated Accountants. *Publications:* Accounting and Banking and Text-books on Auditing, Book-keeping, Business Practice, Law and Secretarial Work; Editor of Longmans, Green & Co.'s Commercial Series. *Recreation:* social and political work. *Address:* Littlecroft, Queen's Road, St. Anne's-on-Sea; 31 Victoria Buildings, Manchester. *T.:* City 2050. *Club:* Reform, Manchester.   *(Died 27 Oct. 1928.)*

NIXON, Maj.-Gen. Arundel James, Col. Commandant R.A. since 1921; *b.* 31 May 1849; *m.* 1876, Maria Lucy, *y. d.* of John Lawrence, Langstone Court, Monmouths. Entered Army, 1868; Maj.-Gen. 1906; retired, 1910; commanded R.A. Gibraltar, 1906-10. *Address:* Clone House, Ballyragget, Co. Kilkenny.
      (Died 9 April 1925.)

NIXON, General Sir John (Eccles), G.C.M.G., *cr.* 1919; K.C.B., *cr.* 1911; C.B. 1902; *b.* 16 Aug. 1857; *m.* 1884, Amy Louisa, *y. d.* of James Wilson, Gratwicke, Billingshurst. *Educ.:* Wellington. Served in 25th, The King's Own, Borderers, and 18th Bengal Lancers; held staff appointments in India; served Afghan War, 1879-80; Zamusht Expedition, 1879 (despatches, medal); Mahsud Waziri Expedition, 1881; Chitral Relief Force, as D.A.Q.M.G. for Intelligence (despatches, medal and clasp, Brevet of Lieut.-Colonel); North-West Frontier of India, 1897-98, as Chief Staff Officer, Tochi Field Force (despatches, clasp); commanded a cavalry brigade in South Africa, 1901-1902 (despatches, medal, four clasps, C.B.); commanded Bengalore Brigade, 1903 to 1906; Inspector-General of Cavalry in India, 1906-8; commanded 7th (Meerut) Division, 1908-10, and 1st Peshawar Division from 1910 to 1912; commanded the Southern Army in India, 1912-15; commanded the Northern Army in India, 1915; commanded the Expeditionary Force in Mesopotamia, April 1915-Jan. 1916. *Publication:* Notes for Staff Officers on Field Service. *Recreations:* cricket, golf, racquets. *Club:* United Service.   *(Died 15 Dec. 1921.)*

NOBLE, Robert, R.S.A.; *b.* Edinburgh, 1857. *Educ.:* Government School of Design. Exhibited first picture R.S.A. 1877; visited Paris following year; afterwards studied at the Scottish Academy Life School, and later at Carolus Duran's Life School in Paris; exhibited Coming from Church, and the Linn Jaws, 1887, in the Royal Academy; gained silver medal for Landscape at Edinburgh International Exhibition; awarded Bronze Medal Paris International, 1900; was the 1st Chairman of the Society of Scottish Artists, and one of the hangers of the Franco-British Exhibition, London. *Address:* East Linton, Prestonkirk, N.B. *Club:* Scottish Arts, Edinburgh.
      (Died 12 May 1917.)

NOBLE, Wilson; *b.* 21 Nov. 1854; *s.* of late Jno. Noble of Park Place, Henley-on-Thames. J.P., D.L.; *m.* 1879, Marian Carolin, *d.* of W. P. W. Dana of Boston, U.S.A.; four *d. Educ.:* Eton;

Trinity Coll. Camb. M.A. M.P. Hastings (C); 1886-95; President of Röntgen Soc. of London, 1899-1900. *Recreations:* scientific pursuits, especially electricity and investigations in Röntgen rays and motoring. *Address:* Park Place, Henley-on-Thames. *Clubs:* Athenæum, Carlton.   (*Died 1 Nov. 1917.*)

NOEL, Lt.-Col. Hon. Edward; D.A.A.G., Ceylon, 1899-1902; *b.* 28 April 1852; 2nd *s.* of 2nd Earl of Gainsborough; *m.* 1884, Ruth, *d.* of late W. H. Lucas, of Trenifle, Cornwall; three *s.* *Educ.:* Oscott College. Entered Rifle Brigade, 1872; Captain, 1880; Major, 1890; Lieut.-Col. 1898, on half-pay; served Ashanti War, 1873-74; N.W. Frontier, India, 1877-78: Burma, 1886-87-88. *Publications:* Natural Weights and Measures, 1889; International Time, 1892; Gustaf Adolf, the father of modern war, 1908. *Address:* Exton Park, Oakham.   (*Died 9 Nov. 1917.*)

NOEL, Evan Baillie; Secretary of Queen's Club, West Kensington, since 1914; *b.* 23 Jan. 1879; 2nd *s.* of Eugene Frederic Noel, J.P., and Ethel Maria Chapman; *m.* 1906, Marjorie Dean Sweeting; one *s.* one *d.* *Educ.:* Evelyns, Hillingdon, Uxbridge; Winchester College; Trinity College, Cambridge. On the staff of The Times, 1903-14; Sporting Editor until 1909; went abroad for a year owing to ill-health; won Amateur Championship of Rackets, 1907, and M.C.C. Silver Racket at tennis, 1908. *Publications:* A History of Tennis; First Steps to Rackets (with Hon. C. N. Bruce); Winchester College Cricket, and numerous articles on tennis, rackets, and other games in periodicals, daily newspapers, etc. *Recreations:* formerly cricket, tennis, rackets, and other ball games, but has not played recently for reasons of health; collecting books and prints on games, especially tennis; bridge. *Address:* 107 Comeragh Road, W.14. *T.:* Fulham 1421. *Clubs:* Bath, M.C.C., Prince's Tennis, and Rackets.   (*Died 22 Dec. 1928.*)

NOEL, Admiral Francis Charles Methuen; retired; 3rd *s.* of Col. E. A. Noel of Clanna, Gloucestershire, D.L., J.P. (*d.* 1899), and Sarah, *d.* of late W. B. Darwin of Elston Hall, Notts; *b.* 1852; *m.* 1886, Wilmot Juliana, *d.* of T. Maitland Snow of Cleve House, Exeter; one *s.* one *d.* *Educ.:* Stubbington House; Royal Naval College. Commanded H.M.S. Partridge in West Indies; Commanded Scout in Red Sea, present at operations round Suakim (Khedive's medal); served with International Expedition, for relief of Kandamos, Crete; Commanded Wallaroo during China War, 1900 (medal); was Deputy Commissioner for Western Pacific, and served on Anglo-French Commission in New Hebrides; was officially present at the inauguration of the Australian Commonwealth; Commanded H.M.S. Hood in home waters; awarded Captain's Good Service Pension; Rear-Admiral, 1907; Admiral on retired list, 1915; is Assessor for Appeals in the House of Lords. *Recreations:* literary. *Address:* 33 Redcliffe Square, S.W. *Club:* Junior United Service.   (*Died 30 Dec. 1925.*)

NOEL, Admiral of the Fleet Sir Gerard Henry Uctred, G.C.B., *cr.* 1913; K.C.B., *cr.* 1902; K.C.M.G., *cr.* 1898; Admiral of the Fleet 1908-15; retired 1915; *b.* 5 Mar. 1845; 2nd *s.* of late Rev. Augustus W. Noel, Rector of Stanhoe, Norfolk; *m.* 1875, Charlotte, *e. d.* of late F. Cresswell and Charlotte, *d.* of 4th Lord Calthorpe. Commanded Naval Guard at Cape Coast Castle, 1873 (promoted, medal, clasp); Rear-Admiral Mediterranean Fleet, 1898-99; a Lord of the Admiralty, 1893-98; A.D.C. to the Queen, 1894-96; commanded Home Fleet, and Admiral-Superintendent, Naval Reserves, 1900-3; Commander-in-Chief, China Station, 1904-6; at the Nore, 1907-8; Gold Medal of Royal United Service Institution. *Address:* Fincham, Downham, Norfolk. *Club:* United Service.   (*Died 22 May 1918.*)

NOEL, Canon John Monk, R.D.; *b.* St. James' Parish. Westminster, 4 June 1840; *m.* 1868, Eliza Anne Le Measurier, St. John's; one *s.* four *d.* *Educ.:* Archbishop Tenison's Grammar School, London; Queen's Theological College, St. John's, Newfoundland. S.P.G. Missionary to Newfoundland, 1860; Incumbent of Ferryland, 1864-67; Upper Island Cove, Conception Bay, 1868-76; Rector of St. Paul's, Harbour Grace, Newfoundland, 1876-1913; Rural Dean of Conception Bay, 1895; Canon of St. Boniface, St. John Baptist Cathedral, 1897. *Recreation:* three months' holiday to England, July to Sep. 1908. *Address:* Harvey Street, Harbour Grace, Newfoundland.   (*Died 1921.*)

NOLAN, Sir Robert Howard, C.B.E. 1918; Hon. Secretary N.Z. Soldiers' Club.   (*Died 13 July 1923.*)

NOPS, Walter, I.S.O. 1902; *b.* 1850; *m.* 1883, Elizabeth Moule; was in Secretary's Office, G.P.O., St. Martin's-le-Grand, E.C. *Address:* Elmdale, Bromley, Kent.   (*Died 26 Feb. 1918.*)

NORBURY, Edwin Arthur, R.C.A.; Director of the Norbury Sketching School and St. James' Life School; Principal of The Henry Blackburn Studio; Painter and Illustrator; *b.* Liverpool, 1849; 2nd *s.* of late Richard Norbury, R.C.A., of Macclesfield; *m.* 1873, Elvira, *e. d.* of D. C. Browne, of Norwich; two *d.* *Educ.:* Dr. Wand's School, Liverpool. At age of 15 began contributing to the Illustrated London News and Illustrated Times; afterwards joined the Graphic as Artist Correspondent, and sketched many passing events; resided chiefly in North Wales, 1875-90; was Vice-President and one of the Founders of the Royal Cambrian Academy; organised the first Technical Art Classes, and received an Exceptional Recognition from the Science and Art Departments; went to Siam to direct the Royal School of Arts and to give Art Instruction in the Raj. Kumara College, 1892; painted two pictures for the King of Siam of the Crown Prince's coming-of-age ceremonies; was Special Artist to the Graphic and Daily Graphic during the Franco-Siamese War of 1893; returned to London, 1896; has exhibited at the Royal Academy, Royal Institute, etc., and chief American Galleries. *Publications:* many illustrations of books, magazines, and papers, including The Kingdom of the Yellow Robe, The Arabian Nights, Animal Arts and Crafts, etc. *Recreations:* sketching, rowing, and walking. *Address:* 241 King's Road, Chelsea, S.W. *Club:* London Sketch.   (*Died 16 Oct. 1918.*)

NORBURY, Inspector-Gen. Sir Henry (Frederick), K.C.B., *cr.* 1897; M.D., F.R.C.S. (Eng.); R.N.; Hon. Surgeon to Kings Edward VII. and George V.; *b.* 1839; *m.* 1868, Mina Legge, *d.* of E. G. Wade-Brown of Burton Bradstock, Dorset; three *s.* five *d.* *Educ.:* Oundle School; St. Bartholomew's Hospital, London; University of Malta. Entered Royal Navy as Surgeon, 1860; promoted Staff Surgeon, 1872; Fleet Surgeon, 1879; Deputy-Inspector-General, 1887; Inspector-General, 1894; was landed in medical charge of the Naval Brigade during Kafir War of 1877-78 (despatches); during Zulu War of 1879 was Principal Medical Officer of General Sir C. Pearson's column; present at the battle of Inyezane and during defence of Ekowe; was afterwards Principal Medical Officer of the Naval Brigade with General Crealock's column (despatches several times; medal with three clasps); promoted and created a Military C.B.; awarded the Blane Gold Medal 1879; K.C.B. (Mil.) 1897; Knight of Grace of St. John of Jerusalem in England, 1895; late Director-General of the Medical Department of the Navy; Jubilee medal of Queen Victoria and Coronation medals of Kings Edward VII. and George V. *Publication:* The Naval Brigade in

South Africa. *Address :* St. Margaret's, Eltham, S.E.9. *T. :* Eltham 1333,

(*Died 10 Dec. 1925.*)

NORDAU, Max Simon, M.D. Paris, Budapesth ; LL.D. *hon. causa,* Athens ; Officier d'Académie, France ; Commander Royal Hellenic Order of St. Saviour ; author and physician ; President Congress of Zionists ; Hon. Mem. of the Greek Acad. of the Parnassos ; Foreign Member of the Royal Academy of Medicine of Madrid ; *b.* Budapesth, 29 July 1849 ; *y. s.* of Gabriel Südfeld, Rabbi, Krotoschin, Prussia, and his 2nd wife ; *b.* Nelkin, Riga, Russia. *Educ. :* Royal Gymnasium and Protestant Gymnasium, Budapesth ; Royal University, Budapesth ; Faculty of Medicine, Paris. Wrote very early for newspapers ; travelled for several years all over Europe ; practised as a physician for a year and a half, 1878-80, at Budapesth ; settled then at Paris, residing there ever since ; *m.* Anna-Elizabeth, 2nd *d.* of State-councillor Captain Julius Dons, Copenhagen, Denmark ; one *d.* *Publications :* Paris, Studien und Bilder aus dem wahren Milliardenlande, 1878 ; Seifenblasen, 1879 ; Vom Kreml zur Alhambra, 1880 ; Aus der Zeitungswelt (together with Ferdinand Gross), 1880 ; Paris unter der dritten Republik, 1881 ; Der Krieg der Millionen 882 ; De la castration de la Femme, 1882 ; Die conventionellen Lügen der Culturmenschheit, 1883 ; Ausgewählte Pariser Briefe, 1884 ; Paradoxe, 1885 ; Die Krankheit des Jahrhunderts, 1887 ; Seelenanalysen, 1891 ; Gefühlskomödie, 1892 ; Entartung, 1893 ; Das Recht zu lieben, 1894 ; Die Kugel, 1895 ; Drohnenschlacht, 1896 ; La funzione sociale dell arte, 1897 ; Doctor Kohn, 1898 ; The Drones must Die, 1899; Zeitgenössische Franzosen, 1901; Morganatic, 1904 ; Mahâ-Rôg, 1905 ; On Art and Artists, 1907 ; Der Sinn der Geschichte, 1909 ; Zionistische Schriften, 1909 ; Märchen, 1910; Der Lebenssport, 1912 ; Franzosische Staatsmanner, 1916 ; Biologia de la Etica (Spanish), 1918 ; Impresiosmes espanolas (Spanish), 1920 ; Los Grandes del Arte espanol (Spanish), 1921 ; Moral and the Evolution of Man, 1922. *Recreations :* foil-fencing, swimming. *Address :* 14 Rue Henner, Paris.   (*Died 22 Jan. 1923.*)

NORDENSKJÖLD, Otto, Ph.D. ; Professor of Geography, University of Gothenburg ; *b.* 6 Dec. 1869 ; *m.* Karen Berg ; one *s.* three *d.* *Educ. :* University of Upsala. Arctic and Antarctic Explorer ; Leader of Scientific Expeditions to Terra del Fuego, 1895-97 ; Alaska and Yukon, 1898 ; the Antarctic Regions, 1901-4 ; West Greenland, 1909 ; South America and Patagonia, 1920 ; also to Spitzbergen, Iceland, etc. Most important studies : former extension of land-ice in South America ; remains of the extinct animal Neomylodon brought to Europe ; Antarctic ice conditions ; Cretaceous Fossils and Tertiary Vertebrates and Plant remains discovered in the Antarctic ; also Swedish Petrology ; Hon. Corresponding Member Royal Geographical Society, London ; Hon. Member Geographical Society, Paris, Berlin, Vienna, Rome, Madrid, Budapest, Brussels, Amsterdam, and others. *Publications :* Antarctica : the Swedish Antarctic Expedition, 1901-4 (in 7 languages) ; Die Polarwelt (Swedish, German, French, Russian) ; La Terre de Feu ; Südamerika ; and many others. *Address :* Göteborg, Sweden.   (*Died 2 June 1928.*)

NORFOLK, 15th Duke of (*cr.* 1483), **Henry FitzAlan-Howard,** K.G., P.C., J.P. Earl of Arundel, 1139 ; Baron Maltravers, 1330 ; Earl of Surrey, 1483 ; Baron Fitzalan, Clun, and Oswaldestre, 1627 ; Earl of Norfolk, 1644 ; Earl Marshal and Hereditary Marshal and Chief Butler of England ; Premier Duke and Earl ; K.G.C. of Order of Christ ; Lt.-Col. 4th Royal Sussex till 1912 ; Lord Lieut., Sussex, since 1905 ; *b.* Carlton Terrace, 27 Dec. 1847 ; *s.* of 14th Duke

and Augusta, *d.* of 1st Lord Lyons ; *S.* father 1860 ; *m.* 1st, Flora, *d.* of 1st Baron Donington and Edith, Countess of Loudoun, 1877 (*d.* 11 Apr. 1887) ; 2nd, 1904, Hon. Gwendolen Constable-Maxwell, now 13th Baroness Herries ; one *s.* three *d.* Special envoy to the Pope, 1887; Mayor of Sheffield, 1895-96 ; first Lord Mayor of Sheffield, 1896-97 ; Postmaster-General, 1895-1900 ; served South Africa, 1900. Owns about 49,900 acres. *Heir : s.* Earl of Arundel. *Address :* Norfolk House, St. James's Square, S.W. ; Arundel Castle, Sussex ; Derwent Hall, Derbyshire ; Beech Hill, Sheffield. *Clubs :* Carlton, Travellers', White's ; Royal Yacht Squadron, Cowes.

(*Died 11 Feb. 1917.*)

NORMAN, Rev. Alfred Merle, M.A., LL.D., D.C.L., F.R.S., F.L.S. ; Medallist of the "Institute" of France ; Gold Medal, Linnean Society, 1906 ; Hon. Canon of Durham since 1885 : late Rector of Houghton-le-Spring, Co. Durham, and Rural Dean ; *b.* 1831 ; *s.* of John Norman, D.L., Iwood House, Somerset. *Educ. :* Winchester; Christ Church, Oxford. A marine zoologist and the author of very many publications on the subject. His extensive collections of the invertebrate fauna of the North Atlantic and Arctic Oceans are now in the British Museum, and his scientific library has been given to the University of Cambridge. Landowner in Somersetshire. *Address :* The Red House, Berkhamsted, Herts.(*Died 26 Oct. 1918.*)

NORMAN, Arthur William, I.S.O., B.A., B.Sc. (Lond.) ; Assistant Secretary, Estate Duty Office, Inland Revenue, 1908-13 ; *b.* 1 May 1850 ; *s.* of late W. J. Norman ; *m.* 1883 ; Irene, *d.* of late Rev. Gideon R. J. Ouseley ; one *s.* one *d.* *Educ. :* private ; University College. Gower Street, and King's College, W.C. Entered Inland Revenue Department, 1867 ; graduated at London University in Arts and Science. *Publications :* A Digest of the Death Duties (3rd ed. 1911) ; Death Duty Tables, etc. *Recreation :* walking. *Address :* Kilfinane, Seafield Road, Southbourne-on-Sea, Hants.   (*Died 24 Nov. 1923.*)

NORMAN, Edward, Banker ; Chairman, Bank of Liverpool and Martin's Ltd., London Board, since 1919 ; *b.* Bromley Common, Kent, 1847 ; *y. s.* of late George Warde Norman, of Bromley Common, Kent ; *m.* 1875, Eleanor Mary (*d.* 1911), *y. d.* of Rev. Aretas Akers of Malling Abbey, Maidstone, Kent ; one *d.* *Educ. :* Eton. Clerk in House of Commons, 1870-81 ; Assistant Secretary to Public Works Loan Board, 1881-83 ; Partner in firm of Martin & Co., Bankers, 1883-1891 ; Director of Martin's Bank, Ltd., 1891 ; Chairman of Public Works Loan Commission, 1908-1921 ; Director of Guardian Assurance Company, Ltd., of Buenos Ayres and Pacific Railway Company, Ltd. ; and of Commercial Bank of Spanish America, Ltd. *Recreations :* formerly lawn tennis, shooting, cricket, hunting and football. *Address :* Chelsfield House, Chelsfield, Kent ; 68 Lombard Street, E.C. *Club :* Windham.

(*Died 5 Feb. 1923.*)

NORMAN, Commander F. M., R.N. ; author, pseudonym Martello Tower ; *b.* 1833 ; *s.* of Robert C. Norman of Kent ; unmarried. *Educ. :* Harrow. Entered Royal Navy, 1848 ; retired as commander, 1863 ; assisted to land allied armies in Crimea ; served for 4 months with the original Naval Brigade before Sebastopol ; wounded in a boat action in China, 1857 ; J.P. for, Hon. Freeman, and twice Mayor of Berwick-on-Tweed ; Fellow of the Botanical Society of Edinburgh. *Decorated :* Crimea—Inkerman and Sebastopol clasps ; Medjidie, 5th class ; China, 1856-58. *Publications :* At School and at Sea ; Martello Tower in China ; History of H.M.S. Havannah ; Manual of School Drill (14 editions) ; Manual of English Grammar for School Teachers (5 editions) ; Guide to the Fortifications of Berwick-on-Tweed. *Recreations:* tastes and employments lie in the direction of natural history and of church work; holds many honorary public offices; has lectured and contributed a number of papers on Natural History matters to Club Proceedings, and on other subjects to the Newcastle Diocesan Conference. *Address:* Cheviot House, Berwick-on-Tweed. (*Died 6 Oct. 1918.*)

NORMAND, Mrs. Ernest (Henrietta Rae), painter of Classical Pictures; *b.* London, 30 Dec. 1859; *y. d.* of late T. B. Rae; *m.* 1884, Ernest Normand (*d.* 1923), the painter; one *s.* one *d. Educ.:* Queen's Square School of Art, Heatherley's, British Museum, Royal Academy Schools; Paris. Medallist at Paris and Chicago Universal Exhibitions. Commenced to study Art at the age of 13. Exhibited first picture at the Royal Academy, 1880; has been represented at the R. A. each succeeding year by important pictures. *Principal paintings:* Ariadne, 1885; A Naiad, 1886; Eurydice, 1886; Doubts, 1887; Zephyrus and Flora, 1888; Death of Procris, 1889; Ophelia, 1890; La Cigale, 1891; Flowers Plucked and Cast Aside, 1892; Mariana, 1893; Psyche at the Throne of Venus, 1894; Apollo and Daphne, 1895; Summer, 1896; Isabella, 1897; Diana and Calisto, 1899. Decoration in Fresco for the Royal Exchange, subject: Sir Richard Whittington and his Charities, 1900; Portrait of first Marquess of Dufferin and Ava, 1901; The Sirens, 1903; Songs of the Morning, 1904; In Listening Mood, 1905; Portrait of The Lady Tenterden and Echo, 1906; Roses of Youth, 1907; Abelard and Heloise, 1908; Hylas and the Water Nymphs, 1910; Spring's Awakening, 1913; Portrait of Sir Robt. Anderson, Bart., ex-Lord Mayor of Belfast, 1912; Portrait of Lady M'Culloch, 1918; Nemesis, and a Portrait of Frederick, third Marquess of Dufferin and Ava, 1919; Portrait of the Rt. Hon. Sir James Johnston, ex-Lord Mayor of Belfast, and a portrait of John Johnston of Lurgan, 1921; Summer, and Portrait of Miss Moyna Macgill, 1922; Portrait of Ald. T. E. McConnell, M.P., 1925. *Recreation:* gardening. *Address:* 4 Fox Hill Gardens, Upper Norwood, S.E.19. *T.:* Sydenham 1949. *M.:* YN 1806. *Club:* Lyceum. (*Died 26 Mar. 1928.*)

NORREYS, Lord; Montague Edmund Henry Cecil Towneley - Bertie; *b.* 2 Nov. 1887; *g. s.* of 7th Earl of Abingdon, and *e. s.* of late Lord Norreys and Hon. Rose Riversdale Glyn, *sister* of 4th Lord Wolverton. Grenadier Guards. Formerly Capt. Royal Anglesey R.E.; Temp. Flight Sub.-Lt., R.N.A.S.; has been employed under the Egyptian Government; served European War (wounded). *Address:* 35 York Terrace, Regent's Park, N.W.1. (*Died 24 Sept. 1919.*)

NORRIS, George Michael, I.S.O. 1902; LL.B.; late First Class Clerk, Board of Education; *b.* 11 Sept. 1841; *s.* of late Wm. Norris of Hornsey Lane; unmarried. *Educ.:* at an Islington School. As Society of Arts' Prizeman received a nomination to compete for a clerkship in the Board of Education, 1864; reorganised the Birkbeck College; was a vice-presidential member of the governing body of the Birkbeck College, one of the first Hon. Secs. of the London Society for the Extension of University Teaching, and a member of the City of London College Council. *Recreations:* reading and walking. (*Died 11 Nov. 1922.*)

NORRIS, William Edward, novelist; *s.* of late Sir William Norris, formerly Chief Justice of Ceylon. *Educ.:* Eton. Barr. Inner Temple, 1874, but has never practised. *Publications:* Heaps of Money, 1877; Mademoiselle de Mersac; Matrimony; My Friend Jim; The Rogue; Adrian Vidal; Matthew Austin; The Dancer in Yellow, 1896; Clarissa Furiosa, 1897; Marietta's Marriage, 1897; The Fight for the Crown, 1898; The Widower, 1898; Giles Ingilby, 1899; An Octave, 1900; The Flower of the Flock, 1900; His Own Father, 1901; The

Embarrassing Orphan, 1901; The Credit of the County, 1902; Lord Leonard the Luckless, 1903; Nature's Comedian, 1904; Barham of Beltana, 1905; Harry and Ursula, 1907; Pauline, 1908; The Perjurer, 1909; Not Guilty, 1910; The Rt. Hon. Gentleman, 1913; Barbara and Company, 1914; Proud Peter, 1916; The Fond Fugitives, 1917; The Obstinate Lady, 1919; The Triumphs of Sara, 1920; Tony the Exceptional, 1921; Sabine and Sabina, 1922; Next of Kin, 1923; The Conscience of Gavin Blane, 1924; Trevalion, 1925. *Recreation:* golf. *Address:* Bellair, Torquay. *Clubs:* National, Windham. (*Died 19 Nov. 1925.*)

NORTH, Col. Dudley, C.B. 1896; *b.* 8 Oct. 1840; *o. surv. s.* of late Dudley North and Sarah, *d.* of Major Lockyer of Lockyersleigh, New South Wales. *Educ.:* Harrow. Joined 47th Regt. 1858; Capt. 1866; Special Service Officer, Gold Coast, 1878-74 (dangerously wounded, despatches, medal and clasp, Brevet Major); A.D.C. to Governor of Malta, 1875-78; commanded the wing North Lancashire Regt. with the Zhob Valley Expedition, 1884; A.A.G. Canada, 1892-97; retired, 1897. *Address:* 23 Down Street, W. *Clubs:* Naval and Military, United Service. (*Died 22 Nov. 1917.*)

NORTH, Colonel Edward, C.B. 1917; retired; late H.M. Army Medical Service; *b.* Dec. 1856; unmarried. *Educ.:* Privately. Served S. African War (despatches); European War, 1914-17 (despatches, C.B.). *Club:* Junior United Service. (*Died 6 June 1927.*)

NORTH, Frederic Dudley, C.M.G. 1902; J.P.; Under Secretary Colonial Secretary's Department, W. Australia, since 1902, and Comptroller-General of Prisons since 1912; four times President of the Civil Service Association: Mayor of Cottesloe for four years in succession, is also President of Civil Service Club for 6th time; *b.* 9 Nov. 1866; *e. s.* of Charles Augustus North and Rachel Elizabeth, *d.* of Sir Francis Grant, P.R.A.; *m.* 1887, Flora Frances, *y. d.* of Edward Hamersley; two *s.* two *d. Educ.:* Rugby. *Address:* Catlidge, Cottesloe, Western Australia. *Clubs:* Carlton; Weld, Civil Service, Perth. (*Died 22 Aug. 1921.*)

NORTH, Sir Harry, Kt., *cr.* 1905; *e. s.* of late Col. John T. North of Avery Hill, Eltham, Kent; *b.* 26 Dec. 1866; *m.* Jessie L., *d.* of late David Evans, J.P., of Cliffden, Saltburn, and Middlesborough, Yorks; one *s.* two *d. Educ.:* Jesus College, Cambridge. Captain and Hon. Major, 4th Batt. (Mil.) Royal Munster Fusiliers; retired, 1905; one of H.M.'s Lieutenants for the City of London; Hon. Lt.-Col. City of London Royal Engineer Cadet Training Corps. *Address:* Lemon Well, Eltham, Kent. *T.:* 187 Lee Green. *M.:* LE 5236. *Clubs:* Carlton, Junior Carlton, Royal Automobile, Royal Thames Yacht. (*Died 26 Nov. 1920.*)

NORTH, John W., A.R.A. 1893; R.W.S. *Address:* Washford, Taunton. *Club:* Arts. (*Died 20 Dec. 1924.*)

NORTHBOURNE, 2nd Baron, *cr.* 1884. **Walter Henry James,** D.L., J.P.; Bart. 1791; Hon. Col. 5th Batt. Durham Light Infantry 1895 - 1921, and Cinque Ports Vol. Artillery; *b.* 25 Mar. 1846; *s.* of 1st Baron and Sarah, *d.* of Cuthbert Ellison, Hebburn Hall, Durham; *S.* father 1893; *m.* Edith, *d.* of John Newton - Lane, King's Bromley Manor, Stafford, and *d.* of 2nd Baron Bagot, 1868; three *s.* one *d. Educ.:* Radley; Christ Ch., Oxford (M.A.). M.P. (L.) Gateshead, 1874-93. Owns about 6700 acres. *Heir: s.* Hon. W. J. James. *Address:* Betteshanger, Dover. *Club:* Travellers'. (*Died 27 Jan. 1923.*)

NORTHCLIFFE, 1st Viscount, of St. Peter in the County of Kent, *cr.* 1917: **Alfred Charles William Harmsworth,** Bt.; *cr.* 1904; Baron Northcliffe of the Isle of Thanet, *cr.* 1905; newspaper proprietor; *b.* 15 July 1865, Chapelizod, Co. Dublin; *e. s.* of late

Alfred Harmsworth, of the Middle Temple, barrister-at-law, and Geraldine Mary, *d.* of William Maffett, Pembroke Place, Co. Dublin; *m.* 1888, Mary Elizabeth, G.B.E., R.R.C., *e. d.* of late Robert Milner, Kidlington, Oxford, and St. Vincent, West Indies; Hon. LL.D.; Rochester University, U.S.A.; Chairman of the British War Mission to the U.S.A. 1917; Chairman British War Mission, 1917-18; Director of Propaganda in Enemy Countries, 1918, and of the Civil Aerial Transport Committee, 1917. *Heir:* none. *Publication:* At the War, 1916. *Address:* 1 Carlton Gardens, S.W.; Elmwood, St. Peter's, Thanet; Buckthorn Hill, Crowborough, Sussex; Chapelizod, Co. Dublin. *Club:* Beefsteak. *(Died 14 Aug. 1922.)*

NORTHCOTE, Rev. the Hon. John Stafford; Chaplain to the King; Prebendary of St. Paul's, 1906; Hon. Sec. of London Diocesan Church Schools Association; Chairman of Grey Coat Hospital Schools; Fellow of King's College, London, 1913; *b.* London, 3 Jan. 1850; 3rd *s.* of 1st Earl of Iddesleigh; *m.* 1881, Hilda (*d.* 1908), 2nd *d.* of Dean Farrar; one *s.* two *d. Educ.:* Eton; King's Coll. London; A.K.C. 1878. Mechanical Engineer, at Beyer and Peacock's Locomotive Factory, Manchester, at Sir W. G. Armstrong and Company, Newcastle, 1867-73; Inspector of Railway Material and Locomotive Engines under the Indian Government, 1873-76; ordained, 1878; Curate of St. Margaret's, Westminster, 1878-81; Rector of Upton Pyne, near Exeter, 1881-89; Vicar of St. Andrew, Westminster, 1889-1916; Chairman of Council, Girls' Public Day School Trust. *Recreation:* Member of the first Rugby football team that played for Manchester. *Address:* 33 Rossetti Garden Mansions, S.W.3. *T.:* Kensington 7098.

(Died 5 June 1920.)

NORTHCOTT, Rev. William, M.A.; Vicar of Atherstone since 1888; Canon of Coventry, 1918; *b.* 16 July 1854; *s.* of James Northcott, late of Fir Lodge, Denmark Hill; *m.* 1880, Nora Catherine Marie, *d.* of Rev. G. F. Mathews, Vicar of Mancetter, and Rural Dean of Atherstone; four *s.* four *d. Educ.:* S. John's College, Cambridge. (Foundation Scholar); 2nd Class, Classical Tripos; Vicar of Hartshill, 1880-88; Chaplain Atherstone Union since 1908. *Publications:* Occasional sermons and hymns. *Recreations:* chess, etc.; formerly golf, lawn tennis, rowing and football. *Address:* The Vicarage, Atherstone. *(Died 12 Oct. 1924.)*

NORTHESK, 10th Earl of (*cr.* 1647), David John Carnegie, D.L., J.P.; Baron Rosehill, 1639; Captain 3rd Batt. Gloucestershire Regt. since 1888; a Representative Peer for Scotland; *b.* 1 Dec. 1865; *s.* of 9th Earl and Elizabeth, *d.* of Admiral Sir George Elliot, K.C.B.; *S.* father 1891; *m.* Elizabeth, *d.* of Maj.-Gen. George Skene-Hallowes, 1894; one *s.* one *d. Educ.:* Eton. A.D.C. to Governor of Victoria, Earl of Hopetoun, 1889-91, and 1892-95. Owns about 10,000 acres. *Heir: s.* Lord Rosehill. *Address:* 6 Hans Crescent, S.W.1; *T.:* Victoria 1092; Ethie Castle, Arbroath, Forfarshire; Whitley Ridge, Brockenhurst, Hants.

(Died 5 Dec. 1921.)

NORTHROP, Cyrus, LL.D. Yale, Wisconsin, Illinois, and South Carolina; President of University of Minnesota, 1884-1911, now Emeritus; *b.* Ridgefield, Conn., 30 Sept. 1834; *y. c.* of Cyrus and Polly B. (Fancher) Northrop; *m.* 1862, Anna Elizabeth, *d.* of Joseph D. Warren of Stamford, Conn.; one *s.* one *d. Educ.:* Yale; B.A., LL.B., LL.D. Clerk of Senate and House of Representatives of Connecticut, 1860-62; Editor of New Haven Daily Palladium, 1862-63; Professor of Rhetoric and English Literature in Yale College, 1863-1884; Candidate for Congress, 1867. *Address:* Minneapolis, Minnesota, U.S.A. *Clubs:* Congrega-

784

tional, Commercial, Publicity, University, Yale. *(Died 3 April 1922.)*

NORTHRUP, William Barton, M.A., K.C., Canada; Clerk Canadian House of Commons, 1918-24; Barrister; Church of England. *Address:* Ottawa, Canada. *Clubs:* Rideau, Country, Ottawa; Royal Canadian Yacht, Albany, Toronto; Belleville. Belleville. *(Died Oct. 1925.)*

NORTHUMBERLAND, 7th Duke of (*cr.* 1766), Henry George Percy, K.G., P.C., LL.D., D.C.L., F.R.S., J.P., D.L.; Earl of Northumberland, Baron Warkworth, 1749; Earl Percy, 1766; Earl of Beverley, 1790; Lord Lovaine, Baron of Alnwick, 1784; Trustee of the British Museum since 1900; Lord-Lieutenant of Northumberland; Chancellor of Durham; *b.* 29 May 1846; *e. s.* of 6th Duke and Louisa, *d.* of Henry Drummond, Albury Park, Surrey; *S.* father 1899; *m.* Lady Edith Campbell (*d.* 1913), *d.* of 8th Duke of Argyll, 1868; three *s.* five *d. Educ.:* Oxford. Hon. Col. 3rd Batt. Northumberland Fusiliers, and 1st Northumberland Artillery Volunteers; M.P. (C.) N. Northumberland, 1868-85; Treasurer of Household, 1874-75; President of Archæological Institute, 1884-92. *Heir:* Earl Percy. *Address:* 2 Grosvenor Place, S.W.; *T.:* Victoria 1462; Albury Park, Guildford; Alnwick Castle, Northumberland; Syon House, Brentford; Kielder Castle, North Tyne. *Clubs:* Athenæum, Carlton, St. Stephen's, Travellers'; Northumberland and Northern Counties. *(Died 14 May 1918.)*

NORTON, 2nd Baron (*cr.* 1878), Charles Leigh Adderley; *b.* 10 Mar. 1846; *e. s.* of 1st Baron Norton and Hon. Julia Anne Eliza Leigh, *e. d.* of 1st Lord Leigh; *m.* 1870, Caroline Ellen, *d.* of Sir Alexander Dixie, 10th Bart.; three *s.* four *d.* Church of England. Conservative. Formerly Assistant Local Government Board Inspector, and Private Sec. to his father as Pres. of Board of Trade. Owns about 4600 acres; Saltley estate came by marriage, *temp.* Charles I., with heiress of Arden family. *Heir: s.* Hon. Ralph Bowyer Adderley. *Address:* Wellington Lodge, Bredon, Worcestershire. *(Died 4 Dec. 1926.)*

NORTON, Major Alfred Edward Marston, D.S.O. 1900; F.R.G.S; *b.* 13 July 1869; *s.* of late John Norton of Golding Hall, Salop; *m.* 1895, Fannie Margaret Stacy. Served South Africa, 1900 (despatches, Queen's medal, 2 clasps, D.S.O.); European War (Bt. Lt.-Col.). *Club:* Naval and Military. *(Died 8 June 1922.)*

NORTON, Edward, J.P., Director of Royal Mail Steam Packet Co., Union Castle S.S. Co., and Nelson Lines; 2nd *s.* of late Edward Norton of Scole, Norfolk; *b.* 1841; *m.* 1st, Edith, *d.* of late Charles Lamport of Bindon House, Somerset; 2nd, Edith Sarah, *d.* of late Rt. Hon. Sir Alfred Wills of Saxholm, Bassett; four *s.* two *d. Address:* Uplands, Fareham, Hants. *Club:* Union. *(Died 20 May 1923.)*

NORTON, Ven. John George, Rector of Christ Church Cathedral, Montreal, and Rector of Montreal since 1902; Archdeacon of Montreal since 1902; *b.* 28 Oct. 1840; 2nd *s.* of late William Norton, Hollybank, Arva, Co. Cavan, and Sarah A. Richmond; *m.* 1st, 1873, Lucy Durham, *d.* of late William Henderson, F.R.H.S.; 2nd, 1902, Amelia Josephine, *d.* of late Stanley C. Bagg, Montreal; one *s.* one *d. Educ.:* Trinity College, Dublin (M.A., D.D.). Ordained, 1865; Curate of Kilmacrenan, 1865-67; Mullabrack, 1867-69; St. Nicholas, Durham, 1869-72; Vicar of St. Giles, Durham, 1872-84; Archdeacon of St. Andrews, P.Q., 1900-1902; Canon of Montreal, 1893-1902. *Publications:* Hearty Services or Revived Church Worship, 3rd ed., 1888; Worship in Heaven and on Earth, 1884. *Address:* The Rectory, 441 University Street, Montreal. *(Died Sept. 1924.)*

NORTON, Rt. Rev. John Henry, D.D., 3rd Bishop of Port Augusta since 1906; *b.* Ballarat, Victoria, 31 Dec. 1855. *Educ.:* private schools and colleges at Ballarat; with the Jesuits at Melbourne; St. Kieran's College, Kilkenny; Propaganda, Rome. Received minor orders from Archbishop Goold at Melbourne, 1876; Deaconship at Rome, 1881; Priest at Rome by Cardinal Monaco la Valetta, 1882; affiliated to the Diocese of Adelaide, and arrived there, 1883; appointed to the Cathedral; first Resident Parish Priest of Petersburg, 1884; Diocesan Consultor; Vicar-General, 1896; Administrator of the Diocese, 1905. *Address:* Bishop's House, Petersburg, South Australia.
(Died 22 Mar. 1923.)

NORTON, Professor Richard; *b.* Feb. 1872; *s.* of Charles Eliot Norton, Professor of the History of Fine Arts at Harvard University, and Susan Sedgwick. *Educ.:* private schools and Harvard University. Studied at American School of Classical Studies in Athens, and the University of Munich, 1892-95; Prof. of History of Fine Arts at Bryn Mawr, Penn. 1895-97; Assistant Director American School of Archæology in Rome, 1897-99; Director, 1899-1907; Director of American Expedition to Cyrene 1910 and 1911; 1914, organised the American Volunteer Motor Ambulance Corps, which has served since then on the French front and has been *cité* twice. *Publications:* Bernini and other Essays, 1915; articles on archæological and kindred subjects in the American Journal of Archæology, Journal of Hellenic Studies, Encyclopædia Britannica, and catalogue of casts in Museum of Fine Arts at Portland, Oregon. *Recreations:* out-door sports. *Address:* c/o Brown, Shipley, and Co., 123 Pall Mall, S.W. *Club:* Brook, New York.
(Died 2 Aug. 1918.)

NORTON, Robert, J.P., D.L.; *b.* 11 Oct. 1838; *s.* of late William Norton of Burcote House, Co. Northampton; *m.* 1st, 1867, Amelia Harriett (*d.* 1900), *d.* of late Rev. John Duncombe Shafto; two s. two d.; 2nd, 1903, Isabel, *d.* of late Hugh Lee Pattinson. Called to Bar at Middle Temple, 1865; M.P. S.W. Kent, 1885-1892; High Sheriff, 1910. *Address:* Downs House, Yalding, Maidstone; St. Mary's, Boscombe, Hants. *Club:* Carlton.
(Died 7 June 1926.)

NOTTER, Colonel J. Lane-, M.A., M.D., D.P.H., R.A.M.C. (retired); *b.* Carrigduve, Co. Cork; *s.* of late Richard Notter of Rock Island and Carrigduve, Co. Cork, and Margaret, *d.* of James Lane of Riverstown, Co. Cork; *m.* Fannie, *d.* of Surgeon-General J. D. McIlree, A.M.S.; one *d. Educ.:* Trin. Coll. Dublin (Fellow Commoner). Entered Army Medical Service, 1866 (First Place); subsequently served in Canada and Malta as Assistant-Surgeon, Royal Artillery; Assistant-Professor, and subsequently Professor, of Military Hygiene, Army Medical School at Netley; on Special Duty at Headquarters, S.A. Field Force; ex-President Epidemiological Society of London; Fellow, Royal Society of Medicine; Governor of Wellington College, Berks.; Fellow and Member of Council, Royal Sanitary Institute; late Examiner in Hygiene, Board of Secondary Education, South Kensington; has been Examiner in Public Health at Cambridge University, Leeds, and Liverpool Universities, Royal Colleges of Physicians and Surgeons, London, and Victoria Universities, and University of Wales; Hon. Member Hungarian Society of Public Health; Delegate to represent Foreign Office and War Office, and H.M. Plenipotentiary to sign the Convention at Venice, 1897; Hon. Associate Order of St. John of Jerusalem; Delegate to following Congresses on behalf of War Office—Berlin, 1890; Chicago, 1893; Rome, 1894; Buda-Pesth, 1894. *Publications:*

The Theory and Practice of Hygiene (with Col. R. H. Firth); Hygiene, 9th edition, 1908; Practical Domestic Hygiene, 5th edition, 1907; editor, 8th edition Parke's Manual of Practical Hygiene; author of sections Air and Military Hygiene in Murphy and Stevenson's Treatise on Hygiene and Public Health, 1892; Hygiene of the Tropics in Davidson's Diseases of Warm Climates; Enteric Fever in the European Army in India, its Etiology and Prevention, Transactions International Hygienic Congress, 1892; section Hygiene, Ency. Brit., Times edition, 1902; and various papers on Hygiene and Preventive Medicine in other works and periodicals. *Recreations:* yachting, photography, travel. *Address:* 3 Kensington Mansions, Earl's Court, S.W.; Rock Island, Co. Cork. *Club:* Athenæum.
(Died 24 Oct. 1923.)

NOTTINGHAM, Rev. Edward Emil, M.A.; Rector of Sutton-upon-Derwent, York, since 1918; *b.* 1866; *s.* of late Edward Nottingham, Pilsgate, Stamford; *m.* Ada Annie, *d.* of late Skelton Smalley, Pilsgate, Stamford; one *s.* two *d. Educ.:* Stratford-on-Avon and Stamford Grammar Schools; St. Catharine's Col., Cambridge. Senior Classical Scholar and Librarian Scholar; 2nd class Classical Tripos, 1888; Second Master, King Alfred's School, Wantage, 1888-89; Loughborough School, 1889-94; Curate of Loughborough, 1893-94; Assistant Master and Chaplain of Eastbourne College, 1894-95; Vice-Principal, Training College, Chester, 1895-98; Principal of Diocesan Training College, York, 1898-1903; Vicar of Acaster Selby with Appleton Roebuck, 1910-18; Assistant Master, St. Peter's School, York, 1917-18 (war work). *Recreations:* golf, travelling. *Address:* The Rectory, Sutton-on-Derwent, Yorks.
(Died 10 Mar. 1921.)

NOVIKOFF, Mme. Olga (*née* Kireeff—"O.K."); Russian political writer; *b.* Moscow, 1848; *d.* of Alexis Kireeff, Hussar-Guards Officer of St. George's Cross, and Alexandra Alabieff (mentioned in poems of Pushkin Lermontoff, etc.); *m.* Lieut.-General John Novikoff (*b.* of the Ambassador at Vienna), Rector of St. Petersburg University (*d.* 1890). Began writing political articles in the hope of continuing the work of her brother who was killed in the Turkish War in defending the Slavonic cause, in addition to which she pleaded for Anglo-Russian alliance and friendship; nicknamed by Disraeli, M.P. for Russia, the title of Mr. W. T. Stead's Biography; co-worker with Mr. Gladstone in the Slavonic Cause. *Publications:* Is Russia Wrong? Friends or Foes; Russia and England; Skobeleff and the Slavonic Cause; Russian Memories; many articles in Pall Mall Gazette, Westminster Gazette, in 1916-17, chiefly in the Asiatic Review and National Opinion, monthly reviews, and French and Russian reviews and papers; Pamphlets: Searchlights on Russia; More Searchlights on Russia. *Address:* 4 Brunswick Place, Regent's Park, N.W.1. *T.:* Langham 2619.
(Died 21 April 1925.)

NUGENT, Algernon John FitzRoy, *e. s.* of 3rd Baron Nugent and Elizabeth, *e. d.* of Theodore Balbazzi, Constantinople; *b.* 5 Oct. 1865; *m.* 1895, Clara, *d.* of Sir George Eliott Meyrick Tapps-Gervase-Meyrick, 3rd Bart.; no *c. Educ.:* Winchester; Trinity College, Cambridge. *Recreations:* captain of first Trinity Boat Club and stroke of the eight in 1887; a keen but only fair golfer; a keen musician; a breeder of Dandie Dinmont terriers, which he exhibits and judges. *Heir:* bro. Albert Beauchamp Nugent, *b.* 12 Feb. 1874. *Address:* Gally Hill, Crookham, Fleet, Hants. *T.A.:* Church, Crookham. *T.:* Fleet 33. *Clubs:* Oxford and Cambridge, M.C.C., Leander.
(Died 15 Mar. 1923.)

NORWOOD, Rev. Reginald. See page xxvii.

NUGENT, Sir Charles, 5th Bt., *cr.* 1795; Count of Holy Roman Empire; Lieut. 17th Lancers; retired, 1869; *b.* 7 Feb. 1847; *S. b.* 1863; *m.* Emily, *d.* of Thomas Walker, Park Lane, W., and Berkswell-Hall, Warwickshire, 1871. Cornet of Regt. 1866. *Heir: g. s.* Hugh Charles, *b.* 26 May 1904. *Address:* Ballinlough Castle, Co. Westmeath. *(Died 22 May 1927.)*

NUGENT, Colonel (Temp. Col. Cmdt.) Charles Hugh Hodges, C.I.E. 1916; C.B.E. 1920; M.I.M.E.; *b.* 11 Dec. 1868; *s.* of late Col. Sir C. B. P. N. H. Nugent, K.C.B., R.E.; *m.* Jessie, *d.* of late Maj.-Gen. Wray, C.B., R.A. 2nd Lieut. R.E. 1888; Captain, 1899; Major, 1907; Lt.-Col. 1915; Col. 1919; Inspector of Iron Structures at War Office, 1899-1905; original member of War Office Mechanical Transport Committee; Inspector of Machinery, Army Headquarters, Simla, from 1911; formerly member of Trials Committee Royal Automobile Club; raised and organised mechanical transport services in India, Aden, Mesopotamia, etc., 1914-18 (despatches); served with North-West Frontier Field Force against Afghans, 1919 (despatches); employed as Assist. Commanding Royal Engineers, Presidency District; Deputy Director Military Works, United Provinces District, Meerut, India. *Clubs:* Junior United Service, Royal Automobile, Ranelagh; United Service, Simla.
(Died 2 Dec. 1924.)

NUGENT, Sir Edmund Charles, 3rd Bt. *cr.* 1806; D.L., J.P.; Capt. Grenadier Guards; retired, 1862; *b.* 12 Mar. 1839; 2nd *s.* of 2nd Bt. and Hon. Maria Charlotte, 2nd *d.* of Lord Colborne; *S.* father 1892; *m.* 1868, Evelyn (*d.* 1922), *d.* of Gen. E. F. Gascoigne; one *s.* two *d.* Entered army, 1857; High Sheriff Norfolk, 1900. *Heir: g.s.* George Guy Bulwer Nugent, *b.* 5 Nov. 1892. *Address:* West Harling Hall, Attleborough. *Clubs:* Carlton, Travellers'.
(Died 4 Dec. 1928.)

NUGENT, Sir Horace Dickinson, K.B.E., *cr.* 1923; C.M.G. 1917; H.M. Consul-General at Chicago, 1909-23; *b.* 26 Feb. 1858; *s.* of Wm. Tasker Nugent, late of the Foreign Office and H.M. Consular Service; *m.* 1893, Antoinette, *y. d.* of late Clement Guion of New York; one *s. Educ.:* Haileybury. Employed in Foreign Office, 1880-81; Vice-Consul attached to British Legation, Bucharest, Roumania, 1881-1886; Junior Vice-Consul, New York, 1886-91; Senior Vice-Consul, 1891-92; Consul for Texas and New Mexico, 1892-1909; Coronation medal, 1911. *Recreations:* golf, fishing. *Club:* Royal Societies. *(Died 30 April 1924.)*

NUGENT. Maj.-Gen. Sir Oliver Stewart Wood, K.C.B., *cr.* 1922; C.B. 1917; D.S.O.; late 60th Rifles; J.P., D.L.; *b.* 9 Nov. 1860; *s.* of late Major-General St. George M. Nugent and Emily, *d.* of Rt. Hon. Edward Litton; *m.* 1899, Catharine Percy, *d.* of late T. Evans Lees and of Mrs. Lees of Beaucroft, Wimborne, Dorset; one *s.* two *d. Educ.:* Harrow. Entered King's Royal Rifles, 1883; Capt. 1890; Maj. 1899; served Hazara Expedition, 1891 (medal with clasp); Samana Expedition, 1891 (despatches, clasp); Izazai Expedition, 1892; Chitral Relief Force, 1895, including Malakand Pass (slightly wounded); engagement at Khar (despatches, D.S.O., medal with clasp); South Africa, 1899-1900 (dangerously wounded, despatches, Queen's medal 2 clasps); European War, 1914-18 (Maj.-Gen.); retired pay, 1920. *Address:* Farren Connell, Mount Nugent, Co. Cavan. *Clubs:* Army and Navy; Kildare Street, Dublin.
(Died 31 May 1926.)

NUGENT, Colonel Robert Arthur, C.B. 1884; C.M.G. 1917; retired; *b.* Bruges, Belgium, 1 Aug. 1853; 2nd *s.* of late Robert Nugent and Emma, *d.* of John Hunter; *m.* Marion (*d.* 1924), *y. d.* of T. Smith, of Weston-super-Mare, and *widow* of F. Hitchcock, of

786

Four Courts, Dublin, 1876. *Educ.:* The Athenée, Bruges; Hartley Coll., Southampton. Joined Control Department, 1872; Ashanti War, 1873-1874 (medal); Egyptian Expedition, 1882-84; Tel-el-Kebir; El Teb; Tamai; Soudan Campaign, 1884-85; Abu Klea and Gubat (medal 5 clasps, 4th class Medjidie, bronze star, despatches); Brevet Colonel, 1898; Substantive Colonel, 1898; Assistant Director Military Transport, Woolwich Arsenal, 1914-18. *Decorated:* Suakim, 1884; Expedition under Sir Gerald Graham, V.C. *Recreations:* golf; fishing. *M.: KL.* 4583. *Club:* United Service. *(Died 12 Aug. 1926.)*

NUNBURNHOLME, 2nd Baron, *cr.* 1905; **Charles Henry Wellesley Wilson;** C.B. 1918; D.S.O. 1900; late Maj. 2nd Vol. Batt. East Yorkshire Regt.; *b.* 1875; *s.* of 1st Baron and Florence, O.B.E., *d.* of Col. W. H. C. Wellesley; *S.* father 1907; *m.* 1901, Lady Marjorie Wynn-Carrington, *d.* of 1st Marquis of Lincolnshire; two *s.* one *d. Educ.:* Eton. Served South Africa, 1900 (Queen's medal, 4 clasps, D.S.O.); European War, Captain R.G.A.; M.P. (L.) Hull, 1906-7; H.M. Lieut. East Riding of Yorkshire. *Heir: s.* Hon. Charles John Wilson. *Address:* 41 Berkeley Square, W.1. *T.:* Mayfair 6591; Hunmanby Hall, Hunmanby, E. Yorks. *Clubs:* Bachelors', National Liberal. *(Died 15 Aug. 1924.)*

NUNN, Rev. Henry Drury Cust; Vicar of Sharow, 1884; Rural Dean, Hon. Canon of Ripon Cathedral, and Proctor in Convocation in Archdeaconry of Ripon; *y. s.* of Rev. Thomas Nunn, Rector of Stansted, Kent; *m.* 1st Eliza Mary, *d.* of R. S. Francis; 2nd, Helena Sophia (*d.* 1909),*d.* of Rev. Canon Worsley; three *s.* one *d. Educ.:* Corpus Christi College, Cambridge (Scholar and Divinity Prizeman, M.A.). Curate of St. Andrew's, Leeds, 1868; Minor Canon and Vicar of Ripon, 1872; Surrogate. *Publication:* Sons of Heaven and Sons of Earth. *Recreations:* Cricket and sketching. *Address:* Sharow Cottage, Ripon. *(Died 7 Jan. 1922.)*

NUTT, Alfred Young. M.V.O. 1906; I.S.O. 1911; late resident architect H.M. Office of Works, Windsor Castle; *b.* 1847; *s.* of late W. Y. Nutt, Rector of Cold Overton; *m.* 1873, Mary, *d.* of J. George; three *d.* Entered Office of Works, 1867; surveyor to Dean and Canons of Windsor, 1874; carried out exterior restoration work at St. George's Chapel and designed Jubilee celebration decorations at Windsor and Eton, 1887-97; architect for Westminster Abbey annexe at Coronation, 1902; also for Coronation annexe, King George V., 1911; retired, 1912. *Address:* Morcott West, Slough, Bucks.
(Died 24 July 1924.)

NUTT, Col. James Anson Francis. Entered army 1866; Capt. 1878; Major, 1884; Lieut.-Col. 1893; Col. 1897; served Afghan War, 1880 (medal); commanded R.A., North-West Frontier of India, 1898 (medal and clasp); commanded R.A., Eastern District. 1899; commanded R.A., Natal Field Force, from Vaal Krantz to relief of Ladysmith (medal and two clasps). *Club:* Naval and Military.
(Died 23 Jan. 1924.)

NUTTALL, Sir Edmund, 1st Bt., *cr.* 1922; A.M.I.C.E., head of the firm of Edmund Nuttall & Co., Civil Engineering Contractors of Trafford Park, Manchester; *b.* 29 May 1870; *s.* of late James Nuttall of Manchester; *m.* 1895, Ethel Christine, 2nd *d.* of Rev. Frederick Lillington, M. A. Oxon; two *s. Educ.:* privately. Articled to the late Sir Edward Leader Williams, M.Inst. C.E., 1887; succeeded to his father's business, 1898; has been responsible for numerous engineering works of national importance. *Recreations:* shooting, and deep sea fishing. *Heir: s.* Edmund Keith, *b.* 27 March 1901. *Address:* Chastefield, Bowdon, Cheshire. *T. A.:* Tunnelling, Manchester. *T.:* Altrincham 1317; Trafford Park 310. *M.:*

NB 5840. *Clubs:* St. Stephen's; Constitutional, Manchester.   *(Died 11 Oct. 1928.)*

NUTTALL, Most Rev. Enos, Bishop of Jamaica since 1880, and Archbishop of the West Indies since 1897 ; B.D. 1879; D.D. 1880 ; Hon. D.D. (Oxòn.) 1897 ; Hon. D.C.L.(Dur.),Hon. LL.D.(Camb.),1908; d. and p. 1866, Kingston ; *b.* 1842. Primate of West Indies, 1898 ; Island Curate of St. George's, Kingston, Jamaica, 1866-80 ; Bishop in charge of Diocese, Honduras, 1881-91. *Publications:* The Churchman's Manual ; Devotions and Catechisms for Children and Young People ; Lectures on the Life of the World to Come. *Address:* Bishop's Lodge, Kingston, Jamaica, West Indies.   *(Died 31 May 1916.)*

NUTTALL, Harry, President Manchester Ear Hospital ; President Manchester Reform Club, 1907 ; M.P. (L.) Stretford, Lancashire,1906 ; retired, 1918; J.P. Manchester and Cheshire; F.R.G.S.; *b.* Manchester, 1849; *s.* of Joseph Nuttall of Manchester ; *m.* 1886, Edith Mary, *d.* of Wm. Smith, J.P., Bolton-le-Moors, Lancashire ; two *d. Educ.:* privately ; Owens College, Manchester. An import and export merchant at Manchester; contested Stretford, 1900 ; President, Manchester Chamber of Commerce, 1905 ; President Manchester Geographical Society, 1910 - 20. *Recreations:* golf and motoring. *Address:* Briarfield, Walton-on-the-Hill, Surrey ; Bank of England Chambers, Manchester. *Clubs:* Reform, Manchester Reform.   *(Died 25 Sept. 1924.)*

NUTTING, Sir John Gardiner, 1st Bt., *cr.* 1902 ; J.P. Co. Dublin ; D.L. Co. Dublin and of City; High Sheriff for Co. Dublin, 1895-96 ; *b.* 24 July 1852; 2nd *s.* of John Nutting, Redlands, Bristol, *s.* of Edward Nutting, Colchester, Essex; *m.* 1879, Mary Stansmore, *d.* of Restel R. Bevis, Manor Hill, Claughton, Cheshire; three *s.* two *d. Educ.:* Clifton College; Germany. Chairman of E. and J. Burke, Ltd., of Dublin. *Recreation:* hunting (member of Meath and Kildare Hunts). *Heir: s.* Harold Stansmore, Captain 17th Lancers, [*b.* 14 Aug. 1882 ; *m.* 1913, Enid Hester Nina, *d.* of F. B. Homan-Mulock, Ballycumber House, King's County ; one *s.* Late A.D.C. to Governor-General, Australia]. *Address:* St. Helens, Booterstown, Dublin. *Clubs:* Carlton, Junior Constitutional ; Sackville Street, Dublin.   *(Died 18 Feb. 1918.)*

NYS, Ernest, Hon. D.C.L. Oxon., Conseiller à la cour d'appel, professeur à l'Université de Bruxelles ; membre de la Cour permanente d'arbitrage ; *b.* Courtrai, Belgium, 27 March 1851. *Educ.:* Universities of Ghent, Heidelberg, Leipzig, Berlin ; Honorary Doctor of Laws of the Universities of Edinburgh and Glasgow ; Member of the Institut de Droit international, Académie royale de Belgique, Académie roumaine de Bucarest, American Philosophical Society, Philadelphia, Reale Istituto Veneto, British Academy. *Publications:* Le Droit de la Guerre et les Précurseurs de Grotius ; L'Arbre des Batailles ; Etudes de Droit international et de Droit politique ; Recherches sur l'Histoire de l'Economie politique (translated into English by A. and N. Dryhurst) ; Le Droit international, Principes, Théories et Faits ; Idées modernes, droit international et franc-maçonnerie ; Le Droit romain, le droit des gens et le Collège des docteurs en droit civil. *Address:* 39 rue Saint Jean, Bruxelles.   *(Died Sept. 1920.)*

O

OAKES, Sir Augustus Henry, Kt., *cr.* 1905 ; C.B. 1902 ; Librarian and Keeper of the Papers, Foreign Office, 1896-1904 ; retired, 1905 ; *b.* 2 Nov. 1839 ; *e. surv. s.* of late Lieut.-Col. Richard Montague Oakes, 22nd Light Dragoons and 1st Life Guards, of Elmsfield, Harrow ; *m.* 1871, Jane Alice, 2nd *d.* of late William H. Cane, M.D., Uxbridge, surgeon, Bucks Yeomanry Cavalry and Royal Elthorne Militia ; one *s.* two *d. Educ.:* abroad. Appointed to a clerkship in the Foreign Office, after passing a competitive examination, 1858 ; an assistant clerk, 1889 ; a Senior Clerk and Librarian and Keeper of the Papers, 1896 ; is a burgess of Newport, Pembrokeshire. *Publications:* chief compiler and editor of the British and Foreign State Papers, and the Collection of Commercial Treaties, 1897-1904 ; joint author of The Great European Treaties of the Nineteenth Century. *Address:* The Nook, Milford, nr. Godalming. *T.A.:* Milford, Surrey.   *(Died 17 Aug. 1919.)*

OAKES, Hon. Charles William, C.M.G. 1922 ; M.L.C. since 1925 ; Nationalist M.P. (for Eastern Suburbs) State Parliament, N.S.W., 1920-25 ; Chief Secretary and Minister for Public Health, 1922 - 25 ; *b.* Wagga Wagga, New South Wales, 1861 ; English parents; *m.* Elizabeth Gregory, New South Wales ; one *s.* one *d. Educ.:* New South Wales State School. Apprenticed to the jewellery trade ; in business afterwards on his own account for 26 years ; Alderman Paddington Council, 1899-1904 ; M.P. (L.) Paddington, 1891-1910 ; Hon. Minister in the Justice Department, 1907-10 ; Senator, New South Wales, 1913-15 ; elected State Member, N.S.W., for Waverley, 1917-20 ; Minister for Housing, Holman Cabinet, 1919-20; Member of Fuller Cabinet, 1922-25 ; Chairman of Prince of Wales Visit Committee to N.S. Wales, 1920. *Recreations:* sailing, numismatics, and early Australian history. *Address:* Quondong, Balfour Road, Belle Vue Hill, Woollahra, Sydney, N.S.W. *T.:* FM 1842, Sydney.   *(Died 3 July 1928.)*

OAKES, Sir Reginald Louis, 4th Bt., *cr.* 1815 ; General Manager of the Cairo Electric Railways and Heliopolis Oasis Co. ; *b.* 29 Sep. 1847 ; *s.* of late Henry Frederick Oakes ; *S.* grandfather, 1850 ; *m.* 1882, Florence, *d.* of Charles de Bela Brounlie, Vice-Consul at Turin. *Educ.:* Ghent University. *Heir:* none. *Address:* Heliopolis, Egypt.*(Died 11 Oct. 1927.)*

OATES, Francis Hamer, C.B., *cr.* 1919 ; Assistant Secretary Board of Education; barrister ; J.P. Notts (Chairman of Quarter-Sessions) ; 2nd *s.* of late W. H. C. Oates, Langford Hall, Notts, and Sophia, 4th *d.* of late L. Domenichetti. *Educ.:* Harrow ; Trinity College, Cambridge. *Address:* Besthorpe, nr. Newark. *Clubs:* Oxford and Cambridge, Boodle's.   *(Died 9 May 1923.)*

OATES, Frederick Arthur Harman, M.V.O. 1922 ; F.S.A.; Keeper of the King's Armoury since 1920; late Keeper, Secretary and Accounting Officer of the London Museum, S.W.1 ; *o. s.* of Frederick Oates, Whitby, Yorks; *m.* 1887, Elizabeth, *d.* of Robt. Grimmer Martins of Worsted, Norfolk; two *s.* three *d. Educ.:* London City School and Private Tutor, Rev. R. Langridge. Lifelong Antiquary ; appointed by Trustees and Keeper as Assistant Secretary on the formation of London Museum, 1911 ; Accounting Officer; Fellow of British Numismatic Society, and of Meyrick Society; Hon. Curator of Swiss Cottage and Museum, Osborne, I. W., 1925. *Publication:* Catalogue of a Collection of Finger Rings, 1917. *Recreations:* search for antiquarian objects, and walking. *Address:* Henry VIII. Gateway, Windsor Castle. *T.:* Windsor Castle 360. *Club:* Athenæum.   *(Died 3 Oct. 1928.)*

OBAIDULLA KHAN, Nowabzada Hafiz Mohamad Bahadur, C.S.I., 1912; Colonel - in - Chief, Bhopal Victoria Imperial Service Lancers ; and Hon. Major, British Army ; *b.* 3 Nov. 1878 ; 2nd *s.* of the Begum,

Ruler of Bhopal; *m.* 1902; three *s.* one *d.* *Educ.:* at home by private tutors; learnt Koran by heart. Joined Bhopal Victoria Imperial Service Lancers, 1904; Commander-in-Chief of the State Forces, 1905; A.D.C. to the Viceroy, 1906; Commission as Captain in H.M.'s Army, 1908; accompanied Her Highness the Begum of Bhopal on pilgrimage to Mecca; Her Highness, who was escorted by Imperial Service Troops, was attacked by Beduin Arabs who fired on the cavalcade; but through his tactful arrangements they were successfully repulsed; took part in Coronation Durbars, 1903 and 1911; attended the Coronation Ceremony at Westminster Abbey, 1910; toured all over Europe; promoted Major, 1911; takes keen interest in education; is Trustee of the M.A.O. College at Aligarh; subscribed 60,000s. to the College Funds. *Recreation:* very keen sportsman. *Address:* Jahan Numa Palace, Bhopal, Central India. *T.:* 18. *Clubs:* Central Indian Residency, Indore; Bhopal Military. *(Died Mar. 1924.)*

O'BEIRNE, Hugh James, C.B. 1905; C.V.O. 1908; J.P., D.L.; Councillor, Petrograd Embassy, since 1906; *b.* Jamestown, Drumsna, Co. Leitrim, 7 Sept. 1866. *Educ.:* Beaumont; BalHol College, Oxford. Attaché at Petrograd, 1892; 2nd Secretary, Washington, 1895-98; Secretary at British Embassy, Paris, 1900-1906. *Address:* British Embassy, Petrograd; Jamestown, Drumsna, Co. Leitrim. *Club:* St. James's. *(Died 5 June 1916.)*

OBRE, Henry, C.B.E. 1919; J.P., partner in the firm of Heatley & Co., 34 Leadenhall Street; *e. s.* of Henry Obré of Fort Villa, Queenstown, Co. Cork; *m.* Emma Eveline Wynn, *d.* of late Lieut. A. E. Wilby (61st) Gloucestershire Regt. *Educ.:* privately; Queen's College, Cork. Entered the firm of Harris Bros. & Co., and became a partner, 1892; retired in 1919 and joined his present firm; Chairman of Baltic and Corn Exchange Red Cross Hospital, Calais, Paris Plage, and Boulogne; Director of the Baltic and Mercantile Shipping Exchange and Trustee for the Baltic and Mercantile Shipping Benevolent Association. *Recreations:* fishing and golf. *Address:* The Manor House, Knebworth, Herts. *T.:* Knebworth 15. *M.:* H 7270. *Clubs:* Union, City of London, Royal Thames Yacht. *(Died 12 July 1922.)*

O'BRIEN, Patrick, M.P. (N.) Kilkenny since 1895; *s.* of James O'Brien, Tullamore; unmarried. Mechanical and marine engineer; M.P. for N. Monaghan, 1886-92. *Address:* House of Commons, S.W. *Clubs:* National Liberal; Leinster, Dublin. *(Died 12 July 1917.)*

O'BRIEN, Richard Barry, Barrister and Author; *b.* Kilrush, Co. Clare, Ireland, 1847; *y. c.* of Patrick Barry O'Brien; *m.* Kathleen Mary, *d.* of Dr. Teevan, of Kensington, W., 1877; five *s.* two *d.* *Educ.:* private tutors and Catholic University, Dublin. Called to Irish Bar, 1874; English Bar, 1875; practised for a short time in England, then glided into politics and literature; one of the founders of the Irish Literary Society; Chairman from foundation 1892-1906, President, 1906-11; Director of National Bank in 1911; LL.D. of National University of Ireland. *Publications:* The Irish Land Question and English public opinion, 1879; The Parliamentary History of the Irish Land Question, 1880; Fifty years of Concessions to Ireland (2 vols.), 1888-85; Irish Wrongs and English Remedies, 1887; Thomas Drummond, Life and Letters, 1889; The Life of Charles Stewart Parnell (2 vols.), 1898; Life of Lord Russell of Killowen, 1901; A Hundred Years of Irish History, 1902; Irish Memories, 1904; England's Title in Ireland, 1905; Dublin Castle and the Irish People, 1909; John Bright—a Monograph, 1910; editor Autobiography of Theobald Wolfe Tone, 1893; editor Children's Study—Ireland, 1896; editor Speeches of John Redmond, M.P., 1910. *Address:* 100 Sinclair Road, Kensington, W. *(Died 17 Mar. 1918.)*

O'BRIEN, William, journalist and author; M.P. (N.) Cork City 1910-18, when he withdrew from public life; *b.* 2 Oct. 1852; *s.* of James O'Brien, Mallow, Co. Cork, and Kate, *d.* of James Nagle; *m.* Sophie, *d.* of Hermann Raffalovich, Paris, 1890. *Educ.:* Cloyne Diocesan Coll.; Queen's Coll., Cork. Reporter on Cork Daily Herald, 1869-75; writer on Freeman's Journal, 1875-80; founded United Ireland, 1880; prosecuted nine times for political offences; spent more than two years in prison; elected to Parliament for native town as a Nationalist, 1883; S. Division Tyrone, 1885-86; N.E. Division Cork, 1887-92; M.P. (N.) Cork City and N.E. Division Cork Co., 1892; was a member of the Land Conference of 1903, which settled the Land Question, and has ever since been an advocate of the Policy of Conciliation for the union of all classes and creeds in Ireland with a view to Home Rule by Consent; founded the All-for-Ireland League and an Independent Parliamentary Party with that object; withdrew from Parliament, with Mr. Healy and the rest of his All-for-Ireland colleagues, at General Election, 1918. *Publications:* When we were Boys, written in prison, 1890; Irish Ideas, 1894; A Queen of Men, 1897; Recollections, 1906; An Olive Branch in Ireland and its History, 1910; Evening Memories, 1920; The Irish Revolution and How it Came About, 1928; Edmund Burke as an Irishman, 1924; The Parnell of Real Life, 1926. *Address:* Bellevue, Mallow, Co. Cork. *(Died 25 Feb. 1928.)*

O'CALLAGHAN, Col. Denis Moriarty, C.M.G. 1917; late A.M.S.; *b.* 11 Dec. 1861; *y. s.* of late Reo Robert O'Callaghan, LL.D., The Rectory, Holton, Suffolk, and *o. d.* of Denis Moriarty, Dingle; *m.* 1912, Katherine, *e. d.* of Mrs. Sayer of Yewtree House, Westfield, Sussex; one *s.* Capt. R.A.M.C. 1886; Major, 1898; Lt.-Col. 1906; Col. 1915; Adjutant Vols. 1894-95; served Ashanti, 1895-96 (Star); Nile Expedition, 1898 (despatches, two medals); S. Africa, 1900-1 (Queen's medal 8 clasps); European War, 1914-1917 (despatches, C.M.G.). *Recreations:* polo, hunting, golf. *Club:* Junior United Service. *(Died 6 Nov. 1926.)*

O'CALLAGHAN, Most Rev. Thomas Alphonsus, R.C. Bishop of Cork; O.P., D.D., cons. coadjutor, 1884; succeeded 1886; *b.* Cork, 1839. *Educ.:* Minerva College, Rome. Prior of St. Clement's, Rome, 1881. *Address:* Farranferris, Cork. *(Died 14 June 1916.)*

O'CONNELL, Captain James Ross; *b.* 28 Aug. 1868; *y. s.* of Sir Maurice O'Connell, 2nd Bart. *Educ.:* The Oratory, Edgbaston. Lieutenant, 85th Regiment 1884; Captain, 85th, 1892; served with the Dongola Expeditionary Force under Sir H. Kitchener, 1896; with 3rd Egyptian Battalion, including engagement at Firkhet and operations at Hafir (despatches, 4th class Medjidie, British medal, and Khedive's medal with four clasps); with 12th Sudanese in the operations 1898, including the battle of Khartoum (despatches, 4th class Osmanieh), Comm. 2nd Egyptian Batt.; and in 1899 in the operations in the final advance against the Khalifa (3rd class of the Medjidie); Governor of Kordofan, Sudan, to 1907. *Recreations:* shooting, fishing, golf. *Club:* United Service. *(Died 25 Feb. 1925.)*

O'CONNELL, Sir Morgan Ross, 4th Bt.; *cr.* 1869; J.P., D.L., Co. Kerry; J.P. Co. Clare; Lord of the Manor of Ballycarbery; *b.* 20 July 1862; *s.* of 2nd Bt., and Emily, *d.* of Rear-Admiral Sir Richard O'Conor; *S. bro.* 1905; *m.* 1884, Mary Pauline, *d.* of Lt.-Col. J. F. Hickie, of Slevoyre, Co. Tipperary; three *s.* one *d.* Owns 18,800 acres. *Heir: s.* Maurice James Arthur, *b.* 24 Dec. 1889; Lieut. 2nd Royal Fusiliers. *Recreations:* shooting, fishing, golfing. *Address:* Lakeview, Killarney, Co. Kerry. *Clubs:*

OBEYESEKERE, Hon. Sir Solomon Christoffel, Kt. See page xxvii.

Royal Automobile ; Kildare Street, Dublin.
(Died 27 April 1919.)

O'CONNELL, Sir Peter Reilly, Kt., *cr.* 1908 ; M.D. ; J.P. Co. Antrim ; *s.* of Patrick O'Connell, Maudabawn, Co. Cavan ; *m.* 1907, Jane Mary, *e. d.* of late Edward Hughes, J.P., Belfast. *Educ. :* St. Patrick's College, Cavan ; Catholic University, Dublin ; Queen's College, Galway ; M.D., M.Ch. Royal University, Ireland. High Sheriff, Belfast, 1907-8 ; D.L. for Co. of City of Belfast ; Member of the Senate, Queen's University, Belfast ; Lecturer and Examiner in Clinical Surgery in Queen's University, 1911 - 12 ; President of the Ulster Medical Association, 1910-11 ; Senior Surgeon, Mater Infirmorum Hospital, Belfast. *Address:* Oatlands, Stillorgan, Co. Dublin.
(Died Sept. 1927.)

O'CONNOR, His Honour Arthur, K.C. ; Judge of County Courts, Durham Circuit, 1901 ; Dorset Circuit, 1911-20 ; Barr. Middle Temple, 1883 ; *b.* 1 Oct. 1844 ; *e. s.* of William O'Connor, M.D., Dingle, Co. Kerry. *Educ.:* Ushaw. M.P. (N.) Queen's County, 1880, and again 1885, when elected simultaneously for East Donegal ; Chairman of Public Accounts Committee, 1895, 1896, 1897, 1898, 1899, and 1900 ; Deputy Chairman of Committees of the House ; member of the panel of Chairmen of the Standing Committees on Trade and on Law ; member of the Royal Commission on Trade Depression, 1885-86 ; on Civil Service Establishments, 1887 ; Public Works Loan Commissioner since 1890 ; member of Home Office Committee on Prisons, 1894 ; Chairman of the Treasury Departmental Committee on the Stationery Department, 1896 ; member Royal Commission on Incidence of Local Taxation ; one of the Panel of Chairmen of the Court of Arbitration under the Conciliation Act of 1896, and Chairman of the Leicestershire Joint District Board under the Coal Mines (Minimum Wages) Act 1912 ; M.P. (N.) E. Donegal, 1885-1900. *Address:* Dunsdale, Bournemouth.
(Died 30 Mar. 1923.)

O'CONNOR, Colonel Arthur Patrick, C.B. 1900 ; F.R.C.S.I., late A.M.S. ; *b.* 9 Aug. 1856 ; *s.* of late Charles A. O'Connor, Acres, Co. Roscommon ; *m.* 1890, Alice, *d.* of Archdeacon Badnall, D.D. ; one *s.* one *d.* Entered army, 1880 ; Lieut. - Colonel, 1900, Col., 1907 : served Burmese Expedition, 1885-86 (medal with clasp) ; South Africa, 1899 - 1902 (despatches, C.B., Queen's medal, 3 clasps, King's medal, 2 clasps). *(Died 25 Jan. 1920.)*

O'CONNOR, Rt. Hon. Charles Andrew, P.C. 1911 ; M.A. and Senior Moderator, Dublin University ; ex-Auditor College Historical Society ; *b.* Roscommon, 1854 ; *s.* of Charles Andrew O'Connor, solicitor, Roscommon ; *m.* Blanche, *d.* of James Scully of Shanballymore, Co. Tipperary. *Educ.:* St. Stanislaus College, Tullamore ; Trinity College, Dublin. Called to Irish Bar, 1883 ; Q.C. 1894 ; Bencher, King's Inns, 1896 ; Solicitor-General, Ireland, 1909-11 ; Attorney-General, 1911-12 ; Master of the Rolls in Ireland, 1912-24 ; Judge of Supreme Court, Irish Free State, 1924-25. *Address:* 48 Thurloe Square, S.W.7. *T.:* Kensington 7024. *Clubs:* Reform, Athenæum ; University, Dublin. *(Died 8 Oct. 1928.)*

O'CONNOR, John, K.C. 1919 ; *b.* 1850 ; M.P. (N.) South Tipperary, 1885 - 92 ; North Kildare, 1905-18. *Address:* 5 Frognal Mansions, Hampstead, N.W.3. *T.:* Hampstead 1496. *Club:* National Liberal. *(Died 27 Oct. 1928.)*

O'CONOR, James Edward, C.I.E. 1891 ; late Financial Department, India ; Registrar Dept. of Agriculture and Commerce, 1873-5 ; Assistant Secretary, 1875 ; transferred as Assistant Secretary in Department of Finance and Commerce, 1879 ; on special duty for Melbourne Exhibition, 1880-81, and in England with Indian Currency Committee, 1898 ;

Director-General of Statistics, India, 1895-1902 ; retired 1902. *Publications:* reports on production, cultivation, and manufacture in India of tobacco, lac, ground nut, eucalyptus, and various other articles ; also annual reviews of the trade of India, 1875-1902. *Address:* Francesco, Church Road, Upper Norwood, S.E. *Club:* Reform. *(Died 8 Jan. 1917.)*

O'CONOR, Sir John, K.B.E., *cr.* 1920 ; M.A., M.D., B.Ch. ; Senior Medical Officer, British Hospital, Buenos Aires, since 1894 ; *b.* 21 Dec. 1863 ; *s.* of late Abraham O'Conor, Carrick-on-Shannon, Ireland ; *m.* 1892, Grace Beatrice Richmond, *d.* of late James Oxley, Welshmill, Frome ; two *s.* two *d. Educ. :* Armagh ; Trinity College, Dublin. House Surgeon, Royal Portsmouth Hospital, 1887 - 89 ; Resident Medical Officer, British Hospital, Buenos Aires, 1890. *Publications:* articles and papers in medical publications. *Recreations:* tennis, golf. *Address:* Mayfair, Freshwater Bay, Isle of Wight ; 1042 Avenida Mayo, Buenos Aires. *Clubs:* Devonshire ; Jockey, Buenos Aires ; Royal Albert Yacht, Southsea. *(Died 8 Oct. 1927.)*

O'CONOR DON, Rt. Hon. Denis Charles Joseph O'Conor, P.C. Ire. ; B.A., LL.B., J.P., H.M.'s Lieut. and Custos Rotulorum for Co. Roscommon ; *b.* Clonalis, 26 Oct. 1869 ; *e. s.* of late Rt. Hon. Charles Owen O'Conor Don and Georgina, *d.* of T. A. Perry, Bitham House, Warwickshire. *Educ. :* St. Gregory's College, Downside ; London University. Member of both the English and Irish Bars. *Recreations:* shooting, motoring, etc. *Address:* Clonalis, Castlerea, Co. Roscommon. *M. :* DI 47 and DI 56. *Club :* Reform. *(Died 23 Feb. 1917.)*

ODDIE, John William, M.A., J.P. ; Senior Fellow of Corpus Christi College, Oxford ; *o. c.* of Thos. Oddie, Hambleton, Lancs. *Educ. :* Preston Grammar School ; Wadham College, Oxford ; B.A. (1st class Classics) 1865. Pupil and friend of B. Jowett and J. Ruskin ; Classical Lecturer of Wadham, 1866 ; Fellow and Tutor of C.C.C. 1867 ; Dean, 1878 ; Vice-President, 1874 ; Public Examiner, 1874 ; Acting Head of C.C.C. 1879-80 ; represented the College on Oxford University Commission, 1879-80 ; resided at Lyzwick Hall, Keswick, 1873-1910 ; J.P. Cumberland since 1879 ; has shown watercolours in Manchester and Liverpool Autumn Exhibitions, in Agnew's galleries, and elsewhere. *Publications:* Vampelectrum : a Fairy Play ; Choice Poems of Heinrich Heine ; Ruskin at Corpus ; curling songs and other contributions to periodicals. *Recreations:* rowing, golfing, curling ; now painting, gardening, and talking with pleasant people. *Address:* Strathmore, St. Leonards-on-Sea. *(Died 19 Jan. 1923.)*

ODDY, Sir John James, Kt., *cr.* 1916 ; mohair spinner and manufacturer ; *b.* 24 Feb. 1867 ; *s.* of James Oddy ; *m.* 1892, Marion, *d.* of John Ambler, Bradford ; one *d. Educ. :* Ley's School, Cambridge. M.P. (U.) Pudsey Division, West Riding, Yorks, 1908-10. *Address:* The Hall, Ilkley, Yorks. *T. :* Ilkley 311. *Clubs:* Carlton ; Bradford ; Leeds.
(Died 20 Feb. 1921.)

O'DEA, Rt. Rev. Thomas, D.D. ; R.C. Bishop of Galway and Kilmacduagh since 1909 ; *b.* 1858 ; *s.* of M. O'Dea of Kilfenora, Co. Clare. *Educ. :* Maynooth. Professor of Theology there, 1882-94, and Vice-President, 1894-1903 ; Bishop of Clonfert, 1903-1909 ; member of the Intermediate Board of Education, Ireland ; of the Governing Body of University College, Galway ; and of the Senate of the National University, Ireland. *Publications:* Maynooth and the University Question ; an unpublished treatise on justice. *Address:* Mount St. Mary's, Galway. *(Died 9 April 1923.)*

ODGERS, William Blake, M.A., LL.D., K.C. 1893 ; F.R.Hist.S. ; *b.* Plymouth, 15 May 1849 ; *s.* of Rev. W. J. Odgers,

Unitarian minister, and Eliza, *d.* of John Collins, Horton, Somerset; *m.* 1877, Frances, *d.* of Charles Hudson, formerly Coroner of Stockport; three *s.* one *d. Educ.*: Bath Grammar School (Exhibitioner); Univ. Coll. London (Scholar); Trinity Hall, Cambridge (Exhibitioner, Scholar, Wrangler, Law Student, M.A., LL.D.); Hon. LL.D., Tufts College, Massachusetts; Middle Temple, Barrister, 1873; Bencher, 1900; Western Circuit; Recorder of Winchester, 1897-1900; of Plymouth, 1900-12; of Bristol since 1912; Director of Legal Studies at the Inns of Court since 1905; Professor of Law at Gresham College, E.C., since 1907. *Publications:* King Arthur and the Arthurian Romances, 1872; Odgers on Libel and Slander, 1881 (now 5th edition); Odgers on Pleading and Practice, 1891 (now 8th edition); An Outline of the Law of Libel, 1897; Odgers on Local Government, 1899 (now 2nd edition); Powell on Evidence (10th edition); Odgers on the Common Law of England, 1911 (now 2nd edition); Bullen and Leake's Precedents of Pleadings (7th edition), 1915. *Address:* 15 Old Square, Lincoln's Inn, W.C.2. *T.:* Holborn 5744; The Garth, 34 Holden Road, North Finchley, N.12. *(Died 16 Dec. 1924.)*

ODLING, William, M.A., M.B., F.R.S.; Fellow of Worcester Coll.; *b.* London, 1829. Fullerian Professor of Chemistry, Royal Institution, 1868-72; Waynflete Professor of Chemistry, Oxford University, 1872-1912. *Publications:* Manual of Chemistry, Descriptive and Theoretical, 1861; Lectures on Animal Chemistry, 1866; Outlines of Chemistry, 1869; A Course of Six Lectures on the Chemical Changes of Carbon, 1869; Chemistry, 1884; Laurent's Chemical Method. *Address:* 15 Norham Gardens, Oxford. *Club:* Athenæum. *(Died 17 Feb. 1921.)*

O'DOHERTY, Philip, M.P. (N.) North Donegal, 1906-18; *b.* 1871. *Educ.*: St. Columba's College, Londonderry. Admitted a solicitor, 1895. *Address:* 11 East Wall, Londonderry. *T.:* 'Derry 224. *(Died 6 Feb. 1926.)*

O'DONNELL, Frank Hugh Macdonald; *b.* 1848; *e. s.* of Captain MacDonald O'Donnell of Tirconnell, Donegal. Unmarried. *Educ.*: The Queen's University, Ireland (M.A. with Gold Medal, 1869); several Continental teachers. An Irish Nationalist in Politics and Advocate of Self-Government for India with Indian Representation in Imperial Parliament; founded so-called Irish Active Policy, 1873; entered Parliament, 1874; collaborated with Messrs. Biggar and Parnell in general policy, until foundation of Land League, which he persistently opposed; organised along with Alexander MacDonald, M.P., the opposition to Flogging in the Army, which produced its abolition in 1879; founded the Farmers' Alliance, 1879; founded the Indian Constitutional Association, 1882; quitted Irish Parliamentary Politics, 1885; co-founder of the National Democratic League, 1899; President of the National Democratic League, 1904-6; many years resident in France, Germany, and Austria. *Publications:* The Message of the Masters; The Ruin of Irish Education and The Irish Fanar; The Stage Irishman of the Pseudo-Celtic Drama; Paraguay on Shannon; The Price of a Political Priesthood; The History of the Irish Parliamentary Party. *Recreations:* yachting and books. *Address:* 38 Tregunter Road, The Boltons, S.W. *(Died 5 Nov. 1916.)*

O'DONNELL, Maj.-Gen. Hugh, C.B. 1911; D.S.O. 1889; Colonel on Staff, India; *b.* 9 Feb. 1858; 2nd *s.* of J. W. O'Donnell P.W.D. Military Works; *m.* 1894, Susan, (*d.* 1908), *d.* of T. G. S. Garnett, J.P., Shifferlands, near Lancaster. *Educ* : privately; Sandhurst. 2nd Lieut. 8th King's, 1878; Lieut. 24th Regiment, 1879; Captain, 1889; Major, 1898; Lieut.-

790

Col., 1904; Bt.-Col. 1907; Substantive Col. in Army, 1907; Maj.-Gen. 1912. Indian Staff Corps, 1880; commanded 42nd (now 6th) Gurkha Rifles, 1899-1907; A A.G. for Musketry and Commandant School of Musketry, Northern Army, 1907-10; served with 24th Foot through Zulu War, 1879 (medal and clasp); raised and commanded Mogoung Levy (Police Batt.) throughout Burma Expedition, 1886-91; served through Mogoung Expedition, 1887-88; commanded Mogoung Field Force, 1888-89, thanks of Govt. of India and Commander-in-Chief in India (wounded, despatches, medal, 3 clasps, D.S.O.); commanded Mogoung column in the Wuntho Expedition, 1890-91 (despatches); Major-General commanding Bannu Brigade, N.W.P., 1911-15. *Recreations:* ordinary games, etc. *Club:* United Service. *(Died 2 Dec. 1917.)*

O'DONNELL, His Eminence Cardinal Patrick, R.C. Archbishop of Armagh since 1924; *b.* Kilraine, Glenties, Co. Donegal, 1856. *Educ.*: Catholic University, Maynooth. Professor of Theology and Prefect of the Dunboyne Establishment, Maynooth; Rector of the Catholic University of Ireland; R.C. Bishop of Raphoe, 1888-1922; Titular Archbishop of Attalia and coadjutor to Cardinal Logue, 1922-24; Cardinal, 1925. *Address:* Ara Coeli, Armagh. *(Died 22 Oct. 1927.)*

O'DONOVAN, John, M.V.O. 1920; I.S.O. 1922; J.P.; *b.* Lisard, Rosscarbery, Co. Cork, 22 May 1858; *s.* of Florence O'Donovan and Mary Haggerty; *m.* 1892, Josephine Whitaker, *widow*; three *s.* one *d. Educ.*: Mount Fachnanus National School, Rosscarbery, County Cork. Teaching Staff of School under Board of National Education, Ireland, 1872-75; emigrated to New Zealand, 1878; joined New Zealand police force as constable, 1879; Serjeant, 1898; Sub-Inspector, 1902; Inspector, 1911; Superintendent, 1915; Commissioner, 1916-21; retired on superannuation with honorary rank and title of Commissioner, 1921; studied law and passed the solicitors' law professional examinations under the University of New Zealand, 1892 and 1893; first instructor in police training college, Police Headquarters, Wellington; accompanied special police contingent which toured New Zealand with the King and Queen as Duke and Duchess of Cornwall, 1901; in command of a similar contingent on the occasion of the visit of the Prince of Wales to New Zealand, 1920. *Address:* c/o Police Headquarters, Wellington, New Zealand. *(Died April 1927.)*

O'DWYER, Right Rev. Edward Thomas, R C. Bishop of Limerick; cons. 1886; *b.* 1842, Holy Cross, Co. Tipperary. *Educ.*: Maynooth. *Address:* The Palace, Corbally, Limerick. *(Died 19 Aug. 1917.)*

O'DWYER, Surgeon-General Thomas Francis, M.D., R.U.I., L.R.C.S. (Edin.); *m.* Henrietta, *d.* of Rev. J. Ringwood; one *s.* one *d.* Entered army, 1864; retired, 1901; served Egyptian Expedition, 1882 (despatches, medal with clasp, bronze star, promoted Surg.-Maj.); Soudan Expedition, 1884-85; Secretary to P.M.O. (despatches, clasp); Late P.M.O. South-Eastern District, Canada and Aldershot. *Address:* Rodney Cottage, Clifton, Bristol. *Club:* Clifton. *(Died 5 Feb. 1919.)*

OELSNER, Herman, sometime Taylorian Professor of the Romance Languages in the University of Oxford (from foundation of Chair, 1909, till resignation, 1913); first holder of the Taylorian Lectureship in Old French and Romance Philology, 1905-9; *b.* 1871; *y. s.* of late Isidor and Eliza Oelsner; *m.* Ethel Mary Fisk. *Educ.*: Dulwich College; Caius College, Cambridge; B.A. 1892; M.A., Cantab., 1898, and Oxon. (by incorporation), 1906; Ph.D. Berlin, 1896. Was recognised as Intercollegiate Lecturer in Romance in the University of Cambridge, 1898; temporarily Prof. of French Language and Literature in the University Coll. of N. Wales, 1903-4;

O'DONOGHUE, David J. See page xxvii.

formerly Examiner in French and other Romance Languages, University of Cambridge; in French and Spanish, University of Oxford; in Italian, University of London and Royal University of Ireland; Member of the Council of the Philological Society; Romance Editor of The Modern Language Review, 1910-13. *Publications:* The Influence of Dante on Modern Thought, 1895 (Cambridge Univ. Le Bas Prize Essay, 1894); Dante in Frankreich, 1898; editions of Dante's Commedia (with Philip H. Wicksteed), 1899-1901, of FitzGerald's Six Dramas of Calderon, 1903, and of Dante's Vita Nuova, 1908; translations of Gaspary's History of Italian Literature to the Death of Dante, 1901, and (with A. W. Baker Welford) of Cervantes' Galatea, 1903; contributions on Romance subjects to numerous periodicals, and on Provençal and Italian Literature to the Ency. Brit. and to Nelson's Ency. *Club:* Savage.   *(Died 26 April 1923.)*

O'FARRELL, Sir Edward, K.C.B., *cr.* 1917; Kt., *cr.* 1915; C.B. 1911; *b.* Dublin, 6 Dec. 1856; *s.* of Michael R. O'Farrell, late of Park, Youghal, Co. Cork, barrister-at-law; *m.* 1895, Dorothy, *d.* of William Richardson Bunbury, of Busselton, W.A.; one *d. Educ.:* Trinity College, Dublin (Scholar, B.A.). Called to Irish Bar, 1882; Registrar to the Irish Land Commission till 1903; Registrar and Assistant Secretary to Estates Commissioners, 1903-8; Assistant Under-Secretary to Lord Lieut. of Ireland, 1908-18; a Census Commissioner for Ireland, 1911; an Estates Commissioner, 1918-23. *Address:* Cuilnagreine, Carrickmines, Co. Dublin. *Club:* University, Dublin.
       (Died 13 Aug. 1926.)

O'FARRELL, Rt. Rev. Michael, Bishop of Bathurst, since 1920; *b.* near Mullingar, 1865. *Educ.:* Navan, Maynooth. Professor All Hallows' College, Dublin, 1892-8; Irish College, Paris, 1898-1903; Mission Work in Ireland, 1903-13; Vice-Rector, St. John's College, University of Sydney, 1915-20. *Address:* Bishop's House, Bathurst, Australia.
       (Died 3 April 1928.)

OGILVIE, Sir Andrew Muter John, K.B.E., *cr.* 1918; C.B. 1912; Officer of the Belgian Order of Leopold, 1919; V.D.; *b.* 1858; *s.* of late R. Annesley Ogilvie, C.B.; unmarried. *Educ.:* University College, London. Private Secretary to successive Postmasters-General, 1891-99; Assistant Secretary, P.O., 1903; a British delegate to International Telegraph Conference, Lisbon, 1908; Col. (retired) R.E. (T.F.); Director of Army Signals (Home Defence), 1913-19; Third Secretary, Post Office, 1911-14; Joint 2nd Secretary of the Post Office, 1914-19; Member of Council Institution of Electrical Engineers, 1913-16 and 1921-4. *Address:* 7 Sheffield Terrace, Kensington, W.8; Golf Cottage, St. John's, Woking. *T.:* Park 60. *Clubs:* Union, Albemarle.
       (Died 26 Dec. 1924.)

OGILVIE, George, B.Sc., M.D., F.R.C.P.; Chevalier de la Légion d'Honneur; Kt. Order Isabel la Catolica; Kt. Order of Nossa Senhora de Villa Viçosa; Senior Physician to the French Hospital, and to the Hospital for Epilepsy and Paralysis, Maida Vale; *b.* 1852; *m.* 1893, Helen, *d.* of Surgeon-General John Houston. *Educ.:* Universities of Edinburgh, Paris, Würzburg, and Vienna. Graduated B.Sc. (Edinburgh) in the Mathematical Sciences, 1875; also Neill-Arnott Prizeman; M.D. Edinburgh, 1876; Fellow Royal Society of Medicine; Membre de la Société de Médecine de Paris. Practises as a Physician, and is medical adviser to the Standard and Scottish Widows' Cos. *Publications:* contributions to the medical journals on Diseases of the Nervous System; Typhoid Fever; The Inheritance of Disease, Germ Infection in Tuberculosis; What is Specific Disease of the Nervous System? 1904; Les descendants des tuberculeux: Hérédo-prédisposition, etc. *Address:* 22 Welbeck Street, Cavendish Square, W. *T.:* 1018 Paddington. *Clubs:* Reform, Caledonian.
       (Died 13 Dec. 1918.)

OGILVIE, Right Rev. James Nicoll, D.D.; Ex-Moderator, Church of Scotland; *b.* 4 April 1860; *s.* of Rev. Alex. Ogilvie, LL.D., Aberdeen; *m.* 1885, Elizabeth Johnston, *d.* of I. Massie, Aberdeen; one *s. Educ.:* Grammar School, Aberdeen; Aberdeen University (M.A. Hon. 1881); Edinburgh University (Gunning Fellow, 1883); Leipsic University (1883-84). Assistant Minister West Parish Church, Aberdeen, 1884; Chaplain, Indian Ecclesiastical Establishment, 1885; served twenty years Madras and Bangalore; Fellow Madras University, Examiner in History; retired as Presidency Senior Chaplain, Church of Scotland, 1904; Minister New Greyfriars Parish, Edinburgh, 1905, resigned 1919; Joint Convener Indian Churches Committee, Church of Scotland, 1907; Convener Foreign Mission Committee, 1909-25; Hon. D.D. Aberdeen University, 1911; Baird Lecturer, 1915; Moderator General Assembly, 1918; Commissioner Church of Scotland to African Missions, 1920, to Indian Missions, 1921; Duff Lecturer, 1923. *Publications:* The Presbyterian Churches of Christendom; Castle Memories, Twenty Tales of Edinburgh Castle; The Greyfriars' Churches; The Apostles of India (Baird Lecture); Afric's Sunny Fountains: an Indian Pilgrimage; Our Empire's Debt to Missions (Duff Lecture). *Recreation:* golf. *Address:* Balgownie, Colinton, Edinburgh. *Club:* University, Edinburgh.
       (Died 9 June 1926.)

OGILVIE-GRANT, William Robert; Assistant Keeper of the Zoological Department, Natural History Museum, S.W., 1913-18; *b.* 25 March 1863; 2nd *s.* of Hon. George H. E. Ogilvie-Grant and Eleanora, 4th *d.* of late Sir William Gordon-Cumming, Bart.; *m.* 1890, Maud Louisa, *e. d.* of Vice-Admiral Mark Pechell; one *s.* three *d. Educ.:* Cargilfield and Fettes College, Edinburgh; private crammer in Edinburgh: studied Zoology and Anatomy. Assistant, 2nd Class Zoological Dept., British Museum, 1882; transferred to Natural History Museum, 1883; Assistant, 1st Class, 1893; studied Ichthyology under Dr. Günther; in 1885 was placed in charge of the Ornithological Section during the absence in India of the late Dr. Sharpe, with whom he afterwards co-operated in raising the collection of Birds from comparative insignificance to its present vast proportions of nearly 800,000 specimens, and in making it by far the finest in any museum in the world; has done extensive work in the field, and made special collecting trips to Arabia, Sokotra, Abd-el-Kuri, the Madeira Group, Canaries, Salvage Island, Azores, etc., and secured many Zoological and Botanical species new to science; has taken a prominent part in organising many expeditions to explore unknown parts of the world and form Zoological collections, and in raising the large funds necessary to defray the expenses, notably Ruwenzori; Snow Mountains, New Guinea, etc.; Editor of Bulletin of the B.O. Club, 1904-14; Fellow Zoological Society (served on Council, 1905-10 and 1911-16); Fellow, Royal Society for Protection of Birds and Avicultural Society (served on Councils of both Societies); joined 1st Batt. County of London Regt. (Vol.) 1914; Invalid since 1916. *Publications:* Catalogue of Birds in the British Museum, vols. xvii. (part), xxii., and xxvi. (part); Allen's Nat. Lib. Handbook to the Game-Birds, vols. i. and ii., 1895-97; The Gun at Home and Abroad; British Game-birds and Wild-fowl, Nat. Hist., 1912; Reports on the B.O.U. Exped. and Wollaston Exped. to Dutch New Guinea, 1909-13 (1915), etc.; large number of monographs and papers on Natural History

791

subjects, chiefly ornithological, published in periodicals such as Ibis, Bulletin, Brit. Orn. Club, Trans. and Proc. Zoological Soc., etc., etc. *Recreations:* natural history in the field, gardening. *Address:* Farley Hill Cottage, near Reading. (*Died 26 July 1924.*)

OGILVY, Mrs. Nisbet-Hamilton (Mary Georgiana Constance); *b.* Dundas, *o. c.* of Rt. Hon. Robert Adam Christopher Nisbet-Hamilton, M.P., and Lady Mary Bruce, *e. d.* of 7th Earl of Elgin; *m.* 1888, Henry Thomas Ogilvy (*d.* 1909), 2nd *s.* of Sir John Ogilvy, 9th Bart. of Inverquharity. Owns 22,000 acres. *Address:* Biel, Prestonkirk; Archerfield, Dirleton; Winton Castle, Pencaitland, East Lothian. (*Died 25 June 1920.*)

OGLE, Sir Henry Asgill, 7th Bt., *cr.* 1816; Capt. R.N. (retired); *b.* Corfu, 12 Sept. 1850; 2nd and *e. surv. s.* of Gen. Sir Edmund Ogle, Bt., R.E., and Catharine, *d.* of H. St. Hill; *m.* 1917, Daisy, *e. d.* of T. L. Boyd, Vista Lieta, San Remo. *Educ.:* Southsea. Entered Royal Navy, 1864. Gained £100 Scholarship at Greenwich, 1877, etc. ; served in West Indies, N. America, Mediterranean, China, Cape, India, West Coast of Africa, Australia, etc.; served with Naval Brigade in Natal; served at Admiralty and at Ordnance Committee, and is a Deputy Commissioner of the Western Pacific. *Recreations:* member of C. T. Club, riding, etc. *Heir: b.* Lieut.-Col. Edmund Ashton Ogle, *b.* 13 Aug. 1857. *Address:* Capo di Monte, San Remo. *Clubs:* United Service; Royal Naval, Portsmouth.
(*Died 5 Mar. 1921.*)

O'GRADY, Lieut.-Colonel John de Courcy, C.B. 1900; J.P., D.L.; late the Connaught Rangers; *b.* 1 Nov. 1856; 3rd *s.* of W. de Courcy O'Grady, Chief of his name; *m.* 1892, Evelyn Wanda, *y. d.* of late Major-Gen. A. Mattei, C.M.G., and Mrs. Mattei, *née* Ceneska Lesczinska. *Educ.:* Windermere College; R.M.C. Sandhurst. Entered army, 1878; Captain, 1881; Major, 1891; Lieut.-Col. 1900; retired 1903; served Zulu War; Secocoeni War (severely wounded, despatches); Boer War, 1879-1881 (medal, despatches, medal, and clasp); S. African War, 1899-1901 (despatches, Queen's medal 5 clasps, C.B.); High Sheriff, Co. Limerick, 1914. *Recreations:* shooting, fishing. *Address:* Kilballyowen, Bruff, Kilmallock, Co. Limerick. *T.A.:* O'Grady, Bruff. *M.:* TI 25. *Club:* County Limerick. (*Died 30 Aug. 1920.*)

O'GRADY, Standish, B.L.; author and publicist; *b.* 18 Sep. 1846; *s.* of Thomas O'Grady and Susanna Dowe; *m.* Margaret, *d.* of Rev. William Fisher: three *s. Educ.:* Tipperary Grammar School; Trinity Coll., Dublin. Scholar Classical; Silver Medallist in Ethics and Psychology; do. Oratory in Undergraduate Philosophical Society; Gold Medallist as Essayist in the same. Relinquished the Bar for journalism in the first instance, and afterwards for literature, chiefly Irish History and Irish Historical Romance; his works in this department of literature generally believed to have been the starting point of the Celtic Renaissance. *Publications:* History of Ireland, Heroic Period, vols. i. and ii.; republished as a romantic Trilogy: (1) The Coming of Cuculain; (2) In the Gates of the North; (3) Triumph and Death of Cuculain; History of Ireland, Critical and Philosophical, vol. i.; The Flight of the Eagle, The Bog of Stars, Finn and His Companions, Ulrick the Ready, The Story of Ireland, Lost on Du-Corrig, The Chain of Gold, The Coming of Cuculain Cycle, 3 vols.; editor of Pacata Hibernia, etc. etc. *Recreations:* golf, cycling. *Address:* The Vicarage, Easton Maudit, Wellingborough, North Hants. (*Died 18 May 1928.*)

O'GRADY, Lt.-Col. Standish de Courcy, C.M.G. 1918; D.S.O. 1917; M.B., R.A.M.C.; *b.* 27 July 1872; *e. s.* of late Capt. S. de C. O'Grady and Charlotte, *d.* of G. P. Houghton, Kilmarnock; *m.* 1911, Esther Alice,

o. d. of Col. P. D. Vigors of Holloden, Co, Carlow; two *s.* one *d.* Served East Africa, 1904 (despatches, medal and clasp); European War (despatches thrice, D.S.O., C.M.G.). *Address:* c/o Holt & Co., 6 Whitehall Place, S.W.1.
(*Died 23 Dec. 1920.*)

O'GRADY, Rev. William Waller, Rector of Kilmocomogue since 1879; Canon of Cork since 1886; Treasurer of St. Finn Barre's Cathedral, Cork, and Rural Dean of Glensalny West; *b.* 7 April 1844; *s.* of Rev. Thomas O'Grady, nephew of 1st Lord Guillamore; *m.* Matilda Kate, *d.* of John Christopher Delmege, Castle Park, Limerick; two *d. Educ.:* Trinity College, Dublin (M.A.). Ordained, 1869; Curate of Drimo-league, 1869-70; Incumbent, 1870-79. *Address:* The Rectory, Bantry, Ireland.
(*Died 18 Mar. 1921.*)

OGSTON, Frank, M.D. and C.M., Aberdeen; Professor of Medical Jurisprudence, University of Otago, Dunedin, New Zealand; *b.* 23 June 1846; *s.* of Dr. Francis Ogston, Professor of Medical Jurisprudence, University of Aberdeen; *m.*; one *d. Educ.:* Aberdeen; Vienna; Prague; Paris. Assistant to Professor of Medical Jurisprudence, Aberdeen University; lately Professor of Hygiene, Otago University; District Medical Officer of Health for the Otago Southland District of New Zealand; Member British Medical Association; Fellow of Society of Medical Officers of Health of England; Member Cor. Etranger de la Société de Médécine Légale de France, etc. *Publications:* editor of Lectures on Medical Jurisprudence by Francis Ogston; Hints to Teachers on Medical Inspection of School Children, 1907. *Recreation:* golf. *Address:* 236 High Street, Dunedin, N.Z. *Clubs:* Dunedin; Otago Golf.

O'HALLORAN, Joseph Sylvester, C.M.G. 1895; Secretary Royal Colonial Institute 1884-1909; *b.* Adelaide, S.A., 28 Mar. 1842; *e. s.* of late Capt. W. L. O'Halloran; *m.* Alice Mary, *d.* of late Henry Simpson, Ridge Park, Adelaide, 1886. *Educ.:* private schools. Clerk, Audit Office, S.A., 1859; Clerk, Executive Council and Court of Appeals, 1869; Private Secretary to Rt. Hon. Sir James Fergusson, Bt., Governor S.A., 1870; Assist. Secretary Royal Colonial Institute, London, 1881; Secretary Geographical Section of the British Association, Montreal, 1884; Aberdeen, 1885. *Publications:* has contributed to the National Dictionary of Biography, Chambers's Encyclopædia, the Field, etc. *Recreations:* has travelled extensively in the Colonies; for some years a volunteer. S.A.
(*Died 25 Jan. 1920.*)

O'HALLORAN, Rev. Richard; a Catholic priest; Rector of the Catholic Church, Mattock Lane, Ealing, which he himself erected; has founded several missions and erected schools and churches. *Educ.:* Mill Hill. Ordained Deacon at Pro-Cathedral, Kensington, and Priest at Belmont Cathedral. Incorporated a secular priest of the diocese of Westminster by Cardinal Manning. *Publications:* Rights of the Secular Clergy Vindicated; Cardinal and Priest. *Recreation:* gardening and flower culture. *Address:* The Catholic Church, Mattock Lane, Ealing, W.
(*Died Oct. 1925.*)

O'HANLON, Rt. Rev. Mgr. Jas., D.D., Vicar-General of Birmingham and Provost of the Chapter since 1905; *b.* 1840. Ordained 1865; Headmaster of St. Chad's Grammar School, 1867-72; Prof. of Theology at Oscott, 1872-77; Rector of Olton Seminary, 1888-89; Domestic Prelate to the Pope. *Address:* 71 Hunter's Road, Birmingham (*Died 25 Feb. 1921.*)

O'HARA, Right Rev. Henry Stewart, D.D.; *e. s.* of Rev. James O'Hara, The Castle, Portstewart, and former Rector of Coleraine; *b.* 6 Sep. 1843; *m.* 1872, Hatton Thomasina, *y. d.* of Thos. Scott, D.L., of Willsboro, Londonderry. *Educ.:* Collegiate School,

Leicester ; Trinity College, Dublin ; B.A. 1865 ;
M.A. 1868 ; D.D. *jure dignitatis*, 1900. Rector
of Coleraine, 1869 ; Vicar of Belfast, 1894 ; Canon
of St. Patrick's Cathedral, Dublin, 1897 ; first
Dean of Belfast, 1899 ; Bishop of Cashel and
Emly, Waterford, and Lismore, 1900 ; res:gned
1919. *Address:* Laurel Hill, Coleraine. *Club:*
Ulster, Belfast.   (*Died 11 Dec. 1923.*)

O'HARA, Colonel James C.B. 1917 ;
b. 16 Nov. 1865 ; *s.* of late Col. James O'Hara,
D.L., late Capt. 2nd D.Gs., of Lenaboy, Galway ;
m. 1902, Margaret (*d.* 1928), *e. d.* of late W.
Chalmers Carmichael ; one *s.* one *d.* *Educ.:*
Wellington ; R.M. College, Sandhurst. Served
in 2nd Dragoon Guards (Queen's Bays), 1886-95 ;
appointed to Army Pay Dept. 1895 ; Col. and
Chief Paymaster, 1913 ; Command Paymaster,
Northern Command ; retired pay, 1925 ; served
South African War, 1899-1902 (despatches twice,
Queen's medal with 2 clasps, King's medal with
2 clasps). *Address:* Lenaboy, Hucclecote,
Gloucester. *Club:* Kildare Street. Dublin.
    (*Died 23 Dec. 1928.*)

O'HARA, John Bernard, M.A., poet ;
b. Bendigo, Victoria, 29 Oct. 1862 ; *s.* of P. K.
O'Hara ; *m.* 1910. Agnes Elizabeth Law, of
Hamilton, Victoria ; two *s.* one *d.* *Educ.:*
Carlton College, and Ormond College (Scholarship), Melbourne University (with first-class
honours, Stawell Exhibition for Engineering
and Mathematical Exhibition ; Lecturer in
Mathematics and Physics at Ormond College,
1886-89 ; Principal of South Melbourne College,
1889-1916. *Publications:* Songs of the South,
1891 ; Songs of the South (second series) 1895 ;
Lyrics of Nature, 1899 ; A Book of Sonnets,
1902 ; Odes and Lyrics, 1906 ; Calypso and Other
Poems, 1912 ; The Poems of J. B. O'Hara,
1918 ; At Eventide, 1922. *Recreations:* tennis,
walking. *Address:* 98 Beaconsfield Parade,
Albert Park, Melbourne. *T.:* 4307 C.
    (*Died 31 Mar. 1927.*)

O'HARE, P., M.P. (N.) North Monaghan,
1906-7 ; a Bailie, Glasgow. *Address:* 25 Circus
Drive, Dennistoun ; Tullygillen House, Monaghan.   (*Died Nov. 1917.*)

O'HIGGINS, Kevin Christopher, Vice-
President and Minister of Justice, late Minister
for Home Affairs, Irish Free State, since 1923 ;
Member of Dail for Dublin County since 1923 ;
M.P. (Sinn Fein) Queen's County, 1918-22 ;
b. 7 June 1892 ; *s.* of late T. F. O'Higgins,
F.R.C.S.I., Stradbally. Leix ; *m.* 1921, Bridget
May Cole. *Educ.:* Clongowes ; St. Patrick's
College, Carlow ; National University of Ire-
land, B.A. *Address:* Woodlands, Timoque,
Stradbally, Queen's Co.   (*Died 10 July 1927.*)

OHNET, Georges; *b.* Paris, 3 April 1848.
Educ.: Sainte Barbe ; lycée Bonaparte. *Pub-
lications:* Serge Panine, 1880 ; Le Maître de
Forges, 1881 ; La Comtesse Sarah, 1883 ; Lise
Fleuron, 1884 ; La Grande Marnière, 1885 ; Les
Dames de Croixmort, 1885 ; Noir et Rose, 1887 ;
Volonté, 1888 ; Le Docteur Rameau, 1889 ; Dernier
Amour, 1890 ; L'Ame de Pierre, 1890 ; Dette de
Haine, 1891 ; Le Lendemain des Amours, 1893 ;
Le Droit de l'Enfant, 1894 ; Nemrod et Cie,
1895 ; La Dame en Gris ; La Fille du Député,
1895 ; L'inutile Richesse, 1896 ; Vieilles Ran-
cunes ; Le Curé de Favières ; Roi de Paris ; Au
Fond du Gouffre, 1899 ; Gens de la Noce, 1900 ;
La Ténébreuse ; Le Brasseur d'Affaires ; Le Cre-
puscule ; La Marche à l'Amour ; Marchand de
Poison ; Le Chemin de la Gloire ; La Con-
quérant ; La Dixième Muse ; La Route rouge ;
L'Aventure de Raymond Dhautel ; Pour tuer
Bonaparte ; La Serre de l'aigle ; Le Revenant ;
Le Partisan. *Plays:* Regina Sarpi ; Marthe ;
Le Colonel Roquebrune ; Les Rouges et les
Blancs. Has dramatised several of his novels
with great success. Elected in 1902 Président
de la Société des auteurs dramatiques. *Address:*
14 Avenue Trudaine, Paris. (*Died 5 May 1918.*)

O'KEEFE, Hon. Michael, M.H.A. ;
Speaker, House of Assembly, since 1925 ; *b.*
Westbury, Tasmania, 12 Sep. 1865 ; *e. s.* of
Edmund O'Keefe and Josephine Thorne ; *m.*
1896, Beatrice Emily Dutton, *g.d.* of late Captain Dutton, R.N., and late Rev. John Copeland Dixon, B.A. ; two *s.* two *d.* *Educ.:* Sel-
bourne, Beconsfield. Farming and mining
until 1912 ; Member of Parliament (Labour)
for Wilmot since 1912. *Recreations:* gardening,
music, reading. *Address:* The Palms, Beaconsfield, Tasmania ; Speakers' Room, Hobart,
Tasmania. *T.:* 41.   (*Died Oct. 1926.*)

O'KELLY, James, M.P. (N.) Co. Roscommon since 1895 ; *b.* 1845 ; *s.* of late John
O'Kelly, Roscommon. *Educ.:* Dublin University ; Sorbonne. Served in French Army (Siege
of Paris), in Cuba, U.S.A. against Indians ;
travelled Mexico ; formerly War Correspondent
of Daily News ; M.P. Co. Roscommon, 1880-85 ;
N. Roscommon, 1885-92. *Address:* 17 Brewster
Gardens, W.   (*Died 22 Dec. 1916.*)

OKUMA, Prince Shigenobu; Prime
Minister, Japan, 1914-16 ; *b.* Saga, Hizen,
1838. A retainer of Lord Nabeshima ; one of
the founders of the new government ; Finance
Minister, 1869-81 ; Foreign Minister, 1888-89 ;
Minister of Agriculture and Commerce, 1896-97 ;
Prime Minister and Foreign Minister, 1898 ;
founder and ex-leader of the Progressive party ;
founder and President of the Waseda University,
Tokio ; founder of the Japanese Women's Uni-
versity. *Recreation:* horticulture. *Address:*
Waseda, Tokio. *T.:* Bancho 177.
    (*Died Jan. 1922.*)

**OLDERSHAW, William James Nor-
man**, C.B.E. 1918 ; V.D. ; Sugar Controller
for the Commonwealth Government ; *b.* Melbourne, 24 April 1856. *Educ.:* Wesley College,
Melbourne. Devoted many years (40) to Rifle
Shooting and Militia work ; Emerald Hill
Artillery, 1877 ; 1st Australian Infantry Regt.,
1886 ; Lt.-Col. commanding, 1900 ; Hon. Secretary Australian War Contingent Association,
London, 1914 ; special work as Commercial
Adviser to Australian Government since 1915.
Recreations: rifle shooting, won Queen's Prize,
1882, Melbourne. *Club:* Bombay.
    (*Died 13 Oct. 1926.*)

OLDFIELD, Sir Francis Du Pre, Kt., *cr.*
1923 ; Professor of Jurisprudence, Manchester,
since 1924 ; Puisne Judge, Madras High Court,
1913-24 ; *e. s.* of Canon C. Oldfield, Stamford ; *b.*
30 June 1869 ; *m.* 1898, Frances, *e. d.* of late Sir
Richard Cayley ; one *s.* one *d.* *Educ.:* Marl-
borough ; Trinity College, Cambridge ; Fellow,
Madras University, 1916 ; Vice-Chancellor, 1918.
Entered the Indian Civil Service, 1890 ; Head
Assistant, Madras, 1897 ; Sub-Collector and
Joint Magistrate, 1904 ; District and Sessions
Judge, 1908. *Address:* 53 Palace Court, W.2.

Club: East India United Service.
(*Died 14 Feb. 1923.*)

OLDFIELD, Sir Richard Charles, Kt. *cr.* 1889; late Indian Civil Service; *b.* 3 Nov. 1828; *e. s.* of Henry Swann Oldfield and Letitia, *d.* of Col. Scott; *m.* 1854, Maria, *d.* of Major Frederick Angelo, (*d.* 1885); one *s.* one *d. Educ.:* Eton; Haileybury. Entered Bengal C.S. 1848; served during Mutiny; wounded near Agra; Judge of the High Court of Judicature, Allahabad, 1878-87. *Club:* Oriental. (*Died 26 Dec. 1918.*)

OLDHAM, Ven. Algernon Langston, D.D.; Archdeacon of Ludlow, 1904-13; Prebendary of Hereford Cathedral; Rector and Rural Dean of Bridgnorth, 1882-1905; *s.* of late James Oldham of Lucastes, Hayward's Heath, and Brighton; two *s. Educ.:* Rugby; Trinity College, Oxford; and Cuddesdon; Canon Residentiary of Hereford Cathedral, 1905-9. *Publication:* Why we are Churchmen. *Address:* The Elms, Shrewsbury. (*Died 23 July 1916.*)

OLDHAM, Charles H., B.A.; Professor of Commerce, University College, Dublin. *Address:* University College, Dublin.
(*Died 20 Feb. 1926.*)

OLDHAM, Sir Ernest Fitzjohn, Kt., *cr.* 1921; senior partner of Vizard Oldham Crowder and Cash, 51 Lincoln's Inn Fields, W.C.2; Vice-President and Deputy-Chairman, Federation of British Industries; *b.* 16 Jan. 1870; *s.* of Frederick Jennings Oldham, Melton Mowbray; *m.* 1899, Margaret Alice, *d.* of late William Tatham, Orpington, Kent, solicitor; one *s.* three *d. Educ.:* Oakham. *Address:* 19 Palace Court, W.2. *Clubs:* Carlton, Conservative, Royal Automobile, Ranelagh.
(*Died 22 Sept. 1926.*)

OLDHAM, Colonel Sir Henry (Hugh), Kt., *cr.* 1897; K.C.V.O., *cr.* 1914; C.V.O. 1902; Lieut. of the Honourable Corps of Gentlemen-at-Arms since 1891; *b.* 17 Sept. 1840; *o. s.* of late Henry Oldham, M.D.; *m.* 1868, Ella (*d.* 1921), *d.* of late Arthur Pigou, B.C.S.; two *s.* two *d. Educ.:* Radley College; Royal Military College, Sandhurst. Entered army, 4 Nov. 1858; served in 48th Regt. and Cameron Highlanders; appointed to Honourable Corps of Gentlemen-at-Arms, 1887; Clerk of the Cheque, same corps, 1887; served in China war (medal and two clasps), 1860; Cossyah and Jyntiah Hill Campaign (mentioned in despatches), 1863-64. *Address:* Cannington, Boscombe, Bournemouth. *Club:* United Service.
(*Died 20 Sept. 1923.*)

OLDHAM, William Benjamin, late I.C.S., C.I.E. 1893; was Member of Bengal Legislative Council; Pres. of Bengal Sanitary Board; Col. commanding Calcutta Vol. Rifles; A.D.C. to the Viceroy of India; *b.* Monkstown, Co. Dublin, 16 April 1845; 2nd *s.* of late Thomas Wilson Oldham, Dublin; *m.* 1879, Maud Julia, 4th *d.* of General Sir A. B. Stransham, G.C.B.; three *s. Educ.:* Kingstown School; Trinity College, Dublin; Exhibitioner; Sizar; 1st Prize, Greek verse. Indian Civil Service, 1865; Orissa Famine, 1866-67; Bihar Famine, 1874; Madras Famine, 1877-78; Bengal Famine, 1897; and Frontier Service; Member of Bengal Board of Revenue to 1900. *Decorated* for Lushai Hills Campaign, 1892, when Inspector-General of Military Police. *Publications:* Some Ethnical and Historical Aspects of the Burdwan District; Hunting and Chasing in the Seventies. *Address:* Owlston, Talbot Avenue, Bournemouth. *T.A.:* Oldham, Bournemouth. *T.:* No. 2230. *Clubs:* Carlyle, W. Bournemouth.
(*Died 14 Oct. 1916.*)

OLDRIEVE, Wm. Thomas, H.R.S.A., F.R.I.B.A.; Architect, Edinburgh; *b.* 1853. *Educ.:* Mansfield Grammar School. Assistant Surveyor in H.M. Office of Works, 1881; Architect for Provincial Post Office buildings in England and Wales, 1892; H.M. Principal Architect for Scotland, 1904; retired, superannuated, 1914; Member of the Royal Commission

794

on the Ancient Monuments of Scotland; Secretary Ministry of Munitions for N. and E. Scotland, 1917-18; Munitions Works Board; Deputy Principal Surveyor for Scotland, 1918. *Address:* Oldrieve, Bell, and Paterson, 22 Ainslie Place, Edinburgh; *T.:* 3859; 13 Braid Avenue; *T.:* Edinburgh 1772.
(*Died Jan. 1922.*)

OLDROYD, Sir Mark, Kt., *cr.* 1909; J.P.; woollen manufacturer; Chairman, M. Oldroyd & Sons; retired, 1920; Alderman; *b.* 30 May 1843; *s.* of late M. Oldroyd, Dewsbury; *m.* 1st, 1871, Maria (*d.* 1919), *d.* of W. Mewburn; 2nd, 1920, A. J. Pattison (*d.* 1926) of Gainsborough. Late Mayor of Dewsbury; M.P. (R.) Dewsbury, 1888-1901; Director of Airedale Collieries, Ltd., Castleford. *Address:* Hyrstlands, Dewsbury.
(*Died 5 July 1927.*)

O'LEARY, Brig.-Gen. Tom Evelyn, C.B. 1914; C.M.G. 1916; C.B.E. 1919; *b.* Aug. 1862; *s.* of late Surg.-Gen. Thomas Conor O'Leary; *m. d.* of late Maj.-Gen. F. W. Ward, C.B.; one *d. Educ.:* Beaumont. Entered army, 1884; served in the Irish Fusiliers; served Miranzai Expedition, 1891 (medal with clasp); Isazai Expedition, 1892; Chitral, 1895 (despatches, Brevet-Major, medal with clasp); South Africa, 1899-1902 (despatches twice, Brevet Lt.-Col., Queen's medal 6 clasps, King's medal 2 clasps); European War, 1914-18 (despatches, C.M.G., C.B.E.). *Address:* West End, Haslemere, Surrey. *T.A.:* Chiddingfold. *Club:* Army and Navy.
(*Died 16 Sept. 1924.*)

OLIVEIRA, Francisco Regis de; Brazilian Ambassador at Lisbon since 1914; *m.* Donna Amelia, *née* da Silva Guimarães. Entered upon his career forty years ago and became Secretary of Legation successively at Paris, Berlin, Vienna, and Montevideo, then Minister in turn in Paraguay, Spain, Russia, Italy, and Austria; Brazilian Minister in London; his grandfather accompanied Dom João VI. when that king fled to Brazil on the invasion of Portugal by Napoleon, and subsequently took a prominent part in proclaiming the independence of the South American Colony. *Address:* Brazilian Embassy, Lisbon.
(*Died 23 Jan. 1916.*)

OLIVER, Daniel, LL.D., F.R.S.; *b.* Newcastle-on-Tyne, 6 Feb. 1830; *e. s.* of Daniel Oliver, Newcastle; *m.* 1861, Hannah, *d.* of James Wall, The Hills, Sheffield; one *s.* two *d. Educ.:* Friends' School, Brookfield, near Wigton, and at private schools. Emeritus Professor of Botany, Univ. Coll. London, 1861-88; Royal Medal of Royal Society, 1884; Linnean Medal, 1893; Keeper of Herbarium and Library, Royal Gardens, Kew, to 1890. *Publications:* Works on Elementary Botany; on African Botany; special Memoirs in Trans. Linn. Soc. London, etc. *Recreations:* painting, gardening. *Address:* 10 Kew Gardens Road, Kew. (*Died 21 Dec. 1916.*)

OLIVER, Rev. George, B.A.; Rector of St. John's, Longton, Staffs. since 1896; *b.* 1848; *e. s.* of Alderman Oliver, Bath; *m.* 1st, 1881, Miss Whitehouse of Sedgley, Staffs.; 2nd, 1894, Miss V. Walker of Brighton; one *s.* two *d. Educ.:* Lansdowne College, Bath; New College, Oxford; Curate of St. Mary's, Sedgley, 1876-80; Hallam Fields, Derbyshire, 1880-85; Vicar of St. George's, Darlaston, 1885-96; Proctor in Convocation for Archdeanry of Stoke-on-Trent; Prebendary of Bishopshull in Lichfield Cathedral; Chairman of Stoke-on-Trent Board of Guardians; Chairman of Longton War Pensions Committee. *Recreations:* cricket and cycling. *Address:* St. John's Rectory, Longton, Staffs. (*Died 17 Dec. 1920.*)

OLIVER, Matthew W. B., O.B.E.; M.A., M.B., B.Ch. Cambridge; F.R.C.S. England; M.R.C.S., L.R.C.P.; Surgeon to the Central London Ophthalmic Hospital; Ophthalmic Surgeon to the Queen's Hospital for Facial

OLIVER, Charles Nicholson Jewel, C.M.G. See page xxvii.

Injuries, Sidcup, and the Royal National Orthopædic Hospital; Ophthalmic Surgeon to the Italian Hospital; Ophthalmic Surgeon to Queen Mary's Auxiliary Hospital, Roehampton; *s.* of late Robert Oliver, of Strathwell, Whitwell, Isle of Wight. *Educ.:* Cheltenham College; Trinity College, Cambridge; St. Bartholomew's Hospital. Held various appointments at St. George's Hospital for two years; held the appointments of Chief Assistant in the Ophthalmic department at St. Bartholomew's Hospital and Assist. Ophthalmic Surgeon to the Miller Hospital, Greenwich; served in the R.A.M.C. in France, Aug. 1914-May 1919 (despatches). *Publications:* various papers on surgical and ophthalmological subjects. *Recreations:* golf, tennis, swimming, motoring. *Address:* 128 Harley Street, W.1. *T.:* Langham 1939. *M.:* DN 4193. *Clubs:* New University, Royal Automobile.
(*Died 10 Feb. 1926.*)

OLIVER, William, I.S.O. 1903; late Senior Principal Clerk, Supreme Court Pay Office. *Address:* Fotheringay, Cumberland Road, Kew.
(*Died 20 Jan. 1917.*)

OLIVEY, Sir Walter Rice, K.C.B.; *cr.* 1887; Col. and Chief Paymaster, retired 1889; *b.* 1831; *e. s.* of late Hugh Oliver Olivey; *m.* Elizabeth (*d.* 1913), *d.* of late R. Goodfellow, Falmouth, 1855; three *s. Educ.:* Truro Gram. School; Falmouth Classical School. Ensign by purchase 91st Argyllshire Regt. 1851; served in New Zealand War (medal) and in Egyptian Campaign of 1882 as Chief Paymaster (C.B. and medal); also in Egyptian Campaign, 1884-85, as Chief Paymaster (clasp, and a K.C.B.); has received distinguished service reward. *Recreations:* shooting, boating, and as an amateur mechanic. *Address:* 51 Blessington Road, Lee, S.E. *T.A.:* Opetide, London. *Club:* Junior Constitutional. (*Died 26 Nov. 1922.*)

OLIVIER, Rev. Dacres, M.A.; Prebendary of Salisbury; Hon. Chaplain to the Earl of Pembroke; *b.* Potterne, 26 Oct. 1831; *s.* of Col. Olivier of Potterne, Manor House, Wilts, and Mary, *d.* of Admiral Sir Richard Dacres; *m.* Emma Selina (*d.* 1908), *d.* of Rt. Rev. Robt. Eden, Primus of the Scottish Episcopal Church; six *s.* three *d. Educ.:* Rugby; Christ Church, Oxford. Curate of Great Yarmouth and of Wilton, 1854-67; Rural Dean, 1885-97; Rector of Wilton, Wilts, 1867-1912. *Address:* The Close, Salisbury, Wilts; The Lea, Grasmere. *Club:* Constitutional.
(*Died 7 Jan. 1919.*)

OLLIVANT, Alfred; *b.* 1874; 2nd *s.* of Col. E. A. Ollivant, Royal Horse Artillery, Elliotts, Nuthurst, Sussex and Catharine, 2nd *d.* of Professor J. J. Blunt; *g.s.* of Rt. Rev. Alfred Ollivant, Bishop of Llandaff; *m.* 1914, Hilda, *d.* of Robert Wigram, *g.s.* of Sir Robert Wigram, Bart., one *d. Educ.:* Rugby; R.M. Academy, Woolwich; passed out Senior Gunner, Toombs' Memorial Scholar, and Winner of the Riding Prize. Commission in Royal Artillery, 1893; resigned, 1895. *Publications:* Owd Bob, 1898; Danny, 1903; The Gentleman, 1908; The Royal Road, 1912; The Brown Mare, 1916; Boy Woodburn, 1917; Two Men, 1919; One Woman, 1920; Boxer and Beauty, 1924. *Address:* 20 Evelyn Gardens, S.W.7. *Club:* Athenæum. (*Died 19 Jan. 1927.*)

OLLIVANT, Brig.-Gen. Alfred Henry, C.M.G. 1916; R.A.; General Staff Officer, 1st grade, Supreme War Council; *b.* 19 Oct. 1871; *s.* of Colonel A. Ollivant, Indian Army, and *g.s.* of Rt. Rev. Alfred Ollivant, late Bishop of Llandaff; unmarried. *Educ.:* Winchester Coll.; Woolwich. Entered Royal Artillery, 1891; Captain, 1899; Major, 1911; Bt. Lieut.-Col. 1914; Lt.-Col., 1917; served with Somaliland Expeditionary Force, 1904 (medal with clasp); passed Staff College, 1908; General Staff Officer, 2nd grade at Colonial Office, 1909-11; 3rd grade

at War Office, 1911-1913; 2nd grade at Admiralty, 1913-14; Bt.-Col. 1918; served European War with Royal Naval Division as General Staff Officer, 1st grade, at Antwerp, 1914 (despatches); Dardanelles, 1915-16 (despatches, C.M.G.); B.E.F. France, 1916-17 (Order of St. Anne of Russia, 2nd Class, despatches). *Club:* Army and Navy. (*Died 31 Aug. 1919.*)

OLLIVANT, Sir (Edward) Charles (Kayll), K.C.I.E.; *cr.* 1892; retired from I.C.S.; *b.* 7 Feb. 1846; *m.* 1st, 1870, Lucy C. (*d.* 1891), 2nd *d.* of Judge Eddis, Q.C.; 2nd, 1899, Edith Margaret, 2nd *d.* of Rev. T. S. Hichens, Hon. Canon Peterborough Cathedral; one *s.* one *d. Educ.:* Marlborough. Entered I.C.S. 1868; Municipal Commissioner, Bombay, 1881-90; Political Agent, Kathiawar, 1890-95; Officiating Commissioner in Sind, 1895; Officiating Chief Secretary to Government of Bombay, 1896; Member of Council of Governor of Bombay, 1897-1902; Member of the Council of Marlborough College; Director of the Bombay, Baroda, and C.I. Railway. *Address:* 2 Westbourne Crescent, W.2. *T.:* Paddington 7225.
(*Died 24 Dec. 1923.*)

OLMSTED, Rt. Rev. Charles Sanford, D.D.; Bishop of Colorado since 1902; *b.* Olmsteville, N.Y., 8 Feb. 1853; *s.* of Levi Olmsted and Maria Beach; three *s.* one *d. Educ.:* St. Stephen's College and General Theological Seminary, N.Y., Missionary, Morley, N.Y., 1876-84; Rector, Cooperstown, N.Y., 1884-96; Archdeacon of Susquehanna, 1886-96; Rector, St. Asaph, Bala, etc., 1896-1902. *Publications:* December Musings and Other Poems; Mediæval Poets. *Address:* The Elms, Saybrook, Connecticut, U.S.A. (*Died 21 Oct. 1918.*)

OLMSTED, Rt. Rev. Charles Tyler, D.D., D.C.L.; Bishop of Central New York since 1904; *b.* 28 April 1842; *s.* of Chas. A. and Ardelia W. Olmsted; *m.* 1876, Catharine Lawrence. *Educ.:* Trinity College Hartford, Conn. Deacon, 1867; Priest, 1868; Prof. Mathematics, St. Stephen's College, Annandale, 1866-68; Assistant Minister, Trinity Parish, New York, 1868-84; Rector, Grace Church, Utica, N.Y., 1884-99; Vicar, St. Agnes' Chapel, Trinity Parish, New York, 1899-1902; Bishop Coadjutor, Central New York, 1902-4. *Publications:* The Rock Whence Ye are Hewn: a Course of Lectures on Early History of English Church; various sermons. *Address:* 1101 Park Ave., Utica, N.Y. *T.:* 250. (*Died 26 Mar. 1924.*)

OLNEY, Richard; *b.* Oxford, Massachusetts, 15 Sept. 1835; *s.* of Wilson Olney; descended from Thomas Olney, who came to America in 1635 from St. Albans, Hertfordshire, England; on mother's side descended from Andrew Sigourney, a French Huguenot, who came to America in 1687 on revocation of Edict of Nantes; *m.* Agnes Park Thomas, 1861. *Educ.:* Leicester Academy (Leicester, Mass.); graduated Brown University (Providence, R.I.), 1856; Harvard Law School, LL.B. 1858; LL.D. Harvard University, 1893; Brown University (Providence, R.I.), LL.D. 1893; Yale University, LL.D. 1901. Admitted to Bar, Supreme Judicial Court, Suffolk County, Mass., 1859; served one term Mass. Legislature, 1874; Attorney-General, United States, March 1893 to June 1895; Secretary of State of the United States, 10 June 1895 to 4 March 1897; declined to be nominated as Ambassador to Great Britain, March 1913; American Member of Commission under treaty between U.S. and France, 1915. *Address:* 710 Sears Building, Boston, Mass. *Club:* Somerset. (*Died 9 April 1917.*)

O'LOGHLIN, Hon. James Vincent; *b.* Gumeracha, South Australia, 25 Nov. 1852; *s.* of pioneer colonist. *Educ.:* Kapunda Classical and Commercial Academy; *m.* 1907, Blanche, *y. d.* of John Besley of Mt. Gambier, S.A.; three *s.* one *d.* Spent earlier years in agricultural and pastoral pursuits, and in the wheat and milling trade; engaged in journalism; in 1884 started Terowi Enterprise, a successful up-country paper; subsequently became editor and managing director of the Southern Cross in Adelaide, with which paper he is still connected; in 1888 was elected member of Legislative Council, and was returned again in 1894 at head of the poll; in 1896 became Chief Secretary and Leader of the Upper House in the Kingston Government, the strongest and longest-lived administration which has held office in South Australia; Senator for S. Australia in Federal Parliament, Session, 1907; elected Senior Member for Flinders, House of Assembly, 1910; Senator for S.A. 1913-20; is Lt.-Colonel in the local forces; ex-Chief President Australian Natives Association; President of the Irish National Association, and for 14 years a trustee of the Savings Bank; has served on several Royal Commissions, and was Chairman of the Public Service Royal Commission; volunteered for active service and took a contingent of the Australian Imperial Force to the Front, Aug. 1915, and again in 1916 (British Empire War Medal, 1914-1918, Gallipoli Star, 1914-15, Victory Medal, 1914-18, Volunteer Decoration); Senator for South Australia, Federal Parliament, since 1922. *Address:* Hawthorn, South Australia. *Club:* Naval and Military.   *(Died 4 Dec. 1925.)*

O'LOUGHLIN, Hon. Laurence; J.P.; *b.* Salisbury, Jan. 1854; *m.* Frances Morris; six *s.* five *d.* *Educ.:* Salisbury; Seven Hills Catholic College. District Councillor in the Port Germain District Council; Member of Vermin Board; Speaker House of Assembly, 1912-14; M.P. district of Frome, 1890-1914; for Burra Burra, 1914; Government Whip, 1894-96; Commissioner of Crown Lands, South Australia, 1896-1902; Minister of Lands, Agriculture, Mines, and Controlling Northern Territory, 1905-9; Minister of Public Works, 1909-10; Speaker, 1912-15. *Address:* Pinnaroo, South Australia. *(Died 27 Jan. 1927.)*

O'LOUGHLIN, Very Rev. Robert Stuart, D.D.; Dean of Dromore; *b.* 30 July 1852; *y. s.* of late Bryan O'Loughlin, of Carrigview, Co. Limerick, and Elizabeth, *d.* of late George Smith, of Brisna, Co. Limerick; *m.* Florence Marie, *d.* of late Hon. J. Burrowes, of New Orleans, U.S.A.; three *d.* *Educ.:* Diocesan School, Limerick; Trinity College, Dublin. *Publications:* The Glory of God, and other Sermons; The Crisis in the Church of England; pamphlets on the Baptismal Controversy; The Priesthood of the Laity; The Doctrines of the Plymouth Brethren; and on other ecclesiastical and religious subjects. *Address:* Lurgan.   *(Died Feb. 1925.)*

OLPHERT, Sir John, Kt.; *cr.* 1902; C.V.O. 1908; D.L.; Gentleman Usher to three Lords Lieut. of Ireland; H.M. Lieut. Co. Donegal; *b.* 2 Sept. 1844; *e. s.* of late W. Olphert of Ballyconnel House, J.P. and D.L.; *m.* 1869, Frances Susan, *o. d.* of late Robert Burrowes, M.P.; one *d.* *Address:* Ballyconnel House; Falcarragh, Co. Donegal.   *(Died 11 Mar. 1917.)*

OLSEN, Dr. Björn Magnusson, Professor of Icelandic Philology in the University, Reykjavik, Iceland. *Address:* Reykjavik, Iceland.

O'MALLEY, Col. William Arthur D'Oyly, C.B. 1909; Indian Army; *b.* 6 Jan. 1853. Entered Army, 108th Foot, 1873; Bengal Staff Corps, 1877; Captain, I.S.C., 1885; Major, 1893; Lt.-Col., Indian Army, 1899; Brevet-Col. 1908; served Mahsood Wuzuree Expedition, 1881 (despatches); Jakht-i-Suleiman Expedition, 1883 (despatches); Zhob Valley Expedition, 1890; Waziristan, 1894-95 (despatches, brevet Lt.-Col., medal with clasp); N.W. Frontier, India, 1897-98 (medal with clasp); also 1902. *Address:* High View, Kintbury, Berks. *Club:* New, Cheltenham.   *(Died 3 April 1925.)*

796

O'MARA, Joseph, operatic tenor; *b.* Limerick; *y. s.* of James O'Mara; *m.* 1896, *o. d.* of M. J. Power, late of Waterford. *Educ.:* Jesuit College, Limerick. Made first appearance in public 1891, in opera Ivanhoe; continued there till close of Royal English Opera House; engaged in 1893 by Sir Augustus Harris, and was retained by him for three years; singing at Drury Lane and Covent Garden as principal tenor in all the grand operas; has sung at all the principal concerts in London and the provinces; toured three years in U.S.A.; at present managing director and principal tenor of The O'Mara Opera Co., Ltd. *Recreations:* cycling, yachting, tennis. *Club:* Savage.   *(Died 5 Aug. 1927.)*

O'MEARA, Capt. Bulkeley Ernest Adolphus, D.S.O. 1900; Kimberley Town Guard; transferred to Intelligence Dept. 1900; *b.* Umballa, India, 1 Feb. 1867; *s.* of late Alfred O'Meara, St. Mark's, Simla, India; *m.* 1899, Edith, *e. d.* of William and Anna Hines. *Educ.:* Dulwich College; King's College School, Somerset House, London. Served as trooper in original Pioneer Force which annexed Rhodesia to the British Empire, 1889-91; Surveyor in De Beers Consolidated Mines, Ltd., Kimberley; served in South African War, 1899-1901, in Kimberley Town Guard; Intell. Officer for Griqualand West, as far as Mafeking; S.O.I. to Vryburg and Carnarvon Columns; Press Censor and Interpreter and Intelligence Officer at Oudtshoorn, under Acting Inspector-General Western (despatches four times); Govt. Surveyor Cape and Transvaal Colonies, practising at Johannesburg. *Decorated* for Siege of Kimberley. *Recreations:* has taken part in all kinds of South African sports, including big game shooting in north. *Club:* Rand, Johannesburg.
    (Died 31 Aug. 1916.)

O'MEARA, Lt.-Col. Charles Albert Edmond, C.I.E. 1917; Indian Army, retired; *b.* 7 Aug. 1668. 2nd Lieut. East Lancs Regt. 1891; Capt. Indian Army, 1891; Major, 1901; Lt.-Col. 1914; Director and Superintendent, Army Clothing Dept., India, 1910; retired, 1922. *Club:* Junior Naval and Military.
    (Died 20 May 1923.)

O'MEARA, Stephen, LL.D. Hon.; Police Commissioner, City of Boston; *b.* Charlottetown, P.E.I., 26 July 1854; *m.* 1878, Isabella M. Squire; three *d.* *Educ.:* Boston Public Schools. Reporter, 1872-79; city editor, 1879-81; managing editor, 1881-91; general manager, 1891-96, Boston Journal; Hon. degree of A.M. from Dartmouth College, 1889; editor and publisher Boston Journal, 1896-1902. *Address:* 585 Beacon Street, Boston, Mass., U.S.A. *Clubs:* Algonquin, Exchange, Press, Union, Boston.
    (Died 14 Dec. 1918.)

OMMANNEY, Sir Montagu Frederick, G.C.M.G., *cr.* 1904; K.C.B., *cr.* 1901; K.C.M.G., *cr.* 1890; I.S.O. 1903; King of Arms Order of St. Michael and St. George, 1908; Secretary, 1900; late Director of London Assurance Co., 1899; Director British North Borneo Co. since 1910; Hon. Treasurer Royal Colonial Institute, 1888-1912; a Vice-President of the Institute since 1912; *b.* 4 Apr. 1842; *m.* 1st, 1867, Charlotte (*d.* 1913), *d.* of O. Ommanney; three *s.* four *d.*; 2nd, 1914, Winifred Rose, *d.* of Harris St. John of West Court, Finchampstead. *Educ.:* Cheltenham; Woolwich. Entered Royal Engineers, 1864; Captain, 1878; Crown Agent for Colonies, 1877-1900; Permanent Under-Secretary of State for Colonies, 1900-7. *(Died 19 Aug. 1925.)*

O'MORCHOE, Rev. Thomas Arthur, M.A.; otherwise O'Morchoe or chief of his Sept of Oulartleigh, Co. Wexford; Rector of Kilternan Parish, Diocese of Dublin, since 1894; *b.* 22 March 1865; *e. s.* of Arthur MacMurrogh Murphy (who was "O'Morchoe") of Oulartleigh, Co. Wexford (*d.* 1918), and Susan

Elizabeth, *s. d.* of Thomas Bradley, M.D., of Kells Grange, Co. Kilkenny, and Sophia, *d.* of Robert Wolfe of Tentower, Queen's Co.; *m.* 1891, Anne, *d.* of John George Gibbon, LL.D., B.L., of Kiltennell, Co. Wexford; four *s.* three *d. Educ.*: Trinity College, Dublin. Member of the Royal Dublin Society, and Royal Society of Antiquaries of Ireland; Member of Dublin County Committee of Agriculture and Technical Instruction, from foundation to 1920, and Board of Education of the General Synod of the Church of Ireland, 1906-11; late Editor of the Dublin University Missionary Magazine. *Publications:* The Evidential Value of the Resurrection; Articles on Reorganisation of Missionary Methods; A Register of Clerical Societies; The Chiefs of Ireland; engaged in historical research, and in particular the origins of Celtic history. Owns property in Co. Wexford. *Heir: e. s.* Capt. Arthur Donel O'Morchoe, [*b.* 3 June 1892. *Educ.*: Trinity Coll., Dublin]. *Address:* The Rectory, Kilternan, Co. Dublin. *T.:* Foxrock, 1x1.
(Died 1921.)

O'NEILL, 2nd Baron (*cr.* 1868), **Edward O'Neill,** J.P., D.L.; *b.* 31 Dec. 1839; *s.* of 1st Baron and 1st wife, Henrietta, *d.* of late Hon. Robert Torrens, Judge of Common Pleas, Ireland; *S.* father, 1883; *m.* Lady Louisa K. E. Cochrane, *d.* of 11th Earl of Dundonald, 1873; one *s.* three *d. Educ.*: Trinity College, Cambridge. M.P. (C.) Co. Antrim, 1863-80. *Heir: g.s.* Shane Edward Robert O'Neill [*b.* 6 February 1907; *s.* of late Hon. Arthur O'Neill, *e. s.* of 2nd Baron, and Lady Annabel Crew-Milnes, *e. d.* of first Marquess of Crewe (she *m.* 2nd, Major J. H. H. Dodds)]. *Address:* 12 Queen's Gate, S.W.7; *T.:* Western 210; Shane's Castle, Antrim, Ireland. *Club:* Carlton. *(Died 19 Nov. 1928.)*

O'NEILL, Charles, J.P. Lanarks; M.P. (N.) South Armagh since 1909; Assist. Prof. of Botany, St. Mungo's College, 1897-99; *b.* 1849, *s.* of Hugh O'Neill, Glenravel, Co. Antrim; *m.* 1874, Margaret, *d.* of Michael M'Killop, Airdrie; *Educ.*: Glasgow University. (M.B. and C.M.) Member of Coatbridge Town Council, Airdrie and Coatbridge Water Trust, etc.; has been Senior Magistrate of Coatbridge; was elected three times for same Parliamentary (a unique circumstance) constituency in one year; the only surviving Nationalist in Parliament associated with Isaac Butt at inception of Home Rule movement. *Address:* Glenravel House, Coatbridge. *Clubs:* National Liberal, Irish.
(Died 14 Jan. 1918.)

ONIONS, Alfred, Alderman Monmouthshire County Council, 1919; J.P.; M.P. (Lab.) Caerphilly Division of Glamorganshire since 1919; General Treasurer for South Wales Miners' Federation; Member of the Parliamentary Committee Trade Union Congress; *b.* St. George's, Salop, 30 Oct. 1858; *s.* of Jabez Onions, miner; *m.* 1887, S. A. Dix, *d.* of a miner; two *s.* one *d. Educ.*: St. George's Church School. Checkweigher Abercarn Colliery, 1887; Member of Mynyddyslwyn School Board, 1888; Bedwelly School Board, 1899; first Chairman of Risca Urban District Council; has been a Member of Monmouthshire County Council 18 years. *Address:* Melrose Villa, Tredegar, Monmouths. *T.:* Tredegar 7. *(Died 6 July 1921.)*

ONNES, Prof. H. Kamerlingh, Ph.D., D.Sc.; Emeritus Professor and Director of the Physical Laboratory, Leyden; *b.* Groningen, 21 Sep. 1853. Foreign Member Royal Societies of London, Dublin, Edinburgh; Hon. Member Royal Institute of Great Britain, Chemical Society; liquefied helium; discovered the possibility of perpetual electric current through metals at certain temperatures; Nobel Prize for Physics, 1913. *Address:* Haagweg 49, Leyden, Holland. *(Died 21 Feb. 1926.)*

ONSLOW, Maj.-Gen. George Thorp, C.B. 1902; Royal Marine Light Infantry; *b.* 17 July 1858; *s.* of late Major Pitcairn Onslow, R.M., of Dunsborough, Ripley, Surrey; *m.* 1887, Ethel Paul, *d.* of Rev. D. Kitcat, Weston-Birt, Gloucestershire; two *d. Educ.*: Clifton Coll.; Wellington College. Entered Royal Marines, 1875; Captain, 1884; Major, 1892; Lieut.-Col., 1898; Colonel, 1902; Col. Commandant, 1906-9; Colonel on Reserved List, 1909; Maj.-Gen. Retired List, 1919; served Soudan, 1884-85 (medal, two clasps, star); South Africa, 1900 (medal, C.B.); Inspector of Marine Recruiting, 1900-5. *Address:* 11 Iverna Gardens, Kensington, W.8. *Club:* United Service.
(Died 14 June 1921.)

ONSLOW, Sir William Wallace Rhoderic, 5th Baronet, *cr.* 1797; D.L., J.P.; Lieut. 12th Regt. (retired); *b.* Simla, 13 Aug. 1845; *S.* father 1876; *m.* Octavia, *d.* of Sir Arthur Knox-Gore, 1st Bt., 1873; two *s.* three *d. Educ.*: Marlborough. Entered 12th Regt. 1864; Capt. 3rd Batt. Duke of Cornwall's Light Infantry, 1875-82. Owns about 10,000 acres. *Heir: s.* Roger Warin Beaconsfield [*b.* 29 Apr. 1880; *m.* 1905, Mildred, *e. d.* of Sir R. R. Wilmot, 6th Bt.; one *s.* Late Lieut. Suffolk Regt.] *Address:* Hengar, St. Tudy, R.S.O., Cornwall. *Clubs:* Carlton, Naval and Military.
(Died 13 Jan. 1916.)

OPPENHEIM, Lassa Francis Lawrence, M.A., LL.D.; Whewell Professor of International Law in the Univ. of Cambridge since 1908; Member of the Institute of International Law; Hon. Member Real Academia de Jurisprudencia, Madrid; Corresponding Member of the American Institute of International Law; Editor of the Series: Contributions to International Law and Diplomacy; *b.* Germany, 30 March 1858; *s.* of Aaron Oppenheim, Frankfort-on-Main; naturalised in England, 1900; *m.* 1902, Elizabeth Alexandra, *d.* of Lt.-Col. Phineas Cowan; one *d. Educ.*: Lycée, Frankfort-on-Main; Universities of Göttingen, Heidelberg, Berlin, Leipzig. Lecturer in the Univ. of Freiburg (Baden), 1886; Extraordinary-professor, 1889; Professor in the University of Basle, 1891; Lecturer at the London School of Economics and Political Science (University of London), 1895; Associate of the Institute of International Law, 1908; Member, 1911. *Publications:* Die Rechtsbeugungsverbrechen, 1886; Zur Lehre von der Untersuchungshaft, 1888; Die Nebenklage, 1889; Das ärztliche Recht zu körperlichen Eingriffen an Kranken und Gesunden, 1892; Die Objekte des Verbrechens, 1894; Gerechtigkeit und Gesetz, 1895; Das Gewissen, 1898; International Law: a treatise, vol. i. Peace, 1905; second edition, 1912; vol. ii. War, 1906; second edition, 1912; The Science of International Law, 1908; International Incidents for discussion in Conversation Classes, 1909; second edition, 1911; The Future of International Law, 1911; The Panama Canal Conflict, 1913; The Collected Papers of John Westlake on Public International Law, 1914. *Address:* Trinity College, or Whewell House, 62 Grange Road, Cambridge. *T.:* Cambridge 753. *Club:* Reform.
(Died 7 Oct. 1919.)

OPPENHEIM, Lieut.-Col. Lawrie, C.M.G. 1918; *b.* 1871; *s.* of Charles Oppenheim, 40 Great Cumberland Place, W., and Isabelle, *d.* of W. P. Frith, R.A.; *m.* 1908, Mary, *d.* of J. Monteith of Carstairs, Lanark; one *s. Educ.*: Harrow; Trinity College, Cambridge, B.A. Served with Tirah Field Force, 1897-98; attached Northampton Regiment and present at actions of Dargai, Maidan, etc.; Nile Expeditionary Force, 1898, present at Battle of Khartoum (medal with clasp); South African War, 1899-1902, with Thorneycroft's Mounted Infantry and Scottish Horse (Queen's medal with seven clasps, King's medal

797

O'NIAL, Surgeon-General John, C.B. See page xxvii.

with two clasps); joined Queen's Bays, 1900; specially employed 1904-9 under War Office and Committee of Imperial Defence in compilation of Official History of South African War; attached 2nd Battalion Highland Light Infantry, 1914; Military Attaché the Hague, Jan. 1915 to April 1920; Military Attaché British Legation, Berne, 1920-22; British Military Representative on Permanent Advisory Commission of League of Nations, Geneva, since 1922 (Brevet-Major, C.M.G., Bt. Lt.-Col., Chevalier Order of St. Vladimir, Commander Order of Orange Nassau, Officier de l'Ordre de Leopold, Commander of the Portuguese Order of Aviz). *Address:* 40 Great Cumberland Place, W. *Club:* Brooks's. (*Died July 1923.*)

OPPENHEIMER, Sir Bernard, 1st Bt., *cr.* 1921; Chairman and Permanent Director South African Diamond Corporation, Ltd.; Chairman of London Committee and Permanent Director Pniels, Ltd.; Chairman New Vaal River Diamond and Exploration Co., and of Kryn & Laby Metal Works, Ltd.; Director of Blaauwbosch Diamonds, Ltd.; *b.* 18 Feb. 1866; *m.* 1890, Lena, *y. d.* of late Michael Straus; one *s.* two *d.* Has founded diamond-cutting factories for disabled soldiers at Brighton, Cambridge, Fort William and Wrexham. *Recreations:* farming and raising pedigree stock. *Heir: s.* Michael, *b.* 26 Dec. 1892. *Address:* 36 Curzon Street, W.1.; *T:* Gerrard 8337; Sefton Park, Stoke Poges, Bucks; Kimberley, S. Africa. (*Died 13 June 1921.*)

ORANGE, George James, C.B.E. 1920; Managing Director since 1912 of Spottiswoode, Dixon & Hunting, Ltd., Regent House, Kingsway, W.C., Advertising Agents and Consultants; *b.* Chester; *e. s.* of late John G. Graves Orange of that city; *m.* 1913, Viola Audrey, *d.* of Walter Stanleigh Phillips, Beauchamps, Rochford, Essex; two *s.* one *d.* Joint Hon. Organiser Official Agents, National War Savings Committee, 1917-18; Hon. Director of activities, Chambers of Commerce, Chambers of Trade, Chambers of Agriculture and kindred organisations, Victory Loan Campaign, 1919; for some years a Member of the Institute of Journalists; formerly assistant editor and leader writer Galignani Messenger, Paris; First Managing Director, Educational Book Co. Ltd., 1908-12; Past President, Thirty Club of London; Past President, Athenæum Debating Society, Manchester; one of the founders Aldwych Club; travelled extensively in America and Canada. *Recreation:* golf. *Address:* 57 Nassau Road, Barnes, S.W. *T.:* Hammersmith 1512. *Clubs:* Authors', Aldwych.
(*Died 16 Mar. 1925.*)

ORANGE, William, C.B. 1886; M.D., F.R.C.P.; retired civil servant; *b* Newcastle-on-Tyne, 1833; *s.* of Rev. John Orange; *m.* 1864, Florence Elizabeth (*d.* 1913), *d.* of Thomas Ingleman Hart, Sevenoaks. *Educ.:* St. Thomas's Hospital Medical School. Assistant Medical Officer Surrey County Lunatic Asylum, 1859-62; Deputy-Superintendent of Broadmoor Asylum at the date of its opening in 1862; Superintendent thereof, 1870-86; member of the Council of Supervision thereof, 1891-1904. *Decorated* for service at Broadmoor under the Home Office. *Publications:* sundry articles bearing upon insanity associated with crime. *Address:* 11 Marina Court, Bexhill-on-Sea, Sussex. (*Died 31 Dec. 1916.*)

ORANMORE and BROWNE, 3rd Baron (Ireland), *cr.* 1836; 1st Baron Mereworth of Mereworth Castle (U.K.), *cr.* 1926; **Geoffrey Henry Browne Browne,** K.P., 1918; P.C. Ireland 1921; a Member of the Irish Convention, 1917-18; appointed a Commissioner of Congested Districts Board, 1919; elected a Senator for Southern Ireland, 1921; D.L., J.P.; a Representative

Peer for Ireland; *b.* 6 Jan. 1861; *o. s.* of 2nd Baron and Christina, *d.* of Alexander Guthrie of the Mount and Bourtree Hill, Ayrshire; S. father, 1900; *m.* 1901, Lady Olwen Verena Ponsonby, Lady of Grace of St. John of Jerusalem, *e. d.* of 8th Earl of Bessborough; two *s.* one *d.* *Educ.:* Trinity College, Cambridge, M.A. Knight of Grace of St. John of Jerusalem; Grand Officer of Order of Crown of Roumania. Owns about 8000 acres. *Heir: s.* Hon. D. G. E. Browne. *Address:* 21 Portland Place, W.1; Mereworth Castle, Kent; Castle MacGarrett, Claremorris, Co. Mayo. *T.:* Langham 1012. *T.:* Wateringbury 43. *Clubs:* Bachelors', Carlton. (*Died 30 June 1927.*)

ORDISH, Thomas Fairman, F.S.A.; *b.* 1855; 2nd *s.* of late Thomas Ordish, London, and Sarah, *e. d.* of late Fairman and Berthalina Mann, Attleborough, Norfolk; *m.* 1880, Ada, *d.* of late John Lamacraft, London; one *d.* *Educ.:* privately; influenced by the late W. F. Ainsworth, F.S.A. Editor of the Antiquary, 1888-90; of The Bookworm, 1888; of the Camden Library, 1891-93; of the London Topographical Record, 1901-6; Communications on Folk-Drama, Folk-Lore Society, 1891-93; Chairman, Entertainment Committee Folk-Lore Congress, 1891; Organised London Topographical Society, 1898; Vice-President, 1906; Founded London Shakespeare Commemoration League, 1902; Director of Commemoration, 1903; Lectures on Shakespeare and London, 1903-1914, passim. *Publications:* Early London Theatres, 1894; Shakespeare's London, 1897—2nd edition, enlarged, 1904; contributed to Colburn's New Monthly Magazine, 1874-77; Contributions to The Antiquary since 1880, including series on London Theatres and on Early English Inventions, 1885-87; to The Bibliographer, 1882; to The Bookworm, 1888; to Book-Song, 1898; on Improvement of Westminster to Cornhill Magazine, 1904; History of London Traffic to the Report of the Royal Commission on London Traffic, 1905; chapter on Elizabethan London to London vols. of Memorials of Counties, 1908; Government and Extension of Washington, U.S.A., and History of Metropolitan Roads to Reports of the London Traffic Branch of the Board of Trade, 1908, 1910; Roads out of London, edited from Ogilby's Survey for London Topographical Society, 1913; London as seen by Shakespeare; William Blake and London, Lond. Topog. Record, vols. v., ix.; on Keats and London, to the John Keats Memorial Volume, 1921. *Recreations:* gardening, conducting rambles in Old London. *Address:* Langdale, Cecil Park, Herne Bay, Kent.
(*Died 5 Dec. 1924.*)

O'REILLY, Rt. Rev. James, Parish Priest of St. Joseph's, Penarth; Dean of St. Illtyds Conference and Vicar-General of the Archdiocese of Cardiff; *b.* Tenode, Westmeath, Ireland, 10 June 1856. *Educ.:* St. Bernard's Grammar School, Granard; All Hallows College, Dublin. Priest, 1879; Swansea, Assistant Priest, 1879; Merthyr, 1881; Dowlais 1881; took charge of the United Missions of Aberdare and Mountain Ash, 1882; resided in the former town for the next 28 years; Vicar General of the Diocese of Newport, 1911; Vicar Capitular and Domestic Prelate to Pope Benedict XV. *Recreation:* golf. *Address:* St. Joseph's, Penarth, Glamorgan. *T.A.:* Penarth. *T.:* Penarth 247.
(*Died 23 Mar. 1923.*)

O'RIORDAN, Rt. Rev. Mgr. Michael, D.Ph., D.D., D.C.L.; Rector of the Irish College, Rome, since 1905; named Protonotary Apostolic by Pius X., 1907; *b.* Co. Limerick, Ireland, 1857. *Educ.:* The Irish College; The Propaganda and The Gregorian University, Rome. Ordained priest, 1883. *Publications:* A Criticism of Draper's History of the Conflict of Religion and Science; Life of St. Columbanus, and of other Irish Saints in Italy; A Reply to

Dr. Starkie's attack on the Managers of Irish National Schools; Catholicity and Progress in Ireland; numerous articles in American, English, Italian, and Irish Reviews. *Address:* Irish College, Rome. *(Died 27 Aug. 1919.)*

ORLEANS, Duc d', Louis Philippe Robert, Head of the Bourbon-Orleans House; *b.* York House, Twickenham, 6 Feb. 1869; *e. s.* of late Comte de Paris, and *n.* of Duc de Chartres; *m.* 1896, Archduchess Marie Dorothea of Austria (*b.* 14 June 1867). *Educ.:* Municipal College, England; College Stanislas, France. Exiled from France, 1886; received commission 60th Rifles; served in India, 1888-9; went to Paris, but again expelled. *Address:* Anjou, near Brussels. *(Died 28 Mar. 1926.)*

ORMATHWAITE, 2nd Baron (*cr.* 1868), **Arthur Walsh**, J.P.; Bt. 1804; Capt. 1st Life Guards, retired 1855; Hon. Col. 3rd Batt. South Wales Borderers since 1876; *b.* 14 April 1827; *s.* of 1st Baron and Lady Jane Grey, *y. d.* of 6th Earl of Stamford and Warrington; *S.* father 1881; *m.* Lady Katherine Emily Mary Somerset (*d.* 1914), *d.* of 7th Duke of Beaufort, K.G., 1858; five *s.* three *d.* *Educ.:* Eton; Trin. Coll. Camb. Entered Army, 1847; Lord-Lieut. for Radnorshire, 1875-95; M.P. (C.) Leominster, 1865-67; Radnorshire, 1868-80. Owns about 26,800 acres. *Heir: s.* Hon. Sir A. H. J. Walsh. *Address:* Strettington House, Chichester. *Club:* Carlton. *(Died 27 Mar. 1920.)*

ORMEROD, Joseph Arderne, M.A., M.D. Oxford; F.R.C.P. London; Registrar Royal College of Physicians, London, since 1909; Consulting Physician to St. Bartholomew's Hospital, Consulting Physician to National Hospital for Paralysed and Epileptic, Queen Square; *b.* 7 April 1848; *e. surv. s.* of Ven. T. J. Ormerod, Archdeacon of Suffolk, of Sedbury Park, Gloucestershire, and Tyldesley, Lancashire (*e. s.* of George Ormerod, D.C.L., F.R.S., historian of Cheshire), and Maria, *e. d.* of Sir Joseph Bailey, 1st Bt., of Glanusk Park; *m.* Mary Ellen, 3rd *d.* of Edward Milner, F.L.S., of Dulwich Wood, Norwood; four *s.* four *d.* *Educ.:* Rugby; Oxford; St. Bartholomew's Hospital. Scholar of C.C.C.; Fellow of Jesus Coll., Oxford; Chancellor's Prizeman Latin Verse; 1st Class Classical Moderations, 2nd Class Literæ Humaniores, 1st Class Natural Science. Formerly Examiner in Medicine to the University of Oxford, and to the Conjoint Board R.C.P. London and R.C.S. Eng.; Harveian Orator, Royal College of Physicians, 1908; Lumleian Lecturer, Royal College of Physicians, 1914; President of Neurological Section of the Royal Society of Medicine; Medical Registrar and Demonstrator of Morbid Anatomy to St. Bartholomew's Hospital; Physician to the City of London Chest Hospital, Victoria Park; Physician to the King George Hospital, Stamford Street, S.E. *Publications:* articles in Clifford Allbutt's System of Medicine; and other contributions to medical literature, chiefly concerning diseases of the nervous system. *Address:* 25 Upper Wimpole Street, W.1; Greenhill, Upham, Hants. *T.:* Paddington 1772. *Club:* Athenæum. *(Died 5 Mar. 1925.)*

ORMONDE, 3rd Marquess of (*cr.* 1825), **James Edward William Theobald Butler**, K.P., P.C. 1902; 21st Earl of Ormonde (*cr.* 1328); Earl of Ossory, 1526; Viscount Thurles, 1537; Baron Arklow, Baron Ormonde (U.K.), 1821; 27th Hereditary Chief Butler of Ireland; H.M.'s Lieut. of Kilkenny since 1878; First Class Crown of Prussia; Commodore Royal Yacht Squadron; Vice-Admiral of Leinster; Hon. Col. 5th Batt. Royal Irish Regt.; *b.* Kilkenny Castle, 5 Oct. 1844; *s.* of 2nd Marquess and Frances Jane, *e. d.* of Sir Edward Paget, G.C.B.; *S.* father 1854; *m.* Lady Elizabeth Harriet Grosvenor, *d.* of 1st Duke of Westminster, 1876; two *d.* Unionist. *Educ.:* Harrow. Joined 1st Life Guards, 1863; retired

as Captain, 1878; commanded Royal East Kent Yeomanry, 1883-94. Owns in Ireland about 24,000 acres; in England about 2500; and a Picture Gallery, Kilkenny Castle. *Recreation:* yachting. *Heir: b.* Lord Arthur J. Wellington Foley Butler. *Address:* Kilkenny Castle; 32 Upper Brook Street, W.1; *T.:* Mayfair 4236; Ballyknockane Lodge Clonmel. *Clubs:* Carlton, Cavalry; Royal Yacht Squadron, Cowes; Kildare Street, Royal Irish, Royal St. George's. *(Died 26 Oct. 1919.)*

ORMROD, Peter, late Major in 6th West Riding Regiment and Lt.-Col. 2/4th Loyal North Lancashire Regt.; *b.* 1869; *e. s.* of late James Cross Ormrod and Edith, *d.* of John Hargreaves of Sillwood Park, Berkshire; *m.* 1895, Gertrude Rose, *d.* of John George Lyon of Pontefract; two *s.* three *d.* Was Capt. 3rd Batt. Loyal North Lancashire Regiment; Lord of the Manor of Nether Wyresdale. *Address:* Picket Post, Ringwood, Hants. *(Died 23 Oct. 1923.)*

ORMSBY, Rt. Rev. George Albert, D.D.; Archdeacon of Lindisfarne since 1914; Hon. Canon, St. Nicholas Cathedral, Newcastle-on-Tyne; Examining Chaplain to the Bishop of Newcastle, 1914; Vicar of Eglingham, 1912; *b.* Dublin, 16 Sep. 1843; *s.* of late Rt. Hon. Henry Ormsby, Chancery Judge of High Court of Justice in Ireland, and Julia, *d.* of late Henry Hamilton, Tullylish House, Co. Down, Ireland; *m.* 1871, Ellie, *d.* of late Canon Scott, Vicar of New Seaham, Durham; six *s.* two *d.* *Educ.:* Trinity College, Dublin. B.A. 1865; Divinity testimonium, 1st Class, 1866; Prizeman in Hebrew, Syriac, and Chaldee, 1864-66; M.A. 1868 B.D. and D.D. Jure Dignitatis, 1893; Ad eundem, Durham M.A. 1877; Fellow of the Royal Colonial Institute, 1895; sub-prelate of the Order of St. John of Jerusalem in England, 1908. Curate of Eglingham, Northumberland, 1866-69, Rector of Jarrow, 1869-75; of Rainton, 1875-85; Vicar of St. Stephen's, Walworth, London, 1885-93; chaplain to the Duke of Manchester, 1869-91; Lecturer in St. Swithin's, London Stone, 1890-93; organising secretary for C.E.T.S. diocese of Rochester, 1889-93; Bishop of Honduras and Central America, 1893-1907; President of the Y.M.C.A., Paris Branch, 1909-12; Chaplain of British Embassy Church, Paris, 1907-12; Rural Dean of Glendale, 1912-1914; Assistant Bishop in the Diocese of Newcastle, 1912-15. *Address:* Eglingham Vicarage, Alnwick, Northumberland. *Club:* National.
(Died 14 Feb. 1924.)

ORMSBY, Sir Lambert Hepenstal, Kt., *cr.* 1903; B.A., M.D., M.B. Dublin University; L.R.C.P.I.; F.R.C.S.I.; J.P., D.L., Co. Dublin; Col. and Hon. Consulting Surgeon, New Zealand Expeditionary Force, 1915; *b.* Onehunga Lodge, Auckland, New Zealand, 19 July 1850; *o. s.* of George Owen Ormsby, C.E., Surveyor-General of the Colony of New Zealand; *m.* 1st, 1874, Anastatia (*d.* 1911) *o. d.* of John Dickinson; one *s.* one *d.*; 2nd, 1921, Geraldine Matthews, R.R.C., O.B.E. *Educ.:* Grammar School, Auckland, N.Z.; Royal School, Dungannon; T.C.D. and R.C.S.I. Articled apprentice to the late Sir George Porter, Bart.; studied at the Meath Hospital and School of the Royal College of Surgeons; late Senior Demonstrator and Surgical Teacher, Examiner in Surgery, R.C.S.I., President, 1902-4; Secretary, 1921; is a Member of the Senate, University of Dublin, Fellow and Member of the Council of the Royal College of Surgeons; late Representative of the College on General Medical Council; Senior Surgeon of the Meath Hospital and County Dublin Infirmary; Senior Surgeon National Children's Hospital; Consulting Surgeon to the Drummond Military School, Bray, Co. Wicklow; Hon. Consulting Surgeon to the Dublin Branch of the Institute of Journalists; Fellow of the Royal

Medico-Chirurgical Society of London ; Fellow of the Royal Academy of Medicine, Ireland ; Chairman of the Board of Superintendence of Dublin Hospitals, and Governor of the Lock Government Hospital ; was formerly Surgeon to the Royal Longford Rifles ; Chairman of the Association for the Housing of the Very Poor, Dublin ; Founder of the Dublin Red Cross Order of Nursing Sisters. *Publications :* Deformities of the Human Body ; Medical History of the Meath Hospital and County Dublin Infirmary ; Surgical Operation Chart ; Red Cross Nursing Chart ; Lectures on Surgical Emergencies ; Lectures on the Causes, Symptoms, and Treatment of Varicose Veins ; Lectures on the Diseases of the Rectum ; The Study of Diseases peculiar to Children : Inventor of Ormsby's Ether Inhaler ; Pile Clamp ; New Form of Rectal Speculum ; Aseptic Glass Drainage-tube ; New Form of Chest Bandage. *Address :* 92 Merrion Square, Dublin. *T.A. :* Ormsby, Merrion Square, Dublin. *T. :* 1088. *Clubs :* Constitutional ; United Service Dublin. *M. :* RI 1296, RI 4163.   (*Died 21 Dec. 1923.*)

ORMSBY, Lt. - Col. Vincent Alexander, C.B. 1915 ; 3rd Queen Alexandra's Own (Gurkha Rifles) ; Indian Army ; *b.* 17 July 1865. Entered army, 1885 ; Captain Indian Army, 1896 ; Major, 1903 ; Lt.-Col. 1910 ; served N.-W. Frontier, India, 1897-98 (medal, 2 clasps) : Tirah, 1897-98 (clasp) ; European War, 1914-15 (C.B.).   (*Died 2 May 1917.*)

ORNSTEIN, John Isidore Maurice, C.M.G. 1892 ; *b.* 1854. Late Dep. Director General Customs ; acting Under Secretary of State and Assistant Financial Adviser, Egypt (1st class Medjidie, 2nd class Osmanieh). *Address :* 1 Rue de Courcelles, Paris. *Club :* St. James's.   (*Died 22 April 1919.*)

O'RORKE, Rev. Benjamin Garniss, D.S.O. 1917 ; M.A. ; Chaplain to the Forces since 1901 ; *b.* 1875 ; *s.* of W. J. O'Rorke, Nottingham ; *m.* Myra Roberta, *d.* of late Rev. H. MacDougall, Rector of St. Michael's, Stamford, sometime Chaplain to the Forces ; three *d.* *Educ. :* Nottingham High School ; Exeter College, Oxford ; Wycliffe Hall, Oxford. Ordained, 1898 ; Curate of St. Peter's, Tiverton, 1898-1901 ; served S. African Campaign, 1901-2 ; at Aldershot, 1902-4 ; Bloemfontein, 1904-5 ; Pretoria, 1905-9 ; Bordon Camp, 1909-14 ; Hon. Sec. Army Missionary Association, 1910-14 ; Commissary to the Bishop of Accra since 1913 ; went out with British Expeditionary Force, Aug. 1914 ; captured by the Germans during retreat from Mons ; prisoner for ten months ; returned to France, 1915 (despatches, D.S.O.). *Publications :* African Missions, 1912 ; Our Opportunity in the West Indies, 1913 ; In the Hands of the Enemy, 1915 ; The Three Heroes, 1916. *Address :* c/o Sir C. R. M'Grigor, Bart., & Co., 39 Panton Street, S.W.1.   (*Died 25 Dec. 1918.*)

O'RORKE, Hon. Sir George Maurice, Kt., *cr.* 1880 ; Speaker of House of Representatives, New Zealand ; *b.* 1830 ; *m.* Cecilia, *d.* of late Alexander Shepherd of Auckland, first Colonial Treasurer of New Zealand, 1842-56 ; one *s.* *Educ. :* Trin. College, Dublin (B.A. 1852, M.A. and Hon. LL.D. 1896). Barr Auckland, 1868 ; Member of House of Representatives ; eight times elected Speaker of House of Representatives, 1862-92 ; Speaker of Auckland Provincial Council, 1865-1876, and member of New Zealand Ministry, 1872-74 ; Member of the Senate of New Zealand University ; Chairman of Council of Auckland University College, Auckland Grammar School Board ; Member of Legislative Council since 1904. *Address :* Onehunga, Auckland, N. Zealand.   (*Died 24 Aug. 1916.*)

ORPEN, His Honour Richard Theodore ; Chief Justice of Barbados since 1925 ; *b.* 13 Oct. 1869 ; *e. s.* of Right Rev. Raymond d'A Orpen, D.D., formerly Lord Bishop of Limerick and Ardfert,   *y. s.* of Sir Richard Orpen

of Ardtully, Kenmare, Ireland, and Sarah Lucinda, *d.* of D. de C. MacGillycuddy, J.P., of Tralee, Co. Kerry ; *m.* 1909, Victoria Maud, *d.* of Alfred Henshaw, J.P., of St. Philips, Milltoun, Co. Dublin ; no *c.* *Educ. :* privately ; Trinity College, Dublin ; Science Scholar Moderator ; B.A. with honours in Mathematics and Experimental Science. Called to Bar, King's Inns, Dublin, 1898 ; Police Magistrate, Southern Nigeria, Aug. 1903 ; Acting Attorney-General, Aug. 1903-Jan. 1904 ; Acting Solicitor-General for various periods, 1905-10 ; Acting Puisne Judge, June-August 1905, June-July 1908, Sept.-Dec. 1909 ; Resident Magistrate, Jamaica, June 1910 ; Acting Judge, Kingston Court, June 1920-Feb. 1921 ; Acting Puisne Judge, Feb-Aug. 1921, Nov. 1922-Sep. 1923, March-Aug. 1924, and Feb-May 1925 ; Judge, Kingston Court, Dec. 1921. *Recreation :* golf. *Address :* Bridgetown, Barbados, B.W.I.   (*Died 1926.*)

ORR, His Honour James, K.C. ; chairman of Quarter Sessions and County Court Judge of Down since 1897 ; *b.* Ballymena, Co. Antrim, 27 Oct. 1841 ; *e. s.* of late William Orr and Mary, *d.* of late Robert Harrison ; *m.* Annie Disney, *d.* of late Alex. Davison ; four *s.* one *d.* *Educ. :* Bromsgrove Grammar School, Worcestershire ; Jesus Coll. Camb. (scholar). 2nd class Classical Tripos, 1864 ; M.A. Irish Barr. 1867 ; Q.C. Trinity, 1884 ; appointed County Court Judge of Monaghan and Fermanagh, June 1891. *Address :* 87 Upper Mount Street, Dublin. *Club :* University, Dublin.   (*Died 19 Jan. 1920.*)

ORR, Maj.-Gen. John William, Indian Army ; *b.* 7 Dec. 1829 ; *m.* Charlotte (*d.* 1910), *y. d.* of late Lt.-Col. Cubitt, R.A., of Catfield, Norfolk. Entered army, 1850 ; Maj.-Gen. 1890 ; unemployed list, 1888 ; served Burmese War, 1852-53 (medal) ; Indian Mutiny, 1858-59 (medal with clasp). *Address :* 1 Merchiston Crescent, Edinburgh.   (*Died 1 April 1916.*)

ORR, Major Michael Harrison, D.S.O. 1902 ; late 1st Alexandra Princess of Wales' Own (Yorkshire Regt.) ; *b.* Ballymena, Co. Antrim, 23 Dec. 1859 ; *s.* of late William Orr of Hugomont, Ballymena, Co. Antrim ; unmarried. *Educ. :* Trinity College, Stratford - on - Avon ; Royal Military College, Sandhurst. Joined 19th Regt. 1880 ; served Egyptian War, 1884-86 ; Frontier Field Force in Egypt (Egyptian medal and Khedive's Star) ; South African campaign, 1899-1902, in the operations near Colesberg under General Sir John French (severely wounded, despatches) ; served in Lord Roberts's march from Bloemfontein to Pretoria ; present at the engagements of Brandfort, Vet River, Zand River, and the operations near Johannesburg and Pretoria, also Diamond Hill and Belfast (despatches, D.S.O., South African medal 5 clasps, King's medal 2 clasps). *Recreations :* cricket, golf, cycling. *Address :* c/o Glyn. Mills & Co., 3 Whitehall Place, S.W.1. *Clubs :* Golfer's ; Royal Portrush Golf.   (*Died 17 Mar. 1926.*)

ORR-EWING, Sir Archibald Ernest, 3rd Bt. ; *cr.* 1886 ; D.L., J.P. Stirlingshire ; *b.* 22 Feb. 1853 ; 2nd *s.* of Sir Archibald Orr-Ewing, 1st Bart. ; *S.* brother 1903 ; *m.* 1879, Hon. Mabel Addington, *y. d.* of 3rd Viscount Sidmouth ; one *s.* two *d.* *Educ. :* Harrow. Late Captain 3rd Batt. Argyll and Sutherland Highlanders ; Royal Archers (King's Bodyguard for Scotland). *Heir : s.* Col. Norman Archibald Orr-Ewing, D.S.O. *Address :* 7 Hereford Gardens, Park Lane, W. *Clubs :* Carlton, Boodle's, Hurlingham ; Royal Yacht Squadron, Cowes ; New, Edinburgh.   (*Died 21 April 1919.*)

ORR-LEWIS, Sir Frederick Orr, 1st Bart., *cr.* 1920 ; President of Lewis Brothers, Ltd., President and Founder of Canadian Vickers, Ltd., Director of Merchants Bank of Canada, Montreal Cotton Company and Bankers' Trust Company, Montreal ; 2nd *s.* of late William Thomas Lewis of Swansea, Co. Glamorgan and

Montreal, Canada; b. Hamilton, Canada, 11 Feb. 1866; m. 1896, Maud Helen, o. d. of William Booth, London, Ontario, Canada; one s. two d. Heir : s. John Duncan, b. 21 Feb. 1898. Address: Whitewebbs Park, near Enfield, Middlesex ; 20 Bleury Street, Montreal, Canada. Clubs: Junior Carlton, Wellington, Ranelagh ; Mount Royal, St. James, Forest and Stream, Jockey, Hunt, Mount Royal Golf, Montreal; Rideau, Ottawa. (Died 18 Nov. 1921.)

ORSMAN, W. J., J.P. Co. of London : b. 13 Aug. 1838 ; twice married ; widower ; one s. one d. Educ.: Cambridge. Assistant to Florence Nightingale in the Crimean War; entered G.P.O. London, 1856; retired from the position of Supervisor of H.M. Mails, 1889; elected to L.C.C. 1889; retired, 1895 ; Founder of the Golden Lane and Hoxton Costers' Christian Mission, 1861, and now the Consulting Superintendent ; Member of the Council of the Ragged School Union and Shaftesbury Society ; was one of the first Governors of the City Parochial Foundation. Publications: Golden Lane Mission Magazine, 12 vols., etc. Recreations: interested in costermongers and street-traders, and their donkeyshows ; also in the evangelistic work at Costers' Hall, Hoxton, N. ; girls' and boys'- Guilds, poor children's meals, holiday homes, etc. Address : 53 Forest Road, Tunbridge Wells.
(Died 4 Jan. 1923.)

OSBORNE, Rt. Rev. Edward William, D.D. ; b. Calcutta, 5 Jan. 1845 ; s. of Rev. J. F. Osborne, Priest of the English Church. Educ.: Gloucester, England. Deacon, 1869 ; Priest, 1870 ; Curate of Highworth, Wilts, 1869 ; Kenn, Devon, 1872 ; Society of St. John Evangelist (Cowley Fathers), 1875 ; worked in Boston, U.S.A., 1877-89 ; S. Africa, 1889-96 ; Missions in India, 1897-98 ; worked in Boston, 1899-1904 ; consecrated Bishop Coadjutor of Springfield, 1904 ; succeeded as Bishop, 1906 ; resigned on account of ill-health, Oct. 1916. Publications: The Children's Saviour : The Saviour King; The Children's Faith; The Story of Daniel; Wonderful Things in the Church Catechism ; Our Wonderful Faith; Woman—God's Gift to Man ; Boys and Girls I have Known ; Chapters for Church-goers. Address : 3915 Falcon Street, San Diego, California, U.S.A. (Died 5 July 1926.)

OSBORNE, Lord Francis Granville Godolphin, s. of 9th Duke of Leeds ; b. 11 March 1864 ; m. 1896, Ruth, e. d. of late Vice-Admiral Grieve, Commander Royal Navy. Address : Ord House, Berwick-on-Tweed. Club : Naval and Military. (Died 17 Oct. 1924.)

OSBURN, Commander Francis ; b. 1834 ; 3rd s. of late William Osburn, Royal Society of Literature, Egyptologist, Leeds ; m. 1859, Victoria Pauline, d. of Captain Richard Bushelle, R.N., Dover ; five s. four d. Entered Royal Navy as Naval Cadet, 1848 ; joined H.M.S. Victory ; served as Midshipman in H.M.S. Desperate on relief expedition for Sir John Franklin, 1852; as Lieutenant in H.M.S. Ajax during Russian War (Baltic medal); present at bombardment of Bomarsund ; promoted and served in H.M.S. Curacoa in Crimea; Stipendiary Magistrate, Jamaica, 1879 ; J.P. Dominion of Canada. Address: Winsley, Southbourne, Sussex. (Died 29 Mar. 1917.)

O'SHAUGHNESSY, Patrick Joseph, M.P. (N.) West Limerick 1900-18 ; b. 1872. Educ.: Rathkeale ; French College, Blackrock. Address : Rathkeale, Co. Limerick.
(Died 20 Dec. 1920.)

O'SHAUGHNESSY, Richard, C.B. 1903 ; M.V.O. 1900 ; Commissioner of Public Works, Ireland, 1891-1903 ; b. 1842 ; s. of James O'Shaughnessy, M.R.C.S.E., D.L., Limerick City ; m. 1867, Ellen, d. of James Potter, Farm Lodge, Limerick ; graduated Trinity College, Dublin. Called to the Bar, Ireland, 1866 ; M.P. Limerick City, 1874-83 ; Registrar, 27

Petty Sessions Clerks, 1883-91 ; Commissioner of Public Works, Ireland, 1891-1903. Address : 8 Palmerston Park, Dublin. Club : Stephen's Green, Dublin. (Died 17 Aug. 1918.)

O'SHEA, Lucius Trant, M.Sc. (Sheffield), B.Sc. (London) ; Professor of Applied Chemistry in the University of Sheffield ; e. s. of late Major Rodney Payne O'Shea, 20th Regiment of Foot, and late Elizabeth Caroline, d. of late Admiral of the Fleet Sir Lucius Curtis, 2nd Bart., K.C.B. ; m. Mary, 2nd d. of late F. M. Tindall; one s. one d. Educ.: Manchester Grammar School; Owens College, Manchester. Assistant Lecturer and Demonstrator in Chemistry in Firth College, Sheffield, 1880 ; Lecturer in Mining Chemistry, 1890 ; Fellow of the Chemical Society, and Member of the Society of Chemical Industry ; Honorary Secretary of the Institution of Mining Engineers ; went to South Africa in command of detachment of the 1st West York Royal Engineer Volunteers, 1901, and was attached to 17th Field Coy. R.E. at Standerton ; remained in South Africa till the declaration of peace (Queen's medal, 5 clasps ; granted rank of Hon. Lieut. in the army) ; Officer Commanding the University of Sheffield O.T.C., 1911-17. Publications: Elementary Chemistry for Coal Mining Students ; papers read before learned societies ; A Contribution to the History of the Constitution of Bleaching Powder ; Retention of Lead by Filter Paper ; Note on the Woolwich Testing Station ; A Testing Station for Mining Explosives ; The Safety of High Explosives, with Special Reference to Methods of Testing. Recreations: golf and volunteering. Address: The Department of Applied Science, The University, Sheffield. T. : 335 Broomhill, Sheffield.
(Died 18 April 1920.)

O'SHEA, Lt.-Col. Timothy, D.S.O. 1916; b. 1856. Major and Quartermaster (retired pay) the King's Royal Rifle Corps ; Lt.-Col. and Quartermaster 9th Batt. London Regt.; retired; served Burma, 1891 (medal with clasp); South African War, 1902 (despatches, Queen's medal with 2 clasps); European War, 1914-18 (despatches twice, D.S.O., 1914 Star, Allies medal and Victory medal, Coronation medal (King George). Address: 15 Berkeley Road, Crouch End, N.8. (Died 7 July 1921.)

OSLER, Sir Edmund Boyd, Kt., cr. 1912; Member Dominion House of Commons for West Toronto 1896-1917 ; b. Tecumceth Parsonage, Co. Simcoe, Ontario, 1845; 4th s. of late Rev. F. L. Osler; m. 1873, Annie Farquharson (d. 1910), d. of late F. J. Cochran of Balfour, Aberdeenshire ; three s. three d. Educ.: Grammar School, Dundas, Ont. Is head of financial firm of Osler & Hammond, Toronto ; President, Toronto Bond Trade, 1896 ; one of representatives of Canada at Congress of Chambers of Commerce, London, 1896 ; Director of and member of the Executive of Canadian Pacific Rly. Co. ; President of Dominion Bank of Canada ; Chairman, Endowment Committee, Trinity University, and a member of Governing Body of Univ. of Toronto. Address: Craigleigh, Toronto, Canada. Clubs : York, Toronto, Toronto Golf, Toronto ; Mount Royal, Montreal.
(Died 4 Aug. 1924.)

OSLER, Featherston, D.C.L. (hon.) Trinity University ; b. 4 Jan. 1838 ; e. s. of late Rev. F. L. Osler, M.A. (Cantab.), formerly of Falmouth, Eng., and Ellen Free Pickton ; m. 1861, Henrietta (d. 1902), d. of late Capt. Henry Smith, H.E.I.C.S.; three s. three d. Bar, 1860; Bencher Law Society of Upper Canada (elected), 1875-79, 1879, and ex-officio since 1910 ; Puisne Judge, Common Pleas, 1879-83 ; Justice of Appeal for Ontario, 1883-1910; declined appointment to Supreme Court of Canada, 1888 and 1909 ; Commissioner for revising Ontario Statutes, 1887, 1897, and 1907-14 (Chairman) ; Trustee of

801

O'SHEA, Sir Henry, Kt. See page xxvii.

Corporation of Trinity College; Senator of University of Toronto (elected); President Toronto General Trusts Corporation since 1910. *Address:* 80 Crescent Road, Toronto. *Clubs:* York, Empire, Toronto.   (*Died 17 Jan. 1924.*)

OSLER, Sir William, 1st Bt., *cr.* 1911; M.D., F.R.S., F.R.C.P. (Lond.); Student (Fellow) of Christ Church; Regius Professor of Medicine, Oxford; Hon. Prof. of Medicine, Johns Hopkins Univ.; *b.* Bond Head, Canada, 12 July 1849; 6th *s.* of late Rev. F. L. Osler; *m.* 1892, Grace, *e. d.* of late John Revere of Boston, Mass. *Educ.:* Trinity College School; Trinity College, Toronto; Toronto University; M'Gill University, Montreal; Univ. Coll. London; Berlin and Vienna. Hon. D.Sc. Oxford, Cambridge, Dublin, Liverpool, and Leeds; LL.D. M'Gill, Toronto, Aberdeen, Edinburgh, Yale, Harvard, Johns Hopkins Universities; D.C.L. Durham and Trin. University, Toronto. Hon. M.D., Christiania; Hon. F.R.C.P., Dublin; Foreign Associate of the Academy of Medicine, Paris; President of the Bibliographical Society, 1913-1918; President of the Classical Association, 1918-19; Professor of the Institutes of Medicine, M'Gill University, 1874-84; Professor of Clinical Medicine, University of Penna, 1884-89; Professor of Medicine, Johns Hopkins University, 1889-1904. *Publications:* Cerebral Palsies of Children, 1889; Chorea and Choreiform Affections, 1894; The Principles and Practice of Medicine, 8th ed. 1912; Lectures on Abdominal Tumours, 1895; On Angina Pectoris and Allied States, 1897; Monograph on Cancer of the Stomach, 1900; Science and Immortality, 1904; Æquanimitas and other Addresses, 1904; Counsels and Ideals, 1905; editor of A System of Medicine, 2nd edition, 1915; Thomas Linacre, 1908; An Alabama Student and other Biographical Essays, 1908; A Way of Life, 1914. *Heir:* none. *Recreation:* bibliography. *Address:* 13 Norham Gardens, Oxford. *Club:* Athenæum.
    (*Died 29 Dec. 1919.*)

O'SULLIVAN, Most Rev. Charles, R.C. Bishop of Kerry and Aghadoe since 1917; *b.* East Kerry, 1862. *Educ.:* Killarney Seminary; Maynooth. Served Mission at Millstreet, 1887-1907; Dean of Kerry and Pastor of Tralee, 1907-17; Member of Congested Districts Board, 1918. *Address:* The Palace, Killarney.
    (*Died 29 Jan. 1927.*)

O'SULLIVAN, Ven. Leopold, D.D., Archdeacon of Killaloe since 1909; Rector of Clough-Jordan since 1877. *Educ.:* Trinity Coll., Dublin. Ordained, 1870; Curate of Dunkerren, 1870-75; Canon of Killaloe, 1888-89. *Address:* The Rectory, Clough-Jordan, Co. Tipperary.
    (*Died 22 Oct. 1919.*)

O'SULLIVAN-BEARE, Daniel Robert (The O'Sullivan-Beare), Consul-General at Rio de Janeiro, 1913-15, and since 1919; *b.* 1865; *o. s.* of late The O'Sullivan-Beare. *Educ.:* French schools; Dublin University (T.C.D.), graduate in Arts and in Medicine, First Senior Moderator, and Gold Medallist in Natural Science. Attached to Army Medical Department during Egyptian Campaign, 1885; subsequently travelled during several years in various parts of the world; was shipwrecked in Straits of Magellan; Medical Officer in the Gold Coast Colony, 1893; acting Medical Officer to Agency at Zanzibar, 1893-94; Vice-Consul for the Island of Pemba, East Africa, 1894; was engaged during several years in suppressing the slave trade; received personal rank of Consul, as reward for services in that connection, 1906; while in Africa, introduced to the notice of the medical profession a native remedy for cure of Blackwater Fever, which has since proved to be a specific for the disease in question; Consul at Bahia, Brazil, 1907; acting Consul-General at Rio de Janeiro, 1907-8; transferred, as Consul,

to São Paulo, Brazil, 1907; seconded by Foreign Office for military service and gazetted Lt.-Col., R.A.M.C., Nov. 1915; served throughout the duration of the war; has received the Order of the Brilliant Star of Zanzibar. *Recreations:* riding, tennis. *Address:* c/o H. S. King & Co., 9 Pall Mall, S.W.1. *Club:* Royal Thames Yacht.
    (*Died 13 June 1921.*)

OSWALD, Richard Alexander, J.P. for Ayrshire, Kirkcudbright, and Dumfriesshire; D.L. for Ayrshire and Kirkcudbright; Vice-Lt. of Ayrshire; Convener of Ayrshire, 1901-13; *e. s.* of late George Oswald and 1st wife, Lydia Margaret, *d.* of late Frederick Homan of Ardenwood, Co. Kildare; *b.* 1841; *m.* 1868, Maude, 2nd *d.* of late James Hugh Smith Barry of Marbury Hall, Cheshire, and Fota, Co. Cork; *S.* father 1871. *Educ.:* Radley; Harrow. Late Lieut. 29th Foot; owns 11,540 acres in Ayrshire, and 24,160 in Kirkcudbright. *Heir: half-b.* Major Julian Oswald, late 16th Lancers. *Address:* Auchincruive, Ayr, N.B.: Cavens, Kirkcudbright, N.B.   (*Died 13 April 1921.*)

OSWALD, William Digby, D.S.O. 1902; *b.* 20 Jan. 1880; *s.* of T. R. Oswald; *m.* 1905, Catherine Mary, *d.* of late Rev. J. S. Yardley; two *d.* Served South Africa with Railway Pioneer Regiment, 1902 (despatches, medal, 5 clasps, D.S.O.).   (*Died 16 July 1916.*)

OULTON, George N., K.C.; Bencher of King's Inns; late Conveyancing Counsel to the Master of the Rolls; Scholar and Moderator T.C.D. *Address:* 19 Upper Mount Street, Dublin.
    (*Died 30 Dec. 1928.*)

OUTCAULT, Richard Felton, artist; *b.* Lancaster, Ohio, 14 Jan. 1863; *s.* of J. P. Outcault and Catherine Davis; *m.* 1890, Mary Jane Martin, Lancaster, O. *Educ.:* McMicken University, Cincinnati. On staff New York Journal since 1905. *Publications:* Buster, Mary Jane and Tige, 1908; Buster Brown, the Busy Body, 1909; Real Buster and the only Mary Jane, 1909; Buster Brown in Foreign Lands, 1912; Buster Brown—the Fun Maker, 1912; Buster Brown and his Pets, 1913. *Address:* Flushing, L.I., New York.
    (*Died 25 Sept. 1928.*)

OUTRAM, Sir James, 3rd Bt.; *cr.* 1858; *b.* 13 Oct. 1864; *o. s.* of 2nd Bt. and Jane Anne (*d.* 1903), *e. d.* of late P. Davidson, Inchmarlo, Kincardineshire; *S.* father, 1912; *m.* 1921, Lilian Mary, *d.* of late Joseph Balfour, Athelstone House, Brighton. *Educ.:* Haileybury; Pembroke College, Cambridge. *Heir: b.* Francis Davidson, O.B.E., Bt. Major (formerly) Royal Engineers [*b.* 4 Aug. 1867; *m.* 1st, 1893, Maud Charlotte (*d.* 1913), *d.* of late J. P. Kitchin, The Manor House, Hampton; one *d.* ; 2nd, 1915, Isabel Mary, *d.* of late H. C. Berry. *Address:* Lyss-na-Greyne, Aboyne, Aberdeenshire]. *Address:* 98 Bouverie Road West, Folkestone.   (*Died 12 Mar. 1925.*)

OUTTRIM, Hon. Alfred Richard, late Member of the Legislative Assembly, representing Maryborough, Victoria, Australia; *s.* of James Outtrim and Elizabeth Rosa Stephenson, both of London; *b.* Mile End Road, London, 30th March 1845; *m.* 1871, Jane Lavinia Tutcher; one *s.* three *d.* *Educ.:* Denominational School, Maryburgh, Victoria. Left London Docks with members of the family in the sailing ship Eliza for Melbourne, 1852; has held office in three Governments in Victoria; has held eight portfolios, viz. Minister of Mines in the three Governments, Minister of Forests in two Governments, Minister of Water Supply in one Government, Minister of Defence in one Government, and Minister of Railways in one Government; Mayor of Maryborough, Victoria, twice; Member of the Borough Council for many years; acting Chairman of Committee of the Legislative Assembly, Victoria. *Recreation:* no time for recreation in his young days. *Address:*

OUIMET, Hon. Joseph Alderic. See page xxvii.

State Parliament House, Melbourne, Victoria, Australia. *(Died Dec. 1925.)*

OUTTRIM, Frank Leon, V.D., I.S.O. 1904; Lt.-Col. Victorian Garrison Artil. Militia (retired); J.P.; *b.* London, 22 Aug. 1847; *s.* of James Outtrim and Rosa Elizabeth Stephenson; *m.* Frances Caroline, *o. d.* of Captain William Henry Litchfield, Williamstown, Victoria; one *s. Educ.:* Church of England School, Maryborough, Victoria. Came to colony with parents, 1852; joined Public Service, 1863; filled various positions in Postal Department; selected for First Deputy Commissioner Income Tax, 1895; connected with local military forces for many years, and was Major in command of North Melbourne Battery Garrison Artillery for seven years, promoted Lieutenant - Colonel on retirement; Deputy Postmaster-Gen., State of Victoria, 1897; retired 1907. *Address:* Minyonge, 78 Holmes Road, Moonee Ponds, Melbourne, Victoria.

OVENDEN, Very Rev. Charles T., D.D.; Dean of St. Patrick's Cathedral, Dublin, 1911; Canon of St. Patrick's Cathedral, Dublin, since 1889; *b.* Enniskillen, 11 Sep. 1846; *s.* of William C. Ovenden, M.D., and Isabella Parkinson; *m.* 1871, Isabella Mary, *d.* of late John Robinson, J.P., Uplands, Co. Wicklow; two *d. Educ.:* Portora Roy. School, Enniskillen; Mannheim, Germany; T.C.D. Dublin. Ordained 1870 for Curacy of Magdalene Church, Belfast; Rector of Dunluce, Co. Antrim, 1872-1879; Succentor of St. Patrick's Cathedral, Dublin, 1879-84; Rector of Portrush, 1884-86; Chaplain to the Lord Lieutenant and Precentor of Clogher, 1886-1903; Dean of Clogher, 1903-11; Rector of Enniskillen, and Rural Dean, 1886-1911. *Publications:* Edited 1st edition of the Cathedral Anthem Book of Words; In the Day of Trouble; To Whom shall we go?; The Church Navvy; The Enthusiasm of Christianity; The Face of Nature; Marvels in the World of Light; The Foundation of a Happy Life; Problems in Life and Religion; Deep Questions; Popular Science for Parochial Evenings; Modern Criticism of the Holy Scriptures; Morning and Evening Service with office of Holy Communion. Anthems—I will alway give Thanks; For the Rain cometh down; Processional Anthem—The Son of God goes forth to War. *Recreations:* oil-painting and music. *Address:* The Deanery, St. Patrick's Close, Dublin. *T.A.:* The Deanery, Dublin. *T.:* Dublin 2901. *M.:* IK 4094. *Clubs:* Hibernian Catch Club, Friendly Brothers, Dublin. *(Died 9 July 1924.)*

OVERTON, Robert; author, dramatist, journalist; lecturer on literary and philosophical subjects; *b.* 8 Dec. 1859; *y. surv. s.* of late Charles Overton, H.M. Customs, and Marler Sulyard Talbot. *Educ.:* privately. Royal Defence Corps, late Honourable Artillery Company. *Publications:* Queer Fish; A Round Dozen; Ten Minutes; The Overton Reciters; Overton Entertainer; Water-Works; Nine and Three; After School; Lights Out; The King's Pardon; Far from Home; Friend or Fortune?; The Son of the School; The Orphan of Tor College; Decoyed across the Seas; A Chase Round the World; Dangerous Days; Saturday Island; The Three Skippers; The Secret of the Caves; The Clue of the Cloak. *Dramas:* Hearts of Oak; Next of Kin; The Mills of God; No Quarter. *One-act plays:* The Man in Possession; Purgatory; Fortune Favours Fools; Splendid Silence; A Mad Marriage; The Lady Secretary; Santa Claus; Gertie's Convict; Mrs. Seton's Secret; Two Negatives; pantomimes, operettas, monologues. *Recreations:* boating, field sports, voyaging in tramp steamships, chess. *Address:* c/o Sampson Low, Limited, 100 Southwark Street, S.E.1. *(Died 28 Nov. 1924.)*

OWEN, Col. Arthur Allen, M.V.O. 1911; gentleman-at-arms; *b.* 19 Jan. 1842; *m.* Jennie *(d.* 1905), *d.* of Edwin Lewis, of Goldthorn Hill, Wolverhampton. Entered Army, 1859; Major,

1877; retired, 1881; served S. Africa, 1877-79 (despatches, medal with clasp, brevet Lt.-Col.); Jubilee medal and clasp; Coronation medal of King Edward VII. and King George V.; Order of Mercy. *Address:* Polesdon, Datchet. *Club:* Naval and Military. *(Died 29 April 1917.)*

OWEN, Major-Gen. Charles Henry; *b.* 1880; *s.* of Henry Owen, who was *n.* of Henry Owen Cunliffe of Wycoller; *m.* Emily Linzee *(d.* 1908), *d.* of W. A. Hunt of Burleigh, near Plymouth; three *s.* three *d. Educ.:* R.M. Acad. Woolwich. Obtained a commission in the Royal Artillery, 1848; joined Royal Artillery as Lieutenant, 1849; served Crimean Campaign, 1854-55, at Inkerman, and in all the six bombardments, throughout the siege, and at the fall of Sebastopol (despatches, Chevalier Legion of Honour, 5th class Medjidie, Crimean medal and two clasps, Turkish war medal, Brevet Major for distinguished service in the field); Professor of Artillery at the R.M. Academy, Woolwich, 1859-73; Member of Ordnance Select Committee, and of the Committee on Ordnance; served in command of 2 or 3 field batteries from 1873, and commanded the Field Artillery at Aldershot, 1879; retired, full pay, 1881. Decorated for service in the Crimea. *Publications:* Motion of Projectiles, Lectures on Artillery, Modern Artillery (Class Book in the service); papers on military and scientific subjects in the Proceedings of the R.A. Institution, and the R.U.S. Institution, and in the U.S. Magazine. *Recreations:* art; member of the Water Colour Society of Ireland, and of the Lancashire and Cheshire Antiquarian Soc.; hunted regularly in England and Ireland. *Address:* Hanley, Camberley, Surrey. *T.A.:* Camberley. *Clubs:* Army and Navy; West Surrey, Camberley. *(Died 6 Nov. 1921.)*

OWEN, Lieut.-Col. Charles William, C.M.G. 1887; C.I.E. 1881; L.R.C.P., M.R.C.S.; J.P. Sussex; *b.* 28 Jan. 1853; *m.* 1st 1878, Mary Elizabeth *(d.* 1920), *e. d.* of late Horace Barry; 2nd, 1921, Mabel Howard, *e. d.* of Rev. H. Hopley, Goodrest, Uckfield, formerly Vicar of Westham. Surgeon, 1876; Lt.-Col. 1896; served on Headquarter Staff, Afghan War. 1879-80 (despatches), including operations round Cabul, 1879 (slightly wounded, despatches, C.I.E., medal with two clasps); Egyptian War, on Headquarter Staff, I.E.F., 1882, including Tel-el-Kebir (medal with clasp, Khedive's star); served on Afghan Boundary Commission (C.M.G.); Mohmund Expedition, 1898, on Headquarter Staff (medal and clasp); formerly Surgeon to H.E. the Commander-in-Chief in India, Lord Roberts; Medical Adviser to late H.H. Maharaja of Patiala; Vice-Chairman of Eastbourne Rural District Council and Member of Board of Guardians; Member of East Sussex Education Committee; Chairman of Hailsham Grouped Council Schools; Member of St. John's Hospital; Land Tax Commissioner; Order of Hurmat, 1886, etc.; Conty Director B.R.C.S., Sussex; Member East Sussex War Pensions Committee. *Recreations:* educationalist, amateur photographer, motorist. *Address:* The Horns, Hankham, Westham, Sussex. *T.A.:* Owen Hankham. *T.:* Pevensy 1X1. *M.:* AP 2371. *Clubs:* Services; The Lewes and County; Sussex County and Eastbourne Automobile, Eastbourne. *(Died 23 May 1922.)*

OWEN, Sir Douglas, Kt., *cr.* 1915; K.B.E., *cr.* 1917; Chevalier de la Legion d'Honneur, France; Officier de l'Ordre de la Couronne, Belgium; Barrister, Inner Temple; Lecturer London School of Economics, Army Class (Ocean Transport); Lecturer, Royal Naval War Colleges; Chairman, Advisory Committee State War Risks Insurance Office; Chairman of Coal Exports Committee; Member of Panel of Advisers on School Commercial Certificates, University of London; 4th *s.* of Dr. W. B. Owen, Cleveland Square, W.; *b.* 1850; *m.* 1889, Eliz.

OVEREND, Walker, M.D. See page xxvii.

803

Charlotte, *d.* of A. W. Surtees. *Educ.* : King's College School ; private. Represented Colonial Office at Shipping Freights Conference at Johannesburg, 1904 ; Hon. Secretary Mansion House Committee on Port of London, 1902 ; Member of Admiralty Small Committee of Experts re Naval Manœuvres, 1906 ; Member Lord Herschell's Special Committee on Marine Insurance Bill, 1895 ; Hon. Sec. Budget Protest League, 1909 ; Hon. Sec and Treasurer Society for Nautical Research ; Chairman, Paddington Green Children's Hospital, and member of House Committee, London Hospital. *Publications*: (with Sir M. Chalmers, draughtsman of Bill) Digest of the Law of Marine Insurance ; Declaration of War, a Survey of the Position of Belligerents and Neutrals in Maritime War ; Ocean Trade and Shipping ; London, the Port of the Empire ; Ports and Docks. *Recreations* : literature, fishing, and shooting. *Address* : 44 St. George s Court, Gloucester Road, S.W.7. *T.* : Kens. 3125. *Clubs* : Savile, Ranelagh. (*Died* 15 *Nov.* 1920.)

OWEN, Edward Cunliffe, C.M.G. 1886 ; Secretary to Metropolitan Electric Supply Co. ; *b.* 1857 ; *s.* of late Col. Cunliffe Owen, R.E., C.B. ; *m.* 1882, Emma, *d.* of late Sir Philip Cunliffe Owen, K.C.B. *Educ.* : Wellington ; Trinity Coll. Cambridge. *Address* : 16 Stratford Place, W. *Club* : Oxford and Cambridge.
(*Died* 27 *Dec.* 1918.)

OWEN, Henry, D.L., J.P. ; D.C.L. Oxford ; F.S.A. London ; Treasurer of the National Library of Wales ; Chairman of the Hon. Society of Cymmrodorion, and Pembrokeshire Quarter Sessions ; High Shoriff, Pembrokeshire, 1902 ; Member of Royal Commission on Public Records. *Publications*: Gerald the Welshman ; Old Pembroke Families ; Owen's Pembrokeshire, etc. *Address*: Poyston, Haverford West. *Clubs*: Athenæum, Savile, New University.
(*Died* 14 *April* 1919.)

OWEN, Col. Henry Mostyn, C.B. 1902 ; M.V.O. 1904 ; Dragoon Guards ; late Assistant Director Remounts ; *b.* 26 April 1858 ; *m.* 1894, Hilda Mary, 3rd *d.* of Sir Robert Gunter, 1st Bt. ; one *s.* two *d.* Entered army, 1878 ; Captain, 1886 ; Major, 1895 ; Lieut.-Col. 1898 ; served with the Carabiniers, Afghanistan, 1879-80 (medal) ; South Africa, 1901-2 (despatches, Queen's medal 5 clasps, C.B.). *Address* : Hambleton House, Norton-Malton. *T.A.* : Malton 189 *Club* : Yorkshire, York. (*Died* 18 *Nov.* 1927.)

OWEN, Sir Hugh, G.C.B., *cr.* 1899 ; K.C.B., *cr.* 1887 ; C.B. 1885 ; *b.* 1835 ; *s. s.* of Sir Hugh Owen, knighted for services in connection with education in Wales ; *m.* 1865, Charlotte Elizabeth, *d.* of late Charles Burt of Tufnell Park, N. ; two *s.* three *d.* Barr. Middle Temple, 1862 ; Assistant Secretary of Local Government Board, 1876-82 ; Permanent Secretary, 1882-98 ; Chairman of the Commissioners under the London Govt. Act, 1899-1907 ; one of the Commissioners forming the Court of Arbitration under the Metropolis Water Act, 1902. In consideration of his services in connection with public health and poor law administration was presented with the honorary freedom of the Plumbers' Company, which was followed by the freedom of the City of London, and was elected Honorary Fellow of the Royal Institute of Public Health, and a Lodge of Freemasons adopted the name of the Hugh Owen Lodge. *Publications*: Education Acts Manual ; Municipal Corporation Act, 1882 ; and other legal works relating to duties of local authorities. *Address* : South Grove, Highgate, N. ; 1 Pump Court, Temple, E.C.
(*Died* 28 *Jan.* 1916.)

OWEN, Sir Isambard, Kt., *cr.* 1902 ; Hon. D.C.L. Durham, 1905 ; LL.D. Wales, hon. causâ, 1911 ; Hon. LL.D. Bristol, 1912 ; M.D., M.A., F.R.C.P. ; Hon. Fellow of Downing College, Cam-

bridge ; Hon. Fellow of the University of Bristol ; Vice-Chancellor of the University of Bristol, 1909-21 ; *b.* Bellevue House, near Chepstow, Mon., 28 Dec. 1850 ; *s.* of the late William George Owen, Chief Engineer of the Great Western Railway ; *m.* 1905, Ethel, *d.* of late Lewis Holland - Thomas of Caerffynnon, Merioneth ; two *d.* *Educ.*: King's School, Gloucester; Rossall; Downing College, Cambridge ; St. George's Hospital. Late Physician to and Lecturer in Medicine at St. George's Hospital ; Hon. Fellow and late Vice - President Medical Society of London ; Senior Deputy-Chancellor University of Wales 1895-1910 ; late Vice-President of University Coll., Bangor ; Member of Council of Univ. Coll. Cardiff ; Gov. Univ. College, Aberystwyth ; late Member of Central Welsh Board ; late Examiner in Medicine, Universities of Cambridge, London, and Durham, Royal Army Medical Corps, and Royal College of Physicians of London ; late President of Teachers' Guild of Great Britain and Ireland, 1898-99 ; Vice-Dean of Faculty of Medicine of Univ. of London, 1901-4 ; Consulting Physician to and Hon. Governor of St. George's Hospital ; Member of the General Medical Council, 1910-25 ; Principal of Armstrong College, Newcastle, 1904-9 ; took the leading part in the establishment of the University of Wales, 1891-93, and in the reconstruction of the University of Durham, 1907-9 ; Hon. Lieut.-Col. Volunteer Force. *Publications*: various papers on education and on professional subjects. *Recreation*: chiefly cycling. *Address*: c/o Faithfull, Owen, Blair and Wright, Dacre House, Westminster, S.W.1. *Club* : Athenæum.
(*Died* 14 *Jan.* 1927.)

OWEN, Jean A. (Mrs. Owen Visger), author and journalist ; *b.* Staffordshire ; *e. d.* of late Thomas Pinder, Burslem and Endon ; *m.* 1st, 1863, George Newton Owen ; 2nd 1883, Harman Visger, Bristol ; one *d.* *Educ.* : Elgin, Scotland ; Neuwied, Germany. Sailed for New Zealand, June 1868 ; lived near Auckland for five years ; voyages to Tahiti, Hawaiian Islands, etc. ; in England again, 1869-72 ; through West Indies, across Panama, and again arrived in the Hawaiian Islands, 1873 ; from Honolulu (after Mr. Owen's death) by San Francisco and New York to England again, 1876 ; shipwrecked in the R.M.S. "Douro" off Cape Finisterre, 1882 ; travelled much in various parts of Europe, and has made many voyages in the North and South Pacific ; lived in Australia and Honolulu, 1910-13, when she returned to England. *Publications*: From San Francisco to New York, 1869 ; Our Honolulu Boys, 1877 ; Silver Linings, Ethel's Comforter, Under Palm and Pine, Sea Blossom, A Runaway, Make the Best of Yourself, Candelaria—between 1877 and 1883 ; After Shipwreck, 1882 ; Forest, Field, and Fell, 1892 ; The Country Month by Month, 1894 ; The Story of Hawaii, 1898 ; Birds in their Seasons, 1904 ; Facing the World, 1905 ; (with Otto Herman) Birds Useful and Hurtful, 1909 ; Love Covers All, 1911 ; Ruth Thornton, 1913 ; Editor and collaborateur of On Surrey Hills, Drift from Longshore, and of all books that have been published under the signature of "A Son of the Marshes"—that title having been chosen by Mrs. Visger to cover the collaborated work of a working naturalist in Surrey and herself. *Recreations* : the tending of plants, music, and travel. *Club* : Writers'
(*Died* 30 *July* 1922.)

OWEN, Rt. Rev. John, Bishop of St. David's since 1897 ; *b.* 24 Aug. 1854 ; *s.* of Griffith Owen, Ysgubor-wen-Llanengan ; *m.* 1882, Amelia, *d.* of J. Longstaff, Appleby, Westmorland ; four *s.* six *d.* *Educ.* : Bottwnog Grammar School ; Jesus College, Oxford (Scholar), M.A. ; Double 2nd class Honours in Moderations, 1874 ; 2nd class Mathematics Honours Finals. Deacon, 1879 ; Priest, 1880 ; Welsh Professor and

Classical Lecturer St. David's College, Lampeter, 1879-85 ; Warden and Headmaster of Llandovery College, 1885-89 ; Dean of St. Asaph, 1889-92 ; Principal of St. David's College, Lampeter : Canon of St. Asaph, 1892-97. *Publications :* various articles and addresses on the Church in Wales. *Address :* The Palace, Abergwili, R.S.O., Carmarthenshire. *T.A. :* Carmarthen. *Club :* Athenæum. *(Died 4 Nov. 1926.)*

OWEN, Gen. Sir John Fletcher, K.C.B., *cr.* 1906 ; C.B. 1902 ; b. 9 April 1839 ; 3rd *s.* of Rev. Canon Owen of Hendrevinws, M.A., Rector of Llaniestyn; J.P., D.L. Carnarvonshire, N. Wales; unmarried. *Educ. :* Rossall Hall; R.M. Acad., Woolwich. Graduate of the Artillery Coll. *p.a.c.* Assist. Supt. Royal Gun Factories, 1877-78; served with Wood's Column in Zulu War, 1879, commanding a mounted Gatling battery at battle of Ulundi (despatches, brevet of Lieut. - Col.) ; Commandant Mil. Forces South Australia, 1885-1888 ; Commandant Camp and School Coast Defences, Golden Hill, 1889-90 ; Commandant Defence Forces, Queensland, 1891-94 ; Major-General on the Staff commanding Artillery Brigade, Malta, 1895-99 ; promoted to Lieut.-General, February 1899 ; received Reward for Distinguished Service, Nov. 1896 ; President Ordnance Committee, 1902 - 4 ; General, 1904 ; Colonel Commandant, Royal Artillery, 1906. *Publications :* various professional papers and lectures. *Recreations :* shooting, fishing, cycling, etc. *Club :* United Service. *(Died 10 June 1924.)*

OWEN, Rev. John Smith, Hon. Canon, Norwich. *Educ. :* Trinity College, Dublin (M.A., LL.D.). Curate of St. Stephens, Norwich, 1863-69 ; Vicar of St. Matthew's, Thorpe Hamlet, 1869-74 ; North Walsham, 1874-1905 ; Witton, 1905-16. *Address :* Lyndhurst, Mundesley-on-Sea. *(Died 20 Mar. 1922.)*

OWEN, Lt.-Col. Robert Haylock, C.M.G. 1916 ; Australian Military Forces ; *s.* of Colonel Percy Owen, V.D., R. Australian Artillery ; *m.* Hilda Grace, *d.* of Thomas Irvine Rowell, M.D., C.M.G. ; one *s.* one *d.* *Educ. :* Sydney Grammar School. Lieutenant Australian Soudan Contingent, 1888 ; Lieutenant to Major in H.M. South Lancashire Regt. ; Lt.-Col. and Chief Staff Officer New Zealand Forces ; Lt.-Col. commanding 3rd Battalion A.I.F., Gallipoli Campaign (despatches twice, C.M.G.). *Address :* Woodmancote, Dursley, Glos. *(Died 5 April 1927.)*

OWEN, Lt.-Col. Sydney Lloyd, D.S.O. 1916 ; late R.E. ; *a. s.* of late Dr. and Mrs. Lloyd Owen of Southsea ; *b.* 27 Feb. 1872. *Educ. :* Portsmouth Grammar School ; Royal Military Academy, Woolwich. Entered Army, 1891 ; served South African War, 1899 - 1902 (despatches, 2 medals and 7 clasps) ; European War, 1914 - 18 (despatches, D.S.O.) ; retired pay, 1921. *Recreations :* cricket, football, golf, amateur theatricals. *Address :* Cox & Co., 16 Charing Cross, S.W.1. *Club :* United Service.

OWEN, Sir Thomas David, Kt., *cr.* 1921 ; *b.* Halton, Cheshire, 18 Nov. 1854 ; unmarried. *Educ. :* Brynford House School, Holywell, Flintshire. Served articles as Chemist and Metallurgical Chemist at Flint Chemical; Head Chemist to Works of John Hutchinson & Co., Chemical Works, Widnes; Manager of Grasselli Chemical Works, U.S.A. ; joined father's firm in Liverpool, Chemical merchants, of which firm now sole partner ; Vice - President, Etablissement Union, Paris and Rouen, Chemical Manufacturers ; member of Council of University College of North Wales, Bangor. *Recreations :* cricket, golf, bowls and motoring. *Address :* Fowell House, Albion Street, Wallasey, Cheshire ; *T.A. :* Filtered, Liverpool. *Club :* Wallasey 900, Central 421 Liverpool. *M. :* HF 87. *Clubs :* New Brighton Cricket ; Leasowe Golf. *(Died 22 Sept. 1921.)*

OWEN, William, I.S.O. 1902; late Chief Clerk, Exchequer and Audit Department ; *b.* 1837 ; *s.* of Sir Hugh Owen, knighted for services in connection with education in Wales. Barr. Middle Temple, 1862. *Address :* 6 Clyde Road, St. Leonards-on-Sea. *(Died 17 Mar. 1918.)*

OWEN-LEWIS, Lieut.-Col. Arthur Francis, O.B.E. 1918 ; D.S.O. 1900 ; D.L., Co. Monaghan; Inspector of Prisons for Ireland; late Yorkshire Regt. and Reserve of Officers ; *b.* 6 Aug. 1868 ; *e. s.* of late Henry Owen-Lewis, D.L. of Inniskeen, Co. Monaghan, M.P., Co. Carlow ; *m.* 1896, Kathleen, *d.* of late William Henry, of Tivoli, Co. Dublin. Entered Army, 1889 ; served South Africa, 1900-2 (despatches, Queen's medal 3 clasps, King's medal 2 clasps, D.S.O.) ; European War, 1914-18 as G.S.O. Irish Command and A.Q.M.G. France (despatches twice, O.B.E.). *M. :* IY 212. *Clubs :* Army and Navy ; United Service, Dublin. *(Died 22 Dec. 1926.)*

OWEN - SMYTH, Charles Edward, C.M.G. 1920 ; I.S.O. 1903 ; Permanent Head Works and Buildings of South Australia 1886-1920 ; *b.* Ferrybank, Co. Kilkenny, Ireland, 1 Jan. 1851 ; *s.* of Stephen Smyth of Ferrybank, and Emma Gaynor, *g.d.* of William Lewys Owen of Egryn Abbey and Caerbelleran, Co. Merioneth ; *m.* 1889, Bessie Saunderson Laidlaw, *d.* of late John Davidson, Galashiels ; one *s.* one *d.* *Educ. :* Erasmus Smith School, Dublin. Entered the Public Service of South Australia, 1876 ; Architect in Chief Department, 1878 ; Founder of the Adelaide Branch Royal Society of St. George, 1908 ; President League of Empire and All British League ; Vice-President Navy League. *Recreation :* field shooting. *Address :* Egryn, Hazelwood Park, Marryatville, Adelaide. South Australia. *(Died 1 Oct. 1925.)*

OWENS, Hon. Wm., Senator, Dominion of Canada, since 1896 ; *s.* of Owen Owens, Denbigh, Wales, and Charlotte Lindley of Brantford, England ; *b.* Argenteuil Co., 15 May 1840 ; *m.* 1st, 1862, Catherine M., *d.* of O. Powers, La Chute, Quebec ; one *d.* ; 2nd, 1890, Margaret C., *d.* of John M'Martin, Chicago ; one *s.* one *d.* *Educ. :* Argenteuil Co. Was for twenty-five years member of the firm of T. & W. Owens and Owens Brothers, operating general stores and lumber business at Stonefield and Montebello, Que., and later head of the Owens Lumber Co., also Riverside Stock Farm at Montebello ; was Mayor, Councillor, and Postmaster of Chatham, P.Q. ; Member Legislative Assembly, 1881-91 (C.); Member Church of England ; President of the Ottawa River Navigation Co., of the Ottawa Valley Railway, and of the Carillon and Granville Railway ; Vice-President Central Railway of Canada ; Conservative. *Address :* 4026 Dorchester Street, Montreal. *T. :* 4026 Mount. *(Died 8 June 1917.)*

OXENDEN, Sir Percy (Dixwell Nowell Dixwell-), 10th Bt., *cr.* 1678 ; J.P. ; *b.* 6 June 1888 ; *S. b.* 1895 ; *m.* Isabella, *d.* of Hon. and Rev. Daniel Finch-Hatton, *g. d.* of Countess of Mansfield, 1868 ; two *d.* *Educ. :* Harrow ; Christ Church, Oxford. Late Captain Royal East Kent Yeomanry. *Heir :* none. *Address :* Craigmore, Leigh-on-Sea, Essex. *(Died 12 July 1924.)*

OXFORD AND ASQUITH, 1st Earl of, *cr.* 1925; **Herbert Henry Asquith ;** Viscount Asquith of Morley, *cr.* 1925 ; K.G. 1925 ; P.C. 1892 ; P.C. Ire. 1916 ; F.R.S. ; K.C. ; B.A. ; Member of Judicial Committee of Privy Council since 1925; Lord Rector Glasgow University, 1905 ; Rector Aberdeen University, 1908 ; High Steward of Oxford, 1927 ; Elder Brother Trinity House since 1909 ; *b.* Morley, Yorkshire, 12 Sep. 1852 ; 2nd *s.* of Joseph Dixon Asquith, Croft House, Morley, and Emily, *d.* of W. Willans, of Huddersfield ;

m. 1st, 1877, Helen (d. 1891), d. of F. Melland, of Manchester; three s. one d.; 2nd, 1894, Emma Alice Margaret,

    d. of Sir C. Tennant, 1st Bt. ; one s. one d. *Educ.* : City of London School; Balliol Coll., Oxford (Scholar, Fellow; Craven University Scholar; 1st class Lit. Hum. 1874). Barr. Lincoln's Inn, 1876; Q.C. 1890; Secretary of State for Home Dept., 1892-95; Ecclesiastical Commissioner, 1892-95; Chancellor of the Exchequer, 1905-8; M.P. (L.) East Fife, 1886-1918; M.P. (L.) Paisley, 1920-24; Secretary of State for War, 1914; Prime Minister and First Lord of the Treasury, 1908-16; Hon. D.C.L. Oxford and Durham; Hon. LL.D. Edinburgh, Glasgow, Cambridge, Leeds, St. Andrews, Bristol. Specially awarded War Star, 1914; War Medal, 1914-18; Victory Medal, 1919. *Publications :* Occasional Addresses (1894-1916), 1918 : The Genesis of the War, 1923; Studies and Sketches, 1924; Fifty Years of Parliament, 1926; Speeches, 1927 *Recreation :* golf. *Heir : g.s.* Viscount Asquith. *Address :* 44 Bedford Square, W.C.1; *T. :* Museum 6464; The Wharf, Sutton Courtney. *Clubs :* Brooks's, Athenæum, Reform.

                               (*Died* 15 *Feb.* 1928.)

OXLEY, Adm. Charles Lister, J.P. ; *b.* 1841; *e. s.* of Charles Christopher Oxley, Ripon Hall, and Mary, *d.* of late Rev. W. J. D. Waddilove; *m.* Emily (d. 1897), d. of Robert Kearsley, Highfield, 1878; two s. five d. Served in attack on Peiho Forts; A.D.C. to Queen Victoria, 1892-95. *Address :* The Hall, Ripon. *Club :* United Service. (*Died* 21 *July* 1920.)

OYAMA, Iwao, Field-Marshal Prince, O.M. 1906; a Samurai of Satsuma; *b.* Oct. 1842. Studied military tactics in Europe; attaché with Prussian army in Franco-Prussian War. Served with the Imperial Forces during the Satsuma Rebellion, 1877; General, 1891; Minister of War, 1880-95; commanded the 2nd Army during the China-Japan War, 1895; Field-Marshal, 1898; Chief of General Staff, 1899-1906; Commander-in-Chief in Manchuria, Russo-Japan War, 1904-5. *Address :* Aoyama, Tokio.

                               (*Died* 11 *Dec.* 1916.)

P

PACKARD, Lt.-Col. Henry Norrington, D.S.O. 1915; R.F.A.; *b.* 12 March 1870. Entered army, 1890; Captain, 1900; Major, 1908; served European War, 1914-15 (D.S.O.).

                           (*Died* 12 *April* 1916.)

PADDISON, Sir George Frederick, K.B.E., *cr.* 1926; C.S.I. 1923; M.A. Oxon; I.C.S.; Commissioner of Labour, Madras; *s.* of C. F. Paddison, Ingleby, Lincoln; *m.* Eleanor Letitia Roberts; two s. *Educ. :* Richmond School, Yorks; Queen's College, Oxford. Indian Civil Service, Madras, since 1897. *Recreations :* shooting, lawn tennis. *Address :* Labour Commissioner's Office, Madras, India. *T.A. :* Labdep, Madras. *T. :* 5260. *M. :* 5780. *Club :* Madras. (*Died* 24 *Oct.* 1927.)

PADDON, Rev. William Francis Locke, B.A.; Incumbent of Parish of the Gulf Islands, formerly Mission District of Mayne, B.C., 1896-1922; 3rd *s.* of Rev. T. H. Paddon, sometime Vicar of High Wycombe, and Anne, *d.* of Wadham Locke, Rowdeford, Wilts. *Educ. :* Rugby; Marlborough; Wadham College, Oxford. Missionary C.M.S., Nazareth, 1868; Incumbent of Ballyconree and Priest, 1871; Incumbent of Roundstone, 1876-77; Kilmain, 1878-87; Prebend of Kilmeen, 1887; emigrated to British Columbia, 1889. *Address :* Mayne Island, British Columbia.

                           (*Died* 28 *Aug.* 1922.)

PAGE, Lieut.-Col. Cuthbert Frederick Graham, D.S.O. 1916, R.A.; *b.* 21 Jan. 1880; *m. o. d.* of Col. C. E. Wyncoll. Served Ashanti War, 1900 (medal); South African War, 1901-2 (medal); European War, 1914-16 (despatches, D.S.O., Bt. Lt.-Col., Italian Silver Medal for valour). (*Died* 6 *Nov.* 1919.)

PAGE, Lt.-Col. F., D.S.O. 1915 ; Hertfordshire Regt. (T.F.) Served South African War, 1900-1901; European War, 1914-15 (wounded, D.S.O.). *Address :* Hertford. (*Died Aug.* 1917.)

PAGE, Frederick, D.C.L., M.A. Dunelm, M.D. Edinburgh, J.P., F.R.C.S.; late Member of Senate, Durham University; Emeritus Professor of Surgery, Durham University; Registrar, University Durham, College of Medicine, Newcastle-on-Tyne; Representative Coll. of Med. in Armstrong Coll. Newcastle; Consulting Surgeon, Royal Infirmary, Fleming Memorial Hospital, Northumberland and Durham Eye Infirmary, Throat and Ear Hospital, The N.E.R. Co.; Surgeon, Northumberland Coal Owners' Mutual Protection Association, Newcastle; The Knight Memorial Hospital, Blyth; *e. surv. s.* of Frederick Page, M.D., F.R.C.S., Surgeon, Royal Portsmouth, Portsea and Gosport Hospital; *m.* 1876, Margaret, *e. d.* of late John Graham and *niece* of late T. Graham, F.R.S., Master of Mint; one s. two d. *Educ. :* Edinburgh Univ. ; Colonial Hospital, Perth, Western Australia. Late House Physic., Royal Infirmary, Edinburgh; Senior House Surgeon, Assist. Surgeon, and Surgeon, Royal Infirmary, Newcastle-on-Tyne; Surgeon, Fleming Memorial Hospital for Sick Children, Newcastle; Med. Referee, Workmen's Compensation Act; Extern. Examiner Clinical Surgery, Edinburgh University; Lord of the Manor of Nethershall Tindalls-Soham, Cambridge, etc. ; Chairman of Visiting Justices H.M.'s Prison and of the Discharged Prisoners' Aid Society; Chairman of the Licensing Committee for the City and County of Newcastle-upon-Tyne; an additional Land Tax Commissioner and member of the Lord Chancellor's Committee *in re* Justices of the Peace. *Publications :* Surgery of the Thyroid Gland; Results of Major Amputations treated Antiseptically in the Newcastle Infirmary, 1878-98; Excision of Varicose Aneurism of the Femoral Artery; Twelve Successful Cases of Ligature of Femoral Artery for Popliteal Aneurism, etc. *Recreations :* literature and the drama. *Address :* 20 Victoria Square, Newcastle-on-Tyne. *T. :* 344, Nat. 7. (*Died* 3 *July* 1919.)

PAGE, Gertrude (Mrs. Dobbin), authoress; *d.* of John E. Page, J.P., of Woburn Sands and Bedford; *m.* George Alexander, *s.* of Captain R. A. Dobbin, Indian Staff Corps, of Armagh, Ireland. *Publications :* Love in the Wilderness; The Edge of Beyond; The Silent Rancher; Paddy the Next Best Thing; Two Lovers and a Lighthouse; Winding Paths; The Rhodesian; The Great Splendour; Where the Strange Roads go down; The Pathway; Follow After; The Supreme Desire; Some There Are; The Veldt Trail; The Course of my Ship (with R. A. Foster-Melliar); Paddy the Next Best Thing, dramatised by Robert Ord and Gayer Mackay; The Edge o' Beyond, dramatised by Roy Horniman and R. Miller. *Address :* Salisbury, Rhodesia. *T.A. :* Pagina Bedford. *Club :* Empress. (*Died* 1 *April* 1922.)

PAGE, Herbert Wm., M.A., M.C. Cantab., F.R.C.S. Eng.; J.P. Surrey; *b.* 1845; *e. s.* of W. B. Page, F.R.C.S., J.P. Cumberland; *m.* 1905, Kathleen, *d.* of Rev. Canon Houghton; Consulting Surgeon to St. Mary's Hospital and to Cumberland Infirmary; ex-Member of Council, Royal College of Surgeons; ex-Consulting Surgeon Great Western Railway Co. and London and North-Western Railway Companies; ex-Pres. Neurological Soc. of London; Assistant Surgeon Hessian Division of German Army in war of 1870-71; formerly Member of Court of Examiners, Royal College of Surgeons, and Examiner in Surgery, Universities of Oxford, Cambridge, and Birmingham. *Publications*: numerous contributions to medical and surgical literature. *Address*: Sedgecombe House, Farnham. *Club*: New University.(*Died 9 Sept. 1926.*)

PAGE, Hon. James, M.P.; Federal Representative for Maranoa, Queensland, since 1901; *b.* London, 1860; *s.* of William Page; *m.* 1881, Elizabeth Mary Sutherland; one *s.* Service with Royal Field Artillery, 1877-81; South African War, 1877-78-79 (medal with bar); came to Australia, 1888; followed pastural pursuits in Queensland central district; J.P. Queensland. *Address*: Federal Parliament House, Melbourne; Brisbane, Queensland. (*Died 3 June 1921.*)

PAGE, John Lloyd Warden, author; *b.* Minehead, Somerset, 26 Aug. 1858; *e. s.* of late John Theodore Page, R.N.; *m. d.* of Rev. Charles Parsons, M.A.; one *d.* *Educ.*: Grammar School, Tavistock. *Publications*: An Exploration of Dartmoor and its Antiquities, 1889; An Exploration of Exmoor and the Hill Country of West Somerset, 1890; The Rivers of Devon from Source to Sea, 1893; The Coasts of Devon and Lundy Island, 1895; Okehampton, Its Castle, etc., 1891; The North Coast of Cornwall, 1897; In Russia without Russian, 1898; The Church Towers of Somersetshire (in collaboration with E. Piper, R.P.E.), The Isle of Skye, 1898-1900, and magazine work. *Recreations*: boat-sailing, cycling tours, foreign travel. *Address*: Derrymore, Parkstone. *T.A.*: Parkstone. (*Died Nov. 1916.*)

PAGE, Thomas Nelson, B.L., D.L., LL.D.; Member of American Academy of Arts and Letters; *b.* Oakland Plantation, Virginia, 28 April 1853; 2nd *s.* of Major John Page (late C.S.A.), and Elizabeth Burwell Nelson; *m.* Florence (*d.* 1921); two *d.* *Educ.*: Washington and Lee University; University of Virginia. Practised law in Richmond, Va., 1875-93; United States Ambassador to Italy, 1913; delivered lectures on subjects connected with history of Southern States; wrote and published stories and essays. *Publications*: In Old Virginia, or Marse Chan and other stories, 1887; Two Little Confederates, 1888; On New-found River, 1891; Among the Camps, 1891; The Old South; Essays, Social and Historical, 1891; Elsket and other stories, 1892; Befo' de War: Poems in Negro Dialect (with A. C. Gordon), 1888; Pastime Stories, 1894; The Burial of the Guns, 1894; The Old Gentleman of the Black Stock, 1896; Red Rock, 1898; Santa Claus Partner, 1899; Social Life in Virginia before the War, 1901; Two Prisoners, 1903; A Captured Santa Claus, 1902; Gordon Keith, 1903; Bred in the Bone and other stories, 1904; The Negro: The Southerner's Problem, 1904; The Coast of Bohemia; Poems, 1906; Under the Crust, Stories, 1907; The Old Dominion; Her Making and Her Manners, 1908; Robert E. Lee: Man and Soldier, 1908; Tommy Trot and his Visit to Santa Claus, 1908; John Marvel, Assistant, 1909; The Land of the Spirit, 1913; Thomas Jefferson, The Apostle of Liberty, 1918; Italy and the World War, 1921. *Recreations*: golf; living in the country. *Address*: Southboro', Mass., U.S.A. *Clubs*: Metropolitan, Cosmos, Chevy Chase, Washington; Westmoreland, Richmond, Va.; Southern Society, University, Century, Authors', New York; Tavern, Boston. (*Died 1 Nov. 1922.*)

PAGE, Walter Hines; American Ambassador to England, 1913-18; member of publishing firm of Doubleday, Page and Co.; *b.* North Carolina, U.S.A., 15 Aug. 1855; *e. s.* of A. F. Page; *m.* Alice, *d.* of Dr. John Wilson of Michigan; three *s.* one *d.* *Educ.*: Johns Hopkins University, LL.D. (Randolph-Macon College, Virginia, Tulane University, La., Aber-

deen, Edinburgh, Sheffield, and Cambridge (Eng.)); D.C.L. (Oxon.). Editor of The Forum (New York), 1890 - 95; The Atlantic Monthly (Boston), 1896-99; The World's Work (New York), 1900-13. *Publications*: The Rebuilding of Old Commonwealths; The Southerner, a novel. *Address*: Garden City, Long Island, New York. *Clubs*: University, Authors', National Arts, New York. (*Died 23 Dec. 1918.*)

PAGET, Lt.-Col. Albert Edward Sydney Louis, M.V.O., 1904; 11th Hussars; *b.* 23 May 1879; *e. s.* of General Sir A. H. F. Paget. Entered army, 1900; Capt. 1909; A.D.C. to Major-Gen., Infantry Brigade, S. Africa, 1900-1; served S. Africa, 1900-1 (Queen's medal, 4 clasps); A.D.C. to Lord-Lieut. of Ireland, 1905-6; Adjutant, 11th Hussars, 1906-8; A.D.C. to G.O.C. in C. Eastern Command, 1908-12; served European War, 1914-15 (wounded, despatches, Bt. Major). *Clubs*: Cavalry, Bachelors', Turf. (*Died 2 Aug. 1917.*)

PAGET, Admiral Sir Alfred (Wyndham), K.C.B., *cr.* 1911; K.C.M.G., *cr.* 1905; C.M.G. 1899; D.S.O. 1917; temp. Capt. R.N.R.; *b.* 20 March 1852; 2nd *s.* of late Gen. Lord Alfred Henry Paget, C.B., 5th *s.* of 1st Marquis of Anglesey; *m.* 1906, Viti, *e. d.* of Sir W. Macgregor; one *d.* Entered R.N. 1865; Captain, 1896; Rear-Admiral, 1906; Vice-Admiral, 1911; Senior Officer Coast of Ireland, 1908-11; served Egyptian War, 1882 (medal, Khedive's star); Eastern Soudan, 1884 - 85; Suakim, 1888 (despatches, promoted Commander, clasp, 3rd class Medjidie); Naval Attaché to Paris, Petrograd, and Washington, 1896-99; China, 1900-1; Officer Legion of Honour. *Address*: 33 Seymour Street, W. *T.*: Mayfair 5303. *Clubs*: United Service, Turf, Bachelors'. (*Died 17 June 1918.*)

PAGET, General Rt. Hon. Sir Arthur (Henry Fitzroy), P.C. Ireland, 1912; G.C.B., *cr.* 1913; K.C.B., *cr.* 1907; K.C.V.O., *cr.* 1906; C.B. 1904; C.V.O. 1901; King at Arms, O.B.E.; *b.* 1 Mar. 1851; *e. s.* of late Gen. Lord Alfred H. Paget, C.B., and Cecilia (*d.* 1914), 2nd *d.* and co-heir of G. T. Wyndham, Cromer Hall, Norfolk; *m.* 1878, Mary (*d.* 1919), *s. d.* of late Paran and Marietta Stevens; two *s.* one *d.* Entered Scots Guards, 1869; Lt.-Col. 1882; Col. 1895; Maj.-Gen. 1900; served Ashanti War, 1873 (medal with clasp); Soudan, 1885 (medal with clasp, Khedive's star); Burmah, 1887-88 (medal with clasp); Soudan, 1888-89, including action of Gemaizah (clasp); commanded 1st Scots Guards, South Africa; 20th Brigade (despatches, medal 6 clasps); 1st Div. 1st Army Corps, 1902-6; Eastern Command, 1908-11; Officer commanding the Forces in Ireland, 1911-17; holds Order of the Red Eagle (first class), Grand Cross of the Dannebrog, Legion of Honour (Grand Officer); Order of St. Alexander Nevsky (Russia); Order of the White Eagle (Serbia). *Address*: Warren House, Coombe Wood, Kingston Hill. *T.*: Kingston 0600. *Club*: Turf. (*Died 9 Dec. 1928.*)

PAGET, Very Rev. Edward Clarence, D.D.; Rector since 1900 and Dean of Calgary since 1901; *b.* Swithland Rectory, Leicestershire, 14 Aug. 1851; 3rd *s.* of Rev. E. J. Paget, and *g.s.* of Vice-Admiral Sir Charles Paget, G.C.H.; unmarried. *Educ.*: Keble College, Oxford, First Class in Modern History, M.A.; Cuddesdon College. Ordained 1875; Curate of Frampton Cotterell, 1875-77; Assistant Master, St. Paul's Cathedral Choir School, 1877-78; Principal, Dorchester Missionary College, 1878-84; Assist. Minister, Davenport Cathedral, Iowa, 1886-87; Rector of Holy Trinity, Muscatine, 1887-99; Vicar of Revelstoke, B.C., 1899-1900. *Publications*: A Year under the Shadow of St. Paul's Cathedral; Ideal of Christian Priesthood; The True Motive of Missionary Work, 1882; Memoir of the Hon.

Sir Charles Paget, 1913. *Address:* The Rectory, Calgary, Canada. (*Died Mar. 1927.*)

PAGET, Sir (George) Ernest, 1st Bt. *cr.* 1897 ; D.L. ; Lt.-Col. ; chairman Midland Railway, 1890-1911 ; *b.* 10 Nov. 1841 ; *o. s.* of George Byng Paget ; *m.* 1866, Sophia (*d.* 1913), *d.* of Col. Charles Holden ; one *s.* one *d. Educ.:* Harrow. Joined 7th Hussars, 1860 ; transferred to Royal Horse Guards, 1861 ; retired, 1867 ; retired as Lieut.-Col. Leicestershire Yeomanry. *Heir: s.* Cecil Walter. *Recreation:* Won the Cambridgeshire Stakes with Re-Echo, 1922. *Address:* Sutton, Bonington, Loughborough. *T.A.:* Kegworth Rail. *Clubs:* Turf, Carlton.
(*Died 30 Dec. 1923.*)

PAGET, Lady, *wife* of Sir A. H. F. Paget ; *b.* America ; *o. d.* of late Paran Stevens and Mrs. Marietta Stevens. *Educ.:* New York ; Paris. *Address:* 35 Belgrave Square, S.W. ; Warren House, Coombe Wood, Kingston Hill. *T.A.:* Fitzroy, London. *T.:* Victoria 1754.
(*Died 18 May 1919.*)

PAGET, Stephen, F.R.C.S. ; Consulting Aural Surgeon, Middlesex Hospital ; Vice-Chairman Research Defence Society ; *b.* 1855 ; 4th *s.* of Sir J. Paget, 1st Bt.: *m.* 1885, Eleanor Mary, 2nd *d.* of Edward Burd, M.D., of Shrewsbury ; two *d. Educ.:* Shrewsbury ; Christ Church, Oxford ; St. Bartholomew's Hospital. *Publications:* The Surgery of the Chest, 1896 ; John Hunter, 1897 ; Ambroise Paré and his Times, 1897 ; Essays for Students, 1899 ; Experiments on Animals, 3rd edition, 1906 ; Memoirs and Letters of Sir James Paget, 1901 ; Selected Essays and Addresses by Sir James Paget, 1902 ; Chronicles of the Royal Medical and Chirurgical Society, 1905 ; The Young People, 1906 ; Confessio Medici, 1908 ; The Faith and Works of Christian Science, 1909 ; I Wonder, 1911 ; For and Against Experiments on Animals, 1912 ; Another Device, 1912 ; Francis Paget, Bishop of Oxford (with Rev. J. M. C. Crum), 1912 ; Pasteur and After Pasteur, 1914 ; The New Parents' Assistant, 1914 ; Essays for Boys and Girls, 1915 ; I Sometimes Think, 1916 ; Sir Victor Horsley, 1919 ; Henry Scott Holland, 1921 ; I have Reason to Believe, 1922. *Address:* Furzedown, Limpsfield, Surrey. *T.:* New Oxted 151.
(*Died 8 May 1926.*)

PAGET, Brig.-General Wellesley L. H., C.M.G. 1915 ; C.B. 1914 ; M.V.O. 1904 ; *b.* 2 Mar. 1858 ; 6th *s.* of late Col. Leopold G. Paget and Mrs. L. Paget, Park Homer, Wimborne ; *m.* 1888, Isabelle Louise, *d.* of late W. H. Swire ; one *s.* one *d. Educ.:* Wellington College ; Woolwich. Lieut. R.A. 1878 ; Adjutant Royal Horse Artillery, 1895-97 ; served in S. African War, 1899-1900 ; commanded 2nd Brigade Division R.F.A. 1900 ; Relief of Ladysmith and operations in Natal and the Transvaal ; appointed to command A Battery (The Chestnut Troop) R.H.A. 1900 ; operations in N.E. Transvaal (despatches three times, Bt. Lt.-Col., Queen's medal with 6 clasps) ; European War, 1914-16 (despatches twice, C.M.G.). *Recreations:* hunting, shooting, fishing. *Address:* Cheriton Manor, Templecombe, Somerset. *Club:* Army and Navy. (*Died 11 June 1918.*)

PAGET, William Edmund, J.P., Leicestershire ; Lord of the Manor of Wymeswold ; *b.* 1879 ; *s.* of late William B. Paget of Loughborough ; *m.* 1905, Barbara, 3rd *d.* of late W. S. Hunter, Gilling Castle, York ; one *s.* one *d. Educ.:* Winchester ; Trinity College, Cambridge, B.A. *Recreations:* hunting, Joint Master Quorn Hounds, 1919, shooting. *Address:* Nanpantan, Loughborough. *Club:* Windham.
(*Died 27 Mar. 1923.*)

PAGET-COOKE, Sir Henry, Kt. *cr.* 1906 ; *b.* 16 May 1861 ; *s.* of late William Major Cooke of Westbourne Terrace, W., and Bellecroft, Newport, Isle of Wight, Metropolitan Police Magistrate, and Maria Bartlett, *d.* of

late Dr. Ashwell of Grafton Street, W. ; *m.* Grace Bernard, *d.* of late Arthur Hathaway, H.E.I.C.S.; one *s. Educ.:* Cheltenham College. Admitted a Solicitor, 1886 ; joined firm of Russell-Cooke and Co., 1890 ; senior partner, 1903 ; is legal adviser to Princess Beatrice as Governor of the Isle of Wight, and to the Liberal Central Association ; his firm has acted in most of the Parliamentary and Municipal Election Petitions since 1890 ; coronation medal, 1911. *Recreations:* Cheltenham College Eleven, 1879-80 ; won the Fives Championship Cup, open to the College, in 1880 ; plays golf ; boats, and shoots. *Address:* 25 Orsett Terrace, Hyde Park, W.2 ; 11 Old Square, Lincoln's Inn, W.C.1. *T.A.:* Rusellanum, London. *T.:* Paddington 1400, Holborn 1924. *Clubs:* Reform, Eighty.
(*Died 7 Mar. 1923.*)

PAICE, Rev. Arthur; Vicar of St. Mary, Lichfield, since 1918 ; Rural Dean of Lichfield, 1918 ; Prebendary of Lichfield Cathedral ; *b.* 8 Oct. 1857 ; *s.* of Henry Charles and Eliza Paice of Egham, Surrey ; *m.* 1895, Mabel Frederica (*d.* 1918), *d.* of Rt. Rev. Sir Lovelace Tomlinson Stamer, 3rd Bt., Lord Bishop Suffragan of Shrewsbury ; no *c. Educ.:* privately ; Corpus Christi College, Cambridge ; Westcott's Clergy Training School. B.A. 1881 (Theol. Trip.) ; M.A. 1884 ; Deacon, 1881 ; Priest, 1882 ; Curate S. Matthew, Walsall, 1881-83 ; Vicar and Rural Dean, 1901-18 ; Curate of Hartshill, Stoke-on-Trent, 1883-87 ; Vicar, 1887-1901 ; Proctor in Convocation Archdeaconry of Stafford. *Recreations:* cricket, golf, tennis. *Address:* St. Mary's Vicarage, Lichfield.
(*Died 3 July 1923.*)

PAIN, Rt. Rev. Arthur Wellesley, D.D. *jure dig.* ; Hon. Sec. C.M.S. of Australia and New Zealand since 1917 ; Canon of Sidney since 1918 ; *b.* Felmersham, Beds, 21 Aug. 1841 ; *s.* of Joseph and Mary Pain ; *m.* 1871, Annie Bisdee, *e. d.* of George Thorne of Sydney ; three *s.* three *d. Educ.:* St. Catharine's College, Cambridge. Ordained, 1866 ; Curate of Holbrook, Suffolk, 1866-67 ; Incumbent of Narellan, N.S.W., 1868-83 ; with Cabramatta, 1877-83 ; R. D. of Camden, 1872-88 ; Rector of St. John, Darlinghurst, Dio. Sydney, 1888-1902 ; R. D. of East Sydney, 1885-1902 ; Chaplain to Archbp. Sydney, 1893-1902 ; Canon of Sydney, 1897-1902 ; Bishop of Gippsland, 1902-17. *Address:* Felmersham, Beecroft, N. S. Wales. *T.:* Beecroft.
(*Died 14 May 1920.*)

PAIN, Barry, B.A. ; author ; *m.* Amelia Nina Anna (*d.* 1920), *d.* of Rudolf Lehmann. *Educ.:* Sedbergh ; Corpus Christi Coll. Camb. (classical scholar). Was one of the best-known contributors to Granta, the University magazine at Cambridge. Served in the A.A.C., R.N.V.R., 1915-1916, afterwards on the London Appeal Tribunal. *Publications:* In a Canadian Canoe, 1891 ; Playthings and Parodies, 1892 ; Stories and Interludes, 1892 ; Graeme and Cyril, 1893 ; Kindness of the Celestial, 1894 ; The Octave of Claudius, 1897 ; Wilmay and other Stories of Women, 1898 ; The Romantic History of Robin Hood, 1898 ; Eliza, 1900 ; Another Englishwoman's Love Letters, 1901 ; The One Before, 1902 ; Little Entertainments, 1903 ; Lindley Kays, 1904 ; Curiosities, 1904 ; The Memoirs of Constantine Dix, 1905 ; Wilhemina in London, 1906 ; First Lessons in Story-Writing, 1907 ; The Shadow of the Unseen (with J. Blyth), 1907 ; The Gifted Family, 1909 ; Proofs before Pulping, 1909 ; The Exiles of Faloo, 1910 ; Here and Hereafter, 1911 ; Eliza Getting On, 1911 ; An Exchange of Souls, 1911 ; Exit Eliza, 1912 ; Stories in Grey, 1912 ; Stories without Tears, 1912 ; The New Gulliver, 1913 ; Eliza's Son, 1913 ; Mrs. Murphy, 1913 ; One Kind and Another, 1914 ; The Short Story, 1915 ; The Problem Club, 1919 ; The Death of Maurice, 1920 ; Marge Askinfort, 1921 ; This

Charming Green Hat Fair, 1925 ; Essays of To-day and Yesterday, 1926. *Club :* Arts.
(*Died 5 May 1928.*)

PAIN, Brig.-Gen. Sir William Hacket, K.B.E., *cr.* 1919 ; C.B. 1900 ; the Queen's, Royal and the Worcestershire Regiments ; M.P. (C.U.) South Londonderry since 1922 ; *b.* 5 Feb. 1855 ; *m.* 1898, Saidie, *y. d.* of late Sidney Merton, Sydney. Entered army 1875 ; Captain, 1886 ; Major, 1894 ; Lieut.-Col. 1900 ; served Soudan, 1888 (medal with clasp, Khedive's star) ; Nile Frontier Field Force, 1889 (3rd class Medjidie) ; capture of Tokar, 1891 (3rd class Osmanieh, clasp to star) ; Dongola Expeditionary Force, 1896 (despatches, brevet of Lieut.-Col., British medal, Khedive's medal two clasps) ; Nile Field Force, 1897 ; Acting A.G. to Egyptian Army to end of campaign ; Brevet Colonel, 1901 ; South Africa, 1901-2 (despatches, C.B., medal 3 clasps, King's medal 2 clasps) ; Col. 1907 ; commanding a District, 1908-11 ; retired 1912 ; raised and commanded 108th Infantry Brigade, Ulster Division, 1914 (Bronze Star, 1915, General Service and Victory medals) ; commanded 15th Reserve Infantry Brigade in Belfast, 1916 ; Northern District Irish Command during Irish Rebellion, 1916-Nov. 1919 ; Divisional Commissioner Royal Irish Constabulary until truce, 1921 (despatches, K.B.E.). *Recreations :* hunting, all field sports. *Clubs :* Royal Automobile, United Service ; Kildare Street, Dublin.
(*Died 14 Feb. 1924.*)

PAINE, Major James Henry, D.S.O. 1898 ; R.G.A., Native Mountain Artillery, India ; *b.* 8 Sep. 1870 ; *m.* 1896, Caroline Mary, *d.* of Dep. Insp.-Gen. Henry Piers, R.N. *Educ. :* Marlborough. Entered army, 1890 ; Captain, 1899 ; served operations at Mekran, 1898 (despatches, D.S.O.). *Address :* 26 Mountain Battery, Abbottabad, India.(*Died 25 July 1918.*)

PAINTER, Sir Frederic George, Kt., *cr.* 1914 ; *b.* 18 Dec. 1844 ; *m.* 1911, Marion, *d.* of Stuart Boyd Connolly, Manchester. Sheriff of City of London, 1913-14 ; Chevalier of the Legion of Honour ; Commander of the Order of the Danebrog ; Order of the Crown of Belgium. *Address :* 8 The Boltons, S.W.10. *T. :* Kensington 4829. (*Died 9 June 1926.*)

PAKENHAM-MAHON, Capt. Henry, late Scots Guards ; D.L. Co. Roscommon ; *b.* 13 July 1851 ; *o. s.* of H. Sandford Pakenham, *e. s.* of Hon. and Very Rev. H. Pakenham, Dean of St. Patrick's, Dublin, *b.* of 2nd Earl of Longford ; *m.* 1890, May, *o. d.* of Col. Sidney Burrard, Grenadier Guards ; one *d. Educ. :* Eton. Has shot in the Rockies and up the Pacific coast ; Member of several of the Royal Societies ; Bibliographical, etc. ; has greatly improved the extensive Strokestown estates and planted the country round, like his predecessors since King Charles II. granted Nicholas Mahon the lands and deer park. *Recreations :* shooting, farming, forestry, gardening. *Address :* Strokestown Park, Longford, Ireland ; 33 Pont Street, S.W.1. *T.A. :* Strokestown. *T. :* Ken. 2016 *Clubs :* Guards, Carlton ; Kildare Street, Dublin.
(*Died 12 Jan. 1922.*)

PALANPUR, H.H. Diwan Sir Shere Mahommed Khan, Lohani Zubdat-ul-Mulk, Nawab of, G.C.I.E., *cr.* 1898 ; K.C.I.E., *cr.* 1893 ; *b.* 1852 ; *S.* father 1877. Hereditary title of Nawab and personal two additional guns, 1910. The State has an area of about 1750 square miles and a population of over 200,000. *Address :* Palanpur, Bombay Presidency. (*Died Nov. 1918.*)

PALEY, Frederick John, M.D. (Lond.) ; M.R.C.S. (Eng.) ; L.R.C.P. (Lond.) ; Hon. Surgeon to Royal Sussex County Hospital, Brighton, since 1907, and in general practice ; *b.* Peterborough, 26 Sept. 1859 ; *s.* of Frederick Apthorp Paley, LL.D., M.A., and Ruth, *d.* of

George Matthew Burchell of Scotsland, Bramley, Surrey ; *m.* 1892, Maude Cecil, *d.* of George Cook Attfield, M.R.C.S., of 17 Salisbury Road, Hove ; two *s.* one *d. Educ. :* The Oratory School, Edgbaston ; St. Bartholomew's Hospital ; qualified to practise, 1888 ; after holding positions of Resident Medical Officer at St. George's Retreat, Burgess Hill, House Surgeon to the Women's Hospital, Brighton, and the Royal Sussex County Hospital, Brighton ; commenced practice in Brighton, 1890 ; Hon. Consulting Surgeon to Royal Sussex County Hospital, 1922 ; Hon. Surgeon to the Women's Hospital, 1890 ; Hon. Surgeon to Royal Sussex County Hospital, 1907 ; President of the Brighton and Sussex Medico-Chirurgical Society, 1900, after holding office as Hon. Secretary in 1889 and 1890, and serving on the Council subsequently for four years ; Lt.-Col. R.A.M.C. (T.F.) (despatches). *Recreation :* motoring. *Address :* 18 Brunswick Place, Hove. *T. :* Hove 8891. *M. :* CD 1961. (*Died 12 Nov. 1924.*)

PALGRAVE, Sir Robert Harry Inglis, Kt. *cr.* 1909, F.R.S. ; J.P. Suffolk ; Knight of the Order of Wasa of Sweden : Yarmouth director of Barclay and Co., bankers, Ltd. ; *b.* Westminster, 11 June 1827 ; 3rd *s.* of late Sir Francis Palgrave, K.H., and Elizabeth, *d.* of Dawson Turner, F.R.S. ; *m.* 1859, Sarah Maria, *d.* of George Brightwen (*d.* 1898) ; one *d. Educ. :* The Charterhouse. Taylor Prize Essay of the Statistical Society, 1871 ; was in 1875 one of three representatives of the English Issuing Country Bankers to give evidence on their behalf before the Select Committee of the House of Commons on Banks of Issue : editor of *Economist* newspaper, 1877-83 ; President of Section F of the British Association, Southport, 1883 ; served on Royal Commission to inquire into the Depression of Trade and Industry, 1885 ; received Hon. Freedom of Great Yarmouth, 1910. *Publications :* The Local Taxation of Great Britain and Ireland, 1871 ; Notes on Banking in Great Britain and Ireland, Sweden, Denmark, and Hamburg, 1873 ; An Analysis of the Transactions of the Bank of England for the years 1844-72 (1874) ; Bank Rate and the Money Market in England, France, Germany, Holland, and Belgium, 1844-1900 (1903) ; An Enquiry into the Economic Condition of the Country, 1904 ; editor of Dictionary of Political Economy (3 vols. 1894-1914) ; Appendix, 1908 ; is preparing a collected edition of the historical works of the late Sir Francis Palgrave. Lord of the Manor, and patron of the living of Henstead. *Recreation :* gardening. *Address :* Henstead Hall, near Wrentham, Suffolk. *Club :* Athenæum.
(*Died 25 Jan. 1919.*)

PALK, Major the Hon. Lawrence Charles Walter, D.S.O. 1915 ; 1st Batt. the Hampshire Regiment ; *b.* 28 Sept. 1870 ; 2nd *s.* of 2nd Baron Haldon and Hon. Constance Mary Barrington, *d.* of 7th Viscount Barrington. *Educ. :* Wellington College. Enlisted 8th H.R.I. Hussars, 20 May 1890 ; 2nd Lieut. Hampshire Regt. 1894 ; Captain, 1900 ; Major, 1914 ; served S. African War, 1901-2 (Queen's medal, 5 clasps) ; European War, 1914-15 (despatches twice, D.S.O.) ; holds Legion of Honour. *Clubs :* Army and Navy, Junior Naval and Military. (*Died 1 July 1916.*)

PALLES, Rt. Hon. Christopher, J.P., hon. LL.D. (Dub. and Cantab), P.C. (England and Ireland) ; Lord Chief Baron of Exchequer in Ireland, 1874-1916 ; *b.* 25 Dec. 1831 ; *s.* of Andrew Christopher Palles, Little Mount Palles, Cavan ; *m.* 1862, Ellen (*d.* 1885), *o. d.* of late Denis Doyle, Dublin. *Educ. :* Clongowes Wood College and Trin. Coll. Dublin (B.A. Univ. Dub. 1852). Irish Barr. 1853 ; Q.C. 1865 ; Solicitor-General for Ireland, 1872 ; Attorney-Gen. 1872-74. *Address :* Mount Anville House, Dundrum, Co. Dublin. *Club :* University, Dublin. (*Died 14 Feb. 1920.*)

809

PALADINI, Grande Ufficiale Prof. Carlo. See page xxviii.

PALMER, Capt. Alexander Edward Guy, D.S.O. 1917; M.C.; Green Howards; *b.* 1886; *e. s.* of Lt.-Com. C. B. Palmer (retired), R.N.; *m.* 1919, Jeanne Léonie, *e. d.* of M. Baratoux; one *d. Educ.:* Eton. Served European War, 1914-18 (despatches, D.S.O.). *T.:* Yateley 25. *Club:* Junior United Service.
(Died 9 Jan. 1926.)

PALMER, Charles, M.P. the Wrekin Division of Salop since Feb. 1920; *b.* 9 Sep. 1869; *m.* 1894, Annie Dudley Smith; one *d.* Parliamentary Journalist on the Globe, 1886-1915; Editor of the Globe, 1912-15; Dramatic and Musical Critic of the People for 20 years; Assistant Editor of John Bull and joint Editorial control with Mr. Bottomley, of the National News and Sunday Evening Telegram; one of the founders of the Society of Dramatic Critics now merged in the Critics Circle of the Institute of Journalists, and a member of the Committee of the Critics Circle; associated with Mr. Kennedy Jones, in raising the £1,000,000,000 Victory Loan; originator of the idea which resulted in the formation of the Federation of British Industries. *Recreations:* work, tennis, and gardening. *Address:* 21 Ridgmont Gardens, W.C.1. *T.:* Museum 121. *Clubs:* Constitutional, Services. *(Died 25 Oct. 1920.)*

PALMER, Charles Felix; Recorder of Richmond, Yorks, since 1910; Assistant Recorder of Leeds since 1910; 2nd *s.* of late Rev. F. Palmer. Called to Bar, Middle Temple, 1884. *Address:* Shadwell Lane, Moor Allerton, Leeds. *(Died 11 Dec. 1919.)*

PALMER, Rev. Charles Samuel, M.A., Prebendary and Treasurer of Hereford Cathedral; *b.* 29 May 1830; *s.* of Rev. H. Palmer, Withcote Hall, Leicestershire; *m.* 1854, Ellen, *d.* of Rev. H. Douglas, Canon of Durham; one *d. Educ.:* Exeter Coll. Oxford (M.A. 1855). Deacon, 1854; Priest, 1855; Proctor in Convocation for Chapter of Hereford, 1859-1916; Rector of Eardisley, 1866-1906; Canon of Hereford, 1892-1909. *Address:* Hampton Manor, Hereford.
(Died 10 Mar. 1921.)

PALMER, Sir Edward Geoffrey Broadley, 10th Bt., *cr.* 1660; J.P.; *b.* 14 June 1864; *o. s.* of late Col. F. Palmer. *S.* cousin, 1909; *m.* 1891, Sibyll Caroline, *e. d.* of late Capt. W. J. Smith Neill; two *s.* one *d. Educ.:* Eton; Magdalene College, Cambridge (M.A.). Late Major 3rd Leicester Regt.; J.P. Leicestershire; High Sheriff, Rutland, 1910. *Heir:* s. Geoffrey Frederick Neill [Capt. Coldstream Guards; *b.* 20 Sep. 1893. *Educ.:* Repton; Trinity College, Cambridge]. *Address:* Withcote Hall, Oakham; Carlton Park, Northants; Carlton Curlieu Hall, Leicestershire. *Club:* Junior Carlton.
(Died 15 May 1925.)

PALMER, Sir Francis Beaufort, Kt. *cr.* 1907; *b.* 7 July 1845; *s.* of Rev. William Palmer (one of the originators of the Oxford Movement) and Sophia, *d.* of Admiral Sir Francis Beaufort, K.C.B., F.R.S.; *m.* 1898, Georgiana Elizabeth, *d.* of 8th Baron de Hochepied Larpent; three *s. Educ.:* University College, Oxford. Bar, 1873; Bencher Inner Temple, 1907. *Publications:* Company Precedents; Private Companies; Company Law; Peerage Law in England; and other works. *Address:* 29 Bryanston Square, W.; *T.:* Paddington 1946; 5 New Square, Lincoln's Inn, E.C. *Clubs:* Athenæum, Burlington Fine Arts.
(Died 15 June 1917.)

PALMER, Frederick Stephen, M.D., Univ. College, Durham; F.R.C.P. (Lond.); M.R.C.S. and L.S.A.; Consulting Physician West End Hospital for Diseases of the Nervous System; Fellow of Royal Society of Medicine, and Medical Society of London; *b.* East Sheen, Surrey; *e. s.* of Henry Smith Palmer, M.R.C.S. and L.S.A., of East Sheen, Surrey;

m. Mary Georgiana, *d.* of Charles Edward Fry of Compton House, Compton Bishop, Somersetshire; one *d.* Formerly Senior House Surgeon, Westminster Hospital, and Resident Medical Officer (4 years) Radcliffe Infirmary, Oxford; Vice-President Medical Society of London; President and Hon. Secretary for the South Durham University Medical Graduates Association; ex-President of the West London Medico-Chirurgical Society; many years in general medical practice at East Sheen, Surrey. *Publications:* various contributions to Medical Journals and Hospital Reports. *Address:* 11 Wimpole Street, W.1; 28 Kew Gardens Road, Kew, Surrey. *T.:* Mayfair 8412. *Club:* Royal Societies. *(Died 21 April 1926.)*

PALMER, Rear-Admiral George; *b.* 1829; *e. s.* of Rev. George Palmer, Rector of Sullington, Sussex; *m.* 1859, Ellen Douglas of Cowes, Roxburghshire; two *s.* two *d. Educ.:* Royal Naval School. Entered navy as Naval Cadet in H.M.S. Thunder, 1844; surveying in the West Indies to 1848; then in the Plumper, Encounter, Britannia Flagship in Mediterranean; Lieut. in President Flagship in Pacific; severely wounded at Petropaulski; 1st Lieut. of Amphitrite; then to the Monarch Flagship; 1st Lieut. of the Edinburgh, then in command of the Procris gunboat; Inspecting Commander of Coast Guard, from N. to S. Foreland; Commander to Aurora, Captain Sir Leopold Maclintock; Commander of Rosario; Captain, 1870; retired, 1873. *Publications:* The Migration from Shinar; Scripture Facts and Scientific Doubts; Kidnapping in the South Seas. *Address:* c/o Countess of Moray, Kinfauns Castle, Perths. *(Died 1 Jan. 1917.)*

PALMER, Rev. George Herbert; Hon. Doctor of Music; *b.* 9 Aug. 1846. *Educ.:* Trinity College, Cambridge; B.A. Ordained, 1869; Curate of St. Margaret, Toxteth Park, Liverpool, 1869-76; St. Barnabas, Pimlico, 1876-83. *Publications:* The Antiphoner and Grail, 1881; Harmonies to the Office Hymn Book, 1891; The Sarum Psalter, 6th ed. 1920; Sarum Vespers, 1908; Antiphons to Magnificat and Nunc. dim., 1911; Requiem Services, 1903; The Hymner, 2nd ed. 1905; Sarum Grails, Alleluias and Tracts, 1908; Introits, 2nd ed. 1918; Sarum Diurnal, pt. i. 1918, pt. ii. 1921; Sarum Compline, 3rd ed., 1922. *Address:* 18 Fairacres Road, Oxford. *(Died 20 June 1926.)*

PALMER, Sir George Hudson, 5th Bt.; *cr.* 1791; *b.* 9 Aug. 1841; *s.* of 3rd Bt. and Emily Elizabeth, *y. d.* of S. P. Holford of Westonbirt, Gloucestershire; *S.* brother 1906. *Educ.:* Eton; Balliol College, Oxford. *Heir:* c. Frederick Archdale [*b.* 25 Aug. 1857; *m.* 1892, Lilian, *d.* of late Gen. E. A. Somerset, C.B. *Address:* Barton, Martinhoe, Devon]. *Address:* Wanlip Hall Leicester. *Club:* St. James's. *(Died 22 Oct. 1919.)*

PALMER, Admiral Norman Craig, C.V.O. 1913; M.V.O. 1909; R.N.; *b.* 20 Aug. 1866; *s.* of late E. C. Palmer; *m.* 1895, Winifred J. R. Livingstone-Learmonth. Entered Navy, 1880; Lieut., 1888; Commander, 1899; Captain, 1904; Rear-Admiral 1915; Vice-Admiral 1919; promoted to Lieutenant for special service in capture of slave dhow, East Coast of Africa, 1888; First Superintendent of Physical Training, H.M. Navy, 1902-5; Naval A.D.C. to H.M. while commanding H.M. Yachts, 1909-13; Commanded H.M. ships Royal Arthur, Highflyer, Suffolk, Aboukir, Conqueror, 1913-14; Adm. retired, 1924. *Clubs:* United Service; R.Y.S. (hon.), Cowes.
(Died 12 Jan. 1926.)

PALMER, Mrs. Potter (Bertha Honoré); *o.* Louisville Ky.; *d.* of Henry H. Honoré; *m.* 1871, Potter Palmer (*d.* 1902). *Educ.:* Convent School, Georgetown. Became social leader; elected President, Board of Lady Managers, World's Columbian Exposition, 1891;

visited Europe and interested foreign Governments there in the Fair; appointed by President only woman member of National Commission for Paris Exposition, 1900; awarded Legion of Honour. *Address:* 100 Lake Shore Drive, Chicago. *(Died May 1918.)*

PALMER, Ralph Charlton; *b.* 1839; 3rd *s.* of Colonel George Palmer, of Nazeing Park, Essex. *Educ.:* Winchester; Balliol College, Oxford. Barrister Lincoln's Inn, 1864; J.P. Essex, 1898; Secretary to Public Schools Commission, 1868; Principal Secretary to Lord Chancellor Selborne, 1881; Clerk of the Crown in Chancery, 1880-85; Lord Chancellor's Legal Visitor in Lunacy, 1885-1910; Deputy Chairman Executive Committee of City and Guilds Institute for Advancement of Technical Education; Member of Senate, University of London, 1912-20. *Address:* Hubbards, Nazeing, Waltham Cross. *T:* 11 Nazeing; 9 Little Stanhope Street, Mayfair, W.1. *Club:* United University. *(Died 8 Sept. 1923.)*

PALMER, W. Howard, J.P. Berks; Chairman, Huntley & Palmers, Ltd., Reading; *b.* 1865; 3rd *s.* of late Samuel Palmer of Northcourt, Hampstead, N.W.; *m.* Ada Morgan, 4th *d.* of late William Reed, Onslow Gardens, S.W.; one *s. Educ.:* Cholmeley School, Highgate. High Sheriff for Berks, 1903. *Recreations:* hunting, shooting. *Address:* Heathlands, Wokingham, Berks; 22 Down Street, Piccadilly, W.1. *Clubs:* Junior Carlton, Royal Automobile, Ranelagh.
(Died 17 Mar. 1923.)

PALMES, Rev. George, M.A., J.P.; *e. s.* of late Rev. W. L. Palmes and Marion, *e. d.* of A. Empson of Spellow Hill; *b.* 1851; *m.* 1882, Eva Blanche, *y. d.* of Henry Dalbiac Harrison of Holbrook Park, Sussex; two *s. Educ.:* Lincoln College, Oxford. Rector of Elston, Notts, 1887-93; Vicar of Naburn, 1904. *Address:* Naburn Hall, York. *(Died 30 July 1927.)*

PANAGAL, Rajah of, The Hon. Rajah Sir Panaganti Ramarayaningar, K.C.I.E., *cr.* 1926; *b.* 1866. *Educ.:* Hindu High School, Triplicane; The Presidency College, Madras. Fellow of Madras University, 1919; Member of the Imperial Legislative Council, 1912-15, and Member of the Madras Legislative Council since 1920; invited to the Imperial War Conference, 1918; visited England as representative of the Landed Aristocracy, and gave evidence before the Parliamentary Joint Committee; appointed as Minister of the Madras Government, under the Reforms Act, 1920; Chief Minister to the Govt. of Madras in charge of Local Self-Government Dept., 1921; Title of Hereditary Rajah conferred in 1922; President of the South Indian Liberal Federation; elected Leader of the Justice Party; presided over the All-India Non-Brahmin Congress, Amraoti, 1925. *Address:* Tawker's Gardens, Royapettah, Madras. *(Died Dec. 1928.)*

PANK, Sir John Lovell, Kt., *cr.* 1922; D.L., Hertfordshire; J.P., Herts and Middlesex; Alderman and Vice-Chairman, Herts C.C.; Chairman Herts Education Committee from formation; Chairman Barnet County Bench; *b.* 1846. *Recreation:* the mountains. *Address:* Somerset Road, New Barnet. *Club:* Junior Constitutional. *(Died 18 Oct. 1922.)*

PANKHURST, Emmeline, Hon. Treasurer W.S.P.U.; *d.* of Robt. Goulden, Manchester; *widow* of R. M. Pankhurst, LL.D., Barrister-at-law; three *d. Educ.:* private schools, Manchester and Paris. Always active Suffragist, also worked in many Reform movements; elected on School Board and Board of Guardians, Manchester; after abolition of School Board co-opted member of Education Committee; resigned all other work to devote life to winning votes for women; on outbreak of war devoted all her time to National Service;

took active part in recruiting work and made many speeches on the war. *Publications:* My Own Story, 1914; Women's Suffrage pamphlets, etc.; Poor Law Reform pamphlets.
(Died 14 June 1928.)

PANTON, Mrs. J. E., F.Z.S.; *b.* London, 18 Oct. 1848; *d.* of William Powell Frith, R.A.; *m.* 1869, James Panton, Wareham, Dorset; three *s.* two *d.* Pioneer of Home Decoration and Management by Correspondence, and Journalist, 1882-1900. *Publications:* One Year in His Life, etc., 1881; Country Sketches in Black and White, 1882; Jane Caldecott, 1882; Less than Kin, 1885; Listen! Poems for Children's Hour, 1885; Curate's Wife, 1886; Dear Life, 1886; From Kitchen to Garret, 1887, 11th ed. 1897; Tangled Chain, 1887; By-paths and Cross-roads, 1889; Nooks and Corners, 1889; Homes of Taste, 1890; Having and Holding, 1890; Within Four Walls, 1893; Suburban Residences, 1896; The Way They Should Go, 1897; Simple Homes, 1898; A Dream House, 1898; A Short Cut to Comfort, 1907; Leaves from a Life, 1908, 5th ed. 1908; A Cannibal Crusader, 1908; Fresh Leaves and Green Pastures, 1909; Leaves from a Garden, 1910; More Leaves from a Life, 1911; Most of the Game, 1911; Round about a Rectory, 1912; The Year's Mind, 1913; Leaves from a Housekeeper's Book, 1914; Leaves from the Countryside, 1914; The Building of Whispers, 1915; The River of Years, 1916; An Eclipse of the Sun—Leaves from my War Book, 1917; For Kitchen and Garret: Hints for the Lean Year, 1919. *Address:* c/o Miss Panton, 26 Southsea Avenue, Watford, Herts.
(Died 13 May 1923.)

PANZERA, Lt.-Col. Francis William, C.M.G. 1911; Reserve of Officers, retired; F.R.S.A.; late Resident Commissioner, Bechuanaland Protectorate; now Commandant, Knockaloe Alien Detention Camp, Peel, Isle of Man; *b.* 1851; *s.* of J. G. I. A. Panzera, Civil Engineer, and *g. s.* of J. G. Panzera, formerly Minister of War, and afterwards British Consul, Naples; *m.*; one *s.* two *d.* Served for some years with Royal and Militia Artil.; appointed to serve as Acting Engineer with R.E. in Eastern District to raise, organise, and train Harwich Militia Division, and 1st Class Army Reserve (Submarine Miners) R.E., 1888; commanded troops, Harwich and Landguard, 1890-91; nominated by War Office to serve under Colonial Office in South Africa, 1892; Government Engineer Officer and Superintendent Public Works, Bechuanaland and Protectorate, and Engineer Officer, Bechuanaland Border Police, 1893; Member Protectorate Concessions Commission, 1893; commanded Imp. Base, Macloutsie; and southern line of Communications, under Colonel Goold-Adams, Matabele War, 1893-94 (promoted Major Reserve of Officers, medal); Magistrate, Macloutsie and Tati Districts, 1893-94; Secretary, Khama Southern Boundary Commission, 1894; Imp. Govt. Engineer and Representative, Vryburg-Palapye Sect. (subsidised), Rhodesia Railways, since 1894; Expert to Treasury for Jameson Trial, 1896; British Member and President British-Transvaal Joint Boundary Commission, 1897; Special Commissioner, Ngamiland, 1898-99; served throughout South African War, 1899-1902; D.A.A.G., commanded artillery, etc., Defence of Mafeking; subsequently as D.A.A.G. on Staff of D.I.G. of Communications; Assistant Commissioner Bechuanaland Protectorate, 1901; and Commandant Northern Protectorate; Imperial Military Member Western Section War Losses Compensation Commission (despatches twice, medal with 2 clasps, King's medal with 2 bars, promoted Lt.-Col. Reserve of Officers). *Publications:* Questions and Answers on Gunnery; The Officering of the Artillery Militia. *Address:* Gatewick, Dovercourt, Essex. *Clubs:*

British Empire, Junior Army and Navy ; Royal Harwich Yacht.   (*Died 14 June 1917.*)

PAPE, Archibald Gabriel; Master of Fox-hounds (Silverton), Master of Beagles (Stoke Hill); *b.* Weymouth, 29 Sep. 1876 ; *s.* of Gabriel Pape and Emily Julia Pape; *m.* 1905, Lily Lynette Aplin ; two *s. Educ.*: Kingston School, Yeovil. *Address*: Hillcot, Stoke Hill, Exeter. *T.A.*: Stoke Hill, Exeter. *M.*: TT 9775.   (*Died 3 Dec. 1927.*)

PAPILLON, Rev. Thomas Leslie; Hon. Canon of St. Albans since 1907 ; Vicar of Writtle, Essex, 1884-1909 ; *b.* Lexden, Essex, 12 April 1841 ; *s.* of Rev. John Papillon, Rector of Lexden, and Frances Anne Prudentia, *d.* of Rt. Rev. John Leslie, Bishop of Kilmore, Ireland; *m.* 1st, 1871, Edith Mary (*d.* 1908), *d.* of Rev. Charles B. Dalton, Prebendary of St. Paul's and Vicar of Highgate ; one *s.* two *d.* ; 2nd, 1909, Laura Mary, *d.* of Samuel Dickson, of Writtle. *Educ.*: Marlborough ; Balliol College, Oxford (Scholar). Fellow of Merton College, 1865-70, and of New College, Oxford, 1870-84 ; 1st class Moderations (Classics), 1862 ; 1st class Final Classical School, 1864 ; Hertford Scholar, 1862 ; Latin Verse Prize, 1863 ; Assist. Master at Rugby, 1868-69 ; Tutor and Dean, New College, 1870-84 ; Junior Bursar, 1877-84 ; Moderator (Honours), 1877-79 and 1885-1887 ; Whitehall Preacher, 1877-79 ; Examiner at Victoria Univ. 1892-94 ; at Leeds Univ. 1905 ; and at various times for Sandhurst, Woolwich, and the Civil Service ; member of the Mosely Educational Commission to the United States, 1903. *Publications*: Commentary on Virgil, 1882 ; revised, 1892 ; articles Campanology in the Times supplement to Encycl. Britannica (9th ed.), Bell in Encycl. Brit. (11th ed.) ; A Manual of Comparative Philology (3rd ed. 1882) : edited Dean Bradley's Aids to Writing Latin Prose. *Address*: 41 Brittany Road, St. Leonards-on-Sea.   (*Died 28 Dec. 1926.*)

PAPPRILL, Rev. Frederick, Vicar of Holy Trinity, Leicester, since 1906 ; Hon. Canon of Peterborough, 1919 ; Hon. Canon, Leicester, 1922 ; *b.* 9 April 1859 ; *s.* of William Fogg Papprill ; *m.* 1889, Alice Jane Smith ; two *s.* three *d. Educ.*: Thanet College, Margate. Ten years' experience in the commercial world in London ; ordained, 1887 ; missionary on Afghan Frontier, 1887-1900 ; Simla, 1900-1904 ; invalided home, 1904 ; Assist.-Priest, Hoddesdon, 1904-6. *Recreations*: fishing and bowls. *Address*: Holy Trinity Vicarage, Leicester. *T*: 954.
     (*Died 25 Mar. 1924.*)

PARDO-BAZAN, Countess Emilia, Spanish novelist and critic ; Counsellor of Public Instruction (the first woman this honour was accorded to) ; *b.* La Corunna, Galicia, 16 Sep. 1852 ; *m.* Don José Quiroga of Orense, 1868 (*d.* 1912); one *s.* two *d.* (title granted by King Alphonso XIII.]. *Decorations*: Banda de Damas Nobles de Maria Luisa ; Pro Ecclesia et Pontifice. *Publications*: Pascual Lopez ; A Wedding Trip ; The Tribune ; The Swan of Vilamorta ; Ulloa's Manor ; Our Mother Nature ; Midsummer Madness ; Morrina ; A Christian Woman ; The Trial ; Thou wilt be King ; Angular Stone ; Adan and Eva ; Guzman's Child ; Mystery ; The Treasure of Gaston ; The Chimera ; The Black Syrene ; Sweet Master (novels) ; Bucolique ; Tales of Marineda ; Into the Tramway ; New Tales ; Mystic Tales ; Tales of the Patrie ; Tales of Love ; The Profound Soul ; Tragic Tales (eight volumes of tales) ; Short Novels : The Naturalism ; Novel and Revolution in Russia ; From Galice ; Polemics and Essays ; Portraits and Sketches ; The Epic Poets ; The Holy Francis of Assisi ; French Modern Literature : The Romantics, The Transition (critique and story); My Pilgrimage ; From the Old Spain ; From the Catholic Europe ; Near the Tour Eiffel (travels); Theatre (five plays); The Old Spanish Cockery (a volume) ; The Modern Spanish Cockery (a

volume). A well-known lecturer and speaker ; the Hispanic Society of New York granted to her First Prize Medal of Literature and Art. *Address*: Madrid, San Bernardo, 37. *Clubs*: Lyceum ; Ateneo de Madrid ; Sociedad Economica de Amigos del pais (the first woman that has entered in).   (*Died 12 May 1921.*)

PAREKH, Sir Gokuldas Kahandas, Kt., *cr.* 1921 ; Vakil High Court, Bombay, since 1871 ; *b.* Umreth, Kaira, 24 Jan. 1847 ; *s.* of Kahandas Kalidas Parekh, School Master ; *m.* 1868, Parsanbai, *d.* of Hargovandas T. Mehta. *Educ.*: Elphinstone College, Bombay. Mathematical Teacher, High School, S'urat, 1867-68 ; Deputy Edl. Inspector, Gujarati Schools, Bombay, 1868-1871 ; Head Master, Alfred High School, Mandvi and Inspector of Schools, Kachh, 1871 ; Deputy Inspector of Gujarati Schools, Bombay, 1871-80 ; Member of Bombay Legislative Council representing the Municipalities of the Northern Division, Bombay Presidency, 1897-1920. *Address*: New Queen's Road, Bombay, India.   (*Died Mar. 1925.*)

PARENT, Hon. Simon Napoleon, K.C. ; Chairman, Transcontinental Railway Commission ; *b.* 12 Sept. 1855 ; *s.* of Simon Polycarpe Parent ; *m.* 1877, Marie Louise Clara, *d.* of Ambroise Gendron ; four *s.* four *d. Educ.*: Laval University. Admitted to practise law, 1881 ; member Quebec City Council, 1890-94 ; Mayor, 1894-1906 ; elected to Legislature, 1890-1905 ; Minister of Crown Lands, 1897 - 1906 ; Premier and Minister of Lands, Mines, and Fisheries, Quebec, 1900-5. *Address*: Ottawa, Ont. *Clubs*: Rideau, Laurentian, Garrison, Ottawa.   (*Died Sept. 1920.*)

PAREPARAMBIL, Rt. Rev. Dr. Aloysius, Vicar Apostolic of Ernakulam, *b.* Pulingundu, Travancore, 25 March 1847. *Educ.*: Seminary. Priest, 1870 ; Professor of Latin, and subsequently vice-Rector or a seminary ; a parish priest in his native place for seven years ; was always in office of counsellor and secretary to his Bishop, Dr. Lavigne, S.J. ; Bishop, 1896 ; travelled through France, Belgium, and Italy, 1895, and 1905 ; Bishop of Tio, and Vicar Apostolic for the Syrian Catholics of the Vicariate of Ernakulam in the Malabar Coast. *Address*: Ernakulam, Malabar, India.   (*Died 9 Dec. 1919.*)

PARFITT, His Honour James John, K.C. 1908 ; B.A. ; Judge County Court, Circuit No. 41 Clerkenwell, since 1921 ; Bencher of Middle Temple, 1917 ; *b.* Slwch Villa, near Brecon, S. Wales, Dec. 1857 ; *m.* 1900, Elizabeth Mary, 4th *d.* of late F. W. Reynolds, of Hillside, Woolton, near Liverpool. *Educ.*: Prior Park College, Bath ; London University. Was for about 3 years a tutor in Cardinal Newman's School at Edgbaston ; called to the Bar, 1887 ; practised on the Midland Circuit ; formerly Junior Counsel to the Post Office on his Circuit and Standing Counsel to the Assay Authorities in Birmingham ; Recorder of Northampton, 1916-18; County Court Judge, Leeds and Wakefield (Circuit 14), 1918-21 ; Sussex Circuit 1921, and Commissioner at Manchester Assizes, July 1921 ; Commissioner of Assize on S. Wales Circuit, Jan. 1924, and on Oxford Circuit, June and July 1924 ; played cricket for Surrey, 1881-82, for Somersetshire, 1883-85 ; formerly one of the Governors of Birmingham University, and formerly a member of the General Council of the Bar. *Recreations*: formerly cricket, now golf, bicycling, and walking. *Address*: Lamb Building, Temple, E.C. ; 17 The Grange, Wimbledon, S.W.19. *T.*: Wimbledon 2168.   (*Died 17 May 1926.*)

PARGITER, Frederick Eden, M.A. ; *b.* 1852 ; 2nd *s.* of Rev. R. Pargiter ; *m.* Florence, *e. d.* of Henry Beverley, Judge of High Court, Calcutta ; one *s.* one *d. Educ.*: Taunton Grammar School ; Exeter College, Oxford (1st class Math. in Mods. 1871 and

Finals, 1873 ; Boden Sanskrit Scholar, 1872). Entered I.C.S. (Bengal), 1875 ; Under-Secretary, Government of Bengal, 1885 ; District and Sessions Judge, 1887 ; Judge of High Court, Calcutta, 1904 ; retired, 1906 ; Secretary Bengal Asiatic Society 1884-85 ; President, 1903-5 ; Fellow of Calcutta University, 1905-6 ; Member of Council, Royal Asiatic Society, 1907-1911, 1912-16, and 1921-5 ; Vice-President, 1916-1921. *Publications :* Bengal Municipal Acts ; Revenue History of the Sundarbans ; Beverley's Land Acquisition Acts ; Translation of the Markandeya Purana with Notes ; Dynasties of the Kali Age ; Ancient Indian Historical Tradition ; Centenary Volume (1923) of the Royal Asiatic Society ; Papers in Journals of Bengal and Royal Asiatic Societies, Epigraphia Indica, etc. *Address :* 12 Charlbury Road, Oxford. *(Died 18 Feb. 1927.)*

PARISET, Georges, Agrégé d'histoire, 1888 ; Litt. D., 1897 ; Professor of Modern History in the University of Nancy since 1891, of Strasbourg since 1919 ; *b.* 8 July 1865 ; *m.* Jeanne Schmidt ; four *c. Educ. :* Sorbonne. *Publications :* Church and State in Prussia, 1713-40, 1897 ; The Anglo-Venezuelan Dispute about Guiana, 1900 ; La Révolution, le Consulat et l'Empire, Lavisse, Hist. de France Contemporaine II-III, 1920-21 ; France under the Consulate and the Empire, Cambridge Modern History, IX, 1906, etc. *Address :* 3 rue de la Monnaie, Strasbourg, France. *(Died 25 Sept. 1927.)*

PARK, Col. and Hon. Col. James Smith, M.V.O. 1905 ; V.D. ; Member of Town Council, Glasgow, since 1914 ; late commander 1st Lanarkshire R.E. Vols., and Scottish Group Telegraph Coys. R.E. Territorial Force ; member of the Corporation and of the Territorial Force Association of the County of City of Glasgow ; J.P. County of City of Glasgow ; *b.* Glasgow, 25 Dec. 1854 ; *s.* of late Robert Ballantyne Park of Glasgow ; unmarried. *Educ. :* Western Academy and University, Glasgow. Late Managing Director at Glasgow of Allan Line, also principal owner and manager of The Park Steamship Company, Limited, and an underwriter at Lloyd's ; Chairman, Dominion of Canada Investment and Debenture Company, Ltd.; and J. Broadfoot & Sons, Ltd. ; Director of W. Beardmore & Co., Ltd., and R. and J. Dick, Ltd. ; and Forth and Clyde Junction Railway Company ; member of the Board of Trade Committee on New Lighthouse Work ; Director in many philanthropic and educational institutions ; has given important evidence on behalf of shipowners before Royal and other commissions ; has raised and successfully contested very important points connected with shipping with the Board of Trade ; was a member of Board of Trade Committee to consider question of Boy Sailors, and of War Office Committees *re* Auxiliary Forces ; long an advocate of universal physical and military training. *Recreations :* riding, cycling, golf, and other athletics. *Address :* 20 Park Terrace, Glasgow, W. ; Auchenkyle, Monkton, Ayrshire. *T.A. :* Parque, Glasgow. *T. :* Charing Cross 115, Glasgow. *Clubs :* Constitutional : New, Conservative, Glasgow. *(Died 1 Feb. 1921.)*

PARK, Sir Maitland Hall, Kt. cr. 1914 ; M.A., LL.D. Glas. 1909; Chief Editor Cape Times, since 1902 ; *b.* Cumbernauld, Dumbartonshire, N.B., 10 Oct. 1862 ; *y. s.* of late Rev. Hugh Park, Established Church, Cumbernauld ; *m.* 1st, Alice, *d.* of late Robert Orr, Helensburgh, N.B. ; 2nd, 1892, Anna, *d.* of Peter Baillie, Inverness; one *s. Educ. :* Glasgow High School and University. Sub-Editor of the Glasgow Herald, 1885-86 ; joined staff Pioneer, Allahabad, N.W.P., India, 1886, as Assistant Editor, and remained as Assistant Editor, Acting Editor, and Chief Editor until 1902. *Recreations :*

nshing, golfing, lawn tennis, bowling. *Address :* Fairlight, Orangezicht, Cape Town. *Clubs :* Imperial Colonies : Civil and City, Cape Town. *(Died 15 Mar. 1921.)*

PARK, Rev. Philip Lees, Hon. Canon of Gloucester Cathedral; *b.* Plymouth, 7 April 1860 ; *s.* of Thomas Park, Surgeon, Royal Artillery, and Emma Lees; *m.* ; two *s.* one *d. Educ. :* Winchester ; Trinity College, Oxford. Assistant Curate of Quebec Chapel, Marylebone, London, 1883-87; St. Paul's, Clifton, Bristol, 1887-92 ; Vicar of Highnam, Gloucester, 1892-1922 ; Rural Dean of the North Forest, Dio. Gloucester, 1909-22. *Publications :* Notes on the Occasional Prayers and Thanksgivings (Book of Common Prayer). *Address :* Parkfield Lawn, St. Stephen's Road, Cheltenham. *T.A. :* Cheltenham. *(Died 20 Mar. 1925.)*

PARK, Rev. William, A.M., D.D., LL.D.; Senior Minister, Rosemary Street Presbyterian Church, Belfast; *b.* Stewartstown, Co. Tyrone, 29 Mar. 1844 ; *m.* 1874, Susan, *y. d.* of Rev. John Edgar, D.D. ; two *s.* three *d. Educ. :* Royal School, Armagh ; Queen's College, Belfast ; New College, Edinburgh ; Assembly's College, Belfast. Ordained Minister of First Ballymena Presbyterian Church, 1866 ; installed as Minister of Rosemary Street Church, Belfast, 1873 ; Convener of Committee of General Assembly on Statistics for fifteen years ; Convener of Continental Mission, two years ; Convener and Joint Convener of Foreign Mission, sixteen years ; Moderator of General Assembly, 1890-91 ; resigned the full charge of Congregation, 1923 ; President of the Alliance of Reformed Churches holding the Presbyterian System, for eight years, 1913-21 ; presided at the eleventh General Council of the same in Pittsburg (U.S.A.), Sep. 1921. *Publications :* ephemeral —sermons, etc. *Recreation :* walking. *Address :* Garthowen, Sans Souci Park, Belfast. *(Died 5 June 1925.)*

PARK, Col. William Urquhart, M.V.O. 1905 ; V.D. ; *b.* 1846 ; *m.* 1891, Margaret, *e. d.* of James W. Black, Greenock. *Educ. :* Cambridge (M.A.). Lt.-Col. and Hon. Col. 1st V.B. Argyll and Sutherland Highlanders, 1903-8. *Address :* 61 Finnart Street, Greenock. *(Died April 1917.)*

PARKER, Baron (Life-Peer), **of Waddington,** *cr.* 1913 ; **Rt. Hon. Robert John Parker,** Kt., *cr.* 1906 ; a Lord of Appeal in Ordinary since 1913 ; *s.* of late Rev. R. Parker of Claxby, Alford, Lincs ; *b.* 25 Feb. 1857 ; *m.* 1884, Constance, *d.* of John Trevor Barkley; three *s.* two *d. Educ. :* Eton ; King's College, Cambridge. B.A. 1880 ; M.A. 1883 ; called to Bar, Lincoln's Inn, 1883 ; Junior Counsel to the Treasury in Equity matters, 1900-6 ; Judge of the High Court, 1906-13. *Address :* 28 Wellington Court, S.W. ; Aldworth, Haslemere. *Clubs :* Athenæum, United University. *(Died 12 July 1918.)*

PARKER, Charles Sandbach, of Fairlie, C.B.E. 1917 ; Order of St. Stanislav (Russia), 2nd class, with star, 1918 ; Chairman and Managing Director, Demerara Co., since 1908, and British Empire Producers' Organisation since 1916 ; *b.* 1 Nov. 1864 ; *e. s.* of Samuel Sandbach Parker, Aigburth, Liverpool ; *m.* 1906, Harriette Dorothy, *y. d.* of E. G. B. Meade Waldo, of Stonewall Park, Kent ; two *d. Educ. :* Eton ; University College, Oxford. Partner of Sandbach, Tinne & Co., Liverpool, and Sandbach, Parker & Co., Demerara, 1890-1908 ; Unionist Candidate for Barnstaple Division of Devonshire since 1910 ; contested Division, 1910 and 1911 ; Head of Russian Metals Dept., Commission Internationale de Ravitaillement, 1915-17 ; Member of Executive Committee, West India Committee, since 1898 ; of Trade and Industry Committee, Royal Colonial Inst., since 1917. *Recreations :* cricket, golf, shooting. *Address :* Fairlie, Ayrshire, N.B.; 45 Cadogan Place, S.W.1. *T. :*

Victoria 6170. *Clubs:* Athenæum, Brooks's.
                          (Died 9 May 1920.)

PARKER, Edward Harper, M.A. (Manc.); Prof. of Chinese, the Victoria Univ. of Manchester, since 1901; Reader in Chinese, University College, Liverpool, since 1896; *b.* 3 Jan. 1849; 2nd *s.* of Edward Parker, surgeon, Liverpool (*d.* 1887), and Mary (*d.* 1860), *d.* of Wm. Rushton, Liverpool; *m.* ; one *d. Educ.:* Dr. Brunner's Preparatory School, Everton; Royal Institution School, Liverpool. Barrister-at-law, Middle Temple. In the cotton-broking, silk, and tea trades, Liverpool and London, 1864-66; studied Chinese under Dr. J. Summers, George Yard, E.C., 1867; student-interpreter in Peking, 1869-1871; served at Tientsin, Taku, Hankow, Kewkiang, and Canton consulates, 1871-75; studied at Middle Temple, 1875-77; served at Foochow, Pagoda Island, Chinkiang, and Canton consulates, 1877-80; consular-agent at Chungking, 1880-81; called to Bar, 1882; acting-consul at Wênchow, 1883-84; temporary vice-consul at Fusan and Chemulpo, 1885-86; acting consul-general at Sôul, 1886-87; served in Shanghai consulate, 1887-88; at Pagoda Island and Hoihow consulates, 1889-94; commissioned H.M. Consul, Kiungchow, 1892; Adviser on Chinese Affairs in Burma, 1892-93; at Hoihow, 1893-94; retired on a pension, 1895. *Publications:* Comparative Chinese Family Law, 1879; The Opium War, 1887; China's Relations with Foreigners, 1888; Up the Yangtsze, 1892; Burma, 1893; A Thousand Years of the Tartars, 1895; 2nd enlarged edition, 1925; China, 1901 (enlarged edition, 1917); John Chinaman, 1901; China, Past and Present, 1903; China and Religion, 1905; Ancient China Simplified, 1908; Studies in Chinese Religion, 1910; etc. *Recreations:* travelling, walking. *Address:* 14 Gambier Terrace, Liverpool. *Club:* Athenæum, Liverpool.
                        (Died 26 Jan. 1926.)

PARKER, Sir Henry, Kt., *cr.* 1908; K.C.M.G., *cr.* 1914; K.C.; Chief Justice of Western Australia, 1906-13; *b.* York, W.A., 7 Nov. 1846; *s.* of Stephen Stanley Parker; *m.* 1872, Amy Katherine, *d.* of G. W. Leake, Q.C.; nine children. *Educ.:* Bishop's College, Perth, W.A. Called to Bar, W.A., 1868; Q.C., 1890; Puisne Judge, 1901; represented Perth, in Legislative Council, 1878-88; Busselton, 1888-90; Member Legislative Assembly for York, 1890-92; Member Legislative Council, 1892-97; Delegate from Legislature to Imperial Parliament to advocate Responsible Government, 1890; represented W.A. in London on the delegation relative to the Federation of Australia, 1900; Mayor of Perth, 1878, 1880, 1881, 1892, 1901; Colonial Secretary, 1892-4; President Weld Club, 1899-1906; President of the Arbitration Court, 1904-6. *Address:* Melbourne
                        (Died 13 Dec. 1927.)

PARKER, Horatio William, Organist; Professor Music, Yale, since 1894; *b.* Auburndale, Mass., 15 Sep. 1863; *m.* 1886, Anna Ploessl, Munich. *Educ.:* Royal Conservatoire, Munich. Hon. A.M. Yale, 1892; Mus. Doc., Camb. 1902; Organist Holy Trinity, New York, 1888-93; Trinity Church, Boston, 1893-1901. *Publications:* (Oratorios) Hora Novissima, 1898; St. Christopher, 1898; A Wanderer's Psalm, 1900; (Cantatas) King Trojan; The Kobolds; (Operas) Mona, 1912; Fairyland, 1915. *Address:* Yale University, New Haven, Conn., U.S.A.
                        (Died 18 Dec. 1919.)

PARKER, Joseph, C.S.I. 1896; *b.* Chislehurst, 12 Aug. 1831; *e. s.* of late Joseph Timothy Parker, Vicar of Wyton, Huntingdonshire, and Mary, *d.* of Gen. F. Campbell (Melfort). R.A.; *m.* 1st, 1865, Bessie (*d.* 1892), *d.* of John Moxon Clabon; 2nd, 1894, Eva, *d.* of late Col. Edmund Campbell (Melfort), Bom. S.C.; two *s.* three *d. Educ.:* Cheltenham. Entered H.E.I.C.S. 1851; senior clerk in Store Dept. 1866; Director-Gen. of Stores at India

814

Office, 1891; retired, 1896. *Recreation:* golf. *Address:* Trelawneys Cottage, Sompting. *Club:* Primrose.   *(Died 6 July 1924.)*

PARKER, Maj.-Gen. Neville Fraser, Bengal Infantry; *b.* 30 July 1841; *m.* ; two *s.* Entered army, 1859; Maj.-Gen. 1897; transferred to unemployed supernumerary list, 1900; served Hazara Campaign, 1868 (medal); Afghan War, 1878-79 (despatches, medal). *Address:* Craymead, Highview Road, Sidcup.
                        (Died 4 Jan. 1916.)

PARKER, Percy Livingstone; Editor and Proprietor of Public Opinion; *b.* Ipswich, 1867; *s.* of M. P. Parker; *m.* 1894 Hilda, *d.* of late Rev. W. H. Tindall, Weybridge. Private Sec. to late Rev. Hugh Price Hughes, 1889-93; to late Sir John Hutton, as Chairman of the L.C.C., 1893-4; Sub-editor The New Age, 1894-1897; Assistant Editor and Editor of Harmsworth Magazine, 1898-1902; Editor of Daily Mail Year-Book, 1901-12. *Publications:* Edited John Wesley's Journal, with Introduction by Hugh Price Hughes and Augustine Birrell; George Fox's Journal, with Introduction by Sir W. R. Nicoll. *Address:* Baston Lodge, St. Leonards-on-Sea; 44 Essex Street, Strand, W.C. *T.:* Central 948. *(Died 1 April 1925.)*

PARKER, Brig.-Gen. Robert Gabbett, C.B. 1919; C.M.G. 1918; D.S.O. 1915; late The King's Own (Royal Lancaster Regiment); *b.* 4 Dec. 1875. *Educ.:* Clifton College; R.M.C. Sandhurst. Entered army, 1896; Captain, 1900; Major, 1910; Lt.-Col., 1915; Col., 1919; served S. African War, 1899-1902 (despatches twice; Queen's medal 6 clasps, King's medal 2 clasps); European War, 1914-18 (despatches six times, D.S.O., C.M.G., C.B., French Croix de Guerre, Officer of the Order of the Crown of Italy); retired pay, 1926. *Address:* Bally Valley, Killaloe, Co. Clare.   *(Died 26 June 1927.)*

PARKER, William Frye, F.R.A.M.; Fellow and Professor Royal Academy of Music; *b.* 10 Sep. 1855; *m.* 1879; two *s.* one *d. Educ.:* Royal Academy of Music. Principal Violin (Leader) at Philharmonic Society's Concerts, Leeds Musical Festival, etc., 1895-1910. *Address:* 17 Luxemburg Gardens, W.6. *T.:* Hammersmith 355. *Club:* Arts.

PARKER, William Newton, Ph.D., F.Z.S; Professor of Zoology at the University College of South Wales and Monmouthshire in the University of Wales; 2nd *s.* of late Prof. W. Kitchen Parker; *m.* Hedwig, 2nd *d.* of late Professor August Weismann; one *s.* two *d. Educ.:* Royal College of Science, London; Morphological Laboratory, Cambridge; University of Freiburg-in-Baden. Formerly Assistant to late Professor Huxley; Deputy-Prosector to the Zoological Society; Lecturer on Biology at University College, Aberystwyth. *Publications:* On the Structure and Development of Lepidosteus (in conjunction with late Professor F. M. Balfour); On the Anatomy and Physiology of Protopterus; Elementary Course of Practical Zoology (with late Professor T. Jeffery Parker); Translations of Wiedersheim's Comparative Anatomy of Vertebrates and Weismann's Germ-Plasm. *Address:* University College, Cardiff. *(Died 22 Feb. 1923.)*

PARKES, Sir Edward E., Kt., *cr.* 1917; M.P. (L.U.) Birmingham, Central, since 1895; ironmaster; Magistrate for Birmingham; *b.* 1848; *s.* of late Israel Parkes, Edgbaston; *m.* Louise, *d.* of late Henry H. Hartshorne; two *s.* two *d. Address:* Oak Grange, Hermitage Road, Edgbaston, Birmingham. *T.A.:* Edward E. Parkes, M.P., Birmingham. *T.:* Edgbaston, Birmingham, 53. *Clubs:* Constitutional, Royal Automobile.   *(Died June 1919.)*

PARKIN, Sir George Robert, K.C.M.G., *cr.* 1920; C.M.G., 1898; LL.D., D.C.L. hon. Oxon.; Organising Representative of Rhodes Scholarship Trust since 1902; author and lecturer on Imperial Federation; *b.* Salisbury,

PARKER, Rt. Rev. Edward Melville, D.D., D.C.L. See page xxviii.

New Brunswick, 8 Feb. 1846; *m.* 1878, Annie Connell, *d.* of Wm. Fisher of Fredericton; one *s.* four *d.* Principal of Upper Canada College, Toronto, Canada, 1895 - 1902. *Publications:* Imperial Federation, 1892; Round the Empire, 1892; The Great Dominion, 1895; Life and Letters of Edward Thring, 1898; Life of Sir John A. Macdonald, Prime Minister of Canada, 1906; The Rhodes Scholarships, 1912. *Address:* Seymour House, Waterloo Place, S.W.; 7 Chelsea Court, S.W.3. *Club:* Athenæum.
(Died 25 June 1922.)

PARKINGTON, Sir John Roper, Kt., *cr.* 1902; D.L. and J.P. Co. London; *b.* 1845; *s.* of late John Weldon Parkington; *m.* 1873, Marie Louise (gold medal, 1st Order of Mérite Civile, and Red Cross decoration—both of Montenegro), *d.* of late A. Sims Silvester of the Stock Exchange, London; three *d. Educ. :* private Catholic schools in England and France. Hon. Col. 7th V.B. Essex Regiment; Major 3rd Batt. East Surrey Regiment (Militia), 1891-98; Chevalier de la Légion d'honneur; Officier d'Académie Francaise, 1906; Commandeur Royal Orders of Montenegro and Servia; Red Cross of Spain; Knight Commander of Our Lady of Conception of Villa Viçosa, Portugal; F.R.G.S.; Fellow Royal Col. Institute; Vice-President Anglo-Portuguese Chamber of Commerce; one of H.M. Lieutenants for the City of London; founder l'Entente Cordiale, Anglo-French Association, 1896. *Address:* Broadwater Lodge, Wimbledon, S.W.19. *M.:* PC 5719. *Clubs:* United Service, Royal Automobile, West Indian City Carlton.
(Died 14 Jan. 1924.)

PARKINSON, Rt. Rev. Mgr. Henry, D.D., Ph.D. (Gregorian University, Rome); Rector of St. Mary's College, Oscott; *b.* Cheadle, Staffordshire, 1852. *Educ. :* Sedgley Park School, nr. Wolverhampton; Douai; Olton; English College, Rome. Ordained, 1877; Vice-Rector of Olton Seminary, 1877-87; and Professor of Philosophy, Senior Curate, and Choirmaster at St. Chad's Cathedral, Birmingham, 1887-89; Vice-Rector and Professor of Philosophy at Oscott College, 1889; first Rector of the Central Seminary at Oscott, 1897, when he was created a Domestic Prelate; Protonotary Apostolic, 1917; President of the Catholic Social Guild, of the Birmingham Society of St. Cecily; Assistant General (for England) of the Apostolic Union of Secular Priests; Canon of Cathedral Chapter of Birmingham since 1913. *Publications:* Definitiones Philosophiæ Universæ; Refectio Spiritualis; A Primer of Social Science. *Address:* Oscott College, Birmingham. *T. :* East 890.
(Died 22 June 1924.)

PARKINSON, John Wilson Henry, Colonial Civil Service; *b.* 13 July 1877; *e. s.* of W. H. Parkinson, The Hall, East Ravendale, Lincs; *m.* 1919, Winifred Mary, *o. d.* of J. A. Forster, Croslands Park, Barrow-in-Furness; one *s. Educ. :* Brighton College. Solicitor Supreme Court, 1900; Administrator-General, East African Protectorate, 1909; Curracy Commissioner, East Africa, 1909-19; Secretary, Wakf. Commission, East Africa. *Recreations:* cricket, golf. *Address:* Mombasa, Kenya Colony. *Club:* Sports.
(Died 17 June 1923.)

PARKINSON, William Edward, A.R.C.A. London, F.S.A.M.; Principal of the School of Arts and Crafts, York; *b.* 1 Jan. 1871; *s.* of late James Hy. Parkinson, Chester; *m.* 1899, Rosemary, *d.* of late Joseph R. Curnow, Chester; two *s. Educ. :* School of Art, Chester; Royal College of Art, London. Formerly Art Master at Barnard Castle; Member of the Soc. of Yorkshire Artists. *Recreations:* caravaning and boating. *Address:* 103 High Petergate, York.
(Died 26 May 1927.)

PARKS, Sir John, Kt., *cr.* 1914; D.L., J.P.; Mayor of Bury, 1914, and three previous times; *b.* 24 Nov. 1844; *m.* 1868, Rachel, *d.* of Samuel

Grundy of Bridge Hall, Bury; three *s.* two *d.* Director, Manchester and Liverpool Bank and Burnley Paper Works Co., Ltd.; Chairman, Smallman's Ltd., Vulcan Spinning and Manufacturing Co., Ltd., and Liverpool Storage Co., Ltd.; contested Bury, 1892. *Address:* Bank House, Bury. *Club:* National Liberal.
(Died 9 Jan. 1919.)

PARKYNS, Sir Thomas Mansfield Forbes, 7th Bt., *cr.* 1681; *b.* 30 April 1853; *S.* father, 1895; *m.* 1886, Beatrice, *d.* of late Arthur Travers Crawford, C.M.G.; one *d. Educ. :* Eton; Brasenose Coll., Oxford. Barr. Inner Temple, 1879. *Recreations:* shooting, golf. *Heir:* none. *Address:* 12 Westminster Palace Gardens, S.W.1. *T. :* Victoria 1495. *Club:* Garrick.
(Died 2 Feb. 1926.)

PARMELEE, William Grannis, I.S.O. 1903; Ex-Deputy-Minister of Trade and Commerce, and Chief Controller of Chinese Immigration, Canada; *b.* 27 Aug. 1833; *s.* of Rotus Parmelee, M.D., Waterloo, Quebec, and Sarah M., *d.* of William Grannis; *m.* 1st, 1856, Marcella A., *d.* of William Whitney of Montpelier, Vermont; 2nd, 1901, Jessie B., *d.* of late Samuel Christie of Ottawa, Ontario. *Educ. :* Waterloo. Engaged several years in insurance and railway offices and as Bank Manager; entered Civil Service, 1876; was Commissioner of Customs; transferred to new Department of Trade and Commerce, which he organised, 1892; served with and on several Commissions; retired, 1908. *Address:* Ottawa, Canada. *T.A. :* Parmelee. Ottawa. *T. :* 408.
(Died 15 Jan. 1921.)

PARNELL, John Howard; *b.* 1843; *s.* of late J. H. Parnell, Avondale, and Delia (*d.* 1898), *d.* of Capt. C. Stewart, U.S. Navy; *b.* of late Charles S. Parnell, M.P.; *m.* 1907, Olivia Isabella, *e. d.* of late Colonel James Smythe, 69th Regt., and widow of Archibald Matier, J.P., The Grove, Carlingford, Co. Louth; one *s.* M.P. (N.) Co. Meath, S., 1895-1900. *Address:* Lion House, Glenegary, Kingstown; Laragh Castle. Co. Wicklow.
(Died 3 May 1923.)

PARR, Cecil Francis, J.P.; *b.* 1847; *y. s.* of late Thomas Parr, of Grappenhall Heyes, Cheshire, and 2nd wife Alicia, *d.* of late Philip Charlton, of Wytheford Hall, Shropshire; *m.* 1882, Amy Ursula, 2nd *d.* of late Hon. Robert, 7th Baron Dinsdale, of Essendon Place, Hertfordshire; one *s. Educ. :* Harrow; Exeter College, Oxford (B.A.). Called to Bar, Inner Temple, 1874. *Address:* Kimpton Grange, near Welwyn. *T. :* Kimpton 3. *T.A. :* Kimpton. *Clubs:* United University, Royal Automobile.
(Died 13 Jan. 1923.)

PARR, Maj.-Gen. Sir Harington Owen, Kt., *cr.* 1926; C.B. 1922; C.M.G. 1919; Military Secretary, A.H.Q., India, 1924; retired, 1926. *Club:* United Service. *(Died 1 Oct. 1923.)*

PARR, Joseph Charlton, J.P., D.L.; 3rd and *e. surv. s.* of late Thomas Parr and 2nd wife, Alicia, *d.* of Philip Charlton of Wytheford Hall, Co. Salop; *b.* 2 June 1837; *m.* 1872, Jessie Maria, *e. d.* of late Lt.-Col. George Lister Kaye; one *s.* three *d. Heir:* s. Roger C. Parr. *Address:* Grappenhall Hayes, Warrington; Staunton Park, Staunton-on-Arrow. *Clubs:* Carlton, Junior Carlton, Constitutional.
(Died 27 Feb. 1920.)

PARRATT, Sir Walter, Kt., *cr.* 1892; K.C.V.O. *cr.* 1921; C.V.O. 1917; M.V.O. 1901; M.A.; Mus. Doc. (Hon.) R.A.M.; Hon. Fellow of Magdalen College, Oxford; Hon. Mus. Doc. Oxford, Cambridge, and Durham; Member of the Associated Board of the Royal Academy and Royal College of Music; Professor of Music, Oxford, 1908-18; Dean of Faculty of Music, London University, since 1916; late Private Organist to Queen Victoria; Organist St. George's Chapel Royal, Windsor; Master of the King's Music; Professor at Royal College of Music; Past Examiner in Music to Universities of Oxford, Cambridge, London, and Wales;

Past President, Royal College of Organists; Past President, Union of Graduates in Music; *b.* 10 Feb. 1841; *s.* of Thomas Parratt, Huddersfield; *m.* 1864, Emma, *d.* of L. Gledhill, Huddersfield: one *s.* three *d.* *Educ.*: Coll. School, Huddersfield; privately. Organist of Armitage Bridge Church; afterwards of Great Witley; Wigan Parish Church; Magdalen College, Oxford; St. George's Chapel Royal, Windsor; Past Grand Organist of the Freemasons. *Publications:* the article on Music in Ward's Reign of Queen Victoria; contributor to Grove's Dictionary of Music and other works; music for the Tale of Troy, etc. *Recreation:* chess (President Oxford University Chess Club; two years Captain of the eight chosen to play against Cambridge). *Address:* Cloisters, Windsor Castle. *Club:* Athenæum.

                       (*Died 27 Mar. 1924.*)

PARROTT, Sir (James) Edward, Kt., *cr.* 1910; Editor to publishing house of Thomas Nelson & Sons since 1898; *b.* 1 June 1863; *e. s.* of E. B. Parrott, Marple, Cheshire; *m.* Elizabeth S., *y. d.* of late John Shirley, Derby (Lady Parrott was for seven years Inspectress of Schools in Liverpool); three *d.* *Educ.*: St. Paul's College, Cheltenham; Trinity College, Dublin; M.A. (senior prizeman in English) and LL.D. (head of examination list, Dec. 1900); F.E.I.S. Had scholastic experience in Sheffield and Liverpool; chairman of S. Edinburgh Liberal Association, 1904-17; chairman of Edinburgh United Liberal Committee, 1908-19; J.P. County of City of Edinburgh. *Publications:* A Pageant of British History; A Pageant of English Literature, 1914; Children's Story of the War (ten volumes); Allies, Foes, and Neutrals, 1918; Editor of Funk & Wagnall's Standard Encyclopædia and of Nelson's New Age Encyclopædia, 1920; numerous school books, including the Highroads Series, etc.; M.P. (L.) South Division of Edinburgh, 1917-18; Life Governor of Cheltenham Training College; Palms in Gold of the Order of the Crown, Belgium; Officer of the Order of St. Sava. *Recreation:* golf. *Address:* 12 Cumin Place, Edinburgh. *Club:* National Liberal.   (*Died 5 April 1921.*)

PARRY, Sir Hubert Hastings; 1st Bt., *cr.* 1902; Kt., *cr.* 1898; C.V.O. 1905; M.A., Mus. Doc., D.C.L., LL.D., J.P.; Director Royal College of Music; Fellow of the Univ. of London; Hon. Fellow of Exeter Coll. Oxford; *b.* Bournemouth, 27 Feb. 1848; 2nd *s.* of T. Gambier Parry, Highnam Court, Gloucester; *m.* Lady Elizabeth Maud Herbert, *sister* of 14th Earl of Pembroke, 1872; two *d.* *Educ.*: Eton; Exeter Coll. Oxford. Professor of Music, Oxford, 1899 - 1908. *Publications:* Studies of Great Composers, 1886; Evolution of the Art of Music; many articles in Grove's Dictionary of Music; Summary of Musical History; Music of the 17th Century; Style in Musical Art, 1912; Life of John Sebastian Bach. *Works:* Music to the Birds of Aristophanes, 1884; Music to the Frogs of Aristophanes; Music to the Clouds of Aristophanes, 1905; Music to the Agamemnon of Æschylus, 1900; Judith, 1888; Ode for St. Cecilia's Day, 1889; The Lotos Eaters; L'Allegro and Penseroso; Blest Pair of Sirens; Invocation to Music; De Profundis, 1891; Job, 1892; King Saul, 1894; Magnificat, 1896; Song of Darkness and Light, 1898; Processional Anthem for the Coronation of King Edward VII.; Te Deum, 1900; War and Peace, 1903; Voces Clamantium, 1903; The Love that Casteth out Fear, 1904; The Pied Piper of Hamelin, 1905; The Soul's Ransom, 1906; The Vision of Life, 1907; Beyond these Voices, 1908; Te Deum for the Coronation of King George V.; Hymn to the Nativity, 1913; Music to the Acharnians of Aristophanes, 1914. *Heir:* none. *Address:* Highnam Court, Gloucester; 17 Ken-

816

sington Square, W.; Knight's Croft, Rustington, Worthing; Royal College of Music, S.W. *T.A.:* Initiative, London. *M.:* A 7838. *Clubs:* Athenæum, Savile, National Liberal, Royal Thames Yacht; Royal Yacht Squadron, Cowes.

                       (*Died 7 Oct. 1918.*)

PARRY, Admiral Sir John Franklin, K.C.B., *cr.* 1919; C.B. 1916; F.R.G.S.; *b.* 15 Aug. 1863; *s.* of Rt. Rev. Edward Parry, Bishop Suffragan of Dover (*d.* 1890); *m.* 1898, Emily Lempriere, *d.* of Hon. Henry Dobson, then Premier of Tasmania; one *d.* Entered Navy, 1877; Sub-Lieut. 1883; Lieut. 1885; Commander, 1899; Captain, 1905; Rear-Admiral, 1916; Vice-Admiral retired, 1920; Chief Assistant to Hydrographer, 1900-1903; Assist. Hydrographer, 1910-14; Hydrographer of the Navy, 1914-19; served in Suakin campaign, 1885 (Egyptian medal and star); served on many technical Committees in connection with Hydrography and Navigation; has been in command of surveys in many parts of the world. *Recreations:* fishing, boating. *Address:* Palais de la Terrasse, Monte Carlo. *Club:* United Service.   (*Died 21 April 1926.*)

PARRY, Alderman William John, C.B.E. 1920; F.C.A.; chartered accountant; *b.* 28 Sep. 1842; *s.* of John Parry and Elizabeth Jones; *m.* 1st, 1864, Jane Roberts; 2nd, 1878, Mary Pughe; 3rd, 1902, Mary Guy; two *s.* one *d.* *Educ.:* British and National Schools, Bethesda; Grammar School, Llanrwst. Liberal agent for his district, 1862-79; took an active part in the Penrhyn strikes of 1865 and 1874, and the lockouts at Llanberis and Glynrhonwy; elected on the Bethesda Board of Commissions, 1867; established the North Wales Quarrymen's Union, 1874, and acted as its first Secretary for 2½ years; its President for nine years; and its Umpire for 22 years; took an active part for establishing the North Wales University College at Bangor; edited the Werin and Genedl Newspapers for 4½ years; visited Canada and the United States in the interest of quarrymen five times, and South America twice; given evidence before Government Committees on Towns Holdings, Quarries Bill, Royal Commission on Labour, Bankruptcy and Building Societies and Quarries Bills; a member of first County Council, and filled the chairs of the County Council, and the Standing Joint Police Committee; a frequent contributor to the national and religious periodicals of his native country during the last sixty years, and acted continuously without a break for sixty years on public bodies. *Publications:* Gyiansoddiadau Eisteddfod Cymreigyddion, Bethesda, 1864; Ymdrafodaeth Caebrae-chycefn, 1875; Helyntion y3 Undebwr, 1885; Cofiant Tanymarian, 1886; Review of Evidence before Royal Commission on Labour, 1893; the same in Welsh, 1893; Chwareli and Chwarelwyr in 1896; Cyfrol y Jiwbili Capel Bethesda, 1900; the Penrhyn Lockout, 1901; Telyn Sankey, 1901; The Penrhyn Quarry Dispute, 1902; Ail Argraffiad Tanymarian, 1901; The Cry of the People, 1906; The English Hymnal, 1907; Cofiant Hwfa Mon, 1909; Ail Argraffiad Telyn Sankey, 1915; Ail Argraffiad o Gofiant Hwfa Mon, 1916. *Recreations:* collecting books, reading and writing, and the company of friends. *Address:* Coetmor Hall, Bethesda. *T.A.:* Coetmor, Bethesda. *T.:* 6. *M.:* 1530. *Club:* National Liberal.

                       (*Died 1 Sept. 1927.*)

PARRY-OKEDEN, William Edward, I.S.O. 1903; J.P.; *b.* Monaro, N.S.W. 13 May 1840; *o. s.* of late David Parry-Okeden, J.P., late R.N., last survivor battle Navarino; *m.* 1873, Gertrude, *e. d.* of late Rev. J. Pilgrim Wall, St. Vincent and Barbados, W.I.; three *s.* four *d.* *Educ.:* Melbourne Diocesan and St. Kilda Grammar Schools; studied law under articles and had training Victoria Volunteer

Rifles, 1857-60; migrated to Queensland; after ten years pioneering and pastoral pursuits, appointed Inspector Police and Customs Border Patrol, 1870; Police Magistrate various towns, 1872-86; when appointed Immigration Agent for Queensland; established Government Labour Bureau; Commission of Inquiry into Gaols Management, 1887; Under Colonial Secretary, 1889; subsequently first Principal Under-Secretary, Queensland; District Magistrate under special Peace Preservation Act, 1894; Commissioner Queensland Police, 1895; retired on pension, 1905; appointed 1906-7, by Commonwealth Government of Australia, Royal Commissioner, to Visit and Report on Present Conditions and Methods of Government in British New Guinea (Papua), and Best Means for Improvement; First Aboriginal Protector for whole State. *Recreations:* riding, driving, cricket. *Address:* Okewall, Redcliffe, Queensland, Australia. *Club:* Queensland.

(Died 30 Aug. 1926.)

PARSONS, Alfred, R.A. 1911; A.R.A. 1897; R.W.S. 1905 (President 1914); landscape painter; *b.* Beckington, Somersetshire, 2 Dec. 1847; 2nd *s.* of Joshua Parsons. *Educ.:* private schools. Clerk in Savings Bank Department of Post Office, 1865-67; since then painting; exhibitor at Royal Academy, Grosvenor, New Gallery, etc.; picture — When Nature painted all Things Gay, bought by Chantrey Fund, 1887; special exhibitions of the Warwickshire Avon, Gardens, Japanese Flowers, etc.; illustrations for Harper's Magazine and other publications, and for The Genus Rosa, by Ellen Willmott. *Publications:* illustrations (with E. A. Abbey, R.A.) for Herrick's Poems; She Stoops to Conquer; Old Songs; The Quiet Life. Alone —for Wordsworth's Sonnets; The Warwickshire Avon; Notes in Japan, the last written by the artist; The Danube, from the Black Forest to the Black Sea (with F. D. Millet). *Recreations:* canoeing, gardening. *Address:* Broadway, Worcestershire. *Clubs:* Athenæum, Arts.

(Died 16 Jan. 1920.)

PARSONS, Major - General Sir Charles, K.C.M.G., *cr.* 1899; C.B. 1906; F.R.G.S.; *b.* 9 May 1855; *e. s.* of late John Parsons, Ringmore, Shaldon; *m.* Margaret, *o. d.* of late Alfred Christian, C.M.G., 1898; two *d.* *Educ.:* Rugby; R. Military Academy. Served in Gaika and Zulu campaigns, including battles of Isandhlwana and Ulundi (despatches, medal with clasps for 1877-78-79); served in Transvaal war, including actions at Laing's Nek and Ingogo (despatches and general orders for gallantry), severely wounded, horse shot; served in Egyptian campaign, 1882, including actions at Mahsama, Kassassin, and Tel-el-Kebir (despatches, horse shot, Brev. Majority, medal with clasp, and 5th class Medjidieh and 4th class Osmanieh); served in Dongola campaign in command of Egyptian Artillery, including action at Hafir (despatches, and Brev. Lieut.-Colonel, medal with clasp); appointed Governor of Red Sea Littoral, 1896; employed on special mission in Eritrea when Kassala was handed over to Egyptian Government (2nd class Medjidieh); commanded at capture and defence of Gedaref, 1898 (despatches, Brev. Colonel, and K.C.M.G., clasp to medal); Assistant Adjutant-General, Woolwich, 1898-99; Col. on Staff R.A., Ireland, 1899; Assistant Inspector-General Lines of Communication, South Africa, 1900-1901 (despatches); Commanded Regular Forces Canada, 1902-6; a Commissioner for the Royal Hospital, Chelsea. *Address:* 28 Onslow Square, S.W.7. *T.:* Kensington 1760. *Club:* Naval and Military.

(Died 25 June 1923.)

PARSONS, Lieut.-Gen. Cunliffe McNeile, C.B. 1915; *b.* India, 15 Feb. 1865; *s.* of late Gen. J. E. B. Parsons, I.S.C., and late

Mrs. Parsons of Southbourne, Hants; *m.* 1903, Christian Jeannette Paton, *d.* of late Colonel E. H. Thomas, I.S.C.; two *d.* *Educ.:* Dulwich College. Entered R.M.L.I. 1883; served in China, 1900 (medal); commanded Chatham Battalion Royal Marines in operations round Antwerp, 1914, and on Gallipoli Peninsula from 29 April till wounded, 28 June 1915; Colonel, 2nd Commandant, Royal Marines, 1915 (despatches thrice, C.B.); command 181st Infantry Brigade at home, and with Expeditionary Force 1916, and 63rd (Royal Naval) Division Reserves, 1917-18; Commandant, Depôt, Royal Marines, 1918; Maj.-Gen. R.M., 1920. *Address:* c/o Stilwell and Sons, 42 Pall Mall, S.W.1. *Club:* Junior Army and Navy.

(Died 21 Jan. 1923.)

PARSONS, Maj. - Gen. Sir Harold Daniel Edmund, K.C.M.G. *cr.* 1918; C.B. 1915; C.M.G. 1900; late Royal Army Ordnance Corps; *b.* London, 3 July 1863; *s.* of late Maj.-Gen. J. E. B. Parsons, late I.S.C.; *m.* 1892, Julia, *d.* of late Thomas Archer, C.M.G.; one *s.* *Educ.:* Dulwich College. Lieut. The Queen's Regt. 1882; Captain, 1891; Major, 1898; Lieut.-Colonel A.O.D. 1904; Ordnance Officer, 3rd Class, 1900; Ordnance Officer, 2nd Class, 1904; Ordnance Officer, 1st Class, and Colonel, 1910; Principal Ordnance Officer, 1920; retired pay, 1923; served Burmese Campaign, 1885 - 89 (medal with two clasps); South African War, 1899-1902 (despatches, C.M.G., Queen's medal with 3 clasps, King's medal with 2 clasps); European War, 1914-18 (despatches five times, 1914 Star, C.B., prom. Maj.-General, K.C.M.G., Commander of Belgian Order of Leopold, Russian Order of St Stanislaus 2nd Class with Swords, American Distinguished Service Medal, Belgian Croix de Guerre, British War Medal, Allied Victory Medal). *Club:* United Service.

(Died 13 Feb. 1925.)

PARSONS, John Inglis, M.D., M.R.C.P., M.R.C.S., etc.; Hon. Fellow of two medical societies abroad, and Fellow of several others; Consulting Surgeon to Chelsea Hospital for Women; *b.* Melbourne House, Holbrooke, Kent, 1857; 3rd *s.* of late Percival Parsons (the inventor of manganese bronze). *Educ.:* private tuition; Guy's Hospital; Durham University. Entered Guy's, 1879; M.B. 1883; M.R.C.S. 1884; M.D. 1886; M.R.C.P. 1892; House Surgeon, 1884; Assistant Physician to Chelsea Hospital for Women, 1886; Fellow of the Royal Society of Medicine; Hon. Fellow of the American Electro-Therapeutic Association, 1891; Corr. Member de la Société Française d'Electrothérapie, 1893. *Publications:* Evolution Explained, 1925; The Disintegration of Organic Tissue by High Tension Discharges; Changes Produced by the Constant Current in Uterine Fibromata; A New and Bloodless Operation for Prolapsus Uteri. *Recreations:* shooting, golf, music, gardening. *Address:* Azalea Cottage, Howard Road, Bournemouth. *M.:* LN 51.

(Died 2 July 1928.)

PARSONS, Lieut.-Gen. Sir Lawrence Worthington, K.C.B., *cr.* 1912; C.B. 1900; *b.* 23 Mar. 1850; *o. s.* of Lawrence Parsons of Parsonstown, King's County; *m.* 1880, Florence Anna, *d.* of Robert Graves, M.D., of Cloghan Castle, King's County; one *d.* *Educ.:* Cheltenham. Served South Africa, 1899 - 1900 (despatches thrice, Queen's medal 6 clasps, C.B.); Inspector-Gen. Artillery, India, 1903-6; Major-General, 1903; Lt.-Gen. 1909; Commanded 6th Division, Cork, 1906-1909; 16th (Irish) Division, 1914-15; Colonel Commandt. R.A. 1917. *Club:* Army and Navy.

(Died 30 Aug. 1923.)

PARSONS, Philip Harry, L.R.C.P., L.R.C.S., L.R.F.P.S.G.; Anæsthetist University College Hospital; Physician Australian Auxiliary Hospital; Anæsthetist Masonic War Hospital; Anæsthetist Kensington General

817

Hospital; Surg. Major 1st C.B. London Scottish Regt.; s. of George Parsons; m. Mary, d. of T. B. M. Richards. *Educ.:* Melbourne University; R.C.S., Edinburgh. Resident Medical Officer Manchester Hospital for Consumption and Diseases of Throat; House Surgeon Royal Edinburgh Infirmary; Surgeon in charge Ear, Nose, and Throat Dept. Kensington General Hospital; District Medical Officer L.C.M.; Fellow Royal Society of Medicine; Hon. Sec. Ass. Med. Dip. Scot.; Sec., Treas., Chairman, Chelsea Division; Vice-President Met. Counties Branch; Member of Council British Medical Association; Member Manchester Pathological and Medical Society. *Publications:* A Simple Inhaler, Lancet, 1902; Case of Recklinghausen's Disease, Medical Press, 1906; New Ethyl Chloride Inhaler, British Medical Journal, 1910. *Address:* 6 Foulis Terrace, Onslow Gardens, S.W.7. *T.:* Ken. 1915. *Club:* Junior Athenæum.

(*Died 27 April 1920.*)

PARSONS, Hon. Richard Clere; 3rd *s.* of 3rd Earl of Rosse; *b.* 21 Feb. 1851; *m.* Agnes Elizabeth (*d.* 1922), *d.* of J. F. La Trobe Bateman, F.R.S.; five *s. Educ.:* privately; Trinity College, Dublin. Senior Moderator and Gold Medallist Physical Science and Chemistry, and Engineering degree with honours, 1873; contested University of Dublin, 1887; partner in Kitson & Co., Leeds, and took an active part in the development of the Yorkshire College, now the University of Leeds, 1880-87; partner of J. F. La Trobe Bateman, F.R.S., 1887-89; amongst other works superintended the design and construction of the Water and Drainage Works of the city of Buenos Ayres; Engineer to the Congested Board for Ireland, 1893-95; invited and subsequently prepared complete designs for a drainage system for the city of Petrograd, 1898; is Engineer to the Consolidated Waterworks Company of Rosario, Limited, the Montevideo Waterworks Company, Limited, and has designed and carried out numerous works abroad; a Director of the Mersey Railway Company; Member of the Institution of Civil Engineers (Millar Scholarship for researches in connection with Centrifugal Pumps); a Telford Gold Medal and a Manby Premium; Membre de la Societé dés Ingenieurs Civils de France; Member of the Institution of Mechanical Engineers; Treasurer and Deputy Chairman of the Delegacy of King's College University of London; a Governor of the Imperial College of Science and Technology, nominated by the University of London; a Vice-President of the Royal Society of Arts; a Vice-President and a Manager of the Royal Institution of Great Britain. *Publications:* has contributed numerous papers to scientific societies. *Address:* 48 Prince's Gardens, S.W.7. *T.:* Kensington 3410. *Clubs:* Athenæum, Junior Carlton, British Empire. (*Died 26 Jan. 1923.*)

PASCAL, Rt. Rev. Albert, O.M.I.; R.C. Bishop of Prince Albert since 1907; *b.* Languedoc, 1848. Indian Missionary in the North-West, 1874-91; Bishop of Mosynopolis and Vicar Apostolic of Saskatchewan, 1891. *Address:* Paina Albert, Saskatchewan.

(*Died July 1920.*)

PASLEY, Thomas Hamilton Sabine, M.V.O. 1904; Secretary Royal Yacht Squadron; *e. s.* of late Captain Hamilton Sabine Pasley; *b.* 1861; *m.* 1899, Alice Marion Margaret, *d.* of Thomas Conolly. *Educ.:* privately. Served in Egyptian War, 1882 and 1884; retired, 1898, as Staff Paymaster, R.N. *Address:* Northlands, Cowes, Isle of Wight. *Clubs:* Naval and Military, Beefsteak.

(*Died 25 Feb. 1927.*)

PASTURE, 4th Marquis, Gerard Gustavus Ducarel de la; [*g.-grandfather* came over from France and settled in England, 1791); *b.* 1 March 1836; *m.* 1st, 1864, Leontine Standish (*d.* 1869); one *d.*; 2nd, 1873, Georgina, Mary, *d.* of Robert J. Loughnan, an Indian

818

Judge; one *s.* one *d.*; *S.* father, 1840. *Heir: s.* Gerard Hubert, *b.* 8 May 1886. *Address:* Cefn Ila, Usk, Monmouthshire. (*Died 28 Jan. 1916.*)

PATCH, Col. Robert, C.B. 1896; H.M. Indian Army; retired; *b.* 25 July 1842; 3rd *s.* of late Lieut.-Col. Henry Revel Patch, H.E.I.C.S., and Charlotte, *d.* of Captain Robert Davies; *m.* Frances Maria, *d.* of James Lloyd of Compton, Dundon Rectory, Somerton, 1867; four *s. Educ.:* Cheltenham College. Ensign 55th Foot (now 2nd Battalion Border Regt.), 1863; Capt. B.S.C. (now Indian Army), 1875; Major, 1883; Brevet Lieut.-Colonel, 1888; Colonel, 1891; served with Bhootan Expedition, 1865 (medal with clasp); during Afghan war, 1879-80 (despatches, medal); Hazara Expedition, 1888 (despatches, Brevet Lieut.-Colonel); Miranzai Expedition 1891 (mentioned by Government of India and in despatches); Chitral Relief Expedition, 1895 (despatches, medal and clasp); Com.-General, Punjab, 1887-95; granted Good Service Pension, 1902. *Recreations:* hunting and gardening. *Address:* Fersfield, Newton Abbot, Devon.

(*Died 25 Feb. 1927.*)

PATERSON, Andrew Melville, M.D. (Edin.), M.B., F.R.C.S.; Assistant Inspector of Military Orthopædics; Major, R.A.M.C.; Professor of Anatomy, University of Liverpool since 1894; ex-President of the Anatomical Society of Great Britain and Ireland; F.R.A.I., F.R.A.M.; member of the Association of American Anatomists; *b.* 7 Mar. 1862; *s.* of late Rev. J. Carruthers Paterson, minister of St. Andrew's Pres. Church, Manchester; *m.* Beatrice, *d.* of late Richard Eadson, Manchester; two *s.* three *d. Educ.:* Manchester Grammar School; Owens College; Edinburgh University (M.B. and C.M. with 1st class Hons. 1883; M.D., gold medallist, 1886). Demonstrator of Anatomy, Edinburgh University and Owens College; 1st Professor of Anatomy, University College, Dundee, 1888; Dean of Medical Faculty, Liverpool, 1895-1904; Examiner in Anatomy, Universities Oxford, Cambridge, Durham, London, Wales, Indian Medical Service, Conjoint Board, the College of Surgeons, etc.; Hunterian Professor, the Royal College of Surgeons, 1903. *Publications:* Duval's Artistic Anatomy; The Human Sternum; articles in Cunningham's Text-Book of Anatomy; The Anatomist's Note Book; Manual of Embryology; numerous articles on anatomical subjects. *Recreation:* golf. *Address:* 21 Abercromby Square, Liverpool. *T.:* Royal 918. *Clubs:* Royal Societies; Royal Liverpool Golf, Racquet, Liverpool; Royal and Ancient Golf, St. Andrews. (*Died 13 Feb. 1919.*)

PATERSON, Arthur Henry; novelist; *b.* Bowdon, Cheshire, 15 July 1862; *y. s.* of late Alexander Henry Paterson, M.D.; also *b.* to late Mrs. Allingham; *m.* 1894, Mary, *d.* of late Lieut.-Col. G. Kellie M'Callum, late 92nd Gordon Highlanders, Gentleman-at-Arms; one *s. Educ.:* Univ. Coll. School, Lond. Sheep-rancher, New Mexico, U.S.A., 1877-79; farmer in Western Kansas. 1879-80; clerk and afterwards sub-manager in merchant's office, Birkenhead, 1881-1884; District Secy., Charity Organization Society, London, 1885-96; Secretary Social Welfare Association for London since 1910; Secretary, National Alliance of Employers and Employed, 1917; Grand Scribe, Order of Crusaders, 1923. *Publications:* The Better Man, 1890; A Partner from the West, 1892; The Daughter of the Nez Percés, 1894; A Man of his Word, 1894; A Son of the Plains, 1895; For Freedom's Sake, 1896; Father and Son, 1897; The Gospel writ in Steel, 1898; Cromwell's Own, 1899; Oliver Cromwell: a Biography, 1899; Colonel Cromwell, an Historical Drama, 1900; The King's Agent, 1902; The Homes of Tennyson, 1905; John Glynn, 1907; Administration of Charity, 1908; The Metropolitan Police, 1909; Our Prisons, 1911; Public Health and the Insurance Act, 1912; The

PASCAL, Jean Louis. See page xxviii.

Weapon of the Strike, 1922; Crusaders, 1925; Man or Beast? 1926. *Recreations:* entomology, cycling. *Address:* 6 Thurlow Road, Hampstead, N.W.3. *T.:* Hampstead 1358. *Club:* Reform.   (*Died 16 Jan. 1928.*)

PATERSON, Surg.-Maj.-Gen. Henry Foljambe, M.D., F.R.C.S., F.R.G.S.; *b.* 9 July 1836; *m.*; two *d.* Entered army, 1857; Principal Medical Officer, Aldershot, 1894-96; retired, 1896. *Address:* 99 Alexandra Road, South Hampstead, N.W. (*Died 11 May 1920.*)

PATERSON, Lt.-Col. Norman Fitzherbert; Registrar of the Court of Appeal, 1908, and clerk of the Supreme Court, of Ontario; *b.* 3 Sep. 1843; *m.* 1872, Sarah Vernon (*d.* 1909), 2nd *d.* of late George Currie, Port Perry, Ont; one *s.* two *d.* Barrister, 1874; K.C. 1883. *Address:* 489 Rushton Road, Toronto. *T.:* Hillcrest 6480.
(*Died 22 July 1925.*)

PATERSON, Thomas Wilson; Lieut.-Gov. British Columbia, 1909-14; *b.* Ayrshire, 6 Dec. 1851; *s.* of William P. Paterson; *m.* 1886, Emma E., *d.* of Senator George Riley; no *c.* *Educ.:* Oxford schools. Commenced career on Public Works, Ontario, 1869; went to British Columbia, 1885; elected for North Victoria to British Columbia Legislature in 1902 and 1903. *Recreations:* golf and motoring. *Address:* Victoria, B.C. *Clubs:* Union, Pacific, Victoria.

PATERSON, William Bromfield, F.R.C.S., L.D.S.; Dental Surgeon; *s.* of William Paterson of Ridge Stockland, Devon; *m.* Agnes Stirling, *d.* of late David Gillies, J.P., Londonderry; one *s.* *Educ.:* Merchant Taylors' School; St. Bartholomew's and Royal Dental Hospitals. Late Senior Dental Surgeon to St. Bartholomew's Hospital, and Dental Surgeon and Lecturer on Dental Surgery, Royal Dental Hospital of London; late Examiner in Dental Surgery, Royal College of Surgeons of England; Past President British Dental Association; Hon. President International Dental Federation; Past President Odontological Sect. of Royal Society of Medicine; Past President Representative Board, British Dental Association; late Examiner in Dentistry, Royal Army Medical Corps, and Dental Expert Advisory Board R.A.M.C.; Fellow Royal Society of Medicine, British Medical Association; Member Dental Tribunal (War), 1916-17. *Publications:* various addresses and contributions to medical and dental societies and journals. *Recreations:* shooting and outdoor sports. *Address:* 7A Manchester Square, W.1. (*Died 2 Sept. 1934.*)

PATON, Diarmid Noel, F.R.S. 1914; M.D., B.Sc., F.R.C.P.Ed., LL.D.; Physiologist; *b.* Edinburgh, 19 March 1859; *e. s.* of late Sir J. Noël Paton, R.S.A.; *m.* 1898, Agatha H., *d.* of late Alex. Balfour and Mrs. Balfour of Dawyck, Peeblesshire; one *s.* one *d.* *Educ.:* Edinburgh Academy and University; Vienna; Paris. Baxter Scholar in Natural Science, 1882; Biological Fellow of Edinburgh University, 1884; Superintendent of Research Laboratory, Royal College of Physicians, Edinburgh, 1889; Lecturer on Physiology, School of Medicine of Royal Colleges, Edinburgh, 1886; late Member of Royal Commission on Salmon Fisheries, 1900, and of the Medical Research Council, 1918-23; Regius Professor of Physiology, Glasgow University, 1906-28. *Publications:* large number of papers on physiological and fishery subjects. *Recreations:* golf, fishing, sailing. *Address:* The University, Glasgow. *T.:* Hillhead 3999. *Club:* Athenæum.   (*Died 30 Sept. 1928.*)

PATON, Hugh; Hon. A.R.E.; retired; *b.* Glasgow, 5 Feb. 1853; *e. s.* of late Alexander Paton, a Glasgow merchant; *m.* Jeannie Black; one *s.* one *d.* *Educ.:* Glasgow Academy. A business man; no particular art training beyond a little drawing at school, and some painting lessons after leaving; inspired by Lalanne's Treatise on Etching; began the practice of that art about

1880; has exhibited regularly in Manchester, Liverpool, Leeds, etc., once at the R.A. and many times at the Paris Old Salon, as well as at the Painter Etchers' regularly since election as an Associate, 1887; has lectured on Etching for the Manchester Art Committee, and given a series of Printing Demonstrations, 1914; presented the Manchester City Art Gallery with a case of copper plates and proofs illustrating the art of the etcher. *Publications:* Etching, Drypoint, Mezzotint, 1895; Colour Etching, 1909. *Recreations:* art, golf. Art has been his chief hobby for forty years. *Address:* Ardenadam, Marple by Stockport. *Club:* Athenæum, Manchester.   (*Died 24 Oct. 1927.*)

PATON, James, Supt. of Museums and Art Galleries of Corporation of Glasgow, 1876, retired; *b.* Auchtergaven, Perthshire, 15 April 1848; *m.* Mary D. (*d.* 1903), *d.* of James Kesson, Fordoun, Kincardineshire, 1866; three *s.* two *d.* *Educ.:* Parish School; private tuition; Edinburgh University. Trained for legal profession in Perth; Assistant in Museum of Science and Art, Edinburgh 1861-76; Pres. of Museums Association of United Kingdom, 1896; Hon. Secretary, Fine Art and Historical Section, Glasgow International Exhibition, 1901. *Publications:* numerous contributions to Encyclopædia Britannica and Chambers's Encyclopædia; The Fine Art Collection of Glasgow, 1906; journalistic work; edited and largely wrote Scottish National Memorials, fol., 1890; wrote Glasgow: its Municipal Organisation and Administration (with Sir James Bell, Bt.), 4to, 1896; edited and partly wrote Scottish History and Life, fol., 1902. *Recreations:* golf, fishing. *Address:* Camphill House, Glasgow. *T.:* Queen's Park 185. *Club:* Art, Glasgow.   (*Died 26 Feb. 1921.*)

PATRON, Joseph Armand, C.M.G. 1911; *b.* 1856; 3rd *s.* of Joseph Patron, M.D.; *m.* 1885, Clemence, *y. d.* of Chevalier Jerome Saccone. Barrister-at-law, Inner Temple, 1877; Acting Police Magistrate, 1894-95; Sanitary Commissioner since 1895; Chairman Exchange Committee since 1898; J.P.; deputed by the Chamber of Commerce and Exchange Committee as Representative of the Civil Community at H.M.'s Coronation. *Address:* Gibraltar. *Club:* Mediterranean, Gibraltar.
(*Died 25 Feb. 1922.*)

PATTERSON, Alexander Blakeley, C.I.E. 1895; *b.* Ballymena, Co. Antrim, 17 Feb. 1842; *s.* of late Rev. Alexander Patterson, and Emily Gaston, *d.* of Rev. Robert Stewart; *m.* 1863, Charlotte Maria (*d.* 1917), *d.* of late John Black, J.P., of Annaskea House, Co. Louth; two *s.* three *d.* *Educ.:* Royal Belfast Academical Institution; Queen's College, Belfast (two scholarships). Entered Indian Civil Service, 1863; appointed to North-West Provinces as Assistant Magistrate and Collector, 1864; Settlement Officer of Fatehpur, 1870, of Karwi, 1878; Magistrate and Collector of Allahabad, 1882; Magistrate and Collector of Saharanpur, 1887-90; Commissioner of Jhansi, 1890; Commissioner Northern India Salt Revenue, 1891-98. *Publications:* Settlement Reports of Fatehpur and Karwi. *Address:* Buckleigh House, Buckleigh, N. Devon. *Club:* East India United Service.
(*Died 9 Nov. 1919.*)

PATTERSON, James Kennedy, A.M., Ph.D., LL.D., F.R.Hist.S., F.S.A. Scot.; Fellow American Geographical Society, American Historical Society, National Tax Association, and American Academy of Political and Social Science; *b.* Glasgow, Scotland, 26 March 1833; *e. s.* of Andrew Paterson and Janet Kennedy, both of Dumbartonshire; *m.* 1859, Lucelia W., *d.* of Captain Chas. F. Wing. *Educ.:* Hanover College, Indiana, A.B. 1856, Ph.D. 1875; LL.D. Lafayette College, Penn., 1896; LL.D. Vermont, 1910, Kentucky, 1916. Principal, Greenville Presbyterian Academy, 1856-59; Prof. Stewart College, Tennessee, 1859-61;

819

PATTERSON, George, K.C. See page xxviii.

Principal, Transylvania High School, Lexington, Kentucky, 1861-65 ; Prof. Latin and Civil History, Agri. and Mech. College of Kentucky, 1865-69 ; Delegate to International Congress Geographical Sciences, Paris, France, 1875, and British Association, Bristol, England, 1875 ; Delegate to British Association Advancement of Science, Leeds, England, 1890 ; obtained from Legislature of Kentucky ½ cent tax on each $100 of taxable property for maintenance of State University, 1880 ; defended tax when assailed by all the denominational colleges, 1882 ; before the Legislature and Appellate Court, and won ; assisted in obtaining additional endowment from Congress, 1890 and 1907, and from State Legislature, 1900, 1904, and 1908 ; President, Association of State Colleges and Universities in 1903 ; of State University of Kentucky, 1869-1910, now President Emeritus ; Trustee of the University, Hanover Coll., Indiana, and Vice-Pres. of American Civic Alliance ; Member of National Tax Association ; President, University of Kentucky, 1869-1910. *Publications:* numerous newspaper articles, etc. *Recreations:* travelling at home and abroad. *Address:* Lexington, Kentucky State University Grounds, U.S.A. *Club:* Authors' ; Beta Theta Pi, New York ; Filson, Louisville, Ky. *(Died 15 Aug. 1922.)*

PATTERSON, John Edward ; litterateur ; *b.* Deepcar, Yorkshire, *s.* of Joseph and Mary Patterson ; *m.* 1902, Ida Harrylynn Pittendreigh. *Educ.:* the village school, Normanton, and at similar houses of correction, till he ran away to sea under the age of 13 ; was in the deep-sea fishery, merchant service, R.N.R., and about the world generally for 17 years, during which he had some adventures, and passed through 6½ years of rheumatism that left him a cripple for long afterwards ; in 1897 Sir Henry Irving invited him to the Lyceum, where he served in a humble capacity while obtaining a footing in London journalism ; he was 2 years on the staff of the Westminster Gazette, and has edited some periodicals. *Publications:* The Mermaid ; The Lure of the Sea (poems) ; Ballads and Addresses ; Fishers of the Sea ; Watchers by the Shore ; Tillers of the Soil ; Love Like the Sea ; The Story of Stephen Compton ; His Father's Wife ; Hillary Marrtyn ; Bond Slaves (novels) ; My Vagabondage ; Sea-Pie ; Epistles of the Sea (autobiography) ; The Sea's Anthology. *Recreations:* gardening, walking, boat sailing, etc. *Address:* c/o Simpkin, Marshall and Co., 4 Stationers' Hall Court. E.C. *(Died 4 April 1919.)*

PATTI, Madame Adelina (Baroness Rolf Cederstrom), prima donna ; *b.* Madrid, 19 Feb. 1843 ; *d.* of Salvatore Patti of Catania, Sicily, and Caterina Chiesa, a well-known opera singer ; *m.* 1st, 1868, Marquis de Caux ; 2nd, 1886, Signor Nicolini ; 3rd, 1899, Baron Rolf Cederström. Studied under Ettore Barili ; début, Academy of Music, New York, Nov. 1859 ; Italian Opera House, Covent Garden, in La Sonnambula, May 1861. *Compositions:* song, On Parting ; waltz, Fior di Primavera. *Address:* Craig-y-Nos Castle, Penycae, S.O., Breconshire, South Wales. *(Died 26 Sept. 1919.)*

PATTINSON, Rev. Canon Joseph Alfred, M.A. ; Headmaster King's School, Parra Matta, since 1916 ; *b.* Yorkshire, 24 Dec. 1861 ; *s.* of Thomas Pattinson, engineer and ironfounder ; *m.* Gertrude Teresa Lucy, *d.* of Canon Lysons of Hempstead Court, Gloucester ; no *c.* *Educ.:* St. John's College, Cambridge. (Scholar and Hare Exhibitioner and Wright's Prizeman) ; First Class Mathematical Honours, B.A. 1884, M.A. 1888, Cambridge ; M.A. University of Queensland, 1912 ; Deacon, 1885 ; Priest, 1886 ; Christ Church, Salford, 1885-90 ; Vicar of St. George, Chorley, 1890-1903; Volunteer Chaplain, 1890-1903; Rector of St. Bartholomew, Salford, 1903-7 ; Vicar of

820

St. James, Hope, Manchester, 1907-10 ; Chaplain to the Forces, Australia, 1910 ; Sub-Dean of Brisbane, 1910-15 ; Warden of St. Paul's College, 1915-16. *Recreations:* tennis, chess. *Address:* King's School, Parra Matta, New South Wales. *T.:* U 8064. *M.:* 553. *Club; Uni*versity. Svdney. *(Died 1 May 1919.)*

PATTISSON, Admiral John Robert Ebenezer ; *b.* Witham, Essex, 10 Dec. 1844 ; 4th *s.* of Jacob Howell Pattisson, I.L.M., and Charlotte Garnham Luard, sister of Admiral Sir William Garnham Luard, K.C.B. ; *m.* 1874, Emma Agnes Streeten (*d.* 1923) ; one *d.* *Educ.:* Royal Naval Academy, Gosport. Entered the navy as a naval cadet, 1859 ; went to sea first in Donegal, a wooden steam battleship ; Sub-Lieutenant, 1864 ; Acting Lieutenant of the Wasp, 1864, and proceeded from East India Station to East Coast of Africa, where he was actively engaged in the suppression of the slave trade ; was carried across a tight-rope on Blondin's back ; Lieut. 1867 ; landed from Wasp at taking of Nicobar Islands ; served in Hart on coast of Spain during Intransigeant War ; Commander, 1879, on Minotaur, flagship of the Channel Squadron ; was in the Thalia during the Egyptian War of 1882 ; Captain, 1886 ; had command of the Euphrates, an Indian troopship, for three years, and later was in command of the Crocodile, the Amphion, the Edinburgh, the Rodney, and the Sans Pareil ; Rear-Admiral, 1899 ; Vice-Admiral, 1904, in which year he retired ; Admiral, 1908. Is entitled to wear the Egyptian medal, the Khedive's bronze star, and the Jubilee medal. Since his retirement has been actively interested in municipal work at Tonbridge. *Address:* Rodbourne, Tonbridge. *(Died 13 Feb. 1928.)*

PAUL, Sir George Morison, Kt., *cr.* 1911 ; *b.* 18 Aug. 1839 ; *s.* of Rev. William Paul, D.D., Minister of Banchory Devenick ; *m.* 1872, Mary (*d.* 1914), *d.* of Alexander John Kinloch of Park, Aberdeenshire ; one *d.* *Educ.:* Aberdeen and Edinburgh Universities. M.A. 1858 ; LL.D. 1908 ; Writer to the Signet, 1867 ; Deputy Keeper of the Signet in Scotland and President of the Society of Writers to His Majesty's Signet, 1905 ; a Governor of Donaldson's Hospital, Edinburgh ; one of the Walker Trustees for the Episcopal Church in Scotland ; Chairman of Fettes College Trust : also of the Dick Bequest Trust for Higher Education in the Counties of Aberdeen, Banff, and Moray ; and of John Watson's and Miss Mary Murray's Educational Institutions, Edinburgh ; a Deputy Governor and Ordinary Manager of the Royal Asylum for the Insane, Edin. ; Mem. of Royal Commission on the Civil Service, 1915 ; a Member of Council of the Scottish History Society, and of the New Spalding Club ; an Extraordinary Director of the Royal Bank of Scotland ; a Director of the Scottish Provident Institution ; a member of the King's Bodyguard for Scotland (Royal Company of Archers) ; D.L., J.P. Edinburgh ; knighted on the occasion of the Coronation of King George V. *Recreation:* travelling. *Address:* 9 Eglinton Crescent, Edinburgh. *T.:* Central 4609. *M.:* S 1382. *Clubs:* Junior Carlton ; University, Edinburgh. *(Died 4 May 1926.)*

PAULTON, James Mellor, M.P. (L.) Bishop Auckland, Durham, 1885-1910 ; Assistant Paymaster-General Supreme Court 1909-21 ; *b.* 1857 ; *s.* of late A. W. Paulton, Manchester, London Chairman of the Anti-Corn Law League, and 1st editor of Manchester Examiner. *Educ.:* privately ; Trinity Hall, Cambridge. War Correspondent for Manchester Examiner in Soudan Campaign ; Private Secretary to James Bryce, Hugh Childers, Home Dept., 1886, and Assistant Private Secretary to H. H. Asquith, Home Dept., 1893-95 ; present at Battle of El Teb, Egypt, 1884. *Address:* 2 Bolton Street, W.1. *T.:* Grosvenor 1027. *Clubs:* Brooks's, Turf, Beefsteak. *(Died 6 Dec. 1923.)*

PAYNE, John Bruce, M.A.; Headmaster, Bishop Stortford School since 1904; *e. s.* of late Rev. Canon D. Bruce Payne, D.D.; *m.*; one *d. Educ.*: King's School, Canterbury; Rossall School (Capt.); Cambridge. Head Mathematical Master, Ascham School, Bournemouth: Headmaster, St. Aubyn's, Lowestoft. *Recreations*: rowing, fives, cricket, now motor-driving only. *Address*: The School, Bishop Stortford, Herts. *T.A.*: Bruce Payne, Bishop Stortford. *M.*: NK 7136. *(Died 4 Feb. 1923.)*

PAYNE, John Horne, K.C., M.A.; *e. s.* of Reuben Craven Payne, Bridgewater, Somerset; *b.* 12 Nov. 1837; *m.*-1868, Georgiana (*d.* 1911), widow of G. Sergent Atwood, U.S.A.; one *s. Educ.*: Univ. College, London (double hons.). Special Correspondent of Morning Herald and Standard in Hungary, 1861; called to Bar, Inner Temple, 1868; joined Home Circuit and Sussex Sessions; admitted Jamaica Bar, 1866; Assist. Boundary Commissioner, S.E. District, 1867; for several years acted as Commissioner for Spanish Government to take evidence in England in cases pending in Spanish Courts;—contested Mansfield Div. Notts (C.), 1885; Q.C. 1886. *Publications*: The Hungarian Diet of 1861; contributes occasional articles to the daily press. *Recreations*: Egyptian- and Assyrian archæology; long country walks. *Address*: Westow Lodge, Upper Norwood. S.E. *Club*: Junior Carlton. *(Died 9 Sept. 1920.)*

PAYNE, Maj.-Gen. Richard Lloyd, C.B. 1905; D.S.O. 1886; *b.* 24 May 1854; 2nd *s.* of late John Selwyn Payne; *m.* 1884, Clara Fripp Agnes, *o. d.* of late Brig.-Gen. Henry Bethune Patton; one *s.* Gazetted 13th Light Infantry, 1876; Lieut.-Col., 1900; commanded 3rd Division, N. Army, India, 1912-13; served Sekuki Campaign, Transvaal, 1878; Zulu War, 1879 (medal with clasp); 'Burmese Exp. 1885-86 (despatches, D.S.O., medal with clasp); N.W. Frontier of India, 1897 (medal with clasp); served South Africa, 1900-2 (despatches twice, Queen's medal with 8 clasps, King's medal 2 clasps, Brevet Col.); retired pay, 1917. *(Died 20 Dec. 1921.)*

PAYTON, Sir Charles Alfred, Kt., *cr.* 1914; M.V.O. 1906; *b.* York, 12 Nov. 1843; *s.* of late Rev. Charles Payton; *m.* 1st, 1880, Eliza Mary (*d.* 1909), *d.* of late John Olive; six *d.* (one *s.* killed in battle, 1915); 2nd, 1913, Mary Stuart, *d.* of Joseph Elliott, Monken Hadley, Barnet. *Educ.*: Scarborough; New College, London; Bonn; matriculated University College, London, 1860, with Honours in Classics. Consul at Mogador, 1880; passed examination before Civil Service Commissioners; Genoa, 1893; Calais, 1897; H.B.M. Consul-General at Calais, 1911; retired on a pension, 1913; Field angling correspondent, 1867-1914. *Publications*: The Diamond Diggings of S. Africa, 1872; Moss from a Rolling Stone, 1879; Days of a Knight, 1924. *Recreations*: fishing and shooting. *Clubs*: Flyfishers'. Authors'. *(Died 11 Mar. 1926.)*

PEACE, Sir Walter, K.C.M.G., *cr.* 1897; I.S.O. 1905; *b.* 19 Oct. 1840; 2nd *s.* of late James Peace, Prof. of Music, Huddersfield; *m.* 1869, Caroline, *y. d.* of William Tilbrook, Woodham Lodge, near Chelmsford, 1869; one *d. Educ.*: Huddersfield; privately. Went to Natal, 1863; in business there as a merchant and shipper till 1879; travelled often to Cape Colony and Mauritius for business purposes; took active interest in public affairs of Natal; became Natal Government Emigration Agent, and agent for Natal Harbour Board in England, 1880; was Belgian Consul in Natal, 1870-79; Portuguese Vice-Consul, 1870-78; member Tariff Commission, 1904; Agent-General for Natal, 1893-1904; Royal Commissioner for the Paris Exhibition, 1900; an original member of the Advisory Committee of the Board of Trade; member of the Tariff Reform Commission.

Publications: Our Colony of Natal; Notes on Natal; Emigration Literature. *Address*: 88 Victoria Street, S.W.; The Yarrows, Camberley. *Clubs*: St. Stephen's; Durban.
(Died 31 Jan. 1917.)

PEACH, Benjamin Neeve, A.R.S.M., LL.D., F.R.S., F.G.S., F.R.S.E.; *b.* Gorran Haven, Cornwall, 1842; *widower*, twice married; two *s.* two *d. Educ.*: Academy, Peterhead; Academy, Wick; Royal School of Mines, London. Retired District Geologist H.M. Geological Survey; Murchison Medal and Wollaston Medal of Geological Society of London; Neill Medal of Royal Society of Edinburgh. *Publications*: The Silurian Rocks of Britain, vol. i. Scotland, 1899; The Geological Structure of the North-West Highlands of Scotland, 1907. *Address*: 33 Comiston Drive, Edinburgh.
(Died 29 Jan. 1926.)

PEACOCK, Major Frederick William, C.B. 1919; D.L., J.P.; Chairman, Territorial Force Association. *Address*: Vernons Oak, Somersall Herbert, Derby. *(Died 8 May 1924.)*

PEACOCK, Sir Robert, Kt., *cr.* 1919; M.V.O.; Chief Constable of Manchester since 1898; *b.* 1859; *s.* of William Peacock, Guisborough, Yorks. Chief Constable of Canterbury, 1888-92; of Oldham, 1892-98; Order of the Redeemer (Greece). *Address*: Town Hall, Albert Square, Manchester. *(Died 18 Nov. 1926.)*

PEACOCKE, Most Rev. Joseph Ferguson, D.D.; late Primate of Ireland; *b.* Queen's Co., Ireland, 5 Nov. 1835; *y. s.* of late George Peacocke, M.D., Longford; *m.* 1865, Caroline Sophia, *y. d.* of late Major John Irvine of Killadeas, Co. Fermanagh; four *s.* one *d. Educ.*: Trin. Coll. Dublin. 1st Senior Moderator History, English Lit., and Political Economy, 1856; 1st Divinity Prizeman, 1858. Ordained 1858; Rector of St. George's, Dublin, 1873-78; Rector of Monkstown, 1878-94; Professor of Pastoral Theology, Dublin Univ., 1893; Bishop of Meath, 1894-97; Archbishop of Dublin, 1897-1915. *Publications*: Sermons: Charges, 1895-1901. *Club*: University, Dublin.
(Died 26 May 1916.)

PEAKE, Hon. Archibald Henry, Premier and Treasurer, S.A., since 1919; *b.* London, 1859; *s.* of late Robert and Mary Peake; *m.* Annie, *e. d.* of late Rev. Henry Byron Thomas; three *s.* four *d. Educ.*: public schools and by private tuition. Left England with parents, 1862; for several years was Clerk of District Council of Narracoorte; entered Parliament, 1897; Treasurer and Attorney-General, 1905; Premier, Treasurer, and Minister of Education, 1909 and 1912-15; Premier, Commissioner of Crown Lands, and Minister of Education, 1909-10; Premier and Chief Secretary, 1917-19. *Recreations*: tennis, golf, and bowls. *Address*: Parkside, Adelaide, South Australia. *Club*: Liberal.
(Died April 1920.)

PEAKE, Brig.-Gen. Malcolm, C.M.G. 1900; A.A.G. War Office since 1914; *b.* 27 Mar. 1865; 3rd *s.* of F. Peake of Burrough, Melton Mowbray, Leicestershire; *m.* 1900, Louisa, *e. d.* of P. H. Osborne, N. S. Wales. *Educ.*: Charterhouse. Entered army, 1884; Capt. 1895; Major, 1900; served Dongola, 1896 (4th class Medjidie, British medal, Khedive's medal with two clasps); in operations 1897 in command of a battery of Egyptian Artillery (despatches, clasp); Atbara and Khartoum, 1898 (despatches, brevet major, two clasps); operations against Khalifa, 1899 (4th class Osmanieh, clasp); opened the Upper Nile 1900 (3rd class Medjidie, C.M.G.); Bt.-Col. 1915; Officer Legion of Honour. *Address*: 17 Thurloe Square, S. W. T.: Kensington 3519. *Club*: Naval and Military.
(Died 27 Aug. 1917.)

PEARCE, Charles E.; Editor South London Press, 1878-82; Funny Folks, 1882-86; serial stories, Answers, 1896-97; novelettes, upwards of seventy, 1896-1910 : novels (Indian Mutiny Trilogy)—Love Besieged ; Red Revenge ; A Star of the East : The Bungalow under the Lake, 1910 ; The Eyes of Alicia, 1913 ; The Crimson Mascot, 1914 ; Criminology Series, 1908-13 ; Unsolved Mysteries ; Remarkable Clues ; Romances of Crime ; The Deadly Hand ; Dark Dramas of Life ; boys' books—The Ball of Fortune, 1896 ; Frank the Fisher Boy ; The Golden Island ; Billy Bos'n ; The Boojum Club and Others ; Biography, The Amazing Duchess, 1910 ; The Beloved Princess, 1911, Polly Peachum and the Beggar's Opera, 1913 ; The Jolly Duchess (Harriot Mellon), 1915 ; Marching Songs, 1914 ; War Up-to-date, 1915 ; Mascot Series—Vengeance is Mine ; Dragged from the Dark ; A Foe in the Shadow, 1918. Stirring Deeds of the Great War—Our Boys' History of British Heroism, 1919 ; Love's Masquerade ; Corinthian Jack ; A History of Perfumes and Cosmetics, 1920 ; Lloyds' Boys' Adventure Stories ; A Queen of the Paddock, 1921 ; Madam Flirt, a Romance of the Beggar's Opera, 1922 ; Polly Peachum (revised edition) ; The Beautiful Devil ; Madame Vestris and her Times, 1923 ; Sims Reeves, Fifty Years of Music in England, 1924 ; Unsolved Murder Mysteries, 1924. *Address :* 37 Homefield Road, Chiswick, W.   *Club :* Whitefriars.

           (*Died 9 Nov. 1924.*)

PEARCE, Charles William, Mus.D. Cantab. ; M.A. (Hon.), Dunelm ; F.R.C.O., F.T.C.L. ; Director of Examinations, Trinity College of Music, 1902-1916 ; Director of Studies, 1916-24 ; Hon. Treasurer Royal College of Organists, 1909-26 ; Vice-President, 1926 ; *b.* Salisbury, 5 Dec. 1856 ; *m.* Agnes, 4th *d.* of late Frederick Bird, J.P., of Norton House, Midsomer Norton, near Bath ; one *s.* three *d.* *Educ. :* Salisbury ; London. Organist of St. Martin's Church, Salisbury, 1871 ; St. Luke's, Middlesex, 1874-85 ; St. Clement's, Eastcheap, 1885-1919 ; Mus.B., Cambridge, 1881 ; Mus.D., 1884 ; M.A. Hon. ; Professor at Trinity College of Music, 1882 ; Examiner for Musical Degrees at Cambridge University, 1888-91 and 1895-97 ; London University, 1901-4, and 1921-25 ; Victoria University, Manchester, 1905-7, and 1921-22 ; Durham University, 1911-13 ; Dean of the Faculty of Music in London University, 1908-12. *Publications :* Editor of Organist and Choirmaster, 1893-1917 ; Trinity College Text-Books of Musical Knowledge ; Modern Academic Counterpoint ; Students' Counterpoint ; Composers' Counterpoint ; Voice-Training Exercises and Studies, twelve books ; The Art of the Piano-teacher : The Priest's Part in the Anglican Liturgy ; Organ Accompaniment to Plainchant ; Organ Versets and Descants ; The Evolution of the Pedal Organ ; Life and Work of E. J. Hopkins ; Biographical Sketch of E. H. Turpin ; composer of Church cantatas, anthems, organ and piano music, and songs. *Recreations :* archæology and architecture. *Address :* The Paddocks, Ferndown, Wimborne, Dorset. *Club :* Bristol Musical.

           (*Died 2 Dec. 1928.*)

PEARCE, Sir Edward Charles, Kt., *cr.* 1922 ; Chevalier Legion d'Honneur, Chinese Order of Merit, Chinese Decoration of the Chiaho, 4th grade ; *b.* 9 April 1862 ; *s.* of late John Swayne Pearce ; *m.* 1894, Marion Everett ; no *c.* *Educ. :* Charterhouse. Went to China, 1884 ; merchant ; Chairman Shanghai Municipality, 1913-20 ; Chairman of Shanghai General Chamber of Commerce, 1921 and 1923 ; Chairman China Association, Shanghai, 1921 and 1923. *Recreations :* in earlier years, riding, rowing, now plays golf. *Club :* Thatched House.

           (*Died 8 Sept. 1923.*)

PEARCE, Major Francis Barrow, C.M.G. 1904 ; Brilliant Star of Zanzibar 1st Class, 1922 ; British Resident, Zanzibar, 1914-22 ; *b.* London, 16 Sep. 1866. *Educ. :*

822

Cheltenham ; Sandhurst. Appointed Lieutenant 2nd Batt. West Yorkshire Regiment, 1886 ; Captain, 1893 ; served Ashanti Campaign, 1895 (star) ; British Central Africa, 1898 (medal and clasp) ; Commanded British Force in combined Anglo-Portuguese operations in East Nyasaland, 1899 (medal, clasp, despatches, Brevet Majority) ; South Africa, 1900 (medal and clasp) ; seconded and appointed Assistant Deputy Commissioner B.C.A. Protectorate under Foreign Office, 1897 ; Deputy Commissioner, 1901 ; acted as Commissioner, Commander-in-Chief, and Consul-General B.C.A. Protectorate, 1903 ; Deputy Governor, Nyasaland, 1907 ; acted as Governor and Commander-in-Chief, 1913-14 : Acting High Commissioner for Zanzibar, 1917-18-21. *Publications :* Zanzibar ; The Island - Metropolis of Eastern Africa ; Rambles in Lion-Land, etc. *Address :* Lennox Lodge, Shanklin.   (*Died 11 June 1926.*)

PEARCE, Henry, J.P. ; *b.* 7 Dec. 1869 ; 2nd *s.* of late Frederick Pearce ; *m.* Lily Blanche, 2nd *d.* of late Joseph Gould, C.E. ; two *d.* Prior to the Boer War, was a well-known traveller in South Africa and took an active interest in politics ; joined the Intelligence Department as special service officer at the outbreak of hostilities, Boer War ; commercial adviser to the Military Governor of the Orange River Colony (Sir G. T. Pretyman) ; Director of Civil Supplies for the O.R.C. ; resigned position in Civil Service, 1902, and travelled extensively ; has written many articles for magazines, reviews, and newspapers ; during European War initiated the Superfluity movement. *Address :* The Chaundrye, Eltham, Kent. *Clubs :* Authors' ; Royal Wimbledon ; Union, Victoria, B.C.

           (*Died 10 Jan. 1925.*)

PEARCE, Sir Robert, Kt., *cr.* 1916 ; F.R.A.S. ; Solicitor ; M.P. (L.) Leek Division, 1906-10, and 1910-18 ; *b.* 15 Jan. 1840 ; *s.* of Joseph Pearce of Ipswich, Suffolk, and Frances Margaret Hayward ; *m.* 1st, 1880, Elizabeth Deane (*d.* 1910) ; one *d.* ; 2nd, 1914, Margaret Exton. *Educ. :* privately ; Ipswich Grammar School. Began business life as an accountant ; admitted Solicitor, 1865 ; practised in Ipswich till 1872, then in London in the firm now Baylis, Pearce and Co., 116 Fore Street, E.C. ; Clerk to the Cripplegate Charities ; Vestry Clerk of Cripplegate ; Solicitor to the City Parochial Foundation ; a member of the Carmen's Company. *Address :* 9 Downside Crescent, Hampstead, N.W.3. *T. :* Hampstead 7359. *Club :* National Liberal.   (*Died 29 Sept. 1922.*)

PEARCE, Rev. Robert John, M.A., D.C.L. ; Rector of Beachampton, Bucks, since 1914 ; *b.* Bury St. Edmunds, 22 Sep. 1841 ; *m.* Lydia Freeman, *d.* of Roger Moser, Kendal, 1870 ; two *s.* five *d.* *Educ. :* Commercial School, Bury St. Edmunds ; Caius Coll. Camb. 3rd Wrangler, 1864 ; Fellow of Caius Coll. Camb. Head Mathematical Master at Rossall and Blackheath Proprietary Schools ; Professor of Mathematics at Durham University ; sub-Warden of Durham University, 1883-1895 ; Vicar of Bedlington, Northumberland, and Rural Dean, 1895-1914 ; Hon. Canon of Newcastle, 1899-1914. *Recreation :* photography. *Address :* The Rectory, Beachampton, Stony Stratford. *T.A. :* Rector, Beachampton.

           (*Died 8 Aug. 1920.*)

PEARCE-SEROCOLD, Brig.-Gen. Eric, C.M.G. 1918 ; K.B.B.C. ; *b.* 1870 ; 2nd *s.* of late Charles Pearce-Serocold of Taplow, Bucks ; *m.* 1st, 1901, Beatrix Lucy (*d.* 1906), *d.* of Admiral Sir Ernest Rice ; 2nd, 1912, Hon. Blanche Florence Daphne Stanley, 4th *d.* of 4th Baron Sheffield. Served South African War, 1899-1900 (Queen's medal and three clasps) ; European War, 1914-18 (despatches, C.M.G., Order of St. Maurice and St. Lazarus, Italy). *Club :* Brooks's.   (*Died 26 June 1926.*)

PEARD, Frances Mary; *d.* of Captain Peard, R.N. *Publications*: One Year; Unawares; The Rose Garden; A Madrigal; Near Neighbours; The Baroness; Mother Molly; Contradictions; Madame's Granddaughter; Alicia Tennant; The Swing of the Pendulum; Paul's Sister; An Interloper; Jacob and the Raven; The Career of Claudia; Donna Teresa; Number One and Number Two; The Ring from Jaipur; The Flying Months; and other novels. Also several boys' books: Scapegrace Dick; The Blue Dragon; The Abbot's Bridge, etc. *Address*: St. James, Torquay.   *(Died 1 Oct. 1923.)*

PEARS, Sir Edwin; Kt., *cr.* 1909; *b.* York, 1835; *m.* Mary, *d.* of J. Ritchie Hall. *Educ.*: privately. Graduated LL.B. London University, first of first class in Honours, Roman Law and Jurisprudence; called to Bar, Middle Temple (Exhibitioner in Constitutional Law and Legal History); General Secretary, Social Science Association, 1868-73; of International Prison Congress, 1872; Editor of Transactions of S.S.A. and Congress; settled in Constantinople, 1873; practising in Consular Courts, became President of European Bar in that city, 1881; as correspondent of Daily News sent letters in May and June 1876 on Moslem atrocities in Bulgaria, two of which were published in Blue Books and awakened widespread interest, which was followed by popular demonstrations led by Mr. W. E. Gladstone. *Publications*: Editor, Law Magazine, 1872; The Fall of Constantinople, being the Story of the Fourth Crusade, 1885; The Destruction of the Greek Empire, 1908; Turkey and its People, 1911; Forty Years in Constantinople, 1915; Abdul Hamid, 1917; Contributions to English Historical Review; and to other periodical literature. *Address*: Pera, Constantinople. *Club*: Reform.   *(Died 27 Nov. 1919.)*

PEARS, Maj. (Temp. Lt.-Col.) M. L., C.M.S. 1916; Res. of Officers; commanding 17th Batt. Northumberland Fusiliers. Served N.W. Frontier, India, 1897-98 (medal, 2 clasps); Tirah, 1897-98 (clasp); S. African War, 1899-1902 (despatches, Queen's medal, 2 clasps, King's medal, 2 clasps); European War, 1914-16 (C.M.G.).   *(Died 20 Oct. 1916.)*

PEARSE, Colonel Hugh Wodehouse, D.S.O. 1900; *b.* 13 Aug. 1855; *s.* of late Rev. Robert W. Pearse; *m.* 1889, Ada Gordon, *d.* of late Walter Scott, of Goldielea, Kirkcudbrightshire, N.B.; one *s.* one *d.* Entered army, 1875; Col. 1904; Assistant Director on Headquarter Staff of the Army, 1907-11; retired, 1911; served Afghan War, 1878-79 (medal); South Africa, 1899-1902 (despatches, Queen's medal four clasps, King's medal two clasps, Brevet of Lieutenant-Colonel, D.S.O.). *Publications*: Memoirs of Col. Alexander Gardner; The Crimean Diary of Lieut.-Gen. Sir Charles Windham; The Hearseys, 1905; Life of General Viscount Lake, 1908. *Address*: 58 Elm Park Gardens, Chelsea, S.W   *Club*: Army and Navy.   *(Died 23 Oct. 1919.)*

PEARSON, Sir Arthur, G.B.E., *cr.* 1917; 1st Bt., *cr.* 1916; President National Institute for the Blind, and Fresh Air Fund; Vice-President Tariff Reform League, and Vice-Chairman of Tariff Commission, 1903; Joint Hon. Sec. Collecting Committee National Relief Fund, 1914; Chairman Blinded Soldiers and Sailors Care Committee, 1914; *b.* Wookey, near Wells, 24 Feb. 1866; *o. s.* of late Rev. A. Cyril Pearson, and Phillippa Maxwell-Lyte; *m.* 1897, Ethel, D.B.E., *cr.* 1920, 3rd *d.* of W. J. Fraser; one *s.* three *d. Educ.*: Winchester. Founded business of C. Arthur Pearson, Ltd., of which still Chairman; Proprietor of various newspapers until failure of sight. *Publications*: Victory over Blindness, 1919; Conquest of Blindness, 1921. *Heir*: *s.* Neville Arthur, *b.* 13 Feb. 1898. *Address*: 15 Devonshire Street, W.1. *T.*: Langham 2508. *Clubs*: Carlton, Bath; Travellers', Paris.   *(Died 9 Dec. 1921.)*

PEARSON, Aylmer Cavendish; C.M.G. 1919; Governor of N. Borneo, 1915-22, and since 1925; *b.* 5 Aug. 1876; 2nd *s.* of late Col. Hugh Pearson, C.B., and Ellen Thomas; *m.* 1907, Violet, *d.* of Edward Gueritz, late Governor of N. Borneo; one *d. Educ.*: Felsted School; Trinity College, Dublin. Cadet British North Borneo Civil Service, 1897; Resident, 1901; Sessions Judge, 1905; Acting Judicial Commissioner, 1908; Acting Commissioner Lands, 1908; Government Secretary, 1909; Acting Governor, 1910, 1911. *Address*: c/o B.N. Borneo (Chartered) Coy., 87 Threadneedle Street, E.C.*(Died 15 Mar. 1926.)*

PEARSON, Sir Edward Ernest, Kt., *cr.* 1917; J.P.; Director of S. Pearson & Son, Ltd., and S. Pearson & Son (Contracting Dept.), Ltd., Contractors for Public Works; *b.* 10 May 1874; 2nd *s.* of late George Pearson. (*b.* of Viscount Cowdray); *m.* 1904, Susannah Grace, *y. d.* of late Richard Benyon Croft of Fanhams Hall, Ware; three *s.* three *d. Educ.*: Rugby. Joined the firm of S. Pearson & Son, and became a Director, 1900; had charge of numerous works, amongst them Malta Dry Docks and Breakwater for the Admiralty, and Port of Valparaiso for the Chilian Government; during the war responsible for construction of H.M. Factory, Gretna; travelled extensively; joined the 1st Middlesex Royal Engineers (Vol.), 1895; retired with rank of Capt. 1911; High Sheriff for Herts, 1909; Mayor of Hereford, 1921-23; interested in agriculture, breeder of Shire Horses, Shorthorns, etc. *Recreation*: shooting. *Address*: 10 Victoria Street, Westminster, S.W.; Brickendonbury, Hertford, Herts. *Clubs*: Reform, Bachelors'.   *(Died 19 Nov. 1925.)*

PEARSON, Henry Harold Welch, M.A., Sc.D., F.L.S.; Harry Bolus Professor of Botany, South African College, and Hon. Director, National Botanic Gardens, Kirstenbosch, Cape Town; *b.* Long Sutton, Lincolnshire, 28 Jan. 1870; *o. s.* of Henry Jackson Pearson; *m.* 1902, Ethel, *y. d.* of late William Pratt of Little Bradley, Suffolk. *Educ.*: privately; Cambridge. Scholar of Christ's College; visited Ceylon as Wort's Travelling Scholar, 1897-98; Frank Smart Student of Botany at Gonville and Caius College, 1898; Assistant Curator of the Herbarium of the University of Cambridge, 1898-99; Walsingham Medallist, 1899; Assistant for India, Royal Botanic Gardens, Kew, 1899-1901; Assistant (Director's Office), Royal Botanic Gardens, Kew, 1901-3. *Publications*: various botanical and geographical papers. *Address*: National Botanic Gardens, Kirstenbosch, Cape Town. *Club*: Savile.   *(Died 3 Nov. 1916.)*

PEARSON, Hugh Drummond, Lt.-Col. Royal Engineers; Director of Surveys, Sudan Government, since 1904; *b.* 17 Feb. 1873; *s.* of David Ritchie Pearson, M.D. (*d.* 1901), and Jean Rae; *m.* 1919, Blanche, *d.* of late Colonel E. E. Grigg. *Educ.*: St. Paul's School; R.M.A. Woolwich. Commissioned 2nd Lieut. R.E. 1892; Chatham, 1892-94; India, 1894-1902; Tirah Expedition, 1897-98; China Field Force, Relief of Pekin, 1900-1902; served European War, 1914 (despatches, D.S.O., Bt. Lt.-Col.); 4th Class Osmanieh, 1911; Beir Expedition, 1912; Murchison Award, R.G.S. 1913; 2nd class star of Ethiopia, 1916; 3rd class Nile, 1916; 2nd class Nadha, 1920. *Recreations*: golf, lawn-tennis. *Address*: Chestnuts, Beckley, Sussex; Khartoum. *Club*: Naval and Military.   *(Died 23 Dec. 1922.)*

PEARSON, Colonel Michael Brown, C.B. 1902; commanded the 2nd Middlesex Royal Garrison Artillery (Volunteers), 1890-1904; *b.* London, 8 April 1840; 2nd *s.* of late William Pearson, formerly of Newcastle-on-Tyne and London; *m.* 1870, Sarah Jane, *d.* of late Henry Thomas Bird of Boulogne-sur-Mer; three *s.* one *d. Educ.*: privately. Served in the

Vol. Artillery, 1860-1904; V.D. 1892; Chairman of Council L. and M. Archæological Society. President of Council National Artillery Association. *Address:* 31 Burnt Ash Road, Lee, Kent. *Club:* Junior Army and Navy.

(Died 12 Nov. 1923.)

PEARSON, Robert Hooper, 3rd s. of late William Pearson of Brewood, Staffs; *b.* 18 July 1866; *m.* Mary, *e. d.* of late James Evans of Llangattock-Lingoed, Monmouthshire; one *d. Educ.:* privately and trained for horticultural career. Joined editorial staff of Gardeners' Chronicle, 1892; Assistant Editor, 1903; Managing Editor, 1908; member of Scientific and Floral Committees of Royal Horticultural Society, Executive Committee of Royal Gardeners' Orphan Fund; Hon. Secretary of Horticultural Club. *Publications:* Garden Pests and Plant Diseases; general editor of the Present-Day Gardening series, My Garden series, and other works. *Address:* Braewyn, Earlsfield Road, S.W. *T.:* Gerrard 1543.

(Died 11 June 1918.)

PEARSON, Thomas Bailey, C.B.E. 1922; late Director of Audit, Exchequer and Audit Department; *b.* Epworth, Lincolnshire, 1864; *s.* of late J. R. Pearson, Doncaster; *m.* 1891, Gertrude Effie, *d.* of late John Nutt, London; three *d. Educ.:* Doncaster Grammar School. Entered Exchequer and Audit Department, 1883; service in France, 1915-16; in Canada, 1916. *Address:* 48 Tetherdown, Muswell Hill, N.10. *(Died 11 May 1927.)*

PEARY, Robert Edwin, Discoverer of North Pole; Rear-Adm. U.S.N. retired; Chairman U.S. Aero Coast Patrol Commission; Ex-President Am. Geographical Society; President 8th International Geog. Congress 1904; Hon. Vice-Pres. 9th and 10th Congresses; Hon. and Cor. Member various Geog. Societies; LL.D. Edin. University; Bowdoin College; Tufts College; *b.* Cresson Springs, Penn., U.S.A., 6 May 1856; *o. c.* of Charles N. and Mary Wiley Peary; *m.* Josephine C. Diebitsch of Washington, D.C., 1888; one *s.* one *d. Educ.:* Bowdoin Coll. Brunswick, Maine, U.S.A. (class of '77). Entered U.S. Navy, 1881; assist. engineer Government Surveys Nicaragua Ship Canal, 1885-86; reconnaissance Greenland Inland Ice, 1886; sub-chief engineer Nicaragua Canal Co., 1887; superintending engineer U.S. Naval Dry Dock, League I., 1888-1891; first expedition to North Greenland; determination of insularity of Greenland, 1891-92; second expedition to North Greenland, 1893-95; Arctic summer voyages, 1896, 1897; discovery and securing of the Cape York meteorites, the largest known meteorites in the world; third Arctic expedition for discovery of the North Pole, 1898-1902; rounded northern end of Greenland, the most northerly known land in the world, and reached 84° 17' N. lat., the highest latitude up to that time attained in the Western Hemisphere; Expedition in S.S. Roosevelt, 1905, 1906, attaining 87° 6' N. lat., the farthest north; second Roosevelt expedition, 1908-9; reached North Pole, 6 Apr. 1909; Gold Medallist of the Royal, Royal Scottish, Paris, Marseilles, Berlin, Normandy, Italian, Belgian, Swiss, Hungarian, Austrian, American, National, and Philadelphia Geographical Societies, the City of Paris, and the Explorers Club (President); promoted Rear-Admiral and given thanks of American Congress by special act, 1911; Grand Officier of Légion d'Honneur, 1913. *Publications:* various papers in geographical and other journals; Northward Over the Great Ice, 1898; Nearest the Pole, 1907; The North Pole, 1910. *Recreations:* boating, riding, hunting. *Address:* Navy Department, Washington, D.C., U.S.A.

(Died 19 Feb. 1920.)

PEASE, Sir Arthur Francis, 1st Bt., *cr.* 1920; D.L.; J.P.; High Sheriff, Co. Durham, 1920; Chairman, Durham County Council, 1922; 2nd Civil Lord of the Admiralty, Jan.

824

1918-March 1919; a Director of Pease Partners, Limited, Lloyds Bank, Ltd., and the London and North-Eastern Railway Company; *b.* 11 March 1866; *e. s.* of late Arthur Pease, M.P., of Hummersknott, Darlington, and Cliff House, Marske-by-Sea, and late Mary Lecky, *d.* of Ebenezer Pike, Besborough, Co. Cork; *m.* 1889, Laura Matilda Ethelwyn, *d.* of late Charles Peter Allix, Swaffham Prior House, Cambridge; one *s.* three *d. Educ.:* Brighton College; Trinity College, Cambridge. B.A. (Historical Tripos) 1888; M.A. 1893. *Heir: s.* Richard Arthur [*b.* 1890; Capt. Northumberland Hussars Yeomanry; *m.* 1917, Jeannette Thorn, *d.* of late Gustav Edward Kissel, Wheatsheaf House, Morristown, New Jersey, U.S.A.; three *s.* one *d.* Served European War, 1914-18 (wounded twice)]. *Address:* Middleton Lodge, Middleton Tyas, Yorks; 12 Montagu Square, W.1. *T.:* Mayfair 6772. *Club:* Brooks's.

(Died 23 Nov. 1927.)

PEASE, Joseph Gerald, C.B.E. 1920; the Umpire under the Unemployment Insurance Act 1923; Reader in Common Law to the Council of Legal Education since 1925; Assistant Reader, 1903-25; *b.* 17 April 1863; 4th *s.* of late Thomas Pease of Cote Bank, Westbury-on-Trym; *m.* 1904, Winifred, 2nd *d.* of late Col. Josiah Hudleston, Madras Staff Corps; two *d. Educ.:* University College, London, B.A. Called to Bar, Inner Temple, 1887; practised on the Western Circuit; Chairman of Court of Referees (the Unemployment Insurance Act) for Metropolitan District, 1915-1922; Chairman of Local Munitions Tribunal for Cambridge District, 1916-19. *Publications:* A Treatise on the Law of Markets and Fairs; A Summary of the Law on Contract, and other legal works. *Address:* 36 Downshire Hill, Hampstead, N.W.3. *T.:* Hampstead 6472. *Clubs:* Athenæum, Royal Cruising.

(Died 3 Mar. 1928.)

PEASE, Colonel Sir Thales, K.C.B., *cr.* 1901; *b.* 1835; *s.* of late William Pease of Woolwich; late Storekeeper-General Naval Ordnance, Admiralty, Whitehall; retired 1902; *m.* 1st, Lavinia (*d.* 1902), *d.* of Robert Jolly of Woolwich; 2nd, 1904, Flora Louise, *d.* of Mons. Hubert; two *s.* two *d.* Entered Ordnance Store Department, 1855; Assist. Comm.-General, 1880; Deputy Commissary-General, 1885; retired, 1892; served Soudan Expedition, 1884-85 (despatches, prom. Colonel, medal with clasp, Khedive's star); was Senior Ordnance Store Officer, S. Dist. 1887-91; Storekeeper-General Naval Ordnance, 1891; retired, 1902. *Address:* 58 Drayton Gardens, South Kensington, S.W.

(Died 26 Feb. 1919.)

PEASE, William Edwin, J.P.; M.P. (C.) Darlington since 1923; *b.* 1865; *e. s.* of Edwin Lucas Pease of Mowden, Darlington. *Educ.:* Clifton College; Trinity College, Cambridge. Director of Cleveland Bridge and Engineering Co., Darlington; Consett Iron Co., and Durham and N. Yorks Public House Trust; Mayor of Darlington, 1917-24. *Address:* Mowden, Darlington. *Club:* Boodle's. *(Died 23 Jan. 1926.)*

PECK, Sir William, Kt., *cr.* 1917; F.R.S.E., F.R.A.S.; Director of City Observatory, Calton Hill, Edinburgh; *b.* Castle Douglas, 3 Jan. 1862; *m.* 1889, Christina (*d.* 1922), *e. d.* of late James Thomson, Roseburn House, Edin. *Educ.:* Edinburgh. Patented inventions in internal combustion engines, propellers, pumps, astronomical instruments, optical instruments, electric ignition devices, etc. *Publications:* Handbook of Astronomy; Constellations and how to find them; Observers' Atlas of the Heavens; An Introduction to the Celestial Sphere, etc. *Recreation:* motoring. *Address:* City Observatory, Calton Hill, Edinburgh; 51 Inverleith Row, Edinburgh. *T.:* Edinburgh 1984. *M.:* S 1516. *(Died 7 Mar. 1925.)*

PECKOVER, 1st Baron of Wisbech (*cr.* 1907), **Alexander Peckover**, LL.D., F.S.A., F.L.S., F.R.G.S., J.P.; President of Essex Hall Asylum, Colchester; Vice - President of Hakluyt Society, Biblical Archæological, British Numismatic, etc.; *b.* Wisbech, 16 Aug. 1830; is directly descended from Edmund Peckover, who served in Cromwell's army, and whose landed property he possesses; *m.* 1858, Eliza (*d.* 1862), *o. d.* of J. Sharples, Hitchin; three *d.* *Educ.:* Grove House School, Tottenham. Partner many years in bank of Gurney, Peckover, and Co.; now retired; takes a special interest in collections of ancient MSS., early Bibles, and maps, also early printed books, especially English; also in meteorology; Lord-Lieut. of Cambridgeshire, 1898-1906. Owns about 4000 acres. *Heir:* none. *Recreations:* chess, cricket, tennis. *Address:* Bank House, Wisbech.

(*Died 21 Oct. 1919.*)

PEDLER, Sir Alexander, Kt., *cr.* 1906; C.I.E. 1901; F.R.S., F.C.S., F.I.C.; *b.* 21 May 1849; *s.* of late G. S. Pedler, Dulwich; *m.* 1st, 1878, Elizabeth Margaret, *d.* of C. K. Schmidt of Frankfurt; 2nd, 1905, Mabel, *y. d.* of late W. Warburton, R.N., of Dedham. *Educ.:* City of London School; Royal Coll. of Science. Formerly Director of Public Instruction for Bengal, Vice-Chancellor University of Calcutta, and additional Member of Legislative Council of Governor - General of India; retired 1906; Member of three Government Total Eclipse Expeditions of 1868, 1875, and 1898. *Publications:* various papers in Proceedings Royal Society; Journal Chemical Society; Journal As. Society, Bengal; Indian Metl. Memoirs; etc. *Recreations:* lawn-tennis, golf. *Address:* 28 Stanhope Gardens, Queen's Gate, S.W. *T.:* 3685 Western. *Clubs:* Constitutional, Ranelagh, Royal Automobile.

(*Died 13 May 1918.*)

PEEK, Sir Wilfrid, 3rd Bt.; *cr.* 1874; D.S.O. 1918; Major, late Royal 1st Devon Yeomanry; *b,* 9 Oct. 1884; *s.* of 2nd Bt. and Hon. Augusta Louisa Brodrick, *d.* of 8th Viscount Midleton; *S.* father, 1901; *m.* 1913, Edwine Warner, *d.* of late W. H. Thornburgh, St. Louis, U.S.A.; one *s.* *Educ.:* Trinity College, Cambridge; served European War, 1914-18 (D.S.O.). *Heir:* *s.* Francis Henry Grenville Peek, *b.* 16 Sep. 1915. *Address:* Rousdon, Devon. *T.A.:* Rousdon. *Clubs:* Carlton, Cavalry.

(*Died 12 Oct. 1927.*)

PEEL, Algernon Robert, M.V.O. 1904; 5th *s.* of late Sir Charles Lennox Peel, G.C.B., and Hon. Caroline Georgina, *e. d.* of 1st Baron Templemore. *Educ.:* Marlborough. Private Secretary to 6th Duke of Richmond and Gordon when Secretary for Scotland; Private Secretary to 5th Earl Cadogan, 1885-1904.

(*Died 26 June 1920.*)

PEEL, Rev. Hon. Maurice Berkeley, B.A.; Vicar of Tamworth since 1915; *y. s.* of 1st Viscount Peel; *b.* 23 Apr. 1878; *m.* 1909, Emily (*d.* 1912), *d.* of late Julius Alington; one *s.* one *d.* *Educ.:* New College, Oxford; Wells College. Ordained 1899; Curate of St. Simon Zelotes, Bethnal Green, 1899-1906; Rector of Wrestlingworth, 1906-9; Vicar of Eyeworth, 1906-9; Vicar of St. Paul's, Beckenham, 1909-15; Chaplain to Forces, 1915 (severely wounded). *Address:* Tamworth Vicarage, Stafford.

(*Died May 1917.*)

PEEL, Sir Robert, 4th Bt.; *cr.* 1800; *b.* 12 April 1867; *e. s.* of 3rd Bt. and Lady Emily Hay (*d.* 1924), *d.* of 8th Marquess of Tweeddale; *S.* father, 1895; *m.* 1897, Mercedes, *d.* of Baroness de Graffenried, Thun, Switzerland; one *s.* *Educ.:* Harrow; Balliol College, Oxford. Formerly Lieut. Staffs Yeo. Cavalry. *Publications:* A Bit of a Fool, 1896; An Engagement, 1897. Owns about 10,000 acres. *Heir:* *s.* Robert [*b.* 8 April 1898; *m.* 1920, Beatrice Gladys Lillie. *Educ.:* Harrow]. *Address:* Drayton Manor, Tamworth. (*Died 12 Feb. 1925.*)

PEEL, Col. Robert Francis; C.M.G.1922; Governor and Commander-in-Chief, St. Helena, since 1920; *b.* 30 April 1874; *m.* 1903, Alice, 2nd *d.* of late Sir Thomas Charlton-Meyrick, 1st Bart. *Educ.:* Harrow. Entered Coldstream Guards, 1898; Captain, 1906; served S. Africa, 1899-1902 (Queen's medal, 6 clasps, King's medal, 2 clasps); retired, 1909; Lt.-Col. and Bt. Col. 4th Battalion (Special Reserve) East Surrey Regt.; M.P. (U.), Woodbridge Division of Suffolk, 1910-20; served European War, 1914-1919. *Address:* Government House, St. Helena. *Clubs:* Carlton, Guards', Windham.

(*Died Aug. 1924.*)

PEEL, Rt. Rev. William George, D.D. (Hon.); Bishop of Mombasa since 1899; *b.* India, 1854; *s.* of late Capt. Peel, H.M. 53rd Regiment; *m.* Agneta Jane Bryan, Monkton Combe, Somerset; three *s.* four *d.* *Educ.:* Blackheath Proprietary School; C.M.S. Theological Coll., Islington, London. Ordained, 1879; Curate of Trowbridge, Wilts, 1879-80; Rugby Fox Master of C.M.S. Noble Coll. Masulipatam, 1880-87 (acting Principal three years); Sec. C.M.S. Madras, 1888-89 and 1892; Sec. C.M.S. W. India, 1892-99. *Address:* Bishop's Court, Mombasa, British East Africa; The Walnuts, Buntingford, Herts. *T.A.:* Peel, Mombasa. (*Died 15 April 1916.*)

PEGLER, Louis Hemington, M.D., M.Ch. Edin., M.R.C.S.; Consulting Surgeon, Metropolitan Throat, Nose, and Ear Hospital, Fitzroy Square; late Surgeon in charge of Ear and Throat Dept., Mile End Military Hospital; Surgeon Laryngologist and Aurist to the Governesses' Benevolent, Clergy Orphan Corporation, and London College of Music; Fellow of Royal Society of Medicine, and Vice-President of Laryngological Section of same; Member of Council and Curator of Museum, Laryngological Section of International Medical Congress, London, 1913; compelled for health reasons to refuse Presidency of Oto-Laryngological Section, British Medical Association Meeting, 1921; *b.* 1852; *s.* of Daniel Pegler of Colchester, pianist and musical composer; *m.* Maude Edith, *y. d.* of F. W. Palmer of Bedford; no *c.* *Educ.:* Royal Grammar School, Colchester; University College, London; Edinburgh University. Commenced practice in London, 1892; Registrar and Pathologist to Central London Throat Hospital, 1893-95; Hon. Secretary to British Lar. Rhin. and Otol. Assoc., 1893-96; organised the International meeting of same in 1895. *Publications:* The Surgical Treatment of some Common Forms of Nasal Insufficiency; The Pathology and Treatment of Discrete Nasal Angioma; Headaches in association with Nasal Obstruction; A Map Scheme of the Fifth Nerve and its Connections, 1913, with book; On the Desirability for a More Discriminative Nomenclature for the Nasal Nerves, Transactions, XVII. International Congress of Medicine, London, 1913. *Recreations:* botany, geology, music; member of several Archæological and Geological Societies, and British Bryological Society; presented his collection of fossil trees and ferns to British Museum of Natural History, South Kensington; has large herbarium and collection of prehistoric flint implements. *Address:* 7 Bartholomew Terrace, Exeter. *M.:* TT 1945. *Club:* Edinburgh University. (*Died 26 Feb. 1927.*)

PELHAM, Rev. Sidney; *b.* 16 May 1849; 3rd *s.* of late Hon. John T. Pelham, Bishop of Norwich, 1857-93; *m.* 1897, Caroline E., *d.* of late Canon John Patteson, Rector of Thorpe St. Andrew, Norfolk. *Educ.:* Harrow; Oxford. Ordained Deacon, 1873; Priest, 1874; Curate at Stalbridge, Dorsetshire, 1873-74; Redenhall, Norfolk, 1874-79; Vicar of St. Peter, Mancroft, Norwich, 1879-81; Private Secretary to the Bishop of Norwich, 1890-1901; Rural Dean of Norwich; Hon. Canon,

1896-1901, and since 1916 ; Chaplain of the Norfolk and Norwich Hospital, 1901-6 ; Archdeacon of Norfolk 1901-16. *Recreations:* Captain of Harrow Eleven, 1868 ; played for the University of Oxford, 1871. *Address:* 85 Newmarket Road, Norwich. *(Died 14 July 1926.)*

PELHAM, Hon. Thomas Henry William, C.B. 1905 ; Assistant Secretary (Harbour Department) Board of Trade, 1895-1913 ; *b.* 1847 ; *s.* of 3rd Earl of Chichester ; *m.* 1883, Louisa Keith Bruce ; one *s.* two *d. Educ.:* Eton ; Trinity College, Cambridge. 2nd Class Law Tripos, 1869. Barrister, Inner Temple, Home and S.E. Circuits, and Sussex Sessions, 1871-82 ; legal adviser to Veterinary Department of Privy Council, 1882-89, and to Board of Agriculture, 1889-95 ; held inquiries for Privy Council, for Local Government Board, and other Departments, 1879-95 ; Boundary Commissioner for Redistribution of Seats Bill, 1884-85 ; Glasgow Boundary Commissioner, 1887 ; Boundary Commissioner under Local Government (Scotland) Act, 1889 ; appointed by Board of Trade to settle canal rates, 1893, and railway rates, 1895 ; Treasurer and Hon. Secretary of Homes for Working Boys ; a Governor of the Polytechnic, Regent Street. *Recreations:* golf, cycling, lawn-tennis. *Address:* Deene House, Putney Hill, S.W. *T. :* 823 Putney. *(Died 23 Dec. 1916.)*

PELL, Maj. Albert Julian ; *b.* 19 Nov. 1863 ; *e. s.* of Rev. Beauchamp Henry St. John Pell, Rector of Ickenham, Uxbridge (*d.* 1907), and Julia Caroline (*d.* 1902), *d.* of late Edward Tyndall, R.N. ; *m.* 1897, Catherine Marion, 3rd *d.* of Sir Walter Greene, Bart., of Nether Hall, Bury St. Edmunds ; two *d. Educ. :* Winchester College ; Merton College, Oxford (B.A.), 1886. Barrister, Lincoln's Inn, 1890 ; D.L. Cambridgeshire ; J.P. Isle of Ely, and Chairman of Quarter Sessions ; Vice-chairman Isle of Ely County Council ; Vice-chairman of Cambs., and Isle of Ely Territorial Forces Association ; was Captain (Hon. Major, 1898), 4th Batt. (Militia) Suffolk Regiment, till 1908. *Publication :* Article on William Cobbett, in Vol. lxiii. (1902), of Journal of Royal Agricultural Society. *Heir :* nephew, Beauchamp Stuart Pell. *Address:* Wilburton Manor, Ely. *T.A. :* Wilburton. *Club:* Carlton.
(Died 28 Aug. 1916.)

PELLETIER, Lt.-Col. J. M. J. Pantaleon, M.D., F.R.C.I., Agent General for the Province of Quebec in London since 1911 ; *b.* River Ouelle, Co. of Kamouraska, 27 July 1860 ; *s.* of Joseph Pelletier and Henriette Martin ; *m.* 1st, 1888, Alice Hudon of Quebec (*d.* 1910) ; 2nd, 1912, Cecile Belleau, *widow* of late J. Boivin, Assistant-Secretary of the Province of Quebec. *Educ.:* Ste. Anne College and Laval University, Quebec. Began to practice at Sherbrooke, 1887 ; studied in New York, 1897 ; continued the study in Paris of surgery and gynæcology ; belonged to the 9th Battalion of Quebec, 1885 ; and took part in the quelling of the Reil rebellion ; acted as coroner of the district of St. Francois, 1890-1900 ; elected to represent the county of Sherbrooke at the Quebec Parliament, re-elected in 1904 and 1908 ; was director of the Sherbrooke Lumber Co. ; Member of the Provincial Office of Health ; President of Trustees of Catholic Schools ; Hon. President and Director of the Canadian Agricultural Association ; unanimously elected Speaker of the Legislative Assembly, Quebec, 1909 ; Liberal ; Roman Catholic. *Address:* Quebec Government Offices, 38 Kingsway, W.C.2. *Clubs:* Royal Automobile, British Empire, Overseas, Canadian, Canada.
(Died 20 Oct. 1924.)

PELLETIER, Hon. Louis Philippe, K.C., M.P. ; Judge of the Court of Appeals, Quebec, since 1914 ; *b.* Trois Pistoles, Quebec, 1857 ; *s.* of Hon. Thos. P. Pelletier and Caroline Casault ; *m.*

1883, Adele Lelièvre. *Educ. :* St. Anne Coll. Laval Univ. Called to Bar, 1880 ; Legislative Council of Province of Quebec, 1888 ; elected County of Dorchester, 1890 ; Provincial Secretary, 1891 ; Attorney-General for his native province, 1896 ; retired from provincial politics, 1904 ; elected for county of Quebec, 1911 ; Postmaster-General, 1911-14 ; an LL.D. and Professor in Laval University. *Address :* 38 Garden Street, Quebec. *Clubs:* Rideau, Ottawa ; Garrison, Quebec. *(Died Feb. 1921.)*

PEMBERTON, Rev. Thomas Percy, M.A., Canon and Prebendary of Bilton, York Minster, since 1879 ; J.P. ; *s.* of William Hudson, Ousecliffe, York ; *m.* 1870, Patience Frances Sophia, *d.* of Capt. William Huntly Campbell, 20th Regt., and Frances Maria Sophia, *o. c.* of Colonel Francis C. J. Pemberton, Trumpington Hall, Cambridge ; one *d.* Surname changed to Pemberton by Royal Warrant, 1900. *Educ. :* St. Peter's School, York (Scholar and Exhibitioner) ; Trinity College, Cambridge, Scholar. 6th Wrangler and 3rd class Cl. Tripos ; Fellow of Trinity, 1856-70 ; Assistant Tutor, 1856-66 ; Tutor, 1866-70 ; Rector of Gilling East, Malton, Yorks, 1870-1901 ; Succentor, York, 1883 ; Proctor in Convocation, 1874-1880 ; Rural Dean of Helmsley, 1890-1901. *Publications:* Works on Arithmetic and Trigonometry. *Recreations:* Founder and conductor of Hovingham Musical Festival, 1887-1905 ; Conductor of York Musical Society, 1896-1900. *Address:* Trumpington Hall, Cambridge. *T.A. :* Trumpington. *T. :* Trumpington 1. *(Died 31 Jan. 1921.)*

PEMBERTON, Major-General Sir Wykeham Leigh, K.C.B., *cr.* 1910 ; C.B. 1879 ; J.P. ; *b.* 4 Dec. 1833 ; *s.* of late Edward Leigh Pemberton of Torry Hill, Kent ; *m.* 1884, Jessie Graham, *d.* of late John Graham, Skelmorlie, N.B. ; one *s.* two *d. Educ.:* Rugby. Served in Royal Navy, 1845-46 ; joined 60th Rifles, 1852 ; served in Indian Mutiny, 1857 ; severely wounded at Cawnpore, 27 Nov. (medal) ; commanded 3rd Batt. 60th Rifles in Zulu War, 1879, and brigade at Ginghiloro (medal and clasp) ; A.Q.M.G. Headquarters, 1880-85 ; A.D.C. to H.R.H. Duke of Cambridge, 1885-90 ; promoted Major-General in 1890 ; Colonel Commandant 60th Rifles, 1906. *Decorated* for command of brigade in active service. *Recreations:* cricket, shooting, etc. *Address:* Abbots Leigh, Haywards Heath, Sussex. *Club:* Army and Navy. *(Died 2 Mar. 1918.)*

PEMBREY, John Cripps, Hon. M.A. ; *b.* 1831 ; *m.* 1863 ; three *s.* four *d.* Entered service of University Press, Oxford, 1846 ; with his father was the first to set up Sanskrit in type for first vol. of the Rig-Veda, 1849 ; since then and until 1916 has been responsible for the reading of most of the Oriental books printed at Oxford ; among others, Rig-Veda (4to and 8vo editions), Sacred Books of the East (50 vols.), Anecdota Oxoniensia, Semitic and Aryan series (21 vols.) ; Dictionaries—Sanskrit (Williams), Syriac (Payne Smith), Compendious Syriac (Mrs. Margoliouth), Vernacular Syriac (Maclean), Hebrew (Gesenius, Ed. Driver, and others), Yonah's Hebrew Roots (Neubauer), Tamil (Pope) ; Grammars—Sanskrit by Wilson (1847), by Williams, by M. Müller, by Macdonell (1914), Arabic (Green), Hebrew (Gesenius), Tenses in Hebrew (Driver) ; Catalogues—Syriac, Sanskrit, Hebrew, Persian, Japanese and Chinese for the Bodleian Library, Persian for India Office ; also edited and published Gospel Banner, monthly, 1872-1916, Pastoral Letters of Rev. J. Hobbs, Life, etc., of Joseph Tanner, Life and Ministry of Bernard Gilpin, and several other devotional books. *Address:* 164 Walton Street, Oxford.
(Died 1 May 1918.)

PENBERTHY, John, J.P. ; late Major Devonshire Regiment ; *b.* Treruffe, Redruth, Cornwall, 19 Apr. 1858 ; *e. s.* of late William

P. of Treworgie, Redruth, and Mary, *d.* of John Boskean; *m.* Eleanor, *e. d.* of John Rees, J.P., Neath, Glamorganshire; one *d. Educ.:* Fowey School; University College. Member of Hon. Soc., Inner Temple, 1885; Inspector of Privy Council under Contagious Diseases (Animals) Act, 1882; Professor of Pathology, 1888, of Medicine, 1892-1908, Royal Veterinary College; president of Royal College of Veterinary Surgeons, 1897; Fellow Royal Society of Medicine; Member Council Central and Gloucestershire Chambers of Agriculture; Governor Royal Agricultural College, Cirencester; Member Court University of Bristol; Advisory Council on Horse Breeding; Departmental Committee on Swine Fever and Foot and Mouth Disease., *Publications:* Text-book of Equine Medicine; Pain, its Indications and Significance in the Lower Animals; Diseases Communicable from the Lower Animals to Man; Protective Inoculation against Anthrax, etc. *Recreation:* gardening. *Address:* Dean Hall, Newnham, Gloucestershire. *T.:* Newnham - Glos. 26. *Clubs:* Royal Societies, Farmers'; Gloucester.

(*Died 23 May 1927.*)

PENDAVIS, Ven. Whylock, M.A.; Rector of Fringford since 1921; *m.;* one *s. Educ.:* Trinity College, Dublin. Curate of St. Philip's, Chorley, 1875-77; St. James's, Collyhurst, 1877-81; Incumbent of St. Augustine, Monsall, 1881-86; Moka, Mauritius, 1886-99; Religious Instructor, R. College, Mauritius, 1899-1907; Hon. Canon of Mauritius, 1899-1907; Archdeacon, 1903-7; Sub-Dean, 1905-7; Examining Chaplain to Bishop, 1903-7; Chaplain at Havre, 1907-9; Rector of Hethe, 1900-21. *Address:* The Rectory, Fringford, Bicester.

(*Died 29 Oct. 1924.*)

PENDER, Sir James, 1st Bt., *cr.* 1897; J.P.; Director of Globe, Telegraph, and Trust Co., Telegraph Construction and Maintenance Co.; *b.* Sep. 28, 1841; *e.s.* of late Sir John Pender, G.C.M.G., M.P. Wick; *m.* 1867, Mary Rose, 3rd *d.* of E. Gregge Hopwood, Hopwood Hall, Lancashire. *Educ.:* Univ. Coll. London. Formerly Lieut. King's Own Borderers; M.P. (C.) Mid Northamptonshire, 1895-1900. *Recreations:* hunting, yachting. *Heir:* none. *Address:* Donhead House, Donhead St. Andrew, Wilts. *Clubs:* Turf, Naval and Military; Royal Yacht Squadron, Cowes. (*Died 30 May 1921.*)

PENDLETON, Alan O'Bryan George William, C.M.G. 1905; *b.* 17 May 1837, Collon, Co. Louth, Ireland; *s.* of Henry Latham Pendleton of Lough Derry, Co. Monaghan, Ireland; *m.* 1877, Agnes, 2nd *d.* of John Edis of Cambs. Entered service of Manchester, Sheffield, and Lincolnshire Railway, 1856; made joint representative in Ireland of the G.N.R. (England) and the Manchester, Sheffield, and Lincolnshire Railway, 1860. Manager and Agent of the Calcutta and South-Eastern Railway, Bengal, 1861; Assistant Superintendent of the G.N.R. England, 1870; General Manager of Railways, South Australia, 1876; Commissioner of Railways, S. Australia, 1895-1909. *Address:* Carnagoen, Mount Lofty, Adelaide, South Australia. (*Died 18 Nov. 1916.*)

PENFOLD, Very Rev. John Brookes Vernon, B.D.; Dean of the Island and Bailiwick of Guernsey and its Dependencies (Alderney, Sark, etc.); *b.* 1864; *s.* of Rev. Wm. Penfold, M.A., Rector of Ruardean, Gloucestershire, and Chaplain to the Duke of Beaufort; *m.* 1st, Maude Frances, o. *d.* of Francis Edward Carey, M.D., Insp.-Gen. R. Guernsey Militia, etc., of Villa Carey, Guernsey; one *s.;* 2nd, 1918, Janet Lily, 2nd *d.* of P. F. Carey, Constable of St. Peter Port, etc. *Educ.:* St. John's School, Leatherhead; Jesus College, Cambridge. Chaplain King William's College, Isle of Man, 1888; Assistant Minister St. James', Welbeck Street, W., 1890; Editor Church of England Pulpit, and occasional contributor to various papers and magazines; Vicar of St. James', Guernsey, 1893; A./G. Chaplain to Forces, 1895; Chaplain Royal Guernsey Artillery, 1901; Dean of Guernsey (Patron, the Crown), Commissary-General of the Bishop of Winchester, and Judge of the Ecclesiastical Court, 1917; Rector of St. Peter Port, 1918; a Freemason, Past Senior Grand Warden of the Province of Guernsey and Alderney, and Past Grand Chaplain of England; Chairman of the Board of Directors of the Royal College of Queen Elizabeth in Guernsey; Chairman of Ladies' College; President of Intermediate Education Committee, and St. Peter Port Education Committee; chiefly interested in Church and Social Reform; a strong supporter of the proposals of the Archbishops' Committee on relations between Church and State has taken a prominent part in the development of Trades Unions in Guernsey; principal work outside ecclesiastical duties concerns education, in the advancement of which he has been actively engaged for twenty years, having at some time or other directed most of the Educational Departments of Guernsey. *Publications:* Inaugural Address to the Decanal Conference of the Deanery of Guernsey; Memoir of the Very Rev. Thos. Bell, M.A., Dean of Guernsey and Canon of Winchester. *Address:* The Deanery, Guernsey.

(*Died 4 May 1922.*)

PENFOLD, Lieut.-Col. Sir Stephen, Kt., *cr.* 1915; V.D.; Mayor of Folkestone for the twelfth time; J.P. for the Borough and the County Kent; *b.* 17 May 1842; 4th *s.* of John Penfold, Folkestone, and Susannah, 2nd *d.* of Henry Jeffery, Folkestone; *m.* 1874, Margaret Elizabeth, o. *d.* of Henry Acton Hall, East Hanney, Berks; one *d. Educ.:* private school. Thirty - five years' volunteering, afterwards municipal work in the Borough and County of Kent; Officer of the Order of the Crown of Belgium; Croix de Chevalier de la Légion d'Honneur, France; Cavalieri of the Order of the Crown of Italy. *Recreation:* gardening. *Address:* Canadian Villa, 70 Cheriton Road, Folkestone. *Clubs:* Constitutional; Radnor, Folkestone. (*Died 9 Jan. 1925.*)

PENNEFATHER, Sir (Alfred) Richard, Kt., *cr.* 1909; C.B. 1896; Diamond Jubilee Silver Medal, King Edward's Coronation Silver Medal; J.P. Essex; *b.* 10 March 1846; *s.* of John Pennefather, Q.C.; paternal grandfather, The Rt. Hon. Baron Pennefather; maternal grandfather, The Hon. Edward de Moleyns; *m.* 1867, Sina, *y. d.* of T. C. Savory. *Educ.:* private school. Home Office Clerk, 1868; Receiver Metropolitan Police District, 1883-1909; Visiting Justice H.M. Prison, Chelmsford; Member of Essex Standing Joint Committee; Member of House of Layman for Province of Canterbury; Member Central Board Finance of Church of England. *Decorated* for public services. *Address:* Little Waltham Hall, near Chelmsford; 30 Westminster Mansions, S.W.1. *T.:* Little Waltham 8. *M.:* LL 3541. *Club:* Union. (*Died 14 Aug. 1918.*)

PENNEFATHER, Rev. Preb. Somerset Edward, M.A., D.D.; Vicar of Kensington since 1897; *b.* Dublin, 1 March 1848; *y. s.* of late John Pennefather, Q.C., *s.* of Baron Pennefather, and Elizabeth Jemima, *d.* of Hon. Edward de Moleyns, *g. d.* of 1st Lord Ventry; *m.* Catherine Emily, *d.* of late T. C. Savory, 1870; three *s.* one *d. Educ.:* King's College, London; Trinity College Dublin, (M.A.). M.A. (*ad eun.*) Durham University; D.D. (Hon.) Aberdeen. Ordained, 1871; Curate, East Claydon, 1871-74; Vicar of Christ Church, Wakefield, 1874-75; Kenilworth, 1875-82; Jesmond, Newcastle-on-Tyne, 1882-88; St. George's, Jesmond, 1888-97; Hon. Canon of Newcastle, 1888-1907; Fellow of King's College, London; Hon. Chaplain 4th Middlesex West London Rifles, 1898; Chaplain to H.M. Troops, Kensington Barracks,

1898 ; Chaplain (2nd Class) Territorial Forces ; Alderman of the Royal Borough of Kensington, 1898 ; Rural Dean of Kensington, 1901 ; Prebendary of St. Paul's Cathedral, 1907 ; Chaplain, Kensington Barracks, 1908 ; Proctor for Diocese of London, 1909. *Address :* The Vicarage, Kensington, W. *T.A. :* Pennefar, London. *T. :* Park 3519.   (*Died 29 Aug. 1917.*)

PENNELL, Arthur, Registrar of Criminals, Home Office ; *b.* Nov. 1852 ; *s.* of Sir Henry Pennell, of the Admiralty, and Harriet Francis, *g.d.* of Sir Philip Francis, M.P. (Junius Letters) ; *m.* 1875, Louisa Erica, 2nd *d.* of H. H. Hungerford, D.L., of Dingley Park, and Maydwell Hall, Northamptonshire, and *g.d.* of Lady Louisa Forester, *d.* of Duke of Cleveland ; one *s. Educ. :* Jesus College, Cambridge. Entered the Admiralty, and subsequently appointed to the Home Office ; contested Elland Div. of Yorkshire, 1900 ; Rotherhithe Div. of London County Council, 1901. *Recreations :* hunting, shooting, golf, and fishing. *Address :* 4 Foulis Terrace, Onslow Square, S.W.7. *T. :* 2542 Kensington. *Clubs :* Wellington, Portland ; Sunningdale ; Westward Ho !
      (*Died 25 Aug. 1926.*)

PENNELL, Joseph, artist and author ; *b.* Philadelphia, Penna., U.S.A. ; *m.* Elizabeth R. Pennell. *Educ. :* School of Industrial Art, Phila ; Penna. Academy of Fine Arts. *Publications :* A Canterbury Pilgrimage, 1885 ; An Italian Pilgrimage, 1886 ; Two Pilgrims' Progress, 1887 ; Our Sentimental Journey through France and Italy, 1888 ; Pen Drawing and Pen Draughtsmen, 1889 ; Our Journey to the Hebrides, 1889 ; The Stream of Pleasure, 1891 ; The Jew at Home, 1892 ; Play in Provence, 1892 ; To Gipsyland, 1893 ; Modern Illustration, 1895 ; The Illustration of Books, 1896 ; The Alhambra, 1896 ; The Work of Chas. Keene, 1897 ; Lithography and Lithographers, 1900 ; The Life of James M'Neill Whistler, 1907 ; Pictures of the Panama Canal, 1912 ; The Wonder of Work, 1916 ; Etchers and Etching, 1919 ; The Whistler Journal, 1921 ; The Graphic Arts, 1922 ; Adventures of an Illustrator, 1925. Member American Academy Arts and Letters ; National Academy Designs, N.Y., and Royal Belgian Academy ; Hon. A.R.I.B.A., Hon. A.A.I.A. ; represented in National Art Galleries of Europe and America. *Address :* Century Club, New York. *Club :* Reform.
      (*Died 23 April 1926.*)

PENNINGTON, Brig.- Gen. Arthur Watson, M.V.O. 1907 ; retired ; late 9th Hodson's Horse ; *b.* 20 March 1867 ; *s.* of late Lieutenant - General Sir Charles Pennington, K.C.B. ; *m.* Helen Bethea, *d.* of late Colonel J. B. Hutchinson, C.S.I. ; one *d. Educ. :* Haileybury ; Oxford Military College. Entered Border Regt. 1888 ; Captain, Indian Army, 1899 ; Major, 1906 ; Lt.-Col. 1914 ; served Chitral, 1895. (medal with clasp) ; Tirah, 1897-98 (two clasps) ; D.A.A.G. Indian Coronation Contingent at King Edward's Coronation ; in charge of King Edward's Indian Orderly Officers, 1907 ; served European War in Egypt, France, and Mesopotamia, 1914-18 (despatches thrice) ; retired, 1922. *Address :* Mylncroft, Frimley Green, Surrey.   (*Died 8 May 1927.*)

PENNY, Edmund, C.I.E. 1900 ; Superintending Engineer and Sec. to Chief Commissioner, Central Prov. Public Works Dept. 1899 ; invalided 1900 ; retired 1902 ; *b.* 23 April 1852 ; *s.* of Alfred Penny, M.I.C.E., and Sarah, *d.* of W. A. Weightman ; *m.* 1881, Ellen Margaret, *d.* of Major-Gen. P. S. Cunningham. *Educ. :* Cheltenham College. Appointed Public Works Department, India, 1874 ; executive engineer Central Provinces, 1883 ; planned and carried out scheme for Nagpur Waterworks, 1890. *Address :* India Office, S.W.   (*Died 13 Aug. 1919.*)

PENRHYN, 3rd Baron, *cr.* 1866 ; **Edward Sholto Douglas-Pennant**, J.P., D.L. ; *b.* 10 June 1864 ; *e. s.* of 2nd Lord Penrhyn and Pamela Blanche, *d.* of Sir C. Rushout-Rushout, 2nd Bt. ; *m.* 1887, Hon. Blanche Georgiana Fitzroy, *d.* of 3rd Lord Southampton ; one *s.* three *d.* ; *S.* father, 1907. *Educ. :* Eton ; Sandhurst. Lieut. 1st Life Guards, 1885-91 ; M.P. (C.) Northamptonshire, S., 1895-1900 ; Member of Jockey Club. *Heir : s.* Hon. Hugh Napier Douglas-Pennant.   *Address :* Penrhyn Castle, Bangor ; Wicken Park, Stony Stratford. *Clubs :* Carlton, Bachelors' ; Royal Yacht Squadron, Cowes.
      (*Died 22 Aug. 1927.*)

PENRHYN, Rev. Oswald Henry Leycester ; Rector of Winwick, 1890-1917 ; Canon of Liverpool since 1880 ; Proctor in York Convocation since 1880 ; Chaplain to the Bishop ; *b.* East Sheen, 6 May 1828 ; 2nd *s.* of Edward Penrhyn, J.P., D.L., and Lady Charlotte, *e. d.* of 13th Earl of Derby ; *m.* Charlotte Louisa Jane, 4th *d.* of Edmund G. Hornby, J.P., D.L., of Dalton Hall, Burton, Westmoreland ; one *s.* three *d. Educ. :* Eton ; Balliol, Oxford ; Wells. B.A. 3rd class, 1849 ; M.A., 1852 ; Ordained, 1852 ; Priest, 1853 ; Curate of Upton St. Leonard's, Gloucestershire, 1852-56 ; Curate of Winwick, Lancashire, 1856-57 ; Incumbent of Bickerstaffe, 1857-69 ; Vicar of Huyton, 1869-90 ; Proctor Archdry. of Warrington, 1887-1908 ; Rural Dean of Winwick, 1892-1910. *Recreation :* cricket in early life. *Address :* Lymm, Warrington, Lancashire. *Club :* Athenæum, Liverpool.   (*Died 3 Dec. 1918.*)

PENROSE, Brigadier-General Cooper, C.B. 1910 ; C.M.G. 1917 ; *b.* 8 Mar. 1855 ; 3rd *s.* of Rev. J. D. Penrose, of Woodhill, Co. Cork ; *m.* 1885, Sylvia Alice, 2nd *d.* of late Thomas Greene, 49 St. Stephen's Green, Dublin ; three *d. Educ. :* Haileybury ; Woolwich. Obtained commission in Royal Engineers, 1873 ; Captain, 1885 ; Major, 1893 ; Lt.-Col., 1900 ; Colonel, 1904 ; Brig.-Gen., 1910 ; served South African War, 1879 ; China, 1900 ; employed with local forces, N.S. Wales, 1885-89 ; Assistant Inspector of Submarine Defences at War Office, 1891-96 ; Inspector, 1897 ; employed on Survey of Wei-Hai-Wei and C.R.E., 1898-1901 ; C.R.E., Gosport, 1901-5 ; Chief Engineer, Southern Coast Defence, 1906-10 ; Chief Engineer Southern Command, Salisbury, 1910-12 ; retired 1912 ; Temp. Chief Engineer, Scottish Command, 1915-16 ; employed under Admiralty, 1917 - 19. *Club :* Junior United Service.   (*Died 12 April 1927.*)

PENTECOST, Rev. George F., M.A., D.D., LL.D. ; *b.* Illinois, U.S.A., 23 Sept. 1841 ; *e. s.* of Hugh L. Pentecost, Virginia, and Emma, *e. d.* of George Flower, Herts, England ; *m.* Ada, *y. d.* of Augustus Webber, M.D., Kentucky ; two *s. Educ. :* Georgetown College, U.S.A. Private Secretary to Governor of State of Kansas, 1857 ; Clerk U.S. District Court, 1858 ; Captain 8th Kentucky Cavalry, U.S.A., 1862-64 ; ordained to Gospel ministry, 1862 ; Boston, Mass., 1868-71 ; Brooklyn, 1868-71, 1880-87 ; evangelical work in Scotland, 1887-88 ; special mission to English-speaking Brahmins in India, 1888-91 ; minister Marylebone Pres. Church, London, Eng., 1891-97 ; 1st Presbyterian Church, Yonkers, N.Y., 1897-1902 ; Special Commissioner of American Board and Presbyterian Board of Foreign Missions to China, Japan, and Philippine Islands, 1902-3 ; since then Bible teaching and evangelistic work ; pastor Bethany Presbyterian Church, Philadelphia, Pa., 1914. *Publications :* In the Volume of the Book, 1884 ; Out of Egypt, 1885 ; A South Window, 1886 ; Bible Studies (10 vols.), 1881-91 ; Birth and Boyhood of Christ, 1896 ; Forgiveness of Sin, 1896 ; Systematic Beneficence, 1897 ; Precious Truth, 1900 ; Christian Imperialism, 1902 ; Fighting for Faith. *Recreation :* gardening. *Address :* Bethany Church. Philadelphia, Pa., U.S.A.   (*Died Aug. 1920.*)

PENTLAND, of Lyth, Caithness, 1st Baron, *cr.* 1909 ; **John Sinclair**, G.C.S.I., *cr.* 1918 ;

G.C.I.E., *cr.* 1912; *b.* 1860; *e. s.* of late Capt. George Sinclair, and *g.s.* of late Sir John Sinclair, Bt., Dunbeath; *m.* 1904, Lady Marjorie Gordon, **D.B.E.,** *o. d.* of 7th Earl of Aberdeen; one *s.* one *d. Educ.*: Edinburgh Academy; Wellington; Sandhurst. Entered army, 1879; served in Soudan Expedition, 1885 (medal and clasp); retired as Captain, 1887; A.D.C. to Lord-Lieutenant of Ireland (Aberdeen), 1886; contested (G.L.) Ayr Burghs, 1886; L.C.C. 1889-92; M.P. for Dumbartonshire, 1892-95; secretary to Governor-General of Canada (Aberdeen), 1895-97; M.P. (L.) Forfarshire, 1897-1909; Secretary for Scotland, 1905-12; Governor of Madras, 1912-19. *Heir : s.* Hon. Henry John Sinclair, *b.* 6 June 1907. *Address :* Frognal End, Frognal Gardens, Hampstead, N.W.3. *T. :* Hampstead 6184. *Clubs :* Brooks's, Athenæum. *(Died 11 Jan. 1925.)*

PENTON, Maj.-Gen. Arthur Pole, C.M.G. 1917; C.B. 1910; C.V.O. 1909; Member Executive Council since 1909; *b.* 6 Oct. 1854; entered R.A. 1873; Capt. 1882; Major, 1889; Lieut.-Col. 1898; Col. 1904; Inspector of Warlike Stores, 1888-1891; Assistant to Director of Artillery, 1891-93; Brig.-Major R.A. 8th District, 1893-96; Commandant Defence Forces, New Zealand, 1896-1901; Commandant Ordnance College, 1904-1907; Commander Coast Defences, Scotland, 1907-1908; Vice.-Pres.Ordnance Board, 1908; served Afghanistan, 1878-80 (despatches, medal); commanding R.A., Malta, 1908-12; South-West Coast Defences, 1912-16. *Clubs :* Junior United Service, Ranelagh. *(Died 23 Aug. 1920.)*

PEPYS, Rev. Charles Sidney, B.D., Vicar of Aylesbury; *b.* 1875; *m.* 1913, Adelaide Mary Elizabeth, *d.* of late Charles Duncan Cutts of Buenos Aires; one *s.* four *d. Educ. :* Winchester; Oriel College, Oxford. English Chaplain at Iquique and Rosario; Hon. Canon of St. John's, Buenos Aires; Chaplain to the Forces, European War, 1917-19 (despatches). *Address :* Vicarage, Aylesbury, Bucks. *(Died 21 Sept. 1927.)*

PEPYS, Rev. Herbert George, M.A., Hon. Canon of Worcester Cathedral since 1878; *b.* 31 Oct. 1830; *y. s.* of Rt. Rev. Henry Pepys, D.D., Lord Bishop of Worcester; *m.* 1863, Louisa Harriet, *d.* of J. Whitmore Isaac of Boughton Park, Worcestershire; two *s.* five *d. Educ. :* Trinity College, Cambridge; Wells Theological College. Curate of Kidderminster, 1853-54; Vicar of Grimley, 1854-77; Vicar of Hallow, 1854-1900. *Address :* Florence Court, Torquay. *T.A. :* Torquay. *(Died 21 Feb. 1918.)*

PERAK, H.H. The Sultan of, G.C.V.O. (hon.), 1913; G.C.M.G. (hon.), 1901; K.C.M.G. 1892. *Address :* Perak, Straits Settlements. *(Died Mar. 1916.)*

PERCEVAL, Sir Westby (Brook), K.C.M.G., *cr.* 1894; *b.* at Launceston, Tasmania, 11 May 1854; *s.* of Westby Hawkshaw Perceval, late of Knightsbrook, Co. Meath, and Carrickmakegan, Co. Leitrim, and Sarah Brook, *d.* of John Bailey, M.D., Brooklands, Essex; *m.* Jessie, *d.* of Hon. John Johnston. M.L.C., Wellington, New Zealand, 1880; two *s.* two. *d. Educ. :* Christ's Coll. Gram. School, Christchurch, New Zealand; Stonyhurst Coll. Barr. Middle Temple, 1878; practised in Christchurch; represented Christchurch in Colonial Parliament, 1887-91; Chairman of Committees, 1891; Agent-General in London for New Zealand, 1891-96; Agent-General for Tasmania, 1896-98; created Knight of St. Gregory the Great by Pope Leo XIII. 1891; Member of Royal Commission for Chicago Exhibition, 1894-95; also Paris Exhibition, 1900; Member of Tariff Commission, 1904. *Publications :* Farming and Labour in New Zealand; Productions of New Zealand; New Zealand Timbers and Forest Products. *Recreations :* golf, motoring. *Address :* Southdown, Wimbledon, S.W.19. *T. :* 196 Wimble-

don. *Clubs :* Union, City of London. *(Died 23 June 1928.)*

PERCIVAL, Rt. Rev. John, D.D.; *b.*1834; *s.* of William Percival, Brough Sowerby, Westmoreland, and Jane, *d.* of William Longmire, Bolton, Westmoreland; *m.* 1st, 1862, Louisa *d.* of James Holland (*d.* 1896); 2nd, 1899, Mary Georgina, 2nd *d.* of late Frederick Symonds, F.R.C.S. Oxford; one *s.* one *d. Educ.*: Grammar School, Appleby, Westmoreland; Queen's Coll. Oxford (Scholar). Junior Mathematical University Scholar, 1855. Double First Mods. and Finals. M.A. 1861. Fellow of Queen's Coll. Oxford. Ordained 1860; Assistant Master, Rugby; Headmaster, Clifton Coll. 1862-78; Prebendary of Exeter, 1871-82; Canon of Bristol, 1882-87; President Trin. Coll. Oxford, 1878-87; Headmaster, Rugby, 1887-95; Bishop of Hereford, 1895-1918. *Publications :* The Universities and the Great Towns; Some Helps for School Life (Clifton College Sermons); Sermons at Rugby. *Address :* 64, Banbury Road, Oxford. *Club :* Athenæum. *(Died 3 Dec. 1918.)*

PERCY, Sir James Campbell, Kt., *cr.* 1921; D.L., J.P.; Chairman, Sackville Press, Dublin; Managing Director, Mecredy, Percy & Co., Ltd.; Director, Central Hotel, Dublin, and Grand Hotel, Greystones; Switzer & Co. Ltd., and Car and General Insurance Co. Ltd. (London); *b.* 15 Feb. 1869; *m.* 1898, Harriet Constance, *d.* of Richard Topham; one *s.* two *d. Educ. :* St. Enochs, Belfast. Has been associated with journalism and the production of technical papers for over thirty years. *Publications :* Bulls, Ancient and Modern; Bulls and Blunders; More Bulls and Blunders. *Recreations :* played international for Ireland Association, 1889; golf and motoring. *Address :* Failte, Totterage Lane, Herts. *M. :* Crossley 27628. *Clubs :* Savage, Engineers; Royal Automobile, Dublin. *(Died 26 Oct. 1923.)*

PEREIRA, Brig.-Gen. George Edward, C.B. 1917; C.M.G. 1905; D.S.O. 1900; late Grenadier Guards; *b.* 26 Jan. 1865; *s.* of Edward and Hon. Margaret Pereira; unmarried. *Educ. :* The Oratory School, Edgbaston, Birmingham. Home service, 1884-99; attached to Chinese regiment till 1900; served China, 1900 (slightly wounded, medal with clasp, D.S.O.); South Africa, 1902 (Queen's medal, 3 clasps); Military Attaché, Peking, 1905-10; served European War (despatches, C.B., Hon. Brig.-Gen.). *Recreations :* travelling, racing, cricket. *Clubs :* Guards', Travellers', Bachelors'. *(Died 20 Oct. 1923.)*

PEREIRA, Rt. Rev. Henry Horace, D.D.; Hon. Canon of Canterbury Cathedral; Rector of All Hallows, Lombard Street, since 1904; *b.*16 Jan. 1845; *s.* of Dr. Pereira; *m.* 1874, Adela, *e. d.* of Col. and the Hon. Mrs. Stretton; one *s.* one *d. Educ. :* Trinity College, Dublin. Theological Prizeman, and Prizeman in Hebrew and Modern Languages. After serving curacies at Eston, Yorkshire, and Holy Trinity, Southampton, he became the first Warden of the Wilberforce Memorial Mission in South London; then Rector of St. Lawrence, Southampton, from whence he was appointed by the Bishop of Winchester, Rector of Chilbolton and Rural Dean of Stockbridge; Vicar and Rural Dean of Croydon, 1894-1903; Bishop of Croydon, 1904-24; Proctor in Convocation for Diocese of Canterbury; formerly Chaplain to Queen Victoria and to King Edward. *Recreation :* reading. *Address :* 18 Collingham Place, S.W.5. *T. :* 314 Western. *(Died 1 Jan. 1926.)*

PERFECT, Captain Herbert Mosley, C.B.E. 1919; O.B.E. 1918; Royal Navy (retired); *b.* 14 October 1867; *s.* of late Henry Goodwin Perfect, Pontefract, Yorks; *m.* Esther Sophia, *o. d.* of late Major-General Rainey, Madras Cavalry, of Rostrevor, Co. Down; one *s. Educ. :* privately; H.M.S. Conway. Served in Boxer rebellion, 1900; North China medal and two clasps); served in Naval Transports as acting Captain R.N. 1914-19; Divisional Naval Transport Officer at Folkestone, Hull, and Southampton (O.B.E., C.B.E.); awarded by President of U.S.A. Distinguished Service Medal for embarkation of U.S.A. troops and service during the War; J.P. Co. Down. *Address:* Rathturret, Warrenpoint, Co. Down. *Club:* Junior Naval and Military.

(Died 27 Mar. 1928.)

PERKIN, Frederick Mollwo, C.B.E. 1920; Ph.D.; F.I.C.; Consulting and Technical Chemist; *y. s.* of late Sir William Perkin, F.R.S.; *m.* Elizabeth Margaret, 4th *d.* of late Geo. Mackay of Edinburgh; one *s.* two *d. Educ.:* Amersham Hall School, Reading; Royal College of Science; Edinburgh University; Owens College; University of Würzburg (Ph.D.). Specially interested himself in study of electrochemistry and carbonization of coal, particularly production of smokeless fuel, also peat and its utilization; Head of Chemistry Department Borough Polytechnic Inst., London, 1897-1909; one of Founders of Faraday Society (Treasurer, 1908-17); President, Paint and Varnish Society; President, Oil and Colour Chemists' Association, 1918-20; Hon. Member Institution of Gas Engineers; Interested in Technology of Oils; Technical Adviser to the Committee on the Production of Oil from Cannel Coal and Allied Minerals; Hon. Sec. British Science Guild, 1908-1916; Vice-President of Jury, Franco-British Exhibition, 1908; Member of Jury, Brussels International Exhibition, 1910; Vice-President Jury, Turin International Exhibition, 1911; and Vice-President Group Jury, Ghent International Exhibition, 1913. *Publications:* Cantor Lectures on Oils, 1915; Qualitative Chemical Analysis; Practical Methods of Electrochemistry; Practical Methods of Inorganic Chemistry; The Metric System; Textbook of Elementary Chemistry; also a number of original papers before Chemical and Faraday Society and Society of Chemical Industry. *Recreations:* gardening, breeding cocker spaniels. *Address:* 91 Talgarth Road, Barons Court, W.; Laboratories, Sudbury, Harrow; Albion House, 59 New Oxford Street, W.C.1. *T.:* Museum 2854; Wembley 108. *(Died 24 May 1928.)*

PERKINS, Lt.-Col. Alfred Edward, D.S.O. 1900; N.S.W. Bearer Company; *b.* 21 Feb. 1863; *m.* 1884, Elizabeth, *d.* of late Richard Shortlands, Sydney. Served South Africa, 1900 (despatches, Queen's medal 6 clasps, D.S.O.). *Address:* Wyoming, Macquarie Street, Sydney, N.S. Wales. *T.:* 2996.

PERKINS, Brig.-Gen. Arthur Ernest John, C.B. 1918; R.A. Served Hazara Expedition, 1891 (clasp); European War, 1914-18 (C.B.). *(Died 20 July 1921.)*

PERKINS, George Walbridge, Director International Mercantile Marine Co. and U.S. Steel Corporation; *b.* Chicago, 31 Jan. 1862; *s.* of George Walbridge Perkins and Sarah Louise Mills; *m.* 1889, Evelyn Ball, Cleveland, O. *Educ.:* Public schools, Chicago. Partner in J. P. Morgan & Co., 1901-10. *Address:* Riverdale, N.Y. *(Died 18 June 1920.)*

PERKINS, Harry Innes, F.R.G.S., F.G.S., I.S.O. 1904; *b.* Simla; *s.* of late Maj.-Gen. E. N. Perkins, B.S.C.; *m.* 1889, Josephine, *d.* of George Monkhouse; one *s.* three *d. Educ.:* Privately; Kings' School, Rochester. Clerk to Director of Public Works and Surveys, Trinidad, 1880-81; Third Assistant Crown Surveyor, Crown Lands Dept., British Guiana, 1881; 2nd, 1884; 1st, 1889; made first ascent of Mt. Roraima in 1884 with E. F. im Thurn; Acting Crown Surveyor, 1890, 1892-1893; Commissioner for settlement of East Indian immigrants in Colony in lieu of return passages to India, 1895; Acting Commissioner of Mines,

1895-1901; Acting Crown-Surveyor in addition during 1896; Commissioner to delimit boundary between British Guiana and Venezuela, 1900; Senior Commissioner January 1903; completed delimitation, 1904; sometime member of the Institution of Mining and Metallurgy; Surveyor-General British Honduras, 1905; Member of the Executive Council, 1908; Acting Director of Public Works, and Member of the Legislative Council, 1915; retired 1919. *Publications:* (with Professor J. B. Harrison) Geology of the Barima, Barama, Potaro, Essequibo, Demerara, and Mazaruni Rivers, 1897-99; Papers on the natural history and mining industries of the Colony. *Recreations:* photography, natural history, travel. *Address:* c/o Lloyds Bank, Ltd., 9 Pall Mall, S.W.1. *(Died 24 Oct. 1924.)*

PERKINS, Lt.-Col. John Charles Campbell, D.S.O. 1902; Military Accounts Depart., India, since 1894; *b.* London, 2 April 1866; *s.* of late Surgeon-General R. H. Perkins, Indian Medical Service, Hon. East India Company's Service, and Anne Bowden Campbell of Inverneill and Ross; a direct descendant in eldest line of John Perkins, senior partner Barclay and Perkins, brewers; *m.* 1st, 1895, Emma Victoria Augusta (*d.* 1912), *d.* of General Douglas Seafield Grant, I.S.C.; 2nd, 1913, Charlotte Mary, *d.* of Harold Beauchamp, Wellington, New Zealand. *Educ.:* Stamford Grammar School; Rossall School. Militia 4th Batt. Shropshire Light Infantry; Commission in 1st Leinster Regt. 1887; joined 1st Batt. in India, 1888; joined Indian Staff Corps, 1890; 44th Gurkha Rifles, also served with 43rd Gurkha Rifles in Assam and Manipur; then short while with 10th Bengal Infantry; Field Service, S.A., 1900-1903; held conjointly appointments Controller Military Accounts and Field Paymaster Indian Contingent, and Officer Commanding Indian Details, S.A. Force (despatches, D.S.O.). *Recreations:* cricket, football, racquets, sport of all kinds; reading books of travel. *Address:* Grindlay and Co., 54 Parliament Street, London, S.W. *Clubs:* Caledonian, East India United Service.

(Died 28 Feb. 1916.)

PERKINS, Joseph John, M.A., M.B. (Cantab.), F.R.C.P.; Consulting Physician St. Thomas's Hospital; Consulting Physician, Brompton Hospital for Consumption and Diseases of the Chest; Consulting Physician, King Edward VII. Sanatorium, Midhurst. *Educ.:* Owens College, Manchester; Emmanuel College, Cambridge (Scholar); St. Thomas's Hospital; 1st Class Natural Sciences Tripos; late Assistant Physician and Pathologist to the City of London Hospital for Diseases of the Chest, Victoria Park. *Publications:* contributions to various medical journals. *Address:* 57 Harley Street, W.1. *(Died 13 Sept. 1928.)*

PERKINS, Surg.-Capt. Robert Clerk, D.S.O. 1900; M.R.C.S., L.R.C.P.; Medical Officer to Swaziland Administration. *Address:* Headquarters, Swaziland. *(Died 7 May 1916.)*

PERKINS, Robert George, *b.* Southampton, 1850. *Educ.:* Springfield, Chelmsford. Early training as journalist on Chelmsford Chronicle and Essex Herald; subsequent experience on South Durham Herald, Worcester Herald, and Worcestershire Chronicle; News Editor Worcestershire Echo; District Representative of The Times, Daily Sketch, Central News Agency, etc. *Address:* Verona Villas, Worcester. *T.:* Worcester 117. *T.A.:* 72 High Street, Worcester. *(Died 25 Jan. 1922.)*

PERKINS, Rev. William; *b.* Haverfordwest, Pembrokeshire, 21 March 1843; *s.* of Thomas Perkins; *m.* 1868, Margaret, *o. d.* of Joseph Whicher of Milford Haven; one *s.* five *d. Educ.:* Grammar School, Haverfordwest. Entered Civil Service as clerk and draughtsman R.E. Dept.; Wesleyan Minister, 1864; churches have been almost entirely in Staffordshire, Lancashire, and

Gloucestershire; Pres. of Wesleyan Methodist Conference, 1909; Sec. Wesleyan Methodist Missionary Society, 1898-1914. *Publications:* contributions to magazines and journals. *Address:* Nolton, Audley Road, Hendon, N.W.
(Died 19 Dec. 1922.)

PERKINS, William Turner, Editor House of Commons Official Report; Assistant Editor, 1908-16; *e. s.* of late Henry Johnson and Mary Ann Perkins; *m.* 1st, Hannah Maria Spears (*d.* 1921), Manchester; four *s.* four *d*; 2nd, Edith Helen, *o. d.* of Alfred Garry, Beckenham, Kent. *Educ.:* Dr. Halley's School; Manchester Grammar School. Reporter, Manchester Courier, and first Parliamentary representative of that paper, 1881-92; also London correspondent, Manchester Evening Mail; leader writer and special correspondent, Shipping Gazette, 1891-1895; Secy., Gallery (Masonic) Lodge, 1893-1898; Worshipful Master, 1891-92; joined Times Parliamentary staff, 1892; Secretary, Gallery Committee, Houses of Parliament, 1888-90; Chairman, 1892-94; editor, Parliamentary Debates, for the Times and Waterlow & Sons, Ltd., 1895-98; special correspondent, Standard, 1900; literary secretary, Channel Tunnel Company, for Bill promoted in Parliament, 1907; editor, Railway Magazine, 1909-13. *Publications:* Popular Illustrated Guide to South-Eastern and Chatham Railway, 1906; local Guides to Dorset, Devon, and Cornwall; contributions to Engineering Wonders of the World. *Address:* House of Commons, S.W.
(Died 14 May 1927.)

PERRIER, Edmond, Membre de l'Institut de France et de l'Académie de Médécine de Paris; Directeur honoraire du Museum National Français d'Histoire Naturelle; Commandeur de la Légion d'Honneur; *b.* Tulle, Corrèze, 9 mai 1844; *s.* of Antoine Perrier, Directeur d'Ecole normale, Chevalier de la Légion d'Honneur, et Jeanne Roche; *m.* Cécile Henry-Bertin; two *s.* *Educ.:* Collège de Tulle; Lycée Bonaparte, Paris; Ecole normale supérieure. Professeur au Lycée d'Agen, Maître de Conferences à l'Ecole normale supérieure, Assistant, puis Professeur et Directeur du Mus. d'Hist. Nat.; Directeur et Président du Comité de Patronage de la section des Sciences naturelles de l'Ecole pratique des Hautes Études; Membre de l'Institut de France (Academie des Sciences), de l'Academie de médecine et de la Societé de Biologie; Président de la Société nationale d'Acclimatation; Membre at ancien Président de la Commission Centrale de la Société de Géographie; Vice-Président de l'Institut général de Psychologie, etc. *Publications:* Mémoires nombreux de Zoologie sur les Echinodermes, sur les Vers, sur l'Embryogénie générale; Les Colonies animales et la Formation des Organismes, 1881; Les Explorations sous-marines, 1884; La Philosophie zoologique avant Darwin, 1886; Le Transformisme, 1888; La Femme dans la nature et l'évolution du sexe féminin, 1908; Traité de zoologie, 1890-1900, La vie dans les Planètes, 1911; France et Allemagne, 1914—A Travers le mondé vivant, 1916; La vie en action, 1918; La bene avant l'Histoire, 1919, etc. *Address:* Jardin des Plantes, 57 rue Cuvier, Paris. *T.:* Gobelins 808, 89. *Club:* St. Hubert, Paris. *(Died 1 Aug. 1921.)*

PERRING, Rev. Sir Philip, 4th Bt.; *cr.* 1808; *b.*15 July 1828; 2nd *s.*of 3rd Bt.and Frances, *o. d.* of late Henry Roe, Ganton, Devon; S. father 1866. *Educ.:* Trin. Coll. Camb. (Scholar, Brown Medallist, 4th in Classical Tripos 1852, M.A.). Late Curate of St. James's, Westminster; The National Party: Christian. *Publications:* Churches and their Creeds; Hard Knots in Shakespeare; Work-days of Moses; Spirit and the Muse; Verse—translation of Florian's Fables; Air Raids from Dreamland. *Heir:* none. *Address:* 7 Lyndhurst Road, Exeter.
(Died 8 June 1920.)

PERRIS, George Herbert; C.B.E., 1920; writer and speaker, especially on international affairs; *b.* Liverpool, 1866; *s.* of Rev. H. W. Perris; *m.*; two *d.* Journalist from 1883; Editor Hull Express, 1885; ten years on editorial staff of The Speaker under Wemyss Reid; Editor of Concord, 1898-1906; one of founders and Hon. Sec. of Anglo-German (1905) and Anglo-Russian (1906) Friendship Committees; Secretary Cobden Club, 1903-5; Foreign Editor of The Tribune, 1906-7; and of Daily News, 1908-10; Originator and Assistant Editor Home University Library, 1912-14; War Correspondent of the Daily Chronicle in France, 1914-18; Chevalier of the Legion of Honour, 1918. *Publications:* Eastern Crisis and British Policy, 1897; Leo Tolstoy the Grand Mujik, 1898; Short History of the First Hague Conference, 1899; Further Memoirs of Marie Bashkirtseff, 1901; Life and Teaching of Tolstoy, 1901; Blood and Gold in South Africa, 1902; Protectionist Peril, 1903; Russia in Revolution, 1905; R. W. Emerson, 1910; Short History of War and Peace, 1911; Our Foreign Policy; Germany and the German Emperor, 1912; The Industrial History of Modern Europe, 1914; The Campaign in France and Belgium, 1915; The Battle of the Marne, 1920. *Address:* 5 Ashburn Place, South Kensington, S.W. *T.:* Western 8655. *Clubs:* National Liberal, Whitefriars. *(Died 23 Dec. 1920.)*

PERROTT, Sir Herbert Charles, 6th Bt., *cr.* 1716; C.H. 1918; C.B. 1902; late Lt.-Col commanding and Hon. Col. 3rd Batt. The Buffs (East Kent Regiment); *b.* Charlton, Kent, 26 Oct. 1849; *e. surv. s.* of 5th Bt., Plumstead, and Emma, *d.* of Commander Charles Evelyn Houghton, R.N.; *S.* father 1886; *m.* 1901, Ethel Lucy, *d.* of late Capt. Marcus S. Hare, R.N., of Court Grange, Newton Abbot; [R.R.C. first-class; Médaille de la Reine Elizabeth; 1911 Coronation Medal; Lady of Justice St. John of Jerusalem; Lady - Superintendent - in - Chief of Nursing Divisions, St. John Ambulance Brigade; Hon. Secretary Queen's War Committee of Ladies of the Order of St. John; late Lady-Commandant-in-Chief of Women's V.A.D. Territorial Branch St. John Ambulance Association]; two *d.* *Educ.:* Ipswich Grammar School. Formerly Ensign 21st K.R.V., and Capt. Reserve of Officers; Assistant Secretary Order of St. John of Jerusalem, 1875-88; Secretary 1894-1910; Secretary-General 1910-15; Knight of Justice St. John of Jerusalem since 1876; Titular Bailiff of Egle since 1915; Chief Secretary of St. John Ambulance Association from its formation, 1877 to 1915; Member, late Vice-Chairman of the Joint War Committee of the Order of St. John and British Red Cross Society; member Executive Committee Standing Council of the Baronetage; was Hon. Secretary of the Eastern War Sick and Wounded Relief Fund; late Vice-Chairman and now Vice-President of the British College for Physical Education; President or Patron of several cricket, football, and other athletic clubs. *Recreations:* riding, shooting, etc., formerly cricket and football (has compiled Regimental Records). *Heir:* none. *Address:* 44 Queen's Gate, S.W.7. *T.:* Kensington 2186. *Club:* United Service. *(Died 15 Feb. 1922.)*

PERROTT, Maj.-Gen. Sir Thomas, K.C.B., *cr.* 1914; C.B. 1900; Royal Artillery; *b.* 5 May 1851; *m.* 1880, Gertrude Louisa Grace, *d.* of late W. C. Cornwall of Richmond, Monkstown, Co. Dublin; one *s.* Entered army, 1870; Captain, 1880; Major, 1886; Lieut.-Col. 1896; Colonel, 1900; Major-General, 1906; served South Africa, 1899 - 1900 (despatches, Queen's medal, 4 clasps, C.B.); China, 1900 (medal); Brig.-Gen. Commanding Scottish Coast Defences, 1906; commanding troops in the Straits Settlements, 1907-10; commanding Royal Artillery, Gibraltar, 1910-13; retired 1913; re-employed Inspector Royal Horse and Field Artillery, Oct. 1914; retired, Oct. 1915. *Club:* United Service. *(Died 3 Nov. 1919.)*

PERRY, Rev. Arthur John, Hon. Canon of Truro, 1918; Vicar of Gwinear. *Address:* St. Gwinear Vicarage, Hayle, Cornwall.
(Died 13 Jan. 1926.)

PERRY, John, M.E., D.Sc., LL.D., F.R.S.; Emeritus Professor of Mechanics and Mathematics, Royal College of Science. S. Kensington; *b.* Ulster, 14 Feb. 1850; 2nd *s.* of Samuel Perry, Garvagh; *m.* Alice Jowitt (*d.* 1904) of Sheffield. *Educ.:* Queen's Coll. Belfast. Assistant-master Clifton College, 1870-74; Professor of Engineering, Japan, 1875-79; electrical engineer and inventor, 1879-96; Professor of Engineering and Mathematics, City and Guilds London Technical College, Finsbury, 1881-96; past President of the Institution of Electrical Engineers; past President Physical Society of London; General Treasurer, British Association; educational reformer, especially in Mathematics and Physical Science; Member S. African University Commission, 1914. *Publications.* The Steam Engine, 1874; Practical Mechanics, 1883; Spinning Tops, 1890; Cantor Lectures, Hydraulics, 1882; Calculus, 1897; Applied Mechanics, 1897; Steam, 1899; Practical Mathematics 1899; England's Neglect of Science, 1901; about 100 scientific papers published before the Royal and other societies. *Address:* 25 Stanley Crescent, Notting Hill, W.11. *T.:* Park 4311. *Club:* Athenæum.
(Died 4 Aug. 1920.)

PERRY, Hon. John; *b.* Sydney, July 1845; *m.* 1870, Susan M'Auslan, 2nd *d.* of late Thomas Alston, Sydney. *Educ.:* Fort St. Model School. Member Legislative Assembly, Richmond River, 1889; Minister of Public Instruction, Labour, and Industry, 1899-1904; Chief Secretary, 1904; Minister for Mines, 1907-8; Minister for Agriculture to 1910. *Address:* George Street, Marrickville, Sydney. *(Died 1922.)*

PERRY, Rear-Adm. John Laisné, R.N. Entered navy, 1852; Commander, 1858; Captain, 1865; retired, 1873; Rear-Adm. 1881.
(Died 16 Nov. 1917.)

PERRY, John Tavenor; *b.* Chelsea, 1842. *Educ.:* St. Peter's Collegiate School and King's College, London. Entered profession of architect as pupil to Professor Hayter Lewis, 1859; Associate of R.I.B.A., 1864; Fellow, 1896; retired, 1901; Medallist and First Pugin Student; designed and executed, among other buildings, schools and vestry to the Chapel Royal, Savoy, for Queen Victoria; school buildings for Dean and Chapter of Rochester; church of Thurville Heath, Bucks.; north wing and Physiological Schools to University College, London; the Alhambra Theatre; Union Assecuranz Societät Office, Berlin; Hotel Metropole, Swansea; Hotel Cecil, London. *Publications:* The Mediæval Antiquities of the County of Durham; An Account of the Priory of St. Martin's, Dover; A Chronology of Mediæval and Renaissance Architecture; Dinanderie; editor of Memorials of Old Middlesex; and writer of numerous articles published in the Transactions of the R.I.B.A., the Old County Memorials series, and the Burlington, Connoisseur, English Illustrated, Reliquary, Antiquary, Christian Art (U.S.A.), and Home Counties Magazines, and the Builder, Architect, and Architectural Review. *Address:* 5 Burlington Gardens, Chiswick, W.

PERTAB SINGHJI, Gen. Sir, G.C.B., *cr.* 1918; G.C.V.O. 1911; G.C.S.I., *cr.* 1886; K.C.B., *cr.* 1901; LL.D., Grand Officer Legion of Honour; Hon. A.D.C. to H.M. the King-Emperor; *b.* 1845; *m.* Maharani Bhatianiji (*d.* 1907); four *s.* one *d.* Hon. Commandant of the Imperial Cadet Corps; placed at the head of the Jodhpur administration; under the guidance of H.H. Maharaja Sir Jaswant Singh he introduced far-reaching reforms in every department of the State and suppressed crime and dacoities which were then rife; by introducing railways and constructing large irrigational

bundhs substantial additions were made to revenue, and the country has been protected against famines to which it is chronically subject; he was one of the Kabul Mission of 1878, an extra A.D.C. to General Ellis in the Mohmand Expedition in 1897, and to General Sir William Lockhart in the Tirah Campaign in 1898 (wounded, and despatches); in 1900 he went with the British Force to China in command of the Jodhpur Imperial Service Troops and saw active service; was made the Ruling Chief of Idar State in Guzerat in 1902, which he abdicated in favour of his son; made Lt.-Col. and subsequently Lieut.-General in the British Army; European War, 1914-15 (despatches). *Address:* Jodhpur, Rajputana. *(Died Sept. 1922.)*

PERTWEE, Rev. Arthur, M.A.; Vicar of Brightlingsea since 1872; Hon. Canon of Chelmsford, 1917. *Educ.:* Pembroke College, Oxford. Ordained, 1861; Curate of Brancepeth, 1861-64; St. Margaret's, Leicester, 1865-72. *Address:* Brightlingsea Vicarage, Colchester.
(Died 14 Jan. 1919.)

PERUGINI, Charles Edward, artist; *b.* Naples; *s.* of late Leonardo Perugini; *m.* Kate Perugini. *Educ.:* in Italy under Giuseppe Bonolis and Giuseppe Mancinelli; in Paris under Ary Scheffer, 1855. *Works:* Hero, 1914, R.A.; An Offering to Pan, 1915, R.A. *Address:* 32 Victoria Road, Kensington, W. *Clubs:* Garrick, Arts. *(Died 22 Dec. 1918.)*

PETERKIN, Rt. Rev. George William, D.D., LL.D.; First Bishop of West Virginia since 1878; *b.* Clearspring, Maryland, 21 March 1841; *s.* of Rev. J. Peterkin, D.D., and Elizabeth Howard Hanson; *m.* 1st, 1868, Constance Gardner Lee (*d.* 1877); 2nd, 1884, Marion M'Intosh Stewart; one *s.* three *d.* *Educ.:* Episcopal High School of Virginia; University of Virginia; Theological Seminary of Virginia. Served in Confederate Army, 1861-65; private in Co. F. 21 Virginia Infantry; corporal, sergeant, and lieut.-adjutant of regiment; 1st lieut. and A.D.C. staff of General W. A. Pendleton, Chief Artillery Army, Northern Virginia; assistant to his father at St. James's Church, Richmond, Va., 1868; Rector St. Stephen's Church, Culpeper, Va., 1869; Memorial Church, Baltimore, Md., 1873; organised Mission in Brazil, 1893; Porto Rico, 1901; founded Sheltering Arms Hospital, 1886; member of Board of Missions since 1886. *Publications:* Records of Protestant Episcopal Church in Western Virginia and West Virginia; addresses at Church conferences and fugitive articles. *Address:* Parkersburg, West Virginia, U.S.A. *(Died 22 Sept. 1916.)*

PETERS, Major John Weston Parsons, D.S.O. 1916; O.B.E.; Reserve of Officers, 7th Dragoon Gds.; *m.* Mary Bertram (*d.* 1922). *Educ.:* Winchester; R.M.C. Sandhurst. Served Chin-Lushai Expedition, 1889-90 (medal with clasp); Hazara Expedition, 1891 (clasp); S. African War, 1900-2 (Queen's medal 4 clasps, King's medal 2 clasps); Brigade-Major, 4th Cavalry Brigade; District Comm. Middleburg; Assistant Military Governor, Pretoria; European War, 1914-19 (despatches four times, D.S.O., O.B.E., 1915 medal, War medal, Victory medal). *Address:* 5 Palmer Street, Westminster, S.W.1. *T.:* Victoria 2072. *Clubs:* Naval and Military; Royal Southern Yacht.
(Died 21 July 1924.)

PETERSEN, Sir William, K.B.E., *cr.* 1920; Chairman of Petersen & Co., Ltd., London, Shipowners; *b.* 29 May 1856; *m.* 1889, Flora M'Kay (*d.* 1918), *e. d.* of George Sinclair, J.P., Aberdeen; three *d.* *Educ.:* Roskilde and Copenhagen, Denmark. Founder and Director of London-American Maritime Trading Co., Ltd., and Director of several other shipping companies; Founder of the Royal and Uranium Passenger Lines to Canada and U.S.A.; Chairman of the British Committee of the

International Shipping Registry, Bureau Veritas (nominated by the Board of Trade); Hon. Comdr. R.N.R.; proprietor of the Hebridean Island, Eigg; owns over 18,000 acres. *Publications:* Numerous contributions to Standard Shipping and other magazines; The Alien in our Midst; The Kiel Canal Problem. *Recreations:* yachting, shooting. *Address:* 80 Portland Place, W.1; Herons G'hyll, Uskfield, Sussex; The Lodge, Eigg, Inverness-shire. *T.:* Mayfair 6022. *Clubs:* Junior Carlton, Constitutional, Royal Societies, Ranelagh; Royal Clyde Yacht; Royal Highland Yacht.

(Died 12 June 1925.)

PETERSON, Sir Arthur Frederick, Kt., *cr.* 1915; **The Hon. Mr. Justice Peterson,** Judge of the High Court of Justice, Chancery Division, since 1915; *b.* 1859; Bar. Lincoln's Inn and Inner Temple. *Address:* 39 Cheyne Walk, S.W.3. *T.:* Kensington 5195. *Clubs:* Athenæum, Albemarle.

(Died 12 May 1922.)

PETERSON, Brig.-Gen. Frederick Hopewell, C.B. 1916; D.S.O. 1895, I.S.C.; *b.* 1864; *s.* of F. V. W. Peterson; *m.* 1896, Mary Elizabeth, *d.* of H. Howard. Entered army (Yorks Light Infantry), 1885; Capt. 1896; Major 1903; Lt.-Col. 1909; Col. 1914; served Sikkim Expedition, 1888 (medal with clasp); Hazara, 1891 (clasp); relief of Chitral Fort, 1895 (despatches, D.S.O., medal with clasp); Tibet, 1903-4 (despatches, medal and clasp); Abor Expedition, 1911-12 (despatches, Brevet Col., medal and clasp); retired, 1919.

(Died 25 Jan. 1925.)

PETERSON, Sir William, K.C.M.G., *cr.* 1915; M.A., C.M.G. 1901; *b.* Edinburgh, 29 May 1856; 5th *s.* of John Peterson, merchant, Leith; *m.* 1885, Lisa, *e. d.* of late Wm. Ross of 12 Hyde Park Gardens, W., and Glenearn, Perthshire. *Educ.:* High School and University, Edinburgh; Univ. of Göttingen; Corpus Christi College, Oxford (Scholar); Ferguson scholar in classics, 1876; M.A. Edin. and Oxford; F.R.S.C.; Hon. LL.D. St. Andrews (1885); Princeton, N.J. (1896); University of New Brunswick (1900); Yale (1901); Johns Hopkins (1902); Pennsylvania, Queen's (1908); Aberdeen (1906); Toronto (1907); Harvard (1909); Trinity College, Dublin (1912); Hon. D.Litt. Oxford and Durham (1912); Doctor Litterarum Classicarum, Groningen, 1914. Assist. Professor of Humanity in the University of Edinburgh, 1879-82; Principal of University College, Dundee, 1882-95; Principal of McGill University, 1895-1919; Chairman of the Protestant Committee of the Council of Public Instruction, Province of Quebec; one of the Vice-Presidents of the Archæological Institute of America. *Publications:* Quintilian's Institutes of Oratory, 1891; The Dialogus of Tacitus, 1893 (and in the Loeb Classical Library, 1914); The Speech of Cicero for Cluentius, 1895; (critical ed., 1899); The Cluni MS. of Cicero, 1901; Cicero's Verrine Orations, 1907; Canadian Essays and Addresses, 1915; Longman's School Poetry Books, etc. *Recreations:* golf, billiards, curling, etc. *Address:* Wildwood, North End, Hampstead, N.W.3. *Clubs:* Athenæum, Savile; Royal and Ancient, St. Andrews; University, Mount Royal, Montreal.

(Died 4 Jan. 1921.)

PETHEBRIDGE, Colonel Sir Samuel Augustus, K.C.M.G. *cr.* 1917; C.M.G. 1913; Naval and Military Expeditionary Force; Commonwealth Commissioner N.-W. Pacific Islands, Nov. 1914-Jan. 1915; Administrator late German New Guinea and Islands since 1915; Secretary Dept. of Defence, Australia, since 1910; *b.* Brisbane, 3 Aug. 1862; *s.* of late Henry Lander Pethebridge and Elizabeth Mary Symons; *m.* 1887, Mary Ada Simmonds; two *s.* one *d. Educ.:* Brisbane and Townsville Public Schools. Entered Public Service, Queensland, 1876;

28

Secretary Marine Board and Dept. to 1901; Chief Clerk Commonwealth Defence Dept., 1901; Sub.-Lieut., Lieut., and Commander, Queensland Navy, 12 years. *Address:* Defence Dept., Melbourne; Rabaul, New Britain. *Clubs:* Athenæum; Naval and Military, Melbourne.

(Died 24 Jan. 1918.)

PETHERAM, Sir William Comer, Kt., *cr.* 1884; K.C.; *b.* 1885; *m.* Isabel, *d.* of Sir W. Congreve, 2nd Bt., 1863. Special Pleader, 1862; Barrister Middle Temple, 1869; Q.C. 1880; Chief Justice of N.W. Provinces of India, 1884; of Bengal, 1886-96. *Address:* 49 York Terrace, Regent's Park, N.W. *Club:* St. Stephen's.

(Died 15 May 1922.)

PETRE, Hon. Albert Henry, *b.* 15 March 1832; *y. s.* of 11th Baron Petre; *m.* 1883, Elsie, *d.* of Rev. Professor William Robinson Clark, D.C.L., Director National Bank, Limited. Member of Stock Exchange; Director of Argentine Land and Investment Company, Limited. *Address:* 9 Rosary Gardens, S.W. *Club:* Reform.

(Died 5 April 1917.)

PETRE, Francis Loraine, O.B.E. 1920; *o. s.* of late Hon. Edmund Petre; *b.* 1852; *m.* 1887, Maud Ellen, *d.* of Rev. W. C. Rawlinson; one *s.* two *d. Educ.:* Oscott College. Called to Bar, Lincoln's Inn, 1873; joined Indian Civil Service, 1874; served in N.W.P. and Oudh up to grade of Commissioner of Division; also in Secretariat of Board of Revenue and of Foreign and Revenue Departments of Govt. of India; in Political Department (Central India and Hyderabad), 1885-89; retired, 1900; Ministry of Munitions (Finance Dept.), 1915-20. *Publications:* Napoleon's Campaign in Poland, 1806-1807; Napoleon's Conquest of Prussia, 1809; Napoleon and the Archduke Charles, 1809; Napoleon's Last Campaign in Germany, 1813; Napoleon at Bay, 1814; The Republic of Colombia; Simon Bolivar, El Libertador; History of the Norfolk Regiment; numerous articles in The Times and other journals. *Address:* Bekyngton, Farnham Royal, Bucks. *T.:* Farnham Common 9. *Club:* East India United Service.

(Died 9 May 1925.)

PETRE, Francis William; *b.* 26 Sep. 1847; *s.* of late Hon. Henry Petre, D.L., and Mary, *d.* of Richard Walmesley; *g.s.* of 11th and *c.* and *heir-pres.* of 17th Baron Petre; *m.* 1881, Margaret, *e. d.* of E. Bowes Cargill of Dunedin, N.Z.; two *s.* one *d. Educ.:* Mt. St. Mary's; H.M.S. Britannia; Ushaw. Studied architecture; went to New Zealand and practised engineering. *Works:* Catholic Cathedral, Christchurch, N.Z., etc. *Address:* Writtle House, St. Clair, Dunedin, New Zealand.

(Died 10 Dec. 1918.)

PETRE, Sir Charles, 1st Bt., *cr.* 1918, Kt., *cr.* 1903; Member of Liverpool City Council, *b.* 23 Feb. 1853; *s.* of Alexander Petrie; *m.* 1880, Hannah, *d.* of late William Hamilton; two *s. Educ.:* Wesley College, Dublin. Lord Mayor of Liverpool, 1901-2; Alderman, J.P., D.L.; President of the Liverpool Constitutional Association. *Recreations:* golf, shooting. *Heir:* *s.* Edward Lindsey Haddon, *b.* 1884. *Address:* Oakfield, Grassendale, Liverpool. *T.:* Garston Liverpool 396. *M.:* K 4030. *Clubs:* Junior Carlton; Conservative, Liverpool.

(Died 8 July 1920.)

PETRIE, Lt.-Col. Charles Louis Rowe, D.S.O. 1902; late the Manchester Regiment; *b.* 15 Dec. 1866; *m.* 1912, Dorothy Frances, *e. d.* of late Rev. E. P. Dew. *Educ.:* Marlborough. Entered army, 1887; Captain, 1896; served with Uganda Rifles, 1902 (despatches, medal with clasp, D.S.O.); Somaliland, 1902-3 (despatches); retired, 1907; Temporary Lt.-Col. commanding 16th (Service) Batt. Manchester Regiment; European War, 1914-18; France, 1916-18 (despatches); Lt.-Col.;

retired. *Club:* Army and Navy.
(*Died 24 Oct. 1922.*)

PETRIE, Sir Edward (Lindsay Haddon), 2nd Bt., *cr.* 1918; *b.* 1881; *s.* of 1st Bt. and Hannah, *d.* of late William Hamilton; *m.* 1912, Blanche, *d.* of C. J. Allen, Stanbury, Spencer's Wood, Berks; two *d.*; *S.* father, 1920. *Heir: b.* Charles Alexander [*b.* 1895: *m.* 1st, 1920, Ursula Gabrielle, *er. d.* of Judge Dowdall; one *s.*; 2nd, 1926, Jessie Cecilia, *er. d.* of F. J. G. Mason, 14 Thurleigh Road, S.W.]. *Address:* Dorincourt, Leatherhead, Surrey. *Clubs:* Windham, St. Stephen's, Royal Automobile.
(*Died 13 Dec. 1927.*)

PETRIE, Col. Ricardo Dartnel, C.B. 1915; late R.E.; *b.* 15 Sep. 1861; *m.* 1906, Inez, *d.* of late B. Horace Wood, Claremont, Natal. Entered army, 1881; Captain, 1889; Major, 1899; Lt.-Col. 1905; Colonel, 1918; Chief Engineer Northern Command, 1912; served Burma, 1886-1888 (despatches, medal 2 clasps); Chin-Lushai Expedition, 1890 (despatches, clasp); China, 1900 (medal); European War, 1914-15 (C.B.). *Club:* Naval and Military. (*Died 27 Dec. 1925.*)

PEYTON, Sir Algernon Francis, 6th Bt., *cr.* 1776; J.P.; High Sheriff, 1896; Capt. 11th Hussars (retired); Hon. Lt.-Col. Imp. Yeomanry; *b.* 24 Nov. 1855; *S.* father 1888; *m.* Ida, *d.* of James Mason, Eynsham Hall, Oxfordshire, 1888; two *s.* one *d.* Owns about 4000 acres. *Heir: s.* Algernon [Lieut. 11th Hussars; *b.* 4 Jan. 1889. Served European War, 1914-15 (wounded)]. *Address:* Swift's House, Bicester, Oxfordshire.
(*Died 11 April 1916.*)

PEYTON, Rev. Thomas Thornhill, M.A., J.P.; Rector of St. Mary's, March, since 1882; Rural Dean of March, 1909-24; Hon. Canon of Ely Cathedral, 1915; *b.* 8 Dec. 1856; 2nd *s.* of Sir Thomas Peyton, 5th Bart.; *m.* 1884, Mary Louisa (*d.* 1909), *d.* of Sir William M. H. Style, 9th Bt.; one *d.* *Educ.:* Wellington College; Magdalen College, Oxford. *Address:* St. Mary's Rectory, March, Cambridge.
(*Died 29 Sept. 1927.*)

PHEAR, Rev. Samuel George, M.A., D.D.; *b.* 30 March 1829, 3rd *s.* of Rev. John Phear, M.A., Rector of Earl Stonham, Suffolk; unmarried. Master of Emmanuel College, Cambridge, 1871-95; Chaplain to Bishop of Winchester, 1878-75; Vice-Chancellor of Cambridge, 1874-75. *Address:* Emmanuel College, Cambridge. *Club:* Athenæum. (*Died 26 Nov. 1918.*)

PHELAN, Major Ernest Cyril, D.S.O. 1918; M.C., R.A.M.C.; *m.* 1926, *widow* of Ian MacDonald, Highfield, Southampton. *Educ.:* Trinity College, Dublin (M.B., C.M., 1906). Served European War, 1914-18 (despatches, M.C., D.S.O.). *Address:* c/o Glyn, Mills & Co., 3 Whitehall Place, S.W.1.

PHELAN, Rt. Rev. Patrick, R.C. Bishop of Sale (Victoria) since 1913; *b.* Co. Kilkenny, 1860. *Educ.:* Mount Melleray Seminary and St. Patrick's College, Carlow. Priest, 1888; Administrator of St. Patrick's Cathedral, 1900-1913. *Publications:* The Holy Sacrifice of the Mass; The Mission of St. Ignatius Loyola; Christian Marriage; The Episcopate; Refutation of Protestant Calumnies; Priesthood of Christ; Martyrdom of Blessed Oliver Plunket; The Twin Evils of Society—Race Suicide and Divorce. *Address:* Sale, Victoria, Australia.
(*Died 5 Jan. 1925.*)

PHELIPS, William Robert, J.P., D.L. Somerset; *b.* 30 March 1846; *s.* of William Phelips of Montacute and Ellen Harriett, *d.* of William Helyar of Coker Court, Somerset; *m.* 1st, Cicely Grace Augusta, *d.* of Frederick Fane of Moyles Court Hants; one *d.*; 2nd, Constance Louisa, *d.* of Rt. Hon. Sir Spencer Ponsonby Fane; two *s.* one *d.* *Educ.:* Harrow; Trin. Coll. Cambridge. Lieut. in 6th Dragoon Guards, 1866-70; Alderman of Somerset C.C. since 1894; twenty-six years Chairman of Yeovil Board of

834

Guardians; twenty years Chairman of the South Somerset Conservative Association. *Heir: s.* Edward, *b.* 1882. *Recreations:* golf, shooting. *Address:* 18 Brompton Square, S.W.3. *T.:* Kens. 5133. *Clubs:* Carlton, Naval and Military.
(*Died 23 Nov. 1919.*)

PHELPS, Lt.-Gen. Arthur, Bombay Infantry; President National Anti-Vaccination League; *b.* 24 Oct. 1887; *m.* 1868, Caroline Ann (*d.* 1904), *d.* of late Abel Peyton, Edgbaston; three *s.* one *d.* Entered army, 1853; Lt.-Gen. 1892; U.S. list, 1893; served Indian Mutiny, 1858-60. *Publication:* Lord Dunchester. *Recreation:* gardening. *Address:* Woodbourne Grange, Edgbaston, Birmingham. *T.:* Edgbaston, 492. *Clubs:* Union, National Liberal.
(*Died 4 Oct. 1920.*)

PHILIPPS, Sir Charles (Edward Gregg), 1st Bt., *cr.* 1887; Lord-Lieutenant and Custos Rotulorum of Co. Haverfordwest, 1876-1925; J.P. for Carmarthenshire and Pembrokeshire (High Sheriff, 1882); Chairman of Pembrokeshire County Council, 1898-1908; three times Mayor of Haverfordwest; Lieut.-Col. (Hon. Col.) commanding Pembroke Yeomanry, 1898-1900; Member of the Governing Body of the Church in Wales; *b.* Huddersfield, 6 Oct. 1840; *e. s.* of late Edward Fisher, Spring Dale, Yorkshire, and Jane, *d.* of Dominick Gregg, Lisburn, Ireland; *m.* 1868, Mary Philippa, *e. d.* and co-heiress of Rev. James H. A. Philipps, M.A., and *niece* of late Baron Milford, Picton Castle; two *s.* four *d.* Assumed name of Philipps by Royal licence, 1876, in compliance with testamentary injunction of his father-in-law. *Educ.:* Cheltenham Coll. Barr. Middle Temple, 1868. Contested Pembrokeshire (C.), 1880, 1885, 1886, and 1892; Military Member of Pembrokeshire Territorial Force Association. Owns, with Lady Philipps, about 20,000 acres. *Recreation:* shooting. *Heir: s.* Capt. Henry Erasmus Edward Philipps, J.P., D.L. [*b.* 9 March 1871; *m.* 1909, Victoria Gladys Elizabeth, *o. c.* of late J. W. Gwynne Hughes of Tregeyb, Llandilo, Lord Lieutenant of Carmarthenshire; one *s.* one *d.* *Club:* Junior Carlton]. *Address:* Picton Castle, Haverfordwest. *T.:* Haverfordwest 42. *Clubs:* Carlton, Junior Carlton, Cavalry; Pembrokeshire County, Haverfordwest. (*Died 5 June 1928.*)

PHILIPS, Lieut.-Col. Burton Henry, C.M.G. 1899; A.D.C. to Sir H. Chermside; reserve of officers; late Royal Welsh Fusiliers; *b.* 1 Oct. 1858; *e. s.* of late John Capel Philips and Hon. Fanny Esther, 2nd *d.* of 5th Viscount Ashbrook; *m.* 1904, Lucy Madeline, 2nd *d.* of Col. Marton, Capernwray, Lancs; one *s.* two *d.* *Educ.:* Eton; Cambridge. Entered army, 1879; Capt. 1887; Major, 1898; served South Africa, 1900; prom. Lt.-Col. *Address:* The Heath House, Tean, Stoke-on-Trent. *Club:* Naval and Military.
(*Died 30 Mar. 1927.*)

PHILIPS, F. C., novelist, dramatist; *b.* Brighton, 3 Feb. 1849; *y. s.* of Rev. George Washington Philips, Ruxley Park, Surrey, and Charlotte, *d.* of late Thomas Jesson, Hill Park, Sevenoaks, Kent; *m.* 1st, Maria, *d.* of Charles Jones of Llanelly, Carmarthenshire; one *s.*; 2nd, Eva, *y. d.* of W. Trevelyan Kevill-Davies, Croft Castle, and Wigmore Hall, Herefordshire; one *s.* two *d.* *Educ.:* Brighton Coll.; R.M.C. Sandhurst. Gazetted 2nd Queen's Royal Regt. 1868; served in Regt. three years. Barr. 1884, and shortly afterwards novelist and dramatist, and contributor to many leading London newspapers and magazines; Knight Commander of the Order of St. Sava. *Publications:* novels—As in a Looking-Glass; A Lucky Young Woman; Jack and Three Jills; The Dean and His Daughter; A Question of Colour; A Full Confession; Social Vicissitudes; One Never Knows; Mrs. Bouverie; Constance; Young Mr. Ainslie's Courtship;

The Luckiest of Three; An Undeserving Woman; A Doctor in Difficulties; A Devil ir Nun's Veiling; The Strange Adventures of Lucy Smith; Little Mrs. Murray; Poor Little Bella; Men, Women and Things; A Woman of the World's Advice; The Matrimonial Country; My Varied Life (F. C. Philips' Reminiscences); with C. J. Wills—The Fatal Phryne, The Scudamores; A Maiden Fair to see, and others; with Percy Fendall — Margaret Byng; A Daughter's Sacrifice; My Face is My Fortune; Disciples of Plato; A Honeymoon and After; (with A. R. T. Philips)—Judas the Woman; Life; The Man and the Woman; and others; with Rowland Strong—A White Sin. As in a Looking-Glass was adapted for the stage, and was played by Mrs. Bernard Beere and Madame Sarah Bernhardt, it being the first English production in Paris by the latter; plays—The Dean's Daughter (with Sydney Grundy); Husband and Wife (with Percy Fendall); Godpapa (with Charles H. E. Brookfield); John Chetwynd's Wife; A Woman's Reason (with Charles H. E. Brookfield); The Fortune of War; A Free Pardon (with Leonard Merrick); Lady Paddington (with Walter Parke); The Burglar and the Judge (with Charles H. E. Brookfield); Papa's Wife (with Seymour Hicks), founded on F. C. Philips s story, In the Third Capacity, and others. *Recreations*: field sports, and the theatre. *Address*: 1 Elm Court, Temple, E.C. *T.A.*: Philps, 21 Temple.   *(Died 21 April 1921.)*

PHILIPSON, Sir George Hare, Kt., *cr.* 1900; M.A., M.D., D.C.L., LL.D., F.R.C.P., J.P.; Vice-Chancellor of the Univ. of Durham, 1912 and 1913; President Univ. of Durham Coll. of Medicine, Newcastle; Prof. of Medicine, Univ. of Durham, since 1876; a Pres. of and Consulting Phys. to Newcastle Royal Victoria Infirmary; member of the General Medical Council; Fellow of the Royal Society of Medicine; Member of Association of Physicians, Great Britain; Cor. Royal Coll. of Physicians, London, 1901-2-3; Hon. Col. R.A.M.C. (T.), Northumbria, 1908-13; *b.* Newcastle, 18 May 1836; 3rd *s.* of late George Hare Philipson, J.P. *Educ.*: Univ. Coll. London; Caius College, Cambridge (Mecklenberg Scholar, Thruston Speaker); Hon. Assoc. of the G.P. of the Order of St. John of Jerusalem in England; Bradshaw Lecturer, Royal Coll. of Physicians, London, 1884; President British Medical Association, 1893. *Publications*: Pathological Relations of the Absorbent System; Investigation of the Prevalent Diseases of the District by a System of Registration; Health and Meteorology of Newcastle and Gateshead. *Recreation*: Art. *Address*: 7 Eldon Square, Newcastle-upon-Tyne. *T.*: Nat. 1202. *Clubs*: Royal Societies, Northern Counties; Durham County, Durham. *(Died 24 Jan. 1918.)*

PHILIPSON, Robert; *b.* 1860, *s.* of William Philipson, Stocksfield, Northumberland; *m.* 1st, Annie, *d.* of John Patterson, Alnwick; one *s.* one *d.*; 2nd, Edith Mary, *d.* of Charles Jackson of Newcastle-on-Tyne. *Educ.*: privately. Commenced official career in the service of the Tyne Improvement Commissioners at Newcastle-on-Tyne; advanced to the position of Assistant Secretary to that undertaking; Secretary to the Thames Conservancy, 1900; Secretary of the newly constituted Port of London Authority, 1909; General Manager of the Port of London Authority, 1909-13. *Recreations*: golfing and motoring. *Address*: 9 Chelsea Court, Chelsea Embankment, S.W. *T.*: 6507 Western. *(Died 14 Aug. 1918.)*

PHILLIMORE, John Swinnerton, M.A., LL.D. (St. Andrews); D.Litt. (Dublin); J.P.; Professor of Humanity, Glasgow University, since 1906; *b.* 26 Feb. 1873; 4th *s.* of late Admiral Sir Augustus Phillimore, K.C.B., D.L., and Lady Phillimore; *m.* 1900, Cecily,

o. *d.* of Rev. S. C. Spencer Smith; one *d.* one *s.* *Educ.*: Westminster; Christ Church, Oxford. 1st Class Classical Moderations; 1st Class Literæ Humaniores; Hertford, Craven, and Ireland Univ. Scholarships; Chancellor's Prize for Latin Verse. Was a Lecturer of Christ Church, 1895, Tutor and Student, 1896-99; Professor of Greek at Glasgow University, 1899-1906; appointed by the University of California to hold the Sather Professorship of Classics there for the year 1914-15. *Publications*: Musa Clauda, or Latin Versions; Propertius (text), 1901 and (Riccardi Press) 1911; Index Verborum, 1906, translation, 1906; Sophocles (3 plays translated), 1902; Poems, 1902; Statius Silvæ text, 1905, 2nd ed. 1917; Philostratus Apollonius of Tyana, translated with Introduction and Notes, 2 volumes, 1912; Things New and Old, 1918; Remarks on Translation, 1919; *Ille Ego* or Virgil and Professor Richmond, 1920; The Hundred best Latin Hymns, 1925; The Silver Latin Book, 1925; collaborated in Essays in Liberalism by Six Oxford Men, 1897; an occasional contributor to Dublin Review, Classical Review, Mnemosyne and G. K.'s Weekly. *Address*: 5 The University, Glasgow. *T.*: Western 167. *Clubs*: Athenæum; Western. Glasgow.   *(Died 16 Nov. 1926.)*

PHILLIPPS, Maj.-Gen. Henry Pye; retired; J.P. Suffolk; *b.* 6 Nov. 1836; 2nd *s.* of Charles Phillipps; *m.* Emily Hester St. Albyn, *d.* of Wm. Savage Wait, Woodborough, Somersetshire. *Educ.*: Sandhurst. Entered 2nd Queen's Regt. 1854; served in British Kaffraria; as Adjutant throughout China War, 1860 (Medal for Taku Forts and Pekin); in Ionian Islands, Gibraltar, Bermuda, Halifax Malta; commanded 2nd Batt. in India; retired as Major-General, 1882. *Club*: United Service.   *(Died 25 July 1927.)*

PHILLIPPS, Lt.-Gen. Picton, C.B. 1924; C.M.G. 1919; M.V.O. 1912; late Royal Marines; late A.D.C. to the King; *b.* Aldershot, 3 March 1869; 2nd *s.* of late Maj. C. B. Phillipps, Barham Hall, Suffolk, and Mrs. Phillipps, Claydon, Suffolk; *m.* Monica Gabrielle, 4th *d.* of late Thomas Neale Fonnereau, Christchurch Park, Ipswich; two *s.* *Educ.*: Aldeburgh; Oxford Military College. Joined R.M.A. 1886; Lieut.-Gen., 1926; Retired List, 1926. *Recreation*: shooting. *Address*: The Lodge, Claydon, Ipswich.   *(Died 2 April 1928.)*

PHILLIPPS-WOLLEY, Sir Clive, Kt., *cr.* 1914; J.P., F.R.G.S.; *e. s.* of R. A. L. Phillipps, M.A., F.R.G.S., F.R.S.C. *b.* England, 1854; *m.* 1879, Jane, 2nd *d.* of Rear-Admiral Fenwick. *Educ.*: Rossall. Was H.B.M.'s Vice-Consul at Kertch; Bar. Middle Temple; went Oxford Circuit; formerly Captain 4th Batt. S.W.B.; assumed name Wolley on succeeding to estates of the Wolleys of Woodhall, Shropshire; explored in the Caucasus; settled in British Columbia; ran unsuccessfully twice for the Commons in the Conservative interest; Vice-President Navy League. *Publications*: Sport in the Crimea and Caucasus; Big Game volumes of Badminton Library; Gold, Gold in Cariboo; The Chicamon Stone; Songs of an English Esau, etc. *Address*: The Grange, Somenos, British Columbia. *Clubs*: Authors', Shikar; Shropshire County; Union, B.C.   *(Died 9 July 1918.)*

PHILLIPS, Sir Claude, Kt., *cr.* 1911; B.A.; Barrister-at-Law; Keeper of the Wallace Collection, 1897-1911; Barr. Inner Temple, 1883; Chevalier of the Order of Leopold; Hon. Member Royal Academy of Milan; Art critic of Daily Telegraph; contributor to Quarterly, Edinburgh, Nineteenth Century, Fortnightly, and North American Reviews, the Burlington Magazine, and the Gazette des Beaux-Arts of Paris. *Publications*: Life of Sir Joshua Reynolds, Life of Frederick Walker, Life of Antoine Watteau, Picture Gallery of Charles I., The Earlier Work of Titian, and The Later Work of Titian. *Address:* 40 Ashburn Place, S.W. *Club:* Beefsteak.   (*Died 9 Aug. 1924.*)

PHILLIPS, Rev. Forbes Alexander; *pseudonym,* "Athol Forbes"; Vicar of Gorleston, Gt. Yarmouth; Rector of Southtown; novelist, dramatist; *b.* 1866; *s.* of George Phillips, H.M. Civil Service; *m.* Helena Bell of Blyth, Co. Northumberland; two *d.* *Educ.:* Durham Univ. and private tutors. Ordained to All Saints', Newcastle, 1889; senior curate to Tynemouth Parish Church, 1891-93; vicar and rector, Gorleston, 1893; surrogate for Norfolk and Suffolk, 1894; select speaker Church Congress, 1895; past provincial grand chaplain of Norfolk and Suffolk; prelate of the Order of Knights Templar; Plantagenet preceptory; chaplain to Church Actors' Union; chaplain, V. Norfolk Territoral. *Publications:* Some Mysteries of the Passion, 1898; Gorleston and its Parish Church, 1894; Cassock and Comedy, 1898; A Son of Rimmon, 1899; Odd Fish, 1901; If Love were All, 1902; The Romance of Smuggling, 1909; What was the Resurrection?; Is Death the End? *Plays:* Her First Proposal, produced in Dublin; Church or Stage? produced by Mrs. Brown-Potter; Lord Danby's Affair; A Maid of France, 1905; When it was Dark, 1906; The Last Toast. *Recreations:* writing for magazines, shooting. *Address:* Gorleston Vicarage, Great Yarmouth. *T.A.:* Vicar, Gorleston.
     (*Died 29 May 1917.*)

PHILLIPS, Francis, C.B. 1903; late assistant comptroller and auditor, Exchequer and Audit Dept.; *b.* 8 Sept. 1835; *o. surv. s.* of late Charles Henry Phillips, F.R.C.S., surgeon to H.M.'s household; *m.* 1868, Mary, *e. d.* of late George Addison, 2nd partner in the Bank of Messrs. Child & Co. *Address:* 5 Porchester Square, Hyde Park, W.   (*Died 8 June 1925.*)

PHILLIPS, Brig.-Gen. George Fraser, C.B. 1918; C.M.G. 1916; *b.* 14 May 1863; *s.* of H. W. Phillips, artist. *Educ.:* Uppingham. Joined West Yorkshire Regt. 1885; A.D.C. to the Governor, Hong Kong, 1897; commanded 2nd Batt. West Yorkshire Regt.; commanded International Force in Scutari, Albania, and Governor of Scutari, 1913 until war broke out, 1914; commanded 2nd Batt. West Yorkshire in France, 1914; Military Attaché, Servia and Montenegro, in 1915-16 (C.M.G.); commanded 10th District, 1916; Head of British Military Mission, Greece, and member of Allied Military Control Mission, Athens, 1916-17 (C.B.); Commandant, Paris Area, 1917-18; Albania, 1918-20; retired 1920. *Clubs:* Junior United Service, Travellers', Beefsteak.   (*Died 2 Dec. 1921.*)

PHILLIPS, Sir John, Kt., *cr.* 1918; M.A., M.D. (Cantab.), F.R.C.P. (London); Hon. Physician to Queen Mary, 1918; J.P. Hants; Professor Emeritus of Obstetric Medicine, King's College, London, and Consulting Obstetric Physician King's College Hospital; *b.* 6 July 1855; *e. s.* of late L. Phillips of Birchmoor Manor, near Bedford, and Ann, *d.* of Robert Ayres of Barford; *m.* 1890, ·Rachel Rattray (*d.* 1917), *d.* of late Robert Tweedie Middleton, M.P, and D.L., of Hillfoot, Kilpatrick, Dumfrieshire; one *s.* three *d.; m.* 1926, Beatrice Margaret, *e. d.* of Rev. Clement Naish, Vicar of Upnor, Kent. *Educ.:* Bedford; St. John's College, Cambridge; Fellow, King's College, London. *Publications:* papers in obstetric medicine and gynæcology; Outlines of Diseases of Women (4th edition). *Recreations:* literature, fishing, shooting, gardening. *Address:* 24 Queen's Road, St. John's Wood, N.W.8. *T.:* Primrose Hill 4422.   (*Died 8 Dec. 1928.*)

PHILLIPS, John, M.P. (N.) South Longford since 1907; J.P.; *b.* Corboy, Co. Longford.

Educ.: Tertiary Carmelites School, Clondalkin; Queen's College, Galway. *Address:* House of Commons, S.W.   (*Died 2 April 1917.*)

PHILLIPS, J. S. Ragland; editor of the Yorkshire Post since 1903; Chairman of the Press Association, 1912; President of the Newspaper Society, 1914; magistrate, City of Leeds; *b.* Pendleton, Manchester, 1850, of Welsh-Norse descent; *y. s.* of Richard Ayres Phillips; *m.* 1875, S. J. C. More; three *s.* *Educ.:* Owens College (evening classes). Editor Kendal Mercury, 1878; worked as a journalist in Worcester, Belfast, York, Newcastle-on-Tyne, Edinburgh (leader writer and reviewer on The Scotsman, 1887-89); editor Manchester Examiner, 1889-91; assistant editor Yorkshire Post, 1891-1903; lectures on travel scenes, and on the Elizabethan drama and stage; contributed to the Cambridge History of English Literature the chapter dealing with Journalism in the Nineteenth Century, 1916. *Recreations:* reading, music, farming, gardening, bee-keeping, walking, is a Cumberland "statesman" at Knot End, Ravenglass, viâ Carnforth, and spends holidays at that postal address. *Address:* Shaw Lane, Headingley, Leeds. *T.:* 160 Headingley. *Clubs:* Authors', Leeds, Leeds Conservative, Leeds.   (*Died 4 Nov. 1919.*)

PHILLIPS, Lawrence Barnett, F.S.A. 1885; F.R.A.S., 1865; A.R.E.; artist and author; *b.* London, 29 Jan. 1842; *s.* of late Barnett Phillips, of Bloomsbury Square, diamond merchant; *m.* Judith, *d.* of M. Cohen, of Clifton Gardens, W.; two *s.* *Educ.:* Dr. Pinches' School; private tuition. Inventor of the rocking bar keyless work for winding watches; patent sketching boxes and palette; simplified mechanism for chronographs; perpetual calendars and calculating machines; since 1882 has devoted himself to art, and exhibited at Royal Academy, New Gallery, Institute, Grosvenor, and the principal provincial galleries; he is an Associate of the Royal Society of Painter-Etchers. *Publications:* Autographic Album, 1866; Horological Rating Tables, 1871; The Dictionary of Biographical Reference, 1873. *Recreation:* travel. *Address:* Chesham House, Sutherland Avenue, W.9. *T.:* Hampstead 1960. *Club:* Royal Societies.   (*Died 14 April 1922.*)

PHILLIPS, Llewellyn Powell, M.A., M.D., B.C. Cantab.; F.R.C.S., F.R.C.P.; Emeritus Professor of Medicine, Royal School of Medicine, Cairo; Consulting Physician, Kasr-el Ainy Hospital, Cairo; *b.* 28 July 1871; *s.* of late James Mathias Phillips, M.D., of Cardigan, South Wales; *m.* 1904, Edith Helen, *d.* of late Alfred Coxon; three *d.* *Educ.:* Epsom College; Gonville and Caius College, Cambridge; St. Bartholomew's Hospital, London. Formerly house surgeon and extern midwifery assistant St. Bartholomew's Hospital, and Demonstrator of Anatomy, Medical School, St. Bartholomews' Hospital; house physician, Royal Free Hospital, Gray's Inn Road; resident surgical officer, Kasrel Ainy Hospital, Cairo; principal medical officer Gresham Life Office for Egypt, Palestine, and Syria; late Hon. Commandant British Red Cross Hospital, Giza, Egypt; Lt.-Col. R.A.M.C. (temp. and honorary); despatches four times, 3rd Class Order of the Nile, 3rd Class Order of Medjieh. *Publications:* Amœbiasis and the Dysenteries; papers in various medical journals and hospital reports. *Recreations:* numismatics, motoring. *Address:* Kasr-el-Dubara, Cairo, Egypt. *T.A.:* Nyllewell, Cairo (Eastern Telegraph Co. only). *T.:* en ville 400. *M.:* C 21. *Clubs:* Garden; Turf, Cairo. (*Died 1 Jan. 1927.*)

PHILLIPS, Reginald William, M.A., D.Sc., F.L.S.; late Professor of Botany, University College, N. Wales, 1884-1922; *b.* Talgarth, 15 Oct. 1854; *s.* of Thomas Phillips, Registrar; *m.* Esther, *d.* of Henry Lloyd Jones, Solicitor, Bangor; three *d.* *Educ.:* Normal Coll., Bangor; St. John's Coll., Camb. Formerly Tutor at Bangor Normal Coll.; graduated while at St. John's College, taking first-class Honours in Natural Science Tripos; Foundation Scholar and Prizeman of the College; appointed Lecturer in Biology in the North Wales University College, Bangor, at its foundation, 1884; has taken D.Sc. degree (London) for a thesis on Algæ; interested in educational questions; formerly Member and Vice-Chairman of the late Bangor School Board; former President of the North Wales Congregational Union; member of the Merionethshire Education Committee; J.P. County of Carnarvon. *Publications:* Memoirs on Algæ. *Recreations:* golf, fond of collecting as a field botanist. *Address:* University College, Bangor. *T.A.:* Dr. Phillips, Bangor.

(*Died 2 Dec. 1926.*)

PHILLIPS, Rev. Sidney, M.A.; Hon. Canon of Worcester; *b.* 30 June 1840; *s.* of Sidney James and Fanny Phillips; *m.* 1868, Alice Margaret, *d.* of Rev. Edward and Lady Harriet Moore; three *s.* five *d. Educ.:* Radley, Oxford. Deacon, 1864; priest, 1866; Vicar of Castle Hedingham, Essex, 1868-75; Vicar of Monmouth, 1875-79; Rector of Nuneham Courtenay, 1879-87; Vicar of Kidderminster, 1887-1909. *Publications:* The Conflict; A Faithful Servant; The Heavenward Way; Communion of Sick. *Recreations:* travelling abroad and motoring. *Address:* The Blanquettes, Worcester. *T.A.:* Worcester. *T.:* Worcester 324. (*Died 21 Mar. 1917.*)

PHILLIPS, Rev. Stephen, D.D. *Educ.:* St. Albans Hall; Merton Coll., Oxford (M.A.). Curate of St. Saviour, S. Hampstead, 1870-73; All Saints, Hampstead, 1873-74; St. Andrews, Deal, 1874-76; Farnborough, Warwickshire, 1875; Chaplain and Sub-Vicar, Stratford-on-Avon, 1876; Minor Canon of Peterborough, 1876-83; Reader and Chaplain of Gray's Inn, 1884-1892; Precentor, Peterborough, 1892-1906; Hon. Canon, 1906-17. (*Died 30 Oct. 1919.*)

PHILLIPS, Rear-Admiral Thomas Tyacke, retired; *b.* Bermuda, 10 March 1832; *m.* 1866, Ellen Annie, *e. d.* of Thomas Hand, Richmond, Surrey; no *c. Educ.:* Helston Grammar School. Entered Navy, 1846; served in H.M.S. Fury at the destruction of a large piratical Fleet in China, 1849 (despatches); while serving in H.M.S. Hastings as mate commanded an armed schooner on the Irrawaddy, 1850 (medal and clasp, Pegu); served in Queen's yacht, 1854 (promoted to Lieutenant); served in H.M.S. Esk, Baltic Campaign, 1855 (medal); Gunnery Lieut. for 9½ years; arrested at the Havana, Austin Bidwell, the great bank forger, who was evading justice, 1873. *Recreation,* gardening. *Address:* The Hermitage, Paignton, Devon. (*Died 26 Aug. 1920.*)

PHILLIPS, William Lambert Collyer, O.B.E. 1918; B.A.; Colonial Treasurer, Barbados, since 1899; *b.* Oct. 1858; *s.* of late John Randal Phillips and Mary Anne Evelyn of Mt. Clapham Plantation, Barbados; *m.* Emily Lovell; *d.* of Joseph Lovell Canfield of Morris Plains, New Jersey, U.S.A.; one *s.* one *d. Educ.:* Lodge School and Codrington College, Barbados; B.A. (Dunelm), 1877. Deputy Clerk, House of Assembly, Barbados, 1879; Clerk, House of Assembly, 1891; Commissioner of Probates and J.P. 1882; Acting Colonial Secretary in 1911 and successive years; Acting Governor of Barbados, 1913; Delegate from Barbados to the Canada-West India Conference held in Ottawa, 1920. *Recreations:* various. *Address:* Innismoyle, Barbados. *Clubs:* West Indian; Bridge Town; Savannah. (*Died 24 Mar. 1924.*)

PHILLPOTTS, Arthur Stephens, J.P., Captain R.N. (retired); *b.* Torquay, 13 Oct. 1844; 2nd *s.* of late Henry Phillpotts, Torquay, *g. s.* of late Bishop of Exeter; *m.* Camilla, *d.* of Rt. Hon.

Sir B. Samuelson, Bt., 1883. *Educ.:* Chudleigh Grammar School; Royal Naval Academy, Gosport. Entered R.N. 1858; sub-lieut. on board H.M.S. "Bombay," in Dec. 1864, when that ship was destroyed by fire off the mouth of the Rio de la Plata, on which occasion 92 officers and men perished; served in Abyssinian Expedition, mentioned in despatches; and also noted for services in connection with the suppression of the slave trade on the East Coast of Africa; M.P. (C.) Torquay Div. Devon, 1895-1900. *Address:* Phillpottstown, Navan; Chelston Cross, Torquay. *Club:* Carlton.

(*Died 12 Aug. 1920.*)

PHILLPOTTS, Lt.-Col. Louis Murray, D.S.O. 1900; R.F.A.; *b.* 3 June 1870. Entered R.A. 1890; Capt. 1900; served South Africa, 1899-1901 (despatches, Queen's medal, three clasps, D.S.O.); European War, 1914-15 (despatches).

(*Died 8 Sept. 1916.*)

PHILP, Hon. Sir Robert; K.C.M.G., *cr.* 1914; *b.* Glasgow, 28 Dec. 1851; *m.* twice; two *s.* five *d. Educ.:* Anderston U.P. Church School, Glasgow; Normal School, Brisbane. With the firm of Bright Bros. & Co., Brisbane, for 11 years; one of the founders of the firm of Burns, Philp, and Co.; first entered Parliament, 1886; joined the M'Ilwraith Ministry, 1893; Minister for Mines and Works; and has also had portfolios of Education, Railways, and the office of Treasurer; Premier and Secretary for Mines, Queensland, 1899-1903; and Home Secretary, 1900-1903; Leader of the Opposition, 1903-8, 1909; Premier and Chief Secretary, 1908-9. *Recreation:* bowls. *Clubs:* Brisbane, Queensloo; Townsville, Queensloo.

(*Died June 1922.*)

PHILPOT, Frederick Freeman, a Master of the Supreme Court. *Address:* Royal Courts of Justice, Strand, W.C.

(*Died May 1916.*)

PHIMISTER, Rev. Alexander, M.A.; minister of John Knox Church, Newcastle-on-Tyne, 1882-1919. *Educ.:* Irvine Academy; Edinburgh University. Minister of the Free Church, Gordon, Berwickshire, 1874; Moderator of the Presbyterian Church of England, 1908. *Address:* 50 Beech Grove Road, Newcastle-on-Tyne. (*Died 5 Jan. 1921.*)

PHIPPS, Rev. Constantine Osborne, M.A. Oxon; Vicar of The Lee, Bucks, since 1914; Hon. Canon of Christ Church Cathedral, Oxford; Surrogate for the Diocese of Oxford; Chaplain to the Territorial Forces, 1914; Rural Dean of Wendover, 1919; *b.* 28 March 1861; *e. s.* of Rev. Pownoll William Phipps, M.A. Oxon; *m.* 1886, Jessie Mabel, *d.* of Joseph Challinor, Compton House, Leek; two *d. Educ.:* Marlborough College; Exeter College, Oxford. Deacon, 1885; Priest, 1886; Assistant Curate of All Saints, Fulham, S.W., 1885-88; Vicar of Cookham Dean, Berks, 1888-1895; Diocesan Inspector of Schools in Religious Knowledge, 1891-95, 1901-9, 1914-17; Vicar of Aylesbury, 1895-1914; Rural Dean of Aylesbury, 1906-11, 1912-14; Commissioner under the Pluralities Act Amendment Act for the Archdeaconry of Buckingham; Assessor under the Clergy Discipline Act for the Archdeaconry of Buckingham; Member of the Bucks County Cricket Club Committee. *Recreations:* golf and fly-fishing. *Address:* The Vicarage, The Lee, Great Missenden, Bucks. *T.:* The Lee 5.

(*Died 7 Nov. 1921.*)

PHIPPS, Hon. Harriet Lepel, *y. d.* of late Col. Hon. Sir C. B. Phipps, K.C.B. Formerly Maid of Honour to the Queen. *Address:* Kensington Palace, W.8. *T.:* Park 4687.

(*Died 7 Mar. 1922.*)

PICK, Thomas Pickering, F.R.C.S.; H.M. Inspector of Anatomy in England and Wales; Consulting Surgeon to St. George's Hospital and to the Victoria Hospital for

Children; *b.* 13 June 1841; *m.* 1873, Adeline, *d.* of late John Lawrence of Liverpool. *Educ.*: Royal Institution School, Liverpool. Late Hunterian Professor of Surgery and Pathology; member of the Court of Examiners and Vice-President, Royal College of Surgeons of England; Examiner in Surgery, University of Durham. *Publications*: Treatise on Surgery; Fractures and Dislocations; editor of Gray's Anatomy and Holmes's Principles and Practice of Surgery; author of numerous papers and lectures in the medical journals. *Recreation*: photography. *Address*: The Nook, Great Bookham, Surrey.   (*Died 6 Oct. 1919.*)

PICKARD-CAMBRIDGE, Rev. Octavius, M.A., F.R.S.; *b.* 1823; *m.* Rose (*d.* 1910), *d.* of Rev. James Lloyd Wallace of Sevenoaks, Kent, 1866; five *s. Educ.*: University College, Durham. Rector of Bloxworth since 1868. *Publications*: Specific Descriptions of Trap-Door Spiders, 1873; The Spiders of Dorset, 1879-81; Art. Arachnida, 9th edition Encyclop. Britannica; Araneidea Biologia Centrali Americana; etc. *Recreations*: general natural history, especially entomology and arachnology. *Address*: Bloxworth, Wareham, Dorset.   (*Died 9 Mar. 1917.*)

PICKERING, Edward Charles; Director of the Astron. Observatory of Harvard College since 1877; *b.* Boston, 19 July 1846; *s.* of Edward Pickering and Charlotte Hammond; *m.* 1874, Lizzie Wadsworth, *d.* of Jared Sparks. *Educ.*: Boston Latin School; Lawrence Scientific School, Harvard (A.M. 1880; LL.D. California, 1886; Michigan, 1887; Chicago, 1901; Harvard, 1908; Pennsylvania, 1906; D.Sc., Victoria Univ., England, 1900; Ph.D. Heidelberg, 1903); L.H.D. Pittsburgh, 1912; Foreign Associate of Royal Society, Institut de France, dei Lincei, Royal Prussian, Imperial Petrograd, Royal Institution, Connaissance des temps, Upsala, Royal Irish, Royal Swedish, Lund, Cherbourg, Toronto, Mexico, Edinburgh, etc.; Kt. German Order pour le mérite; has received the Bruce, Draper, Rumford and two Royal Astronomical Society's gold medals Instructor Mathematics, Lawrence Scientific School, 1865-67; Thayer Professor of Physics, Mass. Institute of Technology, 1867-77; established first physical laboratory in U.S. Study of light and spectra of the stars have been special features of his work. Has made nearly a million and a half measures of the light of the stars. By establishing an auxiliary station in Arequipa, Peru, southern stars are also observed. Founder and first President of the Appalachian Mountain Club; Ex-President Amer. Association; Member National Academy, Amer. Philos. Soc., Amer. Academy; President American Astronomical Society. *Publications*: Elements of Physical Manipulation, and eighty volumes of annals and other publications of Harvard College Observatory. *Recreations*: music, formerly mountain climbing and bicycling. *Address*: Harvard College Observatory, Cambridge, Mass. U.S.A. *T.A.*: Observatory, Boston. *T.*: Cambridge, 2286 W. *Club*: Century Association, New York.

(*Died 3 Feb. 1919.*)

PICKERING, Percival Spencer Umfreville, M.A., F.R.S. 1890; Director of the Woburn Experimental Fruit Farm; Investigator in Chemical Physics; *b.* 1858; *s.* of Percival A. Pickering, Q.C., and Anna Maria, *d.* of John Spencer Stanhope, Cannon Hall, Barnsley; *m.* 1898. *Educ.*: Eton and Balliol Coll. Oxford. 1st class Honours in Science, 1880. Lecturer on Chemistry at Bedford College, 1881-1888. *Publications*: The Pickerings of Barlby, York, and Wetherby; (with the Duke of Bedford) Reports of the Woburn Experimental Fruit Farm; Science and Fruit-growing; edited Memoirs of Anna Maria Pickering, and author of about 150 papers on chemical and physical

investigations in the Journals of the London and Berlin Chemical Societies, the Philosophical Magazine, Proceedings of the Royal Society, etc. *Recreation*: horticulture. *Address*: Harpenden, Herts; Woolacombe, N. Devon. *Club*: Athenæum.   (*Died 5 Dec. 1920.*)

PICKETT, Jacob, M.D. St. And., M.R.C.S. Eng., and L.R.C.P. Ed.; Consulting Surgeon to the Metropolitan Ear, Nose, and Throat Hospital, Fitzroy Square, London; *b.* 1835; 2nd *s.* of late Samuel Ballard Pickett of Wroughton, Wiltshire; *m.* 1879, Maria Ann Hopper, 2nd *d.* of late R. J. Chaplin, J.P. Kent, and D.L. City of London; no. *c. Educ.*: Private; Saint Bartholomew's Hospital. Late Senior Surgeon to the Metropolitan Ear, Nose, and Throat Hospital, London; Member of British Medical Association; Member and Vice-President of the West London Medical and Chirurgical Society; Member of St. Andrew's Graduates Society; Vice-President Medical Sick Insurance Society. *Publications*: articles in the British Medical Journal and Lancet at different times. *Recreations*: travelling and outdoor sports generally. *Address*: 18 Worthing Road, Southsea.

(*Died 3 Mar. 1922.*)

PICKETT, Rev. James; President of Primitive Methodist Conference, 1908-9; *b.* Berwick Bassett, Wiltshire, 19 Dec. 1853; two *s.* four *d. Educ.*: Wootton Bassett, Wiltshire. Business in London 17 to 23 years of age; entered Primitive Methodist ministry, 1876; minister at Bognor, 1876-78; Southwark, 1878-1881; Forest Hill, 1881-85; Leicester, 1885-97; Hull, 1897-1903; Harringay, N., 1903-13; Chesterfield, 1913-16; General Missionary Secretary, 1903-8. *Publications*: The Hartley Lecture, 1913; The Modern Missionary Crisis; various sermons. *Address*: 17 Morrill Street, Hull.

PICKOP, Rev. James, B.A., Hon. Canon of Manchester; *b.* 26 April 1847; *s.* of James Pickop, Solicitor, Blackburn; *m.* 1888, Sara T. Greer; two *s.* three *d. Educ.*: London University. Curate of Walmersley, Bury, 1875-79; St. Luke's, Heywood, 1879-88; Rector of Hatcliffe, Lincolnshire, 1888-1903. *Address*: Winston Hall, Blackburn. *T.*: 538.

(*Died 7 Mar. 1919.*)

PIELOU, Douglas Percival, M.P. (C.) Stourbridge Division since 1922; *b.* 17 Oct. 1887; *e. s.* of Percival Gaberial Pielou, retired Civil Servant; *m.* 1914, Nora, *d.* of late Joseph Pitchford, Dudley; two *s. Educ.*: Marling School, Gloucestershire. Entered bank, 1903; resigned, 1914; joined Cameron Highlanders (severely wounded Battle of Loos, Sep. 1915); Accountant H.M. Ministry of Munitions, Whitehall; Registrar for Tipton, Staffs; Member Tipton Council and Education Committee; President Tipton Branch and Club, British Legion; Chairman West Midland Area British Legion; Vice-Chairman British Legion throughout Country; Member of Ministry of Pensions Advisory Committee; Vice-President (elected) British Empire Services League; Hon. Secretary House of Commons Branch British Legion; served in Worcestershire Hussars Yeomanry and Warwickshire Royal Garrison Artillery (Vols.); late Commissioner B.P. Boy Scouts; Governor Birmingham University. *Recreations*: hunting, hockey, swimming, etc. (pre-War, now on crutches). *Address*: 103 Dudley Road, Tipton, Staffs. *T.*: Tipton 130.

(*Died 9 Jan. 1927.*)

PIERCE, Rev. Francis Dormer; Vicar of Brighton since 1916; 2nd *s.* of J. Timbrell Pierce, J.P., D.L. of Frettons, Danbury, Essex; *m.* Mabel, *y. d.* of P. Woolley of the Brokes, Reigate; no *c. Educ.*: Bedford Grammar School; Bury St. Edmunds; St. David's College, Lampeter. Deacon, 1894; Priest, 1895; Curate of St. Andrew's, Manchester, 1894-99; St. Mark's, Reigate, 1897-99; Rector of Wickford, Essex, 1899-1908; Vicar of

St. John's, Southend, 1908-14 ; Chaplain to the Forces (Territorial), 1910 ; Vicar of Prittlewell, Essex, and Rural Dean of Southend, 1914-16 ; Hon. Canon of Chelmsford, 1915 ; Prebendary of Chichester, 1917 ; Rural Dean of Brighton, 1918 ; Proctor in Convocation ; has travelled widely and is much interested in the missionary work of the Church ; F.R.Hist.S. *Publications:* History of Wickford ; Problems of Pleasure Towns ; magazine articles. *Recreations:* travelling, tennis, croquet. *Address:* Vicarage Lodge, Brighton. *Clubs:* Reform, Royal Societies ; Authors' ; New Brighton.

(*Died 2 Dec. 1923.*)

PIGGOTT, Sir Francis (Taylor), Kt., cr. 1905 ; b. 25 Apr. 1852 ; s. of Rev. Francis Allen Piggott, of Worthing ; m. 1881, Mabel Waldron, e. d. of Jasper Wilson Johns, J.P., D.L. ; two s. *Educ.:* Paris ; Worthing College ; Trinity Coll., Cambridge, M.A., LL.M. Called to Bar, 1874 ; special mission to Italy, 1887 ; Legal Adviser to Prime Minister of Japan, 1887-91 ; Secretary to the Attorney-General, Sir Charles Russell, M.P., on the Behring Sea Arbitration, 1893 ; Acting Chief Judge, Mauritius, 1895-97 ; Procureur and Advocate - General, Mauritius, 1894-1905 ; Chief-Justice Supreme Court, Hong-Kong, 1905 12. *Publications:* Foreign Judgments, 3rd ed. 1908 ; Principles of Law of Torts, 1885 ; Exterritoriality and Consular Jurisdiction, 2nd ed. 1907 ; Behring Sea Letters, 1893 ; Revised Edition of Laws of Mauritius, 6 vols., 2nd ed. 1904 ; Nationality and Naturalisation and the English Law on the High Seas and beyond the Realm, 1904 ; Extradition, 1911 ; The Garden of Japan, 1892 ; Music and Musical Instruments of the Japanese, 1893 ; Huafeng Lao Jen, Letters on the Chinese Constitution,1913; The Neutral Merchant; many publications on the rights of Belligerents and Neutrals and the Freedom of the Sea, 1914-17; The Law of the Sea Series, dealing with the Armed Neutralities, the French Wars, and the Declaration of Paris, 1919 ; The Freedom of the Seas. *Recreation:* golf. *Address:* 7 Stone Buildings, Lincoln's Inn, W.C.

(*Died 12 Mar. 1925.*)

PIGOT, His Honor Judge John H., K.C ; Circuit Judge for the City and County of Dublin ; b. 1868 ; s. of Master D. R. Pigot, sometime County Court Judge of West Cork, and g.s. of Right Hon. D. R. Pigot, Chief Baron of the Exchequer in Ireland ; m. Alice Maud Knox (d. 1914). *Educ.:* Trinity College, Dublin. *Address:* Avondale, Blackrock, Co. Dublin. (*Died 14 April 1923.*)

PIGOT, Rev. William Melville; b. Cromford, Matlock, 23 Mar. 1842 ; s. of Henry Becher Pigot, B.C.L. ; m. 1st, 1867, Eleanor Anne (d. 1887), d. of Rev. Arthur Roberts, Rector of Woodrising ; 2nd, Ada Mary, d. of John Woodland, J.P., of Taunton ; five c. *Educ.:* Islington Proprietary School, London ; Brasenose College, Oxford. Ordained by the Bishop of Norwich to the curacy of Hardingham, 1865 ; Vicar of Eaton, Norwich, 1875-1904 ; Rural Dean of Humbleyard, 1897-1904 ; Hon. Canon of Norwich Cathedral, 1901 ; Vicar of St. Mary-le-Tower, Ipswich, 1904 ; Rural Dean of Ipswich, 1908 ; editor Norwich Diocesan Gazette and Diocesan Calendar ; Diocesan Inspector of Schools in the Deanery ; Member of Standing Committee of S.P.G. ; Chaplain to Actors' Church Union ; Battalion Chaplain to Church Lads' Brigade ; retired, Jan. 1915. *Publication:* Service for Children. *Recreations:* rowing and running at Oxford, tennis, golf, etc. *Address:* Garwich Lodge, Felixstowe. *Clubs:* Junior Army and Navy ; Ipswich and Suffolk, Ipswich.

(*Died 25 Oct. 1916.*)

PIGOTT, John Robert Wilson, y. s. of late Rev. John R. Pigott, Rector of Ashwellthorp-with-Wreningham, Norfolk ; b.

27 Nov. 1850 ; m. 1893, Louisa, 2nd d. of late Richard Young Bazett, of Hon. E.I.C. Civil Service, Bombay, and of Highfield, Reading, Berks. *Educ.:* King Edward VI. School, Norwich. Planting, Ceylon, 1877-85 ; exploration, Australia, 1886-88 ; Assistant Administrator, Imperial British E. Africa, 1888-89 ; Acting Administrator, 1891, and from 1 Jan. 1893 to 30 June 1895 ; Sub-Commissioner, British E. Africa, 1895-96 ; Vice-Consul in Zanzibar, and for British Sphere E. Coast of Africa, 1896 ; H.M. Consul for Sicily, 1896 ; for Surinam and Cayenne, 1898-1911. *Address:* Frankfort Manor, Sloley, Norfolk. *T.:* Coltishall 31. *T.A.:* Smallburgh. (*Died 6 Feb. 1923.*)

PIGOTT, Montague Horatio Mostyn Turtle, M.A., B.C.L. ; Barrister of the Middle Temple; author and journalist; b. 9 Aug. 1865; s. of late Robert Turtle Pigott, D.C.L.; unmarried. *Educ.:* Westminster School ; University College, Oxford. 2nd class honours in classical moderations and in law ; scholarship in international and constitutional law at the Middle Temple; for ten years coached pupils for the Bar examination. *Publications:* contributor to many papers and magazines, particularly The World ; author and composer of many songs ; author of various lyrics and of a play entitled All Fletcher's Fault, produced at the Avenue Theatre, and of Common Room Carols, Two on a Tour, and Songs of a Session ; Founder and first editor of The Isis. *Recreations:* anything that comes along. *Clubs:* Savage, Beefsteak.

(*Died 26 Aug. 1927.*)

PIGOTT, Sir (Thomas) Digby, Kt., cr. 1906 ; C.B. 1890 ; J.P. Norfolk ; b. 1840 ; s. of Rev. John Pigott and Emma, d. of Abbot Upcher, of Sheringham ; m. 1878, Julia, d. of the Hon. A. H. Macdonald-Moreton, Largie, Argyllshire, M.P. West Gloucestershire ; one s. four d. *Educ.:* Marlborough ; abroad. A clerk in War Office, 1859 ; Private Secretary to Lord Northbrook, 1871-72; to Marquis of Lansdowne, 1872-74: to Earl of Pembroke, 1874-75 ; Secretary to Royal Commission on promotion and retirement for the Army, 1874-76 ; for a short time as private secretary to Mr. Gathorne-Hardy (Earl of Cranbrook), Secretary of State for War, 1877 ; Controller of H.M.'s Stationery Office, 1877-1905: printer to H.M. of all Acts of Parliament, and held under H.M.'s letters patent the copyright in all Government publications, 1888-95. *Publications:* London Birds, and other Sketches; The Changeling ; various magazine articles, chiefly ornithological, etc. *Recreations:* member of British Ornithological Union ; has visited the Shetlands, Holland, Finland, etc., in pursuit of favourite hobby. *Heir:* s. Charles Moreton [b. 1879 ; m. 1909, Renea Leighton, d. of Adm. Sir A. D. Fanshawe]. *Address:* The Lodge, Sheringham, Norfolk. *Club:* Carlton.

(*Died 26 Jan. 1927.*)

PIGOTT, Vice-Adm. William Harvey, J.P. ; b. 8 Mar. 1848 ; o. s. of George Grenville Wandesford Pigott, M.P. (d. 1865), and Charlotte (d. 1883), y. d. of late William Lloyd of Aston Hall, Shropshire ; m. 1886, Edith, 3rd d. of late Richard Thomas Lloyd of Aston Hall, Shropshire ; one d. Vice-Admiral, retired, R.N. ; patron of one living; Order of the Osmanieh, 4th Class. *Address:* Doddershall Park, Aylesbury. (*Died 1 Sept. 1924.*)

PIGOU, Very Rev. Francis, D.D. ; Dean of Bristol since 1891 ; president of Church Choir Guilds ; b. Baden-Baden, 8 Jan. 1832 ; m. 1st, 1859, Mary Somers ; two d. ; 2nd, 1869, Harriet Maude, d. of William and Mrs. Gambier. *Educ.:* Neuwied ; Ripon Grammar School ; Cheltenham Coll. ; Edinburgh Academy ; Trin. Coll. Dublin ; Curate of Stoke Talmage, Oxon. 1855-56 ; Chaplain at Marbœuf Chapel, Paris, 1856-58 ; Readership at St. Peter's, Vere Street, 1858-59 ; Incumbent of St. Philip's, 1862-73 ; Vicar of

Doncaster, 1869-75; Vicar and Rural Dean of Halifax, 1875-88; Hon. Canon of Ripon, 1885-88; Dean of Chichester, 1888-91; Hon. Chaplain-in-Ordinary to Queen Victoria, 1871-74; Chaplain-in-Ordinary, 1874-89. *Publications:* Addresses on Holy Communion; Addresses to my District Visitors, 1895; Addresses to Clergy and Workers; Phases of my Life, 1899; Odds and Ends, 1903; Acts of the Holy Ghost, 1908. *Recreations:* science, especially the microscope. *Address:* Deanery, Bristol. (*Died 25 Jan. 1916.*)

PIKE, Vice-Adm. Frederick Owen (Temp. Capt. R.N.R.); C.M.G. 1918; D.S.O. 1917; *b.* 1851; *s.* of late Capt. T. W. R. Pike, R.N.; *m.* 1893, *d.* of late Judge Pohlman, Melbourne. Vice-Adm., retired, 1911; served European War with R.N.R. (C.M.G., D.S.O.). *Address:* 2 Clifton Villas, Alverstoke, Gosport.
(*Died 5 April 1921.*)

PILCHER, Maj.-Gen. Thomas David, C.B. 1901; *b.* 8 July 1858; *s.* of T. W. Pilcher of Harrow; *m.* 1st, 1889, Kathleen, *d.* of Col. F. Gonne, 17th Lancers, 2nd, 1913, Mrs. J. C. L. Knight-Bruce; two *s.* one *d.* *Educ.:* Harrow. Joined 5th Fusiliers, 1879; Major, 1897; served Niger, 1897-98; raised 1st Batt. W.A.F.F., 1899; commanded expedition to Lapai and Argeyah (despatches, brevet of Lieut.-Col., medal with clasp, promoted to command 2nd Bedfords Regiment; received thanks of H.M.'s Government); South Africa, 1899-1902, in command of a column of mounted men (despatches, prom. Col.); A.D.C. to the King, 1901; Major-Gen. 1907; held various commands in India until 1914; commanded 17th Division B.E.F. in England and France, Jan. 1915-July 1916 (wounded, despatches); contested Thornbury Division, Gloucestershire, Dec. 1918. *Publications:* Lessons from the Boer War; The Writing on the Wall; A General's Letters to his Son; A General's Letters on Minor Tactics; War according to Clausewitz; East is East. *Recreations:* hunting, shooting, fishing, polo. *Club:* Naval and Military.
(*Died 14 Dec. 1928.*)

PILKINGTON, Sir George Augustus, Kt.; *cr.* 1898; J.P.; D.L.; *b.* Upwell, Cambridgeshire, 7 Oct. 1848; *s.* of Robert Gorton Combe, surgeon; *m.* Mary, *d.* of James Pilkington, 1875; two *d.* *Educ.:* privately; Guy's Hospital. Practised medicine in Southport, 1870-84; Mayor of Southport, 1884-85, 1892-93; M.P. Southport Division of Lancashire, 1884-85, 1899-1900; Hon. Lieut. R.N.V.; High Sheriff, Lancashire, 1911-12. *Recreations:* shooting, yachting, cycling; athletics generally. *Address:* Bellevue, Southport; Swinithwaite Hall, Yorks. *T.A.:* Bellevue. *T.:* 177. *M.:* 698. *Clubs:* Reform, National Liberal, Royal Automobile. (*Died 28 Jan. 1916.*)

PIM, Frederic William, Director, and from 1896-1917 Chairman, Dublin and South-Eastern Railway; *b.* Dublin, 1839; *s.* of late Jonathan Pim, M.P., City of Dublin, 1865-74; *m.* 1865, Hannah (*d.* 1876), *d.* of late Joshua Beale of Cork; 2nd, 1882, Mary S. (*d.* 1884), *d.* of late Erasmus C. Pratt of Philadelphia, U.S.A.; two *s.* three *d.* *Educ.:* Bootham School, York; Grove House, Tottenham. *Publications:* The Health of Dublin (three Presidential addresses to the Dublin Sanitary Association, 1890-92); Private Bill Legislation—Suggestions for Devolution to a Permanent Commission, 1896; The Early Friends and War, 1910; The Railways and the State, 1912; The Sinn Fein Rising, 1916; The Mites in the Cheese (the War and the Struggle for Existence), 1918; Home Rule through Federal Devolution, 1919. *Recreation:* gardening. *Address:* Lonsdale, Blackrock, Co. Dublin. *Club:* Royal Irish Yacht, Kingstown. (*Died Jan. 1925.*)

PINE-COFFIN, Major John Edward, D.S.O. 1900; North Lancashire Regt.; *e. s.* of

John Richard Pine-Coffin, J.P. and D.L., of Portledge (*d.*1890),and Matilda, *y. d.* of William Speke, of Jordans, Somerset; *b.* 24 Dec. 1866; *m.* 1894, Louisa Gertrude Douglas, *y. d.* of John Barre Beresford, J.P. and D.L., of Learmount and Ashbrook, Co. Londonderry; two *s.* two *d.* *Educ.:* Eton; Cambridge. Entered army, 1888; Captain, 1898; served South Africa, commanding Mobile Column (despatches, Brevet-Major, Queen's medal, 2 clasps, King's medal, 2 clasps, D.S.O.); appointed to command Mounted Infantry, Egypt, served four years, 1904-8; commanded 2nd Batt. L.N. Lancashire Regiment, Mauritius, 1908-9; retired 1909. *Address:* Portledge, nr. Bideford. (*Died 22 Aug. 1919.*)

PINE-COFFIN, General Roger; *b.* 22 Feb. 1847; *m.* 1876, Flora Isabella, *y. d.* of late Andrew Wilson, Inspector-General of Hospitals, India; one *s.* Entered Royal Marines, 1864; Capt. 1880; Major, 1886; Lt.-Col. 1893; Col. 1901; Major-Gen. 1903; Lt.-Gen. 1910; General, 1911; served Egypt, 1882 (despatches twice, medal with clasp, bronze star, Bt.-Major; Soudan, 1885 (two clasps). *Address:* The Old Hall, Brackley, Northants.(*Died 25 Mar. 1921.*)

PINHEY, Lt.-Col. Sir Alexander Fleetwood, K.C.S.I., *cr.* 1915; C.S.I. 1911; C.I.E. 1901; Indian Army; Resident in Hyderabad; Political Department; *b.* 10 July 1861; *m.* 1891, Violet Beatrice, *d.* of late Gen. Sir Henry Gordon, K.C.B.; three *s.* two *d.* Lieutenant, King's Liverpool Regt., 1882; served in Banswara as Assistant Political Agent and as Supt. Moghia operations, 1886; Political Agent Baghel Khand, 1895; Resident in Mewar, 1900; Resident in Gwalior, 1907; Officiating A.G.G. Rajputana, 1908-9; Private Secretary to Viceroy, 1910. *Address:* The Residency, Hyderabad. *Club:* Junior United Service.
(*Died 7 April 1916.*)

PINK, Sir Thomas, Kt., *cr.* 1904; *b.* London, 5 April 1855; 2nd *s.* of Edward Pink, Portobello Road, Kingsdown, Sevenoaks; *m.* 1st, 1878, Ellen Amelia (*d.* 1917), *o. d.* of Edmund Purssey, Camberwell; two *s.* one *d.*; 2nd, 1918, Minnie Jane, 2nd *d.* of George Brown Davis, A.I.M.E., Westminster. *Educ.:* London. Pres. Grocers' Benevolent Society; Trustee London Commercial Travellers' Benevolent Society; was interested in political work in West Newington, 1895-98. *Recreations:* shooting, tennis, motoring. *Address:* 4 Whitehall Court, S.W.1; *T.:* Victoria 2122; Hambleden Place, Henley-on-Thames; *T.:* Henley 154. *Clubs:* Constitutional, Royal Automobile.
(*Died 23 Jan. 1926.*)

PINKHAM, Rt. Rev. William Cyprian, D.D., D.C.L.; *b.* 1844; *s.* of William Pinkham, Teignmouth, Devon, and St. John's, Newfoundland; *m.* 1868, Jean Anne, 2nd *d.* of late William Drever, Winnipeg; four *s.* four *d.* *Educ.:* St. Augustine's Coll. Canterbury. Incumbent of St. James's, Manitoba, 1868-82; Superintendent of Education for Protestant Public Schools of Manitoba, 1871-83; B.D. by Archbishop of Canterbury, 1880; Archdeacon of Manitoba and Canon of St. John's Cathedral, Winnipeg, 1882-87; Acting Rector, All Saints', Winnipeg, 1888-84; Secretary of Synod, 1882-1887; Bishop of Saskatchewan, 1887-1903; Bishop of Calgary, 1888-1926; Chairman Board of Education, N.W.T., from 1887 for several years. Hon. D.C.L., Trinity University, Toronto; University of Alberta; Hon. D.D. University of Manitoba, 1887. *Address:* 603 13th Avenue, Calgary, Alberta, Canada.
(*Died July 1928.*)

PIPON, Maj.-Gen. Henry, late R.A., C.B. 1900; Major of the Tower of London, 1909-28; *b.* 4 Dec. 1843; 2nd *s.* of Colonel Pipon of Noirmont Manor, Jersey; *m.* 1872, Louisa Anne (*d.* 1921), *d.* of Admiral Sir William Edmonstone, 4th Bt., C.B., of Duntreath, Stirling-

840

PILLANS, Charles Eustace. See page xxviii.

shire. *Educ.:* Woolwich. Entered Royal Artillery, 1861; served in Fenian Raid, Canada, 1866 (medal and clasp); in R.H.A. during Afghan Campaign of 1879-81, including actions at Shutagandau, Charasia, and subsequent operations at Kabul; Adjutant R.A. on march to Kandahar; battle of Kandahar (medal and three clasps and bronze star, despatches thrice); commanded R.A., China Field Force, 1900-1901 (despatches, medal). *(Died 14 Jan. 1924.)*

PIRIE, Major Arthur Murray, D.S.O. 1898; late serving with Egyptian Army; *b.* 3 May 1869; 3rd *s.* of Gordon Pirje of Waterton; *m.* 1907, Marie Valerie, *d.* of Philip Gurdon and widow of Claude Loraine; one *d.* Entered 21st Lancers, 1889; Captain, 1899; served Soudan, 1898, including Khartoum (despatches, D.S.O., British medal, Khedive's medal with clasp, 4th class Medjidie); retired, 1906. *Club:* Cavalry. *(Died 21 Nov. 1917.)*

PIRRIE, 1st Viscount, *cr.* 1921; **William James Pirrie,** 1st Baron, *cr.* 1906; K.P.; P.C., 1897; LL.D.; D.Sc.; Controller-General of Merchant Shipbuilding, March 1918; H.M.'s Lieut. Co. of City of Belfast, 1911; J.P. for the City of Belfast and also for Co. Antrim and Co. Down; Ex-Comptroller of the Household of the Lord-Lieutenant of Ireland; Pro-Chancellor of Queen's University, Belfast; *b.* Quebec, 31 May 1847; *o. s.* of late James Alex. Pirrie of Little Clandeboye, Co. Down, and Eliza, *d.* of Alexander Montgomery of Dundesart, County Antrim; *m.* 1879, Margaret Montgomery, *d.* of John Carlisle, M.A., of Belfast. *Educ.:* Belfast Royal Academical Institution. Entered Harland and Wolff's shipbuilding and engineering establishment, 1862; became partner in 1874, and is now chairman; Lord Mayor of Belfast, 1896-97; High-Sheriff of Co. Antrim, 1898, and Co. Down, 1899; first Hon. Freeman of the City of Belfast, 1898. *Heir:* none. *Address:* 24 Belgrave Square, S.W.1; *T.:* Victoria 278; Witley Park, Godalming; Ormiston, Strandtown, Belfast. *Clubs:* Reform; Kildare Street, Dublin; Ulster, Belfast.
(Died 7 June 1924.)

PITCHER, Colonel Duncan George; *b.* 2 Nov. 1839; *e. s.* of late Lt. and Adjt. St. Vincent Pitcher, 6th Madras Lt. Cavalry, and Rose, *d.* of Admiral George Le Geyt, C.B.; *m.* 1867, Rose, *d.* of Capt. J. C. Evison, R.N.; one *s.* six *d. Educ.:* Christ's Hospital; Victoria College, Jersey; R.N. College, Portsmouth. Joined H.M.S. Excellent as marine cadet, 1856; 2nd Lt. R.M.L.I. 1856; qualified for the R.M. Artillery (1st class certificates in naval gunnery and steam); Ensign 5th Fusiliers, 1858; passed at Sandhurst for a direct Commission in November 1855, but elected to remain with R.M.A.; resigned Commission in R.M.A. on being appointed Cornet Bombay Lt. Cavalry, 1859; proceeded to India, 1859, and served successively with 6th Inniskilling Dragoons, 3rd Bombay Lt. Cavalry, 3rd Southern Maratha Horse, and 21st Hussars (1862 - 68); Interpreter, Adjt., and Musketry Instructor, 1865-67; qualified as Military Engineer and Surveyor; transferred to Bengal S.C. and to 5th Bengal Cavalry, 1868; various Revenue, Judicial, and Magisterial posts in the United Provinces, 1868 - 90; special thanks from Secretary of State, 1872, for a scheme of Agricultural Banks, and of Govt. of India for unravelling a pension fraud at Lucknow, and saving for Govt. £5000 a year, 1872; also thanks from Govt. of India and Local Govt. on many occasions, particularly for special inquiries and reports on Forest Consy. in Oudh, 1876; famine mortality in Rohilkand, 1878; working of Oudh Rent Acts, 1883; emigration of natives from India to the Colonies, 1882; effecting an economy in printing and stationery of 1 Lakh rupees p.a. (1889), and for work in connection with Indian Arts and Crafts,

carried out on behalf of the U.P., for exhibitions held in various years at Amsterdam, Vienna, Paris, Calcutta, Lucknow, and London; in 1890 deputed by Indian Foreign Office to the Maratha State of Gwalior to organise a Dept. of Land Records, Cadastral Survey, and Revenue Settlement; remained so employed until departure from India in 1903; famine commissioner for Gwalior through two famines; Kaiser-i-Hind medal, 1st class, for public service in India, 1901; Medaille du Roi Albert, 1921, for services during the war to the Belgian cause; Hon. Secretary Huguenot Society of London; Member Genealogical Society; Fellow Royal Colonial Institute; Member R.U.S. Institution. *Address:* c/o Child and Co., 1 Fleet Street, E.C.4.

PITCHER, William J.C., R.I.; *b.* Northfleet, Kent, 21 March 1858; *s.* of Henry Sotheby Pitcher, ship-builder; artist and designer for the stage under pseudonym of C, Wilhelm; self trained as draughtsman; while still a youth, keenly interested in the art of the theatre; was recommended by J. R. Planché to E. L. Blanchard, to design costumes for Drury Lane Pantomime, resulting in a wide connection for similar work on fantastic and romantic lines, not only in long series with big spectacular scenes at Drury Lane for Sir Augustus Harris, but also the ballets, often entirely invented and produced by him, at the Empire Theatre from 1887-1915, including among many others Orféo, Faust, The Press, Les Papilious, Old China, Féte Galante, The Débutante, The Vine, Cinderella; and similar works at the Crystal Palace and the Lyceum for Mr. Oscar Barrett; was associated with Mr. Seymour Lucas, R.A., in the spectacular drama, The Armada, at Drury Lane, 1888; designed the important Olympia productions Nero and Venice for Imre Kiralfy, 1889 - 91; the Gilbert and Sullivan operas at the Savoy, Iolanthe, Princess Ida, The Mikado, and Ruddigore; Mr. Courtneidge's productions of Midsummer Night's Dream and As You Like It; Edward German's Opera Tom Jones, 1907; The Arcadians, 1909; The Mousmé Japanese Opera, 1911; Young England, Elizabethan Opera, 1917; wrote and decorated historical ballet, La Camargo, for Mlle. Genée, at Coliseum, 1912; Elected Member of the Royal Institute of Painters in Water Colours, 1919. *Publications:* The Art of the Theatre in several articles in The Magazine of Art. *Recreations:* listening to good music; contemplating beauty in Nature; congenial work. *Address:* 122 Coleherne Court, Earls Court, S.W.5. *T.:* Kensington 4187. *(Died 2 Mar. 1925.)*

PITMAN, Captain Robert, R.N., O.M.G 1903; *b.* 15 Feb. 1836; *m.* 1869, Elizabeth (*d.* 1917), *d.* of Andrew Howard of Ringmore, Devon. Entered Navy, 1849; Lieut. 1856; Commander, 1867; Captain retired, 1882; served Baltic, 1854-55 (medal); Chief Superintendent under Board of Trade for carrying out the scheme (originated by him) for transmitting seamen's wages and sending them to their homes from English and Continental ports, 1875-1908. *Address:* 122 Inverness Terrace, W.2. *T.:* Park 259. *Club:* United Service. *(Died 4 Jan. 1921.)*

PITTAR, Sir Thomas John, K.C.B., *cr.* 1905; C.B. 1899; C.M.G. 1903; *b.* 29 Oct. 1846; 3rd *s.* of late Thomas J. Pittar, Hove, Sussex, and Margaret Waring, Waringstown, Ireland; *m.* 1870, Annie Frances, 2nd *d.* of late Thomas Letts of Chale, Isle of Wight; three *s.* one *d.* Late Member of Council, Royal Statistical Society; Commissioner of Customs, 1900; Principal expert to the British Delegation at the Brussels Sugar Conference, 1901-1902; Assistant British Delegate to the Brussels Permanent Commission, 1908; Principal of the Statistical Office, Board of Customs, 1889-1900; edited the Board of Trade Returns relating to the trade of the United Kingdom, 1889-1900; Chairman, Board of Customs, 1908-1908. *(Died 20 July 1924.)*

PITTS, Thomas, C.B. 1908; Assistant Secretary Local Government Board, 1897-1917; *b.* 1857; *s.* of late John Pitts, of Inland Revenue Department, London. *Address:* Taplow, Bucks. *Club:* Isthmian. *(Died 5 Sept. 1919.)*

PLANT, Morton F.; *s.* of late H. B. Plant. Chairman of Board and Director Southern Express Co.; Vice-President and Director Chicago, Indianapolis, and Louisville Ry. Co.; Vice-President and Director Peninsular and Occidental Steamship Co.; Director Atlantic Coast Line R.R. Co.; Interborough Rapid Transit Co.; Interborough-Metropolitan Co.; Lincoln Trust Co.; Windsor Trust Co.; Bowling Green Trust Co.; National Bank of Commerce of New London Casualty Company; of America. *Address:* 2 East 52nd Street, New York; Groton, Conn., U.S.A.
(Died 5 Nov. 1918.)

PLATT, J. Arthur, M.A.; Professor of Greek in University College, London, since 1894; *b.* 11 July 1860; *m.* 1885, Mildred Barham, *d.* of Sir Edward Bond, K.C.B., LL.D. *Educ.:* Harrow; Trinity College, Cambridge (Fellow). Worked at Wren's, 1886-94. *Publications:* an edition of Homer's Iliad and Odyssey; translations of Aristotle's De Generatione Animalium and Aeschylus' Agamemnon; various papers on classical subjects. *Address:* 5 Chester Terrace, N.W.1. *T.:* Museum 5477.*(Died 16 Mar. 1925.)*

PLATTS, Thomas, I.S.O. 1902; *b.* Chatham, 24 Oct. 1843; *s.* of Thomas Platts, of Chatham, and *g. s.* of Thomas Platts, R.M.L.I.; *m.* 1870. *Educ.:* private schools; Chatham. Clerk, Paymaster's Department, 1st Division Royal Engineers, Chatham and Southampton, 1861-64; Writer, Chatham Dockyard, 1864-70; Admiralty, 1870-76; 2nd Division Clerk, 1876-95; Staff Clerk, 1895-1908. *Address:* Claremont Villa, 15 Decimus Burton Road, Thornton Heath, Surrey.
(Died 13 Mar. 1919.)

PLAYFAIR, Arthur Wyndham, actor; *b.* Elichpoor, India, 20 Oct. 1869; *y. s.* of late Maj.-Gen. A. L. Playfair; *m.* 1912, Laurie (*d.* 1917), *d.* of Alexander Stevens. *Educ.:* The Oratory, Edgbaston; Oxford Military College. Started on stage, August bank holiday, 1887; favourite part — Preserving Mr. Panmure. *Recreations:* golf, lawn tennis. *Address:* 109 Park Road, N.W. *(Died 28 Aug. 1918.)*

PLAYFAIR, George Macdonald Home, M.A.; H.B.M. Consul, Foochow, 1899; retired, 1910; *b.* Shahjehanpore, India, 22 Aug. 1850; *s.* of Surg.-Gen. George R. Playfair, M.D.; *m.* 1884, Winifred May Fraser; one *d. Educ.:* Cheltenham; Trinity College, Dublin. Entered Consular Service in China, 1872; Vice-Consul, Shanghai, 1891; Consul at Pakhoi, 1894; at Ningpo, 1894. *Publication:* Cities and Towns of China. *Address:* c/o Keymer, Son & Co., 1 Whitefriars Street, E.C. *Clubs:* Thatched House; Royal and Ancient Golf, St. Andrews.
(Died 29 Aug. 1917.)

PLAYFAIR, Rev. Patrick M., M.A. (Edin.), D.D. (St. Andrews); T.D.; Minister of the First Charge, St. Andrews, since 1899; Chaplain to the 7th Batt. The Black Watch, 1899-1921; Officiating Chaplain to Presbyterians on ships of the R.N. at St. Andrews; Chaplain to the Royal and Ancient Golf Club since 1899; *b.* 5 Nov. 1858; *y. s.* of Rev. D. Playfair (B.A. Cantab.), Abercorn, Linlithgowshire; *m.* 1888, Eliza Anne, *d.* of late John Walker, W.S.; one *s.* one *d. Educ.:* Blair Lodge; Edinburgh University (Neil Arnott Scholar in Physics, Herbarium Gold Medalist). Assistant Minister in St. Stephen's Parish, Edinburgh, 1882-86; Minister of Glencairn Parish, Dumfriesshire, 1886-99; occasional preacher to Queen Victoria and King George in Scotland. *Recreations:* field botany and gardening. *Address:* Wyvern,

842

St. Andrews, Fife. *T.:* St. Andrews 63. *Club:* Royal and Ancient Golf, St. Andrews.
(Died 6 Oct. 1924.)

PLEYDELL-BOUVERIE, Rev. Hon. Bertrand, M.A., Hon. Canon of Salisbury; J.P. Wilts. Clerk in Holy Orders—retired; *b.* 23 April 1845; 4th *s.* of 4th Earl of Radnor; *m.* 1870, Lady Constance Jane (*d.* 1922), 2nd *d.* of 3rd Earl Nelson. *Educ.:* Harrow; Trinity Col., Cambridge. Curate, Halesowen, nr. Birmingham, 1869-70; Rector of Stanton St. Quentin, nr. Chippenham, 1870-80; Rector of Pewsey, Wilts, 1880-1910; has held winter chaplaincies at S. Raphael, 1910-11; Beaulieu, 1911-12-13; Madeira, 1914-15. *Publication:* A Children's Service Book—with Hymns. *Recreations:* water-colour sketching, wood and marble carving, etc. *Address:* 32 Stourcliffe Avenue, West Southbourne, Hants. *(Died 7 Nov. 1926.)*

PLIMMER, Henry George, F.R.S., F.L.S., F.R.M.S., M.R.C.S. (Eng.); Professor of Comparative Pathology in the Imperial College of Science and Technology, S. Kensington; *b.* Melksham, Wilts; *m.* 1887, Helena, *d.* of Alfred Aders. *Educ.:* Guy's Hospital. Fellow Royal Society of Medicine; Member Royal Institution; Fellow Philharmonic Society; late President of the Royal Microscopical Society, 1911-12, Prosector Royal College of Surgeons, Pathologist and Lecturer on Pathology and Bacteriology, St. Mary's Hospital, London. *Publications:* various papers in Proceedings of the Royal Society; Reports of Sleeping Sickness Committee of the Royal Society; Centralblatt für Bakteriologie; Proceedings of Zoological Society, Lancet, Nature, Revue Scientifique, Science Progress, etc. *Address:* 32 Queen's Road, N.W.8. *Club:* Savile.
(Died 22 June 1918.)

PLOWDEN, Sir Henry Meredyth, Kt., *cr.* 1887; *b.* 26 Sep. 1840; *m.* 1887, Helen, *e. d.* of late Sir Cecil Beadon, K.C.S.I.: two *d. Educ.:* Harrow; Trinity College, Cambridge (B.A. 1863). Barr. Lincoln's Inn, 1866; Government Advocate at Lahore, 1870-77; Judge of Chief Court, Punjab, 1877; Senior Judge, 1880-94. *Recreations:* Harrow XI., 1858; Cambridge University XI., 1860-63; Captain, 1862-63; University Challenge Racquet, 1862; Cambridge and Oxford Racquet, 1863. *Club:* Royal Societies.
(Died 8 Jan. 1920.)

PLUMMER, Rev. Alfred, D.D.; *b.* Heworth, near Gateshead, 17 Feb. 1841; 3rd *s.* of Rev. Matthew Plummer and Louisa, *d.* of late J. D. Powles; *m.* 29 Dec. 1874, Bertha Katharine, *d.* of Rev. W. F. Everest, Canon of Truro; one *s.* one *d. Educ.:* Lancing Coll.; Exeter Coll. Oxford. Fellow Trinity Coll., Oxford, 1865-75; Tutor and Dean, 1867-74; Master of University College, Durham, 1874-1902; Sub-Warden University of Durham, 1896-1902. *Publications:* Translations of several of Dr. Döllinger's works, 1870-75; Commentaries on 2 St. Peter and St. Jude, 1879; St. John's Gospel and Epistles, 1880-86; The Pastoral Epistles, 1889; Epistles of St. James and St. Jude, 1890; Introduction to Joshua and Nehemiah, 1881; Handbook on the Church of the Early Fathers, 1887; Commentary on St. Luke's Gospel, 1896; 2 Corinthians, 1903, enlarged 1914; St. Matthew, 1909; St. Mark, 1914; Lectures on English Church History (1575-1649), 1904; Lectures on English Church History (1509-1575), 1905; Lectures on English Church History (1649-1702), 1906; The Church of England in the 18th Century, 1910; The Churches in Britain before A.D. 1000, 1911; The Humanity of Christ, and other Sermons, 1913; 1 and 2 Thessalonians, 1918; Philippians, 1919. *Address:* Dulany, Bideford, Devon. *(Died 17 April 1926.)*

PLUMMER, Rev. Charles, Fellow and Chaplain of Corpus Christi College, Oxford; *b.* St. Leonards-on-Sea, 24 Jan. 1851; 5th *s.* of Rev. Matthew and Louisa Plummer. *Educ.:*

PITTI, Sir Thyagaraya Chetti Garum, Diwan Bahadur, Kt. See page xxviii.

St. Michael's College, Tenbury; Magdalen College School, Oxford; Corpus Christi College, Oxford (Scholar). 1st Class Classical Moderations, 1871; 1st Class Final Classics, 1873; B.A., S.C.L. and Fellow of C.C.C., 1873; M.A., 1876; Deacon, and Chaplain of C.C.C., 1875; Senior Proctor of University of Oxford, 1890-91; Ford's Lecturer in English History, 1901; Select Preacher, 1918-20; Hon. D.D. Durham, 1921; Hon. D.Litt. Dublin, 1923; Fellow of the British Academy, 1924; Hon. Member of the Royal Irish Academy, 1925; Hon. D.Litt. Celt. National University of Ireland, 1925; various College offices at different times. *Publications*: Life and Times of Alfred the Great, 1902; Editor of Fortescue's Governance of England, 1885; Elizabethan Oxford, 1887; Baedae Venerabilis Opera Historica, 2 vols., 1896; Vitae Sanctorum Hiberniae, 2 vols., 1910; Bethada Naem nErenn (Lives of Irish Saints), 2 vols., 1922; Miscellanea Hagiographica Hibernica, 1925; Irish Litanies, 1925; Colophons and Marginalia of Irish Scribes, 1926; Devotions from Ancient and Mediaeval Sources, 1916; Joint Editor two of the Saxon Chronicles Parallel, vol. i., 1892; vol. ii., 1899. *Recreations*: walking, music. *Address*: Corpus Christi College, Oxford; 95 London Road, Salisbury.
(Died 8 Sept. 1927.)

PLUMMER, Sir Walter Richard, Kt., cr. 1904; D.C.L.; J.P.; Plummer and Co., merchants; Alderman of Newcastle; Director N.E.R. Co., Northern Counties Newspaper Co., Newcastle and Gateshead Gas Co., and of The Wallsend Slipway and Engineering Co., Ltd.; b. Newcastle, 8 Nov. 1858; M.P. (C.) Newcastle-on-Tyne, 1900-1906; contested same Division 1906 and 1910. *Address*: 4 Queen Square, Newcastle. *Clubs*: Carlton, Constitutional.
(Died 10 Dec. 1917.)

PLUMMER, William Edward, Director of Liverpool Observatory; Astronomer to the Mersey Docks and Harbour Board; Hon. Reader in Astronomy, University of Liverpool, since 1900; late President of Liverpool Astronomical Society; b. Deptford, 26 March 1849; y. s. of John Plummer; m. Sarah (d. 1927); two s. one d. *Educ.*: privately; Oxford (Hon. M.A.); F.R.A.S. Entered Royal Observatory, Greenwich; assistant to Dr. J. R. Hind at Mr. Bishop's Observatory, Twickenham; senior assistant at Oxford University Observatory; appointed Examiner in Astronomy to the University of Edinburgh, 1895. *Publications*: On the Motion of the Solar System; Researches in Cometary Astronomy; Annual Reports from the Liverpool Observatory; Examination of Anemometer Records, 1896; Great Cluster in Hercules, 1905. *Recreation*: chess. *Address*: Liverpool Observatory, Bidston, Birkenhead. *T.A.*: Neptune, Liverpool. *T.*: 455 Birkenhead.
(Died 22 May 1928.)

PLUNKET, 5th Baron (cr. 1827), **William Lee Plunket**, G.C.M.G., cr. 1910; K.C.M.G., cr. 1905; K.C.V.O.; K.B.E., cr. 1918; D.L., J.P. Co. Dublin; J.P. Co. Wicklow; b. 19 . December 1864; s. of 4th Baron (Archbishop of Dublin and Primate of Ireland) and Anne Lee, o. d. of Sir Benjamin Lee Guinness, Bt., and sister of Lords Ardilaun and Iveagh (d. 1889); S. father 1897: m. 1894, Victoria Alexandrina, y. d. of Frederick, 1st Marquess of Dufferin and Ava, K.P.; three s. four d. *Educ.*: Harrow; Trin. Coll., Dublin (B.A.). Honorary Attaché to the Embassy at Rome, 1889-92, Constantinople, 1892; retired 1894; Private Sec. to Lords-Lieut. of Ireland, 1900-4; Governor of New Zealand, 1904-10. *Heir*: s. Hon. Terence Conyngham Plunket. *Address*: 40 Elvaston Place, S.W.7; Old Connaught House, Bray, Co. Wicklow. *Clubs*: Carlton; Kildare Street, Dublin: Royal St. George's Yacht, Kingstown.
(Died 24 Jan. 1920.)

PLUNKET, Hon. Emmeline Mary; b. 1835; d. of 3rd Baron Plunket. *Publications*: Merry Games in Rhyme from the Olden Time, 1886; Very Short Stories in Very Short Words, 1887; Ancient Calendars and Constellations, 1903; The Judgment of Paris, and some other legends astronomically considered. *Address*: 19 The Grove, Boltons, S.W.
(Died 6 April 1924.)

PLUNKETT, Brig.-Gen. Edward Abadie, C.B.E. 1919; s. of late Lt.-Col. G. T. Plunkett of Belvedere Lodge, Wimbledon; b. 1870; m. Grace Mary, d. of Col. T. Morgan Martin; one d. Served in Nile Expedition, 1898 (despatches); Balkan War, 1912-13, as Military Attaché; Great War, 1914-19 (despatches); employed in Persia under foreign department Govt. of India, 1903-4; Military Attaché at Belgrade, Sofia, Athens, and Bucharest, and chief of military missions at Belgrade, Athens, and Sofia, 1913-22; formerly Lincolnshire Regt.; retired with hon. rank of Brigadier-General. *Address*: 8 Moore Street, Cadogan Square, S.W. *Club*: Naval and Military.
(Died 8 June 1926.)

PLUNKETT, Lt.-Col. George Tindall, retired R.E.; C.B. 1901; Director of Science and Art Institutions, Dublin, 1895-1907; b. 8 Aug. 1842; s. of late V. W. Plunkett, Blackheath Park; m. 1865, Emily Marian (d. 1912), d. of late G. B. Richardson, Blackheath; one s. one d. *Educ.*: R.M.A. Woolwich. M.R.A.S., F.R.G S. Entered army, 1862; Lt.-Col. 1889; retired, 1894; served Soudan, 1885. *Address*: Belvedere Lodge, Wimbledon. *Club*: Travellers'.
(Died 2 May 1922.)

PLYMOUTH, 1st Earl of, cr. 1905, **Robert George Windsor-Clive**; Viscount Windsor (U.K. 1905); 14th Baron Windsor (Eng., cr. 1529); G.B.E., cr. 1918; C.B. 1905; P.C., D.L., J.P.; Lord-Lieutenant of Glamorganshire since 1890; High Steward of Cambridge University, 1919; Hon. Col. of 2nd Glamorganshire Vol. Artillery since 1890; of 2nd Batt. Worcestershire Regt. since 1891; of 3rd Batt. Welsh Regt.; b. 27 Aug. 1857; s. of Hon. Robert Windsor Clive, M.P.; g.s. of Baroness Windsor, and of Mary, d. of 2nd Earl Bradford; S. grandmother, 1869; m. 1883, Alberta, d. of Rt. Hon. Sir Augustus Berkeley Paget; one s. one d. *Educ.*: Eton; St. John's Coll. Camb. (M.A., Hon. LL.D.). Mayor of Cardiff, 1895-96; Paymaster-General, 1891-92; 1st Commissioner of Works, 1902-5; Sub-Prior Order of St. John of Jerusalem. *Publication*: John Constable, R.A., 1903. Owns about 30,500 acres. *Heir*: s. Viscount Windsor. *Address*: Hewell Grange, Redditch; St. Fagan's Castle, Cardiff. *Clubs*: Carlton, Bachelors', Marlborough, St. Stephen's.
(Died 6 Mar. 1923.)

POCOCK, Sir Charles Guy Coventry, 4th Bt.; cr. 1821; b. 3 Nov. 1863; s. of Alfred George Drake Pocock, 3rd s. of 2nd Bt., and Mary, d. of Charles Culverhouse; S. uncle 1915. *Heir*: none. *(Died 31 Mar. 1921.)*

PODMORE, Edward Boyce; b. 13 June 1860; s. of Rev. J. Buckley Podmore, B.A., Rector of Cowfold, Sussex. Hunts own hounds, riding nearly 18 stone; won prizes at boxing, rowing, riding, running, and bicycle riding; a pilot certificate of Shoreham Harbour, and Master of his own yacht; and recognised as one of the leading amateur four-in-hand whips of the day; ran his own coach, the "Star," between Kenilworth and Stratford-on-Avon 5 years, without being late, into either place; and late Master of Vine and Cotswold Foxhounds; joint Master, with Earl De La Warr, of Bexhill Harriers. *Address*: Petworth, Sussex. *T.A.*: Podmore, Petworth. *T.*: Petworth 18.
(Died 15 Jan. 1928.)

POE, Admiral Sir Edmund (Samuel), G.C.V.O. cr. 1912; K.C.B., cr. 1908; K.C.V.O., cr. 1906; C.V.O. 1903; M.V.O. 1896; J.P. for

Queen's County; Commander - in - Chief, Mediterranean Station, 1910-12; *s.* of William T. Poe, barrister-at-law, Glen Ban, Abbeyleix, and Curraghmore, Co. Tipperary; *b.* 11 Sept. 1849; *m.* 1877, Frances, *e. d.* of late Gen. Sir Justin Sheil, K.C.B.; two *s.* one *d.* *Educ.:* Royal Naval Academy, Gosport. Entered navy, 1862; served in H.M.S. "Bombay" when destroyed by fire off Monte Video, 1864; Captain, 1888; Naval Adviser to Inspector-General of Fortifications, 1889-90; has commanded H.M.S. "Imperieuse," "Blenheim," "Victorious," "Active," "Raleigh," and "St. George"; in command of the Training Squadron as Commodore, 2nd class, 1897-1900; second in command of the Home Fleet, 1903; Commanding First Cruiser Squadron, 1904-5; Commander-in-Chief, East Indies, 1905-7; Cape of Good Hope, 1907-8; received Royal Humane Society's bronze medal for saving life in 1875, and the clasp in 1876; Queen's Jubilee medal, 1897; King's Coronation medal, 1911; has received the Grand Cordon of the Osmanieh, and is a Grand Officer of the Legion of Honour; attached to Prince Arthur of Connaught's Funeral and Garter Mission to Japan, 1912; Grand Cordon of the Rising Sun of Japan with Paulownia Flower; A.D.C. to the Queen, 1899: to the King, 1901. First and Principal Naval A.D.C. to the King, 1912-14; retired, Sep. 1914; Member of the Imperial War Graves Commission, 1917. *Recreations:* shooting, fishing, cycling. *Address:* Black Hill, Abbeyleix, Queen's Co. *T.A.:* Black Hill, Abbeyleix. *T.:* Maryborough Area, Abbeyleix 11. *Clubs:* United Service; Royal Naval, Portsmouth; Kildare Street, Dublin. (*Died 4 April 1921.*)

POLACK, Rudolph, J.P., LL.D. (St. Andrews); ex-President, Dundee Chamber of Commerce; Councillor, Dundee University College; Director, Dundee Orphan Institution; *b.* 1842; *m.* Franziska, *d.* of Gustav Weil, Professor of Oriental Languages; one *s.* one *d.* Mercantile education and career. *Address:* Glamis House, Dundee. *T.A.:* Polack, Dundee. *T.:* 2450. *Club:* Eastern, Dundee. (*Died 17 Feb. 1917.*)

POLAND, Sir Harry (Bodkin), Kt., *cr.* 1895; K.C.; J.P., D.L.; *b.* London, 9 July 1829; 6th *s.* of late Peter Poland, merchant, London and Highgate; unmarried. *Educ.:* St. Paul's School. Barr. 1851; Bencher Inner Temple, 1879; for many years one of the counsel to the Treasury and Home Office; retired from practice, 1895; Recorder of Dover, 1874-1901; for some years Alderman of the L.C.C.; Hon. Freeman of Dover. *Publications:* has written various articles and letters on the reform of the law *Address:* 28 Sloane Gardens, S.W.; 5 Paper Buildings, Temple, E.C. *Clubs:* Garrick, Junior Carlton. (*Died 2 Mar. 1928.*)

POLAND, Vice-Adm. James Augustus; *b.* 1832; *m.* 1883, *d.* of late W. O. Markham, F.R.C.P.; two *d.* Naval Cadet, 1846; served as Lieutenant and Gunnery Officer in the Baltic and Black Sea during the Russian War, 1854-56; in China War, 1857-60; in Naval Brigade at capture of Canton; also against the Taiping rebels around Shanghai, 1860; engaged as Senior Lieutenant in H.M.S. Pearl in the attack and destruction of the forts and batteries of Kagosima, Japan, 1863; (promoted Commander); commanded H.M.S. Plover on West Coast of Africa, 1868-71; Captain, 1871; commanded H.M.S. Juno, China, 1875-79; Valiant, Coast Guard District on West Coast of Ireland, 1880-83; Duncan Flagship at Sheerness, 1883-86; retired, 1886; Rear-Admiral, 1888; Vice-Admiral, 1893. *Address:* 4 Cresswell Gardens, South Kensington, S.W. *T.:* 1660, Kensington. *Clubs:* United Service, Junior Carlton. (*Died 14 Mar. 1918.*)

POLE, Sir Frederick Arundell de la, 11th Bt.; *cr.* 1628; *b.* 25 Dec. 1850; *s.* of 9th

Bt. and Margaret Victorioaa, 2nd *d.* of Admiral Hon. Sir John Talbot, G.C.B.; *S.* brother, 1912. J.P. Devon, 1916; High Sheriff, Devon, 1917. Owns about 4600 acres. *Heir: c.* John Gower Pole-Carew, *b.* 1902. *Address:* Shute House, Kilmington, Devon. (*Died 12 Feb. 1926.*)

POLIGNANO, 6th Duke of, **James Edwin-Cole,** F.R.Hist.S., J.P., Barrister-at-Law of the Inner Temple; 2nd but *o. surv. s.* of John Cole (*de jure,* Duke and Marquis of Polignano) of Easthorpe Court, Co. Lincoln, and Susanna, *d.* of Capt. John Bourchier, R.N., Lieut.-Gov. of Greenwich Hospital, and 2nd wife, Charlotte, *d.* of Thomas Corbett of Darnhall, Cheshire, and Elsham, Lincolnshire, and Elizabeth, sole heiress of Humphrey Edwin of Lincoln's Inn and St. Albans. As sole heir and direct lineal representative of Elisabeth, *e. d.* of Don Gaetano de Leto, who inherited the Marquisate of Polignano (*cr.* 1495), confirmed to him 1729 by the Emperor Charles VI. of Austria, and who was in 1730 by that monarch created Duke of Polignano, with remainder to his descendants of both sexes in order of primogeniture, established his right in 1905 to these dignities, which had been dormant since the death in 1854, without issue, of Don Camillo de Leto, Duke of Polignano; *m.* Mary Barbara (*d.* 1910), *d.* of G. Huddleston. *Publications:* The Genealogy of the Cole Family; A Genealogical Memoir of the Family of Bourchier; Memoir of the Family of Edwin; contributor under pseudonyms to The Herald and Genealogist, The Genealogist, Notes and Queries, etc. *Recreations:* historical and genealogical researches, horticulture, riding, continental travel. *Address:* Brampton Manor, near Huntingdon.
(*Died 18 Sept. 1920.*)

POLLARD, Rear-Adm. Geo. Northmore Arthur, R.N.; *b.* 17 March 1847; *s.* of G. A. Pollard of Castlepollard, Ireland, and A. D. Smith of Leicester; *m.* 1880, N. E. Wright, *widow* of Major Wright, 70th Regiment, and *d.* of Rev. G. Garrett of Kilmeagne, Co. Kildare. *Educ.:* Exeter. Entered Royal Navy, 1861; Lieutenant, 1871; Commander, 1885; Captain, 1894; Rear-Adm., 1905; served Canada, 1861 (medal with clasp); Ashantee War, 1873-74 (despatches, medals); Captain in charge, Ascension Island, 1899-1902; held the usual commands to the time of his retirement, 1902, under the age clause; no opportunity for special distinction. *Address:* Parkmount, Kent Road. Southsea.
(*Died Dec. 1920.*)

POLLEN, John, C.I.E. 1903; Lt.-Col. B.V.R.; V.D.; Barrister-at-Law; M.T.; B.A.; LL.D., T.C.D.; Hon. Fellow Bombay University; Commissioner of Customs, 1898, and additional member of Legislative Council, Bombay, 1902; President of Civil and Military Exam. Board in Arabic, Persian, Marathi, etc., 1898; *b.* 3 June 1848; *m.* 1880, Mary, 3rd *d.* of Colonel T. Haggard, R.A.; two *s.* two *d.* *Educ.:* Stackpooles; Trin. Coll. Dublin. Entered I.C.S. 1871; served as Assistant Collector and Magistrate in Khandesh, 1871; on famine relief duty in Bengal, 1874; on special settlement duty, 1876; Acting Under-Sec. to Govt. of Bombay, 1880; Assist.-Commissioner and Inspector-General of Registration and Stamps, Sind, 1881; Sindi translator to Government, 1882; Political Supt. and Civil Judge, Thar and Parkar; Acting Collector and Magistrate, Hyderabad, 1887, of Broach, Ratnagiri, and Panch Mahals; Interpreter in Russian and Reporter General External Commerce, 1890; Junior Collector and Magistrate, 1892; Political Agent, Rewa Kantha; Senior Collector, 1896; Political Officer in charge of the fifteen Indian representative guests of Crown at Coronation of King Edward VII. (thanks from Secretary of State); Special Correspondent Daily Mail, St. Petersburg, 1905; President British Esperanto Association, 1904; on special duty with H.H. the

Nawab of Radhanpur, 1906-7 ; President of Third International Congress of Esperantists, Cambridge, 1907 ; Hon. Sec. East India Association, 1909-20 ; Kaiser-i-Hind Gold medal. *Publications:* Rhymes from the Russian ; Omar Khayyám ; Russian Songs and Lyrics. *Clubs:* National Liberal, Northbrook, Polyglot.
(Died June 1923.)

POLLEN, Rev. John Hungerford, S.J. ; writer on English Catholic history ; *b.* London, 1858 ; *s.* of late J. H. Pollen, M.A., artist. *Educ.:* Germany ; Oratory School ; B.A. Lond. Entered Society of Jesus, 1877 ; Priest, 1891 ; has made prolonged archive studies at the Vatican, Paris, and elsewhere ; a founder of the Catholic Record Society. *Publications:* Papal Negotiations with Queen Mary Stuart, M.S. and the Babington Plot (Scottish History Society, 1901, 1922) ; Letter of Queen Mary to the Duke of Guise *(ibid.,* 1904) ; Unpublished Documents relating to the English Martyrs (Catholic Record Society, 1908, 1919) ; Institution of Archpriest Blackwell, 1916 ; Acts of English Martyrs, 1891 ; English Catholics in the Reign of Queen Elizabeth, 1920 : The Counter-Reformation in Scotland, 1921 : also many contributions to The Month and the Catholic Encyclopædia. *Recreation :* sketching. *Address :* 31 Farm Street, W.1. *(Died 23 April 1925.)*

POLLEN, Sir Richard Hungerford, 4th Bt. ; *cr.* 1795 ; J.P. ; Hon. Lieut.-Col. 4th Batt. Gloucestershire Regt. 1891 ; *b.* London, 6 Oct. 1846 ; *S.* father 1881 ; *m.* Frances, *d.* of William Savage Wait, Woodborough, Somersetshire, 1875 ; two *s.* one *d. Educ. :* Eton ; Christ Church, Oxford. Owns about 1400 acres. *Heir : s.* Richard [*b.* 23 June 1878 ; late Lieut. 4th Batt. Gloucester Regt.]. *Recreations :* hunting, shooting. *Address :* Rodbourne, Malmesbury. *T.A. :* Rodbourne. *Clubs :* Carlton, New University.
(Died 5 May 1918.)

POLLOCK, Lt.-Col. Arthur Williamson Alsager, retired ; late Major The Prince Albert's (Somersetshire L.I.) ; *b.* 3 July 1853 ; *o. s.* of late Major W. P. Pollock, R.A. ; *m.* 1881, Edith Laura, *d.* of Copleston Lopes Radcliffe, Derriford, Devon ; one *s.* two *d. Educ. :* Shrewsbury ; B.N.C. Oxford. Served S. African campaigns, 1878-79 (medal with clasp) ; and Suakin, 1885 (medal with two clasps and bronze star) ; special correspondent of The Times in the Boer War ; editor United Service Magazine, 1898-1920 ; conducted the training of the Spectator Experimental Company, March to September 1906 ; appointed to command 10th (Service) Battalion King's Own Yorkshire Light Infantry, 19 Sep. 1914 ; Commanded the battalion at the battle of Loos, 25-26 Sep. 1915 ; invalided home on account of gas - poisoning ; subsequently attached to various units to assist in training ; served on the lines of communication in France, June 1917-Jan. 1919 (despatches). *Publications:* With Seven Generals in the Boer War ; Simple Lectures for Company Field-Training ; Elementary Military Training ; Lord Roastem's Campaign in North - Eastern France ; In the Cockpit of Europe ; has contributed to many magazines and newspapers. *Recreations :* (formerly) hunting, shooting, and rowing ; rowed in B.N.C. Torpid, 1873 and 1874. *Address :* Eastway, Bishop's Waltham, Hants. *Club :* Junior United Service. *(Died 2 July 1923.)*

POLLOCK, J. Arthur, F.R.S. 1916 ; D.Sc. ; Professor of Physics, Sydney University, since 1899 ; Major, A.E., A.I.F., France, 1916-18 (despatches). *Address :* The University, Sydney.
(Died 24 May 1922.)

POLLOCK, Rev. Jeremy Taylor, M.A. ; Vicar of Brigham ; Hon. Canon of Carlisle ; Rural Dean of Cockermouth and Workington ; Chaplain to Bishop of Carlisle ; *b.* 18 May 1850 ; *s.* of Ven. W. Pollock, Archdeacon of Chester ; *m. d.*

of E. Waugh, M.P., Cockermouth ; two *s.* three *d. Educ. :* Haileybury ; St. John's College, Cambridge. *Recreations :* fishing, golf, chess. *Address :* Brigham Vicarage, Cockermouth. *T.A :* Brigham. *(Died 11 Dec. 1916.)*

POLLOCK, Walter Herries ; Barrister and author ; *b.* 21 Feb. 1850 ; 2nd *s.* of late Sir Frederick Pollock, 2nd Bt. ; *m.* 1876, Emma Jane (*d.* 1922), *d.* of late Col. Pipon, Seigneur de Noirmont of Jersey ; one *s. Educ. :* Eton (King's Scholar) ; Trinity Coll. Camb. M.A., Classical Tripos. Called to the Bar, Inner Temple, but taking to journalism, became firstly sub-editor, then (1883) editor, of the Saturday Review, which he left 1894. *Publications:* The Modern French Theatre, 1878 ; Verse, Old and New ; Sealed Orders and Other Poems ; Lectures on French Poets, republished from lectures given at the Royal Institution ; A Nine Men's Morrice ; King Zub ; The Paradox of Acting (from Diderot with full annotations) ; The Charm and Other Drawing-Room Plays (with Sir Walter Besant) ; Mémoires Inédits du Marquis de —— (in French) ; Jane Austen, her Contemporaries and Herself ; The Ballad-Monger (stage version with Sir Walter Besant of Banville's Gringoire) ; Fencing, in the Badminton Library with F. C. Grove and Camille Prevost ; Animals that have Owned Us ; Hay Fever (story with Guy C. Pollock) ; Impressions of Henry Irving, Alfred de Musset, and Thackeray in Encyclopædia Britannica, etc. *Recreations :* various outdoor sports, fencing and sword-play. *Address :* Chawton Lodge, Alton, Hants ; 13 Old Square, Lincoln's Inn, W.C. *Club :* Athenæum. *(Died 21 Feb. 1926.)*

POLLOK, Rev. Dr. Allan, Hon. Principal Presbyterian Coll. Halifax ; *s.* of late Dr. Pollok, minister of Kingston ; *b.* 19 Oct. 1829 ; *m.* 1854 ; one *d. Educ. :* Glasgow University. Licensed by Presbytery of Dunoon, 1852 ; went to Nova Scotia, 1852 ; in New Glasgow, 1852-78 ; Prof. of Ecclesiastical History and Practical Theology, 1875. *Publications:* Studies in Practical Theology, 1907 ; Short Family Prayers, 1916. *Address :* Halifax, N.S. *(Died 7 July 1918.)*

POLTIMORE, 3rd Baron *(cr.* 1831), **Coplestone Richard George Warwick Bampfylde**, D.L., J.P. ; Bt. 1641 ; *b.* 29 Nov. 1859 ; *e. s.* of 2nd Baron and Florence, *d.* of Richard Brinsley Sheridan, M.P., Frampton Court, Dorsetshire ; *m.* 1881, Hon. Margaret Harriet, *d.* of 1st Baron Allendale ; three *s.* one *d. ; S.* father 1908. Owns about 20,000 acres ; possesses some good pictures, Gainsborough, Godfrey Kneller. *Heir : s.* Hon. George W. Bampfylde. *Address :* Poltimore Park, Exeter ; Court Hall, North Molton, Devonshire ; 8 Belgrave Square, S.W. *T. :* Gerrard 3380. *T.A. :* Broadclyst. *Club :* Marlborough.
(Died 2 Nov. 1918.)

POLWARTH, 6th Baron *(cr.* 1690), **Walter Hugh Hepburne - Scott**, D.L. ; Representative Peer for Scotland, 1882 - 1900 ; Lord-Lieutenant of Selkirkshire since 1878 ; late Convener of Roxburghshire ; *b.* Mertoun House, 30 Nov. 1838 ; *s.* of 5th Baron and Georgina, *d.* of George Baillie of Jerviswood and Mellerstain, and *sister* of 10th Earl of Haddington ; *S.* father 1867 ; *m.* 1st, 1863, Lady Mary Hamilton Gordon (*d.* 1914), *d.* of 5th Earl of Aberdeen ; five *s.* five *d.* ; 2nd, 1915, Katherine Grisell, *d.* of Hon. John Baillie, Canon Residentiary of York Cathedral, and *b.* of 10th Earl of Haddington. *Educ. :* Harrow. Owns about 6000 acres. *Heir : s.* Master of Polwarth. *Address :* Harden, Hawick, Roxburghshire ; Humbie, Upper Keith, Haddingtonshire.
(Died 13 July 1920.)

POMEROY, F. W., R.A. 1917 ; A.R.A. 1906 ; Sculptor ; *m.* 1913, Patricia Morrison Coughlan of Douglas, Co. Cork ; two *s.* Commenced studying at Lambeth School of Art ;

entered R.A. Schools, 1881; Gold Medal and Travelling Studentship for Sculpture, 1885; Medallist at Chicago Exhibition and the International Exhibition of Paris, 1900; has made many public monuments in Great Britain and the Colonies, notably Robert Burns, centenary statue for Paisley, N.B., and for Sydney, N.S. Wales; W. E. Gladstone for Houses of Parliament, Westminster, Duke of Westminster for Chester Cathedral, Archbishop Temple for Canterbury Cathedral, Dean Hole for Rochester Cathedral, Bishop Ridding for Southwell, Dr. Guthrie for Princes Street, Edinburgh, the monument to Lord Dufferin and Ava, Belfast; Lord Curzon of Kedleston for Calcutta; General John Nicholson for Lisburn; also decorated many important public edifices. *Address:* 15 Kensington Square, W.8. *T.:* Western 1135. *Club:* Arts.

(*Died 26 May 1924.*)

PONSONBY, Noel Edward, M.A., B.Mus. (Oxon) ; Organist of Christ Church Cathedral, Oxford, since 1926; *e. s.* of Rev. Chancellor Ponsonby, and Mary, *d.* of late Sir T. Fowell Buxton, Bart. ; *b.* 14 Jan. 1891 ; *m.* 1925, Mary Adela White-Thomson, *o. d.* of Bishop of Ely; one *s. Educ.:* St. George's, Windsor Castle ; Repton ; Trinity College, Oxford. Organist, Royal Naval College, Dartmouth, 1912 - 14 ; Director of Music, Marlborough College, 1914-1918 ; Organist and Magister Choristarum of Ely Cathedral, 1919 - 26. *Publications:* Five Short Pianoforte Pieces, 1917 ; Church Music, etc. *Address:* Christ Church, Oxford

(*Died 10 Dec. 1928.*)

PONSONBY, Capt. William Rundall, D.S.O. 1900 ; late 3rd Dragoon Guards ; retired ; *b.* Aug. 1874 ; *e. surv. s.* of Col. J. G. Ponsonby; *m.* 1902, Lilian Patteson, *d.* of late Sir P. Nickalls ; one *d.* Served South Africa in Thorneycroft's Mounted Infantry and S.A.C.

(*Died 18 Jan. 1919.*)

PONTYPRIDD, 1st Baron, *cr.* 1912 ; **Alfred Thomas ;** Kt., *cr.* 1902 ; J.P., D.L., LL.D. ; retired merchant ; Ex-President of University College of South Wales ; *b.* 1840 ; *s.* of late D. Thomas, Penylan, Cardiff. Was President Baptist Union of Wales ; Mayor of Cardiff, 1882 ; freedom of Cardiff conferred on him, 1888 ; M.P. (G.L.) Glamorganshire, E., 1885-1910 ; Chairman of Welsh Members, 1897-1910 ; First President, National Museum of Wales. *Heir:* none. *Address:* Bronwydd, Cardiff. *Clubs:* Reform, National Liberal.

(*Died 14 Dec. 1927.*)

POOLE, Rev. Frederic John, M.A. ; Rector of S. John-sub-Castro, Lewes, since 1910 ; Rural Dean of Lewes, and Prebendary of Bishop Hurst in Chichester Cathedral ; *b.* 15 June 1852 ; *y. s.* of Rev. T. Poole, Rector of Letwell, Worksop, and Mary, *e. d.* of Rev. T. Guy, Vicar of Howden ; *m.* 1881, Eleanor, *d.* of Thomas Charington of Chislehurst ; two *s.* two *d. Educ.:* Forest School, Walthamstow ; Lincoln College, Oxford. Rector of Telscombe, 1901-10 ; Chairman, Newhaven Rural District Council, and J.P., 1909. *Address:* St. John's Rectory, Lewes. (*Died 10 Dec. 1923.*)

POOLE, Henry, F.R.B.S. ; A.R.A. 1920 ; sculptor ; *b.* Westminster, 28 Jan. 1873 ; *s.* of Samuel Poole ; *m.* Ethel Cogswell. *Educ.:* King's College School ; Lambeth School of Art ; Royal Academy Schools. Studied under the late Harry Bates, A.R.A., and G. F. Watts, R.A., O.M. Works on Public Buildings—Deptford, Cardiff Town Halls, Obach and Colnaghi's Art Gallery, Bond Street ; the Wesleyan Hall at Westminster ; Memorials to Lord de Vesci, Earl Cowper, Sir Daniel Cooper, and the statue and fountains of the King Edward VII. Memorial, Bristol ; The Sculpture on the Naval Memorials at Portsmouth, Plymouth and Chatham ; The Marble

Statue Giraldus Cambrensis for the City Hall, Cardiff ; Captain Ball, V.C., Memorial, Nottingham, and many other works. *Recreations:* lawn tennis, badminton, billiards. *Address:* 1 Wentworth Studios, Manresa Road, Chelsea, S.W.3. *T.:* Kensington 0570. *Clubs:* Arts, Chelsea Arts. (*Died 15 Aug. 1928.*)

POOLE, Hon. Thomas Slaney ; Judge of Supreme Court of South Australia since 1919 ; *b.* Strathalbyn, South Australia, 3 July 1873 ; *e. s.* of Rev. Canon F. Slaney Poole, M.A., of Adelaide ; *m.* 1903, Dora Frances, 2nd *d.* of Rev. Francis Williams, M.A. ; three *d. Educ.:* St. Peter's Collegiate School, Adelaide ; Trinity College, University of Melbourne (Prizeman, Exhibitioner and Scholar) ; Scholarship in Final Honours Classics and Comp. Phil. Univ., Melbourne. B.A. 1894 ; M.A. 1896 ; LL.B. 1897 ; Lecturer in Classics, University, Adelaide. 1896 ; admitted Victorian Bar, 1897 ; S.A. Bar, 1900 ; Lecturer in Wrongs, University of Adelaide, 1909-18 ; Chancellor, Diocese, Adelaide, 1916-19 ; K.C. 1919 ; Warden, Senate, University of Adelaide, 1922 ; Member Council University of Adelaide, 1924 ; Administrator of the Government and Acting Chief Justice, 1925. *Address:* Judge's Chambers, Supreme Court, Adelaide, South Australia. *Club:* Adelaide.

(*Died 2 May 1927.*)

POOLE - HUGHES, Rev. W. Worthington, M.A. ; Warden of Llandovery College since 1901 ; Canon of St. David's Cathedral, 1923 ; Rural Dean of Llangadock, Carmarthenshire ; *b.* Aberayron, 26 Nov. 1865 ; *s.* of late William Poole Hughes ; *m.* 1914, Bertha Cecil, *y. d.* of late Richard Rhys ; one *s.* one *d. Educ.:* Llandovery College ; Balliol College, Oxford (Scholar). 1st Class Mathematical Moderations, 1886 ; 2nd Class Mathematical Finals, 1888 ; Master, Uppingham Lower School, 1888-1891 ; Army Class Master, Sherborne School, 1892-1900. *Recreations:* fishing, fives. *Address:* The College, Llandovery.

(*Died 7 July 1928.*)

POOLER, Ven. Lewis Arthur, D.D. ; Rector of Down with Hollymount ; Archdeacon of Down ; Hon. Canon St. Patrick's Cathedral, Dublin, since 1916 ; Examining Chaplain to Bishop of Down ; Rural Dean, Lecale East ; Member Representative Church Body ; Hon. Secretary General Synod ; *s.* of Rev. Canon Pooler, D.D. ; descended from Captain Robert Pooler ; *b.* 1541, who settled at Tyross, Co. Armagh ; and Angelica Leslie, *d.* of Edward Leslie, B.D., and *g.d.* of Charles Powell Leslie, M.P., Glasslough, Co. Monaghan ; *b.* 29 Jan. 1858 ; *m.* 1885, Augusta, *d.* of Ven. John Charles Wolfe, of Forenaghts and Bishopland, Co. Kildare ; one *s.* one *d. Educ.:* Armagh Royal School ; Trin. College, Dublin. Classical Scholar, 1879 ; Double First Prizeman, Classics and Modern Literature ; B.A., 1881 ; M.A., 1885 ; B.D., 1897 ; D.D., 1904 ; Select Preacher, Dublin University, 1897, 1914, 1915, 1918 ; Donellan Lecturer, 1902-3 ; Senior Resident Master, Royal School, Armagh, 1882-84 ; Curate, St. James', Belfast, 1884-89 ; Incumbent of Hollymount and Residentiary Preacher, Down Cathedral, 1889-1899. *Publications:* History of the Church of Ireland, 2nd ed., 1902 ; Studies in the Religion of Israel, 1904 ; Eschatology of the Psalms, 1904 ; St. Patrick in Co. Down, a Reply to Professor Zimmer, 1904 ; Down and its Parish Church, 1907 ; Social Questions, 1910 ; Urgent Social Problems, 1912. *Recreations:* tennis, sailing, fishing. *Address:* The Rectory, Downpatrick, Ireland. *Clubs:* Down County ; Dublin University. (*Died June 1924.*)

POORE, Maj.-Gen. Francis Harwood ; retired ; Royal Marine Artillery ; *b.* 10 Nov. 1841 ; 4th *s.* of Commander John Poore, R.N. ; *m.* 1885, Harriot Elizabeth (*d.* 1888), *e. d.* of 2nd Earl of Verulam, Lady-in-Waiting to H.R.H. The Duchess of Edinburgh ; one *s.* two *d.*

Educ.: Royal Naval School, New Cross. Entered H.M. service, 1858; served in expedition to Mexico in alliance with French and Spanish Forces, 1861-62; served in H.M. ships Racoon, Galatea, Sultan, Black Prince, and Minotaur; Equerry to the late Duke of Saxe-Coburg-Gotha (Duke of Edinburgh), 1881-91; Extra Equerry, 1891-1900; Colonel Commandant, Royal Marine Artillery, 1896-99; Retired List with honorary rank of Maj.-Gen. 1899. *Address*: Priory Lodge, Andover. *Clubs*: United Service; Royal Naval, Portsmouth.   (*Died 19 Feb. 1928.*)

POORE, Major Roger Alvin, D.S.O. 1900; Royal Wilts Yeomanry; *b.* 8 July 1870; 3rd *s.* of Major R. Poore of Old Lodge, Salisbury; *m.* 1913, Lorne Margery, *d.* of late Major R. F. W. Dennistoun; one *s.* Served S. Africa, 1899-1902 (despatches, Queen's medal, 7 clasps, D.S.O.); afterwards Resident Magistrate in the Transvaal; Deputy Commissioner of Police at Pretoria. *Clubs*: Cavalry, Arthur's.   (*Died 26 Sept. 1917.*)

POPE, Arthur William Uglow, C.I.E. 1906; V.D. 1907; *b.* 1858; *s.* of Rev. G. U. Pope, D.D., M.A.; *m.* 1886, Annie C., *d.* of Rev. J. T. Becher of Ballygiblin, Co. Cork. Late General Manager, Imperial Chinese Railways; Lt.-Col. (retired) Indian Volunteer Service; late of Oudh and Rohilkhand Batt. ; Royal Engineer Volunteers (Railways). *Address*: Clyda, Bath Road, Devizes, Wilts.   (*Died 14 Dec. 1927.*)

POPE, Lt.-Col. Edward Alexander, D.S.O. 1917; Commanding 3rd Batt. Welsh Regt. and 12th Service Batt. S. Wales Borderers; *b.* 1875; 2nd *s.* of Alfred Pope, of South Court and Wrackleford, Dorchester; *m.* 1904, Sybil Aline, *d.* of Lt.-Col. C. J. Briggs, J.P., D.L., of Hilton Castle, Co. Durham; no *c.* *Educ.*: Winchester College. Served in S. African War, 1900-1 (Queen's medal 2 clasps); Assistant Provost Marshal, Vryburg; European War, 1914-17, France, 1916-17 (despatches, D.S.O.); J.P., Dorset, 1915; C.C., Dorset, since 1904. *Recreations*: golf, fishing, shooting, etc. *Address*: Woodbridge, Branksome Park, Bournemouth. *Clubs*: United Service; Bournemouth and County.   (*Died 9 April 1919.*)

POPE, Sir Joseph, K.C.M.G., *cr.* 1912; C.V.O. 1908; C.M.G. 1901; I.S.O. 1906; holds the Grand Cordon of the Rising Sun of Japan, also the 2nd Class of the Japanese Order of the Sacred Treasure; late Under-Sec. of State for External Affairs, Canada, 1909 - 25; *b.* Charlottetown, Prince Edward Island, 16 Aug. 1854; *e. s.* of late Hon. W. H. Pope and Helen Des Brisay; *m.* 1884, Henriette, *e. d.* of late Chief-Justice Sir Henri Taschereau, Montreal; five *s.* one *d.* *Educ.*: Prince of Wales College, Charlottetown. Entered Civil Service of Canada, 1878; Private Secretary to Rt. Hon. Sir John Macdonald, Prime Minister of Canada, 1882-91; Assistant Clerk of the King's Privy Council for Canada, 1889; Under-Secretary of State and Deputy Registrar-General of Canada, 1896; attached to the staff of the British Agent on the Behring Sea Arbitration at Paris, 1893; was Agent of the Canadian Government at the proceedings of the Joint High Commission which met at Quebec and Washington, 1898-99; Associate Secretary to the Alaska Boundary Tribunal, London, 1903; H.M. Plenipotentiary at the Pelagic Sealing Conference, Washington, 1911; deputed by the Government to make arrangements for the tour of the Prince and Princess of Wales in Canada in 1901 (C.M.G.); for similar services on the occasion of the Quebec Tercentenary Celebrations received C.V.O., 1908; attended Prince Arthur of Connaught in his tour through Canada in 1906, and Prince Fushimi of Japan, 1907. *Publications*: Memoirs of Sir John Macdonald; The Royal Tour in Canada, 1901; The Day of Sir John Macdonald;

The Federal Government; The Story of Confederation; Selections from the Correspondence of Sir John Macdonald, 1840-1891, etc. *Address*: 286 Stewart Street, Ottawa, Canada. *Club*: Rideau, Ottawa.   (*Died 2 Dec. 1926.*)

POPE, Colonel Philip Edward, J.P.,D.L.; *b.* 14 Dec. 1842; *m.* Alice Mary, 3rd *d.* of Charles Taylor of Horton Manor, Bucks. Entered army, 1863; served Egyptian expedition, 1882 (medal, bronze star); Col. retired (1893); Sheriff of Bucks, 1906. *Address*: Churchmead House, Datchet, Windsor. *Clubs*: United Service, Cavalry, Junior United Service; Royal Yacht Squadron, Cowes.   (*Died 10 May 1916.*)

POPE, Rev. Richard William Massey, D.D.; *b.* Bangor, 10 Feb. 1849 2nd *s.* of late Rev. Richard Thomas Pembroke Pope, M.A.; *m.* 1878, Cecilia Mary (*d.* 1918), *d.* of Horatio Tennyson. *Educ.*: Friars' School, Bangor; Worcester Coll. Oxford (Scholar). Curate of Marston, 1872-74; of St. Giles', Oxford, 1874-86; Lecturer of Worcester College, 1874-87; Chaplain of Balliol, 1879-88; Senior Proctor, 1884-85; Select Preacher, 1890-92; Censor of non-collegiate students, Oxford, 1887-1919; Censor Emeritus by Decree of Convocation, 1920. *Address*: 4 Keble Road, Oxford. *Club*: Oxford and Cambridge.   (*Died 6 Jan. 1923.*)

POPE, Lieut.-Colonel William Wippell, C.M.G. 1917; *s.* of John Pope, Baring Lodge, Exeter; *m.* 1917, Mabel Jennie, *o. c.* of George Whitwell, Durham. *Educ.*: Sherborne School. Joined R.A.M.C. 1881; served Egyptian War, 1882 (Tel-el-Kebir medal with clasp, Khedive's star); Bechuanaland Expedition, 1884-85; operations in Zululand, 1888; N.W. Frontier of India, 1897-98, with Terah Expeditionary Force (medal with clasp); S. African War, 1897-1900, operations in Natal, defence of Ladysmith (Queen's medal with clasp); European War, 1914-17 (C.M.G.). *Address*: 93A Warwick Road, S.W.5. *T.*: Western 3317. *Clubs*: Junior United Service; Devon and Exeter, Exeter. (*Died 31 Jan. 1926.*)

PORRAL, Albert, I.S.O. 1903; C.M.G. 1912; Chairman of Chamber of Commerce, Gibraltar, since 1910; late Commissioner of Crown Property, Gibraltar; Local Adviser of Anglo-Egyptian Bank, Ltd., Gibraltar, and Consul for Russia; *b.* 27 Aug. 1846; *s.* of Michael Porral; *m.* 1873, Mary, *d.* of Jerome Saccone; one *d.* *Educ.*: privately. *Address*: Gibraltar.   (*Died 7 Jan. 1918.*)

PORRITT, Edward; journalist and author; *b.* Bury, Lancashire, 8 Dec. 1860; *s.* of John Porritt and Elizabeth Longshaw; *m.* 1891, Annie Gertrude, *d.* of John S. Webb, Darwen, Lancs; two *s.* two *d.* *Educ.*: People's College, Warrington. Entered journalism on Warrington Guardian; reporter, Liverpool Daily Mail, 1881; chief reporter, London Echo, 1882-1884; reporter and special correspondent, Globe-Democrat, St. Louis, 1884-85; in gallery of House of Commons, 1886-92; London editor, Manchester Examiner, 1888-92; settled at Farmington, Conn., as history writer and contributor to press, and correspondent, writing on political subjects and giving personal attention and investigation to industrial developments in U.S. and Canada; visited S. Africa to investigate trade and economic conditions after the war, 1902; Corr. with Canadian Tariff Revision Commn., 1905-6; lecturer at Harvard, 1908-9, 1909-10; University of California, summer session, 1910; Johns Hopkins University, Baltimore, 1916; member Society of Friends. *Publications*: Englishman at Home, 1894; Breakup of English Party System, 1895; The Unreformed House of Commons (2 vols.), with Mrs. Annie G. Porritt, 1903; Sixty Years of Protection in Canada, 1846-1906, 1907; Revolt against the New Feudalism in Canada, 1911; Barriers against Democracy in the British

Electoral System, 1911 ; The Evolution of the Dominion of Canada : its Government and its Politics, 1918 ; Associate Editor Sell's Dictionary World's Press 1890-1912. *Address* : 63 Tremont Street, Hartford, Conn., U.S. *T.A.* : Porritt, Hartford. (*Died 8 Oct. 1921.*)

PORTELLI, Rt. Rev. Angelo, O.P. ; S. Th. M. Titular Bishop of Selinonte, Vicar-General of the Archbishop of Malta ; *b.* Valetta, 1852. Joined Dominican Order, 1869 ; Priest, 1874. *Address* : The Palace, Valetta, Malta.

PORTER, Surgeon-Colonel Alex., M.D. ; F.R.C.S.I. ; M.R.I.A. ; *b.* 7 April 1841 ; *s.* of Alexander Porter, Beech-hill, Belfast ; *m.* Maud Mary D'Arcy, *d.* of General M. K. Atherley, Colonel, the Gordon Highlanders ; one *s.* two *d. Educ.* : Queen's College, Belfast. Entered Indian Medical Service, 1865 ; Civil Surgeon, Akola, 1873 ; Sanitary Commissioner, Berar, 1870-71 ; Surgeon, 4th District, and Professor, Medical College, Madras, 1874-86 ; Fellow, Madras University, 1883 ; Principal, Medical College, 1886-90 ; Deputy Surgeon-General, 1890 ; retired, 1895. *Publication* : Notes on the Pathology of Famine Diseases. *Address* : 26 Collingham Place, S. Kensington, S.W. *Club* : East India United Service. (*Died 20 May 1918.*)

PORTER, Sir Alexander, Kt., *cr.* 1912 ; Barrister-at-law ; J.P. City of Manchester ; City Councillor for Manchester ; *b.* Manchester, 27 Feb. 1853 ; *s.* of James Porter of Manchester ; *m.* 1880, Mary Rachel, *d.* of Robert Nuttall of Bury ; three *s.* three *d. Educ.* : Owens College, Manchester. Lord Mayor of Manchester, 1916-17 ; called to Bar, Middle Temple, 1905. *Address* : 60 King Street, Manchester. *Clubs* : National Liberal ; Manchester Reform. (*Died 11 Oct. 1926.*)

PORTER, Rt. Hon. Sir Andrew Marshall, 1st Bt., *cr.* 1902 ; P.C. (Ireland) ; Master of the Rolls, Ireland, 1883-1906 ; *b.* 27 June 1887 ; *s.* of Rev. John Scott Porter, Belfast ; *m.* Agnes, *d.* of late Col. Horsbrugh, Peeblesshire, 1869 ; two *s.* two *d. Educ.* : Queen's Coll. Belfast. Irish Barr. 1860 ; Q.C. 1872 ; M.P. Co. Londonderry, 1881-83 ; Solicitor-General for Ireland, 1881-82 ; Attorney-General, 1882-83. *Heir* : *s.* John Scott, B.A. [*b.* 18 July 1871 ; *m.* 1906, Elaine Maud, *y. d.* of Thomas Jefferies, J.P. of Newbay, Co. Wexford, and Los Buyos, Buenos Ayres ; one *s. Educ.* : Oxford]. *Address* : Donnycarney House, Dublin. *Club* : Kildare Street, Dublin. (*Died 9 Jan. 1919.*)

PORTER, Gene Stratton- ; *b.* Wabash Co., Ind., 1868 ; *d.* of Mark Stratton and Mary Shellenbarger ; *m.* 1886, Charles Darwin Porter ; was Editor Camera Department of Recreation ; on Natural History Staff of Outing ; Specialist in Natural History Photography on Photographic Times Annual Almanac. *Publications* : The Song of the Cardinal, 1902 ; Freckles, 1904 ; What I have done with Birds, 1907 ; At the Foot of the Rainbow, 1908 ; A Girl of the Limberlost, 1909 ; Birds of the Bible, 1909 ; Music of the Wild, 1910 ; The Harvester, 1911 ; Moths of the Limberlost, 1912 ; Laddie, 1913 ; Michael O'Halloran, 1915 ; Morning Face, 1916 ; A Daughter of the Land, 1918 ; Homing with the Birds, 1919 ; Her Father's Daughter, 1921 ; narrative lyric poem, The Fire Bird, 1922 ; Friends in Feathers, 1922 ; The White Flag, 1923 ; Jesus of the Emerald, 1924. *Address* : Limberlost Cabin, Rome City, Ind., U.S.A. ; 356 South Serrano Avenue, Los Angeles, California, U.S.A. *T.* : 560223. *M.* : 529216. (*Died Dec. 1924.*)

PORTER, John, trainer of racehorses ; *b.* Rugeley, Staffordshire, 2 Mar. 1838 ; *s.* of John Porter of that place ; *m.* 1st, Emily Jane (*d.* 1902), *d.* of Edward Moodie, Findon, Sussex ; 2nd, 1903, Isabel, *d.* of Herbert Pilsbury, Bedford. *Educ.* : Mr. Joseph Brittons, Etchinghill, Rugeley. Trainer of 7 Derby winners, and

848

winners of stakes amounting to £794,617, the largest amount ever won by any trainer of racehorses, eight times second for the Derby and twice third. *Publication* : Kingsclere. *Recreations* : all kinds of sport. *Address* : Ormonde House, Newbury, Berks. *Club* : South Berks, Newbury. (*Died 21 Feb. 1922.*)

PORTER, Dr. John Fletcher, C.B.E. ; J.P. (County of London) ; M.B. (Lond.) ; *b.* 7 Jan. 1873 ; *e. s.* of Rev. John Fletcher Porter ; *m.* 1901, Ida, 2nd *d.* of late Rev. T. H. Richards ; two *d. Educ.* : Elmfield College, York ; Yorkshire College, Leeds (Victoria University) ; London Hospital ; London University. General Practitioner ; Specialist in Medico-Legal Work ; Major, R.A.M.C. (1916) ; on Special Army Board for Functional Nervous Diseases, Neurasthenia, Epilepsy, etc. ; Acting Chairman of Board ; with Sir John Collie formed the Medical Service of Ministry of Pensions, 1917, as a whole-time pensionable Civil Servant ; resigned, 1920. *Address* : 206 Upper Clapton Road, E.5. *T.* : Clissold 1686. *M.* : XO 8891. (*Died 17 Feb. 1927.*)

PORTER, Captain John Grey Archdale, D.S.O. 1915 ; 9th (Queen's Royal) Lancers ; *b.* 9 June 1886 ; *e. s.* of J. Porter Porter, D.L., of Belleisle, Lisbellaw ; *m.* 1915, Enid Mary, *o. d.* of late G. W. Assheton-Smith, Vaynol, Carnarvon. *Educ.* ; Harrow ; Sandhurst. Entered army, 1906 ; Captain, 1912 ; served European War, 1914-15 (twice wounded, D.S.O.). *Address* : Belleisle, Lisbellaw, Ireland. *Clubs* : Cavalry, Bath, Ranelagh. (*Died 22 Nov. 1917.*)

PORTER, The Hon. Mr. Justice, William Thomas ; *b.* 21 June 1877 ; *e. s.* of William Porter, Preston Park, Sussex ; *m.* 1908, Edith, *o. d.* of late J. Johnson, Southport, Lancs ; one *s. Educ.* : privately ; Jesus College, Cambridge. Barrister Inner Temple ; went N.E. Circuit ; Stipendiary Magistrate East African Protectorate, 1907 ; President District Court, Cyprus, 1911 ; Judge Supreme Court, Gold Coast Colony, 1915-21 ; Acting Puisne Justice, Cyprus, 1915-16 ; Justice Supreme Court, Ceylon, 1921 ; Acting Chief Justice, 1921 ; retired, 1924. *Recreations* : golf, tennis, yachting. *Address* : 47 Carlisle Road, Eastbourne. *Clubs* : West Lancashire and Corinthian Yacht. (*Died 14 Jan. 1928.*)

PORTER, Sir Ludovic (Charles), K.C.S.I., *cr.* 1923 ; K.C.I.E., *cr.* 1921 ; C.S.I. 1916 ; C.I.E. 1911 ; O.B.E. ; *b.* 27 Nov. 1869. *Educ.* : Eton ; Trinity College, Cambridge. Entered I.C.S. 1887 ; City Magistrate, Lucknow, 1895 ; Magistrate and Collector, 1904 ; temporary Member Governor-General's Council, 1915-18 ; Secretary to Government of India, Department of Education, 1910-15 ; Executive Member of Council, U.P. Govt., 1921-24 ; Finance Member U.P. Govt., 1921-23 ; O.B.E. for services in Mesopotamia, 1918-19 ; retired from I.C.S., 1924. *Address* : 26 Devonshire Place, Wimpole Street, W.1. *T.* : Paddington 2635. *Clubs* : United University, Oriental. (*Died 9 Mar. 1923.*)

PORTER, Maj.-Gen. Sir Robert, K.C.B., *cr.* 1921 ; M.B., C.B. 1916 ; C.M.G. 1919 ; late D.M.S. 2nd Army ; *b.* Co. Donegal, 31 Jan. 1858 ; *s.* of late Andrew Porter ; *m.* 1903, Mary Phillipa, *d.* of late John Johnstone, Barnard Castle ; three *s. Educ.* : Foyle College, Londonderry ; Glasgow University ; Paris. Entered R.A.M.C. 1881 ; served Ashanti, 1895-96, including capture of Coomassie (hon. mention, Star) ; S. African War, 1899-1902 (Queen's medal 5 clasps, King's medal 2 clasps) ; European War, 1914-18 (despatches 6 times, promoted Maj.-Gen. for distinguished service) ; Commander of the Order of the Crown, Belgium ; Croix de Guerre, Belgium. *Recreation* : golf. *Club* : Royal Automobile. (*Died 27 Feb. 1928.*)

PORTER, Robert P.; Journalist and Writer on Economic Subjects; special correspondent to The Times in South America and the Far East; *b.* Norwich, 30 June 1852; *s.* of late James Winearls Porter, Marham, Norfolk. *Educ.:* King Edward VI. School, Norwich; privately in America. Engaged in journalism, Chicago Inter Ocean, 1872; expert U.S. Census, reporting on wealth, debt, taxation, and on transportation, 1880-81; U.S. Tariff Commissioner, 1882; editorial staff, New York Tribune and Philadelphia Press, 1884-87; founded New York Press, 1887-94; Director of Eleventh U.S. Census; Special Fiscal and Tariff Commissioner of President McKinley to Cuba and Porto Rica, 1898; negotiating the arrangement with the late General Maximo Gomez for the disbandment of the Cuban army in 1899; joined the staff of The Times as editor of the Engineering Supplement, 1904; and as principal correspondent for North America, 1906-9; in charge of the Special Supplement Department of that journal; has travelled extensively in North and South America, Mexico, Japan, China, Russia, the Balkans, Roumania, Turkey, and other countries. *Publications:* The West in 1880, 1882; Breadwinners Abroad, 1884; Free Trade Folly, 1886; Life of William McKinley, 1896; Industrial Cuba, 1899; Dangers of Municipal Trading, 1907; The Full Recognition of Japan, 1911; The Ten Republics, 1911; Japan a World Power, 1915; Editor of Porter's Progress of Nation Series; contributor to numerous reviews, articles, and addresses before various scientific and educational associations in Great Britain and the United States. *Address:* Queen Anne's Mansions, St. James's Park, S.W. *Club:* Authors'. (*Died 26 Feb. 1917.*)

PORTER, Rev. Robert Waltham; Rector of Steeple Aston, Oxfordshire, since 1926; Hon. Canon of Chelmsford since 1914; *m.* 1917, Monica, 3rd *d.* of Rev. C. M. McAnally; one *s.* two *d. Educ.:* Brasenose College, Oxford. Vicar of East Ham, 1908-26. *Address:* The Rectory, Steeple Aston, Oxon.
(*Died 30 Sept. 1927.*)

PORTER, Colonel Thomas William, C.B. 1902; Colonel Commanding Canterbury District, N.Z.; *b.* 2 Aug. 1844; *s.* of late Major J. W. Porter of Demerara; *m.* 1st, Herewaka Te Rangi Pala, a Maori chieftainess (*d.* 1905); 2nd, 1906, Florence Ellen, *e. d.* of late J. H. Sheppard. Served N.Z. War, 1863-72 (medals); South Africa, 1901-2, commanding 7th and 9th N.Z. Mounted Rifles (despatches, medal and clasps, C.B.); Under-Secretary for Defence, 1904; Judge of Native Land Court, 1905. *Address:* Heatherlea, Gisborne or Wellington, New Zealand. (*Died 12 Nov. 1920.*)

PORTER, William Smith, M.D.; L.R.C.P.; M.R.C.S.; Consulting Physician, Royal Infirmary, Sheffield; Consulting Physician, Sheffield Royal Hospital; Lt.-Col. R.A.M.C. (Territorial) (retired), 3rd Northern Hospital; *b.* 24 Dec. 1855; *s.* of late John Taylor Porter, F.R.C.S. (Eng.), and Sarah, *d.* of William Smith of Sheffield, Barrister-at-Law, J.P.; *m.* 1893, Jessie, *d.* of late Charles Lockwood of Greno House, Grenoside, near Sheffield; three *d. Educ.:* Repton School; Leeds Medical School; King's College Hospital; Durham University. Former House Surgeon, Royal Infirmary, Sheffield; Lecturer on Physiology and Medicine, Sheffield School of Medicine; Examiner 1st M.B. Examination, Durham University; Hon. Secretary and President of the Sheffield Medico-Chirurgical Society; President of the Sheffield Microscopical Society, and President of the Sheffield and District Press Club; President of Sheffield Literary and Philosophical Society, 1926. *Publications:* Sheffield Lit. and Phil. Society: a Centenary Retrospect, 1922; Notes from a Peakland Parish, 1923; some contributions to medical papers and pamphlets

on local archæological subjects; Handbook and Guide to Sheffield, 1908; edited same, 1910. *Address:* 8 Sale Hill, Broomhill, Sheffield. *T.:* Broomhill 61489. (*Died 5 Oct. 1927.*)

PORTMAN, 2nd Viscount (U.K.); *cr.* 1873; **William Henry Berkeley Portman,** G.C.V.O., *cr.* 1918; J.P., D.L.; M.F.H. (Portman Hunt); *b.* London, 12 July 1829; *e. s.* of 1st Viscount; *S.* father 1888; *m.* 1st, 1855, Hon. Mary Selina Charlotte Wentworth-Fitzwilliam (*d.* 1899), *d.* of late Viscount Milton, five *s.* three *d.*; 2nd, 1908, *d.* of Boyd Cunninghame and widow of A. T. Livingstone Learmonth. *Educ.:* Eton; Merton College, Oxford. Sat in House of Commons as a Whig, 1852-85; followed 8th Duke of Devonshire in his secession from Home Rule party; 18 years Col. West Somerset Yeomanry. *Heir:* *s.* Hon. Henry Portman. *Address:* Bryanston, Blandford, Dorset; Wentworth Lodge, Boscombe; 22 Portman Square, W. *Clubs:* Brooks's, Travellers', Hurlingham.
(*Died 16 Oct. 1919.*)

PORTMAN, 3rd Viscount (U.K.), *cr.* 1873; **Henry Berkeley Portman,** *b.* 16 Feb. 1860; *e. s.* of 2nd Viscount and Hon. Mary Selina Charlotte Wentworth-Fitzwilliam (*d.* 1899), *d.* of late Viscount Milton; *S.* father 1919; *m.* 1901, Dowager Countess of Portarlington (Emma Andalusia Frere), *d.* of Lord Nigel Kennedy, *s.* of Earl of Cassilis, and *g.s.* of 1st Marquess of Ailsa; one *d. Educ.:* Eton; Christ Church, Oxford. *Heir:* *b.* Hon. Claud B. Portman. *Address:* Bryanston, Blandford, Dorset; 22 Portman Square, W.1. *T.:* Mayfair 1711. *Clubs:* Brooks's, Travellers', Bachelors'; Royal Yacht Squadron, Cowes. (*Died 18 Jan. 1923.*)

PORTMAN, Hon. Edwin Berkeley, B.C.L.; Barrister-at-Law; *b.* 3 Aug. 1880; *s.* of 1st Viscount Portman; *m.* 1887, Caroline Ella, *d.* of D. W. Chapman; one *d. Educ.:* Oxford (B.A.). M.P., North Dorset, 1885-92. *Address:* 46 Cadogan Place, S.W.1. *T.:* Vic. 1796. *Clubs:* St. James's, Wellington, United University.
(*Died 27 April 1921.*)

PORTSMOUTH, 6th Earl of (*cr.* 1743), **Newton Wallop,** D.L., J.P., F.S.A.; Viscount Lymington, Baron Wallop, 1720; Hereditary Bailiff of Burley, New Forest; *b.* 19 Jan. 1856; *s.* of 5th Earl and Lady Eveline Alicia Juliana Herbert, *d.* of 3rd Earl of Carnarvon; *S.* father 1891; *m.* Beatrice, *d.* of Edward Pease, Greencroft, Darlington, and Wribbenhall, Bewdley, *niece* of Sir Joseph Whitwell Pease, 1st Bt., 1885. *Educ.:* Eton; Balliol Coll. Oxford (M.A. 1881). M.P. (L.) Barnstaple, 1880-1885; for N. Devonshire, 1885-86; and L.U. 1886-91; Parliamentary Under Secretary for War, 1905-8; an Ecclesiastical Commissioner, 1909. Owns about 66,000 acres. *Heir-pres.:* *b.* Hon. John F. Wallop. *Address:* 16 Mansfield Street, W.; *T.:* Paddington 4105; Eggesford House, Wembworthy, N. Devonshire; Hurstbourne Park, Hampshire; Guisachan, Beauly, N.B. *Clubs:* Brooks's, Garrick, Travellers', M.C.C., Burlington Fine Arts.
(*Died 4 Dec. 1917.*)

PORTSMOUTH, 7th Earl of (*cr.* 1743), **John Fellowes Wallop,** D.L., J.P., F.S.A.; Viscount Lymington, Baron Wallop, 1720; Hereditary Bailiff of Burley, New Forest; *b.* 27 Dec. 1859; *s.* of 5th Earl and Lady Eveline Alicia Juliana Herbert, *d.* of 3rd Earl of Carnarvon; *S.* brother, 1917. *Educ.:* Eton; Cambridge (B.A.). Formerly private secretary to Governor of Tasmania. *Heir:* *b.* Hon. Oliver Henry Wallop. *Address:* Morchard Bishop, N. Devon. *Clubs:* Brooks's, Wellington.
(*Died 7 Sept. 1925.*)

POSTGATE, John Percival, Litt.D. Cambridge; Hon. Litt.D. Dublin and Manchester; F.B.A.; Fellow Trin. Coll., Camb.; *b.* 24 Oct. 1853; *s.* of late John Postgate, F.R.C.S., and Mary Ann, *d.* of late Joshua

Horwood, surgeon, R.N. ; *m.* Edith, *d.* of late T. B. Allen, 1891 ; four *s.* two *d.* *Educ.* : King Edward's School, Birmingham ; Trinity College, Cambridge (Scholar). 1st class in Classical Tripos and Chancellor's medallist, 1876 ; Deputy-Reader in Comparative Philology in Univ. of Camb. 1889 - 90 ; Classical Lecturer, Trin. Coll., Camb., 1884-1909 (Senior Lecturer 1903 - 9) ; Professor Comparative Philology, Univ. Coll., Lond., 1880-1908 (Univ. of London, 1908-10) ; editor of Classical Review, 1899-1907, Classical Quarterly, 1907-10 ; Prof. of Latin (now Emeritus), Univ. of Liverpool, 1909-20 ; Corresponding Member of Virgilian Academy of Mantua, 1910 ; Hon. Editor of Riccardi Classical Texts, 1913 ; President of the Philological Society, 1922-26, and of the Classical Association, 1924-25. *Publications:* Select Elegies of Propertius, 1881 ; editor-in-chief of the Corpus Poetarum Latinorum, vol. i. 1893 - 94, vol. ii. 1900-5, including critical eds. of Catullus, Propertius, Grattius, Columella X., Nemesianus Cynegetica, and (with Mr. G. A. Davies) Statius Silvae ; Lucan, book vii., 1896 ; Silva Maniliana, 1897 ; Selections from Tibullus, 1903 ; critical ed. of Tibullus, 1905 ; Preface and Appendix to English trans. of Bréal's Sémantique, 1900 ; How to Pronounce Latin, 1907 ; Dead Language and Dead Languages, 1910 ; text and translation of Tibullus in Loeb Library, 1913 ; Lucan, viii. (text and commentary), 1917 ; editor of New Latin Primer (completely revised edition, 1918) ; Sermo Latinus (enlarged edition, 1913) ; critical edition of Phædrus' Fables, 1920 ; Translation and Translations, 1922 ; Prosodia Latina, 1923 ; Guide to Greek Accentuation, 1924 ; On Ancient Greek Accentuation (Proc. Br. Acad.), 1925 ; articles on Latin literature, textual criticism, etc., in Encyclopædia Britannica (11th ed.) ; numerous papers in classical and philological journals, English and foreign. *Recreations:* cycling, walking. *Address:* 16 Brookside, Cambridge. *Clubs:* Authors', University of London. (*Died 15 July 1926.*)

POTTER, Frank, General Manager, Great Western Railway, since 1912. Entered service of Company, 1869 ; was engaged for many years in various departments ; Chief Assistant to General Manager, 1904-12 ; Member of Railway Executive Committee since 1914. *Address:* G. W.R., Paddington, W. (*Died 23 July 1919.*)

POULETT, 7th Earl (*cr.* 1706), **William John Lydston Poulett ;** Baron Poulett, 1627 ; Viscount Hinton of Hinton St. George, 1706 ; late 2nd Lieut. 4th Battalion Royal Welsh Fusiliers ; 2nd Lieut. R.H.A. ; *b.* 11 Sept. 1883 ; *s.* of 6th Earl and 3rd wife, Rosa, *d.* of Alfred Hugh de Melville ; *m.* 1908, Sylvia Lilian, *d.* of Fred Storey ; one-*s.* one *d.* *Educ.* : Cheltenham. *Heir :* s. Viscount Hinton. *Address:* Hinton St. George, Crewkerne, Somerset. (*Died 11 July 1918.*)

POUNDS, Charles Courtice, F.R.A.M. ; actor and vocalist ; *b.* London, 30 May 1862 ; *e. s.* of Charles Pounds ; mother well-known singer, under name Mary Curtice. *Educ.* : St. Mark's Coll., Chelsea ; Royal Academy of Music. Solo treble at St. Stephen's, South Kensington, and Italian Church, Hatton Garden ; created parts of Fairfax in Yeomen of the Guard and Marco in The Gondoliers at Savoy Theatre ; appeared at that theatre in all subsequent productions till 1892 ; returned 1894 for Mirette and Chieftain ; joined Williamson and Musgrove's Opera Company in Australia, 1895 ; returned to London, 1896 ; played The Novice in La Poupée, following with the tenor parts in The Royal Star, The Coquette, in The Snowman, and as Wilder in a revival of Dorothy ; as the Clown in Twelfth Night, Ferdinand in the Last of the Dandies, The Minstrel in Ulysses, and Sir Hugh in Merry Wives, Touchstone, the name part in a revival

of Chilperic, and Papillon in London and New York productions of Duchess of Dantzic ; The Blue Moon ; The Cherry Girl, and the Belle of Mayfair ; visited Berlin with Mr. Tree ; appeared in Lady Tatters in 1907 ; Charles, his Friend ; played Touchstone at His Majesty's, 1908 ; also in The Two Pins, The Dashing Little Duke, The Merry Peasant, A Modern Othello ; The Spring Maid, Orpheus in the Underground, Princess Caprice, and Oh ! oh ! Delphine, The Laughing Husband, Chez Nous, The Bos'n's Mate, Lady Frayle, Chu Chin Chow, Abu in Cairo, Franz Schubert in Lilac Time ; The First Kiss, Spring Time, and Just a Kiss, and Jed, in Shavings, The Toymaker, on Tour. *Recreation :* golfing. *Clubs :* Savage, Green Room. (*Died 21 Dec. 1927.*)

POWEL, Thomas, M.A. (Oxon.) ; Professor of Celtic in the University College of South Wales and Monmouthshire 1884-1918 ; now Emeritus ; *o. s.* of Thomas Powell of Llanwrtyd, Breconshire, and Elizabeth Rowland of Penybont, Tregaron, Cardiganshire ; *m.* 1890, Gwenny Elizabeth, *d.* of late Rev. Samuel Jones, Penarth, Glam; one *s.* *Educ.* : Llandovery College ; Jesus College, Oxford. B.A. (Classical Honours), 1872 ; Second Master, Independent College, Taunton, 1878-80 ; Head Master, Bootle College, 1880-83 ; Editor of Journal and publications of London Cymmrodorion Society, 1880-86 ; Examiner in Welsh, University of London. *Publications:* various articles and papers, *inedita,* etc. in Transactions of Cymmrodorion Society, Philological Society, etc. ; edited (with notes) The Gododin of Aneurin, by Thomas Stephens, 1888 ; edited (with introductions) Collotype facsimile of Bishop Morgan's Welsh Psalter of 1588, 1896. *Recreations:* cycling, golf, gardening. *Address:* University College, Cardiff ; Aberystwyth.

POWELL, Arthur, O.B.E. ; B.A., M.D., M.S. ; consulting Physician ; *b.* 10 May 1864 ; *s.* of John Donor Powell ; unmarried. *Educ.* : Trinity College, Dublin ; Royal College of Surgeons, Dublin ; Queen's College, Belfast. Professor of Medical Jurisprudence, Fellow and Syndic in Science, Bombay University ; Prof. of Biology, Medical College, Bombay ; Captain Indian Mounted Infantry, S. African War ; arrested in Germany, outbreak of war ; escaped Switzerland, returned England, Sep. 1914 ; Lieut.-Col. Indian Defence Force ; Officer commanding Byculla Officers' Hospital, 1915-1919 ; Steward, Western India Turf Club, 1904-16 ; consulting Physician for Tropical Diseases, Ministry of Pensions. *Publications:* Practical Biology for Indian Students, four editions ; Chapters in Lyons' Medical Jurisprudence, 6th edition. *Address:* 9 Harley Street, W.1 ; The Firs, Sutton. *T.:* Langham 1777 ; Sutton 1508. *Club:* Oriental. (*Died 23 Aug. 1926.*)

POWELL, Rt. Rev. Edmund Nathanael, D.D. ; Vicar of St. Columba, Wanstead Slip, since 921 ; Hon. Canon of Chelmsford, 1921 ; *o.* Buckhurst Hill, 2 Sep. 1859 ; *s.* of Nathanael Powell, J.P., D.L. ; unmarried. *Educ.* : Winchester ; Trinity College, Oxford (M.A.) ; Hon. D.D., 1907 ; Curate of Chelmsford, 1883 - 87 ; Priest - in - charge, Beckton East, 1887-91 ; Vicar of St. Stephen, Upton Park, 1891-98 ; Bishop of Mashonaland, 1908-10 ; Vicar of St. Saviour, Poplar, 1910-17 ; Vicar of Castle Hedingham, Essex, 1917 - 21. *Address:* The Vicarage, Wanstead Slip, Essex. (*Died 11 April 1928.*)

POWELL, Ellis Thomas, LL.B. (Lond.), D.Sc. (Lond.) ; Fellow of the Royal Historical and Royal Economic Societies, and of the Institute of Journalists and Royal Colonial Institute ; for many years a Member of Council of Newspaper Proprietors' Association and of Empire Press Union ; of the Inner Temple, Barrister - at - Law ; *b.* Ludlow, Salop, 1869 ; *o.*

s. of Thomas Powell and Harriet, *d.* of Ellis Stanier Jones ; *m.* Rose Alberta, *d.* of William Badams ; one *s.* two *d.* *Educ.* : Ludlow Grammar School (Langfordian Scholar). Gave evidence before Marconi Committee ; one of the London delegates to Imperial Press Conference, Ottawa, 1920 ; Member of London Diocesan Conference; Editor of the Financial News, 1909-20. *Publications:* The Essentials of Self-Government; The Management of Parliamentary Elections ; The Mechanism of the City; The Sheaves of Empire; The Evolution of the Money Market ; the Practical Affairs of Life; How to Pass your Exam ; numerous popular manuals on investment and banking ; The Psychic Element in the New Testament ; thousands of leading and other articles. *Recreations :* music, public speaking, psychic research, electioneering (chief Unionist agent in the longest election petition on record, and in Thanet, 1904-6), and the microscope and telescope. *Address:* Rosedene, Brondesbury Park, N.W. *T. :* Willesden 489. *Club:* University of London.   *(Died 1 June 1922.)*

POWELL, Admiral Sir Francis, K.C.M.G., *cr.* 1902 ; C.B. 1894, R.N.; *b.* 15 Sep. 1849 ; 4th *s.* of late Arthur Powell of Milton Heath, Dorking ; *m.* 1875, R. W., *d.* of late J. W. Glynn of Cape Town, South Africa ; three *s.* three *d. Educ. :* St. Andrew's Coll., Bradfield. Joined Royal Navy as Cadet, 1862 ; Midshipman, 1864 ; Sub-Lieut. 1868 ; Lieut. 1872 ; Commander, 1883 ; Capt. 1889 ; Rear-Admiral, 1903 ; Commodore, Hong-Kong, 1899-1902 ; Vice-Admiral, 1907 ; retired, 1907 ; C.B. for services in Benin River ; K.C.M.G. for services in China. *Address:* Clapton, Shanklin.

     (Died 5 Oct. 1927.)

POWELL, George Herbert ; *b.* 1856 ; 2nd *s.* of Rev. T. E. Powell, 52 years Vicar of Bisham, Berks.; *m.* 1904, Beatrice Mary Harding ; one *s. Educ. :* Uppingham ; Trinity (migr. King's) College, Cambridge, Classical Exhibitioner and Greek Verse Prizeman ; B.A. 1879 ; Inner Temple, Barrister 1885 ; Associate Toynbee Hall (15 years Anti-socialist Campaign). *Publications:* Rhymes and Reflections, 1892 ; Excursions in Libravda, 1895 ; Duelling Stories from French of Brantome ; La France Monarchique (40 selections from contemporary Memoirs) ; Burlesques and Parodies (Pelopidæ Papers), 1912 ; Crown Prince's First Lesson Book (Rhymes on the War) ; Articles in Quarterly, Fortnightly, Contemporary, English-woman, and other magazines. *Recreations :* book-hunting, singing, reading aloud, fives, croquet (manual), hockey (on ice), Guidebook Alpine climbing ; first ascent of Pitz Albina, Engadine, out in famous and fatal Matterhorn storm (21 hours on Finster Aarhorn and glacier), 1881. *Club:* Savile.   *(Died 28 July 1924.)*

POWELL, Colonel James Leslie Grove, C.B.E. 1918 ; V.D., T.D., D.L., J.P. Surrey ; retired Territorial Force ; *b.* 26 April 1853 ; *e. s.* of late James Powell, Chichester ; *m.* 1875, Harriette Charlotte (*d.* 1908), *d.* of Henry Huish, M.D., Surgeon-Major 3rd King's Own Hussars ; one *s.* one *d. Educ. :* Prebendal School, Chichester ; Cheltenham College. Admitted a solicitor, 1874 ; C.C. 1910, and Alderman, 1919, Surrey ; Lieut.-Colonel and Hon. Col. commanding 6th Batt. East Surrey Regiment, 1898-1909 ; Hon. Colonel of the battalion since 1909 ; Lieut.-Colonel (temp.), 1914 ; Master of the Coachmakers' and Coach Harness Makers, Livery Company of London, 1922-23 ; Chairman Richmond Royal Hospital ; Director of Richmond Royal Horse Show Society ; Member of Board of Thames Conservancy. *Address :* Tapton House, Richmond, Surrey. *T. :* Richmond 245. *M. :* P 8037. *Clubs:* St. Stephen's, Royal Automobile.   *(Died 28 Feb. 1925.)*

POWELL, Rt. Hon. Mr. Justice John Blake, P.C. Ireland, 1920 ; K.C. ; Judge of the High Court of Justice in Ireland, Chancery Division, since 1918. *Address :* 41 Fitzwilliam Place, Dublin.   *(Died 13 Sept. 1923.)*

POWELL, Sir Richard Douglas, 1st Bt., *cr.* 1897 ; K.C.V.O., *cr.* 1901 ; M.D., F.R.C.P., M.R.C.S. ; M.D. ; F.R.C.P. Dublin ; LL.D. Aber., Birmingham ; D.Sc. Oxon (hon.); Physician in Ordinary to the King since 1910 ; Consulting Physician and Emeritus Lecturer on Medicine to Middlesex Hospital ; Consulting Physician to Brompton and Ventnor Hospitals; Knight of Grace of the Order of St. John of Jerusalem since 1898 ; Deputy-Chairman of the Clerical, Medical, and General Life Assurance Society ; *b.* Walthamstow, 25 Sep. 1842 ; 2nd and *o. surv. s.* of late Captain Scott Powell, formerly 23rd Royal Welsh Fusiliers ; *m.* 1st, 1873, Juliet (*d.* 1909), 2nd *d.* of Sir John Bennett, Kt.; three *s.* one *d.*; 2nd, 1917, Edith Mary Burke, *d.* of late Henry Wood. *Educ. :* Streatham, Univ. Coll. Hospital ; graduated in Honours. University of London, 1866 ; Hon. Fellow Royal Society of Medicine ; Pres. Royal College of Physicians 1905-10 ; late President Royal Medical Chir. Clinical and Medical Societies ; Physician in Ordinary to Queen Victoria, 1899, and King Edward VII., 1907. *Publications :* On Diseases of the Lungs and Heart ; Harveian Oration, 1914, On Advances in Knowledge regarding the Circulation and Attributes of the Blood since Harvey's Time, etc. *Recreation:* outdoor exercise. *Heir: s.* Douglas, C.B.E. *Address :* 10 Cleveland Square, W.2. *T. :* Padd. 20. *Club :* Athenæum.   *(Died 15 Dec. 1925.)*

POWER, Sir George, 7th Bt., *cr.* 1836 ; Prof. of voice production and singing ; *b.* Dublin, 24 Dec. 1846 ; 4th *s.* of Sir John Power of Kilfane, Co. Kilkenny, Ireland, 2nd Bart.; *S.* brother, 1903 ; *m.* 1915, Eva, *d.* of Sir Samuel Boulton, 1st Bt. *Educ. :* Cheltenham College ; Trinity College, Dublin. Went on the stage as tenor ; sang in Malta, Italy ; then in first production of H.M.S. Pinafore at the Opéra Comique ; first studied singing in Milan and Florence, 1873-76. *Recreations:* music and travelling. *Heir:* cousin, Gervase Parker Power. *Address:* 31 Addison Road. W.14.

     (Died 17 Oct. 1923.)

POWER, Hubert ; *b.* 1860 ; *s.* of late P. J. M. Power and Lady Olivia Jane Nugent, *d.* of 9th Earl of Westmeath ; *m.* 1888. Marie Thérèse Aimée, *y. d.* of M. Alexis Charles Toussaint Bourges ; *S.* father 1913. High Sheriff of Co. Waterford, 1888. *Address:* Faithlegg House, Waterford.

POWER, Sir James Talbot, 5th Bt. ; *cr.* 1841 ; D.L. ; *b.* 23 June 1851 ; *s.* of 2nd Bt. and Jane Anna Eliza, *d.* and *co-heir* of John Hyacinth Talbot, Castle Talbot, Co. Wexford ; *S.* nephew, 1914 ; *m.* 1877, Gertrude Frances, *d.* of Thomas Hayes, Grenville House, Cork ; no *c. Educ. :* Oscott College, Warwickshire. Owns about 1300 acres in Co. Wexford ; Chairman of Sir John Power & Son, Distillers, Dublin, established 1791. *Heir: b.* Thomas, *b.* 3 May 1863. *Recreation:* coaching. *Address:* Leopardstown Park, Stillorgan, Co. Dublin. *T.A. :* Power, Dublin. *T. :* 100. *Clubs:* St. Stephen's Green, United Service, Dublin.   *(Died 4 July 1916.)*

POWER, John Danvers, M.V.O. ; Member of Council of the British Red Cross Society and of Malvern College ; J.P. Bucks ; *b.* 1858 ; *m.* 1st, 1891, Edith Ethelston (*d.* 1924), *d.* of late T. O. Wethered of Seymour Court, Marlow ; one *s.* one *d.* ; 2nd, 1925. Mary Gertrude, *d.* of late Sir Juland Danvers, K.C.S.I. *Educ. :* Malvern Coll. ; Downing Coll., Camb. ; Barrister, 1887 ; contested East Leeds (U.), 1895 ; Chairman of the National Hospital for the Paralysed and Epileptic, 1903-5 ; Hon. Secretary of Sir Edward Fry's Committee on Medical Schools, 1904-5 ; of Queen's Unemployed Fund, 1905-6 ;

of King Edward's Hospital Fund, 1904-7; Chairman International Red Cross Conference Committee, 1907; Editor of Red Cross Official Journal, 1914-18, and of the Official Report of the Red Cross and St. John on Voluntary Aid during the War, 1921. *Address:* 8 Eccleston Square, S.W,1. *T.:* Victoria 1861. *Club:* Carlton.
(*Died 3 June 1927.*)

POWER, Admiral Sir Laurence Eliot, R.N.; K.C.B., *cr.* 1921; C.B. 1916; C.V.O. 1917; M.V.O. 1907; A.D.C. to H.M. 1915; Director of Dockyards 1917-23; *b.* Bramley, 7 May 1864; *s.* of Rev. H. B. Power, *g.s.* of Maj.-Gen. Sir Manley Power, K.C.B.; *m.* 1900, Muriel, *e. d.* of Sydney A. Want, Sydney, N.S.W.; one *s.* two *d. Educ.:* East Sheen, Burney's. Entered Royal Navy, 1877; Midshipman, 1879; Lieut. 1887; Commander, 1899; Captain, 1905; Rear-Adm., 1916; Vice-Admiral, 1920; retired, 1920; Admiral, retired, 1925; Shadwell testimonial, 1890; commanded H.M.S. Dryad (navigation school), 1907-10; Master of the Fleet, King Edward VII. Review of Fleet off Cowes, 1907. *Recreations:* various. *Address:* The Old Vicarage, Corsham, Wilts. *Club:* United Service.   (*Died 20 Jan. 1927.*)

POWER, Hon. Lawrence Geoffrey, K.C.; P.C. 1905; LL.D.; Senator of Canada since 1877; *b.* Halifax, Nova Scotia, 9 Aug. 1841; *e. c.* of late Patrick Power, formerly M.P. for Halifax County, and Ellen Gaul; *m.* 1880, Susan, *d.* of M. O'Leary of West Quoddy, Halifax County; two *d. Educ.:* St Mary's Coll. Halifax, N.S.; Carlow Coll.; the Catholic University, Dublin; Harvard Law School. Admitted to Bar, 1866; an Alderman of Halifax, 1870-76; School Commissioner for thirteen years; Member of Senate of University of Halifax, 1876; Speaker of Senate, 1900; a.Director of School for the Blind, of Institution for Deaf and Dumb, of Halifax Visiting Dispensary, of Legislative Library, of Nova Scotia Historical Society, and of Game Society of Nova Scotia, of which last he was for several years president. *Publications:* The Manitoba School Question from the Point of View of a Catholic Member—a pamphlet, 1896; The Whereabouts of Vinland, New England Magazine, Oct. 1892; Canadian Opinion on the Home Rule Question, Dublin Review, July 1886; Richard John Uniacke: a Sketch; a frequent contributor to the press. *Recreations:* former, rowing, fishing, lawn tennis. *Address:* Halifax, Nova Scotia. *T.:* 992. *Club:* Halifax.
(*Died 17 Sept. 1921.*)

POWER, Sir William Henry, K.C.B., *cr.* 1908; C.B. 1902; F.R.S.; *b.* 1842; *m.* 1875, Charlotte Jane, *d.' of* B. C. Godwin; two *d. Educ.:* St. Bartholomew's. Chairman Royal Commission on Tuberculosis; Member Royal Commission on Sewage Disposal; holds Buchanan Medal Royal Society for services to Sanitary Science; Member of the General Council of Medical Education, 1900-8; late Principal Medical Officer to Local Government Board. *Address:* Holly Lodge, East Molesey; 5 Old Palace Yard, S.W. (*Died 28 July 1916.*)

POWLETT, Admiral Armand Temple, retired, 1901; *b.* 17 March 1841; *s.* of Rev. Percy W. Powlett and Isabella, *d.* of C. Wheler; *m.* 1870, Horatia Frances Janet, *d.* of F. A. Powlett; three *s.* two *d. Educ.:* Southampton. Entered Navy, 1855; in H.M.S. Terrible during Russian War; in H.M.S. Cambrian in China, operations in Canton river, 1858 (wounded dangerously at Taku Forts, 24 June 1859); commanded H.M.S. Champion, 1888-87; commanded H.M.S. Benbow, 1887-89; commanded Training Squadron (Active) as commodore, 1889-91; Superintendent Sheerness Dockyard, 1892-94; second in command Channel, 1896-97. *Address:* The Manor House, Frankton, nr. Rugby.   (*Died 22 Jan. 1925.*)

852

POWNALL, George Henry, President of the Institute of Bankers; Member Foreign Trade Debts Committee; Member of the American Dollars Committee; 3rd *s.* of James Pownall, Manchester; *b.* 3 March 1850; *m.* 1877, Margaret Haines Adin; no *c. Educ.:* Home; Owens College. Union Bank of Manchester (Junior); Manchester and Salford Bank, Manager, St. Ann Street, Secretary of Bank; London Manager, Williams Deacons Bank; pupil of Jevons; President Manchester Statistical Society; first Chairman Council Manchester and District Bankers' Institute. *Publications:* Banking Statistics as a Measure of Trade; The Relations of Capital and Labour; Local Taxation and Government; Bank Reserves, the Central Stock of Gold and £1 Notes; The Insufficiency of our Cash Reserves; The Relative Use of Credit Documents and Metallic Money; Savings Banks and their Relation to National Finance; English Banking; Lectures at London School of Economics, and numerous occasional articles on economic and social subjects. *Address:* Croham Mount, Selsdon Road, South Croydon. *T.:* Croydon 2391. *Club:* Royal Societies.   (*Died 16 Dec. 1916.*)

POYNTER, Sir Ambrose Macdonald, 2nd Bt., *cr.* 1902; Lieut. R.N.V.R., 1916-19; *b.* 26 Sep. 1867; *s.* of 1st Bart. and Agnes (*d.* 1906), *d.* of Rev. George B. Macdonald. *S.* father 1919; *m.* 1907, Cherry Margaret, *o. c.* of Lt.-Col. J. J. Burnett, late South Wales Borderers and Army Pay Department; no *c. Heir: b.* Hugh Edward, *b.* 1882. *Address:* Botley, Hants. *Club:* St. James's.   (*Died 31 May 1923.*)

POYNTER, Sir Edward John, 1st Bt., *cr.* 1902; Kt., *cr.* 1896; G.C.V.O. *cr.* 1918; K.C.V.O., *cr.* 1913; President Royal Academy since 1896; D.C.L., Litt.D.; *b.* Paris, 20 Mar. 1836; *s.* of Ambrose Poynter, architect; *m.* 1866, Agnes (*d.* 1906), *d.* of Rev. George B. Macdonald; two *s. Educ.:* Westminster; Ipswich Grammar School. Studied Art in English Schools, 1854-56; Paris under Gleyre, 1856-59; an Associate of the Royal Academy 1869; Slade Professor of Art, Univ. Coll. London, 1871-75; Royal Academician, 1876; director for Art and principal of National Art Training School, South Kensington (resigned, 1881); director of the National Gallery in succession to Sir F. Burton, 1894-1905. *Pictures:* Royal Academy—Israel in Egypt, 1867; Perseus and Andromeda, 1872; Atalanta's Race, 1876; The Fortune Teller (diploma picture), 1877; A Visit to Æsculapius, 1880; The Meeting of Solomon and the Queen of Sheba, 1891; Horae Serenae, Idle Fears, 1894; The Ionian Dance, 1899; The Cave of the Storm Nymphs, 1903; The Nymphs' Bathing Place, 1904; The Cup of Tantalus, 1905; Lesbia and her Sparrow, 1907; Brewing a Storm, 1909; A Naval Disaster, 1912; At Low Tide, 1913; The Sea Bath, or The Champion Swimmer, 1914; Portraits of King Edward VII.; The Duke and Duchess of Northumberland; E. Pember, K.C.; Sir Edward Maunde Thompson, G.C.B.; Mrs. Dubose Taylor, Sir Frederick Eaton, Sec. R.A., 1913; Miss Doris Peterson, 1915, and others; and numerous watercolours, figure and landscape. Two sets of designs for the new coinage, 1894; cartoons for mosaics of St. George and St. David in Westminster Palace; designed architectural and tile decorations for grill-room at South Kensington. *Publication:* Ten Lectures on Art, 1879; Editor of The National Gallery. *Heir: s.* Ambrose Macdonald [*b.* 26 Sep. 1867; *m.* 1907, Cherry Margaret, *o. c.* of Major J. J. Burnett, late South Wales Borderers and Army Pay Department. *Clubs:* Athenæum, St. James's]. *Address:* 70 Addison Road, W. *Clubs:* Athenæum, Burlington Fine Arts.   (*Died 26 July 1919.*)

POYSER, Arthur Horatio, M.A., K.C.; *b.* 21 Jan. 1849; *s.* of Charles Povser of Summer

Hill, Gwersyllt; *m.* 1872, Alice, *d.* of William Whytehead of Clifton, York; one *s.* four *d.* *Educ.*: Shrewsbury School; Christ Church, Oxford. Second class in Honour School of Jurisprudence; B.A. 1872; M.A. 1876; called to Bar, 1873. *Recreations*: golf and chess. *Address*: Burneston, Sydenham, S.E.26; 1 Temple Gardens, Temple, E.C.4. *T.A.*: 70 Temple. *T.*: Sydenham 642 and Central 9514.
(Died 6 June 1923.)

POYSER, Colonel Richard, F.R.C.V.S., D.S.O. 1896; *b.* 1842; *s.* of Joseph Poyser, Wirksworth, Derbyshire; *m.* 1870, Annie Maria, *d.* of John Cruikshank of Ecclefechan, Dumfries; one *s.* two *d.* Gazetted 1865; 7th Dragoon Guards, Royal Horse Artillery, and 6th Dragoon Guards (Carabiniers), with which latter regiment he served through the Afghan War, 1879-80 (medal); principal Veterinary Officer, Chitral Relief Force, 1895 (despatches, D.S.O., medal and clasp); subsequently, till retirement, 1897, principal Veterinary Officer, Punjab Army, India; rewarded by promotion from Lieut.-Col. to Col. (1902) for services during operations in South Africa, and received the thanks of Earl Roberts, Commander-in-Chief. *Address*: 155 Victoria Road, Old Charlton, S.E.
(Died 4 June 1919.)

POZZI, Prof. Jean Samuel; Professor to the Faculty of Medicine, Paris; Surgeon of Hospital Broca; Member of the Academy of Medicine; *b.* Bergerac, Dordogne, 3 Oct. 1849; *m.* Thérèse Loth-Cazalis; two *s.* one *d.* *Educ.*: Lycée of Pau and of Bordeaux; Faculty of Medicine, Paris. Grand Officer Legion of Honour. *Publications*: Clinical and Operative Gynæcology, etc. *Address*: 47 Avenue d'Ie'na, Paris. *T.*: 660-18; La Graulet, near Bergerac.
(Died 1918.)

POZZONI, Mgr. Dominico, R.C. Bishop of Tavia and Vicar Apostolic of Hong-Kong since 1905; *b.* Paderno d'Adda, Italy, Dec. 1861. Went as Missionary to Hong-Kong, 1885; engaged in mission work in Kwang-tung, 1885-1905. *Address*: Caine Road, Hong-Kong.
(Died 1924.)

PRAED, Sir Herbert Bulkley Mackworth-, 1st Bt., *cr.* 1905; J.P., D.L.; *b.* 2 May 1841; 2nd *s.* of late Bulkley John Mackworth-Praed, and 2nd wife, Elizabeth Colthurst, *e. d.* of late Patrick Persse FitzPatrick. *Educ.*: Harrow. Formerly Lt. King's Own Scottish Borderers; High Sheriff, Suffolk, 1886; Patron of Owsden; late a banker in London; M.P. Colchester, 1874-80; Treasurer of Charity Organisation Society, and assisted in its formation; Chairman of Victoria Dwellings Association for Working Men; Treasurer and one of Founders of Working Men's Club and Institute Union, and has been interested in many other philanthropic endeavours; Chairman of Association of Conservative Clubs. *Heir*: none. *Recreations*: hunting, shooting, fishing, deerstalking, yacht-racing, golf, tennis, and fencing. *Address*: 29 St. James's Place, S.W. *T.*: Regent 1083; Owsden Hall, Newmarket. *Clubs*: Arthur's, Carlton, Bachelors', Turf, Beefsteak. *(Died 21 Nov. 1921.)*

PRAGNELL, Sir George, Kt., *cr.* 1912. Com. Lieutenancy, City of London; J.P. London (Newington); Managing partner, Cook, Son, & Co., St. Paul's Churchyard; chairman, National Patriotic Association, Employers' Territorial Association and Wholesale Textile Association; *b.* 1863; *s.* of late W. G. Pragnell, Sherborne; *m.*; one *s.* one *d.* *Recreation*: deepsea fishing. *Address*: Grove Park, Kent. *T.*: Lee Green 1351. *Club*: Royal Automobile.
(Died 14 Feb. 1916.)

PRATT, Edward Roger; landowner, J.P., D.L., C.C., Co. Norfolk; *e. s.* of Rev. Jermyn Pratt of Ryston Hall; *b.* 3 Dec. 1847; *m.* 1881, Hon. Louisa Frances Mulholland, 2nd *d.* of 1st Baron

Dunleath; three *s.* two *d.* *Educ.*: Eton; Trin. Coll. Camb.; B.A. 1869. In boats at Eton; rowed for 3rd Trinity, Cambridge; travelled in N. and Central America, N. Africa, Caucasus, Armenia; Special Commissioner for Stafford House Ottoman Relief Committee, 1879; Russo-Turkish War (received war medal; 3rd class Osmanie; 3rd class Medjidie); Order of St. John of Jerusalem; Colonel (retired) P.W.O. Norfolk Artillery; Past President Royal English Arboricultural Society. *Recreations*: shooting, estate management, and forestry. *Address*: Ryston Hall, Downham. *Club*: Brooks's. *(Died 20 Nov. 1921.)*

PRATT, Brig.-Gen. (Ernest) St. George, C.B. 1916; D.S.O. 1902; Durham L.I.; Inspector of Infantry; *b.* 3 Sep. 1863; *y. s.* of late Spencer Pratt of Stanwick House, Higham Ferrers; *m.* 1902, Edith, *d.* of late Capt. H. P. Andrew, 8th Hussars; one *d.* Entered army, 1884; Captain, 1894; Major, 1903; Lt.-Col. 1910; Col. 1913; served South Africa, 1899-1902 (despatches three times, D.S.O., brevet Major). *Address*: 15 Wilton Street, S.W.1. *Club*: Naval and Military.
(Died 24 Nov. 1918.)

PRATT, Col. Henry Marsh, C.B. 1889; U.S. list; *b.* 24 Oct. 1888; *s.* of Rev. Wm. Pratt of Harpley, Norfolk; *m.* 1891, Evelyn Margaret, 2nd *d.* of Clayton Glyn, Durrington House, Harlow; two *d.* *Educ.*: Marlborough. Arrived in India as Direct Cadet, 1856; present at mutiny of his regt., 51st Bengal Infantry, 1857 (medal); served in campaign, N. China, 1860 (medal and 2 clasps, "Taku Forts" and "Pekin"); served in Afghanistan, 1878-79-80 (medal 4 clasps, "Piewar," "Charasiab," "Kabul, 1879," "Kandahar," despatches); Brevet of Lieut.-Col., bronze star, for Roberts' march; commanded column in Black Mountain expedition, 1888 (medal and clasp, despatches). Decorated for distinguished service in the field; granted a good service pension for distinguished and meritorious service, 1898. *Recreations*: country sports in general. *Address*: 24 Sussex Mansions, South Kensington, S.W. *T.*: Kensington 6103. *Club*: United Service. *(Died 16 April 1919.)*

PRATT, Surg.-Gen. William Simson, C.B. 1906; M.B., late P.M.O. Southern Command; *b.* 21 Jan. 1849. Lt.-Col. R.A.M.C. 1898; Col. 1902; P.M.O. Gibraltar, 1900-2; Administrative Medical Officer, 1902; served Soudan, 1884-85 (despatches, medal with clasp, bronze star, promoted Surgeon-Major). *Club*: Junior United Service. *(Died 8 Sept. 1917.)*

PRATTEN, Herbert Edward; Minister for Trade and Customs Commonwealth of Australia since 1924; *b.* Downland, near Bristol, 7 May 1865; *m.* Agnes, *d.* of late J. P. Wright, Sydney; two *s.* three *d.* *Educ.*: Merchant Venturers School, Bristol. Left England for Australia when 20 years old; has had a successful mercantile, manufacturing and mining career there; 7 years in municipal life; 3 times a Mayor; 3 years President of the Manufacturers Association; member of the British Parliamentary Munitions Committee, 1915-16; elected to the Commonwealth Senate, 1917; resigned; elected to the House of Representatives, 1921. *Publications*: (Brochures) Asiatic Impressions and Through Orient to Occident. *Recreation*: fishing. *Address*: Canberra, Australia. *(Died 7 May 1928.)*

PREECE, John Richard, C.M.G. 1899; F.R.G.S.; *b.* 1843; *s.* of late R. M. Preece; *m.* 1916, Mary, *d.* of David Graham-Allardice and *widow* of G. G. Duncan. *Educ.*: Private School; Imperial College, France. Assistant Traffic Manager, Indo-European Telegraph Department, Teheran, 1868; joined consular service, 1891; British Consul at Ispahan, 1891; Consul-General, 1900-1906; Member Electrical Engineers Society;

read papers in the societies he belongs to on Persian travel and telegraphs. *Address:* 46 Bullingham Mansions, Kensington, W. *Clubs:* Royal Societies', Junior Constitutional. M.C.C. and S.C.C.   *(Died 25 Feb. 1917.)*

PRENDERGAST, Maj.-Gen. Guy Annesley, Indian Army; Colonel, 15th Lancers, since 1904; *b.* 11 Mar. 1834; *m.* 1858, Catherine (*d.* 1902), *d.* of late Major Philip Cortlandt Anderson. Entered army, 1850; Maj.-Gen. 1891; unemployed list, 1893; served Indian Mutiny, 1858 (despatches, medal); Afghan War, 1879 (medal). *Address:* 6 Bramham Gardens, S.W.   *(Died 5 July 1919.)*

PRENDERGAST, Hon. Sir James, Kt., *cr.* 1881; *b.* 1826. *Educ.:* St. Paul's School; Queen's Coll. Camb. (B.A. 1850); Barr. Middle Temple, 1856; Chief Justice of New Zealand, 1875-99. *Address:* Bolton Street, Wellington, New Zealand.   *(Died 1 Feb. 1921.)*

PRENDERVILLE, Arthur de, LL.B., M.R.C.S.; Anæsthetist to Charing Cross Hospital, the Throat Hospital, Golden Square, W., the Acheson Military Hospital, N.W.; *b.* St. Helena, South Atlantic; *s.* of Major J. H. de Prenderville, late of St. Helena Regt., and afterwards Inspector-General of Constabulary, Jamaica, W.I. *Educ.:* Stonyhurst; St. Mary's Hospital, London. Formerly Medical Staff Imperial Maritime Customs, Amoy, S. China; Port Surgeon, Perim, Red Sea; later on staff of Prince of Wales's Hospital, N., and Teacher of Anæsthetics in North-West London Post-Graduate College; Examiner to the British Red Cross Society, London; Acting Medical Officer to the Marconi Company, Ltd.; Fellow Royal Society of Medicine; Member British Medical Association. *Publications:* The Place of Ether in General Practice; Anæsthetic Technique for Operations on Nose and Throat; Reports of Chinese Hospital, Amoy, 1892-97; Anæsthesia and the Nurse's Duties, 1917; A Life Tragedy and Other Verses; Lyrics of the Streets; Versiculi Medicinæ, etc.; contributions to various professional journals. *Recreations:* music, historical research. *Address:* 54 Wimpole Street, W.1.   *T.:* Mayfair 566.   *(Died 4 Jan. 1919.)*

PRESCOTT, Ven. John Eustace, D.D.; Archdeacon and Canon of Carlisle since 1883; Chancellor of Diocese of Carlisle since 1900; *b.* Wakefield, Yorkshire; *e. s.* of George Prescott, Gibraltar, and Phœbe, *d.* of Rev. Dr. Naylor, Crofton, Yorkshire; *m.* Rosalie (*d.* 1919). *Educ.:* Peterborough; Corpus Christi Coll. Cambridge. 12th Wrangler, 1855; Scholar and Fellow Corpus Christi College. Ordained, 1858; Vicar of St. Edward's Camb. 1868-71; examining chaplain to Bishop of Carlisle (Goodwin), 1869-91; St. Mary's, Carlisle, 1877-79. *Publications:* Statutes of Carlisle Cathedral, 2nd ed. 1903; Christian Hymns and Hymn Writers, 2nd ed., 1886; Visitations in Ancient Diocese of Carlisle, 1888; Register of Wetherhal, 1897. *Address:* The Abbey, Carlisle.   *(Died 17 Feb. 1920.)*

PRESGRAVE, Col. Edward Robert John, C.B. 1908; D.S.O. 1895; *b.* London, 29 June 1855; *o. s.* of late Lieut. Edward Presgrave, H.E.I.C.S. (retired). *Educ.:* Wellington College. Joined 21st Regiment, 1875; admitted to Madras Staff Corps, 1879; Adjt. 15th Madras Infantry, 1882-86; Capt. 1886; Brevet Major, 1893; Major, 1895; temporary Lieut.-Col., 1895; Lt.-Col. 1901; Col. 1904; Commandant 10th Gurkha Rifles, 1893-1902; Brigade Staff, India, 1900-1; Divisional Staff, India, 1902-6; employed Rumpa Rebellion, 1879; Afghan Campaign, 1879-80 (medal); Burma, 1886-87-89 (medal and 2 clasps); Manipur Expedition, 1891 (clasp); Chin Hills, 1892-94 (despatches, Bt. Maj., D.S.O., clasp); special appointment Nov. 1914 —graded as G.S.O. 3rd Class 1017 (despatches). *Club:* East India United Service.   854   *(Died 12 Sept. 1919.)*

PRESSLY, David Leith, editor Yorkshire Herald and allied newspapers, York, since 1903; *b.* Stuartfield, Aberdeenshire, 14 July 1855; father, carpenter and crofter; married; two *s.* five *d.* *Educ.:* Old Deer Public School; Aberdeen schools. Reporter in Aberdeen, 1872; connected with Aberdeen Free Press and People's Journal till 1880; went out to Cape Colony; was on staff of Cape Times; 14 years in Ulster as editor Londonderry Sentinel, and leader-writer on Evening Telegraph, Belfast; editor of Aberdeen Daily Journal and Aberdeen Evening Express, 1894-1902; managing editor of East of England Newspaper Company's series of daily and weekly papers, Norwich, 1902-3; organized and edited the King's Book of York Heroes as war memorial, 1920. *Recreations:* painting, sketching, gardening. *Address:* Holgate House, York.   *T.:* York 452.   *(Died 11 April 1922.)*

PRESTON, Henry Edward; J.P. East and West Riding of Yorks.; *b.* July 1857; *o. s.* of Thos. Preston of Moreby, Yorks, and Georgina, 3rd *d.* of Sir Guy Campbell, 1st Bart.; *m.* 1886, Beatrice, 3rd *d.* of Archbishop Thomson of York; one *s.* one *d.* *Educ.:* Eton. *Publication:* editor of Foxhound Kennel Stud Book. *Address:* Moreby Park, York. *Club:* Yorkshire.   *(Died 5 June 1924.)*

PRESTON, Sir Jacob, 4th Bt., *cr.* 1815; partner firm of Loewen, Harvey, and Preston, Ltd., Vancouver, British Columbia; *b.* 6 May 1867; *s.* of 3rd Bt. and Mary Hope, *d.* of late Edmund Lewis Clutterbuck, Hardenhuish Park, Wiltshire; *S.* father 1897. *Educ.:* Eton; Trinity College, Cambridge; B.A., LL.B. Owns about 6000 acres. *Heir:* *b.* Edward Hulton, Lieut. 2nd Batt. Royal Sussex Regt., *b.* 17 Sept. 1888. *Address:* Barton Hall, Neatishead, Norwich. *Club:* Bath. *(Died 12 Feb. 1918.)*

PRETYMAN, Major-Gen. Sir George Tindal, K.C.M.G., *cr.* 1900; C.B. 1896; *b.* 1 March 1845; *e. s.* of late Rev. J. R. Pretyman, M.A., formerly Vicar of Aylesbury, and Amelia, *d.* of Thomas Tindal, of Prebendal House, Aylesbury; *m.* 1889, Winifred, *d.* of late F. Locke, J.P., D.L., Kent, of Dane House, Hartlip, Sittingbourne; two *s.* *Educ.:* Wimbledon School; R.M.A. Woolwich. Joined R.A. 1865; served Canada during Fenian Raids, 1866 and 1870 (medal and 2 clasps); A.D.C. to Gen. Sir F. Roberts during Afghan War, 1878-80 (despatches thrice, Afghan medal and three clasps, bronze star for march from Kabul to Kandahar, brevets of Major and Lieut.-Colonel); Military Secretary to Sir F. Roberts in Madras, 1881-84; A.A.G. for R.A. in India, 1887-89; commanded a 2nd class district, Bengal, 1889-94, with rank of Brigadier-General; commanded 1st Infantry Brigade, Isazai Expedition, 1892; Major-Gen. 1897; Commandant at Headquarters, South Africa, 1899-1900 (despatches twice); Military Governor, Bloemfontein, 1900; commanded Kimberley District, 1901 (medal, 4 clasps, K.C.M.G.); commanded Secunderabad District, India, 1902-3; Forces in Madras, 1904; Burma Division, 1906; retired 1907; Colonel Commandant, Royal Artillery, 1908; Distinguished Service Reward, 1903. *Recreations:* shooting, riding, sport generally. *Address:* Beech Hurst, Camberley. *Club:* United Service.   *(Died 3 Aug. 1917.)*

PRICE, Sir Charles Rugge-, D.L., J.P.; 6th Bt., *cr.* 1804; late Hon. Col. 3rd Batt. E. Surrey Regt.; *b.* 26 May 1841; *o. s.* of 5th Bt. and 1st *cousin,* Mary, *d.* of Richard Price, South Lambeth; *S.* father, 1892; *m.* 1867, Antonia (*d.* 1918), *d.* of William James Harvey, of Carnousie, Co. Banff; one *s.* four *d.* *Educ.:* Harrow. *Heir:* *s.* Charles Frederick (late Lt.-Col. Royal Field Artillery, *b.* 5 Feb. 1868; *m.* 1901, Isabella Napier Keith, *e. d.* of Maj.-Gen. Sir J. Keith Trotter, K.C.B.; two *s.* two *d.*]. *Address:* Spring Grove, Richmond, Surrey.   *(Died 4 May 1927.)*

PRICE, Commander George Edward, R.N., retired ; *s.* of late George Price, *s.* of Sir Rose Price, 1st Bart., of Trengwainton, and Hon. Emily Valentine Plunkett, *d.* of 14th Lord Dunsany ; *b.* 1842 ; *m.* 1878, Gertrude Laurence, adopted *d.* of Phoebe, *widow of* Joseph Locke, M.P. ; three *d.* M.P., Devonport, 1874–92. *Address :* Thorpe Place, Chertsey. *Clubs :* Carlton, Wellington. (*Died 29 June 1926.*)

PRICE, Sir (John) Frederick, K.C.S.I., *cr.* 1898 ; C.S.I. 1893 ; *b.* 3 Oct. 1889 ; *e. s.* of late John Price, 4th *s.* of Sir Rose Price of Trengwainton, 1st Bt., and Mary, *d.* of Major Franklin ; *m.* 1863, Alice, *y. d.* of Hon. H. D. Phillips, Member of Council, Fort St. George, Madras ; two *s.* three *d. Educ. :* Melbourne University. Entered Madras Civil Service, 1862; retired, 1897. *Publications :* Ootacamund, a History ; Editor of the first three volumes of Ananda Ranga Pillais Diary. *Address :* Trengwainton, Exmouth, South Devon. (*Died 12 June 1927.*)

PRICE, Julius Mendes, F.R.G.S. ; Knight of the Order of the Crown of Italy; artist, author, war correspondent ; Official War Correspondent to Italian Govt. 1917 ; *b.* London ; *s.* of Simon Price, merchant, London. *Educ. :* Univ. Coll. School ; Brussels ; École des Beaux-Arts, Paris. Special war artist-correspondent of the Illustrated London News ; was in the Bechuanaland campaign, South Africa, 1884–1885, on which occasion enlisted for journalistic purposes as a trooper in Methuen's Horse, and served with the regiment till it was disbanded ; with Exploration Expedition to open up the Nordenskiold route to the interior of Siberia via the Kara Sea, the Arctic coast of Siberia, and up the Yenesei river, afterwards unaccompanied traversing Siberia, Mongolia, the Gobi Desert, and Northern China to Pekin, 1890–91 ; Expedition through the Western Australian Goldfields, 1895 ; with the Greek Army during the Græco-Turkish War, 1897 ; Expedition across N.-W. Territory, Canada, and down the Yukon River to Klondike, 1898 ; with the Russian Army in Manchuria, Russo-Japanese War, 1904–5, acting in a dual capacity as special artist of the Illustrated London News and war correspondent of the Daily Telegraph ; in the Great War, on the French Front in the early months and later with the Italian Army ; G.H.Q. Lecturer, British Army of Occupation, Germany, 1919 ; Italian Military Medal, 1918. *Publications :* From the Arctic Ocean to the Yellow Sea, 1892 ; The Land of Gold, 1896 ; From Euston to Klondike, 1898 ; Dame Fashion, 1913 ; My Bohemian Days in Paris, 1913 ; My Bohemian Days in London, 1914 ; Six Months on the Italian Front, 1917 ; On the Path of Adventure, 1919 ; writer Fortnightly Review and innumerable magazine articles illustrated from his own sketches ; exhibitor at the Royal Academy and Paris Salon ; medal, Paris Exhibition, 1900. *Address :* 21 Golden Square, W.1. *T.A. :* Pricellum, London. *T. :* Gerrard 2575. *Club :* Savage.
(*Died 29 Sept. 1924.*)

PRICE, Richard John Lloyd, F.R.A., F.A.S., F.I.D., F.Z.S. ; J.P., D.L., Merionethshire ; J.P. Carnarvons. and Denbighs. ; Deputy Chairman of Quarter Sessions for Merionethshire ; High Sheriff, Merionethshire, 1868 ; Temp. Deputy Chairman of Dee Conservations at Chester during European War : still on Committee ; served on County Advisory Committee, mostly Acting Chairman during strenuous portion of war ; *b.* 17 April 1843 ; *m.* 1869, Evelyn, *y. d.* of late Capt. Gregge-Hopwood of Hopwood Hall, Lancs ; one *s. Educ. :* Eton ; Christ Church, Oxford. *Publications :* Rabbits for Profit and Rabbits for Powder ; Practical Pheasant Rearing ; Grouse Driving ; Dogs Ancient and Modern ; The Valley of the Welsh Dee ; Walks in Wales ; Dogs' Tales ; Whist over a Sandwich ; Bridge over a Sandwich. *Recreations :* literature and journalism, judging at Field Trials and Dog Shows, shooting, fishing, and the study of dogs, animals, and birds generally. Owns 64,000 acres in Merionethshire and property in Denbighshire. *Heir : s.* Robert Kenrick [*b.* 3 June 1870. *Educ. :* Eton ; Sandhurst. Captain 3rd Buffs, East Kent Regt. since 1899 (retired July 1901) ; rejoined on declaration of war ; Transport Officer at Woolwich and Bedford until Armistice signed ; *m.* 1905, May, 3rd *d.* of late Albert Brassey of Heythrop Hall, Oxon. ; one *s.* two *d.*]. *Address :* 40 Albemarle Street, W.1. *T. :* Regent 5299 ; *T.A. :* Canis, St. James's, London ; Rhiwlas, Bala, N. Wales ; *T.A. :* Price, Rhiwlas, Bala. *M. :* FF 46. *Clubs :* Turf, Carlton, Union, Eccentric, M.C.C., City University ; Grosvenor, Chester.
(*Died 9 Jan., 1923.*)

PRICE, Sir Robert John, Kt., *cr.* 1908 ; M.P. (L.) East Norfolk 1892–1918 ; *b.* 26 Apr. 1854 ; *y. s.* of late Edward Price, Highgate, railway contractor ; *m.* 1881, Eva, 2nd *d.* of late J. W. Johns, formerly M.P. for N.E. Warwickshire. *Educ. :* Cholmeley School, Highgate ; Univ. Coll. Hospital. M.R.C.S. 1876 ; Barr. Middle Temple, 1883. *Recreations :* golf, bicycling. *Address :* 6 Sussex Mansions, S.W.7. *T. :* Kensington 3254; The Thatched House, Wroxham, Norfolk ; Bank, Lyndhurst, Hants. *Club :* National Liberal.
(*Died 18 April 1926.*)

PRICE, Sir Thomas Rees, K.C.M.G., *cr.* 1908 ; C.M.G. 1901 ; Railway Commissioner South African Railways, Johannesburg, 1902–16; a Public Debt Commissioner for the Union of South Africa ; *b.* Merthyr Tydvil, 20 Feb. 1848 ; *o. s.* of late Rees Price of Llandovery, Carmarthenshire, South Wales, and Hannah Rhys, of Llandilo, Carmarthenshire ; *m.* 1872, Mary, *d.* of Matthias Howell, of Neath ; one *s.* one *d. Educ. :* private school, Ballarat, Victoria ; Melbourne ; Normal College, Swansea, South Wales. Trained for railway service by late Joshua Williams, General Manager of Vale of Neath Railway, etc. ; filled various positions on Great Western Railway until 1880 ; entered service of Cape Government as District Traffic Superintendent at Grahamstown ; Acting Assistant Traffic Manager, Cape Town, 1880 ; Assistant Traffic Manager, Port Elizabeth, 1881 ; Traffic Manager of the Eastern System, 1882 ; Traffic Manager, Northern System, 1892 ; Cape Government Railway Agent in the Transvaal and Orange Free State, 1892 ; Chief Traffic Manager, 1893 ; Assistant General Manager of Railways, 1901 ; General Manager Central South African Railways, 1902, and a Commissioner of Railways and Harbours of the Union of South Africa on the establishment of Union, 1910 ; acted as railway adviser to Sir James Sivewright in the negotiations with the Transvaal Government, which resulted in the Railway Convention of 1891 ; J.P. Cape Colony and Transvaal ; Hon. Associate of the Order of St. John of Jerusalem ; member of Geographical Society of Lisbon. *Address :* Glyn Neath, 19 Union Street, The Gardens, Cape Town. *Clubs :* Royal Societies ; Civil Service, Cape Town ; Pretoria ; East London. (*Died 26 Sept. 1916.*)

PRICE, Sir William, Kt., *cr.* 1915 ; President and Managing Director, Price Bros. & Co., Ltd., Lumber and Paper Manufacturers ; *b.* Talca, Chile, 30 Aug. 1867 ; *s.* of Henry Ferrier Price and Florence S. Rogerson ; *m.* 1904, Amelia Blanche, *d.* of late R. H. Smith, President, Quebec Bank ; four *s.* two *d. Educ. :* Bishop's College School, Lennoxville ; St. Mark's School, Windsor, England. Entered firm, 1886 ; sole partner, 1899 ; Chairman, Quebec Harbour Commission, 1912 ; M.P. Quebec West, 1908 ; Conservative ; Anglican. *Recreations :* yachting and fishing. *Address :* 145 Grand Allee, Quebec. *Clubs :* Garrison, Rideau, Quebec, Ottawa ; Mt.

Royal, Montreal ; St George's, Sherbrooks.
(*Died 2 Oct. 1924.*)

PRICE, Rev. William James, Hon. Canon, Birmingham, 1905. *Educ.* : Jesus College, Oxford (Scholar). Curate of Shelton, Staffs, 1870-1872; Mirfield, 1872-75; St. Peter's, Wolverhampton, 1875-79 ; Vicar of Lilleshall, Salop, 1879-91 ; Vicar and Rural Dean of Harborne, 1891-1915. *Address* : Salterton Road, Exmouth.
(*Died 11 Feb. 1928.*)

PRICHARD, Arthur William, V.D. Member Royal College of Surgeons of England ; Lt.-Col. R.A.M.C. (T.F.) ; retired ; late Commanding 3rd South Midland Field Ambulance ; Consulting Surgeon to Bristol Royal Infirmary ; Consulting Surgeon to the British Eye Dispensary ; late Surgeon to Clifton College ; *s.* of late Augustin Prichard of Clifton, and *g.s.* of Dr James Cowles Prichard, F.R.S., the Ethnologist; *m.* Sarah Anne, *e. d.* of late Dr. William Adye of Bradford-on-Avon ; two *s.* three *d. Educ.* : Clifton College ; Bristol Medical School and University College, London. Practices as a Surgeon in Clifton ; was for 28 years on the active staff of the Bristol Royal Infirmary, and Lecturer on Practical Surgery ; Surgeon to the Bristol Rifles for many years, and Brigade Surgeon to the Portland Volunteer Infantry Brigade ; when the Territorials came into existence in 1908 he was asked to raise and command a Field Ambulance for Bristol ; this unit was one of the first completed to its full establishment of officers and men. *Address* : 6 Rodney Place, Clifton. *T.* : Bristol 689. (*Died Jan. 1926.*)

PRICHARD, Maj. H. Hesketh, D.S.O. 1918 ; M.C. ; *b.* Nov. 1876 ; *s.* of Lieutenant Hesketh Brodrick Prichard, and Kate, *d.* of Gen. Ryall ; *m.* 1908, Lady Elizabeth Grimston, 4th *d.* of 3rd Earl of Verulam;   two *s.* one *d. Educ.* : Fettes. Has travelled and shot big game in Patagonia, Labrador, Canada, Sardinia, Spain, Mexico, Newfoundland, Haiti, etc. ; leader of Patagonian Expedition, 1900-1 ; played cricket for Hampshire, 1899-1913, and Gentlemen *v.* Players, 1903-4-5 ; A.D.C. to Lord Lieutenant of Ireland, 1907 ; served European War, 1914-18 (despatches twice, Commander of the Military Order of Avis). *Publications* : Where Black Rules White: a Journey across and about Haiti, 1900 ; Through the Heart of Patagonia, 1902 ; Hunting Camps in Wood and Wilderness, 1910 ; Through Trackless Labrador, 1911 ; and in collaboration with his mother, Mrs. K. Hesketh Prichard, A Modern Mercenary, 1898 ; Karadac, Count of Gersay, 1900 ; Tammer's Duel, 1901 ; Roving Hearts, 1903 ; Don Q, 1904 ; New Chronicles of Don Q, 1906 ; Sniping in France, 1920. *Recreations* : cricket, shooting, natural history and fishing. *Address* : Prae Wood, St. Albans. *Clubs* : M.C.C., Authors'. (*Died 14 June 1922.*)

PRICHARD-JONES, Sir John, 1st Bt., *cr.* 1910 ; LL.D., D.L., J.P. ; *b.* 31 May 1845 ; *m.* 2nd, 1911, Marie, *y. d.* of late Charles Read ; two *s.* Sheriff of Anglesey, 1905 ; Treasurer, Welsh National Museum ; Appointments Board of Wales and The Roberts Marine Mansions, Bexhill-on-Sea ; Member of the Council of the North Wales University College, Bangor, and Vice-President of the Council, 1909. *Heir* : *s.* John Prichard-Jones, *b.* 20 Jan. 1913. *Address* : Maes yr Hâv, Elstree, Herts ; Bron Menai, Dwyran, Anglesey. *Club* : Royal Automobile.
(*Died 17 Oct. 1917.*)

PRIDEAUX, Sir Walter Sherburne, Kt., *cr.* 1891, for services on various occasions and especially with the repeal of the gold and silver plate duties ; *b.* London, 23 Feb. 1846 ; *e. s.* of Walter Prideaux, Goldsmiths' Hall, London, and Faircrouch, Wadhurst, and Elizabeth, *d.* of General S. H. Williams, R.E.; *m.* 1873, Catharine Mary (*d.* 1924), *er. d.* of Rev. J. V. Povah, minor Canon of St. Paul's ; three *s.* two *d. Educ.* : Eton. Admitted solicitor (Honours),

1870 ; assistant clerk of the Goldsmiths' Co., 1871-82 ; Clerk of the Goldsmiths' Company, 1882-1918. *Publications* : Memorials of the Goldsmiths' Company, 2 vols. 1896 (printed for private circulation). *Recreations* : formerly Capt. of Eton Cricket and Football Elevens, and President of Eton Debating Society ; shooting, natural history. *Address* : Goldsmiths' Hall, E.C. *Club* : Junior Carlton.
(*Died 29 Jan. 1928.*)

PRIDMORE, Albert Edward; President of the Society of Architects, 1905-6, 1906-7 ; Fellow of the Surveyors Institution ; *b.* Coventry, 1864 ; 3rd *s.* of George Alexander Pridmore ; *m.* 1893, Edith Maud, 2nd *d.* of late Tom Bonsell Shepperson. *Educ.* : private schools. Member of Court of Common Council of City of London, 1894-1907 ; Chairman of Guildhall School of Music Committee, 1899 ; Billingsgate and Leadenhall Markets Committee, 1905 ; Member Hon. Irish Society, 1904-5 ; Past President Bishopsgate Ward Club; Chairman Watford Town Council, 1900 ; First Chairman of Executive Committee Society of Warwickshire Folk in London : late An Estates Governor of Dulwich College ; Past Master of Painter Stainers' Company; architect of many important buildings of a public, commercial, and private character ; as a surveyor, a recognised authority on rating matters and valuations for parochial assessments. *Publication* : Rating and City Assessments. *Recreation* : fishing. *Address* : 3 Broad Street Buildings, E.C.2; 35 Ashworth Mansions, Elgin Avenue, W. *T.* : London Wall 1374. (*Died 1 Nov. 1927.*)

PRIMROSE, Rt. Hon. Sir Henry, K.C.B., *cr.* 1899 ; C.S.I. 1885 ; I.S.O. 1904 ; P.C. 1912 ; *b.* 22 August 1846 ; *s.* of late Hon. Bouverie F. Primrose, C.B., 2nd *s.* of 4th Earl of Rosebery ; *m.* 1888, Helen Mary (*d.* 1919), *d.* of G. McMicking of Miltonise, Wigtownshire. *Educ.* : Trinity College, Glenalmond ; Balliol College, Oxford. Entered Treasury, 1869 ; Private Secretary to Viceroy of India (Marquis of Ripon), 1880-84 ; and to Mr. Gladstone, 1886 ; Secretary to H.M. Office of Works, 1886-95 ; Chairman Board of Customs, 1895-99 ; Board of Inland Revenue, 1899-1907 ; Chairman Pacific Cable Board, 1907-14 ; Welsh Church Commission, 1914. *Address* : 44 Ennismore Gardens, S.W.7. *T.* : Western 1565.
(*Died 17 June 1923.*)

PRIMROSE, Sir John Ure; 1st Bart., *cr.* 1903 ; LL.D., Glasgow ; J.P. ; Lord Provost of Glasgow, 1902, and Lord Lieutenant of the County of the City of Glasgow ; senior partner William Primrose and Sons, Flour Millers, Centre Street, Glasgow ; *b.* 16 Oct. 1847 ; *e. s.* of late William Primrose, merchant miller in Glasgow, and Annie (*d.* 1913), *d.* of John Ure, baker and merchant miller in Glasgow, and *:. .* of late John Ure, LL.D., ex-Lord Provost of Glasgow ; *m.* 1st, 1877, Margaret Jane (*d.* 1896), *d.* of James Adam, merchant, Glasgow ; one *s.* ; 2nd, 1897, Anna (*d.* 1913), *d.* of Alexander Spence Wylie, merchant, Glasgow ; 3rd, 1915, Muriel, *widow* of James Donald, shipowner, Glasgow, and *d.* of late Edwin Pilling of Rochdale and Liverpool. *Educ.* : Collegiate School. Entered Town Council of Glasgow 1886 ; magistrate, 1891 ; Chairman of the Clyde Navigation Trustees ; president of numerous public institutions in the city. *Heir* : *s.* William Louis Primrose [*b.* 1 June 1880 ; *m.* 1907, Elizabeth Caroline, *d.* of Hugh Dunmuir, Glasgow ; two *s.*]. *Recreations* : music, photography. *Address* : Redholme, Dumbreck, Glasgow. *Clubs* : Constitutional, Art, Glasgow.
(*Died 29 June 1924.*)

PRIMROSE, Rt. Hon. Neil (James Archibald) ; P.C. 1917 ; M.P. (L.) Wisbech Division, Cambridge, since 1910 ; *b.* 14 Dec. 1882 ; *y. s.* of 5th Earl of Rosebery ;   *m.* 1915, Lady Victoria Alice Louise Stanley, *o. d.* of

17th Earl of Derby;   one *d.*   *Educ.:* Eton; Oxford. Capt. Bucks Yeomanry; Parliamentary Under-Secretary to Foreign Office, Feb.-May 1915; Parliamentary Military Sec. to Min. of Munitions, Sep.-Dec. 1916; Parliamentary Secretary to Treasury Dec. 1916-May 1917. *Address:* 5 Great Stanhope Street, W.; The Manor House, Postwick, Norwich. *T.:* Mayfair 2560.   (*Died 17 Nov. 1917.*)

PRING, Hon. Robert Darlow, Judge of Supreme Court of New South Wales since 1902; *b.* N.S.Wales, 29 Jan. 1853; *s.* of John and Elizabeth Newnham Pring; *m.* 1882, Mary Jane King; three *s.* one *d. Educ.:* The King's School and Sydney University. B.A. 1873; M.A. 1876; admitted to Bar, 1874. *Recreations:* reading, walking. *Address:* Supreme Court, Sydney, N.S.W. *T.:* Ashfield 356. *Club:* Australian, Sydney.   (*Died Aug. 1922.*)

PRINGLE, Sir John, K.C.M.G., *cr.* 1911; C.M.G. 1900; Member of Privy and Legislative Councils, Jamaica; landowner; *b.* 26 July 1848; *s.* of John Pringle of Whaup, Co. Roxburgh; *m.* 1876, Amy Zillah, *d.* of late Hon. J. Levy of St. Jago Park, Spanish Town, Jamaica; four *s.* two *d. Educ.:* University, Aberdeen. *Address:* The Manor House, Conostant Spring, Jamaica. *Clubs:* Constitutional, Empire, West Indian; Jamaica, Kingston.   (*Died 15 Mar. 1923.*)

PRINGLE, John James, M.B., C.M., F.R.C.P.; 3rd *s.* of late Andrew Pringle of Borgue, Kirkcudbrightshire, N.B. *Educ.:* Edinburgh, Dublin, Vienna, Paris, Berlin. Consulting Physician, Skin Department, Middlesex Hospital; late President of Dermatological Section, Royal Society of Medicine; Physician, Royal Scottish Corporation and Royal Caledonian Asylum. *Publications:* numerous articles on Diseases of the Skin. *Address:* 23 Lower Seymour Street, W.1. *T.:* Paddington 3205.   (*Died 18 Dec. 1922.*)

PRINGLE, Sir Norman Robert, 8th Bt., *cr.* 1683; *b.* 18 Oct. 1871; *o. s.* of 7th Bt. and Louisa, *y. d.* of Robert Steuart, M.P., Alderston; *S.* father, 1897; *m.* 1902, Madge, *d.* of T. Vaughan; three *s.* one *d. Heir: s.* Norman Hamilton; *b.* 13 May 1903. *Address:* Newhall, Galashiels, N.B.   (*Died 18 April 1919.*)

PRINGLE, Maj.-Gen. Sir Robert, K.C.M.G., *cr.* 1917; C.B. 1909; D.S.O. 1902; Army Vet. Dept. Vet. Surg. 1878; Vet. Lt.-Col. 1901; *b.* 25 Aug. 1855; *s.* of Gilbert Pringle of Stanraer; *m.* 1898, Sophie, *e. d.* of George Moir Byres of Tonley. Served Afghan War, 1879-80 (medal); Wuzeree Expedition, 1881 (despatches); Zhob Valley Expedition, 1884; South Africa, 1900-1 (despatches, D.S.O., medal 3 clasps); European War (K.C.M.G., medal); Colonel, 1907; Director-General A.V. Service, 1910-17. *Address:* Fairbourne, Farnham, Surrey.   (*Died 30 June 1926.*)

PRINGLE, William Mather Rutherford, M.P. (L.) N.W. Lanarkshire, 1910-18, and Penistone Division of Yorks, 1922-24; *b.* Berwickshire, 1874. *Educ.:* Glasgow University. Bar. Middle Temple; contested Camlachie Division, Glasgow, 1906. *Address:* 1 Garden Court, Temple, E.C.: 17 Enmore Road, Putney, S.W.   (*Died 1 April 1928.*)

PRIOR, Colonel Hon. Edward Gawler, P.C. (Victoria City); Lieutenant-Governor of British Columbia since 1919; *b.* Dallowgill, near Ripon, Yorkshire, 21 May 1853; 2nd *s.* of late Rev. Henry Prior; *m.* 1st, 1878, Suzette (*d.* 1897), *y. d.* of Hon. John Work, of Hillside, Victoria; 2nd, 1899, Genevieve, *e. d.* of Capt. J. Wright; one *s.* three *d. Educ.:* Leeds Grammar School. Mining engineer and surveyor for the Vancouver Coal Mining and Land Company, 1878; Government Inspector of Mines, 1878-80; resigned to commence business as an iron and hardware merchant; Lieut.-Col. commanding the 5th Reg. Canadian Artillery,

1888-96; Hon. A.D.C. to the Governors-General of Canada, 1889, under Lords Stanley and Aberdeen; commanded the Canadian rifle team at Bisley, 1890; twice President of the Dominion Artillery Association; one of the Canadian contingent present at the late Queen's Jubilee, 1897; Legislature, British Columbia, 1886-88, resigned at the request of his constituents, and was elected by acclamation the same day to Dominion House of Commons; re-elected, 1891 and 1896; Controller of Inland Revenue and a member of the Cabinet in the administrations of Sir Mackenzie Bowell and Sir Charles Tupper; Minister of Mines in Local Legislature of British Columbia, 10 March 1902 to 31 May 1903; Premier of B.C. from 21 Nov. 1902 to 31 May 1903; a Conservative. *Recreations:* riding, driving, fishing. *Address:* Victoria, British Columbia. *Clubs:* Constitutional; Union, Victoria; Vancouver, Vancouver.   (*Died 12 Dec. 1920.*)

PRIOR, Maj.-Gen. George Upton; *b.* 27 Oct. 1843; *s.* of Col. Prior of Sydney Place, Bath, and Maria Louisa, *d.* of late Colonel Way, Denham Place, Bucks; *m.* 1893, Kathleen, Lady of Grace St. John of Jerusalem, *d.* of Captain Dickinson, Ashton Keynes, Wilts, and *widow* of late Col. Sinclair, 38th Staff. Regt. *Educ.:* Sandhurst. Joined 100th Royal Canadians, exchanging later to 1st Royals; passed Staff College; served on the staffs of the Western, Southern, and Aldershot Districts; was D.A.Q.M.G. during the Afghan campaign of 1879 on the staffs of Generals Sir Donald Stewart and Sir Michael Biddulph (despatches twice, brevet of Lieut.-Col.); commanded 2nd Batt. Royal Scots, 1886; A.A.G. Gibraltar, 1891; commanded Curragh District, 1900, and was at intervals Commander of the Forces in Ireland; member of the South African Deportation, 1901; received thanks of Government; retired 1904; Colonel of the Prince of Wales's Leinster Regiment, Royal Canadians, 1910; is a Knight of Grace of the Order of St. John of Jerusalem; F.R.G.S. *Address:* Ethorpe, Gerrard's Cross, Bucks. *T.A.:* Gerrard's Cross. *T.:* Gerrard's Cross 39. *Clubs:* Army and Navy, Turf, etc.   (*Died 12 Oct. 1919.*)

PRITCHARD, Robert Albion, D.C.L.; Senior Registrar, Probate Registry. *Address:* 21 Dealtry Road, Putney, S.W.; Higham St. Mary, near Colchester. *Club:* Reform.   (*Died 13 Jan. 1916.*)

PRITCHARD, Urban, M.D., F.R.C.S., Emeritus Professor of Aural Surgery, King's Coll., London; *b.* 21 Mar. 1845; 5th *s.* of Andrew Pritchard, F.R.S.E.; *m.* 1872, Lottie, *e. d.* of Blades Pallister; two *s.* two *d. Educ.:* King's College, London; University of Edinburgh. M.D. Edinburgh (gold medallist and scholar); F.R.C.S. Eng.; Fellow, King's College, London. Over twenty-five years Aural Surgeon to King's College Hospital, and Consulting Aural Surgeon to the Royal Ear Hospital; formerly House Physician King's College Hospital; Surgical Registrar, Demonstrator of Physiology, Pathologist, King's College; ex-President of the Otological Society of the United Kingdom; President of 6th International Congress of Otology, 1899. *Publications:* Handbook of Diseases of the Ear, 3 eds.; Cochlea of the Ornithorhynchus-Platypus, Roy. Society's Philosophical Transactions; co-editor for United Kingdom of Archives of Otology. *Address:* St. Teresa, Chesham Bois, Bucks. *T.:* Amersham 79. *Clubs:* National Liberal; University, Edinburgh.   (*Died 16 Oct. 1925.*)

PROBYN, Rt. Hon. Sir Dighton Macnaghten, P.C. 1901; G.C.S.I., *cr.* 1911; G.C.B. (civil), *cr.* 1902, (mil.) 1910; G.C.V.O., *cr.* 1896; K.C.B., *cr.* 1887; K.C.S.I., *cr.* 1876; C.B. 1858; V.C. 1857; I.S.O. 1903; General retired; Comptroller to Queen Alexandra since

857

PRINCE, J.-E., LL.D., K.C. See page xxviii.

1910; **Extra Equerry to the King** since 1910; *b.* 21 Jan. 1833; *s.* of late Captain G. Probyn and Alicia, *d.* of the late Sir F. Workman-Macnaghten, 1st Bt.; *m.* 1872, Letitia (*d.* 1900), *d.* of T. R. Thellusson. Entered army, 1849; Gen. 1888; served Trans-Indus Frontier, 1852-57; Indian Mutiny, 1857-58; China, 1860; Umbeyla Campaign, North-West Frontier, 1863; Col. 11th King Edward's Own Lancers (Probyn's Horse); Equerry to King Edward when Prince of Wales, 1872-77; Comptroller and Treasurer, 1877-91; Keeper of the Privy Purse and Extra Equerry to King Edward, 1901-10; member of Council of Duchy of Lancaster 1901-10; retired from office of Governor of Wellington Coll., 1919. *Address:* Marlborough House, S.W.; Sandringham, Norfolk. *Clubs:* United Service, Marlborough. (*Died 20 June 1924.*)

PROBYN, Sir Lesley Charles, K.C.V.O., *cr.* 1906; *b.* 1834; 4th *s.* of late Captain George Probyn; *m.* 1859, Victoria Charlotte Isabella (*d.* 1911), *d.* of late J. J. Kinloch of Kair, Kincardineshire. *Educ.:* Finchley; Haileybury. Entered Bengal Civil Service, 1854; served as Assistant Magistrate in the Ghazeepore district with the military forces during the Indian Mutiny (medal); joined Financial Department Government of India, 1860, serving for ten years at Lahore as Accountant-General of the Punjab; during this time was for five years Lt.-Col. Commandant of the 1st Punjab Volunteer Rifle Corps; retired from Indian Civil Service, 1879; sent by the Colonial Office on a Special Commission to British Guiana, 1882; Director of Great Northern Railway since 1883; Auditor Duchy of Cornwall, 1891-1915; Member of Council of Prince of Wales since 1897. *Publications:* papers read before, and published in, the Journals of, the Institute of Bankers, the Royal Statistical Society, the East India Association, and the Royal Colonial Institute, on financial and monetary questions. *Address:* 79 Onslow Square, S.W. *Club:* East India United Service. (*Died 20 Oct. 1916.*)

PROCTER, Rev. Charles James, M.A.; Prebendary of St. Paul's Cathedral, 1917-23; Chairman of Peache Trustees; *s.* of late George Procter, of Wakefield and Ebor House, Cambridge; *m.* Emily E., *d.* of Rev. Walter Scott Dumergue, Vicar of Fareham, godson of Sir Walter Scott; no *c. Educ.:* Owens College, Manchester; Trinity College, Cambridge. Formerly Vicar and Rural Dean of Islington. *Recreations:* gardening and literature. *Address:* 10 Scroope Terrace, Cambridge.

(*Died 24 Nov. 1925.*)

PROCTER, Sir Henry Edward Edleston, Kt., *cr.* 1911; C.B.E. 1918; *b.* 30 April 1866; *s.* of late Charles Edward Procter, of Macclesfield; *m.* 1897, Helen Matilda, C.B.E., *d.* of late Lieut.-Col. Thomas Arthur Freeman, East Surrey Regiment; one *s.* two *d. Educ.:* Birkenhead School. Late Commandant of the Bombay Light Horse. *Address:* 36 Princes Gardens, S.W.7. *Clubs:* Royal Automobile, Oriental. (*Died 11 July 1923.*)

PROCTER, Henry Richardson, F.R.S.; D.Sc.; F.I.C.; F.C.S.; Emeritus Professor of Applied Chemistry (Leather Industries), University of Leeds; Hon. Member of Leathersellers Company; *s.* of John Richardson Procter of North Shields; *b.* 6 May 1848; *m.* 1874, Emma Lindsay, *d.* of late James Watson of Newcastle; two *s.* one *d. Educ.:* Boothain School, York; Royal College of Chemistry. Late Head of Leather Industries Dept., Univ. Leeds, 1891; Hon. Editor of Journal of Society of Leather Trades Chemists; Hon. Director of Procter International Research Laboratory, Leeds. *Publications:* joint translator of Kohlrausch's Physical Measurements; article on Aurora, Encyclopædia Britannica, ninth edition; Textbook of Tanning; Cantor and Cobb Lectures on Leather Manufacture; Leather Industries

858

Laboratory Book; Principles of Leather Manufacture; Leather Chemists Pocket Book; The Making of Leather, etc. *Recreations:* gardening, photography, sketching. *Address:* Fradgen, Newlyn, Penzance; The University, Leeds. *T.:* 20251. *M.:* AF 4882. *Club:* Authors.
(*Died 17 Aug. 1927.*)

PROCTER, Rev. John Mathias, M.A.; Hon. Canon of St. Albans since 1882; *b.* 7 Sep. 1835; 2nd *s.* of Edward Procter, Solicitor, of Macclesfield; *m.* 1864, Marian Marden, *o. d.* of Samuel Mitchell of Great Newbury, Ilford; two *s.* one *d. Educ.:* Macclesfield Grammar School; Trinity College, Oxford (Exhibition) 2nd class Mods. 1856, 2nd class Lit. Hum. 1858. Fellow of Jesus College, Oxford, 1859-64; Deacon, 1859; Priest, 1860; Curate of Barkingside and Aldborough Hatch, 1862-64; Vicar of Barkingside and Aldborough Hatch, 1864-79; Rector of Laindon cum Basildon, 1879-88; Hon. Secretary of Bishop of Rochester's Fund, 1870-78; Bishop of St. Albans Fund, 1878-1910; Rural Dean of Bishop's Stortford, 1893-1904; Proctor in Convocation for the Diocese of St. Albans, 1895-1906; Rector of Thorley, 1888-1909. *Address:* Thorley Rectory, Bishop's Stortford.
(*Died 22 Jan. 1917.*)

PROCTOR, Capt. Andrew Weatherley Beauchamp, V.C.; D.S.O. 1918; M.C., D.F.C.; Royal Air Force. Served European War, 1914-18 (despatches, M.C. with bar, D.F.C., D.S.O., V.C.). (*Died 21 June 1921.*)

PROE, Thomas, C.M.G. 1901; Mayor of Brisbane, 1901; is a Mechanical Engineer; *b.* 21 Jan. 1852; *m.* 1881, Mary Kurth. *Address:* Merthyr Road, Brisbane. (*Died 17 Dec. 1922.*)

PROTHERO, Sir George Walter, K.B.E., *cr.* 1920; M.A., Litt.D. (Cambridge), Hon. LL.D. (Edinburgh and Harvard); Hon. Fellow of King's College Cambridge; Fellow of the British Academy; Corresponding Member of Massachusetts Historical Society; Foreign Honorary Member of the American Academy of Arts and Sciences (Boston); Member of Société d'Histoire Moderne (Paris); Vice-President Royal Historical Society; editor of the Quarterly Review; *b.* Wiltshire, 14 Oct. 1848; *e. s.* of late Rev. Canon Prothero, Whippingham, Isle of Wight, and Emma, *d.* of Rev. William Money-Kyrle, Homme House, Herefordshire; *m.* Mary Frances, *d.* of late Dr. Samuel Butcher, Bishop of Meath, 1882. *Educ.:* Eton; King's Coll. Camb. (Scholar) M.A.; Univ. of Bonn. Bell Scholar, 1869; 1st class in the Classical Tripos, 1872. Fellow of King's Coll. Camb.; assistant master at Eton; Lecturer under University Extension Scheme at Nottingham, Leicester, etc.; University Lecturer in History and tutor of King's College, 1876-94; Prof. of History, University of Edinburgh, 1894-99; President of the Royal Historical Society, 1901-5; Rede Lecturer (Cambridge), 1903; Lowell Lecturer (Boston), and Schouler Lecturer (Johns Hopkins), 1910; Chichele Lecturer (Oxford), 1920; Governor of Holloway College, 1916; Member of Royal Commission for Ecclesiastical Discipline, 1904-6; Director of the Historical Section, F.O., 1918-19; Member of the British Peace Delegation, 1919; Officer of the Crown of Belgium, 1919. *Publications:* Life and Times of Simon de Montfort, 1877; edition of Voltaire's Louis Quatorze, with notes, 1879; translation of vol. i. of Ranke's Weltgeschichte, 1888; Memoir of Henry Bradshaw, 1889; Select Statutes and other documents bearing on the reigns of Elizabeth and James I., 1894; British History Reader, 2 vols. 1898; School History of Gr. Britain and Ireland (to 1910), 1912; German Policy before the War, 1916; editor of Sir J. R. Seeley's Growth of British Policy, 1895, and of the Cambridge Historical Series, and co-editor of the Cambridge Modern History; editor of the series of Peace Handbooks issued by the Foreign Office, 1920; contributor to Encyclopædia Brit-

annica and the Dictionary of National Biography. *Recreations:* mountaineering. fishing, cycling. *Address:* 24 Bedford Square, W.C.1. *T.:* Museum 1495. *Clubs:* Athenæum, Alpine; Rye Golf.
(*Died 10 July 1922.*)

PROTHERO, Vice - Adm. Reginald Charles, R.N., C.B. 1900; M.V.O.; *s.* of Charles Prothero, Newport; *b.* 15 June 1849. *Educ.:* Royal Navy. Entered Navy, 1863; Captain, 1895; retired, 1904; Rear-Admiral, 1906; served South Africa, 1900 (C.B.); Commanded Naval Brigade at battles of Belmont and Graspan (wounded). (*Died 26 Mar. 1927.*)

PROVIS, Sir Samuel Butler, K.C.B., *cr.* 1901; C.B. 1887; Companion of Honour, 1918; *b.* Warminster, 9 Feb. 1845; *e. s.* of Samuel and Mary Provis. *Educ.:* Queens' Coll., Camb. Barr. Middle Temple, 1866; Junior Legal Assistant to the Local Government Board, 1872; Assistant Secretary, 1882 - 89; Permanent Secretary, 1898 - 1910. *Address:* 2 Whitehall Court, S.W. *Clubs:* Union, New Oxford and Cambridge. (*Died 11 July 1926.*)

PROWSE, Arthur Bancks, Lt.-Col. R.A.M.C.(T.); lately Administrator and Officer Commanding 2nd Southern General Hospital, Bristol; M.D. (Lond.), F.R.C.S. (Eng.); Consulting Physician, Bristol Royal Infirmary; County Organiser for Devonshire, English Place-Name Society; *b.* Millbrook, Plymouth, 1856; *e. s.* of Dr. William Prowse; *m.* 1896, Margaret W. (*d.* 1921), *y. d.* of late G. Mitchell of Glasgow and Helensburgh; two *s.* one *d.* *Educ.:* Amersham Grammar School, Bucks; Amersham Hall School, nr. Reading; Liverpool Medical School; St. Mary's Hospital, London; M.B. Lond. with Honours in Medicine, Obstetric Medicine and Forensic Medicine, 1878. Assistant Physician, Bristol Royal Infirmary, 1883; Physician, 1888; Consulting Physician since 1919; Dean of the Faculty, 1888-1910; Lecturer in Materia Medica, Pharmacology, and Therapeutics, Bristol Medical School, 1888-1905; Churchwarden, Clifton Parish Church, 1888-1917; President, Bristol Naturalists' Society, 1901-3; President, Bristol Anti-Narcotic League, 1902-4; Pres., British-Israel National Union, 1909-10; abstainer, non-smoker, and spelling reformer. *Publications:* papers on medical and archæological subjects (especially upon Dartmoor). *Recreations:* gardening, family history, and prehistoric archæology. *Address:* 5 Lansdown Place, Clifton, Bristol. *T.:* 1947 Bristol. (*Died 26 April 1925.*)

PROWSE, Richard Thomas, C.B. 1897; J.P. for Hertfordshire; *b.* Swanage, Dorset, 1835; 2nd *s.* of late Captain William Prowse, R.N., Weymouth; unmarried. *Educ.:* Christ's Hospital, London. Entered the Customs Service, 1853; Surveyor-General of the Customs, 1883-1888; Secretary to the Board of Customs, 1888-1900. *Address:* Howton, Bushey Heath, Hertfordshire. *T.A.:* Bushey Heath. *M.:* AR 2278.
(*Died 17 Dec. 1921.*)

PRUDDEN, T. Mitchell, M.D.; LL.D. Emeritus Professor of Pathology, College of Physicians and Surgeons, Columbia University, New York; member of Board of Directors of the Rockefeller Institute for Medical Research; *b.* 7 July 1849. *Publications:* A text-book on Pathology; various researches in Experimental Pathology; popular works on Sanitation and Travel. *Address:* 160 West 59th Street, New York. (*Died 10 April 1924.*)

PRYCE, Rev. R. Vaughan, D.D.; Principal and Professor of Theology, New College, London University, 1889-1907; now Principal Emeritus; *b.* Bristol, Dec. 1834; *s.* of late George Pryce, F.S.A., Librarian of the city of Bristol. *Educ.:* Queen Elizabeth's Hospital, Bristol; New College, London. Graduated in the University of London, B.A. 1859, LL.B. 1860, M.A. 1861; is a D.D. of the University of Glasgow; was Congregational minister in

Brighton, 1862-71; Worcester, 1871-77; London (Stamford Hill), 1877-89; was elected on the Brighton School Board (1870) to represent the advocates of the view that State - supported education should be free, compulsory, and secular; was Lecturer in Logic and Mental and Moral Science in Cheshunt College, Herts, 1877-85; formerly a member of the Faculty of Theology and of the Senate of the University of London. *Recreation:* foreign travel. *Address:* 68 Bethune Road, Stamford Hill, N.
(*Died 20 Sept. 1917.*)

PRYCE-JONES, Colonel Sir Edward, 1st Bt., *cr.* 1918; T.D.; J.P.; D.L.; *b.* Newtown, N. Wales, 1861; *e. s.* of late Sir Pryce Pryce-Jones, and Eleanor, *d.* of E. Rowley Morris; *m.* 1886, Beatrice, *d.* of Herbert Hardie of Orford House, Cheshire; one *s.* one *d.* *Educ.:* Liverpool College; Jesus College, Cambridge (M.A.) Barrister, Inner Temple, 1892; County Councillor and D.L. Montgomeryshire; High Sheriff, 1923; Joint Hon. Secretary-General of Commercial Committee of Allied Inter-Parliamentary Groups, 1917 - 18, and Joint Hon. Treasurer International Parliamentary Union (British Group), 1911-18; Past Master No. 1 Grand Masters' Lodge (London); Junior Dep.-Chancellor of Univ. Court of Wales, 1911-1913; retired from Montgomeryshire Yeomanry Cavalry as Hon. Maj. after 15 years, 1895; raised 5th Vol. Batt. South Wales Borderers, becoming its first and last commanding officer, 1897-1908; Hon. Col. 7th Royal Welsh Fusiliers, 1908; M.P. (C.) Montgomery District, 1895-1906, 1910-18. *Heir:* *s.* Capt. Pryce Victor Pryce-Jones, *b.* 10 June 1887. *Address:* Dolerw, Newtown, North Wales. *Clubs:* Carlton, 1900, Phyllis Court. (*Died 27 May 1926.*)

PRYCE-JONES, Sir Pryce, Kt.; *cr.* 1887; J.P.; *b.* 1834; *m.* 1859, Eleanor (*d.* 1914), *d.* of Edward Rowley Morris, Newtown; four *s.* four *d.* M.P. Montgomery, 1885-86; 1892-95; High Sheriff for Montgomeryshire, 1891 *Address:* Dolerw, Newtown, Wales. (*Died 11 Jan. 1920.*)

PRYKE, Rev. William Emmanuel, M.A.; Canon and Chancellor of Exeter Cathedral; *b.* 10 March 1843; *m.*; one *s.* *Educ.:* St. John's College, Cambridge. Foundation Scholar and Naden Divinity Student; 14th Wrangler, 1866; Curate of Stapleford, Cambs, 1867-71; St. Andrew the Great, Cambridge, 1871-72; Headmaster, Lancaster School, 1872-93; Select Preacher, Cambridge University, 1873, 1887, and 1912; Rector of Marwood, N. Devon, 1893-1900; Vicar of Ottery St. Mary, 1900-8; Rural Dean of Ottery, 1900-8; Canon of Exeter Cathedral, 1908; Treasurer, 1910; Chancellor, 1915; Chaplain to Bishop of Exeter, 1903; Examining Chaplain, 1907; Proctor in Convocation of Canterbury, 1906-10; re-elected, 1911; resigned, 1918; Member of Devon County Education Committee. *Address:* The Close, Exeter.
(*Died 1 Feb. 1920.*)

PRYNNE, E. A. Fellowes, R.B.A.; painter of portraits and subject pictures, chiefly sacred, church decorations and stained-glass designs and sculpture; *b.* 14 Oct. 1854; 3rd *s.* of Rev. George Rundle Prynne, M.A., and Emily, *d.* of Admiral Sir Thomas Fellowes, K.C.B., D.C.L.; *m.* 1888, Emma Mary Joll; two *s.* three *d.* *Educ.:* Eastman's Royal Naval Academy, Southsea; London; Antwerp; Florence; Paris. Has exhibited at R.A., R.B.A., New Gallery, Grosvenor Gallery, Brussels International, Liverpool, Birmingham, and at Dusseldorf International Exhibition of Religious Art, etc.; command visit to Osborne by Queen Victoria, 1891. *Address:* 1 Woodville Road, Ealing. (*Died 28 Dec. 1921.*)

PRYOR, Arthur Vickris, J.P., D.L.; *b.* 3 Aug. 1846; *e. s.* of late Arthur Pryor of Hylands and Elizabeth Sophia, *e. d.* of late Tomkyns Dew of Whitney Court, Herefordshire; *m.* 1886, Elizabeth Charlotte Louisa

859

PROUT, Henry Goslee. See page xxviii.

(d. 1919), e. d. of 2nd Earl of Craven, and widow of 3rd Earl of Wilton. Educ.: Eton; Christ Church, Oxford; B.A. 1867. Address: Egerton Lodge, Melton Mowbray. Clubs: Carlton, Travellers', Turf, St. James's.

(Died 18 June 1927.)

PRYOR, S. J.; b. Clifton, Derbyshire, 8 June 1865; m. 1894, Laura A. Wells, b. Clifford, Pa., U.S.A.; one d. Editor The Gleaner, Kingston, Jamaica, West Indies, 1889; on various newspapers in America, including five years on editorial staff New York Sun; correspondent in London for New York Journal, 1896; Managing Editor and Director of the Daily Mail for four years to Nov. 1900; Managing Editor Daily Express, 1900-4; Editor St. James's Gazette, 1904, and Evening Standard and St. James's Gazette, 1905; Editor and Managing Director The Tribune, 1907; Day Editor of The Times, 1909, and Director of The Times Publishing Company until 1918; Press Secretary, Buckingham Palace, 1918-20. Address: 2 The Grove, Highgate Road, N.W.5. T.: Hampstead 1244. Club: Whitefriars. (Died 25 Mar. 1924.)

PRYSE, Sir Edward John Webley-Parry-; 2nd Bt., cr. 1866; o. s. of 1st Bt. and Louisa Joan, d. of Capt. John Lewes, Llanlear, Cardiganshire; S. father, 1906; b. 10 July 1862; m. 1891, Nina Katharine, o. d. of D. K. W. Webley-Parry. Formerly Captain 1st Batt.. Welsh Regiment. Heir: b. Lewes Thomas Loveden. Address: Gogerddan, Bow Street R.S.O., Cardiganshire. Club: Army and Navy.

(Died 20 Oct. 1918.)

PTOLEMY, William John, I.S.O., C.A., J.P.; Deputy Treasurer of the Province of Manitoba since 1886; b. 1850; s. of late John Ptolemy, and Elizabeth M'Waters, Hamilton, Ontario; m. 1877, Isabella Muir (d. 1915); three s. three d. Educ.: Public Schools; Smithville Grammar School, Ontario. G.W. Rly. Co. of Canada, 1873-75; C.P. Rly. Dominion Govt. Telegraph Construction, 1875; in Mercantile life, 1876-82; Manitoba Government Service (accountant), 1883-85; Municipal Commissioner, 1886; District Deputy Grand Master (Masonic) District No. 1, 1887; Presbyterian, Treasurer of Church Boards, 1880-1914. Publications: contributor to the Public Press. Address: Winnipeg, Manitoba, Canada. Club: Canadian, Rotary, Winnipeg.

PUCCINI, Giacomo, music composer; b. Lucca, 22 Dec. 1858. Educ.: Milan, Conservatorio di Musica, under Bazzini, Ponchielli. Principal works: Le Villi, 1884; Edgar, 1889; Manon Lescaut, 1893; La Bohème, 1896; La Tosca, 1900; Madame Butterfly, 1904; La Fanciulla del West, 1910; La Rondine, 1916; Il Tabarro, Suor Angelica, Gianni Schicchi, 1918. Address: c/o G. Ricordi & Co., Milan; Torre del Lago, Tuscany, Italy. (Died 29 Nov. 1924.)

PUCKLE, Lt.-Col. John, D.S.O. 1900; A.S.C.; b. 6 Oct. 1869; s. of Col. H. G. Puckle, Worthing; m. 1896, Mary, d. of late Hon. James Fellows. Educ.: Westward Ho!; Bedford; Malvern; St. Peter's College, Cambridge; Sandhurst. Entered army, 1893; Capt., 1899; Major, 1906; Lt.-Col., 1914; served S. Africa, 1899-1902 (despatches, D.S.O.); European War, 1914-15 (despatches). Address: Wyndham House, Sloane Gardens, S.W. Clubs: Naval and Military, Junior Naval and Military.

(Died 15 April 1917.)

PUCKLE, Richard Kaye, C.I.E. 1878; b. 1830; m. 1864, Caroline Victoria, d. of C. J. F. Combe, Stoke D'Abernon. Educ.: Tonbridge School; Haileybury. Entered Madras Civil Service, 1851; Collector and Magistrate, Tinnevelly, 1866; Director of Revenue Settlement, 1874; member of Board of Revenue, 1879; retired, 1881. Address: Lingmoor, Gratwicke Road, Worthing. (Died 29 July 1917.)

860

PUDUKOTA, H.H. Raja Martand Bhairava Tondiman Bahadur, Raja of, G.C.I.E., cr. 1913; b. 1875; S. grandfather, 1886; m. 1915, Esmé Mary Sorrett. y. d. of late W. Fink, M.A., LL.D., Melbourne, Australia. one s., Marthanda Sydney, b. Australia, 1916; The State has an area of 1179 square miles and population of 426,813, and has been ruled by Tondiman dynasty from time immemorial. The Raja has granted his people a representative assembly for consultative and legislative purposes. His salute is 11 guns. Address: La Favorite, Cannes, South France.

(Died 28 May 1928.)

PUGSLEY, Hon. William, Lieut.-Gov., New Brunswick, 1917-23; b. Sussex, K. Co., New Brunswick, 27 Sept. 1850; s. of William Pugsley, farmer; m. 1st, 1876, Fannie J. (d. 1914), d. of Thomas Parks of the City of St. John, merchant; two s.; 2nd, 1915, Gertrude Macdonald. Educ.: Public School in Sussex, K. Co.; University of New Brunswick. Alumni Gold Medallist in Junior Year; graduated at head of class, 1868; second in competition for Gilchrist Scholarship, University of London, 1868 (B.C.L., D.C.L.). Admitted Attorney at Law, 1871; Barrister, 1872; Reporter of the Supreme Court, 1873-83; Q.C., 1891; elected to Legislative Assembly of New Brunswick, 1885; elected Speaker of the House, 1887; resigned 1890, and went into the Government as Solicitor-General; resigned and retired from politics, 1892; again elected to the Legislature for Kings, 1899; entered the Provincial Govt. as Attorney-Gen. 1900; Minister of Public Works, Canada, 1907-1919. Address: Rothesay, New Brunswick, Canada. Clubs: Rideau, Country, Ottawa; Union, St. John, Riverside Golf and County.

(Died Mar. 1925.)

PULFORD, Col. Russell Richard, C.I.E. 1897; retired; b. 20 Dec. 1845. Entered R.E. 1866; Col. 1895; joined India Dept. 1870; served Afghan War, 1878-80; Superintending Engineer, 1892; Officiating Chief Engineer and Secretary to Government N.W. Prov. and Oudh, 1894; Rajputana and Central India, 1896; Chief Engineer, India Public Works Dept. 1899-1901.

(Died 29 Mar. 1920.)

PULLAR, Rufus D., J.P., F.C.S.; Chairman of J. Pullar & Sons, Ltd., Cleaners and Dyers, Perth; President Society of Dyers and Colourists, 1914; b. Perth, 1861; e. s. of late Sir Robert Pullar; m. 1890, Rose Lindsay, d. of late Robert Morison, accountant, Perth; two s. Educ.: Sharp's Institution, Perth; Craigmount School, Edinburgh; Universities of Edinburgh and Leeds. Interested in scientific pursuits; devoted special atten on to chemistry as applied to cleaning and dyeing; travelled on the Continent, Canada, and United States. Address: Brahan, Perth. Clubs: Royal Automobile, Royal Societies; Royal, Perth; University, Edinburgh. (Died 22 Sept. 1917.)

PULLEN, William le Geyt, C.B. 1917; Paymaster-Rear-Admiral retired; b. 1 Sep. 1855; s. of Captain T. C. Pullen, R.N.; m. Harriette, d. of George E. Fox, of Hillside, Plymouth; one s. one d. Entered Royal Navy, 1872; Paymaster-in-Chief, 1910; has served as Secretary to the Admiral commanding Coast of Ireland, 1885, the Naval Commanders-in-Chief in Australia 1889, China 1895, and at Plymouth 1900; Secretary to the Admiral commanding Coastguard and Reserves, 1904, and to the Naval Commander-in-Chief, The Nore, 1911-15, including the early part of the War. Club: Royal Western Yacht, Plymouth.

(Died 18 Jan. 1922.)

PULLEY, Col. Charles, C.B. 1904; Indian Army, retired; b. 1851; m. 1st, 1880, Edith Marion (d. 1888); 2nd, 1896, Rachel, d. of Rev. J. White, Stevenston, Ayrshire; one s. one d.

Served Afghanistan, 1878-80 (medal and clasp); Burma, 1886-7 (wounded, despatches, Bt.-Major; medal and clasp); Lushai, 1892-3 ; N.-W. Frontier India, 1897-8 (despatches, medal 2 clasps); Tirah, 1897-8 (despatches, Bt.-Col. ; clasp). *Address:* Llanberis, Langton Green, Kent.
(*Died 30 Oct. 1925.*)

PULLING, Rev. Edward Herbert, C.B.E. 1919 ; *b.* Traine House, Modbury, Devon, 23 Jan. 1859 ; *y. s.* of Rev. F. W. Pulling, Vicar of Pinhoe, Devon ; *m.* 1892, Emily Frances, *e. d.* of Oswald Cornish Arthur of Gascoigne Place, Plymouth ; three *s.* *Educ.:* Royal Academy, Gosport (Burneys); Oxford University : Salisbury Theological College. Curate of Melksham, 1883-90 ; Chaplain to the Forces, 4th class, 1900 ; 1st class, 1910 ; retired list, 1919 , served at Aldershot, 1890-93 ; Cavalry Depot, Canterbury, 1893-98 ; Sudan Expedition, 1898 ; Alexandria, 1898-1903 ; Plymouth, 1903-6 ; Senior Chaplain, Dublin, 1906-12 ; Portsmouth, 1912-1916 ; Humber Garrison, 1916-19 ; with Lincolnshire Coast Defences, 1918-19 ; brought to notice twice, 1917 and 1919, of Secretary of State for War for valuable services rendered in connection with the war; Vicar of Morgan's Vale, Salisbury, 1919-23. *Address:* c/o Westminster Bank, Ltd., Salisbury. *Club:* Church Imperial.
(*Died 25 Jan. 1926.*)

PULLINGER, Frank, C.B. 1912 ; M.A. (Oxon.), B.Sc. (Lond.); H.M. Chief Inspector of Technical Schools; *b.* 19 March 1866 ; *m.* 1896 ; one *s.* one *d.* *Educ.:* Manchester Grammar School ; Corpus Christi College, Oxford. Oxford University Extension Lecturer, 1891 ; Education Secretary to the Devon County Council, 1891-94. *Address:* Board of Education, Whitehall, S.W. (*Died 23 Dec. 1920.*)

PUMPELLY, Raphael, author, geologist ; *b.* Owego, N.Y., 8 Sep. 1837 ; *s.* of William Pumpelly and Mary H. Welles Pumpelly ; *m.* 1869, Eliza Frances Shepard ; one *s.* two *d.* *Educ.:* Owego Academy ; private schools in America ; Royal School of Mines, Freiberg, Saxony. Made geological explorations in Corsica ; had charge of Mines in Arizona, 1860-1861 ; made scientific explorations for Japanese Govt., 1861-63 ; private Geol. Expdn. through Central, Western, and Northern China and Mongolia, 1863-64 ; explored northern coalfields for Imperial Chinese Govt., 1864 ; journey of exploration across the Gobi Desert ; returned to Europe through Siberia, 1864-65 ; Professor of Mining, Harvard, 1866-73 ; State Geologist, Mich. 1869-71 ; Dir. Mo. Geol. Survey and in charge of mineral industries, the Tenth census, 1879-81 ; organised and directed Northern Transcontinental Survey, 1881-84 ; made the explorations of discovery inaugurating the development of the iron ore industry of most of the iron ore ranges of Michigan and Western Ont., 1867-1901 ; initiated and directed a physical-geographical and archæological exploration of Central Asia, 1903-4, under auspices of Carnegie Inst. of Washington. *Publications:* Geological Researches in China, Mongolia, Japan, 1866 ; Across America and Asia, 1870; Geology of the Upper District of Michigan, 1873 ; Iron ores and Coal Fields of Missouri, 1873 ; Bulletins and Maps of the Northern Transcontinental Survey, 1882-83 ; Mineral Industries of the U.S., vol. xv., Tenth Census, 1886 ; Geology of the Green Mountains, 1894 ; Explorations in Central Asia, 1905 ; Prehistoric Civilisations of Anau, 1908 ; Reminiscences, 1918. *Address:* Newport, Rhode Island, U.S.A.; Dublin, New Hampshire. *T.:* Newport 1541. *Clubs:* Authors, Century, University, New York. (*Died 10 Aug. 1923.*)

PUNCHARD, Rev. Elgood George, D.D. Oxon. ; Hon. Canon of Ely since 1895 ; *b.* Framlingham, Suffolk, 18 April 1844 ; 2nd *s.* of John Elgood Punchard and Elizabeth ; *m.*

1879, Catherine Mary, *y. d.* of Joseph and Ann Johnson of Windsor ; one *s.* one *d.* *Educ.:* New Inn Hall, Oxford, 1868-72 ; transferred to Balliol Coll. 1887. Second class, Law and History, 1872 ; B.A. 1872 ; M.A. 1874 ; B.D. 1880 ; D.D. 1884 ; *proxime accessit* for the Newdigate, 1871 ; prize for English Sacred Poem, 1875 ; deacon, 1872 ; priest by Bishop Mackarness of Oxford, 1878 ; Curate of Wendover, 1872-77 ; Oriental Fellow of St. Augustine's College, Canterbury, 1878 ; Curate in charge of Shalbourne, 1879 ; Vicar of Linslade, 1880-83 ; Vicar of Christ Church, Luton, 1883-1902 ; Rural Dean of Luton, 1897-1902 ; elected Bishop of Antigua, 1896, but declined ; Chaplain to Bishop of Truro, 1906 ; Vicar of Ely St. Mary's, 1902-15. *Publications:* King Saul and other Poems, 1877 ; Commentary on St. James, in the New Testament for English Readers, edited by Bishop Ellicott, 1879 ; Christ of Contention (three essays), 1885 ; The Organisation and Work of a Parish, 1889 ; Records of an Unfortunate Family — Punchard of Heanton-Punchardon, 1894 ; reviews and various articles in the Church Quarterly, Asiatic Quarterly, Indian Church Quarterly ; editor of Ely Diocesan Remembrancer, 1906-9. *Address:* Ely, Cambs. *T.A.:* Punchard, Ely. (*Died 2 Mar. 1917.*)

PURCELL, Rev. Handfield Noel, M.A., V.D. ; Vicar of Fowey, 1867-1920 ; Canon of Truro Cathedral ; J.P. Cornwall ; late Chairman of St. Austell Board of Guardians ; *b.* Dundalk, Co. Louth ; *s.* of late Admiral Edward Purcell ; *m.* 1st, Annie Ellen Treffry (*d.* 1877); 2nd, 1899, Elizabeth Anna Adams ; four *s.* three *d.* *Educ.:* Bath College ; Exeter College, Oxford. Curate of St. Kenelms, Halesowen, Worcester ; Senior Chaplain, R.G.A., Cornwall. *Address:* Lisnawilly, Fowey. *Club:* Royal Fowey Yacht.
(*Died 15 April 1925.*)

PURCELL, Sir John, K.C.B., *cr.* 1900; Director of Industrial and General Trust; *b.* Carrick-on-Suir, Ireland, 1839 ; *s.* of late Dr. Purcell, sometime a Commissioner of Irish Poor Laws; *m.* 1868, Alice Fanny, *d.* of Captain Charles Leighton Kennett ; two *s.* four *d.* *Educ.:* private school. Entered secretariat of Inland Revenue Department, 1856 ; appointed Principal Clerk, 1867 ; Controller of Stamps and Registrar of Joint-Stock Companies, 1883 ; retired from public service, 1900 ; was a member of the Joint Committee on Postage Stamps which sat in 1885-86; and his name is much identified with the series of those stamps issued in the Jubilee Year 1887 ; was one of the six promoters and original members of the London Irish Rifle Volunteers, in which corps he served for some years with the rank of Major. *Decorated* for official services. *Address:* Glebe Lodge, Blackheath, Kent. *T.A.:* Blackheath. *T.:* Lee Green 140. *Club:* Constitutional.
(*Died 7 Dec. 1924.*)

PURCELL, Major Raymond John Hugo, J.P. ; *b.* 1885 ; *s.* of late M. J. Purcell, J.P., Burton Park, Co. Cork. *Educ.:* Beaumont ; Christ Church, Oxford, M.A. Succeeded 1906 ; entered King's Royal Rifle Corps from Oxford, 1907 ; retired as Major, 1921 (owing to severe wounds received in European War). *Recreations:* yachting, hunting, big-game shooting. *Address:* Burton Park, Churchtown, Co. Cork. *Clubs:* Arthur's, Army and Navy; Royal Yacht Squadron, Cowes ; Kildare Street, Dublin.
(*Died 24 July 1925.*)

PURCHASE, Edward James, K.C. 1923 ; *o. s.* of late James Purchase; *m.* Charlotte, 3rd *d.* of late Edwin Guy; one *s.* *Educ.:* Wadham College, Oxford ; M.A. Formerly in Holy Orders ; Rector of Owsden, Newmarket, 1903-5 ; student of Middle Temple, 1905 ; called to Bar, 1908 ; Western Circuit. *Address:* 1 Brick Court, Temple, E.C. *T.:* Temple 97 ; Central 1596. (*Died 3 Feb. 1924.*)

861

PURCHASE, Sir William Henry, Kt., cr. 1921; member of W. H. Purchase & Co.; b. 19 July 1860; m. 1890, Jane Norman, d. of Randal G. Vogan; one s. Chairman National Appointments Committee, Ministry of Labour; Chairman London Telephone Advisory Committee; Member of Council and Member of Commercial Education Committee, London Chamber of Commerce; Member Board of Management, Throat Hospital, Golden Square, W.; Member of City of London Court of Arbitration. Address: The Old Vicarage, Wrotham, Kent. Clubs: Royal Automobile, City Carlton.
(Died 2 July 1924.)

PURDIE, Thomas, Associate Royal School of Mines; B.Sc. Lond.; Ph.D. Würzburg; LL.D. Aber and St Andrews; F.R.S.; b. Biggar, Lanarks, 27 Jan. 1843; e. s. of late James Purdie, writer and banker, Biggar; m. Marianne, d. of late John Rotherham, Coventry, 1878. Educ.: Edinburgh Academy; Royal School of Mines; Universities of St. Andrews and Würzburg. Demonstrator in Chemistry, Royal College of Science, 1875-78; Science Master at the High School, Newcastle, Staffs, 1881-83; Professor of Chemistry, United College University of St. Andrews, 1884-1909; Professor Emeritus since 1909. Publications: A series of researches in Journal of Chemical Society 1881-1910. Recreations: angling, golfing, cycling. Address: University, St. Andrews. Club: Savile. (Died 14 Dec. 1916.)

PURDOM, Thomas Hunter, K.C.; Member of legal firm, Purdom & Purdom, Barristers; b. London, Canada, 25 July 1853; s. of Alexander Purdom, Builder, and Margaret Hunter, who came to Canada from Hawick, Scotland, 1849; m. 1st, 1886, Isabella (d. 1897), d. of John C. Craig; 2nd, 1893, Nellie (d. 1901), d. of David Davies; 3rd, 1902, Marion, her sister; one s. one d. Educ.: Joint Grammar and Common School, London, Ont. Called to Bar, 1876; Solicitor, 1875; Bencher, Law Society at Osgoode Hall, Toronto, 1885-90; President—Dominion Savings and Investment Society; Fidelity Trusts Co. of Ontario; The Northern Life Assurance Co. of Canada; The London Advertiser Co., Ltd.; The Advertiser Job Printing Co., Ltd; Director—The Masonic Temple Co.; The London and Lake Erie Railway Transportation Co.; The Purdom Hardware Co., Ltd. Recreation: golf. Address: 383 King Street, London, Canada. T.: 387. Clubs: London Golf, Rotary, London. (Died 14 Nov. 1923.)

PUREFOY, Richard Dancer, M.D., Hon. LL.D., F.R.C.S.; President, Royal Academy of Medicine in Ireland; Consulting Gynaecologist, Rotunda Hospital, Dublin. Educ.: Trinity College, Dublin. Address: 62 Merrion Square, Dublin. (Died 27 June 1919.)

PURVES, (William) Laidlaw, M.D.; Consulting Aural Surgeon, Guy's Hospital; Consulting Ophthalmic and Aural Surgeon, Hospital for Diseases of Nervous System; Aural Surgeon to Royal Normal College and Academy of Music for the Blind; s. of William Brown Purves, Surgeon, Edinburgh; m. Elizabeth, d. of Patrick Adie of Worton Hall, Isleworth. Educ.: Universities Edinburgh, Berlin, Leipzig, Vienna, Utrecht, Paris. Publications: Enlargement of the Thyroid, a Beneficial Physiological Action; Endothelium en Emigratie; Determination of the Anomalies of Refraction of the Human Eye; A Contribution to Ophthalmoscopy; Method of Determining the Focal Distance of Single or Combined Lenses; An Optometer; An International Calculating Scale for Ophthalmological Purposes; Paracentesis of the Tympanic Membrane; Hearing and the Examinations for the Public Services; The True Value of Artificial Tympanic Membranes; The Determination of the Hearing Power; The Authorship of Robinson Crusoe; The "O"

862

Edition of Robeson Cruso; The First English Translation of Gil Blas, etc. Address: 20 Stratford Place, W. (Died 29 Dec. 1917.)

PURVIS, Brig.-General Alexander Burridge, J.P., D.L. Fife; b. 21 Sep. 1854; e. s. of John Purvis of Kinaldy, and Wilhelmina, d. of William Berry of Tayfield; m. 1894, Bertha, d. of Rev. E. R. Pitman. Educ.: Glenalmond; Marlborough; R.M.A., Woolwich. Commissioned Royal Artillery, 1874; Col., 1907; Commanding Volunteer Infantry Brigade, 1906; retired, 1908; Brigadier-General commanding 17th Divisional Artillery, 1914-15; County Commandant Fifeshire Volunteer Corps, 1916-19. Clubs: Junior United Service, M.C.C.; Royal and Ancient, St. Andrews; New, Edinburgh. (Died 4 April 1923.)

PURVIS, Sir Robert, Kt., cr. 1905; LL.D.; b. Roxburghshire, 1844; m. Elizabeth (d. 1913), e. d. of W. H. Peat, late of Mincing Lane, London, 1874. Educ.: Marlborough School; Downing College, Cambridge (M.A.). Barr. Inner Temple, 1873. Contested Abingdon Div. of Berks, 1885; Edinburgh (South), 1886; Peterborough, 1889-92; M.P. (U.) Peterborough, 1895-1906; contested same Division, 1910. Publication: Sir William Arrol, a Memorial. Club: Oxford and Cambridge.
(Died 23 June 1920.)

PYE, Joseph Patrick, J.P., M.D., F.R.U.I.; Professor of Anatomy and Physiology, Queen's Coll. Galway; Hon. Surgeon, Galway Hospital. Educ.: Queen's Coll. Galway; London; Paris. Address: Rusheen-na-curra, Clifton. Co. Galway.
(Died 25 Mar. 1920.)

PYE-SMITH, Rutherford John, Ch.M. (Sheffield), F.R.C.S.; Consulting Surgeon, Sheffield Royal Hosp.; Emeritus Professor of Surgery, University, Sheffield; J.P. City of Sheffield; formerly President Yorks. Branch, British Medical Association; President and Treasurer Sheffield Medico-Chirurgical Society; Member of the Sheffield Education Committee; Medical Referee Workmen's Compensation Act; Member of General Medical Council; b. London, 1848; 3rd s. of Ebenezer Pye-Smith, F.R.C.S.; m. Barbara, 4th d. of John Edgcumbe Gill. Educ.: Amersham Hall; Guy's Hospital. Commenced general medical practice at Sheffield, 1876; consulting surgical practice, 1895; retired 1919. Publications: Address in Surgery, Annual Meeting, British Medical Association, 1908; Arsenic Cancer (Lancet), 1913. Address: Clvda. Ampthill, Bedfordshire. (Died 23 Mar. 1921.)

PYM, Charles Guy, F.G.S., J.P., D.L. Beds.; Grand Councillor Primrose League; b. Willian, Herts, 11 Feb. 1841; y. s. of Rev. W. W. Pym, Willian Rectory, and Sophia, d. of late Samuel Gambier, Commissioner of Navy; and g. s. of Francis Pym, M.P., Hasells Hall, Beds.; m. d. of late Henry Sykes Thornton, banker, 1885. Educ.: Rossall School. Naval Service, 1855-58; War Office, 1859-74; mercantile pursuits to 1886; M.P. Bedford, 1895-1906; High Sheriff for the County of London, 1911. Recreations: athletics, founder of Civil Service sports, cricket, yachting, golf, captain of Royal Wimbledon, 1884. Address: 35 Cranley Gardens, S.W.; T.: Western 4078; Cæsar's Camp, Sandy, Beds. Clubs: Carlton, Junior Carlton.
(Died 13 Nov. 1918.)

PYM, Francis, J.P., D.L.; b. 6 Dec. 1849; e. s. of late Francis Leslie Pym and Mary Jemima, d. of Rev. Henry Palmer of Withcote Hall, Leicester; m. 1891, Alice, y. d. of Sir George Conway Colthurst, 5th Bart., M.P., of Blarney Castle, Cork. Educ.: Eton; Oxford. Patron of one living; late Sub-Lieut. 1st Life Guards; High Sheriff, Beds, 1903. Address: Hasells Hall, Sandy, Bedfordshire. T.: Sandy 12. Clubs: Travellers', Carlton; Royal Yacht Squadron, Cowes. (Died 7 June 1927.)

PYNE, Sir (Thomas) Salter, Kt., *cr.*
1894; C.S.I. 1894; M.Inst.C.E.; M.Inst.M.E.;
formerly Chief Engineer to Government of
Afghanistan; *b.* 1860; *s.* of John Pyne and
Alice, *d.* of Thomas Salter, Rochdale. *Educ.:*
private tutors. Engineer's apprentice, 1875-
1878; manager of foundry and engineering
works, 1879-83; with a mercantile firm in
India, 1883-85; introduced into Afghanistan
many and various industries, including works
for the manufacture of guns, rifles, ammunition,
swords, coining, distilling, soap, candles, etc.;
was ambassador for His Highness the Amir to
His Excellency the Viceroy of India in 1898,
and at the satisfactory conclusion of the
negotiations was awarded a K.B. and C.S.I.
and was thanked by Her Majesty's Government; has been awarded an Afghan decoration
by His Highness the Amir, with other presents
at various periods; granted a commission in
the K.O.Y.L.I.; employed at the Ministry of
Munitions, 1915. *Recreations:* riding, fishing,
shooting. *Club:* Badminton. (*Died Sept. 1921.*)

Q

**QUARRINGTON, Rev. Edwin
Fowler,** Prebendary of Lincoln. *Address:*
Welby Lodge, Woodhall Spa, Lincs.
(*Died 3 Sept. 1923.*)

QUEENSBERRY, 10th Marquess of (*cr.*
1682), **Percy Sholto Douglas;** Viscount
Drumlanrig and Baron Douglas, 1628; Earl of
Queensberry, 1633; Bt. (Nova Scotia), 1668;
b. 13 Oct. 1868; *s.* of 9th Marquess and Sybil,
d. of Alfred Montgomery, *g. d.* of 1st Lord
Leconfield; *S.* father 1900; *m.* 1st, 1893, Anna
Maria (*d.* 1917), *d.* of Rev. T. Walters, Vicar of
Boyton, Cornwall; two *s.* one *d.*; 2nd, 1918,
Mary Louisa, *d.* of late Richard Bickel, Cardiff,
and widow of Ernest Morgan. Formerly mid-
shipman R.N. and Lieut. 3rd Mil. Batt. King's
Own Scottish Borderers. *Heir: s.* Viscount
Drumlanrig. *Address:* 14 Brook Green, W.
(*Died 1 Aug. 1920.*)

**QUENINGTON, Viscount; Michael
Hugh Hicks-Beach,** M.P. (U.) Tewkes-
bury Div. Gloucestershire since 1906; *b.* 19 Jan.
1877; *o. s.* of 1st Earl St. Aldwyn; *m.* 1909,
Marjorie, *d.* of H. Dent Brocklehurst, Sudeley
Castle, Gloucs.; one *s.* one *d. Educ.:* Eton;
Christ Church, Oxford, (M.A.). Was Captain
4th (Militia) Batt. Gloucester Regt.; 2nd Lt.
Royal Gloucestershire Yeomanry, 1908; served
St. Helena during South African War; acted as
Assist. Private Secretary to Chancellor of Ex-
chequer (his father), 1901-2; to Sir Alexander
Hood, Chief Unionist Whip, 1904-5; travelled
round the world, 1902-3; J.P. Gloucs.; Member
of Northleach Board of Guardians and R.D.C.
Recreations: hunting, shooting, fishing. *Ad-
dress:* Coln St. Aldwyns, Fairford, Gloucs.; 11
Eaton Place, S.W. *Clubs:* Carlton, Bachelors'.
(*Died 23 April 1916.*)

QUERIPEL, Hon. Col. Alfred Ernest,
C.B. 1917; retired pay, late A.V.D.; *b.* 27 Aug.
1870; *m.* Retired 1901. *Address:* c/o Holt &
Co., 3 Whitehall Place, S.W.(*Died 23 April 1921.*)

QUIGLEY, Most Rev. James Edward,
D.D., LL.D.; Archbishop of Chicago (R.C.)
since 1908; *b.* Oshawa, Ontario, 15 Oct. 1854;
s. of James Quigley and Mary Lacey. *Educ.:*
St. Joseph's College, Buffalo, N.Y.; Niagara
University, Niagara Falls, N.Y.; University of
Innsbruck, Austria; Propaganda Coll., Rome.
Ordained, 1879; Rector, St. Vincent's Church,
R.C., Attica, N.Y., 1879-84; St. Joseph's
Cathedral, Buffalo, N.Y., 1884-96; St. Bridget's
Church, Buffalo, N.Y.. 1896-97; Bishop of
Buffalo, 1897-1908. *Address:* 1555 N. State

Street, Chicago, Ill., U.S.A. *T.:* North 815.
(*Died July 1916.*)

QUILL, Maj.-Gen. Richard Henry;
C.B. 1917; A.M.S.; *b.* 8 June 1848; *e. s.* of late
Jerome Quill, J.P. of Kilmolly, Co. Kerry; *m.*
1886, Marion, *o. d.* of Deputy Inspector-General
W. Gunn, R.N.; one *s. Educ.:* Trinity College
Dublin. B.A., 1869; M.B., M.Ch., 1871. Entered army as Assistant Surgeon, 1872; served
with R.A. Afghanistan, 1879-1880 (medal);
was Senior Medical Officer, Thames District
at Chatham, and subsequently Senior Medical
Officer, Ceylon Command, 1898-1902; Administrative Medical Charge of South Eastern District,
1902-5; 2nd Class of the Royal Prussian Order
of the Red Eagle with the Star, 1907; Principal
Medical Officer, Royal Victoria Hospital, Netley,
1905-8; retired, 1908. *Recreations:* formerly
hunting and athletics of various kinds; latterly
golf; won Amateur Golf Championship of
Ceylon, 1899, besides many subsequent golf
trophies. *Address:* Craigleith House, Cheltenham. *T.:* Cheltenham 1014. *Clubs:* Junior
United Service; Cinque Ports Golf, Deal;
New, Cheltenham. (*Died 18 Oct. 1924.*)

QUIN, Maj.-Gen. Thomas James,
Bengal Infantry; *b.* 1 May 1842; *m.* 1870
Mary (deceased), *e. d.* of late Major James
Wemyss. Entered army, 1859; Officiating As-
sistant Commissioner and Cantonment Officer,
N.-W. Provinces, 1869-89; Deputy Commis-
sioner, 1889; Maj.-Gen. 1898; retired, 1898;
served Bhootan Expedition, 1865 (medal).
(*Died 24 Oct. 1919.*)

QUINLAN, Hon. Timothy Francis,
C.M.G. 1913; J.P.; *b.* Tipperary, Ireland, 18
Feb. 1861; arrived in Australia with his parents,
1863; *m.* 1883 (wife died 1904); four *s.* three *d.*
M.L.A., West Perth, in first West Australian
Parliament, 1890; represented Tooday, 1897-
1911; Minister for Works in Morgan's Govern-
ment, 1901; Chairman of Committees, 1905;
Speaker from 1905 (re-elected 1908) until 1911,
when he retired; gazetted Honourable, 1912;
created Knight of Order of St. Silvester by Leo
XIII.; City Councillor of Perth for 12 years;
Director of South British Insurance Co.,
Southern Cross Life Co., and Chairman Perth
Building Society; has extensive landed in-
terests. *Address:* Avoca, Adelaide Terrace,
Perth, W.A. (*Died 8 July 1927.*)

QUIRK, Rev. James Francis, M.A., J.P.;
Rector of Great Coates and Vicar of Aylesby;
Canon of Lincoln Cathedral; Surrogate; *b.*
Willoughby, near Rugby, 5 March 1850; *s.* of
late Rev. J. R. Quirk, M.A., Rector of Blandford-
Forum, Dorset; *m.* 1880, Dora, *o. d.* of late
Rev. W. H. Parson, Vicar of Lynchmere,
Surrey; four *s.* one *d. Educ.:* Atherstone
Grammar School; Milton Abbas, Dorset;
Queen's College, Oxford; B.A. and M.A. 1876.
Curate of Haslemere, 1876-79; Vicar of Grasby,
near Caistor, Lincolnshire (on the presentation
of the late Lord Tennyson, Poet Laureate),
1879-92; Chaplain to High Sheriff of Lin-
colnshire, 1901-2, 1903-4, and 1920-21; Immigra-
tion Board, Grimsby; Chairman of Grimsby
County Bench of Magistrates. *Publication:*
article on Shooting in Victoria History of the
Counties of England, vol. ii. *Recreations:*
shooting and fishing. *Address:* Great Coates
Rectory, Lincolnshire. *T.A.:* Grimsby. *T.:*
2Y3 Healing. *M.:* FU 2929.
(*Died 20 Mar. 1927.*)

**QUIRK, Right Rev. Canon John
Nathaniel,** D.D., D.Litt.; Suffragan Bishop
of Jarrow since 1914; Archdeacon of Durham
and Canon Residentiary of Durham Cathedral
since 1922; Canon Residentiary of York
Minster, 1912-14; of Durham Cathedral since
1914; Proctor in Convocation for Chapter
of Durham, 1914; *b.* 1849; *s.* of Rev. Charles
Thomas Quirk, M.A., Rector of Golborne,

863

QUINN, John. See page xxviii.

Lancs; *m.* 1880, Mary Jane, *d.* of Rev. John Clay, M.A., Vicar of Stapenhill, Derbyshire; two *s.* *Educ.*: Shrewsbury School; St. John's College, Cambridge; trained for Holy Orders by Dean Vaughan, The Temple, 1873-74. 9th Junior Optime and B.A. 1873; M.A. 1876; D.D. Jure Dignitatis, 1902; Hon. D.Litt. Sheffield University, 1914. Ordained, 1874; curate St. Leonard's, Bridgnorth, 1874-78; Doncaster, 1878-81; Vicar of St. Thomas's, Douglas, 1881-82; Rotherham, 1882-89; St. Mary, Beverley, 1889-94; St. Paul, Lorrimore Square, S.E., 1894-95; Canon and Prebendary of York, 1888; Rector of Bath and Rural Dean, 1895-1901; Proctor in Convocation, 1898-1901; Vicar of Doncaster, 1901-1905; Vicar of St. Mark's, Sheffield, 1905-11; Bishop-Suffragan of Sheffield, 1901-14. *Address*: Lake End, Greenodd, Ulverston; The College, Durham. *Clubs*: Royal Societies; Durham County, Durham.

(*Died 26 April 1924.*)

QUIRK, Col. John Owen, C.B. 1897; D.S.O. 1886; retired; late commanding 41st Reg. Dist.; *b.* 18 Aug. 1847: 3rd *s.* of late Philip Quirk, Knockaloe House, Bromboro, Cheshire; *m.* 1875, Eugenie Marie, *y. d.* of late Octavius O'Brien, Kildare St., Dublin. *Educ.*: private school; Trinity College, Dublin (B.A., C.E.). Joined the 41st (The Welsh) Regt., 1869; Colonel, 1897; served in South African War, 1881; Egyptian Expedition, 1884, on transport duties; present at the battles of El Teb and Tamai, and advance on Tamanieb (despatches, medal with clasp, and bronze star); Soudan Expedition, 1884-85, as A.A.G. to E.A. (despatches, clasp, 3rd class Medjidie); Soudan Expedition, 1885-86, as A.A.G. to E.A., present at action of Geniss (horse shot, despatches, D.S.O.); Soudan with Nile Field Force, 1889, as Commandant Korosko (3rd class Osmanieh) *Recreation*: shooting. *Club*: Army and Navy.

(*Died 29 Jan. 1928.*)

R

RABAN, Brig.-Gen. Sir Edward, K.C.B., *cr.* 1906; K.B.E. *cr.* 1919; C.B. 1902; R.E.; *b.* 8 Aug. 1850; *s.* of late Maj.-Gen. H. Raban; *m.* 1873, Edith, *e. d.* of Col. H. W. P. Welman; two *d.* *Educ.*: Sherborne; R.M.A., Woolwich. Entered Army, 1871; Capt. 1883; Major, 1889; Lt.-Col. 1896; Col. 1900; served expedition against Naga Hill tribes, 1879-80 (despatches, medal with clasp); retired, 1900; recalled to Army, 1914; Brig.-Gen. 1917; reverted to retired list, 1918; served on Staff of Viscount French, 1916-17; Deputy Director at War Office, 1917; Director of Works, Admiralty, 1895-1912; Past President The Junior Institution of Engineers; Fellow Society of Engineers. *Address*: 35 Elm Park Gardens, S.W.10. *T.*: Kensington 3040. *Club*: United Service.

(*Died 8 Feb. 1927.*)

RABY, Joseph Thomas, F.J.I. 1910; J.P. and Alderman for City of Lichfield; District Manager of the Staffordshire Advertiser at Lichfield; *b.* 28 Oct. 1853; *e. s.* of Samuel Raby, marble mason of Derby; *m.* 1872, Hannah Lord, step-*d.* of John Newsome, woollen manufacturer, Batley, Yorkshire; five *s.* five *d.* *Educ.*: King Street School, Derby; private academies at Leicester. Journalist; engaged on first daily paper published in Leicester, 1870; afterwards in Lancashire, Yorkshire, Berkshire, and South Wales; Editor of local paper at Lichfield 1882; a correspondent of the Press Association since 1871; took an active part in movement which led to formation of National Association of Journalists; Chairman of Birmingham and Midland Counties District (Inst. of Journalists), 1902; Vice-President, 1903; Member of British

864

Press Tour in Sweden, 1906; Member of Lichfield City Council and Lichfield Board of Guardians since 1898; Sheriff, 1908; Mayor, 1915; one of the founders of the Johnson Library and Museum at Lichfield. *Publications*: Lichfield and Dr. Johnson; Johnsonian Memorials at Lichfield; numerous pamphlets and papers. *Recreations*: billiards and bowls. *Address*: The Tower House, Lichfield, Staffs. *T.A.*: Raby, Lichfield. *T.* : 126 Lichfield.

(*Died 30 May 1916.*)

RADCLIFFE, His Honour Francis Reynolds Yonge, K.C. 1904; J.P.; Barrister; Judge of County Courts Circuit 36 (Oxfordshire) since 1914; *b.* Westminster, 20 Sep. 1851; *e. s.* of late John Alexander Radcliffe and Fanny Johnson, *d.* of Rev. W. J. Yonge; *m.* Helen, *o. d.* of Edward Harbord Lushington of Brackenhurst, Cobham, Surrey; three *s.* three *d.* *Educ.*: Eton; Corpus Christi Coll. Oxford (Exhibitioner); 1st class Classical Moderations, 1872; 1st class Final Classical School, 1874; Fellow of All Souls Coll. 1874-82. Barr. 1876; Revising Barr. 1894; Recorder of Devizes, 1887-1904; Recorder of Portsmouth, 1904-14; a Chairman of Quarter Sessions; Chevalier de l'Ordre de Léopold. *Publications*: The New Politicus; Cases illustrative of the Law of Torts, etc. *Recreations*: rowing, fishing, shooting. *Address*: Headington Rise, Oxford. *T.*: Oxford 601. *Club*: Athenæum.

(*Died 23 April 1924.*)

RADCLIFFE, Henry, Senior Partner in Evan Thomas, Radcliffe & Co., Cardiff.

(*Died 16 Dec. 1921.*)

RADCLIFFE, Major Jasper Fitzgerald, D.S.O. 1900; the Devonshire Regiment; *b.* 18 Aug. 1867; *s.* of late W. C. Radcliffe, of Warleigh; *m.* 1893, Emily Maude, *d.* of Rev. E. C. Orpen, of Exleigh, Starcross, Devon. *Educ.*: Cheltenham. Entered army, 1889; Captain, 1898; served South Africa (despatches twice, Queen's medal with clasp, D.S.O.); European War, 1914-15 (despatches, wounded). (*Died 2 Feb. 1916.*)

RADCLIFFE, John Ed., Christian minister of the United Methodist Church, and President of Conference in the year 1899; *b.* Saddleworth, West Riding of Yorkshire, 11 Nov. 1846; *m.* 1st; 1875 (*d.* 1892), *d.* of late Alderman Garside of Leeds; 2nd, 1898, *o. d.* of S. Naylor of Adwalton, Yorkshire; two *s.* two *d.* *Educ.*: in the fields, by the streams, on the moors, at "an elementary school," with the assistance of evening classes, and at Ranmoor Coll., Sheffield. Upon leaving college in 1870 served four years as a probationary minister; was ordained in 1874; has since ministered in Hunslet (Leeds), Guernsey, Leicester, Ashton-under-Lyne, Forest Hill (London), Manchester, Hanley, Batley, Leeds, Lindley, Halifax and Bradford; retired, 1917. *Publications*: magazine articles. *Recreation*: choicest, a country walk. *Address*: Batley, Yorkshire. (*Died 22 April 1919.*)

RADCLIFFE, Wyndham Ivor, M.A.; *s.* of late Henry Radcliffe, J.P., of Druidstone, Michaelston-y-Vedw, Cardiff. *Educ.*: privately; Christ Church, Oxford. Barr. Inner Temple, 1919; formerly Lieut., Special Reserve of Officers and R.F.A. (T.F.); Sheriff of Glamorgan, 1924. *Address*: 1 Park Lodge, Park Place, Knightsbridge, S.W.1; *T.*: Kensington 8265; Druidstone, Michaelston-y-Vedw, nr. Cardiff; *T.*: St. Mellons (Mon.) 7. *Clubs*: United University, Royal Automobile, Queen's; Cardiff and County, Cardiff. (*Died 15 April 1927.*)

RADFORD, Sir Charles Horace, Kt.; *cr.* 1907; Mayor of Plymouth; *b.* 31 May 1854; 3rd *s.* of late George David Radford of Plymouth; *m.* 1893, Bessie, *d.* of late William May of Devonport. *Educ.*: Amersham Hall, Caversham, Reading. Member of Plymouth County Borough

Council since 1892 ; Alderman since 1896 ; Mayor during Diamond Jubilee Year, 1896-97 ; again elected, 1907 ; J.P. Devonshire, 1895 ; and County Borough of Plymouth, 1906. *Address :* 4 The Crescent, Plymouth ; Polbream, Mullion, Cornwall. *Club :* National Liberal.
(*Died 19 Feb. 1916.*)

RADFORD, Edward, A.R.W.S. ; *b.* Devonport, Devon, 22 April 1881 ; 4th *s.* of William Radford, Civil Engineer, of Irlam, Buglawton, Cheshire ; *m.* Hester Blunden Helsham (*d.* 1877) ; one *s. Educ.:* Stock's School, Poplar ; Tredegar Square Grammar School, Bow. Indentured pupil of Thomas Wickstead, civil engineer ; in employ of J. and C. Rigby, Government contractors, Holyhead and Portland breakwaters ; assistant to his brother William, engineer to Regent's Canal, and under J. M. Rendel, P.I.C.E. ; practised as architect at Toronto, Canada West ; afterwards with W. Tinsley, architect, Cincinnati, Ohio ; Acting-Lieutenant 11th Ohio Battery, United States Artillery, under Major A. G. A. Constable, Bengal Horse Artillery, early in Secesh War ; member of Liverpool Society of Painters in Water Colours ; for many years member of Society of Arts. *Recreations :* at present country walks, and a good novel ; when young, fond of rowing, yachting, shooting, and sparring. *Address:* Morley House, Southwick, Brighton. (*Died 9 June 1920.*)

RADFORD, Sir George Heynes, Kt., *cr.* 1916 ; M.P. (L.) East Islington since 1906 ; J.P. Surrey ; Chairman National Liberal Club Buildings Company, Ltd. ; Senator University of London ; L.C.C. 1895-1907 ; Solicitor ; *b.* 1851 ; *e. s.* of G. D. Radford of Plymouth ; *m.* 1882, Emma Louise, *d.* of Daniel Radford, J.P. ; three *d. Educ.:* London Univ. (LL.B.). *Publications:* Occasional Verses ; Shylock and Others. *Address:* 27 Chancery Lane, W.C. ; Chiswick House, Ditton Hill, Surrey. *T.A.:* Radland, Holb. London. *T. :* Holborn 90. *Clubs :* National Liberal, Reform.
(*Died 5 Oct. 1917.*)

RADFORD, Col. Oswald Claude, C.B. 1905 ; C.I.E. 1900 ; Indian Army ; *b.* 4 Nov. 1850 ; *m.* 1st, 1883, Alice Sarah, *d.* of H. Herdon ; 2nd, 1917, Margaret, *d.* of Thomas Fleming. Served Jowaki-Afridi Expedition, 1877-78 (despatches, medal with clasp) ; Afghanistan, 1879-80 (medal) ; Takht i Suliman, 1883 (despatches) ; Zhob Valley Expedition, 1884 ; Black Mountain, 1888 (wounded, despatches, brevet of Major, clasp) ; Miranzai, 1891 (despatches) ; Waziristan, 1894 (clasp) ; China, 1900 — commanded force of British, French, and Japs at Tai-Tao-Ting (despatches twice, medal, C.I.E.) ; Kabul Kheyl Expedition, 1901—commanded a column (despatches) ; retired, 1910. (*Died 23 Sept. 1924.*)

RAE, Sir Alexander, Kt., *cr.* 1911 ; J.P. Caithness ; Hon. Sheriff of Caithness, Orkney, and Shetland ; *s.* of late William Rae, publisher, Provost of Wick, 1874-86 ; *m.* Mary, *e. d.* of late William Crowe, Factor for the British Fisheries Society. *Educ.:* Wick ; Royal High School, Edinburgh. Was in business as publisher with his father, and, on the latter's death in 1893, conducted the business until 1910, when he retired ; Provost of Wick, 1904-6 ; President of Wick Liberal Association since 1894. *Recreations :* golf, bowls, chess. *Address :* Langhills, Wick, Scotland. *Club :* Scottish Liberal, Edinburgh. (*Died 1924.*)

RAE, Sir (Henry) Norman, Kt., *cr.* 1922 ; M.P. (Co. L.) Shipley Division of Yorks, Dec. 1918 - 23 ; wool merchant ; *b.* 20 Jan. 1860 ; *m.* 1883, Emily (*d.* 1927), *d.* of Joshua Cass, Mirfield, Yorks. Contested Ripon Division, 1910. *Address:* Rossett Green, Harrogate. *Club :* Reform. (*Died 31 Dec. 1928.*)

RAE, Captain Sir James Robert, K.B.E. *cr.* 1920 ; O.B.E. 1918 ; Master, S.S. City of Exeter. *Address:* 73 Caledonia Road, Saltcoats, Scotland. (*Died 29 Dec. 1928.*)

RAEBURN, Sir Ernest Manifold, K.B.E., *cr.* 1920 ; late Director-General, British Ministry of Shipping, New York ; *b.* 13 Dec. 1878 ; *s.* of Sir William H. Raeburn, M.P.; *m.* Greta Mary Alison, *d.* of Eng.-Capt. J. H. Watson, R.N. ; one *s.* one *d. Educ.:* Kelvinside Academy, Glasgow. With his father's firm, Raeburn & Verel, Ltd., Shipowners, Glasgow ; a partner for 10 years ; Commercial Advisor, Transport Dept. of Admiralty shortly after outbreak of war ; then Private Secretary to Sir Joseph P. Maday, Bt., P.C., Shipping Controller ; then assistant to Sir Thos. Royden, Bt., in Washington, D.C. ; then Director of Transport Dept. Ministry of Shipping, New York. *Recreations:* fishing, golf, tennis, badminton, etc. *Address:* 45 West Nile Street, Glasgow. *T.A.:* Vernay Glasgow. *Clubs :* Caledonian, Royal Societies ; Conservative, Glasgow ; London and Press, New York.
(*Died 1 June 1922.*)

RAFFAELLI, J. F.; chevalier de la Légion d'honneur ; Officier de la Couronne royale d'Italie ; chevalier de l'ordre de Léopold de Belgique ; médaille d'or Exposition Universelle de Paris, 1889 - 1900 ; artiste, peintre ; Inventeur des "couleurs solides à l'huile" ; *b.* Paris, 20 avril 1850 ; *m.* Aglaè Rosine Héran ; grand'mère est une de Giuli ; les de Giuli sont alliés à la grande famille des Gonzague. *Address:* Rue Chardin I., Paris. (*Died Feb. 1924.*)

RAFFLES, Rev. Thomas Stamford ; Rector of Lexden, Essex ; *b.* 11 July 1853 ; *m.* 1884, Cecil Helen, 2nd *d.* of Col. Lovett of Henlie, Shropshire ; two *s. Educ.:* Rugby ; Clare College, Cambridge (M.A.) ; Cuddesdon Theological College. Curate of Hawarden, 1880 ; Whittington, Salop, 1880-82 ; Ashton-on-Mersey, 1882-83 ; Rector of Owmby, 1883-87 ; Langham, 1887-1914. *Address:* Lexden Rectory, Colchester. *T. :* Colchester 57. *T.A.:* Lexden.
(*Died 1 Mar. 1926.*)

RAFFLES-FLINT, Ven. Stamford R.; F.Z.S. ; Archdeacon of Cornwall since 1916 ; Canon Residentiary and Treasurer of Truro Cathedral ; *b.* 6 Feb. 1847 ; *s.* of Rev. W. C. Raffles Flint, *n.* of Sir T. Stamford Raffles, and Jenny Rosdew, *d.* of Col. Mudge of Beechwood, S. Devon ; *m.* 1884, Ethel Maud, *d.* of Major Quentin, late 10th Hussars, *g.d.* of Col. Sir George Quentin, 10th Hussars ; two *d. Educ. :* Eton ; University Coll., Oxon. (M.A.). Curate of Alverstoke, Hants, 1871-79 ; Ladock, 1879-1885 ; Rector of Ladock, Cornwall, 1885-1920. *Publication :* Memoir of the Mudge Family. *Address :* Nansawsan, Ladock, Cornwall. *T.A.:* Ladock. *Club :* Athenæum.
(*Died 15 Aug. 1925.*)

RAGHAVA RAU, G. Pantulu; Member of the Legislative Council of Madras, and Vakil of the Madras High Court ; *b.* 1862 ; three *s.* five *d. Educ. :* Presidency College, Madras. Practising as lawyer in Ganjam District ; Member of Municipal Council and Talug and District Boards in Ganjam ; was Chairman of Berhampore for six years. *Recreations:* tennis and riding. *Address :* Anandabag, Vepery, Madras. *Club:* Cosmopolitan, Madras.
(*Died 1921.*)

RAGHUNATH DAS RAI BAHADUR, Diwan Bahadur Sir Chaube, Kt., *cr.* 1923 ; C.S.I. 1912 ; *b.* Nov. 1849 ; *s.* of Pande Jagannath Dasji-a Chaturvedi Brahman of Etawah-a District, U.P., India ; *m.* ; three *s. Educ.:* Humes High School, Etawah ; Government Coll., Agra. Entered Native State Service in Rajputana ; was Assistant Superintendent of Revenue, Kotah, 1877-1893 ; Vice-President of the Kotah Municipality, 1885-93 ; Revenue Superintendent 1894, and soon after a Member of the State Council, Kotah ; Diwan (Minister), Kotah State, since 1896 ; a "Tazimi" Sardar of Kotah State ; holds landed property in Etawah District, paying annually under 4000 rupees as revenue to British Government; Rai Bahadur, 1897; Diwan Bahadur, 1906. *Address:* Kotah State, Rajputana, India. (*Died 1 Dec. 1923.*)

RAGHUNATH RAO DINKAR, Rao Raja, Mashir - i - Khas Bahadur, Madar-ul-Moham, C.I.E.; Political Secretary to H.H. the Maharaja Scindia ; is a member of His Highness' Majlis-i-Khas; ranks as a first-class Sardar in Bombay ; is above Raja Bahadurs in the U.P. ; *b.* 4 Aug. 1858 ; *s.* of Rao Raja Sir Dinkar Rao, K.C.S.I., late Prime Minister to H.H. the Maharaja Scindia of Gwalior; *m.* ; two *s. Educ.:* privately, under the tuition of Mr. K. Deighton, Principal, Agra College. Private Secretary to late Maharaja, and was Additional Accountant-General; Famine Commissioner, 1896 ; member of the Council of Appeal, and member of the Board of Revenue, Gwalior, 1901. *Recreations:* music, photography. *Heir: s.* Col. G. R. Rajwade, Adjutant-General of the Gwalior Army. *Address:* Gwalior, Central India. *Club:* Elgin, Gwalior.

RAGLAN, 3rd Baron (*cr.* 1852), **George Fitz-Roy Henry Somerset,** G.B.E., *cr.* 1919; C.B.; Lieut.-Governor, Isle of Man, 1902-1919; *b.* London, 18 Sep. 1857; *m.* 1883, Lady Ethel Jemima Ponsonby, *d.* of 7th Earl of Bessborough; three *s.* three *d.* Tory. *Educ.:* Eton; Sandhurst. Page of Honour to the Queen, 1868-74 ; Sub-Lieut. unattached, 1875; joined Grenadier Guards, 1876 ; Captain, 1886 ; R.E. (Militia), Monmouthshire, 1887 ; Lieut. - Colonel and Hon. Colonel till 1908 ; A.D.C. to Sir James Fergusson, Bt., Governor of Bombay, 1880-1883 ; Orderly Officer to Major - General Sir R. Phayre in 2nd phase of Afghan War (medal, despatches) ; Under Secretary for War, 1900 - 1902. *Publications:* various magazine articles, letters, etc., on military and sporting subjects. Owns about 1100 acres, and Cefntilla Court. *Recreation:* shooting. *Heir: s.* Hon. Fitz-Roy Richard Somerset. *Address:* 24 Sloane Gardens, S.W.1 ; *T.:* Victoria 9435 ; Cefntilla Court, Usk, Monmouthshire. *Clubs:* Guards', Carlton. (*Died 24 Oct. 1921.*)

RAIKES, Arthur Stewart; *b.* 16 June 1856; 5th *s.* of Henry Raikes of Llwynegrin, Flintshire. *Educ.:* Winchester; Trinity Coll. Cambridge. 1st class History Tripos, 1877; B.A. 1878 ; M.A. 1882. Entered diplomatic service ; attaché at Athens, 1880 ; 3rd sec., Copenhagen, 1882 ; 2nd sec., Buenos Ayres, 1885 ; Berlin, 1887 ; Rome, 1892 ; 1st sec., Rio de Janeiro, 1896 ; Brussels, 1898 ; Washington, 1901-4 ; H.B.M.'s Minister, Santiago, 1904 ; retired 1907. *Address:* The Gate House, Ingatestone, Essex. *Club:* Travellers'. (*Died 22 Mar. 1925.*)

RAIKES, Maj.-Gen. Charles Lewis; Retired List, Indian Staff Corps ; *b.* 20 July 1837 ; *s.* of late Henry Thomas Raikes, Judge High Court, Calcutta ; *m.* 1893, Maude Caroline, *d.* of Deputy-Surgeon-General Fowler ; one *s. Educ.:* Temple Grove, East Sheen ; private tutor ; Addiscombe College. Entered Madras Army, 1855 ; transferred to the Indian Staff Corps ; retired with hon. rank of Major-General, 1887. *Address:* 18 Albany Road, Bedford. *Club:* Junior Conservative. (*Died 25 July 1919.*)

RAIKES, Francis Edward, C.V.O. 1922; M.V.O. 1917 ; O.B.E. 1918; *b.* 7 June 1870; 2nd *s.* of late Rt. Hon. Henry Cecil Raikes and Charlotte Blanche, 4th *d.* of Charles Blayney Trevor-Roper of Plasteg, Flintshire ; *m.* 1906, Iris Veronica, *d.* of late Thomas Sopwith, C.E.; one *d. Educ.:* Haileybury. Held a Commission in 3rd Batt. Cheshire Regt. 1888 - 91 ; Private Secretary to Postmaster General, 1890 - 91 ; Queen's Foreign Service Messenger, 1892 ; Senior King's Foreign Service Messenger; resigned, ill-health, 1921 ; received the Coronation Medals of Kings Edward VII. and George V. *Address:* Moy Lodge, Datchet. *T.:* Windsor 196. *Club:* Carlton.
(*Died 11 Sept. 1923.*)

866

RAIKES, Rev. Walter Allan, M.A.; *b.* Madras, 1852; *s.* of Major R. W. Raikes, commanding Madras Governor's Bodyguard; *m.* 1884, Catherine Amelia, *d.* of William Cotton Oswell of Hillside, Groombridge ; three *s.* three *d. Educ.:* Wellington College ; Trinity College, Cambridge. Master at Wellington College, 1875 ; Curate at Christ Church, Folkestone, 1879 ; Vicar of Ide Hill, Sevenoaks, 1880 ; Hon. Canon of Rochester, 1908-12 ; Vicar of Goudhurst, 1911-28 ; Rural Dean of West Charing, 1920-24. *Address:* Goudhurst, Kent.
(*Died 25 Nov. 1923.*)

RAINSFORD, Col. Stephen Dickson, C.B. 1917 ; late R.A.; *b.* 12 Aug. 1853 ; *s.* of Rev. Marcus Rainsford of Belgrave Chapel, W.; *m.* 1890, Annie Marion, widow of Captain Jourdier, 20th Dragoons, French Army; one *d.* Entered army, 1873 ; Lt.-Col. 1899 ; Bt. Col. 1904 ; retired, 1905 ; served Afghan, 1878-79 (medal and clasp). *Address:* Pond House, Boxted, nr. Colchester, Essex.
(*Died 2 Oct. 1920.*)

RAJAGOPALA, Sir Chariyar, Perun-gavur, M.A., B.L., K.C.S.I., *cr.* 1920 ; C.I.E., 1909 ; *b.* 1862 ; Member of Council of India since Jan. 1924. *Educ.:* Madras University. Entered Civil Service, 1888 ; Diwan to Raja of Cochin, 1896-1902 ; Diwan of Travancore, 1907-1914 ; Secretary to Government, Madras, 1914-1917 ; Member of the Madras Executive Council, 1917-20 ; President of the Madras Provincial Legislature, 1921. *Address:* c/o India Office, S.W.1. (*Died 1 Dec. 1927.*)

RALEIGH, Hon. Sir Thomas, K.C.S.I., *cr.* 1904 ; C.S.I. 1902 ; K.C.; Member of Council of India, 1909-13 ; *b.* Edinburgh, 2 Dec. 1850 ; *e. s.* of Samuel Raleigh, manager Scottish Widows' Fund ; unmarried. *Educ.:* Edinburgh ; Tübingen; Oxford (M.A., D.C.L.; Lothian Prize, 1873). Fellow All Souls College, 1876 ; Barr. 1877 ; Reader in English Law at Oxford, 1884-96 ; contested South Edinburgh, 1885 ; and West Edinburgh, 1888 ; Registrar of the Privy Council, 1896-99; Legal Member of Viceroy's Council in India, 1899-1904. *Publications:* Elementary Politics, 1886 ; Outline of the Law of Property, 1889. *Address:* All Souls' College, Oxford. *Clubs:* Athenæum, Savile.
(*Died 8 Feb. 1920.*)

RALEIGH, Sir Walter, Kt., *cr.* 1911; Professor of English Literature, Oxford, since 1904 ; Fellow of Merton College, 1914 ; *s.* of late Dr. Alexander Raleigh ; *b.* 1861 ; *m.* 1890, Lucie Gertrude, *d.* of Mason Jackson ; three *s.* one *d. Educ.:* University College, London ; King's College, Cambridge. Late Professor of Modern Literature, University College, Liverpool, and of English Literature, Glasgow. *Publications:* The English Novel, 1894 ; Robert Louis Stevenson : an Essay, 1895; Style, 1897 ; Milton, 1900 ; Wordsworth, 1903 ; Shakespeare, 1907 ; The English Voyagers, 1904 ; Six Essays on Johnson, 1910 ; Romance, 1917 ; sundry articles. *Address:* Oxford. *Club:* Athenæum.
(*Died 13 May 1922.*)

RALLI, Pandeli, J.P., D.L. ; *b.* 23 May 1845 ; *o. s.* of late Thomas Ralli of London, and Mary, *d.* of Pandeli Argenti of Marseilles. *Educ.:* King's College, London ; M.P. Bridport, 1875 - 80 ; Wallingford, 1880 - 85. *Address:* 17 Belgrave Square, S.W.1; *T.:* Victoria 436. *Clubs:* Athenæum, Carlton, Bath.
(*Died 21 Aug. 1928.*)

RAM, Abel John, K.C.; barrister-at-law; Recorder of Wolverhampton 1900-18 ; *b.* Ilam, Staffs, 21 Sept. 1842 ; 2nd *s.* of late Rev. A. J. Ram of Clonatin, Co. Wexford, and Lady Jane Stopford, *d.* of 3rd Earl of Courtown ; *m.* 1874, Hon. Mary Grace (*d.* 1912), *d.* of 13th Lord Inchiquin ; one *s.* two *d. Educ.:* Repton ; Corpus Christi College, Oxford. 2nd class Moderations ; 3rd class Natural Science. B.A. 1865 ; M.A. 1867; Barrister 1873 ; joined the Oxford Circuit, of which he is Leader; Revising Barrister, 1879-1896; Bencher of the Inner Temple, 1897; formerly member of the Bar Council; Recorder of Hanley, 1891-1900; Chairman of Royal Commission on Vivisection; member of East Coast Raid Commission, 1915; Knight of Grace of St. John of Jerusalem; J.P. County Herts. *Recreations:* golf, fishing. *Address:* Berkhampstead Place, Great Berkhampstead; Chambers, 3 Paper Buildings, Temple, E.C.; Palace Chambers, Bridge Street, S.W. *T.:* Victoria 1040; Berkhampstead 59. *Club:* Oxford and Cambridge.   (*Died 8 Aug. 1920.*)

RAM, Rev. Robert Digby, M.A.; late Prebendary of St. Paul's; *b.* 24 Jan. 1844; *s.* of Rev Canon Ram, Clonatin, County Wexford, Ireland, and Lady Jane Ram, *d.* of 3rd Earl of Courtown; *m.* 1877, Mary, *o. c.* of late George Edward Anson, C.B., Keeper of Privy Purse to late Queen Victoria; one *s.* one *. d. Educ.:* Repton; Corpus Christi College, Cambridge. Deacon, 1867; Priest, 1868; Curate of Dunchurch, Warwickshire, 1867-73; of Rolleston, Staffordshire, 1873-77; Vicar of Teddington, 1878-82; of Hampton, 1882-1911. *Address:* 93 Eaton Terrace, Eaton Square. S.W.1. *T.:* Victoria 6439. (*Died 18 Oct. 1925.*)

RAM, Rev. Stephen Adye Scott; Canon and Prebendary of Fenton in York Cathedral, 1916; *b.* London, 16 Aug. 1864; *s.* of Stephen Adye and Susan Amelia Ram; *m.* Margaret King, *d.* of John Woodcock, Oakley, Rawtenstall; three *s.* one *d. Educ.:* Charterhouse; St. John's College, Cambridge. 1st class, 3rd division, Classical Tripos, 1886; B.A. 1886, M.A. 1890; Deacon, 1887; Priest, 1888; Curacies—Haslingden, Bolton-le-Sands, and S. Augustine's, Fendlebury; Vicar of S. Mary, Hull, 1899-1926. *Address:* 8 St. Peter's Grove, York. *T.:* 3231. *M.:* DN 9298.   (*Died 28 Nov. 1928.*)

RAMACIOTTI, Maj.-Gen. Gustave, C.M.G. 1917; V.D., J.P.; *b.* Leghorn, 13 March 1861; *s.* of late A. Ramaciotti; *m.* 1882, Ada, *d.* of late W. G. Wilson, of Hawick, Scotland; one *s.* one *d. Educ.:* Italy. Commanded 2nd Australian Infantry Regt. 1909-13; 11th Australian Infantry Brigade, 1914-15; 2nd Military District, N.S.W. 1915-17; Inspector-General of Administration, 1917-20. *Publications:* Tripoli (Turco-Italo War); various military text-books. *Recreations:* tennis, yachting, motoring. *Address:* Australia House, Strand, W.C.; 33 Hunter Street, Sydney, N.S.W. *T.A.:* Rami. *Club:* Royal Automobile.   (*Died 6 Dec. 1927.*)

RAMAKRISHNA, T., B.A.; The South Indian Poet; *b.* 1854. *Educ.:* Madras Christian College. Fellow and Chairman of the Board of Studies in Dravidian Languages, Madras University; visited England, 1911. *Publications:* Life in an Indian Village; Tales of Ind and other Poems; Padmini, an Indian Romance; The Dive for Death; My Visit to the West; Early Reminiscences, etc. *Address:* Thottakkadu House, Madras.

RAMBAUT, Arthur Alcock, M.A. (Dub. et Oxon.); D.Sc., F.R.S., F.R.A.S.; Radcliffe Observer, Oxford, since 1897; *b.* Waterford, 21 Sep. 1859; 3rd *s.* of Rev. E. F. Rambaut; *m.* 1883, Emily Longford; three *s. Educ.:* Arlington House, Portarlington; Royal School, Armagh; Trinity College, Dublin. 1st Science Scholar, 1880; Senior Moderator and Gold Medallist Mathematics and Mathematical Physics, 1881. Senior Science Master, Royal School, Armagh, 1881. Assistant Astronomer Trinity College, Dublin, at Dunsink, 1882-92; Andrew's Professor of Astronomy in the University of Dublin and Royal Astronomer of Ireland, 1892-1897. *Publications:* Biographical Notices of Astronomers in the Ency. Brit.; four Catalogues of Stars published in Astronomical Observations and Researches, Dunsink, and in the publications of the Radcliffe Observatory, Oxford; papers published in the Philosophical Transactions and Proceedings of the Royal Society, the Monthly Notices of Royal Astronomical Society, the Transactions and Proceedings of the Royal Dublin Society, the Royal Irish Academy, the Publications of the Radcliffe Observatory, Astronomische Nachrichten, etc. *Address:* Radcliffe Observatory. Oxford.   (*Died 14 Oct. 1923.*)

RAMSAY, Sir George Dalhousie, Kt.; *cr.* 1900; C.B. 1882; retired Civil Service; *b.* Montrose, 23 May 1828; 7th *s.* of Sir Alexander Ramsay, 2nd Bt. of Balmain, M.P. Kincardine, and Elizabeth. *d.* of 1st Baron Panmure, *sis.* of 11th Earl of Dalhousie; *m.* 1864, Eleanor (*d.* 1918), *d.* of late John Crawford, F.R.S., Governor of Singapore. *Educ.:* France and Germany. War Office, 1846-93; private secretary to Secretary at War, 1849-52, 1853-55; to President Board of Control, 1852; to Secretary of State for War, 1855; Secretary to Royal Commission on Promotion in the Army, 1854; Assistant Director Army Stores and Clothing, 1855-63; Director Army Clothing, 1863-93. *Decorated* for services at War Office. *Publication:* The Panmure Papers. *Recreations:* literature, art collector. *Address:* 7 Manson Place, Queen's Gate, S.W.7. *T.:* Kensington 3545. *Club:* Arthur's.   (*Died 16 Jan. 1920.*)

RAMSAY, George Gilbert, LL.D. Edinburgh, Aberdeen, and Glasgow; Litt.D. Dublin; F.R.L.S.; *b.* 1839; 3rd *s.* of Sir George Ramsay, 9th Bt. of Bamff; *m.* Gertrude Schuyler (*d.* 1911), *d.* of Robert Graham, Ayrshire, 1865; three *s.* two *d. Educ.:* Rugby School (Scholar); Trinity College, Oxford, First Class (Classics), 1861; M.A. 1862; Professor of Humanity Glasgow University, 1863-1906. *Publications:* Selections from Tibullus and Propertius, 1887; Manual of Latin Prose Composition in three vols. (1) Elementary, (2) Introduction and Selected Passages, (3) Latin Versions by selected scholars (4th edition 1897); The Annals of Tacitus, i.-vi.; Trans. with Introduction, Notes, and Maps, 1904; vol. ii. of above, containing Annals, xi.-xvi. 1909; The Histories of Tacitus, 1915; Translation of Juvenal and Persius for the Loeb Library, 1918. *Recreations:* shooting, golf, cycling, skating, mountaineering. *Address:* Drumore, Blairgowrie, Perthshire. *T.A.:* Blacklunans. *Clubs:* Oxford and Cambridge, Alpine; New, Edinburgh; Western, Glasgow.   (*Died 8 Mar. 1921.*)

RAMSAY, Sir Herbert, 5th Bt.; *cr.* 1806; *b.* 9 Feb. 1868; *S.* father 1902; *s.* of 4th Bt. and Octavia, *d.* of Thomas Haigh, Elm Hall, Liverpool; *m.* 1902, Mabel, *d.* of Rev. J. Hutchinson, Australia; two *s.* two *d. Educ.:* Cheltenham College. *Heir: s.* Alexander Burnett, *b.* 26 March 1903.   (*Died 22 Mar. 1924.*)

RAMSAY, Maj.-Gen. Herbert Maynard; *b.* 1843. In Indian Service, 1863, as Assistant Superintendent, District Superintendent, and Personal Assistant to Inspector-General; one of the Commissioners to report on Chaukidari System, 1890-91; Maj.-Gen. 1899; retired, 1903.   (*Died 13 Sept. 1917.*)

RAMSAY, Sir James (Henry), 10th Bt., *cr.* 1666; D.L.; *b.* 21 May 1832; *S.* father 1871; *m.* 1st, 1861, Mary (*d.* 1868), *d.* of W. Scott-Kerr; 2nd, 1873, Charlotte (*d.* 1904), *d.* of William Stewart of Ardvorlich; one *s.* six *d. Educ.:* Rugby; Christ Church, Oxford (M.A.). Barr. Lincoln's Inn, 1863; Hon. LL.D. Glasgow University, 1906; Litt.D. Cambridge University; Fellow British Academy. Owns about 13,900 acres. *Heir: s.* James Douglas. *Publications:* Lancaster and York; The Foundations of England, 1898; The Angevin Empire, 1903; The Dawn of the Constitution, 1908; The Genesis of Lancaster, 1914; Bamff Charters, 1915. *Address:* Bamff, Alyth, Perth. *Clubs:* Alpine,

London Skating ; New, Edinburgh.
(*Died 17 Feb. 1925.*)

RAMSAY, Major-Gen. Sir John George, K.C.B., *cr.* 1911 ; C.B. 1900 ; I.A., retired ; Colonel 24th Punjabis ; *b.* 5 Nov. 1856 ; *s.* of Commander J. D. Ramsay, R.N. ; *m.* 1878, Ethel, *d.* of Major-Gen. G. N. Cave, I.S.C. *Educ.:* Queen Elizabeth's School, Ipswich ; Stubbington House, Stubbington, Hants. Joined 14th Foot, 1875 ; joined 24th Punjab Infantry, 1877 ; Afghan War, 1878-80 ; Action of Kandahar, 1 Sep. 1880 ; Kabul-Kandahar march (medal, clasp, bronze star) ; Hazara Expedition, 1888 (medal and clasp) ; North-West Frontier, 1897-98 ; Malakand (despatches, medal, 2 clasps) ; served China, 1900 ; Relief of Pekin, Action at Peitsang, Action at Yangtsun (despatches, medal, clasp, C.B.) ; Mohmand Expedition, 1908 (despatches, medal, clasp) ; commanding 24th Division, 1914-15. *Address :* Twyford House, Dereham, Norfolk. (*Died 31 Mar. 1920.*)

RAMSAY, Sir William, K.C.B., *cr.* 1902 ; LL.D., D.Sc., M.D., Ph.D., F.R.S., F.C.S. ; Commander of the Crown of Italy ; Knight of the Prussian Order Pour le mérite ; Officier de la Légion d'Honneur ; Nobel Prizeman, 1904 ; Honorary Member of the Institute of France, Hon. Member Royal Academies of Ireland, Berlin, Bohemia, Holland, Rome, Petrograd, Turin, Roumania, Vienna, Norway, and Sweden ; of Academies of Geneva, Frankfort, and Mexico ; and of German Chemical Society ; of Royal Medical and Chirurgical Society ; of the Académie de médecine of Paris ; of Pharmaceutical Society ; of Philosophical Societies of Manchester, Philadelphia, and Rotterdam ; *b.* Glasgow, 2 Oct. 1852 ; *o. s.* of late William Ramsay, C.E., and Catherine Robertson ; *m.* 1881, Margaret, *d.* of late George Stevenson Buchanan ; one *s.* one *d. Educ.:* Glasgow Academy and University ; Tübingen University. Assistant "Young" Laboratory of Technical Chemistry, 1872-74 ; Tutorial Assistant of Chemistry, Glasgow University, 1874-80 ; Professor of Chemistry University Coll. Bristol, 1880-87 ; Principal University Coll. Bristol, 1881-87 ; Professor of Chemistry, University Coll. London, 1887-1913 ; Professor Emeritus since 1913. *Publications :* numerous papers, the most important of which are perhaps The Molecular Surface-Energy of Liquids ; Argon, a New Constituent of the Atmosphere (in conjunction with Lord Rayleigh) ; and Helium, a Constituent of Certain Minerals ; also Neon, Krypton, and Xenon, three new atmospheric gases ; also the transmutation of radium into helium (with Mr. F. Soddy) ; three text-books of Chemistry, and of The Discovery of the Constituents of the Air. *Recreations :* languages, travelling. *Address :* Beechcroft, Hazlemere, Bucks. *Club :* Athenæum. (*Died 23 July 1916.*)

RAMSDEN, Sir William, Kt., *cr.* 1926 ; J.P. ; Solicitor ; senior partner in firm of Ramsden, Sykes and Ramsden, Solicitors, Huddersfield ; *b.* 7 April 1857 ; *s.* of James Ramsden, Dudd House, Meltham, Yorkshire ; *m.* 1894, Ethel H., *e. d.* of T. H. Ramsden, Oakwell House, Golcar, Yorkshire ; no *c. Educ.:* Huddersfield College. President of Huddersfield Law Society, 1902-4 ; Governor since 1906 ; Director and President of Halifax Building Society ; Director of Union Bank of Manchester (Yorkshire Board) ; Director of Hopkinsons Ltd., Huddersfield ; Chairman of Munitions Court for Huddersfield, 1915-1920 ; Chairman, Huddersfield Interviewing Board for Officers, 1920-24 ; Chairman, Court of Referees for Huddersfield, since 1912 ; Chairman, Huddersfield Insurance Committee ; Chairman, Huddersfield Employment Committee ; Chairman, Huddersfield War Pensions Committee ; Chairman of Huddersfield King's Roll Committee ; Chairman of Huddersfield Juvenile Employment Committee. *Address :*

Marshfield, Huddersfield. *T.:* Huddersfield 4. *T.A.:* Ramsden, Marshfield, Huddersfield. *Clubs :* Junior Athenæum ; Huddersfield.
(*Died 22 Oct. 1923.*)

RAMSEY, Colonel Colin Worthington Pope, C.M.G. 1916 ; consulting engineer ; *b.* Bury, Quebec, Canada, 15 Jan. 1883 ; *s.* of W. A. Ramsey, C.E. ; *m.* 1918, Dorothy Elsie, *d.* of late Sir John Jackson ; one *s.* one *d. Educ.:* Dufferin Grammar School ; Royal School of Infantry, St. Johns ; private tuition. Entered service Canadian Pacific Railway Co., 1901 ; employed in various capacities (chiefly engineering depart.) until 1911 ; Chief Engineer of Construction, Canadian Pacific Railway, Montreal, 1911-15 ; Lt.-Col. C.E.F. Feb. 1915-April 1917 ; promoted Colonel 13 April 1917 ; Superintendent Canadian Pacific Railway, Montreal, 1919-20 ; 1921, Dominion Construction Co. Ltd., and Ramsey, engineers and contractors ; Consulting Engineer and Director Greyville Crushed Rock Co. Ltd. ; member Canadian Society Civil Engineers, American Railway Engineering Association, and Canadian Railway Association. *Recreations :* golf, curling. *Address :* Lancaster, Ontario. *Clubs :* St. James's, Canadian, Montreal. (*Died Sept. 1926.*)

RANBIR SINGH, Raja Sir, Sahib of Patiala, K.C.S.i., *cr.* 1903 ; uncle of H.H. the Maharaja of Patiala ; *m.* ; one *s.* one *d.* Has given his residence and estates at Kasauli for the use of the Indian Pasteur Institute there. Appointed member of the Punjab Legislative Council, 1904, and of the Imperial Council, 1910 ; title of " Raja " was conferred by the Maharaja of Patiala Feb. 1915. *Address :* Patiala, Punjab.
(*Died 18 Jan. 1916.*)

RANDALL, Rt. Rev. James Leslie, M.A., D.D. ; 2nd *s.* of Archdeacon James Randall and Rebe, *o. d.* of Richard Lowndes ; *m.* Ann Harriet (*d.* 1899), *d.* of G. A. Bruxner ; one *s.* three *d. Educ.:* Winchester ; New College, Oxford (Fellow). Rector of Newbury, 1857-78 ; Hon. Canon of Christ Church, 1878-95 ; Rector of Sandhurst, Berks, 1878-80 ; Rector of Mixbury, Oxford, 1882-85 ; Prebendary of Chichester, 1894-95 ; Archdeacon of Buckingham, 1880-95 ; of Oxford and Canon of Christ Church, 1895-1902 ; Suffragan Bishop of Reading, 1889-1908. *Address :* Abbey House, Abingdon. (*Died 17 Jan. 1922.*)

RANDOLPH, Rev. Berkeley William, D.D. ; *b.* 10 March 1858 ; *s.* of Rev. Cyril Randolph, M.A., Rector of Chartham, Kent. *Educ.:* Haileybury ; Balliol College, Oxford. Hebrew (minor) Exhibitioner ; B.A., 2nd class Theol. Schools, 1879 ; Denyer and Johnson Theological Scholar, 1880 ; M.A., 1884 ; D.D., 1901. Ordained deacon, 1881 (Canterbury) ; Priest, 1882 ; Fellow of St. Augustine's Coll. Canterbury, 1880-83 ; Principal of St. Stephen's House, Oxford, 1884-85 ; Domestic Chaplain to Bishop (King) of Lincoln, 1885-90 ; Examining Chaplain, 1890-1910 ; Vice-Principal of Ely Theological College, 1890-91 ; Hon. Fellow of St. Augustine's College, Canterbury, 1884 ; Principal of Ely Theological College, 1891-1911 ; Canon of Ely, 1910 ; Warden of the Community of St. Mary, Wantage, 1911. *Publications :* The Law of Sinai, 1896 ; The Threshold of the Sanctuary, 1897 ; Meditations on the Old Testament for Every Day of the Year, 1899 ; The Example of the Passion, 1901 ; The Prayer-Book Psalter with Notes, 1901 ; Meditations on the New Testament for Every Day of the Year, 1902 ; The Virgin-Birth of Our Lord, 1903 ; Ember Thoughts, 1903 ; The Empty Tomb, 1906 ; Christ in the Old Testament, 1907 ; The Precious Blood of Christ, 1909 ; Confession in the Church of England, 1911 ; Memoir of Arthur Douglas, 1912 ; (joint) The Mind and Work of Bishop King, 1918 ; The Seven Sacraments of the Universal Church, 1916 ; A Communicant's

Manual, 1917; The Plain Man's Book of Religion, 1919; The Coming of the Lord, 1920; The Person of Christ in the First Three Gospels, 1922; Meditations on the Psalms, 1922; Meditations on the Holy Spirit, 1923; Editor of Mowbray's Devotional Library; A Revised Liturgy, 1914; Bishop King's Spiritual Letters; etc. *Address:* The Almonry, Ely.

(*Died 9 Jan. 1925.*)

RANKIN, Guthrie, M.D. Glas.; F.R.C.P. Lond. and Edin.; Physician to the Dreadnought and Royal Waterloo Hospitals; *b.* 1854; *s.* of David Rankin, Kilmarnock, N.B.; *m.* 1883, Janet Hutcheson (*d.* 1916), *d.* of John Guthrie. *Educ.:* Kilmarnock Academy; Neuchatel; Glasgow University; London. Is a native of Ayrshire; a Fellow of several learned Societies; was for several years Examiner in Medicine at Glasgow University; lecturer on medicine London School of Clinical Medicine. *Publications:* medical lectures and papers contributed to current medical literature. *Recreations:* yachting; fishing. *Address:* 9 Harley Street, Cavendish Square, W. *T.A.:* Rankigen, London. *T.:* Paddington 2949; The Orchard, Helford, Cornwall. *M.:* LD 3792. *Clubs:* Union, Royal Automobile; Royal Clyde Yacht.

(*Died 14 Sept. 1919.*)

RANKIN, John, LL.D., J.P.; High Sheriff, Westmorland, 1910; *b.* New Brunswick, 1845. *Educ.:* Dr. Ihne's, Liverpool; St. Andrews University. Shipowner; Chairman, Rankin Gilmour & Co. Ltd.; member Mersey Docks and Harbour Board, 1900-12; Director Bank of Liverpool, 1900, Chairman, 1906-9; Director Royal Insurance Co., 1892, Chairman, 1909-12; Director British and Foreign Marine Insurance Committee, 1909; Pacific Steam Navigation Co., 1898-1910; member of Committee of the Liverpool and London Steamship Protection Association, 1896-1911; Lloyd's Registry of Shipping (Liverpool), 1880-1910, Chairman, 1890-91; member of Liverpool Shipwreck and Humane Society, 1880-96, Chairman, 1891-96; on Council of Liverpool University, 1902-7; Governor of Sedbergh School, 1911; Chairman Soldiers and Sailors' Club, 1915; LL.D. University of Liverpool, 1920; Hon. Freedom of City conferred, 1921. *Address:* St. Michael's Mount, St. Michael's Hamlet, Liverpool.

(*Died 23 Dec. 1928.*)

RANKINE, Sir John, Kt., *cr.* 1921; K.C., LL.D., J.P.; Professor of Scots Law, University of Edinburgh, 1888; *b.* Scotland, 18 Feb. 1846; *s. s.* of Rev. John Rankine, D.D., Minister of Sorn, Ayrshire; unmarried. *Educ.:* Sorn; Ayr and Edinburgh Academies; Edinburgh (M.A.) and Heidelberg Universities. Scottish Barr. 1869; Advocate-Depute, 1885; Q.C. 1897. *Publications:* The Law of Landownership in Scotland, 4th ed. 1909; The Law of Leases in Scotland, 3rd ed. 1916; The Law of Personal Bar in Scotland, 1921; editor of Erskine's Principles of the Law of Scotland, 18th-20th ed., and general editor of the 21st ed., 1911; editor of Scots Revised Reports, House of Lords and Court of Session; and joint consulting editor of the Scots Style Book. Owner of 1000 acres. *Recreations:* travel, shooting. *Address:* 23 Ainslie Place, Edinburgh; Threepwood, Lauder. *Clubs:* Royal Societies; University, Conservative, Edinburgh.

(*Died 8 Aug. 1922.*)

RANKSBOROUGH, 1st Baron, *cr.* 1914, of Ranksborough, **Maj.-Gen. John Fielden Brocklehurst,** C.B. 1900; C.V.O. 1902; Lord-in-Waiting to H.M., 1915; Lord-Lieut. Co. Rutland, 1906; commanded 3rd Cavalry Brigade, Natal (Ladysmith), 1899; Equerry to Her Majesty Queen Alexandra since 1901; Equerry to Queen Victoria from 1899 to her death; *b.* 13 May 1852; *s.* of late Henry Brocklehurst, of Foden Bank; *m.* Louisa

Alice, *d.* of Hon. Lawrence Parsons, 1878. *Educ.*. Rugby; Trinity College, Cambridge; B.A. 1873. Entered army 1874; Colonel, 1899; commanded Royal Horse Guards, 1894-99; served Egyptian War, 1882 (medal with clasp, Khedive's star); Nile Expedition, 1884-85 (despatches, brevet of Major, clasp). *Heir:* none. *Address:* Thatched House Lodge, Richmond Park; Ranksborough, Oakham. *Clubs:* Brooks's, Turf, Carlton. (*Died 23 Feb. 1921.*)

RANSOME, Arthur, M.D., M.A., F.R.C.P., F.R.S. See Addenda, page xxix.

RAPHAEL, Sir Herbert Henry, 1st Bt., *cr.* 1911; M.P. (L.) S. Derbyshire, 1906-18; *b.* 23 Dec. 1859; *s.* of late H. L. Raphael, Banker, chief partner in R. Raphael & Sons, and Henriette Raphael; a Trustee of the National Gallery; *m.* 1884, Rosalie, *o. d.* of G. F. Coster, Upper Chine, Shanklin, Isle of Wight. *Educ.:* Hanover; Vevey; Trinity Hall, Cambridge (Hons. in Law, LL.B., B.A.). Was a Member of the first London County Council, and for three years a Member of the London School Board; was a Member of the Essex County Council; stood twice for Romford Div. of Essex, once for North St. Pancras, and once for South Derbyshire; practised at the Bar for some years, gave it up for public work; enlisted in the Royal Fusiliers; afterwards raised the 18th and 23rd K.R.R.C.; promoted Major and second in command of each of these Battalions; now retired with Hon. rank of Major; Trustee of National Portrait Gallery; Governor of Guy's Hospital; J.P. Essex and Derbyshire. *Heir:* none. *Recreations:* fishing, shooting, golf, motoring. *Address:* Hockley Sole, nr. Folkestone. *T.:* Folkestone 660. *Club:* Reform.

(*Died 24 Sept. 1924.*)

RAPHAEL, John N. (Percival) Paris correspondent of The Referee, The Bystander, and The Era; *b.* 16 May 1868; *s.* of Charles and Rosalie Raphael; *m.* Eugénie (Aimée) Gobillet. *Educ.:* Charterhouse. A false start; then, Paris by Day and Night, for Illustrated Bits; the Dreyfus Case, for the Daily Mail, and journalistic work of all kinds. *Plays:* The Jesters, an adaptation in English Alexandrines of Les Bouffons by Zamacois, 1908; Cochon d'Enfant (with André de Lorde); adaptation of La Femme X by Bisson, Madame X, 1909; The Uninvited Guest, from the French of Tristan Bernard, 1911; Peter Ibbetson, from the novel by the late George du Maurier, 1915; an adaptation in French of Potash and Per. utter, 1916; a number of sketches for music halls. *Publications:* Bookland and its Inhabitants; An English Version of the Songs of Yvette Guilbert; Pictures of Paris and some Parisians; Paris in Pen and Picture; Up Above; The Caillaux Drama, 1914; English translations of Marie Claire, and Valserine and Other Stories, by Marguerite Audoux; Jean and Louise, by Antonin Dusserre; etc. *Recreations:* things theatrical in every sense, other people's automobiles, and a lazy life. *Address:* 62 Boulevard de Clichy, Paris. *T.:* Marcadet, 15-16 Paris.

(*Died 23 Feb. 1917.*)

RASHDALL, Very Rev. Hastings; Dean of Carlisle since 1917; *b.* 1858; *s.* of

WHO WAS WHO, 1916-1928

Rev. J. Rashdall, Vicar of Dawlish; *m.* 1905, Constance, *d.* of late H. F. Makins. *Educ.:* Harrow; New College, Oxford. 2nd class in Classical Moderations and in Litt. Hum. ; B.A. 1881 ; M.A. 1884 ; D.Litt. 1901 ; D.D. 1921 ; Hon. D.C.L. Durham, 1898 ; LL.D. St. Andrews, 1911; Hon. D.D. Glasgow, 1920 ; Stanhope Prize, 1879 ; Chancellor's English Essay, 1883. Lecturer in St. David's College, Lampeter, 1883 ; ordained, 1884 ; Tutor in the University of Durham, 1884-1888 ; Fellow and Lecturer of Hertford Coll, Oxford, 1888-95 ; Chaplain and Theological Tutor of Balliol Coll., 1894-95 ; Fellow of New College, Oxford, 1895 - 1917 ; Tutor, 1895-1910 ; Lecturer, 1910-17 ; Select Preacher in Univ. of Oxford, 1895 - 97 ; Hon. Fellow, 1920 ; Public Examiner at Oxford in Litt. Hum. 1896-1899 ; Preacher at Lincoln's Inn, 1898-1903 ; Bampton Lecturer, 1915 ; Fellow of the British Academy, 1909 ; Canon of Hereford, 1910-17. *Publications:* The Universities of Europe in the Middle Ages, 1895 ; Doctrine and Development (University Sermons), 1898 ; (with R. S. Rait) New College (College Histories Series), 1901 ; Christus in Ecclesia, 1904 ; The Theory of Good and Evil, 1907 ; Philosophy and Religion, 1909 ; Is Conscience an Emotion? 1914 ; Conscience and Christ, 1916 ; The Idea of Atonement in Christian Theology, 1919 ; contributor to Contentio Veritatis, 1902. *Address:* The Deanery, Carlisle. *Club:* Athenæum. (*Died 9 Feb. 1924.*)

RASON, Hon. Sir Cornthwaite Hector, Kt., *cr.* 1909 ; *b.* Somerset, 18 June 1858 ; father medical officer, R.N. ; *m.* 1884, Mary Evelyn, *e. d.* of John Terry, York. *Educ.:* Brighton ; Reading. Emigrated to Western Australia, 1881 ; entered local Parliament, 1889, and since sat almost continuously ; Minister for Works and Railways, 1902-4 ; Treasurer, 1904-5 ; Premier, 1905-6 ; Agent-Gen. in London for Western Australia, 1906 - 9 ; J.P. for the State. *Address:* Valetta, Palace Park Road, Sydenham, S.E. (*Died 15 Mar. 1927.*)

RASON, Ernest Goldfinch. Entered Navy, 1865 ; Lieutenant, 1875 ; Commander, 1890 ; retired Captain, 1898 ; First Lieut. of Ready during Egyptian War ; in command of Ready on the occasion of the capture of the Suez Canal (Egyptian medal and bronze star) ; First Lieut. of Sphinx at Suakin (Suakin clasp) ; passed interpreter in Russian, the first in the Royal Navy, 1887 ; when in command of H.M.S. Plover received the thanks of the Admiralty three times ; brought home the first live specimen of the smaller Orantutan ; when in command of Cockatrice was elected Commodore of the Stationaires assembled to do honour to the King of Roumania at the opening of a branch of the Danube ; when in command of Royalist received the thanks of the Royal Society for assistance rendered to Science ; first British Commissioner to New Hebrides ; in conjunction with French Commissioners quieted the natives and obtained the Anglo-French Protectorate ; retired on its proclamation ; member of Royal United Service Institution and of Royal Colonial Institute ; F.Z.S. *Recreation:* Languages.

RATCLIFFE-ELLIS, Sir Thomas Ratcliffe, Kt., *cr.* 1911 ; assumed the additional surname of Ratcliffe, 1911 ; *b.* 31 Dec. 1842 ; *s.* of Thomas Ellis, late of Wigan, builder and timber merchant, and Elizabeth, *d.* of Thomas Ratcliffe, of Haigh, farmer ; *m.* 1868, Mary Dean (*d.* 1917), *d.* of late Matthew Barton, of Wigan, merchant ; three *s.* four *d.* *Educ.:* Wigan Grammar School. Solicitor, admitted 1865 ; Law Clerk and Secretary to the Mining Association of Great Britain, 1892 - 1921 ; Member of the Royal Commission on Mines, 1906, and of the Royal Commission on the Railways Conciliation Scheme of 1907, 1911 ;

870

Member of the Board of Trade Railway Conference, 1909 ; and Industrial Council, 1911 ; Law Clerk and Secretary to the Lancashire and Cheshire Coal Association since 1892 ; Secretary to the Lancashire and Cheshire Coal Owners' Defence Association ; Member of the Governing Body of the Wigan Mining and Technical College ; Clerk to Wigan Borough Justices, 1874-1900 ; Capt. 21st Lancs. Rifle Volunteers, retired 1880. *Address:* The Hollies, Wigan. *T.A.:* Lex, Wigan. *T.:* 22 Wigan. (*Died 6 Mar. 1925.*)

RATHBONE, William (Gair), B.A., F.R.G.S., Kt. of Grace of the Order of St. John of Jerusalem ; *b.* 1849 ; *e. s.* of late William Rathbone, M.P., D.L., LL.D. of Greenbank, Liverpool ; *m.* 1877, Blanche Marie, *e. d.* of Charles Luling, New York ; one *s.* one *d.* *Educ.:* Rugby ; University College, Oxford (B.A. 1872). Director of Royal Exchange Assurance Corporation ; London County and Westminster Bank ; P. and O.S.N. Co. ; British India Steam Navigation Co. ; Hong-Kong and Shanghai Bank (London Committee) ; is a Commissioner of Income Tax for the City of London ; Hon. Secretary to the Council of Queen Victoria's Jubilee Institute for Nurses. *Address:* 39 Cadogan Gardens, S.W. *Clubs:* Athenæum, St. James's, Savile. (*Died 9 April 1919.*)

RATHMORE, 1st Baron (*cr.* 1895), David Robert Plunket, P.C., LL.D. ; *b.* 3 Dec. 1838 ; 3rd *s.* of 3rd Baron Plunket and Charlotte, *d.* of Rt. Hon. Charles Kendal Bushe, Lord Chief Justice of King's Bench, Ireland. *Educ.:* Trin. Coll. Dublin (LL.D. 1875). Barr. King's Inn, Dublin, 1862 ; Q.C. 1868 ; Law Adviser to Irish Government, 1868-69 ; Solicitor-General Ireland, 1875-77 ; late Professor of Law at King's Inn, Dublin ; M.P. Dublin University, 1870-95 ; Paymaster-General, 1880 ; first Commissioner of Works, 1885-92. *Heir:* none. *Address:* Southfield House, Wimbledon Park, S.W. *Clubs:* Athenæum, Carlton, Garrick ; Kildare Street University, Dublin. (*Died 22 Aug. 1919.*)

RATHOM, John Revelstoke, Editor and General Manager, Providence Journal, Providence, R.I., U.S.A. since 1912 ; *b.* Melbourne, Australia, 1868 ; *m.* Florence Mildred Campbell of New Cumberland, West Virginia ; no *c.* *Educ.:* Whinham College, Adelaide, S.A.; Scotch College, Melbourne, Victoria ; English Public Schools. War Correspondent, Soudan, 1886 : Member Bunbury Expedition to New Guinea, 1888 ; Schwatka's Alaska Expedition 1890 ; for several years Staff Correspondent San Francisco Chronicle and Chicago Herald ; War Correspondent Cuba 1898 and South Africa, 1909-2 ; Managing Editor Providence Journal, 1905-12 ; Member of Board of Directors and Executive Committee, The Associated Press, 1917-23 ; an authority on Immigration and Sociological Subjects and on International Relations ; Commander of the Crown of Italy ; Chevalier of the Order of Leopold (Belgium) ; Trustee American Defence Society, and honorary member of numerous patriotic societies. *Recreations:* an authority on trout-fishing and angling generally. *Address:* 89 Brown Street, Providence, R.I., U.S.A. *T.A.:* Kalyptus, Providence. *M.:* 1424, 8000. *Clubs:* Pilgrims, Austral, Authors, Hope, Providence.
(*Died 11 Dec. 1923.*)

RATTIGAN, Hon. Mr. Justice, Sir Henry Adolphus Byden ; Kt., *cr.* 1918 ; Chief Justice, High Court, Punjab, since 1919 ; *b.* 11 Oct. 1864 ; *s.* of late Sir William Rattigan, K.C., M.P. ; *m.* 1891, Edith Nellie Maud, *e. d.* of late Captain C. Thorne, R.N. ; two *d.* *Educ.:* Harrow ; Balliol College, Oxford. B.A. Oxford, 1888 ; called to Bar, Lincoln's Inn, 1888 ; joined the Bar as an Advocate of the Chief Court, Punjab, 1889 ; Legal Remembrancer to Punjab Government, 1900 ; officiated several times as

Judge of the Chief Court until 1909 ; Judge, 1909-19. *Publications:* Law of Divorce in India; joint author of Tribal Law in the Punjab; editor of The Digest of Customary Law of the Punjab (7th ed.). *Recreations:* golf, fishing. *Address:* Lawrence Road, Lahore, Punjab. *Club:* East India United Service.

(Died 11 Jan. 1920.)

RATTRAY, Lt.-Col. Haldane Burney, D.S.O. 1898; I.C.S.; Wing Officer 45th Bengal Infantry; *b.* 27 May 1870; *s.* of late Col. Thomas Rattray, C.B., C.S.I.; *m.* 1905, Ethel Marguerite, *d.* of late W. Piper of Ackleton Hall, Shropshire; one *s.* one *d.* Entered Derbyshire Regt. 1890; served N.-W. Frontier, India,1897-98 (wounded); Tirah Expeditionary Force (despatches, D.S.O., medal with three clasps). *Address:* Dera Ismail Khan, Bengal.

RAU, Bhimanakunté Hanumanta, B.A., I.S.O.; Fellow and Syndic.; Chairman of the Board of Studies and the Board of Examiners in Mathematics in the University of Madras; *b.* 1855 ; *s.* of B. Bhima Rau of Tangore; *m.* 1873 : three *s.* three *d.* *Educ.:* S.P.G. High School, Tangore; Government College, Kumbakonam. B.A., 1874; Headmaster London Mission School, Negapatam, 1874-75 ; Maharajah's College, Mysore, and Central College, Bangalore, 1875-77 ; Calicut College, 1877-79 ; Lecturer in Mathematics, Government College, Kumbakonam, 1879-93 ; Professor of Mathematics, College of Engineering, Madras, 1894-1912. *Publications:* First Lessons in Geometry ; Hall and Steven's Elementary Algebra, fully revised, etc. *Address:* Martinivas, Mylapur, Madras, India.

(Died 3 Dec. 1922.)

RAVEN-HART, Rev. William Roland, Hon. Canon of St. Edmundsbury and Ipswich. *Address:* Fressingfield Vicarage, Harleston, Suffolk.   *(Died 20 Nov. 1919.)*

RAVENSHAW, temp. Maj.-Gen. Hurdis Secundus Lalande, C.M.G. 1915 ; 1st Batt.the Connaught Rangers; *b.*16 June 1869. *m.* 1898, Rose Constance, O.B.E., *d.* of Col. Sir H. R. Thuillier. Entered army (East Yorks Regt.), 1888 ; Captain Devonshire Regt., 1897 ; Major, 1907 ; Lt.-Col. Connaught Rangers, 1914 ; D.A.A. and Q.M.G., Straits Settlements, 1910-12 ; Coast Defences, Southern Command, 1912-14 ; served Chitral, 1895 (medal with clasp); Malakand, 1897-98 (clasp); Tirah, 1897-98 (clasp); S. African War, 1899-1902 (despatches, five times, Queen's medal, 5 clasps, King's medal, 2 clasps, Bt.-Major); European War, 1914-16 (despatches twice, C.M.G., Bt.-Col.). *Club:* Naval and Military.

(Died 6 June 1920.)

RAVENSWORTH, 5th Baron (cr. 1821), Arthur Thomas Liddell, Bt. 1642 ; *b.* 1887; *s.* of Rev. Hon. Robert Liddell, 5th *s.* of 1st Baron Ravensworth; *S. c.* 1904; *m.* 1866, Sophia Harriet (*d.* 1918), *d.* of Sir Thomas Waller, 2nd Bt. ; three *s.* two *d.* *Heir: s.* Hon. Gerald Wellesley Liddell. *Address:* Eslington Park, Whittingham, R.S.O., Northumberland; Ravensworth Castle, Gateshead. *T.:* Newcastle 574. *Club:* Junior Carlton.

(Died 12 Nov. 1919.)

RAWDON, Rev. J. Hamer, M.A.; Hon. Canon of Manchester; retired ; *s.* of late Joshua Rawdon of Larchwood, Cheshire, and Everilda Sarah, *d.* of James Hamer of Hamer Hall, Lancashire ; *m.*1875, Frances, *d.* of George Bramwell; one *s.* three *d.* *Educ.:* Brasenose College, Oxford; B.A. 1858 ; M.A. 1861. Ordained, 1863 ; Fellow of St. Peter's, Radley, 1861-62 ; Vicar of Preston, Lancs, 1877-1899 ; Rector of Yelverton, Norfolk, 1900-7. *Address:* The Hermitage, Stockton-on-Forest, York.

(Died 19 Jan. 1916.)

RAWLING, Brig.-Gen. Cecil Godfrey, C.M.G. 1916 ; C.I.E. 1909 ; F.R.G.S.;

Somerset Light Infantry ; *b.* 16 Feb. 1870 ; *s.* of late S. B. Rawling, Beaumont, Stoke. *Educ.:* Clifton College. Entered army, 1891 ; Captain, 1901 ; Major, 1914 ; Bt. Lieut.-Colonel, 1917 ; served N.W. Frontier, India, 1897-98(medal with clasp); Tibet Mission, 1904 (medal with clasp); explored and surveyed 40,000 square miles of Western Tibet, 1903 ; Commanded the Gartok Expedition across Tibet,1904-5; awarded the Murchison Bequest by the Royal Geographical Society, 1909 ; received the thanks of the Government of India ; Chief Survey Officer and afterwards leader of the British Expedition to Dutch New Guinea, 1909-11; received the thanks of the Netherlands Government ; received 1917 the Patrons' Gold Medal, Royal Geographical Society, for his explorations in Western Tibet and Rudok, 1903, for his journey from Gyantse via Gartok, 1904, and for his New Guinea, 1908. *Publications:* The Great Plateau, 1905 ; The Land of the New Guinea Pygmies, 1913. *Address:* 16, Montagu Street, Portman Square, W. *T.:* Mayfair 1201. *Club:* Army and Navy.   *(Died 23 Oct. 1917.)*

RAWLINGS, Edmund Charles, J.P.; Alderman, Hammersmith ; *b.* Wallingford, 1854 ; *s.* of Rev. Edmund Rawlings. One of the four Representatives of the Free Churches selected to be received by late King Edward at the time of his Coronation ; contested North Islington ; late Mayor of Hammersmith ; took active part in relief of unemployed and assistance of cripples; senior partner in firm of Rawlings, Butt, and Bowyer of Walbrook. *Publications:* The Free Churchman's Legal Handbook; other legal handbooks. *Address:* 6 Gunnersbury Avenue, W.; *T.:* Ealing 1106 ; Winkfield, Berks. *Clubs:* The New City, National Liberal.

(Died Dec. 1917.)

RAWLINS, Maj.-Gen. Alexander Macdonell, R.A. ; *b.* 29 Aug. 1838. Entered army, 1857 ; Maj.-Gen. 1893 ; retired, 1894 ; served Indian Mutiny, 1857-58 (medal). J.P. Kirkcudbrightshire. *Address:* Laghall, Dumfries. *Club:* United Service.   *(Died 28 July 1916.)*

RAWLINS, Francis Hay; Assistant Master at Eton College, 1875-1905 ; Lower Master of Eton, 1905-16 ; Vice-Provost of Eton since 1916 ; *b.* Moseley, Worcestershire, 2 Oct. 1850 ; *s.* of late Samuel Rawlins and Catherine Anne, *d.* of Stuart Donaldson. *Educ.:* Eton (Newcastle Scholar, Tomline Prizeman); King's College, Cambridge (Scholar, 1870, Fellow, 1875) ; Bracketed Senior Classic and Chancellor's Medallist, 1874; Browne's Medallist, 1871, 1872, 1873 ; Governor of Radley, Royal Holloway, and Imperial Service Colleges. *Publications:* The Advanced Eton Latin Grammar (with the Dean of St. Paul's); editions of portions of Livy. *Address:* The Cloisters, Eton College. *Clubs:* Athenæum, Wellington, Cavendish, Royal Automobile, M.C.C.; Leander.

(Died 13 April 1920.)

RAWLINS, Col. (temp. Col.-Comdt.) Stuart William Hughes, C.B. 1924; C.M.G. 1918 ; D.S.O. 1915 ; Director of Artillery at the War Office, 1924-27 ; commanding Royal Artillery, 2nd Division, Aldershot, since Feb. 1927 ; *b.* 11 May 1880 ; *s.* of late W. Donaldson Rawlins and Elizabeth Margaret, *d.* of late Charles King; *m.* 1910, Dorothy Pepys, *d.* of late J. B. Cockerell, Madras C.S.; four *s.* *Educ.:* Eton. Entered Army, 1898 ; Captain, 1910 ; Major, 1914; served King's African Rifles, 1903-8 ; served S. African War, 1902 (Queen's medal 3 clasps); European War, 1914-18 (despatches ten times, D.S.O., Bt. Lt.-Col., Bt. Col., Croix de Guerre, C.M.G., Legion of Honour, Order of Leopold, Belgian Croix de Guerre, 1914 Star). *Address:* White Waltham Grove, near Maidenhead, Berks. *T.:* Littlewick Green. 75. *T.A.:* White Waltham; Carwythenack, Downderry, Cornwall. *M.:* YN 6608. *Club:* Sports.

(Died 16 Dec. 1927.)

RAWLINS, William Donaldson, K.C., M.A.; *b.* Moseley, Worcestershire, 20 July 1846; *e. surv. s.* of late Samuel Rawlins (*d.* 1884) and Catherine Anne, *d.* of Stuart Donaldson; *m.* 1873, Elizabeth Margaret, *o. d.* of late Charles John King; three *s. Educ.:* Eton; Trinity Coll. Camb. (scholar, 1866; Fellow, 1869); Third in 1st class Classical Tripos, 1868. Assistant Master at Eton, 1868-69; Barr. Lincoln's Inn, 1872; Q.C. 1896; Bencher, 1900; Commissioner for Income Tax, Lincoln's Inn; Alderman Holborn Borough Council; Mayor of Holborn, 1906-1907; J.P. County of London and County of Berks. *Publications:* Rawlins on Specific Performance; (joint) Rawlins and Macnaghten on Companies; editor of 4th and 5th editions of Fry's Specific Performance of Contracts, and of Treatises on the Law of Landlord and Tenant, and on Receivers. *Recreations:* riding, cycling, rowing, tennis. golf. *Address:* White Waltham Grove, nr. Maidenhead, Berks; 1 New Square, Lincoln's Inn. W.C. *Club:* Athenæum . *(Died 21 May 1920.)*

RAWLINSON, 1st Baron, *cr.* 1919, of Trent, Dorset; **Henry Seymour Rawlinson,** 2nd Bt., *cr.* 1891; G.C.B., *cr.* 1919; G.C.S.I., *cr.* 1924; G.C.V.O., *cr.* 1917; K.C.B., *cr.* 1915; K.C.M.G., *cr.* 1918; C.B. 1900; Commander-in-Chief of the Army in India since 1920; Member of the Executive Council of the Governor-General of India since 1920; General late 60th Rifles and Coldstream Guards; Member of Army Council, 1918; *b.* 20 Feb. 1864; *e. s.* of Maj.-Gen. Sir Henry Creswick Rawlinson, Bt., and Louisa, *d.* of H. Seymour, Knoyle, Wilts; *S.* father, 1895; *m.* 1890, Meredith, *o. d.* of Coleridge J. Kennard. *Educ.:* Eton; R.M.C., Sandhurst; Staff College, Camberley (P.S.C.). Entered 60th K.R. Rifles, 1884; A.D.C. to Sir Frederick Roberts, Commander-in-Chief in India, 1887-90; served with Mounted Infantry, Burma campaign (medal and clasp); entered Staff College, 1892; exchanged into Coldstream Guards, 1892; served in Soudan campaign as D.A.A.G. to Lord Kitchener, 1898; present at battles Atbara and Khartoum (medal and two clasps, despatches twice); served war in S. Africa (two medals and eight clasps); A.A.G. (Ladysmith siege) Natal, 1899; A.A.G. Headquarters, S. Africa, 1900; commanded Mobile Column, 1901-2 (despatches three times); European War, 1914-18 (despatches eight times, K.C.B., G.C.B., K.C.V.O., G.C.V.O., K.C.M.G.; promotion to Gen. and Lt.-Gen.); commanded 4th Corps and 4th Army; commanded Forces in N. Russia, 1919; G.O.C. Aldershot, 1920; Commandant Staff College, 1903-6; commanded 2nd Brigade, Aldershot, 1907-9; commanding 3rd Division, Salisbury Plain, 1910; A.D.C. to the King; Grand Officer Legion of Honour; Order of Danilo (Montenegro), 1st Class, 1917; French Croix de Guerre; Belgian Croix de Guerre; Rising Sun of Japan, 2nd Class; Order of St. George, Russia. *Publication:* The Officers' Note-book. *Recreations:* hunting, polo, cricket, rackets, drawing. *Heir to Baronetcy: b.* Alfred [*b.* 17 Jan. 1867; *m.* 1890, Margarette Kennard (*d.* 1907), 5th *d.* of W. B. Greenfield; one *s.* one *d.*]. *Clubs:* Guards', Turf, Travellers', Hurlingham.
(Died 28 Mar. 1925.)

RAWLINSON, Lieut.-Col. Charles Brooke, C.I.E., 1905; Revenue Commissioner, N.W. Frontier Province, 1910; *b.* 10 April 1866. *Educ.:* Marlborough. Entered Army, 1885; Captain, 1896; Major, 1903. Assistant Commissioner, Punjab, 1889; Deputy Commissioner, 1899; Political Agent, 1906; Additional Revenue Commissioner, 1907.
(Died 15 Jan. 1919.)

RAWLINSON, Rt. Hon. John Frederick Peel, P.C. 1923; K.C., LL.D.; M.P. (U.) Cambridge University since 1906; Re-

corder of Cambridge since 1898; Commissary of Cambridge University since 1900; J.P. Cambridgeshire since 1901; Deputy High Steward Cambridge University since 1918; Fellow of Eton College since 1919; Hon. Fellow Pembroke College, Cambridge; *b.* 21 Dec. 1860; *y. s.* of late Sir C. Rawlinson, Chief Justice of Madras, 1850-59; unmarried. *Educ.:* Eton; Trinity Coll., Cambridge. LL.B., LL.M.; 1st class Law Tripos, 1882; Prizeman in Common Law. Barr. Inner Temple, 1884; South-Eastern Circuit; sometime Lecturer and Examiner in Law, Pembroke College, Cambridge; represented the Treasury in Inquiry in South Africa as to circumstances connected with Jameson Raid, 1896; Q.C. 1897; contested Ipswich (C.), 1900; Member General Council of Bar since its formation, now Vice-Chairman; Bencher of Inner Temple, 1907; a temporary Chairman of Committees in the House of Commons since 1916; Hon. LL.D. Cambridge; Member of the Governing Bodies of Eton, Malvern, and Brighton College. *Publication:* Rawlinson's Municipal Corporations' Acts, tenth edition. *Address:* 5 Crown Office Row, Temple, E.C.4. *T.:* Central 731. *Clubs:* Carlton, United University, Travellers', Princes'; Cambridge County.
(Died 14 Jan. 1926.)

RAWNSLEY, Rev. Hardwicke Drummond, Canon of Carlisle; Proctor in Convocation; Hon. Chaplain to H.M. since 1912; *b.* Shiplake Vicarage, Henley-on-Thames, 28 Sep. 1851; 2nd *s.* of Canon R. D. B. Rawnsley and Catherine Ann, *o. d.* of Sir Willingham Franklin, and niece of the Arctic explorer; *m.* 1st, 1878, Edith (*d.* 1916), *d.* of late John Fletcher, Croft, Ambleside; one *s*; 2nd, Eleanor Foster, *d.* of late Frederick W. Simpson, The Wray, Grasmere. *Educ.:* Uppingham; Balliol College, Oxford (M.A.). Ordained, 1875; Curate in charge of Clifton College Mission; Vicar of Wray, Windermere, 1878-88; Vicar of Crosthwaite, Keswick, and Rural Dean, 1883-1917; Hon. Secretary of the National Trust for Places of Historic Interest and Natural Beauty; Hon. Secretary of Secondary Schools Association; Chairman, St. George's School, Harpenden; Vice-President of the Holiday Association of National Home Reading Union; Vice-President of the Sunday Imperial Alliance; Chairman, Secondary School Committee, Cumberland Education Authority. *Publications:* Sonnets Round the Coast; Sonnets at the English Lakes; Edward Thring, Teacher and Poet; St. Kentigern of Crosthwaite; Ballads, Lyrics, and Bucolics; Valete and other Poems; Notes for the Nile; Idylls and Lyrics of the Nile; A Coach Drive at the Lakes; Literary Associations of English Lakes (another ed. illus. 1901); Harvey Goodwin, Bishop of Carlisle, a Biographical Memoir; The Darkened West; Ballads of Brave Deeds; The Revival of the Decorative Arts at Lucerne; Editor of revised edition of Jenkinson's Guide to the Lakes; The Sayings of Jesus: Six Village Sermons on a Papyrus Fragment; Henry Whitehead: a Memoir; Life and Nature at the English Lakes, 1899; Sonnets in Switzerland and Italy, 1899; Ballads of the War, 1900 (ill. ed. 1901); Memories of the Tennysons, 1900; Ruskin and the English Lakes, 1901; Illustrated Edition of the Literary Associations of the English Lakes, 1902; A Rambler's Note-book at the Lakes, Illustrated, 1902; A Coach Drive at the Lakes and the Buttermere Round, 1902; Sketches at the English Lakes, 1903; Flowertime in the Oberland, 1904; The Sacrum Commercium of St. Francis, 1904; Sermons on the Sayings of Jesus, from the Oxyrhyncus Papyri, 1905; Months at the Lakes, 1906; A Sonnet Chronicle, 1900-1905, published 1906; Round the Lake Country; Poems at Home and Abroad; By Fell and Dale at the English Lakes, 1911; Memories of the Tennysons, 1912;

Chapters at the English Lakes, 1918; The European War: Poems, 1915; Past and Present at the English Lakes, 1916. *Recreations:* chiefly literary and travel, observations of scenery, bird life, and habits of animals, and local history and traditions. *Address:* Allan Bank, Grasmere. *T.A.:* Grasmere. *Club:* Royal Societies.
(*Died 28 May 1920.*)

RAWORTH, Benjamin Alfred, Whitworth Scholar; Member Institution Mechanical Engineers; Member of the Iron and Steel Institute; Member of Institute of Metals; Joint-editor of Engineering; *b.* Chesterfield, 1 June 1849; *s.* of B. J. Raworth, Sheffield; *m.* 1886, Florence May, *d.* of Charles Tysoe Harvey, M.D.; one *s.* one *d. Educ.:* Chesterfield Grammar School; Owens College, Manchester. Professional training at Wren and Hopkinson, Manchester; private assistant to Sir Joseph Whitworth, Manchester; Departmental Works Engineer to Siemens Bros., Woolwich; in practice as an engineer in Manchester; joined staff of Engineering, 1882. *Address:* 36 Bedford Street, Strand, W.C.; Dorleon, Mayfield Road, Sutton, Surrey. *T.A.:* Engineering, London. *T.:* Gerard 3663. *Club:* St. Stephen's. (*Died 30 Sept. 1919.*)

RAWSON, Frank, C.M.G. 1903; was acting Manager on Uganda Railway; *b.* 16 Dec. 1856; *s.* of late Samuel Rawson. *Club:* Oriental.
(*Died 30 Sept. 1928.*)

RAWSON, Col. Herbert Edward, C.B. 1902; J.P.; R.E., retired 1909; *b.* 3 Sep. 1852; 2nd *s.* of late Sir Rawson W. Rawson, K.C.M.G., C.B., and Sophia, *d.* of Hon. Rev. H. Ward; *m.* 1875, Elizabeth Stuart Armstrong (*d.* 1885), *d.* of late Richard Owen, J P Co. Dublin. *Educ.:* Westminster; Royal Military Academy, Woolwich. Royal Engineers, 1872; submarine mining,1874; Bermuda defence, 1877, Malta, 1885; Treasury, 1880-84; Secretary of R.E. committee and War Office Ordnance committee, 1890-94; Canada, 1885-89, raising a submarine mining militia; selected to command the Royal Engineers in Natal, 6 Oct. 1899, and served on the staff throughout the Boer War, returning to England, Nov. 1902; was present at the engagements Tugela Heights, Relief of Ladysmith, Laing's Nek; commanded district Natal and Zululand Frontier during operations 1901, battle of Itala (medals and 4 clasps, brevet-colonelcy, C.B., despatches 8 times); Member of Natal Defences Commission, 1902; Natal Native Affairs Commission, 1906-7; Chief Engineer and commanding R.E., S. Africa, 1905-7; Chief Engineer Northern Command, 1907-9. *Publications:* Selective Screening (Brit. Ass. 1908, 1913; S. African Ass. 1906; Linnean, 1919, and R.H.S. 1916); Migration of Belts (Journal Meteorological Soc. 1899-1908-10); Journals United Service and Royal Aero-Society. *Recreations:* played cricket for Kent, 1874; International Football (Association) for England, 1874; in the final matches for the Cup, 1874, 1875; member of Loriss and of Free Foresters C.C.; President of the Old Westminsters' C.C.; Freemason (London Rank); is or has been Vice-President of Meteorological Society, Councils of African Royal Aeronautical Societies, Standing Committee of Emigration and Council Royal Colonial Institute; F.R.G.S., F.R.H.S., Linnean, Physical, Herts. Nat. Hist. Societies, Diocesan Finance Board, Herts. and Beds; holder of the Royal Engineer Fowke Medal. *Address:* Home Close, Heronsgate, Herts. *T.:* Chorleywood West. *Club:* Junior United Service. (*Died 18 Oct. 1924.*)

RAWSON, Colonel Richard Hamilton, J.P., D.L. Sussex; M.P. (U.) Reigate Division, Surrey since 1910; Colonel Commanding Sussex Yeomanry since 1908; *b.* 21 Feb. 1863; *e. s.* of Philip Rawson, J.P., D.L., of Woodhurst, Sussex; *m.* 1890, Lady Beatrice Anson, 2nd *d.* of 2nd Earl of Lichfield; one *s.* two *d. Educ.:* Eton; B.N.C., Oxford. Served nine years in the 1st Life Guards, and retired with the rank of Captain,1892; has served since in the Yeomanry; High Sheriff of Sussex, 1899; contested (U.) Reigate Division of Surrey, 1896. *Recreation:* hunting. *Address:* Gravenhurst, Haywards Heath; 64 Cadogan Square, S.W. *T.:* Kensington 4169. *Clubs:* Bachelors', Arthur's, Carlton.
(*Died 18 Oct. 1918.*)

RAY, Mahendranath, C.I.E. 1914; M.A., B.L.; Vakil, Calcutta High Court; Member, Bengal Legislative Council since 1911; *b.* Oct. 1862; *s.* of late Girija Charan Ray of Tazpur, Howrah, India; *m.* 1878, Probodhmoyi Dassi; two *s.* two *d. Educ.:* Presidency College, Calcutta; Burdwan, Vizianagram and Ishan Scholarships; B.A. 1883; Haris Chandra Prize; Gwalior Medal and Gold Medal for Mathematics; M.A. 1st Class Honours, 1884; B.L. 1885; Vakil, 1886; Vice-Chairman, Howrah District Board, 1888-96; Fellow, Calcutta University, 1891; Professor of Mathematics and Law, Calcutta City College, 1886-98; Member of the Syndicate, Calcutta University, 1910-18; Hon. Magistrate, Municipal Commissioner, and Member, District Board, Howrah; Chairman Howrah Municipality, 1916-20. *Publication:* Algebra, Parts I. and II. *Address:* 8 Khooroo Road, Howrah, and 2 Boloram Bose's 1st Lane, Bhawanipur, Calcutta. *T.:* Calcutta 3242. *M.:* 777. *Club:* India, Calcutta. (*Died Aug. 1925.*)

RAY, Prithwis Chandra; Editor, Indian World; *b.* 1870; *m.;* two *s.* three *d. Educ.:* The Mymensingh Zilla School; Presidency College, Calcutta. Editor, Bengalee, 1921-24; Secretary, 21st and 26th sessions of the Indian National Congress, held in Calcutta in 1906 and 1911; Secretary, Bengal Social Reform Association, 1908-14; Founder of the National Liberal League, Bengal, 1918; Member of the Moderate Deputation to England, 1919, and Bengal Landholders' Delegate to England, 1920; Donor of the Gokhale Library to the Indian Association of Calcutta, 1920. *Publications:* Poverty Problem in India, 1896; Indian Famines, 1901; The Map of India, 1904, and reprinted 1927; Our Demand for Self-Government, 1917; A Scheme of Indian Constitutional Reforms, 1918; Life and Times of C. R. Das, 1927. *Address:* 5 Rifle Road, Ballygunge, Calcutta. *Club:* National Liberal.
(*Died Dec. 1927.*)

RAYLEIGH, 3rd Baron (*cr.* 1821**), John William Strutt,** P.C. 1905; J.P., D.C.L. (Hon. Oxon.), LL.D., F.R.S., Hon. C.E., Sc.D. (Cambridge and Dublin); Order of Merit; Past-President Royal Society; Nobel Laureate; Chancellor Cambridge University; Scientific Adviser to Trinity House since 1896; *b.* 12 Nov. 1842; *e. s.* of 2nd Baron and Clara, *d.* of Captain Vicars, R.E.; *S.* father 1873; *m.* Evelyn, *d.* of James Maitland Balfour, Whittingehame, and Blanche, *d.* of 2nd Marquis of Salisbury; two *s. Educ.:* Trin. Coll. Camb. Senior Wrangler and Smith's Prizeman, 1865; Fellow, 1866; Professor of Experimental Physics, Cambridge, 1879-84; Secretary to Royal Society, 1887-96; Lord-Lieut. of Essex, 1892-1901; Prof. of Natural Philosophy, Royal Institution, 1887-1905; Officer Legion of Honour. *Publications:* Theory of Sound; numerous scientific papers recently republished. Owns about 7000 acres. *Heir: s.* Hon. Robert John Strutt. *Address:* Terling Place, Witham, Essex. *T.A.:* Terling. *Club:* Athenæum. (*Died 30 June 1919.*)

RAYNER, Henry, M.D., M.R.C.P.; *s.* of W. Rayner, Hythe; *b.* Nov. 1841; *m.* Rosa, *d.* of A. Field of Leam, Leamington; two *s.* one *d. Educ.:* private schools; St. Thomas's Hospital; Aberdeen University (highest Academical honours, with M.B.). Late Editor of Journal of Mental Science; Late Lecturer

and Physician for Mental Diseases at St. Thomas's Hospital; Assistant Physician Bethlehem Hospital; Medical Superintendent Hanwell; former President of Medical Psychological Assoc.; Lecturer on Mental Diseases, Middlesex Hospital. *Publications:* Melancholia and Hypochondriasis (Allbutt's System of Medicine); Sleep in relation to Narcotics (Jour. Med. Sci.); Early Treatment of Mental Defects in Children (Med. Mag.); Gout and Insanity (Trans. Int. Med. Congress); Moral Insanity (Brain); Temperaments, Journal of Mental Science, 1921. *Recreation:* golf. *Address:* Upper Terrace House, Hampstead, N.W.3. *T.:* Hampstead 378. *Club:* Reform.
(Died 8 Feb. 1926.)

RAYNOR, Sir William (Pick), J.P., Kt., *cr.* 1912; sole proprietor of Thomas Hirst & Co., wool merchants, Huddersfield, Bradford, London and Australia; *b.* 25 Oct. 1854; 2nd *s.* of late John and Hannah Raynor; *m.* 1877, Janet (*d.* 1921), *d.* of Robert Kirk, Huddersfield; no *c.* Entered the service of Thomas Hirst & Co., 1868; partner, 1888; on the Commission of the Peace for Huddersfield, County Boro., 1906; West Riding, Yorks, 1910. *Address:* Rein Wood, Huddersfield. *T.A.:* Reinwood. *T.:* 206. *Clubs:* Huddersfield; Union, Bradford. *(Died 26 Aug. 1927.)*

REA, Right Hon. Russell, P.C. 1909; a junior Lord of the Treasury since 1915; M.P. (L.) South Shields since 1910: shipowner and merchant; Founder and Head of firm R. & J. H. Rea; late Deputy Chairman Taff Vale Railway; Chairman of Departmental Committee appointed to consider the economic effect of an Eight-Hour Day for Miners, 1906; Chairman of the Liberal Publication Depart ment; of the Joint-Committee on the Port of London Bill; of Departmental Committee on Railway Amalgamations, 1909; Member of Royal Commission on Malta, 1911; Chairman of Coal Exports Committee; *b.* 11 Dec. 1846; 3rd *s.* of late Daniel K. Rea of Eskdale, Cumberland, and Elizabeth, *d.* of late Joseph Russell, shipbuilder, of Liverpool; *m.* 1872, Jane Philip, *d.* of P. L. MacTaggart of Liverpool; two *s. Educ.:* privately. Contested Exchange Division, Liverpool, 1897; M.P. (L.) Gloucester, 1900-10. *Publications:* Insular Free Trade; Free Trade in Being; various articles and pamphlets on economic subjects. *Address:* Dean Stanley Street, S.W.; *T.:* Victoria 4649; Tanhurst, Dorking. *M.:* P 6702, P 7033. *Clubs:* Reform, National Liberal; Liberal, Newcastle.
(Died 5 Feb. 1916.)

READ, Brig.-Gen. Hastings, C.B. 1904; *b.* 19 Aug. 1852; *s.* of late Hastings Read, I.C.S.; *m.* 1899, Ada Mary, 3rd *d.* of Maj.-Gen. H. Tod Stuart. *Educ.:* Cheltenham. Entered army, 1873; Captain. 1893; Major, 1899; served Afghanistan, 1879-80 (medal); Burmah, 1887 (medal with clasp); Thibet, 1903-4 (despatches, C.B.); Commanding Belgaum Brigade. 1906-8.
(Died 24 Oct. 1928.)

READE, Sir George, 10th Bt., *cr.* 1660; *b.* 22 Nov. 1869; *s.* of 9th Bt. and Melissa, *d.* of Isaac Ray, Michigan; *s.* father, 1908; *m.* 1893, Carrie Nixon; two *s.* two *d. Heir: s.* John [*b.* 1897. Served European War.] *Address:* Howell, Livingstone, County Michigan, U.S.A.
(Died 24 May 1923.)

READE, John, LL.D., F.R.S.C.; Assoc. Editor, Gazette, Montreal, since 1870; *b.* Ballyshannon, Co. Donegal, Ireland, 13 Nov. 1837. *Educ.:* Enniskillen; Belfast. Arrived in Canada, 1856; has been mostly engaged in journalism and literature; has consistently advocated the conciliation of race and religion in Canada, Canadian Confederation and the unity of the Empire; 1882, one of the original Members, Royal Society of Canada, founded by Marquis of Lorne, and Pres. of Hist. and Archæol. Section (English). *Publications:* Volumes of Verse, 874

1870 and 1906; The Making of Canada, 1884; The Half-breed, 1885; The Basques in North America, 1887; etc. *Address:* 340 Laval Avenue, Montreal.
(Died 1919.)

REAL, Hon. Patrick, Judge of Supreme Court of Queensland 1890-1922; *b.* Limerick, 1847; went to Australia, 1851; called to Bar, 1874; was Crown Prosecutor in Central District, and Member of Royal Commission on Establishment of Queensland University. *Address:* Ulalie, M'Ilwraith Avenue, Coorparoo, Brisbane, Queensland. *(Died 9 June 1928.)*

REAY, 11th Baron (*cr.* 1628), Donald James Mackay, K.T. 1911; G.C.S.I., G.C.I.E., LL.D. Edin.; D.Litt. Hon. Oxon.; P.C., 1905; D.L., J.P.; Bt. 1627; Baron Reay (U.K.), 1881; naturalised, 1877; Baron Mackay of Ophemert, Holland; Lord-Lieut. of Roxburghshire, 1892-1918; Chief of Clan Mackay; *b.* The Hague, 22 Dec. 1839; *s.* of 10th Baron and Maria, *d.* of Baron Fagel; *S.* father 1876; *m.* 1877, Fanny (*d.* 1917), C.I., *d.* of late Richard Hasler, Aldingbourne, Sussex. Rector of St. Andrews University, 1884-86; Governor of Bombay, 1885-90; Under-Secretary for India, 1894-95; Chairman London School Board, 1897-1904; President Royal Asiatic Society and University College, London; 1st President British Academy, 1901-7. *Heir:* (to Scottish titles) cousin, Baron Eric Mackay [*b.* 2 Apr. 1870; *s.* of Baron Æneas Mackay and Baroness Elizabeth de Lynden; *m.* 1901, Baroness Maria Johanna Bertha Christina Van Dedem; three *s.* one *d.*]. *Address:* 35 Berkeley Square, W.1. *Clubs:* Athenæum; New, Edinburgh. *(Died 1 Aug. 1921.)*

REAY, 12th Baron (*cr.* 1628), Eric Mackay, Bt. 1627; Baron Mackay of Ophemert, Holland; Chief of Clan Mackay; *b.* 2 Apr. 1870; *s.* of Baron Æneas Mackay and Baroness Elizabeth de Lynden; *S. cousin*, 1921; *m.* 1901, Baroness Maria Johanna Bertha Christina Van Dedem; three *s.* one *d.* *(Died 2 Nov. 1921.)*

RECKITT, Sir James, 1st Bart., *cr.* 1894; J.P., D.L.; chairman of Reckitt and Sons, Ltd.; Garden Village Co.; Priestman Bros.; and the Hull Royal Infirmary Board; *b.* 14 Nov. 1833; *s.* of Isaac Reckitt and Ann, *d.* of Charles Coleby, Hempstead, Norfolk; *m.* 1865, Kathleen (*d.* 1923), *d.* of Robert Saunders, Lilling, York; two *s.* two *d. Educ.:* Ackworth School, the principal public school of the Society of Friends. Chiefly known from his long and prosperous business career, his interest in most philanthropic and educational work, his gifts of free library, orphan home, convalescent home, new wing to Royal Infirmary, and other gifts to Hull; the building of a complete Model Garden Village in Hull of 600 houses. *Recreations:* an Art collector; has a fine collection of modern pictures and other works of art. *Heir: s.* Harold J. *Address:* Swanland Manor, Hull. *T.A.:* North Ferriby. *T.:* Ferriby 19. *M.:* BT 695, AT 470. *Club:* National Liberal. *(Died 18 Mar. 1924.)*

REDDY, Michael, M.P. (N.) Birr Division of King's County since 1900; farmer. *Address:* Shannon Bridge, King's County.
(Died 30 July 1919.)

REDESDALE of Redesdale, 1st Baron (*cr.* 1902), **Algernon Bertram Freeman-Mitford**, G.C.V.O., *cr.* 1905; K.C.B., *cr.* 1906; J.P., D.L.; *b.* 24 Feb. 1837; 3rd *s.* of Henry Reveley Mitford, Exbury, Hants, and Georgina Jemima, *d.* of 3rd Earl of Ashburnham; *m.* Lady Clementine Gertrude Helen Ogilvy, *d.* of 7th Earl of Airlie, 1874; four *s.* four *d. Educ.:* Eton; Christ Church, Oxford. 2nd class Moderations. Entered Foreign Office, 1858; 3rd Secretary of Embassy, St. Petersburg, 1863; appointed to Peking, 1865; transferred to Japan, 1866; 2nd Secretary of Legation, 1868; Secretary to H.M.'s Office of Works, 1874-86; accompanied H.R.H. Prince Arthur's Mission to Japan, 1906. M.P. for South-West Warwickshire, 1892-95 ; member of Royal Commission on Civil Services, 1887 ; trustee of Wallace Collection ; trustee of National Gallery ; governor of Wellington College. *Decorated for public services. Publications :* Tales of Old Japan, 1871 ; The Bamboo Garden, 1896 ; The Attaché at Peking, 1900 ; The Garter Mission to Japan, 1906 ; A Tragedy in Stone, 1912. *Heir: s.* Hon. David Bertram Ogilvy Freeman-Mitford. *Address :* Batsford Park, Moreton in Marsh, Gloucs. *Clubs :* Travellers', Carlton, Marlborough ; Royal Yacht Squadron, Cowes.   *(Died 17 Aug. 1916.)*

REDFERN, Rev. Thomas, M.A. ; Rector and Rural Dean of Denbigh since 1907 ; Canon of St. Asaph ; Chaplain of North Wales Asylum ; *b.* 1853 ; *s.* of Absalom Redfern, Halkyn, Flintshire ; *m.* 1st, Jane, *d.* of John Roberts, Rhyl ; 2nd, Henrietta Maria, *d.* of Major-General Connolly M'Causland, R.E., Bessbrook, Newtown, Limavady, Co. Derry ; two *s.* three *d. Educ. :* Clare College, Cambridge. Deacon, 1879 ; Priest, 1880 ; Curate of Oswestry, 1879-82 ; Rector of Trefonen, 1882, 1887 ; Vicar of Holy Trinity, Oswestry, 1887-1907 ; Rural Dean of Oswestry, 1903. *Address :* The Rectory, Denbigh.
    (Died Feb: 1924.)

REDFERN, Thomas William, M.V.O. 1908; representative of International Sleeping Car Co. at Paris. *Address :* 40 rue de l'Arcade, Paris.
    (Died 2 Sept. 1924.)

REDFORD, George Alexander, Examiner of Plays, 1895-1911 ; *e. s.* of late George Redford, F.R.C.S. *Educ. :* Clewer House School, Windsor. Was a bank manager for many years ; became Licenser of Plays, 1875 ; formerly assistant and deputy to late Mr. Pigott, Examiner of Plays, 187 Queen's Gate, S.W. *Recreations :* formerly cricket ; now, punting, sculling, and occasionally golf. *Address :* 38 Harrington Gardens, S.W.
    (Died 12 Nov. 1916.)

REDMAN, Rev. Alfred ; Vicar of St. James', Heywood, since 1884 ; Hon. Canon of Manchester. Deacon, 1876 ; Priest, 1877 ; Curate of Royton, 1876-78 ; Vicar of High Crompton, Manchester, 1878-84. *Address :* St. James's Vicarage, Heywood, Lancs.
    (Died 15 Feb. 1927.)

REDMOND, John Edward, M.P. (N.) Waterford since 1891 ; Chairman of Irish Parliamentary Party ; *b.* 1851 ; *s.* of late W. A. Redmond, M.P. Ballytrent ; *m.* Johanna, *d.* of late James Dalton, New South Wales, 1883 ; one *s.* one *d. Educ. :* Clongowes ; Trinity College, Dublin. Barr. Gray's Inn, 1886 ; Irish Barr. 1887 ; M.P. New Ross, 1881-85 ; N. Wexford, 1885-91. *Address :* 18 Wynnstay Gardens, S.W.   *(Died 6 Mar. 1918.)*

REDMOND, Sir Joseph Michael, Kt., *cr.* 1911 ; K.C.H.S., M.D.N.U.I. *(hon. causŭ),* F.R.C.S., L.R.C.S. ; Physician to Mater Misericordiæ Hospital ; Physician to the Castle Red Cross Hospital ; Consulting Physician to Coombe Hospital, St. Michael's Hospital, Kingstown, National Hospital and Cottage Hospital, Drogheda ; Consulting Physician to the Royal College of St. Patrick, Maynooth ; *s.* of late Denis Redmond and Bridget Emily Gorman ; *m.* Oswaldina, *d.* of late James Nelson, J.P. President Royal Coll. of Physicians, 1906-8 ; Vice - President, 1900 - 2 ; has been President, State Medicine Section, Royal Academy of Medicine ; formerly Lecturer on the Practice of Medicine and Pathology in the Ledwich School of Medicine, and Pathologist to the Coombe Hospital ; late Senior Physician to Fever Hospital, Cork Street, etc. *Publications :* Cancer of the Liver ; Acromegaly ; Ulcer of Stomach ; Multiple Small Abscesses of the Liver ; Tumour of the Brain, etc. *Address :* 41 Merrion Square, Dublin ; Gortmore, Dundrum, Co. Dublin. *T. :* 1690. *M. :* IK 932. *Club :* Stephen's Green, Dublin.   *(Died 25 Nov. 1921.)*

REDMOND, Maj. Wm. Hoey Kearney, M.P. (F.) Clare, E., since 1892 ; barrister-at-law ; *b.* 1861 ; 2nd *s.* of late W. A. Redmond, M.P. ; *m.* 1886, Eleanor, *d.* of James Dalton, Orange, N.S.W. *Educ. :* Clongowes. M.P. Wexford, 1883-85 ; Co. Fermanagh, 1885-92. *Publications :* A Shooting Trip in the Australian Bush, 1898 ; Through the New Commonwealth. *Address :* Glenbrook, Delgany, Co. Wicklow. *Club :* Leinster. Dublin.   *(Died 9 June 1917.)*

REDWOOD, Sir Boverton, 1st Bt., *cr.* 1911 ; Kt., *cr.* 1905 ; D.Sc. (hon.), F.R.S.E., Assoc. Inst. C.E., M. Inst. M.E., Member Inst. of Chem., Pres. Society Chemical Ind., 1907-1908 ; Pres. Junior Institution of Engineers, 1913 ; Institution Petroleum Technologists, 1914-16; Member of Council and Past Vice-Pres. Royal Society of Arts ; Fellow of Chem. Geol. and R. Geog. Soc. ; Member of Institute Mining Engineers ; of Am. Philosophical Soc. (hon.) ; Hon. Corres. Mem. Imp. Russian Tech. Soc. ; Chevalier of the Order of Leopold ; Consulting Chemist and Engineer ; Adviser on Petroleum to the Admiralty, the Home Office, the India Office, and the Colonial Office (Consulting) ; Consulting Adviser to the Corporation of London under the Petroleum Acts, Adviser on Petroleum Transport to the Port of London Authority, and Adviser to the Thames Conservancy ; *b.* London, 26 April 1846 ; *e. s.* of late Professor Theophilus Redwood, Ph.D., of Boverton, Glamorganshire ; *m.* 1873, Mary Elizabeth, *e. d.* of late Frederick Letchford ; two *d. Educ. :* Univ. Coll. School ; Pharmaceutical Society of Great Britain Accompanied late Sir Vivian Majendie on visits of inspection to chief centres of petroleum distribution in ·this country, the principal European countries, the United States and Canada, and gave evidence before Committees of Lords and Commons ; was member of several juries at International Inventions and Health Exhibitions ; president of International Jury for lighting appliances and materials at Brussels Exhibition, 1897 ; member of Jury, Paris Exhibition, 1900 ; Home Office Committee on Acetylene Generators, 1901 ; Royal Commission St. Louis Exhibition, 1904 ; Chairman Liberal Arts Committee, and member of Superior Jury, Franco - British Exhibition, 1908 ; Royal Commission Brussels, Rome, and Turin Exhibitions ; Chairman Chemical Industries Committee ; member of Superior Jury, Brussels, 1910 ; member of Delegacy, City and Guilds (Engineering) Coll., Imperial College of Science and Technology ; Royal Commission on Fuel and Engines, 1912 ; Director of Technical Investigations, H.M. Petroleum Executive ; Chairman, Gas Traction Committee. *Publications :* Cantor Lectures on Petroleum and its Products, 1886 ; Petroleum : its Production and Use, 1887 ; Report (with Sir Frederick Abel) on Accidents with Mineral Oil Lamps, 1890 ; also on the Transport of Petroleum through the Suez Canal, 1892 ; articles on Petroleum in Professor Thorpe's Dictionary of Applied Chemistry, 1893 ; The Transport of Petroleum in Bulk (Telford Premium), 1894, Inst.C.E. ; articles on the Petroleum Industry, and Lamps in Chemical Technology, 1895 ; A Treatise on Petroleum (2 vols.), 1896, 3rd ed. (3 vols.), 1913; The Detection and Estimation of Inflammable Gases and Vapours in the Air, 1896 (with Prof. Clowes) ; Handbook on Petroleum (with Captain J. H. Thomson), 1901, 2nd ed. 1906, 3rd ed. (with Major A. Cooper-Key), 1913 ; The Petroleum Lamp (with Captain J. H. Thomson), 1902; Petroleum, in Ency. Brit. (supplement), 1902, and Ency. Brit. 11th ed., 1911 ; Petroleum Technologist's Pocket-Book (with Arthur W. Eastlake), 1915. *Heir : g. s.,* T. Boverton Redwood ; *b.* 15 Oct. 1906. *Address :* The Cloisters, 18 Avenue Road, Regent's Park, N.W. ; Wayside Cottage, Cooden Down, Little Common, Sussex. *T. :* Hampstead 1127. 4 Bishopsgate, E.C. *T.A.:* Olefiant, London. *T.:* Avenue 5814. *M.:* LD 8484. *Clubs:* Savage, Royal Thames Yacht, City of London, Royal Automobile; Royal Motor Yacht.

(Died 4 June 1919.)

REECE, Surgeon - Colonel Richard James, C.B. 1917; M.A., M.D. Cantab.; M.R.C.P.; M.R.C.S.; D.P.H.; Senior Medical Officer, Ministry of Health; *b.* 1862; *o. s.* of late George Reece, Kensington; *m.* 1894, Ada Eleanor, *o. d.* of James Watt Perkins, Edgware; two *s.* two *d. Educ.:* Kensington School; Downing College, Cambridge; St. Bartholomew's Hospital. First Assistant Medical Officer of Health, Port Sanitary Authority of London; entered Local Government Board as Medical Inspector, 1893; Surgeon-Colonel, A Battery, Horse Artillery Division, Honourable Artillery Company: late Senior Examiner State Medicine, Cambridge University; President Epidemiological Section Royal Society of Medicine, 1922 and 1923; Vice-Pres. Public Health Section, B.M.A. Meeting. Glasgow, 1922. *Publications:* Reports on Acute Poliomyelitis, Cerebrospinal Fever, Infectious Disease, etc.; contributions to the Epidemiological Section of the Royal Society of Medicine. *Address:* Ministry of Health, Whitehall, S.W.1; 62 Addison Gardens. W.14; Basketts, Birchington-on-Sea, Kent. *Clubs:* Savage, Leander.

(Died 20 April 1924.)

REED, Herbert Parker, K.C.; *b.* London; *e. s.* of Herbert Adolphus Reed, solicitor. *Educ.:* Brighton, privately. Solicitor, 1873; never practised; engaged in literature; entered Inner Temple, 1874; called, 1877; admitted Gray's Inn, 1887; bencher, 1896; Treasurer, 1902. *Publication:* The Law of Bills of Sale, etc. *Recreation:* The cares of a garden. *Address:* Watcombe, nr. Torquay. *T.:* Torquay 189.

(Died 30 Jan. 1920.)

REED, Rev. Martin, Hon. Canon of St. Albans, 1915; Rural Dean of Ware, 1914-22; Proctor in Convocation, 1920-21; *b.* Brussels, 10 Dec. 1856; 3rd *s.* of B. B. Reed, Managing Director of the Great Luxemburg Railway and later of The Knowle, Reigate, Surrey; *m.* 1888, Annie Elizabeth, *d.* of Rev. D. C. Neary, D.D., Vicar of South Ossett, Yorks; no *c. Educ.:* Trinity College, Cambridge. Went nearly blind when entered for Public School, and had to prepare for the University under private tuition; was Secretary and a frequent speaker at the Union, and took Honours in Theology, 1879; ordained to H. Trinity, Leicester, 1879; Vicar, 1882; Rector of Eastwell, Kent, 1890-94; St. Thomas', Nottingham, 1894-1907; Vicar of Ware, Herts, 1907-24; elected Guardian for city and served ten years; Secretary of Housing Committee for Diocese of Southwell; member of Standing Council of Diocese since 1916; member of County Council Education Committee; much interested in Housing Reform. *Publications:* Papers on The Housing Question in Town and Country. *Recreation:* golf. *Address:* 18 Cunningham Avenue, St. Albans, Herts. *(Died 11 Mar. 1926.)*

REES, Ven. David John, L.Th.; Archdeacon in Diocese of Mombasa; Principal of Huron Training College, C.M.S.; *b.* 16 Dec. 1862; *m.* Agnes, *d.* of late W. B. Cooper, Aberdeen; one *s. Educ.:* University College, Durham. *Address:* Huron Training College, Kongwa, Gulwe Station, Dar - es - Salaam, Tanganyika Territory. *(Died 24 Mar. 1924.)*

REES, His Honour Griffith Caradoc, County Court Judge for North Wales since 1921; *b.* Birkenhead, 1868; *s.* of Griffith Rees, Cilgerran, Cardiganshire, and Sarah Rees, Llangynog, Montgomeryshire; unmarried. *Educ.:* Liverpool Institute. Solicitor, 1895-1905; Barrister, Middle Temple, 1905-21; contested Denbigh Boroughs, Dec. 1910; M.P.

Carnarvon, 1915-18; Parliamentary Secretary to Home Office, 1916-17. *Recreation:* golf. *Address:* 5 Elm Court, The Temple, E.C.

(Died 20 Sept. 1924.)

REES, Rev. Henry, M.A.; Canon and Precentor, Bangor Cathedral, 1892; *b.* 4 March 1844; *s.* of David Rees, Llandovery; *m.* 1879, Harriet (*d.* 1919), *y. d.* of Andrew Schofield, Tanyrallt, Llandudno; one *s. Educ.:* Llandovery College; Sidney Sussex College, Cambridge; B.A., 1866; M.A., 1883. Ordained, 1867; Surrogate, 1870; licensed to officiate in diocese of Winchester, 1896; Curate of Conway, 1867-70; Vicar, 1870-93; Chaplain to Bishop of Bangor, 1891-98. *Publication:* The Welsh Clergyman's Vade Mecum. *Recreations:* golf, fishing, and cycling. *Address:* The White Cottage, Shanklin, I.W. *(Died 5 Feb. 1924.)*

REES, Sir John David, 1st Bt., *cr.* 1919; K.C.I.E., *cr.* 1910; C.V.O. 1908; C.I.E. 1890; Commander Imperial Russian Order of St. Stanislaus; Director Prisoners of War Information Bureau, 1915-20; Cons. candidate, L.C.C. Peckham, 1901; J.P. Middlesex, 1907; M.P. (L.I.) Montgomery District, 1906-1910; M.P. (U.) East Div. of Nottingham since 1912; contested Kilmarnock (U.), 1911, candidate (U.), Walworth, 1911-12; *b.* 16 Dec. 1854; *e. s.* of the late Lodowick William Rees; *m.* 1891, Hon Mary, sister of 14th Lord Dormer; one *s.* one *d. Educ.:* Cheltenham Coll. Indian Civil Service, 1875; Under Secretary Madras Government; private secretary, Sir M. Grant Duff, Lord Connemara, and Lord Wenlock, Governors of Madras; Government Translator in Tamil, Telugu, Persian, and Hindustani; Russian interpreter; H. S. Arabic; on special duty with Duke of Clarence in Madras Presidency, 1889-90; British Resident in Travancore and Cochin; Additional Member of Governor-General of India's Council, 1895-1900; retired I.C.S. 1901; travelled in Corea, Manchuria, China, Arabia, Persia, Siberia, Asia Minor, Mesopotamia, Japan, and America; Chairman British Central Africa Coy., Ltd.; Director, South Indian Ry. Coy., Ltd.; Mysore Gold Mining Co.. Ltd.; Champion Reef Gold Mining Coy., Ltd.; Port Madryn (Argentina) Coy., Ltd.; Chubut Ry. Coy., Ltd.; Kolar Power Coy., Ltd.; Bengal - Dooars Ry. Coy., Ltd. Oregum Gold Mining Co., Ltd.; Consolidated Tea and Lands Co., Ltd.; Anglo-American Direct Tea Trading Co., Ltd.; Kanan Devan Hills Produce Co., Ltd.; Amalgamated Tea Estates Co. *Decorated:* Indian services. *Publications:* Tours in India; Duke of Clarence in S. India; The Mahommedans; The Real India, Modern India; Current Political Problems, Articles in Ninth Ceneteentury, Fortnightly; and other Reviews. *Heir: s.* Richard Lodowick, *b.* 1900. *Address:* 9 Chesham Place, S.W.1; Thames House, Queen Street Place, E.C.; 5 Burton Street, Nottingham. *T.:* City 3497; Victoria 7831. *M.:* LL 676. *Clubs:* Carlton, Travellers', Bachelors', Hurlingham.

(Died 2 June 1922.)

REES, Rev. Thomas, M.A. Ph.D. (Lond.); B.A. (Oxon); Principal of BalaBangor Independent College, Bangor, since 1909; *b.* Llanfyrnach, Pembrokeshire, 1869; *m.* 1902, Charlotte Elizabeth, *d.* of Michael Davies, Bridgend, Glams; five *s.* one *d. Educ.:* Presbyterian College, Carmarthen; University College, Cardiff; Mansfield College, Oxford. Professor of Theology at the Memorial College, Brecon, 1899-1909. *Publications:* Duw, ei Fodolaeth a'i Natur; Hanes Ymneilltuaeth yng Nghymru; Esboniad ar yr Epistol at yr Hebreaid (2 vols.); The Holy Spirit in Thought and Experience; Cenadwri'r Eglwys a Phroblemau'r dydd; Editor of Geiriadur Beiblaidd and of Y Dysgedydd. *Recreation:* mountaineering. *Address:* Independent College, Bangor. *(Died 20 May 1926.)*

REESE, Frederick Focke, D.D. (Univ. of Georgia, 1900 ; Univ. of the South, 1908) ; Bishop of Georgia Episcopal Church since 1908 ; *b.* Baltimore, Maryland, 23 Oct. 1854 ; *s.* of John S. and Arnoldina O. Focke Reese ; *m.* 1879, Ella, *d.* of I. M. and Mary B. Parr, Baltimore ; five *d.* *Educ.:* University of Virginia and Berkeley Divinity School. Deacon, 1878 ; Priest, 1879 ; Priest in Charge, All Saints, Balto., 1878-85 ; Rector, Trinity Church, Portsmouth, Va., 1885-90 ; Rector, Christ Church, Macon, Ga., 1890-1903 ; Christ Church, Nashville, Tenn., 1903-8 ; elected, and declined Missionary Bishop, Wyoming, 1907 ; Deputy to General Convention from Ga., 1892-1901 ; from Tennessee, 1904 and 1907 ; Trustee, University of the South, Sewanee, Tenn., 1893 till now ; other positions of trust in Church ; representative of the Province of Sewanee in the Executive Council of the National Church ; Phi Beta Kappa. *Publications :* occasional sermons. *Recreation :* golf. *Address :* Christ Church, Savannah, Georgia. *Clubs :* Delta Psi College Fraternity ; Savannah Golf ; Colonade, Univ. of Va. *(Died 29 Nov. 1924.)*

REEVE, Henry Fenwick, C.M.G. 1900, M.I.C.E., F.R.G.S., F.S.A.; *b.* Kent, 7 Apr. 1854. *Educ.:* privately; St. Peter's College ; Melbourne University. Served under Government of New South Wales, Victoria, Fiji, Windward Islands, Gambia, and Lagos, West Africa; was Chief Commissioner, Anglo-French Boundary Commission, 1895-96, and 1898-99 ; Acting Governor, Lagos, 1902. *Publication:* The Gambia, 1912. *Recreations:* general shooting, fishing, yachting. *Clubs:* Royal Societies, St. Stephen's. *(Died 18 Jan. 1920.)*

REEVE, Simms, D.L., J.P. Norfolk ; J.P. Norwich ; *e. s.* of Joseph N. Reeve and Mary, *d.* of late Law Simms, Brancaster ; *b.* 1826 ; *m.* 1854, Annie, *d.* of late William Browne. Recorder of Great Yarmouth, 1872-1908 ; High Sheriff for the county of Norfolk, 1898. *Address :* Brancaster Hall, King's Lynn ; St. Helen's Lodge, Norwich. *Club :* Norfolk County. *(Died 29 Oct. 1919.)*

REEVE, Rt. Rev. William Day, D.D., Assistant Bishop of Toronto since 1907 ; *b.* Harmston, Lins., 3rd Jan. 1844; *e. s.* of James Reeve ; *m.* 1st, 1869, Emily (d. 1906), *s. d.* of George Parker ; three *s.* four *d.* ; 2nd, 1907; Alice Mary, *d.* of late R. R. Grindley of Montreal. *Educ.:* National School, Harmston; C.M.S. College, Islington. After two years on a farm, followed by a business training, entered C.M.S. College in 1866 ; C.M.S. Missionary since 1869 ; Fort Simpson, 1869-79, including one year at Fort Rae ; Fort Chipewyan, 1879-89, including one year's furlough, 1880-81 ; Deacon, 1869 ; Priest, 1874 ; Bishop's Chaplain and Registrar, 1874 ; Archdeacon of Chipewyan, 1883 ; consecrated Bishop in Winnipeg, 1891. *Publications:* editor of New Testament, Book of Common Prayer, Hymnal, etc., in Slavi Language. translated by Bishop Bompas. *Recreations:* chess, draughts, shooting. *Address:* Assistant Bishop's Room ; Synod Office ; and 544 Huron Street, Toronto, Canada. *T. :* 0123 Hillcrest. *(Died 12 May 1925.)*

REFALO, His Hon. Sir Michelangelo, Kt., *cr.* 1921; C.B.E. 1918; Chief Justice and President of H.M. Court of Appeal ; *b.* Malta, 1 Mar. 1876 ; *s.* of late Notary Vincenzo Refalo; *m.* 1900, Mary (deceased), 2nd *d.* of late G. D. Debono, architect; three *s.* two *d.* *Educ.:* Malta University ; B.A. 1894 ; LL.D. 1898. Called to Malta Bar, 1899 ; Examiner in Italian Literature, 1902 ; Prof. of Commercial Law, 1907 ; Assistant Crown Advocate, 1910 ; Crown Advocate, Member of the Legislative and Executive Council, Malta, Legal Adviser to the Naval and Military Authorities, and Proper Officer of the Crown in Prize Cases, 1915 ;

Examiner in Faculty of Law, 1915 ; Member of the Control Board, 1916 ; Vice-President of the Council of Government of Malta, 1919-21. *Publications:* contributed an account of the Commercial Laws of Malta in a work dealing with the Commercial Laws of the British Possessions and Protectorates, 1912. *Address:* Valletta, Malta. *T.A.:* Chief Justice, Malta. *Club :* Casino Maltese, Valletta.
(Died 20 Dec. 1923.)

REHAN, Ada, actress ; *b.* Limerick, 22 Apr. 1860. *Educ.:* Brooklyn, New York. *Début,* Newark, New Jersey, 1874 ; during the seasons of 1875-78 enacted nearly 200 different characters in Philadelphia, Louisville, Albany, Baltimore ; playing the heroines of Shakspere with Edwin Booth, Laureuce Barrett, John M'Cullough, etc. ; engaged by Augustin Daly for his New York theatre 1879 ; has since played under Mr. Daly's management in London, Berlin, Paris, etc., as well as New York and San Francisco ; creating a *furore* with her impersonations of Katherine (Taming of the Shrew) ; Rosalind (As You Like It); Viola (Twelfth Night); Lady Teazle (School for Scandal), etc. *Recreations:* cycling, travelling, reading; preferences for Balzac and Thackeray. *Address:* 164 West Ninety-third Street, New York City.
(Died 9 Jan. 1916.)

REIACH, Herbert, Publisher; Editor of the Yachting Monthly ; Joint-Editor of the Badminton Magazine since 1916; Manager of the Saturday Review ; Managing Director of Herbert Reiach, Ltd., Publishers; Naval Architect ; Associate Member I.N.A. *b.* Greenock, 22 Jan. 1873; *y. s.* of late George Reiach, Edinburgh, H.M. Inspector of Scottish Fisheries. *Educ.:* Royal High School and George Watson's College, Edinburgh. Studied and practised Shipbuilding, Naval Architecture and Yacht Designing, 1890-1902; founded the Yachting Monthly in 1906 and edited it since its commencement; Business Editor of the Field, 1908-10 ; Writer on Naval Architecture and Yachting under the pseudonym of "Mina." *Recreation:* Yachting. *Address:* 9 King Street, Covent Garden, W.C.2. *T. :* Gerrard 8157. *Club:* Royal Thames Yacht.
(Died 16 July 1921.)

REICHEL, Rev. Oswald Joseph, M.A., B.C.L., F.S.A.; *b.* 2 Feb. 1840; *e. s.* of late Rev. Samuel Rudolph Reichel of Ockbrook, Co. Derby, and 2nd wife, Matilda, *d.* of Joseph Hurlock of Oxted, Co. Surrey ; *m.* 1887, Julia Maria Harriet Louisa, *d.* of F. Ashenden and *g. d.* of Thos. Lestock Ashenden of Old Barn Court, Nonington, Co. Kent. *Educ.:* Queen's College, Oxford. Taylorian Scholar ; Ellerton Theological Essayist and Johnson and Denyer Theological Scholar in University of Oxford, and Vice-Principal of Cuddesdon Theological College ; Member of St. Thomas' Board of Guardians, Devon; Public Preacher in the Diocese of Exeter. *Publications:* The See of Rome in the Middle Ages, 1870 ; Sparsholt Feast, an antiquarian sermon, 1882 ; contributor to the Devon Association of articles on Domesday, the Pipe Rolls, the Hundreds, Manors, and Churches of Devon ; The Rise of the Parochial System, 1906 ; The Treasury of God and the Birthright of the Poor, 1907 ; Domesday Survey, the Feudal Baronage, and Translation of Domesday text for the Victoria History of the County of Devon ; A Complete Manual of Canon Law ; Editor of Devon Feet of Fines for Devon and Cornwall Record Society, and of Bishop Lacy of Exeter Episcopal Registers. *Address:* A la Ronde House, near Lympstone, Devon.
(Died 30 April 1923.)

REID, Surg.-Gen. Sir Adam Scott, K.C.B., *cr.* 1911; C.B. 1903; M.B., M.Ch., I.M.S.; retired; lately P.M.O. Punjab command; Assistant-Surgeon, 1872 ; Surg.-Gen., 1902 ; *b.* 4 April

1848; *m.* 1875, Sidney Vaughan (*decd.*), *d.* of Sidney Vaughan Jackson of Ballina, Mayo; one *s.* two *d.* Served Afghan War, 1879-80 (medal); Chin Lushai Expedition, 1889 - 90 (medal with clasp); N.W.F., India, 1897-98 (despatches, medal with two clasps). Formerly Administrative Medical Officer, C.P. India, and Inspector-General Civil Hospitals, Punjab; initiated and was President of a Malaria Conference held at Nagpur, 1901; granted a Good Service Pension in recognition of his services to the State. *Publications:* Chin Lushai Land; and numerous contributions to the lay and medical Press. *Recreations:* fishing, shooting, golf, billiards, travel, and literature. *Address:* 10 Zetland House, Cheniston Gardens, Kensington. W. *T.:* Western 1658. *Club:* East India United Service.
(Died 2 Feb. 1918.)

REID, Lt.-Col. Alexander, D.S.O. 1900; V.D.; *b.* 2 Oct. 1865; *s.* of Thomas Reid, Hampstead; *m.* 1906, Margaret Frederica, *widow* of late Major Harry Chalmers Hudson, I.M.S., 16th Bengal Cavalry; one *s. Educ.:* Highgate School. Served South Africa, 1900 (despatches, Queen's medal 4 clasps, D.S.O.); served European War, 1914-20, England, France, and Flanders (despatches); commanded P.O.W. Camp, Queensferry, Chester; 20th Batt. Lancashire Fusiliers; 18th Cheshire; 37 Lab. Group. *Address:* 39 St. Paul's Avenue, Willesden Green, N.W. *(Died 25 Feb. 1927.)*

REID, Alexander, I.S.O. 1904; Under Treasurer of Tasmania, 1895-1914; *b.* 12 Aug. 1848. Entered Civil Service, 1857; Accountant, 1882; retired on pension, 1914. *Address:* Mount Nelson Road, Hobart, Tasmania.

REID, Sir Archibald Douglas, K.B.E., *cr.* 1919; C.M.G. 1915; R.A.M.C., M.R.C.S., L.R.C.P.; D.M.R. and E. (Cambridge); Superintendent Radiological Dept. St. Thomas's Hospital; *b.* 1871; *s.* of Dr. Douglas A. Reid, J.P., of Tenby; *m.* Annie Allan, *d.* of late John Clapperton of Greenock. *Educ.:* Bradfield College; King's College Hospital; Capt. R.A.M.C. (T.F.); temp. Lt.-Col. R.A.M.C.; President of War Office X - Ray Committee, 1914-19; President Electrotherapeutic Section of Royal Society of Medicine, 1911-12. *Address:* 30 Welbeck Street, W.1. *T.:* Paddington 4501.
(Died 15 Jan. 1924.)

REID, Clement, F.R.S., F.L.S., F.G.S.; late District Geologist on survey of England and Wales; *m.* E. M. Wynne Edwards, B.Sc. Studied tertiary formations in the South of England, pliocene deposits, glacial phenomena of the east and south coasts, pliocene and pleistocene botany, Cornish geology. *Publications:* Geology of the Country around Cromer, 1882; Geology of Holderness, 1885; Pliocene Deposits of Britain, 1890; Origin of the British Flora, 1899; The Island of Ictis, 1905; Geology of Newquay, 1906; Geology of Land's End, 1907; Geology of Mevagissey, 1907; reports on the botany of Roman Britain; many contributions to geological journals; Submerged Forests, 1913; jointly with Mrs. Reid — Pre-Glacial Flora of Britain, 1907; Fossil Flora of Tegelen, 1907-1910; The Lignite of Bovey Tracey, 1910; The Pliocene Floras of the Dutch - Prussian Border, 1915. *Address:* One Acre. Milford-on-Sea, Hampshire. *(Died 10 Dec. 1916.)*

REID, Colonel Ellis Ramsay, C.B. 1907; D.S.O. 1902; Chief Paymaster A.P.D.; *b.* 23 Jan. 1850; *s.* of Lestock Robert Reid, late Bombay C.S.; *m.* 1901, Helena Kate Risley. *Educ.:* Hampstead; Harrow; Sandhurst. Joined 108th Regiment as ensign, 1869; exchanged as cornet to 44th Foot, 1878; joined A.P.D. 1881; served Bechuanaland campaign, 1884-85 (honourably mentioned); S. African war from Nov. 1899 to the end (despatches, D.S.O.). *Address:* Blenheim, Blackheath, Colchester.
(Died 14 Oct. 1918.)

REID, Colonel Francis Maude, D.S.O. 1917; retired pay; late the Highland Light Infantry; *b.* 17 June 1849; 6th *s.* of late William Reid, of The Node, Welwyn, Herts; *m.* 1874, Katharine Elizabeth Julia, *e. d.* of late Colonel George Ross, of Cromarty; no *c. Educ.:* Harrow. Joined 71st the H.L.I. as Ensign by Purchase, 1868; went as Adjutant Sutherland Highland Rifles, 1884-89; commanded 1st Batt. the H.L.I., 1894-99; saw service in Cretan rising at Kandia, 6 Sep. 1898 (despatches); joined up for European War, 6 Sep. 1914; commanded 7th S.B. the Lincolnshire Regt.; transferred May 1915 to 13th S.B. the Worcestershire Regt.; again transferred April 1916 to 34th Labour Batt. Royal Fusiliers; went to France with it (despatches twice, D.S.O.). *Recreations:* sporting generally; once Master of Pack of Beagles; Master of Harriers, 1885-88; and 1903-7. *Address:* 45 Earl's Court Square, S.W.5. *T.:* Western 589. *Club:* Naval and Military.
(Died 27 Feb. 1922.)

REID, George, O.B.E. 1918; M.D., D.P.H.; Consulting Medical Officer of Health for Staffordshire. *Address:* County Public Health Offices, Martin Street, Stafford.
(Died 6 Nov. 1925.)

REID, Rt. Hon. Sir George Houstoun, G.C.B., *cr.* 1916; G.C.M.G., *cr.* 1911; K.C.M.G., *cr.* 1909; P.C. 1897; D.C.L., LL.D. Adelaide; K.C.; M.P. (U.) St. George's, Hanover Square, since Jan. 1916; *b.* Johnstone, Renfrewshire, 25 Feb. 1845; *m.* 1891, Flora (G.B.E., *cr.* 1917), *d.* of John Bromby, Thornton, Cressy, Tasmania; Presbyterian. Barr. New South Wales, 1879; elected to Legislative Assembly, 1880; Member for East Sydney, with break in 1884-85, until 1901; after Federation Member for East Sydney, 1901-09; Leader of Federal Opposition during same time, except 1904-5, when Prime Minister of Australia; Prime Minister and Colonial Treasurer of New South Wales. 1894 - 99, during which period as senior Premier he carried the Federal movement to a successful issue; High Commissioner for Australia, 1910-16; Gold Medal, Cobden Club. *Publications:* Five Free Trade Essays; New South Wales, The Mother Colony of the Australias, My Reminiscenses, etc. *Address:* 1 Melbury Road, Kensington, W. *T.:* Park 4265. *Clubs:* Athenæum, British Empire.
(Died 12 Sept. 1918.)

REID, Rev. Henry M. B., M.A., B.D., D.D., F.E.I.S.; Prof. of Divinity, University of Glasgow, since 1903; *b.* Glasgow, 22 March 1856; *s.* of Rev. A. F. Reid, Chaplain to H.M. Prison, Dundee, and Elizabeth Jane, *d.* of Rev. James Beckwith. *Educ.:* High School, Dundee; St. Andrews University. First Class in Classics; Assistant to Professor of Humanity in St. Andrews, 1878-79; licensed by Presbytery of St. Andrews, 1879; appointed Assistant first in Anderston Parish, Glasgow, latterly in Glasgow Cathedral; ordained Minister of the parish of Balmaghie, Kirkcudbrightshire, 1882. *Publications:* Songs for the use of St. Andrews Students, 1876; About Galloway Folk, by a Galloway Herd, 1889, 2nd ed. 1901; The Kirk Above Dee Water, 1895; Lost Habits of the Religious Life, 1896; Books that Help the Religious Life, 1897; A Cameronian Apostle, 1897; One of King William's Men, 1898; Historic Significance of Episcopacy in Scotland, Lee Lecture, 1899; A Country Parish (studies in Pastoral Theology and Church Law), 1908; The Professor's Wallet: essays theological and historical, 1910; The Layman's Book, 1900 to 1911; The Divinity Principals in the University of Glasgow, 1917; A Text - book of Dogmatics, 1919; The Divinity Professors in the University of Glasgow, 1923; The Holy Spirit and the Mystics (Croall Lectures, 1925). *Address:* 12 The University, Glasgow. *T.:*

REID, George Ogilvy. See page xxix.

Western 2019. *Clubs:* University, Edinburgh; Western, Glasgow. *(Died 18 Oct. 1927.)*

REID, Sir James, 1st Bt., *cr.* 1897; G.C.V.O., *cr.* 1901; K.C.B., *cr.* 1895; M.D., LL.D.; Physician-in-Ordinary to the King; *b.* Scotland, 23 Oct. 1849; *e. s.* of late James Reid, M.D., Ellon, Aberdeenshire, and Beatrice, *d.* of late John Peter, of Canterland, Kincardineshire; *m.* 1899, Hon. Susan Baring, formerly Maid of Honour to Queen Victoria, *d.* of 1st Baron Revelstoke; two *s.* two *d. Educ.:* Aberdeen Gram. School (Dux and Gold Medallist, 1865), and Aberdeen Univ. M.A. Aberdeen (Honours in Natural Science and Gold medallist, 1869; M.B. and C.M. (highest Honours), 1872; M.D. 1875; LL.D. 1895; M.R.C.P. Lond. 1887; F.R.C.P. 1892; Hon. M.D. Roy. Univ. Ireland, 1900; Hon. F.R.C.P. Ireland, 1900; Hon. LL.D. Glasgow, 1901; Surg.-Lieut.-Col. (retired) 2nd Vol. Batt. Gordon Highlanders, V.D.; J.P. Aberdeenshire. Consulting Physician to Convalescent Home for Officers, Osborne; to King Edward VII. Sanatorium, Midhurst; and to the Prince of Wales's General Hospital, Tottenham, Fellow of Royal Society of Medicine; studied Vienna, 1876-77; practised Scotland, 1877-81; Resident Physician to Queen Victoria, 1881-1901; Physician Extraordinary, 1887-1889; Physician - in - Ordinary, 1889 - 1901; Physician-in-Ordinary to King Edward VII., 1899-1910; C.B. 1889; has Red Eagle of Prussia (1st Class); Royal Order of the Crown of Prussia (1st Class), and Ernestine Order of Coburg; Commander of the Legion of Honour. *Publications:* papers to medical journals. *Heir: s.* Edward James [*b.* 20 April 1901, godson of King Edward VII.; Page of Honour to the King, 1911-17; Scholar King's College, Cambridge; Browne Medallist, 1920, 1921, and 1922; First Class Classical Tripos, 1922]. *Address:* 72 Grosvenor Street, W.1; The Chestnuts, Ellon, Aberdeenshire. *T.:* 1147 Mayfair. *Club:* Athenæum. *(Died 28 June 1923.)*

REID, James Smith, M.A., LL.M., Litt.D.; Professor of Ancient History, Cambridge, 1899, Emeritus Professor since 1925; Fellow (1878) and Tutor (1885) of Gonville and Caius College, Camb.; *b.* Scotland, 3 May 1846; *e. s.* of John Reid; *m.* 1872, Ruth, *d.* of T. Gardner; two *s.* one *d. Educ.:* City of London School; Christ's Coll., Camb. Browne's Medal (Camb.), 1868; Chancellor's Medal (Camb.), 1869; Whewell Scholarship (Camb.), 1870; Classical Medal (London), 1869. Fellow of Christ's Coll. Cambridge, 1869-72; Classical Lecturer of Christ's College, 1870-80; Hon. Fellow of Christ's College; Classical Lecturer of Pembroke College, Cambridge, 1873 - 78, 1880-85; Hon. Litt.D. Dublin; Hon. LL.D. St. Andrews; Fellow of the British Academy; late President of the Roman Studies Society. *Publications:* editions of Cicero's Academica, De Amicitia, De Senectute, Pro Archia, Pro Balbo, Pro Milone, Pro Sulla; translations of De Finibus and Academica; contributions to the Encyclopædia of Religion and ethics; Municipalities of the Roman Empire, 1913; many scattered papers on classical subjects. *Address:* Gonville and Caius College, and Lysmore, West Road, Cambridge. *T.:* Cambridge 56. *(Died 1 April 1926.)*

REID, John R., R.I. *Address:* 62 Parkhill Road, Hampstead, N.W.; Polperro, Cornwall. *(Died 10 Feb. 1926.)*

REID, Sir Marshall (Frederick), Kt., *cr.* 1916; C.I.E. 1902; East India Merchant; partner Wyer and Hawke, 4 Crosby Square, E.C.; Member of Council of India, 1916-20; Director Anglo - Egyptian Bank and National Bank of India; Member Indian Currency Committee, 1919; Delegate (India) Financial Conference of League of Nations, Brussels, 1921; Chairman of Bombay Chamber of Commerce, 1914-15;

Member of the Imperial Legislative Council of India, 1914-15; Member of Legislative Council, Bombay, 1912-1914, and Director Presidency Bank of Bombay; *b.* 3 Aug. 1864; *s.* of late Daniel Reid, Glasgow; *m.* 1912, H. Mabel, *d.* of J. Tait - Burton, Scotstoun, South Queensferry; two *d. Educ.:* Loretto. *Recreations:* riding, shooting, golf. *Address:* Woodcote Lodge, Epsom, Surrey. *T.:* Epsom 321. *Clubs:* City of London, Oriental, Royal Automobile. *(Died 20 Mar. 1925.)*

REID, Lt.-Col. Richard, Agent-General for Ontario in London; *b.* Millbank, Ontario; *s.* of James and Esther Reid; *m.* 1st, 1886, Alice Woodsend, Nottingham, England; four *s.* one *d.*; 2nd, 1913, Alice Mulholland, Toronto; one *s: Educ.:* St. Catherine's Collegiate Institute and Normal College, Ottawa. Career, mainly scholastic and agricultural; initiated many educational reforms and was President of Teachers' Association of Ontario; an authority on agriculture and live-stock; one of the founders of the Canadian Jersey Cattle Club; Fellow Royal Colonial Institute; Hon. Colonel 108th Canadian Battalion. *Recreations:* golf, motoring, and riding. *Address:* 163 Strand, W.C. *T.A.:* Burocolon. *T.:* Gerrard 5793. *Clubs:* British Empire, Constitutional, Royal Automobile. *(Died 21 Oct. 1918.)*

REID, Robert Lawrence; Assistant Mining Engineer, Memba Minerals, Mozambique, Portuguese East Africa; *b.* near Ballarat, Victoria, 1858; father, Scotch, station owner; mother, English; unmarried. *Educ.:* Queensland State Schools and private tutors. Brought up to the career of pastoralist on his father's station, Echo Hills, in Queensland; left this and started contracting, then mining, both successfully; went to West Australia when goldfields broke out, and was interested in several successful enterprises; left West Australia, 1900, and came to Africa big game shooting; made map of part of Portuguese East Africa, published by Royal Geographical Society; entered Congo Free State service, 1904; engaged in mining work in the Congo up to 1910; mapped the Aruwimi River, award from Royal Geographical Society; was engaged in mineral research work and survey in the Mozambique country, and later mining work for Nigerian New Territories Syndicate. *Publications:* (by the Royal Geographical Society) Map and Notes of Portuguese East Africa; Map and Notes of the Aruwimi River, Belgian Congo. *Recreations:* big game shooting, travel and exploration. *Address:* c/o Union Bank of Australia, 71 Cornhill, E.C. *(Died 16 April 1918.)*

REID, Samuel, R.S.W.; painter and author; *b.* Aberdeen, 4 July 1854; 6th *s.* of late George Reid and Esther Tait; *y. b.* of Sir George Reid, P.R.S.A.; *m.* 1883, Agnes, *e. d.* of late Charles Stewart, Liverpool; one *s.* one *d. Educ.:* Grammar School, Aberdeen. Has exhibited R.A., New Gallery; N.E.A.C., R.S.A., Glasgow Inst.; gold medal, Crystal Palace, 1899; member of Royal Scot. Water-Col. Soc. *Publications:* contributed poems and tales, Blackwood, Chambers's, Cornhill; collected poems, Pansies and Folly-Bells, 1892; has contributed numerous illustrations to Black and White, Good Words, Magazine of Art, etc. *Recreations:* singing and the Georgi flute. *Address:* Caversham Lodge, Chorley Wood, Herts.

REID, Stuart J., D.C.L. (Durham, 1907); J.P. Sussex; 4th *s.* of late Rev. Alex. Reid, Newcastle-on-Tyne, and *y. b.* of late Sir Wemyss Reid; *m.* 1882, Mary Emily, *d.* of late Alfred Fryer, Wilmslow, Cheshire; Director of Sampson, Low & Co., 1891 - 98; editor of Queen Victoria's Prime Ministers Series, of the Essays of Dr. Johnson; The Memoirs of Sir Edward Blount, 1815-1902; The Memoirs of Sir Wemyss Reid, 1842-1885, 1905. *Publica-*

tions : Representative Men in Reign of Queen Victoria, 1878-79 ; Life and Times of Sydney Smith (5th edit. 1901) ; Life of Lord John Russell (4th edit. 1905) ; The Life and Letters of the first Earl of Durham, 1792-1840 ; Life of Sir Richard Tangye, 1908 ; an Annotated Catalogue of Historical Tracts from the reign of Queen Elizabeth to that of George III. (six hundred pages—being the clue to the Redpath Collection of many thousand pamphlets presented to the McGill Univ., Montreal, 1901 : privately printed) ; John and Sarah, Duke and Duchess of Marlborough (from the Blenheim Archives). 1914. At the request of the 8th Duke of Marlborough, arranged and catalogued the Blenheim State and Family Manuscripts at Blenheim Palace, and drew up a report which remains unprinted, 1889-90 ; he has also created a Historical Library at Blenheim for the present Duke, to take the place of the old Sunderland Library, 1896-1900 ; literary adviser to Cassell's, 1903 ; literary director and editor-in-chief to Isbister & Company (Sir Isaac Pitman & Sons), 1904-6 ; joined forces with Duckworth and Co., 1907 ; retired,1914 ; Wrote " First Impressions " in the Speaker, 1890-99 ; between 1887 and 1901 chief literary critic to the Leeds Mercury ; and was for thirty years on the literary staff (non-political) of the Standard ; a Director of British Equitable Assurance Company since 1914, and of the Kelani Valley Rubber Produce Co. since 1919. *Address :* Blackwell Cliff, East Grinstead, Sussex. *T.A. :* Stuart Reid, East Grinstead. *Clubs :* Athenæum, Royal Societies.

(*Died 27 Aug. 1927.*)

REID, Walter, proprietor of Western Daily Press, Bristol Evening News, and Bristol Observer ; *m.* Newcastle-on-Tyne, Charlotte, 2nd *d.* of William Latimer. Started (with the late P. S. Macliver) Western Daily Press, 1858 ; Fellow of Journalists' Institute. *Address :* The Woodlands, Woodland Road, Tyndall's Park, Clifton, Bristol. *T. :* 3565, 492 and 1217. *Clubs :* National Liberal ; Bristol Liberal.

(*Died 18 Feb. 1917.*)

REID, Sir William Duff, Kt., *cr.* 1916 ; a Director of British Empire Steel Co. ; *b.* N.S.W., 20 Nov. 1869 ; *s.* of late Sir Robert G. Reid and Harriet Duff ; *m.* 1894, Minnie, *d.* of late John H. Cormack, Ottawa ; three *s.* one *d. Educ.:* Galt Collegiate Institute ; went to Newfoundland, 1890 ; *Recreations :* motoring, fishing. *Address :* Bartra, Circular Road, St. John's, Newfoundland. *Clubs :* Royal Automobile ; City, St. Johns ; St. James, Royal St. Laurence Hunt, Forest and Stream, Montreal. (*Died Mar. 1924.*)

REILLY, Col. Charles Cooper, C.B. 1917 ; late A.M.S. ; *b.* 18 July 1862. Major, R.A.M.C. 1897 ; Lt.-Col. 1905 ; Col. 1914 ; Assist. Director of Medical Services, 1915 ; Deputy Director, 1915 ; served Sudan, 1885-86 (medal, bronze star) ; S. Africa, 1900-1 (Queen's medal 4 clasps). *Address :* The Cottage, Countess Wear, near Exeter. (*Died 5 May 1926.*)

REILLY, Very Rev. Thomas, Dean of Ardagh since 1913. *Educ. :* Trinity College, Dublin. Ordained, 1876 ; Curate of Killashee, 1876-77 ; Incumbent, 1882-1900 ; Cashel, 1878-1882 ; Rathaspeck, 1900. *Address :* The Glebe, Rathowen, Co. Westmeath. (*Died April 1921.*)

REINACH, Joseph ; contributor to the Figaro under the name Polybe, and to the Revue de Paris ; Vice-President de la Commission supérieur des services de santé ; *b.* Paris, 30 Sep. 1856 ; *m.* 1st, Henriett Reinach (*d.* 1918) ; one *s.* (Adolphe, killed Aug. 1914) one *d.* ; 2nd, Mme. Pierre Goujon, widow of P. Goujon, deputy (killed Aug. 1914). *Educ. :* Lycée Condorcet, Paris. Lawyer ; Secretary to Gambetta, 1881-82 ; Chief Director of the République Française, after Gambetta's death, till 1893 ; articles against Boulanger ; Deputy

for the Basses-Alpes, 1889-97 ; promoter of the revision of the Dreyfus case ; was not re-elected in 1897 on account of his prominent part in that affair ; re-elected in 1906 and 1910 ; Vice-President of the Army Commission ; President of the Commissions against Alcoholism and against Tuberculosis ; a considerable number of speeches on the electoral reform, etc. ; one of the promoters of the law on the three years' military system ; during the war, for six months, on the staff of General Gallieni. *Publications :* Voyage en Orient ; Les Récidivistes ; Le Ministère Gambetta ; La Logique parlementaire ; La Politique opportuniste ; Le Ministère Clemenceau ; Le Scrutin de liste ; Gambetta orateur ; Les Grandes Manœuvres de l'Est ; Histoire de l' Affaire Dreyfus ; Contre l'alcoolisme ; La Réforme électorale ; Discours et Plaidoyers politiques de Gambetta ; Discours choisis de Gambetta ; Discours, Proclamations et Dépêches de Gambetta pendant la Défense Nationale ; Les Commentaires de Polybe (séries 1 à 19) ; La Guerre sur le front occidental (1914-15) ; La Serbie et le Monténégro ; Les Petites Catilinaires ; Pages républicaines ; Démagogues et Socialistes ; Essais de Littérature et d'Histoire ; Essais de Politique et d'Histoire ; Diderot ; Manuel de l'Enseignement primaire ; Le " Conciones " français ; La France et l'Italie devant l'Histoire ; Histoire d'un Idéal ; Raphaël Lévy ; Vers la Justice par la Vérité ; Le Crépuscule des traitres ; Tout le Crime ; Les Blés d'hiver ; La Réorganisation de l'Artillerie ; L'Armée toujours prête ; La Fixité des effectifs ; Mes Comptes rendus ; Récits et Portraits contemporains ; Histoire de Douze Jours ; Discours de Challemel-Lacour ; Les Origines diplomatiques de la Guerre de 1870-71 ; La Vie politique de Gambetta. *Recreations :* Cavalry Officer in the Reserve, travels in the West and Russia. *Address :* 6 avenue van Dyck, Paris. *T. :* Elysée 09.85. *Club :* Interallié. (*Died 18 April 1921.*)

REINOLD, Arnold William, C.B. 1911 ; M.A., F.R.S. ; late Professor of Physics, Royal Naval College, Greenwich ; *b.* Hull, June 1843 ; *s.* of John Henry Arnold Reinold, shipbroker ; *m.* Marion Studdy (*d.* 1918). *Educ. :* St. Peter's School, York ; Brasenose Coll. Oxford (M.A.). Fellow of Merton Coll. Oxford, 1866 ; Lee's Reader in Physics at Christ Church, 1869 ; sometime Lecturer in Physics, Guy's Hospital ; Past President of the Physical Society ; Hon. Member Yorkshire Phil. Soc. *Publications :* papers on the Properties of Thin Films in Phil. Trans. *Address :* East Cosham House, Cosham, Hants. (*Died 11 April 1921.*)

RÉJANE, Madame (Gabrielle Réju), actress ; *b.* Paris, 6 June 1857 ; *m.* M. Porel, Director of the Vaudeville (*div.* 1905). *Educ. :* Conservatoire (under Régnier). *Début* at Vaudeville in Revue des Deux Mondes, 1875 ; left the Vaudeville for Théâtre des Variétés, 1882 ; passed to L'Ambigu in order to create la Glu in 1882 ; afterwards created Ma Camarade, Palais Royal ; Clara Soleil, Vaudeville ; Les Dem. Clochard, Variétés ; Germinie Lacerteux, l'Odéon ; Marquise, Vaudeville ; Ma Cousine, Variétés ; Amoureuse, l'Odéon ; Lysistrata, Grand Théâtre ; Madame Sans Gêne, Vaudeville in 1893 ; and Maison de Poupée, 1894 ; toured in America in 1895, and obtained an enormous success ; one of Madame Réjane's later successes at the Vaudeville is La Passerelle. *Address :* Avenue d'Antin (VIII), Paris.

(*Died 14 June 1920.*)

REMSEN, Ira ; President, 1901-13, and Professor of Chemistry, 1876-1913, now President Emeritus and Professor Emeritus, Johns Hopkins University ; *b.* New York, 10 Feb. 1846 ; *m.* 1875, Elizabeth H. Mallory, New York ; two *s. Educ. :* College City of New York ; College Physicians and Surgeons, New York ; Universities of Munich, Göttingen, and Tübingen. Professor, Williams College, Massachusetts,

1872-76. *Publications*: many scientific articles and books—almost wholly in the field of Chemistry. *Address*: Johns Hopkins University, Baltimore, Md., U.S.A. *Clubs*: University, Baltimore; Chemists', New York.
(*Died Mar. 1927.*)

RENARD, Samuel, I.S.O. 1913; late a Principal Clerk, Supreme Court Pay Office. *Address*: 91 Addison Road, Kensington, W.
(*Died 29 Mar. 1924.*)

RENAULT, Louis, Hon. D.C.L. Oxford; G.C.M.G. (hon.); Professor of International Law, University of Paris; Commander of Legion of Honour; Member of the Institute; Fellow of British Academy; *b.* 21 May 1848. Nobel Peace Prize, 1907. *Publications*: several papers. *Address*: 5 Rue de Lille, Paris; Villa des Troenes, Barbizon, Seine-et-Marne.
(*Died Feb. 1918.*)

RENDEL, Sir Alexander Meadows, K.C.I.E.; *cr.* 1887; civil engineer; consulting engineer to the India Office, the East Indian and other Indian railways, since 1874; *b.* 1829; *e. s.* of late James Meadows Rendel, F.R.S.E.; *m.* 1853, Eliza (*d.* 1916), *d.* of Capt. Hobson, R.N., Governor of New Zealand. *Educ.*: King's School, Canterbury; Trinity College, Cambridge (Scholar and Wrangler). Engineer London Dock Co., 1856; visited India, 1857-58; Member of Commission to determine narrow gauge for Indian Railways, 1870. *Principal Works*: Shadwell basin Royal Albert Dock; the Albert and Edinburgh Docks at Leith; the Workington Dock and Harbour; the Sukker Bridge over the Indus, etc. *Address*: Rickettswood, Charlwood, Surrey. *Club*: Athenæum.
(*Died 23 Jan. 1918.*)

RENDELL, Rev. Arthur Medland; Rector of Eydon, Northants, since 1908; Hon. Canon of Peterborough Cathedral since 1899; *b.* Steyning, Sussex, 7 March 1842; *s.* of John Rendell, Commander, R.N., of Tiverton, and Sophia Medland of Exeter; *m.* 1877, Helen Bliss Barrett (*d.* 1887), of Shenley, Bucks. *Educ.*: Steyning Grammar School; Sir Roger Cholmeley's School, Highgate; Trinity College, Cambridge. Foundation Scholar, Twenty-third Wrangler, 1865; B.A. 1865; 2nd class in Honours, Theological Examination, Easter 1866. Ordained Deacon, 1866; Priest, 1867; M.A. 1868; assistant master of Highgate School, 1865-72; Curate of St. James', Muswell Hill, 1866-72; Rector of Coston, Leicestershire, 1872-1889; Vicar of St. Margaret's Leicester, 1889-1908; Rural Dean of Leicester, 1899-1908; Vice-Chairman of the Coston and Garthorpe School Board, 1874-89; member of the School Board for Leicester, and Chairman of the School Management Committee, 1894-1908; a co-opted member of the Education Committee of the Leicester Borough Council, 1908-8. *Recreation*: gardening. *Address*: Eydon Rectory, Byfield, Northants.   (*Died 7 May 1918.*)

RENDELL, Rev. James Robson, B.A. Lond.; late Minister of New Church (Swedenborgian), Accrington; *s.* of Rev. Elias de la Roche and Elizabeth Rendell; *b.* Preston, 1850; *m.* 1877, Anne Bannister (*d.* 1902), *d.* of James Bannister of Tarleton; two *s.* two *d. Educ.*: Preston Grammar School (Scholarship); Owens College, Manchester; University College, London. Minister of the New Church, Bradford, 1875-90; Lecturer and Demonstrator in Physics in the Yorkshire'College (now Leeds University), 1882-90; ordained, 1878; became an Ordaining Minister, 1899; went to Accrington, 1890; President of the New Church College (1892, '93, '97, 1902, '04, '05, '12); President of the Science Section of the Swedenborg Congress, 1910; President New Church Conference, 1891, 1899, at the Centenary, 1907, and 1917; President of the New Church Sunday School Union, 1917. *Publications*: translator of Swedenborg's Prin-

cipia, Heaven and Hell, Dicta Probantia, and Arcana Coelestia, vols. i. and ii.; Editor of the New Church Magazine since 1900 and a frequent contributor to New Church Journals. *Recreation*: mechanical arts. *Address*: Whinside, Accrington.   (*Died 8 Mar. 1926.*)

RENNENKAMPFF, General-Lieut. Paul Charles von; Commandant of 3rd Corps of Russian Army; *b.* Estlande, 17 April, 1854; *m.*; two *d. Educ.*: Reval Gymnasium; Military School of Finland; Nicolas Academy, Petrograd. Entered 5th Ulan Regiment; commanded Acktizsky Regiment of Dragoons; Chef d'Etat-Major East Baykal district; commanded First Brigade of Cavalry; 3rd Cossack Division of West Baykal; 7th Siberian Corps; 3rd Siberian Corps; served Macedonia, 1900 (Cross of St. George); commanded Siberian Cossack Division, and Chief of the 5th Siberian Corps, Russo-Japanese War (Chevalier, Order of St. Stanislas, General-Lieutenant, sabre of gold and diamonds from the Emperor); in command during European War, 1914-15. *Address*: Petrograd, Russia.   (*Died May 1918.*)

RENNIE, Edward Henry, M.A., D.Sc.; Professor of Chemistry, Adelaide University, since 1885; *b.* Sydney, 19 Aug. 1852; *s.* of E. A. Rennie, late Auditor-General, N.S.W.; *m.* Agnes, *d.* of Dr. J. G. Cadell, Sydney; one *s.* two *d. Educ.*: Grammar School and University, Sydney; Royal College of Science, London. Master, Sydney Grammar School, 1870-75; Brisbane Grammar School, 1876-77; came to London, 1877; Assistant in Chemical Dept., St. Mary's Hospital Medical School; graduated D.Sc. London, 1882; returned to Australia; twice President of Royal Society, S. Australia; Fellow, Institute of Chemistry, Great Britain and Ireland. *Publications*: Papers on Chemistry of several Australian Natural Products in the Journal of the Chemical Society. *Address*: 178 Childers Street, North Adelaide.
(*Died 8 Jan. 1927.*)

RENNIE, Major John George, D.S.O. 1900; The Black Watch (Royal Highlanders); *b.* 25 Feb. 1865; *m.*; one *s.* one *d. Educ.*: Cheltenham. Entered army 1896; Captain, 1903; Adjutant 5th V.B., H.L.I. since 1902; served Soudan, 1898 (despatches, 4th class Medjidie, British medal, Khedive's medal with clasp); South Africa, 1899-1902 (despatches D.S.O., two medals with clasps). *Address*: 29 Dorset Road, Bexhill.
(*Died 22 Feb. 1920.*)

RENNY, Maj.-Gen. Sidney Mercer, C.I.E. 1914; C.S.I. 1919; Director General of Ordnance, India; Director of Ordnance Factories, Woolwich, 1906; *b.* 3 June 1861; *s.* of late Maj.-Gen. G. A. Renny, V.C., R.A.; *m.* *d.* of Rev. W. W. Cazalet; two *s.* one *d. Educ.*: Cheltenham College; Woolwich. Entered Army, 1880; Assistant Superintendent gun carriage factory, Fatehgarh, 1888; foundry and shell factory, Cossipore, 1891; Superintendent, 1899; Ordnance Consulting Officer for India, India Office, 1905; Inspector-General of Ordnance Factories in India, 1906; served Burmese War, 1885-6. *Club*: United Service.
(*Died 27 April 1921.*)

RENSHAW, Arthur Henry; *y. s.* of Thomas Charles Renshaw, Q.C., of Sandrocks, Hayward's Heath, Sussex, a Bencher of Lincoln's Inn; *m.* 1899, Lady Winifred Edith Clements, *e. d.* of 4th Earl of Leitrim; three *s.* two *d. Address*: Watlington Park, Oxon.; 37 Portman Square, W. *T.*: Mayfair 4765. *Club*: Garrick.
(*Died 25 Dec. 1918.*)

RENSHAW, Sir Charles Bine, 1st Bt., *cr.* 1902; D.L.; manufacturer; chairman A. F. Stoddard and Co., Limited, Elderslie, and of Caledonian Railway; Chairman Board of Referees for Excess Profits Tax, since 1916; *b.* 9 Dec. 1848; 3rd *s.* of Thomas Charles Renshaw, Q.C.; *m.* 1872, Mary Home, *d.* of A. F. Stoddard,

881

RENALS, Sir James Herbert, 2nd Bt. See page xxix.

Broadfield, Renfrewshire; one s. four d. *Educ.*: St. Clere, Sevenoaks; Germany. M.P. (C.) W. Div. Renfrewshire, 1892-1906. *Heir*: s. Charles Stephen Bine, b. 9 Dec. 1883 [m. 1911. Edith Mary, 4th d. of late Rear-Adm. Sir Ed. Chichester, 9th Bt., of Raleigh, Devonshire; one s. two d.]. *Address*: 82 Cadogan Square, S.W.; *T.*: Victoria 2114; Barochan, Houston, Renfrewshire; Garvocks, Greenock. *Clubs*: Carlton, Garrick; Western, Glasgow. (*Died 6 Mar. 1918.*)

RENSHAW, Walter Charles, K.C., LL.M.; b. 24 Sep. 1840; e. s. of Thomas Charles Renshaw, Q.C., and Elizabeth, d. of George Blaker, Patcham; m. 1870, Elizabeth, d. of late John W. Wilson of Elsbrock, Holland, Officer of the Legion of Honour and Knight of Belgian Order of Leopold; one d. *Educ.*: King's College, London; Trinity Hall, Cambridge. LL.B. 1862. Barrister, Lincoln's Inn, 1864; Bencher, 1890; practised at Chancery Bar; for some years member of the Supreme Court Rule Committee and of the Council of Law Reporting; member of the Bar Committee many years; member of Baronetage Committee; Chairman of Councils of Sussex Archæological and Sussex Record Societies, and late President and now on Council of Selden Society; J.P. Sussex. *Publications*: has written several genealogical works and many articles in the Sussex Archæological Collection and The Genealogist. *Recreations*: formerly cricket, rowing and shooting; now, reading. *Address*: Sandrocks, near Hayward's Heath, Sussex. *Club*: New University. (*Died 16 July 1922.*)

RENTON, James Crawford, M.D., F.F.P.S.G.; Surgeon and Lecturer on Clinical Surgery, Western Infirmary, Glasgow; b. Auchtermuchty, Fifeshire; s. of Rev. J. Renton, U.F. Manse, Auchtermuchty; m. Margaret Annie, d. of Dr. James Mill, Thurso; two s. one d. *Educ.*: Abbey Park, St. Andrews; Edinburgh University; Paris and Vienna. Resident-Surgeon to Sir Patrick Heron Watson in the Royal Infirmary, Edinburgh; Senior President of Royal Medical Society, Edinburgh University; Assistant to late Professor George Buchanan, Professor of Clinical Surgery, University of Glasgow; Examiner in Surgery and Clinical Surgery in the Universities of Edinburgh and Aberdeen; Surgeon to the Eye Infirmary, Glasgow. *Publications*: Contributions to Clinical Surgery; Notes of Surgical Cases, Lancet and British Medical Journal, etc. *Recreations*: sport, fishing, and shooting. *Address*: 1 Woodside Terrace, Glasgow. W. *T.*: 116 Charing Cross, Glasgow, and 2153 Post Office. *Clubs*: Royal Societies; Western, Glasgow. (*Died 1919.*)

RENTOUL, His Honour James Alexander, K.C., LL.D.; Judge of City of London Court and Judge of Central Criminal Court since 1901; e. s. of late Rev. Alexander Rentoul, D.D., M.D., Manor Cunningham, Co. Donegal, and Erminda, e. d. of James Chittick, Manor Cunningham; m. 1882. Florence (d. 1914), y. d. of late D. W. Young, Wallington Lodge, Surrey, and London; two s. *Educ.*: Queen's College, Galway; Queen's University; University of Berlin; Brussels, B.A. (Honours); LL.B. (Honours and first exhibitioner); LL.D. (first place by examination); first prizeman, Senior Scholarship in Modern Continental Languages and Literature; Senior and Junior Scholarships in Law. Member first London County Council and member of the Belfast Chamber of Commerce; English Bar, 1884; obtained first place and scholarship of one hundred guineas; Q.C. 1895; M.P. (C.) East Down, 1890-1902. *Recreation*: reading Who's Who. *Address*: 44 Lexham Gardens, Kensington, W. *T.*: Western 2332; City of London Court, E.C. *Clubs*: Carlton, Royal Temple Yacht. (*Died 12 Aug. 1919.*)

RENTOUL, Rt. Rev. John Laurence, A.M., D.D.; Professor of Biblical Greek, and of Christian Philosophy, President of Senatus of Ormond College, Melbourne University, since 1888; Ex-President Melbourne College of Divinity; ex-Moderator Presbyterian Church of Australia; b. 1846; s. of late Rev. James B. Rentoul, D.D., Garvagh, Co. Derry, Ireland, and Sara, y. d. of late Rev. W. Wilson, D.D., Coleraine; m. Annie Isobel, 3rd d. of late D. T. Rattray, The Elms, Southport, and Chile; two s. two d. *Educ.*: Queen's College, Belfast; Queen's University, Dublin; Leipzig University. B.A. 1867, M.A. 1868; First Honours, Gold Medallist in Literature, History, and Economic Science, Queen's University, Ireland; Early English Text Society's Prizeman, London. Incumbent of St. George's Church (Presbyterian), Southport, Lancashire, 1872-79; St. George's Church, St. Kilda, Melbourne, 1879-84; Professor of Hebrew and Sacred Languages, Ormond College, Melbourne University, 1884; delegate from Australia to General Assemblies and Councils in the three kingdoms and America; has taken a leading part in vindication of the toiling masses, settlement of strikes, protection of the Australian aborigines, Chaplain-General Commonwealth Military Forces, 1913-19; Australian Imperial Forces at War Front, 1916-17. *Publications*: From Far Lands: Poems of North and South, 1914; Rome and the Early Church (six editions); The Church At Home; Prayers for Australian Households; sermons; and many articles; The Sign of the Cross, 1915; At Vancouver's Well, and Poems, 1917. *Recreations*: angling (in New Zealand, etc.) and cycling. *Address*: St. Oswald's, Ormond College, Melbourne. *Club*: Victorian N. and M. (*Died April 1926.*)

REPINGTON, Lieut.-Col. Charles A'Court-, C.M.G. 1900; Commander of the Order of Leopold; Officer of Legion of Honour; b. 29 Jan. 1858. *Educ.*: Eton; Sandhurst. Entered army (Rifle Brigade), 1878; Lieut.-Col. 1898; served in Afghanistan, 1878-79 (medal, 3 clasps); Burma, 1888-89; Soudan, 1898 (despatches twice, Brevet Lieut.-Col., British and Khedive's medals, 3 clasps); South Africa, 1899-1900 (despatches twice, medal 3 clasps, C.M.G.); Military Attaché, Brussels, and the Hague, 1899-1902. *Publications*: Vestigia, 1919; Diary, 1920; After the War, 1922. *Address*: Amington Hall, Tamworth, Warwickshire. *Club*: Naval and Military. (*Died 25 May 1925.*)

RESTLER, Sir James William, K.B.E., cr. 1918; Chairman Metropolitan Munitions Committee; Chairman Rickmansworth and Uxbridge Valley Water Co., St. Albans Water Co., and of Fire Brigade Co-ordination Committee. *Address*: 17 Queen's Gate, S.W.7. *T.*: Kensington 184. (*Died 11 Nov. 1918.*)

RESZKE, Jean de, operatic singer; M.V.O. (4th class); b. Varsovie, 1853. Appeared in London, 1875; m. la Comtesse Maria de Goulaine. *Recreations*: riding, shooting, tennis; breeding race horses. *Address*: Rue de la Faisanderie, 53, Paris; Chateau Skrzydlom, Poland. (*Died 3 April 1925.*)

RETZIUS, Magnus Gustaf; Dr. of Med.; late Professor of Anatomy; b. Stockholm, 17 Oct. 1842; s. of Professor of Anatomy and Physiology, Anders Retzius, at the Caroline Med. Chir. Institute in Stockholm; m. 1876, Anna Hierta; no c. *Educ.*: The Medical Schools in Stockholm and Upsala. Doctor of Medicine in Lund, 1871; Professor of Histology at the Caroline Institute, Stockholm, 1876; Professor of Anatomy, 1889; Member of the Academies of Science of Berlin, Petrograd, Paris, Rome, Washington, Vienna, Munich, Copenhagen, Christiania, Philadelphia, of the Academies of Medicine, Petrograd, Budapest, Bruxelles, Paris, Torino, etc.; Foreign Member of the Royal Societies of London,

RENTELL, Henry William Sidney. See page xxix.

Edinburgh, Göttingen, etc.; Hon. Dr. of Medicine and Philosophy and Jurisprudence of Bologna, Würzburg, Upsala, Harvard, Geneva, etc. *Publications :* Anatomical Researches, 1872 ; Anatomy of Nervous System, 1875-76 ; Finnish Craniology, 1878 ; Hearing Organs of Vertebrates, 1881 - 84 ; Human Brain, 1896 ; Ancient Swedish Skulls, 1898 ; Swedish Anthropology, 1902 ; Brain of Apes, 1906 ; Biological Researches, 1890-1912 ; various contributions. *Address :* Stockholm, 116 Drottninggatan, Sweden.   (*Died 21 July 1919.*)

KEVILLE, Rt. Rev. Mgr. Stephen, R C. Bishop of Sandhurst, Australia, since 1901 ; *b.* Wexford, 9 May 1844. *Educ. :* St. Peter's College, Wexford. Became a Member of the Order of St. Augustine, and proceeded to Belgium to prosecute his studies; after his ordination he was appointed to the Convent of his Order in Dublin ; during seven years he had charge of St. Laurence O'Toole's Seminary, Usher's Quay ; accompanied Most Rev. Dr. Crane to Australia, 1875 ; Coadjutor Bishop of Sandhurst, 1885 - 1901 ; Assistant Pontifical Throne, 1910 ; Knight of Holy Sepulchre, 1910. *Address :* Bendigo, Victoria (*Died 19 Sept. 1916.*)

REWAH, His Highness Maharaja Venkat Raman Singh Bahadur, G.C.S.I. ; Hon. Lieut. - Col. in Army, 1915 ; *b.* 22 July 1876 ; *s.* of His Highness Maharajah Raghuraj Singh Bahadur, G.C.S.I. ; *m.* Princesses of Dumraon and Rutlam, and daughter of a Parihar Thakur in Oudh. *Educ. :* in his own capital at Rewah. Invested with full powers as Ruling Chief of Rewah State in November 1895, at the age of 19 : had to combat three severe famines which strained the resources of the State to the utmost; Rewah a model State from an administrative point of view. *Decorated* for arrangements for relief of the sufferers in the Indian Famine of 1896-97 ; gave 5000 rupees for purchase of vaseline for Indian Troops during European War, 1915 ; placed all resources of the State at the disposal of the King-Emperor at the commencement of the War ; has presented a number of horses and two aeroplanes to Government ; is one of the Chiefs who have fitted up the Hospital Ship Loyalty. *Heir :* Maharajkumar-Prince Gulab-Singhji ; *b.* 12 March 1903. *Recreations :* an excellent sportsman and shot ; takes deep interest in many exercises, and army drill and discipline. *Address :* Rewah, Central India. (*Died 3 Nov. 1918.*)

REYMONT, Wladislaw, Polish novelist; Nobel Literary Prize, 1924 ; Chairman of the Polish Literary and Press Syndicate ; *b.* near Piotrkow, 1868. *Publications :* The Peasants ; The Promised Land ; The Comedian ; The Year 1793 ; Insurrection ; Autumn. 1925. *Address :* Warsaw.   (*Died 5 Dec. 1925.*)

REYNARD, Robert Proding, I.S.O. 1904 ; Secretary and Registrar of the Imperial Service Order since 1904 ; *b.* 22 June 1857 ; *y. s.* of late Charles Reynard, Nether Hall, Nafferton, Yorkshire ; *m.* 1885, Agnes, *e. d.* of late William Peter of Rockbank, Gisborne, Victoria ; one *d.* Appley, Uppingham ; Germany and France. Entered Civil Service, Class I., Open Competition, 1878 ; Clerk in Home Office 1885 - 1921. *Address :* 54 Cambridge Terrace, Hyde Park, W.2. *T. :* Paddington 6539. *Clubs:* Boodle's, Hurlingham. (*Died 6 Dec. 1926.*)

REYNARDSON, Col. Charles Birch-, J.P. ; *e. c.* of late Charles Thomas Samuel Birch Reynardson and Anne, *d.* of late Simon Yorke of Erddig, Co. Denbigh ; *b.* 10 Dec. 1845 ; *m.* 1875, Emma Maria, *d.* of Rev. William Stracey of Buxton, Norfolk ; two *d. Educ. :* Eton. Late Grenadier Guards ; A.D.C. to Viceroy of India, 1872-74 ; Egypt, 1882 ; High Sheriff of Rutland, 1895 ; patron of one living. *Address :* Holywell Hall, near Stamford. *Clubs:* Carlton, Guards'. (*Died 14 Nov. 1919.*)

REYNOLDS, Major Douglas, V.C. 1914 ; 37th Battery R.F.A. ; Knight of Legion of Honour ; *b.* 21 Sep. 1881 ; 2nd *s.* of late Lt.-Col. H. C. Reynolds, R.E. ; *m.* 1915, Doris, *d.* of William Petersen, Cherkley Court, Leatherhead. Entered army, 1900 ; Captain, 1908 ; served S. Africa, 1902 (Queen's medal, 3 clasps); European War, 1914-15 (severely wounded, D.S.O.). (*Died 23 Feb. 1916.*)

REYNOLDS, Ernest Septimus, B.Sc. (Manch.), L.S.A., M.R.C.S. (Eng.), M.D. (Lond.), F.R.C.P. (Lond.); D.L. Co. Lancaster; Consulting Physician to the Manchester Royal Infirmary; Lt.-Col. R.A.M.C.T. ; Fellow of Royal Society of Medicine ; Emeritus Professor of Clinical Medicine, Manchester University ; *b.* 7 Apr. 1861 ; *s.* of John Henry Reynolds, Manchester ; *m.* Rosa Maud, *d.* of Thomas Hooker ; one *d. Educ. :* Owens College, Manchester. Various appointments in teaching of hygiene and medicine ; resident medical officer for several years in asylums and general hospital ; late Senior Physician to the Ancoats Hospital, and Visiting Physician for sixteen years to Manchester Workhouse Infirmary ; Bradshaw Lectures, 1917 ; late Member of Council British Medical Association ; Past President of the Owens College Union, Pathological Society and Clinical Society of Manchester, the Manchester Medical Soc., and Neurolog. Section Royal Soc. of Medicine ; discoverer of arsenic as cause of epidemic beer poisoning in N. England in 1901. *Publications :* Hygiene for Beginners ; many medical publications, especially relating to nervous diseases, and numerous essays and reviews. *Address :* 2 St. Peter's Square, Manchester ; Platt Cottage, Rusholme, Manchester. *T. :* Manchester, Central 2893 ; Rusholme 72. *M. :* NC 2743 and NC 9783. (*Died 22 May 1926.*)

REYNOLDS, Sir Francis Jubal, Kt., *cr.* 1921 ; J.P. of County of Stafford ; *b.* 22 July 1857 ; 3rd *s.* of late Thomas Reynolds, Birmingham ; *m.* 1st, 1884, Julia (*deceased*), *d.* of Samuel Kirkby, London ; 2nd, 1919, Catherine, *widow* of George Trentham, Birmingham, *d.* of James Austin, Abberley, Worcestershire ; one *d. Educ. :* Birmingham. Admitted Solicitor, 1885 ; Commissioner for Oaths ; Perpetual Commissioner for taking acknowledgments of Deeds by Married Women ; Notary Public ; Organizer and Expert in Transport for Parliamentary and other Elections ; Brewery Director, and practises as a Solicitor, principally in brewery matters and licensed trade generally, in which he has been engaged throughout professional career, and regarded as having made a speciality therein. *Recreations :* fishing, photography, farming. *Address :* Cow Hayes, Solihull. *T. :* 159 ; 1 Lancaster Gate, W.2. *T. :* Paddington 3526 ; Antield Hey, Douglas, Isle of Man. *T. :* 460 ; Muchall Manor Farm, Wolverhampton ; 17 Waterloo Street, Birmingham. *T. :* Central 3422 ; 12 Queen Street, E.C.4. *T. :* City 7550. *Clubs:* Constitutional, Royal Thames Yacht. (*Died 23 Oct. 1924.*)

REYNOLDS, Herbert John, C.S.I. 1885 ; late I.C.S. *Educ. :* King's Coll. Cambridge ; *b.* 1832 ; *m.* 1856, Margaretta Catherine, *d.* of late H. F. Waring of Lyme Regis. Entered service, 1855 ; retired, 1889 ; sometime Member of Bengal Legislative Council and Board of Revenue. *Address :* Southcliff Tower, Cliff Cottage Road, Bournemouth, W. (*Died 30 Nov. 1916.*)

REYNOLDS, James Emerson, M.D., D.Sc., F.R.S. 1880 ; mem. of Roy. Coll. of Phys. Dublin and Edin. ; Pres. Chemical Soc. London, 1902-3 ; Vice-Pres. Roy. Soc. of London, 1902 ; *b.* Booterstown, Co. Dublin, 1844 ; *s.* of Dr. James Reynolds ; *m.* Janet, *o. c.* of Canon Finlayson, Christ Church Cathedral, Dublin, 1875. *Educ. :* Dublin University (M.D. and D.Sc., *causa honoris*). Became Keeper of Minerals at National Museum, Dublin, 1867 ; Professor of

Analytical Chemistry to Royal Dublin Society, 1870 ; Professor of Chemistry to Royal Coll. of Surgeons, Ireland, 1873 ; President Society of Chemical Industry, 1891 ; President of Section British Association, 1893 ; Professor of Chemistry and Chemical Philosophy Dublin University, 1875 - 1903 ; discovered a large number of chemical substances, including the primary Thiocarbamide and many of its allies, a new class of colloids, and later, several groups of organic and other derivatives of the element silicon ; these are described in a series of papers in Trans. Chemical Society and to Royal Society ; also papers on the Periodic Law, Spectrum Analysis, and Electro-Chemistry. *Publications:* Lectures on Experimental Chemistry, 1874 ; General Experimental Chemistry, 1880. *Recreations:* horticulture. *Address:* 3 Inverness Gardens, Kensington, W.   (*Died 19 Feb. 1920.*)

REYNOLDS, J. H. ; M.Sc. ; late Director of Higher Education and Principal, Municipal School of Technology, Manchester ; *m.* 1868, Ellen Ferguson ; one *s.* two *d.* Hon. Member Association of Directors of Education ; President of the Association of Technical Institutions, 1913 - 14 ; Vice - President National Association of Teachers of Manual Training ; Vice-President of Union of Lancashire and Cheshire Institutes ; Vice-President of the Old Owensian Association of the Victoria University of Manchester ; Member of the British Science Guild, and of the Teachers' Guild of Great Britain and Ireland ; Member and ex-Governor of the Manchester Whitworth Institute ; *b.* 8 Feb. 1842. *Address:* Glyn Malden, Cheadle Hulme, nr. Manchester.   (*Died 17 July 1927.*)

REYNOLDS, Stephen, B.Sc. ; Adviser on Inshore Fisheries to Development Commission since 1913, and Resident Inspector of Fisheries, S.W. area, since 1914 ; Member Fish Food and Motor Loan Committee, 1917 ; *b.* Devizes, Wilts, 16 May 1881. *Educ.:* The College, Devizes ; All Saints' School, Bloxham ; Manchester University. Left the Ecole des Mines, Paris, to become sub-editor of an Anglo-French Review, 1902 ; became associated with the Woolley brothers, fishermen, of Sidmouth, 1903 ; worked for one of them for several years, but gradually drifted from fishing into fishery affairs and controversies ; member Committee of Inquiry into Devon and Cornwall Fisheries, 1912 ; member Departmental Committee on Inshore Fisheries, 1913. *Publications:* Devizes and Roundabout, 1906 ; A Poor Man's House, 1908 ; The Holy Mountain: a Novel, 1909 ; Alongshore, 1910 ; Seems So ! a Working-Class View of Politics (in collaboration with Bob and Tom Woolley), 1911 ; How 'Twas : Short Stories and Small Travels, 1912 ; The Lower Deck, the Navy and the Nation, 1912 ; contributions, fictional, literary, on social questions from the working-class point of view, and on fisheries. *Address:* Sidmouth, S. Devon. *T.A.:* Stephen Reynolds, Sidmouth. *T.:* Sidmouth 95.   (*Died 14 Feb. 1919.*)

REYNOLDS, Warwick ; R.S.W. ; Black and White Artist ; *b.* Islington, 1880 ; *s.* of Warwick Reynolds, Black and White Artist, and Martha A. Dunhill ; *m.* 1906, Mary F. L. Kincaid ; two *d.* *Educ.:* private school, Stroud Green ; Life - drawing, Grosvenor Studio, Vauxhall Bridge Road, and St. John's Wood ; Julian's, Paris, 1908 ; studied animals at the Zoological Gardens, Regent's Park, 1895-1901. Working for the Press since 1895 ; contributor to London, Strand, Pearson's, Royal Windsor, Quiver, and other magazines ; exhibitor Royal Academy, Royal Scottish Academy, Royal Glasgow Institute of Fine Arts. *Recreations:* walking, reading. *Address:* 26 West Princes Street, Glasgow, C.4.   (*Died 15 Dec. 1926.*)

REYNOLDS, William George Waterhouse, J.P. ; Company Director ; M.P. (U.)

Southern Division of Leicester, 1922-23 ; *b.* 1860 ; *s.* of T. L. Reynolds, late of Southsea, and Ruth Augusta, of Australia ; *m.* Ida Maud (*d.* 1927), *d.* of late Joseph Roberts of Leicester ; one *d.* *Educ.:* Vicary's School, Southsea. A member of many War Committees, including Military Service Tribunal ; Vice-Chairman of War Pensions Committee at Leicester until 1921 ; Income Tax Commissioner for Leicestershire ; President of Leicester Central Conservative Association. *Recreations:* shooting, golf, fishing. *Address:* The Gables, St. Mary's Road, Leicester. *Clubs:* Junior Carlton, Constitutional, Unionist, 1900. (*Died 3 Sept. 1928.*)

REYNOLDS-BALL, Eustace Alfred, B.A., F.R.G.S. ; *e. s.* of late Rev. A. W. Ball, M.A., and Julia Maria, *e. d.* of late Rev. Anthony Ely, Vicar of Whitminster, Glos. ; *b.* Bridgewater, Somerset ; *m.* 1893, Mary Hannah, *d.* of late Edwin Andrew Chudleigh, Liverpool ; three *s.* one *d.* *Educ.:* Clifton College ; St. John's College, Oxford. Hon. Mod. Hist. 1882. Barrister-at-law, Inner Temple, 1891, but never practised. Travelled extensively in Europe, the Western Mediterranean, North Africa, Palestine, Canada, and Australasia ; Literary Editor, Court Journal, 1907-8 ; Editor, Travel and Exploration, 1909-11 ; employed temporarily by the War Office as Assistant Cable Censor, 1915 ; transferred to another Dept. of the Censorship, 1916 ; part owner of the Manor of Madeley Wood, Shropshire. *Publications:* Mediterranean Winter Resorts, 7th ed. 1914 ; South Italy and Egypt in the Picturesque Mediterranean, 1891 ; Cairo : The City of the Caliphs, 1897 ; Cairo of To-day, 10th ed. 1926 ; Paris in its Splendour, 2 vols. 1900 ; Jerusalem, 3rd ed. 1925 ; Practical Hints for Travellers in the Near East, 1903 ; Rome, 3rd ed. 1913 ; The Tourists' India, 1907 ; The Levantine Riviera (with Dr. W. T. Beeby), 1908 ; Sport on the Rivieras (with Sir C. A. Payton, "Sarcelle"), 1911 ; Oufit and Equipment for the Traveller, Explorer, and Sportsman (Ed.), 1912 ; Bradshaw's Through Routes to the Chief Cities of the World (Ed.), 1913 ; Unknown Italy : Piedmont and the Piedmontese, 1927 ; occasional articles. *Recreations:* cycle-touring, chess, and reading novels. *Address:* Villa Osella, Borgo Osella, Carmagnola, N. Italy. *Clubs:* Authors'; Turin Chess.
           (*Died 30 Mar. 1928.*)

RHEAD, George Woolliscroft, R.E., Hon. A.R.C.A. (Lond.); Member of the Art-Workers' Guild ; ex-Member of the Arts and Crafts Society and Royal Society of Arts ; Art Examiner to the Board of Education ; Honorary Freeman of the Worshipful Company of Fanmakers ; designer of H.M. Queen Mary's Coronation Fan ; painter, etcher and illustrator ; writer on art educational subjects. National Art scholar ; gold and silver medallist ; studied under Legros and Ford Madox Brown ; *m.* 2nd, 1914, Annie French, artist, Glasgow. *Paintings:* O Salutaris Hostia ; Vespers ; The Wise and Foolish Virgins ; A Sacrifice to Neptune ; The Sisters. *Etchings:* The Foundation of Manchester by the Romans ; The Dream of Sardanapalus ; and Crabtree ; after Ford Madox Brown ; also works by Watts, Pettie, Fildes, Boughton, Marcus Stone, John Philip, and others. *Publications:* A Handbook of Etching ; Studies in Plant Form ; The Principles of Design ; The Treatment of Drapery in Art ; Chats on Costume ; A History of the Fan ; Nature Studies for Schools ; British Pottery Marks ; Staffordshire Pots and Potters ; Modern Practical Design. *Illustrated works:* Bunyan's Pilgrim's Progress, and Life of Mr. Badman ; Tennyson's Idylls of the King. *Recreations:* music and shooting. *Address:* Doune Lodge, Oxford Road, Putney, S.W. (*Died 30 April 1920.*)

RHEAM, Henry Meynell, R.I. ; artist ; *b.* Birkenhead, 13 Jan. 1859 ; *m.* 1900, Alice

Elliott; one *s.* one *d.* *Educ.:* Cassel; Düsseldorf. Began to study painting at Heatherleys, 1884; afterwards in Paris under Bouguereau and Tony Robert Fleury; Member Royal Institute Painters in Water Colours, 1893; has worked mostly in Cornwall. *Address:* West Lodge, Alverton, Penzance. (*Died Nov. 1920.*)

RHIND, Lt.-Col. Sir (Thomas) Duncan, K.B.E., *cr.* 1919; C.B.E. 1918; T.D.; The Royal Scots; Statistical Adviser to Ministry of Pensions; *b.* 14 July 1871; *s.* of late John Rhind, Sculptor, A.R.S.A.; *m.* 1902, Mary Elizabeth, *d.* of late W. Matthews Gilbert, Edinburgh. *Educ.:* George Watson's College, Edinburgh. *Address:* 8 Gunsterstone Road, W.14. *T.:* Western 4497. *Club:* Scottish Artists', Edinburgh. (*Died 24 April 1927.*)

RHOADES, James; Hon. D.Litt. Durham University; *b.* 9 April 1841; *s.* of Rev. J. P. Rhoades, Rector of Clonmel, Ireland, and Philadelphia Palmer Tull; *m.* 1st, Charlotte Elizabeth, *d.* of late Major-Gen. F. P. Lester, Bombay Artillery; two *s.* two *d.*; 2nd, Alice, *d.* of late John Hunt, 22 Lancaster Gate, W. *Educ.:* Rugby; Trinity College, Cambridge (Scholar); Chancellor's Medallist for English Verse; B.A. Classical Tripos, 1864; M.A. 1865. Assistant Classical and House Master, Haileybury College, 1865-73; Sherborne School, 1880-93. *Publications:* Poems, 1870; Timoleon, a Dramatic Poem, 1875; translated Virgil's Georgics in English verse, 1881; ditto Æneid, vol. i. 1893, vol. ii. 1896; now re-issued with Eclogue added as The Poems of Virgil in The World's Classics, 1921; Dux Redux, or a Forest Tangle, a Comedy, 1887; Teresa, and other Poems, 1898; The Little Flowers of St. Francis in English Verse, 1904; Out of the Silence, 1906; The Training of the Imagination; An Essay; O Soul of Mine! a Poem, 1912; The City of the Five Gates: a Poem, 1913; Narrative Choruses in Pageants of Sherborne, Warwick, Bury St. Edmunds, Dover, Colchester, and York; numerous verse contributions to The Times and other journals; Words by the Wayside (Poems), 1915. *Recreations:* cycling and lawn tennis. *Address:* Kingsthorpe, Kelvedon, Essex. *Club:* Omar Khayyam. (*Died 16 Mar. 1923.*)

RHODES, Sir George, 1st Bt., *cr.* 1919; J.P. Cheshire; Chairman Dukinfield Petty Sessions; Chairman and Managing Director Thomas Rhodes, Ltd.; *o. surv. s.* of Thomas Rhodes, J.P.; *b.* 4 Sep. 1860; *m.* 1st, 1883, Margaret Catherine, *o. d.* of John Phillips, Liverpool; two *s.* one *d.*; 2nd, 1922, Diana, *widow* of H. Morgan Hill, of Washington, and *d.* of Dan Murphy, California. *Educ.:* Rugby and abroad. Contested (L.) Hyde Division of Cheshire, 1895. *Recreations:* travelling, golf. *Heir: s.* Lt.-Col. J. P. Rhodes. *Address:* 37 Pont Street, S.W.1; *T.:* Kens. 1910; Hollingworth, Cheshire; *T.A.:* Hollingworth, Colossus, Manchester; *T.:* Manchester City 1906. *M.:* EC 574, LY 5409. *Clubs:* Union, Baldwin, Ranelagh. (*Died Feb. 1924.*)

RHODES, George, K.C., 1909; Recorder of Oldham since 1914; *b.* Manchester, 1851; *s.* of John Rhodes, Manchester; *m.* 1882, Bessie (*d.* 1919), *niece* of Dr. Lancashire of Stand, near Manchester; three *s. Educ.:* Private School; Owens College, Manchester. In business as a merchant in Manchester up to 1889; Member Manchester City Council, 1890-1892; called to Bar, Gray's Inn, 1892; Bencher, 1909; J.P. Cheshire and Lancashire; Chairman, Shireoaks Colliery Co., Ltd., and Director, Thos. Rhodes & Son, Ltd., Hadfield Mills, near Manchester, and Lunderston Rubber Co., Ltd. *Publication:* Manchester Municipal Code. *Recreations:* golf, motoring, etc. *Address:* Allandale, Bowdon, Cheshire. *T.A.:* Allandale, Altrincham. *T.:* 224 Altrincham. *M.:* MA 9561. *Clubs:* National Liberal; Manchester Reform. (*Died 23 Sept. 1924.*)

RHODES, James Ford; writer of history; Lecturer on the History and Institutions of the United States of America in Oxford University, 1912; *b.* Cleveland, Ohio, 1 May 1848; *s.* of Daniel P. Rhodes and Sophia Russell; *m.* 1872, Ann Card; one *s. Educ.:* New York Univ.; Univ. of Chicago; School of Mines, Univ. of Berlin; LL.D. Adelbert, 1893, Harvard, Yale, 1901; Litt.D. Kenyon, 1908; Member of Massachusetts Historical Society; American Academy of Arts and Letters; American Philosophical Society; Corresponding Fellow British Academy; LL.D. Wisconsin, 1904; New York University, 1908; D.Litt. hon. Oxford, 1909; LL.D. Princeton, 1912, California, 1916; Litt.D. Brown, 1914; President American Historical Association, 1899; engaged in coal-mining and the manufacture of pig-iron, 1870-85; since 1885 in study and the writing of history; Loubat prize, American History, Berlin Academy of Science, 1901; Gold medal National Institute Arts and Letters, 1910; Harvard Phi Beta Kappa orator, 1915; Pulitzer prize, Columbia University, 1918. *Publications:* vols. i. to vii. of the History of the United States from the Compromise of 1850, to the Final Restoration of Home Rule at the South in 1877, 1892-1906; Historical Essays, 1909; Oxford Lectures on the American Civil War, 1913; History of the Civil War, 1917; From Hayes to McKinley, 1877-1896, 1919; The McKinley and Roosevelt Administrations, 1897-1909, 1922. *Recreation:* walking. *Address:* 392 Beacon Street, Boston, Mass. *T.:* Back Bay 692. *Clubs:* Tavern, Somerset, Algonquin, Boston; University, Authors', New York. (*Died 22 Feb. 1927.*)

RHONDDA, 1st Viscount, *cr.* 1918, of Llanwern; **David Alfred Thomas**, M.A., D.L., Glamorganshire; senior in the firm of Thomas and Davey, coal sale agents; Food Controller since 1917; *b.* Aberdare, 26 March 1856; *s.* of late Samuel Thomas, Yscyborwen, Aberdare; *m.* 1882, Sybil Margaret, *d.* of G. A. Haig, Penithon, Radnorshire; one *d. Educ.:* privately; Caius College, Cambridge (M.A.). Scholar of Jesus and Caius Colleges. President Cardiff Chamber of Commerce, 1895; President South Wales Liberal Federation, 1893-97; M.P. (L.) for Merthyr Burghs, 1888-1910; for Cardiff, 1910; President of Local Government Board, 1916-17; Managing Director of Cambrian Combine and other colliery companies in South Wales. *Recreation:* farming. *Heir:* none. *Address:* Llanwern, Newport, Monmouthshire; 122 Ashley Gardens, S.W. *T.:* P.O. Newport 512, and P.O. Victoria 327. *Clubs:* Reform, National Liberal, Argentine. (*Died 3 July 1918.*)

RIBBLESDALE, 4th Baron (*cr.* 1797), **Thomas Lister**, P.C., J.P.; *b.* Fontainebleau, 29 Oct. 1854; *s.* of 3rd Baron and Emma, *d.* of Col. Wm. Mure, Caldwell, Ayrshire; *S.* father, 1876; *m.* 1st, 1877, Charlotte Monckton (*d.* 1911), *d.* of Sir Charles Tennant, 1st Bt.; three *d.*; 2nd, 1919, Ava, *d.* of Mr. Willing, Philadelphia, and *widow* of Col. J. J. Astor. Sub.-Lieut. 64th Regt. 1873; Lieut. Rifle Brigade, 1874; Major, retired, 1878; Lord-in-Waiting, 1880-85; Master of Buckhounds, 1892-1895. Owns about 4800 acres. *Publications:* The Queen's Hounds and Stag-hunting Recollections, 1897; Charles Lister, 1917. *Heir:* none. *Address:* Gisburne Park, near Clitheroe. *Club:* Brooks's. (*Died 21 Oct. 1925.*)

RIBOT, Alexandre F.; Member of Senate; *b.* St. Omer, 1842; *m.* 1877, Minnie Burch of Chicago; one *s. Educ.:* Lycée of St. Omer. Admitted to Bar, 1864; became substitut du tribunal de la Seine, 1870; appointed by M. Dufaure secretary-general of ministère de la Justice, 1878; elected a member of chambre des deputes, 1878; Minister for Foreign Affairs in M. de Freycinet's ministry, 1890-93; during that period the alliance between France and

Russia was concluded ; President of Cabinet during stormy period of Panama case, and became, for second time, Prime Minister after resignation of M. Casimir-Perier ; Minister of Finance, 1914-17 ; Prime Minister, March-September 1917 ; during last few years has strongly opposed policy of retaliation against religious orders ; his most important speeches have been delivered on finance, foreign affairs, and the question of liberté d'enseignement ; Member of Académie française et Académie des Sciences Morales et Politiques ; Corresponding Fellow British Academy. *Publications:* Life of Lord Erskine, a speech delivered before the conférence des avocats, 1866 ; Réforme de l'enseignement secondaire, edited 1900 ; Discours Politiques, edited 1905.   *Address:* 11 Quai d'Orsay, Paris.   *(Died 13 Jan. 1923.)*

RICARDO, Lieut.-Col. Ambrose St. Quintin, C.M.G. 1917 ; C.B.E. 1919 ; D.S.O. 1900 ; Royal Inniskilling Fusiliers ; retired 1904 ; *b.* 21 Nov.1866 ; 4th *s.* of late Henry D. Ricardo of Gatcombe ; *m.* 1893, Elizabeth Alice, 2nd *d.* of Emerson T. Herdman of Sion House, Co. Tyrone. Entered army, 1888 ; Capt. 1897 ; served North-West Frontier, India, 1897-98 (medal with 2 clasps) ; S. Africa, 1899-1902 (despatches thrice, Queen's medal 3 clasps, King's medal 2 clasps, D.S.O.) ; Temp. Lt.-Col. Commanding 9th Service Batt. Royal Inniskilling Fusiliers in France, since Sep. 1914-18 (despatches, Bt. Major, C.M.G., Bt. Lt.-Col.) ; Brigadier (despatches seven times, C.B.E.).   *Address:* Sion Mills, Co. Tyrone.   *M.: J1 57.*   *(Died 9 July 1923.)*

RICARDO, Col. Francis Cecil, C.V.O. 1902 ; C.B.E.1920 ; retired pay, 1909 ; J.P., D.L., Berkshire ; *b.* 3 July 1852 ; *s.* of late Percy Ricardo of Bramley Park, Surrey ; *m.* May (*d.* 1907), *d.* of T. Littlefield. *Educ.:* Eton (Capt. of the Boats and Keeper of the Field, 1870-71). Entered army, 1872 ; Capt. 1884 ; Major, 1890 ; Lieut.-Colonel, 1897 ; Colonel, 1903 ; Adjutant Grenadier Guards, 1880-85 ; Brigade-Major, Home District, 1885-90 ; A.A.G. Home District, 1900-4 ; High Sheriff of Berkshire, 1913. *Address:* Lullebrook Manor, Cookham, Berks. *T.:* 26 Bourne End.   *Clubs:* Guards', Vikings', Leander, I Zingari ; Berkshire County.

    (Died 17 June 1924.)

RICARDO, Halsey Ralph, Architect ; Fellow of Royal Institute of British Architects ; Past Master Art Workers' Guild ; Member of the Arts and Crafts Society ; *b.* 6 Aug. 1854 ; *s.* of Harry Ralph and Anna (*née* Halsey) Ricardo ; *m.* 1882 ; one *s.* two *d. Educ.:* Rugby. Was articled for two years to Mr. John Middleton of Cheltenham ; afterwards served as pupil and clerk to Mr. Basil Champneys ; commenced individual practice in 1878 after some time spent abroad ; designed various houses, etc., including the coloured house in Addison Road, Kensington ; was also architect of the Terminal Railway Station at Howrah, Calcutta. *Publications:* various articles for the Arts and Crafts Exhibition Society, the Magazine of Art, and the Architectural Review. *Recreations:* listening to music ; idling in the country. *Address:* 13 Bedford Square, W.C.1 ; *T.:* Museum 0159 ; Graffham, Petworth, Sussex.   *(Died 15 Feb. 1928.)*

RICE, B. Lewis, C.I.E. 1884 ; late Director of Archæological Researches, Mysore ; *b.* 1837 ; *m.* 1869, Mary Sophia, *d.* of late John Garrett of Chorlton Lodge, New Hampton ; six *s.* four *d.* Was Director of Public Instruction in Mysore and Coorg ; Secretary to the Education Commission under Sir W. W. Hunter ; Secretary to Government of Mysore in Education and Miscellaneous Departments ; Hon. Fellow of University of Madras ; Acting Secretary Police Department. *Publications:* Mysore, 2 vols. (revised edition) ; Bibliotheca Carnatica, 6 vols. ; Epigraphia

Carnatica, 12 vols. ; Mysore and Coorg from the Inscriptions ; Mysore and Coorg in the Imperial Gazetteer of India ; Coorg Inscriptions (revised edition). *Address:* Greenhalgh, Maxted Park, Harrow-on-the-Hill. *T.:* Harrow 0779.   *(Died 10 July 1927.)*

RICE, Admiral Sir Ernest ; K.C.B., *cr.* 1914 ; *b.* 24 Feb. 1840 ; *s.* of Edward Royds Rice, of Dane Court, Kent ; *m.* 1st, 1870, Laura (*d.* 1899), *d.* of Edward York, of Wighill Park, Tadcaster ; 2nd, 1903, Fanny (*d.* 1923), *d.* of Clinton George Dawkins, and *widow* of Lt.-Col. Gunning, K.R.R. ; two *d.* Present in H.M.S. Odin, bombardment and taking of Bomarsund, 1855 ; severe boat action Gamla Carleby ; bombardment of Sveaborg (medal) ; Commander, 1870 ; Assistant Director of Naval Ordnance at Admiralty, 1870-74 ; Captain, 1878 ; Naval Attaché, 1879-83 ; Rear-Admiral, 1893 ; Vice-President Ordnance Select Committee, 1894-96 ; Admiral Supt. H.M. Dockyard, Portsmouth, 1896-99 ; made all the arrangements in Paris with French Minister of Marine for joint occupation of Egypt, 1882 ; ordered to Egypt same year ; present at battle of Tel-el-Kebir (medal and bronze star) ; Vice-Admiral, 1899 ; commanding Coastguard and Naval Reserves, 1904. *Decorated:* Baltic medal, 1854-55 ; Egyptian medal, 1882 ; Khedive's star, 1882. *Recreations:* hunting, shooting, golf. *Address:* Dane Court, Dover, Kent ; Bramber, Steyning, Sussex.   *Club:* United Service.

    (Died 15 April 1927.)

RICH, Alfred William, Water Colour Painter, and Teacher ; *b.* at Gravely, Sussex, 4 March 1856 ; 2nd *s.* of Stiles Rich of Tetbury, Glos. ; *m.* 1884, Cassandra Philippa, *e. d.* of Edward Berney, F.R.C.S., Croydon ; no *c.* Brought to London by his parents, 1860 ; lived in various parts of the North of London till 1874, when removed to Croydon ; apprenticed to an heraldic draughtsman, 1871, and practized that work till 1890 ; entered the Slade School under late Professor Legros, and later Professor F. Brown till 1896 ; Member of the New English Art Club, 1898, and of late years a Member and on the Council of the International Society of Sculptors, Painters, and Gravers ; most of his work is executed direct from nature ; his paintings are at the Print Room, British Museum the Victoria and Albert Museum, The Tate Gallery, the Musée du Luxembourg, the Walker Art Gallery, Liverpool, the Corporation Galleries of Birkenhead, Oldham, Dudley, Brighton, the Fitzwilliam Museum, Johannesburg, Pietermaritzburg, and private collections. *Publication:* Water-Colour Painting. *Recreations:* very fond of all sports, and practised them in a casual way ; played football (Rugby Union) for Croydon as a young man ; devoted to bicycling as a touring rider, but ever raced. *Address:* Ovingdene, Carlisle Avenue, St. Albans, Herts.   *Clubs:* Savile, Chelsea Arts.   *(Died Sept. 1922.)*

RICH, Rev. Leonard James, Hon. Canon of Liverpool. *Address:* St. Margaret's Anfield, Liverpool.   *(Died 30 Aug. 1920.)*

RICHARD, Timothy, D.D., Litt.D., Missionary and Mandarin; General Secretary Society for Diffusion of Christian and General Knowledge among the Chinese, now called the Christian Literature Society for China ; *b.* Carmarthenshire, 1845 ; parents farmers ; *m.* 1878, Mary Martin, Edinburgh (*d.* 1903). *Educ.:* Swansea Normal College ; Haverfordwest Baptist College, Pembrokeshire. Missionary in China under Baptist Missionary Society ; Public Almoner in the greatest famine in History ; Lecturer to Mandarins ; Adviser of the Governor of Shansi ; Editor of Daily, Weekly, and Monthly Organs ; Publisher, with his colleagues, of more than three hundred books ; Reformer, appointed as one of the Emperor Kuang

Hsu's advisers; Arbitrator, chosen by the Chinese plenipotentiaries to settle affairs after the Boxer massacres; Educator, founded the Modern Imperial University in Shansi; Mandarin, appointed religious adviser to the Chinese Government, and given the rank of mandarin of the first grade; Double Dragon Decoration, 2nd order, 2nd grade. *Publications:* in English— Historical Evidences of Christianity; Conversion by the Million, 2 vols.; The Awakening of Faith in New Buddhism (a translation); Guide to Buddhahood (a translation); The New Testament of Higher Buddhism, 1910; A Mission to Heaven, being a translation of an ancient Chinese epic and allegory, 1913; books and pamphlets on the forces which make for the rise and progress of nations, in Chinese. *Recreations:* none, if not electricity, petrol engines, and flying machines. *Address:* 143 North Szechuen Road, Shanghai. *T.A.:* Literature, Shanghai. *T.:* 303.   (*Died 17 April 1919.*)

RICHARDS, Hon. Albert Elswood, Puisne Judge of Court of Appeal, Manitoba, since 1906; *b.* Toronto, 10 July 1848; *s.* of late Hon. Stephen Richards, Q.C., of Toronto; *m.* 1877, Harriet Edith, *d.* of late J. A. Henderson, Q.C., of Kingston, Ontario. *Educ.:* Upper Canada College, Toronto; University College, Toronto. Called to Bar of Ontario, 1874, and to Bar of Manitoba, 1882; practised at Brockville, Ontario, 1874-82, and at Winnipeg, Manitoba, 1882-99; Puisne Judge of Court of King's Bench, Manitoba, 1899-1906. *Address:* Winnipeg, Canada. *Club:* Manitoba. (*Died 27 May 1918.*)

RICHARDS, Edward Windsor, J.P., D.L.; Past President Iron and Steel Institute, and of Institution of Mechanical Engineers; High Sheriff of Monmouthshire, 1902. *Address:* Plâs Llecha, Tredunnock, Caerleon, Monmouthshire. *Clubs:* Junior Carlton, Royal Societies, Royal Automobile. (*Died 12 Nov. 1921.*)

RICHARDS, Rear - Admiral G. E.; retired; *b.* 10 Dec. 1852; *e. s.* of late Admiral Sir G. H. Richards, K.C.B.; *m.* Emily, *y. d.* of late John de Courcy Bremer of N.S.W., Australia; two *a.* *Educ.:* Stubbington House, Fareham. Employed on Surveying Service in Japan, Australia, N. America, and coast of England during career in Navy. *Recreations:* shooting and fishing. *Address:* Silverton Grange, Silverton, Devon. (*Died 8 Dec. 1927.*)

RICHARDS, Sir Henry Erle, K.C.S.I. *cr.* 1909; K.C. 1905; *b.* 6 Dec. 1861; *e. s.* of late Rev. Prebendary Richards; *m.* 1897, Isabel, *e. d.* of late Spencer Butler of Lincoln's Inn; four *d.* *Educ.:* Eton; New College, Oxford. Called to Bar, 1887; joined Oxford Circuit; was Counsel for Great Britain in Samoa arbitration, 1902, and in Venezuela arbitration at Hague, 1903; legal member of Viceroy of India's Council 1904-1909; Counsel for Newfoundland and Canada in North Atlantic Coast Fisheries Arbitration at the Hague, 1910; Counsel to the India Office, 1911-21; Chichele Professor of International Law and Fellow of All Souls College, Oxford, B.C.L., M.A., 1911. *Publications:* lectures and articles on legal subjects. *Address:* 4 Temple Gardens, E.C.; Baysworth Corner, Foxcombe Hill, Oxford. *Club:* United University. (*Died 23 April 1922.*)

RICHARDS, Sir Henry George, K.B.E., *cr.* 1919; Kt. *cr.* 1911; K.C., M.A.; Puisne Judge High Court of Judicature for the North - Western Provinces of India, 1905 - 11; Chief Justice 1911; retired, 1919; *e. surv. s.* of late John Henry Richards, Chairman of Quarter Sessions for County for County of Mayo, Ireland; *g.s.* of the late Right Hon. John Richards, Baron of Court of Exchequer in Ireland; *b.* 21 Sep. 1860; *m.* 1891, Frances Maud Lyster, O.B.E., *y. d.* of late Henry M. Smythe of Barbavilla, Co. Westmeath. *Educ.:* Trinity College, Dublin. Called to Irish Bar, 1888; joined Connaught Circuit;

extensive and varied practice in Irish Courts; Senior Crown Prosecutor for Counties of Roscommon and Mayo. *Recreations:* riding, hunting, shooting, polo. *Address:* Ballygueni, Hluhluwe, Zululand, S. Africa. *Clubs:* East Indian United Service; University, Dublin.   (*Died 10 Mar. 1928.*)

RICHARDS, Herbert Paul; Subwarden, Fellow since 1870, and Lecturer (late Tutor), Wadham College, Oxford; *b.* Kensington, 15 Oct. 1848; 2nd *s.* of Thomas Richards, printer. *Educ.:* Kensington Grammar School; Balliol College, Oxford (Scholar). Examiner at various times in Honour Moderations and Literæ Humaniores, Oxford; Senior Proctor, 1886-87. *Publications:* Notes on Xenophon and Others, 1907; Aristophanes and Others, 1909; Platonica, 1911; Aristotelica, 1915; articles and reviews in Classical Review and Classical Quarterly. *Address:* Wadham College, Oxford.   (*Died 18 Feb. 1916.*)

RICHARDS, John Morgan; Chairman, John Morgan Richards & Sons, Ltd., London, E.C.; *b.* Aurora, New York, U.S.A., 16 Feb. 1841; 2nd *s.* of Rev. James Richards, D.D., late of Charlestown, West Virginia, U.S.A.; *m.* Laura Hortense (*d.* 1914); two *s.* one *d.* *Educ.:* public schools in U.S.A. Connected with commercial firms in U.S.A. until 1867; in 1867 came to England, and resided here since; proprietor of The Academy, 1888-1905. *Publications:* With John Bull and Jonathan; Sixty Years of an American's Life in England and United States, 1905; The Life and Letters of Mrs. Craigie (John Oliver Hobbes), 1911; Almost Fairyland, 1914. *Recreations:* walking and driving. *Address:* Steephill Castle, Ventnor, Isle of Wight. *T.A.:* Steephill, Ventnor. *T.:* 53 Ventnor. *Clubs:* Reform; County and Castle, Isle of Wight.   (*Died 11 Aug. 1918.*)

RICHARDS, Col. Samuel Smith Crosland, C.B. 1897; *b.* 1841; 2nd *s.* of late Samuel Richards, M.D.; formerly Lieut.-Col. Comdg. and Hon.Col. 19th Middlesex Vol. Rifles,V.D.; received the Jubilee Decoration, being in command of the North London Vol. Inf. Brigade during Procession of 22 July 1897; J.P. for Leicestershire; *m.* 1884, Josephine, *d.* of late Charles Thomson, New York; two *s.* *Educ.:* Univ. Coll. School and Coll. London. *Address:* 3 Brunswick Court, Brunswick Place, Hove. *Clubs:* Constitutional; New, Brighton.   (*Died 6 Oct. 1918.*)

RICHARDSON, Sir Alexander, Kt., *cr.* 1922; M.P. (C.) Gravesend, 1918 - 23; *b.* Dumbarton, 27 March 1864; *s.* of James Richardson; *m.* 1886, Georgina, *d.* of Capt. George Fleming, merchant marine; one *s.* one *d.* A student of engineering in all its applications; was a member of the editorial Staff of Engineering from 1888, being successively Assistant Editor, Joint Editor, and sole Editor, and a Managing Director of Engineering, Ltd.: retired in 1924, and became Consulting Editor of Shipbuilding and Shipping Record, Marine Engineering and Motor Shipbuilder, and other technical journals; is an Associate of the Institution of Naval Architects; Vice - President of the Junior Institution of Engineers and Companion of the Institution of Marine Engineers. *Publications:* The Evolution of the Parsons Steam Turbine; The Man Power of the Nation, and other works, as well as contributions on engineering, shipbuilding, naval and economic subjects; has contributed to the Naval Annual since 1908, principally on machinery of all types for war, including airships and aeroplanes, and in 1921 became Governing Director and Joint-Editor, the title becoming Brassey's Naval and Shipping Annual. *Address:* 33 Tothill Street, Westminster, S.W.1; *T.:* Victoria 8836; Garshake, Clarence Road, Clapham Park, S.W.4; *T.:*

887

RICHARDS, Theodore William, Hon. LL.D. See page xxix.

Brixton 1666. *Clubs:* Carlton. Authors.
(*Died 30 Mar. 1923.*)

RICHARDSON, Ven. Edward Shaw,
M.A. (Cantab.); Vicar and Rural Dean of
Blackburn; Archdeacon of Blackburn, since
1920; Proctor in Convocation and Honorary
Canon of Manchester, 1919; *b.* 1862; *s.* of Rev.
William Richardson and Mary Anne Shaw;
one *s.* three *d. Educ. :* Rossall School; Trinity
College, Cambridge. Curate of Corbridge-on-
Tyne; St. Paul's, Kersal; and St. Philip's,
Ancoats, Manchester; Rector of St. Paul's,
Hulme, Manchester; Vicar of St. Matthew's,
Bolton, 1895-1909; Rector of St. George's,
Hulme, and Canon Residentiary of Manchester,
1909-19. *Recreations :* games and sports, played
football for Northumberland and hockey for
Lancashire. *Address:* The Vicarage, Blackburn.
(*Died 15 Nov. 1921.*)

RICHARDSON, Maj. Francis James,
D.S.O. 1900; late A. and S. Highlanders; Major
4th Batt.; D.A.D. of Remounts, Eastern
Command; *b.* 6 March 1866; *s.* of late Francis
Richardson; *m.* 1899, Rhoda Dagmar, *d.* of
Rastell Bevis; one *s.* one *d. Educ. :* Charter-
house; Jesus Coll. Cambridge. Joined 2nd Batt.
A. and S. Highlanders, 1888; served with 1st
Battalion in South Africa, 1899-1901; Modder
River, Paardeberg, Driefontein, Johannesburg,
and Diamond Hill (despatches, medal six clasps,
D.S.O.). *Address:* The Coombes, Marston
Trussell, Market Harboro. *Clubs:* Naval and
Military; Kildare Street, Dublin.
(*Died 11 Dec. 1917.*)

RICHARDSON, Frank; Barrister and
Novelist; *b.* 1870. *Educ.:* Marlborough; Christ
Church, Oxford; called to Bar, 1891. *Publica-*
tions : King's Counsel, 1902; Semi-Society, 1903;
The Man who Lost his Past, 1903; The Bayswater
Miracle, 1903; There and Back 1904; The
Secret Kingdom, 1905; 2835 Mayfair, 1907;
Love and all about it, 1907; Bunkum, 1907;
The Worst Man in the World, 1908; The
Other Man's Wife, 1908; More Bunkum, 1909;
Whiskers and Soda, 1910; Shavings, 1911; Love
and Extras, 1911. *Recreation :* The Whisker
Question. *Address:* 4 Albemarle Street, W.
T. : 2835 Mayfair. *Clubs:* Garrick, Devonshire.
(*Died 31 July 1917.*)

RICHARDSON, Ven. James Banning,
M.A., D.C.L., Rector of St. John's, London
Township, 1899-1919; retired from parochial
service, 30 June 1919; Archdeacon of London
since 1903; *b.* 23 Nov. 1843; *s.* of James
Richardson; *m.* 1869, Mary Jane, *d.* of Laurence
Tremain, M.D.; two *s.* four *d. Educ. :* privately;
Collegiate School and University, King's College,
Windsor, Nova Scotia. Ordained, 1866; Rector
of Dartmouth, N.S., 1868-74; St. Thomas, Hamil-
ton, Ont., 1874-77; Memorial Church, London,
Ont., 1877-99; Hon. Canon, Saskatchewan, 1885;
Canon of S. Paul's Cathedral, London, Ont.,
1889. *Publications :* Concerning the Church,
1901; Diocese of Huron, its past fifty years,
1907. *Address:* 1095 Richmond Street, W.,
London, Ontario. (*Died 3 May 1923.*)

RICHARDSON, James Nicholson;
Liberal Unionist; chairman of Bessbrook
Spinning Co.; member of Armagh Grand Jury;
b. 1846; *e. s.* of late John G. Richardson;
m. 1st, 1867, Sophia Malcomson, Portlaw,
Co. Waterford; 2nd, 1893, Sara Alexander,
d. of Samuel Alexander Bell, Lurgan, Co.
Armagh. *Educ.:* Tottenham. Spent earlier
years assisting father and uncles in linen business
of Ulster, in which the family has been engaged
from father to son for 150 years; M.P. Co.
Armagh, 1880-85. Sold 5000 acres to tenants
under Wyndham Act. *Publications:* The Quakers
at Lurgan and Grange; O'Neill of Mourne; Concerning Servants. *Recreations:* riding, golf,
water-colour sketching. *Address:* Mount Caulfield, Bessbrook, Co. Armagh. *T.A:* Richardson, Bessbrook. *T.:* Newry 14. *M.:* O 1558.
Club: Reform. (*Died 11 Oct. 1921.*)

**RICHARDSON, Engineer-Rear-Adm.
John,** R.N., C.B. 1916; *b.* 1862; *s.* of late
John Strachan Richardson; *m.* 1896, Elizabeth Maria, *e. d.* of late A. B. M. C. Chiappini,
M.I.A., Cape Town; three *s. Educ. :* Peterhead Academy; privately. Joined H.M.S.
Marlborough, Training School for Engineer
Officers, R.N., 1878; R. N. College, Greenwich,
1884-5; Engineer-Comdr., 1903; Engineer-Capt.,
1912; Engineer-Rear-Adm. 1917. Served Benin
Expedition 1894, landed from H.M.S. Philomel
(despatches, promotion, medal and clasp); S.
African War, 1899-1902 (despatches, promotion,
2 medals 3 clasps); European War, 1914-
1917, including Jutland Bank (despatches,
C.B.); on staff of Vice-Admirals commanding
4th Battle Squadron, 1912-17; on staff of Vice-
Admirals commanding East Coast of England,
1917-19; Coronation Medal, 1911; Order of St.
Anne (Russia), 2nd class, with crossed swords;
retired, 1919. *Recreations :* cricket, golf, fishing, shooting. *Club:* Caledonian United Service, Edinburgh. (*Died 7 July 1923.*)

**RICHARDSON, Major - Gen. John
Booth,** Colonel Commandant Royal Artillery;
b. 1838; *e. s.* of Sir John Richardson, C.B.,
F.R.S., etc., Arctic Traveller and Naturalist;
m. 1878, Annie Leslie, *d.* of R. Dalglish; one *s.*,
Capt. late Lincolnshire Regt. *Educ. :* Chol-
mondeley School; R.M.A., Woolwich. Served
in West and East Indies, Burmah, and Mediter-
ranean; Commanded R.A., Western District;
Commandant School of Gunnery; G.O.C., R.A.
Gibraltar, etc. *Publications :* many professional
pamphlets and works; Silver Medallist R.A.
Institute, etc. *Address:* Halton House,
Spilsby. (*Died 31 Oct. 1923.*)

RICHARDSON, Ven. John Gray, M.A.;
b. 1849; *e. s.* of Samuel Richardson, Sheffield;
m. 1878, Jane Temple (*d.* 1923), *d.* of Rev.
W. H. Perkins, Tunbridge Wells; one *s.* one *d.*
Educ. :, Trin. Coll., Camb. (Scholar and Fellow).
Vicar of St. Michael, Cambridge, 1877-78; of
Monk's Kirby, Withybrook, and Copston, War-
wickshire, 1878-84; of St. John Evangelist,
Darlington, 1884-86; Select Preacher at Cam-
bridge, 1882-84-85; Chairman Nottingham School
Board, 1889-92, 1892-95; Vicar, St. Mary's,
Nottingham, 1886-1900; Archdeacon of Notting-
ham, 1894-1913; Rector of Southwell St. Mary's,
1900-13. *Address:* Combe Fishacre, Newton
Abbot. (*Died 13 July 1924.*)

RICHARDSON, Spencer William,
D.Sc., M.A.; F.Inst.P.; *b.* 13 Dec. 1869; 2nd
s. of Alfred Spencer Richardson, D.D. *Educ. :*
The School of Malvern Link; The High
School, Newcastle, Staffs; University Col-
lege, Aberystwith; Trinity College, Cambridge.
D.Sc. London (First in First Class Honours
in Physics at B.Sc.); Research Student of
Trinity College, Cambridge; Certificate of
Research and M.A., Cambridge; late 1851
Exhibition Research Scholar, etc.; formerly
Lecturer in Physics and Mathematics at Uni-
versity College, Nottingham; at the request of
the Southampton Education Authority, pre-
pared a scheme for the co-ordination of educa-
tion in Southampton, 1906; Principal of the
University College, Southampton, 1902-12; Pro-
fessor of Physics at the University College,
Southampton, 1902-12; for four years a Mem-
ber of the Council of the Association of
Technical Institutions of Great Britain and
Ireland; Research Worker in the Davy Faraday Research Laboratory, Royal Institution.
Publications: contributions to scientific societies
and journals on Electricity and Magnetism;
Captain (R.), T.F. *Recreations :* lawn tennis,
rifle-shooting, theatre, etc. *Address:* Royal
Institution, 21 Albemarle Street, W.
(*Died 10 April 1927.*)

RICHARDSON, Thomas, Labour candidate, Federal by-election, 1920, in Yale constituency, British Columbia ; M.P. (Lab.) Whitehaven, 1910-18 ; *b.* Usworth, Durham, 6 June 1868 ; *m.* 1888, Mary E. Purvis. Late member Durham Miners Executive and Durham Coal Conciliation Board. *Address :* 10 Denny Crescent, S.E.11. (*Died 22 Oct. 1928.*)

RICHARDSON - GRIFFITHS, Major Charles Du Plat, D.S.O. 1900 ; late the Gloucestershire Regiment ; *b.* 2 June 1855 ; *m.* 1894, Florence, *d.* of late H. Schwabe. Entered army, 1875 ; Captain, 1885 ; Major, 1896 ; served Afghan War, 1879-80 (medal) ; South Africa, 1900 - 2 (despatches, Queen's medal three clasps, King's medal two clasps) ; European War, 1914-19. (*Died 1 July 1925.*)

RICHEPIN, Jean ; poet, romancer, conférencier, dramatist ; Commandeur de la Légion d'honneur ; Chancellor of French Academy since 1923 ; *b.* Medéah, Algérie, 1849 ; *s.* of Dr. Richepin, army surgeon ; *m.* 1st, 1879 ; divorced, 1902 ; 2nd, 1902 ; four *s. Educ.:* Ecole Normale Supérieure. *Publications :* Poetry—La Chanson des gueux, 1876 ; Les Caresses, 1877 ; Les Blasphèmes, 1884 ; La Mer, 1886 ; Mes Paradis, 1894 ; La Bombarde, 1899. Théâtre—La Glu, 1883 ; Nana-Sahib, 1883 ; Le Chien de garde, 1889 ; Monsieur Scapin (Comédie-Française), 1886 ; Le Flibustier (*idem*), 1888 ; Par le glaive (*idem*), 1892 ; Vers la joie (*idem*), 1894 ; La Martyre (*idem*), 1898 ; Don Quichotte (*idem*), 1905 ; Le Chemineau, 1897 ; Les Truands, 1899 ; Le Mage (Opéra, avec Massenet), 1897 ; Miarka (Opéra-Comique, avec Alexandre Georges, 1905 ; Théâtre Chimérique (27 actes), 1896 ; La Belle-au-bois-dormant, 1907 ; La Route d'émeraude, 1908 ; Le Tango, 1913 ; Macbeth, 1914. Roman—Jules Vallés, 1872 ; Madame André, 1877 ; Les Morts bizarres, 1877 ; La Glu, 1881 ; Le Pavé, 1883 ; Miarka la fille à l'Ourse, 1884 ; Braves Gens, 1886 ; Césarine, 1888 ; Le Cadet, 1890 ; Truandailles, 1890 ; Cauchemars, 1892 ; La Miseloque, 1893 ; L'Aimé, 1893 ; Flamboche, 1895 ; Les Grandes Amoureuses, 1896 ; Contes de la décadence romaine, 1898 ; Lagibasse, roman magique, 1900 ; Contes espagnols, 1901 ; L'Aile, 1911 ; Proses de Guerre, 1916 ; La Clique, 1917 ; Le Coin des Fous, 1921 ; Poetry, Les Glas, 1922 ; Interludes. 1923. *Recreations :* chase, fencing, gymnastics, yachting. *Address :* 8 Villa Guibert, 83 rue de la Tour, XVIᵉ, Paris ; La Carriere au Val-André (C. du N.) ; Palma de Mallorca (Iles Baléares).
(*Died 11 Dec. 1926.*)

RICHMOND, 7th Duke of (*cr.* 1675), **Charles Henry Gordon-Lennox,** K.G. 1905 ; G.C.V.O. 1904 ; C.B. 1902 ; Earl of March, Baron of Settrington, Duke of Lennox, Earl of Darnley, Baron Methuen, 1675 ; Duke of Gordon, Earl of Kinrara, 1876 ; Duke d'Aubigny (France), 1683-84 ; Hereditary Constable of Inverness Castle ; *b.* London, 27 Dec. 1845 ; *e. s.* of 6th Duke of Richmond and Frances, *d.* of Algernon Frederick Greville ; *S.* father, 1903 ; *m.* 1st, Amy, *d.* of Percy Ricardo, 1868 (*d.* 1879) ; two *s.* two *d.* ; 2nd, Isabel, *d.* of William George Craven, 1882 (*d.* 1887) ; two *d. Educ. :* Eton. Entered Grenadier Guards, 1865 ; Col. 3rd R. Sussex Regt. ; A.D.C. to Queen Victoria, King Edward and King George ; M.P. West Sussex, 1869-85 ; S.W. Sussex, 1885-88 ; served S. Africa, 1901-2 (despatches) ; Chancellor, Aberdeen University, 1917. *Recreations :* hunting, shooting, fishing, racing. Owns about 286,500 acres. *Heir : s.* Earl of March. *Address :* 67 Cadogan Square, S.W.1 ; *T. :* Victoria 4360 ; Goodwood, Chichester ; Gordon Castle, Fochabers, Banffshire ; Glenfiddich Lodge, Dufftown, Scotland. *Clubs :* Carlton, Turf. (*Died 13 Jan. 1928.*)

RICHMOND, Maurice Wilson ; Professor of English Law, Victoria College, Welling-

ton, since 1906 ; *b.* 26 April 1860. *Educ. :* Nelson College ; University Coll., London ; University of New Zealand. Barrister and Solicitor, 1883. *Address :* Wellington, New Zealand.
(*Died 26 Feb. 1919.*)

RICHMOND, Sir William Blake, K.C.B., *cr.* 1897 ; M.A., R.A. 1895 ; painter ; *b.* London, 29 Nov. 1842 ; *s.* of George Richmond, R.A., D.C.L., LL.D. ; *m.* 1867, Clara Jane (*d.* 1915), *d.* of William Richards, Cardiff ; four *s.* one *d.* Student Royal Acad. (2 silver medals) ; A.R.A. 1888 ; exhibited at R.A. portrait of his two brothers, 1860 ; Slade Professor at Oxford, 1878-83 ; President of Society of Miniature Painters, 1899 ; has spent much time in Italy, Greece, and Egypt. *Publications :* The Silver Chain, 1917 ; Assisi ; Impressions of Half a Century, 1919. *Address :* Beavor Lodge, Beavor Lane, Hammersmith, W. *T. :* Hammersmith 758. *Club :* Athenæum. (*Died 11 Feb. 1921.*)

RICHTER, Dr. Hans, M.V.O. 1904 ; Conductor to the Hallé Concerts Society, 1900-11 ; *b.* Raab, Hungary, 4 April 1843 ; *m.* a Hungarian lady. *Educ. :* Louenburg School, Vienna ; studied under Kleinecke (the horn) and Sechter at the Conservatorium in Vienna. Assumed direction of the Court Opera Theatre, Vienna, 1875 ; in 1876 directed Bayreuth Festival ; commenced orchestral concerts in London from 1879 ; created Doctor of Music (*honoris causa*) by the University of Oxford, 1886. (*Died 5 Dec. 1916.*)

RICKARD, Rev. Herbert, M.A., Vicar of Amberley with Houghton since 1918 ; Prebendary of Chichester Cathedral since 1905 ; *s. s.* of late John Rickard of Derby and London ; *m.* 1890, M. R. Spanoghe (*d.* 1900). *Educ. :* Derby School ; King's College School, London ; Jesus College, Oxford. Open Classical Scholar ; First Class Mods., 1883 ; Second Class Greats, 1886. Ordained, 1886, to Curacy of St. Paul's, Lozells, Birmingham ; Assist. Org. Secretary of A.C.S., 1890 ; Curate of Christ Ch., Epsom, 1892 ; Vice-Principal of Chichester Theological College, 1897 ; Principal, 1899-1918. *Recreation :* cycling. *Address :* Amberley Vicarage, Sussex. *T.A. :* Chichester. (*Died 1 Dec. 1926.*)

RICKARDS, Artnur George, K.C. ; V.D. ; *o. s.* of Sir George Kettilby Rickards, K.C.B. ; *b.* 1848 ; *m.* 1882, Elinor Frances, *y. d.* of Charles Butler of Warren Wood, Herts ; two *s.* two *d. Educ. :* Eton ; Brasenose College, Oxford (M.A.). Called to Bar, Inner Temple, 1875 ; Member of Midland Circuit ; Q.C. 1899 ; Bencher of Inner Temple, 1909 ; served 23 years in the Volunteer Forces, retiring as Major, 1896 ; Vice-Chairman of the Central (Unemployed) Body for London ; J.P. Gloucestershire ; a member of Executive Committee of the National Service League ; and of the Military Appeal Tribunals for London and Gloucestershire. *Publications :* the Metropolis Water Act, 1902 ; and Social Reform and National Military Training. *Address :* 20 Southwell Gardens, S.W.7. *T. :* Western 2964 ; Barn's Close, Amberley, Glos. *Clubs :* Athenæum, British Empire. (*Died 28 July 1924.*)

RICKARDS, Rev. Marcus Samuel, Canon, poet and naturalist ; *b.* Exeter, 28 April 1840 ; *y. s.* of late Robert Hillier Rickards, J.P. and D.L., of Llantrissant House, Glamorganshire, and Caroline, *d.* of late Col. Andrew Knox, M.P., of Prehen, Co. Londonderry ; *m.* 1865, Edith Elizabeth (*d.* 1927), *d.* of late Charles Anson ; two *s.* one *d. Educ. :* Merton College. Oxford. B.A. (Theological Honours), 1875 ; M.A. 1878. Admitted a Solicitor (with Honours of the Incorporated Law Society). 1862 ; practised for many years in Bristol ; Deacon, 1875 ; Priest, 1876 ; Curate of Holy Trinity, Clifton, until 1889 : Vicar of Twigworth, Gloucester, 1889-1913 ; a Vice-President of the Poetry Society ; F.L.S. 1871. *Publications :* Sonnets and Reveries, 1889 ; Creation's Hope, 1890 ; Songs of Universal Life, 1891 : Lyrical Studies,

1892; Lyrics and Elegiacs, 1893; Poems of Life and Death, 1895; The Exiles: a Romance of Life, 1896; Poems of a Naturalist, 1896; Music from the Maze, 1899; Gleams through the Gloom, 1900; The Clock of Arba: a Romance, 1901; Musings and Melodies, 1902; Soliloquies in Song, 1903; Poems, Old and New, 1905; Lyrics of Life and Beauty, 1906; Musical Imaginings, 1908; Twilight Music, 1909; Echoes of the Infinite, 1909; Garnered Beauty, 1910; Musical Echoes, 1911; Reflected Radiance, 1912; A Soul's Symphony, 1913; Echoes from the Gospels, 1914; Echoes from the Epistles, 1915; Echoes from the Psalms, 1915; Echoes from the Prophets, 1916; Echoes from the Pentateuch, 1918; contributions on Ornithological Subjects to Natural History Periodicals. *Recreations:* music, reading, study of nature and art. *Address:* The Retreat, Clevedon. *Club:* Clifton.   (*Died 26 Feb. 1928.*)

RICKETTS, Sir Frederick William Rodney, 5th Bt., *cr.* 1827; *b.* 27 Sep. 1857; *s.* of 2nd Bt. and 2nd wife, Lady Caroline Pelham Clinton, *d.* of 4th Duke of Newcastle; *S.* nephew, 1909; *m.* 1879, Alice Eve Grace, *d.* of late Charles Fox Webster; three *s.* one *d.* Formerly Lieutenant Scots Guards. *Heir: e. s.* Claude Albert Frederick [*b.* 27 Apr. 1880; *m.* 1907, Lilian Helen Gwendolen, *d.* of Arthur M. Hill, of Silver Birches, Waltham, and Goodanevy, South Devon; one *s.* two *d.*].(*Died 18 Sept. 1925.*)

RICKETTS, George William, Barrister-at-law; Recorder of Portsmouth since 1914; *b.* Allahabad, India, 2 June 1864; *e. s.* of late G. H. M. Ricketts, C.B.; *m.* 1909, Evelyn Annie, *widow* of Edward Hastings Buckland and *d.* of Thomas Watson Parker of Blackheath. *Educ.:* Winchester; Oriel College, Oxford (Scholar). Oxford University XI., 1887; Barrister-at-law, Inner Temple, 1889; Bencher, 1920. *Address:* 1 Pelham Crescent, S.W.7; *T.:* Kensington 5796; 2 Hare Court, Temple, E.C.4. *Clubs:* Oxford and Cambridge; Hampshire, Winchester.
    (*Died 16 June 1927.*)

RICKMAN, Lt.-Col. Arthur Wilmot, D.S.O. 1917; *b.* Leicester, 25 Sep. 1874; *s.* of late Lieut.-Gen. William Rickman and Mary Pulsford Rickman; *m.* Muriel Joicey Fulton; *Educ.:* Winchester College; served South African War, 1899-1902 (Queen's medal and three clasps, King's medal and two clasps); European War, 1914-18 (wounded twice, despatches four times, D.S.O. and bar). *Address:* The Old House, Coombe Bissett, nr. Salisbury. *Club:* Junior United Service.
    (*Died 16 Oct. 1925.*)

RICKMAN, Capt. William Edward, D.S.O. 1900; Imperial Light Horse; *b.* 1855; *m.* 1895, Margaret Menzies Haliburton. *Educ.:* Haileybury. Served S. Africa, 1900 - 2 (despatches, Queen's medal 3 clasps, King's medal 2 clasps).   (*Died 1 June 1927.*)

RIDDEL, James, A.R.S.A., R.S.W.; *b.* Glasgow, 1857; parents Scotch; *m.* Margaret G. Shepherd, Perthshire; one *s. Educ.:* Wellington Academy. Glasgow; Glasgow University; Glasgow School of Art; Edinburgh Royal Institution and Royal Scottish Academy. Began life in merchant's office; for 20 years Headmaster of Art Department of Heriot-Watt College, Edinburgh: during these years continued to practice painting, landscapes and portraits; regularly exhibited in the Royal Scottish Academy, Royal Glasgow Institute, and other art centres in Scotland; also from time to time in the R.A., Liverpool, Manchester, and other exhibitions in England; Chairman of the Society of Scottish Artists, 1904; found subjects for landscape work mostly in Scotland and Belgium, and has also painted a little in Canada. *Publications:* article on The Art of the Forth in A Guide to the Forth; articles on Perspective, Water-colour Painting,

890

and Drawing; Handbook on Practical Plane and Solid Geometry; article on Teaching of Drawing in the Teachers' Encyclopedia. *Recreations:* golf, billiards. *Address:* Balvonie, Balerno, Midlothian. *T.:* Balerno 28. *Clubs:* Scottish Arts, Edinburgh; Art, Glasgow; Baberton Golf.   (*Died 14 Mar. 1928.*)

RIDDELL, Sir Alexander Oliver, Kt., *cr.* 1904; *b.* Edin.. 1844; 3rd *s.* of late Alex. Oliver Riddell, C.E., Edin.; *m.* 1880, Jane Fazackerley, 2nd *d.* of late Henry Hornby of Seaforth, near Liverpool. D.L. of the City and County of the City of Edinburgh; LL.D. Edinburgh University; J.P. for the County of Midlothian; a member of the Royal Company of Archers, the King's Bodyguard for Scotland; proprietor of the Estate of Bavelaw Castle on the northern slope of the Pentlands, Midlothian, and also of Craiglockhart. *Recreations:* formerly hunting, now shooting. *Address:* Craiglockhart, Slateford, Midlothian. *T.:* Central 4610. *M.:* SY 366. *Clubs:* Caledonian United Service, Scottish Unionist, Edinburgh.   (*Died 10 Oct. 1918.*)

RIDDELL, Sir John Walter Buchanan-, 11th Bt., *cr.* 1628; J.P.; *b.* 14 Mar. 1849; *S. u.* 1892; *m.* Sarah Isabella, *d.* of Robert Wharton, barrister, 1874; one *s.* three *d. Educ.:* Eton; Christ Church, Oxford (M.A.). Barr. Inner Temple, 1874. *Heir: s.* W. R. Buchanan-Riddell. *Address:* 8 Elm Park Gardens, S.W.10. *T.:* Kensington 2985; Hepple, Northumberland.   (*Died 31 Oct. 1924.*)

RIDEING, William Henry, associate editor of the Youth's Companion, Boston, Mass., since 1881; *b.* Liverpool, 1853, of a line of seafaring men, his great-uncle having been Admiral Sir Edward Walpole Browne, R.N., and his father a well-known Cunard officer; *m. d.* of Margaret Elinor, C. E. Bockus, editor Boston Herald. *Educ.:* privately. Went to the United States in 1869; at the age of nineteen became an assistant-editor New York Tribune; afterwards special correspondent of New York Times with United States Geographical Surveys for three years; a frequent contributor to Harper's publications, The Century, Scribner's Magazine, etc.; appointed managing editor North American Review, 1888; resigned 1899. *Publications:* sixteen volumes of fiction, travel, and criticism, including A Little Upstart; A-saddle in the Wild West; Thackeray's London; In the Land of Lorna Doone; How Tyson came Home, 1904; Many Celebrities, 1912; A Young Folks' Life of George Washington, 1916, etc. *Recreations:* rural walks and drives, and ocean steamers, about which he has written much, and of which his knowledge may be said to be "extensive and peculiar." *Address:* c/o The Youth's Companion, Boston, Mass.; c/o Baring Brothers, Co.. E.C. *Club:* Authors'. (*Died 23 Aug. 1919.*)

RIDER, Thomas Francis, M.V.O., 1918; *b.* 12 April 1843; *o. surv. s.* of Thomas and Mary Rider of Union Street, Southwark; *m.* Elizabeth (*d.* 1919), *d.* of William Low of Southwark; two *s.*, one *d. Educ.:* Clarendon House, Lambeth, Dr. Pinches. Member of Corporation of City of London, 1897-99 and since 1902; Chairman of Assessment Committee since 1915 and received special vote of thanks from Common Council; Chairman of Reception Committee on King and Queen's visit to Guildhall on their Silver Wedding Anniversary; Order of Sacred Irasam, 4th Class, from Emperor of Japan on occasion of visit of Prince Fushimi; Estates Governor of Dulwich College; Trustee of Crystal Palace; Governor of St. Olave's and St. Saviour's Grammar School; Deputy Chairman of Belgrave Hospital; Corporation Representative on Sunday Hospital Fund; Chairman of Builders Accident Insurance Company; Past-President of National Federation of Builders, Institute of Builders and London Master Builders; also of Builders' Benevolent and

Builders Clerks Benevolent. *Recreations:* reading and watching cricket; Member of Surrey County Club since 1870. *Address:* Stanstead House, Durand Gardens, S.W.9. *T.:* Brixton 769. *Clubs:* St. Stephen's, City Carlton.
(Died 13 Mar. 1922.)

RIDGEWAY, Rt. Rev. Charles John, D.D.; *b.* 14 July 1841; *s.* of Rev. Joseph Ridgeway, M.A., Vicar of Christ Church, Tunbridge Wells; *m.* 1st, 1868, Susan Jane, *o. d.* of Rev. Gerald S. FitzGerald; one *s.* one *d.*; 2nd, 1899, Katharine Margaret, *e. d.* of late Rev. Canon Johnston, Rector of North Cray. *Educ.:* St. Paul's School; Trinity College, Cambridge. Perry Exhibitioner. B.A., 1863; Theological Tripos, 2nd Class, 1865; Curate of Christ Church, Tunbridge Wells, 1866; Vicar of North Malvern, 1868; Rector of Buckhurst Hill, 1875-80; Inspector of Schools, St. Albans, 1876-1880; Incumbent of St. Paul's, Edinburgh, 1880; Select Preacher, Camb., 1890 and 1907; Golden Lecturer, 1895; Vicar of Christ Church, Lancaster Gate, 1884-1905; Prebendary of St. Paul's Cathedral; Rural Dean of Paddington, 1901; Surrogate Commissary of Archbishop of Cape Town and Bishop of North China; Dean of Carlisle, 1905-8; Past Chaplain of Grand Lodges of Masons both in England and Scotland; Bishop of Chichester, 1908-19; retired, 1919. *Publications:* What Think Ye of Christ?; The Mountain of Blessedness; What does the Church of England Say?; Manual on Holy Communion; How to Prepare for Confirmation; Foundation Truths, In Paradise, etc., etc. *Address:* 169 Queen's Gate, S.W.5; Drumsell, Limpsfield. *T.:* Western 4455. *Club:* Athenæum.
(Died 28 Feb. 1927.)

RIDGEWAY, Major Edward William Crawfurd, C.I.E. 1916; 1st Batt. 2nd King Edward's Own - Gurkha Rifles; Recruiting Officer for Gurkhas; served N.W. Frontier, India, 1897-98 (medal with clasp); S. Africa, 1900-2 (Queen's medal, 4 clasps); European War, 1914-16 (C.I.E.). *(Died 23 Feb. 1917.)*

RIDGEWAY, Right Rev. Frederick Edward, Bishop of Salisbury since 1911; *b.* 1848; *m.* 1875, Pauline Josephine, *d.* of late John Vibart, I.C.S.; four *s.* *Educ.:* Tonbridge School; Clare Coll. Cambridge (M.A.). Hon. D.D. Glasgow, 1890; Priest, 1872; Incumbent of St. Mary Virgin, Glasgow, 1878-90; Dean of Diocese, Glasgow and Galloway, 1888-90; select preacher, Cambridge, 1891 and 1903; select preacher, Oxford, 1913-14; Vicar of St. Peter's, S. Kensington, 1890-1900; Rector of St. Botolph, Bishopsgate, 1900; Bishop of Kensington, 1901-1911; Prebendary of St. Paul's Cathedral, 1901-3; chaplain H.A.C., 1900-11. Precentor of the Province of Canterbury. *Address:* The Palace, Salisbury; Bishop's Cottage, Broadstone, Dorset. *(Died 4 May 1921.)*

RIDGEWAY, Col. Richard Kirby, V.C., 1879; C.B. 1905; Indian Army Staff Corps; retired; *b.* County Meath, Ireland, 18 August 1848; 2nd *s.* of R. Ridgeway, F.R.C.S., and Annette, *d.* of R. Adams; *m.* 1871, Emily Maria (Amy) (*d.* 1917), *d.* of S. W. Fallon. *Educ.:* private school; R.M.C., Sandhurst. Joined 96th Regt. 1868; Indian Staff Corps, 1872; Adjt. 44th Gurkha Rifles, 1874 - 80; passed Staff College, 1883; D.A.Q.M.G., 1884; A.Q.M.G., Army Headquarters, India, 1889-90; comd. 44th Gurkha Rifles, 1891-95; A.Q.M.G. Army Headquarters, India, 1895-98; A.A.G. Peshawar, 1898-1900; Naga Hills Expedition, 1875; Naga Hills Expedition, 1879-80 (despatches, medal, V.C.); Manipur, 1891 (clasp); Tirah, as A.A.G. 2nd Division, 1897 (medal, three clasps). *Clubs:* United Service, Sports. *(Died 11 Oct. 1924.)*

RIDGEWAY, Sir William, Kt., *cr.* 1919; M.A., Sc.D. Camb.; F.B.A., F.Z.S.; Professor of Archæology, Cambridge University, since 1892; Brereton Reader in Classics since 1907;

Fellow of Caius College, Cambridge, 1880; *b.* Ireland, 6 Aug. 1853; *y. s.* of Rev. J. H. Ridgeway, M.A., Ballydermot, King's Co., and Marian, *d.* of S. Ridgeway, Aghanvilla, King's Co.; *m.* 1880, Lucy, *d.* of A. Samuels, Kingstown; one *d.* *Educ.:* Portarlington School; Trinity College, Dublin, Berkeley Greek Medal, Vice-Chancellor Latin Medal, Greek Essay, and Greek Verse (with 3 Greek Comedies) Prizes (graduated Sen. Moderator in both Classics and Modern Literature); and Cambridge (5th Classic); Hon. D.Litt. Dublin, 1902; Hon. D.Litt. Manchester, 1906; Hon. LL.D. Aberdeen, 1908; Hon. LL.D. Edinburgh, 1921; Corresponding Member Archæological Society, Athens; French Assoc. pour les Sciences Anthropologiques; Foreign Member of Sociétés d'Anthropologie of Paris and Brussels, 1909; and of the Deutsche Gesellschaft f. Anthropologie, 1913; Hon. Mem. Bihar and Orissa Research Society; Professor of Greek, Queen's College, Cork, 1883-94; Gifford Lecturer in Natural Religion, University of Aberdeen, 1909-11; Stokes Lecturer in Irish Archæology, Dublin, 1909; Hermione Lecturer in Art, Dublin, 1911; Pres. of Royal Anthropological Inst. 1908-10; Pres. of Anthropological Section, British Association, 1908; Member of Council of Cambridge Senate, 1900-4; took leading part in founding Cambridge Departments of Anthropology and Architecture, and in reforming Classical Tripos; President of Classical Association of England and Wales, 1914; has been President of Cambridge Philological, Antiquarian, Classical, and Anthropological Societies. *Publications:* Origin of Metallic Currency and Weight Standards, 1892; The Early Age of Greece, 1901; The Origin and Influence of the Thoroughbred Horse, 1905; Homeric Land System; Who were the Romans? 1907; The Oldest Irish Epic, 1907; The Origin of Tragedy, 1910; Minos the Destroyer, 1910; The Differentiation of the Chief Species of Zebras, 1909; The Dramas and Dramatic Dances of Non-European Races in special reference to the origin of Tragedy, 1915; various articles in Encyclopædia Britannica, Encyclopædia Biblica, etc. *Recreations:* boating, collects ancient and mediæval coins, precious stones, Greek, Roman, Anglo-Saxon, and mediæval objects, and prehistoric and savage implements. *Address:* Caius College, Cambridge; Flendyshe, Fen Ditton, Cambridge. *(Died 12 Aug. 1926.)*

RIDLEY, 2nd Viscount (*cr.* 1900), **Matthew White Ridley,** 3rd Baron Wensleydale *cr.* 1900; 6th Bt. *cr.* 1756; *b.* 6 Dec. 1874; *e. s.* of 1st Viscount Ridley and Hon. Mary Georgiana Marjoribanks, *d.* of 1st Lord Tweedmouth; S. father 1904. M.P. (C.) Stalybridge since 1900; Lt.-Col. Northumberland Yeo.; D.L.; J.P.; *m.* 1899, Hon. Rosamond Guest, *y. d.* of 1st Baron Wimborne; one *s.* two *d.* *Educ.:* Eton; Balliol Coll. Oxford (B.A. with honours). Owns about 10,200 acres. *Heir:* s. Hon. Matthew White Ridley. *Address:* 10 Carlton House Terrace, S.W.; *T.:* Regent 727; Blagdon, Cramlington, Northumberland. *Clubs:* Turf. Carlton.
(Died 14 Feb. 1916.)

RIDLEY, Rt. Hon. Sir Edward, Kt., *cr.* 1897; P.C. 1917; Judge of the King's Bench Division of the High Court of Justice, 1897 - 1917; *b.* Blagdon, Northumberland, 1843; 2nd *s.* of Sir M. W. Ridley, 4th Bt., and Cecilia Ann, *e. d.* of Baron Parke, afterwards Lord Wensleydale; *m.* 1882, Alice; two *s.* *Educ.:* Harrow; Corpus Christi College, Oxford. First class Moderations, 1864; First class Final Schools, 1866; Fellow of All Souls, 1866-82. Barr. 1868; went Northern and North-Eastern Circuits; M.P. for South Northumberland, 1878-80; Official Referee, 1886-97; Q.C. 1892. *Publication:* A Translation of Lucan's Pharsalia. *Recreations:* shooting, cycling, reading. *Address:* 48 Lennox Gardens,

S.W.1.   *T.*: Kensington 4968.   *Clubs*: Carlton, Oxford and Cambridge, Athenæum.
(*Died 14 Oct. 1923.*)

RIDSDALE, Sir Edward Aurelian, G.B.E., *cr.* 1920 ; F.G.S. ; J.P. Pembrokeshire, High Sheriff 1921 ; *b.* 23 Feb. 1864 ; *e. s.* of late Edward Lucas Jenks Ridsdale and Esther Lucy Thacker ; *m.* 1900, Susan Stirling, 3rd *d.* of late John Ritchie Findlay of Aberlour, Banffshire ; one *s.* one *d. Educ.*: University Coll. School ; Royal School of Mines ; M.P. (L.) Brighton, 1906-10 ; Chairman Executive Committee British Red Cross Society, 1912-14 ; Deputy Chairman, 1914-19 ; Special Commissioner Salonika and Mesopotamia, 1915-16 ; Member of Commission of Enquiry into Medical arrangements in Mesopotamia, 1916 ; Acting Red Cross Commissioner, France, 1916. *Publication*: Cosmic Evolution. *Address*: 14 Ennismore Gardens, S.W.7 ; *T.*: Western 6478 ; Waterwynch, Tenby, Pembrokeshire. *Clubs*: Reform, Bath, Brooks's.
(*Died 6 Sept. 1923.*)

RIGG, Herbert Addington, M.A., J.P. Sussex ; K.C. 1906 ; Deputy Chairman of Quarter Sessions for West Sussex ; Alderman West Sussex County Council ; F.S.A. ; 2nd *s.* of Jonathan Rigg of Wrotham Hill Park, Kent ; *m.* Dora, *y. d.* of late William Chappell, F.S.A. *Educ.*: Tonbridge School ; Trinity College, Cambridge. Barrister, Inner Temple, 1871 ; went Northern Circuit ; and practised at Parliamentary Bar. *Recreation*: hunting, shooting, farming. *Address*: Wallhurst Manor, Cowfold, Sussex. *T.A.*: Cowfold. *T.*: Cowfold 11. *Clubs*: New University, Athenæum.
(*Died 7 Mar. 1924.*)

RILEY, James Whitcomb ; poet and public reader ; *b.* Greenfield, Indiana, U.S.A., 1849 ; *s.* of Reuben A. Riley and Elizabeth Marine ; unmarried. Began life as a journeyman signwriter ; joined a theatrical troupe, rewrote their plays and improvised songs for them ; in 1872 began to publish in local papers poems in the Hoosier dialect ; for some years travelled about giving entertainments with the late "Bill Nye," and later by himself ; connected with the Indianapolis Journal for a number of years ; member of American Academy of Arts and Letters, and awarded by them the gold medal for poetry in 1912. *Publications*: The Old Swimmin'-Hole and 'Leven More Poems, 1883 ; The Boss Girl and other Sketches, 1885 ; Afterwhiles, 1887 ; Pipes o' Pan at Zekesbury, 1887 ; Old-Fashioned Roses (in England), 1888 ; Rhymes of Childhood, 1890 ; The Flying Islands of the Night, 1891 ; Neighborly Poems, on Friendship, Grief, and Farm-Life, 1891 ; Green Fields and Running Brooks, 1892 ; Poems Here at Home, 1893 ; Armazindy, 1894 ; A Child - World, 1896 ; Rubaiyat of Doc Sifers, 1897 ; The Golden Year (in England), 1898 ; Riley Child Rhymes, 1898 ; Riley Love Lyrics, 1899 ; Home-Folks, 1900 ; Riley Farm Rhymes, 1901 ; An Old Sweetheart of Mine, 1902 ; The Book of Joyous Children, 1902 ; His Pa's Romance, 1903 ; Out to Old Aunt Mary's, 1904 ; A Defective Santa Claus, 1904 ; Riley Songs o' Cheer, 1905 ; While the Heart beats Young, 1906 ; Morning, 1907 ; Home Again with Me, 1908 ; Riley Song of Summer, 1908 ; The Orphant Annie Book, 1908 ; Riley Roses, 1909 ; Riley Songs of Home, 1910 ; The Lockerbie Book, 1911 ; The Complete Works of James Whitcomb Riley, Biographical Edition, 1913. *Address*: c/o Union Trust Co., Indianapolis, Ind., U.S.A.   (*Died 22 July 1916.*)

RILEY, Engineer Rear-Adm. William Henry, C.B. 1916 ; was at the Admiralty, 1899-1905 ; in Engineering Branch of Controller's Dept., 1899-1901 : employed on special service, the Admiralty, in connection with watertube boilers, 1902-3 ; with oil-fuel experiments, 1907-1917. Engnr. Rear-Adm., 1907 ; retired, 1912. *Address*: Beechin Wood, Platt, Borough Green, Kent.   (*Died Mar. 1926.*)

RIMINGTON, A. Wallace, A.R.E., R.B.A., Hon. F.S.A. ; artist ; *b.* London ; *e. s.* of Alexander Rimington, descendant of William de Rimington of 13th century of Rimington in Yorks ; *m.* 1st, Charlotte (*d.* 1913), *d.* of G. A. Haig ; 2nd, Evelyn, *d.* of Rev. F. Whyley. *Educ.*: Clifton Coll. Studied art in London and Paris ; frequent exhibitor at Royal Academy, Royal Society of Painter Etchers, and Royal Society of British Artists, and an occasional one at Paris Salon, New Gallery, and international exhibitions of the Continent and America, etc. ; has had seven special exhibitions of his watercolours in the Fine Art Society's Galleries ; Hon. Mention at Berlin International ; ex-Professor of Art at Queen's College, London ; has carried out original researches upon the relations between colour and music ; inventor of the Colour Organ, an instrument for producing Colour-Music, and other forms of the art of Mobile Colour, which has been used in Colour-Music concerts and lectures given in London and elsewhere. His theory has been recently adopted and employed by Scriabine the composer in his Prometheus and other works. *Publications*: Architecture seen through the Painter's Glasses, 1891 ; Colour-Music, 1912. *Recreations*: troutfishing, chess. *Address*: 11a Pembridge Crescent, W. *T.*: 2606 Park. *Clubs*: Arts, Odd Volumes.   (*Died 14 May 1918.*)

RIMINGTON, Major-General Sir Michael Frederic, K.C.B., *cr.* 1921 ; C.B. 1900 ; C.V.O. 1912 ; Hon. Col. 6th Inniskilling Dragoons ; *b.* 23 May 1858 ; *s.* of Michael Rimington of Tynefield, Penrith ; *m.* 1888, Agnes, *d.* of late Henry F. Cunningham of Oakley Park, Co. Galway ; one *s. Educ.*: Oxford University (B.A.). Entered 6th (Inniskilling) Dragoons, 1881 ; Major, 1897 ; served Bechuanaland Expedition, 1884-5 ; Zululand, 1888 ; South Africa, 1899-1900 (despatches 5 times, Queen's medal 8 clasps, King's medal 2 clasps, C.B., Brevet Col.) ; Inspector of Cavalry in India ; Commander Legion of Honour, 1915. *Publications*: Our Cavalry ; Hints on Stable Management. *Club*: Naval and Military.
(*Died 19 Dec. 1928.*)

RIND, Col. Alexander Thomas Seton Abercromby, C.M.G. 1887 ; late Assistant Commissary-General, 1st class, Naini Tal ; I.S.C., late 102nd Foot ; *b.* 1847. Entered army, 1866 ; Capt. 1878 ; Major, 1881 ; Lieut.-Col. 1892 ; Col. 1898 ; served Afghan War, 1879-80 (despatches twice, brevet of Major, medal with clasp, bronze decoration) ; Egyptian War, 1882 (medal, Khedive's Star).   (*Died 29 Sept. 1925.*)

RING, George Alfred, Attorney-General, Isle of Man, 1897-1921 ; 3rd *s.* of late Dr. C. P. Ring, Scholar of Trinity College, Dublin ; *m.* Helena de Guise, *e. d.* of late Ven. Archdeacon Hughes-Games. *Educ.*: privately. Called to the Manx Bar, 1873 ; Chairman of the Douglas School Board, 1883-97. *Publications*: The Legislature and Judicature of the Isle of Man ; Land Tenure in the Isle of Man ; The West Riding Judgment ; Communicants and the Deceased Wife's Sister's Act 1907 ; The Legal Aspect of Vestments. *Address*: 8 Palmeira Court, Hove, Sussex.   (*Died 1 Feb. 1927.*)

RIPON, 2nd Marquess of (*cr.* 1871), Frederick Oliver Robinson ; G.C.V.O. 1909 ; K.C.V.O. 1902 ; Treasurer in the Household of H.M. Queen Alexandra since 1901 ; Bt. 1690 ; Baron Grantham, 1761 ; Earl de Grey, 1816 ; Viscount Goderich, 1827 ; Earl of Ripon, 1833 ; *b.* 29 Jan. 1852 ; *e. s.* of 1st Marquess of Ripon and Henrietta Anne Theodosia, C.I., *d.* of Capt. Henry Vyner, Gautby Hall, Lincolnshire, *g.d.* of 1st Earl de Grey ; *S.* father 1909 ; *m.* 1885, Constance Gladys (*d.* 1917), *sister* of 14th Earl of Pembroke and *widow* of 4th Earl of Lonsdale. M.P. (L.) for Ripon, 1874-80 ; a Trustee of the Wallace Collection. Owns about 21,800 acres.

Heir : none. *Address :* Studley Royal, Ripon. *Clubs :* Marlborough, White's(*Died 22 Sept. 1923.*)

RISSIK, Hon. Johann Friedrich Bernhardt, Member of the S.A. Railway Board; was Administrator Province of the Transvaal; *m.*; two *s.* Was Minister for Lands and Native Affairs, Transvaal; Member, Transvaal Legislative Assembly for North Central Pretoria; Member, Executive Council. *Address :* Linschoten, Sunnyside, Pretoria.

(*Died Aug. 1925.*)

RITCHIE, Lady (Anne Isabella), writer of stories and magazine articles; *e. d.* of W. M. Thackeray; *m.* Sir Richmond Ritchie, K.C.B. (*d.* 1912); one *s.* one *d. Educ. :* Paris; Kensington. Lived at home in her father's house and with her sister for many years until her marriage in 1877; has a son and a daughter. Appointed to the Academic Committee of the Royal Society of Literature, 1911. *Publications :* The Story of Elizabeth, 1863; The Village on the Cliff, 1865; To Esther, and other Sketches, 1869; Old Kensington, 1873; Toilers and Spinsters, 1873; Bluebeard's Keys, 1874; Miss Angel, 1875; Anne Evans, 1880; Madame de Sévigné, 1881; A Book of Sibyls, 1883; Mrs. Dymond, 1885; introductions to editions of Cranford, Our Village, and The Fairy Tales of Madame d'Aulnoy; Alfred Lord Tennyson and his Friends, Portraits and Reminiscences (folio), 1893; Chapters from some Memoirs, 1894; an edition of the works of W. M. Thackeray, 1898; Blackstick Papers, 1908. *Address :* 9 St. Leonard's Terrace, Chelsea, S.W. *T. :* Kensington 4858. *Club :* Sesame.

(*Died 20 Feb. 1919.*)

RITCHIE, Sir George, Kt., *cr.* 1910; merchant; President of the Dundee Liberal Association; J.P. Forfarshire; D.L., J.P. County of City of Dundee; *b.* Kingsmuir, 1849; *s.* of Alex. Ritchie; *m.* 1877, Agnes, *d.* of David Scringeour. *Educ. :* Kingsmuir Parish and Forfar Burgh School. Served on the City Council for nearly 20 years; for the greater part of that time Finance Convener and Hon. City Treasurer; Director of the High School and Technical College; a director of several financial and industrial local companies; takes a keen interest in social and religious work, and serves on various boards. *Address :* Dundee. *T.A. :* Mars, Dundee. *T :* 1055 and 873.

(*Died 3 Dec. 1921.*)

RITCHIE, Major Hon. Harold, D.S.O. 1918; *b.* 30 Oct. 1876; 3rd *s.* of 1st Baron Ritchie of Dundee; *m.* 1907, Ella, *o. d.* of R. C. Priestley; two *s.* two *d. Educ. :* Winchester. Partner of Brightwen & Co., Bill Brokers, Nicholas Lane, E.C. *Address :* 13 Kensington Court, W.8. *T. :* Western 3605. *Club :* Union.

(*Died 28 Oct. 1918.*)

RITCHIE, James, M.A., B.Sc. (Edin. and Oxon.), M.D. (Edin.), F.R.C.P.E.; Irvine Professor of Bacteriology, University of Edinburgh, since 1913; *b.* 1864; *s.* of Rev. William Ritchie, D.D., Duns; *m.* 1898, Lily, *d.* of James Souttar, Aberdeen; three *d. Educ. :* Edinburgh; Oxford. Studied Arts and Medicine in University of Edinburgh; engaged in bacteriological and pathological research in University of Oxford, 1892-1907; successively Lecturer, Reader, and Professor of Pathology there; Hon. Physician, Radcliffe Infirmary, Oxford, 1897-1906; Pathologist to same, 1900-7; Fellow of New College, 1902-7; Superintendent, Royal College of Physicians Laboratory, Edinburgh, 1907-20. *Publications :* Joint Author, Muir and Ritchie's Manual of Bacteriology; Joint Editor, Pembrey and Ritchie's General Pathology; papers on Bacteriology and Pathology in Scientific Journals. *Address :* 10 Succoth Gardens, Murrayfield, Edinburgh, W. *T. :* Central 4042. *Clubs :* Royal Societies; University, Edinburgh.

(*Died 28 Jan. 1923.*)

RITCHIE, Major-General John; retired, late R.A.; *b.* 31 Jan. 1834; *y. s.* of John Ritchie, Calcutta, merchant; *m.* 1st, 1859, Jane Craig (*d.* 1859); 2nd, 1862, Janet (*d.* 1900), *d.* of Archibald Sharp; 3rd, 1904, Louisa Mary, *widow* of Alfred Slocock, Montagu House, Southsea; one *s. Educ. :* Glasgow Academy; Addiscombe. Served in Indian Mutiny, 1857 (despatches). *Recreations :* hunting, golf, yachting. *Address :* Montagu House, 10 Clarence Parade, Southsea. *Club :* Royal Albert Yacht, Southsea. (*Died 20 Nov. 1919.*)

RIVAZ, Hon. Sir Charles Montgomery, K.C.S.I., *cr.* 1901; *b.* 1845; *s.* of late John Theophilus Rivaz, Bengal Civil Service, and Mary, *d.* of late William Lambert, Bengal Civil Service; *m.* 1874, Emily, *d.* of late Major-General Agnew, Bengal Staff Corps; three *s. Educ. :* Blackheath Proprietary School. Entered I.C.S., 1864; served in the Punjab till 1898; Member of Viceroy's Executive Council, 1898-1902; Lieut.-Gov. of Punjab, 1902-6. *Address :* 21 Hyde Park Street, W.2. *T. :* Padd. 1194. (*Died 7 Oct. 1926.*)

RIVAZ, Col. Vincent, C.B. 1900; I.S.C.; *b.* 26 June 1842; *s.* of J. Theophilus Rivaz, late Beng. Civil Service, of Watford Place, Watford; *m.* 1877, Louisa Caroline, *d.* of late Rev. E. R. Eardley Wilmot; two *d.* Entered army, 1860; Col. 1890; served Hazara Campaign, 1868 (medal with clasp); Dour Valley Expedition, 1872; Afghan War, 1878-79 (despatches, medal); Mahsood Wuzeeree Expedition, 1881 (despatches); Hazara Expedition, 1891 (despatches, clasp). *Address :* Millfield, Leamington Spa.

(*Died 1 Mar. 1924.*)

RIVERS, Baroness(Emmeline Laura); *o. d.* of Captain Bastard; *m.* 1st, 1873, 6th and last Baron Rivers (*d.* 1880); 2nd, 1881, M. G. Thorold, *s.* of Sir J. C. Thorold, 11th Bt. *Address :* 1 Abbot's Court, Kensington Square, W.; Honington Hall, Grantham. (*Died 1 Oct. 1918.*)

RIVERS, William Halse R., M.A., M.D., Hon. LL.D. St. Andrews, D.Sc. Manchester, F.R.S., F.R.C.P.; Fellow and Prælector in Natural Sciences, St. John's Coll. Cambridge; President Royal Anthropological Institute and Folklore Society; late temp. Capt. R.A.M.C.; Medical Officer, Craiglockhart War Hospital, and Military Hospital, Maghull; Psychologist, Central Hospital, R.A.F.; *s.* of Rev. H. F. Rivers; *b.* 1864. *Educ. :* Tonbridge; St. Bartholomew's Hospital. Formerly Lecturer on Psychology, Guy's Hospital; Lecturer on Physiological and Experimental Psychology, Univ. of Camb.; Croonian Lecturer, Royal Coll. of Physicians, 1906; FitzPatrick Lecturer, 1915-16; President Section for Anthropology, British Association, 1911; Royal Society's Royal Medal, 1915. *Publications :* The History of Melanesian Society; Kinship and Social Organisation; The Todas; The Influence of Alcohol and other Drugs on Fatigue; Dreams and Primitive Culture; Mind and Medicine; Instinct and the Unconscious; various papers in Reports of Cambridge Expedition to Torres Straits, and in scientific journals. *Address :* St. John's College, Cambridge. (*Died 4 June 1922.*)

RIVETT - CARNAC, Colonel John Henry, C.I.E., 1878; V.D., J.P., A.D.C. to the King; Kt. Grand Commander Austrian Order of Francis Joseph, North Star of Sweden, and of Albrecht the Bear; Grand Cordon of the Lion and Sun; Indian Civil Service (retired), Hon. Commandant Ghazipur Light Horse and Volunteer Rifles; Lord of the Manor of Stanstead Hall, Suffolk; *b.* London, 1838; 2nd *s.* of late Admiral Rivett-Carnac, R.N., and Maria, *d.* of J. S. Davis, R.E., F.R.S., and *sister* of Sir J. F. Davis, Bart., K.C.B.; *m.* 1868, Marian, *d.* of Gen. Sir H.M. Durand, R.E. *Educ. :* abroad for diplomatic service; E.I. Coll. Haileybury. F.S.A.; Fellow of the University of Bombay, the Royal Academies of Spain and Sweden; Royal Society of Northern Antiquaries, and Honorary Fellow of several Antiquarian Societies; Bengal Civil Service, 1859-94; Ad. Secy. to Sir Richard Temple in Central Provinces; Commissioner of Cotton and Commerce with Government of India; Special Commissioner in Bengal Famine of 1874; Opium Agent; extra Private Secretary to Lord Lytton at Delhi; A.D.C. to Commander-in-Chief F. M. Sir Donald Stewart; raised and commanded the Ghazipur Volunteer Light Horse and Rifles; commanded the Volunteer Brigade at the Grand Manœuvres, Delhi, 1888, and Indian Rifle Team at Wimbledon, 1885 and 1887; Vice-Pres. East Anglican Society. *Decorated:* C.I.E., as Special Commissioner for Transport in Bengal Famine of 1894. *Publications:* Report on Indian Cotton Supply Indian Railway Traffic; Indian Antiquities; Archaic Rock Markings in India and Europe; Many Memories, 1910, etc. *Recreations:* sport of all sorts; Winner of the Regimental Silver Cup for Rifle Shooting, 1880. *Club:* United Service. (*Died 11 May 1923.*)

RIVETT-CARNAC, Sir William Percival, 5th Bt., *cr.* 1836; *b.* 1847; *g. s.* of 1st Bt.; *S.* cousin 1924 on presumption of latter's death in 1909; *m.* 1885 Frances Maria, *d.* of late Francis Charles Forbes, B.C.S.; two *d.* (*Died 21 Mar. 1924.*)

RIVIERE, Briton, R.A., D.C.L.; painter; Hon. Fellow of Oriel College, Oxford; *b.* London, 14 Aug. 1840; *y. c.* of William Riviere, London, and Ann, *d.* of Joseph Jarvis, Warwickshire; *m.* Mary Alice, *d.* of John Dobell of Detmore, Gloucestershire, and *s.* of Sydney Dobell, the poet, 1867; five *s.* two *d.* *Educ.:* Cheltenham Coll.; St. Mary Hall, Oxford (M.A.) A.R.A. 1879. Began work as an artist while still a boy, and exhibited at British Gallery and Roy. Academy while at Cheltenham and Oxford; went to live in Kent; there he worked at illustrating for various English and American publications, and exhibited in oils and water-colours at Dudley Gallery and Royal Academy; came to live in London, 1870, and remained there; has been a constant exhibitor at Royal Academy and various international exhibitions abroad; a great number of his works have been engraved. *Works:* The Poacher's Nurse, 1866; The Long Sleep, 1868; Prisoners, 1869; Charity, 1870; Circe, 1871; Daniel, 1872; Argus, 1873; War Time, 1875; Pallas Athene and Dogs, 1876; Lazarus, 1877; Sympathy, Persepolis, and An Anxious Moment, 1878; In Manus tuas, 1879; The Last Spoonful and the Night Watch, 1880; The Magician's Doorway, 1881; Miracle of the Swine, 1883; Actaeon, The King and his Satellites, The Sheep-Stealer, 1884; Vae Victis, Union is Strength, 1885; Rizpah, 1886; Adonis Wounded, An Old-World Wanderer, 1887; Requiescat, Adonis' Farewell, 1888; Pale Cynthia, A Fool and His Folly, Prometheus, 1889; Daniel's Answer to the King, 1890; A Mighty Hunter before the Lord, 1891; Dead Hector, 1892; King's Libation, 1893; Beyond Man's Footstep and Ganymede, 1894; Apollo, 1895; J. F. H. Read, Esq. and Dogs, Aggravation, and a bronze, The Last Arrow, 1896; Lady Wantage, Mrs. F. Methold and her Deerhounds, 1897; The Temptation in the Wilderness, 1898; Lady Tennyson and the Poet's Old Wolf Hound, Karenina, 1899; St. George and The Heron, 1900; To the Hills, 1901; Aphrodite, 1902; The Rt. Hon. Lord Tennyson and Hark! hark! the Lark, 1909. *Address:* Flaxley, Finchley Road, N.W.8. *T.:* Hampstead 4966. *Club:* Athenæum. (*Died 20 April 1920.*)

RIVINGTON, Charles Robert, J.P. and D.L. Westmorland; *b.* 7 Dec. 1846; *s.* of late Charles Rivington, solicitor, London, and Emily, *d.* of Wm. Chadwell Mylne, F.R.S., of Great Amwell, Herts; *m.* 1st, 1869, Fanny Anne (*d.*

1875), *d.* of Duncan Campbell of Adpar, Cardiganshire; 2nd, 1881, Amy, *d.* of Wm. Ghippindale of Dulwich, Surrey; three *s.* one *d.* *Educ.:* King's College, London. Admitted a Solicitor, 1869; Master of Stationers Co. 1921-22; Governor of St. Bartholomew's Hospital, and London Hospital: Treasurer of Eastern Dispensary, Whitechapel; formerly member of Victoria Rifles, and subsequently Captain in 2nd Vol. Batt. Durham Light Infantry; Mayor of Appleby, 1894-95; High Sheriff of Westmorland, 1908; Past Master of Lodge of Antiquity and Vale of Eden Lodge (Freemasons), P.G.S.; Director of the Equity and Law Life Assurance Society. *Publications:* Records of the Stationers Co. *Recreation:* shooting. *Address:* Castle Bank, Appleby, Westmorland; 74 Elm Park Gardens, S.W.10. *T.:* Kensington 1894. *Clubs:* Conservative, Ranelagh. (*Died 22 Aug. 1928.*)

ROACH, Rt. Rev. Frederick; D.D.; Assistant Bishop of Natal since 1913; Vicar General, Natal, 1916; *b.* 1856. *Educ.:* Earl of Ducie's School, Tortworth; Cheltenham Training College. Ordained, 1886; Schoolmaster, Kwamagwaza, Zululand, 1881; Isandhlwana, 1885; Canon of St. Peter's Pro-Cathedral, Vryheid, 1904; Archdeacon of Eshowe, 1905-13; missionary at Etalaneni, 1886-1913. *Address:* 15 Burger Street, Maritzburg, Natal. (*Died June 1922.*)

ROBARTS, Abraham John, J.P., D.L.; *b.* 1838; *e. s.* of late Abraham George Robarts, banker, London, and Elizabeth Sarah, *d.* of late Col. John Henry Smyth, M.P., of Heath Hall, Co. York; *m.* 1869, Hon. Edith Barrington, *d.* of 8th Viscount Barrington. *Educ.:* Eton; Christ Church, Oxford. High Sheriff, Bucks, 1869; late Capt. Bucks Yeomanry. *Heir:* John [b. 1872; *m.* 1898, Margaret Georgina Louisa, *e. d.* of Sir Hugh Arthur Henry Cholmeley, 3rd Bt.]. *Address:* 29 Hill Street, W.1; *T.:* Mayfair 1451; Tile House, Buckingham. (*Died 24 Jan. 1926.*)

ROBBINS, Sir Edmund; K.B.E., *cr.* 1917; *b.* Launceston, 4 April 1847; 2nd *s.* of late R. Robbins; *m.* 1870, Jeannette, *o. d.* of Wm. Pearson, Plymouth; three *s.* six *d.* *Educ.:* Eagle House Academy, Priory House Academy, Launceston. Served apprenticeship (1858-65) with Mr. J. Brimmell at office of Launceston Weekly News; joined Central Press Agency, 1865; appointed sub-editor on the Press Association on its formation, 1870, simultaneously with the taking over of the telegraphs by the State; became secretary and assistant manager in 1874; chief of the Staff in 1878; manager, 1880-1917; secretary of the Provincial Newspaper Society from Oct. 1870 to May 1881; was an active member of the Executive of the Liberator Relief Fund, and was Chairman when in 1917 the Fund was transferred to the Public Trustee; has been Secretary of the Admiralty, War Office, and Press Committee since its formation; a Vice-President of the Newspaper Press Fund, 1917. *Address:* 168 Peckham Rye Common, S.E.22. (*Died 21 Dec. 1923.*)

ROBERTS, Hon. Charles James, C.M.G. 1882; M.L.C.; *b.* 29 Mar. 1846; *e. s.* of late Charles Warman Roberts of Sydney; *m.* 1867, Lucretia, *d.* of late Abraham Abraham of Sydney; one *s.* five *d.* *Educ.:* Sydney Grammar School. M.L.A. for Hastings and Manning, 1882-90; M.L.C. of N.S.W. since 1890; Postmaster-General, 1887-89; Mayor of Sydney, 1879. *Address:* Rockmore, Elizabeth Bay, Sydney, Australia. (*Died 14 Aug. 1925.*)

ROBERTS, Rev. Charles Philip, M.A., Hon. Canon of Manchester; *b.* 1842; *s.* of Rev. Philip Roberts, M.A., of Coleshill, Warwickshire; *m.* 1875, Lilias, *d.* of J. Scholes Walker, Bury, Lancs; three *s.* one *d.* *Educ.:* Marlborough; Trinity College, Oxford. Assistant Master,

Rossall School, 1864-68 ; Curate of Walmersley, Lancs, 1868-71 ; Vicar of Peel, Little Hulton, 1871-87 ; Rector of Longsight, 1887-1915 ; Chairman of Urban District Council of Little Hulton ; Chairman of Education Committee of Bolton Board of Guardians ; P. Prov. Grand Chaplain, East Lancs F.M. *Recreations :* angling, golf, rowing (Oxford University eight, 1864). *Address :* 6 Egerton Road, Fallowfield, Manchester. *Club :* Old Rectory, Manchester. (*Died 21 Sept. 1918.*)

ROBERTS, David Lloyd, M.D., F.R.C.P., F.R.S.E. ; Consulting Obstetric Physician, Manchester Royal Infirmary ; Physician to St. Mary's Hospitals, Manchester ; Lecturer on Clinical Obstetrics and Gynæcology in Manchester University ; *b.* Stockport ; *s.* of Robert Roberts, cotton spinner ; *m.* Martha, *d.* of W. H. Oceleshaw, of Plymouth Grove, Manchester. *Educ.:* Ripponden College (formerly Making Place Hall) ; Royal School of Medicine and Surgery, and Royal Infirmary, Manchester ; articled pupil to William Smith, F.R.C.S., the first Prof. of Physiology in Owens College. Fellow of Royal Medico-Chirurgical Society and Medical Society, London ; and member of other professional and scientific bodies ; late President of North of England Obstetrical and Gynæcological Society ; Vice-President of London Obstetrical Society ; President of Manchester Medico-Ethical and Medical Societies ; President in 1902 of Section of Midwifery, British Medical Association. *Publications :* The Practice of Midwifery, 1876, 4th edition 1896 ; various professional papers ; editor of Sir Thomas Browne's Religio Medici, 1892, revised edition 1898 ; The Scientific Knowledge of Dante, 1914. *Recreations :* reading ; collecting objects of art, books, bindings, etc. *Address :* Broughton Park, Manchester. (*Died 20 Sept. 1920.*)

ROBERTS, Rev. Edward Dale, M.D., Canon of Birmingham ; Vicar of Hill, Four Oaks ; *b.* 1848 ; *m.* ; one *s.* *Educ. :* Oxford. Curate of St. George's, Birmingham, 1872-77 ; Vicar of St. Paul's, Lozells, forty years. (*Died 8 Sept. 1927.*)

ROBERTS, Frederick Thomas, M.D., F.R.C.P. ; Hon. D.Sc. University of Wales ; Consulting Physician to University College Hospital and to Brompton Hospital. *Educ. :* University College, London. Emeritus Professor of Medicine and Clinical Medicine, University College, London. *Publications :* A Handbook of the Theory and Practice of Medicine, 10th ed. ; formerly assistant editor of Quain's Dictionary of Medicine. *Address :* 95 North Gate, Regent's Park, N.W. (*Died 28 July 1918.*)

ROBERTS, Rt. Hon. George Henry, Director of Companies ; P.C. ; J.P. ; M.P. (Lab.) Norwich, 1906-18, (Independent) 1918-1923 ; *b.* Chedgrave, Norfolk, 27 July 1869 ; *m.* 1895, Anne, *d.* of Horace Marshall, Norwich. Was Secretary Typographical Association and President Trades Council, Norwich ; joined I.L.P. 1886 ; Norwich School Board, 1889 ; a Lord Commissioner of the Treasury, 1915-16 ; Parliamentary Sec. to Board of Trade, 1916-18 ; Minister of Labour, 1917-18 ; Food Controller, Jan. 1919-Feb. 1920 ; Chairman National Advisory Committee on the Blind, Ministry of Health, since 1920 ; contested Norwich as Unionist, 1923. *Address :* 56 Abbey House, Victoria Street, Westminster, S.W. ; Westminster House, 104 Earlham Road, Norwich. (*Died 25 April 1928.*)

ROBERTS, Lieut.-Col. Henry Roger Crompton-, D.S.O. 1902 ; retired ; late Grenadier Guards ; *b.* 18 May 1863 ; *e. s.* of Charles Henry Crompton-Roberts of Drybridge, Monmouthshire, and Mary, *d.* and *heiress* of Roger Crompton of Kearsley, Lancs ; *m.* 1905, Blanche Alexandra, *d.* of Lieut.-Col. E. A. Hannay of Ballylough, Co. Antrim ; one *s.* two *d.* *Educ. :* Eton. Entered Army, 1884 ; Capt. 1895 ; Major, 1899 ; Lieut.-Col. 1905 ; served S. Africa

(despatches twice). *Address :* 10 Park Street, Mayfair, W.1 *Club :* Guards'.
(*Died 16 Sept. 1925.*)

ROBERTS, Col. Sir Howland, 12th Bt., *cr.* 1620, and 5th Bt., *cr.* 1809 ; V.D., D.L. ; and J.P. for County of London ; late commanding London Irish Rifles ; *b.* 2 Sep. 1845 ; 2nd *s.* of 10th (3rd) Bt. and Anne Elliott, *d.* of Hon. Captain William Langdon, R.N., M.L.C. ; *S.* half-b. 1899 ; *m.* 1895, Elizabeth Marie, *d.* of late W. T. La Roche, M.D. ; two *s.* *Educ. :* King's College, London. Ensign London Irish Rifles, 1868 ; Colonel, 1896-1906 ; a Freemason. *Heir :* *s.* Thomas Langdon Howland, *b.* 18 June 1898. *Address :* 75A Lexham Gardens, W. *T. :* Western 6206. *Clubs :* St. Stephen's ; Royal Cork Yacht.
(*Died 19 Dec. 1917.*)

ROBERTS, James Frederick, C.M.G. 1912 ; F.R.G.S. ; *b.* 13 Sep. 1847 ; *o. s.* of late J. F. Roberts, of Waston, near Bath, Barrister-at-law ; *m.* 1874, Mary Beatrice, 2nd *d.* of Sankey Gardner, J.P., of Eaglesbush, Neath ; one *d.* *Educ.:* Tonbridge School ; France and Germany. Deputy Commissioner and Vice-Consul, Oil Rivers Protectorate, 1891 ; Consul, Guatemala, 1894 ; Consul, Barcelona, 1897 ; Consul-General, 1901-14 ; Acting Commissioner and Consul-General for the Niger Coast Protectorate, March to June 1898 ; was also in charge of the British Legation at Guatemala as Chargé d'Affaires, 1895-96 ; Consul-General, Odessa, 1914 ; retired, 1916. Coronation medal, 1911. *Club :* St. James's. (*Died 10 Mar. 1927.*)

ROBERTS, Sir John, Kt., *cr.* 1911 ; Mayor of Carnarvon, 1910 ; *b.* 9 Jan. 1861 ; *m.* 1887, Evelyn Augusta, *d.* of Evan Evans ; one *s.* one *d.* Solicitor, 1884 ; Clerk to Carnarvonshire County Council, 1903. *Address :* Plas Llanwnda, Carnarvon. (*Died 7 April 1917.*)

ROBERTS, Sir John Reynolds, Kt., *cr.* 1911 ; J.P. ; C.C. Essex and Co. boro' of West Ham ; *b.* Camberwell, Surrey, 14 June 1834 ; *e. s.* of Thomas Roberts of Dulwich, and Elizabeth, *d.* of Thomas Pring of Bradninch, Somerset ; unmarried. *Educ. :* Dulwich Grammar School. Member of the Worshipful Company of Framework Knitters ; Essex Sewer Commissioner ; Freedom of City of London ; Life-Governor of Cancer Hosp., Brompton, London. *Recreations :* shooting, motoring, golf. *Address :* Salway House, Woodford Green. *T. :* 506 Woodford. *M. :* F 5296. *Clubs :* National Liberal, Royal Automobile. (*Died 25 Sept. 1917.*)

ROBERTS, John Varley, Organist and Director of the Choir at Magdalen College, Oxford, 1882-1918 ; *b.* Poplar House, Stanningley, near Leeds, 25 Sep. 1841 ; *s.* of Joseph Varley Roberts ; *m.* 1866, *e. d.* of Rev. P. J. Maning, Vicar of Farsley, Leeds ; one *d.* *Educ.:* privately. Mus.Bac. Oxon, 1871 ; Mus.D., 1876 ; Hon. M.A., 1916 ; F.R.C.O., 1876. Organist of St. Bartholomew's, Armley, 1862-68 ; Halifax Parish Church, 1868-82 ; St. Giles', Oxford, 1885-93 ; Conductor of Oxford Choral and Philharmonic Society, 1885-93 ; Examiner for Degrees at Oxford in 1883-86, 1889, 1890-99-1900. *Publications :* Church Cantatas : The Story of the Incarnation ; Advent ; The Passion, for Organ and Voices ; Jonah, for Full Orchestra and Chorus ; very considerable Organ Voluntaries ; Practical Method for Training Choristers ; about sixty Anthems ; five Morning and Evening Church Services ; two Full Communion Services ; Part Songs, Tunes, etc. *Address :* 18 Holywell, Oxford. (*Died 9 Feb. 1920.*)

ROBERTS, Rt. Hon. Sir Samuel, 1st Bt., *cr.* 1919 ; P.C. 1922 ; Kt., *cr.* 1917 ; M.A., J.P., D.L. ; *b.* 1852 ; *e. s.* of late Samuel Roberts, M.A., J.P., of Queen's Tower, Sheffield ; *m.* 1880, Martha Susan, *o. d.* of late Archdeacon Blakeney ; four *s.* one *d.* *Educ. :* Repton ; Trinity College, Cambridge. Called to the Bar,

895

Inner Temple, 1878; Lord Mayor, Sheffield, 1899-1900; Deputy - Chairman West Riding Quarter Ses.; contested High Peak Division of Derbyshire, 1900; M.P. (C.) Ecclesall Division of Sheffield, 1902-23. *Recreations:* shooting, fishing, golf. *Heir: s.* Samuel. *Address:* Queen's Tower, Sheffield; 4 Whitehall Court, S.W. *Clubs:* Carlton, Oxford and Cambridge.
(*Died 19 June 1926.*)

ROBERTS, Sir Thomas Edwards, Kt., *cr.* 1911; J.P., D.L.; High Sheriff of Carnarvonshire; *b.* 1851; *s.* of Pierce Roberts, Llyndy, Beddgelert; *m.* 1888, Emily, *d.* of Jas. Taylor, Greenley, Manchester. Commercial career in Manchester and Director of several large companies in England and Wales. *Address:* Plasybryn, Carnarvon. *T.:* 47 Carnarvon. *M.:* CC 12, 371 and 116. *Clubs:* Brasenose, Reform, Manchester. (*Died 29 Aug. 1926.*)

ROBERTS, Thomas Francis, Principal, University College of Wales, Aberystwyth, since 1891; *b.* 25 Sept 1860; *e. s.* of Thomas Roberts, Aberdovey, Merioneth; *m.* Mary Elizabeth, *o. c.* of Robert Davies, Cardiff, 1893; one *s.* *Educ.:* Towyn Academy; Univ. Coll. of Wales, Aberystwyth (Scholar and Associate, 1874-1879); St. John's Coll. Oxford (Scholar, 1879-83); 1st Class Classical Moderations, Oxford, 1881: 1st Class Lit. Hum. 1883; M.A. 1886; Hon. LL.D. Victoria Univ., Manchester, 1902; Professor of Greek, University College of South Wales and Monmouthshire, Cardiff, 1883-91; Chairman of the Cardiganshire County Governing Body of Intermediate Schools, 1896-99, 1901-2; Vice-Chancellor of the Univ. of Wales, 1897-98, 1901-3, 1907-9, 1913-15; Fellow of Jesus College, Oxford, 1915-16; Member of Cardiganshire Education Committee; Member of Council of St. David's College, Lampeter; President of Baptist Union of Wales and Monmouthshire, 1907-8; Member of the Council of the National Library of Wales, of the Executive Committee of the Central Welsh Board of Intermediate Education, and of the Joint Board of Legal Education for Wales. *Publications:* addresses and articles in English and Welsh, mainly on education. *Address:* Treathro, Aberystwyth. *T.A.:* Principal Roberts, Aberystwyth. *T.:* Aberystwyth 115. (*Died 4 Aug. 1919.*)

ROBERTS, Sir Thomas Lee, Kt., *cr.* 1918; *b.* Stockport, 8 Aug. 1848; *s.* of Thomas Roberts, J.P., Civil Engineer, and Ellen Lee, Bolton, Lancashire; *m.* 1st, Mima Horten, Warrington; eight *s.*; 2nd, 1920, Emily Sarah Davis, *d.* of late W. Davis, Odiham, Hants. *Educ.:* Grammar School, Stockport. Early in life entered the legal profession; served his articles in a firm of London Solicitors; entered the Inner Temple as a Barrister; called to the Bar, 1879; joined the Northern Circuit. *Recreations:* indoor games, but chiefly in the enjoyment of a well-stocked library. *Address:* Doddington Lodge, near Ludlow. *Clubs:* Devonshire, National Liberal. (*Died 16 Jan. 1924.*)

ROBERTS, His Hon. Sir Walworth Howland, Kt., *cr.* 1921; C.B.E. 1920; J.P. Staffs; formerly Judge of the Marylebone County Court; retired, 1921; was member (Chairman) of standing County Courts Rules Committee; served 1918-19 as one of the Chairmen Committee on Production, and of Court of Arbitration under Wages (Temporary Regulation) Acts; Standing Arbitrator under Ministry of Transport Act 1922; *b.* 1855; 3rd *s.* of Sir Thomas Howland Roberts, Bt.; *m.* 1890, Katherine, *d.* of John Gibson Thomson of Aitechuan, Ardrishaig, and Catherine, *d.* of John Sinclair of Lochaline, Co. Argyll; one *s.* one *d.* *Educ.:* Highgate School; King's College, London. Called to Bar, Middle Temple, 1878; went Western Circuit and Devon and Exeter Sessions; an Examiner of the Court, and a Revising Barrister for London and Middlesex,

1889-1900; Lieut. 3rd Vol. Batt. Rifle Brigade, 1873-78; Judge Circuit 25, 1900-5; Circuit 37, 1905-11; Circuit 41, 1912-19; President Walsall and District Board of Conciliation and Arbitration, 1904-5. *Publications:* joint author of Roberts' and Wallace's Duty and Liability of Employers, and joint editor of Amos' and Ferard's Law of Fixtures. *Address:* Curtesden, Camberley, Surrey. (*Died 21 Dec. 1924.*)

ROBERTS, Rev. William Henry, D.D., LL.D.; Stated Clerk, General Assembly Presbyterian Church in U.S.A., since 1884; American Secretary of The Alliance of the Reformed Churches throughout the World since 1888; *b.* Holyhead, Wales, 31 Jan. 1844; *s.* of Rev. William Roberts, D.D., and Katherine Parry; *m.* 1867, Sarah E. M'Lean, Washington; two *s.* two *d.* *Educ.:* College, City of New York, 1863. Statistician U.S. Treasury Dept., 1863-65; Assist. Librarian, Congress, Washington, 1866-71; graduated Princeton Theological Seminary, 1873; D.D., Western University of Pennsylvania, 1884: Lafayette College, 1907; LL.D., Miami University, 1887; Pastor, Presbyterian Church, Cranford, N.J., 1873-7; Librarian, Princeton Theological Seminary, 1878-86; Professor Practical Theology, Lane Theological Seminary, Cincinnati, 1886-93; Acting Pastor, 4th Presbyterian Church, Trenton, N.J., 1895-1900; Treasurer, Centennial Fund, 1888-89; President, Glasgow, Scotland, Pan - Presbyterian Council, 1896; Secretary, American Inter-Church Conference on Marriage and Divorce, 1903-10; President, Inter-Church Conference on Federation, New York City, 1905, and of Federal Council of the Churches of Christ in America, 1908; Moderator, Presbyterian General Assembly, 1907; Treasurer, Sustentation Fund, 1906-1912; first Chairman, Executive Committee Federal Council of American Protestant Churches, 1908-12; Chairman, Presbyterian Committee on Church Co-operation and Union since 1903; Member, American Deputation to Great Britain for World Conference of Churches, 1914; Chairman, Armenian Relief Committee. etc., Philadelphia, 1915-19; Secretary, National Service Commission Presbyterian Church, 1917-1918; Chairman, Conference of American Churches on Organic Union, 1918-19. *Publications:* History of the Presbyterian Church, 1888; The Presbyterian System, 1895; Laws Relating to Religious Corporations, 1896; Manual for Ruling Elders, 1897, etc.; Editor, Minutes of General Assembly, 34 vols., 1884-1917; Addresses at the 250th Anniversary of the Westminster Assembly, 1898; Proceedings, Presbyterian Inter-Church Conference on Federation, 1905; Presbyterian Handbook, 1896-1919; many magazine articles. *Address:* Witherspoon Building, Philadelphia, Pa. *T.A.:* Alliance, Philadelphia. *T.:* Walnut 44-83. *Club:* City.
(*Died 26 June 1921.*)

ROBERTS, Col. William Henry, J.P.; *b.* 1848; *o. s.* of late Capt. William Henry Roberts, R.E., and Anne, *e. d.* of late William Lee, M.P., of Holborough Court; *m.* 1870, Edith, *y. d.* of John Jerdein, London; *S.* grandfather, 1881. *Educ.:* Eton. Patron of one living; Major and Hon. Lt.-Col. Queen's Own West Kent Yeomanry. *Address:* Holborough Court, near Rochester. *Clubs:* United Service; Royal Yacht Squadron, Cowes. (*Died 7 April 1926.*)

ROBERTS, William Lee Henry, J.P. Kent; *e. s.* of late Col. W. H. Roberts; *b.* 15 Jan. 1871; unmarried. *Educ.:* Eton College; R.M.C., Sandhurst. Late Lt. Royal Dragoons; Captain West Kent Yeomanry; High Sheriff, Kent, 1920. *Address:* Holborough Court, Rochester, Kent. *Clubs:* Army and Navy, Carlton. (*Died 18 Oct. 1923.*)

ROBERTS, Rev. William Masfen, Rector of Luddesdown since 1893; Hon. Canon of Rochester, 1895. *Educ.:* Jesus College,

Cambridge (M.A.). Curate of St. John and Ladywood, Birmingham, 1869; Upton-on-Severn, 1869-74; Fellow of St. Augustine's College, Canterbury, 1874-75; Curate of Melton, Hants, 1875-78; St. Cross, Winchester, 1878-81; Shoreham, Kent, 1881-89; Hayes, 1889-92; Luddesdown, 1892-93. *Address:* Luddesdown Rectory, Gravesend.   (*Died 9 Feb. 1927.*)

ROBERTS, Very Rev. William Page-, Dean of Salisbury, 1907-19; *b.* 2 Jan. 1836; *s.* of W. Roberts, Brookfield, Lancashire; *m.* 1878, Hon. Margaret Grace (*d.* 1926), 6th *d.* of 5th Lord Rivers; three *d. Educ.:* Liverpool College; St. John's College, Cambridge (M.A.); D.D. Glasgow. Vicar of Eye, Suffolk; Minister of St. Peter's, Vere Street, London, 1878-1907, and Canon of Canterbury, 1895-1907. *Publications:* Law and God, 5th ed.: Reasonable Service, 3rd ed.; Liberalism in Religion, 2nd ed.; Conformity and Conscience. 1899, 3rd ed. *Address:* Highlands, Shanklin, Isle of Wight. *Club:* Albemarle.   (*Died 17 Aug. 1928.*)

ROBERTSON, Rev. Charles, Hon. Canon of Newcastle. *Address:* Belford, Northumberland.   (*Died Jan. 1921.*)

ROBERTSON, Rev. David, M.A.; Honorary Canon of Worcester, 1905; Hon. Chaplain to the King; Chaplain to Bishop of Bath and Wells; *b.* 1888; *s.* of late Hon. Lord Benholme; *m.* 1871, Eleanora Charlotte Dalrymple, *y. d.* of Sir Charles Dalrymple Fergusson, 5th Bart.; one *s.* two *d. Educ.:* Edinburgh Academy; Trinity College, Cambridge; Senior Opt., 1861. Formerly Vicar of Lye, Worcestershire; Rector of Market Deeping, Lincolnshire; Rector of Hartlebury. *Address:* Benholme, Malvern Wells.   (*Died 11 April 1916.*)

ROBERTSON, David, A.R.S.A., F.R.I.B.A. *Address:* 23 St. Ronan's Terrace, Edinburgh. *Club:* Scottish Art, Edinburgh.   (*Died 20 Feb. 1925.*)

ROBERTSON, Sir Frederick Alexander, Kt., *cr.* 1913; K.B.E., *cr.* 1918; *b.* 28 Feb. 1854; *s.* of James R. Robertson and Mary Elizabeth Campbell of Bragleen, Argyllshire; *m.* 1st, Beatrice Mary Angelo; 2nd, Dorothy, *d.* of Colonel E. R. Bromhead; one *d. Educ.:* privately; King's College. Entered Indian Civil Service, 1876; Barrister-at-law; Director of Department of Agriculture, Punjab, 1889-96; Vice-Chancellor of the Punjab University, 1909-1910; LL.D.; Puisne Judge, Chief Court, Punjab, India, 1898-1913; Fellow of King's College, London, 1915; Lecturer on Hindu and Mahomedan Law to the Council of Legal Education; Lecturer on Mahomedan Law at Imperial Institute. *Publications:* Report on the Settlement and Forest Settlement of the Rawal Pindi District; Customary Law and Gazetteer of the Rawal Pindi District; Report on the Tenures of the Maler Kotla State. *Recreations:* cricket, golf, shooting, etc. *Address:* 1 Eaton Terrace, S.W. *T.:* Victoria 7070. *Clubs:* East India United Service, M.C.C.; Royal and Ancient, St. Andrews.   (*Died 20 Dec. 1919.*)

ROBERTSON, Sir George Scott, K.C.S.I., *cr.* 1895; C.S.I. 1892; M.P. (L.) Central Bradford since 1906; *b.* London, 22 Oct. 1852; 2nd *s.* of T. J. Robertson (*o. s.* of Thomas J. Robertson, Rousay, Orkney), and Robina Corston, 2nd *d.* of late Robert Scott, Kirkwall, Orkney; *m.* 1st, 1882, Catharine, *e. d.* of Colonel A. J. C. Birch; 2nd, 1894, Mary, *d.* of Samuel Laurence the painter; one *d. Educ.:* Westminster Hospital Medical School. Entered Indian Medical Service, 1878; served through Afghan campaign, 1879-80, including siege of Sherpur; from June 1888 passed into the employment of the Indian Foreign Office, and was continually employed on Gilgit frontier of Kashmir, and eventually became British Agent of Gilgit; travelled in Kafiristan, 1890-91,

30

living for a year amongst the wild hillmen; chief political officer Hunza-Nagar Expedition, 1891-1892; installed the Mir of Hunza in presence of Chinese envoys, 1892; besieged in Thalpen entrenchment, and present at capture of Chilas, 1892; conducted a political mission to Chitral, 1893; besieged in Chitral, where he was severely wounded, during March and April 1895; installed the present ruler of Chitral, Sept. 1895; for services has been granted three war medals, etc.; he is an Hon. D.C.L. of Trinity University, Toronto; contested Stirlingshire (L.), 1900. *Publications:* The Kafirs of the Hindu Kush, 1896; Chitral: the Story of a Minor Siege, 1898. *Address:* 14 Cheyne Walk, Chelsea, S.W. *T.:* Kensington 3695. *Clubs:* Athenæum, Savile, National Liberal, Burlington Fine Arts.   (*Died 3 Jan. 1916.*)

ROBERTSON, Sir Helenus Robert, Kt.; *cr.* 1913; Chairman Mersey Docks and Harbour Board since 1911, and Union Marine Insurance Co.; Director Phœnix Assurance Co. and Bank of Liverpool; *b.* Greenock, 1841; *s.* of James Hunter Robertson of Bagatelle, Greenock; *m.*; one *s.* one *d. Educ.:* Upper Canada College, Toronto. Formerly partner in the firm of Finlay, Robertson & Co., cotton brokers; President of the Cotton Association, 1882; retired from business, 1883; Member of the Mersey Docks and Harbour Board since 1883. *Recreation:* golf principally. *Address:* Upton Grange, Chester. *Clubs:* Union, Alpine.   (*Died 22 Mar. 1919.*)

ROBERTSON, Henry Robert, R.E., R.M.S.; *b.* Windsor, 1839; *m.* Agnes Lucy Turner; one *s.* three *d.* Academy student; exhibitor at R.A. in oil, water-colour, and etching; picture "Winter" now in the Sheffield Municipal Gallery. *Publications:* wrote and illustrated Plants We Play with; Life on the Upper Thames, etc.; Handbooks on Etching, Pottery-Painting, and Pen-and-Ink Drawing. *Address:* 1 Steele's Studios, Haverstock Hill, N.W.; 9 Elsworthy Terrace, N.W.   (*Died 6 June 1921.*)

ROBERTSON, Herbert; Barr. Lincoln's Inn; J.P.; *b.* 26 Apr. 1849; *s.* of late Thomas Storm Robertson, M.D., F.R.C.S., and Maria, *d.* of Robert Manning; *m.* Helen, *e. d.* of Alexander Durdin, Huntington Castle, Clonegal, Co. Carlow, 1 Jan. 1880; three *s.* one *d.*; M.P. (C.) South Hackney, 1895-1906. *Educ.:* Magdalen Coll. Oxford (M.A.) *Address:* Huntington Castle, Clonegal, Ireland; 36 Bedford Square, W.C. *Clubs:* Athenæum, Carlton, Savile.   (*Died 11 July 1916.*)

ROBERTSON, Very Rev. James, D.D., Parish Minister of Whittingehame, 1865-1918; *b.* 1837; *s.* of Charles Robertson, Schoolmaster, Lethendy, Perthshire; *m.* 1885, Elizabeth Mary, *d.* of Robert Scott-Moncrieff of Fossaway. *Educ.:* St. Andrews. Assistant Minister at Kinghorn, 1861-65; Chaplain to the Lord High Commissioners, 1883-85, 1907-8; Lecturer on Pastoral Theology, 1899-1900, 1902-4; Chairman of Christian Unity Association, 1908-17; Moderator of the General Assembly of the Church of Scotland, 1909. *Publications:* Our Lord's Teaching; The Christian Minister, His Aims and Methods; Lady Blanche Balfour, a Reminiscence; Christian Upbringing; Spiritual Power in the Church, closing address of General Assembly, 1909. *Address:* 36 Queen's Crescent, Newington, Edinburgh.   (*Died 27 May 1920.*)

ROBERTSON, Rev. James, D.D., LL.D.; *b.* Alyth, Perthshire, 2 Mar. 1840; *m.* Catherine, *d.* of John Martin, manufacturer, Dundee, 1864; one *s.* two *d. Educ.:* Alyth Parish School; Grammar School, Aberdeen; Univ. and King's College, Aberdeen; St. Mary's Coll. St. Andrews. M.A. with 1st class Honours in Philosophy, Aberdeen, 1859; Missionary Church of Scotland, Constantinople, 1862-64; Beyrout, Syria, 1864-75; minister of Mayfield Church, Edin-

897

burgh, 1875-77 ; Officier d'Académie, 1906 ; Professor of Hebrew and Semitic Languages (late Oriental Languages), Glasgow Univ., 1877-1907. *Publications :* translation of Müller's Outlines of Hebrew Syntax, 1882 ; The Early Religion of Israel, 1892 ; The Old Testament and its Contents, 1893, enlarged ed. 1896 ; The Poetry and the Religion of the Psalms, 1898 ; The First and Second Books of the Kings (Temple Bible), 1902. *Recreations :* gardening, walking. *Address :* 161 Mayfield Road, Edinburgh. *T. :* 5559 Central.
(Died Dec. 1920.)

ROBERTSON, Lt.-Col. James Currie ; C.M.G. 1917 ; C.I.E. 1914 ; M.B., M.A., B.Sc., D.P.H. Entered Indian Medical Service, 1896 ; Captain, 1899 ; Major, 1907 ; Lt.-Col., 1915 ; served with Dongola Expedition (Suakin) 1896 (medal, Khedive's medal) ; South Africa, 1902, on special duty under the Director of Burgher Camps, Transvaal (Queen's medal with two clasps, despatches) ; Deputy Sanitary Commissioner, United Provinces, 1901 ; Sanitary Commissioner with the Government of India, 1912. *Address :* Simla, India. *(Died 13 May 1923.)*

ROBERTSON, Dr. James Edwin ; Senator since 1902, and Medical Doctor since 1865 ; *b.* New Peith, P.E. Island, Canada 1840 ; *m.* 1879, Elizabeth M'Farlane of Charlottetown, P.E. Island. *Educ. :* Charlottetown Academy ; McGill University, Montreal. A Member of local Parliament of P.E.I., 1870-82 ; a Member of House of Commons, Canada, 1882-90. *Address :* Montague, Prince Edward Island.

ROBERTSON, James Logie (pen-name, **Hugh Haliburton**), First English Master, Edinburgh Ladies' College, 1891 ; retired 1914 ; *b.* Milnathort, Kinross-shire ; 2nd *s.* of William Robertson and Mary Logie ; *m.* Janet, *d.* of P. Simpson, S.S.C., 1881 ; two *s.* three *d. Educ. :* Orwell Parish School ; Edinburgh University. Medallist in Rhetoric, 1870 ; Gray prizeman, 1871 ; M.A. 1872 ; Murchison prizeman in Geology, 1873 ; Glasgow St. Andrew's Society prizeman, 1874 ; Assistant Master Heriot's Hospital, 1871 ; Assist. Master George Watson's College (Boys), 1872 ; Edin. Ladies' College, 1876 ; travelled in Norway (Sætersdal) and Sweden (Swedish Lapland). *Publications :* Poetry — Poems, 1878 ; Orellana and other Poems, 1881 ; Our Holiday Among the Hills (conjointly with his wife), 1882 ; Horace in Homespun, 1886, new ed. illus. 1900 ; Ochil Idylls, 1891. Prose—The White Angel, and other Stories, 1886 ; For Puir Auld Scotland, 1887 ; In Scottish Fields, 1890 ; Furth in Field, 1894 ; A History of English Literature, 1894 ; Outline of English Literature for Young Scholars, 1897. Editorial work —Poems of Allan Ramsay, 1887 ; Burns's Letters, 1888 ; Selections from Burns, 1889 ; Thomson's Seasons and The Castle of Indolence, 1891 ; Scott's Poetical Works, 1894 ; Burns's Poetical Works, 1896 ; Milton's Paradise Lost, books i.-iv., 1900 ; The Select Chaucer, 1902 ; The Select Tennyson, 1903 ; Excursions in Prose and Verse, 1905 ; Campbell's Poetical Works, 1907 ; Thomson's Poems, and The Seasons, a variorum edition, 1908 ; Nature in Books, 1914 ; Petition to the De'il and Other War Verses, 1917. *Recreations :* travelling, angling, geologising. *Address :* 1 Braidburn Crescent, Edint'rgh.
(Died June 1922.)

ROBERTSON, Colonel James Peter, C.B. 1858 ; retired ; *s.* of Hon. Duncan Robertson and Susan Stewart, of the Royal House of Fincastle ; *m.* 1862, Louisa (*d.* 1910), *y. d.* of John Churchill, J.P., Oakfield, Wimbledon. *Educ. :* High School, Edinburgh ; Edinburgh Military Academy. Served in 31st Regt. throughout Sutlej campaign ; also the Crimean campaign ; and commanded a regiment of Light Cavalry throughout the Indian Mutiny ; retired in 1870, having 11 decorations for active service. *Decorated* for

898

capture of Lucknow. *Publication :* Personal Adventures and Anecdotes of an Old Officer. *Address :* Callander Lodge, Callander. N.B.
(Died 11 Feb. 1916.)

ROBERTSON, John, M.B.E. 1918 ; M.P. (Lab.) Bothwell Division of Lanarkshire since 1919 ; Chairman Scottish Miners' Union ; *b.* 1867. Worked in coal mines as a boy of thirteen ; a Lord Commissioner of the Treasury, 1924. *Address :* Cadzowbury House, Hamilton, Lanarkshire. *T. :* Hamilton 223. *(Died 14 Feb. 1926.)*

ROBERTSON, Rev. John, Hon. Canon of Newcastle. *Address :* The Vicarage, Acklington S.O., Northumberland.

ROBERTSON, Thomas, I.S.O. 1903 ; *b.* Edinburgh, 17 Aug. 1842 ; *s.* of Alexander Robertson and Eliza Dryden ; *m.* 1867, Helen Graham (*d.* 1912), *d.* of James Leask, Kirkwall ; three *s.* four *d. Educ. :* Parish School of Shapinshay, Orkney. Apprenticeship in law office, Kirkwall, 1859 - 63 ; entered Inland Revenue Department, 1863 ; Chief Clerk, solicitor's office, Inland Revenue, Edinburgh, 1876 - 1904. *Address :* Stromberry Villa, Newhaven Road, Edinburgh. *(Died 25 Oct. 1925.)*

ROBERTSON, Sir William, Kt., *cr.* 1910 ; linen manufacturer ; Lord Lieut., Co. Fife ; Vice-Chairman of the Carnegie Trusts, Dunfermline ; Member of Extra Parliamentary Panel under Scottish Provisional Orders Bill ; *b.* 7 Oct. 1856 ; *m.* 1887, Elizabeth, *e. d.* of William Berry, Scotston, Aberdeen. *Address :* Benachie, Dunfermline. *Clubs :* Reform ; Scottish Liberal, Edinburgh. *(Died 27 Feb. 1923.)*

ROBERTSON, William Chrystal, I.S.O. 1902 ; was Secretary, Fishery Board for Scotland, 1892-1909. *Address :* 47 Colinton Road, Edinburgh. *(Died 31 Aug. 1922.)*

ROBINS, Rev. William Henry, D.D., Rural Dean and Hon. Canon of Rochester, 1907 ; *b.* 17 Mar. 1847 ; *s.* of William Robins of The Limes, Buxton, Derbyshire ; *m.* 1874, Annie Maria Isabella, *e. d.* of William Rumney, Stubbins House, Lancashire ; three *s.* one *d. Educ. :* College for Blind Sons of Gentlemen, Worcester ; Trinity College, Dublin ; B.A., 1872 ; Div. Test, 1873 ; M.A., 1876 ; B.D. and D.D., 1889. Curate of Tickenhall, Derbyshire, 1875 - 78 ; Vicar of Gillingham, 1878-1915. *Recreations :* music, walking, reading. *Address :* The Restoration House, Rochester. *T. :* Chatham 373.
(Died 27 Mar. 1923.)

ROBINSON, Rev. Arthur William, D.D. (Cantab.) ; Residentiary Canon, Canterbury Cathedral, since 1916 ; *b.* Keynsham Vicarage, Somerset, 19 Jan. 1856 ; *s.* of Rev. George and Henrietta Cecilia Robinson ; *m.* 1918, Mary Beatrice, *d.* of late Rev. Dr. Moore, Canon of Canterbury ; two *s.* one *d. Educ. :* Bristol Grammar School ; Liverpool College ; Jesus College, Cambridge ; Carus University prize, 1st class Theological Tripos. Ordained as Curate to his father at St. Augustine's, Liverpool, 1879 ; Rector of East Shefford, Berks, 1881 ; Vicar of Bilton, Harrogate, 1884 ; joined the Mission Staff of Allhallows Barking, 1888 ; Vicar of Allhallows Barking, E.C., 1895 ; Rural Dean of the East City, 1908 ; Six-preacher of Canterbury Cathedral, 1896 ; Examining Chaplain to the Bishop of London, 1909 ; Proctor in Convocation for Clergy of London, 1910 ; for the Chapter of Canterbury, 1919. *Publications :* The Church Catechism Explained ; A Commentary on Tennyson's In Memoriam ; The Epistle to the Galatians Explained ; The Personal Life of the Clergy ; Co-operation with God ; The Voice of Joy and Health ; Spiritual Progress ; God and the World, a Survey of Thought ; The Trend of Thought in Contemporary Philosophy ; The Christ of the Gospels ; The Christianity of the Epistles ; The New Learning and the Old Faith ;

etc. *Address :* The Precincts, Canterbury.
(*Died 7 Dec. 1928.*)

ROBINSON, Rev. Charles Henry, D.D.; Hon. Canon of Ripon since 1897; Editorial Secretary to the Society for the Propagation of the Gospel. 1902 ; Lecturer in Hausa, University of Cambridge, 1896-1906 ; *b.* Keynsham, 1861 ; *s.* of Rev. G. Robinson, Monaghan, Ireland ; *m.* 1st, 1896, Clare, *d.* of Joseph Arnold, Tunbridge Wells, one *d.* ; 2nd, 1907, Cecily, *d.* of Sir Ernest George ;   one *s.* one *d.* *Educ. :* Liverpool College ; Trinity College, Cambridge. College and University Prizeman ; B.A. 1883 ; M.A. 1888 ; Hon. D.D. Edinburgh, 1910 ; Deacon, 1884 ; Priest, 1885 ; Fellow and Tutor of St. Augustine's College, Canterbury, 1889 ; Vice-Chancellor of Truro Cathedral, 1890-93 ; travelled in Armenia in order to report to Archbishop of Canterbury on the condition of Armenian Church, 1892 ; conducted pioneer expedition to Kano, the commercial centre of the Central Soudan, starting by way of the river Niger, after first making an ineffectual attempt to reach Kano by crossing the Great Sahara from the north, 1893-95. *Publications :* The Church and Her Teaching, 1893 ; Hausaland, or Fifteen Hundred Miles through the Central Soudan, 1896, 3rd ed. 1900 ; Specimens of Hausa Literature, 1896 ; Grammar of the Hausa Language, 5th ed. 1925 ; Mohammedanism : Has it any Future ? 1897 ; the Gospel of St. John in Hausa, 1899 ; Dictionary of the Hausa Language, 4th ed. 1924 ; Studies in the Character of Christ, 8th ed. 1920 ; Nigeria, our latest Protectorate, 1900 ; Human Nature a Revelation of the Divine, 3rd ed. 1910 ; Studies in the Resurrection, 3rd ed. 1911 ; Studies in Worship, 3rd ed. 1910 ; The Interpretation of the Character of Christ to Non-Christian Races, 4th ed. 1913 ; Studies in the Passion of Jesus Christ, 3rd ed. 1916 ; Our Bounden Duty, 1912 ; A Devotional Psalter, 1912 ; The Missionary Prospect, 2nd ed., 1912 ; History of Christian Missions, 1915 ; The Conversion of Europe, 1918 ; How the Gospel spread through Europe, 1917 ; Life of Otto, Apostle of Pomerania, 1920 ; Life of Auskar, the Apostle of the North, 1921. *Address :* S.P.G. House, 15 Tufton Street, S.W. 1. *T. :* Victoria 1398 ; 11 Croham Park Avenue, S. Croydon. *T. :* Croydon 1721   (*Died 23 Nov. 1925.*)

ROBINSON, Major - General Sir Charles Walker, K.C.B., *cr.* 1923 ; C.B. 1887 ; retired (late Rifle Brigade); *b.* Toronto, Canada, 3 April 1836 ; *y. s.* of Sir John Beverley Robinson, Bt., C.B., and Emma, *d.* of Charles Walker of Harlesden, Middlesex ; *m.* 1884, Margaret Frances, *d.* of Gen. Sir Archibald Alison, 2nd Bt. ; one *s.* two *d.* *Educ. :* Upper Canada Coll. ; Trin. Coll., Toronto. B.A. and Hon. LL.D. Joined Rifle Brig., 1857 ; passed through Staff College, 1865 ; served in the Indian Mutiny (medal) ; in Ashanti Expedition, 1873-74 ; Brigade-Major, European Brigade (despatches, medal with clasp and Brev. of Major); Zulu War, 1879 (A.A.G. 2nd Div.) (despatches, medal with clasp, brevet of Lt.-Colonel) ; held appointments of Brigade Major, D.A.A. Gen. and A.A.G. at Aldershot ; Assistant Military Secretary Headquarters of the Army, 1890-92 ; commanding the troops, Mauritius, 1892-95 ; Lt.-Governor and Secretary Royal Hospital, Chelsea, 1895-98 ; retired 1898. *Decorated* for military service. *Publication :* Strategy of the Peninsular War ; Life of Sir John Beverley Robinson, Bt. ; Wellington's Campaigns, 1808-15 ; Canada and Canadian Defence. *Recreations :* riding, cycling. *Address :* 5 Stanford Road, Cottesmore Gardens, Kensington, W.S. *Club :* Army and Navy.
(*Died 20 May 1924.*)

ROBINSON, Edward Kay; President of the British Empire Naturalists'

Association ; projector and editor of The Country-side, and Country Queries and Notes, both being now incorporated, with Science Gossip, in the monthly Country - side ; naturalist and author ; *b.* Naini Tal, 1857 ; *s.* of late Rev. Julian Robinson, Indian Army Chaplain, and Harriet Woodcocke Sharpe ; *m.* 1887, Florence Theresa Gordon ; two *s.* *Educ. :* Cheltenham College. Originator of the " By the Way " column in The Globe ; editor of the Civil and Military Gazette, Lahore, 1887-95 ; on staff of Globe, 1896-98 ; contributor to the Nineteenth Century, Fortnightly Review, etc. *Publications :* To-day with Nature, 1889 ; My Nature Notebook, 1901 ; In the King's County, 1903 ; The Country Day by Day, 1905 ; The Religion of Nature, 1906 ; The Meaning of Life, 1915 ; At Home with Nature (wireless talks), 1925. *Recreation :* natural history. *Address :* Warham, Hampton Wick.
(*Died 20 Jan. 1928.*)

ROBINSON, Sir Ernest William, 5th Bt. ; *cr.* 1823 ; *b.* 22 May 1862 ; *s.* of late Major-General John Innes Robinson ; *S. u.* 1895; *m.* 1st, 1897, Christina Eleanor (*d.* 1916), *d.* of Major Grant of Glen Grant, Rothes, N.B. ; one *d.* ; 2nd, 1920, *widow* of Col. Gordon Watson. *Heir :* *b.* Douglas Innes [*b.* 1863 ; *m.* 1903. *c.* Violet, *d.* of late Charles Herbert Ames, H.E.I.C.S.]. *Address :* Jersey.   (*Died 21 Dec. 1924.*)

ROBINSON, Frederic Cayley-, A.R.A. 1921 ; R.W.S. 1919 ; R.B.A. 1888 ; R.O.I. 1906 ; New English Art Club, 1912 ; Artistic Adviser, Haymarket Theatre, 1911 ; *b.* Brentford-on-Thames, 18 Aug. 1862 ; *s.* of Frederic Robinson ; *m.* 1896, Winifred Lucy Dalley ; one *d.* *Educ. :* Dr. Head, Cliftonville ; Lycée de Pau ; Royal Academy Schools : lived on a small yacht, 1888-90 ; painted The Outward Bound, The Ferry, Drifting, and other works ; studied at Julian's, 1890-92 ; painted Souvenir of a Past Age (exhibited Royal Academy 1894, now in the Adelaide permanent collection), The Close of Day (exhibited Paris International Exhibition), 1892-98 ; The Foundling, Romance, and other works, 1900 ; studied in Italy, painted Fata Morgana, The Depth of Winter, Twilight, and other works, 1898-1902 ; worked in Paris, painted The Deep, Midnight, Dawn, and other works, 1902-6 ; Youth, now in Cape Town permanent collection, The Farewell, Reminiscence, Waning Day, and other works, 1906-10 ; A Winter Evening and The Fisherman, both now in Italian National Collections ; The Death of Abel, now in the Luxembourg Gallery, Paris ; illustrated Genesis for the Medeci Society, and has done Mural decorations for the Middlesex Hospital, 1910 - 14 ; painted The Word, 1922, purchased for the Canadian National Gallery, 1922 ; painted Pastoral, 1924, purchased for the nation under the terms of the Chantry Bequest. *Address :* 1 Lansdowne House, Lansdowne Road, W.   (*Died 4 Jan. 1927.*)

ROBINSON, Rev. Henry; Rector of Badsworth, Yorks, since 1910 ; Canon and Prebendary of Ulleskelf in York Cathedral, 1908 ; Proctor and Synodal Secretary, York Convocation, 1904 ; *b.* 1849 ; *s.* of Mark A. and Sophia Robinson ; *m.* 1880, Caroline C. S., *d.* of late Archibald Sturrock, V.D., J.P., Cadogan Place ; two *d.* *Educ. :* Pembroke College, Oxford ; B.A. 1875 ; M.A. 1878. Took Holy Orders, 1875 ; Curate, St. James's, Doncaster, 1875-79 ; Vicar, Grosmont, 1879-93 ; Rector, St. Maurice, etc., York, 1893-1910 ; Hon. Chaplain to Archbishop of York, 1904-9. *Recreation :* motoring. *Address :* Badsworth Rectory, Pontefract. *M. :* O 4365 and U 2206. *Clubs :* Junior Constitutional ; Yorkshire, York.
(*Died 4 May 1918.*)

ROBINSON, Right Hon. Sir Henry Augustus, 1st Bt., *cr.* 1920 ; K.C.B., *cr.* 1900 ; P.C. Ireland ; Vice - President of the

Local Government Board for Ireland, 1898-1920.; *b.* 20 Nov. 1857; *s.* of late Sir Henry Robinson, K.C.B., and Eva, *d.* of 10th Viscount Valentia; *m.* 1885, Harriet, *d.* of Sir R. Lynch Blosse, 10th Bt., of Athavallie Balla, Co. Mayo, and Harriet, *d.* of 2nd Marquis of Sligo; three *s. Publication*: Memoirs: Wise and Otherwise, 1923; Further Memories of Irish Life, 1924 *Heir: s.* Christopher Henry Robinson, late Resident Magistrate, Co. Louth [*b.* 18 Oct. 1884; *m.* 1912, Dorothy, *d.* of Henry Warren, of Carrickmines, Co. Dublin; one *s. Educ.*: Wellington. *Address*: Highmoor, Parkstone]. *Clubs*: Carlton; Kildare Street, Dublin.

(Died 16 Oct. 1927.)

ROBINSON, Henry Betham, M.D., M.S. Lond., F.R.C.S. England; Surgeon to, and Lecturer on Surgery and Teacher of Operative Surgery at St. Thomas's Hospital; Consulting Surgeon to East London Hospital for Children, Shadwell, and to Children's Hospital, Plaistow; Major R.A.M.C. (T.F.); *b.* 6 Aug. 1860; *s.* of Henry Robinson of West Norwood; *m.* Eveline Louise, *y. surv. d.* of John Milling of Harrogate. *Educ.*: Dulwich College; St. Thomas's Hospital. Graduated as Bachelor of Medicine and Bachelor of Surgery in the University of London, 1885, obtaining the Scholarship and Gold Medal in Medicine and Gold Medal in Surgery; has been Surgeon for Diseases of the Throat, and Lecturer and Demonstrator of Anatomy at St. Thomas's; Hunterian Professor of Surgery and Pathology at the Royal College of Surgeons, England, giving lectures on Diseases of the Breast, 1892; Examiner in Surgery, Universities of London and Manchester. *Publications*: St. Thomas's Hospital Surgeons and the Practice of their Art in the Past; papers relating to Surgery and Diseases of the Throat in medical periodicals. *Recreations*: golf and motoring. *Address*: 1 Upper Wimpole Street, W. *T.*: Mayfair 5363. *M.*: Y 732. *Club*: Sports. *(Died 31 July 1918.)*

ROBINSON, Captain Henry Harold, D.S.O. 1916; R.A.M.C.; M.R.C.S., L.R.C.P. Lond.; Hon. Med. Officer Birkenhead Children's Hospital. *Educ.*: Owen's College, Manchester. Late Senior House Surgeon Southport Infirmary; House Surgeon Infirmary, Burton-on-Trent; served European War, 1914-17 (D.S.O.). *Address*: 39 Park Road, South Birkenhead, and 38 Woodchurch Road, Birkenhead. *T.*: 318. *(Died 1919.)*

ROBINSON, Sir John Holdsworth, Kt., *cr.* 1924; J.P.; Chevalier, Legion of Honour; a member of Council, Yorkshire Provincial Division, National Unionist Association; *b.* 1855; *s.* of James Robinson. Bradford. *Address*: Greenhill Hall, Bingley, Yorks.

(Died 19 April 1927.)

ROBINSON, Rev. John J., D.D. Dublin; Warden of St. John's College, and Head Master of Collegiate School, Winnipeg, since 1913; *b.* Dublin; *s.* of John Robinson, owner of Daily Express newspaper, and Isabella Boyd of Ballymacool, Co. Donegal; *m.* H. Harriet, *y. d.* of Sir John Lubbock, 3rd Bt.; and sister of 1st Lord Avebury; four *s.* two *d. Educ.*: Blackheath School; Trinity College, Dublin. Ordained, 1875; held curacies in England and Ireland; subsequently rector of Delgany, Co. Wicklow, and other places; Dean and Vicar of Belfast, 1903-11; Incumbent of St. Andrew, Edmonton, Alberta, 1911-12; Rector of Christ Church, Edmonton, 1912-13. *Address*: St. John's College, Winnipeg, Canada. *Club*: University, Dublin. *(Died 14 June 1916.)*

ROBINSON, Rev. Ludovick Stewart, Vicar of Pershore, Worcestershire; Hon. Canon of Worcester, 1922; *b.* 1864; *s.* of Rev. Canon Robinson, D.D., Master of St. Catharine's College, Cambridge; *m.* Ellen Duval. *d.* of E. J. Mortlock, Banker, Cambridge; three *s.* two *d. Educ.*: Haileybury College; St. Catharine's College, Cambridge; Clergy Training School. Curate St. Andrew's, Haverstock Hill, N.W.; Chaplain to Bishop of Ripon and Inspector of Schools; Chaplain to Marquis of Zetland; Rector of Richmond, Yorks.; Rural Dean of Richmond, W.; Vicar of Bingley, Yorks.; Rural Dean of South Craven; Rector of Keighley, Yorks.; Hon. Canon of Ripon; Rural Dean of Pershore, 1920. *Recreations*: golf and lawn tennis. *Address*: Pershore Vicarage. *T.*: Pershore 36. *M.*: NP 1454. *(Died 12 Oct. 1923.)*

ROBINSON, Sir Richard Atkinson, Kt., *cr.* 1916; D.L., J.P.; *b.* 16 Oct. 1849; *e. s.* of Henry Robinson, shipowner, Whitby; *m.* 1876, Jeanie, *d.* of Thomas Thistle. Whitby; two *s.* three *d. Educ.*: Pickering; Manchester. Chairman, London County Council, 1908-9; has been member Thames Conservancy, Governor Imperial College of Science, London County Territorial Association, Alderman of Kensington; Hon. Treasurer, London Municipal Society, and taken a prominent part in political and municipal work for many years; was leader of the Municipal Reform Party on L.C.C., 1907, when it came into power for the first time. *Recreation*: outdoor life. *Address*: 19 Bagdale, Whitby. *(Died 28 April 1923.)*

ROBINSON, Robert Thomson, K.C. 1914; *b.* Ireland, 1867; *s.* of John Robinson of Albany, W.A. *Educ.*: Prince Alfred College, Adelaide. Bar, Western Australia, 1889; Formerly Attorney-General, Minister for Mines, and Minister for Industries and Woods and Forests, Western Australia. *Address*: Howard Street, Perth, Western Australia.

(Died 19 Sept. 1926.)

ROBINSON, Col. Stapylton Chapman Bates, C.B. 1917; O.C. Queen Mary's Military Hospital, Whalley, 1914-19; *s.* of late Maj.-Gen. Stapylton Robinson, R.A.; *b.* 21 May 1855; *m.* 1899, Constance Mary, *e. d.* of T. H. Harrison, J.P., of Broxbourne, Herts; two *s. Educ.*: privately. St. Thomas's Hospital; Surgeon, Army Medical Department, 1881; retired as Col. 1912; was in India, Mediterranean, and South Africa; served South African Campaign (Queen's medal with 7 clasps, King's medal 2 clasps); Hon. County Director Hertfordshire V.A.D.'s, 1913-14; volunteered, and was recalled to the Service, 14 Dec. 1914 (despatches, C.B.). *Address*: Roden Lodge, Hoddesdon, Herts. *Club*: Army and Navy. *(Died 7 Mar. 1927.)*

ROBINSON, Sir Thomas, K.B.E., *cr.* 1917; steam trawler owner, etc.; C.C. for the Parts of Lindsey; J.P. County Division; *b.* 23 Jan. 1855; *s.* of John and Betsy Robinson; *m.* 1876, Cornelia Agnes Wheeler; one *s.* three *d. Educ.*: Humberstone Grammar School. Left school 1869; started as sea, followed the sea, fishing fourteen years; commenced business on the Fish Dock, 1883, and has continued as Owner, Salesman, Fish-merchant; has acted for some considerable time as Technical Adviser to the Board of Agriculture and Fisheries, Fisheries Dept., and the Fish Food Committee. *Recreations*: motoring, cycling, billiards. *Address*: Southlands, Cleethorpes; Fish Docks, Grimsby. *T.A.*: Reliance, Grimsby. *T.*: Grimsby 615.

(Died 8 Feb. 1927.)

ROBINSON, Tom, M.D.; Consulting Physician; *b.* East Keal, Spilsby, Lincolnshire; *m.*; one *s. Educ.*: Peterborough; The London Hospital. House Physician, House Surgeon, and Clinical Assistant; Gold Medallist in Medicine, Surgery, and Midwifery. *Publications*: works on Eczema, Syphilis, Acne, Baldness and Greyness. *Recreation*: country life. *Address*: 9 Princes Street, Cavendish Square, W. *Clubs*: Authors', Green Room.

(Died 7 May 1916.)

ROBINSON, William Edward, M.P. (L.) Burslem, 1923-24; *s.* of William Robinson,

Stoke-on-Trent; *b.* 1863; *m.* 1892, *d.* of Thomas Cope. *Address:* The Mount, Porthill, Stoke-on-Trent. *(Died 10 May 1927.)*

ROBINSON, Major-Gen. William Henry Banner, C.B. 1915; Indian Medical Service; Hon. Surgeon to the King; *b.* 7 Dec. 1863; *m.* Elsie Marian, *d.* of Wm. Deane Butcher, M.R.C.S. Entered service, 1886; served Burma, 1885-87 (despatches, medal, 2 clasps); Waristan Expedition, 1894-95 (clasp); Chitral, 1895 (medal with clasp); Tirah, 1897-98 (two clasps); European War, 1914-16 (C.B., despatches twice); served under Foreign Department, Govt. of India, as Residentiary Surgeon, Alwar, Bikanir, Jaipur, Marwar, Mount Abu, and as Chief Medical Officer in Rajputana; as Inspector-General Civil Hospitals, Central Provinces, and Sanitary Commissioner Surgeon-General-Govt. of Bengal; officiating D.G.I.M.S. *Clubs:* East India United Service: United Service. Calcutta. *(Died 7 Feb. 1922.)*

ROBINSON, William Leefe, V.C. 1916; Worcestershire Regt. and R.F.C.; *b.* Tollidetta, S. India, 14 July 1895; *s.* of Horace Robinson and *g. s.* of W. C. Robinson, R.N., Chief Naval Constructor, Portsmouth Dockyard. *Educ.:* St. Bee's School; Sandhurst. Entered army, 1914; joined Royal Flying Corps, March 1915; served European War (France), 1915 (wounded); was night pilot in England for seven months before bringing down first Zeppelin on English soil, at Cuffley, near London, on the morning of Sunday, 3 Sep. 1916 (V.C.).
(Died 31 Dec. 1918.)

ROBSON, of Jesmond. Lord (Life Peer, *cr.* 1910); **Rt. Hon. William Snowdon Robson,** Kt., *cr.* 1905; P.C. 1910; K.C.; G.C.M.G., *cr.* 1911; a Lord of Appeal in Ordinary 1910-12; 3rd *surv. s.* of late Robert Robson, J.P., Newcastle; *m.* 1887, Catherine, *d.* of late Charles Burge, of 7 Park Crescent, Portland Place; one *s.* three *d.* *Educ.:* privately; Caius College, Cambridge (Hon. Fellow, M.A.); Hon. D.C.L., Durham, 1906. Barrister, 1880; Q.C. 1892; Bencher, Inner Temple, 1899; M.P. Bow and Bromley, 1885-86; Recorder of Newcastle, 1895-1905; M.P. (L.) South Shields, 1895-1910; Solicitor-General, 1905-8; Attorney-General, 1908-10. *Address:* 26 Eaton Square, S.W.; T. Victoria 1886; 11 King's Bench Walk, Temple, E.C. *Clubs:* Brooks's, Reform, Athenæum.
(Died 11 Sept. 1918.)

ROBSON, Edward Robert, F.R.I.B.A., F.S.A., F.S.I.; *b.* 2 March 1835; *e. s.* of late Robert Robson, J.P., of Durham; *m.* Marian, *e. d.* of late Henry Longden, Sheffield. *Educ.:* private schools. Three years in shops for practical building construction; pupil, first of John Dobson, Newcastle-on-Tyne, then of G. Gilbert Scott, R.A.; has travelled much in Europe, America, and Canada; built Piccadilly Art Galleries, New Gallery, Regent Street, the People's Palace, with its Library and Queen's Hall, several hundred schools in London, also churches and mansions; was architect in charge of Durham Cathedral six years; surveyor to the Corporation of Liverpool seven years; then first architect to the School Board for London, and so continued until offered posts under Government; now in private practice at Westminster as architect and surveyor. *Publications:* School Architecture; numerous articles and essays. *Recreations:* golf, bicycling, billiards. *Address:* Palace Chambers, Westminster, S.W.; T.: Victoria 4292; Blackheath, S.E. *Club:* St. Stephen's. *(Died 22 Jan. 1917.)*

ROBSON, Henry Naunton, M.R.C.S. (Eng.), L.R.C.P. (Lond.); Doctor, retired; a Vice-President of the Society for the Prevention of Venereal Disease; *b.* Richmond, Surrey, 1861; father and mother English; unmarried. *Educ.:* Westminster School; St. Thomas's Hos-

pital, London. R.M.O. at Stroud Hospital, Glos.; spent several years travelling in Europe, Asia, America, and Australia trying to find a preventative remedy for venereal disease; the first doctor on the British Register to publish a book advocating the medical prevention of venereal diseases. *Publication:* Sexual Disease and its Medical Prevention, 1909. *Recreations:* formerly golf, rifle-shooting, and rowing. *Address:* 6 Vale Road, Bournemouth. *Club:* Junior Constitutional.

ROBSON, Robert, I.S.O. 1906; *b.* 15 Feb. 1845; *s.* of late Thomas Robson, formerly of Great Ayton in Cleveland; *m.* 1st, 1870, Margaret Ann, *o. d.* of late James Kelly, Newcastle-on-Tyne; 2nd, 1892, Helen Julia (*d.* 1913), *e. d.* of James J. Hicks, K.C.S.G., Highbury Grove and Hatton Garden; four *s.* one *d. Educ.:* private tuition; B.A. Honours, 1865. Entered Customs Service as Clerk and Examining Officer at Middlesbrough, 1866; transferred to Secretary's Office of Department, 1867; nominated by Secretary of State to reorganise the Customs Service in the Island of Trinidad, 1876; and on staff of Lord Wolseley to organise Customs and Excise Services in Cyprus, 1878; Private Secretary to Deputy Chairman of Customs, 1888-86; Principal Clerk, 1886-90; Committee Clerk, 1890-1900; Surveyor-General, 1900-6; Collector of the Port of London and Chief Registrar of Shipping, 1906; retired, 1910; President of the Customs Annuity and Benevolent Fund Incorporated, 1916; retired, 1917. *Address:* 56 York Road, Tunbridge Wells. *(Died 15 Aug. 1923.)*

ROCHE, Alexander, R.S.A., painter; corresponding member of Munich Secession; *b.* Glasgow, 17 Aug. 1861; *m.* 1906, Jean, *d.* of Robert Alexander, R.S.A. *Educ.:* Glasgow; Paris. Started as an architect, but liking painting better, went to Paris and studied there. Has tried all sorts of subjects, landscape and figure. His best works are — Tête-a-tête (Gold Medal, Munich), 1891; Squall on the Clyde (Honourable Mention, Salon), 1892; Idyl (bought by the Aukland Picture Gallery), 1892; Spring (Medal, Paris International, 1900); Margaret (Scottish National Gallery), 1900; Landscape (Gold Medal, Dresden), 1897; The Window-Seat (Medal, Pittsburg, and bought for Permanent Gallery), 1898; Prue (bought by Munich Gallery), 1902; An Old Song (bought for Stuttgart Public Museum), 1902; Nancy (bought by Walker Art Gallery, Liverpool), 1904; frescoes decorating Banqueting Hall, Glasgow Municipal Buildings, 1900; Mrs. Andrew Carnegie and daughter, 1903; Portrait of Miss Flora Stevenson, LL.D. (National Portrait Gallery, Edinburgh), 1905; In Maiden Meditation Fancy Free (Museum, Odessa), 1905; The Building of the Ship (Municipal Gallery of Modern Art, Dublin), 1905; Landscape (bought by the Modern Arts Association, Scotland), 1908; Pittenweem Harbour (Presented to the Modern Arts Association, Scotland), 1908; The Prison Gate, Mogador; self-portrait bought by Modern Arts Association, 1916; Here Ouse slow winding thro' a Lonely Plain, bought by Glasgow Corporation, 1918. *Publications:* Finish in Art (Transactions of the National Association for the Advancement of Art, 1889); several essays and lectures on art subjects. *Club:* Scottish Arts, Edinburgh; Glasgow Arts. *(Died 10 Mar. 1921.)*

ROCHE, Colonel Hon. Ulick de Rupe Burke, C.B. 1900; late commanding South Wales Borderers; retired 1903; *b.* 16 Jan. 1856; 4th *s.* of 1st Baron Fermoy; *m.* 1st, 1882, Agnes Blair (*d.* 1905), *e. d.* of General Jasper Otway Mayne, R.E.; 2nd, Dorothea Blanche, *d.* of John Jones of Ynysfor, Penrhyndeudraeth, N. Wales; one *s.* Entered army, 1876; Capt. 1881; Major, 1891; Lt.-Col. 1899. Served Kaffir War, 1877-78 (medal with clasp); Burmese Expedition, 1886-89 (medal with two clasps);

South Africa, 1900-2 (despatches, Queen's medal, 3 clasps, King's medal, 2 clasps, D.S.O.); D.A.A.G. Bengal, 1890 - 95 ; command ed 11th Service Batt. Royal Welsh Fusiliers, 1914-15. *Address:* Saffronhill, Doneraile, Co. Cork.
(*Died 13 April 1919.*)

ROCHE, Hon. William, Senator since 1910 ; *b.* Halifax, N.S., 1842. *Educ.:* Halifax, N.S. M.P., 1900-1908 ; Pres., Halifax Fire Insurance Company. *Address:* Halifax, Nova Scotia.
(*Died 19 Oct. 1925.*)

ROCHFORT, Major-General Sir Alexander Nelson, K.C.B., *cr.* 1911 ; R.A.; C.B. 1900 ; C.M.G. 1904 ; Lt.-Governor and Commanding troops, Jersey, 1910 - 16 ; *b.* 3 June 1850 ; 5th *s.* of late Horace W. N. Rochfort, D.L., of Clogrenane, and Hon. Charlotte, *d.* of 2nd Lord Bridport. Entered army, 1871 ; Captain, 1881 ; Brevet Major, 1885 ; Lieut.-Col. 1886 ; Colonel, 1900 ; Maj.-Gen. 1907 ; served Soudan, 1885 (despatches, Brevet Major, medal with clasp, Khedive's star); South Africa, 1899-1902 (severely wounded, despatches twice, Queen's medal, 4 clasps, King's medal, 2 clasps, C.B.); special service, Somaliland, 1902-1904 (despatches, and general service African medal with clasp, C.M.G.); Inspector Horse and Field Artillery, 1904-10. *Address:* Government House, Jersey. *Clubs:* Naval and Military, Arthur's.
(*Died 5 Dec. 1916.*)

ROCHFORT-BOYD, Lt.-Col. Henry Charles, D.S.O. 1915 ; R.H.A.; *b.* 18 Oct. 1877; *s.* of Col. C. A. Rochfort-Boyd ; *m.* 1908, Dorothy, *d.* of Arthur Nicholson ; one *s. Educ.:* Charterhouse ; R.M.A. Woolwich. Entered army, 1897 ; Captain, 1904 ; Major, 1914 ; served S. African War, 1899-1900 (despatches twice ; Queen's medal 3 clasps); European War, 1914-1917 (despatches thrice, D.S.O., three times wounded). *Address:* Belvedere House, Farnborough, Hants. *Club:* Army and Navy.
(*Died 4 Dec. 1917.*)

RODDICK, Sir Thomas George, Kt., *cr.* 1914 ; M.D., C.M., Hon. LL.D. Edin. and Queen's; Hon. F.R.C.S. Eng.; *b.* Harbour Grace, Newfoundland, 31 July 1846 ; *m.* 1st, 1880, Marion (*d.* 1890), *d.* of late William Mackinnou ; 2nd, 1906, Amy, *o. d.* of late J. J. Redpath, Montreal. *Educ.:* McGill University. Surgeon, Montreal General Hospital, 1874 ; Consulting Surgeon to Montreal General and Royal Victoria Hospital ; Governor, McGill University ; Professor of Surgery, 1890-1907 ; Dean of Medical Faculty, 1901 - 8 ; President, British Medical Association, 1896 - 98 ; Hon. President Medical Council, Canada ; Hon. President Canadian Medical Association ; served N.W. Rebellion, 1885 (despatches, medal); Fenian Raid, 1870 (medal and clasp); Member for Montreal West, 1896-1904. *Address:* 705 Sherbrooke Street West, Montreal. *Clubs:* University, Mount Royal, Montreal.
(*Died 20 Feb. 1923.*)

RODIN, Auguste, D.C.L. Oxon.; sculptor; President International Society Painters, Sculptors, Engravers ; *b.* Paris, 1840 ; *m.* Rose Beurre (*d.* 1917). A workman in ateliers of Barye and Carrier-Belleuse, 1864 - 70 ; Associé de Van Rasbourg (Brussels), 1871-77. *Works:* L'Homme au Nez Cassé, 1864 ; L'Age d'Airain, 1877 ; St-Jean prêchant and The Creation of Man, 1882 ; busts of Jean Paul Laurens, Carrier-Belleuse, Victor Hugo, Antonin Proust, Dalou, 1882-85 ; busts of Puvis de Chavannes, La Cariatide, La Danaïde, Le Penseur, Monument to Victor Hugo, Balzac, Le Baiser, l'Eve ; busts of Falguière, Rochefort, Becque ; Octave Mirbeau, Madame M. V.; Les Bourgeois de Calais, 1889 ; La Porte de l'Enfer ; Le Frère et la Sœur ; Le Printemps ; L'éternelle Idole ; La Guerre ; Psyche ; Amor Fugit ; L'Homme qui s'éveille ; Art ; etc. *Address:* rue de l'Université, No. 182 Paris ; Meudon-Val-Fleury, Seine-et-Oise. (*Died 18 Nov. 1917.*)

RODWAY, James, F.L.S., Curator British Guiana Museum ; Librarian and Assistant Secretary Royal Agricultural and Commercial Society of British Guiana, 1888-1926 ; *b.* Trowbridge, Wilts, 1848 ; *m.* 1873, Kate Reedon, creole of Demerara ; eleven *c. Educ.:* Trowbridge. Chemist until 1888 ; naturalist from boyhood ; studied British Flora before leaving for British Guiana, 1870 ; has made a special study of the Colony from every standpoint, the people, history, geography, fauna and flora, as well as the economic products which may be developed ; is specially interested in the life histories of plants and animals, and their interdependence. *Publications:* History of British Guiana, 3 vols.; Handbook of British Guiana ; In the Guiana Forest ; Story of Forest and Stream ; West Indies and Spanish Main (Story of the Nations Series); In Guiana Wilds (a story); Guiana, British, Dutch, and French ; Papers in Longman's Magazine, Cornhill, Popular Science Monthly, etc. *Recreations:* change of work, collecting, gardening—from the study to the field and forest. *Address:* Georgetown, British Guiana. (*Died 19 Nov. 1926.*)

ROE, 1st Baron, *cr.* 1916 ; **Thomas Roe ;** Kt., *cr.* 1894 ; *b.* 13 July 1832 ; *m.* 1903, Emily (*d.* 1909), *d.* of late Matthew Kirtley. Mayor of Derby, 1867-68, 1896-97, and 1910-11 ; M.P. Derby, 1883-95 and 1900-16 ; J.P. for Derby and Derbyshire. *Heir:* none. *Address:* Litchurch, Derby. *Club:* National Liberal.
(*Died 7 June 1923.*)

ROE, Sir Charles, Kt., *cr.* 1897 ; *b.* 24 Sep. 1841 ; *s.* of John B. Roe, of Blandford, Dorset ; *m.* 1865, Elizabeth (*d.* 1891), *d.* of late Frederick Gaskell ; two *s.* one *d. Educ.:* Merton College, Oxford. Entered Bengal Civil Service, 1863 ; retired 1898 ; was Chief Judge of Chief Court of the Punjab and Vice-Chancellor of the Punjab University (Hon. LL.D. 1899); represented the University of Oxford at the opening of the New Law Schools of the University of Pennsylvania, 1900, and received from the latter University the degree of LL.D. *Publication:* Tribal Law in the Punjab. *Address:* 1 Holywell Street, Oxford.
(*Died 28 Jan. 1927.*)

ROE, Brig.-Gen. Cyril Harcourt, C.M.G. 1919 ; C.I.E. 1916 ; *b.* 15 Oct. 1864. Lieut. R.E. 1884 ; Capt. 1892 ; Major, 1901 ; Lt.-Col. 1908 ; Col. 1912 ; D.A.A.G. Bangalore District, 1904-8 ; served Burma, 1886-87 (medal, two clasps); Burma, 1893 (clasp); European War, 1914-19 (despatches twice, C.M.G., C.I.E.); retired on Indian pension. *Address:* Rydal Mount, Kidderminster Road, Bromsgrove, Worcestershire.
(*Died 26 Nov. 1928.*)

ROE, Rev. Robert Gordon, M.A.; Rector of Acle since 1923 ; Hon. Canon of Norwich, 1918 ; Rural Dean, Walsingham, 1919 ; *o.* 1860 ; *s.* of Robert Roe (Artist in Miniatures) and Maria, *d.* of Rev. W. G. Plees, Vicar of Ash Bocking, Suffolk ; *m.* 1885, Isabel Alice, *d.* of Lt. Col. John Anthony Kysh, 5th Northumberland Fusiliers ; two *s.* three *d. Educ.:* the Perse School, Cambridge ; St. Catharine's College, Cambridge. Ordained, 1885 ; Priest, 1886 ; Curacies at Weaverham, Cheshire ; Teddington, Middlesex ; Vicar of Badwell Ash, Suffolk, with Hunston, 1888 ; Priest in charge of St. Stephens, Buckhurst Hill, 1890 ; Rector of Blo' Norton, Norfolk, 1895-99 ; Vicar of King's Lynn, 1855-1909 ; Rural Dean of Lynn, Marshland ; Rector of Leiston, Suffolk, 1909-15 ; Rector of Blakeney with Glandford and Cockthorpe, 1915-23. *Publications:* article on Old Stained Glass of St. Edmundsbury, etc. *Recreations:* archæological. and painting in water-colours. *Address:* The Rectory, Acle, Norfolk. (*Died 19 May 1927.*)

ROE, Rev. Robert James, Hon. Canon of Truro. *Address:* Lanteglos Rectory, Camelford, Cornwall. (*Died 29 July 1921.*)

ROE, Deputy Surgeon-General William Carden; *b.* 1834; 3rd *s.* of William Roe of Lismore House, Queen's Co. (*d.* 1844); *m.* 1864, Emily Louisa (*d.* 1894), 3rd *d.* of General William Twistleton Layard. Served in the Crimea and Indian Mutiny Campaigns; retired, 1880. *Address:* Loran Park, Roscrea; Shackenhurst, West Cliff, Bournemouth. *M.:* EL 996.   (*Died 8 Oct. 1922.*)

ROE, Lt.-Col. William Francis, D.S.O. 1916; late R.A.M.C., T.F.; L.R.C.S.I.; Surgeon White Star Line since 1923; *e. s.* of late William Roe, M.D., Dublin; *b.* 4 May 1871; *m.* Emma, 3rd *d.* of late Benjamin Ormsby, Blackrock, Co. Dublin; one *d.* Acted as surgeon on Bibby Line, had practice in Northampton Square, E.C., previous to War; Volunteer Bloomsbury Rifles, 1903 (Queen Victoria Rifles (amalgamated), T.F.); Lecturer and Examiner First Aid, L.C.C.; Major, 1915; Temp. Lt.-Col. 1916; served European War, 1914-19 (despatches twice, D.S.O.); resigned commission 1922. *Address:* 35 Ladbroke Road, W.11. *Club:* Royal Automobile.
    (*Died 23 June 1925.*)

ROFF, William George, I.S.O. 1911; late Inspector of Dockyard Accounts, Admiralty; retired, 1918; *b.* 20 May 1858; *s.* of late William Roff, R.N. *Educ.:* privately; Admiralty School, Portsmouth Dockyard. Entered Admiralty Service, 1872; Yard Accounts Branch of the Admiralty Office, 1882; professional assistant to Inspector of Dockyard Accounts, 1891; officer in charge of accounts of Chatham Dockyard, 1895; Senior Assistant Inspector, Admiralty, 1901-4; Member of the Bournemouth County Borough Council since 1920. *Address:* St. Faith, Castlemain Avenue, Bournemouth.   (*Died 25 Aug. 1926.*)

ROGER, Captain Archibald, I.S.O. 1913; District Magistrate, St. Kitts, Leeward Islands; *b.* Tortola, Virgin Islands, 27 Nov. 1842; *s.* of late James Dean Roger, St. Kitts, West Indies and Bridge of Allan, Scotland; *m.* Alicia Julia, *d.* of late William Henry Hall, Nassau, Bahamas; two *d. Educ.:* Collegiate School, Glasgow; College, Brunswick, Germany. Ensign 2nd Royal Lanark Militia, 1859; joined 2nd West India Regiment, 1860; Lieut. 1861; Captain, 1866; exchanged to 1st Batt., 17th Regiment, 1867; sold out, 1870; private secretary to Mr. Bayley, Governor of the Bahamas, 1860-63; Fort-Adjutant, Jamaica, 1863-64; Police Magistrate, Rural District, St. Christopher, 1873; District Magistrate, 1874; Commissioner of Oaths; Official Member, Legislative Council, 1896-1900; Executive Council, 1914; Acting Administrator, St. Kitts-Nevis, in 1912, 1913, 1914, and 1915. *Address:* Romneys, St. Kitts, West Indies.

ROGERS, His Honour Benjamin, President of Rogers & Co., Ltd., General Merchants; *b.* 7 Aug. 1837; parents immigrants from Caermarthenshire, Wales, about 1831; *m.* 1st, 1862, Susannah Abell (*d.* 1897), *d.* of late Capt. Wm. Hubbard, Tignish, P.E.I.; three *s.* three *d.*; 2nd, 1898, Annie M., *d.* of late James Hunter of Kilmahumaig, Argyleshire. *Educ.:* District School Course at Bedeque, P.E.I. Member Legislative Council, 1878-93; President of Council, 1890/93; Member of Amalgamated Council and Assembly, 1893-97, 1900-4; Member of several Administrations, and Provincial Secretary, Treasurer, and Minister of Agriculture, 1900-4; Lieut.-Gov. Prince Edward Island, 1910-15. *Address:* Alberton, Prince Edward Island.   (*Died 16 May 1923.*)

ROGERS, Rev. Charles Pursdon, M.A. Oxon; Hon. Canon Truro; retired; licensed preacher and Surrogate Dio. Truro; *b.* 19 June 1848; *s.* of John Jope Rogers of Penrose, Co. Cornwall; *m.* 1877, Frances Fox (*d.* 1926), *d.* of Preb. Harvey, Rector of Truro; one *s.* three *d. Educ.:* Winchester College; Trinity College, Oxford; 2nd. Cl. Mathematics. Assistant Curate, Loughton, Essex, 1872-75; St. Mary, Truro, 1875-77; Organising Secretary, National Society, 1877-88; Vicar of Mithian, Cornwall, 1888-91; Sithney, 1891-1901; Penzance, 1901-16; Rural Dean of Kirrier, 1898-1901; Penwith, 1913-16. *Address:* The Manor Cottage, Goldsithney, Marazion, Cornwall. *Club:* Cornwall County, Truro.
    (*Died 15 Aug. 1928.*)

ROGERS, Francis Edward Newman, Commissioner, Board of Agriculture, 1911; J.P. Wilts; *b.* 26 Dec. 1868; *s.* of Walter Lacy Rogers of Rainscombe, Pewsey, Wilts, and Hermione, *sister* of Sir E. A. Hamilton, 4th Bart., Iping House, Midhurst; *m.* 1893, Louisa Annie, *d.* of Ed. Jenning of Gellidég, Carmarthenshire; one *s.* one *d. Educ.:* Eton; Balliol College, Oxford. Contested E. Wilts, 1900; contested S. Wilts, Dec. 1910; M.P. (L.) East Wilts, 1906-1910; worked on Wilts C.C., 1884-1911, and other local bodies; farms. *Recreations:* shooting, fishing, nature study. *Address:* Rainscombe, Marlborough, Wilts. *Club:* Brooks's.   (*Died 28 Mar. 1925.*)

ROGERS, Ven. George Herbert, Archdeacon of Rockhampton and Examining Chaplain since 1907; *s.* of Rev. Thomas Percival Rogers, Vicar of Batheaston, and Mary Robinson, *d.* of C. E. Broome, of Elmhurst, Batheaston; unmarried. *Educ.:* Lancing (Exhibitioner); Magdalen College, Oxford (demy M.A.); Leeds Clergy School. Ordained, 1896; Curate of Holy Trinity, Leeds, 1896-99; St. Hugh's Missioner, 1899-1900; Vicar of Hainton, 1900-6; Rector of St. Paul's Cathedral, Rockhampton, 1907-16; Organizing Secretary Home Mission Fund, 1917. *Address:* Lis Escop, Rockhampton, Queensland, Australia. *T.A.:* Archdeacon, Rockhampton.   (*Died 6 Dec. 1926.*)

ROGERS, Col. George William, D.S.O. 1889; *b.* 1843; *m.* 1892, Janie Isabella, *d.* of Maj.-Gen. J. S. Rawlins; D.A.A.G., Bengal, 1884-86. Served Lushai Expedition, 1871-72 (medal with clasp); Afghan War, 1878-80 (despatches, medal, three clasps, bronze star); Sikkim Expedition, 1888. (*Died 27 April 1917.*)

ROGERS, Henry Wade, A.M., LL.D.; Judge of U.S. Circuit Court of Appeals, 2nd Jud. Circuit, since 1913; Emeritus Professor of Law at Yale Univ. since 1921; *b.* Holland Patent, New York, 10 Oct. 1853; *m.* 1876, Emma Ferdon Winner (*d.* 1922). *Educ.:* Univ. of Michigan. Barr. 1877; Professor in Michigan University Law School, 1883; Dean, 1885-90; President of Northwestern University, Evanston-Chicago, Illinois, 1890-1900; Prof. in Yale Law School since 1900; Dean of Yale University Law School 1903-16; Former Chairman of American Bar Association's Section on Legal Education; Former President of Association of American Law Schools; late Chairman of American Bar Association's Committee on Legal Education and Admissions to the Bar; late Chairman of Council on Legal Education; Hon. Member of the Bar Associations of Connecticut, Kansas, Illinois, Missouri, New York; President of the Peace Congress of New England States, Hartford, Conn., May 1910; Chairman, World's Congress on Jurisprudence and Law Reform, Chicago, 1893; President of the Layman's Association of the Methodist Episcopal Church in the United States. Methodist Episcopal; President of National Council of Schools of Religion. *Publications:* Treatise on Expert Testimony. *Address:* New Haven, Connecticut, U.S.A. *T.:* 691. *Clubs:* Graduates, New Haven; University, Evanston, Illinois; Alpha Delta Phi, Yale, N.Y.   (*Died 16 Aug. 1926.*)

ROGERS, Lt.-Col. Sir John Godfrey, K.C.M.G. *cr.* 1898; C.M.G. 1896; D.S.O. 1886; late Director-Gen. Sanitary Department, Egypt; *b.* 11 Apr. 1850; *m.* 1883, Edith Louisa Julie,

C.B.E., Lady·of Grace St. John of Jerusalem. *d.* of late Major Sykes, Bombay Cavalry. *Educ.:* Trin. Coll. Dublin. B.A., M.B., M.Ch. Entered Army Medical Department, 1871 ; Surg. - Major, 1882 ; Surg. Lieut.-Col., 1891 ; retired, 1892 ; Lt.-Col. R.A.M.C. 1896 ; served Afghan War, 1878-81 (medal) ; Egypt, 1882 ; present at Kassassin and Tel - el - Kebir (despatches, medal with clasp, bronze star, promoted Surg.-Maj.) ; Nile Expedition, 1884-85 (despatches, 3rd Cl. Osmanieh) ; Soudan Frontier Field Force, 1885-86 (despatches, clasp, D.S.O.) ; Suakin Field Force, 1888-89, as P.M.O. of Force (despatches, clasp, 2nd Cl. Medjidie) ; Principal Medical Officer Egyptian Army, 1888-1892 ; Director-General Sanitary Department, 1892-99 (2nd class Osmanieh, Grand Cordon Medjidie) ; Commissioner of the British Red Cross, Cairo, 1915-18 ; Bt. Col. 1 Jan. 1919 ; 2nd class Order of the Nile, 1918 ; Knight of Grace St. John of Jerusalem, 1918. *Publications:* Sport in Vancouver and Newfoundland, 1912. *Recreations:* fishing, shooting. *Address:* Whitelands, Edenbridge, Kent. *Clubs:* Junior United Service ; Turf, Cairo.

(*Died 10 Jan. 1922.*)

ROGERS, Sir Robert Hargreaves, Kt., *cr.* 1897 ; Sheriff of London, 1896-97 ; Deputy-Alderman ; Member of Common Council ; Chairman of R. H. & S. Rogers, Ltd. ; Governor of St. Thomas's Hospital ; *b.* 20 Jan. 1850 ; *s.* of Thomas Rogers, Sevenoaks ; *m.* Jane, *d.* of William Stark, Croydon, 1877. *Educ.:* Roxborough House, Liverpool Road, Islington. Entered Common Council, 1886 ; made Deputy, 1890 ; Chairman of City School of Music, 1891 ; Deputy-Governor of Irish Society, 1894 ; Chairman of Finance and Improvement Committee, 1900 ; Chairman of the Gresham Committee, 1901 ; has the Jubilee Medal, 1897, and Officers' Order of Leopold of Belgium. *Recreation:* gardening. *Address:* Marl House, Bexley, Kent. *T.A.:* Producing, London. *T.:* 97 Bexley Heath. *M.:* D 5881. *Clubs:* City Carlton, Royal Automobile ; Dartford Conservative.

(*Died 30 Nov. 1924.*)

ROGERS, Roland, Mus. Doc. Oxon ; Organist, Bangor Cathedral ; *b.* West Bromwich, Staffordshire, 17 Nov. 1847. *Educ.:* privately. Organist, St. John's, Wolverhampton, 1862 ; Tettenhall Parish Church, 1867 ; Bangor Cathedral, 1872 ; resigned, 1891 ; reappointed, 1906 ; choir trainer and adjudicator. *Publications:* Cantatas : Prayer and Praise, The Garden, Floribel ; a large number of part songs, including The River Floweth ; organ compositions and anthems. *Address:* Cibrhedyn, Bangor, N. Wales. (*Died July 1927.*)

ROGERSON, Capt. John Edwin, O.B.E. 1919 ; D.L., J.P.; M.P. (U.) Barnard Castle Div. of Durham, 1922-23 ; *b.* 8 Jan. 1865 ; *e. s.* of late John Rogerson, C.E., Croxdale, Durham ; *m.* Frances Mary, *y. d.* of Pierse Creagh, Mount Elva, Co. Clare ; one *s.* two *d. Educ.:* Durham ; Trinity College, Cambridge. B.A. Hist. Tripos, 1886 ; M.A. 1892 ; Associate Institute Civil Engineers ; Director of various Iron and Coal Companies on North - East Coast ; Alderman for County Durham ; Sheriff, 1905-6 ; Secretary Durham County Territorial Force Association, 1914-19, Chairman, 1920 ; Master of North Durham Foxhounds since 1888. *Recreations:* hunting, shooting, racing. *Address:* Mount Oswald, Durham. · T.: Nat. 67. *M.: J.* 1248. *Clubs:* Carlton, Boodle's ; Durham County, Durham ; Yorkshire, York.

(*Died 23 Mar. 1925.*)

ROHAN, Duchess de (dowager) ; Herminie de Verteillac, *o. c. of* Marquis de Verteillac ; Superintendent of the Nursing Staff of military hospital V. G. 81 Hôtel-Rohan in Paris ; Chevalier de la Légion d'Honneur ; decorated with the Medaille de Vermeil des Épidemies,

904

de L'Insigne Spécial et de la Reconnaissance Italienne ; Commandeur de l'Ordre Serbe de St. Sava de celui de la Charité Serbe ; *widow* of Duke de Rohan, deputy conseillergénéral major of Jasselin, Morbihan; one *s.* (Vicomte de Rohan, lieutenant pilote aviateur) two *d.* (Princess Lucien Murat and Marchioness de Caraman) ; eleven grandchildren, including the Duke de Rohan. Before the War wrote four books, three of poetry, one in prose ; has since written Le chant du Cygne and new lectures, held lectures and painted in water-colours ; member of the Société des Gens de Lettres des Poètes français, des Artistes français, de l'Union des Femmes peintres et sculpteurs, de la Société Internationale du Syndicat des Femmes peintres et sculpteurs (medaille de Vernueil à l'exposition de Vichy), de la Société d'Histoire de France, de la Société diplomatique, du Comité de Prix Femina ; présidente des gymnastes de S. E. le cardinal archevêque de Paris, des comités belges et serbes et des cantines anglaises; et du comité France Amerique; et presidente des femmes alliées de la grande guerre. *Address:* 35 boulevard des Invalides, Paris. *Clubs:* Lyceum, Interallié, Paris. (*Died April 1926.*)

ROLFE, Rev. Harry Roger ; Vicar of St. Michael's, Derby, since 1885; Hon. Canon, Southwell Cathedral ; Surrogate ; Hon. Secretary Derbyshire D.P.A.S. ; Chairman, Derby Board of Guardians ; Assessor under the Clergy Discipline Act ; *b.* 1851 ; *s.* of William Rowland Rolfe, Sudbury, Suffolk. Ordained Curate of Beighton and Staveley, Derbyshire, 1874 ; Vicar of Misson, Notts, 1884 ; Rural Dean of Derby, 1908-10. *Address:* St. Michael's Vicarage, Derby. *T.A.:* Canon Rolfe, Derby.

(*Died 18 Aug. 1924.*)

ROLL, Sir James, 1st Bt., *cr.* 1921 ; Lord Mayor of London, 1920-21 ; *b.* 9th Dec. 1846 ; *s.* of Nathaniel Roll; *m.* 1867, Emma, *d.* of James Gilding ; two *s.* Fifty years with Pearl Assurance Company ; commenced as a representative and became Chairman (retired, 1916) ; Common Councilman for Bridge Ward, Sheriff of the City, 1909-10 ; was Alderman of Billingsgate Ward, Member of the Paviors', Horners', Glovers' and Carmen's Companies ; a prominent Freemason, holding the craft rank of Past Grand Treasurer ; President of the Pickwick Coaching Club; Chairman of Charles Webster, Ltd., and Chapman & Sons, Eastbourne, Ltd. *Recreation:* coaching. *Heir: s.* Frederick James, *b.* 20 Sep. 1873. *Address:* The Chestnuts, Wanstead, E.11. *T.:* Wanstead 134.

(*Died 30 Jan. 1927.*)

ROLLAND, Brig. - Gen. Stewart Erskine, Indian Army ; *b.* 1846 ; *s.* of Capt. C. W. Rolland, Madras Artillery ; *m.* E. S. Cammerer ; one *s.* two *d. Educ.:* Edinburgh Academy ; Bonn ; Kensington Grammar School ; Sandhurst. Ensign, 2/19th Yorks Regt., 1866 ; 26th M.I., 1868-95 ; on Staff, 1887-96; commanding Chin Hills, 1894-95 ; A.Q.M.G., Headquarters, Madras, 1895-96 ; Brig.-Gen. Southern, Rangoon, and Belgaum Dist., 1896-99 ; thanks of Government (Bom.) for services during plague while commanding Belgaum District ; received thanks of O.C. Lines of Communications and Chief of Staff, Upper Burma Field Force ; Burmese War, 1885-89, commanding Western Frontiers and Movable Column, Action at Segu (severely wounded, despatches twice, Bt. Lt.-Col., medal 2 clasps); Hon. Brig.-Gen. and Col. 86th Carnatic Infantry, 1912 ; Inspector, Ealing Special Constabulary, X Division, 1914-16. *Address:* 8 Woodville Road, Ealing, W.5. (*Died 11 Jan. 1927.*)

ROLLESTON, Sir John Fowke Lancelot, Kt., *cr.* 1897 ; M.P. (U.) Hertford 1910 - 16 ; J.P., D.L. ; *b.* 26 **March** 1848 ; *e. s.* of Rev. William Lancelot Rolleston and Mary Sophia, *e. d.* of late Sir Frederick

Gustavus Fowke, Bt. ; *m.* 1892, Eliza, *d.* of late George Morant, Farnborough, Hants. *Educ.*: Repton School ; Applied Science Department, King's College, London. President Surveyors' Institution, 1901 ; Chairman Investment Registry, Ltd. ; Director Law Union and Rock Assurance Co. ; Chairman Leicester Conservative Association, 1889-1909 ; contested (C.) Leicester borough, 1894, 1895, 1900, and twice in 1906 ; Liveryman of the city and Master of the Spectacle Makers' Company ; Knight of Grace, St. John of Jerusalem ; member of Grand Council Primrose League since 1896 ; Senior Deacon, Grand Lodge of Freemasons; M.P. (C.) Leicester, 1900-6. *Recreations:* arboriculture, travel ; President Fosse Football Club, 1896. *Address:* Glen Parva Grange, Leicester ; '54 Curzon Street, W. *T.:* Gerrard 8115. *Clubs:* Carlton, Junior Carlton, Royal Automobile. *(Died 9 April 1919.)*

ROLLESTON, Thos. William, author and journalist; *b.* Glasshouse Shinrone, King's Co., 1857 ; 3rd *s.* of Chas. Rolleston-Spunner, Q.C., and Elizabeth, *d.* of Rt. Hon. John Richards, Chief Baron of the Court of Exchequer, Ireland ; *m.* 1st, 1879, Edith, *d.* of Rev. Wm. de Burgh, D.D. ; 2nd, 1897, Maud, *d.* of late Rev. Stopford A. Brooke; five *s.* three *d.* *Educ.:* St. Columba's College, Rathfarnham ; Trinity College, Dublin. Lived in Germany, 1879-83 ; Editor, Dublin University Review, 1885-6 ; First Hon. Secretary, Irish Literary Society, London, 1892-3 ; Taylorian Lecturer, Oxford, 1892 ; Assistant-Editor, New Irish Library, 1893 ; Managing Director and Secretary, Irish Industries' Association, 1894-97 ; Leader-writer, Dublin Daily Express, and Dublin Correspondent, Daily Chronicle, 1898-1900 ; Organiser of Lectures, etc., to the Department of Agriculture and Technical Instruction, Ireland, 1900-5 ; Organiser Irish Historic Loan Collection, St. Louis Exhibition, 1904 ; Hon. Secretary, Irish Arts and Crafts Society, 1898-1908 ; Hon. Secretary India Society, 1910. *Publications:* The Encheiridion of Epictetus (translated with Introduction and notes), 1881 ; The Teaching of Epictetus, 1888 ; Grashalme (German translation of Walt Whitman) with Dr. K. Knortz, 1889 ; Life of Lessing, 1889 ; Treasury of Irish Poetry, edited with Stopford Brooke, 1900 ; Imagination and Art in Gaelic Literature, 1900 ; Parallel Paths : A Study in Biology, Ethics and Art, 1908 ; Sea Spray (poems), 1909 ; The High Deeds of Finn, 1910 ; Myths and Legends of the Celtic Race, 1911. *Address:* 16 Prince Arthur Road, Hampstead, N.W.3. *T.:* Hampstead 6700.

(Died 5 Dec. 1920.)

ROLLIT, Sir Albert Kaye, Kt., *cr.* 1885 ; Grand Cross of the Order of St. Sava, 1907 ; Consul-General for Roumania in London since 1911 ; *b.* Hull, 1842 ; *s.* of Mr. Rollit of Hull, Solicitor, and Eliza, *d.* of Joseph Kaye, J.P., of Huddersfield, Architect ; *m.* 1st, 1872, Eleanor Anne, 2nd *d.* of late Wm. Bailey, J.P., of Winestead Hall, Holderness (*d.* 1885); 2nd, 1896, Mary, Duchess of Sutherland (*d.* 1912), *d.* of late Rev. Dr. Michell, Principal of Hertford College, Oxford. *Educ.:* King's College (Fellow); University of London (Fellow and Member of Senate); B.A. 1st class honours, 1863 ; LL.B. 1st class honours Principles of Legislation, etc., 1864 ; LL.D. 1st and University Gold Medallist, 1866 ; D.C.L. Durham, 1891 ; LL.D. Victoria, 1902 ; D.C.L. Montreal, 1870. A Solicitor in Mincing Lane and at Hull ; a prizeman of the Incorporated Law Society, 1863, and President of the Society ; Director National Telephone Co.; is also a steamship owner (firm, Bailey and Leetham) at Hull, Newcastle, and London ; Sheriff of Hull, 1875-76, and Mayor, 1883-84-85 ; contested (L.) Epsom Div., Surrey, 1910 ; Hon. Freeman of Hull and Huddersfield ; Elder

Brother, Trinity House, Hull ; Ex-President of Associated Chambers of Commerce, U.K., and of London and Hull Chambers of Commerce ; late a Director of the British Chamber of Commerce, Paris ; Member of the Commercial Intelligence Committee of the Board of Trade ; President Municipal Corporations Association ; Chairman of Savings Bank Inspection Committee ; Lieut.-Col. Engineer Militia (Humber Div. Submarine Miners) ; J.P. Co. of London and Co. of Berks, and D.L. London and Yorks, and Lieut. of City of London ; Officer of the Legion of Honour and of the French Academy ; Knight Commander of Leopold (Belgium), of Crown of Italy, of Danebrog (Denmark), of Rising Sun (Japan), etc. ; a "progressive and independent Conservative," and in favour of wide local government for both England and Ireland ; M.P. Islington (South), 1886-1906. *Address :* St. Anne's Hill, Chertsey ; Manar, Inverurie, N.B. ; 18 Avenue d'Antin, Paris. *Clubs:* Carlton, Junior Naval and Military.

(Died 12 Aug. 1922.)

ROLLO, 10th Baron (*cr.* 1651), **John Rogerson Rollo**, D.L., F.R.G.S., F.S.A. ; Baron Dunning (U.K.), 1869 ; *b.* 24 Oct. 1835 ; *s.* of 9th Baron and Elizabeth, *o. d.* of John Rogerson, Wamphray and Dumcrieff ; S. father 1852 ; *m.* 1857, cousin Agnes (*d.* 1906), *d.* of late Colonel Trotter and Mary, *d.* of 8th Baron ; four *s.* three *d.* *Educ.:* Trinity College, Cambridge (M.A.). Representative Peer, Scotland, 1860-68. Owns about 17,400 acres. *Heir: s.* Master of Rollo. *Address :* Duncrub Castle, Dunning, Perthshire ; Dumcrieff House, Moffat, N.B. ; Wilmington, Ryde, Isle of Wight. *Clubs :* Athenæum, United University.

(Died 3 Oct. 1916.)

ROLT, Very Rev. Cecil Henry, M.A. ; Chaplain of Hornchurch since 1925 ; *b.* 1865 ; *s.* of Rev. H. G. Rolt, Harbledown, Canterbury ; *m.* 1910, Mary Foxley, *e. d.* of Very Rev. William Foxley Norris ; three *s.* *Educ. :* Winchester ; New College, Oxford. Deacon, 1888 ; Priest, 1890 ; served curacies at St. Thomas's, Sunderland, Christ Church, West Hartlepool, St. Hilda's, South Shields, St. Cuthbert's, Bensham ; Vicar of Holy Trinity, Darlington, 1897 ; took part in the Mission of Help to S. Africa, 1904 ; Vicar of Batley, Yorkshire, 1905 ; Vicar of Huddersfield, 1910 ; Dean of Cape Town, 1917-24 ; late Hon. Canon of Wakefield. *Address :* The Chaplaincy, Hornchurch. *(Died 14 Sept. 1926.)*

ROMANES, Ethel (Mrs. G. J. Romanes) ; *b.* Liverpool ; *d.* and *heiress* of late Andrew Duncan ; *m.* 1879, late George John Romanes, F.R.S. ; three *c.* *Educ.:* privately. Is on several committees of work for women ; has lectured for some years on Theology and on Dante, etc., to educated women ; has lectured by request in New York, Boston, etc., on the same subjects ; entered the Catholic Church, 1919. *Publications:* Life and Letters of George John Romanes, 1896 ; The Hallowing of Sorrow, 1896 ; Story of Port Royal, 1907 ; Meditations on the Penitential Psalms, 1902 ; Meditations on the Epistle of St. James, 1903 ; How to Use the Prayer Book, 1905 ; Bible Readings, 1908 ; Charlotte Yonge, an Appreciation ; A Great Mistake, a novel, 1921 ; Anne Chichester, a novel, 1925 ; several smaller devotional books, reviews, etc. *Recreations :* reading, music. *Address:* 52 Ashley Gardens, S.W.1 ; Pitcalzean, Ross-shire. *T.:* Victoria 8984. *Club:* Sesame. *(Died 30 Mar. 1927.)*

ROMER, Sir Robert, Kt., *cr.* 1890 ; G.C.B., *cr.* 1901 ; F.R.S. ; **The Rt. Hon. Sir Robert Romer**; a Lord Justice of Appeal, 1899-1906 ; Judge of the Chancery Division of the High Court of Justice, 1890-99 ; *b.* 23 Dec. 1840 ; 2nd *s.* of late composer Frank Romer and Mary Lydia Cudworth; *m.* 1864,

WHO WAS WHO, 1916-1928

Betty (d. 1916), d. of Mark Lemon, editor of Punch. *Educ.* : private schools; Trinity Hall, Camb. (Scholar; M.A.). Senior Wrangler Mathematical Tripos, 1863; Smith's Prizeman, 1863; Professor of Mathematics, Queen's Coll. Cork, 1865-66; Fellow of Trin. Hall, 1867; Barr. Lincoln's Inn, 1867; Q.C. 1881; Bencher, Lincoln's Inn; P.C. 1899. *Recreations :* shooting, cycling, rowing. *Address :* 21 Queens Gate Gardens, S.W., T. Western 6486. *Club :* Athenæum.
(*Died 19 Mar. 1918.*)

ROMER, Thomas Ansdell, Senior Master of the Supreme Court, Chancery Division; b. 16 Dec. 1848; s. of late Thomas Romer of Kensington: m. 1892, Leila Harriette, d. of late John Harding Robinson, Examiner of Standing Orders, House of Lords; one d. *Educ.* : Kensington Grammar School; Brighton; Frankfort-on-the-Maine; Paris. Admitted a Solicitor, 1873; Certificate of Honour, Final Examination, 1872. *Publications :* The Judicial Trustees' Guide; paper on Copyright Law Reform read at Meeting of Law Society, 1882; and various articles on these subjects. *Recreations :* music, shooting, and fishing. *Address :* 14 Oakwood Court, Kensington, W.; Room 292 Royal Courts of Justice, W.C.(*Died 1 Sept. 1917.*)

RONAN, Rt. Hon. Stephen, Lord Justice of Appeal and Privy Councillor in Ireland, latterly for Irish Free State, 1915-24; b. 1848; s. of Walter Ronan, of Cork, solicitor; unmarried. *Educ.* : Queen's College, Cork; M.A. Q.U.I. Called to Irish Bar, 1870; Q.C. 1889; Bencher, King's Inns, Dublin, 1892; Queen's Advocate-General for Ireland, 1892; called to English Bar, Inner Temple, 1888; K.C. (England), 1909. *Address :* 45 Fitzwilliam Square, Dublin. (*Died 3 Oct. 1925.*)

RONAYNE, Thomas, I.S.O. 1914; Colonel, Railway Transport Service, 1905-14; b. Youghal, 1848; father Irish, mother English; three s. three d. *Educ.* : Corsham; Wakefield. Served apprenticeship at the Inchicore Works, Great Southern and Western Railway, Ireland; subsequently had experience with Sharpe, Stewart and Co., Manchester; went to New Zealand, 1875; appointed General Manager, Kaipara Railway; General Manager, Greymouth Brunner Railway, 1876; Resident and Locomotive Engineer, Wellington and Masterton Railway, 1886; Locomotive Engineer, Hurunui Bluff Railway, 1888; General Manager, Greymouth Brunner Railway, 1900; a Railway Commissioner, 1904; General Manager, New Zealand Railways, 1905-14. *Recreations :* fishing, shooting, gardening. *Address :* 50 Tinakori Road, Wellington, New Zealand. *Club :* Wellington.
(*Died 7 Sept. 1925.*)

ROOKE, Col. Harry William, J.P.; b. 1842; e. surv. s. of late Rev. Canon George Rooke, of Embleton, Northumberland, and Clara Frances, d. of late William Moffat; m. 1881, Jane Henrietta, o. d. of late Thomas Rowlandson Dunn, of Hazelwood, Rylands, and Langthwaite, Lancashire. *Educ.* : Ordnance School, Carshalton; Woolwich. Col. retired, late R.A.; commanded the R.A. in Scotland, 1895-9. *Heir :* s. Douglas Giles, Coldstream Guards [b. 1882; m. 1915, Blanche, d. of late Commander Casberd-Boteler, R.N., and widow of Francis Salwey Winnington]. *Address :* Haynford Hall, Norwich; Villa Constance, Biarritz. *Clubs :* Army and Navy; Norfolk County, Norwich.
(*Died 29 Nov. 1921.*)

ROOKE, Ven. Henry, b., 16 Oct. 1829; s. of Henry Rooke and Elizabeth Warburton; m. 1859, K. E. Lloyd; three s. one d. *Educ.* : Trinity College, Dublin (M.A.). Ordained, 1853; Chancellor's Vicar of St. Patrick's Cathedral, Dublin, 1860-1904; Rector of Wicklow, 1873-1906; Canon of Christ Church Cathedral, Dublin, 1892-1905; Archdeacon of Glendalough, 1905-14; retired; Chaplain of Troops,

Wicklow, 1877; Rural Dean, 1879; Good Service Pay, 1885. *Address :* 4 Belgrave Square, Monkstown, Dublin. (*Died Mar. 1926.*)

ROOKE, Maj.-Gen. William, R.A.; F.R.G.S.; b. 29 Dec. 1836. Entered army, 1854; Col. 1885; retired, 1886; served Crimean War, 1855 (medal with clasp; Turkish medal). *Address :* Ellerslie, Ryde, Isle of Wight.
(*Died 7 Sept. 1919.*)

ROONEY, Rt. Rev. John, D.D.; Bishop of Sergiopolis and Vicar-Apostolic of the Western Districts of the Cape of Good Hope since 1908; Administrator of the Central Prefecture and of the Islands of St. Helena and Ascension; b. Ireland. *Educ.* : All Hallows College, Dublin; Propaganda, Rome. Colonial and Naval Chaplain at Simonstown for about twenty years; Coadjutor Bishop, Cape Town, 1886-1908. *Address :* St. Mary's, Bouquet Street, Cape Town, S.A. (*Died Feb. 1927.*)

ROOS, Gustaf Ehrenreich, Grand Officier du Merite Militaire d'Espagne, Commandeur de St. Stanislas de la Russie, du Medjidié du la Turquie, Chevalier du Wasa de la Suède, du Christ de Portugal; b. Sweden, 15 Sep. 1838; s. of O. G. Roos, Director of Ordnance, Stockholm, and Ulrica Euphrosyne von Keppel; m. Annie (d. 1926), d. of George Roffey of Twickenham. *Educ.* : Gothenburg. Associated with Thorsten Nordenfelt, 1880-90 (the inventor of the guns), and introduced the Nordenfelt guns in the following countries—Russia, Austria-Hungary, Turkey, Roumania, Servia, Bulgaria, Greece, Montenegro, Italy, Spain, and Portugal; travelled a great deal in nearly every country in Europe, Asia Minor, Morocco, United States, and Canada. *Publications :* A Travers L'Orient et L'Occident; L'Emploi des Mitrailleuses et Canons à Tir Rapide, and several other minor publications connected with artillery and powder. *Address :* 7 Queen's Gate Terrace, S.W.7. *T. :* Western 1839.
(*Died 7 Dec. 1928.*)

ROOSEVELT, Col. Theodore, Associate Editor New York Outlook; Progressive; b. New York, 27 Oct. 1858; father of New York (Knickerbocker), mother of Georgian (Scotch) family; m. Edith Kermit Carow. *Educ.* : Harvard. Member of the New York Legislature, 1882-84; leader of the minority in 1883; leader of House in 1884; U.S. Civil Service Commissioner, 1889-95; President, New York Police Board, 1895-97; appointed Assist. Secy. of Navy, April 1897; organised 1st U.S. Cavalry Volunteers (Roosevelt's Rough Riders) and commanded it in Cuba, 1898; Governor of New York State, 1898-1900; Vice-President of the United States, 4 March to 14 Sept. 1901; President, 1901-8; went big-game shooting, British East Africa, 1909. *Publications :* War of 1812, 1882; Hunting Trips of a Ranchman, 1885; Life of Thomas Hart Benton, 1886; Life of Gouverneur Morris, 1887; Ranch Life and the Hunting Trail, 1888; The Winning of the West, 1889-95; The Wilderness Hunter, 1893; American Ideals, 1898; The Rough Riders, 1899; The Strenuous Life; Life of Cromwell; The Deer Family (with others): The Outdoor Pastimes of an American Hunter, 1905; African Game Trails, 1910; Theodore Roosevelt: an Autobiography, 1913; History as Literature, 1913; Life Histories of African Big Game, 1914; A Hunter Naturalist in the Brazilian Wilderness, 1914; Life Histories of African Game Animals (with E. Heller), 1915; Fear God and Take Your Own Part, 1916; A Book-Lover's Holidays in the Open, 1916. *Recreations :* ranching and big-game hunting on the great plains and in the Rocky Mountains; much interested in zoology, especially mammalogy, and field natural history generally. *Address :* Sagamore Hill, Oyster Bay, Long Island, New York. *Clubs :* Century, Union League, Boone and

Crockett, New York; Metropolitan, Washington.
(*Died 6 Jan. 1919.*)

ROOTH, Henry Goodwin; Metropolitan Police Court Magistrate and J.P. for the six Home Counties since 1917 ; *b.* London, 1861 ; *o. s.* of late Goodwin Rooth of Weatherall House, Hampstead, N.W., and Monyash, Derbyshire, shipowner, West Indian merchant, and proprietor of West India Plantations, and Augusta Anne, *e. d.* of Henry Smith, D.P.G.M. Bristol ; *m.* 1897, Beatrice Mary, 4th *d.* of late Edmund Tattersall of Colherne Court (now demolished), S. Kensington ; one *s. Educ. :* Harrow ; Trinity College, Cambridge (B.A.). Called to Bar, Inner Temple, 1887 ; joined and practised on the South Eastern Circuit, C.C.C., Kent and London Sessions, representing the Director of Public Pros. frequently both on Circuit and at Courts Martial ; appointed to H.Q. Staff and Discipline Board of Special Constabulary at Scotland House, Jan. 1915 ; Junior Treasury Counsel in Appeals at London Sessions, 1916. *Recreations:* travelling, painting, golf, and shooting. *Address:* Weatherall House, N.W.3. *T. :* Hampstead 2126. *Clubs :* Garrick, Arts, Royal Automobile.
(*Died 12 Oct. 1928.*)

ROPER, Freeman, M.A. ; *b.* 8 Sep. 1862 ; *e. s.* of late Freeman Clarke Samuel Roper of Palgrave House, Eastbourne ; *m.* 1898, Elizabeth Harriot, *o. d.* of late George Wildman Yates FitzGerald of Maperton, County Somerset, and *heiress* of William Herbert Evans of Forde Abbey, Dorset ; one *s.* one *d. Educ. :* Radley College ; New College, Oxford. Practised for 15 years as a solicitor in London, and retired 1903 ; High Sheriff of Dorset, 1917 ; Alderman Dorset County Council ; J.P. for Dorset and Somerset. *Address:* Forde Abbey, Chard, Somerset. *T.A. :* Forde Abbey, Winsham. *Clubs:* Oxford and Cambridge, Bath.
(*Died 17 Feb. 1925.*)

ROPER, Henry Basil, I.S.O. 1908 ; *b.* Highgate ; *e. s.* of Rev. Thos. H. Roper, late of Puddlehinton Rectory, Dorset, and Mary Emma, *d.* of Basil G. Woodd, late of Hillfield, Hampstead, and Oughtershaw Hall, Yorks ; *m.* Emilie Bessie Earle, *d.* of William Hicks, late of Penryn, Falmouth. *Educ. :* Eton. Joined Colonial Service, 1872 ; at various times Civil Commissioner and Resident Magistrate of Kimberley, Herbert, and Hay ; Commissioner of Police and Chief of Criminal Investigation Department ; Commandant of Burghers in 1878 war (medal) ; Member of Treason Court, 1901-1902 ; Chief Inspector of Prisons for Cape Colony, retired, 1907. *Address:* Beechworth, Havant, Hants. *Club:* Royal Albert Yacht, Southsea.
(*Died 18 Mar. 1918.*)

ROPNER, Col. Sir Robert; 1st Bt., *cr.* 1904 ; Kt. *cr.* 1900 ; M.P. (C.) Stockton, 1900-1910 ; *b.* 16 Dec. 1838 ; *m.* 1858, Mary Anne (*d.* 1921), *d.* of J. Craik, of Newton Stewart, N.B.; five *s.* four *d.* Late Colonel 1st Volunteer Batt. Durham L.I. (V.D.) ; J.P., D.L. Co. Durham ; J.P. Co. York (North Riding) ; Director North-Eastern Banking Co.; Sheriff of Durham, 1896. *Heir : s.* John Henry [*b.* 7 Sep. 1860 ; *m.* 1888, Margaret, *d.* of John Macgregor; two *d. Address:* Ragworth, Norton, Stockton]. *Address:* Preston Hall, Stockton-on-Tees ; Skutterskelf, Yarm, Yorks. *Clubs:* Carlton, Constitutional.
(*Died 26 Feb. 1924.*)

ROSE, Frank Herbert; M.P. (Lab.) North Aberdeen since Dec. 1918 ; Author, Dramatist, Journalist ; *b.* Lambeth, 5 July 1857 ; *s.* of late Thomas Rose of Lambeth ; *m.* 1880, Ellen Mary, 2nd *d.* of late Noah Bishop of Lambeth ; three *s. Educ. :* British School, George Street, Lambeth ; evening classes afterwards. Operative Engineer until 1893 ; Trade Union organizer until 1900 ; journalism and other literary pursuits since ; best known as indus-

trial and labour authority and statistician. *Publications :* The Coming Force ; Our Industrial Jungle ; numerous pamphlets and voluminous press work, stories, sketches ; also author of The Whispering Well, Trouble in the House, The Second Mrs. Banks, The Young Guv'nor, and other plays. *Recreations:* reading, walking. *Address:* House of Commons, S.W.1. *Club:* Manchester Press. (*Died 10 July 1928.*)

ROSE, George Pringle, C.I.E. 1892 ; late Public Works Department, India ; *b.* 1855 ; *s.* of Rev. Donaldson Rose, M.A., of Brechin, Forfarshire. *Educ. :* Aberdeen University ; Wren's ; Cooper's Hill. Assistant Engineer, 1877 ; State Railways, 1878 ; Executive Engineer, 1891 ; Sind Peshni State Railway, 1884-87 ; Chapper Rift Works and Bridge (thanks of Government of India) ; Superintendent of Works, Extension Railway and Kojak Tunnel ; in executive and afterwards administrative charge, 1888 - 91 ; thanks of Secretary of State, Viceroy, Government of India, and Commander-in-Chief (decorated) ; Deputy Manager N.W.S. Railway, 1892-93 ; lent to Nizam's Government to advise as to Railway Policy, 1895 ; Nizam's State Railway Co. as Engineer-in-Chief of Hyderabad-Godavery Valley Railway, 1897-1900 ; Junior Consulting Engineer for Railways, Calcutta, to Government of India, 1902 ; retired, 1904 ; Director, Hyderabad (Deccan) Co., etc. *Address:* Tilthams, near Godalming, Surrey.
(*Died 20 Nov. 1918.*)

ROSE, Major Hugh Alexander Leslie, D.S.O. 1917 ; R.A. ; *s.* of late Hugh Rose. *Educ. :* Wellington College. Entered R.F.A. 1901 ; Capt. 1914 ; Major, 1916 ; served European War in France since 15 Aug. 1914 (despatches twice, D.S.O.). *Club:* Junior United Service.
(*Died 18 April 1918.*)

ROSE, John, *b.* 1841 ; *s.* of J. R. Rose, Stoke-upon-Trent ; *m.* 1882, Janet, *o. d.* of late Charles Darling, Langham Hall, Essex. Barrister, Gray's Inn, 1868 ; Bencher, 1885 ; Metropolitan Police Magistrate, 1891; resigned, 1912. *Address :* Marlows, Westmonkton, Somersetshire.
(*Died 5 Feb. 1926.*)

ROSE, Sir Philip Frederick, 2nd Bt., *cr.* 1874 ; J.P. and D.L. Co. Bucks ; High Sheriff of Bucks, 1898-99 ; *b.* London, 4 Nov. 1848 ; *e. s.* of Sir Philip Rose, Rayners, Penn, 1st Bt., and Margaretta, *d.* of Robert Ranking; *m.* Rose Annie, *d.* of Rev. W. W. Pym, 1866 ; one *s.* three *d. ; S.* father 1883. *Educ. :* Harrow. Commenced life as junior partner in well-known firm of Parliamentary solicitors, Baxter, Rose, and Norton ; for many years legal adviser to the Brighton Railway Co., but has retired from legal practice ; director of several large public companies. *Recreations:* farming, country sports, motoring. *Heir : g.s.* Philip Humphrey Vivian, *b.* 16 Mar. 1903. *Address :* Rayners, Penn, Bucks. *T.A. :* Penn, Bucks. *T. :* High Wycombe 29. *M. :* BH 1163 and BH 2891. *Clubs:* Junior Carlton, Royal Automobile. (*Died 23 Oct. 1919.*)

ROSE-INNES, His Honour Sir Patrick, Kt., *cr.* 1918 ; K.C. 1912 ; Barrister ; J.P. Middlesex, Aberdeenshire, and Kent ; *b.* 1853 ; 2nd *surv. s.* of late George Rose-Innes, J.P., D.L., of Blachrie, Aberdeenshire ; *m.* 1897, Jane (*d.* 1914), *y. d.* of Wm. Palmer, Cote Hill, Cumberland. *Educ. :* University of Aberdeen. Called to Bar, 1878 ; member of South Eastern Circuit ; Recorder of Sandwich and Ramsgate 1905-20 ; Judge of County Courts (Circuit 18), 1920-22 ; contested Elgin Burghs (U.), 1905 ; West Lothian, 1906 ; Jarrow, 1907 ; Middleton Division, Lancs, 1910 ; Major West London Rifles ; Bencher, Lincoln's Inn, 1915 ; sat as Commissioner of Assize S. E. Circuit, 1914-15. *Recreations:* shooting, golf. *Address:* 2 King's Bench Walk, Temple, E.C.4 ; Vale Court, W. ; Blachrie, Aberdeenshire ; The Cottage, St.

Margaret's Bay, Kent. *T.*: Central 754. *Clubs:* Carlton, Junior Carlton, Junior Constitutional; University, Aberdeen. (*Died 2 Oct. 1924.*)

ROSEDALE, Capt. Rev. Honyel Gough, M.A., D.D., F.S.A., F.R.S.L.; Rector of Copford, Colchester, since 1924; P. Grand Chaplain of Grand Lodge of England; Chaplain to Sheriffs of London; Hon. Treasurer London Association for the Blind; Past Master and Chaplain of the Worshipful Company of Coachmakers; Past Master and Chaplain, Worshipful Company of Horners; late Chaplain City of London National Guard, 5th Batt.; President Sette of Odd Volumes, 1920; Editor of The Blind Record; Public Lecturer; *b.* 17 May 1863; *s.* of W. L. Rosedale, LL.D., Vicar of S. Saviour's, Brockley Hill, and of Middleton, Norfolk, and Caroline, *d.* of R. Gough, J.P., of Gorsebrook House, Wolverhampton; *m.* Ada, *e. d.* of P. L. Pelly, J.P., of Oakley, Merstham, and *g.d.* of Sir Henry Pelly, Bart.; two *s.* *Educ.*: Merchant Taylors' School; Christ Church, Oxford; Guy's Hospital; Curate, S. Andrew's, Stockwell, 1886; Spitalfields, 1888; Holy Trinity, Canning Town, 1890; Vicar of Middleton, Norfolk, 1891; S. Peter's, Bayswater, 1894; resigned, 1909; Acting Chaplain, Middlesex R.E. Vols. (resigned); late Hon. Foreign Secretary of Royal Society of Literature; President of C.C.C., 1913-1914; Vice-Pres. Ethological Society; Principal, S. Peter's, Bayswater, Church School, Brompton Boys' School. *Publications:* Life of S. Agnes; Book of Verses; Growth of Religious Ideals in the Great Poets, 1902 and 1926; Queen Elizabeth and the Levant Company, 1904; Celano's Lives of S. Francis, 1904; With the British Association through South Africa; The Spanish Match, 1908; Milton's Religious Views, Milton Tercentenary Lecture, 1908; some notes on the Old Book of the Worshipful Company of Horners, 1910; A Short History of the Horners' Company, 1912; Some Notes on the History of the Worshipful Company of Coach and Coach-Harness Makers; contributor to Ars Quatuor Coronatorum and other Masonic periodicals; and numerous other smaller works. *Recreations, etc.*: travel, golf, and outdoor games; collector of prints, china, curios, old books, and MSS.; Freemasonry. *Address:* The Rectory, Copford, near Colchester; 7 Gloucester Street, Victoria, S.W.; 22 Grafton Road, Worthing; Rosedale House, Warwick Street, S.W.1. *T.*: Marks Tey 32; Victoria 6720 and 5682.

(*Died 14 Jan. 1928.*)

ROSEVEARE, Rev. Richard Polgreen, Vicar of Lewisham since 1917; Hon. Canon of Southwark Cathedral, 1919; Canon residentiary since 1922; *b.* 11 Nov. 1865; *m.*; four *s.* one *d.* *Educ.*: Cambridge University. Ordained, 1889. *Address:* The Vicarage, Lewisham. *T.*: Lee Green 560. (*Died 24 Feb. 1924.*)

ROSS, Alexander, M.Inst.C.E., Consulting Engineer, Westminster; Lieut.-Col. Engineer and Railway Staff Corps; *b.* 20 April 1845; married; one *s.* one *d.* *Educ.*: Aberdeen; Manchester. Pupil, Great North of Scotland Railway, 1862-1871; on Engineering Staff, London and North-Western Railway, 1871-75; District Engineer, Liverpool, 1875-84; Assist. Engineer, Lancs. and Yorks. Railway, 1884-90; Chief Engineer, Great Central Railway, 1890-97; Chief Engineer, Great Northern Railway, 1897-1911; President Institution of Civil Engineers, 1915-16. *Address:* 36 Fellows Road, N.W 3; 23 Abingdon Street, S.W. *T.*: Hampstead 4188; Victoria 1004. *Club:* St. Stephen's.

(*Died 3 Feb. 1923.*)

ROSS, Andrew; Ross Herald; *b.* Rosskeen, Ross-shire, 3 Sep. 1849. *Publications:* Old Scottish Regimental Colours; The Nisbet Plates; The Lyons of Cossins and Wester Ogill, cadets of Glamis. *Address:* 14 Blacket Place, Edinburgh. (*Died 21 Feb. 1925.*)

ROSS, Rt. Rev. Arthur Edwin, D.D.; Bishop of Tuam since 1920; *b.* 1869; *s.* of David Ross, Glenagarey, Co. Dublin; *m.* Mary Elizabeth Linzee, *d.* of Lieut.-Col. R. J. Hezlet, Bovagh, Aghadowey, Co. Derry. *Educ.*: Trinity College, Dublin. T.C.F. 1916-18 (M.C. and bar). *Address:* The Palace, Tuam. *Club:* University, Dublin. (*Died 24 May 1923.*)

ROSS, Rev. David Morison, D.D.; Minister of Westbourne Church, Glasgow, since 1898; Senior Minister since 1912; *b.* 1852; *s.* of Peter Ross, Leithie, Perthshire; *m.* 1885, Isabel, *e. d.* of George Smith, LL.D., C.I.E., Edinburgh. *Educ.*: Edinburgh High School and University (M.A., with 1st class honours in Philosophy, D.D.); studied also at Tübingen and Paris. Assistant to Professor of Logic and Metaphysics, Edinburgh University, 1874-77; Minister of St. John's Free Church, Dundee, 1878-98; Lecturer on Moral Philosophy in Dundee College in 1887. *Publications:* The Cradle of Christianity: chapters on Modern Palestine; Christ and the Home; The Teaching of Jesus; A Plea for Temperance Legislation; Scottish Minister and Soldier: Rev. Peter Ross Husband; The Christ of Faith and the Jesus of History; The Faith of St. Paul: A Study of St. Paul as the Interpreter of Jesus; The Spiritual Genius of St. Paul. *Recreation:* fishing. *Address:* Ivy Knoll, Crieff. *Club:* Liberal, Edinburgh. (*Died 27 Sept. 1927.*)

ROSS, Colonel George, J.P., I.S.O.; General Superintendent of Post Service Branch, Dominion of Canada, 1921-23; Officer Administering Canadian Postal Corps; *b.* Hamilton, Ontario, 21st Feb. 1853; *e. s.* of late John and Mary Ross; *m.* 1874, Rebecca, 2nd *d.* of late John and Letitia Chapman; seven *s.* six *d.* *Educ.*: Hamilton, Ontario. After leaving school was engaged in the printing business for about ten years; accepted a position in the Hamilton, Ontario, Post Office in 1875, and was promoted through the various grades to the Chief Clerkship of that office; Assistant Postmaster at Toronto, Ontario, 1900; Past Officer of the Grand Lodge of Masons, G.R.C., an Oddfellow, a Member of the Ancient Order of United Workmen, and a Past President of the Irish Protestant Benevolent Society of Hamilton. *Address:* P.O. Box 485, Toronto. *T.*: Kenwood 180. (*Died July 1926.*)

ROSS, Major (Temp. Lieut.-Col., Hugh Alexander, D.S.O. 1915; 2nd Batt. The Gordon Highlanders; *b.* 19 Feb. 1880; 2nd *s.* of late John MacDonald Ross, of Ledgowan, Ross-shire; *m.* 1917, Winifred, *d.* of S. Giles, Chatham; one *s.* *Educ.*: Loretto. Captain and played in School XV. for five seasons; played in the Scottish Trial Internationals; joined the 3rd Scottish Rifles, 1900; the Gordon Highlanders, 1901; Captain, 1910; Major, 1916; Adjutant of 3rd Batt. and Depot; served South African War (Queen's medal, 5 clasps) and European War (despatches thrice, D.S.O., and Order of Danilo of Montenegro, 1916); commanded 2nd Battalion in the Battle of Loos. *Recreations:* all sports. *Address:* c/o Holt & Co., 3 Whitehall Place, S.W. *Clubs:* United Service, Royal Automobile. (*Died Oct. 1918.*)

ROSS, Hugh Campbell, Director of the McFadden Research Foundation; Lister Institute of Preventive Medicine; *b.* 1875; *s.* of Sir Campbell C. G. Ross, K.C.B. *Educ.*: Isle of Wight College; St. Thomas' Hospital. Qualified as a doctor 1898, and travelled in Egypt and China; served as surgeon S. African War (Queen's medal five clasps); served in Royal Navy as surgeon, 1902-6, when new methods of microscopical study of living human cells were devised; acted as Medical Officer of Health, Cairo, 1906-8, and started mosquito extermination there under Lord Cromer's administration; resumed investigation of cellular pathology at Royal Southern

Hospital and School of Tropical Medicine, Liverpool, 1908; Director McFadden Research Fund, Lister Institute, Chelsea, 1910, since when new methods were developed for cancer research; conducted research with and advised Factory Department Home Office on industrial cancer, and on certain miner's diseases, 1910-19; inventor of the molybdeno-tungsten ultra-violet light processes for the prevention of industrial cancer in South Wales, of new medical tests, and of tungsten drugs. *Publications:* Induced Cell-Reproduction and Cancer, Vols. I.-IV., and papers published in Proceedings of Royal Society, Royal Society of Medicine, Physiological Society and Medico-Legal Societies; also read papers before the Pathological Society, Philadelphia, and Rockfeller Institute, New York, and American Association for Cancer Research. *Recreations:* motoring and sailing. *Club:* Bath.   *(Died 14 Dec. 1926.)*

ROSS, Mrs. Janet Anne; *b.* London, 24 Feb. 1842; *e. c.* of Sir Alexander Cornewall Duff Gordon, Bt., and Lucie, *o. c.* of John and Sarah Austin; *m.* Henry James Ross, banker, Alexandria, Egypt 1860; one *s. Educ.:* home. Lived six years in Egypt, during three of which was Times correspondent; since 1867 has lived in Italy. *Publications:* Italian Sketches, 1887; Three Generations of English Women, 1888; The Land of Manfred, 1889; Early Days Recalled, 1891; Leaves from our Tuscan Kitchen, 1899; Florentine Villas, 1901; Old Florence and Modern Tuscany, 1904; Florentine Palaces, 1905; Lives of the Early Medici, 1910; The Fourth Generation: Reminiscences, 1912; Letters of Principal J. M. Lindsay to Janet Ross, with Preface by Janet Ross, 1922. *Recreations:* viticulture, music. *Address:* Poggio Gherardo, Settignano, Florence, Italy.
            (Died 23 Aug. 1927.)

ROSS, Sir John, Kt., *cr.* 1922; F.R.G.S.; late Chairman of Directors, Ross & Glendining, Ltd., chief towns of New Zealand; *b.* Halkirk, Caithness, 24 Nov. 1834; *m.* Margaret Watson Cassels; three *s.* three *d. Educ.:* local schools. Founder of firm, Ross & Glendining (as above); founder of Knox College, Dunedin, N.Z.; part founder Ross Home for Aged, Dunedin; Member Knox College Council; former Member of University Council, Otago, and High Schools Board, Dunedin. *Address:* Morven, 3 Newington Avenue, Maori Hill, Dunedin, N.Z.   *(Died 5 Jan. 1927.)*

ROSS, Major John Alexander, D.S.O. 1916; Canadian Infantry; *b.* Kenora, Ont., 20 Oct. 1893; *s.* of Walter Inkerman Ross; unmarried. *Educ.:* Trinity College School, Port Hope, Ont.; Royal Military College, Kingston, Ont. Lieut. in Victoria Rifles of Canada, 1914; temp. Capt. 1915; temp. Maj. in C.E.F. 1915; temp. Maj. B.E.F. 1915; served European War, 1914-16 (D.S.O.). *Recreations:* all sports. *Address:* Lethbridge, Alberta, Canada. *Clubs:* Chinook, Lethbridge,
            (Died 17 Feb. 1917.)

ROSS, John M. E., M.A.; Editor of the British Weekly since 1923; *s.* of Rev. William Ross; *b.* Rothesay, 1870; *m.* 1897, Margaret (*d.* 1923), *yr. d.* of late Rev. Thomas Macadam. *Educ.:* Glasgow High School; University and Free Church College. Minister of the Free Church of Scotland, 1896-1900; of the Presbyterian Church of England, 1900-21; Editor Presbyterian Messenger, 1913-21; Editorial Secretary, Scottish Churches Press Bureau, 1922-1923. *Publications:* The Self Portraiture of Jesus; William Ross of Cowcaddens; The Christian Standpoint; 3 vols. of Devotional Commentary; edited Church Praise; many newspaper and magazine articles. *Recreations:* music, motoring, travel. *Address:* North Hall, Mortimer Crescent, N.W.6. *T.:* Maida Vale 1255. *Clubs:* Royal Societies, National Liberal, Savage, Whitefriars.   *(Died 3 Aug. 1925.)*

ROSS, Hon. Mr. Justice Reginald James Blair, Judge of the Supreme Court of Nigeria; 3rd *s.* of late Sir David Palmer Ross, C.M.G., Surgeon-General of British Guiana; *b.* 19 Sep. 1871; unmarried. *Educ.:* Ipswich School; Gonville and Caius College, Cambridge. Barrister-at-Law, Inner Temple, 1894: entered Colonial Civil Service as District Commissioner at Lagos, 1898; subsequently Police Magistrate, Solicitor-General. *Address:* Lagos, Nigeria, W. Africa. *Club:* Royal Societies, Sports.

ROSS, Robert Baldwin; Additional Trustee of the National Gallery; Executor and Administrator for the literary and dramatic Estate of the late Oscar Wilde; Adviser for the purchase of works of art to the Felton Bequest Committee, Melbourne, Australia; *b.* Tours, France, 25 May 1869; *s.* of Hon. John Ross, Q.C. Attorney-General for Upper Canada, and Augusta Elizabeth, *d.* of Hon. Robert Baldwin, C.B., First Premier of Upper Canada under responsible government. *Educ.:* private schools; King's College, Cambridge. After leaving university without taking a degree, from 1889 contributed signed and anonymous articles on art, literature, and drama to Scots Observer, Saturday Review, Pall Mall Gazette, Cornhill, Daily Chronicle, and more recently to Lancet, Burlington Magazine, The Times, Westminster Gazette; assistant editor of The Author, under late Sir Walter Besant, 1891; Director of Carfax and Co. Ltd., picture dealers, 1900-8; staff of Morning Post, 1908-12; Adviser to the Inland Revenue on picture valuations for estate duty, 1912-14. *Publications:* Life of Charles Robert Maturin, in collaboration with More Adey, 1892; Aubrey Beardsley, 1908; edited Oscar Wilde's posthumous work, De Profundis, 1905; Wilde's Complete Works, 1908; Masques and Phases, 1909; Really and Truly, 1915. *Recreation:* editing new editions of Wilde's works. *Clubs:* Reform, Burlington Fine Arts, Royal Automobile.   *(Died 5 Oct. 1918.)*

ROSS, Sir Thomas MacKenzie, Kt. *cr.* 1927; late Chairman Madras Chamber of Commerce. *Address:* Best & Co., First Line Beach, Madras, India.   *(Died 12 Aug. 1927.)*

ROSS, of Cromarty, Brig.-Gen. Sir Walter Charteris, K.B.E., *cr.* 1919; C.B. 1900; C.M.G. 1918; (late) Durham Light Infantry; retired pay; *b.* 5 Aug. 1857; *s.* of Col. G. W. H. Ross of Cromarty, and Adelaide, *d.* of late Duncan Davidson of Tulloch, N.B.; *m.* 1st, 1887, May (*d.* 1891), *d.* of F. M. Sir Donald Stewart, 1st Bt.; 2nd, 1897, Gertrude May Gathorne, *d.* of Charles Hill of Clevedon Hall and Hazel Manor, Somerset; two *s.* four *d.* Served Afghan War, 1879 (medal); South Africa, 1899-1900 (despatches three times, Queen's medal 5 clasps, C.B.); European War, 1914-19 (K.B.E., C.M.G., despatches four times); J.P., D.L. Ross and Cromarty. *Address:* Cromarty House, Cromarty, Scotland. *T.:* Cromarty 2. *Club:* Naval and Military. *(Died 9 Feb. 1928.)*

ROSS, Hon. William, M.P.C., J.P., V.D.; Member Provincial Council, Cape Province; *b*, Stranraer, Scotland, 6 May 1850; *m.* Jeannette, *d.* of late George Page, Bloemfontein, bank manager; three *s.* one *d. Educ.:* Stranraer Academy. First elected Griqualand West for Legislative Council, 1883; representative for 28 years, never opposed at any election; Chairman Legislative Council Committees, 1904-1908; has acted as President of Council; Honourable for life conferred for long Parliamentary services; after Union, was returned unopposed for Beaconsfield as Member Provincial Council, selected unopposed as one of the four Executive members; again in 1914 and 1917 and 1920; first Captain in command of Kimberley Highlanders (Volunteers), now amalgamated with Kimberley Regiment, of which he is

Hon. Lieut.-Colonel. *Recreations:* very keen sportsman all round—athletics, shooting, fishing, boxing, horse-racing, etc. *Address:* Lochinch, The Gardens, Cape Town. *Clubs:* Kimberley, Kimberley; Rand, Johannesburg; Civil Service, Cape Town.   (*Died Oct. 1925.*)

ROSS-OF-BLADENSBURG, Sir John Foster George, K.C.B., *cr.* 1903; K.C.V.O., *cr.* 1911; L.L.D., D.L., J.P.; Lieutenant-Colonel, 1896; *b.* Ireland, 27 July 1848; 2nd *s.* of David Ross-of-Bladensburg, Rostrevor, Co. Down, and Harriet, *e. d.* of 2nd Viscount Ferrard and Harriet, 9th Viscountess Massereene in her own right; *g.s.* of Maj.-Gen. Robert Ross, who defeated the Americans at the battle of Bladensburg, and captured Washington immediately afterwards, 1814; *m.* 1870, Hon. Blanche Amelia Skeffington, *d.* of 10th Viscount Massereene and Ferrard. *Educ.:* Radley; R.M.A., Woolwich; Gold Medallist (military) Royal United Service Institution, 1876. Joined R.A.; transferred Lieut. to Coldstream Guards, 1873; served in Suakin Campaign, 1885 (medal and clasp, Khedive's star); served on International Boundary Commission as assistant British Commissioner in Turkey, 1878-79; Secretary to Rt. Hon. R. Bourke (Lord Connemara), Financial Commission, Constantinople, 1881; Assistant Private Secretary to Rt. Hon. W. E. Forster, Chief Secretary for Ireland, 1881-82; served on staff of Earl Spencer and Earl of Carnarvon when Lord-Lieut. of Ireland, 1882-85; Secretary to two British Missions to the Holy See (Duke of Norfolk's), 1887, and (Field-Marshal Sir Lintorn Simmons'), 1889-90; Chief Commissioner, Dublin Metropolitan Police, 1901-14. *Publications:* The Marquess of Hastings, K.G. (Rulers of India Series), 1893; History of the Coldstream Guards from 1815 to 1885, 1896; The Coldstream Guards in the Crimea, 1897. *Recreation:* collector of trees and shrubs. *Address:* Rosstrevor House, Co Down. *Clubs:* Guards'; Kildare Street, Dublin.
    (*Died 10 July 1926.*)

ROSS-LEWIN, Ven. Richard S., Archdeacon of Limerick, 1919; Rector of Kilmurry, Limerick, 1886; Rural Dean of St. Mary's, 1900; *b.* 1848; *s.* of Rev. George Ross-Lewin, J.P., Ross-Hill, Co. Clare; *m.* 1877; no *c. Educ.:* Bristol; Durham University. Served in Royal Navy, 1864-1873; took Holy Orders, 1877; Rector of Killscully, 1883; Prebend of Croagh, Limerick Cathedral, 1908-12. *Publications:* West Briton (Poems), 1907; In Britain's Need, 1917. *Recreations:* cricket, golf, lawn tennis. *Address:* Kilmurry Rectory, Limerick.   (*Died Nov. 1921.*)

ROSS-LEWIN, Rev. Robert O'Donelan, M.A., retired chaplain Royal Navy; Hon. Canon of Newcastle Cathedral, 1900; Rural Dean of Bellingham, 1904; Rector of Wark-on-Tyne; *b.* 26 March 1850; *s.* of late Rev. George Ross-Lewin, Rector of Thorneyburn, and of Ross Hill, Co. Clare, Ireland; *m.* 1897, Katherine Mary Beatrice, *d.* of J. W. Walton-Wilson, J.P. of Shotley Hall, Northumberland; one *s.* one *d. Educ.:* Bristol Grammar School; private tuition; Durham University. Curate of Ponteland, Northumberland, 1874-76; Chaplain in Royal Navy, served in H.M.S. "London" (at Zanzibar), 1876-77; "Jumna" (Indian Troop Service), 1878-80; "Audacious" (Home Station), 1880-81, and in "Audacious" (China Station), 1886-88; H.M.S. "Repulse" (Hull), 1881-83; "Duncan" (Sheerness Flagship of Prince Leiningen), 1883-86; "Indus" (Devonport), 1888-91; "Swiftsure" (Flagship of Duke of Edinburgh), 1891-92; Royal Marines, Walmer, 1892. *Publications:* articles in various journals and papers; illustrations in Graphic, Daily Graphic, and Illustrated London News; several military

and naval songs. *Recreations:* drawing, painting, golf. *Address:* Achnamara, Oban, Argyllshire.
    (*Died 11 Mar. 1922.*)

ROSSE, 5th Earl of (*cr.* 1806), **William Edward Parsons;** Bt. 1677; Baron Oxmantown, 1792; Major Irish Guards; H.M. Lieut. King's County; Representative Peer for Ireland since 1911; *b.* 14 June 1873; *s.* of 4th Earl and Hon. Frances Cassandra Harvey-Hawke, *o. c.* of 4th Baron Hawke; *S.* father, 1908; *m.* 1905, Lois, *d.* of Cecil and Lady Beatrice Lister-Kaye; two *s.* one *d. Educ.:* Eton; Oxford University. Late Lieut. 1st Batt. Coldstream Guards; served S. Africa 1899-1900 (Queen's medal, three clasps); European War, 1914-15 (wounded). Owns about 26,500 acres. *Heir: s.* Lord Oxmantown. *Address:* Birr Castle, King's Co.; Womersley Park, Pontefract.   (*Died 10 June 1918.*)

ROSSETTI, William Michael, author; Government - pensioner (Assistant Secretary, 1869-94, Board of Inland Revenue); *b.* 25 Sept. 1829; *s.* of Gabriele Rossetti, author and Prof. of Italian, King's College, London, and Frances Mary Lavinia Rossetti; *m.* Emma Lucy, *d.* of the painter, Ford Madox Brown, herself an author and painter, 1874 (*d.* 1894); four *c. Educ.:* King's College School London. Entered Excise Office, 1845. *Publications:* blank-verse translation of Dante's Comedy, The Hell, 1865; Fine Art, chiefly Contemporary, 1867; Lives of Famous Poets, 1878; Life of Keats, 1887; Dante G. Rossetti as Designer and Writer, 1889; Memoir of Dante G. Rossetti, 1895; Gabriele Rossetti (translated autobiography), 1901; Some Reminiscences, 1906; various minor publications; editor of The Germ, 1856; of Shelley's Poems, 1870, etc.; of Chaucer's Troylus and Cryseyde, 1875, etc.; of Moxon's Popular Poets, 1870, etc.; of Wm. Blake's Poems (Aldine edition), 1874; of Poems by Dante and Christina Rossetti, 1886, 1896, 1904; of Ruskin, Rossetti, Præraphaelitism, 1898; of Præraphaelite Diaries and Letters, 1900; of Rossetti Papers, 1862-1870, 1903; Dante and his Convito, 1910; art-critiques in Encyclopædia Britannica (lives of Painters, mostly Italian), etc. *Recreation:* chess occasionally. *Address:* 3 St. Edmund's Terrace, Regent's Park. *T.:* 2085 Post Hampstead.
    (*Died 5 Feb. 1919.*)

ROSSMORE, 5th Baron, *cr.* 1796; **Derrick Warner William Westenra,** J.P.; H.M.'s Lieut. of the County of Monaghan since 1897; Lieut. 1st Life Guards, retired, 1876; *b.* 7 Feb. 1853; *s.* of 3rd Baron and 2nd wife, his cousin Josephine, *d.* of Henry Lloyd, Farrinrory, Co. Tipperary, and Harriet, *d.* of Sir John Craven Carden, Bt.; *S. b.* 1874; *m.* 1882, Mittie, *d.* of Richard Christopher Naylor, Hooton, Chester; two *s.* one *d.* Sub-Lt. 9th Lancers, 1872; 1st Life Guards, 1874; Hon. Col. Monaghan Militia; 4th Batt. R. I. Fus. *Heir: s.* Hon. William Westenra [*b.* 1892; Lieut. R.N.V.R., Royal Naval Division, personal Staff]. *Publication:* Things I can Tell, 1912. *Address:* Rossmore Park, Monaghan; The Stud House, Hampton Court, nr. London. *T.:* Kingston 1492; *Clubs:* Carlton; Kildare Street, Dublin.
    (*Died 31 Jan. 1921.*)

ROSTAND, Edmond, dramatist; Member Académie Française since 1901; *s.* of Eugene Rostand (*d.* 1915); *b.* Marseilles, 1 Apr. 1868; *m.* Rosemonde Gérard; two *s. Educ.:* Lycée de Marseilles; Collège Stanislas. *Plays:* Les Romanesques, 1894; La Princesse Lointaine, 1896; La Samaritaine, 1897; Cyrano de Bergerac, 1898; L'Aiglon, 1900. *Poems:* Les Musardises, 1890; Pour la Grèce; Un Soir à Hernani; Les Mots; Chantecler, 1910; Le Cantique de l'Aile, 1911; Le Printemps de l'Aile, 1912, etc. *Address:* Arnaga, Cambo, Basses-Pyrénées. *T.:* 4.   (*Died 2 Dec. 1918.*)

ROSS, Hon. William Roderick, K.C. See page xxx.

ROTH, Brig.-Gen. Reuter Emerich, C.M.G. 1917; D.S.O. 1900; *b.* 20 March 1858; *s.* of Mathias Roth and Anna Maria Collins; *m.* 1883, Lily May Hart, Christchurch, New Zealand. *Educ.:* University College School, Univ. Coll. and Hospital, London. M.R.C.S. England. J.P. for N.S.W.; served South Africa, 1899-1900 (medal and six clasps); European War, 1915-17 (C.M.G.); C.O. 5th Australian Field Amb. Gallipoli; D.D.M.S. 1st A.N.Z.A.C., Egypt, then D.D.M.S. 2nd A.N.Z.A.C., Egypt and France (despatches); Kt. of Grace St. John of Jerusalem. *Recreation:* country walks. *Club:* Imperial Service, Sydney.

(Died 3 Sept. 1924.)

ROTHERHAM, 1st Baron, of Broughton, *cr.* 1910; **William Henry Holland,** Bt., *cr.* 1907; Kt., *cr.* 1902; *b.* 15 Dec. 1849; *y. s.* of late William Holland, J.P., of Manchester; *m.* 1874, Mary, *e. d.* of late James Lund, D.L., Malsis Hall, near Leeds; one *s.* two *d.* M.P. North Salford, 1892-95 (L.), Rotherham (W.R. Yorks), 1899-1910; temp. Chairman of Ways and Means; J.P. Manchester and Cheshire; member of Advisory Committee of the Board of Trade on Commercial Intelligence, 1900, of the Indian Currency Committee, 1898, of the Joint-Stock Companies' Committee, 1905; Chairman of the Regimental Canteens' Committee, 1913; Commissioner Paris, Milan, and Brussels Exhibitions Pres.; Associated Chambers of Commerce, 1904-7; Past President, Institute of Directors, Machinery Users' Association, and Textile Institute; Officer of the Order of Leopold, Belgium; Hon. Freeman of the Borough of Rotherham; for many years Chairman of the Fine Cotton Spinners and Doublers Association. *Heir:* o. *s.* Captain Hon. S. L. Holland. *Address:* Lothersdale, Rottingdean, Sussex. *Club:* Royal Automobile. *(Died 26 Dec. 1927.)*

ROTHES, 19th Earl of, *cr.* before 1457; **Norman Evelyn Leslie;** Baron Leslie and Ballenbreich, 1457; Lieut. 4th Batt. Devonshire Regt.; retired; Captain, Fife R.G. Artillery Militia 1906; formerly a Representative Peer for Scotland; *b.* 13 July 1877; *o. s.* of Martin Leslie Leslie and Georgina Francis, *d.* of H. Studdy of Waddeton Court, Brixham, Devon; *g.s.* of Mary, Countess of Rothes; *S.* grandmother, 1893; *m.* 1900, Noelle Lucy Martha, *d.* of late T. Dyer Edwardes of Prinknash Park, Gloucester; two *s.* *Educ.:* Eton. *Heir:* s. Lord Leslie. *Address:* 45 Draycott Place, Chelsea, S.W.3; *T.:* Kensington 6617; Leslie Lodge, Iver Heath, Bucks. *Clubs:* Windham; New, Edinburgh.

(Died 29 Mar. 1927.)

ROTHSCHILD, Alfred Charles de, C.V.O. 1902; partner in the firm of Messrs. N. M. Rothschild and Sons; *b.* London, 20 July 1842; 2nd *s.* of late Baron and Baroness Lionel de Rothschild. *Educ.:* King's College School, London; Trin. Coll. Camb. Engaged in banking business; for some years a director of the Bank of England, and now a trustee of the National Gallery, and of the Wallace Collection, Hertford House. Holds Legion d'honneur of France. *Address:* 1 Seamore Place, Mayfair, W.; *T.:* Mayfair 2947; Halton House, Tring, Herts. *Clubs:* Turf, Marlborough, St. James's, Bachelors', Boodle's, Pratt's.*(Died 31 Jan. 1918.)*

ROTHSCHILD, Baron Henri de, Officier de la Légion d'Honneur; Docteur en Medecine et Homme de lettres: Medecin-chef de la Polyclinique H. de Rothschild; *b.* Paris, 26 July 1872. *Educ.:* Lycées Louis le Grand et Janson. *Publications:* La Sauvegarde, La Rampe, etc.; et ouvrages techniques. *Address:* 33 Faubourg St. Honoré, Paris: T. Elysées 09-33; Abbaye des Vaulx-de-Cernay, Seine et Oise. *Clubs:* Automobile, Aero., Bois de Boulogne, Interallié, Yacht de France, Paris; Royal Yacht Squadron, Cowes.

(Died 3 May 1922.)

ROTHSCHILD, Leopold de, D.L., J.P., C.V.O. 1902; *b.* 22 Nov. 1845; 3rd *s.* of Baron Lionel de Rothschild, M.P.; *m.* Marie, *d.* of A. Perugia, Trieste, 1881; three *s.* *Address:* 5 Hamilton Place, W. *T.:* 4237 Gerrard; Ascott, Leighton Buzzard; Palace House, Newmarket; Gunnersbury Park, Acton. *T.:* 129 Ealing. *Clubs:* Turf, Bachelors', Jockey.

(Died 29 May 1917.)

ROTHSCHILD, Hon. Nathaniel Charles; partner in N. M. Rothschild & Sons; *b.* 9 May 1877; *s.* of 1st Lord Rothschild; *m.* 1907, Rozsika, 3rd *d.* of Captain Alfred Edler von Wertheimstein of Nagy-Varad, Hungary; one *s.* three *d.* *Educ.:* Harrow; Trinity College, Camb. B.A. Nat. Science, 1898; M.A. 1901; Chairman of Alliance Assurance Co., Ltd. *Publications:* several papers on Entomology. *Recreations:* shooting, travel, entomology. *Address:* Arundel House, Kensington Palace Gardens, W.8; Ashton Wold, Oundle. *T.A.:* Eightfold, Notting, London, Oundle. *Clubs:* Bachelors', and Rothschild, Oundle. *Clubs:* Bachelors', Savile, Union, Beefsteak. *(Died 12 Oct. 1923.)*

ROTTON, Sir John Francis, Kt., *cr.* 1899; M.A., LL.B., K.C. 1891; *b.* 1837; *s.* of Richard Rotton, London. Called to Bar, Lincoln's Inn, 1860 (certificate of honour); Legal Adviser to Local Govt. Board, 1883: Asst.-Secy., 1876-83; Legal Asst. Medical Dept., 1869-76; Member of Council Univ. Coll., London, 1869; Vice-Pres. of Senate, 1878 and 1882. *Address:* Lockwood, Frith Hill, Godalming. *(Died 9 April 1926.)*

ROUND, Francis Richard, C.M.G. 1887; of East Hill House, Colchester; *b.* 22 Jan. 1845; *s.* of late Rev. J. T. Round, Colchester; *m.* 1881, Frances Emily, *d.* of the late J. J. Tufnell, Langleys, Essex; three *s.* one *d.* *Educ.:* Marlborough; Balliol College, Oxford. Clerk, Office of Secretary of State for Colonies, 1869; accompanied Sir P. Julyan to Mauritius, 1873; Private Secretary to Sir M. Hicks-Beach, 1880; to the late Sir R. Herbert, 1881; First-class Clerk, 1881; on special service to British Bechuanaland and Mauritius, 1886; Acting Colonial Secretary, Mauritius, 1886-87; Principal Clerk, 1896; retired on pension, 1905; J.P. Essex, 1906. *Address:* Avenue House, Witham, Essex. *Club:* United University.

(Died 24 Nov. 1930.)

ROUND, Rt. Hon. James, P.C. 1902; J.P.; *b.* Colchester, 6 April 1842; *s.* of late Rev. J. T. Round, B.D.; *m.* 1870, *c.* Sybilla (*d.* 1912), *d.* of late Rev. H. Freeland; one *s.* five *d.* *Educ.:* Eton; Christ Church, Oxford (M.A.). Barr. 1868; M.P. E. Essex, 1868-85; (C.) N. E. Essex or Harwich, 1885-1906; owner of 8000 acres in Essex and Middlesex. *Address:* Birch Hall, near Colchester; 31 De Vere Gardens, W.; *T.:* Kensington 2748. *Club:* Carlton. *(Died 25 Dec. 1916.)*

ROUND, John Horace, D.L.; Hon. LL.D. ('Edin.); late Hon. Historical Adviser to the Crown in Peerage Cases: President Essex Archæological Society, 1916-21; now Vice-President: Vice-President English Place-Name Society; *b.* 22 Feb. 1854; *o. s.* of John Round, landowner. *Educ.:* Balliol College, Oxford; M.A., 1st class in modern history. *Publications:* Geoffrey de Mandeville, 1892; Feudal England, 1895; The Commune of London, 1899; Calendar of documents preserved in France, 1899; Studies in Peerage and Family History, 1900; Peerage and Pedigree, 1910; The King's Serjeants, 1911; and smaller works; contributor to Domesday Studies, Dictionary of National Biography, The Complete Peerage, Victoria County History, etc.; also to English Historical Review, Archæological Transactions, etc. *Address:* 15 Brunswick Terrace, Brighton. *Club:* Carlton.

(Died 24 June 1928.)

ROUNDWAY, 1st Baron, *cr.* 1916, of Devizes; **Charles Edward Hungerford Athol Colston,** J.P., D.L.; *b.* 16 May 1854; *s.* of late E. Colston, Roundway Park; *m.* Rosalind, d. of Col. Gostling-Murray, Whitton Park, Hounslow, Middlesex, 1879 ; one s. Educ. : Eton ; Christ Church, Oxford. M.P. (C.) Thornbury Div. Gloucestershire, 1892-1906. Heir : s. Brig.-Gen. Hon. E. M. Colston. Address : Roundway Park, Devizes. Clubs : Carlton, Arthur's. (Died 17 June 1925.)

ROUNSEVELL, Honourable William Benjamin ; b. Sep. 1842 ; s. of William Rounsevell who went to South Australia in 1839 ; m. 1864, Louisa Ann Carvosso. Educ. : John Whinham's ; St. Peter's Colleges, S.A. Devoted himself to breeding stud stock (merino sheep and shorthorn cattle), Corryton Park, Mt. Crawford ; carried on Moolooloo Sheep Station, Cowarie Cattle Run ; sold out in the early 'eighties and retired ; purchased the wine and spirit business of Johnstone & Furness ; floated it with the Kent Town and West End Breweries as a public company called S.A. Brewing Co. (Chairman) ; Chairman of Directors of Cotton, Palmer & Preston, Ltd. ; entered Parliament as Member for Burra, 1875 ; Treasurer, Morgan Ministry, 1882 ; Treasurer, Cotton Ministry, 1884 ; Treasurer, Downer Ministry, 1892-93 ; Commissioner Public Works, Playfond Government, 1890-92 ; Commissioner Public Works, Johnson Government, 1899. Recreations : fond of all sports, shooting particularly—all game ; coursing—bred scores of greyhounds ; racing—Committeeman on S.A.J.C. for a number of years. Address : Tremere, Glenelg, S. Australia. Clubs : Adelaide, Adelaide.

ROUTH, Amand J. McC., M.D., B.S. (Lond.); F.R.C.P. (Lond.); Consulting Obstetric Physician to Charing Cross Hospital and Consulting Physician to the Samaritan Free Hospital for Women ; Past Pres. Obstetric and Gynæcological Section of Royal Society of Medicine ; retired from practice : b. London, 1853 ; e. s. of C. H. F. Routh, M.D., and Mary Anne, d. of James McConnel of Ardwick ; m. 1st, 1880, Blanche, d. of Richard Routh of Constantinople ; 2nd, 1917, Mrs. Carline E. Tocher. Educ. : King's College School, London ; Holbrook, Ipswich ; University College and Hospital, London. Elected to Obstetric staff of Samaritan Free Hospital for Women, 1880, and to Charing Cross Hospital, 1883 (now consulting) ; Obstetric Physician (now consulting) St. Marylebone General Dispensary, 1882 ; Consulting Obstetric Physician to St. John's Hospital, Twickenham ; Examiner in Midwifery, Royal Coll. of Surgeons, England, 1894-99 ; Royal Coll. of Physicians, 1900-1905 ; Examiner in Obstetric Medicine University of London, 1900-1903, and University of Cambridge, 1913-17 ; University of Birmingham, 1906-8 ; Councillor on Municipal Council, Folkestone, 1923. Publications : Cæsarean Section ; Antenatal Hygiene ; numerous papers and articles on Midwifery and Gynæcology. Address : Grimston Court, Folkestone. T. : Folkestone 480. Club : Athenæum. (Died 18 Dec. 1927.)

ROUTHIER, Hon. Sir Adolphe Basile, President of the Court of Admiralty for the Province of Quebec ; b. St. Placide, County of Two Mountains, Province of Quebec ; s. of Charles Routhier and Angélique Lafleur ; b. 8 May 1839 ; m. 1862, Marie Clorinde, o. d. of Jean Mondelet, a lawyer of Three Rivers ; one s. two d. Educ. : Ste. Therese College ; Laval University (L.D. and LL.D., and became a Professor of International Law). Called to Bar, 1861 ; Queen's Counsel, 1872 ; a Judge of the Superior Court for the Province of Quebec, 1873 ; Chief Justice, 1904 ; was made a Knight Commander of the Order of St. Gregory the Great by Pope Pius IX., and Grand Cross of the same order by Leo XIII., and a Knight of St. Michael and St. George by King George the Fifth ; has travelled much in Europe and the Eastern countries. Publications : many volumes,

912

speeches, critical essays, travels, and poetry ; author of the Canadian National Song, O Canada ; A travers l'Europe ; A travers l'Espagne ; Les Echos, poems ; Quebec ; Conférences et Discours ; Le Centurion, a novel of the Messianic times, translated into five languages ; De l'Homme à Dieu, an apology of Christianism ; Paulina (novel) ; Montcalm and Levis (drama). Address : Quebec, Canada ; St. Irénie les Bains, County of Charlevoix.
(Died June 1919.)

ROW, Canchi Sarvothama, I.S.O. ; (retired) District Registrar of Assurances ; b. 1856 ; m. ; one d. Educ. : Saidapet High School ; Madras Presidency College. Graduated, 1876 ; employed as a clerk in the Madras Board of Revenue, 1878-84 ; in the office of the Inspector-General of Registration, 1884-96 ; Personal Assistant to the Dewan of Baroda, 1897-1901 ; District Registrar, Madras Presidency, 1901 - 14. Address : Saidapet, Madras Presidency, India.

ROWBOTHAM, Rev. John Frederick, M.A. Oxon ; poet and historian ; b. Bradford, Yorkshire, 18 April 1859 ; s. of Rev. Frederick Rowbotham, M.A., Rector of St. James's, Edin. Educ. : Edinburgh Acad. ; Rossall ; Balliol Coll. Oxford. Captain of Rossall School ; Scholar of Balliol College ; 1st class Classical Moderations and Finals ; Taylorian University Scholar in Italian. Travelled for some years in Spain, Italy, Austria, Germany, and France ; collected materials for the History of Music ; ordained, 1891 ; Vicar of Ratley, 1892 ; Rector of Huntley, 1895 ; British Chaplain of Buda-Pesth and Hungary, 1896 ; Vicar of Abbotsley, 1897 ; Editor and Proprietor of The Bard, 1910 ; Vicar of Sutton Cheney, 1916. Publications : The History of Music (3 vols.), 1887 ; The Death of Roland, an Epic Poem, 1888 ; The Human Epic, 1890 ; A Short History of Music, 1891 ; The Private Life of the Great Composers, 1892 ; The History of Rossall School, 1894 ; The History of the Troubadours and the Courts of Love, 1895 ; The God Horus, a novel of Ancient Egypt, 1898 ; The Epic of London, 1908 ; The Epic of God and the Devil, 1911 ; The Epic of the Swiss Lake Dwellers, 1913 ; The Epic of the Empire, 1914 ; The Epic of Semiramis, Queen of Babylon, 1920 ; Epic of the Globe, 1921. Recreations : travelling and driving. Address : The Vicarage, Sutton Cheney, Leicestershire. (Died 20 Oct. 1925.)

ROWCROFT, Major Ernest Cave, D.S.O. 1900 ; I.A. ; 35th Sikhs ; retired 1907 ; b. 6 Oct. 1866 ; s. of Major- Gen. G. C. Rowcroft ; unmarried. Educ. : private school, Eastbourne ; Sandhurst. Served China, 1900 ; present at taking of Tientsin and advance from Tientsin on Pekin, and at the relief of the Legations. Address : Srinagar, Kashmir. Clubs : United Empire, Junior Conservative(Died 27 July 1916.)

ROWCROFT, Major-General George Cleland, Indian Army ; b. 17 Sept. 1831 ; s. of late Lt.-Gen. F. E. R. Rowcroft, C.B. ; m. 1860, Oriana Rachel (d. 1921), d. of late Hon. P. D. Souper, Registrar-General of Mauritius ; one s. four d. Educ. : private schools. Entered army 1849 ; Maj.-Gen., 1890 ; unemployed list, 1889 ; served Scind Frontier Expedition, 1852 ; N.W. Frontier of India Campaign, 1852-53 (medal with clasp) ; Indian Mutiny, 1857 (medal) ; N.W. Frontier of India Campaign, 1858 (despatches). Recreations : formerly, shooting, polo, etc. Address : Chinnor, Oxon.
(Died 5 June 1922.)

ROWDEN, Aldred William, K.C. ; s. of late Rev. G. Croke Rowden, D.C.L. Educ. : Rugby ; Balliol College, Oxford. Called to Bar, 1874 ; Q.C., 1899 ; Bencher, Lincoln's Inn, 1906. Publication : The Primates of the Four Georges, 1915. Address : 34 Courtfield Gardens, S.W. T. : Western 3911. Club : New University.
(Died 12 Feb. 1919.)

ROWE, Rev. Alfred William ; Principal Lincoln College, 1892-1912 ; Canon of Lincoln and Prebendary of Biggleswade since 1896 ; *m. Educ. :* Trinity College, Cambridge (M.A.). Assist. Master, Felstead School, 1860-88 ; Vicar of New Brentford, 1888-92. *Address :* 3 St. Giles Avenue, Lincoln.   *(Died 10 Mar. 1921.)*

ROWE, Charles Henry, C.M.G. 1918 ; Paymaster Capt., Royal Navy (retired) ; *b.* 13 July 1869 ; *s.* of Major W. A. S. Rowe, R.M.L.I ; *m.* 1898, Margaret, *d.* of late Edwin Hills, J.P., Deal ; one *s.* one *d. Educ. :* Portsmouth Grammar School. Entered Navy, 1885 ; Secretary to Vice-Admiral, Channel Fleet, 1904-5 ; to Commander-in-Chief, China, 1906-8 ; served in H.M.S. Lion, 1912-17 ; present at actions of Heligoland Bight, 28 Aug. 1914, Dogger Bank, 24 Jan. 1915, and Jutland, 31 May 1916 (despatches) ; Order of Crown of Italy (Officer), conferred 11 Aug. 1917 ; specially promoted for distinguished services rendered during the war. *Address :* 11 Victoria Road, Deal.   *(Died 31 Jan. 1925.)*

ROWE, S. Grant, R.O.I. ; *b.* London, 1861 ; 3rd *s.* of late Charles J. Rowe, lyric author. *Educ. :* private school, and finished at City Middle Class Schools, City, E.C. After leaving school studied from the antique at British Museum and St. Martin's School of Art, and, acting on good professional advice, adopted art as a profession ; first exhibited at R.A., and has been represented at all the most important Art Galleries and Museums. *Recreations :* walking, cycling. *Address :* 6 The Studios, Camden Street, Oakley Square, N.W.
                                         (Died 22 July 1928.)

ROWE, Chief Engineer William, R.D., R.N.R., D.S.O. 1915. Served European War, 1914-15 (D.S.O., despatches for services in patrol work).   *(Died Feb. 1924.)*

ROWELL, Sir Herbert Babington, K.B.E., *cr.* 1918 ; M.Inst.C.E. ; M.I.N.A. ; *o. surv. s.* of Robert Rowell, Newcastle-on-Tyne ; *b.* 1860 ; *m.* 1891, Mary Dobree, *d.* of John N. Robin, Naples ; two *s.* two *d. Educ. :* Mill Hill School ; in Switzerland. President Shipbuilding Employers' Federation, 1912-14 ; President N.E. Coast Inst. of Engineers and Shipbuilders, 1915-17 ; Chairman, R. & W. Hawthorn, Leslie & Co., Ltd. ; J.P. (1906), Co. Durham ; Vice-President Federation of British Industries. *Address :* The Manor House, Jesmond, Newcastle ; Redesmouth House, Northumberland ; 242 St. James' Court, S.W.1. *Clubs :* Royal Automobile, Royal Societies.
                                         (Died 23 June 1921.)

ROWELL, John Soulsby, I.S.O., 1907 ; Agent to the Corporation of Lloyds', the Liverpool and Glasgow Underwriters' Associations for the port and district of Havre, France ; *b.* Hexham, 9 Aug. 1846 ; *s.* of Soulsby Rowell. *Educ. :* France ; Germany. Was Acting-Consul at Havre on various occasions, 1867-83 ; Vice-Consul, 1870 ; passed an examination before the Civil Service Commissioners, 1874 ; H.M. Vice-Consul for Havre to reside at Havre, 1898 ; Acting Consul-General on various occasions, 1884-1906 ; retired on a pension, 1906. *Publications :* French Port Charges ; Souvenirs de voyages, in the Harz Mountains. *Recreation :* fishing. *Address :* 23 Place Gambetta, Havre, France. *T.A. :* Rowell, Havre. *Clubs :* Northern Counties ; Association des anciens élèves du Collège et Lycée, at Havre.
                                         (Died 3 Oct. 1916.)

ROWETT, John Quiller, Managing Director, Rowett Leaky & Co. Ltd., 19 Eastcheap, E.C. ; Chairman, Jude, Hanbury & Co., Ltd., Wateringbury ; *b.* 19 Sep. 1876 ; *s.* of late John Quiller Rowett. Polperro, Cornwall ; *m.* Helen Graham, *d.* of John Jackson Coats, Glasgow ; one *s.* two *d. Educ. :* Mannamead School, Plymouth ; Dulwich College. Founded Rowett Institute of Research in Animal Nutrition in connection with Aberdeen University and North of Scotland College of Agriculture ; mainly financed Shackleton-Rowett Expedition of the Quest to the South Antarctic, 1921-22 ; Master of the Worshipful Company of Fruiterers, 1921 ; Hon. LL.D. University of Aberdeen, 1922. *Recreations :* farming, shooting, billiards. *Address :* 9 Hyde Park Terrace, W.2 ; Ely Place, Frant, Sussex. *T.A. :* Roquille London. *T. :* Paddington 1465, Frant 17. *Clubs :* Junior Carlton, Royal Automobile.   *(Died 2 Oct. 1924.)*

ROWLAND, Rev. Alfred, LL.B., B.A. (Lond. Univ.) ; Member of Convocation ; D.D., C.C. of Canada ; Minister of the Congregational Church, Park Chapel, Crouch End, 1875-1911 ; Ancient Merchants Lecturer, Chairman of London Congregational Union, 1892 ; Chairman of the Congregational Union of England and Wales, 1898 ; *b.* Henley-on-Thames, 1840 ; *s.* of late Rev. James Rowland ; *m.* Ellen Mary (*d,* 1909), *d.* of William Trewent, Pembroke, 1868 ; six *s.* two *d. Educ. :* Crauford College, Maidenhead ; New College, London. Pastor of the Congregational Church in Zion Chapel, Frome, 1865. *Publications :* Half-hours with Teachers ; Paul's First Letter to Timothy ; The Burdens of Life, 1898 ; Open Windows, 1903 ; Possibilities of Obscure Lives, 1904 ; The Exchanged Crowns ; After Death—What ? 1910 ; An Independent Parson, 1923 ; various sermons and addresses ; articles in magazines, Pulpit Commentary, etc. *Recreation :* golf. *Address :* Brightlands, Etchingham Park Road, Church End, Finchley, N.
                                         (Died 3 Sept. 1925.)

ROWLAND, John William, C.M.G. 1897 ; M.B., C.M. : *b.* 30 Dec. 1852 ; *e. s.* of Colonel John Christian Rowland, and *g.s.* of Col. George Tempest Rowland, R.A. *Educ. :* Edinburgh University. Served in India, 1877-1878 ; Assistant Colonial Surgeon, Gold Coast and Lagos, 1880 ; acted also as District Commissioner ; chief medical officer, 1896 ; was on several occasions an extraordinary member of the Council ; acted as botanist to the expedition of Sir Gilbert Carter in 1893. *Decorated for* services in West Africa. *Recreation :* yachting.
                                         (Died 18 Oct. 1925.)

ROWLANDS, James ; M.P. (Lib. and Lab.) N.W. or Dartford Division of Kent, 1906-1910, and since 1910 ; *b.* 1 Oct. 1851 ; *s.* of William Bull Rowlands ; *m.* 1879, Kate (*d.* 1905), *d.* of Joseph Boyden. *Educ. :* Working Men's College, and similar institutions. Apprenticed to watch-case making ; early took interest in politics ; organised registration in old borough of Finsbury ; member of London Municipal Reform League, organised Finsbury branch of it, and became its Hon. Secretary ; M.P. East Finsbury, 1886-95 ; President of the Gas Consumers' Protection League, 1893 ; Secretary of Leaseholds Enfranchisement Association ; took active part in the international arbitration movement ; was a member of the last London School Board ; at present Hon. Secretary of Land Law Reform Association ; takes an active part in Parliament in promoting Bills for reform of the land laws for town and country, and the housing question. *Publications :* pamphlets and articles. *Address :* 119 Mercers Road, Tufnell Park, N.19. ; 8 Buckingham Street, Strand, W.C.2. *Club :* National Liberal.
                                         (Died 1 Mar. 1920.)

ROWLEY, Admiral Charles John, J.P. ; Royal Navy, retired 26 Dec. 1897 ; *b.* Weeting Hall, Brandon, Norfolk, 24 Dec. 1832 ; 2nd *s.* of late Capt. Richard F. Rowley, R.N., and Elizabeth Julia, *d.* of late John Angerstein, Weeting Hall, Brandon ; *m.* 1867, Alice M. A., 3rd *d.* of late George Cary Elwes ; one *s.* one *d. Educ. :* at home. Entered Royal Navy, 24 Dec. 1844 ; served in Black Sea and Sea of Azoff, 1854-55 (medals and clasps and 5th class Medjidie); Naval A.D.C. to the Queen, 1882-84 ; 2nd in command Channel Squadron, 1887-88 ; Admiral, 1895 ; retired, 1897 ; J.P. Bucks and Hants. *Address:* Holmesland, Botley, Hants. *T.A.:* Botley, Hants. *Clubs:* United Service ; Royal Navy, Portsmouth ; Royal Southern Yacht, Southampton.

(*Died 11 Nov. 1919.*)

ROWLEY, Sir George (Charles Erskine), 3rd Bt., *cr.* 1836 ; Hon. Lt.-Col. in Army, retired 1885 ; *b.* 26 Sept. 1844 ; *S. u.* 1884 ; *m.* 1st, 1867, Alicia (*d.* 1888), *d.* of Capt. Hollis, 1st Dragoon Guards ; 2nd, 1890, Amy Isabel, O.B.E., *d.* of William Foster Batt, Cae Kenfy, Abergavenny ; two *s.* *Educ.:* Cheltenham ; Sandhurst. Captain 1st Batt. Royal Welsh Fusiliers, 1879-85 ; retired. *Heir: s.* Rev. George Charles Augustus, resigned Living [*b.* 18 Mar. 1869 ; *m.* 1891, Caroline, *o. d.* of late Rev. John Cuming ; one *s.* two *d.*]. *Address:* Eastfield Lodge, Epsom Road, Guildford. *T.:* Guildford 149. *Club:* Army and Navy.

(*Died 15 Jan. 1922.*)

ROWLEY, Rev. Sir George Charles Augustus, 4th Bt., *cr.* 1836 ; *b.* 18 Mar. 1869 ; *s.* of 3rd Bt. and Alicia (*d.* 1888), *d.* of late Capt. R. Hollis, 1st Dragoon Guards ; *S.* father 1922 ; *m.* 1891, Caroline, *o. d.* of late Rev. John Cuming, M.A. ; one *s.* two *d.* *Educ.:* Trinity College, Cambridge. Ordained deacon, 1893 ; priest, 1894 ; Curate of Scunthorpe, 1893-1895 ; Brabourne, 1895-97 ; Vicar of Harmston, Lincs., 1897-99 ; Rector of Eastwick, Herts, 1899-1916. *Heir: s.* George William, Captain Essex Regt., *b.* 1896. *Address:* Wrottesley House, Mount Ephraim Road, Streatham, S.W.16. *T.:* Streatham 1153. (*Died 7 Sept. 1924.*)

ROWNTREE, Joseph; *b.* 1836 ; *s.* of Joseph Rowntree ; *m.* 1867, Emma Antoinette Seebohm ; three *s.* one *d.* *Educ.:* Friends' School, York. Engaged in business, and in social, political, and literary work. *Publications:* (Joint) The Temperance Problem and Social Reform, British Gothenburg Experiments ; Public Control of the Liquor Traffic, etc. *Recreations:* natural history, gardening. *Address:* Clifton Lodge, York. *T.:* 1060 York.

(*Died 24 Feb. 1925.*)

ROWSELL, Mary Catharine, novelist ; essayist ; dramatist ; *b.* London ; *o. d.* and *y. child* of Charles John Rowsell, London. *Educ.:* Queen's College, Harley St. ; Brussels ; Bonn. *Publications:* Love Loyal ; Traitor or Patriot, 1884 ; The Silver Dial, 1886 ; Thorndyke Manor, 1887 ; Miss Vanbrugh, 1887 ; Richard's Play, comedietta, collaborated, produced, 1894 ; The Friend of the People, 1894 ; The Pedlar and his Dog, Honour Bright, Dick of Temple Bar, with other stories for children ; History of France (volume of "Children's Study" Series), 1897 ; Haunted, 1911 ; The Heir of Willowcote, 1901 ; Red House, and many serials and short stories for magazines, The Wild Swans, 1902 ; joint translator of Murger's Latin Quarter ; Life-Story of Charlotte de la Tremoille, Countess of Derby ; The Song of Liberty (drama) (translated and produced in Sweden) ; The Secret of the Ivory Room ; Monsieur de Paris, 1907 ; Ninon de L'Enclos, 1910 ; Friend of the People, 1908 (new issue) ; Portraits of Robespierre (translation) ; Robin Hood (drama) (collaborated). *Recreation:* music. *Address:* 11 Clarence Avenue, Bickley, Kent.

ROWSELL, Rev. Walter Frederick, M.A. ; *b.* 1837 ; 2nd *s.* of Rev. Evan Edward Rowsell, M.A., Rector of Hambledon, Surrey ; *m.* 1867, Catherine Harriet (*d.* 1923), *o. d.* of Major George Fulljames, late Commander of the Guzerat Horse and Political Agent at Rewa Kanta, India. *Educ.:* Elstree ; Sedbergh ; St. John's College, Cambridge (Scholar), B.A. ; Classical Tripos, 1860 ; M.A. 1863. Deacon, 1863 ; Priest, 1864 ;

914

Curate of Hove with Preston, 1863-7 ; Vicar of Copmanthorpe, Yorkshire, 1867-76 ; Rural Dean of Bishopthorpe, York, 1874-84 ; Vicar of St. Paul's, Sculcoates, Hull, 1876-91 ; Vicar of Topcliffe, Yorkshire, 1891-1902 ; Rural Dean of Thirsk, Yorkshire, 1892-1902 ; Hon. Secretary of the York Diocesan Conference, 1876-1902 ; Prebendary of York Cathedral since 1882. *Recreations:* reading, cycling, etc. *Address:* Meadowcroft, St. Margarets-on-Thames.

(*Died 15 Mar. 1924.*)

ROXBURGHE, Duchess of, Lady Anne Emily Innes Ker, V.A. ; *d.* of 6th Duke of Marlborough and widow of 7th Duke of Roxburghe ; three *s.* three *d.* Late Mistress of the Robes and Lady of the Bedchamber to Queen Victoria. *Address:* Broxmouth Park, Dunbar, Scotland. (*Died 20 June 1923.*)

ROY, Most Rev. Paul Eugene, Archbishop of Quebec since 1925 ; *b.* 9 Nov. 1859 ; *s.* of Benjamin Roy and Desanges Gosselin. *Educ.:* Quebec ; Paris. Professor at Laval University, 1886-90 ; Pastor at St. Ann's Church, Hartford, Conn., 1890-99 ; Missionary at Quebec, 1899-1901 ; Cure de Jacques Cartier à Quebec, 1901-7 ; Directeur de l'Action Sociale Catholique, 1907-1908 ; Bishop of Eleutheropolis, 1908 ; Archbishop of Séleucie, 1914 ; Coadjutor cum futura successione, 1920. *Address:* Archbishop's Palace, Quebec. (*Died Feb. 1926.*)

ROY, Commander Robert Stewart, C.M.G. 1918 ; Royal Navy (retired) ; *b.* 2 March 1878 ; *s.* of late Rev. James Roy of Appleton Roebuck, Yorkshire ; *m.* 1912, Marjorie, *d.* of late Henry Pigeon of Furzedown, Hythe, Southampton ; two *s.* one *d.* *Educ.:* St. Peter's School, York ; H.M.S. Britannia. Naval Cadet, 1892 ; served all over the world ; Commander, 1914 ; served European War (despatches, C.M.G.) ; invalided and placed on retired list, Aug. 1919. *Recreations:* all kinds of outdoor sport. *Address:* The Mount, Chobham, Surrey. *T.:* Chobham 20. *M.:* IO 381. *Club:* Junior United Service.

(*Died 3 Dec. 1924.*)

ROYCE, William Stapleton, M.P. (Lab.). Holland-with-Boston since Dec. 1918 ; *b.* 1857 ; *m.* 1882, Emma Louisa, *d.* of O. L. Broedelet, Rotterdam. *Educ.:* Pretty's Preparatory School, Spalding. Twice contested the Spalding Division (U.); late President of the Holland-with-Boston Unionist Association. *Address:* Pinchbeck Hall, Spalding, Lincs. (*Died 23 June 1924.*)

ROYDEN, Sir Thomas Bland, 1st Bt., *cr.* 1905 ; D.L., J.P., Co. Chester ; *b.* 20 Feb. 1831 ; *s.* of late Thomas Royden of Frankby Hall ; *m.* Alice Elizabeth, *d.* of late Thomas Dowdall ; two *s.* six *d.* High Sheriff of Cheshire, 1903-4 ; Ex-Chairman of Liverpool Conservative Association ; M.P. (C.) West Toxteth, 1885 ; 1886, unopposed, retired 1892 ; moved reply to Queen's Speech ; was Member of Royal Commission on Tonnage and on Unseaworthy Ships, also represented Liverpool upon the Load Line Committee ; head of firm T. B. Royden, steamship owners, 20 Brown's Buildings, Liverpool. *Heir: s.* Thomas, J.P. [*b.* 22 May 1871. Deputy Chairman Cunard Steamship Co. ; Director, Lancs. and Yorks. Railway, and the London, City, and Midland Bank.] *Address:* Frankby Hall, Frankby, Cheshire. *Clubs:* Carlton, Constitutional, Conservative. (*Died 29 Aug. 1917.*)

ROYDS, Col. Sir Clement Molyneux, Kt., *cr.* 1906 ; C.B. ; T.D., D.L., Co. Lancashire, F.S.A., late Col. Commanding Duke of Lancaster's Own Imperial Yeomanry ; Hon. Col. 2nd Vol. Batt. Lancashire Fus. ; Knight of Justice of the Order of St. John of Jerusalem in England ; *b.* 3 April 1842 ; *e. s.* of William Edward Royds, Greenhill, Rochdale, and Danehill Park, Sussex, and Mary Ann, *e. d.* of Anthony Molyneux, Newsham House, Lancashire ; *m.* 1882, Annette Nora Jane, 2nd *d.* of Thomas Littledale of Highfield, Lancs,

Lady of Grace of the Order of St. John of Jerusalem in England. *Educ.* on the Continent. Contested Rochdale, 1892; M.P. (C.) Rochdale, 1895-1906. *Address:* 71 Eaton Place, S.W.; *T.:* Victoria 4275; Greenhill, Rochdale. *Clubs:* Carlton, United Service. (*Died 28 Jan. 1916.*)

ROYLE, Arnold, C.B. 1884; Gentleman Usher to the King, 1901; *b.* 30 Aug. 1887; *s.* of W. Royle, solicitor, Lymington; *m.* 1880, Cecily Jane Longueville, 2nd *d.* of Thomas Snow, Blundellsands, Liverpool; one *s.* two *d. Educ.:* King's Coll. London. Joined army as assistant surgeon on the Staff, 1859; served five years in India; retired half pay, 1871; appointed medical attendant to late Duke of Albany, 1875, and remained with him till his death, 1884; appointed temporary Medical Inspector Local Government Board, 1884; confirmed as permanent inspector, 1893; late Clerk of the Robes and Groom of the Privy Chamber to Her Majesty Queen Victoria. *Recreations:* yachting, golf, etc. *Address:* Albany Lodge, Esher. *M.:* Q 281. *Club:* Naval and Military.

(*Died 16 Feb. 1919.*)

ROZE, Madame Marie; Officier de l'Instruction Publique; *b.* Paris, 2 Mar. 1846. *Educ.:* Paris Conservatoire, under Auber and Mocker; first prize singing, 1865; gold medal, 1866. Made début at Opéra Comique; in Paris at the Grand Opera, 1870; presented with gold medal by M. Thiers for her gallant conduct during siege of Paris; Medaille de 1870; first appearance England, 1872; America, 1877; has a school for singing and lyric declamation. *Address:* Chateau du Belvédère, 3 rue du Pavillon, Parc des Princes, Boulogne sur Seine, France. (*Died 21 June 1926.*)

ROZE, Raymond (J. H. Raymond Roze-Perkins); *b.* London, 1875; *m.*; one *d.* 1st prize with honours of Brussels Royal Conservatoire of Music; Musical Director to late Sir Henry Irving at Lyceum Theatre; and to Sir Herbert Tree at His Majesty's Theatre; composer of Overture and Incidental Music to Shakespeare's plays: Julius Caesar, King John, Henry IV., Henry V., Much Ado About Nothing, Tempest, Merry Wives of Windsor, Taming of the Shrew, Antony and Cleopatra, also to Trilby, and many other plays; Conducted Symphonic Concerts of his own works at Spa, Dieppe, Aix-les-Bains, Monte Carlo, Paris, etc.; Director of the Royal Opera House, Covent Garden, autumn season, 1913, when he produced his own opera Joan of Arc; wrote and composed the fantastic opera Arabesque, produced at Coliseum, 1916; conducted his own music Julius Caesar at Command Performance, Drury Lane, 1916. Founded July 1914, organised and directed, by the special permission of the Army Council, the first new Volunteer Home Defence Corps, the United Arts' Rifles, recruited entirely from members of the fine Arts, now recognised by the War Office under the title of 1st Central London Regiment; invited by Special Committee of House of Commons to act as Hon. Secretary to the Inter-Parliamentary Commercial Conference, 1918 (official thanks of House of Commons Committee). *Address:* 18 Palace Gardens Terrace, W.8. *Club:* Bath.

(*Died 31 Mar. 1920.*)

RUBENS, Paul Alfred, Dramatic Author and Composer; *b.* 29 April 1875; *s.* of Victor Rubens, 8A Kensington Palace Gardens, W. *Educ.:* Winchester College; University College, Oxford. Student at Inner Temple, 1898; gave up career of Barrister for Dramatic and Musical Work; at one time an ardent amateur actor, and still a Member of the O.U.D.S., Oxford; Wrote some of the incidental music for Mr. Tree's revival of Twelfth Night, but has chiefly written music to his own lyrics and librettos; Author of two comedies to be produced in near future. *Publications:* Three Little Maids; Lady Madcap; Young Mr. Yarde (with Harold Ellis); The Dairymaids (with Frank Tours); The Blue Moon (with Howard Talbot); Mr. Popple; Miss Hook of Holland; The Balkan Princess; The Girl from Utah; The Sunshine Girl; Author and Composer of numerous songs in The Country Girl, The Cingalee, Florodora, The Messenger Boy, The Orchid, The Girl from Kay's, etc.; many other songs and ballads. *Recreations:* motoring, golfing, shooting, working, and getting up late —anything, in fact, except London and social functions. *Address:* 27 Shaftesbury Avenue, W. *T.A.:* Sleepy, London. *T.:* Gerrard, 6700. *Clubs:* Garrick, Royal Automobile, Aero.

(*Died 5 Feb. 1917.*)

RUDDOCK, Ven. David; Archdeacon of Hawkes Bay since 1907; *m.*; (two *s.* killed in the War). *Educ.:* St. Catherine's College, Cambridge; Lichfield College. Ordained 1879; Missionary, Melanesia, 1879-84; Curate of Redmire, N.S.W., 1885; All Saints', Parramatta, 1886; St. Mary's, Kangaroo Point, 1886-87; Priest in charge, Rockhampton, 1887-1888; Rector of Holy Trinity, Wooloongabba, 1888-93; S.P.G., 1894-1900; Curate of Shefford Magna, 1901-3; Vicar of Wairoa, 1904-7. *Address:* Napier, N.Zealand. (*Died 30 Jan. 1920.*)

RUFF, Howard, Founder (1894) and Hon. Secretary of the Royal Society of St. George; Founder (1908) and Hon. Editor of the English Race; through his exertions all of the Royal Navy, Army, and Air Force now wear their National Emblems on their respective Saints' days; Fellow of Huguenot Society of London; Royal Colonial Institute; Royal Geographical Society and other Associations; has visited Australia, Canada, U.S.A. *Recreations:* reading, freemasonry; formerly farming and country sports. *Address:* 5 Bloomsbury Square, W.C.1. *T.A.:* Georgical, London. *T.:* Museum 5654. *Club:* Royal Societies. (*Died 29 Oct. 1928.*)

RUFFER, Sir Marc Armand, Kt., *cr.* 1916; C.M.G. 1905; M.A., M.D., F.L.S.; President of Sanitary, Maritime, and Quarantine Council of Egypt, Alexandria; President of the Municipal Delegation, and Vice-President of the Municipality, Alexandria; Commissioner British Red Cross Society and Order of St. John; Egyptian Representative International Bureau of Hygiene, Paris; *b.* 1859; *s.* of late Baron Alphonse Jacques de Ruffer; *m.* Alice Mary, *e. d.* of late Captain Greenfield, R.A.; three *d. Educ.:* Brasenose College, Oxford; University College, London. Formerly Director of Brit. Inst. of Preventive Medicine; Prof. of Bacteriology at Cairo Medical School; Member of Indian Plague Commission; Egyptian Delegate to Sanitary Conferences, Paris, 1908 and 1911, and Rome, 1907; Grand Cross Medjidieh and Grand Officer Osmanieh; Commander Order of Saviour of Greece, St. Anne of Russia, and Cross of Italy. *Publications:* various papers in scientific and medical journals. *Recreation:* billiards. *Address:* Villa Ménival, Ramleh, Egypt. *T.A.:* Ruffer, Alexandria. *Clubs:* Savile, Royal Societies; Khedivial, Union, Alexandria.

(*Died 2 May 1917.*)

RUGGLES, Major-General John, Retired List Indian Army; *b.* 21 July 1827; *e. s.* of late W. H. Ruggles, Lewisham, Kent; *m.* 1885, Ellen Sophia (Nellie), *y. d.* of late G. F. Johnson, H.M.C.S.: no *c. Educ.:* Addiscombe Mil. Coll. First Commission Indian Service, 1845; at siege and capture of Fort Kanysu, 1846; Indian Mutiny, 1857, one of the Lucknow garrison; served in China as volunteer in 1860; in Bhootan, 1865; commanded column of attack which resulted in capture of Bula stockades (thanks of Commander-in-Chief, 3 medals 2 clasps). Colonel 19th Punjabis. *Publication:* Recollections of a Lucknow Veteran. *Address:* Montana, Swanage.   (*Died 26 July 1919.*)

RUGGLES-BRISE, Maj.-Gen. Sir Harold Goodeve, K.C.M.G., *cr.* 1919; C.B. 1915; M.V.O. 1910; *b.* 17 March 1864; 5th *s.* of late Sir S. B. Ruggles-Brise, K.C.B., and *d.* of Sir E. Bowyer-Smyth, 10th Bt.; *m.* 1895, Lady Dorothea Stewart-Murray, *e. d.* of 7th Duke of Atholl. *Educ.:* Winchester; Balliol College, Oxford. Joined Grenadier Guards, 1885; Captain, 1897; Major, 1902; Lt.-Col. 1907; Colonel, 1911; Maj.-Gen., 1917; Brigade-Major, Gibraltar, 1899, S. Africa, 1899-1900, Brigade of Guards, 1901-3; Commandant, School of Musketry, 1911; served S. African War, 1899-1900 (despatches, five times; Bt. Major, Queen's medal 7 clasps); European War, France and Flanders, 1914-18; Brigade Commander, severely wounded, Divisional Commander, and Mil. Sec. G.H.Q. (C.B., promotion to Major-General, K.C.M.G., despatches five times), Commander Legion of Honour, Croix de Guerre, Commander Order of Leopold, Belgian Croix de Guerre. *Address:* 5 Bickenhall Mansions, Gloucester Place, W.1. *T.:* Mayfair 6369. *Club:* Guards'.   (*Died 24 June 1927.*)

RUMSEY, Robert Murray, I.S.O. 1903; *b.* 1849; *m.* 1892, Francesca, *d.* of W. B. Treacher, Carlisle Mansions, Westminster. Entered Royal Navy, 1862; Lieut. 1873; Commander (retired), 1882; served on North America, East India and Pacific and Home Stations; Canadian (Fenian Raid) and Abyssinian medals; Commissioner of Volta District, Gold Coast, 1880; Assistant Colonial Secretary, Lagos, 1883; Deputy Governor, 1884; Assistant Harbour-master, Hong-Kong, 1884; Harbour-master, 1888; Member of Executive and Legislative Councils; pensioned 1904. *Address:* Lavethan, Blisland, Bodmin, Cornwall. *Club:* Naval and Military.
          (*Died 18 Nov. 1922.*)

RUNTZ, Sir John (Johnson), Kt., *cr.* 1903; *s.* of late John Runtz of Stoke Newington; *b.* 14 March 1842; *m.* 1st, Emma (*d.* 1911), *d.* of W. Westwood of Ventnor, Isle of Wight; two *s.* one *d.*; 2nd, 1914, Adeline, *e. d.* of late William Jenkinson. First Mayor of Stoke Newington; J.P. Co. London; a prominent figure in the Conservative cause in Stoke Newington and North Hackney, and also an active worker in the municipal and church life of that district for over thirty years; a member of the Corporation of the City of London and City of London Conservative Association; Hon. Treasurer of the Metropolitan Division of National Union of Conservative Associations; President of N. Hackney Conservative Association; President (first) of the Corporation of Insurance Brokers of United Kingdom. *Address:* Tunnel Woods, nr. Watford, Herts; 33 Nicholas Lane, E.C. *T.A.:* Runtz, London, *T.:* 1216 Avenue; 175 Watford. *Clubs:* City Carlton, Constitutional.   (*Died 4 Nov. 1922.*)

RUSHBROOKE, William George, B.A. Lond., LL.M. Camb., F.R.S.L.; Senior Classical Master, City of London School, 1872-93; Headmaster of St. Olave's Grammar School, 1893-1922; President of the Headmasters' Association, 1918; Dean of the College of Preceptors since 1911; Chairman, Soc. of Schoolmasters; *b.* 21 Jan. 1849. *Educ.:* City of London School; St. John's College, Cambridge (Scholar and Fellow). First in Classics in London B.A.; sixth in first class of Classical Tripos, 1872. *Publications:* First Greek Reader; the Common Tradition of the Synoptic Gospels (with Dr. Abbott); Synopticon, an attempt to set forth the inter-relations of the three Synoptic Gospels, and occasionally their relation to the Fourth Gospel; Olivetum Olavianum, and the Olavian Hymnal. *Address:* 13 Cathcart Hill, N.19. *T.:* Hampstead 412. *Club:* Overseas.
          (*Died 30 Jan. 1926.*)

RUSHTON, William S., I.S.O. 1902; Surveyor, General Post Office, since 1890; *b.* 1850; *s.* of William Rushton, of Eversley, Southsea; *m.* 1891, Gertrude Jurin, 2nd *d.* of William Bache Roberts, of Exchequer and Audit Office; one *s.* one *d.* *Recreations:* golf, cycling, boating. *Address:* Landguard, Granada Road, Southsea. *Clubs:* Constitutional; United Service Golf.   (*Died 20 Feb. 1924.*)

RUSSELL, 1st Baron, *cr.* 1919, **Edward Richard Russell,** Kt., *cr.* 1893; editor of Liverpool Daily Post since 1869; *b.* London, 9 Aug. 1834; *s.* of Edward Haslingden Russell and Mary Ann Crook; *m.* 1st, 1858, Eliza Sophia (*d.* 1901), *d.* of Stephen Bradley and Mary Sophia Ede, Bridge, Canterbury; 2nd, 1902, Jean Stewart, widow of Joseph M'Farlane and *d.* of late Alexander Macdonald of Campbeltown, Argyllshire. *Educ.:* privately. Secretary of Whittington Club, 1858; assistant editor Liverpool Daily Post (now Daily Post and Mercury), 1860; writer of leading articles and dramatic critic, Morning Star, London, 1866; M.P. Glasgow, Bridgeton Division, 1885-87; Life Member of the Court of Liverpool University and Life Governor of University College, Aberystwith; Treasurer Newspaper Press Fund; was first Chairman of the Liverpool Reform Club. *Publications:* A volume of reminiscences under the title of That Reminds Me; also many pamphlets on Shakespearian, Literary, and Philosophical subjects; An Editor's Sermons, 1901; Arrested Fugitives, 1912; A Speculation on Hypothesis in Religion, 1915. *Recreations:* theatre, music, travel. *Heir:* none. *Address:* The Gables, Croxteth Road, Liverpool. *T.A.:* 5 Croxteth Road, Liverpool. *T.:* Royal 2171. *Clubs:* Reform, National Liberal; Liverpool Reform, Liverpool Junior Reform, Liverpool University.
          (*Died 20 Feb. 1920.*)

RUSSELL, Hon. Sir Charles, 1st Bt., *cr.* 1916; K.C.V.O., *cr.* 1921; Solicitor; 2nd *s.* of late Lord Russell of Killowen; *b.* London, 1863; *m.* 1889, Adah Walmsley Williams, *g.d.* of Sir Joshua Walmsley; one *d.* *Educ.:* Beaumont College, near Windsor; abroad. Contested (L.) Hackney and South Salford; in 1893 acted as Solicitor for the British Agent in the Behring Sea Arbitration between Great Britain and the United States; Solicitor for the Government of the Dominion of Canada; Solicitor for the Stewards of the Jockey Club; Director of the Equity and Law Life Assurance Society and the Law Reversionary Society; Chairman of the Board of Management of the Hospital of St. John and St. Elizabeth; Chairman of the Collections Committee of the British Red Cross Society and the Order of St. John, Knight of Grace of the Order of the Hospital of John of Jerusalem in England, 1921. *Recreation:* golf. *Heir:* nephew, Alec Russell, R.H.A., *b.* 1894. *Address:* 37 Norfolk Street, Strand, W.C.2; 18 Dean's Yard, Westminster Abbey, S.W.1; Littleworth Corner, Burnham, Bucks. *T.A.:* Toilful, London. *T.:* Gerrard 7979; Victoria 6631; Burnham 18. *Clubs:* Turf, Beefsteak, Garrick.   (*Died 27 Mar. 1928.*)

RUSSELL, Charles Alfred, K.C.; *b.* 1855; 2nd *s.* of late J. A. Russell, Q.C.; *m.* 1882, Amy Mary, 4th *d.* of late J. S. Westmacott. *Educ.:* University College School and College. Barr. Gray's Inn, 1878; Bencher, 1894; Q.C., 1896. *Address:* 2 Harcourt Buildings, Temple, E.C.
          (*Died 21 June 1926.*)

RUSSELL, Rev. Charles Dickinson; Canon of Kildare, 1889; Curate of Geashill since 1888. *Educ.:* Trinity College, Dublin (M.A.). Ordained 1855; Curate, Clontibret, 1855-58; St. Ann, Dublin, 1858-88; Canon of Christ Church Cathedral, Dublin, 1883-1908. *Address:* Geashill, King's County, Ireland.

RUSSELL, Charles Gilchrist, LL.D. ; J.P. ; *b.* Edinburgh, 1840 ; *s.* of late Thomas Russell ; *m.* 1865, Annie, *e. d.* of J. Best Davidson, for many years chief sub-editor of Leeds Mercury ; two *s.* two *d. Educ.*: Northern District School ; Edinburgh Univ. Was for some years teacher in public schools and tutor in private families. Studied medicine Edinburgh University, 1860-1863 ; reporter Caledonian Mercury, 1862-64 ; Leeds Mercury, 1864-66 ; London correspondent Leeds Mercury, 1866-67 ; literary editor Sportsman, 1867-75 ; assistant editor Glasgow Herald, 1875-87 ; Editor of Glasgow Herald, 1887-1906 ; President Institute of Journalists, 1892-93. *Address:* 11 Buckingham Terrace, Glasgow. *T.:* 203 Western, Glasgow. *Clubs:* Press ; New, Glasgow. *(Died 22 Dec. 1916.)*

RUSSELL, Charles Taze (Pastor Russell) ; independent minister ; *b.* Pittsburgh, 16 Feb. 1852 ; *s.* of Joseph L. Russell and Ann Eliza Birney ; *m.* 1879, Maria Frances, *d.* of Mahlen and Salena Ackley. *Educ.*: private tutors. Began in independent ministry Pittsburgh, 1878 ; now regularly elected pastor of numerous congregations from Me. to Cal., U.S.A., and also in Great Britain, chiefly serving London and Brooklyn Tabernacles ; travels upward of 50,000 miles each year in his work ; disclaims being the founder of a religious sect ; interprets the punishment of the Bible as eternal death and not eternal torture ; President Watch Tower Bible and Tract Society of Pa., People's Pulpit Association of New York, International Bible Students' Association, London. *Publications:* a series of books, Studies in the Scriptures, issued since 1886 ; Editor of The Watch Tower and Herald of Christ's Presence ; his Sunday sermons published by many English, German, French, Swedish, etc., newspapers. *Address:* Brooklyn Tabernacle, 13-17 Hicks Street, Brooklyn, N.Y.; London Tabernacle, Lancaster Gate, W. *(Died Nov. 1916.)*

RUSSELL, Hon. Cyril, *b.* 1866 ; 3rd *s.* of late Lord Russell of Killowen ; *m.* 1894, Helen Mary, *d.* of late Alexander George Pirie of Leckmelm, Ross-shire ; four *s.* two *d. Educ.*: Beaumont College ; University College, Oxford (B.A.). Partner in Helbert Wagg and Russell, Bankers ; retired 1913. *Publications:* Stilts, 1914 ; Wren's Wife, 1918. *Address:* Kensington House, Bayswater Hill, W.2. *T.:* Park 4993. *Club:* Garrick. *(Died 14 May 1920.)*

RUSSELL, Rev. Edward Francis, M.A. ; *b.* 1 Jan. 1844 ; *o. s.* of late Lord Edward Russell, C.B. ; unmarried. *Educ.*: Victoria College, Jersey ; Trinity College, Cambridge ; Cuddesdon Theological College. Assistant Curate of St. Alban's, Holborn, 1867-1917 ; Chaplain-General to the Guild of St. Barnabas for Nurses since 1876 ; Chaplain to the Sisters of Bethany from 1870-86. *Publications:* Lest We Grow Hard, a volume of Addresses to Trained Nurses. *Recreation:* travel. *Address:* 7 Gray's Inn Square, W.C.1. *(Died 7 Nov. 1925.)*

RUSSELL, Senator Hon. Edward John ; *b.* Warrnambool, Victoria, 1879 ; Vice-President, Federal Executive Council, Commonwealth of Australia, 1918-21 ; Minister in Charge of Shipping ; President of the Commonwealth Board of Trade ; and Chairman of the Australian Wheat Board. *Address:* Federal Parliament House, Melbourne. *(Died 18 July 1925.)*

RUSSELL, Rt. Hon. George William Erskine, P.C. 1907 ; LL.D., St. Andrews, 1899 ; *b.* London, 3 Feb. 1853 ; *y.* *s.* of Lord Charles Russell, M.P., 6th *s.* of 6th Duke of Bedford, K.G. *Educ.*: Harrow ; University College, Oxford (Scholar, Prizeman), M.A. M.P. (L.) Aylesbury, 1880-85 ; North Beds., 1892-95 ; Parliamentary Secretary to the Local Government Board, 1883-85 ; Under-Secretary of State for India, 1892-94 ;

for the Home Department, 1894-95 ; Alderman, County Council of London, 1889-95 ; Chairman of Churchmen's Liberation League ; Lay-Reader in the Diocese of Southwark. *Publications:* A Londoner's Log-Book ; The Household of Faith ; Collections and Recollections (two series), 1898 ; St. Alban the Martyr, Holborn ; Fifteen Chapters of Autobiography ; Edward King, 60th Bishop of Lincoln, 1912 ; The Spirit of England, 1915 ; A Short History of the Evangelical Movement, 1915 ; Portraits of the Seventies, 1916 ; Arthur Stanton, 1917, Politics and Personalities, 1917 ; Basil Wilberforce ; etc. *Address:* 18 Wilton Street, S.W. *Clubs:* Reform, Eighty. *(Died 17 Mar. 1919.)*

RUSSELL, Admiral Gerald Walter, J.P.: *b.* 1850 ; 6th *s.* of Lieut.-Col. A. H. Russell, late 58th Regiment ; *m.* 1893, Katherine, 2nd *d.* of H. G. Gatman, Fernden, Haslemere, Surrey ; one *s.* two *d. Educ.*: privately ; H.M.S. Britannia. Naval Cadet, 1863 ; Lieutenant H.M.S. Tourmaline during Egyptian Campaign, 1882 ; Superintendent, Pembroke Dockyard, 1902-4 ; Retired List, 1908 ; Admiral, 1912. *Address:* Hatchfield, nr. Haslemere, Surrey. *T.:* Haslemere 393. *M.:* PX 4318. *Club:* United Service. *(Died 7 Nov. 1922.)*

RUSSELL, Harold John Hastings ; Recorder of Bedford since 1912 ; *e. s.* of Lord Arthur Russell and Laura, *d.* of Viscount de Peyronnet ; *b.* 23 Jan. 1868 ; *m.* 1896, Lady Victoria Alberta Leveson-Gower, *d.* of 2nd Earl Granville ; one *s.* two *d. Educ.*: Balliol Coll., Oxford. F.L.S. ; F.Z.S., M.B.O.U. ; called to Bar, Inner Temple, 1894 ; has practised on the Midland Circuit, the Aylesbury, Bedford, and Northampton Sessions, the Railway Commission Court, and as a Parliamentary draughtsman ; Admiralty War Staff ; Intelligence Division, Feb. 1915 ; Foreign Office, Political Intelligence Department, 1919 ; Joint-Secretary to Anglo-German Mixed Arbitral Tribunal under Act 304 of Peace Treaty, 1920. *Publications:* The Law of Railway Rates and Charges Orders, 1906 ; Chalkstream and Moorland, 1911 ; The Flea, 1913. *Recreations:* natural history, walking, fishing, fox-hunting. *Address:* 16 Beaufort Gardens, S.W.3 ; *T.:* Western 4517 ; 12 King's Bench Walk, Temple, E.C.4. *T.:* Central 2758. *Clubs:* Brooks's, Athenæum. *(Died 22 Aug. 1926.)*

RUSSELL, James, I.S.O. 1903 ; *b.* 15 June 1839 ; *m.* Georgina Waddell (*deceased*), *d.* of late Alexander Waddell ; one *s.* one *d. Educ.*: Torphichen Parish School ; Edinburgh University. Entered Civil Service (Inland Revenue, Stamps and Taxes) ; Supernumerary Surveyor of Taxes, 1858 ; Surveyor of the District of Banff, 1868 ; Surveyor of the Elgin District, 1871 ; Aberdeen I. Survey, 1883 ; Aberdeen II. Survey, 1891 ; Surveyor of Edinburgh II. Survey, 1893 ; Inspector of Stamps and Taxes, 1895 ; Superintending Inspector in Scotland, 1902 ; retired, 1903. *Address:* 16 Blacket Place, Newington, Edinburgh. *(Died 25 Mar. 1923.)*

RUSSELL, Sir James Alexander, Kt., *cr.* 1894 ; M.A., M.B., B.Sc. Pub. Health, LL.D., J.P., D.L., F.R.S. Ed. ; F.R.C.P. Ed. ; Chairman Burgh Committee on Secondary Education, 1893-1902 ; member of George Heriot's Trust, 1880-1903 ; and of Corporation of Edinburgh, 1880-1900 ; *b.* 6 Apr. 1846 ; *m.* 1st, Marianne Rae (*d.* 1882), *d.* of James Wilson, F.R.S. ; 2nd, 1897, Mary Ruth, *d.* of late Capt. G. B. Prior, R.A., and *widow* of Captain Mackenzie, Bombay Cavalry ; two *d. Educ.*: Edinburgh University. Lord Provost of Edinburgh, and Lord-Lieut. of Co. of City of Edinburgh, 1891-94. *Address:* Woodville, Edinburgh. *T.:* 518 Central. *Clubs:* Reform ; Scottish Liberal, Edinburgh. *(Died 22 Jan. 1918.)*

RUSSELL, Right Rev. Dr. James Curdie ; *b.* 19 June 1830 ; *s.* of Archibald

Russell, proprietor, Ardrossan ; *m.* 1858, Martha Stevenson (*d.* 1916), *d.* of William Watson, Banker, Campbeltown ; one *d. Educ. :* Irvine Academy; Glasgow Univ. Licensed by the Presbytery of Kintyre, 1854 ; presented to the First Charge, Campbeltown, and ordained and inducted, 1854 ; still minister of the same parish ; was member of both School Boards, Burgh and Landward, and for several years, Chairman of the former ; was Chaplain of Argyll and Bute Artillery Vols., and has medal ; Member of Synodal Board of Glasgow University, 1872-1903 ; Convener of Highland Committee of Church of Scotland since 1893 ; was Clerk of the Presbytery of Kintyre for 41 years, and has been Clerk of Synod of Argyll since 1880 ; Member of many Committees of the Church ; Member of the Classical Association of Scotland, Brit. Archæological Association, Brit. Astronomical Association, Royal Scottish Geographical Society, and Society of Scottish Artists; F.S.A. Scot.; Fellow of the Zoological Society of Scotland ; Moderator, General Assembly, Church of Scotland, 1902 ; present at Coronation of their Majesties, 1902, as Moderator ; was special preacher on 21 Sep. 1902, when His Majesty was at Balmoral, and received the coronation medal ; presented the address of the Commission of the General Assembly of the Church of Scotland to the King at the Palace of Holyrood House, 12 May 1903 ; Fellow of the Zoological Society of Scotland ; Father of the Church of Scotland. *Address :* 9 Coates Gardens, Edinburgh.

(*Died 18 Mar. 1925.*)

RUSSELL, James George, I.S.O. 1903 ; Commissioner of Insolvency and of Taxes for South Australia, and President of the State Board of Conciliation ; *b.* England, Mar. 1848 ; *m.* 1875, Annie P., *d.* of Alfred France, Adelaide. Went S. Australia, 1860 ; Barrister, 1873 ; Commissioner of Inland Revenue, 1878-84. *Address :* Park Terrace, Parkside, Adelaide.

(*Died 5 Jan. 1918.*)

RUSSELL, Captain James Reginald, D.S.O. 1914 ; Royal West Kent Regiment ; *b.* 9 Oct. 1893 ; *m.* 1919, Gwendolen Edith, *d.* of Rev. G. W. Lawson. Entered army, 1914; served European War, 1914 - 17 (despatches twice, D.S.O.). (*Died 9 Feb. 1920.*)

RUSSELL, Reginald Pemberton, C.S.I. 1915 ; Secretary to Government of India Public Works Dept. since 1913 ; Member of Legislative Council of Governor General ; *b.* 1 Nov. 1860 ; *s.* of late Rev. S. F. Russell, M.A., Rector of Isfield parish, Sussex ; *m.* 1897, Mary Mason ; no *c. Educ. :* Queen Elizabeth's School, Cranbrook, Kent; R.I.E. College, Egham. Passed open competition for entry to Royal Indian Engineering College, Cooper's Hill, 1879 ; College career, 1879-82 ; practical training, St. Alban's and Bethesda Sewerage Works, 1882-83 ; appointed to P.W.D. in India, 1882 ; posted to Punjab Irrigation Branch, 1888 ; served on Irrigation Works, Punjab, 1883-1907 ; Under-Secretary to Punjab Government, 1899-1904 ; Officiating Superintending Engineer, 1906 ; transferred to Burma, P.W.D., 1907 ; Superintending Engineer, 1908 ; Chief Engineer and Secretary to Government, Burma, March, 1912. *Address :* The Shrubbery, Simla. *Club:* United Service, Simla. (*Died 22 Nov. 1917.*)

RUSSELL, Rt. Hon. Sir Thomas Wallace, 1st Bt. *cr.* 1917 ; P.C. ; *b.* Cupar, Fife, 28 Feb. 1841· *s.* of late David Russell and Isabella Wallace ; *m.* 1st, 1865, Harriet (*d.* 1894), *d.* of late Thos. Agnew, Dungannon ; 2nd, 1896, Martha, *d.* of the late Lieut.-Col. Keown, 15th Hussars. *Educ. :* Madras Academy, Cupar Fife. Settled in Ireland, 1859 ; secretary to various Temperance organisations, 1864-82 ; contested Preston (L.), 1885 ; took an active part in the House and in the country against the early Home Rule movement; principal promoter

of the Land Acts Committee in 1894, which resulted in the passing of the Land Act of 1896 ; founder of the New Land Movement in Ulster ; Parliamentary Secretary Local Government Board, 1895-1900 ; M.P. (L.) S. Tyrone, 1886-1910 ; N. Tyrone, 1911-18 ; Vice-Pres. Dept. of Agriculture and Technical Instruction for Ireland, 1907-18. *Publications:* Ireland and the Empire, a Review, 1800-1900 ; The Irish Land Question Up to Date. *Address :* Olney, Terenure, Co. Dublin. *Club:* National Liberal.

(*Died 2 May 1920.*)

RUSSELL, Sir William Fleming, Kt., *cr.* 1922 ; President Glasgow Chamber of Commerce, 1921-2 ; Member of the Glasgow Town Council for many years ; J.P. 1906 ; Honorary President of the Scottish Unionist Association and past Chairman of its Western Divisional Council. *Address:* 90 Mitchell Street, Glasgow. *Clubs :* Constitutional, Royal Automobile ; London Conservative, Glasgow.

(*Died 29 May 1925.*)

RUSSELL-WELLS, Sir Sydney, Kt., *cr.* 1921 ; M.D., B.Sc., F.R.C.P., M.R.C.S. ; M.P. (U.) University of London since 1922 ; Representative of the University of London on the General Medical Council; Senior Physician Seaman's Hosp., Greenwich ; Lecturer on Practice of Medicine, London School of Clinical Medicine ; Physician National Hospital for Diseases of the Heart ; Hon. Physician to Dioceses of Lebombo, Rangoon, and Zululand ; Vice-Chancellor University of London, 1919-22 ; *b.* Kensington, 25 Sep. 1869 ; *s.* of late Benjamin Weston Wells ; *m.* 1895 Harriett, 3rd *d.* of late Stephen Smith ; one *s.* two *d.* Studied science at Royal College of Science, London, and at Univ. College (B.Sc. 1889) ; studied medicine at St. George's Hospital, University of London ; obtained Pollock Prize in Physiology, Treasurer's prize, Brackenbury prize in medicine ; William Brown £100 exhibitioner for two years ; house surgeon ; house physician ; Assistant Curator of Museum ; Medical Registrar at St. George's Hospital ; takes an active interest in University and scientific education. *Publications :* various contributions to scientific and medical journals. *Recreations :* various scientific and mechanical pursuits. *Address :* 126 Wigmore Street, Portman Square, W.1; Riverside Cottage, Irstead, Norfolk. *T. :* Paddington 687. *Club :* Athenæum. (*Died 14 July 1924.*)

RUTHEN, Sir Charles Tamlin, Kt., *cr.* 1919 ; O.B.E. ; Director-General of Housing, Ministry of Health, 1921-26 ; Consulting Chief Inspector of Government Official Accommodation, H.M. Office of Works, F.R.I.B.A. ; Architect and Surveyor ; *b.* 22 Oct. 1871 ; *s.* of late John Ruthen, South Shields ; *m.* 1894, Matilda Jane, *d.* of late William Bondfield Westlake, Swansea ; one *d. Educ. :* Public School, South Shields, and privately. Entered office of Matthew Hall, South Shields, as a pupil 1886 ; served 4 years ; Assistant Surveyor, Swansea County Council, 1890-96 ; began practice in Swansea, 1896 ; designed Hotel Cameron, Mond Buildings, Carlton Restaurant, New Exchange Buildings, Pantygwydir Baptist Chapel, etc., and many private houses ; J.P. Swansea ; Inspector War Cabinet Committee on Accommodation, 1917-18 ; Chief Inspector and Deputy Controller of Accommodation (London Area), 1918-20 ; President of the Institute of Arbitrators ; Pres. of the Institution of Structural Engineers ; Mem. of the Council of the London Society; President of the Society of Architects, 1920-21; Member of the Grants Committee of the Ministry of Labour and of the General Advisory Committee of the Empire Timber Exhibition, 1920 ; Chairman of Government Commission to Belgium to inquire into housing and labour conditions, 1921; Member of Inter-departmental

Committee to inquire into the effect of trade combinations upon prices in the Building Industry, 1928; Member of Government Committee to inquire into new methods of house building, 1924; and of Committee appointed by the Board of Education to consider methods of building as applied to schools, 1925. *Publications*: An Architect's Holiday with a Camera in Northern Italy; The Timber-Frame House —its possibilities; Urban Housing, National Housing, Housing in the Netherlands, and many articles upon housing, town-planning and kindred subjects. *Recreations*: music and foreign travel. *Address*: Bank Chambers, Heathfield Street, Swansea; 44 Bedford Row, W.C.1; Y Dderwen-Fawr, Blackpyl, Swansea. *T.*: Swansea 2594, Sketty 8118, and Holborn 1655. *M.*: CY 405. *Clubs*: National Liberal, 1920; Swansea Liberal; Swiss Alpine.
(*Died 19 Sept. 1926*.)

RUTHERFOORD, Capt. J. B., D.S.O. 1900; Behar Light Horse; Hon. Captain in Army; *b.* 11 Oct. 1864; *s.* of John Rutherford. Served S. Africa with Lumsden's Horse, 1900 (D.S.O.). *Address*: Pepperstone, Ardee, Louth.

RUTHERFORD, Col. Charles, C.B. 1911; C.M.G. 1900; F.R.C.V.S. 1886; *s.* of Richard Rutherford, Edinburgh; *b.* 20 Jan. 1858; *m.* 1890, Kate, *d.* of Thos. Turner, solicitor, Leeds. *Educ.*: Watson's College, Edinburgh. Gazetted to Army Vety. Dept. 1879; Captain, 1889; Major, 1899; Lt.-Col. 1902; Col. 1907; District Veterinary Officer, Natal Command, 1900-1 and 1902-3; Principal Veterinary Officer, India, 1908-13; served Transvaal War, 1881; Bechuanaland Expedition, 1884-85; S. African War, 1899-1901 (despatches, Queen's medal 6 clasps, C.M.G.); retired 24 March 1918. *Address*: c/o Holt and Co., 3 Whitehall Place, S.W.1. (*Died 2 April 1922*.)

RUTHERFORD, John Gunion, C.M.G. 1910; D.V.S.; H.A.R.C.V.S.; Commissioner, Board of Railway Commissioners for Canada; membre correspondant to the Société Centrale de médecine vétérinaire de France, 1922; Superintendent of Agriculture and Animal Industry, Department of Natural Resources, Canadian Pacific Railway, 1912-18; Veterinary Director-General, 1902-12, and Live Stock Commissioner, 1906-12, for the Dominion of Canada; *b.* 25 Dec. 1857; *s.* of Rev. Robert Rutherford, M.A., Mountain Cross, Peeblesshire; *m.* 1887, Edith, *d.* of Washington Boultbee, Ancaster, Ontario, Canada; three *d.* *Educ.*: High School, Glasgow; private tuition; Ontario Agricultural College; Ontario Veterinary College. Practised veterinary medicine, Canada, United States, and Mexico; settled Portage la Prairie, Manitoba, 1884; engaged there in practice and horse-breeding operations; Veterinary Inspector, Manitoba Government, 1887-92; member for Lakeside, Manitoba Legislature, 1892 and 1896; member for Macdonald, Canadian House of Commons, 1897; Delegate for Canada to International Institute of Agriculture at Rome and to International Congress on Tuberculosis at Washington, D.C., 1908; President American Veterinary Medical Association, 1908-9; President Civil Service Association of Canada, 1909-11; Chairman International Commission on Control of Bovine Tuberculosis; Pres. Western Canada Live Stock Union, 1914-18; was for many years President of the Horse Breeders' Association of Manitoba and the North-West Territories; served as Veterinary Officer to the North-West Field Force under General Middleton during the Riel Rebellion, 1885. *Publications*: various monographs on veterinary subjects, also on horse-breeding and care of horses. *Recreations*: riding, driving, fly-fishing. *Address*: Ottawa, Canada. *Clubs*: Rideau, Hunt, Country, Ottawa: Ranchmen's, Calgary.
(*Died 24 July 1923*.)

RUTHERFORD, Sir (William) Watson, 1st Bt., *cr.* 1923; Kt., *cr.* 1918; M.P. (C.) Edge Hill Division, Liverpool, 1903-23; J.P. Liverpool; head of firm of Rutherfords, formerly Miller, Peel, Hughes & Rutherford, 43 Castle Street, Liverpool, and 48 Cannon Street, E.C.; *b.* Liverpool, 1853; *e. s.* of late William Rutherford; *m.* 1878, Elspeth Rose (*d.* 1914), 2nd *d.* of Captain Alexander Strachan, Great Crosby; one *s.* three *d.* *Educ.*: Merchant Taylors' School, Great Crosby. Admitted Solicitor, 1875; elected to Liverpool City Council, 1895; contested Scotland Division, Liverpool, 1900; Lord Mayor, Liverpool, 1902-3. *Address*: 49 Stanhope Gardens, S.W.7. *T.A.*: Roffrid, Liverpool; Roffrid, London. *T.*: City 3116. *Clubs*: Carlton, Constitutional.
(*Died 3 Dec. 1927*.)

RUTHERFURD, James Hunter, M.F.H., Linlithgow and Stirlingshire Hounds, since 1915; *b.* 13 June 1864; *s.* of Andrew Rutherfurd, Sheriff of The Lothians and Peebles, and *g.s.* of Major J. H. Rutherfurd, R.E. *Educ.*: Edinburgh Academy; Sherborne School; Edinburgh University. Became Writer to His Majesty's Signet, 1887; Hon. Secretary to Linlithgow and Stirlingshire Hunt, 1902. *Publications*: The History of the Linlithgow and Stirlingshire Hunt, 1911. *Recreations*: hunting, fishing, etc. *Address*: 17 Great Stuart Street, Edinburgh. *T.*: Central Edinburgh 22514. *Clubs*: New, University, Edinburgh. (*Died 7 Oct. 1927*.)

RUTHERFURD, Maj.-Gen. Thomas Walter, Indian Army; *b.* 4 Sep. 1832. Entered army, 1851; Maj.-Gen. 1892; unemployed list, 1891; 2nd *s.* of Thos. Rutherfurd of Fairnington, Roxburgh, N.B. *Recreations*: reading, travelling. *Address*: 145 Oakwood Court, Kensington, W. (*Died 15 Dec. 1918*.)

RUTHVEN, 8th Baron, *cr.* 1651 (1st creation 1487), **Walter James Hore-Ruthven,** D.L., J.P.; G.O. Crown of Belgium; Lt.-Col. Rifle Brigade, 1916; *b.* 14 June 1888; *s.* of Hon. Wm. Hore, 75th Regt., *s.* of Mary, Baroness Ruthven, and of Dells, *d.* of Lt.-Col. Pierce Lowen, K.H.; *S.* grandmother, 1864; *m.* 1869, Lady Caroline Annesley Gore (*d.* 1915), *d.* of 4th Earl of Arran, K.P.; four *s.* one *d.* *Educ.*: Mr. Murray, Wimbledon. Entered Rifle Brigade, 1854; has served in Crimea, India, Abyssinia, and S. Africa (medals for all); Capt. 1st Batt. Rifle Brigade; Maj. 9th Batt. Rifle Brigade (London Scottish), 1878-86; Lt.-Col. Rifle Brigade, 1819. Extra King's Messenger during European War, and Assistant Provost-Marshal, London. *Heir: s.* Walter, Master of Ruthven. *Address*: Newland, Gorebridge, Midlothian: Harperstown, Taghmon, Wexford; 11 Clarges Street, W. *T.*: Mayfair 5647. *Clubs*: Carlton; New, Edinburgh. (*Died 28 Feb. 1921*.)

RUTLAND, 8th Duke of (*cr.* 1703); **Henry John Brinsley Manners,** K.G. 1918; T.D.; Marquess of Granby, 1703; Earl of Rutland, 1525; Baron Manners of Haddon, 1679; Baron Roos of Belvoir, 1896; Hon. Col. 3rd and 4th Batts. Leicestershire Regt. 1897; President Leicestershire Territorial Assoc. since 1908; Lord Lieut. of Leicestershire since 1900; President of University College, Leicester; J.P. Leicestershire; *b.* London, 1852; *s.* of 7th Duke and Catherine Louisa Georgina, *o. d.* of Lieut.-Col. George Marlay, C.B., Belvedere, Co. Westmeath; *S.* father, 1906; *m.* 1882; one *s.* three *d.* *Educ.*: Eton; Trin. Coll., Camb. 3rd Batt. Leicestershire Regt. 1872-83; Captain, 1878; principal Private Secretary to Marquess of Salisbury, 1885-86, 1886-88; M.P. Leicestershire (Melton Division), 1888-95. Conservative. *Publications*: various magazine articles on sporting subjects, and a volume on Trout Fishing. *Recreations*: shooting, fishing, golfing; very fond of natural history, especially

919

as regards English wild birds. Owns 18,000 acres; minerals in Leicestershire and Derbyshire; picture gallery at Belvoir Castle. *Heir:* s. Marquis of Granby. *Address:* Belvoir Castle, Grantham; 16 Arlington Street, S.W,1; *T.:* Gerrard 2010. *Clubs:* Carlton, Turf, Beefsteak.   (*Died 8 May 1925.*)

RUTLEDGE, Hon. Sir Arthur, Kt., *cr.* 1902; *b.* 29 Aug. 1843; *s.* of late James Rutledge of Sydney; *m.* 1st, 1869, Mary Thomas, 5th *d.* of late Rev. Stephen Rabone; three *s.* four *d.*; 2nd, Rose Ann, *d.* of late Robt F. Davey, Victoria. *Educ.:* New South Wales. Called to Bar, Queensland, 1878; M.P. Enoggera, 1878-83; Kennedy, 1883; Attorney-General, 1883-88; M.P. Charters Towers, 1888-93; M.P. Maranoa, 1899 and 1902; was one of the delegates for Queensland at the first Federal Convention held in Sydney, 1891; was confirmed in the title of Honourable by despatch, 1889; Attorney-General, Queensland, 1899-1903; Q.C., 1899; D.C. Judge, 1906. *Address:* Tamavua, Toowong, Brisbane, Queensland.
     (*Died 1 Feb. 1917.*)

RUVIGNY and RAINEVAL, 9th Marquis of (France) 1651. **Melville Amadeus Henry Douglas Heddle de La Caillemotte de Massue de Ruvigny;** Baron of Raineval before 1080, Baron of Ruvigny about 1524, Baron of La Caillemotte about 1598, Marquis of Raineval,'1621, Viscount of Ruvigny, 1637, Count of La Caillemotte, 1651; *b.* London, 26 April 1868; *s.* of 8th Marquis and Margaret Melville, *o. d.* of George Moodie, of Cocklaw and Dunbog, Co. Fife; *S.* father 1883; *m.* 1893, Rose Amalia (*d.* 1915), *d.* of Poncrazio Gaminara of Tumaco; one *s.* President of the Legitimist Jacobite League of Great Britain and Ireland, 1893-94 and 1897-99; a member of the Council of the Catholic Record Society since 1908; Knight of the Royal and Distinguished Order of Charles III. of Spain, 1898; member of several learned Societies. *Publications:* The Blood Royal of Britain, 1903; The Jacobite Peerage, etc., extracted from the Stuart Papers at Windsor Castle, 1904; The Plantagenet Roll of the Blood Royal, Clarence Vol. 1905, Exeter Vol. 1906; Essex Vol. 1908; Mortimer-Percy Vol., pt. i. 1911; The Moodie Book, 1906; The Nobilities of Europe, 1908; Compiler and Editor of The Titled Nobility of Europe, an International Peerage, 1914, etc. *Recreation:* genealogical researches. *Clubs:* Wellington, Royal Automobile.   (*Died 6 Oct. 1921.*)

RYALL, Sir Charles, Kt., *cr.* 1921; C.B.E. 1918; F.R.C.S., Sen. Surgeon to the Cancer Hospital, and Senior Surgeon to the Bolingbroke Hospital; Consulting Surgeon London Lock Hospital and Rescue Home; Consulting Surgeon to the Gordon Hospital for Diseases of the Rectum, and also to the Leatherhead Cottage Hospital; Fellow of the Royal Society of Medicine and of the Medical Society of London; Member of the Société Internationale de Chirurgie; *b.* Brading, I. Wight. Of Cromwellian Irish descent, *s.* of late E. C. Ryall, M.R.C.S., A.M.D., who served in the Crimean War and Indian Mutiny, surgeon, 18th and 86th Regiments, and Elizabeth, *d.* of Wm. Phayer, J.P.; *m.* 1901, Frances Mary, *d.* of late Thomas Collier, J.P. of, Alderley Edge. *Educ.:* Dublin, Paris, Westminster and King's College Hospitals. Member of Council of the Royal College of Surgeons of England. During the War; Member of the Special Medical Appeal Board; Assessor in Charge of the Board of Medical Assessors to Appeal Tribunals; Member of the Advisory Medical Board to National Service, Surgeon to the King George V. Hospital. *Publications:* various papers on Cancer and Abdominal Diseases. *Recreations:* all field sports, shooting, fishing, and golf. *Address:* 62 Harley Street, W.1; *T.:* Langham, 1612, 2708; Aldenham Corner, Radlett, Herts. *Clubs:* Ranelagh, Reform, Pilgrims, etc.   (*Died 5 Sept. 1922.*)

RYAN, Sir Charles Lister, K.C.B., *cr.* 1887; J.P.; late Comptroller and Auditor-General; *b.* Worcester, 30 Sept. 1831; 5th *s.* of Rt. Hon. Sir Edward Ryan and Louisa, *d.* of W. Whitmore, Dudmaston Hall; *m.* 1862, Jane (*d.* 1914), *d.* of Sir John Shaw-Lefevre, . K.C.B.; two *d. Educ.:* Eton. Entered Civil Service as a junior examiner in Audit Office, 1851; clerk in the Treasury, 1852-65; private secretary to Mr. Disraeli when Chancellor of the Exchequer, to Sir Stafford Northcote, and to Mr. Gladstone, 1859-65; secretary to Board of Audit, Assistant Comptroller, and Comptroller and Auditor-General till March, 1896; a commissioner of the Exhibition of 1851; Governor of Wellington and Royal Holloway Colleges. *Address:* Burley Bushes, Ascot, Berks. *T.:* 271 Ascot. *Club:* Athenæum.
     (*Died 20 Nov. 1920.*)

RYAN, Maj.-Gen. Sir Charles (Snodgrass), C.B. 1916; K.B.E., *cr.* 1919; C.M.G. 1919; Consul-General for Turkey; Consulting Surgeon Melbourne and Children's Hospitals; *b.* 20 Sep. 1853; *s.* of the late Charles Ryan of Derriwatt, Upper Macedon, and *g.s.* of Henry Ryan, Kilfera, Co. Kilkenny, Ireland; *m.* 1884, Alice (*d.* 1923), *d.* of late Hon. Theo. Sumner; one *s.* one *d. Educ.:* Melbourne Grammar School. Graduated as Surgeon in Edinburgh University, 1875; spent two years in Turkish Army as Surgeon; served through the Servian and Russo-Turkish Wars, through the sieges of Plevna and Erzeroum; also European War, 1914-18 (C.B.). *Publication:* Under the Red Crescent. *Recreations:* golf, shooting, fishing. *Address:* 37 Collins Street, Melbourne, Australia. *Club:* Oriental; Melbourne, Australia.
     (*Died 23 Oct. 1926.*)

RYAN, Major Denis George Jocelyn, D.S.O. 1915; 6th Gurkha Rifles; *b.* 1885; *s.* of late Major C. A. Ryan, R.A., and Thomasine Caroline, *d.* of Maj.-Gen. George Shaw, C.B.; *m.* 1922, Aileen, *d.* of Stephen Grehan, Clonmeen, Co. Cork; one *s.* one *d. Educ.:* Stonyhurst. Entered army, 1905; Major, 1920; served European War (despatches six times, D.S.O. and bar). *Address:* Grindlay & Co., Bombay. *Club:* United Service.
     (*Died 18 July 1927.*)

RYAN, Edward Joseph, I.S.O.; Civil Servant, Upper Division, retired; *b.* 1845; *s.* of late Daniel Ryan, Rowan House, Blackrock, Co. Dublin; unmarried. *Educ.:* private academies; Dublin University. Appointed, 1866; rewarded, 1870 and 1874, for performing special duties to the satisfaction of the Lords of the Treasury; promoted, 1884; retired, 1910; holds Queen Victoria's Commemoration Medal, 1900; and King Edward the Seventh's Commemoration Medal, 1903. *Recreation:* gardening. *Address:* Rowan House, Blackrock, Co. Dublin.
     (*Died 1 June 1923.*)

RYAN, Thomas Joseph; Premier, Chief Secretary and Attorney-General of Queensland since 1915; *b.* Port Fairy, Victoria, 1 July 1876; *m.* 1910, Lily Virgina Cook; one *s.* one *d.* Graduated Melbourne University, B.A. 1897; LL.B. 1899; admitted to Queensland Bar, 1900; elected to Queensland Parliament, 1909; leader of Parliamentary Opposition, 1913. *Address:* Auchenflower House, Toowong, Brisbane, Queensland.   (*Died 1 Aug. 1921.*)

RYCROFT, Bt. Major Julian (Neil Oscar), D.S.O. 1918; M.C.; Black Watch; *b.* 22 Feb. 1892; *o. s.* of late Major-Gen. Sir W.H. Rycroft, K.C.B., K.C.M.G.; *m.* 1920, Elizabeth Mildred, *yr. d.* of Sir Ralph Anstruther; two *d. Educ.:* Eton. 2nd Lieut. Royal Highlanders, 1911; Capt. 1915; A.D.C. 1914-15; commanded 12th Batt. H.L.I. 1918; served European War (D.S.O., M.C., Belgian Croix de Guerre); Brevet Major, June 1919. *Address:*

Tinsley House, Musgrave Road, Durban, Natal. *Club :* Naval and Military. *(Died 12 Jan. 1928.)*

RYCROFT, Sir Richard Nelson, 5th Bt., *cr.* 1784; J.P., D.L.; *b.* 12 Dec. 1859; *e. s.* of 4th Bt. and Juliana, *e. d.* of Sir John Ogilvy, 9th Bt., of Inverquharity ; *S.* father, 1894; *m.* 1st, 1886, Lady Dorothea Hester Bluett-Wallop (*d.* 1906), *d.* of 5th Earl of Portsmouth, 1886; two *s.*; 2nd, 1911, Emily Mary, *d.* of Col. Hon. Henry Corry. Edwardstone Hall, Boxford; two *s.* two *d.* *Educ.:* Eton; Trinity Coll. Camb. Maj. Hampshire Carabiniers Yeo.; Capt. 3rd Batt. Hampshire, 1891-95; late Lieut. 2nd Batt. Rifle Brigade ; served with Yeomanry Cavalry in South Africa (despatches); High Sheriff of Hampshire, 1899. *Heir: s.* Nelson [*b.* 19 Dec. 1886; *m.* 1912, Ethel Sylvia Nurton ; one *s.*]. *Address:* Dummer House, Basingstoke. *T.A. :* Dummer House, Dummer.

(Died 25 Oct. 1925.)

RYCROFT, Maj.-Gen. Sir William Henry, K.C.B., *cr.* 1919; K.C.M.G., *cr.* 1918; C.M.G. 1915; C.B. 1910; Governor of British North Borneo, 1922-25; *b.* 17 Feb. 1861; 2nd *s.* of late Sir Nelson Rycroft, 4th Bart., Kempshott Park, Basingstoke; *m.* 1887, Grace Ronald, *o. c.* of late F. N. Menzies of Menzies; one *s.* one *d.* *Educ. :* Eton ; Sandhurst. Joined 71st H.L.I. 1879; served in Nile Expedition (including desert march to Metemmeh), 1884-85 (medal and clasp and bronze star) ; with Egyptian Army, 1886-87 ; action of Sarras (despatches, 4th Class Medjidie); promoted into 7th Dragoon Guards, 1888 ; Staff College, 1891-92 ; D.A.A.G., York, 1895-96; promoted into 11th Hussars, 1896 ; commanded 11th Hussars, 1904-8 ; Staff, S. Africa, 1911-12 ; A.Q.M.G., Southern Command, 1913-14; service, North-West Frontier of India, 1897-98 (medal and clasp); D.A.A.G., Cairo, 1898-99 ; served in S. Africa on Staff, 1899-1900 (despatches, medal and 2 clasps) ; Somaliland, 1902-3 (despatches, medal) with clasp); European War, 1914 - 18 (despatches 7 times), C.M.G., prom. Major-General, K.C.M.G., Knight of Grace, St. John of Jerusalem, Legion of Honour, Croix de Commandeur, Orders of White Eagle of Serbia, Redeemer of Greece, Star of Roumania, Greek Order of Merit 2nd Class); retired pay, 1921. *Recreation :* shooting. *Address:* Rosebank, Perth. *Clubs:* Naval and Military ; New, Edinburgh.

(Died 4 Nov. 1925.)

RYDER, Rev. Alexander Roderick, D.D. ; Canon of Down Cathedral; formerly Rector of Drumbeg ; Prebendary of Durnsford ; Donellan Lecturer ; *b.* 21 Feb. 1852 ; *s.* of Rev. Roderick Ryder, Rector of Errismore, and Sarah M. Bailey ; *m.* 1917, Beatrice L., *d.* of George Bennett, Holland Park, London. *Educ. :* Abbey School, Tipperary ; Trinity College, Dublin (scholar); Vice - Chancellor's Latin Medal, 1872 : Jun. Mod. Classics, 1873 ; Archbishop's King's Div. Prize, 1874 ; Div. Test, 1877; Downe's Prize (first), Written Compo. 1877; reading of Liturgy, Downe's Prize (first), 1878; M.A. 1878 ; B.D. 1895 ; on publication of a volume of lectures, D.D. 1911 ; Ennis College. Deacon, 1877 ; Priest, 1878 ; Master of Armagh College, 1874-76 ; Curate of Sea Patrick, 1877-80 ; Rector of Scarva, 1880-82 ; Tullylish, 1882-88 ; Rural Dean of Aghaderg, 1883. *Publications:* Priesthood of the Laity, 1911 ; The Vision of Christ, 1919. *Recreation:* golf. *Address:* 48 Osborne Park, Belfast. *(Died 29 Nov. 1919.)*

RYDER, Col. Francis John, C.M.G. 1916 ; 3rd Dragoon Guards ; Deputy Director of Remounts (temp.); *b.* 21 March 1866. Served S. African War, 1899-1902 (despatches, Bt. Lt.-Col., Queen's medal, 3 clasps ; King's medal, 2 clasps); European War, 1914-17 (despatches twice, C.M.G.); retired, 1920. *Club:* Army and Navy.

(Died 8 Nov. 1920.)

RYERSON, Major-Gen. George Sterling, M.B., M.D., L.R.C.P. and S. Edin. ; Founder and President of the Canadian Red Cross Society ; *b.* 21 Jan. 1854 ; *s.* of late Rev. George Ryerson ; *m.* 1st, 1882, Mary (lost Lusitania, 1915), *d.* of late James Crowther, Toronto ; two *s.* one *d.*; 2nd, 1916, Mrs. Elizabeth T. Mann, *d.* of E. R. Thomas, Buffalo, N.Y. *Educ. :* Galt Grammar School; Trinity University (M.B. 1875, M.D. 1876); Victoria University (M.D., C.M. ad eun. 1892). L.R.C.P. and S. Edin. and Mem. of Coll. P. and S., Ont., 1878 ; Senator Toronto University, 1895 ; General Secretary Canadian St. John's Ambulance Association ; Pres. United Empire Loyalists, 1896-8 ; Hon. Associate Order of St. John of Jerusalem, 1893, Esquire 1897, Knight of Grace, 1901 ; Surgeon Royal Grenadiers, Toronto, 1881 ; served North West Rebellion, 1885 (medal and clasp) ; Fenian Raid, 1870 (general service medal and clasp); deputy surg.-gen., 1895 ; Lt.-Col., 1900 ; served S. African War, 1900-2 ; Canadian Red Cross commr., and British Commr. at Lord Roberts' Headquarters (Queen's medal and two clasps) ; Hon. Col., 1902 ; Hon. Surg.-Gen., 1915 ; Hon. Col.-in-Chief, A.M.C. 1917 ; made tour of inspection Red Cross work, European War, 1915 ; founder St. John Ambulance Association in Canada, 1895 ; founder Canadian Red Cross Society, 1896 ; President, 1914-16. Freemason, Anglican. *Publications:* Looking Backwards (an autobiography); articles on professional subjects. *Address:* Peaceacres, Niagara on the Lake, Ontario. *Clubs:* York, Toronto, Royal Canadian Yacht, Toronto. *(Died May 1925.)*

RYLAND, Henry, R.I. ; *b.* Biggleswade, Bedfordshire ; *s.* of John Benjamin and Elizabeth Ryland ; *m.* 1901, Mabel Louise Mann ; one *s.* one *d.* *Educ. :* South Kensington Art Schools ; West London and Heatherley's ; Paris under Benjamin Constant, and at Julian's Academy under Boulanger and Lefebvre. Spent some time designing stained glass, and was a contributor to the English Illustrated Magazine from its commencement until it changed hands. *Works:* exhibited first at the Grosvenor Gallery ; has exhibited water-colours fairly regularly at the Royal Academy and New Gallery, and at the Royal Institute of Painters in Water-Colour ; a great number of his pictures have been engraved, or published in other ways. *Recreations:* chiefly reading and bicycling. *Address:* 32 Fairfax Road, Bedford Park, W.

(Died 23 Nov. 1924.)

RYLE, Rt. Rev. Herbert Edward, K.C.V.O., *cr.* 1921 ; C.V.O. 1911 ; D.D. 1895 ; Hon. D.D. Oxford, 1908 ; Glasgow, 1914 ; Dean of Westminster since 1911 ; *b.* London, 25 May 1856 ; 2nd *s.* of late Bishop of Liverpool ; *m.* Nea, *d.* of Maj.-Gen. G. Hewish Adams, late Royal Irish Rifles, 1883 ; one *s.* *Educ. :* Eton, on foundation ; Newcastle Scholar, 1875 ; Classical Scholar of King's Coll., Cambridge, 1875 (B.A. Aegrot, 1879) ; Fellow, 1881. 1st class in Theol. Trip. 1881 ; Carus Prize (undergrad.), 1875, (B.A.) 1879 ; Jeremie Prize, 1877 ; Winchester Reading Prize, 1878 ; Crosse Scholarship, 1880 ; Hebrew, Evans, and Scholefield Prizes, 1881. Divinity Lecturer at Emmanuel Coll., Camb. 1881-84 ; at King's Coll., 1882-86 ; Deacon, 1882 ; Priest, 1883 ; Principal of St. David's Coll., Lampeter, 1886-1888 ; Professorial Fellow of King's Coll., Camb., 1888 ; examining chaplain to late Bishop of St. Asaph, 1887-89, and to Bishop of Ripon, 1889 ; Hon. Canon of Ripon, 1895 ; Chaplain to the Queen, 1898-1901 ; Hulsean Professor of Divinity, Camb. Univ., 1887-1901, and President of Queen's College, Cambridge, 1896-1901 ; Warburton Lecturer, 1899-1903 ; Hon. Fellow of King's, and of Queens' College, Cambridge ; Fellow of British Academy ; Chaplain of Royal Academy of Arts, 1919 ; Prolocutor to the

Lower House of Convocation of Canterbury, 1919-25; Bishop of Exeter, 1901-3; Bishop of Winchester, 1903-11; Chairman of the House of Clergy, 1920-25. *Publications:* joint-editor (with Dr. M. R. James) The Psalms of Solomon, 1891; author, The Canon of the Old Testament, 1892; The Early Narratives of Genesis, 1892; Commentary on Ezra and Nehemiah, 1893; Philo and Holy Scripture, 1895; On the Church of England, 1904; On Holy Scripture and Criticism, 1904; Commentary on Genesis, 1914; Life after Death, 1916; among other literary work article Apocrypha in Smith's Bible Dictionary, ed. 2, and contributions to Camb. Companion to the Bible, 1893; Hastings' Dictionary of the Bible; Charles' Apocrypha and Pseudepigrapha, 1913. *Address:* The Deanery, Westminster, S.W.1. *Club:* Athenæum.

(*Died 20 Aug. 1925.*)

RYLE, Reginald John, M.A., M.D. Oxon., M.R.C.S., J.P. County Borough of Brighton; physician; *b.* 1854; *s.* of J. C. Ryle (Bishop of Liverpool); *m.* Catherine, *d.* of late S. K. Scott, surgeon, Brighton; five *s.* five *d. Educ.:* Repton School; Oxford University; Guy's Hospital. In medical practice at Barnet (Herts) for 10 years; subsequently in practice at Brighton; President of Medico-Sociological Section at Annual Meeting of the British Medical Association, Brighton, 1913. *Publications:* Origin of Feeble-mindedness, in Report of National Association for the Feeble Minded, 1911. *Recreations:* walking, swimming, etc. *Address:* Tutt's Clump, Bradfield, Berks.

(*Died 4 Dec. 1922.*)

RYMER, Sir Joseph Sykes, Kt., *cr.* 1901; *s.* of Matthew Rymer, merchant, York, and Ann Rymer, *d.* of Joseph Sykes, of Huddersfield; *b.* 27 Feb. 1841; *m.* 1864, Sarah, *d.* of John Leetham, steamship owner, of York; four *s.* one *d. Educ.:* York. Sheriff of York, 1882-83; Lord Mayor of York, 1887-88, 1899-1900, 1907-8, and 1912-13; J.P. for the City of York and for the North Riding. *Recreations:* bowls, chess, whist, bridge. *Address:* The Mount, York. *T.:* York 1192.   (*Died 18 Feb. 1923.*)

S

SABATIER, Paul; *b.* St-Michel de Chabrilanoux, dans les Cévennes, 3 Aug. 1858. *Educ.:* Faculté de Théologie de Paris; devint immédiatement, 1885, vicaire de l'église St. Nicolas de Strasbourg. En 1889, le gouvernement allemand lui ayant offert une situation supérieure par laquelle il serait devenu citoyen allemand, il demanda à rester simple vicaire. Cette demande fut considérée comme une manifestation politique et il fut expulsé. Revint dans ses montagnes natales et se fit nommer pasteur à St-Cierge, village qui depuis quinze ans était sans pasteur. Mais sa santé était ruinée et, après quatre ans d'efforts, il dut renoncer à la parole, et se consacrer entièrement aux études historiques. *Publications:* En 1885 avait déjà publié le texte grec de la "Didachè" accompagné d'un commentaire qui attira l'attention des spécialistes, mais c'est la "Vie de St-François" qui a rendu son nom populaire. La première édition française parut en novembre 1893. Un an plus tard avaient déjà paru des éditions en presque toutes les langues de l'Europe, même en Suédois et en Polonais. La première avait été la traduction russe faite sous la direction de Tolstoï. Quelques érudits allemands ayant contesté certains points de cette œuvre, Paul Sabatier commença alors pour les spécialistes une série de travaux destinés à montrer le travail scientifique dont la "Vie de St-François" n'était que le résultat.

Delà la "Collection d'études et de documents sur l'histoire littéraire et religieuse du moyen âge," pour laquelle il fit appel à la collaboration de ses contradicteurs eux-mêmes. C'est un spectacle nouveau que cette union d'érudits de toutes nations et de tous cultes travaillant sur le même chantier qu'un Huguenot français. Le t. i., publié en 1898, a provoqué de tous côtés d'autres travaux qui deviennent chaque jour plus nombreux et plus importants. Il est intitulé, "Speculum Perfectionis seu sancti Francisci Assisiensis Legenda Antiquissima, auctore fr. Leone. Nunc primum edidit Paul Sabatier." Le t. ii. est intitulé, "Fr. Francisci Bartholi Tractatus de Indulgentia Portiunculae. Nunc primum integre edidit Paul Sabatier." Le t. iii.: "Fr. Elie de Cortone, étude biographique par le Dr. Ed. Lempp." Le t. iv.: "Actus b. Francisci et Sociorum eius. Edidit Paul Sabatier." En mai 1901, il découvrit à Capestrano, dans les Abruzzes, la "Regula Antiqua Tertii Ordinis," qui depuis des siècles avait échappé à toutes les recherches. Il en profita pour commencer les "Opuscules de Critique Historique" qui paraissent par fascicules trimestriels. Enfin vers la même époque il retrouva le texte Latin original du fameux recueil des Fioretti dont il donna deux éditions, une pour les érudits, mentionnée plus haut "Actus," etc., l'autre populaire, "Floretum S. Francisci Assisiensis. Liber aureus qui italice dicitur I Fioretti di san Francesco." Enfin en 1902 a organisé la "Société Internationale des études Franciscaines" inaugurée solennellement à Assise le 2 juin. En 1898 la Ville d'Assise par un vote unanime de son "Consiglio Comunale" lui a décerné un titre qu'elle n'avait plus conféré depuis Garibaldi, celui de "Cittadino d'onore." Disestablishment in France, 1907; Lettre ouverte à S.E. le cardinal Gibbons, 1907; Modernism: the Jowett Lectures, 1908, translated by C. A. Miles; France To-day: Its Religious Orientation, translated by H. B. Binns, 1913; A Frenchman's Thoughts on the War, 1915. En 1899, il a été nommé membre de l'Académie Royale de Rome; nommé professeur d'histoire de l'Eglise à l'Université de Strasbourg, 1919. *Adresse:* 3 Ile Sainte Hélène, à Strasbourg.   (*Died Mar. 1928.*)

SACHS, Edwin O.; Architect; F.R.S.E. A. Inst. M.E., F.R.G.S., etc.; Chairman of British Fire Prevention Committee; *b.* London, 5 April 1870; *e. s.* of late G. Sachs, London. *Educ.:* University College School, London; travelled extensively and studied practical side of fire protection; commenced architectural practice, London, 1892; in 1898 he applied electrical power to the working of the stage for the first time in England, at Drury Lane; technical adviser to Royal Opera, Covent Garden, since 1899; founded British Fire Prevention Committee, 1897, and first fire-testing station established in Europe, 1899; organised the technical side of the Int. Fire Exhibition at Earl's Court, acting as Vice-Pres.; organised first Int. Fire Prevention Congress, London, 1903; organised Special Fire Survey Force in connection with the War, acting as its Commissioner; Member Home Office Departmental Committee on Celluloid Dangers; Vice-President of International Fire Service Council; Hon. Member Imperial Russian Society of Architects; French, Italian, Belgian, and other Fire Service Corporations; Knight of the Swedish Wasa Order (1st class); French Gold Medal of Merit; is an officer d'Academie (France), an officer of the Order of the Oaken Crown (Luxemburg); holds Russian insignia of St. Anne, Gold Medals of St. Andrew and of St. Valdimir, and Russian Imperial Fire Service Insignia, and Coronation Medal, 1911. *Publications:* Modern Opera Houses and Theatres, 1896-1898; Stage Construction, 1898; Fires and Public Entertainments, 1897; Facts on Fire Prevention, 1902; The Int. Fire Exhibition, 1903; The Iroquois Theatre Fire, 1903; The Baltimore Fire, 1904; The Brussels Exhibition Fire, 1910; Fire-Protection in Paris, 1911; Fire-Protection in Russia, 1913; numerous essays and papers. *Recreations:* attending fires and travel. *Address:* 8 Waterloo Place, S.W. *T.:* Gerrard 5164. (*Died 9 Sept. 1919.*)

SACKVILLE, 3rd Baron, *cr.* 1876; **Lionel Edward Sackville-West**, formerly Lt.-Colonel West Kent Yeomanry; J.P., D.L.; Vice-Chairman of Kent County Council; Chairman Kent Territorial Army Association; *b.* 15 May 1867; *s.* of Col. Hon. W. E. Sackville-West, Grenadier Guards, and Georgina, *y. d.* of George Dodwell, Kevinsfoot, Co. Sligo; *S.* uncle, 1908; *m.* 1890, *cousin*, Victoria Sackville-West; one *d.* [*m.* 1913, Hon. Harold Nicolson, 3rd *s.* of Lord Carnock]. *Educ.:* Wellington; Christ Church, Oxford (M.A.). Served European War, Gallipoli, Egypt, Palestine, France, 1914-18. *Heir:* *b.* Maj.-Gen. Hon. Sir Charles Sackville-West. *Address:* 9 Bentinck Street, Manchester Square, W.1; *T.:* Mayfair 5030; Knole, Sevenoaks. *Clubs:* Carlton, White's; Royal Yacht Squadron, Cowes. (*Died 28 Jan. 1928.*)

SACKVILLE, Major Lionel Charles Stopford, D.S.O. 1915; Rifle Brigade; *b.* Belfast, 30 April 1891; *s.* of late Colonel Lionel Stopford Sackville, the Rifle Brigade. *Educ.:* Eton; Sandhurst. 2nd Lt. the Rifle Brigade in 1910; Lt. 1912; Capt. 1915; served European War, France and Flanders, 1914-15, and at Salonika, 1915-18 (despatches, D.S.O., Bt. Major, Croix de Guerre avec Palme). *Recreations:* polo and racing. *Address:* 33 Brunswick Gardens, Kensington, W.8. *Clubs:* Travellers', Army and Navy. (*Died 31 Dec. 1920.*)

SACKVILLE, Sackville George Stopford, Hon. Colonel, late Lieut.-Colonel Commandant, 3rd Battalion Northants Regiment; late Chairman of Northants Quarter Sessions; late Chairman County Council; *b.* 19 Mar. 1840; *s.* of William Bruce Stopford (who assumed by Royal Licence the additional name of Sackville) and Caroline Harriet, *niece* and *heiress* of Charles Sackville, last Duke of Dorset; *m.* 1875, Edith Frances (*d.* 1905), *o. d.* of W. Rashleigh of Menabilly. *Educ.:* Eton; Christ Church, Oxford (M.A.). J.P. and D.L. Northants; M.P. (C.) North Northants, 1867-80, 1900-1906. *Address:* Drayton House, Thrapston. *T.:* Lowick 2. *Clubs:* Travellers', Carlton, Royal Automobile. (*Died 6 Oct. 1926.*)

SADASIVA AIYAR, Sir Theagaraja Aiyar, Diwan Bahadur; Kt., *cr.* 1921; **Mr. Justice Aiyar**, Judge of High Court, Madras, 1914-21. *Address:* c/o High Court, Madras. (*Died 1 Dec. 1927.*)

SADLER, Lieut.-Col. Sir James Hayes; K.C.M.G., *cr.* 1907; C.B. 1902; H.M. Governor and Commander-in-Chief Windward Islands, 1909-14; *b.* 1851; *s.* of late Sir J. H. Sadler; *m.* 1875, Rita Annie (*d.* 1918), *d.* of Col. Wemyss Smith, Indian Army; one *s.* Joined 61st Regt. 1870; served with 40th Regt. and 83rd Bengal Infantry; joined Political Department in 1877, in which held various appointments; Consul, Muscat, 1892-96; Consul-General, Somali Protectorate, 1898; Commissioner, etc., in Uganda, 1901-5; Governor British East Africa Protectorate, 1905-9; Governor of the Windward Islands, 1904-14; received Coronation medals, 1902 and 1911. *Club:* Junior United Service. (*Died 21 April 1922.*)

SADLER, Walter Dendy, artist; *b.* Dorking, Surrey, 12 May 1854; 5th *s.* of John Dendy Sadler, solicitor, Horsham. *Educ.:* private school, Horsham. Studied in London and Düsseldorf; exhibited at Royal Academy since 1873. *Pictures:* Thursday; Pegged down Fishing Match; Darby and Joan; The Widow's

Birthday; The New Will; London to York; The End of the Skein; Dummy Whist; Toddy at the Cheshire Cheese; For Weal or Woe; Nearly Done. *Recreation:* fishing. *Address:* Hemingford Grey, St. Ives, Hunts.
(*Died 13 Nov. 1923.*)

SAFONOFF, Wassily, Conductor and Pianist; *b.* Caucasus, 1852; *m.* Warwara Yschnegradski. *Educ.:* Petrograd Conservatoire; was four years Professor there, then Professor, Moscow Conservatoire; Conductor, Moscow Imperial Musical Society for seventeen years; directed the Philharmonic Society, New York, for six years. *Club:* English, Moscow.
(*Died 1918.*)

SAILANA, H.H. Sir Jeswant Singhji Bahadur, K.C.I.E. 1903; **Raja of**; *b.* 1864; *s.* of Maharaj Bhawani Singhji, late Jagirdar of Semlia; adopted by H.H. Raja Duleh Singhji; *S.* 1895; *m.* 1st, Ranawatji, *d.* of late Rao of Dhariawad; 2nd, Kachhawaiji (*d.* 1906), *d.* of late Raja of Machhand; 3rd, Sisodniji, *d.* of late Rana of Barwani; five *s.* three *d.* *Educ.:* Daly (Rajkumar) College, Indore. The State has an area of 450 square miles, and a population of 30,000, the Chief receiving a salute of 11 guns; for his efficient administration of famine relief in 1900, when the State suffered from drought, he received the Kaiser-i-Hind Gold Medal. Gave contribution of 50,000 rupees to British war expenses and various charitable funds pertaining to war. *Recreations:* riding, driving, sauntering, and especially reading. *Address:* Sailana, Malwa.
(*Died 4 Aug. 1919.*)

SAINT, Sir Thomas Wakelin, Kt., *cr.* 1927; J.P.; Alderman of Islington since 1906; Chairman East Islington Conservative Association; member of Metropolitan Water Board; *b.* 1861. *Address:* Bank Chambers, Finsbury Park, N. 4; The Woodlands, Sewardstone, Essex. (*Died 1 June 1928.*)

ST. ALBANS, Grace, Duchess of; *d.* of late Ralph Bernal Osborne, M.P.; *m.* 1874 (2nd wife), 10th Duke of St. Albans (*d.* 1898); two *s.* three *d.* *Address:* Newtown Anner, Clonmel, Ireland. *T.:* Victoria 3180.
(*Died 18 Nov. 1926.*)

ST. ALDWYN, 1st Earl, *cr.* 1914, of Coln St. Aldwyn, **Rt. Hon. Michael Edward Hicks-Beach**, Viscount Quenington, *cr.* 1915; Bt. *cr.* 1619; Viscount, *cr.* 1906; P.C., J.P., D.L., High Steward of Gloucester; Prov. Grand Master, Gloucester, since 1880; An Ecclesiastical Commissioner since 1908; *b.* 1837; *s.* of 8th Bt. and *d.* of John Stratton, Farthinghoe Lodge, Northamptonshire; *S.* father 1854; *m.* 1st, 1864, Caroline Susan (*d.* 1865), *d.* of J. H. Elwes, Colesbourne Park; 2nd, Lucy Catherine Fortescue, *d.* of 3rd Earl Fortescue, 1874; one *s.* three *d.* *Educ.:* Eton; Christ Ch. Oxford (M.A.), Hon. D.C.L. M.P. E. Gloucestershire, 1864-85; W. Bristol, 1885-1906; Under-Secretary Home Department, and Secretary of Poor Law Board, 1868; Chief Secretary for Ireland, 1874-78, 1886-87; Secretary for the Colonies, 1878-80; Chancellor of the Exchequer, 1885-86 and 1895-1902; President of Board of Trade, 1888-92. *Heir:* *s.* Viscount Quenington. *Address:* Coln St. Aldwyn, Fairford, Gloucestershire. *T.A.:* 81 Eaton Place, S.W. *Clubs:* Athenæum, Carlton. (*Died 30 April 1916.*)

ST. AUBYN, Alan (Frances Marshall), novelist; *b.* Surrey; *y. c.* of George Bramstone Bridges, lawyer and dramatist; *m.* Matthew Marshall, St. Aubyn's, Tiverton, N. Devon. *Educ.:* Essex; Cambridge. Author and archæologist; member of Cambridge Antiquarian Society, and Somerset Archæological Society. *Publications:* Old English Embroidery, its Technique and Symbolism. Novels: A Fellow of Trinity; The Junior Dean; The Master of St. Benedict's; Trollope's Dilemma; An Old Maid's

Sweetheart ; Broken Lights ; Orchard Damerel ; To His Own Master ; In the Face of the World ; The Tremlett Diamonds ; A Tragic Honeymoon ; Modest Little Sara ; To Step Aside is Human ; A Proctor's Wooing ; Mary Unwin ; Fortune's Gate ; A Fair Impostor ; Under the Rowan Tree ; Gallantry Bower ; Bonnie Maggie Lauder ; Mrs. Dunbar's Secret ; In the Sweet West Country ; The Bishop's Delusion ; The Wooing of May ; The Loyal Hussar ; A Prick of Conscience ; May Silver ; The Maiden's Creed ; The Scarlet Lady ; A Coronation Necklace ; The Greenstone ; The Red Van ; Purple Heather ; The Ordeal of Sara ; The Harp of Life. Juvenile Books : Joseph's Little Coat ; The Dean's Little Daughter ; With Wind and Tide ; Wapping Old Stairs ; Lizzy's Shepherd ; A Silver Cord ; The Squire of Bratton ; Little Lady Maria ; Jenny Dear ; Antonia's Promise ; The Squire's Children ; The Harvest of the Year ; The Trivial Round ; Footprints, etc. *Recreation:* gardening. *Address:* c/o Dr. Rygate, Hunstanton. *Club :* Lyceum.
(Died 22 Oct. 1920.)

ST. AUBYN, Geoffrey Peter ; Judge of Turks and Caicos Islands since 1898 ; *b.* London, 7 June 1858 ; 2nd s. of Geoffrey St. Aubyn of the Civil Service ; *m.* 1897, Edith, *e. d.* of Edgar Sydney of Greenwich. *Educ.:* St. Charles Coll. Notting Hill. Bar. Middle Temple, 1880 ; went Western Circuit ; appointed Magistrate, Kingstown, St. Vincent. W.I. 1891 ; Acting Chief Justice, St. Vincent, Nov. 1896 to July 1898. *Recreations :* tennis, reading. *Address :* Grand Turk, Turks Islands, W.I.

ST. AUDRIES, 1st Baron, *cr.* 1911 ; **Rt. Hon. Sir Alexander Fuller-Acland-Hood,** 4th Bt. ; *cr.* 1809 ; P.C. 1904 ; Vice-Chamberlain to H.M. ; B.A. ; *b.* at St. Audries, 1853 ; *e. s.* of 3rd Bt. and Isabel, *d.* of Sir Peregrine Palmer Fuller Palmer Acland. Bt. (ext.) ; *S.* father 1892 ; *m.* Hon. Mildred Rose Eveleigh-de-Moleyns, 2nd *d.* of 4th Baron Ventry, 1888 ; two *s.* two *d. Educ.:* Eton ; Balliol Coll. Oxford (B.A.). Entered Grenadier Guards, 1875 ; Adjutant, 1881-1886 ; served in Egyptian campaign, 1882 (medal and clasp) ; 5th class Medjidieh and bronze star ; A.D.C. ; Governor, Victoria, 1889-91 ; retired from army, 1892 ; M.P. (C.) W. Somerset, since 1892 ; Parliamentary Sec. to the Treasury, 1902-6. *Recreations:* cricket, hunting, shooting, fishing, rowing. *Heir :* s. Hon. Alexander Peregrine Fuller-Acland - Hood, [*b.* 1893. *Educ.* Magdalen College, Oxford ; Lieut. Somerset Light Infantry]. *Address:* St. Audries, Bridgwater. *Clubs:* Guards', Carlton, Pratt's.
(Died 4 June 1917.)

ST. CLAIR, Lieut.-Col. William Augustus Edmond, C.M.G. 1918 ; R.E. ; Brevet Col. (retired) ; *b.* 1854 ; *y. s.* of James Louis St. Clair of Staverton Court, Gloucester ; *m.* 1886, Louise, *d.* of Walter Crawshay, of Le Chasnay, Fourchambault, Nièvre, France ; one *d. Educ.:* Private School ; R.M.A., Woolwich. Entered the Royal Engineers, 1873 ; served in Afghan War, 1880 (medal) ; Soudan, 1885 (Suakin, medal with clasp and bronze star) ; South African War, 1902 (Queen's medal with four clasps) ; retired, 1905 ; re-employed, 1914-18, as commanding Royal Engineers, Dublin district ; J.P. Surrey. *Address:* The Beacon, Dormansland, Surrey. *(Died 12 Sept. 1923.)*

ST. CLAIR, Major William Lockhart, D.S.O. 1918 ; R.H.A. ; *e. s.* of Hon. L. M. St. Clair ; *b.* 1883. *Educ.:* Royal Military Academy, Woolwich. Served Togoland and Cameroons, 1914-16 ; European War, 1916-18 ; (despatches, D.S.O.). *Address:* Derriana, Mayfield Road, Sutton, Surrey. *Clubs:* Army and Navy, Cavalry. *(Died 23 Feb. 1920.)*

ST. CYRES, Viscount ; Stafford Harry Northcote ; *b.* 29 Aug. 1869 ; *o. s* of 2nd Earl of Iddesleigh ; *m.* 1912, Dorothy

[Lady of Grace of St. John of Jerusalem. *Publication:* The Holy City, 1922], *y. d.* of late Alfred Morrison of Fonthill Park, Wilts. *Educ.:* Eton ; Merton College, Oxford ; 1st class Modern History ; Senior Student of Christ Church (D.Litt.). Clerical Assistant at Queen Alexandra Military Hospital, Millbank, Nov. 1915 April 1917, when he entered H.M. Diplomatic Service as Hon. Secretary at Berne ; promoted Hon. Counsellor there April 1918 ; resigned through ill-health, Dec. 1918. *Publications:* François de Fenelon, 1901 ; Pascal, 1909. *Recreation:* formerly unskilled agricultural labour. *Address:* 54 Prince's Gate, S.W.7.; Walhampton Park, Lymington, Hants. *T. :* Kensington 8210. *(Died 1 Feb. 1926.)*

SAINT - GEORGE, Henry ; violinist, composer, conductor, and writer on musical subjects ; *b.* London, 1866 ; *s.* and pupil of George Saint-George, composer of violin music ; *m.* Lilly, *d.* of Capt. F. W. von Kornatzki and *g. d.* of late Joseph Lilly the antiquarian ; one *s. Educ.:* privately. *Publications:* The Bow, its History, Manufacture, and Use, 1895 ; The Place of Science in Music, 1905 ; Fiddles, their Selection, Preservation, and Betterment, 1910 ; The Young Man from Stratford, 1911 ; A Musical Zoo, 1913 ; a number of serial articles in the musical press, amongst them being Observations on the Principles of Modulation ; the Symphonies of Beethoven ; composer of Advanced Studies for the Pianoforte ; edited the Strad for 4 years ; known as an expert in the history of ancient instruments, and especially as a performer on the Viola da Gamba and Viola d' Amore ; with his father has introduced to the British public three hitherto unknown works by J. S. Bach, and was the first to give in England a recital solely of Bach's works ; Colonial Examiner to Trinity College. *Recreations:* painting, photography, debating. *Address:* Eldon House, Walterton Road, W. *Club:* Authors'. *(Died 29 Jan. 1917.)*

ST. GERMANS, 6th Earl of, *cr.* 1815 ; **John Granville Cornwallis Eliot ;** Baron Eliot, 1784 ; D.L., J.P. ; Captain Royal Scots Greys ; *b.* 11 June 1890 ; *s.* of 5th Earl and Hon. Emily Harriet Labouchere, *y. d.* of 1st and last Baron Taunton ; *S.* father, 1911. Church of England ; *m.* 1918, Lady Blanche Somerset, *d.* of Duke of Beaufort ; two. *d Educ. :* Eton. Served European War, 1914-17 (M.C., wounded) ; owns about 7000 acres. *Heir :* c. Granville John Eliot. *Address :* Port Eliot, St. Germans, Cornwall.
(Died 31 Mar. 1922.)

ST. JOHN of Bletsoe, 17th Baron (*cr.* 1558), **Henry Beauchamp Oliver St. John ;** Bt. 1660 ; D.L., J.P. Beds. ; *b.* 24 June 1876 ; *s.* of 16th Baron and Helen Charlotte, *d.* of Harry Thornton, Kempston Grange, Beds. ; *S.* father 1912. Church of England. Conservative. *Educ.:* Wellington College ; Magdalene College, Cambridge. Owns about 8000 acres. *Recreations:* country pursuits, country business. *Heir :* b. Hon. Moubray St. A. T. St. John. *Address:* Melchbourne Park, Bedford. *Club:* Junior Carlton. *(Died 17 Oct. 1920.)*

ST. JOHN, Sir Frederick (Robert), K.C.M.G., *cr.* 1901 ; *b.* 2 March 1831 ; 4th *s.* of late Hon. Ferdinand St. John ; *m.* 1882, Isabella Annie, 2nd *d.* of Hon. J. T. Fitzmaurice ; three *s.* three *d. Educ.:* Cheltenham. Attaché at Florence and at Stuttgardt ; 2nd Secretary at Peking, Constantinople, and Vienna ; Secretary of Legation at Buenos Ayres and Rio Janeiro ; Secretary of Embassy at Constantinople ; Minister Resident in Central America, Colombia, and Venezuela ; Envoy Extraordinary and Minister Plenipotentiary at Belgrade and at Berne ; retired on a pension. *Publication:* Reminiscences of a Retired Diplomat, 1906. *Address:* 9 Elm Park Road, S.W.3. *(Died 27 Feb. 1923.)*

ST.. JOHN, Henry Percy, formerly a Clerk in the House of Lords; *b.* 23 March 1854; *e. s.* of late Canon Ferdinand St. John, *g. s.* of 3rd Viscount Bolingbroke, and late Charlotte Lucy Hamilton, *d.* of John Dalyell of Lingo; *heir-pres.* to 6th Viscount Bolingbroke; *m.* 1887, Maud Louisa, *d.* of Hon. Pascoe Charles Glyn; one *s.* two *d. Address:* 64 Eccleston Square, S.W.1. *T.:* Vic. 2725.
(Died 9 Sept. 1921.)

ST. LEGER, Col. Henry Hungerford, D.S.O. 1886; *b.* 26 April 1833; *m.* 1860, Florence Stuart (*d.* 1892), *d.* of late John Moore. Entered army, 1854; Colonel, 1885; served Indian Mutiny, 1858-59 (medal with clasp); Egypt, 1882 (medal with clasp, Khedive's star); Nile Expedition, 1884-85 (clasp); Soudan, 1885-86 (despatches, D.S.O.). *Club:* Junior United Service. *(Died 24 Jan. 1925.)*

ST. MAUR, Lord Ernest; *b.* and *heir-pres.* to 15th Duke of Somerset; *b.* 11 Nov. 1847; *m.* 1907, Dora, *d.* of late Rev J. Constable. *Educ.:* Harrow; Trinity Hall, Cambridge. *Address:* Wilcot Manor, Marlborough, Wilts. *Clubs:* New University, Wellington *(Died 21 May 1922.)*

ST. OSWALD, 2nd Baron (*cr.* 1885), **Rowland Winn,** D.L., J.P.; *b.* 1 Aug. 1857; *s.* of 1st Baron and Harriet, *d.* of Col. Henry Dumaresq and Elizabeth, *sister* of 5th Earl of Lanesborough; *m.* Mabel, *d.* of Sir Charles Forbes, 4th Bt., 1892; three *s.* one *d. Educ.:* Eton. Capt. 2nd Batt. Coldstream Guards, 1889; retired 1893; served in Soudan Expedition, 1885; M.P. (C.) Pontefract, 1885-93. *Heir: s.* Hon. Rowland G. Winn. *Address:* 19 Hill Street, Berkeley Square, W.; Nostell Priory, Wakefield; Appleby Hall, Doncaster. *T.:* Mayfair 1384. *Clubs:* Carlton, Turf, Guards', Bachelors'. *(Died 13 April 1919.)*

SAINT-SAENS, Camille, LL.D. Camb.; D.Mus. Oxford; composer; *b.* Paris, 9 Oct. 1835. *Educ.:* under Stamaty and Maleden, and at the Conservatoire under Benoist and Halévy. Organist of Church of St. Merri, 1853; of the Madeleine, 1858. *Publications:* Les Noces de Prométhée, 1867; La Princesse Jaune, 1872; Le Timbre d'Argent, 1877; Samson et Dalilah. 1877; Etienne Marcel, 1879; Rouet d'Omphale; Danse Macabre; Jeunesse d'Hercule; Symphonies en *mi*, en *la* et en *ut*; Henry VIII., 1883; Ascanio, 1890; Phryné, 1893; Chœurs d'Antigone, 1893; Javotte, 1896; Déjanire, 1898; Les Barbares, 1901; Parysatis, 1902; Hélène, 1906; L'Ancêtre, 1906; concertos de piano, de violon, de violoncelle, sonates, trios, quatuors, quintette, septuor, etc. *Publications littéraires:* Harmonie et Mélodie; Portraits et Souvenirs; Ecole Buissonnière; Au Courant de la vie; Germanophilie, Problèmes et Mystères; Rimes familieres; Comédies, etc.; elected member of the Institute, 1881; grand croix de la Légion d'Honneur, 1913. *Address:* 83bis Rue de Courcelles, Paris. *(Died 16 Dec. 1921.)*

SALE, George S.; *b.* 1831; 3rd *s.* of John Shaw Sale of Rugby; *m.* Margaret, 2nd *d.* of James Bonwell Fortune, of Cobourg, Canada; one *s.* two *d. Educ.:* Rugby, Trinity College, Cambridge (Scholar, Fellow, and Classical Lecturer); went to New Zealand, 1860; at the request of the Canterbury Provincial Govt., took charge of the West Coast Goldfields as Commissioner, 1865; Classical Professor, University, Otago, New Zealand, 1870-1908. *Publications:* Various contributions to the Classical Review and other magazines.
(Died 25 Dec. 1922.)

SALE-HILL, Gen. Sir Rowley Sale, K.C.B., *cr.* 1902; unemployed Supernumerary List Indian Army; *b.* India, 6 Nov. 1839; 2nd *s.* of late Capt. Rowley John Hill, H.E.I.C.S. (*d.* 1850), and Caroline Catherine, 2nd *d.* of Major-Gen. Sir Robert Sale, G.C.B.; *m.* 1872, Caroline Sophia, 2nd *d.* of Colonel Robert Sale, H.E.I.C.S.

Educ.: King William's College, Isle of Man; Dr. Behr's, Winchester. Entered Bengal Army, 1856; joined 66th Gurkhas, now 1st Gurkha Rifles, till 1882; Maj.-Gen. 1885; Lieut.-Gen. 1890; Gen. 1896; served with regt. during Indian Mutiny, 1857-58-59 (medal); Bhutan Campaign, 1865-66; in Huzara Campaign 1868 (medal with 2 clasps); with Malay Peninsula Expedition, 1875-76 (despatches, clasp); throughout Afghan Campaigns, 1878-79-80—(1) in command 1st Gurkhas; (2) brigade on Khyber line; (3) line of communications and movable column (medal, C.B.); and in command of Akka Expedition N.E. Frontier, 1883-84 (thanked by Government and Com.-in-Chief), 1889; added the name of Sale to his patronymic; commanded Rawal Pindi Brigade, 1882; E.F. District, 1882-86. Distinguished service pension for war services. *Recreations:* fishing, riding, rowing. *Address:* Folkestone. *Clubs:* East Indian United Service; Radnor, Folkestone. *(Died 23 Mar. 1916.)*

SALISBURY, Francis, C.B.E. 1918; I.S.O. 1911; J.P.; late Postmaster Surveyor of Liverpool; *b.* Brixton, 1850. *Educ.:* Stockwell Grammar School. *Club:* Athenæum.
(Died 4 Feb. 1922.)

SALMON, Alfred; Managing Director and Chairman of the Board of J. Lyons & Co. Ltd.; Director, Strand Hotel, Ltd.; *b.* 20 July 1868; *e. s.* of Barnett and Lena Salmon; *m.* 1894, Frances Abrahams; three *s. Educ.:* privately. Member of House Committee of London Hospital and of the Board of Management of West London Hospital. *Recreations:* golf and Bridge. *Address:* 24 Albert Court, Kensington Gore, S.W.7. *T.:* Western 4536. *Clubs:* Constitutional; Walton Heath Golf.
(Died 11 Oct. 1928.)

SALMON, Prof. Amédée Victor; Officier de l'Instruction Publique; Lauréat de l'Institut de France; Professor of Romance Philology at the University of London, King's College, and Professor of French Language and Literature at Univ. Coll. Reading; Examiner at the University of London; former Examiner in the Universities of Liverpool, Manchester, Birmingham, St. Andrews, and Glasgow; *b.* Drouilly (Seine-et-Marne), France, 1857; *m.* C. Huss; one *s.* three *d. Educ.:* Lycée de Versailles; Univ. of Paris. Editor of Godefroy's Dictionary of Old French; general editor of the Dictionnaire des Dictionnaires, now Encyclopédie du XXe Siècle; co-editor of La Romania, Le Moyen Age, La Grande Encyclopédie, etc.; Fellow of the Ecole des Hautes Etudes (Romance Philology and History); President of the Federation of the British Branches of the Alliance Française; Chairman of Committee of the British Bureau of the Office National des Universités et Ecoles Françaises. *Publications:* Remèdes populaires du moyen age (XIIIe Siècle), d'après un MS. de Cambrai; Trois Poèmes de Jean Brisebarre, de Douai (XIVe Siècle), d'après un MS. de Charleville; critical ed. of Philippe de Beaumanoir's Coutumes de Clermont en Beauvaisis; Chevalerie Vivien; Les Manuscrits de la Bibliothèque du Tribunal de Beauvais; Deux Rédactions abrégées des Coutumes de Beauvaisis de Philippe de Beaumanoir; Lexique de l'Ancien Français; Grammaire sommaire de l'Ancien Français; Extraits de Montaigne; L'Explication française; Deux mois en France au début de la guerre, etc. *Recreations:* rowing and cycling. *Address:* 54 Western Elms Avenue, Reading. *Clubs:* University of London, Carlyle. *(Died 11 Nov. 1919.)*

SALMON, Lt.-Col. Hon. Charles Carty, L.R.C.P. et S. Edin., L.F.P.S.G., J.P., M.P.; Speaker House of Representatives, 1909-1910; Chairman of Committees and Deputy-Speaker, 1904, 1905, 1906; Lt.-Col. Australian Army Medical Corps, attached 9th Light Horse; *b.* Daisy Hill, Amherst, Victoria: *s.* of

Frederick Browne Salmon, and Susannah Carty Arnell; *m.* 1900, Nancy, *d.* of Sir Matthew Harris; three *s. Educ.:* Scotch Coll., Melbourne; Trinity Coll., University of Melbourne; Medical School, Edinburgh. Elected Member for Talbot and Avoca in Victorian Parliament, 1893, 1894, 1897, and 1900; Member for Laanecoorie in Commonwealth Parliament, 1901-13; Vice-President Imperial Federation League, 1905; President Australian Natives' Assoc. 1898; Chairman Platform Committee, Australian Federation, 1898; Minister for Public Instruction, 1899-1900; Member Council Diocese of Melbourne; Lay Canon St. Paul's Cathedral, Melbourne; Lay Representative, Church Synod Diocese, Ballarat; Trustee Trinity College, University of Melbourne; Chairman Trinity College Council; Grand Master, Fr.A.M., 1914. *Recreations:* cricket, rowing, golf. *Address:* Warrane, Walsh Street, South Yarra; Daisy Hill Park, Talbot, Victoria. *(Died Sept. 1917.)*

SALMON, John Cuthbert, R.C.A.; landscape painter, oil and water-colour; *b.* Colchester, Essex, 28 Feb. 1844; *m.* 1869; four *d. Educ.:* Birbeck Institution, London. First exhibited at the British Institute, Pall Mall, 1865; Suffolk St. Gallery; R.S.A., Edinburgh, for many years; at the Royal Academy, London, and nearly all the provincial exhibitions for many years, including the Liverpool Autumn, Walker Art Gallery, for forty-one years; elected full Member of the Liverpool Academy of Arts, 1901; one of the first members of the Royal Cambrian Academy of Art, Conway, and has served on its Council since the foundation of that Academy. *Recreations:* walking, cycling. *Address:* Westhope, Deganwy, Llandudno.
(Died 2 Oct. 1917.)

SALMOND, The Hon. Sir John William, Kt., *cr.* 1918; M.A., LL.B.; a Judge of the Supreme Court of New Zealand; *b.* North Shields, 3 Dec. 1862; *s.* of Professor W. Salmond, University of Otago, N.Z.; *m.* 1891, Anne Bryham, *d.* of late James Guthrie, Newcastle-on-Tyne, England; one *s.* one *d. Educ.:* University of Otago; University College, London. Barrister of Supreme Court of New Zealand, 1887; Professor of Law in University of Adelaide, 1897-1906; Victoria University College, Wellington, N.Z., 1906-7; Counsel to the Law Drafting Office of New Zealand Government, 1907-10; Solicitor-General for New Zealand, 1910-20; Member of British Delegation, Washington Conference on Armaments, 1921. *Publications:* Essays in Jurisprudence and Legal History, 1891; Jurisprudence, 1902; 7th edition, 1923; Law of Torts, 1907; 6th edition, 1923. *Address:* Wellington, N.Z. *(Died Sept. 1924.)*

SALMOND, Rev. William, D.D.; Professor of Mental and Moral Philosophy, 1886-1914; Emeritus Professor, 1914; *b.* Edinburgh, 9 Feb. 1835; *m.* 1861, Jane Panton Young, Dunfermline. *Educ.:* Heriot's Hospital, High School, and University, Edinburgh; Berlin. Minister, English Presbyterian Church, North Shields, 1858-75; Professor of Theology to the Presbyterian Church, New Zealand, 1875-86. *Address:* 186 Queen Street, Dunedin.

SALOMONS, Sir David Lionel Goldsmid-Stern-, 2nd Bt.; *cr.* 1869; J.P., D.L.; past Vice-President and Treasurer Institution Electrical Engineers; A.I.C.E.; Barr. Middle Temple; Engineer; Director South-Eastern Railway; *b.* 28 June 1851; *s.* of Phillip Salomons, Brighton, and Emma, *d.* of Jacob Montefiore; *S. u.* 1873; *m.* Laura, *d.* of Baron de Stern, 1882; three *d. Educ.:* privately; short time Univ. Coll.; Caius Coll., Camb. (M.A.); Natural Science Honours. Contested (L.) Mid Kent, 1874; St. George's-in-the-East, 1885; was Mayor of Tunbridge Wells, 1895; late Alderman of Tunbridge Wells;

County Councillor of Kent for Tonbridge Division, etc.; Fellow of Royal Astro. Soc., Geolog. Soc., Physical Soc. of London, and many others; served on Jury at International Exhibition, Paris, 1900; Hon. Col. Kent (Fortress) R.E. *Publications:* Electric Light Installations, 11th ed., 3 vols.; Photographic Formulæ; many pamphlets and papers on electrical and other subjects; also on horseless carriages, being one of the pioneers of the movement in England. *Recreations:* scientific research; four-in-hand driving; designing motor carriages; mechanical work generally. *Heir:* none. *Address:* Broomhill, Tunbridge Wells; 47 Montagu Square, W. 1. *Clubs:* Carlton, Athenæum, City of London, Grosvenor, Savage, Royal Societies.
(Died 19 April 1925.)

SALT, Rev. Enoch, Wesleyan Minister; *b.* 20 Jan. 1845; *s.* of Joseph and Anne Salt, Butterton, Staffordshire; *m.* Sabina Chambers, Scarborough; one *s.* four *d. Educ.:* privately; Richmond College. Entered Ministry at age of 20 in City of Manchester, and for 44 years held positions in London, Birmingham, Bradford, Oxford, and Southport; member of Legal Conference, 1896; Chairman of Oxford District, 1893-96; Chairman of Birmingham and District F.C. Council, 1900; is Ministerial Treasurer of Wesleyan Education Fund, Deputy Treasurer of London Mission and Extension Fund, and holds the following Secretaryships: Wesleyan Education Committee, Board of Management of Secondary Schools, Connexional Funds Office, Committee of Privileges, and Committee of Aged Ministers' and Widows' Fund; for 11 years Convener of Committee on Memorials, and for 12 years Examiner in Theology in Richmond, Didsbury, and Handsworth Colleges; Member of three Methodist Œcumenical Conferences held at Washington, London, and Toronto. *Recreation:* golf. *Address:* Central Buildings, Westminster, S.W.; 18 Blenheim Crescent, Croydon. *T.:* 6148 Victoria, 2178 Croydon. *Clubs:* Croham Hurst, Croydon.
(Died 15 July 1919.)

SALT, Sir Shirley Harris, 3rd Bt.; *cr.* 1869; J.P.; *b.* 4 May 1857; *o. s.* of 2nd Bt. and Emma Dove Octavæana, *o. c.* of J. D. Harris, of Ratcliffe Hall, Leicestershire; *S.* father 1892; *m.* Charlotte, *d.* of Very Rev. John Cotter Mac-Donnell, D.D., Canon of Peterborough, Rector of Misterton, 1880; two *s.* two *d. Educ.:* Trin. Coll. Camb. (M.A.) Barr. Inner Temple, 1882. *Heir: s.* John William Titus [Lieut. Commander, R.N.; *b.* 30 Nov. 1884; *m.* 1913, Dorothy, *a. d.* of Col. W. Baker Brown, late R.E.]. *Address:* 5 East Pallant, Chichester. *Club:* Junior Carlton. *(Died 11 Feb. 1920.)*

SALTER, Sir Arthur Clavell, Hon. Mr. Justice Salter, Kt., *cr.* 1917; Judge of the King's Bench Division High Court since 1917; *b.* 30 Oct. 1859; *s.* of late Dr. Hyde Salter, F.R.S.; *m.* 1st, 1894, Mary Dorothea (*d.* 1917), *d.* of late Major J. H. Lloyd, R.A.; 2nd, 1920, Nora Constance, *er. d.* of late Lt.-Col. T. H. Ouchterlony, R.A., Guynd, Forfarshire. *Educ.:* King's Coll., London; B.A. and LL.B. Univ. of London. Called to Bar, Middle Temple, 1885; joined the Western Circuit, 1886; M.P. (U.) Basingstoke Div., Hants, 1906-17; K.C 1904; Recorder of Poole, 1904-17. *Address:* Queen Anne's Mansions, St. James's Park, S.W.1. *Clubs:* Carlton, Garrick, Bath.
(Died 30 Nov. 1928.)

SALTER, Mortyn de Carle Sowerby, F.R.Met.Soc., Assoc. Inst. W.E.; Superintendent, British Rainfall Organization, Meteorological Office, Air Ministry; *b.* 17 Nov. 1880; *s.* of M. J. Salter, F.I.C., F.C.S., of Bank House, Mickleton, Glos.; *m.* 1908, Leila Margaret, *d.* of Edward F. Willoughby, M.D., D.P.H., London; one *s. Educ.:* Bancroft's School.

Assistant to late G. J. Symons, F.R.S., Founder of the British Rainfall Organization; Chief Assistant to Dr. H. R. Mill, 1907; Assistant Director, 1914: Joint Director with Dr. Mill, 1918; Superintendent in charge on the transfer of the Organization to Government in 1919; Joint-Editor of British Rainfall, 1913-18; Editor since 1919; Joint Editor of the Meteorological Magazine; Vice-President, Royal Meteorological Society, 1915-17. *Publications:* The Relation of Rainfall to Configuration (Pres. Premium, Inst. W.E. 1919); The Rainfall of the British Isles, 1921; Numerous papers on meteorological subjects. *Address:* 5 Stanhope Gardens, S.W.7; Meteorological Office, Exhibition Road, S.W.7. *T.:* Kensington 5810. *Club:* Royal Societies.
(*Died 21 May 1923.*)

SALTMARSH, John, I.S.O. 1902; *b.* 9 April 1848; *m.* 1st, Harriott Fanny, *o. d.* of Captain George Ingram; 2nd, Emily Mary, *o. c.* of Charles Stevens of Surbiton and Las Palmas, Grand Canary; one *s.* one *d.* *Educ.:* privately in Guernsey. Assistant Royal Commission for the Paris Universal Exhibition, 1867; late of the Board of Education; Member of governing body of Wandsworth Technical Institute. *Recreations:* gardening, educational work. *Address:* The Rowans, Fairdene Road, Coulsdon, Surrey. (*Died 5 Dec. 1916.*)

SALTUS, Edgar Evertson, publicist; *b.* New York, 8 Oct. 1858. *Publications:* The Philosophy of Disenchantment, 1884; The Anatomy of Negation, 1885; Mr. Incoul's Misadventure, 1886; The Truth about Tristrem Varick, 1887; Eden, 1888; A Transaction in Hearts, 1888; The Pace that Kills, 1889; Mary Magdalen, 1890; Imperial Purple, 1892; A Transient Guest, 1893; Love and Lore, 1894; Enthralled, 1895; When Dreams come True, 1896; Purple and Fine Women, 1903; The Pomps of Satan, 1903; The Perfume of Eros, 1904; Vanity Square, 1905; Historia Amoris, 1906; The Lords of the Ghostland, 1907; The Monster, 1912; Oscar Wilde, 1917; The Paliser Case, 1919; The Imperial Orgy, 1920. *Recreation:* work. *Address:* 25 Madison Avenue, New York. *Club:* Manhattan, New York. (*Died 31 July 1921.*)

SALVIDGE, Rt. Hon. Sir Archibald Tutton James, Kt., *cr.* 1916; K.B.E., *cr.* 1920; P.C. 1922; J.P.; Managing Director, Bent's Brewery Co. Ltd.; Liverpool Alderman; *b.* 4 Aug. 1863; 2nd *s.* of Archibald Tutton Salvidge; *m.* 1885, Alice Margaret, *d.* of late Thomas McKernan; two *s.* one *d.* *Educ.:* Liverpool Institute. Chairman of Council National Unionist Assoc. of Conservative and Liberal Unionist Organisations, 1913; President Liverpool Constitutional Association; declined Lord Mayoralty (Liverpool), 1910; promoted Mersey Road Tunnel Scheme, 1925; Hon. Freeman of Liverpool, 1925; Hon. LL.D. Liverpool, 1928; Leader of Liverpool City Council. *Recreation:* golf. *Address:* Braxted, Hoylake. *M.:* TU 7814. *Clubs:* Constitutional; Conservative, Royal Golf, Liverpool.
(*Died 11 Dec. 1928.*)

SALVIN, Gerard Thornton; *b.* 16 Sep. 1878; *e. s.* of late Henry Thomas Thornton Salvin and Agnes Jane, *y. d.* of Herman Julias Schier, Newcastle-on-Tyne. *Educ.:* Beaumont College. Lord of the Manor of Croxdale. *Address:* Croxdale Hall, Durham. *M.:* Y 1504. *Club:* Durham County. (*Died 15 Sept. 1921.*)

SALVIN (Marmaduke) Henry, D.L.; *b.* 1849; 2nd *s.* of late Marmaduke Charles Salvin, and Caroline, *y. d.* of Sir Charles Wolseley, 7th Bart.; *m.* 1897, Annette Mary, 2nd *d.* of Sir William Edward Vavasour, 3rd Bart. *Educ.:* Oscott College. *Address:* 21 South Street, Park Lane, W.1; *T.:* Mayfair 5757; Burn Hall, Durham. *Clubs:* Turf, Arthur's; Jockey, Newmarket.
(*Died 2 Nov. 1924.*)

SAMARTH, Narayan Madhav; a Member of the Council of India since 1924; Lawyer, Journalist, and Politician. Was a member of the Royal Commission on the Superior Public Services in India, 1924; Member, Legislative Assembly, 1921-24. *Address:* India Office, Whitehall, S.W.1.
(*Died 18 Sept. 1926.*)

SAMMAN, Sir Henry, 1st Bart of Routh, *cr.* 1921; Chairman of Hull Underwriters Association; Hon. Elder Brother Hull Trinity House; *b.* 14 July 1849; *s.* of late Alban Samman; *m.* ; one *s.* two *d.* *Educ.:* Brunswick House, Kelvedon, Essex. Master Mariner, Shipowner, and Underwriter; patron of one living. *Recreations:* hunting, shooting, salmon fishing. *Heir: s.* Henry, M.C. [*b.* 18 Feb. 1881; *m.* 1914, Ellis Watson, *d.* of B. Boyes of King's Mill, Driffield; Lieut. R.F.A. (T.A.)]. *Address:* Manor House, Willerby, E. Yorks. *T.A.:* Samman Hull. *T.:* Kirkella 44 Hull. *Club:* Junior Athenæum. (*Died 7 Mar. 1928.*)

SAMPAYO, Sir Thomas Edward de, Kt., *cr.* 1924; K.C. 1903; LL.B. Cantab.; Puisne Judge of Supreme Court of Ceylon 1915-24; *b.* 1855; *s.* of Gabriel de Sampayo, Mahavidane Mudaliyar, and Philippa Perera Karunaratne, native of Ceylon, Sinhalese by race; unmarried. *Educ.:* St. Benedict's Institute and Royal College, Colombo: Clare College, Cambridge. Winner of the Government University Scholarship, 1877; proceeded to Cambridge University; graduated in the Law Tripos, 1880; called to Bar, Middle Temple, 1881; Advocate of the Supreme Court of Ceylon, 1881; acted as Commissioner of Assize and Puisne Judge of the Supreme Court; Member of the Council of Legal Education, Ceylon; President of the Catholic Union of Ceylon; Delegate from Ceylon to the Eucharistic Congress at Westminster, 1908, and to the Jubilee celebration of Pope Pius X., 1908; Kt. Commander of St. Gregory the Great. *Publications:* co-editor of the Ceylon Law Reports; translator of J. Voet's Title on Donations. *Address:* Colombo, Ceylon. *Clubs:* Orient, Catholic, Colombo.
(*Died 1 Dec. 1927.*)

SAMPSON, Rev. Gerald Victor, M.A.; Vicar of New Beckenham, since 1915; *b.* Moor Hall, Battle, Sussex, 23 May 1864; *s.* of Thomas Sampson, Lt.-Col. R.H.V., and Julie de Méric Sampson; *m.* 1st, 1887, Evelyn (*d.* 1888), *d.* of Edward Bonham, H.M. Consul Calais and Boulogne; 2nd, 1890, Amy Constance Alleyne, widow of H. Alleyne, *d.* of George Bright, I.C.S., Bengal Presidency, Clifton, Bristol; five *s. Educ.:* Westminster School, Queen's Scholar; Exeter College, Oxford. Graduated B.A. (Classical Honours), 1887; M.A. 1896; Deacon, 1887; Priest, 1888; Curate of St. Barnabas, Pimlico, 1887; Curate-in-Charge of St. John's, Pimlico Road, 1893; Vicar of France Lynch, Stroud, Glos., 1895; Rector of Staunton, Coleford, Glos., 1897; Gloucester Diocesan Missioner, 1899; Canon Missioner and Residentiary, Truro Cathedral, 1902; Vicar of St. Winnow with St. Nectan, 1911-15; late Chaplain of St. Faith's House of Mercy, Lostwithiel; Sub-Warden of Truro Diocesan Mission Society, 1911. *Address:* The Vicarage, New Beckenham. (*Died 27 Sept. 1928.*)

SAMPSON, John, C.B.E. 1918; Director of John Brown & Co., Ltd., of Sheffield and Clydebank, and other steel production, shipbuilding, engineering, electricity and ordnance companies; Member of Inst. of Civil Engineers; Member of Inst. of Naval Architects; *b.* London, 1859; *s.* of John Sampson of Hayle, Cornwall; *m.* 1890, Lucy Elizabeth, *d.* of John Pearce Sawyer, of Filham House, Ivybridge, South Devon; one *s.* *Educ.:* Private School. Was British Representative Anglo-Russian Commission in New York during War, and

Member of Financial Facilities Committee. *Recreations:* golf, sketching, travel. *Address:* Queen Anne's Mansions, St. James Park, S.W.1; Granard Lodge, Folkestone, Kent. *Clubs:* Athenæum, Reform. (*Died 11 May 1925.*)

SAMPSON, Major Patrick, D.S.O. 1914; R.A.M.C.; *b.* 4 Jan. 1881; *s.* of M. Sampson, Knocklong, Limerick; *m.* 1917, Dorothea, *e. d.* of Comdr. H. D. Kirwan, R.N; one *s.* one *d,* Entered army, 1906; Captain, 1909; Major, 1918; served European War, 1914-17 (despatches twice, D.S.O., wounded). *Address:* Brook House, Cricklade, Wilts. (*Died 30 Aug. 1922.*)

SAMPSON, Hon. Victor, K.C.; Ex-Attorney-General, Cape Colony; Member of Jameson Ministry; late Acting Judge Eastern Districts Courts. *Club:* Civil Service, Cape Town.

SAMSON, Charles Leopold, Solicitor; Senior Partner in the firm of Grundy, Kershaw, Samson & Co., of London and Manchester; *b.* Manchester, 1853; *s.* of late Leopold Samson; *m.* 1881, Margaret Alice, 2nd *d.* of late William Rumney of Stubbins House, Lancashire; four *s.* *Educ.:* privately. Admitted a Solicitor, 1874; Law Society's Prizeman and Stephen Heelis Gold Medallist. Was President of Manchester Law Society; Vice President, 1911-12; and President of the Law Society, 1912-13; contested (U.) Northwich Division of Cheshire, 1900. *Publication:* Treatise on the Law of Bankruptcy. *Recreation:* literature. *Address:* 121 Ashley Gardens, S.W.1. *T:* Victoria 3517. *Clubs:* Thatched House, Royal Automobile. (*Died 8 June 1923.*)

SAMUEL, Jonathan, J.P.; M.P. (L.) Stockton-on-Tees, 1895-1900, and since 1910; Alderman of Durham County Council; Member of the Tees Conservancy Board; J.P. Stockton-on-Tees, 1893; *b.* 1853; *s.* of late Thomas Samuel, Tredegar, Monmouth; *m.* Hannah Exley, 5th *d.* of late Joshua Mellor, Huddersfield, 1892; four *d.* Mayor of Stockton, 1894-95 and 1902; Hon. Freeman, 1904. *Address:* Lorne Terrace, Stockton-on-Tees. *Club:* National Liberal. (*Died 22 Feb. 1917.*)

SAMUEL, Sir Stuart Montagu, 1st Bart., *cr.* 1912; M.P. Whitechapel Div. of Tower Hamlets, 1900-16; J.P. County of London; late member of Samuel Montagu and Co., foreign bankers; *b.* 24 Oct. 1856; *s.* of Edwin L. Samuel and Clara, *d.* of Ellis S. Yates, Liverpool; *m.* 1893, Ida, *d.* of Alphonse Mayer of London; two *d.* *Educ.:* Liverpool Institute; University College School, London. *Heir:* none. *Address:* 12 Hill Street, Mayfair, W.1; *T.:* Grosvenor 2122; Chelwood Vetchery, Nutley, Sussex. *T.:* Nutley 10. *M.:* A 1150; FY 1001. (*Died 13 May 1926.*)

SAMUELS, Rt. Hon. Arthur Warren, P.C. 1918; K.C., Iré., LL.D., J.P.; M.R.I.A. Judge of the High Court of Justice in Ireland, King's Bench, since 1919; Bencher, Gray's Inn, 1919; Bencher, King's Inns; *b.* 19th May 1852; 2nd *s.* of late Arthur Samuels, Langara, Kingstown, M.A., and Katharine, *d.* of Owen Daly, Mornington, Co. Westmeath; *m.* 1881, Emma Margaret (*d.* 1904), 2nd *d.* of Rev. James Irwin, M.A., Sharon, Co. Donegal, and Florine Griffiths-Lloyd, *o. sis.* of late Sir Herbert Edwardes, K.C.B., K.C.S.I.; one *d.* *Educ.:* Royal School, Dungannon; Trinity Coll., Dublin. 1st Classical Scholar; Royal Scholar; Sen. Exhibitioner; 1st Honours Classics, Modern Literature, History, and Political Economy; Vice-Chancellor's Prizeman; gold medallist Historical Society. Called Irish Bar, 1877; Prizeman, King's Inns; Bacon Scholar, Gray's Inn; Professor Personal Property, King's Inns, 1891-94; Q.C. 1894; called English Bar, 1896; contested Dublin University, 1903; Pres. Social and Statistical Society of Ireland, 1906-8; M.P. (U.) Dublin University, 1917-19; Attorney-General,

928

1918; Solicitor-General for Ireland, 1917-18; Member of Senate and Council of Dublin University; Chancellor of Armagh; Chancellor of United Dioceses of Limerick, Ardfert, and Aghadoe; Unionist; took a prominent part in movements for Irish Private Bill Procedure Reform, and on the Irish Political Financial and Social Questions. *Publications:* pamphlets on Irish Financial Questions; The Expenditure Account, The Financial Report, What it Finds; The Fiscal Question; Features of Recent Irish Finance; Home Rule: What is It?, 1910; Home Rule Finance, 1912; articles on Private Bill Procedure and Devolution, and against Home Rule; Articles in Quarterly and other Reviews; edited, 1923, Edmund Burke's Early Life and Writings, by Arthur P. I. Samuels. *Recreations:* sailing, rowing, angling, ex-Captain Dublin University Rowing Club. *Address:* Cloghereen, Howth, Co. Dublin. *T.:* Howth 56. *Clubs:* Carlton, Constitutional, University, Dublin. (*Died 11 May 1925.*)

SAMUELSON, Berhard Martin, C.I.E. 1918; M.I.C.E.; Chief Engineer, Public Works Department, Burma; *b.* 1874; *m.* Eleanor Mary, *d.* of late A. D. Dufty. *Educ.:* Rugby; Cooper's Hill. Entered I.C.S. 1894. *Address:* T. Cook & Son, Rangoon, Burma. (*Died 20 Feb. 1921.*)

SAMWELL, Ven. Frederick William; Archdeacon of Adelaide; Senior Chaplain Australian Military Forces, V.D.; Sec. General Synod Church of England in Australia; *b.* Leicester, England, 18 Feb. 1861; *s.* of Robert Owen Samwell; *m.* 1888, Marion, *d.* of A. W. Richardson, J.P., Mount Barker, S.A.; one *s.* two *d.* *Educ.:* St. Augustine's College, Canterbury. A founder of the District Trained Nursing Society of South Australia; Past Grand Chaplain of Grand Lodge of Freemasons of South Australia; served in World War as Senior Chaplain Australian Imperial Forces, 1914-15. *Publications:* editor, Adelaide Diocesan Year Book, 1896-1902; editor, Official Report of Adelaide Church Congress, 1902; Editor of Adelaide Church Guardian, 1908-15. *Recreations:* tennis. *Address:* Adelaide, South Australia. (*Died April 1925.*)

SANDARS, John Drysdale, J.P., D.L., C.C.; *b.* 15 Dec. 1860; *s.* of J. E. Sandars, North Sandsfield, Gainsbro.; *m.* Maud Evelyn, *o. d.* of 5th Lord Graves; one *s.* one *d.* *Educ.:* Wellington College; Trinity Hall, Cambridge; Bar, Inner Temple. Served 12 years in North Linc. Militia, retiring as Captain; served as High Sheriff; S. father, 1890; gave up the Bar and took up the malting business, which his father had conducted, and extended this considerably; opened maltings on the Manchester Ship Canal in the early days of this enterprise; took great interest in all local County work and politics; is member for S. Ward, Gainsbro., on County Council, and president of the West Lindsey Conservative Association. *Recreations:* takes interest in all sports, particularly hunting and shooting, though latterly the former has given way to golf. *Address:* Gate Burton Hall, Lincs. *T.A.:* Sandars, Gainsborough. *T.:* 7 Gainsborough. *M.:* BE 1, BE 303. *Clubs:* Boodle's, Wellington, Hurlingham, Ranelagh. (*Died 18 Feb. 1922.*)

SANDAY, Rev. William, D.D., LL.D., Litt.D. Cambridge; Lady Margaret Professor of Divinity and Canon of Christ Church, Oxford, 1895-1919; Chaplain in Ordinary to H.M. since 1903; *b.* Holme Pierrepont, Nottingham, 1 Aug. 1843; *e. s.* of William Sanday, Holme Pierrepont (well known as breeder of Leicester sheep and shorthorns), and Elizabeth Mann, Scawsby, Doncaster; *m.* Marian C. A. (*d.* 1904), *e. d.* of W. H. Woodman Hastings, J.P., Twyning, Tewkesbury (eldest direct descendant of the sister of Warren Hastings), 1877. *Educ.*: Repton; Balliol; Corpus (Scholar), Oxford. 1st class Mods. 1863; 1st class Lit. Hum. 1865. Fellow of Trinity, 1866; Lecturer, 1866-69; ordained, 1867; in charge of Navestock, Romford, 1869-71; Lecturer at St. Nicholas, Abingdon, 1871-72; Vicar of Great Waltham, Chelmsford, 1872-73; Rector of Barton-on-the-Heath, Shipston-on-Stour, 1873-76; Principal of Bishop Hatfield's Hall, Durham, 1876-88; Examining Chaplain to Bishop Lightfoot, 1879-81; Dean Ireland's Professor of Exegesis and Tutorial Fellow of Exeter, 1883-1895; Hon. Fellow, 1898; last of the Oxford preachers at Whitehall. *Publications:* Authorship and Historical Character of the Fourth Gospel, 1872; The Gospels in the Second Century, 1876; Romans and Galatians (in Bishop Ellicott's Commentary), 1878; Appendices ad Novum Testamentum Stephanicum, 1889; The Oracles of God, 1891; Two Present Day Questions, 1892; Inspiration (the Bampton Lectures), 1893; The Life of Christ in Recent Research, 1907; Christologies, Ancient and Modern, 1910; Personality in Christ and in Ourselves, 1911; The Primitive Church and Reunion, 1913; joint-editor, Variorum Bible, 1880-89; joint-editor with the Bishop of Salisbury, Old Latin Biblical Texts, Part II. 1886; Commentary on the Epistle to the Romans, 1895; articles God (in N.T.) and Jesus Christ in Hastings' Dictionary of the Bible, vol. ii. etc. *Address:* Christ Church, Oxford. *Club:* Athenæum. (*Died 16 Sept. 1920.*)

SANDBACH, Major-Gen. Arthur Edmund, D.S.O. 1900; C.B. 1910; b. 30 July 1859; 3rd s. of late H. R. Sandbach of Hafodunos, Co. Denbigh, and Elizabeth, d. and co-heir of Martin Williams of Bryn Gwyn, Co. Montgomery; m. 1902, Hon. Ina Douglas-Pennant, 5th d. of 2nd Baron Penrhyn; one d. *Educ.:* Eton; Royal Military Academy, Woolwich. Entered Army, 1879; Colonel, 1904; Brig.-Gen. 1910; Maj.-Gen. 1914; Commandant 1st Sappers and Miners, Indian Army, 1904-7; Commanding R.E. Troops, Aldershot, 1908-10; Chief Engineer in Ireland, 1910-14; served Egyptian War, 1882, including Tel-el-Kebir (medal with clasp, Khedive's star); Soudan Campaign, 1885 (clasp); Burmese Expedition, 1886-87, horse shot in action (medal with clasp); Sikkim Expedition, 1888 (clasp); Hazara, 1891, as A.D.C. to Major-Gen. Elles commanding (despatches, clasp); Nile Expedition, 1898, as A.A.G., Egyptian Army, including Khartoum (despatches, Brevet Lieut.-Colonel, medal with clasp, Khedive's medal with clasp); Military Secretary to Lord Curzon of Kedleston, Viceroy of India, 1898-99; A.A.G. South Africa, 1899-1901 (despatches, medal with six clasps, D.S.O.); European War, 1914-1915 and 1917 (despatches thrice, wounded, promoted Major-General for distinguished service in the field); D.L., J.P. Montgomeryshire; High Sheriff, 1919; Chairman of County Territorial Force Association, 1908-20. *Address:* Bryn Gwyn, Bwlch-y-Cibau, Montgomeryshire. *Clubs:* Naval and Military, Athenæum.
(*Died 25 June 1928.*)

SANDEMAN, Albert George, Chairman of Geo. G. Sandeman, Sons, and Co., Limited, London; late Director of the Bank of England (Governor 1895-96); one of H.M.'s Commissioners of Lieutenancy for the City of London; Commissioner of Income Tax for City of London; President of the London Chamber of Commerce, 1898; J.P. for Hertfordshire; b. 21 Oct. 1833; s. of George Glas Sandeman, merchant of London and Oporto, and Elizabeth, d. of Albert Forster; m. Maria Carlota Perpetua de Moraes Sarmento, d. of Viscount Moncorvo, Portuguese Ambassador to Court of St. James's, 1856; two s. four d. High Sheriff of Surrey, 1872; late Major 12th Middlesex (Prince of (Wales's Own Civil Service) R.V. *Address:* Greylands, Bexhill-on-Sea. *T.:* Bexhill 381.
(*Died 6 Jan. 1923.*)

SANDEMAN, Rear-Admiral Henry George Glas, C.M.G. 1918; b. 18 June 1868; y. s. of late Lt.-Col. J. G. Sandeman, M.V.O.; m. 1908, Nina, d. of late Alfred Evans. *Educ.:* Cordwalles, Maidenhead. Joined H.M.S. Britannia as Naval Cadet, 1881; served as Flag-Lieut. to Admiral Sir J. O. Hopkins, G.C.B., in N. America and West Indies, and in Mediterranean; commanded H.M.S. Britannia, European War; Commodore and Senior Naval Officer at Hong-Kong, 1916-18; retired, 1918. *Address:* Chicksgrove Mill, Tisbury, Wilts.
(*Died 16 May 1923.*)

SANDEMAN, John Glas, M.V.O., 1902; F.S.A.; late sub-officer and Senior Member H.M. Bodyguard Hon. Corps of Gentlemen-at-Arms; b. 18 Aug. 1836; 2nd s. of late George Glas Sandeman of Westfield, Hayling Island; m. 1862, Eliza Victoire Cormick, e. d. of late Captain Henry C. Lynch of Galway, and Leigh Park, Hants; two s. three d. *Educ.:* King's College, London. Served in 1st Royal Dragoons, 1853-59; Crimean Campaign, 1854-56, battles of Balaklava, Inkerman, and Tchernaya, and siege of Sebastopol; afterwards Lt.-Col. commanding Essex Yeomanry Cavalry, and Hon. Lieutenant Royal Naval Reserve; Cavalheiro of the Order of Christ in Portugal. *Publications:* The Spears of Honour and the Gentlemen Pensioners; Compiler of the Sandeman Genealogy; Editor of the Clan Sandeman Family Magazine; a short account of the Select Knot of Friendly Brothers in London. *Recreations:* Collector of Greek and Roman objects of art. *Address:* Whin-Hurst, Hayling Island, Havant. *T.:* Hayling Island 27. *Clubs:* Junior United Service (Hon.); Royal St. George Yacht, Kingstown; Union, Brighton.
(*Died 7 Dec. 1921.*)

SANDERS, Rev. Charles Evatt, Hon. Canon of Southwark Cathedral, 1906; b. 1846; s. of Evatt Sallows and Hannah Sanders; m. Evelyn Augusta Gilliat; one s. three d. *Educ.:* Worcester College, Oxford. Deacon, 1870; Priest, 1871; Curate of Kingstone, Herefordshire; Whitchurch, Salop; Englefield Green, Surrey; Vicar of Betchworth, 1880-1910; Rural Dean of Reigate, 1905-10. *Publication:* Necessary to Salvation. *Address:* 33 Argyll Road, Kensington, W. (*Died 6 Jan. 1927.*)

SANDERS, Rev. Ernest Arthur Blackwell, M.A.; Vicar of Edmonton, Middlesex, since 1900; Rural Dean of Enfield, 1904; Prebendary of St. Paul's Cathedral, 1911; b. 1858; s. of Frederick Sanders, Freeman of City of London; m. 1882, Jane, d. of John Biggs of Dallington, Sussex; one d. *Educ.:* Highgate School; Worcester College, Oxford. Curate of St. John's, Holloway, 1882-84; Vicar of All Saints', Holloway, 1884-91; Rector of Whitechapel, 1891-96; Vicar of St. Mark's, Dalston, 1896-1900. *Publication:* The Record of a Noble Life (a biography of his father), 1901. *Recreations:* walking. In former years rowing, athletics; holds public school record for 100 yards under 18. *Address:* Edmonton Vicarage, Middlesex. *T.A.:* Vicar, Edmonton. *T.:* 1871 Tottenham. *Clubs:* Primrose, Church Imperial. (*Died 24 Sept. 1917.*)

SANDERS, Rev. Canon Henry S., M.A.; Canon of Chelmsford since 1917; b. 1864; s. of late Rev. W. S. Sanders, M.A.; m. 1906, Elsie Marion Mitchell, Upwood, Bingley, Yorkshire; one s. one d. *Educ.:* Selwyn College, Cambridge. B.A. 1886; M.A. 1890; Deacon, 1887; Priest, 1888; Curate of Portsea, 1887-90; St. Mary's, Southampton, 1890-94; St. John's, Westminster, 1894-97; Rector of Eastnor and Hereford Diocesan Missioner, 1897-1901; Vicar of Bromley by Bow, E.; Rural Dean, 1916-19; Rector of Woodford, 1906-20. *Address:* Chelmsford. *T.:* Chelmsford 334. (*Died 26 Nov. 1920.*)

SANDERS, Thomas W., F.L.S., F.R.H.S., etc.; Kt. of First Class of Royal Order of Vasa

(Sweden), 1906 ; Editor of Amateur Gardening ; Lecturer and Writer on Scientific and Practical Horticulture, Agriculture, etc. ; *b.* Martley, Worcestershire, 6 Nov. 1855 ; *m.* Annie, *d.* of late Richard Hoare ; one *s.* one *d. Educ.:* village school, and afterwards by self instruction. Had a practical training in gardening and farming, and written a great deal on both subjects ; was chairman of party of experts invited by Swedish Government to inspect agricultural industries of Sweden, 1906. *Publications:* Garden Calendar ; An Encyclopædia of Gardening ; Garden and Grounds ; The Amateur's Greenhouse ; Roses and their Cultivation ; Vegetables and their Cultivation ; Book of the Potato ; A Garden of Annuals ; Hardy Perennials and Biennials ; Alphabet of Gardening ; Bulbs and their Cultivation ; Lawns and Greens ; Window and Indoor Gardening ; The Flower Garden ; Hardy Fruits and their Cultivation ; revised edition of Rustic Adornments ; Mushrooms and their Cultivation ; Carnations, Picotees, and Pinks ; Garden Foes ; Popular Hardy Perennials ; Salads and their Cultivation ; Allotment and Kitchen Gardens, etc.; also edited the following Handbooks—Chrysanthemums for Garden and Greenhouse ; Vegetables for Profit ; Ducks, Geese, and Turkeys for Profit ; Rabbits for Profit ; Pigs for Profit ; Horse, its Care and Management ; Dairy Cows and Dairying ; Incubation ; Grape Growing ; The Goat ; Sheep, their Breeding and Management ; Pansies and Violets ; Small Holder's Guide ; Bees for Profit and Pleasure ; Tomatoes, and How to Grow them ; Rock Gardens and Alpine Plants ; Orchids for Amateurs. *Recreations:* natural history, especially British botany ; entomology and geology ; also freemasonry ; is P.M. of Caxton Lodge, 1858, also of Philanthic Lodge, 3082 ; London rank. *Address:* 124 Embleton Road, Lewisham, S.E. *Club:* Horticultural. (*Died 13 Oct. 1926.*)

SANDERSON, 1st Baron (*cr.* 1905), of Armthorpe, York, **Thomas Henry Sanderson,** G.C.B., *cr.* 1900 ; K.C.B., *cr.* 1893 ; K.C.M.G., *cr.* 1887 ; C.B. 1880 ; I.S.O. 1902 ; *b.* 11 Jan. 1841 ; *s.* of Richard Sanderson, M.P., and Hon. Charlotte Matilda Manners Sutton, *d.* of 1st Viscount Canterbury ; unmarried. *Educ.:* Eton. Passed a competitive examination, and appointed Junior Clerk Foreign Office, 1859 ; attached to Lord Wodehouse's (Earl of Kimberley) special Mission to King of Denmark, 1863-64 ; Assistant Protocolist for Conferences on the affairs of Denmark, 1864, and on the Black Sea, 1871 ; Private Secretary to Parliamentary Under-Secretary of State, Mr. (Sir A. H.) Layard, 1866 ; Assistant Agent of H.M. Government at Geneva, in the Arbitration on the Alabama Claims, 1871 ; Private Secy. to late Earl of Derby, Secretary of State for Foreign Affairs, 1866-68, 1874-78 ; Private Secretary to late Earl Granville, Secretary of State for Foreign Affairs, 1880-85 ; Senior Clerk, 1885 ; Assistant Under-Secretary of State for Foreign Affairs, 1889 ; permanent Under-Sec. of State for Foreign Affairs, 1894-1906 ; Hon. D.C.L. Oxford, 1907 ; Chairman of Committee on Indian Emigration to the Crown Colonies, 1909-10 ; Chairman of Council of Royal Society of Arts, 1911-13. *Heir:* none. *Address:* 65 Wimpole Street, W.1. *T.:* Langham 2168. *Clubs:* Athenæum, Travellers', St. James's
(*Died 21 Mar. 1923.*)

SANDERSON, Frederick William, M.A.; Headmaster of Oundle School since 1892 ; J.P. Co. Northants ; *b.* 13 May 1857 ; *y. s.* of late Thomas Sanderson, Brancepeth, Durham ; *m.* Jane, *d.* of L. T. Hodgson, Broughton Hall ; one *s.* one *d. Educ.:* Univ. of Durham (Van Mildert Theological Scholar) ; Christ's Coll., Camb. ; Fellow of Durham Univ. ; bracketed 11th Wrangler, 1882 ; Lecturer at Girton Coll. 1882-85 ; Assistant Master at Dulwich College,

1885-92. *Publications:* Elementary Hydrostatics ; Elementary Electricity ; Introduction to Modern Geometry ; Essays on Education ; A Synopsis of the Life of Christ. *Recreations:* walking, bicycling, climbing. *Address:* Oundle School, Northants. *Club:* Royal Societies.
(*Died 15 June 1922.*)

SANDERSON, Oswald, Managing Director Ellermans Wilson Line, Hull ; Director Suez Canal Co. ; Director, Lloyds Bank, Ltd., London and North Eastern Railway ; Director North British and Mercantile Insurance Company ; Director Earles Shipbuilding and Engineering Co. Ltd., Hull ; Chairman Wilsons and North-Eastern Railway Shipping Co., Hull ; Chairman Humber Conservancy, 1915-25 ; Director United Shipping Co. Ltd., London ; Hull Underwriters' Association, Ltd. ; Hull Mutual S.S. Protection Society ; Hon. Elder Brother Trinity House, Hull ; Member Lloyd's Register, Shipping Federation, Chamber of Shipping ; *b.* 3 Jan. 1863 ; *s.* of Richard Sanderson, Liverpool ; *m.* Beatrice M. F., *d.* of E. F. Beddall, New York ; three *s.* one *d. Educ.:* King's School, Ely. President of Chamber of Shipping of United Kingdom, 1906 ; Member of Royal Commission on Shipping Rings, 1907 ; Hon. Lt.-Col. East Yorkshire Regiment ; Hon. Colonel 73rd Northumbrian Brigade R.F.A. (T.) ; D.L. East Riding, Yorkshire. *Address:* 2 Mansfield Street, W.1 ; Hessle Mount, Hessle, East Yorks. *T.A.:* Hessle. *T.:* Hessle 15. *M.:* BT18. *Clubs:* Carlton, White's ; Royal Yacht Squadron, Cowes. (*Died 25 Dec. 1926.*)

SANDERSON, Sir Percy, K.C.M.G., *cr.* 1899 ; C.M.G. 1886 ; *b.* London, 7 July 1842 ; *s.* of late Richard Sanderson and Charlotte Matilda, *d.* of 1st Viscount Canterbury. *Educ.:* Eton ; Addiscombe. Lieut. Royal Madras Artillery, 1859 ; appointed to Royal Horse Artillery, 1864 ; A.D.C. to Sir William Denison, Governor of Madras, 1865-66 ; 3rd class Commissary of Ordnance, 1866 ; acting A.D.C. to Lord Napier, Governor of Madras, 1868 ; acting 1st class Commissary of Ordnance, Fort St. George, 1868 ; retired on half-pay, 1870 ; Consul at Galatz, 1876 ; Consul-General for Roumania, to reside at Galatz, and Commissioner for the navigation of the Danube, 1882 ; employed on public service in London during the Danube Conference, 1883 ; acting Chargé d'Affaires at Bucharest at intervals in 1881, 1883, 1884, 1885, 1886 ; Consul-General, New York, 1894-1907 ; retired, 1907 ; J.P. Oxfordshire, 1908 ; Reading, 1915. *Address:* Grove Hill, Caversham. *Club:* East India United Service.
(*Died 11 July 1919.*)

SANDFORD, Capt. Francis Hugh, R.N., D.S.O. 1915 ; Assistant-Director of the Plans Division of the Naval Staff ; *b.* 10 Oct. 1887 ; 6th *s.* of late Ven. E. G. Sandford, Archdeacon of Exeter, and Ethel, *d.* of Gabriel Poole, Brent Knoll, Somerset. *Educ.:* Clifton College ; Balliol College, Oxford ; B.A. Served Dardanelles, 1915 (severely wounded, despatches, D.S.O.) ; prom. Comdr., and Croix de Guerre with palm, 1918, for services in raids closing Zeebrugge and Ostend harbours ; Capt. 1924. *Club:* United Service.
(*Died 15 Feb. 1926.*)

SANDHURST, 1st Viscount, *cr.* 1916, of Bath, **William Mansfield,** Baron, *cr.* 1871, G.C.V.O. 1917 ; G.C.S.I., G.C.I.E., P.C. 1906 ; J.P.; Hon. Col. Bombay Rifles since 1895 ; Lord-Chamberlain since 1912 ; Lieut. Coldstream Guards ; retired 1879 ; Knight of Grace, Order of St. John of Jerusalem, 1898 ; *b.* 21 Aug. 1855 ; *s.* of 1st Baron and Margaret, *d.* of Robert Fellowes, Shotesham Park, Norfolk ; *S.* father 1876 ; *m.* 1881, 1st, Lady Victoria Alexandrina Spencer, C.I. (*d.* 1906), *d.* of 4th Earl Spencer, K.G. ; 2nd, 1909, Eleanor, *d.* of Matthew Arnold and *widow* of Hon. Armine

Wodehouse. *Educ.*: Rugby. Sub-Lieutenant, Coldstream Guards, 1873 ; Lord-in-Waiting, 1880-85 ; Under-Secretary for War, 1886, 1892-1894 ; Governor of Bombay, 1895-99 ; was one of a small committee sent by Government to S. Africa in 1906 to report on the subject of Representative Government for S. Africa ; Treasurer, St. Bartholomew's Hospital since 1908 ; holds Grand Cross Order of Dannebrog. *Heir*: *b.* Hon. John William Mansfield. *Address*: 60 Eaton Square, S.W.1. *T.*: Gerrard 3280. *Clubs*: Brooks's, Turf, Garrick.

(*Died 2 Nov. 1921.*)

SANDIFORD, Charles Thomas, C.B. 1903 ; M.I.C.E., M.I.M.E. ; Engineer on Uganda Railway ; *b.* 1840. Worked on Sind, Punjab, and Delhi Railway ; Locomotive Superintendent N.W. State Railway, 1886 ; retired, 1899. *Address*: c/o Henry S. King & Co., Pall Mall, S.W.

(*Died 1 Mar. 1919.*)

SANDS, Rev. Hubert, M.A. ; Vicar of Burbage, near Marlborough, Wilts, since 1913 ; Rural Dean of Bordesley, 1905-13 ; Hon. Canon of Birmingham, 1906-13 ; *b.* Bleasby, Notts, 1855 ; *s.* of T. B. Sands of Liverpool ; *m.* 1889, Lucy Mary, *e. d.* of Samuel Blakemore Allport of Moseley ; four *s.* one *d.* *Educ.*: Bedford School ; Oriel College, Oxford. Curate of Solihull, 1878-1885 ; Moseley, 1886-89 ; Vicar of St. Oswald's, Bordesley, 1889-1913. *Publications*: The First Miracle ; Eucharistic Doctrine. *Recreations*: cycling, fly-fishing. *Address*: Burbage Vicarage, Marlborough, Wilts.

(*Died 5 Oct. 1922.*)

SANDS, Sir James Patrick, Kt., *cr.* 1917 ; President Legislative Council, 1916-23, Member Executive Council, 1901-28, Bahama Islands ; *b.* 7 Oct. 1859 ; *e. s.* of late Thomas Hilton Sands ; *m.* 1884, Laura Louisa, 3rd *d.* of late John Robert Hall, Bahamas ; seven *s.* one *d.* *Educ.*: Private Schools. Merchant ; Member of the House of Assembly, Bahamas, 1889-1916 ; Leader of the Government in the House of Assembly, 1909-16. *Recreation*: boating. *Address*: George Street, Nassau, N.P., Bahamas.

(*Died 11 Mar. 1925.*)

SANDS, William Southgate, M.V.O. 1914 ; Inspector of Buckingham Palace since 1906 ; *b.* 26 Nov. 1853 ; *e. surv. s.* of Thomas S. Sands, Slough ; *m.* Lucy (*decd.*), *o. d.* of J. Crissall, London ; no *c.* *Educ.*: London ; Windsor. Entered the Lord Chamberlain's Dept. 1873 ; Inspector of Holyrood Palace, Edinburgh, 1893-1906 ; Queen Victoria's Jubilee Medal and bar ; King Edward's and King George's Coronation Medals, and various foreign Orders. *Recreations*: painting and antiques. *Address*: Buckingham Palace. S.W.1.

(*Died 13 Dec. 1924.*)

SANDWICH, 8th Earl of (*cr.* 1660), **Edward George Henry Montagu;** Viscount Hinchingbrooke and Baron Montagu of St. Neots, 1660 ; K.C.V.O. 1906 ; Lord-Lt. of Huntingdonshire since 1891 ; J.P. ; Col. late Grenadier Guards ; Hon. Col. 5th Batt. King's Royal Rifles, 1886 ; Knight of Justice, St. John of Jerusalem ; Chairman Hunts County Council ; *b.* 13 July 1839 ; *s.* of 7th Earl and Lady Mary Paget, *d.* of 1st Marquess of Anglesey ; *S.* father 1884. Church of England. Unionist. *Educ.*: Eton. Entered Grenadier Guards, 1857 ; Lieut. and Capt. 1862 ; Adj. 2nd Batt. 1864 ; Capt. and Lieut.-Col. 1870 ; Col. 1881 ; Military Secretary at Gibraltar, 1875-1876 ; Hon. Col. 5th K.R. Rifles, 1884 ; Brig.-Gen. S. Midland Vol. Brigade, 1888-94 ; attached to special Embassies to Constantinople, 1858 ; Berlin, 1861 ; Petrograd, 1874 ; Morocco, 1875 ; M.P. Huntingdon, 1876-84 ; Mayor of Huntingdon, 1897-99. Owns about 20,000 acres. Picture gallery, Hinchingbrooke. *Heir*: *n.* George Charles Montagu. *Publication*: My Experiences in Spiritual Healing, 1915. *Address*: 18 Buckingham Gate, S.W. ; *T.*: Victoria 8489 ;

Hinchingbrooke, Huntingdon ; Hooke Court, Beaminster, Dorset. *Clubs*: Travellers', Turf, United Service. (*Died 26 June 1916.*)

SANDWITH, Fleming Mant, C.M.G. 1916 ; Temp. Col. A.M.S. ; Consulting Physician with H.M. troops in Alexandria ; *b.* 11 Oct. 1853 ; 2nd *s.* of Col. J. W. F. Sandwith ; *m.* Gladys, *d.* of Dr. Humphry Sandwith of Kars ; two *s.* two *d.* *Educ.*: Charterhouse ; St. Thomas's Hosp. ; M.D. Durham ; F.R.C.P. Lond. Knight of Grace Order of St. John of Jerusalem ; Gresham Professor of Physic ; Lecturer at London School of Tropical Medicine and St. Thomas's Hospital ; Senior Physician, Albert Dock Hospital ; Examiner in Tropical Medicine, London and Liverpool Universities ; served as Ambulance Surgeon in the Turco-Servian War, 1876 (Order of Takova and war medal) ; and Russo-Turkish Campaign, 1877-1878 ; present at the fighting at Shipka Pass, and served on Baker Pasha's staff during his retreat across the Rhodope Mountains (Order of Medjidieh and war medal) ; proceeded to Egypt for cholera epidemic, 1883 ; became Vice-Director of the Public Health Department of the Egyptian Government until 1885 ; and Professor of Medicine, Egyptian Government School of Medicine, till 1903 (3rd Order of Osmanieh) ; was Senior Physician of the Imperial Yeomanry Hospital at Pretoria during South African War, 1900 (medal and 3 clasps) ; served European War, 1914-17 (C.M.G.). *Publications*: Egypt as a Winter Resort ; Medical Diseases of Egypt, 1905 ; History of Kasr el Ainy, A.D. 1466-1901 ; and various papers, mostly on medical subjects. *Address*: 31 Cavendish Square, W. *T.*: 679 Mayfair. *Club*: Athenæum. (*Died 17 Feb. 1918.*)

SANDWITH, Major Ralph Leslie, C.M.G. 1900 ; late the Leicestershire Regt. ; *b.* 19 Mar. 1859 ; *s.* of late Major-General John P. Sandwith, Bombay Army ; *m.* 1901. Mabel Ellison Manisty; one *s.* *Educ.*: Harrow. Entered army in 17th Foot, 1880 ; served Boer War at Talana Hill ; commanded Base Depot, Natal, with rank of Lieut. Col. (despatches. C.M.G., medal with clasp). *Recreations*: genealogical research, croquet. *Address*: Mount Side, Harrow-on-the-Hill. (*Died 16 Sept. 1920.*)

SANDYS, Sir John (Edwin), Kt., *cr.* 1911; Litt. D. Cambridge, 1886 ; Hon. Litt.D. Dublin, 1892 ; Hon. LL.D. Edinburgh, 1909, and Athens, 1912 ; Commander in the Order of the Saviour, 1914 ; Fellow of the British Academy, 1909 ; F.R.S.L., 1914; Fellow of St. John's College, Cambridge, since 1867 ; Public Orator in the University of Cambridge, 1876-1919 ; Orator Emeritus, Hon. LL.D. Cambridge, Hon. D.Lit. Oxford, 1920; *b.* 19 May 1844 ; *s.* of late Rev. T. Sandys; *m.* Mary Grainger, *d.* of late Rev. H. Hall, 1880. *Educ.*: Repton ; St. John's, Camb. (Scholar). Bell Scholar, 1864; Browne's Medallist for Greek Ode, 1865 ; Porson Prizeman, 1865, 1866; Members' Prizeman for Latin Essay, 1866, 1867 ; Senior Classic, 1867 ; Classical Lecturer at Jesus, 1867-77, and at St. John's, 1867-1907 ; Tutor, St. John's, 1870-1900 ; Lane Lecturer at Harvard, 1905. *Publications*: editor of Isocrates, ad Demonicum et Panegyricus, 1868 ; Demosthenes, Select Private Orations, 1875, 4th ed. 1910 ; Leptines, 1890 ; Philippic Orations, (1) First Philippic and Olynthiacs, 1897, (2) Second and Third Philippics, De Pace, and De Chersoneso, 1900 ; Euripides, Bacchae (with illustrations from works of ancient art), 1880, 4th ed. 1900 ; Cicero's Orator, 1885 ; Aristotle's Constitution of Athens, 2nd ed. 1912 : Cope's Commentary on Aristotle's Rhetoric, 3 vols. 1877 ; Jebb's translation of the Rhetoric, and the new ed. of Jebb's Theophrastus, 1909 ; joint-editor (with Prof. Nettleship) of Seyffert's Dictionary of Classical Mythology, Religion, Literature, Art, and Antiquities, 1891; editor and translator of Pindar (Loeb Library), 1915, 2nd ed. 1919. author of History of Classical Scholarship, in 3 vols., with Chronological Tables, Facsimiles

Portraits, and other Illustrations; vol. i., From the Sixth Century, B.C., to the End of the Middle Ages, 1903 (3rd ed. 1921); vol. ii., From the Revival of Learning to the End of the Eighteenth Century (in Italy, France, England, and the Netherlands), 1908; vol. iii., The Eighteenth Century in Germany and the Nineteenth in Europe and the United States of America, 1908; Short History of Classical Scholarship, 1915; Harvard Lectures on the Revival of Learning, 1905; Introduction to Latin Epigraphy, 1919; Ancient University Ceremonies in Fasciculus J. W. Clark dicatus, 1909; Orationes et Epistolæ Cantabrigienses (1876-1909), 1910; contributor to "Social England," 1896-97, and Cambridge Companion to Greek Studies, 1905; editor of (and contributor to) Cambridge Companion to Latin Studies, 1910, 3rd ed. 1921; writer of chapter on Latin Literature, from John of Salisbury to Richard of Bury, in Cambridge History of English Literature, vol. i. 1907, and on Scholars, Antiquaries, and Bibliographers, vol. xii. 1915; also on Education and Scholarship, in Sharespeare's England, 1916; Literary Sources of Milton's Lycidas (Royal Society of Literature), 1914; Roger Bacon (British Academy), 1914; Tincommius (Numismatic Chronicle), 1913; contributor of articles on Pausanias and the elder and younger Plinies, and on Greek Law, and the History of Classical Studies, in the 11th edition of the Encyclopædia Britannica. *Recreation:* travelling. *Address:* St. John's House, Grange Road, Cambridge. *Club:* Athenæum. *(Died 6 July 1922.)*

SANFORD, Col. Edward Charles Ayshford, C.M.G. 1902; late 3rd Batt. Wilts Regt.; *b.* 6 June 1859; *s.* of W. A. Sanford, Nynehead Court, Wellington, Somerset, and Ellen, *d.* of Henry Seymour, Knoyle House, Semley, Wilts; *m.* 1904, May, *e. d.* of Lloyd Griffith of Hurst Court, Ore, Hastings; three *s. Educ.:* Eton. Gazetted 3rd Wilts Regt. (Roy. Wilts Militia), 1878; Captain, 1881; Hon. Major, 1893; Lieut.-Col. 1894; Hon. Col. 1898; retired, 1903. Served with Sir Charles Warren's Field Force in Bechuanaland, 1884-85; embodied 17 Jan. 1900, being quartered in Cork command, Ireland; went to St. Helena to guard prisoners of war, 20 June 1901; disembodied, 1902; J.P. Somerset, Devon, and St. Helena. *Club:* Brooks's. *(Died 22 Mar. 1923.)*

SANKEY, Capt. Matthew Henry Phineas Riall, C.B. 1916; C.B.E. 1920; R.E. (retd.); Director and Consulting Engineer to Marconi's Wireless Telegraph Co., Ltd., the Marconi International Marine Communication Co., Ltd., and other Companies; *b.* Nenagh, 9 Nov. 1853; *s.* of late Gen. W. Sankey, C.B.; *m.* E. M., *d.* of General E. L. Pym, R.M.L.I.; one *s.* three *d. Educ.:* Morges and Schaffhausen, Switzerland; Mr. Rippin's School, Woolwich; R.M.A., Woolwich; S.M.E., Chatham. First Commission, Royal Engineers, 1873; assisted at Railway Continuous Brake Experiments, 1875; Gibraltar, 1878-79; Instructor in Fortification at the R.M.C., Kingston, Canada, 1879 - 82; Ordnance Survey, Southampton, in charge of Trigonometrical Division, Stores and Workshops, 1882-89; retired, and joined the Board of Willans and Robinson, Ltd., 1889 - 1905; Vice - President, Institution of Civil Engineers; Past President, Institution of Mechanical Engineers; Member of the following Institutions: American Mechanical Engineers, Electrical Engineers, Iron and Steel, Naval Architects, and Gas Engineers; Member of the Governing Board, National Physical Laboratory; Member of several Committees of the Institutions of Civil Engineers and Mechanical Engineers on Steam and Gas Engine Research; Member of several Sub - Committees of the Engineering Standardisation Committee; Member of two Committees of the British Associa-

tion, Wireless Telegraphy and Gaseous Explosions; Chairman of the Heat Engine Committee of the Institution of Civil Engineers and other Institutions; Director, Marconi's Wireless Telegraph Co. Ltd., and other companies. *Publications:* The Energy Chart, Practical Application to Reciprocating Steam Engines; Part IV. of Rimington's Construction (anonymously); author of papers read before the Institutions referred to above, and others. *Address:* 57 Castlebar Road, Ealing, W.5. *T.A.:* c/o Expanse Estrand, London. *T.:* Ealing 998; City 8710. *Club:* St. Stephen's.
(Died 3 Oct. 1925.)

SANT, James, C.V.O. 1914; R.A. 1870-1914, when he resigned; late principal Painter-in-Ordinary to Queen Victoria; Corresponding Member of La Regia Accademia Raffaello in Urbino; *b.* Croydon, 1820; *m. d. (d.* 1907) of R. M. M. Thomson, staff-surgeon, Bengal; one *s.* four *d. Educ.:* pupil of John Varley and Sir Augustus Calcott, R.A.; studied at R.A. for four years. A collection of his works at Strawberry Hill, painted for the Countess Waldegrave, was exhibited at French Gallery, 1861; he contributes frequently to R.A. exhibitions. *Paintings:* Dick Whittington; Little Red Riding Hood; Infant Samuel; Mother's Hope; Infant Timothy; Morning; Evening; Light of the Cross; She Never Told Her Love; Harmony; Young Minstrel; Retrospection; Saxon Women; The Boy Shakespere; The Walk to Emmaus; The Miller's Daughter; Young Steele; The Soul's Awakening; The Last Phase. *Address:* 43 Lancaster Gate, Hyde Park, W. *T.:* Padd. 7210.
(Died 12 July 1916.)

SANTLEY, Sir Charles, Kt., *cr.* 1907; baritone singer; *b.* Liverpool, 28 Feb. 1834; *m.* 1st, 1859, Gertrude, *g. d.* of Charles Kemble; 2nd, 1884, Elizabeth Mary, *d.* of George Rose-Innes; one *d. Educ.:* England and Italy. First appeared in London, 1857; his first great success was in the opera Dinorah, at Covent Garden, 1859; first appearance in Italian Opera, Covent Garden, three nights, 1862; remainder of same season engaged with Mapleson at Her Majesty's Theatre (burned, 1867), Italian Opera; Valentine in Faust, first representation in England, 1863; Drury Lane, Mapleson management, 1868; Covent Garden—Gye and Mapleson coalition—Hamlet, in production of Ambrose Thomas' Opera, 1869; Drury Lane, Mapleson management, Vanderdecken, in Flying Dutchman, the first opera of Wagner produced in England, 1870; visited America, 1871, 1891; Australia, 1889-90; the Cape, 1893, 1903; Knight Commander of St. Gregory. *Publications:* Student and Singer, 1892; Art of Singing, 1908; Reminiscences of My Life, 1909. *Address:* 13 Blenheim Road, N.W.
(Died 22 Sept. 1922.)

SAO, Sir Moung, K.C.I.E., *cr.* 1916; C.I.E. 1906; Sawbwa of Yawng Hwe, Southern Shan States, Burma; Member of Federated Shan States; *b.* 1847; two adopted *s.*, three adopted *d. Address:* Yawng Hwe, Southern Shan States, Burma. *(Died 3 Dec. 1926.)*

SAPARA - WILLIAMS, Hon. Christopher Alexander, C.M.G. 1914; Barrister-at-law; Member of Legislative Council, Nigeria, since 1901; of Municipal Board of Health, Lagos; Licensing Justice for the Municipal Area, Lagos; Leader of the Nigerian Bar; *b.* 19 July 1854; *s.* of Alexander Charles and Nancy Sapara-Williams, Lagos; *m.* 1886, Anna Sophia (*d.* 1904), *d.* of Hon. Robert Hutchison of Cape Coast, Gold Coast. *Educ.:* Wesleyan School, Buxton Chapel, Freetown, Sierra Leone; C.M.S. Grammar School, Sierra Leone; Wesley College, Sheffield, England. Called to Bar, Inner Temple, 1879; practised on the Gold Coast, Lagos, and Nigeria since 1880; Counsel for the Government in several cases, and as

Junior to Attorney-General in several important cases. *Address:* The Nest, Customs Street, Lagos, Nigeria. *T.A.:* Sapara, Lagos. *Club:* National Liberal.   (*Died 14 Mar. 1915.*)

SARAWAK, Rajah of, H.H. Sir Charles Johnson Brooke, G.C.M.G., *cr.* 1888; 2nd " Rajah " of Sarawak; *S. u.* Sir James (Rajah) Brooke, 1868; *b.* 1829; *m.* Margaret, *d.* of Clayton de Windt, Blunsden Hall, Wilts. Joined H.M.'s Navy 1840; resigned commission to serve under his uncle in Sarawak, 1851; was prominent in helping to restore the country to order and put down piracy and head-hunting. Rules over a population of 500,000 souls and a country 40,000 sq. miles in extent. *Recreations:* hunting, reading. *Heir: s.* Charles Vyner Brooke. *Address:* The Palace, Sarawak, Borneo; Chesterton House, Cirencester; Villa Raffo, Bogliasco, nr. Genoa, Italy.
    (*Died 17 May 1917.*)

SARGANT, Ethel, F.L.S. 1904; *b.* 28 Oct. 1863; 3rd *d.* of Henry Sargant of Lincoln's Inn and Emma Beale; unmarried. *Educ.:* North London Collegiate School for Girls; Girton College, Cambridge. Natural Sciences at Cambridge; worked under Dr. D. H. Scott, F.R.S., at the Jodrell Laboratory in Kew Gardens, 1892-93; since then has worked at home on various botanical subjects; on Council of Linnean Society, 1906-10; President of Section K (Botany) at British Association Meeting, Birmingham, 1913; Hon. Fellow Girton College, 1913. *Publications:* several papers in the Annals of Botany from 1893 onwards. *Address:* The Old Rectory, Girton, Cambs. *T.A.:* Girton, Histon. *Club:* Ladies' University.
    (*Died 16 Jan. 1918.*)

SARGEAUNT, John, Sixth Form Master at Westminster, 1890-1918; *b.* Irthlingborough, Northamptonshire, 12 Aug. 1857; *e. s.* of John Barneby Sargeaunt, Barrister-at-Law. *Educ.:* Bedford (head of the school); University College, Oxford. First Class Classical Moderations, 1878; 2nd Class Classical Finals, 1880; President of the Oxford Union Society; Past Prior of the Johnson Club; Member of the Council of Brighton College. *Publications:* Annals of Westminster School, 1888; Virgil's Pastorals in English Verse, 1900; Pope's Essay on Criticism, 1909; Dryden's Poems (the restored text), 1910; Terence in English prose (Loeb Classics), 1912; The Trees, Shrubs, and Plants of Virgil, 1920; several Latin and English schoolbooks and many reviews. *Recreations:* gardening and bridge. *Address:* Arnolds, Fairwarp, Sussex. *Club:* Reform.
    (*Died 20 Mar. 1922.*)

SARGENT, Very Rev. John Paine, Dean, St. Peter's Pro-Cathedral, Diocese of Qu'Appelle, 1903; *b.* Dublin, 16 Jan. 1838; *s.* of R. S. Sargent, M.D., Fellow of King and Queen's Colleges of Physicians, Ireland; *m.* Elizabeth, *d.* of Harry King, D.C.L., Judge of Probate Windsor. Nova Scotia: two *s.* two *d. Educ.:* King's College University, Windsor, Nova Scotia, 1864; B.A. Formerly Ensign in H.M. 62nd Regiment of Foot, 1855-1861; S.P.G. Missionary, Nova Scotia and N.W. Canada, 1864-1900; Archdeacon of Assiniboia. 1898-1903; Chaplain, No. 2 Field Hospital, N.W. Canadian Field Force, 1885 (medal); Hon. D.D. University of Manitoba; Secretary, Synod Diocese of Qu'Appelle, 1892-1911; Deputy-Prolocutor, Provincial Synod of Rupert's Land, 1899-1902; Prolocutor, 1902-1905; Chaplain Masonic Grand Lodge of Saskatchewan, 1910-1911. *Address:* Qu'Appelle, Canada.
    (*Died 11 Dec. 1919.*)

SARGENT, John Singer, R.A. 1897; R.S.W. 1908; D.C.L. Hon. Oxon; Hon. LL.D. Camb.; Officier de la Légion d'Honneur; portrait painter; *b.* Florence, 1856; *s.* of a physician of Boston, U.S.A. *Educ.:* Italy; France. Studied

under Carolus Duran; exhibited at Salon, 1879; since then exhibited continually at Salon and Academy; A.R.A. 1894. *Principal works:* El Jaleo; Portraits—Carolus Duran; Ellen Terry; Rt. Hon. Joseph Chamberlain; Mrs. Carl Meyer and Children; Octavia Hill; Lady Fandel Phillips; and many others. *Address:* 31 Tite Street, Chelsea, S.W.3. *T.:* Western 4849. *Club:* Athenæum. (*Died 15 April 1925.*)

SARTORIS, Francis Charles; *b.* 1857; *e. s.* of late Alfred Sartoris, and Hon. Mary Frances Barrington, 2nd *d.* of 6th Viscount Barrington. Late Lieutenant Royal Fusiliers. *Address:* 11 Chesham Street, S.W.1. ·*T.:* Victoria 1771. *Clubs:* Naval and Military, Orleans; Royal Yacht Squadron, Cowes.

SARTORIUS, Major-General Euston Henry, V.C., C.B. 1896; *b.* Cintra, Portugal, 1844; 3rd *s.* of late Admiral of the Fleet Sir G. R. Sartorius, G.C.B.; *m.* 1874, Emily (*d.* 1915), *d.* of Sir F. Cook, 1st Bt.; two *d. Educ.:* Royal Naval School, New Cross; Woolwich; R.M.C., Sandhurst. Joined 59th Regt. 1862; passed Staff College; Afghan War (twice mentioned in despatches, thanked by Indian Government for work on the Survey; Brevet of Major, and V.C.); D.A.A.G. and D.A.Q.M.G. Aldershot; Egyptian Campaign, 1882 (D.A.A.G., class Osmanieh, Brevet of Lieut.-Col., despatches); C.S.O. Portsmouth; Military Attaché, Japan; C.B.; Humane Society's bronze medal; attached to Crown Prince of Siam at celebration of H.M. Jubilee and Coronation of King Edward; attached Prince Chakrabhong of Siam, Coronation of H.M. King George. *Decorated* for taking a hill at Shahjui in possession of Ghazis (leading the attack). Bears the title of Conde de Penhafirme while in Portugal. *Address:* 17 Chelsea Embankment, S.W.3; Hurtwood, Holmbury St. Mary, Surrey. *T.A.:* Penhafirme, Sloane. *T.:* Kensington 861; Ewhurst 14. *Clubs:* Naval and Military, Royal Automobile.
    (*Died 19 Feb. 1925.*)

SARZANO, 11th Marquis of; *cr.* 1695, Frank James Carandini; Major, retired, 5th Royal Irish Lancers; *b.* 20 May 1847; *s.* of late 10th Marquis (*d.* 1870); *m.* 1887, Florence Annie, *y. d.* of late Lt.-Gen. C. D. Clementson, Indian Army; one *d.* Granted His Majesty's Royal Licence and authority to bear and use in this country the titles of Marquis of Sarzano, Patrician of Modena, and Noble of Bologna, 1910; Captain in 8th Hussars to 1893; served Afghan War, 1879-80 (medal).   (*Died 6 Aug. 1920.*)

SASSOON, Sir Edward Elias, 2nd Bt., *cr.* 1909; chief partner in E. D. Sassoon & Co., merchants and bankers of India, London, and China; *b.* 1853; *g.s.* of David Sassoon of Baghdad; *S.* brother, 1916; *m.* 1880, Leontine, *d.* of A. Levy; one *s.* two *d. Heir: s.* Ellice Victor [*b.* 1881; late Capt. R.A.F.]. *Address:* 46 Grosvenor Place, W.1. *T.:* Victoria 176.
    (*Died 2 Dec. 1924.*)

SASSOON, Sir Jacob Elias, 1st Bt., *cr.* 1909; *g. s.* of David Sassoon of Baghdad; *b.* 1844; *m.* 1880, Rachel Simon (*d.* 1911), *d.* of Simon H. Isaacs of Calcutta. Established a Central College of Science in Bombay; built first mill, 1883, and has since constructed several others; chief partner in E. D. Sassoon and Co., merchants and bankers of India, London, and China. *Heir-pres.* (special remainder), *b.* Edward Elias Sassoon [*b.* 1853; *m.* 1880, Leontine, *d.* of Abraham Levy; two *s.* two *d. Address:* 46 Grosvenor Place, W.]. *Address:* Braganza Hall, Bombay; Ashley House, Poona; Glen Ogle, Mahableshwar, India. *Clubs:* Bombay Yacht; Poona Gymkhana; Mahableshwar.   (*Died 23 Oct. 1916.*)

SASSOON, Joseph S., J.P.; *b.* 31 Dec. 1855; *e. s.* of late Sassoon David Sassoon, and Flora, *d.* of Solomon Reuben, of Baghdad;

m. 1884, Louise, *e. d.* of Baron Horace de Gunzburg of Petrograd; five *s.* *Educ.:* Christ Church, Oxford (M.A.). *Address:* Ashley Park Walton-on-Thames. *(Died 4 Jan. 1918.)*

SASSOON, Meyer Elias, *brother* of Sir E. E. Sassoon, 2nd Bart. and *g. s.* of David Sassoon of Baghdad; *b.* 7 July 1855; *m.* 1892, Mozelle, *d.* of late A. M. Gubbay, and *g.d.* of Sir Albert Sassoon, 1st Bart.; one *s.* one *d.* *Address:* 6 Hamilton Place, W.1.; *T.:* Grosvenor 2624; Port Breton, Dinard, France. *Clubs:* Cavalry, Baldwin. *(Died 5 Nov. 1924.)*

SATOW, Samuel Augustus Mason; late a Master of the Supreme Court; *s.* of H. D. C. Satow; *b.* 1847; *m.* 1875, Kathrin (*d.* 1907), *d.* of J. Dakin. *Address:* Berkhamsted, Herts. *(Died 30 May 1925.)*

SAUNDBY, Robert, M.D. Edin.; LL.D. M'Gill; LL.D. St. Andrews; F.R.C.P. Lond.; F.R.C.P.I. Hon.; M.Sc. Birm.; J.P. Co. Warwick; Emeritus Professor of Medicine, University of Birmingham; Lt.-Col. R.A.M.C.T. Physician to 2nd Southern Military Hospital; Consulting Physician, General Hospital, Birmingham; formerly member of General Medical Council of Education for the United Kingdom; Harveian Orator R.C.P., 1917; *b.* London, 9 Dec. 1849; *m.* 1880, Mary Edith Spencer; three *s.* one *d.* *Educ.:* Edinburgh University. Emeritus Senior President, Royal Medical Society; House Physician, Edinburgh Royal Infirmary, 1874; House Physician to the Royal Hospital for Diseases of the Chest, 1875; Pathologist to the General Hospital, Birmingham, 1876; Assistant Physician, 1877; Physician, 1885; retired, 1912; Examiner in Medicine, English Conjoint Board, 1894-1897; President British Medical Association, 1911-12; President of the Council, British Medical Association, 1896-99; President, Birmingham Medical Institute, 1895-99, and Birmingham Library, 1904-1908. *Publications:* Treatment of Diseases of the Digestive System, 2nd ed., 1914; Lectures on Renal and Urinary Diseases, 4th ed. 1900; The Common Forms of Dyspepsia in Women, 1894; Medical Ethics, 2nd. ed., 1907; article Diabetes, in Allbutt's System of Medicine, 1907; Old Age, its Care and Treatment in Health and Disease, 1913; Urgent Symptoms in Medical Practice, 1915; numerous contributions to the medical press. *Address:* 68 Hagley Road, Edgbaston; 140B Great Charles Street, Birmingham. *T.:* C. 905. *Clubs:* Reform; Union, Birmingham.*(Died 28 Aug. 1918.)*

SAUNDERS, Major Frederick John, D.S.O. 1901; Royal Marine Light Infantry; *b.* 18 Sep. 1876; *s.* of William Saunders, Sydenham; *m.* 1902, Muriel, *d.* of late Alexander Maxwell Tod, Walmer; one *s.* Entered Royal Marine Light Infantry, 1895; landed from H.M.S. Powerful, and joined Naval Brigade in South Africa, 1899-1900 (medal and 4 clasps, despatches, D.S.O.); Captain, 1901; Major, 1914; served European War in Gallipoli (despatches). *Club:* United Service. *(Died Nov. 1916.)*

SAUNDERS, George, O.B.E., B.A. Oxford; LL.D. Glas.; *b.* Rattray, Perthshire 1859; *e.*, *s.* of late David H. Saunders, J.P., Dundee and Craigmill, Blairgowrie, N.B.; *m.* 1893, Gertruda, *d.* of late Oscar Hainauer, Berlin; three *s.* two *d.* *Educ.:* Dundee High School; Universities of Glasgow, Bonn, Göttingen, and Oxford (Snell exhibitioner of Balliol College). Buchanan prizes for Moral Philosophy, English Literature, Rectorial prize for essay on Constantine the Great, Monteath Bursary for German, etc., Glasgow University. First foreign correspondence was contributed to Scotsman; series of letters to Pall Mall Gazette from Paris and Departments during General Boulanger's electoral campaign; Berlin Correspondent, Morning Post, 1888-97; many special missions for that journal to German army manœuvres; and in France, Austria, Italy, Greece, Turkey, Bulgaria, Russia; Berlin Times Correspondent, 1897-1908; Paris Times Correspondent, 1908-14; served in Department of Political Information and other War Departments, 1915-18; a temporary Senior Clerk in the Foreign Office, March 1918-Feb. 1920 and Aug. and Nov. 1920. *Recreation:* golf. *Address:* Pontsarn, Woking. *Clubs:* St. James's, Athenæum. *(Died 10 Sept. 1922.)*

SAUNDERS, Captain (Temp. Major) Harold Cecil Rich, D.S.O. 1917; E. York Regt.; *b.* Kingston, Jamaica, 28 April 1882; *e. s.* of A. R. Saunders, M.B., F.R.C.S., and Louise, *e. d.* of Dr. J. C. Phillippo; *m.* 1915, Dorothy, *e. d.* of Brig.-General C. P. Triscott, C.B. *Educ.:* Clifton College. Joined East Yorkshire Regt. from Tasmania Militia Infantry, 1905; in Burma and India; seconded 3rd King's African Rifles, 1909-12; served East Africa (medal and clasp, Somaliland); served European War, 1914-17; arrived France, Jan. 1915; wounded, Feb. 1915 (despatches, D.S.O.) *Recreations:* sketching, usual field sports and games. *Club:* Junior Naval and Military. *(Died 30 Mar. 1919.)*

SAUNDERS, Thomas Bailey, M.A.; author; *b.* Alice, Cape Colony, 2 Dec. 1860; 2nd *s.* of late Deputy-Inspector-Gen. George Saunders, C.B. (*s.* of Lieut.-Colonel Richard Saunders, Co. Kerry), and Isabella, *d.* of Thomas Bailey, J.P., Co. Fermanagh, Ireland; *m.* 1887, late Contessa Elena Alberti di Poja, *o. c.* of late Conte Gustavo Alberti di Poja, Rovereto, S. Tyrol. *Educ.:* King's College, London; University College, Oxford. 2nd class Lit. Hum. 1884; Fellow and Member of Council of King's College, and of the Senate of the University of London, 1913-21; Chairman of the Trustees of the Sladen Memorial Fund for assisting scientific research, since 1904. After leaving Oxford spent some time in Germany; Barr. Inner Temple, 1888; from Aug. 1898 to June 1900 Sec. of the Statutory Commission for the Reorganisation of the University of London. *Publications:* several volumes of translation from Schopenhauer's essays, The Wisdom of Life, Studies in Pessimism, The Art of Literature, On Human Nature, etc., 1889-96; Goethe's Maxims and Reflections (selected in part by Huxley and Leighton), 1893; The Life and Letters of James Macpherson, 1894; Notes on Technical Instruction in the German Universities, 1899; versions of Prof. Harnack's Christianity and History, 1896, Thoughts on Protestantism, 1899, and What is Christianity? 1901; The Quest of Faith, 1899; Schopenhauer, 1901; Prof. Harnack and his Oxford Critics, 1902; contributions to the Quarterly Review, the Athenæum, the Dict. of Nat. Biog., etc. *Recreation:* music. *Address:* Staveley Corner, Eastbourne. *T.:* 1766. *Club:* Athenæum. *(Died 8 Feb. 1928.)*

SAVAGE, Sir George Henry, Kt., *cr.* 1912; M.D., F.R.C.P., F.R.A.M.I.; Consulting Physician Guy's Hospital, and to Earlswood Idiot Asylum; *b.* Brighton, 12 Nov. 1842; *m.* 1st, Margaret, *d.* of Jacob Walton of Greenends, Alston Moor; 2nd, *d.* of Dr. Sutton, Physician to London Hospital; one *s.* one *d.* *Educ.:* Brighton Schools; Sussex County Hospital; Guy's Hospital (Treasurer's Gold Medal). Former Physician-Superintendent of Bethlem Royal Hospital; former President of Medico-Psychological Association of Great Britain; and of Neurological Society; Examiner in Mental Physiology, University of London; former Lecturer on Mental Diseases, Guy's Hospital. *Publications:* Manual on Insanity; former Editor of Journal of Mental Science. *Recreations:* mountaineering, fishing, fencing. *Address:* 26 Devonshire Place, W.1; The Island, Hurstbourne Priors, Whitchurch, Hants. *T.:*

934

SAUZIER, Anatole. See page xxx.

2075 Paddington. *Club:* Athenæum.
(*Died 5 July 1921.*)

SAVAGE-ARMSTRONG, Major Francis Savage Nesbitt, D.S.O. 1915; 1st Batt. S. Staffs Regt.; *b.* 5 July 1880. Entered army, 1900; Captain, 1909; Major, 1915; Lieut.-Col. (temp.) 1916; served South Africa, 1900-2 (Queen's medal, 3 clasps; King's medal, 2 clasps); European War, 1914-15 (despatches, D.S.O.). *Address:* Strangford House, Strangford, Co. Down, Ireland. *Club:* Army and Navy. (*Died April 1917.*)

SAVARY, Alfred William; Retired Judge; *b.* Plympton, Digby County, Nova Scotia, 10 Oct. 1831; *s.* of Sabine Savary and Olive, *d.* of Samuel Marshall, M.P.P., Yarmouth, N.S.; a lineal descendant from Thomas Savory who came to Plymouth, Mass., 1633, from Hannington or vicinity, Wilts.; *m.* 1st, 1877, Elizabeth Crookshank (*d.* 1887), *d.* of H. P. Otty; 2nd, 1892, Eliza T., *d.* of late Rev. Abraham Spurr Hunt; two *s.* *Educ.:* King's College, Windsor, N.S. (M.A. 1857, D.C.L. Hon. 1909). Attorney, New Brunswick, 1857; Barrister, N.S., 1860; M.P. Digby, 1867-73; K.C. 1872; Judge of County Courts, N.S., 1876-1907; a Vice-President N.S. Historical Society and regular or corresponding member of several other historical, antiquarian, and genealogical societies. *Publications:* finished and published Calnek's inchoate History of the County of Annapolis, 1897; other publications, Savery and Severy Genealogies, with biography of William Savery, eminent Quaker minister, 1893; Supplement to same, 1905; Narrative of Col. David Fanning, Loyalist, American Revolution, 1908; Ancestry of Gen. Sir Fenwick Williams, with sketch of allied historic families of Annapolis Royal, 1911, and other short genealogical compilations; Supplement to History of Annapolis, 1913. *Address:* Annapolis Royal, Nova Scotia. *Club:* Halifax, Halifax.
(*Died 23 Feb. 1918.*)

SAVILE, Colonel Henry Bourchier Osborne; C.B. 1902; Hon. Col. of the Wessex Royal Engineers; *b.* 5 May 1819; 3rd *s.* of Albany Savile of Oaklands, Devon, and Eleanor Elizabeth, *d.* of Sir Bourchier Wrey, 7th Bt.; *m.* 1st, 1842, Katherine (*d.* 1846), *o. d.* of Rev. J. Law; one *s.*; 2nd, 1848, Mary (*d.* 1870), *e. d.* of Cornelius O'Callaghan of Ballynahinsh, Co. Clare; two *s.*; 3rd, 1872, Ellen Lucy, *o. d.* of Richard Sisson Darling of the Lothians, Trinidad; one *s.* *Educ.:* Royal Military Academy, Woolwich. Received 1st Commission, 1837, in the Royal Artillery, in which he served fifteen years; became Major of the Royal North Gloster Militia, 1853, and served with them till the commencement of the Volunteer Movement, when he raised and commanded the Artillery Corps of Gloster and Somerset; J.P. for the City and County of Bristol, and High Sheriff of the same, 1883-84. *Address:* Clifton, Bristol. *Club:* National.
(*Died 17 Aug. 1917.*)

SAVILE, Brig.-Gen. Walter Clare, C.B. 1917; D.S.O. 1900; *b.* 4 July 1857; *s.* of late Col. H. B. O. Savile, C.B.; *m.* 1881, Helen, 4th *d.* of William Ruxton, Ardee House, Co. Louth; one *s.* one *d.* *Educ.:* Clifton College. Entered R.A. 1877; Captain, 1885; Major, 1894; Lt.-Col. 1904; Col. 1909; Assistant to Director of Artillery, 1888-92; occupation of Crete, 1898; Boer War, 1899-1901, including defence of Ladysmith (despatches thrice, medal and four clasps, and D.S.O.); Col. Commanding Harwich Coast Defences, 1906-9; Assistant Director of Artillery, 1909-12; commanding South Irish Coast Defences, 1912-14; retired, 1914; re-employed War Office, 1914-15; Ministry of Munitions, 1915. *Address:* 35 Cadogan Gardens, S.W.3. *T.:* Kensington 4415. *Club:* Army and Navy.(*Died 13 Nov. 1928.*)

SAVORY, Vice-Admiral Herbert Whitmore, R.N., M.V.O. 1906; *b.* 15 July 1857; *m.* 1890, Miss Gregory of New York; one *s.* one *d.* Entered Navy, 1870; Commander, 1895; Captain, 1901; Rear-Admiral, 1911; Ashanti War, 1873-4 (medal and clasp); Flag Captain in China, H.M.S. Diadem, conveyed Prince Arthur of Connaught and Garter Mission to Japan; (M.V.O. and Order of Rising Sun); Flag Capt. in Mediterranean to H.S.H. Prince Louis of Battenberg, 1907; Inspecting Captain of Training Establishments, 1909; Vice-Adm., retired, 1916. *Address:* 10 Eaton Terrace, S.W. *T.:* Vic. 5763. *Club:* Naval and Military.
(*Died 23 Feb. 1918.*)

SAVORY, Sir Joseph, 1st Bt., *cr.* 1891; D.L., J.P.; Lieut. and Alderman of City of London, 1883; Chairman of Almoners of Christ's Hospital since 1891; Chairman of Princess Helena College; Governor of Queen Anne's Bounty; Royal Holloway College, St. Bartholomew's, and St. Thomas's Hospitals; *b.* 23 July 1843; *m.* 1888, Helen, *d.* of late Col. Sir G. A. Leach, K.C.B. *Educ.:* Harrow. Sheriff of London and Middlesex, 1882-83; member of School Board for City, 1885-88; Lord Mayor, 1890-91. M.P. (C.) Westmorland (Appleby), 1892-1900. *Heir:* none. *Address:* Wyndham House, Sloane Gardens, S.W.; Buckhurst Park, Sunninghill. *Clubs:* Carlton, National.
(*Died 1 Oct. 1921.*)

SAWARD, Maj.-Gen. Michael Henry; *b.* London, 22 Dec. 1840; *e. s.* of late M. Saward, Croydon, Surrey, and Westbarrow Hall, Essex, and Harriet, *d.* of Rev. J. Morbeck Sumner, J.P., D.L.; *m.* 1877, Katherine Isabella (*d.* 1919), *d.* of late Gen. F. C. Maisey; one *s.* (Captain R. Scots, killed in Great War) one *d.* *Educ.:* Merchant Taylors' School; Addiscombe Mil. Coll. Lt. Bengal Art. 1859; Lt. Royal Art. 1861; Col. Army, 1889; Major-Gen. 1896; Col. Com. R.A. 1905 and R.H.A. 1926; Hon. Col. Royal Guernsey and Alderney Militia, 1914; A.D.C. to Gen. Sir H. Tombs, V.C., K.C.B. 1871-74, and to Gen. Sir Crawford Chamberlain, G.C.I.E., C.S.I., 1875-76; A.Q.M.G., 1874; D.A.A.G. R.A. in India, 1877-82; I.G. School of Gunnery, 1982-87; A.A.G. R.A. India, 1889-94; Col. on Staff C.R.A.T.D., 1895-96; Lieut.-Governor and Comg. Guernsey and Alderney Dist., 1899-1903. *Address:* 29 Brechin Place, S.W.7. *Club:* United Service. (*Died 13 Feb. 1928.*)

SAWBRIDGE, Rev. John Sikes, Hon. Canon of St. Edmundsbury and Ipswich. *Address:* Thelnetham Rectory, Diss, Norfolk.
(*Died 9 May 1925.*)

SAWYER, Sir James, Kt., *cr.* 1885; M.D., F.R.C.P., F.S.A., F.R.S.E., J.P.; consulting physician and Consulting Physician to Queen's Hospital, Birmingham; *b.* Carlisle, 11 Aug. 1844; *s.* of late James Sawyer, Carlisle, and Ann, *e. d.* of William George, Ross; *m.* Adelaide, *d.* of Rev. J. H. Hill, Rector of Cranoe, Leicestershire, 1873; two *s.* two *d.* *Educ.:* Queen's College, Birmingham; London University. Lumleian Lecturer, R.C.P., 1908; Professor of Pathology, Queen's College, Birmingham, 1875-78; Prof. Materia Medica, 1878-85; Prof. Medicine, 1885-91; Chairman of Warwicks Chamber of Agriculture, 1898-99. V. P. Therapeutics Section International Medical Congress, London, 1913. *Publications:* Diagnosis of Diseases of the Lungs, Heart, and Kidneys, 1870; Notes on Medical Education, 1889; Causes and Cure of Insomnia, 1904; Contributions to Practical Medicine, 4th ed. 1904; Maladies of the Heart (Lumleian Lectures), 1908; Coprostasis, 1912; many papers in medical periodicals. *Recreations:* literature, archæology, agriculture. *Address:* Haseley Hall, Warwick; 29 Old Burlington Street, W. *T.A.:* Consultant, Birmingham. *T.:* Central 3477. *Clubs:* Junior Conservative; Midland Conservative, Birmingham.
(*Died 27 Jan. 1919.*)

SAWYER, Maj.-Gen. Richard Henry Stewart, C.B. 1918; C.M.G. 1915; M.B.,

935

F.R.C.S.I.; *b.* 9 Oct. 1857; *m.* Flora Murray, *y. d.* of late Malcolm MacGregor, S.S.C., Edinburgh. *Educ.*: Trinity College, Dublin. Maj.-1898; Lt.-Col. 1901; Col. 1910; Assist. Director of Medical Services, Irish Command, 1910; served Nile Expedition, 1898 (Egyptian medal with clasp, medal); South African War, 1899-1902 (despatches, Queen's medal 4 clasps, King's medal 2 clasps); European War, 1914-1918 (despatches 5 times, C.M.G., C.B.); Grand Officer, Military Order of Aviz, Portugal, 1919. *Address*: c/o Lloyds Bank, Ltd., Cox and King's Branch, 6 Pall Mall, S.W.1.   *Clubs*: Junior United Service; University, Dublin.
(Died 23 April 1926.)

SAYER, Dr. Ettie; Hon. Medical Officer to the Society for Distressed Gentlefolks; and Consulting Physician to the National Society for the Welfare of the Feeble-minded; *d.* of William Sayer, Bacton, Norfolk. *Educ.*: Rossell School (Mrs. Nall), Paignton, Devon; University College, London; Royal Free Hospital; Queen Charlotte's Hospital. Qualified London University (M.B., B.S., 1899); Chesterfield Medallist; Fellow of the Royal Society of Medicine; House Surgeon, Tunbridge Wells Eye and Ear Hospital, 1899; Physician to the Cowley Mission to Mohammedan and Kaffer women; Medical Officer for Plague to the Cape Colonial Government in 1901; Visited Concentration Camps during the Boer War, and later on the Lepers in Robben Island; Assistant Medical Officer, London County Council (Education Department); Lecturer on First Aid to the Injured to L.C.C. and to the Church Army Nurses; Medical Examiner to International Safety Emigration Society. Member of the Council of the Psycho-Medical Society; and the National Society for the Welfare of the Feebleminded. A Fellow of the Royal Society of Medicine, and of the American Electro-Therapeutical Society. *Publications*: Effects of Electric Currents upon Blood-Pressure; Deterioration of Vision during School Life; Morally Defective Children; Textbook for Nurses on Medical Electricity and Light. *Address*: 4 Ennismore Gardens, Knightsbridge. *T.*: Kensington 39.   *M.*: PB 6523.   *Clubs*: Lyceum, Ladies' Army and Navy.
(Died 7 July 1923.)

SAYER, Captain M. B., C.B.E., R.D., R.N.R.; Royal Naval Reserve A.D.C. 1928; Captain Superintendent, Thames Nautical Training College, H.M.S. Worcester, off Greenhithe, Kent; *s.* of Edmund Barcham Sayer of Thurlton, Norfolk; *m.* Elaine Constance, *d.* of Alfred Talbot, Seacroft, Southend-on-Sea; no *c.* *Educ.*: Mr. Lowe's, Stranraer, Bournemouth; H.M.S. Worcester. Served in Mercantile Marine, 1890-95; Colonial Office Service, Southern Nigeria Marine, 1895-1914; served on Kuno Patrol Expedition, 1912; Royal Naval Reserve, Sub-Lieut., 1903; Lieut. 1906; Lieut.-Commander, 1914; Commander, 1916; Captain, 1921; served in Navy, 1914-16, then lent to War Office for Service; Lt.-Colonel R.E.; Marine-Supt. War Office in Inland Water section, responsible for despatch of all War Office vessels to Mesopotamia; Younger Brother Trinity House, 1919; surveyed and charted Lagos Harbour and Bar, S. Nigeria, 1912. *Recreations*: yachting, golf, tennis. *Address*: H.M.S. Worcester, off Greenhithe, Kent.   *T.A.*: Worcester, Greenhithe.   *T.*: Greenhithe 39. *M.*: T 9315.   *Club*: Junior Army and Navy.
(Died 24 Dec. 1928.)

SCAFE, General Charles, Royal Marines; *b.* 1844; *s.* of late Capt. W. Scafe, Madras, N.I.; *m.* 1874, Sarah Ann, *e. d.* of G. Morris. Entered Royal Marines, 1862; Major General, 1900; Lieut.-Gen. 1902; General, 1908. *Address*: 2 Clarence Cottages, Auckland Road, West, Southsea.   *(Died 15 July 1918.)*

936

SCALES, Francis Shillington, M.A., M.D., M.B., B.Ch. (Cantab.); Univ. Lecturer in Medical Radiology and Electrology; Hon. Physician in charge of X-ray and Electrical Department, Addenbrooke's Hospital, Cambridge; Secretary for the Cambridge Diploma in Medical Radiology and Electrology; *b.* London; 3rd *s.* of George Johnston Scales, London, and Mary, 2nd *d.* of W. R. Carter, Nottingham; *m.* 1892, Marion, *y. d.* of late Thomas Shillington, J.P., of Tavanagh House, Portadown, Ireland; two *d.* *Educ.*: privately; Jesus College, Cambridge; Middlesex Hospital, London. Raymond Horton Smith Prize, University of Cambridge, 1912; Fellow of the Royal Microscopical Society (late Curator. Hon. Secretary and Vice-President); Fellow of the Cambridge Philosophical Society; Member of the Council of the British Institute of Radiology; Fellow of the Royal Society of Medicine; Member of the British Medical Association; Examiner for the Cambridge Diploma in Medical Radiology and Electrology since 1920; late Lecturer in Microscopy at Westminster Hospital. *Publications*: Elementary Microscopy, 1905; Practical Microscopy, 1909 and 1926; contributions to various scientific journals dealing with microscopy and radiology. *Recreations*: shooting, fishing, travel, books, music. *Address*: Redcourt, Adams Road, Cambridge.   *T.*: Cambridge 441.   *M.*: ER 6. *Clubs*: New University, Royal Automobile; Cambridge Union Society. *(Died 28 Feb. 1927.)*

SCANNELL, Rev. Canon Thomas Bartholomew, D.D.; theological and historical writer; *b.* London, 8 July 1854. *Educ.*: St. Edmund's College, Ware (10th in Honours, London University Matric., 1873; 1st LL.B. Honours in Jurisprudence and Roman Law); English College, Rome (B.D. 1877; D.D. 1898). Professor of Philosophy, St. Edmund's College, 1878-85; appointed by Leo. XIII. to Commission in Rome on Anglican Orders, 1896. *Publications*: Manual of Catholic Theology, 3rd ed.; Priests' Studies in the Westminster Series; articles in Catholic Dictionary, of which he is Editor; numerous articles, including those on Pastor's History of the Popes, Lamennais, Maury, De Maistre, Fénelon, Bossuet, and Rosmini, in the Dublin Review and Irish Ecclesiastical Record, etc. *Address*: St. Charles's Cottage, Weybridge.   *(Died 11 Feb. 1917.)*

SCARISBRICK, Sir Charles, Kt., *cr.* 1903; J.P.; late Mayor of Southport; *b.* 20 Apr. 1839; *m.* 1860, Bertha Petronella (*d.* 1915), *d.* of Ernest Marquard Schonfeld, of Hanau-on-Main and Dusseldorf; one *s.* two *d.* *Address*: Scarisbrick Lodge, Southport, Lancs. *Club*: Junior Carlton.   *(Died 15 Jan. 1923.)*

SCARLETT, Lieut.-Col. James Alexander, D.S.O. 1915; R.A.; *b.* 16 June 1877; *o. s.* of late Rev. G. W. Scarlett, Rossington, Yorks; *m.* 1922, Muriel, *o. d.* of Walter Blease, F.C.A., J.P., of Sefton Park, Liverpool; one *s.* Entered army, 1900; Captain, 1908; Adjt., 1913-14; Maj., 1914; Lt.-Col., 1922; served European War, 1914-18 (despatches, D.S.O.).
(Died 29 Dec. 1925.)

SCARSDALE, 4th Baron (*cr.* 1761), **Rev. Alfred Nathaniel Holden Curzon,** J.P.; Bt. 1641; Rector of Kedleston, 1856; *b.* 12 July 1831; 2nd *s.* of Hon. and Rev. Alfred Curzon, *s.* of 2nd Baron and Sophia, *d.* of R. Holden, Nuttall Temple, Nottinghamshire; *S. uncle* 1856; *m.* 1856, Blanche (*d.* 1875), *d.* of J. Pocklington-Senhouse, Netherhall, Cumberland; four *s.* six *d.* *Educ.*: Rugby; Oxford (M.A.). Owns 11,000 acres. *Heir*: *s.* Earl Curzon of Kedleston. *Address*: Kedleston, Derby.   *Clubs*: Carlton, Arthur's.   *(Died 23 Mar. 1916.)*

SCARTH, Sir Charles, Kt., *cr.* 1914; Head of the firm of Charles Scarth and Sons, Ltd.; *b.* Morley, 5 Jan. 1846; *e. s.* of Henry and

Grace Scarth; *m.* 1st, 1869, Jane (*d.* 1885), *d.* of James and Ann Pears of East Cottingwith, Yorks; two *s.* seven *d.* ; 2nd, 1887, Jessie Glendinning Watson; one *s.* two *d.* *Educ.:* locally. Has always taken a deep interest in educational work; Member of School Board for seventeen years, nine years Chairman; entered Town Council on its formation, 1885; been a member ever since; several times Mayor; Hon. Freeman of the Borough of Morley, 1903; J.P. for West Riding of Yorkshire, also for Borough of Morley; Liberal. *Address:* Scarthingwell House, Morley, Yorks. *M.:* 4078. *Club:* National Liberal.   (*Died 3 Feb. 1921.*)

SCATCHERD, Felicia Rudolphina, (Felix Rudolph); *b.* London; *d.* of Watson Scatcherd, I.C.S., and Emily Frances, *o. d.* of Rev. Augustus Crofton. Some time Editor Asiatic Review and still associated therewith as Hon. Co-Editor; Member of Council, East India Association; Life Member Sociological Society, and British Association for the advancement of Science; has travelled extensively in the Near East, and lectured on Social Science, Psychology, and the oppressed nationalities; was one of late W. T. Stead's helpers in the founding of Julia's Bureau, hailed by him and others as the M.P. for Humanity; Vice-President of the Stead Bureau, and Member of the Society for Psychical Research; Vice-President Greek Socialist Party and Greek Labour League; Delegate, International Conference of Housing and City-Planning, New York, 1925; International Psychic Congress, Paris, 1926. *Publications:* Human Radioactivity; Sir William Crookes as Psychical Researcher; articles on the Near East, Armenia, Russia, etc. ; Friends of India: Wise and Otherwise; Originator of the Literary Silhouette. *Recreations:* walking in hilly country, psychical research. *Address:* Ringmore House, Hastings; 14 Park Square (East), N.W.1; 3 Victoria Street, S.W.1. *T. :* Victoria 1201.   (*Died 12 Mar. 1927.*)

SCEBARRAS, Sir Filippo, Kt., *cr.* 1921; M.D.; *m.* 1881, Teresa Testeferrata Abela. *Address:* 70 Strada Mercato, Floriana, Malta.   (*Died 28 Aug. 1928.*)

SCHELPHAUT, Mgr. Philip, C.Ss.R.; Fifth Bishop of Roseau, Dominica, since 1902; *b.* Belgium, 27 Sep. 1850. *Educ.:* The Seminary in his native town, and The Redemptorist House of Studies at Wittem (Holland). Professed, 1873; consecrated priest, 1878; Professor of Poesy at St. Trond, Belgium, 1879-80; Superior, St. Thomas, West Indies, 1881-94; went to Montreal for 3 years on account of health; Superior at St Croix for 4 years; Superior at St. Thomas 1 year. *Publications:* founded The Ecclesiastical Bulletin of Roseau; The Dominica Chronicle. *Address:* Bishop's House, Roseau, Dominica, B.W.I.   (*Died 22 May 1921.*)

SCHIFF, Sir Ernest Frederick, Kt., *cr.* 1911; *b.* 25 Dec. 1840; *s.* of Leopold Schiff, Trieste. Founded a Convalescent Home; Knight of Imperial Austrian Order of Iron Crown; Commander Order of Francis Joseph, with the Star; Knight of Grace of the Order of St. John of Jerusalem. *Address:* 1 Carlos Place, W. *T. :* Gerrard 3354. *Club:* Devonshire.   (*Died 5 Nov. 1918.*)

SCHINDLER, Gen. Sir A. Houtum, C.I.E.; General in the Persian Army. *Publication:* Eastern Persian Irak. *Address:* Teheran, Persia.   (*Died 15 June 1916.*)

SCHLESWIG-HOLSTEIN, H.R.H. Gen. Prince Frederick Christian Charles Augustus of, K.G., P.C., G.C.V.O.; High Steward of Windsor; *b.* 22 Jan. 1881; *m.* 1866, H.R.H. Princess Helena, 3rd *d.* of Queen Victoria; A.D.C. to the King; Colonel 3rd Batt. Royal Berkshire Regiment; D.C.L., Oxford, 1910; Ranger of Windsor Great Park. *Address:* Cumberland Lodge, Windsor Park; Schomberg House, Pall Mall, S.W.   (*Died 28 Oct. 1917.*)

SCHLETTER, Colonel Percy, C.B. 1902; late the King's Liverpool Regiment; *b.* 4 Aug. 1855; *m.* 1896, Edith M., *d.* of late W. Eills; one *d.* Entered army, 1874; Captain, 1882; Major, 1891; Lieutenant-Colonel, 1900; Colonel, 1904; served Afghan War, 1878-80 (medal); South Africa (medal, clasps, despatches, and C.B.), 1900-1902; European War, France and Italy, 1917-19 (despatches twice). *Club:* Junior United Service.(*Died 26 Aug. 1922.*)

SCHLICH, Sir William, K.C.I.E., *cr.* 1909; Ph.D. 1867; F.R.S. 1901; M.A. Oxon 1905; Professor of Forestry, University of Oxford, 1905; retired, 1919; *b.* 1840; *s.* of late Kirchenrath Schlich, Hesse-Darmstadt; naturalised in England, 1886; *m.* 1st, 1874, Mary Margaret (*d.* 1878), *d.* of William Smith, C.E.; 2nd, 1886, Mathilde, *d.* of late Herman Marsily; one *s.* four *d.* *Educ.:* Darmstadt: University of Giessen. Appointed to the Indian Forest Department, 1866; Conservator of Forests, 1870; Inspector-General of Forests to the Government of India, 1881; organised the first School of Forestry in England at Coopers Hill, 1885; transferred to Oxford University, 1905. *Publications:* A Manual of Forestry, in 5 volumes; The Outlook of the World's Timber Supply; Afforestation in Great Britain and Ireland; Forestry in the United Kingdom, three editions. *Address:* 29 Banbury Road, Oxford.

    (*Died 28 Sept. 1925.*)

SCHOLDER, Dr. Charles Albert, Directeur-propriétaire de l'Institut médico-mécanique et orthopédique de Lausanne (Suisse); né le 26 mai 1861 à Zurich. *Educ.:* aux universités de Zurich, Berne, Vienne, Berlin. Docteur et médecin diplômé de l'université de Zurich. Assistant d'anatomie, de médecine interne et de chirurgie à Zurich; fait deux voyages aux Indes; au retour assistant à la clinique chirurgicale universitaire de Berne. Pratiqué la médecine générale pendant 6 ans, puis fondé l'Institut médico-mécanique et orthopédique de Lausanne après études spéciales faites en Suède; inventé l'Arthromoteur, machine pour déraidir les articulations ankylosées et une machine pour traitement de la Scoliose. *Publications:* Dissertation inaugurale; La traitement médico-mécanique; L'arthromoteur; Les Déviations de la colonne vertébrale dans les Ecoles de Lausanne (avec les Dr. Weith et Combe). *Address:* Boulevard de Grancy No. 39, Lausanne (Suisse) *T. A.:* Scholder, Lausanne. *T.:* 751.

    (*Died Aug. 1913.*)

SCHOOLING, John Holt; Actuary, Statistician, and Author; *b.* London, 25 March 1859; *s.* of late Henry Schooling and Harriet Maria Holt; *g.s.* of Captain John Schooling, H.A.C.; *g.-g.s.* of James Schooling, London; *m.* Jessie Ellen Sanders; one *s.* one *d.* *Educ.:* Elizabeth College, Guernsey. Fellow of the Royal Statistical Society; Associate of the Institute of Actuaries; Consulting Actuary to various assurance bodies; formerly Chairman of the Richmond Surrey Division of the National Service League; strongly in favour of Tariff Reform. *Publications:* The British Trade Book; Mr. Chamberlain's Proposal; Local Rates and Taxes; London County Council Finance; A Peep into Punch; contributed to Nineteenth Century, Fortnightly Review, Monthly Review, National Review, Morning Post, Pall Mall Gazette, etc., mainly on economic subjects, and to Pall Mall Magazine, Strand Magazine, etc., on miscellaneous subjects; short stories in English Illustrated Magazine, The Sketch, etc. *Recreations:* fishing, music, chess, lathe and bench work. *Address:* 19 Linton Road, Hastings.   (*Died 14 July 1927.*)

SCHREIBER, Sir Collingwood, K.C.M.G., *cr.* 1916; C.M.G. 1893; C.E.; General Consulting Engineer to the Government of Canada, and Chief Engineer of the Western Division of the National Transcontinental Railway since 1905; *b.* Essex, 14 Dec. 1831; *s.* of late Rev. Thomas Schreiber of Bradwell Lodge, Essex, and Sarah, *d.* of Adm. Bingham; *m.* 1st, Caroline (*d.* 1892), *d.* of late Col. Allan Maclean, 41st Foot; four *d.*; 2nd, 1898, Julia Maud, *d.* of late Mr. Justice Gwynne. Went to Canada 1852; Assistant Engineer, Hamilton & Toronto Railway, 1852-1855; in private practice in the firm of Fleming, Ridout, and Schreiber, Civil Engineers, Toronto, 1855-60; Supt. Engineer Northern Railway, 1860-62; Chief Engineer of Govt. Railways in operation, 1873; Chief Engineer of Canadian Pacific Railway, 1880; Deputy Minister and Chief Engineer, Railways and Canals, Canada, 1893-1905. *Address:* 192 Argyle Avenue, Ottawa. *Clubs:* Rideau, Golf and Country, Ottawa.
(*Died 20 Mar. 1918.*)

SCHREINER, Olive (Mrs. S. C. Cronwright Schreiner) (pseudonym **Ralph Iron**), author; *b.* in Basutoland; *d.* of late Rev. G. Schreiner, who was a missionary sent out by the London Missionary Society; her mother was Rebecca Lyndall of London; *m.* 1894, S. C. Cronwright. *Publications:* The Story of an African Farm; Dreams; Dream Life and Real Life; Trooper Peter Halket of Mashonaland, 1897; An English South African's View of the Situation, 1899; Women and Labour, 1911; also (jointly with her husband) The Political Situation, 1895. *Address:* De Aar, Cape Colony. (*Died Dec. 1920.*)

SCHREINER, Rt. Hon. William Philip, P.C. 1917; K.C.,C.M.G. 1891; politician and barrister; High Commissioner for Union of S. Africa in England, 1914; *b.* Cape Colony, 1857; *bro.* to Olive Schreiner; *m.* 1884, Frances Hester, *sister* of ex-Pres. Reitz of Orange Free State. *Educ.:* Cape Univ. (Univ. and Porter Scholarships, 1877); Lond. Univ. and Downing Coll. Cambridge (Fellow). Senior in Law Tripos and Chancellor's Legal Medal, 1881; Senior Studentship Inns of Court, 1880; Bar Inner Temple, 1882; Parliamentary Draftsman, 1885-1891; Legal Adviser to High Commissioner, 1887-93; Member of Mr. Rhodes's second ministry, 1893; twice Attorney-General; delegate at various conferences between Cape and other S.A. States and Colonies regarding railways and customs; witness before British South Africa Committee of House of Commons, 1897; sat in Legislative Assembly for Kimberley, 1893; Barkly West, 1894-98; Malmesbury, 1898-1900; Queenstown, 1908-14; Senator South African Union, 1910-14; Prime Minister of Cape Colony, 1898-1900. *Recreation:* golf. *Address:* 32 Victoria Street, S.W. *Clubs:* Civil Service, Cape Town; Kimberley. (*Died 28 June 1919.*)

SCHÜDDEKOPF, Albert Wilhelm, Ph.D., M.A. (Göttingen); Professor of German Language and Literature at the University of Leeds; Examiner in German in various Universities; *b.* Göttingen, 19 Nov. 1861; *m. d.* of late Wilhelm Blau, Berlin; one *s. Educ.:* Gymnasium and University of Göttingen. Staatsexamen 1887; Professor of German at Bedford College, London, 1888; Lecturer in German at Yorkshire College, Leeds, 1890; Professor of German at Yorkshire College, 1897; Dean of the Faculty of Arts and Member of the University Council, 1912-14. *Publications:* Sprache und Dialekt des me. Gedichtes William of Palerne, 1886; Ancient German Glass in Wragby Church (Yorkshire Arch. Journal); many literary articles in the Literarische Echo, etc. *Recreations:* music, foreign travel. *Address:* 32 Springfield Mount, Leeds. *T.:* Central 180. (*Died 11 Sept. 1916.*)

SCHULER, Gottlieb Frederick Henry, Editor, Age, Melbourne, since 1900; *b.* Stuttgart, Germany, 26 Feb. 1854; *m.* Sarah, *d.* of Richard Strahan, of Dublin, Ireland; two *d. Educ.:* privately. Arrived with parents in Melbourne, 1860; joined Age literary staff, 1877; has remained continuously on active service of that journal. *Recreations:* painting, music. *Address:* Age Office, Melbourne.
(*Died 11 Dec. 1926.*)

SCHUSTER, Ernest Joseph, Barrister-at-Law since 1890; K.C. 1922; *b.* 7 July 1850; *e. s.* of Francis Joseph Schuster, London; *m.* 1876, Hilda, *e. d.* of Sir Hermann Weber, M.D.; two *s. Educ.:* Frankfort; Geneva; Doctor of Laws in the University of Munich. A managing partner in firm of Schuster, Son & Co. of Cannon Street, E.C., 1873-88; Member of Executive of Society of Comparative Legislation; Member of Council of International Law Association; has lectured for Institute of Bankers and for School of Economics and Political Science. *Publications:* The Principles of German Civil Law; The Wife in Ancient and Modern Times; The Effect of War on Commercial Transactions; numerous contributions to legal and other periodicals, and to Palgrave's Dictionary of Political Economy. *Recreations:* formerly cycling and rowing; now walking. *Address:* 33 Albert Court, S.W.7. *T.:* Western 513. *Club:* Savile.
(*Died 16 Dec. 1924.*)

SCHWAB, John Christopher, Professor of Political Economy, Yale, 1898-1905; Librarian, Yale, 1905; *b.* New York, 1865; *s.* of Gustav Schwab and Catherine Elizabeth von Post; *m.* 1898, Edith A. Fisher. *Educ.:* Yale; Berlin University; Göttingen University (Ph.D.). Editor of Yale Review, 1892-1911. *Publications:* History of New York Property Tax, 1890; The Confederate States of America, 1901; various articles in historical reviews and magazines. *Address:* 310 Prospect Street, New Haven, Conn. *Clubs:* Century, New York; Graduates', New Haven. (*Died 12 Jan. 1916.*)

SCHWARZ, Ernest H. L., A.R.C.S., F.G.S.; Professor of Geology, Rhodes University College, Grahamstown, since 1905; *b.* 27 Feb. 1873; *s.* of F. M. Schwarz, Basinghall Street, South American merchant; *m.* Daisy Murray Bowen, *d.* of J. C. O'Halloran, late of the Colonial Service; no *c. Educ.:* Westminster; Royal College of Science, London. Went to Johannesburg, 1895; editor Scientific African; joined Geological Survey of Cape Colony, 1896; with Dr. A. W. Rogers, carried out first Systematic Geological Survey of South Africa. *Publications:* Causal Geology; Handbook of South African Geology; South African Geography; The Kalahari, or Thirstland Redemption; Brendavale; articles in Geographical Journal, Geological Magazine, Quarterly Journal Geological Society, Science Progress, Annals and Mag. Natural History, Journal of Geology, American Journal of Science, Records Albany Museum, etc. *Recreations:* tennis, driving. *Club:* Authors'. (*Died 19 Dec. 1928.*)

SCLATER, Lady; Edith (Harriet), D.B.E., *cr.* 1918; *d.* of late Sir Walter Barttelot, 1st Bart.; *m.* 1884, General Sir Henry Crichton Sclater (*d.* 1923). *Address:* 2 Ovington Gardens, S.W.3. (*Died 29 Mar. 1927.*)

SCLATER, General Sir Henry Crichton, G.C.B., *cr.* 1916; G.B.E., *cr.* 1919; K.C.B., *cr.* 1913; C.B. 1902; Col. Commandant, R.A.; *b.* 5 Nov. 1855; *s.* of late James Henry Sclater of Newick Park, Sussex; *m.* 1884, Edith Harriet, D.B.E., *d.* of late Sir Walter Barttelot, 1st Bart. *Educ.:* Cheltenham. Entered army, 1875; Captain, 1883; Brevet Major, 1885; Lieut.-Col. 1900; General 1919; served Nile Expedition, 1884-85, as staff-officer, and afterwards as D.A.A.G. at headquarters (despatches, brevet of Major, medal with clasp, Khedive's star);

Egyptian Frontier Field Force, 1885 - 86; D.A.A.G., Cairo, 1885-90; South Africa, 1899-1902, as A.A.G. for R.A., and Col. on Staff for R.A. (despatches thrice, Brevet Colonel, Queen's medal 6 clasps, King's medal 2 clasps, C.B.); Director of Artillery, War Office, 1903-4; Quarter-Master General in India, 1904-8; commanded Quetta Division, 1908 - 12; G.O.C. - in - Chief Southern Command, 1916-19; Adjutant-General to the Forces and Member of H.M.'s Army Council, 1914-16; retired pay, 1922. *Address:* Holmwood, Edenbridge, Kent.(*Died 26 Sept.1923.*)

SCOBELL, Ven. Edward Chessall, M.A.; Archdeacon of Gloucester since 1908; Residentiary Canon of Gloucester since 1912; Examining Chaplain to the Bishops of Gloucester since 1888; *b.* 27 Jan. 1850; *s.* of Rev. S. G. Scobell, Vicar of Market Rasen; *m.* 1879, Dora M., *d.* of C. Sumner, Judge of County Court. *Educ.:* Marlborough; Pembroke Coll. Oxford (second class, Theology). Deacon, 1873; Curate, Horsham, 1873-77; Curate, St. Luke's, Gloucester; Lecturer Gloucester Theological Coll., 1877-81; Vicar, St. Luke's, Gloucester, 1881-89; Rector of Upton St. Leonards, 1889-1912; Rural Dean of Gloucester, 1890-1908; Hon. Canon, 1895-1912; Governor Gloucester Endowed Schools, 1901; member of Gloucestershire Education Committee; Sec. Gloucester Diocesan Conference, 1890-92. *Publications:* sermons, addresses, etc. *Recreations:* travel, Swiss mountain climbing, cycling. *Address:* 7 College Green, Gloucester. *Clubs:* New Oxford and Cambridge; Gloucester.

(*Died 8 Feb. 1917.*)

S C O B L E, Right Hon. Sir Andrew Richard, K.C.; K.C.S.I., *cr.* 1890; P.C.; *b.* London, 25 Sept. 1831; 2nd *s.* of John Scoble, Kingsbridge, Devon sometime member Provincial Parliament of Canada; *m.* 1868, Augusta Harriette, *o. d.* of Joseph Nicholson. *Educ.:* City of London School. Barr. Lincoln's Inn, 1856; Advocate-General, and Member of Legislative Council, Bombay, 1872-77; Q.C. 1876; Member Council of the Gov.-Gen. of India, 1886-1891; Treasurer of Hon. Society of Lincoln's Inn, 1899; M.P. (C.) Hackney, Central Div., 1892-1900; Member of Judicial Committee of Privy Council, 1901. *Publications:* translations of Mignet's History of Mary Queen of Scots, Guizot's History of the English Revolution, and other works. *Address:* Chivelston, Wimbledon Common. *Clubs:* Athenæum, Carlton.

(*Died 17 Jan. 1916.*)

SCOTT, Alexander MacCallum, M.A., Barrister-at-law; *b.* Boathouse, Blantyre, 16 June 1874; 3rd *s.* of late John Scott, of Millhill, Polmont; *m.* 1910, Jessie, *e. d.* of Dr. John Hutchison, ex-Rector of the Glasgow High School; one *s. Educ.:* Polmont Public School; Falkirk High School; Glasgow University. President of the Union, Glasgow University, 1896-97; graduated, 1897; engaged in journalistic and political work in London; Secretary League of Liberals against Aggression and Militarism, 1900-3; Secy. New Reform Club, 1903-6; Member of Lewisham Borough Council, 1903-6; called to Bar, Middle Temple, 1908; Private Secy. to Lord Pentland; Secretary for Scotland, 1909-10; Member of the Speaker's Committee on Electoral Reform, 1916-17; Parliamentary Private Secretary to Mr. Churchill, Minister of Munitions, 1917-19; to Mr. Churchill, Secretary of State for War, 1919; Member of Interim Forest Authority, 1918; Coalition Liberal Whip for Scotland, 1922; M.P. (L.) Glasgow (Bridgeton) 1910-22; joined Labour party, 1924; made frequent visits to Russia and Finland. *Publications:* Winston Spencer Churchill, a Biography, 1905; The Truth about Tibet, 1905; Through Finland to St. Petersburg, 1908; Licensing in Scandinavia, 1908; Winston Churchill in Peace and War, 1916; Barbary, 1921; Bits of Chelsea, 1922;

Clydesdale, 1924; Beyond the Baltic, 1925; Suomi, the Land of the Finns, 1926. *Recreations:* walking, cycling, Northern travel. *Address:* 13 Wellington Square, Chelsea, S.W.3. *Clubs:* Devonshire, Savage, Whitefriars.

(*Died 25 Aug. 1928.*)

SCOTT, Arthur William, M.A.; Phillips Professor (Science), St. David's College, Lampeter, since 1872; *b.* Dublin, 1846; *s.* of late David Scott, Dublin. *Educ.:* Trinity College, Dublin. B.A. 1868; Senior Moderator and Gold Medallist in Mathematics, and Senior Moderator and Gold Medallist in Experimental and Natural Science; M.A. 1872; Fellow of the Physical Society of London; Fellow of the American Association for the Advancement of Science; Mayor of Lampeter, 1910-11; Fellow of the Institute of Physics. *Recreation:* travelling. *Address:* St. David's College, Lampeter. *Club:* St. Stephen's. (*Died 7 Mar. 1927.*)

SCOTT, Ven. Avison Terry, Archdeacon of Tonbridge since 1906; Vicar of St. James', Tunbridge Wells, since 1886; *b.* 18 July 1848; *s.* of late Rev. Canon Scott, Vicar of Wisbech, Cambs; *m.* 1874, Dora, *d.* of late Rev. R. H. Tillard, Rector of Blakeney, Norfolk; four *s.* two *d. Educ.:* Trinity College, Cambridge; M.A. Curate of Swaffham, 1871-73; Wimbledon, 1873-79; Vicar of Christ Church, Bootle, 1879-1886; Hon. Canon of Canterbury Cathedral, 1904; Rural Dean of Tunbridge Wells, 1894. *Address:* St. James' Vicarage, Tunbridge Wells. *T.:* Tunbridge Wells 518. (*Died 18 June 1925.*)

SCOTT, Sir Basil, Kt., *cr.* 1909; M.A.; *b.* June 1859; 2nd *s.* of late Henry Scott of Bombay; *m.* 1914, Gertrude Gwendoline, *d.* of late H. W. Villiers-Stuart, J.P., D.L., Dromana, Co. Waterford; two *s. Educ.:* Haileybury; Balliol College, Oxford. Called to Bar, 1883; admitted Advocate of High Court, Bombay, 1885; Acting Advocate-General of Bombay, 1899; Advocate-General of Bombay, 1900-8; Chief Justice of Bombay, 1908-1919. *Club:* New University.

(*Died 1 May 1926.*)

SCOTT, Sir Benjamin, Kt., *cr.* 1904; J.P. City of Carlisle and County of Cumberland; *b.* Carlisle, 1841; *e. s.* of late Hudson Scott of Carlisle; *m.* 1874, Sarah, *d.* of late Joseph Hope of Whooff House, Cumberland; one *d. Educ.:* Society of Friends' School, Wigton. Mayor of Carlisle, 1885, 1891, 1892, 1902, 1911, and 1912. *Address:* Linden House, Stanwix, Carlisle. *T.A.:* Stanwix, Carlisle. *T.:* Carlisle 24.

(*Died 10 July 1927.*)

SCOTT, Col. Bertal Hopton, C.M.G. 1917; late A.M.S.; *b.* 12 Aug. 1863; *s.* of late Rev. G. H. Scott and Frances S. Armstrong; *m.* 1898, Hilda A., *d.* of late C. Hamilton Jackson, formerly Administrator-General, Jamaica; two *s. Educ.:* Cholmeley School, Highgate; Trinity College, Toronto; London Hospital. Surgeon, M.S., 1887; Maj. 1889; Lt.-Col. 1911; Col. 1915; D.A.D.G.; A.M.S. 1910-14; Assist. Director of Medical Services, 1915; served Chitral, 1895 (medal with clasp); Sierra Leone, 1898 - 99 (severely wounded, medal with clasp); European War, 1914-17 (despatches thrice, C.M.G.); *Address:* 29 Amherst Road, Ealing, W.

(*Died 24 Oct. 1926.*)

SCOTT, Charles Clare, K.C. 1910; Bencher of the Middle Temple, 1898; Treasurer, 1920; *b.* 2 Sep. 1850; *e. s.* of late John Scott, Inspector - General of Hospitals, Bombay; unmarried. *Educ.:* Rugby; King's College, London; Wren's; Student of the Middle Temple, 1871. Called to Bar, 1874; joined the Home (now South-Eastern) Circuit. *Address:* 69 Inverness Terrace, W.2. *T.:* Central 1240.

(*Died 4 May 1925.*)

SCOTT, Maj.-Gen. Sir Charles Henry, K.C.B., *cr.* 1909; C.B. 1898; Col.-Commandant R.A.; *b.* 15 June 1848; *s.* of late Edward

939

John Scott of Portland Lodge, Southsea; *m.* 1872, Frances (*d.* 1889), *d.* of Gen. J. G. Halliday; two *s.* two *d.* *Educ.:* privately; Woolwich. Entered R.A. 1868; became Captain, 1879; Major, 1885; Lieutenant-Colonel, 1892; Col. 1896; Maj.-Gen. 1902; retired 1910; served with Tirah Expedition, 1897-98, including capture of Sampagha and Arhunga Passes, and Bazar Valley Expedition (despatches, C.B., medal, 2 clasps); was Superintendent, Gunpowder Factory Bengal, 1881-92; Ordnance Consulting Officer for India, 1892-95; Dep. Director-Gen. of Ordnance, 1895; Inspector-Gen. of Ordnance, India, 1895-1900; Ordnance Consulting Officer for India (2nd time), April 1900-1902; Director-General of Ordnance in India, 1902-5; Member of Council of Governor-General of India, 1905-9. *Decorated* for service with the Tirah Expeditionary Force. *Address:* Colleens, Cousley Wood, Wadhurst. *Club:* United Service. (*Died 6 Oct. 1919.*)

SCOTT, Rt. Rev. Charles Perry, D.D.; *b.* 1847; *s.* of Rev. J. Scott, Hull; *m.* 1889, Frances (*d.* 1900), *d.* of late Capt. Montagu Burrows, M.A., Chichele Professor of Modern History, Oxford. *Educ.:* Charterhouse; Jesus College, Cambridge (B.A.). Ordained, 1870; Missionary at Chefoo, 1874-80; Bishop in North China, 1880-1913. *Address:* Chung Te School, Pekin, N. China. (*Died 13 Feb. 1927.*)

SCOTT, Rt. Hon. Sir Charles (Stewart), P.C. 1898; G.C.B., *cr.* 1899; G.C.M.G., *cr.* 1899; K.C.M.G., *cr.* 1896; C.B.; *b.* Ireland, 17 Mar. 1838; 4th *s.* of late Major Thomas Scott, Willsborough, Co. Londonderry, and second wife Ann, *d.* of Rev. E. Lucas, Coote Hill, Co. Monaghan; *m.* 1875, Christian Crauford (*d.* 1922), *d.* of James Macknight, W.S., Edinburgh; one *s.* four *d.* *Educ.:* Cheltenham College; Trinity College, Dublin. Entered Diplomatic Service, Dec. 1858; employed as Attaché at Paris, Dresden, and Copenhagen; 3rd Secretary, Madrid, 1865; 2nd Secretary, Mexico, 1866; subsequently at Lisbon, Stuttgart, Munich, Vienna, St. Petersburg, and Darmstadt, 1879; appointed Secretary of Legation and Chargé d'Affaires, Coburg, 1879, also accredited to Prince of Waldeck, 1883; Secretary of Embassy, Berlin, where he was repeatedly acting Chargé d'Affaires; created C.B. 1886; appointed Envoy Extraordinary and Minister Plenipotentiary to Swiss Confederation, 1888; 2nd Plenipotentiary to Samoan and Labour Conferences, Berlin, 1889, 1890; Envoy Extraordinary at Copenhagen, 1893-98; H.M. Ambassador to the Court of Russia, St. Petersburg, 1898-1904; Hon. LL.D. Trinity College, Dublin, 1898. *Address:* Glengair, Rosneath, Scotland. (*Died 26 April 1924.*)

SCOTT, Hon. David Lynch, K.C.; Chief Justice of the Appellate Division, Supreme Court of Alberta, and Chief Justice of Alberta since 1921; *b.* 21 Aug. 1845; *m.* 1883, Mary, *d.* of Thomas M'Vittie; two *s.* two *d.* *Educ.:* Brampton Grammar School. Barrister, 1870; Mayor of Regina, 1883; K.C. 1885; raised to Bench, N.W.T., 1894. *Address:* 9825 106th Street, Edmonton, Alberta, Canada. *T.:* 1979. *Club:* Edmonton. (*Died 26 July 1924.*)

SCOTT, Maj.-Gen. Douglas Alexander, C.V.O. 1901; C.B. 1897; D.S.O. 1886; F.G.S.; *b.* 14 Dec. 1848; *s.* of late John Scott, M.D.; *m.* 1894. Mary (*d.* 1918), *d.* of late Capt. C. B. Cardew, 74th Highlanders, and late Hon. Mrs. Cardew (*d.* of 1st Baron Westbury), East Hill, Liss; one *s.* two *d.* *Educ.:* Milton Abbas Grammar School; R.M.A., Woolwich. Deputy Consulting Engineer to Government of India for Guaranteed Railways, 1876-77; in charge of Royal train on Govt. Railways on occasion of Prince of Wales's visit to India, 1876 (received thanks of Govt. of India); Afghan War, 1878-80 (medal); Egyptian Campaign, 1882 (despatches,

940

medal, bronze star, brevet of Maj.); Director of Railways Soudan Expedition, 1884-85 (despatches, clasp, brevet Lieut.-Colonel); Soudan, 1885-86, D.A.A. and Q.M.G. (despatches, D.S.O.); Colonel, 1889; A. A.-Gen. R.E. Head Quarters, 1894-99; C.R.E. Southern District, 1899-1902; Maj.-Gen. on the Staff, C.R.E., II. A.C. 1902-4; Chief Engineer, Southern Command, 1904-5; Hon. Col. Engineer and Railway Staff Corps; Commanded Eastern Coast Defences, 1906-9; Colonel Commandant Royal Engineers, 1921. *Recreations:* golf, music, cycling. *Club:* Army and Navy. (*Died 4 Feb. 1924.*)

SCOTT, Edward John Long, M.A., D. Litt. Oxon., M.R.A.S.; late Keeper of MSS. and Egerton Librarian, British Museum; now Keeper of Muniments at Westminster Abbey; *b.* Bridgwater, 11 April 1840; 2nd *s.* of late George H. C. Scott, Rector of Rhôs-Crowther, co. Pembroke, and Mary Favell Dehany, Jamaica; *m.* 1869, Anna F. K., *o. d.* of Edward T. Donoghue; three *s.* two *d.* *Educ.:* Marlborough; Lincoln Coll. Oxford; Classical Scholar, 1859; Senior Exhibitioner, Goldsmith Company, 1861; Boden Sanskrit Scholar, 1862; in College eight and eleven; B.A. 1862; M.A. 1866; D. Litt. 1902. Assistant MSS. Department, British Museum, 1868; Assistant Keeper, 1879; Keeper, 1888. *Publications:* Introduction to Reprint of Eikon Basilike, 1880; The Eclogues of Virgil, translated into English verse, 1884; Letter-Book of Gabriel Harvey, edited for Camden Society, 1884; Private Diary of Shakespeare's Cousin, Thos. Greene, Town-Clerk of Stratford-upon-Avon, 1885; Records of Harrow School, 1886; William Harvey's Original Lectures on the Circulation of the Blood, 1886; The Eclogues of Calpurnius, translated into English verse, 1890. *Recreations:* bridge, gold. *Address:* 37 Culverden Road, Balham, S.W. *Club:* United Sports. (*Died 19 May 1918.*)

SCOTT, Lt.-Col. George John, D.S.O. 1900; *b.* 7 May 1858; *m.* 1886, Mary Ethel (*d.* 1906), *d.* of J. F. Christy, J.P., of Upton, Alresford, Hants. *Educ.:* Marlborough. Joined Shropshire Militia, 1875; Sub.-Lt. 2nd Dragoon Guards, 1879; served with 7th Dragoon Guards in Egypt, 1882 (medal with clasp, Tel-el-Kebir, and Khedive's star); exchanged to 18th Hussars 1885; retired, 1889; served with 19th Batt. Imperial Yeomanry in South Africa, 1900-1 (medal 2 clasps, despatches, D.S.O.); City of London Yeomanry, 1901-13; 3rd Middlesex Yeomanry, 1915-16. *Recreations:* shooting, fishing. *Clubs:* Cavalry, Marlborough. (*Died 4 May 1925.*)

SCOTT, Sir James, Kt., *cr.* 1911; engineer; *b.* Broughty Ferry, 11 Nov. 1838; *s.* of David Scott; *m.* 1862, Jeannie, *d.* of Robert Brough; five *s.* one *d.* *Educ.:* Broughty Ferry. Trained a mechanical engineer at Monifieth; six years in Royal Gun Factories, Woolwich; ten years Manager of the Paragon Works, S. Queensferry, and for last forty years Prospector of the Tayport Engine Works; a member of the Engineers' and Shipbuilders' Association in Scotland; a Fellow of the Society of Antiquaries of Scotland; twice elected Provost of Tayport; a J.P. for the county, and member of the St. Andrews Licensing Bench. *Address:* Rock Knowe, Tayport, Scotland. *T.A.:* Scott, Tayport. *M.:* SP 194. *Club:* Liberal, Dundee. (*Died 12 May 1925.*)

SCOTT, James, I.S.O. 1905; *b.* 11 Oct. 1850. Student Interpreter, China, 1872; 1st Class Assistant, 1886; Vice-Consul in charge of shipping business, Shanghai, 1892; Senior Vice-Consul, 1893; Consul, Chin Kiang, 1898; Swatow, 1899; Consul-General, Canton, 1902-6. *Publications:* English-Corean Vocabulary; Corean Manual for Students. *Address:* 54 Birch Grove, West Acton, W.3. (*Died 10 May 1920.*)

SCOTT, Sir John, 2nd Bt., *cr.* 1907; Proprietor of Tyne Brass and Tube Manufactur. Co., Jarrow; Member Walter Scott and Middleton, Ltd., Contractors, and of the Walter Scott Publishing Co., Ltd.; *b.* 23 Aug. 1854; *s.* of 1st Bt. and Ann, *d.* of John Brough of Branfield, Cumberland; *S.* father 1910; *m.* 1st, 1882, Elizabeth (*d.* 1911), *d.* of Mark Garbutt, of Saltburn; no *c.*; 2nd, 1919, Emily, *d.* of late Thomas Cotes, Benwell, Darlington. *Heir: n.* Walter, Lieut. A.S.C. [*b.* 31 March 1895; *m.* 1915, Mancie Margaret (Margot), *d.* of Samuel Herbert March, Châlet du Parc, Cannes]. *Address:* Danby Lodge, Darlington.   (*Died 29 April 1922.*)

SCOTT, John, R.I. *Address:* 47A Stanley Gardens, Belsize Grove, Haverstock Hill, N.W.   (*Died 1919.*)

SCOTT, John Halliday, M.D., M.R.C.S.; Professor of Anatomy, Otago University, since 1877; Dean of the Faculty of Medicine; *b.* Edinburgh. *Educ. :* Edinburgh Institution and University. *Address:* Garfield Street, Roslyn, Australia.   (*Died 25 Feb 1914.*)

SCOTT, John Healey; Chief Magistrate, East Griqualand; *b.* Gravesend, Kent, 23 May 1843; *s.* of Rev. George Scott, Wesleyan Minister; *m.* 1870, Elizabeth Ann, *d.* of Rev. George H. Green, Wesleyan Minister. *Educ. :* Grammar School, Preston, Lancashire. With Messrs. H. Pooley & Sons, weighing-machine makers, 1857; emigrated to South Africa, 1859; engaged as farm tutor and teacher of Wesleyan Mission schools; Wesleyan Minister, 1867-76; entered Government Service as Magistrate with Bacela, 1876; served in Gealeka War and Northern Border War, 1878-80; retired on pension, 1902. *Recreation :* mechanics. *Address:* Kokstad, East Griqualand. *Club:* Kokstad.   (*Died Jan. 1925.*)

SCOTT, Commander John Wilfred, D.S.O. 1919; R.N., retired; *s.* of late Ven. Avison Terry Scott; *b.* 1881; *m.* Primrose Helen, *d.* of late Robert Turner; one *s. Educ. :* H.M.S. Britannia. Served European War, 1914-19 (despatches, D.S.O.); retired list, 1924. *Address:* St. James' Vicarage, Tunbridge Wells. *T. :* 518. *M. :* KK 5963.   (*Died 8 Aug. 1926.*)

SCOTT, Dr. Kenneth, M.D., C.M.. F.R.C.S. (Edin.), M.R.C.S.(Eng.); Consulting Ophthalmic Surgeon, St. Mary's Hospital for Women and Children, E.; Medical Officer, City of London Branch, British Red Cross Society; *b.* Morton, Bingley, Yorkshire; *s.* of Thomas Graham Scott, Edinburgh, and Ann, *d.* of James Whitley, Morton, Bingley; widower; no *c. Educ. :* Edinburgh Academy; University of Edinburgh; King's College, London. Graduated Edinburgh University, with Honours in Final, 1887; Lecturer, and Professor later, of Ophthalmology, Egyptian Government Medical School, Cairo; and Ophthalmic Surgeon, Kasr-el-Aïni Hospital, Cairo, Egypt, 1889-99; Lecturer on Ophthalmology, West London Post-graduate College, 1907-9; Organiser and Hon. Secretary, Cairo Blind School, 1900-6; Membre de l'Association Valentin Haüy pour le Bien des Aveugles, Paris. *Publications:* Refraction and Visual Acuity; numerous articles and contributions on ophthalmic work. *Recreations:* water-colour painting, gardening. *Address:* 7 Manchester Square, W. *T. :* Mayfair 487.   (*Died 19 Feb. 1918.*)

SCOTT, Lieut.-Col. Lothian Kerr, C.B. 1897; late R.E.; *b.* 24 May 1841; *s.* of George Scott, formerly of Glendowran, Lanarkshire; mother, *d.* of General Graham, Governor of Arcot; *m.* A. H., *d.* of G. A. Anstey; two *s. Educ. :* Winchester for seven years, which he joined at the age of 9½ years. Entered the R. M. Academy by competition and obtained comm. in the R.E.; joined at Chatham, 1862; served at the Curragh till 1868; volunteered for service in India, and was employed in the public works, railways and irrigation; was invalided in 1869; returned, 1871; invalided again; joined at Dover; musketry instructor Chatham till 1877; instructor in fortifications, Sandhurst, till 1882; Prof. of fortifications and artillery, 1882-89; inspector of telescopic sights, and instructor to the R.A. in artillery sights, 1889-91; made many inventions relating to improvement in the shooting of artillery. In 1872 invented telescopic sight which was adopted for all our guns; invented automatic sights in 1878; has taken out several patents for various improvements relating to the service; retired from the service on account of ill-health. *Decorated* for services regarding telescopic sights. *Recreations:* cricket (capt. of cricket at the R.M.C.); represented his Corps for years in racquet matches *v.* R.A.; boating, skating, hunting, shooting. *Address:* Forest Lodge, Farnboro, Hants. *Club :* Junior United Service.   (*Died 7 July 1919.*)

SCOTT, Margaret; *m.* Colonel Courtenay Scott; *b.* 1841; maiden name, Colquhoun. *Publications:* Every Inch a Soldier; Invasion of India from Central Asia; Under Orders; Primus in Indis. *Address:* Pennant Hall, Abermule, R.S.O., Montgomeryshire.   (*Died 14 Sept. 1917.*)

SCOTT, Hon. Mrs. Maxwell (Mary Monica); *b.* 2 Oct. 1852; *d.* of late J. R. Hope Scott, Q.C., and Charlotte Harriet Jane Lockhart, *d.* of John Gibson Lockhart; *g. g. d.* of Sir Walter Scott; *m.* Hon. Joseph Constable-Maxwell, 3rd *s.* of Baron Herries of Terregles, 1874; three *s.* one *d. Publications:* The Tragedy of Fotheringay, 1895; Abbotsford and its Treasures, 1893; The Making of Abbotsford, and Incidents in Scottish History, 1897; Henry Schomberg Kerr, Sailor and Jesuit, 1901; Joan of Arc, 1905; Garcia Moreno; Madame Elizabeth de France, 1908; Madame de La Rochejacquelin, 1911; St. Francis de Sales and his Friends, 1913. *Address:* Abbotsford, Melrose, Roxburghshire.   (*Died 15 Mar. 1920.*)

SCOTT, Owen Stanley; Curator and Sec. of the Bowes Museum, Barnard Castle, since 1884; *b.* Devonport, Sept. 1852; *m.* 1878, Isabella Christy, *d.* of late James Collins; one *s.* four *d. Educ. :* Ardingly. Technical Assistant in South Kensington Museum, 1872; Assistant Secretary, Fine Art Section, Glasgow International Exhibition, 1901; P.M. Barnard Lodge of Free masons; P.P.S.G.D., Durham. *Publications:* Raby, its Castle and its Lords, etc. *Recreations:* photography, golf. *Address:* Bowes Museum, Barnard Castle. *T. :* 35 P.O.

    (*Died 22 Jan. 1922.*)

SCOTT, Admiral Sir Percy, 1st Bt., *cr.* 1913; K.C.B., *cr.* 1910; K.C.V.O., *cr.* 1906; C.V.O. 1902; C.B. 1900; Hon. LL.D., Cambridge; in charge of gunnery defences of London against aircraft attacks, 1915-16; late Inspector of Target Practice; *b.* 10 July 1853; *s.* of Montagu Scott; *m.* 1894, Roma (whom he divorced 1911), *e. d.* of Sir Frederic Dixon Hartland, 1st Bt.; one *s.* one *d.* Entered Navy 1866; Captain, 1893; Admiral, 1913; served Ashanti War, 1873-74 (medal); Congo Expedition, 1875 (despatches, special promotion); Egyptian War, 1882 (despatches, medal); South Africa, 1899-1900 (C.B., despatches, medal); China War, 1900 (despatches, medal); has served on Ordnance Committee, on Committee on Naval Uniforms, and Naval Exhibition Committee; inventor of night signalling apparatus now used in the R.N. and of various appliances for improving heavy gun shooting; also invented the gun carriages which enabled 6-inch and 4·7-inch guns to be used in South Africa; retired, 1913; Medjidie 3rd class, Khedive's Bronze Star. *Publication :* Fifty Years in the Royal Navy, 1919. *Heir: s.* Douglas Winchester, *b.* 4 Feb. 1907. *Address:* 52 South Audley Street, W.1; *T. :* Grosvenor 1043; The Warren, Ascot. *Clubs:*

United Service; Royal Yacht Squadron, Cowes.
(Died 18 Oct. 1924.)

SCOTT, Robert George, V.C. 1879; D.S.O. 1900; Lieut.-Col. Cape Colonial Forces; late Cape Mounted Rifles; *b.* 1857; *s.* of Fleet-Surg. R. C. Scott, R.N.; *m.* Constance, *d.* of Lt.-Col. C. A. Daniell. Served Kaffir Wars, 1877-79; with Kimberley Light Horse, Scott's Railway Guards, and Cape Railway Sharpshooters, S. Africa, 1900-2 (despatches, Queen's medal, 3 clasps, King's medal, 2 clasps, D.S.O.). *Address:* Kimberley, S. Africa. *(Died 3 Oct. 1918.)*

SCOTT, Robert Henry, M.A., D.Sc., F.R.S.; *b.* Dublin, 28 Jan. 1833; *y. s.* of James Smyth Scott, Q.C., and Louisa, *d.* of Hon. Charles Brodrick, D.D., Archbishop of Cashel; *m.* Louisa (*d.* 1901), *d.* of Hon. W. Stewart, Island Secretary, Jamaica, 1865. *Educ.:* Rugby; Trin. College, Dublin; studied also at Berlin and Munich, 1856-58. Classical Scholar Trin. Coll. Dublin, 1853; 1st Senior Mod. Exp. Physics, 1855; M.A. 1859; D.Sc. 1898; Keeper of Minerals Royal Dublin Society, 1862-67; superintended Meteorological Office, 1867-1900; Officer Legion of Honour. *Publications:* Weather Charts and Storm Warnings, 1876, 2nd ed. 1887; Elementary Meteorology, 1883; numerous papers in the Proceedings Royal Society, Quarterly Journal Royal Meteorological Society, etc. *Recreations:* cricket and football up to 1860. *Address:* 6 Elm Park Gardens, S.W. *Club:* Athenæum.
(Died 18 June 1916.)

SCOTT, Sir Robert Townley, Kt., *cr.* 1909; I.S.O. 1903; *b.* Dawney, Berks, 30 Dec. 1841; *m.* 1868, Ellen, *d.* of George Parkinson Wright, Brisbane; four *s.* one *d.* *Educ.:* private schools, Brisbane. Went to Australia, 1848; entered General Post Office, Brisbane, 1862; Under Secretary and Superintendent of Telegraphs, Queensland, 1899-1901; Secretary, Postmaster-General's Dept. and Permanent Head of Commonwealth Telegraph Service since 1901. *Address:* Brisbane, Queensland.
(Died Aug. 1922.)

SCOTT, Rev. Samuel Cooper, M.A.; Vicar of St. John Baptist, Chester, 1875-1915; Hon. Canon of Chester, 1896; Rural Dean, 1905; *b.* Kingston-upon-Hull, 12 March 1838; *s.* of Rev. John Scott, Vicar of St. Mary's, Kingston-upon-Hull, and *g.g.s.* of Thomas Scott the Commentator; *m.* 1875, Susannah Jane, *d.* of Dr. Leggett, H.E.I.C.S., and *g.d.* of General Bell; two *s.* two *d.* *Educ.:* private school; Trinity College, Cambridge. Clerk in Smith's Bank, Derby, 1854-63; Trinity College, Cambridge, 1863-66; Deacon, 1866; Priest, 1867; Curate of Wisbeach; in charge of St. James', Derby, 1869-70; Curate of St. George's, Bloomsbury, 1870-74; Minister of St. Peter's, Battersea, 1874. *Publications:* Lectures on the History of the Parish and Church of St. John Baptist, Chester; Guide-book to ditto. *Recreation:* carpentry. *Address:* 19 Clifton Dale, York.
(Died 12 Aug. 1923.)

SCOTT, Rev. Samuel Gilbert, Rector of Havant, 1892-1916, and Rural Dean, 1900-16; Hon. Canon of Winchester, 1905; *b.* 1847; *s.* of Samuel King and Georgina Scott; *m.* 1874, Louisa, *d.* of late William Aldwin Soames, Tramore Lodge, Brighton; three *s.* four *d.* *Educ.:* Brighton College; Magdalen College, Oxford. Curate of Battersea, 1873; Vicar of S. Saviour's, Battersea, 1877-83; Rector of Woolwich, 1883; Rural Dean of Woolwich, 1885; Rural Dean of Landport, 1896-1900; Hon. Secretary, Portsmouth Church Extension Fund, 1897-1904; Bishop of Winchester's Fund, 1904-11; Grand Chaplain of England for Freemasons, 1916; Director Hants Friendly Society, 1916; Surrogate. *Publication:* History of S. Faith's Church, Havant. *Recreations:* walking, cycling, angling, member of British Ornithological Union. *Address:* Belmore House, Upham, Hants. *(Died 5 Nov. 1916.)*

942

SCOTT, Thomas Bodley, M.R.C.S., L.R.C.P.Ed.; Physician; J.P. Bournemouth; Member of Borough Council; 3rd *s.* of late S.K. Scott, M.R.C.S., Brighton; *m.* Adeline, *d.* of Albert Savory, Potters Park, Chertsey; eight *s.* two *d.* *Educ.:* Brighton College; House Physician St. Bartholomews, 1873; since in practice at Bournemouth. *Publications:* The Religion of a Doctor; The Road to a Healthy Old Age; Why do we Die? Modern Medicine; Endocrine Therapeutics. *Address:* 7 Poole Road, Bournemouth. *T.:* 37. *Club:* Junior Constitutional; Bournemouth.
(Died 2 Feb. 1924.)

SCOTT, Tom, R.S.A., hon. retired list; water-colour painter; *b.* Selkirk, 12 Oct. 1854; *e. s.* of T. Scott, clothier, Selkirk. *Educ.:* Selkirk Grammar School. Commenced studying at the Royal Institution, Edinburgh, 1877; afterwards in Royal Scottish Academy life classes; had sketching trips to the following places—Grez, near Paris; Florence, Rome, Naples, and Capri; Naples, Ravello, and Salerno; Tunis; Holland. *Publications:* The Otter Hunt; Meet of Foxhounds at Riddell; Mosstroopers returning from a Raid; Return to Selkirk after Flodden; The Legend of Ladywood; Return to Hawick from Hornshole, 1514; Newark Castle; St. Mary's Loch; The Trysting Tree; Daybreak; Reparabit Cornua Phœbe; A Stronghold of the Scots; A Hayfield in Ettrick; A Witch lived here in days gone by; Canal Scene near Dordrecht; After the Battle of Philiphaugh; Ettrick Pen, Selkirkshire; Goldielands Tower, near Hawick; Whin-burning, Gordon, Berwickshire; The Warrior's Rest, Yarrow; November in Liddesdale; Carnoustie; Tweed at Abbotsford; Auld Wat O'Harden; The Crofter's Mare; Sir Walter's Gate; Bemersyde Hill. *Recreation:* collecting stone and flint implements; possesses a good collection of Border Antiquities. *Address:* Leslie Cottage, Selkirk. *Club:* Scottish Arts, Edinburgh. *(Died July 1927.)*

SCOTT, Walter Montagu, J.P. Glos. 1906; M.A. Cantab.; *y. s.* of late John Scott, M.D., of 8 Chandos Street, Cavendish Square, W.; *b.* 1867. *Educ.:* Harrow; Jesus College, Cambridge. *Recreations:* hunting, shooting, and fishing. *Address:* Nether Swell Manor, Stow on the Wold. *T.:* 17 Stow on the Wold. *Clubs:* Carlton, Junior Carlton, Royal Automobile.
(Died 14 Aug. 1920.)

SCOTT, William A., A.R.H.A., A.R.I.B.A., M.S.A., F.R.I.A.I., Architect in private practice; Professor of Architecture, National University of Ireland, since 1911; *b.* Dublin, 1 Sep. 1871; *s.* of Anthony Scott, M.S.A., F.R.S.A.I., architect, and Catherine Hayes; *m.* 1900, Catherine, *d.* of Patrick Crumley, J.P., M.P., D.L., Fermanagh; no *c.* *Educ.:* Classical School, Manorhamilton; St. Finian's Seminary, Navan; Metropolitan School of art, Dublin. Apprenticed to Sir T. Newenham Deane and Son, 1891; engaged on reparation of National Monuments; design selected, and executed Enniskillen Town Hall, open competiton; 3 years various London offices and staff appointment in London C.C.; returned Dublin, 1902; late Hon. Examiner Planning and Design, London Society of Architects, since 1903; Member of Council and Past Hon. Treas. R.I.A.I.; Past President, Architectural Association of Ireland; has designed and carried out Spiddal Church; O'Growney Mausoleum, Maynooth; Garden Village, Kilkenny; Town Hall, Cavan; Spiddal House for Lord Killanin; Convent Chapel and Schools, Enniskillen; Church and Convent, Edenderry; Irvinstown Church; St. Mary's College, Galway; designed Cathedral for Galway; studied and sketched in British Isles, Belgium, France, Germany, Austria, Italy, Constantinople, Asia Minor. *Publications:* Papers and Lectures at various Architectural Society's Meetings. *Recreations:* fishing, yachting, motoring, nature study. *Address:* 45 Mountjoy Square, Dublin. *T.A.:* Scott, Mountjoy Square, Dublin. *T.:* Dublin 2380. (*Died 20 April 1918.*)

SCOTT, Ven. William Edward, Chaplain Holy Trinity, Geneva, 1915 - 18 ; Rector of Bradwell - by - Braintree, 1909 - 14 ; Chairman of the Committee of Women's Work-S.P.G., 1910. *Educ. :* Keble College, Oxford (M.A.). Fellow of Bombay University; Curate of Merton, Surrey, 1875-77 ; Headmaster Northallerton Grammar School, 1877-1880 ; curate of Yafforth, 1879-80 ; Rector of Hawthorn, Durham, 1880-85 ; chaplain Nasirabad, 1885 - 87 ; Deolali, 1888 ; Christ Church, Byculla, 1888-91 ; chaplain to Bishop of Bombay, 1894-95 ; at Colaba, 1895-97 ; Archdeacon of Bombay, 1897-1907 ; chaplain of Kirkee, 1901 ; Rector of Tolleshunt Knights, Essex, 1907-9. *Address:* Hotel Beau Séjour, Vevey. *Clubs:* New Oxford and Cambridge ; Alpin Suisse.
(*Died 29 Dec. 1918.*)

SCOTT-GATTY, Sir Alfred Scott, Kt., cr. 1904 ; K.C.V.O., cr. 1911 ; C.V.O. 1906 ; Commander of the Royal Norwegian Order of St. Olaf ; F.S.A. ; Garter Principal King-of-Arms since 1904 ; *b.* Ecclesfield Vicarage, Co. York, 26 Apr. 1847 ; 2nd *s.* of Rev. Alfred Gatty, D.D., Sub-Dean of York Cathedral and Vicar of Ecclesfield, and Margaret, *d.* and *heir* of Rev. Alexander John Scott, D.D., sometime Private Secretary to Horatio, Viscount Nelson. Assumed by Royal Licence, 1892, the additional surname and arms of Scott ; *m.* Elizabeth, *d.* of John Foster, Newhall Grange, Laughton-en-le-Morthen, Co. York, 1874 ; one *s. Educ.:* Marlborough ; Christ's Coll. Cambridge. Rouge-Dragon Pursuivant of Arms, 1880 ; York Herald of the College of Arms, London 1886-1904 ; Acting Registrar of the same, 1899 - 1904 ; Knight of Justice of the Order of St. John of Jerusalem and Genealogist of that Order ; at an early age showed a great love for music, and commenced musical compositions in mother's magazine, entitled Aunt Judy's Magazine, 1868. *Publications:* Little Songs for Little Voices, 3 vols. ; Musical Plays for Children ; Rumpelstiltskin ; The Goose Girl : The Three Bears ; Plantation Songs, 4 vols. and hundreds of songs sentimental and humorous ; in many instances both words and music. *Address:* Wendover Lodge, Welwyn, Herts ; The College of Arms, Queen Victoria Street, E.C. *Clubs:* Athenæum, Garrick. (*Died 18 Dec. 1918.*)

SCOTT-MONCRIEFF, Sir Colin Campbell, K.C.S.I., cr. 1903, K.C.M.G., cr. 1887 ; C.S.I. 1878 ; LL.D. (Edinburgh) ; *b.* Scotland, 3 Aug. 1836 ; 6th *s.* of late Robert Scott-Moncrieff. Fossaway, and Susan, *d.* of A. Pringle, Whytbank ; *m.* 1st, 1860, Lucy (*d.* 1874), *d.* of late John Sturge ; 2nd, 1879, Margaret (*d.* 1885), widow of L. J. Sturge ; 3rd, Mary Deborah, *d.* of Arthur Albright, Mariemont, Birmingham, 1890 ; two *d. Educ.:* Edin. Academy ; H.E.I.C. Military College, Addiscombe. 2nd Lieut. Bengal Engineers, 1856 ; retired with rank of Col., 1888 ; engaged in suppression of Indian Mutiny (medal) ; Irrigation Depart. N.W. Provinces ; Chief Engineer Burmah ; Under-Secretary of State Public Works, Cairo, 1883-92 ; Under-Sec. for Scotland 1892-1902 ; President of Indian Irrigation Comm., 1901-1903. *Publication:* Irrigation in Southern Europe, 1868. *Address:* 11 Cheyne Walk, Chelsea, S.W. *Club:* Athenæum.
(*Died 6 April 1916.*)

SCOTT-MONCRIEFF, Major-General Sir George Kenneth, K.C.B., cr. 1915 ; K.C.M.G., cr. 1918 ; C.B. 1907 ; C.I.E. 1900, R.E. ; *b.* 3 Oct. 1855 ; *s.* of Major A. P. Scott-Moncrieff, I.S.C. ; *m.* 1886, Helen (*d.* 1916), *d.* of R. Moubray, of Cambus, N.B. *Educ.:* Edinburgh Academy ; R.M.A. Woolwich. Commanded R.E. China Expeditionary Force, 1900-1 (despatches, medal and clasp) ; served

Afghanistan, 1878-80 (despatches, medal with clasp) ; served Waziristan Expedition, 1901 (medal and clasp) ; Instructor School of Military Engineering, 1893 - 98 ; Chief Engineer, Aldershot, 1909 - 11 ; Vice - President, C.M.S. ; Hon. Memb. Inst. C.E. ; retired, 1918 ; Director of Fortifications and Works, War Office, 1911-18 (medal for European War). *Address:* 31 Ladbroke Square, W.11. *T.:* Park 5177. *Club:* National. (*Died 4 June 1924.*)

SCOTT - MONCRIEFF, William George, M.A. ; Advocate ; F.S.A. Scot., F.Z.S.Scot. ; Sheriff-Substitute of Lanarkshire at Lanark, 1900-17, now Hon. Sheriff ; *b.* 15 April 1846 ; *s.* of late Rev. William Scott-Moncrieff ; *m.* 1878, Jessie Margaret, *d.* of Robert Scott-Moncrieff, Edinburgh ; three *s. Educ.:* privately ; Edinburgh University. M.A. 1866 ; called to Scottish Bar, 1870 ; appointed Sheriff-Substitute of Banffshire, 1877 ; Stirlingshire, 1887 ; Inverness-shire, 1897 ; served on Scottish Departmental Commission relating to the Inebriate Laws, 1908. *Publications:* contributor to legal journals, and editor of Nimmo's Narrative and Justiciary Proceedings for the Scottish History Society. *Address:* Whitchurch Rectory, Edgware, Middlesex. *Club:* University, Edinburgh.
(*Died 2 Jan. 1927.*)

SCOUGAL, Andrew E. ; *b.* 1846 ; *s.* of late James Scougal, one of H.M. Inspectors of Schools in Scotland. *Educ. :* Cheltenham Grammar School ; Edinburgh Academy, Institution, and University ; Aberdeen Free Church College. M.A. Edin. 1865 ; LL.D. Edin. 1908 ; F.R.S.E. Acting Inspector of Schools, 1868-69 ; H.M. Inspector, 1869 ; Chief Inspector, Western Division of Scotland, 1899 ; Senior Chief Inspector and Inspector of Training Colleges, 1904 ; H.M. Chief Inspector for the Training of Teachers in Scotland, 1910-11 ; retired, 1911. *Address:* 1 Wester Coates Avenue, Edinburgh. *Club:* Northern, Edinburgh.
(*Died Nov. 1916.*)

SCOURFIELD, Sir Owen Henry Philipps, 2nd Bt., cr. 1876 ; D.L., J.P. ; *b.* 10 Oct. 1847 ; *e. s.* of 1st Bt. and Augusta Lort, 2nd *d.* of J. Lort Phillips of Lawrenny Park, Pembrokeshire ; *S.* father 1876 ; *m.* 1st, 1877, Gertrude Katharine (*d.* 1894), *o. d.* of Seymour Philipps Allen of Cresselly, Pembrokeshire ; 2nd, 1896, Frances Katharina (*d.* 1914), *d.* of late Rev. J. Turner Lea, of Orchardlea, Droitwich, and Vicar of Far Forest, Bewdley. *Educ.:* Harrow ; Christ Church, Oxford. Owns about 8000 acres. *Heir:* none. *Address:* Williamston, Neyland, R.S.O., Pembrokeshire. *T.A.:* Houghton, Pembrokeshire. *Clubs:* Carlton, Boodle's, United University. (*Died 5 Feb. 1921.*)

SCOVELL, Sir Augustus Charles, Kt., cr. 1907 ; J.P. Co. of London ; *b.* 1840 ; *s.* of George Scovell, J.P., D.L., Grosvenor Place, London ; *m.* 1865, Arabella Barrington (*d.* 1916), *y. d.* of Captain Vincent Frederick Kennett of the Manor House, Dorchester - on - Thame, Oxfordshire ; one *s.* four *d. Educ. :* Harrow ; Christ Church, Oxford (B.A. 1862). A manager of the Metropolitan Asylums Board since 1882 ; Chairman, 1904-7 ; has taken an active part in Poor Law and other public work, metropolitan and local ; for many years chairman of the Guarantee Society, Birchin Lane, London. *Address:* 8 Primrose Mansions, Battersea Park, S.W. *Club:* Oxford and Cambridge.
(*Died 28 May 1924.*)

SCRATCHLEY, Herbert Arthur, M.V.O. 1905 ; British Vice-Consul and Lloyd's Agent at Bona, Algeria, since 1906 ; Proprietor of corkwood forests near Bona ; *b.* 1855 ; 3rd *s.* of late Arthur Scratchley, M.A. (Cantab.), Barrister-at-Law, and Marian Beaumont, *d.* of T. Beaumont, R.N., of Bath ; *m.* Maria Matilde Elena Prax y Prax, *e. d.* late Señor Don Victoriano Prax y Roca of La Junquera, Catalonia,

Spain, and Philippeville, Algeria ; one s. *Educ. :* Brighton College ; University College School, London. Went to Algeria as mining engineer to an English company established near Bona ; Assoc. M.Inst.C.E., 1884 ; British Vice-Consul at Philippeville. 1892-1906 ; Vice-Consul for Portugal at Philippeville, 1898-1906 ; for Norway, 1906 ; Lloyd's Agent at Philippeville, 1898-1903 ; acting Vice-Consul for Norway, June 1916-18 ; for Portugal, 31 May 1919. *Publications:* newspaper articles ; consular reports ; guide-book of Algeria. *Recreations:* reading and walking. *Address:* Bona, Algeria. *T.A.:* Scratchley, Bona. *Club:* Cercle de l'Union, Bona.
(Died 22 April 1920.)

SCRIVEN, Ven. Augustine, Archdeacon of Vancouver since 1884. *Educ.:* St. Mary Hall, Oxford (M.A.). Ordained 1875 ; Curate of Kirkham, 1875-78 ; Frindsbury, 1879-80 ; Martinhoe, 1880-81 ; St. Peter, Rochester, 1882-84. *Address:* Victoria, British Columbia.
(Died 21 July 1916.)

SCULLARD, Rev. Herbert Hayes, M.A., D.D. ; Professor of Church History, Christian Ethics, and History of Religions, Hackney and New Colleges, London University ; *b.* 1862 ; *s.* of Rev. H. H. Scullard, who for more than 50 years was a Congregational Minister ; *m.* 1901, Barbara Louisa, *e. d.* of G. W. Dodds, Sydenham, and *g.d.* of Ebenezer Viney, for many years Treasurer of Hackney College ; one *s. Educ.:* Pembroke House School, Lytham ; Lancashire Independent and Owens Colleges ; St. John's College, Cambridge. At Owens College distinctions in Modern Philosophy, Ethics, Political Economy, Psychology, Logic, and other subjects ; at London University, M.A. in Mental and Moral Science, 1885 ; B.D. (first division), 1903 ; D.D. 1907 (the first Nonconformist to obtain a D.D. degree from any English University) ; at St. John's Coll., Cambridge, Foundation Scholar, Hughes Exhibitioner, Naden Divinity Student, and Greek Testament prizeman ; also honours in 1st and 2nd parts of Theological Tripos, Cambridge, and Hulsean prizeman, Cambridge ; B.A. 1888 ; M.A. 1891. Pastor of Congregational Churches at York Street, Dublin, and Howard Church, Bedford, the latter of which John Howard the Philanthropist was a founder. *Publications:* St. Martin : Apostle of Gaul ; John Howard ; Christian Ethics in the West ; Essays in Christ and Civilization, and London Theological Essays ; articles in Contemporary Review, Hibbert Journal, London Quarterly Review, etc. *Address:* 10 Wessex Gardens, Golders Green, N.W. *(Died 21 Mar. 1926.)*

SEAFORTH of Brahan, 1st Baron, *cr.* 1921 ; **James Alex. Francis Humberston Stewart-Mackenzie,** F.R.G.S., F.Z.S. ; J.P. ; *o. s.* of late Keith William Stewart-Mackenzie, J.P., and 1st wife, Hannah Charlotte (*d.* 1868), *e. d.* of late James Joseph Hope-Vere of Craigie Hall, ?Midlothian ; *b.* 1847 ; *m.* 1890, Mary.   Was Military Secretary to Governor of Madras ; served Afghan War, 1878-80 (wounded, despatches twice, Bt.-Major, medal with two clasps, and bronze star) ; Vice-Lieut. of Cos. Ross and Cromarty ; Col. ret., late commanding 9th Lancers ; Hon. Col. 4th Batt. Seaforth Highlanders. *Heir:* none. *Address:* Brahan Castle, Cononbridge, Ross-shire ; 47 Berkeley Square, W.1. *T.:* Mayfair 3358 ; Lydhurst, Hayward's Heath. *Clubs:* Carlton, Army and Navy, Turf.
(Died 3 Mar. 1923.)

SEAGER, Philip Samuel, I.S.O. 1906 ; Registrar of Supreme Court, Tasmania ; Registrar of Deeds and Commissioner of Stamp Duties since 1894 ; *b.* 1845 ; *s.* of late Charles Seager, of Tasmanian Civil Service ; *m.* 1869, *d.* of late J. T. Smales, Hobart. *Educ.:* privately. Entered public service Tasmania, 1863 ; is a member of

several Public Boards ; was associated with the experiment of introducing Salmonidæ into Tasmanian waters ; is a Commissioner of Fisheries ; Chairman of Tasmanian Tourist Association, and a Justice of the Peace for Tasmania. *Address:* Hobart, Tasmania.
(Died Jan. 1924.)

SEAMAN, Colonel Edwin Charles, C.M.G. 1917 ; R.E. ; *b.* 4 Nov. 1867. Entered R.E. 1886 ; Capt. 1896 ; Major, 1904 ; Lt.-Col. 1912 ; Col. 1916 ; Assist. Instructor, School of Military Engineering, 1890-92 ; School of Submarine Mining, 1892-97 ; Supt. Brennan Torpedo Factory, 1902-4 ; Inspector of Electric Lights, Hdqtrs. of Army and War Office, 1904-12 ; Assistant Director of Fortifications and Works War Office, 1916 ; served European War, 1914-17 (C.M.G.) ; White Eagle (Servia), 4th Class.
(Died 10 May 1919.)

SEARLE, Maj.-Gen. Arthur Thaddeus, Indian Army ; *b.* 29 Dec. 1830. Entered army, 1849 ; Maj.-Gen., 1890 ; unemployed list, 1888.
(Died 15 Aug. 1925.)

SEARLE, Sir Malcolm William, Kt., *cr.* 1923 ; **Mr. Justice Searle,** Judge President of Cape Provincial Division of Supreme Court of South Africa. *Address:* Highlands, Wynberg, Cape Province.
(Died 9 June 1926.)

SEATON, Rev. Douglas; Vicar of Goodrich since 1875 ; Prebendary of Bartonsham, Hereford Cathedral, since 1893 ; Rural Dean of Archenfield since 1902 ; *b.* 1 May 1839 ; 2nd *s.* of George and Eleanor Seaton, of the Yorkshire branch of the Seaton family ; *m.* 1866, Catherine Mary (*d.* 1920), *d.* of late Frederick Hale Thomson ; one *s.* three *d. Educ.:* Hyde Abbey School, Winchester ; Brighton ; Trinity Coll. Camb. B.A. 1861, and M.A. 1875. Deacon, 1862 ; Priest, 1863 ; Curate, Bishop's Hatfield, Herts, 1862-64 ; Chertsey, 1864-66 ; All Saints, Hereford, 1866 ; Goodrich, 1866-75 ; Vicar of Breinton, 1875 ; Secretary and Treasurer of the Hereford Archidiaconal Board of Education 1875 ; Secretary of the Archdeaconry of Hereford Voluntary Schools Assoc. ; Member of the Herefordshire County Council Committee on Education ; Past Provincial Grand Chaplain and Senior Grand Warden of Herefordshire ; Past M. W. Scr. Rouge Croix Chapter (St. Thomas) ; prelate of Rouge Croix Chapter 18 St. Thomas, Gloucester. *Publications:* Handicraft or Manual Training ; Guide to Goodrich Castle ; History of Goodrich Castle ; History of the Deanery of Archenfield. *Address:* Goodrich Vicarage, Ross, Herefordshire. *T.A.:* Goodrich. *(Died 25 Feb. 1923.)*

SEAVERNS, Joel Herbert, foreign and colonial merchant ; partner of the firm of Henry W. Peabody & Co. of London ; *b.* Boston, U.S.A., 13 Nov. 1860 ; *o. s.* of Joel Seaverns, M.D., and Jane M. Seaverns ; *m.* 1892, Helen, *d.* of H. B. Brown of Portland, Me., U.S.A. *Educ.:* Harvard University (B.A., with honours, 1881). Has been a resident of London since 1884 ; M.P. (L.) Brixton Division of Lambeth, 1906-1910 ; Member of Territorial Force Association of the County of London, and Joint Committee of County and City Associations ; ex-President Harvard Club of London ; D.L. ; J.P. County of London. *Recreation:* golf. *Address:* 25 Grosvenor Road, S.W.1. *T.:* Victoria 2172 ; 16 Eastcheap, E.C. *Club:* Reform.
(Died 11 Nov. 1923.)

SEBRIGHT, Sir Edgar Reginald Saunders, 11th Bt. ; *cr.* 1626 ; J.P. Herts ; Major and Hon. Lieut.-Col. (retired) 4th Batt. (Militia) Bedfordshire Regt. ; *b.* 8 Nov. 1854 ; 3rd *s.* of 8th Bt. and 2nd wife, Olivia, *y. d.* of J. J. Henry, of Straffan ; *bro.* of Sir John Sebright, 9th Bt. ; *S nephew* 1897. *Educ.:* Eton ; Magdalen College, Oxford. Equerry to late Duchess of Teck, 1885-97 ; Aide-de-Camp

to Governor of Victoria, Earl of Hopetoun, 1892-94; Private Secretary to Governor of South Australia, Earl of Kintore, 1894-95; High Sheriff, Herts, 1902. [*Heir:* b. Guy Thomas Saunders, b. 19 Aug. 1856; m. 1882, Olive Emily, d. of Arthur Frederick. *Address:* 82 Eaton Place, S.W. *Clubs:* Travellers', Bachelors'.] *Address:* Cheverells, Dunstable; 14 Arlington Street, S.W. *Clubs:* Carlton, Marlborough, Bachelors', United Service, Beefsteak, Pratt's.
(*Died 25 Dec. 1917.*)

SECCOMBE, Thomas; Prof. of English Literature, Queen's University, Kingston, Ontario, since 1921; b. Terrington, 1866; s. of Dr. J. T., and *g.s.* of Sir Thomas L. Seccombe, G.C.I.E.; m.; one s. two d. *Educ.:* Felsted; Balliol, Oxford (Stanhope prize, 1887). Assistant editor Dictionary of National Biography, 1891-1901; Lecturer, Owens, 1901; East London College, 1907-12; Professor in English, R.M.C., Sandhurst, 1912. *Publications:* Twelve Bad Men, 1894; The Age of Johnson, 1900; The Age of Shakespeare (with J. W. Allen), 1903; Bookman History of English Literature, 1905-6; George Meredith, 1913, etc.; editor of Smollett's Miscellanies and Travels; Constable's English Garner and Religions Ancient and Modern; Borrow's Isopel Berners and Lavengro; George Gissing, an Introductory Survey; Parkman and Prescott; Mrs. Gaskell's novels; Florio's Montaigne; Boswell's Letters; Dr. Johnson and Mrs. Thrale; Goldsmith's Plays and Poems; Adlington's Golden Ass; In Praise of Oxford. *Address:* Queen's Univ., Kingston, Ontario. *Club:* Athenæum.
(*Died 20 June 1923.*)

SECKHAM, Lt.-Col. Bassett Thorne, D.S.O. 1900; J.P. Staffordshire; late Lt.-Col. Commanding 4th Battalion South Staffordshire Regiment; b. 22 Nov. 1863; e. s. of late Samuel Lipscomb Seckham, J.P., D.L.; m. 1888, Alice Dorothy, d. of W. F. Moore of Cronkbourne, Douglas; one s. two d. Served South Africa, 1900-1 (despatches, Queen's medal 3 clasps, D.S.O.). *Address:* Whittington Old Hall, Staffs. *Club:* Junior United Service.
(*Died 29 June 1925.*)

SEDGWICK, Rev. Gordon, Hon. Canon of Coventry; Vicar of Sherbourne, Warwick, since 1893; b. 1840; m.; four s. five d. *Educ.:* Brighton College; Gonville and Caius College, Cambridge (Scholar); 6th Senior Optime, 1863, B.A., M.A. Ordained, 1866; Assistant Curate, Holy Trinity, Coventry, 1866-70; Monks Kirby, Warwickshire, 1871-77; Vicar of St. Mark's, Coventry, 1877-98. *Address:* Barford-Warwick. *M.:* AC 2662.
(*Died 11 Oct. 1921.*)

SEDGWICK, William Thompson, Ph.D.; Sc.D.; Professor of Biology, Massachusetts Institute of Technology, since 1883; Curator, Lowell Institute, since 1897; b. West Hartford, Conn., 29 Dec. 1855; s. of William and Anne (Thompson) Sedgwick; m. 1881, Mary Katrine Rice. *Educ.:* Yale (Ph.B., 1877). Johns Hopkins Univ. (Ph.D. 1881). Instructor Yale Univ., 1878-79; Fellow, Assistant, Associate, Johns Hopkins University, 1879-83; Biologist State Board of Health, Mass., 1888-96; Pres. Soc. American Bacteriologists, 1900; Pres. American Soc. of Naturalists, 1901; President New England Water Works Association, 1906, and American Public Health Association, 1915; Member Advisory Board, U.S. Public Health Service; Member Public Health Council, Mass. State Dept. Health; Member International Health Board, Rockefeller Foundation. *Publications:* General Biology (with E. B. Wilson), 1896; Principles Sanitary Science and Public Health, 1902; The Human Mechanism (with T. Hough), 1907; A Short History of Science (with H. W. Tyler), 1917; and numerous special papers. *Address:* Mass. Institute of Technology, or Lowell Institute, Boston.
(*Died 25 Jan. 1921.*)

SEELY, Sir Charles (Hilton), 2nd Bt., cr. 1896; J.P.; M.P. (Lib.) Mansfield Division of Notts, 1916-18; colliery owner; b. 7 July 1859; e. s. of Sir Charles Seely, 1st Bt., and Emily, d. of William Evans and sis. of Sir F. Evans, 1st Bt.; S. father, 1915; m. 1891, Hilda, d. of R. T. A. Grant; three s. two d. *Educ.:* Harrow; Trinity Coll. Camb. Contested Mid-Derbyshire, 1886; Rushcliffe Division, Nottinghamshire, 1892; M.P. (U.L.) Lincoln, 1895-1906; Lt.-Col. and Hon. Col. 5th V. Batt. Hants Regt. (Isle of Wight Rifles, Princess Beatrice's), 1900-8. *Heir:* s. Hugh Michael. *Address:* Sherwood Lodge, Arnold, Notts; Gatcombe House, Newport, Isle of Wight; 25 Belgrave Square, S.W.1. *T.:* Victoria 20. *Clubs:* Brooks's, Athenæum; Royal Yacht Squadron, Cowes.
(*Died 26 Feb. 1926.*)

SEGUR, Marquis de Pierre Marie Maurice Henri, Membre de l'Académie Française; b. Paris, 18 Feb. 1853; m. Thérèse Hely d'Oissel; one s. *Educ.:* Collège Stanislas. *Publications:* Le Maréchal de Segur, 1895; Le Royaume de la rue St-Honoré, 1897; La Dernière des Condé, 1899; Gens. d'autrefois, 1900; Le Maréchal de Luxembourg, 1904; Le Tapissier de Notre Dame, 1906; Julie de Lespinasse, 1906; Au Couchant de la Monarchie (2 vols.), 1913. *Address:* 45 avenue d'Iéna, Paris. *T.:* 1662-09. Château de Villiers par Poissy, Seine-et-Oise. (*Died 14 Aug. 1916.*)

SEIGNE, John Thomas, M.V.O. 1904; Agent to Marquess of Ormonde and other landowners in Ireland; b. 14 Dec. 1844; o. s. of late Thomas Seigne; m. 1877, Elizabeth, d. of Richard Barter, St. Ann's Hill, Co. Cork; two s. one d. High Sheriff of the County of Kilkenny, 1912. *Address:* Grenane House, Thomastown, Co. Kilkenny. *T.A.:* Seigne, Kilkenny.
(*Died 7 Jan. 1922.*)

SELBY, 2nd Viscount, cr. 1905; **James William Herschell Gully;** b. 4 Oct. 1867; e. s. of 1st Viscount and Elizabeth Ann Walford, e. d. of Thomas Selby; S. father 1909; m. 1st, 1893, Ada Isabel (who obtained a divorce, 1909), d. of late A. G. Pirie of Stoneywood House, Aberdeen; one d.; 2nd, 1909, Dorothy Evelyn, y. d. of late Sir William Grey, K.C.S.I.; one s. three d. *Educ.:* Winchester; Balliol Coll. Oxford. Called to Bar, Inner Temple, 1892; practised at Parliamentary Bar. *Heir:* s. Hon. Thomas Sutton Evelyn Gully, b. 16 Feb. 1911. *Address:* 18 Brunswick Square, Brighton. *Club:* Oxford and Cambridge.(*Died 2 Feb. 1923.*)

SELBY, Francis Guy, M.A.; C.I.E. 1908; Hon. LL.D., Bombay, 1908; b. 8 Dec. 1852. *Educ.:* Durham School; Wadham College, Oxford (Scholar and Hody Greek Exhibition 1st Class Mods. and 1st Class Lit. Hum., 1875). Formerly Director of Public Instruction, Bombay Presidency; Fellow of the University of Bombay; Vice-Chancellor of the University of Bombay, 1906. *Publications:* The Metaphysic of Aristotle, an Introduction to the Study of Kant; edited Bacon's Advancement of Learning, and Essays; Burke's Reflections on the French Revolution; American Speeches and Letters to the Sheriff of Bristol; Thoughts on the Cause of the Present Discontent. *Recreations:* gardening and bicycling. *Address:* Bridstow, Worcester Park, Surrey.
(*Died 7 May 1927.*)

SELBY, Lt.-Col. William, D.S.O. 1898; Indian Medical Service (Bengal); Hon. Surgeon to the Viceroy; Principal King George's Medical College, Lucknow; Dean of the Faculty of Medicine, and Member of the Syndicate, Allahabad University; b. Dunedin, New Zealand, 16 June 1869; y. s. of late Prideaux Selby, Koroit, Park Hill, Croydon, and Rose Anne, 3. of late John Wise; m. Eliza Kinsman, d. of late Frederick Benjamin, Wood Lane, Falmouth, 1896. *Educ.:* Whitgift Grammar School; St. Bartholomew's Hospital. M.R.C.S. England ; L.R.C.P. Lond. 1892 ; F.R.C.S. England, 1905. Joined Indian Medical Service, 1894 ; served in Chitral Relief Force, 1895 (medal with clasp) ; North-West Frontier and Tirah Expeditionary Force, 1897-98 (three clasps, despatches, D.S.O.). *Decorated* as above. *Address :* Lucknow, U.P. India. *Club :* East India United Service. *(Died 8 Sept. 1916.)*

SELFE, Sir Robert Carr, Kt., *cr.* 1910 ; *b.* 4 Dec. 1840 ; *s.* of late John Selfe of Stockwell ; *m.* 1864, Rosetta (*d.* 1917), *d.* of late Benjamin Priest. Entered office of Ecclesiastical Commission, 1860 ; Accountant and Assistant Financial Adviser, 1891 ; Assistant Secretary, 1897 ; Secretary and Financial Adviser, 1908 ; retired, 1909. *Address :* Cedarlea, Parklands, Surbiton Hill. *(Died 28 Sept. 1926.)*

SELFE, His Honour Sir William Lucius, K.B., *cr.* 1897 ; *b.* London, 11 June 1845 ; 3rd *s.* of late Henry J. Selfe Selfe, Metropolitan Police Magistrate (*d.* 1870), and Anna Maria, *e. d.* of Venerable William Spooner, Archdeacon of Coventry ; *m.* Ellen, 2nd *d.* of late Henry S. Bicknell, 10 August 1876. *Educ. :* Rugby ; Corpus Christi Coll., Oxford. Scholar, 1863 ; 1st class Moderations, 1865 ; Final Classics, 1867 ; B.A. 1868. Barr. Inner Temple, June 1870 ; practised as conveyancer and equity draftsman ; engaged in the preparation of Statute Law Revision Bills, the publication of the Revised Edition of the Statutes, the Chronological Table and Index to the Statutes, and in the office of the Parliamentary Draftsman ; principal Secretary to Lord Chancellor, Earl Cairns, 1880 ; Judge of County Courts, Monmouthshire and Cardiff, 1882 - 84 ; East Kent, 1884-1905 ; Chairman East Kent Quarter Sessions, 1893 - 1905 ; Marylebone and West London, 1905-19 ; retired, 1919 ; member of County Courts Rules Committee, 1894 - 1919. *Address :* 13 Connaught Square, W.2. *Club :* Athenæum. *(Died 19 Mar. 1924.)*

SELINCOURT, Agnes de ; Principal of Westfield College (University of London) since 1913 ; *b.* Streatham, 1872 ; *d.* of Charles Alexander de Sélincourt and Theodora Bruce Bendall. *Educ. :* Notting Hill High School ; Girton College, Cambridge ; Somerville College, Oxford. First Class in Mediæval and Modern Languages Tripos, Cambridge, 1894 ; engaged in educational missionary work in India, 1896-1909 ; Principal of the Lady Muir Memorial Training College, Allahabad, 1901-9 ; Central Volunteer Secretary of the Student Christian Movement, 1910-12 ; Member of the Board of Oriental Studies of the University of London. *Address :* Westfield College, Hampstead, N.W. *T.A. :* Discipula, Kilfort, London. *T. :* Hampstead 734. *Club :* University of London.
(Died 31 Aug. 1917.)

SELKIRK, Countess of, Cecely Louisa, peer's widow (*cr.* 1646) ; *d.* of Sir Philip de Malpas Grey-Egerton, 10th Bt. ; *m.* 1878, Dunbar James, 6th Earl of Selkirk (*d.* 1885). *Address :* Balmae, Kirkcudbright, Scotland ; 50 Berkeley Square, W.1. *T. :* Mayfair 507.
(Died 10 Jan. 1920.)

SELLAR, Lieut. - Colonel Thomas Byrne, C.M.G. 1916 ; D.S.O. 1918 ; commanded 8th Batt. K.O.S.B. ; *b.* 2 March 1865 ; *s.* of late Thomas Sellar, Hall Grove, Bagshot ; *m.* 1902, Evelyn, *d.* of late L. P. Pugh, J.P., D.L., Abermead, Cardiganshire. *Educ. :* Fettes. Served Chitral, 1895 (medal with clasp) ; N.W. Frontier, India, 1897-98 (clasp) ; Tirah, 1897-98 (clasp) ; South Africa, 1899-1900 (Queen's medal, 4 clasps) ; European War, 1914-17 (despatches, C.M.G., D.S.O.) ; Order of St. Michael and St. Lazarus (Chevalier). *Address :* Eirianfa, Aberdovey, N. Wales. *Club :* Army and Navy.
(Died 11 April 1924.)

946

SELLHEIM, Maj.-Gen. Victor Conradsdorf Morisset, C.B. 1900 ; C.M.G. 1916 ; Administrator of Norfolk Island since 1926 ; Permanent Staff Australian Military Forces ; *b.* Sydney, New South Wales, 12 May 1866 ; *s.* of late P. F. Sellheim, Permanent Under-Secretary for Mines, Queensland, and Laura Theresa, *d.* of late Lt.-Col. Morisset, His Majesty's 48th Regiment ; *m.* 1890, Susan Henrietta, *d.* of late Rev. E. M. and Harriett Howell-Griffith, Clocaenog Rectory, North Wales. *Educ. :* Brisbane Grammar School. Adjutant Kennedy Regiment, 1896 ; extra A.D.C. to Right Hon. Baron Lamington, G.C.M.G., 1896 ; Staff Officer Northern Mihtary District (Queensland), 1897 ; officiating D.A.A.G., Queensland, 1900 ; D.A.A.G. and D.Q.M.G. Queensland Mil. Dist., 1902 ; attended special courses of military instruction in England during 1899 ; special service in South Africa, 1899-1900 ; served with 2nd Batt. Northampton Regiment, Queensland Mounted Infantry, staff of Pilcher's Mounted Infantry Brigade, staff of Chauvel's Mounted Infantry (despatches, medal and 6 clasps) ; Staff Officer Central Military District (Queensland), 1900 ; D.A.A.G. and D.A.Q.M.G. District Headquarters, Queensland, 1902-7 ; attached Headquarters, 3rd Infantry Brigade, Aldershot, 1906 ; Headquarters, Aldershot Army Corps, 1906 - 7 ; 4th Division Indian Army at Quetta, 1907 ; A.A.G. Victoria, 1907-11 ; A.A.G., N.S.W., 1911-12 ; Quartermaster-General and 3rd Military Member Military Board, 1912-14 ; Adjutant-General and 2nd Military Member Military Board, Australian Military Forces, 1914-16 ; A.A. and Q.M.G. 1st Division A.I.F., 1914 - 15 ; G.O.C. A.I.F. Troops in Egypt, Jan. 1915-May 1916 ; Commandant Administrative Headquarters, London, and G.O.C. Australians in England, 1916 (despatches, C.M.G., 1914-15 Star, British War Medal and Victory Medal) ; commanding 3rd Military District, 1917 ; reappointed Adj. - General Australian Military Forces, 1917-24 ; A.D.C. to the Governor-General, 1917-20. *Address :* Norfolk Island. *Clubs :* Melbourne ; Australasian Pioneers', Sydney.
(Died 25 Jan. 1928.)

SELOUS, Frederick Courteney, D.S.O. 1916 ; Captain Royal Fusiliers ; *b.* London, 31 Dec. 1851 ; of mixed French and English parentage on father's side, and Scotch and English on mother's ; *m.* Marie Catherine Gladys, *d.* of Canon Maddy, Down Hatherley Parish, Gloucestershire ; two *s.* *Educ. :* Bruce Castle, Tottenham ; Rugby ; Neuchatel, Switzerland ; Wiesbaden, Germany. Awarded by the Royal Geographical Society the Cuthbert Peek grant, the Back Premium, and the Founder's Gold medal ; also elected a Corresponding Member by the Zoological Society. Left England for South Africa on 25 July 1871 ; proceeded to Matabeleland in the following year, and from that time until 1890 travelled continually all over South Central Africa, making a living by elephant hunting and the collection of specimens of natural history. In 1890 took service under the B. S. A. Company, and acted as guide to the Pioneer Expedition to Mashonaland ; returned to England in Dec. 1892, but went back the following year in order to take part in the first Matabele war. After another visit to England, again got back to Matabeleland just in time to witness the outbreak of the rinderpest and the late native insurrection in that country ; served European War. with Legion of Frontiersmen, East Africa (D.S.O.) *Publications :* A Hunter's Wanderings in Africa, 1881 ; Travel and Adventure in South-East Africa, 1893 ; Sunshine and Storm in Rhodesia, 1896 ; Sport and Travel, East and West, 1900 ; Recent Hunting Trips in British North America, 1907 ; African Nature Notes and Reminiscences, 1908. *Recreations :* football and birds'-nesting when young ; at present hunting big game, shooting, cricket, lawn tennis, cycling, collecting specimens of natural history. *Address:* Heatherside, Worplesdon, Surrey, England.

(*Died 4 Jan. 1917.*)

SELWYN, Rev. Edward Carus, D.D.; Hon. Canon of Peterborough Cathedral, 1905; *b.* Blackheath, 25 Nov. 1853; *o. s.* of Rev. E. J. Selwyn, Principal of Blackheath Proprietary School; *m.* 1st, Lucy Arnold, *adop. d.* of J. W. Cropper, Dingle Bank, Liverpool, *g. d.* of Dr. Arnold of Rugby; 2nd, Maud Stuart Dunn, *d.* of James A. Dunn; four *s.* two *d. Educ.:* Eton; King's Coll. Camb. Newcastle Scholar; King's Scholar; Bell Scholar; Carus Prizeman; Browne's Medallist thrice; Fellow of King's Coll.; Lecturer there, 1876-78; Curate of St. Paul's, Jarrow-on-Tyne, 1879; Dean of King's Coll. 1880-82; Lecturer there and at Emmanuel Coll.; Principal of Liverpool Coll. 1882-87; Headmaster of Uppingham School, 1887-1907; Select Preacher, Cambridge, 1881, etc. *Publications:* The Christian Prophets; St. Luke the Prophet; The Oracles in the New Testament; contributions to The Expositor, J.T.S., etc. *Address:* Undershaw, Hindhead. *Clubs:* Alpine, Athenæum. (*Died 8 Nov. 1918.*)

SEMON, Sir Felix, Kt., *cr.* 1897; K.C.V.O. *cr.* 1905; C.V.O. 1902; M.D., F.R.C.P.; late Physician Extraordinary to King Edward VII.; Commander of Order of Isabella la Catolica; Grand Officer Order of Medjidie; Grand Cordon of Star of Zanzibar; Consulting Laryngologist and Vice - President National Hospital for Epilepsy and Paralysis; *b.* Dantzic, 8 December 1849; *s.* of S. J. Semon, stockbroker; *m.* Augusta, *d.* of late H. Redeker, 1879; three *s. Educ.:* Berlin, Heidelberg, Vienna, Paris, London (St. Thomas's). Studied medicine in Germany, 1868-73; having finished his studies at home, travelled to Vienna, Paris, London; became attached first to Throat Hospital (Golden Square), later to St. Thomas's Hospital, and held the post as Physician for Diseases of the Throat at that hospital from 1882-97; one of the founders and (3 years) President of the Laryngological Society of London; had on his retirement the Semon Lectureship in Laryngology founded in his honour at the University of London; Hon. and Corresponding Member of many learned Societies. *Publications:* numerous physiological and clinical contributions to scientific medicine in Philos. Trans., Proc. of Royal Soc.; Forschungen und Erfahrungen, 1880 - 1910, etc. *Recreations:* music, gardening, travelling, shooting, fishing. *Address:* Rignalls, Great Missenden, Bucks. *T.A.:* Semon, Great Missenden. *T.:* Great Missenden 33. (*Died 1 Mar. 1921.*)

SENIER, Alfred, M.D., Ph.D., D.Sc.; Professor of Chemistry since 1891, Member of Council, 1893-1908, of Governing Body since 1908, Dean of the Faculty of Science since 1912, University College, formerly Queen's College, Galway; Member of Senate, National University of Ireland, since 1908; President of the Chemical Section of the British Association, 1912; Fellow of Chemical Societies of London, 1875, Berlin, 1885; Fellow of Institute of Chemistry, 1878; Member of Royal Irish Academy, 1907; Hon. Member of Aristotelian Society, 1902; *b.* Burnley, 24 Jan. 1853; *e. s.* of late Alfred Senier and Jane, *e. d.* of Donald Sutherland; *m.* Elsbeth Ida, *e. d.* of late Justizrath Heinrich Friedrich Wagner, of Berlin; two *d. Educ.:* privately; Universities of Wisconsin, Michigan, and Berlin. Demonstrator and Assist. in Chemistry, Pharmaceutical Society, 1874-82; Lecturer on Chemistry, St. John's College, Battersea, 1881-84; Research Student with the late Professor von Hofmann, Berlin, 1884 - 87; in charge of Chemistry, Queen's College, Cork, 1890-91; Hon. Secretary and Treasurer Aristotelian Society, from foundation till 1884. *Publications:* Scientific

memoirs; mainly devoted to organic chemistry, in Transactions of London and Berlin Chemical Societies and in other journals; Essays, notably A Visit to Giessen, 1898, Bonn on the Rhine, 1901, and The University and Technical Training, 1910; Address, Section B, British Association, 1912; article on Cyanic Acids in Watt's Dictionary of Chemistry, and articles on Chemistry of Drugs in Thorpe's Dictionary of Applied Chemistry. *Recreations:* Treasurer, from its foundation, 1893 - 94 till 1910, Univ., formerly Queen's, College Athletic Union; Conservator of Fisheries, Galway, since 1900. *Address:* 28 Herbert Park, Donnybrook, Co. Dublin; University College, Galway. *Clubs:* Galway County; United Service, Dublin.

(*Died 29 June 1918.*)

SENIOR, Mark; Member of the National Portrait Society; *b.* Hanging Heaton, Yorkshire, 1863. *Address:* 15 Park Row, Leeds.

(*Died Jan. 1927.*)

SENIOR, William, author; adopted journalism as a profession, 1858; was a regular lecturer at literary and mechanics' institutions in the South and Western counties; joined staff of Daily News, 1866, and became a contributor to serial literature; in 1875 went to Queensland to establish and edit a Parliamentary Hansard for that colony; resumed connection with Daily News as special correspondent on returning home, 1881-99; succeeded Francis Francis as angling editor of the Field, 1883; editor-in-chief of Field, 1900-1909; Fellow of Institute of Journalists; ex-President of Fly-fisher's Club. *Publications:* Notable Shipwrecks, 1873; Waterside Sketches, 1875; By Stream and Sea, 1877; Anderton's Angling, 1878; Travel and Trout in the Antipodes, 1880; Angling in Great Britain, 1883; Near and Far, 1888; The Thames from Oxford to the Tower, 1889; A Mixed Bag, 1895; new edition of Blakey's Angling, 1898; Pike and Perch volume of Fur, Feather, and Fin series, 1900. *Recreations:* angling, cycling, golf. *Clubs:* Authors', Savage, Fly-fishers'.

(*Died 7 Oct. 1920.*)

SERAO, Matilde; *b.* Patras, Greece, 1856; *m.* Edoardo Scarfoglio. Founded with her husband Il Corriere di Roma, Il Corriere di Napoli, and Il Mattino; founded and still directs Il Giorno in Naples. *Publications:* La Conquista di Roma; Il Paese di Cuccagna (The Land of Cockayne); The Ballet Dancer, and On Guard Sentinel, 1901; In the Country of Jesus, 1905; Farewell Love; Castigo; Sister John of the Cross; After the Pardon; Fantasy; Evviva la Vita; Ella non respose, and others. *Address:* Il Giorno, Naples. (*Died 25 July 1927.*)

SERENA, Arthur; J.P., F.R.G.S.; Knight Grand Cross of the Crown of Italy; Commendatore of the Order of San Maurizio and Lazzaro; Senior Partner in the Firm of Galbraith, Pembroke & Co., Shipowners, Underwriters at Lloyd's, Ship and Insurance Brokers; *s.* of late Chevalier Leon Sereua, the Venetian Patriot of 1848-49; unmarried. *Educ.:* London University School; Bonn. Visiting Justice of Holloway Prison; Past Vice-Chairman and Treasurer of the London Chamber of Commerce, Member of the Council; Member of Council of Association of British Chambers of Commerce; Member of the Military Appeal Tribunal, County of London; of Council of the Chamber of Shipping United Kingdom; Hon. Vice-President Italian Chamber of Commerce; Executive Committee London Savings Bank; on the Committee of Management Royal Academy of Music; contested (L.) Penryn and Falmouth (1892); on the Committee of the London Hospital; Consul - General for the Republic of San Marino; Envoy Extraordinary and Minister Plenipotentiary at the Coronation of King George; founded Chairs of Italian at the Universities of Oxford, Cambridge, Manchester, and Birmingham; established an annual Gold Medal for Italian Studies in the gift of the British Academy; Founded Chairs in English in Italy; Representative on Commerce Degrees Committee, University of London. *Address:* 36 York Terrace, Regent's Park, N.W.1. *T.A.:* Serena, London. *T.:* Paddington 1755, Avenue 5014. *Clubs:* Reform, City of London, Arts, Bath, Ranelagh.

(Died 31 Mar. 1922.)

SETH, Arathoon, I.S.O. 1905, J.P.; Registrar of the Supreme Court of Hong-Kong since 1908; Official Administrator; Official Trustee; Registrar of Companies; *b.* 1852; *s.* of late Seth Aviet Seth, merchant, Hong-Kong; *m.* 1878, Katherine, *d.* of late Peter Aviet Seth, merchant, Singapore; three *s.* two *d. Educ.:* St. Paul's College, Hong-Kong. Called to Bar, Lincoln's Inn, 1893; entered Magistracy, Hong-Kong, 1868-69; Third Clerk, 1872; Second Clerk, 1873; First Clerk, 1875; Clerk of Councils, and Chief Clerk Colonial Secretary's Office, 1881; Valuer under Rating Ordinance, 1875, 1881-83; Superintendent of Opium Revenue, 1883-85; Imports and Exports, 1887; Secretary to Board under Taiping-shan Resumption Ordinance, 1894-95 (thanks of Government); Secretary to Sanitary Properties Commission, 1896; Acting Deputy Land Officer, 1894-95, and 1895-96; Deputy Registrar and Appraiser Supreme Court, and Commissioner for Oaths, 1895; Commissioner for taking Acknowledgments of Married Women, 1896; Secretary to Squatter's Board, Official Receiver in Bankruptcy, 1895-96; Acting Assistant Registrar-General, 1897; Acting Registrar, Supreme Court, Acting Land Officer, Acting Registrar of Companies, Official Administrator and Official Trustee, 1898-1900; Member of Board of Examiners, 1902; retired, 1909. *Address:* 1 Upper Addison Gardens, Kensington, W.; Common Room, Lincoln's Inn, W.C.; Norman Cottage, Peak Road, Hong-Kong. *T.A:* Adash, London; Cottager, Hong-Kong. *Club:* Hong-Kong, Hong-Kong.

(Died 30 Dec. 1918.)

SETH, James, M.A.; LL.D., Professor of Moral Philosophy in the University of Edinburgh since 1898; *bro.* of Prof. Andrew Seth; *b.* Edinburgh, 1860. *Educ.:* George Watson's College; University of Edinburgh (M.A. 1881); Leipzig, Jena, Berlin. Asst. to Prof. Campbell Fraser (Logic and Metaphysics), 1883-85; Prof. of Philosophy, Dalhousie Coll. Halifax, Nova Scotia, 1886-92; Brown University, U.S.A., 1892-96; Sage Professor of Moral Philosophy in Cornell University, U.S.A.. 1896-98; co-editor of the Philosophical Review. *Publications:* A Study of Ethical Principles, 1894, 14th ed. 1918; English Philosophers and Schools of Philosophy, 1912. *Address:* 3 Queen's Crescent, Edinburgh. *Club:* University, Edinburgh.

(Died 24 July 1924.)

SETH-SMITH, W. H., F.R.I.B.A.; architect; *b.* London, 1852; *e. s.* of late William Seth-Smith; *m.* 1887, Beatrice, 3rd *d.* of Colonel H. Brabazon, Urmston. Past President Society of Architects, 1888-91; President Architectural Association, 1900-2; Fellow and late member of Board of Examiners, R.I.B.A. *Address:* 46 Lincoln's Inn Fields, W.C.2. *T.:* Holborn 4924.

(Died 30 Aug. 1928.)

SETON, Miles Charles Cariston, C.B. 1915; M.B., C.M., F.R.C.S., Edin. Univ.; Hon. Anæsthetist, Alfred Hospital, Melbourne; *b.* 1874; *e. s.* of late William Carden Seton of Cariston and Treskerby, Capt. 32nd Regiment. and Amy Isobel, 3rd *d.* of James Forsyth of Dunach and Glengorm, Argyllshire. Served South Africa, 1901-2; late Captain Cape Medical Staff Corps; is in line male the representative of the Setons of Cariston, and of the family of Cocke of Treskerby, Cornwall. *Recreations:*

walking, shooting, and bridge. *Address:* Hotham Street, East St. Kilda, Melbourne, Australia: 24 Collins Street, Melbourne. *Club:* Melbourne Savage. *(Died 13 Jan. 1919.)*

SETON, Walter, M.A., D.Lit. (London); D.Jr. Padua: Ph. Dr. Prague; F.S.A.; Fellow Royal Historical Society; Fellow of University College, London; Secretary of University College, London, since 1903; Lecturer in Scottish History, University College, London, since 1923; *b.* 4 Oct. 1882; 4th *s.* (3rd *surv.*) of late Col. Alexander R. Seton, R.E., *brother* of Sir Bruce Gordon Seton, Bt., of Abercorn, Co. Linlithgow; unmarried. *Educ.:* privately miseducated; subsequently educated at University College, London, 1899-1903. Assisted in foundation of University College Hall, Ealing, 1903; Warden of University College Hall, 1912-23; Political Secretary to Ministry of Information, with charge of propaganda in Balkans, 1918; Knight Gold Cross, Order of the Redeemer, Greece, 1919; Knight Officer of the Order of the Crown of Italy, 1921; represented University of London at celebrations of seventh centenary of Padua University, 1922, and at similar celebrations at Naples University, 1924; Secretary of the Ramsay Memorial Fund, 1917-1923, and is now Secretary to the Ramsay Fellowship Trust; responsible for securing for Scotland the Penicuik Jewels of Mary Queen of Scots, 1923; Secretary and Treasurer British Society of Franciscan Studies since 1923. *Publications:* Two Fifteenth-Century Franciscan Rules, 1914; Blessed Agnes of Bohemia, 1915; Blessed Giles of Assisi, 1918; Vita di S. Chiara Vergine, 1921; Nicholas Glassberger and his Works, 1923; Penicuik Jewels of Mary Queen of Scots, 1923; numerous articles in Archivum Franciscanum Historicum, Scottish Historical Review, Antiquaries' Journal. *Recreations:* collecting books and MSS. *Address:* 20 Stafford Place, Buckingham Gate, S.W.1. *T.:* Victoria 9333. *Clubs:* Athenæum, Union.

(Died 26 Jan. 1927.)

SETTLE, Lieut.-General Sir Henry Hamilton, R.E.; K.C.B., *cr.* 1900; C.B. 1898; D.S.O. 1891; *b.* 27 Jan. 1847; *m.* 1875, Edith, *o. d.* of late John Rigg of Wrotham Hill Park, Kent; one *d. Educ.:* Cheltenham College. Entered army, 1867; Col. 1893; p.s.c.; served Nile Expedition, 1884-85 (despatches, brevet of Major, medal with clasp, Khedive's star); as Senior Staff Officer, operations, Suakim, 1888 (despatches, brevet of Lieut.-Col. and clasp); Toski, 1889 (despatches, clasp, 2nd class Medjidieh); Tokar, 1891 (despatches, clasp); South Africa Field Force, 1899-1902 (despatches twice, K.C.B., promoted Maj.-Gen. for distinguished service in the field); Surveyor-General and Q.M.S., Egyptian Army, 1886-92; Insp.-Gen. Police of Egypt, 1892-94; Assistant Insp.-General of Fortifications, War Office, 1895; G.O.C. Cape Colony, 1902-1904; Portsmouth Defences, 1905-1908; retired, 1911; Colonel Commandant R.E. 1921; has rank of Pacha, 2nd class Osmanieh, 1st class Medjidieh. *Address:* 7 Park Street, Bath. *Club:* United Service.

(Died 22 April 1923.)

SETTRINGTON, Lord; Frederick Charles Gordon-Lennox; *o. surv. s.* and *heir* of Earl of March; *b.* 15 Feb. 1904. *Address:* Molecomb, Chichester.

(Died 24 Aug. 1919.)

SEWALL, Mrs. May Wright (*née* Montague Wright) Founder and Hon. Pres. International Council of Women; Chairman of Committee to organise a World's Conference of Internationalists for 1915, and a Director of the National Conservation League of Childhood; Hon. Pres. International New Thought Alliance; *b.* Milwaukee, Wisconsin; *m.* 1880, Theodore Lovett Sewall. *Educ.:* by private tutors;

at Bloomington Academy ; and the North-Western University. M.L. and M.A. Member of National Historical Association and of the National Geographical Society, U.S.A. ; of the Union Universelle de Lettres et Sciences (Paris) ; Founder of Propylæum Association, and Art Association, Indianapolis. *Publications:* Higher Education of Women in the Western States ; many monographs on subjects of Education and Reform ; Historical Resume of the World's Congress of Representative Women, 2 vols. ; The Open Mind ; The New Internationalism, etc. Editor of Transactions of the Third Quinquennial International Council of Women, Berlin, 1904 (2 vols.) ; The Genesis of the International Council of Women, 1888-93 ; Women, World War and Permanent Peace. *Recreations:* walking, rowing, the theatre. *Address:* Indianapolis, Indiana, U.S.A. *T.A.:* Maydore, Indianapolis, U.S.A. *Clubs:* Lyceum ; Sorosis, Artists, New York ; Women's, Contemporary, Art Association, Indianapolis.
(Died 22 July 1920.)

SEWARD, Edwin, F.R.I.B.A., R.C.A. ; *b.* Yeovil, Somerset, 1853 ; *s.* of William Seward of Hendford Hill, Yeovil ; *m.* 1884, Edith Jessie, *e. d.* of late Thomas Maddox, Surveyor, Hereford ; two *d.* *Educ.:* Aldridge's Grammar School, Yeovil. Articled as Architect at Yeovil, 1867 ; Cardiff, 1870 ; winner of various medals, National Competitions, South Kensington ; Architect of the Cardiff Original Municipal Buildings ; the Wye Bridge, Monmouth ; Cardiff Coal and Shipping Exchange ; Glamorgan and Monmouth Infirmary ; Cardiff Workhouses and Hospitals ; Library, Museum ; Art Schools of Cardiff ; Harbour Trust Offices and Council Chamber, Swansea ; Exhibitor Royal Academy, etc. ; First President South Wales Architects' Society ; Member, Royal Cambrian Academy of Arts ; Founder South Wales Art Society ; Past-President Naturalists' Society of Cardiff. *Publications:* pamphlets on antiquarian, artistic, and scientific subjects connected with professional matters and archæology, and as delegate to and Hon. Secy. of Sections of the British Association and British Archæological Association. *Recreations:* landscape gardening, collector of works of art and antiquities. *Address:* 12 Victoria Esplanade, Weymouth. *Club:* Royal Dorset Yacht.
(Died 21 June 1924.)

SEWELL, Col. Thomas Davies, F.R.A.S. ; senior proprietor of the Broad Arrow ; the Naval and Military Gazette ; clerk of the Spectacle-makers' Company, and Secretary of its diploma scheme ; *b.* London, 21 Sep. 1832 ; *s.* of late Henry William Sewell, sword-bearer of the City of London, and late Mary Davies ; two *s.* one *d.* *Educ.:* City of London School. Formerly clerk of the Fanmakers', Shipwrights', and Loriners' Companies ; clerk of the Chamberlains Court, Guildhall, London ; Past Grand Sword-bearer of England ; Major and Lt.-Col. Royal London Militia (4th Batt. Royal Fusiliers) ; Col. Commanding 4th Batt. Essex Regiment, R.V. ; Major and Lt.-Col. Tower Hamlets Volunteers, R.E. ; Senior Captain London Rifle Volunteer Brigade ; Member National Reserve, City of London Section ; Senior Churchwarden of St. John the Evangelist, Westminster, since 1894 ; formerly Master of the Loriners' and Pattenmakers' Companies in the City of London. *Address:* 9/11 Temple House, Temple Avenue, E.C. ; 29 Grosvenor Road, S.W. *T.A.:* Sagittaria, London. *T.:* 4883 Holborn. *Club:* Junior Army and Navy. *(Died 13 April 1916.)*

SEXTON, Col. Michael John, LL.D., M.D. ; C.B. 1916 ; late A.M.S. ; *b.* 1860 ; *s.* of John Sexton, Cork ; *m.* Katherine, *e. d.* of Capt. J. Conway, Duke of Cornwall's L.I. ; one *d.* *Educ.:* Queen's College,

Cork. Served Burma, 1889 (medal with clasp) ; Chin Lushai Expedition, 1888-90 (clasp) ; S. Africa, 1901-2 (Queen's medal 3 clasps) ; European War, 1914-18 (despatches twice, C.B.). *Address:* Holt & Co., 3 Whitehall Place, S.W.1.
(Died 29 April 1922.)

SEYMOUR, Dr. Edgar William; M.V.O. 1912 ; M.A., M.B., B.C. (Cantab.); M.R.C.S. ; late Surgeon in Ordinary to Princess Beatrice, *b.* 1868 ; *s.* of late Dr. William Hoffmeister, M.V.O. [changed name to Seymour by deed poll dated 6 June 1918]. *Educ.:* Cambridge ; St. Bartholomew's. Late Consulting Physician, Royal Convalescent Home for Officers, Osborne, and Surgeon Royal Yacht Squadron ; retired. *Address:* Debourne, Cowes, I. of W. *(Died 24 July 1926.)*

SEYMOUR, Lord Edward Beauchamp, 2nd Lieut., 4th Batt. Royal Warwicks Regt. ; 3rd *s.* of 6th Marquess of Hertford ; *b.* 22 Nov. 1879 ; *m.* 1914, Elfrida Adelaide, 2nd *d.* of S. C. De Trafford. Served South African War, 1900-1 (wounded). *(Died 5 Dec. 1917.)*

SEYMOUR, Sir Michael Culme-, 3rd Bt., *cr.* 1809 ; G.C.B., G.C.V.O.; Admiral 1893 (retired 1901) ; Vice-Admiral of the United Kingdom, 1901-20 ; *b.* Northchurch, Berkhampstead, 18 Mar. 1836 ; *S.* father 1880 ; *m.* 1866, Mary (*d.* 1912), *d.* of Hon. Richard Watson, M.P., Rockingham Castle, and *g.d.* of 2nd Baron Sondes ; two *s.* one *d.* *Educ.:* Harrow. Entered Navy, 1850 ; served Burmah War, 1852 ; Baltic, 1854 ; Black Sea, 1854-55, including Naval Brigade in Crimea ; China War, including Fatshan, Canton, and Peiho, 1858 ; Naval A.D.C. to Queen, 1869 ; Private Secretary to First Lord of Admiralty, Rt. Hon. G. Ward Hunt, 1874-76 ; Rear-Admiral, 1882 ; Vice-Admiral, 1888 ; in command of Pacific Squadron, 1885-87 ; Channel Squadron, 1890-92 ; Mediterranean Squadron, 1893-97 ; Commander-in-Chief, Portsmouth, 1897-1900 ; First and Principal A.D.C. to the late Queen, 1899-1901 ; Grand Commander, Order of the Redeemer (Greece), 1920. *Heir:* *s.* Rear-Adm. Sir Michael. *Recreations:* shooting, hunting, fishing, golf. *Address:* Wadenhoe House, Oundle. *T.A.:* Wadenhoe. *Club:* United Service.
(Died 11 Oct. 1920.)

SEYMOUR, Vice - Admiral Sir Michael Culme-, 4th Bt., *cr.* 1809 ; K.C.B., *cr.* 1920 ; C.B. 1916 ; M.V.O. 1912 ; Second Sea Lord and Chief of Naval Personnel since 1924 ; *b.* 29 Aug. 1867 ; *e. s.* of Sir M. Culme-Seymour, 3rd Bt. and Mary (*d.* 1912), *d.* of Hon. Richard Watson, M.P., Rockingham Castle, and *g.d.* of 2nd Baron Sondes ; *S.* father, 1920 ; *m.* 1896, Florence Agnes Louisa, *y. d.* of late A. L. Nugent ; one *s.* one *d.* Lieut., 1889 ; Captain, 1905 ; Rear-Adm. 1916 ; Vice-Adm. 1920 ; served Battle of Jutland, 1916 (despatches, C.B.) ; Rear-Admiral Commanding Black Sea and Caspian Squadron, 1919 ; Second-in-Command in the Mediterranean, 1920 ; Commander-in-Chief North America and West Indies Station, 1923-24. *Heir:* *s.* Michael, *b.* 26 April 1909 (naval cadet). *Address:* Tothill, Christchurch, Hants. *Clubs:* Naval and Military, Carlton. *(Died 2 April 1925.)*

SEYMOUR, Comm. Ralph Frederick, R.N. ; C.M.G. 1919 ; D.S.O. 1916 ; *b.* 6 Jan. 1886 ; *e. s.* of late Sir Horace (Alfred Damer) Seymour, K.C.B., and Elizabeth Mary, *d.* of Col. Frederick Romilly. Served European War, 1914-19, on personal staff of Admiral Sir David Beatty including battles of Heligoland, Dogger Bank, and Jutland Bank (despatches, D.S.O.) ; prom. Commander, 1917 ; Commander H.M. Yacht Victoria and Albert, 1920. *Address.* 19 Chesham Road, Brighton *Clubs:* Turf, United Service. *(Died 5 Oct. 1922.)*

SEYMOUR, Gen. Sir William Henry, K.C.B., *cr.* 1904 ; C.B. 1859 ; General ; and Col. Queen's Bays ; *b.* 1829 ; *s.* of Sir William Seymour and *e. d.* of Lieut.-Gen. Sir H. Oakes, Bt. ; *m.* 1875, Anne Charlotte, *d.* of Ven. Archdeacon Bowles. Entered army, 1847 ; served in the Crimea, 1854-55 (medal 4 clasps, Turkish medal) ; Indian mutiny, 1857-59 (despatches three times, brevet major, medal with clasp, C.B.).   (*Died 20 June 1921.*)

SHACKLETON, Major Sir Ernest (Henry) Kt., *cr.* 1909 ; C.V.O. 1909 ; M.V.O. 1907 ; O.B.E. 1919 ; Explorer ; *b.* Kilkee, 15 Feb. 1874 ; *e. s.* late Henry Shackleton, M.D. ; *m.* 1904, Emily Mary, 2nd *d.* of late Charles Dorman ; two *s.* one *d. Educ. :* Dulwich Coll. 3rd Lieut. National Antarctic Expedition, 1901 ; Commander British Antarctic Expedition, 1907 ; Antarctic Expedition, 1914 ; Director Equipment and Transport Mobile Forces North Russia Winter Campaign, 1918-19 ; Commander British Oceanographical and Sub-Antarctic Expedition, 1921. *Publications :* The Heart of the Antarctic ; The Diary of a Troopship. *Address :* 14 Milnthorpe Road, Eastbourne. *Clubs :* Marlborough, Royal Yacht Squadron, Cowes.   (*Died 5 Jan. 1922.*)

SHADWELL, Dr. Charles Lancelot, Provost of Oriel College, 1905-14 ; late Fellow of Winchester College ; *b.* London, 16 Dec. 1840 ; *e. surv. s.* of Lancelot Shadwell, barrister-at-law, and *g. s.* of late Vice-Chancellor of England. *Educ. :* Westminster School (Q.S.) ; Christ Church, Oxford ; 1st class Moderations, 1861 ; 1st class Final Classical School, 1863 ; B.A. 1863 ; M.A. 1866 ; D.C.L. 1898. Fellow of Oriel College, Oxford, 1864-98 ; Senior Proctor 1875-76 ; called to the Bar, Lincoln's Inn, 1872. *Publications :* The Purgatory of Dante, translated into English verse, 1892 ; The Earthly Paradise, 1899 ; The Paradise, 1915 ; Quaestio de Aqua et Terra, 1909 ; History of Oriel College, in Clark's series, 1891 ; Registrum Orielense, vol. i. 1893, vol. ii. 1902 ; The Laudian Statutes, 1888 ; The University and College Estates Acts, 1898 ; edited W. H. Pater's Greek Studies, 1895 ; Miscellaneous Studies, 1895 ; Gaston de Latour, 1896. *Recreations :* punting, billiards, chess problems, chronograms. *Address :* 108 Banbury Road, Oxford. *Club :* Athenæum. (*Died 13 Feb. 1919.*)

SHADWELL, Lionel Lancelot, M.A. ; Commissioner of the Board of Control, 1918-1920 ; *b.* 1845 ; *e. surv. s.* of Lancelot Shadwell, barrister-at-law, and *g.s.* of late Vice-Chancellor of England. *Educ. :* Winchester ; New College, Oxford ; 1st class Moderations, 1866 ; 1st class Final Classical School, 1868 ; barrister, Lincoln's Inn, 1873 ; Secretary to Commissioners in Lunacy, 1901-4 ; Commissioner in Lunacy, 1904-14. *Publications :* Enactments in Parliament specially concerning the Universities of Oxford and Cambridge, the Colleges and Halls therein, and the Colleges of Winchester, Eton, and Westminster, 1912 ; Odes of Horace translated into English Verse, 1920. *Recreation :* golf. *Address :* La Pastorelle, Icart, Guernsey. *Clubs :* Union, Albemarle.   (*Died 2 Dec. 1925.*)

SHAH, Hon. Sir Lallubhai Asharam, Kt., *cr.* 1920 ; M.A., LL.B. ; a Judge of H.M. High Court of Judicature, Bombay, since 1913 ; acted as Chief-Justice in 1922, 1923 and 1924 ; *b.* 4 Feb. 1873 ; *s.* of Asharam Dalichand Shah of Ahmedabad, late Karbhari of several Native States in Kathiawar. *Educ. :* The Gujerat College, Ahmedabad ; Government Law School, Bombay. Practised as Pleader of the Bombay High Court since 1895 ; Fellow of the Bombay University, 1904-11, and since 1915 ; officiated as Government Pleader, 1910, 1911, and 1912-13. *Recreations :* billiards and tennis. *Address :* Malabar Hill, Bombay. *Clubs :* Orient, Hindu Union, Willingdon, Bombay.   (*Died Nov. 1926.*)

SHAKESPEAR, Maj.-Gen. George Robert James, Indian Army ; *b.* 14 Oct.

950

1842 ; *m.* 1873, Lily Alice, *e. d.* of Maj.-Gen. Charles Stuart Lane. Entered army, 1860 ; Maj.-Gen. 1899 ; served Soudan, 1885 (despatches, medal with clasp, bronze star, brevet Lieut.-Col.) ; Hazara Expedition, 1891 (despatches, medal with clasp). *Address :* South View, Denville, Havant.   (*Died 2 Sept. 1926.*)

SHAKESPEARE, Rev. John Howard, M.A. (London) ; D.D. (Glasgow) ; LL.D. (McMaster, Toronto) ; Secretary of the Baptist Union of Great Britain and Ireland, 1898-1924 ; European Secretary of the Baptist World Alliance ; President of the National Council of Evangelical Free Churches, 1916 ; Moderator of the Federal Council of the Evangelical Free Churches of England, 1919-21 ; Joint Secretary of the Federal Council of the Evangelical Free Churches of England ; ex-Chairman of United Navy, Army, and Air Force Board ; *b.* Malton, Yorkshire, 1857 ; *m.* Amy, *d.* of late Rev. William Goodman, B.A. *Educ. :* University Coll., London ; Regent's Park Baptist College. B.A. (Honours), 1881 ; M.A. 1882. Minister, St. Mary's Baptist Church, Norwich, 1883-98. *Publications :* Baptist and Congregational Pioneers ; The Churches at the Cross-Roads, 1918. *Recreation :* golf. *Address :* Fallowhurst, Finchley, N. *T. :* Finchley 1527.   (*Died 12 Mar. 1928.*)

SHAMS-UL-HUDA, The Hon. Mr. Justice (Nawab Sir Syed) K.C.I.E., *cr.* 1916 ; M.A., B.L. ; President of the Bengal Provincial Legislature since 1921 ; *b.* 1864 ; belongs to well-known family of Syeds in Tippera, East Bengal ; grandfather was Judicial Officer in Chittagong, and father was a distinguished Arabic and Persian scholar, and for some time editor of the now defunct Persian newspaper Doorbeen. *Educ. :* The Presidency College, Calcutta ; Calcutta University (M.A., Fellow 1894). Commenced practice as a Vakil in the High Court at Calcutta ; Member of Eastern Bengal Legislative Council, 1908 ; elected to represent the Mahomedans of Eastern Bengal in the Imperial Legislative Council, 1909 ; Member Bengal Executive Council, 1912-1917 ; Vice-President Bengal Executive Council, April-June 1917 ; Judge, Calcutta High Court, 1917-21 ; held the office of Secretary of the Bengal Provincial Moslem League and that of Bengal Landholders' Association ; President-Elect of the All-India Moslem League, 1912 ; received the title of Nawab as a personal distinction, 1918. *Recreations :* gardening and Persian poetry. *Address :* 220-2 Lower Circular Road, Calcutta. *Clubs :* Calcutta, India, Calcutta.   (*Died Oct. 1922.*)

SHAND, His Honour Sir Charles Lister, Kt., *cr.* 1922 ; J.P. County of Lancaster ; *b.* Liverpool, 2 Dec. 1846 ; *o. s.* of late Alexander Shand, Warmsworth, Doncaster, and Mary Anne, *d.* of James Lister, Ousefleet Grange, Goole ; *m.* 1892, Isabel Eleanor Louisa, *d.* of Rev. John Richardson, Knowsley, Prescot ; one *s.* two *d. Educ. :* Harrow ; Trin. College, Oxford. Barr. Inner Temple, 1870, and joined the Northern Circuit ; Revising Barr. 1884-89 ; Judge of County Courts, Circuit No. 6 (Liverpool), 1889-1921. *Recreations :* shooting, fishing. *Address :* Stand House, Childwall, Liverpool. *T.A. :* Stand House, Broadgreen. *T. :* 170 Wavertree. *Club :* Junior Carlton.   (*Died 4 April 1925.*)

SHANN, Sir Thomas Thornhill, Kt., *cr.* 1905 ; J.P. ; Lord Mayor of Manchester, 1903-4, 1904-5 ; *b.* 1846 ; *m.* Hannah (*decd.*), *d.* of late William Sutcliffe, Stansfield Hall, Todmorden. Alderman of Manchester City Council ; Chairman Manchester Education Committee ; Trustee and Treasurer of the John Rylands Library ; Treasurer of the Manchester Industrial Schools ; Chairman of Mayes Charity. *Address :* Lincluden, Formby, Lancs ; *T. :* Formby 169 ; Manchester 1291 and 1132. *T.A. :* Bundles,

SHAH, Khan Bahadur Sir Sayyid Mehdi, K.C.I.E. See page xxx.

SHAMSHER SINGH, Sir Sardar, Sardar Bahadur, K.C.I.E. See page xxx.

Manchester. *Clubs:* Constitutional; Constitutional, Manchester.   *(Died 14 July 1923.)*

SHANNON, Sir James Jebusa, Kt., *cr.* 1922, R.A. 1909; R.B.C. 1920; A.R.A. 1897; R.H.A.; portrait painter; *b.* Auburn, New York, 1862. Came to England in 1878; worked 3 years at South Kensington School, where he took gold medal for painting the figure; first important picture at R.A. portrait of Hon. Horatia Stopford in 1881; at R.A. in 1887 with full length of Henry Vigne Esq.—a picture which has since gained 1st class medals at Paris, Berlin, and Vienna Exhibitions; medal at Chicago Exhibition for full length of Mrs. Charlesworth; has painted a large number of portraits and a few subject pictures; was an original member of the New English Art Club, and remained a member for some years; a member of Chelsea Arts Club; President Society of Portrait Painters. *Address:* 3 Holland Park Road, Kensington, W.14. *T.:* Park 4670. *Club:* Athenæum.

     (Died 6 Mar. 1923.)

SHANSFIELD, William Newton; partner in The Press Agency; *b.* Mistley; *s.* of late William Jarrold Shansfield. Trained on the East Anglian Daily Times; Parliamentary Sketch Writer; contributor to British Medical Journal, and to leading provincial dailies; Hon. Secretary, Whitefriars Club; Editor, National Press Agency, 1905-9. *Recreations:* chess, sidelights on psychology. *Address:* Albany Chambers, Queen Anne's Gate, S.W. *T.:* Victoria 484. *Clubs:* National Liberal, Savage, Whitefriars.   *(Died 27 July 1925.)*

SHAPCOTT, John Dufour, I.S.O. 1913; *b.* 6 Nov. 1857; *s.* of late George Guy Shapcott, Perth, N.B. *Educ.:* St. Xavier's College, Calcutta. Entered Government of India Service, 1877; Department of Revenue and Agriculture, 1881; Registrar, Department of Revenue and Agriculture, 1910-17. *Address:* Simla, India.

     (Died 1923.)

SHAPURJI, Sir Burjorji Broacha, Kt., *cr.* 1911; Sheriff of Bombay. *Address:* Bombay.   *(Died 24 June 1920.)*

SHARFUDDIN, The Hon. Mr. Justice Syed; one of the Puisne Judges of the Patna High Court since 1915; Member of Executive Council, Governor-General of Behar; *b.* Neora (Dis. Patnà), 10 Sep. 1856; *y. s.* of Syed Farzand Ali Pleader of Chupra; *m.* 1882; one *s.* one *d.* *Educ.:* Patna College. Called to the Bar in 1880; practised at Patna, Behar; Puisne Judge, Calcutta, 1907 - 15; Member of the Senate of Calcutta University, 1904; Bengal Legislative Council, 1905, for Behar Landholders' Association; President of All India Mahomedan Educational Conference, 1906. *Address:* High Court, Patna. *Club:* Calcutta.

SHARP, Cecil J., B.A.; musician, writer, and lecturer; *b.* 1859; *m.* 1893; one *s.* three *d.* *Educ.:* Uppingham; Clare College, Cambridge. Mus. M. (hon.) Cambridge, 1923. Associate to the Chief Justice of South Australia, 1883-89; Principal of the Hampstead Conservatoire of Music, 1896-1905; Director of English Folk-Dance Society, 1911; Occasional Inspector, Board of Education, 1919-23. *Publications:* A Book of British Song; English Folk-Song, Some Conclusions; Folk - Songs from Somerset, Series 1-6 (with Rev. C. L. Marson); English Folk-Carols; English Folk-Chanteys; Songs, Dances, and Incidental Music to A Midsummer Night's Dream; The Country Dance Book, parts 1-6 (with George Butterworth); The Morris Book, parts 1-5 (with Herbert MacIlwaine and George Butterworth); The Sword Dances of Northern England, parts 1-3; English Folk-Songs from the Southern Appalachians; Folk-Songs collected in the Appalachian Mountains, parts 1 and 2, etc. *Address:* 4 Maresfield Gardens, Hampstead, N.W.3. *T.:* Hampstead 5791. *Club:* Savile.   *(Died 23 June 1924.)*

SHARP, David, M.B., C.M., M.A., F.R.S., F.Z.S.; Past President of Entomological Society of London; Hon. Member of the Institute of New Zealand, and of the Entomological Societies of France, Germany, The Netherlands, Russia, Washington, and Hawaii; Editor Zoological Record; *b.* 1840; *s.* of W. Sharp. *Educ.:* privately. Curator of Museum of Zoology, Cambridge, to 1909. *Publications:* Aquatic Carnivorous Coleoptera, 1882; Cambridge Natural History, "Insects," 1895 and 1899; Insects and Termites (Ency. Brit.), 1902; A Scheme for a National System of Rest-Funds (or Pensions) for Working People, 1892. *Address:* Lawnside, Brockenhurst.   *(Died 27 Aug. 1922.)*

SHARP, Ernest Hamilton, O.B.E., K.C., B.C.L., M.A.; *m.* 1900, Sarah, *d.* of Roger Cunliffe, of Tunbridge Wells. *Educ.:* Lincoln College, Oxford. Called to Bar, Inner Temple, 1891; Midland Circuit; acting Attorney - General, Hong - Kong, 1902 and 1904-5; Member of Executive Council, Hong-Kong; Chairman of War Charities Executive Committee, Hong-Kong, 1915-18; of Military Service Commission, Hong - Kong, 1917; of General Military Service Tribunal, Hong-Kong, 1918; of Hong-Kong University Commission, 1920. *Address:* The Peak, Hong-Kong; Great Bookham, Surrey; 5 Stone Buildings, Lincoln's Inn, W.C. *Clubs:* Junior Carlton, New Oxford and Cambridge; Hong-Kong.*(Died 8 Feb. 1922.)*

SHARP, Lt.-Col. Frederick Leonard, C.M.G. 1915; R.A.; *b.* 18 May 1867. Entered army, 1886; Captain, 1896; Major, 1901; Lieut.-Col., 1913; served European War, 1914-15 (C.M.G.).   *(Died 13 Aug. 1916.)*

SHARP, Rev. John, M.A.; *b.* Bradford, Yorkshire, 13 March 1837; *e. s.* of late Wm. Sharp, M.D., F.R.S.; *m.* 1864, Elizabeth *(d.* 1906), *d.* of late Dr. Lachlan M'Lean of Oban; one *s.* one *d.* *Educ.:* Rugby (Taberdar) Queen's College, Oxford (graduated in honours, B.A. 1860, M.A. 1863). Deacon, 1861; Priest, 1864; Missionary, C.M.S., in S. India, 1861-70, and 1872-78; Rugby Fox Master, 1861-65, and Principal of the Noble College at Masulipatam, 1865-78; curate in charge of Langton, by Partney, Lincs, 1870-72; first University Lecturer in Telugu and Tamil at Cambridge, 1878-80; Sec. British and Foreign Bible Society, London, 1880-1900; Sunday Evening Lecturer, St. Catherine Cree, Leadenhall Street, 1881-89; Editorial Superintendent of Translations and Editions of the Holy Scriptures, and Consulting Secretary of the British and Foreign Bible Society, 1901-8; Vice-President, B. and F.B.S., 1908. *Publications:* detached sermons on some special occasions; reports and pamphlets for B.F.B.S. *Address:* 32 Harold Road, Upper Norwood, S.E.

     (Died 20 May 1917.)

SHARP, Major John Reuben Philip, V.D., I.S.O. 1908; Chief Clerk of the Ordnance Survey (Board of Agriculture), 1873-1907; 2nd *s.* of William Sharp of Freemantle, Southampton. *Educ.:* privately. Commanded the Civil Service Company 2nd V.B. Hampshire Regt. from its formation in 1882 until 1904. *Address:* Red Hill House, Bassett, Southampton. *Clubs:* Overseas; Royal Southampton Yacht.

     (Died 8 Oct. 1922.)

SHARP, Sir Milton Sheridan, 1st Bt., *cr.* 1920. Chairman of Bradford Dyers' Association. *Heir: s.* Milton, *b.* 1880. *Address:* Spring House, Norristhorp, Heckmondwike, Yorks.

     (Died 22 May 1924.)

SHARP, Thos. Herbert, I.S.O. 1902; late Dep. Assist. Paymaster-Gen. for Supreme Court business; retired; *b.* 4 June 1840; *s.* of Thomas Sharp, sculptor, Royal Academy Silver Medallist, 1830; *m.* 1st, Katharine Frances, 2nd *d.* of Edmund Jones of Mirzapore, India (div.); three *d.*; 2nd, Florence, 3rd *d.* of Chester Cheston, F.S.I., of Upper Clapton; one *s.* one *d.* *Educ.:*

Hurstpierpoint; King's Coll. Evening School. Appointed Clerk in Accountant-General's Office in Chancery by Lord Chancellor on nomination of William Russell, Accountant-General, 1857; transferred to Paymaster-General under Chancery Funds Act, 1872; Civil Service Volunteer Corps, 1860-80; Captain, 1877-80; received Long Service Medal, 1894; late Member of Committee, Civil Service Benevolent Fund; People's Warden, Holy Trinity, Lamorbey, Bexley, from 1895-1903; Hon. Treasurer and Correspondent, Lamorbey National Schools, 1893-1905; late Member Council Sidcup Conservative Polling Association, Dartford Division of Kent. *Address:* Chaumont, Prospect Road, Tunbridge Wells. *Club:* Junior Constitutional.
(Died 12 Nov. 1918.)

SHARP, Rev. Canon William Hey, M.A.; Canon of St. Andrew's Cathedral, Sydney, since 1884; *b.* Hull, Yorkshire 21 Sep. 1845; *s.* of Wm. Sharp, M.D., F.R.S.; *m.* 1876, Mary E. P., *d.* of late Archdeacon Farr. LL.D., of Adelaide, South Australia; two *s. Educ.:* Rugby School (Exhibitioner); Lincoln College, Oxford (Scholar). Deacon, 1869; Priest, 1870; Warden of St. Paul's College within the University of Sydney, 1878-1908; examining Chaplain to Bishop Barry at Sydney, 1884-89; Chaplain to Archbishop of Sydney, 1893-1909; Fellow and Registrar of Australian College of Theology, 1896-1927. *Publications:* Sermons at St. Paul's College; Papers at Australian Church Congresses, etc. *Address:* Horton, Gordon, Sydney, Australia. *(Died 6 Feb. 1928.)*

SHARPE, Reginald Robinson, D.C.L.; Records Clerk to the Corporation of the City of London, 1876-1914; Barrister-at-Law of the Inner Temple; *b.* 1848; *s.* of Rev. Lancelot Arthur Sharpe, B.D., late Rector of Tackley, Oxon, and Ellen Elizabeth, *d.* of William Robinson, LL.D., and *g.s.* of Rev. Lancelot Sharpe, M.A., F.S.A., sometime Rector of All Hallows, Staining, in the city of Lond. *Educ.:* Merchant Taylors' School, Lond.; St. John's Coll., Ox. Appointed Dr. Andrew's Civil Law Scholar, St. John's Coll. Ox. 1866; a senior assistant in the Department of MSS. in the British Museum, 1871-76; Barr. 1888. *Publications:* London and the Kingdom (3 vols.); editor of Calendar of Letters, City of London, 1350-70; Calendar of Wills, Court of Husting, London, 1258-1688 (2 vols.); Calendar of Letter Books (A-L.) of the Corporation of London from A.D. 1275-1497; Calendar of City Coroners' Rolls, A.D. 1300-1378. *Recreation:* golf. *Address:* Tresco, York Road, Sutton, Surrey. *Club:* Constitutional.
(Died 3 Feb. 1925.)

SHARPE, Maj. Wilfred Stanley, C.M.G. 1900; Resident, Northern Nigeria; 4th Battalion Royal Irish Rifles, 1893; *b.* Richmond, Surrey, 29 April 1860; *s.* of J. C. Sharpe (*d.* 1913), of Gosling & Sharpe, 19 Fleet Street, E.C.; unmarried. *Educ.:* Radley; Oxford University. Served with the 9th Lancers in India, 1883; promoted into 19th Hussars, and transferred to Inniskilling Dragoons, 1890; District Commissioner Sierra Leone, 1894-1900; served Sierra Leone rebellion, 1898-99 (medal and clasp, C.M.G.); Dakkakari Expedition, 1903 (medal and clasp). *Recreations:* shooting and yachting. *Address:* Sutton Court, Chiswick, W. *Clubs:* Sports, Junior Naval and Military.
(Died 20 April 1917.)

SHARPIN, Ven. Frederick Lloyd, M.A.; 4th *s.* of late Henry Sharpin of Blofield, Norfolk, formerly of the 4th Light Dragoons; *b.* 1868, Helen Georgiana, *d.* of General Sealy, R.A.; three *s.* three *d. Educ.:* Bedford School; Exeter College, Oxford. Graduated 1860; Ordained, 1862, to the Curacy of Northill, Beds; Chaplain on Bombay Ecclesiastical Establishment, 1865; after serving a few years at Nasirabad and elsewhere, was ap-

952

pointed to the Cathedral as Junior Chaplain and afterwards as Senior Chaplain, until in 1886 he became Archdeacon of Bombay, having previously acted in that office for several years on different occasions; on resigning the Archdeaconry in 1888, was appointed to the living of Millbrook, Beds, which he held for 21 years. *Address:* 37 Eversley Road, Bexhill-on-Sea. *Club:* New, Bexhill-on-Sea.
(Died 2 June 1921.)

SHATTOCK, Prof. S. G., F.R.S. 1917; F.R.C.S., Fellow of University College, London; Pathological Curator, Royal College of Surgeons, London; joint-teacher in Pathology, St. Thomas's Medical School, London. *Educ.:* University College, London. External Examiner in Pathology, Victoria University, 1898-1901; External Examiner in Pathology, University of London, 1900-8; Editor and General Secretary Pathological Society of London, 1900-7; Hunterian Lecturer, Royal College of Surgeons, 1908-9; Member of Committee for the Revision of the Nomenclature of Diseases, Royal College of Physicians, 1902-13; President, Pathological Section, Royal Society of Medicine, 1907; President, Pathological Section, British Medical Association Meeting, held in London, 1910; President, Section of General Pathology and Morbid Anatomy, International Congress of Medicine, held in London, 1913. *Address:* Royal College of Surgeons, Lincoln's Inn Fields, W.C.2. *(Died 11 May 1924.)*

SHAUGHNESSY, 1st Baron, *cr.* 1916, of Montreal; **Thomas George Shaughnessy,** Kt., *cr.* 1901; K.C.V.O., *cr.* 1907; *b.* Milwaukee, 6 Oct. 1853; parents Irish; *m.* 1880, Elizabeth, *d.* of M. Nagle, Wisconsin; one *s.* two *d.* General purchasing agent C.P.R., 1882; subsequently Assistant General Manager and President; President and Director of a number of Railway Companies, all of which are directly or indirectly connected with the C.P.R. *Heir:* *s.* Hon. W. J. Shaughnessy. *Address:* 905 Dorchester Street, W., Montreal.
(Died 10 Dec. 1923.)

SHAW, Sir Alexander (William), Kt., *cr.* 1906; Head of firm W. J. Shaw and Sons, Limerick; *b.* Oct. 1847; *s.* of late Wm. John Shaw; *m.* Eleanor R. Gubbins, *d.* of late Wm. Gough-Gubbins; three *s.* four *d. Educ.:* St. Mary's College, Limerick. *Publications:* Irish Trade; Irish Canals and Waterways. *Recreations:* golf, motoring, fishing. *Address:* Derravoher, Limerick. *T.A.:* Limerick. *T.:* Limerick 246. *M.:* TI 393. *Club:* Limerick County.
(Died 28 Nov. 1923.)

SHAW, Rev. Sir Charles (John Monson), 8th Bt., *cr.* 1665; Rector of Wrotham, Kent, since 1913; *b.* 24 Nov., 1860; *s.* of Rev. C. J. Kenward Shaw and Julia, *d.* of Captain J. H. Boteler, R.N.; *S.* nephew, 1909; *m.* 1893, Louisa, *d.* of J. W. Bosanquet; one *s. Educ.:* Haileybury; Hertford College, Oxford. Ordained, 1884; Curate, Bexley, 1884-89; Swanley, 1890-92; Vicar, 1892-1902; Vicar of Margate, 1902-12. *Heir:* *s.* John James Kenward, Lieut. R.N.; [*b.* 11 June 1895; *m.* 1921, Elizabeth Mary Theodora, *e. d.* of Robert Hughes, Stowford Lodge, Ivybridge, S. Devon.] *Address:* Wrotham, Kent. *(Died 11 Sept. 1922.)*

SHAW, Sir Doyle Money, K.C.B., *cr.* 1911; C.B. 1882; Inspector-General of Hospitals, R.N., retired 1892; *b.* 1880; 5th *s.* of late Dr. David Shaw, H.E.I.C.S. *Educ.:* Edinburgh Academy and University. Entered navy as Assist.-Surgeon, 1854; served during Crimean War in H.M.S. "Spiteful" (medal, with clasp for Sebastopol, and Turkish medal); with battalion of Marines in China, 1857-61 (mentioned in despatches, promoted to Staff Surgeon, medal with 3 clasps); on board "Octavia" flagship during Abyssinian War (medal); Senior Medical Officer on board flagship "Alexandra" at bombardment of forts of Alexandria, 1882 (medal with clasp, C.B., and promoted to Deputy-Insp.-Gen.); in charge of R.N. Hospitals at Plymouth, Malta, and Haslar between 1884 and 1892.   *(Died 30 Sept. 1918.)*

SHAW, Edward Wingfield, D.S.O. 1915; 1st Batt. The Duke of Cambridge's Own (Middlesex Regiment). *b.* 19 Feb. 1895; *s.* of Col. G. J. Shaw; unmarried. *Educ.:* Lancing and Dulwich College. Served European War, 1914-15 (despatches, D.S.O.). *Address:* 14 Richmond Bridge Mansions, E. Twickenham, Middlesex. *Club:* Junior United Service.
         (Died Dec. 1916.)

SHAW, Sir Frederick William, 5th Bt.; *cr.* 1821; D.S.O. 1900; D.L., J.P.; *b.* Dublin, 15 Mar. 1858; *e. s.* of 4th Bt. and Kate, *d.* of William Barton, Grove, Co. Tipperary; *S.* father, 1895; *m.* Eleanor, *d.* of Major Horace de Vere, R.E., of Curragh Chase, 1885; two *s.* four *d.* *Educ.:* Harrow; Oriel College, Oxford. Lieut. Royal Dragoons, 1879-85; Lieut.-Col. 5th Batt. Royal Dublin Fusiliers; served South Africa, 1900-1902 (despatches); commanded 8th (S.) Batt. Royal Dublin Fusiliers. *Recreations:* hunting, shooting, fishing, golf, cycling. *Heir: s.* Robert de Vere [*b.* 24 Feb. 1890; M.C.; Capt. R.F.A.; served European War, 1914-18 (despatches, M.C.)]. *Address:* Bushy Park, Terenure, Co. Dublin. *Club:* Kildare Street, Dublin.   *(Died 15 July 1927.)*

SHAW, J. Byam; A.R.W.S.; Partner with Rex Vicat Cole in School of Art, Campden Hill, W.; *b.* Madras, 13 Nov. 1872; *s.* of John Shaw, Registrar High Court, Madras, and Sophia Alicia Byam Gunthorpe; *m.* 1899, Evelyn Pyke-Nott; four *s.* one *d.* *Educ.:* privately. Came to England, 1878, and London, 1879; went to St. John's Wood School of Art; entered Royal Academy Schools, 1889; first picture, Rosé Mary, Royal Academy, 1898. *Publications:* illustrated Browning's Poems, 1898; Tales from Boccaccio, 1899; Chiswick Shakespeare, 1900; Old King Cole's Book of Nursery Rymes, 1901; Pilgrim's Progress, 1904; Coronation Book, 1902; Cloister and the Hearth, 1909; Tales of Mystery and Imagination, E. A. Poe, 1909; The Garden of Kama, Laurence Hope, 1914. *Recreation:* boating. *Address:* 62 Addison Road, W. *T.:* Park 4198. *Club:* National Sporting.
         (Died 26 Jan. 1919.)

SHAW, Sir James Dods, Kt., *cr.* 1913; Manager of House of Commons Official Staff for recording the Parliamentary proceedings since 1908, and Editor of the Commons Debates; *s.* of late Andrew Shaw of Garliestown and Glasgow; *m.* Kate Mary, *d.* of late Francis Wood. Was on literary staffs of Liverpool Daily Post, Leeds Mercury, and Manchester Guardian; Managing Editor of Nottingham Daily Express; acted for many years as political representative of Press Association in Parliamentary Lobbies; is a life member of the Imperial Society of Knights Bachelor; has written on holiday travels in Canada, Egypt, Siberia, Japan, China, Malaya, Ceylon, as well as on social, political and antiquarian subjects. *Recreation:* golf. *Address:* House of Commons, S.W.
         (Died 14 Nov. 1916.)

SHAW, Lauriston Elgie, M.D., F.R.C.P.; Consulting Physician to Guy's Hospital, and to the Royal Buckinghamshire Hospital; *b.* London, 1859; *s.* of Archibald Shaw, of St. Leonards; *m.* May, *d.* of late Howard Spalding; one *s.* *Educ.:* City of London School; Univ. College, London; Guy's Hospital. *Publications:* contributions to medical literature. *Address:* Oatlands Chase, Weybridge. *T.:* Walton-on-Thames 293.   *(Died 25 Dec. 1923.)*

SHAW, Thomas Claye, B.A., M.D. (Lond.); Fellow of the Royal College of Physicians, London; consulting practitioner; *b.* 1841; *m.*

Hannah Gratrix (*d.* 1925), *d.* of late J. Ridgway of Kytes, Leavesden, Herts; two *d.* *Educ.:* King's College, London (Senior Warneford Scholar). Formerly Medical Director of the London County Asylum at Banstead; Examiner in Mental Physiology at the University of London, and to the Board of Studies, Army Medical Service; Emeritus Professor of Psychological Medicine at St. Bartholomew's Hospital, and on Clinical Insanity at St. Luke's Hospital; Ex-President of the Society for the Study of Inebriety; Member of the Medico-Legal, Harveian Society; was one of the earliest co-operators (with Rev. H. Hawkins) in foundation of After-Care Association. *Publications:* Ex Cathedra—Essays on Insanity, 1905; articles in St. Bartholomew's Hospital Reports and in Tuke's Dictionary of Insanity, etc. Medical Journalist. *Recreations:* fishing, bicycling, music. *Address:* 29 Queen Anne Street, W.1. *T.:* Langham 2187. *Club:* Garrick.   *(Died 14 Jan. 1927.)*

SHAW, Captain Walter William; M.P. (C.) Westbury Division since 1924; *b.* 1868; *y. s.* of late Edward Dethick Shaw of Oaklands, Wolverhampton; *m.* 1893, Mary Louise, *y. d.* of William Webb Wakeman, New York; one *s.* one *d.* *Educ.:* private school; Jesus College, Cambridge. Served European War; sent on Special Mission to the United States by the War Office, 1917; Captain in the 3rd Queen's; Sheriff for county and town of Poole, 1913; C.C. for Dorset; contested the Houghton-le-Spring Division, Durham, 1922, and the Westbury Division, 1923. *Address:* Rood Ashton, Trowbridge, Wilts. *Clubs:* Carlton, Ranelagh, Royal Automobile, Pilgrims.
         (Died 10 May 1927.)

SHAYLOR, Joseph; one of the directors of Simpkin, Marshall, Hamilton, Kent & Co., Ltd., since 1894; also a director of other companies; *b.* Thrupp, near Stroud, Gloucestershire, 1844; *s.* of Charles and Hepzebah Shaylor; *m.* 1870, Emily Lark; two *s.* two *d.* *Educ.:* privately. Was apprenticed to a bookseller at Stroud, 1857; entered the firm of Simpkin, Marshall & Co., 1864; is a Livery man of the city of London and a member of the Stationers' Company; a vice-president of the Booksellers' Provident Institution, and also of the Gloucestershire Society in London. *Publications:* The Fascination of Books, and other Essays; The Pleasures of Bookland, with Introduction by Andrew Lang; In Friendship's Garden; In Nature's Garden; Some Favourite Books and their Authors; Saunterings in Bookland. *Recreations:* books and gardening. *Address:* Gloucester House, Holden Road, Woodside Park, N.12. *T.:* Finchley 803. *Club:* Whitefriars.   *(Died 22 Dec. 1923.)*

SHEARD, Thomas Frederick Mason, M.A., R.B.A. 1896; Professor of Art, Queen's College, London, since 1915; *b.* 16 Dec. 1866; *s.* of T. J. W. Sheard, Oxford; *m.* 1901, Mabel, *o. d.* of late T. G. Harrison, of St. George's East; one *s.* one *d.* *Educ.:* Magdalen College School, and Keble College, Oxford. Grove Exhibitioner, 1888; Second Class in Modern History, 1889. Went to Paris, 1889; studied painting under Courtois, Rixens, Lefebvre and Rigolot; began exhibiting at Royal Academy, the Salon, the R.I., etc., in 1891; Hon. Sec. R.B.A., 1899-1904. *Publications:* represented in British section at Brussels International Exhibition, 1896; at Paris Exhibition, 1900 (bronze medal); at St. Louis International Exhibition, 1905; New Zealand International Exhibition, 1907, and International Exhibition, Rome, 1911. Pictures often of Oriental subjects, with effects of strong sunlight, as in A Market Morning in a City of the Sahara, An Arab Blacksmith, An Arab Fète, Desert Tribesmen returning from a Raid, etc.; also Birds of a Feather, The Outcast, Parted, The Price of Victory, Hull Docks.

End of the Day, and many portraits; member of the Pasel Society. *Recreations:* the garden and motor bike. *Address:* Ye Monk's Orchard, East Hendred, Berks; 49 Hugh Street, S.W.1.
(Died 4 Oct. 1921.)

SHEARER, Colonel Johnston, C.B. 1908; D.S.O. 1898; M.B. I.M.S., retired; *b.* Aberdeen, 22 Oct. 1852; *s.* of J. Shearer; *m.* Elizabeth, *d.* of late J. Kinghorn, J.P., Aberdeen, 1890; two *s. Educ.:* Grammar School and University Aberdeen. M.A. (honours in Nat. Sc.), 1873; M.B. and C.M. (honours), 1877; Maclaine Prizeman in Military Surgery, Army Medical School, Netley, 1881; D.P.H. Aberd., 1897. Joined I.M.S. 1880; Egyptian Expedition, 1882 (medal and bronze star); Burmese Expedition, 1887-88 (medal and 2 clasps); Hazara Expedition, 1891 (clasp); Miranzai (2nd) Expedition, 1891 (clasp); Waziristan Expedition, 1894-95 (clasp, despatches); Tirah Expeditionary Force, 1897-98 (medal and 2 clasps, D.S.O. despatches); retired, 1910. *Decorated* for Tirah Expedition. *Recreations:* shooting, reading. *Address:* c/o H. S. King & Co., 9 Pall Mall, S.W. *Clubs:* East India United Service; United Service, Simla.
(Died 6 Feb. 1917.)

SHEARME, Edward, J.P., F.S.A.; late Master of the Supreme Court of Judicature; J.P. Cornwall, 1879; *e. s.* of late Edward Shearme, Stratton, Cornwall; *m.* Caroline, *d.* of W. Major Cooke, late Metropolitan Police Magistrate. *Educ.:* Marlborough College. *Address:* West Cliff, Bude, Cornwall.*(Died 11 Sept. 1920.)*

SHEARME, Paymaster - Captain Edward Haweis, C.B.E. 1920; O.B.E. 1917; Royal Navy, retired; Anglo-Persian Oil Company, Ltd., London, since 1920; *b.* Dublin, 21 June 1876; *s.* of John Shearme, Bude, Cornwall; *m.* 1913, Angela Mallaby, *d.* of Rev. Prebendary R. H. Barnes, Exeter; no *c. Educ.:* Plymouth College. Joined Navy, 1893; retired, 1912; served as Secretary to the late Admiral Lord Milford-Haven, 1904-11; served at Admiralty during World War as Assistant Chief Naval Censor; specially promoted to Paymaster-Captain (retired list), Nov. 1918, for services; Ministry of Labour, 1919. *Recreations:* golf, tennis, sailing. *Address:* Campden House Chambers, W.8. *T.A.:* Pulmonary, London. *T.:* Park 2641. *Clubs:* Junior United Service, Roehampton. *(Died 11 Nov. 1925.)*

SHEARME, Rev. John, M.A.; Hon. Canon of Winchester since 1903; *b.* 1842; 2nd *s.* of Edward Shearme, of Stratton, N. Cornwall; *m.* 1881, Mary Stewart, 3rd *surv. d.* of Henry Fowler Broadwood of Lyne, Surrey; one *s. Educ.:* Exeter; Pembroke College, Oxford. Ordained to Toddington, Bedfordshire, 1866-68; Curate of Linslade, Bucks, 1868-71; Curate of Cranleigh, Surrey, 1871-79; Rector of Holmbury St. Mary, Surrey, 1879-91; Vicar of Ryde, I.W., 1891-1905; Vicar of Oakwood, Surrey, 1905-18. *Publication:* Lively Recollections, 1917. *Address:* Upwood, Ryde, I. of W.
(Died 7 Jan. 1925.)

SHEDLOCK, John South; *b.* Reading, 29 Sep. 1843; *s.* of Rev. John Shedlock. Studied at Paris, the piano under Ernst Lübeck, and composition under Edouard Lalo; B.A. at London University, 1864; many years teacher of the pianoforte and of harmony; musical critic of the Academy; and of the Athenæum, 1900-15. *Publications:* The Pianoforte Sonata, 1895; A Translation of Beethoven's Letters, 1909; Beethoven-Cramer Studies; two of Kuhnau's Bible Sonatas; pieces by Pasquini, etc. *Address:* 36 Brondesbury Road, N.W.6.
(Died Jan. 1919.)

SHEEPSHANKS, William, J.P.; Chairman of Aire & Calder Navigation; *b.* 1851; *s.* of Rev. T. Sheepshanks of Arthington Hall, Leeds; *m.* 1876, Emily Florence, *d.* of

954

Rev. Henry Blunt; one *s.* one *d. Educ.:* Cheam School; Eton College; Trinity College, Cambridge. Called to the Bar, 1874; West Riding County Council, 1888-1907; Chairman of Petty Sessions, 1895-1913; Director and Chairman of Yorkshire Penny Bank, 1894-1911; Chairman of Pateley Bridge District Council and Board of Guardians, 1904-7; Chairman of Quarter Sessions (West Riding of Yorkshire), 1915-24; represents Ripon Diocese in the Church National Assembly. *Recreation:* shooting. *Address:* Arthington Hall, Leeds. *Clubs:* Carlton, Oxford and Cambridge; Yorkshire, York.
(Died 21 July 1928.)

SHEHYN, Hon. Joseph, *b.* Quebec, 10 Nov. 1829, of Irish and French parentage; *m.* 1st, 1858, Marie Zoé Virginie (*d.* 1892), *e. d.* of late Ambroise Verret, coachmaker, of Quebec; 2nd, Josephine Beliveau, widow of N. Leduc; four *s.* two *d. Educ.:* Quebec Seminary and privately. Sole proprietor of the firm M'Call, Shehyn & Co., now converted into M'Call, Shehyn & Son, Ltd., wholesale dry goods merchants; has been in business for 50 years; several years President of the Quebec Board of Trade, and a member of the Harbour Commission; Provincial Treasurer, 1887-91; Minister without portfolio, 1897-1900; elected to Legislature, 1875, and re-elected up to 1900; called to Senate, 1900; a Liberal; Knight Commander of Order of the Great; Officer of the Order of Leopold III. *Publication:* Railways *versus* Canals (pamphlet). *Recreations:* reading and outdoor exercise. *Address:* Quebec, Canada. *(Died 15 July 1918.)*

SHEILD, Arthur Marmaduke, M.B., B.C., Cantab., F.R.C.S.; consulting surgeon to St. George's Hospital, London; late surgeon in charge of Throat Department; consulting surgeon Hospitals of St. John and St. Elizabeth; and to Hospital for Women and Children, Waterloo Bridge Road; *b.* 1858; *s.* of William Henry Sheild, Gilfach, Pembrokeshire. *Educ.:* privately; Downing College, Cambridge, Bachelor of Medicine, Cambridge; Fellow of the Royal College of Surgeons, England. Was House Surgeon to St. George's and Addenbrooke's Hospital, Cambridge; Assistant Surgeon and Aural Surgeon to Charing Cross Hospital, and Lecturer on Operative Surgery; Surgeon and Lecturer on Practical Surgery to St. George's Hospital; late additional Examiner in Surgery to University of Cambridge; late Examiner to Apothecaries Company; late Secretary Medical Society of London, and of Dermatological Society; Surgical Secretary British Medical Association; late Member of Council of Royal Medico-Chirurgical Society. *Publications:* A treatise on diseases of the breast; diseases of the ear; nasal obstruction and its treatment; articles—diseases of breast, Quain's Dict. Med.; dislocations and joint injuries, Treves' System of Surgery; many other papers on surgical subjects. Retired from London practice through ill-health. *Club:* New University.
(Died 4 Aug. 1922.)

SHEPHARD, Sir Horatio Hale, Kt., *cr.* 1908; M.A., L.L.D. Glasgow; late Legal Adviser and Solicitor to Secretary of State for India; *s.* of John Shephard of Doctors' Commons; *m.* 1876, Agnes, *d.* of Maj.-Gen. J. W. Rideout; two *s. Educ.:* Eton; Balliol College, Oxford. Called to Bar at Inner Temple, 1867; went to Madras, 1872, and there held various legal appointments, including that of Advocate-General, until appointed Judge of the High Court; resigned office of Judge, 1901, and returned to England. *Publications:* Commentary on the Indian Contract Act; Commentary on the Transfer of Property Act; Commentary on Limitation. *Address:* 58 Montagu Square, W.1. *T.:* Paddington 4028. *Club:* Athenæum.

(Died 19 April 1921.)

SHEPHARD, Rev. John, M.A.; Hon. Canon of Christ Church, Oxford, since 1902; *b.* 8 Dec. 1837; *s.* of John Shephard of Castlehill, Englefield Green; *m.* 1867, Caroline Emily (*d.* 1895), *d.* of Captain Brownlow Layard of Windsor; one *s.* six *d. Educ.*: Eton, 1850-56; Balliol College, Oxford, 1856-60. 2nd class Mod.; 2nd class Lit. Hum. 1860. Private Tutor at Eton, 1860-62; ordained, 1862; acted as voluntary Curate to Canon T. T. Carter at Clewer; Curate of Rev. C. W. Furse (afterwards Archdeacon) at Staines, 1863; Conduct of Eton College, 1863-75; Vicar of Eton, 1875-1905; Member of Oxford Diocesan Conference, 1876-1905; Member of Whitelands College Council, 1903-24. *Publication:* Old Days of Eton Parish, 1908. *Address:* 33 Craven Hill Gardens, Hyde Park, W.2. *T.:* Paddington 6189.
(*Died 13 Mar.* 1926.)

SHEPHERD, Col. Charles Herbert, C.B.E. 1918; D.S.O. 1889; 1st Garrison Batt. Lincs. Regt.; late commanding 9th Regt. Dist.; *b.* 4 Apr. 1846; 2nd *s.* of late Thomas Shepherd, Beverley, Yorkshire; married. *Educ.*: Rugby. Gazetted Ensign 9th Foot, 1865; Lieutenant, 1871; Captain, 1880; Major, 1888; Lieut.-Colonel, 1893; Colonel, 1897; served Burmese Expedition, 1887-89; operations in Chin Hill (despatches, medal with clasp, D.S.O.); Chin-Lushai Expedition, 1889-90 (clasps). *Club:* Naval and Military. (*Died 2 Jan.* 1920.)

SHEPHERD-CROSS, Herbert; *b.* Bolton, 1 Jan. 1847; 2nd *s.* of Thomas Cross, Ruddington Hall, Nottinghamshire; *m.* 1st, 1870, Lucy M. Shepherd (*d.* 1891), *o. d.* and heir of late Rev. John Shepherd Birley, M.A.; 2nd, 1895, P. Penelope, *d.* of James Hortor. *Educ.*: Harrow; Exeter College, Oxford (M.A.). Late Major, Duke of Lancaster's Own Yeomanry; M.P. (C.) Bolton, 1885-1906. *Address:* Hamels Park, Buntingford. *Club:* Junior Carlton.
(*Died 9 Jan.* 1916.)

SHEPPARD, Rev. Canon Edgar, D.D. Oxon.; K.C.V.O., *cr.* 1914; C.V.O., 1902; Canon and Precentor of St. George's Chapel, Windsor Castle, since 1907; Sub-Dean of Chapels Royal since 1884; Deputy Clerk of the Closet to H.M.; Sub-Almoner to H.M. since 1901, and Domestic Chaplain since 1910; Domestic Chaplain to Queen Alexandra, 1910; Chaplain of Order of St. John of Jerusalem; Hon. Chaplain to Royal Society of Musicians; Hon. Chaplain to Royal Academy of Music; Hon. Chaplain 4th Batt. V.B. Royal Fusiliers (Brigade Chaplain); *b.* 10 August 1845; *s.* of Edgar Sheppard, M.D., D.C.L., Professor of Psychology at King's College; *m.* 1874, Mary, *e. d.* of Richard White, of Instow; two *s.* one *d.* Formerly Curate of Marlow and Hornsey; Minor Canon of St. George's, Windsor, and Priest-in-Ordinary to Queen Victoria,1878-84; Chaplain to late Duchess of Cambridge; Sub-Almoner and Chaplain-in-Ordinary to Queen Victoria, and Duke of Cambridge; Chaplain-in-Ordinary to King Edward, 1901-9; Domestic Chaplain, 1908-10; Knight of the Order of Danebrog. *Publications:* Memorials of St. James's Palace; The old Royal Palace of Whitehall; Life of the Duke of Cambridge; various sermons and addresses. *Address:* St. James's Palace, S.W. *T.A.:* Subdean, St. James's Palace, S.W.; Cloisters, Windsor Castle. *Club:* Oxford and Cambridge.
(*Died 30 Aug.* 1921.)

SHEPPERSON, Claude Allin, A.R.W.S., A.R.A. 1919; painter and illustrator; *b.* Beckenham, Kent, 25 Oct. 1867; 2nd *surv: s.* of late Allin Thos. Shepperson of Winsland Harberton, S. Devon, and Florence Mary, *e. d.* of late William Hinkes Cox, J.P.; *m.* Mary Isabel, *o. d.* of Arthur W. G. Adey of the Indian Medical Service; one *s.* one *d. Educ.*: privately. First studied Law, and afterwards studied Art in Paris and London,

1891. *Address:* 5 Mulberry Walk, Chelsea, S.W.3. *T.:* Kensington 6472. *Club:* Arts.
(*Died 30 Dec.* 1921.)

SHEPSTONE, John Wesley, C.M.G. 1888; J.P. Colony of Natal; late judge of the Native High Court of Natal, 1884-95; *b.* Grahamstown, Cape Colony, 29 Mar. 1827; 3rd *s.* of late Rev.William Shepstone; *m.* Mary Maria, 2nd *d.* of late Capt. James Geary, R.N. *Educ.*: Salem, Cape Colony. Entered Civil Service of Natal, 1846; proceeded 1847 and 1850 on Mission of Zulu King and Chief of Pondo Nation, 1850; Assist. Magistrate, Pietermaritzburg, 1851; commanded native forces against native chiefs, 1857; on two occasions carried out vaccination of 60,000 natives, 1863; acted as Secretary for Native (and Judicial Assessor) Affairs for the Colony in 1861, 1874, 1876-83; member Zulu-Transvaal Boundary Commission, 1878; delivered High Commissioner's Ultimatum to the Zulu Delegates, 1878; accompanied Sir Garnet (now Lord) Wolseley as adviser to arrange settlement of Zululand after Zulu War, 1879 (mentioned in despatches); British Commissioner Native Reserve, Zululand, 1882. *Decorated* for long service. *Recreations:* shooting, riding. *Address:* Cliff House, Pietermaritzburg, Natal. (*Died 23 Jan.* 1916.)

SHERARD, 11th Baron, *cr.* 1627; **Philip Halton Sherard;** *b.* 2 May 1851; *S.* brother, 1902. *Heir:* c. Robert Castell Sherard [*b.* 1858. *Address:* South Perth, Western Australia.
Address: Roscrea, Paignton, Devon.
(*Died 1 May* 1924.)

SHERARD, Colonel Ralph Woodchurch; Indian Army (retired); *b.* 11 Nov. 1860; *s.* of late Rev. Simon Haughton Sherard, *b.* of 9th Lord Sherard, and Mary Halton, *d.* of Sir Simon Haughton Clarke, 9th baronet of Shirland; *m.* 1895, Juliet Valentine, *y. d.* of late Robert Raynsford Jackson, 81 Harrington Gardens, S.W.; one *d.* Entered 15th Foot, 1879; transferred to Indian Staff Corps, 1881; commanded 36th Jacob's Horse, 1901-8; retired 1911; served Afghan War, 1880 (medal); employed under War Office, 1917-19; heir presumptive to brother, 11th Lord Sherard. *Address:* 3 Douro Terrace, Jersey, C.I.
(*Died 14 Mar.* 1922.)

SHERBORNE, 4th Baron (*cr.* 1784), **Edward Lenox Dutton,** J.P.; *b.* Bibury, Co. Gloucester, 23 April 1831; *s.* of 3rd Baron and Elizabeth, *d.* of 16th Earl of Suffolk; *S.* father 1883; *m.* Emily (*d.* 1905), *d.* of late Baron de Stern, 1894. Church of England. Sits on cross benches. *Educ.*: Harrow; Balliol College, Oxford, B.A. Diplomatic Service. Owns about 15,773 acres. *Recreations:* gardening and estate management. *Heir:* *b.* Rev. Hon. Canon F. G. Dutton. *Address:* Sherborne House, near Northleach. *T.A.:* Sherborne, Glos.; 9 St. James's Square, S.W.; Bibury Court, Fairford, and Standish House, Stonehouse, Gloucester. *Clubs:* Bachelors', Boodle's, Travellers', Athenæum, Portland; Union, Brighton.(*Died 20 July* 1919.)

SHERBORNE, 5th Baron (*cr.* 1784), **Frederick George Dutton,** *b.* 28 May 1840; *s.* of 3rd Baron and Elizabeth, *d.* of 16th Earl of Suffolk; *S.* brother 1919. *Educ.*: Christ Church, Oxford (M.A.). Ordained 1869; Vicar of Sherborne, 1870-74; Hon. Canon of Gloucester, 1901; Vicar of Bibury, 1874-1916. Owns about 15,775 acres. *Heir:* *n.* Major James Huntly Dutton, D.S.O. *Address:* Mosborough, Cheltenham. *Club:* Athenæum.
(*Died 3 Jan.* 1920.)

SHERBROOKE, Rev. Henry Nevile; 2nd *s.* of late Henry P. Sherbrooke, of Oxton Hall, Notts; *b.* 1846; *m.* 1st, Lady Harriet Curzon (*d.* 1875), *o. d.* of 2nd Earl Howe; 2nd, 1878, Lady Lilias Charlotte (*d.* 1889), *e. d.* of 1st Earl Cairns; 3rd, 1892, Alice, 4th *d.* of late Henry Abel Smith, of Wilford House, Nottingham;

two s. five d. Was Captain 43rd Foot ; incumbent of Portman Chapel, 1877-91 ; Vicar of Clifton, Bristol, 1891-1897. *Address:* 15 Paragon, Clifton. *(Died 2 Oct. 1916.)*

SHERBURN, Sir John, Kt., *cr.* 1902 ; M.B., C.M. (Edin.); M.R.C.S. (Eng.) ; J.P. East Riding of Yorks and City of Hull ; *b.* 3 March 1851 ; *s.* of late John Sherburn of Howden ; *m.* 1884, Louisa Ainley, *y. d.* of late William Bailey, J.P., Winestead Hall, Holderness ; two *s.* three *d. Educ.:* Edin. Univ. Hon. Consulting Surgeon, Hull Royal Infirmary and Victoria Hospital for Children, Hull ; Lt.-Col. Northumbria Brigade, R.F.A. (retired), V.D. ; Sheriff of Hull, 1886-87 ; entered Hull Council, 1887 ; Mayor, 1888-89, 1889-90 ; Alderman since 1889 ; contested Gateshead (U.), 1900 ; West Hull, 1906 and 1910 ; Rep. Member E.R. Yorks Territorial Force Association. *Address:* Brantingham Thorpe, East Yorks. *T.A.:* Brough. *T.:* Brough No. 11. *(Died 7 July 1926.)*

SHERIFF, Rev. Thomas Holmes, M.A.; Hon. Canon of Chester, 1911 ; Rural Dean of Mottram since 1921. *Address:* St. Paul's Vicarage, Stalybridge.*(Died 20 Nov. 1923.)*

SHERLOCK, Ven. William; Member of the Senate of T.C.D. ; Member of General Synod ; *b.* Canada ; *s.* of Richard T. Sherlock of Sherlockstown, Co. Kildare ; *m.* Adelaide, *d.* of Col. Francis Sherlock, K.H. of Southwell, Notts. *Educ.:* privately. Senior Moderator and Gold Medallist, Ethics and Logic ; Junior Moderator and Silver Medallist in History, Law, and Political Economy ; M.A., T.C.D. ; formerly Canon of Christ Church Cathedral, Dublin ; of St. Brigid's Cathedral, Kildare, and Archdeacon of Kildare. *Publications:* The Constitutions of the American and Colonial Churches ; Articles in Co. Kildare Archæological Society's Journal ; The Bible and the Young ; The Vindictive Psalms, etc. *Address:* Sherlockstown, Sallins, Ireland. *(Died 17 Mar. 1919.)*

SHERRARD, Col. James William, C.B.E. 1924 ; Indian Army (retired) ; *s.* of Col. C. W. Sherrard, R.E. (retired) ; *m.* 1905, Margaret Craig ; one *s.* two *d. Educ.:* Monkton Combe School ; Sandhurst. Served North-West Frontier, India, Mohmand and Buner operations, 1915-16 ; Mesopotamia, 1916-18 ; Palestine, 1918-19 ; Razmak operations (N.W.F.), India, 1922-23 (despatches thrice, Bt. Lt.-Col., C.B.E.) ; has Order of the Nile, 3rd Class. *Address:* 65 Dorset Road, Bexhill-on-Sea.
(Died 9 Feb. 1926.)

SHERSTON, Colonel William Maxwell, D.S.O. 1901 ; J.P. for Somerset ; *b.* 14 April 1859 ; *s.* of late J. D. Sherston, J.P., Somerset, of Evercreech, near Bath ; *m.* 1894, Evelyn Maude Maitland, *e. d.* of late J. Maitland Spencer, of Oakhill, near Bath. *Educ.:* Marlborough ; Pembroke College, Cambridge. Enlisted 7th Dragoon Guards, 1877 ; promoted Lieut. Rifle Brigade, 1882 ; Captain 18th Hussars, 1888 ; served Boer War, 1881 ; Egypt, 1884-85 (medal 2 clasps) ; Burmah, 1887 (medal 1 clasp, despatches) ; S. Africa, 1900-1 (medal 5 clasps, despatches, D.S.O.). A.D.C. to Com.-in-Chief, 1901-4 ; commanded North Somerset Yeomanry, 1904-9 ; served European War, Egypt and France, 1914-18. *Address:* Shore Lodge, Lilliput, Dorset. *M.:* FX 1554. *Clubs:* Army and Navy ; Royal Dorset Yacht.*(Died 18 Aug. 1925.)*

SHERWOOD, Wm. Albert, A.R.C.A., C.N.A. ; Life Member Canadian Institute ; President Anglo-Saxon Union ; *b.* Omemee, Canada, 1 Aug. 1855 ; father, English ; mother, Irish ; unmarried. *Educ.:* Omemee Grammar School. Began the study of portrait painting at an early period of life ; has painted many Canadian genre pictures, amongst which are The Gold Prospector (Ontario Government) ; The Negotiation (Dominion Government) ; The Canadian Rancher ; The Canadian Backwoods-

man. Exhibited at The International Exhibition, Chicago, 1893 ; San Francisco, 1894 ; International, Paris, 1900 ; Pan-American, Buffalo, 1902 ; World's Fair, St. Louis, 1905 ; the British Colonial Art Exhibition, London, England, 1902. Chief portraits — Hon. Sir G. W. Ross, Rev. Canon Scadding, Lt.-Col. Sir Henry Pellatt, Rev. Geo. F. Sherwood, Dr. Samuel Passmore May, Col. Gunsaulus, John G. Griffin, Lt.-Col. A. E. Belcher, Abraham Levy, O. B. Sheppard, Capt. Geo. H. Capron Brooke, T. Arthur Kirvan, John W. McCullough, K.C., Flight Sub-Lieut. C. L. Calvert, R.N. *Publications:* articles in leading magazines of Canada and in Encyclopædia of Canada ; Lectures upon the National Spirit in Art. *Recreations:* walking, swimming, canoeing. *Address:* 31 Queen Street, W., Toronto.

SHERWOOD, Rev. William Edward ; Hon. D.C.L. Oxon, 1915 ; *b.* Cumberland, April 1851 ; *e. s.* of Thomas Sherwood ; widower. *Educ.:* Magdalen Coll. School ; Christ Church, Oxford (M.A.); 1st class Math. - Mods. ; 3rd Math.-Final Schools. Mathematical Master, Magdalen School, 1875 ; Vice-Principal Sidney College, Bath, 1878 ; remaining after that school was absorbed by Bath College ; Chaplain of the School, 1881 ; Headmaster Magdalen College School, Oxford, 1888-1900 ; Vicar of Sandford-on-Thames, 1901-10 ; Mayor of Oxford, 1913-15 ; Divinity Lecturer and Assistant Chaplain, C.C.C., Oxford, 1912-20. *Publications:* Oxford Rowing ; Oxford Yesterday. *Recreations:* rowing (Putney, 1873-74) ; cycling. *Address:* 260 Iffley Rd. Oxford.
(Died 23 Sept. 1927.)

SHIFFNER, Sir John Bridger, 6th Bt., *cr.* 1818 ; *e. s.* of 5th Bt. and Elsie, *d.* of Ogden Hoffman Burrows, of Rhode Island, U.S.A. ; *b.* 5 Aug. 1899 ; S. father 1914 ; *m.* 1918, Sybil Helen, *y. d.* of Sills Clifford Gibbons, Staynes Hill, Sussex. *Heir:* b. Henry Burrows, *b.* 29 July 1902. *Address:* Coombe Place, Lewes, Sussex. *(Died 24 Sept. 1918.)*

SHIPLEY, Sir Arthur Everett, G.B.E., *cr.* 1920 ; F.R.S. 1904 ; M.A. ; Sc.D. ; Hon. D.Sc. Princeton ; Hon. LL.D. Michigan ; Hon. M.Sc. Drexel Institute, Philadelphia ; F.Z.S., F.L.S. Vice-Chancellor of Cambridge University, 1917-1919 ; Master, Christ's College, Cambridge, since 1910 ; Reader in Zoology in University, 1908 ; late Vice - President Linnean Society ; Vice President of the Research Defence Society ; Chairman of Council of Marine Biological Association ; Chairman of the Governing Body of the West Indian Agricultural College ; Member of the Central Medical War Committee ; Foreign Member American Association of Economic Entomologists and of the Helminthological Society of Washington ; Hon. Mem. of the Soc. Roy. Zool. et Malacologique, Belg. and of the Yorkshire Phil. Soc. ; Hunterian Trustee ; Tancred Trustee ; Beit Trustee ; Member of the Royal Commissions on the Civil Service, Trinity College, Dublin, and the Importation of Store Cattle and the Departmental Enquiry into Grouse Disease ; and other Colonial Office Commissions ; *b.* 10 March 1861 ; 2nd *s.* of late Alex. Shipley, of the Hall, Datchet, Bucks. *Educ.:* University College School ; Bartholomew's Hospital ; Christ's College, Cambridge, 1st class Natural Sciences Tripos, Part I., 1882 ; 1st class, Part II., 1884 ; Demonstrator of Comparative Anatomy in the University, 1885-94 ; Lecturer on Advanced Morphology of the Invertebrata, 1894 - 1908 ; Fellow of Christ's College, 1887 ; sent on a mission by Colonial Office to investigate plant disease in the Bermudas, 1887 ; appointed Secretary of the Museums and Lecture Rooms Syndicate, 1891 ; Member of the Council of the Senate, 1896-1908, 1917 - 19. *Publications:* Zoology of the Invertebrata, 1893 ; Pearls and Parasites, 1908 ;

" J," a Memoir of John Willis Clark, 1913; The Minor Horrors of War; More Minor Horrors, 1916; The Voyage of a Vice-Chancellor, 1919; Life, 1923; Cambridge Cameos, 1924; Islands; part translator of Weismann on Heredity, 2 volumes, 1889-92; Studies in Insect Life, 1916; (with A. Schuster)   Britain's Heritage of Science, 1917; joint-editor and part-author of the Cambridge Natural History; Grouse in Health and in Disease; editor of the Pitt Press Natural Science Manuals, Biological Series; and of the Fauna of British India Series; part author and editor of A Text-book on Zoology and Handbook to Natural History of Cambridgeshire; author of articles in the Encyclopædia Britannica, the Encyclopædia of Sport, Allbutt and Rolleston's System of Medicine, and the Ency. Biblica; formerly co-editor of Parasitology and of the Journal of Economic Biology, and author of numerous zoological papers in various scientific journals. *Address:* Christ's College Lodge, Cambridge. *T.:* Cambridge 894.   *Clubs:* Athenæum; Pitt, Cambridge.   (*Died 22 Sept. 1927.*)

SHIPLEY, Orby; *y. s.* of Rev. Charles Shipley, Twyford House, Hampshire; *b.* 1 July 1832; *m.* 1868, Zoë, 4th *d.* of Rt. Hon. James Wilson. *Educ.:* Jesus College, Cambridge (Rustat Scholar). B.A. 1854; M.A. 1857. Worked as a clergyman of the Church of England for 23 years, and was received into the Catholic Church in 1878. As an Anglican, wrote articles, reviews, and essays in contemporary periodicals, and published lectures and sermons, *e.g.* Four Cardinal Virtues, 1871; Theory about Sin, 1872; Principles of the Faith, 1878. Edited 3 vols. of Sacred Lyra, 1863-65; 3 yearly vols. of Church and the World, 1867-69; Tracts for the Day, 1867; Glossary of Ecclesiastical Terms, 1871; Essays on Ecclesiastical Reform, 1873; 2 vols. of Studies in Modern Problems, 1874. Adapted foreign and Catholic devotional works, *e.g.* 4 vols. of Ascetic Library, 1868-70; Quesnel on St. Matthew, 1869; Spiritual Exercises of St. Ignatius, 1870. Also reprinted Anthony Stafford's Female Glory (Life of the B.V.M. 1635), 1860; and published in 1870 and in 1878 Ritual of the Altar, an edition of the Anglican Communion Service, supplemented from the Roman Missal. All these books are out of print. As a Catholic, has contributed to Catholic and other papers and reviews; reprinted Old English ascetical books; and published Truthfulness and Ritualism, 1879-80; Annus Sanctus, Hymns of the Church, 1884; and Carmina Mariana, anthologies in honour of B.V.M., in 1893 and 1902, a third and final volume of which is in preparation; as is also a reprint of Lyra Eucharistica (1863), revised, with additions. *Address:* Colway, Lyme Regis, Dorset.
            (*Died 12 July 1916.*)

SHIPLEY, Lieut.-Col. Reginald Burge, C.M.G., 1915; T.D.; late 9th London Regiment (Queen Victoria's Rifles) (T.F.); *y. s.* of late Alexander Shipley, The Hall, Datchet; *m.* 1907, Flora Marion, *d.* of D. F. Wallace, Kansas City, U.S.A.; one *s.* one *d.* Served South Africa, 1900 (despatches); European War, 1914-15 (despatches, C.M.G.). *Address:* The Manor Cottage, Englefield Green, Surrey.   (*Died 11 Mar. 1924.*)

SHIPLEY, Sir William Alexander, Kt., *cr.* 1905; Mayor of Windsor, 1902; C.C. for Berkshire, 1905; *s.* of the late Alexander Shipley, of The Hall, Datchet, Bucks; *m.* 1882, Edith, *d.* of Thomas Hirst. *Recreation:* golf. *Address:* Riverbank, Datchet, Windsor. *T.:* 71 Windsor. *M.:* 352 BL. *Clubs:* Constitutional, Royal Thames Yacht; Berkshire, Reading.   (*Died 6 Oct. 1922.*)

SHOLL, Richard Adolphus, I.S.O. 1903; *b.* 18 Dec. 1846; *s.* of Robert John (late Govt. Resident, N.W. Territory) and Mary Sholl.

Educ.: Bishop Hale's College, Perth, W.A. Entered General Post Office, Perth, 1863; Chief Clerk, 1873; Chief Clerk and Accountant, Treasury, 1879; Postmaster-General and General Superintendent of Telegraphs, 1889; Deputy Postmaster-General under Commonwealth of Australia, 1901; retired, 1904; Lieutenant of Local Forces, 1875; Captain, 1883; Capt. Commandant, 1888; Major, 1893. *Recreations:* amateur sport of every kind, horse-racing especially. *Address:* 156 Aberdeen Street, Perth, Western Australia. *T.:* 4333. *Clubs:* Weld, Masonic, Civil Service, Perth. (*Died May 1919.*)

SHOOLBRED, Frederick Thomas, C.B. 1911; *b.* 1841. *Address:* Thames Bank, Goring.   (*Died 30 April 1923.*)

SHORE, Brig.-Gen. Offley Bohun Stovin Fairless, C.B. 1914; C.I.E. 1916; D.S.O. 1901; Indian Army, retired; *b.* 9 Aug. 1863; *o. s.* of Offley Bohun Shore; *m.* 1908, Caroline Perry, *d.* of Charles P. Sinnickson, Philadelphia, U.S.A. Entered West Yorks Regt. 1882; transferred to Bengal Cavalry, 1884; Capt. 1893; Bt.-Maj. 1898; Major, 1901; Lt.-Col. 1906; Bt.-Col. 1910; Col. 1911; D.A.A.G., India, 1895-1900; passed Staff Coll.; served North-West Frontier, India, 1897-98 (despatches, brevet of Major, medal with two clasps); S. Africa, 1900-2; D.A.A.G Army, Brig.-Maj. Mounted Infantry, Yeomanry and Mounted Troops; actions Poplar Grove, Driefontein, entry into Bloemfontein; operations in Orange River Colony, Western Transvaal, and Griqualand West; District Commandant, Cape Colony; Staff Officer to cavalry column, operations Eastern Transvaal and Orange River Colony (despatches, D.S.O., Queen's medal, three clasps, King's medal, 2 clasps); Director of Staff Duties and Military Training, Army Headquarters, India, 1913-15; Head of British Military Mission to the Caucasus, 1917-18; retired 1919. *Club:* United Service.
            (*Died 26 Oct. 1922.*)

SHORT, Richard, R.C.A.; marine artist; *b.* St. Ives, Cornwall, 29 Dec. 1841; *s.* of Richard Short (Master Mariner), and Grace Ninnes Short; *m.* Charlotte Martin Noall; three *s.* three *d.* *Educ.:* Navigation School, St. Ives. Went to sea for about twelve years; served through various grades in the merchant service, including Master in Steam; gave up sea life and turned to art; exhibited at many of the leading exhibitions, including about twelve years at the Royal Academy. *Publication:* after visiting the ruins of Ephesus, wrote and published a book entitled Saronia: a Romance of Ancient Ephesus. *Recreations:* a voyage at sea or acting as a nautical assessor (Admiralty jurisdiction). *Address:* 22 The Walk, Cardiff.   (*Died 8 Dec. 1916.*)

SHORT, Thomas Sydney, M.D. (London), D.P.H. (Cambridge), M.R.C.P. (London); Senior Physician to the General Hospital; Consulting Physician to the General Dispensary, Birmingham; *b.* Sheffield; *s.* of William Short of Sheffield and Birmingham. *Educ.:* Sheffield Royal Grammar School; King's College School and King's College, London. House Physician to King's College Hospital; Resident Medical Censor, King's College; Resident Medical and Surgical Officer, Jaffray Hospital; Resident Medical Officer, General Hospital, Birmingham; Chairman of William Dudley Charity Trust, Birmingham; Major R.A.M.C. (T.); President Birmingham Branch of British Medical Association, 1921-22. *Publications:* On a Special Form of Dilatation of the Stomach; papers and articles on medical subjects in the Medical Press; On some of the Characteristics of George Meredith's Prose Writing, 1907. *Recreations:* cycling, motoring. *Address:* 85 Edmund Street, Birmingham. *T.:* Central 6969. *Clubs:* Union, University Graduates', Birmingham.   (*Died 27 Aug. 1924.*)

SHORT, Lt.-Col. William Ambrose, C.M.G. 1916; R.A. Served European War, 1914-16 (despatches twice, C.M.G.). *Address:* 12 Inglis Road, Colchester. (*Died 21 June 1917.*)

SHORTALL, Sir Patrick, Kt., *cr.* 1916; High Sheriff of Dublin, 1915; *b.* 1872; *e. s.* of late James Shortall, Kilkenny; *m.* Mary, *e. d.* of late P. Coyle, Dublin; four *s.* Member Municipal Council, Dublin, and Royal Institute Public Health; Building Contractor. *Address:* Wilford, St. Lawrence Road, Clontarf, Dublin.
(*Died 27 June 1925.*)

SHORTER, Clement King; *b.* 19 July 1857; editor of The Sphere, 1900-26, and a Director of The Sphere and Tatler Company since 1900, and of The Illustrated London News and Sketch Company since 1922; *b.* London; of Hunts and Norfolk ancestry; *m.* 1st, 1896, Dora (*d.* 1918), *d.* of late George Sigerson, M.D.; 2nd, 1920, Doris, *y. d.* of late John Banfield and Mrs. Banfield, of Alverton Vean, Penzance; one *d.* *Educ.:* Downham Market. Civil servant, Exchequer and Audit Department, Somerset House, 1877-1890; Assistant Editor Penny Illustrated Paper, 1890; Editor Illustrated London News, 1891-1900; founded The Sketch for Illustrated London News Company, 1893, and edited it for seven years; also, during same period, Illustrated London News and English Illustrated Magazine; founded The Sphere, 1900, and The Tatler, 1903. *Publications:* Charlotte Brontë and her Circle, 1896; Sixty Years of Victorian Literature, 1897; edited Mrs. Gaskell's Life of Charlotte Brontë, with many new letters; also an edition of the Waverley Novels; Charlotte Brontë and her Sisters, 1905; The Brontës: Life and Letters, 2 vols., 1907; Immortal Memories, Essays and Addresses, 1907; Napoleon's Fellow Travellers, 1909; Highways and By-ways of Buckinghamshire, 1910; Napoleon in his Own Defence, 1910; The Complete Poems of Emily Brontë, 1911; George Borrow, 1913; an edition of Boswell's Johnson, 1922; the Complete Works of George Borrow, 1923; C.K.S., an Autobiography, 1926; was one of the founders of the Omar Khayyam Club, and is an ex-President of the Johnson Club. *Address:* Knockmoroon, Great Missenden, Bucks. *T.:* 9. (*Died 19 Nov. 1926.*)

SHORTER, Dora, *b.* Dublin; *d.* of George Sigerson, M.D.; *m.* 1896, Clement Shorter. *Publications:* Verses, in 1894; The Fairy Changeling and other Poems, 1897; My Lady's Slipper and other Poems, 1898; Ballads and Poems, 1899; The Father Confessor, 1900; The Woman who went to Hell, 1902; As the Sparks Fly Upward, 1904; The Country House Party, 1905; The Story and Song of Earl Roderick, 1906; Through Wintry Terrors, a Novel, 1907; Collected Poems, 1909; The Troubadour, 1910; New Poems, 1912; Madge Lindsey and other Poems, 1913; Do-Well and Do-Little, a Fairy Story, 1914; Love of Ireland: Poems and Ballads, 1916. *Address:* 16 Marlborough Place, N.W. *T.:* Paddington 1386; Knockmoroon, Great Missenden, Bucks. *T.:* 9 P.O. *Club:* Lyceum. (*Died 6 Jan. 1918.*)

SHOUBRIDGE, Maj.-Gen. (Thomas) Herbert, C.B. 1918; C.M.G. 1916; D.S.O 1898; *b.* 15 June 1871; *s.* of late Lieut.-Colonel H W. Shoubridge, Indian Army; *m.* 1910, Gladys Constance, *e. d.* of late Major H. Dugdale, 16th Lancers; one *s.* one *d.* *Educ.:* Blundell's School, Tiverton. Entered Dorset Regiment, 1893; Captain Northumberland Fusiliers, 1900; Brevet Lieut. Colonel, 1914; Brevet Colonel, 1917; served Tirah Expedition, 1897-98 (despatches, D.S.O., medal with two clasps); served South Africa as Staff Captain and D.A.A.G. with the Natal army, 1899-1902 (despatches twice, Bt. Major, Queen's medal four clasps, King's medal two clasps); European War,

958

1914-18 (despatches six times, C.M.G., Bt. Col., C.B., 1914 Star); D.A.Q.M.G. Headquarters S.A. Command, 1902-5; Brigade Maj. 13th Inf. Brig., 1926-10; commanded East Lancs. Div. (T.F.), 1919-23; Commandant, Royal Military College, Sandhurst, 1923; resigned Oct., 1923. *Club:* United Service. (*Died 27 Oct. 1923.*)

SHOWERS, Lt.-Col. Herbert Lionel, C.S.I. 1911; C.I.E. 1902; Indian Staff Corps; British Commissioner, Mewar Enquiry Committee; *b.* London, 16 June 1861; *s.* of General C. L. Showers, I.S.C.; *m.* 1903, Christian, 2nd *d.* of James Stirling of Garden, Port of Menteith, N.B.; one *s.* one *d.* *Educ.:* private schools. Entered army, 1883; joined the Welsh Regiment in Natal; transferred to Norfolk Regiment and arrived in India, 1884; entered Staff Corps, 1885, and served with 17th Bengal Infantry, 4th Gurkhas, Meywar Bhil Corps, and Erinpura Irregular Force; entered the Political Department, 1890; served Soudan Campaign, 1885 (medal with two clasps, Khedive's star); the assault and capture of Nodiz Fort, Mekran, 1901. *Address:* Udaipur, India. *Clubs:* East India United Service, Ranelagh.
(*Died 2 Feb. 1916.*)

SHREWSBURY, 20th Earl of (*cr.* 1442), **Charles Henry John Chetwynd-Talbot;** K.C.V.O. 1907; Earl of Waterford, 1446; Baron Talbot, 1733; Earl Talbot, Viscount Ingestre, 1784; Premier Earl of England., Hereditary Great Seneschal or Lord High Steward of Ireland; Lord High Steward of Stafford since 1892; *b.* London, 13 Nov. 1860; *o. s.* of 19th Earl and Anna Theresa, *d.* of Commander Richard Howe Cockerell, R.N., and Theresa, afterwards Countess of Eglinton; *S.* father 1877; *m.* 1882, Ellen Mary, *d.* of Charles Rowland Palmer - Morewood, Ladbroke Hall, Warwick; Alfreton Hall, Derbyshire; one *d.* *Educ.:* Eton. Protestant. Conservative. Very fond of coaching; ran the Greyhound Coach from Buxton to Alton Towers daily for several seasons; first person to start cabs fitted with noiseless tyres in London and Paris. *Heir: g.s.* Viscount Ingestre. *Address:* Ingestre, Stafford; 67 Portland Place, W.1. *T.:* Mayfair 6018. *T.A.:* Wexford, London. *Club:* White's.
(*Died 17 May 1921.*)

SHUCKBURGH, Sir Stewkley Frederick Draycott, 10th Bt., *cr.* 1660; *b.* Shuckburgh, 20 June 1880; *e. s.* of 9th Bt. and Ida Florence Geraldine, *o. d.* of Rev. Frederick W. Robertson of Brighton; *S.* father 1884. *Heir: b.* Gerald Francis Stewkley, *b.* 28 Feb. 1882 [*m.* 1909, Honor Zoe, *d.* of Neville Thursby, of Harlestone, Northamptonshire; two *s.* one *d.*]. *Address:* Shuckburgh, Daventry. *T.A.:* Daventry. *T.:* 23 Daventry. (*Died 17 Nov. 1917.*)

SHUTTLEWORTH, Alfred, J.P., D.L.; *b.* 1843; *e. s.* of late Joseph Shuttleworth, Hartsholme Hall, and Old Warden Park, Beds; *m.* 1869, Mary (*d.* 1880), *y. d.* of Nathaniel Clayton, East Cliff, Lincoln. High Sheriff, Lincoln, 1889. *Address:* Eastgate House, Lincoln. *Clubs:* Wellington; Royal Yacht Squadron, Cowes.
(*Died 22 Nov. 1925.*)

SHUTTLEWORTH, George Edward, Hon. Associate of the Order of St. John of Jerusalem; Fellow and Hon. Associate of King's College, London; M.R.C.S. (Eng.) and L.S.A.; Member of Society of Apothecaries, London; *b.* Edgbaston, Warwickshire, 16 Nov. 1842; *s.* of Charles Edward Shuttleworth; *m.* Edith Mary, *d.* of Henry Hadwen, Lancaster; one *s.* one *d.* *Educ.:* Philological and City of London Schools; King's College, London; B.A. (Honours in Physiology); Heidelberg University (M.D.). Medical Superintendent, Royal Albert Asylum, Lancaster, 1870-93; Medical Examiner of Defective Children, School Board for London, 1899-1901; Medical Expert (M.A.B.), Rochester House Institution for Improvable Imbeciles,

1901-5, and Consulting Medical Officer, National Association for Feeble-minded, 1900-10 ; Hon. Consulting Physician, Royal Albert Institution for the Feeble-minded of the Northern Counties, Lancaster; late Medical Officer for Schools for Mentally Defective Children, Willesden Education Committee; Member of Royal Medico-Psychological Association of Great Britain and Ireland; Vice-President of the National Association for the Feeble-minded ; of the Central Association for Mental Welfare; of the Child Study Society, London ; Examiner St. John Ambulance Association; formerly Hon. Secretary of Asylum Workers' Association and instrumental in obtaining the Asylum Officers' Superannuation Act of 1909 ; Member of Departmental Committee, Board of Education, on Report of which Elementary Education (Defective and Epileptic Children) Act 1899 was framed. *Specialty:* Psychological medicine (specially in respect of mentally deficient children). *Publications:* Mentally Deficient Children : their Treatment and Training (1st edition 1895, 5th edition 1922) ; Articles : Mental Deficiency, Encyclopædia Medica, vol. viii.; Idiocy (joint author), Allbutt's New System of Medicine ; Educational Training of Idiots and Imbeciles, Hack Tuke's Dictionary of Psychological Medicine ; Aetiology of Idiocy and Imbecility (joint author), ibid. ; Education of Exceptional Children, Teachers' Encyclopædia, and Encyclopædia of Education, etc. *Recreations:* travel and literature. *Address:* 36 Lambolle Road, Hampstead, N.W.3. *T.:* Primrose Hill 2578.   (*Died 28 May 1923.*)

SIAM, H.M. the King of, RAMA VI., G.C.V.O., *cr.* 1902 ; Hon. General British Army ; *b.* 1 Jan. 1881 ; *S.* father, 1910. *Educ.:* private tutor; Royal Mil. Coll., Sandhurst; Christ Church, Oxford. Came to England, 1898 ; proclaimed heir to the throne of Siam on the death of elder brother, 1895 ; represented the King of Siam at the Jubilee of Queen Victoria, 1897 ; joined R.M. College, Sandhurst, 1898 ; attached to 1st Battalion Durham L.I., 1899 ; during same year was attached to No. 6 Mountain Battery during training at Okehampton ; in November and December 1899 joined School of Musketry at Hythe, and obtained officer's extra certificate ; went up to Oxford, January 1900, and remained till end of 1901 ; represented the King of Siam at the funeral of Queen Victoria, represented King of Siam at King of Spain's Coronation in May and King Edward's Coronation in June 1902. *Publications:* The War of the Polish Succession, 1901, and others on History, Archæology, and the Drama ; also some 30 Plays in Siamese and English. *Recreations:* riding and driving. *Address:* Bangkok, Siam. *Clubs:* United Service, Army and Navy, Junior United Service, Travellers', Bachelors'.

    (*Died 26 Nov. 1925.*)

SIDDALL, Joseph Bower, M.D., C.M. (Aberd.) ; graduated with Highest Academical Honours, M.R.C.S., L.S.A., D.P.H. (Camb.) ; retired ; 4th *s.* of late George Siddall and Mary Oldham of Matlock ; *b.* 4 March 1840 ; *m.* 1870, Mary Elizabeth (*d.* 1906), 2nd *d.* of late Charles Binns, J.P., of Clay Cross Hall, Chesterfield ; no *c. Educ.:* Chesterfield Grammar School ; St. Thomas's Hospital, London ; University of Aberdeen. House Surgeon, St. Thomas's Hospital, 1864 ; Prosector, Royal College of Surgeons, 1864 ; House Surgeon to Bristol General Hospital, 1867-68 ; Medical Officer to H.M. Legation, Japan, 1868 ; was in charge, till the conclusion of the War of Restoration in Japan, of the first Military Hospital at Tokio, where he attended large numbers of the wounded soldiers ; subsequently founded the Dai-Biyoin (Great Hospital), the first civil hospital, and generally assisted in the earliest development of modern medical science

in Japan (Order of the Rising Sun) ; returned to England, 1874 ; Physician to the Bristol General Hospital, 1876. *Publications:* Surgical Experiences in Military Hospitals in Japan ; St. Thomas's Hospital Reports, 1875. *Recreations:* formerly cricket, at present golf. *Address:* Oriel House, Malvern. *Clubs:* Malvern ; Royal North Devon, Royal Eastbourne, Worcestershire Golf. (*Died 4 July 1925.*)

SIDEBOTHAM, Joseph Watson ; *b.* 1857 ; *s.* of late J. Sidebotham, Erlesdene, Bowdon, Cheshire; *m.* Marian, *d.* of late Rev. E. Dowling, 1886 ; two *s.* two *d. Educ.:* Owens Coll.,Manchester. M.P. (C.) Hyde Div. Cheshire, 1886-1900 ; J.P. County of Chester. *Address:* Merlewood, Bowdon, Cheshire.

    (*Died 10 June 1925.*)

SIDGREAVES, Rev. Walter, S.J. ; Director of Observatory, Stonyhurst College ; *b.* Preston, 1837 ; *s.* of Edward Sidgreaves of Grimsargh. *Educ.:* Stonyhurst College. Professor of Physics in same College 25 years ; served on the expeditions for observing the Transits of Venus across the sun's disc—1874 Kerguelen Land, and 1882 Madagascar ; awarded Gold Medal at the St. Louis Exposition 1904. and Grand Prix at the Franco-British Exhibition 1908, for photographic work on Stellar Spectra. *Publications:* In the Memoirs and Monthly Notices of the Royal Astronomical Society and other Scientific periodicals. *Address:* Observatory, Stonyhurst College, Blackburn. *T.A.:* Stonyhurst. *T.:* 23 Whalley.

    (*Died 12 June 1919.*)

SIDGWICK, Arthur, Fellow of Corpus Christi College, Oxford, 1882-1902, and since 1903; *m. Educ.:* Rugby; Trinity College, Cambridge (Fellow); Bell Scholar, 1860 ; Porson Scholar, 1861 ; Member's Prizeman, 1862, 1863, 1864 ; 2nd Classic and Senior Chancellor's Medallist, 1863 ; Hon. LL.D., Glasgow, 1892 ; Hon. Litt.D.. Leeds, 1910 ; formerly Reader in Greek, Oxford University, 1894-1906. *Publications:* Edition of Virgil, 1890 ; of Æschylus (text and five annotated plays), 1880-1903 ; Greek Prose Composition, 1876 ; Greek Verse Composition, 1882 ; other school-books, and a few educational essays. *Address:* Woodstock Road, Oxford.   (*Died 25 Sept. 1920.*)

SIDNEY, Herbert (Sidney Herbert Adams), F.S.A.; portrait and historical painter ; *s.* of Fred. W. Adams, art dealer, Piccadilly, London ; assumed surname of Sidney by deed-poll; unmarried. *Educ.:* Royal Academy, London ; Royal Academy, Antwerp, under de Keyser and Van Lérius ; Beaux Arts, Paris, under Gérôme. Exhibitor, Royal Acad. London, and Salons, Paris, Brussels, etc. ; commanded by the late King Edward, and by King George and Queen Mary, to submit some of his works for inspection at Buckingham Palace in 1909, 1911, and 1919 ; painted portrait of Crown Prince Olav of Norway, Royal Academy, 1913, and memorial portrait of late Prince Francis of Teck ; portraits of Mayors of Westminster, 1914 (R. W. Granville-Smith) and 1915 (G. Booth-Heming), for the City Hall, Westminster ; painted "The Sorrow of the Mothers" for War Relief Fund Exhibition, Royal Academy, 1915. *Recreations:* music, literature, historical research. *Address :* 4 St. Paul's Studios, W.14.

    (*Died 30 Mar. 1923.*)

SIDNEY, Thomas Stafford, K.C., 1911 ; Attorney-General, Leeward Islands, since 1909 ; *b.* 1863 ; *e. s.* of late Thomas Sidney, Lord Mayor of London, 1853-54 ; and some time M.P. for Stafford. *Educ.:* Harrow ; Trinity Hall, Cambridge ; M.A. 1888. Barrister Middle Temple, 1885 ; S.E. Circuit, Surrey and South London Sessions ; for some years practised in India and engaged in journalism ; Advocate of the High Court of Madras, 1894 ; was a District Commissioner, Lagos 1901-3. *Recreations:*

walking and golf. *Address:* St. John's, Antigua, B.W.I. *Clubs:* M.C.C., British Empire.
(*Died 16 Nov.* 1917.)

SIEMENS, Alexander; *b.* Hanover, 22 Jan. 1847; *s.* of Gustav Siemens and Sophie Heise; *m.* 1881, Frances Dodwell, of Campden, Glos.; three *d. Educ.:* Hanover; Berlin. Came to England to work in the shops of Siemens Brothers at Woolwich, 1867; went to Persia to assist in building Indo-European Telegraph Line, 1868; assisted in laying cable in the Black Sea for same Co., 1869; went through the Franco-Prussian War as a private in an infantry regiment, and received the Iron Cross, 1870-71; after the war returned to England and worked as a pupil of the late Sir Wm. Siemens, assisting in building regen. gas furnaces for various purposes, in laying submarine cables from 1875 onwards; built furnaces for Sir Wm. Siemens in Canada and the U.S.A. in 1876-77; was released formally from German citizenship and became a naturalised British subject, 1878; took over the management of the Electric Light Depart. of Siemens Bros., 1879; Pres. Institute Electrical Engineers, 1894 and 1904; Pres. Institute Civil Engineers, 1910-11. *Publications:* Papers read before the British Association, the Society of Arts, and the Institution of Electrical Engineers, and some other Societies. *Address:* Westover, Milford - on - Sea, Hants. *Clubs:* Athenæum, Royal Automobile.
(*Died 16 Feb. 1928.*)

SIENKIEWICZ, Henryk, Polish novelist; *b.* Okreya, Podlasia; family originally Lithuanian; removed to Poland in consequence of Russian War; Hon. Member Russian Academy of Sciences. *Educ.:* Warsaw Gymnasium and University. Travelled in U.S. of America, 1877; Central Africa, 1891. *Publications:* Hania, 1874; Sketches in Charcoal, 1877; Fire and Sword, 1884; The Deluge, 1885-87; Pan Michael, 1888; Without Dogma, 1891; Children of the Soil, 1894; Quo Vadis. 1896: The Knights of the Cross, 1900; Monte Carlo; Through the Desert, etc. (*Died 16 Nov. 1916.*)

SIFTON, Rt. Hon. Arthur Lewis, P.C. 1920; M.A., LL.B., D.C.L., K.C.; Secretary of State, Canada, since 1920; *b.* 26 Oct. 1858; *s.* of late Hon. John W. Sifton, formerly Speaker of Manitoba Assembly, and Kate Sifton; *m.* 1882, Mary H. Deering; one *s.* one *d. Educ.:* various public schools; Wesley College, Winnipeg; Victoria University, Cobourg. Called to Bar, Manitoba, 1883; practised law; first elected North-West Assembly, 1898; Treasurer and Commissioner Public Works N.W.T. 1901; Chief Justice N.W.T., 1903-5; Chief Justice, Alberta, 1905-10; portfolios of Public Works and Treasury, 1910-12; Premier of Alberta; Minister of Railways and Telephones, 1912-18; Minister of Customs and Inland Revenue, Canada, 1917-20; Minister of Public Works, 1919. *Address:* Château Laurier, Ottawa, Canada. *Clubs:* Rideau, Country, Ottawa; Ranchmen's, Calgary; Edmonton, Edmonton. (*Died 21 Jan. 1921.*)

SIGERSON, George, M.D., M.Ch.; Hon. Fellow, R.C.P.I.; Professor of Biology, D.U. Coll., Dublin; Senator, National Univ., Ireland; *m.*; one *s.* two *d. Educ.:* Queen's Coll., Cork; Dublin; Paris. Member of Senate, Irish Free State, 1922-3. *Publications:* Microscopical Researches on the Atmosphere; Heat as a Factor in (so-called) Vital Action; Cause of Buoyancy of Bodies of Greater Density than Water; Changes in the Physical Geography of Ireland; Additions to the Flora of 10th Botanical District; Relationship of the Inflorescences; trans. with notes, Prof. Charcot's Lectures on Diseases of the Nervous System; On Alternate Paralyses; History of Land Tenures and Land Classes; Modern Ireland; Bards of the Gael and Gall, The Last Independent Parliament of

Ireland. *Recreations:* collecting miniatures, pastels, etc. *Address:* 3 Clare Street, Merrion Square, Dublin. (*Died 17 Feb. 1925.*)

SIGSBEE, Rear - Adm. Charles Dwight, U.S. Navy; *b.* Albany, New York, 16 January 1845; *s.* of Nicholas Sigsbee and Agnes Orr Sigsbee; *m.* Eliza Rogers Lockwood, *d.* of General Henry H. Lockwood, 1870. *Educ.:* United States Naval Academy. Entered the Naval Academy, 1859; served in the Civil War, 1863-65; China Station, 1865-69; head of several departments of the Naval Academy; has commanded the "Kearsage," "Dale" (twice), "Constellation," "Portsmouth," "Maine," "St. Paul," and "Texas"; commanded the "Maine" when she was destroyed in Havana, 15 Feb. 1898; from 1874-78 engaged in deep sea exploration in command of U.S. Coast Survey Steamer "Blake" (gold medal and two diplomas of honour for deep sea inventions at the International Fisheries Exhibition, London; Red Eagle of Prussia, 1880); in charge of the U.S. Hydrographic Office, 1893-97; commanded "St. Paul" in war with Spain, 1898; advanced for extraordinary heroism, 11 Feb. 1901; retired 1907. *Publications:* Deep Sea Sounding and Dredging, U.S. Coast and Geodetic Survey, 1880; The Story of the "Maine," 1898; Graphical Method for Navigators, U.S. Hydrographic Office. *Address:* 539 W. 112th Street, New York. (*Died July 1923.*)

SILCOCK, Thomas Ball; *b.* Bradford-on-Avon, 19 Sept. 1854; *s.* of T. B. and Amelia Silcock; *m.* 1881, Mary Frances, *d.* of Rev. H. Tarrant of Bath; three *s.* two *d. Educ.:* Bristol Grammar School. B.Sc. of London University; Mayor of Bath, 1900-1 and 1910-11; M.P. (L.) Wells Division of Somerset, 1906-10; J.P.; Architect and Surveyor *Address:* Walden, Bath. *T.:* Bath 1090.
(*Died 1 April 1924.*)

SIM, Henry Alexander, C.I.E. 1901; F.R.G.S.; *b.* 1856; *s.* of J. D. Sim, C.S.I., of Moxley, Surrey; unmarried. *Educ.:* Cheltenham. I.C.S. 1876; went to India, 1878; served in Revenue, Judicial, Forest, and Account branches; Private Sec. to Governor, 1897-1901; Memb. Board of Revenue, Madras, 1901; Memb. of Gov.-General's Legislative Council, 1904-8; retired, 1908. *Address:* c/o Lloyds Bank, 6 Pall Mall, S.W. *Club:* East India United Service.
(*Died 21 April 1928.*)

SIM, The Honourable Sir William Alexander, Kt., *cr.* 1924; Judge of Supreme Court of New Zealand since 1911; *b.* Wanganui, N.Z., 13 Sep. 1858; *e. s.* of late P. L. Sim; *m.* 1886, Frances Mary, *d.* of late Joseph Walters, of Victoria; three *s.* one *d. Educ.:* Wanganui Grammar School; Otago University. Admitted as barrister and solicitor, November 1879; Judge of Arbitration Court, 1907-14; temporary Judge of Supreme Court, 1909. *Publications:* Divorce Act and Rules (New Zealand); (with Sir Robert Stout) The Practice of the Supreme Court and Court of Appeal of New Zealand. *Address:* Dunedin, New Zealand. *Club:* Authors'; Dunedin, Dunedin; Christchurch, Christchurch; Wellington, Wellington. (*Died Aug. 1928.*)

SIMM, Matthew Turnbull, M.P. (Coal. Lab.) Wallsend Division of Northumberland, Dec. 1918-22; *b.* 4 Jan. 1869; father a miner; *m.* 1895, *d.* of George Dodds; one *s. Educ.:* Colliery School. *Recreation:* walking. *Address:* 29 Otterburn Avenue, Gosforth, Newcastle. (*Died 8 Oct. 1928.*)

SIMMONDS, Frederick, V.D.; M.V.O. 1906; *b.* 4 Dec. 1845; late Crown Receiver of Windsor Parks. *Address:* 16 Abingdon Court, Kensington, W.8. *T.:* Western 8100. *Club:* Junior Army and Navy.
(*Died 14 July 1921.*)

SIMMONS, Sir Anker, K.B.E., *cr.* 1920; C.B.E. 1918; J.P., Berks; *e. s.* of late Charles Simmons, J.P., of Crandem Gate, Henley - on - Thames; *b.* 5 Oct. 1857; *m.* 1883; Edith Nora, *o. d.* of Edward Smith Beddome, of Lloyd's; one *s.* three *d. Educ.:* privately; Henley Old Grammar School. Fellow of Surveyors' Institution and Auctioneers' and Estate Agents' Institute; Vice - President of Auctioneers' Institute; late senior partner and now Adviser and Consultant to Simmons & Sons, chartered surveyors, of Henley-on-Thames, Reading, and Basingstoke; an authority on agricultural and land questions; Agricultural Adviser, from its formation, to the Ministry of Food; Official Arbitrator under the Acquisition of Land (Assessment of Compensation) Act 1919, 1924-26; Past Chairman of the Farmers' Club; has taken an active part in political, masonic, and local government matters; Alderman and senior member of Henley Town Council (39 years); four times Mayor of Henley; five times P.M.; has read several papers at the Farmers' Club, and spoken all over England on land questions; was invited to stand as agricultural candidate for S. Oxon, 1918. *Recreations:* an old athlete; rowing, swimming, cycling, running; winner of many races. *Address:* Bird Place, Henley-on-Thames. *T.:* 146. *M.:* BW 6696. *Clubs:* Constitutional, Farmers'.   (*Died 20 Oct.* 1927.)

SIMMONS, Arthur Thomas, B.Sc. (Lond.), A.R.C.Sc. (Lond.); author; joint editor of The Journal of Education and School World; Inspector of Secondary Schools for University of London; Examiner in Science for various public examinations; *b.* Devonport, 26 June 1865; 2nd *s.* of Thomas Simmons of Southampton; *m.* 1909, Winifred Mabel, *y. d.* of late Thomas Mortimer Jacombs; two *s. Educ.:* Hartley University Coll. Southampton; Royal College of Science, London. 1st class Honours in Physical Geography and Geology at B.Sc. London University, 1890; 1st class Associateship in Physical Division of Royal College of Science, London, 1886. Lecturer in Physics, Chemistry, etc., at Southport Science and Art Institute, 1887-90; science master and second master of Tettenhall College, Staffs, 1891-97; contributor to educational and other periodicals since 1889. *Publications:* Physiography for Beginners; Physiography for Advanced Students,; joint author of the following among other text-books: Elementary General Science; Exercises in Practical Physics; Science of Common Life; Introduction to Practical Geography: Class-Book of Physical Geography. *Address:* Passaic, Kew, Surrey. *T.:* Richmond 1878. *Club:* University of London.   (*Died 19 Aug.* 1921.)

SIMMS, Ven. Arthur Hennell, Archdeacon of Totnes since 1910; Canon residentiary of Exeter Cathedral, 1920; *b.* 1853; *s.* of William Simms, F.R.S.; *m.* 1896, Jenny, *d.* of John Marks, of Newton Abbot. *Educ.:* Trinity College, Cambridge. Ordained, 1878; Curate of Lifton, 1878-81; St. John, Clifton, 1881-82; Vicar of Churchstow, 1882-8; Rector of Wolborough, 1888-96; Vicar of St. Michael, Cambridge, 1896-1902; Holy Trinity, Ely, 1902-3; St. Luke, Torquay, 1903-20; Select Preacher, Cambridge, 1897 and 1898. *Address:* The Close, Exeter.   (*Died 15 Jan.* 1921.)

SIMONS, Admiral Ernest Alfred, *b.* Lucknow, 3 Sep. 1856; *s.* of Capt. A. Parmenter Simons, Bengal Artillery (killed defending Lucknow Residency, 1857); *m.* 1881, Florence Isabella (*d.* 1922), 2nd *d.* of late Philip George, Redland Bank House, near Bristol, one *d.* Entered Navy, 1870; specially promoted to Lieut. for proficiency in examinations, and as Lieut. was a Gunnery Staff-Officer; as Com-

mander was Senior Naval Officer, Suakim, during the Dongola Expedition, 1896 (Khedive's medal and thanks of Govt. of India); Captain, 1896; sometime Assistant to Director of Naval Ordnance at the Admiralty, 1901; received the acknowledgments of the Govt. of India for Service as Senior Naval Officer at Koweit; Admiral Superintendent Malta Dockyard, 1910-1912; A.D.C. to the King, 1906-7; Rear-Adm. 1907; Vice-Adm. 1911; Admiral, 1914; retired, 1915; Officer Legion of Honour, Redeemer of Greece. *Address:* 50 Charlwood Street, S.W.1.   (*Died 30 Aug.* 1928.)

SIMONS, Very Rev. William Charles; 3rd *s.* of Rev. John Simons, Vicar of Dymock, Gloucestershire; *m.* Emily Martha, *d.* of Thos. Harding, Wick House, Brislington, Bristol; one *s. Educ.:* private schools; Oxford (M.A. 1866). Deacon, 1867; Priest, 1868; Curate Kirby Underdale, Yorks, 1867; Priest-in-Charge Knowle, Bristol, 1870; Chaplain to Lord Kinnaird, Rossie Priory, Scotland, 1873; Chaplain to Frances Lady Kinnaird and Knapp Chapel, 1878; Dean of Brechin, 1913; Canon, St. Paul's, Dundee, 1905; Examining Chaplain to Bishop of Brechin, 1906; Rector of All Souls, Invergowrie, Dundee, 1883; retired. *Publication:* Some things hard to be understood. *Address:* Lynchmere, Petersfield, Hants.

    (*Died 7 Jan.* 1921.)

SIMPSON, Sir Alexander Russell, Kt., *cr.* 1906; M.D., D.Sc. (causa honoris), LL.D.; *b.* Bathgate, West Lothian, 30 Apr. 1885; 2nd *s.* of Alexander Simpson, bank agent; *m.* Margaret Stewart (*d.* 1911), *d.* of George Freeland Barbour, Bonskeid and Gryffe Castle, 1872; four *s.* one *d. Educ.:* Bathgate Academy; Edinburgh Univ.; apprenticed to Prof. John Goodsir. Whilst still a student elected one of the Presidents Royal Medical Society; studied at Univ. of Montpellier and Berlin; Assistant seven years to his uncle, Sir James Young Simpson, Bt.; five years in private practice in Glasgow; formerly Dean of the Faculty of Medicine and Emeritus Professor of Midwifery and the Diseases of Women and Children, Univ. of Edinburgh, 1870-1905. *Publications:* editor of Sir James Y. Simpson's Lectures on Diseases of Women; author of Contributions to Obstetrics and Gynecology; and of an Atlas of the Frozen Section of a Cadaver in the Genu-pectoral Position (along with Dr. Berry Hart), and many memoirs. *Recreations:* travel; takes an interest in Evangelistic work in Edinburgh, and especially in the mission movement among students. *Address:* 52 Queen Street, Edinburgh. *T.A.:* Chloroform, Edinburgh. *T.:* 2580.   (*Died 6 April* 1916.)

SIMPSON, Alfred Muller, Australian Manufacturer; *b.* London, 4 April 1843; *s.* of Alfred Simpson, afterwards of Adelaide, S.A. (*d.* 1891); *m.* 1st, 1871, Catherine, *e. d.* of James Allen, Unley, S.A.; 2nd, 1888, Violet Laura, *d.* of John Sheridan, M.D., Edinburgh, N.B.; two *s.* three *d.* Arrived in Colony, 1849; has introduced six or more different industries into the Colony since 1869; Member of Legislative Council for metropolitan district, 1887-93; member of the State Board of Conciliation, 1895; President of the Royal Agricultural Society of S.A., 1898, 1899; Governor of Botanic Gardens, 1899; one of the equippers of the Bushmen's Contingent in the South African War, 1900; Trustee of the State Bank of South Australia, 1902; Associate of Order of St. John of Jerusalem for services in connection with ambulance work, 1910. *Address:* Young House, Parkside, South Australia.   (*Died 20 Sept.* 1917.)

SIMPSON, Hon. Archibald Henry, Chief Judge in Equity, New South Wales, since 1896; of Lincoln's Inn; *b.* 1843; *s.* of George Simpson, Barrister. *Educ.:* Tonbridge School; Christ's Coll. Cambridge (Fellow). Went to

Australia, 1881 ; Fellow of the University of Sydney, 1897 ; Vice-Chancellor, 1902-1904. *Address :* Chancery Square, Sydney, New South Wales. *Clubs :* Savile ; Australian, Sydney.
(*Died* 1918.)

SIMPSON, Sir Benjamin, K.C.I.E., *cr.* 1887 ; *b.* 1831 ; *m.* Jane, *d.* of Brigadier Hugh Sibbald, C.B., 1859 ; one *s.* one *d. Educ. :* Dublin University (B.A., M.D.). Late Surgeon-Gen. and Sanitary Commissioner with Govt. of India, 1885-90. *Address :* 77 Ashley Gardens, S.W.1. *T. :* Vic. 5582. (*Died 27 June 1923.*)

SIMPSON, Miss Evelyn Blantyre ; *b.* Edinburgh, Dec. 1856 ; *d.* of Sir James Y. Simpson, Bt. (discoverer of chloroform). *Publications :* Dogs of Other Days ; Sir J. Y. Simpson's Biography in Famous Scot Series ; R. L. Stevenson's Edinburgh Days, 1898 ; R. L. S., 1905 ; R. L. S.'s Originals. *Recreations :* cycling, walking, gardening. *Address :* 15 Inverleith Row, Edinburgh. (*Died 23 Jan. 1920.*)

SIMPSON, Frederick Moore, Emeritus Professor of Architecture in the University of London ; F.R.I.B.A. ; Knight, first class, of the Order of S. Olav ; *s.* of James Moore Simpson ; *m.* 1894, Maud Mary Sandilands (*d.* 1914). Articled to G. F. Bodley, R.A., 1876 ; was admitted a student of the Royal Academy, 1880 ; gained the R.A. Travelling Studentship, 1884 ; President of the Liverpool Architectural Society for Sessions 1900-1 and 1901-2 ; Member Council, R.I.B.A. 1917-20 ; first Prof. of Architecture, Univ. Coll., Liverpool, 1894-1903 ; started School of Architecture there, 1894 ; elected a member of the Art Workers' Guild, 1887 ; Member of Commission appointed by Norwegian Government on Trondhjem Cathedral, 1922. Buildings : Laboratories at University College, London, for Physiology, Pharmacology, Chemistry, Eugenics, and Applied Statistics, Anatomy (Rockefeller gift) Engineering, and School of Architecture, etc. ; Queen Victoria Memorial, Liverpool (in collaboration) ; School of Oriental Studies, Finsbury Circus ; various country houses, etc. *Publication :* A History of Architectural Develop. nt (3 vols.) ; editor The Architect's Library. *Address :* 10 Campden Grove, W.8 ; *T. :* Park 7910 ; Chelwood Gate, Sussex. *Club :* Athenæum. (*Died 13 June 1928.*)

SIMPSON, Henry Fife Morland, M.A., LL.D., J.P. ; Rector of Aberdeen Grammar School since 1893 ; *b.* Newcastle-on-Tyne, 25 Nov. 1859 ; *s.* of late Wm. Graham Simpson ; *m.* 1893, Jenny F. Dohm, Eutin, Holstein ; two *s.* two *d. Educ. :* Oundle ; Pembroke Coll., Cambridge (1st class Classical Tripos, 1882). Private Tutor in Germany ; Assistant Master, Marlborough College, and at Fettes College, Edinburgh, 1883-93. *Publications :* Prehistory of the North (trans. from Worsaae) ; Southesk and other Rune Prime Staves (Proc. Ant. Scot., etc.) ; Wishart's Deeds of Montrose (joint - editor) ; Scott's Legend of Montrose ; Selections from Ovid ; Bon Record, Records and Reminiscences of Aberdeen Grammar School, 1256-1906, etc. *Address :* Amatola, Aberdeen.
(*Died 15 May 1920.*)

SIMPSON, Sir James Hope, Kt., *cr.* 1917 ; Director and formerly General Manager, Bank of Liverpool, and Martin's, Ltd. ; *b.* 4 Nov. 1864 ; *s.* of John Hope Simpson ; *m.* 1895, Mary, *y. d.* of late Isaac Whitwell Wilson, J.P., Kendal ; two *s.* one *d. Educ. :* Liverpool College ; the Continent. Banking — in the service of Williams Deacons Bank, Ltd., Bank of Egypt, Bank of Liverpool, Ltd. *Address :* The Firs, London Road, Guildford. *T. :* Guildford 972.
(*Died 6 Oct. 1924.*)

SIMPSON, Sir James Walter Mackay, 3rd Bt., *cr.* 1866 ; *b.* 6 Sep. 1882 ; *e. s.* of 2nd Bt. and Anne Fitzgerald, *d.* of late Alexander Mackay ; *S.* father, 1898. An ardent

962

supporter of temperance ; interested in social problems ; C.O.S. Finsbury Industrial Improvement Committee, City Council, etc. Has travelled extensively in Europe and America. *Educ. :* Eton ; Balliol College, Oxford. *Publication :* work on Training for Games. *Recreations :* walking, gardening (specially interested in trees), and deep-sea fishing. *Heir :* none. *Address :* Ballabraes of Ayton, Berwickshire ; Strathavon, Linlithgowshire, Scotland ; Oxford House, Bethnal Green Road, E. *T.A. :* Candour, London. *T. :* Kensington 2484. *Club :* Sports.
(*Died 16 Mar. 1924.*)

SIMPSON, Sir Robert Russell, Kt. ; *b.* 1840 ; *y. s.* of Alexander Simpson, banker, Bathgate, and *nephew* of Sir James Young Simpson, Bart., M.D., etc. ; *m.* 1877, Helen Dymock (*d.* 1923), *d.* of Samuel Raleigh, Manager of the Scottish Widows' Fund Life Assurance Society ; four *s.* one *d. Educ. :* Bathgate Academy ; Edinburgh University. Admitted a member of H.M. Society of Writers to the Signet, 1869 ; a J.P. for the City of Edinburgh ; Depute (Lay) Clerk (Emeritus) of the General Assembly of the United Free Church of Scotland ; Chairman of Dr. Guthrie's Industrial Schools ; Vice-President of the Edinburgh Industrial Brigade ; Vice-President of the National Bible Society of Scotland, and Director of various philanthropic and other Institutions in Edinburgh. *Recreations :* golf and travelling. *Address :* 23 Douglas Crescent, Edinburgh. *T.A. :* Simla, Edinburgh. *T :* 2636. *Club :* University, Edinburgh.
(*Died 14 Dec. 1923.*)

SIMPSON, Col. Thomas Thomson, C.B. 1893 ; *s.* of late John Simpson of Findermore, Co. Tyrone ; *b.* 1 June 1836 ; *m.* 1879, Margaret, *y. d.* of late Robert Batt of Pundy's Burn, Co. Down ; no *c. Educ. :* Nutgrove School, Dublin ; privately. Entered army, 1857 ; Captain, 1864 ; Major, 1878 ; Lt.-Col. N. Staffordshire Regt., 1880 ; Col. 1884 ; served Indian Mutiny, 1858 ; against Cabul Kal Wazeerees, 1860 (medal with clasp) ; Zhob Valley Field Force, 1884 (despatches, C.B.) ; commanded 98th Regiment, 1880-85 ; Regimental District 33, 1886-91 ; J.P. for Cos. of Waterford and Kerry. *Recreation :* salmon-fishing. *Address :* Glenmore, Glencairn, S.O., Co. Waterford. *Club :* Army and Navy.
(*Died 30 Dec. 1916.*)

SIMS, Charles ; R.W.S. ; R.A. 1916 ; A.R.A. 1900 ; Keeper and Trustee of Royal Academy, 1920-26 ; Trustee of National Gallery of British Art, 1920 (Tate Gallery) ; *b.* Islington, 1873 ; *m.* 1896, Agnes Helen, *d.* of late John MacWhirter, R.A. ; two *s. Educ. :* private schools. Entered commission agent's office in Paris, 1887, and three other offices subsequently ; began to study art at South Kensington (National Art Training School), 1890 ; Academie Julian, under J. Le Febvre and Benjamin Constant, 1891 ; Royal Academy Schools, 1893 ; exhibited R.A. 1894 ; exhibited The Vine and a portrait at Royal Academy, 1895 ; Childhood, 1896, purchased in 1900 for the Musée du Luxembourg, Paris, and obtained medal at Salon ; Gold medal (International Exhibition), Amsterdam, 1912 ; Gold medal (International Exhibition), Pittsburg, 1912 ; The Fountain and The Wood Beyond the World, Tate Gallery (Chantrey Bequest) ; pictures in the Permanent Municipal Collections of Leeds, Christchurch, New Zealand ; Bristol, Durban, and Pietermaritzburg (S.A.), and N.S.W. *Recreations :* chamber music for strings, golf. *Clubs :* Athenæum, Garrick.
(*Died 13 April 1928.*)

SIMS, George Robert, journalist and dramatic author ; *b.* 2 Sep. 1847 ; *m.* 1901, Florence Wykes. *Educ. :* Hanwell College and Bonn. Journalist and playwright since 1874 ; writer of Mustard and Cress columns in the Referee, under the pen - name of Dagonet, from the irth of the paper in 1877; Knight of the Roy. Norwegian Order of St. Olaf, 1st class, 1905. *Publications:* How the Poor Live; The Dagonet Ballads; Rogues and Vagabonds; Three Brass Balls; Memoirs of Mary Jane; Memoirs of a Landlady; Social Kaleidoscope; Ten Commandments; As it was in the Beginning; Dorcas Dene, Detective, 1897; In London's Heart; Once upon a Christmas Time, 1898; Without the Limelight; A Blind Marriage; Living London; The Cry of The Children; The Black Stain; The Death Gamble; Young Mrs Caudle; Among my Autographs; The Life we Live; For Life—and After; Joyce Pleasantry; His Wife's Revenge; Anna of the Underworld; My Life; Glances Back, etc.; author or part-author of following plays—Lights of London; In the Ranks; Harbour Lights; Master and Man; Mother-in-Law; Faust up to Date; Member for Slocum; Merry Duchess; Golden Ring; Little Christopher Columbus; Grey Mare; Guardsman; The Trumpet Call; The English Rose; Two Little Vagabonds; In Gay Piccadilly; The Elixir of Youth; Romany Rye; My Innocent Boy; Dandy Fifth; Gipsy Earl; Gay City; Golden Ladder; For Life and After; Hop o' my Thumb; Sleeping Beauty; Puss in Boots; Ever-Open Door, etc. *Recreations:* battledore and shuttlecock, bull-dogs, and motoring. *Address:* 12 Clarence Terrace, Regent's Park, N.W.1. *T.A.:* Hybiscus, London. *T.:* Padd. 70. *Clubs:* Devonshire, etc.

(*Died 4 Sept. 1922.*)

SIMSON, Colonel William Amor, C.M.G. 1919; D.S.O. 1916; *b.* 1872; *m.* 1911, Louise, *d.* of late E. L. Du Barry, Norfolk, Virginia. Served European War, 1st Divisional Train, Canadian Force, 1914-18 (despatches, C.M.G., D.S.O.). (*Died 17 Nov. 1925.*)

SINCLAIR, 15th Baron (*cr.* 1449), **Charles William St. Clair;** Representative Peer for Scotland since 1885; *b.* 8 Sep. 1881; *e. s.* of 14th Baron and Jane, *d.* of Archibald Little, Shabden Park, Surrey; *S.* father 1880; *m.* 1870, Margaret, *d.* of James Murray, Ancoats Hall. Conservative; one *s.* three *d. Educ.:* R.M.C. Sandhurst. Entered army, 1848; served in 57th Regt. in Crimean War, Indian Mutiny, and New Zealand War; retired with rank of Col., 1878; J.P., D.L., Berwickshire. *Heir: s.* Master of Sinclair. *Address:* Herdmanston, Pencaitland; Nisbet House, Duns, N.B.; 55 Onslow Square, S.W.7. *T.A.:* Stonedge, London. *T.:* Western 4163. *Clubs:* Carlton, United Service; New, Edinburgh. (*Died 25 April 1922.*)

SINCLAIR, Archibald, journalist and author; *b.* 11 Jan. 1866; *e. s.* of Archibald Sinclair, Lanark; *m.* 1888, Helen Elizabeth Miller. *Educ.:* St. Mark's College, Chelsea. Hon. Assoc. Order of St. John of Jerusalem in England; Vice-President, Royal Life-Saving Society, and joint Hon.-Secretary, 1891-96; sub-editor The Referee since 1897; was sporting editor of The Morning, and on the staff of The Sportsman for several years. *Publications:* (joint) Swimming, Badminton Library; various publications dealing with swimming and amateur sport. *Recreations:* angling, shooting, swimming, and trotting; for many years an official of the Amateur Athletic and Amateur Swimming Associations. *Address:* Twickenham, Middlesex. (*Died 24 Mar. 1922.*)

SINCLAIR, Surg.-Gen. David, M.B., C.M. (Aberdeen), C.S.I., 1899; Indian Medical Service; retired; *b.* 26 Jan. 1847; 2nd *s.* of William Sinclair, Milltimber, Peterculter; *m.* 1876, Jane Birnie, 2nd *d.* of late John Ferguson, advocate, Aberdeen; one *s.* five *d. Educ.:* Aberdeen Grammar School and University (M.B., C.M.). *Decorated* for services in Burma. *Address:* 11 Mortonhall Road, Edinburgh. *Club:* Caledonian United Service, Edinburgh.

(*Died 11 Oct. 1919.*)

SINCLAIR, Deputy Surgeon-General Edward M., C.B. 1907; M.D. St. Andrews, 1853; M.R.C.S. 1853; *s.* of Martin Sinclair, M.D., F.R.C.S.E., of Edinburgh; *b.* 1832; *m.* 1870, Annie Catherine, 2nd *d.* of Andrew Hamilton, Co. Donegal; one *d.* Entered Army Medical Service, 1854; retired 1888; served Crimea, 1854-56, Fall of Sebastopol; Indian Mutiny, 1857-59, several actions in Oude with Gen. Frank's force, Capture of Lucknow, operations in Bundelcund; South Africa, Transvaal Campaign, 1881 (despatches). *Address:* 30 Nevern Square, S.W. *Club:* Junior United Service.

(*Died 14 June 1916.*)

SINCLAIR, George Robertson, Mus. Doc. Cantuar., Hon. F.R.C.O., Hon. R.A.M., L.R.A.M.; Hon. Fellow of St. Michael's College, Tenbury; Organist and Master of the Choristers, Succentor and Sub-Canon at Hereford Cathedral since 1889; *b.* Croydon, 28 Oct. 1863. *Educ.:* St. Michael's College, Tenbury. Studied music under Rev. Sir Fred. Ouseley, Sir Robert Stewart, and Dr. C. H. Lloyd, 1879. Assistant organist of Gloucester Cathedral, and organist and choirmaster of St. Mary de Crypt Church, Gloucester, 1880; appointed at 17 years of age organist and choirmaster of Truro Cathedral; conducted the Festivals of the Three Choirs at Hereford in 1891, 1894, 1897, 1900, 1903, 1906, 1909, and 1912; Conductor Birmingham Festival Choral Society, Hereford Choral Society, Herefordshire Orchestral Society, and Diocesan Choral Union, and Ross Musical Society; Grand Organist to the Grand Lodge of England, 1902; Grand Organist to the Grand Lodge of Mark Master Masons, 1908; Grand organist in the Supreme Grand Chapter of the Royal Arch, 1909. *Recreations:* motor cycling and photography. *Address:* The Close, Hereford. *T.A.:* Hereford. *T.:* 1370. *Clubs:* Junior Constitutional; Herefordshire County.

(*Died 7 Feb. 1917.*)

SINCLAIR, Col. Hugh Montgomerie, C.B. 1910; C.M.G. 1917; C.B.E. 1919; F.R.G.S.; *b.* 23 Feb. 1855; *s.* of Rev. Canon W. Sinclair, Rector of Pulborough, and *g.s.* of Rt. Hon. Sir John Sinclair, 1st Bt., P.C.; *m.* 1905, Rosalie Sybil, *d.* of late Sir John Jackson, M.P.; two *s.* two *d. Educ.:* Malvern; Repton; Woolwich (Pollock medallist). Private Secretary to High Commissioner, Cyprus, 1881-86; passed Staff College with honours, 1890; served Ashanti Campaign, 1895-96 (despatches); Military Secretary to G.O. C.-in-C., Bengal, 1899; A.A.G. in India, 1899-1901; S. Africa, 1900 (despatches); A.Q.M.G. Western District and Southern Command, 1903-7; Chief Engineer Scottish Command, 1908-12; retired, 1912; Commandant Railway Troops, R.E., Longmoor, 1914-19 (despatches, C.M.G., C.B.E.). *Recreations:* hunting, painting, music. *Address:* Barming House, Maidstone. *Club:* Junior United Service.

(*Died 10 July 1924.*)

SINCLAIR, Sir John Rose George, 8th Bt., *cr.* 1631; D.S.O. 1901; J.P., D.L., V.L.; *b.* Slough, 10 Aug. 1864; *e. s.* of Col. A. Y. Sinclair, 26th B.N.I.; *S.* grandfather, 7th Bt., 1873; *m.* Edith, *o. d.* of Lieut.-Col. W. M. Dunbar, 1885. *Educ.:* Military College, Oxford. Lieut. 4th Batt. Cheshire Regt. 1881-85; Lieut.-Col. Commandant, 1892-1900; Hon. Colonel, 1900, 1st Caithness Volunteer Artillery; President Caithness Territorial Force Association, 1908-20; has farmed since 1885; served South Africa (Imp. Yeo.), 1900-1 (despatches); European War, 1914-19, with 14th Batt. King's Liverpool Regt. Owns 6800 acres. *Recreations:* cycling, horses, turning. *Heir: n.* Ronald Norman John Charles Udny Sinclair, *b.* 30 June 1899. *Address:* Barrock House, Wick. *T.A.:* Lyth. *M.:* SK 838. *Club:* Constitutional.

(*Died 3 Nov. 1926.*)

SINCLAIR, Ven. John Stewart; Archdeacon of Cirencester; Hon. Canon of Gloucester; *b.* 15 May 1853; *s.* of Prebendary Wm. Sinclair, Rector of Pulborough, Sussex; *g.s.* of Rt. Hon. Sir John Sinclair, 1st Bt., P.C., of Ulbster; *m.* Clara Sophia, *d.* of John Dearman Birchall of Bowden Hall, Gloucestershire; two *s.* two *d.* *Educ.:* Repton School; Oriel College, Oxford. 2nd class Mod. History (rowed in the Oxford boat, 1874). Curate of Pulborough; Curate of All Saints', Fulham; Vicar of St. Dionis, Fulham; elected Chairman of the Fulham Vestry, 6 years; Vicar of Cirencester, 1898-1908; P.G. Chaplain of England. *Publications:* Civic Duties, and other sermons. *Recreations:* archæology, riding, fishing. *Address:* The Greenway, Shurdington, nr. Cheltenham. *Club:* Oxford and Cambridge.

(*Died 30 April 1919.*)

SINCLAIR, Louis; *b.* Paris, 1861, of English parents, who returned to England in 1864; *m.* 1886, Nina, *d.* of Daniel de Pass, of Natal and London; three *s.* one *d.* *Educ.:* University Coll., London; Continental-Colleges. Went to Australia, 1878, and started life on the staff of the Argus, Melbourne; subsequently engaged in commercial pursuits, and retired from business at twenty-five years of age; deeply interested in commercial questions, and was entirely instrumental in forming the Commercial Committee of the House of Commons, 1899, of which he was Hon. Secy.; initiated the Anglo-French Interparliamentary visits; M.P. (C.) Romford Div. Essex, 1897-1906; was the appellant in the Birkbeck Bank disaster,and secured equal and proper treatment to the depositors; reformed the Commercial Committee of the House of Commons, 1913; was entirely responsible for the formation of Commercial Committees in the Parliaments of Europe; appointed Permanent Hon. Secy. General of the Commercial Inter-Parliamentary Congress, in recognition of his services; during the War served in the R.A.C. War Transport Service, in which he was Emergency Officer; visited the Australasian Dominions and formed Commercial Committees in the Federal Parliament, and also in the Queensland, New South Wales and South Australian Parliaments, 1920. *Publications:* Our Commercial Disabilities; Ministry of Justice instead of Home Office; Our Poor Laws and their Degrading Operation. *Address:* Daydawn, 7 Netherhall Gardens, N.W.3; *T.:* Hampstead 145; 28 Castle Hill Avenue, Folkestone. *Clubs:* Carlton, Royal Automobile. (*Died 4 Jan. 1928.*)

SINCLAIR, Ven. William Macdonald, Hon. D.D. Glasgow; F.R.S.L., F.R.G.S., F.R.H.S.; examining chaplain to Bishop of London; honorary chaplain to H.M. the King; *b.* Leeds, 3 June 1850; *e. surv. s.* of late Rev. William Sinclair, Prebendary of Chichester (5th *s.* of Rt. Hon. Sir John Sinclair, 1st Bt., and Diana, *d.* of Alexander, 1st Lord Macdonald). *Educ.:* Repton; Balliol Coll. Oxford (Scholar); 2nd class Moderations and Classics. President Oxford Union Society, 1873; assistant minister of Quebec Chapel, 1876; resident chaplain to Bishop of London, 1877; Vicar of St. Stephen's, Westminster, 1880; member London School Board, 1885; Grand Chaplain of England, 1894; Chaplain to Order of St. John of Jerusalem, 1900; chaplain-in-ordinary to Queen Victoria; Hon. Chaplain to King Edward VII.; Archdeacon of London and Canon of St. Paul's, 1889-1911; Rector of Shermanbury, Henfield, Sussex, 1911-15. *Publications:* The Psalms in the original Rhythm, 1879; Commentary on the Epistles of St. John, 1880; Lessons on the Gospel of St. John, 1882; The Servant of Christ, 1891; The Christian's Influence, 1892; Christ and our Times, 1894; Words to the Laity, 1895; Leaders of Thought in the English Church, 1896; Simplicity in Christ, 1896; The New Law, 1897;

The Happy Life, 1897; Unto You, Young Men, 1900; Words from St. Paul's (first series), 1900; Likewise the Younger Women, 1901; Words from St. Paul's (second series), 1902; John MacWhirter, R.A., 1903; Difficulties of our Day, 1905; Memorials of St. Paul's Cathedral; The Chapels Royal, 1912; Joseph Farquharson, A.R.A., 1912; short edition of Memorials, 1913; charges—Condition of the People; The Church, Visible, Invisible, Catholic, National; Sacred Studies; The English Church and the Canon Law; Points at Issue between the Church of England and the Church of Rome; The Ancient British Churches; The Churches of the East, 1898; Church Courts, 1899; The Duties of Archdeacons, 1901; The Church and the Nonconformists, 1902; The Authority of Sunday, 1903; Catholic and Protestant, 1906; The Catholic Faith and the New Theology, 1907; The Part of Faith in the Healing of the Sick, 1910. *Recreations:* riding, cycling, and swimming. *Clubs:* Athenæum, Authors'.

(*Died 4 Dec. 1917.*)

SINCLAIR-LOCKHART, Sir Robert Duncan, of Castle Hill, Co. Lanark, 11th Bt., *cr.* 1636; holds Sinclair of Stevenson Baronetcy; *b.* 12 Nov. 1856; *s.* of late George Duncan and Elizabeth Amanda Lockhart; *S.* uncle 1904; *m.* 1895, Flora Louisa Jane Beresford, *d.* of Captain Edward Power; five *s.* one *d.* Heir: *s.* Graeme Duncan Power, *b.* 29 Jan. 1897. *Address:* Kanoulla, Remuera, Auckland, N.Z.

(*Died 8 Nov. 1919.*)

SINDING, Stephan; sculptor; *b.* of Christian Sinding, composer, and late Otto Sinding, painter; *b.* Drontheim, 1846; has studied and worked in Berlin, Paris, Rome, and Copenhagen. *Works:* May; Mother Earth; The Joy of Life; The Barbarian Mother; Man and Woman; Walküre; The Eldest of Her Kin; Grave Monument of the Isenberg Family.

(*Died 24 Jan. 1922.*)

SINGLETON, Rev. John J., M.A.; Hon. Canon of Southwell since 1885; *b.* 1838; *s.* of Rev. W. Singleton, M.A.; *m. e. d.* of Rev. W. Calder, M.A., Headmaster of the Chesterfield Grammar School, and afterwards Rector of Wingerworth, Derbyshire. *Educ.:* Ipswich Grammar School; Pembroke College, Cambridge. Ordained Deacon, 1861; Priest, 1862; Assistant Curate of Chesterfield, 1861-70; Vicar of Ogley Hay, 1870-73; Rector of Brimington, 1873-88; Vicar of Melbourne, Derbyshire, 1888-1908. *Address:* Southwell, Notts.

(*Died 27 Dec. 1917.*)

SINHA, 1st Baron of Raipur, *cr.* 1919; **Rt. Hon. Sir Satyendra Prassano Sinha,** K.C.S.I., *cr.* 1921; Kt., *cr.* 1914; K.C. 1918; P.C. 1919; Member of Judicial Committee of Privy Council since 1926; late Member of Viceroy's Executive Council, India (1st native); *b.* 1864; *s.* of Babu Siti Kantha Sinha; four *s.* three *d.* *Educ.:* Birbhoom Zilla School; Presidency College, Calcutta (Scholar). Came to England, 1881; Lincoln's Inn; called to Bar, 1886; Barrister, Calcutta High Court; Standing Counsel, Government of India, 1903; Advocate-General, Bengal, 1907-9, 1915-17; a Representative of India in Imperial War Conference, 1917; Member Imperial War Cabinet, 1918; Freeman of City of London, 1917; Under-Secretary of State for India, 1919-20; Governor of Bihar and Orissa, Dec. 1920-21. *Address:* Queen Anne's Mansions, S.W.1. *Clubs:* Reform, Marlborough, National Liberal.

(*Died 6 Mar. 1928.*)

SINNETT, Alfred Percy; *b.* 18 Jan. 1840; *s.* of E. W. P. Sinnett, journalist (*d.* 1845), and Mrs. Percy Sinnett, author of Byways of History, etc.; *m.* 1870, Patience (*d.* 1908), *d.* of Richard Edensor of Shaw Wood, Derbyshire. *Educ.:* London University School. Assist. sub-editor of the Globe, 1859; afterwards sub-editor and leader-writer on various London papers; appointed editor of the Hong-Kong Daily Press, 1865; returned London, 1868; leader-writer on Standard; appointed editor of the Pioneer of India, 1872; became interested in theosophical movement, 1879; wrote The Occult World, 1881; Esoteric Buddhism, 1883; Vice-President of the Theosophical Society; author of two novels founded on occult ideas, Karma and United; in 1896 published The Growth of the Soul. Brought out new monthly review called Broad Views, 1904; ceased publication, 1907; author of play, Married by Degrees, produced London, 1911. *Club:* Junior Carlton.

(Died 26 June 1921.)

SIVEWRIGHT, Hon. Sir James, K.C.M.G., *cr.* 1892; C.M.G. 1880; *b.* 1848; *s.* of William Sivewright, Fochabers, N.B.; *m.* Jennie, *d.* of George Page, Bloemfontein, 1880. *Educ.:* Aberdeen University (M.A. 1866; LL.D. 1893). General Manager South African Telegraphs, 1877-85; Commissioner of Crown Lands and Public Works, Cape Colony, 1890-92; Commissioner of Public Works, 1896-1898. *Address:* Tulliallan Castle, Kincardine-on-Forth; Lourensford, Somerset West, Cape Colony. *(Died 9 Sept. 1916.)*

SKEGGS, Rev. Thomas Charles, M.A.; Chaplain at Palermo, 1900-26; Canon of Gibraltar, 1899-1926. *Educ.:* Hertford College, Oxford. Deacon, 1879; Priest, 1880; Curate of St. Thomas, Pendleton, 1879-81; St. Ambrose, Pendleton, 1881-85; Chaplain of Marseilles, 1885-1900. *Address:* Homes of St. Barnabas, Dormans, Surrey. *(Died 25 Sept. 1927.)*

SKEMP, Arthur Rowland, M.A., Ph.D.; Winterstoke Professor of English, University of Bristol, since 1911; Lecturer on Military Training; adjcapt. unattached list T.F., attached No. 3 Officer Cadet Batt.; *b.* Eccles, 1882; 2nd *s.* of Thomas Rowland Skemp, cotton manufacturer, and later, Unitarian minister; *m.* 1909, Jessie, *d.* of J. Clarkson, J.P., of Barrow-in-Furness; one *s.* one *d. Educ.:* Universities of Manchester (1st class English, 1904, M.A. 1907, Univ. Scholar, Falconer Fellow in Arts), Berlin, Strassburg i/E (Ph.D. summa cum laude, 1908). Editor (joint), Manchester University Magazine, 1902-5; President, S.R.C. 1904; Lektor of English in University of Strassburg, 1906; Lecturer, University of Sheffield, 1909. *Publications:* (creative): Guenevere, tragedy in three acts. produced by Miss Muriel Pratt at the Theatre Royal, Bristol, 1914; (critical): Tragedy of Messallina (Bang's Materialen), 1910; Francis Bacon, 1912; Robert Browning, 1916; articles and reviews. chiefly on Old English poetry or on subjects connected with the drama, in Modern Philology, Jahrbuch der deutschen Shakespeare-gesellschaft, Modern Language Review, Essays and Studies by members of the English Association, etc. *Recreations:* boxing, lacrosse, the theatre. *Address:* 8 Cavendish Road, Westbury-on-Trym.

(Died 1 Nov. 1918.)

SKERRINGTON, Lord; William Campbell, of Skerrington, Ayrshire; one of the Senators of the College of Justice in Scotland, 1908-25; Q.C., 1898; *b.* 27 June 1855; *o. s.* of the late Robert Campbell of Skerrington, and Anne, *d.* of late John Carr of Dunston Hill, County Durham; *m.* 1880, Alice Mary, 2nd *d.* of late Patrick Fraser, one of the Senators of the College of Justice in Scotland; two *s.* one *d.* Dean of the Faculty of Advocates, 1905-8; Knight Commander of Gregory the Great. *Address:* 12 Randolph Crescent, Edinburgh.

(Died 21 July 1927.)

SKETCHLEY, Major Ernest Frederick Powys, D.S.O. 1915; General Staff Officer 2nd Grade, Royal Naval Division, since 1914; *b.* 6 Aug. 1881; *s.* of Rev. E. Powys Sketchley; *m.* Phyllis, *d.* of J. F.

Campbell, Deputy Master of the Mint, W. Australia; one *s.* one *d. Educ.:* Dulwich College. 2nd Lieut. R.M.L.I. 1900; Lieut. 1901; Capt. 1911; A.D.C. and private secretary to H.E. Governor of Western Australia, 1905-8; Adjutant Portsmouth Division R.M.L.I. 1910-14; served European War in France and Antwerp with R.M. Brigade as Brigade Major; through whole of Gallipoli campaign in present position, including landing and final evacuation of Cape Helles (despatches, D.S.O.). *Recreations:* riding, golf, tennis, etc. *Address:* Forton Barracks, Gosport, Hants. *T.A.:* Marine Gosport.

(Died Oct. 1916.)

SKILBECK, William Wray, Editor of the Nineteenth Century and After since 1908; *b.* 12 July 1864; *s.* of William Skilbeck, solicitor, Bedford Row, and Janet, *d.* of Stuart Donaldson; *m.* 1894, Beatrice Isabel, *y. d.* of Sir James Knowles, K.C.V.O.; two *d. Educ.:* Harrow; Trinity College, Cambridge. B.A., LL.B. 1886; solicitor, 1890; called to Bar, Inner Temple, 1898; Private Secretary to Sir James Knowles, founder and editor of the Nineteenth Century, from 1893 until his father-in-law's death in 1908. *Recreations:* boating, lawn tennis, bicycling (formerly captain of the Clapham Rovers and East Sheen Rugby Football Teams, and member of the Surrey Fifteen). *Address:* Queen Anne's Mansions, S.W. *Club:* Oxford and Cambridge. *(Died 17 July 1919.)*

SKINNER, Col. Edmund Grey, C.B. 1891; *b.* 29 Jan. 1850; *s.* of Russell Morland Skinner, B.C.S., sometime Judge of Kishnagur; *m.* 1st, 1878, Alice Augusta (*d.* 1902), *d.* of F. Gilliat Smith of The Oaks, Surrey; five *d.*; 2nd, 1904, Amy, *d.* of T. H. Foreman, Breadsell, Battle; two *s. Educ.:* Wimbledon School; R.M.C. Sandhurst. Joined Army Ordnance Department, 1867; Perak Exhibition, 1875-76 (medal); Egypt, 1882-85; including actions Kassassin, Tel-el-Kebir, and Suakin, 1885, when he was C.O.O. of the expedition (medal and clasps, 4th class Medjidie, bronze star); Major, 1882; Bt. Lt.-Col. 1885; Col. 1894; retired, 1901. *(Died 18 Nov. 1917.)*

SKINNER, Rev. John, D.D.; Emeritus Principal; Professor of Old Testament Language and Literature and Apologetics, Theological College of Presbyterian Church of England, 1890-1922; Principal, 1908-22; *b.* 18 July 1851; *e. s.* of James Skinner, Inverurie, Aberdeenshire; *m.* 1885. Jessie Elizabeth, *d.* of James Niven, Mills of Echt. *Educ.:* Gymnasium, Old Aberdeen; Aberdeen University and Free Church College, Aberdeen; New College, Edinburgh; Leipzig; Gottingen. M.A. and D.D. Aberdeen; D.D. St. Andrews; Hon. M.A. Cambridge; Hon. D.D. Oxford; Minister of Free Church of Scotland: St. Fergus, 1880-86; Kelso, 1886-90. *Publications:* Historical Connection between the Old and New Testaments; The Book of Ezekiel (Expositor's Bible); The Book of the Prophet Isaiah, 2 vols.; articles in Hastings' Dictionary of the Bible; I. and II. Kings (Century Bible); A Critical and Exegetical Commentary on the Book of Genesis, 1910; The Divine Names in Genesis, 1914; Prophecy and Religion. 1922. *Address:* 55 Hartington Grove, Cambridge. *(Died 20 Mar. 1925.)*

SKINNER, Sir Thomas, 1st Bt., *cr.* 1912; J.P. Middlesex; *b.* 1840; *m.* 1st, 1866, Sara Margaret (*d.* 1902), *d.* of Jonas D. Hewitt; three *s.* three *d.*; 2nd, 1903, Martha Lauretta (*d.* 1924), *d.* of Job Long, and *widow* of C. J. Williamson. Founder and editor of the Stock Exchange Year - Book, The Stock Exchange Gazette, The Directory of Directors, The Bankers' Almanac and Year Book, The Canadian Gazette, etc.; is a Director of the Canadian Pacific Railway, the Canadian Pacific Ocean Services, the Bank of Montreal, and the Com-

mercial Cable Company. *Heir: s.* Thomas Hewitt Skinner [*b.* 12 June 1875; *m.* 1899, Ellen Constance, *d.* of James Hay Hall; two *s.* two *d. Address:* Falconhurst, Wimbledon, S.W.]. *Address:* 330 Gresham House, E.C.2; 22 Pont Street, S.W.1; The Gables, Worthing *T.A.:* Desollar, London. *T.:* 506 Victoria, 2886 Central, and 394 Worthing. *M. :* LF 6206. *Clubs:* City of London, Junior Athenæum.
(Died 11 May 1926.)

SKINNER, Walter Robert; Journalist; Editor and Proprietor of The Mining Manual, and Mining Year-Book, established 1887; Oil and Petroleum Manual, established 1910; The Capitalist, established 1885; *b.* 1851; *s.* of James Skinner, Bristol; *m.* 1876; two *s.* one *d. Educ.:* privately. *Address:* 15 Dowgate Hill, Cannon Street, E.C.4; *T.:* Central 1929; 29 Palmeira Square, Hove, Sussex.
(Died 12 May 1924.)

SKOTTOWE, Britiffe Constable, 4th Baron Skottowe in the peerage of France (creation by Louis XVIII. 1814); *b.* 1857; *o. s.* of Thomas Britiffe Skottowe of Harrow Weald House, 3rd Baron, and Lœtitia Mourgue, *d.* of John Constable of Wassand; *m.* 1899, Jane Margaret Phillips (*d.* 1923), *o. c.* of John Orwell Phillips, Lieutenant City of London, of 44 Grosvenor Street, W., and The Common, Weybridge. *Educ.:* Harrow; New College, Oxford (M.A.); 1st class Modern History, 2nd class Jurisprudence; F.R.G.S. *Publications:* Our Hanoverian Kings; A Short History of Parliament; Sudden Death, etc. *Recreations:* many. *Address:* 64 Prince's Gate, S.W.7. *T.:* Kensington 5545. *Clubs:* Carlton, Wellington, Hurlingham; Mid-Surrey Golf.
(Died 22 Feb. 1925.)

SKRINE, Rev. John Huntley, D.D.; Vicar of St. Peter in the East, Oxford, since 1908; *b.* Somerset, 3 April 1848; 3rd *s.* of Henry Duncan Skrine, Warleigh, Somerset, and Susanna C. Mills, *d.* of Thomas Mills, Saxham House, Suffolk; *m.* Mary, *d.* of Rev. T. H. Tooke, 1878; one *d. Educ.:* Uppingham; Corpus Christi College, Oxford (Scholar, M.A.); D.D. 1912. 1st class (Classics) in Mods. and in Final Schools; Newdigate Prize Poem, 1870. Fellow of Merton Coll. Oxford, 1871-79; ordained, 1874; assistant master, Uppingham, 1873-87; canon of Perth Cathedral, 1897-1902. Warden of Trinity College, Glenalmond, 1888-1902; Vicar of Itchenstoke, 1903-7; select preacher to University of Oxford, 1907; Bampton Lecturer for 1911. *Publications:* Margaret of Anjou (Newdigate Prize Poem), 1870; Uppingham by the Sea, 1878; Under Two Queens (Lyrics), 1884; The Ocean Throne (a Jubilee Masque), 1887; A Memory of Edward Thring, 1890; Columba (a Poem), 1892; Joan the Maid (a Dramatic Poem), 1895; Songs of the Maid, and other Ballads and Lyrics, 1896; A Goodly Heritage (School Sermons), 1897; The Heart's Counsel (General Sermons); Thirty Hymns for Public School Singing, 1899; The Queen's Highway, lyrics of the war, 1900; Saints and Worthies (General Sermons), 1901; Pastor Agnorum, a Schoolmaster's Afterthoughts; The Mountain-Mother (Glenalmond Sermons), 1902; The Christ in the Teacher (Addresses), 1905; What is Faith? (Theology), 1907; Pastor Ovium, 1909; Problems of Hope and Love; Village Hymns and Litanies; Sermons to Pastors and Masters, 1910; Creed and the Creeds, Bampton Lectures, 1911; Miracle and History, 1912; Pastor Futurus (Dramatic Idyll); Eucharist and Bishop, 1914; The Survival of Jesus (study in telepathy), 1917; The Gospel of the Manhood, 1922. *Address:* 1 Church Road, Oxford. *(Died 8 May 1923.)*

SLACK, Captain Charles, F.R.G.S., F.R.C.I., M.R.U.S.I.; served for sixteen years as Commissioned Officer in Lancashire and

Middlesex Artillery, retaining rank on retirement; Captain in National Reserve. *Educ.:* privately. Has travelled through all the countries of Europe, also in Algeria, Tunis, Egypt, United States, Canada, Siberia, China, and Japan; Councillor for borough of Lambeth in the Conservative interest since 1906; Chairman of Education Committee, 1911, and of Libraries Committee, 1916; on staff of Army and Navy Gazette and Brixton Free Press. *Publications:* Handbook of Company Drill, 48 editions; Handbook of Infantry Drill; Handbook of Artillery Drill; Attack Formations; Military Models for Instruction in Drill and Tactics; Military Essays; Manual of Languages (22) for Tourists and Students; also Manual of Burmese; Introduction to Swahili; My Tour in the Far East; Federation of the British Empire; The New Europe; Ireland and its Traditions; contributions to the public press on Naval, Military, Political, and Social Subjects, etc. *Recreation:* foreign travel. *Address:* 45 Medora Road, Brixton Hill, S.W.2. *(Died Dec. 1925.)*

SLADDEN, Sir Julius, Kt., *cr.* 1926; Chairman of Conservative and Unionist Association, Evesham Division; County Councillor, Worcestershire; Chairman of Governors, Prince Henry's Grammar School, Evesham; Commissioner of Income Tax; *b.* 25 June 1847; *y. s.* of late John Sladden, M.R.C.S., of Ashnext-Sandwich; *m.* 1877, Eugénie Narcisse, *d.* of John Mourilyan of Paris, and formerly of Sandwich, Kent; four *s.* four *d. Educ.:* Epsom College. *Address:* Seward House, Badsey, Evesham. *T.A.:* Sladden, Badsey. *T.:* Badsey 11. *M.:* UY 70. *(Died 21 Dec. 1928.)*

SLADE, Admiral Sir Edmond John Warre, K.C.I.E., *cr.* 1011; K.C.V.O., *cr.* 1911; M.V.O. 1908; R.N.; Vice-Chairman Anglo-Persian Oil Company, Ltd.; *b.* 20 March 1859; *s.* of Rev. George Fitzclarence and Eleanor Frances Slade; *m.* 1887, Florence Madeleine, *e. d.* of late James Carr Saunders; two *d. Educ.:* Eton. Entered Navy, 1872; Lieut. 1879; Commander, 1894; Captain, 1899; served in H.M.S. Hecla during the Egyptian War, 1882; Commander-in-Chief, East Indies, 1909-12; retired, 1917. *Address:* 63 Bedford Gardens, Campden Hill, W.8. *T.:* Park 4959. *Clubs:* United Service, Royal Automobile, City of London.
(Died 20 Jan. 1928.)

SLADEN, Brig.-Gen. David Ramsay, C.M.G. 1915; D.S.O. 1898, 1st Batt. King's Own Scottish Borderers; *b.* 7 Feb. 1869; *s.* of late Major-General John Ramsay Sladen; *m.* 1911, Isabel, *d.* of late John Blakiston-Houston of Orangefield, Co. Down; two *s.* one *d.* Entered army, 1888; Capt. 1897; Major, 1907; Lt.-Col. 1914; served Suakim Field Force, 1888 (medal with clasp, Khedive's star); Soudan Frontier, 1889; North-West Frontier of India, 1897-98 (slightly wounded, despatches, D.S.O., medal with two clasps); South Africa, 1899-1902 (despatches, Queen's medal, 3 clasps, King's medal, 2 clasps); European War, 1914-18 (wounded twice, despatches, C.M.G.); Commanded 2/K.O.S.B. France, 1915-17; Brig.-Gen. France, 1917; J.P., D.L., Radnorshire. *Address:* Rhydoldog, Rhayader. *Club:* Naval and Military.
(Died 21 June 1923.)

SLATER, John, B.A., F.R.I.B.A.; architect; surveyor to the Berners Estate, London; *b.* Bishop's Stortford, 28 July 1847; *e. s.* of late John Slater, J.P.; *m.*; one *s.* two *d. Educ.:* Collegiate School, Bishop's Stortford; Univ. Coll., London. Articled to Professor T. Roger Smith, 1868; President Architectural Association, 1887; Vice-President Royal Institute of British Architects, 1900-4; Member of Tribunal of Appeal London Building Acts. *Publications:* A Short History of the Berners Estate; (with Professor Roger Smith) Classic and Early Christian Architecture.

Address: 46 Berners Street, W.1 ; 13 Welbeck Mansions, West Hampstead, N.W.6.   *T.* : Museum 1433.   *Club :* Athenæum.

(Died 1 Dec. 1924.)

SLATER, Rev. William Fletcher, M.A.; late Professor of Biblical Literature, Didsbury College ; *b.* Uttoxeter, Staffordshire, 25 Aug. 1831 ; *m.* 1860, Mary, *d.* of W. C. Arnison, M.R.C.S., Allendale ; three *s.* four *d.* *Educ. :* Wesleyan College, Didsbury ; Cambridge University. Wesleyan Minister at Allendale, Newcastle-on-Tyne, Sunderland, Harrogate, Cambridge, Leeds, Edinburgh, Liverpool, London. *Publications:* Methodism in the Light of the Early Church (Fernley Lecture, 1885) ; The Faith and Life of the Early Church, 1892 ; Manual of Modern Church History, 1895 ; St. Matthew (Century Bible), 1901. *Address:* 49 Redbourne Avenue, Finchley, N.

(Died 30 Mar. 1924.)

SLAUGHTER, Sir William Capel, Kt., *cr.* 1915 ; partner in the firm of Slaughter and May, Solicitors, 18 Austin Friars, E.C. ; *b.* 1857, *y. s.* of late Mihill Slaughter ; *m.* 1st, Ida (*d.* 1890), 3rd *d.* of Loraine Weaver, 2nd, Hester Mary, *e. d.* of William Duff Bruce ; three *s.* one *d.* *Educ. :* privately. *Address:* 3 Berkeley House, Berkeley Square, W. ; *T.:* Gerrard 8420 ; White Ness, Kingsgate, Thanet. *Club:* Bath.

(Died 10 Mar. 1917.)

SLEIGHT, Sir George Frederick, 1st Bt., *cr.* 1920 ; Kt., *cr.* 1918 ; J.P. Lincolnshire ; steam trawler owner, and general wholesale merchant and gentleman farmer ; *b.* Cleethorpes, 26 March 1858 ; 3rd *s.* of Joseph Sleight, wholesale merchant, Grimsby and Cleethorpes ; *m.* 1872 ; four *s.* three *d.* *Educ. :* Cleethorpes School. Owner of the largest private steam trawler fishing business in the world ; formerly the principal fishing-smack owner ; saw possibilities of steam ; became a pioneer in effecting a change from the old to the new order ; was the first merchant to finance a privately-owned steam trawler in Grimsby ; during the war lent the Government between fifty and sixty steam ships ; lost over thirty boats by enemy action ; purchased a number of obsolete ships, altered these, and refitted and equipped them on modern lines to keep up the fishing fleet ; so contributed to the nation's food supply ; is an extensive farmer, cattle breeder, and rearer of pigs and sheep ; has bred a herd of the noted Lincolnshire red shorthorns ; believes in applying the most modern methods to farming as to other businesses, and has considerably increased food crops on land brought under his control. *Recreations:* farming, motoring, and outdoor country life. *Heir: e. s.* Major Ernest Sleight, O.B.E. *Address:* Weelsby Hall, near Grimsby, Lincs. *T.A.:* Sleight, Grimsby. *T.:* Grimsby 830. *Club:* County, Grimsby.

(Died 19 Mar. 1921.)

SLOAN, John MacGavin ; *b.* Scotland ; *m.* 1880, Mary Jane, *d.* of late Thomas Helme, wood merchant ; one *d.* *Educ. :* privately ; University of Glasgow. Withdrew from ministry to become a *littérateur* ; Editor of Dumfries and Galloway Courier and Herald, 1897-1900) ; thereafter settled in London. *Publications:* Quintin Doonrise, a Study in Human Nature, 1892 ; Fallacies of State Socialism, 1894 ; The Carlyle Country, with a Study of Carlyle's Life, 1903 ; edited Lockhart's Lives of Burns and Scott in Library of Standard Biographies, 1904 ; Galloway, in Black's Colour-book Series, 1908 ; Studies in Burns contributed to T.P.'s Weekly ; Our Referee on many Matters in Yorkshire Weekly Post since 1907 ; contributor to Saturday Review, Fortnightly Review, Chambers's Journal, Landmark, John o' London's Weekly. *Recreation:* bowling. *Address:* 9 Bonham Road, Brixton Hill, S.W.   *(Died 15 Nov. 1926.)*

SLOANE, William Milligan, A.M., Ph.D., L.H.D., LL.D. ; Seth Low Professor of History,

Columbia Univ. New York City ; *b.* Richmond, Ohio, U.S.A., 12 Nov. 1850 ; *e. s.* of Rev. James Renwick Sloane of New York (*d.* 1886), and Margaret Milligan (*d.* 1854) ; *m.* 1877, Mary Espy Johnston ; two *s.* two *d.* *Educ. :* Columbia Coll., New York ; Berlin and Leipzic Univs. Classical Master of the Newell School, Pittsburgh, 1868-1872 ; Secretary to George Bancroft, U.S. Ambassador in Berlin, 1872-75 ; Professor of Latin (1876-84), and of History (1884-96), Princeton University ; Director of Historical Studies, Columbia University, 1896-1916 ; Member of International Olympic Committee, 1894 ; Chancellor of the American Academy of Arts and Letters, 1908-20, President 1920 ; ex-Vice-President N.Y. Historical Society ; Member American Historical Society and ex-President ; Officier de la Légion d'Honneur, 1910 ; Commander of the North Star, Sweden, 1912. *Publications :* The Poet Labid, 1876 ; The Life and Work of J. R. W. Sloane, 1887 ; The French War and the Revolution, 1892 ; The Life of James M'Cosh, 1895 ; The Life of Napoleon Bonaparte, 1897 ; The French Revolution and Religious Reform, 1901 ; Parteiherrschaft in Amerika, 1913 ; The Balkans, 1914 ; Party Government in the United States, 1914 ; The Powers and Aims of Western Democracy, 1919 ; Greater France in Africa, 1924. *Recreations:* golf, walking. *Address:* Columbia Univ., New York. *Clubs:* Century, Univ., New York ; Nassau, Princeton, N.J.

(Died 12 Sept. 1928.)

SLOMAN, Rev. Arthur, M.A. ; Hon. Canon of Ely, 1907-14 ; Hon. Canon of St. Albans, 1914 ; Rural Dean of Huntingdon, 1908-14 ; Rector of Sandy ; *b.* Farnham, Surrey, 18 Oct. 1851 ; 2nd *s.* of S. G. Sloman, Surgeon, and *d.* of Dr. W. Newnham ; *m.* 1884, Bessie, *d.* of late Wm. Penrose of Glenmore, Queenstown ; two *s.* *Educ. :* Epsom College ; Pembroke College, Oxford (Scholar). 1st Class Honours in Classical Moderations ; 2nd Class in Final Classical School ; President of Union Society, 1875 ; Assistant Master, Rossall, 1876-77 ; Westminster, 1877-86, and Master of the King's Scholars from 1881 ; Headmaster of Birkenhead School, 1886-97. *Publications:* Trinummus of Plautus, and the Andria, Adelphi, and Phormio of Terence (two former with C. E. Freeman) ; St. Matthew, Greek text with notes ; A Grammar of Classical Latin ; An Elementary Latin Grammar ; Latin Prose for Middle Forms (with W. H. Spragge). *Recreations:* keen mountaineer, member of Alpine Club since 1879, cricket, tennis. *Address:* Sandy Rectory, Beds. *T.A.:* Sandy. *Club:* Alpine.

(Died 20 Dec. 1919.)

SLOMAN, Very Rev. Ernest ; Dean of Georgetown, 1910 ; Rector of St. George's Cathedral, Georgetown, since 1910 ; Archdeacon of Demerara, 1914 ; Vicar-General, 1910-14. *Educ. :* St. Edmund Hall, Oxford (M.A.) ; Leeds Clergy School. Ordained 1878 ; Curate of S. Hackney, 1878-83 ; Christ Church, Georgetown, 1883-84 ; Principal of Belair Training Institute, 1884-89 ; Rector of St. Patrick's, Berbice, 1889-1910. *Address:* The Deanery, Georgetown, British Guiana. *Club:* New Oxford and Cambridge.   *(Died 8 July 1918.)*

SLY, Sir Frank George, K.C.S.I., *cr.* 1918 ; C.S.I. 1911 ; Hon. D.Litt. (Nagpur), 1924 ; Chief Commissioner, Central Provinces and Berar, 1920 ; Governor of Central Provinces, 1921-25 ; *b.* 1866. *Educ. :* Balliol College, Oxford. Entered I.C.S. 1885 ; Under-Secretary, Government of India, 1895-98 ; Political Agent, Chattisgarh Feudatories, 1899 ; Commissioner of Settlements and Agriculture, 1901 ; Inspector-General of Agriculture, 1904-5 ; Commissioner of Berar, 1908-12 ; Member of Royal Commission on Indian Services, 1912-1914 ; Chairman of P.W.D. Reorganisation Committee, 1916-17 ; Chairman of Champaran En-

quiry, 1917 ; Vice - Chairman, Lord South-borough's Committee on Franchise, 1918-19. *Address:* c/o Lloyds Bank, 6 Pall Mall, S.W.1. *Club:* East India United Service.
(*Died 16 July 1928.*)

SLYNE, Denis, C.B.E. 1919 ; Barrister-at-law ; Lord O'Hagan medallist and David Lynch medallist, King's Inns, Ireland ; *m.* ; two *d.* Entered Imperial Inland Rev. Dept., 1880 ; Treas. and Receiver-General, Trinidad, 1903 ; Member of Legislative and Executive Councils, Trinidad ; Commissioner of Currency ; Member of Port of Spain Sewerage Board and Water Authority, and Member of Port of Spain Town Board, 1904-7 ; Chairman of Committee for Liquidation of Enemy Businesses, 1914 ; Custodian of Enemy Property, 1916 ; Chairman of Public Officer's Guarantee Fund and of Board of Management of Agricultural Banks, Trinidad ; Controller of Enemy Debts Clearing House, 1920 ; Commissioner of Income Tax, 1922 ; retired from public service, 1923. *Address:* 19 Collingham Place, Earl's Court, S.W.5. (*Died 27 Feb. 1928.*)

SMALE, Morton Alfred, M.R.C.S., L.S.A., L.D.S.; Hon. Dental Surgeon, King George's Hosp. ; Consulting Dental Surgeon, Royal Dental Hospital and St. Mary's Hospital ; Dental Surgeon to St. Mary's Hospital, 1891-1907 ; *b.* London, 1847 ; *m.* 1897, Madeline, widow of Dr. Andrew Miller, Hampstead. *Educ.:* Philological School, London ; St. Mary's Hospital ; Royal Dental Hospital. First appointment was Dental Surgeon to West London Hospital, subsequently to Westminster Hospital, and St. Mary's Hospital ; was Dean of the School Royal Dental Hospital for 20 years, and instrumental in causing the new hospital to be erected ; was a member of Dental Board of Examiners at Royal College of Surgeons for 12 years ; President Stomatological Section International Medical Congress, 1913 ; was Hon. Secretary of the British Dental Association ; refused the office of president both of that Association and of the Odontological Society ; was President of Dental Section of British Medical Association for 1905 ; is a member of many of the medical and dental societies. *Publications:* joint-author of Injuries and Diseases of the Teeth ; and of many communications to Lancet, British Medical Journal, etc. *Recreations:* boating and swimming. *Address:* 22a Cavendish Square, W. ; *T.:* Gerrard 2696 ; Henley-on-Thames. *T.:* Henley 55. (*Died 4 Aug. 1916.*)

SMALLEY, George Washburn, M.A. ; American correspondent of the Times from 1895 to 1906 ; now retired from active journalism, but writing for the New York Tribune and for Reviews ; *b.* Franklin, Norfolk Co., Mass., 2 June 1833 ; *s.* of Rev. E. Smalley and Louisa, *d.* of Hon. A. Washburn. *Educ.:* Yale University (B.A. and M.A.) and Harvard Law School. Barr. Boston, Mass. 1856-61 ; J.P. and Commissioner of Insolvency ; war correspondent, Nov. 1861 to Oct. 1862 (Civil War), for New York Tribune ; then on editorial staff till 1867 ; organised its European Bureau in London, 1866-67 ; in charge European correspondence during Franco-German War, and till 1895 ; special Commissioner for U.S. at Paris Exposition, 1878. *Publications:* Bright's Speeches, 1868 ; London Letters, 1890 ; Studies of Men, 1895 ; Life of Sir Sydney Waterlow, Bart., 1909 ; Anglo-American Memories, 1st series 1911, 2nd series 1912. *Address:* 4 Down Street, W. *T.:* 3684 Mayfair. *Clubs:* Garrick, Beefsteak. (*Died 4 April 1916.*)

SMALLMAN, Sir (Henry) George, Kt., *cr.* 1906 ; one of H.M. Lieutenants of the City of London ; Commander of the Order of the Redeemer of Greece ; Knighthood (First Class) of the Royal Order of Saint Olaf of Norway ; a Governor of St. Bartholomew's Hospital ; Past Master of the Fanmakers' Company ; *b.* 1854 ; *s.* of late Henry Smallman ; *m.* 1880, Louisa,

968

e. d. of Richard Strong, J.P. ; four *s.* *Educ.:* Thanet College, Margate, Kent. Articled to Messrs. Nash and Field, solicitors, 12 Queen Street, E.C., and admitted a Solicitor, 1879 ; practised for several years at Queen Street, E.C. ; retired, 1893 ; entered Corporation of London as representative of the ward of Cheap, 1888 ; Alderman and J.P. for the City of London, 1898-1909 ; Sheriff of the City of London, 1905-1906 ; retired, 1909. *Address:* Eliot Lodge, Beckenham, Kent. *T.:* Bromley 866. *Club:* Constitutional. (*Died 2 April 1923.*)

SMALLWOOD, Lieut.-Col. Frank Graham, C.V.O. 1911 ; M.V.O. 1905 ; Ordnance Officer, Rawalpindi ; *b.* 10 Feb. 1867 ; *m.* 1900, Isobel, *d.* of Sir James Thomson ; one *s.* Entered R.A. 1886 ; Capt. 1897 ; Major, 1905 ; Lt.-Col. 1914 ; served Sikkim Expedition, 1888 (medal with clasp) ; Chitral, 1895. *Club:* Army and Navy. (*Died 30 Dec. 1919.*)

SMEATON, Lt.-Col. (Charles) Oswald, C.B. 1915 ; retired ; holds Pilot-Aviator's Certificate No. 115, 1911 ; F.Z.S. 1909 ; F.R.S.A. 1909 ; *b.* 3 Aug. 1862 ; *s.* of David James Smeaton of Letham and Abbey Park, N.B., and great-grand-nephew of John Smeaton, C.E. ; *m.* 1913, Evelyn Marion Rashleigh, *o. c.* of Rev. Francis R. Burnside, Rector of Great Stambridge, Essex. *Educ.:* R. Military Academy, Woolwich. Entered R.A., 1882 ; Lieut.-Col. 1911 ; in conjunction with Captain Fred Harvey, solved the problem of the cure of Trypanosomiasis in Animals, 1907-12 ; served Bechuanaland Expedition, 1884-85 ; Zululand, 1888 ; Crete, 1897 ; Nile Expedition, 1898 (despatches, medal) ; European War, 1914-17 (despatches, C.B.). *M.:* LB 5955. *Clubs:* Royal Aero ; Royal and Ancient Golf, St. Andrews.
(*Died 23 April 1923.*)

SMEETON, Captain Samuel Page, I.S.O. 1903 ; late Registrar-General and Deputy-Keeper of Records, Jamaica ; *b.* 25 Jan. 1842 ; *s.* of Thomas Smeeton ; *m.* 1st, 1863, Emma, *d.* of Edward Moore (*decd.*) ; 2nd, 1899, Jean, *d.* of John Henderson ; two *s.* four *d.* *Educ.:* private tuition. Extra Clerk, Colonial Office, 1862-70 ; First-Class Clerk, Colonial Secretary's Office, Jamaica, 1870 ; Registrar-Gen. Jamaica, 1878-1908 ; Lieutenant, Jamaica Militia Garrison Artillery, 1885 ; Captain, 1887 ; now retired. *Publications:* Reports on Jamaica Census, 1881 and 1891 ; Annual Reports Jamaica Vital Statistics, 1878-1908. *Recreations:* principal, rifle-shooting. *Address:* Edmonton, Alberta, Canada.
(*Died 19 July 1916.*)

SMELLIE, Alexander, M.A., D.D., minister, Original Secession Church ; *b.* 1857 ; *m.* 1897 ; two *s.* *Educ.:* Edinburgh Royal High School ; George Watson's College, Edinburgh ; Edinburgh University. Ordained minister at Stranraer, 1880 ; edited Sunday School Chronicle, 1896 ; ordained at Carluke, 1900 ; received D.D. from Senatus of Edinburgh University, 1908. *Publications:* Men of the Covenant ; In the Hour of Silence ; In the Secret Place ; Out of the Desert, a Gift ; The Well by the Way ; Lift up your Heart ; Torch-Bearers of the Faith ; Talks about Jesus ; Service and Inspiration ; Robert Murray McCheyne ; Evan H. Hopkins, a Memoir. *Address:* O.S. Manse, Carluke, Lanarkshire.
(*Died 23 May 1923.*)

SMIJTH, Sir William Bowyer-, 12th Bt., *cr.* 1661 ; *b.* 1 Sept. 1840 ; *e. s.* of 11th Bt. and Marianne Frances, 2nd *d.* of Sir Henry Meux, 1st Bt. ; *S.* father 1883. *Educ.:* Eton. Entered Diplomatic Service, 1858 ; Secretary of Legation at Yeddo, 1881. Owns about 9300 acres. *Heir:* c. Alfred John [late Major and Hon. Lt.-Col., 3rd Batt. Hampshire Regiment; *b.* 12 Sep. 1850]. *Address:* Hill Hall, Theydon Mount, Epping. *Club:* Carlton.
(*Died 22 July 1916.*)

SMITH, Adam, C.M.G. 1916; Unofficial Member of Legislative Council, Trinidad; *b.* Scotland, 1854; *e. s.* of Adam Smith, M.A.; *m.*; two *s.* two *d.* *Educ.:* private school. Hon. Secretary Chamber of Commerce, Trinidad, since 1902; Commissioner of Currency since 1908; Chief, Commissioner, Port of Spain, 1907-14; Mayor of Port of Spain, 1919-20. *Recreations:* reading, billiards. *Address:* St. Clair, Port of Spain, Trinidad. *Club:* Trinidad Union, Port of Spain. *(Died 3 Oct. 1920.)*

SMITH, Hon. Alfred Lee, Member of Legislative Council of New Zealand; *b.* Sutton-on-Hull, Yorkshire, England, 1838; *y. s.* of late John Lee Smith, of Sutton, near Hull, Yorkshire; *m.* 1864, Elizabeth, *d.* of John Sharp, of Hedon, Yorkshire; one *s.* *Educ.:* privately; Beverley. Was for some years in business in London; emigrated to New Zealand, 1868; is interested in various commercial and industrial undertakings; represented New Zealand at the Colonial Conference held at Ottawa, Canada, 1894; chairman of three companies. *Recreation:* farming. *Address:* Anderson's Bay, near Dunedin, N.Z. *T.A.:* Dunedin.

SMITH, Allan Ramsay, M.A.; Headmaster, Loretto School, Musselburgh, since 1908; *b.* 10 Jan. 1875; *s.* of James Smith of Craigielands, Beattock, and Merle Dene, Bidston, Birkenhead, Cotton Broker; *m.* Violet, 4th *d.* of Champion Russell; one *s.* one *d.* *Educ.:* Loretto School; Trin. Coll., Oxford. Graduated with second-class honours Lit. Hum.; Captain of Oxford University Rugby Football team; also captained Scottish International Football team; travelled round the world; and after two years as House Tutor at the Borough Road Training College, became one of H.M.'s Inspectors of Schools. *Recreations:* shooting, fishing, and outdoor games. *Address:* Loretto School, Musselburgh, N.B. *T.:* 100 Musselburgh. *Clubs:* Bath; Liverpool University; Edinburgh University. *(Died 31 Mar. 1920.)*

SMITH, Arthur Lionel, M.A.; LL.D. St. Andrews; successively Jowett Fellow, and Tutor and Dean, and now Master (1916) of Balliol College, Oxford; *b.* 4 Dec. 1850; *s.* of W. H. Smith, civil engineer; *m.* 1879, Mary Florence, *e. d.* of John Forster Baird of Bowmont Hill, Northumberland; two *s.* seven *d.* *Educ.:* Christ's Hospital; Balliol College; 1st c. Cl. Mods. and Lit. Hum. Lothian Prizeman. Fellow of Trinity College, Oxford, 1874-79; Examiner in Modern History in Universities of Oxford, Cambridge, Manchester, Liverpool, Birmingham, Bristol, Glasgow, and Wales; Ford's Lecturer in English History, 1905; Curator of Bodleian Library; Trustee of Oxford University Endowment Fund; Delegate for University Extension; Member of Hebdomadal Council, 1920. *Publications:* Notes on Stubbs' Charters; Life and Bibliography of F. W. Maitland, 1908; Church and State in the Middle Ages, 1913; contributor to Dictionary of English History, Dictionary of Political Economy, Cambridge Modern History, Social England (ed. Traill). *Address:* Balliol College, Oxford. *T.:* Oxford 354. *(Died 14 April 1924.)*

SMITH, Ven. Augustus Elder, Rector of Holy Trinity. Port of Spain, since 1888; Archdeacon of Trinidad since 1902; *Educ.:* Codrington College, Barbados. Ordained, 1868; Curate of St. Silas, Barbados, 1870-71; Checkleigh, Staffs., 1877-79; Holy Trinity Cathedral, 1871-88. *Address:* Deanery, Port of Spain, Trinidad. *(Died 8 Jan. 1916.)*

SMITH, Basil Guy Oswald, M.A.; *b.* 28 Sep. 1861; *e. s.* of late Oswald Augustus Smith of Hammerwood Lodge, Sussex, and Rose Sophia, *d.* of late Arthur Vansittart of Foots Cray, Kent, and Shottesbrooke Park, Berkshire; *m.* 1893, Rose Marguerite, 3rd *d.* of late Charles Bruce Henry Somerset and Victoria Alice Anne, *d.* of late William Fitz-Gibbon of Sydney House, Cork; one *d.* *Educ.:* Eton; Trinity College, Cambridge. *Address:* Shottesbrooke Park, Berkshire; 19 Hill Street, W.1. *Clubs:* Travellers', Windham.
(Died 13 July 1928.)

SMITH, Rt. Hon. Sir Cecil Clementi, G.C.M.G., *cr.* 1892; K.C.M.G., *cr.* 1886; P.C. 1906; retired 1893; *b.* London, 23 Dec. 1840; *s.* of Rev. John Smith, M.A., and Cecilia, *d.* of Muzio Clementi, the composer; *m.* Teresa, *d.* of A. Newcomen, Kirkieatham Hall, Redcar, 1869; three *s.* four *d.* *Educ.:* St. Paul's School; Corpus Christi Coll. Camb. (M.A.). After competitive examination 1862, was elected one of the first student interpreters, Hong-Kong; served in various offices; promoted from Colonial Treasurer, Hong-Kong to Colonial Secretary, Straits Settlements, 1878; administered Government, 1884-85; and then appointed Lieutenant-Governor and Colonial Secretary, Ceylon; Governor and Commander-in-Chief of the Straits Settlements, 1887; H.M. High Commissioner and Consul-General for Borneo and Sarawak, 1889; British Commissioner under the F.O. to settle certain marine claims at Manila, and received the thanks of H.M. Government, 1878; as also for the "Nisero" case, 1884; revived the Volunteer Corps in Singapore under the style of the Singapore Volunteer Artillery, and is Hon. Col. of the Corps; Master of the Mercers' Company, 1897-8; one of the Royal Commissioners for the Paris Exhibition, 1900; Member of the Advisory Committee, Imperial Institute, 1902; Member of Tariff Commission, 1904; Head of the British Delegation to the International Opium Commission, Shanghai, 1909 (received the thanks of H.M. Government); Chief British Delegate to the International Opium Conference at The Hague, 1911 (received the thanks of H.M. Government); Hon. Fellow Corpus Christi College, Cambridge, 1912. *Address:* The Grange, Welwyn, Herts. *Clubs:* National, Sports.
(Died 6 Feb. 1916.)

SMITH, Charles, M.A.; Master of Sidney Sussex College, Cambridge, 1890; Vice-Chancellor University of Cambridge, 1895-96, 1896-97; *b.* Huntingdon, 11 May 1844; *m.* Annie, *o. d.* of late Lt. E. B. Hopkins, R.N., 1882; four *s.* *Educ.:* Sidney Sussex Coll. Camb. (B.A.). 3rd Wrangler, 1868; Fellow of Sidney Sussex Coll. 1868; tutor, 1875; Governor of Eton Coll., 1896-1909. *Publications:* An Elementary Treatise on Conic Sections. 1882; An Elementary Treatise on Solid Geometry, 1884; Elementary Algebra, 1886; Treatise on Algebra, 1887; Arithmetic, 1891; Geometrical Conics, 1894; Euclid (Smith and Bryant), 1901. *Address:* The Lodge, Sidney Sussex College, Cambridge. *(Died 13 Nov. 1916.)*

SMITH, Hon. Sir (Charles) Abercrombie, Kt., *cr.* 1903; *b.* 12 May 1834; *y. s.* of Andrew Smith; *m.* 1897, Christina Caroline, *y. d.* of H. Remington Horne. M.A. and Breadalbane Scholar, Glasgow Univ.; M.A., 2nd Wrangler and 2nd Smith's Prizeman, 1858, Cambridge; Fellow of St. Peter's College. 1860-97; Hon. Fellow since 1897; LL.D. Cape University, 1917. Member of Legislative Assembly, Cape of Good Hope, 1866-75; Member of Executive Council since 1872; Minister of Crown Lands and Public Works, 1872-75; Controller and Auditor-General, 1875-1903; Commissioner for reduction of Public Debt, 1872-74, and 1897-1903; Member of University Council since 1873; Vice-Chancellor Cape University, 1877-79, 1905-11; Science Examiner for 25 years; Chairman of Meteorological Commission, 1874-1911; Chairman of Tender Board, 1875-1903; Chairman War Expenditure Commission, 1881; Chairman of Civil Service Examining Commission, 1887-1910; served also on a number of important Commissions, such as Federation Commission 1871. Civil Service

SMITH, Alfred John, F.R.C.S.L See page xxx.

969

Enquiry Commissions 1882-3 and 1904-6, etc. *Publications:* Schemes of Account-books and Accounts for the several departments of the Civil Service; a number of Blue-books every year, 1875-1911; Financial, Public Debt, and other Regulations, etc. *Recreations:* rambles to the habitats of the magnificent Cape flora. *Address:* St. Cyrus, Wynberg, near Cape Town. *Club:* Civil Service, Cape Town.

(Died May 1919.)

SMITH, Captain Charles Appleton, C.B.E. 1919; R.D., R.N.R. (retired); *b.* Liverpool, 3 March 1864; *s.* of William Charles Smith, Master Mariner, and Caroline Smith; *m.* 1885, Edith Strawbridge, Liverpool; three *s,* two *d. Educ.:* Southport Grammar School. Served European War, Commander of Caronia and Captain of Aquitania (despatches). *Address:* 106 Mortlake Road, Kew Gardens, Surrey. *(Died 17 Nov. 1928.)*

SMITH, Capt. Charles Futcher, D.S.O. 1902. Served South Africa with Driscoll's Scouts, 1900-2 (despatches, Queen's medal 4 clasps, King's medal 2 clasps, D.S.O.).

(Died 17 Aug. 1925.)

SMITH, Maj.-Gen. Sir Charles Holled, K.C.M.G., *cr.* 1892; C.B. 1891; retired; *b.* 12 Sep. 1846; *s.* of Charles Sergison Smith, late of Consall Hall, Leek, and Georgiana, *d.* of Hon. Herbert Gardner; *m.* 1883, Maud Mary (*d.* 1917), *d.* of Major Fearnley Whittingstall; one *s. Educ.:* Shrewsbury. Entered army, 1865; Captain, 1877; Brevet Major, 1882; Brevet Lt.-Col., 1885; Brevet Colonel, 1888; Major-Gen. 1900; served Zulu and Boer Wars, 1879-81 (despatches, medal with clasp); Egyptian War, 1882 (despatches, brevet of Major, medal with clasp, Khedive's star); Nile Expedition, 1884-1885 (despatches, Brevet Lieut.-Col., clasp); Soudan, 1885-86; Suakin, 1888 (despatches, Brevet Col., clasp); Tokar, 1891 (clasp, Khedive's star, 2nd class Medjidie). Governor of Red Sea Littoral (2nd class Osmanieh); Commandant at Suakim, 1888-92; Commandant of Forces in Victoria, 1894. *Club:* Naval and Military.

(Died 18 Mar. 1925.)

SMITH, Charles Michie, B.Sc., F.R.A.S., F.R.S.E., C.I.E. 1910; Director of the Kodaikánal and Madras Observatories, 1899-1911; *b.* Keig, Aberdeenshire, 13 July 1854 *, s.* of Rev. Dr. W. Pirie Smith; unmarried. *Educ.:* home; Aberdeen and Edinburgh Universities. On Electrical Staff of Thomson & Jenkin, 1874-75; Professor of Physical Science, Madras Christian College, 1877; Government Astronomer, Madras, 1891. *Publications:* Publications of the Madras and Kodaikánal Observatories and various scientific papers. *Recreations:* golf, fishing, gardening. *Address:* Winsford, Kodaikánal, S. India. *Clubs:* Savile, Royal Societies; Madras. *(Died 27 Sept. 1922.)*

SMITH, Rev. Clement, M.V.O. 1901; M.A.; Chaplain-in-Ordinary to the King; Canon of Windsor; *b.* 1845; 3rd *s.* of late Henry Smith, Accountant-General of the War Office: *m.* 1871, Mary Eliza, *d.* of late Stephen Spurling. *Educ.:* St. Paul's School; Christ Church, Oxford. *Address:* Whippingham Rectory, East Cowes, Isle of Wight; The Cloisters, Windsor.

(Died 22 May 1921.)

SMITH, Brig.-Gen. Clement Leslie, V.C. 1904. Entered Army, 1900; Captain, 1911; Maj. 1916; with Egyptian Army 1905-15; served S. Africa, 1901-2 (medal with 3 clasps); Somaliland, 1904 (despatches, medal with two clasps); Soudan, 1910 (medal with clasp); European War, 1914-17 (Bt. Lt.-Col.); Brig.-General, Dec. 1916-Jan. 1921; Colonel Comdt. Jan.-Oct. 1921; commanded 2nd Duke of Wellington's Regt., 1921-25; retired pay, 1925. *Club:* United Service. *(Died 14 Dec. 1927.)*

SMITH, Lt.-Col. Douglas Kirke, D.S.O. 1917; *b.* 24 May 1883; 2nd *s.* of Rev. A.

970

Kirke Smith, Boxworth Rectory, Cambridge; *m.* 1906, Mary Ellen Beadle; one *s.* two *d. Educ.:* Haileybury College. Joined Territorial R.A. 1908; served European War in France, 1914-17 (despatches, D.S.O.). *Recreations:* hunting, shooting, and fishing. *Address:* Knowle House, Westcombe Park Road, Blackheath, S.E.3. *T.:* Greenwich 479. *Club:* Devonshire.

(Died 21 May 1923.)

SMITH, Edgar Albert, I.S.O. 1903; *b.* 1847. Late Assistant Keeper, The Natural History Museum, Cromwell Road, S.W.; retired, 1913. *Address:* Mill Hill Park, Acton, W.

(Died 22 July 1916.)

SMITH, Major-General E. Davidson-, on retired pay; *s.* of late S. Smith of 23 Westbourne Terrace Road, Hyde Park; *m.* 1863, Mary Matilda, *d.* of late Wm. Cooke-Collis of Castle Cooke, Co. Cork, and niece of late John Hyde of Castle Hyde, Co. Cork; two *s.* three *d.* Served in Bulgaria, 1854; with the 95th Regt. in Crimea, present at battles of Alma and Inkerman, at the affair of 26th October, and at the siege of Sevastopol (dangerously wounded in the trenches before Sevastopol; medal with 3 clasps and Turkish war medal); served Indian Mutiny, 1857-58; present at capture of the fortress of Awah, Rajpootanah, siege and capture of Kotah, battle of Kotah-Ke-Serai, siege and capture of city and fortress of Gwalior, Capture of Chindaree, and other minor affairs, Central India (medal with clasp); served on the staff in Jersey; was Assistant Adjutant-General, West Indies, and Assistant Quartermaster-General, Dublin district; reward for distinguished and meritorious services, 1903. *Address:* Allen House, Allen Street, Kensington, W. *Clubs:* Carlton, United Service, Junior United Service, Constitutional, Albemarle.

(Died 8 Sept. 1916.)

SMITH, Sir Edward, Kt., *cr.* 1916; J.P.; Vice-Pres. National Liberal Club and Crystal Palace Trustees; Chairman Tower Bench of Magistrates; Standing Joint Committee of London; *b.* 20 Oct. 1857; *s.* of William and Sophia Smith; *m. Educ.:* private school. Member Lord Chancellor's Advisory Committee J.P.'s, London. *Recreations:* golf, driving. *Address:* 75 Gore Road, N.E.; Ganbrook, Frinton-on-Sea, Essex. *Club:* National Liberal.

(Died 20 Sept. 1926.)

SMITH, Edward; *b.* Dunstable, 1839. Official life in London; leisure almost entirely given to historical studies. *Publications:* The Peasant's Home, 1875 (first Howard medal of Statistical Society); William Cobbett, a Biography, 1878; The Story of . the English Jacobins, 1881; Foreign Visitors in England, 1889; England and America after Independence, 1900; a Life of Sir Joseph Banks, P.R.S. 1911. An Index Locorum to Birch's Cartularium Saxonicum; items in bibliography, English topography and antiquities. *Recreations:* pedestrian touring, chess-play. *Address:* 42 Rosehill Road, Wandsworth Common, S.W.

(Died Nov. 1919.)

SMITH, Hon. Sir Edwin Thomas, K.C.M.G., *cr.* 1888; *b.* 6 Apr. 1830; *s.* of late Edwin Smith of Walsall; *m.* 1st, 1857, Florence (*d.* 1862), *d.* of late Robert Stock of Clifton; 2nd, 1869, Elizabeth, *d.* of Edward Spicer of Adelaide. *Educ.:* Queen Mary's Grammar School. Mayor of Kensington and Norwood, 1868, 1869, 1870, 1872, and 1873; of Adelaide, 1880, 1881, 1882, 1887, and 1888; Minister of Education, 1884; Commissioner of International Exhibitions at Philadelphia, 1876; Paris, 1878; Sydney, 1880; Melbourne, 1881; Colonial and Indian Exhibition, 1886; Melbourne Centennial Exhibition, 1888; Vice-President and Promoter of Adelaide Jubilee Exhibition, 1887; Member of House of Assembly of South Australia, 1872-93; M.L.C. of South Australia since 1894; J.P. of the Colony; Chairman of Trustees of Savings Bank of South

Australia, of National Park Commissioners, and of Old Colonists' Association; Member of numerous Institutions. *Address:* The Acacias, Martyatville, S. Australia. *Clubs:* Adelaide, Commercial Travellers. (*Died 25 Dec. 1919.*)

SMITH, Frederick Bonham, I.S.O. 1903; *b.* Codrington College, Barbados, West Indies, 31 March 1837; *s.* of Rev. E. P. Smith, M.A. of Pembroke College, Oxford, who was Tutor of Codrington College; *m.* 1869; a widower; two *s.* one *d.* *Educ.:* Lodge School, Barbados, and subsequently completed education at Codrington College, having obtained an Island Scholarship there. Entered the Public Service of Barbados, 1859; Senior Police Magistrate of Bridgetown and St. Michael, 1873; Acting Judge Assistant Court of Appeal, 1878-80; Acting Col. Secretary, Barbados, in 1879; Provost-Marshal, 1882; and Inspector of Prisons in Island of Barbados, West Indies, 1878; retired on pension, 1917. *Recreations:* captained the Barbados team in first intercolonial cricket match, Barbados *v.* Demerara, played in Barbados about 1865; also acted as captain in return match played in Demerara about 1868. *Address:* Bridgetown, Barbados, W.I.

SMITH, Fred John, M.A., M.D. Oxon. 1891; F.R.C.P. Lond. 1895; Consulting Physician; *b.* Castle Donington, Leicestershire, 17 Aug. 1857; *m.* 1889. *Educ.:* Christ's Hosp. Balliol Coll., Oxford. Scholar, 1876; B A. 1880; Radcliffe Trav. Scnolar, 1885-88; M.B. 1886; Assist. Physician, Lond. Hosp., 1891; full Physician, 1902; Lect. on Forensic Medicine since 1895; Referee under the Workmen's Compensation Act; Exam. University Leeds and Society of Apothecaries; Hunterian Society's Orator, 1901; Pres. 1904. *Publications:* Differential Diagnosis of Diseases; Lectures on Forensic Medicine; Domestic Hygiene for Nurses; editor of Taylor's Principles and Practice of Medical Jurisprudence, 6th ed. 1910, and many contributions to Hunterian Society's Transactions, etc.; article on the Treatment of Typhoid Fever, etc. *Recreations:* botanising, billiards, cycling, rowing, and golf. *Address:* 138 Harley Street, W. *T.:* Padd. 1168. (*Died 30 April 1919.*)

SMITH, Sir Frederick William, Kt., *cr.* 1910, J.P.; Mayor of Capetown, 1908-12; merchant; sole partner, Smith, Webster & Co., Capetown; *b.* 30 Oct. 1861; 7th *s.* of William James Smith of London and Capetown; *m.* 1890, Lillie Edith, O.B.E., *d.* of John A. Mathew; two *d.* *Educ.:* S. African College, Capetown. Chairman, S. African Association, and Southern Life Association; Director, Atlas Fire Company; S.G.I.G. 33rd Degree of Scottish Freemasonry in Western Province of the Cape; President United Municipal Associations of S. Africa and Municipal Association of Cape Province, 1909-1910, 1910-11, and 1911-12. *Recreations:* tennis, mountain-climbing. *Address:* c/o Smith, Webster & Co., St. George's Street, Capetown. *T.A.:*

Dorodith. *T.:* 177. *Club:* City, Capetown. (*Died June 1926.*)

SMITH, George, C.I.E. 1878; LL.D., F.R.G.S., F.S.S.; Foreign Sec. U.F. Church of Scotland, 1878-1910; *b.* Leith, 28 April 1833; *s.* of Adam Smith, Fillyside; *m.* 1st, 1855, Janet C. (*d.* 1888), *d.* of Robert Adam, Edinburgh; 2nd, 1890, Mary Agnes, *d.* of William Mackintosh, Inshes House, Inverness-shire; five *s.* five *d.* *Educ.:* High School; Univ. Edinburgh. Principal of Doveton College, Calcutta, 1854-59; Fellow and Examiner Univ. of Calcutta, 1856-77; editor of Calcutta Review, 1857-64; editor of The Friend of India (weekly newspaper), Serampore, Bengal, and of the Annals of Indian Administration (19 vols.); India correspondent of The Times, 1860-75; J.P. of Bengal-Behar, and Orissa; a Vice-President of the Royal Scottish Geographical Society. *Publications:* Student's Geography of British India; The Conversion of India; Short History of Christian Missions (8th ed.); Bishop Heber, Poet and Missionary; Henry Martyn, Saint and Scholar; Twelve Indian Statesmen (2nd ed.); Twelve Pioneer Missionaries; Life of William Carey, D.D. (4th ed.); Life of John Wilson, D.D., F.R.S. (2nd ed.); Life of Alexander Duff, D.D., LL.D. (4th ed.); Stephen Hislop, Missionary and Naturalist (2nd ed.); A Modern Apostle (2nd ed.); Physician and Friend; articles in Encyclopædia Britannica, Dict. of Nat. Biography, and Quarterly Review, etc. *Recreation:* travel. *Address:* 10 South Learmonth Gardens. Edinburgh. *T.:* 2809. (*Died 24 Dec. 1919.*)

SMITH, Brig.-Gen. George Barton, C.B. 1918; C.M.G. 1915; Army Pay Department; *b.* 10 Aug. 1860; *m.* 1899, Kathleen, *d.* of Col. F. Haynes, A.P. Dept.; one *d.* *Educ.:* Tonbridge School; private tutor; Caius College, Cambridge. Entered army (North Staffs. Regt.), 1884; Captain, 1893; Major, 1901; Lt.-Col. 1900; Colonel, 1910; Paymaster, 1892-1901; Chief Paymaster, 1910; served European War, 1914-18 (despatches thrice, C.M.G., C.B.); placed on retired pay with hon. rank of Brigadier-General. *Club:* Army and Navy. (*Died 15 Nov. 1921.*)

SMITH, Rev. George Herbert, M.A. Oxon; late Principal of the S.P.G. Theological College, Madras; Secretary of the Madras Diocesan Committee of S.P.G. 1901-20; Hon. Canon of St. George's Cathedral, Madras, 1910; late Incumbent of St. Thomas' Church, San Thome, Madras; *b.* Bishopthorpe, York, 31 Aug. 1851; *s.* of Rev. Charles Francis Smith, Rector of Beaford, Yorks, and Ellen Smith; *m.* 1879, Mary Elinor, 2nd *d.* of Edward Donkin of Sleights Old Hall, Yorks; one *s.* two *d.* *Educ.:* Richmond School, Yorks; Queen's College, Oxford (Lady Elizabeth Hastings Exhibition 1870, first-class Classical Mods., fourth-class Lit. Hum.). Senior Classical Master, Forest School; Walthamstow, 1875; Curate of Leytonstone, Essex, 1878; Vice-Principal of Theological School, Ambataharanana, Madagascar, 1879; founded new Mission at Mahanoro, Madagascar, 1884; Organisin Secretary S.P.G. for Dioceses of Lichfield and Chester, 1887; Pioneer Missionary on West Coast of Madagascar, 1891; returned to Mahanoro as Missionary-in-charge, 1898; Principal S.P.G. College, Trichinopoly, 1897; Examiner University of Madras, 1900-04; Examining Chaplain to the Bishop of Madras, 1902. *Publications:* Among the Menabe (thirteen months on the West Coast of Madagascar). *Recreations:* golf, cricket, tennis, boating. *Address:* Chesmead, Belmont Park Avenue, Maidenhead. Berks. (*Died 1 July 1925.*)

SMITH, George Hill, Barrister-at-Law; Father of Bar of Northern Ireland, 1922; Crown Prosecutor on Northern Circuit for Down, Antrim, and Belfast; *b.* 7 July 1833; 7th *c.* of George Smith and Elizabeth Lee; *m.* 1858.

Eliza Graham (d. 1895); three s. three d. Educ.: private schools, Dublin; matriculated at Queen's College, Belfast, 1874. For some years managing assistant in solicitor's office, Dublin; acting registrar, Probate Court, Dublin, 1867; district registrar, Armagh, 1873-1886; called to Bar, 1877; joined N.E. Circuit, 1878; K.C. 1914. Publications: Torrens Registration Scheme; Rambling Reminiscences; Concise Guide to Probate Practice; Concise Guide to Matrimonial Court Practice: Forms of Indictments; Sketch of the North-East Bar; etc. Address: Glenmona, Cregagh Road, Belfast. (Died 1 April 1926.)

SMITH, r George John, Kt., cr. 1897; J.P., C.A., D.L.; Managing Director, Bickford, Smith and Co., Ltd., etc.; b. 24 June 1845; s. of Geo. Smith, J.P., LL.D., Trevu, Camborne, and Elizabeth Burrall, d. of William Bickford; m. Jane Symons, e. d. of Edward Burgess, Mountroy, Wells, 1871; seven s. four d. Educ.: privately; University. London. Succeeded to management of his father's business in 1870; a Conservative; younger brother of late William Bickford-Smith, Trevarno, Helston, formerly M.P. Truro-Helston Div.; Hon. Col. 4th Batt. Duke of Cornwall's L.I., formerly commanding 1st Vol. Batt. D.C.L.I. Recreations: formerly cricket; music. Address: Treliske, Truro. T.: 75 Truro and 65 Camborne. M.: AF 709. Club: Constitutional.
(Died 9 Oct. 1921.)

SMITH, Rt. Rev. George John; R.C. Bishop of Argyll and the Isles since 1893; b. Cuttlebrae, Banffshire, 1840. Ordained 1864. Address: Bishop's House, Oban.
(Died 18 Jan. 1918.)

SMITH, Rev. George Maberly, M.A. b. 5 June 1831; m. 1863, Emily Harriet, d. of Maxwell Macartney, M.D., of Rosebrook, Armagh; one s. Educ.: Tonbridge School; Gonville and Caius College, Cambridge. Curate of Penshurst, 1856-69; engaged in tuition at Tonbridge Wells, 1869-78; Hon Canon of Canterbury; Rural Dean of Tonbridge, 1884-1912; Rector of Penshurst, Kent, 1878-1916. Address: Grenville Lodge, Henley on Thames. T.: 166. (Died 7 Nov. 1917.)

SMITH, George Munro, M.D. (Br.), L.R.C.P. Lond.; M.R.C.S.; Hon. Consulting Surgeon Bristol Royal Infirmary since 1909; b. 17 June, 1856; s. of William Smith, M.R.C.S., L.S.A.; m. 1889, Amy Elizabeth Hassell; one s. one d. Educ.: Clifton College; Bristol Medical School; University College, London. Suple Gold Medals, Medicine and Surgery. Bristol Royal Infirmary; Clarke Scholarship; 2nd and 3rd years Prizeman, Bristol Medical School; Medical Tutor, Bristol Med. School, 1879; Demonstrator of Physiology, 1881-87; Lecturer on Physiology, 1887-93; Professor of Physiology, University College, Bristol, 1893-99; Acting Surgeon, 2nd Gloucestershire Engineer Vol., 1886-87; Hon. Surgeon, Clifton Dispensary, 1896; Assistant Surgeon, Bristol Royal Infirmary, 1889; Hon. Surgeon, 1897-1909; Hon. Secretary Bristol Med. Chirurgical Society, 1888; President, 1902; President Bath and Bristol Branch British Med. Assoc., 1909; President Association of Alumni, Bristol University, 1909; President Bristol Naturalists' Society, 1910; Lieut.-Colonel 'à la suite' 2nd Southern General Hospital Royal Army Corps, 1910. Publications: The Medical Life; The Vis Medicatrix Naturae; various articles in British Medical Journal, Bristol Medico-Chirurgical Journal, and other periodicals. Address: 18 Apsley Road, Clifton, Bristol. T.: 616. (Died 13 Jan. 1917.)

SMITH, George Murray; Chairman Midland Railway since 1911; Alderman Leicestershire County Council; D.L. and J.P. Leicestershire; b. 4 Feb. 18 ; e. s. of George M. Smith, publisher and founder of Dictionary

of National Biography, and Elizabeth, d. of J. Blakeway; m. 1885, Hon. Ellen Strutt, y. d. of 1st Baron Belper; one s. one d. Educ.: Harrow; Jesus College, Cambridge. Was associated with his father's publishing firm, Smith, Elder & Co., for 10 years; Captain in South Notts Yeomanry Cavalry; Member of the Leicestershire County Council; was Vice-Chairman of Leicester Infirmary and Member of Market Harborough Board of Guardians for many years; contested (U.) Rushcliffe Division of Notts, 1895. Recreations: shooting, fishing, hunting. Address: Gumley Hall, Market Harborough. T.A.: Gems, Leicester. T.: 1 Kilworth. Clubs: Brooks's, Athenæum.
(Died 18 April 1919.)

SMITH, Lieut.-Col. Sir Gerard, K.C.M.G., cr. 1895; J.P.; Scots Fusilier Guards (retired); b. 12 Dec. 1839; s. of late M. T. Smith, M.P.; m. 1871, Isabella Chatelaine (d. 1915), d. of Canon Hamilton; two s. three d. Groom-in-Waiting to Queen Victoria, 1883-85; M.P. High Wycombe, 1883-85; Governor of West Australia, 1895-1900. Address: 237 Cromwell Road, S.W.5. Club: Brooks's.
(Died 28 Oct. 1920.)

SMITH, Granville, a Master of the Supreme Court; b. Dartmouth, 17 May 1859; s. of late William Smith, Solicitor, Dartmouth; m. 1900, Nellie Claire, d. of Alfred Mead, London. Educ.: Blundell's School, Tiverton. Member of the Law Society; a Member of the Court of the Worshipful Company of Woolmen; a Vice-President of the London Devonian Association. Address: 288 Royal Courts of Justice, W.C. Club: Royal Automobile. (Died 13 April 1925.)

SMITH, Colonel Granville Roland Francis, C.B. 1911; C.V.O. 1911; late A.A.G. and Q.M.G., London District; half-pay; e. s. of late Roland Smith and Constance Henrietta Sophia Louisa, d. of late Lord Granville Charles Henry Somerset; b. 1860; m. 1883, Lady Blanche Catherine, 2nd d. of 8th Earl of Kintore; two s. Heir: s. Rev. Roland Aubrey [b. 31 Jan. 1887; m. 1913, Margaret Halcro Erskine, o. d. of R. A. Hill, Bridge of Allan]. Educ.: Eton; Sandhurst. Late Coldstream Guards; Patron of one living. Address: Duffield Hall, near Derby; 6 Grosvenor Square, W. Clubs: Carlton, Guards'.
(Died 4 Mar. 1917.)

SMITH, Sir Harold, Kt., cr. 1921; K.C. 1923; Recorder of Blackburn since 1922; M.P. (C.) Warrington (Lancs.) Division, 1910-22, Wavertree Division of Liverpool since 1922; J.P. Co. Northants; barrister-at-law, Gray's Inn; b. 18 Apr. 1876; s. of Frederick Smith, Birkenhead, Cheshire, barrister-at-law, Middle Temple; m. 1914, Joan, y. d. of late Rev. and Mrs. Furneaux; one s. Educ.: Birkenhead School, Cheshire. Until the end of 1908 a partner in firm of surveyors and valuers in Liverpool and Birkenhead; entered Gray's Inn, 1908; called to Bar, 1911; Bencher, 1920; contested (C.) Huddersfield, 1910. Recreations: golf, lawn tennis. Address: 4 Elm Court, Temple E.C.4; T.: Central 3110; 68 St. James's Court, S.W.1; Middleton House, Middleton Cheney, nr. Banbury. Clubs: Carlton, Constitutional.
(Died 10 Sept. 1924.)

SMITH, Sir Henry, Kt., cr. 1916; J.P. Norfolk, and one of H.M.'s Lieutenants for City of London; Adviser to Quartermaster-General's Department, Equipment and Stores, 1914. Address: Luxor Lodge, Elsworthy Road, N.W.3; Uplands, Sheringham.
(Died 1 Nov. 1919.)

SMITH, Lieut.-Col. Sir Henry, K.C.B., cr. 1897; b. 15 Dec. 1835; s. of Rev. George Smith, D.D., Edinburgh; m. 1909, Annie, d. of late John Graham. Chief Superintendent of Police in City of London, 1885-90; Commissioner of Police, 1890-1901; resigned 1901. Publication:

From Constable to Commissioner, 1910. *Club:* New, Edinburgh. *(Died 2 Mar. 1921.)*

SMITH, Sir Henry Babington, G.B.E., *cr.* 1920; K.C.B., *cr.* 1908; C.B. 1905; C.S.I. 1897; Companion of Honour, 1917; *b.* 29 Jan. 1863; *s.* of late Archibald Smith, F.R.S., of Jordanhill, Renfrewshire; *m.* 1898, Lady Elisabeth Bruce, *d.* of 9th Earl of Elgin; four *s.* five *d. Educ.:* Eton; Trinity Coll., Cambridge. Fellow; 1st class in Classical Tripos (Parts I. and II.): Chancellor's Medallist (M.A.); Examiner in the Education Dept. 1887; principal private sec. to the Chancellor of the Exchequer (Mr. Goschen), 1891; clerk in the Treasury, 1892; sec. to the British delegates at the Brussels Monetary Conference, 1892; private secretary to Earl of Elgin, Viceroy of India. 1894 - 99; Represented Treasury in Natal, 1899; British Representative on Council of Administration of Ottoman Public Debt, 1900; President, 1901; British Delegate at Postal Congress, Rome, 1906; at Radio-Telegraph Conference, Berlin, 1906; at Telegraph Conference, Lisbon, 1908; at Radio-Telegraph Conference, London, 1912; Secretary to Post Office, 1903-9; President, National Bank of Turkey, 1909; Member of Financial Mission to United States, 1915; Chairman, Royal Commission on Civil Service, 1915; Fellow of Eton; Assistant Commissioner for Great Britain in United States, 1918-19; Chairman, Committee on Indian Currency, 1919; Chairman, Railways Amalgamation Tribunal, 1921 - 23; Deputy - Governor British Trade Corporation; Director of the Bank of England. *Address:* 121 St. James' Court, S.W.; Vineyards, Saffron Walden. *T.:* Saffron Walden 61. *Clubs:* Brooks's, Athenæum. *(Died 29 Sept. 1923.)*

SMITH, Colonel Henry Robert, C.M.G. 1911, L.S.O. 1903; J.P.; Sergeant-at-Arms House of Commons, Ottawa, since 1892; *b.* 30 Dec. 1843; *e. s.* of the Hon. Sir Henry Smith, K.B., of Roselawn, Kingston, Canada; *m.* 1887, Mary Gurley, widow of Major Barrow, Royal Canadian Rifles. *Educ.:* Kingston Grammar School. Entered Civil Service, 1859; Deputy Sergeant-at-Arms, 1872; Extra A.D.C. to the Earl of Derby, Governor-General; served on Canadian Frontier, 1866 and 1870 (medal and 2 clasps); North-West Campaign, 1885 (despatches, medal); was A.D.C. to Lt.-Gen. Sir E. Selby-Smyth, and Lt.-Gen. Luard, C.B.; Hon. A.D.C. to Earl of Minto, Governor-General, 1899-1903; was Extra A.D.C. to Earl Grey, Governor-General; Extra A.D.C. to H.R.H. The Duke of Connaught; President Frontenac Loan and Investment Society, Kingston, and a Commissioner of Parliament. *Recreations:* shooting and fishing. *Address:* House of Commons, Ottawa, Canada. *Clubs:* Rideau, Canadian, Country, Ottawa. *(Died 20 Sept. 1917.)*

SMITH, Horace, J.P., Metropolitan Magistrate, Westminster, 1888-1917; *b.* London, 18 Nov. 1836; 5th *s.* of Robert Smith, merchant, Westbourne Terrace, and Hannah, *d.* of John Boden, Ednaston, Derbyshire; *m.* Susan, *d.* of Rev. C. Watkins, 1870; three *s.* three *d. Educ.:* private schools; Highgate Grammar School; King's College, London; Trinity Hall, Cambridge (B.A. in Mathematical Honours; prize essays each year at Trinity Hall). Barr. 1862; counsel to the Mint; revising barrister on Midland Circuit; secretary to Oxford Bribery Commission; Recorder of Lincoln, 1881; Bencher of the Inner Temple, 1886. *Publications:* Treatises on Landlord and Tenant, and Negligence; editor of Addison on Contracts, Addison on Torts; Roscoe's Criminal Evidence; Russell on Crimes; Poems, 1860; Poems, 1890; Interludes, 1892; Interludes (2nd series), 1894; Poems, 1897; Interludes (3rd series), 1899; Hymns and Psalms, 1903; Interludes (4th series), 1905; Collected Poems, 1908; Inter-

ludes (5th series), 1910; Interludes (6th series), 1913. *Recreations:* literature, painting, gardening, golf. *Address:* Keston, The Avenue, Sherborne, Dorset. *(Died 25 Nov. 1922.)*

SMITH, Hugh Bellingham; Member New English Art Club since 1894; *b.* London, 1866; *m.* 1915; one *d. Educ.:* Slade School under A. Legros; Paris under Benjamin Constant. *Works:* The Viaduct, Hampstead; On the Arun; Romance; Teesdale; Barnard Castle; The Dream Fan; The Downs, Lewes; The Crinoline, etc. *(Died 3 April 1922.)*

SMITH, Rev. Dr. Isaac Gregory, M.A. Oxford, Hon. LL.D. Edinburgh; Rector of Gt. Shefford to 1900; *b.* Manchester, 21 Nov. 1826; *s.* of Rev. Jeremiah Smith, D.D., High Master of the Free Grammar School, Manchester; *m. d.* of Rev. Canon G. W. Murray. *Educ.:* Rugby; Trin. Coll. Oxford (Scholar). Hertford University Scholar; Ireland University Scholar; Fellow of Brasenose Coll. Rector of Tedstone Delamere, Herefordshire; afterwards Vicar of Gt. Malvern; successively Prebendary of Hereford Cathedral, and Honorary Canon of Worcester, and while in Worcestershire Rural Dean of Powick; in Herefordshire he was Diocesan Inspector of Schools; Bampton Lecturer, 1873; Examining Chap. to Bp. of St. David's, 1880-1900. *Publications:* Faith and Philosophy; Fra Angelico and other Lyrics (3rd ed.); Aristotelianism (Ethic) and Modern Thought (3rd ed.); History of Worcester Diocese (with Rev. Phipps Onslow); History of Christian Monasticism; The Silver Bells (2nd ed.); The Holy Days (Vignettes in verse); The Athanasian Creed; What is Truth? Practical Psychology, 1908; Riullera (In Memoriam); On Assent to Creeds; Thoughts on Education, etc. *Address:* The Howdah, Horsell, Woking. *(Died 17 Jan. 1920.)*

SMITH, Very Rev. James Allan, D.D.; Dean of St. David's since 1908; and Chaplain to Bishop of St. David's; Surrogate for granting marriage licences; *b.* Pyecombe, Sussex, 2 Aug. 1841; *s.* of late Rev. James Allan Smith, Rector of Pyecombe, and *d.* of late William Catt of Bishopston; *m.* 1st, 1865, Charlotte Isabella (dec.), *d.* of late Rev. Henry Linton, M.A., of Stirtloe, Huntingdon, and Hon. Can. of Christ Church, Oxford; 2nd, 1902, Annie (*d.* 1916), *d.* of late Thomas Hawksley, Surgeon, of Nottingham; two *s.* one *d. Educ.:* as pupil of late Rev. Charles Shorting, Rector of Stonham Aspall, Suffolk, and Hon. Canon of Norwich; Wadham College, Oxford, 1860-63; B.A. 1863; M.A. 1867; B.D. and D.D. 1898. Curate, Trinity Church, St. Marylebone, 1864 - 66; Lecturer of Boston, Lincs., 1866-71; Vicar of Holy Trinity, Nottingham, 1871-84; Prebendary of Sanctæ Crucis, Lincoln Cathedral, 1875; Vicar of Swansea and Rural Dean of E. Gower, 1884-92; Vicar of Hay, 1902-3; Chancellor of St. David's Cathedral and Canon Residentiary, 1898-1903. *Publications:* several Sermons. *Address:* The Deanery, St. Davids, R.S.O. *(Died Nov. 1918.)*

SMITH, Most Rev. James A., D.D., Ph. D., R.C. Archbishop of St. Andrews and Edinburgh since 1900; *b.* Edinburgh, 18 Oct. 1841. *Educ.:* St. Mary's Coll., Blairs, Aberdeen, and Gregorian Univ., Rome. Ordained priest, 1866; Prof. at Blairs, 1867-90; cons. Bishop of Dunkeld, 1890. *Address:* St. Bennet's, 42 Greenhill Gardens, Edinburgh. *(Died 25 Nov. 1928.)*

SMITH, Lieut.-Col. Sir James Robert Dunlop, K.C.S.I., *cr.* 1910; C.S.I. 1909; K.C.V.O., *cr.* 1916; C.I.E. 1901; Knight of Grace of the Order of St. John of Jerusalem; Knight Commander of the North Star of Sweden; Political A.D.C. to Secretary of State for India; *b.* 24 Aug. 1858; *s.* of late George Smith, C.I.E.; *m.* 1887, Beatrice Clementina (*d.* 1902) *e. d.* of Sir Charles Umpherston Aitchison, K.C.S.I.; two *d.*

Educ.: Edinburgh University (M.A.); Royal Military College, Sandhurst. 2nd Lieut. 22nd Regiment, 1879; Lieut. Indian Staff Corps, 1882; Private Secy. to Lt.-Governor, Punjab, 1883; Settlement Officer, Sialkot, 1887; Deputy-Commissioner, Hissar, 1896; Director of Land Records and Agriculture, Punjab, 1897; Famine Commissioner, Rajputana, 1899; member of Horse and Mule-Breeding Commission, India, 1900; Political Agent, Phulkian States and Bhawalpur, 1901; Private Secretary to Earl of Minto, Viceroy of India, 1905-10. *Address:* 25 Ovington Square, S.W.3. *T.:* Western 170. *Clubs:* Bath, Brooks's.   (*Died 24 April 1921.*)

SMITH, John, C.B. 1895; *b.* 9 July 1837; *s.* of late David Smith of Edinburgh; *m.* 1867, Annie Grant, 5th *d.* of late Peter Nicolson of Adelphi. Berbice, British Guiana; one *s.* five *d.* *Educ.*: High School and University, Edinburgh. Admitted a Member of the Society of Chartered Accountants in Edinburgh, 1861; engaged in banking in Bombay, 1862-67; a merchant in Hull, Yorkshire, 1868-72; General Manager and Director of the London and Yorkshire Bank, Ltd. (since incorporated with the Union of London and Smith's Bank, Ltd.), 1872-83; first Inspector-General in Bankruptcy, 1888; Inspector-General in Companies Liquidation, 1890; retired 1904. *Publications:* Official Reports to Board of Trade for presentation to Parliament, on the working of the Bankruptcy and Companies (Winding-up) Acts from 1884 to 1903. *Address:* Dunedin, Chichester Road, Croydon. *T.:* Croydon 720.   (*Died 25 Feb. 1922.*)

SMITH, Very Rev. John, M.A.; B.D., D.D.; Hon. F.E.I.S.; J.P., T.D.; Minister of Partick Parish, Church of Scotland; Moderator, General Assembly of Church of Scotland, 1922; *b.* Tollcross, Lanarkshire, 14 Oct. 1854; *s.* of Robert Smith, iron merchant, and Jean Wright; *m.* Helen, *d.* of late Rev. Gilbert Johnston of Shettleston; three *s.* one *d.* *Educ.*: Annfield Academy, High School, and University of Glasgow. Studied in Germany; ordained, 1881; after a brief ministry in North Parish, Stirling, called to Partick Parish; formerly Convener of the Business Committee of Glasgow University Council, and Member of the University Court; Vice-Chairman of Glasgow Education Authority; formerly Chairman of Govan Parish School Board, and President of the Scottish School Boards Association since its inception; Chairman of National Committee and Chairman of Glasgow Provincial Committee for Training of Teachers; Convener of the Church of Scotland Education Committee; formerly Convener of Committee on Sabbath Schools; Convener of Examining Board; formerly Convener of Committee on Education for the Ministry; Chaplain, 6th H.L.I. (Terr.); Member of Advisory Board in Scotland for the Blind. *Publications:* Broken Links in Scottish Education; Andrew Melville; George Heriot; Short Studies in the Gospels; one of the authors of Scottish Sabbath School Teachers' Books; The Hebrew Psalmist and the Scottish Bard; articles on education; frequent contributor of expositions and reviews to journals and magazines. *Recreations:* travelled on the Continent, France, Germany, Denmark and Sweden, and South Africa; golf. *Address:* The Manse, Partick, Glasgow. *T.:* Western 1502.

   (*Died 9 June 1927.*)

SMITH, Major-General John Blackburne, C.B. 1918; C.I.E. 1922; B.A., M.B., M.Ch. (R.U.I.), D.P.H., D.T.M. and H. (Camb.); Indian Medical Service, retired; President, Medical Board India Office, and Medical Adviser to the Secretary of State for India; *b.* 21 Jan. 1865; *s.* of Rev. J. A. Smith, M.A., Cork; *m.* 1896, Leta Mayne, *d.* of late W. R. Nelson, Belfast; three *s.* one *d.* *Educ.*: Queen's College, Cork. Civil Surgeon various stations Bombay Presi-

974

dency; A.D.M.S. Poona Division; D.D.M.S. Eastern Command, India; served European War (despatches, C.B.). *Address:* 51 Gordon Road, Ealing, W.5. *T.:* Ealing 2727. *Club:* East India United Service. (*Died 2 Nov. 1928.*)

SMITH, Lt.-Col. John Manners, V.C. 1891; C.I.E. 1894; C.V.O. 1911; Political Department, Government of India; a Political Resident, 1st class; *b.* Lahore, 30 Aug. 1864; 5th *s.* of late Charles Manners Smith, F.R.C.S. (Surg.-Gen. I.M.S.); *m.* 1896, Bertha Mabel, *e. d.* of late Philip Arderne Latham. *Educ.*: Trin. Coll. Stratford-on-Avon; King Edward VI. School, Norwich; R.M.C. Sandhurst. Lieut. Norfolk Regt. 1883-85; joined Indian Staff Corps, and served with 3rd Sikhs (infantry) and 5th Gurkha Rifles, 1885-87; appointed Military Attaché, Foreign Office, Govt. of India, and admitted Political Department, 1887; accompanied Sir Mortimer Durand on his Missions to Sikkim, 1888, and Kabul, 1893; held Political appointments in Kashmir, Bundhelkand, Baluchistan, Rajputana, Central India and Nepal, 1889-1918; served in N.W. Frontier Expeditions—capture of Nilt Position (medal with clasp, V.C.); Hunza-Nagur, 1891; Isazai, 1892; Punjab Frontier and Tirah, 1897-98 (medal with 3 clasps). *Address:* The Residency, Mt. Abu, Rajputana, India. *Clubs:* Junior United Service, M.C.C. (*Died 6 Jan. 1920.*)

SMITH, Rev. John Reader; Vicar of Edgbaston since 1916; Hon. Canon of Birmingham Cathedral since 1906; Rural Dean of Edgbaston, 1913; unmarried. *Educ.*: Bishop Hatfield's Hall, Durham, M.A. Curacies at Bangor and St. Hilda's, Darlington; clerical secretary of the Church Lads' Brigade, 1900-2; Chaplain to Rt. Rev. Dr. Gore when appointed Bishop of Worcester, 1902; Chaplain to Bishop of Birmingham, 1905-10; Hon. Chaplain to present Bishop of Birmingham, 1911; Vicar of St. James's, Edgbaston, 1910-16; Chaplain (2nd Class) 3rd S. Midland Brigade, R.F.A. *Address:* The Vicarage, Edgbaston. *T.:* Edgbaston 368.

   (*Died 13 Jan. 1923.*)

SMITH, John William, D.L. Lancashire; T.D., M.Ch., M.B., F.R.C.S.; Emeritus Professor of Surgery, University, Manchester, 1922; Consulting Surgeon, Manchester Royal Infirmary; Lieut.-Col. (Bt. Col.) R.A.M.C., T.F., retired; *b.* 1864; *e. s.* of Thomas Davidson Smith and Mary Gorrill; *m.* Irène Maud, *o. d.* of H. J. Iason, Holland Park, W.; one *s.* one *d.* *Educ.*: Lancaster School; Edinburgh Univ.; Vienna. M.B. Edinburgh (with first-class honours), 1886; Resident Surgeon, Edinburgh Royal Infirmary, 1887; Demonstrator of Anatomy, University of Edinburgh and Victoria University of Manchester, 1888-91; Resident Surgical Officer, Manchester Royal Infirmary, 1891-94; Visiting Surgeon, Withington Hospital, and Assistant Surgeon, Cancer Hospital, Manchester; served South Africa, 1900 (Hon. Lieut. in the Army, Queen's medal two clasps); commanded 3rd East Lancashire Field Ambulance, Territorial Force, 1908-12; Lecturer in Operative Surgery, 1904-11. *Publications:* various surgical and anatomical papers. *Address:* Richmond Road House, Ingleton (via Carnforth); *T.:* Ingleton 10; Gamblesholme, Tatham, Lancaster. (*Died 13 April 1926.*)

SMITH, Maj.-Gen. Joseph Barnard, Indian Army; *b.* 12 June 1889; *m.* 1871, Edith Olivia (*d.* 1920) *d.* of late Joseph Mansfield, M.A. Entered army, 1856; Maj.-Gen. 1895; retired list, 1898; served N.-W. Frontier of India, 1863 (medal with clasp) Tooshai Expedition, 1871-1872 (clasp); Afghan War, 1878-80 (medal, brevet Lieut.-Col.). (*Died 2 Jan. 1925.*)

SMITH, Rt. Rev. Joseph Oswald, O.S.B.; first Abbot of Ampleforth since 1900; *b.* St. Helens, 1854. *Educ.*: Ampleforth; Belmont; Rome. Was Prefect of Studies at Ampleforth.

Professor of Philosophy at Belmont, and Canon of the Cathedral Chapter of St. Michael's Priory, Hereford ; Prior of Ampleforth, 1898. *Publications:* An Easy Way to use the Psalms ; The Ordinary of the Mass the Food of Prayer ; The Spirit of Our Lady's Litany ; Our Lord's Own Words in the Gospel of St. John ; Meditations on the Passion ; Meditations on the Litany of the Holy Name ; Meditations on the Litany of the Sacred Heart. *Address:* Ampleforth Abbey, York.   (*Died 4 Nov. 1924.*)

SMITH, Sir Lumley, Kt., *cr.* 1914 ; M.A., K.C. ; J.P. Sussex ; Chairman of Quarter Sessions for West Sussex, 1904-14 ; Vice-Chairman Sussex Territorial Force Association, 1908-10 ; Bencher (since 1881) and late Treasurer (1906) of Inner Temple ; a Lieut. for City of London since 1877 ; *y. b.* of Richard Horton-Smith, K.C. ;   *b.* 1834 ; *m.* 1874, Jessie (*d.* 1879), 2nd *d.* of late Sir Thomas Gabriel, 1st and last Bt. *Educ.:* University College School ; University College, London ; Trinity Hall, Cambridge. Ninth Wrangler, 1857 ; Le Bas Prize, 1858 ; and late Fellow of Trin. Hall, Camb. Called to Bar, 1860 ; Q.C. 1880 ; Recorder of Sandwich, 1883-94 ; Judge of Shoreditch and Bow County Courts, 1892-93 ; Judge of the Westminster County Court, 1893-1901 ; Judge of City of London Court, and a Judge of Central Criminal Court, 1901-13. *Publications:* The Koran in India, 1858 ; Editor of Mayne on Damages. *Address:* 25 Cadogan Square, S.W. ; 4 Paper Buildings, Temple, E.C. *Clubs:* Athenæum, Oxford and Cambridge.   (*Died 7 June 1918.*)

SMITH, Lyman Cornelius; organised L. C. Smith and Bros. Typewriter Co. of which he is now President, 1908 ; also L. C. Smith Transit Co., U.S. Transportation Co. and American Transit Co. of Great Lakes ; Rochester, Syracuse, and Eastern Railway ; National Bank of Syracuse ; Chairman Managing Directors of Halcomb Steel Company, Syracuse ; Treasurer and Vice-President Toledo Ship Building Co. ; Vice-President Board of Trustees, Syracuse Univ. ; Chevalier French Legion of Honour. *Address:* Syracuse, New York. *Clubs:* Century, Citizen's, Syracuse ; Hardware, New York.

SMITH, Maynard, C.B. 1918 ; M.B., B.S. (Lond.), F.R.C.S. (Eng.) ; Knight of Grace of the Order of St. John of Jerusalem ; Surgeon to St. Mary's Hospital ; Surgeon to London Fever Hospital ; Consulting Surgeon, St. Luke's House ; Hon. Surgeon Royal Masonic Institute for Girls ; Consulting Surgeon, King Edward VII. Memorial Hospital, Ealing ; formerly Senior Assistant Surgeon, Victoria Hospital for Children, and Surgeon in charge of the Orthopædic Department, St. Mary's Hospital ; Fellow of the Association of Surgeons of Great Britain and of the Société Internationale de Chirurgerie ; *b.* 20 Sep. 1875 ; *s.* of W. H. Smith, Admiralty ; *m.* 1917, Isabel, *d.* of F. I. Pitman ;   one *s.* one *d. Educ.:* Epsom College. Civil Surgeon South African Field Force (medal and two clasps) ; went to France 1915 as Surgeon-in-Chief to the St. John Ambulance Brigade Hospital (Hon. Major, R.A.M.C.) ; Colonel, A.M.S., and appointed Consulting Surgeon to the Fifth Army, 1916 (despatches thrice, C.B., Croix de Guerre). *Publications:* Fractures of Lower Extremity, Official History of War ; articles, Head Injuries and Dislocations, Index of Treatment ; Surgical Infective Diseases, etc., System of Treatment ; Inflammation, Choyce's System of Surgery ; and papers in medical journals and Transactions of societies. *Address:* 49 Wimpole Street, W.1. *T.:* Langham 2030.   (*Died 18 Mar. 1928.*)

SMITH, Morton William, Barrister-at-law, Recorder of Rochester since 1897 ; *b.* 29 Mar. 1851 ; *e. s.* of late F. J. Smith,

Recorder of Margate ; *m.* Adrienne Ernestine Blanche, *d.* of M. A. Blonet of Paris. *Educ.:* Cowbridge Grammar School. Recorder of Gravesend, 1889-97 ; J.P. Cornwall ; Chancellor Diocese of Sierra Leone ; Member of the Diocesan Conference for Rochester. *Address:* Sunset House, Atlantic Road, Newquay, Cornwall ; 4 Essex Court, Temple, E.C. (*Died 5 Feb. 1925.*)

SMITH, Lt.-Gen. Octavius Ludlow, Indian Army ; *b.* 31 July 1828 ; *m.* Mary Harriett Mackenzie Eyre ; two *s.* Entered army, 1847 ; Lt.-Gen. 1892 ; unemployed list, 1886 ; served Indian Mutiny, 1857-59 (twice severely wounded, thanked by Govt. of India, medal with 2 clasps). *Address:* 7 Manson Place, S.W.7. *T.:* Kensington 3828.(*Died 7 May 1927.*)

SMITH, Peter Caldwell, C.B.E. 1919 ; Medical Officer of Health, Metropolitan Borough of Wandsworth, since 1901 ; *b.* Uddingston, Lanarkshire, 1858 ; *s.* of James Smith, LL.D., J.P. ; *m.* 1883, Ina, *d.* of A. S. Macdonald, J.P., Sutherlandshire ; two *s.* one *d. Educ.:* Glasgow University, M.A. 1878 ; M.B., C.M. 1881 ; M.D. 1884 ; D.P.H., Cambridge, 1888. Lecturer on Public Health, Anderson's College, Glasgow, 1890-93 ; Medical Officer of Health, Parish of Wandsworth, 1894-1901 ; Major and O.C. 2nd London Sanitary Coy., R.A.M.C., T.F. 1909-13 ; Lt.-Col. 1915 ; President Travelling Medical Board, London District, 1916-18 (despatches, C.B.E.). *Publications:* numerous papers on Public Health in Lancet, British Medical Journal, Glasgow Medical Journal, and The Hospital, etc. *Address:* 79 East Hill, Wandsworth, S.W.18. *T.:* Battersea 290. *Clubs:* Caledonian, Yorick.   (*Died 21 Feb. 1923.*)

SMITH, Philip, Principal Clerk of the Vote Office, and Sub-Accountant, House of Commons; retired 1918 ; *b.* 1853 ; *s.* of late J. G. Smith, Clerk to the Librarian of House of Commons ; *m.* 1878, Catherine Laslett Dane ; one *s.* three *d.* Assistant Clerk in Vote Office, 1875 ; has made a special study of Parliamentary customs and the interesting features of the old and new Palaces of Westminster. *Publications:* part author of Parliament Past and Present, a popular and picturesque history of 1000 years in the home of the Mother of Parliaments. *Address:* Hillfield, Broadway, Dorset.
    (*Died 29 Aug. 1922.*)

SMITH, His Honour (Philip) Howard, Judge of County Courts, Circuit 25, since 1905 ; *e. surv. s.* of late Sir Wm. Smith, D.C.L., LL.D. ; *b.* 27 Dec. 1845 ; *m.* 1879, Mary Beaumont, 3rd *d.* of late Richard O'Shaughnessy. one *s. Educ.:* St. Paul's School ; Trinity College, Cambridge, M.A. Called to Bar, 1870 ; member of the Oxford Circuit ; a revising barrister ; Recorder of Bridgnorth, 1900-5. *Address:* The Ford House, Wolverhampton. *Clubs:* New University, Savile.   (*Died 13 May 1919.*)

SMITH, His Honour Philip H. Law, M.A., LL.D., K.C. 1906 ; County Court Judge of City and County of Limerick since 1908 ; *b.* 1866 ; 2nd *s.* of late Philip Smith, J.P., Kevit Castle, Co. Cavan ; *m.* 1914, Ellen, *o. d.* of Col. Sir Wm. Henry Dunn, Bart. *Educ.:* St. Patrick's College, Cavan ; Trinity College, Dublin. Called to Irish Bar, 1887 ; Senior Crown Prosecutor, North-West Circuit. *Publications:* (joint) Practice of Supreme Court of Judicature in Ireland. *Address:* 22 Ailesbury Road, Dublin. *Clubs:* Reform ; County, Limerick.
    (*Died 6 Jan. 1920.*)

SMITH, Sir Prince, 1st Bt., *cr.* 1911 ; J.P. West and East Ridings of Yorkshire ; Chairman of Bradford District Bank ; worsted machinery maker ; *b.* Keighley, Yorks, 3 Sep. 1840 ; *s.* of late Prince Smith, of Holly House, Keighley, worsted machinery maker, and Martha, *d.* of John Edmondson, of Keighley, contractor ; *m.*

1864, Martha Ann (*d.* 1913), *d.* of John Greenwood, of Skipton-in-Craven. Yorks; one *s.* two *d.* *Educ.:* Wesley College, Sheffield. Been engaged in business as worsted machinery maker all his life. *Heir: s.* Prince Smith, jun. [*b.* 13 Oct. 1869; *m.* 1894, Maud Mary, *d.* of Henry Wright, of Mayfield, Keighley; one *s.* two *d.* *Address:* Whinburn, Keighley]. *Address:* Hillbrook, Keighley; Southburn, Driffield. *T.A.:* Prince, Keighley. *T.:* 236 Keighley (*Died 20 Oct. 1922.*)

SMITH, Reginald, R.B.A., R.W.S., A.R.C.A. *Educ.:* Manchester Branch of Royal College of Art: afterwards abroad. Has exhibited pictures at Royal Academy for many years; also an exhibitor at Paris Salon. *Address:* 92 Pembroke Road, Clifton, Bristol.

SMITH, Reginald John, K.C.; principal of Smith, Elder, and Co., publishers; editor Cornhill Magazine since 1897; President Publishers' Association, 1904-5 and 1915-16; Member of Council, Royal Geographical Society; Member of Executive Committee of Royal Literary Fund, and Chairman of Anniversary Committee; on Employers' Panel of Board of Trade Conciliation; Treasurer and Member of Management Committee Poplar Hospital for Accidents; *b.* 30 May 1857; *s.* of late John Smith, Britwell House, Oxfordshire; *m.* Isabel Marion, *d.* of late George Murray Smith, 40 Park Lane, W., 1893. *Educ.:* Eton; King's College Cambridge (1st class Classics; distinguished in examination for Chancellor's Medals, B.A., LL.M.). Barr. 1883; assisted late Lord Russell of Killowen in his work at the Bar, 1886-94; Q.C. 1894. *Address:* 11 Green Street, W.; *T.:* Mayfair 1395; 15 Waterloo Place, S.W. *Clubs:* Athenæum, Brooks's, New University, Burlington Fine Arts.
(*Died 26 Dec. 1916.*)

SMITH, Robert Addison, C.V.O. 1917; M.V.O. 1908; Senior partner of the firm of R. Addison Smith & Co., W.S., Edinburgh; Hon. Treasurer, Queen Victoria School, Dunblane, N.B., the Scottish National Memorial to the late Queen; Solicitor to Edinburgh Parish Council and Board of Control; Clerk and Treasurer Midlothian and Peebles Board of Control, etc.; *m.* Mary, *d.* of David Lind, Edinburgh, who built the Scott Monument, Edinburgh; four *s.* three *d.* *Educ.:* private schools; Edinburgh University (honours Logic and Law); took a prominent part in the movement for the Secretary for Scotland (1885) Bill, and the Private Legislation (Scotland) Bill 1889. *Recreations:* cricket, golf. *Address:* 3 Belgrave Crescent, Edinburgh.
(*Died 2 April 1925.*)

SMITH, Robert Cooper, K.C., D.C.L.; LL.D.; Professor of Commercial Law, McGill University, since 1899; *b.* Montreal, 1859; *s.* of Robert Smith; *m.* 1890, Charlotte Florence Elizabeth, *d.* of Milton Pennington. *Educ.:* Montreal High School; McGill University. Called to Bar, 1882; Q.C. 1897; Ex-Batonnier of the Bar; Officier d'Académie, France, 1917; practising as senior member of legal firm of Smith, Markey, Skinner, Pugsley and Hyde. *Address:* 112 St. James Street, Montreal. *T.A.:* Smar, Montreal. *Clubs:* National Liberal; St. James, Forest and Stream, Mount Royal, University, Royal St. Lawrence Yacht, Montreal; Quebec Garrison, Quebec; Rideau, Ottawa.
(*Died 22 Sept. 1917.*)

SMITH, Robert Macaulay, M.A., LL.B.; Advocate; Sheriff-Substitute of Berwickshire since 1908; *b.* Dalry, Ayrshire, 1859; *s.* of David Smith, merchant, Dalry; *m.* 1898, Jean, *d.* of John Wylie, merchant, Largs, Ayrshire; no *c.* *Educ.:* Public School, Ayrshire; Edinburgh University. Called to Scottish Bar, 1889; Advocate-Depute in Sheriff Court, 1895; held position of Prosecutor for Public Interest for City of Edinburgh, 1899-1908;

976

known during period at Bar as platform speaker and worker in Liberal interest in politics. *Publication:* edited The Liberal Platform, 1895. *Recreations:* golf and cycling. *Address:* Duns, Berwickshire. *Club:* Scottish Liberal, Edinburgh.
(*Died 13 Jan. 1927.*)

SMITH, Robert Murray, C.M.G. 1884, M.A.; one of the leaders of Constitutional Party in Victoria; a Trustee of the Melbourne Argus; Trustee of Public Library; *b.* 29 Oct. 1831; *s.* of late Alexander Smith, Liverpool; *m.* 1858, Jane (*d.* 1913), *d.* of Hon. J. F. Strachan, M.L.C.; three *d.* *Educ.:* Repton; Oriel College, Oxford (Scholar). Hon. M.A. Oxford, 1888. Emigrated to Victoria, 1854; elected M.L.A. for St. Kilda, 1873; for Boroondara, 1877; as joint leader of the Conservative opposition in 1881, he helped to carry Sir B. O'Loghlen's vote of want of confidence in the Berry Ministry—but did not take office; appointed Agent-General for Victoria in London, 1882; renewed in 1885; returned to Victoria, 1886; elected member for Hawthorn. 1894-1897. *Recreation:* literature. *Address:* Repton, Toorak, Australia. *Club:* Melbourne. Victoria.
(*Died 31 Aug. 1921.*)

SMITH, Robert Shingleton, M.D. (Lond. and Bristol), F.R.C.P., B.Sc., F.R.H.S.; Consulting Physician Bristol Royal Infirmary, 1905; *b.* 1845; *m.* Eliza Mary Dowson; one *s.* *Educ.:* Queen's College, Taunton; King's College, London. Physician Bristol Royal Infirmary, 1873-1905; Consulting Physician Bristol Dispensary and Hospital; Fellow Royal Society of Medicine; Fellow and Associate King's College, London. *Publications:* late Editor Bristol Medico-Chirurgical Journal; many contributions to various medical journals. *Address:* Deepholm, Clifton Park, Clifton, Bristol. *T.:* 553. (*Died 15 April 1922.*)

SMITH, Sir Ross Macpherson, K.B.E., *cr.* 1919; M.C., D.F.C., A.F.C.; Aviator; *b.* Adelaide, Australia, 4 Dec. 1892; unmarried. *Educ.:* Queen's School, Adelaide; Warriston School, Moffat, Scotland. Served on Gallipoli and Sinai with Australian Light Horse; two years with Australian Flying Corps in Palestine (M.C. and bar, D.F.C. and 2 bars, Order of el Nahda); first flight from Cairo to Calcutta, 1918 (A.F.C.); first flight England to Australia, 1919 (K.B.E.). *Recreations:* golf, tennis, etc. *Address:* Gilberton, South Australia. *Club:* Junior Naval and Military. (*Died 13 April 1922.*)

SMITH, Samuel, F.R.Hist.Soc., F.L.A.; Consultant Librarian, Sheffield Public Libraries, since 1921; *b.* Harrogate, 14 Aug. 1855; *e. s.* of Thomas Smith; *m.* 1st, Jane Hustler, 2nd, Olivia Flint; one *s.* *Educ.:* privately; Yorkshire College. Assistant Librarian, Leeds Public Libraries, 1872; City Librarian, Worcester, 1880; Ex-President of the Sheffield Branch of the Dickens Fellowship; President of the North Midland Library Association; member of many of the leading literary societies, and lecturer on literary and social subjects. *Publications:* History of the Parish and Church of Leigh, in Transactions of Worcester Diocesan Architectural and Archæological Society; papers contributed to the Library Association, various magazines, and the press. *Recreations:* raconteur, photography, and reading. *Address:* Allendale. Barnsley Road, Sheffield.

SMITH, Sir Swire, Kt.; *cr.* 1898; M.P. (L.) Keighley Div., Yorks, since 1915; J.P.; *b.* Keighley, 4 Mar. 1842; *e. s.* of George Smith, Keighley, and Mary, *d.* of Thomas Swire, Keighley. *Educ.:* Keighley; Wesley College, Sheffield. Member of Royal Commission on Technical Instruction, 1881-84; Vice-Chairman Royal Commission on International Exhibitions, 1909; LL.D. University of Leeds, 1912. *Publications:* pamphlets and magazine articles on technical education. *Address :* Steeton Manor, near Keighley.   *(Died 16 Mar. 1918.)*

SMITH, Rev. Sydney Fenn, S.J. ; on the staff of writers attached to the Jesuit Residence at Farm Street, Berkeley Square, W., since 1891 ; *b.* Margate, 11 March 1843 ; *e. s.* of Rev. Sydney Smith, M.A., Cantab., Vicar of Worth, Sandwich, and Frances Mary, *d.* of James Mellcott Richardson. *Educ. :* private school. Received into the Catholic Church, 1864 ; entered the Society of Jesus, 1866 ; Priest, 1877 ; Professor of Ethics at Stonyhurst College, 1878-9 ; of Dogmatic Theology and Holy Scripture at St. Beuno's College, 1888-9 ; editor of the Month, 1897-1901. *Publications :* many articles in exposition and defence of Catholic doctrine and history in the Month and other periodicals, also for the Catholic Encyclopædia ; the article on Ordinations Anglicanes in the Dictionnaire apologetique de la foi Catholique ; numerous tracts for the Catholic Truth Society ; editor of Scripture Manuals for Catholic Youth. *Address :* 31 Farm Street, Berkeley Square, W.   *(Died 1921.)*

SMITH, Vernon Russell, K.C. ; *b.* 7 April 1849 ; *s.* of Thomas Smith, Highgate ; *m.* E. Gertrude, *d.* of Charles H. Lovell, Highgate, 1879 ; one *s. Educ. :* Highgate School ; St. Peter's College, Cambridge (M.A.). Barrister, Inner Temple, 1872 ; Q.C. 1894 ; retired, 1904. *Club :* Oxford and Cambridge.*(Died 5 Dec. 1921.)*

SMITH, Vincent Arthur; C.I.E. 1919 ; Litt.D. Dublin ; M.A. Dublin and Oxford ; M.R.A.S. ; Indian Civil Service, retired ; *b.* Dublin, 1848 ; *s.* of Aquilla Smith, M.D. ; *m.* 1871, *d.* of W. C. Tute ; three *s.* one *d. Educ. :* Trinity College, Dublin. Classical Scholar ; 1st Senior Moderator in English Literature and Mod. History ; 2nd Senior Moderator in Classics ; University Student ; some time Lecturer in Indian History and Hindustani at T.C.D., and in Indian History at Oxford ; Fellow of the Allahabad University ; Gold Medallist of the Royal Asiatic Society, 1918 ; served in I.C.S. 1871-1900 as Assistant Magistrate, etc. ; Settlement Officer ; Magistrate and Collector ; District and Sessions Judge ; Commissioner of Division ; and Chief Secretary to Govt. of U.P. and Oudh ; retired, 1900 ; then devoted life to work on Indian history, numismatics, art, and archaeology. *Publications :* Asoka, 2nd ed., 1909 ; Early History of India, 3rd ed., 1914 ; History of Fine Art in India and Ceylon, 1911 ; Akbar, the Great Mogul, 1917 ; Oxford History of India, 1919 ; many minor books and editions and innumerable papers in Quarterly Review and various journals. *Recreation :* reading. *Address :* 6 Fyfield Road, Oxford. *Clubs :* Oxford and County.   *(Died 6 Feb. 1920.)*

SMITH, Rev. Walter Percy, M.A. ; Hon. Canon of Winchester Cathedral since 1910 ; *b.* 1848 ; 2nd *s.* of Nathaniel Smith of Cheltenham ; *m.* 1874, Annie Maria, *d.* of H. D. Martin of Cheltenham. *Educ. :* Marlborough ; New College, Oxford. 1st Class Classical Moderations, 1869 ; 1st Class Law and Modern History, 1871 ; Assistant Master at Marlborough, 1872 ; Winchester, 1873-1901 ; Chaplain to Winchester College,1883-1901 ; Secretary to Winchester Diocesan Conference, 1903 - 20 ; to Winchester Clergy Sustentation Fund, 1904-13 ; Gen. Sec. to Church Congress, Southampton, 1913 ; Chairman of the Council of the University College, Southampton, 1917. *Publications :* Sir Thomas Browne's Religio Medici ; pamphlet on Father Henry Garnet, S.J. ; papers in Winchester College, 1393-1893 ; and Memorials of Old Hampshire. *Address :* Wychbury, Winchester.   *(Died 11 Sept. 1922.)*

SMITH, Rev. Walter R. ; *b.* Parsonage, King's Cove, Bonavista Bay, Newfoundland, 5 July 1845 ; *s.* of Rev. Benjamin Smith, Rural Dean, and S.P.G. Missionary, Newfoundland ; *m.* 1871, Mary (*d.* 1910), 2nd *d.* of George H. Le

Messurier, Deputy Postmaster-General, Newfoundland ; two *s.* one *d. Educ. :* Queen's College, St. Johns, Newfoundland. Matriculated, 1865 ; Deacon, 1869 ; Priest, 1871 ; Incumbent of Greenspond, 1869-70 ; S.P.G. Missionary at Exploits, 1870 - 73 ; Rector of Tilt Cove, great mining centre, Notre Dame Bay, Newfoundland, 1874-9 ; Assistant Priest to his father at Trinity East, 1880-85 ; Clerical Member, Executive Committee Diocesan Synod, 1894, and re-elected to same office at every biennial session of Synod since that date ; Vice-President, Newfoundland Historical Society, 1905 ; Canon of the Cathedral and Rural Dean of Avalon, 1905 ; Incumbent of Portugal Cove, 1886 ; Clerical Member Executive Committee Diocesan Synod ; Member of Council of Queen's College (Theological), 1906 ; also of Corresponding Committee Colonial and Continental Church Society ; Episcopal Commissary, 1912 ; retired 1914. *Publications :* many articles on both religious and secular subjects for Newfoundland newspapers and magazines. *Address :* Episcopal Commissary, 44 Angel Place, S. John's, Newfoundland.   *(Died 24 April 1921.)*

SMITH, Watson, Editor, Journal Society of Chemical Industry, 1881-1915 ; F.C.S., F.I.C. ; *b.* Stroud, Gloucestershire, 16 June 1845 ; *s.* of late Rev. Watson Smith ; *m.* 1st, 1880, Susanne Felber of Zürich ; five *s.* two *d.* ; 2nd, 1915, Dorothy Gertrude Orchard. *Educ. :* Owens College, Manchester ; Heidelberg University ; Polytechnikum, Zürich. Chemist and manager in works and factories, 10 years ; Examiner, Institute of Chemistry ; Lecturer in Technical Chemistry, Owens College, Victoria University, Manchester, and Professor of Applied Chemistry in University College, London ; on first staff of abstractors for Journal of Chemical Society. Discoverer of true cause of flour-mill explosions, 1876 ; also of dinaphthyls and phenylnaphthalene ; Discoverer of arsenide of Eucalyptol and glycerol phthalate ; Investigator of Milke coal and its high resinoid constituents. *Publications :* Contributions to Journal of Chemical Society, etc. on the Destructive Distillation of Wood ; Resinoid Coals, Ammonium Salts, Bye-products of Coke Ovens, also of Blast Furnace Gases and Tars, etc. to the Journal of Society of Chemical Industry. *Recreation :* musical composition. *Address :* 34 Upper Park Road, Haverstock Hill, N.W.*(Died 1 May 1920.)*

SMITH, Sir William, Kt., cr. 1913 ; J.P., Co. Derby ; in business as corn miller since 1859 ; senior partner in Smith and Son, Ltd., Langley Mill, Derbyshire ; Smith Brothers, Ltd., Walsall, Staffordshire ; Smith Brothers, Ltd., Worksop, Notts. ; *b.* 1843 ; *s.* of Wm. and Hannah Smith, of Milnhay House, Langley Mill ; married ; six *s.* three *d. Educ. :* Wesley College, Sheffield ; Mansfield Grammar School. Visited Australia in old sailing-ship days, 1868 ; America, 1893 ; New Zealand, 1903 and 1911 ; Wesleyan local preacher ; temperance and political speaker. *Recreations :* horse-riding, historical reading. *Address :* Dunstead House, Langley Mill. *T.A. :* Smith, Langley Mill. *T. :* 13.   *(Died 12 Jan. 1916.)*

SMITH, Major-General William, Royal Artillery, retired ; *b.* 1835 ; 5th *s.* of late William Smith of Carbeth - Guthrie, Stirlingshire ; *m.* 1869, Emma Corrie, *d.* of Francis Henry Crozier, H.E.I.C.S. ; three *s.* two *d. Educ. :* Edinburgh and Glasgow Universities. Joined Royal Artillery and appointed to a field battery at Ipswich, 1855 ; served Indian Mutiny, 1857-59 ; relief of Lucknow (horse shot), battle of Cawnpore, actions of Serai Ghat, Chanda, Umeerpore and Sultanpore, siege and capture of Lucknow, attack of the Moosabagh and action of Baree, Trans-Gogra campaign (despatches, medal with two clasps) ; served in the Horse Artillery, 1859-63 ; New

Zealand War, 1864; campaigns on the Waikato and at Te Ranga, and attack on the Gate Pah (medal); Garrison Artillery, 1865-71; Gunnery-Instructor at the School of Gunnery at Shoe-buryness, 1871-74; Garrison Instructor at Luck-now and Rawal Pindi, 1875-79; commanding a Field Battery in India, 1879-82; commanding Auxiliary Artillery in Dublin district, 1882-87; retired, with rank of Maj.-Gen. 1887. *Address:* Balcarras House, Charlton Kings, Cheltenham.
(*Died 25 Dec. 1922.*)

SMITH, Col. William Apsley, C.B. 1900; C.M.G. 1918; retired; late Royal Artil-lery; *b.* 11 Mar. 1856; *e. s.* of late John Smith, Britwell House, Oxfordshire; *m.* 1885, Mary, 2nd *d.* of late Gen. Sir John Adye; one *d. Educ.:* Eton; R.M.A., Woolwich. Passed Staff Col-lege, 1886, Honours, etc.; Staff Captain S.E. District, 1886-88; Brig. Major, Aldershot, 1888-1891; Assistant Military Secretary to G.O.C. Canada, 1894-96; Special Service Officer at Headquarters, 1896-98; Ordnance Committee, 1906-8; Brig. General, Commanding R.A. 3rd Division, 1908-9; A.Q.M.G. Eastern Command 1914-18; served Afghan War, 1880 (medal); Egyptian War, 1882 (medal, star, and de-spatches, 5th class Medjidie); S. African War, 1899-1900 (despatches, medal, and four clasps, C.B.); Military Attaché Russo-Japanese War, 1904-5; Japanese War medal; 3rd Class Rising Sun. *Address:* Ashdown House, Danehill, Sussex. *T.:* Chelwood Gate 11. *Club:* United Service. (*Died 1 May 1927.*)

SMITH, Sir William Frederick Haynes, K.C.M.G.,; *cr.* 1890; C.M.G. 1897; *b.* 1839; *m.* 1867, Ellen Parkinson (*d.* 1923), *d.* of J. T. White. Barr. Middle Temple; Sol.-Gen. of Brit. Guiana, 1865; Attor.-Gen. 1874; Governor of British Guiana, 1884-87; Leeward Isles,1888-1895; the Bahamas, 1895-97; High Comr. and Comdr.-in-Chief of the Island of Cyprus, 1897-1904. *Address:* 26 Chester Terrace, Regent's Park, N.W. *Clubs:* Athenæum, Garrick.
(*Died 17 Dec. 1928.*)

SMITH, W. Harding, R.B.A., Hon. Sec-retary Japan Society. *Address:* White Lodge, 209 Brixton Hill, S.W. (*Died 9 Jan. 1922.*)

SMITH - DORRIEN, Rev. Walter Montgomery, B.D., M.A.; Prebendary of Exeter; Vicar of Crediton since 1901. *Educ.:* Harrow School; Magdalen, Oxford. President O.U.A.C. 1874; Curate, Parish Church, Leeds, 1876-79; St. Martin's, Brighton, 1881-85; Minor Canon of Durham, 1885-93; Precentor, 1886-7; Chaplain, St. Mary's Chapel, Dalkeith, N.B., 1893-99. *Address:* The Vicarage, Crediton.
(*Died 17 Dec. 1924.*)

SMITH-MARRIOTT, Sir William Henry, 5th Bt.; *cr.* 1774; J.P.; *b.* Horse-monden, 7 Aug. 1835; *S.* father 1864; *m.* 1868, Eliza (*d.* 1904), *d.* of Hon. Richard Cavendish, Thornton Hall, Buckinghamshire; two *s.* two *d. Educ.:* Harrow; Balliol Coll. Oxford. Owns about 3900 acres. *Heir: s.* William John, *b.* 6 Nov. 1870. *Address:* The Down House, Blandford, Dorsetshire. *Club:* Windham.
(*Died 30 Nov. 1924.*)

SMITHERS, Sir Alfred Waldron, Kt., *cr.* 1919; M.P. (Co.U.) Chislehurst Division of Kent Dec. 1918-22; J.P.; late Deputy Chairman South-Eastern and Chatham Rail-way; Chairman of the English Association of American Share and Bondholders; *b.* 4 Oct. 1850; *s.* of late William Henry Smithers of the Bank of England; *m.* 1880, Emma Roberta, *d.* of R. M. Theobald, M.A., M.R.C.S. *Address:* Knockholt, Sevenoaks, Kent. *Clubs:* Devon-shire, City of London. (*Died 22 Aug. 1924.*)

SMYLY, William Cecil, K.C.; LL.B.; J.P.; *b.* Dublin, 2 Jan. 1840; *y. s.* of John George Smyly, Q.C., D.L., Castlederg and Camus, and Eliza, *d.* of Sir Andrew Ferguson, Bt., M.P. Londonderry; *m.* Alice, *o. d.* of

978

Samuel Wm. Brooks, Watford, 1884; two *s.* two *d. Educ.:* Harrow; Trin. Coll. Camb. Judge of County Courts, Derbyshire, and part of Stafford-shire, 1895-1902; Judge of C.C. Bow and Shore-ditch, 1902-15. *Publications:* late editor of County Court Practice. *Recreations:* rowing; Captain Cambridge University Boat Club, 1862-1863; Capt. 1st Trinity Boat Club, 1861-62. *Address:* Heathfield, Windlesham, Surrey. *Clubs:* New University, Alpine.
(*Died 4 Mar. 1921.*)

SMYTH, Sir Alfred John Bowyer-, 13th Bt., *cr.* 1661; late Major and Hon. Lt.-Col., 3rd Batt. Hampshire Regiment; *b.* 12 Sep. 1850; *s.* of late Rev. A. J. E. Smyth, Rector of Attle-borough, and Mary, *d.* of late Major.-Gen. Sir J. Rolt; *S.* cousin, 1916. *Heir: n.* Lieut.-Commr. Philip Weyland, R.N., *b.* 4 Feb. 1894. *Address:* 4 The Crescent, Winchester. *Clubs:* Junior United Service; Hampshire, Winchester.
(*Died 4 Aug. 1927.*)

SMYTH, Col. Charles Coghlan, C.B. 1891; *b.* 1842; retired, 1896. Entered army, 1861; Col. 1889; served Red River Expedition, Canada, 1870; Jowaki Campaign, 1877 (medal with clasp); Afghan War, 1877-80 (despatches, medal with clasp); Nile, 1884-85 (despatches, brevet of Lieut.-Col., medal with clasp, Khedive's star); Suakin, 1888 (despatches, clasp, 3rd class Medjidie). (*Died 3 Mar. 1920.*)

SMYTH, Capt. Gerald Brice Fer-guson, D.S.O. 1914; R.E.; *b.* 7 Sep. 1885. Entered army, 1905; Captain, 1914; served European War, 1914-17 (severely wounded, despatches four times, D.S.O. and bar).
(*Died July 1920.*)

SMYTH, Rear-Adm. Harry Hesketh, C.M.G. 1917; D.S.O. 1917; Royal Navy (re-tired); *b.* 28 April 1872; *s.* of late Charles Robert Knox Smyth, Commander Royal Navy (ret.); *m.* 1923, Helen Irene Carlyle, *widow of* late Captain S. J. Lovegrove, K.A.R. Joined H.M.S. Britannia, 1885; Captain, 1914; Com-manded M.H. Ships Intrepid, Orvieto, Wahine, Ariadne, Amphitrite, Princess Margaret, during the European War (despatches twice, D.S.O., C.M.G., Officier Legion d'honneur); Rear-Admiral, 1925. *Recreations:* golf, lawn-tennis. *Address:* Pitmore Cottage, Sway, Hants. *T.:* Sway 33. *Club:* Naval and Military.
(*Died 9 July 1926.*)

SMYTH, Major Humphrey Etwall, D.S.O. 1917; O.B.E. 1919; R.A.O.C.; *b.* Sial-kot, India, 1884; 2nd *surv. s.* of Col. E. W. Smyth, C.B.; *m.* 1908, Kathleen, *e. d.* of Aubrey Robinson; one *s. Educ.:* Royal Military Academy, Woolwich. First commissioned in the R.G.A. 1902; transferred to R.A.O.C. 1918; served European War, 1915-19 (despatches four times, D.S.O., O.B.E.). *Address:* Lloyds Bank, Ltd. (Cox's Branch), 6 Pall Mall, S.W.1.
(*Died 1 Nov. 1927.*)

SMYTH, John, M.A., D.Phil.; Professor of Education, University of Melbourne, since 1918; Principal of the Teachers' Coll., State of Victoria, since 1902; *b.* Lanarkshire, Scotland, 1864; *m.*, 1891; one *s. Educ.:* Otago University; Edin-burgh University; Heidelberg and Jena Uni-versities. Educated and trained to be a teacher in the National Schools, Ireland; commenced teaching career N. Zealand, 1882; gained the M.A. degree with scholarship in Mental Science, 1892; Rector district High School, Waimate, N.Z.; relieved Prof. Salmond, Mental Science classes, Otago University, N.Z., 1897; studied Edinburgh, Heidelberg, Jena, 1898-1900, gain-ing Doctor of Phil. degree, Edinburgh; Chief Inspector of Schools, Wanganui District, N.Z., 1900-2; Principal of Teachers' College, Melbourne, and Lecturer in Education, Uni-versity of Melbourne, 1902-18. *Publications:* Truth and Reality; Guide to a Modern Infant

Room; The Rural School in Australasia. *Recreation*: golf. *Address*: 632 St. Kilda Road, Melbourne. *T.*: Windsor 6731.
(Died 20 Aug. 1927.)

SMYTH, Col. Owen Stuart, D.S.O. 1886; late commanding mountain batteries Jutogh; *b.* 1853; *m. Educ.*: R.M.A. Woolwich. Entered Royal Garrison Artillery, 1873; Lieut.-Col. 1898; served Afghan War, 1878-80 (despatches); Candahar (medal, two clasps, bronze decoration); Burmah,1885-86(despatches, D.S.O., medal with clasp); Wuntho Expedition, 1891 (despatches, clasp); Manipur (despatches, clasp).
(Died 30 Jan. 1923.)

SMYTHE, His Honour Charles John; *b.* 21 April 1852; 2nd *s.* of late W. Smythe, Methven Castle, Perthshire, N.B.; *m.* 1876, Margaret, *y. d.* of late J. King of Lynedoch, Natal; seven *s.* five *d. Educ.*: Glenalmond College, Perthshire. Came to Natal, 1872; began stock farming in Nottingham Road district, 1876; J.P. for colony, 1887; elected Member of Legislative Assembly for Lion's River Division on the introduction of Responsible Government, 1893; Speaker, 1897-99; Colonial Secretary, Natal, 1899-1903; Prime Minister, Natal, and Colonial Secretary, 1905-6; one of the delegates for Natal to S. Africa National Convention, 1908-9; Administrator, Natal, 1910. *Address*: Strathearn, Nottingham Road, Natal. *Club*: Victoria, Maritzburg. *(Died May 1918.)*

SMYTHE, Col. David Murray, retired Colonel; *b.* 17 Nov. 1850; *e. s.* of William Smythe of Methven and Emily, *d.* of Sir John Oswald of Dunnikier; *m.* 1898, Hon. Katherine, *d.* of 3rd Lord Bagot and Lucia, *d.* of Lord Dover; one *d. Educ.*: Trinity College, Cambridge; Sandhurst. Joined Royal Perth Rifles (Militia), 1870; joined Cameron Highlanders, 1872; joined 3rd Batt. Royal Highrs. (Militia), 1880; commanded 3rd Royal Highrs. 1893-97; served in the Zulu War in the Natal Native Contingent, 1879; D.L. and J.P. Perthshire. *Address*: Moulin Almond, nr. Perth. *T.A.*: Almondbank. *T.*: Methven 6. *Club*: New, Edinburgh.
(Died 10 Feb. 1923.)

SMYTHE, Sir (John) Walter, 8th Bt., *cr.* 1660; late Captain Louth Rifles; J.P., Shropshire; D.L., Monmouthshire; *b.* 7 Nov. 1827; 4th *s.* of 6th Bt.; S. brother, 1898; *m.* 1864, Marie Louise, 2nd *d.* of William Herbert, Clytha Park, Monmouth; one *s.* two *d.* Owns about 8700 acres. *Heir*: *s.* Edward Patrick Herbert Walter [*b.* 20 March 1869. *Educ.*: Downside]. *Address*: Acton Burnell Park, Shropshire; Eshe Hall, Durham. *Clubs*: Hurlingham, Wellington. *(Died 5 Mar. 1919.)*

SMYTHE, Lionel Percy, R.W.S., R.A. 1911; A.R.A., 1898; *b.* 1840. Germinal, painted 1890, is in the Chantrey Collection. *Address*: 40 Dover Street, W.; Château d'Honvault. Wimereux, Pas de Calais, France. *(Died 10 July 1918.)*

SNEYD, Major Gen. Thomas William; *b.* 14 Jan. 1837; *s.* of Thomas Sneyd, 2nd *s.* of William Sneyd of Ashcombe, and Emma, *d.* of George Whitley of Norley Hall, Cheshire; *m.* 1879, Charlotte Marion, *d.* of late Capt. W. W. Repton; one *s.* two *d. Educ.*: Harrow. Served in the Queen's Bays in the Indian Mutiny; commanded the Regiment, 1877-82. *Address*: Ashcombe Park, nr. Leek, Staffs. *T.A.*: Cheddleton. *(Died 1 May 1918.)*

SNOWDEN, Sir Arthur, Kt., *cr.* 1895; *b.* Dartford, 1829; *m.* 1856, Elizabeth (*d.* 1900), *d.* of Benjamin Jarvis. Went to Australia, 1852; Mayor of Melbourne, 1892-93, 1893-94, 1894-95; M.L.C. Victoria, 1895-1904. *Address*: St. Heliers, Abbotsford, Melbourne, Victoria.
(Died 18 June 1918.)

SOARES, Sir Ernest Joseph, Kt., *cr.* 1911; M.A., LL.D.; *b.* 20 Oct. 1864; *m.* 1893, Kate Carolyn, *d.* of late Samuel Lord; one *d. Educ.*:

St. John's Coll., Camb. Formerly Solicitor in Manchester; Parliamentary Private Secretary to the Home Secretary, 1906-7; Charity Commissioner, 1908-10; Junior Lord of the Treasury, 1910-11; Assistant Comptroller Reduction of National Debt and Life Annuity Office, 1911-16; M.P. (L.) North-West or Barnstaple Division of Devonshire, 1900-11. *Address*: Corriemoillie, Garve, Ross-shire. *Club*: Oxford and Cambridge. *(Died 15 Mar. 1926.)*

SODEN, Thomas Spooner, Barrister-at-Law; *b.* Bath, 15 May 1837; *y. s.* of late John Smith Soden, F.R.C.S.; *m.* Isabella Clavering (*d.* 1911); *y. d.* of late Edward Cator Seaton, of Local Government Board, F.R.C.P., 1873. *Educ.*: privately; Exeter Coll. Oxford (M.A.). Called to Bar, Middle Temple, 1862; goes Midland Circuit; was a Revising Barrister in 1868, and from 1875 to 1901; Assistant Recorder at Birmingham, 1882-1912; Recorder of Grantham, 1897-1914; formerly Counsel for Mint at Warwick Assizes and Sessions. *Publications*: joint author of Smith and Soden's Landlord and Tenant. *Address*: 1 Courthope Road, Wimbledon. *Club*: Athenæum. *(Died 5 Aug. 1920.)*

SOLOGUB, Feodor (Feodor Kuzmich Teternikov); *b.* 1864. *Educ.*: Petrograd. *Publications*: The Old House, 1915; The Sweet Scented Name, 1915. *(Died 5 Dec. 1927.)*

SOLOMON, Solomon Joseph, P.R.B.A., R.A.: painter; *b.* London, 16 Sep. 1860; *s.* of Joseph Solomon; *m. d.* of late Hyman Montague, F.S.A., 1897; one *s.* two *d. Educ.*: school of Mr. Thomas Whitford; privately by Rev. Mr. Singer. Studied Art at Heatherly's, the R.A. schools, Munich Academy, and the Beaux Arts, Paris; worked in Italy, Spain, and Morocco; Vice President of the Maccabæans Society; and President R.B.A., 1918; at the beginning of the War drew attention to the need for camouflage in modern warfare, and initiated it in the British Army; was a Lieut.-Col., R.E.; introduced fishing net, the base of our effective camouflage during the War, 1916. *Paintings*: Cassandra, 1886; Samson, 1887; Niobe, 1888; The Judgment of Paris, 1890; Portrait of Mrs. Patrick Campbell, 1893; I. Zangwill; Echo and Narcissus, 1894; Birth of Love, 1895; decoration for Royal Exchange; Laus Deo; and the Houses of Parliament. *Publications*: Strategic Camouflage, 1920; The Practice of Painting. *Recreation*: horseriding. *Address*: 18 Hyde Park Gate, S.W.7; *T.*: Western 3869; Whitecliffe, Birchington. *Clubs*: Athenæum, Arts, Omar Khayyam.
(Died 27 July 1927.)

SOLTAU-SYMONS, George William Culme, J.P., D.L.; *b.* 29 May 1881; *e. s.* of George William Soltau (*d.* 1884) and Frances, *d.* of late Rev. Thomas Culme, of Tothill, Devon; *m.* 1st, 1859, Hon. Adèle Isabella (*d.* 1869), 2nd *d.* of 3rd Lord Graves; 2nd, 1875, Mary Elizabeth, *d.* of Lt.-Col. Frederick William Todd, and widow of St. John Coventry. *Educ.*: Winchester; Christ Church, Oxford. High Sheriff, Devon, 1875. *Heir*: *s.* George Algernon James, Capt. Reserve of Officers (late Capt. K.R.R. Corps.; *b.* 1867; *m.* 1898, Eleanor, *e. d.* of late Lt.-Gen. Sir William Howley Goodenough, K.C.B.; one *d. Educ.*: Eton]. *Address*: Chaddlewood Plympton, Devon. *(Died 24 Oct. 1916.)*

SOLVAY, Ernest, Ministre d'Etat de Belgique; Inventor of Soda; *b.* 1839; *m.*; Grand Officer Order of Leopold; President of the Bureau of International Institute of Bibliography, Brussels; hon. member Royal Institute of Great Britain; holds Lavoisier Medal, Institute of France; Grand Medal, University of Paris; established Solvay Society of Brussels; founded International Solvay Institutes of Physic, of Chemistry and of Sociology; was a member of Belgian Senate. *Address*: 43 rue des Champs Elyseés. Brussels. *(Died 26 May 1922.)*

SOMERSET, 15th Duke of (*cr.* 1547), **Algernon St. Manr,** J.P.; Baron Seymour, 1547; Bt., 1611; Lieutenant 60th Rifles (retired); Lieut.-Colonel 1st Wiltshire Rifle Volunteers; *b.* 22 July 1846; *s.* of 14th Duke and Horatia, *d.* of John Philip Morier, minister, Dresden; *S.* father 1894; *m.* Susan, *d.* of Charles Mackinnon, 1877. Owns about 25,400 acres. *Heir:* c. Brig.-Gen. Sir Edward Hamilton Seymour. *Address;* 35 Grosvenor Square, W.1; *T.:* Mayfair 6872; Maiden Bradley, Bath; Berry Pomeroy, Totnes, Devon. *Clubs:* Carlton, Army and Navy; Royal Yacht Squadron, Cowes.
(*Died 22 Oct. 1923.*)

SOMERSET, Lady Henry (Isabel) ; late President National British Women's Temperance Association and World's Women's Christian Temperance Union ; *e. d.* of 3rd Earl Somers ; *m.* 1873, Lord Henry Somerset; *o. c.* H. C. S. A. Somerset. Established the Woman's Signal, and edited that paper in the interest of woman's work ; founded in 1895 the industrial farm colony for inebriate women at Duxhurst, Surrey (the first institution opened in England for women on those lines); had for 15 years a home for training workhouse children, and has The Children's Village, Duxhurst, for saving child-life. *Publications:* edited the Woman's Signal ; leaflets on different phases of woman's work ; a book of stories ; Studies in Black and White ; Under the Arch of Life; magazine articles; A Book for Children, illustrated and written by her ; Our Village Life ; and a book on reform for women, Beauty for Ashes. Formerly owned properties in Surrey, and in Herefordshire and Worcestershire, but has made them over to her heirs. *Recreations:* modelling, painting. *Address:* 4 Gray's Inn Square, W.C.1 ; *T.:* Holborn 5646 ; The Homes of the Holy Redeemer, Duxhurst, Reigate.
(*Died 12 Mar. 1921.*)

SOMERVELL, James, J.P., D.L.; *b.* 19 Sep. 1845 ; *e. s.* of late Graham Somervell and Henrietta Jane, *d.* of William Stirling ; *m.* 1892, Kathleen Emilie, *e. d.* of Maclaine of Lochbuie; one *s.* two *d.* *Educ.:* Harrow. Called to Bar, Inner Temple, 1870 ; Major and Hon. Lieut.-Col. late Ayrshire Yeomanry ; M.P. Ayr Burghs, 1890-92. (*Died 10 Feb. 1924.*)

SOMERVILLE, David Hughes, I.S.O. 1902 ; retired Civil servant; *b.* 20 June 1840 ; *y. s.* of late William Somerville of Castlecomer, Co. Kilkenny, Ireland ; *m.* Anne Elizabeth (*d.* 1914). *Educ.:* private schools. Appointed Clerk in General Post Office, London, 1860; held appointment of Head-Postmaster of several London districts in succession, 1885-1905. *Recreations:* country walks and sketching. *Address:* 18 Queenswood Road, Forest Hill, S.E.
(*Died 5 Feb. 1918.*)

SOMERVILLE, William Dennistoun; heir-pres. to Baronetcy held by his cousin, 2nd Baron Athlumney; *b.* 8 June 1842 ; *s.* of late Tenison Alan Somerville, and Cecilia, *d.* of Daniel O'Connor of Shoreham, Sussex. *Address:* Clermont, Rathnew, Co. Wicklow.
(*Died 10 Mar. 1917.*)

SONNINO, Baron Sidney ; *b.* Pisa, 11 March 1847 (mother English); single ; LL.D. Univ. of Pisa, 1865. Diplomacy, 1867-72 ; entered Parliament, 1880 ; Minister of Finance, 1893-94 ; Minister of the Treasury, 1894-96 ; Premier and Minister of Interior, Italy, during 1906, and 1909-10 ; Minister for Foreign Affairs, 1914-19 ; Member of Parliament (Italy), 1880 - 1919; Senator, 1920. *Publications:* Contadini in Sicilia, 1876 ; editor of the Rassegna Settimanale, 1878-1882 ; several articles in the Nuova Antologia of Rome on Politics and Economics. *Address:* 1 A. Via delle Tre Cannelle, Rome. *T.:* 13-63.
(*Died 24 Nov. 1922.*)

SOOTHILL, Alfred, B.A. (Lond.); Headmaster of Ashville College, Harrogate, since 980

1905; *b.* 25 July 1863 ; *s.* of William Soothill, Halifax ; *m.* Emma, *y. d.* of late Rev. Richard Gray, Darlington ; one *s.* one *d.* *Educ.:* private School, Halifax; London University; United Methodist College, Victoria Park, Manchester. United Methodist Minister from 1885-1905 ; having Pastorates at Bow, Sunderland, Leeds, Newcastle-on-Tyne. *Recreations:* music, tennis. *Address:* Ashville College, Harrogate. *T.:* Harrogate 234. (*Died 12 Sept. 1926.*)

SOUTHAM, Frederick Armitage, M.B. (Oxon), F.R.C.S.; late Examiner in Surgery, Victoria Univ.: late Examiner in Surgery, Univ. of Oxford ; Consulting Surgeon, Manchester Christie Hospital ; Consulting Surgeon, Manchester Royal Infirmary ; Consulting Surgeon, Northern Hospital for Women and Children ; Consulting Surgeon. Victoria Jewish Hospital, Manchester ; Emeritus Professor of Surgery, Victoria Univ., Manchester. *Educ.:* Oxford ; Owens College, Manchester. *Publications:* Regional Surgery, including Surgical Diagnosis ; A Manual for Students. *Address:* 13 St. John Street, and 10 Kinnaird Road, Withington, Manchester. *T.:* Manchester 1480. *M.:* ND 5871.
(*Died 9 Mar. 1927.*)

SOUTHEY, Senator Hon. Charles William, J.P., C.M.G. 1902 ; *b.* 1832 ; *s.* of late Sir Richard Southey, K.C.M.G., of Southfield, Plumstead, Cape Colony ; *m.* 1864, Georgina Greaves ; two *s.* three *d.* *Educ.:* Diocesan College, Cape Town. Entered Cape Civil Service, 1855 ; Commissioner and Resident Magistrate, Richmond, 1865 ; Alexandria, 1866 ; Middelburg, 1868 ; retired, 1870 ; farmer-thorough-bred horses, shorthorn cattle, and ostriches ; served South Africa, 1900-2 (C.M.G.) ; nominated to the Senate, 1910; received King's Medal on Act of Union. *Address:* Culmstock, Schoombie, Cape Province, South Africa. *Clubs:* Rand, Johannesburg ; Civil Service, Cape Town ; Port Elizabeth.
(*Died 30 July 1924.*)

SOUTHWARD, Rev. Walter Thomas, M.A., Mus.B. Camb. ; Fellow, Tutor, Chaplain of St. Catharine's Coll. Camb. Inter-Collegiate Lecturer in Theology ; *b.* Liverpool, 1851 ; *s.* of Jackson Southward, printer ; *m.* 1st, Ellen Bartlett, 1889 (*d.* 1898); 2nd, 1904, Ellen Banks; one *s.* *Educ.:* Liverpool Coll. 1862-71; St. Cath. Coll. Cambridge, 1871 - 75. First Class in Classics and highly distinguished in Chancellor's Medals, 1875. Master at Dulwich, 1875 ; private tutor in Liverpool, 1876 ; ordained, 1876 ; curate of Fairfield, S. Mich., Liverpool ; Huyton, 1879 ; returned to Cambridge, 1884 ; Examiner for Bell Scholarships, local examinations, previous examinations ; took charge of choir of St. Cath. Coll., 1887 ; Senior Proctor and Select Preacher, 1889 and 1898, ; Tutor of St. Cath., 1892 ; has travelled in Germany, Italy, France. *Publications:* Commentary on Acts of the Apostles in Greek ; Analysis of History of Church of England ; Musical Setting of Evening Service ; songs ; musical essays. *Recreations:* amateur photography, chamber music. *Address:* St. Catharine's College, Cambridge ; Brookfield, Newnham, Cambridge.
(*Died 4 July 1919.*)

SOUTHWELL, Rev. Herbert Burrows, Canon of Worcester Cathedral since 1912 ; married. *Educ.:* Charterhouse ; Pembroke Coll. Oxford (2nd class Lit. Hum. ; 2nd class Theology ; Denyer and Johnson Theological Scholar, 1881). Ordained 1881 ; Curate of St. Mary the Virgin, Oxford ; Chaplain to the late Bishop Lightfoot, 1881 ; Principal of Lichfield Theological College, 1885, and Prebendary of Lichfield Cathedral, 1887 ; Principal of Bishop Jacob Hostel, and Canon of the Cathedral, Newcastle-on-Tyne, 1901-12. *Address:* The College, Worcester. (*Died 9 April 1922.*)

SOWTEE, Ven. Francis Briggs; Prebendary of Highworth Sarum, 1903-27 ; Canon

SOMERSET, John Henry William. See page xxx.

Residentiary of Sarum, 1910 - 16 ; Bishop's Chaplain, 1903 ; *m.* 1877. *Educ. :* Corpus Christi Coll., Camb. (Scholar). Rector of Corscombe, Dorset, 1877-84 ; Vicar of Holy Trinity, Weymouth, 1884-90 ; Vicar of Fleet, Dorset, 1886-90 ; Archdeacon of Dorset, 1889-1901 ; Rector of Holy Trinity, Dorchester, 1895-98 ; Rural Dean, 1895-98. *Address :* 17 The Close, Salisbury.

(*Died 10 Sept.* 1928.)

SPALDING, Colonel Warner, C.M.G. 1885 ; *b.* Portsmouth, 1 May 1844 ; *e. s.* of late Col. R. C. Spalding, Royal Marines; *m.* 2nd,1884, La Valette, *d.* of late James Keele of Sydney ; three *s.* four *d. Educ. :* Royal Naval School, New Cross. Royal Marine Cadet, H.M.S. Excellent, 1860-61 ; Lieutenant Royal Marines, 1862-69 ; Captain New South Wales Permanent Artillery,1871, and Adjutant Volunteer Artillery, Colonel commanding New South Wales Artillery Forces, 1892-96 ; Acting Commandant New South Wales Forces, 1892 ; Chief Magistrate Norfolk Island, 1896-98 ; present at bombardment of batteries by English and French fleets at Simonoseiki, Japan ; carried colours—Royal Marines—during assault and capture of batteries, etc., 1864 ; Soudan Expedition (Suakim), 1885, second in command New South Wales contingent (despatches, brevet of Colonel, C.M.G., medal with clasp, Khedive's star). *Recreations :* motoring, shooting. *Address :* Valetta, Macksville, Nambucca River, N.S. Wales, Australia. (*Died 22 Aug.* 1920.)

SPEAR, Sir John Ward, Kt. *cr.* 1911; M.P. (L.U.) West or Tavistock Division of Devonshire, 1900-6 and 1910-18 ; Alderman of Devon County Council ; J.P. ; President of Poor Law Union Association for England and Wales ; Trustee of Tavistock Hospital ; Member of Tavistock Board of Guardians ; Nonconformist ; Income Tax Commissioner ; *b.* 1848; *m.* 1877, *d.* of John Willcock of Kingsbridge; one *s.* two *d. Educ. :* Duke of Bedford's School, Milton Abbott; Bodmin. *Address :* Venn, Tavistock. *Club :* St. Stephens'.(*Died 27 April* 1921.)

SPEARMAN, Edmund Robert, C.M.G. 1901 ; Acting 1st Secretary in Diplomatic Service ; Vice-Consul at Chantilly since 1901 ; *b.* 10 May 1837 ; 2nd *s.* of Rt. Hon. Sir A. Y. Spearman, 1st Bt. ; *m.* 1859, Lady Maria Louisa Fitzmaurice, 3rd *d.* of 5th Earl of Orkney ; two *d. Educ. :* Eton ; France ; Germany. Entered Public Service, 1854 ; Assist. Secretary Public Works Loan Board and West Indian Islands Relief Board, 1860 ; Secretary, 1880-85; Assist. Delegate, International Penitentiary Congress, Paris, 1895 ; Representative in Paris of the Royal Commission for Paris Exhibition, 1898-1901; late Capt. Middlesex Yeomanry ; J.P. Middlesex, 1863. *Publications:* articles in most of leading English and American Reviews. *Recreations :* gardening, shooting. *Address :* Chantilly, France. *Club :* Sports.

(*Died 6 Oct.* 1918.)

SPEARMAN, Sir Joseph Layton Elmes, 2nd Bt., *cr.* 1840 ; J.P., D.L. ; *b.* Holmer, near Hereford, 22 Sep. 1857 ; *s.* of late A. Y. Spearman and Betha, *d.* of late Sir Joseph Bailey, 1st Bt. ; *S.* grandfather 1874 ; *m.* 1st, 1878, Ethel (*d.* 1909), *d.* of William Leask, 48 Queen's Gate ; three *s.* five *d.* ; 2nd, 1914, Carrie, *d.* of late F. Eastwood and *widow* of Richard Sykes, Denver, U.S.A. *Educ. :* Eton ; Brasenose Coll. Oxford. *Recreations :* hunting, shooting, golf. *Heir :* s. Joseph William [*b.* 22 Aug. 1879]. *Address :* Grove House, Bexhill. *Club :* Junior Carlton.

(*Died 11 Feb.* 1922.)

SPECK, Rev. Jocelyn Henry, Hon. Canon of St. Alban's ; Vicar of St. Paul's, Bedford, and Hon. Warden of Diocesan Deaconesses Home ; Chaplain at Depôt, Kempton Barracks ; *s.* of Rev. Edward J. Speck and Anna Katherine Lally ; *m.* Rosalie Dalrymple ; one *s.* two *d. Educ. :* Marlborough ;

Worcester College, Oxford, M.A. Formerly Proctor in Convocation ; resigned, 1919. *Address :* St. Paul's Vicarage, Bedford.

(*Died 9 July* 1922.)

SPEER, Rear-Adm. F. Shirley Litchfield-, R.N., C.M.G. 1917 ; D.S.O. 1916 ; Superintendent of Sheerness Dockyard since 1919 ; *b.* 24 Mar. 1874 ; *e. s.* of Frederick Litchfield [assumed additional name of Speer by Royal Licence, 1915] ; *m.* 1902, Marianne Frances Cecilia, *e. d.* of late Edward F. Sandys; five *s. Educ. :* Stubbington House, Fareham ; H.M.S. Britannia. Entered R.N. 1887 ; Commander, 1905 ; Capt. 1911 ; in Command of Mine-layer Squadron, 1915-17 (despatches); Deputy Director of Mining, Admiralty, 1918-19. *Address :* Wateringbury Place, Wateringbury, Kent. *Club :* United Service. (*Died 31 May* 1922.)

SPEIGHT, Thomas Wilkinson, novelist and magazinist; *b.* Liverpool, 3 Apr. 1830 [of North Country parentage, progenitors for several generations being natives of Cumberland or Westmorland]. *Educ. :* Sandys' School, Kendal. Forty years in the service of the Midland Railway Company, retired 1887. *Publications :* Brought to Light, 1867 ; In the Dead of Night, 1874 ; A Secret of the Sea, 1875 ; Mysteries of Heron Dyke, 1880 ; Fate of the Hara Diamond, 1891 ; A Guilty Silence, 1892 ; The Grey Monk, 1895 ; Master of Trenance, 1896 ; Heart of a Mystery, 1896 ; A Minion of the Moon, 1897 ; The Secret of Wyvern Towers, 1898 ; Mora, 1899 ; Juggling Fortune, 1900 ; A Late Repentance, 1901 ; As it was Written, 1902 ; The Sport of Chance, 1903 ; By Fate's Caprice ; Stepping Blindfold ; The Celestial Ruby, 1904 ; The Plotters, 1905 ; Under a Cloud, 1906 ; Time Bargains, 1907 ; Price of a Secret, 1908 ; Ursula Lenorme, 1909 ; Tangled Lives, 1910 ; Foiled, 1911 ; Oh the Fringe 1911 ; one-act plays—Salt Tears, and A Close Shave ; writer of The Gentleman's Annual from 1885-1902, each number containing a complete novel. *Address :* 212 Mount Pleasant Road, Tottenham. (*Died 1 Jan.* 1915.)

SPEIR, Robert Thomas Napier, J.P., D.L. Renfrewshire and Perthshire, of Culdees, Co. Perth, and Blackstone and Burnbrae, Co. Renfrew ; *o. s.* of Robert Speir of Culdees and Burnbrae, and Mary, *d.* of Sir William Milliken Napier of Milliken ; *b.* 15 Oct. 1841 ; *m.* 1868, Hon. Emily Gifford, 3rd *d.* of 2nd Baron Gifford ; four *s.* two *d. Educ. :* Eton ; Christ Church, Oxford. For forty years Chairman of the Executive Committee and Home Mission Board of the Scottish Episcopal Church ; was Captain in 4th Batt. Argyll and Sutherland Highlanders. *Publications:* one of the Essays on Church Reform, edited by the Bishop of Birmingham. *Address :* Culdees, Muthill. Perthshire.

(*Died 3 April* 1922.)

SPENCE, Col. Gilbert Ormerod, C.B. 1921 ; D.S.O. 1917 ; T.D. ; J.P. N.R. Yorks, 1914 ; D.L. County of Durham ; Vice-Chairman Durham Territorial Association ; *b.* 1879 ; *o. s.* of Henry Grant Spence, J.P., of Elmwood, Hartburn, Stockton-on-Tees ; unmarried. *Educ. :* Uppingham. Col.-Commandant commanding the Durham L.I. Brigade, T.A. ; Hon. Col. 5th Batt. Durham L.I. ; served European War, 1914-18 (wounded, despatches thrice, D.S.O.); formerly Director of Richardson, Duck & Co., shipbuilders. *Recreations :* agricultural and county pursuits. *Address :* Far End, Kirklevington, Yarm - on - Tees. *T. :* Eaglescliffe 50. *Clubs :* Junior Army and Navy, Kennel.

(*Died 28 Nov.* 1925.)

SPENCE, James Knox, C.S.I. 1898 ; *b.* 10 Dec. 1844 ; *s.* of Gen. J. K. Spence, I.S.C. ; *m.* 1882, Emma, *d.* of G. W. Hemming, K.C. *Educ. :* Cheltenham. Bombay Civil Service, 1865-1900 ; from 1878-80 was in Postal Department ; Political Agent, Koluba, 1885 ; Senior Collector,

Bombay, 1888 ; Commissioner. 1891 ; Member, Legislative Council, 1895, 1897, and 1898 ; Member of Gov.-Gen.'s Legislative Council, 1899-1900. *Address :* 6 Connaught Square, W.
(Died 15 Feb. 1919.)

SPENCE, John Bowring ; H.B.M.'s Consul-General, Tripoli of Barbary, since 1914 ; *b.* 26 Feb. 1861 ; *s.* of late B. E. Spence, Sculptor, Rome, and Rosina Gower : *m.* 1895, Costanza (*d.* 1912), *d.* of Count Bentivoglio Middleton of Rome ; two *s. Educ. :* Dulwich College. Pro-Consul, Leghorn, 1887-90 ; International Customs Tariffs Bureau, Brussels, 1891-95 ; Vice-Consul, Madrid, 1895-97 ; Consul, Madeira, 1897-1905 ; Consul and Consul-General, Trieste, 1905-14. *Address :* British Consulate-General, Tripoli, N. Africa. *Club :* Constitutional.
(Died 26 Feb. 1918.)

SPENCE, Thomas William Leisk, C.B. 1912 ; J.P. ; *b.* 1845 ; *s.* of late Basil Spence, Raefirth, Shetland ; *m.* 1876, Henrietta Fanny, 3rd *d.* of R. J. Hebden, of Eday, Orkney ; and Ely Grange, Sussex. Was Secretary to General Board of Lunacy for Scotland, 1888-1911. *Address :* 30 Comely Bank, Edinburgh ; Uyea, Uyeasound. Shetland.*(Died 9 Nov. 1923.)*

SPENCE-JONES, Very Rev. Henry Donald Maurice, D.D. ; Dean of Gloucester since 1886 ; Professor of Ancient History in the Royal Academy, 1906 ; *b.* Pall Mall, 14 Jan. 1836 ; *e. s.* of late George Spence, Q.C., M.P. ; *m.* Louise, *d.* of David Jones, M.P. Pantglás, Carmarthenshire, 1871 ; one *s. Educ. :* Westminster School ; Cambridge (M.A.) ; D.D. honoris causâ. 1st class Theological Tripos, 1865 ; Carus University Prizeman, 1862 ; Carus and Scholefield University Prizeman, 1865 ; Professor Eng. Lit. and Hebrew Lecturer, St. David's Coll. Lampeter, 1865-70 ; Rector of St. Mary de Crypt, Gloucester, 1870-77 ; Principal Gloucester Theol. Coll. 1875-77 ; Hon. Canon Gloucester, 1875 ; Examining Chaplain to Bishop of Gloucester and Bristol, 1871-86 ; Vicar and Rural Dean of St. Pancras, London, 1877-86; Select Preacher, Camb. 1883, 1887, 1901, 1905 ; Oxford, 1892, 1903 ; J.P. Cardiganshire. *Publications :* editor of Pulpit Commentary (47 vols.), author of Commentary on St. Luke (2 vols., Pulpit Commentary) ; on 1 Samuel, and Pastoral Epistles in Bishop Ellicott's Commentary ; on Acts, in Anglo-American Commentary ; The Teaching of the Apostles, Greek Text, with Translation and Notes ; Introduction to Talmudical Commentary on Genesis ; Dreamland and History, the Chronicle of the Norman Dukes ; Cloister Life in Days of Cœur de Lion ; The Church of England : a History for the People—vol. i. British or Saxon Church ; vol. ii. The Mediæval Church ; vol. iii. the Reformation ; vol. iv. The Anglican Church ; The White Robe of Churches of the Eleventh Century ; Early Christianity and Paganism : a History, A.D. 64-320 ; The Golden Age of the Church (studies in the 4th century) ; The Early Christians in Rome, 1910 ; contributor to Quarterly Review, Contemporary, Good Words, Quiver, English Illustrated Magazine, etc. *Recreation :* favourite amusement is working at mediæval ecclesiastical architecture, in his leisure moments. *Address :* The Deanery, Gloucester ; Pantglás, Caermarthenshire. *Club :* Athenæum.
(Died 2 Nov. 1917.)

SPENCER, 6th Earl (*cr.* 1765). **Rt. Hon. Charles Robert Spencer,** P.C., M.A. ; G.C.V.O., *cr.* 1911 ; K.G. 1913 ; Lord Chamberlain to H.M., 1905-12 ; Baron Spencer, Viscount, 1761 ; Viscount Althorp, 1765 ; Lord-Lieutenant of Northants, 1908 ; *b.* 30 Oct. 1857 ; *o. s.* of 4th Earl by his second wife, Adelaide, *o. d.* of late Sir Horace Beauchamp Seymour ; *S. half-b.* 1910 ; *m.* 1887, Hon. Margaret Baring (*d.* 1906), *d.* of 1st Baron Revelstoke ; three *s.* three *d. Educ. :* Harrow ; Trin. Coll.

Cambridge (M.A.). M.P. N. Northants, 1880-1885 ; Mid Northants, 1885-95 ; contested East Herts, 1898 ; Parliamentary Groom-in-Waiting to the Queen, 1886 ; Vice-Chamberlain, 1892-95 ; M.P. (L.) Mid Northants, 1900-5 ; *cr.* Viscount Althorp, 1905 ; Grand Cross, Danebrog, 1906. Owns about 20,000 acres. *Heir : s.* Viscount Althorp. *Address :* Althorp, Northampton ; North Creake, Fakenham, Norfolk ; 28 St. James's Place. S.W.1. *T. :* Regent 1089. *Clubs :* Brooks's. Turf. *(Died 26 Sept. 1922.)*

SPENCER, Rev. Arthur John, M.A., F.R.G.S. ; Rector of Drayton with Hellesdon, Norwich, since 1904 ; Rural Dean of Taverham ; Hon. Canon of Norwich ; Chaplain 1st Class, Territorials, T.D. ; Surrogate ; *b.* 18 June 1850 ; *s.* of John Spencer, barrister-at-law, and afterwards Vicar of Eastwood, Essex, and Margaret, *d.* of Rev. E. Penny, Master at Charterhouse, and afterwards Rector of Great Stambridge, Essex ; *m.* 1st, Jane Anne (*d.* 1914), *d.* of John Hugh Bainbridge of Frankfield, Co. Cork ; 2nd, Agnes Elizabeth, widow of Rev. Thomas Carpenter, Rector of Thwaite. *Educ. :* Uppingham ; Trin. Coll. Camb. ; Wells Theological College. Curate in Charge of St. John's, Great Yarmouth ; Vicar of Hinckley ; Vicar of Christ Church, Chelsea ; Vicar of Eye, Suffolk. *Recreations :* golf, etc. *Address :* Drayton Rectory, Norwich. *T.A. :* Rectory, Drayton, Norfolk. *T. :* Drayton 4. *M. :* 714. *Club :* Norfolk, Norwich. *(Died 24 Aug. 1922.)*

SPENCER, Augustus, A.R.C.A. London ; Principal and Headmaster of the Royal College of Art, Board of Education, South Kensington ; 1900-20 ; *b.* Silsden, Yorkshire, 18 April 1860 ; 7th *s.* of John Spencer ; unmarried. *Educ. :* Keighley Grammar School and School of Art. Entered Royal College of Art with a Scholarship, 1881 ; Headmaster of the School of Art, Coalbrookdale, Shropshire, 1885 ; Headmaster of the School of Art, Leicester, 1888 ; New School of Art erected 1897, when the School became municipalized ; same year all Board Schools in Leicester affiliated to School of Art, from which a new Drawing Syllabus was issued for them. *Club :* Arts. *(Died 3 Oct. 1924.)*

SPENCER, Hugh, C.I.E. 1909 ; F.R.G.S., F.Z.S., I.C.S., retired ; *b.* 1867; *s.* of late Charles Innes Spencer, M.I.C.E. ; *m.* 1911, Mowbray, *d.* of late William Smith, J.P., Sundon House, Clifton, Gluco. *Educ. :* Bristol Grammar School ; Magdalen College, Oxford. Entered I.C.S. 1888 ; Magistrate and Collector, retired 1915 ; Hindustani and Hindi Censor, Cairo, 1915-19. *Address :* 5 Clifton Gardens, W.9. *T. :* Paddington 718. *Club :* East India United Service.
(Died 14 Jan. 1926.)

SPENCER-SMITH, Michael Seymour, D.S.O. 1919 ; M.C. ; partner in H. S. Lefevre & Co., 16 Bishopsgate, E.C. ; a Director of the Bank of England since 1920 ; *b.* 1881 ; *y. s.* of late Rev. Spencer Compton Spencer-Smith, Kingston Vicarage, Dorset ; *m.* 1907, Evelyn Penelope, *y. d.* of Rev. Arthur Delmé-Radcliffe ; two *s.* one *d. Educ. :* Eton ; New College, Oxford. Started in business, 1903 ; spent nine years in Japan ; joined Army, Aug. 1914 ; served in King's Royal Rifle Corps and on staff of Canadian Corps Heavy Artillery ; Promoted Lt.-Colonel and employed as A.A. and Q.M.G. Murmansk 1918 (despatches, D.S.O., M.C.). *Address :* Norman House, Stansted, Essex. *Club :* Bath. *(Died 20 Jan. 1928.)*

SPENDER, Arthur Edmund, Editor of the Shrewsbury Chronicle since 1922 ; *b.* London, 26 Oct. 1871 ; *surv. s.* of late Edward Spender (known as the Prince of the Lobby, founder of the first London Letter for the provincial newspapers, co-founder of the Western Morning News), and Mrs. Ellen Spender, *d.* of late Dr. Edmund E. Rendle,

SPENCER, Ven. George.   See page xxx.

Plymouth; *m.* 1905, Helen Frances, *d.* of late Arthur Champernowne, Dartington Hall, Devon; four *s.* three *d. Educ.:* Radley; Christ Church, Oxford. Honours in History finals, 1894; called to Bar, Inner Temple, 1895; Tour round the world, 1896; Managing Director Western Morning News, 1900-22; Member of the Moseley Education Commission to the United States, 1903; Special Correspondent for the Winter Sports in Norway, 1902; Mayor of Plymouth, 1908-9; Magistrate of Plymouth, 1911; President Port of Plymouth Chamber of Commerce, 1912; Captain Territorial Reserve Force, Devon Regiment, 1915; President of the Newspaper Society, 1916; Chairman of the Press Association, 1917. *Publications:* Two Winters in Norway; Random Notes on the Moseley Education Commission; Impressions on Finland (pamphlet), 1920. *Recreation:* gardening. *Address:* The Limes, Shrewsbury. *T.:* Shrewsbury 162.   *(Died 6 July 1923.)*

SPENDER, E. Harold; Commander Greek Order of the Redeemer; LL.D.(Athens); F.R.G.S.; author, journalist and lecturer; *b.* Bath, 22 June 1864; *s.* of late Dr. and Mrs. J. K. Spender, novelist; *m.* 1904, Violet Hilda (*d.* 1921), *d.* of late Ernest Schuster, K.C.; three *s.* one *d. Educ.:* Bath College (Head Boy, 1882 - 83); Exhibitioner of University College, Oxford. 1st in Mods. 1884; 1st in Lit. Hum. 1887; M.A.; on staff of the Echo, 1887-89; Lecturer for Oxford Univ. Extension Delegacy, 1889-92; on staff of the Pall Mall Gazette, 1891-93 : Westminster Gazette, 1893-95 ; Daily Chronicle, 1895-99 ; Manchester Guardian, 1899-1900 ; Daily News, 1900-14. During the war gave himself up to war savings propaganda, volunteering, and other war activities, 1914-1918; contested Bath as United Liberal candidate, General Election, Nov. 1922; Chairman of Social Welfare Council, Hampstead. *Publications:* Story of the Home Rule Session, 1893; At the Sign of the Guillotine, 1895 ; Through the High Pyrenees, 1898 ; The Arena, 1906 ; Home Rule, 1912; In Praise of Switzerland, 1912; The Call of the Siren, 1913 ; One Man Returns, 1914 ; The Flame of Daring, 1915 ; The Dividing Sword, 1916 ; The Man Who Went, 1919 ; three biographies—Herbert Henry Asquith, 1915; General Botha, 1916 ; David Lloyd George, 1920 ; A Briton in America, 1921; Byron and Greece, 1924; Men and Mansions, 1924; The Cauldron of Europe, 1925; numerous short stories and magazine articles. *Recreations:* mountaineering, travelling, golfing. *Address:* 10 Frognal, Hampstead, N.W.3. *T.:* Hampstead 3137. *Clubs:* National Liberal, Alpine, Whitefriars ; Wimbledon Park Golf.
                (Died 15 April 1926.)

SPICER, Sir Howard, K.B.E., *cr.* 1918; papermaker and wholesale stationer; Vice-Chairman and Joint Managing Director of Spicers, Limited; Director of United Newspapers, Ltd., and Edinburgh Evening News; *b.* 1872 ; *e. s.* of late James Spicer of Eltham; *m.* 1st, 1896, Muriel, *d.* of Rev. S. B. Handley; 2nd, 1923, Ethel Anne, *o. d.* of Frederick Marsh. *Educ.:* Leys School, Cambridge; privately on the Continent. *Publications:* editor, Sandow's Magazine, 1899-1901; resigned to edit Boys of Our Empire, 1901 ; co-founder, Boys Empire League ; editor, Sports Library, The Girls' Empire ; author of Sports for Boys, Sports for Girls ; general articles. *Recreations:* riding, travelling. *Address:* 12 Elm Tree Road, St. John's Wood, N.W.8. *Clubs:* Reform, Kennel, Royal Automobile, 1920. *(Died 16 Aug. 1926.)*

SPICER, John Edmund Philip, J.P. ; *b.* 1850 ; *e. s.* of late John William Gooch Spicer and Juliana Hannah Webb, *d.* of late Rev. Edmund Probyn, of Longhope, Co. Gloucester ; *m.* 1888, Lady Margaret Mary Fane, *y. d.* of 12th Earl of Westmorland ; five *s. Heir: s.* Anthony Napier Fane, *b.* 1891. *Educ.:* Wellington. High Sheriff, Wilts, 1889 ; Patron of one living ; late Captain, 1st Life Guards. *Address:* Spye Park, Chippenham. *T. A.:* Spye Park, Bromham. *Club:* Arthur's[*Died 31 Mar. 1928.*]

SPICER, Rev. Canon John Maurice, Vicar of Kirk-Malew since 1895 ; Canon of St. Columba since 1912 ; ordained 1885 ; Curate of Kirk-Michael, 1885-87 ; Chaplain, Laxey, 1887-95. *Address:* Malew Vicarage, Ballasalla, Isle of Man.   *(Died 12 Aug. 1930.)*

SPICER, Robert Henry Scanes, M.D. London : specialist for nose, throat, and ear affections : Consulting Surgeon Diseases of the Throat, St. Mary's Hospital ; Hon. Phys. Royal Soc. of Musicians of Great Britain ; President Sect. of Laryng. and Otol. British Med. Assoc. 1900 ; *e. s.* of late Robert H. S. Spicer, M.D., of North Molton, Devon, and *g.s.* of late Robert Spicer of Exeter ; *m.* Mary Wilhelmina Huelin ; one *s.* two *d.* Won Open Natural Science Scholarship at St. Mary's Hospital; Anatomical Scholar and Demonstrator; Gold Medal Society of Apothecaries ; graduated M.B. and B.Sc. in honours ; afterwards visited leading throat clinics in Vienna, Berlin, and Paris ; M.R.C.S. ; Fellow Royal Society of Medicine ; one of the founders, jointly first Secretary, and later Vice-Pres. Laryng. Soc. of Lond.; one of founders of Otolog. Society of Great Britain. *Publications:* numerous technical pamphlets and contributions to medical press on diseases of throat, nose, and ear, cancer, and physical education. *Recreations:* country life, travel, literature, music, and theatre. *Address:* 26 Graham Street, Eaton Square, S.W.1. *T.:* Victoria 9309.
                (Died 18 June 1925.)

SPIELMANN, Sir Isidore, Kt., *cr.* 1905 ; C.M.G. 1907; F.S.A.; Commander of Order of the Crown of Belgium; Grand Cordon of Order of the Crown of Italy ; Officer of Order of Leopold; *b.* London, 21 July 1854; *e. surv. s.* of Adam Spielmann; *m.* 1879, Emily, *d.* of Sir J. Sebag-Montefiore ; one *s.* three *d. Educ.:* privately in England. Director for Art, Board of Trade (Exhibitions Branch) ; Executive Committe National Art-Collections Fund ; Member of Advisory Council, Victoria and Albert Museum ; a Governor, British Institute Industrial Art, Boards of Trade and Education ; assisted the promotion of the Stuart, Tudor, Guelph, Early Italian, Venetian, Spanish, and other Art Exhibitions ; Hon. Sec. and Delegate of the British Commission Fine Art Section, Brussels Intl. Exhibition, 1897 ; Sec. and Delegate of the British Fine Art Section Royal Commission, Paris Intl. Exhibition, 1900, and British Juror for Decoration ; Hon. Sec. (London) Fine Art Section, Glasgow Intl. Exhibition, 1901 ; Representative in Great Britain for the Belgian Govt. Exhibitions of Early Flemish Art, Bruges, 1902 ; the Toison d'Or, Bruges; Early Belgian Art, Brussels, 1910 ; International Miniature Exhibition, Brussels, 1912 ; Hon. Sec. and Member Art Committee, and Hon. Assist. Sec. Royal Commission St. Louis Intl. Exhibition, 1904 ; Member British Government Committee and Director for Art, British Government Exhibit and an Executive Commissioner New Zealand International Exhibition, 1906-7 ; Member Departmental Committee to inquire into and report to Government upon British participation in International Exhibitions, 1907; Commissioner for Art, Franco-British Exhibition, 1908 ; Member of Royal Commission for the Brussels International Exhibition, 1910, and Turin International Exhibition, 1911 ; Commissioner-General for Great Britain, Rome International Fine Arts Exhibition, 1911 ; Director, Exhibition of British Arts and Crafts, Louvre, Paris, 1914 ; Member Spanish Art Exhibition, Burlington House, 1920 ;

Council British Empire Exhibition, 1924; an Executive Commissioner New Zealand Exhibition, 1926; Member of Council of Imperial Society of Knights Bachelors. *Publications:* The Royal Pavilion (illustrated), Paris International Exhibition, 1900; The British Section at the St. Louis Exhibition, 1904, at the New Zealand International Exhibition, and International Fine Art Exhibition, Rome, 1911 (all illustrated); The Fine Art Section, Franco-British Exhibition (illustrated); The Germans, as others see them; Open letters to Herr Max Harden, 1917 and 1918; Germany's Impending Doom, 1918. *Recreation:* interest in Art Exhibitions, especially for the furtherance of British Art. *Address:* 56 Westbourne Terrace, Hyde Park, W.2. *T.:* Paddington 1931. *Club:* Arts.   (*Died 10 May 1925.*)

SPIERS, R. Phene, F.S.A., F.R.I.B.A.; architect; Corresponding mem. of the Institute of France; Associate and Fellow of King's Coll. London; Past President of Architectural Association; Hon. and Corresponding member of the Société centrale des Architectes, Paris; Sociedad de los Arquitectos, Madrid, and Hon. Associate American Institute of Architects. *Educ.:* King's Coll. London; École des Beaux Arts, Paris. Gold Medallist; Scholar and Travelling Student of the Royal Academy; Soane Medallist and Travelling Student of the Royal Institute of British Architects; architect of two Board Schools, London—Lord Monkswell's house on Chelsea Embankment—Locke Park, Barnsley—and of painters' studios in various parts of London. *Publications:* re-edited Pugin's Normandy in 1870; Fergusson's History of Architecture, 1893; author of works on Architectural Drawing, 1887; The Orders of Architecture, 1902; The Architecture of Greece and Rome, 1907; Architectural Essays on Sassanian Architecture; Domed Churches in Périgord; Mosque at Damascus; Architecture, East and West; and other subjects. *Recreations:* archæology, chiefly of eastern lands; delineation in pencil and colour of ancient architecture; study of Japanese art. *Address:* 21 Bernard Street, Russell Square, W.C. *Club:* Arts.   (*Died 3 Oct. 1916.*)

SPINNEY, George Franklin; President and manager Daily and Sunday Globe, St. Paul, Minnesota, U.S.A.; *b.* Great Falls, New Hampshire, 9 July 1852; *m. Educ.:* Public Schools, Lawrence, Massachusetts. Printer; proofreader; foreman; reporter; political correspondent; managing editor and publisher of The New York Times, New York City. *Recreation:* newspaper business. *Clubs:* Press, New York; Minnesota. Commercial, St. Paul.

SPITTA, Edmund Johnson, L.R.C.P. (Lond.), M.R.C.S.(Eng.), 1874; President of Quekett Microscopical Club, 1904-8; Past Pres. Brighton and Hove Natural History and Philosophical Society; Past Vice-President Royal Astronomical Society, and of Royal Microscopical Society; Chairman of the Sussex County Survey; *b.* Clapham, 1853; *s.* of R. J. Spitta, M.D. (London); *m.* 1876, Francis Catherine Dacre; one *s.* two *d. Educ.:* Clapham Grammar School; privately. Entered St. George's Hospital, 1870; Senior Demonstrator of Anatomy, 1873-74; four years prizeman, St. George's Hospital Medical School; Ophthalmic Assistant, St. George's Hospital, 1874; made hon. perpetual pupil, St. Thomas's Hospital, 1874; also studied at Middlesex Hospital and Children's Hospital, Great Ormond Street; commenced practice at Clapham, 1875; retired from Clapham, 1905. *Publications:* article Kidney, Gray's Anatomy, 1874; (joint-author) An Atlas of Bacteriology, 1898; Photomicrography, 1899; Microscopy, 1907, 1909, and 1920; silver medal for contributions to Photomicrography, Paris Exhibition, 1900;

984

and gold medal, St. Louis Exhibition, 1908. *Address:* 41 Ventnor Villas, Hove, Sussex. *T.:* Hove 8876.   (*Died 21 Jan. 1921.*)

SPITTELER, Carl Friedrich Georg; Author; Winner of Nobel prize for literature, 1919; *b.* Liestal, Baselland, Switzerland, 24 April 1845; *m.* Marie Op den Hooff of The Hague; two *d. Educ.:* Basel, Zürich and Heidelberg Universities. Hon. Ph.D. Zürich and Lausanne Universities; Hon. Member of Société des gens de lettres, Paris; Officer of Order of Leopold II., Belgium, Commandeur de la Légion d'Honneur, France, etc.; tutor in Russia, 1871-79, afterwards contributor to various leading Swiss newspapers. *Publications:* Prometheus and Epimetheus, 2 vols., 1881; Schmetterlinge (Butterflies, lyrics); Conrad der Leutnant (French trans.); Imago (a novel, French trans.); Literarische Gleichnisse (Literary Parallels); Balladen (poems); Die Mädchenfeinde (French trans., Les Misogynes); Glockenlieder; Der Olympische Frühling, (1st ed. 1900-3), several times revised; Lachende Wahrheiten, 1898; Meine frühesten Erlebnisse, (autobiography, 1914); Unser Schweizer Standpunkt (Our Swiss Standpoint, a warning to Swiss against the influence of the foreign press), 1914. *Recreation:* pianoforte playing. *Address:* 12 Gesegnetmatt Strasse, Lucerne, Switzerland.   (*Died 29 Dec. 1924.*)

SPOKES, Arthur Hewett, Recorder of Reading since 1894; *b.* 28 June 1854; 2nd *s.* of late Sir Peter Spokes; *m.* Ethel Mary, *d.* of Arthur Gurney, Russell House, Balham, 1892. *Educ.:* University College, London (Fellow); B.A., B.Sc., LL.B., London. Matriculated 3rd in Honours, University of Lond., 1870; Gilchrist Scholarship, Univ. Hall, 1870; Andrews Entrance Scholarship, Univ. Coll. 1870; 1st year, 1871; 2nd year, 1872; Jews' Commemoration Scholarship, Univ. Coll. 1870; Studentship Jurisprudence and International Law, Inns of Court, 1875; called to the Bar, 1875; Recorder of Newbury, 1893. *Address:* 6 St. Andrew's Place, Park Square, N.W.1; *T.:* Museum 574; 5 Pump Court, Temple, E.C.4; *T.:* Central 2532.   (*Died 7 Dec. 1922.*)

SPONG, Major Charles Stuart, D.S.O. 1898; *b.* Faversham, Kent, 12 June 1859; *s.* of W. Nash Spong, F.R.C.S.; *m.* 1900, Mary Barnsley, *o. d.* of late Henry Y. Pickering of Titusville, Penn.; one *d. Educ.:* Epsom College; Guy's Hospital. F.R.C.S. Eng.; B.Sc. London. Joined army as surgeon, 1887; seconded to Egyptian Army, 1890; served through Soudan Campaign as S.M.O. to 1st Egyptian Brigade (despatches four times, D.S.O., English Soudan medal, 4th class Medjidie and Egyptian Soudan medal with 6 clasps); World War, 1916 (despatches). *Address:* Saugata, Clarens, Vaud, Switzerland. *Club:* Army and Navy.   (*Died 12 July 1925.*)

SPOOR, Rt. Hon. Benjamin Charles, P.C. 1924; O.B.E. 1918; M.P. (Lab.) Bishop Auckland Division of Durham since Dec. 1918; a Member of the Executive Council of the Labour Party, 1919; *b.* 2 June 1878; *m.* 1st, 1900, Annie Louisa (*d.* 1920), *d.* of William Leyburn, Bishop Auckland; 2nd, 1923, Ann Mary, *d.* of James Fraser, Wrexham. Parliamentary Secretary to Treasury, 1924; Chief Whip of Labour Party, 1924-25.   (*Died 22 Dec. 1928.*)

SPRAGGE, Lt.-Col. Basil Edward, D.S.O. 1887; Gentleman-at-arms; J.P. County of Suffolk; *s.* of late F. H. Spragge, J.P., of Paignton, Devon; *b.* 9 Oct. 1852; *m.* 1892, Anne Ingham, *d.* of late Edward Brook of Hoddom, Dumfriesshire; three *s.* one *d. Educ.:* Cheltenham College; Trinity College, Cambridge. Joined 51st Light Infantry, 1872; Major, 1889; retired, 1894; adjutant of regiment, 1879-85; on staff Quartermaster - General's Department, India, 1885 - 89; served in Jowaki Expedition, 1877, as orderly officer to Brig.-Gen. Doran (medal with clasp); in 1st Afghan War, 1878-79, as Supt. Army Signalling (despatches); 2nd Afghan War, 1879-80, as adjutant to regiment (despatches, medal with clasp); Burmah War, 1885-89, as D.A.A.G. (despatches twice, medal with two clasps, Brevet Major, and D.S.O.); served with Yeomanry Cav. in S. Africa, 1900, in command of a regiment (medal 3 clasps); raised and commanded 2/1 Loyal Suffolk Hussars, 1914-16; served on the Staff IV. Army Corps B.E.F. 1917-18. *Address:* Denbie, Lockerbie, Dumfriesshire. *Clubs:* Naval and Military, Royal Cruising, Garden. *(Died 12 Feb. 1926.)*

SPRAGGE, Brig.-Gen. Charles Henry, C.B. 1898; J.P.; *b.* 8 March 1842; *s.* of F. H. Spragge, J.P. Co. Devon; *m.* 1st, 1869, Esther E. (*d.* 1903), *d.* of Hon. George Moss; two *s.* two *d.*; 2nd, F. J., widow of W. H. Rawson of Bramhope. *Educ.:* Cheltenham College. Entered Royal Artillery, 1860; retired, 1899; was General commanding the Royal Artillery during the Tirah Campaign, 1897-98; present at the actions of Chagra Kotal, Sampagha, and Arhunga Passes, occupation of Maidan, operations in Bazaar Valley and Khyber Pass (medal and two clasps, despatches, C.B.). Special reward for distinguished and meritorious service: Hon. Col. 4th Wessex Brigade R.F.A. since 1909. *Address:* The Quinta, Babbacombe, South Devon; 8 Pont Street, S.W. *T.:* Victoria 5897. *Club:* Wellington.
(Died 9 Jan. 1920.)

SPRAGUE, Thomas Bond, M.A. Camb.; LL.D. St. Andrews; F.I.A., Hon. F.F.A.; *b.* 29 Mar. 1830; *s.* of Thomas Sprague, London, wholesale stationer; *m.* 1st, Margaret Vaughan, *y. d.* of James Steains, Liverpool, tea merchant; four *s.* four *d.*; 2nd, Jean Elizabeth, 3rd *d.* of Morris Forsyth Stuart, Edinburgh, army and navy contractor. *Educ.:* private schools; St. John's College, Cambridge. Senior Wrangler and First Smith's prizeman, 1853; Fellow and Assistant Tutor at St. John's; formerly Actuary Liverpool and London Insurance Company; Actuary and Sec. Equity and Law Life Assurance Society, 1861-73; Manager of the Scottish Equitable Life Assurance Society, Edinburgh, 1873-1900. *Publications:* A Treatise on Life Insurance Accounts, and many papers in the Journal of the Institute of Actuaries. In particular, he invented a new form of Mortality Tables, applicable to lives selected for Insurance or otherwise, and showing the gradual disappearance of the benefit of Selection. Also papers in the Transactions of other Societies—the Edinburgh Mathematical, the Philological, Naturalists' Field Club, Edinburgh, Scottish Natural History Society. *Recreations:* the microscope, especially in connection with the study of the Entomostraca, novel - reading, mathematics. *Address:* West Holme, Woldingham, Surrey. *Club:* Scottish Unionist.
(Died 29 Nov. 1920.)

SPRECKELS, John Diedrich; *b.* Charleston, S.C., 16 Aug. 1853; *s.* of late Claus Spreckels. *Educ.:* Oakland College, California; Polytechnic School, Hanover, Germany. Founded J. D. Spreckels and Bros. Co., shipping and commission merchants, owning large fleet of tugs and vessels trading with Hawaii, 1880; President of the Oceanic Steamship Co., mail and passenger line to Hawaii, Australia, and New Zealand; the Beaver Hill Coal Co.; Western Sugar Refining Co.; proprietor San Francisco Morning Call, etc *Address:* 327 Market Street, San Francisco. *(Died June 1926.)*

SPRIGG, Alfred Gordon, editor and manager of the Leicester Mail; *b.* 1861; *y. s.* of late James Sprigg, Coventry; *m.* Laura, *e. d.* of late William Smith, Coventry, a journalist and writer of stories for young people. *Educ.:* privately. Articled on the Coventry Herald; for some years on the reporting, and afterwards on the editorial staff of daily newspapers in Sheffield and Leeds, and took a prominent part in exposing false marking of foreign cutlery as of Sheffield origin; managing editor of the Scarborough Post, 1898-1909; Vice-President, The Newspaper Society, 1919 - 21. *Address:* Eversley, Stoneygate, Leicester. *T.:* Leicester 1745. *(Died 7 Mar. 1921.)*

SPRING-RICE, Rt. Hon. Sir Cecil Arthur, P.C. 1913; G.C.M.G., *cr.* 1916; K.C.M.G., *cr.* 1906; G.C.V.O., *cr.* 1908; British Ambassador to the United States since 1912; *b.* 27 Feb. 1859; 2nd *s.* of Hon. C. Spring-Rice; *m.* 1904, Florence, *d.* of Rt. Hon. Sir Frank Lascelles; one *s.* one *d. Educ.:* Eton; Balliol Coll. Oxford. Exhibitioner; 1st class moderations and final classical school; clerk in War Office, and Foreign Office; Assist. Priv. Secretary to Earl Granville, precis writer to Earl of Rosebery; Secretary at Brussels, Washington, Tokio, Berlin, and Costantinople; Chargé d'Affaires, Teheran, 1900; British Commissioner of Public Debt, Cairo, 1901; 1st Secretary of Embassy at Petrograd, 1903-5; Minister and Consul - General, Persia, 1906-8; Minister to Sweden, 1908-12; Hon. LL.D. M'Gill University, Montreal, Princeton University, Harvard University, 1917. *Decorated:* 1st class Medjidie; 1st class Polar Star. *Address:* British Embassy, Washington, U.S.A. *Clubs:* Travellers', St. James's, Savile, Beefsteak.
(Died 14 Feb. 1918.)

SPRINGETT, Rev. William Douglas, D.D. Oxon; Hon. Canon of Canterbury, 1919; Diocesan Preacher, 1924; Rural Dean of East Charing, 1914; *b.* 14 Sep. 1850; *e. s.* of late Rev. W. J. Springett, M.A.; *m.* 1887, Katharine Henrietta, 2nd *d.* of late Sir Edwyn Sandys Dawes, K.C.M.G.; no *c. Educ.:* Queen's College, Oxford, M.A. Deacon, 1873; Priest, 1874; Curate of St. Mary, Nottingham, 1873; St. Stephen-at-Hackington, Canterbury, 1876; Vicar of Hernhill, Kent, 1883; West Tarring, Sussex, 1892; Brixton, Surrey, 1898; Rector of Pluckley - cum - Pevington, 1905-24; Lecturer at St. Margaret Lothbury, 1912; Member of Diocesan Conference; and Diocesan Finance, Education, Building and Missionary Committees; formerly Member of Committee for forming the Diocese of Southwark; Hon. Fellow of the G.C. Mus., 1896. *Publications:* Prize Essay on the Sabbath, 1891; Statistical Tables on British Church History, 1886; Apocalyptic Prophecies, 1912; assisted editing Murray's Guides (Kent, 1890; Sussex, 1892); Papers in Chambers's Journal; Literary Churchman and Archæologia, 1887-97; Music: Part Song, The Sunbeams; Tunes to Hymns with unusual Metres; Easter Hymn, By the Grave, 1922; Easter Chorale; Good Old Kent (County Song), 1925. *Recreations:* formerly rowing, rifle corps, mountain climbing, walking tours; music, organ, piano; foreign travel. *Address:* 7 Ethelbert Road, Canterbury. *(Died 21 Sept. 1928.)*

SPROULE, Thomas Simpson, M.D., M.P. East Grey since 1878; Speaker of the House of Commons, Canada, since 1911; parents both Irish from Tyrone; *b.* Township of King, County of York, Ontario, 25 Oct. 1843; *m.* 1881, Mary Allice, *d.* of W. K. Flesher, M.P.; one *d. Educ.:* Common Schools, Co. Grey; University of Michigan; Victoria University, Toronto. Graduated in Medicine, 1868. Was engaged in commercial life for about 4 years, before study in medicine; carried on farming for 30 years; also in drug and stationery business for 12 years, and in flour and saw-milling for some time; served in Municipal Council, and connected with agricultural societies for 30 years; practised medicine and surgery for 40 years; 5 years Chairman of Standing Committee on Agriculture and Immigration, and for some years Chairman of Committee, Miscellaneous Private Bills; was M.G. Master of the L.O. Association of British America for 10 years; and President, Triennial Orange Council of the World, for 3 years; a Methodist, a Conservative. *Address:* Markdale, Ontario, Canada; Speaker's Chambers, House of Commons, Ottawa, Canada.

(*Died 10 Nov. 1917.*)

SPURGEON, Rev. Thomas, President of Pastors' Coll. and of Stockwell Orphanage; *b.* London, 20 Sept. 1856; *twin s.* of late C. H. Spurgeon (*d.* 1892); *m.* Lila M'Leod, *e. d.* of Gideon Rutherford, Dunedin, New Zealand, 1888; one *s.* one *d. Educ.:* the Pastors' Coll.; Metropolitan Tabernacle. Studied Art at South Kensington, and wood-engraving at Fetter Lane; visited Australia and Tasmania, 1877; second visit to Australasia, 1879; accepted pastorate of Baptist Church, Auckland, New Zealand, 1881; Evangelist of New Zealand Baptist Union, 1889-93; commenced ministry at Metropolitan Tabernacle, 1893; resigned through ill-health, 1908. *Publications:* The Gospel of the Grace of God (sermons), 1884; Scarlet Threads and Bits of Blue (poems), 1892; Down to the Sea (sea sermons), 1895; Light and Love (sermons), 1897; God save the King (sermons), 1902; My Gospel (sermons), 1902. *Recreation:* sketching. *Address:* San Remo, 40 Prentis Road, Streatham, S.W. *T.:* Streatham 1384.

(*Died 20 Oct. 1917.*)

SQUAIR, John; *b.* Bowmanville, Ont., 1850 of Scotch parents; *m.* 1886, Laura Prout; one *d. Educ.:* Public and High Schools in Clarke, Newcastle, and Bowmanville; Univ. of Toronto. Began to teach Public School in Darlington, Ontario, 1874; matriculated into University of Toronto, 1879; graduated from University of Toronto, 1883, with gold medal in Modern Languages; has been Fellow, Lecturer, Associate Professor and Professor of French in University College, Toronto; Emeritus, 1916; was Lecturer in School of Pedagogy, Toronto, and Examiner in French and German for the Education Department; has been Secretary of the Modern Language Association of Ontario; has been Chairman of College and High School Dept. of Ontario Educational Association; President of Higher Education Section of the Dominion Educational Association; Officier de l'Instruction Publique, 1914; Chevalier de la Légion d'Honneur, 1924. *Publications:* joint author, with Prof. W. H. Fraser, of High School French Grammar, 1891; revised eds. of same, 1900 and 1921; joint author with same of High School French Reader, 1891, and of Shorter French Course, 1913; joint author with Mr. J. H. Cameron of Exercises in French Prose, 1895; editor of several French texts for High Schools; En Temps de Guerre, 1916; John Seath, and the School System of Ontario, 1920; Alumni Associations in the University of Toronto, 1922; Admission of Women to the University of Toronto, 1924; The Townships of Darlington and Clarke, including Bowmanville and Newcastle, Province of Ontario, Canada, 1927. *Address:* 368 Palmerston Avenue, Toronto, Canada. *Club:* York, Toronto.

(*Died 15 Feb. 1928.*)

SQUIRE, John Edward, C.B. 1904; M.D. (Lond.), F.R.C.P., M.R.C.S., D.P.H. (Camb.); Consulting Physician, Mount Vernon Consumption Hospital; National Sanatorium for Workers, Benenden; Medical Adviser (Sanatorium Benefits), London Insurance Committee; Consulting Medical Officer, Pearl Life Assurance Company; Member of Council, National Association for Prevention of Consumption; Member of Sanitary

Inspectors' Examination Board; Corresponding Member, International Association for the Prevention of Tuberculosis, Berlin; *b.* 20 Dec. 1855; *s.* of William Squire, M.D., F.R.C.P.; *m.* 1894, Mary Lilian Youngman; two *d. Educ.:* University College, London. House Physician, University College, London; Senior Medical Officer to Red Cross in Soudan Campaign, 1885 (Egypt medal, clasp Suakin, 1885, Khedive's Bronze Star); commanded London Companies R.A.M.C. Vols., 1898-1904 (C.B. (civil), V.D.); Knight of Grace Order of St. John of Jerusalem; Queen Victoria Jubilee medal; King Edward VII. Coronation medal; King George V. Coronation medal. *Publications:* Essays in Consumption; The Hygienic Prevention of Consumption; Medical Hints for Medical Officers with Troops. *Address:* 2 Bentinck Terrace, North Gate, Regent's Park, N.W. *T.:* Paddington 2824. *Club:* Savage.

(*Died 2 May 1917.*)

SQUIRE, Sir Peter Wyatt, Kt., *cr.* 1918; *b.* 6 Feb. 1847; *s.* of late Peter Squire; *m.* Mabel Jane, *d.* of late Alexander Bramwell Bremner; two *d. Educ.:* King's College School. Chemist on the Medical Staff of the Royal Household since 1867; Hon. Secretary Thames Punting Club since 1894. *Publications:* Squire's Companion to the British Pharmacopœia; Squire's London Hospital Pharmacopœias; Methods used in the Preparation of Tissues for Microscopical Examination; Punting section of the Badminton Library. *Recreations:* punting and golf. *Address:* The Ryepeck, Shepperton. *T.A.:* Squire, Shepperton. *T.:* Weybridge 65. *M.:* A 8161. (*Died 16 Sept. 1919.*)

SQUIRE, William Barclay, M.V.O. 1926; M.A., F.S.A., F.R.C.M., F.R.G.S.; Knight of Grace, Order of Hospital of St. John of Jerusalem; Hon. Fellow Pembroke College, Cambridge; Hon. Curator of the Royal Music Library; Librarian Royal College of Music; *b.* 1855; *o. s.* of late William Squire of Feltham Hill, Middlesex. *Educ.:* privately; Germany; Pembroke College, Cambridge; Honours (Hist.) Tripos, 1878. Admitted a Solicitor, 1883, but has not practised since 1885; awarded Silver Medal for assistance at Musical Historical Exhibition, South Kensington, 1885; in charge of Printed Music in British Museum; Deputy Keeper, Department of Printed Books, British Museum, 1912-20; Musical Critic of the Saturday Review, 1888-94; Westminster Gazette, 1893; Globe, 1894-1901; and Pilot, 1900-1904; worked for the War Intelligence Department of the Admiralty, 1916-18; on Editorial Staff of the Historical Section of the Foreign Office, 1918-20. *Publications:* Articles in Grove's Dictionary of Music, Dictionary of National Biography, Archæologia, Encyclopædia Britannica, Music and Letters, etc.; Catalogue of Music in Chapter Library, Westminster, 1908; Catalogue of Printed Music in Royal College of Music, 1909; Catalogue of Pictures in the Collection of the Earl of Radnor (with Helen, Countess of Radnor, 2 vols., 1909); Catalogue of old Printed Music in the British Museum, 2 vols., 1912; The Tribes of Tunisia, 1916; Librettos of Veiled Prophet of Khorassan (opera by Sir C. V. Stanford, 1881) and Callirhoe (cantata by Sir F. Bridge, 1888); edited Palestrina's Stabat Mater; Purcell's Harpsichord Music, 4 vols., 1918; Byrd's Masses; R. Jones's Muses' Garden for Delights, 1901; the Fitzwilliam Virginal Book (1894-90), Fourteen Pieces by William Byrd, Twenty-five Pieces from Cosyn's Virginal Book (all with J. A. Fuller Maitland); and many old madrigals and motets. *Address:* 14 Albert Place, Kensington, W.8. *Club:* Athenæum.

(*Died 13 Jan. 1927.*)

STACEY, Major Gerald Arthur, D.S.O. 1916; 2nd in Command, 2nd Batt. London

Regt. ; *b.* 26 Dec. 1881 ; *s.* of late Arthur Stacey, of Leigh Place, Surrey ; *m.* 1907, Annette Hope Neild ; two *s.* two *d.* *Educ.:* privately. Passed final exam. of Institute of Chartered Accountants, 1906 ; practised as Chartered Accountant in London, 1907, until outbreak of war ; obtained Commission in 2nd V.B. Royal Fusiliers, 1902 ; Capt. 1905 ; Major, 1915 ; served European War, 1914-15 (despatches, D.S.O.) ; Legion d'Honneur, 1915. *Recreations :* soldiering, golf, sailing. *Address :* The Haven, Rottingdean. Sussex.
(Died 11 Oct. 1916.)

STACK, Maj.-Gen. Sir Lee Oliver Fitzmaurice, G.B.E., *cr.* 1923 ; K.B.E., *cr.* 1918 ; C.M.G. 1914 ; Governor-Gen. of Sudan and Sirdar of the Egyptian Army since 1919 ; *b.* 15 May 1868 ; *m.* 1902, Flora C. Moodie ; one *d.* *Educ.:* Clifton ; Sandhurst. Joined the Border Regt. 1888 ; Major, 1909 ; temp. Lieut.-Col. 1914 ; temp. Maj.-Gen. 1917 ; Staff Officer to the British Military Commissioner and General Officer commanding H.M. troops in Crete, 1899 ; joined Egyptian Army, 1899 ; retired, 1910 ; commanded Shambe Field Force, 1902 (despatches, medal and clasp, 4th class Osmanieh) ; Sudan Agent and director of Military Intelligence, 1908 ; Civil Secretary, Sudan Government, 1913-16 ; Acting Governor-General of the Sudan and Sirdar of the Egyptian Army, 1917-19 ; 1st Class Orders of the Nile, 1917 ; The Nahda, 1920, and 3rd Class Medjidieh. *Address :* The Palace, Khartoum. *Clubs :* United Service, Travellers'. *(Died 20 Nov. 1924.)*

STACPOLE, Col. John, C.V.O. 1901 ; C.M.G. 1902 ; J.P. Hants ; *b.* 27 Dec. 1849 ; 2nd *s.* of late Thomas Stacpole, of Ballinahow, co. Tipperary ; *m.* 1st, 1876, Leila (*d.* 1906), 3rd *d.* of late George Smith, Iping, Sussex ; 2nd, 1907, Isabella, 2nd *d.* of late M. P. Grazebrook, Holly Grove, Hagley, Worcester. Entered army, 1874 ; Captain, 1884 ; Major, 1891 ; Lieut.-Col. 1895 ; Colonel, 1900 ; retired, 1904. Served Soudan, 1885 (medal with clasp, bronze star). *Address :* Sharvells, Milford-on-Sea, Hants. *Club :* United Service. *(Died 30 Dec. 1916.)*

STAGNI, Most Rev. Pellegrino Francesco, D.D., O.S.M. ; Titular Archbishop of Ancyra, Apostolic Delegate to Canada and Newfoundland since 1910 ; *b.* Budrio, Italy, 1859. *Educ.:* Italy ; England, where he spent youth as a member of the English Province of the Servite Order ; professed, 1875 ; Priest, 1881 ; for some years Parish Priest at Fulham ; Professor of Philosophy at the College of Propaganda, 1893 ; Prior-General of the Order, 1901-1907 ; Archbishop of Aquila, in the Abruzzi, 1907 ; Apostolic Delegation, Ottawa.
(Died 23 Sept. 1918.)

STAINFORTH, Lt.-Col. Herbert Graham, C.M.G. 1915 ; Indian Army ; Commandant 4th Cavalry ; *b.* 18 May 1865 ; *s.* of late Maj.-Gen. C. R. Stainforth, Madras Cavalry ; *m.* Georgina Helen, 3rd *d.* of Maj.-Gen. Pipon, Major of Tower of London ; two *s.* one *d.* *Educ.:* Tonbridge ; R.M.C. Sandhurst. Entered army, 1885 ; Captain Indian Army, 1896 ; Major, 1903 ; Lt.-Col. 1911 ; served European War, 1914-15 (C.M.G.). *Address :* c/o H. S. King & Co., 9 Pall Mall, S.W. *Club :* Cavalry. *(Died 11 May 1916.)*

STALKER, Rev. James, M.A., D.D. ; Professor of Church History in the United Free Church College, Aberdeen, 1902 ; Emeritus since 1924 ; *b.* Crieff, 21 Feb. 1848 ; *m.* 1884, Charlotte Melville (*d.* 1920), *d.* of Francis Brown-Douglas, Edinburgh ; one *s.* four *d.* *Educ.:* Univs. of Edinburgh, Halle, and Berlin ; New College, Edinburgh. Minister of St. Brycedale Church, Kirkcaldy, 1874 ; St. Matthew's, Glasgow, 1887 ; delivered the Lyman Beecher Lectures on Preaching at Yale Univ. U.S.A., 1891 ; was Cunningham Lecturer at Edinburgh in 1899 ; Gay Lecturer at Louisville, Kentucky,

1904 ; James Sprunt Lecturer at Richmond, Virginia, 1914. *Publications :* The Life of Jesus Christ ; The Life of St. Paul ; Imago Christi ; The Preacher and his Models ; The Trial and Death of Jesus ; The Two St. Johns ; The Four Men ; Christ's Teaching about Himself ; The Seven Deadly Sins ; The Seven Cardinal Virtues ; John Knox, His Ideas and Ideals ; Three Lectures on the Atonement ; The Ethic of Jesus ; How to read Shakspeare ; Christian Psychology ; The Beauty of the Bible, etc. *Recreations :* reading publishers' catalogues and cutting open new books. *Address :* Balbegno, Crieff, Perthshire. *T. :* 201. *Club :* Liberal, Edinburgh.
(Died 5 Feb. 1927.)

STANDAGE, Lt.-Col. Robert Fraser, C.I.E. 1922 ; F.R.C.S., M.R.C.P. (Lond.) ; I.M.S. (retired) ; an Esquire of the Order of the Hospital of St. John of Jerusalem, 1926 ; *b.* 5 April 1868 ; *s.* of late Alfred Standage of Hurcott House, Worcestershire ; *m.* 1902, Gwendolen, *d.* of late William Lonsdale of Hutton Roof, Eastbourne and Mysore State ; one *s.* *Educ.:* St. Bartholomew's Hospital ; Bentley Surgical Prize, 1890 ; House Surgeon and Physician, 1891-93 ; Lieutenant I.M.S. 1894 ; Capt. 1898 ; Major, 1906 ; Lieut.-Colonel, 1915 ; M.O. 2nd Bombay Lancers (now 32nd Lancers), 1895-97 ; Famine duty, Bombay, 1897 (thanks of Government) ; Uganda Mutiny, 1897-99 (despatches, medal and clasp) ; East Africa Field Force, 1917-19 (despatches) ; Consulting Surgeon, East Africa Field Force, 1918-1919 ; under Foreign and Political Dept., India, 1908-26 as Residency Surgeon in Mysore ; retired, 1926. *Publications :* contributions on surgical and gynæcological subjects to Lancet, British Medical Journal, Journal of R.A.M.C., Journal of Gynæcology, Indian Medical Gazette. *Recreations :* cricket, tennis, big and small game shooting. *Clubs :* East India United Service, M.C.C.
(Died 16 Jan. 1927.)

STANDEN, Edward James, C.B. 1891 ; *b.* 1836 ; *s.* of late Edward Standen ; *m.* *Educ.:* King's College, London. Served Crimea with Turkish contingent Engineers, 1855-56 (medal) ; Secretary to British Commissioner on European Commission of the Danube, 1857-72 ; Resident Director in Paris to represent H.M.'s Government on Council of Suez Canal Company, 1876-1891 ; made Member of Managing Committee, 1888. *Address :* 37 Queen's Gate Gardens, South Kensington, S.W. *(Died 1 Nov. 1921.)*

STANDFORD, Col. William, M.V.O. 1911 ; D.S.O. 1902. Served South Africa, 1877-1878 (medal with clasp) ; Transkei, 1880-81 (medal with clasp) ; South Africa with Cape Town Highlanders, 1899-1902 (despatches, Queen's medal with clasp, King's medal two clasps, D.S.O.). *Address :* Cape Town.
(Died 7 April 1926.)

STANDISH, Henry Noailles Widdrington ; *b.* 2 Nov. 1847 ; *e. s.* of late Lionel C. H. Standish and Sabine de Noailles, *d.* of le Duc de Foix, France ; *m.* 1870, Hélène de Perusse, *d.* of le Comte des Cars, France. *Address :* Standish Hall, Wigan. *Clubs :* Marlborough ; Royal Yacht Squadron, Cowes.
(Died 31 July 1920.)

STANDISH, Major William Pery ; J.P. Hants and Cumberland ; O.B.E. 1919 ; Major, Army Remount Service, 1915-19 ; *b.* 3 Aug. 1860 ; *o. s.* of late William Cecil Standish, and *nephew* of late Rowland E. W. Pery Standish of Marwell, Hants, and Scaleby, Cumberland ; *m.* 1901, Evelyn Cecilia *d.* of late C. N. P. Phipps of Chalcot, Wilts ; two *s.* four *d.* *Educ.:* Eton. Joined 15th Regt. 1881 ; Capt. E. York Regt. 1888-93 ; Capt. Royal Reserve Regt. 1900-1901 ; High Sheriff of Cumberland, 1902 ; Master Hambledon Foxhounds 1900-21. *Recreations :* all country pursuits. *Address :* Marwell Hall, Owslebury, Winchester ; Scaleby

Castle, Carlisle. *Clubs:* Naval and Military, Boodle's. (*Died 11 Nov. 1922.*)

STANFORD, Sir Charles Villiers, Kt., cr. 1902; M.A., Mus.D., D.C.L., LL.D.; Prof. of Music, Camb. Univ.; Prof. of Composition and Orchestral Playing in the Roy. Coll. of Music; b. Dublin, 30.Sep. 1852; o. s. of late John Stanford, Examiner to Court of Chancery in Ireland, and Mary, 3rd d. of William Henn, Master in Chancery; m. 1878, Jennie, 4th d. of late Champion Wetton, Joldwynds, Surrey; one s. one d. *Educ.:* privately; Cambridge (Queen's Coll. 1870-72 and Trin. Coll. from 1872); afterwards studied at Leipzig under Reinecke, and at Berlin under Kiel. B.A. Cambridge Classical Tripos, 1874. Organ and Classical Scholar at Queen's College, Cambridge, 1870-72; Organist of Trinity College, Cambridge, 1872-93; Conductor of Cambridge University Musical Society, 1872-93; Conductor of Bach Choir, 1885-1902; of the Leeds Philharmonic Society; Conductor of the Leeds Festival, 1901-10; has produced operas in Germany (Hanover, Hamburg, Breslau, and Leipzig), and conducted concerts in Berlin, Amsterdam, Brussels, and Paris; of Maatschappij der Toonkunst, Amsterdam, 1906; many works have been produced at the Festivals of Birmingham, Leeds, etc., and on the London stage, and at the Albert Hall, Richter Concerts, Crystal Palace, etc. *Publications:* most recent musical—Cushendall, a Fire of Turf (Song-Cycles); Symphony No. 7 in D minor; Irish Rhapsody, No. 4 and 5; Pianoforte Quartet and Trio; 5 Organ Sonatas; Verdun, for Orchestra, etc.; Capriccios, Fairy Day Cantata for Women's Voices, etc.; Literary—Studies and Memories, 1908; Musical Composition, 1911; Pages from an Unwritten Diary, 1914. *Address:* 9 Lower Berkeley Street, Portman Square, W.1. *T.:* Mayfair 2696. *Clubs:* Athenæum, Savile. (*Died 29 Mar. 1924.*)

STANHOPE, Ven. Hon. Berkeley Lionel Scudamore, M.A.; b. 1824; 3rd s. of Sir Edwyn F. Scudamore Stanhope, bro. of 9th Earl of Chesterfield; m. Caroline S., e. d. of J. Arkwright, of Hampton Court, Herefordshire, 1858; one d. *Educ.:* Balliol Coll. Oxford. Fellow of All Souls' College, 1846-58; Vicar of Bosbury, Herefordshire, 1856-66; Archdeacon of Hereford, 1887-1910; Rector of Byford, 1866-1908. *Address:* The Grange, Much Wenlock. (*Died 21 Mar. 1919.*)

STANHOPE, Hon. Evelyn Theodore Scudamore, D.L.; Chief Constable of Herefordshire, 1895-1923; b. 9 Jan. 1862; 5th s. of 9th Earl of Chesterfield; m. 1888, Julia, y. d. of J. Gerald Potter; one s. one d. Late Lieut. King's Royal Rifle Corps, and Captain Army Service Corps. *Club:* Naval and Military. (*Died 9 Nov. 1925.*)

STANHOPE, Hon. Richard Philip, J.P.; C.C., Lindsey Division of Lincolnshire; Lieut. Lincolnshire Yeomanry; heir to b. 7th Earl Stanhope; b. 1885; y. s. of 6th Earl Stanhope; m. 1914, Lady Beryl Le Poer Trench, o. d. of 5th Earl of Clancarty. *Educ.:* Eton; Magdalen College, Oxford; B.A. 1907; M.A. 1910. *Recreations:* rowing, shooting, hunting, fishing. *Address:* Revesby Abbey, Boston, Lincolnshire. *T.A.:* Revesby. *M.:* BE 912. *Clubs:* Bachelors', Cavendish, Leander. (*Died Sept. 1916.*)

STANIER, Sir Beville, 1st Bt., cr. 1917; M.P. (U.) North Shropshire, 1908-18, and Ludlow since Dec. 1918; D.L., J.P. Shropshire; Deputy Chairman of North Staff. Railway; Deputy Chairman Trent and Mersey Canal; Director Home Grown Sugar; M.R.A.C. of Cirencester; b. 12 June 1867; m. 1894, Constance, d. of late Rev. B. Gibbons; three s. one d. C.C. 1902-12; Governor Harper Adams Agricultural College; Captain in Territorial Reserve; Hon. Secretary Shropshire Territorial Association, 1914-18; Chairman of British Sugar Beet Growers' Society; Director Farmers' Land Purchase Co. *Heir:* s. Alexander Bevi le Gibbons; b. 1898. *Address:* The Citadel, Weston, Preston Brockhurst, nr. Shrewsbury; 21 Buckingham Gate, S.W.1. *Club:* Carlton. (*Died 15 Dec. 1921.*)

STANIFORTH, Joseph Morewood, Artist, Western Mail, Cardiff; b. 16 May 1863; 4th s. of Joseph and Mary Staniforth, Cardiff; m. 1891, Emily, d. of J. Chidgey, Somerset. *Educ.:* St. John's School, Cardiff; apprenticed to the Lithographic Department of the Western Mail, Ltd., 1878. After about ten years' experience of this trade, joined the Editorial Staff of the paper and was engaged in Illustrating Current Events; during some years contributed Daily Cartoons to the Evening Express, and in 1893 commenced the Daily Cartoon in the Western Mail, which has continued to the present day; practices Painting in Oil and Water-Colours; and has been a Member of the South Wales Art Society since its inception, 1888, exhibiting regularly at its annual exhibitions. *Recreations:* sketching and gardening. *Address:* The Bungalow, Lynton, Devon. (*Died 17 Dec. 1921.*)

STANLEY, Hon. Right Rev. Monsignor Algernon Charles, Bishop of Emmaus; 4th s. of 2nd Baron Stanley of Alderley; a Canon of St. Peter's, Rome, 1919; b. 16 Sep. 1843. *Educ.:* Harrow; Rugby; Trinity College, Cambridge; B.A. 1865; M.A. 1868. Formerly curate of Kidderminster, West Bromwich, and St. Mary's, Soho; incumbent of Holy Cross, St. Pancras; is in holy orders of the Church of Rome; Bishop Assistant at Pontifical Throne; Canon of St. Peter's; was at St. James's, Spanish Place, 1883-93; resident in Rome; consecrated in Rome, 1903; appointed Auxiliary Bishop to Cardinal Vaughan, Archbishop of Westminster. *Address:* 1 Via Giulia, Rome. *Club:* Athenæum. (*Died 23 April 1928.*)

STANLEY, Lady (Dorothy); d. of late C. Tennant of Cadoxton Lodge, Vale of Neath, Glamorganshire; m. 1st, 1890, Sir H. M. Stanley, African Explorer (d. 1904); 2nd, 1907, Henry Curtis, F.R.C.S. *Publications:* London Street Arabs, 1890; Autobiography of Henry M. Stanley (edited), 1909. *Address:* 2 Richmond Terrace, Whitehall, S.W.1. (*Died 5 Oct. 1926.*)

STANNARD, Henry, R.B.A.; landscape and sporting painter; married; two s. two d. *Educ.:* South Kensington. Exhibitor of the Royal Academy and of the Royal Institute of Painters in Water Colours for several years. Established the Academy of Arts, Bedford, 1887, where he receives a number of students; Member of the Dudley Art Society. *Publications:* Illustrated his own manuscripts of Outdoor Common Birds, Master Bob Robin, and other books; Artist for The Encyclopædia of Sport; The Badminton Magazine; Baily's Magazine; The Illustrated London News; Sporting and Dramatic News. *Recreation:* shooting. *Address:* Harpur Place, Bedford. (*Died 15 Nov. 1920.*)

STANSFELD, Capt. John, J.P.; b. 16 Jan. 1840; o. surv. s. of late Robert Stansfeld, of Field House, and Hannah Lætitia (d. 1864), o. c. and heiress of late Lewis Farley Clogstoun Johnston; m. 1871, Eliza (d. 1916), y. d. and co-heiress of late Patrick Arkley, of Dunninald Castle; no c. Late Capt. Royal Scots Greys. *Address:* Dunninald Castle, Montrose. *Clubs:* Junior United Service; New, Edinburgh. (*Died 22 Jan. 1928.*)

STANSFIELD, Sir Charles Henry Renn, Kt., cr. 1922; C.B. 1911; b. 8 Feb. 1856; s. of late Henry Penn Stansfield; m. 1881, Agnes Helen Sargent; three s. Entered Admiralty, 1876; was Private Secretary to

Admirals Sir R. Vesey Hamilton, Sir Henry Fairfax, Sir Frederick Richards, and Lord Walter Kerr; Director of Greenwich Hospital, 1903-21; Member of the Royal Patriotic Fund Corporation; of Executive Committee of Royal Naval Fund; and Committee of Seamen's Hospital Society. *Address:* The Hollies, Bromley Common, Kent. *Club:* Union.
(*Died 29 May 1926.*)

STANTON, Major Harold James Clifford, M.V.O.1919; *b.* 1859; *s.* of late James Thomas Stanton and Louisa Loveday Stanton of The Leaze, Eastington, Gloucestershire; *m.* Henrietta, 3rd *d.* of late Sir Alexander Jardine of Applegarth, 8th Bart.; one *s. Educ.:* Harrow; Christ's College, Cambridge. Joined King's Own Scottish Borderers, 1881; Captain, 1890; Adjutant, 1st Roxburgh and Selkirk Rifle Volunteers, 1895-1901; retired, 1901; joined the War Office Staff in the Department of the Military Secretary, 1902; gazetted a Staff Captain at Headquarters on the outbreak of the War, 1914; resigned that appointment, 1917; promoted Brevet Major on the retired list, 1918; finally retired, 1919. *Club:* Naval and Military.
(*Died 22 Feb. 1927.*)

STANTON, Lionel William, I.S.O.; J.P.; *b.* England, 1843; *e. s.* of late Rev. L. W. Stanton, M.A., Incumbent of St. Mary's, Kooringa, S.A.; *m.* 1st, 1873, Catherine, *e. d.* of Edward William Hitchin, Auditor-General of South Australia; four *s.* three *d.*; 2nd, 1892, Alice Mary, *y. d.* of late William Giles, Melbourne; no *c. Educ.:* S. John's Foundation School, Kilburn, London; City of London School, Cheapside. Second Master of Lichfield Grammar School of King Edward VI.; went to South Australia, 1868; Head Master of Clare Grammar School, 1870-75; Inspector of Schools, 1876; Assistant Inspector-General of Schools, 1892; Chairman of the Board of Inspectors of Schools, 1896; Inspector-General of Schools, 1902; Secretary to the Minister Controlling Education, South Australia, 1906; retired, 1916. *Recreation:* gardening. *Address:* Adelaide S. Australia. *T.:* 1732.
(*Died 15 Aug. 1925.*)

STANTON, Rev. Vincent Henry, D.D.; Regius Professor of Divinity, University of Cambridge, 1916-22; *b.* Victoria, Hong-Kong, 1 June 1846; *s.* of Rev. V. J. Stanton, late Rector of Halesworth, Suffolk, and formerly Colonial Chaplain of Victoria, Hong-Kong; descended, on mother's side, from Robert Barclay of Ury. *Educ.:* Kensington Grammar School; Trin. Coll., Camb. Minor Scholar, 1866; Major Scholar, 1868; B.A. 1870 (20th Wrangler and 2nd class Classical Tripos); M.A. 1873; B.D. 1890; D.D. 1891; Fellow of Trinity College, 1872; Deacon, 1872; Priest, 1874; University Extension Lecturer, 1873; Junior Dean of Trinity College, 1874-76; Senior Dean, 1876-84; Tutor, 1884-89; Divinity Lecturer, 1882-89; Select Preacher before the University of Cambridge, 1874, 1878, etc.; and before University of Oxford, 1896-98; Hulsean Lecturer, 1879; Cambridge Whitehall Preacher, 1880-81; Examining Chaplain to Bishop of Ely, Dr. Woodford, 1875-85; and to Bishop of Ely, Lord Alwyne Compton, 1885-1905; Ely Professor Divinity, Cambridge, and Canon of Ely, 1889-1916. *Publications:* The Jewish and the Christian Messiah, a Study in the Earliest History of Christianity, 1887; The Place of Authority in Matters of Religious Belief, 1891; The Gospels as Historical Documents, Part I. 1903, Part II. 1909, Part III. 1920; articles in Hastings Dictionary of the Bible; the Encyclopædia Britannica; the Dictionary of National Biography (Supplt.). *Address:* Selwyn Croft, Cambridge. (*Died 8 June 1924.*)

STAPLETON-BRETHERTON, Frederick, J.P., D.L.; *b.* 1841; *o. surv. s.* of late Bartholomew Bretherton and Martha, *d.* of late Charles Annesley; *m.* 1869, Hon. Isabella Mary, 2nd *d.* of 12th Lord Petre. Assumed name of Stapleton by Royal Licence, 1884. *Address:* The Hall, Rainhill, near Prescot; Heathfield House, Fareham, Hampshire. *Club:* Windham. (*Died 13 April 1919.*)

STAPLETON - COTTON, Col. Hon. Richard Southwell George, *u.* and *heir-pres.* to 4th Viscount Combermere; *b.* 9 Oct. 1849; *m.* 1870, Hon. Jane Charlotte Methuen (*d.* 1924), *d.* of 2nd Baron Methuen; two *s.* three *d.* Entered army 1868; served Zulu War 1879 (despatches), including Ulundi (despatches, medal with clasp); Bechuanaland Expedition, 1884-85. *Address:* Gambles House, Antigua, B.W.I. *Club:* Carlton. (*Died 24 Nov. 1925.*)

STAPLEY, Sir Richard, Kt., *cr.* 1908; J.P.; Member of Council City of London; *b.* 23 Oct. 1842; *s.* of Robert Stapley, Twineham, Sussex; *m.* 1866, Annie (*d.* 1917), *d.* of Henry Jenner, Brighton. Contested (L.) Brixton Division, Lambeth, 1892, and Holborn Division, Finsbury, 1910. *Address:* 33 Bloomsbury Square, W.C.1. *T.:* Central 8556; Horeham Road, Sussex.
(*Died 20 May 1920.*)

STARK, Rev. James, D.D. Aberdeen; *b.* Glasgow, 24 Dec. 1838; *m.* 1st, 1805, Jean (*d.* 1905), *d.* of George Aimer, St. Andrews; one *s.*; 2nd, 1908, Amelia, 2nd *d.* of late Alexander G. Burnett of Kennay. *Educ.:* Edinburgh University, Scottish Congregational Theological Hall. Called to Elgin, 1864; Edinburgh; 1872; Aberdeen, 1877; retired from pastoral work, 1908; Hon. D.D. Aberdeen University, 1895; Editor of Scottish Congregational Mag., 1872-77; Chairman of Scottish Congregational Union, 1888; represented Union at International Council of Congregationalists in London, 1891, and in Boston, U.S.A., 1899. *Publications:* John Murker of Banff; Dr. Kidd of Aberdeen; The Lights of the North; Comradeship in Sorrow; Priest Gordon of Aberdeen; Lord Cullen, the first of the Monymusk Grants; Spiritualism, a Review; Met by the Way; The Lord is my Strength and Song; and other Sermons. *Address:* Braes o' Benachie, Kemnay, Scotland.
(*Died 15 Nov. 1922.*)

STARKIE, Rt. Hon. William Joseph Myles, P.C. (Ireland) 1914, B.A. (Camb.), M.A., Hon. Litt.D. (Dublin), Hon. LL.D. (Royal University); Resident Commissioner of National Education, Ireland, since 1899; Chairman of the Board of Intermediate Education since 1911; President of Queen's Coll. Galway, 1897-99; late Fellow and Tutor of Trinity College, Dublin; Member of the following Boards—Academic Council Dublin University, National Education, Intermediate Education; President of the British Empire Shakespeare Society (Dublin Branch); President of the Classical Association (Ireland), 1911. Member of Royal Commission on University Education in Ireland, 1901-1902; *b.* Sligo, 10 Dec. 1860; 5th *s.* of late William Robert Starkie, J.P., R.M., Cregane Manor, Rosscarbery (*d.* 1897); *m.* 1893, May, *e. d.* of C. Walsh; one *s.* four *d. Educ.:* Shrewsbury; Trinity College, Cambridge; Trinity College, Dublin. Head boy, Shrewsbury School; Foundation Scholar, Trinity College, Cambridge; 1st class Classical Tripos; 1st Scholar, 1st Senior Moderator and Fellow, Trinity College, Dublin. *Publications:* The Vespæ of Aristophanes, edited, with Introduction, Critical Notes, Commentary, and Appendices, 1897; The Acharnians of Aristophanes, edited, with Translation, etc., 1909; also the Clouds of Aristophanes, 1911; Contributions to Sabrinæ Corolla, Kottabos, Hermathena, Classical Review, Quarterly Review, etc.; Recent Reforms in Irish Education, 1902; A History of Irish Primary and Secondary Education during

the last Decade, 1911 ; Continuation Schools, 1912. *Recreations :* at one time rowing, Alpine climbing, cycling, lawn tennis, and golf. *Address :* Tyrone House, Dublin ; Melfort, Shrewsbury Road, Dublin. *Clubs :* Athenæum ; Dublin University, Royal Irish Yacht, Fellows', Trinity College, Dublin. *T. :* Ballsbridge 134.
(Died 21 July 1920.)

STARLING, Ernest Henry, C.M.G. 1918 ; F.R.S. ; Officier l'Ordre de la Couronne de Belgique ; Foulerton Research Professor of Royal Society ; late Jodrell Professor of Physiology, Univ. Coll., Lond., 1899-23 ; Lt.-Col. R.A.M.C. 1916; *b.* 1866; *e. s.* of late M. H. Starling, Barrister-at-law and Clerk to the Crown, Bombay ; *m.* Florence Amelia, *e. d.* of Sir Edward Sieveking, M.D., 1891 ; one *s.* three *d. Educ. :* King's Coll. School; Guy's Hospital; Heidelberg. M.D., B.S. London ; Hon. D.Sc. Dublin and Sheffield; Hon. Sc.D. Cantab. ; Hon. M.D. Breslau ; Hon. Doctor of Univ. Strasbourg ; F.R.C.P. London. Entered Guy's Hospital as student, 1882; Demonstrator of Physiology, 1889 ; Joint Lecturer on Physiology, 1890-99 ; Lecturer on Physiology at School of Medicine for Women, 1898-99; Croonian Lecturer Royal Society, 1904 ; Croonian Lecturer, Royal College of Physicians, 1905 ; Baly Medallist, 1907; Herter Lecturer, New York, 1908 ; Royal Medal of Royal Society, 1913 ; Linacre Lecturer, Cambridge, 1915 ; Oliver Sharpey Lecturer, R.C.P., 1919 ; Harveian Orator, R.C.P., 1923 ; served European War, 1915-17 (C.M.G.) ; Chemical Adviser, Salonica Force, 1916-17 ; Scientific Adviser Ministry of Food, 1918 ; British Delegate Inter-Allied Food Commission, 1918. *Publications :* Elements of Human Physiology, 8th ed., 1908 ; Primer of Physiology, 1904 ; Lectures on the Physiology of Digestion, 1906 ; The Fluids of the Body, 1909 ; Principles of Human Physiology, 4th ed., 1925 ; Monographs on Physiology, 1918 ; The Feeding of Nations, 1919 ; The Action of Alcohol on Man, 1923 ; editor of Metchnikoff's Lectures on Inflammation ; numerous papers on various physiological subjects, published chiefly in the Journal of Physiology. *Address :* Physiological Institute, University College, W.C.1. *Club :* Athenæum. *(Died 2 May 1927.)*

STARR, Clarence L., M.B. University of Toronto, M.D. University of New York, F.A.C.S. ; LL.D. ; Professor of Surgery, University of Toronto; Surgeon-in-Chief, Toronto General Hospital ; Consulting Surgeon, Hospital for Sick Children, Toronto; Lieut.-Colonel, C.A.M.C. ; Consultant Orthopedic Surgeon, C.A.M.C. in Canada ; *b.* 1 July 1868 ; *s.* of M. H. Starr, M.D., Brooklin, Ont., and Sabra Wilcox ; *m.* Annie Louise, *d.* of Hon. John Dryden, late Minister of Agriculture for Province of Ontario ; four *d. Educ. :* University of Toronto ; Bellevue, N.Y. Graduated Toronto, 1890 ; Resident House Surgeon, Hospital for Ruptured and Crippled, New York ; Assistant, Out-Patient Department, New York Hospital ; Post-graduate work in Germany, France, and England ; Commenced practice in Toronto, 1896 ; Demonstrator in Anatomy, University of Toronto, 1897, subsequently Demonstrator in Surgery. *Publications :* Deformities of the Spine ; American Practice of Surgery ; various contributions to Medical Journals. *Recreations :* motoring and golf. *Address :* 182 Bloor Street West, Toronto. *T. :* Kingsdale 2481. *M. :* 12582-12583. *Clubs :* York, Rosedale Golf, Toronto.
(Died 25 Dec. 1928.)

STATHAM, Rev. Prebendary George Herbert ; Rector of Torwood, Torquay, since 1884 ; Prebendary of Exeter, 1903 ; *b.* Liverpool, 3 Sep. 1842 ; *s.* of H. H. Statham, solicitor ; *m.* 1877, Emily Florence, *d.* of Rev. Alldersey Dicken, D.D. ; one *s. Educ. :* Liverpool Coll. ; Christ's Coll., Cambridge. Second Master, Bury

St. Edmund's Grammar School, 1865-75 ; Tutor at St. Columba's College, Ireland, 1875-77 ; Head Master, Crediton Grammar School, 1877-1884 ; Rural Dean, 1889-94 ; Chairman, Torquay Schools Union, 1887-1904 ; Vice-Chairman, Torquay Education Committee, 1902-4, and since 1909. *Recreations :* cricket and golf. *Address :* Torwood Rectory, Torquay. *T. :* Torquay 575.
(Died 23 Mar. 1922.)

STATHAM, Henry Heathcote, F.R.I.B.A., Architect, and for twenty-five years editor of The Builder ; *b.* 11 Jan. 1839 ; *s.* of H. Heathcote Statham, solicitor, Liverpool ; *m.* 1887, Florence Elizabeth, *y. d.* of W. Stephens Dicken, Deputy General Inspector of Hospitals, East India Co.'s Service; two *s.* two *d. Educ. :* Liverpool Collegiate Institution, under Dr. Howson. Articled to an architect in Liverpool, where he subsequently practised for a time ; at about the age of thirty took up residence in London ; in 1883 appointed editor of The Builder ; is an amateur musician and writer on music, and for many years musical critic to the Edinburgh Review ; for several successive years gave classical organ recitals at the Albert Hall on Sunday afternoons during the London season; was a contributor to Grove's Dictionary of Music, and author of many essays on artistic, musical, and literary subjects, more especially in the Edinburgh and Fortnightly Reviews and the Nineteenth Century ; and of many papers read before the Institute of Architects and the Architectural Association ; Hon. Member the Architectural Association and the Musical Association, and Fellow of the Royal Philharmonic Society. *Publications :* Architecture for General Readers ; Modern Architecture ; Architecture among the Poets ; My Thoughts on Music and Musicians ; Form and Design in Music ; Winged Words, published anonymously, 1907 ; The Organ and its place in Musical Art, 1909 ; Design for remodelling the front of the National Gallery and laying out Trafalgar Square, 1912 ; A Short Critical History of Architecture, 1912 ; What is Music? a short analysis for the general reader, 1913. *(Died 29 May 1924.)*

STAUNTON, Lieut. - Col. Reginald Kirkpatrick Lynch, D.S.O. 1915 ; R.A.; *b.* 9 Apr. 1880 ; *s.* of Capt. G. S. Lynch Staunton, Purbrook House, Hants. Entered army, 1899 ; Captain, 1907 ; Adjutant, 1913-14 ; Major, 1914 ; Bt. Lt. - Col. 1916 ; employed with Egyptian army, 1907 - 11 ; Brigade - Major, 1914 ; served South Africa, 1900 (Queen's medal 3 clasps); Soudan, 1910 (medal with clasp) ; European War, 1914-15 (despatches, D.S.O., wounded) ; Mesopotamia, 1915 - 17 ; Russian decoration, Order of St. Anne and Cross Swords. *Club :* Naval and Military. *(Died 7 Nov. 1918.)*

STEAD, Francis Herbert, M.A. ; Warden of Robert Browning Settlement, Walworth, 1894-1921 ; *b.* Howdon-on-Tyne, 20 Oct. 1857 ; *s.* of Rev. William and Isabella Stead (Independent Church) ; *m.* 1887, Bessie, *d.* of Rev. G. D. Macgregor (Paddington Chapel) ; one *s.* three *d. Educ. :* at home ; Owens Coll., Manchester ; Airedale College, Bradford ; Glasgow Univ. ; at Halle, Göttingen, Giessen, Berlin Universities. Buchanan Medallist in Logic and in English Literature ; graduated with honours in Classics and Philosophy at Glasgow ; Dr. Williams' Divinity Scholar. Reporter on Northern Daily Express, 1874 ; on Northern Echo, 1875-76 ; studied for Congregational Ministry, 1876-84 ; was pastor of Gallowtreegate Church, Leicester, 1884 - 90 ; member of the Leicester School Board, 1888-90; editor of the Independent and Nonconformist, 1890 - 92 ; Assistant Editor of the Review of Reviews, 1894-1912; initiated the series of conferences with Mr. C. Booth which resulted in National Committee on Old Age Pensions, 1898 ; convener of Browning Hall

Conferences on Housing and Locomotion, 1901; initiated Labour Weeks, 1910; Commenced agitation for National Old Age Homes, 1913; Convener of the League to Abolish War, 1916; Convener of International Conference on Labour and Religion, 1919. *Publications:* Handbook on Young People's Guilds, 1889; The Kingdom of God, a Plan of Study, 1894; How Old Age Pensions Began to Be, 1909; Eighteen Years in the Central City Swarm, 1913; No More War. A Novel, 1917; The Proletarian Gospel of Galilee, 1922; The Unseen Leadership, 1922; Story of Social Christianity, 1924; The Deed and the Doom of Jesus, 1927. *Address:* 20 Humber Road, Blackheath, S.E.3.
                (Died 14 Jan. 1928.)

STEAD, John Edward, F.R.S., F.I.C., F.C.S.; J.P., 1903; Hon. D.Sc. Manchester; Bessemer medallist; Hon. Doc. Metallurgy, Sheffield Univ., 1910; Hon. Doc. Science, Leeds Univ., 1912, Manchester Univ., 1914; President of the Iron and Steel Institute, 1920-21; Metallurgical Chemist; Borough Analyst, and senior partner of the firm of Pattinson and Stead, Middlesbro'; *b.* 17 Oct. 1851; *s.* of Rev. W. Stead; *m.* 1887, L. M. Livens (*d.* 1907); one *s.*; President of the Iron and Steel Institute, 1921. *Address:* Everdon, Redcar, Yorkshire; 11 Queen's Terrace, Middlesbro'. *T.A.:* Stead, Middlesbro'. *M.:* NT 7; AJ 12.
                (Died 31 Oct. 1923.)

STEAVENSON, His Honour Judge David Fenwick, J.P., B.A., LL.B.; *b.* 10 Sep. 1844; *y. s.* of John Carpenter Steavenson of Fortrose and Berwick-on-Tweed and Elizabeth, *d.* of John Fenwick, Campville, Northumberland; *m.* 1st, 1873, Eleanor Matilda, *d.* of J. G. Bennett, Isle of Man; 2nd, Gertrude, *d.* of T. Hughes, Caermarthen; two *d.* *Educ.:* private tuition; King William's College; Trinity Hall, Cambridge. Barr. North-Eastern Circuit; County Court Judge, Cumberland and Westmorland, 1891-1912. *Recreations:* rowed in the Cambridge University Eight, 1864-65-66; golf and cycling. *Address:* Dunvegan, Carbis Bay, Cornwall. *T.:* St. Ives 52. *Club:* New University.
                (Died 12 Mar. 1920.)

STEBBING, Rev. Thomas Roscoe Rede, M.A.; F.R.S., F.L.S F.Z.S.; Fellow of King's College, London; a serf to Natural History, principally employed about Crustacea; *b.* London, 6 Feb. 1835; 4th *s.* of late Rev. Henry Stebbing, D.D., F.R.S.; *m.* Mary Anne (F.L.S.), 3rd *d.* of late W. Wilson Saunders, F.R.S., 1867. *Educ.:* King's Coll. School and King's Coll., Lond. Scholar of London; Scholar of Lincoln College, and Scholar and Fellow of Worcester College, Oxford. Engaged in tuition, 1858-84; at the same time and since in literary and scientific pursuits; ordained 1858, 1859; tutor of Worcester College, 1865-67; spent several years in preparing Report on the Amphipoda of the "Challenger" Expedition; Chairman of Conference of Delegates, corresponding societies of British Association, 1899; Zoological Secretary of Linnean Society, 1903-7; gold medallist, 1908; President of South-Eastern Union of Scientific Societies, 1896, 1897, and 1916; Hon. Fellow, Worcester College, 1908. *Publications:* Eventide, a Book of Prayer for the Schoolroom, 1864; Translation of Longinus On the Sublime, 1867; Essays on Darwinism, 1871; "Challenger" Reports, Zoology, vol. xxix. 1888; The Naturalist of Cumbrae, a true Story, being the Life of David Robertson by his Friend, 1891; A History of Crustacea, 1893; Amphipoda Gammaridea of Das Tierreich, 1906; Australian Amphipoda, "Thetis" Expedition, 1910; Cumacea (Sympoda) of Das Tierreich, 1913; contributions to Magazines, etc.; Marine Investigations in South Africa, parts, 1900-1924; On Crustacea brought by Dr. Willey from the South Seas, etc.; Faith in Fetters, 1919; Isopoda and

Amphipoda from Angola and South Africa, in Göteborgs K. Vet. Handlingar, 1922; an Autobiographic Sketch, with Portrait, in the Torquay Natural History Society's Transactions, vol. iv., 1923. *Recreations:* novels with a "good" ending, the morning paper, humorous writings in general. *Address:* Ephraim Lodge, The Common, Tunbridge Wells.
                (Died 8 July 1926.)

STEBBING, William, M.A.; Hon. Fellow of Worcester Coll. Oxford; Fellow of King's Coll. London; Barrister-at-law; author; 3rd *s.* of late Rev. Henry Stebbing, D.D., F.R.S.; *m.* 1870, Anne Pinckard (*d.* 1925), 3rd *d.* of late J. S. Pidgeon of Warley Elms, Essex; three *s.* one *d.* *Educ.:* Westminster School (Queen's Scholar); King's College, London; University of Oxford. Scholar, Lincoln College; Scholar, Fellow, and Hon. Fellow, Worcester College, Oxford; 1st class Moderations, double 1st class in Final Classical and Law and Modern History Schools. Conveyancer and Equity Draftsman, Lincoln's Inn; Evening Lecturer in History at King's College; Examiner for India Civil Service, and for admission to Sandhurst and Woolwich; contributor to Saturday and Edinburgh Reviews, etc.; for nearly thirty years on the staff of The Times as leader-writer, and as second to the late Mr. J. T. Delane in the editorship. *Publications:* Some Verdicts of History reviewed; Biographies of Sir Walter Ralegh and Earl of Peterborough; Memorials of Charles Henry Pearson; Probable Tales; Rachel Wulfstan; Borderland Tales; The Poets: Impressions (new revised edition, Five Centuries of English Verse: Impressions); Truths or Truisms, Parts I., II., and III.; passages translated from Virgil and Lucretius; some Greek Masterpieces thought into English (verse); some Latin Masterpieces; Greek and Latin Anthology, 3 vols. *Recreations:* novel-reading, gardening. *Address:* Frith Park, Walton on the Hill, Surrey. *M.:* XE 2578. *Clubs:* Athenæum, Reform.   *(Died 27 May 1926.)*

STEEL, Charles; General Manager of the Great Northern Railway, 1898-1902; formerly Manager of Highland Railway; *b.* 1847; *m.* 1st, 1870 (*d.* 1887); 2nd, 1903. *Club:* St. Stephen's.
                (Died 4 Nov. 1925.)

STEEL, Major Edward Anthony, D.S.O. 1915; R.F.A.; *b.* 12 Dec. 1880; *s.* of Colonel J. P. Steel, R.E. Entered army, 1900; Captain, 1908; Major, 1914; employed with W. African Frontier Force, 1904-8; with Anglo-Belgian Boundary Commission, N. Rhodesia, 1911-14; served W. Africa, 1904-5 (despatches, medal with clasp); 1905-6 (despatches, clasp); European War, 1914-16 (despatches twice, D.S.O., wounded); Mesopotamia, 1918; Siberia, 1919. *Address:* 17a Longridge Road, S.W.5. *Club:* Royal Automobile.
                (Died 19 Oct. 1919.)

STEEL, Colonel Richard Alexander, C.M.G. 1919; C.I.E. 1916; late 17th Cavalry, Indian Army; *e. s.* of late Col. E. H. Steel, I.S.C.; *m.* 1st. 1902, Adine (*d.* 1923), *d.* of W. Acton, Adams, J.P. of Tipapa, Canterbury, N.Z.; two *s.*; 2nd, 1925, Rosalind, *y. d.* of late Dr. Saumarez Smith, Archbishop of Sydney. *Educ.:* Rugby; Sandhurst. Entered army (7th D.G.), 1892; 87th Royal Irish Fusiliers, 1893; Capt., 1901; Maj., 1910; served Indian Frontier, 1897 (medal); China, 1900; Relief of Peking (despatches, medal); France, 1914 (despatches, Bt. Lt.-Col., C.M.G., Bt. Col., C.I.E.; Legion of Honour; Orders of White Eagle, Serbia, Rising Sun, Japan, Crown, Belgium, St. Maurice and St. Lazarus, Italy, St. Anne and St. Stanislas, Russia); retired, 1921. *Club:* United Service.
                (Died 13 July 1928.)

STEELE, John, C.B. 1899; J.P.; *b.* Drumour, Perthshire, 30 Sept. 1837; *m.* 1862, Janet, *e. d.*

of James Henderson Forrester of Mayfield, Kennoway, Fifeshire; late Chief Inspector in Excise Department of Inland Revenue. *Recreations:* scientific pursuits (mainly chemical), reading, gardening, special fondness for ornithology. *Address:* Laurel Bank, Holders Hill, Hendon, N.W.   *(Died 7 Mar. 1922.)*

STEELE, Maj.-Gen. Julian McCarty, C.B. 1918; C.M.G. 1916; D.S.O. 1918; *b.* 1870; *e. surv. s.* of late General Sir Thomas Montagu Steele, G.C.B.; *m.* Sybil, *d.* of late W. J. Mure, C.B.; two *s.* one *d. Educ.:* Eton; Sandhurst. Entered Coldstream Guards, 1890; Adjutant 2nd Batt., 1896-1900, during S. African War (despatches, Bt. Major, Queen's medal 7 clasps); Commandant Guards Depôt, 1903-5; Brigade Major (Brigade of Guards), 1905-9; D.A.A. and Q.M.G. 1st Territorial London Division, 1912; Lt.-Col., 1915; Col. 1919; Maj.-Gen. 1925; commanded 22nd Infantry Brigade, 1915-19; served European War, 1914-19 (despatches seven times, C.M.G., Bt.-Col., C.B.. D.S.O. and bar, Croix de Guerre, Croce di Guerra); Commendatore St. Maurice and St. Lazarus, Italy; Commanding 1st Guards Brigade, Aldershot, 1920-24. *Address:* 58 Pont Street, S.W. *T.:* Kensington 4928. *Club:* Guards'.   *(Died 13 Mar. 1926.)*

STEELE, Maj.-Gen. Sir Samuel Benfield, K.C.M.G., *cr.* 1918; C.B. 1900; M.V.O. 1901; Maj.-Gen. Canadian Permanent Staff; *b.* Purbrook, Canada, 5 Jan. 1849; 4th *s.* of Capt. Elmes Steele, R.N., of Coleford, Gloucestershire, and 2nd wife, Anne, *y. d.* of Neil Maclan Macdonald, of Islay; *m.* 1890, Marie Elizabeth, *e. d.* of Robert Harwood, a Seigneur of Vaudreuil, P.Q., Canada; one *s.* two *d. Educ.:* Orillia, County Simcoe; British American Commercial School, Toronto. 35th Batt. Simcoe Foresters, 1866; served Red River Expedition, 1870 (medal with clasp); joined Canadian Permanent Artillery, 1871; North-West Mounted Police, 1873; Inspector, 1878; Superintendent, 1885; served campaign of 1885 in North-West Canada, and was present at action of Frenchman's Butte; commanded the Mounted Force in pursuit of Big Bear's Band and the Wood Crees (despatches, medal with clasp); commanded an expedition into Kootenay, British Columbia, 1887 (thanked in General Orders); commanded the North-West Mounted Police posts, White and Chilkoot passes, 1898; was magistrate and had charge of the Customs (thanked by the Governor-General in Council); prom. Lt.-Col.; member of Council Yukon Territory; Commandant of Lord Strathcona's Corps in Boer War, 1899-1901 (despatches twice, Bt. Col., M.V.O., C.B., Queen's medal three clasps); commanded B. Northern Transvaal Division S.A.C., Boer War, 1901-6 (despatches, King's medal, two clasps); commanded Boer cordon round the Rand to suppress the Chinese outrages. (Thanked by Lord Milner and Lord Selborne for services in S. Africa); Inspector General of Forces, Western Canada, 1914; organised, commanded, and trained 2nd Canadian Division, 1915; commanded Imperial and Canadian Troops, 1915-18, Shorncliffe. *Recreations:* takes interest in all sports. *Publication:* Forty Years in Canada, 1915. *Address:* c/o C. A. Harewood, Quebec Bank Building, Place D'Armes, Montreal, Canada; 38 Kingsway, W.C.2. *Clubs:* Constitutional, Services, Junior Army and Navy.   *(Died 30 Jan. 1919.)*

STEEN, Robert Hunter, M.D. London; F.R.C.P. London; Emeritus Professor of Psychological Medicine, King's College, Lond.; Medical Superintendent of the City of London Mental Hospital, Dartford, Kent, 1904-25; *b.* Belfast, 1870; *m.* Alice, *d.* of Lawrence Barnes; one *d. Educ.:* Royal Belfast Academical Institute; Queen's College, Belfast; St. Mary's Hospital. Late Out-patient Physician in Psychological Medicine, King's College Hospital. *Address:* 51 Sutherland Avenue, Bexhill.
    (Died 12 July 1926.)

STEER, Henry Reynolds, R.I. 1884; artist; *b.* London, 25 Aug. 1858; *m. Educ.:* The Priory, Highbury; art education at Heatherley's, 1879-88. Society of Miniature Painters, 1896; Leicester Society of Artists, 1895. *Recreations:* hunting for curios, costumes, etc., necessary to art. *Address:* 60 Clarendon Park Road, Leicester.
    (Died 28 Feb. 1928.)

STEEVENS, Major-General Sir John, K.C.B., *cr.* 1902; K.C.M.G., *cr.* 1917; Colonel Commandant, R.A.O.C., since 1921; *b.* London, 9 June 1855; *s.* of late John Steevens, Henley-on-Thames; *m.* 1st, 1891, Alice Kate (*d.* 1922), *d.* of late H. C. Blackburn; two *s.*; 2nd, 1922, Louise Marguerite Strang, *d.* of late Henry Alphonse Rossel, Eltham, Kent. *Educ.:* St. John's College, Hurstpierpoint; private tuition in Germany. Joined Control Department of Army, 1874, and transferred to Army Ordnance Department, 1880; served Zulu War, 1879, as Senior Ordnance Officer 2nd Division (specially promoted, medal with clasp); Egyptian Expedition, 1882 (present at battle of Tel-el-Kebir, despatches, special promotion, medal with clasp, bronze star, 3rd class Order of the Medjidie); Assistant Director-General of Ordnance at Headquarters, 1893-98 (C.B. 1897); Principal Ordnance Officer, Royal Arsenal, in connec n with the South African War, 1899-1902 (K.C.B.); Insp.-General, Ordnance Stores Headquarters, 1903-5; Inspector of Equipment, India Office, 1905-14 and 1919-23; Director of Equipment and Ordnance Stores, 1914-18: Controller of Salvage, 1918-19; Commander of the Crown of Italy. *Address:* Chieflowmar, Tiverton, Devon. *Club:* Junior United Service.   *(Died 12 June 1925.)*

STEINAECKER, Lieut.-Col. Francis Christian Ludwig, Baron v., D.S.O. 1902; late commanding the Regt. of Steinaecker's Horse; *b.* Berlin, 28 Sept. 1854; mother *née* Baroness v. Thumen; father was colonel German Army (Guards); *m.* 1881, *d.* of Geheimer Ober Regierungs Rath Kegler of Berlin. *Educ.:* Royal Cadet Corps at Wahlstatt and Berlin. Entered German Army (Leib Grenadiers) in the early seventies; resigned commission, 1879, going to Bulgaria with Prince Alexander of Battenberg; during Bulgarian revolution commanded at Plevna; resigned about 1885; led expedition to interior of German South-West Africa; returned, 1888; came out to Pondoland, 1889; settled in Natal, 1890, Port Shepstone district; British subject; was president political association of this district; joined Colonial Scouts at outbreak of war; left Maritzburg beginning of March 1900, to break enemy's communication on Delagoa line; blew up Malalene Bridge, 17 June; took the commandant of that line, Van Dam, prisoner; raised Steinaecker's Horse in the enemy's country without base to draw from, without transport or provisions (despatches, Queen's medal, 3 clasps, King's medal, 2 clasps, D.S.O.). *Publications:* different articles on agriculture, politics, and phylloxera. *Recreations:* fond of books and horse-flesh. *Address:* Bushbank Ridge, near Pilgrim's Rest, Transvaal.

STEINLEN, Theophile Alexander; Artist, Painter and Illustrator; Hon. A.R.E.; *b.* Lausanne, 20 Nov. 1859; *m.*; one *d. Educ.:* College and Academy, Lusanne. *Works:* Illustrations for numerous books, periodicals, posters, etc. *Address:* 21 rue Caulaincourt, Paris; Jouy la Fontaine, Seine-et-Oise, France.   *(Died 14 Dec. 1923.)*

STENNING, Sir Alexander Rose, Kt., *cr.* 1910; J.P.; *b.* 9 Feb. 1846; 5th *s.* of William Stenning of Godstone Court, Surrey; *m.* 1st,

1869, Theresa Marcia (d. 1913), d. of Rev. C. Maberly, Vicar of Owlesbury, Hants; two s.; 2nd, 1914, Emmeline Augusta, d. of Rev. G. O. Vandeleur, Ballinamora, Limerick. Was President of the Surveyors' Institution.
(Died 22 April 1928.)

STENTIFORD, Charles Douglas, J.P.; late Editor and Managing Director of the South Wales Argus. For some years sub-editor of the Western Morning News; subsequently, as editor of the Hampshire Independent, established the Southern Echo, an evening daily, but resigned the editorship of those papers on a change of proprietorship; in 1892 undertook the establishment of the South Wales Argus (daily) and the South Wales Weekly Argus, with the position of Managing Editor; later, appointed Managing Director of the proprietary company, but resigned owing to ill-health, 1917; Life Governor of the Royal Gwent Hospital. Address: 5 Meadfoot Terrace, Plymouth.
(Died 1920.)

STEPHEN, Katharine, Principal of Newnham College, 1911-20; b. 26 Feb. 1856; e. d. of late Sir James Fitzjames Stephen, 1st Bart., formerly Judge of the High Court, and Mary Richenda, d. of the Rev. J. W. Cunningham, formerly Vicar of Harrow; unmarried. Educ.: private school, Brighton; Bedford College, London. Vice-Principal of Newnham College, 1892-1911; Librarian, 1887-1910; Member of the Managing Committee of Stormont House Tubercular School, and of Carlyle School, Chelsea; a Governor of the Horticultural College, Swanley. Publications: French History for English Children; Three Sixteenth-Century Sketches. Address: 4 Rosary Gardens, S.W.7. Club: University Women's. (Died July 1924.)

STEPHEN, Sir (Matthew) Henry, Kt., cr. 1904; b. 5 Dec. 1828; 3rd and e. surv. s. of late Rt. Hon. Sir Alfred Stephen, G.C.M.G.; m. 1st, 1854, Caroline Sibella, d. of H. T. Shadforth; 2nd, Florence Sophia, d. of late A. G. D. Huthwaite, sometime Lieut. R.N. Barr. New South Wales, 1850; Q.C. 1879; member of Legislative Assembly, 1869-71; Puisne Judge, 1887; appointed acting Chief Justice during Sir Frederick Darley's absence, 1902; late Senior Puisne Judge of Supreme Court of New South Wales; retired, 1904. Address: Woollahra, Sydney. Club: Australian, Sydney.
(Died 1 April 1920.)

STEPHENS, Maj.-Gen. Adolphus Haggerston, C.B. 1887; b. 14 June 1835. Entered army, 1851; Maj.-Gen. 1889; served with Rifle Brigade, Crimea, 1855 (medal with clasp, Turkish medal); Indian Mutiny, 1857-58 (medal with clasp); Ashanti, 1874 (slightly wounded, despatches, Brevet Lt.-Col., medal with clasp). Address: 2 Carlisle Place, Victoria Street, S.W.
(Died 24 Oct. 1916.)

STEPHENS, George Henry, C.M.G. 1902; Medjidie, 2nd class, 1902; e. s. of late Samuel Henry Stephens of Clifton, Bristol; m. 1901, Dorothy, 3rd d. of late Thomas Woolner, R.A.; one s. Engaged on construction of railway, harbour, and irrigation works, India, 1879-86; England, America, West Africa, and West Indies, 1887-97; Egypt Superintending Engineer, Assiout Barrage, 1898-1903. Address: 13 Campden Hill Road, W.8. T.: Park 5233. Club: Junior Carlton.
(Died 13 Dec. 1927.)

STEPHENS, Henry Morse, Professor of History, University of California, since 1902; Director of University Extension, 1902-10; b. Edinburgh, Scotland, 3 Oct. 1857. Educ.: Haileybury; Balliol College, Oxford. Lecturer on Indian History, Cambridge, 1892-4; Professor Modern European and English History, Cornell University, 1894-1902; Editor of American Historical Review, 1895-1905; President American Historical Association,

1915; Commander of the Order of Isabel the Catholic of Spain, 1916. Publications: History of French Revolution, 1886; Portugal, 1891; Albuquerque, 1892; Speeches of Statesmen and Orators of the French Revolution, 1892; Revolutionary Europe (1789-1815), 1898; Modern European History (1600-1890), 1899; Select Documents of English Constitutional History, 1901; St. Patrick at Tara (a forest play), 1909; editor, The Pacific Ocean in History, 1916; contributor to Ency. Brit. and Dictionary of National Biography. Address: Berkeley, Cal., U.S.A. Clubs: Savage; Century, New York; Tavern, Boston; Bohemian, University, San Francisco. (Died 16 April 1919.)

STEPHENS, Rev. John Otter, Hon. Canon of Southwark Cathedral, 1914; b. 1882; m. 1887, Emma Charlotte, d. of A. S. Leslie-Melville of Branton Hall, Lincoln, and Hon. Mrs. Leslie-Melville, d. of Charles, Viscount Midleton; two d. Educ.: Winchester College; Brasenose College, Oxford. Deacon, 1854; Priest, 1856; Curate at Steeple Aston, 1857; Belgrave, 1858-61; Vicar of Savernake, 1861-79; founded, with the Marquis and Marchioness of Ailesbury, Savernake Hospital; Rector of Blackney, 1879-1903; founded with others the Alexandra Hospital, Woodhall Spa; left co-trustee with Mr. Nicholl under the will of the late Lady Charles Brudenell-Bruce for £140,000 to found a Parish and erect the necessary buildings in the County of London to the memory of his friend Lord Charles Brudenell-Bruce, 1903; built and endowed All Saints, Tooting - Graveney, and became first Vicar, 1903-12; Chaplain for several seasons at Beaulieu sur Mer, and built the Church of St. Michael and All Angels there; Chaplain at Sorrento, 1912-13, and at Marienbad, 1908-10. Address: 25 Chester Terrace, Chester Square, S.W.1. T.: Victoria 4729. Club: Wellington.
(Died 14 Aug. 1925.)

STEPHENSON, Sir (Albert) Edward, K.C.M.G., cr. 1921; C.M.G. 1914; V.D. 1910; Major (retired) 4th V.B. East Surrey Regt.; Director of Colonial Audit since 1910; b. 1 Feb. 1864. Entered Exchequer and Audit Dept. 1884; Local Auditor, Lagos, 1888; appointed to Colonial Audit Service in London, 1891; has undertaken local official investigations in several Colonies. Address: Colonial Audit Dept., 58 Victoria Street, S.W. Club: Junior Army and Navy. (Died 17 April 1928.)

STEPHENSON, Francis Lawrance, C.B. 1907; M.B.; V.D.; Hon. Col. R.A.M.C.; a Territorial, 2nd London Division; b. 1845; s. of Col. J., Stephenson, late 17th Lancers; m. 1872, Grace, d. of late Rev. C. I. Furlong.
(Died 28 April 1920.)

STEPHENSON, Admiral Sir Henry Frederick, G.C.V.O., cr. 1902; K.C.B., cr. 1897; Gentleman Usher of the Black Rod since 1904; b. 7 June 1842; s. of late H. F. Stephenson and Lady Mary Stephenson; m. 1903, Hon. Charlotte Elizabeth Eleanor Fraser, e. d. of 17th Baron Saltoun, and widow of William H. A. Keppel. Entered R.N. 1855; Vice-Adm. 1896; served Crimean War, 1854-55; China Expedition, 1857; Indian Mutiny, 1857-58; Canada, 1866; Arctic Expedition, 1875-76; Egyptian Campaign, 1882; Naval A.D.C. to Queen Victoria, 1888-90; Equerry to H.R.H. the Prince of Wales, 1878-93; C.B. 1876; Commander-in-Chief, Pacific Station, 1898-96; commanding Channel Squadron, 1897-1898; First and Principal A.D.C. to the King, 1902-4; retired list, 1904. Address: 18 Lowndes Street, S.W.1. T.: Ken 497.
(Died 16 Dec. 1919.)

STEPHENSON, Rev. Jacob, Hon. Canon of Winchester, 1903; b. 21 May 1844; e. s. of Jacob Stephenson of Newton Kyme, Yorkshire; m. 1871, Martha Elizabeth (d. 1920), d. of James Greenwood of Melmerby,

33

Yorkshire; three *s.* four *d. Educ.:* private school; Richmond College; graduated B.A., Lond. Univ., 1867; M.A. (in mental and moral science, fifth in list) 1882; prizeman in Hebrew and New Testament Greek. A Wesleyan minister in London, Waterloo, and Southport, 1867-83; ordained Deacon by Bishop Lightfoot of Durham, 1883; Priest by Bishop Harold Browne of Winchester, 1884; Curate of St. Augustine, Southampton, 1883-85; of Alverstoke, with charge of Christ Church, 1885-88; Vicar of Forton, and Sub-Warden of St. Thomas Home, 1888-1910; Rector of Droxford, 1910-26; Rural Dean of Alverstoke, 1901-10; of Bishop's Waltham, 1912-22; member of the Councils of The Rescue Union, Board of Education, also of the Consultative Committee of the National Society, London. *Publications:* The Prophecies, the Gift, the Warfare, an Ordination Sermon; The Chief Truths of the Christian Faith, 1902. *Address:* 2 Clifton Road, Winchester. *T.A.:* Winchester.

(*Died 1 Feb. 1927.*)

STEPHENSON, Sydney, M.B., C.M., F.R.C.S.E., D.O. (Oxon); late Ophthalmic Surgeon to Queen's Hospital for Children, the Evelina Hospital, Queen Charlotte's Hospital, etc., late Vice-President of the Ophthalmological Society of the United Kingdom; Master of the Oxford Ophthalmological Congress; *b.* 1862; *s.* of Appleby Stephenson, M.D., and Annie Manlove; *m.* Jane Finch, *d.* of J. H. Peck, J.P.; one *s.* one *d. Educ.:* privately; Nottingham High School; Epsom College; University of Edinburgh. Inspector of the Local Government Board for ophthalmic purposes, 1896-97; Visiting Surgeon to the Ophthalmic School, Hanwell, W., 1889-1903; co-founder of the Society for the Study of Disease in Children; Middlemore Prizeman, 1907; Ophthalmic Referee under Workmen's Compensation Act for London and its environs; editor British Journal of Ophthalmology. *Publications:* Epidemic Ophthalmia, 1895; Contagious Ophthalmia, 1899; Ophthalmic Nursing (2nd ed.); translations of Dr. Feuer's Die Beziehungen zwischen Zahn und Augen-Affectionen, and of Dr. Darier's Leçons de Thérapeutique Oculaire, 1903; Report upon the Ophthalmic State of Poor-Law Children in the Metropolis, 1897 (Blue Book). *Address:* 33 Welbeck Street, Cavendish Square, W.1. *T.:* Mayfair 403. *M.:* LR 6861. (*Died 15 Dec. 1923.*)

STEPHENSON, Major-General Theodore Edward. C.B. 1900; *b.* 28 Mar. 1856; *s.* of Rev. Canon Stephenson of Weymouth; *m.* 1889, Philippa Anna Frederica, O.B.E., *d.* of Col. Gordon Watson; one *d. Educ.:* Marlborough College; p.e.c. Joined 56th Regt., 1874; promoted Captain Essex Regt., 1881; Major, 1883; Lieut.-Col., commanding 1st Battalion Essex Regiment, 1895; Brevet Col., 1899; was D.A.A.G. Gibraltar, 1883-86; for N. Dist. 1883-89; N.E. Dist. 1889-1890; served in S.A.; gazetted 18 Feb. 1900, as Major-Gen. on Staff Commanding 18th Brigade; commanded at Barberton with charge of the Portuguese frontier, Oct. 1900; commanded mobile columns in Cape Colony, Oct. 1901 (C.B., despatches four times, 8 clasps); Major-General commanding Bloemfontein District and troops in Orange River Colony, 1902-04; Major-General commanding Transvaal, 1904-06; acted G.O. Commander-in-Chief S. Africa, 1904; rank of Major-General confirmed, 1906; Accredited Agent of Lord Selborne in Zululand to report progress of the rebellion and military operations for its suppression, 1906 (medal); commanded 6th Division, Colchester, 1906; Distinguished Service Reward, 1906; 2nd Division, Aldershot, 1907-10; commanded troops in Straits Settlements and Malay Peninsula, at Singapore, 1910-1914; commanded 65th Division, 1916; served

994

on London Pensions Committee and on Children's Welfare Committee (Foundling Hospital). *Address:* 75 Carlisle Mansions, Westminster, S.W.1. *T.:* Victoria 0224. *Club:* United Service. (*Died 19 Jan. 1928.*)

STEPHENSON, William, M.D., LL.D., F.R.C.S.; Professor of Midwifery, University, Aberdeen, 1875-1912; *b.* Edinburgh, 2 July 1887; *m.* 1909, Alice Irene, 3rd *d.* of late James Lawrance, Melbourne; one *s. Educ.:* High School and University, Edinburgh. Practised in Edinburgh; was Physician to the Royal Hospital for Sick Children; Council Obstetrical Society, London, 1881-83; Vice-President, 1887-89; President Obstetrical Society, Edinburgh, 1908; Obstetric Physician, Maternity Hospital, Aberdeen. *Publications:* numerous papers on professional subjects to medical journals. *Address:* 11 Bonaccord Crescent, Aberdeen. *M.:* TN 1555.

(*Died Feb. 1919.*)

STEPHENSON, Sir William Haswell, Kt., *cr.* 1900; D.L., D.C.L.; Alderman and Magistrate; *b.* 15 May 1836; *s.* of Wm. Stephenson, of Throckley House, Northumberland; *m.* 1862, Eliza Mary (*d.* 1901), *d.* of James Bond; one *d. Educ.:* Wesley College, Sheffield. Was Sheriff, has been four times Mayor of Newcastle, and Lord Mayor, 1909-10, 1910-11, and 1911-12; Chairman of Tyne Commission, and director of several public companies; Chairman of Newcastle Commercial Exchange Co.; presented with the Freedom of Newcastle-upon-Tyne for public service to the community. *Address:* Elswick House, Newcastle-upon-Tyne. *T.A.:* Throckley, Newcastle Tyne. *T.:* P.O. 549 and 37 Nat. *M.:* BB 1059.

(*Died 7 May 1918.*)

STERLING, Maj.-Gen. John Barton; *b.* 12 Oct. 1840; *o. surv. s.* of late Rev. John Sterling, and *g.s.* of late Edward Sterling; *m.* Caroline (*d.* 1917), *e. d.* of Sir John Salusbury Trelawny, 9th Bt. After a short service in the Navy, gazetted to 8th Foot, 1861; transferred to Coldstream Guards in same year; served in that regiment till 1896, and commanded the 2nd Battalion for four and the regiment and North London Volunteer Brigade for five years; present with 2nd Battalion in Egypt, 1882; 2nd in command of 1st Battalion in the Soudan and in Cyprus, 1885; Major-General 1896; retired 1901. *Clubs:* Athenæum; Royal Yacht Squadron, Cowes. (*Died 5 Dec. 1926.*)

STERNBERG, Hon. Joseph, M.L.C. Victoria; *b.* 1855; *s.* of late Alexander Sternberg, J.P., a Victorian pioneer landowner; *m.* Selina, *o. d.* of late B. Lazarus of Bendigo. *Educ.:* private college. Member for Northern Province Legislative Council of Victoria, 1891; Bendigo Province since 1904; was member of the Royal Commission on Old Age Pensions and Shops and Factories Acts; on that to inquire into the Electrification of the Victorian Railways; and on that inquiring into the Housing Conditions in the Principal Cities of Victoria, Australia; first Commissioner of the Campaspe Irrigation Trust; and member of the first Council of Education in Victoria; is a past Grand Warden in the Grand Lodge of Freemasons of Victoria; Past Grand Master of M.U.I.O.O.F. of Victoria; largely interested in Bendigo mining; Director of the following Goldmining Companies:— Clarence, New Prince of Wales, Suffolk, United Moon, and New Moon Consolidated, and others. *Recreations:* athletic sports, cycling, and reading. *Address:* State Parliament House, Melbourne; Kalimna, Bendigo, Australia.

(*Died 15 Jan. 1928.*)

STERNDALE, 1st Baron (*cr.* 1918) of King Sterndale, **William Pickford,** P.C. 1914; Kt., *cr.* 1907; Q.C. 1893; Master of the Rolls since 1919; *b.* 1849; 2nd *s.* of Thomas Edward Pickford; *m.* Alice Mary (*d.* 1884), 2nd *d.* of J. W. Brooke,

Sibton Park, Yoxford, Suffolk. *Educ.*: Liverpool College ; Exeter College, Oxford (M.A., Hon. Fellow). Joined Northern Circuit, 1875 ; Recorder of Oldham, 1901-4 ; Liverpool, 1904-7 ; Commissioner of Assize, N.E. Circuit, 1906 ; Judge of the High Court, King's Bench Division, 1907-14 ; a Lord Justice of Appeal, 1914-18 ; President of the Probate Division, Admiralty Court, 1918-19. *Address* : Queen's House, Cheyne Walk, Chelsea, S.W. ; King Sterndale, near Buxton. *Clubs:* Athenæum, United University, Alpine.   (*Died 7 Aug. 1923.*)

STERRETT, Professor John Robert Sitlington ; Head of the Department of Greek in Cornell University, Ithaca, N.Y. ; of Scotch-Irish descent ; *b.* near Lexington, Virginia, 4 March 1851 ; *s.* of Robert Dunlap Sterrett and Nancy Snyder Sitlington ; *m.* Josephine Moseley, *d.* of Joel Shrewsbury Quarrier and Frances Friend, of Charleston, W. Va., 1892. *Educ.* : Universities of Virginia, Leipzig, Berlin, Athens (Greece), and Munich (Ph.D. 1880). Professor of Greek in Miami University (Oxford, O.), 1886-88 ; same, University of Texas, 1888-92 ; same, Amherst College (Mass.), 1892-1901 leader of various Archæological Expeditions to Asia Minor and Babylonia, 1883-85 ; Professor in American School of Classical Studies at Athens (Greece), 1896-97; Student in the same, 1882-84 ; its Secretary, 1884-85 ; Corresponding Member of the Imperial German Archæological Institute ; Member Board of Managers of American School of Classical Studies at Athens ; Associate Editor of American Journal of Archæology ; joint editor of Cornell Studies ; LL.D. of Aberdeen, 1902. *Publications:* Qua in re Hymni quinque maiores inter se differant aequitate, 1881 ; Inscriptions of Assos, 1884 ; Inscriptions of Tralles, 1884 ; Epigraphical Journey in Asia Minor, 1888 ; Wolfe Expedition to Asia Minor, 1888 ; Leaflets from Note-book of Travelling Archæologist, 1889; Troglodytes of Cappadocia, 1900 ; Glimpses of Asia Minor, 1901 ; The Torch Race, 1902 ; Caravansaries in the Orient, 1904 ; The Iliad of Homer ; and many minor articles. Forthcoming : Historical Geography of the New Testament. *Recreations:* bicycling and golf. *Address:* Cornell Univ., Ithaca, New York, U.S.A.
    (*Died 17 June 1914.*)

STEVEN, Temp. Capt. (John) Fraser, D.S.O. 1916; M.A., B.Sc., M.B., Ch.B.; R.A.M.C.; 2nd *s.* of late Roderick Steven, Glasgow ; *m.* 1916, Gladys, *o. d.* of late Major Fraser ; one *s.* Served European War, 1914-17 (despatches, D.S.O.). *Address:* 43 Lansdowne Crescent, Glasgow. *T.:* W 3575.   (*Died 4 July 1920.*)

STEVENS, Bertram ; joint-editor, Art in Australia (quarterly magazine) ; and The Home (quarterly magazine) ; *b.* Inverell, N.S.W. ; *s.* of W. Matheson Stevens, formerly of London ; *m.* Edith Wogaman ; two *s.* one *d.* *Educ.* : N.S.W. public schools. *Publications:* edited Poetical Works of John Farrell, with memoir, 1904 ; Wine and Roses, verses by Victor Daley, with memoir, 1911 ; Golden Treasury of Australian Verse, 1908 (an enlarged and revised edition of An Anthology of Australian Verse, 1906); Australian Birthday Book, 1907 ; Bush Ballads ; The Charm of Sydney ; Poems of Henry Kendall, 1920 ; The Bulletin Book of Humorous Verse, 1920 ; and several other books. Editor Red Page (Literary) of Sydney Bulletin, 1909-11 ; The Lone Hand (magazine), 1911-18 ; joint-editor—Pen Drawings of Norman Lindsay, 1918 ; Art of J. J. Hilder, 1918 ; Art of Arthur Streeton, 1919 ; and other art publications. *Address:* 24 Bond Street, Sydney, N.S.W.
    (*Died 14 Feb. 1922.*)

STEVENS, Lt.-Col. Cecil Robert, I.M.S., M.D., B.S. Lond., F.R.C.S. Eng. ; Professor of Clinical and Operative Surgery, Medical College, Calcutta ; *b.* 14 Mar. 1867 ; *s.* of Sir

Charles Stevens, K.C.S.I. ; *m.* 1892, Katharine, *d.* of Lt.-Col. James Duff of Knockleith ; one *s.* one *d.* *Educ.*: Malvern ; University College, London ; St. Bartholomew's. Served in Chitral Expedition, 1895 ; operations in Samana, Tirah, and N.W. Frontier, 1897, late Professor of Anatomy, Medical College, Calcutta ; Surgeon to Medical College Hospital ; Member of Governing Body of State Medical Faculty, Bengal ; Member of Council of State Medical Registration, Bengal. *Publications:* Notes on Appendicitis, etc. *Recreations:* shooting, fishing, tennis, golf. *Address:* 5 Middleton Street, Calcutta. *T.:* Calcutta 1059. *M.:* 1421. *Clubs:* Bengal, Bengal United Service, Calcutta.   (*Died 1919.*)

STEVENS, Charles John, J.P. ; Associate Editor of the Register, Adelaide, 1899-1910 ; *b.* London, 16 Aug. 1857 ; *e. s.* of late John Stevens, formerly of Marlborough, Wilts ; *m.* 1st, 1878, Elizabeth, *e. d.* of Henry Brandwood, Walsall ; 2nd, 1884, Julia, 3rd *d.* of W. R. Rashleigh of St. Keverne, Cornwall ; six *s.* one *d.* *Educ.*: Herrold's School, Bermondsey. Spent five years in Law Offices, London ; arrived in Adelaide, 1875 ; after connected with the Register ; Manager of Port Adelaide Office, 1876-86 ; sub-Editor, 1886-92 ; leader of Reporting Staff, 1892-99 ; Associate Editor, 1899 ; Acting Editor, 1905-6 ; regular contributor to Provincial Press ; W. M. of Commercial Lodge No. 39 S.A.C. of Freemasons, 1914 ; President of Masters and Wardens Association, 1915. *Publication:* The Barrier Silver and Tin Fields, 1888—the first work published describing the leading Broken Hill and Euriswie Mines ; Spirit of History ; Masonic Mysteries ; and other addresses. *Recreations:* farming and gardening. *Address:* Glengowan, Enfield. Adelaide, S. Australia.   (*Died 10 Feb. 1917.*)

STEVENS, Hon. E. J., M.L.C., F.R.G.S., F.R.S., F.R.C.I. ; late Chairman Brisbane Newspaper Company, Limited ; Local Deputy Chairman A.M.P. Society ; *b.* Melbourne, Victoria, 10 July 1845 ; *s.* of F. P. Stevens of Melbourne ; *m.* 1877, Ada C., *d.* of J. H. Jackson, Sandford Downs, Victoria ; two *s.* six *d.* *Educ.*: Church of England Grammar School, Melbourne. Went to Queensland to manage Yarronvale for a Victorian company, 1866 ; took up country on Bulloo River for himself, 1868 ; his nearest neighbour was 80 miles distant, the blacks were very treacherous, revolvers being carried for about four years ; elected Legislative Assembly for Warrago, 1878 ; Logan, 1883, 1888, and 1893 ; retiring in 1899, when he was called to the Legislative Council ; founded four schools of arts and established several rifle clubs ; patron or president of many athletic clubs. *Publications:* twenty-two serial stories of life in the Never-Never bush (Bulloo). *Recreations:* shooting and fishing. *Address:* Myninn, Southport, Queensland. *Clubs:* Queensland, Johnsonian, Brisbane.

STEVENS, Frederick, I.S.O. 1902 ; *b.* 1840 ; *s.* of late T. J. Stevens, Cheshunt ; *m.* 1867, Agnes, *d.* of late John Dennett Potter ; one *d.* Formerly Principal of Statistical Department of Local Government Board. *Address:* The Poplars, Mill Road, West Worthing
    (*Died 18 Sept. 1917.*)

STEVENS, Rev. Henry Bingham, M.A. ; Hon. Canon of Rochester, 1906 ; *b.* Wilmington Vicarage, Kent, 1835 ; *s.* of Rev. Henry Stevens, Vicar of Wateringbury (*s.* of Very Rev. Robert Stevens, Dean of Rochester), and Mary Frances Stevens, *d.* of late Colonel Charles Cox Bingham, R.A. ; *m.* 1885, Catherine E., *d.* of Rev. Henry Charles Bartlett, Vicar of Westerham ; two *d.* *Educ.* : Tonbridge School (Foundation Exhibitioner, 1853) ; Emmanuel College, Cambridge (Senior Optime Math. Tripos and B.A., 1857 ; M.A. 1860).

Curate of Thatcham, Berks, 1858-61 ; Curridge, Berks, 1861-67 ; St. Lawrence, Reading, 1867-68 ; Rector of Chatham, 1868-83 ; Rural Dean of Gravesend, 1901-09 ; Vicar of Darenth, Kent, 1883-1911. *Recreations :* captain of the Tonbridge School C.C., 1853 ; captain of Second Emmanuel Boat, 1856. *Address :* The Beck, Wateringbury, Kent.

(Died 14 Jan. 1924.)

STEVENS, Sir John (Foster), Kt., *cr.* 1905 ; *s.* of late Charles Green Stevens ; *b.* 9 July 1845 ; *m.* 1868, Frances Louisa, *d.* of late Capt. W. H. Jeremie, Indian Army ; one *s.* three *d. Educ.* : King Edward's School, Birmingham ; Lycée of Versailles ; and other foreign schools; King's College, London. Entered I.C.S. (Bengal), 1865 ; joint-Magistrate, 1876 ; Acting District and Sessions Judge, 1876, 1878, and 1879-1884 ; District and Sessions Judge, 1884 ; Acting Judicial Commissioner, Central Provinces, 1891 ; Judicial Commissioner, 1894 ; Acting Judge, High Court, Calcutta, 1895 ; Judge, High Court, 1897 ; retired, 1904. *Address :* 2 Lansdown Place West, Bath. *Club :* Bath and County, Bath. *(Died 19 Sept. 1925.)*

STEVENS, Rt. Rev. Thomas, D.D., F.S.A. ; Archdeacon of Essex since 1894 ; *b.* 1841; *m.* 1866, Anne Elisabeth (*d.* 1918), *d.* of G. Bertram, and *s.* of Sir George Clement Bertram, late Bailiff of Jersey ; one *d. Educ.* : Shrewsbury School ; Magdalene Coll. Camb. (Scholar and Exhibitioner). Assistant Master, Charterhouse, 1863-66 ; Vicar of St. Luke, Victoria Docks, 1875-82 ; Vicar of Saffron Walden, 1882-89 ; Vicar of St. John's Stratford, 1889-1901 ; Chaplain of St. Mary's Hospital, Ilford, 1901-4 ; Grand Chaplain of English Freemasons, 1896-97 ; Hon. Canon of St. Albans, 1891-94 ; Bishop of Barking (Suffragan), 1901-19 ; Bishop of Barking, 1901-19 ; President, Essex Archæological Society, 1911-16. *Address :* Orsett. *Club :* Royal Societies.

(Died 24 Aug. 1920.)

STEVENSON of Holmbury, 1st Baron, *cr.* 1924 ; **James Stevenson,** Bt., *cr.* 1917 ; G.C.M.G., *cr.* 1922 ; Commander Legion of Honour ; Chairman of Standing Committee of British Empire Exhibition ; *b.* Kilmarnock, 2 April 1873 ; *e. s.* of Archibald Stewart Stevenson; *m.* 1st, 1897, Jessie Baird Hogarth (*d.* 1917), Ardrossan ; 2nd, 1918, Stella Johnstone, *widow. Educ.* : Kilmarnock Academy ; privately. Is Managing Director of John Walker & Sons, Ltd., Distillers, Kilmarnock ; Director of Area Organisation, Ministry of Munitions, 1915-17 ; Vice-Chm. of Ministry of Munitions Advisory Committee, 1917 ; Member of Central Reconstruction Committee ; Member of Munitions Council for Ordnance 1918, and Chm. of Council Committee on Demobilisation and Reconstruction ; Surveyor-Gen. of Supply, W.O., 1919-21 ; Member of the Army Council, 1919 ; Member of the Air Council, 1919-21 ; Vice-Chairman of Advisory Committee on Civil Aviation ; Chairman of Rubber Investigation Committee ; appointed by Secretary of State for Colonies personal Commercial Adviser, 1921 ; all the above appointments in an honorary capacity; has travelled extensively. *Recreations :* golf, motoring. *Heir :* none. *Address :* Holmbury House, Holmbury St. Mary, Surrey ; *T. :* Ewhurst 3 ; 22 Old Queen Street, S.W.1; *T. :* Victoria 371. *Clubs :* Reform, Royal Automobile. *(Died 10 June 1926.)*

STEVENSON, Sir Edmond Sinclair, Kt., *cr.* 1905 ; J.P. ; M.D., F.R.C.S. (Edin.), etc.; *b.* Geneva, 10 July 1850 ; *s.* of late William Ford Stevenson and Æneas, *e. d.* of Col. Sinclair of Forse, Caithness ; *m.* 1880, Emily Anna d'Urban Musgrave, *d.* of J. Eaton. *Educ.* : Geneva ; Edinburgh; London; Paris; Berlin, Served as Medical Officer during Kaffir War, 1879 (medal); in Natal in last Boer War; late President British Medical Association, Cape Town; late President

996

South African Congress ; late President Council for the Colony ; Physician-in-Ordinary to the late High Commissioner (Lord Milner); Lieut.-Col. S.A.M.C. *Address :* Strathallan and St. Clair, Rondebosch, Cape Colony. *T. A. :* Rondebosch. *T. :* Central 12, Cape Town. *Club :* Civil Service, Cape Town.

(Died April 1927.)

STEVENSON, Edward Snead Boyd, C.I.E. 1905 ; *b.* 1849 ; *m.* 1876, Constance, *d.* of Rev. Thomas Ffoulkes. Entered Service, 1870. Deputy Inspector-General, Madras Police Department, 1895-1904 *Address :* Salem, Madras Presidency, India. *(Died 14 Dec. 1917.)*

STEVENSON, Colonel Francis, C.B. 1906 ; *b.* 8 March 1851. Entered army, 1870 ; Capt. Bombay Staff Corps, 1882 ; Major, I.S.C. 1890 ; Lieut.-Col., Indian Army, 1896 ; brevet Col. 1900 ; A.A.G. Bombay, 1891-94 ; served Afghan War, 1879-80 (despatches, medal with 2 clasps, bronze star); Soudan, 1885. Awarded the Royal Humane Society's Bronze Medal for saving the lives of two lascars who fell overboard the transport Asia, Porebunder, India, 22 Jan. 1874. *(Died 30 May 1922.)*

STEVENSON, Colonel James, C.B. 1905 ; J.P., D.L. ; V.D., T.D. ; *b.* Braidwood, Carluke, N.B., 6 Nov. 1838 ; *e. s.* of late Nathaniel Stevenson, J.P., of Braidwood, and Margaret Jane, *e. d.* of Thomas Rennie Scott, D.L., J.P. ; *m.* 1st, 1866, Eliza Hamilton of Fairholm, *e. d.* of late Jas. Hamilton ; 2nd, 1879, Frances, *e. d.* of late Frederick Richards Leyland of Woolton Hall, Lancashire ; 3rd, 1895, Florence, *o. d.* of Samuel Mountford Gibbs ; three *s.* three *d. Educ.* : Rugby. Cornet 12th Royal Lancers, 1860 ; Lieut. 1862 ; Capt. 1866 ; commanded a squadron in Kerry during Fenian disturbances, 1867 ; Major commanding 3rd Ad. Batt. Lanark Rifle Vols. 1872 ; Lieut.-Col. commanding 9th Lanark Rifle Vols. 1875 ; Colonel in Volunteer forces, 1896 ; Brig.-Gen. commanding H.L.I. Vol. Brigade, 1905 ; retired : A.D.C. to the Queen, 1896-1901 ; A.D.C. to King Edward VII. 1901, and to King George V. 1910 ; retired, 1920. *Recreations :* racing (won Grand Military Steeplechase, 1865), hunting, shooting, fishing, cycling, skating, curling. *Address :* Braidwood, Carluke, Lanarkshire. *T. A. :* Braidwood, Carluke. *T. :* Carluke 34. *Club :* Army and Navy.

(Died 6 Nov. 1926.)

STEVENSON, Sir Malcolm, K.C.M.G., *cr.* 1923 ; C.M.G. 1920 ; Governor and Commander-in-Chief, Seychelles, since 1927 ; *b.* 25 March 1878 ; *s.* of late Alexander Stevenson, Lisburn ; *m.* 1914, Mabel, *d.* of 1st Baron Chalmers ; one *s.* one *d. Educ.* : Trinity College, Dublin ; B.A. 1901 ; M.A. 1907. Entered Ceylon Civil Service, 1901 ; Second Assistant Colonial Secy., 1911 ; Private Secy. to the Governor, 1913 ; Principal Assistant Colonial Secy., 1915 ; Chief Secy. to Government, Cyprus, 1917 ; Administered the Government of Cyprus, 21 November 1918-July 1920 ; High Commissioner and Commander-in-Chief, Cyprus, July 1920 ; Governor and Commander-in-Chief, Cyprus, 1925-26. *Recreations :* tennis, golf, billiards. *Address :* Government House, Mahé, Seychelles. *T. A. :* Mahé-Seychelles. *Club :* Badminton. *(Died 27 Nov. 1927.)*

STEVENSON, Maj.-Gen. Thomas Rennie, C.B. 1882 ; *b.* Braidwood House, Lanarkshire, 26 Oct. 1841 ; 3rd *s.* of N. Stevenson of Braidwood ; *m.* 1870, Isbella, *d.* of J. Banks Friend of Ripple Vale, Kent, and 30 Sussex Square ; one *s.* one *d. Educ.* : private. Joined 67th Regiment, 1861 ; 87th R.I. Fusiliers 1863 ; commanded R.I. Fusiliers, 1882-86 ; commanded 26th and 71st Regt. Dists.,1887-92; retired as Maj.-Gen. 1898 ; Colonel Royal Irish Fusiliers, 1899 ; served during Egyptian Campaign, 1882, including battle of Tel-el-Kebir (despatches, C.B., medal and clasp, and Khedive's star);

D.L., J.P. Lanarkshire. *Recreations:* fishing, shooting. *Address:* Sunnyside, Lanark. *T.A.:* Sunnyside, Lanark. *T.:* Lanark 18. *M.:* V 682. *Clubs:* Army and Navy, United Service; New, Edinburgh. *(Died 19 Nov. 1923.)*

STEVENSON, Major.-Gen. William Flack, C.B. 1900; King's Hon. Surgeon, 1905; late Professor of Military Surgery, R.A.M. College, London; *b.* 29 May 1844; *s.* of John Stevenson, Strawberry Hill, Dalkey, Co. Dublin; *m.* 1871, Marie Teresa, *d.* of G. Riddick, Monkstown, Co. Dublin. *Educ.:* Dublin University. B.A., M.B, M.Ch. Entered Medical Service, 1866; Assist.-Surgeon Royal Artillery; served in West Indies and in India; Army Med. School, 1892; P.M.O. Lines of Communication, S.A., Nov. 1899; P.M.O. Lord Roberts' Headquarter Staff, 6 Feb. 1900 (despatches, C.B., medal and 5 clasps). *Publication:* Wounds in War, the Mechanism of their Production and their Treatment (3rd ed.), 1910. *Clubs:* Junior United Service; Bournemouth. *(Died 7 July 1922.)*

STEVENSON, William Grant, R.S.A., sculptor; *b.* Ratho, 7 March 1849; *m.* Jeanie, *d.* of late John Dickson, Edinburgh, 1885. *Educ.:* parish school, Ratho. Student Royal Institution, Edinburgh; Royal Scottish Academy Life School: A.R.S.A. 1885; R.S.A. 1896; public statues: Burns, Kilmarnock; Burns, Denver; Burns, Chicago; Wallace, Aberdeen. *Publications:* Wee Johnnie Paterson; Puddin'; The M'Crankys, etc. *Recreations:* golf, shooting. *Address:* 8 Osborne Terrace, Edinburgh. *Club:* Scottish Arts, Edinburgh. *(Died 6 May 1919.)*

STEWARD, Major-General Edward Harding, C.M.G. 1887; Late Inspector of warlike stores for Crown Colonies, colony of New Zealand, and Egypt; late R.E.: *b.* 13 July 1835; *e. s.* of late Samuel Steward; *m.* 1862, Jessie, 2nd *d.* of late Henry Baskerville of Crowsley Park, Oxon.; four *s.* two *d. Educ.:* Weybridge; R.M.A. Woolwich. Served in Royal Engineers, 1854-83; quartered in Malta, the Ionian Islands, Halifax N.S., Bermuda, and at home; employed in the Defence Department, War Office, 1865-78; served with South African Field Force as commanding R.E. 1879; Commandant of Colony of Natal, 1880; commanding R.E. at Manchester, 1880-82-83, and commanded the Garrison. *Decorated* for services rendered to the Colonies and Dependencies. *Publication:* Notes on Submarine Mines. *Address:* Newton Lodge, Nailsworth, Glos. *(Died 15 Mar. 1918.)*

STEWART, Lt.-Col. Sir George, K.B.E., *cr.* 1918; C.M.G. 1909; V.D., F.F.I.A., J.P.; Chief Commissioner of Police, Victoria, since 1919; C.O. 50th Battalion Infantry; *b.* Portree, N.B., 17 March 1866; *m.* 1908, Anna Lucas Synnot. *Educ.:* Ipswich; Durham. English Civil Service and Royal Engineers, 1882-92; entered Tasmanian Civil Service, 1892; Chief Clerk and Accountant, Education Department; Chief Inspector of Explosives and Magazines; Secretary to the Premier; Under Secretary for the State; transferred to Commonwealth Service, 1901; Secretary to Federal Executive Council, and Official Secretary to Governor-General, Commonwealth of Australia, 1902-19. *Recreation:* farming. *Address:* Federal Government House, Melbourne; St. Kilda, Victoria, Australia. *Clubs:* Naval and Military, Athenæum, Melbourne. *(Died 10 May 1920.)*

STEWART, Lieut.-Colonel Albert Fortescue, C.M.G., O.B.E.; retired pay, Regular Army; *s.* of late Sir John Marcus Stewart, Bart., D.L., J.P.; *m.* 1902, Margarita Minnie Eva, *d.* of late Rt. Hon. J. Christian, Lord Justice of Appeal, Ireland; no *c. Educ.:* Victoria College, Jersey. Joined Regular Army, 1887; retired on completing command

1st Batt. Suffolk Regiment, 1920; served Aro Expedition, Nigeria, 1901-2 (despatches); Great War (despatches four times, Brevet Lieut.-Colonel, C.M.G., O.B.E., Chevalier de l'ordre de Leopold des Belges). *Recreations:* cricket, tennis, racquets, golf, etc. *Address:* Eastleigh, Greenham, Newbury, Berkshire.
(Died 25 Nov. 1925.)

STEWART, Rev. Alexander, M.A.; Rector of Liverpool since 1870; Hon. Canon, Liverpool since 1880; Chaplain to Bishop of Liverpool, 1900. *Educ.:* Clare College, Cambridge. Ordained, 1849; Curate of Smalley, Derby, 1849-55; South Cadbury, 1855-58; Chilton-Cantelo, Somerset, 1858-68; Vicar of Cogges, Oxford, 1868-70; Chaplain to Bishop Ryle of Liverpool, 1888-1900. *Address:* 29 Sandon Street, Liverpool. *(Died 30 Mar. 1916.)*

STEWART, Maj.-Gen. Alexander Charles Hector, D.L., J.P.; *b.* 15 Nov. 1838; *e. s.* of late John Vandeleur Stewart of Rockhill, Co. Donegal, and Lady Helen Graham-Toler, 4th *d.* of 2nd Earl of Norbury; *m.* 1872, Gertrude Mary, *e. d.* of E. Carrington Smith of Ashfold, Sussex; one *d. Educ.:* Harrow. Entered army, 1856; Lieut.-Col. 1870; retired 1878 as Colonel 2nd Life Guards; High Sheriff, Donegal, 1881. *Address:* 23 Lennox Gardens, S.W. *T.:* Kensington 5050; Rockhill, Letterkenny, Co. Donegal. *Clubs:* Carlton, Bachelors'. *(Died 8 Mar. 1917.)*

STEWART, Major Algernon Bingham Anstruther, D.S.O. 1900; Seaforth Highlanders; *b.* 6 Dec. 1869; *e. s.* of Colonel C. E. Stewart, C.B.; *m.* 1911, Edith Evelyn, *d.* of Sir Arthur Vivian; twin *d.* Entered army, 1890; Capt. 1899; Maj. 1908; Served Chitral Relief Force (medal with clasp); South Africa, 1899-1902 (despatches, Queen's medal, 5 clasps, King's medal, 2 clasps); European War, 1914-15 (despatches); Adjt. 3rd Batt. Seaforth Highlanders, 1903-8; India, 1908. *Address:* 51 Redcliffe Square, S.W.; Ornockenoch, Gatehouse, N.B. *Club:* Naval and Military.
(Died 23 May 1916.)

STEWART, Charles; 4th *s.* of late Duncan John Stewart, and Harriet (*d.* 1884), 3rd *d.* of late Major Anthony Gore, *b.* of Sir Ralph Gore 7th Bart.; *b.* 1840; *m.* 1st, 1870, Eva (*d.* 1872), 4th *d.* of late Henry Robert Kingscote; 2nd, 1874, Alice Louisa, 2nd *d.* of late Robert Johnstone-Douglas of Lockerbie, Dumfriesshire. *Educ.:* Rugby; Edinburgh University. Admitted a Member of the Scottish Faculty of Advocates, 1862; a Solicitor in London, 1872; a retired Member of the Council of the Law Society; proprietor of Castle Stalker (or Stalcaire), Strath Appin, Loch Linnhe; contested (U.) Argyllshire, 1903. *Publications:* Reminiscences of Fifty Years of Legal Life in Edinburgh and London, 1903; In the Evening (Essays), 1910. *Address:* Achara, Duror of Appin, Argyllshire; 38 Eaton Place, S.W. *Clubs:* Carlton, Athenæum; New, Edinburgh.
(Died 2 Aug. 1916.)

STEWART, Lieut.-Col. Charles Edward, C.M.G. 1915; 1st Batt. Royal Highlanders; *b.* 27 Sep. 1868. Entered army, 1889; Captain, 1898; Major, 1908; Lt.-Col. 1914; Brig.-Major, S. Africa, 1900-2; Adjutant, Volunteers, 1903-8; served S. Africa, 1899-1902 (despatches; Queen's medal, 4 clasps; King's medal, 2 clasps); European War, 1914-15 (C.M.G.). *Club:* Army and Navy. *(Died 14 Sept. 1916.)*

STEWART, Rev. Charles Henry Hylton, M.A.; V.D. 1905; Hon. Canon of Chester, 1916; Warden of Special Service Clergy; Assistant County Director B.R.C.S. for City Division, Chester; *m.* Florence Hope, *d.* of Thos. Dixon, Bangor, Chester; four *s.* one *d. Educ.:* St. Catharine's College, Cambridge (choral scholar). Deacon, 1875; priest, 1876; organist of Chichester Cathedral, 1874-75;

curate of Pebmarsh, Essex, 1875-77; minor canon, precentor, and sacrist of Chester, 1877-89; vicar of New Brighton, 1889-1905; rector of Bathwick, 1905-16. *Recreations:* cricket, tennis, rowing. *Address:* 10 Abbey Square, Chester. *Clubs:* Junior Army and Navy; Grosvenor, Chester.
(*Died 7 April 1922.*)

STEWART, Charles Hunter, M.B., D.Sc., F.R.S. Edin.; Professor of Public Health, and Director of the John Usher Institute of Public Health, University of Edinburgh; *b.* Edinburgh, 29 Sep. 1854; *m.* 1st, 1888, Ann Maria (*d.* 1905), *e. d.* of late George Gordon Gibson, civil engineer, Edinburgh; 2nd, 1912, Agnes Millar MacGibbon, *y. d.* of late Robert Somers, Thrushville, Stirling. *Educ.:* Edinburgh. After graduation studied in various foreign laboratories; Assistant to the Professor of Medical Jurisprudence and Public Health, 1884-97; elected first occupant of the Bruce and John Usher Chair of Public Health, 1898. *Publications:* various contributions to the Transactions and Proceedings of Royal Society of Edinburgh, etc. *Recreation:* walking. *Address:* University, Edinburgh. *Club:* Royal Societies. (*Died 30 June 1924.*)

STEWART, Charlotte (*pen name,* **Allan McAulay**); *b.* Cachar, Assam, 30 Sep. 1863; *d.* of late Colonel Robert Stewart of Ardvorlich. *Educ.:* home. *Publications:* The Honourable Stanbury and Others, 1894; The Rhymer, 1900; Black Mary, 1901; Poor Sons of a Day, 1903; The Eagle's Nest, 1910; collaborated with Kate Douglas Wiggin and the Misses Findlater in The Affair at the Inn, 1904: The Safety of the Honours, 1906; Beggars and Sorners, 1912. *Occupation:* knitting socks. *Address:* Ardvorlich Cottage, Balquhidder, Perthshire. (*Died 18 April 1918.*)

STEWART, Sir David, Kt., *cr.* 1896; M.A., LL.D., D.L., J.P.; *b.* 29 July 1835; *s.* of late John Stewart, J.P., Banchory-Devenick and Leggart, and of Mary Irvine; *m.* Margaret Dyce, *d.* of Rev. David Brown, D.D., LL.D., 1860; three *s.* five *d.* *Educ.:* King's College, Aberdeen (M.A.). Chairman Great North of Scotland Railway Company, and Director of Northern Assurance Company and Aberdeen Comb Works Company; Six years Lord Provost of Aberdeen, and nine years in University Court, during which he greatly extended the Aberdeen University Buildings and the City of Aberdeen, so as to include Old Aberdeen, Woodside, and Torry. *Address:* Banchory House, Banchory-Devenick, Kincardineshire. *T.A.:* Banchory House, Aberdeen. *T.:* 1865 Aberdeen. *Clubs:* Carlton, Caledonian; Royal Northern, Aberdeen.
(*Died 11 Oct. 1919.*)

STEWART, David Mitchell, I.S.O. 1915; Superintending Engineer G.P.O., 1895-1918; *b.* 7 Nov. 1853; *s.* of Andrew Stewart, Woodend, Coupar Angus, Perthshire; *m.* Annie Torrance, *d.* of J. T. Weir of Blantyre Park, Lanarkshire; one *s.* one *d.* Entered Post Office Service, 1870; Assistant Superintending Engineer, 1892. *Recreations:* Farming and Shetland pony breeding. *Address:* Blantyre Park, Blantyre, Lanarkshire. *T.:* 60. *M.:* 989. *Club:* Scottish Automobile, Glasgow. (*Died 25 Jan. 1924.*)

STEWART, Sir Francis (Hugh), Kt., *cr.* 1916; C.I.E. 1911; M.A. (Oxon.); partner in Gladstone, Wyllie, & Company, Merchants, London and Calcutta; *b.* Nov. 1869; *s.* of late Robert Stewart of London and Calcutta; *m.* 1906, Frances Henrietta, *e. d.* of A. G. Rickards, K.C.; three *s.* four *d.* *Educ.:* Harrow; Magdalen College, Oxford. Captain Oxford University Golf Club, 1894; Amateur Golf Champion of India, 1897; President Bengal Chamber of Commerce, 1915; Member of Bengal Legislative Council, 1911-12, 1914; Imperial Legislative Council, 1915; a Commissioner for the port of Calcutta, 1909-12, 1914-15: Sheriff of Calcutta, 1914. *Recreations:*

cricket, golf. *Address:* 5 Council House Street, Calcutta. *Clubs:* Union; Bengal, Calcutta.
(*Died 29 Dec. 1921.*)

STEWART, Major - General George, C.B. 1887; Colonel Q.O. Corps of Guides; *b.* 20 July 1839; *s.* of late Major W. Murray Stewart, H.E.I.C.S., of Ardvorlich, N.B.; *m.* 1881, Mary (*d.* 1924), *d.* of J. Monteath Douglas. *Educ.:* St. Andrews; London. Entered Bengal Army, 1856; Capt. Bengal Staff Corps, 1868; Major, 1876; Lieut.-Col. 1879; Colonel, 1883; Major-General (retired), 1887; served throughout Indian Mutiny, 1857-59; present at Havelock's relief of Cawnpore and Lucknow, and its final capture (despatches, medal with two clasps); in China War, 1860 (despatches, medal with two clasps); in Ambeyla Campaign (medal and clasp); with Jawaki Expedition, 1878 (despatches, clasp); in Afghan War, 1878-80; present at Ali Masjid; actions about Kabul; siege of Sherpur and Charasiab (despatches, medal and two clasps). *Address:* Baldorran, College Road, S.E.19. *T.:* Sydenham 764.
(*Died 2 Feb. 1927.*)

STEWART, Right Hon. George Francis, P.C. Ireland, 1921; J.P., D.L., F.S.I.; *b.* 1 Nov. 1851; 8th *s.* of James Robert Stewart of Gortleitragh, Co. Dublin, D.L., and Martha, *e. d.* of Richard Benson Warren, Serjeant-at-law; *m.* 1881, Georgiana Lavinia, 2nd *d.* of Admiral R. R. Quin; two *s.* one *d.* *Educ.:* Marlborough College; Trinity College, Dublin. Senior Moderator and Gold Medallist, 1872; Member of University Senate; had very extensive agencies in Co. Leitrim, of which county he was twice High Sheriff, 1893 and 1913; Director of Bank of Ireland, 1902; Governor of the Bank, 1914 and 1915; Chairman of Irish Branch of Surveyors Institution, 1899; President of the Surveyors Institution, 1916-17; senior partner in the firm of J. R. Stewart & Sons, Dublin, and member of boards of public companies and hospitals; elected as a Representative of the Southern Unionists to Irish Convention, 1917. *Recreations:* travelling and yachting. *Address:* Summerhill, Killiney, Co. Dublin. *M.:* IK 51. *Clubs:* Kildare Street, Dublin; Royal St. George Yacht, Kingstown. (*Died 12 Aug. 1928.*)

STEWART, Sir James Watson, 1st Bt., *cr.* 1920; Chartered Accountant; Member of the Chartered Institute of Accountants and Actuaries; Fellow of the Chartered Insurance Institute, and Senior Partner of J. W. Stewart & Co., C.A., Glasgow; *b.* Rome, 1852; *s.* of late Alexander Stewart, J.P., Springhill, Muirkirk, and late Marion Watson; *m.* 1883, Marion Symington, *e. d.* of late Rev. Alexander Young, of Darvel, Ayrshire; three *s.* five *d.* *Educ.:* Irvine Academy; privately. Member of County Council of Dumbartonshire, 1890-1910; Chairman of Eastern District Committee of the County for seventeen years; Chairman of Dumbartonshire Secondary Education Committee for twenty-seven years; Vice-Chairman of the County of Dumbarton for twelve years, and thereafter Convener of the County and Chairman of the County Council, 1908-10; Member of Glasgow Provincial Committee for the Training of Teachers, and Chairman of Finance Committee, 1905-18; Member of Corporation of Glasgow, 1904-20; acted as Magistrate of the City, and as Convener of the Electricity Committee, and of the Health Committee; Lord Provost of Glasgow, and Lord-Lieutenant of the County of the City of Glasgow, 1917-20; a Governor of the West of Scotland Agricultural College since 1899, and a Member of the Clyde Navigation Trust since 1905; J.P., D.L., City of Glasgow; D.L., County of Lanark; J.P., County of Dumbarton; LL.D., Glasgow University; a Commander of the Legion of Honour, and of the Order of the Crown of Belgium. *Heir:* *s.* Alexander Stewart, *b.* Nov. 1886. *Ad-*

dress: Balgownie, Bearsden, Dumbartonshire.
Clubs: New, Art, Conservative, Royal Scottish
Automobile, Glasgow ; Royal Clyde Yacht.
(Died 3 Nov. 1922.)

STEWART, Sir John, 1st Bt., *cr.* 1920 ;
D.L., J.P. ; partner of Messrs. Alex. Stewart
& Son. of Dundee ; *b.* 1877 ; *s.* of Alexander
Stewart ; Freeman of the City of London.
Address: Fingask Castle, Errol, Perthshire.
(Died 6 Feb. 1924.)

STEWART, John Graham, K.C. 1906.
Educ.: Edinburgh University, M.A., L.L.B. ;
Forensic Prizeman, 1885 ; Vans Dunlop Scholar
in Scots Law and Conveyancing, 1887 - 1890 ;
admitted to Faculty of Advocates, 1887 ; Advocate Depute, 1905 ; contested East Perthshire
(C.), 1900. *Publication:* A Treatise on the Law
of Diligence in Scotland. *Address:* 17 Abercromby Place, Edinburgh. *Clubs:* Conservative,
Barnton, Edinburgh. *(Died 21 May 1917.)*

**STEWART, Sir Mark John Mac-
Taggart,** 1st Bt. of Southwick, Ardwell ; *cr.* 1892 ; D.L., J.P. Wigtownshire ;
D.L., J.P. Stewartry of Kirkcudbright ; *b.*
Stevenson House, East Lothian, 12 October 1834 ;
e. s. of late Mark Hathorn Stewart of Southwick (*s.* of Robert Hathorn Stewart of Physgill)
and Janet, *d.* of John Sprot of Riddell ; *m.* 1866,
Marianne Susanna (*d.* 1914), *o. d.* of late John
Orde Ommanney and Susanna, *d.* and heiress of
Sir John MacTaggart, Bt., of Ardwell, in accordance with whose will the surname of MacTaggart
prior to that of Stewart was assumed, 1895 ;
one *s.* five *d. Educ.:* Winchester Coll. ; Christ
Church, Oxford (M.A.). Barr. Inner Temple,
1862 ; Hon. Col. 1st Administrative Brig. Ayr
and Galloway Artillery Volunteers (medal) ;
M.P. (C.) Wigtown Burghs, 1874-80 ; Stewartry
of Kirkcudbright, 1885-1906 and 1910 ; Chairman of School Board since 1874 ; has travelled
in East and West. The landed properties
extend over 18,000 acres. *Recreations:* travelling, and possesses celebrated herd of pedigreed
Ayrshire cattle. *Heir:* s. Edward Orde [*b.*
31 Jan. 1883 ; *m.* 1917, Hon. Margaret, *e. d.*
of 3rd Lord Donnington. *Educ.:* Eton ;
Christ Church, Oxford. Lieut. Gren. Guards].
Address: Southwick, Dumfries, N.B. *Clubs:*
Carlton, Athenæum ; New, Scottish Conservative, Edinburgh. *(Died 26 Sept. 1923.)*

STEWART, Sir Norman (Robert),
2nd Bt., *cr.* 1881 ; C.B. 1901 ; *b.* 27 Sep. 1851 ;
s. of 1st Bt. and Marina, *d.* of Comm. Thomas
Dymock Dabine, R.N. ; *S.* father, 1900 ; *m.* 1875,
Ada, *d.* of P. Hewitt of Bombay ; one *s.* two *d.*
Entered Army, 1871 ; Capt. 1879 ; Col. 1890 ;
served Afghan War, 1878-80 (despatches, Brevet
Major, medal with clasp) ; Nile Expedition,
1884-85 (despatches, Brevet Lieut.-Col., medal
with two clasps, Khedive's star) ; commanding 1st Infantry Brigade, China, 1900 (despatches) ; retired ; late commanding 2nd class
District, India. *Publication:* My Service Days,
1909. *Heir: s.* Douglas [*b.* 1 July 1878 ; *m.* 1903,
Lilian Dorothea, *d.* of F. W. Quarry].
(Died 6 Nov. 1926.)

STEWART, Rev. Ravenscroft ; Arch-
deacon of N. Wilts 1910-19 ; *b.* 23 June 1845 ;
s. of James Stewart, J.P., D.L., of Cairnsmore,
Newton Stewart, N.B. ; *m.* 1871, Lucy Pene-
lope, *d.* of R. W. M. Nesfield. Castle Hill,
Bakewell ; six *s.* one *d. Educ.:* Loretto ;
Uppingham ; Trinity College, Cambridge.
B.A. 1869 ; M.A. 1879 ; Deacon, 1869 ; Priest,
1870 ; Curate of Bakewell, 1869-71 ; Rector of
Pleasley, Derbyshire, 1871-83 ; Vicar of All
Saints Ennismore Gardens, S.W., 1883-1904 ;
Canon of Bristol, 1903 ; Archdeacon, 1904-10.
Club: Athenæum. *(Died 16 Aug. 1921.)*

**STEWART, Gen. Sir Robert Mac-
gregor,** G.C.B., *cr.* 1911 ; K.C.B., *cr.* 1902 ;
C.B. 1881 : Col.-Comdt. R.A. ; *b.* 1842 ; *s.* of late
John Stewart ; *m.* 1st, 1868, Caroline, *o. c.* of late

Rev. A. Glasse ; one *d.* ; 2nd, 1889, Jessie, *d.*
of 1st Baron Playfair (widow of Capt. Peel).
Served in Hazara campaign, 1868 ; Afghan War.
1878-79 ; Soudan, 1885 ; A.D.C. to the Queen,
1887-97 ; late G.O.C. Royal Artillery, Southern
District, Portsmouth ; Governor of Bermuda,
1904-7 ; Lieutenant of the Tower 1907-09. *Address:* 41 Egerton Crescent, S.W.
(Died 22 Oct. 1919.)

STEWART, Major William, of Ardvor-
lich, Lochearnhead, Perthshire ; Governor,
H.M. Prison, Edinburgh ; *b.* 8 Oct. 1859 ; *m.*
1891, Lily, *d.* of Doctor A. C. MacLaren, 60
Harley Street, W. ; one *s.* two *d. Educ.:*
Cheltenham ; Sherborne. Joined the York and
Lancaster Regt. 1879, and the 10th Lancers,
Hodson's Horse, 1882 ; served through the
Malakand Campaign, 1897 (medal) ; retired to
join the Scottish Prison Dept. 1899. *Recrea-
tions:* shooting and golf. *Address:* The
Governor's House, The Calton, Edinburgh.
T.: Central 4961. *Clubs:* New, Caledonian
United Service, Edinburgh ; Royal and Ancient
Golf, St. Andrews. *(Died 8 June 1918.)*

STEWART, William, D.D., LL.D. ; Dean
of Faculties in Glasgow University since
1911 ; *b.* Annan, 15 Aug. 1835 ; *e. s.* of William
Stewart, Registrar of Births, etc., district of
Dalbeattie, Kirkcudbrightshire ; *m.* 1868 ; three *s.*
Educ.: Dalbeattie Parish School and Glasgow
University ; B.A., 1861 ; M.A., 1862 ; B.D., 1867 ;
D.D., 1874 ; LL.D., 1911. Examiner in Mental
Philosophy for Degrees in Arts, Univ. of Glas.,
1867-70 ; Minister of Church and Parish *quoad
sacra* of St. George's-in-the-Fields, Glasgow, 1868-
1875 ; Professor of Divinity and Biblical Criticism
in University of Glasgow, 1873-1910 ; Clerk of
Senate in University of Glasgow, 1876 - 1911 ;
one of the Governors of the Glasgow City
Educational Endowments Board since 1885 ;
one of the Governors of the Glasgow General
Educational Endowments Board since 1885 ;
Member of the University Court, 1889-1909 ;
Dean of the Faculty of Theology, 1895-1910 ;
one of the Governors of the Glasgow and West of
Scotland Agricultural College, 1899-1908 ; Re-
presentative of Glasgow University on Carnegie
Trust, 1901-11. *Publications:* The Plan of St.
Luke's Gospel, 1873 ; Editor of The University
of Glasgow, Old and New, 1891. *Address:* 3
Annfield Road, Partickhill, Glasgow. *T.:* 182
Partick. *(Died 18 Sept. 1919.)*

**STEWART-BAM of Ards, Lt. - Col.
Sir Pieter Canzius van Blommes-
tein,** Kt., *cr.* 1907 ; O.B.E. 1918 ; J.P. ; M.L.A.
Cape Town. 1904-10 ; *b.* Cape Town, 29 July 1869 ;
e. surv. s. of late J. A. Bam, M.L.A. ; *m.* 1910, Ena
Dingwall Tasca, *d.* and *co-heir* of late Alexander
G. J. Stewart of Ards, Co. Donegal : by Royal
consent added name of Stewart, 1910 ; two *s.*
three *d. Educ.:* Cheltenham ; Normal College and
South African College, Cape Town ; Diocesan
College, Rondebosch ; Cheltenham College.
Entered Cape Garrison Artillery, 1892 ; retired
with rank, 1901 ; served South African War
(medal) ; contested Cape Town, 1904 ; Victoria
West, 1904 ; Chairman of the General Executive
of South African Exhibition, 1907; Originator in
1910 of the British Empire Exhibition ; raised
in 1915, and in command of the 37th Batt.
the London Regt. : Chief Recruiting Officer
City London Territorials, May - Sep. 1915 ;
Founder and first Chairman and present Vice-
President of the South African National Union ;
special medal granted in 1910 by King Edward
for services rendered in connection with formation of the Union of South Africa ; Originator
and Chairman of the Executive of the British
National Union ; connected with many Imperial organisations in England and S. Africa ;
J.P. Co. Donegal. *Recreations:* all sorts of
sport. *Address:* Launcetown House, Ducks
Hill, Northwood ; *T.:* Northwood 216 : Ards,

629

Cashelmore, Co. Donegal; **Sea Point, Cape Town.** *Clubs:* Sports, Royal Automobile; City, Civil Service, Cape Town.
(*Died 20 Dec. 1928.*)

STEWART-CLARK, Sir John, 1st Bt., *cr.* 1918; J.P. and D.L. Linlithgowshire; Director Clark & Co., Ltd., and Scottish Provident Institution; a member of the Royal Company of Archers, King's Bodyguard for Scotland; *b.* 14 Sep. 1864; *o. s.* of late Stewart Clark of Dundas and Cairndhu, and Annie, *d.* of John Smiley, Larne, Co. Antrim; *m.* 1903, Marie Gertrude, *d.* of Major Marcell Conran of Brondyffryn, Denbigh; four *s.* two *d. Educ.:* Merchiston Castle School, Edinburgh; Jesus College, Cambridge. On the Boards of the Queen Victoria Institute for Jubilee Nurses, Edinburgh; Governesses Benevolent Society (Scotland); Royal Victoria Eye Infirmary, Paisley; Edinburgh Agricultural and Fat Stock Societies. *Recreations:* shooting, fishing, golf, and motoring. *Heir: s.* Stewart, *b.* 4 July 1904. *Address:* Dundas Castle, South Queensferry, N.B. *T.A.:* Chateau, Corstorphine. *T.:* 21 Corstorphine. *Clubs:* Royal Automobile, Caledonian, Royal Thames Yacht; Western, Glasgow; New, Edinburgh; Royal Northern and Royal Clyde Yacht; Royal and Ancient, Prestwick, and Hon. Company of Edinburgh Golfers. (*Died 3 Mar. 1924.*)

STEWART-SMITH, Sir Dudley, Kt., *cr.* 1917; Vice-Chancellor of the County Palatine of Lancaster, 1912; K.C. 1902; *b.* 3 Feb. 1857; *s.* of Alexander Stewart - Smith, of London and Hong-Kong; *m.* Katherine, *d.* of Henry Cautley, of Burton Pidsea; two *s.* three *d. Educ.:* University College, London; LL.B. London University. Called to the Bar, 1886; Bencher Middle Temple; Chairman Lancaster Quarter Sessions (Salford Hundred); on the Council of the Victoria and Liverpool Universities; Royal Commissioner (Land Transfer); J.P. Westmorland, Lancashire, and Cheshire; M.P. (L.) Kendal Division, Westmorland, 1906-1910; contested Kendal and East Nottingham, 1910. *Publication:* Law of Winding-up and Reconstruction of Joint-Stock Companies. *Address:* Assize Courts, Manchester; 42 Albert Court, Kensington Gore, S.W.7. *T.:* Western 2280. *M.:* EC 186. *Clubs:* Reform; Westmorland County; Union, Manchester; Athenæum, Liverpool. (*Died 9 May 1919.*)

STEYN, Martinus Theunis; barrister-at-law, Inner Temple, London; *b.* Winburg, O.R.C., 2 Oct. 1857; 3rd *s.* of Martinus Steyn, Bloemfontein, O.R.C., and Cecilia Johanna Wessels, *d.* of Commandant Wessels, Winburg, O.R.C.; *m. e. d.* of Rev. Colin J. Fraser of Philippolis, O.R.C. *Educ.:* Grey Coll. Bloemfontein; Wevente, Holland; Inner Temple, London. Advocate, Bloemfontein, 1883-89; State Attorney, 1889; Second Puisne Judge, 1889-93; First, 1893-96; State President, Orange Free State, 1896-1900. *Recreations:* shooting, riding. *Address:* Bloemfontein, O.R.C.
(*Died 28 Nov. 1916.*)

STIGAND, Major Chauncey Hugh, F.R.G.S. F.Z.S.; Fellow Royal Anthropological Institute; *s.* of William and Agnes Catherine Stigand; *m.* 1913, Nancy Yulee, *d.* of Major Wallace Neff, Washington, D.C.; one *d. Educ.:* Radley; Army tutors. Entered The Queen's Own Royal West Kent Regiment, 1899; served Burmah and Aden; Special Service Officer, Somaliland, 1900; served with King's African Rifles in Nyasaland, British East Africa and Zanzibar, 1902-7; Captain R.W. Kent Regt., 1904; attached East Africa Survey, 1907; Egyptian Army, 1910; Major, 1915; Governor, Upper Nile, 1916. *Publications:* The Game of British East Africa; The Land of Zinj; To Abyssinia through an Unknown Land; Scouting and Reconnaissance in Savage Countries;

Hunting the Elephant in Africa; Administration in Tropical Africa; A Comparative Grammar of Swahili Dialects, etc. *Address:* c/o Cox and Co., Charing Cross, S.W.1. *Club:* Naval and Military. (*Died 20 Dec. 1919.*)

STIKEMAN, William Rucker, C.I.E. 1911; retired merchant; *b.* Lee, Kent, 2 March 1854; *s.* of Henry Frederic Stikeman; unmarried. *Educ.:* Uppingham School. Merchant in Calcutta and Rangoon; recently additional Member of the Burma Legislative Council; Chairman of the Burma Chamber of Commerce. *Recreations:* riding, golf. *Address:* 61 Onslow Gardens, S.W. *Club:* Oriental.
(*Died 3 June 1927.*)

STILEMAN, Rt. Rev. Charles Harvey; Secretary Church Pastoral Aid Society since 1918; Vicar of Emmanuel Church, Clifton, Bristol, 1916-18; *b.* 1863; *s.* of late Major-General W. C. Stileman; *m.* 1887, Frances Dale Fenwick; two *s.* one *d. Educ.:* Repton; Trinity College, Cambridge. Ordained 1887; Curate, North Shields, 1887-89; C.M.S. Missionary, Baghdad, 1889-91; Julfa (Persia), 1891-93; Secretary C.M.S. Persia Mission, 1895-1900, 1901-6; Clerical Secretary C.E.Z.M.S. 1908-12; Bishop in Persia, 1912-16. *Publication:* The Subjects of the Shah. *Address:* Falcon Court, 32 Fleet Street, E.C.4; 37 Lingfield Road, Wimbledon, S.W.19. (*Died 23 Feb. 1925.*)

STILL, William Chester, C.B.E. 1918; Managing Director of W. M. Still & Sons, Ltd., since 1914; *b.* 17 June 1878; *s.* of late William Mudd Still; *m.* Maud Ellen, *d.* of late Edward Bullock, Civil Servant; one *s. Educ.:* Cowper Street Schools. Apprenticed in works of W. M. Still & Sons, Ltd., and became works manager; became a Director, 1907. *Address:* Aberfoyle, Broad Walk, Winchmore Hill, N.21. *T.:* Palmers Green 283. (*Died 12 Aug. 1928.*)

STIRLING, Archibald William, B.C.L.; senior partner in the firm of Maddison, Stirling, and Humm, 13 Old Jewry Chambers, E.C.2, solicitors; *s.* of Charles Stirling of Hamden, S. Australia, and Edith, *e. d.* of John Whitnash of Taunton, Somerset; *m.* 1887, Laura Biddulph, *d.* of John H. Biddulph Pinchard of Taunton; two *s.* and one *d. Educ.:* Taunton; Lincoln Coll., Oxford. 2nd class in Law Honour School, 1878; and 1st class in Civil Law School, 1881; called to Bar but became a solicitor, 1893; visited Australia, 1884, and returned to this country permanently, 1888. *Publication:* The Never Never Land, 1884. *Recreations:* breeds, judges, and shows Dandie Dinmont terriers, and grows sweet peas for exhibition; does some journalism. *Address:* Holmesea, Goring-on-Thames.
(*Died 13 Mar. 1923.*)

STIRLING, Sir Edward Charles, Kt. *cr.* 1917; C.M.G. 1893; M.A., M.D., Sc.D.Cantab., F.R.S., F.R.C.S., C.M.Z.S.; Hon. Fellow Anthropological Institute of Great Britain; Professor of Physiology, Adelaide University; director, South Australian Museum; *b.* South Australia, 8 Sept. 1848; *e. s.* of late Hon. E. Stirling, M.L.C.; *m.* 1877, Jane, *d.* of late Joseph Gilbert, Pewsey Vale, S.A.; five *d. Educ.:* St. Peter's College, S.A.; Trinity College, Cambridge; St. George's Hospital, London. House surgeon, assistant surgeon, lecturer on Physiology, St. George's Hospital; returning to S.A. in 1881 became Lecturer and subsequently Professor of Phys. Adelaide Univ.; consulting surgeon, Adelaide Hospital; late director, S.A. Museum; member, House of Assembly, 1883-86; member, Council Adelaide Univ.; Pres. Australasian Medical Congress, Adelaide, 1905. *Publications:* contributions to medical journals; joint author of article Hydatids in Allbutt's System of Medicine; Notoryctes typhlops, a New Genus and Species of Marsupial (Trans. R.S. of S.A.); Genyornis newtoni, a Fossil Struthious Bird from Lake Callabonna (Trans. R.S. of S.A.); manus and pes of Diprotodon australis (Mem. R.S. of S.A.); Report on the Anthropology of Central Australia, Report Horn Scientific Expedition; and other contributions to Trans. R.S. of S.A., R. Zool. Soc.; etc. *Recreations*: shooting, horticulture. *Address*: St. Vigeans, Mt. Lofty, South Australia. *T.A.*: Adelaide. *Clubs*: Athenæum, New University; Adelaide. (*Died 20 Mar. 1919.*)

STIRLING, Right Hon. Sir James, Kt., cr. 1886; LL.D.; F.R.S.; P.C. 1900; *b.* Aberdeen 3 May 1836; *e. s.* of Rev. James Stirling, George Street U.P. Church, Aberdeen, and Sarah Irvine; *m.* Aby, *e. d.* of John Thomson Renton, Bradstone Brook, Shalford, Surrey, 1868; one *s.* two *d.* *Educ.*: Grammar School and University, Aberdeen; Trin. Coll. Camb. (B.A.) Cambridge (Senior Wrangler and First Smith's prizeman), 1860; M.A. Cambridge, 1863. Barr. Lincoln's Inn, 1862, Bencher, 1886; practised as conveyancer and equity draftsman; Junior (equity) Counsel to the Treasury, 1881; Judge of the Chancery Division of the High Court of Justice, 1886-1900; Lord Justice of Appeal, 1900-6. *Recreations*: interested in physical and natural science. *Address*: Finchcocks, Goudhurst, Kent. *Club*: Athenæum.
(*Died 27 June 1916.*)

STIRLING, James Heron; *b.* Cookstown, Co. Tyrone, 7 Sep. 1867; *s.* of James Stirling, Ayrshire, and Elizabeth Heron, Co. Tyrone; *m.* 1901, Lisette C. Adami, Ashton-on-Mersey; two *d.* *Educ.*: Royal Belfast Academical Institution. Entered York Street Flax Spinng Ltd., Belfast, 1882; remained there since, Senior Managing Director; Hon. Treasurer, Queen's University and Member of Senate; Chairman, Board of Governors R. B. Academical Institution; Vice-Chairman Ulster Hospital; Past President Belfast Chamber of Commerce; Danish Consul for Ireland, Knight of the Dannebrog; Prov. G.M., A.F. and A.M., Antrim. *Recreations*: golf, gardening. *Address*: Mount Randal, Belfast. *T.*: Malone 26. *M.*: XI 2527, OI 7497. *Clubs*: Constitutional; Ulster Reform, Belfast: Royal County Down Golf.
(*Died 23 Nov. 1928.*)

STIRLING, Hon. Brig.-Gen. James Wilfred, C.B. 1918; C.M.G. 1917; *b.* 1855; *o. s.* of late J. Stirling, of Ballawley Park, Dundrum; *m.* 1881, Cecilia Mary, *d.* of late Maj.-Gen. D. E. Hoste, C.B. *Educ.*: Wellington College. Is Lieut.-Col. and Brevet Col. R.F.A. (retired), and a Hon. Brig.-Gen.; served European War, 1914-18 (despatches five times, C.B., C.M.G., Croix de Guerre); D.L., J.P. Devon. *Address*: Hensleigh House, Exeter. *Club*: Army and Navy. (*Died 4 June 1926.*)

STIRLING, John W., M.B. (Edin.), etc.; M.D., McGill, 1913; Professor of Ophthalmology, McGill Univ.; Consulting Surgeon Oculist to Royal Victoria Hospital; *b.* Halifax, N.S., 2 July 1859; *s.* of W. S. Stirling, Manager Union Bank of Halifax; *m.* 1898, Annie, *e. d.* of Howard Primrose, Pictou, N.S.; no *c.* *Educ.*: Halifax; Galt, Ont.; Edinburgh; Vienna; Berlin. After school career in Halifax, short business course, then entered Edinburgh University; graduated 1884; House Surgeon Royal Infirmary; studied in Vienna and Berlin; attached to Royal Moorfields Ophthalmic Hospital; settled in Montreal, 1887. *Publications*: numerous short articles on Ocular Diseases, etc. *Recreation*: golf. *Address*: 388 Sherbrooke Street West, Montreal; Keewaydin, Pointe Claire, P.Q. *T.*: up 1489. *Clubs*: Mount Royal, University, Forest and Stream, Royal Montreal Golf, Beaconsfield Golf. (*Died 11 Dec. 1923.*)

STIRLING, Rt. Rev. Waite Hockin, D.D.; *b.* 1829; *s.* of Captain T. Stirling, R.N. Curate of St. Mary's Church, Nottingham, 1852-56; Secretary to South American Mission, 1857-62; Superintendent of English Church Mission in Tierra del Fuego and Patagonia,

1862-69; 1st Bishop of Falkland Isles, 1869-1901; Assistant to Bishop of Bath and Wells 1901-12; Canon Residentiary, of Wells Cathedral, 1901-20; Precentor, 1903-20. *Publication*: (jointly) The Story of Commander A. Gardiner, R.N., 1867. *Address*: 24 Holland Park, W.11. *T.*: Park 428. (*Died 19 Nov. 1923.*)

STOCK, Eugene; Secy. of Church Missionary Society, 1873-1906; *b.* 26 Feb. 1836; *m.* 1st, 1862, Eliza Mann (*d.* 1882); 2nd, 1902, Hon. Mrs. Isabella Emily Fiennes. *Educ.*: private schools. In mercantile life till 1873; also Editor to Church of England Sunday School Institute, 1867-75; Editor of Church Missionary Society's Publications, 1873-1902; visited the Colonies, 1892 and 1895; India, 1892-93; United States, 1900; Member of London Diocesan Conference from its establishment, 1883; Member of House of Laymen from its establishment, 1885; Member of National Church Assembly from its establishment to 1925; Diocesan Lay Reader for the Diocese of London from 1891, also for Diocese Rochester and Winchester; Hon. D.C.L. Durham, 1908. *Publications*: Lessons on the Life of our Lord, 1871; Steps to Truth, 1878; for nine years, 1873-81, contributed the English Teachers' Notes to the Sunday School Journal, America; Lesson Studies on Genesis, 1880; planned the Church Missionary Gleaner, 1874; Author of History of Church Missionary Soc. (4 vols.), 1899-1916; Short Handbook of Missions, 1904; and several works on Missions; also Story of the Bible, 1906; Talks on St. Luke, 1907; My Recollections, 1909; English Church in 19th century, 1910; The Servant, 1912; An Heroic Bishop (Valpy French), 1913; Plain Talks on the Pastoral Epistles, 1914; Beginnings in India, 1917. *Address*: Melita, Bournemouth West. *T.*: Bournemouth 1846. *Club*: National.
(*Died 7 Sept. 1928.*)

STOCKENSTRÖM, Sir Andries, 3rd.Bt., cr. 1840; Member of the Railway Board; *b.* 22 Sep. 1868; *s.* of late Hon. Andries Stockenström; *m.* 1897, Mabel, *d.* of J. H. Booysen of Klip Drift, Graaf Reinet, S. Africa; two *s.* two *d.*; *S.* uncle, 1912. *Educ.*: Pembroke College, Cambridge. Called to Bar, Middle Temple, 1891; was M.L.A. Transvaal and Union of S. Africa. *Address*: Maaström, Bedford, Cape Province, S. Africa.
(*Died 1 Dec. 1922.*)

STOCKER, Ven. Harry, Vicar of St. John, Invercargill, 1882; Archdeacon of Invercargill 1885, retired; *m.*; one *s.* *Educ.*: Trinity College, Dublin (B.A.). Ordained, 1868; Curate of Kingsclere, Hants, 1868-74; Vicar of Lincoln, N.Z., 1874-79; Incumbent of Akaroa, 1879-82. *Address*: 111 Springfield Road, Christchurch, New Zealand. (*Died 1 Sept. 1922.*)

STOCKLEY, Colonel Charles More, C.B. 1894; *b.* 1845; 2nd *s.* of Captain W. S. Stockley, H.E.I.C.S.; *m.* 1st, 1874, Margaret, *d.* of Stephen Creagh Sandes; 2nd, 1890, Eleanor, *d.* of F. Fryer, and widow of Capt. H. Thornton, R.N. Entered army, 1862; Colonel, 1888; retired, 1897; served N.W. Frontier, India, 1863 (medal with clasp); Jowaki, 1877-78 (clasp); Afghan Campaign, 1880-81 (despatches, medal, Brevet Major); Commanded Regimental District 27, 1892-97. *Address*: Round Oak, Newbury, Berks.
(*Died 18 Oct. 1923.*)

STOCKMAN, Sir Stewart, Kt., cr. 1913; M.R.C.V.S.; Chief Veterinary Officer and Director of Veterinary Research Ministry of Agriculture and Fisheries since 1905; *b.* Edinburgh, 27 Sep. 1869; 4th *s.* of W. J. Stockman, merchant; *m.* 1908, Ethel, *e. d.* of Sir John M'Fadyean; two *d.* *Educ.*: Royal High School, Edinburgh; Royal Veterinary College, Edinburgh; Paris and Brussels. Professor of Pathology and Bacteriology, Royal Veterinary College, Edinburgh, 1892-99; served S. African War, 1900 (medal and four clasps); served in

Indian Civil Veterinary Department, 1902-3; appointed Principal Veterinary Officer, Transvaal Department of Agriculture, 1903-5. *Publications:* A Text-book of Meat Inspection; various Scientific Articles and Reports. *Recreations:* riding, golf. *Address:* 4 Whitehall Place, S.W.1. *T.A.:* Agriti, London.   (*Died 2 June 1926.*)

STOCKS, Rev. John Edward, Residentiary Canon of Peterborough since 1920; Examining Chaplain to Bishop of Peterborough, 1915; *b.* 28 Aug. 1843; *s.* of Samuel Stocks, Leeds; *m.* 1871, Emily Jane, 3rd *d.* of Thomas Mallam, solicitor, Oxford; six *s.* four *d. Educ.:* Christ Church, Oxford (Chaplain, 1867-71). Vicar of Market Harborough, 1871-84; Vicar of St. Saviour's, Leicester, 1884-1902; Rural Dean of Gartree, 1884; of Leicester, 1891-1899; Archdeacon of Leicester, 1899-1920; Hon. Canon of Peterborough, 1893-99; Rector of Misterton, Lutterworth, 1903-14; Prolocutor, Lower House of Convocation, Canterbury, 1913-18. *Address:* Precincts, Peterborough. *Club:* Church Imperial.   (*Died 29 Aug. 1926.*)

STOCKTON, Rear-Admiral Charles Herbert; *b.* Philadelphia, Penn., U.S., 13 Oct. 1845; *s.* of Rev. W. R. Stockton, D.D., and Emma T. Stockton; *m.* 1st, 1875, Cornelia Carter; 2nd, 1880, Pauline Lentilhon, *d.* of Peter V. King of New York; one *s.* two *d. Educ.:* U.S. Naval Acad. Graduated from the Naval Acad. 1865 and went into active service at once as a midshipman, making various cruises, and being promoted to the rank of Commander, 1892; while Lt.-Com. in command of the U.S.S. "Thetis," cruised in the Arctic Ocean from mouth of the Mackenzie to Wrangel land, 1889; in command "Yorktown," Asiatic Station, 1895-97; President U.S. Naval War Coll., 1898-1900; promoted Capt. 1899; in command battleship "Kentucky," Asiatic Station, 1901-3; Naval Attaché to American Embassy, London, 1903-6; promoted Rear-Admiral, 1906; on duty Navy Department, Washington, D.C., 1906-7; in command Special Service Squadron, 1907; retired, 1907; first representative of the United States at International (Naval) Conference which met in London, 1908; LL.D. George Washington Univ., 1909; Pres. of George Washington Univ., 1910-18. *Publications:* History of the United States Naval Asylum; The Laws and Usages of War, a Naval War Code; editor of a Manual of International Law (2nd ed.); Manual of International Law for Naval Officers, 3rd ed. 1921; Outlines of International Law, 1915. *Address:* 2017 O Street N.W., Washington. *T.:* North 6959, Washington. *Clubs:* University, New York; University, Providence; Metropolitan, Washington, etc.
(*Died 31 May 1924.*)

STOKER, Robert Burdon, M.P. (C.) S. Manchester since 1918; Shipowner; Chairman and Managing Director of Manchester Liners, Ltd., 108 Deansgate, Manchester; Director of Manchester Ship Canal Co.; Chairman of s.s. Knutsford, Ltd., of Ocean Dry Docks Co., Ltd., Swansea, and Director of other Companies—Insurance, Shipping, and Engineering; J.P. County Palatine of Chester; President (1916, 1917, and 1918) of Manchester Chamber of Commerce; *m.*; two *s.* two *d. Educ.:* Liverpool College, Liverpool. *Address:* Heather Lea, Green Walk, Bowdon, Cheshire. *Clubs:* Carlton; Constitutional, Clarendon, Manchester.   (*Died 4 Sept. 1919.*)

STOKER, Thomas, B.A., C.S.I. 1898; I.C.S.; *b.* 20 Aug. 1849; 3rd *s.* of late Abraham Stoker; *m.* 1891, Enid, *d.* of late William Robert Bruce; one *d. Educ.:* Trinity Coll., Dublin. Entered I.C.S. 1872; held various appointments, including District and Settlement Officer, Commissioner, Special Famine Secretary, and Chief Secretary to Government, North-Western Provinces and Oudh, 1897-98; retired, 1899; served throughout in N.W.P. and Oudh. Decorated for services in 1897 famine. *Publications:* A Gold Standard for India; Settlement Report, Bulandshahr District, etc. *Address:* 42 Egerton Crescent, S.W.3. *T.:* Western 6697. *Club:* East India United Service.
(*Died 14 June 1925.*)

STOKES, Adrian, M.D., F.R.C.S.I. D.S.O. 1918; O.B.E. 1919; Sir William Dunn Professor of Pathology in the London University since 1922; *b.* Lausanne, 1887; *s.* of Henry John Stokes, I.C.S., and Mary Anne MacDougal; unmarried. *Educ.:* private school; Trinity College, Dublin. Medical School, Honours in Anatomy; Demonstrator in Anatomy; M.B. 1910; M.D. 1911; Medical Travelling Prize; Assistant to Professor of Pathology; Professor of Bacteriology and Preventive Medicine, Dublin University, 1919-22; Pathologist Royal City of Dublin Hospital; Pathologist Adelaide Hospital; Lt. R.A.M.C. !1 Aug. 1914 (despatches, D.S.O., O.B.E., Chevalier Ordre de la Couronne Belgium, 1918); Member Rockefeller Commission on Yellow Fever, West Africa, 1920. *Publications:* Infectious Jaundice, Typhoid Carriers, Dysentery, etc. *Recreation:* cricket. *Address:* Guy's Hospital, St. Thomas's Street, S.E.1; 602 Clive Court, Maida Vale, W.9. *M.:* MI 30. *Clubs:* Athenæum, M.C.C.; University, Dublin.   (*Died 19 Sept. 1927.*)

STOKES, Sir Arthur, 2nd Bt., *cr.* 1889; *b.* 27 Sept. 1858; *s.* of Sir George Gabriel Stokes, 1st Bt., Master of Pembroke College, Cambridge, at one time M.P. for Cambridge University; *m.* 1897, Mary Winifred, *d.* of late Hubert Garbett, of Rushen House, Castletown, Isle of Man; two *d. Educ.:* Charterhouse; King's College, Cambridge. *Heir:* none. *Recreations:* sailing, shooting, skating, travelling, cycling. *Address:* Kingsland, Shrewsbury.
(*Died 12 June 1916.*)

STOKES, Rev. Augustus Sidney; Hon. Canon, Ely, 1891; *m.* 1879, Alice *d.* of John Hill of Wombourn, Staffs; four *s.* four *d. Educ.:* St. John's College, Cambridge (M.A.). Curate of St. John Baptist, Kidderminster, 1872-75; St. Anne's, Soho, 1875; St. Lawrence, Jewry, 1876-77; Diocesan Inspector, Ely, 1877-1896; Vicar of Elm, 1896-1920; Rural Dean of Wisbech, 1916. *Address:* 87 Cheriton Road, Folkestone.   (*Died 24 Sept. 1922.*)

STOKES, Sir (Frederick) Wilfrid Scott, K.B.E., *cr.* 1917; M.Inst.C.E.; Past Pres. of British Engineers' Association, and of the Ipswich and District Engineers Employers' Assoc.; Chairman of Ransomes & Rapier, Ltd.; *b.* 9 April 1860; 5th *s.* of late Scott Nasmyth Stokes, B.A., Barrister, and Emma Louisa, *y. d.* of late Benjamin Walsh, Worcestershire; *m.* 1900, Irene Theodora, 2nd *d.* of Luke Ionides. *Educ.:* Kensington Catholic Public School; Catholic University College, Kensington. Inventor of the Stokes' gun, shell, etc.; has Order of the Osmanieh, 2nd class, and Medjidie, 2nd class. *Address:* Millwater, Ripley, Surrey; 7 Park Lane, W.1. *T.:* Gerrard 3472.
(*Died 7 Feb. 1927.*)

STOKES, Sir Gabriel, K.C.S.I., *cr.* 1909; C.S.I. 1903; *b.* 7 July 1849; *s.* of Henry Stokes, for many years county surveyor of Kerry; *m.* 1st, 1885, Rebecca (*d.* 1886), *d.* of Alfred Horsfall of Formby, Liverpool; one *s.*; 2nd, 1889, May Florence (*d.* 1897), *d.* of James Fuller of Glashuachrse, Kenmare, Co. Kerry; three *s. Educ.:* Kilkenny College; Armagh Royal School; Trinity College, Dublin, Graduated T.C.D. 1871; entered Indian Civil Service, 1871; superintended the census of the Madras Presidency, 1881; Revenue Secretary to Madras Govt., 1896; acting member of Council, 1902; Chief Sec. Government of Madras, 1898-1903; Member of Council, 1903-8; acted as Governor of Madras, 1906. *Club:* University, Dublin.   (*Died 22 Oct. 1920.*)

STOKER, George, C.M.G. See page xxx.

STOKES, Sir Henry Edward, K.C.S.I., cr. 1892; b. 23 July 1841; m. 1st, 1865, Janet (d. 1870), d. of William Stokes, M.D.; 2nd, 1872, Helena Amy (d. 1874), d. of Surg.-Gen. Currie; two s. Educ.: Trinity College, Dublin. Entered Madras C.S. 1863; Secretary to Govt. of Madras, 1883; Member of Council of Governor of Madras, 1888-93. Address: 32 Brunswick Gardens, Campden Hill, W.8. T.: Park 3451.
(Died 20 Oct. 1926.)

STOKES, Leonard (Aloysius Scott), F.R.I.B.A.; b. 1858; 2nd surv. s. of Scott Nasmyth Stokes; m. 1898, Edith Nellie, d. of William Edward Louis Gaine; two s. two d. Vice-President of the Architectural Association, 1887-88; President, 1889; President of the Royal Institute of British Architects for 1910 and 1911; Royal Gold Medalist, 1919; médaille d'argent (Architecture) at Paris Exhibition, 1900; buildings include the Chelsea Town Hall; Lincoln Grammar School; several Exchange Buildings for the National Telephone Co. Ltd., at Birmingham, Glasgow, Aberdeen, etc., and in London; Minterne House (for Lord Digby); additions to Downside School; All Saints Convent, Colney, near St. Albans; churches at Maidenhead, Folkestone, Southampton, Exeter; St. Begbroke and St. Clare's, Sefton Park; Nazareth House, Southsea; and Nazareth House, Bexhill; new quadrangle at Emmanuel College, Cambridge; R.C. Cathedral, Georgetown, Demerara, etc.; member, Royal Commission on Historical Monuments (England), appointed 1908, and a member of the Committee for the King Edward Memorial for London. Address: 3 Mulberry Walk, Chelsea, S.W.3. T.: Gerrard 672. Clubs: Arts, Chelsea, Arts.
(Died 25 Dec. 1925.)

STONE, Ven. Arthure Edward, b. 1852; s. of Rev. Meade Nisbett Stone, H.E.I.C.S.; m. 1897, Elinor Mabel, e. d. of Innes Rogers. Educ.: St. Peter's, York; Trinity College, Dublin; Gloucester Theological College. Chaplain, Bengal Ecclesiastical Establishment, 1877-1902; Chaplain, Upper Burma Field Force, 1886-1888 (despatches, medal, clasp); Commissary-in-Charge of the Diocese of Calcutta; Fellow Calcutta University, 1898; Chaplain, Calcutta Light Horse, 1892-1902; Archdeacon of Calcutta, 1898-1903; Rector of Islip, Oxon, 1902-10; Vicar of Burcombe, 1910-17. Recreation: fishing. Address: 3 Horace Road, Boscombe, Bournemouth. (Died 11 Jan. 1927.)

STONE, Hon. Sir Edward Albert, Kt., cr. 1902; K.C.M.G., cr. 1912; Lieut.-Gov. of Western Australia since 1906; b. 9 Mar. 1844; 2nd s. of late Hon. G. F. Stone, Attorney-Gen.; m. 1867, Susan, d. of late G. Shenton. Educ.: Chigwell, Essex, England. Called to W.A. Bar, 1865; Clerk to Legislative Council, 1870-74; Acting Attorney-General, 1879; Nominee Member of Legislative Council, 1880; Acting Chief Justice, 1881, 1887, 1889, 1890; Crown Solicitor, 1881; Puisne Judge, 1884; Chief Justice, Perth, W.A., 1901-6. Address: Rose Hill, Perth, W.A.
(Died 30 April 1920.)

STONE, George Frederick, Managing Editor and chief leader writer, Western Daily Press, Bristol, since 1921; Director of Walter Reid & Son, Ltd., the company publishing this and other papers; b. Bath, 25 Sep. 1855; s. of late Frederick Stone, Bristol; m. Selina, e. d. of late Richard Upham Rossiter, Bristol; one s. three d. Educ.: Bristol Trade and Mining School (now Merchant Venturers' Technical College). Apprenticed newspaper reporting, Bristol Times and Mirror, 1870; transferred to Western Daily Press, 1877; did much special work for that paper; became chief reporter and deputised for editors; President Bristol Press Fund 1907, 1908, 1922; member Bristol Rotary Club; Bristol Committee of London Press Fund;

Bristol Officers' Association Committee; Council of Bristol Chamber of Commerce and Shipping; Colston Research Society Committee; Bristol and Gloucestershire Archæological Soc. Publications: Bristol as it Was and as it Is; with Mr. C. Wells edited Bristol and Great War. Recreations: cycling, gardening, photography, etc. Address: 18 Logan Road, Bristol. T.: Bristol 5634. Club: Bristol Liberal.
(Died 8 Dec. 1928.)

STONE, Marcus, R.A. 1887; b. 4 July 1840; 2nd s. of late Frank Stone, A.R.A. Educ.: home. Exhibited in 63 consecutive exhibitions of the R.A., rarely elsewhere; has received medals at the international exhibitions of Paris, Berlin, Vienna, Philadelphia, Chicago, Melbourne, and others; when young illustrated books, Dickens, Trollope, Cornhill Magazine, etc.; painter of subjects of human interest and historical genre; A.R.A. 1877. Publications: the greater number of his works have been published as engravings. Recreations: omnivorous reader of books; a player of billiards. Address: 8 Melbury Road, Kensington, W. Clubs: Athenæum. Arts.
(Died 24 Mar. 1921.)

STONE, Rev. W. H., M.A.; Rector of Sevenoaks since 1920; b. 1860; s. of W. Stone, J.P.; m. Helena Jane, d. of late Colonel G. Grant Gordon, C.V.O., C.B., Controller to Prince Christian; three d. Educ.: Rugby; Trinity College, Cambridge. Rector of Charleton, Devon, 1888-91; Vicar of St. James's, Hatcham, 1891-96; St. Mary, Kilburn, 1896-1907; Prebendary in Wells Cathedral, 1911; Rector of Walcot. Bath, 1907-13; Chipstead, Surrey, 1913-20. Recreation: golf. Address: Sevenoaks Rectory, Kent. Club: New Oxford and Cambridge.
(Died 17 Nov. 1920.)

STONE-WIGG, Rt. Rev. Montagu John, D.D.; Commissary in Australia to Bishop of New Guinea, 1910; b. 1861; m. 1907, Elfie Marcia, d. of late James Mort; two d. Educ.: Winchester; University College, Oxford; Ely. Deacon, 1884; Priest, 1885; 1st Canon Residentiary and Subdean of St. John's Cathedral, Brisbane, 1892-98; 1st Bishop of New Guinea, 1898-1908; resigned, 1908; Ramsden Preacher at Oxford, 1908; Fellow, St. Paul's College, Sydney University, 1914. Address: Colonna, Burwood, New South Wales, Australia. (Died 16 Oct. 1918.)

STONEX, Rev. Francis Tilney; Hon. Canon of Chester Cathedral; Vicar of Bowdon since 1919; b. Gt. Yarmouth, 28 Sep. 1857; s. of late Henry Stonex, Gt. Yarmouth; m. Alice Mary Rowe, d. of late Dr. Pring, of Elmfield, Taunton, Somerset; three s. one d. Educ.: Gt. Yarmouth Grammar School; Trinity College, Dublin. Curate of S. Mary's, Taunton, 1880-3; Curate in charge of S. Michael's, Claughton, Birkenhead, 1883-7; Vicar of Holy Trinity, Birkenhead, 1887-91; Surrogate, 1888; Vicar of Bredbury, Stockport, 1891-93; Rector of S. Peter's, Chester, 1893-1905; Vicar of S. James, New Brighton, 1905; Rural Dean of Wallasey, 1914-19. Address: The Vicarage, Bowdon, Cheshire. T.A.: Bowdon.
(Died Jan. 1920.)

STONHAM, Charles, C.M.G., 1901; F.R.C.S., F.Z.S., Senior Surgeon, Lecturer on Surgery, Teacher of Operative Surgery, Westminster Hospital, London; Examiner in Surgery, Society of Apothecaries, and Royal University, Ireland; Hon. Major in the army, and Lt.-Col. in command of London Mounted Brigade F.A.; b. 27 Mar. 1858; 3rd s. of T. G. Stonham, of Maidstone, Kent. Educ.: King's School, Canterbury; Univ. Coll., London; Aitchison Scholarship, Univ. Coll. Lond.; Gold Medallist in Surgery, in Medicine, and in Gynæcology; Member of British Ornithologists' Union; Fellow of Royal Soc. of Medicine. Professional education at University College, London, where held all house posts, and for some years was Senior Demonstrator of Anatomy and Curator of the Pathological Museum; made Assistant Surgeon, Westminster Hospital, 1887, then resigning other surgical posts, promoted to full staff, 1895, and became Senior Surgeon, 1897. *Decorated* for services in South Africa as Chief Surgeon and officer commanding Imperial Yeomanry Field Hospital (medal and 4 clasps). *Publications:* The Birds of the British Islands; A Manual of Surgery, and various other surgical and pathological works; Report of Field Hospital and Bearer Company in South Africa. *Recreations:* mountaineering; natural history, especially ornithology. *Address:* 4 Harley Street, W. *T.:* 1466 Paddington. *M.:* A 1011. *Clubs:* Conservative, Alpine. (*Died 31 Jan. 1916.*)

STOODLEY, Edwin Edward, C.B. 1906; Joint Secretary to Board of Inland Revenue, Stamps and Taxes, 1902-9; *b.* 1844; *m.* 1885, Ada Mary, *d.* of late Francis Ballard, Leominster. *Address:* Oketon, Hampton Road, Teddington. (*Died 13 Feb. 1922.*)

STOPFORD, Hon. Horatia Charlotte Frances, a Woman of the Bedchamber to late Queen Victoria; *b.* 1835; *d.* of Lieut.-Col. Hon. Edward Stopford; *g. d.* of 3rd Earl of Courtown. *Address:* 6 St. Katherine's, Regent's Park. N.W. (*Died 6 Feb. 1920.*)

STORER, Bellamy; *b.* Cincinnati, Ohio, 28 Aug. 1847; *m.* Mrs. Maria Longworth. *Educ.:* Harvard University. Bar, 1869; Representative 1st Dist., Ohio, to U.S. Congress, 1890-95; Minister to Belgium, 1897-99; to Spain, 1899-1902; Ambassador of the United States at Vienna, 1902-6. *Recreations:* engravings, books, golf. *Address:* Cincinnati, U.S.A. *Clubs:* Metropolitan, Washington; Queen City, Cincinnati; Jockey, Vienna. (*Died 12 Nov. 1922.*)

STOREY, Hon. Sir David, Kt., *cr.* 1923; Member Legislative Council, N.S. Wales, since 1920; Governing Director David Storey & Co., Ltd.; Chairman Directors Insurance of Australia, Ltd.; *b.* 18 Aug. 1856; *s.* of late Robert Storey, Monaghan, Ireland; *m.* Rachel Agnes, *o. c.* of late Capt. Andrew Doig, Edinburgh; four *s.* one *d.* *Educ.:* Wattsbridge Academy. Arrived in Australia, 1879, at age of 23; founded firm of David Storey & Co., Ltd., 1880; first elected to N.S. Wales Parliament, as Member for Randwick, in 1894; represented that electorate till resignation, 1920; Hon. Minister in the National Ministry of N.S. Wales, 1916-19; Minister for Public Health, 1919-20. *Recreation:* bowls. *Address:* Sherbrooke, Randwick, Sydney, N.S.W., Australia. *T.A.:* Yerots, Sydney. *T.:* Randwick 12. *Clubs:* New South Wales, Masonic, Randwick Bowling, Sydney. (*Died July 1924.*)

STOREY, George Adolphus, R.A. 1914; A.R.A., 1876; Professor of Perspective, Royal Academy, since 1914; *b.* London, 7 Jan. 1834; 2nd *s.* of James Payne Storey and Emily Fitch; *m.* Emily, *y. d.* of late James Hayward, London; one *d.* *Educ.:* in Paris, under M. Morand, Prof. of Mathematics. Returned to England, 1850; studied at J. M. Leigh's Art School in Newman Street; became a student at Royal Academy; exhibited first picture R.A., 1852; visited Spain, 1862-63; Teacher of Perspective at the Royal Academy, 1900; Examiner in Drawing, Board of Education, 1913. *Pictures:* The Widowed Bride, 1858; The Bride's Burial, 1859; The Annunciation, 1860; War Time, 1862; The Closed House, 1862; The Danaides, 1864; Lady Godiva, 1865; A Royal Challenge; After You, 1867; The Shy Pupil, 1868; The Old Soldier, 1869; Only a Rabbit, 1870; Scandal, 1872; Blue Girls of Canterbury; Little Swansdown; Christmas Visitors, 1874; Dame Octavia Beaumont, 1874; Mrs. Finch, 1875; Caught; Mistress Dorothy; The Pump-Room, Bath; The Connoisseur; The Young Prodigal. etc.;

1004

First Practice, 1894; Double Dummy; Coming Events; Rival Minstrels, 1895; A Love Stratagem, and the Town Gossip, 1896; Summer Days, 1897; In Evening Shade, 1898; The Lost Labour of the Danaides; Philomel, 1900; The Love Letter, 1901; A Love Sonnet; Miss Reynolds, 1902; Pluto's Messenger, 1904; Venus Lamenting the Death of Adonis: Griselda, 1905; Leda, Pamela, etc., 1906; Phryne, 1908; Circe, Pan and Syrinx, and Phillis Meyerstein, 1909; My Mother's Portrait, purchased by the Committee of National Arts Collections Fund, 1912, for the National Gallery of British Art; My Father's Portrait, 1874, now in the National Gallery of British Art, purchased by the Comtemporary Art Society and subscriptions in 1914; Lady in Furs; Miss Gladys Storey, 1912; Her First Letter, 1913; A Young Painter, Edward Cressy; Armida in the Enchanted Wood, 1914; Viola (diploma work), Diana, 1915; Girl in White; A Kentish Garden, 1916; The Mill Stream; Chevening, 1917; Cupid Fishing, 1918. *Publications:* Sketches from Memory, 1899; Theory and Practice of Perspective, 1910. *Recreations:* reading, etc. *Address:* 39 Broadhurst Gardens, Hampstead. N.W. *T.:* Hampstead 7033. (*Died 29 July 1919.*)

STOREY, Samuel, D.L., J.P. Durham County and Berwickshire; *b.* 13 Jan. 1840; *s.* of Robert Storey, of Whitburn; *m.* 1st, 1864, Mary Ann (*d.* 1877), *e. d.* of J. Addison; 2nd, 1898, Sarah (*d.* 1908), *widow* of John Newton; one *s.* two *d.* Mayor of Sunderland, 1876, 1877, and 1880; M.P. (R.) Sunderland, 1881-95, and Jan. 1910 as Ind. T.R.; retired Dec. 1910; Chairman of Durham County Council, 1894-1905. *Recreations:* motoring, salmon-fishing. *Address:* Southill, Chester-le-Street, Co. Durham. *M.:* J 8500. *Club:* Royal Automobile. (*Died 18 Jan. 1925.*)

STORMONTH-DARLING, Major John Collier, D.S.O. 1915; 1st Batt. the Cameronians (Scottish Rifles); temporary Lt.-Col. commanding 9th H.L.I. (Glasgow Highlanders); *b.* 9 Feb. 1878. Entered army, 1900; Captain, 1912; Major, 1915; served S. African War, 1899-1902 (despatches, Queen's medal 3 clasps, King's medal 2 clasps); European War, 1914-15 (despatches, D.S.O.). *Address:* Edenbank, Kelso; Lednathie, Kirriemuir. *Club:* Caledonian. (*Died 1 Nov. 1916.*)

STORR, Francis, B.A.; Officier d'Academie; late editor of Journal of Education; *b.* Suffolk, 28 Feb. 1839; *e. s.* of late Rev. Francis Storr and Caroline, *d.* of Colonel Holland; *m.* Rose, *d.* of late Francis Lloyd; one *s.* three *d.* *Educ.:* Harrow; Trin. Coll., Camb. (Scholar). Bell University Scholar; 6th in Classical Tripos, 1861. Master at Marlborough College, 1864-75; Merchant Taylors', 1875-1901; Authors' Society, College of Preceptors (Fellow). Teachers Guild, Froebel Society, Modern Language Association (Vice-President), Women's Training and Registration Society (Vice-Chairman of Council), University of London Board of Pedagogy. *Publications:* Heine's Travel Pictures; Lermontoff's Demon; Canterbury Chimes; Bacon's Essays; Life and Remains of R. H. Quick; Sophocles, verse translation; and various school-books. *Recreations:* fishing, billiards. *Address:* 40 Mecklenburgh Square, W.C. *Club:* Athenæum. (*Died 8 April 1919.*)

STORRS, Very Rev. John, M.A.; Dean of Rochester since 1913; *b.* Canada; *m.* Lucy (*d.* 1923), *d.* of late Major Cust of Ellesmere, Salop; three *s.* two *d.* *Educ.:* Pembroke College, Cambridge (Scholar); Curate of St. Mary's, Bury St. Edmunds, 1871-73; St. Peter's, Eaton Square, 1873-80; Vicar of St. James', Bury St. Edmunds, 1880-83; Rural Dean of St. George's, Hanover Square, 1891-1902; Rural Dean of Westminster, 1902-13; Prebendary of Brownswood in St.

Paul's Cathedral, 1900-13 ; Vicar of St. Peter's, Eaton Square, with St. John's, Wilton Road, and St. Peter's Chapel, Buckingham Gate, 1883-1913; Hon. Chaplain to Bishop of Salisbury, 1911-13 ; Hon. Chaplain to H.M. the King, 1912-13 ; Surrogate Diocese of London, 1904-1913 ; Select Preacher at Cambridge, 1914 ; took part in the Mission of Help to South Africa, organised by the late Bishop of St. Andrews, 1904 ; visited Egypt and Cyprus as Archbishop's messenger, Jan.–May 1917. *Recreations :* golf, music, chess. *Address:* The Deanery, Rochester. *Clubs:* Athenæum, New University ; County, Rochester.   (*Died 29 Feb. 1928.*)

STORY, Douglas, C.B.E. 1920 ; Author and Journalist ; Captain 5th (Reserve) Batt. Middlesex Regiment; *b.* Edinburgh, 31 Dec. 1872 ; *e. s.* of Dan. F. Story, J.P., Peeblesshire. *Educ. :* George Watson's College, and University, Edinburgh. Daily Mail war correspondent with the Boers, South African War, 1899-1900 ; Daily Express war correspondent with the Russians, Russo-Japanese War, 1904-5 ; New York Herald special correspondent with the present King through Canada, 1901 ; Tribune special correspondent, Egypt, Siam, China, Japan, Russia, and South Africa, 1905-8 ; special correspondent for various syndicated newspapers Russia, Siberia, and India ; editor of various journals in London, New York, Johannesburg, and Hong Kong ; D.A.Q.M.G. Army Headquarters, India, 1916-18 ; Shipping Controller in India, 1918-20 (thanks of the Ministry of Shipping, thanks of the Government of India, C.-in-C.'s despatches, C.B.E.); Director of Bureau of Information, Government of Bengal, 1920. *Publications :* Ten Miles from Anywhere, 1895 ; The Drift of the Day, 1902 ; The Campaign with Kuropatkin, 1904 ; To-Morrow in the East, 1907.   (*Died 8 July 1921.*)

STORY, Mrs. Janet Leith ; *b.* Bombay, 19 Jan. 1828 ; *d.* of Captain Philip Maughan, H.E.I.C.S., and Elizabeth Arnott ; *m.* 1863, Rev. Robert Herbert Story, Minister of Rosneath, Dumbartonshire, afterwards Principal of Glasgow University ; two *d. Educ. :* Edinburgh ; Hampstead. *Publications :* Charley Nugent, or Passages in the Life of a Sub., 1860 ; St. Aubyns of St. Aubyn ; The Co-Heiress, 1863 ; Early Reminiscences, 1911 ; Later Reminiscences, 1913 ; contributions to magazines ; etc. *Recreations :* reading, whist, music. *Address :* 30 Lilybank Gardens, Glasgow.
    (*Died 11 Sept. 1926.*)

STORY, John Benjamin ; Hon. Surgeon Oculist to H.M. in Ireland ; Pres. Royal Coll. of Surgeons in Ireland, 1918-20 ; Pres. of Ophthalmological Soc. of the United Kingdom, 1918-20 ; M.B. Dublin ; Prof. of Ophthalmic Surg. R. Coll. of Surgeons ; President and Hon. Consultant Surgeon, Royal Victoria Eye and Ear Hospital ; *s.* of Rev. William Story of Corick, Clogher, Tyrone, and Sara Bernard, *d.* of John Black, Sligo ; *m.* 1892, Blanche Christabel, *d.* of Rev. J. Hallowell ; two *d. Educ. :* Winchester: Trinity Coll., Dublin ; Zurich ; Vienna. High Sheriff of Co. Tyrone, 1911 ; Pres. of the Irish Med. Association, 1913 ; Hon. Surg. Oculist to Earls Cadogan and Dudley, Lord-Lieuts. of Ireland, during their tenure of this office ; Hon. Secretary Dublin Branch of National Service League from foundation till it closed down during the War. *Publications :* Papers in the various Ophthalmological Journals. *Address :* 4 Carlisle Terrace, Malahide, Dublin ; Corick, Clogher, County Tyrone.   *T. :* 1271. *Club :* Tyrone County, Omagh.   (*Died 18 Feb. 1926.*)

STORY, Lt.-Gen. Philip ; Bengal Infantry ; *b.* 17 Jan. 1840 ; *s.* of late Gen. P. F. Story, C.B., Bengal Cavalry ; *m.* 1879, Elisabeth Louisa, *d.* of Rev. C. J. Waterhouse ; two *s.* two *d.* Entered army, 1857 ; Lt.-Gen. 1893; retired list, 1893 ; served Indian Mutiny, 1858-

59 (medal) ; Bhootan Expedition, 1865-66 (medal with clasp) ; Perak Expedition, 1875-76 (clasp) ; Afghan War, 1878-1880 (despatches, medal). *Address :* The Hill, Stowmarket.
    (*Died 26 Sept. 1916.*)

STOTT, Edward, A.R.A., 1906 ; *b.* Rochdale, Lancashire ; unmarried. *Educ. :* Rochdale Grammar School ; King's School, Ely, Cambridgeshire. In Paris (where he remained some three years), worked for a short time under Carolus Duran, but his studies were conducted chiefly at the Ecole des Beaux Arts under Cabanel. *Recreations :* in winter time, a regular evening walk or horse-ride. *Address :* Amberley, Sussex. *Club :* Arts.
    (*Died 19 Mar. 1918.*)

STOURTON, Right Rev. Monsignor Joseph, Pastor of Oldcotes since 1885 ; Domestic Prelate to the Pope, 1918 ; Priest, 1868 ; *b.* 23 March 1845 ; *y. s.* of late Hon. William Stourton. *Educ. :* Jesuit College, Namur ; St. Cuthbert's College, Ushaw. *Address :* St Helen's, Oldcotes, Rotherham.
    (*Died Mar. 1921.*)

STOWE, Leonard, C.M.G. 1913 ; Clerk of Parliaments since 1889 ; Clerk of the Legislative Council since 1865 ; Examiner of Standing Orders relative to Private Bills since 1888 ; *b.* 11 Mar. 1837 ; *s.* of Dr. W. Stowe, Trolly Hall, Buckingham ; *m.* 1871, Jane, *d.* of Dr. Greenwood, late Sergeant at Arms to the House of Representatives ; two *s.* two *d. Educ. :* Rugby. Went to New Zealand, 1858 ; Clerk to the Provincial Council, 1864 ; invented Stowe's Patent Calculating Machine, exhibited at the Melbourne Exhibition of 1881, and received honourable mention. *Address :* Tiakiwai, Tinakori Road, Wellington.   (*Died 25 April 1920.*)

STOWELL, Rev. Thomas Alfred, M.A., Rector of Chorley, 1890-1907; Hon. Canon of Manchester since 1879 ; *b.* Salford, 15 July 1831 ; 2nd *s.* of Rev. Hugh Stowell, M.A., Rector of Christ Church, Salford, and Hon. Canon of Chester ; *m.* 1861, Emma, 2nd *d.* of Richard Tatham of Lowfields, Burton in Lonsdale ; eight *s.* five *d. Educ. :* Manchester Grammar School ; Queen's College, Oxford. Bridgeman Exhibitioner ; 2nd class in Classical Moderations, 1853 ; B.A. (3rd class Lit. Hum. and hon. 4th Law and Modern History), 1855 ; M.A., 1858 ; ordained, 1857 ; Priest, 1858 ; Curate of Calverley, near Leeds (in sole charge of Bolton) ; Perpetual Curate of St. Stephen's, Bradford, 1860-65 ; Rector of Christ Church, Salford, 1865 ; Rural Dean of Salford, 1876-90 ; Rural Dean of Leyland, 1890-1901 ; Proctor in Convocation for Archdeaconry of Blackburn, 1900-6 ; Hon. Sec. of Manchester Diocesan Bd. of Education, 1870-81 ; Representative on Central Council of Diocesan Conferences, 1882 ; Assessor for Chapter of Manchester Cathedral under Clergy Discipline Act, 1892-1907. *Publications :* The Church Catechism Simply and Clearly Explained, 1882 ; The Church Catechism for the use of Teachers and Students, 1894 ; Hymns chiefly for Children and Sunday Schools, 1898 ; papers in The Churchman. *Address :* Danehurst, 10 Morley Road, Southport.
    (*Died 10 Feb. 1916.*)

STRACHAN, James, C.I.E. 1897 ; late Engineer and Secretary to the Karachi Municipality. *Address :* 47 Kirkdale, Sydenham, S.E. *Club :* Constitutional.   (*Died 7 Feb. 1917.*)

STRACHAN, John, K.C. ; *b.* South Shields, 18 June 1838 ; 3rd *s.* of John Strachan, J.P. ; *m.* Sarah Matilda, *y. d.* of Charles Hayward, Orono, Ontario, 1859 ; one *d. Educ. :* privately. Journalist and dramatic author up to 1876, when called to the Bar ; practised since in London and on North-Eastern circuit ; Q.C. 1896 ; Bencher of Middle Temple, 1904 ; Chairman and Umpire Conciliation Board, Northumberland Coal Trade up to termination in 1911 ; District Probate Registrar, Lincoln, 1914.

Publications: numerous dramatic works up to 1876 ; Northumbrian Masonry, 1898. *Address:* White Hart Hotel, Lincoln. (*Died 3 June 1918.*)

STRACHAN, William **Henry Williams,** C.M.G., 1902 ; L.R.C.P. (Lond.) ; M.R.C.S. Eng. ; F.L.S. ; F.Z.S. ; F.R.A.I. ; Member Royal Sanitary Institute ; Member Royal Society of Arts ; *e. s.* of late Col. W. H. P. FitzM. Strachan. *Educ.:* private schools and private tuition ; Guy's Hospital. Junior resident Medical Officer Public Hospital, Kingston, Jamaica, 1882 ; senior resident, 1885 ; senior medical officer, 1892 ; P.M.O. Lagos, 1897 ; acted as Colonial Secretary, Lagos, 1899-1900 ; P.M.O. of Amalgamated South Nigeria, 1906-11. *Publications:* in various scientific journals. *Address:* c/o Cox & Co., 16 Charing Cross, S.W.1.
(*Died 13 June 1921.*)

STRACHAN - DAVIDSON, James **Leigh,** M.A., Oxford ; Hon. LL.D., St. Andrews and Glasgow ; Master of Balliol College, Oxford, since 1907 ; *s.* of James Strachan, merchant, Manila and Madras (afterwards James Strachan-Davidson of Ardgaith, Perthshire), and Mary Ann Richardson, Penrith, Cumberland ; unmarried. *Educ.:* Leamington College ; Balliol College, Oxford. Exhibitioner (Warner and Jenkyns) ; first-class in Moderations and in Lit. Hum.; Fellow of Balliol, 1866 ; Tutor and Dean, 1872 ; Jowett Fellow, 1906. *Publications:* Selections from Polybius ; Appian Civil Wars, Book I. ; articles on Roman Constitution in Smith's Dictionary of Antiquities ; Life of Cicero in Heroes of the Nations series ; Problems of the Roman Criminal Law. *Address:* Balliol College, Oxford. *Club:* New University.
(*Died 28 Mar. 1916.*)

STRACHEY, Lady, **Jane Maria ;** *d.* of Sir John Peter Grant of Rothiemurchus, G.C.M.G., K.C.B., and Henrietta Chichele Plowden ; *m.* late Lieut.-General Sir Richard Strachey, G.C.S.I., F.R.S. ; four *s.* five *d.* *Publications:* Lay Texts ; Poets on Poets ; Nursery Lyrics ; Memoirs of a Highland Lady. *Address:* 51 Gordon Square, W.C.1. *T.:* Museum 0987. *Club:* Lyceum.
(*Died 14 Dec. 1928.*)

STRACHEY, John St. **Loe ;** journalist ; late Editor and proprietor of the Spectator till Dec. 1925, when he retired ; he continues to be a weekly contributor ; *b.* 9 Feb. 1860 ; 2nd *s.* of Sir Edward Strachey, 3rd Bart., and Mary Isabella, 2nd *d.* of John Addington Symonds, M.D. ; *m.* Amy, *d.* of late C. T. Simpson, 1887 ; one *s.* one *d.* *Educ.:* Balliol Coll. (1st class History), Oxford. Barr.; journalist in London since 1884 ; editor of Cornhill Magazine, 1896-97. *Publications:* From Grave to Gay ; The Manufacture of Paupers, 1907 ; Problems and Perils of Socialism ; The Practical Wisdom of the Bible, 1908 ; A New Way of Life, 1909 ; The Adventure of Living, 1922 ; Economics of the Hour, 1923 ; The Referendum, 1923 ; The River of Life, 1924 ; The Madonna of the Barricades, 1925 ; American Soundings, 1926. *Recreations:* riding, motoring, and cycling. *Address:* 76 Chester Square, S.W. ; *T.:* Victoria 9767 ; Newland's Corner, Merrow, Guildford. *Clubs:* Brooks's, Athenæum.(*Died 26 Aug. 1927.*)

STRAFFORD, 5th Earl of, *cr.* 1847 ; **Rev. Francis Edmund Cecil Byng ;** Baron Strafford (U.K.), 1835 ; Viscount Enfield, 1847 ; *b.* 15 Jan. 1835 ; 3rd *s.* of 2nd Earl of Strafford ; *S.* brother 1899 ; *m.* 1st, 1859, Florence, *d.* of late Sir W. Miles. 1st Bt. (*d.* 1862) ; 2nd, 1866, Emily, *d.* of late Lord F. Kerr ; three *s.* two *d.* *Educ.:* Eton (Prince Albert Prizeman for Modern Languages, 1850-51) ; Christ Church, Oxford (3rd class Law and Modern History). Rector of Little Casterton, Rutland, 1859-62 ; Vicar of Holy Trinity, Twickenham ; Chaplain at Hampton Court, 1862-67 ; Hon. Chaplain to

1006

Queen Victoria, 1867 ; Chap.-in-Ordinary, 1872 ; Chaplain to the Speaker, 1874-89 ; Vicar of St. Peter, Cranley Gardens, 1867-89 ; Grand Chaplain of Freemasonry in England, 1889. *Heir: s.* Viscount Enfield. *Address:* 5 St. James's Square, S.W. ; Wrotham Park, Barnet, Herts. *T.:* Barnet 34. *Club:* Oxford and Cambridge.
(*Died 18 Jan. 1918.*)

STRAFFORD, Alice, Countess of ; *b.* 1830 ; *e. d.* of 1st Earl of Ellesmere, K.G.; *m.* 1854, 3rd Earl of Strafford (*d.* 1898). *Publications:* edited Personal Reminiscences of the Duke of Wellington, by 1st Earl of Ellesmere ; Leaves from the Diary of Henry Greville. *Address:* 51 South Street, Park Lane, W.1.
(*Died 22 Dec. 1928.*)

STRAHAN, Sir **Aubrey,** K.B.E., *cr.* 1919 ; F.R.S. 1903 ; Sc.D., M.A. ; Hon. LL.D. (Toronto) ; F.G.S., F.R.G.S. ; Director Geol. Survey of Great Britain and Museum of Practical Geology, 1913-20 ; *b.* London, 20 April 1852 ; *s.* of William and Anne Strahan (*d.* of Sir G. Fisher) ; *m.* 1886, Fanny Evelyn Margaret (*d.* 1926), *d.* of Edward H. Roscoe ; one *s.* *Educ.:* Eton ; St. John's College, Cambridge. President Geological Society, 1913-14 ; Wollaston Medallist, 1913-14 ; President Section C British Association, 1904 ; Member of Royal Commission on Coal Supplies, 1903 ; Vice-Pres. International Geological Congress, 1913 ; Vice-President Berkshire Archæological Society ; Hon. Member R.E. Inst., North of England Inst. Engin., Institute Mining and Metallurgy, Institute Petroleum Technologists, and Chester Soc. Nat. Sci., Cor. Member Geological Society of Belgium. *Publications:* Geological Survey Memoirs on Chester, Rhyl, Flint, Isle of Purbeck, and Weymouth, South Wales Coal Field, etc. ; and contributions to scientific journals. *Address:* Fairfield House, Goring, Reading. *Club:* Athenæum. (*Died 4 Mar. 1928.*)

STRAHAN, Rev. Professor **James,** M.A., D.D. ; Professor of Hebrew and Biblical Criticism in the Magee College, Londonderry, since 1915 ; *b.* Cardenwell, Fyvie, Aberdeenshire, 1 May 1863 ; *m.* 1909, Catherine Evangeline Booth-Clibborn. *g.d.* of General Booth ; two *s.* one *d.* *Educ.:* Grammar School, Old Aberdeen ; King's College, Aberdeen ; New College, Edinburgh ; Universities of Tübingen and Berlin, Hebrew Tutor, New College, Edinburgh, 1885 ; Minister of St. Fergus Free Church, 1890-1908 ; Belgrave Presbyterian Church, London, 1903-10 ; Cunningham Lecturer, Edinburgh, 1915 ; Smyth Lecturer, Londonderry, 1916 ; Carey Lecturer, 1925. *Publications:* Hebrew Ideals (2 vols.), 1903-6 ; The Captivity and Pastoral Epistles, 1910 ; The Book of Job, 1913 ; The Maréchale, 1914 ; Life of Professor A. B. Davidson, 1917 ; Judges and Ruth, 1919 ; Memoir of Mary Crawford Brown, 1920 ; God in History, 1923 ; contributions to Theological Review, Critical Review, Expository Times, and Hastings' Dictionaries. *Recreations:* travel and mountain-climbing. *Address:* 7 College Avenue, Londonderry. (*Died 24 Mar. 1926.*)

STRANG, Alexander Ronald, C.B.E., J.P. ; *b.* 23 Nov. 1848 ; *e. s.* of Robert Strang, Alloa ; *m.* 1884, Agnes, *e. d.* of Alex. Begg, Paisley ; one *s.* two *d.* *Educ.:* The Academy, Alloa. Late Captain Argyll and Sutherland Highlanders ; Provost of Alloa at outbreak of war ; Chairman of Tribunal and Recruiting Committees ; engaged in initiating and organising the various War Schemes and Relief Committees ; has travelled for a year in China, Japan, and Canada. *Recreations:* golf, curling, bowling. *Address:* North Park Alloa. Scotland. *T.:* 83. (*Died 19 Aug. 1926.*)

STRANG, William, A.R.A. 1906 ; LL.D. Glasgow, 1909 ; painter, etcher ; President of the International Society of Sculptors, Painters, and Gravers since 1918 ; *b.* Dumbarton, 13 Feb.

1859 ; *m.* 1885, Agnes M'Symon, *d.* of David Rogerson, J.P.; four *s.* one *d. Educ.*: Dumbarton Academy ; Slade School ; Univ. College, London. Studied and worked in London since 1875 ; Silver Medal for Etching, Paris International Exhibition, 1889 ; First Class Gold Medal for Painting, Dresden International Exhibition, 1897. *Publications:* The Earth Fiend, a ballad ; Death and the Ploughman's Wife ; Etchings illustrating Kipling's Short Stories, 1901 ; Thirty Etchings of Don Quixote, 1903. *Address:* 7 Hamilton Terrace, N.W.8. *T.:* Paddington 4946. *Club:* Art Workers' Guild.
(Died 12 April 1921.)

STRANG-WATKINS, Watkin, F.Z.S. ; *b.* 4 June 1869; *o. s.* of late George Strang-Watkins and Helen Watkins, heiress of Shotton Hall and Tilley Park, Shropshire, and Calderbank, Lanarkshire ; *m.* 1896, Lady Muriel Lindsay, *o. d.* of 11th Earl of Lindsay ; one *s. Educ.*: Eton ; Cambridge. B.A. 1890 ; called to the Bar (Inner Temple), 1893 ; Member British Ornithologists' Union ; Lieut. Royal Defence Corps, 1914. *Publications:* Birds of Tennyson ; Editor of the Wild Birds' Protection Acts, etc. *Recreations:* shooting and all natural history pursuits. *Clubs:* Wellington ; County, Salop.
(Died 25 Nov. 1921.)

STRANGE, Major - Gen. Thomas Bland, late Royal Artillery ; J.P. Kerry ; Member of Council National Service League ; President Local Branch Tariff Reform League ; *b.* Meerut, 1831 ; 2nd *s.* of Col. H. F. Strange, K.O.S.B., and Letitia, *d.* of Major N. Bland, 47th Regt. ; *m.* 1st, Elinor Maria (*d.* 1917), *d.* of Capt. Robert Taylor, H.E.I.C.S. ; two *s.* three *d.* ; 2nd, 1918, Janet, *d.* of late Rev. J. A. Fell, and *widow* of Col. F. C. Ruxton, Worcesters Regt. *Educ.*: Edinburgh Academy ; R.M.A., Woolwich. Served Indian Mutiny, siege and capture of Lucknow (despatches four times, captured two guns of the Black Horse Sepoy Battery by leading a charge of artillery) ; Commandant R.M. Repository, Woolwich, 1865 ; Inspector Canadian Artillery, 1871 ; Commandant Fortress of Quebec ; commanded Alberta Field Force, 1885 ; fought action of Frenchman's Butte, defeating the Cree Indian Chief, Big Bear (received thanks of Canadian Government). *Publications:* Artillery Retrospect of the War, 1870-1871 ; Military Aspect of Canada ; Gunner Jingo's Jubilee, an Autobiography. *Recreations:* artistic and literary. *Address:* Geraghmeen, Camberley, Surrey. *T.:* Camberley 165. *(Died 9 July 1925.)*

STRATHCLYDE, Baron, *cr.* 1914; **Alexander Ure,** P.C. 1909 ; G.B.E., *cr.* 1917 ; LL.D., K.C. ; Lord President Court of Session and Lord Justice-General for Scotland, 1913-1920 ; *b.* Glasgow. 24 Feb. 1853 ; 2nd *s.* of John Ure, Cairndhu, Helensburgh, ex-Lord Provost of Glasgow ; *m.* 1879, Margaret Macdowall, *d.* of Thomas Steven ; one *d. Educ.*: Glasgow (M.A.) and Edinburgh Universities. Scotch Bar, 1878 ; Lecturer on Constitutional Law and History, Glasgow University, 1878-88 ; contested West Perthshire, 1892, and Linlithgowshire, 1893 ; Solicitor-General, Scotland, 1905-9 ; Lord-Advocate, 1909-13 ; M.P. (L.) for Linlithgowshire, 1895-1913. *Address:* Cairndhu, Helensburgh. *M.:* 4213. *Clubs:* Reform, Royal Automobile ; Western, Scottish Automobile, Glasgow ; University, Edinburgh ; Royal Northern Yacht, Royal Clyde Yacht. *(Died 2 Oct. 1928.)*

STRATHCONA, Baroness, *cr.* 1897 ; **Margaret Charlotte Smith Howard,** *d.* of 1st Baron and late Isabella Sophia, *d.* of late Richard Hardisty, Canada ; *b.* 17 Jan. 1854 ; *S.* father, 1914 ; *m.* 1888, R. J. Bliss Howard, F.R.C.S. (*d.* 1921) ; two *s.* two *d.* Heir: *s.* Hon. Donald Sterling Palmer Howard. *Address:* 46 Green Street, Park Lane, W.1 ; *T.:* Mayfair 4300 ; Glencoe, N.B. ; Colonsay,

N.B.; 911 Dorchester Street, Montreal.
(Died 18 Aug. 1926.)

STRATHEDEN, 3rd Baron, *cr.* 1886 ; **and CAMPBELL, 3rd Baron,** *cr.* 1841 ; **Hallyburton George Campbell,** J.P. ; Bengal C.S., retired 1855 ; *b.* 18 Oct. 1829 ; *s.* of 1st Baron and Mary, Baroness Stratheden, *d.* of Lord Abinger ; *S. b.* 1893 ; *m.* Louisa, *d.* of Rt. Hon. A. J. B. and Lady Mildred Beresford Hope, M.P., Bedgebury Park, Kent ; two *s.* one *d.* Entered Bengal C.S. 1849 ; Associate to Lord Chief Justice, 1853 ; Secretary of Commissions in Court of Chancery, 1860-73 ; Master of Supreme Court of Judicature ; Col. 40th Middlesex Rifles, 1866-72. Heir: *g. s.* Alastair Campbell, *b.* 21 Nov. 1899. *Address:* 17 Bruton Street, W.; Hartrigge, Jedburgh. *Clubs:* Brooks's, Bachelors'.
(Died 26 Dec. 1918.)

STRATON, the Rt. Rev. Bishop Norman Dumenil John, D.D. ; *b.* 4 Nov. 1840 ; *e. surv. s.* of late Rev. George W. Straton, Rector of Aylestone ; *m.* Emily (*d.* 1916), *d.* of J. R. Pease, Hesslewood, Hull, 1873. *Educ.*: Trinity College, Cambridge (B.A. 1862 ; M.A. 1869 ; D.D. 1892). D.D. Durham, 1908 ; Curate of Market Drayton, 1865-66 ; Vicar of Kirkby Wharfe, Yorkshire, 1866-75 ; Vicar and Rural Dean of Wakefield, 1875-92 ; Proctor for Archdeaconry of Craven, 1880-85 ; Hon. Canon of Ripon, 1883 ; Hon. Canon of Wakefield and Archdeacon of Huddersfield, 1888 ; Bishop of Sodor and Man, 1892-1907 ; Dean of Sodor and Man, 1895 ; Bishop of Newcastle, 1907-15 (when he resigned). *Address:* Bishopscourt, Broadwater Down, Tunbridge Wells. *Club:* National.
(Died 5 April 1918.)

STRATTON, Rev. Joseph, M.A. Master of Lucas' Hospital, Wokingham, since 1889 ; *b.* 1 May 1839 ; 2nd *s.* of John Stratton, of Clifton Campville, Staffordshire, and Anne, *d.* of Edward Mousley, of Haunton, near Tamworth ; *m.* 1892, Louise Cecilia Bazalgette Lucas Lucas, *d.* of St. John Welles Lucas, M.R.C.S., and niece of Sir Joseph W. Bazalgette, C.B., C.E. *Educ.*: Appleby Grammar School ; Worcester College, Oxford. Engaged for some years in tuition ; ordained, 1870 ; held Curacies in Swansea, Burton-on-Trent, New Barnet, etc. ; retired from the Church on theological grounds, 1878 ; returned in 1886, and became Curate of Winchfield, Hants ; interested in social questions, education, housing of the people, putting labourers on the land, management of prisons and workhouses, etc. ; of late years an active humanitarian, one of his aims being the abolition of the Royal Buckhounds (presented with a public testimonial in connection with this event, 1 July 1901). *Publications:* Vivisection and Anti-Vivisection, which Side must I Take, 1898 ; Sports Legitimate and Illegitimate, 1898 ; The Decline and Fall of the Royal Buckhounds, 1901 ; Fireside Poems, 1901 ; Ethelfleda and other Poems, 1915 ; Letter to a Friend on Theology : A Defence of the Broad Churchman's Position in the Establishment, 1902 ; innumerable Press letters dealing with the rights of men and animals ; The Attitude, Past and Present, of the R.S.P.C.A. towards such Spurious Sports as Tame Deer Hunting, Pigeon Shooting, and Coursing Rabbits, 1906. *Recreations:* reflective walks, and, when sympathetic companions are at hand, philosophical talks ; fond of music, vocal and instrumental. *Address:* Wokingham, Berks. *(Died 14 Jan. 1917.)*

STRATTON, Hon. J. R.; Publisher ; *b.* 3 May, 1858 ; *s.* of James Stratton and Rosanna Armstrong ; *m.* 1881, Eliza J. Ormond ; no. *c.* ; *Educ.*: Peterborough Collegiate Institute. Elected to the Ontario Legislature as a Liberal for West Peterborough, 1886, 1890, 1894, 1898, 1900, 1902 and 1908 ; Provincial Secretary, 1900 ; President of the Peterborough Examiner, Ltd., publishers of the Daily and Weekly Examiner. *Address:* 751 George Street, Peterborough, Ont. *T.A.:* Peterborough, Ontario. *T.:* 178. *M.:* 84010. *Clubs:* National, Toronto, Toronto; Peterborough, Peterborough.

(*Died 19 April 1916.*)

STRAUS, Oscar S., A.M., LL.D., Litt.D., Member of the Permanent Court of Arbitration at the Hague; Chairman of the Paris Committee of The League to Enforce Peace; *b.* 23 Dec. 1850; *s.* of Lazarus and Sara Straus: married; one *s.* two *d. Educ.:* Columbia University, New York City. Attorney and Counsellor-at-law, 1873-81; afterwards a member of the commercial firm of L. Straus & Sons; Envoy and Minister Plenipotentiary to Turkey, 1887; reappointed to the same position on a special mission to adjust differences between the U.S. and Turkey, 1897; Secretary of Commerce and Labor, 1906; Ambassador to Turkey, 1909; one of the founders of the National Civic Federation, and its Vice-President for a number of years; has acted as arbitrator in a number of labor controversies, and in 1912 was chosen as Chairman of the Board to arbitrate the differences between the fifty-two Railroads east of the Mississippi and their locomotive engineers; late Chairman of the Public Service Commission of the State of New York; Member of President Wilson's Industrial Commission, 1919-20; Member of President's Advisory Committee of the Commission for Relief in Belgium; Member of the Permanent Court of Arbitration at The Hague; Member of Board of Trustees, Carnegie Peace Foundation; late President American Social Science Association and N.Y. Board of Trade and Transportation; one of the founders and Vice-President of the American International Law Association; trustee of the New York Life Insurance Co. *Publications:* The Origin of Republican Form of Government in the U.S.; The Development of Religious Liberty in the U.S.; Roger Williams, the Pioneer of Religious Liberty; The American Spirit, 1913; Under Four Administrations from Cleveland to Taft, 1922. *Recreations:* fishing and reading. *Address:* 5 West 76th Street, New York City. *Clubs:* Authors', City, Bankers', New York.

(*Died 3 May 1926.*)

STRAUSS, Arthur, M.P. (U.) North Paddington 1910-18; partner in A. Strauss and Co., tin merchants; *b.* 1847; *s.* of A. Strauss, Mayence; *m.* Minna Cohen, 1893. M.P. (L.U.) Camborne Div. Cornwall, 1895-1900. *Address:* 1 Kensington Palace Gardens, Bayswater, W.8; *T.:* Park 4520; 16 Rood Lane, City, E.C.3. *Club:* Carlton. (*Died 30 Nov. 1920.*)

STREATFEILD, Frank Newton, C.M.G. 1879; *b.* 2 Feb. 1848; 3rd *s.* of late W. C. Streatfeild of Chart's Edge, Kent; *m.* 1864, Agatha, *d.* of R. Fry: two *s.* one *d.* Commandant of Levies, South African War, 1877-79; Resident Magistrate Transkei, 1878-1884; Civil Commissioner British Bechuanaland, 1887-89. *Publications* Kafirland, a Ten Months' Campaign; The Da chick; Reminiscences of an Old'un, 1910; Sporting Recollections of an Old'un. *Address:* Hever Cottage, Edenbridge, Kent. (*Died 23 Jan. 1916.*)

STREATFEILD, Rev. Henry Bertram, M.A.; Vicar of St. Mark's, Milverton, Leamington, 1901-20; Hon. Canon of St. Michael's, Coventry; *b.* 1852; *y. s.* of Rev. William Streatfeild, Vicar of East Ham, Essex; *m.* 1st, 1880, Agnes Blount, *d.* of late Dr. Mercer-Adam, Boston, Lincs.; 2nd, 1905, Eleanor Mary, *d.* of late Henry Smith Lawford, Solicitor to India Office; one *d. Educ.:* Charterhouse; Exeter College, Oxford. Curate of All Saints, Woodford Wells, 1875-76; Holy Trinity, Louth, Lincs., 1876-80; Vicar of Holy Trinity, Skirbeck, Lincs., 1880-83; Holy Trinity, Louth, Lincs., 1883-1901.

1008

Address: 42 Hamilton Road, Boscombe, Hants. (*Died 25 April 1922.*)

STREATFEILD, Richard Alexander, B.A.; Assistant, Department of Printed Books, British Museum, since 1889; Musical Critic of The Daily Graphic, 1898-1912; *b.* Carshalton, 1866; *e. surv. s.* of late Frank Newton Streatfeild, C.M.G., and Agatha Maria Fry. *Educ.:* Oundle School, 1877-83; Senior Classical Scholar, Pembroke College, Cambridge, 1883; 2nd class, Classical Tripos, 1886. *Publications:* Masters of Italian Music, 1895; The Opera, 1897, 2nd ed. 1902, 3rd ed. 1907; Modern Music and Musicians, 1906 (translated into French by Louis Pennequin as Musique et Musiciens modernes, Paris, 1910); Handel, 1909; Musiciens Anglais Contemporains (translated by L. Pennequin), 1913; and numerous articles and pamphlets on the history of music; has edited George Darley's Nepenthe, 1897; Christopher Smart's Song to David, 1901: Darley's Selected Poems, 1903; T. J. Hogg's Shelley at Oxford, 1904; has translated Henrik Ibsen's Lyrical Poems, 1902; literary executor of Samuel Butler, author of Erewhon, whose posthumous Way of All Flesh, 1903, Essays on Life, Art, and Science, 1904, Sonnets, 1904, and God the Known and Unknown, 1909, he has prepared for publication, and of whose Life and Habit, Evolution Old and New, Unconscious Memory, Alps and Sanctuaries, Humour of Homer, Fair Haven, and First Year in Canterbury Settlement, he has brought out new editions. *Recreation:* golf. *Address:* 26 Great Ormond Street, W.C. *Club:* Sports.

(*Died 6 Feb. 1919.*)

STREET, Captain Edmund Rochfort, D.S.O. 1915; 3rd Battalion the Sherwood Foresters (Nottinghamshire and Derbyshire Regiment). Served European War, 1914-15 (wounded, D.S.O.). (*Died 15 Oct. 1916.*)

STREET, Colonel Harold Edward, C.M.G. 1916; R.A.; *s.* of late Joseph Edward Street of Lloyd's; *m.* 1916, Gladys Mary, *d.* of G. Fenwick Harrison, and widow of Major W. Sholto Douglas, R.E. Served S. Africa, 1899-1902 (despatches thrice, Queen's medal, 6 clasps, King's medal, 2 clasps); European War (Dardanelles), 1914-15 (despatches thrice, C.M.G., Bts. of Lt.-Col. and Col.). *Address:* Woodside, Caterham. (*Died 25 Aug. 1917.*)

STRETCH, Rt. Rev. John Francis, B.A., LL.B. (Melbourne); D.D. (Oxon.); Bishop of Newcastle (New South Wales) since 1906; *b.* Geelong, Jan. 1855; *m.* 1885, Amelia Margaret, *y. d.* of R. H. Weekes, of Chevy, Geelong; four *s.* two *d. Educ.:* Trinity College, Melbourne (B.A.) Ordained, 1878; Assistant Curate, All Saints, Geelong, 1879-80; All Saints, S. Kilda; 1880-81; S. Andrew's, Brighton, 1881-2; L. T., Little Brighton. 1883; V., Holy Trinity, Maldon, 1883; V., S. Mark's, Fitzroy, 1885; V., S. Andrew's, Brighton, 1892; Dean of Ballarat and Vicar of Christ Church Cathedral, Ballarat, 1894-95; Bishop Coadjutor of Brisbane, Queensland, 1895-1900; Dean of Newcastle and Vicar of Christ. Church Cathedral, Newcastle, 1900-6. *Address:* Bishop's Court, Newcastle, New South Wales.

(*Died 19 April 1919.*)

STRETTEN, Charles James Derrickson, M.V.O. 1903; J.P. Cambridgeshire; late Chief Constable of Cambridgeshire; *b.* 1830; *s.* of late Thomas Stretten, Assistant Chief Constable of Wiltshire; *m.* Catherine Wisbey (*d.* 1910). *Address:* 71 Chesterton Road, Cambridge.

(*Died 23 Aug. 1919.*)

STRICKLAND, Algernon Henry Peter; a partner in the banking firm of Hoare & Co.; *b.* 19 Dec. 1863; *e. s.* of late Algernon Augustine de Lille Strickland and late Charlotte Anne. *y. d.* of late Peter Richard Hoare, of Luscombe, Devonshire; *m.* 1890, Mary

Selina, *y. d.* of late Walter Drummond ; one *s.* one *d. Educ. :* Eton : Christ Church, Oxford, B.A. *Heir :* Algernon Walter [Capt. R. Gloucestershire Hussars Yeo. ; *b.* 5 Mar. 1891 ; *m.* 1915, Lady Mary Charteris, 2nd *d.* of 10th Earl of Wemyss.   *Educ. :* Eton ; B.N.C., Oxford]. *Address :* Apperley Court, near Tewkesbury ; 90 Eaton Place, S.W.1.   *T. :* Sloane 4948. *Club :* Carlton   (*Died 22 Feb. 1928.*)

STRICKLAND, Walter G. ; Director, National Gallery of Ireland ; retired, 1916 ; late Hon. Secretary, Royal Society of Antiquaries of Ireland ; Vice-President, Royal Irish Academy; *b.* 3 June 1850; *s.* of Thomas Strickland, of the family of Sizergh, Westmorland ; *m.* Margaret, *d.* of P. Ryan of Sevenhills, South Australia ; one *s.* one *d. Educ. :* Ushaw College, Durham ; King's College, London. *Publications :* A Dictionary of Irish Artists, 1914 ; Georgian Society, vols. i. and ii. ; Catalogue of National Portrait Gallery, Dublin ; Catalogue of Pictures in Trinity College, Dublin, 1916 ; various historical and archæological papers, etc.   *Address :* 63 Merrion Square, Dublin.   (*Died 16 Oct. 1928.*)

STRONG, Herbert A., M.A., LL.D. ; Officier de l'Instruction publique ; formerly President of Liverpool Royal Institution and Liverpool Guild of Education ; Vice-President of Liverpool Devonian Society ; Professor of Latin, University, Liverpool, 1882 - 1909 ; Emeritus Prof. since 1910 ; *b.* at St. Mary's Clyst Rectory, near Exeter ; *s.* of Rev. Edmond Strong ; *m.* 1st, Miss Edmiston ; 2nd, Miss Isabel White, artist ; two *s. Educ. :* Blackheath, Eliot Place School ; Winchester Commoners and College ; Corpus Christi, Oxford. Was Assistant - Professor of Humanity at Glasgow University for six years under Professor Ramsay ; then appointed to the Chair of Classics at the University, Melbourne, Australia ; has for twenty years been employed by the Scottish Education Department as Examiner of Secondary Schools ; elected as Hon. President of the French Society of Liverpool. *Publications* · an edition of Catullus and Juvenal, and work on the History of Language in collaboration with Professors Logeman and Wheeler, and many articles contributed to literary journals. For twenty years President of the University Athletic Club. *Address :* Clyst, Farnham, Slough.   *Clubs :* Albemarle ; Stoke Poges ; University, Liverpool.   (*Died 13 Jan. 1918.*)

STRONG, Hugh W., F.J.I. ; author and journalist ; contributor on antiquarian, literary, industrial, economic, and sociological subjects to reviews and periodicals ; joined Upper Staff, Census of Production (Board of Trade), on its formation, 1907, as Investigator and Examiner ; native of Liskeard, Cornwall ; *b.* 1861 ; *m.* 1891, Agnes Ward, *d.* of William King, Maidstone. President Birmingham Press Club, 1895 ; Vice-President Institute of Journalists, 1895-1900 ; President Birmingham and Midland Cornish Association, 1899-1900. Editor, Daily Argus, Birmingham, 1891-98 ; editor-manager, Oxford Chronicle, 1899-1901 ; editor Newcastle Daily Leader. Evening Leader, Weekly Leader, 1901-1903. *Recreations :* field botany, gardening, cricket, football, and the play. *Address :* 59 Marine Avenue, Whitley Bay, Northumberland. *Club :* National Liberal.   (*Died 21 July 1920.*)

STRONG, John Alexander, I.S.O. 1903 ; Superintending Clerk, Admiralty : *b.* 12 March 1844 ; *s.* of Rev. Clement D. Strong, M.A., Oxon., late Vicar of All Saints, Bristol ; *m. d.* of Lieut. Marcus Hare, R.N., and Hon. Mrs. Hare ; two *s. Educ. :* Marlborough College. Entered Admiralty, 1861 ; Examiner of Indian Accounts at Portsmouth Dockyard, 1885-92 ; Head of Finance Branch Transport Department of Admiralty through Boer War. *Address :* Moorhill, Westend, Hants.   *Club :* National.   (*Died 20 Mar. 1917.*)

STRONG, Right Hon. Sir Thomas Vezey, Kt., *cr.* 1905 ; P.C. 1911 ; K.B.E., *cr.* 1918 ; K.C.V.O., *cr.* 1911 ; Lt. of City of Lond. ; Lord Mayor of City of London, 1910 - 11 ; Senior Sheriff of London, 1904-5 ; An Hon. Col., 1st London Brigade, Royal Field Artillery ; 3rd and *y. s.* of late John Strong ; *m.* 1900, Lillie, *d.* of late James Hartnoll of Ganwic. Barnet ; Lady of Grace. *Educ. :* privately. Chairman Hospital Saturday Fund ; of H.M. Prison. Holloway ; Licensing Magistrates, City of London ; and of London Temperance Hospital ; Director of the United Kingdom Temperance and General Provident Institution ; Officier of the Legion of Honour. France ; Commander of the Order of Isabella the Catholic of Spain ; of the Order of Our Lady of Villa Vicosa of Portugal ; of the Order of the Crown, Belgium. *Recreation :* rowing. *Address :* 197 Upper Thames Street, E.C. *Clubs :* Reform, Bath.   (*Died 3 Oct. 1920.*)

STRONGE, Sir Francis (William), K.C.M.G., *cr.* 1915 ; Envoy Extraordinary and Minister Plenipotentiary, Chile, 1913-19 ; *b.* 22 Nov. 1856 ; *s.* of Sir J. C. Stronge, 4th Bt., and Margaret Zoe Caulfield, *sis.* of 3rd Earl of Charlemont ; *m.* 1909, Mary Elizabeth Florence, *e. d.* of late Gen. Hon. Sir David Fraser, G.C.B. *Educ. :* Dublin University. Attaché, 1878 ; Secretary of Legation, Mexico, 1894 ; Athens, 1899 ; Secretary of Embassy, 1903 ; Consul - Gen. Buda - Pesth, 1903-5 ; Councillor of Embassy, Constantinople, 1905-6 ; Minister Resident, Colombia, 1906-11 ; Minister Plenipotentiary, Mexico, 1911-13. *Address :* Kilbroney House, Rostrevor, Co. Down. *Club :* Travellers'. (*Died 20 Aug. 1924.*)

STRONGE, Rt. Hon. Sir James (Henry), 5th Bt., *cr.* 1803 ; P.C. Northern Ireland, 1924 ; *b.* 8 Dec. 1849 ; *s.* of 4th Bt. and Margaret Zoe Caulfeild, *sis.* of 3rd Earl of Charlemont ; *m.* 1885, Ethel Margaret (*d.* 1926), *d.* of Colonel Y. H. Burges ; five *d. Educ. :* Eton ; Brasenose College Oxford ; 2nd class in Law and Modern History ; M.A. 1875. Barr. Lincoln's Inn, 1874 ; Past Grand Master of the Orangemen of Ireland ; served 15 years in 4th Royal Inniskilling Fusiliers (Tyrone Militia) ; retired as Hon. Major, 1885 ; High Sheriff of Tyrone, 1880 ; High Sheriff of Armagh, 1885 ; Secy. to Ulster Defence Union, 1894 ; Chairman of Armagh Dist. Council, 1899-1900. *Publications :* article in National Review on Irish politics, in reply to Sir Charles Gavan Duffy, 1885 ; article Nineteenth Century, Sep. 1907, on Ireland and the Transvaal; article in Irish Church Quarterly, 1912 ; A Plea for Charity in Irish History. *Recreations :* football till thirty years of age ; played in Old Etonian eleven in semi-final for Association Cup. *Heir :* c. Walter Lockhart, *b.* 5 Sep. 1860. *Address :* Tynan Abbey, Tynan, Co. Armagh.   (*Died 20 May 1928.*)

STRUTHERS, Sir John, K.C.B., *cr.* 1910 ; C.B. 1902 : Secretary, Scotch Education Department 1904-21 ; *b.* 1857 ; *s.* of Robert Struthers, Oban ; *m.* 1912. Gertrude, *d.* of Julian Hill of Dean's Yard, Westminster. *Educ. :* Glasgow and Oxford Universities ; 1st class hons. Lit. Hum. Oxford, 1885. Inspector of Schools, Scotland. 1886-98 ; Assistant, then Principal Assistant Secretary, Scotch Education Dept. 1898-1904 ; LL D. Aberdeen, 1905 ; Member of Royal Commission Manual and Practical Instruction (Ireland), 1898 ; Committee on Physical Deterioration, 1904 ; Committee Local and Imperial Taxation, 1912 ; Joint Board of Insurance Commissioners, 1912. *Address :* 31 Sloane Gardens, S.W.1.   *T. :* Victoria 2716. *Clubs :* Athenæum, Caledonian ; Northern, Edinburgh.   (*Died 25 Oct. 1925.*)

STRUBEN, William Charles Marinus, C.M.G. See page xxx.

STRUTT, Alfred William, A.R.E., R.C.A., R.B.C., F.R.G.S.. etc.; animal-figure and landscape painter; also painter of many portraits: an etcher and painter in oil, water-colour, and pastel; *b.* Taranaki, New Zealand; spent early years in Australia; *s.* of late William Strutt, R.B.C., F.Z.S.; fourth generation of artists of same name; *m.* Nellie Maria, *d.* of B. R. Ketchlee; two *s.* two *d.* *Educ.:* Sutton Valence; Pupil of William Strutt, and at a Kensington school where he was a medallist and prize-winner; exhibitor of fifty-one pictures at R.A. since 1877; exhibitor at all principal galleries of this country, and at Paris Salon and in the Colonies. Painter of In a Fix, They'll want us again, Any Port in a Storm, The Run of the Season, At his Wits' End, Head over Ears in Love, Ilka Lassie ha's her Laddie, See how they Run, Three Offers, Thanks Awfully, Never too Late to Mend, Where's the Field, The Cold Shoulder, Getting it Hot, First Aid to the Wounded, Cavalier and Roundhead, and many others. *Publications:* all the above pictures have been engraved and a great many more. *Recreations:* driving and gardening. *Address:* Afterglow, Wadhurst, Sussex. *T.A.:* Wadhurst. *Club:* Savage.   (*Died 8 May. 1924.*)

STRUTT, Hon. Charles Hedley, B.A., J.P.; Chairman of Essex Quarter Sessions, 1904-21; County Alderman, 1888 - 1925; *b.* 18 April 1849; 4th *s.* of 2nd Baron Rayleigh and of Clara, *d.* of Captain R. Vicars, Royal Engineers; *m.* 1919, Evangeline Bernard, *widow* of Percy Brodrick Bernard of Castle Hacket, Ireland, and *d.* of Henry Hoare of Staplehurst. *Educ.:* Winchester; Trinity College, Cambridge (B.A.); 1st class Moral Science Tripos, 1871; English Essay and old masters' prize, Trinity College, 1871. M.P. (C.) for East Essex, 1883 - 85; Chairman of Anglo - Dutch Plantations, and of other companies; has travelled to North Borneo and Sumatra, etc.; an agriculturist; M.P. (C.) Maldon Div. Essex, 1895-1906. *Recreation:* golf. *Address:* Wevaham, St. Tudy, Cornwall; St. Ermins, Caxton Street, Westminster, S.W.1. *Club:* Carlton.
(*Died 19 Dec. 1926.*)

STRUTT, George Herbert, J.P.; D.L., V.D.; *b.* 21 Apr. 1854; *e. s.* of late George Henry Strutt of Bridgehill, and Agnes Ann, *d.* of Edward Ashton of Prescot; *m.* 1st, 1876, Edith Adela (*d.* 1897), *e. d.* of Major Charles Yelverton Balguy; one *s.* five *d.*; 2nd, 1898, Emily, 2nd *d.* of Rev. Robert Hind, R.N., of Crosby-on-Eden, Cumberland; one *s.* four *d.* *Educ.:* Harrow; Magdalen College, Oxford. High Sheriff, Derbyshire, 1903; Patron of one Living; Capt. and Hon. Major 1st Vol. Batt. Sherwood Foresters, 1877-97. *Heir:* George Ashton [Lt.-Col. Derbyshire Imp. Yeomanry; *b.* 1878; *m.* 1904, Hon. Winifred Cavendish, 2nd *d.* of 4th Lord Waterpark (she obtained a divorce, 1924); 2nd, 1926, Mary Reeve (*m.* Capt. William Rodney Winterbottom, whom she divorced, 1925), *d.* of Gibson Ward, Bermuda]. *Address:* Bridge Hill, Belper; *T.:* 15; Kingairloch, Argyllshire, N.B.
(*Died 17 May 1928.*)

STRUTT, Hon. Richard, 2nd *surv. s.* of 2nd Baron Rayleigh; *b.* 29 Feb. 1848; *m.* 1879, Augusta, *o. c.* of 5th Baron Braybrooke, of Audley End, Essex, and Billingbear, Berks; one *s.* one *d.* *Educ.:* Winchester; Magdalen College, Oxford; M.A. 1876. Entered business in an American Bank in London, and afterwards joined the Stock Exchange; for over thirty years Warden and Choirmaster of St. John's Church, Wilton Road, London; is a member of the London Diocesan Conference; a Fellow of the Philharmonic, Horticultural, and Zoological Societies, and is on the Councils of the Corporation of the Church House, Whitelands Training College, Chelsea, the North China and Shantung Mission, the Gregorian Association, and the

1010

Church Music Society; is an Honorary Member of the London Society of Organists. *Address:* 89 Tite Street, Chelsea, S.W.; The Court, St. Catharine, Bath. *T.A.:* Strutt, Batheaston. *T.:* Batheaston 59.   (*Died 14 Oct. 1927.*)

STUART OF WORTLEY, 1st Baron, *cr.* 1916, of the City of Sheffield, **Charles Beilby Stuart-Wortley,** K.C., P.C. 1896; M.A.; *b.* Escrick Park, York, 15 Sep. 1851; *s.* of Rt. Hon. James Stuart-Wortley, Q.C. (3rd *s.* of 1st Baron Wharncliffe), and Jane, *d.* of Paul Beilby, Lord Wenlock; *m.* 1st, 1880, Beatrice (*d.* 1881), *d.* of Thomas Adolphus Trollope, the historian of Florence; one *d.*; 2nd, 1886, Alice, 3rd *d.* of late Sir John Everett Millais, 1st B., P.R.A.; one *d. Educ.:* Rugby; Balliol Coll., Oxford (M.A. 1879). Barr. 1876; practised North-Eastern Circuit, 1876 - 85; Q.C. 1892; Parliamentary Under-Secretary of State for Home Department, 1885, and again 1886-92; added to Chairman's Panel for Standing Committees, 1895; nominated by Mr. Speaker a Deputy Chairman of Committee of the whole House, 1895; appointed by Archbishop Benson to the office of Ecclesiastical Commissioner and Church Estates Commissioner, 1895; attended as principal Delegate of H.B.M. Government the International Conference at Madrid on the Protection of Industrial Property and the Repression of False Trade Descriptions, 1890; and again at Brussels, December 1897, and December 1900; M.P. (C.) undivided borough of Sheffield. 1880-1885; Hallam Division, Sheffield, 1885-1916; is a director of the Underground Electric Railways Co., Ltd. *Heir:* none. *Address:* 7 Cheyne Walk, Chelsea, S.W.3. *T.:* Kensington 313. *Clubs:* Carlton, Beefsteak, St. Stephen's.
(*Died 24 April 1926.*)

STUART, Hon. Charles Allan, Puisne Judge of the Supreme Court of Alberta, Canada, since 1907; *b.* Caradoc, Middlesex Co., Ontario, 3 Aug. 1864; *s.* of Charles Stuart, emigrant from Blair Atholl, Perthshire, Scotland, and Hannah Campbell, emigrant from Morpeth, England; *m.* 1901, Beatrice Roxburgh, Norwood, Ontario; three *s. Educ.:* University of Toronto; Columbia College, New York; Osgoode Hall, Toronto. Gold Medallist in Classics, University of Toronto, 1891; called to Bar of Ontario, 1896; North-West Territories of Canada, 1898; practised Law at Calgary, Alberta, 1898-1906; Member of First Legislature of Province of Alberta for Gleichen, 1905; Puisne Judge of Supreme Court of North-West Territories, 1906; Chancellor of University of Alberta, 1908. *Recreations:* riding, canoeing, fishing. *Address:* 718 7th Ave., West Calgary, Alberta. *T.A.:* Casjus, Calgary. *M.:* 2563.   (*Died Mar. 1926.*)

STUART, Rev. Edward Alexander; Canon of Canterbury since 1907; Mid-day Lecturer at St. Mary le Bow since 1888; *b.* Calcutta, 17 April 1853; *s.* of James Stuart of Sudbury Hill, Harrow; *m.* Emily Ada, *d.* of John Guy of Catton House, Norwich; four *s.* four *d.* *Educ.:* Harrow, 1866-72 (Capt. of Cricket Eleven, 1872); St. John's Coll., Camb.; Capt. of Lady Margaret Boat Club, 1875; Foundation Scholar. 2nd class Classical Tripos 1876. Ordained, 1876; Curate of St. Andrew's, Thorpe, 1876-77; St. Giles's, Norwich, 1877-79; Vicar of St. James's, Holloway, 1879-93; Select Preacher, Cambridge, 1892, 1899; Jones's Lecturer, St. Margaret's, Lothbury, 1897-98, 1906-7; Vicar of St. Matthew's, Bayswater, 1893-1907; Prebendary of St. Paul's, 1905-7. *Publication:* Children of God, 1892. *Address:* The Precincts, Canterbury.
(*Died 26 Feb. 1917.*)

STUART, Sir Harold (Arthur), G.C.M.G., *cr.* 1922; K.C.S.I., *cr.* 1914; K.C.M.G., *cr.* 1921; K.C.V.O., *cr.* 1906; C.S.I. 1903; I.C.S.; British Commissioner in Allied Administration for the Plebiscite of Upper Silesia, 1921-22 (G.C.M.G.); *b.* York, 29 July

1860; *s.* of late Peter Stuart; *m.* 1885, Alice Catharine, *d.* of late Rev. F. W. Whitehead, of Cambridge; one *s.* one *d.* *Educ.:* Bishop's Stortford; King's College, Cambridge. Entered Indian Civil Service 1881, and was posted to Madras, where he filled from time to time the usual administrative posts, and also served as Under Secretary to Government under Sir M. E. Grant Duff and Lord Connemara, as Secretary under Lord Ampthill, and as Private Secretary to Sir Arthur Havelock; directed the Census operations, 1891, and wrote the report: Inspector-General of Police in Madras, 1898; after officiating as Deputy Secretary to the Government of India, became Secretary to the Police Commission appointed by Lord Curzon, 1902; First Director of Central Criminal Intelligence Department, India, 1904; Home Secretary to the Government of India, 1908-11; Member of Executive Council, Madras, 1912-16; retired Oct. 1916; served in the Ministry of Food, 1916-18; H.M.'s High Commissioner on the Inter-Allied Rhineland High Commission, 1920-1921. *Address:* Oppeln, Germany; 10 Cleveland Gardens, W.2. *Club:* East India United Service.   *(Died 1 Mar. 1923.)*

STUART, John, C.B.E. 1918; Managing Director of Ross, Ltd., Opticians, Clapham Common, S.W.4; proprietor of the British Journal of Photography; *b.* Grantown, 19 July 1836; *s.* of William and Mary Stuart; *m.* Mary Annie, *d.* of George Bacon, St. Albans, Herts; two *d.* *Educ.:* Grantown; Inverness; Aberdeen. Entered business in Edinburgh, 1853; professional photographer, 1860; travelled extensively on the Continent and in America, producing large series of landscapes and architectural photographs; joined Ross and Co. in the management of Photographic Lenses Dept., 1870; associated with Francis Herbert Wenham (the inventor of binocular microscopes); during the following fifteen years introduced several series of new types of photographic lenses, such as the portable and rapid symmetricals, universal lenses, etc.; also several forms of new and improved microscopes, objectives, and apparatus; on the introduction of the new Jena optical glasses, a series of concentric lenses were brought out, being the first anastigmat lenses invented; followed by a number of more rapid anastigmat lenses, such as the homocentric, telecentric, xpres, and combinable lenses; a new form of variable power gun sighting telescope was introduced, 1889 (awarded the Grand Prix and the Gold Medal, Paris Exhibition); this variable power gun sighting telescope has been the forerunner of many types of naval gun sighting instruments and periscopes, and has now become the standard type in the British, Italian, Japanese, and of many other foreign navies. On the outbreak of European war, the entire output of Ross, Ltd. was requisitioned by the Government, necessitating the stoppage of all general trade; special machinery was installed, old buildings were extended, and new buildings erected. *Recreations:* landscape and rock gardening, farming, etc. *Address:* Stonehurst, Ardingly, Sussex. *T.A.:* Stuart, Stonehurst, Ardingly. *T.:* Ardingly 8; Battersea 376 and 702. *M.:* AP 965 and LM 4384. *Club:* Royal Automobile.   *(Died 28 April 1926.)*

STUART, Leslie; *b.* Southport, 15 Mar. 1866; Organist to St. John's R.C. Cathedral, Salford, at age of fifteen, where he remained 7 years; organist to Church of the Holy Name, Manchester, for 7 years; *m.* Composer of Florodora; The Silver Slipper; The School Girl; The Belle of Mayfair; Havana; The Slim Princess; Peggy. *Songs:* Soldiers of the Queen; Little Dolly Day-dream; Louisiana Lou; The Bandolero; Rip Van Winkle; The Vales of Arklow; Is Your Mammie always wid Ye?;

The Lily of Laguna; The Little Octoroon; I May Be Crazy; Sweetheart May; Sheelah Magee: The Willow Pattern Plate; Trilby will be True; The Dandy Fifth; My Little Black Pearl; On the Road to Tipperary; The Old Shield; Mighty Mother England. *Recreation:* billiards.   *(Died 27 Mar. 1928.)*

STUART, Ruth M'Enery; author; *b.* Louisiana, U.S.A.; *d.* of James M'Enery and Mary Routh Stirling; *m.* 1879, Alfred O. Stuart, cotton planter (deceased). *Educ.:* New Orleans. Has been writing since 1888. *Publications:* A Golden Wedding and other Tales; Carlotta's Intended; Solomon Crow's Christmas Pockets; In Simpkinsville; the Story of Babette; Moriah's Mourning; Sonny; Holly and Pizen; Napoleon Jackson, The Gentleman of the Plush Rocker; George Washington Jones, A Christmas Gift that went A-begging; The Rivers' Children; The Second Wooing of Salina Sue; Aunt Amity's Silver Wedding, and other Tales; Sonny's Father; The Haunted Photograph; Daddy Do-funny's Wisdom-Jingles. *Recreations:* mycology, collecting aboriginal baskets, out-doorings, etc. *Address:* 220 Central Park, South, N.Y.; summer, Columbine Cottage, Onteora Park, via Tannersville, N.Y., U.S.A. *Clubs:* Barnard, Wednesday Afternoon, Onteora; Cosmopolitan, New York.   *(Died 6 May 1917.)*

STUART, Sir Thomas Anderson, Kt., *cr.* 1914; M.D.; LL.D. Hon. Edinburgh; D.Sc. Hon. Dunelm.; Professor of Physiology, University of Sydney; Dean of the Faculty of Medicine; Fellow of the Senate since 1883; Chairman of Board of Directors of Royal Prince Alfred Hospital; Member of Board of Health; President of Industrial Blind Institution; President of Civil Ambulance Brigade, etc.; *b.* Dumfries, Scotland 20 June 1856; *s.* of Alexander Stuart, Dean of Guild, and Jane Anderson; *m.* 1893, Dorothy Primrose, *g.-d.* of late Hon. Bouverie F. Primrose, Edinburgh; four *s.* *Educ.:* Dumfries Academy; Gymnasium, Wolfenbüttel; Universities of Edinburgh and Strassburg. M.B. and Ch.M. Edinburgh University, First-Class Honours, First of Year and Ettles Scholarship, 1880; M.D., with Gold Medal, 1882; Hon. Fellow Royal Academy Medicine in Ireland; President Royal Medical Society, Edinburgh, 1882; twice President of Royal Society of N.S.W.; Member of Medical Board of N.S.W.; Physician Children's Hospital; President Board of Health; Medical Adviser to Govt. and Health Officer for Port Jackson; Trustee Australian Museum; President Highland Society; President United Dental Hospital; Councillor of Women's College; President of Zoological Society; President Health Society of New South Wales; and has held many other offices, and is member of many learned Societies; organised Royal Society (London) Expedition to Funafuti, which bored coral reef, proving Darwin's theory of reef formation correct; took principal part in promoting main existing Public Health Legislation of N.S.W.; promoted and planned Medical School, Offices, and Laboratories of Board of Health, Queen Victoria Memorial and extensions of Royal Prince Alfred Hospital; initiated the movement which led to the foundation of the Australian Institute of Tropical Medicine at Townsville, N.Q., 1906. *Publications:* principally papers in Scientific Journals on Anatomical and Physiological subjects. *Recreation:* golf. *Address:* 2 Lincluden Gardens, Fairfax Road, Double Bay, Sydney, N.S.W. *Club:* Union, Sydney.   *(Died 28 Feb. 1920.)*

STUCK, Ven. Hudson, D.D., F.R.G.S.; Archdeacon of the Yukon since 1904; *b.* England, 11 Nov. 1863; *s.* of James Stuck and Jane Hudson; unmarried. *Educ.:* Private schools,

London ; classes at King's College, London, for two years ; University ' of South, Sewanee ; graduated in Theology, 1892. Left England for Texas, 1885 ; schoolmaster in Texas for three years ; ordained, 1892 ; Rector, Gracechurch, Cuero, Texas, 1892-94 ; Dean of St. Matthew's Cathedral, Dallas, 1894-1904. *Publications:* Ascent of Denali (Mt. McKinley), 1914 ; Ten Thousand Miles with a Dog-Sled, 1914 ; Voyages on the Yukon and its Tributaries, 1917. *Address:* Fort Yukon, Alaska, U.S.A. ; 281 4th Avenue, New York. (*Died Oct. 1920.*)

STUCLEY, Sir Edward Arthur George, 3rd Bt., *cr.* 1859 ; Major, 1st South Australian Regiment ; retired ; *b.* 12 Feb. 1852 ; *s.* of 1st Bt. and Elisabeth, *d.* of 2nd Marquis of Thomond. K.P. ; *S.* brother, 1911 ; *m.* 1892, May, *e. d.* of late Hon. Thomas King. *Educ.:* private ; Jesus College, Cambridge. *Recreations:* hunting, fishing, and reading. *Heir: half-b.* Hugh Nicholas Granville [*b.* 22 June 1873 ; *m.* 1902, Gladys, *d.* of W. A. Bankes of Wolfeton House, Dorchester ; one *s.* two *d. Address:* Pillhead, Bideford. *Club:* Travellers']. *Address:* 41 Gwydyr Mansions, Hove. *Club:* Wellington. (*Died 7 Dec. 1927.*)

STUDER, Paul, M.A. (Oxon) ; D.Lit. (Lond.) ; Taylorian Professor of the Romance Languages in the University of Oxford since 1913 ; *b.* Biel, Switzerland, 1879 ; *m.* 1908, Julie Adèle Knoll of Le Locle, Neuchâtel ; two *s.* one *d. Educ.:* Le Locle, Neuchâtel ; Univ. of Berlin ; 1904, M.A. (London), with special distinction ; 1912, D.Lit. (Lond.). Professor of French and German in the Hartley Univ. Coll., Southampton, 1907-13 ; Admiralty War Staff, 1916-18. *Publications:* Studies in Anglo-Norman ; The Oak Book of Southampton (3 vols.), 1910-11 ; The Port Books of Southampton, 1913 ; Le Mystère d'Adam, 1918 ; The Study of Anglo-Norman, 1920 ; An Anglo-Norman Poem by Edward II., King of England, 1921 ; The Franco-Provençal Dialects of Upper Valais, with Texts, 1924 ; Anglo-Norman Lapidaries (in collaboration), 1924 ; A Historical French Reader, Medieval Period (in collaboration), 1924 ; St. Joan of Orleans, scenes from the 15th Century Mystère du Siège d'Orléans (in collaboration), 1926. *Address:* Exeter College and Beech House, Headington Hill, Oxford. (*Died 25 Jan. 1927.*)

STURDEE, Admiral of the Fleet Sir (Frederick Charles) Doveton, 1st Bt., *cr.* 1916, of the Falkland Isles ; G.C.B., *cr.* 1921 ; K.C.B., *cr.* 1913 ; K.C.M.G. *cr.* 1916 ; C.M.G. 1900 ; C.V.O. 1906 ; LL.D. Cambridge ; *b.* 9 June 1859 ; *m.* 1882, Marion Adela, *d.* of W. J. Andrews ; one *s.* one *d. Educ.:* Royal Naval School, New Cross. Entered Navy, 1871 ; Captain, 1899 ; Rear-Admiral, 1908 ; served Egyptian War, 1882 (Egyptian medal, Alexandra clasp, Khedive's bronze star) ; Assistant to Director of Naval Ordnance, 1893-7 ; Assistant Director of Naval Intelligence, 1900-2 ; Chief of the Staff, Mediterranean Fleet, 1905-7 ; and Chief of the Staff, Channel Fleet, 1907 ; A.D.C. to the King, 1907-8 ; Rear Admiral 1st Battle Squadron, 1910 ; Admiral, 1917 ; Admiral of the Fleet, 1921 ; received gold medal of Royal United Service Institution, 1886 and 1894 ; commanded British Force in Samoa, 1899 (C.M.G.) ; commanded 2nd Cruiser Squadron, 1912-13 ; Chief of War Staff, 1914-15 ; Commander-in-Chief H.M.S. Invincible in action off the Falkland Isles, 1914 (despatches, Bart., Parliamentary grant (£10,000) ; battle of Jutland Bank, 1916 (despatches, K.C.M.G.) ; Commander in Chief The Nore, 1918-21 ; Commander, Legion of Honour ; St. Anne of Russia, 1st class with swords ; Grand Officer of St. Maurice and St. Lazarus, Italy ; Grand Cordon of Rising Sun, Japan ; Croix de Guerre with palm, France ;

Striped Tiger, 1st class, China. *Heir: s.* Com. Lionel A. D. Sturdee, R.N. ; *b.* 2 Sep. 1884. *Address:* Wargrave House, Camberley, Surrey. *T.:* Camberley 110. *Club:* United Service. (*Died 7 May 1925.*)

STURGE, William Allen, M.V.O. 1897 ; M.D. University of London ; F.R.C.P. of London ; Member Victorian Order, 4th class ; *b.* Bristol, 1850 ; *s.* of William Sturge ; *m.* 1886, Julia, *d.* of late A. C. Sherriff, M.P. for Worcester. *Educ.:* privately. Formerly Physician Royal Free Hospital, London, and to Hospital for Epilepsy and Paralysis, Regent's Park, London ; practised at Nice, 1881-1907. *Publications:* various papers on medical subjects to different medical societies and publications. *Recreations:* possessor of a large collection of prehistoric implements and weapons in stone and bronze, also of objects (vases, etc.) connected with classical archæology. *Address:* Icklingham Hall, Mildenhall, Suffolk. (*Died 27 Mar. 1919.*)

STURLEY, Major Albert Avern, Professor of Physics, University of King's College, Windsor, N.S. ; *b.* Harbury, Warwickshire, 9 Aug. 1887 ; *s.* of late W. B. Sturley ; *m.* V. W. E. Hill of Dibden, Hants ; two *s. Educ.:* Banbury, Oxon. ; Lennoxville, Quebec ; Christ Church, Oxford ; 193rd Nova Scotia Regt. C.E.F. ; seconded to Imperial Forces. *Recreations:* tennis, cricket, O.C. King's College Contg. C.O.T.C. *Address:* Windsor, Nova Scotia. (*Died 22 Oct. 1922.*)

STURROCK, John, C.I.E. 1900 ; late Indian Civil Service ; *b.* 17 Feb. 1845 ; *m.* 1871, Regina Mary, *d.* of late Major-Gen. George S. Dobbie, Madras Army ; three *s.* one *d. Educ.:* High School, Dundee. Entered I.C.S., 1863 ; served Madras as Assist. Collector and Magistrate ; Acting Secretary of Govt. Revenue Department, 1873 ; Under Secretary to Government in Chief Secretary's Department, 1875 ; additional Sub-Secretary Board of Revenue, 1878 ; Sub-Secretary, 1879 ; Collector and Magistrate, 1883 ; Member, Legislative Council, 1894 ; Member, Revenue Board and Commission Land Tax, 1894 ; Commissioner, Land Revenue, 1898 ; Member, Legislative Council, Madras, 1896 and 1898 ; retired, 1899. *Address:* 12 Greenhill, Weymouth. *Club:* Royal Dorset Yacht. (*Died 12 Feb. 1926.*)

STURT, George (George Bourne) ; author. *Publications:* The Bettesworth Book ; Memoirs of a Surrey Labourer ; The Ascending Effort ; Change in the Village ; Lucy Bettesworth ; William Smith ; A Farmer's Life ; The Wheelwright's Shop. *Address:* Vine Cottage, The Bourne, Farnham, Surrey. (*Died Feb. 1927.*)

STURT, Hon. Gerard Philip Montagu Napier ; Captain Coldstream Guards ; *b.* 9 April 1893 ; *e. s.* of 2nd Baron Alington. Enter army, 1912 ; Lieut. 1914 ; Capt. 1915 ; served European War, 1914-18 (wounded). *Address:* 38 Portman Square, W. *Clubs:* Guards', Bath, Pratt's. (*Died 11 Nov. 1918.*)

STYLE, Rev. George, Rector of Chalbury since 1905. *Educ.:* Queen's College, Cambridge. Fellow of Queen's College, 1864-77 ; Assistant Master Clifton College, 1868-69 ; Headmaster Giggleswick School, Yorkshire, 1869-1904. *Address:* Chalbury Rectory, Wimborne. (*Died 16 Jan. 1923.*)

SUART, Brig.-Gen. William Hodgson, C.M.G. 1918 ; J.P. ; *b.* 17 Dec. 1850 ; *s.* of late Major William Swainson Suart, of Bowles, Chigwell, Essex ; *m.* Mary Catharine, *d.* of late Maj.-Gen. W. C. Lester of Battwick Lodge, Boscombe, Hants ; one *d. Educ.:* Privately ; R.M. Academy, Woolwich. Entered Royal Artillery, 1871 ; served Afghanistan, 1880 (medal) ; retired, 1907 ; commanding Home Counties Divisional Artillery Territorials, April 1909 - Nov. 1913 ; re-employed

Nov. 1914; commanded Training Divisional Artillery at home, ending up with a Field Artillery Reserve Brigade, Dec. 1917. *Address:* Rusthall Cottage, Tunbridge Wells. *Club:* United Service.   *(Died 23 June 1925.)*

SUCKLING, Rev. Robert Alfred J., Vicar of St. Alban's, Holborn, since 1882; Superior-General of the Confraternity of the Blessed Sacrament, 1895 - 1915. *Educ.:* St. Edmund Hall, Oxford. Ordained, 1865; Curate of Rowde, 1865-68; Rector of Barsham, Suffolk, 1868-80; Vicar of St. Peter's, London Docks, 1880-82; Patron and Lord of the Manors of Barsham and Shipmeadow. *Address:* St. Albans Clergy House, Brooke Street, Holborn, E.C.   *(Died 24 Sept. 1917.)*

SUDELEY, 4th Baron (*cr.* 1838), **Charles DouglasRichardHanbury-Tracy,** P.C., F.R.S., D.L., J.P.; Lieut. R.N., retired 1863; *b.* Brighton, 3 July 1840; 2nd *s.* of 2nd Baron and Emma, *d.* of George Hay Dawkins Pennant of Penrhyn Castle, Carnarvon, and Sophia, *d.* of 1st Viscount Hawarden; *S. b.* 1877; *m.* Ada Maria Katharine, *d.* of Hon. Frederick James Tollemache, *n.* of 7th Earl of Dysart, 1868; one *s.* four *d.* Entered Navy, 1854; Lt. 1860; served in Russian War 1854, and was present at siege of Bomarsund, of Fatshan in China and at San Blas in Mexico; was gunnery Lieut. in Mediterranean, 1862; Barr. Inner Temple, 1866; Commissioner Electrical Exhibition, Vienna, 1883; M.P. for Montgomery, 1863-77; Lord-in-Waiting, 1880-85; Captain of Hon. Corps of Gentlemen-at-Arms, 1886. *Publications:* Lectures and various pamphlets and articles in magazines on the Public Utility of Museums. *Heir: s.* Hon. William C. F. Hanbury Tracy. *Address:* Beston Lodge, Petersham, Surrey. *T.A.:* Petersham. *T.:* Richmond 2365.   *(Died 9 Dec. 1922.)*

SUDERMANN, Hermann, dramatist and novelist; *b.* Matzicken, Heydekrug, East Prussia, 30 Sept. 1857. *Educ.:* Elbing and Tilsit; Universities of Königsberg and Berlin. Journalist from 1881 (editor of the Deutsches Reichsblatt); afterwards man of letters; first play put upon the stage, 1889. *Publications:* Im Zwielicht (stories), 1887; Frau Sorge (novel), 1887; Geschwister (stories), 1888; Katzensteg (novel), 1889; Die Ehre (drama), 1890; Sodoms Ende (drama), 1891; Iolanthes Hochzeit (tale), 1892; Heimat (drama), 1893; Es War (novel), 1894; Die Schmetterlingsschlacht (comedy), 1896; Das Glück im Winkel (drama), 1896; Morituri: Teja, Fritzschen, Das Ewigmännliche (three dramas), 1896; Johannes (tragedy), 1898; Die drei Reiherfedern (drama), 1899; Johannisfeuer (drama), 1900; and Es lebe das Leben (drama), 1901; Der Sturmgeselle Sokrates, 1903; Stein unter Steinen (drama), 1905; Das Blumenboot (drama), 1905; The Undying Past, 1906; Das Hohe Lied, 1908; Strandkinder, 1909; Der Bettler von Syrakus (tragedy), 1911; The Indian Lily (stories), 1911; Der gute Ruf (comedy), 1913. *Address:* (winter) Grunewald Bettinastrasse 3, Berlin; (summer) Schloss Blankensee bei Trebbin (Kreis Teltow). *Clubs:* Berliner Presse Verein, Litterarische Gesellschaft.   *(Died 21 Nov. 1928.)*

SUFFIELD, 6th Baron (*cr.* 1786), **Charles Harbord,** Bt. 1745; C.B. 1900; M.V.O. 1902; Scots Guards; Col. retired; Captain of Yeomen of the Guard, 1915-18; *b.* 14 June 1855; *e. s.* of 5th Baron and Cecilia Annetta (*d.* 1911), *d.* of Henry Baring, and *sis.* of 1st Baron Revelstoke, Lady of the Bedchamber to H.M. the Queen; *S.* father 1914; *m.* 1896, Evelyn Wilson-Patten, *d.* of Marchioness of Headfort; two *s.* two *d. Educ.:* Eton. Served on the staff of Lord Lorne in Canada, staffs of Lords Ripon, Dufferin, and Lansdowne, 1881 to 1894; served in S. Africa 1900 to end of war; Groom-in-Waiting to the late Queen. *Heir:*

s. Hon. Victor Alexander Charles Harbord, Capt. Scots Guards [*b.* 12 Sep. 1897; Page of Honour to King George, 1910 - 15]. *Address:* Gunton Park, Norwich. *Clubs:* Guards', Turf.   *(Died 10 Feb. 1924.)*

SUFFOLK and BERKSHIRE, 19th Earl of (*cr.* 1603), **Henry Molyneux Paget Howard,** Viscount Andover and Baron Howard, 1622; Earl of Berkshire, 1626; *b.* 13 Sept. 1877; *e. s.* of 18th Earl and Mary Eleanor Lauderdale, 4th *d.* of Hon. Henry Coventry; commands Wilts Battery 3rd Wessex Brigade (T.); *S.* father 1898. Liberal Unionist; *m.* 1904, Margaret Hyde, *y. d.* of late Levi Z. Leiter; three *s. Educ.:* Winchester. Owns 10,000 acres; celebrated picture-gallery and well-known collection of Old Masters. *Recreations:* hunting, fishing. *Heir: s.* Viscount Andover. *Address:* Chariton Park, Malmesbury. *Clubs:* Turf, Orleans, Carlton.   *(Died 21 April 1917.)*

SUGDEN, Charles, actor; *b.* Cambridge, 24 Dec. 1850; *o. s.* of Charles Langworthy Sugden and Mary, *o. d.* of James Camper Wright, Fellow of Eton and King's Coll. Cambridge; *m.* Helen de la Feuillade, a descendant of an old Bourbon family, herself a well-known actress, known to the playgoing public as Miss Vane. *Educ.:* Beccles Grammar School; and at Rev. Henry Mackaness, Ash, nr. Sandwich, Kent. Theatre Royal, Brighton, 1867; Theatres Royal, Dublin and Edinburgh, 1868-69 and 1870; first appeared in London at Globe Theatre 1871, under management of H. J. Montague, in Partners for Life; afterwards created the parts of King William in Clancarty, Chevalier in Two Orphans, Charles in Our Boys, which he played 600 nights; Captain Bradford in Peril at the old Prince of Wales's Theatre; Allen Villiers in Red Lamp; Judge Brack in Hedda Gabler; and Paillard in A Night Out at Vaudeville Theatre; was the Touchstone in a revival of As You Like it at St. James's Theatre in 1890. *Publications:* The Kite Flyer, comedy, 1894; The Limit of the Law, 1912; Forty Years of Turf and Stage, 1912. *Recreations:* shooting, fishing, racing; owned racehorses, 1879 - 1910; has wonderful collection of birds' eggs, all gathered by himself; famous sprint runner in 1870; won L.A.C. hundred yards challenge cup and beat Roland Upcher in 200 and 100 yards races, winning the former in 21 seconds, the latter in 10½ seconds. *Address:* 5A Hyde Park Mansions, Marylebone Road, W.   *(Died 3 Aug. 1921.)*

SUGDEN, Frank; *e. s.* of late Rev. Hon. Frank Sugden and Henrietta Maria, *d.* of Philip Saltmarshe; *g.s.* of 1st and *c.* and *heir pres.* to 3rd Baron St. Leonards; *b.* 28 Oct. 1852; *m.* 1st, 1894, Edyth Mary (*d.* 1904), *d.* of late General Sir Arthur Becher, K.C.B.; 2nd, 1909, Alice (*d.* 1921), *d.* of late Rev. C. J. Phipps Eyre, formerly Rector of St. Marylebone. *Address:* 2 Ryder Street, St James's, S.W.1. *Club:* Conservative.   *(Died 19 Aug. 1927.)*

SULIVAN, Col. Ernest Frederic, C.B.E. 1919; a Director of the Pacific and Papua Produce, Ltd.; *b.* 1860; *s.* of late Rev. Filmer Sulivan; *m.* 1885, Florence Mary, *d.* of James Houldsworth, of Coltness. Served Afghan War, 1879-80 (medal with clasp); S. Africa, 1902 (Queen's medal with two clasps); European War, 1914-19 (despatches, C.B.E.). *Address:* Wilmington, Woking.   *(Died 14 Oct. 1928.)*

SULLIVAN, Sir Edward, 2nd Bt., *cr.* 1881; *b.* Ireland, 27 Sep. 1852; *s.* of 1st Bt., Lord Chancellor of Ireland, and Bessie Josephine, *d.* of Robert Bailey, Cork; unmarried. *Educ.:* Portora Royal School, Enniskillen; Trin. Coll., Dublin. First Honoursman in Classics; Classical Scholar and Moderator; Vice-Chancellor's Prizeman in Latin Verse, Barr. King's Inns, Dublin, 1879; Middle Temple,

1888; contested (L.U.) St. Stephen's Green Div. of Dublin, 1886; Chester le Street Div. of Durham, 1892; Ex-trustee of National Library of Ireland. *Publications:* Dante's Comedy, in English Prose, part i. Hell, 1893; Tales from Scott, 1894; Buck Whaley's Memoirs; The Book of Kells, 1914; The Introduction to Guazzo's Civile Conversation, translated by George Pettie, 1581 (Tudor Translations); Contributor to Quarterly Review, Nineteenth Century, etc.; Ex-President of Ye Sette of Odd Volumes. *Recreations:* literature, book-cover decoration. *Heir:* b. William [b. 21 Feb. 1860. Barrister, King's Inn, Dublin; Resident Magistrate, Co. Meath; *m.* 1886, Charlotte Anna, *d.* of late Right Hon. Richard Dowse, a Baron of the Exchequer; one *d.*]. *Address:* 26 Queensberry Place, South Kensington, S.W.7. *Clubs:* Reform; Royal Irish Yacht.

(*Died 19 April 1928.*)

SULLIVAN, William Charles, M.D.; Superintendent, Broadmoor Criminal Lunatic Asylum, Crowthorne, Berks; *y. s.* of late W. K. Sullivan, Ph.D. (Giessen), President of Queen's College, Cork; *m.* Mary (authoress of The One Outside, and other Irish stories), *d.* of late John Fitzpatrick; one *s. Educ.:* Cork; Dublin; Paris. Formerly in prison medical service; was Scientific Adviser to Central Control Board (Liquor Traffic), 1915-19; is Lecturer on Criminology and Forensic Psychiatry at the Maudsley Hospital. *Publications:* Alcoholism, 1896; Crime and Insanity, 1924; various contributions to scientific journals on criminology, psychiatry, and alcoholism. *Address:* Broadmoor, Crowthorne, Berks. (*Died 26 Feb. 1926.*)

SULLIVAN, Hon. Sir William Wilfred, Kt. *cr.* 1914; Chief Justice, and Judge of Vice-Admiralty Court, Prince Edward Island, since 1889; *b.* 6 Dec. 1843; *m.* 1872, Alice Maud Mary, *d.* of J. F. Newbery. *Educ.:* Central Academy; St. Dunstan's College, Charlottetown. Called to Bar, 1867; Q.C. 1876; Attorney-General of Province, and Premier, 1879-89; Roman Catholic. *Address:* Brighton Villa, Charlottetown, Prince Edward Island.

(*Died 1923.*)

SULLY, James, LL.D.; Emeritus Professor of Philosophy, University College, London, and late lecturer on Education to the University of Cambridge, the College of Preceptors, etc.; writer on Psychology; *b.* Bridgwater, 3 Mar. 1842; *s. s.* of J. W. Sully, merchant and colliery proprietor; married; one *s.* one *d. Educ.:* Independent College, Taunton; Regent's Park College, London (M.A. and gold medallist of the University of London); Universities of Göttingen and Berlin. *Publications:* Sensation and Intuition, 1874; Pessimism, 1877; Illusions, 1881; Outlines of Psychology, 1884; Teacher's Handbook of Psychology, 1886; The Human Mind, 1892; Studies of Childhood, 1895; Children's Ways, 1897; An Essay on Laughter, 1902; Italian Travel Sketches, 1912; My Life and Friends, 1918. *Address:* 30 Arlington Park Mansions, Chiswick. W. (*Died 1 Nov. 1923.*)

SULTE, Benjamin, F.R.S.C.; retired Civil Servant; *b.* Three Rivers, P.Q., 17 Sep. 1841; *s.* of Benjamin Sulte, navigator, and Marie Antoinette Lefebvre; *m.* 1871, Augustine (*d.* 1918), *d.* of Etienne Parent, Under Sec. of State. *Educ.:* Friars' School, Three Rivers. Engaged in commerce and lumbering business; served as a volunteer at the frontier, 1865; Military School certificate, 1865; served at the frontier, 1866 (medal); Translator in Parliament, 1867; Private Secretary to Minister of Militia and Defence, 1870-73; Clerk in same department, 1870; Chief Clerk and Acting Deputy Minister, 1889; retired on superannuation, 1903; President, Institut Canadien, Ottawa, 1874; President, St. John Baptist Society, Ottawa, 1883; President of St. Joseph Society, 1877; **1014**

President of the Royal Society of Canada, 1904; LL.D. University of Toronto, 1916; Corresponding Member of several historical societies. *Publications:* Les Laurentiennes (poems), 1870; Les Chants Nouveaux (poems), 1876; Mélanges d'Histoire, 1876; Histoire des Canadiens-Français (8 vols.), 1882-84; Pages d'Histoire, 1891; Histoire de la Milice Canadienne, 1897; La Langue Française en Canada, 1898; La Bataille de Châteauguay, 1899; History of Quebec, 1908; Historiettes et Fantaisies, 1910; Cinquante-six ans de vie littéraire, 1916; Mélanges Historiques, 10 vols., 1918-22; besides many small publications; has translated the National Anthem into French, and delivered many lectures on historical subjects. *Address:* 43 Fairmont Street, Ottawa. (*Died 6 Aug. 1923.*)

SULZBERGER, Mayer, Resident Lecturer on Jewish Jurisprudence and Institutes of Government, Dropsie College, Philadelphia; *b.* Heidelsheim, Baden, 22 June 1843. *Educ.:* Central High School, Philadelphia. Admitted to Bar, 1865; Judge, Court of Common Pleas, 1895-1915; Presiding Judge, 1902-15; Member of Constitutional Commission of the State of Pennsylvania, 1919-21. *Publications:* An-ha-Aretz, 1909; The Polity of the Ancient Hebrews, 1912; The Ancient Hebrew Law of Homicide, 1915; The Status of Labor in Ancient Israel, 1922. *Recreations:* walking, reading. *Address:* 1303 Girard Avenue, Philadelphia. *T.:* Poplar 4516. (*Died 1923.*)

SUMMERS, Bt.-Lieut.-Colonel and Temp. Colonel Sir Gerald Henry, K.C.M.G., *cr.* 1925; C.M.G. 1920; F.R.G.S.; Governor and Commander-in-Chief, Somaliland, since 1922; 8th King George's Own Light Cavalry (Indian Army); *b.* 12 Oct. 1885; *s.* of late Rev. Walter Summers, Danehill, Sussex; *m.* 1916, Margaret Frances Troath, *d.* of late Lt.-Col. T. R. Swinburne, of Pontop Hall, Durham; one *s.* one *d. Educ.:* Ashdown House; Bradfield; Sandhurst. Entered Army, 1904; attached 1st Royal Sussex Regt. 1904; 93rd Burma Infantry, Burma, 1905-6; 26th Cavalry, 1907; Capt. 1913; Major, 1919; attached Somaliland Indian Contingent King's African Rifles, 1912; action of Dul Madoba with Somaliland Camel Corps, 1913 (severely wounded three times; Brevet Major); Staff Officer to troops, Somaliland and Intelligence Officer, 1914; Operations at Shimber Berris, 1914-15 (despatches, medal and clasp); Officer commanding troops and Deputy Commissioner Somaliland (despatches, temp. Lt.-Col.), 1916; temp. Col., 1919; commanded Military Force in operations against the Dervishes in Somaliland, Jan.-March 1920 (despatches, clasp, Brevet Lt.-Col.); Acting-Governor Somaliland Protectorate, March-Dec. 1921. *Address:* Government House, Berbera, Somaliland; Slough House, Danbury, Essex. *Club:* Cavalry. (*Died 29 Nov. 1925.*)

SUNDARLAL, Hon. Pandit, Rai Bahadur, C.I.E. 1907; Advocate, High Court, N.W.P., Allahabad; member Legislative Council, United Provinces of Agra and Oudh, since 1895; Fellow of the University of Allahabad since 1889; *b.* May 1857; *s.* of Pandit Gobind Ram Davé of Allahabad. *Educ.:* Muir Central College, Allahabad; University of Calcutta. Graduated, 1881; enrolled as a vakil of Allahabad High Court, 1880; enrolled as an Advocate, 1895; member of Council of Law Reporting, 1888; Vice-Chancellor, University of Allahabad, 1906-8 and 1912-16; reappointed, 1916; Judicial Commissioner of Oudh U.P., 1909; Vice-Chairman, United Provinces Exhibition, 1910-11; Judge, High Court, N.W.P., 1914; reappointed 1916; member Legislative Council of Viceroy and Governor-General of India, 1915; first Vice-Chancellor Benares Hindu University, 1916. *Recreations:* tennis, cycling, etc. *Address:* 9

Elgin Road, Allahabad. *T.:* No. 25. *Club:* Indian, Allahabad. (*Died April 1918.*)

SUPPLE, Col. James Francis, C.B. 1900; R.A.M.C.; *b.* 14 Nov. 1843; *e. s.* of J. Supple, St. Anne's, Glenageary, Co. Dublin, and Feltrim, Cork; *m.* Julia Mary, *e. d.* of R. Lambkin, J.P. Entered army, 1867, Assist. Surgeon 1st Royal Scots; served in Ashanti War, 1873-74 (thanked by Director-Gen., medal with clasp); Afghanistan, 1878-79 (medal); Burmah, 1886-87 as P.M.O. 6th Brigade under Sir Robert Low (despatches, medal with clasp); South Africa, 1899-1901 (despatches, Queen's medal with clasp, C.B.); P.M.O. Durbar Troops, India, 1903 (medal); awarded Distinguished Service Pension. *Recreations:* music, painting, cricket, tennis, and boating. *Address:* c/o Messrs. Holt & Co., 3 Whitehall Place, S.W.1. (*Died 8 Aug. 1922.*)

SUTHER, Gen. Cuthbert Collingwood, Royal Marine Artillery; *b.* 1 Aug. 1839; *m.* 1868, Louise Adelaide (*d.* 1899), *e. d.* of J. W. Jennings. Entered Royal Marines, 1855; General, 1899; retired, 1904. *Address:* Eastney, Heene Road, Worthing. (*Died 29 Sept. 1927.*)

SUTHERLAND, Angus, C.B. 1907; *b.* 1848; 3rd *s.* of late William Sutherland, Helmsdale, Sutherland; unmarried. *Educ.:* parish school; Edinburgh Training College; Glasgow University. M.P. Sutherlandshire, 1886-96; Member of Royal Commission on Highlands and Islands of Scotland, 1892; Chairman of Fishery Board for Scotland, 1896; Member of Congested Districts Board for Scotland, 1892; Member of Royal Commission on Congestion in Ireland, 1906. *Address:* 191 George Street, Edinburgh; Helmsdale, Sutherland. *Club:* Scottish Liberal, Edinburgh (*Died 16 Jan. 1922.*)

SUTHERLAND, Edward Davenport, I.S.O. 1906; Auditor-General of Canada, Ottawa; *b.* 1853; *m.* 1877, Kate, *d.* of W. J. Goodeve. *Address:* Ottawa, Canada. (*Died 8 Jan. 1923.*)

SUTHERLAND, John Ebenezer, M.P. (L.) Elgin Burghs since 1905. *Address:* Durn House, Portsoy, S.O., Banffs, N.B. *Clubs:* Reform, National Liberal.
(*Died 17 Aug. 1918.*)

SUTHERLAND, Rt. Hon. Robert Franklin, B.A., K.C., P.C.; A Puisne Judge of the Exchequer Division of the High Court of Justice for Ontario since 1909; *b.* Newmarket, Ont., 5 April 1859; *s.* of Donald Sutherland (Scotch) and Jane Boddy (Irish); *m.* 1888, Mary Bartlet; two *d.* *Educ.:* Public and High Schools, Newmarket; High School, Windsor; Toronto University; Western University. Called to Bar, 1886; K.C. 1899; has been an Alderman of City of Windsor, President Windsor St. Andrew's Society and President Windsor Library Board; a Presbyterian, and Elder of St. Andrew's Church, Windsor; Liberal; M.P. Essex N., 1900-9; Speaker of House of Commons, 1905-9. *Address:* Toronto, Canada. *Clubs:* York, Toronto Golf, Toronto; Rosedale Golf.
(*Died 17 June 1922.*)

SUTHERLAND, Sir Thomas, G.C.M.G., 1897; K.C.M.G., 1891; LL.D.; Knight of St. John of Jerusalem and of the Legion of Honour; late Chairman Peninsular and Oriental Co., retired 1914; and of London Board of Suez Canal Co., of which he is Vice-President; Director London City and Midland Bank; Chairman Marine and General Assurance Society; *b.* Aberdeen, 16 Aug. 1834; *s.* of Robert Sutherland and Christian, *d.* of Thomas Webster; *m.* 1880, Alice (*d.* 1920), *y. d.* of late Rev. John Macnaught, M.A. Oxon, Vicar St. Chrysostom's, Liverpool; one *d.* *Educ.:* Aberdeen Grammar School and University. Entered service P. and O. Company, and was in China for some years, where represented that Company; was one of founders Hong-Kong Docks and of Hong-Kong and Shanghai Bank; Member of Legislative

Council of that Colony; M.P. (L.U.) Greenock, 1884-1900. *Recreations:* motoring, golf. *Address:* 7 Buckingham Gate, S.W.1; *T.:* Victoria 5821. *Clubs:* Reform, Brooks's.
(*Died 1 Jan. 1922.*)

SUTTON, Sir Abraham, Kt., *cr.* 1903; J.P., Co. Cork; *b.* Aug. 1819; *s.* of late Abraham Sutton of Monkstown, Co. Cork. *Educ.:* Clongowes. High Sheriff of Cork, 1903. *Address:* Windsor, Douglas, Co. Cork. *T.A.:* Sutton, Douglas, Cork. *T.:* 8 Douglas, Cork. *Clubs:* Cork, Cork; R.C.Y.C., Queenstown. *M.:* IF 469.
(*Died 27 Nov. 1921.*)

SUTTON, Col. Alfred, C.B. 1918; C.M.G.; Australian A.M.C. *Address:* 29 Wickham Terrace, Brisbane. (*Died 15 April 1922.*)

SUTTON, Rev. Arthur Frederick, Prebendary of Lincoln; Rural Dean of Loveden; F.S.A.; *s.* of Canon Augustus Sutton, Rector of West Tofts, Norfolk. *Educ.:* Uppingham School; Jesus College, Cambridge; Secretary of Lincolnshire Architectural Society. Member of Agricultural Institute. *Address:* The Vicarage, Earls Colne, Essex. (*Died 18 Nov. 1925.*)

SUTTON, Arthur Warwick, J.P., F.L.S., V.M.H., F.R.H.S.; *b.* Reading, 1854; *s.* of Martin Hope Sutton; *m.* 1881, Arabella Constance, *d.* of Rev. E. Gambier Pym, late Rector of Washington; one *s.* two *d.* *Educ.:* Malvern College; Royal Agricultural College, Cirencester. Became partner in the firm of Sutton & Sons, Reading, 1876; senior partner, 1913; retired owing to illness, 1921. *Publications:* My Camel Ride from Suez to Mount Sinai; several bulletins on Horticultural Research, and papers read before the Linnean Society, the Farmers' Club, the Royal Horticultural Society, the Royal Agricultural Society, the Genetical Society, and Victoria Institute. *Recreations:* Eastern travel, golf, shooting, fishing; special hobby, lecturing on Eastern travels, with original lantern slides. *Address:* 8 Clifton Road, Southbourne, Bournemouth. *T.A.:* Sutton, Southbourne. *T.:* Southbourne 112. *M.:* EL 7056. *Clubs:* Royal Automobile; Berkshire, Reading; Royal and Ancient, St. Andrews.
(*Died 15 April 1925.*)

SUTTON, Charles William, M.A.; Librarian of the Manchester Public Free Libraries; *b.* Manchester, 14 April 1848; *s.* of late Thomas Sutton; *m.* 1st, Sarah H. Evans; 2nd, Marie Pocklington; five *s.* Sub-librarian of Manchester Public Libraries, 1874; chief librarian, 1879; vice-president of Library Association; late treasurer, Manchester Literary Club; hon. librarian, Manchester Statistical Society; hon. secretary of Spenser Society (now defunct); hon. secretary of Chetham Society; past president of Lancashire and Cheshire Antiquarian Society and Manchester Association for Masonic Research; Hon. M.A. of Victoria University, 1902. *Publications:* List of Lancashire Authors, 1876; Special Collections of Books in Lancashire and Cheshire, 1899; editor of Transactions of Lancashire and Cheshire Antiquarian Society since 1885; contributions to Chetham Soc., including Life of Humphrey Chetham; many articles in the Dictionary of National Biography, etc. *Address:* 323 Great Clowes Street, Higher Broughton, Manchester.
(*Died 24 April 1920.*)

SUTTON, Sir Henry, Kt., *cr.* 1906; B.A.; *b.* 1845; 2nd *surv. s.* of James Sutton of Shardlow Hall, Derby; *m.* 1872, Caroline Elizabeth (*d.* 1916), *e. d.* of late John Nanson, Knells, Carlisle; one *s.* four *d.* *Educ.:* Rugby; Cambridge (Scholar Christ's, and Senior Optime). Called to Bar, Lincoln's Inn, 1870. Bencher, formerly Junior Counsel to Treasury; Judge of King's Bench Division of High Court of Justice, 1905-10. *Publication:* Law of Tramways. *Recreation:* fishing. *Address:* 49 Lexham Gardens, S.W.; *T.:* Western 3125.

Clubs: Athenæum, New University.
(*Died 30 May 1920.*)

SUTTON, Rev. Henry, Hon. Canon, Birmingham; *b.* 28 Sep. 1833; 2nd *s.* of Rev. Thomas Sutton, Vicar of Marton, Gainsboro'. *Educ.:* Louth Grammar School Lincolnshire; Trinity College, Dublin. Curate of Tealby and Legsby, Lincolnshire, under his uncle, Rev. Field Flowers, 1858-61; Association Secretary, Church Missionary Society, 1861-64; Vicar of St. Augustine's, Everton, Liverpool, 1864-70; St. Barnabas', Douglas, Isle of Man, 1870-72; St. Cleopas', Liverpool, 1872-79; Central or Home Secretary, C.M.S., 1879-87; Vicar of Holy Trinity, Bordesley, Birmingham, 1887-95; Proctor in Convocation for Diocese of Birmingham, May 1905; Vicar of Aston-juxta-Birmingham, 1895-1917. *Publications:* The Christian's Recreations; Articles in National Review on Church Patronage; The Children of Literature; and many unsigned articles in Church papers. *Recreations:* cricket, cycling. *Address:* 65 Locking Road, Weston-super-Mare.
(*Died 18 April 1921.*)

SUTTON, Maj.-Gen. Hugh Clement, C.B. 1916; C.M.G. 1919; Lieut.-Governor Royal Hospital, Chelsea, since 1923; *b.* 20 Jan. 1867; *s.* of late Henry Geo. Sutton; *g.s.* of Sir R. Sutton, 3rd Bart.; *m.* 1st, Ida, *d.* of Sir Campbell Munro, of Lindertis; one *s.*; 2nd, Hon. Alexandra Mary Wood, *d.* of Viscount Halifax; three *d. Educ.:* Eton; R.M.C., Sandhurst. Joined Coldstream Guards, 1887; Adjutant, 1894-98; served South African War with 2nd Batt. Coldstream Guards (despatches, Brevet of Major), and afterwards was Deputy Assistant Director of Railways; after the war was D.A.A.G. at Cape Town till 1906; Commanded 1st Batt. Coldstream Guards, 1910-13; A.A.G. War Office, 1913-16; D.A. and Q.M.G. with Army in France, 1916; Inspector-General of Communication, Home Forces, 1917; Deputy I.G.C. Mesopotamia, 1918; I.G.C. 1919 (despatches four times, C.M.G., Order of St. Anne of Russia, 2nd Class); Colonel i/c Administration, London District, 1920; Deputy Director Personal Services, War Office, 1921; Order of the Rising Sun, Japan, 3rd Class, 1921. *Address:* Royal Hospital, Chelsea, S.W.3. *T.:* Victoria 7619. *Clubs:* Guards', Arthur's.
(*Died 15 April 1923.*)

SUTTON, Sir Richard (Vincent), 6th Bt., *cr.* 1772; Capt. 1st Life Guards; *b.* 26 April 1891; *o. c.* of 5th Bt. and Constance, *d.* of Sir Vincent Corbet, 3rd Bt. (she *m.* 2nd, H. D. Astley); *S.* father, 1891. *Educ.:* Eton. Served European War, 1914-17. Owns about 13,000 acres, exclusive of London estates. *Heir: u.* Arthur, [*b.* 24 Sep. 1857; *m.* 1885, Cecile Blanche, *d.* of W. D. Dumbleton, Cape Colony; one *s.* one *d. Address:* Shanks, Wincanton, Somerset. *Club:* Junior Conservative.] *Address:* Benham-Valence, Newbury, Berks. *T.:* Newbury 227; 41 South Audley Street, W. *T.:* Mayfair 2992. *Clubs:* Naval and Military, Arthur's, St. James's, Pratt's.
(*Died 29 Nov. 1918.*)

SUYEMATSU, Viscount Kencho; Privy Councillor, Japan; B.A., LL.M. Cantab., D.Litt. LL.D. Tokyo Imperial Univ.; *b.* Aug. 1855, at Buzen, Kiusiu; *m. e. d.* of Prince Ito. Was a civilian staff officer to Commander-in-Chief of the Imperial Force during Satsuma Rebellion, 1877; a Member of House of Commons, elected at the first formation of the Diet, 1890; created Baron, 1895, for distinguished service rendered in connection with the China War, since which time elected to the House of Peers by the Barons; Minister of Communications; Minister of Interior; Viscount, 1907. *Publications:* The Risen Sun; A Fantasy of Far Japan, 1905; English translation of Genji Monogatari; translation of Anderson's Pic-
1016

torial Japan; translations and annotations of Justinian, of Gaius, of Ulpian, etc. *Address:* Shiba, Tokyo.
(*Died 5 Oct. 1920.*)

SWABY, Rt. Rev. William Proctor, D.D., F R. Micro. Soc., F. R.G.S., F.Col. Inst.; Bishop of Barbados and the Windward Islands since 1900; *b.* 1844. *Educ.:* Durham University (Exhibitioner and Barry Scholar). Vicar of Castletown, Durham, 1874-84; St. Mark, Millfield, Durham, 1884-93; Bishop of Guiana, 1893-1900. *Publication:* History of Hylton Castle, 1883. *Address:* Bishop's Court, Barbados, West Indies. *Club:* Royal Societies. (*Died 16 Nov. 1916.*)

SWAIN, Hon. Col. George Llewellyn Douglas, C.M.G. 1914; V.D.; *b.* Corfu, Ionian Islands, 8 June 1858; 2nd *s.* of late Assistant Commissary-General, Charles Olton Swain, and Elisa Dominga Sanchez de Piña of Gibraltar; *m.* 1899, Charlotte Elizabeth Mary Patten (*d.* 1921), of Clone, Co. Wicklow; four *d. Educ.:* schools in England and Ireland and Colonies; Harrison's College, Barbados. Clerk, Colonial Banks, Barbados and British Guiana, 1878-82; Paymaster Police Force, British Guiana, 1882-84; District Inspector of Police, 1884; County Inspector, 1892; Chief County Inspector and Second in Command, 1899; acted Inspector-General and Colonel Commandant Militia, British Guiana, 1902; Deputy Inspector-General, Constabulary, Trinidad, 1903; Inspector-General of Trinidad Constabulary, and Commandant Local Forces, 1907-16; Member of Executive and Legislative Councils, Trinidad and Tobago; served with Ashanti Expedition, 1895-96 (Star, special mention); Colonial Forces Decoration, V.D., 1911; commanded Trinidad Coronation Contingent, 1911 (Coronation medal); Hythe Certificate Musketry, 1887; training with Royal Irish Constabulary, 1890; Member of Commission to inquire into working of Poor Law Board, British Guiana; Member of Medical Inquiry Commission, Trinidad, 1911. *Recreations:* shooting, fishing, etc. *Address:* c/o Capital and Counties Bank, Southsea. *Club:* Royal Albert Yacht, Southsea.
(*Died 1 May 1924.*)

SWAIN, Joseph; Emeritus President Swarthmore College since 1921; *b.* Pendleton, Ind., 16 June 1857; *s.* of Mary A. and Woolston Swain; *m.* Frances Morgan, Knightstown. Ind. *Educ.:* Indiana University; University of Edinburgh. LL.D. Wabash College, 1893, Lafayette College, 1912, University of Penn., 1912, Indiana University, 1920, Swarthmore College, 1921; Professor of Mathematics, Indiana University, 1886-91; Leland Stanford University, 1891-93; President Indiana University, 1893-1902; Swarthmore College, 1902-21; Member National Councils of Education and of Religious Education; President Indiana State Teachers' Association, 1894; President Higher Education Section of N.E.A., 1897; President National Council, 1907-10; President National Education Association, 1913-14. *Publications:* numerous scientific and educational papers. *Recreation:* golf. *Address:* Swarthmore, Pennsylvania. *T.A.:* Swarthmore. *T.:* Swarthmore 200.
(*Died 19 May 1927.*)

SWAIN, Percival Francis, C.B.E. 1919; Principal Clerk Public Trustee Office since 1917; *b.* 1888; *s.* of William Swain of Wynchcroft, Reading; *m.* Winifred, 2nd *d.* of late F. W. Balding, of Padworth, Berks. *Educ.:* Reading School and University College. Qualified as Chartered Accountant, 1909; Entered the office of the Public Trustee, 1910; Assistant Principal Clerk, 1915; *cr.* O.B.E. 1918. *Address:* Dingley, Tilehurst-on-Thames, Berks.
(*Died 19 July 1924.*)

SWAINE, Colonel Charles Edward, C.B. 1897; A.A.G. for Cavalry, Headquarters, 1900-1; retired; *b.* Hamburg, 20 Sep. 1844; *y. s.* of R. V. Swaine, sometime Consul-

General for Belgium in Hamburg. Unmarried. *Educ.*: Louth Grammar School, Lincolnshire; private tutor; and Trin. Coll. Camb. M.A. Joined 17th Lancers, 1868; Lieut. 1870; Zulu Campaign, 1879; battle of Ulundi (medal and clasp); Adjutant 17th Lancers, July to Dec. 1879; Captain 11th Hussars, 1880; A.D.C. to G.O.C. Cavalry Transvaal Campaign, 1881; A.D.C. to G.O.C. Cavalry Egyptian Expedition, 1882; present at action of Mahuta; capture of Mahsameh; both actions of Kassassin; battle of Tel-el-Kebir; pursuit to Belbeis; surrender and occupation of Cairo (medal with clasp, bronze star, 4th class Medjidie; Brev. of Major, despatches, 1882); Major, 1883; served with Light Camel Corps in Nile Expedition, 1884-85 (clasp), A.D.C. and Mil. Priv. Sec. to Viceroy of Ireland, 1886-1888; Lieut.-Col. 1891; commanded 11th Hussars, 1891-96; Colonel, 1895; A.A.G. for Cavalry, 1900-1; retired 1901; 2nd Class Red Eagle of Prussia, 1901; 2nd Class Redeemer of Greece, 1910. *Address:* 88 St. James's Street, S.W.1. *T.:* Regent 2894. *Clubs:* Army and Navy, Turf.   *(Died 2 May 1928.)*

SWAMIKANNU PILLAI, Louis Dominic, M.A.; LL.B.; Diwan Bahadur; C.I.E. 1924; I.S.O. 1917; President, Madras Legislative Council, Fort St. George, since 1924; *b.* 4 Feb. 1865; *m.*; three *s.* ten *d. Educ.:* St. Joseph's College, Negapatam. Assistant and Lecturer, St. Joseph's College, Trichinopoly, 1883-87; Clerk to the Legislative Council and French Translator, Chief Secretariat, Fort St. George, 1888-90; Latin Master, Presidency College, Madras, 1890-91; Deputy Collector and Magistrate, 1892-95; Assistant Secretary, Board of Revenue, Madras, 1895-1906; Secretary, Board of Revenue, Revenue Settlement, Madras, 1906-11; Registrar of Co-operative Societies, 1911-17; Collector and District Magistrate, 1917-19; Secretary to Government and Director of Agriculture, 1920; Secretary, Legislative Council, 1920-23; deputed to England to study House of Commons Procedure, April to July 1922; Fellow of Madras University, 1900; Chairman, Board of Examiners to Madras University in Greek, Latin, French, and German, 1903-17. *Publications:* Indian Chronology, 1911; 2nd edition, 1922; Indian Ephemeris, A.D. 1800-2000, 1915; 2nd edition, 1922; Indian Ephemeris, A.D. 700-1800, 6 vols., (Madras Government publication, 1922); various articles in Indian Antiquary and Epigraphia Indica on Indian Chronology; Credibility of Indian Astrology, 1922; Maximum Age of Dhruva Nadi, 1923; Secret of Memory, 1909; Panchang and Horoscope, 1925. *Address:* Roseville, Royapuram, Madras, India. *Club:* Cosmopolitan, Madras.   *(Died Oct. 1925.)*

SWANN, Frederick Samuel Philip, C.I.E. 1915-17; Magistrate and Collector U.P. 1911. *Educ.:* Berkhampstead School; Magdalen College, Oxford. Entered I.C.S., 1893; Joint-Magistrate, 1903; Commissioner, 1909.   *(Died 30 Nov. 1921.)*

SWANSEA, 2nd Baron (cr. 1893), **Ernest Ambrose Vivian**, D.L., J.P.; Bt. 1882; *b.* 11 Feb. 1848; *s.* of 1st Baron and Jessie, *d.* of Ambrose Goddard, M.P., The Lawn, Swindon. *Educ.:* Eton; Magdalen Coll. Oxford. *S.* father 1894. *Heir: half-b.* Hon. Odo Vivian. *Address:* Singleton, Swansea. *Clubs:* Carlton, Athenæum, Bachelors'.   *(Died 17 July 1922.)*

SWANSON, Sir John Warren, Kt., cr. 1923; *b.* 13 May 1865; *s.* of late William Swanson, Caithness. *Educ.:* Walker's School, Melbourne. Was President of Master Builders' Association, Melbourne, and of Federated Master Builders' Association; Lord Mayor of Melbourne, 1920. *Address:* Town Hall, Melbourne.   *(Died 4 Feb. 1924.)*

SWAYNE, Colonel Charles Henry, D.S.O. 1898; late R.A.M.C.; *b.* Carrick-on-Shannon, Ireland, 18 Sep. 1848; 2nd *s.* of late A. C. Swayne, M.D., J.P., Carrick-on-Shannon, and Anne, *d.* of D. Brown; *m.* Margaret Blakeney, *d.* of late David Gillies, Londonderry, 1896; two *d. Educ.:* private school; Ledwich School of Medicine, Dublin (prizeman in Medicine, Surgery, Midwifery). Appointed Staff Assist.-Surg. 1872; Surg. 1873; Surg.-Maj. 1886; Surgeon Lt.-Col. 1894; Brigade Surgeon Lt.-Col. 1897; Lt.-Col. Royal Army Medical Corps, 1898; Col. 1902; retired Sep. 1905; served with distinction during the yellow fever in Trinidad, W.I., 1881; in the Nile campaign, 1884-85, and thanked for services (medal, clasp, and Khedive's star); Burmese campaign, 1886-1889 (specially reported for services, medal and two clasps); in charge No. 6 B.F.H. and senior Medical Officer, 1st Brigade, Tirah Expeditionary Force, N.W.P., 1897-98 (medal and two clasps, despatches, D.S.O.). *Recreations:* golfing, fishing, tennis. *Address:* 7 Palmerston Park, Dublin. *T.:* Rathmines 670.   *(Died 4 Aug. 1925.)*

SWAYNE, Charles Richard, C.M.G. 1906; *s.* of Rev. C. B. Swayne; *b.* Aug. 1843; *m.* 1898, Frances Edith, *d.* of Thomas Richard Pace. Stipendiary Magistrate, Colony of Fiji, 1878; had various offices of administration and executive in Fiji; Deputy Commissioner and First British Resident of Gilbert and Ellice Islands, 1896; retired, 1906. *Address:* Lifton House, St. Marychurch, South Devon.   *(Died 11 June 1921.)*

SWAYNE, Maj.-Gen. James Dowell; Retired List, Indian Army; *b.* Delhi, 9 Nov. 1827; *s.* of Major Stephen Swayne, H.E.I.C.; *m.* 1877, Mary Morris Cormack; one *s.* one *d. Educ.:* Blackheath New Proprietary School; Addiscombe H.E.I.C. Military College. Joined 11th Bengal Native Infantry; after eight years with the 11th Native Infantry obtained an appointment in the Public Works Department, in which he remained until he retired from the service, 1878. *Recreations:* cricket chiefly. *Address:* 4 Vanbrugh Park, Blackheath, S.E.   *(Died 6 Dec. 1916.)*

SWAYNE, Professor Walter Carless, V.D.; M.D., B.S. (Lond.); M.D., Ch.B. (Bristol); M.R.C.S., L.R.C.P.; Professor of Obstetrics, and Director of Clinical Obstetrics, Bristol University, since 1909; Consulting Obstetric Physician, Bristol Royal Infirmary; Fellow Royal Society of Medicine; Major T.F.R., late commanding 1st Battery Gloucestershire R.F.A. (T. F.); Bristol University Contingent, O.T.C. (S.D.); 3/1st S.M. Gloucestershire Brigade R.F.A. and N.Z. Reserve F.A. (attached); *b.* 1862; *e. s.* of R. A. Swayne, J.P., Tillington Court, Hereford; *m.* Louisa Margaret, *d.* of late Rev. R. F. Heath: one *s.* three *d. Educ.:* King Edward's School, Birmingham; University College, Bristol; Guy's Hospital. *Recreations:* fly-fishing, riding, shooting. *Address:* Clarence House 2 Clifton Park, Clifton. *T.:* Bristol 2620. *Club:* Clifton.   *(Died 14 Aug. 1921.)*

SWAYTHLING, 2nd Baron (cr. 1907), **Louis Samuel Montagu**, 2nd Bt., cr. 1894; J.P.; *e. s.* of 1st Baron Swaythling and Ellen, *y. d.* of late Louis Cohen, of the Stock Exchange; *b.* 10 Dec. 1869; *S.* father, 1911; *m.* 1898, Gladys Helen Rachel, *d.* of late Col. A. E. Goldsmid; three *s.* one *d.* Head of the banking firm of Samuel Montagu & Co., London; 1st Baron assumed name of Montagu by Royal Licence; owns about 1200 acres. *Heir: s.* Hon. Stuart Albert Montagu, *b.* 19 Dec. 1898. *Address:* 28 Kensington Court, W.8; *T.:* Western 800; Townhill Park, Bitterne, nr. Southampton. *Clubs:* Reform, Bath; Royal Southern Yacht.   *(Died 11 June 1927.)*

SWEENY, Lt.-Col. Roger Lewis Campbell, D.S.O. 1916; O.B.E. 1922; M.C.; Indian Army Service Corps; *b.* 21 Nov. 1878; *s.*

1017

SWANN, Harry Kirke. See page xxx.

SWEENEY, Hon. Francis J., K.C. See page xxxi.

of Col. James Fielding Sweeny, British Service ;
m. 1902, Hilda, *d.* of late G. Lumgair, Collector
of Customs, Mauritius ; one *s.* two *d.* *Educ.:*
Montreal, Quebec, and Royal Military College,
Kingston, Ontario, Canada. 2nd Lieut. Unattached List for Indian Army, 1899 ; Lieut.
1901 ; Captain, 1908 ; Major, 1915 ; Lt.-Col. 1924 ;
on field service in Jubaland, B.E. Africa, March-
July 1914 ; in East Africa, Oct. 1914-May 1917
(despatches twice, D.S.O., M.C.) ; Egyptian
Expeditionary Force, June 1918-Dec. 1918 ;
operations against Afghanistan, May 1919-Nov.
1919 ; operations in Waziristan, 1919-20 (despatches, O.B.E.). *Address:* c/o Grindlay &
Co., 54 Parliament Street, S.W.1.
                              (Died Oct. 1926.)

SWETE, Henry Barclay, D.D. (Cambridge
and Glasgow), Litt.D. (Dublin and Oxford) ;
Regius Professor of Divinity, Cambridge,
1890 - 1915 ; Emeritus Professor, 1915 ; *b.*
Redlands, Bristol, 14 March 1835 ; *s.* of Rev.
John Swete, D.D. ; unmarried. *Educ.:* King's
College, London ; Caius College, Cambridge.
Deacon, 1858 ; Priest, 1859 ; Dean, Tutor and
Theological Lecturer, Caius College, 1869-77 ;
Rector of Ashdon, Essex, 1877-90 ; Professor of
Pastoral Theology, King's College, London,
1882-90 ; Examining Chaplain to Bishop of
St. Albans, 1881-90 ; Fellow of Caius College,
1858-77 ; Hon. Fellow, 1886-90 ; re-elected Fellow,
1890 ; Fellow of King's College, London, 1891 ;
Fellow of British Academy, 1902 ; Hon. Canon of
Ely, 1906 ; Hon. Chaplain to H.M. the King,
1911. *Publications:* two essays on History
of the Doctrine of the Holy Spirit, 1873, 1876 ;
Theodore of Mopsuestia's Commentary on the
Epistles of St. Paul, 1880-82 ; contributions to
Smith and Wace's Dictionary of Christian Biography (vols.iii. and iv.),1882-87 ; and to Hastings'
Dictionary of the Bible (vols. ii. and iii.), 1899-
1900 ; The Old Testament in Greek,1887-94 (3rd ed.
1901-7) ; The Akhmim Fragment of the Gospel
of Peter, 1893 ; The Apostles' Creed in Relation
to Primitive Christianity, 1894 (3rd ed. 1899) ;
Faith in Relation to Creed, Thought, and Life,
1895 ; Church Services and Service Books
before the Reformation, 1896 ; The Gospel
according to St. Mark : the Greek Text, with
Introduction, Notes, and Indices, 1898 (2nd
ed. 1902) ; An Introduction to the Old Testament in Greek, 1900 (2nd ed. 1902) ; Patristic
Study, 1902. Studies in the Teaching of our
Lord, 1903 ; The Apocalypse of St. John : the
Greek Text, with Introduction, Notes, and
Indices, 1906 (2nd ed. 1907) ; The Appearances of
our Lord after the Passion, 1907 (2nd ed. 1908) ;
The Holy Spirit in the New Testament, 1909 ;
The Ascended Christ, 1910 ; The Holy Spirit in
the Ancient Church, 1912 ; The Last Discourse
and Prayer of our Lord, 1913 ; The Holy
Catholic Church : The Communion of Saints,
1915 ; Editor of Cambridge Theological Essays,
1905 ; and Cambridge Biblical Essays, 1909.
Recreation : reading works of fiction. *Address:*
23 Old Park Road, Hitchin. *(Died 10 May 1917.)*

SWETENHAM, Clement William ; re-
tired Lieut.-Commander R.N., 1882 ; Chairman
of Congleton Petty Sessional Division ; *b.* 1852 ;
e. s. of Clement Swetenham of Somerford
Booths, Cheshire ; *m.* Louisa, *y. d.* of Ralph
Creyke of Marton and Rawcliffe Halls, York-
shire. *Educ.:* H.M.S. Britannia. *Address:*
Somerford Booths, Congleton. *T.A.:* Lower-
Withington. *M. :* 5712. *Club:* Naval and
Military.   *(Died 12 Dec. 1927.)*

SWIFTE, Sir Ernest Godwin, Kt., cr.
1921 ; Chief Metropolitan Police Magistrate,
Dublin, 1910-21 ; *b.* 3 June 1839 ; *o. s.* of late
William Richard Swifte, of Whitechurch Lodge,
Co. Dublin, and Elizabeth Catherine (*d.* 1887), *d.*
and *co-heiress* of Rev. Daniel Kelly, of Dawson's
Grove, Co. Armagh ; *m.* 1868, Frances (*d.* 1925),
d. of late Robert Coddington, of Kilmoon, Co.

1018

Meath ; three *s.* one *d.* *Educ. :* private school
in England ; Trinity College, Dublin ; M.A.
University of Dublin. Called to Irish Bar,
1863 ; K.C. 1911 ; appointed a Metropolitan
Police Magistrate of Dublin, 1890. *Address:*
18 Fitzwilliam Square, Dublin. *T.:* Dublin
61776.   *(Died 7 May 1927.)*

SWINBURNE, Hon. George, M.I.C.E.,
M.Inst.Mech.E. ; *b.* Newcastle-on-Tyne, 1861 ;
s. of M. W. Swinburne ; *m.* 1890, Ethel, *d.*
of Rev. D. Jones Hamer, Wolverhampton and
Melbourne ; four *d.* *Educ.:* Royal Grammar
School, Newcastle-on-Tyne. Arrived Australia,
1886 ; practised as engineer : initiated several
large hydraulic and gas undertakings ; Member
of Parliament for Hawthorn, 1902-13 ; Minister
of Water Supply and Agriculture, 1904 -8 ;
author of Water Acts on which Government
Irrigation policy is founded, and which national-
ised all the waters in the rivers and streams of
the State ; Member of four Interstate Conferences of State and Federal Ministries to consider financial and other questions ; Member of
the Inter State Commission for the commonwealth, 1913-17 ; Controlled issue of Capital
and Companies, and Chairman Business Board
Defence Department during War ; Member
State of Victoria Electricity Commission ;
Chairman Mount Lyell Railway and Mining
Co. ; Director National Mutual Life Association, Electrolytic Zinc Co. of Australia, etc.
Address: Shenton, Kinkora Road, Hawthorn,
Melbourne. *Clubs:* Melbourne, Australian,
Melbourne.   *(Died 4 Sept. 1928.)*

**SWINBURNE, Lt. - Col. Thomas
Robert,** of Pontop Hall, Durham ; *e. s.* of late
Capt. T. A. Swinburne, R.N., of Pontop Hall, and
Eilean Shona, Inverness-shire ; *b.* 4 Oct. 1853 ; *m.*
1886, Louise Gertrude, *e. d.* of late Robert
Stewart of Kinlochmoidart ; one *d.* Entered the
Royal Marine Artillery, 1872 ; served in Egypt,
1882 (despatches) ; Sudan, 1884-85 (medal and
clasp). *Address:* Reeds, Liss, Hants ; 23 Eaton
Place, S.W.1. *T.:* Vic. 2557. *Club:* United
Service.   *(Died 8 Oct. 1921.)*

SWINDLEY, Maj.-Gen. John Edward,
C.B. 1907 ; *b.* 21 March 1831. Entered army,
1847 ; Lt.-Col. 1874 ; retired, 1884 ; served
Kaffir War, 1852-53 (medal) ; Crimea, 1855-56
(medal with clasp, Turkish medal) ; Indian
Mutiny, 1858-59 (medal) ; Afghan War, 1879
(despatches). *Address:* Raleigh House,
Raleigh Drive, Esher, Surrey. *Club:* Army
and Navy.   *(Died 11 Mar. 1919.)*

SWINEY, Maj.-Gen. John, Indian Army ;
b. 9 Feb. 1832 ; *m.* 1871, Rosa, *d.* of Major J.
Biggs, 4th Dragoon Guards. Entered army,
1849 ; Maj.-Gen. 1890 ; unemployed list, 1890 ;
served Indian Mutiny, 1857-59. *Address:* Sandford Lawn, Bath Road, Cheltenham. *Clubs:*
Primrose, New, Cheltenham (*Died 17 May 1918.*)

SWINFEN, of Chertsey, 1st Baron, cr.
1919.   *(Died 15 Nov. 1919.)*

SWINLEY, Maj. - Gen. George, C.B.
1893 ; late Royal Bengal Artillery ; *b.* 24 Apr.
1842 ; *s.* of late Maj.-Gen. G. H. Swinley, R.A. ;
m. 1873, Alice (*d.* 1922), *d.* of W. G. Probyn ; three
d. *Educ. :* Harrow ; East India Col., Addiscombe. Entered army, 1860 ; Maj.-Gen. 1895 ;
served Bhootan Field Force, 1865-66 (medal with
clasp) ; Black Mountain Expedition, 1868
(clasp) ; Jowaki Afreedee Expedition, 1877-78
(despatches, clasp) ; Afghan War, 1878-80 (despatches several times, brevets of Major and
Lt.-Col., medal with three clasps, bronze decoration). *Address:* 2 Fauconberg Villas, Bayshill
Road, Cheltenham. *T. :* Cheltenham 736.
Club: New, Cheltenham. *(Died 26 July 1925.)*

SWINNY, Shapland Hugh : editor of the
Positivist Review ; *b.* Dublin, 30 Dec. 1857.
Educ.: St. John's College, Cambridge ; M.A.
1884. President of the London Positivist
Society since 1901, and of the English Positivist

Committee since 1904; Member of the Council of the Sociological Society from its foundation (Chairman, 1907-1909); Secretary of the South Africa Conciliation Committee, 1900-1902; Treasurer of the Nationalities and Subject Races Committee, 1908-13; Vice - President Irish Literary Society, London; has visited India, America, the Near East, Portugal, etc., and written on India and in defence of the Portuguese Republic; a life-long advocate of the Anglo - French alliance. *Publications:* The History of Ireland, 1890; The Day of All the Dead, 1892; joint-editor of the New Calendar of Great Men, 1920; a frequent contributor to periodicals. *Recreation:* travel. *Club:* National Liberal.   (*Died 31 Aug. 1923.*)

SWINSTEAD, George Hillyard, R.I., R.C.A.; artist painter; member of The Worshipful Company of Painter Stainers. Vice-President Hampstead Society of Artists; 4th *s.* of Charles Swinstead, artist, and Jane Hillyard of Ipswich; *m.* 1887, Rosalie, 3rd *d.* of late John Sheppard Edmonds of Highgate; two *d.* *Educ.:* Royal Academy Schools, 1881. Chorister in Her late Majesty's Private Chapel Choir, Windsor, from 11 to 16 years of age; exhibited first picture at 17 years of age; first picture exhibited at Royal Academy in 1882. *Works:* By Appointment; When Trumpets Call; When the Heart is Young; The First Step; Baby's Own; Wild Flowers and Thorns; Across the Bridge of Time; Lilies; Reunited; Song of the Sailors, on a Nile Dahabeah; The Road from Gizeh to Cairo; A Wild-Flower; First on the Antarctic Continent; The Early Days of Golf; A Church Window; Poppy Land; Violets; Pomona's Blossom; The Angel's Message; The White Horse; Home from the Meadows; Wanderers; Steady; Blossoms; My Little Bird; Haven under the Hill; Black and Ivory; The Wounded Wanderer: The White Cliff: Hardanger Fjord; The Pathway of Light; Pandora; A Summer Reverie; Polperro Harbour; Francis Belsey; The White Comrade; The Boy Scouts; Boy Scouts Stalking; The Bay of Villefranche; many portraits. *Publication:* My Old World Garden, and how I made it in a London Suburb. *Recreations:* cricket, golf, etc. *Address:* 14 Kidderpore Avenue, Hampstead, N.W.3. *T.:* Hamp. 5214. *Clubs:* M.C.C.; Northwood Golf.   (*Died 16 Jan. 1926.*)

SWINSTEAD, Rev. John Howard, M.A., D.D.; Vicar, St. Peter's, Bayswater, and Surrogate; *b.* 14 July 1864; *s.* of Charles Swinstead, artist; *m.* 1st, Agnes Marion Thomas, *d.* of Elias Squarey, Downton; 2nd, Hannah Sclater, *d.* of George Humphrey, West Dene; two *d.* *Educ.:* City of London School (Saddlers' Company Scholar); St. Catherine's College, Cambridge (Classical Scholar and librarian). B.A. 1886, M.A. 1890; Assistant Master, N.E.C.S., Barnard Castle, and Dover College; Head of Cathedral Choir School, Oxford; Curate St. Mary's, Dover, Marylebone, and Cathedral and Close of Salisbury; St. Andrew's Missioner, Sarum; Chaplain, Christ Church, M.A. and D.D., Oxford; Vicar of Chalgrove-cum-Berrick, Oxon.; Chaplain to H.B.M.'s Legation, Sweden; Fellow of Royal Botanic Society; Liveryman of Guild of Saddlers; Chaplain to the Guild of Showmen; Chaplain to St. Luke's Hospital, W.2; Lecturer, Christian Evidence Society. *Publications:* A Parish on Wheels; Chalgrove Field and John Hampden; In a Wonderful Order; Brought to the Bishop; History of English Church, Stockholm; Through English Eyes; The Cradle of the Swedish Church; The Swedish Church and Ours; After Fifty Years. *Recreations:* cricket, golf, lawn tennis. *Address:* 13 Ladbroke Gardens, W.11. *T.:* Park 1980.
    (*Died 28 Aug. 1924.*)

SWINTON, Lieut.-Colonel Francis Edward, C.I.E. 1919; I.M.S., retired; *e. surv. s.* of late Robert Blair Swinton, Madras Civil Service (late H.E.I.C.S.); unmarried. *Educ.:* St. Bartholomew's Hospital. Medical Officer, 28th Bombay Pioneers; P.A. to P.M.O. Bombay Command; M.S.K. to Government, Bombay; Deputy Director-General I.M.S.; M.S.K. to Government, Madras; retired, 1922. *Recreation:* navigation. *Clubs:* United Service, Simla; Byculla, Royal Bombay Yacht, Bombay; Madras: Western India, Poona.
    (*Died 25 Dec. 1927.*)

SWINTON, Captain George Herbert Tayler (retired); *b.* 25 Dec. 1852; *o. s.* of Archibald Adam Swinton, Bengal Civil Service; *m.* 1885, Mary M'Chlery, *d.* of S. Becher, B.C.S.; one *s.* one *d.* *Educ.:* Cheltenham College. Joined Royal Brecknock Rifle Militia, 1871; transferred as lieutenant in 2nd Batt. 16th Bedfordshire Regt. 1874; Captain, 1884; retired, 1893; J.P. Berwickshire. *Recreations:* shooting and fishing. *Address:* Swinton, Berwickshire. *M.:* SH 327.   (*Died 19 Sept. 1923.*)

SWINTON, John Liulf Campbell, V.D., J.P. and D.L., Berwickshire; *b.* 3 Mar. 1858; *e. s.* of late Archibald Campbell Swinton, LL.D., of Kimmerghame, and 2nd wife, Georgiana Caroline, 3rd *d.* of Sir George Sitwell, 2nd Bart.; *m.* 1893, Agnes Cecil, *y. d.* of late George Towry White, barrister-at-law; one *d.* Late Major 2nd (Berwickshire) V. Batt. King's Own Scottish Borderers; Member Royal Company of Archers, King's Bodyguard for Scotland. *Recreations:* salmon - fishing, shooting, bridge. *Address:* Kimmerghame, nr. Duns, N.B. *Clubs:* Carlton; New, Edinburgh; Royal Highland Yacht, Oban.   (*Died 6 Sept. 1930.*)

SWITHINBANK, Harold William, F.R.S. Edin.; F.R.G.S.; *b.* 1858; *s.* of late George Edwin Swithinbank, LL.D., F.S.A.; *m.* 1883, Amy, *d.* of James Crossley Eno of Wood Hall, Dulwich, Kent; one *s.* two *d.* Late Lieutenant and Adjutant, 11th Hussars; Captain, Middlesex Yeomanry, and Reserve of Officers; Commander R.N.R. for Special War Service, 1914; D.L., J.P. Bucks; High Sheriff, 1891; member of first Buckinghamshire County Council; Governor of Royal Agricultural Society of England; Vice-President of Royal Veterinary College. *Publications:* Bacteriology of Milk; various papers to Royal Society and other kindred bodies. *Address:* Denham Court, Denham, Bucks; 2 Sussex Gardens, W.2. *T.:* Paddington 2829. *Clubs:* Naval and Military, Cavalry; Royal Yacht Squadron, Cowes; Royal Thames Yacht.   (*Died 9 Feb. 1928.*)

SYKES, Sir Henry, 6th Bt., *cr.* 1781; *b.* 9 Dec. 1828; *s.* of 4th Bt. and Henrietta, *d.* of Henry Villebois, of Marham Hall, Norfolk; *S.* brother 1899; *m.* Mary Winifred, *d.* of Henry Tuck. Joined R.N.; late Capt. Royal Dragoons; served in Crimean War (medal). *Heir:* kinsman Arthur, *b.* 2 Sep. 1871. *Address:* 2 Greenhill Terrace, Weymouth, Dorset.
    (*Died 10 April 1916.*)

SYKES, Lt.-Col. Sir Mark, 6th Bt., *cr.* 1783; J.P., F.R.G.S.; M.P. (U.) Central Hull since 1911; *b.* 16 Mar. 1879; *o. s.* of 5th Bt. and Christina Anne Jessica, *e. d.* of Rt. Hon. George Augustus Cavendish-Bentinck, M.P.; *S.* father, 1913; *m.* 1903, Edith Violet, 3rd *d.* of late Rt. Hon. Sir J. E. Gorst; three *s.* three *d.* *Educ.:* Beaumont; Ecole des Jesuites, Monaco; Institut St. Louis, Brussels; Jesus College, Cambridge. C.C. for E.R. Yorks; served South Africa, 1902; Hon. Captain in the Army, 1902; Captain 3rd Battalion Yorkshire Regiment, 1902-7; Major 5th Batt. Yorkshire Regt. 1908, Lt.-Col. 1911; Member N.R. Territorial Force Association. *Publications:* Through Five Turkish Provinces, 1900; D'Ordel's Tactics (with Mr. E. T. Sandars), 1902; Pantechnicon (ditto),

1904 ; Dar-ul-Islam ; Five Mansions of the House of Othman, 1909 ; The Caliphs' Last Heritage, 1915, and contributions to journals and reviews. *Heir : s.* Mark Tatton Richard, *b.* 24 Aug. 1905. *Address :* Sledmere, Malton, Yorks. *Clubs :* Carlton, Marlborough, Beefsteak, Prince's, 1900 ; Yorkshire, York.
(*Died 16 Feb. 1919.*)

SYLVA, Carmen, *nom de plume of* **Elizabeth, Queen of Roumania, Pauline Elizabeth Ottilie Louise ;** *b.* Neuwied, Germany, 29 December 1843 ; *d.* of late Prince Hermann of Wied and the Princess Maria of Nassau ; *m.* 1869, Prince Charles, later King, Roumania, 2nd *s.* of Prince Anthony of Hohenzollern (*d.* 1914). Travelled, 1863-68 ; daughter born, 1870 (*d.* 1874) ; Roumania declared a kingdom, 1881, and on 22 May of same year she was crowned Queen ; member Academy of Sciences of Bucharest, 1882 ; visited England, 1890. *Publications :* Thoughts of a Queen, 1890 ; Edleen Vaughan, 1892 ; Shadows on Life's Dial, 1895 ; A Real Queen's Fairy Book, 1901 ; In Memory's Shrine ; Sweet Hours, and many poems, novelettes, fairy-tales, and dramas. *Address :* Bucharest, Roumania.
(*Died 2 Mar. 1916.*)

SYLVESTER, Assist. Surgeon Henry Thomas, V.C., M.D., L.R.C.S. Edin., L.S.A. Served at siege and fall of Sebastopol, 1855 (despatches, medal with clasp, V.C., Kt. of Legion of Honour) ; Indian Campaign, 1857-58, including relief of Lucknow (medal with two clasps) ; retired, 1861. *Decorated* for dressing wounds of an officer under heavy fire.
(*Died Mar. 1920.*)

SYLVESTER, Rev. Samuel Augustus Kirwan ; Vicar of Roby, near Liverpool, since 1885 ; Rural Dean of Prescot ; Hon. Canon of Liverpool ; Hon. Chaplain to the Bishop of Liverpool ; *b.* 1852 ; 4th *s.* of George Mairis Sylvester of Trowbridge, Wiltshire ; *m.* 1880, Harriet Eliza (*d.* 1917), *e. d.* of Henry H. Hornby of Beechwood, Aigburth, Liverpool. *Educ. :* Epsom College ; New College, Oxford. Curate of Huyton, 1875 ; Priest, 1876 ; Curate of Windermere Parish Church, 1879. *Address :* The Vicarage, Roby, Liverpool. *T.A. :* Roby. *Club :* Athenæum, Liverpool.
(*Died 22 Nov. 1928.*)

S Y M, Major-General Sir John Munro, K.C.B., *cr.* 1908 ; C.B., 1889 ; *b.* Edinburgh, 15 Feb. 1839 ; *o. s.* of Rev. John Sym of Free Greyfriars Church, Edinburgh, and Catharine Glassfurd, *o. d.* of Lieut.-Col. John Munro, H.E.I.C.S. ; *m.* Eliza d'Oyley Vincent, *o. d.* of Major Hugh Rees James, C.B. Indian Staff Corps, 9 August 1870 ; one *s. Educ. :* High School and University, Edinburgh. 58th Bengal Infantry, 1858 ; 5th Gurkha Rifles, 1863 ; Capt. 1870 ; Major, 1878 ; Brevt. Lieut.-Col. 1881 ; Lieut.-Col. 1884 : Col. 1885 ; Major-Gen. 1896 ; Hon. Col. 5th Gurkha Rifles, 1916. *Field Services :* N.W. Frontier of India ; Umbeyla, 1863 (medal with clasp) ; Hazara, 1868 (clasp) ; Afghanistan, 1879-80 (three times in despatches, medal with 3 clasps, bronze star and Brevet of Lieut.-Col.) ; N.W. Frontier of India, Hazara, 1888 ; commanded 1st, Col. 1st Brigade (despatches, clasp and C.B.) ; 2nd, Miranzai, 1891 ; commanded 1st Brigade (despatches, clasp). *Decorated* for services in Hazara. *Recreations :* shooting, fishing, golf. *Address :* 4 Belgrave Place, Edinburgh. *Club :* New, Edinburgh.
(*Died 5 Oct. 1919.*)

SYMES, Rev. John Elliotson ; *b.* London, 31 Dec. 1847 ; 2nd *s.* of E. S. Symes, M.D. *Educ. :* Univ. Coll. School, London ; Downing Coll. Camb. (M.A.). Camb. University Extension Lecturer, 1875-80 ; Second Master Royal Grammar School, Newcastle-on-Tyne, 1880-81 ; Professor of English Literature, etc., University Coll. Nottingham, 1881-96 ;
1020

Principal of University College, Nottingham, 1890-1912. *Publications :* Newcastle Sermons, 1882 ; Political Economy, 12th ed. 1920 ; The Prelude to Modern History, 1890 ; The French Revolution, 2nd edition, 1904 ; Broad Church, 1913. *Address :* 78 Elsham Road, W.14.
(*Died 31 Mar. 1921.*)

SYMINGTON, Johnson, M.D. (Edin.), F.R.C.S. (Eng. and Edin.), F.R.S. 1903 ; late Professor of Anatomy, Registrar and Member of Senate and of Statutory Commission, Queen s University, of Belfast ; LL.D. (Belfast) ; *b.* 1851. *Educ. :* Taunton ; Edin. Univ. ; Ex-Fellow and Examiner in Anatomy, Royal Univ. of Ireland ; President of Section of Anthropology, British Association, Southport, 1903 ; of Anatomical Society of Great Britain and Ireland, 1904-5-6. *Publications :* The Topographical Anatomy of the Child ; an Atlas of Skiagrams of the Teeth (with Dr. Rankin) ; an Atlas on the Topography of the Head and Neck, Thorax and Abdomen ; one of the editors of Quain's Anatomy, and numerous papers on human and comparative anatomy. *Address :* 4 Montague Street, W.C.1.
(*Died 24 Feb. 1924.*)

SYMMONS, Israel Alexander, LL.B. ; Police Magistrate, Greenwich and Woolwich, 1911 ; Clerkenwell, 1916 ; Marylebone since 1922 ; *b.* 1862 ; *m.* 1895, *d.* of Jonas Drucquer ; Barrister, Middle Temple, 1885. *Address :* 31 Sheriff Road, Kilburn, N.W. *Clubs :* Garrick, British Empire.
(*Died 31 July 1923.*)

SYMONDS, Captain F. C. Loder- ; late Royal Artillery ; J.P., Chairman of Faringdon Petty Sessional Division, and Alderman Berks County Council ; *b.* 1846 ; *e. s.* of late James Frederick Symonds, J.P., of Okeleigh, Hereford ; *m.* 1873, Isabel Emily Annette, *d.* of late Captain John Parland, Russian Imperial Guard ; one *s.* two *d.* Succeeded cousin, John Loder-Symonds, of Hinton Manor, and assumed the additional name of Loder by Royal License. *Educ. :* Royal Military College, Woolwich. *Publication :* A History of the Old Berkshire Hunt. *Recreations :* shooting, motoring ; took part in 1912 in the motor contest between the Royal Auto Club and Imperial German Club organised by Prince Henry of Prussia. *Heir : s.* Captain F. P. Loder-Symonds. *Address :* Hinton Manor, Faringdon. *T.A. :* Longworth. *T. :* Kingston Bagpuize 7. *M. :* BL 1, BL 115, and BL 215. *Clubs :* Army and Navy. (*Died 27 Dec. 1923.*)

SYMONDS, Rev. William, M.A. ; Rector and Patron of the Advowson of Stockport Parish Church since 1875 ; *b.* 2 April 1832 ; *s.* of Stephen Symonds of Handforth, Cheshire ; *m.* 1867, Maria (*d.* 1905), *d.* of Charles Sainsbury of Court Hill, Potterne, Wilts ; three *s.* four *d. Educ. :* Privately ; Gonville and Caius College, Cambridge ; Junior Optime. Deacon, 1856 ; Curacies, St. Simon's, Salford, St. Stephen's, Camden Town, Parish Church, Croydon ; Priest, 1859 ; Rector of Greystoke, 1871-75 ; Hon. Can. Chester Cathedral, 1886 ; Rural Dean of Stockport, 1889-1905 ; Assessor Surrogate ; during incumbency Parish Church restored, Almshouses rebuilt, Offerton Schools built, St. Alban's, Offerton, built and endowed, Mission Churches built, St. Stephen's and St. Andrew's National Schools rebuilt. *Publications :* Forty Rectors of Stockport ; Six Weeks in Ægean Sea. *Address :* Stockport. (*Died 15 Mar. 1919.*)

SYMONS, Lt.-Col. Frank Albert, D.S.O. 1915 ; M.B. ; R.A.M.C. ; *b.* 28 April 1869. *Educ. :* Edinburgh. Captain, 1896 ; Major, 1904 ; Lt.-Col., 1915 ; served S. African War, 1899-1900 (Queen's medal, 3 clasp) ; European War, 1914-1915 (despatches, D.S.O.). (*Died 30 April 1917.*)

SYMONS, Capt. Thomas Raymond, J.P., D.L. ; *b.* 30 Mar. 1866 ; *o. s.* of Thomas George Symons (*d.* 1868) and 2nd wife, Mary Hayley, *y. d.* of late Rev. Thomas Edward Allen ; *m.* 1888, Margaret Ethel, 2nd *d.* of Sir

James Rankin, 1st Bart.; one *s. Educ.*: Eton. High Sheriff, Herefordshire, 1894; Patron of Much Birch; late Captain Imperial Yeomanry in S. Africa, and Lieut. N. Somerset Imperial Yeomanry; previously Lieut. Royal Monmouthshire Engineer Militia. *Address*: The Mynde Park, Hereford. *Club*: Badminton.
(*Died 26 July 1922.*)

SYMPSON, Edward Mansel, M.A., M.D. Cantab.; J.P. City of ·Lincoln; Sheriff, 1906-7; F.S.A.; Hon. Lt.-Col. R.A.M.C. (T.F.); Surgeon Lincoln County Hospital; Consulting Surgeon, General Dispensary; Fellow, Medical Society of London; President, Midland Branch, British Medical Association, 1906-7; *b.* 22 March 1860; *o. c.* of Thomas Sympson, F.R.C.S., of Lincoln, and Caroline, *d.* of Rev. E. Peacock, M.A., Fifehead Magdalene, Dorset; *m.* 1888, Florence Mabel, *y. d.* of Joseph Knight, Barrister-at-Law, F.S.A., of 27 Camden Square, N.W.; one *s. Educ.*: Lincoln Grammar School; Shrewsbury School; Gonville and Caius College, Cambridge; St. Bartholomew's Hospital. Edited Cambridge Review; was House Physician and House Surgeon at St. Bartholomew's Hospital; in practice in Lincoln since 1888; associate editor Quarterly Medical Journal; Hon. Local Secretary Society of Antiquaries; editor Lincolnshire Notes and Queries; co-Editor Associated Architectural Societies' Reports and Papers; Hon. Treasurer Lincolnshire Architectural Society; Governor Christ's Hospital and Girls' High School, Lincoln; ex-Chairman of the Lincoln Conservative and Liberal Unionist Association; Member of Council National Union Conservative Associations; Vice-President R. Archæological Institute (Lincoln Meeting). *Publications*: Lincoln, a Historical and Topographical History of; Lincolnshire (Cambridge County Geographies); editor of Memorials of Old Lincolnshire; many articles and papers in professional and archæological journals. *Recreation*: archæology. *Address*: Deloraine Court, Lincoln. *T.A.*: Sympson, Lincoln. *T.*: Lincoln 32. (*Died 15 Jan. 1922.*)

SYNGE, Sir Francis Robert Millington, 6th Bt., *cr.* 1801; *b.* 27 May 1851; *S.* father 1894; *m.* 1st, 1876, Frances (*d.* 1911), *d.* of Robert Evans, Rock Ferry, Cheshire; three *s.* three *d.*; 2nd, 1912, Fanny Cecil, *d.* of late Charles R. Wade-Gery, Wornditch Hall, Kimbolton; one *d.* Adjutant 4th Batt. Liverpool Regt. 1890-95; Major South Lancashire Regt. 1893-99. *Heir*: *s.* Robert Millington Synge [*b.* 17 Nov. 1877; *m.* 1922, Christobel Etienne Liddell; one *d. Address*: 101 Eaton Terrace, S.W.1. *T.*: Victoria 7451]. *Address*: Syngefield, Birr, King's Co. (*Died 1 Mar. 1924.*)

SYNGE, Major Mark, C.I.E. 1919; D.S.O. 1917; Indian Army Supply and Transport Corps; *b.* 25 April 1871; *y. s.* of late Joshua Sing, Aigburth, near Liverpool, J.P.; *m.* 1899, Beatrice Ellen, *d.* of late Sir William White Cooper; one *s.* three *d. Educ.*: Shrewsbury; Christ Church, Oxford. Entered Army, 1894; medals Punjab Frontier, 1897-98; Tibet, 1904; Abor, 1911-12; served European War, 1914-17 (despatches twice, D.S.O.). *Publications*: (1) unofficial, under the nom de plume Powell Millington, In Cantonments, 1898; In and Beyond Cantonments, 1904; To Lhassa at Last, 1905; A Homeward Mail, 1907; On the Track of the Abor, 1912; (2) official (as a publication of the Government of India), Certain Subjects taught to Officers at the London School of Economics, 1909; Elementary Economics as an aid to the Supply and Transport Office, 1918. *Recreations*: golfing, climbing, riding. *Club*: Rawal Pindi.
(*Died 11 July 1921.*)

SYNGE, Sir Robert Follett, K.C.M.G., *cr.* 1919; C.M.G. 1897; His Majesty's Deputy Marshal of the Ceremonies, Foreign Office;

b. 8 Dec. 1853; *e. s.* of late W. W. F. Synge; *m.* 1881, Laura, *d.* of late J. C. Fletcher, Dale Park, Arundel. *Educ.*: Charterhouse. Lieut. in Royal Surrey Militia; appointed to the Treaty Department of Foreign Office, 1884; appointed to assist the Master of the Ceremonies, 1894; Assistant Marshal of the Ceremonies, 1899; Deputy Marshal of the Ceremonies, 1902; Secretary to Lord Wolseley's Special Mission to announce the accession of King Edward VII. 1901; of Lord Roberts' Special Mission to announce the accession of King George V. 1910; received the Jubilee Medal for 1887, and clasp for 1897; Coronation Medal, 1902, and several foreign decorations; Officer Legion of Honour. *Decorated* for services in connection with the Queen's Diamond Jubilee. *Address*: 7 Chester Square, S.W.1. *T.*: Vic. 7899. *Clubs*: St. James's, London Fencing, Prince's Golf. (*Died 22 Jan. 1920.*)

SYNNOTT, Nicholas Joseph, J.P. Co. Kildare; *e. s.* of late Thomas Synnott, J.P., of Innismore, Co. Dublin, and Catherine, *d.* of J. Dunne; *m.* 1891, Barbara, *d.* of J. MacEvoy Netterville, and Hon. Mary Netterville, *d.* and *heiress* of 7th Viscount Netterville of Dowth, Co. Meath; two *s.* four *d. Educ.*: Stonyhurst College; University of London; B.A. 1877. Called to Bar, Middle Temple, 1881; joined the Northern Circuit; contested seat at the London County Council, 1895; High Sheriff of Co. Kildare, 1906; Governor of the Bank of Ireland and director of the Great Southern and Western Railway; chairman of the Naas Board of Guardians, 1899-1905; member of Royal Commission on Income Tax, 1919; has given evidence before the Royal Commissions on University Education in Ireland and the Local Taxation Commission. *Publications*: pamphlets and articles on the Irish University question, on the Valuation of Land, on Irish financial questions. *Address*: Furness, Naas, Co. Kildare. *T.*: Naas 3X. *Clubs*: Garrick; Stephen's Green, Dublin. (*Died 1 Aug. 1920.*)

SZCZEPANSKI, Maj.-Gen. Henry Charles Antony, Indian Army; *b.* 21 Jan. 1841. Entered army, 1857; Maj.-Gen. 1897; retired list, 1897; served Indian Mutiny, 1857-1858 (medal); Assistant Commissioner, Punjab, 1860; Hyderabad, 1864; in turns Cantonment Magistrate and Small Cause Court Judge and Deputy Commissioner; Judl. Commissioner, 1894-95; Officiating Commissioner, 1888-89; reverted to military department, 1895.
(*Died 2 June 1923.*)

SZLUMPER, Sir James Weeks, Kt., *cr.* 1894; J.P. Surrey and J.P. and D.I. Cardiganshire; High Sheriff, 1898-99; M.Inst.C.E.; *b.* 29 Jan. 1834; *m.* 1867, Mary (*d.* 1914), *d.* of James Culliford, Bristol; one *s.* two *d. Educ.*: privately. Has extensively constructed English and Welsh railways; Mayor of Richmond, Surrey, 1894, when Prince Edward was born in that borough, and on two occasions that year received Her late Majesty Queen Victoria when visiting Richmond; again Mayor, 1900-1 and 1904-5; Co-opted Member Surrey Territorial Force Association. *Address*: 17 Victoria Street, Westminster, S.W.1; Glanteif, Kew Gardens. *T.*: 5076 Victoria, and 1433 Richmond.
(*Died 26 Oct. 1926.*)

T

TAAFFE, George Joseph, D.L., J.P. Co. Louth; J.P. Co. Meath; Capt. 3rd Batt. Queen's Own Royal West Kent Regt.; *o. s.* of Stephen Taaffe of Glenkeiran and *g.s.* of George Taaffe of Smarmore Castle, Co. Louth, J.P., D.L.; *m.* Alice Catherine Trevor, *d.* of late Capt. B. T. Griffith-Boscawen, J.P., D.L., Trevalyn Hall, Denbighshire, N. Wales, and Sister of Right

Hon. Sir A. Griffith - Boscawen, M.P.; two s. one d. *Educ.:* Stonyhurst College. Formerly Capt. 4th Batt. King's Own Royal Lancaster Regt.; served as A.D.C. to G.O.C. 26th Division in Salonica during European War; took an active part in the formation of the Irish Land Conference Committee, and also of the Committee for the Settlement of the Irish question along the lines of Devolution; Smarmore Castle has been in possession of the family since the 10th century. *Recreations:* hunting, shooting, golf, tennis. *Address:* Smarmore Castle, Ardee, Co. Louth. Ireland. *Club:* Royal Automobile. (*Died 7 June 1925.*)

TACON, Sir Thomas Henry, Kt., *cr.* 1900; Alderman of the East Suffolk County Council since its formation; J.P. for counties of Suffolk and Norfolk and borough of Eye; High Sheriff, 1898, and Deputy-Lieutenant of Suffolk; Deputy - Chairman of the County Finance Committee; Governor of Eye Grammar School; President of Eye Volunteers; Mayor of Eye, 1892-93, 1893-94, 1905-6, 1906-7, 1907-8, 1913-1914, 1914-15, 1915-16; Unionist; *b.* Eye, 14 March 1838; *s.* of Charles Tacon of Eye, Suffolk; *m.* 1868, Catherine Elizabeth, *e. d.* of R. B. Orford of Occold Hall; one *d.* Alderman Eye Town Council. *Address:* Red House, Eye, Suffolk.
(*Died 19 Feb. 1922.*)

TAFLIA, 4th Marquis or (Malta), Lt.-Col. Frederick Sedley; *b.* 1837; *s.* of F. Sedley, Superintendent of Police at Malta (*d.* 1885), and Catherine (*d.* 1866) *d.* of 2nd Marquis of Taflia; *m.* 1871, Edith (*d.* 1899), *d.* of late Rev. G. H. Langdon, Vicar of Oving, Sussex, and *g.d.* of late Admiral Sir John Acworth Ommanney, K.C.B.; one *d.* Served in China War, 1860 (medal and three clasps); formerly Captain 5th Lancers and 48th Regt.; retired 1880; granted hon. rank of Lieut.-Colonel. 1881. *Address:* Badgergate, Rye, Sussex. *Club:* Constitutional. (*Died 15 Mar. 1921.*)

TAILLON, Hon. Sir Louis Olivier, Kt., *cr.* 1916; *b.* 26 Sept. 1840; *s.* of Aimé Taillon and Marie Josephte Dannais; *m.* 1875, Marie Louise Georgina (*d.* 1876), *d.* of late Hon. P. U. Archambault. *Educ.:* Masson College. Called to Bar, 1865; commenced practice in Montreal; Q.C. 1882; Batonnier, 1892; Member for Montreal East, 1875-86; Speaker of Assembly, 1882-84; Attorney-General, 1884-87; formed an Administration, Jan. 1887, but resigned in two days; Leader of Opposition to 1890; Minister without Portfolio, Dec. 1891; Member for Chambly, 1892; Prime Minister, 1892-96; Postmaster-General, 1896; defeated in General Elections, 1896 and 1900; declined seat on Bench, 1888; Hon. D.C.L., Bishop's College, 1895, and Laval, 1900; has now retired into private life. Roman Catholic. *Address:* 595 St. Denis Street, Montreal. *T.:* 1537. (*Died April 1923.*)

TAIT, Hon. Sir Melbourne McTaggart, Kt., *cr.* 1897; D.C.L.; LL.D. M'Gill University, 1912; *b.* 20 May 1842; *s.* of Thomas Tait, merchant, Melbourne, Canada; *m.* 1st, 1863, Monica (*d.* 1876), *d.* of James Holmes, Montreal; one *s.* two *d.*; 2nd, 1878, Lydia, *d.* of H. B. Kaighn, Newport, R.I.; three *s. Educ.:* St. Francis Coll. School, Richmond, Province of Quebec; University M'Gill Coll. Montreal. Barr. Montreal, 1863; Q.C. 1882; Judge Superior Court, 1887; Acting Chief Justice, Montreal, 1894; Chief Justice of Superior Court for the Province of Quebec, 1906-12. *Address:* 1004 Dorchester Street, W. Montreal, Quebec. *Club:* St. James's, Montreal.
(*Died 19 Feb. 1917.*)

TAKAMINE, Jokichi, chemist; *b.* Takaoka, Japan, 1854; *m.* 1887, Caroline Hitch, New Orleans; two *s. Educ.:* Imperial University of Japan, 1879, as chemical engineer; University of Glasgow, 1879-81. Head chemist, Japanese Department of Agriculture and Commerce,

1881-84; Imperial Japanese Commissioner to Cotton Centennial Exposition at New Orleans, 1884-85; organised first superphosphate works erected in Japan, 1887; removed to United States, 1890, and has since resided there; discovered diastatic enzyme known as takadiastase, used as starch digestant; isolated the active principle of suprarenal glands in product known as adrenalin; consulting chemist, Parke, Davis & Co., Detroit, Michigan; President, Takamine Laboratory, Inc., Takamine Ferment Company, International Takamine Ferment Company, and Sankyo Company (Tokio); Doctor of Chemical Engineering, 1899; and Doctor of Pharmacy, 1906, Imperial University of Japan; Fourth Order of Rising Sun, 1915; Member of Imperial Academy of Science in Japan, 1913; Fellow of Chemical Society, London; Member, Society of Chemical Industry, England; American Chemical Society, Institute of Chemical Engineers, and Electro-Chemical Society, U.S.A.; President Nippon Club, New York; Vice-President Japan Society, New York. *Address:* 334 Riverside Drive, New York City. *Clubs:* Lotus; Chemists; Drug and Chemical; Athletic; Bankers, New York. (*Died 22 July 1923.*)

TALBOT DE MALAHIDE, 5th Baron (*cr.* 1831), **Richard Wogan Talbot,** D.L.; Baron Talbot of Malahide, Baron Malahide of Malahide, 1831; Baron Talbot de Malahide (U.K.), 1856; Hereditary Lord Admiral of Malahide and adjacent seas (15 Edward IV.); late Lieut. 9th Lancers; *b.* London, 28 Feb. 1846; *s.* of 4th Baron and Maria, *d.* of Patrick Murray, Simprin, Forfarshire; *S.* father 1882; *m.* 1st, 1878, Emily (*d.* 1898), *d.* of Sir James Boswell, last Bt.; one *s.*; 2nd, 1901, Isabel Charlotte, D.B.E., *d.* of late R. B. Hunfrey, of Wrexham House, Norwich, and widow of late John Gurney of Sprowston Hall, Norwich. *Educ.:* Eton. Owns 3600 acres. *Heir: s.* Hon. James Boswell Talbot. *Address:* Malahide Castle, Co. Dublin; Auchinleck House, Ayrshire. *Clubs:* Army and Navy, Carlton; Kildare Street, Dublin.
(*Died 4 Mar. 1921.*)

TALBOT, Lieut. - Col. Sir Adelbert (Cecil), K.C.I.E., *cr.* 1895; *b.* 3 June 1845; *s.* of Rev. Hon. W. W. C. Talbot, and *g.s.* of 2nd Earl Talbot, K.G.; *m.* 1870, Agnes Mary (*d.* 1894), *d.* of Rev. W. Clarke; one *s.* three *d. Educ.:* Eton. Lt. R.A., 1867; I.S.C. 1869; Capt. 1879; Major, 1887; Lieut.-Col. 1891; C.I.E. 1885; Resident Persian Gulf, 1891-94; Deputy Secretary Indian Dept., Govt. of India, 1894-96; accompanied Shahzadah Nasrullah Khan of Afghanistan to England, 1895; Resident in Kashmir, 1896-1900; Unemployed Super. list, 1900. *Address:* High Barn, Effingham. *Club:* United Service. (*Died 28 Dec. 1920.*)

TALBOT, Rev. Arthur Henry, Rector of Edgmond; Prebendary of Wellington in Lichfield Cathedral; Provost of Denstone Coll. since 1896; *b.* 27 Sep. 1855; *s.* of Hon. Rev. Arthur Chetwynd Talbot (2nd *s.* of 2nd Earl Talbot); *m.* Eveline Mary, *co-heiress* of Lieut.-Col. Charles Ashton of Little Onn Hall, Stafford; four *s.* two *d. Educ.:* privately; Keble College, Oxford, M.A., 3rd class Theological School. Curate of Stoke-on-Trent; Vicar of Lapley; Rector of Church Eaton; Rural Dean of Stafford; Rural Dean of Edgmond; Chaplain to the late Bishop of Lichfield. *Address:* Edgmond Rectory, Newport, Salop. *T.:* Newport 38. *M.:* AY 8796. *Clubs:* Oxford and Cambridge, Royal Automobile. (*Died 26 Nov. 1927.*)

TALBOT, Charles Henry, J.P.; *b.* 2 Feb. 1842; *o. s.* of late William Henry Fox Talbot, M.P., and Constance, *y. d.* of late Francis Mundy, of Markeaton, Co. Derby. *Educ.:* Harrow; Trinity College, Cambridge (B.A.). *Heir: sister,* Matilda Caroline, who *m.* late John Gilchrist-Clark, of Speddoch, Co. Dumfries.

Address: Lacock Abbey, Chippenham: *Club:* National Liberal.   *(Died Dec. 1916.)*

TALBOT, Emily Charlotte; *e. d.* of late Christopher Rice Mansel Talbot, Lord-Lieutenant of Glamorganshire, and Lady Charlotte Butler, *d.* of 1st Earl of Glengall, *(extinct).* Patron of five livings. *Address:* Margam Park, Port Talbot; Penrice Castle, Reynoldstone, R.S.O., Glamorganshire; 3 Cavendish Square, W.   *(Died Sept. 1918.)*

TALBOT, Rt. Rev. Ethelbert, D.D., LL.D.; D.D. Oxon, 1924; Presiding Bishop of the Protestant Episcopal Church, Feb. 1924-Jan. 1926; Bishop of Bethlehem since 1909; *b.* Fayette, Missouri, U.S.A., 9 Oct. 1848; *s.* of John A. and Alice W. Talbot; *m.* 1873, Dora Harvey; one *d.* *Educ.:* Dartmouth College, Hanover, New Hampshire; General Theological Seminary, New York. Deacon, 1873; Priest, 1873; Rector St. James's Church, Macon, Mo., and Head-master of St. James's Military Academy, Macon, Missouri, 1873-87; Bishop of Wyoming and Idaho, 1887; Central Pennsylvania, 1898. *Publications:* My People of the Plains; A Bishop among his Flock; Tim: the Autobiography of a Dog; A Bishop's Message: What the Episcopal Church Stands For; various addresses and magazine articles. *Recreations:* golf, horseback riding. *Address:* Bishop's House, Bethlehem, Penna. *Club:* University, Philadelphia.   *(Died Feb. 1928.)*

TALBOT, Gustavus Arthur, M.P. (Co.U.) Hemel Hempstead Division of Herts since Dec. 1918; *b.* 24 Dec. 1848; *s.* of Rev. Hon. G. G. Chetwynd-Talbot and Emily Sarah, 2nd *d.* of Henry Elwes; *m.* 1880, Susan Frances, *d.* of Robert Elwes; two *s.* two *d.* *Educ.:* Welling-ton. J.P.; Mayor of Hemel Hempstead; late M.L.C. Ceylon. *Adress:* Marchmount House, Hemel Hempstead. *Clubs:* Carlton, City of London.   *(Died 16 Oct. 1920.)*

TALBOT, Howard; composer and conductor; *b.* New York; *s.* of Lillie and Alexander Munkittrick; *m.* Dorothy Maud, *d.* of late Arthur H. Cross of Sandringham; four *d.* *Educ.:* King's College, London. Received musical education at the Royal College of Music under Sir Herbert Parry, Sir Frederick Bridge, and Dr. F. E. Gladstone; first opera Wapping Old Stairs, 1894; subsequent works include Monte Carlo, 1896; A Chinese Honeymoon, 1899, 1901; Kitty Grey (part composer), 1901; Three Little Maids (part composer), 1902; The Blue Moon (part composer), 1905; The White Chrysanthemum, 1905; The Girl behind the Counter, 1906; The Three Kisses, 1907; The Belle of Brittany, 1908; The Arcadians (part composer) 1909; The Mousmé (part composer), 1911; A Narrow Squeak (operetta), 1913; Simple-hearted Bill (sketch), 1913; The Pearl Girl (part composer), 1913; A Mixed Grill (revue), 1914; A Lucky Miss (musical comedietta), 1914; The Light Blues (part composer), My Lady Frayle (part composer), 1915-16; Mr. Manhattan, 1916; High Jinks (part composer), 1916; Houp-la (part composer), 1916; The Boy (part composer), 1917; Who's Hooper (part composer), 1919; My Nieces, 1921; has conducted at Daly's, The Adelphi, The Prince of Wales' and other theatres since 1900. *Recreations:* motoring and yachting. *Address:* 35 Croydon Road, Reigate, Surrey. *T.:* Reigate 339. *Club:* Green Room.   *(Died 12 Sept. 1928.)*

TALBOT, Sir William Henry, Kt., *cr.* 1906; *b.* Leeds, 1831; *s.* of John Talbot and *g.s.* of Matthew Talbot, both of Leeds; *m.* 1861, Maria Emma *(d.* 1915), *o. d.* of James Winser, Jr., of Ratsbury, Tenterden, Kent; two *s.* *Educ.:* privately; University College School, London. Articled to Mr. Joseph Munn, Town-Clerk of Tenterden, Kent, and admitted a solicitor, 1853; Town-Clerk of Manchester, 1890-1910. *Address:* Woodlands Road, Cheetham Hill, Manchester.   *(Died 9 May 1919.)*

TALBOT, William John, J.P., D.L.; *o. s.* of late John Talbot and 2nd wife, Gertrude Caroline, *d.* of Lt.-Col. Bayly of Ballyarthur; *b.* 1859; *m.* 1897, Julia Elizabeth Mary *(d.* 1922), *o. c.* of Sir Capel Molyneux, 7th Bart. *Educ.:* Eton; Magdalene College, Cambridge. High Sheriff, Co. Roscommon, 1887, Armagh, 1903; H.M. Lieut. of Co. Roscommon; late Capt. Wicklow Artillery, S. Division, R.A. *Address:* Mount Talbot, Roscommon; Castle Dillon, Co. Armagh. *T.A.:* Ballygar, Ireland. *M.:* DI 5, DI 112. *Clubs:* White's; Kildare Street, Dublin; Royal St. George Yacht.
    (Died 7 June 1923.)

TALLBERG, Professor Axel, A.R.E. 1891; Hon. R.E. 1911; Professor and Principal of the School of Etching and Engraving, retired, with a State-pension, 1926, Royal Academy of Arts, Stockholm, Sweden; *b.* Gefle, Sweden, 23 Sep. 1860; *s.* of Carl Erik Tallberg and Christina Johanson, the former owner of an iron foundry and machine works in Falun, Dalecarlia; *m.* 1900, Greta Santesson; one *s.* one *d.* *Educ.:* Grammar School, Falun; Royal Academy of Arts, Stockholm; Royal Academy of Arts, Düsseldorf; Rome, Paris, and other capitals. Started as draughtsman to the Royal Academy of Science, Stockholm (entomological section); illustrator and correspondent to several Swedish and foreign newspapers and magazines; aquarelliste and finally etcher; Member of the Royal Archæological Institute, London, 1892, and of Royal Society of Arts, London, 1907; lived exclusively in England, near Windsor, 1886-95; many travels in Africa, Asia, and the Continent; after many years' endeavours and hard work succeeded in getting the Swedish Parliament to found and maintain a School of Etching and Engraving at the Royal Academy, Stockholm; appointed its first head, 1909; principal study has been the technical ways and means relating to all forms of painting, etching, and engraving, old and new. *Publications:* About Etching and Engraving, 1911; Chemistry of Paints and Painting, 1912; Etchings and Engravings, A Handbook for Print Collectors, 1917; The Etcher, his Ways and Means, 1917; Swedish Etchers and Engravers, 1895-1918, 2 vols., 1918; Zorn: his childhood and youth, 1920; The Etcher, a Practical Handbook for Art Students, 1924; a great number of articles regarding the Arts in The Studio and other magazines; gold medal Literis et Artibus, 1896. *Recreations:* scientific experiments, chemical and physical, reading, angling, and fishing, but above all, study. *Address:* Royal Academy of Arts, Stockholm, Sweden. *Club:* Artists', Stockholm.
    (Died Feb. 1928.)

TALLENTS, George William; Barrister-at-Law; Alderman of the Westminster City Council; a Governor of Harrow School; a Director of the London Assurance; *b.* 26 Sep. 1856; *s.* of late Godfrey Tallents, Newark-on-Trent, and Mary Anne Frances, *d.* of late George William Brande, of H.M. Treasury; *m.* 1883, Hon. Mildred Sophia, *d.* of 1st Baron Ashcombe; three *s.* two *d.* *Educ.:* Harrow (entrance scholar, Head, 1874-75; Lyon Scholar); Balliol College, Oxford (Exhibitioner); 1st class Mods., 2nd class Lit. Hum.; called to Bar, Lincoln's Inn, 1882; Mayor of the City of Westminster, 1906-7 and 1918-19; Knight of the Order of Dannebrog, 1907; Officier de la Légion d'Honneur, 1919; J.P. *Address:* 49 Warwick Square, S.W.1. *T.:* Victoria 6051. *Clubs:* Athenæum, Carlton.
    (Died 17 Dec. 1924.)

TAMPLIN, Herbert Travers, K.C., 1898; Crown Prosecutor since 1903; *b.* 1853; *s.* of R. W. Tamplin, F.R.C.S.; *m. d.* of late John Cooper Forster, F.R.C.S. President Royal College of Surgeons, London; called to Bar, Middle Temple, 1875; Advocate Supreme

Court, Cape Colony, 1880 ; High Court, 1908 ; edited Cape Law Journal, 1885-99 ; M.L.A. Victoria East, 1891-1902 ; Lieut. 1st City Grahamstown Volunteers, 1883 ; commanding officer, 1896 ; served Langeberg Campaign, 1897 ; Boer War, 1899 ; (V.D., Colonial Aux. Forces Officers Decoration : Colonial Forces Field Service medals). *Clubs :* Royal Societies ; Grahamstown ; Kimberley ; Civil Service, Cape Town.
(Died 24 April 1925.)

TANCOCK, Rev. Charles Coverdale, D.D. 1899, Oxford ; *b.* 1 Dec. 1851 ; *s.* of Rev. O. J. Tancock, D.C.L. Oxford, late vicar of Tavistock, son of Rear-Admiral John Tancock, R.N., and Emma, *d.* of W. Davey Sole, Devonport; *m.* Marion Alma Smith, *d.* of Robert Smith of Killcott, Godalming, 1886 ; two *d. Educ. :* Sherborne School ; and Exeter Coll. Oxford ; scholar ; 1st class Classical Moderations, 1872 ; 1st class Literæ Humaniores, 1874 ; B.A., 1874 ; M.A., 1877 ; B.D., 1899. Ordained, 1880 ; Assistant Master at Charterhouse, 1875-86 ; headmaster of Rossall, 1886-96 ; vicar of Leck, Kirkby Lonsdale, 1896-98 ; Headmaster of Tonbridge School, 1899-1907 ; Hon. Canon of Rochester Cathedral, 1905-8 ; Rural Dean of Rutland Second Deanery, 1909-12 ; Member of Rutland Education Committee, 1909-12 ; Trustee of Oakham School, 1911-12 ; Warden of Peterborough Diocese Lay Readers' Association, 1910-12 ; Rector of Little Casterton, 1907-1912. *Address :* Sussex House, Winchester.
(Died 16 April 1922.)

TANNER, Maj.-Gen. Edward, C.B. ; *cr.* 1881 ; retired full pay ; *b.* 1839 ; *s.* of Joseph Bouverie Hussey Tanner, Wexcombe, Wilts ; *m.* 1867, Georgina Wyndham (*d.* 1910), *d.* of Gen. George William Powlett Bingham, C.B., The Vines, Rochester. Entered Army, 1855 ; Captain, 1860 ; Major, 1869 ; Lieut.-Col. 1877 ; Col. 1881 ; Maj.-Gen. (retired) 1886 ; served Afghan Campaign, 1878-80 (despatches, medal with clasp) ; formerly Lieut.-Colonel Commandant 1st Battn. The King's (Liverpool) Regt. ; commanded regiment at the storming of Peiwar Khotal, Afghan Campaign, 1878-80. *Recreations :* golf, cricket, boating, tennis, shooting. *Address :* Woodside, Old Shirley, Southampton. *Clubs :* Junior Conservative, Royal Southern Yacht. *(Died 8 Mar. 1916.)*

TANNER, Brig.-Gen. John Arthur, C.B. 1911 ; C.M.G. 1916 ; D.S.O. 1888 ; retired ; *b.* Tidcombe, Wilts, 27 Feb. 1858 ; *e. s.* of late John Tanner, Poulton, Marlboro' ; *m.* 1916, Gladys Helen, *d.* of late Charles Townshend Murdoch, M.P. *Educ. :* Cheltenham College ; R.M.A. Woolwich. Lieut. R.E. 1877 ; Captain, 1888 ; Major, 1895 ; Lt.-Col. 1903 ; Col. 1906 ; served Waziristan, 1881 ; Suakin, 1885 ; Burma, 1885-1888 ; Chitral, 1895 ; Punjab Frontier, 1897. *Decorated* for services in Burma. *Address :* South View, Aldbourne, Wilts. *Club :* Junior United Service. *(Died 23 July 1917.)*

TANNER, John Arthur Charles, M.A. ; Taxing Master of the Supreme Court (Bankruptcy) since 1887 ; *b.* 6 Aug. 1854 ; *s.* of late John Tanner, of Yatesbury, Calne, Wilts ; *m.* Grace Mann, *d.* of late W. W. Aldridge, 31 Bedford Row, W.C., Solicitor ; two *s.* one *d. Educ. :* Marlborough ; St. John's College, Oxford. Assistant Solicitor to the Official Receiver in Bankruptcy, 1885-87. *Recreations :* shooting and golf. *Address :* 31 Orsett Terrace, Hyde Park, W.2 ; *T. :* Paddington 2582 ; Bankruptcy Buildings, Carey Street, W.C. ; *T. :* Holborn 6700, Bankruptcy Extension, 126.
(Died 12 Mar. 1928.)

TARLETON, Captain Alfred Henry, M.V.O. 1904 ; *b.* 16 May 1862 ; *o. s.* of late Admiral Sir Walter Tarleton, K.C.B., A.D.C., and late Lady Tarleton, *d.* of 4th Baron Dimsdale ; *m.* 1888, Henrietta, *o. c.* of late Admiral E. C. Tennyson d'Eyncourt, C.B., of Bayons Manor, Lincs.,

and late Lady Henrietta Tennyson d'Eyncourt, *y. d.* of 4th Duke of Newcastle ; three *d.* ; served on Admiralty War Staff, 1914-19 ; specially promoted to Captain for War Service ; Captain, R.N. ; J.P., D.L., Middlesex ; Sheriff, 1903 ; Hon. Equerry to Duchess of Albany ; Order of Mercy ; Knight of Grace, St. John of Jerusalem. *Address :* Breakspears, Uxbridge. *T.A. :* Tarleton Harefield. *T. :* Harefield 17. *Clubs :* Marlborough, Carlton, Travellers', Constitutional. *(Died 7 June 1921.)*

TARLETON, Francis Alexander, LL.D., Sc.D. ; Fellow of Trinity College, 1866 ; Professor of Natural Philosophy, University of Dublin, 1890 ; co-opted a Senior Fellow, 1901 ; Commissioner of Intermediate Education for Ireland, 1901 ; President, Royal Irish Academy, 1906 ; *b.* Co. Monaghan, 28 April 1841 ; *y. s.* of late Rev. J. R. Tarleton, Rector of Tyholland, and Judith, *d.* of F. Falkiner, Congar House, Tipperary ; *m.* Gertrude, *d.* of late Rev. Charles Fleury, D.D. *Educ.* by his father ; Trin. Coll. Dublin (Scholar). Senior Moderator in Mathematics, Junior Moderator in Logics and Ethics, 1861. Assistant to Professor of Applied Chemistry, 1876 ; Church of Ireland ; Unionist. *Publications :* An Introduction to the Mathematical Theory of Attraction, 1899, vol. ii. 1913 ; A Treatise on Dynamics (in conjunction with Dr. Williamson), 3rd ed. 1900. *Address :* 24 Upper Leeson Street, Dublin. *Clubs :* Royal Societies ; University, Dublin.
(Died 19 June 1920.)

TARRANT, Rev. William George, B.A. (Lond.) ; Unitarian Minister and Journalist ; Editor of The Inquirer 1887-97, and since 1918 ; *b.* 1853 ; *s.* of Matthew Tarrant, Worcestershire ; *m.* Alice, *d.* of Henry Stanley, Manchester ; one *d.* two *s. Educ. :* Birmingham ; Owens College, Manchester ; Manchester New College, London ; University College, London. Minister at Wandsworth, 1883-1920 ; Member of Executive of British and Foreign Unitarian Association since 1887 ; Lecturer and Representative in Canada, United States, South Africa, and several European Congresses ; Examiner and Visitor to Carmarthen College and Unitarian Home Missionary College ; Elementary Education Manager to L.C.C. and L.S.B. since 1886. *Publications :* Hymns, in various hymnals ; several volumes on Early Christianity and Modern Religion, including The Story and Significance of the Unitarian Movement (Essex Hall Lecture), 1910 ; Unitarianism, 1912 ; also Bee Songs, 1906 ; Songs Devout, 1912 ; John Milton, 1908, etc. *Recreations :* walking, cycling, verse. *Address :* 53 Westover Road, S.W.18. *(Died 15 Jan. 1928.)*

TARRING, Sir Charles James, Kt. ; *cr.* 1906 ; *b.* London, 17 Sep. 1845 ; *s.* of John Tarring, architect ; *m.* 1883, Edith, *d.* of J. B. Carlill, M.D. Lond. ; one *s.* one *d. Educ. :* City of London School ; Trinity College, Cambridge (B.A. 1868 ; M.A. 1881). Called to Bar (Inner Temple), 1871 ; Professor of Law in Imperial University of Japan, 1878-80 ; Assistant Judge and subsequently Judge of H.B.M. Supreme Consular Court at Constantinople, 1883-97 ; Chief Justice of Grenada, West Indies, 1897-1905 ; J.P., County of London. *Publications :* Chapters on the Law relating to the Colonies ; Analytical Tables of the Laws of Real Property ; British Consular Jurisdiction in the East ; A Practical Turkish Grammar ; article on Dependencies and Colonies (other than India) in Lord Halsbury's Laws of England. *Address :* S. Godric, 18 Arkwright Road, Hampstead, N.W.3. *Club :* National Liberal.
(Died 31 Mar. 1923.)

TARVER, J. C. ; *b.* Filgrave, Bucks. *Educ. :* Eton ; Cambridge ; Heidelberg. Was a master at King's School, Canterbury ; Clifton College. Headmaster of High School at Gateshead *Publications :* Tiberius the Tyrant ; Observations of a Foster Parent : Life and Letters of Gustave Flaubert ; Muggleton College. *Address :* Brookside, Woburn Sands.

(*Died 6 Nov. 1926.*)

TASADDUK RASUL KHAN, Raja Sir, K.C.S.I. 1898 ; Taluqdar of Jahangirabad, Bara Banki, Oudh ; member of Legislative Council of United Provinces ; title of Raja, conferred in 1893, made hereditary in 1897 ; member British Indian Association, Oudh ; Hon. Magistrate, 1st class ; Chairman Municipal Board, Bara Banki, till 1917 ; President Hockey Club, Bara Banki, Oudh ; awarded a Sword of Honour for services during the war, 1919. *Address :* Bara Banki. *T. :* 65. *Club :* United Service, Lucknow. (*Died Sept. 1928.*)

TATA, Sir Ratan, cr. 1916 ; *b.* Bombay, 20 Jan. 1871 ; *y. s.* of Jamshedji Nusserwanji Tata ; *m.* 1892, Naja, *y. d.* of Ardesir Merwanji Sett, Bombay. *Educ. :* St. Xavier's College, Bombay. Partner of Tata, Sons, and Co., Bombay ; Director of Indian Hotels Co., Ltd., Bombay ; Director of Tata Limited, London ; Tata Iron and Steel Works, Sakchi ; the Tata Hydro-Electric Power Supply Co., Ltd., India ; besides various cotton-spinning and weaving mills, and other industrial concerns in India. *Recreations :* travelling, gardening, riding, tennis. *Address :* York House, Twickenham, Middlesex. *T. :* Richmond 1665 ; Tata House, Bombay, India. *Clubs :* Carlton, Queen's ; Automobile of France, Paris ; Western India Turf, Bombay.

(*Died 5 Sept. 1918.*)

TATE, James William ("That "); Composer and Partner on the Variety Theatres and Music Halls with Clarice Mayne ; *b.* July 1875 ; *s.* of Jacob Tate, Wolverhampton ; *m.* 1912, Clarice Mayne. *Educ. :* St. Wilfred's College, Gatton, Cheadle, Staffs. Musical Director of Carl Rosa Opera Company ; composer many successful and popular songs, including A Broken Doll, Every Little While, etc. *Recreations :* golf, horse-riding, tennis, river, flying. *Address :* 65 Gordon Mansions, Francis Street, W.C.1. *T. :* Museum 3298 ; Clarijin Bungalow, The Lammas, Staines ; 5 Lisle Street, W.C.2. *T.A. :* Funniosity, Westrand, London. *M. :* LU 5680, KN 7191. *Clubs :* Eccentric, Durham Yacht. (*Died 5 Feb. 1922.*)

TATE, Walter William Hunt, M.D., F.R.C.P., Obstetric Physician to St. Thomas's Hospital ; Gynæcologist to the National Hospital, Queen's Square ; Consulting Gynæcologist to the Radium Institute ; *b.* 18 Dec. 1865 ; *s.* of late Dr. George Tate ; *m.* Flora Dalzell, widow of late Dr. Anthony Dalzell. *Educ. :* University College School and Hospital. *Publications :* various contributions to scientific societies. *Recreations :* motoring, archery. *Address :* 1 Queen Anne Street, Cavendish Square, W. *T.A. :* Tatendish, London. *T. :* Paddington 1085. *Club :* British Empire. (*Died 5 July 1916.*)

TATE, Sir William Henry, 2nd Bt., cr. 1898 ; Sheriff of Co. Palatine of Lancaster, 1907 ; D.L., J.P. Lancs ; *b.* 23 Jan. 1842 ; *e. s.* of 1st Bt. and June, *d.* of John Wignall, Aughton, Lancs. ; *S.* father 1899 ; *m.* 1863, Caroline H. R. Glasgow, adopted *d.* of late John Glasgow, Old Trafford, Manchester ; two *s.* seven *d. Educ. :* privately. Director of Henry Tate and Sons, Ltd., Sugar Refiners, Liverpool and London. *Heir : s.* Ernest William Tate [*b.* 7 Jan. 1867 ; *m.* 1892, Mildred Mary, 2nd *d.* of F. H. Gossage of Camp Hill, Woolton, Liverpool ; one *s.* two *d.*] *Address :* Highfield, Woolton, Lancashire ; Bodrhyddan Rhuddlan, Flintshire. (*Died 21 Dec. 1921.*)

TAVERNER, Hon. Sir John William, Kt., cr. 1909 ; K.C.M.G., cr 1913 ; *b.* 1856 ; *m.* 1879, Elizabeth A. Bassett, *d.* of James and Mary Luxton. *Educ. :* Melbourne. Member of Swan Hill Shire Council, Victoria, 1879 ; twice President and resigned 1889 ; Member of Legislative Assembly for Donald and Swan Hill, 1889-1904 ; Member of first Railway Standing Committee, 1890-94 ; Minister of Agriculture, Commissioner of Public Works, and Vice-President of Board of Lands and Works, 1894-99 ; Minister of Lands and Agriculture and President of Board of Lands and Works, 1902-1904 ; President of Royal Commission for Victoria, Greater Britain Exhibition, 1899 ; Agent-General for Victoria, 1904-13. *Recreations :* cricket, cycling, and boating. *Address :* General Buildings, Aldwych, W.C.2. *T.A. :* Jerukian, Estrand. *T. :* City 1968. *Clubs :* Empire, Overseas, Royal Automobile.(*Died 17 Dec. 1923.*)

TAWNEY, Charles Henry, M.A., C.I.E. ; retired, 1903 ; *b.* 1837 ; *s.* of Rev. Richard Tawney, Vicar of Willoughby, and Susan James, *d.* of Dr. Bernard, Clifton ; *m.* 1867, Constance Catharine (*d.* 1920), *d.* of Charles Fox, M.D. *Educ. :* Rugby ; Trinity College, Cambridge. Bell University Scholar, 1857 ; Davies University Scholar, 1858 ; Scholar of Trinity, 1858 ; bracketed Senior Classic, 1860 ; Fellow of Trinity, 1860. Appointed Assist. Professor in the Presidency Coll., Calcutta, 1864 ; served for many years as Prof. in and Prin. of the Presidency College, and as Registrar of the Calcutta University ; officiated three times as Director of Public Instruction, Bengal ; late Librarian, India Office. *Publications :* has translated from the Sanskrit the Kathā Sarit Sāgara ; the Kathā Koša ; the Mālavikāgnimitra ; the Uttara Rāma Charita ; the Prabandha Chintāmani ; and two Centuries of Bhartrihari ; has edited Richard III. *Address :* Chartley, Camberley, Surrey.(*Died 29 July 1922.*)

TAY, Waren, F.R.C.S., L.S.A. ; late Consulting Surgeon, Queen's Hospital for Children, Hackney Road, Bethnal Green ; also London Hospital, Royal London Ophthalmic Hospital, and Hospital for Diseases of the Skin, Blackfriars. *Educ. :* London Hospital. *Address :* 61 Oakfield Road, West Croydon.

(*Died 15 May 1927.*)

TAYLER, Albert Chevallier, R.B.C. ; *b.* 5 April 1862 ; 7th *s.* of late Wm. M. Tayler, solicitor ; *m.* 1896, Mrs. Cotes, *d.* of Mr. Allingham, surgeon. *Educ. :* Bloxham ; Slade School ; Paris. Spent twelve years in Cornwall ; awarded medal of the 2nd Class, Paris Salon, 1891 ; Hors concours, etc. *Principal works :* The Last Blessing ; La vie Boulounaise ; Gentlemen, the Queen ; Honi soit qui mal y pense ; Royal Exchange panel, The Vintners' Company entertaining the five Kings ; since painter for the permanent Collection of the Corporation of London ; Guildhall Art Gallery portraits of Admiral Earl Beatty and Field-Marshal Earl Haig ; represented in the Corporation Galleries of Liverpool, Birmingham, Hartlepool, Preston, Bristol, Kettering, Durban, Adelaide, Bendigo, etc. *Address :* 23 Orsett Terrace, Hyde Park, W.2. *T. :* Paddington 1198. *Club :* Devonshire.

(*Died 20 Dec. 1925.*)

TAYLOR, Alexander ; Sheriff-substitute of Forfarshire at Forfar since 1912 ; Captain 9th Battalion (Highlanders) The Royal Scots ; *b.* Carrickfergus, Co. Antrim, 1872 ; *s.* of James Taylor, of James Taylor & Sons, Limited, Barn Mills, Carrickfergus, Flax Spinners ; *m.* 1905, Rhoda, *d.* of James Macintyre of J. & J. Macintyre, Glasgow, Manufacturers ; no *c. Educ. :* Glasgow Academy and University. Called to the Scottish Bar, 1896 ; 2nd Lt. 9th Battalion (Highlanders) The Royal Scots, 1900 ; retired as Captain, 1912 ; Re-gazetted, 1914 ; wounded near Ypres, 23 Apr. 1915. *Recreations :* shooting, walking, cycling. *Address :* Rosehill, Brechin. *T. :* Brechin 10. *Clubs :* New, Brechin ; Scottish Liberal, Edinburgh.

(*Died 21 April 1917.*)

TAYLOR, Charles Edward, J.P., M.F.H. Sedbergh ; *b.* 1853 ; *s.* of Robert Taylor, Lan-

34   **TAVEGGIA, Rt. Rev. Santino.** See page xxxi.

1025

caster; *m.* 1880, Alice, *e. d.* of James Turner, Lancaster. *Address:* Akay, Sedbergh S.O.,Yorks.
(*Died 5 Nov. 1924.*)

TAYLOR, Lt.-Col. Edward Harrison Clough, J.P., York E.R.; *b.* 1849: *m.* 1st, 1880, Lady Elizabeth Campbell (*d.* 1896), *d.* of 8th Duke of Argyll; 2nd, 1898, Lady Mary Stuart, *y. d.* of 5th Earl of Castlestuart; three *s.* one *d. Educ.:* Harrow. Formerly Royal Welsh Fusiliers; retired 1886; A.D.C. to Viceroy of India (Marquis of Ripon), 1880-84; re-employed and commanded Details Royal Welsh Fusiliers, 1900-1901. *Address:* Firby Hall, York. *T.A.:* Firby, Kirkham-Abbey. *Clubs:* Naval and Military, Yorkshire.
(*Died 1 April 1921.*)

TAYLOR, Edward Henry, M.D., D.Sc.; Professor of Surgery, Dublin. *Educ.:* Trinity College, Dublin; Vienna. *Address:* 77 Merrion Square South, Dublin. *T.:* Dublin 1953.
(*Died April 1922.*)

TAYLOR, Col. Francis Pitt Stewart, C.M.G. 1915; late R.A.S.C.; *b.* 15 June 1869; *m.* 1903, Anne Isabel, *d.* of late Capt. Frederick Allhusen and *widow* of C. P. Hall. Entered army (South Lancs Regt.), 1889; Captain A.S.C., 1898; Major, 1903; Lt.-Col., 1912; Deputy Asst. Director of Supplies and Transport, Eastern Command, 1905-6; Brig.-General commanding British Adriatic Mission, 1915-16; served Nile expedition, 1898 (Egyptian medal; medal); S. African War, 1900-2 (Queen's medal 3 clasps, King's medal 2 clasps); European War, 1914-17 (Bt. Col., despatches twice, C.M.G.); retired pay, 1919; Grand Cordon White Eagle of Serbia, 1916; Officer Crown of Italy.
(*Died 22 Dec. 1924.*)

TAYLOR, Franklin; pianist and teacher of pianoforte; Professor at Royal College of Music; *b.* Birmingham, 5 Feb. 1843. *Educ.:* Leipzig Conservatoire. Professor at National Training School, 1876; member of Associated Board of R.A.M. and R.C.M. *Publications:* Primer of Pianoforte Playing, 1877; Technique and Expression in Pianoforte Playing, 1897; articles in Grove's Dictionary, etc. *Address:* 49 Iverna Court, Kensington, W.
(*Died 19 Mar. 1919.*)

TAYLOR, Sir Frederick, 1st Bt., *cr.* 1917; M.D., F.R.C.P.; Consulting Physician to Guy's Hospital; Physician to Seamen's Hospital, Greenwich; Member of Senate of University of London; late Representative of Univ. of London on General Medical Council; *b.* 1847; *s.* of David Taylor, M.R.C.S., of Kennington; *m.* Helen Mary (*d.* 1917), *d.* of Frederic Manby of East Rudham, Norfolk; two *s.* one *d. Educ.:* Epsom College; Guy's Hospital. M.D. University of London; University Scholar in Obstetric and in Forensic Medicine; late President, Royal College Physicians, Royal Society of Medicine; Examiner in Medicine, Universities of London, Durham, Birmingham, Cambridge, and Belfast; Harveian Orator, 1907. *Publications:* The Practice of Medicine, 11th ed.; Lumleian Lectures; On some Disorders of the Spleen; contributions to medical societies and journals. *Heir: s.* Eric Stuart, M.D., Cantab.; *b.* 28 June 1889. *Club:* Athenæum.
(*Died 2 Dec. 1920.*)

TAYLOR, Hon. George; Senator since 1911; President and Manager of the Ontario Wheel Co., also President of the Pease River Land and Investments Co.; *b.* 31 Mar. 1840; 2nd *s.* of William Taylor and Ann Graham, both of the north of Ireland; *m.* 1863, Margaret Ann Latimer; no *c. Educ.:* common school at Lansdown in county of Leeds. Began life in mercantile business as clerk in country general store when eleven years of age; continued with same firm afterwards as partner over twenty-five years; first elected as Reeve of Gananoque, 1872; held office for seven years, then elected Warden
1026

of united counties of Leeds and Grenville; Member of House of Commons, 1882, 1887, 1891, 1896, 1900, 1904, 1908, and 1911; Chief Whip of the Conservative Party in House of Commons for over twenty-five years. *Address:* Gananoque, Ontario. *T.:* 37.
(*Died Mar. 1919.*)

TAYLOR, George Paul, metropolitan police magistrate, Marylebone, since 1905; *b.* 1860; *m.* 1900, Rosa, *d.* of Henry Williamson, Chasetown, Staffordshire. *Educ.:* Downside Coll.; Catholic University College, Kensington. Barr. Middle Temple, 1885; contested (L., Ince Div., Lancs, 1886; M.P.M. N. London, 1895-97; metropolitan police magistrate, Greenwich, 1897-98; Southwark, 1898-1905. *Address:* 7 Lancaster Gate Terrace, W. *Club:* Reform.
(*Died 4 May 1917.*)

TAYLOR, Harry Mead, C.B. 1923; Assistant Secretary for Finance, Board of Trade, 1920-27; *b.* 1872; *e. s.* of late Henry Taylor; *m.* 1896. Katie, *y. d.* of late Alfred Maynard; no *c. Educ.:* privately. Entered Board of Trade Department of the Official Receivers in Companies Liquidation, 1891; resigned on joining S. Allsopp & Sons of Burton-on-Trent, 1900; Manager, 1901-7; associated with commercial and financial undertakings until 1914, and travelled in Canada and U.S.A.; on outbreak of war appointed Secretary of Foreign Trade Debts Committee, and in 1916 of Enemy Debts Committee; Controller of Trading Accounts, Board of Trade, 1918. *Club:* Royal Societies.
(*Died 19 July 1928.*)

TAYLOR, Henry Martyn, J.P.; F.R.S., F.R.A.S.; Barrister-at-law; Fellow of Trinity Coll., Cambridge; *b.* Bristol, 6 June 1842; 2nd *s.* of Rev. James Taylor, D.D. *Educ.:* Wakefield Grammar School; Trin. Coll. Camb.; 3rd Wrangler and 2nd Smith's Prizeman, 1865; B.A. 1865; M.A. 1868. Vice-Principal of the Royal School of Naval Architecture and Marine Engineering, 1865-69; assistant tutor, Trin. Coll. Camb. 1869-74; tutor, 1874-84; lecturer, 1884-94; Mayor of Cambridge, 1900-1. *Publications:* editor of Pitt Press Euclid. *Recreations:* formerly cricket, tennis, shooting, fishing. *Address:* The Yews, Cambridge. *T.:* 118.
(*Died 16 Oct. 1927.*)

TAYLOR, Colonel H. Brooke, C.B.E. 1919; V.D.; D.L.; Senior Partner in the firm of Brooke Taylor & Co., Solicitors, Bakewell, Derbyshire; *b.* 6 Oct. 1855; *s.* of John and Catherine Ann Taylor, of Darley-in-the-Dale, Derbyshire; *m.* 1884, Mary Taitt, *o. d.* of Rev. W. Mallalieu of Ockbrook, Derbyshire; four *s.* one *d. Educ.:* Ockbrook; Lausanne. Admitted a Solicitor, 1878; has taken part in public duties of various kinds; Colonel Commanding 2nd V.B. Sherwood Foresters (retired 1904); Member Derbyshire Territorial Force Association from commencement; Hon. Secretary and Organiser, Derbyshire Branch of British Red Cross Society prior to war; served on Recruiting Staff 45th Recruiting Area and No. 6 District, 1914-17; Assistant Director of National Service, Derbyshire, 1917-18; Hon. Secretary Derbyshire Volunteer Training Corps (eight Battalions) and C.S.O., 1914-15. *Recreations:* cricket, golf. *Address:* The Close, Bakewell, Derbyshire. *T.:* Bakewell 9. *Club:* County, Derby.
(*Died 20 Feb. 1923.*)

TAYLOR, James Henry, I.S.O.; late Deputy Commissioner, Angul District, Orissa, Bihar and Orissa, India; *b.* 20 Aug. 1861; *s.* of William Colebrooke Taylor; *m.* 1884, Hélène Berthe, *d.* of late Henry Augustus Cowper, H.M. Consular Service; two *s. Educ.:* Western Coll., Brighton; Rev. C. Jenkins, Brussels. Studied medicine, Charing Cross Hospital; gave up this profession; proceeded India; obtained post in Forest Department of Baramba and Narsingpur Feudatory States; appointed to Government post, Tahsildar, Koudmals, Orissa, 1887;

promoted Sub-Deputy Collector, Deputy Collector, Assistant Settlement Officer, Orissa; Settlement Officer of Darpan, Porahat, Midnapur and Revision Settlement of Orissa; held listed appointment of Magistrate and Collector in Indian Civil Service; retired, 1919. *Recreations:* a keen shikari and fisherman; interested in natural history, pisciculture, agriculture, gardening. *Address:* c/o The National Bank of India, 26 Bishopsgate, E.C. *Club:* Overseas.
(*Died 14 Jan. 1926.*)

TAYLOR, James Monroe, A.B., D.D., LL.D.; president of Vassar College, 1886-1913; *b.* Brooklyn, 5 Aug. 1848; 3rd *s.* of E. E. L. Taylor, D.D., and Mary Jane Perkins; *m.* Kate Huntington, 1873; three *s.* one *d.* *Educ.:* Rochester, N.Y.; Germany. Pastor, South Norwalk Ct. 1873-82; pastor, Providence, R.I., 1882-86. *Publications:* various essays; privately printed for classes, a volume on Psychology; also, for classes, a Syllabus of Ethics, 1907; printed address on A New World and an Old Gospel; Practical, or Ideal; Before Vassar opened. *Address:* c/o Brown, Shipley and Co. *Clubs:* University, A.Δ.Φ., Century, New York; Adirondack League. (*Died 19 Dec. 1916.*)

TAYLOR, John, M.V.O. 1909; British Vice-Consul, Cannes, since 1884; *b.* 20 Oct. 1834; *s.* of William Taylor, of Coddenham, Suffolk; *m.* Harriett Taylor (*d.* 1908); one *d.* *Educ.:* Coddenham village school. *Recreation:* gardening. *Address:* 43 rue de Frejus, Cannes. *T.A.:* Taylor, Cannes. *T.:* 1,32.(*Died 21 April 1922.*)

TAYLOR, Luke, R.E. 1910; Fellow of the Royal Society of Painter-Etchers and Engravers; *b.* 20 Sep. 1876; unmarried. *Educ.:* Royal College of Art, South Kensington. *Address:* Hawley Grange, Dartford.
(*Died 3 June 1916.*)

TAYLOR, Rev. Malcolm Campbell, D.D.; LL.D.; Extra Chaplain-in-Ordinary to the King in Scotland since 1901; Professor of Ecclesiastical History, Edinburgh University, 1876-1908; Ex-Secretary of University Court. *Address:* 6 Greenhill Park, Edinburgh.
(*Died 10 Mar. 1922.*)

TAYLOR, Rev. Richard; Hon. Canon of Carlisle, 1906. *Address:* Bromfield Vicarage, Carlisle. (*Died 10 Feb. 1922.*)

TAYLOR, Sir Richard Stephens, Kt., *cr.* 1919; Solicitor, Gray's Inn; senior partner, R. S. Taylor, Son & Humbert; Chairman Equity and Law Life Assurance Society; President of the Law Society, 1915-16; J.P. Bucks; *b.* 19 July 1842; *s.* of R. S. Taylor, of Gray's Inn, Solicitor; *m.* 1st, Clara (*d.* 1877), *d.* of Charles Humbert; 2nd, 1885, Anna Gordon (*d.* 1923), *d.* of J. Geddes, Orbliston, Morayshire; three *s.* three *d.* *Educ.:* Merchant Taylors' School. *Address:* 38 Lennox Gardens, S.W.1. *T.:* Ken. 151. *Clubs:* Garrick, Conservative. (*Died 30 Mar. 1928.*)

TAYLOR, Sir Robert, Kt., *cr.* 1920; Partner in the Firm of John Taylor & Sons, Civil and Mining Engineers; *b.* 1855; *s.* of John Taylor, Great Cumberland Place, W.; *m.* Blanche G., *d.* of Thomas Borrow Myers, Porters Park, Shenley, Herts; one *s.* two *d.* *Address:* 28 Lennox Gardens, S.W. *Club:* Windham.
(*Died 4 April 1921.*)

TAYLOR, Thomas, J.P.; M.P. (L.) Bolton since 1912; *b.* Bolton, 1851; *s.* of late William Taylor, corn merchant; *m.* 1874, Mary E., 3rd *d.* of late Robert Lomax, manufacturer, of Bolton; two *d.* *Educ.:* Bolton Church Institute. Apprenticed at age of 15 to Barlow and Jones, Ltd., cotton manufacturers; retired and founded a business of his own at the Saville Mill, 1894; Examiner in Cotton Weaving to the City and Guilds of London Institute, 1888-94; formerly Member Bolton School Board. *Address:* Saville Mill, Bolton. (*Died 17 Dec. 1916.*)

TAYLOR, Hon. Sir Thomas Wardlaw, Kt., *cr.* 1897; M.A.; *b.* Auchtermuchty, Fife, 25 Mar. 1833; *o. s.* of late Rev. John Taylor, M.D., D.D., and Marion Antill, *d.* of late John Wardlaw, Banker, Dalkeith; *m.* 1st, Jessie, *d.* of late John Cameron, M.D., Wilmington, U.S.A., 1858 (*d.* 1863); 2nd, Margaret, *d.* of late Hugh Vallance, 1864. *Educ.:* privately; Edinburgh University. Barr. Upper Canada, 1858; Q.C. 1876; Master in Chancery, 1872-83; Puisne Judge Court of Queen's Bench for Manitoba, 1883-87; Chief Justice, 1887-99; Administrator of the Government of the Province in 1890, and again in 1893. *Publications:* Chancery Statutes and Orders; Commentaries on Equity Jurisprudence; Investigation of Titles; Public Statutes relating to the Presbyterian Church in Canada. *Recreations:* fishing, golf. *Address:* 67 Victoria Avenue, Hamilton, Canada.
(*Died 1 Mar. 1917.*)

TAYLOR, Surg.-General Sir William, K.C.B., *cr.* 1902; C.B. 1898; retired 1904; *b.* Moorfield, Ayrshire, 5 April 1843; 3rd *s.* of late James Taylor, Etruria, Staffordshire, and Moorfield, Ayrshire, and Mary Hamilton, *d.* of the late William Hamilton, Purroch. *Educ.:* Carmichael, Lanarkshire; Glasgow University. Joined Army Medical Staff, 1864; served in Canada, 1865-69, and took part in the operations against the Fenian raiders on the Vermont frontier (medal); in India, 1870-80, and again, 1882-1898; was in the Jowaki Expedition (medal); served on the staff of the Commander-in-Chief in India, and was with him during the Burman Campaign, 1886-87 (despatches, clasp); sent as Militaro-Medical Attaché to the Japanese army during the war with China (Japanese war medal); P.M.O. of the Ashanti Expedition, 1895-96 (Queen's star and specially promoted to Surgeon-General); P.M.O. of expedition to Khartoum, 1898; and was present at the battle of Omdurman (despatches, C.B., 2nd class of the Medjidie, English and Egyptian medals); P.M.O. H.M. forces in India, 1898-1901; King's Hon. Physician, 1901; Director-General Army Medical Service, 1901-4; is a Knight of Grace of the Order of St. John of Jerusalem in England; Hon. LL.D., Glasgow. *Club:* Conservative. (*Died 10 April 1917.*)

TEALE, Major Joseph William, D.S.O. 1916; R.E.; *b.* 1876; *s.* of Goodman Teale of Allendale, Toorak, Melbourne; *m.*; one *s.* one *d.* *Educ.:* Elizabeth College, Guernsey; Crystal Palace School of Engineering; Camborne School of Mines. Member of Institution of Mining and Metallurgy, and American Institute of Mining Engineers; served European War, 1914-19 (despatches three times, D.S.O.); has visited the following countries professionally—Africa, Australia, Brazil, Burma, Canada, Ceylon, France, Mexico, Spain, Turkey, United States. *Recreations:* shooting, fishing, and golf. *Clubs:* Royal Automobile, Mining.
(*Died 11 April 1926.*)

TEALE, Thomas Pridgin, M.A., M.B., Hon. D.Sc., University of Leeds; F.R.S.; Consulting Surgeon, General Infirmary, Leeds; *b.* Leeds, 28 June 1831; *s.* of Thomas Pridgin Teale, F.R.S. and Frances, *d.* of Rev. Charles Isherwood, sometime Fellow of Magdalene Coll. Camb.; *m.* 1st, Alice (*d.* 1891), *d.* of Rev. W. H. Teale; 2nd, Jeanie, 2nd *d.* of late D. C. Jones of Tamworth; four *s.* four *d.* *Educ.:* Leeds Grammar School; Winchester; Brasenose Coll. Oxford; King's Coll., London. Lecturer on Anatomy and Surgery, Leeds School of Medicine, 1856-76; Surgeon, General Infirmary, Leeds, 1864-84; Crown Member General Medical Council, 1876-1901; Hon. Fellow Royal Society of Medicine. *Publications:* Dangers to Health: a Pictorial Guide to Domestic Sanitary Defects, 1879 (translated into German by H.R.H. the Princess Christian); Economy of Coal in House Fires; The Princi-
1027

ples of Domestic Fireplace Construction; Hurry, Worry, and Money, the Bane of Modern Education; Dust and Fresh Air: how to keep out the one, and let in the other; besides publications on surgical subjects. *Recreation:* trout-fishing. *Address:* North Grange, Headingley, Leeds. *T.A.:* Teale, Headingley 92. *T.:* Headingley 92.
(*Died 13 Nov. 1923.*)

TEALL, Sir Jethro Justinian Harris, Kt., *cr.* 1916; M.A., F.R.S., F.G.S.; D.Sc. (Oxon., Camb., and Dublin); LL.D. (St. Andrews); *b.* Northleach, Gloucestershire, 5 Jan. 1849; *o. c.* of Jethro and Mary Teall (*née* Hathaway); *m.* 1879, Harriet, *d.* of G. R. Cowen; two *s. Educ.:* Berkeley Villa School, Cheltenham; St. John's College, Camb. Sedgwick Prizeman; Fellow, St. John's College, 1875-79. Some time Lecturer on the Cambridge University Extension Scheme; Director H.M.'s Geological Survey and Museum of Practical Geology, 1901-13; Bigsby Medallist, 1889, and Wollaston Medallist, 1905, of the Geological Society of London; President Section C, British Association, 1893; President Geological Society of London, 1900-1902; Vice-President Royal Society of London, 1900-1901; Delesse Prizeman, Academy of Science, Paris, 1907; Member of Royal Commission on Coal Supplies, 1901-5. *Publications:* British Petrography, a Description of the Rocks of the British Isles, 1888; scientific papers on Geology and Petrology. *Recreations:* cycling, golf. *Address:* 174 Rosendale Road, Dulwich, S.E.21. *T.:* Brixton 1306. *Club:* Athenæum.
(*Died 2 July 1924.*)

TEBB, William, F.R.G.S.; *b.* Manchester, 22 Oct. 1830; *m.* 1856, Mary Elizabeth Scott of Hopedale, Massachusetts, U.S.; one *s.* three *d. Educ.:* private school. Chairman, Burstow Parish Council, 1894-1903. *Publications:* Compulsory Vaccination in England, 1884; The Recrudescence of Leprosy and its Causation, 1893; Premature Burial and How it may be Prevented (with late Col. E. P. Vollum), 1896; 2nd edition, 1905 (edited by Dr. Walter Hadwin). *Recreations:* travel and change of occupation. *Address:* Rede Hall, Burstow, Horley, Surrey. *T.A.:* Shipleybridge.
(*Died 23 Jan. 1918.*)

TEDDER, Henry Richard, F.S.A.; late Secretary since 1889, and Librarian since 1874, of the Athenæum Club; retired 1922; *b.* South Kensington, 25 June 1850; *e. s.* of late William Henry Tedder and Elizabeth, *d.* of Richard Ferris; *m.* 1st, Alice (*d.* 1915), *d.* of D. Callan; two *d.*; 2nd, 1916, Violet, *d.* of late Frederick H. Anns. *Educ.:* privately, and in France. From early life devoted himself to librarianship; librarian to 1st Lord Acton, 1873-74; one of the organisers and joint-sec. of 1st International Conference of Librarians, 1877; joint hon. sec. of Library Association, 1878-80; hon. treas. of the same, 1889-97, and from 1898; President, 1897-98; treas. and sec. Metropolitan Free Libraries' Committee, 1878-80; organising sec. of Pope Commemoration Committee, Twickenham, 1888; hon. treas. second International Conference of Librarians, 1897; hon. treas. and hon. sec. Advanced Historical Teaching Fund from 1902; hon. treasurer Royal Historical Society from 1904; V.P., 1923; Secretary to Herbert Spencer's Trustees; Member of Royal Commission on Public Records, 1910-19. *Publications:* joint-editor of first three volumes of Transactions of Library Association, and of Reports of 1st and 2nd International Library Conference; editor of continuation of Descriptive Sociology (Herbert Spencer Trust); author of many papers in publications of Library Association, some printed separately, articles in reviews, and contributions to Encyclopædia Britannica, Dictionary of National Biography, and Palgrave's Dictionary of Political Economy. *Club:* Athenæum.   (*Died 1 Aug. 1924.*)

TEELING, Bartholomew; K.C.P.; Private Chamberlain to the Pope; head of family of Syddon and Mullagha; *b.* 27 June 1848; *e. surv. s.* of Charles George Teeling; *m.* 1st, 1879, *d.* (*d.* 1906) of Rev. Thomas Clarke, Rector of Woodeaton, Oxford; three *s.* two *d.*; 2nd, 1911, Florence, *y. d.* of late T. R. Auld. Served in the Pontifical Zouaves during the Campaign of 1867 (Cross Fidei et Virtuti); received a medal for special service in 1870 from Pope Pius the Ninth, and the Bene Merenti medal from Pope Leo XIII.; served as Captain in 8th Batt. Rifle Brigade and 3rd Batt. Royal Irish Rifles; retired as Hon. Captain in the Army; in conjunction with Cardinal Cullen and the Earl of Granard organised The Catholic Union of Ireland in 1872, of which Association he was Secretary; possesses historical family relics of 1798, and the bureau which stood in the Irish House of Lords. *Publications:* Military Maxims and Apophthegms of Commanders Ancient and Modern; My Weatherwise Companion; My First Prisoner; contributes to literary magazines. *Recreations:* riding on horseback, and making genealogical research.
(*Died 4 Jan. 1921.*)

TEELING, Charles Hamilton, K.C., Ireland; called to Bar, 1868; Q.C. 1894.
(*Died 1921.*)

TEETZEL, Hon. James Vernal; retired Justice of the Supreme Court of Judicature for Ontario, Common Pleas Division; *b.* 6 Mar. 1853; *m.* 1880, Priscilla, *d.* of late John Darling; no *c. Educ.:* Woodstock, Galt, Toronto. Called to Bar, 1877; Q.C. 1889; Bencher Law Society, Upper Canada, 1891, 1896, and 1901; Mayor of Hamilton, 1899-1900; contested Hamilton for Dominion Parliament, 1900; LL.D. MacMaster University, 1907. *Recreations:* golf and riding. *Address:* The Alexandra Apartments, Toronto. *T.A.:* Teetzel, Toronto. *T.:* Main 4991. *Clubs:* Toronto; York; Hamilton.
(*Died 24 Aug. 1926.*)

TEIGNMOUTH, 4th Baron (*cr.* 1797), **Frederick William John Shore**, Bt., 1792; *b.* 27 Aug. 1844; *s.* of 2nd Baron and Caroline, *d.* of William Browne, Tallantire Hall, Cumberland; *S.* brother 1915; *m.* 1894, Anne Louisa, *d.* of late Peter Connellan. *Educ.:* Harrow. Joined R.A. 1867; Lieut.-Col. 1894. *Heir:* *b.* Henry Noel, *b.* 29 Aug. 1847. *Address:* Ballyduff, Thomastown, Co. Kilkenny.
(*Died 11 Dec. 1916.*)

TEIGNMOUTH, 5th Baron, *cr.* 1797; **Commander Henry Noel Shore**, R.N., Bt., 1792; *b.* 29 Aug. 1847; *s.* of 2nd Baron and Caroline, *d.* of William Browne, Tallantire Hall, Cumberland; *S.* brother, 1916; *m.* 1880, Mary Aglionby, *d.* of Rev. Canon Porteus; two *s. Educ.:* Edinburgh Academy. H.M.S. Britannia as naval cadet, 1861; served in several ships; Inspecting Officer of Coastguard, 1881-89; retired on account of ill-health, 1891; studied art under Professor Legros at University College, 1879-80; exhibited pictures at Royal Institute of Painters in Water Colours, Royal Scottish Academy, Royal Irish Academy, and other galleries. *Publications:* read paper on China and Japan by request of Council of Society of Arts, Commerce, and Manufactures, 1882; The Flight of the Lapwing in China, Japan, and Formosa; Smuggling Ways and Smuggling Days; Old Foye Days; Three Pleasant Springs in Portugal; (with Charles G. Harper) The Smugglers (2 vols.); many magazine and newspaper articles, and contributions to professional journals. *Recreations:* painting, motoring, magic. *Heir:* *s.* Hon Hugh Aglionby Shore, late India, P.W.D. [*b.* 12 July 1881; *m.* 1915, Caroline, *d.* of Col. Marsh, R.E.; two *s.* one *d.*]. *Address:* Mt. Elton, Clevedon, Somerset.   (*Died 15 Feb. 1926.*)

TEIXEIRA DE MATTOS, Alexander Louis; Chevalier of the Order of Leopold II.,

1920; F.Z.S.; author and translator; *b.* Amsterdam, 9 April 1865 ; *s.* of late Jacques Teixeira de Mattos and Bertha, *d.* of Augustus Mendes; *m.* 1900, Lily, *d.* of late William Armit Lees and widow of W. C. K. Wilde. *Educ.:* Kensington Catholic Public School ; Beaumont ; private tuition under Monsignor Capel. Settled in England, 1874 ; editor of Dramatic Opinions, 1891 ; assistant-editor and afterwards editor of the Candid Friend, 1901-2 ; Head of Intelligence Section, War Trade Intelligence Dept., 1915-18 ; Secretary of the Dept., 1918-19 ; represented the Dept. on Main Licensing Committee, 1917-19 ; has translated many books and plays from the French, Flemish, German, Danish and Dutch ; is a liberal and a Catholic. *Publications* · Tyltyl; translations of Melati van Java's Resident's Daughter, Couperus' Ecstasy (with John Gray), Majesty (with the late Ernest Dowson), Books of the Small Souls and all later works, Zola's Curée, van Hoytema's Happy Owls, Arthur Byl's Yvette Guilbert, Israëls' Spain, the Souvenirs of Léonard, Memoirs of Marshal Oudinot, the Recollections of Alexis de Tocqueville, the Memoirs of Chateaubriand, the Memoirs of President Kruger, Rompel's Heroes of the Boer War, Maeterlinck's Double Garden and all later works, Georgette Leblanc-Maeterlinck's Choice of Life and Children's Blue Bird, Grenard's Tibet, Vicomte R. d'Humières' Through Isle and Empire, Stijn Streuvels' Path of Life, Ewald's, My Little Boy, the Old Room and all the fairy-tales, Marius' Dutch Painting in the Nineteenth Century, Leblanc's Exploits of Arsène Lupin and all later works, Leroux's Phantom of the Opera and Balaoo, Fabre's Life of the Spider and all later works, Weissl's Mystery of the Green Car, Paoli's Their Majesties, etc. *Plays :* Zola's Thérèse Raquin and Heirs of Rabourdin, Van Nouhuijs' Goldfish, Josine Holland's Leida, Maeterlinck's Joyzelle, Blue Bird and all later plays, the Cradle (from the Flemish), etc. *Recreation :* bridge. *Address :* 9 Cheltenham Terrace, Chelsea, S.W.3. *T.A.:* Teixeira, Sloane, London. *T. :* Victoria 643. *Clubs :* Reform, Cleveland, Pilgrims.   *(Died 5 Dec. 1921.)*

TEMPERLEY, Rev. Canon Arthur, M.A.; late Rector of South Willingham, Lincolnshire ; Hon. Secretary, Lincoln Diocesan Board of Education; Canon and Prebendary of Lafford in Lincoln Cathedral; *b.* 1850; *m.* 1880, Frances G. Howard Tripp; two *s.* five *d.* *Educ.:* Sidney Sussex College, Cambridge. Mathematical master at Hereford Cathedral School ; Headmaster of De Aston School, Market Rasen ; Examiner for Cambridge Local Examination Syndicate; Member of the Education Committee of the Lindsey County Council. *Recreations :* cycling, woodcarving, tennis. *Address :* Heighington, Lincoln. *T.A.:* Branston. *M.:* FU 947.   *(Died 21 Feb. 1927.)*

TEMPEST, Sir Percy Crosland, K.B.E., *cr.* 1923 ; C.B.E. 1918; M.Inst.C.E. ; General Manager, Southern Railway, since 1923 ; Belgian Croix d'Officer de l'Ordre de Leopold ; Chevalier of the Legion of Honour ; Member of the Order of Dannebrog, Denmark ; *b.* 1861 ; *s.* of Charles Tempest, solicitor, Leeds ; *m.* 1897, Evelyn, *d.* of Alfred Willis, D.L., J.P.; two *d.* *Educ.:* Grammar School and University, Leeds. Joined the S.E. and Chatham Railway Engineers Department, 1882; Assistant Engineer, 1896; Chief Engineer, 1899; General Manager and Chief Engineer S.E. and Chatham Railway, 1920-23 ; Engineer to the English Channel Tunnel Co. since 1916. *Address :* 77 Carlisle Mansions, S.W.1. *T. :* Victoria 896.   *(Died 3 Nov. 1924.)*

TEMPEST - HICKS, Brig. - Gen. Henry, C.B. 1900 ; J.P. Herts and Middlesex ; *b.* 25 November 1852 ; *s.* of late George Henry Tempest-Hicks of Hillgrove, Wells, Somerset ; *m.* 1885, Anne Clara Georgiana, *d.* of late

Charles Hemery of Gladsmuir, Monken Hadley, Herts ; one *s.* one *d.* *Educ.:* Harrow ; Trinity College, Cambridge. Joined 2nd Royal Dublin Fusiliers, 1872 ; commanded his regiment in Boer War, 1899-1902 (despatches, Queen's medal, 5 clasps, King's medal, 2 clasps, C.B.) ; served in the Aden Hinterland ; Brevet Col. 1904 ; retired, 1904 ; commanded Coast Defences and 2nd South Wales Infantry Brigade, 1915. *Recreations :* won Freshman's 100 yards and hurdles at Cambridge. *Address :* Gladsmuir, Monken Hadley, Herts ; Hillgrove, Wells, Somerset. *Clubs :* Arthur's, Army and Navy.   *(Died 10 Nov. 1922.)*

TEMPLE, Sir Alfred (George). Kt., *cr.* 1920 ; F.S.A. ; Director of the Guildhall Gallery; *b.* 27 Oct. 1848; *m.* 1880, Elizabeth Mary Harriot (*d.* 1926), *e. d.* of late Edwin Undecimus Crosley, C.E.; one *s.* Knight Commander of Order of the Dannebrog, Denmark ; Knight Commander of Order of Alfonso XII. of Spain ; Officier de l'Instruction Publique de France, Chevalier of the Order of Leopold of Belgium, Officier of Order of the Crown of Belgium ; Commander of the Royal Order of Isabel the Catholic of Spain, and of the Inca of Peru ; corresponding Member of the Royal Academy of San Fernando, Madrid ; Member of Executive Committee of the National Trust, and of Council of Royal Drawing Society; Chairman of Fine Art Section Irish International Exhibition, 1907 ; Member of British Art Committee Franco-British Exhibition, 1908, of International Exhibition, Rome, 1911, of Exhibition of Miniatures, Brussels, 1912, and of the Exhibition of Spanish Painting at the Royal Academy, 1920, etc. Has organised at the Guildhall since 1890 special exhibitions, which have embraced the works of British artists, including a separate exhibition of the works of J. M. W. Turner, and of those of France, Spain, Holland, Belgium, and Denmark. The sixteenth exhibition was of naval and military works by painters of the allied nations —Great Britain, France, Russia, and Belgium. Contributor to various Art periodicals, and author of the Art of Painting in the Queen's Reign, 1897 ; Sacred Art, 1898 ; The Nation's Pictures, 1901 ; Great Pictures in Private Galleries, 1905 ; the Wallace Collection, 1903 ; Modern Spanish Painting, 1908 ; By Rochford Town, and other Poems, 1926; Guildhall Memories, 1918, etc. *Address :* The Guildhall, E.C. ; 31 College Road, Dulwich Village, S.E.21. *T. :* Sydenham 4530 ; London Wall 6400. *Club :* Conservative.   *(Died 8 Jan. 1928.)*

TEMPLE, John, C.B. 1917 ; Chairman, Warrington Wire Rope Works, Ltd. ; Director, Horden Collieries Ltd., North Brancepeth Coal Co., Ltd. ; Trustee for Debenture Holders, United Alkali Co., Ltd. ; *b.* 18 April 1839 ; *s.* of Robert Temple, Banker, Colne, Lancashire ; *m.* 1st, 1867, Mary Anne (*d.* 1917), *d.* of late Humphrey Roberts, Queen's Gate Place, S.W.; one *d.* three *s.* ; 2nd, Katherine Mary, *d.* of Walter Hull of Staley, near Manchester. *Educ.:* privately. Entered the telegraph service in Leeds, Manchester, and London, 1852; joined the Atlantic Telegraph Company upon its formation, 1856, and worked on the staff of Sir Charles Bright, Engineer-in-Chief, subsequently obtaining a post on the Agamemnon during the laying of the first cable across the Atlantic ; engaged by Glass, Elliot and Co. 1859 ; afterwards the Telegraph Construction and Maintenance Company, and acted over four years as Engineer for the Malta and Alexandria Cable and other Mediterranean Cable Companies, having his Headquarters at Malta ; returned to England in time for the laying, in the summers of 1865-66, of the Second Atlantic Cable, and was Third Engineer-in-Charge in these expeditions on the Great Eastern, under Sir Samuel Canning ;

was in charge of the grappling ship Albany, which picked up the first piece of the lost 1865 cable; Managing Director of the Warrington Wire Rope Works, 1867; for some years a Director of the West India Pacific Company, and acted as liquidator on its final sale; has large interests in coal, particularly in Durham. *Address:* Mossley Bank, Aigburth, Liverpool. *T.A.:* Temple, Aigburth. *T.:* Mossley Hill 158. *M.:* K 7003. *Clubs:* Constitutional; Exchange, Liverpool. *(Died 17 May 1922.)*

TEMPLE, Lieut.-Col. William, V.C., B.A., M.B., L.R.C.S.I.; Army Medical Staff, retired pay; *b.* 7 Nov. 1833; *o. s.* of late William Temple, M.D., of Monaghan, and Anne, *d.* of Hugh Hamill of Rooskey; *m.* 4th *d.* (*d.* 1918) of late Maj.-Gen. T. R. Mould, C.B., R.E.; three *s.* five *d.* *Educ.:* private school; Trinity College, Dublin. Entered the service, 1858; served in Royal Artillery in New Zealand Wars, Taranaki Campaign, 1860-61, and Waikato Campaign, 1863-65; present in actions of Teairei, Rangiriri, Rangiawhia, etc. (despatches, V.C. "for gallant conduct during the assault on the enemy's position at Rangiriri, in exposing his life to imminent danger in crossing the entrance to the Maori keep at a point on which the enemy had concentrated their fire, with a view to render assistance to the wounded, more especially the late Capt. Mercer, R.A."); Hon. Surgeon to Viceroy, in recognition of services in that country. *Recreations:* takes an interest in photography, mechanical work, field sports, etc. *Address:* c/o Cox and Co., Charing Cross, S.W. *(Died 13 Feb. 1919.)*

TEMPLE-GORE-LANGTON, Hon. Chandos Graham; *b.* and *heir-pres.* 5th Earl Temple; *b.* 8 Sept. 1873; *m.* 1907, Frances Ethel, *y. d.* of late Rev. A. L. Gore; two *s.* one *d.* *Educ.:* Eton. Was Captain 1st Dragoon Guards, North Somerset Imperial Yeomanry. *Address:* The Mount, Newton St. Loe. Bristol. *(Died 19 Aug. 1921.)*

TEMPLEMORE, 3rd Baron (*cr.* 1831), **Arthur Henry Chichester,** late Major (Mil.) Irish Regt.; *b.* 1854; *e. s.* of 2nd Baron and Laura, *d.* of Rt. Hon. Sir Arthur Paget, G.C.B., *bro.* of 1st Marquis of Anglesey, K.G.; *m.* 1st, 1879, Evelyn (*d.* 1888), *d.* of late Rev. W. J. Stracey-Clitherow; one *s.*; 2nd, 1885, Alice, *d.* of C. J. Augustus Dawkins, D.L. and J.P. for Co. Wexford; one *s.*; *S.* father 1906. *Educ.:* Eton. Private secretary to Rt. Hon. R. A. Cross, Home Secretary, 1875-78. Owns about 26,700 acres. High Sheriff, Co. Wexford, 1890. *Heir: s.* Hon. A. C. Chichester. *Address:* 4 Portman Square, W.1; *T.:* Paddington 2698; Dunbrody Park, Arthurstown, Co. Wexford. *(Died 28 Sept. 1924.)*

TEMPLER, His Honour Judge Frederic Gordon, County Court Judge, York Circuit, since 1898; *b.* Greenwich, 12 June 1849; 3rd *s.* of late John Charles Templer, Master of the Court of Exchequer, and Hannah Frances, *e. d.* of Admiral of the Fleet Sir James Alexander Gordon, G.C.B.; *m.* 1876, Alice Blanche (*d.* 1914), 5th *d.* of late Rev. W. C. Templer, Rector of Burton Bradstock. *Educ.:* Harrow; Trin. Coll. Camb., B.A., 1870. Barr. 1872; Inner Temple, Western Circuit, Dorset Sessions; appointed District Judge, Cyprus, 1882; Queen's Advocate, 1893. *Publications:* Summary Jurisdiction Act, 1878. *Recreations:* cricket, golf, shooting, fishing, skating, astronomy, chess. *Address:* The Hall, Eaglescliffe. Yorks. *Club:* The Yorkshire. *(Died 28 Aug. 1918.)*

TEMPLER, Col. J. L. B.; formerly Adviser in Ballooning to the Government, and Superintendent Balloon Factory at Aldershot; *b.* 1846; *s.* of John Templer, Master in H.M. Court of Exchequer; *m.* 1889, Florence Gilliat, of Chorleywood Cedars, Herts; one *d.* *Educ.:* Harrow; Trinity College, Cambridge. Director

1080

of Steam Road Transport in South Africa, 1900; in command of Balloon Detachment, Egypt, 1885; organiser of steam road transport for the army. *Address:* Laughton Grange, Lewes, Sussex. *(Died 2 Jan. 1924.)*

TENNANT, Charles Coombe, J.P.; *o. s.* of late Charles Tennant, M.P., and late Gertrude Barbara Rich, *e. d.* of Adm. Henry Theodosius Brown Collier, R.N.; *b.* 30 July 1852; *m.* 1895, Winifred Margaret, *y. d.* of George Pearce-Serocold of Cherry Hinton, Cambridgeshire; two *s.* *Educ.:* Harrow; Balliol College, Oxford (B.A.). Called to Bar, Inner Temple, 1882. *Address:* Cadoxton Lodge, Vale of Neath, South Wales. *Club:* Brooks's. *(Died 5 Nov. 1928.)*

TENNANT, Hercules; C.M.G., 1906; Secretary to the Law Department of the Transvaal Government, 1901-8; J.P. for the Transvaal; of the Inner Temple, Barrister-at-Law, 1871; *b.* Cape Town, 3 March 1850; *e. s.* of the Hon. Sir David Tennant, K.C.M.G.; *m.* 1874, Mary Cathcart, *d.* of Robert Graham, 14th of Fintry. Member of Cape House of Assembly, for several years representing the division of Caledon; Advocate of the Supreme Courts of Cape Colony and Transvaal; was Lieutenant in the Duke of Edinburgh's Own Volunteer Rifles, Cape Town; Extra A.D.C. to Governor of Cape Colony (The Rt. Hon. Sir Bartle Frere); served Basuto War, 1880-81 (medal), with rank of Captain as A.S.O. to G.O.C.; held various positions in Cape Civil Service since 1882, such as Registrar and Taxing Officer of Cape Supreme Court, Acting Master of Supreme Court, and High Sheriff of Cape Colony, from which latter position he was transferred to his post in the Transvaal. *Publications:* editor and compiler of a number of legal text-books. *Address:* Royal Colonial Inst., Northumberland Avenue, W.C. *Club:* British Empire. *(Died 21 May 1925.)*

TENNYSON, 2nd Baron (*cr.* 1884), **Hallam Tennyson,** G.C.M.G., *cr.* 1903; K.C.M.G. 1899; P.C. 1905; Grand Cross of the Japanese Order of the Rising Sun, 1905; Litt.D. Camb., Melbourne, and Adelaide; D.C.L. Oxford; Hon. Col. South Australian Artillery, and 7th Victorian Light Horse; D.L. and J.P., Hants; Deputy-Governor of the Isle of Wight since 1913; member Marlborough Coll. Executive Council; President of the Folk Song Society; Gordon Boys' Home Executive Council, etc.; *b.* 11 Aug. 1852; *m.* 1st, 1884, Audrey (*d.* 1916), *d.* of Charles Boyle, and *g.d.* of Admiral the Hon. Sir Courtenay Boyle; one *s.*; 2nd, 1918, widow of Andrew Hichens, Monks Hatch, Compton, Guildford, and *d.* of Charles Prinsep (Advocate-General, India). Unionist. *Educ.:* Marlborough; Trinity College Cambridge; Inner Temple. After that he lived with his father as his private secretary; Governor and Commander-in-Chief of South Australia, 1899-1902; first Acting Governor-General of the Commonwealth of Australia, 1902, and Governor-General of Australia, 1902-04. *Publications:* Jack and the Beanstalk, illustrated by R. Caldecott; Alfred, Lord Tennyson: a Memoir, 1897; edited Charles Turner's Collected Sonnets (with preface); Poems by Two Brothers (with preface); In Memoriam (with Notes); Eversley Edition of complete works of Tennyson (with own and father's notes), 1908; contributed articles and poems to magazines; Tennyson and his Friends. Owns important modern pictures by G. F. Watts, R.A., Briton Riviere, R.A., Hubert Herkomer, R.A., Holman Hunt, R. Doyle, E. Lear. *Heir: s.* Hon. Lionel Hallam Tennyson. *Address:* Farringford, Freshwater, Isle of Wight. *Club:* Athenæum. *(Died 2 Dec. 1928.)*

TENNYSON-D'EYNCOURT, E. C.; Metropolitan Police Magistrate, 1897-1924; Marylebone, 1916-22; Marlborough Street, 1922-1924; *e. s.* of late Louis Chas. Tennyson

d'Eyncourt of Bayons Manor, Market Rasen, Metropolitan Police Magistrate ; *m*. 1892, Ruth (J.P. Lindsey, Lincs), *o. c.* of Sir A. F. Godson ; three *s.* three *d.* *Educ.* : Eton ; University College, Oxford (M.A.). Barr. Inner Temple, 1881 ; formerly Hon. Secy. United Club ; Captain Lincs Imperial Yeomanry ; Chairman Lincs Lindsey Quarter Sessions. *Recreations* : riding, shooting, golf. *Address* : Bayons Manor, Tealby, Lincoln. *T.A.* : Tealby ; *T.* : Tealby 2 ; 57 Lowndes Square, S.W.1 ; 4 Lyall Street, S.W.1 ; *T.* : Victoria 6342 and 6476. *Club* : United University.
(*Died* 29 *Oct.* 1924.)

TERRELL, Thomas, K.C. 1895. Called to Bar, Gray's Inn and Middle Temple, 1879 ; Bencher ; Treasurer of the Gray's Inn, 1904. *Address* : 1 New Court, Temple, E.C.4. *T.* : Central 1724. (*Died* 27 *April* 1928.)

TERRINGTON, 1st Baron, *cr.* 1918, of Huddersfield, **James Thomas Woodhouse,** Kt., *cr.* 1895 ; J.P., D.L. ; one of H.M. Railway Commissioners, 1906 ; M.P. (L.) Huddersfield, 1895-1906 ; *b.* 16 July 1852 ; *e. s.* of James Woodhouse ; *m.* Jessy, *d.* of W. J. Reed, of Skidby, Yorks, 1876 ; two *s.* two *d.* *Educ.* : Hull College ; Univ. College, London. LL.B. (Lond.) Mayor of Hull, 1891 ; J.P. and D.L. East Riding, Yorkshire ; J.P. Co. Buckingham ; Ex-President of Association of Municipal Corporations ; Director of London City and Midland Bank, of the Hull and Barnsley Railway Company ; Chairman of Governors of Hymers College, and late Chairman of Grand Committee on Law, House of Commons ; Chairman of Royal Commission under Defence of the Realm Acts. *Heir* : *s.* Hon. H. G. S. Woodhouse. *Address* : 42 North Gate, Regent's Park, N.W.8 ; 105 Pall Mall, S.W.1. *T.* : Hampstead 3620. *Clubs* : Reform, Bath, Ranelagh Royal Automobile. (*Died* 8 *Feb.* 1921.)

TERRY, Ellen (Mrs. James Carew) ; G.B.E., *cr.* 1925 ; *b.* 27 Feb. 1848 ; *m.* Made first appearance at Princess's, under Charles Kean ; played first with Sir Henry Irving in The Taming of the Shrew, Queen's Theatre, Long Acre ; joined Mr. Bancroft at Prince of Wales's, 1875 ; joined Mr. John Hare at the Court in Lord Lytton's The House of Darnley, 1876 ; on 30 Dec. 1878 made her first appearance at the Lyceum (as Ophelia) ; visited America with Sir H. Irving, etc. *Recreations* : reading, driving, motoring. *Address* : 35 Burleigh Mansions, W.C.2 ; The Farm, Small Hythe, Tenterden, Kent.
(*Died* 21 *July* 1928.)

TERRY, Rev. Canon George Frederick, F.S.A. 1898 ; F.R.S.L. 1890 ; F.R. Hist. S. 1892 ; Rector of St. John's Church, Princes Street, since 1909, and Canon of St. Mary's Cathedral, Edinburgh ; *b.* 1864 ; *e. s.* of late C. F. Terry ; *m.* 1901, Alice Taylor, *e. d.* of John Musker, Shadwell Court, Thetford ; two *s.* three *d.* *Educ.* : University College, Durham ; L.Th. 1891. Educated as an architect ; Deacon, 1892 ; Priest, 1893 ; Curate St. Saviour, Nottingham, 1892-94 ; Senior Curate St. Peter, Kensington, W., 1894-1901 ; Vicar All Souls, South Hampstead, N.W., 1901-09. *Publications* : Religion in Modern Thought, 1899 ; The Old Theology in the New Age, 1904 ; Memorials of the Church of St. John the Evangelist, Edinburgh, 1911, 2nd Edition, 1918 ; Essays in Constructive Theology, 1914, etc. *Address* : 10 Learmonth Terrace, Edinburgh. *T.* : Central, Edinburgh, 6286. *Club* : University, Edinburgh. (*Died* 7 *Feb.* 1919.)

TERRY, Stephen Harding ; M.I.C.E., Member Inst. Mech. Engineers ; *b.* Dummer, Hants, 15 April 1853 ; *e. s.* of late Stephen Terry of Dummer and Anne Margaret, *d.* of late Rev. Charles Shrubsole Bonnett, Rector of Avington, Hants. *Educ.* : King's College, Lon-

don. Apprenticed to Aveling and Porter, engineers, Rochester ; employed by them and by Clayton and Shuttleworth at Lincoln and Vienna ; Engineering Inspector to the Local Govt. Board, 1878-89 ; made the Type Drawings adopted by the Board, and conducted some 800 Inquiries and reported on Water Supply, Sewerage, and other matters under the Public Health Act ; equipped the First National Vaccine Station ; managing partner in Engineering Works in the Midlands, 1890-93 ; for some 20 years in practice as Consulting Engineer ; advising in numerous Engineering Works connected with Gas, Water and Electricity, Heating and Warming, Steam Cars, Cranes, Petroleum Storage and Transport, Refuse Destructors, Forced Draught and Ventilation of Ships, Rating Valuations ; with Sir Fortescue Flannery, M.P., devised and patented the system universally adopted of Petroleum Ship Ventilation ; wrote the pioneer letter in The Lancet, 10 June 1882, which eventually led to The Standard Bread Movement. *Publications* : The Foundering of Steam-ships, 1882 ; many papers read before Societies ; Monograph : The Crime of Docking Horses. *Recreations* : sailing, swimming, photography, carpentry. *Address* : Upcott, Seaton, Devon. *M.* : T 27. *Club* : Royal Automobile (Founder Member). (*Died* 16 *Dec.* 1924.)

TETLEY, Rev. James George, Canon of Bristol, 1892-1922 ; Examining Chaplain to Bishop of Bristol, 1900 ; *b.* Torquay, 6 July 1843 ; *o. surv. s.* of late James Tetley, M.D., F.R.C.P., and Sarah Anne, *d.* of William Langmead, Elfordleigh, Devon ; *m.* 1868, Mary Anne Grace (*d.* 1918), *d.* of late George Milward, Barrister-at-Law, of Lechlade Manor, Gloucestershire. *Educ.* : Magdalen Coll., Oxford (D.D.). D.Litt. Bristol 1919 ; curate of Caldicot, Monmouthshire, 1867 ; Badminton, 1868-75 ; Henleyon-Thames, 1875-76 ; Vicar of Highnam, 1876-1892 ; Rural Dean of North Forest, 1888-92 ; Proctor in Convocation for Chapter of Bristol, 1894 - 1910 ; Archdeacon of Bristol, 1910 - 21. *Publications* : Old Times and New, 1904 ; Forty Years Ago and After, 1910. *Address* : Belmont, Torre, Torquay. *Club*. United University. (*Died* 10 *Mar.* 1924.)

TEUNON, Sir William, Kt., *cr.* 1921 ; *b.* 23 May 1863 ; *s.* of William Teunon, Aberdeen ; *m.* 1888, Alice Charlotte Lovell (*d.* 1922) ; one *s.* one *d.* *Educ.* : King's College, Aberdeen ; King's College, Cambridge. Entered the Indian Civil Service and posted to Bengal (Lower Provinces), 1883 ; to Assam, 1887 ; reposted to Bengal, 1895 ; to Eastern Bengal and Assam, 1905 ; again to Bengal, 1912. Appointments held : Assistant and Joint-Magistrate, Bengal ; Assist. Deputy - Commissioner, Assam ; District and Sessions Judge, Bengal and Eastern Bengal ; Legal Remembrancer and Secretary to Lieut.-Governor's Legislative Council, Eastern Bengal and Assam ; Puisne Judge of the High Court, Calcutta ; retired, 1922. *Publication* : Report on Civil Judicial Offices, Eastern Bengal and Assam. *Recreation* : golf. *Clubs* : East India United Service ; United Service, Calcutta.
(*Died* 29 *April* 1926.)

TEW, Percy, J.P., D.L., West Riding of York ; *b.* Heath, nr. Wakefield, 3 July 1840 ; *y. s.* of late Edward Tew, J.P., D.L., Wakefield ; *m.* 1868, Madeline Elizabeth, *o. d.* of Rev. Canon Thomas Lowe, Vicar of Willingdon, Sussex, and Canon of Chichester ; one *s.* five *d.* *Educ.* : Exeter College, Oxford (B.A. 1862 ; M.A. 1865). Became a Member of the Firm of Leatham, Tew & Company, Bankers of Wakefield, Pontefract, and elsewhere, 1862 ; upon the amalgamation of the above firm with Barclay's Bank of 58 Lombard Street, E.C., became a Director of the latter Company, 1906 ; a Director of the Aire & Calder Navigation ; Chairman of the Justices of the Petty Sessions at Division of Lower

Agbrigg in the West Riding of Yorkshire. *Address:* Heath, Wakefield, Yorkshire; Brightling Park, Sussex. *M.: C* 4300. *Club:* Carlton.
(Died 24 Mar. 1921.)

THACKERAY, Col. Sir Edward Talbot, K.C.B., *cr.* 1897; V.C.; *b.* 19 Oct. 1836; *s.* of Rev. Francis Thackeray of Broxbourne, Herts, and Mary Anne, *d.* of John Shakespear, Singleton, Sussex; *m.* 1st, 1862, Amy Mary Anne (*d.* 1865), *d.* of Eyre Evans Crowe; 2nd, 1869, Elizabeth, Lady of Grace, Order of St. John of Jerusalem, *d.* of Major T. B. Pleydell; four *s.* two *d.* *Educ.:* Marlborough; H.E.I.C. Military Coll., Addiscombe. Entered R.E. 1854; Capt. 1865; Major, 1872; Lt.-Col. 1880; Col. 1884; retired, 1888; served throughout Indian Mutiny, 1857-58 (medal two clasps, V.C. at siege of Delhi); Afghan War, 1879-80 (severely wounded, despatches, medal); held various posts in P.W.D., 1858-71; commanded Bengal Sappers and Miners, 1879-85; Chief Commissioner Order of St. John of Jerusalem, 1893-98, and Knight of Grace of the Order; C.B. (Mil.) 1886; Commissioner, Bordighera branch British Red Cross Society, Italy, 1917-19 (despatches, War and Victory Medals). *Publications:* Two Indian Campaigns; Biographies of Officers of the Bengal Engineers; Reminiscences of the Indian Mutiny and Afghanistan. 1916; History of Sieges in the XIXth Century; etc. *Address:* c/o H. S. King & Co., Pall Mall, S.W.1. *Club:* Athenæum.
(Died 3 Sept. 1927.)

THACKERAY, Rev. Francis St. John, F.S.A.; F.G.S.: M.A.; Vicar of Mapledurham since 1883; *b.* 13 Dec. 1832; *s.* of Rev. Francis Thackeray, author of Life of Chatham, and Mary Anne, *d.* of John Shakespear, of Singleton, Sussex; *m.* 1860, Louisa Katharine, *d.* of Rev. A. Irvine, Vicar of St. Margaret's, Leicester; one *s.* three *d.* *Educ.:* Eton; Merton College, Oxford. First Class (Classics), 1854, Moderations; First Class, 1856, Lit. Hum.; Fellow and Tutor of Lincoln College, 1857; Assistant Master of Eton College, 1858-83. *Publications:* Anthologia Latina, 8th ed., 1900; Anthologia Græca, 9th ed., 1900; Eton College Library, 1881; Guide to the Roman Coins at Eton, 1882; Translations from Prudentius into English verse, with Introduction and Notes, 1890; Memoir of Provost Hawtrey, 1896; Sermons preached in Eton College Chapel, 1897; Christian Biographies through Eighteen Centuries, 1908; Joint Editor with Rev. E. D. Stone of Florilegium Latinum, vol. i., 1899, vol. ii., 1902; Three Lectures on the Psalms, 1917; *Recreations:* Fossilising in England and France, 1890-1906. *Address:* Mapledurham Vicarage, Reading. *Clubs:* A.lenæum, Authors'. *(Died 14 July 1919.)*

THACKERAY, Lance, Painter and Illustrator; has held one-man exhibitions at the Leicester Galleries, 1908; Fine Art Society, 1910; Walker's Galleries, 1913. *Publications:* The Light Side of Egypt, 1908; The People of Egypt, 1910. *Clubs:* Savage, Arts; Turf, Cairo.
(Died 11 Aug. 1916.)

THACKERSEY, Sir Vithaldas Damodher, Kt., *cr.* 1908; J.P.; millowner; *b.* 1 Dec. 1873: *s.* of late Damodher Thackersey Mooljee, a Bhattia millowner in Bombay. *Educ.:* Elphinstone College, Bombay. Caste Bhattia Hindu; controls five of the largest cotton mills in Bombay; Member of Corporation, 1898-1910; Non-official Member of the Bombay Legislative Council, 1903-10; Chairman of Standing Committee and President of Corporation, 1907; was Chairman of Millowners' Association; Chairman, National Congress Exhibition Committee, 1904; President of the Second Industrial Conference held at Calcutta, 1906; takes deep interest in Indian mining and railways promotion; Chairman Bombay Central Co-operative Bank, Ltd.; Director of many Joint-Stock Companies; representative

Bombay Chamber of Commerce and Bombay Millowners' Association on the Indian Factory Commission, 1907-8; Member of Bombay Improvement Trust, 1909-15; Member of Imperial Legislative Council, Calcutta, 1910-13; Trustee the Grant Medical College since 1908; Trustee of the Sir Sassoon David Trust for Agricultural and Educational Fund, 1912; millowners' representative on Bombay Port Trust, 1913-17; Chairman of Committee on proposed Reclamation of the foreshore of Bombay, 1912; Chairman Indian Merchants' Chamber and Bureau, 1917-18. *Address:* Damodher Bhuvan, Warden Road, Mahaluxmi. *T.A.:* Dragonnade. *T.:* 811 and 811A. *M.:* 1003, 1115, 1665, and 2209.
(Died 12 Aug. 1922.)

THARP, Arthur Keane, Deputy Chairman National Mutual Life Assurance Society; Chairman of Bullers, Limited; *b.* Chippenham, 1848; *s.* of Rev. Augustus James Tharp, of Chippenham, Cambridgeshire; *m. y. d.* of Rev. H. Jodrell. *Educ.:* Haileybury College; Gonville and Caius College, Cambridge (B.A.). Served in the Derbyshire Yeomanry Cavalry. *Recreations:* shooting, yachting, golf, etc. *Address:* Midanbury, Bitterne Park, Hants. *T.:* Southampton 2893. *Clubs:* Marlborough; Naval and Military; M.C.C., Beefsteak; Royal Motor Yacht; Royal Yacht Squadron, Cowes.
(Died 17 Nov. 1928.)

THESIGER, Hon. Sir Edward (Peirson), K.C.B., *cr.* 1911; C.B. 1886; Clerk Assistant at House of Lords, 1890 - 1916; *b.* London, 19 Dec. 1842; *y. s.* of 1st Baron Chelmsford, Lord Chancellor of Great Britain, and Anna, *d.* of William Tinling, Southampton, *niece* of Maj. Peirson the defender of Jersey; *m.* Georgina (*d.* 1906), *d.* of William Bruce Stopford Sackville, 1869; three *s.* one *d* *Educ.:* Eton. A clerk in Parliament Office, 1862; secy. of Presentations to successive Lord Chancellors, 1866-90; Clerk Assistant of the Parliaments, 1890; Chairman of the United Westminster Schools; Member of the London Diocesan Conference; Treasurer of the Queen Victoria Clergy Fund and Church House. *Recreations:* member I Zingari Cricket Club; for twelve years secretary Civil Service Cricket Club; golf, cycling; plays the violin; late member of the orchestra of tne Wandering Minstrels, Imperial Institute; member of Handel Society. *Address:* 142 Sloane Street, S.W.1. *T.:* Victoria 1349. *Club:* Junior Carlton.
(Died 11 Nov. 1928.)

THESIGER, Capt. Hon. Wilfred (Gilbert), D.S.O. 1900; Consul-General, New York, since 1919; *b.* 25 Mar. 1871; 3rd *s.* of 2nd Baron Chelmsford; *m.* 1909, Kathleen, *d.* of T. M. C. Vigors, Burgage, Co. Carlow; four *s.* *Educ.:* Cheltenham. Nominated Vice-Consul, Algiers, but did not proceed; transferred to Taranto, Italy, 1897; Vice-Consul at Belgrade, Servia, 1901-6; given local rank of 2nd Secretary in Diplomatic Service since 1902, and was in charge of Legation, 1903-6; served 15th Batt. Imperial Yeomanry, South Africa, 1900-1 (despatches, D.S.O.); European War, 1914-15 (despatches); Consul for N. and N.E. Russia, 1906-7; H.B.M.'s Consul for Congo, 1907-9; Consul-General Abyssinia, 1909-14, with local rank of Envoy Extraordinary and Minister Plenipotentiary; General Staff, War Office, 1914-19. *Address:* British Consulate-General, New York. *Club:* St. James's.
(Died 31 Jan. 1920.)

THIBAUDEAU, Hon. Alfred Arthur; Senator since 1896; head of Thibaudeau Freres et Cie, Montreal; *b.* 1 Dec. 1860; *m.* 1894, Marie Therese Irene Eva, *d.* of late Hon. E. Rodier, Montreal. *Educ.:* Quebec High School. *Club:* St. James's, Montreal. *(Died Aug. 1926.)*

THICKNESSE, Rt. Rev. Francis Henry, D.D.; Canon of Peterborough, 1875-1920; Rector of Oxendon, Northamptonshire,

1032

1892-1914 ; *b.* 14 May 1829 ; 2nd *s.* of Rev. W. E. Coldwell, Prebendary of Lichfield, and Mary, *d.* of E. Norman ; *m.* 1st, Anne, *d.* of Ralph Thicknesse, M.P. ; two *s.* two *d.* ; 2nd, Beatrice, *d.* of Marsham Argles, D. D., Dean of Peterborough. *Educ. :* Brasenose College, Oxford. Hon. Canon of Manchester, 1863-75 ; Bishop of Leicester, 1888-1902 ; Archdeacon of Northampton, 1875-1911. *Address :* South Luffenham Hall, Rutland. *Club :* United University.

(*Died 2 Nov. 1921.*)

THISELTON-DYER, Sir William Turner, K.C.M.G. 1899 ; C.I.E. 1892 ; M.A., B.Sc., LL.D., Sc.D., D.Sc., Ph.D. ; F.R.S. retired ; J.P. Glos. ; *b.* Westminster, 28 July 1843 ; *s.* of late William George Thiselton-Dyer, M.D. ; *m.* 1877, Harriet Ann, *d.* of late Sir Joseph Dalton Hooker, O.M., G.C.S.I. ; one *s.* one *d. Educ. :* King's College ; Christ Church, Oxford (Hon. Student, 1899). Professor of Natural History at R.A.C. Cirencester, 1868 ; Professor of Botany, Royal College of Science for Ireland, 1870 ; Assistant Director Royal Gardens, Kew, 1875-85 ; Fellow University of London, 1887-90 ; V.P.R.S. 1896-97 ; Royal Commissioner Melbourne Centennial Exhibition, 1888 ; Paris International Exhibition, 1900 ; St. Louis Exhibition, 1904 ; Botanical Adviser to Secretary of State for Colonies, 1902-6 ; Director Royal Botanic Gardens, Kew, 1885-1905 ; Representative of University of Oxford on Gloucestershire Education Committee, 1908-1916 ; Member of Court of University of Bristol since 1909. *Publications :* joint author of Flora of Middlesex, 1869 ; edited English edition of Sachs's Text-book of Botany, 1875 ; editor of Flora Capensis and Flora of Tropical Africa. *Address :* The Ferns, Witcombe. Gloucester.

(*Died 23 Dec. 1928.*)

THOM, Donaldson Rose, M.A. ; secretary of the University of Aberdeen ; advocate ; *b.* and *educ.* in Aberdeen. *Recreation :* Golf. *Address :* 42 Albyn Place, Aberdeen ; Hazlehead House, near Aberdeen. *Clubs :* Royal Northern, University, Aberdeen. (*Died 23 Jan. 1920.*)

THOMAS, Rev. David Alexander ; Canon of Killaloe, 1913 ; Incumbent of Nenagh since 1888 ; ordained, 1875 ; Curate of Castleconnor, 1875-9 ; Rector of Kilcolman Erris, 1879-82 ; Tubbercurry, 1882-8. *Address :* Nenagh, Co. Tipperary.

(*Died 9 June 1918.*)

THOMAS, Annie (Mrs. Pender Cudlip), novelist ; *b.* Aldborough, Suffolk ; *o. d.* of Lieut. George Thomas, R.N. ; and *widow* of the Rev. Pender Cudlip. *Educ. :* at home. *Publications :* beginning with Sir Victor's Choice, and Denis Doune, in 1862, has since written upwards of 100 novels and innumerable stories, sketches, etc. ; Comrades True, 1900 ; The Diva, 1901 ; The Cleavers of Cleaver, 1902 ; Social Ghosts, 1903 ; Penholders of the Past, 1913.

(*Died 24 Nov. 1918.*)

THOMAS, Colonel Arthur Havilland, C.B. 1902 ; D.S.O. 1900 ; retired 1910 ; *b.* India. 31 July 1860 ; 3rd *s.* of Henry S. Thomas, retired, Indian Civil Service ; *m.* 1903, Louie Marion, *d.* of Edward Druce, Dover. *Educ. :* Cheltenham Coll. ; Royal Military Coll., Sandhurst. Joined 31st Regt., 1880 ; promoted Captain, 1887 ; joined Army Service Corps, 1887 ; promoted Major, 1895 ; Lt.-Col. 1900 ; Colonel, 1904 ; D.A.A.G. China and Hong-Kong, 1893-96 ; in charge of supply and transport Sierra Leone Rebellion, 1898, and Sierra Leone Protectorate Expedition, 1898-99 (despatches, medal with clasp, and D.S.O.) ; D.A.A.G. Field Army, South Africa 1899-1900 ; A.A.G. and Director of Supplies, 1901-2 (despatches, S.A. medal, 3 clasps, King's medal, 2 clasps, C.B.) ; served European War as A.D.S.T. *Recreations :* fishing, golf. *Address :* Dunmow, Fleet, Hants. *Club :* Army and Navy. (*Died 8 Nov. 1919.*)

THOMAS, Major-General Charles Frederick, Indian Army ; *m.* Edith Eliza (*d.* 1917), *e. d.* of late Rev. Weston Joseph Sparkes. Maj.-Gen. 1899. *Address :* Oakcliff, Dawlish.

(*Died Mar. 1922.*)

THOMAS, Ven. David Richard, M.A., F.S.A. ; Hon. Fellow R.S.A. Ireland ; Archdeacon of Montgomery and Canon of St. Asaph since 1886 ; Rector of Llandrinio since 1892 ; *m.* Louisa, *e. d.* of Wm. Goodenough Bayly, D.C.L., Vicar of Fittleworth ; two *s.* two *d. Educ. :* Ruthin School ; Jesus College, Oxford (Scholar). Rector of St. M. Cefn, 1864-77 ; Vicar of Meifod, Montgomeryshire, 1877-92. *Publications :* History of the Diocese of St. Asaph, 1874, new enlarged and illustrated edition, 1906-13 ; A History of the Church in Wales (in Welsh). 1874 ; The Life and Work of Bishop Davies and William Salesbury, 1902, etc. *Recreations :* The Archæology and History of Wales. *Address :* Llandrinio Rectory, Oswestry ; The Canonry, St. Asaph. *T. :* Llandrinio.

(*Died 4 Oct. 1916.*)

THOMAS, Edward ; *b.* 1878 ; Corporal in Artists' Rifles. *Educ. :* St. Paul's School ; Lincoln College, Oxford. Always a writer. *Publications :* Horæ Solitariæ ; Beautiful Wales ; The Heart of England ; The South Country ; Life of Richard Jefferies ; Maurice Maeterlinck ; George Borrow ; Lafcadio Hearn ; Swinburne ; Pater ; Keats ; The Icknield Way ; In Pursuit of Spring ; Rest and Unrest ; Light and Twilight ; The Happy-go-lucky Morgans ; Four and Twenty Blackbirds ; The Duke of Marlborough *Address :* Steep, Petersfield.

(*Died April 1917.*)

THOMAS, General Sir Francis William, K.C.B., *cr.* 1911 ; *b.* 10 May 1832 ; *o. s.* of late Capt. J. W. Thomas, R.M. ; *m.* 1857, Virginia (*d.* 1905), *e. d.* of late A. Stodart ; two *s.* three *d. Educ. :* privately. Entered R.M. 1849 ; Gen. 1889 ; retired, 1897 ; served Crimea, 1854-55, at Eupatoria, Balaklava, and Kinburn (despatches, medal with clasp, 5th class Medjidie, Turkish medal) ; Col. Commandant, R.M.L.I., Plymouth, 1885-86. *Recreations :* photography, music. *Address :* 14 New Road, Rochester.

(*Died 25 June 1925.*)

THOMAS, Sir George Sidney Meade, 6th Bt., *cr.* 1766 ; *b.* 12 Feb. 1847 ; *S.* father 1867 ; *m.* Edith Margaret, *d.* of Morgan Hugh Foster, C.B., Brickhill, Bedfordshire, 1874, one *s.* two *d. Educ. :* Caius College, Cambridge. *Heir :* *s.* George Alan. *b.* 14 June 1881. *Address :* 11 Kenilworth Court, Putney, S.W.

(*Died 9 Mar. 1918.*)

THOMAS, Brig.-Gen. Sir Godfrey Vignoles, 9th Bart., *cr.* 1694 ; C.B. 1904 ; D.S.O. 1900 ; D.L., late Brig.-General, R.A. 3rd Division ; *b.* Hafod, Cardiganshire, 27 March 1856 ; *e. s.* of 8th Bt. and Emily, *d.* of late W. Chambers, Hafod ; *S.* father 1861 ; *m.* 1887, Isabelle, *e. d.* of late C. Oppenheim, 40 Great Cumberland Place, W. ; one *s. Educ. :* Brighton Coll. ; Woolwich (medal with clasps, Khedive's star), 1882 ; Soudan (medal with clasps), 1884 ; 4th class Order of Medjidie ; South Africa, 1899-1901 (despatches, medal 7 clasps, D.S.O.) ; European War as Brig.-Gen. R.A. 1914-17. *Recreations :* field sports generally. *Heir :* *s.* Godfrey John Vignoles [*b.* 14 April 1889. *Educ. :* Harrow. Third Secretary, Diplomatic Service, 1914. *Clubs :* Marlborough, Bachelors']. *Address :* Wynters, Harlow, Essex. *T. :* Potters Street 5. *M. :* OA 39. *Clubs :* Junior United Service, Royal Automobile. (*Died 17 Feb. 1919.*)

THOMAS, Sir Griffith, Kt., *cr.* 1904 ; J.P. Glamorgan ; *s.* of late John Thomas, of Court Herbert, Neath, and Mary, *d.* of late Griffith Griffiths. *Educ. :* Swansea Grammar School ;

Cheltenham College; King's College, London. High Sheriff, Glamorgan, 1901; Mayor of Swansea, 1901, 1902, 1903; Mayor of Neath, 1908. *Address:* Court Herbert, Neath, Glamorgans.
(Died 9 Feb. 1923.)

THOMAS, Grosvenor, R.S.W.; Landscape Painter; Chevalier of the Order Crown of Italy, 1910; Gold Medal of Honour for Art and Science, Holland, 1912 (Order of the House of Orange); Associate of International Society of Sculptors, Painters, and Gravers; Royal Scottish Society of Painters in Water Colours; Corresponding Member Royal Society des Beaux-Arts, Brussels; Pastel Society; *b.* Sydney, Australia, 1856; *m.* 1884; one *s.* one *d. Educ.:* Warminster Grammar School, England. Adopted art as a profession about 1892; self-taught; gold medal, Munich, 1901; gold medal, Dresden, 1901; served on Jury at International Art Exhibition, Amsterdam, 1912. Represented in following Museums: Oldham Corporation Art Gallery; Municipal Gallery of Modern Art, Venice; Hungarian National Gallery, Buda-Pest, Bohemian National Gallery, Prague; Permanent Gallery, Weimar; Fine Arts Academy, Buffalo, U.S.A.; in private collections of King of Italy, late Prince Regent Luitpold of Bavaria, late Herr Krupp, late James Staats Forbes, etc. *Recreations:* collecting old stained glass, billiards. *Address:* St. Anne's, 13 Leonard Place, W.8. *T.;* Western 226. *M.:* LB 4638.
(Died 5 Feb. 1923.)

THOMAS, Harold, recorder of Hull since 1904; *b.* 1847; *s.* of Henry Thomas of Sheffield, surgeon. Called to the Bar, Lincoln's Inn, 1874; Recorder of Rotherham, 1901-4. *Address:* 9 Bank Street, Sheffield. *(Died 1 April 1917.)*

THOMAS, Henry Arnold, M.A. (Camb. and London); minister of Highbury Congregational Church, Bristol, 1876-1923; Chairman of the Congregational Union, 1899; *b.* 13 June 1848; *s.* of Rev. David Thomas, thirty-one years minister of Highbury Church; *m.* Emily Georgina, 2nd *d.* of late G. H. Newall, formerly of Dundee. *Educ.:* Mill Hill School; Univ. Coll., London; Trin. Coll., Camb. 1st class in Moral Science Tripos, Camb. Formerly minister at Ealing. *Publications:* Memorials of Rev. David Thomas, 1876; Three Questions, 1892; The Way of Life, 1899. *Address:* Seafield Lodge, Stoke Bishop, Bristol.
(Died 28 June 1924.)

THOMAS, Major Sir Hugh James Protheroe, Kt., *cr.* 1922; O.B.E., D.L., J.P.; *b.* 22 Apr. 1879; *s.* of James Thomas, J.P., Haverfordwest; *m.* 1904, Charlotte Eveline, *d.* of late Bayly Matthews; two *s.* two *d. Educ.:* Haverfordwest Grammar School. Sole surviving partner of James Thomas & Son, land and estate agents, Haverfordwest; Mayor of Haverfordwest, 1909-1910, 1918-19; Alderman of Pembrokeshire County Council, and a trustee of the Haverfordwest charities for many years; a Governor of the Pembrokeshire County Hospital; a member of the Pembrokeshire Territorial Force Association. *Address:* Castle Hall, Milford Haven. *T.A.:* Sir Hugh Thomas, Milford Haven. *T.:* Milford Haven 75. *M.:* DE 2. *Clubs:* Junior Carlton, Royal Automobile. *(Died 30 Dec. 1924.)*

THOMAS, James Jonathan, C.M.G. 1908; Legislative Council, Sierra Leone; *b.* 1850; *m.* 1st, Patience, *d.* of Thomas Joe; 2nd, Rhoda, *d.* of Abram Hebron. *Address:* Wilberforce House, Gloucester Street; Freetown, Sierra Leone. *(Died 4 Nov. 1919.)*

THOMAS, Sir John, Kt., *cr.* 1907; J.P.; C.A.; paper manufacturer; *b.* 1834; *s.* of late William Thomas of the Elms, Wooburn; *m.* 1st, 1857, Sarah Eleanor Elizabeth (*d.* 1878), *d.* of Benjamin George of West Malling; 2nd, 1879, Ada (*d.* 1915), *e. d.* of late William Stimson, of
1034

Marston Morteyne, Beds.; 3rd, 1916, Helen Mary, *d.* of late J. W. B. Cattle, Norbury, Surrey. *Address:* Brook House, Wooburn, Bucks. *Club:* National Liberal. *(Died 15 Mar. 1920.)*

THOMAS, J. Havard, M.A., R.B.S., R.W.A.; Sculptor and Draughtsman; Member of the International Society of Sculptors, Painters, and Gravers; *b.* 22 Dec. 1854; *m.* Sofia, *d.* of Sig. Milano Gennaro; three *s.* three *d. Educ.:* National Scholar, South Kensington; Ecole des Beaux-Arts, Paris. Worked for many years in the South of Italy. *Public Statues:* Samuel Morley, Bristol; Rt. Hon. W. E. Forster, Bradford; Edmund Burke, Bristol; S. Morley, Nottingham; many portrait-busts, poetical statues and bas-reliefs and drawings, including bronze statues Lycidas, Tate Gallery, and Thyrsis, Johannesburg; Manchester City Gallery by wax models, and Bradford Corporation Gallery by bas-reliefs and drawings; teacher of sculpture, Slade Schools, University College *Address:* 21A Upper Cheyne Row, Chelsea, S.W. *Club:* Chelsea Arts. *(Died June 1921.)*

THOMAS, Principal (Emeritus) **John Owen,** M.A., D.D.; Acting Principal and Professor of New Testament at the United Theological College, Aberystwyth, 1922-26; *b.* Bangor, 18 Sep. 1862; *e. s.* of Rev. Josiah Thomas, M.A.; unmarried. *Educ.:* Liverpool Coll.; Glasgow University (M.A. 1885, Hon. D.D. 1924); New College, Oxford; Berlin and Strassburg Universities. 2nd class Honours Classical Mods. and 2nd class Honours Lit. Hum. Oxford; B.A. 1887; M.A. 1890; Minister of Presbyterian Church of Wales successively at Everton Brow, Liverpool, 1887-91, Aberdovey, 1892-99, and Menai Bridge, 1899-1907; Secretary of North Wales Quarterly Association (or Synod), 1902-7; Moderator, 1921; Secretary of General Assembly, 1907; served with the Y.M.C.A. in France, 1916-18; Professor of New Testament at the Theological College, Bala, North Wales, 1907-22; Member of the University Court and of the Faculty of Theology (Wales); and of the Council and of the Court of Governors of Aberystwyth University College. *Publications:* occasional contributions to periodicals. *Address:* Bronygraig, Bala, North Wales. *(Died 15 Feb. 1928.)*

THOMAS, Percy; Painter and Etcher; The Royal Society of Painter-Etchers, of which he was an original Member; *b.* London; 3rd *s.* of Ralph Thomas, Serjeant at Law; *m.* Alice Tree; two *s.* four *d. Educ.:* Schools – Oxford, London, Paris; Royal Academy of Arts. One of the earliest friends and first pupil of J. A. M. Whistler, from whom he learnt etching, and learnt printing of Auguste Delatre; exhibited at the R.A. since 1876; picture entitled Relics exhibited in the R.A. 1886, was reproduced in the only illustrated catalogue issued by the Royal Academy. *Publications:* etched the portrait of Whistler for Ralph Thomas's catalogue of Whistler's Etchings, 1874; for the Art Union of London, Windmill by John Crome; a series of The Temple, London; the text written by Canon Ainger. *Recreations:* boating, swimming, walking. *Address:* 16 Seafield Road, Hove, Sussex.
(Died July 1922.)

THOMAS, Philip Henry, I.S.O. 1902; *b.* Tredegar, Monmouthshire, 1854; *s.* of Henry Eastaway Thomas; *m.* 1877, Mary Elizabeth, *d.* of Edward Thos. Townsend of Newport, Monmouthshire; five *s.* [father of the poet, Edward Thomas, killed in action.] *Educ.:* Sirhowy and Swindon. Entered Board of Trade, by open competition, 1873; promoted to Tramway, Gas, and Water business, 1879; special allowance for services in connection with Provisional Orders, 1885; Secretary of a Committee appointed by the President of the Board of Trade to advise on further Light Railway legislation, 1901; Staff

Clerk for Light Railways, 1904; retired, 1914 ; secretary of a Special Committee H.M. Treasury dealing with Naval and Munition matters, 1917; Liberal Candidate for Clapham, 1918; Leader of Church of Humanity, Chapel St., Holborn, 1909-19. *Publications:* A Religion of this World, with numerous articles and lectures on questions of political, social, and religious reform. *Recreation:* a day at the Oval. *Address:* Rusham Gate, Rusham Road, S.W.12.   (*Died 18 Dec. 1920.*)

THOMAS, Rev. William Henry Griffith, A.K.C., M.A., D.D. (Oxon.) ; Fellow of the College and Member of the Corporation, King's College, London, since 1913 ; *b.* 1861 ; *o. s.* of late William Thomas, *s.* of Thomas Thomas, Coton.Ruyton XI. Towns, Salop, and Annie, *o.d.* of late William Griffith, M.D., Oswestry, Salop ; *m.* Alice, *d.* of late Alfred Monk ; one *d.* *Educ.:* King's College, London ; Christ Church, Oxford. Ordained, 1885 ; Curate of St. Peter's, Clerkenwell, 1885-88 ; St. Aldate, Oxford, 1888-96 ; Vicar of St. Paul, Portman Square (formerly Portman Chapel), 1896-1905 ; Principal of Wycliffe Hall, Oxford, 1905-10 ; Professor, Wycliffe College, Toronto, 1910-19. *Publications:* The Catholic Faith ; The Apostle Peter ; A Sacrament of Our Redemption ; Methods of Bible Study ; Handbook to The Acts ; Commentary on Genesis (3 vols.) ; Life Abiding and Abounding ; Christianity is Christ ; Commentary on Romans (3 vols.) ; The Work of the Ministry ; The Holy Spirit of God ; The Prayers of St. Paul ; The Power of Peace ; Grace and Power ; The Christian Life ; Christ Pre-eminent (Studies in Colossians) ; The Apostle John ; " Let us go on " (Studies in Hebrews). *Address:* 129 Maplewood Avenue, Philadelphia, U.S.A. *Club:* City, Philadelphia.   (*Died 2 June 1924.*)

THOMAS, William Thelwall, M.B.E., Ch.M.(Liverpool) : F.R.C.S. (Eng.) ; Consulting Surgeon, Royal Infirmary, Liverpool; Emeritus Professor of Regional Surgery, and Clinical Lecturer in Surgery, University, Liverpool ; Consulting Surgeon King Edward VII. Memorial for Wales ; Fellow Royal Society of Medicine ; Member of Council, Royal College of Surgeons ; Member of General Medical Council ; Member of University Council, Liverpool ; *b.* Liverpool, 1865 ; *s.* of late John and Eliz. Thomas ; *m.* 1892, Anabel, *d.* of late Alexander Spence, Huntly, Aberdeen. *Educ.:* Liverpool Institute ; Glasgow Royal Infirmary ; University College, Liverpool. House Surgeon and House Physician, Royal Infirmary, Liverpool ; Holt Scholar at Anatomy, University of Liverpool, 1887 ; Assistant Surgeon, Royal Infirmary, late Assistant Lecturer on Anatomy and Lecturer in Operative Surgery ; President of Surgery Section B.M.A. 1913 ; President, Liverpool Medical Institution, 1918 - 19. *Publications:* many articles on Surgical subjects in Medical Journals and Encyclopædia Medica. *Address:* 84 Rodney Street, Liverpool; Verdala Tower, Allerton. *T.:* Royal 2501; Mossley Hill 39. *M.:* K 998. *Clubs:* Royal Automobile ; University, Reform, Athenæum, Liverpool.
    (*Died 10 Sept. 1927.*)

THOMPSON, Alfred Corderoy ; Chairman The Prudential Assurance Company, Ltd. ; Director since 1918. *Address:* Chetnole, Oatlands Avenue, Weybridge. (*Died 9 Nov. 1928.*)

THOMPSON, Lt.-Gen. Arnold Bunbury, *b.* 15 June 1822 ; *m.* Charlotte Wilkinson (*d.* 1910), *o. d.* of Robert Dent, Flass House, Crosby, Ravensworth. Entered army, 1839 ; Maj.-Gen. 1870 ; retired 1880 ; served Crimea, 1855-56. *Address:* Northfield, Maidenhead. *Clubs:* United Service, Army and Navy.
    (*Died 7 Feb. 1917.*)

THOMPSON, Lieut.-Colonel Cyril Powney, C.B.E. 1919 ; *b.* 21 Aug. 1864 ; *e. s.* of late Fendall Thompson, B.C.S. ; *m.* 1892, Mary

(M.B.E.), *e. d.* of Lieut.-General R. C. R. Clifford, C.B.   *Educ.:* Charterhouse ; R.M.C., Sandhurst. Joined Wiltshire Regt. 1885 ; 3rd Sikhs P.F.F. 1888 ; Panjab Commission, 1889 ; Commissioner Multan Division, 1915-19 ; retired, 1919. *Club:* East India United Service.
    (*Died 27 Oct. 1924.*)

THOMPSON, Edward Raymond (E. T. Raymond) ; Journalist ; Editor of the Evening Standard since 1923 ; *b.* 1872 ; *y. s.* of late Ephraim Thompson, solicitor ; *m.* Elsie Mabel, *d.* of George Watts ; one *s.* one *d.* *Educ.:* privately. Received training of a journalist at Brighton, Leeds and elsewhere ; joined staff of Star, 1897 ; associated with late Captain Brinkley, R.A., of Tokyo, on Japan Mail, 1898 - 1900 ; Editor Japan Gazette, Yokohama, 1900-2 ; Night Editor Daily Mirror, 1904-7 ; on staff of the Standard, first as Night Editor, afterwards as News Editor, and finally as leader-writer, 1907-16 ; Edited the Outlook, 1919-20 ; chief leaderwriter of Evening Standard since 1916. *Publications:* Uncensored Celebrities, All and Sundry, 1919 ; Mr. Balfour, 1920 ; Portraits of the Nineties, 1921 ; Mr. Lloyd George, 1922 ; The Man of Promise (Lord Rosebery), 1923 ; Disraeli : The Alien Patriot, 1925 ; Portraits of the New Century, 1927 ; numerous contributions, chiefly on political subjects, to British and American periodicals. *Address:* 44 Clarges Street, W.1 ; Waltham St. Lawrence, Twyford, Berks. *T.:* Grosvenor 2197, Shurlock Row 13.
    (*Died 9 April 1928.*)

THOMPSON, Frederick Chas., Secretary, Public Works Department, India Office, 1901-11. *Club:* Reform.

THOMPSON, Gibson. *Educ.:* privately ; King's College, London. Engaged in municipal government work before journalism ; now part proprietor and editor of Surveyor and Municipal and County Engineer. *Publications:* Wolfe-Land : Westerham and District, 4th ed. 1911 ; Picturesque Kent. 1900 ; Picturesque Surrey, 1902. *Recreations:* archæology, philately, and lawn tennis ; in Upton Park F.C. team that won London Cup in two consecutive years ; played for Surrey and for London. *Address:* St. Bride's House, 24 Bride Lane, Fleet Street, E.C. ; *T.:* City 1046 ; Thames Ditton, Surrey. *T.A.:* Municipium, London.
    (*Died 12 Mar. 1917.*)

THOMPSON, Captain Harold, D.S.O. 1916 ; 21st Royal Scots Fusiliers ; *b.* 17 Nov. 1881 ; *m.* 1912, Sophia Hepburn ; one *d.* *Educ.:* Ardvreck, Crieff ; Fettes College, Edinburgh. Joined 3rd Royal Scots Fusiliers (Militia), 1900 ; 2nd (Line). 1901 ; served S. Africa, 1902 (Queen's medal, 3 clasps) ; European War, 1914-16, Cape Helles, Egypt (D.S.O.). *Recreations:* shooting, fishing, golf. *Club:* Army and Navy.
    (*Died 22 April 1917.*)

THOMPSON, Major-Gen. Sir Harry Neville, K.C.M.G. *cr.* 1919 ; C.B. 1918 ; C.M.G. 1916 ; D.S.O. 1902 ; B.A., M.B., B.Ch. ; A.M.S. ; *b.* 15 Mar. 1861 ; *s.* of late Rev. Mungo Neville Thompson, Rector of Clonmany, Donegal. *Educ.:* Trinity College, Dublin ; B.A., M.B., B.Ch. 1883 ; M.D. (Hon.) 1919. Surgeon, 1884 ; Surgeon-Major, 1896 ; Major lt. A.M.C. 1898 ; Lt.-Col. 1904 ; Colonel Army Medical Service, 1913 ; Maj.-Gen. 1917 ; retired pay, 1920 ; served Nile Expedition, 1898 (medal and Khedive's medal) ; South Africa, 1900-2 (despatches, Queen's medal 5 clasps ; King's medal 2 clasps, D.S.O.) ; European War, 1914-18—as A.D.M.S. 2nd and 48th Div. ; D.D.M.S. 6th Corps, 29 May 1915 ; D.M.S. First Army, July 1917 ; British Army of the Rhine, 1918 (despatches seven times, C.B., C.M.G., K.C.M.G., French Croix de Guerre with two palms ; American Distinguished Service Medal ; Portuguese Grand Officer of

the Order of St. Aviz); Coronation and Delhi Durbar medals, 1903; King George's Coronation medal, 1911. *Club:* Army and Navy.
(Died 21 June 1925.)

THOMPSON, Rev. Henry; Hon. Canon, Norwich. *Educ.:* Corpus Christi College, Cambridge. Mawson Scholar; B.A. 1863; Curate, Christ Church, Lee, 1805-67; Perpetual Curate, Farnham, Suffolk, 1869-74; Vicar of Aldeburgh, 1874-1904; Rural Dean of Orford, 1891; Select Preacher, University, Cambridge, 1901; Proc. for Convocation, 1903; Bishop's Commissary for Suffolk, 1904; Vicar of Eaton in Norwich, 1904-10. *Address:* 68 Mill Hill Road, Norwich. *(Died 6 Aug. 1916.)*

THOMPSON, Henry Yates, J.P.; Officer of the Legion of Honour, 1907; *b.* 1838; *e. s.* of late S. H. Thompson of Thingwall Hall, Lancs. *Educ.:* Harrow; Trinity College, Cambridge (B.A.). Barrister Lincoln's Inn, 1867; formerly proprietor of Pall Mall Gazette; Officer Legion of Honour. *Address:* 19 Portman Square, W.1.
(Died 8 July 1928.)

THOMPSON, Rt. Rev. James Denton, M.A.; Bishop of Sodor and Man since 1912; Rural Dean of Birmingham (Central) and Hon. Canon of Birmingham Cathedral; *b.* Liverpool, 20 July 1856; *s.* of John Roper Thompson and Jane Denton; *m.* Isabella Susannah, *d.* of Alfred Roberts Arnold of Bournemouth; two *s.* three *d. Educ.:* Liverpool Instit. and Coll.; Corpus Christi Coll. Camb. B.A. (*Aeg.*) Greek Test. Prize, 1882; M.A. 1886; Deacon, 1882; Priest, 1883; Hon. Canon of Liverpool, 1895; Curate of Didsbury, Manchester, 1882-84; St. Saviour's, Liverpool, 1884-86; Clerical Sup. of Church of England Scripture Readers' Soc., 1886-89; Vicar of St. Leonard's, Bootle, 1889-94; Member of Bootle School Board, 1891-94. Rector of North Meols (Southport), 1894-1905; Rector of Birmingham 1905-12. *Publications:* God and the Sinner; Church and the People; Problems of Church Work; Central Churchmanship; Missions, Parochial and General; Revived Churchmanship; Vision and Vocation; The Holy Communion; Peace, Perfect Peace, etc. *Recreation:* golf. *Address:* Bishop's Court, Isle of Man. *(Died 31 Oct. 1924.)*

THOMPSON, Rev. Sir Peile, 2nd Bt., *cr.* 1890; Barr. Inner Temple; *b.* 19 July 1844; *e. s.* of 1st Bt. (Mayor of Bradford and M.P.), and *c.* Mary Ann, *d.* of Benjamin Thompson, of Parkgate, Guiseley; *S.* father 1891; *m.* Jessie, *d.* of Joseph Beaumont, Huddersfield, 1871; three *s.* one *d. Educ.:* Rugby; Trinity College, Cambridge (M.A.). Ordained 1877; Curate of Monken Hadley, 1877-81; Christ Church, Marylebone, 1881-85. *Heir:* [*s.* Matthew William, *b.* 28 June 1872; *m.* 1909, Harriet Kathleen, *o. d.* of Colonel S. Hamilton-Grace. *Educ.:* Trinity College, Cambridge. *Address:* Salters Hall, Sudbury, Suffolk. *Club:* Oxford and Cambridge]. *Address:* Howard Square, Eastbourne; Great Yeldham, Sussex.
(Died 8 April 1918.)

THOMPSON, Peter, M.D. (Vict.), Professor of Anatomy Birmingham University since 1909; and Dean of the Faculty of Medicine, 1912-1919; *b.* Earlestown, Lancs, 13 Feb. 1871; *o. s.* of late Peter Thompson; *m.* 1906, Nessy, *d.* of late G. L. Davies. The Old Hall, Helsby, Cheshire; two *s. Educ.:* Upholland Grammar School; Owens College, Manchester. M.B., Ch.B. (Honours) in 1894; M.D. (Gold Medallist), 1899; formerly Senior Demonstrator of Anatomy in the Owens College, Lecturer on Anatomy in the Victoria University, Manchester, and Lecturer on Anatomy at the Middlesex Hospital, London; Hon. Secretary of the Anatomical Society of Great Britain and Ireland, 1901-4; Professor of Anatomy, and Dean of the Faculty of Medicine, King's College, London, 1905-9; Fellow of King's College, London.

1036

Publications: The Myology of the Pelvic Floor, 1900, and other papers dealing with Human Anatomy, Morphology, and Embryology in the Journal of Anatomy and Physiology. *Address:* Tai Bach, Penmaenmawr, N. Wales.
(Died 16 Nov. 1921.)

THOMPSON, Rev. Ralph Wardlaw, Foreign Secretary London Missionary Society, 1881-1914; now Secretary emeritus; Chairman Congregational Union of England and Wales, 1908; *b.* Bellary, South India; *s.* of Rev. William Thompson and Jessie Crawford, *d.* of late Rev. Ralph Wardlaw, D.D., of Glasgow; *m.* Mary Stewart, *d.* of late John Brown, jun., J.P., of Glasgow. *Educ.:* South African College, Cape Town; Cheshunt College. B.A. of the Univ. of the Cape of Good Hope; D.D. Glas. and Edin. Universities; Minister of Ewing Place Congregational Church, Glasgow, 1865-70; Norwood Congregational Church, Liverpool, 1871-80; has at various times visited the missions of the Society in India, China, South Africa, Madagascar, New Guinea, and the South Seas. *Publications:* My Trip in the "John Williams"; joint author of British Foreign Missions: The Life of Griffith John, Fifty Years in China; and various articles in magazines and reviews. *Recreation:* fishing, especially trout-fishing. *Address:* 16 New Bridge Street, E.C. *T.A.:* Missionary, London. *T.:* 13737 Central.
(Died 10 June 1916.)

THOMPSON, Rt. Hon. Robert, P.C. Ire. 1916; J.P., D.L.; M.P. (C.) North Belfast since 1910; Chairman of Lindsay, Thompson & Company, Limited, flax spinners and linen thread manufacturers; *b.* Ballylesson, near Belfast, 1839. *Educ.:* Purdysburn Preparatory School and Wellington Academy, Belfast. President Ulster Flax Spinners' Association, 1903-1910; Chairman Belfast Harbour Commissioners; Ex.-President Belfast Chamber of Commerce; President Board of Governors, Campbell College, Belfast. *Address:* Drum House, Co. Down; Bertha House, Malone Road, Belfast. *Clubs:* Carlton, Constitutional, St. Stephen's; Ulster, Union, Belfast. *(Died 3 Aug. 1918.)*

THOMPSON, Sir Robert James, Kt., *cr.* 1908; J.P. Kent; *b.* Northallerton, 29 May 1845. R.E. Dept., Chatham, 1866-71; H.M. Office of Works, 1871-98; Treasury Valuer and Inspector of Rates, 1898-1909; Chief Valuer Inland Revenue, Somerset House, 1909-11. *Address:* 5 Homefield Road, Bromley, Kent.
(Died 11 April 1926.)

THOMPSON, Silvanus Phillips, D.Sc., F.R.S., B.A. Lond., Hon. M.D., LL.D.; Principal and Professor of Physics in the City and Guilds Technical College, Finsbury, since 1885; Professor of Applied Physics, University of London; Past President of Physical Society; Past President of Institution of Electrical Engineers; Past President of Röntgen Society; Past President of Optical Society; Past President of Illuminating Engineering Society; Past President of the Optical Conference, 1912; Past President of the Sette of Odd Volumes; *b.* York, 19 June 1851; *s.* of Silvanus Thompson, York; *m.* 1881, Jane, *e. d.* of late James Henderson, Pollokshields; four *d. Educ.:* Bootham School, York; Flounders' Institute, Pontefract; Royal School of Mines. Science Master, York; Professor of Experimental Physics, Univ. Coll. Bristol, 1876-85. *Publications:* Michael Faraday, 1898; sundry technical works on Electricity, including treatises on Dynamo-electric Machinery, and the Electromagnet; The Life of Lord Kelvin, 1910; Lectures on Light, and other optical works. *Recreations:* walking, water-colour sketching. *Address:* City and Guilds Technical College, Finsbury. *Clubs:* Sette of Odd Volumes. Athenæum. *(Died 12 June 1916.)*

THOMPSON, Hon. Thomas, M.L.C. since 1903 ; M.P. Auckland City North, 1884-1899 ; Minister for Justice and Defence, 1900. *Address:* Mount Eden, Auckland, N.Z..

THOMPSON, Sir William Henry, K.B.E., *cr.* 1918 ; M.D., M.Ch., Sc.D. Dub. Hon. Causa, F.R.C.S. Eng. ; resigned, 1914 ; F.R.C.P.I. ; King's Professor of Institutes of Medicine ; School of Physic, Trinity College, Dublin, since 1902 ; Scientific Adviser, Ministry of Food ; *b.* Co. Longford, Ireland ; 3rd *s.* of William Thompson, Ballynulty House, near Granard, and *g. s.* of Robert Thompson, formerly of Cloncoose,Co. Longford; *m.* 1894, Isabel,*e.d.*of Peter Redfern, M.D., 4 Lr. Crescent, Belfast, and Templepatrick House, Donaghadee ; one *s.* four *d. Educ.:* Dundalk Institution ; Queen's Coll. Galway; medical study,Galway,Dublin,London, Leipsic, Paris, Marburg, Heidelberg. Peel Prize Mathematics, Q.U.I. ; 1st Science Sch. (Mathem.) Q.C.G., 1879 ; 1st Med. Scholar for four years, 1880-83, and Senior Sch. Anat. and Physiol. 1884, Q.C.G. ; 1st of 1st Honours and 1st class Exhibition at Graduation, 1888 ; Special Prize and Diploma in Mental Diseases, 1885 ; Demonstrator of Anatomy, Trinity Coll. Dublin, 1887-91 ; Foreign Study and Research, 1892-93, also 1896, 1900, 1901, 1904, 1905 ; Dunville Professor of Physiology, Queen's College, Belfast, 1893-1902 ; Hon. Member Imperial Military Academy of Medicine, Petrograd, 1899 ; Sc.D. Hon. Causa, Univ. Dublin, 1904. *Publications:* Translation of The Work of the Digestive Glands (Pavlov); Foods and their Relative Nourishing Value ; The Food Value of Great Britain's Food Supply ; Collected Papers from Physiological Laboratory, Queen's College, Belfast, and Trinity College, Dublin ; Papers in Reports, British Association, Journal of Physiology, Archives de Physiologie Normale et Pathologique, British Medical Journal, and elsewhere. *Recreations:* tennis, golf, cycling. *Address:* 14 Hatch Street, Dublin. *T.:* Dublin 3564. (*Died 11 Oct. 1918.*)

THOMPSON, Col. William Oliver, D.S.O. 1895 ; I.S.C. ; retired ; *b.* 14 Nov. 1844 Entered army, 1863 ; Col. 1895 ; served Afghan War, 1878-1879 (medal) ; Mahsood-Wuzeeree Expedition, 1881 ; Hazara Expedition, 1888 (medal with clasp) ; Miranzai, 1891 (despatches, clasp) ; Waziristan (despatches twice, D.S.O., clasp). *Club:* East India United Service.

(*Died 10 Sept. 1917.*)

THOMPSON, William Whitaker, M.A., LL.B.; contested (C.) Otley Division, W.R. Yorks, three times ; Chairman London County Council, 1910-11 ; Mayor of Kensington, 1911-12 ; J.P. London ; 3rd *s.* of Sir Mathew William Thompson, 1st Bt. ; *b.* 1857 ; *m.* 1889, Isabella, *d.* of Spencer Robert Lewin, of The Bourne, Widford, Herts. *Address:* 24 Argyll Road, W.8. *T.:* Park 4132. *Clubs:* Oxford and Cambridge, Carlton. (*Died 2 Mar. 1920.*)

THOMSON, Hon. Alex. Macdonald ; *b.* Turriff, Scotland, 27 Sep. 1863 ; 2nd *s.* of J. W. Thomson, M.A., schoolmaster, and Isabella, *e. d.* of late Alex. Macdonald of Kindrought, Portsoy, N.B. *Educ.:* Aberdeen University (M.A., with 1st class in Mathematics, 1883). Lecturer in Mathematics, Naini Tal College, N.W.P., India, 1884-85 ; Assistant Professor of Mathematics, Aberdeen, 1887 ; entered Hong-Kong Civil Service, and attached for one year to the Colonial Office, 1887 ; Bacon Scholar, Gray's Inn, 1888 ; passed examination in Chinese, 1890 ; has served in following offices in the Colony — Superintendent, Victoria Gaol, Assistant Colonial Secretary, Registrar-General Postmaster-General, Colonial Secretary, and Treasurer ; confirmed in last appointment, 1898, with seat *ex officio* on Executive and Legislative Councils ; retired, 1918. *Recreations:* reading, gardening, golf. *Address:* Crescent Avenue, San Mateo, California, U.S.A. (*Died 28 July 1924.*)

THOMSON, Alexander Stuart Duff, B.A., LL.B. ; Advocate ; Sheriff-Substitute of Lanarkshire 1903-26 ; *b.* New York, 1 May 1854 ; *s.* of Rev. John Thomson, D.D. ; *m.* 1905, Mary Agnes (*d.* 1924), *d.* of Rev. James Brown, D.D., Paisley. *Educ.:* New York and Edinburgh Universities. Admitted to Scottish Bar, 1883. *Address:* Averley, Great Western Road, Glasgow. *Clubs:* Western, Glasgow ; Conservative, Edinburgh. (*Died 9 Sept. 1927.*)

THOMSON, Brig.-Gen. Andrew Graham, C.B. 1911 ; C.M.G. 1916 ; R.E. ; retired, 1919 ; *b.* 8 Feb. 1858 ; *s.* of late Surgeon-Major-General W. A. Thomson, Honorary Physician to Queen Victoria and King Edward VII. ; *m.* Anne, *d.* of late Rev. W. Yalden Thomson. *Educ.:* privately ; Woolwich. Joined Royal Engineers, 1877 ; served Egypt, 1882 ; Suakin, 1885 ; South Africa, 1899-1902 ; European War, 1914-17 (despatches, C.M.G.) ; specially employed Holland, 1918-19 ; on Ordnance Survey, United Kingdom, 1885-90 ; in office of Inspector-General of Fortifications, 1897-99 ; commanded Training Battalion R.E. 1903-8 ; Commandant Royal Military Academy, Woolwich, 1908-12. *Address:* 72 St. George's Square, S.W.1. *T.:* Victoria 2128. *Club:* Junior United Service.

(*Died 14 Feb. 1926.*)

THOMSON, Captain Anthony Standidge, C.B. 1897 ; C.B.E. 1919 ; Commander (retired) Royal Naval Reserve, 1899 ; Elder Brother of Trinity House, 1898-1922 ; F.R.G.S. ; *b.* Blackpool, Lancashire, 1 Aug. 1851 ; *e. s.* of Rev. Anthony F. Thomson, B.A. Oxon., and Betsy Sowter Richardson ; *m.* 1888, Alethea Isabella Evans Davis (*d.* 1912) ; three *d. Educ.:* St. John's Foundation School, Kilburn. First went to sea 1868 ; Mercantile Marine, Royal Mail Steam Packet Co. 1872-1879 ; Orient Steam Navigation Co. 1880-83 ; commanded the "Silvertown" and other telegraph steamships, 1883-95 ; served in the Royal Navy on several occasions as Lieut. R.N.R. ; elected Younger Brother of Trinity House, 1892 ; Lieutenant R.N.R., 1887. Takes much practical interest in the science of oceanography and current surveying ; contributed a paper on Ocean Currents to the Sixth International Geographical Congress, held in London 1895 ; served on the Departmental Committee of B.T. on ship's side lights, 1895. *Address:* Northwood Court, near Ramsgate. (*Died 16 April 1925.*)

THOMSON, David Alexander, C.I.E. 1920 ; Conservator of Forest Utilization Circle, Bombay, since 1920 ; *b.* 4 July 1872 ; *s.* of late James Balfour Thomson ; *m.* Mary Fulton, *d.* of James Mill ; one *s.* two *d. Educ.:* High School, Dundee ; R.I.E.C., Cooper's Hill. Joined Indian Forest Service as Assistant Conservator of Forests, 1894 ; Deputy Conservator of Forests, 1898. *Recreations:* shooting and golf. *Clubs:* Club of Western India, Poona ; Royal Bombay Yacht. (*Died 17 May 1922.*)

THOMSON, Lieut.-Col. David George, C.B.E. 1919 ; M.D. ; late Medical Superintendent, County Mental Hospital, Thorpe, Norwich ; *b.* Edinburgh, 1856 ; *s.* of Thomas Thomson, of Princes Street, Edinburgh ; *m.* 1887, Melina Louisa Stromeyer ; one *s.* one *d. Educ.:* Edinburgh University ; Dresden ; Dunkirk. M.D. with honours, 1881 ; commanded the Norfolk War Hospital during European War (despatches, C.B.E.) ; President of Medico-Psychological Association, 1914-18. *Publications:* articles on Medico-Psychological subjects in Journal of Mental Science ; The Evolution of the Nervous System, Trans. of Norf. and Norwich Naturalists, etc. *Recreations:* music, boating, camping, and natural history on the Norfolk Broads. *Address:* 16 Mount Pleasant, Norwich. *T.:* Norwich 1387. *M.:* S 1319. *Club:* Norfolk, Norwich. (*Died 4 Jun. 1923.*)

THOMSON, Hon. Dugald; Member of the House of Representatives, Parliament of the Commonwealth of Australia; b. London, 1848; s. of John Thomson, Shipbroker. *Educ.:* private schools in Australia and in Liverpool, England. Left England with parents for South Australia, 1850; returned to relatives in Liverpool, 1854; after leaving school was for a short time in the service, ashore and afloat, of Balfour, Williamson & Co., Liverpool; left England for Melbourne, Australia, and there entered mercantile pursuits, 1867; removed to Sydney, New South Wales, opening as managing partner business for a firm of manufacturers and importers, 1877; retired from the firm, 1892; Member for Warringah, New South Wales Legislative Assembly, 1894; Hon. Treas. and one of the platform speakers of the Federal Association until the accomplishment of Australian union; Member for North Sydney, Federal House of Representatives, 1900, 1903, and 1906; Commonwealth Minister for Home Affairs, 1904-5; a Representative of the Commonwealth at the Imperial Conference on Merchant Shipping Legislation, London, 1907; Member of Australian Royal Commission on Food Supplies, Trade and Industry during the war. *Publications:* Federal and Political pamphlets. *Address:* Wyreepi, Kirribilli Point, Sydney. *T.:* 213 North Sydney. *Club:* Royal Sydney Yacht Squadron.

(*Died 27 Nov. 1922.*)

THOMSON, Edward William, F.R.S.L., F.R.S. (Can.); b. near Toronto, Canada, 12 Feb. 1849; s. of William Thomson, banker and littérateur, and Margaret Hamilton Foley; m. A. L. G. St. Denis (d. 1921); one s. *Educ.:* public schools; Trin. Coll. Grammar School. Served under Grant, 3rd and 5th Pa. Volunteer cavalry regiments, last year of American Civil War; served in Queen's Own Rifles, Toronto, and Fenian Raid of 1866; civil engineer until 1878; since then political writer, story writer, versifier, and general journalist. *Publications:* Old Man Savarin; sundry other collections of short stories; versifier in M. S. Henry's translation of Aucassin and Nicolette; When Lincoln Died, The Many-Mansioned House, and other poems. *Recreations:* walking and talking. *Address:* 52 Hereford Street, Boston, Mass., U.S.A. *T.:* Queen 2565. (*Died Mar. 1924.*)

THOMSON, George William, J.P.; retired banker; b. Aberdeen, 11 March 1845; s. of George Thomson and Elizabeth S., o. d. of Peter Duguid, Bourtie, Aberdeenshire, and Auchlumies, Kincardineshire; m. 1st, 1878, Ellen Augusta, d. of A. W. Gadesden, D.L., J.P., Ewell Castle, Surrey; 2nd, 1888, Coralie Louise, d. of Edward John Woollett, of Paris and Brussels; three s. two d. *Educ.:* Aberdeen University. Lieutenant Volunteer Artillery, 1860-62; Oriental Bank, China and Japan, 1870-1888; Volunteer Artillery, Shanghai, 1870; wrecked at Cape Gardafui, published account, 1877; founded first European bank in Persia, 1888 (Order Lion and Sun); founded African Banking Corporation, 1891; Chief Manager for 18 and a Director for 11 years; President Caledonian Society of London, 1906-7; Member Council Japan Society; Fellow Institute of Bankers; has travelled in America, Africa, Persia, India, China, and Japan, and in every country in Europe except Greece; during war equipped and commanded Volunteer Corps; retired from active life, 1920. *Publications:* Verses from Japan, 1884; contributions to Chambers's Journal, etc., The Japan of Forty Years Ago, Persia and its People, and other lectures and speeches. *Recreations:* reading, motoring, and wireless. *Address:* St. Valery, Beaconsfield, Bucks. *T.:* Beaconsfield 80. *Club:* Savile. (*Died 6 Sept. 1928.*)

THOMSON, Harry Redmond, M.A., Barrister-at-Law; late Headmaster, Eastbourne

College; b. St. Leonard's, Sussex, 24 Oct. 1860; y. s. of late H. P. Thomson, Monkton House, Taunton; m. Alice Elizabeth, d. of late Clement Cazalet of Petrograd. *Educ.:* Marlborough; Univ. Coll. Oxford (Scholar). 1st class Classical Moderations, 1881; 2nd class Lit. Hum. 1883; Equity Scholarship, Inner Temple, 1887; Barr. 1887. Assistant master at Sherborne School. *Address:* Beechwood, Lake Road, Wimbledon, S.W. *T.:* Wimbledon 520. (*Died 29 Aug. 1917.*)

THOMSON, Henry, J.P.; b. 1840; 2nd s. of late Henry Thomson of Newry, Co. Down, and Anne, d. of late Rev. William Henry, of Tassagh, Co. Armagh; m. 1866, Alice Cecilia, y. d. of late Henry Corbet-Singleton of Aclare, Co. Meath. *Educ.:* Trinity College, Dublin. M.P. Newry, 1880-85. *Address:* Scarvagle House, Scarva, Co. Newry. *Club:* Carlton. (*Died 30 Dec. 1916.*)

THOMSON, Henry Alexis, C.M.G. 1916; M.D., F.R.C.S.; Professor of Surgery, University of Edinburgh since 1909; and Surgeon to the Royal Infirmary; b. Edinburgh, 1863; m. Ethel Kate, 4th d. of C. Grey Wotherspoon, barrister-at-law, of 18 Great Stuart Street, Edinburgh, and Hillside, Aberdour, Fife. *Educ.:* High School, Edinburgh; Realschule, Hanover; Edinburgh University; London Hospital. Graduated with Honours, Bachelor of Medicine and Master of Surgery; Thesis Gold Medallist, Edin.; Bachelor of Science in Public Health, 1888; served European War, 1914-16 (C.M.G.); Consulting Surgeon to III. Army in France. *Publications:* Neuroma and Neurofibromatosis, 1900; Manual of Surgery (joint author), 1904, etc.; joint editor of Edinburgh Medical Journal. *Address:* 39 Drumsheugh Gardens, Edinburgh. *T.A.:* Deltoid, Edinburgh. *T.:* Edinburgh 2168. Moredun, Gilmerton, Midlothian. *T.:* Central 4237. Edinburgh. *Club:* University, Edinburgh.

(*Died 5 Mar. 1924.*)

THOMSON, Hugh, artist; b. 1 June 1860; m. 1884; one s. *Publications:* illustrated—Cranford; Jane Austen's novels; Peg Woffington; St. Ronan's Well; A Kentucky Cardinal and Aftermath; The Great Hoggarty Diamond; Highways and Byways of London; Evelina; Scenes from Clerical Life; The Fair Hills of Ireland; Highways and Byways in Donegal and Antrim; Esmond; As You Like It; Merry Wives of Windsor; School for Scandal; Highways and Byways of Kent, Surrey, and Middlesex, and the Border; The Vicar of Wakefield; Silas Marner; She Stoops to Conquer; Quality Street; The Famous Cities of Ireland; Tom Brown's School Days. *Recreations:* golf and out-door sketching. *Address:* 8 Patten Road, Wandsworth Common, S.W.

(*Died 7 May 1920.*)

THOMSON, John, M.D., F.R.C.P. Edinburgh; Honorary LL.D. Edinburgh; Consulting Physician to the Royal Edinburgh Hospital for Sick Children, and to the Royal Scottish National Institution, Larbert; formerly University Lecturer on the Diseases of Children; b. Edinburgh, 23 Nov. 1856; s. of Thomas Thomson, W.S., and Elizabeth Cleghorn; m. 1887, Isobel F., d. of Rev. John S. McPhail, U.F.C., Benbecula; three s. two d. *Educ.:* Edinburgh Academy and University; Vienna; Berlin. Elected Hon. Member of American Pediatric Society, 1903; Member of Association of Physicians. *Publications:* Guide to Clinical Study and Treatment of Sick Children (translated into French and Spanish), 4th edit.; articles on Diseases of Children in various textbooks and medical journals. *Address:* 14 Coates Crescent, Edinburgh. *T.:* Central 2271.

(*Died 2 July 1926.*)

THOMSON, John Ebenezer Honeyman, M.A., B.D., D.D.; b. Glasgow, Aug. 1841; s. of Ebenezer Thomson and Catherine Ferguson Honeyman; left Glasgow for reasons of health, 1856; m. 1893, Margaret Dalgleish,

d. of Provost James Gray, J.P., Dalkeith ; no *c.*
Educ. : private schools and private tutor ;
Glasgow University ; United Presbyterian
Divinity Hall, and Divinity Hall of Glasgow
University. Licentiate of U.P. Church, 1867 ;
Missionary to Palestine, 1895 ; retired for reasons
of health, 1899 ; Alexander Robertson Lecturer
to University of Glasgow, 1916 ; stayed in
Dennyloanhead, Stirlingshire, 1856-69 ; Blair-
logie, Perthshire, 1869-74 ; Stirling, 1874-1906,
with the exception of stay in Palestine ; in
Edinburgh from that date. *Publications :* A
short Treatise on New Testament Psychology,
1876 ; Upland Tarn, poem, 1881 ; Memoir of
George Thomson, 1881 ; Books which influenced
our Lord and His Apostles, 1891 ; Modern
Criticism Examined, 1902 ; Commentary on
Daniel in the Pulpit Commentary Series, 1897 ;
edited with Dr. Ewing Temple Dictionary of
the Bible, 1910 ; Memoirs of Rev. Thomas
Dunlop, 1919 ; The Samaritans, 1919 ; The
Pentateuch of the Samaritans, when they got
it and whence ; The Readers for whom Matthew
wrote his Hebrew Gospel, 1922. *Recreation :*
light reading. *Address :* 170 Mayfield Road,
Edinburgh. *T. :* Edinburgh 1885.

(Died 9 June 1923.)

THOMSON, General Sir Mowbray,
K.C.I.E., *cr.* 1911 ; Bengal Infantry ; *b.* April
1832 ; *m.* Mary Ironside (*d.* 1903), *d.* of late Rev.
William Money. Entered army, 1853 ; General,
1894 ; retired list, 1885 ; served Indian Mutiny,
1857-58 (wounded four times, medal with clasp,
brevet Maj., one year's service). *Address :* 19
Victoria Square, Reading. *(Died 25 Feb. 1917.)*

THOMSON, Theodore, M.A. (Aberd.) ;
M.D. (Lond.) ; C.M.G. 1905 ; Barrister-at-
Law ; Inspector H.M. Local Government Board,
1891-1911 ; Assistant Medical Officer since 1911.
Educ. : Aberdeen and Edinburgh Universities. Member of Committee of Inquiry into
the Public Health of the City of Dublin,
1900 ; a British Delegate to the International
Sanitary Conferences of Paris, 1903, and Rome,
1906 ; Plenipotentiary to sign the International Sanitary Conventions of 1903 and 1906 ;
Imperial Delegate to the West Indian Inter-
colonial Sanitary Conference of Barbados, 1904 ,
sent on Special Mission of Inquiry into the
Sanitary Defence of the Persian Gulf, 1906 ;
British representative on the Committee of
the Office International d'hygiène publique.
Publications : numerous official reports on
public health subjects. *Address :* Local Government Board, Whitehall, S.W.

(Died 6 Mar. 1916.)

THOMSON, Trevelyan, M.P. (Ind. L.)
Middlesbro' West since Dec. 1918 ; J.P. County
Boro' of Middlesbro' ; *b.* Stockton-on-Tees, 30
April 1875 ; *s.* of late T. James Thomson, iron
founder and merchant ; *m.* 1907, Hilda Mary,
d. of late Rev. J. G. Tolley, London ; one *s.* one
d. Educ. : Friends' Schools, Ackworth and
Bootham, York. Joined his father in business as
iron and steel merchants, which he still continues at 17 Albert Road, Middlesbro' ; a Member
of Middlesbro' County Boro' Council since
1904 ; served overseas in the ranks of
the R.E. 1917-18. *Address :* The Corner, Old
Battersby, nr. Great Ayton ; 17 Albert Road,
Middlesbro'. *T.A. :* Merchant, Middlesbro'. *T. :*
Middlesbro' 218. *Clubs :* National Liberal ;
Cleveland, Middlesbro'. *(Died 8 Feb. 1928.)*

THOMSON, Walter Henry, B.A., J.P.,
I.S.O. ; Municipal Commissioner, Dumka (Sontal
Pergunnahs) ; *b.* 21 August 1856 ; *m.* 1892 ;
one *s. Educ. :* Hooghly College, Chinsurah ;
Presidency College, Calcutta. Graduated in
1877 with Honours in Mathematics ; three years
Professor of Mathematics and Chemistry at the
Doveton College, Calcutta ; entered the Execu-
tive Branch of the Provincial Civil Service, 1880 ;
rose to its top, 1910 ; retired 1913. *Recreations :*

  practical gardener and builder. *Address :*
Sontal Pergunnahs (Bihar), Dumka, India. *Club :*
Dumka. *(Died 26 May 1917.)*

THORBURN, Septimus Smet, F.R.G.S.,
F.R.A.S. ; Indian Civil Service (retired) ; *b.* 12
Aug. 1844 ; *s.* of late D. Thorburn of Dumfries and
Edinburgh ; *m.* 1881, Mary Melise (*d.* 1917), *d.* of F.
Leeston Smith of Leeston, Weston-super-Mare,
and New Zealand ; two *s. Educ. :* Cheltenham
College. Passed thence direct into the I.C.S. ;
posted to Punjab, 1865 ; served trans-Indus until
1890, when appointed Commissioner of Rawal-
pindi ; afterwards appointed Financial Com-
missioner of the Punjab until retirement, 24 Nov.
1899 ; is a member of the Council of the E.I. As-
sociation. *Publications :* Bannu, or our Afghan
Frontier, 1876 ; David Leslie, a Story of the Afghan
Frontier, 1879 ; Musalmans and Moneylenders,
1886 ; Asiatic Neighbours, 1894 : His Majesty's
Greatest Subject, 1897 ; Transgression, 1898 ;
The Punjab in Peace and War, 1904 ; India s
Saint and the Viceroy, 1908 ; Sir John's Con-
version, 1913. *Address :* Old Bracknell House,
Bracknell, Berks. *T.A. :* Thorburn, Bracknell.
T. : Bracknell 34. *(Died 26 April 1924.)*

THORBURN, Thomas, M.V.O. 1912 ; R.D.,
R.N.R. ; Chief Engineer, P. & O. Steam Naviga-
tion Co. *Address :* Eildon Bank, Melrose, N.B.
(Died 1927.)

THORBURN, Rev. Thomas James,
D.D., LL.D. ; *b.* 24 Feb. 1858 ; *s.* of late Thomas
Charles Thorburn, C.E. (formerly R.E.) of
Claughton, Birkenhead, and Charlotte, *d.* of
James Evans of Kentchurch, Herefordshire ;
m. 1887, Emilie J., *d.* of late Edward Hailstone ;
one *s.* one *d. Educ. :* Birkenhead ; Christ's
College, Cambridge ; Trinity College, Dublin.
Curate of St. Leonard's, Colchester, 1881 ; 2nd
Master, Chesterfield Grammar School, 1882-85 ;
Senior Science Master, Royal Grammar School,
and Curate of Sheffield, 1885-93 ; Headmaster of
Caistor School, 1893-97 ; Odiham School, 1897-
1903 ; Acting Headmaster of Hastings Grammar
School (War Service), 1915-19. *Publications :*
A Critical Examination of the Evidences for the
Doctrine of the Virgin Birth ; The Resurrection
Narratives and Modern Criticism ; Jesus the
Christ : Historical or Mythical ? The Historical
Jesus ; The Mythical Interpretation of the
Gospels (Bross Prize, 1915, Lake Forest Uni-
versity, Ill., U.S.A.). *Recreations :* most active
games, but especially walking. *Address :* 21
St. Helen's Road, Hastings. *(Died 11 Jan. 1923.)*

THORBURN, Sir William, K.B.E.,
cr. 1919 ; C.B. 1916 ; C.M.G. 1919 ; D.L. Co.
Lancaster ; M.D., B.S., B.Sc. London ; F.R.C.S.
England ; B.Sc. (Manchester) ; (hon.) M.D.
Malta ; Emeritus Professor of Clinical Surgery,
University of Manchester, 1910-21 ; Member
of Council and of Court of Examiners, Royal
College of Surgeons ; Honorary Consulting
Surgeon, Manchester Royal Infirmary ; Medical
Referee under Workmen's Compensation Act,
etc. ; Col. late R.A.M.C. (T.), 2nd Western
General Hospital, and Colonel A.M.S., Con-
sulting Surgeon in Malta, Salonika, etc. (de-
spatches) ; Consulting Surgeon to the Forces in
France since Sep. 1917 (despatches) ; *s.* of John
Thorburn, M.D., F.R.C.P., Professor of Obstetric
Medicine, Owens Coll. Manchester, and Annie
Pollok Anderson ; *m.* Augusta (*d.* 1922), *d.* of W.
E. Melland ; three *d. Educ. :* Owens College ;
Manchester Royal Infirmary ; various London
Hospitals. Member of Court and Council of
Victoria University of Manchester ; Past Presi-
dent of Owens College Union, Owens College
Associates, Pathological Society of Manchester,
and Manchester Med. Society, and Neurological
Section of Royal Soc. of Medicine ; Jacksonian
Essayist and Hunterian Professor of Royal
College of Surgeons of England. *Publications :*
Surgery of the Spinal Cord ; many surgical
publications, papers, essays, lectures. *Address :*

8 York Gate, Regent's Park, N.W.1. *Clubs:* Athenæum, Oriental ; Union, Brasenose, Manchester.   *(Died 18 Mar. 1923.)*

THORNE, Edward Henry, Mus.D. ; Organist and Choirmaster of St. Anne's, Soho, since 1891 ; *b.* Cranborne, Dorset., 9 May 1834 ; *m.* 1861, Elise Payn, Jersey ; two *s.* one *d. Educ.:* St George's Chapel, Windsor. Organist and Choirmaster, Henley-on-Thames, 1853 ; Chichester Cathedral, 1863 ; St. Patrick's, Brighton, 1870 ; St. Peter's Cranley Gardens, 1872 ; St. Michael's, Cornhill, 1875. *Publications:* organ music ; church music ; pianoforte music ; songs and part-songs ; A Short Life of John Sebastian Bach. *Recreation:* reading. *Address:* 19 Clarendon Gardens, Maida Vale, W.
     (Died 26 Dec. 1916.)

THORNE, Sir William, Kt., *cr.* 1904 ; M.L.A. ; *b.* Llanstedwell, Pembrokeshire, 27 Jan. 1839 ; *m.* 1863, Ellen, *d.* of Thomas Lane, Chichester ; two *s.* three *d. Educ.:* privately. Went to Cape Town, 1859 ; thrice Mayor of Cape Town ; Director Stuttaford & Co., Merchants, Cape Town and Johannesburg. *Address:* Rusdon, Rondebosch, Cape Town. *Clubs:* Junior Civil Service, City, Cape Town.
     (Died 28 Mar. 1917.)

THORNELY, Hon. Mr. Justice, P. Wilfrid, M.A., LL.D. (Cantab.) ; LL.D., T.C.D., etc. ; Judge of the International Court of Appeal and Adviser to the Ministry of Justice, Bangkok, Siam, since 1911 ; *b.* 1879 ; *o. s.* of late John and Helen Thornely, of Southbourne ; *m.* 1911, Doreen Hammersley, *y. d.* of late Lt.-Col. Beech Johnston, M.D. ; one *s.* two *d.* Member of Trinity Hall, Cambridge, and of the Inner Temple, Barrister-at-law ; practised in London (Fountain Court, Temple) and on the South-Eastern Circuit, 1902-11 ; Siam Coronation Medal 1st Class, 1911 ; Knight Comm. Order of the Crown of Siam ; Commander Order of the White Elephant. *Publications:* History of Negotiability ; The History of a Transition ; Angelus (Libretto of the winning Opera in Ricordi Competition, first produced at Royal Opera House, Covent Garden, in 1909) ; Torrington Towers ; translation with lyrics of Siamese Opera ; various short stories, etc. *Recreations:* writing and motoring. *Address:* Ministry of Justice, Bangkok, Siam. *T.A.:* Thornely, Bangkok. *Club:* Royal Sports, Bangkok.   *(Died 9 Mar. 1926.)*

THORNTON, Canon Herbert Parry, M.A. ; Hon. Secretary Winchester Diocesan Clerical Registry since 1913 ; 3rd *s.* of late Canon Francis Vansittart Thornton and Mary Louisa, *e. d.* of Rev. Horace George Cholmondeley ; *m.* 1890, Alice Mary (*d.* 1913), *y. d.* of late General Edward Darvall ; no *c. Educ.:* Sherborne ; Trinity College, Cambridge, Jun. op. Math. Tripos., 1878. Vicar of Normanton, Yorks, 1889-97 ; Curate, 1897-1900 ; Diocesan Missioner, Grafton and Armidale, N.S.W. ; 1901 ; Vicar of Market Weighton, 1902-8 ; Chaplain of Taormina, 1906-7, 1911-12 ; Chaplain of Patras, 1908-9 ; Hon. Canon, Winchester Cathedral, 1921. *Address:* Wonersh, Guildford. *T.A.:* Wonersh. *T.:* Bramley 44.   *(Died 9 Oct. 1923.)*

THORNTON, Sir James Howard, K.C.B., *cr.* 1904 ; C.B. 1885 ; D. Surg.-Gen., I.M.S. (retired) ; *y. s.* of late Major John Thornton, 78th Regt. ; *b.* 1834 ; *m.* 1861, Mary (*d.* 1918), *y. d.* of late J. Astor of Jersey ; three *s.* two *d. Educ.:* Chatham House, Ramsgate ; King's Coll. London. B.A. University of London, 1854 ; M.B. 1855 ; M.R.C.S. 1855 ; Associate of King's Coll. London, 1855 ; Fellow of King's Coll. Lond. 1898. Entered Indian Medical Service, 1856 ; served throughout Indian Mutiny Campaigns, 1857-59 ; China War, 1860 ; Khasia and Jyntia Hills Campaign, 1862-63 (wounded in action) ; Bhootan War, 1865-66 ; Egyptian Expedition, 1882 ; Suakin Expedition, 1885 (as Principal

1040

Medical Officer) ; Hazara Expedition, 1888 (as Principal Medical Officer) ; was five times mentioned in despatches, and received four war medals with seven clasps, the Khedive's star, and the C.B. ; retired in 1891. *Decorated* for services in the Suakin Expedition, 1885. *Publications:* Memories of Seven Campaigns. *Recreations:* cricket, lawn-tennis, chess.
     (Died 6 Jan. 1919.)

THORNTON, Percy Melville, LL.M. (Camb.) ; *b.* 12 Upper Gloucester Place, London, 29 Dec. 1841 ; *e. s.* of late Rear-Admiral Samuel Thornton and Emily Elizabeth, *d.* of Rev. J. Rice ; *m.* Florence, 3rd *d.* of late Henry Sykes Thornton, 1877. *Educ.:* Harrow ; Jesus Coll Camb. At Cambridge was first secretary of the inter-University sports, and afterwards in London ; during 1866, first amateur champion half mile ; since 1880 has pursued a literary career, which has only been interrupted by parliamentary duties ; M.P. (C.) Clapham and Battersea, 1892-1910 ; one of the Registrars of the Royal Literary Fund ; a Vice-President 1917 ; when war broke out was elected Hon. Commandant of the Veteran Athlete Volunteers. *Publications:* Recovered Thread of England's Foreign Policy, 1880 (5 editions) ; Foreign Secretaries of the Nineteenth Century, 3 vols., 1881 (2 editions) ; Harrow School and its Surroundings, 1883 ; The Brunswick Accession, 1887 ; The Stuart Dynasty, 1890 ; Continental Rulers of the Nineteenth Century ; Some Things we have Remembered, 1912. *Recreations:* a lover of cricket, rowing, and athletics for years ; hon. sec. Middlesex County Cricket Club until 1898. *Address:* 30 Evelyn Gardens, South Kensington, S.W. ; *T.:* Kensington 3059 ; Ryders Wells House, Lewes, Sussex. *Clubs:* Carlton, United University. *(Died 8 Jan. 1918.)*

THORNTON, Right Rev. Samuel, D.D. Oxon. ; M.A. Melbourne ; Assistant Bishop, Diocese of London, and Hon. Diocesan Visitor of the Church Army since 1911 ; *b.* London, 1835 ; 3rd *s.* of Thomas Thornton, F.R.A.S., and Elizabeth, *d.* of H. Robinson, Bagshot, Surrey ; *m.* 1st, *d.* (*d.* 1909) of H. Thornton, 1866 ; one *s.* ; 2nd, 1913, Caroline Wakefield, *widow* of Rev. Dr. Rice. *Educ.:* Merchant Taylors' School ; Queen's College, Oxford (late Michel Fellow). Open Exhibition, 1851 ; Scholarship, 1853 ; 1st class Classics, mods. ; 2nd class in Classics and in Nat. Science, finals. Graduated at 19 ; educational work on leaving Oxford ; ordained Deacon to Fellowship, 1858 ; Priest, 1859 ; London Diocesan Home Mission, 1858 ; Incumbent of St. Jude's, Whitechapel, 1859 ; Rector of St. George's, Birmingham, 1864-75 ; first Bishop of Ballarat, 1875-1900 ; Assistant Bishop to Bishop of Manchester and Vicar of Blackburn, 1901-1910 ; Proctor, York Convocation, 1906-10 ; Chaplain, Langho Female Inebriates Asylum, 1907-10 ; Rural Dean, 1907-10. *Recreations:* his boating, and tennis, and horseback days are over ; reading is his recreation—in all departments : "Humani nihil alienum puto." *Address:* 80 Elsham Road, Kensington, W. *Club:* Church Imperial.
     (Died 25 Nov. 1917.)

THORNTON-DUESBURY, Rt. Rev. Charles Leonard, M.A. ; D.D. 1925 ; Bishop of Sodor and Man since 1925 ; *b.* Glen Helen, Isle of Man, 3 Feb. 1867 ; *s.* of Capt. W. H. Thornton-Duesbury, B.A., J.P., late of Durham Light Infantry, and Catherine Wilkinson, of East Riding, Yorkshire ; *m.* 1896, Ethel Nixon, *d.* of General Baumgartner, C.B., of Island Hall, Godmanchester ; one *s.* one *d. Educ.:* Shattallan Hall, Isle of Man ; Trinity College, Dublin ; B.A. 1890 ; M.A. 1893 ; B.D. and D.D. 1925 ; Catech. Prize, 1889. Deacon, 1890 ; Priest, 1891 ; Hon. Canon of Chelmsford, 1914 ; Rural Dean of Leyton. 1915 ; Curate of St. George-in-the-East, 1890-94 ; Vicar of St.

Mark's, Barrow-in-Furness, 1894-1905 ; Vicar of St. Peter's, Islington, 1905-7 ; Vicar of Leyton, 1907-18 ; Rector of Holy Trinity, St. Marylebone, W., 1919-25 ; Chairman of Church of England Sunday School Institute, 1917-25 ; Vice-Chairman, C.E.T.S., 1920-25 ; Chairman of C.M.S. Home Committee, 1920-25. *Address :* Bishop's Court, Kirknichael, Isle of Man.

(*Died 11 Mar. 1928.*)

THORNYCROFT, Sir John Isaac, Kt., *cr.* 1902 ; LL.D., F.R.S. ; Vice-Pres. of Institute of Naval Architects ; naval architect and engineer ; *b.* Rome, 1843 ; *e. s.* of Thomas and Mary Thornycroft, both sculptors ; *m.* 1870, Blanche, *d.* of Frederick Coules, Gloucester ; two *s.* five *d. Educ.:* private school ; Glasgow University. Diploma, Glasgow Univ. Founded shipbuilding works at Chiswick, 1866 ; introduced improvements in naval architecture and marine engineering, which have promoted the development of high speeds at sea. *Publications :* papers in the Trans. of British Assoc. ; Institution of Naval Architects and Civil Engineers. *Recreations :* small boat sailing and racing, skating, photography, motoring. *Address :* Steyne, Bembridge, Isle of Wight. *M. :* H 99. *Clubs :* Royal Automobile ; Bembridge Sailing.

(*Died 28 June 1928.*)

THORNYCROFT, Sir (William) Hamo, Kt., *cr.* 1917 ; R.A. 1888 ; sculptor ; Hon. Member of Royal Academy of Munich ; *b.* London, 9 March 1850 ; 2nd *s.* of Thomas and Mary Thornycroft ; *m.* 1884, Agatha, 2nd *d.* of Homersham Cox, Tonbridge. *Educ.:* Macclesfield Grammar School ; University College School, London. Gold medallist Royal Academy of Arts, 1875 ; A.R.A. 1881 ; hon. member Royal Academy of Munich, 1889 ; médaille d'Honneur, Paris, 1900. *Statues :* National Monument to General Gordon in Trafalgar Square and in Melbourne ; John Bright in Rochdale ; Sir Steuart Bayley in Calcutta ; Lord Granville in House of Parliament ; Her Majesty the Queen in the Royal Exchange ; Archbishop Thomson in York ; Bishop Goodwin in Carlisle ; Teucer in Chantrey Collection ; Artemis at Eaton Hall ; The Mower, Liverpool Gallery ; Lot's Wife ; Edward I. ; The Sower ; Summer ; Joy of Life ; Cromwell Statue at Westminster ; National Memorial to Gladstone, Strand, London ; Queen Victoria Memorial at Karachi ; War Memorial at Durban ; Armstrong Memorial at Newcastle ; Lord Curzon Memorial, Calcutta ; King Edward Memorial at Karachi, 1915 ; The Kiss, marble group, Tate Gallery, 1916 ; Bronze Statue of Courage as War Memorial at Luton, 1923 ; Bishop Yeatman-Biggs Statue in Coventry Cathedral, 1925. *Recreations :* gardening, bicycling, trout fishing. *Address :* 2A Melbury Road, Kensington, W. ; The Old Farmhouse, Coombe, Handborough, Oxford. *Club :* Athenæum.

(*Died 18 Dec. 1925.*)

THORODDSEN, Prof. Dr. Thorvald, *b.* Flatey, Breidifjord, W. Iceland, 6 June 1855 ; *s.* of Jon Thoroddsen ; poet and author ; *m.* 1887, Thora (*d.* 1917), *d.* of Dr. P. Pjetursson, D.D., Bishop of Iceland. *Educ. :* Coll. in Reykjavik, Iceland. Studied zoology and geology at the Univ. of Copenhagen, 1875-80 ; and geology and physical geography in Germany, 1884-85 ; teacher at the Technical School in Módruvellir, N. Iceland, 1880-84 ; teacher at the College in Reykjavik, 1885-95. Lives since 1895 in Copenhagen, occupied with scientific work, but stays during the summer mostly in Iceland ; travelled in Iceland to explore the geology and geography of that country, 1881-99, and has made a geological survey of the entire island, and for first time mapped parts of the little known deserts and high plateaus in the interior. Hon. Ph.D. Univ. of Copenhagen, 1894 ; Hon. Prof. 1902 ; Member of the R. Acad. Science, Copenhagen,

1909 ; gold medallist of Geographical Societies of Paris, New York, and Copenhagen and of Royal Academies in Copenhagen and Stockholm ; Cuthbert Peek Grant, R. Geographical Society, London, 1897 ; Hon. Corresponding Member and Hon. Member of Geographical Societies of London, Berlin, Berne, Copenhagen, Stockholm, of Geological Societies of London, Brussels, and Copenhagen ; formerly President of Icelandic Liter. Society ; Knight of Dannebrog, 1899. *Publications :* History of Icelandic Geography, 1892-1904 ; Geological Map of Iceland, 1901 ; Description of Iceland, 1881, 1900, 1919 ; Description of Iceland, 1908-21 ; Travels in Iceland, 1913-15 ; Climate Conditions in Iceland During One Thousand Years, 1916-17 ; History of Icelandic Volcanoes, 1882 ; Volcanoes and Earthquakes in Iceland, 1896 ; Earthquakes in Iceland, 1899 ; Iceland, Geography and Geology, 1905-1906, etc. ; many papers on the geology and geography of Iceland in Icelandic, Danish, Swedish, German, and English scientific journals. *Recreations :* has travelled in Sweden, Germany, England, Switzerland, and Italy for recreation and scientific purposes. *Address :* Reykjavik, Iceland.

(*Died Nov. 1921.*)

THOROLD, Sir John Henry, 12th Bt., *cr.* 1642 ; LL.D. Cambridge ; D.L., J.P. ; landowner ; *b.* 9 Mar. 1842 ; *e. s.* of 11th Bt. and *d.* of Colonel Hildyard, Flintham Hall, Notts. S. father 1866 ; *m.* 1869, Hon. Henrietta Alexandrina Willoughby, *e. d.* of 8th Baron Middleton ; two *s.* two *d. Educ. :* Eton. LL.D. (Camb). Late Lieut. Leicestershire Regt. 1888 ; Hon. Col. 2nd Vol. Linc. Regt., 1868-88 ; M.P. (C.) Grantham, 1865-68. Owns about 9000 acres. *Heir : s.* Major John George Thorold, *b.* 2 Oct. 1870. *Address :* Syston Old Hall, Grantham. *Club :* Carlton.

(*Died Oct. 1922.*)

THOROLD, Montague George, J.P., late R.N. ; 2nd *s.* of Sir John C. Thorold, 11th Bt. ; *b.* 22 Aug. 1844 ; *m.* 1881, Emmeline Laura Thorold (*d.* 1918), *d.* of Captain John Bastard, and widow of 6th Baron Rivers. *Address :* Harston House, Grantham. *Club :* Royal Yacht Squadron, Cowes. (*Died 19 Dec. 1920.*)

THORP, Austin, D.S.O. 1917 ; Lieut.-Col. Royal Garrison Artillery, Commanding 82nd Brigade, Royal Field Artillery, since Dec. 1915 ; *b.* Todmorden, 23 Oct. 1873 ; *s.* of late Charles William Thorp, M.D., Dobroyd, Todmorden, and Mrs. Thorp, Foxleigh, Wem ; *m.* 1911, Edith May, *e. d.* of late William Henry Petrie, Rochdale ; one *s.* one *d. Educ. :* Elstow School, Bedford ; Royal Military Academy, Woolwich. 2nd Lieut. Royal Artillery, 1893 ; served in India and Burma in the Royal Field Artillery, Royal Garrison Artillery, and Indian Mountain Artillery, 1893-1901 ; passed through the Gunnery Staff Course, 1902 ; served in Royal Garrison Artillery in Malta, 1903-7, and in Indian Mountain Artillery in India and Burma, 1908-14 ; at the outbreak of the War was commanding the R.G.A. Depot, Plymouth ; joined B.E.F. France July 1915 in command of a 4·5 Howitzer Battery with the 18th Division (despatches four times, D.S.O.). *Recreations :* golf and motoring. *Address :* 7 Dorset Road, Bexhill-on-Sea.

(*Died 30 Oct. 1918.*)

THORPE, Sir Edward, Kt., *cr.* 1909 ; C.B. 1900 ; Ph.D., D.Sc., Sc.D., LL.D., F.R.S. ; Emeritus Professor of General Chemistry in the Imperial College of Science and Technology, S. Kensington ; *b.* near Manchester, 8 Dec. 1845 ; *s.* of George Thorpe, Trafford Bank, nr. Manchester ; *m.* 1870, Caroline Emma, *d.* of John Watts, Manchester. *Educ. :* Owens Coll., Manchester ; Universities of Heidelberg and Bonn. Professor of Chemistry in the Andersonian Institution, 1870 ; Yorkshire Coll. Leeds, 1874 ; Royal Coll. of Science, London, 1885 ; formerly treasurer and president Chemical Society ; president Chemical

Section, British Association, 1890; vice-president, 1900; vice-president Royal Society, 1894-1895; president Society of Chemical Industry, 1895; a Fellow of the Univ. of Lond.; Hon. or Corres. Memb. of the Royal Soc. of Edinburgh, Literary and Phil. Societies of Glasgow, Manchester, Leeds, Haarlem, Berlin, Petrograd, Chemists' Club of New York, etc.; late Director of the Government Laboratories, London: Foreign Secretary Royal Society to 1908; President of the British Association for the Advancement of Science, 1921. *Publications*: Chemical Problems, 1870; Inorganic Chemistry, 2 vols., 1874; Quantitative Analysis, 1874; Qualitative Analysis, 1873; A Dictionary of Applied Chemistry, 7 vols.; Essays in Historical Chemistry; Humphry Davy, Poet and Philosopher; Joseph Priestley; A History of Chemistry, 2 vols.; The Scientific Papers of Henry Cavendish; A Yachtsman's Guide to the Dutch Waterways; The Seine from Havre to Paris, 1913; Alcoholometric Tables, 1915; Life of Sir Henry Roscoe, 1916; Editor of Monographs on Industrial Chemistry; numerous memoirs in the Philosophical Transactions of the Royal Society, and of the Chemical Society. *Address*: Whinfield, Salcombe, S. Devon. *Clubs*: Athenæum; Salcombe Yacht.

(Died 23 Feb. 1925.)

THRIFT, Sir John Edward, Kt., *cr.* 1909; *b.* 30 Jan. 1845; *s.* of late William Thrift; *m.* 1872, Fanny Selina, *d.* of late James Hart, Nottingham; one *s.* one *d.* *Educ.*: privately. Entered Inland Revenue Department, 1866; Superintendent Inspector Stamps and Taxes for the City of London, 1903; knighted for special services in connection with the Finance Act 1907; Chief Inspector of Inland Revenue, 1907-10. *Address*: The Whare, Woodcote Road, Wallington, Surrey. *(Died 15 Mar. 1926.)*

THROCKMORTON, Sir Nicholas William George, 9th Bt., *cr.* 1642; D.L., J.P.; *b.* 25 Apr. 1838; 2nd *s.* of 8th Bt. and Elizabeth, *o. d.* of Sir John Acton, Bt.; *S.* father 1862. Owns about 22,400 acres. *Heir*: *b.* Capt. Richard Charles Acton [*b.* 26 Apr. 1839; late Captain 87th Foot; *m.* 1866, Frances Stewart (*d.* 1895), *d.* of Maj. John A. Moore; four *s.* three *d.*]. *Address*: 17 Clifford Street, W.; Coughton Court, Coughton, S.O., Warwickshire. *Clubs*: Travellers', Boodle's.

(Died 21 Dec 1919.)

THROCKMORTON, Sir Richard (Charles Acton), 10th Bt., *cr.* 1642; *b.* 26 Apr. 1839; *s.* of 8th Bt. and Elizabeth, *o. d.* of Sir John Acton, Bt.; *S.* brother, 1919; *m.* 1st, 1866, Frances Stewart (*d.* 1895), *d.* of Maj. John A. Moore; four *s.* three *d.*; 2nd, 1921, Florence (*d.* 1924), *widow* of Major Charles Allix Lavington Yate, V.C., and formerly wife of late Col. G. Burroughs, 3rd Bombay Cavalry. Late Captain 87th Foot. Owns about 22,400 acres. *Heir*: *g.s.* Robert George Maxwell [*b.* 15 Feb. 1908; *s.* of late Lt.-Col. Courtenay Throckmorton and Lilian, *o. d.* of Col. Langford Brooke, Mere Hall, Cheshire. *Address*: Coughton Court, Coughton, S.O., Warwickshire]. *Address*: 18 Milner Street, Lennox Gardens, S.W.

(Died 28 April 1927.)

THUILLIER, Sir Henry Ravenshaw, K.C.I.E., *cr.* 1895; Col. R.E., retired 1895; *b.* India, 26 Mar. 1838; *e. s.* of late Gen. Sir Henry Landor Thuillier C.S.I.; *m.* Emmeline, 3rd *d.* of Fleetwood Williams, C.S.I., 1867; two *s.* two *d.* *Educ.*: Wimbledon School; Military Coll. Addiscombe. Entered Bengal Engineers, 1857; Survey of India Department, 1859; Surveyor-General of India, 1886-95. *Address*: 10 Philbeach Gardens, South Kensington, S.W.

(Died 4 Mar. 1922.)

THURLOW, 5th Baron (*cr.* 1792), **Thomas John Hovell-Thurlow-Cumming-Bruce,** P.C., F.R.S., D.L., J.P.; *b.* 5 Dec.

1838; *s.* of 3rd Baron and Sarah, *o. d.* of Peter Hodgson; *S. b.* 1874; *m.* Lady Elma Bruce, *o. d.* of 8th Earl of Elgin and Kincardine, K.T., and 1st wife, Elizabeth, *d.* of Major C. L. Cumming-Bruce; two *s.* Entered Diplomatic Service, 1858; at Embassies at Stockholm; at Paris, 1859-60; on Earl of Elgin's Mission to China, 1860-61; present at capture of Taku Forts and of Pekin; Private Secretary to Viceroy of India (Earl of Elgin), 1862-63; 3rd Secretary at Vienna, 1864; Private Secretary to Minister at Washington, 1865-66; 2nd Secretary at the Hague, 1866-70; Lord-in-Waiting, 1880-86; Paymaster-Gen. 1886; Lord High Commissioner of General Assembly of Church of Scotland, 1886; Chairman of Salt Union. *Publications*: The Company and the Crown; Trades Unions Abroad, etc. Owns about 13,900 acres *Heir*: *s.* Rev. Hon. Charles Edward Hovell-Thurlow-Cumming-Bruce. *Address*: Dunphail, N.B.

(Died 1916.)

THURSBY, Sir John (Ormerod Scarlett), 2nd Bt., *cr.* 1887; D.L., J.P.; *b.* 27 April 1861; *s.* of 1st Bt. and Clara, *d.* of Col. Williams; *m.* 1888, Ella Beatrice (*d.* 1915), *d.* of T. Richard Crosse; one *d.*; *S.* father, 1901. *Educ.*: Eton; Trinity College, Cambridge (B.A.). Barrister-at-Law; High Sheriff of Lancashire, 1905; President of British Chess Federation; President of Burnley Chamber of Commerce; Steward of Jockey Club, 1915-18. *Heir*: *half-b.* George James [*b.* 17 Nov. 1869; *m.* 1894, Mary Augusta, *e. d.* of Thomas Hardcastle of Bradshaw Hall, Bolton-le-Moors. *Address*: Fountain Court, Brook, Lyndhurst. *Club*: Arthur's]. *Address*: Ormerod House, Burnley. *Clubs*: Carlton, Garrick, Turf, Savile. *(Died 26 Dec. 1920.)*

THURSFIELD, Sir James Richard, Kt., *cr.* 1920; M.A.; *b.* Kidderminster, 16 Nov. 1840; *y. s.* of late Thomas Thursfield, M.R.C.S.; *m.* Emily, *d.* of late Rev. S A. Herbert, 1880; one *s.* one *d.* *Educ.*: Merchant Taylors' School; Corpus Christi College, Oxford (scholar, 1859); 1st class Moderations (classical), 1861; 1st class Lit. Hum. 1863; Fellow of Jesus College, 1864 to 1881, Tutor, Dean, Librarian, and Lecturer; Classical Moderator (pass), 1870; Public Examiner (classical honours), 1878; Junior Proctor, 1875; Hon. Fellow of Jesus College, 1908. Is a writer on The Times, and has been a frequent contributor to the Naval Annual, and an occasional contributor to the Quarterly, Westminster, and National Reviews, the Athenæum, Academy, and Literature; has acted as correspondent of The Times during naval manœuvres since 1887; is an Hon. Member of the R.U.S.I. and a J.P. for Co. Herts. *Publications*: Peel, in the series of English Statesmen; The Navy and the Nation, conjointly with Sir George S. Clarke, now Lord Sydenham; Nelson and other Naval Studies; Naval Warfare. *Recreation*: walking, fishing, golf. *Address*: 57 Rotherwick Road, N.W.4. *T.*: Finchley 1055. *(Died 22 Nov. 1923.)*

THURSTON, Colonel Hugh Champneys, C.B. 1918; C.M.G. 1900; A.M.S.; *b.* 14 Mar. 1862; *s.* of late O. E. Thurston of Kington, nr. Thornbury; *m.* 1896, Susie, *d.* of Charles Steele, Clifton; one *s.* one *d.* Entered Army, 1887; Major, 1899; served Wuntho Expedition, 1891, under Lt.-Gen. Sir G. Wolseley, K.C.B. (medal with clasp); South Africa, 1899-1902 (despatches, Queen's medal, five clasps, King's medal, 2 clasps, C.M.G.); European War, 1914-18 (despatches, C.B.). *Address*: Thornbury, Co. Gloucester. *(Died 17 Aug. 1919.)*

THYNNE, Lord Alexander George, D.S.O. 1917; Major Royal Wilts Yeomanry; M.P. (U.) Bath since 1910; L.C.C. (M.R.) East Marylebone since 1910; *b.* of 5th Marquis of Bath; *b.* 1873. *Educ.*: Eton; Balliol Coll. Oxford. Contested (U.) Frome Division of Somerset, 1896; City of Bath, 1905; represented the City of London on the London County Council, 1899-1900;

1042

THULRAI, Taluqdar of, Rana Sir Sheoraj Singh Bahadur of Khajurgaon, K.C.I.E. See page xxxi.

Greenwich, 1907-10 ; Chairman of Improvements Committee, 1909-12 ; served South Africa with 1st Batt. Imperial Yeomanry, and on the Staff, 1900-2 (Queen's medal, 3 clasps, King's medal, two clasps) ; Sec. to the Lieut.-Gov. Orange River Colony, 1902-1905 ; accompanied Somaliland Field Force, 1903-4, as Reuter's Special Correspondent (medal and clasp) ; European War, 1914-17 (D.S.O.). *Address :* 15 Manchester Square, W. *T. :* Mayfair 2471. *Clubs :* White's, Turf, Carlton.

(*Died 16 Sept. 1918.*)

THYNNE, Major Algernon Carteret, D.S.O., 1902 ; Major Royal N. Devon Hussars Yeomanry ; *b.* 9 April 1868 ; 2nd *s.* of late Francis John Thynne of Haynes Park, Bedford, and Edith Marcia Caroline, *e. d.* of Richard Brinsley Sheridan of Frampton Court, Dorset ; *m.* 1904, Constance, *d.* of late Edward William Bonham, and *widow* of Francis Philips. Served S. Africa, 1900-2 (despatches, Queen's medal with four clasps, King's medal with two clasps, D.S.O.). *Address :* Penstowe, Kilkhampton, N. Cornwall. *Club :* Travellers'. (*Died 6 Nov. 1917.*)

THYNNE, Col. Hon. Andrew Joseph ; V.D., M.L.C., Queensland, 1882-1922 ; *b.* Ireland, 30 Oct. 1847 ; *m.* 1st, 1869, Mary, *d.* of late William Cairncross ; three *s.* five *d.* ; 2nd, 1922, Christiana J., *widow* of Leslie Gordon Corrie. *Educ. :* private tuition ; Queen's College, Galway. Went to Queensland, 1864 ; Solicitor, 1873 ; Minister of Justice and Attorney-General, 1888-90 ; Delegate to First Federal Convention, Sydney, 1891, and to Colonial Conference, Ottawa, 1894 ; Postmaster-General, 1894-97 ; Secretary for Agriculture, 1896-98 ; President Queensland Ambulance Brigade ; Chairman Queensland Law Society for thirty-five years ; Vice-Chancellor Univ. of Queensland ; Chairman Queensland Recruiting Committee during War ; Vice-Chairman Australian Council of St. John's Ambulance Association. *Recreations :* agriculture and horticulture. *Address :* Thoonbah, S. Brisbane. *Clubs :* Queensland, Johnsonian, Brisbane.

(*Died 28 Feb. 1927.*)

THYNNE, Rev. Arthur Barugh ; Vicar of Seend, 1873-1916 ; Rural Dean of Bradford since 1896 ; Prebendary of Salisbury since 1899 ; *b.* 29 May 1840 ; *m.* ; seven *c. Educ. :* King's College School ; Trinity College, Cambridge. Curate of Northam, Southampton, 1865 ; Thames Ditton, 1865-69 ; Wilsford, Marlborough, 1869-73. *Address :* Seend Vicarage, Melksham.

(*Died 2 Nov. 1917.*)

THYNNE, Maj.-Gen. Sir Reginald Thomas, K.C.B., *cr.* 1902 ; *b.* 23 Dec. 1843 ; *s.* of late Rev. Lord John Thynne, D.D., 3rd *s.* of 2nd Marquis of Bath ; *m.* 1890, Louise, *widow* of Major William Ewing, and *d.* of Douglas Du Bois ; two *d. Educ. :* Radley. Entered army, Grenadier Guards, 1862 ; Maj.-Gen. 1893 ; served Zulu War, 1879 (medal with clasp) ; Egypt, 1882 (medal, 4th class Osmanieh, Khedive's star) ; Soudan, 1885 (despatches, C.B., clasp) ; commanding N.E. District, 1894-1902. *Address :* 24 Park Square, Regent's Park, N.W.1. *T. :* Museum 6262. *Clubs :* Guards', Travellers'.

(*Died 30 Dec. 1926.*)

TIBBLES, William, D.C.L. (Washington), LL.D., M.D. (Chicago), L.R.C.P. (Edin.), M.R.C.S. (Eng.), L.S.A. (Lond.) : *b.* Leicester, 10 April 1859 ; *s.* of William Tibbles, M.D. ; *m.* Selina, *d.* of Thos. Pearson, Goxhill, Lincs ; one *s.* one *d. Educ. :* Charing Cross (London University). Specialty : Dietetics and the Diseases of Nutrition and Metabolism. Acting Assist.-Physician Nottingham General Hospital, 1915-19 ; Member of Pensions Medical Board, Nottingham ; M.O.H. Melton Mowbray R. District ; M.O. 4th District Nottingham Parochial Union ; Fellow Royal Institute of Public Health ; Member British Medical Association ;

Member American Association Physicians and Surgeons, and Nottingham Medico-Chirurgical Society ; late Pathological Assistant, Charing Cross Hospital. *Publications :* Life and Evolution, 1927 ; Food and Hygiene ; Dietetics : or Food in Health and Disease ; Foods : their Origin, Manufacture and Composition ; The Theory of Ions : a Consideration of its Place in Biology and Therapeutics ; Diet in Dyspepsia ; articles on Diet in various medical papers ; works on Diet were largely used by Ministry of Food and by U.S.A. Government in European War. *Recreations :* motoring and travel. *Address :* 119 Derby Road, Parkside, Nottingham. (*Died 26 Feb. 1928.*)

TICKELL, Rr.-Adm. Frederick, Director of Naval Reserves, Australia, since 1911 ; C.M.G. 1900 ; *b.* 7 Mar. 1857 ; *m.* 1886, Mary Elizabeth, *d.* of Edward G. Figg, M.D. Torpedo-Lieut., 1892-97 ; Commander 1897 ; Captain 1900 ; Naval Commandant, Victoria, 1897-1904, and 1907-10. Served with Victorian Naval Contingent, China, 1900-1 ; Naval Commandant, Queensland, 1904-7. *Address :* Delmira, Kew, Victoria, Australia.

(*Died 20 Sept. 1919.*)

TIGHE, Edward Kenrick Banbury, J.P. and D.L., Co. Kilkenny ; Director, Dublin and South-Eastern Railway ; *b.* 24 Aug. 1862 ; *s.* of Lieut.-Col. F. E. B. Tighe and Lady K. Ponsonby, *d.* of 4th Earl of Bessborough ; *m.* 1894, Viola, *d.* of E. Skeffington Smyth, D.L., Queen's Co. *Educ. :* Harrow ; Trinity College, Cambridge. Lieut. Rifle Brigade, 1884-87 ; served in Burmese War, 1886-88 (medal, two clasps) ; Grenadier Guards, 1887-93 ; contested N.W. Norfolk, 1895 ; High Sheriff, Kilkenny, 1895 ; Westmeath, 1903 ; Director Dublin, Wicklow, and Wexford Railway since 1894 ; The Hibernian Bank, Ltd., since 1912. *Recreation :* country life. *Address :* Woodstock, Inistioge, Co. Kilkenny. *Clubs :* Guards', Brooks's, Turf ; Kildare Street, Dublin.

(*Died 17 Nov. 1917.*)

TIGHE, Lieut.-General Sir Michael Joseph, K.C.B., *cr.* 1922 ; K.C.M.G., *cr.* 1916 ; C.I.E. 1912 ; C.B. 1911 ; D.S.O. 1889 ; Colonel-in-Chief 2nd Frontier Force Rifles (I.A.) ; *b.* 21 May 1864 ; *e. s.* of late Captain M. J. Tighe, 70th Regiment ; *m.* 1900, Katharine Helen Mackay-Scott, *d.* of late Hugh Baillie Scott ; one *s. Educ. :* Sandhurst. Joined Leinster Regiment, 1883 ; served in Burmese War, 1886-88 (medal and clasp) ; Red Karen Expedition, 1889 (clasp and D.S.O.) ; Chin-Lushai Expedition, 1889-90 (clasp) ; Chin Hills Expedition, 1890-91 (clasp) ; E. African Expedition, 1895 (medal and Brilliant Star of Zanzibar, 2nd class) ; Uganda, Ankole, and Unyoro Expeditions 1898-99 ; commanded Ankole operations (medal, clasp, and Bt. Maj.) ; operations in Mukran and S.E. Persia ; capture of Nodiz fort (Bt. Lieut.-Col.) ; served European War (East Africa), in chief command, 1914-16 (despatches, 1914 Star, Victory Medal, Allies Medal) ; 3rd Afghan War, 1919-20 (medal) ; Colonel, 1907 ; Major-Gen. 1915 ; Lieut.-Gen. 1920 ; retired, 1921. *Recreations :* big-game hunting, shooting, fishing, hunting, etc. *Address :* Kensington Palace Mansions, W.8. *Club :* Naval and Military. (*Died 5 Sept. 1925.*)

TIGHE, Major Vincent John, D.S.O. 1899 ; late West India Regt. and Manchester Regt. ; *b.* 1865 ; *s.* of late M. J. Tighe, Major 70th East Surrey Regt. ; *m.* 1906, Angela Lucy, 4th *d.* of Osmond Seager ; four *d.* Employed with Royal Niger Co. ; operations on the Niger, 1897-98 ; expeditions to Egbon, Bida, Ilorin (medal and clasp) ; expedition to Eboussa, Benin Hinterland, 1898 (clasp) ; to Siama, 1898 (wounded) ; employed West African Regt. 1899-1908 ; Ashanti Expedition, 1900 ; relief of Kumasi (medal and clasp). *Address :* 12 Leyburn Road, Dover. (*Died 7 June 1919.*)

TILDEN, Sir William Augustus, Kt., cr. 1909; D.Sc. Lond., Sc.D. Dublin, D.Sc. Victoria; LL.D. Birm.; F.R.S.; b. London, 15 Aug. 1842; e. s. of late Augustus Tilden; m. 1st, 1869, Charlotte (d. 1905), d. of late Robert Bush; one s.; 2nd, 1907, Julia Mary, y. d. of late C. W. Ramié. Educ.: various private schools; two years at Bedford school; Pharmaceutical Society; Royal College of Chemistry. Demonstrator at Pharmaceutical Society, 1864-72; Science Master, Clifton College, 1872-80; Professor of Chemistry, Mason College, Birmingham, 1880-94; President In. 'ute of Chemistry, 1891-94; Treas. Chemical Soc. 1899-1903; President, 1903-5; Professor of Chemistry, Royal College of Science, London, 1894-1909; and Dean of the College, 1905; Davy Medal, Royal Society, 1908; Emeritus Professor in the Imperial College of Science and Technology, 1909. Publications: Introduction to Chemical Philosophy, 1876; Practical Chemistry, 1880; Hints on Teaching Chemistry, 1895; A Manual of Chemistry, 1896; A Short History of the Progress of Scientific Chemistry, 1899; The Elements, 1910; Chemical Discovery and Invention in the Twentieth Century, 1917; Life of Sir William Ramsay, 1918; Famous Chemists, 1921; and many scientific papers. Address: The Oaks, Northwood, Middlesex.
(Died 11 Dec. 1926.)

TILLARD, Major-Gen. John Arthur, C.B. 1887; R.A.; retired; b. 13 Sep. 1837; s. of Philip Tillard of Stukeley Hall, county Huntingdon; m. 1st, Eliza Scott (d. 1895), d. of Gen. G. P. Whish, B.S.C.; three s. two d.; 2nd, Annie Jane, d. of G. J. Scott, and widow of H. Buckland, of Kiatoa, Otago, New Zealand. Educ.: Brighton College; Trinity College, Cambridge. 1st commission in the Royal (late Bengal) Artillery, 1857; Major-General, 1891; placed on retired list, 1895; served Afghan War, 1878-80; action of Ahmed Khel; march from Kabul to relief of Kandahar, and battle of 1st Sept. 1880 (despatches thrice, medal with 2 clasps, bronze star, brevet of Lt.-Col.); Burmese Expedition, 1886-87 (despatches, medal, C.B.). Address: c/o Barclay & Co., 54 Lombard Street, E.C. (Died 9 July 1928.)

TINLEY, Col. Gervase Francis Newport, C.B. 1909; C.M.G. 1916; Indian Army; b. 4 Nov. 1857; s. of Maj.-Gen. Robert Newport Tinley; m. 1st, Elsie Benton, d. of Col. W. B. Hughes, D.Q.M.G. U.S. Army; 2nd, Beryl R., d. of Francis Tytherleigh-Easton of Heatherwood House, Farnham; three s. two d. Educ.: Victoria College, Jersey; St. James's Collegiate School, Jersey; Sandhurst. Entered Army, 1875; Captain Indian Staff Corps, 1887; Major, 1896; Lt.-Col. Indian Army, 1902; Col. 1905; A.A.G. India, 1905-8; served Zhob Valley Expedition, 1884; Burmah, 1885-89 (wounded, horse shot, despatches, medal with two clasps); Egypt, 1896 (medal, Egyptian medal); European War, 1914-17 (despatches three times; C.M.G.); Commandant lines of communication, 1914-17. Address: Tower Hill House, Kingsclere, Hants. T.A.: Tinley, Kingsclere. (Died 18 Feb. 1918.)

TIRARD, Prof. Sir Nestor (Isidore Charles), Kt., cr. 1916; M.D., F.R.C.P.; Emeritus Professor of Medicine at King's College; Consulting Physician at King's Coll. Hospital; Consulting Physician to Evelina Hospital for Children, etc.; Crown Nominee on General Medical Council until 1927; Lt.-Col. commanding 4th London General Hospital, R.A.M.C. (T.); Order of St. Sava of Serbia, 2nd Class; b. 23 Sep. 1853; m. 1885, Helen Mary, d. of Rev. R. S. Beloe; one s. two d. Educ.: King's College Hospital. Scholarship and gold medal in Forensic and Obstetric Medicine, and Honours in Medicine at London University. Publications: Diphtheria and Anti-Toxin, 1896; Albuminuria and Bright's Disease, 1899; Medical Treatment (Diseases and Symptoms), 1900;

1044

senior editor, British Pharmacopœia, 1914; editor of King's College Hospital Reports. Recreations: sketching and fishing. Address: 74 Harley Street, W.1. T.: Langham 2646. Club: Athenaeum. (Died 10 Nov. 1928.)

TISDALL, Colonel Arthur Lance, C.M.G. 1914; late Royal Artillery; b. 25 Nov. 1860; s. of Major-General Archibald Tisdall, 85th Royal Sussex Regt.; m. 1898, Katherine Maud, widow of Major Alexander Gzowski, Welsh Regt., and d. of John Gordon Bowen, Burt House, Co. Donegal. Educ.: Clifton College; Woolwich. Lt. R.A., 1880; retired as Lieut.-Colonel, 1914; re-employed in Remount Service, 1915-19; Bt. Col. 1919. Address: Athgaine, Budleigh Salterton. T.: Budleigh Salterton 28. (Died 18 May 1927.)

TISDALL, Rev. William St. Clair, D.D.; b. 19 Feb. 1859; e. s. of Major William St. Clair Tisdall; m. Marian L., d. of Rev. W. Gray, M.A., Sec. C.M.S.; four s. (two killed in the War, one of whom gained the V.C. at the landing from River Clyde, Gallipoli, April 1915) four d. B.A. (1st class Classical Honours) and M.A., University of New Zealand; Hon. D.D. of Edinburgh University, 1903; deacon, 1882; priest, 1883; Vicar of Wakefield, Nelson, N.Z., 1882; Hebrew and Classical Lecturer, Bishopsdale Theological College, Nelson, 1883; Vice-Principal St. John's College, Lahore. Panjab, 1885; Principal Training College, Amritsar, Panjab, 1886; in charge C.M.S. Muhammadan Mission, Bombay, 1887; head of C.M.S. Persia and Baghdad Mission, 1892; James Long Lecturer on Islâm, Hindûism, Buddhism, and Comparative Religion, 1900-5; Hebrew Lecturer, C.M.S. Coll., Islington, 1910; Vicar of St. George-the-Martyr Corporation Church, Deal, Kent, 1913-26; Surrogate for Deal; H.C.F. 1916-1919. Publications: Christianity and Other Faiths; Comparative Religion; The Noble Eightfold Path; Religion of the Crescent; Religio Critici; Original Sources of the Qur'ân; Mythic Christs and the True; numerous pamphlets against Higher Criticism, etc.; translator of Four Gospels into Kirmanshâhi Kurdish; author of numerous works in the Persian language; contributor to Bible Encyclopædias, Victoria Institute Journal, etc.; author of Grammars of Gujarâti, Panjâbi, Urdû, and Persian languages. Recreation: literary work. Address: Ferahabad, Warwick Road, Walmer, Kent. (Died 1 Dec. 1928.)

TITHERIDGE, Lieut. Benjamin, M.V.O. 1909. Was chief gunner on Royal yacht Alexandra. Address: Woolston. Southampton. (Died Feb. 1918.)

TIVEY, Colonel Edwin, C.B. 1917; D.S.O. 1901; C.O. (Brigadier) 8th Infantry Brigade Australian Imperial Force, Foreign Service, 1915; b. 1866; m. 1906, Annie Bird, d. of John Robb, Toorak; one s. one d. Served South Africa, Victorian Imperial Bushmen and 2nd Commonwealth Horse, 1900-1902 (despatches twice, Queen's medal, 6 clasps, D.S.O.); European War, 1914-17 (C.B.). Address: Huntingtower Road, Malvern, Victoria, Australia. (Died Nov. 1917.)

TIZARD, Capt. Thomas Henry, R.N.; C.B. 1899; F.R.S.; Assistant Hydrographer of the Admiralty, 1891-1907; b. 1839; s. of late Joseph Tizard; m. 1881, Mary Elizabeth, d. of W. H. Churchward, C.E.; one s. four d. Joined the Navy as Master's Assist. 1854; served in the Baltic during the Russian War, 1854-56; present at the attack on Hango forts and the bombardment of Sveaborg (Baltic medal); joined the Surveying Service, 1861; was Navigating Officer of the "Challenger" in her expedition, 1872-76; contributed the Hydrographical part of the official narrative of that expedition; was in charge of Surveys in England, 1879-91. Publications: has contributed papers on the Exploration of the Faroe Channel to the Royal Society and

to the Royal Society of Edinburgh. *Address :* 23 Geneva Road, Kingston-on-Thames.
(*Died 17 Feb. 1923.*)

TOD, Hunter F., M.A., M.D., F.R.C.S.; 2nd *s.* of late David Tod, J.P., of *Eastwood* Park and Hartfield, Renfrewshire, N.B. ; Senior Surgeon, the Ear, Nose and Throat Department, London Hospital ; Lecturer in Aural Surgery at London Hospital Medical Coll.; late Surgeon, Throat and Ear Department, Paddington Green Children's Hospital ; *m.* Yvonne Grace, *e. d.* of Stanley Rendall, of Chantmerle, Aix-les-Bains, France ; one *s.* three *d. Educ. :* Clifton College ; Trinity College, Cambridge ; London Hospital ; Leipzig, Vienna, Halle, Berlin. *Publications :* Diseases of the Ear, Oxford Medical Manuals ; Operations on the Ear, Burghard's System of Operative Surgery ; Diseases of the External Auditory Canal and Tympanic Membrane, in Allbutt and Rolleston's System of Medicine. *Address :* 11 Upper Wimpole Street, W.1. *T. :* 4750 Paddington. *M. :* LD 19 ; LH 3265. *Clubs :* Oxford and Cambridge, Royal Automobile.
(*Died 23 Jan. 1923.*)

TODD, Howard, C.B. 1911 ; Hon. Surgeon to the King ; *b.* 20 Sep. 1855 ; *s.* of M. G. Todd, Hove, Brighton, and M. A., *d.* of Capt. Pryce, R.N. ; *m.* 1893, Florence Agnes, *d.* of E. Haynes, Thimbleby, Yorks ; one *s.* two *d. Educ. :* Dr. Seaver's, Brighton ; St. Thomas's Hospital (Prizeman). Served Niger Expedition, 1879 ; yellow fever epidemic, Jamaica, 1885-86 (received thanks of Admiralty) ; thanked by Foreign Office for services rendered at Mapanda's Kraal, acting Consular Surgeon, 1891 ; Surgeon-General Royal Navy ; J.P. Hampshire. *Recreations :* golf, tennis, fishing. *Address :* Anglesey House, Anglesey, nr. Gosport, Hants.
(*Died 6 Nov. 1925.*)

TODD, (John) Spencer Brydges, C.M.G. 1878 ; I.S.O. 1905 ; *b.* Dresden, 28 Aug. 1840 ; *y. s.* of late Col. George Todd and Mary, *d.* of Sir Egerton Brydges, Bart. ; *m.* Susan Margaret, *e. d.* of late Baron Goert van Reede van Oudtshoorn, 1865 ; two *s.* two *d. Educ. :* Blochmann's Gymnasium, Dresden ; and the Imperial Lyceum, St. Omer. Civil Service, Cape of Good Hope, 1860-1904 ; Sec., Department of Agent - Gen. in London, 1882 - 1904 ; Executive Commissioner for the Cape, and an International Juror, Paris Universal Exhibition, 1878 ; C.M.G. for services as such ; I.S.O. on retirement. *Publications :* The Resident Magistrate at the Cape of Good Hope, 1882 ; Handy Guide to Laws and Regulations at the Cape of Good Hope, 1887. *Address :* Hotel Roland, 3 and 4 Roland Houses, South Kensington, S.W.1. (*Died 15 April 1921.*)

TODD, Sir Joseph White, 1st Bt., *cr.* 1913 ; Chairman of Central Argentine Railway and Director Buenos Ayres Western Railway ; Deputy-Chairman Callander and Oban Railway ; Member of the Royal Commission on Sugar Supply, 1917-21 ; Member International Sugar Committee, New York and Washington, 1917-18; *b.* Stirlingshire, 23 June 1846 ; *m.* 1st, 1879, Aline Fannie (*d.* 1924), *d.* of Louis Lefebvre of New York, and *widow* of T. Orihuela ; no *c.* ; 2nd, 1925, Euphemia, *widow* of Charles Day Halsey, of New York, *o. d.* of Ed. Burot Grubb, formerly U.S. Minister to Spain. *Educ. :* privately. Resided in Havana, Cuba, several years, Merchant Banker, and retired in 1885 ; has Grand Cross of Spanish Order of Merit. *Recreations :* shooting, fishing, etc. *Heir :* none. *Address :* 33 Eaton Place, S.W.1 ; *T. :* Victoria 508 ; Morenish Lodge, Killin, Perthshire. *Clubs :* Reform. City of London. (*Died 19 Feb. 1926.*)

TODHUNTER, John, M.D. ; author ; *b.* Dublin, 30 Dec. 1839 ; *e. s.* of late Thomas Harvey Todhunter, merchant ; *m.* 1st, Katharine, *d.* of late Robert Ball, LL.D., Dublin, 1870 ;

2nd, Dora Louisa, *d.* of late William A. Digby, Dublin, 1879 ; one *s.* two *d. Educ. :* York School ; Trinity College, Dublin. M.D. and M.Ch. Dublin ; Vice-Chancellor's Prize for English Verse, 1864, 1865, 1866 ; Gold Medallist Philosophical Society (for Prose Essay), 1866. Studied in Vienna and Paris, and practised Medicine for some years in Dublin ; Professor of English Literature, Alexandra Coll. Dublin, 1870-74 ; travelled on the Continent and in Egypt, and finally settled in London. *Publications :* The Theory of the Beautiful (a lecture delivered in Trin. Coll.), 1872 ; Laurella and other Poems, 1876 ; Alcestis, 1879 ; A Study of Shelley, 1880 ; True Tragedy of Rienzi, and Forest Songs, 1881 ; Helena in Troas, 1885 (performed 1886) ; The Banshee, and other Poems, 1888 ; A Sicilian Idyll (several times performed), 1890 ; The Poison Flower (performed 1891) ; The Black Cat (performed 8 Dec. 1893), pub. 1895 ; A Comedy of Sighs (performed 1894) ; Life of Sarsfield, 1895 ; Three Irish Bardic Tales, 1896 ; Sounds and Sweet Airs, 1905 ; translation of Heine's Book of Songs, 1907. *Recreation :* sketching. *Address :* Orchardcroft, Bedford Park, W. *Clubs :* Savile, Odd Volumes, Poets', Authors', Pepys, Omar Khayyam.
(*Died 25 Oct. 1916.*)

TOLE, Hon. Joseph Augustus, K.C., B.A., LL.B. ; Crown Solicitor and Crown Prosecutor, Auckland, N.Z. ; *b.* Wakefield, Yorkshire, England ; 5th and *y. s.* of late John Tole, land surveyor ; *m.* Eleanor, *d.* of Edward Lewis ; one *s.* three *d. Educ. :* St. John's College, Sydney ; University of Sydney. Admitted Bar, N.S.W., 1871, and N.Z. Bar, 1872 ; M.P. 1876-87 ; Minister of Justice, 1884-87 ; drafted and carried through Parliament, First Offenders' Probation Act, 1886 (the first in the Empire) ; Member of Board, Governors of Grammar School, and of University College, and also a Fellow of University of N.Z. *Recreations :* music, reading, walking, billiards. *Address :* Remuera, near Auckland, N.Z. *T. :* 722. *Clubs :* Northern, Pacific, Auckland.
(*Died 13 Dec. 1920.*)

TOLLEMACHE, Arthur Frederick Churchill, *heir* to Baronetcy of 9th Earl of Dysart; *b.* 1 Aug. 1860 ; *m.* 1888, Susan Eleanor (*d.* 1919), *e. d.* of Capt. J. C. Campbell, R.N., of Ardpatrick, Argyllshire, N.B. ; two *d. Educ. :* Eton ; Christ Church, Oxford (B.A. 1883). J.P. King's Co. ; High Sheriff, 1888. *Clubs :* Arthur's ; Kildare Street, Dublin ; St. George's Yacht. (*Died 18 Aug. 1923.*)

TOLLEMACHE, David, F.R.S.L., Author and Journalist ; *m.* 1913, Grace, *d.* of late W. H. Dodd. *Educ. :* Larchfield, Helensburgh; Andersonian University, Glasgow. Member of Council Royal Society of Literature, 1904-7 ; Freeman of City of London and of the Worshipful Company of Spectacle - Makers ; Assistant Literary Secretary, Tariff Reform League, since 1907. Formerly editor Court Circular, Commercial Traveller, Trade and Industry, Home and Export Trade Review, and Insurance Agents' News ; editor, Cassell's Newspaper Press Agency, 1905; has contributed short stories under the pen-name of Mark Lovell, and political and social articles, to many periodicals; leader-writer and London Correspondent of many provincial newspapers. *Publications :* English Coronations ; The Story of the English Boroughs ; Bible Stories for Young Readers ; Cassell's New Dictionary of Cookery, 1904 ; Wayside Warblings. *Recreations :* the drama, Freemasonry (P.M., P.Z., L.R.) *Address :* 7 Grand Parade Mansions, Muswell Hill, N. *Club :* Constitutional.
(*Died Nov. 1918.*)

TOLLEMACHE, Hon. Lionel Arthur, author ; *b.* 28 May 1838 ; 2nd *s.* of 1st Baron Tollemache and Georgina Best ; *m.* Hon.

Beatrix Lucia Catherine Egerton, 4th *d.* of 1st Baron Egerton of Tatton, 1870 (author of Russian Sketches). *Educ.:* Harrow; Balliol College, Oxford; Balliol Scholar, 1856; 1st class Classics and honorary class in Mathematics, 1860. *Publications:* Safe Studies and Stones of Stumbling, 1891; Benjamin Jowett, a Personal Memoir, 1895; Talks with Mr. Gladstone, 1898; Old and Odd Memories, 1908; Nuts and Chestnuts, 1911. *Recreations:* debarred by extreme near-sightedness from ordinary amusements; hearing poetry and novels read aloud, and studying human nature. *Address:* Dunrozel, Haslemere, Surrey. *Club:* Athenæum.
(Died 29 Jan. 1919.)

TOLLNER, Col. Barrett Lennard, C.B. 1902; R.A.; *b.* 25 Nov. 1839. Entered army, 1861; Captain, 1875; Major, 1881; Lieut.-Col. 1889; Col. 1894; Assistant Inspector of Remounts, Woolwich, 1899-1905; Inspector since 1905. *Address:* 42 Half Moon Street, W.
(Died 25 Nov. 1918.)

TOMASSON, (Capt. Sir William Hugh), K.B.E., *cr.* 1920; C.B.E. 1918; M.V.O. 1906; Chief Constable of Notts since 1892; Assistant Inspector of Constabulary; *b.* 1858; *m.* 1882, Eliza, *d.* of late George Lees. *Educ.:* Clifton. *Address:* Woodthorpe, Nottingham. *Clubs:* Boodle's, Pratt's. *(Died 12 Oct. 1922.)*

TOMBS, Robert Charles, I.S.O. 1902; *b.* 11 Nov. 1842; *s.* of officer in Bengal Horse Artillery, Hon. East India Company's Service; of Gloucestershire family; *m.* Annie Maria, *d.* of William Brown Rooff, of Highgate, London; four *s.* one *d.* *Educ.:* Stratford-on-Avon. Appointed Clerk, Foreign Branch, General Post Office, under competitive system, 1861; Principal Clerk, Circulation Department, 1868; Assistant Controller, London Postal Service, 1884; Controller, 1887; retired through ill-health, 1892; Special Postal Mission to Ireland, 1870-73; served on many Departmental Committees. *Publications:* London Postal Service of To-Day; Visitors' Guide to the General Post Office; Bristol Royal Mail; Service Instruction Books; The King's Post; The Tombs Families of the Cotswolds, etc. *Recreations:* genealogy, archæology, and literature. *Address:* Henleaze, nr. Bristol. *(Died 18 Sept. 1925.)*

TOMES, Sir Charles Sissmore, Kt., *cr.* 1919; M.A., LL.D., F.R.S., F.R.C.S.; *b.* London, 6 June 1846; *s.* of late Sir John Tomes, F.R.S., and Jane Sibley. *Educ.:* Radley; Christ Church, Oxford; Middlesex Hospital. 1st class, Natural Science. Was examiner in dental surgery at Royal College of Surgeons for fourteen years; Inspector of dental examinations in United Kingdom on behalf of General Medical Council, 1895-96; Crown nominee on and Treasurer of General Medical Council; late Vice-President Zoological Society. *Publications:* papers relating to Odontology, in Phil. Trans. of Royal Society, etc.; A Manual of Dental Anatomy, Human and Comparative, 6th ed. 1904. *Recreations:* shooting, fishing, motoring. *Address:* Welbeck House, Wigmore Street, W.; Mannington Hall, Aylsham. *M.:* H 1621. *Clubs:* Savile; Norfolk, Norwich. *(Died 24 Oct. 1928.)*

TOMKINS, Ernest William, C.I.E. 1920; O.B.E. 1919; Inspector-General of Police, North West Frontier Province, since 1920; *b.* 19 May 1872; *s.* of late Rev. G. W. Tomkins, M.A. *Educ.:* privately. Entered the Indian Police, 1893; officiating Inspector-General of Police, North-West Frontier Province, 1919; mentioned in London Gazette for valuable services in connection with the War, 1919; 1914-15 Star and 3rd Afghan War medal, British War medal, 1914-1918 Victory medal. *Address:* Peshawar, North-West Frontier Province, India.
(Died 20 Nov. 1925.)

TOMKINS, Lieut.-Col. Harry Leith, C.M.G. 1916; D.S.O. 1898; late 28th Punjabis,

Indian Army; *b.* 1870; *s.* of late Samuel Leith Tomkins. Entered 4th King's Own (Royal Lancashire) Regt. 1890; Lieut. 1893; joined Indian Army, 19th Punjabis, 1894; 28th Punjabis, 1895; Capt. 1901; Major, 1908; served N.W. Frontier, India, 1894-95, Waziristan (medal and clasp); 1897-98, as Railway Staff Officer, Line of Communications (despatches, D.S.O.); 1901-2, N.W. Frontier, India, Mahsud Waziri (medal and clasp); 1903-4, Somaliland, with 27th Punjabis (medal and clasp); N.W. Frontier, India, 1908; operations in the Zakkha Khel country (medal and clasp); European War, 1914-17 (despatches twice, Bt. Lt.-Col., C.M.G.); Assistant Military Secretary and A.D.C. to G.O.C. Northern Army, India; retired 1920. *Club:* Junior United Service.
(Died 20 Feb. 1926.)

TOMKINS, Gen. William Percival, C.I.E. 1890; Colonel Commandant R.E.; *b.* 11 June 1841; *s.* of late Samuel Tomkins; *m.* 1864, Annie, *d.* of late Robert Thurburn. Entered army, 1860; General, 1898; served Zhob Valley Expedition, 1884. *Address:* 120 Lexham Gardens, S.W. *Club:* East India United Service.
(Died 19 Nov. 1922.)

TOMKINSON, Michael, J.P., D.L., Alderman, C.C. Worcestershire; J.P. Shropshire; *b.* 1841; 2nd *s.* of Michael Tomkinson, of Leamington; *m.* 1871, Annie, *d.* of M. P. Stonehouse, of Wakefield, Yorks; seven *s.* five *d.* *Educ.:* privately. Mayor of Kidderminster, 1887, 1893, 1894, 1895, 1905, 1912; High Sheriff for Worcestershire, 1892; Governor of Birmingham University and Member of Council. *Publication:* A Japanese Collection, 2 vols., 1898. *Recreations:* shooting, fishing, interested in Japanese art, early printed books and manuscripts, member of Roxburghe Club. *Address:* Franche Hall, near Kidderminster, Worcestershire; Chilton, Cleobury Mortimer, Shropshire. *Club:* Burlington Fine Arts. *(Died 28 June 1921.)*

TOMPKINS, Engineer Captain Albert Edward, C.B.E. 1919; R.N.; Royal Navy (retired); Director, Tangential Dryers, Limited; *b.* 30 May 1863; *s.* of late John Tompkins, of Aveley Hall, Essex; *m.* Dorothea Frances, *e. d.* of late Edmund G. Reader, Genoa; one *d.* *Educ.:* private schools. Appointed to H.M.S. Marlborough, Portsmouth, as R.N. Engineer Student, 1878; Engineer Commander, 1901; Engineer Captain (retired), 1913; China, 1885-1886; Mediterranean, 1886-88 and 1890-94; Australia, 1897-1900, including warlike operations in Samoa, H.M.S. Porpoise under Commander (later Admiral) Sturdee, Annexation of Savage Island and Protectorate of Tonga Islands; Engineer Commander of Flagship of Second Cruiser Squadron, 1906-7; Flagship of East Indies Squadron (Admiral Sir E. Slade), 1909-11, during Persian Gulf Blockade (N.G.S. medal, Persian Gulf clasp, and East African medal, Somaliland clasp); Instructor in Marine Engineering at R.N. College, Greenwich, and Lecturer to the R.N. War Colleges, 1902-6; on War service; appointed to Clyde District to supervise Emergency Repairs; transferred to Italy in 1917 in charge of repairs to H.M. ships and vessels by Italian private firms (despatches, C.B.E.). *Publications:* Marine Engineering (a Text-Book), 5th edition; Turbines (Romance of Science Series), 3rd edition. *Address:* Tiptoe, 8way, Hants. *(Died 10 Sept. 1927.)*

TOMPSON, Maj.-Gen. William Dalrymple, C.B. 1879; Colonel of the Leicestershire Regiment, 1912; *b.* 1833; *m.* 1884, Ellen Mary, *d.* of late William Carroll. *Educ.:* Cheltenham. Entered army, 1852; Maj.-Gen. 1884; served Crimea, 1855 (dangerously wounded, despatches, medal with clasp, Turkish medal, Kt. of Legion of Honour); Afghan War, 1878-79 (despatches, C.B., medal with clasp). *Address:* Iver House, Iver, Bucks. *Club:* Army and Navy.
(Died 7 Dec. 1916.)

TOMSON, Rev. John, M.A.; Prebendary of Hereford since 1913. *Educ.:* Magdalene College, Cambridge, M.A. Deacon, 1878; priest, 1879. Rector of Rochford, Worcester, 1892-1919. *Address:* Engleton, Tenbury.
(Died 28 Jan. 1926.)

TOOTH, Howard Henry, C.B. 1918, C.M.G. 1901; Hon. M.D. Malta Univ.; M.A., M.D. Cantab., F.R.C.P., Consulting Physician to St. Bartholomew's, the National Hospital for the Paralysed and Epileptic, and the Metropolitan Hospitals; late Examiner in Medicine, Cambridge and Durham Universities; late Censor, Royal College of Physicians; temp. Col. A.M.S. Consulting Physician to troops in Malta and Italy (despatches twice); Col. A.M.S. (T.F., Res.) retired; late O.C. 1st London General Hospital. and Medical Unit Officers' Training Corps, London University Contingent; *b.* 22 April 1856; *s.* of late Frederick Tooth of Hove, Sussex; *m.* 1st, 1881, Mary Beatrice (*d.* 1905), *d.* of late Edward Price; one *d.*; 2nd, 1908, Helen Katharine, O.B.E. 1920, 2nd *d.* of Rev. C. S. Chilver; one *s.* two *d.* *Educ.:* Rugby School; St. John's Coll., Cambridge. *Decorated for service in South Africa as Physician to the Portland Hospital, and as Physician to troops in Malta. Publications:* Many contribution to scientific and medical societies and journals. *Address:* The Moat, Hadleigh, Suffolk; *T.:* Hadleigh 20; 90 Harley Street, W.1; *T.:* Mayfair 3311. *(Died 13 May 1925.)*

TOOVEY, Rev. Henry, M.A. Oxon. 1868; Canon and Prebendary of Botevant in York Minster since 1898; Master of Lord Leycester's Hospital, Warwick, since 1901; Chaplain to Lord De L'Isle and Dudley since 1880; *b.* 1843; *s.* of John and Marianna Toovey; *m.* Jane, *e. d.* of Robert Hubie of Barlby Grove, Yorkshire; one *d. Educ.:* France; Worcester College, Oxford. Private Sec. and Domestic Chaplain to the Earl of Feversham, 1867-70; Vicar of Ingleby Greenhow, Yorks, 1870-80; Inspector of Schools for the Diocese of York, 1880-1902; Rector of Newton Kyme, Yorks, 1894-1902. *Address:* The Master's Lodge, Lord Leycester's Hospital, Warwick. *Club:* Warwick and County, Warwick. *(Died 17 July 1922.)*

TOPHAM, Frank W. W., R.I.; *b.* London, 1838; *s.* of late F. W. Topham, R.W.S.; *m.* 1870, Helen, *d.* of Mark Lemon, editor of Punch; three *s.* five *d. Educ.:* private schools in England and France; in art Royal Academy Schools and Atelier Gleyre, Paris. Since 1863 constant exhibitor at the Royal Academy and other exhibitions throughout the country; among other pictures, the following are in permanent Public Galleries: Burning the Vanities by order of Savonarola, Sydney, N.S.W., Australia; A Roman Triumph, Leicester; A Prize in the Lottery, Leeds; The Fall of Rienzi, Liverpool; Drawing for the Conscription, Modern Italy, Manchester; The Emigrant's Letter, Reading; Rescued from the Plague. London, 1665. *Recreation:* gardening. *Address:* Coneyhurst, Ewhurst, Guildford. *(Died 25 May 1924.)*

TOPPING, Colonel (Hon. Brig.-Gen.) Thomas Edward, C.B. 1919; C.M.G. 1917; D.S.O. 1900; A.D.C. West Lancashire Territorial Artillery; (retired). Served 1st Brigade Imperial Yeomanry, South Africa (despatches, Queen's medal four clasps, D.S.O.); European War, 1914-18 (C.M.G., C.B.). *Address:* Whitehall Court, S.W. *Club:* White's.
(Died 8 July 1926.)

TORR, Cecil; *b.* 1857; *s.* of late T. S. Torr, and *g.s.* of late John Torr of Wreyland, unmarried. *Educ.:* Harrow; Trinity College, Cambridge. Called to the Bar, 1882. *Publications:* Ancient Ships, and other antiquarian works; also Small Talk at Wreyland. *Address:* Wreyland, near Lustleigh, Devon.
(Died 17 Dec. 1928.)

TORR, Rev. William Edward, M.A.; Vicar of Eastham, 1880-1917; Hon. Canon of Chester Cathedral; *b.* 18 July 1851; *e. surv. s.* of late John Torr, M.P.; *m.* Julia Elizabeth (*d.* 1920), *d.* of John Holmes of Somerfield, Maidstone; two *s.* three *d. Educ.:* Harrow; Trinity College, Cambridge. Vicar of Flamstead, Herts, 1878-80; succeeded to Carlett Park, 1880; Proctor in York Convocation, 1895-1910. *Address:* Carlett Park, Eastham, Cheshire. *T.A.:* Eastham. *T.:* 86 Bromborough (Birkenhead). *M.:* K 4337. *(Died 17 Sept. 1924.)*

TORRE - DIAZ, Count de, Brodie Manuel de Zulueta; G.C.S.G.; G.C.I.C.; retired Banker; *b.* 1842; *s.* of 2nd Count de Torre-Diaz and Sophia Anne, *d.* of Brodie M'Ghie Willcox, M.P.; *m.* 1st, 1873, Constance, *d.* of Hon. Frederick Petre; one *s.* three *d.*; 2nd, 1892, Hon. Bertha Clifford, *d.* of 8th Lord Clifford of Chudleigh. Conservative; Roman Catholic. *Address:* 21 Devonshire Place, W.
(Died 20 Sept. 1918.)

TORREY, Reuben Archer; Special Lecturer Moody Bible Institute, Chicago; *b.* Hoboken, New Jersey, 28 Jan. 1856; *s.* of R. S. Torrey and Elizabeth A. Swift; *m.* 1879, Clara B. Smith, Garrettsville, Ohio; one *s.* two *d. Educ.:* Yale; Leipsic; Erlangen. Entered Congregational Ministry, 1878; was Superintendent of the Minneapolis City Mission Society; joined late D. L. Moody at Chicago, 1889; Superintendent Moody Bible Institute, Chicago, 1889-1906; pastor of Chicago Avenue Church, 1894-1906; conducted Torrey-Alexander Mission in Australia, New Zealand, India, and Great Britain, 1902-5; conducted Torrey Missions in United States and Canada, 1906-11; Torrey Missions in England, Scotland, and Ireland, 1911; Dean of the Bible Institute of Los Angeles, 1912-24; Pastor, Church of the Open Door, Los Angeles, 1914-24; Missions in China and Japan, 1902, 1919, 1921; Torrey Missions in U.S., Canada, and other lands since 1924. *Publications:* How to bring Men to Christ; How to obtain Fulness of Power; The Baptism with the Holy Spirit; What the Bible Teaches; Divine Origin and Authority of the Bible; How to Work for Christ; How to Promote and Conduct a Successful Revival; Revival Addresses; How to Study the Bible for Greatest Profit; Real Salvation; How to Pray; How to Succeed in the Christian Life; The Bible and its Christ; The Gist of the Lessons; Anecdotes and Illustrations; Difficulties and Alleged Contradictions in the Bible; Practical and Perplexing Questions Answered; Studies in the Life and Teachings of our Lord; The Person and Work of the Holy Spirit; The Return of the Lord Jesus; The Joy of Soul Winning; The Fundamental Doctrines of the Christian Faith; The Voice of God in the Present Hour; The Real Christ; Jesus the Prophet, the Priest, the King, the Wonder; The Importance and Value of Proper Bible Study; Is the Bible the Inerrant Word of God?; The Gospel for To-day; New Evangelistic Sermons for a New Age; The God of the Bible; How to be Saved and How to be Lost; The Christ of the Bible; Soul Winning Sermons; The Power of Prayer and the Prayer of Power; Divine Healing; Why God used Dr. L. Moody; The Bible the Peerless Book, God's Own Book, and God's Only Book; How to get the Gold out of the Word of God; The Holy Spirit: Who He Is and What He Does; The Conversion and Christian Training of Children; Exposition Lectures on the First Epistle of John. Some of these books have been translated into thirty - four different languages. *Address:* Asheville, North Carolina, U.S.A.; Chicago, Illinois, U.S.A.; Montrose, Pennsylvania, U.S.A. *T.A.:* Bible, Chicago.
(Died Oct. 1928.)

TOSTI, Sir F. Paolo, K.C.V.O., cr. 1908 composer; Hon. C.V.O., 1906; *b.* Abruzzi, 1847

Educ.: Conservatoire, Naples. Came to England, 1876. *Songs:* Come to my Heart, For ever and for ever, Good-bye, That Day, Let it be soon, Ask me no more, Help me to pray, Yesterday, At the Convent Gate, We have loved, Tell them! *(Died 2 Dec. 1916.)*

TOTHILL, Admiral Sir Hugh Henry Darby, K.C.B., *cr.* 1923 ; K.C.M.G., *cr.* 1918 ; K.C.V.O., *cr.* 1921 ; C.B. 1916 ; A.D.C. ; Admiral commanding Reserves, 1923-25 ; *b.* 14 Mar. 1865 ; *m.* 1892, Hilda Montgomerie, *d.* of late John Beddoe, F.R.S. Served Egyptian War, 1882, including bombardment of Alexandria (medal, star) : European War, 1914-1918, including Battle of Jutland Bank, 1916 (despatches, C.B.) ; Commander-in-Chief, East Indies, 1919-21 ; 4th Sea Lord of the Admiralty, 1917-19 ; Vice-Adm. 1921 ; Admiral, 1926. *Address:* The Chantry, Bradford - on - Avon, Wilts. *Clubs:* Army and Navy, Wellington.
(Died 25 Sept. 1927.)

TOTTENHAM, Col. Charles George, D.L. Co. Wicklow ; J.P. Cos. Wexford and Wicklow ; *b.* 11 April 1835 ; *s.* of Charles Tottenham of Ballycurry and Isabella Catherine, *d.* of Gen. Sir G. Airey ; *m.* 1859, Catherine Elizabeth (*d.* 1905), *d.* of Hon. and Rev. Sir F. Stapleton, 7th Bt. ; four *d.* *Educ.:* Eton. Served in Scots Fusilier Guards ; gained 5th class of Medjidie and British and Turkish medals ; M.P. New Ross, 1863-68, and 1878-80 ; Hon. Col. Wicklow Militia Artillery. *Address:* Ballycurry, Ashford, Co. Wicklow. *T.A.:* Ashford, Wicklow. *Clubs:* Carlton ; Kildare Street, Dublin ; Irish Automobile. *(Died 10 May 1918.)*

TOULMIN, Sir George, Kt., *cr.* 1911 ; *b.* Bolton, 17 March 1857 ; *m.* 1882, Mary Elizabeth, *e. d.* of late Alderman Thomas Edelston, Preston ; two *s.* two *d.* *Educ.:* Preston Grammar School. Newspaper proprietor ; managing director of the Lancashire Daily Post and Preston Guardian ; Chairman Press Association, 1919-20 ; Hon. Treasurer, Newspaper Society ; J.P. Co. Lancaster, 1906, and County Borough of Preston, 1897 ; Fellow Institute of Journalists ; contested Bury (L.), 1900 ; M.P. (L.) Bury, 1902-18. *Address:* 127 Fishergate, Preston. *Clubs:* Reform, National Liberal, Eighty ; Ninety-five, Manchester.
(Died 21 Jan. 1923.)

TOWER, Charlemagne, American Ambassador to Germany, 1902 - 8 ; *b.* Philadelphia, 17 Apr. 1848 ; *s.* of Charlemagne and Amelia Bartle Tower, 8th in descent from John Tower who emigrated from Hingham, in Norfolk, to Massachusetts, in 1637 ; *m.* 1888, Helen, *d.* of G. Frank Smith of San Francisco, California ; three *s.* two *d.* *Educ.:* Exeter Academy, New Hampshire, 1868 ; graduated Harvard Univ. 1872. Called to the Bar at Philadelphia, 1878 ; LL.D. Glasgow and St. Andrews, Chicago, 1903, Hamilton, 1909, Lafayette, 1897 ; attaché, U.S. Legation, Madrid, 1872-73 ; studied history and literature in Spain, France, and Germany, 1873 - 76 ; President, Duluth and Iron Range Railway ; Managing Director, Minnesota Iron Company, 1882-87 ; President, Finance Company of Penna, 1887 ; Member of the Board of City Trusts of Philadelphia, 1915 ; President of the Historical Society of Pennsylvania, 1917 ; Minister to Austria-Hungary, 1897 ; Ambassador to Russia, 1899-1902 ; Member Board of Trustees Carnegie Endowment for International Peace ; Grand Officer of the Legion of Honour of France ; Grand Cordon of St. Alexander Nevsky of Russia. *Publications:* The Marquis de La Fayette in the American Revolution, 1895 ; Essays Political and Historical, 1914 ; The Origin, Meaning, and International Force of the Monroe Doctrine, 1921. *Address:* 228 South Seventh Street, Philadelphia, Pennsylvania, U.S.A. *Clubs:* Metropolitan, University, New York ; Rittenhouse, Union League, Philadelphia. *(Died 25 Feb. 1923.)*

1048

TOWER, Christopher John Hume, J.P., D.L. ; *b.* 20 Jan. 1841 ; *e. s.* of Christopher Tower Huntsmoor, and Lady Sophia Frances Cust, *d.* of 1st Earl Brownlow ; *m.* 1st, 1865, Mary (*d.* 1865), 2nd *d.* of Rev. Delves Broughton, Broughton Hall ; 2nd, 1883, Cecilia, *o. d.* of Rev. R. B. Tower and *widow* of Osgood Hanbury. *Educ.:* Harrow ; Christ Church, Oxford. High Sheriff of Essex, 1876. *Address:* Wealdside, Brentwood. *T.A.:* South Weald.
(Died 11 July 1924.)

TOWERS-CLARK, James ; *b.* 1852 ; *e. s.* of late William Towers-Clark of Wester Moffat and 2nd wife, Isabella, 3rd *d.* of James Curle of Evelaw, Berwick ; *m.* 1880, Annie, 4th *d.* of late Thomas Lever Rushton. Major North Somerset Imperial Yeomanry ; late Captain 1st Royal Dragoons. *Address:* The Hooke, Chailey, Sussex. *Clubs:* Army and Navy ; New, Edinburgh ; Western, Glasgow ; Royal Yacht Squadron, Cowes. *(Died 19 Nov. 1926.)*

TOWNSEND, Surg.-Gen. Sir Edmond, K.C.B., *cr.* 1904 ; R.A.M.C., C.B., C.M.G., 1900 ; M.A., M.D., M.Ch. ; retired ; *b.* 1845 ; *s.* of late W. C. Townsend, M.D. of Cork ; *m.* 1884, Frances Josephine, *d.* of late J. W. MacMullen, J.P. Clontymon, Cork ; one *s.* two *d.* Entered army, 1867 ; Surg.-Gen. 1901 ; served Abyssinian Campaign, 1867-68 (medal) ; Malay Peninsula, 1875-76 (severely wounded ; medal with clasp) ; Zulu War, battle of Ulundi, 1879 (despatches) ; operations against Sekukuni (medal with clasp) ; Egyptian War, 1882, including Kassassin, Tel-el-Kebir (medal with clasp, Khedive's star) ; Burmese Expedition, 1885 - 86 (medal with clasp) ; Ashanti Expedition, 1885 - 86 (despatches, star) ; North-West Frontier of India, 1897-98 ; P.M.O. Mohmund Field Force (despatches) ; P.M.O. 1st Div. Tirah Expeditionary Force (despatches, C.B., medal with two clasps) ; South Africa, 1899-1902, P.M.O. 1st Div., and afterwards P.M.O. Western District, Belmont, Enslin, Modder River, Magersfontein, Paardeberg (despatches, dangerously wounded, C.M.G., Queen's medal four clasps, King's medal two clasps). *Address:* Clontymon, Cork, Ireland. *(Died 3 Jan. 1917.)*

TOWNSEND, Frederick Henry, A.R.E., Artist ; Art Editor, Punch, since 1905 ; *b.* 25 Feb. 1868 ; *m.* ; one *s.* Studied at Lambeth School of Art. *Publications:* Illustrated Kipling's They and Brushwood Boy ; has contributed drawings to Lady's Pictorial, Illustrated London News, Graphic, Sphere, Tatler, Queen, etc. *Recreations:* cricket, golf, fencing. *Address:* 89 Hampstead Way, N.W.4. *T.:* 994 Finchley. *Clubs:* Arts, Chelsea Arts ; Hampstead Golf.
(Died 11 Dec. 1920.)

TOWNSEND, Thomas Sutton, J.P. and C.C. for Warwickshire ; Lord of the Manor, and Lay Rector of Clifton - upon - Dunsmore, near Rugby ; *e.s.* of late William Townsend of Clifton Manor, Warwickshire ; *b.* 1847 ; *m.* 1st, 1877, Mary Alice (*d.* 1896), *d.* of late Thomas Ainsworth, D.L., the Flosh, Cumberland ; 2nd, 1904 Ursula Verelst, 3rd *d.* of Lord Justice Farwell ; one *s.* one *d.* *Educ.:* Rugby. Medical practitioner in London ; landowner in Warwickshire ; a member of many public bodies in the county, Chairman of Income Tax Commissioners for the Rugby and Monk's Kirby Divisions, and has been Chairman of Parish Council since its commencement ; restored the chancel of the Parish Church of Clifton-upon-Dunsmore, and built a Working Men's Club and Village Hall. *Address:* Clifton Manor, near Rugby ; 68 Queen's Gate, S.W. *T.:* 276 Kensington, 85 Rugby. *Clubs:* Athenæum, Reform. *(Died 4 Dec. 1918.)*

TOWNSHEND, 6th Marquess (*cr.* 1786), **John James Dudley Stuart Townshend,** D.L. ; Bt. 1617 ; Baron Townshend, 1661 ; Viscount Townshend, 1682 ; High Steward of Tamworth ; *b.* 17 Oct. 1866 ; *s.* of 5th Marquess

and Lady Anne Elizabeth Clementina Duff, *d.* of 5th Earl of Fife, K.T.; *S.* father 1899; *m.* 1905, Gladys Ethel Gwendolen Eugenie, *e. d.* of late Thomas Sutherst, Barrister; one *s.* one *d.* [The Marchioness Townshend is the author of In the King's Garden (verse); Maxims and Musings; and several other literary works.] Owns about 20,000 acres. *Heir: s.* Viscount Raynham.   *Address:* 78 Avenue Road, Regent's Park, N.W.8.   *T.:* Hampstead 4535.
                         (Died 17 Nov. 1921.)

TOWNSHEND, Hon. Sir Charles James, Kt., *cr.* 1911; D.C.L. King's College University, Windsor, Nova Scotia, 1908; *b.* 22 March 1844; *s.* of Rev. Canon Townshend, Rector of Christ Church, Amherst, Nova Scotia; *m.* 1st, 1867, Laura, *d.* of J. D. Kinnear; 2nd, 1887, Margaret, *d.* of John M'Farlane; three *s.* two *d.* *Educ.:* Collegiate School and King's College, Windsor, Nova Scotia (B.A. 1862, B.C.L. 1872). Barr. Canada, 1866; Q.C. 1881; M.L.A. Cumberland, 1878 and 1882; to House of Commons of Canada, 1884; M.E.C. 1878-82; Judge of Supreme Court of Nova Scotia, 1887-1907; Chief Justice of the Supreme Court of Nova Scotia, 1907-15; Chancellor of King's College, Windsor, Nova Scotia, 1912. *Address:* Halifax, Nova Scotia. *Club:* Halifax, Halifax.   *(Died June 1924.)*

TOWNSHEND, Maj.-Gen. Sir Charles (Vere Ferrers), K.C.B., *cr.* 1916; C.B. 1895; D.S.O. 1898; M.P. (Ind.) Wrekin Division of Salop, 1920-22; *g.s.* of late Lord George Townshend; *cousin* and *heir-pres.* of 7th Marquess Townshend; *b.* 21 Feb. 1861; *m.* 1898, Alice, *d.* of Comte Cahen d'Anvers; one *d.* Entered Royal Marines, 1881; I.S.C. 1886; Capt. 1892; Major, 1895; Lt.-Col. 1896; Col. 1904; Brig.-Gen. 1909; Maj.-Gen. 1911; Royal Fusiliers, 1900; Shropshire Light Infantry, 1908; served Soudan Expedition, at Suakim with Mounted Infantry, and in Nile Expedition with the Guards' Camel Regiment in Desert Column actions of Abu Klea and Gubat, 1884-85 (despatches, medal with two clasps, bronze star); Hunza Nagar Expedition, 1891-92 (despatches, medal with clasp); commanded garrison of Chitral Fort during siege (thanked by Government of India, despatches, medal with clasp, Brevet Major, C.B.); Dongola Expedition, 1898 (despatches, medal with two clasps, Brevet Lt.-Col.); Atbara, 1898 (despatches, clasp); Nile Expedition, 1898 (despatches, D.S.O.) South Africa, 1899-1900; European War (Mesopotamia), 1914-16 (despatches, K.C.B.); commanded 6th Division and Force in Mesopotamia battles of Kurna, Kut-el Amara, Ctesiphon, and Defence of Kut; commanding a Division Territorial Force, 1912-13; resigned, 1920. *Publications:* Life of Field-Marshal 1st Marquis Townshend; My Mesopotamia Campaign, 1920. *Address:* Vere Lodge, Raynham, Norfolk. *Clubs:* Bachelors', Brooks's, White's, Naval and Military; Union, Paris.
                        (Died 18 May 1924.)

TOWNSHEND, Colonel Frederick Trench; *b.* 1838; *y. s.* of late Richard Townshend of Myross Wood, Co. Cork, and Helen, *d.* of Very Rev. T. Trench, Dean of Kildare, *bro.* of Lord Ashtown. *Educ.:* Harrow; Oxford. B.A. 1860; F.R.G.S.; entered 2nd Life Guards, 1861; Capt. 1865; Major, 1877; Lieut.-Col. 1882; Colonel, 1886; commanded 2nd Life Guards, 1888; retired from army, 1895; served Egyptian Campaign, 1882 (wounded, medal, Khedive's star, Brevet Lieut.-Col., order of Osmanieh); with United States troops on staff of General Augur in Sioux Indian War, 1868. *Publications:* three books of travel. *Address:* 6 William Street, Lowndes Square, S.W. *Clubs:* Arthur's, Bachelors', Carlton.   *(Died 3 June 1924.)*

TOWNSHEND, Captain Harry Leigh, J.P. Warwickshire; · *b.* 27 June 1842; *s.* of

Henry Townshend; *m.* 1880, Hon. Annie Ellen, *d.* of 1st Lord Crawshaw; one *s.* *Educ.:* Westminster. Served in the Royal Dragoons and in the 12th Suffolk Regiment; Sheriff for Warwickshire, 1901. *Address:* Caldecote Hall, Nuneaton. *Club:* Arthur's.*(Died 30 April 1924.)*

TOY, Crawford Howell, A.M. (University of Virginia); Professor of Hebrew in Harvard University since 1880; Professor Emeritus since 1909; *b.* Norfolk, Virginia, 23 March 1836; *e. s.* of late Thomas Dallam Toy and Amelia, *d.* of James Rogers; *m.* Nancy, *d.* of Rev. R. M. Saunders, 1888. *Educ.:* University of Virginia. Instructor in Albemarle Institute, 1856-59; attached to the Confederate Army, 1861-64; Professor in University of Alabama, 1864-5; studied at University of Berlin, 1866-68; Professor of Hebrew in Southern Baptist Theological Seminary, 1869-79. *Publications:* Religion of Israel, 1882; Quotations in the New Testament, 1884; Judaism and Christianity, 1890; Ezekiel (revised Hebrew text and translation), 1899; Proverbs (revised translation and commentary), 1899; Introduction to the History of Religions, 1913. *Recreations:* walking, rowing. *Address:* 7 Lowell Street, Cambridge, Massachusetts, U.S.A. *T.A.:* Cambridge, Mass.   *(Died 12 May 1919.)*

TOYNE, Rev. Frederick Elijah; Hon. Canon of Winchester, 1905; Ordained, 1877; Curate of Mudeford, Hants, 1877-81; Vicar of St. Michael's. Bournemouth, 1881-1915. *Address:* 4 Drury Road, Bournemouth.
                       (Died 9 Sept. 1927.)

TOZER, Rev. Henry Fanshawe, M.A.; F.R.G.S.; Hon. Fellow of Exeter College since 1893; *b.* 18 May 1829; *o. s.* of Aaron Tozer, Captain Royal Navy, of Plymouth, and Mary Hutton of Lincoln; *m.* 1868, Augusta Henrietta, *d.* of H. D. C. Satow of Upper Clapton. *Educ.:* Winchester; Univ. and Exeter Coll. Oxford (2nd cl. Lit. Hum. 1850); Fellow Exeter Coll. 1850; Tutor, 1855-93; Classical Moderator in Honours, 1866-68, 1873, 1878-79, 1882-84; Curator of the Taylor Institute, 1869-93; Fellow of the British Academy; Corresponding Member of Historical Society of Greece, and of the United Armenian Educational Societies; Hon. Member of the Parnassus Philological Society of Athens. Has travelled extensively in Greece, and in European and Asiatic Turkey. *Publications:* The Highlands of Turkey, 2 vols. 1869; Lectures on the Geography of Greece, 1873; Primer of Classical Geography, 1877; Turkish Armenia and Eastern Asia Minor, 1881; The Church and the Eastern Empire, 1888; The Islands of the Aegean, 1890; History of Ancient Geography, 1897; An English Commentary on Dante's Divina Commedia, 1901; English Prose Translation of Dante's Divina Commedia, 1904. *Edited:* Finlay's History of Greece, 1877; Wordsworth's Greece, 1882; Byron's Childe Harold, with introduction and notes, 1885; Selections from Strabo, with introduction and notes, 1893; various contributions to Ency. Brit., Journal of Hellenic Studies, Classical Review, the Academy, and other literary periodicals. *Address:* 18 Norham Gardens, Oxford.   *(Died 2 June 1916.)*

TOZER, Hon. Sir Horace, K.C.M.G. *cr.* 1897; Solicitor in Brisbane; *b.* N.S.W., April 1844; *m.* 1st, 1868, Mary Hoyles Wilson; 2nd, 1880, Louisa Lord (*d.* 1908). *Educ.:* Collegiate School, Newcastle, and Sydney, N.S.W. Member of Gympie Social Mining Court, 1868; elected Alderman 1st Municipal Council, Gympie, 1880; Secretary for Public Works, 1890-93; Colonial and afterwards Home Secretary, 1890-98; Acting Prime Minister, Queensland, Mar. to Nov. 1897; Official Representative Queensland Government in London, 1898-1909; under his direction Free Public Library and National Art Gallery were started

in 1896. *Address:* Brisbane. Queensland.
(*Died 21 Aug. 1916.*)

TRACY, Louis ; C.B.E. 1920; author; *b.* Liverpool, 18 March 1863 ; *m.* ; one *s. Educ.:* privately in Yorkshire, and in France. Began journalism on the Northern Echo, Darlington, 1884; thence went to Cardiff, 1886; and to Allahabad, India, 1889 ; returned to England, 1893, and acquired an interest with others in The Evening News, 1894 ; went to United States, 1895 ; revisited States and Delhi, Punjab, 1896-1900 ; Sub - commandant, Whitby District North Riding Regt. of Volunteers, Oct. 1915 ; went to United States, Mar. 1916, and lectured and wrote extensively on the war ; joined the Headquarters Staff of the British War Mission in the U.S.A., 13 Sep. 1917 ; liquidator of British Bureau of Information ; temporarily attached to Foreign Office, July 1919 ; later, while on Editorial Staff of the Times and Daily Mail, became Member of Westminster Abbey Restoration Fund, and collected many thousands of pounds for the Fund in U.S.A. during 1921. *Publications:* The Final War, 1896 ; Rainbow Island, 1904 ; The Pillar of Light, 1905 ; Waifs of Circumstance, 1906 ; The Wheel o' Fortune, 1907 ; The Red Year, 1908 ; The Message, 1909 ; The Stowaway, and A Son of the Immortals, 1910 ; The Silent Barrier ; The Silent House ; Sylvia's Chauffeur, 1911 ; Mirabel's Island, 1912 ; The Only Way, One Wonderful Night, The Terms of Surrender, 1913 ; Diana of the Moors, 1914 ; His Unknown Wife and Number 17, 1915 ; Flower of the Gorse ; The Day of Wrath, 1916 ; The Postmaster's Daughter ; The Revellers, 1917 ; The Second Baronet, 1923 ; The Park Lane Mystery, 1923 ; The Turning Point ; The Token, 1924 ; The Passing of Charles Lanson ; The Black Cat ; The Gleave Mystery, 1925 ; The Law of the Talon, 1926 ; The Third Miracle ; The Woman in the Case, 1927. *Address:* c/o Barclays Bank, Ltd., Whitby, Yorkshire. *Clubs:* Authors, Savage ; Lotos, New York.
(*Died 13 Aug. 1928.*)

TRAIL, James William Helenus, M.A., M.D., F.L.S., F.R.S. ; Regius Prof. of Botany University of Aberdeen since 1877 ; *b.* Birsay, Orkney, 4 Mar. 1851 ; *y. s.* of late Very Rev. Samuel Trail, D.D., LL.D., Professor of Systematic Theology in the University of Aberdeen 1867-87 ; Moderator of the Church of Scotland, 1874 ; *m.* Katherine, *e. d.* of late Very Rev. Wm. Milligan, Professor of Biblical Criticism in the University of Aberdeen, 1860-93 ; Moderator of the Church of Scotland, 1882. *Educ.:* home ; Grammar School, Old Aberdeen ; University of Aberdeen. M.A. with Highest Honours in the Natural Sciences ; M.B. and C.M. with Highest Honours. Travelled in North Brazil as Naturalist of an Exploring Expedition, 1873-75. *Publications:* numerous papers on botanical and zoological subjects in scientific journals. *Recreations:* field botany, zoology, and the mutual relations of plants and animals. *Address:* University, Aberdeen.
(*Died 18 Sept 1919.*)

TRAILL, Major Thomas Balfour, D.S.O. 1914 ; 1st Batt. Royal Scots Fusiliers ; *b.* 21 Nov. 1881 ; *o. s.* of late Major-General George Traill, C.B. ; *m.* 1918, Winifred Jean Bertha, *d.* of Major W. A. Warren. Entered army, 1900 ; Indian army, 1902 ; Captain, 1909 ; served European War, 1914-17 (wounded, despatches, D.S.O., Bt. Major). *Club:* Cavalry.
(*Died 7 July 1920.*)

TRAIN, Rev. John Gilkison ; Moderator of the Synod of the Presbyterian Church of England, 1907-8; *b.* 1847. *Educ.:* Collegiate School and University of Glasgow ; Theological Hall, Edinburgh ; Universities of Leipsic and Tübingen. Ordained, St. David's Church, Buckhaven, 1874 ; Inducted, Prospect Street Church, Hull, 1886 ;
1050

Inducted, St. Andrew's Church, Norwood, 1892 ; Re-inducted, Prospect Street Church, Hull, 1905 ; Inducted, United Free Church of Scotland, Southend, Presbytery of Kintyre, 1914. *Address:* U.F.C. Manse, Southend, Argyll.
(*Died 17 Nov. 1920.*)

TRASK, Katrina ; living in retirement on her estate since the death of her husband ; *d.* of George L. Nichols, English descent, and Christina Cole, Dutch descent : *m.* 1874, Spencer Trask, banker ; no *c. Educ.* ; private schools and tutors. The life of the home and of society, and the education of her children ; later, after her children were taken, devoted herself to literary work ; owns the estate of Yaddo, to be left to literary and other artists. *Publications:* Sonnets and Lyrics ; Night and Morning ; The Mighty and the Lowly, 1915, and various stories, etc., under her own name ; Mors et Victoria and King Alfred's Jewel, published anonymously in England ; the third edition of King Alfred's Jewel published in her own name ; and In the Vanguard, etc. *Recreations:* walking, improvising on the piano. *Address:* Yaddo, Saratoga Springs, N.Y., U.S.A.
(*Died 7 Jan. 1922.*)

TRAVANCORE, H.H. Sir Bala Rama Varma, Maharajah of, G.C.I.E. *cr.* 1903 ; G.C.S.I. *cr.* 1888 ; M.R.A.S.. Officier de l'Instruction Publique ; Hon. Col. of 10th Batt. 3rd Madras Regt., 1923 ; *b.* 25 Sep. 1857 ; *S.* 1885. The State has an area of 6730 square miles and a population of 3,000,000. *Address:* The Palace, Trivendrum, Travancore, South India.
(*Died 7 Aug. 1924.*)

TRAVERS, Graham (*nom de guerre* of **Dr. Margaret Todd**), novelist, and late assistant physician to Edinburgh Hospital for Women and Children ; *b.* 1859 ; *d.* of James Cameron Todd of Glasgow and Rangoon. *Educ.:* Edinburgh and Glasgow University Classes for Women, and in Berlin. Engaged in teaching ; studied at Edinburgh School of Medicine for Women ; L.R.C.P. and S.Ed. ; M.D. Brux. 1894. *Publications:* Mona Maclean, 1892 ; Fellow Travellers, 1896 ; Windyhaugh, 1898 ; The Way of Escape, 1902; Growth, 1906. *Address:* 18 Challoner Mansions, W. *Club:* Lyceum. (*Died 3 Sept. 1918.*)

TRAVIS, Harry, C.B.E. 1920 ; I.S.O. 1911 ; M.I.M.E., M.I.N.A. ; Advising Officer on Boats and Vessels to H.M. Customs ; late Superintending Engineer and Constructor of Shipping, Royal Arsenal ; *b.* 18 July 1858 ; *s.* of John Travis, of Devonport ; *m.* 1881, Emmeline, *d.* of G. Hamlyn, late of Roborough, South Devon; one *s.* one *d. Educ.:* Devonport. Was a pupil for five years with the firm of Robert Napier & Sons, engineers, etc., Glasgow, and student at Glasgow Univ. ; joined the War Dept., 1881 ; Assist. Superintending Engineer and Constructor of Shipping, 1891 ; invented the means for improving the speed of targets used in Royal Artillery practice from fortresses. *Address:* Custom House, E.C. (*Died 5 Nov. 1927.*)

TRAVIS, Rev. James ; *b.* Summit, Littleborough, 6 Mar. 1840 ; *m.* Jane Killip, Lonan, Isle of Man : one *d. Educ.:* privately. Entered ministry, 1858 ; President of National Council of Evangelical Free Churches, 1903-1904 ; President of Primitive Methodist Conference, Norwich, 1892 ; formerly General Missionary Secretary and Superintendent Home Missions ; an Examiner of Candidates for the Ministry for 13 years ; superannuated, 1906. *Publication:* 75 Years. *Address:* 3 Waterloo Road, Chester.
(*Died 5 Dec. 1919.*)

TRAVIS, Rev. William Travis, Hon. Canon of Ripon. *Address:* The Rectory, Ripley, Yorks. (*Died 2 May 1924.*)

TREACHER, Sir William Hood, K.C.M.G., *cr.* 1904 ; M.A. Oxford ; *b.* Wellington, Somerset, 1 Dec. 1849 ; *y. s.* of late Rev.

TRAPANI, Lt.-Col. Alfred, M.V.O. See page xxxi.

J. S. Treacher; *m.* 1881, Cornelia, *d.* of Rev. J. Rumsey; two *d.* Colonial Secretary, Labuan; Acting Consul - General, Brunei; employed on a mission to the Sulu Islands and North Borneo, in connection with Spanish claims; first Governor of British North Borneo, 1881-87; Secretary to Government, Perak, 1888; British Resident, Selangor, 1892; British Resident, Perak, 1896; acted as Resident-General, Federated Malay States, 1897-98, 1900-1901; Resident-General, Federated Malay States, 1902-1904 (retired). *Publication*: British Borneo. *Address*: 97 Cadogan Gardens, S.W. *T.*: Kensington 4959; St. Stephen's Cottage, St. Albans. *T.*: St. Albans 418. *M.*: LO 6494. *Clubs*: Oriental, Sports, City Carlton.

(*Died 3 May 1919.*)

TREANOR, Ven. James, Archdeacon of Tuam since 1898; Rector of Ballinrobe since 1882. *Educ.*: Trinity College, Dublin (M.A.). Ordained, 1870; Curate of Tuam, 1870-74; Rector of Athenry, 1874-77; Kiltullagh, 1877-1882; Canon of Tuam, 1887-90; Provost, 1890-98. *Address*: Ballinrobe, Co. Mayo.

(*Died 15 May 1926.*)

TREASURE, William Houston, I.S.O. 1914; Clerk to Legal Adviser to Secretary of State for India, 1887; to Solicitor of the Supreme Court, 1887; Assist. to the Legal Adviser, 1892; Assist. Solicitor, 1900; Commissioner for Oaths, 1908; retired, 1913. *Address*: India Office, S.W.

(*Died 3 Mar. 1916.*)

TREBLE, Rev. Edmund John; Rector of Morningthorpe, Norfolk, since 1908. *Educ.*: King's Coll. London (Theological Associate, 1st in first class, 1885; Hebrew Prizeman, 1884; Prayer-Book Prize, 1885; Universities' Preliminary Theological Examination, 1st in first class, 1885; Gospeller at Ordination); and Freiburg University (Canon Law and History of Art). Appointed to Board of Trade, Whitehall Gardens, 1873; retired 1884; deacon, 1885; priest, 1886; served curacies in Marylebone and Hackney; chaplain at Freiburg in Black Forest, 1891-1900; travelled in Greece and Egypt, 1899; acted as chaplain at Assouan, winter 1899-1900; English Chaplain, Wiesbaden, 1900-1906; Curate, Hunstanton, 1906-8. *Publications*: Plain Teaching about the Church of England, 1893; Sermons on Sunday Observance, 1893; Anglican Jurisdiction on the Continent, 1898; Notes on Morning and Evening Prayer, 1912; articles in journals and magazines; contributor to the Encyclopædia Britannica (10th ed.), 1902; editor of The Chaplaincy Quarterly Magazine, 1900-1906. *Recreations*: older novels, walking. *Address*: The Rectory, Morningthorpe, Norfolk.

(*Died 19 June 1924.*)

TREDCROFT, Lieut.-Col. Charles Lennox, J.P., Surrey; Hon. Lieutenant-Colonel Royal West Surrey Regiment (2nd Vol. Batt.); *o. s.* of Rev. R. Tredcroft of Tangmere, Sussex, and *d.* of Sir T. Brooke Pechell, 2nd Bart.; *b.* 24 Oct. 1832; *m.* 1st, 1863, Harriette Sophia Louisa (*d.* 1869), *e. d.* of J. H. Woodward; 2nd, 1871, Elizabeth (*d.* 1886), *e. d.* of Sir William Scott, 6th Bart. of Ancrum; 3rd, 1889, Hon. Constance Mary Fitz-Alan Howard, *d.* of 1st Lord Howard of Glossop; two *s.* four *d. Educ.*: Woolwich. Late Capt. R.H.A.; served Crimea, 1855-56 (medal and clasp, and Turkish medal and order of Medjidie); and County Alderman, 1889-1904. *Address*: Glen Ancrum, Guildford. *T.A.*: Guildford. *Club*: Army and Navy. (*Died 20 Dec. 1917.*)

TREE, Sir Herbert Beerbohm, Kt., *cr.* 1909; actor; *b.* London, 17 Dec. 1853; 2nd *s.* of Julius Beerbohm and Constantia Draper; *m.* Maud Holt; three *d. Educ.*: Schnepfenthal College, Germany. Made his first appearance on the stage in 1877; became manager of the

Haymarket Theatre in 1887; relinquished its management in 1896; is now proprietor and manager of His Majesty's Theatre; holds Order of St. John of Jerusalem, also Crown of Italy. *Publications*: lectures on The Imaginative Faculty, and on Hamlet from an Actor's Prompt Book, Henry VIII. and His Court; Thoughts and Afterthoughts, 1913, etc. *Address*: 1 All Souls' Place, Portland Place, W. *T.*: Gerrard 2135. *Clubs*: Garrick, Beefsteak, Green Room, Royal Automobile. (*Died 2 July 1917.*)

TREFFRY, Charles Ebenezer, J.P.; *b.* 1 May 1842; *m.* 1st, 1866, Udney Maria Blakeley, *d.* of Baron von Bretton; one *s.* two *d.*; 2nd, 1905, Henrietta, 2nd *d.* of late John Kingsley, Manchester. High Sheriff of Cornwall, 1886; late Captain 2nd Brigade Western Division R.A., first Mayor of Fowey under new Charter. *Heir*: *s.* Edward. *Address*: Place, Fowey, Cornwall. (*Died 27 Feb. 1924.*)

TREFUSIS, Lady Mary; Woman of the Bedchamber to H.M. the Queen since 1895; *d.* of 6th Earl Beauchamp and Lady Mary Catherine, *d.* of 5th Earl Stanhope; *m.* 1905, Lieut.-Col. Hon. H. W. H.-S.-F.-Trefusis; one *s.* Hon. Secretary Church Music Society since 1906; President English Folk Dance Society since 1912; Member Church Assembly and Missionary Council. *Recreation*: music. *Address*: Trefusis, Falmouth. (*Died 12 Sept. 1927.*)

TREGEAR, Major-General Sir Vincent William, K.C.B., *cr.* 1909; U.S. list, Indian Army; *b.* 25 June 1842; *e. s.* of Vincent Tregear, Educational Department, Government of India; *m.* 1867 (*d.* 1899), Jane Charlotte, *e. d.* of William Oswald Bell; three *s.* one *d. Educ.*: private school. Entered Bengal Army, 1859: served in the 19th P.I., 41st B.I., 29th P.I., and commanded the 9th B.I. Regiment; Colonel on the Staff at Mooltan, Punjab, 1895-1897, when vacated on promotion to Maj.-Gen.; served Afghanistan, 1879-80, with Khyber Field Force (medal); N.E. Frontier of India, Lushai, 1889, commanded the Force (thanks of Government, despatches); Chin-Lushai, 1889-90, commanded the Chittagong Column (mentioned by Government of India, medal with 2 clasps, C.B.). *Address*: c/o Henry S. King and Co., 9 Pall Mall, S.W.1. *Club*: Royal Albert Yacht, Southsea.

(*Died 17 July 1925.*)

TREHERNE, Rev. Charles Albert, M.A.; Vicar of Tintagel, N. Cornwall, since 1919; *b.* 25 July 1856; *m.* 1886, Mabel, *d.* of late Richard Dodd, Calcutta: one *s. Educ.*. Godolphin School; Sheffield Collegiate; Gonville and Caius College, Cambridge (scholar). Curate of St. John the Evangelist, Newbury, 1880; Dilbury Vicar in Hereford Cathedral, 1882; Curate of Tupslev, 1883; Minor Canon, St. George's Chapel, Windsor, 1884; Curate, Eton, 1885; Curate, Clewer, 1892; Divinity Lecturer at St. George's Chapel, 1884; Vicar of All Saints, Hereford, 1895; Chaplain, H.M. Prison, Hereford, 1902; Prebendary of Moreton and Whaddon in Hereford Cathedral, 1918. *Recreations*: music and painting. *Address*: The Vicarage, Tintagel. (*Died 16 Nov. 1919.*)

TRELAWNY, Sir William Lewis Salusbury-, 10th Bt., *cr.* 1628; D.L., J.P.; *b.* 26 Aug. 1844; *S.* father, 1885; *m.* 1st, Jessy, *o. d.* of Sir John Murray, 6th Bt. 1868 (*d.* 1871); one *s.* one *d.*; 2nd, Harriet, *d.* of Rev. James Buller Kitson, Vicar of Morval, Cornwall; two *s.* two *d. Educ.*: Eton; Trin. Coll. Camb. Late Capt. 3rd Batt. Duke of Cornwall's Light Infantry. Owns about 8000 acres. *Heir*: *s.* John William [*b.* 6 May 1869; *m.* 1st, 1891, Agnes Hedewig Helga, *e. d.* of W. B. Braddick (who divorced him); one *d.*; 2nd, 1905, Catherine Penelope (Mrs. W. C. Howard), *d.* of late A. S. Cave-Browne-Cave; one *s.*]. *Address*: Trelawne, Duloe, Cornwall. *Club*: Brooks's

(*Died 30 Nov. 1917.*)

TRELOAR, Sir William Purdie, 1st Bt., *cr.* 1907; Kt., *cr.* 1900; Alderman (Ward of Farringdon Without) since 1892; Principal of firm of Treloar and Sons, Ludgate Hill; Director and Trustee of T. Cook and Son, Egypt, Ltd. ; one of Sheriffs of London, 1899-1900 ; Lord Mayor, 1906 - 7 ; Founder of the Lord Mayor Treloar Cripples Hospital and College, Alton and Hayling Island, Hants ; Hon. Fellow of the British Orthopædic Assoc. ; J.P. Kent, Surrey; and London; *b.* London, 13 Jan. 1843 ; 2nd *s.* of late Thomas Treloar, of Helston, Cornwall ; *m.* 1865, Annie (*d.* 1909), *d.* of G. Blake. *Educ.:* King's College School. Member of the Corporation of the City of London since 1880 ; Chairman of the Commissioners of Sewers, 1891 ; Deputy Chairman Commissioners of Income Tax for City of London ; Presented with the honorary freedom of the City of Truro, the Boroughs of Bury St. Edmunds, Croydon, Helston, and Okehampton ; Knight of several foreign Orders. *Publications:* Ludgate Hill, Past and Present ; Prince of Palms ; Wilkes and the City, 1917 ; A Lord Mayor's Diary, 1920. *Recreation:* reading. *Heir:* none. *Address:* Grange Mount, Upper Norwood, S.E.19. *T.A.:* Treloar, London. *T.:* Sydenham 238. *Clubs:* Carlton, Savage, Press, Whitefriars, Authors'.
(Died 6 Sept. 1923.)

TREMATON, Viscount; Rupert Alexander George Augustus Cambridge; *b.* 24 Aug. 1907 ; *e. s.* of Earl of Athlone. *Educ.:* Eton. *(Died 15 April 1928.)*

TRENCH, Hon. Cosby Godolphin, J.P., D.L.; *b.* 6 Jan. 1844 ; *y. s.* of 2nd Lord Ashtown and Henrietta, *d.* of Thomas Phillips Cosby ; *m.* 1873, Maria, *e. d.* of Sir Richard Musgrave, 4th Bt. ; three *s. Educ.:* Eton ; Sandhurst ; Corpus Christi College, Oxford. High Sheriff, Tipperary, 1886 ; formerly Capt. 1st Royal Dragoons ; contested North Tipperary (L.U.), 1892. *Recreations:* shooting, riding, motoring. *Address:* Sopwell Hall, Cloughjordan, Co. Tipperary. *T.A.:* Ballingary Roscrea. *Clubs:* Naval and Military ; Kildare Street, Dublin. *(Died Dec. 1925.)*

TRENCH, Hon. Frederic Sydney; 2nd Lieut. 3rd Batt. K.R.R.C.; *e. s.* of 3rd Baron Ashtown ; *b.* 9 Dec. 1894. *Educ.:* Eton ; Sandhurst ; Magdalen Coll. Oxford. Entered army, 1914. Served European War, 1914-16 (wounded). *(Died 24 Nov. 1916.)*

TRENCH, Herbert; writer of poems and plays ; late Senior Examiner and Assistant Director of Special Enquiries at Board of Education ; *b.* Avoncore, Co. Cork, Nov. 1865 ; *m.* 1891, Lilian Isabel, *d.* of Robert Fox, of Grove Hill, Falmouth, and Penjerrick, Cornwall ; two *s.* three *d. Educ.:* Haileybury ; Oxford. Fellow of All Souls' College ; Examiner at the Board of Education, 1891 ; went up the Nile, 1888, and has travelled in Syria, Russia, Austria, Spain, Morocco, Algeria, and rural Italy ; retired 1908. While Director of the Haymarket Theatre staged Shakespeare's King Lear, Maeterlinck's The Blue Bird, Bunty Pulls the Strings, etc. ; Hon. Vice-Chairman of the Istituto Britannico, Florence, for which he drew up the scheme that obtained the first grant from the British Government for the promotion, by means of a public library and lectures, of better mutual understanding between Great Britain and Italy, 1918. *Publications:* Deirdre Wedded and nineteen other poems, 1901 : also New Poems ; Apollo and the Seaman, Stanzas to Tolstoy, the Questioners, 1907 ; Lyrics and Narrative Poems, 1911 ; Ode from Italy in time of War, 1915 ; Poems with Fables in Prose (including Bitter Serenade, Battle of the Marne, etc.), 1917 ; Napoleon (a play), 1918. *Address:* Villa Viviani, Settignano, Florence. *Clubs:* Athenæum, United University.
(Died 11 June 1923.)

TRENHOLME, Hon. Norman William; Judge Court of King's Bench, Quebec, since 1904 ; *b.* 18 Aug. 1837 ; *m.* 1st, 1868, Lucy Wilkes (*d.* 1885), *d.* of late Samuel Hedge, Montreal ; 2nd, 1886, Grace Low, *d.* of late Robert Shaw, Quebec. *Educ.:* McGill University. Advocate, 1865 ; K.C. 1889 ; Professor of Roman and Public Law, McGill University, 1868-88 ; Puisne Judge, Superior Court, 1901. *Address:* 65 Rosemount Avenue, Montreal. *Club:* University, Montreal. *(Died 25 June 1919.)*

TREVELYAN, Sir Ernest John, Kt., *cr.* 1909 ; D.C.L. ; Assessor Chancellor's Court, Oxford, since 1910 ; Fellow and Subwarden, All Souls College, Oxford ; Member Oxford University Hebdomadal Council, 1914-1920 ; Chairman Court of Referees under National Insurance Act (Unemployment Insurance), Oxford ; Chairman Local Munitions Tribunal, Oxford and Reading, 1914-19 ; *b.* 7 Dec. 1850 ; 2nd *s.* of late Maj.-Gen. H. W. Trevelyan, C.B., R.A. ; *m.* 1st, 1880, Mary Katherine (*d.* 1885), *d.* of late Patrick Black. M.D.: one *s.* ; 2nd, 1890, Julia Isabel (*d.* 1903), *d.* of E. W. Mark ; four *d.* ; 3rd, 1909, Winifred Helen, *d.* of late Sir C. U. Aitchison, K.C.S.I. Barrister, Middle Temple, 1873 ; Judge, High Court, Calcutta, 1885-98 ; Vice - Chancellor, Calcutta University, 1897-98 ; Reader in Indian Law, Oxford Univ., 1900-23 ; Lecturer in Hindu and Mahomedan Law to the Council of Legal Education, 1910-14 ; Councillor Oxford Town Council, 1905 - 15. *Publications:* Works on Indian Law. *Address:* 1 Marston Ferry Road, Oxford. *T.:* Oxford 399. *Club:* Oriental. *(Died 29 July 1924.)*

TREVELYAN, Rt. Hon. Sir George Otto, 2nd Bt., *cr.* 1874 ; O.M. 1911 ; P.C.; LL.D., D.C.L., D.L. ; resigned as M.P. 30 Jan. 1897 ; *b.* Rothley Temple, Leicestershire, 20 July 1838 ; *o. s.* of 1st Bt. and Hannah More, *d.* of Zachary Macaulay, Secretary of the Anti-Slavery Society, and *sister* of the historian Lord Macaulay ; *S.* father,1866; *m.* 1869, Caroline, *d.* of R. N. Philips, formerly M.P. for Bury, Lancashire, of the Park, Manchester, and Welcombe, Stratford-on-Avon ; three *s. Educ.:* Harrow ; Trin. Coll. Camb. 2nd Scholar and Honorary Fellow of Trin. Coll. Camb. ; Honorary Fellow of Oriel College, Oxford ; M.P. Tynemouth, 1865 ; Hawick Burghs, 1868 ; Bridgeton Division of Glasgow, 1887-97 ; Civil Lord of the Admiralty, 1868 ; Secretary of the Admiralty, 1880 ; Chief Secretary for Ireland, 1882 ; Chancellor of the Duchy of Lancaster, with a seat in the Cabinet, 1884 ; Secretary for Scotland, 1886 ; again Secretary for Scotland, 1892 ; took an active part in furthering the abolition of purchase in the Army, and the extension of Household Suffrage to the counties. *Publications:* The Ladies in Parliament, Horace at the University of Athens, and other pieces, collected and published in 1868 ; The Competition Wallah, 1864 ; Cawnpore, 1865 ; The Life and Letters of Lord Macaulay, 1876 ; Selections from the Writings of Lord Macaulay, 1876 ; The Early History of Charles James Fox, 1880 ; The American Revolution (four vols.), 1909 ; Interludes in Prose and Verse, 1905 ; George III. and Charles Fox, vol i. 1912, vol. ii. 1914. Owns about 14,000 acres. *Recreations:* shooting, country pursuits generally, touring in Italy. *Heir: s.* C. P. Trevelyan. *Address:* Wallington, Cambo, Northumberland; Welcombe, Stratford-on-Avon. *(Died 17 Aug. 1928.)*

TREVES, Sir Frederick, 1st Bt. *cr.* 1902 ; G.C.V.O., *cr.* 1905 ; K.C.V.O. 1901 ; C.B. 1901 ; LL.D., M.D., F.R.C.S. ; Serjeant Surgeon to the King; Surgeon in Ordinary to Queen Alexandra ; Knight of Grace of the Order of St. John of Jerusalem; consulting surgeon to the London Hospital; Lord Rector Aberdeen Univ., 1905-8 ; *b.* Dorchester, 15 Feb. 1853 ; *m.* 1877, Annie, *y. d.* of

A. S. Mason of Dorchester; one *d.* *Educ.*: Merchant Taylors' School. Hunterian Prof. of Anatomy and Wilson Prof. of Pathology, Royal College of Surgeons, 1881-6; Examiner in Surgery, Univ. of Cambridge, 1891-96; Col. A.M.S.; late President of Headquarters Medical Board at War Office; Member of the Army Sanitary Committee, War Office; late Member of the Advisory Board of the Army Medical Service; one of the Founders of the British Red Cross Society, and First Chairman of Executive Committee; Chairman of the Radium Institute; Consulting Surgeon to Forces in South Africa, 1900; was with the Ladysmith relief column (medal and three clasps); performed the operation upon H.M. King Edward VII. on 24 June 1902; Sergeant Surgeon to King Edward VII.; Surgeon Extraordinary to Queen Victoria, 1900-1. *Publications:* Physical Education; System of Surgery; Manual of Operative Surgery: Surgical Applied Anatomy; treatises on Intestinal Obstruction, Peritonitis, and Appendicitis; German - English Dictionary of Medical Terms; Tale of a Field Hospital, 1900; The Other Side of the Lantern, 1905; Highways and Byways in Dorset, 1906; Cradle of the Deep, 1908; Uganda for a Holiday, 1910; The Land that is Desolate, 1912; The Country of the Ring and the Book, 1913; The Riviera of the Corniche Road, 1921; The Lake of Geneva, 1922. *Recreations:* boat - sailing, sea - fishing. *Heir:* none. *Club:* Marlborough.
(Died 7 Dec. 1923.)

TREVOR, 2nd Baron (*cr.* 1880), **Arthur William Hill-Trevor**, J.P.; Lieut.-Col. 1st Life Guards, retired 1895; *b.* 19 Nov. 1852; *s.* of 1st Baron and 1st wife Mary, *d.* of Sir Richard Sutton, 2nd Bt.; *S.* father 1894; *m.* 1st, 1893, Hon. Anne Mary Eleanor Fraser, *d.* of 17th Baron Saltoun (*d.* 1895); 2nd, 1897, Rosamond C., M.B.E., *g. d.* of 11th Baron Petre and widow of 4th and last Earl of Bantry. Owns about 23,700 acres. *Heir:* half-*b.* Hon. Charles Edward Hill-Trevor, *b.* 22 Dec. 1863. *Address:* Brynkinalt, Chirk, Denbigh. *Club:* Carlton.
(Died 19 May 1923.)

TREVOR, Sir Arthur Charles, K.C.S.I., *cr.* 1898; Indian C.S. (Bombay); *b.* Jellalabad, Afghanistan, 6 April 1841; 5th *s.* of late Capt. R. S. Trevor, 3rd Bengal Cavalry (killed at Cabul, Dec. 1841); *m.* 1867, Florence Mary (*d.* 1918), 2nd *d.* of Colonel C. J. Prescott, Bombay Staff Corps; two *s.* four *d.* *Educ.:* St. John's Foundation School and Trinity and Lincoln Colls. Oxford; Scholar of Lincoln. Appointed after examination of 1860; arrived, 1861; served in Bombay as Assistant Collector and Magistrate, and Deputy Commissioner of Customs and Opium; Collector of Customs, Bombay, 1879; Senior Collector, 1884; Collector of Salt Revenue, 1885; Commissioner of Customs, Sat, Opium, and Abkari, and Reporter-General of External Commerce, 1888; also British Delegate for the Portuguese Treaty; Commissioner in Sind, 1890; member of Bombay Council, 1892; C.S.I., 1894; temporary member of Governor-General's Council in charge Railways and Public Works, April to Oct. 1895; confirmed April 1896-1901. *Address:* 16 Harcourt Terrace, West Brompton, S.W.
(Died 22 Sept. 1920.)

TREVOR, Arthur Hill, B.A. Oxon; Barrister - at - Law; Commissioner, Board of Control, since 1914; *o. s.* of Charles Binny Trevor, late I.C.S.; *b.* 1858. *Educ.:* Winchester; Corpus Christi College, Oxford. Called to Bar, Inner Temple, 1884; South - Eastern Circuit; Sussex Sessions; Secretary to Commissioners in Lunacy, 1904-7; Commissioner in Lunacy, 1907-14. *Recreations:* golf and shooting; Winchester XI., 1877; Oxford XI., 1880, 1881; played for Sussex, 1880-84. *Address:* 4 Albemarle Street, W.1. *T.:* Regent 443. *Clubs:* Arthur's, Brooke's, Royal Automobile.
(Died 27 Sept. 1924.)

TREVOR, Sir (Charles) Cecil, Kt., *cr.* 1896; C.B. 1882; *b.* July 1830; *e. s.* of Charles Trevor, Somerset House; *m.* 1863, Mary (*d.* 1892), *d.* of James Weston. *Educ.:* Rugby; St. Catharine's College, Cambridge; Hon. Fellow (M.A.). Barrister Lincoln's Inn, 1855; Assistant Secretary to Board of Trade, 1867-95; a Conservator of the River Thames, 1895-1906; delegate to North Sea Fishery Conference at Hague, 1881-82; to Submarine Cables Conference at Paris, 1882-83 and 1886; to North Sea Liquor Traffic Conference at Hague, 1886; to Channel Fisheries negotiations at Paris, 1886. *Address:* 28 Bramham Gardens, South Kensington, S.W. *Clubs:* Athenæum, Oxford and Cambridge.
(Died 18 Sept. 1921.)

TREVOR, Surg.-Gen. Sir Francis (Woollaston), K.C.S.I., *cr.* 1911; C.B. 1907; Hon. Surgeon to His Majesty; *b.* 11 Dec. 1851; *s.* of E. S. R. Trevor, Trowscoed, Welshpool; *m.* Mary H. Mytton, *d.* of R. H. Mytton, Garth, Welshpool; two *s.* one *d.* *Educ.:* Guy's Hospital; Aberdeen University. Lieut.-Col. R.A.M.C. 1894; Col. 1903; P.M.O. Scottish District, 1903-4; Administrative Medical Officer, India, 1904; P.M.O. 6th Div., India; Principal Medical Officer of H.M.'s Forces in India, 1908; served Afghanistan, 1878-80 (medal two clasps, bronze star); Soudan, 1884-85 (medal with clasp, bronze star); South Africa, 1901-2 (despatches, Queen's medal, five clasps); Colonel Commandant, R.A.M.C. 1921-22. *Address:* Oerley Hall, Oswestry, Salop. *Club:* Naval and Military.
(Died 16 Nov. 1922.)

TREVOR, Frederick George Brunton, C.I.E. 1900; J.P. Surrey; late Director of Funds, India Office; *b.* India, 28 Oct. 1838; 2nd *s.* of late Rev. George Trevor, D.D., Canon of York, and Elizabeth Louisa Garrick; *m.* 1860, Rose (*d.* 1902), 3rd *d.* of William Hudson, of York; four *s.* *Educ.:* Marlborough. Entered India Office, 1858; retired, 1903. *Recreation:* cricket. *Address:* Redholme, Richmond, Surrey.
(Died 20 Feb. 1924.)

TREVOR, Hon. George Edwyn Hill-; Major, Reserve of Officers; *heir-pres.* to 2nd Baron Trevor; *b.* 15 Nov. 1859 at Norwood Park, Notts; 2nd *s.* of 1st Baron Trevor of Brynkinalt, N. Wales, and Mary C., *d.* of 3rd Baron Scarsdale of Kedleston Hall, Derby; *m.* 1st, 1893, Ethel G. M., *d.* of H. Chapman and Ethel, *d.* of Sir Fras. Dugdale Astley, 2nd Bt.; 2nd, 1910, Helen (*d.* 1919); *d.* of Thomas Suart, Edinburgh. Lieut. Shropshire Yeomanry Cavalry, 1882-88; Commanded 4/8th Middlesex Regt. (Duke of Cambridge's Own), June-Dec. 1915. *Recreations:* shooting, foreign travel, numismatics, fire brigade work, soldiering. *Address:* 15 Duke Street, St. James, S.W.1. *(Died 19 July 1922.)*

TREVOR, Col. George Herbert, C.S.I., 1891; Supernumerary List, Indian Army; *b.* 29 Jan. 1840; *s.* of Rev. George Trevor, D.D., Canon of York; *m.* 1870, *d.* of Col. E. K. Elliot, B.S.C.; two *s.* one *d.* *Educ.:* Marlborough College. Served in R.A. 1858-62, when transferred to Indian Staff Corps consequent on entering civil employ; held various posts in the Political Department, 1867-95, ending with that of Agent to Governor-General for Rajputana, and Chief Commissioner of Ajmere and Merwara. *Club:* Union, Brighton.
(Died 10 July 1927.)

TREVOR, Rev. Thomas Warren, M.A.; Rector of Llanfaelog since 1902; Prebendary and Senior Canon of Bangor Cathedral; *s.* of Rev. I. W. Trevor, M.A., Chancellor of the Diocese of Bangor Canon Residentiary, and Rector of Llanfaelog; *b.* 1839; *m.* Caroline Maria, *d.* of C. H. Evans of Plas-gwyn and Henblas, Anglesey; two *s.* three *d.* *Educ.:* Marlborough College: Jesus College, Oxford. Curate of Beaumaris, 1862-65; Dolgelley, 1867-68; Vicar of Penmon and Llanfaes, 1868-89; Rural Dean of Tyndaethwy, 1874-89; Rector of Machynlleth, 1889-

1902 ; Prebendary of Penmynydd and Canon of Bangor Cathedral, 1891 ; Proctor in Convocation for the Clergy, 1892-95; Proctor for the Chapter, 1895-1919 ; Hon. Secretary Diocesan Clergy Charity, 1877 ; Clergy Life Insurance Society, 1882. *Publication:* Church Finance and Aided Life Insurance, 1882. *Address:* c/o Llanfaelog Rectory, Ty-Croes, Anglesey.

(*Died 12 April 1924.*)

TREVOR-BATTYE, Aubyn Bernard Rochfort, M.A., F.L.S., F.Z.S., F.R.G.S. ; *b.* Hever, Kent ; 2nd *s.* of late Rev. William Wilberforce Battye of Tingrith Manor, Beds, and Little Hampden, Bucks [in right of Ruth, *d.* of John Hampden the patriot, who *m.* Sir John Trevor], Rector of Hever, and Harriet Dorothea, *o. d.* of Edmund Wakefield Meade-Waldo, of Stonewall Park and Hever Castle; *m.* 1901, Margaret Amy (*d.* 1906), *y. d.* of late C. North Graham ; two *d.* *Educ.:* St. Edward's School, Oxford ; Christ Church, Oxford ; studied Natural Science under Professor H. N. Moseley of the "Challenger." Has for several years travelled in various countries : N.-W. America, Africa, Arctic Russia, Spitsbergen, Nepal, etc., for exploration and natural history ; was first explorer of Kolguev in Barent's Sea ; Zoologist to the Conway Arctic Expedition, 1896 ; Editor and proprietor of The Artist, 1897 ; Editor-in-Chief of Natural History in the Victoria History of the Counties of England, and Hon. Secy. to Advisory Council, 1899. *Publications:* Pictures in Prose, 1893 ; Icebound on Kolguev, 1895 ; A Northern Highway of the Tsar, 1897 ; editor of Lord Lilford on Birds, 1903 : Camping in Crete, 1913 ; and many scattered papers. *Address:* Ashford Chace, Petersfield, Hants. *M.:* AA 1639.(*Died 20 Dec. 1922.*)

TRICKETT, Hon. William Joseph, M.L.C., J.P.; Deputy Chairman of Committees of the Legislative Council, New South Wales ; *b.* 2 Sept. 1844 ; married ; two *s.* four *d.* *Educ.:* Sydney Grammar School. Went to Australia, 1854 ; M.L.A. Paddington, 1880-89 ; has been Postmaster-General, Minister for Public Instruction, chairman of Committees of the Legislative Assembly, chairman of Committees of Legislative Council, and Acting President, is Vice-President and Parliamentary Founder of the National Art Gallery, member and chairman of the Parliamentary Public Works Committee ; Local Alderman for 33 years ; Member of State Children's Relief Board. *Publication:* Trip to China and Japan. *Recreations:* yachting and touring. *Address:* Shorwell, 121 Queen Street, Woollahra, Sydney, New South Wales. *Club:* Australian, Sydney. (*Died July 1916.*)

TRIGGS, H. Inigo, A.R.I.B.A. ; Architect and Garden Designer ; *b.* Chiswick, 28 Feb. 1876 ; *m.* 1907, Gladys Claire, *y. d.* of late Sir Edward Hill, K.C.B., of Rookwood, Llandaff. *Educ.:* Godolphin School ; Schools of Royal Academy. *Publications:* Some Architectural Works of Inigo Jones, written in conjunction with Henry Tanner, Jun., 1900 ; Formal Gardens in England and Scotland, 1902 ; The Art of Garden Design in Italy, 1906 ; Town Planning, Past, Present, and Possible, 1909 ; Garden Craft in Europe, 1913 ; has devoted special attention to the study of garden planning. *Address:* Little Boarhunt, Liphook, Hants ; 38 Sackville Street, Piccadilly, W.1. *T.:* Liphook 13. *Club:* Arts. (*Died 8 April 1923.*)

TRIMEN, Roland, F.R.S. (1883), F.L.S., F.Z.S., F.E.S. ; Hon. M.A. Oxon. (1899) ; *b.* London, 1840 ; 3rd *s.* of Richard and Mary Ann Trimen ; *m.* 1883, Henrietta Blanche, *d.* of H. E. Boyes Bull of Calcutta, and originator of the League of the Empire, 1901. *Educ.:* private school ; King's Coll. School. Entered Cape Civil Service, 1860 ; served in offices of Auditor-Gen., Colonial Sec., Commis-
1054

sioner of Lands and Public Works, Governor, etc. ; Curator of South-African Museum, Cape Town, 1873-95 ; President of South-African Philosophical Society, 1883-84 ; retired from Cape Civil Service 1895 President of the Entomological Society of London, 1897-98 ; awarded Darwin Medal by Royal Society, 1910 ; Corr. Mem. American Entom. Soc. *Publications:* Rhopalocera Africae Australis : a Catalogue of South-African Butterflies, 1862-66 ; South-African Butterflies : a Monograph of the Extra-tropical Species, 1887-89 ; various memoirs and papers on entomology and other branches of zoology, etc., in the Transactions of the Linnean, Zoological, and Entomological Societies, and other publications. *Address:* Glaslyn, Waterden Road, Guildford. *Club:* Royal Societies. (*Died 25 July 1916.*)

TRIPP, George Henry; C.B. 1913 ; *b.* 28 May 1860 ; *s.* of George Lewis Tripp ; *m.* 1881, Sophia Caroline, *d.* of G. A. F. Freeman ; three *s.* one *d.* *Educ.:* Mercers' School. Clerk in Home Office, 1878 ; Secretary to Home Office Committee on Metropolitan Police Superannuation, 1889 ; Auditor of Royal Patriotic Fund, 1893-98 ; Member of Home Office Committee on Housing of Metropolitan Police, 1903, and Metropolitan Police Finances, 1909 ; Member of Treasury Committee on Education Rates, 1905 ; Receiver for the Metropolitan Police District and Courts, 1910-18 ; Coronation Medal, 1911. *Address:* Pymlicoe House, Hadley Green, Herts. (*Died 18 Feb. 1922.*)

TRISCOTT, Col. Charles Prideaux, C.B. 1910 ; C.M.G. 1917 ; D.S.O. 1888 ; R.A. ; *b.* 2 Sep. 1857 ; *y. s.* of late Joseph Blake Triscott of Plymouth and Helston ; *m.* 1884, Catherine May, 2nd *d.* of Maj.-Gen. M. M. Prendergast ; two *d.* *Educ.:* Royal Military Academy. Lieut. R.A. 1876 ; served in Afghanistan, including action at Charasiab and march from Kabul to Kandahar (medal and bronze star) ; Burma Campaign, 1885-88 ; commanded expedition against Salay Hill Kachins, and also to Lake Endawgyee and Jade Mines (despatches, D.S.O., medal with two clasps) ; served as A.Q.M.G. 2nd Division, Tirah Ex. Force (despatches, medal with 2 clasps) ; Officer Com. Western Coast Defences, 1912-16 ; retired pay, 1916. *Recreation:* fishing. *Club:* Naval and Military.

(*Died 17 Aug. 1926.*)

TRISTRAM, Rev. John William, D.D. ; Canon of St. Patrick's, Dublin, 1908-22 ; Chaplain to the Lord Lieutenant ; Lord Lieut.'s Inspector of Education ; *s.* of Thomas Everard Tristram of Farnley, Wexford, and Alice, *d.* of Major Bolton of the Wexford Yeomanry ; *m.* 1st, C. S. Cavanagh ; 2nd, Gertrude, *d.* of late F. Brook-Hollinshead, 12th Lancers ; one *s.* two *d.* *Educ.:* Tipperary Grammar School ; Trinity College, Dublin. Curate and afterwards Rector in Ossory Diocese ; Organising Secretary of Dublin Board of Education, 1880 ; to him is largely due the present system of Religious Instruction in Protestant Schools in Ireland ; took a prominent part in resisting Home Rule, 1893-95 ; spoke in over 400 meetings in 28 English counties and boroughs ; largely engaged in journalistic work, and for many years a leader-writer in Irish Times. *Publication:* A False Alarm ; a Plea for Toleration in Irish Education. *Recreation:* golf. *Address:* Ardoyne, Bramshott Chase, Hindhead, Surrey. *T.:* Grayshott 121. *Club:* University, Dublin.

(*Died 3 Oct. 1926.*)

TRITTON, Sir (Charles) Ernest, 1st Bt. *cr.* 1905 ; senior partner in firm of Brightwen and Co., bill-brokers and banking agents, London ; Director of the U.K. Temperance and General Provident Institution, 1897 ; *b.* 4 Sep. 1845 ; *s.* of late Joseph Tritton, Lombard Street ; *m.* Edith, 2nd *d.* of late Frederick Green, 1872 ; one *s.* two *d.* *Educ.:* Rugby ; Trinity Hall,

TRICKETT, William, D.C.L., LL.D. See page xxxi.

Camb. (B.A. 1868). M.P. (C.) for Norwood Division of Lambeth, 1892-1906; Vice-Chairman Hospital Sunday Fund and Chairman of Finance Committee; Vice-Chairman London City Mission; Chairman Princess Christian's Hospital for British Wounded, South Norwood; President Norwood Cottage Hospital; Member of Board of Management British Home for Incurables; a Vice-President of British and Foreign Bible Society and of Church Missionary Soc. [*Heir*: *s.* Alfred Ernest, *b.* 8 June 1873; *m.* 1898, Agneta Elspeth, *d.* of W. M. Campbell; one *s.* three *d.*] *Address*: 5 Cadogan Square, S.W.; Bloomfield, Norwood. *Clubs*: Carlton, New University.   (*Died 28 Dec. 1918.*)

TRITTON, Joseph Herbert, one of H.M. Lieutenants for the City of London; *e. s.* of late Joseph Tritton; *b.* 1844; *m.* 1869, Lucy Jane (*d.* 1919) *e. d.* of late Henry Abel Smith of Wilford, Notts; four *s.* four *d. Educ.*: Rugby. Formerly partner in Barclay, Bevan, Tritton & Co., bankers, and Director of Barclay's Bank, Ltd.; Chairman of Indo-European Telegraph Co., Ltd.; member of the Council of Foreign Bondholders, of The Shipwrights' Company, and of the Fellowship of the Russia Company; Hon. Secretary, London Clearing Bankers, 1888-1906; Vice-President of the Committee of English Country Bankers; ex-President Institute of Bankers, and of London Chamber of Commerce; Order of The Lion and the Sun, Persia. *Publications:* Tritton, the Place and the Family; The Assault on the Standard; many Presidential Addresses and Articles on Banking, Financial, and Economic Subjects; volume of Religious Poetry—privately printed; various Religious Addresses and Articles. *Address*: 6 Sloane Court, S.W.3; Lyons Hall, Great Leighs, Chelmsford. *Clubs*: Athenæum, National Liberal.
      (*Died 11 Sept. 1923.*)

TROLLOPE, Sir Thomas Ernest, 11th Bart., *cr.* 1641; Barrister; *b.* 14 Sep. 1858; 3rd *s.* of late General Sir Charles Trollope, K.C.B., and Frances, *o. c.* of John Lord; *S.* brother, 1921. *Educ.*: Eton; Magdalene College, Cambridge (M.A.). *Heir*: cousin Henry Cracroft, *b.* 1860. *Address*: 18 Montpelier Square, S.W.7. *T.*: Kensington 2573. *Clubs*: Junior Carlton, Wellington.   (*Died 23 Sept. 1927.*)

TROLLOPE, Sir William (Henry), 10th Bart., *cr.* 1641; Barrister; *b.* 14 Sep. 1858; 2nd *s.* of late General Sir Charles Trollope, K.C.B., and Frances, *o. c.* of John Lord; *S.* to baronetcy on death of his cousin, 3rd and last Baron Kesteven, 1915; *m.* 1894, Louisa Charlotte Campbell, *d.* of Capt. Frederick Johnston, R.N.; two *d. Educ.*: Eton; Trinity College, Cambridge (M.A.). *Heir*: twin *b.* Thomas Ernest Trollope [Barrister-at-law. *Address*: 18 Montpelier Square, S.W.7. *Club*: Junior Carlton]. *Address*: 5 Montagu Square, W.1. *Club*: Junior Carlton.   (*Died 24 Aug. 1921.*)

TROTTER, Rev. Canon Edward Bush, M.A., V.D., Commissary to Bishop of Trinidad, 1918; *b.* 10 Dec. 1842; 4th *s.* of late Alexander Trotter, and Jaqueline, *d.* of Bp. Otter (of Chichester); *m.* 1870, Gertrude Mary, 2nd *d.* of late Rev. F. Fitch, Rector of Cromer, Norfolk; no *c. Educ.*: Harrow; King's College, London; and Christ's College, Cambridge. B.A. 1865; M.A. 1869; Junior Optime and 3rd Cl. Theol. Tripos. Deacon, 18 6; Priest, 1867; Curate of Holy Trinity, Haberdham Eaves, Lancs., 1866-1869; Vicar of Alnwick, Northumberland, and Domestic Chaplain to Duke of Northumberland; Chaplain to 3rd Artillery Volunteers, and to the Light Infantry Militia, 1869-90; Hon. Canon of Newcastle-on-Tyne, 1884-90; Rector of St. Stephen's Savanna Grande, Trinidad, B.W.I., 1890-1901; Canon of H. T. Cathedral, Trinidad, 1896-1903, and since 1908; Archdeacon

and Vicar-General of Trinidad, 1896-1903; Archdeacon of Western Downs and Canon of Brisbane Cathedral, Queensland, 1903-8; Canon of Port of Spain, Trinidad; Chaplain to H.B.M. Legation, Carácas, Venezuela, and in charge of the Anglican congregations throughout Venezuela, 1908-16. *Publications:* The Church of England: Early History, Property, and Mission, Reformation Period; The Three Days of Grace; The Church Catechism and Bible Story (3 vols.); Two Historical Charts of Church of England; Royal Progress of Our Lord. *Recreations:* walking and climbing, when younger. *Address:* 105 Alumhurst Road, Bournemouth. *Club:* Church Imperial.   (*Died 14 July 1920.*)

TROTTER, Major Edward Henry, D.S.O. 1900; Grenadier Guards; *b.* 1 Dec. 1872; *s.* of late Major-General Sir H. Trotter, G.C.V.O. Entered army, 1893; Captain, 1900; served Soudan, 1898 (British medal, Khedive's medal with clasp); South Africa, 1900-1902 (despatches, medal and 4 clasps, D.S.O.). *Club:* Guards'.   (*Died 8 July 1916.*)

TROTTER, Lieut.-Colonel Sir Henry, K.C.M.G., *cr.* 1906; C.B., *cr.* 1880; *b.* Cowfold, Sussex, 30 Aug. 1841; 3rd *s.* of late Alexander Trotter and Jaqueline, *d.* of late Rt. Rev. William Otter, Lord Bishop of Chichester; *m.* 1890, Olivia Georgiana, *o. d.* of late Adm. Sir George Wellesley, G.C.B.; two *d. Educ.*: Cheltenham College; E.I. Military Coll. Addiscombe. Lieut. R.E. (late Bengal), 1860; retired as Lieut.-Col. 1890; served 1863-75 on great Trigonometrical Survey of India; accompanied Sir Douglas Forsyth's mission to Yarkand and Kashgar, 1873-74, as geographer; employed on special service in China, 1876; was awarded, 1878, the Victoria medal of Royal Geog. Soc. for explorations in Turkestan; appointed additional military attaché at Constantinople during Turko-Russian War, 1877-78; accompanied the Turkish armies throughout the campaign in Asia (siege and relief of Kars, battles of Yeshek Ilias, and Deveh Boyoun, etc.), Turkish war medal; Consul for Kurdistan, 1878-82; superintended International relief operations at Scio after the great earthquake of 1881; military attaché, Constantinople, 1882-89, during which time he was frequently employed on special missions; Consul-General in Syria, 1890-94; has frequently acted as H.M. Chargé d'Affaires at Bucharest; British Delegate on the European Commission of the Danube, and H.B.M. Consul-Gen. for Roumania 1894-1906; Jubilee medal 1897. *Publications:* various papers contributed to the Royal Geog. Soc. *Recreations:* shooting, was the first European to shoot the *Ovis Poli.* or wild sheep of the Pamirs, 5 May 1874. *Address:* 18 Eaton Place, S.W. *Clubs:* Athenæum, United Service. (*Died 25 Sept. 1919.*)

TROTTER, Rev. Henry Eden, M.A.; Hon. Canon of Christ Church, Oxford, since 1898. *Educ.*: Christ Church, Oxford. Ordained, 1869; Curate of St. John, Bedminster, 1869-72; Cobham, Surrey, 1872-73; Vicar of Northam, Hants, 1873-83; Ardington, Berks, 1884-99; Rector of Whitchurch, 1899-1914; Rural Dean of Henley, 1913-17. *Address:* Horton Lodge, Reading.
      (*Died 4 July 1922.*)

TROTTER, Rev. John George, Vicar of Polesworth since 1882; Hon. Canon Birmingham; Rural Dean, Surrogate. *Educ.*: St. John's College, Oxford (M.A.). Curate of Burghfield, Berks, 1872-75; Northden, 1875-78; Ashburn, 1878-82; Assistant Diocesan Inspector of Schools, 1891-93; Hon. Canon Worcester, 1901-5. *Address:* Polesworth Vicarage, Tamworth.
      (*Died Feb. 1917.*)

TROTTER, Lieut.-Col. John Moubray, D.L., J.P., and Convenor of Midlothian; *b.* 6 Sep. 1842; 4th *s.* of Archibald Trotter of Dreghorn, Midlothian (*d.* 1844), and Louisa Jane, *y. d.* of late James Strange of Madras Civil Service; *m.* 1876, Hon. Mary Catherine Elizabeth (*d.* 1908), *o. c.* of Ralph, 2nd Lord Dunfermline, K.C.B.; two *s.* two *d.* *Educ.:* Harrow; Addiscombe. Served for many years on the Staff of the Army in India. *Address:* Colinton House, Midlothian, Scotland. *Clubs:* Naval and Military; New, Edinburgh.

(Died 15 Feb. 1924.)

TROTTER, Col. Sir Philip, Kt., *cr.* 1908; J.P., D.L.; Colonel commanding troops, Stirling Castle; *b.* 13 June 1844; 4th *s.* of A. Trotter of Dreghorn, J.P., Midlothian, and Louisa, *d.* of J. Strange and Hon. Anne Strange, *d.* of Viscount Melville; *m.* 1886, Eliza, *d.* of C. Scott Plummer of Middlestead, and Sunderland Hall, Selkirk; one *s.* one *d.* *Educ.:* Harrow. Joined 93rd Highlanders, 1866; served Nile Campaign, 1884-6 (medal, clasp, bronze star, Bt. Lt.-Col., despatches, 3rd class Medjidie); Commanded 93rd Highlanders, 1891-94; 91st Regimental District, 1898-1902; 34th Field Army Brigade Scot. Border Brigade, etc.; received freedom of Royal Burgh of Stirling, 1902; Chairman Ex-Committee Q.V. School, Dunblane. *Publication:* Our Mission to the Court of Morocco. *Address:* Mainhouse, Kelso. *Clubs:* Naval and Military; New, Edinburgh.

(Died 26 Oct. 1918.)

TROUBRIDGE, Adm. Sir Ernest Charles Thomas, K.C.M.G., *cr.* 1919; C.B. 1911; C.M.G. 1904; M.V.O. 1904; *b.* 15 July 1862; 3rd *s.* of Col. Sir Thomas St. Vincent H. C. Troubridge, 3rd Bt.; *m.* 1st, 1891, Edith (*d.* 1900), *y. d.* of William Duffus, Halifax, N.S.; one *s.* two *d.*; 2nd, 1908, Una (authoress of Guests and Memories, 1925), *y. d.* of late Capt. Harry Taylor, M.V.O.; one *d.* Naval Attaché, Vienna, Madrid, and Tokio, 1901-4; Captain and Chief of Staff Mediterranean, 1907-8; Chief of the War Staff, Admiralty, 1911-12; commanding Mediterranean Cruiser Squadron, 1912; Head of the British Naval Mission to Serbia, 1915; Admiral Commanding on the Danube, 1918; Admiral, 1919; retired list, 1921; President of the International Commission of the Danube, 1919-24; Grand Officer of the Rising Sun; Officer of Legion of Honour; Grand Cordon of Star of Roumania, with Swords, 1919; Grand Officer of S.S. Maurice and Lazarus, 1917; Grand Officer of Redeemer of Greece, 1918; Croix de Guerre with Palms, 1918; 2nd Class of Red Eagle; 2nd Class of Spanish Naval Merit; Gold Medal of Order of Imtiaz; Grand Officer of Kara George with Swords, 1915; First Class Order of White Eagle, 1916. *Address:* 6 Cheltenham Terrace, S.W.3. *T.:* Kensington 3346. *Clubs:* Travellers', Beefsteak.

(Died 28 Jan. 1926.)

TROUP, James; Consul-General, retired; *b.* 15 April 1840; *s.* of late Alexander Troup, grain merchant, Aberdeen; *m.* 1st, Hannah (*d.* 1903), *d.* of late Robert Scott, Gilston, Herts; 2nd, Catherine, *d.* of late Donald Macpherson, Inverness; three *s.* one *d.* *Educ.:* Gymnasium, Old Aberdeen; Aberdeen University, M.A. Entered H.M. Consular Service, Japan Establishment, 1863; Vice-Consul, 1873; Consul, 1877; Consul-General at Yokohama, and Assistant Judge of H.M. Court for Japan, 1896; Jubilee Medal; retired, 1898. *Publications:* Trade Reports; Papers on Buddhistic and other subjects in Transactions Asiatic Society of Japan, Japan Society, and Royal Asiatic Society, London, etc. *Recreations:* travelling, fishing, studies. *Address:* Wollescote, Springhill, Ventnor, Isle of Wight.

(Died 26 July 1925.)

TROUTON, Frederick Thomas, F.R.S.; *b.* Dublin, 24 Nov. 1863; *y. s.* of Thomas Trouton, of that city; *m.* Annie, *d.* of George Fowler, Liverpool; two *s.* three *d.* *Educ.:* Dungannon Royal School; Trin. Coll. Dublin; and also Engineering School, Trinity College,
1056

Dublin; M.A., D.Sc. (Dublin); assistant to the Professor of Physics, Trin. Coll. Dublin, 1884-1901; Lecturer in Experimental Physics, Trinity College, Dublin, 1901-1902; Quain Professor of Physics, University College, London, 1902-14. *Publications:* On Molecular Latent Heat (Phil. Mag. vol. xviii.), commonly referred to as "Trouton's Law"; Repetition of Hertz's Experiments and Determination of the direction of the vibrations of Light (Nature, vol. xxxix.); Experiments on Electromagnetic Radiations, including some of the phases of secondary waves (Nature, vol. xl.), and the various other papers. *Address:* The Rookery, Downe, Kent. *T.:* Bromley 1812.

(Died 21 Sept. 1922.)

TROWBRIDGE, John Townsend; *b.* Ogden, N.Y., 18 Sep. 1827; *s.* of Windsor Stone and Rebecca Willey Trowbridge, parents of English stock; *m.* 1st, 1860, Cornelia Warren, of Lowell, Mass.; 2nd, 1873, Sarah Adelaide Newton, of Arlington, Mass.; one *s.* two *d.* Attended common country school in boyhood, but mostly self-taught, in intervals of leisure, while working on father's farm; began to write verses at an early age; one term at a classical school in Lockport, New York, 1844-45; went to prairie country of Illinois, 1845, and spent one year there, farming, hunting, school-teaching, and pursuing private studies; to New York City in spring of 1847, and began writing for the press; to Boston 1848, wrote for the press, edited newspapers, and published first of a series of small books, Father Brighthopes, 1853; spent one year abroad, mostly in Paris, 1855-56; contributor to Atlantic Monthly, 1857; edited Our Young Folk's Magazine, 1870-73; visited Europe, 1888-91, and again, 1908-9. *Publications:* The Vagabonds, and other Poems; The Book of Gold, and other Poems; The Emigrant's Story, and other Poems; A Home Idyl, and other Poems; The Lost Earl, and other Poems; books for the young: The Little Master; The Tinkham Brothers' Tide Mill; His One Fault; His Own Master; The Pocket Rifle; The Prize Cup; Two Biddicut Boys; The Silver Medal; The Kelp Gatherers; Jack Hazard stories (five vols.); The Fortunes of Toby Trafford; A Pair of Madcaps, 1909; novels and tales: Neighbors' Wives; Coupon Bonds; Cudjo's Cave; Neighbor Jackwood; My Own Story (autobiography), and Poetical Works (complete), 1903. *Address:* Arlington, Mass., U.S.A. *(Died 12 Feb. 1916.)*

TROWER, Right Rev. Gerard, D.D.; Rector of Chale, Isle of Wight, since 1927; *b.* 1860; *s.* of Rev. Arthur Trower, Rector of St. Mary-at-Hill, Eastcheap, E.C. *Educ.:* Keble College, Oxford (3rd Class Theological Schools); Ely College. Ordained, 1888; Curate of St. Albans the Martyr, Birmingham, 1888-93; St. Mary Redcliffe, Bristol, 1893-95; Rector of Christ Church, Sydney, 1895-1901; Bishop of Nyasaland, 1901-10; Bishop of North-West Australia, 1910-27. *Address:* Chale Rectory, Isle of Wight. *Club:* New Oxford and Cambridge. *(Died 25 Aug. 1928.)*

TROWER, Sir Walter, Kt. *cr.* 1915; senior partner in the firm of Trower, Still, Parkin & Keeling, of Lincoln's Inn; *b.* 14 Feb. 1853; *y. s.* of late Captain Edward Spencer Trower, of Stansteadbury, Herts, 9th Lancers, and Emma, *d.* of Admiral Gosselin of Bengeo Hall, Herts; *m.* 1884, Mabel, *d.* of late Capt. Phelips, R.A., of Oaten Hill, Canterbury; one *s.* one *d.* *Educ.:* Haileybury. Admitted a Solicitor, 1876; Member of Council of the Law Society, 1902; Vice-President, 1912-13; Chairman of Finance Committee, 1902-20; President, 1913-14; Member of the Council of King Edward's Hospital Fund for London; of the Committee on the Transfer of Land in England and Wales, 1918; of the Royal Commission on Income Tax, 1920; of the

Council of Law Reporting; of the Committee to enquire into Civil Litigation between the Subject and the Crown, 1921-22. *Address:* 8 Westbourne Terrace, Hyde Park, W.2 *Clubs:* Travellers'; Stoke Poges and Woking Golf.
(Died 5 April 1924.)

TUBB, Captain Frederick Harold, V.C. 1915; 7th Batt. Australian Imperial Force; *y. s.* of Harry Tubb, of Longwood East, Victoria. Was some years in Australian Light Horse; Captain, 1915; served European War, 1914-15 (wounded, V.C. for Lone Pine Trenches, Gallipoli).
(Died 22 Sept. 1917.)

TUCK, Sir Adolph, 1st Bt., *cr.* 1910; Chairman and Managing Director Raphael Tuck and Sons, Ltd., Art Publishers to their Majesties the King and Queen; Extraordinary Director, Scottish Equitable Life Assurance Society; President of the Association of Publishers of Christmas Cards and Calendars; President of the Association of Publishers of Picture Postcards; Treasurer of Jews' College; *b.* 30 Jan. 1854; 2nd *s.* of late Raphael Tuck of Highbury, N., and Ernestine (*d.* 1895), *d.* of David Lissner, of Schrimm, Poland; *m.* 1882, Jeanetta, *d.* of late William Flatau of Lusan House, Highbury; two *s.* three *d. Educ.:* Elizabeth Gymnasium (College), Breslau. Entered his father's art business in London, 1869; inaugurated the first of a series of Original Christmas Card Designs Exhibitions at the Dudley Gallery with Sir Coutts Lindsay, John Everett Millais, R.A., and Marcus Stone, R.A., as judges, 1879; introduced Picture Postcards into the British Empire, 1894. *Heir: s.* William Reginald [Major 3rd County of London Yeomanry (Sharpshooters); *b.* 8 July 1883; *m.* 1917, Gladys, 2nd *d.* of N. Alfred Nathan of Wickford, Auckland, N.Z., and *widow* of Desmond Fosberry Kettle, Lieut. Auckland Mounted Rifles; two *d.*]. *Recreations:* riding, walking. *Address:* 29 Park Crescent, Portland Place, W.1. *T.:* Langham 1854. *M.:* F 4431. *Clubs:* National Liberal, City Reform, Empire.
(Died 3 July 1926.)

TUCK, William Henry, M.A.; author and writer for press; *b.* Great Moulton, Norfolk, 3 Oct. 1840; *e. s.* of late Rev. William Gilbert Tuck, Tostock House, and Anne Elizabeth, *o. c.* of Edward Smyth, West Bradenham Hall, Norfolk; *m.* Jane St. John, *o. d.* of late J. W. Budd, M.D., of Plymouth, 1866. *Educ.:* Ipswich; Emmanuel Coll. Camb. (M.A. 1866). *Publications:* The Avi-Fauna of a Suffolk Village; The Aculeate Hymenoptera of Bury St. Edmunds District. *Recreations:* reading, fishing, general entomology. *Address:* 5 Southgate Green, Bury St. Edmunds.

TUCKER, Francis Ellis, I.S.O. 1909; Retired Civil Servant; *b.* 29 May 1844; *e. surv. s.* of late Rev. Francis Tucker, Baptist Minister of Manchester and London; unmarried. *Educ.:* private schools in Manchester and Leatherhead, Surrey; matriculated at London University, 1860. After a short commercial engagement, obtained an appointment on the staff of the British Museum (Director's Office), 1862; Assistant Secretary, 1903; retired, 1908, after a total service of 46½ years; visited Egypt and Palestine, 1871; America, 1878; South Africa, 1909-10. *Publications:* Tourist Notes in Egypt, 1872; Fairy's Rainbow, and other addresses to Sunday Schools. *Recreations:* music and literary study. *Address:* 7 Purbeck Road, West Cliff, Bournemouth.
(Died 28 Oct. 1921.)

TUCKER, Maj.-Gen. Louis Henry Emile, C.I.E. 1891; *b.* 1843; *s.* of Robert Tudor Tucker, formerly B.C.S.; *m.* 1877, Annie Lætitia, *d.* of Sir Robert Henry Davies, K.C.S.I., C.I.E. *Educ.:* Wimbledon School; Addiscombe. Entered Bengal army, 1860; Capt. 1869; Major, 1880; Lieut.-Colonel, 1886; Colonel, 1890; Major-

General, 1899; served N.W. Frontier of India Campaign, 1863 (despatches, medal with clasp); Jowaki Expedition, 1877-78 (despatches, and clasp); Afghan War, 1878-80 (despatches, medal with two clasps); formerly Inspector-Gen. of Police, Punjab. *Address:* Winhaven, The Undercliffe, Sandgate, Kent. *(Died 15 Oct. 1925.)*

TUCKWELL, Rev. W., Unbeneficed Clerk in Orders; *b.* Oxford, 1829; *s.* of William Tuckwell, Surgeon, and Margaret Wood; *m.* 1858, Rosa, *d.* of Captain Stron, H.E.I.C.S.; one *s.* three *d. Educ.:* Winchester; New College, Oxford (Fellow). Master at St. Columba's College, Ireland, 1853-54; Curate, St. Mary Magdalen, Oxford, 1856; Master of New College School, 1857-63; Headmaster of Taunton College School, 1864-77; Rector of Stockton, Warwickshire, 1878-93; Rector of Waltham, Lincolnshire, 1893-1905. *Publications:* Tongues in Trees, 1891; Winchester Fifty Years Ago, 1898; A. W. Kinglake: a Biographical Study, 1902; Reminiscences of Oxford, 1st edition, 1900; 2nd edition, 1907; Reminiscences of a Radical Parson, 1905; Life of Chaucer, 1904; Horace, 1905, Spenser, 1906; Pre-Tractarian Oxford, 1909; Monograph on Lycidas, 1911; Nuggets from the Bible Mine, 1913. *Address:* Pyrford Rough, Woking. *T.A.:* Pyrford Maybury.
(Died 1 Feb. 1919.)

TUDOR, Sir Daniel (Thomas), Kt., *cr.* 1917; K.C.; Chief Justice of Gibraltar since 1922; *b.* Lampeter, South Wales, 21 July 1866; *m.* 1896, Hettie Josephine (*d.* 1924), 2nd *d.* of Gustavus Thompson, Cadogan Gardens, London; three *d.* Called to Bar, Gray's Inn, 1890; went Western Circuit and various local Sessions, 1893-1903; Attorney-General of the Colonies of Grenada and St. Vincent, British West Indies, 1903-11, during which time he acted on several occasions as Chief Justice, also as Colonial Secretary of Grenada, and administered the Government both for Grenada and St. Vincent; Commissioner to revise the laws of Grenada, 1911; acted as Legal Assistant, Colonial Office, London, 1911; Chief Justice of Supreme Court of Bahama Islands, 1911-22; President of the Discharged Soldiers' Commission, 1918-19. *Publication:* The Revised Laws of Grenada, 1911. *Recreations:* swimming and riding. *Address:* The Haven, Gibraltar. *Club:* Boodle's. *(Died 23 Nov. 1928.)*

TUDOR, Hon. Frank Gwynne, M.P.; Minister Trade and Customs, Australia, 1908-13, and 1914-16; *b.* 27 Jan. 1866; 3rd *s.* of John L. and Ellen C. Tudor; two *s.* three *d. Educ.:* State Schools, Williamstown and Richmond, Victoria. Worked in England and America at Felt Hat trade, 1889-94; introduced Trade Union Label into England and Felt Hatters Society, 1892; returned to Victoria, 1894; President Melbourne Trades Hall Council, 1900-1; elected to first Commonwealth Parliament; Whip for (Watson) Labour Ministry; Leader of Australian Labour Party since 1916. *Recreations:* cycling, rowing, lover of football and cricket. *Address:* Aberfoil, Rowena Parade, Richmond, Melbourne.
(Died Jan. 1922.)

TUFNELL, Col. Arthur Wyndham, C.M.G. 1916; *o. s.* of late Rt. Rev. Edward Wyndham Tufnell, D.D., Bishop of Brisbane; *m.* 1897, Frances Mary Adelaide, *d.* of late Capt. John Campion Wells, R.N.; one *d. Educ.:* Eton; Sandhurst. Joined The Queen's Regiment, 1891; Lieut. 1896; Captain, 1900; Major, 1914; Brev. Lt.-Colonel, 1916; passed Staff College, 1904; attached General Staff, War Office, 1904-1906; General Staff, Scottish Command, 1906-1910; General Staff Officer, East Lancashire Division, 1912-14; served with 1st Batt. The Queen's Regt., N.W. Frontier of India and in the Tirah Campaign, 1897-98 (medal with 2 clasps); S. African War with the Natal Field Force, including the Relief of Ladysmith, and

afterwards in the Transvaal and Orange River Colony, 1899-1902, with 2nd Batt. The Queen's Regt., and afterwards as A.D.C. to Brig.-General E. O. F. Hamilton, C.B. (despatches, severely wounded, Queen's medal with 6 clasps, King's medal with 2 clasps) ; European War, 1914-16, as General Staff Officer, Brigade-Commander and Brigadier-General General Staff (despatches thrice, wounded, Brevet of Lt.-Col. and Col., C.M.G., Chevalier of the Legion of Honour) *Clubs:* Army and Navy, Royal Automobile.
(Died 17 May 1920.)

TUFNELL, Col. W. Nevill, D.L. and J.P.; Local Director of Barclay's Bank; 2nd *surv. s.* of late J. J. Tufnell of Langleys, D.L. and J.P.; *m.* 1861, Eleanor Frances (*d.* 1919), *d.* of late Maj.-Gen. C. Gostling, R.A.; four *s.* one *d. Educ.:* Cheam. Entered Royal Navy on board H.M.S. Britannia, Flagship of Admiral Sir D. Dundas, 1852; served through the Russian War in that ship and H.M.S. Niger, and in the batteries at Balaclava; served also in the Boxer Gunboat in Sea of Azof; present at loss of H.M. Steam frigate Tiger, off Odessa; engaged in suppression of slave trade on East Coast of Africa; retired, 1863; commanded 2nd V.B. Essex Regt. for eighteen years, retiring in 1897. *Publication:* Tour in Palestine with Duke of Edinburgh in 1859. *Recreations:* country sports, carving in wood, and painting. *Heir: e. s.* Major De H. Tufnell, Essex Regt. *Address:* Langleys, Chelmsford. *T.:* Little Waltham 4.
(Died 3 Nov. 1922.)

TUFTON, Hon. Charles Henry, C.M.G. 1917; Sec., Foreign Office; 3rd *s.* of 1st Baron Hothfield; *b.* 16 May 1879; *m.* 1903, Stella Josephine, *y. d.* of Sir G. Faudel Phillip 1st Bt.; two *s.* one *d. Address:* 33 Albert Road, N.W.8. *T.:* Hampstead 8491. *(Died 23 Sept. 1923.)*

TUFTS, J. F., B.A., M.A., D.C.L.; Professor of History in Acadia University since 1874, and Dean of the Faculty of Arts and Science; *b.* New Albany, Annapolis County, Nova Scotia; *s.* of Samuel Tufts and Lorisa Kniffin; *m.* 1878, Marie Woodworth (*d.* 1900); two *s.* two *d. Educ.:* Acadia University; Harvard University. Principal of Horton Collegiate Academy, a preparatory school affiliated with Acadia College, 1874-89; Professor of History and Political Economy, 1892-1912. *Recreations:* gardening and care of lawn and grounds. *Address:* Wolfville, Nova Scotia. *T.:* 78. *(Died 7 Feb. 1921.)*

TUITE, James, J.P.; Chairman of Mullingar Town Commissioners; *b.* 1849; *s.* of late J. Tuite, Mullingar. M.P. (N.) Westmeath, N., 1885-1900. *Address:* Greville Street, Mullingar, Co. Westmeath. *(Died 6 Oct. 1916.)*

TULLOCH, Major-General Sir Alexander Bruce, K.C.B., *or.* 1902; C.B. C.M.G.; retired; *b.* Edinburgh, 2 Sept. 1838; 2nd *s.* of late Lieut.-Col. J. G. D. Tulloch and Anne, *d.* of late S. Staunton; *m.* 1st, 1865, Arabella (*d.* 1904), *d.* of late Stephen Heelis; five *s.*; 2nd, 1907, *d.* of late Canon Brandreth, and widow of Mr. Attwood of Glaslyn Court, Brecknocks. *Educ.:* private school; Roy. Military Coll. Sandhurst (cadet 13 to 16 years of age). Joined 1st Royals 1855; passed Staff College 1869; served as acting engineer, gunboat expeditions, and D.A.Q.M.G. South China; D.A.A.G. for instruction; D.A.Q.M.G. Southern District. Intelligence Dept. War Office; several confidential missions for War and Foreign Offices; special service officer to Commander-in-Chief, Mediterranean Fleet, 1882; in charge Intelligence Dept., Egypt; commanded Welsh Regt. South Africa and Egypt; Brigadier-General, Cairo; Major-General commanding Victorian military forces, and general military adviser to Australian colonies; president, Royal Commission on Defence Organisation, Sydney, 1892; served Crimea, 1855-1856; India, 1857-58; China Campaign, 1859-60; Egyptian Campaign, 1882; also for Intelligence

1058

Dept. with Spanish army during Carlist War in Pyrenees, 1874; requested by King of Belgians to undertake Gordon's work in Central Africa when that officer was shut up in Khartoum (not sanctioned); several times mentioned in despatches by both naval and military Commanders-in-Chief, 1882. *Decorated:* C.B. for Intelligence Dept. work, and arrangements made in Egypt for the expected naval and military operations; promoted Lieut.-Colonel on recommendation of Admiralty to War Office; also recommended for Victoria Cross; C.M.G. for arrangements made in Australia whereby the different Colonies at last agreed to furnish the necessary funds to build fortifications and barracks at the important coaling ports of King George's Sound and Thursday Island; president of a joint Naval and Military Committee which decided on the positions of the batteries; Times War Correspondent, Manchuria, 1904; awarded Good Service Pension; Hon. Colonel 5th Federal Regiment, Australia. *Publications:* Recollection of Forty Years' Service, 1903; Recollection of Four Years' Farming, 1905; The Argentine Republic and its Neighbours, 1907; The Highland Rising of the 45, 1901; Elementary Lectures on Military Law, 1871; Possible Battlefields in the next European War, 1890; A Soldier's Sailoring, 1912; and many professional papers. *Recreations:* farming, salmon and trout fishing, keeping bees, antiquarian research. *Address:* Glaslyn Court, Crickhowell. *Club:* United Service.
(Died 25 May 1920.)

TULLOCH, Major Hector, C.B. 1893; late Royal Engineers; late Chief Engineering Inspector, Local Government Board; *b.* 16 April 1885; *s.* of General John Tulloch, C.B.; *m.* 1st, 1855, Sophia Jane (*d.* 1858), *d.* of George Smith; one *s.* one *d.*; 2nd, 1860, Ada (*d.* 1907), *d.* of Edward Morton of Kensington Gate; one *s.* three *d. Educ.:* Kensington Grammar School; Addiscombe. Got his commission in 1855; served in India in Public Works Department up to 1868; appointed Municipal Engineer of Bombay in 1868, and an engineering inspector under the Local Government Board in 1873; made Chief Engineering Inspector in 1888; retired on 31st Dec. 1897. *Address:* 33 Half Moon Lane, Herne Hill, S.E.24. *T.:* Brixton 1197.
(Died 11 July 1923.)

TULLOCH, Rev. W. W., M.A., B.D., D.D.; *b.* Dundee, 22 Sept. 1846; *e. s.* of Very Rev. Principal Tulloch, D.D., LL.D., Principal of St. Andrews University, and Jane Anne Sophia Hindmarsh, Alnwick. *m.* 1st, 1872, Margaret Mather Crawford Hill (*d.* 1879); four *s.*; 2nd, 1884, Esther Proctor Hamilton Adamson; one *s.* two *d. Educ.:* Madras College; St. Andrews University. For twelve years contributor of Tangled Talk by Orion to Glasgow Citizen; Editor of Scots Magazine for four years and of Sunday Talk for five years. Gained Rector's Prize (Mr. J. A. Froude) at University for Essay on the Gowrie Conspiracy. Ordained Minister Old West Kirk, Greenock, 1871; assistant and successor to Parish of Kelso, 1874; Past Grand Chaplain of Freemasons of Scotland; Minister of Maxwell Parish, Glasgow, 1877-1901; Chaplain to Lord High Commissioner, 1891. *Publications:* Biographer of Leyden and editor of his Scenes of Infancy; one of the "... Giles' Lectures on the Creeds of Christendom— The Society of Friends and the Congregational Church; The Story of the Life of Queen Victoria (revised by the Queen); The Story of the Life of the Prince Consort (revised by the Queen; translated into Urdu; The Story of the Life of Emperor William; For the Sorrowful; Life of Tom Morris, 1907; Biographer of A.K.H.B. in Stray Sermons and Essays; Church Union in Scotland. *Recreations:* golf, reading novels and light literature of all kinds, writing *causeries* for newspapers and magazine articles. *Club :* Royal and Ancient, St. Andrews. *(Died Jan. 1920.)*

TUNNICLIFFE, Francis Whittaker, M.D., physician; *b.* Eccleshall, Staffs.; Physician, King's College Hospital, London; Member of the Departmental Committee on Food Preservatives; formerly Professor of Pharmacology, King's College, London. *Publications:* scientific papers upon the physiology and pathology of the respiratory, circulatory, and digestive organs. *Address :* 129 Harley Street, W.1. *T.:* Langham 2538. *Clubs:* Arts. Royal Automobile. *(Died 15 Dec. 1928.)*

TUOHY, James M.; *b.* Cork, 1859 ; *y. s.* of late Patrick Tuohy, manager, Cork Examiner; *m.* 1885, Florence, *d.* of late Jerome Donovan, Cork; two *s.* two *d.* *Educ.:* privately. London correspondent, Dublin Freeman's Journal, 1881-1912; European Manager, New York World, since 1897. *Recreation :* golf. *Address :* 23 Warwick Gardens, Kensington, W.14. *T.A. :* Promulgate, Westrand, London. *T. :* Western 411. *Clubs:* National Liberal, Savage, Pilgrims'. *(Died 7 Sept. 1923.)*

TUPPER, Hon. Sir Charles Hibbert, K.C.M.G., *cr.* 1893; LL.B. Harvard; K.C.; *b.* 3 Aug. 1855; 2nd *s.* of late Sir C. Tupper, 1st Bt.; *m.* 1879, Janet, *d.* of Hon. James Macdonald, C.J., of Nova Scotia; three *s.* three *d.* *Educ.:* McGill Coll., Montreal (Gov.-Gen. Scholarship); Harvard Law School. Barr. Nova Scotia, 1877; Ontario, 1895; British Columbia, 1898; Bencher of B.C. Law Society; elected to House of Commons, 1882, 1887, 1888, 1891, 1896-1900; Member of Canadian House of Commons for Pictou, Nova Scotia, 1882-1904; Minister of Marine and Fisheries, 1888-95; Minister of Justice and Attorney-General for Canada, 1895-96; Agent of H.B.M. Paris Tribunal of Arbitration, 1892 (K.C.M.G.); senior member of legal firm Tupper, Bull & Tupper, Vancouver, B.C. *Address :* Vancouver, B.C. *Clubs:* Union, Victoria; Vancouver, Country, Jericho, Vancouver.
(Died 30 Mar. 1927.)

TUPPER, Sir Daniel Alfred Anley, Kt., *cr.* 1909; M.V.O. 1901; Serjeant-at-Arms in Ordinary to H.M.; *b.* 1849; *m.* 1st, 1882, Mary, *d.* of late Lieut.-Col. C. E. Dering; 2nd, 1894, Rose, *e. d.* of Sir E. J. Reed, K.C.B., M.P., F.R.S. Entered Lord Chamberlain's Office, 1869; Chief Clerk, 1894-1901; Assistant-Controller, 1901-10. *Address:* Doric House, Bath. *T.:* 854. *Clubs:* Athenæum; Bath and County, Bath.
(Died 29 April 1922.)

TURING, Henry, I.S.O. 1913; Coronation Medal, 1911; *b.* 1 Aug. 1843; *s.* of late Sir J. H. Turing, 7th Bart.; *m.* Jeanne Marie Catherine (*d.* 1917), *d.* of late S. A. Chabot, banker, of Rotterdam; one *s.* three *d.* *Educ.:* in Holland; Queen Elizabeth's Grammar School, Sevenoaks. Was Acting British Consul at Rotterdam at different times, 1862-74; Vice-Consul, 1874; Consul for the provinces of South Holland, Zealand, and Limburg, 1882; retired on a pension, 1913. *Address:* Rotterdam. *Clubs:* Amicitia, Royal Rowing and Sailing, De Maas, Rotterdam.
(Died Mar. 1922.)

TURING, Sir James Walter, 9th Bt. *cr.* 1638; *b.* 3 Jan. 1862; *s.* of 8th Bt. and Catherine, *d.* of Walter S. Davidson; *S.* father, 1913; *m.* 1891, Mabel Rose, *d.* of Andrew Caldecott, of Pishiobury, Sawbridgeworth; two *s.* *Heir:* *s.* Robert Andrew Henry [*b.* 13 Sep. 1895; Capt. The Rifle Brigade (Prince Consort's Own). *Club :* Naval and Military]. *Address:* Crocker Hill House, Chichester. *Club :* Junior Carlton.
(Died 21 Feb. 1928.)

TURNBULL, Major Dudley Ralph, D.S.O. 1914; Gordon Highlanders; *b.* 15 Oct. 1891. Entered army, 1912; Adjutant 1st Batt., June-Sep. 1915; Staff Captain 91st Infantry

Brigade, June 1916; served European War, 1914-17 (wounded, despatches, D.S.O., Bt.-Major). *Club :* United Service.
(Died 1 Oct. 1917.)

TURNBULL, Major-General Peter Stephenson, M.D., K.H.S., H.M. Indian Army (retired); *b.* 1836; *m.* 1870, Mary, 2nd *d.* of George Oliver, Hawick; three *s.* four *d.* Joined Iudian Medical Service, 1860; served in Abyssinia under Lord Napier of Magdala, 1867-68 (medal); Secretary to the P.M.O., H.M. Forces, Bombay, 1882-88; Acting Inspector-General of Prisons, Bombay Presidency, 1883-1885; P.M.O. Sind District, 1888-93; Surgeon-General with the Government of Bombay, 1893-1896; retired 1896; Fellow of the University of Bombay, 1893; awarded Good Service Pension, 1896; Hon. Surgeon to King, 1902. *Recreations:* golf, etc. *Address:* 4 Church Hill, Edinburgh.
(Died 7 Oct. 1921.)

TURNBULL, Sir Robert, Kt., *cr.* 1913; M.V.O 1910; *b.* 21 Feb. 1852; *s.* of Rev. Robert Turnbull, Vicar of Wybunbury, Cheshire, and Louisa Phillippina; *m.* 1889, Kate, 2nd *d.* of late James Morten and *widow* of Sidney Humbert; one *s.* *Educ.:* Whitechurch Grammar School, Salop. Joined the London and North-Western Railway, 1868; Assistant to Superintendent of the Line, 1889; Superintendent of the Line, 1893-1914; General Manager 1914; joined the Board, 1915; Lt.-Col. in Railway Engineer and Staff Corps. *Address:* Gallowshill, Kings Langley, Herts. *(Died 22 Feb. 1925.)*

TURNER, Alfred; *b.* Bootham, York, 27 March 1874; *s.* of Charles Turner; *m.* 1897, Annie Elizabeth Davies; no *c.* *Educ.:* Grove School, York; privately. Trained in journalism from the age of seventeen; Dramatic Critic and Special Correspondent on the staff of The Yorkshire Post; Editor Yorkshire Evening Post for seven years; became associated with Carmelite House, 1911. *Publications:* In Faëry Lands Forlorn; Grey Days; Songs of the Sunset (Verse); On Falling in Love (Essays); two short plays produced in London and the Provinces; several short stories. *Recreations:* tramping anywhere in the open country, swimming, trying to play golf, reading. *Clubs:* Authors', Savage. *(Died 13 Dec. 1922.)*

TURNER, Major-General Sir Alfred Edward, K.C.B., *cr.* 1902; Director of British North Borneo Company; of Manchester North Borneo Rubber Co.; Chairman of North Borneo State Rubber, Ltd.; *b.* London, 3 Mar. 1842; *e. s.* of late Richard E. Turner, B.L. Bencher, Inner Temple, and Frances *d.* of Charles Johnstone; *m.* 1st, 1865, Blanche (*d.* 1899), *d.* of Charles Hopkinson of Wotton Court, Gloucester; 2nd, 1902, Juliette Elizabeth Marie, *o. d.* of late Henry Whiting; two *s.* one *d.* *Educ.:* Westminster School; Addiscombe. Joined R.A. 1860; A.D.C. and military private secretary Viceroy of Ireland, 1882-84; D.A.A.G. Nile Expedition, 1884-85 (despatches, medal and clasp, bronze star); assistant military secretary, Commander-in-Chief in Ireland, 1885-86; private secretary Viceroy of Ireland, 1886; Commissioner of Police, Cork Kerry, Clare, Limerick, 1886-92; Assis. Adj.-Gen. R.A. Army Headquarters, 1895-98; Inspector-General of Auxiliary Forces, 1900-4; President of Salon; Member of Japanese Society; Chairman of the Alliance Franco-Britannique. *Decorated* for civil services in Ireland (civil C.B.), for military services and being mentioned in despatches (mil. C.B.). *Publications:* The Retreat from Moscow and Passage of the Beresina; From Weissenburg to Sedan; Sixty Years of a Soldier's Life, 1912. *Recreations:* reading, riding, and Alpine climbing. *Address:* Carlyle House, Chelsea Embankment, S.W. *T. :* 1222 Western. *M. :* LA 8797. *Clubs:* Savage, Junior United

Service, Sesame, Royal Automobile, Swiss Alpine, Polyglot. *(Died 20 Nov. 1918.)*

TURNER, Engineer Rear-Admiral Arthur William, R.N. ; C.B. 1913; *b.* 29 Aug. 1859 ; 3rd *s.* of late Rev. George Turner ; *m.* 1st, Lily Seymour ; one *d.* ; 2nd, Sarah Faulconer. *Educ.:* Kingswood School, Bath ; Royal Naval Colleges, Devonport and Greenwich. Entered Navy as Assistant Engineer, 1880 ; Engineer, 1886 ; Chief Engineer, 1893 ; Engineer Commander, 1902 ; Engineer Captain, 1909 ; Engineer Rear-Admiral, 1912 ; served in Amethyst, Thames, Colossus, Renard, Sharpshooter, on introduction of Belleville boilers, Argonaut, Terrible, Nile, Vengeance, King Edward VII. ; and on the staffs of Admirals Sir A. B. Milne, Sir G. A. Callaghan, Sir J. Jellicoe, all 2nd Division Home Fleet ; Sir G. A. Callaghan, Commander-in-Chief Home Fleet ; retired, 1917. *Recreation:* motoring. *Address:* The Mount, Mannamead Avenue, Mannamead, Plymouth. *M:* CO 723. *Clubs:* Royal Automobile ; Royal Western Yacht, Plymouth. *(Died 30 Oct. 1928.)*

TURNER, Col. Augustus Henry, C.B. 1897 ; Unemployed Supernumerary List Indian Army ; *b.* 12 Oct. 1842 ; *s.* of George Turner, Beacon Downs, Devon. *Educ.:* Marlborough. Entered army, 1861 ; Brev. Col. 1891 ; served Hazara Campaign, 1868 (medal with clasp); Afghan War, 1878-80 (despatches, medal with two clasps) ; Mahsood - Wuzeeree Expedition, 1881 ; Zhob Field Force, 1890 (despatches) ; in command of column, Miranzai Expedition, 1891 (despatches, brevet of Col., clasp) ; in command of brigade, Waziristan, 1894-95 (thanks of Government of India, despatches, clasp). *Address:* Sunnyside, Dulverton, Somerset. *Club:* East India United Service.
(Died 3 April 1925.)

TURNER, Rt. Rev. Charles Henry, D.D., Suffragan to Bishop of London ; Bishop of Islington since 1898 ; *b.* 14 Jan. 1842 ; *s.* of Thomas Turner (barrister-at-law and treasurer of Guy's Hospital, formerly Fellow of Trinity College, Camb.); *m.* 1877, Edith Emma, 2nd *d.* of Bishop McDougall, late Bishop of Labuan and Sarawak ; four *s.* four *d.* Cholmeley School, Highgate ; Trin. Coll. Camb. ; Scholar, 10th Wrangler, 1864 ; M.A. 1867 ; D.D. 1898 ; read for orders with Dr. Vaughan. Ordained deacon, 1868, priest, 1869, Ely ; curate of Godmanchester, Hunts., 1868-73 ; resident chaplain to Bishop Jackson of London, 1873-77 ; Vicar of St. Saviour's, Fitzroy Square, 1877-82 ; Rector of St. George in the East, 1882-97 ; Rural Dean of Stepney, 1893-97 ; Prebendary of St. Paul's, 1898-1912 ; Examining Chaplain to Bishop of London, 1884-98 ; Hon. Chaplain to the Queen, 1895-98 ; Chaplain in ordinary, 1898 ; Rector of St. Andrew Undershaft, 1898-1912. *Address:* Stainforth House, Clapton Common, E.5 *T.:* Dalston 1526. *M.:* 4747. *Club:* Athenæum. *(Died 13 July 1923.)*

TURNER, Dawson, B.A., M.D., F.R.C.P.E., M.R.C.P. Lond. ; F.R.S.E. ; Lecturer on Medical Physics, Surgeons Hall ; Additional Examiner to the University of Edinburgh, and to the Royal Colleges of London and Edinburgh; in charge of radium treatment at the Royal Infirmary ; late President of the Royal Scottish Society of Arts ; Lieut. Army Motor Reserve ; *b.* Liverpool, 1857 ; *s.* of Rev. Dawson Turner, D.C.L. ; *m.* Emily, *d.* of William Barry, of Romford. *Educ.:* Shrewsbury ; Oxford ; Dalhousie ; Edinburgh ; Vienna. After graduating with honours in Edinburgh University, devoted particular attention to medical physics and to electricity, the X-rays and radium ; for thirty years medical electrician to the Royal Infirmary, Edinburgh. *Publications:* A Manual of Practical Medical Electricity, 4th edition ; Radium, its Physics and Therapeutics, 2nd edition ; A Students' Handbook of Diseases of

1060

the Skin ; many original papers to scientific societies. *Recreations:* a motor pioneer of Scotland, and a founder member of the Royal Automobile Club ; golf, motoring. *Address:* Belton, Hydon Heath, Godalming. *T.:* Hascombe 31X. *M.:* 8 11. *Club:* Athenæum.
(Died 25 Dec. 1928.)

TURNER, Rt. Hon. Sir George, K.C.M.G., *cr.* 1897 ; P.C. 1897 ; Premier and Treas. of Victoria ; M.P. for St. Kilda, Victoria ; Councillor and ex-Mayor of St. Kilda ; J.P. for Victoria ; member of Executive Council of Victoria ; *b.* Melbourne, Victoria, 8 Aug. 1851 ; *s.* of Alfred Turner ; *m.* 1872, Rose, *d.* of John Morgan, Bovey, Devon. *Educ.:* Central School, Melbourne. LL.D. Cambridge ; Under-graduate, Melbourne. Practising as solicitor and barrister in Victoria ; entered St. Kilda Council in 1887, and still a member ; elected to Parliament for St. Kilda in 1889 ; has held office in two previous Governments as Minister of Customs, Minister of Health, and Solicitor-General ; has also been Minister of Defence ; became Premier in Sept. 1894 ; Treas. Australian Federal Government, 1901-4, and 1904-5 ; also Pres. of the Federal Council of Australasia, and Chairman of the Standing Committee of such Council ; a member of the Australian National Federation Convention. *Recreation:* bowls. *Address:* 341 Collins Street, Melbourne ; Summerlee, Riversdale Road, Hawthorn.
(Died 14 Aug. 1916.)

TURNER, Rev. Herbert William, M.A. ; Rector of Sutton, Surrey, since 1886. *Educ.:* St. John's College, Oxford. Hon. Canon in Southwark Cathedral, 1918. *Address:* The Rectory, Sutton, Surrey. *(Died 14 June 1922.)*

TURNER, John Andrew, C.I.E. 1916 ; J.P. ; M.D. Edin. ; M.B., C.M., D.Ph. Camb. ; Executive Health Officer, Bombay, 1901-16 ; *b.* 1858 ; *m.* 1881, Vera Marguerite Lambert. *Educ.:* Edinburgh, London, Paris, Bonn. *Publications:* Sanitation in India ; Water Supply for Rural Districts, etc. *Address:* 34a Pembroke Square, W.8. *(Died 21 Aug. 1922.)*

TURNER, John Herbert ; *b.* 7 May 1833 ; *s.* of John and Martha Turner, Ipswich, Suffolk, England ; *m.* 1860, Elizabeth Eilbeck, of Whitehaven, Cumberland ; one *s. Educ.:* Whitstable, near Canterbury. Mercantile ; went to Nova Scotia in 1856 ; subsequently to Charlottetown, Prince Edward Island ; left for British Columbia, 1862 ; commenced in Victoria, 1863 ; elected to the City Council, 1877 ; Mayor of Victoria, 1879, 1880, 1881 ; elected Legislative Assembly of province, 1886 (city of Victoria) ; Minister of Finance and Agriculture, 1887-98 and 1899-1901 ; Premier, 1895-98 ; introduced the Budget for thirteen years, and Acts for encouragement of fruit growing, dairying, and formation of Farmers' Institutes and Farmers' Banks, etc. ; changed the financial system of province, 1888, by issue of 3 per cent inscribed stock in London. Joined the first company of Volunteers, 1864 ; retired into Canadian Reserve Militia, 1881, as Lieutenant-Colonel ; Agent-General for British Columbia in London, 1901 until retirement, 1916 ; whilst in office he arranged the purchase of lease for 99 years of Nos. 1 and 3 Regent Street, and had erected the new British Columbia building thereon ; Fellow of Royal Colonial and Royal Horticultural Societies. *Recreations:* riding, fishing, cricket, etc. *Address:* Bingham House, Richmond, Surrey. *Clubs:* Junior Constitutional, Royal Automobile ; Union, Victoria.*(Died 9 Dec. 1923.)*

TURNER, John Sidney, J.P. (Kent); Chairman, Petty Sessions, Penge Division ; M.R.C.S.Eng. ; F.L.S. ; Fellow Royal Society of Medicine ; Consulting Surgeon, Norwood Cottage Hospital ; Member of Council (a Founder) of Lister Institute of Preventive Medicine ; Member Board of Management,

British Home and Hospital for Incurables; General Editor of The Kennel Encyclopædia; Chairman of The Kennel Club; Chairman of the Society for the Prevention of Hydrophobia; Vice - President Battersea Home for Lost and Starving Dogs; Chairman of Penge and Upper Norwood Conservative Association (Dulwich); Vice-Chairman, Conservative and Unionist Association, Bromley Division of Kent; Member of Executive and Organization Committees of National Unionist Association; *b.* Old Shoreham, 12 Feb. 1843; *s.* of Jas. S. Turner of Chyngton, Seaford, Sussex; *m.* 1st, Isabella (*d.* 1893), *d.* of Arthur Scott of India Office; two *s.* one *d.*; 2nd, 1898, Emily Jane, *d.* of late Dr. John Boyle Barry of Calcutta and Dilkhoosh, Sydenham Hill; one *d. Educ.*: Merchant Taylors' School; Guy's Hospital. Late President South-Eastern Branch British Medical Association; late President of Sydenham District Medical Society; Fellow Obstetrical Society of London (Member of Council, 1893-94). *Publications:* articles in International Journal of Microscopy and Natural Science, Hazell's Annual; contributions to medical societies and journals. *Recreations:* shooting, fishing. *Address:* Stanton, Anerley, S.E.20. *T.:* Sydenham, 1071. *M.:* LT 7394; *Clubs:* Royal Societies, Kennel, Omar Khayyam.
　　　　　(*Died 16 Jan. 1920.*)

TURNER, Percy Frederick, C.B.E. 1920, partner in the firm of Turner, Brightman & Co.; *b.* July 1878; 4th *s.* of late W. H. Turner; *m.* 1918; two *s.* Private Secretary and Personal Assistant to Shipping Controller during European War; represented the Shipping Controller on British Allied Mission to Germany in connection with the interned British steamers in German ports in December 1918. *Address:* 28 Bolton Gardens, S.W.5. *T.:* Kensington 2229. *Club:* Devonshire. 　　(*Died 5 April 1926.*)

TURNER, Sir Samuel, Kt. *cr.* 1914; J.P.; twice Mayor of Rochdale; Senior Partner in cotton mills of S. Turner & Co., Ltd., the Asbestos works of Turner Bros., Ltd., and Chairman of Turner's and Newall, Ltd.; *b.* Rochdale 25 Feb. 1840; *s.* of Samuel Turner of Rochdale and Jane, *d.* of Robert Nuttall of Rochdale; *m.* 1st, 1864, Sarah Jane (*d.* 1896), *d.* of Thomas Fielding of Clitheroe; 2nd, 1900, Arabella (*d.* 1911), *d.* of late William Sothern Bellamy, of Gedney, Lincs; 3rd, 1916, Lavinia Heath, *d.* of William Wilson of Knaresborough, Yorkshire. Mayor of Rochdale, 1901-03; received Hon. Freedom of Borough, 1906. *Address:* Chaseley, Rochdale. 　　(*Died 11 Aug. 1924.*)

TURNER, Sir William, K.C.B., *cr.* 1901; Kt. *cr.* 1886; D.Sc., F.R.S., LL.D., D.C.L.; Principal and Vice - Chancellor of Edinburgh University since 1903; late President Royal Society, Edinburgh; *b.* Lancaster, 1832; *s.* of William Turner, Lancaster; *m.* Agnes (*d.* 1908), *e. d.* of Abraham Logan of Burnhouses, Berwickshire, 1863. *Educ.:* private schools; St. Bartholomew's Hospital. M.B. University of London; Hon. LL.D. Glasgow, St. Andrews, Aberdeen, Montreal, and Western University, Pennsylvania; Hon. D.C.L. Oxford, Durham, and Toronto; Hon. D.Sc. Dublin and Camb.; F.R.S. London and Edinburgh; F.R.C.S. London and Edinburgh; Hon. Member Royal Irish Academy, and of learned societies in Paris, Berlin, Rome, St. Petersburg, Brussels, New South Wales, etc.; Demonstrator of Anatomy, University of Edinburgh, 1854-67; Professor of Anatomy, University of Edinburgh, 1867-1903; Member of General Medical Council, 1873-1905, President 1898-1904; Member of the Medical Acts Commission, 1881; President British Association for advancement of Science, 1900; Hon Lieut.-Col. Queen's R. Vol. Brig. (V.D.); D.L. and Hon. Burgess, City of Edinburgh. *Publications:* numerous

memoirs on human and comparative anatomy, anthropology; several reports in the publications of H.M.S. Challenger; editor of Journal of Anatomy and Physiology. *Recreation:* travel. *Address:* 6 Eton Terrace, Edinburgh. *Club:* Athenæum. 　　(*Died 15 Feb. 1916.*)

TURNER, Sir William Henry, K.B.E., *cr.* 1921; Senior Partner, Turner, Brightman & Co., Shipowners, London; *b.* 6 Dec. 1868; *s.* of William Henry Turner and Sarah Jane Paul; *m.* 1895, Eleanor, *er. d.* of E. L. Ashworth, J.P., Knutsford, Cheshire; one *d. Educ.:* privately; abroad. Entered City in service of Turner, Brightman & Co., 1885; Partner, 1892; Vice-Chairman, Baltic Exchange; President, Institute of Chartered Shipbrokers; Member Committee, Lloyd's Register; Ex-Chairman, London General Shipowners' Society; Governor, London Orphan School, Merchant Seamen's Orphan Asylum; Member of Council, Chamber of Shipping, Committee Lifeboats Institution, etc. *Recreations:* golf, tennis. *Address:* Cranford, Weybridge. *T.:* Weybridge 121. *M.:* PB 8749, LY 5641, PA 6562. *Clubs:* Conservative, Devonshire, Royal Automobile, City.
　　　　　(*Died 19 Oct. 1923.*)

TURNEY, Sir John, Kt., *cr.* 1889; J.P. for the City; J.P. for the County of the City; M.I.M.E.; *b.* 2 Jan. 1839; *m.* 1st, 1866, Mary Eleanor (*d.* 1867), *d.* of Edward Nicholson, Manchester; 2nd, 1870, Juliette Emma (*d.* 1891), *d.* of A. Topham of Calais. Mayor of Nottingham, 1887-89; Member of Chamberlain Tariff Commission; Managing Director and Chairman of Turney Brothers, Ltd.; Chairman of Murray Brothers, Ltd., and of the Walsall Glue Co. Ltd. *Address:* Gedling House, Gedling, Notts. 　(*Died 17 Mar. 1927.*)

TURNOR, Algernon, M.A., J.P., C.B. 1887; *b.* London, 14 Nov. 1845; 4th *s.* of Christopher Turnor of Stoke Rochford, and Caroline, *d.* of 9th E. of Winchilsea; *m.* 1880, Lady Henrietta Caroline Stewart, *d.* of 9th Earl of Galloway; one *s.* three *d. Educ.:* Eton; Christ Church, Oxford. Entered the Treasury, 1867; appointed private secretary to the Permanent Secretary, and in 1874 private secretary to the Prime Minister, Earl of Beaconsfield; attached to the special embassy at Congress of Berlin, 1878; appointed Financial Sec. of H.M. Post Office, 1880; resigned, 1896. *Address:* 9 Clarges Street, Mayfair, W.1. *T.:* 4598 Gerrard. *Clubs:* Carlton, St. James's. 　　(*Died 11 Dec. 1921.*)

TURPIN, Ven. William Homan; Canon of Grahamstown, 1903; Archdeacon of Craddock, 1911. Ordained 1859; S.P.G. Missionary St. Philip's, Grahamstown, 1864-1905. *Address:* Grahamstown, Cape. 　(*Died 30 Nov. 1920.*)

TURQUAN, Joseph; homme de lettres; appartient à une vieille famille parisienne, originaire du Poitou, anoblie en 1413 par le roi Charles VI.; noblesse confirmée en 1777; *m.* 1883, Marie de la Motte de la Motte-Rouge, *nièce* du général de ce nom qui s'illustra dans la guerre de Crimée (1854-55) et celle d'Italie (1859). Paralysé des deux jambes depuis 1885; s'est adonné à la littérature. *Publications:* L'Impératrice Joséphine; Les sœurs de 'Napoléon; La reine Hortense; La citoyenne Tallien; La duchesse d'Abrantès; La duchesse d'Angoulême; Les femmes de l'Emigration; Madame Récamier; Le roi Jérôme; Napoléon amoureux; Le monde et le demi-monde sous Napoléon; Lady Hamilton; La belle Paméla (Lady Edward Fitz-Gerald); Madame de Stäel, etc. *Recreations:* ne quitte jamais sa chaise longue. *Address:* Rue Mignet 1, Paris (16e).
　　　　　(*Died Sept. 1928.*)

TUSON, Sir Henry Brasnell, K.C.B., *cr.* 1895; *b.* 30 Apr. 1836; *m.* Ann Frances, *d.* of the late Major J. Bates, 40th Madras N.I. 1864; one *s.* three *d. Educ.:* Christ's Hospital; King's College, London. Entered army, 1854; Lieut.-Gen. 1893; General, 1899; served China, 1858-60 (despatches, medal with 2 clasps); Egyptian Campaign, 1882 (despatches twice, 2 clasps, 3rd class Osmanieh, 3rd class Medjidie); Soudan Campaign, 1884; holds 1st class Saxe-Ernestine Order. *Address:* 16 Walpole Road, Surbiton, Surrey. *T.:* 315 P.O. Kingston. *(Died 21 Dec. 1916.)*

TUTTLE, Rt. Rev. Daniel Sylvester, S.T.D., LL.D.; Bishop of Missouri since 1886; Presiding Bishop of the Protestant Episcopal Church, U.S.A., since 1903; *b.* Windham, N.Y., 1837; *m.* 1865; three *s.* one *d.* *Educ.:* Columbia University; General Theological Seminary, New York City. Deacon, 1862; Priest, 1863; Missionary Bishop of Montana, Utah, and Idaho, 1867. *Publication:* Reminiscences of a Missionary Bishop, 1905. *Address:* St. Louis, Missouri, U.S.A.
(Died 17 April 1923.)

TWEEDIE, Colonel John Lannoy, D.S.O.; *b.* 6 May 1842; 5th *s.* of late Capt. M. Tweedie of Quarter, Peeblesshire, and Frances, *d.* of late R. W. Forbes of Rawlinson, Kent; *m.* 1891, Emma Constance, 3rd *d.* of late W. G. Murray of Avonmore, Ballybrack, Co. Dublin; two *d.* *Educ.:* privately. Served in Royal West Kent Regt. (97th and 50th); joined the 97th Regt. 1860; Transvaal Campaign; served with the Natal Field Force; Soudan Expedition 1884-85 (Nile medal with clasp, bronze star); Soudan Field Force; action at Giniss (despatches, D.S.O.). *Recreations:* shooting, riding, skating, etc. *Address:* Calder, Dorchester, Dorset.

TWEEDIE, Hon. Lemuel John; K.C., LL.D.; descended from the Tweedies of Drummelzier, Peeblesshire, Scotland; *b.* Chatham, N.B., 30 Nov. 1849; *m. d.* of the late Alexander Loudoun of Chatham; four *s.* two *d.* *Educ.:* At a Presbyterian College. Admitted to the Bar of N.B., 1871; elected to the House of Assembly of N.B. for Northumberland, 1874, and has represented that County ever since, except 1878-1882; Surveyor-General, 1890; Provincial Secretary, 1896; Premier, 1900-7; represented New Brunswick at the King's Coronation in 1901-2; Lieutenant-Governor of New Brunswick, 1907-1912; holds long service medal in Militia of Canada. *Recreations:* yachting, shooting, fishing, curling. *Address:* Elmhurst, Chatham, New Brunswick, Canada. *Club:* Union, St. John.
(Died Sept. 1917.)

TWEEDIE, Major-General Michael, F.R.G.S. (retired); *s.* of Capt. M. Tweedie, R.A., of Rawlinson, Rolvenden, Kent; *b.* 1836; *m.* 1872, Louisa Bateson Hammond. *Educ.:* Royal Military College, Woolwich. Crimea; siege of Sebastopol; battle of Tchernaya, 1855-56; Indian Mutiny, 1858; mutiny at Mooltan; served in India, Ceylon, Canada, Australia, Mediterranean, etc. *Recreations:* riding, boating, shooting, etc. *Address:* Boveney Folkestone. *Club:* Army and Navy
(Died 8 Aug. 1917.)

TWEEDY, Sir John, Kt., *cr.* 1906; Past President of the Royal College of Surgeons the Ophthalmological Society of the United Kingdom, the Medico-Legal Society, the Medical Defence Union and Royal Medical Benevolent Fund; a Trustee of the Hunterian Collection, Royal College Surgeons; Member of Council and formerly of the Distribution Committee of King Edward's Hospital Fund; Emeritus Professor of Ophthalmic Medicine and Surgery in University College London; Consulting Ophthalmic Surgeon to University College Hospital; Consulting Surgeon to the Royal London Ophthalmic Hospital (Moorfields); LL.D. Edinburgh; *b.* Stockton-on-Tees, 1849; *m.* 1885, Mary, *y. d.* of Richard Hillhouse, Finsbury Place; two *s.* one *d.* *Educ.:* Elmfield College, York; University College, London. *Publications:* various articles and papers on ophthalmological subjects, medical history, education, and politics;

1062

Hunterian Oration, Royal College of Surgeons, 1905; The Thomas Vicary Lecture on the History of Anatomy and Surgery, Royal College of Surgeons, 1919; The Annual Oration Medical Society of London, 1919, etc. *Address:* 100 Harley Street, W.1. *T.:* Mayfair 4036. *Club:* Reform. *(Died 4 Jan. 1924.)*

TWEMLOW, Colonel Francis Randle, D.S.O. 1900; commanded 4th Batt. North Staffs. Regiment; retired, 1908; *b.* 20 Dec. 1852; *m.* 1st, 1878, Evelyn Harriet (*d.* 1880), *d.* of Sir John Thomas Buller Duckworth, 2nd Bart.; 2nd, 1882, Annie Mary Gertrude, *o. c.* of Rev. Edward Lewis; one *d.* *Educ.:* Winchester; Christ Church, Oxford. M.A. (first-class honours in Modern History), 1875; Barrister of Inner Temple, 1879; served South Africa, 1900-1902. *Address:* Peatswood, Market Drayton. *Club:* United University. *(Died 21 Jan. 1927.)*

TWIGG, John J., K.C.; *s.* of late Rev. Thomas Twigg, A.M., rector of the parish of Pomeroy, Co. Tyrone, and Sarah Macausland of Streeve, Co. Londonderry; *m.* Eliza, *d.* of late James Corry Lowry, of Rockdale, Co. Tyrone, Q.C. *Educ.:* Armagh Royal School; Trinity College, Dublin. Called to the Bar, 1851; Inner Bar, 1877; Bencher of King's Inns, 1889. *Club:* University, Dublin. *(Died June 1920.)*

TWINING, Maj.-Gen. Sir Philip Geoffrey, K.C.M.G., *cr.* 1919; C.B. 1918; C.M.G. 1915; M.V.O. 1911; late R.E.; Director of Fortifications and Works, War Office; *b.* Halifax, Nova Scotia, 7 Sep. 1862; *s.* of late Edmund Crawley Twining, *s.* of Chas. Twining, Q.C., barrister-at-law, of Halifax, N.S., and Elizabeth Lee Whitman, *d.* of John Whitman of Annapolis, Nova Scotia; *m.* Louise Mary, *d.* of George and Mary Daly of Napanee, Ontario, 1897. *Educ.:* Kingston, Canada. Gazetted Lt. Royal Engineers, 1886; served in England, Canada, East Africa, India, and China; Regimental Employment, Staff and Special Service; Col. 1915; Maj.-Gen. 1 Jan. 1917; served European War, 1914-18 (despatches seven times, C.M.G., C.B., Order of St. Stanislaus) *Publications:* contributions to reviews and periodicals upon military and general subjects. *Recreations:* travel, riding, golf. *Clubs:* Ranelagh; United Service, Simla. *(Died 15 Jan. 1920.)*

TWISADAY, Major C. E. J., I.S.O.; V.D. 1892; *b.* 9 May 1850; *s.* of Rev. J. Twisaday; *m.* 1886, Jose E. S., *d.* of late General Sir A. J. Cloete, K.C.B.; one *s.* *Educ.:* Lewes Grammar School; private tuition. Indo-European Telegraph Dept.; India Office, 1869-1915; accompanied Director-in-Chief to India, Persian Gulf, Persia, and Constantinople; 30 years commissioned service in Queen's Westminster R.V.; retired as Major. *Publications:* joint-author of official translations of three International Telegraph Conventions. *Recreations:* shooting, golf, woodcarving, clockmaking, etc. *Address:* Chichester House, Upper Westbourne Terrace, W.2. *T.:* Paddington 2024. *Clubs:* St. Stephen's, Neasden Golf. *(Died 6 Feb. 1925.)*

TWISS, Lt.-Col. (retired pay) **George Edward,** C.M.G. 1917; R.A.M.C.; M.D., M.K. and Q.C.P.I., F.R.C.S.I.; Hon. Sec. Southampton Centre St. John Ambulance Association; member chapter General Order of St. John and Ambulance Committee; *b.* Dublin, 5 Nov. 1856; *s.* of John Twiss and Ann Willis; *m.* 1912, Ethel Madeline Sprague; no *c.* *Educ.:* Columbia University, New York (M.D.). Graduated 1876; Demonstrator of Anatomy, R.C.S.I. 1878-79; Civil Surgeon Zulu War, 1879-80; Surgeon A.M.D. 1881; Lt.-Col. R.A.M.C. 1901; retired, 1907; re-employed 5 Aug. 1914; relegated to retired pay & June, 1919; Knight of Grace, Order of St. John of Jerusalem, 1908; medals: Zulu with clasp, Egyptian and Khedive's Star, Queen's medal with 3 clasps, King's medal with 2 clasps, despatches twice; European War, 1914-19 (despatches, C.M.G.,' G.S. medal); St. John Ambulance Bde. Coronation medal. *Publication:* Manual for Voluntary Aid Detachments. *Recreations:* masonry and work. *Address:* Mayfield, Oakley Road, Southampton. *Club:* Royal Southampton Yacht. (*Died 27 June 1921.*)

TWISS, Vice-Admiral Guy Ouchterlony; *b.* 19 Oct. 1834; *m.* 1880; three *s.* two *d. Educ.:* Launceston, V.D. Laud. Joined the Navy as Cadet, 1848; served in the Channel, West Indies, China; as Lieut. present at capture of Taku Forts in H.M.S. Pique; served in Excellent and in Royal Oak in Mediterranean; as Commander in Warrior and in Eagle, drill ship R.N.R.; Serapis 3 years, and in Belleisle at Kingstown. *Address:* Lindfield, Hayward's Heath. (*Died 7 Oct. 1918.*)

TWYFORD, Thomas William, J.P., D.L.; *b.* 1849; *e. s.* of Thomas Twyford, of Shelton, Staffordshire (*d.* 1872), and Sarah (*d.* 1874), *d.* of late Robert Jones, of Bordeaux; *m.* 1872, Susannah, *d.* of Edward Whittingham; one *s.* one *d.* High Sheriff, Staffordshire, 1906; has the Order of St. Ann of Russia; Conservative Candidate for N.W. Staffordshire, 1907; Chairman, Twyfords, Ltd., Hanley, Staffordshire Sentinel Newspaper, and North-Western Electricity and Power Gas Co. *Address:* Whitmore Hall, Newcastle, Staffordshire. *Clubs:* Carlton, Junior Carlton. (*Died 21 Mar. 1921.*)

TWYNAM, Col. Philip Alexander Anstruther, C.B. 1882; *b.* Ceylon, 5 May 1832; 5th *s.* of late Thomas Holloway Twynam, R.N., and Mary, *d.* of late Major Somerville, 83rd Regt.; *m.* 1862, Elizabeth Annie, *e. d.* of late Captain Horrocks Whitehead, H.E.I.C.S. *Educ.:* private school. Joined 15th East Yorks Regt. 1851; Captain, 1858; Major, 1868; Lieut.-Col. 1876; Col. 1881; Retired on age clause, 1890. Commanded 15th Regt. 1876-81; passed Staff Coll. 1859; Brig.-Maj. Aldershot, 1860; D.A.Q.M.G. Aldershot, 1861-66; and D.A.Q.M.G. Ireland, 1869; A.A.G. and A.Q.M.G. Egypt, 1882 (medal and clasp, despatches, C.B., 3rd class Osmanieh); commanded 15th Regimental District, 1883-84; A.A.G. and Chief Staff Officer S. District, 1884-1889. *Address:* 55 Elsham Road, Kensington, W. *Club:* Army and Navy. (*Died 27 Dec. 1920.*)

TWYNAM, Sir William Crofton, K.C.M.G. 1896; C.M.G. 1884. Entered Government Service, Ceylon, 1845; Assist. Agent, Jaffa, 1848; Hanbantota, 1854; Manaar, 1858; N.W. Provinces, 1868; Government Agent, Northern Province, Ceylon, 1869-95; retired 1896; widower. *Address:* Jaffna, Ceylon.
(*Died 14 Mar. 1922.*)

TYLER, Maj.-Gen. Trevor Bruce, C.B. 1917; C.S.I. 1903; D.I..; J.P. Co. Glamorgan; Col. Comdt. R.A.; *b.* 7 Jan. 1841; *s.* of Rev. Roper Trevor Tyler, of Llantrithyd, Glamorgan; *m.* 1873, Ada, *d.* of Edward Perkins, Birtley Hall, Durham; one *d. Educ.:* R.M.A. Woolwich. Entered army, 1859; served Fenian Raid, Canada, 1866 (medal and clasp); commanded B Battery, R.H.A., 1881-86; Commandant Okehampton Camp, 1891-93; Colonel on the Staff, Poona, 1893-95; Brigadier-Gen. R.A. Punjab, 1895-97; Maj.-Gen. 1900; Inspector-General of Artillery, India, 1897-1903; retired, 1903; Chairman Glamorgan County Terr. Association. *Address:* Llantrithyd, Glamorgan. *T.A.:* Bouvilston. *Club:* Naval and Military.
(*Died 12 Feb. 1933.*)

TYLOR, Sir Edward Burnett, Kt. *cr.* 1912; D.C.L., LL.D., F.R.S., J.P.; Hon. Fellow of Balliol College; Emeritus Professor of Anthropology, University of Oxford; *b.* London, 2 Oct. 1832; *m.* Anna, *d.* of late Sylvanus Fox, Wellington, Somerset, 1858. *Educ.:* Grove House School, Tottenham. Author and anthropologist. *Publications:* Anahuac, Mexico and the Mexicans, 1859; Researches into the Early History of Mankind, 1865; Primitive Culture, 1871; Anthropology, 1881. *Address:* Linden, Wellington, Somerset. *Club:* Athenæum.
(*Died 2 Jan. 1917.*)

TYMMS, Rev. T. Vincent, D.D.; *b.* London, 1842; *s.* of Ebenezer Tymms; *m.* 1st, 1869, Agnes, *d.* of Ralph Dodds of Berwick-on-Tweed; 2nd, 1888, Louisa I., *d.* of James Doré of Clapton; three *s.* three *d. Educ.:* private school and Regent's Park College, London. Became pastor of the Baptist Church at Berwick-on-Tweed, 1865; removed to Accrington, 1868; first minister of the Downs Chapel, Clapton, London, 1869-91; President, and Professor of Theology, Baptist College, Rawdon, Leeds, 1891-1904; President of the London Baptist Association, 1881, and while in that office built Woodberry Down Chapel, London, N.; Vice-President of the Baptist Union of Great Britain, 1895; President, 1896; D.D. St. Andrews, 1897; Angus Lecturer Regent's Park College, 1908. *Publications:* The Mystery of God, 5th edition; The Christian Idea of Atonement, 1904; The Private Relationships of Christ, 1907; The Evolution of Infant Baptism and Related Ideas, 1912; wrote the first essay in The Ancient Faith in Modern Light. *Recreations:* cricket in earlier years, now golf. *Address:* 82 Marina, St. Leonards-on-Sea. (*Died 25 May 1921.*)

TYNDALL, Lt.-Col. William Ernest Marriott, D.S.O. 1900; West Riding Regt.; D.A.A.G., Western Command; *b.* 2 Feb 1875; *m.* 1908. Alice Lorna, *d.* of late Mr. Sedgwick, Byfleet, Surrey. Entered army, 1895. Served South Africa, 1899-1902 (despatches thrice, Queen's medal, 4 clasps, King's medal, 2 clasps, D.S.O.); European War, 1914-15 (wounded). *Address:* 17 Castellain Road, Maida Vale, W.; Chester. (*Died 1 Aug. 1916.*)

TYRRELL, Lt.-Col. Gerald Ernest, D.S.O. 1915; Royal Garrison Artillery; *b.* 31 Oct. 1871. Entered army, 1892; Captain, 1900; Major, 1912; with Macedonian Gendarmerie, 1907-9; Military Attaché, Constantinople and Athens, 1909-13; served N.W. Frontier, India, 1897-8 (medal, 3 clasps); European War, 1914-15 (despatches twice, D.S.O., Bt. Lt.-Col.). (*Died 17 May 1917.*)

TYRWHITT, Rev. the Hon. Leonard Francis, O.B.E. 1919; M.V.O. 1906; Rector of Rolleston, Burton-on-Trent, since 1907; Canon of St. George's Chapel, Windsor, since 1910; chaplain-in-ordinary to the King; *b.* 29 Oct. 1863; *s.* of Sir H. Tyrwhitt, 3rd Bt., and Baroness Berners. *Educ.:* Marlborough Coll.; Magdalene College, Cambridge (M.A.); Wells Theological Coll. Curate at Henley-on-Thames, 4½ years; Hendon, Middlesex, 2½ years; Chaplain to H.M.S. Renown for tour of T.R.H.'s the Prince and Princess of Wales to India, 1905-6; Vicar of Fenton, 1895-1907; Vice-Provost of Denstone since 1906; Acting-Chaplain to the Forces since 1914 (wounded, despatches); Deputy Assistant Chaplain-General, 1918. *Address:* Rolleston Rectory, Burton-on-Trent; The Cloisters, Windsor Castle. *Club:* Wellington.
(*Died 7 July 1921.*)

TYSER, Sir Charles Robert, Kt., *cr.* 1909; *b.* 24 Dec. 1848; 4th *s.* of George Dorman Tyser; *m.* 1893, Lilian Adelaide, *d.* of Rev. Charles John Kennard Shaw. *Educ.:* Rugby; Trinity College, Cambridge. Called to Bar, Inner Temple, 1873; Attorney-General Leewards, 1886-89; President, District Court, Kyrenia, Cyprus, 1895; Puisne Judge, Cyprus, 1902; Chief Justice Cyprus, 1906-19. *Publications:* Marine Insurance Losses, 1894; translated Omar Hilmi Effendi's Evkaf Law, 1899, and the Mejelle, 1901. *Club:* United University.
(*Died 23 Aug. 1926.*)

TYSON, William Joseph, M.D., F.R.C.P. Lond.; F.R.C.S. Eng.; Hon. Physician, Royal

Victoria Hospital, Folkestone ; J.P. Kent ; Chairman of the Elham Division ; *b.* 9 Sep. 1851 ; *s.* of W. Taylor Tyson, **M.R.C.S.** ; *m.* Lola Houssemayne, *d.* of Julius Houssemayne du Boulay, of West Lawn, Sandgate ; three *d.* *Educ.:* Guy's Hospital. Fellow of the Royal Society of Medicine, etc. ; practises as a Physician ; Member of the Church Assembly of the Church of England. *Publications:* several contributions to medical literature, addresses, etc. *Address:* Kimberley, Jointon Road, Folkestone. *T.:* 361. *M.:* KL 3105.   *(Died 2 Sept. 1927.)*

TYTLER, Maj.-Gen. Robert Francis Christopher Alexander, Indian Army. Major-General, 1895 ; served Afghan War, 1878-1880 (despatches, medal with clasp, Brevet Lt.-Colonel). *Address:* 62 Bedford Gardens, Campden Hill, W.   *(Died 19 Oct. 1916.)*

U

UDNY, Sir Richard, K.C.S.I., *cr.* 1897 ; *b.* 1847 ; *s.* of George Udny, Bengal Civil Service ; *m.* 1st, 1883, Alicia *(d.* 1904), *d.* of Samuel Tomkins, banker, London ; 2nd, 1917, Edith Phyllis, 4th *d.* of late William Davies, Liverpool, and of Mrs. Davies, Prestatyn ; one *d.* *Educ.:* Aberdeen Univ. M.A. 1866 ; 1st class Honours Mathematics ; 2nd class Classics ; Fullerton Mathematical Scholar, 1867 ; Hon. LL.D. 1898. Entered Bengal Civil Service, 1869, retired 1899 ; served as a political officer with following frontier expeditions, viz. : Jowaki, 1877-78 ; Mahsud Waziri, 1881 ; Samana (Miranzai), 1891 (medal and two clasps) ; and Isazai (Black Mountain), 1892 : also as chief of the political staff with the Tirah Expedition against the Afridis and Orakzais, 1897-98 (medal and two clasps) ; was appointed on a special mission to the Kurram Valley, 1888 ; Commissioner of the Peshawar Division, 1891 ; Commissioner for Delimitation of parts of the Indo - Afghan Boundary, 1894-95 and 1896-97. *Address:* 5 Clarendon Road, St. Helier, Jersey.
(Died 24 April 1923.)

UHTHOFF, John Caldwell, M.D., F.R.C.S. ; *b.* 1856 ; *s.* of Edward Uhthoff ; *m.* 1st, 1884, Ellen Aston, *d.* of late Charles King, formerly of North Lodge, Enfield ; one *s.* three *d.* ; 2nd, 1913, Ida, *d.* of late Francis Goode Cuningham, of Bentley House, Hants. *Educ.:* Brighton College ; Guy's Hospital. Knight of Grace St. John of Jerusalem. *Recreations:* golf, travel. *Address:* 7 Branksome Wood Road, Bournemouth. *T.:* 2747. *Club:* Bournemouth.
(Died 19 Jan. 1927.)

UMFREVILLE, Colonel Percy, C.M.G. 1915 ; C.B.E. 1919 ; Royal West Kent Regiment ; *b.* 29 Feb. 1868 ; *s.* of late S. C. Umfreville, Ingress Abbey, Greenhithe, Kent ; *m.* Edith Margaret, *d.* of late J. B. Tracey, I.C.S. ; one *d.* Entered army, 1887 ; Bt. Lieut.-Colonel, 1917 ; Lt.-Col. 1919 ; Col. 1920 ; Adjutant, 1894-7 ; Captain, 1896 ; Major, 1905 ; Adjutant Volunteers, 1897-1902 ; Governor Military Prison, 1902-1912 ; Commandant Detention Barracks, 1912-1914 ; Governor Military Prisons in Field, France, 1914 - 16 ; Director Military Prisons in Field, British Army in France, Aug. 1916–Oct. 1919 ; Temp. Brig.-Gen. Aug. 1916–Oct. 1919 ; Half Pay, Oct. 1919–March 1920 ; Assistant Adjutant General Scottish Command, March 1920 ; served European War, 1914-19 (C.M.G., Bt. Lt.-Col.).
(Died 11 July 1922.)

UMNEY, John Charles, a Managing Director of Wright, Layman, and Umney, Ltd., wholesale druggists, Southwark ; Joint-Managing Director of W. Woodward, Ltd., Nottingham and London ; Managing Director of Thomas Wilkinson, Ltd., London ; Director of

R. Carter & Sons, Ltd., London ; Member of the Pharmaceutical Society ; Past President British Pharmaceutical Conference ; Past President of the Wholesale Druggists' Club ; Ex-Chairman of the Chemical Trades Section of the London Chamber of Commerce, also of the Proprietary Articles Section of the London Chamber of Commerce, also Toilet Soap Trades Section ; Past Pres. of Proprietary Articles Trade Association ; a Member of the Council of the Advertisers' Protection Society ; Member of the Pharmaceutical Committee of Reference for the British Pharmacopoeia ; Silver Medallist of the Royal Society of Arts ; Fellow of the Chemical Society, of the Royal Botanical Society, the Royal Horticultural Society, and of the Society of Public Analysts ; Juror at Franco - British and Imperial International Exhibitions, 1908 - 9 ; *b.* London, 1868 ; 2nd *s.* of late Charles Umney, F.I.C., F.C.S. ; *m.* Constance, *d.* of late John Sloane Carter ; one *s.* one *d.* *Educ.:* Dulwich College (Scholar) ; Pharmaceutical Society's School (bronze and silver medallist). *Publications:* A Short Guide to the British Pharmacopoeia, 1898 ; Essential Oils in their relation to the British Pharmacopoeia and Trade ; Standards for Medicines ; Editor of Perfumery and Essential Oil Record ; etc. *Address:* 27A Sloane Square, S.W.1 ; *T.:* Victoria 2478 ; Berea Court, Yapton, Arundel, Sussex.   *(Died 9 Oct. 1919.)*

UNDERHILL, Admiral Edwin Veale, C.B. 1918 ; R.N. ; *b.* 27 March 1868 ; *m.* ; three *s.* Served Tokar, Eastern Sudan, 1891 (Bronze Star) ; present at bombardment of Sultan of Zanzibar Palace, 1896 ; served in punitive Naval Expedition against King of Benin, 1897 (medal and clasp) ; European War, 1914-18 (C.B.) ; Admiral Superintendent, H.M. Dockyard, Devonport, 1919-22 ; retired list, 1924. *Address:* Bellair House, Havant, Hants. *M.:* PT 3251.   *(Died 22 July 1928.)*

UNDERWOOD, Arthur Swayne, L.D.S., M.R.C.S. ; late Professor of Dental Surgery, King's College, London, Dental Surgeon, King's College Hospital, and Examiner in Dental Surgery, Royal College of Surgeons, 1900-10 ; Inspector of Dental Examinations in the United Kingdom on behalf of the General Medical Council, 1911 ; Hon. Dental Surgeon to King George Hospital for wounded ; Tomes prize for research, Royal College of Surgeons, 1906-8. *Educ.:* King's College, London. *Publications:* Surgery for Dental Students, 1881 ; Aids to Dental Surgery, 1906 (2nd ed.) ; Notes on Anæsthetics, 1893 ; Aids to Dental Anatomy and Physiology, 1914 (3rd ed.) ; Studies in Comparative Odontology, 1903. *Address:* 38 Harley Street, W. *T.:* Mayfair 6848.
(Died 2 Dec. 1916.)

UNWIN, Francis Sydney ; *b.* Stalbridge, Dorset, 11 Feb. 1885 ; *s.* of Rev. C. E. Unwin ; *m.* 1917, Clara Miyadera, *d.* of R. S. Schwabe of Yokohama, Pianist. *Educ.:* D.C.M.S. Cheltenham ; Slade School, London ; Paris ; Italy. Draughtsman, etcher, lithographer, painter ; Member New English Art Club, 1912 ; work in National Gallery of British Art, Millbank, Print Room, British Museum, New York Public Library and Metropolitan Museum ; Sydney National Gallery, etc. *Publications:* Decorative Arts of the Church ; critical articles ; Maloja, Portfolio of Etchings, 1921. *Recreation:* travelling. *Address:* 61 High Street, Hampstead, N.W.3.   *(Died 26 Nov. 1925.)*

UNWIN, Colonel Garton Bouverie, D.S.O. 1908 ; Indian Army ; late 21st Cavalry ; *b.* 9 July 1859 ; *m.* 1898, Katharine, *e. d.* of Sir Arthur Fanshawe, K.C.I.E. ; two *d.* *Educ.:* Wellington. Entered Army, Somerset Light Infantry, 1878 ; Captain, 1889 ; Major, 1898 ; Lieut.-Col. 1904 ; Bt.-Col. 1907 ; served Zhob Valley expedition, 1890 ; Waziristan, 1894-

1895 (medal with clasp) ; N. W. Frontier, 1897-98 (medal with clasp) ; Waziristan, 1901-2 (clasp) ; Mohmund expedition, 1908 (medal and clasp, D.S.O.) ; European War, Remount Dept., and Q.M.G.'s Dept. *Address:* Pin Close, Budleigh Salterton, Devon.   (*Died 4 July 1928.*)

UPCHER, Henry Morris, J.P., D.L. ; B.O.U. ; *e. s.* of late Henry Ramey Upcher and Caroline, *d.* of Joseph Morris of Ampthill ; *b.* 15 Dec. 1839 ; *m.* 1869, Maria Hester, *o. c.* of Rev. Edward Bowyer Sparke, of Feltwell, Norfolk ; two *s.* two *d.* [*Heir :* Henry Edward Sparke ; *m.* 1904, Fanny (Nina), *y. d.* of late T. G. Simpson. *Educ. :* Harrow ; Trinity College, Cambridge (B.A. 1893) ; *b.* 1871.] *Educ. :* Harrow ; Trinity College, Cambridge. *Address :* Sheringham Hall, Norfolk ; East Hall, Feltwell, Norfolk. *Club :* Conservative.
    (*Died 6 April 1921.*)

UPCOTT, Ven. Arthur William, D.D. Oxon. ; Rector of Brightling and Archdeacon of Hastings since 1920 ; *b.* Manor House, Cullompton, Devon, 6th Jan. 1857 ; 4th *s.* of John Samuel Upcott, of Manor House, Cullompton ; *m.* 1888, Sophia Madeline, 3rd *d.* of late Charles Anderson Dalgairns, M.D.. F.R.C.S. ; one *s.* one *d. Educ. :* Sherborne School ; Exeter Coll. Oxford. Scholar,1875; Goldsmiths' Exhibitioner, 1877 ; 1st class Class. Mods., 1876 ; 2nd class Lit. Hum., 1879 ; B.A. 1879 ; M.A., 1882 ; B.D. and D.D. 1906 ; Deacon, 1884, Priest, 1886 ; Assistant Master, St. Mark's School, Windsor, 1880-82, 1884-86 ; Head Master, 1886-91 ; Assistant Master, Westminster School, 1882-84 ; Head Master, St. Edmund's School, Canterbury, 1891-1902 ; Head Master, Christ's Hospital, 1902-1919. *Publications:* Caesar, B. G., Book iv. ; Euripides, Hecuba. *Address :* The Rectory, Brightling, Sussex.   (*Died 22 May 1922.*)

UPCOTT, Sir Frederick Robert, K.C.V.O., *cr.* 1906 ; C.S.I., 1900 ; M. Inst. C.E. ; *b.* 28 Aug. 1847 ; 2nd *s.* of J. S. Upcott, Cullompton, Devon ; *m.* 1878, Jessie, *d.* of late Harold Turner ; one *s. Educ. :* Sherborne School ; King's College, London. Appointed by examination to the Public Works Depart. India, 1868; was engaged on the construction of Indian railways ; appointed consulting engineer to Madras Government for railways,1892 ; Director-General of Railways in India, 1896 ; Secretary in the Public Works, India, 1898-1901 ; Govt. Director of Indian Railways, 1901-1904 ; Chairman Board of Indian Railways, 1904-8 ; *Decorated* for services in the Railway Department of India. *Recreations :* is a Lieut.-Colonel in the Indian volunteer forces. *Address :* c/o Cocks, Biddulph, Bankers, Charing Cross, S.W.1.   (*Died 15 Oct. 1918.*)

UPPERTON, Maj.-Gen. John, C.B. 1882, I.S.C. ; *s.* of late Robert Upperton, of Westburton, Sussex ; *b.* 10 June 1838. Entered Bengal army, 1854 ; Maj.-Gen. 1894 ; served Indian Mutiny, 1857-59 (medal with clasp) ; China, 1860 (thanked by Commander-in-Chief of French forces, medal with two clasps) ; N.-W. Frontier of India (medal with clasp) ; in 1869 accompanied the Ameer Sher Ali, of Cabul, to Umballa, on the occasion of his visit to the Viceroy (thanked by Government) ; appointed to political charge of the Envoy, from the Ameer of Kabul, to India, 1873 ; specially employed on a mission to Beluchistan, 1876 ; Egyptian War, 1882 (despatches, C.B., 3rd class Medjidie, Khedive's star). *Address :* 7 Sloane Street, S.W.1. *T. :* Kensington 1110. *Club :* Naval and Military. (*Died 2 July 1924.*)

UPTON, Professor Charles B., Professor of Philosophy in Manchester College, Oxford, since 1875, now Professor Emeritus ; *b.* Portsea, Hampshire, 19 Nov. 1831 ; *m.* 1663. *Educ. :* Dr. J. R. Beard's School at Higher Broughton, Manchester ; Manchester New College ; University College, London. Graduated in the University of London ; B.A., 1857 ; B.Sc., 1862 ; Minister of Toxteth Park Chapel, Liverpool, 1867-75. *Publications :* many philosophical articles in various Reviews ; delivered the Hibbert Lectures on the Bases of Religious Belief, 1893, published 1894; author of the philosophical portion of the Life and Letters of Dr. James Martineau, later published separately as Dr. Martineau's Philosophy. *Recreation :* cultivation of fruit-trees. *Address :* St. George's, Littlemore, near Oxford.
    (*Died 21 Nov. 1920.*)

UPTON, Florence, Associate Société Nationale des Beaux Arts, Paris ; portrait painter ; *b.* New York, of English parents, Thomas Harborough Upton and Bertha, *d.* of John W. Hudson, architect. *Educ. :* New York and Paris ; Art Education—New York, Paris, and Holland. Exhibitor at Salon, Royal Academy, Continental and American Exhibitions ; Medaille d'honneur Inter. Exp. Nantes, 1905. *Publications:* The Golliwogg Series ; The Vegemen's Revenge ; Borbee and the Wisp, etc., 1895-1909. *Address :* 21 Great College Street, Westminster, S.W.1. *T. :* Victoria 2423.
    (*Died 17 Oct. 1922.*)

UPTON, Rev. William Clement, Prebendary of Lincoln. *Address :* 4 Queensway, Lincoln.   (*Died 6 Aug. 1922.*)

UPWARD, Allen, Barrister-at-law ; *b.* Worcester, 1863 ; *s.* of George Upward, J.P. ; unmarried. *Educ. :* Great Yarmouth Grammar School ; Royal University of Ireland. Brook Scholarship ; O'Hagan Gold Medal for Oratory ; Silver Medal, Dublin ; Inns of Court Studentship ; two 1st class Scholarships, Middle Temple ; Corr. Member Parnassos Philolog. Soc. Athens ; Hon. Bard National Gorsedd (Maenhir); F.R.A.I. Barr. Ireland, 1887; Barr. England, 1889 ; South Wales Circuit ; contested Merthyr-Tydvil, 1895 ; fought as volunteer in Greco-Turkish War, 1897 ; British Resident, Northern Nigeria, 1901 ; Mission to Macedonia, 1907-8 ; volunteered as Scoutmaster at the Front, thanked by General Commanding, 1914 ; Head Master of Inverness College, 1916. *Publications:* Secrets of the Courts of Europe, and International Spy (A.V.) series in Pearson's Magazine, 1895-1905 ; A Flash in the Pan (play), 1896 ; A Day's Tragedy, 1897 ; Treason, 1903 ; The New Word (Geneva), 1907 ; The East End of Europe, 1908 ; Secrets of the Past, 1909 ; The Divine Mystery, 1913 ; Some Personalities, 1921 ; and numerous romances, etc. *Recreation :* bridge. *Address :* c/o A. Wallace, 162 Bath Street, Glasgow. *Club :* Royal Societies.
    (*Died 12 Nov. 1926.*)

URMSON, Rev. Thomas, Hon. Canon of Durham ; Rector of Willington, Co. Durham, 1890-1920 ; Special Service Clergy, Chester, 1921. *Educ. :* Trinity College, Cambridge, M.A. *Address :* Riverside, Boughton, Chester. *Clubs :* Grosvenor. Chester : Durham County.
    (*Died 28 Sept. 1926.*)

URMSTON, Colonel Edward Brabazon, C.B. 1902 ; J.P. Co. Argyll ; *b.* 18 Feb. 1858 ; *m.* 1903, Christina Beatrice, *d.* of late Rev. A. Burn-Murdoch. Entered army, 1878 ; Capt. 1886 ; Major, 1896 ; served South Africa, 1899-1902 (despatches twice, Queen's medal, 4 clasps, King's medal, 2 clasps, brevet Lieut.-Colonel, C.B.) ; late 1st Battalion Argyll and Sutherland Highlanders ; Commanding Highland District, 1908-12 ; retired 1914. *Address :* Glenmorven, Argyllshire.
    (*Died 6 Dec. 1920.*)

URQUHART, Colonel Robert, M.V.O. 1905 ; D.L. ; V.D. (retired) ; 6th Batt. Seaforth Highlanders ; Town Clerk of Forres, Morayshire ; *b.* 10 Dec. 1845 ; *s.* of Alexander Urquhart, Banker, Forres, and Margaret Milne ; *m.* 1874, Finella Hoyes, *d.* of Andrew Smith, Cluny, Forres ; no *c. Educ. :* Forres

Academy; Edinburgh University. Served forty-six years in the Regiment. *Address:* Cluny Forres, Morayshire. *T.A.:* Urquhart, Cluny, Forres. *T.:* Forres, 6.   *(Died 24 Nov. 1922.)*

USHER, James Ward, Art Jeweller and Silversmith; *b.* Lincoln; *s.* of James Usher; unmarried. *Educ.:* Lincoln Grammar School; Totteridge Park, Herts. Has been engaged in the jewellery and plate business during the greater part of his life: a connoisseur of works of art; has formed private collection of miniatures, antique gold watches (generally admitted to be the finest known), old English silver, china, and Battersea enamels, all from famous collections dispersed during the above term at Christie's Rooms, of which he has been a constant habitué; Sheriff of the City of Lincoln, 1916-17. *Publications:* Objects of Art, forming the private collection of James Ward Usher of Lincoln; An Art-Collector's Treasures, illustrated and described by himself, in water colour. *Recreations:* water-colour painting, motoring. *Address:* Lincoln. *M.:* FE 738.   *(Died 20 Sept. 1921.)*

UTTING, Sir John, Kt., *cr.* 1924; ex-Lord Mayor of Liverpool; Alderman; J.P.; D.L. Lancashire; Chairman of the Finance Committee of Liverpool; *s.* of H. A. Utting; *b.* Rackheath, Norfolk; *m.* twice; two *s.* one *d.* *Educ.:* King Edward VI. School, Norwich; Guy's Hospital. General medical practitioner in Liverpool for fifty years; Major, R.A.M.C. (T.); eighteen years Chairman of the Port Sanitary and Hospitals Committee of Liverpool; President of School of Hygiene, Liverpool; Lord Mayor, 1917-18; Chairman of Finance Committee for six years. *Recreations:* shooting and fishing. *Address:* St. Anne's Hill, Anfield, Liverpool. *T.A.:* Anfield 70, Liverpool. *T.:* Anfield 70. *M.:* KB 254 and KB 177. *Clubs:* Conservative, University, Liverpool.   *(Died 17 Feb. 1927.)*

V

VAIZEY, Mrs. G. de Horne. *Publications:* About Peggy Saville; More about Peggy; Pixie O'Shaughnessy; More about Pixie; The Love Affairs of Pixie; The Fortunes of the Farrells; A Houseful of Girls; The Independence of Claire; Betty Trevor; Big Game; A College Girl; The Lady of the Basement Flat. *Address:* 4 Bouverie Street, E.C.4.
  (Died 23 Jan. 1927.)

VALENTIA, *(de jure)* 11th Viscount (*cr.* 1621), **Arthur Annesley,** K.C.V.O., *cr.* 1923; J.P.; C.B. 1900; M.V.O. 1901; Bt. 1620; Baron Mountnorris, 1628; Baron Annesley (U.K.), *cr.* 1917; Premier Baronet of Ireland; *b.* 28 Aug. 1843; *e. s.* of Hon. Arthur Annesley and Flora, *d.* of Lieut.-Col. James Macdonald; *S.* grandfather, 1863; *m.* Laura Sarah, *y. d.* of Sir Hale Webb, Wykham Park, Oxfordshire, and *widow* of Sir Algernon William Peyton, 4th Bt., 1878; two *s.* (eider killed in action, 16 Nov. 1914) six *d.* *Educ.:* Royal Mil. Academy, Woolwich. Entered 10th Hussars, 1864; Lieut. 1868; served with Yeomanry Cavalry, A.A.G., South Africa (despatches); M.P. (C.) Oxford since 1895; Comptroller of H.M. Household, 1898-1905; Lieut. 10th Hussars, retired 1872; formerly a Lord-in-Waiting to H.M. Owns about 7000 acres. *Heir:* s. Hon. Caryl Arthur James Annesley. *Recreations:* fox-hunting, Master of Fox-hounds, 1872-84; shooting, deerstalking. *Address:* Bletchington Park, Oxford. *Clubs:* Carlton, Cavalry. *(Died 20 Jan. 1927.)*

VAN BUREN, Rt. Rev. James Heartt, D.D.; Bishop of Porto Rico, 1902-1912; *b.* 7 July 1850; *s.* of James S. and Harriet A. Van Buren; one *s.* *Educ.:* Yale University; Berkeley Divinity Schools. Deacon, 1876; Priest,

1877; Rector in St. Peter's Church, Milford, Ct.; Trinity Church, Seymour, Ct.; St. Paul's Church, Englewood, N.J.; St. Paul's Church, Newburyport, Mass.; St. Stephen's Church, Lynn, Mass.; Archdeacon in Massachusetts; Examining Chaplain; went as a Missionary to Porto Rico, 1901. *Publications:* Short History of the Christian Church; Confirmation or the Laying on of Hands; Latin Hymns in English Verse; Hunnario Provisional; Sermons That Have Helped; Sermon in Commemoration of King Edward VII.; Pagans, a Missionary Play. *Address:* 9 Trumbull Street, New Haven. Conn.   *(Died 28 July 1917.)*

VANDERBILT, William Kissam; *b.* Staten Island, 12 Dec. 1849; *s.* of William Henry Vanderbilt and Maria Louisa Kissam; *m.* 1st, Alva Smith, Mobile, Ala.; 2nd, 1903, Mrs. L. M. Rutherford. Director of many companies. *Address:* 660 Fifth Avenue, New York.   *(Died 22 July 1920.)*

VAN DER VEER, John Conrad; London Editor of De Telegraaf Amsterdam, 1903-25; President of the Foreign Press Association in London; during the War Voluntary Secretary of the Foreigners Section of National Service; *b.* Friesland, Holland, 5 Feb. 1869; *g.s.* of a Dutch medical man who died in America after being shipwrecked on accompanying as doctor a party of Dutch emigrants to New Orleans; *m.*; no *c.* *Educ.:* Sneek, Holland, at a public school, further self-educated. Worked as youth in a printing office; took leading part in the early Dutch labour movement as speaker, organiser, writer; edited some years a weekly paper at Middelburg; organised afterwards a Tolstoyan movement in Holland; corresponded with the late Count Leo Tolstoy; came in 1899 to England; lived for a time with a Russian colony in Essex; settled two years later in London; studied the life of homeless people; was appointed in 1903 London correspondent of De Telegraaf; took at the outbreak of the Great War openly the side of the Allies in sympathy with their fight for justice and national freedom; gave over 150 voluntary lectures supporting Britain's cause, chiefly under auspices Navy League; elected Life Vice-President, Navy League. *Recreations:* book collecting, reading, diligent writer. *Address:* 15 Rondu Road, Cricklewood, N.W.2. *T.:* Hampstead 4663. *Club:* Savage.
  (Died 30 Aug. 1928.)

VAN DER VLUGT, W., Emerit. Professor of the Philosophy and the Encyclopaedia of Jurisprudence at Leyden University, Prof. 1880-1923; *b.* 12 March 1853; *s.* of Jan Van der Vlugt, banker at Haarlem, and J. H. M. Hinlópen; *m.* 1882, Anna, *d.* of late Dr. L. W. E. Rauwenhoff, Professor of Theology at Leyden, and of F. F. Tobias; two *s.* two *d.* *Educ.:* Haarlem; Leyden Univ. Doctor utriusque iuris, 1879. Member of the 2nd Chamber of the States-General, 1902-1906. *Publications:* De rechtsstaat volgens de leer van Rudolf Gneist (Dissertation), 1879; various papers in the Dutch monthly De Gids, amongst others, in den stryd om het recht, 1889, and Toynbee werk, 1892; In memoriam Dr. Abraham Kuenen in biographies of deceased members of the Maatschappy v. Letterkunde, 1890; idem Dr. James Martineau in Theologisch Tydschrift; article on De geestelyke wetenschappen in Eene halve eeuw. Historisch gedenkboek, 1898; Transvaal versus Great Britain, 1809; Finland, de rechtsvraag (translated into French), and other papers on the same subject; Les vrais coupables; lettre à M. Tallichet, 1900. A series of papers on Crime and the Criminal; articles on Two Varieties of Parliamentary Government: The British Atmosphere and The British School of Political Self-discipline, besides several studies on Dutch politics in the Dutch monthly, Onze Eeuw, since 1901; a

paper on the methods of the study of international law in Rechtsgeleerd Magazyn, 1913; a contribution to the American publication: The Church, The People, and the Age, 1914; a rectorial address on Two Dutch Masters of Jurisprudence (Huber and Noodt), delivered 8 Feb. 1916; two presidial addresses to meetings of the Dutch Lawyers Association, 1919-1920; a study on Samuel von Pufendorf, in the farewell book, dedicated to Professor Greven; Papers read in the Royal Dutch Academy on the Codex iuris canonici and on Christian Thomasius; a study on La question des iles d'Aland, 1921; an answer to the Swedish Livre Bleu concerning the same matter, 1921; two papers on East Carelia in De Gids, 1923; a farewell address to the Leyden students of law, 1923; a selection of the author's principal works was published by his colleagues at the end of his active professorship 1923; since then appeared *inter alia*; a necrology of late Mr. C. Krantz, a remarkable captain of Leyden industry; a couple of papers in De Gids on the history of diplomacy between the end of the Middle Ages and Frederick the Great; an aperçu (in the same monthly) of Rüdolph Stammler's philosophy of law, a study of Dr. D. S. Lohman and the law of nations (1926); lastly, an unfinished introductory volume to the text of his own lectures on the Encyclopædia of Jurisprudence, to be followed by a series of lectures on l'oeuvre de Grotius et son influence sur le développement du droit des gens, in the publications of the Académie du droit des gens de La Haye (1925). *Address:* 28 Oegstgeest, Wilhelmina Park. Leyden. *T.:* 941.
(*Died 5 Nov. 1928.*)

VAN DER WAALS, Prof. J. D.; Professor of Theoretical Physics; Nobel Prize for Physics, 1910. *Address:* The University, Amsterdam.   (*Died 8 Mar. 1925.*)

VAN DEVENTER, Hon. Lt.-Gen. Sir Louis Jacob, K.C.B. cr. 1917; C.B. 1917; served S. African War as second in command to Gen. Smuts, 1899-1902; Commander-in-Chief East Africa 1917-19 (C.B., K.B.E.). *Address:* c/o High Commissioner for South Africa, 32 Victoria Street, S.W.
(*Died 27 Aug. 1922.*)

VAN DYCK, Ernest Marie Hubert, operatic singer; Professor for Dramatic Art at the Conservatoires of Brussels and Antwerp; Officier Order of Leopold, Chevalier Légion d'Honneur, etc.; *b.* Antwerp, 2 April 1861; *m.* Augusta, *d.* of F. Servais, 1886. *Educ.:* Jesuits' College, Antwerp; Universities of Louvain and Brussels. Originally journalist. *Address:* Chateau de Berlaer, nr. Antwerp, Belgium.
(*Died Sept. 1923.*)

VANE, Captain Hon. Henry Cecil, Captain Royal Field Artillery; *e. s.* and heir of 9th Baron Barnard; *b.* 19 Sept. 1882; *m.* 1914, Lady Enid Victoria Rachel Fane, *e. d.* of 13th Earl of Westmorland. *Educ.:* Eton: Christ Church, Oxford. Late Major Yorkshire Hussars Yeo.; A.D.C. to Governor of Madras, 1903-7. *Address:* Raby Castle, Darlington. *Clubs:* Marlborough: Yorkshire, York.
(*Died 9 Oct. 1917.*)

VANE, Hon. Ralph Frederick; *b.* 8 June 1891; 3rd *s.* of 9th Baron Barnard and Lady Catherine Sarah Cecil (*d.* 1918), *d.* of 3rd Marquess of Exeter; *m.* 1917, Kathleen Airini, *o. c.* of late Capt. Gilbert Mair, N.Z.C., formerly Judge of Native Land Court, Tauranga, N.Z. *Educ.:* Eton; Trinity College, Cambridge, B.A. Formerly Captain Durham Light Infantry; served European War, 1914-18. *Clubs:* Travellers'; Devon and Exeter, Exeter. (*Died 6 June 1923.*)

VANE, Hon. William Lyonel, D.L.: *b.* 30 Aug. 1859; 4th *s.* of late Sir Henry Morgan Vane and Louisa, *y. d.* of Rev. Richard Farrer of Ashley, Northamptonshire; *b.* of 9th Baron Barnard; *m.* 1904, Lady Katharine L. Pakenham, *d.* of 4th Earl of Longford; one *s.* two. *d.* Late Major 1st Batt. Durham Light Infantry; Lt.-Col. and Hon. Col. commanding 6th Batt. Durham Light Infantry, 1903-11; Vice-Chairman Durham Territorial Force Association. *Address:* Haughton Hall, Darlington. *Club:* Carlton.(*Died 23 Jan. 1920.*)

VANE-TEMPEST, Lord (Herbert Lionel) Henry, K.C.V.O., cr. 1911; *b.* 1862; *b.* of 6th Marquess of Londonderry. Late Major, 8th Vol. Brigade, N. Division, R.A. *Address:* Plas Machynlleth, Montgomeryshire. *Clubs:* Turf. Bachelors'.   (*Died 26 Jan. 1921.*)

VAN REETH, Right Rev. Joseph, S.J.; Bishop of Galle since 1895; *b.* Antwerp, 1848. *Educ.:* Collége Notre Dame, Antwerp. Entered the Society of Jesus, 1860; Priest, 1875; Secretary of the Provincial Belgian Province, 1877-82; Provincial Belgian Province, 1882-88; Rector and Master of Novices at Tronchiennes, 1888-95. *Address:* Galle, Ceylon.
(*Died 11 Sept. 1923.*)

VANSITTART, Spencer Charles Patrick; J.P. Co. Limerick; *b.* 1860; *s.* of Captain Spencer Vansittart and Emily Teresa, *d.* of Admiral Warde, K.H., of Squerryes Court, Kent; *m.* 1889, Hon. Matilda Isabella Massy, 2nd *d.* of 6th Lord Massy; three *d.* *Club:* Junior United Service.   (*Died 9 Aug. 1923.*)

VANSTON, Sir George Thomas Barrett, Kt., cr. 1917; K.C. 1908; LL.D., M.A. (stip. con.); Legal Adviser to the Local Government Board for Ireland 1900-22; *b.* 31 May 1853; 2nd *s.* of John Davis Vanston, Solicitor, Hildon Park, Terenure, Co. Dublin, and Hacketstown, Co. Carlow, and Catherine, *d.* of George Washington Biggs, Bellevue, Borriskane, Co. Tipperary; *m.* 1899, Clementina Mary, *e. surv. d.* of Marcus Clement Sullivan, 26 Highfield Road, Rathgar, Co. Dublin; two *s.* two *d.* *Educ.:* Kingstown School; Trinity College, Dublin (Classical Scholar; First Senior Moderator and Gold Medallist in History, Law, and Political Economy; Senior Moderator and Gold Medallist in Classics; Vice-Chancellor's Latin Gold Medallist; Gold Medallist in History, College Historical Society); called to Irish Bar, 1878. *Publications:* The Grand Jury Laws of Ireland, 1883; The Law of Public Health in Ireland, 1892; Supplement, 1897, 2nd ed. 1913; The Law relating to Local Government in Ireland, 2 vols., 1899, 1905, 2nd ed. vol. i. 1916; Supplement to vol. ii., 1919; The Law relating to Municipal Towns in Ireland, 1900; The Law relating to Municipal Boroughs in Ireland, 1905. *Recreations:* Travel, cycling, gardening. *Address:* Hildon Park, Terenure, Co. Dublin.   (*Died 6 July 1923.*)

VAN STRAUBENZEE, Maj.-Gen. Turner, C.B. 1882; late R.A.; *b.* 9 Aug. 1888; *e. s.* of late Col. Henry van Straubenzee, J.P., D.L., of Spennithorne, Yorkshire, and Henrietta, *d.* of 1st Baron Wrottesley; *m.* 1877, Florinda, *e. d.* of late W. J. Hamilton; one *s.* one *d.* *Educ.:* R.M.A., Woolwich. Entered Royal Artillery, 1855; A.D.C. to Maj.-Gen. Sir C. T. van Straubenzee, commanding a division in India, 1862-1866; to Governor of Bombay, 1869-72; Instr. in Gunnery, Shoeburyness, 1874-79; in command of Cadet Co. R.M.A., 1879, until promoted Lieut.-Col. in India, 1882; commanded R.A. Indian contingent Egyptian Campaign, 1882; served in R.H.A. in India until 1887; Col. on the Staff R.A. in India, 1888-91; commanded the Madras District as Brig.-Gen., 1891-95, when retired with the honorary rank of Major-General. Decorated for Egyptian Campaign, 1882 (medal and clasp for Tel-el-Kebir, 3rd class Medjidie, Khedive's star, and C.B.). *Address:* Spennithorne, R.S.O., Yorkshire. *Club:* Army and Navy.
(*Died 27 Feb. 1920.*)

VAN WYCK, Robert Anderson, Mayor of New York, 1898-1902 : Democrat ; lawyer ; *b.* New York, 20 July 1849 ; descended from Cornelius Barento Van Wyck, who settled in the New Netherlands in 1650 ; unmarried. *Educ. :* Columbia Law School. Judge, City Court of New York, 1889-97. *Address :* 135 East 46th Street, New York.   (*Died Nov. 1918.*)

VASSAR-SMITH, Sir Richard Vassar, 1st Bt., *cr.* 1917 ; D.L., J.P. ; *b.* 1843 ; *e. s.* of Richard Tew Smith, of Wotton, Gloucester, assumed by Royal Licence additional name of Vassar ; *m.* 1886, Mary, *d.* of John Partridge, Malvern ; one *s.* three *d. Educ. :* College School, Gloucester. Chairman, Lloyds Bank, Ltd., Lloyds and National Provincial Foreign Bank, Ltd., Gloucester Railway Carriage and Wagon Co., Ltd., and Gloucester Gas Light Co. ; Director, Baldwin's, Ltd., Port Talbot Steel Co., Ltd. ; Brymbo Steel Co., Ltd. ; British Mannersman Tube Co., Ltd. ; Yorkshire Penny Bank, Ltd., London and River Plate Bank, Limited ; and the P. and O. Banking Corporation, Ltd. ; Member of Council, Cheltenham College ; Chairman of Council, Cheltenham Ladies' Coll. ; Chairman of Council, St. Hilda's Incorporated Colleges, Oxford and Cheltenham ; late Chairman, Committee of London Clearing Bankers, and of Central Association of Bankers, 1916-17 ; late President and Chairman of the Council of the Institute of Bankers ; Alderman, County Council of Gloucestershire ; Provincial Grand Master, Freemasons, Gloucestershire ; Grand Superintendent, Royal Arch Freemasons, Gloucestershire and Herefordshire ; Deputy Grand Master and Provincial Grand Master, Mark Freemasons, Glos. and Herefordshire. *Recreations :* fishing, shooting, walking, archæology. *Heir : s.* John George Lawley, *b.* Dec. 1886. *Address :* Spiel, Charlton Kings, Glos. ; 16 St. James's Street, S.W.1. *T. :* Regent 1293. *Clubs :* Carlton, Boodle's, British Empire.
    (*Died 2 Aug. 1922.*)

VAUDIN, William Marshall, I.S.O. 1914 ; Superintendent of Public Works and Surveys since 1901, and Chairman of the Local Board of Health since 1902 ; Chairman of the Agricultural Board, 1915, Seychelles ; *b.* 13 Dec. 1866 ; *s.* of late Rev. A. Vaudin of Sark, Channel Islands, and Isabella, *d.* of George Spain Marshall of Northumberland, England ; *m.* Bertha, *e. d.* of Rev. J. Larzen, Vicar of Methwold, Norfolk ; one *d. Educ. :* Royal College, Mauritius. Entered service, 1888 ; Acting-Assistant, Government Surveyor, Mauritius, 1890, 1891-92 and 1897-1900 ; Assistant Surveyor, Seychelles, 1900 ; has been Acting Auditor, Acting Police Magistrate, and Acting Treasurer and Collector of Customs, Seychelles ; Director of Labour Bureau, 1917 ; Controller of Food Stuffs, 1918 ; Member of Executive and Legislative Councils, Seychelles, since 1912. *Address :* Mahe, Seychelles. *Club :* Seychelles.

VAUDREY, Sir William Henry, Kt., *cr.* 1905 ; Solicitor and Notary ; *b.* 26 Feb. 1855 ; *s.* of late Henry Vaudrey of Bayswater, London ; *m.* 1880, Florence Eleanor, *d.* of Septimus Campbell Slade. *Educ. :* City of London School. Has practised in Manchester as a Solicitor since 1878 ; Lord Mayor of Manchester, 1898-99 ; contested (C.) North-east Manchester, 1910. *Recreation :* golf. *Address :* Devon Cottage, Mount Avenue, Ealing, W.5. *T. :* Ealing 0663. *Clubs :* Constitutional ; Conservative, Manchester.
    (*Died 11 Oct. 1926.*)

VAUDREY - BARKER - MILL, William Claude Frederick, J.P., ; *e. s.* of late William Vaudrey, of Langley Manor, Hants, and Marianne, *d.* and heir of Frederick Ibbotson, of Colbury Manor, Hants ; *b.* 1874 ; *m.* 1905, Hon. Mary Brenda Collins, 3rd *d.* of late Lord Collins ; one *s.* one *d. Educ. :* Oxford

University, B.A. *Address :* Mattisfont Abbey, Romsey, Hants.   (*Died 16 Sept. 1916.*)

VAUGHAN, Rev. Bernard, S.J. ; *b.* 20 Aug. 1847 ; *s.* of late Col. Vaughan of Courtfield, Herefordshire, and *bro.* of late Cardinal B. Vaughan. *Educ. :* Stonyhurst. As a professed Father of the Society of Jesus for 18 years, took an active and conspicuous part in the religious and civic life of Manchester ; after which he came to London (1901) to Farm Street, W. ; worker among the poor at Westminster and in the East End ; has organised concerts and bazaars for erection of clubs for working class ; his sermons on The Sins of Society in 1906 drew large audiences ; so too his Lenten course, The Sins of Society gauged by the Passion of Christ, 1907, and the course entitled, Why believe in Christ and Christianity ? 1907 ; Cathedral preacher at Eucharistic Congress, Montreal, 1910 ; toured through the United States and parts of Canada and Alaska ; lectured before Wasada and Imperial Universities of Tokyo, and addressed the House of Peers, and ladies of Society in Japan ; also lectured in China, and in Italy and France ; preached the Lent of 1914 in Dublin on Jesus Christ as Guest and Host ; received letter from Pope Benedict XV. 1916 congratulating him on his religious Jubilee, and giving privilege of Portable Altar. *Publications :* The Roman Claims ; Faith and Reason ; The Triple Alliance ; The Demon of Drink in the Temple of God ; Her Golden Reign ; The Sins of Society, 1906 ; Society, Sin and the Saviour, 1907 ; Life Lessons from Joan of Arc, the Matchless Maid ; Socialism, 1910 ; The Our Father, Our Country's Need To-day, 1911 ; Socialism from the Christian Standpoint, 1913 ; What of To-day ? 1914 ; The Menace of the Empty Cradle, 1917 ; The Worker's Right to Live, 1918. *Address :* 114 Mount Street, W.   (*Died 31 Oct. 1922.*)

VAUGHAN, Charles Edwyn, M.A., Litt. D. ; *b.* 10 Feb. 1854 ; *o. s.* of the late Rev. E. T. Vaughan, Rector of Harpenden, Herts ; unmarried. *Educ. :* Marlborough ; Balliol Coll. Oxford. Assistant Master at Clifton College, 1878-88 ; Professor of English Literature, University College, Cardiff, 1889-98 ; Professor of English Literature, Armstrong College, Newcastle-on-Tyne, 1899-1904 ; Professor of English Literature, University of Leeds, 1904-1913. *Publications :* edited Burke's Reflections on the French Revolution, 1892, and American Speeches, 1893 ; Webster's Duchess of Malfi, 1896 ; English Literary Criticism, 1896 ; Milton's Areopagitica and other Tracts (Temple Classics), 1900 ; The Romantic Revolt, 1907 ; Types of Tragic Drama, 1908 ; The Political Writings of Rousseau, with Introductions and Notes, 2 vols. 1915 ; Rousseau's Essay on A Lasting Peace, translated with Introduction, 1917 ; Rousseau's *Contrat Social,* edited with Introduction and Notes, 1918. *Recreation :* gardening. *Address :* 9 St. Aldwyn's Road, Withington, Manchester.   (*Died 8 Oct. 1922.*)

VAUGHAN, Francis Baynham, J.P., D.L. ; *b.* 18 Mar. 1844 ; 5th *s.* of late Col. John Francis Vaughan, and 1st wife, Louisa Elizabeth, *d.* of late John Rolls of The Hendre, Co. Monmouth ; *m.* 1871, Caroline Ruth, *d.* of Charles Alexander Pope, of St. Louis, U.S.A. ; three *s.* three *d.* Late Col. Commanding Royal Monmouthshire Engineer Militia ; Chamberlain to the Pope. [*Heir : e. s.* Capt. Charles Jerome ; *m.* 1908, Florence, 3rd *d.* of C. E. Lister-Kaye] *Address :* Court-Field, Ross.
    (*Died 9 Aug. 1919.*)

VAUGHAN, Prebendary Henry ; Rector of Wraxall, near Bristol, since 1891 ; Prebendary of Combe II., Wells Cathedral, 1904 ; Rural Dean of Chew, 1900-20 ; Deanery Inspector of Schools, 1892-1912, Surrogate ; *b.* 1848 ; *s.* of Rev. E. P.

Vaughan; *m.* 1874, Ellen Christine Crake, *d.* of late John Crake, of The Lawn, Datchet; two *s.* *Educ.*: Westminster; Clifton; University College, Oxford. Curate of Mere, Wilts, 1871-1872; Datchet, 1872-74; Curate in Charge, Savernake, Wilts, 1874-75; Vicar of Easton Royal, 1875-77; Curate of Wraxall, Bristol, 1877-91. *Address*: Wraxall, near Bristol.   (*Died 31 Dec. 1920*.)

VAUGHAN, Rev. Canon John; Rector St. Andrew's, Summer Hill, Sydney, since 1881; Canon of St. Andrew's Cathedral, Sydney, 1902; Synod Nominator, Member of Standing Com., Provincial and General Synods; Trustee of Moore College and Church Missionary Association; *b.* Hereford, Eng., 28 Oct. 1841; *m.* 1863, Annie Graham; three *s.* one *d. Educ.*: Moore Theological College, Liverpool, N.S.W. Licensed as Lay Reader by Bishop of Sidney, 1860; conducted the first Church of England service held at Botany Bay, 1861; Deacon, 1865; Priest, 1866; Rector St. Thomas', O'Connell, 1866; Rector, St. Stephen's, Penrith, 1868; started to form parish of St. Andrew's, Summer Hill, 1881; first in N.S.W. to start the principle of direct giving in the Lord's House on the Lord's Day. *Publications*: Sermons, Priest and Priesthood, etc.; Lectures, Palestine, Egypt, America, France. *Recreations*: walking, riding. *Address*: The Rectory, Summer Hill, Sydney, N.S.W.
    (*Died 13 Dec. 1918*.)

VAUGHAN, Rev. Canon John, M.A.: Canon Residentiary of Winchester Cathedral since 1909; *b.* 22 Jan. 1855; 2nd *s.* of Rev. Matthew Vaughan, late Vicar of Finchingfield; *m.* 1891, Gertrude Blomfield, *e. d.* of Rev. F. Whyley; two *d. Educ.*: Felstead; Corpus Christi College, Cambridge. Vicar of Porchester, 1890; Vicar of Langrish, 1897; Rector of Droxford, Hants, 1902-10; Hon. Canon of Winchester, 1903-9. *Publications*: has contributed to the Nineteenth Century, Cornhill, Saturday Review, and other publications; articles on the Isle of Wight, and the Botany of Hampshire in Dent's County Guides; The Wildflowers of Selborne and other Papers, 1906; Lighter Studies of a Country Rector, 1909; A Mirror of the Soul, 1913; Winchester Cathedral Close, 1914; Winchester Cathedral, its Monuments and Memorials, 1919; The Music of Wild Flowers, 1920. *Recreations*: botany and archæology. *Address*: The Close, Winchester.
    (*Died 10 July 1922*.)

VAUGHAN, Right Rev. John Stephen, D.D.; Bishop of Sebastopolis and Auxiliary to Bishop of Salford since 1909; Domestic Prelate of the Papal Court since 1896; Rector of St. Bede's College, Manchester, 1912-15; *b.* Courtfield, Ross, 24 Jan. 1853; *y. s.* of late Colonel John Vaughan of Courtfield. *Educ.*: St. Gregory's College, Downside, Bath; Monte Cassino, Italy; Ecclesiastical Studies at Collegio Inglese, Rome, and at Grand Séminaire, Bruges. Priest, 1876; professor of mathematics at St. Bede's College, Manchester; sailed to Australia, and for three years travelled about that colony, preaching and lecturing and doing missionary work; returned and settled down in London, where he undertook parochial work, first under Cardinal Manning, and then under his brother, Cardinal Vaughan; Canon of Westminster, 1898; he organised a series of Free Catholic Evidence Lectures delivered in all the Public Halls in London, 1890-1903; in addition to preaching in all the chief Catholic Churches throughout the Diocese, he gave Spiritual retreats to seminarists and to clergy, both in England and Ireland and United States of America; resided in Rome, 1904-7, when he again went to United States and Canada on a preaching and lecturing tour, visiting the chief Catholic Institutions and places of interest; in 1909 went, as Bishop, to live in Manchester; a writer to papers and periodicals.

Publications: Life After Death; Thoughts for All Times; Earth to Heaven; Faith and Folly; Concerning the Holy Bible; Dangers of the Day; The Purpose of the Papacy; Happiness and Beauty; Time or Eternity; Sermons for All the Sundays and for the Chief Feasts throughout the Year; Life Everlasting; Venial Sin. Some of these books have been translated into several foreign languages, one of them into Japanese. *Address*: Mission House, Brondesbury Park, N.W.6.   (*Died 4 Dec. 1925*.)

VAUGHAN, Mrs. W. W.; *b.* 15 Jan. 1869; Margaret, 3rd *d.* of late John Addington Symonds, Clifton, Bristol, and Janet Catherine, 2nd *d.* of Frederick North, Rougham Hall, Norfolk; *m.* 1898, W. Wyamar Vaughan; two *s.* one *d. Educ.*: home. *Publications*: Our Life in the Swiss Highlands (in conjunction with her father); Days Spent on a Doge's Farm; Melting Snows (translated from the German of Prince Carolath); The Story of Perugia (in conjunction with Lina Duff Gordon) 1898; A Child of the Alps, 1920; Out of the Past, 1925. *Address*: The School House, Rugby.   (*Died 4 Nov. 1925*.)

VAUGHAN-LEE, Admiral Sir Charles Lionel; K.B.E., *cr.* 1919; C.B. 1917; *b.* 27 Feb. 1867; 3rd *s.* of late Vaughan H. Vaughan-Lee of Dillington Park, Somerset; *m.* Rose, *d.* of Llewellyn Llewellyn of Nethway, Devon; one *s.* one *d.* Entered R.N. as Naval Cadet, 1880; served in Egyptian War; European War, 1914-17 (K.B.E., C.B., Legion of Honour; Order of St. Maurice and Lazarus of Italy; Order of Rising Sun, Japan, 2nd Class); Lieut. 1887; Commander, 1899; Captain, 1904; Rear-Adm., 1915; Admiral, 1925; Naval A.D.C. to the King, 1914; Admiral Superintendent of Portsmouth Dockyard; retired list, 1920. *Address*: Bepton, Midhurst. *Club*: Naval and Military.   (*Died 16 Mar. 1928*.)

VAUGHAN-WILLIAMS, Major Francis, J.P., Cos. Denbigh and Staffs.; *b.* 28 Jan. 1856; *e. s.* of late Judge R. Vaughan-Williams, Bodlonfa, Flintshire, North Wales; *m.* Laura, *y. d.* of late Peter Walker, J.P., of Coed-y-glyn, Wrexham, and Auchenflower, Ayrshire. *Educ.*: Shrewsbury. M.F.H. The Tedworth, 1885-88; M.F.H. North Hereford, 1893-1895; M.F.H. Co. Galway, 1895-97; late Major Oxford and Bucks L.I. and Hampshire Carabiniers. *Address*: Donnington Lodge, Newbury. *Club*: Carlton. (*Died 24 Nov. 1920*.)

VAUX, Lt.-Col. Ernest, C.M.G. 1916; D.S.O. 1900; late 7th Durham Light Infantry; *b.* 1865; *s.* of J. S. Vaux, Sunderland; *m.* 1906, Emily L., *d.* of H. Moon-Ord; two *s.* two *d.* Served S. Africa, 5th Imperial Yeomanry, 1900 (despatches, medal 3 clasps, D.S.O.); European War, 1914-18 (C.M.G., despatches twice). *Address*: Brettanby Manor, Barton, R.S.O., Yorks.   (*Died 21 Nov. 1925*.)

VEDDER, Elihu, artist, painter, and modeller; *b.* New York, 26 Feb. 1836; *m.* 1869, Caroline, *d.* of Hon. E. H. Rosekrans of Glen's Falls, N.Y.; one *d. Educ.*: Brinkerhoff School, Brooklyn. Painted with Mattison at Sherburne, N.Y., and in atelier of Picot, Paris, 1856; worked in Italy, 1856-61; returned to U.S. until 1865; then after one winter in Paris went in 1867 to Rome, where he has since had his studio, making frequent visits to the U.S. His subjects are principally imaginative; in 1884 he illustrated the Rubaiyat of Omar Khayyám; five decorative panels and the mosaic Minerva in the New Congressional Library at Washington, large panel in Bowdoin College, Maine, also decorative ceiling in the Huntington house, New York City, are his work; other works are in the Boston Art Museum, Brooklyn Art Museum, Metropolitan Museum, N.Y., and Pittsburg Art Gallery; Academician Nat. Acad. of Design since 1865; member Soc. of American Artists; American Soc. of Mural Decorators;

Century Assoc. of New York; Academician American Institute of Arts and Letters; Gold Medal Columbian Exhibition, Chicago. *Publications:* The Digressions of V., 1910; Miscellaneous Moods in Verse, 1914. *Address:* 4 Via Porta Pinciana, Rome; Torre Quattuo Venti, Capri. *T.A.:* Vedder, Rome.

(*Died 29 Jan. 1923.*)

VEITCH, Sir Harry James, Kt., *cr.* 1912; V.M.H., F.L.S.; *b.* Exeter, 29 June 1840; *s.* of James Veitch, Horticulturist; *m.* 1867, Louisa Mary (*d.* 1921), *d.* of late Frederick W. Johnston. *Educ.:* Exeter Grammar School; France; Germany. Came to London, 1853; Vice-Pres. of Royal Horticultural Society; late head of James Veitch & Sons, Ltd.; Chevalier of the Legion of Honour; Cross of Officer of the Belgian Order of the Crown. *Publications:* Veitch's Orchidaceous Plants and Manual Coniferæ. *Address:* 34 Redcliffe Gardens. S.W.; East Burnham Park, Slough. (*Died 6 July 1924.*)

VELLA, Hon. Tom; retired; *b.* 15 Sep. 1849; *s.* of late Paul Lewis Vella, LL.D., and Irene Magri; *m.* Dolores Borg; one *s.* *Educ.:* Malta. Clerk (Civil Service), 1865-93; Deputy Collector of Customs, 1893-95 and 1897-1902; Deputy Postmaster-General, 1895-97; Collector of Customs, 1902-3; Postmaster-General, 1903-1911; Treasurer and Director of Contracts, 1911; Member of the Executive and Legislative Councils; retired, 1916. *Address:* 161 Strada Stretta, Valetta. *Club:* Casino Maltese, Valetta.

VENIS, Arthur, C.I.E. 1911; M.A., D.Litt. *Educ.:* Edinburgh University; Balliol College, Oxford; Boden Sanskrit Scholar; Fellow of the Asiatic Society of Bengal and of the University of Allahabad. Entered Indian Educational Service, 1881; Professor of English Literature, Queen's College, Benares. 1885; Professor of Philosophy, and Principal, Sanskrit College, Benares, 1888; Principal, Queen's College, Benares, 1897; Professor of Post-Vedic Sanskrit, University of Allahabad, 1914. *Address:* Government Sanskrit Library, Benares, India.

(*Died 5 June 1918.*)

VENKATAGIRI, Rajah of, Unde Rajaha Raje Sri Maharaja Velugoti Sree Rajagopala Krishna yachendra Bahadur, G.C.I.E., *cr.* 1915; K.C.I.E., *cr.* 1888; Panchahazar, Munsubdar, Zamindar; *b.* 25 Nov. 1857; *s.* of Unde Rajaha Raje Sri Rajah Velugoti Kumara yachama Naidu Bahadur, C.S.I., Panchahazar, Mansubdar, Rajah of Venkatagiri; *m.* a Zamindar's daughter in Godavery District, 1875; one *s.* one *d.* *Educ.:* private study at his palace. Belongs to an ancient family of historical renown; now a leading Rajah amongst the Zamindars; succeeded to the estate in 1878; twice Member of Council of Fort St. George; President of Madras Landholders' Association. *Publications:* none in English, but several in vernaculars. *Recreations:* outdoor sports, such as tennis, riding, shooting, etc. *Address:* Venkatagiri Nellore, Madras Presidency. *Clubs:* Madras Cosmopolitan, Racing, Gymkhana, etc.

(*Died 23 July 1916.*)

VENKATASWETA CHALAPATI RUNGA-RAO BAHADUR, Maharajah Sir Ravu, Maharajah of Bobbili, G.C.I.E., *cr.* 1911; K.C.I.E. 1895; Maharajah, 1900; C.B.E. 1917; Ancient Zemindar of Bobbili; *b.* Venkatagiri, 28 Aug. 1862; adopted *s.* of 10th Rajah Seetaramakrishna Rayadappa Runga-Rao Bahadur; *m.* 1st, 1878; 2nd, 1881; 3rd, 1888; two *s.* *Educ.:* Bobbili, privately, under Dr. J. Marsh. Ascended Gaddi in 1881; President of the Madras Landholders' Association: Life-member Royal Asiatic Society; Member Northbrook Society and East Indian Association: visited England, 1893, when he was presented to Her Majesty the late Queen-Empress; represented the Madras Presidency at Corona-

1070

tion of King Edward; Member of Madras Legislative Council, 1896, 1898, 1900, and 1902; First Native Member of the Madras Executive Council, 1910-11; on 6 November 1916 abdicated his Zemindary, together with the Incorporated Estates, in favour of his elder son, and gave away by a Deed of Settlement his landed property in Godavari District to his second son. Decorated for the prudent management of his zemindary, for the charitable institutions he has founded, and for his attention to his public duties. *Publications:* The Rajah of Bobbili's Diary in Europe in 1893; The History of Bobbili Zemindary, 1900: The Maharajah of Bobbili's Diary in Europe, with an Account of the Delhi Durbar, 1902; Advice to the Indian Aristocracy: revised and enlarged History of the Bobbili Zemindary. Owns about 800 square miles of land. *Recreations:* shooting, riding, and other manly sports. *Address:* Bobbili, Vizagapatam, Madras Presidency, India. *M.:* 13648. *Clubs:* Waltair, Madras Race, Madras

(*Died 12 Sept. 1920.*)

VENN, Albert John, M.B. Mch., M.D. Aberdeen, M.R.C.P. London, Graduate University of Chicago; Life Governor of St. Bartholomew's Hospital; the Metropolitan Free Hospital: the West London Hospital; Vice-Patron of the Victoria Hospital for Children, Chelsea; *b.* Colombo, Oct. 1840; 2nd *s.* of John Whatley Venn, the first Municipal Magistrate of Colombo, and Ann Tripp Venn; *m.* Emma, *o. d.* of William and Ellen Maria Stevens of Tulse Hill; two *s.* one *d.* *Educ.:* Bath Rectory School; City of London College; University of Aberdeen; St. Bartholomew's Hospital; University of Chicago. Fellow Royal Society of Medicine; late Midwifery Assistant, St. Bartholomew's ,Hospital; House Physician, Soho Hospital for Women; Obstetric Assistant, St. Bartholomew's Hospital; Assistant Physician, Metropolitan Hospital; Senior Physician, Out-Patients, Victoria Hospital for Children; Obstetrical Physician, Metropolitan Free Hospital, and Physician for Diseases of Women, West London Hospital; Research Student, Marcus Beck Laboratory, Royal Society of Medicine, London. *Publications:* Editor of 5th, 6th and 7th editions of Beasley's Book of Prescriptions, of 11th edit. of Chavasse's Advice to a Mother, of 13th edit. of Chavasse's Advice to a Wife, and of 6th edit. of Chavasse's Counsel to a Mother; Co-Editor of 3rd edit. of Drs. Tanner and Meadows' Diseases of Infancy and Childhood; 4th edit. of Dr. Meadows' Manual of Midwifery, and 5th edit. The Prescribers' Companion. *Recreations:* riding, golf, fishing. *Clubs:* Junior Carlton; The Phi-Chi Fraternity of America, Rho Chapter.

(*Died 13 Nov. 1919.*)

VENN, Rev. Henry; Hon. Canon of Canterbury, 1900; *b.* 27 July 1838; *s.* of Rev. Prebendary Henry Venn; *m.* 1st, Isabel Louisa *d.* of Capt. W. M. De Butts; 2nd, Louisa Jane, *d.* of R. B. and Lady Louisa Wardlaw-Ramsay; three *s.* four *d.* *Educ.:* Gonville and Caius College, Cambridge. Rector of Clare Portion, Tiverton, Devon; Rural Dean of Tiverton, 1870-85; Vicar of Sittingbourne, Kent, 1885-92; Vicar of Walmer, 1893-1908. *Address:* Precincts, Canterbury. (*Died 17 May 1925.*)

VENN, John, Sc.D., F.R.S., F.S.A.; Fellow of Caius College, Cambridge; President, 1903; *b.* Hull, Yorkshire, 4 Aug. 1834; *s.* of Rev. Henry Venn, B.D., and Martha, *d.* of Nicholas Sykes, Swanland, Yorkshire; *m.* 1867, Susanna C., *d.* of Rev. C. W. Edmonstone; one *s.* *Educ.:* Caius Coll. Camb. Lecturer in Logic and Moral Philosophy for many years at Cambridge; Examiner, etc. *Publications:* Hulsean Lectures, 1869; Logic of Chance, 3rd ed. 1888; Symbolic Logic, 2nd ed. 1894; Empirical Logic, 2nd ed.

1907; Biographical History of Gonville and Caius College, 3 vols. 1901; Venn Family Annals, 1904. *Address:* Vicarsbrook and Caius College, Cambridge. *(Died 4 April 1923.)*

VENNING, Alfred Reid, I.S.O.; *b.* 18 May 1846; *m.* 1879, Katherine Henrietta, *d.* of Henry Wilson Reeves, I.C.S. Member of Council, Bombay; four *s.* two *d. Educ.:* St. Andrews; University College School, London; Germany. Late Federal Secretary, Federated Malay States; previously State Treasurer of Selangor; Secretary to Government of Perak. *Address:* The Homestead, Bracknell, Berks. *(Died 22 Aug. 1927.)*

VENNING, Sir Edgcombe, Kt., *cr.* 1906; F.R.C.S.; *b.* 24 April 1837; *s.* of J. Meybohm Venning; *m.* 1873, Francis Edith (*d.* 1916), *o. d.* of Capt. Aylmer Pearson, late 43rd Light Infantry; one *s.* one *d. Educ.:* privately. Late House Surgeon and Surgical Registrar, St. George's Hospital; Surgeon, 1st Life Guards for 15 years. *Address:* Lamorva, Falmouth. *Club:* Athenæum. *(Died 17 Nov. 1920.)*

VENTRY, 5th Baron, *cr.* 1800; **Lt.-Col. Frederick Rossmore Wauchope Eveleigh-de-Moleyns;** Bt. 1797; D.S.O. 1897; late Commissioner of Police, Mashonaland; *b.* 11 Dec. 1861; *e. s.* of 4th Baron and Harriet (*d.* 1906), *d.* of Andrew Wauchope, Niddrie Marischal, Midlothian; *S.* father 1914. *Educ.:* Harrow. Entered army, 1882; Captain, 1890; served South Africa, 1896-7 (despatches twice, D.S.O., Bt. Lieut.-Col.); acted as Extra Staff Officer; in general command of the troops, 1897; retired 1901. Owns about 93,700 acres. *Heir:* b. Hon. Arthur William Eveleigh-de-Moleyns. *Address:* Burnham, Dingle, Co. Kerry. *(Died 24 Sept. 1923.)*

VERDIN, Sir Joseph; 1st Bt., *cr.* 1896; D.L., J.P. Cheshire; J.P. Herefordshire; *b.* 4 Jan. 1838; *e. surv. s.* of Joseph Verdin of Highfield House, Cheshire, and Margaret, *d.* of Wharton Sadler. *Educ.:* privately. Life Trustee of River Weaver; County Alderman for Cheshire; High Sheriff, Herefords, 1903; Lord of the Manor of Dilwyn. *Heir:* none. *Address:* Garnstone Castle, Weobley, Herefordshire. *Club:* Constitutional. *(Died 28 Dec. 1920.)*

VERDON, Rt. Rev. Michael, R.C. Bishop of Dunedin since 1896; *b.* Liverpool, 1838. Was Student and Vice-Rector at the Irish College, Rome; President Holy Cross College, Clonliffe, Dublin; and of St. Patrick's College, Manly, Sydney. *Address:* Dunedin, New Zealand. *(Died 22 Nov. 1918.)*

VERE, Very Rev. Canon Langton George, Rector of St. Patrick's, Soho, since 1885; Member of Westminster Chapter; President of Westminster Diocesan Schools Association; on Council of Catholic Federated Associations; *b.* 1844. *Educ.:* English College, Lisbon; St. Edmund's, Ware. Ordained 1868; Rector of Homerton Mission, 1877-85; sat on the Vestry and old Strand Board of Works; member of the Westminster City Council. *Publications:* For Better, not for Worse; several volumes of Poems, Essays, Recollections and Short Stories. *Address:* St. Patrick's Presbytery, Soho Square, W.1. *(Died 29 Mar. 1924.)*

VEREY, Sir Henry William, Kt., *cr.* 1920; *b.* 1836; *e. s.* of late Henry Verey of Bridge House, Twyford, Berkshire; *m.* Henrietta Maria, *d.* of late Edward Williams Hasell of Dalemain, Cumberland; one *s.* one *d. Educ.:* Trinity College, Cambridge; Mathematical Tripos, 1859. Bar (Inner Temple), 1865; Revising Barrister Mid-Kent, 1875; I.C.R.V. (Devil's Own), Long Service Medal; Official Referee of Supreme Court of Judicature, 1876-1920; J.P. Berkshire. *Recreations:* shooting, boating, yachting. *Address:* Bridge House, Twyford, Berkshire. *T.:* Twyford 7; Royal Courts of Justice, W.C. *Clubs:* New University; Berkshire. *(Died 4 Dec. 1920.)*

VERHAEREN, Emil; *b.* St. Amand, Belgium, 1855, of Flemish Parentage. *Educ.:* Brussels; -Ghent; University of Louvain. *Publications:* Les Flamandes, 1883; Les Moines, 1886; Soirs, 1887; Debacles, 1888; Flambeaux Noirs, 1890; Les Villages Illusoires, 1894; Les Villes Tentaculaires, 1895; Les Visages de la Vie, 1899; Les Forces Tumultueuses, 1902; Les Aubes; Tendresses Premières, 1904; Heures d'Apres Midi, 1905; La Multiple Splendeur, 1907; Toute la Flandre; Deux Drames, 1915; La Belgique Sanglante, 1915.*(Died 28 Nov. 1916.)*

VERNER, Colonel William Willoughby Cole; *b.* 1852; *m.* Hon. Elizabeth Mary Emily Parnell, *d.* of 3rd Baron Congleton, 1881; one *d.* Joined Rifle Brigade, 1873; passed Staff College, taking 1st place and Honours, 1881; Colonel, 1904; served Nile Expedition, 1884-85; actions of Abu Klea and El Gubat, where guided the fighting square in its march to the Nile (despatches), and subsequent fighting on Gordon's steamers near Metemmeh (medal with two clasps, Khedive's star); awarded bronze medal of Royal Humane Society, 1882; Professor of Military Topography, R.M.C. Sandhurst, 1896-99; served South African campaign, 1899-1900, on the Staff; present at battles of Belmont and Graspan (severely injured, medal and clasps). *Inventions:* inventor and patentee of the Luminous Magnetic and Prismatic Compasses adopted into Service, and of the pattern of Cavalry Sketching Case and Plane Tables likewise adopted, and various other Military Sketching and Surveying Instruments. *Publications:* Sketches in the Soudan, 1886; Rapid Field Sketching and Reconnaissance, 1887; Military Topography and Range Finding, 1889; The First British Rifle Corps, 1890; A British Rifle Man, 1899; Map Reading and Field Sketching, 1891, 4th ed. 1906; The Military Life of Field-Marshal H.R.H. the Duke of Cambridge (2 vols.), 1905 (by command of H.R.H.); My Life among the Wild Birds in Spain, 1909; Editor of The Rifle Brigade Chronicle (thirty volumes issued), 1890-1919; History and Campaigns of the Rifle Brigade, Part i. (1800-1809), 1912; Part ii. (1809-1813), 1919. (With the Abbé H. Breuil of the Institut de paléontologie humaine, Paris), La Pileta Cavern (Palæolithic rock drawings in Audalucia), 1915; Cave Exploration (Pre-historic man) in Southern Spain; Battle Cruisers at Falklands Action by late Commander Rudolf Verner, R.N. (edited), 1920. *Recreations:* wild-fowl shooting, boat sailing, ornithology, oology, natural history—photography, sketching. *Address:* Hartford Bridge, Hartley-Wintney, Winchfield; El Aguila, Algeciras, Spain. *T.A.:* Colonel Verner, Hartley-Wintney. *Club:* United Service. *(Died 25 Jan. 1922.)*

VERNHAM, John Edward; Organist and Choirmaster of St. Paul's, Knightsbridge, since 1879; Professor of Music, King's College, London, since 1889; *b.* Lewes, Sussex, 1854; *m.* Julia Augarde, Pianiste, and pupil of Scharwenka in Berlin. *Educ.:* under late George Cooper and the late Dr. Steggall. Played for the first time in Church, Full Choral Evensong, at the age of 13, at St. Paul's, Walworth; appointed Organist of All Saints, Lambeth, at the age of 15. *Publications:* Novello's Primers, Nos. 49 and 58; Boys' Voices; Communion Service in B Flat; Evening Service in A; Xmas Carols, etc. *Recreation:* country walks. *Address:* 5 Warrington Crescent, Maid Hill, W. *(Died 4 Mar. 1921.)*

VERNON, Sir Harry Foley, 1st Bt., *cr.* 1885; J.P. County of Worcester and D.L. and County Alderman; *b.* Worcestershire, 11 Apr. 1834; 2nd *s.* of T. T. Vernon, Hanbury Hall, Worcestershire, and Jessie Anna Laetitia, *d.* of Herbert Foley, Ridgeway, Pembrokeshire; *S. b.* 1859; *m.* 1861, Lady Georgina Sophia Baillie-

1071

Hamilton, d. 10th Earl of Haddington; one s. one d. Educ.: Harrow; Magdalen Coll. Oxford (M.A.). M.P. East Worcestershire, 1861-66; Master of Worcestershire Foxhounds, 1862-68; Col. of 2nd Vol. Batt. Worcestershire Regt. 1873-85; Hon. Col. (retired) of Worcestershire Hussars. Heir: s. Bowater George Hamilton [b. 12 Sep. 1865; m. 1905, Doris, d. of James H. Allan, Wood House, Shrawley. Late Capt. Worcestershire Yeomanry; served S. Africa, 1900-1. Address: Bramfield Hall, Suffolk. Club: Cavalry]. Recreations: hunting, shooting, cycling, skating. Address: Hanbury Hall, Droitwich, Worcestershire. T.A.: Vernon, Stoke Works. (Died 31 Jan. 1920.)

VERNON, Rev. James Edmund, M.A. Oxon; Vicar of Olveston, Glos., 1885-1918; Rural Dean of Stapleton, 1911-13; Hon. Canon of Bristol, 1912; b. 13 April 1837; s. of Rev. W. H. Vernon; m. 1864, Lavinia (d. 1922), d. of Martin Hunnybun, Godmanchester; three s. two d. Educ.: private schools; private tutor; Wadham College, Oxford. B.A. 1859; Mathematical Master, Temple Grove School, 1859-60; Assistant Master, Cheam School, 1860-63; Deacon, 1863; Priest, 1864; Assistant Curate of Leyton, Essex, 1863-67; Vicar of Withiel Florey, Somerset, 1867-1869; Bicknoller, Somerset, 1869-77; Assistant Curate of St. Paul's, Clifton, 1877-85. Publications: Addresses to Children; Bible Truths in Simple Words. Recreations: cricket, rowing, mountaineering, golf, chess. Address: Lynmouth, Reigate, Surrey. (Died 1 Feb. 1928.)

VERNON, Sir William, 1st Bt., cr. 1914; head of W. Vernon & Sons, millers, Liverpool and London; b. 1835; m. 1857, Jane Margaret (d. 1910), d. of Thomas Cooper, Fulford Hall, Staffs; four s. one d. Heir: s. John Herbert [b. 12 July 1858; m. 1889, Elizabeth, d. of J. Bagnall; four s. one d. Address: Eastham House, Cheshire]. Address: Shotwick Park, Chester. Club: Constitutional. (Died 24 June 1919.)

VERNON HARCOURT, Augustus George, M.A., F.R.S., D.Sc., D.C.L., LL.D.; Vice-President of the Chemical Society; Metropolitan Gas Referee; b. London, 24 Dec. 1834; é. s. of Admiral Frederick E. Vernon Harcourt, and Marcia, sister of 1st Lord Tollemache; m. Hon. Rachel Mary, d. of 1st Lord Aberdare, 1872; two s. eight d. Educ.: Harrow; Balliol College, Oxford. First Class in Natural Science, 1858; studentship at Christ Church, 1859. Publications: Exercises in Practical Chemistry (in conjunction with H. G. Madan, Fellow of Queen's College, Oxford); numerous communications to the Royal Society, the Chemical Society, and the British Association. Inventions: two standards of light, of the values one candle and ten candles; an inhaler, for administering chloroform mixed with air in any proportion up to the limit of safety. Address: St. Clare, Ryde, Isle of Wight. T.: Ryde 16. Club: Athenæum. (Died 23 Aug. 1919.)

VERONESE, Senator Giuseppe; Professor of Mathematics, Royal University, Padua; b. Chioggia, Venice, 7 May 1854; s. of Anthony and Octavia Duse; two s. two d. Educ.: Venice, Zürich, Rome, Leipzig. Drawer at Vienna, 1873; Assistant of Mathematics at Rome, 1877-80; Professor at Padua, 1881; Deputy, 1897-1900; Senator of the Kingdom of Italy since 1904; Fellow, R. Academy di Lincei; Ital. Soc. of the XL.; R. Lombard Institute of Sciences; R. Venetian Inst. of Sciences; R. Academy of Turin, of Padua; Hungarian Acad. of Sciences of Budapest; Doctor of Laws of Aberdeen; Vice-President of the Superior Counsel of Waters and Forests; President of the Hydra Technical Institute in Stra (Venice), and R. Technical Institute in R. School of Decoration and Industrial Arts (Padua), etc. Publications: Nuovi teoremi sull' Hexagrammum mysticum, 1877; Behandlung der proiectivischen Verhältnisse der Räume von mehreren Dimensionen, 1881; Interprétations géométriques de la théorie des substitutions de n lettres, 1883; La geometria descrittiva a quattro dimensioni, 1882; Superficie omaloide normale del 4º ordine a due dimensioni dello spazio a cinque dimensioni, 1884; Fondamenti di geometria (trans. into German), 1891; Elementi di geometria, 1897-1913; Notions of Intuitive Geometry, 1900-15; Complements of Algebra and Geometry, 1915; Il Vero nella Matematica (lecture), 1906; La geometria non-archimedea (lecture), 1908; Publications on Hydraulics; Parliamentary speeches and reports. Recreation: amateur in painting. Clubs: Mathematical, Palermo; International Artistic, Rome, etc.

VERRETT, Lt.-Col. Hector Bacon, D.S.O. 1916; Assistant Deputy Postmaster General, Ottawa, Canada, since 1911; b. Loretteville, Quebec, 9 Feb. 1874; s. of J. A. Verrett and E. Bacon; m. 1905, Irene Forbes, Ottawa, Ontario; no c. Educ.: Levis College, Laval University, Quebec. Private Secretary to Sir Charles Fitzpatrick, 1896-1902; to Hon. G. H. Carroll, 1902-4; to Hon. Rodolphe Lemieux, 1904-6; successive Solicitors-General of Canada; to Hon. Rodolphe Lemieux, Postmaster General of Canada, 1906-11; Lieutenant in The Governor General's Foot Guards, Ottawa, 1906-8; Capt. 1908; Major, 1915; came to England with 2nd Battalion, 1st Canadian Contingent, as Captain, 1914; promoted Major in the field, 1915, and Lt.-Col. as above, 1916 (D.S.O., despatches). Address: Ottawa, Canada. Clubs: Laurentian, Royal Golf, Hunt, Connaught Park, Ottawa; Garrison, Laurentides, Quebec; St. Denis, Montreal. (Died Oct. 1926.)

VERULAM, 3rd Earl of, James Walter Grimston; Baronet, 1628; Baron Forrester (Scotland), 1633; Baron Dunboyne and Viscount Grimston (Ireland), 1719; Baron Verulam (Great Britain), 1790; Viscount Grimston and Earl of Verulam (United Kingdom), 1815; b. 11 May 1852; s. of 2nd Earl and Elizabeth, d. of Major Richard Weyland, Wood Eaton, Oxfordshire; S. father 1895; m. 1878, Margaret Frances, d. of Sir Frederic Ulric Graham, 3rd Bt., and Hermione, d. of 12th Duke of Somerset; one s. five d. Educ.: Harrow. Served in 1st Life Guards, 1870-78; Hon. Major, Herts Yeomanry; M.P. (C.) Mid Hertfordshire, 1885-92; County Councillor, Herts; County Alderman, 1912; late Chairman of Q. Sessions, Liberty of St. Albans, Herts. Owns about 40 acres. Heir: s. Viscount Grimston. Address: Gorhambury, St. Albans. T.: St. Albans 5. Clubs: Carlton, Bachelors'. (Died 11 Nov. 1924.)

VETCH, Col. Robert Hamilton, C.B. 1900; J.P., R.E.; Retired List; b. Birmingham, 6 Jan. 1841; e. surv. s. of Capt. James Vetch, R.E., F.R.S., of Haddington, N.B., Conservator of Harbours at Admiralty, and Alexandrina Ogilvie, d. of Robert Auld of Edinburgh; m. Mary Ann, d. of Commissary-General George Darley Lardner, and granddaughter of Dr. Dionysius Lardner, 1863. Educ.: Grammar School, Henley-on-Thames; private schools; Royal Military Academy, Woolwich. Lieut. Royal Engineers, 1857; Capt., 1869; Maj., 1878; Lieut.-Col., 1884; Col., 1888; employed on defences of Bermuda, Bristol Channel, Plymouth Harbour, and Malta, 1861-76; Secretary of R.E. Institute, Chatham, 1877-83; commanded R.E. Submarine Mining Batt., 1884; Assistant Inspector-General of Fortifications at War Office, 1884-89; Deputy-Inspector-General of Fortifications and Secretary of the Defence Committee, and of the Joint Naval and Military Committee on Defence, War Office, 1889-94; Chief Engineer in Ireland and Colonel on Staff, 1894-98. Sent by Government in "Great Eastern" to report on laying of French

Atlantic Cable from Brest to St. Pierre, and thence to Duxbury, Mass., 1869. Distinguished Service Pension. *Decorated* for Services at War Office in connection with the defences of Empire. *Publications:* Gordon's Campaign in China; Life of Lieut.-Gen. Sir Gerald Graham, V.C., G.C.B.; Life of Lt.-Gen. Sir Andrew Clarke, G.C.M.G., C.B., C.I.E.; edited, The Professional Papers of the Corps of R.E., from 1877 to 1884 inclusive; also the R.E. Journal, during same period; contributor to The Dictionary of National Biography, Encyclopædia Britannica, etc., etc. *Address:* c/o Messrs Cox & Co., 16 Charing Cross, S.W. *Club:* Constitutional.
(Died 28 Jan. 1916.)

VIALLS, Lt.-Col. Harry George, C.B. 1900; West Australian Bushmen's Corps; *b.* 7 Nov. 1859. *Educ.:* Cheltenham. Served Afghan War, 1880 (medal); South Africa, 1899-1902 (despatches twice, King's medal, 2 clasps, C.B.). *Address:* Kalharrup Ford, Warren River, via Balbanup, West Australia.
(Died 16 May 1918.)

VIBART, Colonel Henry Meredith, R.E. (retired); *b.* Taunton, 2 March 1839; 2nd *s.* of Henry Vibart, Madras Civil Service; *m.* 1884, Louisa E., *e. surv. d.* of Col. Charles F. Le Hardy, Madras Army, 1st Commissioner of Coorg; one *s.* *Educ.:* private school at Streatham; Addiscombe College. Obtained commission in H.E.I.C. Engineers, 1857; served at Chatham till 1859; arrived in India, 1859; appointed to P.W. Dept., 1861; served in Tinnevelly and Kistna on Irrigation Works, 1861-68; furlough, 1868-71; Kistna Irrigation Works till 1872; Executive Engineer, Bangalore Military Works, 1872-78; special duty to Madura, 1878, and to Trichinopoly, 1878-79; Under Secretary for Irrigation, 1879; Supt. Engineer, 1879-80; Supt. of Works, Madras and Bangalore, 1881; furlough, 1881-84; Supt. Engineer, Bellary, 1884-87; Madras, 1887-1888; 6 months' special leave to England, 1888-89; Supt. Engineer, 1889; left Bombay on leave, 1889; retired from the service, 1891. *Publications:* Military History of Madras Engineers and Pioneers, 2 vols., 1883; Addiscombe, its Heroes and Men of Note, 1894; Richard Baird Smith, the Leader of Delhi Heroes of 1857, 1897; Life of General Sir Harry Prendergast, V.C., G.C.B., R.E., 1914. *Address:* Woodlands, Remenham, Henley-on-Thames. *Clubs:* East India United Service; M.C.C.
(Died 1 Nov. 1917.)

VICARS, Sir Arthur Edward; Kt., *cr.* 1896; K.C.V.O., *cr.* 1903; C.V.O., *cr.* 1900; F.S.A.; *b.* Leamington, 27 July 1864; *y. s.* of late Col. W. H. Vicars, H.M.'s 61st Regt. and Jane, 3rd *d.* of R. Gun-Cuningham, D.L., Mount Kennedy, Co. Wicklow, and widow of P. K. Mahony, of Kilmorna, Co. Kerry; *m.* 1917, Gertrude, *e. d.* of late J. J. Wright, M.D., of Campfield House, Malton, Yorkshire. *Educ.:* Magdalen College School, Oxford; Bromsgrove School. Ulster King-of-Arms and Registrar and Kt. Attendant on Order of St. Patrick, 1893-1908; is a Govt. Trus. Nat. Library of Ireland; F.S.A. London; Hon. Sec. Kildare Archaeological Soc. since its foundation, 1891; besides heraldry and genealogy is generally interested in matters of art, archaeology, Ex Libris, old plate, etc. *Publications:* Index to the Prerogative Wills of Ireland, 1536-1810, 1897; papers in several archaeological serials. *Recreation:* hunting. *Address:* Kilmorna, Co. Kerry. *Club:* Kildare Street, Dublin.
(Died 14 April 1921.)

VICKERS, Albert; late Chairman of Vickers Ltd.; *b.* 16 Sep. 1838; 3rd *s.* of Edward Vickers late of Tapton Hall, Sheffield, and of Thenford, Banbury; *m.* 1st, 1862, Helen Gage of Boston, U.S.A.; 2nd, 1875, Edith, *d.* of John Foster of Newhall Grange, Maltby, Co. York. *Educ.:* Privately. Knight Grand Cross of the

Order of Naval Merit of Spain; Order of the Rising Sun, Japan. *Recreations:* shooting and fishing. *Address:* 14 Cadogan Square, S.W.; *T.:* Kensington 400; Meallmore, Daviot, Inverness. *Clubs:* Junior Carlton, Arts, Royal Automobile.
(Died 12 July 1919.)

VIDAL, Rt. Rev. Julian, S.M.; Vicar Apostolic of the Fiji Islands, and Titular Bishop of Abydus since 1887; *b.* 1846. *Educ.:* Rodez. Went to Fiji Islands. 1873. *Address:* Suva, Fiji Islands. *(Died 2 April 1922.)*

VIGORS, Captain Philip Urban, M.V.O. 1903; late Royal Irish Regt.; *b.* 7 July 1875; 3rd *s.* of Rev. R. W. Vigors, M.A.; *m.* 1912, Gladys Ingledew, *y. d.* of T. J. Jones-Williams. Laughern Hill, Wichenford, Worcester; one *d.* *Educ.:* Marlborough College. Entered Army, 1897; Captain, 1904; served S. Africa, 1899-1902 (despatches, Queen's medal five clasps, King's medal two clasps); resigned commission, 1907.

VILJOEN, Hon. Sir Antonie Gysbert, Kt., *cr.* 1916; M.B., C.M., M.R.C.S.; *b.* 1858; *s.* of Jacobus Johannes Viljoen; *m.* 1887, Margaretha, *d.* of H. P. Beyers. *Educ.:* S. African College; Edinburgh University. Served S. African War, 1899-1901; in German S.W. Africa, 1915; M.L.A.; Director National Bank of S. Africa and several Insurance Companies. *Address:* Oak Valley, Elgin Station, Cape Province, S. Africa. *(Died 25 Oct. 1918.)*

VILLALOBAR, Marquis of, and Marquis of Guimarey, K.C.V.O.; Spanish Ambassador in Brussels; *b.* 1866; *g.s.* of Duke of Rivas, Poet, Politician, and General during the Peninsular War; *m.* 1921, Marquise de Guimarey. *Educ.:* Madrid; England. Has served in the Diplomatic service at the Foreign Office in Madrid, in the United States Spanish Legation, the Embassy in Paris, in London, and as Plenipotentiary Minister in Washington and in Lisbon; Lord Chamberlain to the King of Spain; Maestrante of the Royal Cavalry Order of Saragossa; Grand Cross of Charles III., and of Isabel of Spain; Medal of Alphonse XIII.; Medal of the Regency of Maria Christina; Grand Cross of Leopold from Belgium; Grand Cross of St. Gregory the Great of Rome; Grand Cross of St. Maurice of Italy; Grand Cross of the Rising Sun of Japan; Grand Cross of the Star of Roumania; Grand Cross of St. Savas of Servia; Grand Cross of the Order of Honour and Merit of Cuba; Knight Commander of the Victorian Order of Great Britain; Grand Officier of the Legion of Honour, France; Commander of the Orders of Christ and Villaviçosa, Portugal; Medal of the Coronation of King Edward of Great Britain; Gold Medal of Zaragoza, of the Puente de San Payo, of Liege, of Ghent, of the Universal Exhibition of Paris, 1900; Star of the Red Cross from Spain; Civique Belgian Order, 1914-18; Correspondent of the Royal Academy of History from Madrid; Honorary citizen of Brussels, of Ghent, of Antwerp, of Liege; Doctor (Hon.) of the University of Liege and of Bruges; Minister Protector of the National Committee of Belgium during the war; in charge during the war in Belgium of the interests of France, Russia, Italy, Portugal, the United States, Japan, Brazil, Cuba, Costa Rica, Bolivia, Roumania, Denmark, Servia, etc. *Recreations:* literature, history, and political studies; painting. *Address:* Calle del Duque de Rivas 1, Madrid; Rue Montoyer 26, Brussels. *T.:* 2340. *Clubs:* Marlborough, Turf, Travellers', United Service, Junior United Service; Cercle du Parc, Cercle Gaulois, Brussels: Nuevo, Madrid. *(Died 9 July 1926.)*

VILLIERS, Colonel Ernest, A.D.C. to the King; Hon. Colonel of First Surrey Rifles; *b.* July 1838; *s.* of late Hon. Edward Ernest Villiers, and Hon. Elizabeth Charlotte Villiers, *d.* of 1st Lord Ravensworth; *m.* 1st,

1865, Elizabeth, d. of late Sir Alexander Wood ; 2nd, 1869, Adela, d. of late Col. and Lady Adela Ibbetson. *Educ.:* Harrow. Served for seventeen years in 43rd Light Infantry, now 1st Batt. Oxfordshire Light Infantry ; served as A.D.C. to Sir William Denison when Governor of Madras ; served as A.D.C. to Lord Strathnairn when Commander of the Forces in Ireland ; served as A.D.C. to the Earl Spencer when Lord Lieutenant of Ireland ; Adjutant of 1st V. B. East Kent Regiment ; served in 15th Middlesex Rifle Volunteers and in command of 1st Surrey Rifles. *Recreations:* stalking, shooting, fishing. *Address:* 50 Thurloe Square, S.W.7. *T.:* Kensington 4182. *Clubs:* Travellers', Wellington, Junior Army and Navy.

(Died 23 April 1921.)

VILLIERS, Ernest Amherst; *b.* 14 Nov. 1863 ; *s.* of Rev. Charles Villiers, late Rector of Croft, Yorkshire, and Florence Amherst, *sister* of 1st Lord Amherst of Hackney ; *m.* 1898, Hon. Elaine Guest, d. of 1st Lord Wimborne ; two *s.* two *d.* *Educ.:* Uppingham ; Cambridge ; M.P. (L.) Brighton, 1905-10. *Address:* 111 Gloucester Place, W.1 ; *T.:* Mayfair 1729; Speen Court, Newbury. *(Died 26 Sept. 1923.)*

VILLIERS, Rt. Hon. Sir Francis Hyde, P.C. 1919 ; G.C.M.G., *cr.* 1918 ; G.C.V.O., *cr.* 1909 ; K.C.M.G., *cr.* 1906, C.B. 1894 ; has the Grand Cross of Orders of Christ of Portugal and Leopold of Belgium: *b.* London, 13 Aug. 1852 ; 4th *s.* of 4th Earl of Clarendon ; K.G. ; *m.* 1876, Virginia Katharine, d. of Eric Carrington Smith of Ashfold, Handcross ; two *s.* two *d.* *Educ.:* Harrow. Entered Foreign Office, 1870 ; Private Sec. to Lord Tenterden Sir J. Pauncefote, and Sir P. Currie, Permanent Under-Secretaries for Foreign Affairs ; Acting Secretary in Diplomatic Service, 1885 ; Private Secretary to Earl of Rosebery, Secretary of State for Foreign Affairs, 1886, and 1892-94 ; Acting Private Secretary to Marquess of Salisbury, 1887 ; Assistant Under-Secretary of State for Foreign Affairs, 1896-1905; Envoy Extraordinary and Minister Plenipotentiary to Portugal, 1905-11 ; Envoy Extraordinary and Minister Plenipotentiary to Belgium, 1911-19; Ambassador to Belgium, 1919-20. *Address:* Elm Lodge, Englefield Green, Surrey. *T.:* Egham 45. *Club:* Travellers'. *(Died 18 Nov. 1925.)*

VILLIERS, Francis John, C.M.G. 1880 ; J.P. Herts ; *b.* 1851 ; 2nd *s.* of late John F. Villiers, barrister. *Educ.:* Aldenham School, Elstree, Herts. Private Secretary to Administrator of Griqualand West, S. Africa (Col. Sir W. Owen Lanyon, K.C.M.G., C.B.), 1875, and Clerk of Legislative Council ; acted as Colonial Secretary, 1877-80 ; Auditor-Gen. B. Guiana, 1882-98. *Decorated* for services in S. Africa. *Address:* Stevenage, Herts *(Died 7 Feb. 1925.)*

VILLIERS, Frederic; war artist, correspondent; *b.* London, 23 Apr. 1852 ; 2nd *s.* of Henry Villiers and Caroline, d. of Thomas Bradley; *m.* Louise (d. 1916), d. of George Lister-Bohne ; one *s.* one *d.* *Educ.:* Guines, Pas-de-Calais, France. Studied art at the British Museum and the South Kensington Schools, 1869-70; admitted as student at the Royal Academy, 1871 ; exhibitor of war pictures at the Royal Academy and the Institute of Painters in Oil Colours, Piccadilly; recipient of twelve English and foreign war medals, clasps, and decorations. War artist for the Graphic; in Servia, 1876; with the Russians in Turkey, 1877 ; with the Russians at Passage of the Danube, Biela, Plevna, Shipka; Afghanistan—Gadamuck and the Bazaar Valley, 1878 ; then round the World ; with Lord Beresford on the Condor, El Magfa, Tel-el-Kebir, 1882 ; invited by the Tzar Alexander III. to his coronation in Moscow, 1883 ; the Eastern Soudan—at Tokar, in the Broken Square at Tamai, 1884 ; with Admiral Sir William Hewitt on his Mission to King

John of Abyssinia ; up the Nile for the Relief of Khartoum, twice wrecked, 1884 ; with Stewart across the Desert—the Battles of Abu Klea and Gubat, 1885 ; with the Servians invading Bulgaria, 1886 ; Burma, 1887; across Canada with the Governor-General ; then on a lecture tour through America, Canada, and British Isles, Chicago Exhibition, 1892; with the Japanese army, Battles of Ping Yang and the march on and taking of Port Arthur, 1894 ; a tour round the world lecturing, 1895 ; Coronation of Nicholas II. at Moscow, 1896 ; in April 1897 joined Greek army campaign against Turkey. During armistice visited Crete. Used the cinematograph camera for first time in history of campaigning during the war ; also introduced bicycle for first time in any European campaign; joined Sirdar's army on its march to Omdurman, 1898 ; present at battle which finally crushed the Khalifa ; lectured on that campaign throughout the United Kingdom and the Antipodes; left Australia for South African War, 1899 ; after occupation of Pretoria returned and then for fourth time started for Antipodes; left for Far East beginning of 1904 ; with Jap forces ; only war artist present at the siege of Port Arthur ; joined the Spanish army operating in Morocco, 1909 ; the Italian army on the invasion of Tripoli, 1911 ; the Bulgarian army in the war with the Balkan Allies and the Turks in 1912-13, and was at the siege of Adrianople ; joined the French armies, 1914; was in the retreat in Flanders, Ypres, Neuve Chapelle, La Boiselle, Rheims, the river Aisne, Argonne and Verdun ; after two years and a half with both British and French armies left France for a lecture tour and visits to other fronts ; lectured through Australia, South Africa, Ceylon, India, failing to get into Mescopotamia, visited N.W. frontier, saw fighting on Mohmund territory, then continued lecture tour through the F.M.S., Straits Settlements, China, Japan, Canada, and the U.S.A. *Publications:* Pictures of Many Wars (illustrated by himself), 1902 ; Port Arthur (with original sketches), 1905 ; Peaceful Personalities and Warriors Bold (illustrated by himself), 1907 ; Villiers : His Five Decades of Adventure, 1921 ; painted 20 feet battle picture of siege, called Sap and Shell ; *Recreations:* cycling, golf, motoring. *Club:* Arts. *(Died 3 April 1922.)*

VINCENT, Marvin Richardson, D.D. ; Professor of New Testament Exegesis and Literature, Union Theological Seminary, New York City, since 1888 ; *b.* Po'keepsie, New York, 11 Sep. 1834 ; father a clergyman ; *m.* 1858. Graduated with first honours from Columbia College, New York, 1854 ; Instructor in the Grammar School of Columbia College, 1854-58 ; Principal Instructor, 1856-58 ; Professor of Latin and Greek, Troy University, 1858-61 ; licensed to preach, 1859 ; Pastor of the First Presbyterian Church, Troy, New York, 1863-73 ; Pastor of Church of the Covenant, New York City 1873-1888; Trustee of Columbia University, New York; member Society of Biblical Literature and Exegesis, New York Historical Society, and Religious Education Association ; Director of New York College of Dentistry. *Publications:* translation of Bengel's Gnomon of the New Testament, 1860 ; Amusement a Force in Christian Training, 1867 ; The Two Prodigals, 1876 ; Gates into the Psalm-Country, 1879 ; Stranger and Guest, 1879 ; Faith and Character, 1880 ; The Minister's Handbook, 1882 ; new revised edition, 1900 ; In the Shadow of the Pyrenees, 1883 : The Expositor in the Pulpit, 1884 ; God and Bread, 1884 ; Christ as a Teacher, 1886 ; The Covenant of Peace, 1887 ; Word Studies in the New Testament, 4 vols., 1887-1900 : Student's New Testament Handbook, 1893 ; Biblical Inspiration and Christ, 1894 ; That Monster the Higher Critic, 1894 ; The Age of Hilde-

brand, 1896 ; International Commentary on Philippians and Philemon, 1897 ; A History of the Textual Criticism of the New Testament, 1899 ; fourth and last vol. of Word Studies in the New Testament, 1900 : The Gospel according to Luke, in Temple Bible, 1902 ; Metrical Translation of Dante's Inferno with commentary ; numerous review articles, essays, and addresses. *Address :* No. 20 East Ninety-second St., New York City. *Club :* Century, New York.
(*Died 15 Aug. 1922.*)

VINCENT, Ralph, M.D. ; B.S. ; M.R.C.P. ; Senior Physician and Director of the Research Laboratory, the Infants' Hospital, London ; Hon. Fellow of the Glasgow Obstetrical and Gynæcological Soc. ; Consulting Physician to the Board of Control, Combe Bank Farm ; Hon. Capt. R.A.M.C. (1914-15 medal); *b.* 20 Dec. 1870 : *e. s.* of Ralph Vincent, Solicitor. *Educ. :* privately : Universities of Oxford, Durham, and Vienna ; St. Bartholomew's Hospital, London. *Publications :* The Nutrition of the Infant, 4th ed. 1913 ; On Acute Intestinal Toxæmia in Infants : An Experimental Investigation of Etiology and Pathology of Epidemic or Summer Diarrhœa, 1910 ; Evidence on Infant-Feeding, Milk-Supply, etc., before Privy Council Committee on Physical Deterioration (Minutes of Evidence, 1904) ; The Milk Laboratory and its relation to Medicine, 1906 ; Clinical Studies in the Treatment of the Nutritional Disorders of Infancy, 1906 ; Lectures on Babies, 1908 ; and various contributions on scientific subjects. *Address :* 32 Seymour Street, Portman Square, W.1. *T. :* Paddington 1568. *M. :* E 1394.
(*Died 21 July 1922.*)

VINCENT, Sir William W., Kt. *cr.* 1912 : J.P. Leicester and Leicestershire ; *b.* Bristol, 1843 : *e. s.* of Rev. John Vincent ; *m.* 1866 ; Anne Susannah, *d.* of Wm. Stark of Chard-Somerset ; one *s.* two *d.* ; Chairman of Roberts & Roberts, Ltd., and J. Johnson & Co., Ltd., member of local advisory Board of London City and Midland Bank ; Member of Leicester Town Council since 1891 ; Alderman since 1898 ; Mayor, 1902-3 and 1910-11 ; Chairman of the Derwent Valley Water Board ; Governor of the Leicester Royal Infirmary and of the Wyggeston Hospital. *Recreations :* walking and travelling. *Address :* Knighton Hall, Leicester. *Club :* Leicestershire.
(*Died 27 Oct. 1916.*)

VINCENT-JACKSON, Rev. William, 3rd *s.* of John Jackson, of London ; *m.* Annie (*d.* 1917), *d.* of Thomas Mitchell of West Arthurlie, N.B. ; one *d. Educ. :* King's College, London ; Exeter and Hertford Colleges, Oxford. Scholar of Hertford College. Curate of Holy Trinity, Nottingham, 1868-1869 ; Vicar of St. Stephen's, Nottingham, 1869-95 ; Rector of Bottesford, Leicestershire, and of Kilvington, 1895-1918 ; resigned 1918 ; Hon. Canon of Southwell ; J. P. Leicestershire. *Address :* 49 Campden House Court, W.8. (*Died 8 June 1919.*)

VINE, Rev. Marshall George ; Warden and Chaplain of Philanthropic Society's Farm School Redhill, since 1887 ; *s.* of Rev. Marshall Hall Vine, M.A., late Rector of St. Mary le Bow, Cheapside ; *b.* Deal, Kent, 24 Aug. 1850 ; unmarried. *Educ. :* Christ's Hospital ; Islington Proprietary School ; Hertford College, Oxford. B.A. 1873 ; Curate of Steyning, Sussex, 1874-81 ; Far Headingley, Leeds, 1881-86 ; Incumbent of Micklefield, Yorks, 1886-87 ; Hon. Diocesan Inspector of Schools, Rochester Diocese ; Member of Diocesan Board of Education and of Council of National Association of Reformatory and Industrial Schools ; Hon. Canon of Southwark Cathedral, 1906. *Publications :* In Loco Parentis ; 23 Annual Reports of the Farm School, Redhill ; numerous papers on Reformatory work. *Recreations :* inventions, music, and drama. *Address :* Warden's House, Redhill. Surrey.
(*Died 5 Sept. 1918.*)

VINES, Rev. Thomas Hotchkin, Prebendary of Lincoln ; Rector of Fiskerton, since 1876 ; *m.* Catherine Maria (*d.* 1921). *Address :* Fiskerton Rectory, Lincoln.(*Died 12 June 1928.*)

VINOGRADOFF, Professor Sir Paul, Kt., *cr.* 1917 ; F.B.A. ; Corpus Professor of Jurisprudence, Oxford University, since 1903 ; Dr. of History, M.A., Hon. D.C.L. (Oxford and Durham) ; LL.D. (Cambridge, Harvard, Liverpool, Calcutta and Michigan) ; Dr. juris, Berlin ; Dr. Hon. Causa Paris ; Fellow of the Russian Academy, Petrograd ; Foreign Member of Royal Danish, Royal Belgian and Norwegian Academies ; Corresponding Member of Prussian Academy, Berlin ; of Royal Academy, Bologna ; the Academy dei Lincei in Rome ; and the Society of Sciences, Livów, Poland ; Member of International Academy of Comparative Law, Geneva ; Acting President of Union of Academies, Brussels, 1925 ; *b.* Kostroma, Russia, 1854 ; *m.* 1897, Louise, *d.* of Judge A. Strang, of Arendal, Norway ; one *s.* one *d.* While Professor in Moscow he exerted himself for the spread of instruction in Russia, founded the Moscow Pedagogical Society, and acted as Chairman of the Educational Committee in the City of Moscow ; resigned his chair in consequence of a conflict with bureaucratic authorities and came to England, where he resumed his interrupted studies in English social and legal history. Elected to the Corpus Chair of Jurisprudence in 1903 ; lectured in Harvard and other American Universities in 1907, and in the University of Leiden in 1921 ; Lectured in the University of Calcutta, 1913-14 ; Lectured in the Universities of Columbia, Johns Hopkins, Yale, Michigan, and California in 1923 ; conducted a Round Table Conference at the Institute of Politics, Williamstown, Mass. 1924 ; delivered 10 lectures at the Institute for the Comparative Study of Culture, Oslo, 1924 ; Director of Publications of the British Academy (Series of Records of Social and Economic History) ; Editor of the Russian Section of the Social and Economic History of the War (1914-17) published by the Carnegie Endowment Fund. *Publications :* Villainage in England ; The Growth of the Manor ; English Society in the Eleventh Century ; Roman Law in Mediæval Europe ; Common Sense in Law (Home University Series, 1914) ; Self-Government in Russia, 1915 ; edited (with Mr. F. Morgan) the Survey of the Honour of Denbigh (1st volume of Records of Social and Economic History, published for the British Academy, 1914) ; Outlines of Historical Jurisprudence, vol. i. 1920, and vol. ii. 1922 ; articles on Russia in the 12th edition of the Encyclopædia Britannica ; edited (with Dr. L. Ehrlich) for the Selden Society the 13th and 14th volume of their Year Book Series ; edited eight volumes of Oxford Studies in Social and Legal History, and the Essays in Legal History contributed by the members of Section VIA of the International Congress of Historical Studies held in London, 1913 ; The Rise of Feudalism in Lombard Italy (Russ.) ; Inquiries in the Social History of England (Russ.) ; Historical Types of International Law in Bibliotheca Wisseriana, Leiden, 1928 ; Custom and Right in the Series of the Institute of Comparative Study of Culture, Oslo. *Recreations :* chess, music, travelling, motoring. *Address :* 36 Beaumont Street, Oxford. *Clubs :* Athenæum, Reform.
(*Died 19 Dec. 1925.*)

VIPAN, Major Charles, D.S.O. 1900 ; 3rd Batt. The Buffs ; Hon. Captain in the Army ; *b.* 1849 ; 2nd *s.* of late Thomas Curtis Vipan of The Mansells, Harlington, Beds. ; *m.* Mary Frances, 2nd *d.* of late Alfred Jones of Needingworth, Hunts, *sister* and *co-heiress* to late John Vipan Jones, also of Needingworth. Fellow of the Linnean Society. Served South Africa, 1900 (despatches, medal with clasps);

retired, 1904; J.P. Hastings. *Address:* Ford Bank, St. Leonards-on-Sea. *Club:* United Service.   *(Died 15 Aug. 1921.)*

VISETTI, Albert; F.R.C.M.; member of Board of Royal College of Music; Professor of Singing, R.C.M.: Examiner for Associated Board of R.C.M. and R.A.M. ; *b.* Dalmatia, 1846 ; *m.* an American ; naturalised British subject for the last 40 years. *Educ.:* Royal Conservatoire of Milan. Gained scholarships from Governments both of Austria and Italy ; at Milan his diploma exercise was a cantata written by his fellow-student Arrigo Boito ; later received appointment as Conductor at Nice ; went to Paris, was introduced by Auber to Court of Napoleon ; wrote an opera "Les trois Mousquetaires" to a libretto by Dumas père ; came to England, 1870 ; was musical adviser to Adelina Patti for five years ; wrote specially for her "La Diva," which has been sung in all countries ; on its formation was the first to be placed on the Staff of Professors at the National Training School, now merged into the Royal College ; for several years held the post of Director and Conductor of the Bath Philharmonic Society, for which society he wrote two successful cantatas ; knighted by the King of Italy for his literary attainments ; Member of Worshipful Company of Musicians ; Freeman of City of London. *Publications:* Italian translation of Hullah's History of Modern Music ; Dr. Hueffer's Musical Studies ; and Life of Palestrina, from the Italian into English ; and an Essay on Musical Culture ; Life of Verdi, 1905. *Recreations:* leisure hours are devoted to lecturing and to contributing to musical publications both foreign and English. *Address:* 12 Phillimore Terrace, W.8. *T.:* Western 611. *Clubs:* Arts, O.P.
     (Died 10 July 1928.)

VIVIAN, Sir Arthur Pendarves, K.C.B.; *cr.* 1902 ; Hon. Col. 6th Batt. (Territorial) The Welch Regt. ; J.P., D.L. ; *b.* London, 4 June 1834 ; 3rd *s.* of late John Henry Vivian, M.P. for Swansea ; *m.* 1st, 1867, Lady Augusta Emily (*d.* 1877), 2nd *d.* of 3rd Earl of Dunraven ; one *s.* two'd. ; 2nd, 1880, Lady Jane Georgina (*d.* 1914), *e. d.* of 10th Earl of Stair ; two *d.* *Educ.:* Eton ; Mining Academy at Freiberg in Saxony ; Trin. Coll., Camb. M.P. West Cornwall, 1868 - 85 ; joined the Volunteers, 1859 ; Col. commanding 2nd Vol. Batt. Welsh Regiment, 1872-95 ; Colonel commanding South Wales Volunteer Infantry Brigade, 1895-1901, when given command of South Wales Border Brigade ; retired 1903 ; Hon. Colonel 7th Batt. (Cyclist) Welsh Regiment ; member of Glamorgan County Council, 1892 - 98, since which Alderman of Cornwall County Council. *Decorated* for services in connection with the Volunteers. *Publication:* Wanderings in the Western Land, 1879. *Address:* Bosahan, St. Martin S.O., Cornwall. *T.:* St. Keverne 12. *Clubs:* Brooks's ; Royal Yacht Squadron, Cowes.   *(Died 18 Aug. 1926.)*

VIVIAN, Captain Gerald William, C.M.G. 1918 ; Royal Navy ; *b.* 11 June 1869 ; *s.* of Sir Arthur Vivian ; unmarried. *Educ.:* Farnborough ; H.M.S. Britannia. Entered Royal Navy, 1882 ; Midshipman, 1885 ; Sub.-Lieut. 1889 ; Lieutenant, 1892 ; Commander, 1904 ; Captain, 1912 ; qualified in flying, 1913 ; commanded Naval Flying Base ship Hermes ; commanded, during the War Europa, 1914, Patia, 1915, Liverpool, 1915-17, Roxburgh, 1917-18 ; now commanding H.M.S. Glorious. *Recreations:* cricket, shooting, fishing. *Address:* H.M.S. Glorious, Devonport. *Clubs:* Brooks's, United Service, M.C.C. ; Royal Western Yacht.   *(Died 14 Aug. 1921.)*

VIVIAN, Lieut.-Col. Ralph, F.R.G.S. ; *b.* 25 May 1845 ; *s.* of late George and Elizabeth Anne Vivian of Claverton Manor, Bath ; *m.* Susan Lawrence, *d.* of John Endicott of Salem,

Massachusetts, and widow of Marshall Owen Roberts of New York. *Educ.:* Eton. Entered Scots Guards, 1864 ; served Egyptian Campaign, 1882 (medal and clasp and Khedive's star) ; retired 1883. *Address:* 15 Grosvenor Square, W.1. *T.:* Mayfair 8135. *Clubs:* Marlborough, Travellers'.   *(Died 15 Aug. 1924.)*

VIZETELLY, Ernest Alfred, author, etc. ; Chevalier of the Légion d'Honneur ; French medal of the War of 1870-71 ; *b.* 29 Nov. 1853 ; *e. surv. s.* of late Henry Richard Vizetelly, and Ellen Elizabeth, *d.* of John Pollard, M.D. ; *m.* 1881, Marie Tissot of Albens, Savoy ; one *s.* three *d.* *Educ.:* Lycée impérial Bonaparte, now Condorcet, Paris. During the Franco-German war (1870) he became a newspaper correspondent (youngest on record) and artist for Daily News, Pall Mall Gazette, and Illustrated London News ; was in Paris during part of the German siege ; passed out, joined the Army of the Loire, attached to Staff of 3rd Division 21st Army Corps ; was in Paris throughout the Commune ; continued acting in a journalistic capacity on the Continent until (*cir.* 1886) he became an editor and reader to Vizetelly & Co., publishers. After the liquidation of that business, consequent upon a prosecution for publishing translations of some of Zola's novels, Mr. Vizetelly reverted to journalism ; but in later years prepared or edited English versions of most of Zola's works, besides producing : The Heptameron, English Bibliophilists' edition, 5 vols., 1894 ; The True Story of the Chevalier d'Éon, 1895 ; With Zola in England, 1899 ; Bluebeard, Comorre the Cursed and Gilles de Rais, 1902 ; Emile Zola, Novelist and Reformer, 1904 ; The Anarchists, their Creed and Record, 1911 ; also three novels : The Scorpion, a romance of Spain, 1894 ; A Path of Thorns, a story of French Life, 1901 ; The Lover's Progress, 1902 ; further, as Le Petit Homme Rouge : The Court of the Tuileries, 1907 ; The Favourites of Henry of Navarre, 1910 ; The Favourites of Louis XIV. 1912 ; Republican France (1870-1912), 1912 ; My Days of Adventure, 1914 ; My Adventures in the Commune of Paris, 1914 ; In Seven Lands, 1916 ; The True Story of Alsace-Lorraine, 1918 ; Paris and her People, 1919. *Address:* c/o Victor Vizetelly, 27 Mount Road, New Malden, Surrey.
     (Died 26 Mar. 1922.)

VOGUÉ, Marquis Charles Jean Melchior de; Commandeur de la Légion d'Honneur ; Membre de l'Académie Française et de l'Académie des Inscriptions et Belles-Lettres ; Président de la Société des Agriculteurs de France ; Président de la Croix-Rouge Française ; *b.* Paris, 18 oct. 1829 ; *m.* ; three *s.* three *d.* Ambassadeur à Constantinople, 1871 ; à Vienne, 1875. *Publications:* Les Églises de la Terre Sainte, 1860 ; Le Temple de Jérusalem, 1864 ; La Syrie Centrale, architecture et inscriptions sémitiques, 1865-77 ; Mémoires sur l'archéologie, l'épigraphie et la numismatique de l'orient ; Villars, 1888 ; Le Duc de Bourgogne et le Duc de Beauvilliers, 1900 ; Jérusalem, 1911 ; Une Famille vivaroise, 1912 ; Discours agricoles et académiques. *Address:* 2 rue Fabert, Paris. *T.:* 700-59, Château de Peseau, à Boulleret, Cher. *M.:* 1661 - U2. *Clubs:* Union, Jockey, Union artistique.
     (Died Nov. 1916.)

VON DONOP, Lieut.-Colonel Pelham George, Chief Inspecting Officer of Railways, Board of Trade, 1913-16 ; *b.* 28 April 1851 ; *s.* of Vice-Admiral E. P. von Donop ; *m.* 1890, Ethel Farran, *d.* of J. Orr, the High Court, Bombay. *Educ.:* Somerset College, Bath. Entered Royal Engineers, 1871 ; Captain, 1883 ; Major, 1890 ; Lt.-Col. 1897 ; Inspector Submarine Defences, India, 1889-94 ; Inspecting Officer of Railways, Board of Trade, 1899-1913. *Address:* Heatherdale Lodge, Camberley. *T.:* Camberley 178. *Club:* Junior United Service. *(Died 7 Nov. 1921.)*

VOULES, Sir Gordon Blennerhassett, Kt., *cr.* 1906 ; late of the Admiralty ; *b.* 8 Sep. 1839 ; *s.* of late Rev. F. P. Voules ; *m.* 1866, Frances Cotton (*d.* 1912), *d.* of James Minchin, Judge in India ; two *s.* three *d. Educ. :* Marlborough College. *Address :* Hamslade, Portchester Road, Bournemouth. *Clubs :* Sports, M.C.C. ; Surrey Cricket ; Bournemouth ; Hampshire Cricket. (*Died 24 Mar. 1924.*)

VYVYAN, Rev. Sir Vyell Donnithorne, 9th Bt. ; *cr.* 1644 ; J.P. ; *b.* 16 Aug. 1826 ; *s.* of Rev. Vyell Francis Vyvyan, Rector of Withiel ; *S.* uncle 1879 ; *m.* 1857, Mary Frederica Louisa Bourchier (*d.* 1907) ; three *s.* one *d. Educ. :* St. John's College, Camb. ; St. Aidan's College, Birkenhead. Ordained, 1854 ; Curate of Churchstoke, Montgomeryshire, 1854-55 ; Rector of Winterbourne-Monkton, Dorset, 1856-66 ; Vicar of Broad Hinton, Wilts, and Diocesan Inspector, 1866-77 ; Rector of Withiel, Cornwall, 1877-79. Owns about 13,400 acres. *Heir :* s. Courtenay Bourchier. *Address :* Trelowarren, Mawgan ; Trewan, St. Columb, Cornwall. *T.A. :* St. Martin, Cornwall. *Club :* Junior Carlton. (*Died 27 May 1917.*)

W

WACE, Colonel Ernest Charles, D.S.O. 1886 ; late R.A. : *b.* Goring, 19 March 1850 ; *s.* of Rev. R. H. Wace of Wadhurst, Sussex ; *m.* 1891, Gertrude Mary Hay, *d.* of Charles Nathan, F.R.C.S., of Sydney, N.S.W. ; one *s.* two *d. Educ. :* Marlborough. Joined Royal Artillery, 1871 ; served in Jowaki Expedition, N.W. Frontier, 1877 (medal with clasp) ; Afghanistan, 1878-80 (despatches, medal with two clasps) ; Burmah Campaign, 1885-86 (wounded, despatches, clasp for Burmah, and D.S.O.) ; retired pay, 1926. (*Died 29 June 1927.*)

WACE, Very Rev. Henry, D.D. ; Dean of Canterbury since 1903 ; *b.* London, 10 December 1836. *Educ. :* Marlborough ; Rugby ; King's College, London ; Brasenose College, Oxford (B.A.). 2nd class Hon. Classics and Mathematics ; Hon. Fellow of Brasenose, 1911. Ordained Curate, St. Luke's, Berwick Street, 1861-63 ; St. James's, Piccadilly, 1863-69 ; Grosvenor Chapel, 1870-72 ; delivered Boyle Lectures, 1874, 1875 ; Bampton Lectures at Oxford, 1879 ; Warburton Lecturer at Lincoln's Inn, 1896 ; Select Preacher at Oxford, 1880-81, 1907 ; at Cambridge, 1876, 1891, 1903, and 1910 ; Prof. of Ecclesiastical History in King's College, London, 1875 ; Prebendary of St. Paul's, 1881 ; Principal of King's College, London, 1883-97 ; Chaplain of Lincoln's Inn, 1872-80 ; Preacher of Lincoln's Inn, 1880-96 ; Rector of St. Michael's, Cornhill, 1896-1903 ; Chaplain to Inns of Court R.V., 1880-1908 ; received honorary freedom of the city of Canterbury, 1921. *Publications :* editor, in conjunction with late Sir William Smith, of Dictionary of Christian Biography, Literature, Sects, and Doctrines, during the First Eight Centuries, 4 vols., 1877-1887 ; and, with the Rev. E. Piercy, of Dictionary of Christian Biography during the First Six Centuries, 1 vol., 1911 ; also of The Speaker's Commentary on the Apocrypha ; Boyle and Bampton Lectures ; Lectures on the Gospel and its Witnesses, and on our Lord's Ministry ; editor of Luther's Primary Works ; Sermons on the Sacrifice of Christ, 1898 ; The Bible and Modern Investigations, 1903 ; The Principles of the Reformation, 1910 ; Prophecy : Jewish and Christian, 1911 ; Some Questions of the Day, 1912, and 1914 ; The War and the Gospel, 1917 ; The Story of the Passion, 1922 ; The Story of the Resurrection, 1923. *Address :* The Deanery, Canterbury. *Clubs :* Athenæum, National. (*Died 9 Jan. 1924.*)

WACE, Maj.-Gen. Richard, C.B., 1897 ; retired, 1904 ; *b.* 16 July 1842 ; *s.* of late Rev. R. H. Wace, Wadhurst, Sussex ; *m.* 1875, Gertrude Mary, *d.* of late Major Candy, C.S.I. ; one *s.* one *d. Educ. :* Marlborough. Joined the Royal Artillery, 1864 ; Capt. 1876 ; Major, 1879 ; Lieut.-Col. 1890 ; Col. 1894 ; Maj.-Gen. 1902 ; served in the Afghan Campaign, 1878-81 (despatches twice, brevet of Major) ; Director-General of Ordnance in India, 1897-1902 ; Col. Comdt. R.A. 1913. *Address :* 16 Court Road, Tunbridge Wells. (*Died 25 May 1920.*)

WADDELL, Alexander Peddie-; Convener of Stirlingshire ; *s.* of James Peddie, W.S., of Edinburgh ; *b.* 1832 ; *m.* 1864, Georgina Catherine, *e. d.* of late Geo. Waddell, of Balquhatstone, whose name he assumed. D.L. for Co. Stirling. *Address :* Balquhatstone, Falkirk, N.B. ; 4 Great Stuart Street, Edinburgh. *Club :* University, Edinburgh. (*Died 26 Jan. 1917.*)

WADDELL, John ; Professor of Chemistry and Librarian of the Science Department, Queen's University, Kingston, Canada ; *b.* Pictou County, Nova Scotia ; *s.* of Rev. Jas. Waddell and Elizabeth Blanchard ; *m.* Annie Maud Burrows ; two *d. Educ. :* Pictou Academy, Nova Scotia. B.A. Dalhousie University, Halifax ; B.Sc. London ; Ph.D. Heidelberg ; D.Sc. Edinburgh ; Hope Prizeman and Vans Dunlop Scholar, Edinburgh University ; Professor's Assistant in Chemistry, Edinburgh ; Professor of Science, Royal Military College of Canada ; Member of the American Chemical Society and of the American Association for Advancement of Science ; Fellow of the Canadian Institute of Chemistry. *Publications :* The Arithmetic of Chemistry ; A School Chemistry ; Quantitative Analysis in Practice ; articles in a number of chemical and physical periodicals. *Address :* Queen's University, Kingston, Canada. *Club :* Frontenac, Kingston. (*Died 4 June 1923.*)

WADDILOVE, Sir Joshua Kelley, Kt., *cr.* 1919 ; Wesleyan leader and philanthropist. (*Died 14 Feb. 1920.*)

WADDINGTON, Mary King; widow of late W. H. Waddington, French Ambassador to England. *Publication :* Italian Letters of a Diplomatist's Wife, 1905 ; Letters of a Diplomatist's Wife, 1906 ; Château and Country Life in France, 1908 ; My War Diary, 1917. *Address :* rue Auguste Vacquerie 29, Paris. (*Died 30 June 1923.*)

WADDINGTON, Samuel, B.A. Oxford ; late of Board of Trade (retired 1906), poet and littérateur ; *b.* Boston Spa, Yorkshire, 9 Nov. 1844 ; *y. s.* of late Thomas Waddington. *Educ. :* St. Peter's School, York ; St. John's, Huntingdon ; Brasenose College, Oxford ; a Fellow of the Anthropological Institute ; Private Secretary to Lord Balfour of Burleigh, and afterwards to Mr. Thomas Burt, 1892 ; has travelled on foot through Norway, Holland, the Ardennes, Savoy, Black Forest, etc. *Publications :* English Sonnets by Living Writers, 1881 ; English Sonnets by Poets of the Past, 1882 ; Arthur Hugh Clough, a Monograph, 1883 ; Sonnets and other Verse, 1884 ; Sonnets of Europe, 1886 ; Sacred Song, a Volume of Religious Verse, 1888 ; A Century of Sonnets, 1889 ; Poems, 1896 ; Collected Poems, 1902 ; Chapters of My Life, 1909 ; Some Views respecting a Future Life, 1917 ; contributions to Nineteenth Century, Athenæum, Academy, Literature, Westminster Gazette, Pall Mall Gazette, etc. *Recreations :* rowing, mineralogy, and literature. *Address :* 50 Brondesbury Villas, N.W.6. *Club :* Junior Constitutional. (*Died 7 Nov. 1923.*)

WADDINGTON, Maj.-Gen. Thomas, J.P. ; *b.* 1827 ; *m.* 1862, Emilie Helena (*d.* 1909), *d.* of Major-General Michael Willoughby, C.B. *Address :* The Chestnuts, Pangbourne, Berks. (*Died 31 Jan. 1921.*)

WADDY, Henry Turner; Metropolitan Police Magistrate, since 1917, Tower Bridge Police Court; *b.* 12 Feb. 1863; 2nd *s.* of late Judge Waddy, K.C.; *m.* 1890, Alice Maud, *o. d.* of late William Dingley; one *s.* four *d. Educ.:* Leys School, Cambridge. Called to Bar, Inner Temple, 1885; Member North Eastern Circuit; late a Member of the General Council of the Bar; Recorder of Scarborough, 1913-17. *Address:* 206 Ashley Gardens, S.W.1. *T. :* Victoria 4084. *Clubs:* Garrick, Devonshire.
(Died 4 Nov. 1926.)

WADE, Hon. Sir Charles Gregory, K.C.M.G., *cr.* 1920; Knight, *cr.* 1918; K.C. 1905; K.C. (Eng.) 1920; Justice of Supreme Court, Sydney, since 1920; *b.* Singleton, N.S.W., 26 Jan. 1863; *s.* of W. Burton-Wade, M.I.C.E.; *m.* Ella Louise, *d.* of Francis Bell, M.I.C.E.; two *s.* two *d. Educ. :* All Saints, Bathurst; King's School, Parramatta (Broughton and Forrest Exhibitions); Merton College, Oxford (B.A., Hons. Classics, Hon. Fellow). Called to Bar, Inner Temple, 1886; Crown Prosecutor, N.S.W., 1891; Prosecutor for Western Circuit and Central Criminal Court, 1894-1902; M.L.A. 1903-17; Premier N.S.W. 1907-10; Attorney-General and Minister for Justice, 1904-10; Leader of Liberal Party in N.S.W. 1907-16; Fellow of Royal Historical Society, 1918; Chairman of Australian Canteens for Serbians, 1918-19; Agent-General for N.S.W., 1917-20; l'Ordre de la Couronne (Belgium). *Publications:* Married Women's Property Act and Employer's Liability Act; Australia : Problems and Prospects. *Recreation :* Oxford University XV. 1882-86; English XV. 1883-86. *Address :* Supreme Court, Sydney, N.S.W. *Club:* Australian, Sydney. *(Died 22 Sept. 1922.)*

WADE, Hon. Frederick Coate, B.A., K.C.; Agent-General for British Columbia in Great Britain since 1918; *b.* Bowmanville, Ont.; 26 Feb. 1860; *s.* of William Wade; *m.* 1886, Edith Mabel, *d.* of late D. B. Read. Q.C., Toronto; one *s.* one *d. Educ. :* Toronto University. Editorial Writer Toronto Daily Globe, 1882; called to Manitoba Bar, 1886; editorial writer, Manitoba Free Press, 1886-87; represented Department of Justice of United States in inquiry into claims of compensation made by Jean Louis Legare for surrender of Sitting Bull after Custer Massacre, 1887; first President of the Young Liberal Association, Winnipeg, 1886; re-elected, 1887; Member of the Provincial Board of Education, 1889; Member Council of Manitoba University and Winnipeg Public School Board; appointed by Lord Aberdeen Commissioner to inquire into the management of the Manitoba Penitentiary, 1897; Crown Prosecutor, Legal Adviser, and Member of the Yukon Council, 1897-98; one of British Counsel, Alaska Boundary Commission, 1903; first President Canadian Club, Vancouver, 1906-7; Senator of University of British Columbia, 1912; present by invitation at the Coronation of King George and Queen Mary, Westminster Abbey, June 1911. *Publications:* National Schools for Manitoba; The Klondyke: a Four Years' Retrospect; The Alaska-Yukon Boundary Dispute: its Practical Side; Some Comments on the Alaska Award; Canada at the Grave of General Wolfe; The Early Navigators of the Pacific; The Canadian Flag; A Short History of Liberalism in Canada; The Awakening of the Pacific, etc. *Recreations:* reading, travel, camping. *Address:* British Columbia House, Nos. 1 and 3 Regent Street, S.W. *Clubs:* Canadian (Vice-Pres.), Overseas; Vancouver, Jericho Country Vancouver. *(Died 9 Nov. 1924.)*

WADESON, Maj.-Gen. Frederick William George, C.B. 1915; Indian Army; *b.* 12 July 1860. Entered army, 1880; Captain, I.S.C., 1891; Major, Indian Army, 1900; Lt.-Col. 1906; Col. 1907; Maj.-Gen. 1916; Brig.-

1078

Commander, India, 1918; served European War, 1914-17 (despatches twice, C.B.).
(Died 10 Dec. 1920.)

WADHAM, Arthur; Founder and Editor of the Machinery Market, established 1879; writer on trade economics; *b.* Barnstaple, 7 Sep. 1852; *m.* 1st, 1876, Sarah Marina, *d.* of Wm. Swann of Bradford, Yorks; 2nd, 1916, Eliza Annie, *d.* of late Thomas Summerson, Haughton le Skerne, Darlington. *Educ. :* Society of Friends' Schools. Associate Institute of Mechanical Engineers, 1893; C.I. Mechanical Engineers, 1922; commenced press agitation in 1879 for cheaper patents, ultimately secured by Act of 1883; contributed articles to Manchester Guardian series, Aug. 1903, in defence of Free Trade for Machinery and Engineering interests (reprinted in book form and published under title, "Protection and Industry"); article on the Rise and Progress of the Machinery and Engineering trades for "British Industries under Free Trade," 1903. *Recreations :* watercolour painting, music, golf, tennis. *Address :* Wardrobe Chambers, 146A Queen Victoria Street, E.C.; 11 Ridge Road, N.; Scalebeck, Keswick; *T.A.:* Wadham, London; *T.:* P.O. Central 730. *Clubs:* Highgate and Keswick Golf.
(Died 3 July 1923.)

WADIA, Sir Hormasji Ardeshir, Kt., *cr.* 1918; Barrister; Advocate, High Court, Bombay. *Address:* Bombay.
(Died 10 Nov. 1928.)

WADSON, Hon. Sir Thomas John, Kt., *cr.* 1911; *s.* of John James Wadson and Sarah Perot, *d.* of Forster Cooper; *b.* 22 May 1844; *m.* 1874, Eva Bonnell, *d.* of John Samuel Darrell; one *s. Educ. :* Warwick Academy, Bermuda. Member Board of Public Works, 1888-95; Member House of Assembly since 1875; Speaker since 1895; Chairman of Audit Board since 1898; President Chamber of Commerce, 1907-13; represented the general community of Bermuda at the Coronation, 1911. *Address:* Hamilton, Bermuda. *Club:* Royal Bermuda Yacht.
(Died 4 Feb. 1921.)

WADSWORTH, John, M.P. (Lab.) Hallamshire Div. W.R. Yorks since 1906; *b.* West Melton Fields, near Rotherham, 4 Feb. 1850; *m.* 1872, Annie Eliza Bell of Newbigin, near Sheffield. *Educ. :* Brampton School. Removed to Newbigin, near Sheffield, in the early sixties; was employed at Newton Chambers Co.'s Thorncliffe pit until the great lockout, 1869; worked at Wombwell Main Colliery, Wombwell, during the period of the Thorncliffe dispute; obtained employment at the Wharncliffe Silkstone Colliery, Tankersley, near Barnsley, as a coal miner, 1870; elected by the Wharncliffe Silkstone miners as their checkweighman, 1883-1904; was Secretary, President, and Delegate for the Wharncliffe Silkstone Branch of the Yorkshire Miners' Association for twenty years; Vice-President of the Yorks Miners' Association for fifteen years; President of the Y.M.A., 1904; General and Corresponding Secretary to the Y.M.A., 1905. *Address:* 2 Huddersfield Road, Barnsley.
(Died 10 July 1921.)

WAECHTER, Sir Max Leonard, Kt., *cr.* 1902; D.L.; J.P.; High Sheriff of Surrey, 1902; *b.* 1837, Stettin, Germany; *m.* 1st, Harriet Shallcrass (*d.* 1910), *e. d.* of late Thomas Cave, J.P., M.P.; 2nd, 1912, Armatrude, *d.* of late Colonel Bertie Hobart, R.A., and Mrs. Hobart Grimston, of Grimston Garth, Holderness, East Yorkshire, and *g.d.* of late Hon. and Very Rev. Henry Lewis Hobart, Dean of Windsor. *Educ. :* Stettin. Came to England, 1859; naturalized 1865; published pamphlet on the Federation of the States of Europe (lecture delivered at the London Institution, February 1909), and has personally submitted this scheme to the sovereigns and governments of Europe for approval and support; presented Petersham Ait (formerly Glover's Island), and the freehold of Petersham Lodge and grounds, to the town of Richmond as free gifts, for the preservation of the view from Richmond Hill; founded the Victorian Convalescent Home for Surrey Women, also the Princess Mary Memorial Home of Rest, and the King Edward VII. Memorial Home for Surrey Children, all at Bognor; founded the Queen Mary's Holiday Home for Governesses at Petersham; founder of the European Unity League. *Recreations:* yachting, motoring, and boating. *Address:* The Terrace House, Richmond, Surrey. *T.:* Richmond 387. *Clubs:* Liberal Unionist United Empire Surrey Magistrates'. (*Died 3 Oct. 1924.*)

WAGSTAFF, William George, C.M.G. 1898; *b.* Pembroke, 3 Nov. 1837; *e. s.* of late William Wagstaff, and Elizabeth, *d.* of John Vaughan; *m.* 1st, 1874, Marie Louise (*d.* 1883), *d.* of Georges Nein of Fribourg, Switzerland; 2nd, Sarah Amelia, *w.* of Wm. Brenan of Odessa, *e. d.* of Richard Webster of Jersey, formerly of Leeds, Yorks, 1886; three *d. Educ.:* Greenwich Hospital School. Was present first bombardment of Sebastopol, 17 Oct. 1854 (Crimean medal and clasp, and Turkish medal); appointed clerk to Consulate, Berdiansk, 1861; Vice-Consul, 1874; Vice-Consul, Nicolaieff, 1876; Consul at Taganrog for province of Ekaterinoslav, 1884; and ports of the Sea of Azoff; Consul for Governments of Voronetz, Saratof, Samara, Ufa, Orenburg, Astrakhan, Stavropol, the Don Cossack country, and the Kuban and Ter districts, 1887; Consul at Riga for provinces of Livonia and Courland, 1889; Consul-General at Rio de Janeiro, 1895; received the Jubilee Medal, 1897; Consul-Gen. for the States of Rio de Janeiro, Espirito Santo, Minas Geraes and Matto Grosso, 1899; retired on a pension, Aug. 1900. *Address:* Belmont, De Roos Road, Eastbourne. (*Died 12 May 1918.*)

WAHLSTATT, Blucher von, 3rd Prince, H.S.H. (*cr.* 1814), **Gebhard Gustaw Lebrecht,** Hereditary Member of the House of Lords in Prussia [family old nobility of the German Empire, first mentioned 1214; first Prince was famous Field-marshal, hero of the Katzbach and conqueror of Napoleon]; *b.* 18 March 1836; *e. s.* of 2nd Prince and Mary, Countess Larisch Moennich; *S.* father 1875; *m.* 1st, 1860, Marie, Princess Lobkowitz, Duchess of Raudnitz (*d.* 1870); two *s.* two *d.*; 2nd, 1889, Elisabeth, Countess Perponcher Sedlnitzky (*d.* 1894); one *s.* one *d.*; 3rd, 1895, Wanda, Princess Radziwill, *g. g. d.* of H.R.H. Princess Louise of Prussia; two *s.* two *d. Educ.:* at home. Joined 1st Regiment of Dragoons of the Guard, 1855; Military Attaché to the Prussian Legation, Vienna, 1857-59; served as First Lieut. Cuirassiers of the Guard during the Austro-German War, 1866 (battles of Skalitz and Königgrätz). Owns estates of Krieblowitz and Wahlstatt in Prussia, and of Radun, Stauding, Stielnik, Brosdorf, and Polanka in Austrian Silesia. *Recreations:* shooting, swimming. (*Died 12 July 1916.*)

WAINWRIGHT, Rev. Frederick; Hon. Canon of Chester, 1908. *Address:* Ballington Vicarage, Altrincham.   · (*Died 12 Nov. 1921.*)

WAITHMAN, William Sharp; J.P. and D.L. County Galway; J.P. Cheshire; has served as High Sheriff; *b.* 1853; *s.* of late R. W. Waithman, D.L., of Moyne Park, County Galway, and *d.* of William Sharp, J.P., Linden Hall, Lancashire; *m.* 1st, Lady Philippa Stanhope (*d.* 1920), *d.* of 7th Earl of Harrington; one *s.* one *d.*; 2nd, 1921, Lydia Frances Elizabeth, *widow* of H. Lyon-Smith, M.D., of Harley Street. Served in army as temp. Capt. 1915-16. *Educ.:* Eton. *Address:* Merlin Park, Galway; Gawsworth Old Hall, Macclesfield. *Club:* Kildare Street, Dublin. (*Died 8 Nov. 1922.*)

WAKE, Sir Herewald, 12th Bt.; *cr.* 1621; J.P.; *b.* 19 July 1852; *S.* father 1865; *m.* Catherine, *d.* of Sir Edward St. Aubyn, 1st Bt., St. Michael's Mount, Cornwall, and *sister* of 1st Lord St. Levan, 1874; three *s.* three *d. Educ.:* Eton. Capt. 4th Batt. Northamptonshire Regt. 1882-88. *Heir: s.* Hereward.   Owns about 3200 acres. *Address:* Courteenhall, Northampton. *Club:* Arthur's.   (*Died 5 Jan. 1916.*)

WAKERLEY, Rev. John E.; President Wesleyan Methodist Conference, 1922-23; Chairman of Wesleyan Methodist Church, East Anglia District; *s.* of John and Mary Wakerley, Melton Mowbray; *b.* 12 Nov. 1858; *m.* Essie, *y. d.* of James Illingworth; no *c. Educ.:* Melton Public School; Didsbury and Handsworth Colleges. Entered Wesleyan Ministry, 1882; first appointment to Nottingham; has been Member of Finsbury Borough Council, and of Holborn Board of Guardians; 2nd President National Brotherhood Federation; Secretary of First London District, Wesleyan Methodist Church, for twelve years; now Member of the Legal Conference of the Wesleyan Methodist Church, Chairman Western Section of Methodist Œcumenical Conference; Secretary of Wesleyan Conference, 1917-22. *Publications:* Christianity and Business; Christianity and Amusements; The Making of Moral Manhood. *Recreation:* agriculture. *Address:* Tostock, Bury St. Edmunds. *T.A.:* Drinkstone, Suffolk.   (*Died 4 Sept. 1923.*)

WALCOT, Lt.-Col. Basil, D.S.O. 1915; R.E.; *b.* 3 Dec. 1880; *m.*; two *s.* Entered army, 1900; Capt., 1909; special employ Headquarters, 1906-9; Staff Capt., 1909-11; General Staff Officer, 3rd Grade, 1913; 2nd Grade, 1915; served South Africa, 1902 (Queen's medal 4 clasps); European War, 1914-15 (despatches four times, D.S.O.). *Club:* Army and Navy. (*Died 14 Sept. 1918.*)

WALCOTT, Charles Doolittle, LL.D., Sc.D., Ph.D.; Secretary, Smithsonian Institution, Washington, D.C., since 1907; *b.* 31 March 1850; *s.* of Charles D. Walcott and Mary Lane; *m.* 1st, 1888, Helena B. Stevens (*decd.*); one *s.* one *d.*; 2nd, 1914, Mary Morris Vaux. *Educ.:* Public Schools, Utica, N.Y. Director, United States Geological Survey, 1894-1907; Secretary, Carnegie Institution of Washington, 1902-5; on National Advisory Committee for Aeronautics (Chairman); Member National Academy of Sciences (President, 1917-23), Mary Clark Thompson medal; National Research Council (1st Vice-Chairman); American Association for Advancement of Science; American Academy of Arts and Sciences (President, 1923); Academy of Natural Sciences, Philadelphia (Hayden Medal); American Philosophical Society (President, 1925); Academy of Sciences of Paris; London Geological Society (Bigsby and Wollaston Medals); Royal Geographical Society of London; Gaudry Medal (1917), Société geologique de France; Royal Academy, Stockholm; Christiania Scientific Society; Academy of Sciences, Institute of Bologna; Imperial Society Naturalists (Moscow); Alpine Club of Canada, etc. *Publications:* The Trilobite; Paleontology of the Eureka District; Cambrian Faunas of North America; Fauna of the Lower Cambrian or Olenellus Zone; Fossil Medusae; Pre-Cambrian Fossiliferous Formations; Cambrian Brachiopoda; The Cambrian Faunas of China; Cambrian Geology and Palæontology; The Cambrian and its Problems in the Cordilleran Region; Pre-Cambrian Algonkian Algal Flora; Discovery of Algonkian Bacteria; Cambrian Trilobites; Evidences of Primitive Life; The Albertella Fauna in British Columbia and Montana; Fauna of the Mount Whyte Formation; Appendages of Trilobites; Middle Cambrian

Algae; Middle Cambrian Spongiae; Notes on Structure of Neolenus, etc. *Clubs*: Cosmos, University, Aero of America, New York.
(Died Feb. 1927.)

WALCOTT, Col. Edmund Scopoli, C.B. 1885; J.P., D.L., High Sheriff for Devon, 1902; County Alderman for County of Devon; Hon. Colonel 6th Devon Regiment, T.D.; *b.* Castle Caldwell, Co. Fermanagh, 1842; *e. s.* of John Minchim Walcott; *m.* 1900, Mrs. Vicary, *widow* of J. Vicary, and *d.* of late Lieutenant-Colonel Cox of Manor House, Beaminster. *Educ.:* at home and abroad. Entered Bombay Army, 1860; Captain, 1869; Major, 1880; Br. Lieut.-Colonel, 1881; Br. Colonel, 1885; served in the China War, 1860-63 (medal); Afghan War, 1879-80 (medal with clasp, mentioned in despatches); Soudan Expedition, 1885 (mentioned in despatches, medal, clasp, star, C.B.); belongs to the Geographical, Royal Agricultural, and Horticultural Societies, and the Japanese Society. *Recreations:* on most of the local bodies of the district; his garden. *Address:* Aylwood, Heavitree, Exeter.*(Died 11 Oct. 1923.)*

WALDRON, Rev. Arthur John; Vicar of Brixton, 1906-15; Surrogate for Southwark; Lecturer in City Churches; *b.* 30 Sep. 1868; *s.* of W. Waldron, R.N.; *m.* Lily J. Wilson, *d.* of J. E. Wilson, C.E.; one *s.* *Educ.:* Plymouth; Handsworth College, and Oxford. London and Provincial Lecturer for the Christian Evidence Society from 1892-99; ordained, 1899; Curate, St. Luke's, Camberwell, 1899-1901; a well-known lecturer against secularism in London parks, etc. *Publications:* Problems of Life; Ethics of War; Resurrection of Christ; Modern Spiritualism; contributor to several volumes of sermons. *Plays:* Should a Woman Tell? The Carpenter, etc. *Recreations:* golf. *Address:* 31 Prince of Wales Mansions, Battersea Park, S.W.11. *T.:* Battersea 1738.
(Died 1 Sept. 1925.)

WALDRON, Rt. Hon. Laurence Ambrose, P.C. Ireland, 1911; *b.* Ballybrack, Co. Dublin, 14 Nov. 1858; 4th *s.* of late Laurence Waldron, D.L., M.P. for Co. Tipperary; unmarried. *Educ.:* The Oratory School, Birmingham. Member of the Dublin Stock Exchange since 1881; Director of Grand Canal Co. (Chairman); Director Dublin and Kingstown Railway (Chairman); Director Dublin United Tramways (1896) Co. (Chairman); Director Gt. South. and West. Rly. of Ireland; Director Alliance and Dublin Consumers' Gas Co.; one of the Governors and Guardians of National Gallery, Ireland; a Commissioner of National Education, Ireland; of charitable donations and bequests, Ireland; a Trustee of the National Library of (Ireland); Member of Senate of National University; M.P. (I.L.) St. Stephen's Green, Dublin, 1904-10. *Address:* Marino, Ballybrack, Co. Dublin; and 10 Anglesea Street, Dublin. *Clubs:* Reform, National Liberal, Burlington Fine Arts; Sackville Street, St. Stephen's Green, Dublin; Royal St. George Yacht, Royal Irish Yacht, Kingstown.
(Died 27 Dec. 1923.)

WALERAN, 1st Baron (*cr.* 1905), **of Uffculme, Rt. Hon. Sir William Hood Walrond,** Bt., *cr.* 1876; P.C. 1899; D.L., J.P.; *b.* 26 Feb. 1849; *S.* father, 1889; *m.* 1st, 1871, Elizabeth Katherine (*d.* 1911), *heiress* of late James Pitman, Dunchideock House, Devonshire; two *d.*; 2nd, 1913, Helena Margaret, *d.* of late Mr. Morrison and *widow* of Wilfred Grant. M.P. (C.) E. Devonshire, 1880-85; Junior Lord of the Treasury, 1885-86, 1886-92; late Chief Govt. Whip; Chancellor of Duchy of Lancaster, 1902-1905; Capt. Grenadier Guards, retired 1872; M.P. (C.) Tiverton Div. Devon, 1885-1906; Patronage Secretary to Treasury, 1895-1902. *Heir: g.s.* William George Hood Walrond. *Address:* Casa Picciola,

1080

Roquebrune, Cap Martin, France. *Clubs:* Carlton, Garrick. *(Died 17 May 1925.)*

WALKER, Major-General Albert Lancelot; retired; *b.* 23 Sep. 1839; 5th *s.* of Edwin Walker of The Chase Cottage, Enfield; unmarried. *Educ.:* R.M.C. Sandhurst; received commission, 1857; passed Staff College, 1868. Entered 99th (subsequently Wiltshire) Regiment; served China War, 1860 (medal and clasp); Zulu War, 1879 (Brevet Lt.-Col., medal and clasp). *Address:* 24 Marlborough Buildings, Bath.
(Died 12 Feb. 1918.)

WALKER, Rev. Arthur, M.A.; Prebendary of Wells Cathedral, 1903-11; 3rd *s.* of William Walker of Bolling Hall, Yorkshire; *m.* 1st 1866, Adelaide, *d.* of Archdeacon Sandford; one *d.*; 2nd 1881, Harriet, *d.* of Rev. E. P. Vaughan of Wraxall. *Educ.:* Westminster; Trinity College, Cambridge. Curate of Alvechurch and afterwards of Hammersmith; Rector of Easton in Gordano, and afterwards Rector of Dinder. *Address:* 13 Albert Road, Regent's Park, N.W. *Clubs:* Junior Conservative, New Oxford and Cambridge.
(Died 30 Dec. 1918.)

WALKER, Sir (Byron) Edmund, Kt., *cr.* 1910, C.V.O. 1908, LL.D. (Toronto), D.C.L. (Trinity University, Toronto), F.G.S., F.R.S.C., F.R.C.I.; President Canadian Bank of Commerce since 1907; Chairman, Board of Governors, University of Toronto; Member of the National Battlefields Commission of Canada; President of Board of Trustees of the National Gallery of Canada; President and Founder of the Champlain Society for publishing rare works on Canadian History; *b.* Township of Seneca, Co. Haldimand, Ont., 14 Oct. 1848; *m.* 1874, Mary (*d.* 1923), *d.* of Alex. Alexander, Hamilton, Ont.; four *s.* three *d.* *Educ.:* public schools. Commenced business career in banking office of his uncle, J. W. Murton, Hamilton; he entered service of The Canadian Bank of Commerce, 1868; General Manager, 1886; has filled the offices of Chairman of the Bankers Section of the Toronto Board of Trade; President and Vice-President of the Canadian Bankers' Association. *Publications:* many papers and Addresses on Banking and other subjects. *Address:* Long Garth, Toronto; Broadeaves, De Grassi Point, Lake Simcoe. *Clubs:* Toronto, York, Toronto; Rideau, Ottawa. *(Died 27 Mar. 1924.)*

WALKER, Rear-Admiral Charles Francis, J.P.; 3rd *s.* of Sir James Walker, 1st Bt.; *b.* 1836; *m.* 1873, Edith Frances (*d.* 1906), *d.* of Adm. Hon. Arthur Duncombe; one *s.* Served Crimea (2 medals and clasp); Silver Medal Royal Humane Society. *Address:* The Hall, Beverley, Yorks. *(Died 8 Aug. 1925.)*

WALKER, Edmund W.; a Master of the Supreme Court, 1873-1908; *b.* 1832; *e. s.* of late M. H. Walker, Solicitor; *m.* 1859, Mary, *d.* of Samuel Field, of Thame. *Address:* Vale Cottage, Esher, Surrey. *(Died 18 Oct. 1919.)*

WALKER, Sir Edward Daniel, J.P.; head of firm of E. D. Walker and Wilson, Wholesale Newsagents and Railway Bookstall Lessees; *b.* Brighton, 1840. Ancestor, Sir Henneker Walker, admiral in time of Charles II.; *m.* cousin, *d.* of E. D. Walker, Solicitor, Sheffield. *Educ.:* privately. After establishing on a firm foundation his Wholesale Newsagency and many other commercial undertakings, directed his energies to public affairs; has been a member of the Board of Guardians, Durham County Council, a J.P. of the Boro, and for nearly twenty years sat on the Town Council. Thrice called to the Mayoralty. Two of these occasions were the Jubilee year of the late Queen, and the Coronation year of King Edward VII. Twice stood in the forefront of municipal battles: on the question of Gas management he saved the town £3000 a year, and on that of Water, whilst safeguarding on modern lines a wholesome supply was chiefly instrumental in preventing the adoption of a costly scheme (£80,000 to £100,000), afterwards admitted to be unnecessary. *Recreations:* cricketing, gardening, and latterly a little golf. *Address:* North Rise, Darlington. *T.:* 91 Darlington. *Club:* National Liberal. (*Died 21 May 1919.*)

WALKER, Ernest Octavius, C.I.E. 1891; M.I.E.E.; *b.* Teignmouth, 16 July 1850; *s.* of G. J. Walker, late 18th Light Dragoons, and Anna, *d.* of Bishop Corrie of Madras; *m.* 1881, Rosa, *d.* of Rev. H. C. Deshon, Vicar of East Teignmouth; one *s. Educ.:* Thorn Park School, Teignmouth; Regent's Park College, London; Hartley Institute, Southampton. Entered Indian Telegraph Department in 1871; in charge telegraph in Lushai Expedition, 1889-90 (mentioned in despatches, created C.I.E.); retired, 1892; Superintendent of Telegraphs in Ceylon, 1895-98. *Decorated* for services in Chin Lushai Expedition, 1889-90. *Publications:* papers upon Earth Currents in Journal of Electrical Engineers; A Romance of Ceylon, 1899. *Recreations:* science, antiquities, travel in wild countries. *Address:* 77 Iverna Court, Kensington, W. (*Died 12 Feb. 1919.*)

WALKER, Sir Francis (Elliot), 3rd Bt., *cr.* 1856; *b.* 9 March 1851; *s.* of 1st Bt. and Mary Catherine Sinclair, *o. d.* of Captain John Worth, R.N., of Duren; *S. b.* 1905; *m.* 1883, Helen, Constance (*d.* 1901), *d.* of late Rev. A. Paris; one *d.* Is a retired Lieut. R.N. *Heir: g.s.* Baldwin Patrick, *b.* 1924. *Address:* Swansfield House, Alnwick. (*Died 27 July 1923.*)

WALKER, Francis S., R.H.A., R.E., Painter and Etcher *b.* 1848; *e. s.* of Thomas Walker, Dunshaughlin, Co. Meath. *Educ.:* Catholic University, Royal Dublin Society; Royal Hibernian Academy. Was awarded Taylor Scholarship, and came to London 1868, where for some years was engaged in illustrating books, journals, The Graphic, Illustrated London News, etc., until he began to exhibit in the Royal Academy and other galleries; then turned his attention to etching and mezzotinting his own pictures. *Publications:* over seventy original plates, mostly of places of interest; some of these in book form, viz. The Thames from Oxford to the Tower; Rivers of the West of England; Killarney; and colour books — Ireland and Poet's Country. *Recreation:* walking *Address:* The Firs, Highwood Hill, Mill Hill, N.W.(*Died 17 April 1916.*)

WALKER, Sir George Casson, K.C.S.I., *cr.* 1911; C.S.I. 1906; *b.* 9 July 1854; *s.* of Rev. Joseph Walker and Catherine Mary, *d.* of Admiral Sir William F. Carroll, K.C.B.; *m.* 1883, Fanny (Kaiser-i-Hind decoration, 1910), *d.* of Samuel Coates, M.D.; one *s.* three *d. Educ.:* Winchester College (scholar); New College, Oxford. Mathematical Honours (Moderation). Entered I.C.S. 1877; served in various capacities in the Punjab, up to 1901, when he was deputed to the Native State of Hyderabad (Deccan) as Financial Adviser to the Nizam, in which capacity he served continuously until his retirement on pension in 1911; J.P. Borough of Hove. *Address:* 55 Wilbury Road, Hove, Sussex. (*Died 27 April 1925.*)

WALKER, George Walker, A.R.C.Sc., M.A., F.R.S.; Chief Scientist R.N. Mining School, H.M. Gunwharf, Portsmouth; *b.* Aberdeen, 24 Feb. 1874; *s.* of John Walker, accountant to Messrs. Chalmers, advocates; *m.* 1904, Agnes Elizabeth, *d.* of James Gifford, art dealer, Aberdeen; one *s. Educ.:* Gordon's College, Aberdeen (Foundationer); Royal College of Science, London (1st National Scholar, Mechanics); A.R.C.Sc. 1894; Trinity College. Cambridge (Major Scholar); 4th Wrangler, Mathematical Tripos, 1897; "One One," Part II., 1898; Smith's Prize, 1899;

Isaac Newton Student, 1899; Fellow of Trinity, 1900; Studied at Göttingen, 1901; Lecturer on Physics, Glasgow University, 1903-8; Superintendent of Eskdalemuir Observatory, 1908-12; magnetic re-survey of the British Isles for 1915. *Publications:* papers to scientific journals and societies; Modern Seismology. *Recreations:* fishing and walking. *Address:* 17 Anglesey Cresent, Alverstoke, Hants. (*Died 6 Sept. 1921.*)

WALKER, General George Warren, R.E.; Colonel Commandant, R.E. since 1899; *b.* 6 April 1823; *s.* of Major-Gen. George Warren Walker, commanding 21st Royal North British Fusiliers, formerly of the 8th Royal Irish Light Dragoons; *m.* 1st, 1858, Margaret (*d.* 1904), *d.* of late John Anderson, Inverness; 2nd, 1905, Augusta (*d.* 1918), *w.* of John Turner, Backwell, Bristol; one *s.* two *d.* Entered Army, 1842; General, 1885; unemployed list, 1882; Assistant Civil Engineer. 1847; District Engineer, Kanara, 1859; Superintending Engineer. Coimbatore, 1863; Chief Engineer and Public Works Secretary, Govt. of Madras, 1872-76. *Address:* 4 Forster Road, Bath. (*Died 4 July 1920.*)

WALKER, Henry de Rosenbach, B.A.; *b.* 30 May 1867; *s.* of late R. F. Walker, Shooter's Hill, Kent, and Marie von Rosenbach, of Karritz, Esthonia, Russia; *m.* 1900, Maud Eleanor, *d.* of Rev. D. W. Chute, Rector of Sherborne St. John, nr. Basingstoke; three *d. Educ.:* Winchester; Trin. Coll. Camb. Clerk in the Foreign Office, 1889-92; contested N.W. Suffolk (L.), 1895; Plymouth, 1900; M.P. (L.) Melton Div. Leicestershire, 1906-10; elected to the London County Council for East St. Pancras, 1913; Alderman of the County of London, 1919; Member of London War Pensions Committee, 1916; has travelled extensively in Russia, Central Asia, the Far East, North America, the West Indies,and the Antipodes. *Publications:* Australasian Democracy, 1897; The West Indies and the Empire, 1901; reviews and newspaper articles. *Recreations:* music, travel, shooting. *Address:* 20 Stafford Terrace, W.8. *Club:* Reform. (*Died 31 July 1923.*)

WALKER, James Douglas, K.C.; *b.* 1841; *e. s.* of Jas. Ouchterlony Walker, of London and Blairton, Aberdeenshire, and Jane Charlotte, *d.* of Richard Holden Webb; *m.* Susan Matilda, *d.* of John Forster of Malverleys, Hants, 1871; three *s.* one *d. Educ.:* Rugby; University Coll. Oxford (M.A.). Barr. Lincoln's Inn, 1866; Bencher, 1887; Q.C. 1891; Treasurer of Lincoln's Inn, 1913; contested Bridgwater Division of Somersetshire, 1892; Writer of Prefaces to the Black Books of Lincoln's Inn. *Recreations:* golf, travel. *Address:* 20 Queen's Gate Gardens, S.W.7. *T.:* 406 Western. *Club:* Reform. (*Died 24 June 1920.*)

WALKER, Maj.-Gen. James Grant Duff, Madras Cavalry; *b.* 4 Sept. 1842. Entered army, 1858; Maj.-Gen. 1897; retired, 1898; served Indian Mutiny, 1859; Burmese Expedition, 1887-89 (medal with clasp). (*Died 23 Jan. 1921.*)

WALKER, Sir James (Lewis), Kt., *cr.* 1908; C.I.E. 1888; V.D. 1911; *b.* 1845; *s.* of late John Walker, Punjab Police; *m.* 1st, 1866, Lizzie Marion, *d.* of late W. Hogan, of Simla (*d.* 1892); 2nd, 1893, Catherine Featherston, *d.* of Charles Davey, of Canonbury, N. Lieut.-Col. Comdt. 2nd Punjab Vol. Rifles, 1884-91; a Proprietor of The Pioneer and Civil and Military Gazette newspapers, India. *Address:* Worplesdon Place, Worplesdon, Surrey. *T.:* Mayfair 3115. *Clubs:* Oriental, Junior Carlton; Bengal, Calcutta. (*Died 13 April 1927.*)

WALKER, Hon. James Thomas, J.P. (Queensland), F.R.C.I.; Fellow Institute Bankers, London; Senator of N.S.W. in Commonwealth Parliament, 1901-13; Director Bank, N.S.W. (President, 1898-1901), Australian

Mutual Provident Society (1887-1921), etc.; Chairman Women's College Council, and Councillor St. Andrew's College (both in University of Sydney); Chairman Thomas Walker Convalescent Hospital; Chairman Finance Committee Presbyterian Church, 1889-1919; Director of the Burnside Orphans' Home; Trustee Infants' Home, Ashfield, since 1888; President of Australian Golf Club, 1903-19; *b.* Springfield Place, Leith Walk, Midlothian, 1841; *s.* of John William Walker, who emigrated 1844, taking up Castlesteads Station N.S.W.; *m.* Janette Isabella, *d.* of Thomas Palmer, J.P., Summer Hill, Mayo; three *s.* two *d.* *Educ. :* Circus Place School; Edinburgh Institution; King's College, London. On Staff Bank of N.S.W., London, Sydney, and Queensland, 1860-85; first General Manager Royal Bank of Queensland, 1885-87; Executor of Thomas Walker of Yaralla, N.S.W.; Member of People's Federal Convention at Bathurst, 1896, and Australian Federal Convention, 1897-98; owns Mount Ubi estate, Wide Bay, Queensland. *Publications :* pamphlets on Australian Banking and Federal Finance. *Recreations :* golf, walking, reading. *Address :* Wallaroy, Woollahra, Sydney. *T. :* City 6153. *Clubs :* Queensland, Brisbane; Union, Sydney; Tasmanian, Hobart; Melbourne, Melbourne.   (*Died 18 Jan. 1923.*)

WALKER, John Bayldon ; *b.* 16 Jan. 1854; *e. s.* of late Charles Walker, Dewsbury, and Elizabeth Wood, *d.* of late John Bayldon, Royston; *m.* 1889, Mary Ann Ella, *e. d.* of late Wm. Bayldon, Batley, Yorks. Barr. Inner Temple, 1875; went N.E. Circuit and W.R. Yorks Sess.; Police Magistrate and Coroner, Freetown, S. Leone, 1890; Judge Supreme Court, Turks and Caicos Islands, 1895; Chief Justice, St. Vincent, 1898; S.J.P., Port-of-Spain, Trinidad, 1902; Chief Justice, St Lucia, 1903; of Grenada, 1906-9. *Address :* 53 Breakspears Road, Brockley, S.E.4. *T. :* New Cross 1223.
    (*Died 19 April 1927.*)

WALKER, Maj. Reginald Selby, D.S.O. 1916; R.E.; *b.* 16 April 1871. 2nd Lieut. 1890; Capt. 1901; Major, 1910; Lt.-Col. 1916; Chief Instructor R.M.C. 1904-9. Served S. African War, 1900-2 (despatches, Queen's medal 4 clasps); European War, 1914-18 (despatches, D.S.O.).
    (*Died 30 Sept. 1918.*)

WALKER, Robert, M.A. (Aberd. et Cantab.), LL.D. (Aberd.); Registrar Emeritus of the University of Aberdeen; *b.* 18 Feb. 1842; *y.* of six sons of late Wm. Walker; unmarried. *Educ.:* Grammar School and University, Aberdeen; Clare College, Cambridge. Fellow, 1866-78; Examiner in Mathematics in Universities of Edinburgh, 1872-75, and Aberdeen, 1877-80; Librarian University of Aberdeen, 1877-93; and Secretary of University Court, Registrar and Clerk of the General Council, 1877-1907. *Recreations :* gardening and fishing. *Address :* Tillydrone House, Old Aberdeen. *Club :* University, Aberdeen.   (*Died 27 Oct. 1920.*)

WALKER, Lieut.-Col. Robert Sandilands Frowd, C.M.G. 1891; F.R.G.S.; F.Z.S.; Commandant Malay States Guides; *b.* 1850; *m.* 1896, Beatrice, *d.* of late T. J. Ireland, M.P., and *widow* of Colonel Bolton. *Educ. :* R.M.C. Sandhurst. Ensign, 28th Foot, 1872; Captain, 1881; Hon. Lt.-Col. 1889; A.D.C. to Governor Straits Settlements, 1878-79; attached to Perak Armed Police, 1879; Deputy Commissioner, 1880; Commissioner, 1881; in command of Pahang Expeditionary Force, 1892-94; organised Regt. Malay States Guides, 1896; Acting Assist. Resident, Perak, 1882; Acting Sec. to Govt. Perak, 1894-95. Acting Resident, Selangor, 1899; Acting British Resident, Perak, 1900-1. *Address :* Scott's Lodge, Knockholt, Kent. *Clubs :* Naval and Military, Ranelagh, Wellington, Sports.
    (*Died 16 May 1917.*)

WALKER, Sir Thomas Gordon, K.C.I.E., *cr.* 1908; C.S.I. 1903; Hon. LL.D.

1082

Aberdeen; Lieutenant-Governor of the Punjab; *b.* 14 Sept. 1849; *s.* of late Rev. Henry Walker of Urquhart, Moray; *m.* 1879, Adela, *d.* of Rev. A. Irwin, rector of Napton, Warwicks; two *s.* *Educ.:* Gymnasium and University, Aberdeen. Entered I.C.S. 1872; Settlement Officer, Ludhiana, 1878-84; Registrar Chief Court, 1884-88; Commissioner of Excise and Inspector-General of Registration, 1888; Deputy Commissioner, 1896; Divisional Judge, 1898; Judge, chief court, 1898; Commissioner, Delhi Division, 1901-5; Financial Commissioner, Punjab, 1905-7; member of Viceroy's and Provincial Legislative Councils, 1903-7; Lieutenant-Governor, May-Aug. 1907; Jan.-May, 1908. *Address :* Puckaster, W. Worthing. *Club :* Junior Carlton.   (*Died 25 Nov. 1917.*)

WALKER, Very Rev. Thomas Gordon, Dean of Achonry since 1907. Ordained, 1880; Curate of Emlaghfad, 1880-82; Rector, 1882-1907; Canon of Achonry, 1896-1907. *Address :* The Deanery, Ballymote, Ireland.
    (*Died 9 May 1916.*)

WALKER, William James Dickson, C.B. 1911; *b.* 1854; *s.* of late William Walker of Dungannon, Co. Tyrone; *m.* 1884, Barbara, Paterson; one *s.* one *d.* *Educ. :* Royal School, Dungannon; private tuition; Industrial Inspector and Adviser to Congested Districts Board, Ireland, 1897-1910; Member of the Congested Districts Board, Ireland, 1910. *Address :* Firbeck, Inverary Avenue, Belfast. *Club :* Ulster Reform, Belfast.   (*Died 10 May 1926.*)

WALKER, William Sylvester, F.R.C.I.; F.I.B.P.; ("Coo-ee") author; *b.* Australia, 16 May 1846; *e. s.* of late Hon. W. B. Walker, M.L.C., first Commodore and Founder of the Royal Sydney Yacht Squadron; *m.* twice; three *s.* two *d.* *Educ. :* two English schools; Sydney Grammar School, N.S.W.; Worcester College, Oxford. Sometimes in England, sometimes in Australia, etc.; fifteen years in New Zealand; was three years a pastoralist in interior of Queensland; learned station life at Merungle on the Lachlan after leaving Oxford; was amongst the wild natives in Australia at Humeburne on the Paroo River, with the late Mr. Sylvester John Browne; volunteered for Parihaka in New Zealand; was in South Africa, amongst the first for Diamond Fields, Klipdrift, Pniel. *Publications :* When the Mopoke Calls; From the Land of the Wombat; Native-Born; Virgin Gold; In the Blood; Zealandia's Guerdon; The Silver Queen; What Lay Beneath; Blair's Ken; At Possum Creek; Finished; Koi, or The Thing without any Bones. *Recreation :* boating. *Address :* Soroba House, Oban, Argyllshire. (*Died 6 April 1926.*)

WALKLEY, Arthur Bingham, dramatic critic of The Times; *b.* Bristol, 17 Dec. 1855; *o. s.* of late Arthur H. Walkley of that city; *m.* Frances Eldridge; one *d.* *Educ. :* Warminster; Balliol and Corpus Christi, Oxford (B.A.). F.R.S.L. 1907; entered Secretary's Office, G.P.O. 1877; Assistant Secretary, 1911-1919; Sec. to British Delegation, Washington Congress, 1897; Sec. to Imperial Penny Postage Conference, 1898; a British Delegate, Rome Congress, 1906. *Publications :* Playhouse Impressions, 1892; Frames of Mind, 1899; Dramatic Criticism, 1903; Drama and Life, 1907; Pastiche and Prejudice, 1921; More Prejudice, 1923; Still More Prejudice, 1925. *Recreation :* gardening. *Address :* Bristol House, Southampton Row, W.C.; Brightlingsea, Essex. *Clubs :* Athenæum, Garrick.   (*Died 7 Oct. 1926.*)

WALL, Arthur Joseph, C.B.E. 1924; O.B.E. 1918; late Secretary to the Prison Commissioners for England and Wales; *s.* of late Capt. Michael Wall; *m.* 1st, Jessie Elizabeth Pratt (*d.* 1907); 2nd, 1924, Eleanor Annie, *widow* of late Albert Rutherford; two *s.* one *d.* *Educ. :* Battersea Grammar School. Entered Prison

Commission, 1880; Assistant Secretary, 1910; Secretary and Inspector, 1917. *Recreations:* gardening, sketching in water colours. *Address:* 2 West Parade, Horsham, Sussex.

(Died 7 Dec. 1927.)

WALLACE, Major-General Sir Alexander, K.C.B., *cr.* 1922; C.B. 1908; retired, Indian army; *b.* 22 Aug. 1858; *s.* of late Alexander Wallace, merchant, Calcutta; *m.* 1889, Ethel, *d.* of Colonel G. C. Ross, late Indian Army; three *s.* one *d.* *Educ.:* Framlingham College, Suffolk (governor, 1916). Entered Army, 1876; Capt. I.S.C. 1887; Maj. 1896; Lt.-Col. Indian Army, 1902; Brevet-Col. 1904; Maj.-Gen. 1911; served Afghan War, 1879-80 (medal); Burmah, 1886-88 (medal); Hazara, 1891 (clasp); 2nd Miranzai, 1891 (clasp); in command of Kashmir Imperial Service Troops at occupation of Chilas, 1892 (twice wounded); N.W. Frontier, India, 1897-98 (medal with clasp); Waziristan, 1901-2 (clasp); East Africa, 1903-4 (despatches, brevet-col.); A.A.G. Peshawar Division, 1907; commanded Jubbelpore Brigade, 1908-13; in command 15th Scottish Division on formation, 1914; Suez Canal, 11th Indian Division, 1914-15 (despatches); Mediterranean Force, 1915; Egypt, in command Western Frontier Force, 1915-16 (despatches, Order of the Nile, 2nd class, 1916); Council of the British and Foreign Unitarian Association, 1902. *Publications:* occasional papers in Journal of U.S. Institution of India. *Address:* Fleetwood, Wellington College Station, Berks. *(Died 25 Dec. 1922.)*

WALLACE, Alexander Falconer, O.B.E.; partner in Wallace & Co., Bombay; Director of Wallace Brothers & Co., Ltd., London; *b.* Edinburgh, 30 June 1836; 6th *s.* of late L. A. Wallace, Edinburgh; *m.* Katharine Louisa, 4th *d.* of late Wm. Harter, Hope Hall, Eccles, 1868; one *s.* one *d.* *Educ.:* Edinburgh High School and University. *Address:* 20 Hyde Park Gardens, W.2; *T.:* Padd. 143. *Clubs:* Reform, Oriental. *(Died 24 Jan. 1925.)*

WALLACE, Sir Donald Mackenzie, K.C.I.E., *cr.* 1887; K.C.V.O., *cr.* 1901; *b.* 11 Nov. 1841; *o. surv. s.* of Robert Wallace, Boghead, Dumbartonshire; unmarried. *Educ.:* private schools; Universities of Glasgow, Edinburgh, Berlin, Heidelberg; Ecole de Droit, Paris. Resided and travelled in various foreign countries, chiefly in France, Germany, Russia, and Turkey, 1863-84; Private Sec. to Marquess of Dufferin and Marquess of Lansdowne as Viceroys of India, 1884-89; attached to the Czarewitch as political officer during his tour in India and Ceylon, 1890-1891; Director of the Foreign Department of the Times, 1891-99; Assist. Private Secy. to H.R.H. the Duke of Cornwall and York during his colonial tour, 1901; Extra Groom-in-waiting to King Edward VII., 1909, and to King George V., 1910; attached to Emperor of Russia during his visit to England, 1909; member of Institut de Droit International and Officier de l'Instruction Publique of France; edited 10th edit. Ency. Brit. *Publications:* Russia, 1877; Egypt and the Egyptian Question, 1883; The Web of Empire, 1902; New editions of Russia, rearranged and brought up to date, 1905 and 1912. *Recreation:* change of occupation. *Address:* 26 Park Mansions, Knightsbridge, S.W.1. *Clubs:* Athenæum, Marlborough, St. James's, Reform, Polyglot. *(Died 10 Jan. 1919.)*

WALLACE, George, K.C., M.A. (Cantab.); *e. s.* of late Rev. T. S. Wallace, M.A., Incumbent of St. Paul's, Bolton, Lancs; *b.* 1854; *m.* 1886, Nicolina Maud (*d.* 1904), *e. d.* of late R. G. Deverell of Tullamore, King's Co.; four *d.* *Educ.:* Clergy Orphan (now St. Edmund's) School, Canterbury; Jesus College, Cambridge. Called to Bar, 1879, Lincoln's Inn; now Middle Temple, Bencher, 1918, retiring, 1926; K.C. 1910. *Publication:* joint author of Roberts and Wallace on the Duty and Liability of Employers, 4th ed., 1908. *Address:* 26 Ladbroke Gardens, W.11. *T.:* Park 3272. *(Died 24 Nov. 1927.)*

WALLACE, Lieut.-Colonel Hugh Robert, of Busbie; D.S.O. 1916; J.P., D.L.; late commanding Res. Garrison Batt. Suffolk Regt.; 10th Gordon Highlanders; *b.* 31 Aug. 1861; *s.* of late Capt. Henry Ritchie Wallace, Gordon Highlanders; *m.* 1st, 1886, Matilda Marion Christie (*d.* 1905), *d.* and *heiress* of late Archibald Campbell of Cammo, Midlothian; 2nd, 1908, Isobel M., *widow* of Charles Ralph Dubs, Glasgow, and *d.* of late William Rae Arthur; three *s.* one *d.* *Educ.:* Cheltenham College. Vice-Lieutenant of Ayrshire; ex-Convener of County of Ayr; Hon. Sheriff-Substitute for the County; served European War, 1914-18 (despatches twice, D.S.O.); retired Lt.-Col., 1918. *Address:* Cloncaird Castle, Maybole, Ayrshire. *Clubs:* Carlton, Orleans; New, Edinburgh. *(Died 2 May 1924.)*

WALLACE, Col. Sir Johnstone, K.B.E., *cr.* 1917; Iron and Coal Merchant; *s.* of T. Wallace, Magherafelt; *b.* 20 Oct. 1861; *m.* 1889, Norah, *d.* of John B. Bowes, Newcastle; two *s.* one *d.* Sheriff, Newcastle, 1905-1906; Lord Mayor, 1913-14; Alderman, D.L., J.P., Northumberland; Chairman of British Federation of Iron, Steel and Metal Merchants. *Address:* Parkholm, Newcastle. *T.:* Central 400 and 4780. *Club:* Junior Constitutional.

(Died 14 Nov. 1922.)

WALLACE, Roger William, K.C.; Barrister-at-law; *b.* Glasgow, 28 April 1854; *e. s.* of Hugh Wallace, J.P., Dorset Hall, Merton, Surrey; *m.* 1877, Sarah, *d.* of John Thornton; one *s.* one *d.* *Educ.:* London University. Besides legal pursuits, has taken great interest in chemical, electric, and engineering work; member of Council of Electrical Engineers, 1891, 1899, 1900, 1901, and is an Associate; first Chairman of Royal Automobile Club, 1897-1904; Chairman of Motor Union, 1901-4; Chairman of Royal Aero Club, 1901-12; now a Vice-President; Director Westminster Electric Supply Corporation, Ltd., and other electric light companies, from their inception. *Publications:* The Law of Letters Patent for Invention; numerous articles on motoring and chemistry. *Recreations:* shooting, golf, etc. *Clubs:* Reform, Bath, Ranelagh, Royal Automobile, Royal Aero, Hurlingham.

(Died 13 Dec. 1926.)

WALLACE, Sir William, K.C.M.G., *cr.* 1907; C.M.G. 1897; F.R.G.S.; *b.* 12 Sept. 1856; *s.* of late James Wallace of Aberbrothock; *m.* 1891, Christine Baillie, *d.* of late Joseph Rickard, Dundee; one *d.* *Educ.:* Arbroath High School. Late administrator of the Niger Company's Territories; chiefly occupied during thirty-two years acquiring and consolidating British interests and gaining political influence; concluded numerous treaties with the native potentates and Fulani Emirs; one with the Sultan of Sokoto, 1894; commanded or served with over thirty military expeditions. This work in a great measure led to the subjugation of the Fulani nation and native races, and so to the acquisition of Nigeria for the British Empire; three West African medals, five clasps, coronation medal; at the transfer of the Territories to the Crown in 1900 joined Government Service as Resident General; Deputy High Commissioner and acting Governor, Northern Nigeria, 1900-10; retired from Government Service, 1910; received Murchison grant from Royal Geog. Society for explorations in Nigeria. *Address:* Weycroft Manor, Axminster, Devon. *Clubs:* Devonshire, City Liberal.

(Died 10 July 1916.)

WALLACE, William, M.A., LL.D.; Barrister-at-Law; *b.* 17 Nov. 1843; *s.* of Jasper Wallace, Culross, Perthshire; *m.* 1869, Rebecca,

d. of Peter White, Edinburgh; two s. one d. *Educ.*: Geddes School, Culross; Grammar School and University, Aberdeen; M.A.; Hon. LL.D. of St. Andrews. After college was Classical Master in Ayr Academy for two years; joined journalism in Edinburgh; edited Dumfries Herald 1870-78; on staff of Echo and other papers in London from 1878-89; Assistant Editor Glasgow Herald, 1889-1906; Editor of Glasgow Herald, 1906-9. *Publications*: New Edition of Chambers's Life and Works of Robert Burns, 1896; Burns and Mrs. Dunlop, 1898; Scotland Yesterday, 1891; After the Revolution, and other fantasies, 1891; Life and Last Leaves of Robert Wallace, 1903; articles in various magazines. *Recreation*: golf. *Address*: 106 University Avenue, Glasgow.

(*Died 17 July 1921.*)

WALLACE, William, C.B.E. 1920; Sheriff-Substitute of Argyll, at Oban since 1910; J.P., Argyll; *b.* Glasgow, 1860; *o. s.* of Dr. William Wallace, public analyst for Glasgow and Lanarkshire; *m.* Barbara, *d.* of Alexander Munro; two s. two d. *Educ.*: Glasgow Academy and University (M.A. 1880). Admitted member of Scots Bar, 1888; Advocate-Depute in Sheriff Courts, 1901; Advocate-Depute on Glasgow Circuit, 1902; Counsel for the Crown as *Ultimus Haeres*, 1903; Sheriff-Substitute at Campbeltown, 1904-1910; late Captain 1st Vol. Battalion Highland Light Infantry. *Publications*: Banking Law, with Forms (with A. M'Neill), 4th ed. 1913; The Trial of the City of Glasgow Bank Directors (Notable Scots Trials), 1906; The Scots Law of Bankruptcy, 2nd ed. 1914; The Practice of the Sheriff Court of Scotland, 1909; The Sheriff Court Style Book, 1911; many articles in legal encyclopædias and journals, including Green's Encyclopædia of Scots Law and the articles on Scots Law in Modern Business Practice, The Encyclopædia of Accounting, etc. *Recreations*: golf, yachting. *Address*: Glenlee, Oban, N.B. *Club*: Scottish Conservative, Edinburgh; Royal Highland Yacht, Oban. (*Died July 1922.*)

WALLER, Alfred Rayney, M.A., of Peterhouse, Cambridge; Secy. to the Syndics of the Univ. Press, Cambridge; *b.* York, 1867; *m.* 1890, Emily Mary Hudson, Cherry Hill House, York. Engaged in literary work and journalism in London, 1888-1902. *Publications*: edited Florio's Montaigne, 6 vols., 1897; edited, with Arnold Glover, the collected edition of Hazlitt's writings, 13 vols., 1902-6; translated Molière's plays, 8 vols., 1902-7; edited the works of Butler, Cowley, Crashaw and Prior for the University Press, Cambridge, 1904-8; joint-editor with the Master of Peterhouse of The Cambridge History of English Literature, 14 vols. *Address*: 1 Cavendish Avenue, Cambridge. *T.*: 543 Cambridge.(*Died 19 July 1922.*)

WALLER, Augustus Désiré, M.D., F.R.S., LL.D.; D.Sc. Perth, W.A.; Director of Physiological Laboratory, Univ. of London; Corresponding Member and Memb. Associé of Société de Biologie, Paris, of Physiological Society, Moscow, of Royal Academies of Medicine, Rome and Belgium; Hon. Member Council of University of Tomsk; Lauréat de l'Institut de France, 1889 (discovery of electromotive action of Human Heart, and record by electrocardiogram); Premio Aldini sul Galvanismo R. Acad. d. Scienze d. Instituto di Bologna, 1892; *b* Paris, 12 July, 1856; *s.* of Augustus Volney Waller, M.D., F.R.S.; *m.* Alice Mary, *s. d.* of late George Palmer, formerly M.P., Reading; three s. one d. *Educ.*: Collège de Genève; Universities of Aberdeen and Edinburgh. *Publications*: Introduction to Human Physiology; Animal Electricity, 1897; Signs of Life, 1903; Physiology, the Servant of Medicine, 1910; The Psychology of Logic, 1912; scientific papers in Royal Society and Journal of Physiology. *Recreations*: billiards,

motoring. *Address*: Weston Lodge, 32 Grove End Road, N.W.8 *T.*: Hampstead 788. *M.*: A 220. *Club*: Savile. (*Died 11 Mar. 1922.*)

WALLERSTON, Brig.-Gen. Francis Edward, C.B. 1916; *b.* 14 Oct. 1856; *s.* of late Edward Francis Wallerstein, H.M. Diplomatic Service; *m.* 1913, Phoebe Adeline, *o. d.* of late Henry Simpson of Bowstead, Cumberland, and Sparken, Notts, and *widow* of Thomas Bright Matthews. *Educ.*: Rugby. Entered York and Lancaster Regt., 1876; exchanged to 1st Batt. King's Own Scottish Borderers, which he commanded; commanded No. 6 District Lichfield, 1908-12; retired, 1912; served South African War (Queen's medal 3 clasps); European War, Commanding Infantry Brigade, 1914-17 (despatches, C.B.). *Address*: Sparken, Bournemouth. *Clubs*: Naval and Military, Bath. (*Died 3 Mar. 1926.*)

WALLIS, Charles Edward, M.R.C.S., L.R.C.P., L.D.S. Eng.; Principal Assistant Medical Officer (Public Health Dept.) L.C.C.; Lecturer and Senior Dental Surgeon King's College Hospital; late Dental Surgeon, King George Hospital; late Hon. Dental Consultant, London Military Hospitals; late Dental Surgeon Victoria Hospital for Children, Chelsea; also under London County Council and Metropolitan Asylums Board; Fellow of Royal Society of Medicine; late Vice-President Chelsea Clinical Society and President of School Dentists' Society; Vice-President, Medical Officer of Schools Association; late Member of Representative Board of the British Dental Association; Chairman Marylebone Division, British Medical Association; late Chairman, Editorial Committee, British Dental Association; *b.* London; *e. s.* of Augustus and Fanny Margaret Wallis. *Educ.*: Bedford; King's College; King's College Hospital. On becoming qualified went for a voyage as ship's surgeon in R.M.S. Garth Castle; since then in various vacations has been as ship's surgeon to Arctic regions, the Tropics, Canada, Cape Colony, United States; spent short time in Buffalo, U.S.A. *Publications*: King's College Hospital Dental Reports (with Professor Underwood); The Care of the Teeth in Public Elementary Schools; School Dental Clinics; Dentistry in Ancient Times; T. R. Malthus; Marat, The French Revolutionary; Cagliostro and Dr. Graham; Dog and Duck Water; Richard Partridge and Garibaldi; Why Harley Street, etc. *Recreations*: foreign travel, archæology of London, and French history. *Address*: 26 Welbeck Street, Cavendish Square, W.1. *T.*: Mayfair 6657. (*Died 4 Jan. 1927.*)

WALLIS, Right Rev. Frederic, M.A., D.D.; Fellow of Caius College, Cambridge, since 1878; Canon of Salisbury since 1913; *b.* 1853; *s.* of Rev. Joseph Wallis, M.A.; *m.* 1894, Margaret, *d.* of Col. Sir R. Williams, Bt., M.P. *Educ.*: St. Paul's School; Caius College, Cambridge(Scholar). Carus Prize, 1874, 1877; Scholefield and Evans Prize, 1878; 1st cl. Classical and 1st cl. Theol. Tripos; Dean of Caius Coll. 1878-91; Divinity Lecturer, 1878-94; Examining Chaplain to Bishop of Sarum, 1886-94; Senior Proctor, Camb. 1892-93; Examiner for Theological Tripos, 1883, 1884, 1887, 1889, 1890; Select Preacher to the University, 1897, 1903, 1908; Bishop of Wellington, N.Z., 1895-1911; Archdeacon of Wilts, 1911-12; of Sherborne, 1916-19. *Address*: 3 Studland Road, Bournemouth.

(*Died 24 June 1923.*)

WALLIS, Henry Aubrey Beaumont; *s.* of John Richard Smith Wallis of Drishane Castle, Co. Cork, and Octavia Willoughby, *d.* of 7th Lord Middleton; *m.* 1st, Elizabeth Caroline, *e. d.* of Hon. A. Y. Bingham; 2nd, Julia Mary Catherine (*d.* 1922), *widow* of Capt. E. W. Curtiss and *o. d.* and *heiress* of Mrs. Wright of Mottram Hall, Cheshire;

one d.; 3rd, Annie Christine Cecil, 2nd d. of late Acheson ffrench, Monivea Castle, Co. Galway. *Educ.:* Eton. Travelled on the Continent, India, Australia, New Zealand; farmed extensively in Ireland until the Irish property was sold in the 'nineties; frequently successful in the showyard with light horses; kept hounds in Ireland; Master of the Four Burrow Hounds in Cornwall, 1910-13; Master of the Woodland Pytchley, 1913-20; successful breeder of hounds, black and tans; temporary Major in command of a squadron in the Remount Service; assumed the name of Wright by royal licence on wife succeeding to the Mottram estates, 1916; resumed surname of Wallis, by deed poll, 1923; well known as a judge of hunters and horses. *Publications:* Hunting editor of Land and Water for 2 seasons; Polo editor for 3 seasons; wrote numerous articles on Coaching, also on Hunting and Sport generally. *Recreations:* hunting, coaching, shooting; breeder of Polled Aberdeen - Angus cattle. *Address:* Keythorpe, Leicester. *Club:* Carlton.(*Died 20 April 1926.*)

WALLIS, Mrs. Ransome, Founder and Hon. Directress, the Mission of Hope Incorporated; *b.* Walthamstow, 1858; *d.* of John McCall; *m.* 1883; two *s.* three *d. Educ.:* private schools; Lausanne. Has devoted over thirty years to the practical study of the needs of the illegitimate child and the unmarried mother. *Publications:* various articles and pamphlets treating on the care of tne unmarried mother. *Address:* Roseneath, South Croydon. *T.:* 0817 Croydon. (*Died 14 Feb. 1928.*)

W A L L I S, Sir Whitworth, Kt.; *cr.* 1912; J.P.; F.S.A.; Director, the Corporation Museum and Art Gallery, Birmingham; *b.* Handsworth, 23 June 1855; *y. s.* of George Wallis, F.S.A., senior keeper, South Kensington Museum. *Educ.:* privately in London, Paris, Hanover, and Berlin; Knight of several Continental Orders; Royal British Commission, Paris Exhibition, 1878; in charge of Bethnal Green Museum, 1879-81; in charge Indian collections H.M. Queen Victoria, Prince of Wales (Edward VII.), Duke of Edinburgh, S. Kensington Museum, 1881-84; at India Museum and at Berlin Exhibition, Stockholm, Copenhagen, Amsterdam; and appointed director Birmingham Art Gallery, 1885; well known as lecturer on Pompeii, Sicily, and English pre-Raphaelite art, etc.; delivered special lectures to troops in France, 1917; Hon. Sec. Birmingham and Midland Institute; Trustee National Art Congress Studentship Fund; Member of Council National Art Collections Fund; Life Trustee of Shakespeare's Birthplace; Governor, Memorial Theatre, Stratford-on-Avon, etc. *Publications:* contributor to many art and other magazines on above and other subjects; edited special catalogues, works of David Cox, 1890; pre-Raphaelite Painters, 1891; William Muller, 1896; English masterpieces by Gainsborough, Reynolds, Romney, etc. 1900; masterpieces by Raeburn - Hoppner, etc., 1903. *Recreations:* travel, photography, painting, golf. *Address:* Red Walls, Stratford-on-Avon. *T.:* Central, Birmingham 7003; Stratford 41. *Clubs:* Garrick, Royal Automobile; Clef, Birmingham. (*Died 16 Jan. 1927.*)

W A L L S, Rev. John W.; Secretary, United Methodist Stationing Committee; *b.* Low Norwood, near Gateshead, 7 Oct. 1858; *s.* of John Walls; *m.* Bertha Whitworth, Ashton-under-Lyne; two *d. Educ.:* Whickham, Durham. Entered ministry, 1880; Member of the Uniting Conference held in City Road Chapel, 1907; President of the United Methodist Church, 1918. *Address:* The Avenue, Stone, Staffs.

WALLSCOURT, 4th Baron (*cr.* 1800), **Erroll Augustus Joseph Henry Blake,** D.L., J.P.; Capt. Coldstream Guards, retired 1867; *b.* 22 Aug. 1841; *s.* of 3rd Baron and Elizabeth,

d. of William Lock, Norbury, Surrey; *S.* father 1849; *m.* 1st, Lady Jane Harriet Charlotte Stanhope, *d.* of 7th Earl of Harrington, 1874 (*d.* 1889); one *s.* one *d.*; 2nd, 1896, May, *d.* of Sir William Palliser, M.P. Gentleman Usher to Viceroy of Ireland, Duke of Marlborough, 1876-80; Lieut. in Regt. 1866. *Heir: s.* Hon. Charles William Joseph Blake. *Address:* Ardfry, Oranmore, Co. Galway. *Clubs:* Guards', Marlborough. (*Died 22 July 1918.*)

WALLSCOURT, 5th Baron (*cr.* 1800), **Charles William Joseph Blake;** *b.* 12 Jan. 1876; *o. s.* of 4th Baron and 1st wife, Lady Jane Harriet Charlotte Stanhope, *d.* of 7th Earl of Harrington; *S.* father 1918; *m.* 1897, Ellen, *d.* of Joseph Mayo and widow of M. Boisset. *Heir:* none. (*Died 27 May 1920.*)

WALMSLEY, Right Rev. John, M.A., D.D.; Bishop of Sierra Leone since 1910; Vicar of St. Ann's, Nottingham, 1904-10; late Hon. Canon of Southwell; *s.* of late George Walmsley, of Hereford. Unmarried. *Educ.:* Hereford; Brasenose, Oxford. (Somerset Scholar) 2nd Class. Mods.; 3rd Lit. Hum. 1885; 2nd Theol.; Senior Hall Greek Testament Prize; ordained 1890; Vice-Principal Wycliffe Hall, Oxford, 1894-98; Vicar of Normanton-by-Derby and Acting Chaplain to the Forces, Normanton Barracks, 1898-1904; Member of Diocesan Committees for Central Society of Sacred Study; Higher Religious Education; Sunday School work; Diocesan Mission. *Recreations:* cycling, walking, climbing, etc. *Address:* Bishop's Court, Sierra Leone.
(*Died 9 Dec. 1922.*)

WALMSLEY, Robert Mullineux, D.Sc. (Lond.), F.R.S.E., M.I.E.E., F. Inst. Phy., F.C.S., A.F.R.Ae.S.; Chairman of Convocation and, since 1905, Senator of the University of London; Principal since 1896, and Head of the Electrical Engineering Department of the Northampton Polytechnic Institute, E.C.1; *b.* near Liverpool; *s.* of Robert Walmsley, jun.; *m.* 1896, Emily Victoria, *yr. d.* of Captain Hicks, Chester; two *s.* two *d. Educ.:* private school; Queen's College, Liverpool. Matriculated at the University of London, 1879; B.Sc. 1882; D.Sc. 1886. Engaged in secondary school work, and later as a Technical Assistant to Professors Ayrton and Perry; First Senior Demonstrator in Electrical Engineering in the Finsbury Technical College, 1883; Principal of the Sindh Arts College, 1887; Staff of the City and Guilds (Engineering) College, 1888; First Professor of Electrical Engineering and Applied Physics at the Heriot-Watt College, Edinburgh, 1890-95; Chairman of numerous Senatorial Committees, and for 15 years Chairman of the University Extension Board; Chairman of the Council of the Association of Technical Institutions, 1909; Chairman of the Executive Committee of the Optical Convention, 1912; has been Member of the Council of the Royal Aeronautical Society of Great Britain; Liveryman of the Worshipful Company of Spectacle Makers. *Publications:* The Electric Current, 1894; partly revised and extended the second edition of Dr. Urbanitzsky's Electricity in the Service of Man, and in 1904 entirely re-wrote and extended the book, which has since passed through a much larger edition in four volumes, three dealing with the technology of electricity, the last being published in 1921; has read Papers before the Institution of Electrical Engineers and the Institution of Mechanical Engineers. *Address:* 23 Hilldrop Road, N.7; Northampton Polytechnic Institute, St. John Street, E.C.1. *Club:* University of London.
(*Died 15 June 1924.*)

W A L P O L E, Sir Charles (George), Kt., *cr.* 1897; M.A., F.R.G.S.; *b.* 7 Sep. 1848; *s.* of Charles Vade Walpole, C.B.

(*d.* 1891), and Annette (*d.* 1885), *d.* of late Rear-Admiral James Prevost; *m.* 1st, 1877, Maria Elizabeth (*d.* 1914), *d.* of late Henry Forde of Abbeyfield, Cheshire; one *s.*; 2nd, 1922, Marie Bowles, *d.* of late Percy Hale Wallace, and *widow* of Major H. J. Seton. *Educ.:* Eton; Trin. Coll., Camb. (Classical Honours). Barr. Inner Temple, 1878; President of the District Court of Larnaka, Cyprus, 1882; Attorney-General, Leeward Islands, 1889, and Member of the Executive and Legislative Councils; acting Chief Justice, 1890 and 1891; Chief Justice, Gibraltar, 1892; Chief Justice, Bahamas, 1893; retired, 1897; J.P. and Deputy-Chairman of Quarter Sessions for Surrey, 1903-14; Chairman of Quarter Sessions for Surrey, 1914-25; Chairman of Surrey Standing Joint-Committee; County Councillor for Chobham and Windlesham, 1912 - 22; Chairman Chertsey Bench, 1906-22; Chairman Chertsey Division Conservative Association, 1906-22; Chairman of the Surrey Provincial Division of the National Unionist Association, 1912-23; Member of the Surrey Central Defence Committee, Aug. 1914-Dec. 1918; Chairman of the Guildford Appeal Tribunal, 1916, 1917, 1918. *Publications:* A Rubric of the Common Law; A Short History of the Kingdom of Ireland; A Translation of the Ottoman Penal Code; The Leeward Islands Magistrates Acts. *Address:* 4 Kensington Court, W.8. *T.:* Western 2169. *Clubs:* New University, Surrey Magistrates.
　　　　　　　　　　　(*Died 24 May 1926.*)

WALPOLE, Sir Horatio George, K.C.B., *cr.* 1892; Assistant Under-Secretary for India, 1883-1907; *b.* 1843; 2nd *s.* of Rt. Hon. Spencer H. Walpole, Q.C., and Isabella, *d.* of Rt. Hon. Spencer Perceval, M.P.; *m.* Selina, *d.* of Capt. John T. Perceval, 1870. *Educ.:* Eton. *Address:* Danegate. Eridge Green, Sussex. *Clubs:* Carlton, Athenæum.　　(*Died 29 June 1923.*)

WALPOLE, Ralph Charles, Librarian House of Commons, 1887-1908; *b.* 1844; 3rd *s.* of late Rev. Thomas Walpole, of Stagbury, Surrey. *Educ.:* Radley. *Recreation:* golf. *Club:* Union.
　　　　　　　　　　　(*Died 20 Feb. 1928.*)

WALROND, Col. Henry, J.P.; *co-heir* to the Barony of Welles (*cr.* 1254); Marquis de Vallado, etc., in Spain (*cr.* 1683); *b.* Paris, 9 Nov. 1841; *e. s.* of late Bethell Walrond, Dulford House, Collumpton, and Lady Janet St. Clair Erskine, *d.* of 2nd Earl of Rosslyn; *m.* 1861, Caroline Maud (*d.* 1915), *d.* of late W. J. Clark, Buckland Tout Saints, Devon; five *s.* four *d. Educ.:* Christ Church, Oxford. Joined 4th Batt. Devon Regiment, 1863; Capt. 1872; Major, 1882; Lieut.-Col. and Hon. Col. 1893; retired with hon. rank of Colonel, 1897. *Publications:* Historical Records of 1st Devon Militia (4th Batt. Devon Regt.); joint author of the Archery volume of the Badminton Library; editor, Archers' Register. *Recreations:* shooting, yachting, archery. *Address:* 21 Blomfield Street, W. *Club:* Royal Toxophilite Society.
　　　　　　　　　　　(*Died 19 June 1917.*)

WALROND, Main Swete Osmond, C.M.G. 1901; *b.* 22 Feb. 1870; *s.* of late Rev. Main S. A. Walrond, M.A. *Educ.:* Harrow; Balliol, Oxford. Companion and Tutor to Prince Kemal el dine, *o. s.* of Sultan Hussein, 1892-94; Land Tax Adjustment Commission, Ministry of Finance, Egypt, 1894-97; Private Secretary to High Commissioner, South Africa, 1897-1905; appointed District Commissioner, Cyprus, 1905, but did not proceed; employed in Arab Bureau, Cairo, under High Commissioner for Egypt, 1917-18; resided in Cairo, studying Arabic, advised in private capacity Lord Milner's Mission to Egypt, 1919-21. *Club:* St. James's.
　　　　　　　　　　　(*Died 14 Nov. 1927.*)

WALSH, Hon. Gerald, a General Inspector, Ministry of Health; *b.* 16 Dec. 1864;

s. of 2nd Baron Ormathwaite; *m.* 1916, Averil Constance Antonette Janetta, *d.* of late Col. W. T. Markham, Becca Hall, Yorks. *Address:* Charnwood, Melton Mowbray. *Clubs:* Boodle's, White's.　　(*Died 18 May 1925.*)

WALSH, Colonel Henry Alfred, C.B. 1905, J.P., Somersets.; *b.* 18 Aug. 1853; *e. s.* of late Theobald Walsh; *m.* 1880, Ann Plofexfen, *d.* of late Benjamin Sparrow, of Cleeve, Ivybridge, Devon; one *s.* one *d.* Joined 1st Somerset Militia, 1870; 1st Battalion 13th Light Infantry, 1874; Adjutant, 1880-84; Adjutant 3rd Battalion Somerset Light Infantry, 1885-90; commanded 1st Battalion, 1898-1902; commanded 20th Regimental District, 1902-4; Chief Recruiting Staff Officer, London, 1904; served in the Mounted Infantry in the Sekukuni Campaign, 1877; Zulu War, 1878-79, present at the re-occupation of Isandlwana, and battles of Zlobane, Kambula, and Ulundi (medal with clasp); Nile Campaign, 1884-85, in the Mounted Infantry of the Camel Corps, present reconnaissance to Gakdul Wells, at the battles of Abu Klea and Gubat, and the second Abu Klea (dangerously wounded, despatches, medal with two clasps, bronze star, brevet of Major). *Address:* Hillmore, Bishops Hull, Taunton. *Club:* Army and Navy.　(*Died 25 Nov. 1918.*)

WALSH, Very Rev. James Hornidge, D.D.; Dean of Dublin, commonly called Dean of Christ Church Cathedral, Dublin, 1908-18; *m.* 1875, Jane Mary, *y. d.* of late Francis Alex. Fitzgerald, LL.D., Baron of the Court of Exchequer. *Educ.:* Trinity College, Dublin, Scholar, B.A.; Senior Moderator Classical (First), 1858; Archbishop King's Prizeman (First), 1859; Theological Exhibitioner (First), entitling to Divinity Testimonium, 1861; Deacon, 1860; Priest, 1861; Curate of Dundrum, Dublin; Adare, Limerick; Rector of Chapel Russell, Limerick; Curate of St. Stephen's, Dublin; Rector of St. Stephen's, 1883-1908; Assistant to Archbishop King, Lecturer, T.C.D., 1877-83; to Regius Professor, 1883-1908; Canon of Christ Church, Dublin, 1893-1905; Chancellor of Christ Church, Dublin, 1905-8; Examining Chaplain to late Lord Plunket, Lord Archbishop of Dublin, 1893-97; to Lord Archbishop of Dublin (Peacocke), 1897; Private and Examining Chaplain to late Bishops of Limerick (Graves and Bunbury); Chaplain to the Lord-Lieutenant; member of General Synod and of Representative Church Body. *Address:* 47 Upper Mount Street, Dublin. *Clubs:* University, Stephen's Green, Dublin.
　　　　　　　　　　　(*Died 4 Sept. 1919.*)

WALSH, John, J.P., M.P. (I.N.) Cork County South, 1911-18; *b.* 1856; Chairman of Beamish & Crawford Bottling Co., Bandon; extensive farming; member of Cork County Council. *Recreations:* fox - hunting, golfing, fishing. *Address:* Eversleigh, Bandon, Co. Cork. *T.:* Bandon 30. *T.A.:* Walsh, Bandon.
　　　　　　　　　　　(*Died 25 Aug. 1925.*)

WALSH, Langton Prendergast, J.P., C.I.E. 1890; *b.* 29 Feb. 1856; *e. s.* of late Col. T. Prendergast B. Walsh of Laragh, Co. Cavan, and Ealing, Middlesex; *m.* 1st, 1891, Annie Clementina, *d.* of late Major R. G. Macgregor, R.A. (*d.* 1894); 2nd, 1902, Laura (*d.* 1918), *o. c.* of late John Forbes, K.C.; one *s.* two *d. Educ.:* France; Cowley, Oxford. Entered Marine Postal Service, 1873; transferred to Bombay Political Service, 1879; attached to Staff of Indian Div. in Egypt, 1882; present at Kassassin and Tel-el-Kebir (medal, clasp, and bronze star, despatches); services lent to British Foreign Office, 1884; in Consular and administrative charge Berbera and Zeila, N.E. Africa, 1884-92; raised Somali Coast Protectorate Police; operations against Jibril Abuker tribes, 1886 (thanked by Govt. of Bombay); Esa Expedition, 1890; present at Hussein Zareeba (services commended by

Governments of India and Bombay); served as Political Assistant in Kathiawar, Aden, and Southern Maratha country; Political Agent at Sawant Wadi and Commandant Sawant Wadi Local Infantry Corps, 1896-1903; retired 1903. *Publications:* for many years a contributor to the Indian press. *Recreations:* big-game shooting, travel, billiards, whist. *Address:* Plas Idwal, Gunnersbury Avenue, W.5. *T.:* Ealing 1865. *Clubs:* Carlton, Conservative.   (*Died 17 Mar. 1927.*)

WALSH, Ven. Philip; Canon of Auckland since 1897; Archdeacon of Waimate, 1900-12; *b.* 7 May 1843; 2nd *s.* of late Rev. Edw. Walsh of Kilcooley, Co. Tipperary, Ireland. *Educ.:* privately. Passed most of youth in France; emigrated to New Zealand, 1866; engaged some years in farming, acting as lay-reader for settlement; awarded scholarship, St. John's College, Auckland, 1872; Deacon, 1874; Priest, 1876; first appointment, Waikara, Taranaki, large scattered district, laborious work; after seven years removed to Auckland; temporary charge, St. Mary's, Parnell; thence to Coromandel, a gold-mining district; visited the old country, 1883-84; again in 1899-1900; Vicar of Waimate North, 1884-1909. Waimate Archdeaconry includes numerous native districts worked by Maori clergy. *Publications:* occasional scientific papers for New Zealand Institute; contributions to magazines on social and artistic subjects; short stories. *Recreations:* mechanics, gardening, drawing, painting, etc. *Address:* Cambridge, Auckland, New Zealand.

WALSH, Ven. Robert, D.D.; Archdeacon of Dublin, 1909; Rector of Donnybrook, 1889, Chaplain to the Lord-Lieutenant; Examining Chaplain to the Archbishop of Dublin; *e. s.* of Rt. Hon. John Edward Walsh, LL.D. (*d.* 1869); Master of the Rolls in Ireland and formerly M.P. for the University of Dublin, and Blair Belinda, *o. d.* of late Captain Gordon John M'Neill, 77th Regiment; *m.* 1st, 1873, Elizabeth Sophia (*d.* 1893), *d.* of Rev. Joseph Carson, D.D., Vice-Provost, Trinity College, Dublin; 2nd, 1898, Amy Elinor, *o. d.* of late Most Rev. Robert Samuel Gregg, D.D., Archbishop of Armagh and Primate of all Ireland; three *s.* one *d. Educ.:* Trinity College, Dublin; B.A. Auditor College Historical Society and Gold Medallist, Oratory, 1864; Vice-Pres. 1900; Div. Test., M.A.; D.D. 1889; Member of Senate, 1889; ordained curate of Tamlaght Finlagan, Dio. Derry, 1865; Curate of St. Mary, Dublin, 1867; Rector, Malahide, 1874; Member General Synod, Representative Church Body, and Standing Committee, 1888; Prebendary, St. John, Christ Church Cathedral, 1906. *Publications:* Fingal and its Churches, 1888; sermons. *Address:* St. Mary's Rectory, Donnybrook, Dublin. *Club:* University, Dublin. (*Died 24 Feb. 1917.*)

WALSH, Valentine John Hussey-; *b.* 17 Feb. 1862; *e. s.* of Walter Hussey Walsh, J.P., of Mulhussey, Co. Roscommon, and 81 Onslow Gardens, S.W.; *m.* 1907, Elizabeth Duchesse de La Mothe Houdancourt, grandee of Spain, 1st class, *d.* of Count Artus de Cossé Brissac (*s.* of 10th Duc de Brissac) and Alix *d.* of Louis, Marquis de Walsh-Serrant, Duc de La Mothe Houdancourt, grandee of Spain. *Educ.:* Oratory School, Birmingham; Kalksburg, Austria; Edinburgh University. Called to Bar, Middle Temple, 1885; went the Western Circuit and Wiltshire Sessions, 1886-1907; Private Secretary to Lord Londonderry, Postmaster-General, 1900-2; contested (C.) Carlisle, Jan. 1910; has written for the Quarterly Review, Fortnightly Review, Blackwood's Magazine, and Revue Hebdomadaire. and many papers. *Recreations:* golf, cycling, *Address:* 24 Ennismore Gardens, S.W.; *T.:* Western 4025; 7 Rue Galilée, Paris; *T.A.:* Passy 68.68; Mulhussey, Athlone; Le Fayel

Canly (Oise), France; Anglesqueville, St.-Valery-en-Caux (Seine Inférieure), France. *Clubs:* Athenæum; Union, Interallié, Paris.   (*Died 20 April 1925.*)

WALSH, Rt. Rev. William, M.A., Hon. D.D.; Archdeacon and Canon of Canterbury since 1897; Chaplain of the Cinque Ports, 1901-16; *b.* 1836; *m.* 1865, Catharine Banchory, *d.* of General Pickering, R.A.; two *s. Educ.:* St. Alban's Hall (transferred to Merton Coll.), Oxford. Prebendary of St. Paul's, 1889-91; Bishop of Mauritius, 1891-97; Bishop (Suffragan) of Dover, 1898-1916. *Publications:* Progress of the Church in London, 1887; second edition, 1908. *Address:* The Precincts, Canterbury. *Club:* Athenæum. (*Died 17 Oct. 1918.*)

WALSH, Most Rev. William J., D.D.; Archbishop of Dublin (Roman Catholic) and Primate of Ireland since 1885; *b.* Dublin, 30 Jan. 1841. *Educ.:* St. Laurence O'Toole's Seminary, Dublin; Catholic Univ. of Ireland; St. Patrick's Coll. Maynooth. Professor of Dogmatic and Moral Theology, Maynooth, 1867; Vice-President, Maynooth Coll. 1878; Canon in Diocesan Chapter of Dublin, 1879; President, Maynooth Coll. 1881; Member of Senate of Royal Univ. of Ireland, 1888 (resigned 1884); Vicar-Capitular of Dublin, 1885; Commissioner of Education in Ireland, 1891 (resigned 1917); Commissioner of Intermediate Education in Ireland, 1892 (resigned 1919); Commissioner of Charitable Donations and Bequests, Ireland, 1893; Commissioner of National Education in Ireland, 1895 (resigned 1901); member of Consultative Committee on Education in connection with Department of Agriculture and Technical Instruction for Ireland, 1900-1904; member of Commission on Manual and Practical Instruction in Primary Schools in Ireland, 1897-98; of Commission on Intermediate Education in Ireland, 1898-99; of the Dublin Statutory Commission appointed by the Irish University Act 1908; of the Senate of the National University of Ireland, 1908; First Chancellor of the National University of Ireland, 1908. *Publications:* Tractatus de Actibus Humanis, 1880, 1891; A Plain Exposition of the Irish Land Act of 1881, 1881; The Queen's Colleges and the Royal University of Ireland, 1883, 1884; Ordo Exsequiarum, 1884, 1890, 1900; Harmony of the Gospel Narratives of the Passion, etc., 1885; Grammar of Gregorian Music, 1885; Addresses on Various Subjects, 1886; Two Addresses on the Irish University Question, 1890; Statement of the Chief Grievances of Irish Catholics in the Matter of Education, Primary, Intermediate, and University, 1890; Bimetallism and Monometallism 1893, 1894, 1895, 1896; The Irish University Question, 1897; Trinity College and the Univ. of Dublin, 1902; The Irish University Question: Trinity College and its Medical School, 1906; The Motu Proprio Quantavis Diligentia, and its Critics, 1912; O'Connell, Archbishop Murray, and the Board of Charitable Donations and Bequests. *Address:* Archbishop's House, Dublin.

(*Died 9 April 1921.*)

WALSHAM, Hugh, M.A., M.D. (Cantab), F.R.C.P.; F.R.A.S.; Consulting Physician to the City of London Hospital for Diseases of the Chest, Consulting Radiologist to St. Bartholomew's Hospital; Consulting Radiologist to King Edward VII. Sanatorium, Midhurst; late Medical Officer in Charge of the X-ray Department, St. Bartholomew's Hospital, and Lecturer on Radiology to the Medical School; *b.* London; 2nd *s.* of William Walker Walsham, Wisbech, Cambs.; *m.* 1916, Amy, *d.* of Stephen Bannister, Coventry. *Educ.:* King's College School, London; Caius College, Cambridge; St. Bartholomew's Hospital, and Hospital for Sick Children, Great Ormond Street. Pathologist for some years to the

Victoria Park Chest Hospital; Medical Referee to the National Sanatorium, Benenden, Kent, and Consulting Physician, X-ray Department, Eltham Cottage Hospital; awarded by the Royal College of Physicians the Weber Parkes Prize and First Medal for research work on Tuberculosis, 1903; President of the Radiology Section of British Medical Association, Birmingham, 1911; Vice-President Sec. Radiol. 17th Internat. Cong. Med. Lond., 1913; Fellow Royal Society of Medicine. *Publications:* The Channels of Infection in Tuberculosis, 1904; the Röntgen Rays in the diagnosis of Diseases of the Chest, 1906; numerous papers to medical societies and journals. *Recreations:* astronomy, especially solar physics. *Address:* 114 Harley Street, W.1. *T.:* Langham 2157.   (*Died 13 April 1924.*)

WALSINGHAM, 6th Baron (*cr.* 1780), **Thomas de Grey,** D.L., J.P., M.A.; LL.D. (Cambridge), 1891; F.R.S., F.L.S., F.Z.S., F.E.S. (President, 1889-90); Memb. Soc. Ent. de France; Ent. Ver. zu Berlin; Nederlandsche Ent Ver.; Soc. Ent. de Russie; Linn. Soc. N.S.W.; Am. Ent. Soc. Philadelphia; Br. Ornith. Union, etc.; High Steward of University of Cambridge since 1891, and of the Borough of King's Lynn since 1894; Trustee of British Museum, the Hunterian Museum (Royal College of Surgeons); *b.* 29 July 1843; *s.* of 5th Baron and Augusta, *d.* of Sir Robert Frankland Russell, 7th Bart. of Thirkleby; *S.* father, 1870; *m.* 1st, 1877, Augusta Selina Elizabeth (Leila) (*d.* 1906), *o.c.* of Capt. William Locke, widow of Lord Burghersh, 2nd *s.* of 11th Earl of Westmorland, and afterwards wife of Duc de Santo Teodoro; 2nd, 1909, Marion Gwytherne-Williams (*d.* 1913), F.R.H.S., *d.* of late Thomas Rhys Withers; 3rd, 1914, Agnes, *d.* of late Frederick Shand Hemming, and widow of Richard Dawson. *Educ.:* Eton: Trinity College, Cambridge (M.A.). M.P. (C.) West Norfolk, 1865-70; Lord-in-Waiting, 1874-75. *Publications:* numerous monographs and papers on the Microlepidoptera of the world; the Walsingham collection of Micro-lepidoptera is the largest and most important—with it is incorporated the famous Zeller Collection, the Hofmann, Christoph, and others; the Walsingham collections were conveyed by Deed of Gift, dated 23 Nov. 1901, to the Trustees of the British Museum, to which they were transferred in 1910, together with his valuable entomological library. Owns about 19,200 acres. *Recreations:* is a famous shot—his bag of 1070 grouse to 'his own gun has never been surpassed; contributed the articles on the grouse, the pheasant, and the partridge to the Badminton Library; visited California and Oregon (1870-71) on a sporting and collecting tour, and made extensive collections there and subsequently in S. France, Corsica, Andalusia, Morocco, Algeria, Jamaica, etc.; played in Eton and Cambridge cricket elevens, and in Gentlemen v. Players, I.Z., M.C.C., etc. *Heir: half-b.* Hon. John Augustus de Grey. *Address:* 6 Montagu Place, Portman Square, W. *T.:* Mayfair 4577. Merton Hall, Thetford. *Clubs:* Carlton, Isthmian.   (*Died 3 Dec. 1919.*)

WALSTON (Waldstein), Sir Charles, Kt., *cr.* 1912; Litt.D. (Cantab.); Ph.D. (Heidelb.); Hon. Litt.D. (Col. Univ., New York); Hon. Litt.D. T.C. (Dublin); Knight Commander of the Greek Order of the Redeemer; Knight of the Danebrog; Hon. A.R.I.B.A.; High Sheriff of Cambs. and Hunts, 1922-23; Member of Standing Committee of Advice on Art to Board of Education; Fellow (since 1894) and Lecturer of King's College, Cambridge; Vice-President Hellenic Society and member of Council of British Archæological School, Athens, Rome, etc.; a Vice-President of the English-Speaking Union; *b.* New York, 30 March 1856; 3rd *surv. s.* of late Henry Waldstein, merchant of New York; *m.* 1909, Florence, *e. d.* of late D. L. Einstein, of New York, and *widow* of Theodore Seligman, New York; one *s.* one *d. Educ.:* Columbia College, New York; Heidelberg University, Germany. Lecturer in Classical Archæology in Univ. of Camb. 1880-83; Director of Fitzwilliam Museum, Camb. 1883-1889; Reader in Classical Archæology, 1883-1907; Slade Prof. of Fine Art, 1895-1901, and 1904-1911; Director, American Archæological School, Athens (retaining Readership at Camb.), 1889-1893, retaining Professorship there till 1896; excavated site of ancient Platæa, 1889-90; Eretria (tomb of Aristotle), 1891; the Heraion of Argos, 1892-95. *Publications:* Balance of Emotion and Intellect, 1878; Essays on the Art of Phidias, 1885; The Work of John Ruskin, 1894; The Study of Art in Universities, 1895; The Expansion of Western Ideals and the World's Peace, 1899; The Jewish Question and the Mission of the Jews, 1899; The Argive Heræum, 1902; Art in the Nineteenth Century, 1903; (with L. Shoobridge) Herculaneum, Past, Present, and Future, 1908; What may we Read? 1912; Greek Sculpture and Modern Art, 1914; Aristodemocracy, 1916, new editions 1917 and 1920; What Germany is Fighting For, 1917; Patriotism, National and International, 1917; The Next War, Wilsonism and Anti-Wilsonism, 1918; Truth, etc., 1919; The English-Speaking Brotherhood and the League of Nations, 1919; 2nd ed. 1920; Eugenics, Civics, Ethics, 1920; Harmonism and Conscious Evolution, 1922; Alcamenes and the Establishment of the Classical Type in Greek Art, 1926. *Recreations:* hunting, shooting, golf. *Address:* Newton Hall, Newton, Cambridge. *T.A.:* Harston, Cambs. *T.:* Harston 8; Mayfair House, Carlos Place, W. *T.:* Grosvenor 2452. *Clubs:* Athenæum, Marlborough, Bath.
          (*Died 21 Mar. 1927.*)

WALTER, Arthur; Editor, Parliamentary Debates, House of Lords, since 1898; *b.* Ditcheat, Somersetshire, 20 June 1874; *e. s.* of Benjamin Walter; *m.* 1899, Mabel Mary, *d.* of Richard T. Wooff, of London. *Educ.:* Monmouthshire and South Wales University. Was for several years member of editorial staff South London Press; acted for two Sessions as Parliamentary Correspondent of Echo de Paris; travelled through Europe as Private Secretary to late A. Pulitzer, founder of New York Journal; was one of the representatives of British journalism at International Congress of the World's Press, Antwerp, 1894, and Berlin, 1908; admitted a Freeman of City of London, 1903; Hon. Sec. and Fellow Institute of Journalists; President (1918-19) British International Association of Journalists; Past Master of Duchy of Cornwall Lodge of Freemasons, and Life Governor of the three Royal Masonic Benevolent Institutions; has contributed largely to magazines and weeklies on parliamentary and cognate matters. *Recreation:* touring. *Address:* 12 Calais Gate, Myatts Park, S.E.5. *T.A.:* Sirdar, Phone, London. *T.:* Brixton 2290. *Clubs:* Press, New Oxford and Cambridge, Eccentric, Royal Automobile.   (*Died 27 Jan. 1921.*)

WALTER, Arthur James, K.C., LL.B. Called to Bar, Inner Temple, 1885; *m.* 1891, Florence Maud, 3rd *d.* of Rev. Canon Carver, D.D. Equity Scholar of Inner Temple, 1885; chiefly engaged in Patent Trade Mark and technical litigation; one of the Governors of Dulwich College; a founder member of Automobile Club; a trustee of James Peek charity. *Address:* 5 Fig Tree Court, Temple, E.C.; 6 Rutland Gate, S.W.; *T.:* Kensington 3908; Bryn Goleu, Dolwyddelen, North Wales. *Clubs:* Garrick, Savage, Royal Automobile.
          (*Died 9 April 1919.*)

WALTER, Louis Heathcote, M.A.; Editor of Science Abstracts since 1903; *b.* London; *y. s.* of late D. Henry Walter; *m.* 1900, Rose Mabel, *y. d.* of late Capt. Edward

Williams, late 69th Regt. *Educ.*: privately in England; Hanover; Trinity College, Cambridge (Natural Sciences Tripos). An Associate Member of the Institution of Electrical Engineers; sometime Associate Member of the Institution of Civil Engineers; for some years was experimental assistant to Sir Hiram S. Maxim; in 1907 became associated with the inventors of the Bellini-Tosi system of directive wireless telegraphy, and introduced it into England; later the patents were acquired by the Marconi Company, 1912. *Publications:* Directive Wireless Telegraphy, 1921; acted as reviser of the volumes Electrical Engineering, Steam Engines, and Internal Combustion Engines of the Deinhardt - Schlomann Technical Dictionaries; is hon. indexer in Physics for the International Catalogue of Scientific Literature; author of some twenty papers on electrical subjects communicated to the Royal Society, the Institution of Electrical Engineers, and other societies and the technical press. *Discoveries:* increase of hysteresis loss due to oscillations superposed on rotating field; self-restoring detector action of a tantalum-mercury contact; valve effect of tungsten electrodes; valve action of zirconium anodes. *Inventions:* a selective system of wireless control, 1898; various forms of coherers, magnetic detectors, etc.; for his oscillation galvanometer was awarded the John Scott Medal, 1907. *Address:* Institution of Electrical Engineers, Victoria Embankment, W.C.2.
(*Died Sept. 1922.*)

WALTERS, W. C. Flamstead, M.A.; Professor of Classical Literature, King's College, London, 1901-24, and in the University of London, 1911-24; Fellow of King's College, London; *s.* of Rev. A. V. Walters, B.A. Oxon, of Winchester; *m.* 1st, Ethel (*d.* 1902), *y. d.* of Major-Gen. Skyring, R.E.; one *s.*; 2nd, 1912, Fanny, *e. d.* of late Rev. T. Walters, M.A., Vicar of Boyton, Cornwall, and *sister* of late Marchioness of Queensberry. *Educ.*: Christ's Hospital; Pembroke College, Oxford. Formerly House and Composition Master at Christ's College, New Zealand; late Lecturer in Classics, University College, Cardiff; Professor of Classics in Queen's College, London, 1901-9; Dean of the Faculty of Arts, King's College, 1904-8, 1911-12; formerly Member of Council of the Roman Society; of the Board of Classical Journals, and of the Council of the Hellenic Society; Treasurer of the Classical Association; formerly Examiner in the Universities of New Zealand, Wales, and Manchester. *Publications:* Various school - books and editions of authors; occasional papers and notes in Classical Quarterly, Classical Review, etc.; co-Editor with Prof. Conway of Livy, i.-x. *Recreations:* boating, tennis, golf, etc. *Address:* Limen, Miton Park, Gerrard's Cross.
(*Died 19 Mar. 1927.*)

WALTERS, William Melmoth; Solicitor; senior partner in firm of Walters, Wood & Co., 9 New Square, Lincoln's Inn (founded about 1780); *b.* 28 Jan. 1835; *s.* of John Eldad Walters of Batheaston, Somersetshire, and late of Lincoln's Inn and Ewell, Surrey, and Eleanor, *d.* of late Alexander Radclyffe Sidebottom of the Middle Temple; *m.* 1860, Marian Eleanor, *e. c.* of late Alfred Leggatt, 13 William Street, Lowndes Square, S.W.; two *s.* six *d. Educ.*: tutor, and private school, Bayswater, and King's College, London. Articled with the then firm of Roumieu, Walters & Co., 1852; read in the Chambers of Joshua Williams and of T. K. Kingdon; passed Final Examination (taking 2nd prize), and was admitted Solicitor, 1857; member of firm, 1859; elected to the Council of the Law Society, 1878; President, 1891-92, and late Senior Member of the Council; Director of the Law Fire Insurance Society, the Law Debenture Corporation, the
36

Law Accident Insurance Society, and the Solicitors' Benevolent Association; late Member of the Solicitors' Discipline Committee; a Member of the Committee of Inspection of Trustee Savings Banks from its formation; Member of the Committee of Proprietors of Lincoln's Inn; Member of the Council of Law Reporting; late Member of the Rule-making Committee; late Chairman of the Ewell, Cuddington, and Malden Conservative Association; Governor of St. Thomas Hospital, King's College Hospital, Consumption Hospital, and various other hospitals and philanthropic institutions. *Recreations:* shooting, salmon-fishing, cruising; in earlier life, rowing, swimming, skating, cricket, lawn - tennis, etc. *Address:* 9 New Square, Lincoln's Inn, W.C.; Purberry Shot, Ewell, Surrey. *T.A.*: Various, Holborn, London. *T.*: Holborn 157, Epsom 599. *Clubs:* Constitutional; Golf, Conservative, Epsom. (*Died 20 Nov. 1925.*)

WALTON, Edward Arthur, R.S.A. 1905; Hon. R.W.S.; Hon. R.I.; President of the Royal Scottish Society of Painters in Water Colours; Vice-President of the Imperial Arts League; artist painter; *b.* Glanderston House, Renfrewshire, 15 April 1860; 5th *s.* of late Jackson Walton. *Educ.*: Glasgow. Studied drawing and painting, Glasgow and Düsseldorf; medallist Paris, Munich, and Chicago; works in the following permanent galleries: Munich, Carlsruhe, Budapest, Ghent, Venice, Pittsburg, Leeds, Glasgow, Edinburgh, Melbourne, and Auckland; Member of International Society of Sculptors, Painters, and Gravers, London; Associate Société Nationale des Beaux-Arts, France. *Address:* 7 Belford Park, Edinburgh. *Clubs:* Glasgow Art; Scottish - Arts, Scottish Liberal, Edinburgh. (*Died Mar. 1922.*)

WALTON, Frank, R.I.; R.O.I.; Hon. Member, retired, Royal Institute of Oil Painters, and Royal Institute of Painters in Water Colours; *b.* London, 10 July 1840; *s.* of James Walton, publisher; *m.* Sophia (*d.* 1921), *d.* of John Wichham Flower; one *d. Educ.*: private schools. *Address:* Holmbury St. Mary, Dorking. *T.A.*: Holmbury St. Mary. *Club:* Arts.
(*Died 23 Jan. 1928.*)

WALTON, Frederick Thomas Granville, C.I.E. 1888; M.Inst.C.E.; *b.* 1840; *s.* of William Walton of Hampton, Middlesex; *m.* 1877, Charlotte Eliza (*d.* 1922), 2nd *d.* of Sir Cusack Roney; two *s. Educ.*: privately. Began his professional career as a pupil of R. Johnson, chief engineer G.N. Rly. 1861; served on that railway until 1868, when he went out to India in the service of the Oudh and Rohilkhund Rly. Co., and was employed on the construction of that line until it was purchased by Govt. in 1889; he then entered Govt. service as Engineer-in-Chief of the same railway until 1896, when was sent to construct the railway bridge over the Godavari River on the E.C. Rly.; among other bridges he has constructed the following: Ramgunga, Bareilly; Ramgunga, Moradabad; Kosi, Rampur; Dufferin Bridge, Benares; Godavari Rajamundry. *Address:* 34 St. George's Court, Gloucester Road, S.W.7.
(*Died 21 Dec. 1925.*)

WALTON, James, M.P. (Lab.) Don Valley Division, Yorks., Dec. 1918-22; miner; *b.* 7 Sep. 1867; *m.* 1889, *d.* of William Jackson. *Educ.*: Broomhill Board Schools. Late Secretary of Mexborough Trades Council and Delegate Yorkshire Miners' Association. *Address:* 101 Avenue Road, Wath-on-Dearne, near Mexborough. (*Died Jan. 1924.*)

WALTON, Sir Joseph, 1st Bt., cr. 1910; J.P. Middlesbrough, J.P. and D.L., N.R. Yorks; M.P. (L.) Barnsley Division, W.R. Yorks, 1897-1918; (Co. L.) Borough of Barnsley since 1918; F.R.G.S.; *b.* Bollihope, Co. Durham, 19 Mar. 1849; 2nd *s.* of late Joseph Walton, Frosterley;

m. 1880, Faith Gill, *d.* of late Robert Gill, Middlesbrough; two *d. Educ.:* privately. Commenced commercial career in Middlesbrough, coal and allied trades, 1870; contested (L.) Doncaster Division, 1895; travelled extensively in India, Burma, Africa, America, Canada, Australia, New Zealand, and British Protectorates, also in China, Japan, Persia, Mesopotamia, Russia, Balkans, etc. *Publication:* China and the Present Crisis, 1900. *Recreation:* Alpine climbing. *Heir:* none. *Address:* Rushpool, Saltburn - by - the - Sea. *Clubs:* Reform, Ranelagh, Royal Automobile.   (*Died 8 Feb 1923.*)

WANAMAKER, John; *b.* Philadelphia, 11 July 1838. Started business, April 1861; founder and owner of the largest new kind of Store in the United States, at Philadelphia and New York; Republican; Postmaster-General, 1889-93; founded Bethany School, 1858. *Address:* City Hall Square, Philadelphia.
(*Died 12 Dec. 1922.*)

WANAMAKER, Rodman, C.V.O.; President, John Wanamaker, New York; John Wanamaker, Philadelphia; *b.* Philadelphia; *s.* of John Wanamaker and Mary B. Brown. *Educ.:* Princeton. *Address:* Broadway, 8th, 9th and 10th Streets, New York; City Hall Square, Philadelphia.   (*Died 9 Mar. 1928.*)

WANLISS, Captain Harold Boyd, D.S.O. 1916; 14th Infantry Battalion, Australian Imperial Force; *b.* Ballarat, 11 Dec. 1891; *s.* of Newton Wanliss, M.A., LL.B., formerly solicitor, Ballarat, and Margaret Boyd; unmarried. *Educ.:* Ballarat College (dux, 1908); Hawkesbury Agricultural College, New South Wales. Belongs to one of the oldest pioneer families in the State of Victoria; purchased a landed property in Otway Ranges, Victoria, and was the discoverer of falls on the Upper Erskine River; enlisted in the Australian Imperial Force, April 1915, and left Australia the same year in charge of reinforcements; attached to the 14th Australian Infantry Battalion in Egypt, and accompanied it to France, June 1916; as first lieutenant; led a battalion raid on the German trenches on the night of 2 July 1916; conducted the raid successfully (three times severely wounded, and had to be carried in, D.S.O.); Capt. 1917. *Address:* Little Scotland, Lorne, Victoria, Australia. (*Died 20 Sept. 1917.*)

WANSTALL, Rev. Walter; Canon Non-Residentiary of Lincoln since 1899; Prebendary of Aylesbury in Lincoln Cathedral; Vicar of All Saints, Lincoln, since 1904; *b.* Rochester, 13 Aug. 1847; *o. s.* of Walter Wanstall, L.R.C.P.; unmarried. *Educ.:* Rome House, Rochester; Bromsgrove School; Exeter Coll. Oxford. Ordained by Christopher Wordsworth, Bishop of Lincoln, 1870; Curate of Sneinton, Notts, 1870-81; Vicar of St. Peter at Gowts, Lincoln, 1882-84; Vicar of St. Andrew's, Lincoln, 1884-96; Chaplain to the High Sheriff of Lincolnshire, 1894; Vicar of St. Swithin's, 1896-1904. *Recreations:* music, reading good novels. *Address:* All Saints, Lincoln.
(*Died 4 Dec. 1918.*)

WANTAGE, Lady, Harriet Sarah Loyd-Lindsay, R.R.C., *o. d.* and heir of 1st and only Baron Overstone, and Harriet, *d.* of Ichabod Wright of Mapperly Hall, Notts; *b.* 1837; *m.* 1858, 1st and only Baron Wantage, K.C.B., V.C. (*d.* 1901). *Publication:* Lord Wantage, V.C., K.C.B.: a Memoir. *Address:* Lockinge, Wantage, Berks; Overstone Park, Northampton.   (*Died 7 Aug. 1920.*)

WARBURTON, John Paul, C.I.E. 1911; *b.* 28 Aug. 1840; *s.* of Sirdar Faiz Talab Khan, and *step-s.* of late Col. R. Warburton; *m.* 1863, Mary Whayman. Joined Police Department, Punjab, 1864; District Superintendent, 1873; Assistant Inspector-General, Railway Police, 1894; retired, 1900. *Address:* Gilbert House, Kasauli, Punjab; Warburton, Gujranwalla District, Punjab.   (*Died 21 Oct. 1919.*)

1090

WARD, Sir Adolphus William, Kt., *cr.* 1913; Litt.D.; Hon. LL.D.; Hon. Ph.D.; Master of Peterhouse, Cambridge, since 1900; *b.* Hampstead, 2 Dec. 1837; 2nd *s.* of late John Ward, C.B., Her Majesty's Minister Resident to the Hanse Towns; *m.* 1879, Adelaide Laura, *d.* of Rev. T. B. Lancaster, Rector of Grittleton, Wiltshire; one *d. Educ.:* King Edward VI.'s School, Bury St. Edmunds; Peterhouse, Camb. Fellow of Peterhouse, 1861; held Assistant Lectureships at Peterhouse and in Glasgow University, and a temporary Examinership in the Education Office; Professor of History and English Literature, Owens College, Manchester, 1866; Principal Owens College, Manchester, 1890-97; Honorary Fellow of Peterhouse, 1891; Vice-Chancellor of the Victoria Univ. 1886-90 and 1894-96; Ford Lecturer at Oxford, 1898; received Freedom of the City of Manchester, 1897; Governor of Royal Holloway Coll. 1899-1909; President of Royal Historical Society, 1899-1901; President of the Chetham Society, 1901; Vice-Chancellor of the University of Cambridge, 1901; Governor of St. Paul's School, 1902; of Bury St. Edmunds School, 1903; Fellow of the British Academy, 1902; President of the British Academy, 1911-13, and of English Goethe Society, 1911-22; one of the Editors of the Cambridge Modern History, 1902; of the Cambridge History of English Literature, 1907; Knight of the Prussian Order of the Crown, 2nd class, 1911. *Publications:* E. Curtius' History of Greece, English translation, 5 vols. 1868-73; Globe ed. of Pope's Poetical Works, 1869; The House of Austria in the Thirty Years War, 1869; A History of English Dramatic Literature to the Death of Queen Anne, 2 vols. 1875, 2nd ed. 1899; Marlowe's Doctor Faustus and Greene's Friar Bacon, 1878 (and later editions); Chaucer (1880) and Dickens (1882), in English Men of Letters; The Counter-Reformation (1888); The Poems of John Byrom, 2 vols., Chetham Society, 1894-1895; Sir Henry Wotton, 1897; Great Britain and Hanover (Ford Lectures), 1899; contributions to vols. i., iii.-vi., of the Cambridge Modern History, 1902-7, and vols. v.-x. of the Cambridge History of English Literature; The Electress Sophia and the Hanoverian Succession, 1903; 2nd edition, 1909; The Poems of Crabbe (Cambridge English Classics), 1905-6; Lillo's London Merchant and Fatal Curiosity (Belles Lettres Series), 1906; Knutsford edition of the works of Mrs. Gaskell, 1906; Germany, 1815-1890 (Cambridge Historical Series), vol. i. 1916, vol. ii. 1917, vol. iii. 1918; Collected Papers, Historical, Literary, and Miscellaneous, 1921; five vols., 1921-22; Introduction and contributions to vols. i. and ii. of Cambridge History of British Foreign Policy from 1783, 1922-23; contributions to the Dictionary of National Biography, Encyclopædia Britannica, Edinburgh and Quarterly Reviews, etc. *Address:* Peterhouse Lodge, Cambridge. *Club:* Athenæum.   (*Died 19 June 1924.*)

WARD, Arthur William, M.A.; Professor of Physics, Canning College, Lucknow, since 1889; *b.* Waterloo, 1 Aug. 1858; *y. s.* of late James Ward, and *b.* of Prof. James Ward; *m.* 1st, Edith, *d.* of late J. A. Houston, R.S.A.; 2nd, Annie, *d.* of late Surg.-Maj. Bond; one *s. Educ.:* Liverpool College; Liverpool Institute; St. John's College, Cambridge (Scholar, 1880; B.A. 1882). Lecturer at Borough Road Training College, 1882; worked in Cavendish Laboratory, 1883-84; Lecturer on Physical Science, Kumbakonam College, S. India, 1885-87; invalided home; Fellow and Member of Syndicate, Allahabad University; Member of Senate of Benares Hindu University, 1916. *Publications:* scientific papers in Proceedings Royal Society and Philosophical Magazine; many articles in Indian Press on educational questions; Evidence before Indian University Commission, 1902; Public Service Commission, 1913. *Recreations:*

music, gardening, bridge. *Address:* Badshah Bagh, Lucknow, India.   *(Died July 1919.)*

WARD, Rt. Rev. Mgr. Bernard, R.C. ; Bishop of Brentwood since 1917 ; *b.* Old Hall, Herts, 4 Feb. 1857 ; 3rd *s.* of W. G. Ward of Northwood, Isle of Wight, known at Oxford as "Ideal" Ward, one of the leaders of the Oxford Movement. *Educ.:* St. Edmund's Coll. Old Hall, 1868-75 ; Oscott Coll. Birmingham, 1879-82. Ordained priest by Cardinal Manning, 1882 ; a master at St. Edmund's Coll. 1882-85 ; established new mission, Willesden, 1885-88 ; a master at Oscott, 1888-90 ; Vice-President, St. Edmund's Coll., Old Hall, 1890 ; President, 1893-1916 ; the centenary of the Coll. celebrated July 1893 ; domestic prelate to the Pope, 1895 ; R.C. Canon of Westminster, 1903 ; F.R.Hist.S. 1907 ; Rector of Holy Trinity, Brook Green, 1916-17. *Publications:* History of St. Edmund's College, 1893 ; Commentary on St. Luke's Gospel, 1899 ; Life of St. Edmund of Canterbury, 1903 ; St. Edmund's College Chapel, 1903 ; Catholic London a Century Ago, 1905 ; The Dawn of the Catholic Revival, 1909 ; The Eve of Catholic Emancipation, 1912 ; The Sequel to Catholic Emancipation, 1915 ; The Priestly Vocation, 1918. *Address:* Bishop's House, Brentwood.

(Died 21 Jan. 1920.)

WARD, Lieut.-Gen. Hon. Bernard Matthew, C.B. 1905 ; retired ; *b.* 26 Aug. 1831 ; *s.* of 3rd Viscount Bangor ; *m.* 1st, 1865, Emily Maria, *e. d.* of John La Touche of Harristown, Co. Kildare ; 2nd, 1883, Laura, *d.* of Major-General E. Maberly, C.B. ; four *s.* six *d.* Served Crimea, including Inkerman and Sebastopol, 1854-55 (medal with two clasps, Sardinian and Turkish medals) ; Col. of Suffolk Regt. *Decorated:* Jubilee Crimean War. *Address:* Staplecross, Christchurch, Hants. *Club:* United Service.   *(Died 27 June 1918.)*

WARD, Rev. Charles Triffit ; Hon. Canon of Chelmsford, 1918-25 ; Deacon, 1886 ; Priest, 1887 ; late Vicar of St. Peter's, Colchester. *Address:* St. Peter's, 36 Montalt Road, Woodford, Essex.   *(Died 30 Sept. 1925.)*

WARD, Edward, M.A., M.B., Cantab. ; F.R.C.S. England ; late Professor of Surgery, University of Leeds ; Hon. Consulting Surgeon, Leeds General Infirmary ; formerly Examiner, Universities of Cambridge and Victoria. *Educ.:* Trinity College, Cambridge. *Address:* 30 Park Square, Leeds. *Club:* Leeds.

(Died 30 April 1921.)

WARD, Col. Sir Edward (Willis Duncan), 1st Bt., *cr.* 1914 ; G.B.E., *cr.* 1919 ; K.C.V.O., *cr.* 1907 ; K.C.B., *cr.* 1900 ; late President Union Jack Club ; late President Union Jack Hostel ; Director-General of Voluntary Organisations ; Hon. Commandant in Chief Metropolitan Special Constabulary ; Chairman of Camps Library ; Chairman of Royal Society for the Prevention of Cruelty to Animals ; *b.* Oban, 17 Dec. 1853 ; *o. s.* of late Captain John Ward, R.N., and Mary Hope, *d.* of late John Bowie ; *m.* 1880, Florence Caroline, *d.* of H. M. Simons ; two *s.* *Educ.:* private school. Entered Army, 1874 ; Major Army Service Corps, 1885 ; Lieut.-Col. 1890 ; Brevet Col. 1898 ; served with Soudan Expedition, 1885 (despatches, medal with two clasps, bronze star) ; Major ; on special service with Ashanti Expedition, 1895-96, as A.A.G. (star, C.B.) ; D.A.A.G. Headquarters Staff, Ireland, 1892-95 ; D.A.A.G. Home District Staff 1895-1899 ; A.A.G. Ladysmith, 1899-1900 (despatches thrice, K.C.B.) ; Director of Supplies S. African Field Force, 1900 (Queen's medal 3 clasps) ; A.Q.M.G. Headquarters, Feb. to April 1901 ; Permanent Under-Secretary of State, War Office, 1901-14 ; hon. sec. Royal Military Tournament, 1895-99 ; Knight of Grace, Order of St. John of Jerusalem, 1920. *Publication:* Army Service Corps Duties in Peace and in War. *Re-*

creations: riding, rowing, fishing. *Heir: s.* Edward Simons Ward, late Grenadier Guards [*b.* 11 July 1882. Served European War, 1914-19 (wounded). *Club:* White's]. *Address:* 5 Wilbraham Place, Sloane Street, S.W.1. *T.:* Victoria 2984 ; Furnace Mill, Cowden, Kent ; *T.:* Edenbridge 78. *Clubs:* Carlton, United Service, Ranelagh, Orleans.   *(Died 11 Sept. 1928.)*

WARD, Enoch, R.B.A. 1898 ; M.I.J. ; *b.* Parkgate, near Rotherham, Yorks, 1859 ; went with parents to Chicago at age of eleven, and spent boyhood there ; returned to England 1880, and studied Art at South Kensington ; after which he spent six months in Paris ; *m.* 1890, Elizabeth, *d.* of John Horsfield of Manchester. Has been upon the staff of Black and White since the inception of that paper ; has illustrated books for most of the leading publishers, and has contributed drawings occasionally to The Illustrated London News and The Queen newspapers. *Recreations:* his spare time is spent in his garden or upon his bicycle ; essentially a lover of the country, and cares not overmuch for London. *Address:* 20 Lower Teddington Road, Hampton Wick, Middlesex.   *(Died Feb. 1922.)*

WARD, Major-Gen. Francis William, C.B. 1904 ; Col. Commandant Royal (late Bengal) artillery ; *b.* 6 April 1840 ; *s.* of late John Ward, J.P., of Bodmin ; *m.* 1862, Alice (*d.* 1916), *d.* of Major Macmullen, Bengal Cavalry. Entered Bengal Artillery, 1857 ; Maj.-Gen. 1895 ; served Indian Mutiny, 1857 (medal) ; N.W. Frontier, 1863-64 (medal with clasp) ; Afghan War, 1878-80 (medal). *Club:* Army and Navy.   *(Died 27 Mar. 1919.)*

WARD, Rev. Frederick Hubert, M.A. ; Hon. Canon of Birmingham Cathedral ; Vicar of Sparkhill, Birmingham ; *b.* 1858 ; *s.* of late Rev. Thomas Ward, Vicar of Rowley Regis, Staff., and formerly of Macclesfield, and Agnes Hannah, *d.* of Benjamin Shorthouse, Managing Director of Collieries ; *m.* 1884, Mary St. Maurice, *d.* of late Rev. F. L. Potter, Vicar of St. Leonards ; one *s.* two *d.* *Educ.:* King Edward's Grammar School, Birmingham ; Oxford. After two years' curacy at Cullompton, Devon, settled down to work up the district of Sparkhill. *Address:* Sparkhill, Birmingham.

(Died 17 July 1918.)

WARD, Rev. Frederick William Orde, 'F. Harald Williams," pseudonym ; *b.* Blendworth, 9 April 1843 ; 2nd *s.* of Rev. E. L. Ward, Rector of Blendworth, Hants ; *m.* 1878, Clara, Mary (*d.* 1920), *o. surv. c.* of Samuel Parker, and *n.* of Rt. Hon. John Parker, 1st M.P. for Sheffield ; three *d.* *Educ.:* Tonbridge School (Exhibitioner) ; Wadham College, Oxford (Exhibitioner, 2nd in Classics Moderations). B.A. 1865 ; private tutor at Oxford for some years, and ordained 1868 to Curacy of St. Giles', Oxford ; Vicar of Pishill, 1888-88 ; Rector of Nuffield, 1888-97. *Publications:* Women must Weep (4th ed.), 1887 ; 'Twixt Kiss and Lip, 1890 ; Confessions of a Poet, 1894 ; Baby Pilgrims (2nd ed.), 1895 ; Matin Bells (2nd ed.), 1897 ; English Roses, 1899 ; New Century Hymns for the Church Seasons, 1900 ; The Prisoner of Love, 1904 ; The Keeper of the Keys, 1905 ; Lux Hominum, 1907 ; The World's Quest, 1908 ; Falling Upwards, 1909 ; Songs of Sussex ; Christ and Woman ; Last Crusade ; Songs for Sufferers ; contributor to Hibbert Journal, etc. *Address:* Nunnykirk, Milnthorpe Road, Eastbourne. *T.A.:* Orde Ward, Eastbourne.   *(Died 14 Mar. 1922.)*

WARD, Genevieve, Countess de Guerbel, D.B.E., *cr.* 1921 ; tragedienne ; *b.* New York, U.S.A., 27 Mar. 1837 ; *m.* Count de Guerbel in Warsaw, 10 Nov. 1855. *Educ.:* France, Italy, America. Commenced operatic career under the name of Ginevra Guerrabella, as Lucrezia Borgia at La Scala, Milan, 1856 ; thence to Paris, London, America, and Cuba ; injured voice by overexertion ; taught singing in New York for some years ; later on studied dramatic art, making first appearance as Lady Macbeth, Theatre Royal, Manchester, 1873 ; then starred through Great Britain ; in 1879 first produced the play Forget-me-not at Lyceum Theatre, London, and after a long run at Prince of Wales' Theatre, toured every part of the English-speaking world, acting the same play about 2000 times ; afterwards acting at Lyceum Theatre with Sir Henry Irving in Becket, King Arthur, Richard III., etc.; played in Coriolanus and Richard III. with Benson at various times; played Duchess in Basker at St. James's, 1916; played Duchesse of Hauteveille in The Aristocrat at St. James's, 1917. *Publication:* (with Richard Whiteing)   Before and Behind the Curtain, 1918. *Recreations:* riding, swimming, rowing, painting, modelling. *Address:* 22 Avenue Road, N.W.8.   *T.:* Hampstead 5272.

(*Died 18 Aug. 1922.*)

WARD, Henrietta Mary Ada ; *d.* of George Raphael Ward ; *g.d.* of James Ward, R.A., Animal Painter to the King, *niece* of John Jackson, R.A., portrait painter, *great-niece* of George Morland, also of William Ward, A.R.A., *o. c.* of George Raphael Ward and Mary Webb ; *n.* 1848, E. M. Ward, R.A., at the age of 16 ; two *d. Educ.:* at home ; Cary's Academy, Bloomsbury Street. Exhibited at the Royal Academy consecutively 1849-79, and constantly since, there and other galleries—chiefly historic works. Worked much for Queen Victoria from time to time. *Works:* —The May Queen, God Save the Queen, Joan of Arc, Palissy the Potter, Art Gallery, Leicester ; Mrs. Fry visiting the prisoners in Newgate (dedicated by permission to Queen Victoria) ; Chatterton, Art Gallery, Bristol ; The Princes in the Tower, Museum and Art Gallery, Rochdale, and others ; painted several portraits for Queen Victoria and Royal Family ; exhibited at the Royal Academy, 1903, 1904, 1905, 1906, 1913, and 1921. *Publication:* Reminiscences of Mrs. E. M. Ward, 1918. *Recreations:* sketching, collecting curios and antiquities. *Address:* 59 Sydney Street, Chelsea, S.W.3.   *T.:* Westminster 6010.

(*Died 12 July 1924.*)

WARD, Herbert, sculptor ; Knight of Legion of Honour ; Member of Society of British Sculptors ; *m.* 1890, Sarita, *d.* of Charles H. Sanford ; two *s.* two *d.* Survivor of Stanley's Emin Pacha Relief Expedition ; awarded the Croix de Guerre for work with the British Ambulance and for succouring French wounded in Les Vosges. *Publications:* Five Years with the Congo Cannibals ; My Life with Stanley's Rear Guard, 1891 ; A Voice from the Congo, 1912 ; Mr. Poilu, 1916. *Address:* 102 Eaton Square, S.W. ; 59 Boulevard Berthier, Paris ; Rolleboise, Seine et Oise, France. *Clubs:* St. James's ; Union Artistique, Paris.

(*Died 7 Aug. 1919.*)

WARD, Mrs. Humphry (Mary Augusta) ; *b.* Hobart, Tasmania, 11 June 1851 ; *e. d.* of Thomas Arnold, M.A., 2nd *s.* of Dr. Arnold, Rugby ; *m.* T. Humphry Ward, M.A., 6 Apr. 1872. *Publications:* Milly and Olly, 1881 ; Amiel's Journal (translated), 1885 ; Miss Bretherton, 1886 ; Robert Elsmere, 1888 ; The History of David Grieve, 1892 ; Marcella, 1894 ; Sir George Tressady, 1896 ; Helbeck of Bannisdale, 1398 ; Eleanor (played at Court Theatre, 1902 and 1905), 1900 ; Lady Rose's Daughter, 1903 ; The Marriage of William Ashe, 1905 ; Agatha, a play (produced at His Majesty's Theatre), 1905 ; Fenwick's Career, 1906 ; Diana Mallory, 1908 ; Daphne, 1909 ; Canadian Born, 1910 ; The Case of Richard Meynell, 1911 ; The Mating of Lydia, 1913 ; The Coryston Family, 1913 ; Delia Blanchflower, 1914 ; Eltham House, 1915 ; A Great Success, 1916 ; Lady Connie, 1916 ; England's Effort, 1916 ; Towards the Goal, 1917 ; Missing, 1917 ; A Writer's Re-

collections, 1918 ; The War and Elizabeth, 1918 ; Fields of Victory, 1919 ; numerous articles on West-Gothic Kings and Bishops in vols. ii. and iii. of Smith's Dictionary of Christian Biography ; articles in Macmillan's Magazine, Nineteenth Century, Quarterly Review, etc. ; founded the Passmore Edwards Settlement and the Play Centres for London (1897), and is Chairman of the Committee. *Address:* Stocks House, Tring.

(*Died 24 Mar. 1920.*)

WARD, James ; Fellow of Trinity College, Camb., and Professor of Mental Philosophy, Cambridge ; *b.* Hull, 27 Jan. 1843 ; *e. s.* of James Ward, Great Crosby, Liverpool ; *m. d.* of Rev. H. Martin, Congregationalist Minister ; one *s.* two *d. Educ.:* Liverpool Institute ; Spring Hill College (Congregationalist) ; Universities of Berlin and Göttingen ; Trin. Coll., Camb. M.A. London (gold medal), 1874 ; Senior Moralist, Cambridge, 1875 ; Sc.D. Cambridge, 1887 ; Hon. LL.D. Edinburgh, 1891 ; Hon. D.Sc. Oxford, 1908 ; Hon. LL.D. Cambridge, 1920 ; Fellow of the British Academy, 1902 ; Foreign Member New York Academy of Sciences, 1908 ; Foreign Member of the Royal Danish Society, 1913 ; Corresponding Member of French Institute, 1913. Left school early; articled to a firm of architects, Liverpool ; afterwards prepared for the Congregationalist Ministry ; pastor for a year of Emmanuel Church, Cambridge; resigned because of change in theological opinions and entered the University ; elected scholar of Trinity College, 1872 ; Fellow, 1875 ; Lecturer, 1881 ; Professor in the University, 1897 ; Gifford Lecturer, University of Aberdeen, 1895-97 ; University of St. Andrews, 1908. *Publications:* various articles in Mind, Journal of Physiology, Encyclopædia Britannica, etc. ; Naturalism and Agnosticism, 1899, 4th ed. 1915 ; The Realm of Ends or Pluralism and Theism, 1911. 3rd ed. 1920 ; Heredity and Memory, 1913 ; Psychological Principles, 1918, 2nd ed. 1920 ; A Study of Kant, 1922. *Recreations:* angling, gardening, field natural history, chess. *Address:* 6 Selwyn Gardens, Cambridge. (*Died 4 Mar. 1925.*)

WARD, James, Hon. A.R.C.A.Lond. ; Headmaster Dublin Metropolitan School of Art, 1907-1918 ; artist, author, lecturer ; *b.* Belfast, 17 Nov. 1851 ; *e. s.* of James Ward, decorative artist ; *m.* Elizabeth Ham of London ; four *s.* four *d. Educ.:* Belfast ; at various schools, and private classes. National Scholar at Royal College of Art, 1873-76 ; assistant to Lord Leighton, P.R.A., 1878-86 ; Lecturer on Art Subjects; exhibitor at the Royal Academy ; Membre Correspondant Société Archéologique de France. *Publications:* Elementary Principles of Ornament,1890; Principles of Ornament,1892; Report on the Art and Technical Schools of Crefeld, Zürich, and Lyons, 1895 ; Historic Ornament, in 2 vols., 1897 ; Progressive Design ; Floral Studies for Decorative Design, 1901 ; Colour Harmony and Contrast, 1902 ; translated into Japanese, 1917 ; Fresco Painting, Its Art and Technique, 1909 ; Relation of Schools of Art to Museums, 1912 ; History and Methods of Ancient and Modern Painting, 1913 ; Colour Decoration of Architecture, 1913 ; painted a series of eight frescoes in the City Hall of Dublin, representing important events in the history of the city, 1915-18. *Recreations:* reading, walking, sketching. *Address:* Upland, Newtown Road, Newbury. Berks.

(*Died 18 May 1924.*)

WARD, Sir Leslie, Kt., *cr.* 1918 ; Member of the Royal Society of Portrait Painters ; portrait painter and caricaturist; "Spy" of Vanity Fair, 1873-1909, but now devotes a large proportion of his time to portraiture ; *b.* London, 21 Nov. 1851 ; *e. s.* of late E. M. Ward, R.A., and Henrietta M. A. Ward ; *g.s.* of

James Ward, R.A.; *m.* 1899, Judith Mary Topham-Watney, *b. d.* of Maj. R. Topham, 4th Hussars; one *d. Educ.*: Eton; Barnes. Studied architecture under Sydney Smirke, R.A.; entered Royal Academy Schools as architectural student, and art student: exhibited bust in sculpture-room R.A. when at school; from time to time has exhibited architectural drawings, oil-colour and water-colour portraits in Royal Academy and elsewhere; has drawn for the Graphic. *Publication*: Forty Years of Spy, 1915. *Recreation*: resting when possible. *Address*: 247 Knightsbridge, S.W.; 16 Wellington Square; S.W. *T.*: Western 4899. *Club*: Beefsteak.   (*Died 15 May 1922*.)

WARD, Philip, J.P.; Commissioner of National Education, Ireland, since 1910; *b.* near Carrickmacross, Co. Monaghan, 1845; *m.*; one *s.* one *d. Educ.*: the National School, Carrickmacross; privately. Was teacher of a National school for over forty years, ranking before 1900 as first division of first class, and under the new regulations of the National Board as first division of first grade; the teaching of French, Irish, and mathematics was a feature of his school; was member for many years of the Central Executive of the Irish National Teachers' Organization, and three times President; has contributed a good deal to literary and educational journals. *Recreations*: fond of outdoor exercise, especially walking and cycling. *Address*: Farney Glen Road, Belfast. *Club*: National, Belfast.
     (*Died 5 Nov. 1916*.)

WARD, Thomas Humphry, M.A.; journalist and author; *b.* Hull, 9 Nov. 1845; *s.* of late Rev. Henry Ward, M.A.; *m.* 1872, Mary Augusta (*d.* 1920), *e. d.* of Thomas Arnold, M.A., and *g.d.* of Dr Arnold of Rugby. *Educ.*: Merchant Taylors' School; Brasenose College, Oxford. 1st class Lit. Hum. 1868; Fellow of Brasenose, 1869; Tutor, 1870-81; is a writer on The Times. *Publications*: joint-author of The Oxford Spectator, 1868, and of Romney, 1904; editor of The English Poets, 1881-1918; of English Art in the Public Galleries of London, 1888; of The Reign of Queen Victoria, 1887; of Men of the Reign, 1885; of Men of the Time (12th ed.); author of Humphry Sandwith, a Memoir; engaged on the authorized History of the Athenæum. *Address*: 2 Eccleston Square, S.W.1. *T.*: Victoria 3950. *Club*: Athenæum.   (*Died 6 May 1926*.)

WARD, Wilfrid Philip, F.S.A.; *b.* Old Hall, Ware, 2 Jan. 1856; 2nd *s.* of William George Ward, Northwood Park, Isle of Wight ("Ideal" Ward of the Oxford Movement), and Frances Mary (*d.* 1898), *y. d.* of Rev. John Wingfield, D.D., Headmaster of Westminster, Prebendary of Worcester, and Canon of York; *m.* Josephine Mary, 2nd *d.* of late James Robert Hope-Scott, Q.C., Abbotsford, and Lady Victoria Howard, *d.* of 14th Duke of Norfolk. 1887; two *s.* two *d. Educ.*: St. Edmund's Coll. Ware; Ushaw Coll. Durham; Gregorian Univ. Rome. Select Lec. in Philosophy at Ushaw Coll. 1890; Examiner in Mental and Moral Science in the Royal Univ. of Ireland, 1891-92.; member of the Council of the Catholic Union of Great Britain since 1886; Chairman of Conservative Committee, Freshwater Division, 1887-88; editor of the Dublin Review; member of the Royal Commission on Irish University education, 1901; Lecturer at the Lowell Institute, Boston, 1915. *Publications*: The Wish to Believe, 1884; The Clothes of Religion, 1886; William George Ward and the Oxford Movement, 1889; William George Ward and the Catholic Revival, 1893; Witnesses to the Unseen, 1894; The Life and Times of Cardinal Wiseman, 1897; Problems and Persons, 1903; Aubrey de Vere, a Memoir, 1904; Ten Personal Studies, 1908; Life of John Henry, Cardinal Newman, 1912;

Men and Matters, 1914; also Essays in the Quarterly, Edinburgh, Dublin, Contemporary, National, and New Reviews, and in the Nineteenth Century. *Recreations*: golf, cycling, music. *Address*: Lotus, Dorking. *Clubs*: Athenæum (under Rule II.), Junior Carlton.
     (*Died 9 April 1916*.)

WARD, Sir William, Kt., *cr.* 1900; C.V.O. 1904; K.C.M.G., *cr.* 1910; *b.* 2 June 1841; *y. s.* of late John Ward, C.B., H.M. Minister Resident at Hamburg; *m.* 1872, Jenny Maria (*d.* 1910), *d.* of late Henry Fowler. *Educ.*: partly in Germany and partly in England; British Vice-Consul at Memel, East Prussia, 1866-70; H.M. Consul at Bremen, 1871-80; at Portland (Maine), U.S., 1881-83; at Bordeaux, France, 1884-96; H.M. Consul-General at Hamburg, 1897-1911. *Address*: Glen May, Amhurst Road, Withington, Manchester.   (*Died 23 Dec. 1927*.)

WARD, Sir William Erskine, K.C.S.I., *cr.* 1896; *b.* 1888; *s.* of Hon. J. P. Ward (brother of 3rd Viscount Bangor); *m.* Alicia, *d.* of Edward Palmer, Calcutta, 1866; four *s.* one *d. Educ.*: Trin. Coll. Camb.; Senior Optime, M.A. Entered B.C.S., 1861; Judicial Commissioner of Lower Burmah 1889-91; Chief Commissioner of Assam, 1891-96. *Address*: 8 Kent Gardens, Ealing, W. *T.*: 329 P.O. Ealing. *Clubs*: Oriental; Royal Victoria Yacht, Ryde.
     (*Died 24 Dec. 1916*.)

WARD, Rev. William Hayes, D.D., LL.D.; Editor of the Independent, 1868-1914; Hon. Editor since 1914; *b.* Abington, Mass. 25 June 1835; *s.* of Rev. James W. Ward and Hetta Lord (Hayes) Ward; *m.* Ellen Maria Dickinson; one *s. Educ.*: Amherst Coll. (A.B.,A.M., LL.D.); Andover Theological Seminary. D.D. Rutgers College and University of New York. Pastor, Oskaloosa, Kansas; teacher, Utica, N.Y., Free Academy; tutor, Natural Sciences, Beloit College, Wis.; Prof. of Latin, Ripon College, Wis.; President of American Oriental Society, 1909-10; associate editor of the Independent, 1868; superintending editor, 1873; editor, 1897. *Publications*: Cylinders and other Ancient Oriental Seals, 1909; The Seal Cylinders of Western Asia, 1910; What I Believe, and Why, 1915; articles in reviews, mainly on Oriental archæology; biographical introduction to Poems of Sidney Lanier. *Recreations*: botany and Assyrian archæology. *Address*: South Berwick, Maine, U.S.A. *Club*: Authors'. (*Died 28 Aug. 1916*.)

WARFIELD, Benjamin Breckinridge, D.D., LL.D., Litt.D.; Professor of Didactic Theology in Princeton Theological Seminary since 1887; *b.* near Lexington, Kentucky, 5 Nov. 1851; *s.* of William Warfield and Mary Cabell Breckinridge; *m.* 1876, Annie Pearce, *d.* of George Blackburn Kinkead, Lexington, Kentucky; no *c. Educ.*: private schools; Princeton University, A.B. 1871, A.M. 1874; Princeton Theological Seminary; University of Leipzig. D.D. Princeton, 1880; LL.D. Princeton and Davidson, 1892; Litt.D. Lafayette, 1911; S.T.D. University of Utrecht, 1913. Ordained to the Presbyterian Ministry, 1879; Instructor in New Testament Language and Literature, 1878-79; Professor of same at the Western Theological Seminary, Pittsburgh, 1879-87; Acting President, Princeton Theological Seminary, 1901, 1914; Joint-Editor of The Presbyterian Review, 1888-89; Editor of The Presbyterian and Reformed Review, 1890-1902. *Publications*: Introduction to the Textual Criticism of the New Testament, 1886; Augustine's Anti-Pelagian Treatises, 1887; Two Studies in the History of Doctrine, 1893; The Right of Systematic Theology, 1897; The Significance of the Westminster Confession. as a Creed, 1898; Acts and the Pastoral Epistles (in the Temple Bible), 1902; The Power of God

unto Salvation, 1903 ; The Lord of Glory, 1907 ; Calvin as a Theologian and Calvinism To-day, 1909 ; Hymns and Religious Verses, 1910 ; The Saviour of the World, 1914 ; The Plan of Salvation, 1915 ; Faith and Life, 1916 ; Counterfeit Miracles, 1918. *Address :* 74 Mercer Street, Princeton, New Jersey, U.S.A.
(Died 16 Feb. 1921.)

WARING, Francis John, C.M.G. 1898 ; F.R.G.S. ; M. Inst. C.E. ; Fellow of King's College, London ; one of the consulting engineers to the Crown Agents for the Colonies, 1898-1921 ; *b.* Southsea, 25 Oct. 1843 ; *e. s.* of Francis Waring and Frances Margaret, *d.* of Captain H. Waring, R.N. ; *m.* 1883, Mary Elizabeth Maud, 4th *d.* of late W. M. Harries of Tenby ; four *d. Educ. :* King's College School, London (Fellow, 1908). Served in India professionally, 1863 - 72 ; Brazil, 1873-75 ; entered service of Government of Ceylon as a civil engineer, 1875 ; was from 1882 to 1896 Chief Resident Engineer of Government Railway Extensions in that Colony. *Address :* Uva Lodge, 49 Mount Avenue, Ealing, W.5 ; *T. :* Ealing 487. *Club :* St. Stephen's.
(Died 6 Feb. 1924.)

WARNE, George Henry; M.P. (Lab.) Wansbeck since 1922 ; Trustee of Northumberland Miners' Association ; President of Northumberland and Durham Miners Approved Society ; a Junior Lord of the Treasury, 1924 ; *b.* Cramlington, Northumberland, 15 Dec. 1881 ; *s.* of William Warne, Ashington ; *m.* 1904, Dorothy Isabel, *d.* of George Fenwick, Ashington. *Address :* 18 The Drive, Gosforth, Newcastle upon Tyne. *(Died 24 Dec. 1928.)*

WARNER, Edward Handley, J.P., D.L. ; *b.* 1850 ; *o. surv. s.* of Edward Warner of Quorn Hall (*d.* 1894), and Marianne (*d.* 1892), 4th *d.* of late Rev. J. W. R. Boyer of Swepstone, Leicestershire ; *m.* 1877, Jessie Nancy, *d.* of Thomas Brooks, late of Barkby Hall. Leicestershire. *Educ. :* Rugby ; Trinity College, Oxford (B.A.). High Sheriff, Leicestershire, 1897 ; late Capt., Leicestershire Yeomanry Cavalry. *Heir :* Edward Guy [*b.* 1881 ; *m.* 1908, Gladys Muriel, *y. d.* of late Rev. James Wastie Green ; Lieut. retired pay, late 8th Hussars]. *Address :* Bragbury End, Knebworth, Herts.
(Died 16 Aug. 1925.)

WARNER, Francis, M.D. Lond., F.R.C.P., F.R.C.S. Eng. ; Consulting Physician London Hospital since 1913 ; late Lecturer on the Neuroses and Psychoses of Children ; Lieut.-Colonel, T.F. ; *b.* 10 July 1847 ; *s.* of James Neatby Warner ; *m.* 1880, Louisa Loder, *d.* of William Howard of Hampstead ; one *s.* one *d. Educ. :* private school ; King's College, London. Honours, M.B. London, 1872 M.D. 1873 ; F.R.C.S. Eng. 1873 ; F.R.C.P. 1883 ; Medical Registrar, London Hospital. 1877 ; Assist. Physician, 1879 ; Assist. Physician. East London Hospital for Children, 1878-84 ; Hunterian Prof. of Comparative Anatomy and Physiology, R.C.S. 1887 ; Milroy Lect. R.C.P. London, 1892 ; Fellow Royal Medical Society ; Hon. Member Society Public Health, Budapest ; in residence at London Hospital for war work since Feb. 1916. *Publications :* Mental Faculty Lectures, Cambridge University) ; The Study of Children ; The Nervous System of the Child : its Health and Training : Physical and Mental Condition of Children in 106 Schools, Journal Royal Stat. Soc. 1893-96 ; other articles on Nervous and Defective Children. *Recreations :* literary and scientific. *Address :* Whitbourne, Warlingham, Surrey. *T. :* Upper Warlingham 30. *(Died 26 Oct. 1926.)*

WARRACK, Sir James Howard, K.B.E. ; *cr.* 1919 ; *b.* Montrose, 1855 ; *s.* of James Warrack, shipowner, Montrose ; *m.* 1886, Dorothy Cooper, *d.* of George Todd, C.A., Edinburgh. *Educ. :* Montrose Academy. Received

1094

business training in Montrose and Liverpool ; became a partner in John Warrack & Co., Leith, 1880 ; has been a member of Leith Dock Commission, Leith Chamber of Commerce (Chairman), Leith Nautical College (Chairman) ; Ex-President Edinburgh Chamber of Commerce, Director British Imperial Council of Commerce, Committee of Lloyd's Register of Shipping, Council of Chamber of Shipping of the United Kingdom (President, 1914-15), Council of the Shipping Federation ; during the war served on various Government Advisory Committees ; Vice-President Admiralty Transport Arbitration Board ; Director of the Bank of Scotland, Caledonian Insurance Company, and the North British Rubber Co., Ltd. *Address :* 38 Palmerston Place, Edinburgh. *Clubs :* Junior Constitutional ; University, Edinburgh.
(Died 30 Oct. 1926.)

WARRE, Rev. Edmond, D.D. ; C.B. 1905 ; C.V.O. 1910 ; M.V.O. 1901 ; Hon. Chaplain to the King ; Prebendary of Wells since 1899 ; *b.* London, 12 Feb. 1837 ; 2nd *s.* of late Henry Warre, Bindon, Somerset, and Mary Caroline, 3rd *d.* of Nicolson Calvert, Hunsdon, Herts ; *m.* Florence Dora, 2nd *d.* of Lieut.-Colonel C. Malet, Fontinell Parva, Dorset, 1861 ; five *s.* two *d. Educ. :* Eton ; Newcastle Scholar, 1854 ; Balliol Coll. Scholar, 1855 ; 1st Class Mods. 1856 ; 1st class Lit. Hum. 1859 ; Fellow of All Souls, 1859 ; Hon. Fellow of Balliol, 1896 ; Hon. D.C.L. Oxford, 1907. Assistant Master Eton, 1860 ; Headmaster. 1884-1905 ; Provost, 1909-18 ; Hon. Col. 2nd Bucks (Eton Coll.) R.V. 1884 ; O.T.C. 1910 · V.D. *Recreation :* rowing ; was in Oxford boat, 1857-58-59 ; President O.U.B.C. 1859. *Address :* The Lodge. Eton College. *Club :* Athenæum. *(Died 22 Jan. 1920.)*

WARRE, Rev. Francis, Rector of Bemerton since 1890 ; Canon of Salisbury Cathedral ; *s.* of Henry Warre of Bindon House, Wellington, Somerset, and *d.* of Nicholson Calvert, late M.P. for Hertfordshire Hunsdon House, Ware ; *m.* 1860, Ellin Jane (*d.* 1914), *d.* of Rev. James J. Peach ; four *d. Educ. :* Eton College ; Balliol College, Oxford. Vicar of Bere-Regis, Dorset, 1864 - 76 ; Vicar of Melksham, Wilts. 1876 - 90. *Address :* Bemerton Rectory, Salisbury. *T. :* 166 Southampton Area. *(Died 15 Sept. 1917.)*

WARREN, Sir Alfred Haman, Kt., *cr.* 1918 ; O.B.E. 1918 ; M.P. (Co.U.) Edmonton, Dec. 1918-22 ; *b.* Poplar, 6 Feb. 1856 ; *m.* 1896, Jenny Macey (*d.* 1926), *d.* of George W. Castle, H.M. Customs ; one *s.* one *d. Educ. :* Wesleyan School, Poplar. Mayor of Poplar, 1913-18 ; Past Grand Master, Manchester Unity of Oddfellows ; Past President National Conference of Friendly Societies, and Parliamentary Agent. *Address :* Mountain Ash, Wanstead. *T. :* Wanstead 410. *(Died 1 Aug. 1927.)*

WARREN, Arthur, author and journalist ; *b.* Boston, Mass., 18 May 1860 ; *y. s.* of late Capt. M. H. Warren, U.S.A. ; *m.* 1887, Abbie N., *d.* of late James Gunnison, Scarborough, Maine, U.S.A. ; journalist in London, 1878 - 82 ; a special and editorial writer and critic Boston Herald, 1883-88 ; London correspondent, 1888-97 ; editorial and special correspondent, 1897-1907 ; Editor, 1907-9 ; Dramatic Critic New York Tribune, 1909-12 ; also connected actively, 1897-1903, with the affairs of the late George Westinghouse, and again from 1909 till the latter's death in March 1914. *Publications :* London Days, A Book of Reminiscences, 1920 ; The Charles Whittinghams, a biography, with an account of English printing from 1789 to 1860, 1896 ; many short stories and articles, etc. *Club :* Royal Automobile. *(Died 16 April 1924.)*

WARREN, Gen. Sir Charles, G.C.M.G., *cr.* 1885 ; K.C.B., *cr.* 1888 ; R.E. ; F.R.S. ; Knight of Justice of the Order of St. John of Jerusalem ; *b.* Bangor, North Wales, 7 Feb.

1840; 2nd *s.* of late Major-General Sir Charles Warren, K.C.B.; Col. 96th Regt.; *m.* 1864, Fanny Margaretta (*d.* 1919), *d.* of Samuel Haydon, Guildford ; two *s.* two *d. Educ. :* Bridgnorth ; Cheltenham Coll.; R.M.C. Sandhurst ; R.M.A. Woolwich. Entered R.E. 1857 ; Survey of Gibraltar, 1861-65 ; Assist. Instructor Survey School of Military Engineering, 1856 ; conducted Excavations at Jerusalem and Reconnaissance of Palestine for P.E. Fund, 1867-70 ; School of Gunnery, Shoeburyness, 1871-73 ; H.M. Commissioner for laying down Boundary Line Griqualand West and Orange Free State, 1876-77 (C.M.G.) ; Commissioner Land Claims Griqualand West, 1877 ; commanded Diamond Fields Horse, Kaffir War, and Rebellion in Griqualand West, 1878 ; commanded troops against Bechuanas, 1878 ; Administrator and Com.-in-Chief Griqualand West ; commanded troops Northern Border Expedition, 1879 ; Instructor in Surveying S.M.E. 1880-84 ; special officer attached to Admiralty, Egyptian Campaign, 1882 (K.C.M.G.) ; engaged in Arabia Petræa ; H.M. Special Com. and Maj.-Gen. com. Bechuanaland Expedition, 1884-85, (G.C.M.G.) ; contested Hallamshire, Sheffield, 1885 ; commanded troops Suakim, 1886 ; Commissioner Metropolitan Police, 1886-88 (K.C.B.) ; commanded troops Straits Settlements, 1889-94 ; Thames District, 1895-98 ; Lt.-Gen. in command of 5th Div. S. Africa Field Force, 1899-1900 (despatches). *Publications :* Enlarged General Frome's Outlines of a Trigonometrical Survey, 1873 ; author of part of the Recovery of Jerusalem ; Underground Jerusalem, 1874 ; The Temple or the Tomb, 1880 ; Jerusalem, vol. of Survey of Palestine, with Portfolio of Plates and Excavations, 1884 ; On the Veldt in the Seventies, 1902 ; The Ancient Cubit and our Weights and Measures, 1903 ; The Early Weights and Measures of Mankind, 1914. *Address :* 3 Trinity Mansions, Weston-super-Mare. *Club :* Athenæum.

(Died 21 Jan. 1927.)

WARREN, Admiral Herbert Augustus, M.V.O. 1903 ; *b.* 24 July 1855. Entered Navy, 1869 ; Commander, 1892 ; Capt. 1898 ; Rr.-Adm. 1907 ; served Burmah, 1885-87 (medal with clasp) ; retired Admiral, 1916. *Address :* The Manor House, East Preston, near Littlehampton. *Club :* United Service.

(Died 30 Oct. 1926.)

WARREN, John ; Member Legislative Council and J.P. South Australia ; *b.* 3 Sep. 1830 ; *m.* 1863 ; eight *s.* four *d. Educ. :* New Spynie, Morayshire, Scotland. Engaged in agriculture, pastoral, and horticultural, also mining work ; pastoral on a large scale in the far north ; held office Chairman District Council of Mount Crawford for many years ; Captain in military force for twenty-two years (long service medal). *Address : .* Mount Crawford, South Australia. *Clubs :* Naval and Military, Adelaide.

(Died 13 Sept. 1919.)

WARREN, Vice-Admiral John Borlase ; *b.* 27 March 1838 ; 2nd *s.* of Sir John Borlase Warren, 4th Bt., and *heir-pres.* to 7th Bt. ; *m.* 1874, Mary Elizabeth St. Leger, 2nd *d.* of St. Leger Atkins of Water Park, Co. Cork, Ireland ; three *d. Educ. :* private tutor. Entered Royal Navy as Cadet, 1850 ; Midshipman, 1852 ; Sub-Lieutenant, 1857 ; Lieutenant, 1859 ; Commander, 1871 ; Captain, 1880 ; Rear-Admiral, 1896 ; Vice-Admiral, 1901 ; served in Russian and Chinese Wars of 1855 and 1861 ; granted a Good Service Pension of £150, 1892. *Address :* Carbery, Salcombe, South Devon. *Club :* United Service.

(Died 29 Jan. 1919.)

WARREN, Rev. John Shrapnel, M.A. ; Rector of Willoughby, 1875-1922 ; Rural Dean for Calcewaith, 1889 ; *b.* Beverley, Yorks ; *s.* of Rev. Z. S. Warren, Vicar of Ancaster, Lincs ; *m.* 1st, Caroline (*d.* 1919), *d.* of J. E. Brooke, Hotham House, Yorks ; no *c.* ; 2nd, 1920, Ethel

Adelaide, *d.* of late Rev. H. A. Marsh, Vicar of Luxford. *Educ. :* Rugby ; Cambridge. Vicar of Langtoft, Lincs., 1858-75 ; J.P. Lincs, 1865 ; Prebendary of Lincoln Cathedral, 1895.

(Died 2 May 1925.)

WARREN, Sir Pelham Laird, G.C.M.G., *cr.* 1902 ; C.M.G. 1901 ; H.M. Consul-General, Shanghai, 1901-11 ; *b.* 22 Aug. 1845 ; *s.* of Admiral Richard Laird Warren ; *m.* 1875, Mary Donnithorne Huntfridge. Student Interpreter, China, 1867 ; Vice-Consul, Pagoda Island, 1883 ; Acting Consul, Taiwan, 1883-84, and 1886 ; Consul, Taiwan (now Tainan), 1886 ; Consul, Hankow, 1893 ; Consul-General, Hankow 1899-1901. *Club :* Oriental. *(Died 21 Nov. 1923.)*

WARREN, Philip David, C.M.G. 1908 ; A.I.C.E., F.R.G.S., F.R.Met.S. ; *b.* 7 Feb. 1851 ; *s.* of late John Neville Warren, A.M.I.C.E. ; *m.* 1881, Julia A. M. (*d.* 1915), *d.* of late John Graham, Enniskillen ; one *s.* two *d. Educ. :* Norwich Grammar School ; etc. Served articles to borough engineer, Margate ; six years on engineering and survey work in South Wales ; joined Survey Department, Ceylon, as Assistant Surveyor, 1878 ; District Surveyor, 1879 ; Assistant Surveyor-General, 1897 ; Surveyor-General of Ceylon, 1904-10 ; retired ; Fellow Royal Colonial Institute. *Address :* St. Catherine's, West Hill Road, Woking, Surrey. *Club :* Engineers'. *(Died 28 Jan. 1928.)*

WARREN, William Henry, Hon. LL.D. Glasgow, Wh.Sc., M.Inst.C.E., M.Am.Soc.C.E. ; Member of Council of International Society for Testing Materials ; Challis Professor of Engineering since 1883, and Dean of Faculty of Science since 1908, Dean of the Faculty of Engineering and President of the Professorial Board since 1919 ; University of Sydney ; *b.* Bristol, 1852 ; *m.* 1875 ; one *s. Educ. :* Royal College of Science, Dublin ; Owens College, Manchester. Locomotive Works of the L. and N.W. Railway Co., England, 1866-72 ; studied at the Royal College of Science, Dublin, and Owens College, Manchester, 1872-75 ; occupied various positions in Manchester and London, including chief of drawing office to firm of E. T. Bellhouse and Co., and supervising and designing engineer to Magnall and Littlewoods, Manchester, 1875-80 ; specially engaged by L. and N.W. Co., Euston, to design bridges and roofs for the Victoria Station extensions, Manchester ; occupied in Public Works Dept. of N.S. Wales on roads, bridges, and sewerage, and at the same time organised and directed the Mechanical Engineering Dept., Sydney Technical College, 1881-83 ; has done some consulting work as an engineer in every State of Australia, and has acted on numerous Boards of Inquiry and Royal Commissions ; twice President of the Royal Society of N.S. Wales. *Publications :* Engineering Construction, Part I. in Steel and Timber ; Part II. Masonry and Concrete ; Australian Timbers Testing Materials, Stresses in Structures, and the Physical Properties of Materials used in Engineering Construction ; about fifty pamphlets read before the Royal Society, Sydney, and other scientific societies, on materials used in engineering constructions, including four papers on Reinforced Concrete Constructions ; bridge work, etc. *Recreations :* golf, billiards, music. *Address :* University of Sydney. *Clubs :* Union, Sydney ; Australian Golf.

(Died 9 Jan. 1926.)

WARREN, Hon. William Robertson, K.C. : LL.D. Edin. 1923 ; a Judge of Supreme Court, Newfoundland, since 1926 ; *b.* 9 Oct. 1879 ; *s.* of late William H. Warren ; *m.* 1st, Ethel Alice, *e. d.* of late James Gordon ; one *s.* two *d.* ; 2nd, Emilie Jackson, *d.* of late R. L. Mare ; one *d. Educ. :* Bishop Field College, St. John's, Newfoundland ; Framlingham College, Suffolk. M.P. for Trinity District, 1902 ; for Port de Grave, 1908 and 1909 ; for Fortune

Bay, 1919-24; Speaker of House of Assembly, 1909-13; represented House of Assembly at Coronation of His Majesty King George V., 1911; Attorney-General, 1919-23; retained by Government of Newfoundland in Labrador Boundary Dispute with Canada before Privy Council; Prime Minister, 1923-24; attended Imperial Conference, London, 1923, representing Newfoundland. *Recreations:* golf, curling, salmon-fishing. *Address:* Balsam Aunex, St. John's, Newfoundland. *T.A.:* Warren. *Clubs:* City, St. John's; Bally Haly Golf and Country.
(*Died 31 Dec. 1927.*)

WARRENDER, Vice-Admiral Sir George John Scott, 7th Bt., of Lochend, East Lothian, *cr.* 1715; K.C.B., *cr.* 1913; K.C.V.O., *cr.* 1911; C.B. 1902; C.V.O. 1907; M.V.O. 1904; Commander-in-Chief, Plymouth, since 1916; *b.* Scotland, 31 July 1860; 2nd *s.* of 6th Bt. and Helen, *o. c.* of Sir Hugh Hume Campbell, 7th Bt.; *S.* father 1901; *m.* 1894, Lady Maud Ashley, *y. d.* of 8th Earl of Shaftesbury; two *s.* one *d.* *Educ.:* Rev. John Hawtrey's, Slough. Entered R.N., Naval Cadet, 1873; Commander, 1893; Capt. 1899; with Naval Brigade, Zulu War, 1879; present at battle of Ginghilovo (medal, clasp); C.-in-C. East Indian Station, 1907-9; Rear-Adm. 1908; Vice-Adm. 1913; commanded 2nd Cruiser Squadron, 1910-12; 2nd Battle Squadron, 1912-16; served European War, 1914-15. *Recreations:* golf, cricket. *Heir: s.* Victor Alexander Anthony George, *b.* 23 June 1899. *Address:* 23 Great Cumberland Place, W. *T.A.:* Ecosse, London. *T.:* 1398 Paddington; Bruntsfield House, Edinburgh; Leasam, Rye, Sussex. *Clubs:* Carlton, Turf, Naval and Military; New, Edinburgh; Royal Naval, Portsmouth; Hon. Member Royal Yacht Squadron, Cowes.
(*Died 8 Jan. 1917.*)

WARRENDER, Lieut.-Col. Hugh Valdave, D.S.O. 1916; *b.* 14 Sep. 1868; *y. s.* of late Sir George Warrender, 6th Bt., of Lochend, and Helen, *o. c.* of Sir H. Hume Campbell, 7th Bt. of Marchmont. *Educ.:* Eton; Sandhurst. Joined Grenadier Guards, 1889; retired, 1897; joined Civil Service Rifles. T.F., on outbreak of European War; served in France, 1914-18 (D.S.O.); commanded 1st Batt. Civil Service Rifles; resigned commission, 1920. *Recreations:* fishing, gardening, shooting, golf. *Address:* Berkeley House, Hay Hill, W. 1; *T.:* Gerrard 6114; High Grove, Pinner, Middlesex. *Clubs:* Turf, Garrick. Beefsteak.
(*Died 8 Mar. 1926.*)

WARWICK, 5th Earl of (*cr.* 1759), **Francis Richard Charles Guy Greville,** D.L., J.P. Warwicks., Somerset, and Essex; C.C. Warwicks.; Baron Brooke, 1621; Earl Brooke, 1746; a Trustee of Rugby School; Past Deputy Grand Master, Freemasons of England; Past Provincial Grand Master of Essex since 1882; Lord Lieutenant of Essex; Hon. Colonel Warwickshire Yeomanry; Hon. Colonel Essex Imperial Yeomanry; Hon. Col. Essex Militia; *b.* 9 Feb. 1853; *s.* of 4th Earl and Anne, *d.* of 8th Earl of Wemyss and March; *S.* father 1893; *m.* 1881, Frances Evelyn, *d.* of Col. Hon. Charles Henry Maynard, *s.* of last Viscount Maynard, and Blanche, afterwards Countess of Rosslyn; two *s.* two *d.* *Educ.:* Christ Church, Oxford. M.P. (C.) E. Somersetshire, 1879-85; Colchester, 1888-92; Mayor of Warwick, 1894-95, 1895-96, 1915-1916; Alderman, Warwick Town Council. Owns about 10,200 acres. *Publication:* Memories of Sixty Years, 1917. *Heir: s.* Lord Brooke. *Address:* Warwick Castle, Warwickshire; Easton Lodge, Dunmow, Essex. *Club:* Carlton.
(*Died 15 Jan. 1924.*)

WARWICK, 6th Earl of (*cr.* 1759), **Leopold Guy Francis Maynard Greville,** Baron Brooke, 1621; Earl Brooke, 1746; C.M.G. 1915; M.V.O. 1905; D.L.; J.P. Warwick and

Essex; late Capt. 3rd Batt. Essex Regt.; A.D.C. to Inspector-General of Forces; raised and commanded Warwickshire Horse Artillery Territorial; brevet Lieut.-Col.; Hon. Col. Essex and Suffolk Cyclist Battalion; Brig.-Gen. Canadian Forces, 1914; Life Governor Birmingham University; *b.* 10 Sep. 1882; *e. s.* of 5th Earl and Frances, Countess of Warwick; *S.* father, 1924; *m.* 1909, Marjorie, *d.* of Sir W. Eden, 7th Bt.; three *s.* *Educ.:* Eton. Late Capt. 1st Life Guards; served South Africa, 1900; extra A.D.C. to Lord Milner, 1901-2; acted as Reuter's Special Correspondent during Russo-Japanese War, 1904-5; Private Secretary to the Chief of the Imperial General Staff, 1913-14; holds Order Rising Sun, Japan, and Russian war medal; Prussian Order Red Eagle; commanded 2nd Canadian Cavalry Brigade, 1913: Territorial Force Reserve; commanded Manœuvres, Canada, 1914; A.D.C. to Commander-in-Chief, British Army in France, 1914-15 (despatches twice, C.M.G., Legion of Honour, Order of St. Stanislas, Russia, wounded, Croix de Guerre with palm); commanded 4th Canadian Infantry Brigade Expeditionary Force as Brig.-Gen.; commanded 12th Canadian Infantry Brigade. Owns about 10,200 acres. *Heir: s.* Lord Brooke. *Address:* Warwick Castle, Warwickshire. *Clubs:* Marlborough, Guards'
(*Died 31 Jan. 1928.*)

WASON, Rt. Hon. Eugene, P.C. 1907; *b.* 26 Jan. 1846; *s.* of Rigby Wason, M.P., Ipswich; *m.* 1870, Eleanor Mary, *d.* of C. R. Williams of Dolmelyullyn, Dolgelly, D.L. Merionethshire; three *s.* two *d.* *Educ.:* Rugby; Wadham Coll., Oxford (B.A. 1868, M.A. 1870). Formerly Lieut. in the Rugby School Rifle Corps and 8th Ayrshire Rifle Volunteers; rowed in Trial Eights Oxford, 1865 and 1866; Captain of Wadham College Boat Club, and winner of the University foils, 1868. Called to the Bar, 1870, and went Northern Circuit; disbarred, 1872; admitted solicitor, 1876, a partner in Williams, James & Wason, 1876-85; [struck off the Rolls in 1886, and readmitted a member of the Bar the following week, a unique experience, Mr. Wason having been both disbarred and struck off the Rolls, but each time at his own request]; Chairman of the Scottish Liberal Members, 1908-18; Chairman of Departmental Committee on Food Production, 1915; Member of Committee on Scottish National War Memorial; Assistant Examiner to Incorporated Law Society in Common Law, 1878-82; M.P. S. Ayrshire, 1885-86, 1892-95; Clackmannan and Kinross, 1899-1918; has twice gone round the world, in 1886-87 by India, China, Japan, San Francisco, and America, and in 1896-97 by Australia, New Zealand, Fiji, Hawaii, Vancouver, and Canada; is a Past Master of the University Lodge, a D.L. and J.P. Ayrshire. *Recreations:* formerly football, shooting, rowing, and fishing; now reading, bridge, backgammon, and piequet. *Address:* 8 Sussex Gardens, Hyde Park, W.2; Blair, Dailly S.O., N.B. *T.A.:* Blair, Killochan. *T.:* Paddington 4120. *Club:* Reform.
(*Died 19 April 1927.*)

WASON, John Cathcart, M.P. (L.U.) Orkney and Shetland, 1900; resigned 1902; re-elected as Liberal 1902, 1906, and 1910; *b.* 1848; *y. s.* of Rigby Wason, M.P., and Euphemia Mactier; *m.* 1874, Alice Seymour, *d.* of Edward Bell, C.E.; *bro.* of Rt. Hon. Eugene Wason. *Educ.:* Laleham; Rugby. Barrister, Middle Temple; for many years a farmer in New Zealand; and also member New Zealand Parliament. *Address:* 40 Grosvenor Road, S.W.1; *T.:* Victoria 3104; Craig, Pinlan, Ayrshire. *Clubs:* Reform, Royal Automobile.
(*Died 19 April 1921.*)

WATERHOUSE, Charles Owen, I.S.O. 1910; F.E.S.; *b.* 1843; *s.* of G. R. Waterhouse of the British Museum ; *m.*: one *d.* *Educ.* : University College School. Entered Entomological Department of the British Museum, 1866 ; Assistant keeper, 1905 ; retired, 1910 ; President of the Entomological Society of London, 1908-9. *Publications.* Index Zoologicus ; over 200 papers on Entomological subjects. *Address :* 22 Avenue Gardens, Acton, W.

(*Died 4 Feb. 1917.*)

WATERHOUSE, Edwin, B.A. London ; M.A. (Honoris Causa) Oxon. ; F.C.A. ; J.P. ; Chartered Accountant ; 4th *s.* of late Alfred Waterhouse of Whiteknights, Reading, formerly of Liverpool ; *b.* Aigburth, Liverpool, 1841 ; *m.* 1st, 1869, Georgina (*d.* 1896), *d.* of John Philipp Thöl ; three *d.* one *s.* ; 2nd, 1898, Helen C., *d.* of Frederick Weber, M.D. ; one *s.* *Educ.* : University College, London. Commenced practice as a public accountant, 1864 ; joined the firm of Price, Holyland and Waterhouse, 1865 ; was head of the firm of Price, Waterhouse & Co. from 1887-1906, when he retired from active business as a partner ; was president of the Institute of Chartered Accountants of England and Wales, 1892-94 ; has assisted in various government and public inquiries. *Address :* 3 Frederick's Place, E.C. ; Feldemore, Holmbury St. Mary, Surrey. *Club :* City of London. (*Died 17 Sept. 1917.*)

WATERHOUSE, Major-Gen. James, Unemployed Supernumerary List, Indian Army (retired) ; *b.* 24 July 1842 ; *s.* of late J. W. Waterhouse ; unmarried. *Educ.* : Univ. Coll. School ; King's College, London ; Addiscombe. Royal (Bengal) Artillery, 1859-66 ; Indian Ordnance Department, 1866 ; Assist. Surveyor-General in charge of photographic operations in the Surveyor-General's Office, Calcutta, 1866-97 ; took part in the observation of total eclipses, 1871 and 1875, and of transit of Venus, 1874 ; President of the Asiatic Society of Bengal, 1888-90 ; Trustee of the Indian Museum, Calcutta, 1875-97 ; Chairman, 1888-89 and 1895-97 ; Hon. Sec. Zoological Gardens, Calcutta, 1894-97 ; awarded Roy. Phot. Soc. Progress Medal, 1890, also Vienna Phot. Soc. Voigtländer Medal, 1895, for researches in scientific photography ; Hon. Member Phot. Soc. India, 1897 ; President 1894-97 ; Hon. Member Vienna Photographic Society 1901 ; Hon. Fellow Royal Phot. Society ; President, 1905-6. *Publications :* The Preparation of Drawings for Photographic reproduction : Report on the United States Government Surveys, 1906 ; and numerous papers in the Bengal Asiatic Society's Journal and various photographic journals and publications. *Address :* Hurstmead, Eltham.

(*Died 28 Sept. 1922.*)

WATERHOUSE, J. W., R.A., 1895 ; A.R.A., 1885. *Address :* 10 Hall Road, St. John's Wood, N.W. *Club :* Athenæum.

(*Died 10 Feb. 1917.*)

WATERHOUSE, Paul, M.A. ; F.S.A., architect ; *b.* Manchester, 1861 ; *e. s.* of late Alfred Waterhouse, R.A., LL.D., of Yattendon, Berks ; *m.* 1887, Lucy Grace, *d.* of Sir Reginald Palgrave, K.C.B. ; one *s.* two *d.* *Educ.* : Eton : Balliol College, Oxford. Past President of Royal Institute of British Architects ; formerly Chairman of Board of Architectural Education ; Life Trustee of the Soane Museum ; has designed buildings for the universities of Oxford, Manchester, and Leeds, the Prudential Assurance Co., the Refuge Assurance Co., the Atlas Assurance Co., the London Salvage Corps, the Royal National Pension Fund for Nurses, the National Provincial and Union Bank of England, and (in Paris and Brussels) for Lloyds and National Provincial Foreign Bank ; various houses, and work for churches, banks, schools, and hospitals, including the University College Hospital Medical School. *Publications :* Articles on Architecture in the Edinburgh and many other

Reviews and Journals ; articles on Town-planning ; several lives for the Dictionary of National Biography. *Address :* Staple Inn Buildings, High Holborn W.C.1 ; Yattendon Court, Berkshire. *T.A. :* Aedilis London. *T. :* Holborn 2399. *Clubs :* Athenæum, Arts.

(*Died 19 Dec. 1924.*)

WATERLOW, David Sydney ; *b.* Highgate, 18 Dec. 1857 ; 4th *s.* of Sir Sydney Waterlow, 1st Bt. ; *m.* 1883, Edith Emma, *e. d.* of Mrs. F. Maitland ; three *d.* *Educ.* : Northampton ; Lausanne. Travelled round world, 1879 ; joined firm of Waterlow & Sons, Ltd., printers, 1880 ; retired, 1898 ; Chairman Director, 1922 ; Improved Industrial Dwellings Co., Ltd., since 1885 ; L.C.C., North St. Pancras, 1898-1910 ; M.P. (L.) North Islington, 1906-1910 ; Chairman Governors, United Westminster Schools, 1914 ; J.P. London, 1916. *Address :* Wrydelands, Leatherhead, Surrey. *Clubs :* National Liberal, Reform, Royal Automobile. (*Died 25 Aug. 1924.*)

WATERLOW, Sir Ernest Albert, Kt., *cr.* 1902 ; R.A. 1903 ; late President Royal Society of Painters in Water Colours ; landscape painter ; *b.* London, 24 May 1850 ; *o. s.* of late A. C. Waterlow, lithographer ; *m.* 1876, Mary Margaret Sophia (*d.* 1899), *d.* of late Prof. Carl Hofman ; two *s.* two *d.* ; 2nd, 1909, Eleanor Marion, *widow* of Dr. G. Sealy. *Educ.* : Eltham Collegiate School ; Heidelberg. Entered Royal Academy Schools, 1872 ; obtained Turner gold medal, 1873 ; elected R.W.S. 1880 ; elected Associate R.A. 1890. *Address :* 1 Maresfield Gardens, Fitzjohn's Avenue, N.W. *Clubs :* Athenæum, Arts.

(*Died 25 Oct. 1919.*)

WATERS, James ; a dramatic critic on the Daily Mail ; also the dramatic critic of the Weekly Dispatch. *Address :* Carmelite House, Carmelite Street, E.C. *Club :* Royal Automobile. (*Died 14 Jan. 1923.*)

WATERS, Lieut.-Colonel Robert, M.D., C.B. 1891 ; J.P. ; Army Medical Staff, retired ; *y. s.* of late James Waters, Tobermore. *Educ.* : Royal Academical Institution ; Queen's Coll. ; Belfast (Senior scholar) ; Exhibitioner, Queen's Univ. in Ireland. Entered Army Medical Dept. 1860 ; for special services in the Gambia in 1869 received the thanks of the Colonial Government and of the Sec. of State for the Colonies ; promoted Staff-Surgeon (Surgeon-Major) ; was P.M.O. West African Settlements, 1873 ; served in the Ashanti War of 1873-74 (mentioned in despatches, medal with clasp) ; served with the Nile Expedition, 1884-1885, as chief sanitary officer ; for a time offg. P.M.O. on the lines of communication (mentioned in despatches ; promoted Brigade-Surgeon ; medal with clasp, and Khedive's star) ; was P.M.O., Quetta District, India, 1888 ; and of the Sirhind District, 1889-90. *Recreations :* travelling and visiting every division of the world and places of interest. *Address :* White Fort, Tobermore, Co. Londonderry.

(*Died 5 Aug. 1927.*)

WATERS, Rev. Thomas Brocas, Vicar of Christ Church, Hampstead, since 1917 ; *y. s.* of Edwin Hughes Waters and Sarah Maria Deborah Waters of Chilverton Elms, Dover ; *m.* 1902, Alice Mary, *d.* of James Young and Louisa Anderson of Bunker Hill, Co. Durham ; one *s.* *Educ.* : Tonbridge School ; Trinity College, Cambridge, Deacon, 1888 ; Priest, 1889 ; Curate of Southborough, 1888-95 ; Curate of Holy Trinity, Marylebone, 1895-97 ; Vicar of Jesmond, Newcastle-on-Tyne, 1897-1907 ; Hon. Canon of Newcastle-on-Tyne, 1904-7 ; Vicar of St. Mary's, Bury St. Edmunds ; Officiating Clergyman to the Depot of the Suffolk Regiment, also Chaplain to West-Suffolk General Hospital and Thingoe Union, Bury St. Edmunds, 1907-17 ; Hon. Canon of St. Edmundsbury and Ipswich, 1914-17. *Address :* Christ

Church Vicarage, Hampstead, N.W.3. *T.:* Hamp. 5222. *(Died 16 Sept. 1922.)*

WATKINS, Ven. Henry William, M.A., D.D.; Archdeacon and Canon of Durham; Emeritus Professor of Hebrew, University of Durham; Examining Chaplain to Bishop of Durham; *b.* 19 Jan. 1844; 4th *s.* of late William Watkins, Wern-y-cwm, Abergavenny, and Sarah, *o. d.* of T. Dew, Llanvetherine Court; *m.* 1883, Kate Mary Margaret, *e. d.* of Sir Henry Thompson, 1st Bt.; three *d. Educ.:* King's Coll. London; Balliol Coll. Oxford (Scholar, M.A.); Fellow of King's Coll. London; Hon. Fellow of St. Augustine's Coll. Canterbury. Ordained 1870; Vicar of Much Wenlock, 1873; Censor, Tutor, and Lecturer in Greek Testament in King's Coll. London, 1875; Professor of Logic and Moral Philosophy, 1877; Warden of St. Augustine's Coll. Canterbury, 1879; Bampton Lecturer at Oxford, 1890. *Publications:* Charges addressed to the Clergy; Articles in Smith's Dictionary of the Bible, etc.; Commentary on the Gospel according to St. John; Modern Criticism considered in its Relation to the Fourth Gospel (the Bampton Lectures for 1890). *Recreation:* reading. *Address:* The Archdeaconry, Durham. *Club:* Athenæum.

(Died 31 Aug. 1922.)

WATKINS, Ven. Oscar Daniel, M.A.; *b.* 29 June 1848; *s.* of late Daniel Watkins; *m.* 1876, Elizabeth Martha, *d.* of Rev. T. B. Ferris; two *s.* one *d. Educ.:* North London College School; King's College, London; Merton College, Oxford (Postmaster, 1869-73). Curate of St. Michael and All Angels, Croydon, 1878; Chaplain All Saints, Allahabad, 1876; later at Meerut, Mussoorie, Bareilly, Naini Tal; St. Martin's, Colchester; Holywell, Oxford; Archdeacon of Lucknow, 1897-1902; Examining Chaplain to Bishop of Lucknow; Chaplain on H.M.'s Bengal Establishment, 1881-1903; Vicar of Holywell, Oxford, 1907-21; Commissary to Bishop of Lucknow, 1902-9; retired, 1921. *Publications:* Holy Matrimony, a Treatise on the Divine Laws of Marriage, 1895; The Divine Providence, 1904; A History of Penance (2 vols.), 1920; Holy Marriage, 1925. *Address:* 14 Winchester Road, Oxford.

(Died 19 Feb. 1926.)

WATKINSON, Rev. William L., D.D., LL.D.; Wesleyan Minister; *b.* Hull, 30 Aug. 1838; *m.* Phœbe (*d.* 1911), *d.* of Samuel Swindley, Oldbury; four *s.* two *d. Educ.:* privately. D.D. Wesleyan Univ. Middletown, Conn.; LL.D. North-Western Univ. Chicago; Pres. of Wesleyan Conference, 1897-98; Editor of Wesleyan Church, 1893-1904. *Publications:* The Blind Spot and other Sermons, 1899; Studies in Christian Character, Work, and Experience, 1901; The Bane and the Antidote, and other Sermons, 1902; The Education of the Heart, 1904; The Supreme Conquest, 1907; The Fatal Barter, 1910; The Moral Paradoxes of St. Paul, 1913; The Shepherd of the Sea, 1920; The Fairness of Trial, 1923. *Address:* 29 Exeter Road, Brondesbury, N.W. *(Died 14 Feb. 1925.)*

WATNEY, Sir John, Kt., *cr.* 1900; *b.* 27 Jan. 1834; *s.* of John Watney; *m.* 1864, Elizabeth (*d.* 1896), *y. d.* of Stephen Dendy of Leigh Place, Surrey; two *s.* one *d. Educ.:* Harrow. Chairman of Council of City and Guilds Institute for Advancement of Technical Education; F.S.A.; J.P., Surrey; one of H.M.'s Lieutenants for the City of London. *Publications:* History of the Hospital of St. Thomas of Acon and an account of the Plate of the Mercers' Company; and a short history of the Mercers' Company. *Address:* Shermanbury House, Reigate. *T.:* Reigate 171. *(Died 25 Mar. 1923.)*

WATNEY, Vernon James, M.A.; D.L.; J.P.; F.S.A.; Vice-Chairman Oxfordshire C.C. 1927; *b.* 14 Oct. 1860; *s.* of late James Watney, M.P.; *m.* 1891, Lady (Gwendolen) Margaret

1098

Wallop, *d.* of 5th Earl of Portsmouth; one *s.* two *d. Educ.:* Eton; New College, Oxford. County Councillor for Westminster Division of London, 1889-91; Chairman of Watney & Co.'s Brewery, 1887-98; Master of the Brewers' Company, 1893-94; High Sheriff of Oxfordshire, 1908; Alderman, Oxfordshire C.C., 1905; Chairman of Education Committee, 1908-1914; Chairman of Oxfordshire Finance Committee since 1918; Member of the Rubber and Tin Exports Committee, 1915-19; Member of the Council of Oxford Territorial Force Association, 1907-27; Member of the Advisory Council of the Institute on Research in Agricultural Economics, Oxford, since 1912; a Radcliffe Trustee, Oxford, since 1922. *Publications:* Littlecote, 1900; Cornbury, 1910. *Address:* 11 Berkeley Square, W.1; *T.:* Mayfair 3347; Cornbury Park, Charlbury, Oxfordshire; Fannich, Loch Luichart, Ross-shire. *Clubs:* Brooks's, Garrick. *(Died 27 Aug. 1928.)*

WATSON, Aaron, J.P.; author and journalist; *b.* Fritchley, Derbyshire, 14 Dec. 1850; *m.* Phebe, *d.* of late John Gibling, Norwich, 1871. Editor Newcastle Critic, 1873; assistant editor Newcastle Weekly Chronicle, 1874-78; leader - writer Newcastle Daily Chronicle, 1878-80; editor Echo, London, 1883; editor Shields Daily Gazette, 1885-93; London correspondent Newcastle Daily Leader, 1893-95; editor Newcastle Leader, 1895-1902; Member Northumberland County Council, 1889; Vice-Chairman Northumberland Sea Fisheries Committee; Vice-President Institute of Journalists, 1885; Hon. Secretary, 1894-95; Vice-President, World's Press Parliament, St. Louis, 1904. English Representative, World's Press Congress, San Francisco, 1915. *Publications:* Brown Studies, a book of essays, 1885; Waifs and Strays, with Verses Grave and Gay, 1886; For Lust of Gold, a romance, 1890; Papers on Fishery Questions; More Waifs and Strays; F. C. G., a Sketch; The Savage Club; A Medley of History, Anecdote, and Reminiscence, 1907; Tennyson (The Peoples' Books), 1912; A Great Labour Leader, 1908; A Newspaper Man's Memories, 1925. Part-author of The Royal River, Rivers of Great Britain, etc.; in collaboration, The Marquis of Carabas, a novel. *Recreation:* sketching. *Address:* Bewley House, Lacock, Wilts. *Clubs:* Savage, London Sketch, Wigwam; Pen and Palette, Newcastle-on-Tyne. *(Died 26 June 1926.)*

WATSON, Alfred Edward Thomas, editor of the Badminton Library and Badminton Magazine; for more than 30 years musical and dramatic critic of the Standard; since on staff of The Times; *b.* 10 Mar. 1849; *s.* of Capt. B. L. Watson. After having contributed verse and prose to various magazines, joined the staff of the Standard in 1872; contributed much to the Saturday Review, 1885-94; wrote occasionally for Punch, and edited the Illustrated Sporting and Dramatic News, writing under the signature "Rapier," 1880-95. *Publications:* Sketches in the Hunting Field, 1880; Race Course and Covert Side, 1883; Types of the Turf, 1885; Steeplechasing, 1886; chapters in the Badminton volumes on Hunting, Riding and Driving, Racing and Chasing, 1897; The Turf, 1898, etc.; The Racing World and its Inhabitants, 1904; King Edward VII. as a Sportsman, 1911; A Sporting and Dramatic Career, 1918; sectional editor (Sports and Pastimes) Ency. Brit., and contributor of various articles to the work. *Recreations:* riding, shooting, racing. *Address:* 29 Catherine Street, Westminster, S.W.1. *T.:* Victoria 20. *Clubs:* Junior Carlton, Beefsteak, Bath, Ranelagh. *(Died 8 Nov. 1922.)*

WATSON, Arthur George, D.C.L., J.P.; *b.* London, 30 Nov. 1829; 3rd *s.* of Henry Watson, Barnes, Surrey; *m.* 1864, Caroline Jane, *e. d.* of Hon. and Rev. K. H. Digby; two *s.*

WATKINS, Frederick Henry. See page xxxi.

four d. *Educ.*: Rugby; Balliol College, Oxford. First Class in Classics, 1852; Johnson Theological Scholar. Fellow of All Souls College, 1853-64; Assistant Master at Harrow, 1854-91. *Address*: Uplands, Wadhurst, Sussex. *T.A.*: Wadhurst. *T.*: 66 Wadhurst. *M.*: AP 3361. *Clubs*: New University, National Liberal.
(*Died 21 Oct. 1916.*)

WATSON, Arthur William, C.B. 1923; C.B.E. 1920; O.B.E. 1918; Principal Assistant Secretary and Director of Establishments, Ministry of Labour; *b.* Nieuchwang, China, 16 Nov. 1874; *s.* of J. Watson, M.D., of Dormans House, Dormans Park, Surrey; *m.* 1902, Marion, *d.* of W. H. Ashwin, J.P., D.L., of Bretforten Manor, Worcestershire; one *s.* one *d. Educ.*: Cheltenham College; Uppingham School; Magdalene College, Cambridge. Entered Indian Civil Service, 1897; served in Bihar, Chota Nagpur and Bengal in various executive and judicial capacities, 1899-1909; acting Registrar, Calcutta High Court, 1909-10; Sessions Judge, Calcutta, 1910-12; Secretary to Bengal Legislative Council, 1912; Secretary to Bengal Government in Legislative Department and Secretary to Bengal Legislative Council, 1913; Deputy Assistant Secretary Ministry of Munitions (England), 1916; Assistant Secretary, Ministry of Labour (temp.), 1918; transferred permanently to Home Civil Service, 1919. *Address*: Dormans House, Dormans Park, Surrey. *T.*: Dormans Park 12. *Club*: Travellers'.
(*Died 9 Oct. 1925.*)

WATSON, Colonel Sir Charles Moore, K.C.M.G., *cr.* 1905; C.B. 1902; C.M.G. 1887; M.A.; *b.* Dublin, 10 July 1844; *s.* of late Wm. Watson, Dublin; *m.* Genevieve, Lady of Grace of Order of St. John of Jerusalem in England, *d.* of late Rev. Russell Cook, 1880. *Educ.*: Trinity Coll. Dublin; R.M.A. Woolwich. Lieut. R.E. 1866; served in Soudan under late Gen. C. G. Gordon, C.B., 1874-75; A.D.C. to Field-Marshal Sir Lintorn Simmons, G.C.B., 1878-80; employed in India Office, 1880-82; special service, Egyptian War, 1882 (Brevet Major and 4th class Medjidie); employed in Egyptian Army, 1882-86; with rank of Pasha (3rd class Osmanieh); Assistant Inspector-General of Fortifications, 1891-96; Deputy Inspector-General, 1896-1902; Sec. to Royal Commission for St. Louis Exhibition and Commissioner-General, 1904; British Government Delegate to International Navigation Congresses at Düsseldorf, 1902, Milan, 1905, and Petrograd, 1908; Knight of Grace of Order of St. John of Jerusalem in England; Chairman of Committee of Palestine Exploration Fund since 1905. *Publications*: Life of Maj.-Gen. Sir C. M. Wilson, 1909; British Weights and Measures, 1910; The Story of Jerusalem, 1912; Fifty Years' Work in the Holy Land, 1915. *Recreation*: travelling. *Address*: 16 Wilton Crescent, S.W. *Clubs*: Athenaeum, Junior United Service.
(*Died 15 Mar. 1916.*)

WATSON, Sir Charles Rushworth, 3rd Bt., *cr.* 1866; *b.* 21 Sept. 1865; *s.* of 2nd Bt. and Rosamond (*d.* 1904), *d.* of C. P. Rushworth, Queen Anne Street, Marylebone; *S.* father, 1907; *m.* 1910, Evelyn, *d.* of late Aubrey Cartwright, of Edgcote; two *s.* one *d. Educ.*: Eton. *Heir*: *s.* Thomas Aubrey, *b.* 7 Nov. 1911. *Address*: 15 Eaton Place, S.W.1. *Club*: Travellers', Windham.
(*Died 27 Mar. 1922*)

WATSON, Maj.-Gen. Sir David, K.C.B., *cr.* 1918; C.M.G. 1917; C.B. 1916; Commanding 4th Canadian Division since 1916; *b.* 7 Feb. 1871; *m.* Mary Browning; two *d. Educ.*: Public School, Quebec. In active journalism all his life; owns Quebec Chronicle: in military associations for over 20 years; took command of 2nd Batt. 1st Canadian Division, Aug. 1914; commanded 5th Bde. 2nd Division, Aug. 1915; European War, 1914-18 (despatches seven times, C.B., C.M.G., K.C.B., etc.); Croix de Com-

mander of the Legion of Honor, France; Commander of the Order of Leopold; Croix de Guerre, Belgium and France; D.C.L., Bishops' College, Lennoxville. *Address*: Quebec, Canada. *Clubs*: Junior Carlton, Royal Automobile; Garrison, Quebec; St. James's, Montreal.
(*Died 19 Feb. 1922.*)

WATSON, George, M.A.; *b.* Edinburgh, 24 Sep. 1845; *e. s.* of James Watson, Manager of the Scottish Provident Institution for Insurances on Lives; *m.* 1874, Margaret Campbell (*d.* 1914), *o. c.* of Patrick Campbell MacDougall, Professor of Moral Philosophy in the University of Edinburgh; two *s.* three *d. Educ.*: Edinburgh Academy and University. Graduated with first-class honours in Classics, 1867; called to Scottish Bar, 1871; English Bar, Inner Temple, 1884; Sheriff-Substitute of Dumfries and Galloway, 1890-1925. *Publication*: edited Bell's Dictionary and Digest of the Law of Scotland. *Recreations*: music, fly-fishing, travel. *Address*: Corsbie West, Newton Stewart. *Club*: University, Edinburgh.
(*Died 2 Feb. 1927.*)

WATSON, Gilbert, Political Correspondent of the Yorkshire Post; *s.* of Edwin Watson, late senior clerk at the Admiralty; *m.* Lilian, *d.* of C. F. Pearson, late of Clare, Suffolk; one *s. Educ.*: St. Joseph's College, Clapham; graduate in arts of London University. Has had considerable experience of Parliamentary and organisation work; entered parliamentary journalism, 1904; acted at times as political correspondent of the Manchester Courier, the Standard, the Times, and the Yorkshire Post; Hon. Sec. of the Parliamentary Press Gallery, 1908-10; Chairman, 1911-12; Chairman, Parliamentary Lobby Journalists, 1913. *Recreations*: rowing, sailing, walking. *Address*: 29 Ellesmere Road, Chiswick, W.4. *T.*: 794 Chiswick. *Clubs*: Constitutional, University of London, Thames Rowing. (*Died 5 April 1930.*)

WATSON, Henry Brereton Marriott, B.A.; author; *e. s.* of Rev. H. C. M. Watson, incumbent of St. John's, Christchurch, N.Z.; *b.* Caulfield, Melbourne, 20 Dec. 1863; at age of nine taken to New Zealand; *m.* Rosamund (*d.* 1911). *y. c.* of Benjamin Williams Ball. *Educ.*: Grammar School, Christchurch, New Zealand; Canterbury College. Came to England, 1885; took up journalism, 1887. *Publications*: Marahuna, 1888; Lady Faintheart, 1890; The Web of the Spider, 1891; Diogenes of London, 1893; At the First Corner, 1895; Galloping Dick, 1896; The Heart of Miranda, 1897; The Adventurers, 1898; The Princess Xenia, 1899; The Rebel; Chloris of the Island, 1900; The Skirts of Happy Chance: The House Divided, 1901; Godfrey Merivale, 1902; Alarums and Excursions, 1903; Captain Fortune; Hurricane Island, 1904; Twisted Eglantine, 1905; The High Toby, 1906; A Midsummer Day's Dream; The Privateers, 1907; A Poppy Show; The Golden Precipice, 1908; The Flower of the Heart, 1909; The Castle by the Sea, 1909; The King's Highway; Alise of Astra, 1910; At a Venture, 1911; Couch Fires and Primrose Ways; The Tomboy and Others; The Big Fish, 1912; Ifs and Ans, 1913; Rosalind in Arden, 1913; Once Upon a Time; The House in the Downs, 1914; Chapman's Wares, 1915; As it Chanced, 1916; The Affair on the Island, 1916; Mulberry Wharf, 1917; The Excelsior, 1918; The Pester Finger; Aftermath, 1919; joint-author with J. M. Barrie of Richard Savage, play; has been assistant-editor of Black and White and Pall Mall Gazette; was on the National Observer staff under W. E. Henley. *Club*: Savile.
(*Died 30 Oct. 1921.*)

WATSON, Sir John, 3rd Bt.; *cr.* 1895; Lieut. 16th Lancers; *b.* 24 Feb. 1898; *s.* of 2nd Bt. and Edith Jane, *e. d.* of W. H. Nott, Liverpool; *S.* father 1903. *Educ.*: Eton; R.M.C. Sandhurst. *Heir*: *b.* Derrick William

Inglefield, b. 7 Oct. 1901. *Address:* Earnock, Hamilton, Lanarkshire. (*Died 23 Mar. 1918.*)

WATSON, Gen. Sir John, G.C.B. 1902; K.C.B., *cr.* 1886; V.C.; *b.* 6 Sep. 1829; *m.* 1860, Eliza Jesser (*d.* 1892), *d.* of John Davies of Cranbrook Park, Essex. Entered Bombay Army, 1848; Gen. 1891; served Punjab, 1848-49; Bozdar, 1857; Indian Mutiny, 1857-59; in command of Cavalry of Bombay Field Force despatched to Malta, 1878; in command of Punjab Chief Contingent in Afghan War, 1879-80; Governor-Gen.'s Agent at Baroda, 1881-88. *Address:* Northcourt, Finchampstead, Berks. *Club:* United Service. (*Died 23 Jan. 1919.*)

WATSON, John; founder and principal proprietor of the Northern Newspaper Syndicate; J.P. Westmorland; Alderman, Westmorland County Council: Member Lake District Fishery Board, Lune Conservancy Board, Eden Fishery Board; *b.* Kendal; *s.* of late William Watson; *m.* Emily, *d.* of late Isaac Farrer. *Publications:* Sylvan Folk ; Nature and Woodcraft ; British Sporting Fishes ; The English Lake District Fisheries; Poachers and Poaching ; Annals of a Quiet Valley ; Woodlanders and Field Folk, etc. ; contributor to the Victorian History of England. *Recreations:* shooting, fishing, hound-breeding. *Address:* Eden Mount, Kendal. *T.:* Kendal 122.
(*Died 30 Sept. 1928.*)

WATSON, Reginald George, C.M.G. 1911; *b.* 2 June 1862; *s.* of late Gen. E. D. Watson, Bengal Army; *m.* 1905, Sydney Frances Vivien, *o. d.* of Duncan Presgrave ; three *d. Educ.:* Haileybury. Entered Civil Service, Straits Settlements, 1883; Protector of Chinese Perak, 1891; Senior Magistrate, Selangor, 1896 ; Secretary to Government, 1899 ; Senior Magistrate, Perak, 1901 ; Commissioner of Lands and Mines, Federated Malay States, 1903 ; Commissioner of Lands and Surveys, 1906 ; Federal Secretary, 1909 ; British Resident, Selangor, 1911; Perak, 1912-19; retired, 1919. *Address:* 71 Bickenhall Mansions, Gloucester Place, W.1. *T.:* Mayfair 6845.
(*Died 20 Mar. 1926.*)

WATSON, Rev. Robert A., M.A., D.D. Minister of United Free Church; *b.* Aberdeen, 1845 ; *e. s.* of Patrick Watson, merchant; *m.* 1874, Elizabeth Sophia, (*d.* 1918) *d.* of Rev. John Fletcher, London. *Educ.:* Grammar School; University, Aberdeen. D.D.1891. *Publications:* Gospels of Yesterday, 1888 ; in Expositor's Bible : Judges and Ruth, 1889 ; The Book of Job, 1892 ; The Book of Numbers, 1894 ; In the Apostolic Age, 1894 (new ed. 1912) ; contributor to the British Weekly, Sunday at Home, etc. ; in co-operation with Mrs. Watson, *nom de plume* "Deas Cromarty," edited George Gilfillan : Letters, Journals, and Memoir, 1892, and The Christian Leader, 1900-1. *Recreations:* travel, country life, chess. *Address:* Broomlee, Cults, Aberdeen. (*Died 3 Feb. 1921.*)

WATSON, Lt.-Col. Thomas Colclough, V.C.; R.E.; Military Works Dept. India; *b.* 1867 ; *m.* 1892, Edythe (Royal Red Cross), *y. d.* of late Major-General John Whately Welchman, C.B., Indian Army; one *s.* Entered army, 1888 ; Capt. 1899 ; Major, 1906 ; Lt.-Col. 1914; served North-West Frontier, 1897-98 (wounded, despatches, medal with clasp, V.C.). *Club:* Junior United Service.
(*Died 15 June 1917.*)

WATSON, Sir Thomas Edward, 1st Bt., *cr.* 1918 ; J.P.; colliery owner, shipowner, and coal exporter; *b.* 1 Jan. 1851; *e. s.* of late Edward Watson, West Hartlepool; *m.* 1874, Mary Elizabeth, *e. d.* of late Thomas Harrison and Sarah Jane Lewen, Scarborough ; two *s.* one *d.* High Sheriff, Monmouthshire, 1911; Newport Harbour Commissioner and Chairman of River Usk Dredging Committee, 1893-1917 ; Newport Pilotage Commissioner, 1896-1917 ; President of the Cardiff Chamber of Commerce,
1100

1914-18 ; Chairman of the Board of Trade Coal and Coke Supplies Committee for South Wales and Monmouthshire; Chairman of the Cardiff Committee for the Supply of Coal to France and Italy during the War ; a Member of the Glamorgan Appeal Tribunal on Recruiting ; a Member of the Severn Commission, and of the Committee of Lloyd's Register; a Vice-President of the King Edward Hospital, Cardiff, and of the Royal Gwent Hospital, Newport; a Governor of the Welsh National Memorial to the late King Edward ; owner of the Somerton garden suburb for the better housing of the working-classes ; entered the office of George Pyman & Company, West Hartlepool, 1865 ; built his first steamer the SS. Spray of West Hartlepool, 1873, which the following year effected the salvage of the derelict French Transatlantic steamer Amerique and her cargo, the most valuable salvage which had ever been effected up to that date ; commenced business at Cardiff and Newport in partnership with John William Pyman as steamship owner and coal exporter, 1874 ; purchased the Ffaldau Collieries, 1883 ; established Patent Fuel Works in France, 1902 ; purchased the Fleet of the London and Northern Steamship Company, 1916. *Recreations:* Collection of early printed books and MSS.; hunting; breeding pedigree shorthorns. *Heir: s.* Wilfrid Hood Watson, *b.* 23 July 1875. *Address:* St. Mary's Lodge, Newport, Mon.; Merthyr House, Cardiff; Catsash Farm and Kemeys Folly, Mon. *Clubs:* Devonshire ; Cardiff County ; Newport County.
(*Died 1 May 1921.*)

WATSON, Rev. Wentworth; *o. surv. s.* of late Hon. Richard Watson, J.P., Northants.; *b.* 1 March 1848 ; *m.* 1903, Eveleen Frances, *d.* of Rev. F. M. Stopford. *Educ.:* Eton ; Christ Church, Oxford ; M.A. Formerly Vicar of Monmouth ; of St. Thomas, Oxford ; and Abingdon, Berks. *Address:* Rockingham Castle, Northants. *T.A.:* Rockingham. *T.:* Rockingham 3. *Club:* Travellers'. (*Died 5 July 1925.*)

WATSON, Sir William, Kt., *cr.* 1897 ; J.P., D.L. City of Dublin; M.A. Dublin; Chairman and Managing Director City of Dublin Steam Packet Co. ; *s.* of late William Watson, J.P.; *b.* 28 April 1842 ; *m.* 1868, Janet (*d.* 1876), *d.* of Very Rev. H. B. Macartney Dean of Melbourne. *Address:* 25 Fitzwilliam Place, Dublin. *T.A.:* Watson, Dublin. *T.:* 1239. *Clubs:* National ; St. George's Yacht, Kingstown ; Sackville Street, Dublin.
(*Died 9 Mar. 1918.*)

WATSON, William, C.M.G. 1916 ; F.R.S. 1901 ; D.Sc.; Temp. Lt.-Col. ; Associate and Professor of Physics, Royal College of Science, London ; *b.* 1868. *Educ.:* King's College School ; Royal College of Science. Served European War (C.M.G.). *Publications:* Manual of Elementary Practical Physics ; A Text Book of Physics ; A Text Book of Practical Physics. *Address:* 7 Upper Cheyne Row, S.W. ; Royal College of Science, South Kensington, S.W. *Clubs:* Savile, Royal Automobile.
(*Died 3 Mar. 1919.*)

WATSON, Lt.-Col. William Walter Russell, C.B. 1916 ; C.M.G. 1919 ; V.D.; late 24th Batt., Australian Imperial Force; *b.* 19 May 1875 ; *m.* 1904, Minnie Sarah, *d.* of late Samuel Hordern, Sydney. Served S. Africa, 1900-1 (despatches, Queen's medal 6 clasps); European War, 1914-16 (despatches, C.B.). (*Died 30 June 1924.*)

WATT, Francis; *b.* Haddington, 20 Sep. 1849; *e. s.* of late James Watt, J.P., sometime Provost of Haddington ; *m.* 1895, Edith Mary, *d.* of H. Willis, Sittingbourne ; one *d. Educ.:* Edinburgh University (M.A. with honours); Heidelberg. Barrister-at-law (Gray's Inn, 1886, Middle Temple, 1898); one of the Examiners of the High Court since 1914 ; Deputy Librarian, Middle Temple,

WATSON, Ven. W. C. See page xxxi.

1916-19 (War time work). *Publications:* Life and Opinions of the Rt. Hon. John Bright, 1885; History of Scotland from Robert the Bruce to the Union, 1885; Picturesque Scotland, 1887; The Laws Lumber Room, 1895; 2nd ed. 1896; 2nd series, 1898; Terrors of the Law, 1902; Scotland of To-day (with T. F. Henderson), 3rd ed. 1913; Edinburgh and the Lothians, 2nd ed. 1912; Book of Edinburgh Anecdote, 1912; R.L.S., 2nd ed. 1913; cheap edition, 1918; Canterbury Pilgrims and their Ways, 1917; Our Inns of Court (with Sir D. Plunket Barton and Charles Benham), 1924, etc.; various articles. *Recreations:* Latin, walking. *Address:* 1A Middle Temple Lane, E.C.4. *T.A.:* 102 Temple.   *(Died 4 Oct. 1927.)*

WATT, Henry J., D.Phil.; Reader in Psychology in the University of Glasgow; *b.* Aberdeen, 18 July 1879; *m.* 1909, Nellie Smith (*d.* 1922), pianist, *g.d.* of Rear-Admiral Townsend Dance. *Educ.:* Aberdeen; Berlin; Würzburg; Leipzig. Lecturer on Psychophysiology in the University of Liverpool, 1907; Lecturer in Glasgow since 1908; Principal Lecturer in the Faculty of Arts, 1922; civil prisoner of war in Germany till 6 May 1915. *Publications:* Experimentelle Beiträge zu einer Theorie des Denkens, 1904; various papers in German Psychological Journals till 1907; numerous papers in the British Journal of Psychology, Proceedings of the Royal Society, Mind, Music and Letters, Psyche, etc.; Article Psychology in Hastings' Encyclopedia of Religion and Ethics, 1918; The Psychology of Sound, 1917; The Foundations of Music, 1919; The Functions of Intervals in Songs, British Journal of Psychology; Melody, Music and Letters; The Dimensions of the Labyrinth Correlated, Proceedings of the Royal Society, 1924. *Address:* Hillhead House, The University, Glasgow.   *(Died 1925.)*

WATT, James Crabb, Advocate, K.C., Scotland, 1903; *b.* Muchalls, 1853; *e. s.* of David Watt, Kinneff; *m.* Mary, *e. d.* of Alexander Mackenzie, Elgin; one *s.* one *d.* *Educ.:* Stonehaven; Edinburgh University. Advocate-Depute under the Coalition Government; Honorary Sheriff Substitute of Lanark, and Kincardineshires; Member of General Assembly for many years; began life as journalist, and was youngest editor in this country, at 18; holds record for sustained speed in shorthand; Member of Nexus Committee of International Shorthand Congress, London, 1887, and contributed largely to its printed proceedings; left journalism for law in youth, and has had large practice in teinds, church law, criminal cases, and jury work generally; reporter for 15 years for Scotland for Board of Trade R.P.C.; politician (C.) for forty years; contested Ross-shire, 1900, in absence of the candidate; selected candidate, 1906, when he contested this county; Banffshire, January 1910. *Publications:* Great Novelists; John Inglis, a Memoir; The Mearns of Old; Place-Names of Kincardine, 1914; editor of series of biographies; wrote one of the first articles on Criminal Appeal Courts (National Review, 1890), and many contributions to newspapers and magazines. *Recreations:* antiquities, archæology, golf. *Address:* 2 Heriot Row, Edinburgh. *T.:* 6268. *Clubs:* Scottish Conservative; Burgess Golfing Society.   *(Died 15 July 1917.)*

WATT, Samuel, C.B. 1920; C.B.E. 1923; retired; *b.* 6 April 1876; *s.* of W. D. Watt, Newry, Co. Down; *m.* Jessie Maud, *e. d.* of Joseph Cochrane, Coleraine, Co. Derry; one *s.* two *d.* *Educ.:* Trinity College, Dublin. Entered Civil Service by Class 1 Exam.; served in Public Record Office, Dublin; Local Government Board of Ireland; Chief Secretary's Office, Dublin, and Admiralty, Whitehall; Private Secretary to Rt. Hon. Edward Shortt, K.C., when Chief Secretary for Ireland, 1918, also to Rt. Hon. Ian Macpherson, K.C., M.P., Chief Secretary for Ireland, 1918-20. *Address:*

Ballinavalley, Sandown Road, Knock, Belfast. *T.:* Knock 533. *Club:* Ulster, Belfast.   *(Died 18 Nov. 1927.)*

WATTERSON, Hon. Henry; LL.D., D.C.L.; Vice-President Inter-State Perry Commission; fifty years Editor Louisville Courier Journal; retired; *b.* Washington City, D.C., 16 Feb. 1840; *o. s.* of Hon. Harvey Watterson; *m.* 1865, Rebecca, *e. d.* of Hon. Andrew Ewing; three *s.* two *d.* *Educ.:* chiefly by private tutors. Confederate Staff Officer and Chief of Scouts, 1861-65; member of Congress, 1875-77; member Democratic National Conventions, 1872-92; President of the Convention of 1876; Chairman of Platform Committee, 1880 and 1888; has repeatedly declined office; Chevalier Legion d'Honneur, France; and de la Couronne, Belgium. *Publications:* Oddities of Southern Life, 1881; History of War with Spain, 1898; The Compromises of Life, 1903; Marse Henry, Memoirs, 1919. *Recreations:* music, yachting, and outdoor sports. *Address:* Jeffersontown, Kentucky, U.S.A.   *(Died 22 Dec. 1921.)*

WATTS, Sir (Fenwick) Shadforth, Kt., *cr.* 1919; Chairman of the Shipping Federation; *b.* 1858; *s.* of Edmund H. Watts; *m.* Julia Hamilton, *d.* of late A. T. Macgowan. Late President of the Chamber of Shipping of the United Kingdom; principal Representative of Shipowners on the National Maritime Board. *Address:* 7 Whittington Avenue, E.C.   *(Died 25 April 1926.)*

WATTS, Colonel Sir Philip, K.C.B., *cr.* 1905; LL.D., D.Sc., F.R.S.; *s.* of John Watts of Southsea; *b.* 30 May 1846; *m.* 1875, Elise Isabelle, *d.* of Chevalier Gustave Simonau of Brussels; two *d.* *Educ.:* Kensington School of Naval Architecture. In the Constructive Department of the Admiralty until 1885; Chairman of the Federation of Shipbuilders; Naval Architect and Director of War Shipbuilding Department of Sir W. G. Armstrong, Whitworth & Co., Ltd., 1885-1901. Freemason; C.O. of 1st Northumberland R.G.A. Volunteers; later 1st Northumberland Brigade R.F.A. (T.); equipped and sent out the Elswick Battery to the Boer War, 1900-1; Director of Naval Construction, Admiralty, 1901-12; afterwards Adviser on Naval Construction to the Board of the Admiralty. *Address:* 4 Hans Crescent, S.W. *T.:* 1210 Kensington. *Clubs:* Athenæum, United Service.   *(Died 15 Mar. 1926.)*

WATTS, Colonel Sir William, K.C.B., *cr.* 1910; C.B. 1900; V.D. 1912; D.L.; J.P.; F.S.A.; late Lieut.-Colonel and Colonel commanding 3rd Battalion Welsh Regt.; raised and commanded the Cape Volunteer Rifles; Hon. Col. 1st C.B. King's Royal Rifle Corps; Colonel Commandant City of London Brigade of Military Cadets; raised and commanded in 1914 the 13th Batt. the Welsh Regt.; and in 1915 the 20th Batt. the Welsh Regt.; Knight of Grace Order of St. John of Jerusalem, 1900; Order of Mercy, 1918; *b.* 6 Feb. 1858; *s.* of late V. B. Watts, Melcombe Horsey, Dorchester; *m.* 1883, Emily Annie, *o. d.* of C. H. P. Flower. *Educ.:* Sherborne School. 3rd Batt. the Welsh Regt.; served South Africa, 1900-2 (despatches twice, Queen's and King's medals, C.B.); Commandant of Kenhardt-Prieska and Wynberg districts; Hon. Col. in Army; Deputy Provincial Grand Master of Dorsetshire Freemasons; Grand Superintendent of Royal Arch Masons of Dorset; Provincial Grand Master of Mark Masons of Dorset; Governor, Sherborne School; Vice-President, Society of Dorset Men in London; Governor, United Service College, Windsor; Chairman, Militia Club, 1907-10. *Address:* The Priory, Branksome Wood, Bournemouth, W. *Clubs:* Junior Army and Navy, Public Schools,

Royal Automobile, Bournemouth.
(*Died 4 Aug. 1922.*)

WATTS, William Marshall, D.Sc. (Lond.), B.Sc. (Vict.); *b.* 1844 ; *y. s.* of Rev. Isaac Watts; *m.* 1877 ; Ida, *y. d.* of D. Massey, founder of the Massey-Harris Co. of Toronto; one *d. Educ.:* the Owens College, Manchester; University of Heidelberg. Assistant to Prof. Roscoe at the Owens College, 1864-66 ; Assistant Prof. of Chemistry, University of Glasgow, 1866-68 ; First Science Master, Manchester Grammar School, 1868-72 ; First Science Master, Giggleswick School, 1872-1904. *Publications:* A School Flora ; Introduction to the Study of Spectrum Analysis ; The Index of Spectra. *Recreation:* spectroscopic research. *Address:* Shirley, Venner Road, Sydenham, S.E.
(*Died 13 Jan. 1919.*)

WATTS - DITCHFIELD, Rt. Rev. John Edwin; 1st Bishop of Chelmsford since 1914 ; Hon. M.A. Durham ; D.D. Lambeth ; Victoria University, Manchester, and London College of Divinity ; *b.* 17 Sep. 1861 ; *m.* 1892, Jennie, *d.* of late Thomas Lax Wardell ; one *d.* Ordained, 1891 ; Curate of St. Peter, Highgate, 1891-97 ; Founder of St. Peter's Men's Service, 1892 ; Member of Bethnal Green Board of Guardians since 1899 ; Select Preacher Cambridge University, 1909 and 1913 ; President Council of St. John's Hall, Durham ; Lecturer in Pastoral Theology, Cambridge University, 1912-13 ; C.E.M.S. delegate to Australia, 1912 ; Vicar of St. James the Less, Bethnal Green, 1897-1914 ; Chairman C.E.M.S. *Publications:* Fishers of Men, 1899 ; Liturgies for Men's Services, 1901 ; Here and Hereafter, 1911 ; The Church in Action, 1913 ; Reservation, 1917 ; The Church and Her Problems, 1920. *Address:* Bishopscourt, Chelmsford. *Clubs:* Athenæum, National. (*Died 14 July 1923.*)

WAUGH, Ven. Arthur Thornhill, Canon Residentiary of Ripon Cathedral since 1891 ; Master of the Ripon Hospitals since 1895 ; *b.* 23 Nov. 1842 ; *s.* of Rev. D. J. Waugh, Principal of the Winchester Diocesan Training College ; *m.* 1st, Harriette Margaret, *d.* of Thomas Butcher, of Hampstead ; 2nd, Ethel Maud, *d.* of Rev. W. Gibbon, Canon Residentiary of Ripon ; one *d. Educ.:* Christ's Hospital ; Jesus College, Cambridge (Scholar). Wrangler and 3rd Class Classics ; Head of Modern Department, Rossall ; Vicar of Elmstead, Essex, 1869-1873 ; St. Mary's, Brighton, 1873-95 ; Chaplain to Bishop Carpenter, 1884-1910 ; Archdeacon of Ripon, 1895-1905. *Publications:* occasional sermons and papers. *Recreations:* miscellaneous, active and sedentary. *Address:* Ripon. *M.:* AJ 1731. (*Died 20 Nov. 1923.*)

WAUHOPE, Colonel Robert Alexander, C.B. 1905 ; C.M.G. 1905 ; C.I.E. 1897 ; retired 1905 ; *b.* 14 April 1855 ; *s.* of Lieut.-Col. H. J. Wahab, formerly 94th Regiment. In 1911 resumed family name of Wauhope. Entered army, 1873 ; Major, 1892 ; Col. 1899 ; served Afghan War, 1878-80 (medal) ; Mahsood-Wuzeeree Expedition, 1881 ; Zhob Valley Expedition, 1884 ; Hazara Expedition, 1888 (despatches, medal with clasp) ; Hazara Expedition, 1891 (despatches, clasp) ; Izazai Field Force, 1892 ; Waziristan, 1894-95 (despatches twice, brevet of Lieut.-Col., clasp) ; Anglo-Russian Boundary Commission, Pamirs, 1895 ; Tirah Expeditionary Force, 1897-98 (medal with two clasps) ; H.M. Commissioner Aden Boundary Delimitation, 1902-4. *Address:* The Crescent, Alverstoke, Hants. *Club:* East India United Service.
(*Died 23 Jan. 1921.*)

WAY, Maj.-Gen. Nowell FitzUpton Sampson-, C.B.; late Col. commanding Royal Marines ; *b.* 1838 ; *s.* of late Holroyd Fitzwilliam Way ; *m.* 1st, 1871, Mary Anne Louisa (*d.* 1902), *d.* of late Lieut.-Colonel G. N. Prior ; 2nd, 1903, Lucy Emily (*d.* 1921), *widow* of G. L. Matthews.

1102

Entered Army, 1855 ; Maj.-Gen. 1895 ; served Soudan, 1885 (despatches, C.B., medal with two clasps, Khedive's star). *Address:* Henbury, Bristol. *Club:* Junior United Service.
(*Died 16 May 1926.*)

WAY, Rt. Hon. Sir Samuel James, 1st Bt., *cr.* 1899 ; P.C., 1897 ; Q.C. 1871 ; Chief Justice of South Australia since 1876 ; *b.* Portsmouth, 11 April 1836 ; *m.* Katharine Gollan (*d.* 1914), widow of W. A. S. Blue of Strathalbyn and Hahndorf, S.A., 1898. Attorney-General, 1875 ; Vice-Chancellor of Adelaide University, 1876-83 ; Chancellor since 1883 ; appointed first Lieut.-Governor of South Australia, 1891 ; has administered the government of South Australia ten times, besides frequent short periods of office during absences of the Governor ; became first Representative of Australasian Colonies on the Judicial Committee of Privy Council, 1897 ; Hon. D.C.L. Oxon. 1891 ; LL.D., Adelaide, 1892 ; Queen's Univ., Kingston, Canada, 1895 ; Hon. LL.D. Cantab. 1897 ; Melbourne, 1901. *Heir:* none. *Address:* Montefiore, North Adelaide, S. Australia. *Clubs:* Athenæum ; Melbourne ; Adelaide.
(*Died 10 Jan. 1916.*)

WAY, Captain William, R.N., M.V.O. 1903 ; *b.* 16 May 1847 ; *s.* of late William Way of Scheirstein, Nassau, Germany ; *m.* 1st 1889, Maria Chattock, *d.* of Doctor Shaw, Sutton Coldfield (*d.* 1891) ; one *d.* ; 2nd, 1898, Florence P. D., *o. c.* of late J. W. Foulkes of Sutton Lodge, West Molesley, Surrey. *Educ.:* Ryde Naval School, Isle of Wight ; Ormonde House. Entered Navy, 1862 ; served as navigating sub-Lieut. in Ashanti War, 1873-4 (medal) ; as navigating Lieut. in Egyptian War, 1888 (medal and Khedive's bronze star) ; operations in Eastern Soudan, 1884 (medal and clasp) ; Harbour Master at Bermuda Is., 1891-96 ; Staff Captain, 1900 ; retired as Captain, 1906. *Address:* 9 Nettlecombe Avenue, Southsea, Hants. *T.:* Post Office 3898. *Club:* Royal Albert Yacht, Southsea. (*Died 3 April 1927.*)

WAYMOUTH, Paymaster - Captain Frederick Richard, C.M.G. 1918 ; R.N. ; *b.* 1862 ; *s.* of Henry Waymouth, Plymouth ; *m.* 1890, Beatrice Lily, *d.* of Capt. Edwin Wise, R.N. ; two *d. Educ.:* privately. Served European War, 1914-19 (despatches) ; Legion of Honour ; Retired List, 1920. (*Died 9 Oct. 1927.*)

WAYNFORTH, Harry Morton, Assoc.M.Inst.C.E., M.I.M.E. ; Professor of Engineering, University of London, King's College ; *b.* 19 Dec. 1867 ; *o. s.* of late Henry Waynforth ; *m.* 1898, Florence Julia, *d.* of late J. Hutchings of Ramsgate ; three *s. Educ.:* Haberdashers' Schools ; Finsbury Technical College. Served apprenticeship with Messrs. Bennett and Son, Engineers, London ; Assistant at Finsbury Technical College, 1889 ; Demonstrator in Engineering, Mason College, Birmingham, 1891 ; Demonstrator in Engineering, 1896 ; Sub-Dean of the Faculty of Engineering at King's College. *Address:* 127 Rosendale Road, West Dulwich, S.E. *Club:* St. Stephen's.
(*Died 5 Nov. 1916.*)

WEAKLEY, Ernest, C.M.G. 1908 ; Commercial Attache, Constantinople, 1897-1914 ; *b.* 7 Jan. 1861 ; *o. s.* of late Rev. R. H. Weakley of Alexandria. *Address:* Foreign Office, S.W.
(*Died 23 Dec. 1923.*)

WEALE, W. H. James, Keeper of the National Art Library, South Kensington, 1890-97 ; Hon. Member of Royal Flemish Academy, 1887 ; Associate of the Royal Academy of Belgium, 1896 ; Hon. Member of Royal Academy of Fine Arts, Antwerp, 1901 ; Officer of Order of Leopold ; *b.* Marylebone, 8 Mar. 1832 ; *e. s.* of late James Weale and Susan Caroline Ellis Vesien ; *m.* Helena A. Walton ; four *s.* five *d. Educ.:* King's College, London. *Publications:* Belgium, Aix-la-Chapelle, and Cologne, an Archæological Guide-Book, 1859; Bruges et ses Environs, 1862 (4th ed. 1884); Mémoire sur la Restauration des Monuments publics en Belgique, 1862; Le Beffroi: Arts, Héraldique, Archéologie, 1863-1876; Hans Memlinc: a Notice of his Life and Works, 1865; La Flandre: Revue des Monuments d'Histoire et d'Antiquités, 1867-73; Chronica monasterii S. Andreae iuxta Brugas Ordinis S. Benedicti, 1868; Les Eglises du Diocese de Bruges: Doyenné de Dixmude, 1874; Descriptive Catalogue of Manuscripts and Printed Books exhibited at Albert Hall, 1885; Bibliographia liturgica, 1886; Some Account of an Illuminated Psalter for the Use of the Convent of S. Mary of the Virgins at Venice, 1887; Analecta liturgica, 1889; Gerard David, Painter and Illuminator: a Monograph, 1895; Hans Memlinc: Biography; Pictures at Bruges, 1901; Catalogue de Tableaux des XIVe., XVe., et XVIe. siècles exposés à Bruges, 1902; Hubert and John van Eyck, their life and work, 1907; Peintres Brugeois: L. Blondeel; Les Christus; Les Ryckx; Les Claeissins; Les Prevost, 1907-12. *Address:* 29 Crescent Grove, Clapham Common, S.W   (*Died 26 April 1917.*)

WEARDALE, 1st Baron (cr. 1905), of Stanhope, Co. Durham; **Philip James Stanhope**; *b.* 1847; *y. s.* of 5th Earl Stanhope and Emily Harriet, *d.* of Sir E. Kerrison, Bt.; *m.* 1877, Alexandra, *d.* of Count von Cancrine of the Baltic Provinces, *widow* of Count Tolstoy of Petrograd. Trustee of National Portrait Gallery; President of Inter - Parliamentary Union, 1906; formerly Lieut. R.N.; M.P. (L.) Wednesbury, 1886 - 92; Burnley, 1893 - 1900; Harboro' Div. of Leicestershire, 1904-5. *Heir:* none. *Address:* 3 Carlton Gardens, S.W.1. *T.:* Regent 3833; Weardale Manor, Brasted Chart, Kent. *Clubs:* St. James's, Turf, National Liberal.
       (*Died 1 Mar. 1923.*)

WEATHERALL, Col. Henry Burgess, C.B. 1902; 5th Batt. Royal Fusiliers. *Educ.:* Harrow. Served South Africa, 1901-1902 (despatches, Queen's medal, 5 clasps, C.B.). *Club:* Junior United Service.   (*Died 13 May 1917.*)

WEAVER, Mrs. Baillie (Gertrude) (G. Colmore), novelist; 6th *d.* of late John Thomson Renton, Bradstone Brook; *m.* 1st, the late Henry Arthur Colmore Dunn, B.A., a Barrister-at-law and author of Fencing in the All England Series, 1882; 2nd, 1901, Harold Baillie Weaver (*d.* 1926), Barrister. *Educ.:* school in Frankfort-on-Main; private teaching in Paris and London. *Publications:* Concerning Oliver Knox, 1888; A Conspiracy of Silence, 1889; A Living Epitaph, 1890; A Valley of Shadows, 1892; A Daughter of Music, 1894; Poems of Love and Life, 1896; Love for a Key, 1897; Points of View, 1898; The Strange Story of Hester Wynne, 1899; The Marble Face, 1900; A Ladder of Tears, 1904; The Angel and the Outcast, 1907; Priests of Progress, 1908; The Crimson Gate, 1910; Suffragette Sally, 1911; Mr. Jones and the Governess; The Life of Emily Davison: an Outline, 1913; Whispers, 1914; The Guest, 1917; The Thunderbolt, 1919; The Guardian, 1923; A Brother of the Shadow, 1926. *Address:* Eastward House, Wimbledon Common, S.W.19. *T.:* Wimbledon 2122. *M.:* PE 6604. *Clubs:* Writers', Pioneer.   (*Died 26 Nov. 1926.*)

WEB-GILBERT, Charles; sculptor; *b.* Talbot, Victoria, Australia, 1869; *m.;* two *s.* (twins). *Educ.:* Melbourne. Exhibitor at Royal Academy, Liverpool, etc.; work bought by the Felton Bequest for Melbourne National Gallery, and many private memorials in bronze and marble; Lieut. Australian Imperial Forces Commissioned by Australian Government to execute models of battlefields fought over by the Australian Forces; also executing the memorial to the 2nd Division at Mont St. Quentin, France, replica of which is to go to

Australian War Museum. *Works:* The Vintage Offering, 1897; The Wheel of Life; busts of Sir Thomas Gibson - Carmichael, Sir Edward Holroyd, L. A. Adamson, L. Abrahams, Sir Samuel Gillott Memorial at Melbourne, The Critic, bought by the President and Council of the Royal Academy out of funds of the Chantrey bequest for the Tate Gallery, 1917, etc. *Recreation:* sculpture.   (*Died 3 Oct. 1925.*)

WEBB, Sir Arthur Lewis, K.C.M.G., cr. 1912; C.M.G. 1902; M.I.C.E.; *b.* 27 Oct. 1860. *Educ.:* Royal Engineering College, Cooper's Hill. Public Works Department, India: Irrigation Branch, 1881 - 94; Irrigation Department, Egypt, 1894: Inspector - General of Irrigation, 1899; Director - General of Reservoirs, Egypt; Under - Secretary for Irrigation, 1906; Adviser to the Public Works Ministry, Egyptian Government, 1908. *Decorated* for services on Nile Reservoir; 1st Class Medjidieh (Grand Cordon); 2nd Class Osmanieh. *Address:* 143 Maida Vale, W.9. *T.:* Hampstead 7127. *Clubs:* Oriental; Turf, Cairo.   (*Died 15 Mar. 1921.*)

WEBB, Frederick William, C.M.G. 1894, J.P., F.R.S. (N.S.W. 1897); Clerk of the Legislative Assembly of New South Wales, 1888-1904; *b.* Sydney, N.S.W., 20 Feb. 1887; *o. s.* of late John Webb of H. M. Commissariat and Mary, *e. d.* of late Captain William Bell of the N.S.W. Royal Veteran Corps; *m.* 1st, Charlotte Elizabeth, *e. d.* of Stephen R. Hickson of Cork, 1866; 2nd, 1872, Emily, *y. d.* of late John Piper Mackenzie, official Assignee, Sydney; one *s.* one *d.* Clerk in Legislative Council Depart. (N.S.W.), 1851-53 (before responsible government); clerk, General Post Office, 1854-60; clerk in Legislative Assembly Department, 1860-87; elected by the National Australasian Federal Convention (Sydney) its secretary, 1891; assistant clerk, 1897. *Decorated:* for public services as Clerk of the Legislative Assembly, and as Secretary to Australasian Federation Convention in 1891; retired, 1904. *Recreations:* boating, fishing, shooting. *Address:* Livadia, Balgowlah, nr. Manly, New South Wales. (*Died 17 July 1919.*)

WEBB, Mary (Mrs. Henry Bertram Law Webb); authoress; *b.* Leighton, Cressage, Shropshire; *d.* of George Edward Meredith, schoolmaster, of Welsh ancestry, and Sarah Alice Scott, *d.* of an Edinburgh doctor of the clan of Sir Walter Scott; *m.* 1912, Henry Bertram Law Webb, schoolmaster, B.A. (Cantab.); no *c. Educ.:* chiefly at home; two years at 1 Albert Road, Southport. Began verse writing at ten; afterwards wrote fairy tales and stories; brought up in Shropshire; published verse and prose in various papers and magazines in England and America before coming to London in 1921; at present reviewing for The Bookman, and occasionally for The Spectator, English Review, Nation, and New Statesman; contributing articles to the Daily News and T.P.'s Weekly; poems have been included in various anthologies, and the authoress hopes to publish a collection of them this year; awarded the Femina Vie Heureuse Prize for the best English novel of 1924-25; no literary agent, representative, or secretary. *Publications:* The Golden Arrow, 1916; The Spring of Joy, 1917; Gone to Earth, 1917; The House in Dormer Forest, 1920; Seven for a Secret, 1922; Precious Bane, 1924; Armour Wherein he Trusted, 1926. *Recreations:* nature study, playgoing, social life. *Address:* c/o Society of Authors, 11 Gower Street, W.C.1.
       (*Died 8 Oct. 1927.*)

WEBB, Col. Walter George, C.B. 1898; *b.* 1888; *s.* of Rev. W. Webb, late Rector of Tixall, Staffs; *m.* 1864, 1st, Mary Anne, *d.* of late W. D. Webb of Elford, Staffs; 2nd, Jane Ann, *e. d.* of John Cheesman of Fence, Yorkshire; late Lieut.-Col. Commandant and Hon. Col. 3rd and 4th Battalions South Stafford

Regts. (retired 1898) ; J.P. Co. Stafford. *Address:* The Grange, Malvern. *(Died 7 Mar. 1919.)*

✓EBB, William Seward; President Rutland Railroad Co., St. Lawrence and Adirondack Railway Co., etc. ; *b.* New York, 31 Jan. 1851 ; *s.* of Gen. J. W. Webb ; *m.* Leila Osgood, *d.* of late W. H. Vanderbilt. *Educ.:* private tutors ; military school ; Columbia Coll. Studied medicine in Vienna, Paris, and Berlin, Coll. of Physicians and Surgeons, New York ; practised medicine for some time ; became member of W. S. Webb & Co., stockbrokers, but retired 1883 ; was President of various companies ; Republican Member of Protestant Episcopal Church. *Recreations:* travel, yachting, horse-breeding. *Address:* 680 Fifth Avenue, New York ; Shelburne Farms, Shelburne, Vermont, U.S.A. *(Died 29 Oct. 1926.)*

WEBB-PEPLOE, Rev. Hanmer William, Prebendary of St. Paul's Cathedral since 1893 ; Vicar of St. Paul's, Onslow Square, 1876 ; resigned March 1919 ; *b.* 1837 ; *y. s.* of Rev. J. B. Webb (afterwards Peploe) of Garnstone Castle, Herefordshire, and Mrs. J. B. Webb (afterwards Peploe), authoress of Naomi, etc. ; *m.* 1863, Frances Emily, *e. d.* of late Lord Justice Lush ; two *s.* one *d.* *Educ.:* Marlborough, 1848-51 ; Cheltenham College, 1851-56 ; Pembroke College, Camb., 1856-59. 1st class Poll Degree, 1859 ; Select Preacher before the University, 1896. As champion gymnast had a heavy fall at opening of second session in Camb., which compelled three years to be spent on his back ; all examinations had to be passed (both for degree and ordination) in a recumbent position ; reading was practically forbidden. *Publications:* I Follow After ; All One in Christ Jesus ; The Life of Privilege ; The Victorious Life ; Calls to Holiness ; Christ and His Church ; Within and Without ; Titles of Jehovah ; Remarkable Letters of St. Paul. *Recreations:* travelling and study. *Address:* 1 Evelyn Gardens, S.W.7. *Club:* National.

(Died 19 July 1923.)

WEBBER, William Downes, A.B., J.P. Queen's and Cork Counties ; resident Irish landowner ; *b.* 19 July 1834 ; *e. s.* of Rev. T. Webber, Rector of Castlemacadam, Co. Wicklow, owner of Leckfield and other estates in Co. Sligo, and Frances, *e. d.* and heiress of the Rev. Thomas Kelly of Kellavil, Queen's Co. ; *m.* 1873, Anna (*d.* 1909), Countess of Kingston. *Educ.:* Trinity College, Dublin. *Occupations:* agriculture, estate management. *Recreations:* foreign travelling and country pursuits. *Address:* Mitchelstown Castle, Co. Cork. *Clubs:* Kildare Street, Dublin ; Cork County.

(Died 22 Feb. 1924.)

WEBER, Sir Herman, Kt., *cr.* 1899 ; F.R.C.P. London ; Consulting Physician to the German Hospital, Dalston, and Royal National Hospital for Consumption, Ventnor ; *b.* 1823 ; *s.* of L. Weber, landed proprietor, and Maria Ruperti ; *m.* 1854, Matilda (*d.* 1911), *d.* of J. F. Gruning of Highbury Grove, N. ; two *s.* three *d.* *Educ.:* Marburg ; Bonn (M.D. 1848) ; Guy's Hospital. Fellow of the Royal Society of Medicine, and an Hon. or Corresp. Member of several societies on the Continent and in North America. *Publications:* various works on the treatment by climate and mineral waters, on the prevention and treatment of tuberculosis, prolongation of life, and on other medical and scientific subjects. *Recreation:* Greek numismatics. *Address:* 10 Grosvenor Street, W. *T.:* Mayfair 5165. *(Died 11 Nov. 1918.)*

WEBSTER, Col. Arthur George, C.B. 1884 ; *b.* Cheltenham, 9 Feb. 1837 ; 3rd *s.* of late James Webster, J.P., D.L., Hatherley Court, Cheltenham ; *m.* 1889, Mona, 3rd *d.* of late Col. Wyatt, C.B., 65th Regt. *Educ.:* Cheltenham Coll. Cavalry cornet, 1856 ; Indian Mutiny (mentioned in despatches, 1857-59, medal) ;

1104

Egypt, 1882, Tel-el-Kebir (4th class Osmanieh, despatches, medal with clasp) ; commanded 19th, Queen Alexandra's Own Royal Hussars, 1884, Soudan, Suakin, El-Teb, Tamai, Tokar (2 clasps, C.B.). *Recreations:* shooting, cycling. *Address:* Ravenswell, Banister's Park, Southampton. *Club:* Junior United Service. *(Died 17 May 1916.)*

WEBSTER, Sir Augustus Frederick Walpole Edward, 8th Bt., *cr.* 1703 ; Prov. Grand Master Prov. Hants and Isle of Wight ; Capt. 2nd Batt. Grenadier Guards (retired) ; *b.* 10 Feb. 1864 ; *e. s.* of 7th Bt. and Amelia Sophia, 2nd *d.* of C. F. A. Prosser-Hastings ; S. father 1886 ; *m.* Mabel (*d.* 1917), *o. d.* of late Henry Crossley, Aldborough Hall, Bedale, 1895 ; two *d.* *Educ.:* Eton. Lieut. of Regt. 1884. *Heir:* none. *Address:* Battle Abbey, Sussex ; Hildon, Broughton, Stockbridge. *Clubs:* Guards', Bachelors'.

(Died 13 Aug. 1923.)

WEBSTER, Sir Francis, Kt. *cr.* 1911 ; partner in firm of Francis Webster & Sons, Linen Manufacturers and Merchants, Arbroath and London ; *e. s.* of Francis Webster, Manufacturer, Arbroath ; *b.* 1 Sep. 1850 ; *m.* 1889, Annie (*d.* 1918), *d.* of Joseph Frain, M.D., of South Shields ; three *s.* one *d.* *Educ.:* Arbroath High School ; Edinburgh High School and University. *Address:* Ashbrook, Arbroath.

(Died 6 Feb. 1924.)

WEBSTER, Rev. Francis Scott; Rector of All Souls', Langham Place, W., since 1898 ; Prebendary of Brownswood in St. Paul's Cathedral since 1913 ; *s.* of late Rev. William Webster, M.A. ; *m., e. d.* of late Charles Handfield Jones, M.D., F.R.S., St. Mary's Hospital ; no *c.* *Educ.:* City of London School ; Pembroke College, Oxford (Open Mathematical Scholarship). First Class Mathematical Moderations, 1879 ; First Class Mathematical Greats, 1881 ; Curate of St. Aldate's, Oxford, 1882 ; Head of the Church Army Training Homes in Oxford and London, 1882-88 ; Rector of St. Thomas's, Birmingham, 1888-98 ; Hon. Secretary of the Religious Tract Society, 1909 ; Chairman of the Young Helpers' League of Dr. Barnardo's Homes, 1910 ; Chairman of the Candidates Committee of the Church Missionary Society, 1916. *Publications:* Spiritual Churchmanship ; Christians and Christians ; The Beauty of the Saviour ; The Secret of Holiness ; Elijah the Man of Prayer ; Jonah, Patriot and Revivalist ; Saving Truths of the Gospel ; Trusting and Triumphing ; Enemies Reconciled ; The Second Gospel. *Recreations:* mountaineering and golf. *Address:* All Souls' Rectory, 12 Weymouth Street, Portland Place, W.1. *T.:* Pad. 3420. *Clubs:* Chorley Wood Golf ; Woodhall Spa Golf. *(Died 2 Jan. 1920.)*

WEBSTER, Herbert Cayley, F.Z.S. ; Explorer, Naturalist, Author, Composer ; Captain late 7th Brigade, South Irish Division R.A. ; *b.* Waltham Abbey ; *s.* of late William Cayley Webster, J.P. ; *g.g.s.* of Sir William Cayley, Bart., R.N. ; *m.* 1901, *e. d.* of late Major Charles Fred. Campbell-Renton, J.P., D.L., 87th Royal Irish Fusiliers, of Mordington, Berwick-on-Tweed and Lamberton, Berwickshire. Served in Egypt, Medal and Star, Order of Medjidie (3rd class) ; travelled several years through the South Pacific in a yacht ; also many times round the world ; made two expeditions to New Guinea ; the first white man to penetrate through German New Guinea to the British boundary ; discovered the source of the River Minjim ; serious fights with natives ; discovered also the non-existence of the Bismark Range, 1896-99 ; discoverer of numerous new ornithological and entomological species, etc., now named after the discoverer in Natural History Museum ; late Master of Foxhounds ; founder of the Soldiers' and Sailors' Labour Brigade. *Publications:* Through New Guinea ;

A Quick Riddance ; Melanesia ; Other Cannibal Countries ; The Bay Tree, etc. ; contributor to Wide World, Strand, Black and White, Animal Life, The Living Races of Mankind ; and other magazines ; has also written several waltzes, songs, etc., the most prominent being The Rose of Memories, The Angel's Dream, Love's Desire, Why should we Part ?, March of the King's Colonials, etc. *Address :* 7 Sloane Street, Knightsbridge, S.W. *Club :* Junior Naval and Military.   (*Died 29 July 1917.*)

WEBSTER, Captain John Alexander, R.N. (retired) ; C.B.E. 1919 ; M.V.O. 1908 ; *b.* 23 Nov. 1874 ; *s.* of late John Webster, Barrister, and Jessie, *d.* of late John Miller of Leithen, Peeblesbire ; *m.* 1903, Lalia, *d.* of late Sir Wallace Graham, Halifax, N.S., Canada ; three *s.* one *d.* *Educ. :* H.M.S. Britannia. Midshipman, 1889 ; Sub - Lieut. 1893 ; Lieut. 1895 ; Commander, 1907 ; Captain, 1914 ; navigating officer of H.M.S. Indomitable during H.R.H. the Prince of Wales' voyage to Canada on the occasion of the Quebec Tercentenary (M.V.O.) ; served European War, 1914-16 (prom. Capt.) ; Director of Nav., Admiralty, 1917-19 ; retired list, 1922. *Address :* Braehead, Berkhamsted. *Clubs :* Caledonian, Royal Cruising.
    (*Died 24 June 1924.*)

WEBSTER, Robert Grant, LL.B., J.P. ; Captain R.F.A., 1915-17 ; *s.* of late R. Webster, Montrose ; *m.* Emily, *d.* of B. M. Jalland, Holderness House, East Yorks. ; one *s.* *Educ. :* Radley ; Trin. Coll., Camb. Barr. Inner Temple, 1869 ; M.P. (C.) St. Pancras, E., 1886-99. *Publications :* The Trade of the World ; The Law relating to Canals ; Japan, from the Old to the New, 1905 ; The Awakening of an Empire, 1917. *Address :* 18 Eccleston Square, S.W.1. *T. :* Victoria 2796. *Clubs :* Carlton, Hurlingham.
    (*Died 14 Jan. 1925.*)

WEDDERBURN, Lieut.-Col. Henry Scrymgeour, J.P., D.L. ; Hereditary Standard - bearer of Scotland ; *s.* of late H. Scrymgeour Wedderburn and Juliana, *y. d.* of Thomas Bradell of Coolmelagh, Co. Wexford ; *b.* 28 June 1872 ; *m.* 1901, Edith, *o. d.* of J. Moffat ; two *s.* one *d.* *Address :* Birkhill, Cupar, Fife, N.B.   (*Died 12 May 1924.*)

WEDDERBURN, Sir William, 10th and 4th Bt., *cr.* 1704 and 1803 ; J.P., D.L., and C.C. Gloucestershire ; *b.* Edinburgh, 25 Mar. 1838 ; 3rd *s.* of 2nd Bt. and Henrietta, *d.* of William Millburn ; *m.* Mary Blanche, *o. d.* of H. W. Hoskyns, North Perrott Manor, Somerset, 1878 ; two *d.* *Educ. :* Loretto School ; Edinburgh Univ. Took 3rd place in open competition for Indian Civil Service, 1859 ; served in Bombay C.S., 1860-87; acted as Judge of High Court, Bombay, and retired when acting Chief Secretary to the Government of Bombay ; president of Indian National Congress, 1889 and 1910 ; contested N. Ayrshire, 1892 ; member of Royal Commission on Indian Expenditure, 1895 ; chairman of Indian Parliamentary Committee ; M.P. (L.) Banffshire, 1893-1900. *Publications :* pamphlets on Criminal Procedure, Arbitration Courts, Agricultural Banks, Village Communities, and other matters affecting the condition of the Indian people; Memoir of Allan Octavian Hume, C.B. *Recreations :* gardening, golf, travelling. *Heir :* kinsman, John Andrew Wedderburn-Ogilvy [*b.* 16 Sept. 1866 ; *m.* 1909, Meta Aileen Odette, *e. d.* of Col. E. G. Grogan; three *d.* ; Major Scottish Horse Yeomanry. *Address :* Ruthven, Meigle, N.B.]. *Address :* 84 Palace Chambers, Westminster, S.W.; Meredith, Gloucester. *M. :* 4 B 8517. *Clubs :* Reform, National Liberal.
    (*Died 25 Jan. 1918.*)

WEDDERBURN-MAXWELL, Major James Andrew Colvile, J.P. ; *e. s.* of late Andrew Wedderburn-Maxwell and Joanna, *y. d.* of James Keir, M.D., Moscow ; *b.* 5 Feb. 1849 ; *m.* 1891, Helen Mary Godfrey, *d.* of late Rev.

Henry Godfrey Godfrey-Faussett-Osborne, of Hartlip Place, Kent ; three *s.* two *d.* *Educ. :* Trinity College, Glenalmond. Major, late 54th Regt., 3rd Punjab Infantry, Punjab Frontier Force, 2nd Queen's Own Bengal, and 38th Bengal Infantry ; retired 1889 ; served Jandola Expedition, 1880 (despatches) ; Burmese Campaign, 1886-87 (medal and clasp). *Address :* Glenlair, Dalbeattie.   (*Died 28 Dec. 1917.*)

WEDGWOOD, Major Cecil, D.S.O. 1902 ; Director Josiah Wedgwood & Sons, Ltd. ; first Mayor of Stoke-on-Trent ; *s.* of late Godfrey Wedgwood; late 4th Batt. N. Staffs. Rgt.; Hon. Major in army. Served South Africa, 1900 - 2 (despatches twice, medal with clasp, King's medal, 2 clasps, D.S.O.). *Address :* Hanley. Staffs.   (*Died July 1916.*)

WEDMORE, Sir Frederick, Kt., *cr.* 1912 ; author ; *b.* Richmond Hill, Clifton, 9 July 1844 ; *e. s.* of late Thomas Wedmore, J.P., Druid Stoke, near Bristol ; *m.* Martha, *y. d.* of late John Peele Clapham, J.P., of Burley Grange, Wharfedale, treasurer of County Courts ; one *d.* *Educ. :* Weston - super - Mare, Lausanne, and Paris. Hon. Fellow, Royal Society of Painter-Etchers ; has lectured or given Readings of verse and his own stories in the chief English cities, and at Harvard and Baltimore, and, as a Writer, has been specially an exponent in England of the art of France, from Nattier, Chardin and Latour, to Méryon, Boudin, Fantin, Ribot. *Publications :* his work in Fiction consists of Pastorals of France (1877), Renunciations, English Episodes, Orgeas and Miradou, with other short stories and imaginative pieces, and the novels, The Collapse of the Penitent and Brenda Walks On,—the latter of which—a study of the life of the Theatre—was written as lately as 1916. His Critical writing includes The Life of Balzac (Great Writers Series); Studies in English Art ; Méryon; Etching in England ; Whistler's Etchings ; Fine Prints ; On Books and Arts ; Whistler and Others ; Some of the Moderns, 1909 ; Etchings, 1911 ; Memories—a book of reminiscence, social and literary—1912. Held the post of chief art critic of the Standard for about thirty years ; he is a contributor to the Nineteenth Century : edited the English edition of Michel's Rembrandt, 2 vols. ; Turner and Ruskin, 2 vols. ; and with his daughter Millicent—who is the author of the volumes of poems, A Minstrel in the South and Chiefly of Heroes—he edited the Poems of the Love and Pride of England. *Recreations :* the theatre, collecting. *Address :* White Mill End, Sevenoaks. *Clubs :* Burlington, Fine Arts.   (*Died 25 Feb. 1921.*)

WEEDON, Hon. Sir Henry, Kt., *cr.* 1908; M.L.C.; J.P. ; Member Legislative Council of Victoria ; *b.* 16 March 1859 ; *m.* ; one *s.* *Educ. :* Melbourne. Elected City Corporation, 1899 ; Lord Mayor, 1905-1908 ; M.P. Melbourne East 1906-12 ; appointed and visited England as Commissioner for Franco - British Exhibition, 1908 ; Chairman of Victorian Commissioners, New Zealand Exhibition, 1906 ; Life Governor all leading Hospitals and Charitable Institutions ; Trustee and Treasurer, Victoria Public Library, Museums and Art Gallery ; Member of Faculty, Melbourne University, and of Australian Commonwealth . National War Museum ; President Royal Life Saving Society. etc. *Address :* Yarallah, South Yarra, Victoria. Australia.   (*Died 27 Mar. 1921.*)

WEGUELIN, John Reinhard, R.W.S. ; painter ; *b.* Sussex, 23 June 1849 ; *s.* of Rev. William Andrew Weguelin, Rector of South Stoke ; unmarried. *Educ. :* Cardinal Newman's Oratory School, Edgbaston, Birmingham. Underwriter at Lloyd's, 1870 - 73 ; in which year entered the Slade School under Professor Poynter, and afterwards Professor Legros. *Pictures :* The Labours of the Danaids; Herodias's Daughter : Roman Acrobat ; Bacchus and the

Choir of Nymphs; Cupid Bound; and many water-colours, etc. *Address:* Cleveland, Fairlight Road, Hastings.   (*Died 28 April 1927.*)

WEI YUK, Sir Boshan, Kt., *cr.* 1919; C.M.G. 1908; J.P.; Member of Legislative Council, Hong-Kong; *b.* 1849; *s.* of late Wei Kwong, banker; *m.* 1872, Yuk Hing, *e. d.* of Hon. Wong Shing, M.L.C., J.P., one of the founders of the Tung Wah Hospital, Hong-Kong. *Educ.:* Government Central School, Hong-Kong; Stonygate School, England; Dollar Institution, Scotland. Toured Europe, 1872; entered service of Chartered Mercantile Bank of India, London, and China (now the Mercantile Bank of India, Ltd.), Hong-Kong, of which his father was Compradore, 1872; Compradore since 1882; left the Bank in 1910, and since has carried on own business as exporter and importer; Permanent Committee-man, District Watch Committee, Hong-Kong, 1880; Chairman of the Tung Wah Hospital, 1881-83, 1888-90; originator of Railway Scheme in China, which failed on account of opposition of Chinese officials, 1890; one of the Founders, and permanent Committee-man, of the Po Leung Kuk (Home for Destitute Women and Children, and Women's Protection Society), 1893; unofficial Member of Legislative Council, Hong-Kong, representing the Chinese Community, since 1896; Member Standing Law Committee 1896-1917; Member of Public Works Committee; Member of Hong-Kong Univ. Court; Member of Prize Court; rendered much service in negotiations between Chinese and Hong-Kong Governments on various matters; decorated by Chinese Govt. with 3rd class Order of Chas-ho, in recognition of services rendered to Chinese people, 1912; decorated by King Gustav V. of Sweden with 1st class Order of Wasa, 1918; has also received several gold medals from Chinese Govt. from time to time. *Address:* Atack & Co.'s Building, Des Vœux Road, Hong-Kong. *T.A.:* Weiyuk, Hong-Kong. *T.:* 666.

WEIGALL, Henry, D.L., J.P.; Artist; *b.* 1829; *m.* 1866, Lady Rose (Sophia Mary) Fane (*d.* 1921), 2nd *d.* of 11th Earl of Westmorland. *Address:* Southwood, St. Lawrence, Ramsgate. *Club:* Athenæum.

    (*Died 4 Jan. 1925.*)

WEIGALL, Lady Rose (Sophia Mary); *b.* 1834; 2nd *d.* of 11th Earl of Westmorland; *m.* 1866, Henry Weigall; six *s.* one *d.* *Publication:* Correspondence of Lady Burghersh with the Duke of Wellington; Correspondence of Priscilla, Countess of Westmorland. *Address:* Southwood, St. Lawrence, Ramsgate.

    (*Died 14 Feb. 1921.*)

WEIGALL, Theyre à Beckett, LL.M., K.C. 1907; Barrister-at-law; *b.* Melbourne, 1860; *s.* of Theyre Weigall and Marian à Beckett, both of England; *m.* 1890, Anne S. H., *e. d.* of late Sir R. G. C. Hamilton, K.C.B., then Governor of Tasmania; one *s.* three *d.* *Educ.:* Church of England Grammar School, Melbourne; Trinity College, University of Melbourne. Barrister, Victoria, 1881; Acting Judge of Supreme Court since 1923. *Recreations:* tennis, cycling, golf (President of Lawn Tennis Association of Victoria). *Address:* Supreme Court, Melbourne, Victoria. *T.:* Windsor, Victoria 244. *Clubs:* Melbourne, Bohemians, Royal Melbourne Golf.

    (*Died June 1926.*)

WEIGHT, Rev. Thomas Joseph, Rector of Christian Malford, 1912-26; Hon. Canon of Bristol, 1901; *b.* 19 Oct. 1845; *s.* of Rev. George Weight, Vicar of St. George's, Wolverton; unmarried. *Educ.:* Elstree Hill; King's College, London; Hertford College, Oxford. B.A. and M.A. 1874; Deacon and Priest, 1875; Curate of Blakeney, 1875; Curate in Charge of Newnham-on-Severn, 1875; Vicar, 1881; Vicar of St. Barnabas', Bristol, 1890; Rural Dean of Bristol

1106

East, 1905; Senior Rural Dean of Bristol, 1909; Chief Secretary of Church Congress, 1903. *Address:* Highworth, Wilts.   (*Died 1 Dec. 1922.*)

WEIR, Lt.-Col. Donald Lord, D.S.O. 1916; M.C.; Leicestershire Regt.; *b.* 21 Sep. 1885. Served European War, 1914-18 (despatches twice, M.C., D.S.O. and bar, Serbian Order of Karageorge). *Address:* Deane House, Parkstone, Dorset.   (*Died 21 April 1921.*)

WEIR, Rt. Rev. Mgr. Peter John, Prelate of the Household of the Pope and Canon of Aberdeen (R.C.) Cathedral; *b.* Nether-Buckie, Banffs. 1831. *Educ.:* Blairs College, Aberdeen; Institution Poiloup, affiliated to Sorbonne (University); Vaugirard, Paris, and at Grand Séminaire de St. Sulpice, Paris; Incumbent of Fochabers, 1867. *Address:* Fochabers, N.B.   (*Died 10 Dec. 1917.*)

WEIR, Robert Fulton, M.D.; Professor of Surgery, College Physicians and Surgeons, Columbia University; Senior Surgeon, Roosevelt Hospital, New York; *b.* 16 Feb. 1838; *s.* of James Weir and Mary Anne Shapter; *m.* 1st, 1863, Maria Washington M'Pherson; one *d.*; 2nd, 1895, Mary Badgley Alden. *Educ.:* College of the City of New York. A.B. 1854; A.M. 1857; Corresponding Fellow Société de Chirurgie, Paris, 1892; Honorary F.R.C.S. 1900. Assist. Surg. U.S. Army, 1861-65; Surg. in Charge, U.S.A. General Hospital, Frederick, Md. (thanked in general orders); Surg. St. Luke's Hosp., N.Y., 1865-75; Surg. N.Y. Hosp. 1876-1900; Surgeon, Roosevelt Hospital, 1900-8; President American Surgical Association, 1900; President N.Y. Academy of Medicine, 1900; Chevalier Order of Boilvar. *Publications:* numerous (over one hundred) surgical papers in medical journals, principally on brain, appendical and gastric lesions. *Recreations:* travelling and horticulture. *Address:* 16 E. 96th Street, New York; Bar Harbor, Maine. *Clubs:* University, Century, New York.

    (*Died 6 Aug. 1927.*)

WEIR, Robert Stanley, K.C., D.C.L.; F.R.S.C.; Recorder of Montreal, 1899-1915; Licence Commissioner; *b.* Hamilton, Ontario, Nov. 1856; *s.* of late William Park Weir, Surveyor of Customs, Montreal; *m.* Margaret, *d.* of Alexander Douglas, Montreal. *Educ.:* McGill University, Montreal; called to Bar of P.Q., 1881; revised Charter of Montreal, 1899; Professor Jurisprudence and Liturgics, Congregational Coll. of British N. America, 1890-1904; Representative Fellow in Law, McGill University, since 1909; resumed practice of law, 1915; Elected Fellow Royal Society of Canada, 1923. *Publications:* Administration of the Old Régime; An Insolvency Manual; Bills of Exchange Act, 1890; The Civil Code of I.C.; The Code of Civil Procedure; The Education Act; The Municipal Code, and several Municipal Studies in University of Toronto series; author of O Canada, Canadian National Song; After Ypres and Other Verse, 1917; Poems, Early and Late, 1923. *Recreations:* music, golf; President Outremont Golf Club, 1901-7. *Address:* 96 The Boulevard, Westmount; Cedarhurst, Lake Memphremagog. *Clubs:* Outremont Kanawaki Golf; Reform, Montreal; Newport, Vt.

    (*Died Aug. 1926.*)

WELBY, Edward Montague Earle, Police and Stipendiary Magistrate for Sheffield, 1874-1915; *b.* 12 Nov. 1836; 4th *s.* of late Sir G. E. Welby-Gregory of Denton Hall, near Grantham; *m.* Sarah Elizabeth (*d.* 1909), *d.* of R. Everard, Fulney House, near Spalding, 1870; two *s.* two *d.* *Educ.:* Eton; C.C.C., Oxford. *Address:* Yew Lodge, Spalding, Lincolnshire.

    (*Died 25 Jan. 1926.*)

WELCH, Charles, F.S.A.; late Librarian, Guildhall Library; *b.* 21 July 1848; *s.* of Charles Welch, physician, of Hackney; *m.* 1872, Rose, *y. d.* of late John Jupp; four *s.* six *d.* *Educ.:*

City of London School, under Rev. Dr. Mortimer. Fellow of Library Association ; Member of Council of the Bibliographical Society ; late Member of Council of the Society of Antiquaries and of the Hakluyt Society ; Vice-President and late hon. sec. and hon. editor of London and Middlesex Archæological Society ; late Lecturer for London University Board for Extension of University Teaching ; formerly licensed Lay Reader, Diocese of London; Lecturer for L.C.C. to London teachers ; Past Master of Cutlers' Company ; member of Court of Paviors' Company ; Liveryman of Clockmakers' and Gardeners' Companies. *Publications :* Civic Lives in Dictionary of National Biography ; History of the Tower Bridge; Numismata Londinensia; Modern History of the City of London ; Mediæval London (jointly with Rev. Canon Benham); contributor to Victoria County Histories ; History of the Pewterers' Company ; History of the Paviors' Company ; Coat-armour of London Livery Companies ; History of the Cutlers' Company ; Illustrated Guide to Royal Exchange ; Catalogue of the Guildhall Museum ; editor of facsimile reproduction of Ogilby and Morgan's Map of London, 1677 ; Register of Freemen of City of London, temp. Hen. VIII. ; Churchwardens' Accounts of Allhallows, London Wall, 15th to 16th cent. Various contributions to learned societies, etc. *Recreations :* vocal music, especially choir and part singing, archæological investigations. *Address :* Montrose, 158 Bethune Road, Stamford Hill, N.16. *T. :* Dalston 2574. *Clubs :* John Carpenter, Colophon. *(Died 14 Jan. 1924.)*

WELCH, James, actor ; *b.* Liverpool, 6 Nov. 1865 ; *y. s.* of John Robert Welch, chartered accountant ; *m.* Audrey Ford. *Educ. :* Liverpool. Served articles to chartered accountant ; joined dramatic profession with Mr. Wilson Barrett at Globe Theatre, Dec. 1887 ; since then has played in most London theatres. *Club :* Eccentric. *(Died 11 April 1917.)*

WELD, Reginald Joseph ; *b.* 24 May 1842 ; 2nd *s.* of late Edward Joseph Weld and Ellen Caroline, *e. d.* of Sir Bourchier-Palk Wrey, 8th Bt. *Educ. :* Stonyhurst. *Heir :* *b.* Humphrey Joseph, *b.* 1854. *Address :* Lulworth Castle, Wareham, Dorset. *(Died 13 Aug. 1923.)*

WELD-BLUNDELL, Charles Joseph; *b.* 1845 ; *s.* of Thomas Weld, who succeeded to the Ince Blundell Estates in Lancashire in 1840, and assumed additional name of Blundell ; *m.* 1884, Charlotte Catherine Marcia *(d.* 1926), *e. d.* of Col. Hon. Charles Pierrepoint Lane-Fox, *b.* of Lord Conyers ; two *d. Educ. :* Stonyhurst College, Lancashire ; Christ Church, Oxford. Travelled widely with especial view to Natural History and Botany. After 3 years in Spanish America, where he made a special study of the question Scent *v.* Vision in Birds of Prey, he published a compendium of his arguments in favour of the latter view in the Times, Oct. 1872. In Bolivia he was entrusted with a special mission to report to Lord Clarendon as to the advisability of renewing diplomatic intercourse with that Republic, and held a commission to report upon and examine the country between the Vermejo and Pilcomayo Rivers, and the country of the Abas, from the Government of Melgarejo. At 40 marrying, and soon after succeeding to the Lancashire estates, he abandoned travel for art, politics, and journalism, lecturing on Tithes, writing for Dublin Review, Tablet, Liverpool Mercury, and Catholic Times, for which paper he wrote a series of Polemical Articles, afterwards published in book form, The Church of the Tithe. Contested Preston, 1885. Defeated at Preston, he was offered Chatham as a solatium by the Liberal Caucus ; but through his holding strong views against the then Liberal crusade against the Peers, and in

general against the Newcastle programme, was tabooed by the Liberal Caucus. Since when he has been mainly employed in developing his Lancashire estates, and after a protracted study of the foreign methods of forestry, has succeeded in clothing the bare sandhills of his coast between Southport and Formby Point with pines. He received his late Majesty in Coronation year at Lulworth Castle, the splendid home of his ancestors in Dorset. His Lancashire seat has a European reputation for its art treasures, which comprise by far the largest private collection of antique marbles in the country. *Address :* Ince Blundell Hall, near Liverpool. *Club :* Travellers'. *(Died 5 Aug. 1927.)*

WELDON, Colonel Sir Anthony Arthur, 6th Bt., *cr.* 1723 ; H.M.L. Co. Kildare; D.L. Queen's County and J.P. Queen's County and County Kildare ; C.V.O. 1911 ; D.S.O. 1900 ; State Steward and Chamberlain to Lord Lieutenant of Ireland since 1908 : Lt.-Col. Commanding the 4th Batt. Leinster Regt. (Royal Canadians) ; *b.* London, 1 March 1863 ; *e. s.* of 5th Bt. and Elizabeth, *d.* of late Col. Arthur Kennedy ; *m.* 1902, Winifred, *d.* of late Col. Varty Rogers of Broxmore Park, Romsey, and late of the Royal Dublin Fusiliers and H.M. Bodyguard of Gentlemen-at-Arms; three *s. Educ. :* Charterhouse ; Trin. Coll. Camb. (B.A. 1884). Vice-Chamberlain to Lord Lieutenant of Ireland (the Earl of Aberdeen), 1905. Joined 4th Batt. Leinster Regiment, 1885 ; served as special service officer with the Natal Field Force under Sir Redvers Buller, Boer War, 1899-1900 (despatches) ; A.D.C. to F.-M. Viscount Wolseley, Commander-in-Chief, 1895-1900. Owns 2800 acres. *Recreations :* shooting, fishing, hunting. *Heir :* *s.* Anthony Edward Wolseley Weldon, *b.* 1 Dec. 1902. *Address :* Kilmorony, Athy, Co. Kildare ; Rahinderry, Ballylinan, Queen's County, Ireland. *Clubs :* Bachelors'; Kildare Street, Dublin.
(Died 29 June 1917.)

WELDON, Major Francis Harry, D.S.O. 1900 ; the Derbyshire Regt., retired 1906 ; *e. s.* of Col. Thomas Weldon ; *b.* 24 Apr. 1869 ; *m.* 1902, Eveleen Campbell of Rivermount House, Pangbourne ; one *s.* one *d. Educ. :* Cheltenham. Entered army, 1890 ; Captain, 1896 ; served South Africa, 1899-1902 (despatches, Queen's medal, 3 clasps, King's medal, 2 clasps, D.S.O.). *Address :* Herondean, Pummersdale, Chichester. *Clubs :* Naval and Military, Sports. *(Died 8 April 1920.)*

WELDON, Sir William Henry, Kt. *cr.* 1919 ; C.V.O. 1902 ; F.S.A. ; Clarenceux King-of-Arms since 1911 ; *b.* 1837 ; *s.* of William Weldon of Bramley Hall, Yorks ; *m.* 1st Georgina *(d.* 1914), *e. d.* of Morgan Treherne of Gate House, Sussex ; 2nd, 1914, Annie, widow of Major Stanley Lowe, Whitehall, Churchstow, Devon. *Educ. :* Harrow. Late 18th Hussars ; Rouge Dragon, 1869 ; Windsor Herald, 1880 ; Norroy King of Arms, 1894 ; Registrar of the College of Arms, 1886-94 ; Secretary to Earl Marshal, 1904-11 ; acted as Deputy Garter at Coronation of King Edward VII. *Recreations :* boat-sailing and motor-boating. *Address :* College of Arms, Queen Victoria Street, E.C. ; Orchard, Shiplake, Oxon. *Clubs :* Army and Navy, Garrick. *(Died 25 Aug. 1919.)*

WELFORD, Richard, M.A., J.P.; *b.* Upper Holloway, Middlesex, 29 May 1836 ; *m.* Minnie *(d.* 1903), *d.* of late Thos. Deverell of Hackney ; two *s.* one *d.* Journalist, 1854-61 ; Secretary and Managing Director Tyne Steam Shipping Company, Limited, 1864-1904 ; Foreign Office Passport Agent, 1872-1909 ; Vice-Chairman of Tyne-Tees Shipping Co.; Director of Free Trade Wharf Co.; Hon. M.A., Dunelm., 1897 ; a Vice-president of the Surtees Society, and Newcastle Society of Antiquaries ; Member of the Northumb. History Committee ; a

Governor of the Armstrong College, and of the Newcastle School for the Blind ; one of the Visiting Justices for Co. Northumb. *Publications:* History of Gosforth, 1879 ; History of St. Nicholas' Cathedral, Newcastle, 1880 ; Pictures of Tyneside Sixty Years Ago, 1881 ; History of Newcastle and Gateshead, 3 vols. 1885 ; Men of Mark 'Twixt Tyne and Tweed, 3 vols. 1895 ; Royalist Compositions in Durham and Northumb. (Surtees Society, vol. cxi.), 1905 ; Newcastle Typography and Bibliography, from 1639 to 1800 ; Local Muniments, 5 Series in Archæologia Æliana. *Recreation:* gardening. *Address:* Thornfield, Gosforth, Newcastle. *T.A.:* Welford, Newcastle. *T.:* 54 Gosforth, Nat. *Club:* Newcastle Liberal.
(Died 20 June 1919.)

WELLER-POLEY, Thomas ; J.P., Sussex ; *b.* 8 Nov. 1850 ; 2nd *s.* of J. G. Weller-Poley of Boxted Hall, Suffolk ; *m.* 1878. Eleanor Mary, *o. surv. c.* of late J. J. Johnson, Q.C., of West Broyle, Chichester ; one *s. Educ.:* Eton ; Merton College, Oxford, M.A. Called to Bar, Lincoln's Inn, 1878. *Recreations:* shooting and fishing. *Address:* West Broyle, Chichester. *T.:* Lavant 11. *Club:* United University.
(Died 29 Dec. 1924.)

WELLS, Arthur Collings, J.P., C.C. Hertfordshire ; *b.* 1857 ; 6th *s.* of late Joseph Wells of Broomfield, Essex ; *m.* ; two *s.* two *d.* *Educ.:* Repton. *Recreations:* hunting and shooting. *Address:* Caddington Hall, Hertfordshire. *Club:* Junior Carlton. *(Died 11 May 1922.)*

WELLS, Prof. Charles, M.A. Oxon. ; Ph.D. Leipzig ; Oriental Translator to the Foreign Office since 1892 ; Professor of Turkish, King's College, London, 1889-1916 ; formerly Lecturer on Turkish at the University of Oxford ; *b.* London ; *s.* of J. W. Wells ; *m.* Emma Chardon, *d.* of Imperial " Rentmeister " Louis Chardon ; two *d. Educ.:* King's Coll. London (Oriental Dept.). Turkish Prizeman, King's Coll. London, 1860 ; special correspondent of Daily Telegraph in the Schleswig-Holstein War, 1864 ; Professor of English at Imperial Naval Coll. Constantinople, 1870-74 ; Private Secretary to General Kemball on Turco-Persian Frontier Commission, 1875, and in Turco-Servian War, 1876. *Publications:* " Ilm Tedbir-i-Mulk," an essay on Political Economy in Turkish, 1860 ; Mehemet the Kurd, and other Tales from Eastern Sources, 1865 ; A Practical Grammar of the Turkish Language, 1880 ; a revised and enlarged edition of Redhouse's Turkish Dictionary, 1880 ; The Literature of the Turks, 1890. *Recreation:* philology. *Address:* Emmaburg, Portslade Station, Brighton ; King's College, London.
(Died 5 Oct. 1917.)

WELLS, Eugene ; J.P. for Suffolk ; 3rd *s.* of Joseph Wells, Broomfield, Essex ; *m.* Gertrude, *d.* of Duncan Campbell of Toronto, Canada. *Recreations:* hunting, shooting, golf ; M.F.H. Suffolk, 1898-1903 ; Master Suffolk Staghounds, 1904-6. *Address:* Buxhall Vale, near Stowmarket, Suffolk. *T.A.:* Great Finborough. *Club:* Junior Carlton. *(Died 21 June 1925.)*

WELLS, Rev. James, M.A., D.D., sometime Moderator of United Free Church of Scotland ; *b.* 11 June 1838 ; *s.* of David Wells, farmer, Dumfriesshire ; *m.* 1867, Janet Finlay Simpson, Bathgate ; two *s.* two *d. Educ.:* Torthorwald School ; Dumfries Academy ; Edinburgh and Erlangen Universities. Minister in Glasgow of Wynd Church, Barony Free Church, and Pollokshields West Church ; deputy to the Presbyterian Churches in United States and Canada, and to missions in India, Africa, and Palestine. *Publications:* Life of Dr. Stewart, of Lovedale ; Life of Dr. Hood Wilson ; Travel-Pictures from Palestine ; Rescuers and Rescued ; Christ in the Present Age ; Christ and the Heroes of Heathendom ; Bible Echoes ; The Parables of Jesus ; Bible Images ; Bible Children ; The Child's

Prayer, etc. *Recreations:* Travel and mountaineering. *Address:* Pollokshields, Glasgow. *T.:* Queen's Park 1226. *(Died Feb. 1924.)*

WELLS, Captain John Stanhope Collings, D.S.O. 1917 ; Acting Lt.-Col. 4th Batt. Bedfordshire Regt. ; *b.* 1880 ; *e. s.* of A. Collings Wells, J.P., Caddington Hall, Herts ; unmarried. Served European War, 1914-17 (D.S.O.). *Address:* Caddington Hall, Herts. *Club:* Junior United Service.
(Died 27 Mar. 1918.)

WELLS, Sidney Herbert, C.B.E. 1919 ; Director-General of Department of Technical, Industrial, and Commercial Education, Egypt, since 1907 ; *b.* Cottenham, Cambs, 10 Aug. 1865 ; 2nd *s.* of late Rev. J. C. Wells, Baptist Minister ; *m.* 1st, 1890, Mary Elizabeth (*d.* 1907), *d.* of late George Mathew, Worsted Lodge, Camb. ; two *d.* ; 2nd, 1908, Florence Amelia, *y. d.* of late George Mathew. *Educ.:* private schools ; Birkbeck and King's Colleges, London. Educated for Engineering ; Whitworth Scholarship, 1885 ; founded and for five sessions Chairman of Institution of Junior Engineers, 1889 ; Assistant and Form Master, Dulwich College, Engineering and Science Side, 1889 ; Senior Assistant Engineering Dept. of Leeds University, 1891 ; First Principal of Battersea Polytechnic, 1893 ; is an Associate Member of the Institution of Civil Engineers ; original member of Faculty of Engineering of London University ; Secretary of Board of Studies, 1903-5 ; of Faculty, 1905 ; Member of Incorporated Association of Headmasters and Member of Council 1904-6 ; Member of Council of Association of Technical Institutions, 1894 ; Hon. Secretary, 1903-7 ; Member of Examinations Board of City and Guilds Inst. 1903, of Teachers' Registration Council, 1904, and of Consultative Committee of Board of Education, 1904 ; visited Egypt to report on technical education, 1906. Holds 2nd class Medjidieh and 2nd class Nile Orders ; mentioned in General Allenby's despatches ; was Vice-Chairman of Egyptian Commission of Commerce and Industry, 1916-18 ; Director of Civilian Employment for E.E.F., 1917-19. *Publications:* text-books on Engineering, Drawing, and Design, 2 vols., and on Practical Mechanics. *Recreations:* riding, golf, and gardening. *Address:* Department of Technical Education, Cairo. *T.A.:* Techedu, Cairo. *Clubs:* Royal Societies ; Turf, Cairo. *(Died 28 Mar. 1923.)*

WELLS, William Page Atkinson ; landscape painter ; *b.* Glasgow, 1872 ; *s.* of Andrew Wells, decorator and poet ; *m.* 1897 ; two *s. Educ.:* Glasgow High School. Lived in Glasgow until 1885 ; travelled with parents to Australia ; lived both in Sydney and Melbourne for five years ; returned to England, studied at the Slade School under Professor Legros, also under MM. Bougereau and Ferrier at Paris for a number of years ; returned again to England and exhibited first pictures at the Institute of Painters in Oil, Piccadilly ; worked for some years in North Lancashire, then for ten years settled in the Isle of Man ; after the war migrated to Devonshire ; is now living and working in Appledore, North Devon ; has exhibited in most of the important British and Continental Galleries ; pictures acquired by the Scottish Modern Arts Society and Oldham, Glasgow, and Belfast Corporations and Birkenhead. *Recreations:* various. *Address:* 29 Irsha Street, Appledore, N. Devon. *Clubs:* Glasgow Art, Scottish Automobile, Glasgow ; Ellen Vannin, Douglas. *(Died 1923.)*

WELSH, Elizabeth, Mistress of Girton Coll. Cambridge, 1885-1903. *Address:* 55 Morningside Park, Edinburgh. *Club:* University for Ladies.
(Died 13 Feb. 1921.)

WELSH, Rt. Rev. John Francis, D.D. ; Bishop of Trinidad since 1904 ; *b.* Huddersfield ; *y. s.* of Robert Welsh of Tweedsmuir, Peeblesshire, and Huddersfield ; *m.* 1882, Jane, *e. d.* of Matthew Brown of Scaurbank, Arthuret, J.P. for County of Cumberland. *Educ. :* Christ Church, Oxford (B.A. 1881; M.A. 1886) ; D.D. (hon. causa) 1904. Deacon, 1881 ; Priest, 1882 ; Curate of St. James, Whitehaven, 1881-83 ; Lecturer of St. Bees' Theological Coll. 1883-86 ; Principal of Warminster Missionary Coll. 1887-1904. *Recreations:* music, wellknown chess-player ; was Pres. of Oxford Univ. Club. *Address:* Port - of - Spain, Trinidad. W.I. *T.A. :* Bishop, Port-of-Spain. *T. :* 499. *Club:* West Indian. *(Died 21 July 1916.)*

WENDELL, Barrett, Litt. D. Columbia and Harvard ; Hon. Dr., Strasbourg : Prof. of English at Harvard College, 1898 ; Prof. Emeritus, 1917 ; Clark Lecturer, Trinity College, Cambridge, 1902 ; Lecturer at the Sorbonne and other French universities, 1904; Fellow American Academy of Arts and Letters, 1916 ; *b.* Boston, 23 Aug. 1855 ; *s.* of Jacob and Mary Bertodi (Barrett) Wendell ; *m.* 1880, Edith, *d.* of W. W. Greenough of Boston ; two *s.* two *d. Educ. :* Harvard Coll. A.B. 1877. Student of law, 1877-80 ; Instructor in English, Harvard Coll. 1880-88 ; Assis. Prof. 1888-98. *Publications:* The Duchess Emilia, 1885 ; Rankell's Remains, 1887 ; English Composition, 1891 ; Cotton Mather, 1891 ; Stelligeri, and other Essays concerning America, 1893 ; William Shakspere, 1894 : A Literary History of America, 1900 ; Ralegh in Guiana, etc., 1902 ; The Temper of the Seventeenth Century in English Literature, 1904 ; Liberty, Union, and Democracy ; the National Ideals of America, 1906 ; The France of To-Day, 1907 ; The Privileged Classes, 1908 ; The Mystery of Education, 1909 ; The Traditions of European Literature (from Homer to Dante), 1920. *Address:* 358 Marlborough Street, Boston. *T.A. :* Bwendle, Boston. *T. :* 305 Back Bay. *Clubs :* Somerset and Tavern, Boston ; Century, New York. *(Died 8 Feb. 1921.)*

WENDEN, Henry Charles Edward, C.I.E. 1903 ; M.Inst.C.E. ; *e. s.* of late Henry Wenden, of Barnes, Surrey ; *m.* 1881, Ada Henrietta, *y. d.* of late Major Edward Simpson, 2nd Bombay Cavalry. Engaged on Indian railways, 1859 - 1906, when he retired. *Address:* Summerhill, Horsell, near Woking, Surrey. *Club :* East India United Service. *(Died 31 Jan. 1919.)*

WENLOCK, 4th Baron, *cr.* 1839 ; **Richard Thompson Lawley,** C.B. 1902 ; Bt. 1641 ; *b.* 21 Aug. 1856 ; *s.* of 2nd Baron and Elizabeth, *d.* of 2nd Marquis of Westminster ; *S.* brother 1912 ; *m.* 1909, Rhoda Edith, 2nd *d.* of Rev. Canon Knox - Little, Worcester. Entered army, 1876 ; Lieut.-Col. 1899 : Col. 1903 ; served Nile Expedition, 1884-85 (medal with clasp and Khedive's star) ; South Africa, 1901 - 2 (despatches, medal with five clasps). Owns about 3500 acres. *Heir:* b. Rev. Hon. Algernon G. Lawley. *Address:* Monkhopton, Bridgnorth. *(Died 25 July 1918.)*

WENTWORTH, Baroness (*cr.* 1529), **Ada Mary Milbanke,** *b.* 26 Feb. 1871 ; *o. d.* of 2nd Earl of Lovelace, and Fannie, 3rd *d.* of late Rev. George Heriot, of Fellow Hills, Berwick. *Heir-pres. :* aunt, Lady Anne Blunt. *Address:* White Heather, Sunninghill, Ascot. *(Died 18 June 1917.)*

WENTWORTH, Baroness, *cr.* 1529 ; **Anne Isabella Noel Blunt,** *b.* 1837 ; *d.* of 1st Earl of Lovelace. *S.* niece, 1917 ; *m.* 1869, Wilfred S. Blunt. *Heir. : o. d.* Hon. Mrs. N. S. Lytton. *Address:* Crabbet Park, Three Bridges, Sussex *(Died 15 Dec. 1917.)*

WERE, Major Harry Harris, D.S.O. 1917 ; late East Lancs Regt. ; *b.* 1865 ; *y. s.* of Nicholas Were of Wellington, Somerset ; *m.* 1890, Kathleen, *y. d.* of late Stephen Creagh Sandes of Sallow Glen, Tarbert, Co. Kerry ; no *c. Educ. :*

Kelly College, Tavistock ; Sandhurst. Joined E. Lancashire Regt. 1885 ; retired, 1913 ; served European War, 1916-17 (despatches twice). *Recreations:* shooting and golf. *Address:* c/o Lloyds Bank, Ltd., 6 Pall Mall. S.W.1. *Club:* United Service. *(Died 26 Dec. 1925.)*

WERNER, Professor Alfred; Nobel Prize for Chemistry, 1913 ; Professor of Chemistry at Zurich University ; *b.* Mulhausen, 12 Dec. 1866 ; *m.* 1894, Emma Giesker ; one *s.* one *d. Address:* Freie Strasse 111., Zurich, V., Switzerland.

WERTHEIMER, Professor Julius, D.Sc., B.A., F.I.C., F.C.S. ; Principal of the Merchant Venturers' Technical College, Bristol, since 1890 ; also Professor of Applied Chemistry and Dean of the Faculty of Engineering in the University of Bristol since 1909 ; *b.* Birmingham ; *e. s.* of late Maurice Wertheimer ; *m.* Katharine Eastwood, *o. d.* of late John Eastwood, of Newlaithes Hall, Yorks. *Educ. :* High School of the Liverpool Institute ; University College, Liverpool ; Owens College, Manchester. Late Exhibitioner of the University of London ; Fellow of the Physical Society ; Head Master of the Leeds School of Science and Technology, 1887-90 ; Hon. Secretary of the Association of Technical Institutions, 1893-1903; Chairman of Council, 1904 ; Président d'honneur du Cercle français de Bristol, 1905 - 16 ; Officier d'Académie (de France), 1906; Member of the Council and Senate of the University of Bristol, 1909 ; D.Sc. honoris causa, Bristol, 1911 ; Member of the Court, University of Sheffield, 1912 ; Member of the Teachers' Registration Council, 1912 ; Chairman of the Experience Committee of the T.R.C., 1914 ; Major, Merchant Venturers' Cadet Corps, 1915-19 ; organized W. of England Industrial Reserve for the production of munitions, 1915 ; Member of Council of Engineering Training Organisation and of W. of England (Joint) Disablement Committee, 1917 ; Member Education Committees of the Gloucestershire County Council, Bristol City Council, and British Science Guild ; late Member of Standing Committee of Convocation of University of London ; late Examiner for London County Council Scholarships ; Chairman of Conference of British Navigation Schools, 1918; Chairman, Fairfield Secondary School Committee, 1919. *Publications:* articles in the Nineteenth Century, The Times, Nature, etc. ; Text - Books on Chemistry ; editor of Series of Text-books of Technology ; Experiments with Waterfinders, etc. *Recreations:* golf, motoring. *Address:* 11 The Paragon, Clifton, Bristol ; *T.A.:* Merchants' College, Bristol ; *T. :* Bristol 407 and 1682. *Clubs:* University of London ; Clifton ; Constitutional, Bristol and Clifton Golf, Bristol Rotary. *(Died 9 Aug. 1924.)*

WESBROOK, F. F., President of the University of British Columbia, 1913 ; of American Public Health Association, 1905 ; Member Association of American Physicians; Fellow Royal Sanitary Institute ; Fellow of Royal Society of Canada ; of American Association for Advancement of Science ; Canadian Public Health Association; American Physiological Society ; Society of American Bacteriologists ; Pathological Society of Great Britain and Ireland ; Pathological Section of Royal Society of Medicine, London ; American Medical Association ; National Association for the Prevention and Relief of Tuberculosis, and others ; *b.* 12 July 1868 ; *s.* of Henry Shaver Wesbrook ; *m.* 1896, Annie, *d.* of late Chief Justice Sir Thomas W. Taylor, Winnipeg; one *d. Educ. :* University of Manitoba (B.A. 1887 ; M.A. 1890 ; M.D., C.M. 1890 ; LL.D. 1913); LL.D. Toronto, 1915 ; Alberta, 1915 ; University of California, 1918. John Lucan Walker student in Pathology, Univ.

WELSH, Rev. Thomas. See page xxxi.

of Camb. 1893-95; late Professor of Pathology, University of Manitoba; Dean, College of Medicine and Surgery, 1906, and Professor of Public Health and Bacteriology, University of Minnesota; Director of Minnesota State Board of Health Laboratories, 1896-1911; Member of Minnesota State Board of Health, 1896-99 and 1911-12; President Section on State and Municipal Hygiene, International Congress of Hygiene and Demography, 1912; Member Advisory Board, Hygienic Laboratory, U.S. Public Health Service, 1904-13. *Publications:* numerous technical and educational papers and reports. *Address:* The University of British Columbia, Vancouver, B.C. *Clubs:* Vancouver, University, Jericho Country, Union of B.C.. American, Vancouver.   (*Died Oct. 1918.*)

WESSELS, Hon. Sir Cornelius Hermanus, Kt., *cr.* 1920; Commissioner of Public Works, Lands, etc., O.R.C., since 1907; *b.* Wynberg, 26 April 1851; *s.* of John H. Wessels. *Educ.:* privately. Member of Volksraad for Boshof, 1885; Chairman for 2 years; represented Orange Free State in England as one of the Peace Commissioners. *Address:* 52 Aliwal Street, Bloemfontein, O.R.C.   *Club:* Bloemfontein.   (*Died Mar. 1924.*)

WEST, Rt. Hon. Sir Algernon, P.C., G.C.B., *cr.* 1902; late Alderman L.L.C.; Director of Northern Assurance, and Member of the Council of Foreign Bond-holders; *b.* 4 April 1832; 3rd *s.* of M. J. West and Maria, 3rd *d.* of 2nd Earl of Orford; *m.* Mary, *d.* of Capt. Hon. George Barrington, 1858 (*d.* 1894); three *s.* one *d.* *Educ.:* Eton; Christ Church, Oxford. Was a clerk in the Admiralty; assistant secretary to Sir C. Wood and Duke of Somerset; secretary to Sir C. Wood at India Office, and Mr. Gladstone when Prime Minister; Chairman of Board of Inland Revenue; served on Prison Commission, and was Vice-Chairman of the Licensing Commission. *Publications:* Recollections, 1899; Memoir of Sir Henry Keppel, 1905; One City and Many Men, 1908; Contemporary Portraits: Men of My Day in Public Life, 1920. *Address:* 14 Manchester Square, W.1.   *T.:* 3623 Paddington.   *Club:* Brooks's.   (*Died 21 Mar. 1921.*)

WEST, Charles Henry, C.I.E. 1903; *b.* 20 April 1859; *s.* of late Charles Henry West, Merchant in the Punjab; *m.* 1888, Agnes Lingard, *d.* of late Charles Murphy, Survey of India Department; one *s.* one *d.* Joined the service in 1876; served in Civil Departments of Punjab until 1880; became Personal Assistant to A. G. India, 1890, and Assistant Secretary to Government of India, Army Dept., 1906; served during the Burmah War, 1886-87 (medal with clasp); *Address:* 79 Harcourt Terrace, S.W.   (*Died 15 May 1923.*)

WEST, Prof. George Stephen, M.A., D.Sc., F.I.S., A.R.C.S.; Mason Professor of

1110

Botany, Birmingham University, since 1909; *b.* Bradford, 1876; *m.* 1906. *Educ.:* Bradford Technical College; Royal College of Science, London; St. John's Coll. Cambridge (Scholar; Hutchinson Research Student). 1st class in Natural Science Tripos, Part I. 1897; 1st class, Part II. 1898; obtained the Forbes medal and prize at R.C. Science. London, 1894; demonstrating in Biology at Cambridge, 1899; Prof. of Natural History, Royal Agricultural Coll. Cirencester, 1899-1906; Lecturer in Botany, Birmingham University, 1906-9. *Publications:* various papers on the Anatomical and Histological Characters of Poisonous Snakes, 1895-1900; Freshwater Rhizopods and Heliozoa, 1901-4, etc. ; A Treatise on the British Freshwater Algæ, 1904; various systematic and œcological papers on Algæ dating from 1899; joint-author (with late W. West, F.L.S.) of over twenty publications on Freshwater Algæ and Plankton from all parts of the world; and A Monograph of the British Desmidiaceæ, vol. i. 1904, vol. ii. 1906, vol. iii. 1908, vol. iv. 1911; Cambridge Botanical Handbooks. Algæ, vol. i. 1916. *Recreations:* golf, gardening. *Address:* 13 Pakenham Road, Edgbaston, Birmingham.   (*Died 7 Aug. 1919.*)

WEST, John Henry Rickard, I.S.O. 1908; *b.* 1846; late Assistant-Controller, Savings Bank Department, G.P.O. *Address:* Carlyle, Calton Road, Dulwich Village, S.E.   *Club:* Constitutional.   (*Died 27 Mar. 1920.*)

WEST, Samuel, M.A., M.D., Oxon.; F.R.C.P., London; Consulting Physician St. Bartholomew's Hospital; King George Hospital; Consulting Physician, Royal Free Hospital and New Hospital for Women; Member of the Governing Body of Westminster School and a Busby Trustee; *b.* 1848; *s.* of John West, Deputy Insp.-General of Mails, G.P.O.; *m.* Margaret Nanny, *d.* of Sir Edward Frankland, K.C.B., F.R.S., D.C.L., etc.; three *s.* three *d.* *Educ.:* Westminster School (Queen's Scholar); Christ Church, Oxford (Jun. Student); St. Bartholomew's Hospital; Berlin; Vienna. At Oxford; 1st class Natural Science Demonstrator of Anatomy, Radcliffe Travelling Fellow, Examiner, Member of Board of Faculty of Medicine —at Royal College of Physicians, London; Bradshaw Lecturer, Examiner, Member of Council, Senior Censor—Examiner in Medicine at Universities of Oxford, Cambridge, Birmingham, and London, and for Conjoint Board—at Royal Society of Medicine; President of Medical Section, and President of Clinical Section—at Medical Society; Lettsomian Lecturer and President; President, Royal Medical Benevolent Fund; Physician, Provident Mutual and Phœnix Life Assoc.; Hon. Phys. to Metropol. Convalescent Instit., and to British Orphan Asylum, Slough; Fellow of Roy. Soc. Med., of Medical, and other Socs.; formerly Physician and Lecturer on Medicine, St. Bartholomew's Hospital, Physician to City of London Hospital for Diseases of Chest, Victoria Park, and to Royal Free Hospital. *Publications:* Diseases of the Organs of Respiration, 2nd ed. 1909; How to Examine the Chest, 3rd ed.; Lettsomian Lectures on Granular Kidney and Physiological Albuminuria, 1899; contributions to the various learned societies upon diseases of the heart, lungs, kidneys, diabetes. *Recreations:* country pursuits and sports, music. *Address:* 15 Wimpole Street, W.1; Frankland, S. Leonards, Bucks.   *T.:* Paddington 987. *Club:* Athenæum.   (*Died 2 Mar. 1920.*)

WEST, William Cornwallis Cornwallis-; Lord-Lieut. of Denbighshire since 1872; Hon. Col. 4th Batt. Royal Welsh Fusiliers; J.P. Hampshire; *b.* 1835; 2nd *s.* of late F. R. West, *g. s.* of 2nd Earl Delawarr, and Theresa, *d.* of Capt. Whitby, R.N.; *m.* Mary, *d.* of Mr. and Lady Olivia Fitz-Patrick, and *g. d.* of 2nd Marquis of Headfort; one *s.* two *d.* *Educ.:* Eton.   Barr. Lincoln's Inn, 1862; contested

Lymington, 1874 ; W. Cheshire (L.), 1880 ; M.P. W. Division, Denbighshire, 1885-92, when he joined the Liberal Unionist party, but has since acted with the Conservatives. Owns about 10,000 acres. *Recreations:* painting, shooting, fishing. *Address:* Ruthin Castle, North Wales. *T.:* 21 Ruthin. Newlands Manor, Lymington, Hants. *T.:* 5 Milford-on-Sea. 55 Jermyn Street, W. *Clubs:* Brooks's, Windham, Hurlingham.
(Died 4 July 1917.)

WESTCOTT, Ven. Frederick Brooke, D.D. ; Canon of Norwich since 1909 ; Hon. Canon, Salisbury Cathedral, 1900 ; Archdeacon of Norwich since 1910 ; Chaplain-in-Ordinary to H.M. ; *b.* Harrow, 16 Dec. 1857. [Father, Rev. B. F. Westcott, afterwards Bishop of Durham, at the time Assistant Master in Harrow School.] *Educ.:* Cheltenham College ; Trinity College, Cambridge ; Scholar of Trinity College, Cambridge, 1879 ; Bell (University) Scholar, 1878 ; Senior Classic, 1881 ; Fellow of Trin. Coll. Camb. 1882 ; Assistant Master at Rugby, 1884-92 ; Headmaster of Sherborne School, 1892-1908. *Publications:* St. Paul and Justification, 1913 ; A Letter to Asia. *Recreations:* none. *Address:* The Close, Norwich. *T.:* 522 Norwich. *M.:* CL 984. *Club:* Athenaeum.
(Died 24 Feb. 1918.)

WESTCOTT, Rt. Rev. George Herbert, D.D. ; Bishop of Lucknow since 1910 ; *s.* of late Bishop Westcott of Durham. *Educ.:* Marlborough ; Peterhouse, Cambridge (M.A.). Ordained, 1886 ; Assistant Master of Marlborough, 1886-89 ; Missionary at Cawnpore, 1889-1910 ; Examining Chaplain to Bishop of Lucknow, 1898 ; Member of Syndicate, Allahabad University, 1896 ; Secretary Diocesan Board of Missions and S.P.G. Diocesan Representative Canon, Allahabad Cathedral, 1906. *Publication:* Kabir and Kabir Panth. *Address:* Bishop's Lodge, Allahabad. *(Died Jan. 1916.)*

WESTCOTT, Col. Sinclair, C.B. 1915; C.M.G. 1900; D.P.H. 1809; Knight of Grace, St. John of Jerusalem ; Col. A.M.S., retired pay, 1918 ; *b.* 23 Feb. 1859 ; *m.* 1898, Ethel Constance, *d.* of Col. Hon. Robert Bradshaw, and *widow* of D. Gifford Ottley ; one *d.* Served as P.M.O. South Africa, 1899-1902 ; present in Ladysmith during siege (despatches 3 times, Queen's and King's medals 5 clasps, C.M.G.) ; European War, 1914-18 ; A.D.M.S. 1st Division ; D.D.M.S. First Corps (despatches six times, C.B.) ; Med. Officer of Health, Hong Kong, 1895, during plague epidemic ; Hon. Surgeon to the Viceroy of India, 1910 ; D.C.M.S., Ministry of Pensions, 1818-20 ; Director Metropolitan Association for the Improvement of the Dwellings of the Industrious Classes. *Address:* 59 Cadogan Square, S.W.1. *T.:* Kensington 2530. *Clubs:* New Oxford and Cambridge, Ranelagh.
(Died 6 Nov. 1923.)

WESTCOTT, William Wynn, J.P. ; *b.* 1848 ; *s.* of Dr. Peter Westcott of Oundle ; *m.* Lizzie (*d.* 1921), *d.* of Edmund Crawford Burnett; three *d. Educ.:* University Coll., London. M.B. Univ. London ; D.P.H. ; M.R.C.S. For ten years in medical practice at Martock, Somersetshire ; removed to London, and was appointed Deputy Coroner for Central Middlesex and Central London; H. M.'s Coroner for North-East London, 1894-1920 ; was for a short time Medical Officer of Health for Islington ; Past President of the Society for the Study of Inebriety ; Vice-Pres. of the Medico-Legal Society and National Sunday League ; Past President of Coroners' Society ; Divisional Director for Islington of the Red Cross Society. *Publications:* joint-author of sixteen editions of the Extra Pharmacopoeia ; author of Suicide, its History and Causation ; Numbers ; The Isiac Tablet of Cardinal Bembo ; seven volumes of the Collectanea Hermetica. *Recreations:* Freemasonry (Past Master of Quatuor Coronati Lodge, P.G.D. of England) ; study of Egyptian and Hebrew antiquities ; authority on mediæval Rosicrucian, magical and alchemical books ; chief of Rosicrucian Society of England. *Address:* 39 Rapson Road, Durban, Natal.
(Died July 1925.)

WESTERN, Lt.-Col. James Halifax, C.M.G. 1888 ; late R.E., and India Public Works Department ; *b.* 17 May 1842 ; *m.* 1869, Caroline Sophia, 3rd *d.* of G. N. Atkinson of Cangort. Assistant Engineer, N.W. Provinces, 1863 ; Executive Engineer, 1868 ; Punjab, 1882 ; Superintending Engineer, 1882 ; Officiating Chief Engineer and Joint Secretary for Irrigation, 1884 ; served Egypt, 1885-87 ; retired, 1887. *Address:* Halifax Lodge, Hurstpierpoint, Sussex. *Club:* East India United Service. *(Died 2 April 1917.)*

WESTERN, Sir Thomas Charles Callis, 3rd Bt. of Rivenhall, Essex ; J.P., D.L. ; *b.* 29 Aug. 1850 ; *o. c.* of 2nd Bt. and Giulietta Romana, *e. d.* of Sir Edward Manningham Buller, 1st Bt. ; *S.* father 1877 ; *m.* 1883, Elizabeth Ellen, *d.* of late Isaac Newton. *Educ.:* Eton ; Christ Church, Oxford. Late Lieutenant 2nd Life Guards. *Heir:* none. *Address:* 82 St. George's Square, S.W. ; Rivenhall Place, Essex. *(Died 1 Feb. 1917.)*

WESTLAKE, Colonel Almond Paul, D.S.O. 1887 ; *b.* 1858 ; *m.* 1884, Alice Agnes, *o. surv. d.* of General W. D'Oyly Kerrich, late R.H.A.; one *d.* Entered army, 1877 ; served Afghan War, 1879-80 (medal) ; Burmah, 1886-89 (despatches, D.S.O., medal with two clasps) ; late commanding 26th (K.G.O.) Lt. Cav., I.A.; Commandant Remount Dept., 1914.
(Died 22 Aug. 1927.)

WESTLAKE, Rev. Herbert Francis, M.V.O. 1921; F.S.A. 1917; M.A. 1908; Custodian since 1910, and Minor Canon since 1909, of Westminster Abbey ; *b.* 3 Aug. 1879 ; *s.* of late Alfred Westlake, Gloucester ; *m.* 1913, Edith Mary, *d.* of Rev. A. G. S. Raynor, late Master of King's Scholars, Westminster School ; one *s.* three *d. Educ.:* Christ's Hospital ; Pembroke College, Oxford. Chaplain of Hazelwood School, Limpsfield, 1902-3 ; Senior Mathematical Master, Lancing College, 1903-9. *Publications:* New Guide to Westminster Abbey ; The Palace of Westminster ; Westminster : A Historical Sketch ; The Parish Guilds of Mediæval England — St. Margaret's, Westminster; Westminster Abbey : The Last Days of the Monastery ; The Church, Convent, Cathedral, and College of St Peter, Westminster ; Hornchurch Priory ; articles in encyclopædias, archæological journals, and press *gen* rally. *Recreation:* golf. *Address:* 2 The Cloisters, Westminster Abbey, S.W.1.
(Died 27 Nov. 1925.)

WESTLAKE, Nathaniel Hubert John, F.S.A. ; painter, designer, and writer in Art ; *b.* Romsey, 1833 ; *s.* of John Westlake and Elizabeth Hinves ; *m.* 1858, Frances Lloyd ; two *s.* four *d.* Intended for sea ; scheme fell through ; was a few years with well-known publishers ; studied at Lees's, Newman Street, now called Heatherley's, at Somerset House under Dyce and Herbert, at the British Museum, South Kensington, Antwerp, and Paris for Art ; at the suggestion of late W. Burges, R.A., went to a firm of glass painters to design, afterwards became Art manager and partner about 1880 ; is now the proprietor of the establishment ; designed side windows in St. Martin le Grand, and windows in St. Paul's, Worcester, and Peterborough Cathedrals, and other prominent churches, also the glass for the Gate of Heaven Church, South Boston, U.S.A. ; painted the roof and 14 stations of the chapel of Maynooth College ; did the Mosaics for Newman Memorial, Birmingham ; painted St. Thomas of Canterbury Church, St. Leonard's-on-Sea, and many other churches, besides various altarpieces, etc.; has frequently exhibited at R.A.; Hon. Member of the British and American Archæological Society of Rome. *Publications:* History and Design in Painted Glass, 4 vols.; History and Design in Mural Painting; edited parts of the MS. 2 B. VII., British Museum, with translations; Stations of Cross (the first done by an Englishman, with Preface by Cardinal Manning); Sketches at the Great Malines Ecclesiastical Exhibition; Portraiture of St. Francis: Dancing; and contributions to various publications. *Recreations:* various. *Address:* 20 Clifton Gardens, Maida Hill, W.   (*Died 9 May 1921.*)

WESTMACOTT, Percy Graham Buchanan; J.P. Northumberland; M.I.C.E., past President, Institute Mechanical Engineers, and member of other institutions; *b.* Edinburgh, 11 Sept. 1830; *y. s.* of Henry Westmacott, Whetstone, Middlesex; *m.* Annette Beatrice, 2nd *d.* of Rev. Ralph Berners, Erwarton Rectory, Suffolk; seven *s.* three *d. Educ.:* Edinburgh; Dresden; Chester. Served Millar, Ravenhill, and Co., Marine Engineers, in offices, works, and afloat; joined W. G. Armstrong and Co., Elswick Works, Newcastle-on-Tyne, as draughtsman, 1851; manager of works, 1853; partner, 1863; managing director, upon the formation of the concern into a company; raised and commanded for some years the 1st Newcastle-on-Tyne Engineer Volunteers. *Recreations:* art and golf. *Address:* Rose Mount, Ascot; Benwell Hill, Newcastle-on-Tyne. *T.A.:* Ascot. *T.:* 18 Ascot. *Clubs:* Athenæum, Constitutional.   (*Died 10 Sept. 1917.*)

WESTMACOTT, Major-Gen. Sir Richard, K.C.B., *cr.* 1898; C.B. 1891; D.S.O. 1890; Indian Staff Corps; *b.* 16 Mar. 1841; 2nd *s.* of Rev. Horatio Westmacott; *m.* 1889, Rose Margaret *d.* of Maj.-Gen. F. J. Caldecott, C.B., one *s. Educ.:* Rossall. Entered Bombay Army, 1859; served Indian Mutiny; against rebel Bheels, 1860; Naikras, 1868; Afghan War, 1879-80; Soudan Expedition, 1885; Col. 1889; Major-Gen. 1899; commanded Advance Column Chin-Lushai Expedition, 1889-90 (D.S.O., despatches); commanded 28th Bombay Pioneers, 1887-94; Manipur, 1893-94; A.A.G. Poona, 1894-95; Colonel on Staff, 1895-96; commanded Nagpur District, 1896-99; 1st Brigade Mohmund Field Force, 1897; commanded 4th Brigade Tirah Expedition Force, 1897-98 (K.C.B., despatches); 1st class District Mhow, 1900-1903; now on the Unemployed List. *Recreations:* hunting, shooting, fishing. *Address:* Bishop's Caundle, Sherborne, Dorset. *Club:* United Service.   (*Died 27 Feb. 1925.*)

WESTMORLAND, 13th Earl of (*cr.* 1624), Anthony Mildmay Julian Fane, J.P.; C.B.E. 1919; Baron Burghersh, 1624; *b.* 16 Aug. 1859; *s.* of 12th Earl and Lady Adelaide Ida Curzon, *d.* of 1st Earl Howe; *S.* father 1891; *m.* 1st, 1892, Lady Sybil Mary St. Clair Erskine (*d.* 1910), *d.* of 4th Earl of Rosslyn; two *s.* two *d.*; 2nd, 1916, Catherine Louise, *d.* of late Rev. G. Geale. Col. 3rd Batt. Northamptonshire Regt. 1900; A D.C. to King George V. *Recreations:* very fond of hunting and shooting, and all sports. *Heir:* *s.* Lord Burghersh.   *Address:* Wolverton, Enfield. *Club:* Marlborough.
       (*Died 9 June 1922.*)

WESTMORLAND, Brig.-Gen. Charles Henry, C.B. 1908; *b.* 30 June 1856. Widower. Entered Army, 1874; Captain I.S.C. 1885; Bt.-Major, 1889; Lt.-Col., Indian Army, 1900; Col., 1904; A.A.G. Hyderabad Contingent, 1902-5; India, 1904-7; Commanded Karachi Brigade, 1907-10; retired 1912 with honorary rank of Brig.-Gen.; served Afghan War, 1878-79 (medal with clasp); Burma, 1887-89 (despatches, medal with clasp, Brevet Major); N.W. Frontier, India, 1897-98 (medal with clasp); China, 1900

1112

(despatches, medal). *Club:* United Service.
       (*Died 9 Feb. 1916.*)

WESTON, Dame Agnes; G.B.E. *cr.* 1918; Hon. Doctor of Law, Glasgow University; *b.* London; father a barrister; founder of Royal Sailors' Rests at Portsmouth and Devonport. *Publications:* My Life Among the Blue Jackets; Ashore and Afloat. *Address:* Royal Sailors' Rest, Portsmouth.   (*Died 23 Oct. 1918.*)

WESTON, Right Rev. Frank; Bishop of Zanzibar since 1908; *b.* 13 Sept. 1871; 4th *s.* of R. W. G. Weston; unmarried. *Educ.:* Dulwich College; Trinity College, Oxford (1st class Theology; M.A., B.D., D.D.). Curate of Trinity College (Oxon) Mission, 1894-96; St. Matthew's, Westminster, 1896-98; Chaplain of St. Andrew's Coll., Zanzibar, 1898-99; Warden, St. Mark's Theological Coll., Zanzibar, 1899, 1901; Principal, St. Andrew's Training College, Kiungani, Zanzibar, 1901-8; Chancellor of Zanzibar Cathedral, 1904-8; Major commanding Zanzibar Carrier Corps, 1916 (O.B.E.). *Publications:* The One Christ; Ecclesia Anglicana, An Open Letter; God with Us: The Fulness of Christ; Christ and His Critics; Conquering and to Conquer; The Revelation of Eternal Love; and some books in Swahili. *Address:* Universities' Mission, Zanzibar. *T.A.:* Ulema, Zanzibar: Zanzilik, London. (*Died 2 Nov. 1924.*)

WESTON, Jessie Laidlay, D.Litt. *Educ.:* Brighton; Paris; Hildesheim; studied Art, Crystal Palace Schools. *Publications:* Parzival, by Wolfram von Eschenbach, trans. into English Verse, 1894; Legends of the Wagner Drama, 1896; The Legend of Sir Gawain, 1897; The Legend of Sir Lancelot du Lac, 1901; The Three Days' Tournament, 1902; The Legend of Sir Perceval (vol. i.), 1906, (vol. ii.), 1909 (all published in the Grimm Library); Arthurian Romances unrepresented in Malory (7 vols.); The Soul of the Countess: Romance, Vision and Satire, 1912; Chief Middle-English Poets, 1914; From Ritual to Romance, 1920 (awarded Crawshay Prize for 1920); contributor to the Encyclopædia Britannica, Athenæum, Folk-lore, and Romania (French). *Address:* 85 Biddulph Mansions, Elgin Avenue, W.9. *Club:* Lyceum.   (*Died 29 Sept. 1928.*)

WESTON, Sir John Wakefield, 1st Bt., *cr.* 1926; M.P. (Ind.U.) South Westmorland, 1913-18; (U.) Westmorland, 1918-1924; Chairman of County Council for Westmorland; Chairman Territorial Association, Cumberland and Westmorland; *b.* 13 June 1852; *s.* of Rev. G. F. Weston, Vicar of Crosby Ravensworth, Westmorland; *m.* 1890, Kate, *d.* of J. R. Brougham; two *d. Educ.:* Rugby; University College, Oxford. *Recreations:* golf, hunting, cricket, tennis. *Address:* Enyeat, Endmoor, Kendal. *T.:* 27 Sedgwick. *Club:* Carlton.
       (*Died 19 Sept. 1926.*)

WESTON-STEVENS, Sir Joseph, Kt., *cr.* 1913; J.P., D.L.; *b.* 1861; *s.* of W. J. Y. Stevens; *m.* 1888, Victoria Alice, *d.* of Arthur Keen, Edgbaston; one *s.* one *d. Educ.:* Clifton College. Entered business in the firm of T. and J. Weston, 1881; now sole proprietor of that business and the Bristol Foundry Co.; Chairman of the Taff Vale Railway Co.; Chairman of the Bristol Wagon and Carriage Works Co.; Director of Guest, Keen and Nettlefolds, Ltd., and the London City and Midland, Ltd.; Sheriff of Bristol, 1902-3; President of the Liberal Association, 1897; President of the Bristol Liberal Federation; Chairman of the Executive Committee of the Western Counties Liberal Federation; Chairman of the Bristol Citizens Recruiting Committee; joined Gloucestershire Vol. Artillery, 1883, retiring with rank of Major, 1900. *Address:* Worcester Lodge, Clifton, Bristol. *T.:* Bristol 695. *M.:* AE 1612, AE 2929, AE 4107. *Clubs:* Reform, Royal Automobile: Clifton and Bristol Liberal.   (*Died 7 Feb. 1917.*)

WETHERBEE, George, R.I.; artist; painter; b. Cincinnati, U.S.A., Dec. 1851; s. of J. Q. Wetherbee, Boston, U.S.A. *Educ.:* Boston, U.S.A.; Royal Academy of Arts, Antwerp; and London. Travelled and resided in West Indies, France, Germany, Italy, Belgium. etc. *Recreations:* golf, cycling. *Address:* 18 Redington Road, N.W.3. *Clubs:* Arts, St. John's Wood Arts. *T.:* Hampstead 885. (*Died 23 July 1920.*)

WETHERED, Lt.-Col. Francis Owen, C.M.G. 1916; Chairman, Thomas Wethered & Sons, Ltd., The Brewery, Marlow; b. 13 Dec. 1864; e. s. of late Col. Owen Peel and Mrs. Wethered of El Robado, Puerto Orotava, Teneriffe; m. 1st, 1899, Adeline Harris (d. 1900), e. d. of late W. F. MacTier, M.D., of Kinnessburn, St. Andrews; one s. one d.; 2nd, 1917, Margaret, o. d. of J. M. Dyer, M.A., Farnham Common, Bucks; one s. *Educ.:* Eton; Christ Church, Oxford. M.A.; J.P., D.L., Bucks; 2nd Bucks R.V.C. (Eton College), 1878-82; 1st Bucks R.V.C. 1883-1908; Bucks Batt., Oxford and Bucks Light Infantry, 1908-15; Lt.-Col. 1914-15; Lt.-Col. 1/6 Royal Warwickshire Regt. 1915-16 (V.D., C.M.G.); Bucks C.C. 1910; Thames Conservancy, 1916. *Recreations:* rowed for Oxford, 1885-6-7; Pres. O.U.B.C. 1887. *Address:* Meadside, Marlow, Bucks. *T.:* 26.
(*Died 3 Aug. 1922.*)

WETHERED, Frank Joseph, M.D. (Lond.), 1888; F.R.C.P. (Lond.) 1895; M.R.C.S. (Eng.) and L.S.A., 1885; Consulting Physician to Hospital for Consumption and Diseases of Chest, Brompton, and to the National Hospital for Consumption, Ventnor; Consulting Physician, Royal Cornwall Infirmary, Truro; late Physician to Middlesex Hospital; Consulting Physician to St. Saviour's Hospital; late Physician to the Equity and Law Life Assurance Society; Examiner in Medicine, Royal College of Physicians; Captain R.A.M.C. (T.F.), 3rd London General Hospital; b. 1860; s. of late Joseph Wethered, Clifton; m. 1889, Rose, d. of late Edward How, Devonshire. *Educ.:* Clifton College. Studied at Bristol Medical School, London Hospital, Berlin, and Vienna. *Publications:* essay on A Sanatorium for Consumption, 2nd Prize H.M. the King's competition; two works on the use of the microscope in medicine; various communications to medical journals. *Recreations:* out-door sports, especially sea-fishing. *Address:* Pencaer, Falmouth. *T.:* Falmouth 63. (*Died 28 Oct. 1928.*)

WETHERED, Thomas Owen, J.P. for Bucks; b. 26 Nov. 1832; e. s. of Owen Wethered, J.P., of Remnantz, Marlow, Bucks, and Anne, d. of late Rev. Giles Haworth Peel of The Grotto, Basildon; m. 1856, Edith Grace, d. of Rev. Hart Ethelston, Rector of St. Mark's, Cheetham Hill, Manchester; three d. *Educ.:* Eton; Christ Church, Oxford. M.P. Great Marlow, 1868-81; Conservative; Church of England; was Captain, Bucks R.V. *Address:* Seymour Court, Marlow, Bucks. *T.:* 21. *Clubs:* Carlton, Oxford and Cambridge.
(*Died 22 Feb. 1921.*)

WETMORE, Hon. Edward Ludlow, LL.D.; Chief Justice Supreme Court, Saskatchewan, 1907-12; b. 24 March 1841; s. of Charles P. and Sarah B. Wetmore; m. 1872, Eliza J., d. of Charles Dickson; two s. one d. *Educ.:* Grammar Schools in Fredericton and Gage Town, New Brunswick; King's College, Fredericton, now the University of New Brunswick, Fredericton. Graduated with honours, 1859. Barr. of the Province of New Brunswick, 1864; Mayor of Fredericton, 1874-76; a Commissioner for Consolidating the Statutes of New Brunswick, 1877; Q.C. 1881; President of the Barristers' Society, 1886-87; Representative of Alumni Association in Senate of University, 1886-87; a Member of the Local Legislature of the Province, 1883-86,

and Leader of the Opposition during that time; defeated at the General Election for Provincial Legislature, 1887; Judge of Supreme Court of the North-West Territories, 1887-1907; a Commissioner for Consolidating the Ordinances of the North-West Territories, 1898; Chancellor, University of Saskatchewan, 1907; Chairman of Commission for Consolidating Laws of Saskatchewan, 1908; Hon. LL.D. University of New Brunswick, 1908; Hon. D.C.L., University of Saskatchewan, 1919. *Address:* 604 Linden Avenue, Victoria, British Columbia.

WETTON, Henry Davan, Mus.D. Univ. Coll., Dunelm; Fellow of the Royal College of Organists; Fellow of the Guildhall School of Music; Organist and Director of the Choir at, Christ Church, Lancaster Gate, W., since 1926; Professor of the Organ, Harmony, Counterpoint, and Composition at the Guildhall School of Music; Head of Music Dept. Battersea Polytechnic; retired, 1927; Prof. of Sight Singing, Ear Training, and Examiner, Royal College of Music; Member of the Faculty of Music, University of London; Fellow Incorporated Staff Sight - Singing College; Examiner to the Associated Board of the Royal Academy of Music and the Royal College of Music; e. s. of late Henry Davan and Sarah Wetton, of Hazel - groves Hayward's Heath, Sussex. *Educ.:* The Islington Proprietary School; private tuition. Organist and Choirmaster, All Saints, Stoke-Newington, 1877 - 84; Assistant Organist to Sir Frederick Bridge, Westminster Abbey, 1881 - 96; Organist and Choirmaster, Christ Church, Woburn Square, 1884-86; St. Gabriel's, Pimlico, 1886 - 89 and 1890 - 93; Sub-Organist Wells Cathedral, 1890; Organist and Director of the Music at the Foundling Hospital, 1892-1926; Organist and Chorus-master, Queen's Hall Choral Soc. (season 1893-94); Head of the Musical Department, Northampton Institute, 1896 - 1906; Organist (retired), Alexandra Palace, 1901; Conductor of the Choir, People's Palace, E., 1902-3; London University Musical Society, 1905-8, etc. *Publications:* Cantata, The Fulfilment; Church services, anthems, carols, part songs, pieces for organ and pianoforte, and songs. *Address:* 19 Pembridge Mansions, W.2. *Club:* University of London.
(*Died 2 Dec. 1928.*)

WEYMAN, Stanley John, novelist; b. Ludlow, 7 Aug. 1855; 2nd s. of late Thomas Weyman, solicitor; m. Charlotte, d. of late Rev. Richard Panting, H.E.I.C.S. *Educ.:* Shrewsbury; Christ Church, Oxford; B.A. Oxford; 2nd class Modern History. Barr. at Law, 1881. *Publications:* The House of the Wolf, 1890; The New Rector; The Story of Francis Cludde, 1891; A Gentleman of France, 1893; Under the Red Robe, 1894; My Lady Rotha, 1894; Memoirs of a Minister of France; The Red Cockade, 1895; The Man in Black, 1896; Shrewsbury, 1897; The Castle Inn, 1898; Sophia, 1900; Count Hannibal, 1901; In King's Byways, 1902; The Long Night, 1903; Chippings, 1906; The Abbess of Vlaye, 1904; Starvecrow Farm, 1905; Laid up in Lavender, 1907; The Wild Geese, 1908; The Great House, 1919; Ovington's Bank, 1922; The Traveller in the Fur Cloak, 1925; Queen's Folly, 1925. *Recreations:* riding, cycling. *Address:* Llanrhydd, Ruthin. *Club:* Athenæum.(*Died 10 April 1928.*)

WEYMOUTH, Viscount; John Alexander Thynne; 2nd Lieut. 2nd Dragoons; e. s. of 5th Marquess of Bath; b. 29 Nov. 1895. (*Died 13 Feb. 1916.*)

WHALE, George; solicitor; b. Woolwich, 25 Nov. 1849; s. of George and Ellen Whale; one s. two d.; m. 1st, 1874, Matilda Lawson (d. 1922); 2nd, 1923, Winifred Stephens. *Educ.:* Huntingdon; Woolwich.

Solicitor, 1872; retired from practice, 1913; contested Marylebone, 1892; Oxford City, 1906 and 1910; F. R. Hist. Society; on Council Folk Lore Society; Hon. Chairman Rationalist Press Association; Chairman of Woolwich Polytechnic, 1918-21; Mayor of Woolwich, 1908-9; held various professional and Local Government appointments at Lee, Eltham, etc., and member of several local bodies; one of the Founders of the Omar Khayyam and Pepys Clubs. *Publications:* Greater London and its Government, 1888; Essays in Johnson Club Papers, 1899; magazine articles. *Address:* 49 York Terrace, Regent's Park, N.W.1. *T.:* Langham 2884. *Club:* Reform.

(*Died 4 May 1925.*)

WHARNCLIFFE, 2nd Earl of (*cr.* 1876), Francis John Montagu - Stuart - Wortley; Viscount Carlton, 1876; Baron Wharncliffe, 1826. Commander R.N., retired; J.P. and D.L. for W. Riding, Yorkshire; *b.* 9 June 1856; *e. s.* of Hon. F. D. Montagu-Stuart-Wortley, 2nd *s.* of 2nd Baron Wharncliffe; *S.* uncle, 1899; *m.* 1886, Ellen (*d.* 1922), 2nd *d.* of late Lt.-Gen. Sir T. L. Gallwey, R.E.; one *s.* three *d. Educ.:* Eton; Royal Naval College. Naval cadet, 1869; Lieutenant, 1879; retired, 1889; Commander on Retired List, 1896. *Heir:* Viscount Carlton. *Address:* Wortley Hall, Sheffield. *Clubs:* Carlton; Yorkshire, York.

(*Died 8 May 1926.*)

WHATES, Harry Richard; journalist; Parliamentary Correspondent Birmingham Post (London office); an assistant editor of The Standard, 1896-1905, retired on the change of proprietorship in 1905. Has acted as Special Correspondent. *Publications:* The Politician's Handbook: a Review and Digest of the State Papers, 1899, 1900, 1901, 1902; The Third Salisbury Administration, 1895-1900; Dissolution Dialogues, 1900; His Majesty Edward VII., 1901; Canada, the New Nation, 1906; The Life and Times of Edward VII., 1841 1910 (5 vols.); Midland Regiments in France, 1917; Disaffected Ireland, 1920. *Address:* Cranford, Middlesex. *Club:* Press. (*Died 25 Mar. 1923.*)

WHATMAN, George Dunbar; one of H.M. Lieutenants for the City of London; J.P. Middlesex and London; Director of Lloyds Bank, Bank of British North America, Liverpool, London, and Globe Insurance Co., etc.; *b.* 21 Feb. 1846; *e. s.* of late W. G. Whatman, Banker; partner in firm of Bosanquet, Salt & Co., now absorbed in Lloyd's Bank; *m.* 1872, Frances, *e. d.* of late G. A. Fuller of Rookery, Dorking, and 77 Lombard Street, Banker; one *s. Educ.:* Eton; Exeter College, Oxford; B.A. *Address:* 2 Cranley Gardens, S.W.7. *T.:* Western 2544. *T.A.:* Humdrum, London. *Clubs:* Windham, Hurlingham.

(*Died 26 Dec. 1923.*)

WHEATLEY, Henry Benjamin, Hon. D.C.L. (Durham); F.S.A.; *m.* 1872, Louisa Louise (*d.* 1899), *d.* of late Dr. George Robins; two *s.* three *d. Educ.:* privately. Clerk to Royal Society, 1861-79; Assistant Secretary, Society of Arts, 1879-1908; Assistant Secretary Brit. Royal Commission, Section of Chicago Exhibition, 1893; Hon. Sec. Early English Text Society, 1864-72; Treasurer, 1872-1916; President, Samuel Pepys Club, 1903-16; Prior, Johnson Club, 1906-7; President, Hampstead Antiquarian and Historical Society, 1906-16; President of the Sette of Odd Volumes, 1909; President of the Bibliographical Society, 1911-16; Vice-President of the London Topographical Society, 1900-16; Chairman of Council, Shakespeare Association, 1914 - 16. *Publications:* Anagrams, 1862; Round about Piccadilly and Pall Mall, 1870; What is an Index? 1878; Samuel Pepys and the World he lived in, 1880; How to form a Library, 1886; How to Catalogue a Library, 1889; How

1114

to make an Index, 1902; Remarkable Bindings in the British Museum, 1889; London, Past and Present, 1891; Literary Blunders, 1893; new edition Pepys's Diary, 1894-99; Pepysiana, 1899; Historical Portraits, 1897; Prices of Books, 1898; The Story of London, 1904 (Mediæval Towns); Hogarth's London, 1909. Edited The Romance of Merlin, 1865-99; Levins' Manipulus Vocabularum, 1867; Ben Jonson's Every Man in his Humour, 1877; Wraxall's Historical and Posthumous Memoirs, 1884; Shakespeare's Merry Wives of Windsor, 1886. *Address:* 96 King Henry's Road, N.W. *Club:* Garrick. (*Died 30 April 1917.*)

WHEATLEY, Col. Moreton John, C.B. 1901; R.E.; *b.* 2 Mar. 1837; *e. s.* of late T. R. Wheatley of Gwersyllt Park, Denbighshire; *m.* 1864, Edith Frances, *y. d.* of late Charles Millett of Maiden Erleigh, Berks; three *s.* one *d.* Entered army, 1854; Captain 1861; Major, 1872; Lieut.-Col., 1879; Colonel, 1883; Bailiff of the Royal Parks, 1879-1902. *Address:* 314 St. James's Court, S.W.; Gwersyllt Park, Denbighshire. *T.A.:* Escorted, London. *T.:* 1981 Victoria. *Clubs:* Junior United Service, Union. (*Died 13 May 1916.*)

WHEATLEY, Major William Prescott Ross, D.S.O. 1917; I.A.S.C.; *b.* 1878; *s.* of George Wheatley, 2 Priory Parade, Cheltenham; *m.* 1923, Una, widow of Major E. W. Worrall, Somerset Light Infantry. Served Somaliland, 1903 (medal with two clasps); France and Mesopotamia, 1914-17 (despatches, D.S.O.). *Club:* Naval and Military.

(*Died 6 Sept. 1925.*)

WHEELER, Major Henry Littelton, C.B. 1918; D.S.O. 1900; late Hampshire Regt.; Secretary Territorial Association, Staffordshire, since 1908; *b.* 8 May 1868; *e. s.* of late Rev. T. Littelton Wheeler; *m.* 1908, Vera, *y. d.* of Col. Gillum Webb, of Walton House, Ashchurch; one *s.* one *d.* Joined Militia (Worcestershire), 1887; entered army, 1892; Captain, 1900; served South Africa, 1900-2 (despatches thrice, Queen's and King's medals, four clasps, D.S.O.). *Address:* The Woodlands, Stafford.

(*Died 14 Dec. 1924.*)

WHEELER, His Honour Thomas Whittenbury, M.A., J.P., K.C.; late County Court Judge; resigned 1918; *s.* of late Serjeant Wheeler, LL.D., J.P., County Court Judge and Fanny, *d.* of John Whittenbury, Green Heys, Ardwick; *m.* Henrietta Brooksbank (*d.* 1920), *y. d.* of Edward Lodge Ogle, M.D. *Educ.:* Westminster School; Trinity Hall, Cambridge. Barrister, 1865; revising barrister, 1868; junior counsel to the Post Office, 1873-86; Queen's Counsel, 1886; Bencher Inner Temple, 1894; chairman, Law and Parliamentary Committee, Vestry of Kensington, 1894-97; chairman of Vestry, 1897; chairman Liberal Unionist Association, S. Kensington, 1892-98; Alderman, Borough Council; Hon. Member Surveyors' Institution. *Publications:* The Law of Dilapidation, 1887; Betterment: Transactions of Surveyors' Institution; The Good Old Times, 1888; Contracts Implied by Law, 1897, etc.

(*Died 3 April 1923.*)

WHEELER, William, C.M.G. 1904; O.B.E. 1918; Treasurer, British Central Africa Protectorate, 1892-1920; Acting Chief Secretary, 1912 and 1916-19; retired, 1920; mentioned in Gen. Van Deventer's Despatch, 1919. *Address:* Edingale, Tamworth, Staffs. (*Died 23 Feb. 1926.*)

WHEELER-BENNETT, John Wheeler, C.B.E.; J.P.; Director of Metropolitan Railway and other Companies; High Sheriff of Kent, 1922-24; *m.* 1882, Christine Hill McNutt of Truro, Novia Scotia, Canada; two *s.* one *d. Educ.:* at Vickery's, Hope House, Southsea, Portsmouth. Carried on business at Hibernia Chambers, London Bridge, S.E., for forty years as an import merchant, having large interests in Canada, America, Argentine, and Denmark; was Chairman of the London Home and Foreign Exchange, 1913; retired from active commerce, 1912; engaged in war activities, 1914-19; Chairman Bromley (Kent) Rural Tribunal; an original member of Major Rothschild's City of London Military Advisory Committee; Chairman of Finance, Kent County War Fund, administering nearly 100 V.A.D. hospitals (C.B.E.). *Recreations:* shooting, golf, etc. *Address:* Ravensbourne, Keston, Kent. *Clubs:* City Carlton, Royal Automobile; Bromley and Bickley Golf. (*Died 25 June 1926.*)

WHELER, Sir Granville (Charles Hastings), 1st Bt., *cr.* 1925; C.B.E. 1920; M.P. (C.) North-East Kent, now Faversham Division, since 1910; *b.* 2 Oct. 1872; *s.* of late Charles Wheler Wheler, J.P., D.L., and Elizabeth, *d.* of William Hall of Syndale Park, Faversham; *m.* 1905, Florence Faith, *d.* of late Captain Clarke of Alcombe Cote, Somerset. *Educ.:* Eton; Christ Church, Oxford. Called to Bar, Middle Temple, 1898; Member of West Riding County Council, 1907-10; contested (U.) Osgoldcross Division, West Riding, Yorks, 1906; Colne Valley, 1907; Major on Headquarters Staff, Western Command, 1915-1918; Lt.-Col., 1918; J.P., D.L. *Recreations:* cricket, shooting, hunting. *Address:* Ledston Hall, Yorks; Otterden Place, Faversham, Kent. *Clubs:* Carlton, Royal Automobile.

(*Died 14 Dec. 1927.*)

WHERRY, George Edward, F.R.C.S.; University Lecturer in Surgery; Consulting Surgeon to Addenbrooke's Hospital, Cambridge; Lt.-Col. R.A.M.C. (T.), 1st Eastern General Hospital; Examiner in Surgery, University of Cambridge; Supervisor of Examinations in Surgery; *b.* Bourne, Lincolnshire, 1852; *m.* 1881, Albinia Lucy Cust; one *d.* *Educ.:* St. Thomas's Hospital, London; Downing College, Cambridge (M.A., M.C.). *Publications:* Clinical Notes on Nerve Disorders; Alpine Notes, and the Climbing Foot; Notes from a Knapsack; Cambridge and Charles Lamb, 1925. *Recreations:* walking, climbing, cycling. *Address:* 5 St. Peter's Terrace, Cambridge. *T.A.:* Cambridge. *T.:* 98. *M.:* CE 1484. *Clubs:* Alpine, Junior Constitutional. (*Died 12 Aug. 1928.*)

WHINNEY, Sir Arthur, K.B.E. 1919; J.P.; chartered accountant; senior partner in firm of Whinney, Smith & Whinney, London, Paris, Antwerp, Berlin, etc.; *b.* 16 Dec. 1865; *s.* of Frederick Whinney; *m.* 1892, Amy Elizabeth (*d.* 1923), *d.* of William Golden, late of H.M. Treasury (Solicitor); two *s.* one *d.* Late Adviser on Costs of Production to the Admiralty; late Assistant Accountant-Gen. of the Navy, and Adviser and Consultant to the Admiralty in Accountancy; President, Institute of Chartered Accountants; Chairman of Board of Trade Committees *re* Superphosphates and Worsteds under Safeguarding of Industries Enquiry. *Address:* 80 Gloucester Terrace, W.2; Lee Place, Charlbury, Oxon. *T.:* Paddington 4975. *Clubs:* Marlborough, Reform, Bath, Arts, British Empire, Gresham, Ranelagh. (*Died 30 May 1927.*)

WHIPHAM, Thomas Tillyer, M.A., M.D. Oxon., F.R.C.P.; J.P. Co. Devon; Consulting Physician to St. George's Hospital; member Court of Assistants (late Prime Warden) Goldsmiths' Company; *s.* of Thomas Henry Whipham of Lincoln's Inn, Barrister-at-Law; *m.* Florence, *d.* of Charles Tanqueray; one *s.* *Educ.:* Rugby; Oriel Coll. Oxford. Was Demonstrator of Anatomy, Curator of the Museum, Lecturer on Botany, Pathology, and Medicine; Assistant-Physician and Physician at St. George's Hospital; Examiner in Medicine for the University of Oxford, and for the Conjoint Board of the Royal Colleges of Physicians and Surgeons in England; Censor and Senior Censor of the Royal College of Physicians; Physician to

the Legal and General Life Assurance Society; Junior Physician at the West London Hospital. *Publications:* contributions to the Lancet and other medical publications on various subjects. *Address:* Fishleigh House, Hatherleigh, N. Devon. *Club:* Oxford and Cambridge.

(*Died 3 Nov. 1917.*)

WHITAKER, William, B.A., F.R.S., F.G.S., Assoc. Inst. C.E.; F.R. San. Inst.; Assoc. Soc. M.O.H.; hon. member of many societies (English and Foreign); Consulting Geologist; Past President of Geological Society (Wollaston, Murchison and Prestwich medals); Past President of Geologists' Association; retired Civil Service (Geological Survey); *b.* London, 4 May 1836; one *s.* one *d.* *Educ.:* St. Albans Grammar School; University Coll. London. Geological Survey of England, 1857-96. Has done much work in Geology, especially in South-Eastern England, and in Applied Geology (Water-Supply and other sanitary questions). *Publications:* many Geological Survey Maps and Memoirs; many papers and addresses to Geological Society, to several other societies, etc. *Recreations:* walking, cards. *Address:* Wellesley Court, Wellesley Road, Croydon. *T.:* Croydon 922.

(*Died 15 Jan. 1925.*)

WHITBY, Rev. Thomas, M.A.; *b.* Liverpool, 12 May 1835; *s.* of Thos. Whitby and Mary Bateson; *m.* 1870, Mary Louisa Titley Beverley; three *s.* two *d.* *Educ.:* Liverpool Coll.; St. John's Coll. Camb.; B.A. 1859; M.A. 1866. Vicar of St. Simon's, Leeds, 1865-77; Christ Church, Plymouth, 1877-81; Member of the Plymouth School Board; Vicar of Parish Church, Dewsbury, 1881-90; Member and Chairman of the Dewsbury School Board; Hon. Canon of Wakefield, 1888-1909; Proctor in Convocation for the Archdeaconry of Halifax, 1889-91; Rural Dean of Dewsbury, 1889-90; Vicar of St. John's, Sandown, Isle of Wight, 1891-1905; F.R.G.S. 1868. *Publications:* The Church of England, its Property and its Work. *Recreations:* at Cambridge, boating; now, foreign travel and "rubbing monumental brasses." *Address:* 145 Brondesbury Park, N.W. (*Died 13 Aug. 1918.*)

WHITCOMBE, Right Rev. Robert Henry; Bishop of Colchester since 1909; Archdeacon of Colchester; *b.* 18 July 1862; *s.* of Philip Whitcombe, Gravesend; *m.* 1892, Annie, 2nd *d.* of S. T. G. Evans, of Eton College; six *s.* two *d.* *Educ.:* Winchester; New Coll., Oxford. Assistant Master, Wellington College, 1886-89; Eton College, 1889-99; Rector of Hardwicke, Aylesbury, 1899-1904; Vicar of Romford, 1904-9; C.F. in France, 1918; *Address:* Derby House, Colchester.

(*Died 19 Mar. 1922.*)

WHITE, Andrew Dickson, B.A. and M.A., Yale; Ph.D. Jena; LL.D. Yale, St. Andrews, Michigan, Cornell, Johns Hopkins, Dartmouth, and Hobart; L.H.D. Columbia; D.C.L. Oxon.; Officer of the Legion of Honour of France; Member of the Royal Academy of Sciences of Berlin; Recipient of the Gold Medal in Science and Literature from the Prussian Government, 1902; De Forest Gold Medallist, also Yale Literary Gold Medal; First Clarke Prizeman at Yale; *b.* Homer, Cortland County, New York State, 7 Nov. 1832; *s.* of Horace White and Clara Dickson; *m.* 1st, 1857, Mary A. Outwater (*d.* 1887); 2nd, 1890, Helen, *d.* of Edward Hicks Magill; two *d.* Graduated Yale University, 1853; travelled in Europe; studied at Sorbonne and Collège de France, 1853-1854; attaché to Legation of the United States, Petrograd, 1854-55; studied University of Berlin, 1855-56; Professor of History and English Literature University of Michigan, 1857-63; returned to Syracuse and elected State Senator, in which capacity (1863-67) he introduced reports and bills codifying the school laws, creating a new system of normal schools, establishing new Health Board in the

1115

City of New York, and incorporating Cornell University at Ithaca, all of which became laws; chosen first president of that University, 1866-1885; visited Europe to purchase books and apparatus therefor, and make special study of European educational methods; has in addition to the presidency filled the chair of Modern History; commissioner to Santo Domingo to study and report on question of annexation, 1871; Commissioner to the Paris Exposition, 1878; minister to Berlin, 1879-81; minister to Petrograd, 1892-94; member of the Venezuelan Commission, 1895-96; Ambassador to Berlin, 1897-1903; President of American Delegation at Peace Conference of the Hague, 1899; a Regent of the Smithsonian Institution, a Trustee Carnegie Institution for Research and Peace Foundation, Washington, and of Cornell University; ex-president American Social Science Association, and American Historical Society. *Publications:* Various Essays, Papers, Addresses, and Speeches on Historical, Educational, and Political Subjects; also Paper Money Inflation in France: how it came, what it brought, and how it ended—various editions; The Warfare of Science, 1876 (Swedish abridged translation, 1877); History of the Warfare of Science with Theology in Christendom, 1897 (French, 1907; Italian, 1902; German, 1910; Portuguese, 1911; Spanish, 1911, 1912); Autobiography, 1905 (German translation of the chapters on Diplomatic Life, 1906); Seven Great Statesmen in the Warfare of Humanity with Unreason, 1910; German, 1912; The Work of Benjamin Hale, 1911; Lecture on The Problem of High Crime in the United States. *Address:* Cornell University, Ithaca, New York. *Clubs:* Union League, Century, New York City; Cosmos, Washington.   (*Died 4 Nov. 1918.*)

WHITE, Arnold; author; *b.* 1 Feb. 1848; *m.* 1879, Helen Constance(*d.* 1918), *o. d.* of late Lowell Price of Farnham Royal, Bucks. Has devoted himself to social problems; in connection with colonization has visited South Africa six times and made repeated visits to Canada, the United States, and Russia; acted for Baron de Hirsch in negotiating with Russian Government for Jewish colonization of land in Argentine Republic; contested Mile End, 1886, Tyneside Division, Northumberland, 1892 and 1895, and North Londonderry, 1906; is interested in a strong navy, and especially in gunnery; writes as Vanoc of the Referee. *Publications:* Letters of S.G.O. to the Times; The Modern Jew, 1899; Problems of a Great City; Tries at Truth; English Democracy; Efficiency and Empire; For Efficiency; The Great Idea; The Navy and its Story; Is the Kaiser Insane?; The Hidden Hand. *Recreations:* climbing, travel, shooting, golf, chess, gardening. *Address:* Windmill Cottage, Farnham Common, Bucks. *T.:* Farnham Common 2. *Club:* 1900.   (*Died 5 Feb. 1925.*)

WHITE, Aubrey, C.M.G. 1914; Deputy Minister Lands, Forests, and Mines, Province of Ontario, Canada, since 1883; *s.* of David White, Omagh, Tyrone, Ireland; *m.* 1882, Mary Bridgland, Toronto; one *s.* four *d. Educ.:* Royal School, Raphoe; Royal School, Dungannon. Forest Manager, Geo. Bay Lumber Company, 1871-76; Forest Ranger, Ontario Govt., 1876-78; Crown Lands Agent, Ontario, 1878-82; Clerk in Dept. Crown Lands, 1882-87; President Forestry Association of Canada, 1896; Grand Master A.F. and A.M., Canada, 1911-12. *Publications:* Outlined and put in operation the Forest Fire Protection at present in force in Province of Ontario; The Pioneer System in Canada. *Address:* 35 Admiral Road, Toronto, Canada. *Clubs:* Canada, Royal Canadian Yacht, Toronto.

WHITE, Charles Frederick, M.P. (L.), Western Division of Derbyshire, since Dec. 1918; *b.* Tetbury, Gloucestershire, 11 March 1863; 2nd *s.* of Frederick and Ruth White; *m.*
1116

1881, Alice, 2nd *d.* of Wm. Charlesworth of Bonsall, near Matlock; one *s.* five *d. Educ.:* private school, Tetbury, Gloucestershire. Registration and Political Agent and Secretary; five years Magistrate by virtue of being Chairman of Local Authority; four years Member of Derbyshire County Council; contested West Derbyshire, Dec. 1910; Liberal; Member of Executive, League of Nations, and of Agricultural Committee, House of Commons. *Recreation:* work. *Address:* The Woodlands,Matlock.   (*Died 4 Dec. 1923.*)

WHITE, Charles Percival, M.V.O.; M.A., M.B., B.C. (Cantab.); *s.* of late Robert Owen White of Gestingthorpe Hall, Essex; *m.* Marian Irene, *d.* of Charles Verrall Willett, Brighton; three *d. Educ.:* privately; Clare College, Cambridge; St. Bartholomew's Hospital. In practice in London for thirty years. *Address:* 7 Albany Villas, Hove, Sussex. *Clubs:* Garrick; Union, Brighton. (*Died 11 Dec. 1923.*)

WHITE, Lieut.-Col. Frederick, C.M.G. 1902; Comptroller-General of the North-West Mounted Police in the Dominion of Canada; *b.* Birmingham, 16 Feb. 1847; *m.* Clara Olivia, *e.d.* of late R. W. Cruise of Ottawa; one *d. Educ.:* Birmingham. 3rd Class Clerk, Dept. of Justice, Canada, 1869; Chief Clerk, 1876; on organisation of North-West Mounted Police took charge under Sir John Macdonald of Police Bureau at Ottawa; for some years a Captain in the Governor-General's Foot Guards. *Address* 368 Besserer Street, Ottawa. *Club:* Rideau.
          (*Died 27 Sept. 1918.*)

WHITE, Colonel Frederick, D.S.O. 1900; Royal Marine Light Infantry; *b.* 14 Oct. 1861; *s.* of late Major George White, R.M.L.I. Entered army, 1879; Captain, 1888; Major, 1896; Lieut.-Colonel, 1902; Colonel (Brevet), 1906; D.C.O. 1915-19 (Victory Medal, British War Medal, 1914-15 Star); served Egyptian War, 1882 (medal with clasp, Khedive's Star); Soudan, 1884 (5th class Medjidie, two clasps); South Africa, 1900-2 (despatches, two medals four clasps, D.S.O.); retired, 1909. *Address:* St. John's Park, Blackheath, S.E.
          (*Died 8 Dec. 1924.*)

WHITE, Major Frederick Alexander, D.S.O. 1900; Suffolk Regt.; temp. Lt.-Col.; *b.* 6 Aug. 1872. Entered army, 1894; Lieut. 1897; Capt. 1901; Major, 1914; served S. Africa, 1899-1902 (despatches, Queen's medal, 3 clasps, King's medal, 2 clasps, D.S.O.); European War, 1914-17. (*Died 26 Jan. 1919.*)

WHITE, Sir George; 1st Bart., *cr.* 1904; Hon. LL.D. Bristol; J.P.; *b.* 28 Mar. 1854; *s.* of late Henry White of Bristol and Eliza, *d.* of John Tippetts; *m.* 1876, Caroline Rosena(*d.* 1915), *d.* of William Thomas, Bristol; one *s.* one *d.* Established first manufactory of aeroplanes in England, and introduced the Bristol Biplanes and Monoplanes in 1910. A pioneer of electric street traction, first to introduce it into London, Dublin, Bristol, Middlesbrough, etc.; head of the firm of George White and Company of Bristol; Past President of the Bristol Stock Exchange and of the Council of Associated Stock Exchanges of the United Kingdom; President and Treasurer of the Bristol Royal Infirmary; one of the Charity Trustees, and a Governor of the Bristol Grammar and other Schools; President of the Queen Victoria Memorial Hospital at Nice; Past President of the Dolphin Society; chairman of several important undertakings, and interested in or controlling railway and other industrial concerns in Bristol and South Wales. *Heir:* *s.* George Stanley [*b.* 31 July 1882; *m.* 1908, Kate Muriel, *d.* of late Thomas Baker of Bristol; one *s.*]. *Address:* Old Sneed Park, Bristol. *T.A.:* White, Bristol. *T.:* Stoke Bishop 121. *M.:* AE 8348, AE 3349. *Club:* Carlton.
          (*Died 22 Nov. 1916.*)

WHITE, George Gilbert, C.S.I. 1911; *b.* Grayingham, Kirton Lindsey, Lincs, Jan. 1857; *s.* of late Rev. John White, and of Emily White, Bydews, Lincoln; *m.* 1896, Ethel Maude, *d.* of late Arthur John Hughes C.I.E., M.Inst. C.E.; two *d. Educ.:* Malvern College; Royal Indian Engineering College, Cooper's Hill. Appointed to P.W.D., 1877; Assistant and Executive Engineer Central Provinces, 1878-1901; Superintending Engineer and Secretary to Agents of Governor-General, Rajputana and Central India, 1901-5; Chief Engineer Burma, 1905-6; Chief Engineer and Secretary to Local Government of Burma, 1906-12, Member of Legislative Council, Burma, 1908-12. *Address:* Fontenay, Belvedere, St. Helier, Jersey.

(*Died 9 Dec. 1916.*)

WHITE, Henry, Hon. LL.D. St. Andrews; LL.D. Johns Hopkins and Harvard Universities; *b.* Baltimore, 29 March 1850; *s.* of John Campbell White and Miss Ridgely, of Hampton; *m.* 1st, 1879, Margaret Stuyvesant Rutherfurd (*d.* 1916); one *s.* one *d.*; 2nd, 1921, Mrs. Emily Vanderbilt Sloane. *Educ.:* tutors and private schools in America and France. Secretary of the American Legation at Vienna, 1883-84; transferre² to London as Second Secretary of Legation, 1884; Secretary of Legation, 1886, and American Delegate to the International Conference on Sugar Bounties, London, 1888; recalled by President Cleveland, 1893; Secretary of Embassy at London, 1897-1905; American Ambassador to Italy, 1905-7; Senior Delegate from the U.S. to the International Agricultural Conference at Rome, 1905, which resulted in the foundation of the International Institute of Agriculture there; Senior Delegate from the U.S. to the Algeciras Conference, 1906; American Ambassador to France, 1907-9; Chairman of the American Delegation to the fourth Pan-American Conference at Buenos Aires, 1910; Special Ambassador to Chile for the celebration of the centenary of that country's independence, 1910; Regent of Smithsonian Institution, Washington; Commissioner Plenipotentiary to Peace Conference, Paris, 1919. *Recreations:* hunting, shooting, and golf. *Address:* 1624 Crescent Place, Washington. *Clubs:* Athenæum, Marlborough, Bachelors', Beefsteak, Royal Automobile; Knickerbocker, Metropolitan, New York; Metropolitan, Washington; Cercles de l'Union and de la Rue Royale, Paris.(*Died 15 July 1927.*)

WHITE, Sir Henry Arthur, Kt., *cr.* 1897; C.V.O. 1907; Private Solicitor to King and other members of Royal Family; *b.* 18 June 1849; *s.* of late Henry White, and *n.* of late Sir Arnold Wm. White, with whom he lived as his adopted son from 1856 to the date of his death in 1893; *m.* 1st, Isabel Mary (*d.* 1905), *e. d.* of late Charles Courtenay Colley, 1896; one *d.*; 2nd, Katie, *d.* of late Samuel Seldon, C.B.; one *d. Educ.:* Harrow. Practised as a solicitor from 1873. *Recreations:* fishing, cycling. *Address:* 14 Great Marlborough Street, W.1. *T.:* Gerrard 1310. (*Died 5 Jan. 1922.*)

WHITE, Horace, M.A., LL.D.; *b.* Colebrook, N.H., 10 Aug. 1834; *s.* of Horace White, physician, and Elizabeth Moore; *m.* 1st, 1859, Martha H. Root (*d.* 1873); 2nd, 1875, Amelia J. MacDougall; three *d. Educ.:* Beloit College, Beloit, Wisconsin. Graduated, 1853; went to Chicago, and became city editor of the Chicago Evening Journal, 1854; assistant editor of the Chicago Tribune, 1857; chief editor, 1865-74; removed to New York, 1877; joined others in purchasing the New York Evening Post, 1882; Editor, 1899-1903. *Publications:* Took an active part in supporting the Gold Standard in the monetary struggle following the Civil War, published numerous pamphlets, and also a book entitled

Money and Banking in 1895 (5th edition in 1914); translated from the Greek the Roman History of Appian of Alexandria, 1899; Chairman of Committee to Investigate Speculation in Securities and Commodities in N.Y. City, 1908-9. *Publication:* Life of Lyman Trumbull, 1913. *Address:* 18 West 69th Street, New York. *T.:* 948 Columbus. *M.:* 12292 N.Y. *Club:* Century.

(*Died 6 Sept. 1916.*)

WHITE, James; Managing Director of the Beecham Trust, Ltd.; Chairman, George Edwardes (Daly's Theatre), Ltd.; *b.* Rochdale, 1878. *Address:* 21 Park Street, Mayfair, W.1.

(*Died 29 June 1927.*)

WHITE, James, F.R.G.S., F.R.S.C., M. Eng. Inst. Can.; Technical Adviser to Minister of Justice since 1922; *b.* 3 Feb. 1863; *e. s.* of David White and Christina, *d.* of George Hendry; *m.* 1888, Rachel, *d.* of Thomas Waddell; two *d. Educ.:* Royal Military College, Kingston, Ont. Topographer on the staff of the Geological Survey of Canada, January 1884; made surveys in the Rocky Mountains, 1884 and 1885; in the Madoc, Ont. gold district, 1886; in the Ottawa County, Que. phosphate district, 1887-90; in the Kingston and Pembroke, Ont. district, 1891-93; Geographer and Chief Draughtsman to the Geological Survey, 1894; Member, Geographic Board of Canada, 1898; Chief Geographer of the Department of the Interior, 1899; organized map-work in this branch; employed on the Alaska Boundary Commission 1903; made investigations respecting fast trans-Atlantic passenger steamships (the All-Red Line), 1907; Secretary, Commission of Conservation, 1909; Assistant Chairman and Deputy Minister, 1913; Chairman, Advisory Board on Wild Life Protection since 1917; Chairman Geographic Board since 1925; Prix Alexandre Roquette, 1917; employed on the Labrador Boundary Case, 1921; Vice-President Section C and Section E British Association for Advancement of Science, 1924; President, Section IV. Royal Society of Canada, 1924. *Publications:* Topographical Work of the Geological Survey; Atlas of Canada, 1906; Altitudes in Canada, 1901 and 1915; Dictionary of Altitudes, 1903 and 1916; Maps and Map-making in Canada; Derivation of Place-names in Canada; Treaties and Boundaries affecting Canada; Fuels of Western Canada; Power in Alberta; Senator Lodge and the Alaska Boundary; various articles, etc. *Recreation:* travel. *Address:* 450 Wilbrod Street, Ottawa, Ont. *T.A.:* Conservation. *T.:* Rideau 388. *Clubs:* Anthors; Rideau, Ottawa.

(*Died 26 Feb. 1928.*)

WHITE, James Charles Napoleon; Chairman of the Governing Body and Treasurer of Birkbeck College; Governor of Northampton Polytechnic Institute; Liveryman of Worshipful Company of Basketmakers; *m.* Constance, *d.* of late Captain Douglas Charles Kinnaird Dana; no *c. Educ.:* privately; Birkbeck College; student at St. Martin's School of Art. For fifty years actively engaged in honorary work at Birkbeck College. *Recreations:* the drama, music, and travel. *Address:* 43 Gordon Square, W.C. *Club:* British Empire.

(*Died 16 Nov. 1923.*)

WHITE, James Cobb, M.L.C., J.P.; General Manager for White Brothers, Graziers; *b.* Belltrees, Scone, N.S.W., 29 Nov. 1855; *s.* of Francis White, M.L.A.; *m.* 1882, Emmeline Ebsworth; three *s.* two *d. Educ.:* Grammar School, Newcastle, etc. Twelve months in a bank; thereafter employed in pastoral pursuits, having interests in stations in the Northern Territory, in the Gulf, in Central Queensland, and in New South Wales; a member of the firm of White Brothers, White & Co., The Gulf Cattle Co., and Lorraine and Talawanta Pastoral Co. *Address:* Edinglassie, Muswellbrook, New

South Wales. *Club:* Australian, Sydney.
(*Died 18 Jan. 1927.*)

WHITE, James Martin, J.P.; F.R.S.E.; *b.* 1857; *s.* of J. F. White, Balruddery; M.P. (G.L.) Forfarshire, 1895-96; *m.* 1st, 1898, Mary MacRae; one *s.* one *d.*; 2nd, Priscilla A. M. Leigh, Bristol and New York. *Educ.:* Edinburgh University; Germany; France. Chairman, Governor, Member of Committee on Boards of many Educational Institutions, Elementary to University. *Recreations:* shooting, golf, touring by motor. Owns 1100 acres. *Address:* 1 Cumberland Place, Regent's Park, N.W.1; Balruddery, Dundee. *T.:* Museum 854. *Clubs:* Royal Societies, Authors'.
(*Died 7 July 1928.*)

WHITE, James William, M.D., Ph.D., LL.D. (Aberdeen); *b.* Philadelphia, 2 Nov. 1850; *s.* of Dr. James W. White of Philadelphia; *m.* 1888, Letitia, *d.* of Benj. H. Brown of Philadelphia. *Educ.:* The University of Pennsylvania. Graduated 1871; on Staff of Prof. Louis Agassiz during Hassler Expedition to West Indies, Straits of Magellan, both coasts of South America, Juan Fernandez, the Galapagos Archipelago, the Isthmus of Panama, etc., 1871-72; Resident Physician, Philadelphia Hospital, 1873; Surgeon to Eastern Penitentiary, 1874-77; Surgeon, First Troop Philadelphia City Cavalry, 1878-88; has taught and written on Surgery during whole professional life; was Professor of Genito-Urinary Surgery, Professor of Clinical Surgery, John Rhea Barton Professor of Surger Uni-versity of Pennsylvania, successively; now Emeritus Professor of Surgery; Surgeon to the University Hospital; Consulting Surgeon, Philadelphia and Jewish Hospitals; Member, American Surgical Association, American Genito-Urinary Association, College of Physicians of Philadelphia, American Medical Association, British Medical Association, etc.; one of the Editors of the Annals of Surgery; Trustee, University of Pennsylvania; Advisory Surgeon Pennsylvania Railroad; Commissioner of Fairmount Park. *Publications:* American Text-Book of Surgery; Genito-Urinary Surgery; Human Anatomy; numerous surgical articles in text-books and systems of surgery, and in medical journals. *Recreations:* bicycling, swimming, walking, climbing, rowing, automobiling. *Address:* 1810 South Rittenhouse Square, Philadelphia, Pa., U.S.A. *Clubs:* Reform, Royal Automobile; The Kinsmen; Swiss Alpine; American Alpine; Rittenhouse, Phila.; Corinthian Yacht; Phila. Country.
(*Died 24 April 1916.*)

WHITE, Hon. John; Minister for Agriculture and Stock; Member for Musgrave in Parliament of Queensland, 1903-4, and since 1907; *b.* Dumbartonshire, 1852; arrived in Queensland, 1883; Managing Director, Bundaberg Foundry, Ltd.; Chairman of Harbour Board; Chairman of Bundaberg Co-operative Insurance Association and of the Mercantile Association. *Address:* Bundaberg, Queensland. *Clubs:* Johnsonian, Brisbane; Bundaberg.
(*Died 13 July 1922.*)

WHITE, John Claude, C.I.E. 1904; *Educ.:* Rugby; Bonn; Cooper's Hill. Joined P.W.D. Bengal, 1876; Executive Engineer, 1887; Political Officer, Sikhim, 1889; accompanied Tibet Mission, 1904; Political Agent for Sikhim, Bhutan, and Tibetan affairs, 1905-8. *Publication:* Sikhim and Bhutan, Experiences of Twenty Years on the North-East Frontier of India, 1909. *Address:* Newland, Glos.; 65 Redcliffe Gardens, S.W. (*Died 19 Feb. 1918.*)

WHITE, John Williams, Ph.D., LL.D., Litt.D.; Emeritus Professor of Greek in Harvard University; *b.* Cincinnati, Ohio, 5 Mar. 1849; *s.* of Rev. John Whitney White and Anna Catharine, *d.* of Judge Hosea Williams; *m.* 1871,

1118

Alice, *d.* of Picton Drayton Hillyer; one *s.* three *d.* *Educ.:* Ohio; Germany; Harvard University; Ph.D. 1877; LL.D. Wesleyan University 1896; Ohio Wesleyan Univ. 1905; Litt.D. Cambridge, England, 1900; Harvard, 1913; Princeton, 1914. Fellow of the American Academy of Arts and Sciences; Hon. Member of the Society for the Promotion of Hellenic Studies, and member of the Kaiserlich Deutsches Archäologisches Institut; Hon. President of the Archæological Institute of America; first Chairman of the Managing Committee of the American School of Classical Studies at Athens, 1881-87; former Editor of the Harvard Studies in Classical Philology; Associate-Editor of Classical Philology, and the Classical Review and Classical Quarterly. *Publications:* School and College Text-Books; senior editor of the College Series of Greek Authors (thirty volumes); Monographs on Philological and Archæological Subjects; The Verse of Greek Comedy, 1912; The Old Greek Commentary on Aristophanes; Scholia on the Aves, 1914. *Address:* 18 Concord Ave., Cambridge, Mass. *Clubs:* Royal Societies, Authors'. (*Died 9 June 1917.*)

WHITE, John W.; *m.*; two *s.* two *d.* Past President of The National Federation of Building Trade Employers of Great Britain and Ireland; Member of the Industrial Council; Member of the Sunderland Town Council; Member of Committee on Production. *Address:* High Barnes Works, Sunderland. *T.:* 695 and 696. *T.A.:* Whibild, Sunderland. *M.:* 6 BR. *Club:* Sunderland. (*Died 24 Sept. 1919.*)

WHITE, Lt.-Col. Joshua Chaytor, C.M.G. 1916; I.M.S., ret.; late Director of Public Health, United Provinces of India; *s.* of Albert White, Tower Hill, Waterford; *b.* 21 Oct. 1864; *m.* Helen Eliza, *d.* of G. C. Bright, Cannes; no *c.* *Educ.:* University of Edinburgh (M.D., M.C.); Heidelberg; Bonn. Diplomate in State Medicine (D.P.H.), University of Cambridge. Entered Indian Medical Service, 1889; served with Chitral Relief Force, 1895 (medal and clasp); in charge Camps, Delhi Durbar, 1903; retired, 1912; served European War as Commandant Convalescent Depot for Indian Troops, Barton, Hants, and as Commandant Convalescent Depot for British Troops, Barton, Hants. *Publications:* Two Monographs on Plague in India. *Recreations:* shooting, fishing, golf, tennis. *Address:* Chewton Farm, nr. Christchurch. *Club:* East India United Service. (*Died 20 Jan. 1924.*)

WHITE, Sir Luke, Kt., cr. 1908; D.L., J.P., *b.* Deighton, Yorks, 1 March 1845; *m.* 1869, *d.* (d. 1916) of A. Wood, of York. M.P. (R.) Buckrose Division of East Riding of Yorkshire 1900-18; solicitor, coroner for East Riding District, Yorks *Address:* Driffield. *T.A.:* Driffield. *T.:* Nat. 185. *Club:* National Liberal.
(*Died 17 Aug. 1920.*)

WHITE, Montagu, barrister; *e. s.* of late Henry Fancourt White, of Blanco, near George. Cape Colony; married. *Educ.:* Diocesan College, Cape Town. Entered the Cape Colonial Civil Service, 1874; resigned, 1878; sometime secretary of the Divisional Council, Komgha, Kaffraria; took part in the Gaika War at Draaibosch; left for the Transvaal, 1886; entered Mining Department; Mining Commissioner of Boksburg till 1892; Consul-General in London for South African Republic, 1892-1900. *Recreation:* music. *Address:* The Lodge, Haslemere. *Club:* Wellington. (*Died 18 April 1916.*)

WHITE, Sir Richard; Kt., cr. 1924; Chief Master of the Supreme Court, Chancery Division. *Address:* Room 173, Royal Courts of Justice, Strand, W.C. (*Died 21 Jan. 1925.*)

WHITE, Vice-Admiral Richar William; *b.* 20 Feb. 1849; *s.* of Admiral R. D. White, C.B. Entered Navy, 1862; Captain, 1891; served Straits of Malacca, 1874 (Perak medal and clasp); Assistant to Director of Naval Ordnance, 1884-88 ; commanded H.M.S. Porpoise, 1889-91 ; commanded Naval Forces of Colony of Victoria, 1892-95; Assistant Director of Naval Intelligence, 1895-97 ; commanded H.M.S. Vulcan, 1897-1900 ; District Captain at Queensferry in H.M.S. Rodney, Anson, 1900-1901 ; · commanded H.M.S. Ocean on China Station, 1901-1903 ; Admiral Superintendent Contract-built ships, Tyne and Thames, 1903-6; retired, 1904 ; Rear-Admiral, 1904 ; Vice-Admiral, 1908. *Recreations :* photography, bicycling, golf. *Address:* 3 Manston Terrace, Heavitree, Exeter. *Club :* Devon and Exeter.   (*Died 4 Dec. 1924.*)

WHITE, Lt.-Col. Samuel Robert Llewellyn, D.S.O. 1900 ; late Leinster Regt. ; *b.* 4 June 1863 ; *o.s.* of Robert White of Scotch Rath, Dalkey, Co. Dublin ; *m.* 1st, 1895, Dorothy Hey (*d.* 1903), *d.* of late Rev. B. F. Carlyle, Vicar of Cam, Gloucestershire ; one *s.* ; 2nd, 1913, Louise Mary, *y. d.* of Charles Hughes, Bryndedwydd, Dolgelly. Entered army, 1885 ; Major, 1901 ; served South Africa, 1900-2 (despatches, King's and Queen's medals and 5 clasps, D.S.O.) ; European War, 1914-15 (1914-15 Star, medals). *Address:* Scotch Rath, Dalkey, Co. Dublin. *Clubs:* United Service, Royal Societies.
    (*Died 2 Sept. 1925.*)

WHITE, Sinclair, C.B.E. 1919 ; Senior Surgeon, Sheffield Royal Infirmary ; Professor of Surgery, University, Sheffield, since 1911 ; President British Med. Association, 1909 ; Lt.-Col. R.A.M.C. (T.) ; Administrator 3rd Northern General Hospital (T.) ; *b.* 1858 ; *m.* 1887, Evelyn, *d.* of late Frederick Chalmer, Sheffield. *Educ. :* Queen's College, Galway, M.D. (gold medallist), M.Ch. Royal University ; F.R.C.S. England : D.P.H. Camb. Graduated, 1879 ; medical tutor ; then House Surgeon ; then Medical Officer of Health for the city of Sheffield ; now practising as a Consulting-Surgeon. *Publications:* The Solvent Action of Moorland Waters on Lead Piping, 1886 ; Trade Diseases of Cutlers and File-makers, 1894 ; various articles on surgical diseases in the Lancet, British Medical Journal, and Quarterly Medical Journal. *Recreation :* golf. *Address:* Ranmoor, Sheffield. *T. :* 58 Broomhill. *M. :* W 569. *Club :* Sheffield.   (*Died 8 Aug. 1920.*)

WHITE, T. Charters, M.R.C.S., L.D.S., F.R.M.S. ; s. of a Solicitor ; *b.* Chichester, 11 Nov. 1828. *Educ. :* home, privately. Qualified as Member of the College of Surgeons at King's College, London, and obtained his diploma, 1863 ; Licentiate in Dental Surgery, 1863 ; President of the Odontological Society of Great Britain, 1886 ; President of the Quekett Microscopical Club, 1880-81. *Publications:* An Elementary Manual of Microscopical Manipulation ; The Microscope and How to Use it ; various papers on Dental Histology, Microscopy, Photography, and Photo-micrography in publications ; A Microscopical Analysis of the Dental Tartar or Salivary Calculus on the Teeth of the Stone Age, describing the particles of food found in it. *Recreations :* microscopical investigation, photography, photo-micrography. *Address :* Woodland Villa, 59 Victoria Road South, Southsea.   (*Died 5 Mar. 1916.*)

WHITE, Col. William Westropp, C.B. 1916 ; C.M.G. 1919 ; B.A., M.D., M.Ch., M.A.O. ; I.M.S., retired ; *b.* 10 June 1862 ; *e. s.* of late John Carpenter White, Cork ; Capt. I.M.S. 1887 ; 4th Indian Cavalry, 1891 ; Major, 1899 ; Lt.-Col. 1907 ; Col. 1915. Served Hazara Expedition, 1891 (medal with clasp) ; Chitral, 1895 (medal with clasp) ; N.W. Frontier, India, 1897-98 (2 clasps) ; Tirah, 1897-98 (clasp) ; China, 1900 (despatches, medal with clasp) ; Relief of Pekin ; European War, 1914-18 (despatches four times, 1914 Star (France, Mesopotamia, Palestine), Bt. Col., C.B., C.M.G.) ;

retired, 1921. *Club:* Junior Naval and Military.
    (*Died 21 Mar. 1927.*)

WHITE-THOMSON, Colonel Sir Hugh Davie, K.B.E., *cr.* 1919 ; C.M.G. 1917; C.B. 1915 ; D.S.O. 1900 ; R.H.A. ; *b.* 6 Sep. 1866 ; *y. s.* of late Col. Sir R. T. White-Thomson, K.C.B. ; *m.* 1893, Ela Louisa Agatha (*d.* 1894), *d.* of late Rev. J. S. Ruddach. *Educ. :* Eton. Served South Africa (wounded, despatches thrice, Queen's medal, 5 clasps, D.S.O.) ; European War, France and Balkans, 1914-18 (wounded, despatches six times, C.B., C.M.G., K.B.E., White Eagle, Serbia, 2nd class, Officer of the Legion d'Honneur, France). *Address:* Broomford Manor, Exbourne, Devon. *Club:* Naval and Military.   (*Died 24 Feb. 1922.*)

WHITE-THOMSON, Col. Sir Robert Thomas, K.C.B. ; *cr.* 1897 ; D.L. and J.P. ; Alderman, Devon C.C. ; *b.* Glasgow, 21 February 1831 ; *e. s.* of Robert Thomson, Camphill, Renfrew ; *m.* Fanny Julia, *d.* of Gen. Sir H. Ferguson Davie, 1st Bart. 1857 ; two *s.* two *d.* *Educ. :* Eton. Major late King's Dragoon Guards ; Lieut.-Col. Commandant and Hon. Col. 4th Batt. Devon Regt. from 1867 to 1893 ; contested Tavistock Division, 1892 and 1895. *Address:* Broomford, Jacobstowe, Exbourne, Devon. *T.A. :* Exbourne.
    (*Died 13 Mar. 1918.*)

WHITE-WINTON, Meryon, M.A. ; late Editor of Weekly Notes (The Law Reports) ; *s.* of late Thomas White of 53 Portland Place, W., and of late Louisa Frances, *d.* of late William Winton of Halland Park, Sussex ; assumed mother's maiden name as additional surname, 1905. *Educ. :* St. Paul's School ; Christ Church, Oxford (M.A. 1880). Barr. 1877, Inner Temple and South-Eastern Circuit ; Hon. Sec. of Jurisprudence Department of Association for Promotion of Social Science ; was formerly Captain 3rd Battalion K. O. Yorkshire Light Infantry, and Major 4th Middlesex (West Middlesex) Volunteers. *Publications:* The Conveyancing Acts, 1881-82 (two editions) ; joint-author of White and Blackburn's Married Women's Property Act, 1882 ; The Law of Primogeniture ; The Lunacy Laws ; Law Reports : Ten Years' Digest, 1891-1900 ; Law Reports : Ten Years' Digest, 1901-1910 ; Law Reports : Current Indexes (annually) 1896-1913 ; also contributed to The Laws of England, vols. vi. and vii. (subject, Constitutional Law) 1909. *Recreations:* shooting, golf. *Address:* 97 Cadogan Gardens, S.W. ; 1 Stone Buildings, Lincoln's Inn, W.C. *Clubs:* Athenæum, Authors', Ranelagh.
    (*Died 10 July 1921.*)

WHITEHEAD, Rt. Rev. Cortlandt, S.T.D. ; Bishop of Pittsburgh since 1882 ; *b.* New York City, 30 Oct. 1842 ; *s.* of William Adee Whitehead and Margaret Elizabeth Parker ; *m.* 1868, Charlotte Burgoyne King ; one *s.* four *d.* *Educ. :* Phillip's Academy, Andover ; Yale University ; Philadelphia Divinity School. Deacon, 1867 ; Priest, 1868 ; three years in Colorado as Missionary Priest ; Rector of the Church of the Nativity, South Bethlehem, Penn., 1870 ; Secretary of the Diocesan Convention, Central Pennsylvania ; Deputy to General Convention, 1877 and 1880 ; D.D. Union College, 1880 ; D.D. Hobart College, 1887 ; S.T.D. St. Stephen's College, New York, 1890 ; LL.D. Pittsburgh, 1912. *Publications:* Sermons and addresses, missionary reports and papers ; Revision of Bishop Coxe's Thoughts on the Services. *Recreations :* foreign travel, boating, fishing. *Address:* 4868 Ellsworth Avenue, Pittsburgh, Pennsylvania, U.S.A. *T. :* Schenly 4869.
    (*Died 18 Sept. 1922.*)

WHITEHEAD, Major-Gen. Sir Hayward Reader, K.C.B., *cr.* 1917 ; C.B. 1909 ; F.R.C.S. Eng. ; Col. Commandant R.A.M.C. since 1922 ; *b.* 14 July 1855 ; 2nd *s.* of

late Rev. T. C. Whitehead ; *m.* 1893, Evelyn Wynne, 2nd *d.* of late Colonel Cayley, C.M.G., I.M.S. ; no *c.* Entered the medical profession, 1873, and the Army Medical Department, 1882 ; Assist. Professor of Military Surgery, Medical School, Netley, 1891-96 ; served Tirah Campaign, 1897-8 ; present at the actions of Dargai, and the taking of Sampagha and Arhanga Passes ; expedition against the Chamkanni Khel Afridis ; operations in the Bazar Valley, 1897 (despatches, medal 2 clasps, promoted Lieut.-Colonel) ; Colonel, 1905, and Administrative Medical Officer in India ; Principal Med. Officer, Mohmand Expedition, 1908 (despatches, medal and clasp) ; Surgeon-General, 1909 ; Deputy Director, Medical Service, Southern Command, 1909-12 ; Eastern Command, 1912-15 ; Director Medical Services, Malta, July 1915-March 1916 ; British Salonika Force, March 1916-Sep. 1917 ; Knight of Grace of the Order of St. John of Jerusalem, 1912 ; Commandant of the Legion of Honour, 2nd Class Order of St. Sava, Grand Commander of the Order of the Redeemer, Médaille d'or des Epidémies, Serbian Red Cross. *Publications:* various articles in medical journals. *Address:* Whinfield, Cobham, Surrey, *T.:* Oxshott 17. *Club:* Junior United Service.
(*Died 28 Sept. 1925.*)

WHITEHEAD, Sir Henry, Kt., *cr.* 1922 ; *b.* 12 Jan. 1859 ; *m.* 1887, Alice Mawson, Wath on Dearne ; one *d.* Worsted spinner and manufacturer ; proprietor of Henry Whitehead, Young Street Mills, Bradford and Crystal Mills, Heckmondwike ; Chairman Salts (Saltaire), Ltd. ; Chairman J. & J. Crombie, Ltd., Aberdeen ; Director Yarra Falls, Ltd., Melbourne ; partner in Robert Archibald & Sons, Tillicoultry, Scotland ; President Bradford Chamber of Commerce, 1921-24 ; Pres. Worsted Spinners' Federation ; President Bradford Masonic Association and Permanent Committee ; Chairman Bradford Freemasons Hall Co., Ltd. ; during the War was one of the three representatives of the Worsted Spinners Federation on the Wool Board of Control ; was Deputy Chairman of the Board and Chairman of the Spinners Sectional Committee ; served on every advisory committee on wool and its products which the Government set up. *Recreation:* motoring. *Address:* Stagenhoe Park, near Welwyn ; Hawkswood, Baildon, Yorks. *T.A.:* Rampant, Bradford. *T.:* Shipley 565. *Club:* Union, Bradford.
(*Died 29 Feb. 1928.*)

WHITEHEAD, Henry, M.V.O. 1909 ; D.L., J.P. ; *b.* 1842 ; *e. surv. s.* of John Whitehead (*d.* 1898) and Eliza Ellen, *d.* of late Robert Allanson of Birtle, Lancashire ; *m.* Louisa (*d.* 1918), *d.* of late Peter Priestley of Euxton ; five *s.* two *d. Educ.:* Shrewsbury ; Uppingham. Director Sir W. G. Armstrong Whitworth and Co. ; Vice-Chairman Lancashire and Yorkshire Bank ; Director Bleachers' Association ; Chairman Liverpool Storage Co. ; Director Whitehead Torpedo, Weymouth and Fiume. *Recreation:* shooting. *Address:* Haslem Hey, Bury, Lancashire. *T.A.:* Lowercroft. *T.:* Bury 390. *Clubs:* Carlton, Constitutional ; Constitutional, Union, Manchester.
(*Died 14 Mar. 1921.*)

WHITEHEAD, Sir James, 1st Bt. ; *cr.* 1889 ; D.L., J.P. F.S.A., F.R.Hist.S., F.R.S.S. ; Lord of the Manor of Wilmington or Grandison, Kent ; *b.* 2 March 1834 ; *y. s.* of James Whitehead, Appleby, Westmorland ; *m.* Mercy (*d.* 1911), 4th *d.* of Thomas Hinds, Bank House, Hunts, 1860 ; three *s.* two *d. Educ.:* Appleby Grammar School ; a Bradford merchant in London, 1860-81. Alderman of City of London, 1882-96 ; Sheriff of London and Middlesex, 1884 ; Lord Mayor of London, 1889 ; High Sheriff of County of London, 1890 ; contested North Westmorland, 1885 and 1886 ; M.P. Leicester without contest, 1892 ; retired through illness, 1894 ; one

of H.M. Lieutenants for the City of London ; for many years Chairman of the Board of Visitors to Borstal convict prison ; also for some years a visitor to H.M. Prison, Holloway, and the City of London Asylum, Stone, Kent ; for several years Governor of Christ's Hospital, St. Bartholomew's Hospital, and Queen Anne's Bounty ; Commander of the Legion of Honour, France ; Knight Commander of Servian Order of Takovo ; and Grand Cordon of Royal Order of St. Sava ; Knight Officer of Belgian Order of Leopold ; Lion and Sun of Persia ; Chinese Tablet of Honour ; Founder of Volunteer Equipment Fund ; Gold Medallist Royal Agricultural Society ; first Honorary Freeman of the Borough of Appleby, also of Kendal ; Honorary Freeman Framework Knitters' Company ; Master of the Fruiterers' Company, 1889-90 ; Master Fanmakers' Company, 1885 ; Pres. Brit. Section French Exhibition, 1889 ; for many years President Mansion House Association on Railway Rates, which he founded ; 1st Hon. Member of the Institute of Journalists ; mediated in and settled Great Dock Strike, 1889 ; Founder of the Penny a Week Collection for the Metropolitan Hospitals ; Founder of the Rowland Hill (Post Office) Benevolent Fund ; raised a fund to recompense Pasteur for his gratuitous services to 234 British patients, the surplus from which was devoted to the establishment of the British (now Lister) Institute of Preventive Medicine ; founder of several entrance and leaving scholarships at Appleby Grammar School ; founder of the Self Help Society, the Village Institute, and the Boy Scouts Troop and Club House, Wilmington. *Publications:* pamphlets on Fruit Culture, Technical Education, and Volunteer Equipment. *Recreations:* travel, fruit and flower culture, and farming. *Heir:* *s.* George Hugh. *Address:* Wilmington Manor, near Dartford, Kent. *T.:* Dartford 30. *M.:* LM 4991. *Club:* Reform.
(*Died 20 Oct. 1917.*)

WHITEHEAD, Sir James Beethom, K.C.M.G., *cr.* 1909 ; *b.* 31 July 1858 ; 2nd *s.* of late Robert Whitehead of Fiume ; *m.* 1896, Hon. Marian Cecilia Brodrick, *y. d.* of 8th Viscount Midleton ; five *s.* two *d. Educ.:* Austria ; St. John's College, Cambridge. Graduated in honours, 1880 ; M.A. Entered the diplomatic service, 1881 ; served at Petrograd, Rio de Janeiro, and Berlin ; First Secretary at Tokio, Brussels, and Constantinople ; Councillor of Embassy, Berlin, 1903-6 ; H.M.'s Envoy Extraordinary and Minister Plenipotentiary at Belgrade, 1906-10 ; J.P. Hampshire. *Address:* Efford Park, Lymington, Hants. *T.A.:* Everton, Hants. *T.:* Lymington 103. *Club:* Travellers'. (*Died 19 Sept. 1928.*)

WHITEHEAD, Colonel John Herbert, D.S.O. 1917 ; Hon. Col. R.A.M.C. ; Lieut.-Colonel, S.A.M.C. ; *y. s.* of Walter Whitehead, Shrubbery House, Upper Addiscombe, Surrey, founder of Whitehead, Morris & Co., wholesale stationers, printers, etc. ; *b.* 1 Oct. 1869 ; *m.* Maude, *d.* of Francis Newton Lowe, of Sleaford, Lincs ; two *d. Educ.:* St. Peter's Grammar School, Thanet ; Upper Canada College, Toronto ; University, London (Charing Cross Hospital). M.R.C.S. Eng. 1893 ; L.R.C.P. Lond. 1893 ; House Surgeon and House Physician, Charing Cross Hospital ; Member British Medical Association ; passed into Army Medical Service, 1894 ; resigned, 1896 ; rejoined, 1899 ; served through Siege of Ladysmith and operations Natal and Free State (King's and Queen's medals and 4 clasps) ; transferred to S.A. Constabulary (Baden-Powell's Police) in 1901 with rank Capt. ; retired, 1904, and took up private practice ; served through S.A. Rebellion, 1914, as Capt. S.A.M.C. ; assisted to raise and train

8th Mounted Brigade Field Ambulance, and commanded it in German West Africa Campaign; S.M.O. Line of Communication, Northern Force, German South - West Africa (despatches); in 1915 was S.M.O. Polchefstroon with rank of Lt.-Col.; went to S.E. Africa in command 4th Field Ambulance and S.M.O. 3rd Brigade; A.D.M.S. 2nd Div. (Gen. Van Deventers), 1916, (Colonel, 1916, despatches); returned to South Africa, 1917; A.D.M.S., Durban; retired, 1919. *Address:* The Oaks, Plains, Natal, S.A. *T.:* Plains 2. *Club:* Royal Natal Yacht.

(Died 11 July 1928.)

WHITEHEAD, Rev. Silvester; late Gov. Handsworth College, Birmingham; *b.* 11 May 1841; *m.* 1st, Isabella, *d.* of Francis Foster, Markenfield Hall, Ripon; 2nd, Frances, *d.* of Benjamin Craven, Hazel Head, Penistone; two *s.* two *d. Educ.:* National School, and Wesleyan Coll. Richmond, Surrey. Ordained, 1866; Missionary in Canton, China, 1867-77; Circuit Minister in England, 1877-1905; President of the Wesleyan Methodist Conference, 1904. *Address:* 3 St. Paul's Road, Manningham, Bradford. *(Died 3 Jan. 1917.)*

WHITEHEAD, Spencer; *b.* 1845; *s.* of Edward Bickerton Whitehead of Bristnall, Worcestershire; *m.* 1st, Catherine Ellen, *d.* of Dr. Birt Davies of Birmingham; 2nd, 1881, Gertrude Fanny, *d.* of Austin Piper of The Wilderness, Norwich; one *d. Educ.:* King Edward the Sixth School, Birmingham. A solicitor from 1868-97; a Master of the Supreme Court, 1897 - 1921; Deputy-Chairman of the Surrey Quarter Sessions; J.P.; an Income-tax Commissioner. *Address:* Imber Grove, Esher, Surrey. *T.:* Esher 316. *(Died 10 Jan. 1922.)*

WHITEHOUSE, Rev. Owen Charles, M.A. (London); Hon. D.D. Aber.; M.A. (Camb. Christ's College); Principal and Prof. of Biblical Exegesis and Theology in the Countess of Huntingdon's College, Cheshunt, 1895-1905; Senior Theological tutor after its removal to Cambridge; *b.* Palamcottah, S. India, 15 Nov. 1849; *s.* of Rev. J. O. Whitehouse, formerly missionary in Travancore; *m.* 1877, Annie Margaret, *y. d.* of late Robert Maynard, Tottenham; two *d. Educ.:* Amersham Hall School, near Reading; Univ. Coll. London (1866-70); Cheshunt Coll (1872-74); Univ. of Bonn (1876-77). Matriculated London University, 1866, with Gilchrist Scholarship; M.A. Branch 1. (Classics), 1876; Tutor in Hebrew and Classics in Cheshunt Coll., 1877-95; member of Faculty of Theology, Board of Theological and of Oriental Studies, Univ. of London, 1901-6; Examiner in Hebrew. *Publications.* translated, with additions, Schrader's Cuneiform Inscriptions and the Old Testament (2 vols.); Primer of Hebrew Antiquities, 1895; contributions to Dr. Hastings' Bible Dict., Dict. of Christ and Gospels, Encycl. of Religion and Ethics, to Encyclopædia Biblica, to Ency. Brit. (11th ed.), and to Dr. Charles' Apocrypha; also to Critical Review, Expository Times, Interpreter, and Expositor; Temple Bible (Ezekiel); Commentary on Isaiah in Century Bible; Old Testament Books. *Address:* Morley Lodge, Brooklands Avenue, Cambridge.

(Died 10 April 1916.)

WHITEING, Richard; author and journalist; *b.* London, 27 July 1840; father was in the Inland Revenue Department, Somerset House; *m.* Helen, *n.* of Townsend Harris, first United States Minister to Japan, 1869. *Educ.:* privately. First a pupil of the late Benjamin Wyon, Medallist and Chief Engraver of Her Majesty's Seals; in 1866, first essay in journalism—series of satirical papers, political and social, in Evening Star, afterwards republished as "Mr. Sprouts—his Opinions"; leader-writer and correspondent, Morning Star; editorial department, Press Association; editorial staff, Manchester Guardian; Paris Correspondent, Manchester Guardian, World (London), World

(New York), etc., etc.; returned to London to join editorial staff Daily News; resigned, 1899. *Publications:* The Democracy, 1876; The Island, 1888; No. 5 John Street, 1899; The Life of Paris, 1900; The Yellow Van, 1903; Ring in the New 1906; All Moonshine, 1907; Little People, 1908; My Harvest, 1915; Both Sides of the Curtain (with Dame Geneviève Ward), 1918; Film. No. 5 John Street, 1921. *Address:* Burford Close, 35A High Street, Hampstead, N.W.3.

(Died 29 June 1928.)

WHITELAW, Græme Alexander Lockhart; *b.* 1863; *m.* 1st, 1885, Bessie (*d.* 1900), *d.* of James Reid Stewart; one *s.*; 2nd, 1902, Laura, *d.* of late James Montagu, Melton Park, Doncaster; three *d. Educ.:* Harrow; Trinity College, Cambridge. Late Capt. 3rd Batt. Argyll and Sutherland Highlanders; M.P. Lanarkshire, N.W., 1892-95. *Address:* Brockham Park, Betchworth, Surrey. *Club:* Carlton.

(Died 23 July 1928.)

WHITELAW, Thomas, M.A., D.D.; Senior Minister of King Street United Free Church, Kilmarnock; Moderator of the United Free Church of Scotland, 1912-13; *b.* Perth, 1840; *s.* of Thomas Whitelaw, Grain Merchant there, and Barbara Dron; *m.* 1867, Alice, *d.* of Rev. Thomas M'Creath of Mile-end Road United Presbyterian Church, South Shields; four *s.* two *d. Educ.:* Perth Grammar School; St. Andrews University; United Presbyterian Theological Hall, Edinburgh. Ordained at South Shields, 1864; minister Cathedral Street U.P. Church, Glasgow, 1867; Kilmarnock, 1877; called to Ballarat, Australia, but declined, 1885; special commissioner U.F. Church of Scotland for Union of Presbyterian Churches of Australia, Sydney, 1901; visited churches in Queensland, N.S. Wales, Victoria, W. Australia, New Zealand, and Tasmania; has also travelled extensively on the Continent, in the United States, Canada, and Egypt; served on principal committees of United Presbyterian and United Free Churches; and at present a member of the United Free Committee conferring with the Established Church Committee with regard to Union. *Publications:* The Pulpit Commentary on Genesis; Exegetical and Homiletical Commentary on St. John; Preacher's Commentary on the Acts; Patriarchal Times; How is the Divinity of Jesus depicted in the N.T.?; Old Testament Critics; The Old Lamp, being short studies on the Bible; Jehovah—Jesus; numerous contributions to the Pulpit Commentary on Numbers, Job, 2nd Chronicles, Ecclesiastes, Ezekiel, with various articles in Magazines. *Recreation:* change of work. Celebrated his jubilee as an ordained minister in March 1914. *Address:* 59 Corrour Road, Newlands, Glasgow.

(Died 9 Aug. 1917.)

WHITELOCKE, R. Henry Anglin, M.D., M.Ch., F.R.C.S. (Eng.), M.A. Oxon (Hon.), Surgeon; late Lt.-Col. R.A.M.C. (T.), 3rd Southern General Hospital; Hon. Surgeon Radcliffe Infirmary and County Hospital, Oxford; Litchfield Lecturer on Surgery, University of Oxford; Examiner in Surgery in the Universities of Aberdeen and Liverpool; a Consulting Surgeon to the Great Western and London and North-Western Railway Companies; Fellow Royal Society of Medicine, President Section Children's Diseases; *b.* 1861; 4th *s.* of late Rt. Hon. Hugh Anthony Whitelocke of Bulstrode Park, Westmorland; *m.* Barbara Henry, *e. d.* of late George Lowe Reid, M.I.C.E., Brighton; two *s.* three *d. Educ.:* Owens Coll., Manchester; University of Edinburgh. After graduating and before settling in practice held various resident hospital appointments in Edinburgh, Glasgow, London, and the provinces; was for a time engaged in teaching anatomy. *Publications:* Sprains and Allied Injuries of Joints; Football Injuries; Athletics in Relation

to Disease; The Substitution of Temporary and Absorbable for Permanent and Unabsorbable Sutures in the Operations on Bone; articles, Injuries of Joints, Injuries in Region of Knee and Leg, in Practitioners' Surgery, 1912, 1916, 1919; Treatment of Sprains, System of Treatment, by Hutchinson and Collier, 1914-20; Loose Bodies in the Knee, British Journal of Surgery, 1914; Operation for Outward Dislocation of the Knee-Cap, Ibid. 1914; Movements of the Isolated Human Appendix Vermiformi (with Dr. Gunn), Ibid. 1914; Appendicutomy by a New Route, Proceedings Royal Society of Medicine, and B.M.J., 1920; many papers in medical journals. *Recreations:* collecting antiques, and shooting. *Address:* St. Giles' Gate, Oxford; 11 Upper Wimpole Street, W.1. *T.A.:* Whitelocke, Oxford. *T.:* Oxford 389, Langham 1124. *M.:* FC 4940. *Clubs:* West Indian; Oxford and County, Vincents, Oxford.
(Died 19 Nov. 1927.)

WHITESIDE, Most Rev. Thomas, R.C. Archbishop of Liverpool (Bishop since 1894); *b.* 17 April 1857. *Educ.:* St. Edward's College, Liverpool; Ushaw; English College, Rome. Professor, Vice-President, President, St. Joseph's College, Upholland; Canon of Liverpool, 1893. *Address:* Archbishop's House, Belvidere Road, Liverpool, S. *(Died 28 Jan. 1921.)*

WHITING, William Henry, C.B. 1914; M.I.C.E., Vice-Pres. I.N.A.; *b.* 1854; *s.* of William Whiting, Porchester and Gosport; *m.* 1880, Marian, *d.* of Robert Little, J.P., Slough, Buckinghamshire; three *s.* three *d.* *Educ.:* Royal Naval College, Greenwich. Entered Portsmouth Dockyard as apprentice, 1869; student of naval construction, Royal Naval College, 1873-76; draughtsman and assistant constructor, Admiralty, 1877-90; Instructor in Naval Architecture, R.N. College, 1885-90; Constructor at Chatham and Devonport, 1890-95; Chief Constructor, Hong-Kong Yard, 1895-97; served on Admiralty Committees on Submerged Torpedo Discharge and on Floating Docks; Chief Constructor and Assistant Director of Naval Construction, Admiralty, 1897-1912; Superintendent of Construction Accounts and Contract Work, Admiralty, 1912-17. *Publication:* Influence of Modern Accessories on the Design of War Ships (Gold Medal of Institution of Naval Architects). *Address:* South Corner, Duncton, Petworth. *T.A.:* Whiting Petworth. *T.:* Sutton (Sussex) 10. *M.:* YO 3223. *(Died 22 Aug. 1927.)*

WHITLEY, John Robinson; *b.* Leeds, 13 Dec. 1843; *m.* Ellen Naylor, Manchester; one *s.* three *d.* *Educ.:* France, Germany, and Italy. Associated with Lincrusta (to which he gave name) in Europe and America; creator of Earl's Court a 25-acre exhibition area, and organiser of a series of National Exhibitions —first of their kind—held there: America 1887, Italy 1888, France 1890, Germany 1891; founder and organiser of Le Touquet (Paris-Plage) as an Anglo-French pleasure resort, and then of Hardelot as a sister Pleasance, near Boulogne, as nucleus of which he acquired the historic castle of Hardelot; thanked by M. Clémenceau for placing all resources of Hardelot at disposal of Allies. *Address:* Château de Condette, Pont-de-Briques, Pas-de-Calais. *Club:* Constitutional.
(Died 31 Mar. 1922.)

WHITLEY, Kate Mary, R.I. 1889; artist; *b.* London; *d.* of late Rev. J. L. Whitley, Leicester. *Educ.:* Manchester. Began to exhibit in London and provinces, 1884; exhibited at R.A. several times; also at Dresden, Chicago, and Brussels. *Address:* Leopold House, South Wigston, near Leicester.
(Died 24 Aug. 1920.)

WHITLEY-THOMSON, Sir Frederick Whitley, Kt., *cr.* 1916; *b.* 2 Sep. 1851; *s.* of Jonathan Thomson of Glasgow, and Emma Whit-

ley of Halifax; *m.* 1888, Bertha Florence, 3rd *d.* of late Alderman Matthew Smith, Halifax; one *d.* Received grant by Royal Licence to use surname Whitley-Thomson, 1914. *Educ.:* Glasgow Academy and Andersonian Univ., Glasgow. M.P. (L.) Skipton Div. of West Riding of Yorks, 1900-1906; contested South Herefordshire, 1908; Colchester, 1910; Director of English Card-clothing Co., Ltd.; J.P., County Borough, Halifax; Mayor of Halifax, 1908-11; Alderman, 1908; was instrumental in raising a fund of £10,000 for Royal Halifax Infirmary and Halifax District Nursing Association in memory of King Edward VII.; Chairman Finance Committee of Halifax County Borough Council, 1913-19; Chairman Halifax War Refugees Committee, and received from King Albert the Medaille du Roi in recognition of services to Belgian refugees resident in Halifax and district during the War; President Halifax Chamber of Commerce, 1912-14. *Address:* 19 Addison Road, W.14; *T.:* Park 1838; 40 Prescott Street, Halifax, Yorks. *T.:* Halifax 1750. *M.:* CP 179 and XF 7171. *Clubs:* Reform, Eighty, Ranelagh; Halifax. *(Died 21 June 1925.)*

WHITMAN, Sidney, F.R.G.S.; political writer; *b.* London; *m.* 1st, 1888, Frances Charlotte (*d.* 1907), *e. d.* of late Captain Edmund Francis Austey, 20th Regiment; 2nd, 1910, Annia Henrietta, *widow* of late Edward Derenberg of Evelyn Gardens, S.W. *Educ.:* King's College School, London; Germany, and Brussels. Represented New York Herald at Constantinople during outbreak of Armenian conspiracy, 1896, and at Moscow during revolution, 1905-6; visited Edhem Pacha in same capacity at Turkish headquarters, Elassona, 1897; accompanied Turkish mission through Kurdistan, Anatolia, and Syria from Black Sea to Mediterranean, 1897-98; Austrian Grand Gold Medal for Arts and Sciences, Viribus Unitis; Grand Officer's Cross and Star of the Royal Order of the Crown of Roumania; the King of Roumania's Jubilee Medal, etc., etc. *Publications:* Metrical Translation of Grillparzer's Medea, 1878; Fetish Worship in the Fine Arts, 1885; Conventional Cant, 1887; Imperial Germany, 1888; Realm of the Habsburgs, 1893; Teuton Studies, 1895; English version (for America) of Bruno Garlepp's illustrated work, Germany's Iron Chancellor, 1897; Story of Austria, 1898; Reminiscences of the King of Roumania, 1899; Conversations with Prince Bismarck; Life of the Emperor Frederick, 1900; My Reminiscences of Prince Bismarck, 1902; German Memories, 1912; Turkish Memories, 1914; Things I Remember, 1916; ed. English version of Moltke's Letters, 2 vols.; and various contributions to English, German, and American magazines. *Address:* 25 Gledhow Gardens, S.W. *Club:* Junior Athenæum.
(Died 30 Oct. 1925.)

WHITMARSH, Rev. Robert Thomas, Hon. Canon of Norwich. *Address:* Ashby St. Mary Rectory, Norwich. *(Died 19 July 1921.)*

WHITNEY, Sir Benjamin, Kt., *cr.* 1897; Clerk of the Crown, Clerk of the Peace and Local Registrar of Titles, Co. Mayo; *b.* 23 Dec. 1833; *m.* Annabella (*d.* 1899), *d.* of late Isaac North-Bomford, 1860; two *d.* *Address:* 29 Upper Fitzwilliam Street, Dublin; Brayfort, Bray. *Clubs:* Constitutional; Friendly Brothers, Dublin.
(Died 21 Dec. 1916.)

WHITTAKER, Rt. Hon. Sir Thomas Palmer, P.C. 1908; Kt., *cr.* 1906; M.P. (L.) Spen Valley Division, Yorks, W.R., since 1892; *b.* Scarborough, 7 Jan. 1850; *s.* of Thomas Whittaker, J.P., Scarborough; *m.* Emma Mary, *d.* of Capt. Charles Theedam, Scarborough, 1874. *Educ.:* Huddersfield Coll. In the hardware and iron trade, 1866-82; editor of newspapers, 1882-92, Chairman and Managing Director of Life Assurance Institution; takes active part in Temperance movement; a member of Royal Com-

mission on Licensing, 1896-99; Chairman of Select Committee on Parliamentary Procedure, 1914; Chairman of Royal Commission on Importation of Paper, 1916. *Publications:* The Ownership, Tenure, and Taxation of Land, 1914; has written much in reviews and newspapers on Economical, Financial, Commercial, Statistical, and Social questions. *Address :* 2 Wetherby Gardens, Kensington, S.W. 5. *T. :* Western 2900. *Clubs:* Reform.
(Died 9 Nov. 1919.)

WHITTINGTON, Col. George John Charles, C.B. 1900; Army Pay Department; *b.* 1836; *s.* of George Whittington of Bath. Entered Royal North Gloucestershire Militia, 1856; Royal Canadian Rifles, 1858; Royal Welsh Fusiliers, 1875; and A.P.D., 1878; Hon. Maj. 1882, and Col.1892; served Canada (Fenian Raids), 1866-70 (medal); Egypt, 1882 (medal, Khedive's star); South Africa, 1900-1 (despatches, Queen's medal, 4 clasps, C.B.). *Address :* Codham Hall, Great Warley, Brentwood. *(Died 5 April 1916.)*

WHITTON, James Reid, D.Litt. University of South Africa; *b.* Perthshire. Three years a Resident Master in one of the London Training Colleges; served as an Assistant Inspector of Schools in the South-Eastern District of Scotland; Headmaster of the Public School at Melrose; Rector of the Normal College, Cape Town, 1878-1915; Member of Cape School Board since 1906; Member of the Council of the University of the Cape of Good Hope. *Address :* The University, Cape Town. *(Died 14 Dec. 1919.)*

WHITWELL, Edward Robson, J.P., D.L.; *b.* Sunderland, 1843; *m.* Mary Janet, *d.* of late E. Aldam Leatham, D.L., of Misarden Park, Gloucestershire; two *s.* three *d.* *Educ. :* Grove House, Tottenham. Chairman and Managing Director of the North Brancepeth Coal Co., Ltd.; Vice-Chairman and Managing Director of the Horden Collieries, Ltd.; senior partner Greveson and Whitwell, Darlington. *Address :* The Frisarage, Yarm-on-Tees, Yorks. *Clubs :* Wellington, Alpine; Royal Yacht Squadron, Cowes. *(Died 14 Oct. 1922.)*

WHYHAM, William Henry, I.S.O. 1906; District Magistrate, Antigua, Leeward Islands; *b.* 1848; *s.* of late W. Whyham, R.N.; *m.* 1876, Charlotte, *d.* of C. M. Eldridge. *Educ. :* Royal Naval School, New Cross. Entered R.N. 1864; retired, 1873; entered Colonial Civil Service; District Magistrate, Dominica, 1874; District Magistrate and Inspector of Prisons, Antigua, 1878; President Legislative Council, 1895-98; Member Executive Council, Antigua, 1895; Member Legislative Council, 1898; Member Executive Council Leeward Islands, 1902. *Recreation :* golf. *Address :* St. John's, Antigua, Leeward Islands, W.I.

WHYTE, Rev. Alexander, D.D., LL.D.; Principal New College, Edinburgh, 1909-18; *b.* Kirriemuir (Thrums), Forfarshire, 13 Jan. 1836; *m.* Jane Elizabeth, *d.* of late George Freeland Barbour of Bonskeid, Perthshire, N.B.; three *s.* three *d.* *Educ. :* Aberdeen University; New College, Edinburgh. Ordained as colleague in Free St. John's, Glasgow, 1866; translated to Free St. George's, Edinburgh, as colleague and successor to Dr. Candlish, 1870; retired as senior minister, 1916; freedom of the City of Edinburgh, 1909. *Publications:* Commentary on Shorter Catechism, 1882; Characters and Characteristics of William Law, 1893; Appreciation of Jacob Behmen, 1895; Bunyan Characters, vols. i.-iv.; Samuel Rutherford and some of his Correspondents, 1894; Lancelot Andrewes and his Private Devotions, 1895; Bible Characters, 1897, vols. i.-vi.; Santa Teresa, 1897; Father John, 1898; An Appreciation of Browne's Religio Medici, 1898; Newman, An Appreciation; Bishop Butler, An Appreciation; The Apostle Paul; The Walk, Conversation, and Character of Jesus Christ,

Our Lord; Thomas Shepard; James Fraser, Laird of Brea; Thirteen Appreciations. *Recreation:* walking. *Address :* 22 Church Row, Hampstead, N. W. *(Died 6 Jan. 1921.)*

WHYTE, James Wilkinson, I.S.O. 1915; J.P.; Senior Associate of Arts 1870; Recorder of Titles; Registrar of Public Trusts; Collector of Stamp Duties, 1884; Commissioner of the Public Debts Sinking Fund (State), 1893; of Hobart Corporation, 1910; a Trustee of the Agricultural Bank (State Advances), 1910; Retired from Public Service, 1921; *b.* Hobart, Tasmania, 1852; *s.* of late Hon. James Whyte, born on Scottish Border; *m.* 1st, Julia Helen Coverdale; 2nd, Annie Coverdale; three *s.* *Educ. :* High School, Hobart. Admitted practitioner of Supreme Court, 1876; solicitor to the Lands Titles Commissioners, 1883. *Address :* New-Town-Park, New Town near Hobart, Tasmania *T. :* 1368. *Club :* Tasmanian, Hobart. *(Died 29 May 1923.)*

WHYTE, Ven. Richard Athenry, Canon of Grafton and Armidale, 1911. *Educ. :* Pembroke Coll., Cambridge (B.A.). Ordained 1883 Curate of St. James', Plumstead, 1883-86; St. Stephen, Ballarat, 1886-88; Vicar of St. John, Horsham, Victoria, 1889-92; Rokewood, 1892-99; Coleraine, 1899-1903; Vicar and Archdeacon of Lismore, 1903-11. *Address :* Lismore, N.S.W.

WICKHAM, Rev. Gordon Bolles, Vicar, Bradford Abbas, since 1886; Canon of Salisbury; *b.* 1850; *s.* of Rev. Frederic Wickham, Winchester College; *m.* 1887, Sidney Katherine, *d.* of Admiral Lord Frederic Kerr. *Educ. :* New College, Oxford, M.A. Curate of Newton Ferrers, Devon, 1873-75; Vicar, Church Crookham, 1875-82; Assistant Priest, Winchester College Mission, 1882-86; temp. Chaplain to the Forces, Gibraltar, 1886. *Address :* Bradford Abbas Vicarage, Sherborne, Dorset.
(Died 19 Dec. 1920.)

WICKHAM, Sir Henry, Kt., *cr.* 1920; *b.* 29 May 1846; *e. s.* of late Henry Wickham, of Corbet Court, Capel Court, City of London, and Rose Cottage, Haverstock Hill; *m.* 1871, Violet Cave Carter. Sometime Commissioner for the introduction of the Pará (Hevea) Indian Rubber for the Government of India; also Inspector of Forests, Commissioner of Crown-lands; Acting District Commissioner and J.P. Colonial Service; explorer and pioneer planter for half a century in equatorial belt (east and west), Central America, Orinoco, Amazon Valley, Australia, New Guinea, Pacific Islands, etc. *Publications:* Introduction, Plantation, and Cultivation of Pará (Hevea) Indian Rubber, 1908; Journey through the Wilderness, 1872. *Recreation :* Speciality — pioneer planting. *Address :* 32 Newton Road, W.2. *T. :* Park 8423.
(Died 27 Sept. 1928.)

WICKHAM, Major Thomas Edmund Palmer, D.S.O. 1900; R.F.A.; *b.* 30 Jan. 1879; *e. s.* of R. W. Wickham of Ebley Court, Stroud; *m.* 1908, Elsie, *y. d.* of N. W. Grieve of Coyleigh, Groombridge; two *s.* *Educ. :* Marlborough. Entered R.A., 1898; served South Africa, 1900-1902 (wounded, despatches, Queen's medal, 6 clasps, King's medal, 2 clasps, D.S.O.); European War, 1914-15 (despatches, wounded, Bt. Major). *(Died July 1917.)*

WICKSTEED, Joseph Hartley, J.P., M.Inst.C.E.; Past-President I.Mech.E.; late Chairman J. Buckton and Co., Ltd., Leeds; *b.* 1842; *e. s.* of Rev. C. Wicksteed; *m.* Mary, *d.* of John Hancock, J.P., of Lurgan; four *d.* *Educ. :* Ruthin Grammar School. Inventor of several patents; Member of the Court and Council of Leeds University; late President Leeds Chamber of Commerce; late President of Leeds Philosophical Society. *Publications:* various papers. *Recreation:* golf. *Address:* Weet-
1123

wood, Leeds. *T.:* Headingley 183. *Club:* Leeds.
(*Died 16 Dec. 1919.*)

WICKSTEED, Rev. Philip Henry, M.A.
(Lond. Classics); Litt.D. (Leeds and Manchester); Lecturer and Writer; *b.* 25 Oct. 1844; 2nd *s.* of Rev. Charles Wicksteed of Leeds; *m.* 1868, Emily Rebecca (*d.* 1924), *e. d.* of Rev. Henry Solly; eight *c. Educ.:* Ruthin Grammar School; University College School; University College; Manchester New Coll., Lond. Entered the Unitarian ministry, 1867; settled first at Taunton; removed, 1870, to Dukinfield, near Manchester; Little Portland Street Chapel, London, 1874-97; Univ. Extension Lecturer, 1887-1918; Subjects—Dante, Political Economy, Wordsworth, Greek Tragedy, etc. *Publications:* Translation of Bible for Young People (six vols.); Dante, Six Sermons; Alphabet of Economic Science; Co-ordination of the Laws of Distribution; Henrik Ibsen (lectures); Religion of Time and Religion of Eternity, 1899; Translation and Notes to Paradiso; Translation and Notes to Dante's Convivio; (with Ferrers Howell, M.A.) Translation of Dante's Latin Works, with notes; (with Edmund Gardner, M.A.) Dante and Del Virgilio; The Common Sense of Political Economy; Dante and Aquinas, 1913; Dogma and Philosophy (a study of Aquinas), 1920; From Vita Nuova to Paradiso, 1922; sermons, transiations, etc. *Address:* Childrey, Berks. *Club:* University of London.
(*Died 18 Mar. 1927.*)

WIDDICOMBE, Rev. John, Canon Emeritus of Bloemfontein; *b.* Brixham, 28 Mar. 1839; *s.* of John and Louisa Widdicombe; *m.* 1877, Matilda Anne Sibley (*d.* 1878); one *d.* Ordained, 1863; Curate of George, Cape Colony 1863-70; Rector of Malmesbury, 1870-71; Master St. Andrew's School, Bloemfontein, 1872-4; Vicar of Thaba N'Chu, 1875-7; R.D. Basutoland, 1885-99; S.P.G. Director, St. Saviour's Mission, Hlotse Heights, 1876-1906; Canon of Bloemfontein, 1884-1906. *Publications:* Fourteen Years in Basutoland; In the Lesuto, 1907; Distant Brethren of Low Degree; Memories and Musings, 1915. *Recreation:* gardening, especially rose-growing. *Address:* St. Raphael's, Faure, Cape, South Africa. (*Died 27 June 1927.*)

WIDDRINGTON, Major Shallcross Fitzherbert, J.P., D.L.; *b.* 9 Feb. 1826; 3rd *s.* of late Shallcross Jacson, Capt. 3rd Light Dragoons, and Frances, *e. d.* of late Rev. Joseph Cook; assumed name Widdrington 1856 on *S.* his maternal uncle, Capt. Samuel Widdrington, R.N.; *m.* 1864, Cecilia, *e. d.* of late Edward John Gregge-Hopwood, of Hopwood Hall, Co. Lancaster; two *s.* two *d. Educ.:* Rugby. High Sheriff, Northumberland, 1874; late Major Northumberland Light Infantry Militia. *Address:* Newton Hall, Felton, Northumberland. (*Died Dec. 1917.*)

WIGGIN, Sir Henry Arthur, 2nd Bt., *cr.* 1892; J.P., D.L.; *b.* 3 May 1852; *s.* of 1st Bt. and Mary, *d.* of David Malins, Edgbaston, Birmingham; *S.* father 1905; *m.* 1878, Annie Sarah, *d.* of C. R. Cope of Kinnerton Court, Radnors; one *s.* two *d.* High Sheriff, Co. Stafford, 1896. *Heir: s.* Charles Richard Henry, Captain Staffordshire Yeomanry [*b.* 21 Mar. 1885; *m.* 1916, Mabel Violet Mary, *d.* of late Sir William Jaffray, 2nd Bt. *Educ.:* Eton; Trinity College, Cambridge; B.A. 1906]. *Address:* Walton Hall, Eccleshall. *Clubs:* Reform, Union.
(*Died 2 May 1917.*)

WIGGIN, Kate Douglas (Mrs. George Christopher Riggs), D.Litt. Bowdoin, 1904; American authoress; organised the first free kindergartens for the poor on the Pacific coast, and for several years devoted herself to that work. *Publications:* Timothy's Quest; A Cathedral Courtship; Polly Oliver's Problem; A Summer in a Cañon; The Birds' Christmas Carol; The Story of Patsy; Marm Lisa; Nine Love
1124

Songs and a Carol; A Village Watch Tower; Penelope's Experiences: 3 vols.: England, Scotland, Ireland; The Diary of a Goose Girl; in collaboration with her sister, Nora Archibald Smith, The Story Hour; Children's Rights; The Republic of Childhood, 3 vols.: The Posy Ring Golden Numbers; Rebecca of Sunnybrook Farm; The Affair at the Inn; New Chronicles of Rebecca; Waitstill Baxter, 1913; two books of Verse and five of Fairy and Folk Tales collated for children and youth (with her sister Nora A. Smith); Rose o' the River; The Old Peabody Pew; Susanna and Sue; Robinetta; Mother Carey; The Romance of a Christmas Card, 1916. *Address:* 145 West 58th Street, New; York; 12 Henrietta Street, W.C.
(*Died 24 Aug. 1923.*)

WIGHT-BOYCOTT, Lt.-Col. T. A., D.S.O. 1902; Hon. Lieut.-Col. in Army; Major Staffs Yeo. (Q.O.R. Regt.); *b.* 5 Aug. 1872; *e. s.* of late C. B. Wight-Boycott of Rudge Hall, Shropshire; *m.* 1894, Anne Catherine, *d.* of late Rev. J. Morgan, Rector of Llandudno, N. Wales; one *d. Educ.:* Eton. Served with Imperial Yeomanry in South Africa, 1900-2 (despatches twice, Queen's and King's medals, D.S.O.). *Address:* Rudge Hall, Pattingham, Wolverhampton. *Clubs:* Boodle's, Wellington.
(*Died 30 Mar. 1916.*)

WIGLEY, Frederick George, C.I.E. 1912; of the Inner Temple, Barrister-at-Law; Secretary to the Bengal Legislative Council, 1896-1913; attached to India Office, 1913-17; *b.* 1855, *s.* of late John Gwyn Middleton Wigley, solicitor; *m.* Grace Agnes, *d.* of late George Davidson Mackay; three *s.* three *d. Educ.:* Melbourne, Victoria. Called to Bar, 1889; Parliamentary Draftsman; practised at the Calcutta Bar, 1895-98; Secretary to the Calcutta Building Commission, 1897-98; Coroner of Calcutta, 1898-99. *Publications:* several works on Indian law. *Recreations:* walking, music. *Club:* Constitutional. (*Died 22 Mar. 1918.*)

WIGLEY, Sir George, Kt., *cr.* 1923; J.P.; Chairman George Wigley & Sons, Ltd., silk merchants, Nottingham; *b.* 1837; *s.* of Robert Wigley; *m.* 1870, Clara, *d.* of Jos. Clarke; two *s.* five *d.* President of Savings Bank, Nottingham; President Nottingham Eastern Division Conservative Association; Director of Eagle, Star, and British Dominion Insurance Co.; Chairman of Directors of Nottingham Manufactory Company, *Recreation:* shooting. *Address:* Redcliffe, Mapperley Road, Nottingham. *T.:* 1689. *M.:* 1074. *Clubs:* Conservative, Boro', Nottingham. (*Died 5 Jan. 1925.*)

WIGNALL, James, National Organiser, Dock, Wharf, Riverside and General Workers' Union; M.P. (Lab.) Forest of Dean, Gloucester, since Dec. 1918; *b.* 21 July 1856; *m.* 1876, *d.* of George Rees, Carmarthen; three *s.* one *d. Educ.:* National School. Thirty years Trade Unions organiser; J.P. Borough of Swansea; Member of old School Board; Vice-Chairman four years; Member of Overseas Settlement Delegation, 1923. *Recreations:* no time for anything but work. *Address:* Newnham, 17 Fawnbrake Avenue, Herne Hill, S.E.24.
(*Died 10 June 1925.*)

WILBERFORCE, Ven. Albert Basil Orme, D.D., Archdeacon of Westminster since 1900; Rector of St. John's, Westminster; Chaplain of the House of Commons since 1896; *b.* Winchester, 14 Feb. 1841; *y. s.* of Samuel Wilberforce, Bishop of Oxford, subsequently of Winchester; *m.* Charlotte (*d.* 1909), *e. d.* of Capt. Netherton Langford, R.N., and Caroline St. Leger. *Educ.:* Eton; Exeter Coll. Oxford (D.D.). Ordained 1866 as Chaplain to the Bishop of Oxford; subsequently Curate of Cuddesdon, Oxfordshire; of Seaton, Devonshire; of St. Jude's, Southsea; appointed Rector of St. Mary s, Southampton, 1871; Canon

of Westminster, 1894-1900. *Publications:* The
Trinity of Evil, 1885 ; Sermons preached in
Westminster Abbey, 1898 ; second series 1902 ;
Following on to Know, 1904 ; Speaking Good of
His Name, 1905 ; Sanctification by the Truth,
1906 ; New Theology, 1908 ; The Hope that is
in me, 1909 ; The Power that Worketh in us,
1910. *Address:* 20 Dean's Yard, Westminster
Abbey, S.W. *T.:* Victoria 1800.
                              (*Died 13 May* 1916.)

WILCOX, Ella Wheeler ; poet; *b.*
(Wheeler) Johnstown Centre, Wisconsin, 1855 ;
m. 1884, Robert M. Wilcox (*d.* 1916) of New York.
Educ.: University of Wisconsin. Editorial writer
and contributor New York Journal and Chicago
American. *Publications:* Poems of Passion;
Three Women, 1898 ; An Ambitious Man; Every-
day Thoughts in Prose and Verse ; Maurine ;
Poems of Pleasure : Kingdom of Love and other
Poems ; An Erring Woman's Love ; Men, Women,
and Emotions ; The Beautiful Land of Nod ;
Poems of Power ; The Heart of the New Thought;
Sonnets of Abelard and Héloise ; An Ambitious
Man, 1908 ; The Diary of a Faithless Husband,
1910 ; Poems of Experience ; Yesterday ; Poems
of Progress; 1911 ; Picked Poems ; A Woman's
Letters ; Cameos, 1912 ; Poems of Problems,
1914 ; The Art of being Alive ; Historical
Mother Goose, 1914. *Address:* Granite Bay,
Short Beach, Conn. ; Hotel Belmont, New
York.   (*Died 28 Oct.* 1919.)

WILD, James Anstey ; J.P. ; Registrar,
City of London Court, 1889-1921 ; Barr.-at-Law,
Gray's Inn ; *b.* 2 July 1853 ; *e. s.* of late James
Anstey Wild, 104 Westbourne Terrace, W. ; *m.*
Beatrice Dorothy Margaret, *e. d.* and *co-heiress*
of late Rev. W. S. Preston, of Warcop Hall,
Westmorland, Lord of Manor of Warcop, and
patron of that living ; two *s.* one *d. Educ.:*
privately. *Address:* Warcop Hall, Westmor-
land ; St. James's Court, S.W. ; City of London
Court, E.C. *Club:* Arts. (*Died 19 May* 1922.)

WILD, Rev. Marshall, M.A. (Oxon.) ; Hon.
Canon of Southwell since 1906 ; *b.* 1834 ; *s.* of
Thomas Martyr Wild of Strettit Place, East
Peckham, Kent. *Educ.:* The King's School,
Canterbury ; Queen's College, Oxford. Deacon,
1855 ; Priest, 1858 ; Assistant Curate succes-
sively at Talk - on - the - Hill, Alton, Staffs,
St. Mary's, Wolverhampton, and Newark,
Notts, 1860-64 ; Incumbent of Poynton,
Cheshire, 1864-80 ; Vicar of Newark and Rural
Dean, 1880-1907. *Address:* St. Werburgh's
Vicarage, Derby.   (*Died 6 Jan.* 1916.)

WILDE, Henry, D.Sc., D.C.L., F.R.S. ; *b.*
Manchester, 1833. *Educ.:* private schools. Engaged in scientific pursuits from early age.
Discoveries: indefinite increase of the magnetic
and electric forces from quantities indefinitely
small, 1864 ; the synchronising property of
alternating currents to control the rotations of
a number of dynamos, an essential feature in
the great installation at Niagara and other
electro-generating stations, 1868 ; new multiple
relations among the atomic weights by which
the existence of undiscovered elements and
their properties have been predicted, 1878 ;
that the moving force of celestial bodies is as
the square of the velocity, and inversely proportional to the square of the distance, 1909.
Inventions: the dynamo-electric machine, 1864-
1865 ; generated powerful electric light for the
first time therefrom, 1865 ; applied the dynamo,
with other of his inventions, to the production
of the search-light in the Royal Navy, and to
the electro-deposition of metals from their
solutions, 1868-80 ; magnetarium for reproduc-
ing the phenomena of terrestrial magnetism and
the secular variation of the mariner's compass,
1890. *Publications:* original papers in the Phil.
Trans. and Proc. of the Roy. Soc., Philosophical
Magazine, Memoirs of the Manchester Literary
and Philosophical Society, Comptes Rendus de

l'Académie des Sciences. Interests himself in
the advancement of science and the higher
education, and has given substantial aid to
institutions for the promotion of these objects.
Address: The Hurst, Alderley Edge, Cheshire.
                              (*Died 29 Mar.* 1919.)

WILKIE, Alexander, J.P. ; Companion of
Honour, 1917 ; M.P. (Lab.) Dundee, 1906 - 22 ;
Alderman of Newcastle City Council ; was on
Education Committee, and is a Magistrate ; *b.*
30 Sep. 1850; *s.* of William Wilkie; *m.* 1872, Mary
Smillie (*d.* 1921) ; one *s. Educ.:* Public School,
Fife. Served his apprenticeship to be a ship-con-
structor, after some sea-going experience settled
in Glasgow ; became Secretary of the Glasgow
Shipwrights Society, and for seventeen years
represented it on the Glasgow Trades Council,
of which Council he was President for some
considerable time ; took an active interest in
Glasgow Parliamentary representation ; re-
constituted, 1882, the then self-contained local
Societies into a National and International
Association, now the Ship-constructors' and
Shipwrights' Assoc. (was appointed Gen. Sec.);
has represented the Association since, and has
never missed a single meeting on the Trade
Union Congress ; Member for years of the Parliamentary Committee ; topped the Poll at the
Edinburgh Congress and was Chairman for the
year ; member of the Congress Committee which
instituted the Labour Representative Committee, now the Labour Party ; acted on the
Committee for several years ; one of the Committee who framed the Rules and Regulations
of the General Federation, and has been one of
its Trustees on the Management Committee all
along ; represented the British Congress at the
Detroit Convention of the American Federation of Labour, 1899 ; Member of the Mosely
Industrial Commission to America, 1902 ; contested Sunderland, 1900. *Address:* Wilkie Chambers, Eldon Square, Newcastle ; Leven House,
Lesbury Road, Heaton, Newcastle.
                              (*Died 2 Sept.* 1928.)

WILKIN, Sir Walter (Henry), K.C.M.G.,
cr. 1896 ; Kt., *cr.* 1893 ; D.L. ; *b.* 1 Apr. 1842 ; *s.*
of D. Wilkin, of Kelvedon Hatch, Essex, and
City of London ; *m.* 1870, Margot, *d.* of H. R.
Dale ; two *s.* one *d.* Barrister Middle Temple,
1875 ; Sheriff of London, 1893 ; Lord Mayor of
London, 1895 ; late Colonel 3rd Middlesex A.V.,
V.D. ; is a Knight Commander of several foreign
orders. *Address:* 43 Gloucester Square, Hyde
Park, W.2. *T.:* Paddington 6742; Linton, Cambridgeshire. *Clubs:* City of London, Oriental.
                              (*Died 13 Nov.* 1922.)

WILKINS, Rev. George, B.D. ; Fellow
and Tutor Trinity College, Dublin. *Educ.:*
Trinity College, Dublin. B.A. 1880 ; M.A. 1884 ;
ordained 1891; Fellow, 1891 ; Junior Dean, 1892 ;
Tutor and Junior Proctor, 1893 ; Classical
Lecturer and Examiner, 1892 ; Div. Lecturer,
1893; Univ. Select Preacher, 1895 ; Professor of
Hebrew, 1900. *Publications:* The Growth of
the Homeric Poems, 1880 ; Deuteronomy, 1902.
Address: Trinity College, Dublin.
                              (*Died 11 Feb.* 1920.)

WILKINS, Rev. Henry Russell, Vicar
of St. John's, Clifton ; Hon. Canon of Bristol;
late Rural Dean of Clifton ; *b.* London, Dec. 1859 ;
s. of George Dashwood Wilkins, Bengal Civil Service ; *m.* 1887, Mary Christabel (*d.* 1922), *d.* of
Rev. E. G. Penny, M.A., Vicar of St. Mary-
de-Lode, Gloucester ; two *s. Educ.:* London;
Gloucester Theological College. Deacon, 1885 ;
Priest, 1886 ; worked in or near Bristol ever
since. *Address:* St. John's Vicarage, Clifton,
Bristol.   (*Died 15 Mar.* 1924.)

WILKINS, Col. James Sutherland,
D.S.O. 1891 ; L.R.C.P., M.R.C.S., P.M.O. Aden
District ; *b.* 1851 ; *m.* 1905, Dora Sophia Lee (*d.*
1906), 2nd *d.* of Rev. F. French of Worlingworth
Rectory, Suffolk : one *s.* Entered I.M.S. 1874 ;
                                          1125

served Afghan War, 1880-82 (medal); Burmah, 1886-87 (despatches, medal with two clasps, D.S.O.); Kaiser-i-Hind gold medal for public service in India, and silver cross of the Order of the Hospital St. John of Jerusalem in England for four years' plague work in India; in charge Concentration Camps, Orange River Colony, 1902-3 (medal, three clasps); Coronation Medal when Mayor of Eye, 1910. *Address:* Stayer House. Eye, Suffolk. (*Died 27 Oct. 1916.*)

WILKINSON, Major-General George Allix, R.A. (retired); *b.* 1828; *s.* of Robert Wilkinson, Montague Square, W.; *m.* 1858, Eliza, *d.* of Francis Gosling, Sutton, Surrey; two *s.* two *d. Educ.:* Royal Military Academy, Woolwich. Entered Royal Artillery, 1847; served in Canada, India, and Mediterranean Stations; Passed Staff College; retired as Colonel with honorary rank Major-General, 1880. *Address:* Edenholme, Thorpe Chertsey.

(*Died 22 Nov. 1919.*)

WILKINSON, Sir Hiram Shaw, Kt., *cr.* 1903; Pro-Chancellor Queen's University, Belfast; *b.* Belfast, 13 June 1840; *s.* of late John Wilkinson, Belfast, and Annabella, *d.* of late William Shaw of Holden's Valley, Waringstown, Co. Down; *m.* 1864, Prudie (*d.* 1870), *d.* of late Thomas Gaffikin; one *s. Educ.:* Queen's College, Belfast (B.A., LL.D.); holder of Studentship awarded by Four Inns of Court, 1871; Barrister, 1872. Entered Consular Service in Japan as Student Interpreter, 1864; Vice-Consul, 1877; Acting Assistant Judge, Shanghai, 1879-80; Crown Advocate, 1881; was British Commissioner for Settlement of Claims after Canton Riots, 1888; Judge of H.M. Court for Japan, 1897-1900; Chief Justice H.M. Supreme Court for China and Corea, 1900-1905; retired; D.L., J.P. Co. Londonderry; High Sheriff, 1921. *Address:* Moneyshanere, Tobermore, Co. Derry. *T.A.:* Wilkinson, Tobermore. *Clubs:* Athenæum, Wellington; Ulster, Belfast. (*Died 27 Sept. 1926.*)

WILKINSON, Vice-Admiral Julian Charles Allix; *b.* 1859; *s.* of late Capt. James Allix Wilkinson, 15th Regt. (now East Yorkshire); *m.* Frances, *o. d.* of late J. W. Welby, late of Cromwell Road, S.W. *Educ.:* Rev. Arthur Watson's, Egypt House, Cowes. Joined H.M.S. Britannia as Naval Cadet, 1872; Midshipman, 1874; Sub-Lieut., 1878; Lieut., 1882; Comr., 1895; Capt., 1900; commanded H.M.S. Iris, Hawke, Thetis, London; Inspecting Captain, Western District of Coastguards; Good Service Pension, 1907; Rear-Admiral, 1909; retired 1911. *Club:* United Service.

(*Died 13 Nov. 1917.*)

WILKINSON, Lancelot Craven, F.R.G.S., etc. Adviser to Russian Government on Oriental matters; *s.* of Edward Wilkinson, M.A., Ph.D. *Educ.:* Harrow; Cheltenham; St. Bartholomew's Hospital; abroad. A.D.C. to H.S.M. the Sultan of Morocco, 1908-1910; served South African Campaign, 1899-1902, Warwickshire Imperial Yeomanry; Lieut. Intelligence Department H.Q.S., and later attached to 7th Dragoon Guards (Queen's medal, 3 bars, King's medal, 2 bars); Hispano-Moorish Campaign, 1910, War Correspondent to New York Herald and Daily Mail (medal and clasp); Moorish Civil War, 1908, attached to H.S.M. Sultan (Moulai Hafid) Personal Staff; Belgrade, 1904, present at assassination of King Alexander with British Consul; M.R.C.S. (Eng.), L.R.C.P. (Lond.).; Chief personal adviser to Secretary of State for War on Foreign Political Matters, 1914-15; senior resident surgeon to the Saidieh Hospital, Cairo, 1916. *Publications:* several works on Preventive Inoculation and Autogenous Vaccines as applied to surgery on the field of battle. Inventor and patentee of Mehamo process for economising and rendering fuel smokeless, 1907. *Recreations:* Oriental

1126

literature and travel. *Club:* Sports.
(*Died 28 July 1923.*)

WILKINSON, Rev. Michael Marlow Umfreville: Rector of Reepham St. Mary since 1864; Hon. Canon, Norwich, 1902; *b.* 10 Dec. 1831; *m.* 1866; three *d. Educ.:* Trinity College, Cambridge (Scholar, 5th Wrangler). Fellow and Assistant Tutor, Trinity College, 1855-65; Diocesan Inspector, Norwich, 1875-88. *Address:* Reepham Rectory, Norwich.

(*Died 22 Mar. 1916.*)

WILKINSON, Major Thomas Henry Desvœux, D.S.O. 1887; retired pay; *b.* London, 11 June 1858; *e. s.* of Rt. Rev. the Bishop of St. Andrews, and Caroline, *d.* of Lieut.-Col. Benfield Desvœux, late Scots Guards. *Educ.:* Royal Military Coll., Sandhurst. Joined Rifle Brigade, 1879; served in Mahsood Waziri Expedition, 1881; Burmese Expedition, 1886-88 (despatches, D.S.O., India medal and two clasps); received the Jubilee Decoration of 22 June 1897. *Club:* Naval and Military. (*Died 27 Jan. 1928.*)

WILKS, Rev. William, M.A., V.M.H., F.R.H.S.; *b.* Ashford, Kent, 19 Oct. 1843; *s.* of Dr. G. F. Wilks, of Ashford. *Educ.:* under the great scientist Prof. Charles Pritchard; Pembroke College, Cambridge. After 2 years accepted the Curacy of Croydon; about 1880 became a member of the Floral Committee of R.H.S., and was elected to a seat on the Council and appointed Hon. Sec. 1888; resigned, 1919; Vicar of Shirley, Surrey, 1879-1912. *Publications:* man**'** papers in the Journal of the Society. *Recreation:* growth and study of plants of all kinds. *Address:* The Wilderness, Shirley, Croydon. (*Died 2 Mar. 1923.*)

WILLANS, Lt.-Col., Thomas James, D.S.O. 1915; late 57th Wilde's Rifles, Frontier Force; *b.* 2 Sep. 1872. Entered army, 1893; Capt. Indian Army, 1902; Major, 1911; served N.W. Frontier, India, 1897-8 (medal with clasp); European War, 1914-17 (despatches, D.S.O.); retired 1921. (*Died 11 Dec. 1923.*)

WILLCOCKS, G. Waller, C.B. 1911; M.I.C.E.; Chief Engineering Inspector Local Government Board, 1902-13; *m.* 1884, Mary, *e. d.* of late Rowland Escombe; two *s.* one *d. Address:* Redthorn, Rodway Road, Roehampton. S.W. (*Died 7 July 1918.*)

WILLCOCKS, General Sir James, G.C.B., *cr.* 1921; K.C.B., *cr.* 1914; K.C.S.I., *cr.* 1913; G.C.M.G., *cr.* 1915; K.C.M.G., *cr.* 1900; D.S.O. 1887; C.M.G. 1899; C.B. 1907; Col. Loyal Regt.; *b.* 1 Apr. 1857; 4th *s.* of late Capt. W. Willcocks, H.E.I.C.S.; *m.* 1889, Winifred, 2nd *d.* of Colonel G. A. Way, C.B.; one *s. Educ.:* Tutors; Easton, Somersetshire. Entered Army, 1878; Captain Leinster Regt. 1884; Major, 1893; Lt.-Col., 1899; Colonel, 1902; Maj.-Gen., 1906; Lt.-Gen., 1908; General, 1916; served in Afghan Campaign, 1879-80 (medal); Waziri Expedition, 1881 (despatches); Soudan Campaign, 1885 (medal with clasp and bronze star); Burma Expedition, 1886-89 (medal with 2 clasps, despatches, D.S.O.); Chin Lushai Expedition, 1889-90 (clasp); Munipoor Expedition 1891 (despatches, clasp); as A.A.G. with Tochi Field Force, 1897 (despatches, medal with clasp, Brevet of Lieut.-Col.); as 2nd in command West African Frontier Force, 1898; Borgu, 1898 (medal with clasp); received the special thanks of H.M. Government; temporary Lieut.-Col., Nov. 1897; Commanded West African Frontier Force, 1899-1900; local Colonel. Sept. 1898; in command of Ashanti Field Force; Relief of Kumasi, 1900 (Brevet of Colonel); K.C.M.G.; received the freedom of the City of London, and a sword of honour; mentioned in King's Speech at opening of his first Parliament; joined Field Force in South Africa, 1902 (medal and clasp); commanding Nowshera Brigade, India, 1902-7; Zakka Khel Expedition, 1908; served European War, 1914-

1915 (despatches twice, G.C.M.G.); Governor of Bermuda, 1917-22; retired pay, 1922; Grand Officer Legion of Honour; LL.D. of Amherst College, United States, 1918. *Publications:* From Cabul to Kumassi, 1904; With the Indians in France, 1920; The Romance of Soldiering and Sport, 1925. *Recreations:* big-game shooting, riding, polo. *Club:* Naval and Military.   (*Died 18 Dec. 1926.*)

WILLES, William, M.R.C.S. (Eng.); L.R.C.P. Ed.; Consulting Physician to the Miller General Hospital for South-East London; late Additional Medical Officer to the Royal Naval College and Royal Hospital School, Greenwich; *s.* of late William P. Willes, solicitor, Weymouth, Dorset; *b.* 1855; *m.* Emily Kate, *d.* of late Deputy Inspector of Hospitals, W. W. Rawes, Madras Army; two *s.* *Educ.:* Bath College; St. Bartholomew's Hospital. Resident Medical Officer at Royal Free Hospital, Royal United Hospital, Bath, and Royal Sea Bathing Infirmary, Margate; in practice at Greenwich since 1883. *Address:* Thornleigh, Bodorgan Road, Bournemouth. *T.:* 2815. *Club:* Bournemouth. (*Died 7 May 1924.*)

WILLIAMS, Capt. Albert, M.V.O. 1908 and 1922; Mus. Doc.; late Director of Music, Grenadier Guards; Liveryman, Musicians' Company; Conductor, National Welsh Festival; Member Musical Association and Madrigal Society; retired pay, 1921. *Club:* Savage.
    (*Died 10 Feb. 1926.*)

WILLIAMS, Maj.-Gen. Sir Albert Henry Wilmot, K.C.V.O., *cr.* 1904; Col.-Commandant R.H.A.; *b.* 7 Feb. 1832; *s.* of late J. W. Williams, of Herringston, Dorset. Entered army, 1849; Captain, 1856; Major, 1872; Lieut.-Colonel, 1875; Colonel, 1880. Served Crimea, 1855 (medal with clasp, Turkish medal); Indian Mutiny, 1858 (despatches); Central India (medal). *Address:* 22 Chesham Place, S.W. *Clubs:* United Service, Turf, Marlborough.
    (*Died 29 Oct. 1919.*)

WILLIAMS, Aneurin, J.P.; M.P. (L.) Plymouth, 1910; North-West Durham, 1914; Consett Division, 1918-22; Chairman of House of Commons Committee on Public Accounts, 1921 and 1922; Director, First Garden City, Ltd. Joint Hon. Secy. Labour Copartnership Assoc.; Member of Executive League of Nations Union; Treasurer Proportional Representation Society; *b.* Dowlais, Glamorganshire, 11 Oct. 1859; 2nd *s.* of late Edward Williams, C.E., J.P., of Cleveland Lodge, Middlesbrough, ironmaster; *m.* 1888, Helen Elizabeth (*d.* 1922), *d.* of John Pattinson, J.P., of Shipcote House, Gateshead; one *s.* one *d.* *Educ.:* private school; St. John's College, Cambridge (M.A. Classical Tripos, 1880). Called to Bar, Inner Temple, 1884; one of acting partners, Linthorpe Ironworks, Middlesbrough, 1886-1890; contested Mid-Kent (L.), 1906. *Publications:* Copartnership and Profit-sharing; Twenty-eight Years of Copartnership at Guise; article on Co-operative Societies in the Encyclopædia Britannica, etc. *Address:* Hindhead, Surrey. *T.A.:* Hindhead. *Clubs:* Reform, National Liberal, Eighty.
    (*Died 20 Jan. 1924.*)

WILLIAMS, Anna, Professor of Singing; *b.* 3 Campden Hill Terrace, W., of English parents; *m.* 1910, R. J. Fennessy. *Educ.:* Queen's College; Bedford College. Commenced in 1874 in concerts, oratorios, ballads, also in opera; retired 13 Oct. 1897. *Recreations:* rowing, walking, gymnastics, fencing, cycling. *Address:* 72 Comeragh Road, Baron's Court, W.
    (*Died 3 Sept. 1924.*)

WILLIAMS, Brig.-Gen. Arthur Blount Cuthbert, C.B. 1913; Director of Supplies and Transport, India, since 1912; *b.* 1 Dec. 1860. Entered army, 1881; Captain, I.S.C., 1892; Major, Indian army, 1901; Lieut.-Col., 1907; served Relief of Chitral (medal

with clasp); China, 1900 (despatches, medal); N.W. Frontier, India, 1908 (despatches, medal with clasp). *Address:* Q.M.G.'s Branch, Simla, India.   (*Died 20 June 1918.*)

WILLIAMS, Rt. Rev. Arthur Llewellyn, D.D.; Bishop of Nebraska since 1908; *b.* Canada, 30 Jan. 1856; *s.* of Richard Jones Williams, and Elizabeth Johnstone; *m.* 1880, Adelaide M'Kinstry; one *d.* *Educ.:* Greenwich Academy; Western Theological Seminary. Deacon, 1888; Priest, 1889; Missionary White River, Colorado, 1888-92; Rector Christ Church, Chicago, 1892-99; Bishop Coadjutor of Nebraska, 1899. *Publications:* occasional sermons and current articles. *Address:* 1716 Dodge Street, Omaha, Neb., U.S.A.
    (*Died 29 Jan. 1919.*)

WILLIAMS, Sir (Arthur) Osmond, 1st Bt., *cr.* 1909; J.P.; D.L. Carnarvonshire and Merionethshire; Chairman Quarter Sessions; Lord-Lieut. of Merionethshire; Constable of Harlech Castle, 1909; *b.* 17 Mar. 1849; *s.* of David Williams, first Liberal Member (1868) for Merionethshire since the Commonwealth; *m.* 1880, Frances Evelyn (*d.* 1926), 4th *d.* of J. W. Greaves of Berricote, Warwickshire; one *s.* two *d.* Was Chairman of Merioneth County Council for three years; M.P. (R.) Merionethshire, 1900-10. *Heir:* *g.s.* Michael Osmond, *b.* 22 April 1914. *Address:* Castle Deudraeth, Penrhyn Deudraeth, N. Wales. *Clubs:* Boodle's, Ranelagh, Brooks's.   (*Died 28 Jan. 1927.*)

WILLIAMS, Sir Burton Robert, 6th Bt. *cr.* 1866; *b.* 7 July 1889; 3rd *s.* of 3rd Bt. and Matilda Frances, *d.* of E. B. Beauchamp of Trevince, Redruth; *S.* brother, 1913; late Lieut. 3rd Batt. Devon Regiment; rejoined Aug. 1914; served European War, 1914-17. Owns about 4500 acres. *Heir:* *u.* Captain Frederick Law Williams [*b.* 10 May 1862]. *Club:* Naval and Military.   (*Died 3 Oct. 1917.*)

WILLIAMS, Rt. Rev. Charles David, D.D., L.H.D., LL.D.; Bishop of Michigan, U.S.A., since 1906; *b.* 30 July 1860; *s.* of David and Eliza Williams; *m.* 1886, Lucy Victoria, *d.* of Rev. Samuel Benedict, Rector of St. Paul's Church, Cincinnatti, O.; four *s.* five *d.* *Educ.:* Kenyon College; Bexley Theological Seminary, Gambier, Ohio. Tutor, Kenyon College; 1880-1884; Assistant at Trinity Church, Columbus, O., 1884; Rector, Church of the Resurrection, Fern Bank, O., 1884-89; St. Paul's Church, Steubenville, O., 1889-93; Dean of Trinity Cathedral, Cleveland, Ohio, 1893-1906. *Publications:* various sermons and sociological pamphlets; A Valid Christianity for To-day; The Christian Ministry and Social Problems. *Address:* 24 Eliot Street, Detroit, Michigan, U.S.A. *T.A.:* Woodward 2326 and Detroit, Michigan. *T.:* Glendale 196, Main 9583. *M.:* Mich. 23140 *Clubs:* Cobden; City, New York.
    (*Died 14 Feb. 1923.*)

WILLIAMS, Charles Riby, C.M.G. 1902; *b.* 1857; *m.* 1892; one *d.* Member of the Legislative and Executive Councils; Supervisor of Customs, Gold Coast Colony, 1884; District Commissioner, 1887; Comptroller of Customs, 1890; Chief British Commissioner Anglo-German Boundary Commission, 1892; Treasurer of the Gold Coast Colony, 1895-1909; Acting Colonial Secretary various periods; retired 1909.
    (*Died 13 Dec. 1924.*)

WILLIAMS, Chisholm, F.R.C.S. 1891; Electro-Therapeutist, London Homœopathic Hospital; *b.* London, 10 April 1866; 2nd *s.* of late D. C. Williams, H.M.C.; *m.* 1893, Amy Hannah, *d.* of late W. Woodward, Camberwell; two *d.* *Educ.:* privately; King's College, London; St. Thomas's Hospital. Member Royal College of Surgeons, England, 1892; Past President W. Kent Medical-Chirurgical Society; Past President British Electro-Therapeutic Society; Member,

British Medical Association, British Orthopædic Society, etc.; late Lecturer London School Board; late Electro-Therapeutist and Surgeon late City Orthopædic Hospital; Lecturer on Electro-Therapeutics, West London Hospital Post-Graduate College; St. John's Hospital for Skin Diseases. *Publications*: High Frequency Electrical Currents in the Treatment of some Diseases, 1901; X-Rays in the Treatment of Cancer, Lancet, 1905; and in Archives of Rontgen Rays, 1906; and many other papers on X-Rays and Cancer. *Recreations*: electrical and mechanical experiments, photography. *Address*: Heriot House, Hendon; Breakers, Shoreham, Sussex. *T.*: Mayfair 3815; 295 P.O. Finchley. *Club*: Royal Automobile. (*Died 10 April 1928*.)

WILLIAMS, C. F. Abdy; engaged in musical literary work; *b.* 1855; *s.* of Charles Abdy Williams and Eliza Ellen Windsor; *m.* 1881, Ellen Margaret, *d.* of Frederick Bayard Elton of Whitestaunton Manor, Somerset. *Educ.*: Sherborne; Trinity Hall, Cambridge. Composed music in the Greek modes for the Greek plays at Bradfield College, 1895, 1898, 1900. *Publications*: Historical Account of Degrees in Music at Oxford and Cambridge; Life of J. S. Bach; Life of Handel; Story of Musical Notation; Story of the Organ; Story of Organ Music; The Rhythm of Modern Music; The Aristoxenian Theory of Rhythm; articles and lectures on Ancient Greek Music, Plainsong, etc. *Recreation*: yachting. *Address*: South Mead, Milford-on-Sea, Hants. *Club*: Royal Cruising. (*Died 27 Feb. 1923*.)

WILLIAMS, David, D.A. (Wales), M.A. (Oxon); Professor in Pastoral Theology at the United Theological College, Bala, since 1922; *b.* Holyhead, 4 May 1877; *s.* of Eliezer and Elizabeth Williams; *m.* 1905, Margaret Catherine Owen, Holyhead; no *c.* *Educ.*: Park Board School, Holyhead; High School, Oswestry; University College of Wales, Aberystwyth; Jesus College, Oxford. Pastor of Clifton Street Church (Presbyterian Church of Wales), 1903-5; Professor of Church History at Trevecca College, 1905-6; Professor of New Testament Exegesis at the Theological College, Aberystwyth, 1906-22; Chaplain to H.M. Forces, 1916-18. *Publications*: Commentaries (in Welsh) on Galatians and 2 Corinthians; assistant editor and contributor to Welsh Bible Dictionary; articles in religious and theological magazines. *Recreations*: golf, tennis, walking. *Address*: Theological College, Bala, North Wales.
(*Died 11 July 1927*.)

WILLIAMS, Ven. David Edward, Archdeacon of St. Davids since 1900; Rector of Bosherston, Pembroke, since 1912; M.A. Exeter Coll., Oxford; *y. s.* of Matthew Davies Williams of Cwmcynfelin, Cardiganshire; J.P., D.L.; *b.* 1847; *m.* 1879, Rose (*d.* 1909), *d.* of Joshua Paynter, C.B.; two *d.* Formerly curate of St. David's, Carmarthen; vicar, St. Michael's, Pembroke, 1877-83; All Saints, Glasbury, 1883; Llanfrynach, 1883-89; Llawhaden, 1889-97; Lampeter Velfrey, 1897-1901; Chaplain to late Bishop of St. Davids, 1898-97; Rector of Johnston with Steynton, 1901-12. *Address*: Bosherston Rectory, Pembroke. *Club*: Junior Constitutional. (*Died 23 Mar. 1920*.)

WILLIAMS, Sir Dawson, Kt., *cr.* 1921; C.B.E. 1919; Hon. LL.D. (Glasgow); D.Litt. (Durham); D.Sc. (Sheffield); M.D., F.R.C.P.; editor of the British Medical Journal since 1898; consulting physician to East London Hospital for Children, Shadwell; *b.* Ulleskelf, Yorkshire, 17 July 1854; *e. s.* of Rev. John Mack Williams, formerly Rector of Burnby, Yorks, and Ellen, *d.* of Nicolas Monsarrat; *m.* 1882, Catherine (*d.* 1917), *d.* of Robert Kirkpatrick-Howat, D.L., of Mabie, Kirkcudbrightshire. *Educ.*: Pocklington; Univ. Coll. London.

1128

M.B. (Honours), B.S., 1879; M.D. 1881, University of London; F.R.C.P. London, 1895; Hon. D.Sc. Sheffield, 1908; Hon. D.Litt. Durham, 1921; Fellow of University College, London. *Publications*: Medical Diseases of Infancy and Childhood, 1898. *Address*: British Medical Association House, Tavistock Square, W.C.1. *T.A.*: Aitiology, Westcent, London. *T.*: Museum 9864. *Clubs*: Garrick, Bath.
(*Died 27 Feb. 1928*.)

WILLIAMS, Edith; Professor of English, Ecole Norinale, Fontenay aux Roses; Chevalier Legion of Honour. *Address*: International Guild, 6 Rue de la Sorbonne, Paris.
(*Died 16 Feb. 1919*.)

WILLIAMS, Maj.-Gen. Edward Charles Ingouville, C.B. 1910, D.S.O. 1900; Lieut.-Colonel, The Buffs; Commanding 16th Infantry Brigade since 1912; *b.* 13 Dec. 1861; *s.* of late Gen. Sir J. W. C. Williams, K.C.B., Maj.-Gen., 1915; served Soudan, 1884-1885 (medal with clasp, bronze star); Nile, 1898 (despatches twice, Brevet Major, Egyptian medal with 2 clasps, medal); Nile, 1899 (clasp); S. Africa, 1899-1902 (despatches five times, Brevet Lieut.-Colonel, Queen's medal, 6 clasps, King's medal, 2 clasps, D.S.O.); European War, 1914-15 (despatches twice). *Club*: Naval and Military. (*Died 22 July 1916*.)

WILLIAMS, Sir Frederick Law, 7th Bt., *cr.* 1866; Capt. late Dorset Regt.; *b.* 10 May 1862; *s.* of 2nd Bt. and Mary Christian, *d.* of Rev. V. Law, Rector of Christian Malford, Wilts; *S.* nephew, 1917; *m.* 1899, Emily, *d.* of William Reid, Downpatrick; one *s.* two *d.* *Heir*: *S.* William Law, *b.* 1 May 1907. *Club*: Naval and Military. (*Died 20 Dec. 1921*.)

WILLIAMS, Rev. George H.; Rector of Remenham, Henley-on-Thames; *b.* Bangor, North Wales, 23 May 1859; *s.* of late T. Williams, Caederwen, Upper Bangor; *m.* 1887, Florence Marion, *d.* of late A. Ogle, Burnley; one *s.* one *d.* *Educ.*: Friars School, Bangor; Christ Coll., Brecon; Jesus Coll., Oxford; (Classical Scholar) 2nd Class Classical Mods. 1881; 2nd Class Greats, 1883; B.A. 1883; M.A. 1887; Second Master of Loughborough Grammar School, 1884-89; Curate of Loughborough, 1887-89; Head Master of Kingsbridge Grammar School, 1889-91; Kendal Grammar School, 1891-1901; Carlisle Grammar School, 1901-12; Chief Examiner in Latin for Central Welsh Board, 1913, 1914, 1915, 1916, 1917. *Publication*: Careers for our Sons. *Address*: Remenham Rectory, Henley-on-Thames. *T.*: Henley 191. *Club*: Authors'. (*Died 9 Sept. 1926*.)

WILLIAMS, Rt. Rev. Gershom Mott, A.M., D.D.; Bishop in charge of American Episcopal Churches in Europe since 1913; *b.* Fort Hamilton, N.Y., 11 Feb. 1857; *s.* of Gen. Thomas Williams and Mary Neosho Bailey; *m.* Eliza, *d.* of Wm. S. Biddle; four *s.* three *d.* *Educ.*: Newburgh (N.Y.) Academy; Cornell University. Admitted to Michigan Bar, 1879; Deacon, 1880; Priest, 1882; Rector of Messiah Church, Detroit, 1882-84; St. George's, Detroit, 1884-89; Dean of Milwaukee Cathedral, 1889-1891; Archdeacon of Northern Michigan, 1891-1896; Editor American Church Times, 1888-89; Chaplain Michigan State Troops, 1884-88; Member of the Psi Upsilon Fraternity, the Military Order of the Loyal Legion, the American Historical Association, the Lambeth Conferences, 1897 and 1908; Member of Lambeth Commission of Conference with the Church of Sweden; Bishop of the Diocese of Marquette (the Northern Peninsula of Michigan, U.S.A.), 1896-1919. *Publications*: Sacramental Teachings, 1884; Between Two Christmas Days, Poems, 1888; The Church of Sweden and the Anglican Communion, 1910; Human Questions and Divine Answers, 1913; editor of the Hymnal of the Protestant Episcopal Church as adopted

1916; Sermons, Addresses, and Charges; contributor to The Churchman, The Living Church, The Church Eclectic, etc. *Recreations:* travel and woodcraft. *Address:* 12 Southgate Avenue, Annapolis, U.S.A. *T.:* 351. *M.:* 31760. *Clubs:* Annapolitan; Knickerbocker Yacht, New York.
(Died 14 April 1923.)

WILLIAMS, Col. Henry David, C.M.G. 1918; J.P., D.L., Staffordshire; retired pay; *b.* 1854; *m.* 1888, Ethel Louisa *(d.* 1921), *d.* of late Rev. Canon Montagu Hankey. Served Zhob Valley Expedition, 1884. *Address:* Lambert House, Dorchester. *Club:* Naval and Military.
(Died 21 July 1924.)

WILLIAMS, Herbert; Medical Officer of Health for the Port of London since 1901; *b.* Weymouth, 1862; *s.* of Alderman T. H. Williams, J.P.; unmarried. *Educ.:* privately; London University; St. Bartholomew's Hospital. Graduated M.B. Lond. with honours in Medicine and Physiology, 1888; appointed Medical Officer to the Metropolitan Hospital, and subsequently became House Physician to Dr. Gee at St. Bart. Hosp. for one year; then Resident House Surgeon in charge of the ward for diseases, etc., of the Hyes; M.D. 1890; entered service of Corporation of City of London, 1892, as Assistant Port Medical Officer, took Diploma of Public Health at Cambridge University, and again graduated as M.D. in State Medicine at London University. *Recreations:* golf, rowing; late Major in 1st Kent Royal Garrison Artillery Volunteers, has passed the School of Instruction, Woolwich, and obtained the Artillery certificate; acted as Adjutant of the Corps during the South African War, 1902. *Address:* 51 King William Street, Greenwich. *T.A.:* Medoff Green, London. *T.:* 36 New Cross. *Clubs:* Junior Army and Navy; Walton Heath Golf, Sundridge Park Golf. *(Died 16 Jan. 1916.)*

WILLIAMS, Hugh Noel, author; *b.* Newport, Monmouthshire, 20 Jan. 1870; *s.* of late William Williams of Clifton Down, Bristol; *m.* 1st, Florence Lulu Holdom; one *s.*; 2nd, Eva Kathleen Deane; two.*d. Educ.:* Clifton College; St. John's Col., Oxford. B.A. (honours in Modern History), 1892. *Publications:* Madame Récamier and her Friends, 1901; Madame de Pompadour, 1902; Madame de Montespan, 1903; The Hand of Léonore, 1904; Madame du Barry, 1904; Queens of the French Stage, 1905; Later Queens of the French Stage, 1906; Five Fair Sisters, 1906; Queen Margot, 1906; A Princess of Intrigue, 1907; The Women Bonapartes, 1908; A Rose of Savoy, 1909; The Fascinating Duc de Richelieu, 1910; Henri II.: his Court and Times, 1910; A Princess of Adventure, 1911; The Love Affairs of the Condes, 1912; Unruly Daughters, 1913; A Fair Conspirator, 1913; Rival Sultanas, 1915; Tainted Gold, 1915; The Pearl of Princesses, 1916; The Independence of Belgium, 1916; Sir Douglas Haig's Great Push: The Battle of the Somme, 1917; Life and Letters of Admiral Sir Charles Napier, K.C.B. 1917; The Brood of False Lorraine, 1919; The Grasshamptom Stable, 1921; A Gallant of Lorraine, 1921; The Moneylender Intervenes, 1923; Last Loves of Henri of Navarre, 1925. *Address:* c/o Cree & Turner, 109 Jermyn Street, S.W. *(Died 13 Oct. 1925.)*

WILLIAMS, James Alexander, I.S.O. 1903; District Commissioner, Gold Coast, 1889-1907; *b.* 18 June 1856; *s.* of George Shotan and Maria Williams; *m.* 1st, 1881, Rebecca Elizabeth, 5th *d.* of Rev. Peter William Bernasko, W.M.S., Gold Coast; 2nd, 1913, Kate Otema, *d.* of Chief Kwaku-Adjaye of Akwapim, Gold Coast Colony. *Educ.:* Grammar School, Lagos. Entered public service at Lagos as Messenger and Copyist, Secretariat and Treasury, 1871; Clerk and Keeper Debtors' Prison, 1875; 2nd Clerk Governor's Office, Gold Coast, 1876; Chief Clerk, 1877; Special Interpreter to Benin with the late

Governor Young, 1884; Clerk of Legislative Council, 1886-87; retired 1907. *Address:* 11 Oke Olowogbowo, Lagos; Williamsville, Dodowah, *via* Accra, Gold Coast Colony.

WILLIAMS, Hon. James Rowland, M.A. Oxon.; Director of Education, Jamaica, since 1909; *b.* Jamaica, 1860; *m.* 1888, Margaret Emily Caroline, 3rd *d.* of Major-Gen. W. T. Freke Farewell, retired Indian Army, of Bath; three *s.* three *d. Educ.:* Somersetshire College, Bath; Trinity College, Oxford (Scholar). Inspector of Schools, Jamaica, 1884-1909; Acting Assistant Colonial Secretary, Jamaica, 1906-7; attended as Government delegate at Conference on Trade Relations between West Indies and Canada, at Barbados, 1908, and at West Indian Agricultural Conferences at Barbados and Trinidad as representative of the Jamaica Agricultural Society; member Legislative Council, Jamaica, 1910; acted as Member of Privy Council, Jamaica, 1913. *Publications:* School Gardens, for elementary schools in Jamaica, 1907. *Recreations:* Anything that is going. *Address:* Education Office, Kingston, Jamaica; Kew Park, Westmoreland, Jamaica.
(Died 23 April 1916.)

WILLIAMS, Sir John, 1st Bt., *cr.* 1894; G.C.V.O., *cr.* 1911; K.C.V.O., *cr.* 1902; M.D.; F.R.C.P.; hon. LL.D. Edin., Glas., and Aber.; D.Sc. (Hon.) Wales; President of the University College of Wales; President of the National Library of Wales; Emeritus Prof. Midwifery at Univ. Coll. London, and Consulting Obstetric Physician to the Hospital; Hon. Fellow of the Royal Society of Medicine; *b.* Carmarthenshire, 6 Nov. 1840; 3rd *s.* of Rev. David Williams. Blaenllynant; *m.* 1872, Mary *(d.* 1915), *d.* of Richard Hughes, Ynistawe. *Educ.:* Normal Coll. Swansea; University College, London (Fellow). Grand Cross of Dannebrog; High Sheriff, Carmarthenshire, 1904. *Publications:* papers in Obstetric Medicine. *Heir:* none. *Address:* Blaenllynant, Aberystwyth.
(Died 24 May 1926.)

WILLIAMS, John, M.P. (Lab.) Gower Division of Glamorganshire since 1906; J.P. County Glamorgan; Advisory Agent for the Western Miners Association; Lecturer in Economics; Welsh Poet; Baptist Minister, and a Governor of the Univ. Colls. of Wales; *b.* 1861. General Secretary, Amalgamated Society of S. Wales Colliery Workers, 1890; on Mountain Ash District Council. *Address:* 36 Charlwood Street, S.W.; Swansea. *(Died 20 June 1922.)*

WILLIAMS, John David, J.P.; Farmer; *b.* Blaenclydach Farm, Clydach Vale, Rhondda, 12 July 1853; *s.* of late John and Mary Williams, Flynon Dwyn Farm, Clydach Vale; *m.* 1882, Ann Llewellyn; two *s.* six *d. Educ.:* British School, Trecherburt; Christ College, Cardiff. Has devoted his time and attention chiefly to farming; has been a Director of the Rhondda Valley Brewery Co. upwards of 40 years; a Director of the Cardiff Malting Co. Ltd. for upwards of 23 years, also Director of the Town Hall Co. Ltd., Ton-y-Pandy, for 15 years; ex-Chairman and member of Rhondda District Council for over 25 years, and member of the Pontypridd Board of Guardians for 6 years; was Master of the Ystrad and Pentyrch Foxhounds for 12 years up to 1902; since then master of the Ystrad Foxhounds. *Recreations:* hunting and shooting. *Address:* Clydach Court, Trealaw, Rhondda Valley. *T.:* Porth 126. *(Died 19 Sept. 1923.)*

WILLIAMS, Joseph Grout, J.P.; *e. s.* of late Rev. James Williams, of Pendley, and Elizabeth, *d.* of late James Grout; *b.* 1848; *m.* 1878, Catharine Mary, *d.* of late Robert Tidswell. *Educ.:* Harrow; Trinity College, Cambridge. High Sheriff, Herts, 1889; J.P. Herts and Bucks. *Address:* Pendley Manor, Tring, Hertfordshire. *(Died 9 Oct. 1923.)*

WILLIAMS, Major-General Lawrence Henry, Indian Army ; *b.* 14 Oct. 1834. Entered army, 1850 ; Maj.-Gen. 1891 ; retired list, 1891 ; served Indian Mutiny, 1857 (medal) ; Cossyah and Jyntiah Hills Campaign, 1862-63 ; N.W. Frontier of India, 1863 (medal with clasp) ; Afghan War, 1878 (medal with clasp) ; Mahsud Waziri Expedition, 1881 (despatches). *Address :* 46 Castle Hill Avenue, Folkestone.
(*Died 13 July 1916.*)

WILLIAMS, Colonel Leslie Gwatkin, C.M.G. 1919; D.S.O. 1916; late 5th Cavalry, Indian Army; *b.* 1878 ; *m.* 1921, Helen Mary (*née* Landale), *widow* of Dr. W. B. Grandage ; one *d.* Served South African War, 1900-1 (Queen's medal and five clasps); European War, 1914-18 (despatches, C.M.G., D.S.O., Bt. Lt.-Col., Legion of Honour); retired, 1922. *Address :* 74 Gloucester Road, S.W.7. *Club :* Cavalry. (*Died 28 Jan. 1926.*)

WILLIAMS, Sir Ralph (Champneys), K.C.M.G., *cr.* 1907 ; C.M.G. 1901 ; *b.* 9 Mar. 1848 ; *s.* of Rev. T. N. Williams, of Trefios, Anglesey ; *m.* 1875, Jessie (*d.* 1917), *y. d.* of Samuel Dean ; one *s.* *Educ. :* Rossall. Explored in Patagonia, 1873-74 ; in Central Africa, 1883 - 84 ; head of the Civil Intelligence Department, Bechuanaland Expedition, 1884 - 85 ; was also special correspondent of the Standard, 1884-85 ; appointed British Consular Officer South African Republic, 1887 ; appointed 1st British Agent South African Republic, with letter of credence, 1888 ; appointed Colonial Treasurer of Gibraltar, 1890 ; and also to the associated office of Captain of the Port of Gibraltar, 1895 ; received silver medal and vellum certificate from the Italian Government for services in connection with the wreck of the "Utopia," 1891 ; Colonial Secretary of Barbados, with dormant commission of Governor, 1897-1901 ; Resident Commissioner Bechuanaland Protectorate 1901-1906; Governor Windward Islands, 1906-9 ; Governor of Newfoundland, 1909-13 ; President of the 2nd Line of Defence for the War in British East Africa, Aug. 1914 ; invalided home, April 1915, and received the thanks of the Governor and the General Officer commanding ; is a Governor of Rossall School. *Publications :* The British Lion in Bechuanaland ; How I became a Governor, 1913. *Recreation :* ceaseless travelling to far-away countries. *Clubs :* St. James's, M.C.C., Royal Thames Yacht.
(*Died 22 June 1927.*)

WILLIAMS, Rt. Hon. Sir Roland Lomax Bowdler Vaughan, Kt., *cr.* 1890; P.C. 1897 ; Lord Justice of the Court of Appeal 1897-1914; *b.* 1838 ; *m.* 1865, Laura Susannah, *d.* of Edmund Lomax of Netley and Tanhurst, Surrey ; one *s.* [R.E.L.V. Williams]. *Educ. :* Christ Church, Oxford (B.A. 1860). Judge Supreme Court, Queen's Bench Division, 1890-1897. Barr. Lincoln's Inn, 1861 ; Q.C. 1889. *Address :* 6 Trebovir Road, S.W. ; High Ashe's Farm, Abinger, Dorking. *Club :* Athenæum.
(*Died 8 Dec. 1916.*)

WILLIAMS, Samuel Charles Evans, J.P.; *b.* 20 May 1842; *o. s.* of late Rev. John Williams, of Bryntirion, and Jane, *widow* of John Patterson, of Devon ; *m.* 1867, Mary Caroline, *d.* of Rev. Henry William Robinson Luttman-Johnson, of Binderton House, Sussex ; five *d.* *Educ. :* Westminster ; Christ Church, Oxford, M.A. ; High Sheriff, Radnor, 1880 ; M.P. Radnor, 1880-84. *Address :* 69 Knightsbridge, S.W.1. *Club :* National Liberal.
(*Died 2 Mar. 1926.*)

WILLIAMS, Rev. Thomas Charles, M.A., Minister of the Welsh Presbyterian Church, Menai Bridge, North Wales ; *s.* of Rev. Hugh Williams, and *g.s.* of late Rev. John Charles, Gwalchmai, Anglesey ; the family have been ministers, from father to son, for over a hundred years ; *m.* 1911, Evelyn, *d.* of 1130

David Jones,- Manager, Metropolitan Bank, Conway. *Educ. :* Oswestry High School ; Bala College ; Aberystwyth University College ; Jesus College, Oxford, graduated in Honours, 1898. Brought up to the ministry ; settled in Menai Bridge when he left Oxford, and in spite of calls to English and Welsh churches in the big towns has remained there but travels extensively, both in this country and in America ; preaches often in London in Welsh and in the leading English churches ; late Chaplain 6th Batt. R.W.F. ; Secretary General Assembly, 1913-14, and Member Welsh Theological Board ; Moderator North Wales Presbyterian Synod, 1918-19 ; Moderator of the General Assembly for 1921-22 ; D.D. Edinburgh University, 1923 ; Preached the Council Sermon at the Pan-Presbyterian Alliance in Cardiff, 1925 ; in Liverpool Cathedral, 28 Feb. 1926. *Address :* Menai Bridge, Anglesey.
(*Died 2 Oct. 1927.*)

WILLIAMS, Thomas Jeremiah, M.P. (L.), Swansea District, since 1915 ; J.P. Glamorganshire ; Director of various firms ; Barrister-at-law ; *b.* 1872 ; *e. s.* of late William Williams, former M.P. Swansea District, J.P. Glamorganshire, and Margret Jeremiah ; *m.* 1912, Laura Alice, *y. d.* of late Thomas Marlow, Southport ; one *d.* *Educ. :* University College School, London ; Technical College, Sheffield ; Firth College. Technical and commercial training ; practised at the Bar, South Wales and Chester Circuit, etc. ; travelled Canada, America, Japan, China, India, Egypt, the whole of Europe ; contested West Glamorgan, 1905. *Recreations :* shooting, motoring. *Address :* Maes-y-Gwernen Hall, nr. Swansea. *T. :* Morriston 90. *M. :* CT 1580. *Clubs :* Royal Automobile ; Bristol Channel Yacht ; Swansea and Counties'. (*Died 12 June 1919.*)

WILLIAMS, Lt.-Col. Thomas Samuel Beauchamp ; M.P. (Lab.) Kennington Division of Lambeth, 1923-24 ; I.M.S., retired ; *b.* Bangor, 1877 ; *s.* of late Ven. Thomas Williams, Archdeacon of Merioneth. *Educ. :* Edinburgh University, M.B., Ch.B. Served European War, 1914-19 (despatches, Bt. Lt.-Col.). Contested Bridgwater Division of Somerset, 1922 ; Kennington, 1924 ; Eastbourne, 1925 ; Parliamentary Private Secretary to President of Board of Trade, 1924. *Address :* Imperial Chambers, 3 Cursitor Street, W.C.
(*Died July 1927.*)

WILLIAMS, Surgeon-General Sir William Daniel Campbell, K.C.M.G., *cr.* 1916 ; C.B. 1900 ; Knight of Grace of the Order of St. John of Jerusalem ; Director - General Army Medical Services, Commonwealth Defence, 1902 ; *b.* Sydney, New South Wales, 30 July 1856 ; *s.* of late William James Williams, M.D. ; *m.* 1881, Florence, *d.* of late Henry A. Severn ; one *s.* one *d.* *Educ. :* The New School, Sydney ; Sydney Grammar School ; University College, London. Gold Medallist, Surgery, University College Hospital, London. Staff Surgeon New South Wales Artillery ; Surgeon-Major and P.M.O. Soudan Contingent, 1885 ; P.M.O. Australian and New Zealand Forces, South Africa, and P.M.O. Hamilton's Force and Hunter's Force, South Africa, 1900 ; Surgeon-General (local), South Africa ; European War, 1914 - 16 (K.C.M.G.). *Decorated* for South African services. Consulting Surgeon St. Vincent's Hospital, Sydney, New South Wales. *Address :* Headquarters, Melbourne. *T. :* Melbourne 551. *Clubs :* Melbourne, Melbourne ; Union, Sydney. (*Died 10 May 1919.*)

WILLIAMS, Rt. Rev. William Leonard, B.A., D.D. ; *b.* 1829; *m.* Sarah, *d.* of John Bradshaw Wanklyn of Witherslack, Westmorland, 1853 ; five *s.* four *d.* *Educ. :* Magdalen Hall, Oxford ; B.A., 1852 ; 3rd Class Lit. Hum. ; Hon. D.D., 1897. Archdeacon of

Waiapu, 1862-94; Principal of Maori Theological College, Gisborne, 1883-94; Bishop of Waiapu, 1894-1909. *Publications:* Enlarged Dictionary of the New Zealand Language; First Lessons in Maori. *Address:* Taumata, Napier. N.Z.
(*Died 1 Sept. 1916.*)

WILLIAMS, W. Llewelyn, M.P. (L.) Carmarthen District, 1906-18; K.C. 1912; Barrister; Recorder of Cardiff since 1915; Bencher of Lincoln's Inn; *b.* Brownhill, Co. Carmarthen, 10 March 1867; *m.* Elinor Jenkins, Glansawdde, Co. Carmarthen. *Educ.:* Foundation Scholar, Llandovery College; Open Hulme Exhibitioner (Modern History) and B.C.L.; B.N.C. Oxford Recorder Swansea, 1912-15. *Publications:* The Making of Modern Wales, 1919; numerous essays dealing with Welsh History; editor of Giraldus Cambrensis and Froude's History of England in the Everyman series. *Recreations:* fishing and golf. *Address:* 111 Ashley Gardens, S.W.1; 3 King's Bench Walk, Temple, E.C.4. *T.:* Victoria 5849; City 1948. *Clubs:* National Liberal, Reform.
(*Died 22 April 1922.*)

WILLIAMS, Hon. William Micah, O.B.E. 1920; M.L.C. for Hobart since 1916; *b.* New Norfolk, Tasmania; *m.* 1st, Elizabeth, *d.* of John Hoggins; two *d.*; 2nd, Grace M., *d.* of John Smith, Wellington, Surrey; 3rd, Annie Ellen Winspear, *d.* of Rev. Henry Bath, Melbourne. *Educ.:* Clifton College, New Norfolk. Magistrate for the city of Hobart and the Municipality of New Town, 1908; Alderman of city of Hobart; Mayor, 1915; Fellow of the Royal Colonial Institute; Chairman of Chamber of Commerce, 1911-13; Deputy Chairman of State War Council; Chairman of State Recruiting Committee; Member Red Cross Executive during War: Chairman General Hospital; Chairman Public Library; Trustee of Public Cemetery; President of National Rose Society; Trustee, State Savings Bank; Ex-officio member of Methodist Conference; Representative English Conference, 1905, 1909; also Ecumenical Conference, Toronto, 1911, 1919. *Address:* Papanui, Angusta Road, New Town, Hobart. *T.:* 636. *M.:* 1631. *Club:* Commonwealth, Hobart (President). (*Died 11 Aug. 1924.*)

WILLIAMS, W. Phillpotts; late Master East Cornwall Foxhounds; *b.* 1860; *m. d.* of Canon Simpson of Bexhill; one *d.* Master of Netton Harriers, South Molton Harriers, Hursley Foxhounds, and present pack; always interested in the question of the National Horse Supply; founded the Brood Mare Society, which resulted in present Government grant of £45,000 a year; worked also at the building up of a genuine reserve of horses within the country; supported Mr. Tilling when obtaining the additional grant of £40,000 a year for subsidising 10,000 transport horses; strong advocate of the retaining principle. *Publications:* Poems in Pink; Over the Open. *Recreations:* horses and hounds, and Imperial Federation work for the Colonies. *Address:* Barnfield House, Liskeard, Cornwall. (*Died 31 Aug. 1916.*)

WILLIAMSON, Captain Adolphus Huddleston, R.N., C.M.G. 1917; M.V.O. 1909; Captain H.M.S. Africa, Portsmouth; *b.* 5 July 1869; 2nd *s.* of Sir Hedworth Williamson, 8th Bt., and *heir-pres.* to 9th Bt. Entered Navy, 1882; Lieut. 1891; Commander, 1902; Naval Attaché, Rome, 1908; Officer Legion of Honour. *Clubs:* Brooks's, Naval and Military. (*Died 14 July 1918.*)

WILLIAMSON, The Rt. Rev. Andrew Wallace, K.C.V.O. *cr.* 1926; C.V.O. 1919; M.A., D.D., H.R.S.A.; D.L. Midlothian; *b.* Thornhill, Dumfriesshire, 29 Dec. 1856; *y. s.* of James Williamson and Margaret Wallace; *m.* 1st, 1883, Agnes, 2nd *d.* of Walter Blackstock, Edinburgh; 2nd, 1888, Elizabeth Mary Phoebe, *d.* of Robert Croall, Craigcrook, Mid-Lothian.

Educ.: Morton School and Wallace Hall; University, Edinburgh. Thomson Scholar, 1878; Hepburn Prizeman, 1881; Assistant North Leith, 1881; Minister, North Leith, 1882; St Cuthbert's, Edinburgh, 1883-1909; Univ. Lecturer in Pastoral Theology, 1897-98; Croall Lecturer; Moderator of the Church of Scotland, 1913-14; Dean of the Order of the Thistle and the Chapel Royal in Scotland; Minister St. Giles's, Edinburgh, 1910-25; Chaplain-in-Ordinary to the King in Scotland. *Publications:* Macleod Lecture; Ideals of Ministry; The Person of Christ. *Address:* 44 Palmerston Place, Edinburgh. *Club:* University, Edinburgh. (*Died 10 July 1926.*)

WILLIAMSON, Benjamin, D.Sc., F.R.S., D.C.L.; Vice-Provost, Trinity College, Dublin; *b.* Cork, 1827; *m.* Agnes (*d.* 1899), *d.* of Rev. W. Wright, Vicar of Selston, Nottingham. *Educ.:* Kilkenny College; Trinity College, Dublin. D.Sc. Dublin, 1890; D.C.L. Oxford, 1892. Fellow of Trinity College, Dublin, 1852; F.R.S. 1879; Professor of Natural Philosophy, 1884; Senior Fellow, 1897. *Publications:* Treatise on the Differential Calculus, 1872; Integral Calculus, 1874; Dynamics, in conjunction with Professor Tarleton, 1884; Mathematical Theory of Stress and Strain, 1893; author of the articles "Infinitesimal Calculus," "MacLaurin," "Variations, Calculus of," etc., in 9th ed. of the Encyclopædia Britannica, etc. *Address:* Trinity Coll. Dublin; 1 Dartmouth Road, Dublin. *Clubs:* Royal Societies; University, Dublin. (*Died 3 Jan. 1916.*)

WILLIAMSON, Charles Norris, journalist and author; *b.* Exeter; *s.* of Rev. Stewart Williamson; *m.* Alice Muriel Livingston. *Educ.:* University College, London. Studied science and practical engineering until twenty-two; for eight years on the editorial staff of the Graphic; in 1891 started Black and White. *Publications:* Life of Thomas Carlyle, 2 vols. 1881; newspaper articles (many on travel and automobilism). With Mrs. Williamson; The Lightning Conductor; The Princess Passes; My Friend the Chauffeur; Lady Betty Across the Water; The Car of Destiny; Rosemary in Search of a Father; The Botor Chaperon; Scarlet Runner; Set in Silver; The Motor Maid; Lord Loveland Discovers America; The Golden Silence; The Princess Virginia; The Guests of Hercules; The Heather Moon; The Demon; The Love Pirate; It Happened in Egypt; Secret History: The Shop Girl; The Lightning Conductress; The War Wedding, 1916; Crucifix Corner, 1918; The Lion's Mouse, 1919. *Recreations:* travel, walking, autocaring. *Address:* St. Christopher, Combe Down, Bath. *Clubs:* Savage, Whitefriars, Royal Automobile. (*Died 3 Oct. 1920.*)

WILLIAMSON, Francis John, sculptor; *b.* Hampstead, 17th July 1833; *e. s.* of Francis Edward Williamson; *m.* Elizabeth Patman Smith, 1857; two *s.* two *d. Educ.:* private school, Hampstead. Articled pupil of the late J. H. Foley, R.A.; assistant to him for some years; after which started practising at Esher, where he has resided ever since. *Works:* statues of Queen Victoria, Australia, India, London, etc.; the first statue of Queen Victoria in Ireland; Dean Milman in St. Paul's Cathedral; various public statues in various parts of the British Isles; numerous portraits of many of the Royal Family executed for Queen Victoria, etc.; many ideal and private commissions. *Recreations:* various. *Address:* Faireholme, Esher, Surrey. *T.A.:* Esher.
(*Died 12 Mar. 1920.*)

WILLIAMSON, Rev. Henry Drummond, M.A.; Rector of Brent Eleigh since 1922; Hon. Canon of St. Edmundsbury and Ipswich, 1914; *b.* 17 Dec. 1854; *s.* of late Rev. George Frederick Williamson, M.A.; *m.* 1877,

Alice Jane, *d.* of late Rev. Matthew Collisson, M.A.; two *s.* two *d.* *Educ.:* Rossall; Corpus Christi College, Cambridge (Scholar); 3rd Class Theological Tripos. Went to India under Church Missionary Society, 1878; at Calcutta Cathedral Mission College, 1878; Mandla, Central Provinces, 1878-93; Secretary Bengal Mission, 1893-97; Associate Secretary C.M.S. for Dioceses of Bristol, Gloucester, and Worcester, 1899-1901; Organising Secretary C.E.Z.M.S., 1901-5; Vicar of St. Margaret's, Ipswich, 1905-22. *Publications:* Gondi Grammar; Hindi Church Hymn-book. *Recreations:* golf, cycling. *Address:* Brent Eleigh Rectory, Lavenham.
(Died 21 Mar. 1926.)

WILLIAMSON, Herbert; Physician Accoucheur, St. Bartholomew's Hospital; Obstetric Physician, Royal Hospital for Women; *b.* 1872; *s.* of S. L. Williamson, J.P., of Grantham, Lincs; *m.* 1915, Mrs. Edith Lockwood. *Educ.:* Cambridge University (M.A., M.B., B.C.); St. Bartholomew's Hospital. F.R.C.P. London; Brackenbury Scholar in Surgery, 1897; Surgeon to Imperial Yeomanry Hospital, Pretoria, during Boer War. *Publications:* contributions on obstetric and gynæcological subjects to Journal of Obstetrics, Transactions of the Obstetrical Society, St. Bartholomew's Hospital Reports, Clifford Allbutt's System of Medicine, etc. *Recreation:* riding. *Address:* 8 Queen Anne Street, Cavendish Square, W.1. *T.:* Langham 2288. *M.:* H 4199. *Club:* Reform.
(Died 16 Dec. 1924.)

WILLIAMSON, Victor Alexander, C.M.G. 1882; *b.* 28 June 1838; 4th *s.* of Sir Hedworth Williamson, 7th Bt. of Whitburn Hall, Sunderland, and Hon. Anne Elizabeth, *d.* of 1st Baron Ravensworth; unmarried. *Educ.:* Westminster; sometime student of Christ Church, Oxford. 2nd class in Moderations, 1859. Barr. Inner Temple, 1865; went Northern and, after division of that Circuit, the North-Eastern Circuit; a Royal Commissioner appointed to inquire into the Treatment of Indian Immigrants in Mauritius, 1872-73; chairman of the Lands Commission in Fiji, 1879-82; also M.L.C. and M.E.C. of that colony. *Decorated* for Colonial services. *Address:* Southend House, Whitburn, nr. Sunderland. *T.:* Whitburn 16. *Club:* Brooks's.
(Died 16 Sept. 1924.)

WILLINK, Very Rev. John Wakefield, D.D.: Dean of Norwich since 1919; *b.* 24 Oct. 1858; *s.* of Rev. Arthur Willink, M.A., Vicar of St. Paul's, Tranmere, Cheshire, and Sarah Wakefield, *d.* of John Cropper, of Liverpool; *m.* 1887, Ruth Agnes, *d.* of J. D. Sim, C.S.I., for over thirty years in the Indian Civil Service; two *s.* two *d.* *Educ.:* Clifton College; Pembroke College, Cambridge. Theological Tripos; Winchester Reading Prize; a year of special training was spent with Bishop Lightfoot, Bishop of Durham, at Auckland Castle; Curate of Bishop Auckland, 1881; Vicar of St. John's, Sunderland, 1885-91; St. Helen's, Lancashire, 1891-1904; Hon. Canon of Liverpool, 1898-1905; Hon. Secretary for Liverpool Cathedral, 1901-5; Acting Chaplain 2nd Norfolk R.A. Volunteers, 1904; Vicar of Great Yarmouth, 1903-12; Rural Dean of the Flegg Deanery, 1905-12; Hon. Canon of Norwich, 1905-12; Select Preacher Cambridge University, 1912; Rector of Birmingham and Hon. Canon of Birmingham, 1912-19; Proctor in Convocation, 1917-19. *Publication:* History of the Parish Church of Great Yarmouth. *Recreations:* motoring, formerly rifle shooting, bicycling and tennis. *Address:* The Deanery, Norwich. *T.:* Norwich 1090. *Club:* Norfolk, Norwich.
(Died 22 Sept. 1927.)

WILLIS, Rt. Rev. Alfred, D.D.; Assistant Bishop for Tonga since 1902; *b.* 3 Feb. 1836; 2nd *s.* of late Francis Willis, M.D.; *m.* 1883, Emma Mary, *y. d.* of late Capt. Simeon, and
1132

g. d. of late Sir R. G. Simeon, Bart. *Educ.:* Uppingham; St. John's Coll. Oxford; Wells Theological Coll. Curate of Strood, Kent, 1856-62; Perpetual Curate of St. Mark, New Brompton, Kent, 1863-72; Bishop of Honolulu, 1872-1902. *Publications:* Hawaiian Hymn Book, 1880; Revision of Hawaiian Prayer Book, 1883; Honolulu Diocesan Magazine, 1890-1902; The Unity of the Bible, 1916. *Address:* Nukualofa, Tonga, South Seas. *(Died 14 Nov. 1920.)*

WILLIS, Col. Charles Fancourt, M.D.; C.B. 1911; I.M.S. (retired); *b.* 22 May 1854. Major, Indian Medical Service, 1891; Lt.-Col. 1899; Col. 1908; served Egypt, 1882 (medal with clasp, bronze star); N.W. Frontier, India, 1897-8 (medal, two clasps); Tirah, 1897-8 (despatches, clasp). *Address:* Frith Manor, East Grinstead. *(Died 28 April 1918.)*

WILLIS, Joseph George; C.B. 1911; Inspector-General in Bankruptcy 1908-21; *b.* Sep. 1861; unmarried. *Educ.:* Christ Church, Oxford; 1st class in (Classical) Moderations, 1882; 1st class in Lit. Hum. 1884. Gained 1st place at Civil Service Competitive Examination (Class 1) 1885, and appointed to clerkship in Board of Trade; Private Secretary to Parliamentary Secretary Board of Trade, 1893-1900; Junior Assistant Secretary (Railway Department), 1907. *Address:* 123 Pall Mall, S.W. *Club:* Reform. *(Died 17 May 1924.)*

WILLIS, Ven. William Newcombe de Laval; Vicar of Cambridge, N.Z., 1878-1912; Archdeacon of Waikato, 1882-1913 (retired); *b.* 14 Feb. 1846; 3rd *s.* of late Rev. W. N. Willis, sometime Rector of Kilpeacon and Prebendary of St. Mary's Cathedral, Limerick, Ireland; *m.* 1875, Mary Agnes, *e. d.* of late G. H. Clarke, sometime of Micheldever, Hampshire; three *s.* four *d.* *Educ.:* privately, in Ireland; St. John's College, Auckland. Deacon, 1874; Priest, 1875; Curate of Holy Sepulchre, Auckland, 1875-78. *Publications:* The Battle for the Bible, 1902; Bible Teaching in State Schools, 1911; Hon. Editor of Digest of Ecclesiastical Law of the Church of Province of New Zealand, Diocese of Auckland, and of Statistics and Accounts of the said Diocese. *Recreations:* mechanics, gardening, etc. *Address:* Kilpeacon, Cambridge, Auckland, N.Z. *(Died 10 Feb. 1916.)*

WILLIS-BUND, John William, C.B.E. 1918; F.S.A.; J.P., D.L.; *b.* 1843; *o. s.* of late John Walpole Willis, and 2nd wife, Ann Susannah Kent, *d.* of late Col. Thos. Henry Bund, of Wick Episcopi [assumed name of Bund, 1864]; *m.* 1st, 1872, Harriette Penelope (*d.* 1895), *sis.* of Sir Richard Temple, 1st Bt.; one *s.* two *d.*; 2nd, 1896, Mary Elizabeth (*d.* 1919), *y. d.* of Gen. Frederick Reynell Thackeray, C.B., and *widow* of Col. Alexander E. F. Holcombe, 1st Royal Scots. *Educ.:* Eton; Caius College, Cambridge (B.A., LL.B., 1st class Law, M.A.). Barrister Lincoln's Inn; late Chairman Worcestershire Quarter Sessions and County Council. *Address:* Wick Episcopi, Worcester. *Clubs:* Oxford and Cambridge, Constitutional.
(Died 7 June 1928.)

WILLISON, Sir John (Stephen), Kt., *cr.* 1913; LL.D., F.R.S.C.; *b.* 9 Nov. 1856; *s.* of Stephen Willison, Yorkshire, of Scottish descent; *m.* 1st, 1885, Rachel Wood (*d.* 1925), *d.* of William Turner of Tiverton, Ontario; one *s.*; 2nd, 1926, Marjory, *d.* of Archibald MacMurdy, M.A., Toronto. *Educ.:* Canadian schools. Became Member of London Advertiser Staff, 1881; Editor Toronto Globe, 1890-1902; Toronto Daily News, 1903-17; for years in Parliamentary Press Gallery for Toronto Globe (before 1890). *Publications:* The Railway Question in Canada; The American Spirit; Sir Wilfrid Laurier and the Liberal Party; The New Canada; Personal and Political Reminiscences. *Recreation:* bowling on the green. *Address:* Toronto. *Clubs:* York, Toronto Hunt, Toronto. *(Died 27 May 1927.)*

WILLMORE, Henry Horace Albert, M.V.O. 1910; Chief Gunner, R.N.; officer attending the gun-carriage at funeral of King Edward VII.; *b.* 19 April 1871; *s.* of late Edward Thomas Willmore, Bexley Heath, Kent; *m.* 1900, Mabel, *d.* of late Edward Wilkinson, Portsmouth. *Address:* Laburnum House, 312 Laburnum Grove, Portsmouth. *(Died 29 Sept. 1919.)*

WILLOUGHBY, Maj.-Gen. James Fortnom, Indian army (retired); *b.* 1844; 2nd *s.* of late Admiral J. B. Willoughby; *m.* 1882, Mary Ann (*d.* 1915), *d.* of late Rev. H. R. Harrison, Rector of Elston, Notts; one *s.* (Capt. J. G. W., 33rd Cavalry, killed in action in Mesopotamia, 1915). *Educ.:* Royal Naval School, New Cross. Entered Bombay Army, 1861; Colonel of the 33rd Q.V.O. Light Cavalry, 1908; served Abyssinian Expedition, 1867 and 1868 (medal); Afghan War, 1880 (medal and clasp); Maj.-Gen. 1899; retired, 1899; J.P. Gloucestershire. *Address:* Gabari, Cheltenham; Springfield, Bourton-on-the-Water, Glos. *Clubs:* United Service; New, Cheltenham. *(Died 30 May 1922.)*

WILLOUGHBY, Major Sir John Christopher, 5th Bt., *cr.* 1794; D.S.O. 1917; J.P. Oxon; Major Royal Horse Guards (retired); Director of Willoughby's Consolidated Co.; *b.* 20 Feb. 1859; *e. s.* of 4th Bt. and 2nd wife, Maria Elizabeth, 4th *d.* of Thomas Fawkes of Hemley House, Staffs; *S.* father 1866. *Educ.:* Eton; Trin. Coll. Camb. Lieut. 3rd Batt. Oxford Light Infantry, 1879; 2nd Lieut. 6th Dragoon Guards, and entered Royal Horse Guards, 1880; Major, 1895; served in Egyptian Campaign, 1882, and Nile Campaign, 1884-85 (medals and clasps, despatches); second in command of forces of Imperial British South Africa Co. Matabeleland, 1890-91; Matabeleland Conquest, 1893; accompanied Dr. Jameson, C.B., into the Transvaal, 1896; served South Africa, 1899-1900; was in Ladysmith with Cavalry Headquarter Staff during the siege, and appointed Major under General Hunter, in charge of the transport of the Flying Column for the relief of Mafeking, also employed on the Intelligence Department (medal and clasps, despatches); European War, 1914-17 (D.S.O.). Owns properties in Oxfordshire and Buckinghamshire. *Heir:* none. *Address:* 2 Down Street, W.; *T.:* Mayfair 5797; Fulmer Hall, Slough, Buckinghamshire. *Clubs:* Carlton, Hurlingham, Marlborough, Turf. *(Died 16 April 1918.)*

WILLOUGHBY, Lieut.-Gen. Michael Weekes, C.S.I. 1885; Indian Army; *b.* 18 Mar. 1833; *s.* of Major-General M. F. Willoughby, Bombay Artillery; *m.* 1855, Louisa Frances (*d.* 1921), *d.* of Robert Anderson; one *s.* *Educ.:* Cheltenham. Entered army, 1849; Lt.-Gen., 1893; served Persia, 1856-59 (medal with clasp); Abyssinia, 1868 (despatches, medal). *Address:* 17 Lansdown Place, Cheltenham. *(Died 17 Mar. 1925.)*

WILLOUGHBY DE BROKE, 19th Baron, *cr.* 1492; **Richard Greville Verney,** T.D., D.L., J.P.; Lieut.-Col. in the Warwickshire Yeomanry 2nd Line Regt., which he commanded during the War; M.F.H. Warwickshire since 1900; *b.* 29 March 1869; *e. s.* of 18th Lord Willoughby. de Broke and Geraldine, *d.* of late J. H. Smith-Barry; *S.* father 1902; *m.* Marie Frances Lisette, O.B.E., *y. d.* of C. A. Hanbury, Strathgarve, Ross-shire, 1895; one *s.* *Educ.:* Mr. Rawnsley's, near Winchester; Eton; New College, Oxford (B.A.). M.P. (C.) Rugby, Warwickshire, 1895-1900. Owns about 6000 acres. *Publications:* Hunting the Fox, 1920; The Sport of Our Ancestors, 1921. *Heir: s.* Hon. John Henry Peyto Verney. *Address:* 23 Gilbert Street, Grosvenor Square, W.1; Woodley House, Kineton, Warwickshire.

Clubs: Carlton, Turf, Beefsteak, Garrick. *(Died 16 Dec. 1923.)*

WILLS, Sir Edward Chaning, 2nd Bt., *cr.* 1904; M.A. and F.C.S.; *b.* 25 April 1861; *s.* of 1st Bt. and Mary Ann, *e. d.* of late J. Chaning Pearce, F.G.S., Montague House, Bath; *S.* father 1910; *m.* 1891, Isabella Sommerville, *d.* of P. F. Sparke Evans, J.P., of Trinmore, Clifton Down; no *c.* *Educ.:* Emmanuel College, Cambridge. A Director Imperial Tobacco Company; Ltd. *Heir: b.* Ernest Salter, J.P.; [*b.* 30 Nov. 1869; *m.* 1894, Caroline Fanny Maude, *d.* of late William Augustine de Winton, Westbury Lodge, Durdham Down, Bristol; two *s.* three *d.* *Address:* Ramsbury Manor, Wilts]. *Address:* Harcombe, Chudleigh, Devon. *(Died 14 Oct. 1921.)*

WILLS, Sir George Alfred, 1st Bt., *cr.* 1923; J.P. Somerset; Hon. D.C.L. Oxford University; Hon. LL.D. University of Bristol; President of the Imperial Tobacco Co. (of Great Britain and Ireland), Ltd.; Director of the Great Western Railway; Chairman of the Council and Pro-Chancellor University of Bristol; President Bristol General Hospital; Director British-American Tobacco Co., Ltd.; Chairman, Leigh Woods Land Co., Ltd.; Sheriff of Bristol, 1899-1900; *b.* 3 June 1854; *e. s.* of late Henry Overton Wills, J.P., of Kelston Knoll, near Bath (first Chancellor of the University of Bristol); *m.* 1878, Susan Britton, *e. surv. d.* of late Robert Proctor of Clifton, Bristol; one *s.* four *d.* *Educ.:* private school, Clifton; Mill Hill School, Middlesex. A past President of the Grateful (Colston Society), also a past President of the Colston Research Society. *Recreations:* fishing, shooting. *Heir: s.* George Vernon Proctor Wills. *Address:* Coombe Lodge, Blagdon, Somerset; Burwalls, Leigh Woods, near Bristol. *T.:* Bristol 551. *M.:* YA 5435, HU 9350, AE 4909. *Clubs:* Reform; University and Literary, Bristol *(Died 11 July 1928.)*

WILLS, Henry Herbert, J.P.; Director of the Imperial Tobacco Co. of Great Britain and Ireland, Ltd.; President of Bristol Royal Infirmary; Pro-Chancellor of Bristol University; Member of the Council of Clifton College; *b.* 20 March 1856; 2nd *s.* of late Henry Overton Wills, J.P., of Kelston Knoll, near Bath (first Chancellor of University of Bristol); *m.* 1886, Mary Monica, *d.* of late Sir Philip Cunliffe Owen, K.C.B., K.C.M.G., C.I.E.; no *c.* *Educ.:* Clifton College and University College, Bristol. High Sheriff of Somerset, 1910; a past President of the University Colston Society; formerly an Alderman of the County Council of Somerset; trained as a mechanical engineer. *Recreations:* shooting, fishing, deer-stalking, motoring, bicycling, riding, rowing, lawn tennis, foreign travel, music. *Address:* St. Vincent's, Clifton Park, Bristol. *T.:* Bristol 2699. *M.:* FB 350, Y 1958. *(Died 11 May 1922.)*

WILLSHIRE, Sir Arthur Reginald Thomas Maxwell-, 2nd Bt.; *cr.* 1840; Lieut.-Col. Scots Guards, retired 1885; *b.* 23 Nov. 1850; *S.* father 1862; *m.* Frederica (*d.* 1912), *d.* of late Sir Sanford Freeling, K.C.M.G., 1891; one *s.* *Educ.:* Wellington College. Served in Egyptian campaign, 1882. *Recreations:* fishing, shooting. *Heir: s.* Gerard Arthur Maxwell [*b.* 21 Aug. 1892; *m.* 1912, Lilian, *d.* of Henry Birtles]. *Address:* 61 Elm Park Gardens, S.W. *T.:* 4530 Ken. *Clubs:* Guards', Wellington. *(Died 26 April 1919.)*

WILLSON, Leslie, Writer on Diet and Hygiene; *s.* of William Rivers Willson; *m.* Jessie Mary Guy. *Educ.:* Huish's School, Taunton. Studied at Chiswick School of Art; started work as a book illustrator, 1881; engaged subsequently in journalism in U.S.A. and in London; contributed drawings to various English and American papers, 1883-98; art editor Ladies' Field, 1899-1907; Editor Amalgamated Press Novels Department 1907-9:

General Editor of the Book Department, George Newnes, Ltd., 1901-7; editor of the Thin Paper Classics and Newnes' Art Library. *Publications:* Songs and Lyrics from the Dramatists; Poems of Michael Drayton; Plays and Poems of Ben Jonson, and numerous articles, mainly on health matters. *Address:* 9A Gloucester Place, W.1. *T.:* Langham, 1771.
                  (*Died 8 Dec. 1924.*)

WILLYAMS, Arthur Champion Phillips, J.P., D.L.; *y. s.* of late Humphry Willyams, M.P., J.P., D.L., of Carnanton, Cornwall, and Ellen Frances, (*d.* 1885), *y. d.* of late Gen. William Bridges Neynoe, of Castle Neynoe, Co. Sligo; *b.* 1837; *m.* 1861, Charlotte Elizabeth (*d.* 1887),2nd *d.* and co-heiress of late Rev. Harry Longueville-Jones, of Ty-Maen; two *s.* one *d.* *Heir:* Humphry John [*b.* 1861; *m.* 1890, Margaret, *y. d.* of late Joseph Jowitt, of Bishop Thornton, Ripley, Yorkshire; one *s.* one *d.*]. *Educ.:* New College, Oxford. A Deputy Warden of the Stannaries of Cornwall and Devon; late Capt. Duke of Cornwall's Rifle Vols. *Address:* Tolcarne, St. Columb. *Club:* Isthmian.(*Died 9 Jan. 1917.*)

WILLYAMS, Edward Brydges, J.P. and D.L. Cornwall; Deputy Warden Stanneries, Devon and Cornwall; *b.* 1836; *m.* 1st, 1856, Jane (*d.* 1877), *d.* and *co-heir* of Sir Trevor Whelton, 9th Bart., of Leamington, Hastings, Warwickshire; 2nd, 1882, Emily (*d.* 1901), *sis.* of 1st Lord Burnham. *Educ.:* Merton College, Oxford. High Sheriff for Cornwall; M.P. Truro, 1857-60, 1880-85; East Cornwall, 1868-73. *Recreations:* Master of Hounds for 15 years. *Address:* Carnanton, St. Columb.   (*Died 10 Oct. 1916.*)

WILMOT, Hon. Alexander, K.S.G., K.H.S., F.R.G.S.; belongs to "Progressive" (Rhodes) party; Gazetted Honourable after 21 years' service and has now retired from S. Africa Parliament; created a Papal Count for services to the Church; *b.* Edinburgh, 9 April 1836; *m.* 1860, Alice Mary Slater (*d.* 1922); six *s.* seven *d.* *Educ.:* Univs. of Glasgow and Edinburgh; Prizeman Univ. of Edin. Passed Civil Service Examination head of list in Cape Colony, and served in various offices until 1886, when retired on a pension; Member of Legislative Council, Cape Colony, 1889; successful in passing several bills through Legislature connected principally with social and temperance subjects; elected by the Loyal Congress of South Africa, 1900, one of their delegates to proceed to Europe, and in England and Scotland addressed various meetings; wrote articles for and worked in common with the Imperial S. A. Association. *Publications:* The History of the Cape Colony; The History of the Zulu War; The Story of the Expansion of Southern Africa; Monomotapa (Rhodesia) Map; The History of our own Times in South Africa; The Life of Sir Richard Southey; The Life and Times of Bishop Ricards; The Climate of S. Africa—the Best in the World. *Address:* Wynberg, Cape Province.

WILMOT, Sir Ralph Henry Sacheverel, 6th Bt.; *cr.* 1759; *b.* 8 June 1875; *s.* of Rev. A. A. Wilmot, 4th *s.* of 4th Bt., and Harriet Cecilia, *d.* of Rev. A. Fitzherbert; *S.* uncle, 1901; *m.* 1905, Lady Ada Marian Maitland, *d.* of 18th Earl of Lauderdale; two *s.* one *d.* Joined Coldstream Guards, 1896; Lieut. 1898; Capt. 1903; Capt. Reserve of Officers, 1906. *Heir: s.* Arthur Ralph, *b.* 2nd Feb. 1909. *Address:* Chaddesden Hall, Derby. *Clubs:* Guards', Arthur's. (*Died 14 Jan. 1915.*)

WILSON, Alexander Johnstone, proprietor and editor of Investor's Review since 1892; *b.* Forglen, Banffshire, 20 Oct. 1841; *s.* of late George W. Wilson, H.M. Photographer for Scotland, Aberdeen; *m.* 1862; one *s.* two *d.* *Educ.:* Dr. George Ogilvie's school, Turriff; privately. Junior sub-editor of the Economist, 1872-73; assistant city editor of Times, 1874-81;

1134

city editor of Pall Mall Gazette, 1881-83; city editor of the Standard, 1883-99. *Publications:* The Resources of Modern Countries, 1878; Banking Reform, 1879; Reciprocity, Bimetallism, and Land Tenure Reform, 1880; The National Budget, 1882; edited Supplement to M'Culloch's Dictionary of Commerce, 1882; numerous essays in the Spectator, Fraser, Macmillan, the Fortnightly. *Recreation:* gardening. *Address:* Annandale, Atkins Road, S.W.12. *T.A.:* Unveiling. *T.:* Streatham 671. *Club:* Reform.
              (*Died 22 July 1921.*)

WILSON, Alpheus Waters, Bishop Methodist Episcopal Church South since 1882; *b.* Baltimore, 5 Feb. 1834; *m.*; three *d.* *Educ.:* schools in Md. and Virginia; Columbian College, Washington, D.C. Secretary Board of Missions, 1878-82; delegate to Ecumenical Methodist Conference in London, 1881 and 1901; took episcopal tours round the world, 1886, 1888, 1890, 1898, 1900; went to Brazil on Episcopal duty, 1892 and 1902; to China, 1907-8. *Publications:* Missions; Lectures—Witnesses to Christ, etc. *Address:* 1601 Park Place, Baltimore
              (*Died Nov. 1916.*)

WILSON, Admiral Sir Arthur Knyvet, 3rd Bt., *cr.* 1857; G.C.B., *cr.* 1906; G.C.V.O., *cr.* 1905; K.C.B., *cr.* 1902; V.C.; O.M., 1912; First Sea-Lord, Admiralty, 1909-12; retired, 1912; *b.* 4 March 1842; *s.* of late Rear-Admiral George Knyvet Wilson and Agnes Mary, *y. d.* of Rev. William Yonge, vicar of Swaffham; *S.* brother 1919. Capt. 1880; Rear-Adm. 1895; Vice-Adm. 1901; served Crimean War, 1854; Chinese War, 1865; Egyptian Campaign, 1882; Soudan Campaign, 1884; A.D.C. to the Queen, 1892-95; C.B. 1887; a Lord Commissioner of the Admiralty and Comptroller of the Navy, 1897-1901; Commanded Channel Squadron, 1901-3; Commander-in-Chief of Home and Channel Fleets, 1903-7; Admiral of the Fleet, 1907. *Heir:* none. *Address:* Swaffham, Norfolk. *Clubs:* United Service, Royal Societies.
           (*Died 25 May 1921.*)

WILSON, Rev. Barton Worsley, Hon. Canon of Carlisle, 1898. *Address:* The Rectory, Lazonby, Cumberland. (*Died 30 Dec. 1920.*)

WILSON, Sir Charles Rivers, G.C.M.G.; *cr.* 1895; C.B. 1876; President Grand Trunk Railway, Canada, since 1895; on Council Suez Canal Co. 1876-95; *b.* 1831; *s.* of Melvil Wilson and Louisa, *d.* of Major-General Sir Benjamin Stephenson, G.C.H.; *m.* 1st, 1860, Caroline (*d.* 1888), *d.* of R. Cook; 2nd, 1895, Hon. Beatrice Violet Mary Mostyn, *sister* of 7th Lord Vaux, 1895. *Educ.:* Eton; Balliol Coll. Oxford (B.A. 1853). Entered Treasury, 1856; Comptroller-Gen. of National Debt Office, 1874-94; Finance Minister, Egypt, 1877-79; Medjidie, 1st class. *Address:* 9 Berkeley Square, W.; *T.:* Mayfair 5696; Foxhills, Chertsey. *Clubs:* Arthur's, St. James's, Marlborough, Garrick.
           (*Died 9 Feb. 1916.*)

WILSON, Col. Christopher Wyndham, J.P., D.L.; *b.* 1844; *e. s.* of late William Wilson and 1st wife, Maria Lætitia, *d.* of late Richard Parrott Hulme, of Maisonnette, Devon; *m.* 1st, 1874, Mildred Eyre (*d.* 1878), *y. d.* of late T. S. Spedding, of Mirehouse, Cumberland; 2nd, 1879, Edith (*d.* 1913), *y. d.* of Sir Walter Minto Townsend Farquhar, 2nd Bart.; High Sheriff, Westmorland, 1884; Col. late commanding Westmorland and Cumberland Yeomanry. *Address:* Rigmaden Park, Kirkby Lonsdale. *Clubs:* Carlton, Royal Automobile. (*Died 8 Dec. 1918.*)

WILSON, Clive Henry Adolphus, D.S.O. 1900; 12th Batt. Imperial Yeomanry; 3rd *s.* of late Arthur Wilson of Tranby Croft; *b.* 1876; *m.* 1907, Elvira, *d.* of late Signor Magherini of Florence. Served South Africa, 1900-2 (severely wounded, despatches twice, Queen's medal 4 clasps, King's medal 2 clasps, D.S.O.). Chairman Lambert Parkers Gaines,

WILMER, Canon John Kidd. See page xxxi.

Ltd.; Master of Holderness Hounds. *Address:* Little Tranby, Beverley, E.R. Yorks. *T.A.:* Foxes Beverley. *Clubs:* Bachelors', White's.
(Died 18 Jan. 1921.)

WILSON, Rev. Daniel Frederic, M.A. (Oxon); Hon. Canon of Southwark Cathedral; Vicar of Mitcham, Surrogate; *b.* 10·Nov. 1830; *s.* of Rev. Prebendary Wilson, Prebendary of St. Paul's, Vicar of Islington; *m.* 1st, Katherine, *d.* of Edward Leathes, Lowestoft; 2nd, Sarah Maria, *d.* of Andrew Johnston, M.P. St. Andrews; two *s.* three *d.* *Educ.:* King's College, London; Oxford. M.A. 1854; Chaplain at Serampore, Calcutta; Curate at Calne, Wiltshire, and St. Mary's, Islington. *Address:* Vicarage, Mitcham. *T.:* Mitcham 820. *Clubs:* Primrose; Mitcham Conservative.
(Died 17 Feb. 1918.)

WILSON, Sir David, K.C.M.G., *cr.* 1899; C.M.G. 1890; Hon. Col. (V.D.) Trinidad L.I.V.; *b.* 1838; *s.* of late Very Rev. Dean Wilson, Fyvie, Aberdeen; *m.* 1st, Jane, *d.* of late Alexander Milne, 1870 (*d.* 1874); 2nd, Nora, *d.* of Norval Clyne, Aberdeen, 1881; two *s.* two *d.* Private Sec. to Gov. of N. Brunswick and Trinidad, 1861-1869; Stip. Magistrate, Trinidad, 1870-78; Commissioner of Northern Province and Sub-Intendant of Crown Lands, Trinidad, 1878-97; Acting Colonial Sec. Trinidad on several occasions, 1875-96; Capt. New Brunswick Vol. Militia, 1863; Major St. John Vol. Batt. on frontier service, 1866 (Canadian medal, one clasp); Officer commanding Trinidad Vol. Force, 1879-1890; Col. commanding Light Infantry Vols. 1890-1897; Governor of British Honduras, 1897-1903. *Address:* Clovelly Cottage, Rydens Avenue, Walton-on-Thames, Surrey.*(Died 15 Mar. 1924.)*

WILSON, Lieut.-Col. Edmond Munkhouse, C.B. 1902; C.M.G. 1896; D.S.O. 1898; Knight of Grace of the Order of St. John of Jerusalem, 1903; retired pay; *b.* Oundle, Northamptonshire, 4 Oct. 1855; *y. s.* of late C. T. Wilson. *Educ.:* Sherborne; St. George's Hospital, M.R.C.S. England; L.R.C.P. London; D.P.H. Camb. Served as Civil Surgeon Zulu War, 1879 (medal and clasp); joined Army Med. Dept., 1881; served in Nile Expedition, Egypt, 1884-85 (medal and clasp, Khedive's star); Nile Expedition, 1885-86; Expedition Gambia, West Africa, 1891-92 (medal and clasp); Ashanti Expedition, 1895-96, in command of Base Hospital (honourably mentioned, C.M.G., star); Soudan Expedition to Khartoum, 1898, as Secretary to Surg.-Gen. (despatches, D.S.O., English medal, and Soudan medal and clasp); R.A.M. Corps; D.-A. Director-Gen. of A.M.S. at headquarters, 1899-1904.; R.A.M.C. Record Office, 1905-13, 1914-16; President West London Medico-Chirurgical Society, 1918-19; Secretary R.A.M.C. Fund and Benevolent Society. *Publications:* Notes on Malarial Fever in connection with Meteorological Conditions at Sierra Leone, 1896-98. *Address:* 15 Gilston Road, South Kensington, S.W. *T.:* Victoria 2722. *Club:* Junior United Service.
(Died 9 Oct. 1921.)

WILSON, Col. Edward Hales, C.B. 1896; *b.* 1845. Entered army, 1865; Col. 1895; served Hazara, 1888 (medal with clasp); Chitral Relief Force (despatches, C.B., medal with clasp).
(Died 23 Aug. 1917.)

WILSON, Major-General Erastus William, C.M.G. 1917; Canadian Forces; Provincial Manager, Canada Life Assurance Co., Montreal; *b.* 1860; *m.* 1887, Sara E. L. Bricker; two *s.* *Clubs:* Mount Royal, St. James', Forest and Stream, Montreal.
(Died 15 May 1922.)

WILSON, Hon. Frank, C.M.G. 1911; J.P.; Premier and Colonial Treasurer, Australia, since 1916; *b.* Sunderland, 1859; father a member of the firm of J. and W. Wilson and Sons, of Sunderland; *m.* Annie, *e. d.* of Robert Hall Phillips, Sunderland. *Educ.:* Moravian School, Neuwied on the Rhine.; Wesley College, Sheffield. With his brother founded the firm of J. W. and F. Wilson and Co., marine engineers and boiler manufacturers, at Sunderland in 1878; arrived in Queensland, Australia, 1887; was manager of the firm of A. Overend and Co., railway contractors, engineers, and machinery merchants, Brisbane, until he left for Western Australia, to take up the position of Managing Director of the Canning Jarrah Timber Company, Ltd., 1891; was for four years in succession President of the Perth Chamber of Commerce; President of the Timber Merchants' and Saw Millers' Association for many years; presided over the Coal Owners' Association of Western Australia; sat in Perth City Council, 1895-97; elected member of the Legislative Assembly for Canning, 1897, and for Perth, 1901; Minister for Railways and Mines, 1901; employers' representative on Arbitration Court Bench till June 1904, when he was elected Member of the Legislative Assembly for Sussex, which seat he has won on four successive occasions; Minister for Works, 1905-6 and 1909-1910; Colonial Treasurer, Minister for Education and Agriculture, 1906-9; Premier and Colonial Treasurer of Western Australia, 1910-11; member of Senate of University of W.A. since 1912; Leader of the Opposition, 1911-16. *Address:* Viking House, Perth, Western Australia.
(Died 12 Dec. 1918.)

WILSON, Frederick James, C.I.E. 1910; M.Inst. C.E.; *b.* Edinburgh, 1858; 2nd *s.* of late William Wilson of Pilton, Darling Downs, Queensland, Australia, and Edinburgh; *m.* 1888, Mary Phoebe, *d.* of Col. E. A. Birch, M.D. late I.M.S.; two *s.* one *d.* *Educ.:* Royal Indian Engineering Coll., Coopers Hill. A year's practical course on dock works in England; joined the P.W.D. Madras as Assistant Engineer, 1880; services lent to Madras Harbour Trust, 1892; Assistant to Chief Engineer for Irrigation and Under-Secy. to Government, 1896; Local Consulting Engineer to the Madras Harbour Trust; Superintending Engineer P.W.D., 1902; Chief Engineer Madras Port Trust, 1908-6; Chief Engineer for Irrigation and Joint Secretary of Government, 1905; Chief Engineer and Secretary to Government of Madras Public Works Department, 1906-11; Member of the Legislative Council; President Sanitary Board; retired 1911. *Address:* Meadhurst, Sidmouth, Devon. *Clubs:* East India United Service; Madras; Ootacamund. *(Died 1 Oct. 1926.)*

WILSON, Sir Frederick William, Kt., *cr.* 1907; D.L.; proprietor East Anglian Daily Times; farms his own land in Norfolk; *b.* Scarning, Norfolk, 26 Mar. 1844; 2nd *s.* of William Wilson, Manor House, Scarning, a Liberal tenant farmer, and one of the founders and directors of the Norfolk News, which for many years led the Reform party in Norfolk; *m.* 1870, Mary Elizabeth, *d.* of Edward Cappes of Forest Hill, an early currency reformer, and winner of the 300-guinea prize offered by the Society of Arts for the best essay on the National Debt. *Educ.:* Wymondham Grammar School. Called up as a volunteer to defend Chester Castle against the Fenians in 1866; 29 years after, meeting one of the attacking party as a colleague in the House of Commons; indentured to Mr. J. H. Tillett, editor of Norfolk News and M.P. for Norwich, 1868-80; subsequently assistant to Sir Edward Russell on Liverpool Daily Post; founded the East Anglian Daily Times, 1874; president Newspaper Society of the United Kingdom, 1894, and Institute of Journalists, 1907; J.P. for Suffolk, 1894; in 1897 session rode in Parliamentary steeplechase, and played chess for the House of Commons against the American House of Representatives; one of the founders of the

Norfolk Small Holdings Association, and takes great interest in all movements calculated to keep the villager in the village; M.P. (L.) Mid Norfolk, 1895-1906. *Publications:* articles in his own newspaper. *Recreations:* presided at formation of Felixstowe Golf Club, the 5th club established in England, 1880; has scored 100 at Queen's ranges with Martini rifle, all bulls' eyes at 500 and 600 yards; D.L. for Norfolk, member of the Suffolk Territorial Association. *Address:* The Dale, Scarning, Norfolk. *Club:* Reform.   (*Died 26 May 1924.*)

WILSON, Harry; *b.* 1852; married. *Educ.:* Brighton College; Jesus College, Cambridge (Scholar, M.A.); Ely Theological Coll. Assistant Curate, St. Andrew's, Rugby, 1877-1881; Rector of Over Worton and Vicar of Nether Worton, 1881-88; Vicar of St. Augustine's, Stepney, 1883-1902; received into the Catholic Church, 1917; was Editor of The American Catholic. *Publications:* Why and Wherefore; A Good Communion; Our Dead: Where are They? A Holy Lent: The Third Day; Follow to Calvary, etc. *Address:* 330 So. Vendome Street, Los Angeles, California, U.S.A.   (*Died 21 Sept. 1923.*)

WILSON, Helen Russell, R.B.A. 1911; 6th c. of late James Leonard Wilson and Adelaide Anne, d. of E. B. Fripp. *Educ.:* Slade School; London School, under Frank Brangwyn, A.R.A.; studied Japanese painting in Tokyo. Exhibitor at Royal Academy, Royal Institute of Painters in Oil-Colours, International Society of Sculptors, Painters, and Gravers, Société Nationale des Beaux-Arts, Paris, Liverpool, Leeds, etc. *Recreations:* swimming, reading. *Address:* (studio) The Mountain, Tangier, Morocco.   (*Died 22 Oct. 1924.*)

WILSON, Rev. Henry Austin; Fellow of Magdalen College, Oxford, since 1876; *b.* Ayr, 7 Dec. 1854; 3rd *s.* of Rt. Rev. William Scot Wilson, Bishop of Glasgow and Galloway. *Educ.:* Glenalmond; Wadham College, Oxford. 1st cl. Classical Moderations, 1874; 2nd cl. Lit. Hum. 1876; Examiner in Hon., Sch. of Theol., 1893-95, 1908-10; Curator of the Bodleian Library, 1894-19; Perpetual Curator, 1919; Delegate of the University Press, 1900-19; Hon. Sec. of the Henry Bradshaw Society, 1895-1926; editor of the Journal of Theological Studies, 1902-8. *Publications:* Index to the Roman Sacramentaries of Muratori, 1892; The Gelasian Sacramentary, 1894; History of Magdalen College, in series of Oxford College Histories, 1899; has edited for the Henry Bradshaw Society Liber Eveshamensis, 1893; The Missal of Robert of Jumièges, 1896; The Benedictional of Abp. Robert, 1903; The Order of the Communion of 1548, 1908; The Pontifical of Magdalen College, 1910; The Gregorian Sacramentary under Charles the Great, 1915; The Calendar of St. Willibrord, 1918. *Address:* Magdalen College, Oxford; 55 Dundonald Road, Kilmarnock, Ayrshire.   (*Died 18 June 1927.*)

WILSON, Field-Marshal Sir Henry Hughes, 1st Bt., *cr.* 1919; G.C.B., *cr.* 1915; K.C.B., *cr.* 1915; C.B. 1908; D.S.O. 1901; Rifle Brigade; Chief of Imperial General Staff and Member of War Cabinet since 1918; *b.* 5 May 1864; *s.* of James Wilson, D.L., J.P., Currygrane, Edgeworthstown, Ireland; *m.* 1891, Cecil Mary, *y. d.* of late George Cecil Gore Wray, J.P., Ardnamona, Donegal. *Educ.:* Marlborough Coll.; Graduate at Staff College. Entered Royal Irish Regt. 1884; transferred to the Rifle Brigade, 1884; served Burma campaign, 1885-87 (wounded); served again, 1887-89 (medal with 2 clasps); Staff College, 1892-94; Staff Captain, Intelligence Division, 1894-97; Brigade-Major 2nd Brigade, Aldershot, 1897-99; Brigade-Major Light Brigade, South Africa, 1899-1900; D.A.A.G. Army Headquarters, South Africa, 1900-1 (despatches 4 times, medal with 5

1136

clasps, and Brevet Lieut.-Colonel on promotion to Major, D.S.O.); served European War, 1914-1915 (Lt.-Gen., K.C.B.); commanded 9th Provisional Batt., 1902-3; D.A.A.G. Army Headquarters, 1903; A.A.G. Army Headquarters, 1903-6; Assistant Director Staff Duties, War Office, 1904-1906; Commandant Staff College, 1907-10; Director of Military Operations at Army Headquarters, 1910-14; Assistant Chief of General Staff to Lord French, 1914; Corps Commander; Liaison Officer with the French; Commanded Eastern District; British Military Representative, Versailles, 1917; Field Marshal, 1919; Grand Cross, Legion of Honour; Grand Cross of the Russian White Eagle. *Recreations:* hunting, shooting, polo, lawn tennis. *Heir:* None. *Address:* Currygrane, Edgeworthstown, Ireland; Grove End, Bagshot, Surrey; 36 Eaton Place, S.W.1. *T.:* Victoria 5348. *Clubs:* White's, Travellers'; Royal Yacht Squadron, Cowes.   (*Died 22 June 1922.*)

WILSON, Captain Herbert Haydon, D.S.O. 1901; *b.* 14 Feb. 1875; *y. s.* of late Samuel Wilson of Ercildoune, Victoria. Hon. Captain in Army, 1901; Major, Notts (Sherwood Rangers) Imp. Yeo., 1904; served South Africa, 1900-1901 (despatches twice, Queen's medal, 4 clasps, D.S.O.). *Decorated* for defending posts in Boer attack on Lichtenburg. *Clubs:* White's. Bachelors', Carlton.

      (*Died 11 April 1917.*)

WILSON, Sir James, K.C.S.I., *cr.* 1909; C.S.I. 1901; *b.* 1853; *m.* 1888, Anne Campbell (*d.* 1921), *d.* of late Very Rev. Norman Macleod, D.D., Dean of the Thistle. *Educ.:* Perth Academy; Univ. of Edinburgh; Balliol Coll., Oxford. Entered I.C.S., 1875; served in the Punjab; Secretary to the Government of India in the Dept. of Revenue and Agriculture; Financial Commissioner of Punjab; retired, 1910; Superintending Inspector under the Board of Agriculture and Fisheries, London, 1911-15; a Governor of the Agricultural Organisation Society, 1912-14; Delegate to International Institute of Agriculture, Rome, 1914-1917; Chairman of Central Agricultural Wages Committee for Scotland, 1917-21. *Publications:* Gazetteer of Shahpur District; Settlement Report of Sirsa District; Code of Tribal Custom in Shahpur and in Sirsa; Grammar of Western Panjabi; Lowland Scotch; Farm-workers in Scotland; The Dialect of Robert Burns; Scottish Poems of Robert Burns; Dialects of Central Scotland. *Address:* Annieslea, Crieff, Scotland. *T.:* Crieff 194. *Club:* Caledonian.

      (*Died 22 Dec. 1926.*)

WILSON, Rev. James, M.A., B.D., Litt.D.; Vicar of Dalston since 1888; Hon. Canon of Carlisle; Hon. Chaplain of the Bishop; 3rd *s.* of late James Wilson of Drumgoland and Billis Grove, Co. Cavan; *b.* 28 Aug. 1856; *m.* 1886, Laura, *y. d.* of late T. King Atkinson, J.P., of Cardew Lodge, Dalston, and Reston Hall, Westmorland; one *s.* one *d. Educ.:* privately; Trinity College, Dublin. Deacon, 1879; Priest, 1880; Curate of St. Paul's, Carlisle; during his incumbency the two churches have been restored and beautified at a cost of £5000, and the two church schools have been added to and kept in line with educational requirements, one of which has been recovered for church usage. *Publications:* Editor of the Victoria History of Cumberland, vol. i. 1901, vol. ii. 1905; Register of the Priory of St. Bees, for the Surtees Society; Rose Castle, the Residential Seat of the Bishop of Carlisle; and several local publications; contributor to the Scottish Historical Review. *Address:* Dalston Vicarage, Cumberland.   (*Died 26 Mar. 1923.*)

WILSON, James, I.S.O. 1907; *b.* Ayr, 27 May 1847; *e. s.* of late William Wilson, mineral water manufacturer, Dumfries; *m.* 1875, Grace M'Candlish, *d.* of late Capt. Black, Isle of Whithorn ; three *s. Educ.:* Gemmel's Private School, Dumfries ; Dumfries Academy. Forty-one years in the Post Office Service ; retired from position of Postmaster and Surveyor of Leeds, 1907 ; was previously Postmaster at Hull, Derby, Exeter, and Preston ; and Chief Superintendent (Postal) at Liverpool. *Address :* 4 Edgerton Road, West Park, Leeds.   **(***Died 5 Mar. 1924.***)**

WILSON, Lieut.-Col. (James) Alban, D.S.O. 1912 ; late 8th Gurkha Rifles ; *b.* 12 Feb. 1865 ; *s.* of late James Buck Wilson, J.P., of Firbank ; *m.* 1898, Carrie, *d.* of late Gen. F. J. Priestley. *Educ.:* Uppingham. Joined 3rd Seaforth Highlanders, 1885 ; 2nd Seaforth Highlanders, 1887 ; 44th L.I. (now 8th Gurkhas), 1889 ; Capt., 1898 ; Major, 1905 ; D.A.A.G. Bengal, 1901-6 ; served Manipur, 1891 (medal with clasp); N.E. Frontier, Assam (Abor), 1894 ; Burma, 1895-6 ; Waziristan, 1901-2 (despatches, medal with clasp) ; Abor Expedition, 1912 (medal and clasp, despatches, D.S.O.) ; commanded Naga Hills Expedition, 1913 (Brevet of Lieut.-Col.) ; commanded 1/8th Gurkhas in Mesopotamia, 1916-17 ; raised and commanded 3/8th Gurkhas, 1917 and 1918 ; retired, 1920 ; Knight of the Order of the Red Eagle of Prussia ; Knight of the Order of Merit of Pyrmont-Waldeck. *Publication :* Sport and Service in Assam and Elsewhere, 1924. *Recreations:* shooting and fishing. *Address :* West Burton, Aysgarth, Yorks. **(***Died 27 April 1928.***)**

WILSON, Rev. James Allen, M.A., J.P. ; Rector of Bolton-by-Bolland, 1859-1915 ; Hon. Canon of Ripon Cathedral ; *b.* 3 June 1827 ; *s.* of James Wilson of Brinkcliffe Tower, Sheffield ; *m.* 1860, Catherine (*d.* 1914), *y.d.* of Henry Remington of Aynsome, Grange-over-Sands, and Crow Trees, Melling, Co. Lancaster ; six *s.* three *d. Educ.:* Sheffield Collegiate School; Trinity College, Cambridge (Foundation Scholar), 22nd Wrangler ; Curate of Hornby, Yorkshire, 1854-56 ; Stanwix, Cumb., 1857-59; was Chairman of Clitheroe Board of Guardians ; Rural Dean of West Craven, 1881-1904. *Address:* Taitlands, Stainforth, Settle. *M.:* C 1874. *Club:* New Oxford and Cambridge. **(***Died 14 Dec. 1917.***)**

WILSON, Sir John, of Airdrie, 1st Bt. ; *cr.* 1906 ; J.P. and D.L. Lanarkshire, Glasgow, Fifeshire ; Chairman of Wilson and Clyde Coal Company, Ltd., employing 5000 men ; proprietor of mineral estates in Lanarkshire and Fifeshire, etc. ; is connected with extensive steel and iron works and other industrial undertakings in Lanarkshire ; *b.* 26 June 1844 ; *s.* of late James Wilson, coalowner, Airdrie ; *m.* 1st, Margaret B. M. (*d.* 1885), *d.* of James Robertson, Glasgow ; 2nd, Emma Alexandrina, *d.* of David Binnie, Glasgow ; two *s.* two *d. Educ.:* Airdrie and Glasgow Academies. M.P. (L.U.) Falkirk District of Burghs, 1895-1906. *Recreations:* shooting and golfing; was in final in parliamentary golf match, 1904. Owns about 7000 acres in Lanarkshire, Fifeshire, Perthshire, and Kinross-shire. *Heir : s.* James Robertson [*b.* 5 May 1883 ; *m.* 1908, Helen Rae Fife, *e. d.* of A. Bulloch Graham, Park Gardens, Glasgow ; one *s. Educ.:* Oxford (B.A.)]. *Address:* Airdrie House, Airdrie, N.B. ; Kippen Tower, Dunning, Perthshire. *T.:* Dunning 6. *Clubs:* Reform, Bath, Royal Automobile. **(***Died 23 July 1913.***)**

WILSON, John ; *b.* 1837 ; *m.* 1883, Margaret (*d.* 1917). *d.* of late John Hewetson of Ellergil, Westmorland, M.P. (L.U.) St. Rollox Div. Glasgow, 1900-6 ; D.L. and J.P. Stirlingshire. *Address:* Finnich Malise, Drymen, Stirlingshire. *Club:* New, Glasgow.   **(***Died 5 Jan. 1928.***)**

WILSON, Very Rev. John Skinner, Hon. D.D. Edin. ; *b.* 1849 ; *y. s.* of late Very Rev. David Wilson, Dean of Aberdeen ; *m.* L. Mary, *d.* of Norval Clyne, Advocate, Aberdeen ; five *s.* two *d. Educ.:* Trin. College, Glenalmond ; St. Catharine's Coll. Cambridge (M.A.).

Ordained, 1871 ; Priest, 1873 ; Rector of St. George's, Edinburgh, 1885-96 ; Synod Clerk, 1890 ; Canon of Edinburgh, 1890-97 ; Dean of the Diocese and of St. Mary's Cathedral, 1897 ; retired, 1919 ; has taken a prominent part in the administrative and financial work of the Episcopal Church in Scotland since 1880. *Publications:* editor, Seabury Centenary Report, 1885 ; Scottish Guardian. 1886-88. *Address :* Aros, Strathtay, Perthshire.(*Died 13 Nov. 1926.*)

WILSON, Matthew, K.C. 1880 ; D.C.L. 1917 ; Head of law firm of Wilson, Pike, & Stewart, in Chatham, Ontario ; a Municipal and Corporation Counsel ; practises before all the higher Courts of Canada and in the Privy Council of England ; Hon. Treasurer of the Provincial Synod of Ontario and a member of the highest Court of Appeal for the Church of England in Canada ; a Bencher of the Law Society ; *b.* Harwich, Ontario, Canada, 28 Aug. 1854 ; *s.* of Robert Wilson, and Isabella Waugh ; *m.* Anna Marsden *e. d.* of Charles R. Atkinson, K.C. One *s.* two *d. Educ. :* Chatham, Whitby, and Toronto. Past President of the Western Bar Association, and Past President of the Kent Law Association ; Member of the Council of Huron Divinity College, and a Past Senator of the Western University of London ; Director of the Northern Life Assurance Co. of London, and of the Trusts and Guarantee Co. of Toronto, and President of the Great West Land Co. of Canada ; member of the Board of Management and of the Executive Committee of the Missionary Society for all Canada and for Foreign Missions : in 1918 appointed by Government of Ontario Representative of that Province to attend Inter-Provincial Meetings to promote Uniformity of Legislation throughout Canada. *Publications :* Articles advocating various law reforms. *Recreations :* horseback riding and tennis. *Address :* 325 Wellington Street, Chatham, Ontario. *T.A. :* Wilson, Chatham, Ontario. *T. :* 508. *M. :* 63872. (*Died 1 May 1920.*)

WILSON, Reginald Henry Rimington Rimington-, J.P.; *b.* 3 Nov. 1852 ; *e. s.* of late James Wilson Rimington-Wilson, and Jane, *d.* of Robert Wallas. *Educ. :* Eton ; Trinity College, Cambridge. Patron of one living ; late Lieut. Inniskilling Dragoons. *Heir : n.* Henry Edmund, *b.* 1899. *Address:* Broomhead Hall, Sheffield. *T.A. :* Broomhead, Deepcar. *T. :* 11 Stocksbridge. *Clubs:* Naval and Military, Army and Navy.   **(***Died 31 Mar. 1927.***)**

WILSON, Robert ; Director (Chairman) and Editor, Edinburgh Evening News, Ltd. ; *b.* Manchester, 1871 ; *s.* of late Hugh Wilson (editor of the Manchester Evening News) ; unmarried. *Educ.:* George Watson's College. Edinburgh ; Monmouth Grammar School ; Edinburgh University (M.A.) ; Berlin University. Been on staff of Edinburgh Evening News, of which he is the largest shareholder, for 26 years ; Member of the Consultative Board of the Press Association. *Recreations:* shooting, golf, billiards. *T.:* 718 Central, Edinburgh. *M.:* S 3738. *Clubs:* National Liberal, Savage. Press ; Scottish Liberal, Edinburgh.
(*Died Nov. 1920.***)**

WILSON, Sir Roland Knyvet, 2nd Bt., *cr.* 1857 ; M.A., LL.M. Cantab. ; J.P. Richmond, Surrey ; *b.* Swaffham, Norfolk, 27 August 1840 ; 2nd *s.* of late Rear-Admiral George Knyvet Wilson and Agnes Mary, *y. d* of Rev. William Yonge, vicar of Swaffham ; *S.* uncle 1874 ; *m.* 1873, Christiana (*d.* 1917), *d.* of late Richard Phillips, F.R.S. *Educ.:* Eton (King's Scholar and Newcastle Scholar) ; King's College, Cambridge ; Craven University Scholar, 1861 ; Senior Classic, 1863 ; late Fellow of King's Coll. Camb. Barr. 1867 ; reporter for the Weekly Reporter and Law Journal, 1867-71 ; classical and historical lecturer for Mr. Walter Wren (afterwards Wren and Gurney), 1871-78 ; Reader in Indian Law to

1137

WILSON, P. Macgregor. See page xxxi.

the University of Cambridge, 1878-92 ; Pres. of the National Dwellings Soc. Ltd. 1905. *Publications:* A Short History of Modern English Law (Rivington's Historical Handbooks), 1874 ; an annotated edition of Sir G. C. Lewis's Use and Abuse of Political Terms, 1877 ; An Introduction to the Study of Anglo-Muhammadan Law, 1894 ; A Digest of Anglo-Muhammadan Law, 1895 ; 4th ed. 1912: The Province of the State, 1911 ; The First and Last Fight for the Voluntary Principle in Education, 1915 ; articles, etc. *Heir: b.* Admiral Sir A. K. Wilson. *Address:* 86 Church Road, Richmond, Surrey.
(Died 29 Oct. 1919.)

WILSON, Surg.-General Sir William Deane, K.C.M.G., *cr.* 1900 ; M.B., L.R.C.S.I.; *b.* 27 Aug. 1842 ; *s.* of J. Deane Wilson, Rathdowney, Queen's County ; *m.* 1880, Anna Wilhelmina Elizabeth, *e. d.* of late Rev. Henry Smythe ; five *s.* Entered army, 1867 ; served Afghan War. 1878-80 (medal) ; Egyptian Expedition, 1882-84 (medal, bronze star) ; Soudan, 1884, battles Teb and Tamai (despatches, 2 clasps, promoted Surgeon-Major, ranking Lt.-Colonel) ; S. African War, 1899-1902 ; P.M.O., S. Africa ; advance on Kimberley ; operations in Orange Free State, April and May 1900 ; operations in Transvaal, June 1900 ; operations in Transvaal, east and west Pretoria, July to 29 Nov. 1900 ; operations in Orange River Colony, May to 29 Nov. 1900 ; operations in Cape Colony, south Orange River, 1899-1900 ; operations in Transvaal, Orange River Colony, Cape Colony, 30 Nov. 1900 to 31 May 1902 (despatches thrice, Queen's medal 3 clasps, King's medal 2 clasps). *Address:* Moorside, Westfield, Sussex. *(Died 19 Oct. 1921.)*

WILSON, Very Rev. William Hay, Dean of the United Diocese of Moray, Ross, and Caithness ; Rector of St. James' Church, Dingwall, and Chaplain of St. Anne's Memorial Church, Strathpeffer Spa, N.B., 1889 ; retired; *m.* 1889, Lucy, *e. d.* of William Rhodes, M.I.C.E. *Educ.:* Edinburgh and Durham Universities ; Edinburgh Theological College. B.A. 1885; M.A. 1889, of Durham Univ. ; F.S.A. (Scot.) 1887 ; Deacon, 1884 ; Priest, 1885 ; Chaplain, Diocese Moray, 1884 ; Senior Chaplain Inverness Cathedral, 1885 ; with charge of Holy Spirit Mission, 1887 ; Chaplain to late Primus Kelly, 1901-4 ; Synod Clerk of the Diocese and Canon of Inverness Cathedral, 1902 ; Chaplain to Bishop of Moray, 1904 ; Grand Chaplain of Scotland (Masonic), 1903-5 ; J.P. *Publications:* After the Change called Death ; several Masonic writings. *Address:* Kinnoull, Bridge of Allan, Stirlingshire. *(Died 7 Oct. 1925.)*

WILSON, Major William Herbert, D.S.O. 1917 ; Royal Field Artillery ; *s.* of late Colonel Thomas Wilson, C.B., of Liverpool, and Gadlys, Cemaes, Anglesey ; *m.* Florence Kerr, *y. d.* of late David Fernie, of Blundellsands, Lancs, shipowner ; no *c.* *Educ.:* Wellington College. Formerly in business; held commission in Auxiliary Forces, 1885-1902, retiring with rank of Major ; R. S. Clare & Co. Ltd. ; Gunner's Venture, Ltd., Kenya Colony ; joined Royal Field Artillery shortly after outbreak of war, with temporary rank of Major (D.S.O., despatches). *Recreations:* hunting, shooting, travelling. *Address:* Runnymede, Nanyuki, Kenya Colony. *Club:* Bath. *(Died 19 Nov. 1928.)*

WILSON, William Robert, I.S.O. 1903 ; *b.* 26 July 1844 ; *s.* of late Henry Charles Wilson, Superintendent Registrar of Births, Deaths, and Marriages for Marylebone ; *m.* Mary, *d.* of late J. G. Barrow, M.R.C.S., of Davies Street, W. ; one *s.* four *d.* *Educ.:* The Philological School, Marylebone. Entered the British Museum, 1863 ; Superintendent of Reading Room, 1896 ; Assistant-Keeper of Printed Books in the British Museum, 1899-1909 ; retired, 1909. *Recreations:* whist, angling. *Address:* 28 Steele's Road, Hampstead, N.W. *(Died 21 June 1928.)*
1138

WILSON, William Tyson, J.P., M.P. (Lab.) West Houghton Div. of Lancs since 1906 ; one of the founders of Bolton Building Trades Federation ; *b.* 1855. Whip to Labour Party, 1915 ; Chief Labour Whip, Jan. 1919. *Address:* 98 Mornington Road, Bolton, Lancs.
(Died 14 Aug. 1921.)

WILSON, William Wright, J.P., F.R.S., (Edin.) F.R.C.S. (Edin.), M.R.C.S. (Eng.) ; Consulting Surgeon to the Birmingham and Midland Ear and Throat Hospital ; *b.* Aston Juxta, Birmingham, 1843 ; *e. s.* of Joseph and Ann Wilson ; *m.* 1st, 1873, Emily Sarah Whitfield (*d.* 1902), 2nd, 1909, Amy Hurlston ; no *c.* *Educ.:* King Edward's Grammar School ; Edgbaston Proprietary School and Queen's College, Birmingham. Has written on Botany, Archæology, Heraldry, Physics, Natural History, Anatomy, and Freemasonry ; was a Fellow of the Linnean Society ; Hon. Secretary and Editor of the Midland Record Society ; Hon. Secretary to the Birmingham Naturalist and Microscopical Society ; Hon. Librarian to the Birmingham Archæological Society, etc. ; was a representative of Birmingham University on the Yardley Charity Estates, of which he was chairman, 1911 ; Deputy Provincial Grand Mark Master for Warwickshire, 1902 ; Grand Mark Overseer, 1914 ; is a Knight of the 30°, etc. ; J.P. Co. Warwick ; is consulting Surgeon to the Hospital for Diseases of the Ear, Throat, and Nose. *Publications:* The Physical Education of Girls ; Fashions and Habits, especially with Regard to Children ; Notes on Bordesley Manor ; Notes on Maxstoke ; Life of George Dawson ; History of Christ Church, Birmingham ; The Ancient Deeds of the Yardley Charity Estates ; The Creation and other verses, etc. *Recreations:* angling, antiquarian pursuits, bibliophile, numismatics, a reader of old deeds, and horticulture. *Address:* Cottesbrook, Acocks Green, Birmingham. *(Died 26 Feb. 1919.)*

WILSON, Woodrow, Ph.D., Litt.D., LL.D. ; President of the United States, 1913-20 ; *b.* Staunton, Virginia, 28 December 1856, of Scots-Irish parents ; *m.* 1st, 1885, Ellen Louise Axson (*d.* 1914), Savannah, Georgia ; three *d.* ; 2nd, 1915, Mrs. Norman Galt. *Educ.:* private schools, Princeton University, University of Virginia, Johns Hopkins Univ. Practised law, Atlanta, Georgia ; but, finding study more congenial, gave up practice to enter academic life ; Professor of History and Political Economy, Bryn Mawr College, 1885-88 ; Wesleyan University, 1888-90 ; Professor of Jurisprudence and Politics, Princeton University, 1890 - 1910 ; President of the University, 1902 - 1910 ; Governor of New Jersey, 1911-13 ; writer and public lecturer. *Publications:* Congressional Government : a Study in American Politics, 1885 ; The State : Elements of Historical and Practical Politics, 1889 ; Division and Reunion, 1829 - 89, 1893 ; An Old Master, and other Political Essays, 1893 ; Mere Literature, and other Essays, 1896 ; George Washington, 1896 ; A History of the American People, 1902 ; The New Freedom, 1916. *Recreations:* bicycling, rowing, golf. *Address:* 2340 S. Street, Washington, U.S.A. *(Died 3 Feb. 1924.)*

WILSON-TODD, Captain Sir William Pierrepoint, 2nd Bt., *cr.* 1903 ; *b.* 3 May 1857 ; *s.* of 1st Bart. and Jane, *o. c.* and *heiress* of late J. Todd, Halnaby, whose name 1st Bart. took in addition to his own ; S. father, 1910 ; *m.* 1887, Catharine James Crawford, *d.* of late James Russel. Late Capt. 4th Q.O. Hussars. *Heir:* none. *Address:* Halnaby Hall, Croft, Darlington. *Clubs:* Naval and Military, Arthur's, Turf, Boodle's. *(Died 13 Feb. 1925.)*

WILTON, 6th Earl of, *cr.* 1801 ; **Seymour Edward Frederic Egerton ;** Viscount Grey de Wilton, 1801 ; late Lieut. R.N. ; *b.* 1 Aug. 1896 ; *s.* of 5th Earl and Hon. Mariota Thellusson, *d.* of 5th Baron Rendlesham ; *S.*

father, 1915; *m.* 1917, Brenda, *d.* of late Sir William Petersen, K.B.E.; one *s.* one *d.* Served European War. Conservative. Owns about 9900 acres. *Heir:* s. Viscount Grey de Wilton.   *Address:* 43 Park Street, W.1. *T.:* Mayfair 7047.   (*Died 12 Oct. 1927.*)

WIMBLE, Sir John (Bowring), K.B.E., *cr.* 1919; Director of C. T. Bowring & Co., Ltd., of Liverpool, London, Cardiff, New York, and St. John's, Newfoundland; Hon. Treasurer King George's Fund for Sailors; *b.* 24 Aug. 1868; *s.* of John Wimble and Harriet, *d.* of late C. T. Bowring, Liverpool; *m.* 1893, Anne Mason, *d.* of late William Fothergill Batho; two *s.* two *d.* *Educ.:* Clifton College. Chairman London Shipowners' and Transport Workers' Military Service Committee; Chairman London Port Labour Committee; Chairman London General Shipowners' Society, 1916-17; Member of the Port of London Authority; Member of Committee of Lloyd's Register; Chairman Metropolitan Life Assurance Society; Member of the Port and Transit Executive Committee, 1917-19; J.P. Oxfordshire. *Recreations:* shooting, golf. *Address:* 23 Cambridge Square, Hyde Park, W.2; Huntercombe, near Henley-on-Thames. *T.:* Padd. 4748; Nettlebed 14. *Clubs:* Union; Bath, City of London, Ranelagh. (*Died 25 Nov. 1927.*)

WINANS, Walter, Chevalier of the Imperial Order of St. Stanislas of Russia; Commander of the Royal Spanish Order of Isabel the Catholic, and of the Crown of Roumania; Officer of the Star of Roumania; *s.* of William L. Winans of Ferry Bar Estate, Baltimore, Maryland, U.S.A. *Educ.:* Petrograd, Russia. *Publications:* The Modern Pistol; Hints on Revolver Shooting; Automatic Pistol Shooting: The Sporting Rifle; Practical Rifle Shooting; The Art of Revolver Shooting; Shooting for Ladies; Deer Breeding; Animal Sculpture. *Address:* Carlton Hotel: 17 Avenue de Tervueren, Brussels. (*Died 12 Aug. 1920.*)

WINCHILSEA, 13th Earl of (*cr.* 1628), and NOTTINGHAM, 8th Earl of (*cr.* 1675), **Henry Stormont Finch-Hatton;** Bart. 1611; Viscount Maidstone, 1623; Bart. English, 1660; Baron Finch, 1674; Hereditary Lord of Royal Manor of Wye; *b.* 3 Nov. 1852; *s.* of 10th and *b.* of 12th Earl; *S.* brother, 1898; *m.* 1882, Anne (*d.* 1924), *d.* of late Admiral of the Fleet Sir Henry J. Codrington, K.C.B.; two *s.* one *d.* *Educ.:* Eton; Balliol Coll., Oxford. Owns about 5000 acres. *Heir:* s. Viscount Maidstone. *Address:* Haverholme Priory, Sleaford. *T.A.:* Haverholme, Ruskington. *T.:* Ruskington 10. *M.:* FF 135. *Clubs:* White's, Carlton. (*Died 14 Aug. 1927.*)

WINDER, Captain Robert Cecil, C.B. 1918; D.L.; V.D.; Secretary East Lancs. T.F. Association. *Address:* Wenderholme, Boltonle-Moors, Lancs.   (*Died 15 Jan. 1920.*)

WINDER, Very Rev. Thomas Edward, Rector of Ulcombe, Maidstone. *Educ.:* Trinity College, Dublin (M.A.). Ordained, 1889; Curate Great Sankey, Lancs, 1889-92; Succenter, St. Patrick's Cathedral, 1892-99; Rector, Aghade, 1899-1902; Incumbent, Fiddown, 1902-8; Canon of Kilkenny, 1907-8; Incumbent of Kilkenny, 1908; Dean of Ossory, 1908-23. *Address:* Ulcombe Rectory, Maidstone. *Club:* University, Dublin. (*Died 12 June 1926.*)

WINDHAM, Vice-Admiral Charles, R.N., C.V.O. 1901; Gentleman Usher to H.M. since 1907; *b.* 1 March 1851; *e. surv. s.* of General Sir Charles Ashe Windham, K.C.B., and *g. s.* of Admiral William Windham, of Felbrigg Hall, Norfolk. *Educ.:* Lee's School, Brighton, and H.M.S. Britannia. Entered Navy, 1865; served in Abyssinian Expedition, 1868; Ashanti, 1874; Egypt, 1882; Captain of Royal Yacht Osborne, 1896-1901; H.M.S. Isis, 1901-2; Amphitrite, 1902; Rear-Admiral, 1905. *Clubs:* Marlborough, Naval and Military, Sports. (*Died 20 May 1916.*)

WINDSOR-CLIVE, Lieut.-Col. Hon. George Herbert Windsor, D.L.; Retired List; *b.* 12 Mar. 1835; 2nd *s.* of late Baroness Windsor and Hon. R. H. Clive, s. of 1st Earl of Powis; *m.* 1876, Hon. Gertrude Albertina Trefusis (*d.* 1878), *d.* of 19th Baron Clinton; one *s.* *Educ.:* Eton. M.P. (C.) Ludlow, 1860-85; served in 52nd Light Infantry, 1852-60; Coldstream Guards, 1860-70. *Address:* 12 Stratford Place, W. *Clubs:* Carlton, Travellers'. (*Died 26 April 1918.*)

WINGATE, Sir J. Lawton, Kt., *cr.*, 1920; P.R.S.A. Associate, 1878; Academician, 1887; President, 1919; *b.* 1846. Father, Manufacturing Chemist; *m.*; one *s.* five *d.* Attended Glasgow School of Art, Edinburgh School of Art, and Academy Life School. *Address:* 39 Mansionhouse Road, Edinburgh. (*Died 22 April 1924.*)

WINGATE, Captain Malcolm Roy, D.S.O. 1915; M.C.; 26th Field Co. R.E.; now Staff Captain, General Headquarters, British Expeditionary Force; *b.* 28 Aug. 1893; 2nd *s.* of Gen. Sir F. R. Wingate. Entered army, 1912; served European War, 1914-15 (D.S.O., Military Cross, and Croix de Guerre). *Address:* Knockenhair, Dunbar, Scotland. *Club:* Caledonian. (*Died 21 Mar. 1918.*)

WINGFIELD, Rev. Lt.-Col. William Edward, D.S.O. 1916; Rector of Broome, Norfolk, since 1920, and of Thwaite Norfolk since 1922; *b.* 1867; *s.* of late Captain Richard Wingfield, 52nd Light Infantry, of Abbeyleix, Queen's Co.; *m.* 1896, Elizabeth Mary, *d.* of late George J. Trench of Ardfert, Co. Kerry; two *s.* two *d.* *Educ.:* Wellington; R.M.A., Woolwich; Ridley Hall, Cambridge. Received commission in R.A. 1886; retired, 1907; Deacon, 1909; Priest, 1911; Curate St. Paul, Portman Square, 1911-13; recalled from Reserve of Officers, 1914; served 3½ years overseas in European War (promoted Lt.-Col. in Gallipoli; wounded in France, 1918; D.S.O., despatches 3 times). *Recreations:* mountaineering, skiing, yachting. *Address:* Rectory, Broome, Norfolk. (*Died 25 Jan. 1927.*)

WINKS, William Edward, Baptist minister, retired; *b.* Leicester, 1842; *y. s.* of late J. Foulkes Winks; *m.* Annie, *d.* of Lewis Whitehead, Chatham; one *s.* four *d.* *Educ.:* Rev. T. Carrier's Private School, New Walk, Leicester; Chilwell College, Notts. Minister Allerton, Bradford, 1865-67; Wisbech, 1867-76; Cardiff, 1876-1914; Hon. Curator Cardiff Museum, 1876-1913; Member Public Library Committee since 1876; erstwhile Governor and Councillor of S. Wales University College, Cardiff. *Publications:* Thoughts on Prayer, 1879; Lives of Illustrious Shoemakers, 1883; A Pastoral Medley; Prayer in the Four Gospels, 1897; The Gospel of Prayer in St. Luke, 1897; Christian Hymns and Songs, 1897, 2nd ed. 1906; History of Bethany Baptist Church, Cardiff; An Attempt to solve the School Library Problem; Library Association Record, 1900, Part I.; Danish Place-Names in S. Wales; Proceedings of Cardiff Naturalist Society; Sketch of History of the English Bible, 1911. *Address:* Eaton Cottage, Llanishen, Cardiff. (*Died 21 Dec. 1926.*)

WINN, Lieut.-Commander Sydney Thornhill, D.S.O. 1914 (retired); *o. s.* of late Dr. Winn, R.N.; *m.* 1919, Mary *e. d.* of A. H. A. Knox-Little, Garth House, Dorking. Served European War, 1914-15 (D.S.O.); was in Submarine B11 in her dash into the Dardanelles. *Address:* 23 Lyndale Avenue, Finchley Road, N.W.2.   (*Died 16 May 1924.*)

WINNINGTON, Lt.-Col. John Francis Sartorius, D.S.O. 1915; 4th Batt. Worcestershire Regt.; A.I.R. Headquarters Western Command, Chester; *b.* 17 Sep. 1876; *m.* Joyce Mary, *d.* of D. Marriage, J.P., Boughton Park, Worcester; two *d.* Entered army, 1897 ; Captain, 1901 ; Adjutant 1st Batt. 1912 ; Major, 1914 ; Adjutant 5th Worcestershire Regt. 1906-10 : served South Africa with 2nd Batt. Dublin Fusiliers and 2nd Worcestershire Regt. 1899-1900 (Queen's medal, 4 clasps) ; European War, 1914-15 (despatches twice, Bt. Lt.-Col., D.S.O.). *Recreations:* cricket (has played for County), shooting, hunting, fishing. *Address:* Boughton Park, Worcester.

(*Died 22 Sept. 1918.*)

WINSLOE, Lieut. - Col. Herbert Edward, C.M.G. 1920 ; D.S.O. 1917 ; R.E. ; *s.* of late Col. R. W. C. Winsloe, C.B. ; *b.* 1873 ; *m.* 1921, Aileen Marie Constance Venables. *Educ.:* University College School ; Dover College ; R.M. Academy, Woolwich. Joined R.E. as 2nd Lieut., 1892 ; served in India, 1894-1914 ; Tirah Campaign 1898 (medal and clasp) ; Zakka Khel Campaign 1908 (medal and clasp) ; Mesopotamia Expeditionary Force 1914-16, including Siege of Kut (despatches thrice, D.S.O., promoted Bt. Lt.-Col.). *Recreations:* shooting, riding. *Club:* Naval and Military.

(*Died 1 Dec. 1921.*)

WINSLOE, Colonel Richard William Charles, C.B. 1889 ; retired pay ; *b.* Innerleithen, 20 April 1885 ; 2nd *s.* of Richard Winsloe (*d.* 1878), Mount Nebo, Wilton, Somerset, and Isabella Wyld, *d.* of late Captain Richard Dawson, The Buffs ; *m.* 1861, Constance Edwards, 2nd *d.* of late F. M. Cromartie, Supt. of Stores, Ordnance Department ; four *s.* five *d.* *Educ.:* Edinburgh Academy. Joined 15th Regt. 1853 ; volunteered to the Royal Scots Fusiliers, 1854 ; served with them during the latter part of the Crimean Campaign, 1855-56 ; present siege and fall of Sebastopol and Expedition to Kinburn (medal and clasp and Turkish medal) ; Zulu Campaign, 1879 ; present at Battle of Ulundi (severely wounded, mentioned in despatches, medal and clasp, brevet of Lieut.-Col.) ; Transvaal Campaign, 1880-81 ; commanded troops at siege of Potschefstrom, being thanked in district orders (wounded, mentioned in despatches, A.D.C. to Her Majesty) ; Burmese Expedition, 1886-87 ; in command of the Royal Scots Fusiliers and Thayetmyo District ; commanded the troops at the relief of Thabybin in Upper Burmah (mentioned in despatches, medal) ; A.D.C. to H.M. 1882-90 ; Jubilee Medal 1887, and clasp 1897 ; reward for distinguished service. *Publication:* Siege of Potschefstrom. *Recreations:* gardening, cricket, carpentering. *Address:* 20 Guilford Terrace, Dover. *Club:* Union, Malta.

(*Died 5 June 1917.*)

WINSLOW, Rev. William Copley, D.D., S.T.D., Ph.D., Sc.D., Litt.D., D.C.L., LL.D. ; founder of American branch of Egypt Exploration Fund in 1883 ; its Hon. Sec., and Vice-President for America till 1902 ; archeologist-historical writer, and journalist ; former ed. of Christian Times and assoc. ed. World ; formerly assoc. ed. of The Hamiltonian and University Quarterly, and on staff of Biblia ; late assoc. ed. of American Antiquarian, and of American Historical Register ; now assisting work of Egyptian Research Account under Petrie, and as V.P. of Research in the United States, by raising funds in the United States and writing articles for journals on the discoveries ; *b.* Boston, 13 Jan. 1840 ; *s.* of Rev. Hubbard Winslow, D.D., author ; *m.* 1st, Harriet S. (*decd.*), *d.* of Hon. Joseph Hayward ; one *d.* ; 2nd, Elizabeth Bruce Roclofson, author. *Educ.:* Hamilton Coll. ; General Theol. Seminary (Episcopal), New York City. On executive committees of various leading societies ; executive secretary Free Church Association, Massachusetts, since 1883 ; V.P. Hamilton College Alumni Association of the U.S.A. at its centennial, 1912 ; Ex - President New England Alumni Association ; hon. member of leading Canadian Association and 23 of the State historical societies, including five of the six New England States ; Hon.

Fellow of Oriental Research Society (U.S.A.) ; university lecturer, etc. *Publications:* A Greek City in Egypt ; Pithom and Zoan ; Pilgrim Fathers in Holland ; Gov. Edward Winslow of Plymouth ; Egyptian Antiquities in American Museums ; Egypt at Home ; Distribution of Papyri in the United States ; published papers before Amer. Oriental Soc., Amer. Hist. Assoc. Arch. Inst., New Eng. Hist. Soc., N.Y. Biog. Soc., American Statistical Association, etc. *Recreations:* summers in the woods of Maine and New York, where he has explored ; and also on Cape Cod by the sea. *Address:* 525 Beacon Street, Boston, U.S.A. *Clubs:* University, Clerical, Boston. (*Died 2 Feb. 1925.*)

WINTER, Lieut.-Col. Ernest Arthur, D.S.O. 1918 ; M.C. ; Surveyor of H.M. Customs and Excise, Grimsby ; 3rd *s.* of late James Winter, Civil Servant, The Lodge, Torrington ; *m.* 1914, Mary Madeline Jung, Bewdley, Worcs ; two *d.* *Educ.:* privately. Entered Civil Service, 1895 ; served in Cumberland, Devonshire, Ireland, and Worcestershire ; joined H.M. Forces, 1914 ; served with 23rd Batt. Royal Fusiliers, 1914-19 ; commanded the Batt. 1917-19 ; commanded British Base Camp, Antwerp, 26 May - Oct. 1919 (M.C., D.S.O. and bar, despatches thrice) ; demobilised, 1919. *Recreations:* hunting, fishing, shooting. *Address:* Brooklands Avenue, Cleethorpes, Lincs. *T.A.:* Winter, Brooklands Avenue, Cleethorpes. *M.:* EE 4666. (*Died April 1925.*)

WINTER, Hon. Sir Francis Pratt, Kt., *cr.* 1900 ; C.M.G. 1892 ; *b.* Colony of Victoria, Australia, 23 Feb. 1848 ; *e. s.* of George Winter, King's County, Ireland, and Elizabeth, *d.* of James Cox of Tasmania ; *m.* 1903, Edith, *d.* of Hon. George Moore of Fiji. *Educ.:* private school, London. A solicitor, Colony of Queensland ; barrister and solicitor, Colony of Fiji ; acting Attorney-General, Colony of Fiji ; First Chief Judicial Officer, British New Guinea, 1888-1903. *Decorated* for services in British New Guinea.

(*Died 29 Mar. 1919.*)

WINTER, Hon. Henry Daniel, J.P. ; *b.* 26 Oct. 1851 ; *s.* of J. E. F. Winter of Pietermaritzburg, Natal ; *m.* Janet, *d.* of William Leslie of Campsie Glen, Estcourt. *Educ.:* Pietermaritzburg, Natal. Began farming in Weenen County, Natal, 1875 ; Member of the Legislative Assembly, 1893 ; Minister of Agriculture, Natal, under Binns Ministry, 1899 ; under Hime Ministry, 1899-1903 ; under Smythe Coalition Ministry, 1905-6. *Address:* Loch Sloy, Estcourt, Natal.

(*Died 4 Nov. 1927.*)

WINTER, William, author ; *b.* Gloucester, Massachusetts, U.S.A., 15 July 1836 ; 2nd *s.* of Captain Charles Winter and Louisa Wharff ; *m.* 1860, Elizabeth Campbell, of the Campbells, formerly of Ederline, Loch Awe, N.B. ; two *s.* one *d.* *Educ.:* Boston and Cambridge Schools ; Dane Law School ; Harvard Coll., B.L. 1857 ; Litt. Doc. from Brown Univ., 1895. Lecturer, political speaker, 1856 ; writer for the press, poet, essayist, traveller, editor, biographer, etc. ; first visited England in 1877 ; founded the Arthur Winter Memorial Library in 1886 ; dramatic editor and reviewer for N.Y. Tribune, 1865-1909 ; President of Staten Island Academy, 1891-1907. *Publications:* Shakespeare's England ; Gray Days and Gold ; Old Shrines and Ivy ; Brown Heath and Blue Bells ; Wanderers (Poems) ; Shadows of the Stage (Three Series) ; Life and Art of Edwin Booth ; Life and Art of Joseph Jefferson ; Orations ; Life of John Gilbert ; Brief Chronicles ; The Actor and other Speeches ; The Press and the Stage ; The Stage Life of Mary Anderson ; Henry Irving ; A Wreath of Laurel ; George William Curtis ; Life of John McCullough ; Life of Ada Rehan ; Life and Letters of William Law Symonds ; Other Days, being Chronicles and Memories of the Stage ; Old Friends, being Literary Recollections ; Poems, def. ed. ; Life and Art of Richard

Mansfield ; Over the Border; Shakespeare on the Stage ; Lives of the Players—1. Tyrone Power; The Wallet of Time; Shakespeare on the Stage (Second Series) ; Vagrant Memories, 1915. *Recreations:* study of Shakespeare, antiquarian research, and travel. *Address:* 46 Third Avenue, New Brighton, Staten Island, N.Y. ; Ederline Cottage, Mentone, California. *T.:* Tompkinsville 62 J. *Clubs:* Lotos, New York ; Bohemian, San Francisco. *(Died 30 June 1917.)*

WINTER, W. Tatton, R.B.A. ; *b.* Ashton-under-Lyne. *Educ.:* various elementary and private schools. Entered business at an early age in Manchester ; studied Art at the Board School classes, in evening, and Manchester Academy of Fine Arts ; gave up business later. toured through Belgium and Holland ; studied under Verlat at Antwerp ; exhibitor at Royal Academy since 1889 ; at New Gallery, Royal Institute of Painters on Water Colours, The Salon, and Munich, etc.; elected to London Sketch Club, 1902. *Recreations:* gardening walking, and literature. *Address:* Avondale, South Park, Reigate. *(Died 22 Mar. 1928.)*

WINTERBOTHAM, Canon Rayner. *Educ.:* University of London (B.Sc., M.A., LL.B.); Wells College. Ordained 1865 ; Chaplain to Bishop of Grafton, 1867-68 ; Incumbent of Christ Church, Grafton, N.S.W., 1867-72 ; of St. Peter's, Fraserburgh, N.B., 1878-86 ; Rector of Holy Trinity, Dean Bridge, Edinburgh, 1886-99 ; Synod Clerk of the Diocese of Edinburgh and Canon of St. Mary's Cathedral, 1897-1900 ; Hon. Canon of St. Mary's Cathedral, 1900. *Address:* Melmoth, Zululand, Natal, S. Africa. *(Died 7 May 1924.)*

WINTERBOTHAM, Sir William (Howard), Kt., *cr.* 1919 ; Official Solicitor to the Supreme Court, 1895-1919 ; *b.* 13 Dec. 1843 ; *y. s.* of Lindsey Winterbotham, Stroud, Gloucestershire ; *m.* 1875, Elizabeth, *d.* of Thomas Micklem, Hoddesdon, Herts ; four *s.* one *d. Educ.:* Amersham School, Buckinghamshire ; University College, London ; Pembroke College, Cambridge. Graduated B.A. (1st class with honours) at London University, 1862 ; B.A. (1st class Mathematical Tripos) at Cambridge, 1866 ; admitted a Solicitor, 1869 ; senior partner in the firm of Waterhouse & Co., 1 New Court, Lincoln's Inn, until his retirement in 1919 ; Member of the Council of the Law Society, 1895 ; President, 1909. *Recreations:* yachting and gardening. *Address:* 51 Ladbroke Grove, Notting Hill, W.11 ; *T.:* Park 62 ; Craig-y-Môr, Abersoch, Carnarvonshire. *Club:* National Liberal. *(Died 24 Jan. 1926.)*

WINTRINGHAM, T., M.P. (Ind. Lib.) Louth since 1920. *Address:* House of Commons, S.W.1. *(Died 8 Aug. 1921.)*

WIRGMAN, Ven. Augustus Theodore, D.D., D.C.L. ; Archdeacon of Port Elizabeth ; Hon. Chaplain to His Majesty ; Canon of Grahamstown Cathedral since 1899 ; Vice-Provost of St. Mary's Collegiate Church, Port Elizabeth, since 1888 ; Senior Chaplain and Hon. Lieut.-Col. Colonial Forces, Cape Colony ; V.D. 1896 ; S. African General Service Medal, 1880 ; on active service during Boer War, 1899-1900 (medal and clasp) ; Coronation medal, 1911 ; *b.* Bradbourne, Derbyshire, 22 Sept. 1846 ; *e. s.* of Rev. Augustus Wirgman, M.A., Vicar of Hartington, Co. Derby, and Jane, *d.* of Thomas Pearson of Wingfield ; *m.* Rose, *d.* of A. J. Worthington of Ball Haye Hall, Leek, Co. Stafford, 1874. *Educ.:* Rossall ; Magdalene College, Cambridge (Scholar, 1866). B.A. Classical Tripos, 1870 ; 2nd class Theological Tripos, 1871 ; M.A., 1873 ; M.A. University of the Cape, 1875 ; Hon. D.C.L. University of the South, U.S.A. 1877 ; B.D. Cambridge, 1893 ; D.D. Cambridge, 1899. Deacon, 1870 ; Priest, 1871 ;

Curate of Hartington, Alton, and St. Michael's, Handsworth, Birmingham, 1870-73 ; Vice-Principal of St. Andrew's College, Grahamstown, Cape Colony, 1873-75 ; Rector of St. Mary's, Port Elizabeth, 1875 ; Rural Dean of Port Elizabeth, 1884-96 ; Examining Chaplain to Bishop of Grahamstown, 1883-92 ; to Bishop of Mashonaland, 1899 ; Secretary of Theological Faculty of Church in South Africa, 1898 ; Prov. Secretary for South Africa of the Church House, Westminster, 1892 ; Select Preacher at Cambridge, 1911. *Publications:* The Prayer Book with Historical Notes and Scripture Proofs, 1873 ; The Beatitudes and the Lord's Prayer, 1877 ; The Sevenfold Gifts, 1889 ; The Church and the Civil Power, 1893 ; The Spirit of Liberty, 1893 ; The English Reformation, etc., 1890 ; The History of the English Church and People in South Africa, 1894 ; The Doctrine of Confirmation, 1896 ; The Constitutional Authority of Bishops, 1899 ; articles in Nineteenth Century on Boer War, 1900 ; The Blessed Virgin and all the Company of Heaven (an Eirenicon), 1905 ; The Life of James Green, D.D., Dean of Maritzburg, 1909 ; History of Protestantism, 1911. *Recreations:* rowing, cricket, football, golf, sketching, painting. *Address:* St. Mary's Rectory, Port Elizabeth, South Africa. *Club:* Authors'. *(Died 16 Oct. 1917.)*

WIRGMAN, T. Blake, Member of the Royal Society of Portrait Painters. *Address:* 24 Dawson Place, W.2. *T.:* Park 2112. *(Died 16 Jan. 1925.)*

WISE, Alfred Gascoyne, LL.B. ; *b.* Colombo, Ceylon, 15 August 1854 ; *s.* of late Alfred Wise ; *m.* Augusta Frances (*d.* 1911), *d.* of A. N. C. R. Nugent ; two *s. Educ.:* Repton ; Trinity College, Cambridge. Called to Bar, Lincoln's Inn, 1878 ; Police Magistrate, Hong-Kong, 1884 ; Registrar of the Supreme Court, etc., 1892 ; Puisne Judge of the Supreme Court, Hong-Kong, 1895-1909. *Address:* Valroy, Camberley. *Club:* Conservative. *(Died 25 June 1923.)*

WISE, Hon. Bernhard Ringrose ; Agent-General for N.S.W. in London since 1915 ; *b.* Sydney, N.S.W., 10 Feb. 1858 ; 2nd *s.* of Mr. Justice Wise of Sydney ; *m.* 1884, Lilian Margaret, *d.* of John Forster Baird of Beaumont Hill, Northumberland. *Educ.:* Rugby ; scholar of Queen's Coll. Oxford ; Cobden Prize, 1878 ; Proxime for the Lothian Historical Essay, 1880 ; 1st class in Law, 1880 ; President of the Oxford Union and O.U.A.C. 1880 ; one of the founders and first Vice-President Amateur Athletic Association of Great Britain ; amateur mile champion, 1879-81 ; called to the Bar by the Middle Temple, 1883 ; Attorney-General of New South Wales, 1887-88 ; Q.C. 1898 ; Attorney-General of New South Wales, 1899-1904 ; one of the delegates from New South Wales to the Australian Federal Convention. His Majesty approved of his retention for life of the title of Honourable, 1907. *Clubs:* Garrick ; Australian, Sydney. *(Died 19 Sept. 1916.)*

WISE, Francis Hubert, Master Co. Limerick Hounds, 1899-1908 ; *b.* 6 Feb. 1869 ; *s.* of late Charles W. Wise of Rochestown, Cahir, Co. Tipperary ; *m.* 1898, Jean Orme, *y. d.* of late General Sir Archibald Little, G.C.B., of Upton House, Tetbury, Gloucestershire. *Educ.:* Harrow. Served as lieutenant in 3rd Durham L.I., 1888-90 ; gazetted to 2nd lieutenant, 13th Hussars, July 1890 ; lieutenant, 1891 ; retired, 1901 ; served with 13th Hussars during South African War, and was present at all engagements up to Relief of Ladysmith (despatches) ; awarded Humane Society's Bronze Medal for saving life of trooper, 13th Hussars, in River Tugela, Jan. 1900 ; hunted 13th Hussars Harriers when regiment quartered at Dundalk, 1895-96 ; Major, South of Ireland Imperial Yeomanry, 1903. *Recreations:* hunting, shooting, fishing. *Address:* Rochestown, Cahir. *Clubs:* Naval and Military; Kildare Street, Dublin. (*Died 5 June 1917.*)

WISE, Sir Fredric, Kt., *cr.* 1924; D.L., J.P., M.P. (U.) for Ilford since 1920; *b.* 1871; *e. s.* of Alexander Wise, of Belleville Park, Cappoquin, Waterford, and Julia, *d.* of John Anthony Woods, of Benton Hall, Newcastle-on-Tyne; *m.* Lucy, *d.* of late Sir Thomas Wrightson, Bt.; one *s.* one *d. Educ.:* Marlborough College; abroad. Started life in a bank, and in 1903 founded present stockbroking firm of Wise, Speke & Co., of Newcastle-on-Tyne; has travelled a great deal all over the world in interests of his business; during war gave his services voluntarily—in County as Chairman of Volunteers and Military Representative, in London to National Service, Food Ministry, Treasury; sent to France to lecture to troops on food position; sent to Berlin in March 1919 by Peace Conference to report on Financial Position of Germany; is Financial Adviser to Lord Byng's Committee of United Service Fund; Director of Daily Express, Director of Sudan Plantation Syndicate, Ltd. *Address:* Holwell Court, Hatfield. *Clubs:* Carlton, Oriental. (*Died 26 Jan. 1928.*)

WISEMAN, Very Rev. Dr. James, Dean of Aberdeen and Orkney since 1910; Rector of St. Machar since 1874. *Educ.:* University of Aberdeen (M.A., Hon. D.D.). Ordained, 1870; Incumbent of Alford, 1870-74. *Address:* The Rectory, Bucksburn, Aberdeen.

WITHAM, Philip; *y. s.* of Sir Charles Witham, R.N.; *m.* Louisa, 2nd *d.* of Marmaduke Charles Salvin of Burn Hall, County Durham; two *d. Educ.:* Mount St. Marys, Derbyshire; abroad. Head of the firm of solicitors; 1 Grays Inn Square, W.C. *Recreations:* shooting, fishing, and golf. *Address:* Whitmoor House, Sutton Park, nr. Guildford. *T.A.:* Sutton Green. *T.:* Worplesdon 34. *(Died 4 May 1921.)*

WODEHOUSE, Edmond Henry, C.B. 1897; *b.* Norton, Kent, 17 Feb. 1837; 7th *s.* of Rev. T. Wodehouse, Canon of Wells, and Anne, *d.* of Walker King, Bishop of Rochester; *m.* Louisa Clara, *d.* of Rev. N. Wolehouse, Vicar of Worle, Somerset, 1864. *Educ.:* Westminster; Christ Church, Oxford (Student). M.A.; 1st class Classical Mods. 1857; 2nd class Final School Litt. Hum. 1859. Inspector of Poor Law Schools, 1863-71; Poor Law and Local Govt. Board Inspector, 1871-86; Chief General Inspector and assist. sec. Local Govt. Board, 1886-91; Commissioner of Inland Revenue, 1891-1902. *Recreations:* cricket (as a spectator), bicycling. *Address:* Plomer Hill House, West Wycombe, Bucks. *Club:* Oxford and Cambridge.

(*Died 27 Mar. 1923.*)

WODEHOUSE, Rev. Preb. Philip John, M.A.; Rector of Bratton Fleming, Devon, 1875-1913; Rural Dean of Shirwell, 1887-1908; Prebendary of Exeter Cathedral since 1903; *b.* Malvern, 6 Oct. 1836; *s.* of late Col. Philip Wodehouse, of Wribbenhall, Bewdley, Worcestershire; *m.* 1st, 1876, Constance Helen (*d.* 1877), 3rd *d.* of Wade Brown, of Monkton Farleigh, Wilts; 2nd, 1879, Marion Bryan, *d.* of Rev. Gilbert I. Wallas, Rector of Shobrooke; two *s.* two *d. Educ.:* Harrow; Caius College, Cambridge (Eighth Wrangler); Deacon, 1859; Priest, 1860; Curate of Halesowen, Worcestershire, 1859-60; St. John, Ladywood, Birmingham, 1860-65; St. Mary, Nottingham, 1865-66; Vicar of St. Margaret's, Lynn Regis, 1866-71; Diocesan Inspector, Manchester, 1871-75. *Address:* Wheatridge, Chelston, Torquay. (*Died 8 Dec. 1917.*)

WOLFE-MURRAY, Lt.-Col. Arthur Alexander, C.B. 1915; Highland Light Infantry; *b.* 22 May 1866; *s.* of late James Wolfe-Murray and Louisa Grace, *d.* of Sir Adam Hay, 7th Bt.; *m.* 1904, Evelyn Mary Hay, *e. d.*

1142

of late Colin Mackenzie, Lord Lieutenant for Peeblesshire; one *s. Educ.:* Harrow. Entered army, 1886; Captain, 1893; Major, 1904; Lt.-Col., 1912; served S. African War, 1899-1900 and 1902 (despatches twice; Queen's medal, 2 clasps; King's medal with clasp); European War, 1914-15 (C.B.). *Recreations:* shooting, fishing, golf. *Address:* 20 George Square, Edinburgh. *Clubs:* Naval and Military; New, Edinburgh. (*Died 7 Dec. 1918.*)

WOLLASTON, Sir Arthur Naylor, K.C.I.E., *cr.* 1908; J.P. Kent and Cinque Ports; *b.* Norwood, 14 Oct. 1842; *y. surv. s.* of late Henry Francis Wollaston, Southsea; *m.* 1873, Caroline Marianne (*d.* 1902), *o. d.* of late Sir Albert William Woods; one *s. Educ.:* Stockwell Grammar School. Entered India Office by open competition, 1859; junior clerk, 1860; senior clerk, 1878; assistant secretary, 1884; succeeded Sir F. J. Goldsmid as examiner in Persian at Royal Staff College, Sandhurst, 1880; selected in 1881 by the Science and Art Department to superintend the translation of Oriental inscriptions in S. Kensington Museum; C.I.E. 1886; Registrar and Superintendent of Records, India Office, 1898-1907. *Decorated* for Oriental scholarship. *Publications:* translation of Anvar-i-Suhaili, or Fables of Bidpai, 1877; Sir Lewis Pelly's Miracle Play of Hasan and Husain, 1879; English - Persian Dictionary, 1882; a larger work of the same kind, 1889; Half-Hours with Muhammad, 1886; Sword of Islam, 1905; The Religion of the Koran, 1905; The Scroll of Wisdom, 1906; Tales within Tales, 1909; and jointly with Sir Roper Lethbridge, Gazetteer of the Territories under the Government of India. *Recreations:* literature, music. *Address:* Glen Hill, Walmer, Kent. *T.A.:* Walmer. *Club:* Northbrook.

(*Died 8 Feb. 1922.*)

WOLLASTON, Sir Harry Newton Phillips, LL.D., K.C.M.G., *cr.* 1912; C.M.G. 1907; I.S.O. 1903; J.P.; Barr.-at-Law; late Permanent Head of Department of Trade and Customs, Commonwealth of Australia and Comptroller-General of Customs, retired 1911; *b.* W. Australia, 17 Jan. 1846; *s.* of Rev. H. N. Wollaston, Trinity Church, E. Melbourne; *m.* 1st, 1868, Mary Annie Harker (*d.* 1902); one *s.* three *d.*; 2nd, 1914, Mary, *d.* of late Maj.-Gen. Price-Dent, Hallaton Manor, Leicesters. *Educ.:* St. John's College, Auckland; Nelson College, N.Z.; Melbourne University. Entered Civil Service of Victoria after examination as a junior, 1863; rose through all grades and became Secretary for Trade and Customs in that state, 1891; Standing Counsel to Marine Board, 1886-1901; graduated with honours in Law, 1884; called to Bar, 1885; admitted as Master of Laws, 1886; Doctor of Laws, 1891; transferred to Commonwealth service, 1901; matriculated at University, and completed University course after entering the Civil Service; attended Imperial Conference on Shipping Laws in London in 1907 as an official delegate from Australia. *Publications:* Trade Customs and Marine Law of Victoria; Customs Law of Australia; Marine Board Act of Victoria with Notes; Customs Handbook, etc. *Recreations:* riding and cycling, reading. *Address:* Toorak, Melbourne, Victoria. *Club:* Melbourne.

(*Died 14 Feb. 1921.*)

WOLRIGE-GORDON, Col. John Gordon, of Hallhead and Esslemont, Aberdeenshire; C.M.G. 1918; retired pay; Lt.-Col. commanding 3rd Batt. A. and S. Highlanders, 1914-1919; *b.* 20 Dec. 1859; *m.* Isabel (*d.* 1911), *o. c.* of William Hervey Woodhouse of Irnham Hall, Lincolnshire; one *s.* two *d. Educ.:* Eton; Royal Military Coll., Sandhurst. Entered Army, 1879; retired (A. and S. Highlanders), 1907; served N.W. Frontier India, 1897-98 (medal and clasp); S. Africa, 1899-1902 (despatches twice,

Bt. Lt.-Col., Queen's and King's medals 6 clasps). *Address:* Esslemont, Ellon, Aberdeenshire ; 58 Queen's Gate, S.W.7. *Clubs:* Carlton ; New, Edinburgh.   (*Died 30 Sept. 1925.*)

WOLSELEY, Sir Capel Charles, 9th Bt., *cr.* 1744 ; F.R.G.S. ; *b.* 24 Aug. 1870 ; *s.* of late Major W. C. Wolseley ; *m.* 1907, Beatrice, *d.* of late Col. W. Knollys. *S.* kinsman 1890. Lieut. Royal West Surrey Regiment, 1891-93 ; Vice-Consul at Archangel, 1900-1909 ; joined 3rd Batt. East Surrey Regt. Dec. 1914 ; Captain, Feb. 1915 ; served European War, 1914-18 ; with the British Expeditionary Force in North Russia, 1919. *Heir:* cousin, Reginald Beatty, *b.* 31 Jan. 1872. *Address:* 32 Knightsbridge, S.W.   (*Died 27 Aug. 1923.*)

WOLSELEY, General Sir George Benjamin, G.C.B., *cr.* 1907 ; K.C.B., *cr.* 1891 ; Col. York and Lancaster Regt. ; *b.* 11 July 1839 ; 4th *s.* of late Major Garnet J. Wolseley, King's Own Borderers, and brother of 1st Viscount Wolseley ; *m.* 1867, Esther Louise (*d.* 1902), *d.* of W. Andrews. *Educ.:* private tuition. Ensign Cheshire Regiment, 1857 ; Lieut. York and Lancaster Regiment, 1858 ; by purchase Capt. North Staffordshire Regiment, 1868 ; Maj. York and Lancaster Regiment, 1878 ; Lieut.-Col. 1879 ; Col. and A.D.C. to Queen Victoria for Egyptian War, 1882 ; Maj.-Gen. by selection, 1892 ; served with 84th Foot in Indian Mutiny (medal) Assistant Adj.-Gen. in Afghan campaign (medal and Brevet Lieut.-Col.) ; Assistant Adj. and Quartermaster-Gen. Egyptian campaign, including Tel-el-Kebir (medal and bronze star) ; A.D.C. to Queen Victoria ; Assistant Adj. and Quartermaster-Gen. the Nile campaign, and subsequently as Col. on the Staff commanding troops at Abu Gus (clasp and C.B.) ; Brig.-Gen. in Burmese campaign, and commanded expedition which annexed Wunthoo (thanked by Government of India, medal, and K.C.B.) ; ' commanded the Forces, Punjab, India, with rank of Lieut.-Gen. 1897-98 ; Madras Forces, 1898-1903 ; retired, 1906. *Publications:* magazine articles. *Recreations:* shooting, cycling, tennis. *Address:* Thatched Cottage, Wateringbury, Kent. *T.A.:* Wateringbury. *Club:* United Service.
    (*Died 10 May 1921.*)

WOMBWELL, Capt. Sir Henry (Herbert), 5th Bt., *cr.* 1778 ; *b.* 24 Sep. 1840 ; 3rd *s.* of 3rd Bt. and Georgiana, *d.* of Thomas Orby Hunter, Crowland Abbey, Co. Lincoln ; *S. b.* 1913 ; *m.* 1902, Hon. Myrtle Mabel Muriel Mostyn, *sister* of 7th Baron Vaux of Harrowden ; no *c. Educ.:* Harrow. Late 7th Hussars and Royal Horse Guards. *Heir: g.-n.* Frederick Philip Alfred William Wombwell, *b.* 6 July 1910. *Address:* 85 Vincent Square, S.W.1. *T.:* Victoria 5402. *Clubs:* Boodle's, Orleans.
    (*Died 1 Feb. 1926.*)

WOOD, Sir Alexander, Kt., *cr.* 1922 ; J.P. ; *b.* Partick ; *m. d.* of late Alexander Mathers ; one *s.* one *d. Educ.:* Partick Academy ; Glasgow University. Was a partner in Alexander Wood & Sons, weighing machine makers ; Provost of Partick, 1898 ; during S.A. War acted as Chairman to the Advisory Committee on recruiting for the Partick Division of Lanarkshire. *Address:* Woodlands, Partickhill, Glasgow. *T.A.:* Exprownd, Glasgow. *T.:* Western Glasgow 501. *Club:* Conservative, Glasgow.   (*Died 19 April 1924.*)

WOOD, Ven. Alfred Maitland ; Archdeacon of Macclesfield since 1904 ; Vicar of Bowdon since 1911 ; *b.* 1840 ; *s.* of Alfred Wood, Basinghall Street, E.C. ; *m.* Sarah (*d.* 1913), *d.* of W. Topham, The Limes, Tarvin, Cheshire ; one *s. Educ.:* Christ's Hospital, Times' scholar, 1859 ; Trinity Coll. Cambridge ; B.A., 31st Wrangler, 1863 ; Mathematical Master, Furness's Rugby, 1863-65 ; Curate of Tarvin, 1865-71 ; Wallasey, 1871-78 ; Vicar of St. Mary's, Liscard, 1878-

1887 ; Vicar of Runcorn, 1887-1911 ; Hon. Canon of Chester, 1890-1904 ; Rural Dean of Frodsham, 1891-1905 ; Proctor in Convocation, 1892-1904 ; Member of Archbishops' Committee upon Elementary Education, 1894-95 ; Examining Chaplain to Bishop of Chester, 1895 ; Archdeacon of Macclesfield, 1904. *Address:* The Vicarage, Bowdon. *M.:* M 6257.
    (*Died 28 Dec. 1918.*)

WOOD, Rev. Andrew, M.A. ; Rector of Great Ponton ; Prebendary of Lincoln ; *b.* India 1833 ; *s.* of Andrew and Caroline Wood ; *m.* 1858, Caroline Colpoys ; six *s.* four *d. Educ.:* Blackheath ; Trinity College, Cambridge. Assistant Master, Blackheath, 1855 and 1858-62 ; Curate, Droxford, Hants, 1856-58 ; Ruddington, Notts, 1862-66 ; Vicar, Skillington, Lincs, 1866-82 ; Diocesan Inspector of Schools, 1874-1909 ; Association Secretary, C.M.S. 1878 ; a V.P. of Midland Evangelical Association. *Publications:* The Hebrew Monarchy ; Sermons to Children, and Wedding Leaflet ; Promise and Performance, etc. *Recreations:* school inspection and pupil teacher examinations. (*Died 30 Sept. 1917.*)

WOOD, Lieut.-Col. David Edward, C.B. 1917 ; retired pay ; Inspector of Remounts, 1903-1921 ; *b.* 22 August 1853 ; *m., Educ.:* Harrow ; Cambridge. Protestant. Entered Army, 1874 ; Lt.-Col. 1900 ; retired, 1903 ; served Afghanistan, 1879-80 (medal) ; S. Africa, 1900-1 (slightly wounded, despatches, Queen's medal 4 clasps). *Address:* Kibworth, Leicester. *Clubs:* Cavalry ; Kildare Street, Dublin.   (*Died 29 July 1927.*)

WOOD, Sir Edward, Kt. ; *cr.* 1906 ; J.P. ; *b.* 1839 ; *s.* of W. Wood ; *m.* 1862, Annie (*d.* 1907), *d.* of Thomas Sewell, Uppingham ; three *d.* Founded firm of Freeman, Hardy, and Wills, Ltd., Boot and Shoe Manufacturers, Leicester. *Address:* Shirley Lodge, Knighton, Leicester. *Clubs:* City Liberal, National Liberal.
    (*Died 22 Sept. 1917.*)

WOOD, Field-Marshal Sir Evelyn, G.C.B., *cr.* 1891 ; G.C.M.G., *cr.* 1882 ; K.C.B., *cr.* 1879 ; D.L., V.C., 1855 ; D.C.L. Oxon. ; Constable of the Tower since 1911 ; *b.* Cressing, Braintree, Essex, 9 Feb. 1838 ; *y. s.* of late Rev. Sir John Page Wood, 2nd Bt., and Caroline, *y. d.* of Admiral Sampson Michell, Croft West, Cornwall ; *m.* 1867, the Hon. Mary Paulina Southwell (*d.* 1891), *sis.* of 4th Viscount Southwell. *Educ.:* Marlborough Coll. Barr. Middle Temple, 1874 ; passed Staff Coll. ; entered Navy, 1852 ; served in Crimea with Naval Brigade 1 Oct. 1854 to 18 June 1855, when he was severely wounded while carrying a scaling ladder to the Redan ; mentioned in Lord Raglan's despatches ; medal and 2 clasps ; Knight of Legion of Honour, Medjidie, Turkish medal ; joined 13th Light Dragoons, 1855 ; served in 17th Lancers in India campaign, 1858 ; mentioned in despatches twice ; granted Victoria Cross, December 1859 ; Ashantee, Kaffir, Zulu, and Transvaal Wars, 1879-81 ; commanded Chatham District, 1882-88 ; 2nd Brigade (2nd Division) Expedition to Egypt, 1882 ; raised the Egyptian Army, 1883 ; served in N le Expedition, 1884-95 ; commanded Eastern District, 1886-88 ; Aldershot Division, 1889-98 ; Quartermaster-Gen. to the Forces, 1893-97 ; Adjutant-General to Forces, 1897-1901 ; 2nd Army Corps District, 1901-5. *Publications:* The Crimea in 1854-94 ; Cavalry at Waterloo, 1896 ; Achievements of Cavalry ; From Midshipman to Field Marshal, 1906 ; The Revolt in Hindustan, 1908 ; Our Fighting Services and How they Made the Empire, 1916 ; Winnowed Memories, 1917. *Recreations:* hunting, shooting, cycling, lawn-tennis. *Address:* Millhurst, Harlow. *T.:* Harlow 35. *Clubs:* United Service, Army and Navy.   (*Died 2 Dec. 1919.*)

WOOD, Francis Derwent ; R.A. 1920 ; A.R.A. 1910 ; Cavaliere of the Order of the Crown of Italy, 1911 ; sculptor ; *b.* Keswick, 1871 ; *f.* American, *m.* English ; *m.* 1903, Florence Schmidt,

Australian singer; one s. *Educ.*: Switzerland, Germany. Began his artistic career at Karlsruhe, returned to Eng., 1889; National Scholar under Prof. Lanteri at South Kensington; Assistant to Professor Legros at Slade School for two years; Royal Academy Student, Gold Medallist and Travelling Studentship, 1895; Assistant to Thos. Brock, R.A., 1894-95; Award at Paris Salon, 1897; appointed Modelling Master at Glasgow Art Schools; returned to London, where now resides; enlisted R.A.M.C. (T.), March 1915; commission, March 1916; general services—in charge of Masks for Facial Wounds Dept.; late Prof. of Sculpture at Royal College of Art, South Kensington. *Principal Works*: Queen Victoria for Patiala, India; statue Sir Titus Salt, Saltaire; statue Rev. C. H. Spurgeon, Baptist Church House; four statues of the Arts in Glasgow Art Galleries; Chamberlain bust in the Guildhall; Pitt statue for Washington, to celebrate 100 years' peace; bust of Henry James, bought for the Tate Gallery (Chantry Bequest), 1914; also statue Atalanta; Machine Gun Corps War Memorial, Hyde Park Corner; exhibitor at Royal Academy of ideal works since 1894. *Address*: 27 Glebe Place, S.W.3; 18 Carlyle Square, S.W.3. *T.*: Ken. 530. *Clubs*: Chelsea Arts, Garrick.   (*Died 19 Feb. 1926.*)

WOOD, Frederick Benjamin, O.B.E. 1920; I.S.O. 1910; *b.* 1849; *s.* of Thomas Wood, British Consul for Morea; *m.* Mary (*d.* 1926), *d.* of late A. L. Crowe, British Consul, Zante; two *s.* four *d. Educ.*: abroad. Entered Consular Service, 1874; late H.M.'s Consul for the Morea and Provinces of Etolia and Acarnania; retired from Consular Service, 1922; Gold Cross of the Redeemer, Greece. *Recreations*: shooting, yachting. *Address*: Aroe, Patras, Greece.   (*Died 25 Dec. 1928.*)

WOOD, George Arnold, M.A.; Professor of History in the University of Sydney since 1891; *b.* Salford, 1865; *s.* of G. Stanley Wood, Manchester; *m.* Eleanor Madeline Whitfeld, Sydney; three *s.* one *d. Educ.*: Owens College, Manchester; Balliol College, Oxford. Brackenbury History Scholarship, 1886; Stanhope Essays, 1889. *Publications*: The Discovery of Australia, 1922; The Voyage of the Endeavour, 1926. *Address*: Sydney University.
     (*Died 14 Oct. 1928.*)

WOOD, Colonel Henry, C.B. 1889; *b.* 26 Mar. 1835; *m.* 1st, 1866, Charlotte Frances Smith (*d.* 1869); 2nd, 1871, Helen Mary, *d.* of Rev. Henry Brown; five *d.* Entered army, 1853; Colonel, 1884; served in Crimea, 1855; North-West Frontier, 1862; Afghan War, 1878-1879; Expedition against Mahsood Wuzeerees, 1881 (despatches); commanded 9th Regimental District, 1887. *Address*: 71 Thorpe Road, Norwich. *Club*: United Service.(*Died 17 Mar. 1919.*)

WOOD, Rev. Henry Thellusson, M.A.; Rector of Aldbury since 1890; Hon. Canon St. Albans, 1904; Chaplain to Bishop of St. Albans since 1913. *Educ.*: St. John's College, Cambridge; Curate of Baldock, 1874-77; Vicar of Great Chishall, Essex, 1877-84; Biggleswade, 1884-90; Rural Dean, Berkhampstead, 1902-22; Surrogate, 1904. *Address*: Aldbury Rectory, Tring.   (*Died 21 July 1928.*)

WOOD, Lt.-Col. John Bruce, D.S.O. 1918; M.C.; late 4th Batt. Royal Scots; Solicitor and bank agent. *Educ.*: Fordyce Academy; Edinburgh University. Served European War with Gordon Highlanders, 1914-18 (despatches thrice, D.S.O., M.C., Croix de Guerre). *Address*: National Bank House, Bathgate.   (*Died 20 Oct. 1927.*)

WOOD, Lt.-Col. John William Massey, M.V.O. 1907; *s.* of late John Henry Wood; *b.* 3 Sep. 1855; *m.* 1895, Ethel Maria, *d.* of Capt. H. L. Webb. *Educ.*: King's College, London; Caius College, Cambridge. Served in the Royal Dragoons, 1878-98; Provost Marshal and

1144

Commandant Military Police Corps, 1898; retired 1910. *Club*: Junior Constitutional.
     (*Died 9 Dec. 1916.*)

WOOD, Rev. Joseph, D.D., M.V.O. 1905; Canon Residentiary of Rochester Cathedral since 1910; and Vice-Dean since 1914; *b.* 1842; *m.* 1868, Caroline, *d.* of W. S. Pryce-Hughes, Northwick Hall, Worcester. *Educ.*: Balliol College, Oxford; 1st class Classical Mods.; 1st class Final Classical School. Deacon, 1865; Priest, 1873; Fereday Fellow of St. John's Coll. 1865-68; Headmaster of Leamington College, 1870-90; Classical Examiner at Oxford, 1876-77; Headmaster Tonbridge School,1890-98; collated to the Prebend of Mapesbury in St. Paul's Cathedral, 1907-11; Headmaster of Harrow School, 1898-1910. *Address*: The Precincts, Rochester.
     (*Died 13 July 1921.*)

WOOD, His Honour Josiah; *b.* 18 April 1843; *e. s.* of Mariner and Louisa C. Wood; *m.* 1874, Laura S. Trueman; two *s.* three *d. Educ.*: Mount Allison University, Sackville, N.B. (M.A.). Merchant; represented Westmorland County, New Brunswick, in Dominion House of Commons, 1882-96; Mayor of Sackville, 1903-8; Treasurer Mount Allison University Board of Regents, 1875; Senator of the Dominion of Canada, 1896-1912; Lieut.-Governor of New Brunswick, 1912-17; resigned, 1922. *Address*: Sackville, New Brunswick.
     (*Died May 1927.*)

WOOD, J. S., Co-proprietor, Chairman and Managing Director of The Gentlewoman and other newspapers; Chairman of The Press Printers, Ltd.; *b.* 4 Jan. 1853; *m.* Elena Maria Umilta, *d.* of late Torello Ambuchi of Florence; one *s.* three *d.* Has initiated and organised, as a voluntary worker, charitable schemes which have raised nearly half a million of money for hospitals and various philanthropic institutions; Member of Council, Chelsea Hospital for Women, 1886-1920; Hon. Sec. for five years at Foundation of Bolingbroke Hospital (the first pay hospital); late Member, Council Hospitals Association; founder two political associations; founder The Children's Salon, 1890 (which has endowed 11 cots in children's hospitals); founder The Society of Women Journalists, 1893; for 14 years Member of Grand Council of Primrose League; Deputy Chairman, The Royal Irish Industries Association, 1888-1916, by which means £300,000 has been sent to cottage workers in Ireland; Member of Visiting Committee of King Edward's Hospital Fund. *Recreations*: shooting, golfing. *Address*: 29 Kensington Court, W.8. *T.A.*: Jayswood, London. *T.*: Western 3684 and Gerrard 9026. *Clubs*: Carlton, Cecil, Savage.
     (*Died 20 Dec. 1920.*)

WOOD, Sir Lindsay; 1st Bart.. *cr.* 1897; J.P., D.L. Co. Durham; High Sheriff, 1889; *b.* 21 June 1834; 4th *s.* of Nicholas Wood (*d.* 1865) and Maria Foster Lindsay, *d.* of Collingwood Foster Lindsay; *m.* Emma, 4th *d.* of Samuel Gooden Barrett, Heighington House, Co. Durham, 1873; three *s.* two *d. Educ.*: Royal Kepier Grammar School, Houghton - le - Spring; King's Coll. London. Made several elaborate and exhaustive experiments in respect of the pressure of gas in coal; member of the Royal Commission on Accidents in Mines, 1879-86. *Publications*: Institute of Mining Engineers, of which he was President, 1875-78. *Heir*: *s.* Arthur Nicholas Lindsay Wood [*b.* 29 March 1875; Captain Northumberland Artillery]. *Address*: The Hermitage, Chester - le - Street, N. Durham. *Clubs*: Carlton, Junior Carlton.
     (*Died 22 Sept. 1920.*)

WOOD, Rev. Theodore, Vicar of St. Mary Magdalene, Wandsworth Common, since 1902; Hon. Canon of Southwark, 1920, and Rural Dean of Wandsworth; *b.* 6 Aug. 1862; *s.* of Rev. J. G. Wood, M.A., author of many works on natural history; *m.* 1898, Helen

Louisa, *e. d.* of late **Commander E. F. Clarke**, R.N., of St. Peter's, Kent. Deacon, 1889; Priest, 1890; Curate of Baldock, 1889-93; Curate of St. Mary Magdalene, Wandsworth Common, 1898-1902. *Publications:* Our Insect Allies, 1884; Our Insect Enemies, 1885; Our Bird Allies, 1886; Nature and her Servants, 1886; The Farmer's Friends and Foes, 1887; Life and Work of the late Rev. J. G. Wood, 1890; Out-of-the-way Pets, 1896; Young People's Natural History, 1905; The Zoo, Past and Present (with A. T. Elwes), 1905; The Sea-Shore, 1907; Dwellers in the Garden, Wood, etc., 1908; Butterflies and Moths, 1909; Birds One Should Know, 1921; The Second Adam (theological), 1911. *Recreation:* collecting British beetles. *Address:* The Vicarage, Lyford Road, Wandsworth Common.
(*Died 13 Dec. 1923.*)

WOOD, Rt. Hon. Thomas M'Kinnon, P.C. 1911, D.L.; LL.D. (St. Andrews); M.P. (L.) St. Rollox Division, Glasgow, 1906-1918; *b.* London, 26 Jan. 1855; *o. s.* of the late Hugh Wood and Jessie M'Kinnon, *d.* of Rev. Thomas M'Kinnon; *m.* 1883, Isabella, *d.* of Alex. Sandison, J.P.; four *s.* one *d. Educ.:* Mill Hill School; Univ. College, London (B.A.). L.C.C. Central Hackney, 1892-1907; Alderman L.C.C. 1907; chairman, 1898-9; chairman Parliamentary Committee, 1895-8; leader of progressive party; Parliamentary Sec. to Board of Education, 1908; Parliamentary Under-Secretary, Foreign Office, 1908-11; Financial Secretary to the Treasury, 1911-12; Secretary for Scotland, 1912-16; Chancellor to the Duchy of Lancaster and Financial Secretary to the Treasury, 1916. *Publications:* articles in Ency. Brit. and reviews. *Address:* 24 Queen's Gate, S.W.7: *T.:* Western 3016; Starfield, Crowborough. *Clubs:* Reform, National Liberal; Liberal, Glasgow; Scottish Liberal, Edinburgh.
(*Died 26 Mar. 1927.*)

WOOD, Rev. William, D.D.; Rector of Rotherfield Greys, Henley, since 1901; Hon. Canon, Christ Church, Oxford; *b.* 1829; *s.* of A. Wood, F.R.C.S.; *m.* 1862, Emma, *e. d.* of Col. R. Moorsom, Scots Guards; five *s.* three *d. Educ.:* Trinity Coll. Oxford. Matriculated at Brasenose Coll. Oxford, 1847; elected Scholar of Trinity Coll.; Second for Hertford (Univ.) Scholarship, 1848; 2nd class Litt. Hum. 1851; B.A. 1851; Elected Fellow of Trin. Coll. 1851; Lecturer, 1852; ordained Deacon, 1852; M.A. 1853; Priest, 1853; Sub-Warden of Radley Coll. 1853-63; Perpetual Curate of Prestwood, Bucks, 1864; Warden of Radley, 1866; B.D. and D.D. 1868; Vicar of Radley, 1868; Vicar of Cropredy, 1870; Diocesan Inspector of Schools, 1877-88; Rural Dean of Deddington, 1881-98; Rector of Monks Risborough, 1898; Examiner of Training Colleges for National Society, 1895-1906; travelled in Egypt and Palestine in 1861, and visited Ceylon in 1888. *Publications:* various papers and reviews in Cornhill Magazine, Temple Bar, Newberry House, Ludgate, 19th Century, Quarterly, etc. *Address:* Rotherfield Greys Rectory, Henley-on-Thames.
(*Died 28 Oct. 1919.*)

WOOD-MARTIN, William Gregory, J.P., D.L., High Sheriff, Co. Sligo, 1877; A.D.C. to late Queen Victoria, to late King Edward, and now to the King (Militia); Colonel commanding the Duke of Connaught's Own Sligo Artillery, R.G.A. 1883-1902; *b.* Woodville, Co. Sligo, 16 July 1847; *o. surv. s.* of late James Wood of Woodville and Anne, *e. d.* of Abraham Martin of Cleveragh, Sligo; *m.* 1873, Frances Dora (*d.* 1905), *e. d.* of Roger Dodwell Robinson of Wellmont, Co. Sligo; two *s.* one *d. Educ.:* private schools, Switzerland and Belgium; R.M.C. Sandhurst. *Publications:* Sligo and the Enniskilleners, 1880 (2nd ed. 1881); History of Sligo County and Town (3 vols.), 1882-92; The Lake Dwellings of Ireland,

1886; The Rude Stone Monuments of Ireland (Co. Sligo), 1888; Pagan Ireland, 1895; Traces of the Elder Faiths of Ireland, 1902; sometime editor of the Journal of the present Society of Antiquaries of Ireland; member Royal Irish Academy. Owns 7062 acres. *Heir: s.* Henry R. B. Wood-Martin, F.S.I., Stephen Street, Sligo. *Recreations:* archæological pursuits. *Address:* Cleveragh, Sligo. *T.A.:* Sligo. *Club:* Army and Navy. (*Died 1917.*)

WOOD-SEYS, Roland Alex.; novelist; *b.* Stourbridge, Worcestershire, 5 Nov. 1854; *m. y. d.* of John Hebden, The Hollies, Bolton, Lancs, and Woodlands, Siverdale, *via* Carnforth. *Educ.:* privately. Abroad in 1876; literary work, home in 1884-96, reading (publishers), reviewing, and contributing to most of the leading London journals; travelling; 1903 California, olive-growing. *Publications:* The Blacksmith of Voe; Woman with a Secret; Bull i' th' Thorn; Cut with His Own Diamond; The Shepherdess of Treva; God's Lad; The Hon. Derek, The Device of the Black Fox, etc. *Recreations:* golf, shooting. *Address:* The Hermitage, Oceanside, San Diego Co., California. *Club:* Authors'.
(*Died Dec. 1919.*)

WOODALL, Sir Corbet, Kt., *cr.* 1913; D.Sc., M.Inst. C.E., J.P.; Governor of the Gas Light and Coke Company; President twice of Institute of Gas Engineers; Hon. Col. 12th Batt., Co. of London Regiment; *b.* 1841; *m.* 1865, Anne, *d.* of W. H. Whiteman, Croydon; five *s.* five *d.. Address:* Walden, Chislehurst; Palace Chambers, Westminster, S.W. *T.:* Bromley 942. *Clubs:* Reform, National Liberal.
(*Died 17 May 1916.*)

WOODARD, Rev. Lambert, M.A.; Hon. Canon of Ely; *b.* 26 Aug. 1848; *s.* of Canon Woodard, D.C.L., Founder and Provost of Lancing College; *m.* 1879, Emily, *d.* of Henry Perkins, J.P., of Thriplow Place, Cambs.; three *s.* three *d. Educ.:* Lancing; Jesus College, Cambridge. Vicar of Thriplow, 1878-1886; St. Paul's, Bedford, 1886-1913; Heath, 1916-19; Vicar of St. Stephen's, Shepherd's Bush, 1919-21. *Recreations:* cricket, football, lawn tennis, bowls. *Address:* 91 Warwick Road, Thornton Heath. (*Died 1 Nov. 1924.*)

WOODFALL, His Honour Judge Robert, Judge of County Courts Circuit 58, 1898; transferred to Westminster Co. Court, 1902; *b.* 1855; 4th *s.* of late Henry Woodfall of Stanmore; *m.* 1887, Mary Helena, *d.* of Lt.-Col. E. Galt, J.P., of Southsea; one *s.* one *d.* Called to Bar, Inner Temple, 1883; revising barrister, 1891-97; secretary to president Probate Division and Admiralty Div. High Court of Justice, 1892-98. *Publications:* Law of Railway and Canal Traffic, 1889. *Address:* Nutfield, Weybridge. *Club:* Junior Carlton.
(*Died 6 Feb. 1920.*)

WOODFORD, Charles Morris, C.M.G. 1912; *b.* Gravesend, 1852; *s.* of late Henry Pack Woodford; *m.* 1889, Florence, *d.* of late John Palmer of Bathurst, N.S.W; two *s.* (second son, Harold Vivian, 2nd Lieut. 8th Royal Berkshire Regt., killed in France, 13 Oct. 1915). *Educ.:* Tonbridge School. Fellow of Royal Geographical Society, and was awarded the Gill Memorial in 1890 for travels and exploration in Solomon Islands. Travelled and explored in Western Pacific, particularly in Solomon Islands, 1882-89; Acting Consul and Deputy Commissioner at Samoa, 1895; Resident Commissioner, the British Solomon Islands, 1896-1914; Fellow of Royal Anthropological Institute; member of Hakluyt Society; Member of British Ornithologists' Union. *Publications:* Naturalist among the Head Hunters; various papers in Geographical Journal, and Journal of Royal Anthropological Institute. *Address:* Bramley, Steyning, Sussex.
(*Died 4 Oct. 1927.*)

WOODGATE, Walter Bradford; Barrister; *b.* 20 Sep. 1840; *e. s.* of late Canon H. A. Woodgate, Rector of Belbroughton (Bampton Lecturer, 1838), and Maria Bradford. *Educ.:* Radley; Brasenose College, Oxford. Rowed in Oxford University (winning) Eight, 1862, 1863; amateur (aquatic) champion, 1862 *et seq.*; Diamond Sculls, 1864 (*inter alia* at Henley Regattas). *Publications:* (Badminton Library) Boating; A Modern Layman's Faith; (Novels) O.V H.; Ensemble; Tandem; Oars and Sculls and how to use them; Reminiscences. *Recreations:* aquatics, hunting, shooting. *Address:* Clovelly, Henley-on-Thames. *Clubs:* Isthmian, Leander.   (*Died* 1 *Nov.* 1920.)

WOODHEAD, Sir German Sims, K.B.E., *cr.* 1919; M.A. Cantab. (Honoris Causa); Hon. LL.D. (Toronto); Hon. LL.D. Birmingham; M.D. Edinburgh, F.R.C.P. Edinburgh, F.R.S.E.; Fellow of Trinity Hall, Cambridge; Professor of Pathology, Cambridge University, since 1899; Captain, V.M.S.C., 1886; Major, 1902; Lt.-Col. R.A.M.C. (T.); Bt. Col. A.M.S. 1917; Inspector of Laboratories in Military Hospitals in U.K.; formerly Adviser in Pathology (U.K.) to the War Office, and M.O. i/C Irish Command Depôt, Tipperary (twice mentioned for special war services); Member of the Royal Commission on Tuberculosis, 1902; Member of Executive Committee Imperial Cancer Research Fund, Member Scottish Universities Committee (Treasury); Hon. Fellow Henry Phipp's Inst. Philadelphia, 1902; Hon. Fellow Institute of Sanitary Engineers; Superintendent of the Laboratory of the Royal Coll. of Physicians, Edinburgh, 1887-90; Director of the Laboratories of the Conjoint Board of the Royal Colleges of Physicians (London) and Surgeons (England); President of the Royal Microscopical Society, 1890-99; *b.* Woodland Mount, Huddersfield, 29 April 1855; *e. s.* of late Joseph Woodhead (formerly M.P. for Spen Valley), editor Huddersfield Examiner, and Catherine, *e. d.* of James Booth Woodhead, The Ridings, Holmfirth; *m.* 1881, Harriett Elizabeth St. Clair Erskine, 2nd *d.* of James Yates, Edinburgh. *Educa.:* Huddersfield Coll. Edin. Univ., Berlin, and Vienna. President Royal Medical Society, 1878; Assist. Com. to the Royal Commission on Tuberculosis, 1892-1895. *Publications:* Practical Pathology, 1883; Pathological Mycology (with Arthur W. Hare, M.B.), 1885; Bacteria and their Products, 1891; Report to the Royal Commission on Tuberculosis, 1895; Report on Diphtheria to the Metropolitan Asylums Board; Village Settlements for the Tuberculous (with P. C. Jones Varrier); contributions to Medical Journals; formerly editor of the Journal of Pathology and Bacteriology. *Recreations:* golf: for many years President of the Edinburgh University Athletic Club; Pres. British Medical Temperance Association and President British Temperance League. *Address:* Dysart House, Luard Road, Cambridge. *T.:* 174 and 639. *Clubs:* Athenæum, Savage, National Liberal.

      (*Died* 29 *Dec.* 1921.)

WOODHOUSE, Sir Stewart, Kt., *cr.* 1908; M.D. (Dub.); retired Medical Member of General Prisons Board (Ireland); *b.* 1846; *s.* of late George Woodhouse of Dublin (retired Bank Manager) and Margaret, *d.* of John Cochrane of Londonderry; *m.* 1879, Charlotte, 4th *d.* of Isaac Corry, D.L. of Newry, Co. Down; one *d.* *Educ.:* Royal School, Dungannon; Trinity College, Dublin. Classical Scholar and first Senior Moderator in Ethics and Logic in University of Dublin; became Lecturer on Pathology to Carmichael School of Medicine, and Assistant Physician to House of Industry Hospitals, Dublin; a Local Government Board Inspector, 1880; Medical Member of the General Prisons Board (Ireland), 1890; Member of Vice-Regal

1146

Commission on Irish Milk Supply, 1911. *Publications:* Hints on Improvement of the Working Man's Life, etc.; various reviews, official reports, etc. *Address:* 67 Ailesbury Road, Dublin. *Clubs:* University, Dublin; Royal St. George Yacht, Kingstown. (*Died* 2 *Nov.* 1921.)

WOODLAND, Col. Arthur Law, C.B. 1900; Commanded an Infantry Regimental District to 1905; Officer in charge of Records, Newcastle, 1905-6; *b.* 24 June 1849; *s.* of Richard Reynolds Woodland. Served South Africa, 1899-1900; action at Colenso; operations Vaal Krantz; Tugela, Pieters Hill, and in Transvaal; relief of Ladysmith (despatches thrice, Queen's medal, 4 clasps, C.B.) *Address:* 59 Eaton Terrace, Eaton Square, S.W. *Club:* Naval and Military.   (*Died* 26 *May* 1921.)

WOODS, Henry, R.A. 1893; *b.* Warrington, 22 April 1846; *e. s.* of late William Woods of that town; *s.* of George Woods. *Educ.:* The Grammar School, Warrington. Began Art education in the School of Art, Warrington; afterwards at South Kensington; worked afterwards for illustrated periodicals; one of original members of Graphic staff; has exhibited pictures at Royal Academy from the first exhibition at Burlington House; worked principally in Venice since 1876; A.R.A., 1882; Member of College of Academicians, Royal Academy, Venice, 1908. *Address:* Calcina, Zattere, Venice, Italy. *Clubs:* Athenæum, Arts.

      (*Died* 27 *Oct.* 1921.)

WOODS, Hon. Henry John Bacon, Postmaster-General of Newfoundland since 1902; *b.* 20 Oct. 1842; *s.* of John Woods and Anne Lang; *m.* 1870, Hannie L., *d.* of late John Bemister, Sheriff of Newfoundland; seven *d.* *Educ.:* General Protestant Academy, St. John's, Newfoundland. Entered his father's office, and in 1880 became partner under the firm of John Woods and Son, shipowners; elected Liberal for Bay de Verde district and appointed a member of Cabinet with the portfolio of Surveyor-General, 1889; re-elected and took a seat in the Cabinet without portfolio, 1899; resigned 1902; title of Honourable, 1902; has been identified with the educational interests of Newfoundland for many years; President Newfoundland Auxiliary British and Foreign Bible Society. *Address:* St. John's, Newfoundland.   (*Died Aug.* 1916.)

WOODS, Joseph Andrews; Member of Senate, Northern Ireland, 1921; Secretary National Health Insurance Society, Belfast. *Address:* 161 Templemore Avenue, Belfast.

      (*Died* 6 *Oct.* 1925.)

WOODS, Matthew Snooke Grosvenor, K.C.; Bencher of Lincoln's Inn; *b.* 14 March 1838; *o. s.* of Matthew Snooke, Chichester, and Elizabeth, *d.* of Francis Smith, M.D., Maidstone (adopted name of Woods in compliance with directions in father's will); *m.* 1877, Mary Amabel (*d.* 1915), *d.* of John Vincent Thompson, Serjeant-at-Law. *Educ.:* Prebendal School, Chichester; Trinity College, Cambridge (Fellow, 1860; assistant tutor for three years). Barr. (Chancery Bar) 1865; Q.C. 1894.

      (*Died* 5 *April* 1925.)

WOODS, Percy, C.B. 1902; *b.* 5 July 1842; *s.* of late C. J Woods, Godalming; *m.* 1881, Helen Maria (*d.* 1888), *d.* of late Rev. R. Trimmer; two *d.* *Educ.:* Cheltenham. Entered Admiralty, 1863; transferred to Treasury, 1880; retired, 1902.   (*Died* 7 *April* 1922.)

WOODS, Richard Lennox, I.S.O., retired Civil Servant; *s.* of late William Whitfield Woods, late of Colonial Office; *m.* Emily, *e. d.* of J. B. Ellis. *Educ.:* Dublin. In the Exchequer and Audit Department, 1857-1903; late Captain Civil Service Volunteers. *Address:* Grove House, Falmouth.   (*Died* 10 *June* 1918.)

WOODVILLE, Richard Caton, artist (battle-painter); *b.* Stanhope Gardens, London, 7

Jan. 1856 ; father *b.* Baltimore, artist, *d.* London ; English extraction. *Educ.:* Düsseldorf, Germany. Went through Egyptian War, 1882 ; Turkish, 1878 ; as well as minor warlike operations in Albania and the East generally ; has the Grand Cross of the Red Cross of Spain ; Commander of the Medjidie of Turkey ; the Daniello of Montenegro ; and the Academy Palms of France. Exhibited first picture Royal Academy, 1879, since then annually. Painted several large pictures in Windsor Castle for the Queen : Wedding at Whippingham Church, Death of Gen. Sir Herbert Stewart, The Guards at Tel-el-Kebir. *Publications :* Random Recollections, 1913 ; magazine articles on sport and travel. *Recreations :* shooting, big-game hunting, travel. *Address :* Dudley Mansions, 29B Abbey Road, N.W.8. *T. :* Maida Vale 3840. *Club :* Junior Army and Navy.
(Died 17 Aug. 1927.)

WOODWARD, Colonel Francis Willoughby, D.S.O. 1900 ; late 1st Loyal Regiment (North Lancashire) ; *b.* Bombay, 5 Dec. 1872 ; *s.* of Willoughby Woodward. *Educ.:* Shrewsbury School ; R.M.C., Sandhurst. Entered Army, 1893 ; Lieut. 1896 ; Capt. 1901 ; Adjutant, 1st Loyal North Lancashire Regiment, 1901-4 ; served South Africa, 1899-1902 (despatches twice, S.A. medal 3 clasps) ; defence of Kimberley, Orange Free State, Transvaal (King's medal, 1901 and 1902 ; clasps) ; Egyptian Army, 1906-15 (3rd class Mejidieh, 3rd class Order of the Nile) ; European War (Bt. Lt.-Col., Croix de Guerre and Croce de Guerra ; Officer of St. Maurice and St. Lazarus ; Col. 1924 ; retired on retired pay, 1924. *Club :* United Service. *(Died 27 Dec. 1926.)*

WOODWARD, Henry, LL.D., F.R.S., F.G.S. ; President Palæontographica-Society since 1896 ; Past-President of the Royal Microscopical and Geological Societies ; *b.* Norwich, 24 Nov. 1832 ; *y. s.* of Samuel Woodward, Norwich, antiquary and geologist ; *m.* Ellen Sophia (*d.* 1913), *o. d.* of Fountain Page, Norwich ; five *d. Educ. :* Norwich Grammar School ; Rev. George Haddock's, Botesdale, Suffolk ; Royal Agric. College, Cirencester. Entered bank, Norwich, 1850-57 ; British Museum, 1858 ; keeper of geology, 1880-1901 ; pres. Geologists' Assoc., 1878-74 ; Murchison medallist, 1884 ; Wollaston Medallist, 1906 ; pres. Geological Section British Assoc., 1887 ; pres. Geol. Soc., 1894-96 ; pres. and founder Malacological Soc., 1893-95 ; Pres. Museums Association, 1900. *Publications :* contributions to scientific journals 300 ; a monograph on the Merostomata, 1866-78 ; on Carboniferous Trilobites, 1883-84 ; article Crustacea, Ency. Brit. (9th ed. vol. vi. 1877) ; articles Mollusca and Crustacea (Cassell's Nat. Hist.), and numerous addresses and lectures ; editor of the Geological Magazine, a monthly journal of Geology and Palæontology since 1864. *Address :* Tudor Cottage, Clay Hill, Bushey, Herts.
(Died 6 Sept. 1921.)

WOODWARD, Col. John Henry, C.B. 1911 ; V.D. ; Treasurer Society of Merchant Venturers, Bristol ; *b.* 10 Aug. 1849 ; 4th *s.* of George Rocke and Ellen Woodward, of Clifton, Bristol ; *m.* 1876, Mary Alice Hamilton, 2nd *d.* of Admiral and Mrs. Thomas Fisher, of Clifton, Bristol ; one *s.* four *d. Educ. :* Windermere College, Westmorland. Enrolled in Bristol Rifle Volunteer Corps, 1869 ; commanded 4th Batt. Gloucestershire Regiment, 1905-11 ; Master of the Society of Merchant Venturers, Bristol, 1886 ; J.P. Bristol 1894 ; Director of Bristol Wagon Works Co., Limited ; Director Bristol and South Wales Building Society and Portishead Gas Co., Ltd. *Address :* Upton Lea, Bitton, N. Bristol. *Club :* Constitutional, Bristol. *(Died 18 May 1918.)*

WOODWARD, Sir Lionel Mabbott, Kt., *cr.* 1922 ; Chief Justice Federated

Malay States since 1921 ; *b.* 9 Sep. 1864 ; *s.* of Lionel Mabbott Woodward, of Harrow ; *m.* 1897, Kathleen Tarifa, *d.* of Col. Frederick Fitzroy Gibbons, late of Devonshire Regt. ; three *s. Educ. :* Harrow ; Trinity College, Cambridge, B.A. 1st Class Honours Classical Tripos, 1886 ; M.A. 1892. Bar Inner Temple, 1897 ; Cadet Straits Settlements, 1888 ; Magistrate and J.P. Singapore, 1890 ; Sheriff and Deputy Registrar Supreme Court, 1896 ; Magistrate and J.P. Penang, 1898 ; Assistant Registrar Supreme Court, 1902 ; Deputy Public Prosecutor, 1904 ; Judicial Commissioner, Federated Malay States, 1906 ; Senior Puisne Judge Straits Settlements, 1915 ; acting Chief Justice, S.S. 1914-15 and 1919. *Recreations :* tennis, golf, riding. *Address :* Kwala Lumpor, Federated Malay States. *T.A. :* Kwala Lumpor. *Club :* Constitutional.
(Died 5 Sept. 1925.)

WOODWARD, Robert Simpson, Ex-President of the Carnegie Institution of Washington, Washington, D.C. ; *b.* Rochester, Michigan, 1849 ; of New England ancestry ; *m.* Martha Gretton Bond, 1876 ; three *s. Educ. :* Rochester Academy ; Univ. of Michigan (C.E. 1872 ; Ph.D. 1892) ; Hon. LL.D. Wisconsin, 1904 ; Michigan, 1912 ; Johns Hopkins, 1915 ; Hon. Sc.D. Univ. Pennsylvania and Columbia Univ., 1905. Assistant engineer, U.S. Lake Survey, 1872-82 ; astronomer, U.S. Transit Venus Commission, 1882-84 ; astronomer, U.S. Geological Survey, 1884-90 ; assistant, U.S. Coast and Geodetic Survey, 1890-93 ; Professor of Mechanics and Mathematical Physics, Columbia Univ., 1893-1905 ; Dean School Pure Science, Columbia Univ. 1895-1905. *Publications :* numerous papers and addresses on subjects in astronomy, geodesy, mathematics, mechanics, and geophysics ; Administrative Reports in Year-Books of Carnegie Institution of Washington 1905-20 ; editor (with Mansfield Merriman) of Mathematical Monographs. *Recreations :* boating, motoring, farming. *Address :* Carnegie Institution of Washington, Washington, D.C. *Clubs :* Century Association, New York ; Cosmos, Washington. *(Died 29 June 1924.)*

WOOLDRIDGE, Harry Ellis, M.A. ; of Trinity Coll. Oxford ; Slade Professor of Fine Art, Oxford University, 1895-1904 ; *b.* 1845 ; *m.* Julia Mary, *d.* of late Stephen Olding, 1894. *Educ. :* privately. Student of the Royal Academy 1865, and about the same time commenced the study of music, chiefly antiquarian. *Principal artistic works :* large reredos in the Church of St. Martin, Brighton, and frescoes in parish Church of St. John, Hampstead. *Principal works on music :* new edition of Chappell's Popular Music of the Olden Time with new title—Old English Popular Music, 1893 ; and The Polyphonic Period, Parts I. and II. (vols. I. and II. of the Oxford History of Music). *Address :* 90 Oakwood Court, Kensington, W. *Club :* Savile. *(Died 13 Feb. 1917.)*

WOOLLEN, James, Journalist and Editor ; *b.* Westminster, 3 Mar. 1854 ; 3rd *s.* of Frederick Woollen of N.W. Somerset, and Damaris, *e.d.* of John Booth of North Lincolnshire ; *m.* 1879, Alice Eugenie (*d.* 1915), *y. d.* of Thomas Carpenter, Westminster ; one *s. Educ. :* St. Michael's Schools, Chester Square, S.W. ; privately. Was for three and a half years in Civil Service (Inland Revenue) ; became a clerk in weekly newspaper office, and taking interest in journalism generally, contributed constantly to various publications ; becoming early in life associated with some of the earliest temperance reformers and many leading politicians, has taken prominent part in temperance and political movements since 1874 ; was Hon. Sec. of Labour Representation Union, founded 1884, and of the Gladstone Election Fund (1886) at N.L.C., and acted as Hon. Election Agent for several candidates returned to Parliament and to the L.C.C. ;

1147

contested L.C.C. in 1888, City of Perth (Advanced Radical), 1892. *Publications:* contributes extensively to periodical literature on political, social, and art subjects; was one of the originators and founders of the Burlington Magazine (1903); edited Metropolitan Temperance Advocate, Lady's Gazette, etc., etc., and the Crown, the Court, and County Families newspaper, 1906-8; Vanity Fair, Favourite Home Journal, Glass Section Pottery and Glass Record, etc. *Recreations:* gardening, walking, cycling, collecting.   (*Died Nov. 1921.*)

WOOLLEY, Charles, F.R.G.S.; *b.* 30 Nov. 1846; *s.* of late Nathaniel Woolley of Ecton, Northamptonshire, and Piccadilly, W.; *m.* Elizabeth, 2nd *d.* of late Henry Bone of 5 Pall Mall East, and Clapham, S.W.; one *s.* two *d.* *Educ.:* privately; King's Coll. London. Sec. National Discount Company, Ltd., 1890-1910; Director Consolidated Electrical Company, Ltd., and Anglo-Portuguese Telephone Company, Ltd.; Fellow Incorporated Society of Accountants and Auditors, and Institute of Bankers; past President and Fellow Chartered Institute of Secretaries; Fellow Chartered Institute of Directors; is an expert in Company Law Procedure, and appeared before Select Committee of House of Lords to give evidence in respect of Company Law Amendment, in connection with Lord Dudley's Bill, which came into operation 1 Jan. 1901; Member London Press Club, and Chartered Institute of Journalists; Conservative. *Publications:* Phases of Panics; A Cruise round the British Isles; A Voyage to Viking Land; a contributor to the Press and to Magazines. *Recreations:* fond of sport and art, being a book collector and numismatologist; is a patentee of pneumatic tyres for cycles and vehicles. *Address:* Verulam, Dulwich Road, Herne Hill, S.E. *Club:* Savage.
(*Died 5 Aug. 1922.*)

WOOLLEY, Samuel Walter, F.C.S.; Editor of The Chemist and Druggist, 1917-27; *b.* Stamford, Lincs, 1865; unmarried. *Educ.:* Stamford Grammar School. Pharmaceutical Chemist, 1887; Assistant Editor of The Chemist and Druggist, 1898; Fellow of the Spectaclemakers Company; Corresponding Member of the Société Royale de Pharmacie de Bruxelles. *Publications:* The Chemist - Optician; Pharmaceutical Formulas, etc. *Recreations:* archæology and photography. *Address:* Tresham Lodge, Barnack, Stamford. *Club:* National Liberal.   (*Died 25 Nov. 1927.*)

WOOLRYCH, H. R., M.A.; Headmaster, Blackheath School, 1895 - 1905; *b.* 1858; *s.* of Rev. W. H. Woolrych, Vicar of Crowle, Worcester; *m.* 1885, Elizabeth Beatrice, *d.* of George Owen of Copenhagen; five *s.* two *d.* *Educ.:* Rossall School; Pembroke Coll. Oxf. (Classical Scholar). 1st Class Moderations, 1879; 2nd Class Lit. Hum. 1882; B.A. 1882; M.A. 1884; Assist. Master, Rossall School, 1883-84; 2nd Master, Blackheath School, 1884-94. *Publication:* Ovid Tristia, Bk. iii. *Recreations:* tennis, golf. *Address:* 31 Redcliffe Gardens, S.W. *T.:* Western 2076.   (*Died 30 Aug. 1917.*)

WOOLS-SAMPSON, Col. Sir Aubrey, K.C.B., *cr.* 1902; C.B. 1900; M.P. Braamfontein; partner in Wools-Sampson and Mullins, financial and estate agents. Founded Imperial Light Horse; Hon. Col. in Army; served S. Africa, 1899-1902 (severely wounded, despatches four times, Queen's medal 4 clasps, King's medal 2 clasps, K.C.B.). *Address:* Cape Town.
(*Died May 1924.*)

WOOLSTON, Thomas Henry, C.B.E. 1918; D.L.; J.P.; *b.* 10 Mar. 1855; *s.* of late Samuel Hames Woolston, Wellingborough; *m.* 1910, Florence Katherine, *d.* of William Moxon, M.R.C.S., J.P., Northampton. *Educ.:* St. Paul's, Stony Stratford. Knight of Grace of Order of St. John of Jerusalem in England;

1148

was County Controller V.A.D.'s, Northamptonshire, and County Director Northants. Auxiliary Hospitals and V.A.D.'s during War, 1914-19; Member of Northamptonshire Territorial Army Association; Member of Board of Management and Vice-Chairman of Finance Committee of the Northampton General Hospital; Member of Board of Management and Chairman of House Committee, Manfield Orthopædic Hospital, Northampton; Chairman of the Northampton and County Crippled Children's Fund; Commissioner (Reserve) St. John's Ambulance Brigade. *Address:* 53 East Park Parade, Northampton; The White Cottage, Caister-on-Sea, Norfolk. *T.:* Northampton 794.   (*Died 19 Mar. 1927.*)

WOOTTEN, Aubrey Francis Wootten, K.C., 1921; *s.* of William Wootten Wootten, Banker, Oxford, and Sarah Wootten Wootten; *b.* Headington House, Oxford, 19 Sep. 1866; *m.* 1893, Gertrude, 2nd *d.* of D. Tremewen, Solicitor, Falmouth; one *s.* two *d.* *Educ.:* Rugby; Oriel College, Oxford; Captain of School XV. and shooting VIII. Rugby; B.A. Oxford, 2nd Class Honours Jurisprudence, 1889. Called to Bar, Inner Temple, 1892; Chief Inspector V. Division, Special Constabulary 1914-1919; Assistant Commander 1920; Medal of O.B.E. for Police Work during war, 1921; Chairman Epsom Division Constitutional Association, 1921. *Recreations:* horticulture, bowls. *Address:* 1 Temple Gardens, Temple, E.C.4; Sunningdale, Downs Road, Epsom. *T.A.:* Aubrey Wootten, Epsom. *T.:* Central 851, Epsom, 576. *Clubs:* New University, Surrey County Cricket, Royal Automobile.
(*Died 4 Aug. 1923.*)

WOOTTON, Hubert A., Head - Master Kingswood School, Bath; *b.* Nottingham, 1 Feb. 1884; *m.* 1917, Eileen Mary Masaroon; two *d.* *Educ.:* Nottingham High School; Clare College, Cambridge. Thirteen years Chief Science Master, Westminster School; during War Captain Special List, Commandant Young Officers Training School, Sub-Section Technical Director of Shell Filling, Ministry of Munitions (despatches). *Publication:* Journal of the Chemical Society. *Recreation:* golf. *Address:* Kingswood School, Bath. *T.:* Bath 440.
(*Died 18 Jan. 1922.*)

WORDINGHAM, Charles Henry, C.B.E. 1918; Consulting Engineer; engaged in advising on large electric power supply schemes for London, East Midlands and elsewhere, and electrical work generally; *b.* Twickenham, Middlesex, 1866; *s.* of William Hales Wordingham and Madeline West; *m.* 1912, Emily Anne, *e.* *d.* of late Charles John West, J.P. of Goodwood, Maryboro', Queensland; one *s.* four *d.* *Educ.:* King's Coll. School, London; King's College, London. Articled to Dr. John Hopkinson, F.R.S., as civil engineer, 1885-87; United Telephone Co., 1887-89; on engineering staff of the London Electric Supply Corporation, 1889-92; Assistant to Dr. J. Hopkinson, 1892-1894; City Electrical Engineer to Manchester Corporation, 1894-1901; consulting engineer, advising numerous local authorities and private clients on electrical questions, giving Parliamentary and law court evidence, and acting generally as electrical expert, 1901-3; Director of Electrical Engineering, Admiralty, responsible for the entire electrical equipment of all H.M. ships and for advising on electric light and power questions in H.M. dockyards and shore establishments, 1903-18; Member of Institution of Civil Engineers and Institution of Mechanical Engineers and Institution of Electrical Engineers (Past President of the Institution and Past Chairman of Manchester Section); F.S.A.; Associate of Institution of Naval Architects; Past President and Hon. Member Incorporated Municipal Electrical Association; Past President of Junior Institution of Engineers; President of Illuminating Society; Fellow of King's College, London, 1912, and Member of Council and of Delegacy; Membre de la Société des Ingénieurs Civils de France; Member of Main and Chairman of Electrical Sectional Committee of the British Engineering Standards Association; one of the British representatives on the International Electro-technical Commission; President and Past Chairman of the British Electrical and Allied Industries Research Association, and one of the founders of the Electrical Development Association and of the Society of Radiographers. *Publications:* Central Electrical Stations; numerous papers on Engineering subjects presented to Engineering Institutions of which a member; also articles and reviews in technical journals. *Recreations:* photography, cycling, travelling abroad. *Address:* 7 Victoria Street, Westminster, S.W.1; *T.:* Victoria 7292; 33 Brazennose Street, Manchester; *T.:* Central 828; Beechgrove, Ridgeway Road, Redhill, Surrey; *T.:* Redhill 453. *T.A.:* Outguards, Sowest London, and Outguards Manchester. *Clubs:* St. Stephen's, Engineers'; Engineers', Old Rectory, Manchester. *(Died 28 Jan. 1925.)*

WORDSWORTH, William, C.I.E. 1887; *b.* 1835; *m.* 1st, 1862, Mary Emma (d. 1898), *d.* of late Morris Reynolds, Ambleside; 2nd, 1900, Maria Schonnard (d. 1903), *e. d.* of late Gen. Hayes, U.S. Army, and *widow* of Lieut.-Col. Bille, U.S. Army Medical Corps. Entered I.C.S. 1861; was Principal of Elphinstone College, Bombay; retired, 1890. *Address:* Villa Wordsworth, Capri. *(Died 7 Mar. 1917.)*

WORKMAN, Fanny Bullock, F.R.G.S., F.R.S.G.S., Member Royal Asiatic Society; Corresponding Member American Geographical Society; Hon. Member American Alpine Club; Officier de l'Instruction Publique, 1904; authoress and lecturer; *d.* of ex-Governor Bullock of Massachusetts; *m.* Dr. W. H. Workman. *Educ.:* New York and Germany. Travelled extensively in Spain, North Africa, Palestine, Asia Minor, Egypt, Greece, India, Ceylon, Java, Sumatra, and Cochin China; in 1899 made three first record ascents for women in the Karakoram Mountains, the highest of which was Mount Koser Gunge, 21,000 feet; explored Choge Lungma glacier, Baitistan, 1902; made another expedition to Himalayas, 1903; made two first ascents of 21,500 feet and 22,568 feet; made expedition to Himalayas, 1906; climbed one of Nun Kun peaks, 23,300 feet—a first ascent, which gives her the world record for mountaineering for women; explored and surveyed Hispar glacier and branches, 1908; First ascent of Biafo Watershed Peak, 21,350 ft.; crossed Hispar Pass and descended Biafo glacier to Baltistan in 1911, explored and mapped seven glaciers of the Hushe and Kondus systems, Karakoram, and made first ascent of peak 21,000 feet; 1912, explored and surveyed 50 mile long Siachen glacier and affluents; made seven new ascents of peaks and cols from 19,000 to over 21,000 feet; discovered the water-parting between the Indus and Chinese-Turkestan regions; has lectured before geographical and scientific societies and Alpine clubs in America, Scotland, France, Germany, and Italy. *Publications:* joint author of Algerian Memories; Sketches Awheel in Fin de Siècle, Iberia (for remainder see under W. H. Workman); contributor to magazines and papers. *Recreations:* mountaineering and cycling. *Address:* c/o The American Express Company, 6 Haymarket, S.W.1. *Clubs:* Lyceum French, German-Austrian, Italian Alpine, Appalachian and American Alpine (Hon. Member). *(Died 22 Jan. 1925.)*

WORKMAN, Walter Percy, M.A., B.Sc., Headmaster of Kingswood School, Bath, since 1889; *b.* Peckham, S.E., 2 Nov. 1863; *s.* of Rev. John Sansom Workman, Wesleyan minister; *m.* 1897, Amelia, *d.* of Rev. Edward Workman; one *d. Educ.:* Kingswood School, Bath; Trin. Coll. Camb. (M.A.). Second Wrangler in Camb. Math. Tripos, 1884; 1st Smith's prizeman, 1886; Fellow of Trin. Coll. Camb. 1887; Assistant Master, Leys School, 1888. *Publications:* History of Kingswood School, 1898; Tutorial Arithmetic, 1902; Geometry, Theoretical and Practical, 1905; Register of Kingswood School, 1910; Memoranda Mathematica, 1912; Kingswood Sermons, 1917. *Recreations:* golf, motoring. *Address:* Kingswood School, Bath. *T.A.:* Kingswood, Bath. *T.:* Bath 440.
(Died Sept. 1918.)

WORLLEDGE, Rev. Arthur John, M.A.; Canon and Chancellor of Truro Cathedral; principal of Divinity School 1887-1901; Acting Treasurer of Cathedral since 1904; *b.* London, 29 May 1848; *e. s.* of late John Worlledge, Judge of the County Courts (Circuit 33), and Mary, *d.* of Rev. J. D Wastell, Risby, Bury St. Edmunds; unmarried. *Educ.:* Queen Elizabeth's Grammar School, Ipswich; Caius Coll. Camb. (Scholar). 2nd class Classical Tripos; 1st class Theol. Hon.; Carus Gk. Test. prizeman; curate of St. Andrew's, Enfield, 1872-76; Prebendary in Lincoln Cathedral, 1878-87; tutor in the Schol. Cancell. Lincoln, 1876-83; principal of the Leeds Clergy School, and lecturer in Leeds Parish Church, 1883-87; examining chaplain to Bishop Wilkinson, Truro, 1890; to Bishop Gott, 1891; Bishop Stubbs, 1906; Bishop Burrows, 1912; select preacher at Cambridge, 1879, 1885, 1892, 1899, 1900, 1906, and 1909. Proctor in Convocation for Truro Chapter since 1892; Commissary to Bishop of Brisbane, 1885-1903; to Bishop of Natal, 1901-15; Hon. Sec. Conferences on Training of Candidates for Holy Orders, 1881-1912; Member Central Advisory Council of Training for the Ministry, 1913. *Publications:* vol. on Prayer (Oxford Library of Practical Theology); section on Romanism, Dissent, and Unbelief, in S.P.C.K. Manual of Parochial Work; edited sermons preached at the Benediction of the Nave of Truro Cathedral; Editor (assistant) The Letters of Bishop Gott; Editor Truro Diocesan Magazine, since 1904. *Recreations:* study of architecture (specially ecclesiastical), and antiquities. *Address:* 4 Strangways Terrace, Truro, Cornwall.
(Died 20 Feb. 1919.)

WORRELL, John Austin, K.C., D.C.L.; Barrister and Solicitor; head of firm of Worrell, Gwynne & Beatty; *b.* Smith's Falls, Ont., 1852; *s.* of Rev. Canon Worrell, late Rector of Oakville, Ont. *Educ.:* Smith's Falls Grammar School; Trinity College School, Weston; Rev. W. Stennett's Private School, Keswick; Trinity University, Toronto. B.A. and Prince of Wales Prizeman and Wellington Scholar, 1871; M.A., 1875; B.C.L., 1880; D.C.L. (honoris causâ), 1898. Called to Bar, 1878; Q.C., 1889; President of York Law Association, 1895; Solicitor to Bank of Montreal; etc. Member of Church of England; Delegate Assessor to Prolocutor and formerly Lay Secretary of General Synod of Canada; Hon. Treasurer, Missionary Society, Church of England, in Canada Chancellor of Diocese of Toronto, 1897; member of Corporation of Trinity University, Toronto, of Council of St. Hilda's College, and of Governing Body of Trinity College School, Port Hope; Member of Senate of University of Toronto; Chancellor, Trinity University, 1914; Liberal Conservative; has been President of Young Men's Liberal-Conservative Association of Toronto and of Ontario; member of British Empire League and formerly Secretary of Imperial Federation League of Canada. *Address:* 39 Prince Arthur Avenue, Toronto. *T.:*

1149

Kingsdale 3347. *Clubs:* Toronto, University Toronto.   (*Died 27 Feb. 1927.*)

WORSLEY, Rev. Edward, M.A.; Hon. Canon of Peterborough, 1913; *b.* 4 Jan. 1844; *s.* of late Rev. Charles Worsley, M.A.; *m.* 1880, Ethel Adela, *d.* of late Edward Knight, of Chawton House, Alton, Hants.; five *s.* three *d.* *Educ.:* Radley; Magdalen College, Oxford (Exhibitioner). 2nd Cl. Mods.; 2nd Cl. Lit. Hum. and B.A.; Fellow of Magdalen College, 1867-72; 2nd Master of Magdalen College School, 1867-68; ordained, 1868; Sub-Warden of Radley, 1868-72; Vicar of Evenley, Northants, 1871-1920. *Recreations:* rowing, cricket, racquets, Alpine climbing, lawn tennis, bell-ringing, played racquets for Oxford *v.* Cambridge 1864.
              (*Died 16 April 1923.*)

WORSLEY, Lt.-Col. Richard Stanley, D.S.O. 1916; Assistant Director of Supplies, Egyptian Army; *b.* Harrington Hall, Spilsby, Lincolnshire, 7 Sep. 1879; *s.* of Major-General Richard Worsley; unmarried. *Educ.:* Wellington College; Sandhurst. Entered A.S.C. 1900; served S. African War from 1900 (King's medal, Queen's medal and 5 clasps); remained there till 1905; at Woolwich, 1905-8; Adj. East Lancs. Transport and Supply Column T.F. (when T.F. Act introduced) to 1912; at Aldershot, 1912-13; joined the Egyptian Army Nov. 1913; served European War, attached to New Zealand Div. Train as Senior Supply Officer, Apr.-Sep. 1915; present at Anzac including original landing and attack on Sari Bair ridge (D.S.O.). *Recreations:* Football XV. at Sandhurst; polo, cricket. *Address:* c/o Mrs. Worsley, 7 St. George's Court, Gloucester Road. S.W   (*Died 4 May 1917.*)

WORSLEY-TAYLOR, Sir Henry Wilson, 1st Bt., cr. 1917; J.P., D.L., K.C.; Recorder of Preston (resigned 1898); Chairman Lancashire Quarter Sessions held at Preston, 1893-1917; *b.* 25 July 1847; *o. s.* of late James Worsley, The Laund, Accrington, Lancashire; *m.* 1871, Harriette Sayer (*d.* 1913), *o. d.* of Sir E. W. Watkin, 1st Bt.; two *s.* two *d.* *Educ.:* Harrow; Exeter College, Oxford. Barr. Middle Temple, 1871; Bencher, 1893; acting for a few years on the Northern Circuit, and at Preston Sessions; after that exclusively at the Parliamentary Bar; assumed the name of Taylor in accordance with the will of his cousin Miss Pilling-Taylor, 1881; M.P. (C.) Blackpool Div. Lancashire, 1900-6. *Recreations:* shooting, fishing, golf. *Heir:* *s.* James, *b.* 10 July 1872. *Address:* Moreton Hall, Whalley, Lancashire. *Clubs:* Carlton, Conservative.   (*Died 27 June 1924.*)

WORTHINGTON, Albert Octavius, J.P., D.L. Staffordshire; represents Lichfield (City) on County Council; High Sheriff, 1889-1890; Capt., hon. Major, (late) Queen's Own Regt. Imperial Yeomanry; Lord Manor Pype-cum-Membris; Patron of Seals, Derbyshire; on Governing Body of Repton School; Director of North Staffordshire Railway Co.; *b.* 20 Nov. 1844; *s.* of William Worthington, J.P., Newton Park, Derbyshire, and Mary Anne, 2nd *d.* of Francis Calvert of Houndhill, Staffs; *m.* 1871, Sarah Elizabeth (*d.* 1913), *o. d.* of John Etty; one *s.* four *d.* *Educ.:* Repton. *Publication:* Birds of Derbyshire in Wild Flowers, etc., of Repton. *Recreations:* hunting, shooting, fishing, and cricket. *Address:* Maple Hayes, nr. Lichfield. *M.:* E 765. *Clubs:* Junior Carlton, Hurlingham.   (*Died 9 May 1918.*)

WORTHINGTON, Arthur Mason, C.B. 1902; M.A., F.R.S., F.R.A.S.; *b.* Manchester, 11 June 1852; *y. s.* of Robert Worthington, Crumpsall Hall, Manchester, and Elizabeth, *e. d.* of Robert Brewin, Birstall Hall, nr. Leicester; *m.* 1877, Helen, *y. d.* of Thomas Solly, Barrister of Middle Temple, and Professor in the Univ. of Berlin; one *s.* one *d.* *Educ.:* Rugby; Trin. Coll. Oxford (M.A.); Owens

1150

Coll. Manchester; University of Berlin, in the Laboratory of Professor Helmholtz. Headmaster of the Salt Schools, Shipley, Yorks, 1877-79; assistant master, Clifton College, 1880-85; headmaster and Professor of Physics in H.M. Dockyard School, Portsmouth, 1887-88; and in Royal Naval Engineering College, Devonport, 1888-1908; Professor of Physics, Royal Naval College, Greenwich, 1909-11. *Publications:* various papers on physical subjects; Physical Laboratory Practice, Dynamics of Rotation; The Splash of a Drop; A Study in Splashes. *Address:* Exmouth.   (*Died 5 Dec. 1916.*)

WORTHINGTON, Henry Hugo; J.P.; High Sheriff for Bucks, 1917-18; *b.* 19 July 1857; *e. surv. s.* of late James Worthington of Sale Hall, Cheshire, and Mary, *d.* of Henry McConnel of Cressbrook, Derbyshire; *m.* 1883, Amelia Maud, 3rd *d.* of late Matthew Kennedy of Low Nook, Ambleside; three *c.* *Educ.:* Clifton; Oriel College, Oxford. *Recreation:* gardening. *Address:* Grantlands, Uffculme, Cullompton. *T.A.:* Uffculme.   (*Died 23 Mar. 1921.*)

WORTLEY, Rev. Edward Jocelyn; Hon. Canon, Jamaica, 1909; Rector of St. Andrew, Halfway Tree, 1901-21. *Educ.:* Gen. Theological Seminary, New York. Curate of Catherine, 1883; Incumbent of Holy Trinity, Montego, 1883-86; Rector of St. Peter, Port Royal, 1886-88; Curate of Cathedral, Spanish Town, 1890-92; Rector, 1892-1900. *Address:* Maurice Hill, Constant Spring P.O., Jamaica.
               (*Died 4 Sept. 1928.*)

WRAGGE, Clement Lindley, F.R.G.S., F.R.Met.S.; F.R.C.I.; *b.* Stourbridge, 18 Sep. 1852; father Solicitor. *Educ.:* Uxxoxeter Grammar School. First educated for a solicitor; then took to travel and scientific research; joined Surveyor-General's Department, Adelaide, 1876; established three observatories, chiefly for problems of climatology, at different heights in the Churnet Valley and moorlands of Northern Staffs; established and worked Ben Nevis Observatory, 1881 (gold medal); also Torrens Observatory near Adelaide, 1884; that of Mount Lofty, S.A., 1884; he inaugurated the chief Australasian weather bureau at Brisbane, 1887; established Meteorological Stations throughout Queensland; Mount Wellington (Tasmania) High Level Station; reorganised meteorological service of Tasmania, 1895; Mount Kosciusko Observatory, New South Wales (highest point in all Australia), and correlative low level station at Merimbula, 1897-98; in the practical pursuit of scientific meteorology has been many times to Australia; has travelled on the Continent, through Syria, Palestine, Egypt, North America, India, and the South Seas; presented a collection of shells, native Australian weapons, etc., to the town of Stafford, where it is known as the Wragge Museum; Hon. Mem. N. Staffs Naturalists' Field Club; Hon. Corres. Mem. Scottish Geographical Society, Italian Meteorological Society, etc.; attended International Meteorological Conferences on behalf of Queensland at Munich 1891, Paris 1896 and 1900; established Capemba Botanical Gardens, near Brisbane, 1889-1900; Government Meteorologist of Queensland, 1887-1902; scientific lecturer; settled in New Zealand, 1910, and established Wragge Scientific Institute Museum and Waiata Botanical Gardens. *Publications:* The Romance of the South Seas, 1905; several brochures and papers on meteorological and other scientific subjects. *Address:* Wragge Museum, Stafford, England; Waiata, Birkenhead, Auckland, New Zealand.
               (*Died Dec. 1922.*)

WRAY, Captain Kenneth Mackenzie, D.S.O. 1900; 1st Australian Horse; *b.* 7 June 1855; *s.* of late George Cecil Gore Wray of Ardnamona, Co. Donegal; *m.* 1882, Grace, 4th

d. of Benjamin Lloyd Edwards of Molonglo, N.S. Wales; two *s.* four *d.* Served in South African War as Capt. 6th Imperial Bushmen, 1900-1 (despatches, D.S.O.). *Address:* 8 Roslyndale Avenue, Woollahra, Sydney, N.S.W.
(Died 5 Oct. 1927.)

WREFORD, George, Barrister-at-Law; *b.* Exeter, 3 Feb. 1843; 2nd *s.* of William Wreford; *m.* 1864, Susan Annie, *d.* of late Robert Churchward, Exeter; three *s.* one *d. Educ.:* Hele's Foundation and Mansion House Schools, Exeter. Junior clerk, Exeter Court of Bankruptcy, 1858-1862; assistant clerk, Education Department, Whitehall, 1863-65; chief clerk, Exeter Court of Bankruptcy, 1865-70; Public Accountant, Exeter, 1870-72; Senior Examiner and Inspector Comptroller in Bankruptcy's Department, London, 1872-88; Senior Assistant-Receiver in Bankruptcy (Board of Trade), 1884-90; Senior Official Receiver in Bankruptcy (Board of Trade and High Court of Justice), 1890-96; Barr. Gray's Inn, 1893. *Publications:* Review of Bankruptcy Legislation, 1875; prize essay, Bankruptcy of Members of the Legal Profession, 1879; late Fellow of Society of Accountants and Auditors. *Address:* 30 Marine Parade, Dover. *T.:* Dover 365. *(Died 2 April 1919.)*

WRENCH, Rt. Hon. Frederick Stringer, P.C. Ire. 1902; D.L., J.P.; *b.* 4 Nov. 1849; *m.* 1872, Charlotte Mary, 3rd *d.* of Sir Alan E. Bellingham, 3rd Bt.; one *s.* two *d. Educ.:* Haileybury; Exeter College, Oxford. Irish Land Commissioner, 1887: Senior Estates Commissioner, 1903; was member of the Congested Districts Board for Ireland (representing agriculture), 1891-1903; past President Hackney Horse Society; Vice-President Royal Dublin Society, Past President Irish Shorthorn Breeders' Association; Past President of the Shorthorn Society of Great Britain and Ireland; Member of the Council of the Royal Agricultural Society of England, and Chairman of the Food Control Committee for Ireland. *Recreations:* shooting, stalking, travelling, photography, and breeding pedigree stock. *Address:* Killacoona, Hythe, Kent. *Clubs:* Carlton, Overseas League, English-Speaking Union; Kildare Street, Dublin. *(Died 7 June 1926.)*

WREY, Sir Bourchier Robert Sherard, 11th Bt.; *cr.* 1628; Hon. Lieut.-Col., Royal North Devon Hussars; J.P., D.L. Devon; *b.* Sidmouth, 23 May 1855; *e. s.* of late Sir H. B. T. Wrey, 10th Bt., and late Hon. Marianne Sherard, *d.* of Philip Castel, 9th Baron Sherard; *m.* 1905, Jessie Maud, *d.* of late W. T. Fraser.; one *d.* Formerly in Royal Navy; served in Zulu War, 1879 (medal with clasp); in Egyptian Campaign, 1882 (Egyptian medal, Khedive's bronze star); Burmah, 1885-1886 (medal with clasp). Patron of three livings; President Unionist Association for N.W. Devon. Owns about 8000 acres. *Co-heir* to Barony of Fitzwarine (abeyant since 1636). *Recreations:* yachting, shooting, and hunting. *Heir:* b. Philip Bourchier Sherard [*b.* 28 June 1858; *m.* 1889, Alice Mary, *d.* of late Captain Borton, R.H.A.; two *d. Club:* Union]. *Address:* 20 Cadogan Place, S.W.; *T.:* Victoria 7591; Tawstock Court, Barnstaple. *Clubs:* Naval and Military, Cavalry, Boodles; Royal Yacht Squadron, Cowes. *(Died 26 Jan. 1917.)*

WREY, Capt. William Bourchier Sherard, C.M.G. 1917; C.B.E 1919; R.N.; retired; served in the Great War as Principal Naval Transport Officer, Southampton; *b.* 2 April 1865; 4th *s.* of Sir Henry Bourchier Toke Wrey, 10th Bt.; *m.* 1897, Flora Bathurst, *d.* of Vice-Adm. W. S. Greive, Ord House, Berwick-on-Tweed. Midshipman of the Superb at bombardment of Alexandria and Suakin, 1882 (medal 2 clasps, bronze star); promoted Commander for services; as 2nd in Command Naval Brigade Relief of Pekin, 1900 (medal

and clasp); Officer of Order Crown of Belgium, 1917, and Japanese Order of the Sacred Treasure; Distinguished Service Medal of U.S. America, 1919; British War and Victory Medals. *Address:* Taw Green, Westbourne, Sussex. *Club:* Naval and Military. *(Died 8 Jan. 1926.)*

WRIGHT, Rev. Arthur, M.A.; Rector of Low Toynton since 1913; Prebendary of Melton Ross with Scamblesby in Lincoln Cathedral, 1875: late Treasurer Linc. Dioc. Conf.; Surrogate, 1892; b. Wrangle, near Boston, Co. Lincoln, 1831; *s.* of Rev. Thomas Bailey Wright, Vicar of Wrangle, and Henrietta Weekes Wright, *s.* of Sir John Franklin, the Arctic navigator; *m.* Harriet Maria (*d.* 1895), *d.* of James Hairby, M.D., of Hundleby, near Spilsby, Co. Lincoln; one *d. Educ.:* St. John's Coll. Camb. Scholar and Exhibitioner; 2nd class Classical Tripos, 1853; Curate of S. Ormsby, 1854; Vicar of Welton le Marsh, 1857: Rector of Gunby, St. Peter, 1866; Rural Dean of Candleshoe, 2nd Div. 1871; J.P. for Parts of Lindsey, 1879; late Chairman Horncastle Bench; late Vice-Chairman Horncastle Board of Guardians, 1880; Governor of Horncastle Grammar School, 1874; Rector of Coningsby, 1873; Rural Dean of Gartree, 1890. *Publications:* In Memoriam Franklin, 1882; late Editor Lincoln Diocesan Calendar, 1866; various pamphlets. *Address:* Low Toynton Rectory, Horncastle. *T.A.:* Horncastle. *(Died 7 Aug. 1920.)*

WRIGHT, Rev. Arthur, D.D.; Vice-Pres. Queen's College, Cambridge, since 1900; *b.* Birmingham, 16 Aug. 1843; *s.* of Rev. B. Wright, Vicar of St. Matthew's, Wolverhampton. *Educ.:* Wolverhampton Grammar School; Queens Coll. Cambridge (Fellow). 1st class Classical Tripos 1867. Curate of Trinity, Islington, 1867-68, Trinity, Marylebone, 1868-72; Resident Fellow and Lecturer of Queen's College, Cambridge, 1872; Dean, 1872-82; Tutor, 1878. *Publications:* Introduction to Greek and Latin Syntax, 1875; The Composition of the Four Gospels, 1890; A Synopsis of the Gospels in Greek, 1896; 3rd annotated edition, 1906; Some New Testament Problems, 1898; St. Luke's Gospel in Greek, 1900. *Recreations:* travel, golf, shooting. *Address:* c/o Mrs. Partridge, Warley House, Bescot, Walsall. *T.:* Walsall 334.
(Died 12 April 1924.)

WRIGHT, Frank, J.P.; Treasurer of the National Liberal Federation; *b.* 1853; 4th *s.* of late John Skirrow Wright of Birmingham, M.P.; *m.* 1882, Alice, *d.* of John Whitehouse of Moseley Worcestershire. *Address:* Seven Gables, Streetly. Birmingham. *Club:* National Liberal.
(Died 11 Jan. 1922.)

WRIGHT, Lieut.-Colonel Frederick William, D.S.O. 1887; C.M.; M.C. Edin.; *b.* 1850; *s.* of late Robert John Wright, Norwich; *m.* 1914, Edith Bella Freeman of Dover. Entered Indian Medical Service, 1873; Surg. Lieut.-Col. 1893; served Afghan War, 1878 - 80 (medal with clasp for Candahar, bronze decoration); Burmah, 1886-87 (despatches, D.S.O., medal with clasps); British Contingent, China Expeditionary Force, 1900-1 (medal); Waziristan, 1901-2 (medal and clasp); retired, 1905. *Recreations:* golf, fishing. *Address:* 127 Cromwell Road, Queen's Gate, S.W. *T.:* Kensington 1893. *Club:* East India United Service.
(Died 9 Sept. 1927.)

WRIGHT, Alderman Sir George, Kt., *cr.* 1926; J.P.; 21 years Chairman of the Willesden Bench; 20 years Chairman of the Central Conservative Council for the Ealing Division, and 38 years Chairman and then President of the Acton Conservative Association; 38 years Member of the Middlesex County Council. *Address:* Marlow House, 470 Uxbridge Road, W.12. *(Died 16 Feb. 1927.)*

WRIGHT, George Arthur, M.B., B.A. Oxon.; F.R.C.S.; Consulting Surgeon Royal

Infirmary, Manchester ; Emeritus Professor of Systematic Surgery, Victoria University, Manchester ; late Member Council R.C.S.; Consulting Surgeon, Hospital for Children, Pendlebury; Consulting Surgeon, Cancer Pavilion, Manchester ; Lieut.-Col. R.A.M.C. ; Consulting Surgeon Queen Mary's Military Hospital, Whalley, Lancashire ; late Lieut.-Col. R.A.M.C. (T.); late C.O. 2nd Western General Hospital. *Educ.:* Marlborough ; Oxford ; Guy's Hospital. *Publications:* Hip Disease in Childhood, 1887 ; (with Dr. Ashby) Diseases of Children, Medical and Surgical, 5th ed. 1905 ; (with Mr. Preston) Surgical Anatomy, 1903. *Address:* The Old Orchard, Bickwell Valley, Sidmouth, S. Devon.
(*Died 23 Mar. 1920.*)

WRIGHT, Rev. Harold Hall, M.A.; Hon. Canon and Precentor of Chester Cathedral ; *b.* Scarborough, 7 Feb. 1859 ; *o. s.* of late Henry Wright, J.P., M.R.C.S., Scarborough ; *m.* Ethel Beatrice, 2nd *d.* of W. J. Foskett, Adelaide Crescent, Hove. *Educ.:* privately; Caius College, Cambridge. Honorary Assistant Curate of Scarborough Parish Church, 1882-85 ; Curate of S. John's, Darlington, 1885-86 ; Curate and Precentor of S. Patrick's, Hove, 1886-90 ; Minor Canon and Precentor of Chester, 1890 ; presented to an Honorary Canonry by Bishop of Chester, 1923. *Address:* The Precentory, Chester. (*Died 20 Sept. 1926.*)

WRIGHT, James Brown, C.B.E. 1918; Chief Constable of Newcastle-upon-Tyne, 1889-1925; *s.* of late Samuel Wright, J.P., of Newbliss, Co. Monaghan ; *b.* 1861; *m.* 1897, Zara, *d.* of late Trevor Corry of Belmont, Newry. *Educ.:* Trinity College, Dublin (B.A., LL.B. 1881, LL.D. 1906); joined R.I. Constabulary as a Cadet, 1887 ; District Inspector, 1888, serving as such in Counties Cork and Limerick and City of Belfast; Mobilizing Officer of Fire Brigades, N.E. Area, since 1917 ; Member of Commission on Irish Police Pay, 1919 ; Member of Police Council, 1920-22 ; King's Police and King's Coronation Medals. *Address:* 84 Osborne Road, Newcastle-upon-Tyne.(*Died 20 June 1926.*)

WRIGHT, Col. Sir John Roper, 1st Bt., *cr.* 1920 ; J.P., D.L.; Director of Baldwins, Ltd.; Hon. Lt.-Col. in the Army; *b.* 12 March 1843 ; *m.* 1st, 1870, Jane Eliza (*d.* 1896), *d.* of Charles Wilson, Birmingham ; one *s.* ; 2nd, 1897, Alice, *d.* of Bryan William Stevens, of Aldwinckle, Edgbaston. Contested (L.U.) Swansea District, 1895 ; Swansea Town, 1910. *Heir :* *s.* Sir W. C. Wright. *Address:* Widcombe Manor, Bath. (*Died 25 July 1926.*)

WRIGHT, Col. Robert Wallace, C.M.G. 1917; A.M.S., L.R.C.P. Lond., M.R.C.S. Eng. ; *b.* 5 Oct. 1863. *Educ.:* St. George's Hospital. Served European War, 1914-19 (C.M.G.). ; retired from army, 14 March 1919. *Address:* Testbourne House, Totton, Hants.
(*Died 20 June 1923.*)

WRIGHT, Thomas Rowland Drake, LL.B., Trinity Hall, Cambridge ; Recorder of Bradford, 1905-26 ; *b.* 1853 ; *e. s.* of Rev. Thomas Booth Wright; *m.* 1884, Marianne, *d.* of R. Nesfield; two *s.* Recorder of Pontefract, 1891-1905. *Address:* St. Gregory's, Bedale.
(*Died 25 Oct. 1926.*)

WRIGHT-HENDERSON, Rev. Patrick Arkley, D.D., M.A. ; Hon. Fellow, Wadham College ; *b.* 18 June, 1841 ; *m.* 1870, Anne Wood, *d.* of Major Gray of Carse Gray, Forfarshire ; one *s.* three *d. Educ.:* Balliol College, Oxford. Fellow and Tutor, Wadham College, 1867-1903 ; Chaplain, 1869-1903 ; Sub-Warden, 1881-1903 ; Warden, 1903-13. *Publications:* occasional contributions to Blackwood's Magazine. *Address:* Broom, Hinksey Hill, Oxford. (*Died 7 Jan. 1922.*)

WRIGHTSON, John ; President of the College of Agriculture, Downton. 1880-1906 ; *y.s.* of late Thomas Wrightson of Neasham Hall,

Darlington ; *b.* 9 Sep. 1840 ; *m.* Maria Isabel, *d.* of late Charles Norleigh Hulton, 3rd *s.* of William Hulton of Hulton Park, Lancashire ; seven *s.* four *d.* Hon. Professor in the Royal Agricultural College, Cirencester ; Professor of Agriculture, Royal College of Science, London, 1882-98. *Publications:* numerous works on agriculture. *Address :* 13 Charleville Mansions, West Kensington, W. *Clubs:* Authors', Farmers'.
(*Died 30 Nov. 1916.*)

WRIGHTSON, Sir Thomas, 1st Bt., *cr.* 1900 ; J.P., D.L. ; Chairman of firm of Head, Wrightson & Co., Stockton-on-Tees ; Chairman of Cramlington Colliery Co., Northumberland ; Chairman of Small Dwellings Acquisition Co., London ; *b.* 31 Mar. 1839 ; *s.* of Thomas Wrightson of Neasham Hall, Durham ; *m.* 1869, Elizabeth, *d.* of Samuel Wise of Ripon ; three *s.* six *d.* Contested Stockton, 1885 and 1886, 1888, 1892, and 1895 ; contested L. St. Pancras, 1899, 1900, and 1906 ; M.P. (C.) Stockton, 1892-1895 ; M.P. (C.) East St. Pancras, 1899-1906. *Publications :* scientific papers on physical changes in iron and other metals, also on accoustics and an enquiry into the analytical mechanism of the internal ear, 1918. *Heir :* *s.* Thomas Garmondsway, *b.* 21 Aug. 1871 [*m.* 1909, Gwendolen Cotterill, *d.* of G. Harding Neame ; four *s. Educ.:* Trinity College, Cambridge (M.A.). *Address :* The Manor House, Eryholme, nr. Darlington]. *Address :* Neasham Hall, Darlington. *Club :* Carlton.
(*Died 18 June 1921.*)

WRONG, Edward Murray, M.A.; Fellow and Tutor, Magdalen College, Oxford, 1920 ; *b.* 14 April 1889 ; *e. s.* of Prof. G. M. Wrong; *m.* 1915, Rosalind Grace, 6th *d.* of late A. L. Smith; two *s.* four *d. Educ.:* St. Andrew's College, Toronto; University of Toronto; Balliol College, Oxford. 1st Class, Modern History, 1913 ; Fellow of Magdalen College, 1914 ; Beit prizeman, 1915 ; Vice-Principal, Manchester College of Technology, 1916-1919 ; Beit Lecturer in Colonial History, Oxford University, 1919-24 ; Vice-President, Magdalen College, 1924-25 ; Junior Proctor, 1927-28. *Publications:* Charles Buller and Responsible Government ; History of England, 1688-1815. *Address :* Holywell Ford, Oxford.
(*Died 15 Feb. 1928.*)

WROUGHTON, Major Philip Musgrave Neeld, M.A. ; Berks Yeomanry ; *e. s.* of late Philip Wroughton and Evelyn Mary, 2nd *d.* of Sir John Neeld, 1st. Bt. ; *b.* 30 Aug. 1887. *Educ.:* Christ Church, Oxford. *Address:* Woolley Park, Wantage, Berks. *Club:* Carlton.
(*Died 19 April 1917.*)

WROUGHTON, William Musgrave ; *b.* 24 Sep. 1850 ; 3rd *s.* of late Philip Wroughton and Blanche, 5th *d.* of John Norris, Hughenden House, Bucks ; *m.* two *d.* M.F.H., Pytchley, 1894-1902 ; of Woodland Pytchley, 1903-8. *Address:* Creaton Lodge, Northampton; 77 Chester Square, S.W.1. *T.:* Victoria 151.
(*Died 29 Dec. 1928.*)

WYATT, Major Francis Ogilvy, M.V.O. 1906 ; *b.* 11 July 1871. Entered R.A. 1892 ; Captain, 1899 ; Adjutant Volunteers, 1901-7 ; R.A. 1910 ; Major 1912 ; served N.W. Frontier, India, 1897-8 (medal, two clasps, slightly wounded). *Address :* Rawal Pindi, India.
(*Died 16 Dec. 1919.*)

WYATT, Harold Frazer ; speaker and writer on Naval and Imperial matters ; *y. s.* of late Rev. H. H. Wyatt, J.P., Rector of Conington, Hunts. *Educ.:* privately ; Exeter College, Oxford. Joined Executive Committee, Navy League, 1895 ; Navy League Honorary Envoy to Colonies, 1902-4 ; Hon. Sec. Navy League, 1905 ; Joint Founder and late Joint Hon. Secretary Imperial Maritime League ; Unionist candidate, Rushcliffe Division, Notts, 1906. *Publications:* England's Threatened Rights at Sea, 1909 ; God's Test by War, 1912; many articles in the Nineteenth Century and After, The English Review and (joint) The Passing of the Great Fleet, 1909 ; The True Truth about the Navy, 1909 ; Keep the Flag Flying, 1910 ; Britain's Imminent Danger, 1912 ; engaged (1915) in effort to promote independent movement in favour of compulsory national service ; head of Speaking Staff, Naval Intelligence Division, Admiralty, 1917; National Party Candidate for North Leeds, 1918 ; a Director of The English Review, 1923. *Recreations:* bicycling and chess. *Clubs:* United University, Services (Hon.).   (*Died 20 May 1925.*)

WYATT, Thomas Henry, M.V.O. 1902 ; I.S.O. 1902, V.D. ; late Chief Civil Assist. in Quartermaster-General's Dept., War Office ; Secretary, Army Railway Council, 1900-3 ; *b.* 19 Oct. 1841 ; *s.* of Thomas Henry Wyatt, a former president of Royal Institute of British Architects ; *m.* 1865, Julia Lucy Mervyn, *d.* of Rev. T. W. Wrench, Rector of St. Michael's, Cornhill, E.C. ; six *s.* three *d.* *Educ.:* King's College, London. Served in the War Department, 1859-1908 ; formerly in the 19th Middlesex R.V., and retired 1883 with the rank of Hon. Major. *Address:* Weston Corbett, Winchfield, Hants. *T.A.:* Upton Gray.
(*Died 21 Sept. 1920.*)

WYKES-FINCH, Rev. William Robert ; Honorary Canon of Newcastle Cathedral ; *b.* 17 May 1855 ; *s.* of late John Finch ; *m.* 1881, Frances Christiana, *d.* of John Wilkinson Edwards of Baddiley Rectory, Cheshire ; no *c.* *Educ.:* King's College, Cambridge. Formerly Lecturer, St. Augustine's College, Canterbury, 1878 ; Chaplain, Lichfield Theological College, 1879 ; Curate, St. Peter's, Leicester, 1880 ; Christ Church, Luton, 1883 ; Vicar of Rennington with Rock, 1886 ; Vicar of Chatton, Northumberland, 1896-1917 ; Warden of the Duke of Northumberland's School, Alnwick, 1898-1919 ; Proctor in Convocation for Archdeaconry of Lindisfarne, 1910-21. *Recreations:* gardening, motoring, continental travel. *Address:* St. Cuthbert's Lodge, Wells, Somerset ; North Wyke, North Tawton, Devon. *M.:* X 365, X 999. *Club:* Church Imperial.
(*Died 2 April 1922.*)

WYLD, Rev. Edwin G. ; Vicar of Melksham since 1890 ; Canon of Salisbury, 1900 ; *s.* of Rev. William Thomas Wyld of Woodborough ; *m.* 1872, Mary (d. 1911), *d.* of Sir Hungerford Pollen, 3rd Bt. ; three *d.* *Educ.:* Marlborough ; Exeter College, Oxford. Curate of Hullavington, 1870 ; Rector of Gratwich and Kingston, 1872 ; Rector of Woodborough, 1873 ; Vicar of Mere, 1881. *Address:* The Vicarage, Melksham. *T.:* 48. *M.:* AM 2425. *Club:* New Oxford and Cambridge.
(*Died 27 Dec. 1919.*)

WYLDE, General Edward Andrée ; Royal Marines, Light Infantry ; *b.* 29 April 1858 ; *e. s.* of late Major-General E. A. Wylde, R.M.L.I. ; *m.* 1881, Theresa Mary, 4th *d.* of late James Sutherland Mitchell, of Etham, Sydney, N.S.W. ; three *d.* *Educ.:* Lausanne College ; Sydney College, Bath. Joined Royal Marines as Lieutenant, 1876 ; Captain, 1885 ; Major, 1892 ; Lieut.-Col. 1899 ; Col. 2nd Commandant, 1905 ; Col. Commandant Depôt, Royal Marines at Deal, 1908 ; Maj.-Gen. 1910 ; Lieut.-General, 1912 ; General, 1922 ; served in H.M.S. Raleigh, Mediterranean Station, 1877-80 ; H.M.S. Wolverene, Australian Station, 1880-82 ; H.M.S. Shannon, west coast of Ireland, 1886-88 ; H.M.S. Pembroke at Chatham, 1897-99 ; Instructor of Gunnery at Chatham, 1890-95 ; Member of Committee, Royal Humane Society ; J.P. Somerset. *Address:* 11 Evelyn Mansions, Carlisle Place, S.W.1. *T.:* Victoria 9326. *Club:* United Service.   (*Died 12 Oct. 1925.*)

WYLDE, John Truro ; I.S.O. 1906 ; *b.* Swellendam, Cape Colony ; *s.* of Clarence

Thomas Wylde and Elizabeth Palmer ; *m.* Iris Calland ; two *s.* two *d.* *Educ.:* Grammar School, Exeter. Joined Cape Civil Service as a clerk in Colonial Secretary's Office, 1866 ; appointed Civil Commissioner and the Resident Magistrate, Queenstown, East London, Port Elizabeth, and other districts of the Colony ; was Commandant of European Mounted Volunteers Basuto War, 1880-81, and Colonel Commanding Town Guard at East London, subsequently also Port Elizabeth during Anglo-Boer War, 1899-1908 ; Resident Magistrate, Cape Town and Cape District. *Club:* Civil Service, Cape Town.
(*Died 9 May 1927.*)

WYLDE, Rev. Robert, Hon. Canon of Worcester. *Address:* The Warden's Lodge, Newland, Malvern.   (*Died 23 May 1927.*)

WYLIE, Alexander, J.P., D.L. retired Turkey-red Dyer and Calico Printer ; *s.* of late J. Wylie ; widower ; M.P. (C.) Dumbartonshire 1895-1906. *Publication:* Labour, Leisure, and Luxury ; Future of the British Army, etc. *Address:* Condale, Renton, Dumbartonshire. *Clubs:* Carlton, National ; Western, Conservative, Glasgow.   (*Died 13 Feb. 1921.*)

WYLIE, Major-Gen. Henry, C.S.I. 1881 ; retired 1900 ; *b.* 1844 ; *m.* 1st, 1871, Melian Rebecca (d. 1905), *d.* of late John Massy, J.P., of Kingswell House, Co. Tipperary ; one *s.* two *d.* ; 2nd, 1907, Anna Maude, *e. d.* of Capt. F. L. Tottenham, Coolmore, Crowborough, Sussex. Entered army, 1861 ; Major-General, 1899 ; served North-West Frontier of India, 1863 (medal and clasp) ; Bhutan, 1865 (clasp) ; Abyssinia, 1868 (medal) ; Hazara, 1868 (clasp) ; on special duty in Baluchistan, and Assistant to Governor-General's Agent, 1875-78 ; served Afghan War, 1878-80 (medal) ; as Chief Political Officer in Peshin, and with Gen. Sir R. Phayre's column (despatches twice, medal, C.S.I.) ; Assistant to Resident in Mysore, and Secretary to Chief Commissioner of Coorg, 1882-85 ; Political Agent successively at Bhopawar, Jhallawar, and Bhopal ; resident at Nepaul, 1891-1900 ; Officiating Agent to the Governor-General of India for Baluchistan, 1898-1900. *Address:* Glenfarne, Farnham Common, Bucks. *Club:* United Service.   (*Died 5 Oct. 1918.*)

WYLLIE, Lt.-Col. Alexander Keith, C.B. 1900 ; Hon. Col. 3rd Batt. West Riding Regt. since 1906 ; Barrister-at-law, Inner Temple ; *b.* May 1853 ; *o. surv. s.* of late James Wyllie, 3 King's Gardens, Hove, and Eilenroc, Antibes, France ; *m.* 1906, Mrs. A. Fellowes Gordon (d. 1912), *d.* of late John Green. Served S. Africa, 1900-2 ; operations in Cape Colony (despatches, Queen's and King's medals with clasps) ; Chairman R.S.P.C.A. since 1926 ; a Director of the Tredegar Iron and Coal Co. Ltd., Oakdale and Markham Collieries. *Address:* 39 Princes Gate, S.W.7. *Clubs:* Boodle's, United Service.   (*Died 9 Oct. 1928.*)

WYLLIE, Charles W., Member of Society of Oil Painters.   (*Died 28 July 1923.*)

WYLLIE, John, M.D. 1865 ; F.R.C.P. Ed. 1870 ; LL.D. Ed. 1897 ; late Principal Medical Officer to Scottish Equitable Assurance Company ; *b.* Midlothian. *Educ.:* Edinburgh and Paris. Formerly Senior President of the Royal Medical Society, Edinburgh, 1866 ; Resident Physician in the Edinburgh Royal Infirmary, 1865-66 ; House Physician to the General Hospital, Birmingham, 1866-68 ; Pathologist to the Royal Infirmary, Edinburgh, 1875-1877 ; Assistant Physician in charge of Fever Wards, 1876-82 ; Ordinary Physician to the Royal Infirmary, 1882-97 ; Consulting Physician to the City Hospital for Fevers, 1896-1900 ; Professor of Medicine and of Clinical Medicine, Edinburgh University, 1900-14. *Publications:* The Disorders of Speech, 1894 ; various papers in medical journals. *Address:* 44 Charlotte Square, Edinburgh.   (*Died 25 Jan. 1916.*)

WYLSON, Oswald Cane, M.B.E. ; Architect, F.R.I.B.A., M.S.A. ; *b.* 6 April 1858 ; *s.* of James Wylson, architect, London ; *m.* 1st, Edith Oakley (*d.* 1900); 2nd, Katherine, *d.* of B. Murgatroyd, Yorkshire ; two *s.* *Educ.:* King's College School, London. Articled to late Arthur Cates ; student of Royal Academy ; Donaldson Silver Medallist in Fine Art and Construction at University College ; carried out many important architectural works, chiefly theatres and entertainment buildings, restaurants, etc. ; served for many years on Strand Board of Guardians ; Chairman of the Building Committee of that body, and their representative on the Metropolitan Asylums Board ; on the Executive of the British Fire Prevention Committee ; Hon. Deputy Chief Surveyor of B.F.P.C. in relation to prevention of fires in hospitals and camps during the War, and also served during same period on the Concrete Research Committee ; Hon. Member Fédération Royale des Pompiers, Belgique ; Hon. Member Fédération Nationale des Sapeurs Pompiers, France. *Recreations :* yachting, travel. *Address :* 22 Buckingham Street, Strand, W.C. ; Beacondene, Tankerton, Whitstable, Kent. *T.A.:* Optically, Westrand, London. *T. :* Gerrard 1443. *Clubs :* Royal Automobile, Royal Corinthian Yacht.
(Died 28 April 1925.)

WYNDHAM, Sir Charles, Kt., *cr.* 1902 ; actor ; lessee and manager of Criterion Theatre since 1876 ; *b.* 25 Mar. 1837 ; *m.* 1860, 1st, Emma, *d.* of J. Silberrad (*d.* 1916) ; one *s.* one *d.* ; 2nd, 1916, Mary Moore, *widow of James Albery. Educ.:* Neuwied, Germany ; St. Andrews ; Dublin. Intended for medical profession ; fought in American Civil War ; made first appearance in America with John Wilkes Booth, brother of Edwin Booth and assassin of President Lincoln ; made first appearance in London, 1865 ; has acted in German as well as English ; brother-in-law of American dramatist, Bronson Howard ; built and opened with Mary Moore, Wyndham's Theatre at the corner of Charing Cross Road, and The New in St. Martin's Lane, 1899. *Address :* 43 York Terrace, Regent's Park, N.W.1. *T. :* Mayfair 4321. *Clubs :* Garrick, Savage, Beefsteak, Eccentric, Green Room.
(Died 12 Jan. 1919.)

WYNDHAM, Sir Hugh, K.C.M.G., *cr.* 1894 ; C.B. 1878 ; J.P. Sussex ; *b.* 18 Nov. 1836 ; *m.* 1863, Charlotte, *d.* of Hon. and Rev. W. H. Scott ; two *s.* two *d. Educ.:* Harrow, Oxford. Entered Diplomatic Service, 1857 ; Sec. of Legation, Athens, 1875 ; Madrid, 1878 ; of Embassy, Petrograd, Constantinople, 1881 ; Envoy Belgrade, Rio de Janeiro, and Bucharest ; retired on pension, 1897. *Recreations :* riding and shooting ; owns about 2000 acres. *Address :* Rogate Lodge, Petersfield. *T.A. :* Rogate. *Club :* Travellers'.
(Died 10 Feb. 1916.)

WYNNE, Maj. Francis George, D.S.O. 1916 ; Capt. (Temp. Major), L. N. Lancashire Regt. ; *b.* 7 Nov. 1885 ; *s.* of Major M. S. Wynne, late 81st Regt. ; unmarried. *Educ. :* United Services College, Westward Ho ! Joined Militia, 1905 ; granted commission Regular Army, 1907 ; served in Colonies and India with 2nd Batt. L. N. Lancashire Regt. till 1913, when came to the depot ; on outbreak of war went to France as Adjutant with 8th L. N. Lanc. Regt. (wounded July 1916, D.S.O., despatches). *Recreations:* shooting, tennis.' *Address:* Mellaston, Pembroke. *Club:* Junior United Service.
(Died April 1918.)

WYVILL, Marmaduke D'Arcy, J.P. North and East Ridings ; D.L. W. Riding ; *b.* London, 5 Mar. 1849 ; *e. s.* of Marmaduke Wyvill, Constable Burton, and Denton Park, Yorks, and Laura, *d.* of Sir Charles Ibbetson, 4th Bt. ; *m.* 1st, 1871, Isabella (*d.* 1895), *e. d.* of John Banner

1154

Price ; three *d.* ; 2nd, 1898, Elizabeth, *e. d.* of Sir W. H. Wilson-Todd, 1st Bt. *Educ. :* Eton. M.P. (C.) for Otley Division, Yorks, W.R., 1895-1900. *Recreations :* shooting, driving. *Address :* Constable Burton, S.O., Yorkshire. *Clubs :* Carlton, Travellers' ; Yorkshire, York.
(Died 23 Sept. 1918.)

Y

YAMAGATA, Aritomo, Field - Marshal Prince, O.M. 1906 ; President of Privy Council ; *b.* Choshu, April 1838. Junior Vice-Minister of War, 1870 ; Senior Vice-Minister of War, 1871 ; Lieut.-General, 1872 ; Minister of War, 1873 ; Chief of Staff, Imperial Army, during Civil War, 1877 ; Chief of General Staff, 1878 ; Count, 1884 ; Minister of Home Affairs, 1885 ; visited Europe and America, 1888-89 ; Prime Minister, 1889 ; General, 1890 ; Minister of Justice, 1892 ; President of Privy Council, 1893 ; commanded First Army, China-Japan War ; Inspector-General, 1894 ; Marquis, 1895 ; attended Coronation of Czar Nicholas, 1896 ; Field-Marshal, Prime Minister, 1898 ; Chief of General Staff, 1904 ; President of Privy Council, 1905 ; Prince, 1907. *Address :* Goban-cho, Kōjimachi, Tokyo, Japan. *(Died 1 Feb. 1922.)*

YARDE-BULLER, Brig.-Gen. Hon. Sir Henry, K.B.E., *cr.* 1919 ; C.B. 1917 ; D.S.O. 1900 ; M.V.O. 1908 ; *b.* 2 Nov. 1862 ; 4th *s.* of 1st Baron Churston ; *m.* 1902, Adelaide Maude Sophia, *d.* of late Col. Charles Meeking of Richings Park, Colnbrook. *Educ. :* Radley. Joined Rifle Brigade, 1884 ; Captain, 1893 ; Major, 1901 ; Lieut.-Col. 1907 ; Col. 1911 ; served Waziristan Expedition, 1894-95 (medal and clasp) ; Soudan, 1898, including Battle of Khartoum (medal and clasp, Egyptian medal) ; in Crete as Governor of a District, 1898-99 ; South Africa, 1899-1902 (despatches thrice, Queen's medal with five clasps, King's medal two clasps, D.S.O.) ; European War, 1914-16, as Brig.-Gen. on General Staff and Head of British Mission at French Army Headquarters ; A.D.C. to Duke of Connaught, comdg. Aldershot, 1898 ; Military Secretary to Commander-in-Chief of Forces in Ireland, 1910-12 ; Military Attaché, Northern European Courts, 1906 - 10 ; Commander 2nd Class Dannebrog, 1906 ; Military Secretary to G.O.C., Ireland, 1910 ; Military Attaché, Paris, Madrid, and Lisbon, 1912, Christiania, 1917, Christiania and Stockholm, 1918 - 19 ; Commander 2nd Class Epée ; Commander 2nd Class St. Olaf ; Commander 2nd Class Leopold ; Commander of the Legion of Honour. *Address :* 14 Hobart Place, S.W.1. *T. :* Victoria 7156. *Clubs :* Travellers', Naval and Military, Marlborough. *(Died 15 Mar. 1928.)*

YARDLEY, Col. John Watkins, C.M.G. 1918 ; D.S.O. 1917 ; District Remount Officer, Glos. ; *b.* 17 July 1858 ; *s.* of late John Yardley, Chesterfield Lodge. Staff. ; unmarried. *Educ. :* Repton ; Trinity College, Cambridge (B.A.) ; R.M.C., Sandhurst. Entered 6th Inniskilling Dragoons, 1882 ; served Bechuanaland Expedition, 1884-85 ; Zululand, 1888 ; A.D.C. to Governor of Natal, 1887-90 ; served South Africa, 1899-1900 (despatches, seriously wounded, Queen's medal, five clasps, promoted Lieut.-Col. Reserve of Officers) ; European War, 1914-19, as Deputy-Director of Remounts with Cavalry Corps, Fourth and Fifth Armies (despatches, D.S.O., C.M.G.). *Publication :* With the Inniskilling Dragoons. *Recreations :* steeplechasing, member of National Hunt Committee, hunting, big-game shooting, fishing, polo, tennis. *Address :* 15A Motcomb Street, Belgrave Square, S.W.1. *Clubs :* Naval and Military, Prince's ; New, Cheltenham.
(Died 28 Nov. 1920.)

YATES, Joseph Maghull, K.C.; Chairman of Quarter Sessions Salford Hundred, and Stipendiary Magistrate, Manchester Division of Lancashire, since 1894; *b.* 19 June 1844; *e. s.* of late Joseph St. John Yates, Wellbank, Sandbach, Judge of County Courts, and Emily Augusta Scott; *m.* 1873, Wilhelmina Elizabeth, *d.* of W. H Wylde, C.M.G.; three *s.* one *d. Educ.:* Westminster (exhibition Cambridge); Trinity College, Cambridge (3rd class Classical Honours). Barrister, Jan. 1869·; Q.C. 1893; Recorder of Salford, 1889-1904. *Recreations:* shooting, fishing, golf. *Club:* Union, Manchester. *(Died 17 April 1916.)*

YEAMES, William Frederick, R.A.; late Librarian Royal Academy; late Curator Painted Hall, Greenwich Hospital; *b.* Russia, 18 Dec. 1835; 3rd *s.* of William Yeames, H.B.M. Consul in Taganrog, and Mary, *d.* of John Henley; *m.* Anne, *d.* of Major James Stainbank Winfield, late of the H.E.I.C.S., *niece* of Sir David Wilkie, R.A. *Educ.:* home; studied art with G. Scharf and F. Westmacott, and in Florence with Professor Pollastrini and R. Buonajuti. A.R.A. 1866 and R.A. 1878. Exhibited in R.A. and other exhibitions, 1860; also in Paris, Berlin, Brussels, etc.; done much teaching in the schools of the R.A.; and examiner's work in the Department of Science and Art, South Kensington. *Recreation:* golf. *Address:* 1 Brimley House, Teignmouth, South Devon. *(Died 3 May 1918.)*

YEATMAN-BIGGS, Rt. Rev. Huyshe Wolcott, M.A., D.D., F.S.A.; Bishop of Coventry since 1918; Dean of the Cathedral, Coventry; Hon. Fellow Emmanuel College, Cambridge; Select Preacher to the Universities of Oxford and Cambridge; *b.* Manston House, Dorset, 2 Feb. 1845; *y. s.* of Harry Farr Yeatman, J.P., and Emma, *d.* and *heiress* of Harry Biggs, Stockton House, Wilts; *m.* 1875, Barbara *(d. 1909), d.* of 4th Earl of Dartmouth; two *s.* one *d. Educ.:* Winchester; Emmanuel College (Dixie Scholar), Cambridge (M.A.). Played in Winchester football six for commoners; shot two years in the eleven at Wimbledon; trained for holy orders by the Master of the Temple, Dr. Vaughan; ordained 1869; curate of St. Edmund, Salisbury; chaplain to the Bishop, 1875; clerical secretary of the Diocesan Synod; vicar of Netherbury, Dorset, 1877; vicar of Sydenham, 1879; Proctor for Diocese of Rochester in convocation; examining chaplain to Bishop of Winchester; Bishop Suffragan of Southwark, diocese Rochester, 1891-1904; Bishop of Worcester, 1904-18; represented the Church of England at American Convention, 1916; inherited the estates of his brother, General Yeatman-Biggs, C.B., and assumed the name of Biggs by Royal licence, 1898. *Publications:* The Efficiency and Inefficiency of a Diocese; Life in an English Diocese; Lay work, Handbooks for Clergy; American Addresses; various papers on parochial work, education, etc. *Recreations:* horticulture, history, archæology, art. *Address:* The Bishop's House, Coventry. *Clubs:* Athenæum, Burlington Fine Arts. *(Died 14 April 1922.)*

YEATS, John Butler, R.H.A.; *b.* Tullylish, 1839; *s.* of Rev. William Butler Yeats, M.A., Rector of Tullylish, County Down; *m. d.* of late Wm. Pollexfen, merchant and shipowner, Sligo; two *s.* two *d. Educ.:* Athol Academy; Douglas, Isle of Man; Honourman and Political Economy Prizeman; B.A. Trin. Coll. Dublin. Called to Irish Bar; attended R.A. Schools and Slade School; has exhibited at R.A., R.H.A., etc. *Publications:* Extracts from Letters by John Butler Yeats, R.H.A., edited by Ezra Pound; Further Letters of John Butler Yeats, edited by Lennox Robinson; Essays, Irish and American, by John Butler Yeats, R.H.A.; articles in American and Irish papers. *Address:* Gurteen Dhas, Dundrum, Dublin; 317

W. 29th Street, New York City, U.S.A. *(Died 3 Feb. 1922.)*

YEATS - BROWN, Montagu, O.M.G. 1892; *b.* Island of Palmaria, Italy, 2 Aug. 1834; *e. s.* of late T. Yeats Brown, formerly H.M. Consul at Genoa, and the Hon. Stuarta Erskine; *m.* 1875, Agnes Matilda, *y. d.* of Sir Alan Bellingham, 3rd Bart.; three *s. Educ.:* Marlborough. Employed in Consulate at Genoa from 1854; Vice-Consul there 1856; H.M. Consul at Genoa, 1858; transferred to Boston, 1893; retired on pension, 1896. *Decorated* for consular services. *Recreations:* yachting, sailing, rowing, bicycling. *Address:* 11 Castello, Portofino, Italy. *(Died 22 Feb. 1921.)*

YELD, Edward; I.S.O. 1902; *b.* 1839; *m.* Victoria Louisa *(d.* 1913), *d.* of Thomas Walker, Edgbaston, Birmingham. Entered General Post Office, 1859; Assist.-Sec., 1896-1903. *Address:* 17 Oak Hill Avenue, Hampstead, N.W. *(Died 5 Aug. 1921.)*

YEO, Sir Alfred William, Kt., *cr.* 1918; J.P., M.P. (L.) Poplar, 1914-22; Vice-Chairman Tower Bench; *b.* 13 Oct. 1863; *s.* of Geo. R. J. Yeo, Devon; *m.* 1st, 1886, Mary Ann Brown *(d.* 1911), *d.* of Mrs. Stevens; one *s.*; 2nd, 1911, Florence J. Stevens, Poplar. *Educ.:* Marner Street and High Street Schools, Bromley. Started work in iron foundry; thirty years also in business in music trade; Member of Vestry, Board of Works and Boro Council for 25 years; Member of Poplar Board of Guardians 10 years, Chairman 6 years; Chairman Poplar Distress Committee 10 years; Mayor, Poplar, 1908-4; Chairman over 20 years under L.B.S. of Managers of Local Schools in St. Leonard's Road, Hay Currie, and Bromley Hall Road Groups; 9 years a member of the L.C.C.; Chairman of Lord Buxton's Committee dealing with distress during great Dock Strike, and Chairman, Claybury Mental Hospital; caused Government to bring in a Bill to prevent increase of rents during war and six months after; caused Government to bring in regulations for Tribunals dealing with one-man businesses. *Publications:* Pamphlets—Trade After the War; On Character; The Cross and the Crossways, etc. *Recreations:* much interested in brass bands and all sports. *Address:* 86-88 St. Leonard's Road, Poplar, E.14. *T.:* East 3371; Leamington, King s Road, Westcliff-on-Sea. *T.:* Southend 687. *Club:* National Liberal. *(Died 14 April 1928.)*

YERBURGH, Robert Armstrong, M.P. (C.) Chester, 1886-1906, and 1910-16; D.L.; J.P. Lancashire; J.P. Kirkcudbrightshire; President Navy League since 1900; late Major 2nd Volunteer Battalion Cheshire Regt.; *b.* 17 Jan. 1853; 3rd *s.* of Rev. Richard Yerburgh, Vicar of Sleaford, Lincolnshire, and Susan, *d.* of John Higgin, Greenfield, Lancaster; *m.* 1888, Elma Amy, *o. c.* of Daniel Thwaites, Woodfold Park, Blackburn, formerly M.P.; two *s. Educ.:* Rossall; Harrow; Univ. Coll. Oxford. *Barr.* Middle Temple, 1880; Private Secretary to Mr. Akers-Douglas when Patronage Secretary, 1885-86; Assistant Private Sec. to Mr. W. H. Smith, First Lord of Treasury, 1887; President Agricultural Organisation Society; President Urban Co-operative Banks Association; Hon. Sec. Recreation Evening Schools Association; Vice-Chairman National Home Reading Union. *Publications:* articles advocating National Granaries for storage of corn to complete our system of home defence, and articles on British imperial interests in China; pamphlets on agricultural banks. *Recreations:* hunting and country pursuits generally. *Address:* 25 Kensington Gore, S.W.; Woodfold Park, Blackburn; Barwhillanty, Parton, N.B. *Clubs:* Travellers', Carlton, Wellington. *(Died 18 Dec. 1916.)*

YEW, Loke, C.M.G. 1915. *Address:* Selangor, Malay States. *(Died 23 Feb. 1917.)*

YONGE, Lt.-Col. Philip Caynton, D.S.O. 1918; T.D., 1919; late 5th Batt. The Essex Regt.; Bank of England; Hon. Secretary Essex County Rifle Association; b. 29 May 1877; s. of Rev. Denys Nelson Yonge; m. 1914, Doris Evelyn, d. of Rev. J. S. Barrass; one s. two d. *Educ.:* Forest School, Walthamstow. Served European War, 1914-18 (despatches, D.S.O.). *Address:* 27 The Ridgeway, Chingford.
(Died 14 Oct. 1928.)

YORKE, Hon. Alfred Ernest Frederick, late Lieut. Grenadier Guards; b. 11th July 1871; s. of 7th and *heir-pres.* to 8th Earl of Hardwicke; m. 1905, Gladys (who obtained a divorce, 1918), o. c. of Andrew Vans Dunlop Best; one s. Late Lieut. 5th Batt. Royal Inniskilling Fusiliers and Royal Fusiliers. *Heir:* s. Philip Grantham, b. 1906.
(Died 24 Aug. 1928.)

YOUNG, Charles Edward Baring; b. 1850; e. s. of late Charles Baring Young of Oak Hill, Herts, and Elizabeth, d. of late Stephen Winthrop of Little Bounds, Tunbridge, Kent. *Educ.:* Eton; Trinity Coll., Cambridge (M.A.). Called to Bar at Inner Temple, 1876; M.P. Christchurch, 1885-9°. *Address:* Daylesford House, Chipping Norton. *Club:* Oxford and Cambridge
(Died 22 Sept. 1928.)

YOUNG, Daniel Henderson Lusk, C.B.E. 1918; J.P., D.L., County of the City of Glasgow; b. Glasgow, 1861; married; one s. one d. *Educ.:* Glasgow Academy and University (M.A.). Entered service of James Templeton and Co., carpet manufacturers, 1884, now managing partner; Deputy Commissioner National Service (Scotland), 1916; Director National Service (Northern Region), 1917; prospective Unionist candidate for Dumbartonshire. *Address:* Overtoun, Dumbarton, Lanarkshire. *Clubs:* Reform; Western, Glasgow.
(Died 26 May 1921.)

YOUNG, Colonel Frederick de Bude, C.M.G. 1916; Substantive Col., Indian Army; b. 31 March 1865; s. of Col. H. C. Young, Indian Army, of Cleish Castle, Fifeshire; m. Alice Maude Mary, d. of Alexander Pirie, of Stoneywood, Aberdeenshire; two s. *Educ.:* Cheltenham College; R.M.A., Woolwich. Entered Royal Artillery, 1884; served in Black Mountain Expedition, 1888, with British Mountain Battery (medal and clasp); transferred 6th Bengal Cavalry, 1890; served as Squad. Comdr. and on Staff in Tirah Campaign, 1897 (despatches, medal and 4 clasps); Passed Staff College, 1895-96; served in South African War on Staff, and as Adjutant and 2nd in command, and sometime in command of 4th N.Z. Rifles (despatches, medal and 4 clasps); commanded 32nd Lancers; many Staff appointments: Deputy Secretary, Military Finance, to Lord Kitchener; Commandant of Anzacs in Gallipoli Peninsula (C.M.G., despatches); Chief Staff Officer, 1st Cyclist Division and Outpost Troops, Norfolk and Suffolk, 1916. *Recreations:* big-game shooting, polo, golf, tennis, fishing. *Clubs:* Cavalry, Devonshire.
(Died 1 Nov. 1920.)

YOUNG, Capt. Sir Frederic William, K.B.E., cr. 1920; C.B.E. 1919; Commodore 2nd class R.N.R.; M.I.Mech.E.; Honorary Naval Salvage Adviser; Officer of the Crown of Belgium; United States Navy Cross; 36 years Chief Surveyor and Salvage Officer to the Liverpool Salvage Association; Head of Admiralty Salvage Section during the War, and afterwards Commodore in charge of Salvage Operations on the Belgian Coast for the removal of the Vindictive and Blockships sunk in the Zeebrugge Canal; Managing Director Sir Frederic W. Young & Co. Ltd., salvage experts and consulting engineers, 101 Leadenhall Street; Managing Director of the Young Accumulator Co. Ltd., Burlington Works, Rigault Road, Fulham. *Address:* Cheyne Cottage, Cheyne

1156

Row, S.W.3. *T.:* Kensington 6244. *Club:* Royal Thames Yacht. *(Died 20 Dec. 1927.)*

YOUNG, Brig.-Gen. George Frederick, C.B. 1897; late D.A.G. Bengal; b. 5 May 1846; e. s. of late Sir Frederick Young. *Educ.:* Marlborough. Entered army, 1865; Col. 1891; served Afghan War, 18.9 80 (despatches, medal); Mahsood-Wuzeeree Expedition, 1881 (despatches); Hazara, 1888 (Brevet Lieut.-Col., medal with clasp). *Publications:* The Medici; East and West through Fifteen Centuries, 1916. *Address:* Leny, Cobham, Surrey.
(Died 8 Nov. 1919.)

YOUNG, James Carleton, F.R.G.S.; L.L.D.; Litt.D.; capitalist; President Western Mortgage Co.; James C. Young Land Co.; Imperial Investment Co.; Central Trackage Co.; Treasurer North Dakota Clay and Coal Co.; Vice-President Guaranty Investment Co.; Trans-Empire Real Estate and Mortgage Co.; b. Marion, Iowa, 29 July 1856; s. of Joseph Barris Young and Jane M. Carter; m. 1888, Etta May Rogers; one d. *Educ.:* Cornell College (B.S. 1876; M.S. 1879). Engaged in real estate business; President National Association Real Estate Dealers, 1884-6; Hon. Commissioner of U.S. to Paris Exposition, 1878; time now mostly devoted to formation of a library, which shall contain all the best books of the most celebrated living authors in the world, each book characteristically inscribed by the writer — this library is already the most remarkable of its kind in existence; Cross Legion of Honour, 1910; Member Loyal Legion. *Recreations:* travel, shooting, and fishing. *Address:* 1819 Ninth Avenue South, Minneapolis, Minnesota, U.S.A. *T.A.:* Young, Minneapolis. *Clubs:* Authors'; Grolier, New York City; Rowfant, Cleveland; Caxton, Chicago. *(Died 8 Jan. 1918.)*

YOUNG, Maj.-Gen. James Charles; C.B. 1917; b. 1 May 1858; s. of late H. L. Young, D.L., Lee Mount, Co. Cork; m. 1896, Madeline, d. of J. G. Leeb, Cape Town; one d. *Educ.:* Shrewsbury School. Entered Army, 1876; joined 35th Royal Sussex Regt. 1877; Lt.-Col. commanding 2nd Batt. The Royal Sussex Regiment, 1899-1903; Egyptian War, 1882 (medal and Khedive's star); Nile Expedition, 1884-85, including operations of the Desert Column (clasp); D.A.A.G. South Africa, 1892-97; A.A.G. Deesa, 1903-4; A.A.G. 4th Div. India, 1904-7; Brig.-Gen. commanding a Brigade in India, 1907-10; Maj.-Gen. commanding a Brigade in India, 1910-12; commanded Home Counties Division Territorial Force, 1912; a Division on Home Service, 1914-17 (despatches twice, C.B.); Colonel The Royal Sussex Regiment, 1914; retired from the Army, 1919. *Address:* 7 Portland Court, W.1. *T.:* Museum 3268. *Club:* United Service.
(Died 7 Jan. 1926.)

YOUNG, General James Nowell; b. 4 Feb. 1824; m. 1854, Lady Francis Erskine (d. 1887), sis. of 33rd Earl of Mar. Entered army 1840; General, 1891; unemployed list, 1886; served Afghan War, 1842; Judge Advocate; General, Bengal, 1877-81. *Address:* 13 Jevington Gardens, Eastbourne. *(Died 13 Jan. 1917.)*

YOUNG, John; b. Fulwood, 13 June 1845; 3rd s. of John Young, Fulwood, Renfrewshire, and Marion Carruth; m. 1880, Jessie Currie, d. of late John Graham, accountant, Glasgow; three s. *Educ.:* Paisley Grammar School. Studied and practised estate management and agriculture; entered service of Glasgow Corporation, 1875; was first General Manager and organiser of Glasgow Corporation Tramways as a municipal undertaking, firstly under horse traction, and later under electric traction; following upon this pioneer work was called upon to advise many of the largest Corporations in kingdom, and to assist them in obtaining Parliamentary powers to municipalise and

YOUNG, Ernest Herbert. See page xxxii.

operate their tramways; was first President of Municipal Tramways Association of Great Britain; became Assistant to Chairman of Underground Electric Railways Company of London, Limited, and General Manager of the Metropolitan District Railway, and later a Director of the District Railway; is a Director of the Lancashire Light and Power Company, Ltd., and the Lancashire Electric Power Company; for some years resided on and interested himself in his Wilts property of Fisherton de la Mere Manor, Wylye, and was a member of the Wilts County Council, also of the Wilton Rural District Council, and Parish Chairman. *Recreations:* curling, golf, and motoring. *Address:* Wolstan, The Grange, S.W.19. *T.:* Wimbledon 2043.   (*Died 3 June 1925.*)

YOUNG, Rt. Hon. Robert, P.C. Ireland; J.P. Co. Antrim; Architect and Civil Engineer; *b.* Belfast, 22 Feb. 1851; *e. s.* of late James Young, Abbeyville, Co. Antrim; *m.* Sara, *o. d.* of Rev. Robert Magill, M.A., Antrim (*d.* 1870); one *s.* two *d.* *Educ.:* Belfast Academy; Glasgow College. Articled with late Sir Charles Lanyon, M.P., C.E., and afterwards was his chief assistant in carrying out important engineering works, including the Belfast and Ballymena Railway; subsequently acted for several years as engineer to late William Dargan on the Dublin and Galway Railway; commenced practice as architect and civil engineer in Belfast on his return early in the 'fifties, and was joined in partnership by John Mackenzie and later by his son, R. M. Young, in the firm of Young and Mackenzie, of which he is still a member; Chairman of the Lagan Navigation Company and ex-President of Linenhall Library, Belfast; an ex-President of both the Belfast Literary Society and Belfast Natural History Society. *Publications:* some papers on geological and antiquarian subjects read at British Association and before various learned societies. *Recreations:* bowling, water-colour sketching and Irish music. *Address:* Rathvarna, Belfast.   (*Died 21 Jan. 1917.*)

YOUNG, Robert Magill, M.A., F.R.I.B.A., and Member of Council; Member of Royal Irish Academy; F.R.S.A., Ireland; J.P.; Senator Q.U.B.; senior partner, Young & Mackenzie, architects, 7 Donegall Square West, Belfast; Hon. Secretary, Royal Victoria Hospital, Belfast; *b.* 1851; *s.* of Rt. Hon. Robert Young, P.C., Rathvarna, Belfast; *m.* 1878, Eleanor, *d.* of James Reid; two *s.* two *d.* *Educ.:* Belfast Royal Academy; Queen's College (now Queen's University, Belfast). Pupil of Young & Mackenzie, of which his father was founder; for many years made sketching tours on the Continent; in connection with his firm has designed numerous Presbyterian churches, manses, and schools throughout Ulster; the Presbyterian Assembly Buildings; Belfast Royal Academy; Scottish Provident Institution and Ocean Insurance offices, mansions and large warehouses; hospitals for several public authorities. *Publications:* various papers on Architectural and antiquarian subjects to several learned societies; in 1870 described the Antiquities of Bute in his uncle's (Dr. James Bryce) Guide to Arran; edited Town Book of Belfast, 1892; Ulster in '98, 1893; Historical Collections relative to Old Belfast, 1896; Belfast and the Province of Ulster in XXth Century, 1908. *Address:* 7 Donegall Square West, and Rathvarna, Belfast. *T.:* Belfast 1491; Fort William 52. *Club:* Ulster Reform.   (*Died 19 Nov. 1925.*)

YOUNG, Samuel, J.P.; M.P. (N.) East Div. Co. Cavan, since 1892; head of Young, King, and Co., Ltd., distillers, Belfast and Limavady; Chairman of Bernard Hughes, Ltd., bakers and millers; was Member of Royal Commission on Royal Licensing Laws; *b.* 1822; *s.* of late Samuel Young, Dunavaly, Portaferry, Co. Down; *m.* 1846, *d.* of late Edward Allen, shipowner, Fenchurch Street; three *s.* two *d.* *Educ.:* Old Presbyterian College, Belfast. Devoted greater part of his life to business; has devoted himself to the advocacy of self-government for Ireland. *Recreation:* omnivorous reader. *Address:* Avonmore, Derryvolgie, Belfast. *Club:* National Liberal.   (*Died 18 April 1918.*)

YOUNG, Sir William Lawrence, 8th Bt., *cr.* 1769; *b.* 3 Aug. 1864; *s.* of Sir Charles Lawrence, 7th Bt. and 1st wife, Mary Florence, *y. d.* of Henry Hayman Toulmin of Childwick Bury, Herts; *S.* father 1887; *m.* 1887, Helen, *d.* of Hon. Henry William Petre. *Educ.:* Charterhouse. *Heir:* *b.* Sir Charles Alban Young. *Address:* 85 Lower Seymour Street, W. *Clubs:* Brooks's, Beefsteak, Garrick, Orleans.   (*Died 11 June 1921.*)

YOUNG, Sir William Mackworth, K.C.S.I., *cr.* 1897; J.P.; *b.* 15 Aug. 1840; 3rd *s.* of Capt. Sir George Young, R.N., 2nd Bt., of Formosa Place; *m.* 1st, 1869, Isabel Maria (*d.* 1870), 3rd *d.* of Rev. C. B. Elliott, F.R.S.; one *d.*; 2nd, 1881, Frances Mary, *d.* of Sir R. E. Egerton, K.C.S.I.; four *s.* one *d.* *Educ.:* Eton; King's College, Cambridge (M.A. and Fellow). Additional Member of Legislative Council of India for making Laws and Regulations, 1893; Financial Commissioner, Punjab, 1889-95: Resident of Mysore and Chief Commissioner of Coorg, 1895-97; Lieut.-Governor of the Punjab, 1897-1902; Vice-President Church Missionary Society; C.S.I. 1890. *Address:* Lerryn, Weybridge. *T. A.:* Lerryn, Weybridge.   (*Died 10 May 1924.*)

YOUNGMAN, Annie Mary, R.I. 1887; artist; *b.* Saffron Walden, Essex; *o. d.* of John Mallows Youngman, formerly member of New Water-Colour Society. *Educ.:* South Kensington School of Art and Royal Academy. Queen's Prize Holder at South Kensington; 1st Silver Medallist at R.A. Schools, 1883; exhibitor at Melbourne International, 1888; Paris International, 1889; Chicago International, 1893; Brussels International, 1897; also at Royal Academy, etc. *Address:* 19 Hyde Vale, Greenwich, S.E.10.   (*Died 11 Jan. 1919.*)

YOXALL, Sir James Henry, Kt., *cr.* 1909; M.P. (L.) Nottingham Boro West, 1895-1918; General Secretary, National Union of Teachers, 1892-1924; *b.* 15 July 1857; *e. s.* of late Henry Houghton Yoxall and late Elizabeth, *o. d.* of late James Smallwood; *m.* Elizabeth, *e. d.* of late Lt.-Col. Coles, R.E., 1886; one *s.* two *d.* *Educ.:* Wesleyan School, Redditch; Westminster Training Coll. Became a certificated teacher, 1878; President National Union of Teachers, 1891; Royal Commissioner on Secondary Education, 1894, 1895; Committee on Modern Language Teaching, 1916-1918; J.P.; Hon. M.A. Cambridge, 1899; M.A. Oxon 1907; Officier d'Académie, France. *Publications:* Nutbrown Roger and I, 1891; The Lonely Pyramid, 1892 (edition in German, 1899); Secondary Education, 1896; The Girl from St. Agneta's, 1902; The Rommany Stone, 1902; Alain Tanger's Wife, 1903; Smaliou, 1904; Beyond the Wall, 1906; Château Royal, 1908; The Wander Years, 1909; The A B C about Collecting, 1910; The Courtier Stoops, 1911; More about Collecting, 1913; The Villa for Coelebs, 1914; Collecting Old Miniatures, Collecting Old Glass, 1916; The Patriotic Reader, 1919; contributions to reviews, magazines, and newspapers on literary and artistic subjects; Editor of The Schoolmaster, 1909. *Recreations:* travel, collecting. *Address:* Springfield, Kew Gardens Road, Kew. *T.:* Richmond 1942. *Club:* Reform.   (*Died 2 Feb. 1925.*)

YPRES, 1st Earl of, *cr.* 1921; Viscount, *cr.* 1915, of Ypres and of High Lake; **Field-Marshal**

John Denton Pinkstone French, O.M.,
K.P. 1917 ; K.C.M.G., *cr.* 1902 ; G.C.B., *cr.* 1909 ;
K.C.B., *cr.* 1900 ; G.C.V.O., *cr.* 1905 ; D.C.L. Hon.
Oxon. ; LL.D. Camb. ; Captain of Deal.Castle
since 1923 ; A.D.C. General to H.M. 1911 ; Col.
19th Hussars since 1902 ; Col. Irish Guards,
1916 ; Colonel-in-Chief Royal Irish Regiment ;
b. Ripple Vale, Ripple, Kent, 28 Sep. 1852 ; *o. s.*
of Captain French, R.N., and Margaret, *d.* of
Wm. Eccles ; *m.* 1880, Eleanora, *d.* of R. W.
Selby-Lowndes of Elmers, Bletchley ; two *s.*
Educ. : Joined H.M.S. Britannia, 1866, and
served as a naval cadet and midshipman in
Royal Navy for 4 years. Entered army (8th
Hussars), 1874 ; transferred to 19th Hussars,
in which regiment served in Soudan Campaign,
1884-85, and in actions of Abu Klea, Gubut,
Metemmeh ; commanded 19th Hussars, 1889-
1893 ; employed as A.A.G. of Cavalry on the
staff, 1893-94 ; appointed A.A.G. at Headquarters
of Army, 1895 ; served there till 1897, when
appointed Brigadier to command 2nd Cavalry
Brigade ; transferred as temporary Maj.-Gen. to
1st Cavalry Brigade at Aldershot, 1899 ; appointed Maj.-Gen. to command Cavalry Division
in Natal, 1899 ; commanded troops at battle of
Elandslaagte, and commanded the cavalry in
Sir G. White's forces in the battles of Reitfontein and Lombard's Kop ; Lieut.-Gen. commanding Cavalry Division in South Africa, 1900-
1902 (despatches, promoted Maj.-Gen.) ; commanded the troops in operations round Colesberg from 10 Nov. 1899 to 31 Jan. 1900, including several important engagements ; commanded
cavalry force in the operations culminating in
the relief of Kimberley in Feb. 1900 ; commanded
Cavalry Division in Lord Roberts's forces
throughout the operations ending in the capture
of Bloemfontein and Pretoria ; commanded left
wing of Lord Roberts's forces in the battles east
of Pretoria on 10 and 12 June 1900 (despatches
8 times) ; commanded forces in operations culminating in capture of Barberton, also forces in
Eastern Transvaal during operations in spring
of 1901, also operations against rebels in Cape
Colony up to end of war ; General, 1907 ;
commanding 1st Army Corps, 1901-7 ; Field-
Marshal, 1913 ; Chief of Imperial-General Staff,
1911-14 ; Inspector-General of the Forces, 1907-
1911 and 1914 ; Commander-in-Chief of the
Expeditionary Forces in France, 1914-15 ; Com-
mander-in-Chief the troops stationed in the
United Kingdom, 1915-18 ; Lord-Lieut. of
Ireland, 1918-21 ; First Military Member Army
Council ; Grand Cross, Legion of Honour ;
Order of St. George, Russia ; Médaille Militaire
of France ; Freedom of City of London and
sword of honour, 1920. *Heir: s.,* Viscount
French.   *Address:* Deal Castle, Drumdoe,
Co. Roscommon, Ireland.   *Clubs:* Athenæum,
Marlborough, Cavalry.   (*Died 22 May 1925.*)

YULE, Sir David, 1st Bt., *cr.* 1922 ; Kt., *cr.*
1912 ; member of Andrew Yule & Co. Ltd. ;
Director Midland Bank, Mercantile Bank of
India, Ltd., Vickers, Ltd., and of Royal
Exchange Assurance ; *b.* 4 Aug. 1858 ; *s.* of
David Yule, Edinburgh ; *m.* 1900, Annie
Henrietta, *o. d.* of late Andrew Yule, Cal-
cutta. *Heir:* none. *Address:* Clive Row,
Calcutta.   (*Died 3 July 1928.*)

YULE, Col. James Herbert ; C.B. 1900 ;
retired ; *b.* 26 April 1847 ; *m.* 1898, Katharine
Burch, *y. d.* of Rev. Edward Burch Field, of
Moreland, Kinross-shire, N.B., J.P. and D.L. for
county, and widow of Brig.-Surg. B. C. Kerr.
Entered army, 1865 ; Colonel, 1898 ; served
Afghan War, 1879-80 (medal) ; Burmese Ex-
pedition, 1891-92 (despatches, brevet of
Lieut.-Col., medal with clasp) ; Tirah Expedi-
tionary Force, 1897-98 (despatches, brevet of
Col., medal with two clasps) ; South African
War, action Talana Hill ; commanded retire-
ment of force from Dundee to Ladysmith, 1899-

1158

1900 (despatches twice, medal with clasp, C.B.).
Address: 14 Hobart Place, S.W.   *T.:* Vic. 7156.
Clubs: Junior United Service ; New, Edinburgh.
      (*Died 7 May 1920.*)

YVES-GUYOT, Editor of Journal des Eco-
nomistes since 1909 ; Editor of L'Agence
Economique et Financière since 1911 ; *b.* Dinan
(Côtes-du-Nord), 6 Sep. 1843 ; *s.* of Prosper
Guyot, barrister, Rennes ; *m.* Mlle. H. Fontaine ;
two *d.* Republican ; publicist ; manager of the
Independant du Midi, Nîmes, 1868-69 ; contributor to the Rappel, 1870 ; Secretary of
the Anti-plebiscite Committee, 1870 ; member
of the Ligue des Droits de Paris sous la Commune ; Municipal Councillor of Paris, 1874 ;
editor of the Bien public et de la Réforme
économique ; published the letters of the Vieux
petit employé against the Prefecture of Police,
1878 ; hon. member of the Cobden Club, 1879 ;
deputy, 1885 ; rapporteur général du budget,
1887 ; Minister of Public Works, 1889-92 ;
political editor of Le Siècle, 1892-1903 ;
campaign against Socialism, defeated at the
election of 1893 ; has advocated the revision
of the Dreyfus case since 1894 ; wounded by
anarchists when attempting to prevent masons
attending a meeting of Louise Michel, 1882 ;
président de la Société d'Economie Politique, etc. ;
président de la Ligue du Libre Echange, 1911 ;
ancien président de la Société d'Anthropologie,
de la Société de Statistique, et de la Société
de Navigation aërienne ; a reçu en 1902 the
Guy medal from Royal Statistical Soc. (hon.
Fellow) ; American Statistical Society, hon.
Fellow, 1914 ; Political Economic Club, hon.
Member, 1919 ; LL.D. St. Andrews University ;
American Economic Assoc., Hon. Fellow, 1921.
Publications: La Science économique, 1st ed.
1881, 6th ed. 1925 ; La Prostitution, 1882 ; La
Tyrannie socialiste, 1893 (all these have been
translated into English) ; Les Principes de 89
and le socialisme, 1894 ; The Boer Politics,
1900 ; The Sugar Question, 1901 ; Le Bilan de
l'Eglise, 1902 ; L'Economie de l'effort, 1897 ;
several pamphlets on the affaire Dreyfus ; Le
Dictionnaire du commerce, de l'industrie et de
la banque, with M. A. Raffalovich ; Les Conflits
du travail et leur solution, 1908 ; La Comédie
protectionniste, 1905 (translated into English :
The Comedy of Protection) ; La Démocratie
individualiste, 1907 ; Sophismes socialistes et
faits economiques, 1907 (translated into English,
1909) ; Histoire de rapports économiques entre
la France et l'Angleterre (introduction to the
Catalogue of the French Section of the Franco-
British Exhibition), 1908 ; Le Commerce, un
vol., 1909 ; Les Préjugés économiques, 1909 ;
translated into English, Economic Prejudices ;
Les Chemins de fer et la grève, 1911 ; La Gestion
par l'Etat et les municipalités, 1912 (translated
in English under this title : Where and Why
Public Ownership has Failed) ; L'ABC du libre
échange, 1913 ; L'industrie et les industriels
1914 ; The Cause and Consequences of the War,
1916 (British edit.) ; La Province Rhénane
et la Westphalie, 1915 ; La Question de
l'alcool, 1917 ; Les Garanties de la paix,
1918 ; Inflation et Déflation, 1921 (avec M. A.
Raffalovich) ; Les Problémes de la Déflation,
1923 ; Politique Parlementaire et Politique
atavique, 1924. *Address:* 95 rue de Seine, Paris.
T.: Fleurus 08.19.   (*Died Feb. 1928.*)

Z

ZAMMIT, Salvatore Cachia, C.M.G.
1913. Was unofficial member of Executive
Council and elected member, Council of Government, Malta. *Address:* Malta.
      (*Died 15 July 1918.*)

ZANGWILL, Israel, man of. letters ; *b.* London, 1864 ; *s.* of late M. Zangwill : *m.* 1903, Edith (authoress of The First Mrs. Mollivar, The Rise of a Star, The Call, etc.), *d.* of late Professor W. E. Ayrton ; two *s.* one *d. Educ.* : elementary schools ; practically self-educated. B. A. (Honours) London.　Teacher, then journalist ; edited Ariel ; has written novels, essays, poems, and plays ; has lectured in Great Britain and Ireland, Jerusalem, Holland, and the United States ; President of the Jewish Historical Society of England ; ex-President and Hon. Member Playgoers' Club ; President of the Jewish Drama League ; Member of the Dramatists' Club, etc.　*Publications :* The Premier and the Painter, 1888 ; The Bachelors' Club, 1891 ; The Big Bow Mystery, 1892 ; The Old Maids' Club, 1892 ; Children of the Ghetto, 1892 ; Merely Mary Ann, 1893 ; Ghetto Tragedies, 1893 ; The King of Schnorrers, 1894 ; The Master, 1895 ; Without Prejudice, 1896 ; Dreamers of the Ghetto, 1898 ; Ghetto Tragedies, 1899 ; The Mantle of Elijah, 1900 ; The Grey Wig, 1903 ; Blind Children (verse), 1903 ; Ghetto Comedies, 1907 ; Italian Fantasies, 1910 ; The War for the World, 1916 ; The Principle of Nationalities, 1917 ; Chosen Peoples, 1918 ; Jinny the Carrier, 1919 ; The Voice of Jerusalem, 1920 ; Ibn Gabirol's Poems (from the Hebrew), 1923 ; Watchman, What of the Night? (Address to American Jewish Congress), 1923. *Plays* (the majority obtainable in book form) : Six Persons, 1892 ; Children of the Ghetto, 1899 ; The Moment Before, 1900 ; The Revolted Daughter, 1901 ; Merely Mary Ann, 1903 ; The Serio-Comic Governess, 1904 ; Jinny the Carrier, 1905 ; Nurse Marjorie, 1906 ; The Melting Pot, 1908 ; The War God, 1911 ; The Next Religion, 1912 ; Plaster Saints, 1914 ; Too Much Money, 1918 ; The Cockpit, 1921, The Forcing House, 1922 ; We Moderns, 1923. *Address :* Far End, East Preston, Sussex ; 3 Hare Court, Temple, E.C.　*T.A. :* Zangwill, East Preston.　*(Died 1 Aug. 1926.)*

ZEPPELIN, Count Perdinand, German aeronaut ; *b.* Constance, 8 July 1888 ; *s.* of late Friedrich J. W. K. Graf von Zeppelin, and Amelie F. P. Macaire d'Hoggner ; *m.* 1869, Isabella Freiin von Wolff ; one *d. Educ. :* Polytechnik, Stuttgart ; Kriegsschule, Ludwigsburg ; Tübingen University.　Took part in American War of Secession ; served Franco-German War, 1870 ; made first ascent in dirigible airship, 1900. Holds Order "pour le Mérite." *Address :* Stuttgart, Herdwegg 66 ; Manzell, nr. Friedrichshafen, Lake Constance Germany.
(Died 8 Mar. 1917.)

ZIMMERMANN, Agnes Marie, F.R.A.M. ; *b.* Cologne ; came to England at age of four ; naturalised British subject, 1872. *Educ. :* Royal Academy of Music, London ; made her début at Crystal Palace Saturday Concerts ; played in London at Monday and Saturday Popular and Philharmonic Concerts, at Liverpool Phil., Manchester (Hallé), and chief Provincial Concerts ; in Germany, at Leipsic (Gewandhaus), Frankfurt, Berlin, etc. *Publications :* suite for pianoforte, violin, and violoncello ; three Sonatas for pianoforte and violin, pianoforte Solos, Songs, etc. ; edited Schumann's pianoforte works, Beethoven's Sonatas, Mozart's Sonatas. *Address :* 16 Devonshire Street, Portland Place, W.1.　*T. :* Langham 1924.　*Club :* Albemarle.　*(Died 14 Nov. 1925.)*

ZORN, Anders Leonard ; *b.* Mora, province of Dalarne, Sweden, 18 Feb. 1860 ; *s.* of peasants ; *m.* 1885, Emma Lamm, Stockholm ; no *c. Educ. :* School of Enköping ; Academy of Fine Arts, Stockholm.　Travelled in Spain, Italy, and England painting water-colours ; learnt the art of etching in London from the Swedish artist Axel Haig ; painted his first oil-pictures, 1888, in England, and sold his Fisherman from St. Yves to the Luxembourg Museum ; painted portrait of himself for the Uffizi, Florence, 1889 ; gold medal, Paris Exhibition, 1889 ; since 1893 has several times visited America to paint portraits of Americans ; two medals of honour at the Paris Exhibition, 1900, as painter and etcher ; his most important work as a sculptor is the statue of Gustavus Vasa in Mora ; has painted the portraits of nearly all the members of the Swedish royal family.　*Recreations :* ski-ing and yachting. *Address :* Mora, Dalarne, Sweden.
(Died 22 Aug. 1920.)

PRINTED BY PHOTO-LITHOGRAPHY BY
MORRISON & GIBB, LTD., EDINBURGH & LONDON